A

GENEALOGICAL AND HERALDIC HISTORY

OF THE

LANDED GENTRY

OF

IRELAND

BY

SIR BERNARD BURKE

© 2010 Benediction Classics

Preface

EIGHT years having passed, obviously it had become necessary that a new edition of the "Landed Gentry of Ireland" should be issued, in order that the genealogical records of the various families appearing in the book might be revised to date, and the happenings of birth, marriage and death, in the interval, be added to the pedigrees. But one is now confronted with the problem whether there still remains a Landed Gentry at all in that country, so great has been the compulsory alienation of land in Ireland during the last decade.

Whatever may be the decision as to future editions, in the present one there has been no violent disqualification of families because the broad acres of their estates have been contracted to the lands about the mansion house; in fact, but very few pedigrees have been removed. Although the fascination of the ownership of land—land hunger—is still a dominant characteristic of the British race, it cannot be said to possess its ancient importance; and the interest of the public, it seems to me, lies in the families themselves rather than in the extent of their ownership of land. The growth of the new landless plutocracy has shifted the importance of things, and is a factor that must weigh in the future, and be considered in conjunction with absenteeism. But the problem is for the next edition.

Although a number of new and interesting pedigrees are now included in "Burke" for the first time the changes in the present volume are chiefly caused by the revision of pedigrees and the occurrences of the interval. The latter have been exceedingly numerous, and I am chiefly indebted to the very many members of the families concerned with whom I have been in correspondence or to whom I have submitted proofs, for an enormous amount of assistance generously given to me. For that my grateful thanks.

In the revision of the pedigrees there will be found a number of important alterations. Some of my most vehement correspondents seem to fancy that "Burke" is edited by Hans Andersen. That really is quite a mistake. Of course, one knows that every Irishman is the descendant of countless kings, princes and other minor celebrities.

One admits it—the thing is unquestionable. One knows, of course, also, that every family is the oldest in Co. Galway, or Co. Sligo, or somewhere else, and that, for some reason or other, every Irishman is the "head" of his family, and I am growing weary of reading letters which assure me that the mushroom families included in the Landed Gentry pale into insignificance beside the glories of those which are omitted, and I am slowly learning—so often am I so assured—that all the pedigrees herein are hopelessly wrong. But although I may not have included quite so much as has been desired, I think I may claim that what is inserted may be relied upon. All genealogical works started upon a model of narrative, in which a place might properly be found for supposition and tradition. There has been a gradual transition to exactitude of fact, which is the aim in view, and which I claim has now been reached.

For the present edition every coat-of-arms has been carefully scrutinized and compared with the original records in Ulster's Office. I believe I can now claim for the Irish volume that, apart from unintentional error, every single one which is quoted herein can be relied upon as borne by unquestionable right. Families to whom no armorial bearings are assigned have none recorded to them in Ulster's Office.

The publishers have consented to incur the expense of bringing the Landed Gentry into line with the PEERAGE and BARONETAGE by illustrating every coat-of-arms in the book. This must add very greatly to its interest, and I trust their lavish expenditure on this point will receive the reward it merits in the increased appreciation of the public.

I am indebted to Mr. Farnham Burke, C.V.O., C.B., Norroy King of Arms, for much assistance in the preparation of this edition, and I have profited greatly from the kind help and from the labours of Mr. Ashworth Burke, who has resigned the editorship of the present edition, whilst many others have taken much trouble with the single-minded desire for the improvement or the accuracy of the volume. To all I tender my thanks, but above all I am under a deep debt of gratitude to Mr. G. D. Burtchaell, Athlone Pursuivant. His able and willing assistance have been acknowledged in former editions, but on the present occasion I have had the advantage of his help to an extent little short of a scrutiny of every line in the book. He it is who has examined the arms, and has gone to endless trouble to solve doubts and difficulties as they have become apparent in the pedigrees. I really think his name should be on the title page as editor. Mere words of thanks seem a feeble acknowledgment of what this edition owes to his untiring assistance.

THE EDITOR.

A GENEALOGICAL AND HERALDIC DICTIONARY OF THE LANDED GENTRY OF IRELAND.

ACHESON. *See* BURKE'S PEERAGE, **GOSFORD, E.**

ACTON OF KILMACURRAGH.

CHARLES ANNESLEY ACTON, of Kilmacurragh, Rathdrum, co. Wicklow, J.P., late Capt. Royal Welsh Fusiliers, *b.* 14 Feb. 1876; *s.* his uncle 25 Aug. 1908.

Lineage.—THOMAS ACTON, of Bog Hall, Ballygannonbeg (part of the lands of West Aston), *m.* Alice Coventry. His will is dated 1645 and witnessed by his wife. He had a son,
 THOMAS ACTON, of Bog Hall, co. Wicklow, who left issue, a son,
 THOMAS ACTON, who commenced building the house at West Aston in 1697, the same year that Lord Acton built Aldenham Hall. He obtained from Richard, Viscount Rosse, leases for lives renewable for ever of lands in co. Wicklow, by deeds dated 13 Feb. and 10 May, 1716. He *m.* Elinor, dau. of Nicholas Kempston, of Dunmurray, co. Cavan, Colonel in Oliver Cromwell's Army by Grace his wife, dau. of Thomas Maule, Commissioner of Customs, and *d.* 2 Jan. 1750, leaving issue,
 1. WILLIAM, his successor.
 1. Grace, *m.* Thomas Ball, Barrister-at-Law, of Sea Park, co. Wicklow.
 2. Elinor, *m.* Rev. John Blachford, D.D., who *d.* 1748.
 3. Alice, *m.* Henry Kempston.
Mr. Acton, whose will is dated 23 Oct. 1731, and was proved 7 Jan. 1750, was *s.* by his son,
 WILLIAM ACTON, entered Trin. Coll. Dublin, 14 Nov. 1726, and was Keeper of the Writs of the Court of Common Pleas, and Serjeant of the Coif (holding the ring appertaining to that office), *b.* 1711; *m.* 4 March, 1736, Jane, dau. of William Parsons, eldest son of Sir William Parsons, 2nd bart., of Birr Castle, and had issue,
 1. William, *d.s.p.* 2. THOMAS, his successor.
 1. William, *unm.*
 2. Maria, *m.* by licence, dated June, 1783, Thomas Walker, of Tagunnan, co. Wexford, Master in Chancery.
 3. Jane, *d. unm,* 1794.
Mr. Acton was *s.* by his only surviving son,
 THOMAS ACTON, of West Aston, co. Wicklow, *m.* 1780, Sidney, dau. of Joshua Davis, Barrister-at-Law, Dublin, and *d.* 1817, leaving issue,
 1. WILLIAM, his successor.
 2. Thomas (Rev.), of Dunganstown Glebe, co. Wicklow, *m.* by licence, dated 16 Sept. 1818, Sidney, dau. of Hampden Evans, of Portrane, co. Dublin, and *d.* 16 Aug. 1846, having by her (who *d.* Aug. 1867) had issue,
  1. Thomas, *d.* 12 Aug. 1843.
  2. Hampden, of Chàlet Lucia, Pau, France, Col. Madras Staff Corps (ret.), *b.* 21 April, 1822; *m.* 22 Jan. 1868, Lucy, dau. of William Jackson Greer, of Rhone Hill House, co. Tyrone, J.P., and widow of Henry Davis, of Waterford. He *d.* April, 1901, leaving issue,
   (1) Hampden, *b.* 31 Dec. 1870; *d.* 6 Feb. 1888. I.L.G.

   (2) Fitzmaurice Massey, Commander, R.N., *m.* 7 May, 1910, Ruby, widow of Lieut. Percy Crabtree, R.N.
   (3) William Maxwell.
   (1) Margaret Usher.
  3. William, of Brookville, co. Dublin, J.P., High Sheriff co Leitrim, 1875, *b.* 5 Oct. 1824; *m.* 16 Jan. 1852, Georgina (*d.* 31 Oct. 1905), dau. of James Lowry, of Rockdale, co. Tyrone, and *d.* 9 Jan. 1896, leaving issue,
   (1) Thomas Hampden Evans, Lieut.-Col. R.A. (*Knockeadar*, Bray, *co. Wicklow*), *b.* 9 Dec. 1855; *m.* 18 Jan. 1882, Olivia Charlotte Jessie, eldest dau. of Right Hon. George Augustus Chichester May, Lord Chief Justice of Ireland, and has issue,
    1. William Hampden May, Lieut. R.F.A., *b.* 23 Oct. 1882.
    2. Philip James Barrington, *b.* 1 May, *d.* Sept. 1884.
    3. Theodore John Chichester, *b.* 18 Aug. 1886.
    1. Mary Olivia Barrington, *b.* 21 May, 1890; *d.* July, 1891.
    2. Stella Mary Georgina.
   (2) James Lowry Cole, Lieut.-Col. late Connaught Rangers, *b.* 6 Nov. 1856; *m.* 7 April, 1888, Matilda Julia, youngest dau. of Henry Salisbury Milman, and has issue,
    1. Armar Edward, *b.* 25 April, 1889.
    2. Owen Henry, *b.* 7 Sept. 1890.
    1. Sydney Georgina.
    2. Ruth Margaret.
    3. Bertha Joice. 4. Leonora Janet.
   (3) William George, *m.* Dec. 1887, Louisa Joice Leslie, dau. of the late Henry Lowry Barnwell, and *d.* Oct. 1891, leaving issue,
    1. William George Henry, *d.* young, July, 1896.
    2. Edward Leslie Lowry, *b.* Oct. 1889.
   (4) Henry Lowry Barnwell, Maj. Indian Army, Ass. Judge Advocate-Gen., India, *b.* 30 Aug. 1861; *m.* 1st, May, 1886, Nora Prudentia, dau. of late Gen. W. Fuller, Madras Staff Corps. She *d.* 21 June, 1901, leaving issue,
    Ethel Jessie Muriel.
   He *m.* 2ndly, 16 Oct. 1907, Louise Vereker, dau. of Col. Dickson, R.A.
   (1) Harriette Mary Louisa. (2) Georgina Elizabeth.
   1. Margaret, *m.* 9 Dec. 1851, Henry Lambert Bayly, and has issue (*see* BURKE'S *Peerage,* ANGLESEY, M.).
   2. Sidney Anna, *d.* Oct. 1864.
   3. Anna Sophia, *m.* her cousin, Capt. George Warburton Drought, Yorks. L.I., of Cargins, co. Roscommon, J.P., who *d.* Nov. 1880,
  1. Anna Maria, *m.* 6 July, 1806, Major George Warburton, of Augherim, co. Galway.
  2. Jane, *m.* George Mears John Drought, of Glencarrig, co. Wicklow, who *d.* 4 March, 1844, leaving issue (*see that family*).
 His elder son,
  LIEUT.-COL. WILLIAM ACTON, of West Aston, M.P. co. Wicklow, Lieut.-Col. of Militia, and High Sheriff of the county, 1820, also Vice-Lieutenant, D.L. and J.P., *b.* 1789; *m.* 16 June, 1818, Caroline, dau. of Thomas Walker, of Tagunnan, co. Wexford, Master in Chancery, and *d.* 10 April, 1854, having by her (who *d.* 11 April, 1879) had issue,

A

1. THOMAS, his successor.
2. William Molesworth Cole, Col. late 77th Regt., served in the Crimea, present at Inkerman, b. 29 Dec. 1827; d. 22 April, 1904; m. 7 Aug. 1861, Elizabeth Frances, only child of Capt. Frederick Adolphus Robinson, 5th Fusiliers.
3. Charles BALL-ACTON, C.B., of Syddon, co. Meath, and Egginton House, Leighton Buzzard, Col. King's Own Yorkshire L.I., assumed the prefix surname of BALL 1875, b. 17 Dec. 1830; m. 31 July, 1869, Georgina Cecilia (*Kilmacurragh, Rathdrum*), dau. of George Annesley (*see* BURKE's *Peerage*, VALENTIA, V.), and d. 3 Feb. 1897, leaving issue,
  1. William Parsons Annesley, b. 21 March, 1871; d. April, 1884.
  2. CHARLES ANNESLEY, now of Kilmacurragh.
  3. Reginald Thomas Annesley, Capt. late King's Own Yorkshire L.I., b. 2 Oct. 1877.
  4 Vere Annesley, 2nd Lieut. Oxford L.I., b. 22 April, 1879, killed in action near Paardeberg, South Africa, 18 Feb. 1900.
  1. Evelyn Caroline Annesley; m. 3 Nov. 1808, Edward Nixon Wynne, J.P., of Wentworth House, Wicklow, and has issue (*see* WYNNE *of Hazlewood*).
  2. Grace Annesley.
  3. Irene Annesley.
1. Jane, d. unm. 5 Nov. 1906.

His eldest son,

THOMAS ACTON, of West Aston, J.P., D.L., co. Wicklow, High Sheriff 1857, b. 1826; d. unm. 25 Aug. 1908, being s. by his nephew.

Seat—Kilmacurragh, Rathdrum, co. Wicklow. Club—Kildare Street, Dublin.

ADAMS OF NORTHLANDS.

SAMUEL ALLEN ADAMS, of Northlands, co. Cavan, J.P., formerly 1st Lieut. Tipperary Militia Artillery, educated Trin. Coll. Dublin, b. 1 March, 1847; m. 13 June, 1871, Frances Dorothea, dau. of Rev. Decimus W. Preston, M A., Rector of Killinkere, and granddau. of William Preston, Judge of Appeal, and Hon. Frances Dorothea, dau. of John, 5th Lord Carbery (*see* BURKE's *Peerage*), and has issue,
  1. JOHN HERVEY STUART, b. 30 Dec. 1875.
  2. Samuel Allen Adams, b. 11 April, 1882.
  3. Ambrose Douglas, b. 9 May, 1889.
  1. Emily Maude Elizabeth, d. 29 May, 1891.
  2. Felicia Preston, d. 24 June, 1887.
  3. Olive Mildred.
  4. Mary Henrietta Mabel.
  5. Frances Dorothea Kathleen, d. 2 Sept. 1887.
  6. Hazel Gertrude.

Lineage.—COL. JAMES ADAMS m. Catherine, dau. of Arthur Magennis, 1st Viscount Iveagh, by Sarah his wife, dau. of Hugh O'Neill, Earl of Tyrone, and was father of

CAPT. JAMES ADAMS, an officer in the Army of WILLIAM III, who distinguished himself at the battle of the Boyne, and was granted the freedom of the borough of Drogheda for himself and his heirs, which privilege the family still enjoys. His son,

JAMES ADAMS, of Monaghan, and Corranearry House, co. Cavan, b. 1673; m. 1694, Jane, dau. of William Allen, of Kilmore, co. Monaghan, and d. 19 Nov. 1744, leaving by her (who d. 17 March, 1752, aged 75) an only son,

ALLEN ADAMS, of Corranearry House, b. 1708; m. about 1735, Martha, dau. of William Higginbotham, and grand-dau. of Capt. Thomas Higginbotham, by his wife, Miss Williams, maid of honour to MARY II., and dau. of General Scurlog Williams, of Clongill Castle, co. Meath. He d. 15 Dec. 1755 (his will was proved in Dublin, 24 Jan. 1756), and by her (who d. 1807, aged 105) had issue,
  1. RICHARD, of Shercock House, co. Cavan, J.P., High Sheriff 1783, and of Monaghan in 1785, b. 1736; m. 13 April, 1761, Amelia, dau. of Thomas Cosby, of Beeks Court, and d. 1789, leaving issue.
  2. James, of Corranearry House, b. 1745; d. unm. 15 June, 1809.
  3. William, of Castletown House, co. Cavan, b. 1746; m. 1st, about 1769, Olivia, dau. of Neason Wildridge, and by her, who d. 1781, had issue; he m. 2ndly, 6 July, 1783, Anne, widow of George MacDaniel, and d. 28 Feb. 1815, leaving further issue.
  4. Samuel, b. 1750; m. 10 March, 1779, Elizabeth, dau. of Alexander Leslie, and d. 7 June, 1709, having had issue.
  5. BENJAMIN (Rev.), of whom hereafter.

His 5th son,

REV. BENJAMIN ADAMS, Rector of Killinick, J.P. for co. Cavan, b. 1756; m. 14 April, 1777, Elizabeth, dau. of John Clarke, grandson of the celebrated metaphysician, Dr. Samuel Clarke, Rector of St. James, London, and Chaplain to Queen ANNE, and d. 10 June, 1840, leaving issue,
  1. William Allen, b. 15 May, 1783; d. 3 March, 1784.
  2. John, J.P. co. Cavan, High Sheriff for Cavan in 1811, b. 16 May, 1785; m. 2 Nov. 1806, Joyce, eldest dau. of his uncle Richard, and d.s.p. Feb. 1827.
  3. SAMUEL, succeeded his father.
  4. Charles James, of Shinan House, Capt. R.N., J.P. co. Cavan, High Sheriff 1833 (*vide* O'BYRNE's *Naval Biography*), b. 29 April, 1792; m. 29 Sept. 1821, Anne Jane (who d. 4 March, 1834, aged 36), dau. of Capt. William Foster, of Fosterstown, co. Meath, and d. 23 Aug. 1854, having had issue.
    1. Elizabeth, d. 25 April, 1780.
    2. Elizabeth, d. 28 Oct. 1780.
    3. Emelia, d. 5 Sept. 1782.
    4. Charlotte, d. 26 Aug. 1790.
    5. Matilda, d. 15 July, 1794.
    6. Caroline, m. 1 Jan. 1812, John J. A. Leonard, of Claremont House, J.P., and d. 22 June, 1858, leaving issue.

His 3rd son,

THE VERY REV. SAMUEL ADAMS, M.A., of Northlands, co. Cavan, Dean of Cashel, and Prebendary of Terebrine, J.P. cos. Cavan and Monaghan, b. 15 Feb. 1788; m. 4 Jan. 1809, Frances, youngest dau. of Capt. John Harvey, of Killiane Castle, co. Wexford (*see that family*), and d. 7 Dec. 1856, having by her (who d. 28 Nov. 1869) had issue,
  1. Benjamin William, b. 13 Feb. 1816; d. 4 March, 1822.
  2. JOHN HARVEY, late of Northlands.
  3. Charles Stuart, of Glynch House, Newbliss, J.P. for cos. Meath and Cavan, b. 12 July, 1820; m. 1st, 6 June, 1850, Eliza, only dau. of Charles McMahon, of Rockfield, co. Monaghan, and by her (who d. 5 May, 1860) had issue four sons,
    1. Samuel Stuart, b. 21 March, 1851.
    2. Richard Hervey, b. 27 Sept. 1852.
    3. Charles Allen, b. 12 June, 1857; d. 22 March, 1860.
    4. William Vigors, b. 28 Oct. 1859; d. 23 Dec. 1867.

Mr. C. S. Adams m. 2ndly, 23 Oct. 1862, Jane Henrietta, eldest dau. of Rev. Charles Sheridan Young. She d. 21 July, 1888. He d. 30 April, 1876, having by her bad issue,
    5. Charles Sheridan, b. 29 July, 1863; d. 19 Dec. 1867.
    6. Douglas Gerald, of Aubawn, Killeshandra, co. Cavan, b. 20 March, 1868; m. 1st, 23 Jan. 1897, Eleanor Anna, dau. of Lieut.-Gen. Clifford, C.B., and by her has issue,
      Violet Eleanor Sheila, b. 5 Dec. 1897.
He m. 2ndly, 8 Oct. 1902, Edna Olivia Mant, only dau. of Edward Dobbs, LL.D.
    7. Claude Stuart Alexander, b. 16 March, 1874; d. 15 Sept. 1875.
    1. Marie Stuart, m. 16 Oct. 1890, Rev. William Knox, Rector of Killeshee.
    2. Frances Florence, m. Aug. 1897, W. J. Hamilton, of Castle Hamilton, D.L., and has issue (*see that family*).
    3. Eva Adeline, m. 26 Nov. 1891, R. Claude Hamilton, of Dunmany House (*see* HAMILTON *of Castle Hamilton*).
    4. Lilian Maude, d. 10 Sept. 1875.
    5. Nora Cathleen, m. 21 June, 1905, Joseph C. C. Martin.
    6. Violet Blanche, d. 14 Sept. 1875.
    7. Irene Gwendoline, m. Rev. Herbert Hughes.
  4. Benjamin William, D.D. (Rev.), of Kinnea, co. Cavan, b. 31 March, 1827, Rector of Santry, Diocese of Dublin; m. 1st, 14 Dec. 1854, Georgina Roberts (who d. 16 May, 1863), dau. of John Drew Atkin, and grand-dau. of Sir Thomas Roberts, Bart., and had issue,
    1. Samuel Arthur, b. 12 Sept. 1857; d. 10 March, 1869.
    1. Georgina Roberts.
    2. Frances Hervey, m. Dr. G. W. T. Clarke, and d. 7 July, 1908.
He m. 2ndly, 11 Aug. 1864, Louisa Jane, dau. of William O'Brien Adams, M.D., and d. 26 June, 1886, leaving issue,
    2. William Augustus ADAM, of Kinnea, co. Cavan, Major 5th Lancers, M.P. for Woolwich 1910, educated at Harrow, Dublin University and Sandhurst, and assumed by Deed Poll 16 Aug. 1907, the name of ADAM, b. 27 May, 1865.
    3. Herbert Algernon ADAM, Capt. R.N., assumed by Deed Poll 16 Aug. 1907, the name of ADAM, b. 3 Jan. 1872; m. 21 Dec. 1898, Emily Banner Clough, dau. of Somerset James Johnstone, late R.N. (*see* BURKE's *Peerage*, JOHNSTONE, Bt.), and has issue,
      Alastair Somerset Graham, b. 1904.
    3. Constance Louisa.
  1. Dorothea Anne, m. 11 Nov. 1833, Le Chevalier Charles A. Zander, of Munich, and d. 7 Feb. 1864, having had issue.
  2. Elizabeth Frances, m. 21 March, 1833, John J. D. McDonald, Lieut. 47th Regt., and d. 29 Jan. 1865.
  3. Caroline Matilda, m. 2 May, 1837, Thomas R. Barry, and has issue.

The eldest surviving son,

JOHN HERVEY ADAMS, of Northlands, Barrister-at-Law, J.P. cos. Cavan and Monaghan, and High Sheriff 1854, b. 28 April, 1818; m. 1st, 30 April, 1846, Elizabeth Frances, 3rd dau. of Ambrose Going, J.P., of Ballyphilip, co. Tipperary, and by her (who d. 25 July, 1867) had issue,
  1. SAMUEL ALLEN, now of Northlands.
  2. Ambrose Going, J.P., b. 22 March, 1850; m. 3 Oct. 1872, Anne Jane Foster, dau. of Rev. William Watkyns Deering, M.A., and had issue,
    1. Clara Elizabeth Charlotte.   2. Ethel Annie.
  1. Margaret Anna, m. 4 April, 1871, Ormsby Colville McClintock Jones, J.P., of Mount Edward, co. Sligo, and has issue.
  2. Elizabeth Frances, m. 3 Sept. 1872, Robert Edward Follett Jones, son of Major James Jones, of Mount Edward, co. Sligo, and has issue.

Mr. Adams m. 2ndly, 24 Sept. 1869, Sarah Mary, dau. of Lieut.-Col. Owen Loyd Ormsby, 88th Regt., and d. 8 May, 1871.

Arms—Gu., a heart, between three cross-crosslets fitchée or. Crest—On a mount vert, a cross-crosslet fitchée or, charged with a bleeding heart, gu. Motto—In cruce salus.
Seat—Northlands, Carrickmacross.

ADAMS OF JAMESBROOK.

MAJOR WILLIAM RICHARD GOOLD-ADAMS, of Jamesbrook, co. Cork, J.P., late 1st Dragoon Guards, b. 30 Aug. 1853.

Lineage.—MICHAEL GOOLD-ADAMS, of Jamesbrook (son of WALLIS ADAMS, and Frances Goold his wife), m. 1800, Martha, sister of the 1st Earl of Bantry, and dau. of Simon White, of Bantry House, co. Cork, by Frances Jane his wife, dau. of Richard Hedges Eyre, of Mount Hedges, and d. 1817, having by her (who d. 1841) had issue,
1. RICHARD WALLIS, his heir.
2. Michael, Lieut.-Col. in the Army, of the Scots Greys, d. unm.
3. Robert Hedges, d. unm. 1875.
4. Samuel Hamilton, of Salisbury, co. Tipperary, J.P., m. 1st, in 1846, Frances Margaret, dau. of Col. Richard Wellesley Bernard, of Castle Bernard, King's Co. (see that family), and by her (who d. March, 1850) had a dau.,
  Charlotte Katharine, d. unm. 30 Oct. 1905.
He m. 2ndly, Nov. 1852, Frances Louisa (d. 13 Sept. 1905), dau. of Very Rev. Thomas John Burgh, Dean of Cloyne, by Lady Anna Burgh, his wife (see DE BURGH of Oldtown). He d. Dec. 1884.
1. Frances Jane, d. Nov. 1884.

His eldest son,
RICHARD WALLIS GOOLD-ADAMS, of Jamesbrook, J.P., High Sheriff 1868, b. 27 March, 1802 ; m. 4 Nov. 1852. Mary Sarah, dau. of Sir William Wrixon Becher, Bart., of Ballygiblin. She d. 31 Dec 1899. He d. 5 May, 1873, leaving issue,
1. WILLIAM RICHARD, now of Jamesbrook.
2. Francis Michael, b. 20 Dec. 1854 ; Capt. R.A., Assistant Superintendent of the School of Gunnery at Shoeburyness, m. 2 Nov. 1881, Evelyn, dau. of Rev. Edward P. Wynne, Rector of Shoeburyness, and was killed in the explosion at that place, 26 Feb. 1885, leaving three daus.,
  1. Evelyn St. Bride Mary, m. Edward W. Scrutton.
  2. Lynette.
  3. Beatrice, m. Francis Rowe, I.C.S.
3. Richard Eyre, Major late Highland Light Inf., b. 22 July, 1856 ; m. 8 Jan. 1891, Zoe, dau. of Charles Douglas Burnett, of Hawley, Hants, and d. 31 Oct., 1910.
4. Hamilton John (Sir), G.C.M.G. (1907), K.C.M.G. (1902), C.B., Maj. (ret.) Roy. Scots Regt., Lieut.-Gov. of Orange River Colony 1901, Gov. and Com.-in-Chief 1909-10, High Commissioner and Com.-in-Chief of Cyprus from 1911 (Government House, Nicosia, Cyprus. Club—Army and Navy), b. 27 June, 1858 ; m. 4 July, 1911, Elsie, youngest dau. of Charles Riordan, of Montreal, Canada.
5. Henry Edward Fane, C.M.G., Colonel R.A. (United Service Club), b. 16 May, 1860.
6. Edward Eyre (Rev.), Rector of Beelsby, Grimsby, M.A. Camb. b. 5 April, 1862 ; d. unm. 24 April, 1900.
7. Arthur Chaloner (Corbally, Glanmire, co. Cork), b. 7 Dec. 1864 ; m. 25 April, 1893, Lilian Sarah, dau. of the late Charles Weldon, of Morden Hill, Lewisham, and has issue,
  Aileen Lilian, b. 30 Oct. 1895.

Seat—Jamesbrook, near Ballinacurra.

ADAMSON OF GLENFARNE HALL.

LIEUT.-COL. JOHN GEORGE ADAMSON, of Linden Hall, Co. Northumberland and of Glenfarne Hall, co. Leitrim, D.L., J.P., High Sheriff 1908, late King's Own Yorkshire Light Infantry, b. 8 Jan. 1855 ; m. 9 Aug. 1883, Caroline Sara, only dau. of the late Rev. James Timothy Bainbridge Landon, M.A. Oxford, Hon. Canon of York, and Vicar of Ledsham, Yorks., formerly Fellow of Magdalen Coll. Oxford, and has issue,

1. Muriel Annie Pearl, b. 25 May, 1884.
2. Catharine Evelyn, b. 8 Dec. 1890.

Lieut.-Col. Adamson is the elder son of the late Lawrence William Adamson, LL.D., D.L., of Linden, Long Horsley, co. Northumberland (see BURKE'S Landed Gentry), and Anne Jane, his first wife, who d. 16 Dec. 1869, dau. of John Thomas Edward Flint, of Filleigh, co. Devon.

Lineage.—See ADAMSON of Linden.

Arms—Vert goutté d'eau a cross invected, in the first quarter a key in pale and in the second a talbot passant all or. Crest—A talbot passant az. collared and charged on the shoulder with a cross invected and holding in the dexter paw a key in pale all or. Motto—Watch and ward.

Seats—Glenfarne Hall, co. Leitrim, and Linden Hall, Long Horsley, Northumberland. Clubs—Naval and Military ; Kildare Street, and Royal St. George Yacht.

ALCOCK OF WILTON.

CAPT. PHILIP CLAYTON ALCOCK, of Wilton, co. Wexford, J.P., D.L., High Sheriff 1900. late Capt. Gloucester Regt., b. 26 June, 1861 ; s. his uncle 1893.

Lineage.—JOHN ALCOCK, of Downpatrick, had issue, with three daus. (Elizabeth, m. Oct. 1680, her kinsman, John Alcock, of Kells, co. Meath, another m. Godfrey Williamson, and another m. Robert Rowan), three sons, viz.,
1. WILLIAM, his heir.
2. Alexander (Rev.), b. 1665, entered Trin. Coll. Dublin, 2 Jan. 1684, aged 19, B.A. 1688, M.A. 1692, Chancellor of the Diocese of Waterford 1699, Dean of Lismore 22 July, 1725 ; m. Jane, dau. of Sir John Mason, Knt., of Waterford (and sister to Aland John Mason M.P., who m. in 1739, Elizabeth, created 1746, Viscountess Grandison, of Dromana, co. Waterford), and d. 1747, leaving issue,
3. Simon, of Dublin, m. Aug. 1680, Rose Kelly, and d.s.p. His will, dated 8 April, 1725, was proved 27 April, 1727.

The eldest son,
WILLIAM ALCOCK, of Wilton, co. Wexford, m. Aug. 1670, Jane, dau. of John Bamber, of Bamber Hall, co. Lancaster, and had issue,
1. Richard, b. 1675 ; d.s.p.   2. WILLIAM, his successor.
3. John, b. 1682.
1. Mary, m. Richard Leigh, of Collinmore, co. Westmeath.
2. Elizabeth, m. Robert Haly.
3. Alice, m. Aug. 1695, Michael Moore, of Drogheda.
4. Jane, m. Patrick Luttin, of Dublin.

The eldest son,
WILLIAM ALCOCK, of Wilton, b. 1681 ; m. 13 May, 1701, Henrietta, 3rd dau. of Sir John Mason, Knt., of Waterford, and had issue seven daus., Elizabeth ; Anna Maria ; Alice ; Susannah ; Anne ; Hannah ; Mary ; and two sons,
1. WILLIAM, his heir.
2. Henry, of Nymphall, co. Waterford, b. 1716 ; m. 7 Sept. 1748, Jane Sheppard, and d. s.p. His will, dated 13 April, 1779, was proved 8 June, 1784 ; his widow d. 1806, aged 84.

Mr. Alcock's will, dated 1738, was proved 1739. The eldest son,
WILLIAM ALCOCK, of Wilton, Col. of the Waterford Regt. of Militia, m. May, 1734, Hon. Mary Loftus, eldest dau. of Nicholas, Viscount Loftus, and in her descendants co-heir to her brother Henry, Earl of Ely ; and had issue, three sons and two daus.,
1. HENRY, his heir.
2. William (Major), of Springfield House, co. Wexford (will dated 8 July, 1808), m. 1st, Miss Goldfrap, by whom he had issue,
  1. William Henry.   2. Henry Loftus.
  1. Ada, m. — Stepney.   2. Jane Evans.
He m. 2ndly, Beata, sister of Edward Turner, and by her left issue,
  3. Sarah Beata.   4. Anne.
  5. Mary Catherine.
3. John (Sir), of Waterford, Knt. (whose will, dated 22 Feb. 1792, was proved 7 May, 1799). He m. 4 April, 1777, Sarah, dau. of Rev. William Dennis, of Coolroebeg, co. Waterford, by whom (who d. 4 April, 1825) he had issue,
  1. William, b. 1778, d. unm.
  1. Jane, m. Thomas Carew, of Ballinamona.
  2. Marianne, m. Ven. Strange Butson, Archdeacon of Clonfert.
  3. Henrietta, m. Edward William Tottenham, of Woodville, co. Wexford.
  4. Sarah, d. young.
1. Mary, m. James Kearney, of Waterford.
2. Henrietta, m. Dec. 1785, John Burchall, of Waterford.
Col. Alcock d. 19 March, 1779. His will, dated 14 March, 1779, was proved 15 May, 1779. His eldest son,
HENRY ALCOCK, of Wilton, M.P. for Waterford, an officer in the 13th Light Dragoons, m. 1 June, 1764, Philippa Melosina, dau. of the Right Rev. Richard Chenevix, Bishop of Waterford and Lismore ; she d. with her infant son, 14 May, 1765. He m. 2ndly, 6 Sept. 1766, Elizabeth Catharine, dau. of Beverley Ussher, M.P. for co. Waterford for 36 years, and by her had issue,
1. William Henry, d. unm.   2. Ussher, d. unm.
3. WILLIAM CONGREVE, b. 1771, M.P. for co. Wexford, s. his father 1811, and d. unm. 1812, when Wilton devolved on his only surviving brother.

Alcock.   THE LANDED GENTRY.   **4**

4. HARRY, s. his brother.
1. Eliza Jane.   2. Mary Anne.
3. Henrietta, *m.* Jan. 1804, James Wallace, of Waterford.
Mr. Alcock *d.* 1811; his son,
HARRY ALCOCK, of Wilton, *b.* 22 Feb. 1792, *s.* his elder brother in 1812, and *m.* 10 Sept. 1818, Margaret Elinor, dau. and heir of James Savage, of Kilgibbon, co. Wexford, a descendant of the old Anglo-Norman family of Savage, of Portaferry. She *d.* 24 March, 1867. He *d.* 3 Dec. 1840, having had issue,
  1. HARRY, late of Wilton Castle.
  2. Ussher William, late Lieut. 83rd Regt., *b.* 7 April, 1825; *m.* 14 Sept. 1857, Aphra Belinda, dau. of Richard Daxton, and has issue,
    1. Harry, *b.* 30 April, 1861.
    2. Arthur Augustus, *b.* 14 Oct. 1867.
    3. Ussher William, *b.* 29 March, 1866.
    1. Sarah Aphra, *d.* young.
    2. Henrietta Mary, *m.* 9 Aug. 1883, Edward John Wolfe, son of Ven. John Charles Wolfe, Archdeacon of Clogher (*see* WOLFE *of Forenaghts*).
  3. Philip Savage, of Park House, Wexford, *b.* 24 May, 1828, late Capt. 95th Regt., Hon. Col., J.P. co. Wexford, *m.* 16 April, 1857, Katherine Annette, 2nd dau. of Richard Clayton Browne Clayton, of Adlington Hall, co. Lancaster, and Carigbyrne Lodge, co. Wexford (*see* BROWNE-CLAYTON *of Browne's Hill*). She *d.* 3 April, 1909. He *d.* 28 May, 1886, leaving issue.
    1. PHILIP CLAYTON, now of Wilton.
    2. Arthur Henry, *b.* 14 June, 1872.
    1. Katherine Annette Pauline, *m.* 24 April, 1879, Rev. Thomas J. Yarde, of Culver House, Chudleigh, and *d.* 1893.
    2. Clotilde Henrietta.   3. Edith Mary.
  4. George Augustus (Rev.), *b.* 12 Aug. 1829; *d.* 9 April, 1905; *m.* 30 July, 1860, Katharine, dau. of Rev. Robert Fishbourne, Rector of Ferns, co. Wexford, and had issue,
    James Augustus, *b.* 25 July, 1861.
  1. Elinor Catherine, *d. unm.* 1 Nov. 1908.
  2. Henrietta, *m.* 1853, William Russell Farmar, of Bloomfield, co. Wexford, who *d.* 20 Sept. 1871.
  3. Elizabeth Louisa, *m.* July, 1856, Henry Eckersal Wynne, and *d.* 16 May, 1888.
  4. Margaret Charlotte, *m.* 1851, David Beatty, of Borodale, co. Wexford, who *d.* 5 April, 1881.
  5. Sarah, *m.* 1848, Sir Thomas John Fetherston, 5th bart., of Ardagh, who *d.* 21 Sept. 1869. Lady Fetherston *d.* 27 Jan. 1872.
The eldest son,
HARRY ALCOCK, of Wilton, J.P. and D.L., Hon.-Col. Wexford Militia, High Sheriff 1846, *b.* 27 July, 1821; and *d.s.p.* 12 July, 1893, leaving his property to his nephew.

Arms—Arg., a fess, between three cocks' heads, erased sa.
Crest—On a pomeis, charged with a cross pattée or, a cock statant sa. *Motto*—Vigilate.
Seat—Wilton Castle, Enniscorthy. *Club*—Kildare Street, Dublin.

ALCOCK-STAWELL-RIVERSDALE. *See* STAWELL.

ALDWORTH OF NEWMARKET.

JOHN CHARLES OLIVER ALDWORTH, of Newmarket Court, co. Cork, formerly Lieut. 3rd Batt. King's Shropshire Lt. Inf., Capt. and Hon. Major late 9th Batt. King's Royal Rifle Corps, served in S. Africa (Queen's Medal and four clasps and King's Medal), *b.* 2 Dec. 1869; *s.* his cousin 12 March, 1907; *m.* 27 Aug. 1901, Lena Stephanie Cecil, elder dau. of late John Stephen Collins, J.P., of Ardnalee (*see that family*), and has issue, three daus.,

1. Dorothy Agnes St. Leger.   2. Susan Stephanie Cecil Letitia.
3. Mary Katherine Elizabeth.

Lineage.—RICHARD ALDWORTH obtained a grant of part of the Earl of Desmond's forfeited estate near Short Castle, Mallow, *temp.* ELIZABETH. He *m.* Ellen Poer, and was father of
SIR RICHARD ALDWORTH, Knt., Provost-Marshal and Vice-President of Munster, to whom the manor and estate of Newmarket were granted, 1 March, 1621. He *m.* Anne Mervin, and *d.s.p.* 21 June, 1629 (Fun. Ent.). That property devolved in succession to
SIR RICHARD ALDWORTH, Knt., of Newmarket, eldest son of William Aldworth (who was the elder brother of Sir Richard Ald-

worth, the Provost-Marshal). Sir Richard *m.* Martha, dau. of Sir Robert Travers, niece of Michael Boyle, the Primate, and widow of Capt. Robert Stannard, and had a son and heir,
BOYLE ALDWORTH, of Newmarket, who *m.* Elizabeth, dau. of William Culliford, and had an only son,
RICHARD ALDWORTH, of Newmarket, *b.* in 1694; *m.* Elizabeth (the only lady ever made a Freemason), dau. of Arthur, 1st Lord Doneraile, and had issue,
  1. BOYLE, his heir.
  2. ST. LEGER, who was created *Lord Doneraile* (*see* BURKE'S *Peerage*).
Mr. Aldworth *d.* 25 April, 1776, and was *s.* by his eldest son,
BOYLE ALDWORTH, of Newmarket, *m.* 1st, Jane, dau. of Robert Oliver, of Cloughnodfoy, co. Limerick, and by her had issue,
  1. RICHARD, of Newmarket, of Rockmill Lodge, and of Ann's Grove, co. Cork, *b.* 1741; *m.* 1 Feb. 1770, Anne (relict of Admiral Thomas Cotes), dau. of John Ryder, D.D., Archbishop of Tuam, by Alicia, dau. of John Wilmot, of Osmaston (she was *b.* 8 June, 1743, and *d.* 10 May, 1827), and *d.s.p.* 4 April, 1824, aged 83.
  2. Robert, *d.* young.
  1. Jane, *m.* Phineas Bury.
  2. Elizabeth, *m.* John Flood.
  3. Mary.   4. Susan.
He *m.* 2ndly, Oct. 1755, Martha, dau. of Col. Christopher Rogers, of Lota, co. Cork, and by her had issue,
  3. St. Leger, *d.s.p.* 1823.   4. Christopher, *d.s.p.* 1796.
  5. ROBERT ROGERS, who carried on the line.
Mr. Aldworth *d.* 7 Dec. 1788. His youngest son,
ROBERT ROGERS ALDWORTH, of Newmarket, *m.* 12 March, 1793, Elizabeth, dau. of the Ven. John Oliver, Archdeacon of Ardagh, and had issue,
  1. RICHARD OLIVER, late of Newmarket.
  2. John (Rev.), Rector of Glanworth, co. Cork, *b.* 28 Dec. 1800; *m.* 1st, 5 May, 1826, Anne, dau. of Charles Deane Oliver, of Rockmill Lodge, co. Cork. She *d.* 7 Nov. 1845, leaving issue. He *m.* 2ndly, 10 June, 1847, Mary, dau. of William Jackson, of Youghal. She *d.s.p.* 12 Dec. 1864. He *d.* 12 June, 1878, having by his 1st wife had issue,
    1. Charles Oliver, of Poulacurra and Ballybrack, co. Cork, *b.* 3 Aug. 1829; *d.* 7 Nov. 1896; *m.* 13 Feb. 1868, Sarah, dau. of William Crooke Ronayne, of Cork, and widow of Robert James Martin, of Dublin, and had issue,
      (1) JOHN CHARLES OLIVER, now of Newmarket.
      (2) William Ronayne Oliver, *b.* 23 March, 1874.
    2. Robert St. Leger (Rev.), Rector of Athnowen, co. Cork, *b.* 8 July, 1832; *d.* 1893; *m.* 9 Sept. 1871, Sarah Pratt, dau. of Noblett Dunscombe Parker, of Carrigrohan Lodge, co. Cork, M.D.
    3. Richard FitzJohn, District Inspector Royal Irish Constabulary, *b.* 22 Oct. 1836; *m.* 1st, 7 April, 1869, Elizabeth MacGregor, dau. of William Hutton, of Headview House, co. Waterford, and by her (who *d.* 3 May, 1889, had issue,
      Oliver Fitzmaurice, *b.* 5 March, 1870; *d.* 9 April, 1884.
He *m.* 2ndly, 9 Nov. 1891, Maria Louisa, dau. of Rev. E. Loftus FitzGerald, and *d.s.p.s.* 10 Feb. 1893.
    4. St. Leger Hewitt, *d.* 19 June, 1850.
    1. Elizabeth Katherine, *m.* 20 May, 1871, Rev. Percival Walsh Jordan, Rector of Drayton, co. Oxford, and had issue. She *d.* 17 April, 1908.
    2. Sarah Maria.   3. Letitia Agnes.
  3. St. Leger, Comm. R.N., of Dunmabon, Carrigdownane and Dungansillagh, co. Cork, J.P., *b.* 4 Sept. 1806; *m.* 20 Oct. 1836, Alicia Susan Deane, dau. of Charles Deane Oliver, of Rockmill Lodge, and *d.* 6 Jan. 1877, having by her (who *d.* 23 Nov. 1874) had issue,
    Robert Oliver, Capt. 49th Regt., *b.* 14 May, 1839; *d. unm.* 31 July, 1874.
    Alicia Emily Hester St. Leger, of Beechmount and Carrigdownane, co. Cork.
  4. Robert, of Glouncaume and Meenkeragh, co. Cork, Col. (retired) N. Cork Rifles, late Capt. 94th Regt., *b.* 31 Oct. 1809; *m.* 29 April, 1852, Olivia Catherine, dau. of Rev. James Morton, Rector of Clonfert, and widow of George Wood, of Edghill, Liverpool. and *d.* 1 Sept. 1899, having had issue,
    1. Robert Morton, *b.* 29 July, 1854; *d.* 29 Aug. 1868.
    2. William, *b.* 3 Oct. 1855, D.S.O., Lieut.-Col. Duke of Cornwall's L.I., formerly Beds. Regt., killed in action at Paardeberg, S. Africa, when gallantly leading his regiment, 18 Feb. 1900, *d. unm.*
    3. St. Leger Boyle, of Meenkeragh, co. Cork, late District Superintendent Burmah Police, and Deputy Commissioner, Arakan Hill Tracts, *b.* 18 May, 1863.
    4. John James Richard Oliver, Malay Federated States Civil Service, *b.* 18 Sept. 1866; *m.* 24 May, 1905, Dorothea Anne Harvey, dau. of Richard W. Drew, of Bechingley House, Surrey, and has issue,
      Robert Harvey, *b.* 17 Nov. 1906.
      Kathleen Olivia, *b.* 14 Nov. 1908.
    1. Olivia (*Claremont, Dorking*).
    2. Adelaide Louisa, *m.* 24 June, 1880, Rev. Charles James Ferguson, D.D., Rector of Clondalkin co. Dublin, and has issue, three sons and two daus.
    3. Letitia Charlotte, *d.* young, 1861.
    4. Jane Dorothea Sophia.
Mr. Aldworth *d.* 28 Jan. 1836. His eldest son,
RICHARD OLIVER ALDWORTH, of Newmarket, co. Cork, J.P. and D.L., High Sheriff 1832–33, *b.* 2 Feb. 1794; *m.* 22 Jan. 1824, Lady Letitia Hare, eldest dau. of Richard, Viscount Ennismore (eldest son of William, 1st Earl of Listowel), and *d.* 27 Feb. 1887, having by her (who *d.* 19 Sept. 1874) had issue,
  1. RICHARD WILLIAM, late of Newmarket.

2. ROBERT, late of Newmarket.
3. William St. Leger (Rev.), Vicar of Eardisley, co. Hereford, b. 21 Feb. 1829 ; m. June, 1853, Mary, 3rd dau. of William Stark Dougall, of Scotscraig, co. Fife, and d.s.p. 29 Dec. 1865.
4. John (Rev.), b. 8 Sept. 1832 ; d. 18 April, 1896.
1. Katherine Anne.
The eldest son,
COL. RICHARD WILLIAM ALDWORTH, of Newmarket Court, co. Cork, Col. late 7th Royal Fusiliers, J.P. for cos. Cork, Kerry, and Limerick, D.L. co. Cork, High Sheriff co. Cork, 1869 ; b. 31 Jan. 1825 ; m. 30 July, 1863, Lady Mary Catherine Henrietta Bernard, eldest dau. of Francis, 3rd Earl of Bandon, and d.s.p. 4 Feb. 1899. He was s. by his brother,
ROBERT ALDWORTH, of Newmarket Court, co. Cork, and Westlake, co. Somerset, J.P. for both cos., Barrister-at-Law, formerly Capt. and Hon. Major 9th Batt. King's Royal Rifles, b. 11 June, 1827 ; m. 23 May, 1867, Louisa Mary (who d. 13 May, 1903), eldest dau. and co-heir of Major-Gen. Henry Dunbar Tolley, C.B., by Frances his wife, sister of 6th and 7th Viscounts Midleton. He d. 12 March, 1907, being s. by his kinsman.
Arms—Arg., a fess engrailed between six billets, gu. *Crest*— A dexter arm embowed in armour, the hand grasping a straight sword, all ppr. *Motto*—Nec temere, nec timide.
Seat—Newmarket Court, co. Cork.

ALEXANDER OF MILFORD.

JOHN ALEXANDER, of Milford House, co. Carlow, J.P., High Sheriff 1891, formerly Major King's Dragoon Guards, b. 23 Sept. 1850 ; s. his father 1885 ; m. 22 April, 1896, Ethel, dau. of Kennett Bayley, of Sevenoaks, Inchicore, co. Dublin, and has issue,
1. JOHN, b. 9 July, 1898.   2. Kennett, b. 22 March, 1900.
3. William, b. 13 May, 1901.   4. George, b. 21 Dec. 1907.
1. Jane.
Lineage.—THE REV. ANDREW ALEXANDER, D.D., Presbyterian minister, went from Scotland and settled in the north of Ireland, A.D. 1618. He m. Dorothea, dau. of Rev. James Caulfeild, D.D., and dying circa 1641, left a son,
ANDREW ALEXANDER, of Ballyclose, Newtownlimavady (attainted by JAMES II., 1689), m. 1st, a dau. of Sir Thomas Phillips, called Governor Phillips, and had a son and heir, JACOB. He m. 2ndly, a dau. of the Laird of Hilles, and had a son, JOHN, of whom alter as ancestor of ALEXANDER of Milford. The eldest son,
JACOB ALEXANDER, of Newtownlimavady, m. 1692, Margaret (or Jane), dau. and heiress of John Oliver, of The Lodge, Newtownlimavady, chief magistrate appointed to administer the oath of allegiance on the accession of WILLIAM and MARY, and had issue. The eldest son,
JAMES ALEXANDER, of Newtownlimavady, merchant, m. Elizabeth Ross, of Newtownlimavady, and had issue. Mr. Alexander (whose will was proved 4 July, 1786) was s. by his eldest son,
LESLEY ALEXANDER, of Newtownlimavady, who m. Anna Simpson, of Armagh, and had issue,
1. John, of Newtownlimavady, m. Margaret, dau. of Samuel Maxwell, and dying 1853, left issue,
  1. Lesley, 11th Hussars, d. unm.
  2. Alexander, d. unm.
  3. Samuel Maxwell, of Roe Park, J.P. and D.L., High Sheriff co. Londonderry, b. 1834 ; m. 22 April, 1884, Henrietta Constance, dau. of Sir Frederick William Heygate, Bart., and d.s.p. 10 June, 1886.
  4. John, of Newtownlimavady, b. 1836 ; d. unm.
  1. Anna, m. 1857, Alfred John Stanton, M.P., and d. 1858.
  2. Jane, m. 1850, E. F. C. Ritter. He d. 1891, leaving issue. She d. 23 March, 1903.
2. James, of Gortinesson, co. Derry.
3. Lesley, of Foyle Park, J.P. and D.L., m. 1835, Amelia Maria, dau. of Col. Bates, but d.s.p.
4. Alexander, d. 1832.
5. THOMAS, late of Buncrana.
  1. Louisa.   2. Jane, m. William Moody.
  3. Elizabeth.
The youngest son,
THOMAS ALEXANDER, of Frowick House, Essex, and Buncrana, co. Donegal, and 70, Lancaster Gate, Hyde Park, High Sheriff co. Donegal 1852, b. 1791 ; m. 1836, Jane, eldest dau. of William Haigh, of Westfield House, Doncaster (who d. 12 May, 1828), and Rosetta Alethea Martin his wife (who d. 1834). She d. 24 Feb. 1875. He d. 17 Feb. 1867, having had issue,
1. LESLEY WILLIAM, of Buncrana, co. Donegal, and of Ahilly, b. 15 Aug. 1841 ; d. unm. 15 July, 1909.
2. James, b. 1843 ; d. 19 Aug. 1869.
3. Thomas, d. 2 Sept. 1877.
4. Edward Merydeth Edgworth, d. unm.
1. Anna Louisa, m. Capt. S. S. Bristowe, of Hutoft, Lincolnshire.
2. Rosetta, m. 7 May, 1861, Algernon Bathurst, son of Sir James and Lady Caroline Bathurst. He d. 16 Feb. 1895.
3. Elizabeth Frances, d. unm. Oct. 1897.
We now return to JOHN ALEXANDER above mentioned. This JOHN ALEXANDER, of Ballyclose, Newtownlimavady, co. Londonderry, and Gunsland, co. Donegal, son of Andrew Alexander, of Ballyclose, by his second wife, m. Anne, dau. of John White, of Cady Hall, co. Londonderry, and d. 12 March, 1747, leaving issue,
1. JOHN, of whose line we treat.
2. NATHANIEL, ancestor of the ALEXANDERS of Portglenone, and of the EARLS OF CALEDON.

3. William, ancestor of ALEXANDER, Bart., of Dublin.
1. Martha, m. Alexander Kellie.
The eldest son,
JOHN ALEXANDER, of Londonderry, b. 1689 ; m. Sarah, dau. of Alexander Macaulay, of Drumnagisson, co. Antrim. He d. 1766, leaving, with other issue, a son,
JOHN ALEXANDER, of Ardmoulin, co. Down, b. 26 Jan. 1736 ; m. 29 May, 1760, Anne, dau. of George Portis, and dying 23 Dec. 1821, was s. by his son,
JOHN ALEXANDER, of Milford, co. Carlow, b. 27 Feb. 1764 ; m. 8 Sept. 1801, Christian, dau. of Lorenzo Nickson Izod, of Chapel Izod, co. Kilkenny. She d. 13 Dec. 1864, leaving issue,
1. JOHN, of Milford.
2. Lorenzo William, b. 22 Oct. 1810 ; m. 25 June, 1857, Harriet, dau. of Col. Henry Bruen, of Oak Park, co. Carlow, and d. 21 Sept. 1867, leaving
  1. Henry Bruen, b. 8 Nov. 1860.
  1. Christian.
  2. Anne, m. 21 Dec. 1886, Henry E. W. de Robeck, Wicklow Art., late Capt. R.A., eldest son of Baron de Robeck.
3. George, of Erindale, co. Carlow, J.P., Barrister-at-Law, b. 17 Feb. 1814 ; m. 28 Feb. 1861, Susan Henn (d. July, 1895), dau. of Stephen Collins, Q.C., of Merrion Square, Dublin (see COLLINS of Ardnalea), and d. 1893, leaving issue,
  1. John Stephen, b. 4 Jan. 1862.   2. Frank, b. 26 Jan. 1864.
  3. James Leslie, Major Indian Army, b. 1 May, 1868 ; m. 17 Oct. 1903, Emily Shakespear, youngest dau. of Gen. Sir Robert Cunliffe Low, G.C.B., and has issue a son, b. 17 April, 1907.
  4. Walter Lorenzo, Capt. Yorks. Regt., b. 8 Sept., 1872 ; m. and has issue, a son, b. 18 April, 1905.
  1. Christian Izod.
4. James, b. 8 March, 1818 ; m. 12 July, 1855, Lucia Margaret, dau. of Sir William Clarke Travers, Bart. She d. 7 Feb. 1893. He d.s.p. 9 Feb. 1882.
5. Charles Leslie (Rev.), b. 28 April, 1820 ; m. 26 Jan. 1882, Hon. Emily Caroline Fremantle, dau. of 1st Lord Cottesloe, and d.s.p. 1888.
6. Henry, Gen. in the Army, b. 17 Aug. 1822.
1. Anne, m. 6 Oct. 1828, John Cranstoun, and d.s.p. 10 April, 1862.
2. Lucia, d. unm. 7 Oct. 1877.
3. Fanny, m. 19 Oct. 1847, Rev. Charles Henry Travers.
Mr. Alexander d. 16 Aug. 1863. His eldest son,
JOHN ALEXANDER, of Milford House, co. Carlow, M.A., High Sheriff 1824, and M.P. for Carlow 1853 to 1859, b. 26 July, 1802 ; m. 18 Oct. 1848, Esther, eldest dau. of Matthew Brinkley, of Parsonstown, co. Meath, 2nd son of Right Rev. John Brinkley, Bishop of Cloyne, and d. Oct. 1885, leaving issue,
1. JOHN, now of Milford.
2. William Cranstoun, b. 5 Nov. 1851 ; m. 8 Feb. 1879, Edith Caroline, dau. of Col. William Longfield, of Ashgrove, co. Cork.
3. Lorenzo, of Sandon, British Columbia, b. 28 Aug. 1833 ; m. 28 Dec. 1899, Charlotte Catherine Louisa, dau. of Arthur John Campbell Gwatkin (see BURKE'S *Family Records*), and has issue,
  A son, b. 30 May, 1901.
  A dau., b. 13 Oct. 1902.
4. Charles Henry, Maj. R.A., b. 2 June, 1856 ; m. 17 March, 1891, Isabel Annie, dau. of Gen. Sir Campbell Claye Ross, K.C.B., of Lothian House, Ryde.
5. George, Barrister-at-Law, b. 20 June, 1858.
1. Harriet Lucia, m. 8 July, 1875, Lieut.-Col. E. G. M. Donnithorne, late Scots Greys, and has issue.
Seat—Milford House, near Carlow. Clubs—Naval and Military, and Kildare Street.

ALEXANDER OF FORKILL.

GRANVILLE HENRY JACKSON ALEXANDER, of Forkill House, co. Armagh, J.P. and D.L., High Sheriff, 1883, late Lieut. 83rd Regt. and Capt. 3rd Batt., Royal Irish Fus., b. 26 June, 1852 ; m. 25 Feb. 1880, Daisy, dau. of M. Mathews, of San Francisco.
Lineage.— NATHANIEL ALEXANDER, of Gunsland, co. Donegal, b. 1689, 2nd son of JOHN ALEXANDER, of Ballyclose, co. Londonderry, and of Gunsland, co. Donegal (see ALEXANDER *of Milford*), and grandson of ANDREW ALEXANDER, of Ballyclose. He was admitted an alderman of Londonderry 1755. He m. Elizabeth, dau. of William McClintock, of Dunmore, co. Donegal (see BURKE'S *Peerage*, RATHDONNELL, B.), and d. 22 Sept. 1761, having had issue,
1. WILLIAM, of London, Barrister-at-Law, m. 1 Jan. 1753, Charlotte, dau. of Messenger Monsey, M.D., of Chelsea Hospital. She d. 11 Oct. 1798. He d. 1774, leaving issue,
  1. Monsey (Rev.), incumbent of Moville, co. Derry, m. Susan

Alexander. THE LANDED GENTRY. 6

Maria, dau. of James McClintock. He d. 1790, having by her (who m. 2ndly, Rev. Samuel Law Montgomery) had an only dau., Dorothea, m. 1816, Rev. Alexander Staples, D.D., rector of Gowran. She d. 1859. He d. 1864, leaving issue.
2. William, d. unm. 3. John, d. unm.
4. Robert, E.I.C.S., and member of council at Madras, b. April, 1771; m. 1st, dau. of — Williams, and had a son,
(1) James Williams, B.S.C., d.s.p.
He m. 2ndly, 6 May, 1809, Grace, dau. of Rev. St. John Blacker, D.D. She d. 19 Oct. 1835. He d. 15 July, 1861, aged 90, having had,
(2) Robert, of Holwood, Kent, C.B., B.S.C., b. 2 July 1813; m. 1st, 8 Oct. 1846, Caroline Skelton, dau. of George Murray. She d.s.p. 29 July, 1859. He m. 2ndly, 13 Dec. 1870, Emmeline Bethia, dau. of R. K. Greville, LL.D., and widow of Major-Gen. H. Drummond. He d.s.p. 16 Aug. 1882.
(1) Charlotte, m. 17 Aug. 1850, John Muddelle.
(2) Mary, m. 6 April, 1837, Rev. Sir St. Vincent Love Hammick, 2nd bart., who d. 19 Feb. 1888. She d. 17 July, 1902, leaving issue (see BURKE's *Peerage*).
1. Charlotte Grace.
2. Elizabeth, m. 27 Dec. 1803, Henry Harmer, of Bicton Hall, Salop. 3. Mary.
4. Anne, m. William Dalton, and d.s.p. 1840.
5. Jemima, m. 1789, Rev. John Edward Rolfe. She d. 25 June, 1827. He d. 24 July, 1795, leaving issue.
6. Catherine, m. 1800, Ven. John Bedingfeld Collyer, archdeacon of Norwich, and had issue.
2. ROBERT, of Boom Hall.
3. JAMES, 1ST EARL OF CALEDON (see BURKE's *Peerage*).
1 Mary Jane, m. 1st, Joseph Weld, and 2ndly, Hamilton Maclure, and had issue.
2. Rebecca, m. 1766, Josias Du Pré, of Wilton Park, Bucks, and d. 1800.
Alderman Alexander d. 22 Sept. 1761. His 2nd son,
ROBERT ALEXANDER, of Boom Hall, co. Londonderry, m. Anne, dau. and coheir of Henry McCulloch. She d. 20 Jan. 1817. He d. 27 March, 1790, leaving issue.
1. NATHANIEL (Right Rev.), of whom presently.
2. Henry, of Glentogher, co. Donegal, M.P. in several Parliaments, b. 1763, m. 14 Feb. 1807, Dorothy, dau. of Francis Rivers. She d. 10 Dec. 1864. He d. 6 May, 1818, leaving issue,
1. James, B.C.S., b. 12 Jan. 1813; m. 6 Nov. 1849, Catherine, dau. of Richard Harvey. She d. 6 Dec. 1879. He d.s.p. 28 Feb. 1851.
1. Mary.
2. Ann, m. 1838, Maj.-Gen. George Rowlandson. He d. 31 May, 1875. She d. 6 April, 1851, leaving issue.
3. Catherine. 4. Fanny.
3. William, Lieut.-Gen. in the Army, b. 1768; m. 1793, Matilda, dau. of Sir Robert Waller, Bart. She d. 1850. He d. 1 Jan. 1824, leaving a son and a dau.,
1. Robert (Rev.), Prebendary of Derry and Rector of Aghadoe, b. 17 Sept. 1795; m. 16 Oct. 1820, Dorothea, dau. and heir of Henry McClintock, of Rathdonnell House, co. Donegal (see BURKE's *Peerage*, RATHDONNELL, B.). She d. 17 May, 1877. He d. 11 May, 1872, leaving issue,
(1) William (Most Rev.), D.D., D.C.L., Archbishop of Armagh (see BURKE's *Peerage*), b. 13 April, 1824; d. Aug. 1911; m. 15 Oct. 1850, Cecil Frances, dau. of Maj. John Humphreys, D.L., of Miltown House, co. Tyrone. She d. 12 Oct. 1895, leaving issue,
1a. Robert Jocelyn, B.A. Oxford, b. 11 June, 1852; m. 5 Jan. 1876, Alice Rachael, dau. of J. J. H. Humphreys, of Lincoln's Inn, and had issue,
William Harold, b. 26 Feb., d. 5 Dec. 1880.
2a. Cecil John Francis, b. 16 March, 1855; d. 28 March, 1910; m. 27 July, 1882, Eva Frances, dau. of Right Hon. Arthur MacMurrough Kavanagh, of Borris, co. Carlow (see that family), and by her (who d. 27 Sept. 1896), had issue,
Arthur Cecil, d. unm., 29 Oct., 1907.
1a. Eleanor Jane.
2a. Dorothea Agnes, m. 22 July, 1893, George John Bowen.
(2) Henry McClintock, Rear-Adm. R.N., b. 7 Oct. 1834; m. 1st, 22 Oct. 1864, Eliza Frances Charlotte, only dau. of Sir W. S. Wiseman, 8th bart. She d. 1 April, 1875 leaving issue,
1a. Robert William Wiseman, b. 11 Jan. 1870.
1a. Kathleen Henrietta, d. 6 Feb. 1877.
2a. Charlotte Marion.
3a. Agatha Frances Mary, m. Christopher B. L. Lefroy, and d. 27 June, 1903.
He m. 2ndly, 16 Jan. 1877, Agnes, widow of Col. J. Wray, and dau. of Capt. J. Hannay. He d. 17 Dec. 1896.
(1) Mary, m. 17 Sept. 1845, Wm. Keown, M.P. (who assumed the name of Boyd), of Ballydugan, co. Down, and by him (who d. 19 Jan. 1877) had issue. She d. 15 Nov. 1905.
(2) Matilda, m. 10 July, 1845 Maximilian Hammond Dalison, of Hamptons, Kent. He d. 30 March, 1902. She d. 15 April, 1903, leaving issue.
(3) Elizabeth, m. 10 Jan. 1856, Very Rev. A. Ferguson Smyly, Dean of Derry. She d. 9 May, 1875, leaving issue (see SMYLY of *Camus*).
(4) Catherine, m. 4 June, 1861, Jas. Sinclair (see SINCLAIR of *Holyhill and Bonnyglen*), and d. his widow 15 Jan. 1906, having had issue.
(5) Dorothea, m. 10 Jan. 1856, Lieut.-Col. H. Keown, late R.I Rifles.
2. William Ferguson.

1. Catherine, m. George Thompson, of Clonskeagh Castle, co. Dublin and d. 1836.
4. James, of Somerhill, Kent, D.L., M.P. in many Parliaments, b. 1769; m. 1st, Eliza, dau. of Capt. Dundas, of Manour, co. Stirling, by whom he had,
1. Eliza Charlotte, m. 3 Sept. 1825, Stratford Canning, Viscount Stratford de Redcliffe, G.C.B. She d. 25 Nov. 1882. He d. 14 Aug. 1880.
He m. 2ndly, 8 March, 1813, Charlotte Sophia, dau. of Thomas Dashwood, and widow of the Hon. Charles Andrew Bruce (see BURKE's *Peerage*, ELGIN, E.). She d. 11 April, 1870. He d. 12 Sept. 1848, leaving issue,
1. Robert, of Uphaven, Wilts, b. 10 Feb. 1815; m. 23 July, 1844, Julia Charlotte, dau. of W. Fane, Bengal C.S. She d. 1903. He d. 23 Oct. 1863, having had issue,
(1) James Fane, of Uphaven, formerly Capt. 17th Lancers, b. 1 Jan. 1846; m. 16 Sept. 1884, Aurea Otway, dau. of Major Henry Otway Mayne (of Mayne's Horse), and d. 31 Dec. 1891, leaving issue,
1a. Paul Robert Mayne, b. 16 Sept. 1885.
2a. Charles Otway, b. 1 Jan. 1888.
3a. William James, b. 6 July, 1891.
(1) Amy Louisa, d. 7 June, 1870. (2) Emily Maude.
2. James, of Oak Bank, Sevenoaks, b. 7 May, 1822; m. 13 May, 1845, Anna Maria Julia, dau. of Maximilian D. D. Dalison, of Hamptons, Kent (who d. 30 May, 1910), and d. 8 Aug. 1899, leaving issue,
(1) James Dalison, of Oakbank, near Sevenoaks, late Capt. West Kent Yeomanry Cavalry, D.L. for Kent (70, *Cadogan Square, S.W.*), b. 5 March, 1846; m. 27 Jan. 1885, Lady Emily Harriet Catherine Boyle, eldest dau. of Earl of Cork and Orrery, K.P., and has issue,
1a. James Ulick Francis Canning, Lieut. Coldstream Gds., b. 10 Feb. 1889.
2a. James Cedric St. Lawrence, b. 15 July, 1897.
1a. Evelyn Catherine, b. 21 March, 1887; m. 5 Jan. 1909, Claud Alfred Victor Sykes, Grenadier Gds., of West Ella, near Hull, and d. 27 April, 1909.
2a. Jacqueline Harriet, b. 7 June, 1892.
(2) Charles Robert, Barrister-at-Law, b. 8 Nov. 1847; d. 17 Feb. 1902.
(3) Evelyn Ferguson (Rev.), B.A. Oxon., b. 23 March, 1850; d. unm. 24 Feb. 1887.
(1) Mabel Emma.
2. Charlotte Sophia, d. unm. 1897.
3. Anne, d. unm. 1886.
4. Emma, d. unm. 1843.
5. Josias Du Pré, an East India Director, and for some years M.P. for Old Sarum, b. 1771; m. 1 Feb. 1808, Mary, dau. of the Rev. Thomas Bracken. She d. 13 Nov. 1868. He d. 20 Aug. 1839, having had issue,
1. Caledon Du Pré, of Auberies, Essex, D.L., Capt. 1st Life Guards, b. 16 Nov. 1817; m. 1843, Caroline, 2nd dau. of James Ewing, and d. 18 July, 1884, having by her (who d. 15 Dec. 1891) had issue,
(1) Caledon James, Capt. Coldstream Guards, m. 17 Sept. 1874, Nina Stewart, eldest dau. of Col. Sir John Stewart Wood, K.C.B., and d. 21 Sept. following.
(2) Francis, Lieut. R.N., m. 31 Jan. 1883, Caroline Mary, dau. of Lieut.-Col. Arthur Tremayne, of Carclew, formerly 13th Light Dragoons.
(3) William Merk, drowned in the River Tweed, 2 May, 1885, aged 23.
(4) Harvey, D.S.O., Lieut.-Col. 10th Hussars (*Res.—The Grange, Chetnole, Sherborne*), b. 3 June, 1859; m. 17 April, 1890, Mildred Maria, youngest dau. of Charles Prideaux-Brune, of Prideaux Place, Cornwall, and has issue,
1a. Caledon James, b. 1895.
2a. Robert Dudley, b. 1899.
1a. Constance Isolda.
(5) Reginald.
(1) Janet, m. 17 June, 1871, Maj.-Gen. E. A. Wood, C.B., who d. 22 May, 1898, leaving issue.
(2) Mary (3) Louisa.
(4) Margot.
2. Josias Bracken Canning, b. 12 Dec. 1826; m. 11 Jan. 1848, Agnes Cecilia, dau. of Sir William Curtis, 2nd bart., and d. 1882, leaving issue,
(1) Josias William, I.C.S., b. 14 May, 1849; d. unm.
(2) Frederick, late R.N., b. 13 Dec. 1852.
(3) Atwell Lake, b. 8 June, 1856.
(4) Henry Charles, b. 25 March, 1858.
(5) Horace Bracken, b. 30 Aug. 1859.
(6) Charles, b. 7 Nov. 1860.
(7) George Frank, b. 15 Jan. 1862.
(8) William Montague, b. 24 June, 1865.
(9) Edward Stewart, b. 6 Nov. 1867.
(10) Frank Beaufort, b. 13 May, d. 17 Oct. 1869.
(1) Agnes Mary.
(2) Jessie Louisa, m. G. S. Everard.
(3) Caroline Isabella.
(4) Gertrude Mary Ann (twin with Charles).
(5) Madelina Louisa. (6) Ellen Augusta.
(7) Lucy Georgina. (8) Constance Maud.
1. Mary Anne, m. 1837, J. Pratt Barlow, who d. 21 Aug. 1871.
2. Lucy Emma.
3. Eliza, m. 22 Jan. 1842, Robert Holbeche Dolling, of Magheralin, co. Down, and d. 2 Jan. 1870. He d. 28 Sept. 1878, leaving issue.
4. Charlotte Maria, d. unm. 5. Ellen Louisa, d. unm.
6. Madeline, m. 2 Sept. 1845, Admiral Frederick William

IRELAND. Ancketill.

Pleydell-Bouverie, late R.N., and has issue (*see* BURKE'S *Peerage*, RADNOR, E.). He *d.* 17 July, 1898.
7. Fanny Selina, *m.* 22 Jan. 1846, Rev. Francis Simpson, M.A., vicar of Foston-on-the-Wolds, Yorkshire, and left issue.
8. Agnes Henrietta.
1. Elizabeth, *m.* Sir And. Ferguson, Bart., of The Farm, Londonderry, M.P., who *d.* in 1808, leaving issue.
2. Anne, *m.* Col. Alexander Scott, Royal Artillery, and had issue.
The eldest son,
THE RIGHT REV. NATHANIEL ALEXANDER, D.D., P.C., Bishop of Meath, *b.* 12 Aug. 1760, *m.* 18 May, 1785, Anne, dau. of the Right Hon. Richard Jackson, M.P., of Coleraine. She *d.* Aug. 1837. He *d.* 21 Oct. 1840, leaving issue,
1. Robert (Rev.), of Portglenone, co. Antrim, *b.* 19 June, 1788 ; *m.* 1st, 21 Aug. 1813, Catherine, youngest dau. of the Right Hon. John Staples, M.P. She *d.* 12 March, 1830, leaving issue. He *m.* 2ndly, 1837, Hester Helena, dau. of Col. Alexander McManus. She *d.s.p.* 23 June, 1874 He *d.* July, 1840, having by his first wife had issue,
   1. Nathaniel, of Portglenone House, co. Antrim, M.P., *b.* Aug. 1815 ; *m.* 7 April, 1842, Florinda, 2nd dau. of Richard Boyle Bayley, by Alicia his wife, dau. of Richard, 2nd Lord Castlemaine, and *d.* 5 Jan. 1853, having by her whc *m.* 2ndiy, 1855, Edmund F. Leslie, of Donaghadee. co. Dcwn, and *d.* 24 May, 1861) had issue.
     (1) Robert Jackson, of Portglenone, J.P. and D.L., High Sheriff co. Antrim 1875, and Londonderry 1870, *b.* 18 Jan. 1843 ; *d. unm.* 1884.
     (2) John Staples, of Portglenone, J.P. and D.L., late R.N., *b.* 14 June, 1844 ; *d. unm.* 10 Oct. 1901.
   2. Robert, H.E.I.C.S., *b.* Nov. 1823 ; *m.* 17 Feb. 1863, Louisa, dau. of R. B. Bayley, and had issue,
     Robert Arthur Molony, *b.* 16 Feb. 1867.
   Florinda.
   1. Harriet, *m.* John Wakefield, and *d.s.p.* 1853.
   2. Grace, *m.* Thomas Gilbert Nicholson.
   3. Charlotte, *d. unm.* 1878.
   4. Catherine, *m.* Molyneux Pooley Shuldham.
2. James (Rev.), LL.D., *b.* 22 July, 1794 ; *m.* 14 Aug. 1833, Alicia Louisa, dau. of Samuel Dopping, of Lotown House, and *d.* 2 April, 1857, leaving issue,
   1. Samuel, *b.* 5 April, 1840.
   2. James, Lieut.-Col. late 38th Regt., *b.* 3 Jan. 1844 ; *d.* 8 May, 1907.
   1. Anna.   2. Mary Jane.
   3. Clarissa.
3. Nathaniel, *b.* 6 Dec. 1796 ; *m.* Sophia, dau. of N. Hickey, and widow of J. Young ; and *d.* 14 Oct. 1880, leaving issue,
   1. Nathaniel, *d. unm.* 24 Aug. 1864.
   2. Robert Hugh, *d.* in India.
   3. William James, *b.* 1836 ; *m.* Lucy, dau. of W. Gray, and *d.* 1885.
   4. John Henry, Col. R.II.A. (ret.), *b.* 22 May, 1839 ; *m.* 3 Nov. 1880, Katharine Mary, dau. of Gen. J. Francis, and *d.* 3 Feb. 1900, leaving issue,
     (1) Dorothy Katharine, *d.unm.* 1889.
     (2) Norah Katharine.   (3) Enid Rosamund.
   5. George Caledon, Barrister-at-Law (19, *Bury Street, S.W.*), *b.* 1842.
   1. Sophia Charlotte, *m.* Rev. Charles Rae Hay.
   2. Annie.
   3. Mary. *m.* 5 Dec. 1866, Arthur Thompson.
   4. Henrietta, *m.* Robert Scott.
4. HENRY, of whom presently.
5. George, Bengal C.S., *b.* 20 Jan. 1805 ; *m.* 1833, Rebecca, dau. of W. Molloy, and had issue,
   1. George.   2. William.
   3. James.
6. William Stuart, of Ballyarton, Londonderry, Bengal C.S. *b.* 29 Oct. 1807 ; *m.* 15 July, 1834, Janet Bethia, dau. of Brig.-Gen. Charles Dallas. She *d.* 13 Oct. 1876. He *d.* 9 July, 1883, leaving issue,
   1. William Stuart, *b.* 3 June, 1836 ; *m.* 5 Jan. 1862, Emma Sophia, dau. of S. Steward, and *d.* 13 Sept. 1868, leaving issue,
     William Frederick, *b.* 6 Feb. 1864.
     Bethia Emma.
   2. Nathaniel Stuart, J.P. Sussex, late Ind. C.S. (*Cecil House, Church Road, St. Leonards-on-Sea*). *b.* 14 June, 1838 ; *m.* 9 July, 1873, Dora, dau. of Edward Currie, and has issue,
     (1) William Nathaniel Stuart, Capt. Connaught Rangers, *b.* 8 May, 1874.
     (2) Edward Currie, D.S.O., Capt. Indian Army, *b.* 15 Sept. 1875.
     (3) Robert Dundas, Capt. Indian Army, *b.* 28 Aug. 1880.
     (1) Mary Bethia Isabel, *b.* 20 May, 1878.
     (2) Dora, *b.* 23 Dec. 1881 ; *d.* 5 Jan. 1882.
   3. Charles Dallas, M.A. Camb., *b.* 25 Dec. 1839 ; *m.* 19 Sept. 1874, Helen, dau. of Molyneux Shuldham, and has issue,
     William Dallas, *b.* 5 Aug. 1875.
   4. James Edward, Capt. R.A., *b.* 30 June, 1841 ; *m.* 19 July, 1870, Mary Elizabeth, dau. of A. R. Webster, and *d.s.p.* 9 June, 1873.
   5. Richard Dundas, *b.* 26 May, 1846 ; *m.* 17 Nov. 1870, Charlotte Augusta, dau. of Rev. A. R. Webster, and *d.* June, 1885, leaving issue,
     (1) Edward Bruce, *b.* 3 March, 1872.
     (2) Kenneth Bruce, *b.* 11 March, 1874.
     (1) Marion Bethia.
     (2) Charlotte Dora.

   6. Ernest Bruce, Bengal C.S., *b.* 13 Sept. 1849 ; *m.* 27 Oct. 1881, Ella Sarah, dau. of John William Williamson.
   1. Anne, *m.* Sept. 1813, Rev. John Molseworth Staples, Rector of Upper Moville. She *d.* 23 July, 1869. He *d.* 4 April, 1859, leaving issue (*see* BURKE'S *Peerage*).
   2. Mary.
   3. Eliza, *m.* 21 July, 1824, John A. Nicholson, of Balrath Bury. She *d.* 1860. He *d.* Dec. 1872, leaving issue (*see that family*).
   4. Henrietta Frances, *m.* 20 May, 1830, Robert Smyth, of Gaybrook, co. Westmeath. He *d.* 29 July, 1878.
The 4th son,
HENRY ALEXANDER, of Forkill House, co. Armagh, High Sheriff 1856, Barrister-at-Law, *b.* 16 Feb. 1803 ; *m.* 14 Aug. 1839, Louisa Juliana, 2nd dau. of Thomas, 2nd Earl of Ranfurly. She *d.* 31 March, 1896. He *d.* 1 Dec. 1877, leaving issue,
1. GRANVILLE HENRY JACKSON, now of Forkill House.
2. Henry Nathaniel, Inspector-Gen. of Prisons, Bombay, late Indian C.S., *b.* 7 June, 1854 ; *m.* 1883, Mary Stuart, dau. of Claude Erskine, B.C.S., and has issue,
   Constance Mary.
3. Claud Henry, Major late Wiltshire Regt. (*Bolton Lodge, Winchester*). *b.* 31 May, 1856 ; *m.* 1 Oct. 1896. Irene Christine, dau. of Col. William C. Tamplin, of Lennox Place, Brighton and has issue,
   1. Dorothy Alice, *b.* 8 Oct. 1897.
   2. Rosemary Irene, *b.* 18 Dec. 1900.
   3. Nancy Stuart, *b.* 11 Sept. 1902.
4. Ronald Henry, *b.* 15 Aug. 1858.
5. Frederick Henry Thomas, late Capt. Leicester Regt. and Army Pay Department, *b.* 30 Nov. 1860 ; *m.* 7 June, 1899, Blanche, dau. of Lieut.-Gen. W. C. Bancroft, of Knellwood, Farnborough, and has issue,
   1. Elisabeth Maud, *b.* 22 July, 1902.
   2. Freda Alice, *d.* an infant 25 March, 1905.
6. Dudley Henry, C.M.G., Major West Yorkshire Regt. (6. *St. James's Place, S.W. Club—United Service*), *b.* 13 Jan. 1863.
1. Blanche Catherine, *m.* 4 Sept. 1877, Rev. Frederick Anthony Hammond, of Loureston House, Dover, and *d.* 16 June, 1878.
2. Alice Mary Juliana.
3. Constance Henrietta Georgina, *m.* 3 Oct. 1867, Col. Gregory Colquhoun Grant, Indian Army, and has issue.
4. Emily Louisa, *m.* 25 March, 1874, Col. Arthur M. Hogg, Indian Army, and *d.* Aug. 1900, leaving issue.
5. Edith Ellen, *m.* 15 Aug. 1891, Henry Herbert Southey, 7th Bombay Lancers, and *d.* 27 May, 1892, leaving a dau.
Arms—Per pale arg. and sa. a chevron between in chief an annulet and in base a crescent, all counterchanged. *Crest*—An arm in armour embowed, the hand grasping a sword all ppr., on the elbow with an annulet sa. *Motto*—Per mare, per terras.
Seat—Forkill House, co. Armagh. *Clubs*—Carlton and White's, S.W., and St. George's Yacht.

ANCKETILL OF ANCKETILL'S GROVE.

WILLIAM ANCKETILL, of Ancketill's Grove, co. Monaghan, D.L. co. Monaghan, late Lieut. Royal Tyrone Fus., *b.* 16 March, 1851 ; *m.* 13 July, 1875, Jean Laing, dau. and co-heir of Robert Falkner, of Broughton Park, co. Lancaster, and has issue.
   Olive Maud, *b.* 28 Oct. 1876 ; *m.* 1st, 24 Oct. 1901, Reginald George Petre Wymer, late Lieut. Argyll and Sutherland Highlanders, only son of Capt. Reginald Augustus Wymer, 3rd Batt. Cameron Highlanders, late Ensign 91st Foot, and grandson of Sen. Sir Henry George Petre Wymer, K.C.B., and has issue a dau., Lovice Vivian Petre. She *m.* 2ndly, 1 Nov. 1907, Michael Linning Henry Melville, late Egyptian Civil Service. She *d.* 6 March, 1909, having had issue, a dau.
   Monica Agnes Ancketill, *b.* 2 July, 1908.
Lineage.—CAPT. OLIVER ANCKETILL, J.P. co. Monaghan, High Sheriff 1662, son of William Ancketill, of Shaftesbury, bapt. there 9 April, 1609 ; *m.* Rebecca, probably of the family of Bullingbrooke, of Galway, and *d.* 26 June, 1666, having had issue,
1. MATTHEW, his heir.
2. William, *b.* 1652, from whom the Anketells of Dernamuck trace their descent.
3. Richard, *b.* 1654.
1. Sarah, *m.* 1660, James Corry, ancestor of the Earls of Belmore.
2. Elizabeth, *b.* 1648.
The eldest son,
MATTHEW ANCKETILL, of Ancketill's Grove, co. Monaghan, *b.* 1651, to whom that estate was confirmed by patent, 19 CHARLES II. He was High Sheriff for the co. 1682, but was attainted by JAMES II. He *m.* Matilda, dau. of Robert Moore, of Ravella and Garvey, co. Tyrone, and was killed at the battle of Drumbanagher, 13 March, 1688, having had, with other issue,
1. WILLIAM, his heir.   2. OLIVER, *s.* his brother.
3. Robert.
1. Catherine, *b.* 1653 ; *m.* Thomas Singleton, of Fort Singleton.
The eldest son,
WILLIAM ANCKETILL, of Ancketill's Grove, co. Monaghan, High Sheriff 1707, *b.* 1677 ; *d. s.p.* 1709, and was *s.* by his next brother,
OLIVER ANCKETILL, of Ancketill's Grove, *b.* 1680, M.P. for borough of Monaghan, 1754 to 1760 ; M.A. and LL.B. Trinity Coll. Dublin, 1703 ; one of the original founders of the Royal Dublin Society ; High Sheriff for co. Monaghan, 1703 ; *m.* 1st, 28 Feb. 1716, Hon. Sarah Caulfeild, 2nd dau. of William, 2nd Viscount Charlemont, and by her (who *d.* Dec. 1742) had (with three daus., 1. Ann, *m.* 6 Nov. 1752, Rev. Edward Lill, D.D., brother of Godfrey Lill, Justice of the Court of Common Pleas ; 2. Rebecca, *m.* Samuel

Anderson. THE LANDED GENTRY. 8

Coulston, M.D.; 3. Catherine, *m.* Thomas Singleton, jun., of Fort Singleton) an only surviving son,
  1. WILLIAM, *b.* 18 March, 1724, who *d.v.p.* 1756; he *m.* 11 March, 1748, Anne, eldest dau. of Charles Coote, of Bellamont Forest, M.P. for co. Cavan, and sister of Charles, Earl of Bellamont, K.B., and had issue,
    1. CHARLES, successor to his grandfather, of whom presently.
    2. Richard, *b.* 1775; *d.s.p.* 1814.
    3. Matthew, of Arlington Castle, Portarlington, *b.* 1756, J.P., Capt. in 57th Regt., of which he obtained the Light Company in 1778; Lieut.-Col. Monaghan Militia, High Sheriff co. Monaghan, 23 GEORGE III.; *m.* 1st, Prudentia Martha, dau. of John Corry, of Rockcorry, by whom (who *d.* Oct. 1781) he had an only dau.,
      Prudentia Catherine, who *d.* aged 8 years.
Col. Anketill *m.* 2ndly, Mary (who *d.* Aug. 1838), only child of the Rev. Richard Norris, D.D., and *d.* 11 April, 1828, leaving
    (1) WILLIAM, of whom presently.
    (1) Maria, *d.* 28 April, 1842, *unm.*
    (2) Matilda, *d.* 28 June, 1819, *unm.*
    (3) Caroline, *m.* 1817, Augustus Woodville Amyatt, Lieut. Royal Irish Dragoon Guards, and *d.* three weeks after her marriage.
He *m.* 2ndly, when about 80 years of age, Anne Stephens (*née* Tuton), and *d.* immediately after, on 27 May, 1760, and was *s.* by his grandson,
  CHARLES ANKETELL, of Anketell Grove, *b.* 1754; *d. unm.* 20 Nov. 1828, and was *s.* by his nephew,
  WILLIAM ANKETELL, of Anketell Grove, J.P. and D.L., High Sheriff 1830, *b.* 10 Oct. 1790; *m.* 23 June, 1809, Sarah, dau. of Lieut.-Col. John C. F. Waring-Maxwell, of Finnebrogue, co. Down, M.P., and *d.* 23 April, 1851, having by her (who *d.* 2 April, 1874) had issue,
  1. MATTHEW JOHN, his heir.
  2. William Robert, of Quintin Castle, Portaferry, co. Down, *b.* 31 March, 1820, formerly Capt. Monaghan Militia, J.P. for co. Down; *m.* 8 Oct. 1844, Madelina Selina, 2nd dau. of David Ker, of Portavo, co. Down, M.P., and Lady Selina Sarah Juliana, his wife, dau. of Robert, 1st Marquis of Londonderry, and *d.* 9 March, 1889, having by her (who *d.* 8 April, 1878) had issue,
    1. Amyatt William, now of Quintin Castle, *b.* 4 Aug. 1853; late Lieut. 83rd Foot.
    2. David Fitz Ameline Robert, *b.* 27 May, 1855, Lieut. 3rd Belooch Regt. (N.I.) and formerly Lieut. 1st Royal Scots (the Lothian Regt.), served in Afghan War 1880 (medal) and Egyptian War 1882 (medal and Khedive star); *d.* at Kurachi, Scinde, 26 Aug. 1885.
    3. William Frederick, *b.* 18 Feb. 1858; *d.* 14 Dec. 1858.
    1. Edith Matilda, *m.* 1st, 8 Aug. 1871, Thomas John Knox, who [*d.* 5 Dec. 1875, leaving issue (*see* BURKE's *Peerage*, RANFURLY, E.). She *m.* 2ndly, 10 Feb. 1880, John Lewis Vaughan Henry, late Capt. 2nd Dragoons, eldest son of Mitchell Henry, M.P., of Kylemore Castle, co. Galway (*see that family*).
    2. Constance.   3. Ada.
    4. Celia Selina, *d. unm.* 18 Oct. 1883.
  3. Oliver Charles, 37th Madras N.I., H.E.I.C.S., *b.* 18 Aug. 1821; *d.* at Hong-Kong, China, while with his regiment, 13 July, 1841.
  4. Fitz Ameline Maxwell, of Killyfaddy, Clogher, co. Tyrone, J.P., High Sheriff 1881, *b.* 14 April, 1825; *d.* 24 Aug. 1905; *m.* 8 Nov. 1859, Laura Valetta (*d.* 21 July, 1907), 2nd dau. and co-heiress of Henry Ranking, of Eaglehurst, Bathford, Somerset (by his wife Frances Helen, dau. of the Rev. W. Heath, Vicar of Inkberrow, co. Worcester), and had issue,
    1. REGINALD, of Killyfaddy, *b.* 23 March, 1861.
    2. Henry, *b.* 21 Dec. 1863; *d.* 9 Jan. 1864.
    3. Charlemont Fitz Ameline, *b.* 15 March, 1872.
    1. Maud Mary, *d.* young 11 May, 1882.
  5. Maxwell, of Leatherhead, Surrey, *b.* 24 Oct. 1826; *m.* 1st, 29 Sept. 1857, Julia Elizabeth, only surviving child of the late Gustavus Whitaker, of St. Petersburg, Russia; she *d.* 1869; 2ndly, 1878, Mary Louisa, 3rd dau. of the late Henry Ranking, of Eaglehurst, Bathford; and *d.* 22 Feb. 1888, having (by his 1st wife) had issue,
    1. Oliver George, *b.* 5 Sept. 1860; *d.* 25 Feb. 1889.
    2. Arthur Cecil, *b.* 25 July, 1863; *d.* 28 Jan. 1885.
    3. Charles Edward, *b.* 3 June, 1869.
    1. Frances Julia.
    2. Isabella Sara, *m.* 26 May, 1904, William, 2nd son of Rev. William Blennerhassett, of Iwerne Minster, Dorset (*see* BLENNERHASSETT *of Ballyscedy*).
  6. Moutray, *b.* 18 April, 1829, Capt. R.A. (ret.); *d. unm.* 3 April, 1899.
    1. Anne Dorothea, *m.* 10 Dec. 1833, Rev. Robert Loftus Tottenham, 2nd son of Right Rev. Lord Robert Loftus Tottenham, Bishop of Clogher. She *d.* 16 Oct. 1891. He *d.* 5 Feb. 1893, leaving issue (*see* BURKE's *Peerage*. ELY, M.).
    2. Maria, *m.* 5 Dec. 1838, Rev. Sir John Richardson-Bunbury, 3rd Bart., of Augher Castle, co. Tyrone, and *d.* 2 March, 1888, leaving issue. He *d.* 19 Feb. 1909.
    3. Matilda Jane, *d. unm.* 14 March, 1840.
The eldest son,
  MATTHEW JOHN ANKETELL, of Anketell Grove, J.P. and D.L., High Sheriff, co. Monaghan, 1834, Major Monaghan Militia, *b.* 31 Oct. 1812; *m.* 6 Feb. 1840, Catherine Anne Frances, eldest dau. David Ker, M.P., of Portavo and Montalto, co. Down, by the Lady Selina, his wife, dau. of the 1st Marquess of Londonderry. He *d.* 8 May, 1870. She *d.* 28 Feb. 1887, leaving issue,
  1. MATTHEW DAVID, his heir.
  2. Oliver Frederick, *b.* 27 Feb. 1850; *d. unm.* 10 Feb. 1872.
  3. WILLIAM, successor to his brother.

4. Henry, M.L.A. Natal, late R.N., *b.* 4 May, 1855; *m.* 7 Dec. 1900, Oona, dau. of R. Reeson, of Maritzburgh, S. Africa, and has issue.
  1. Matthew David, *b.* 27 Dec. 1907.
  2. Henry George, *b.* 5 Jan. 1911.
5. Robert Waring Maxwell, *b.* 19 Nov. 1856; *d.* 1866.
1. Selina Sarah.   2. Ada, *d.* young.
3. Frances Emmeline, *m.* 1st, 22 Jan. 1867, Newton Haworth Wallace, Capt. Royal Bengal Fusiliers, 101st Regt.; and 2ndly, Clement Cordner, J.P., of Greenmount, Muckamore, co. Antrim, He *d.* 18 Aug. 1905.
4. Gertrude Madelina, *m.* 1 July, 1873, Anketell Moutray, D.L., of Favour Royal, and has issue (*see that family*).
5. Bertha Grace Phœbe, *d. unm.* 10 Jan. 1898.
6. Octavia Mary, *m.* 19 Feb. 1879, Frederick Augustus Morse-Boycott, of Sennowe Hall, Norfolk, and Sennoweville, Bushey, Herts (*see that family*).   7. Augusta, *d. unm.* 8 May, 1908.
The eldest son,
  MATTHEW DAVID ANKETELL, of Anketell Grove, *b.* 5 Jan. 1841; was killed by a fall from horseback, 17 July, 1872; *d. unm.* and was *s.* by his next surviving brother.
  Seat—Ancketill's Grove, Emyvale, co. Monaghan. *Residence*—Killyfaddy, Clogher, co. Tyrone.

ANDERSON OF GRACE DIEU.

THOMAS WILLIAM ANDERSON, of Grace Dieu, co. Waterford, J.P. and D.L., High Sheriff for co. Waterford in 1885, and J.P. co. Kilkenny, B.A. Cantab., *b.* 26 June, 1852; *s.* his father, 22 Oct. 1867; *m.* 10 Nov. 1879, Constance Agnes Jane (who *d.* 9 Aug. 1881); and 2ndly, on 2 Oct. 1907, Ellen Blanche Carew, both daus. of Very Rev. Anthony Latouche Kirwan, D.D., Dean of Limerick, by Susan his wife, 2nd dau. of William Blacker, of Woodbrook, Wexford, and by his first wife has a dau., Susan Alice.

Lineage.—JOHN ANDERSON, of Ardbrake, in Botriphnie Parish, Banffshire, *m.* Ann Gordon (who *d.* 19 Nov. 1670), "A matron of — years" (see tombstone in Parish church), and had issue,
  1. JAMES, of whom next.
  2. Arthur, Chaplain to WILLIAM III, *d.s.p.* 1714, bur. in the Rower Churchyard, co. Kilkenny.
  3. Alexander, admitted an Advocate 9 Jan. 1666.
  1. Susannah.   2. Margaret.
The eldest son,
  JAMES ANDERSON, *m.* 1st, Katharine (*d.* 9 March, 1667), 4th dau. of Robert Leslie, of Findrassie; and 2ndly, Isabell Douglas widow of Rev. Alex. Cant. He is described in *Sasines* and other records as "of Wester Ardbrake" which sometimes appears as "Westertoun"). By his 1st wife he had issue,
  1. JOHN, of whom next.
  2. Alexander, Major in Col. Sir John Hill's Regt. of Foot, afterwards of Grace Dieu.
    1. Elizabeth, *m.* 16 Oct., 1675, John Gordon, jun., of Carroll, in Sutherlandshire, Sheriff Depute of Sutherland in 1685. He *d.* in 1701, leaving issue.
    2. Anna, *m.* J. Gibson, of Linkwood.
    3. Mary, *m.* Thomas Baker, of Ballytobin, co. Kilkenny.
The eldest son,
  JOHN ANDERSON, of Westerton, *m.* Jean Gordon, and had issue,
  1. James, chirurgeon, bapt. at Botriphnie, 26 March, 1684.
  2. John, bapt. at Botriphnie, 30 Sept. 1686.
  3. ALEXANDER, of whom next.
  1. Katharine, bapt. at Botriphnie.
  2. Jean, bapt. at New Machar, *d.* 25 March, 1710.
  3. Isabell, bapt. at Botriphnie.
  4. Elizabeth, bapt. at Botriphnie.
  5. Anna, bapt. at Botriphnie.
The 3rd son,
  ALEXANDER ANDERSON, bapt. at Botriphnie, 4 July, 1688; *m.* 2 Feb. 1721, a dau. and co-heir of William Brewster, son of Sir Francis Brewster, twice Lord Mayor of Dublin. By her (who *d.* 1754) Alexander left (with two daus., one of whom *m.* Robert Carew, of Woodenstown, co. Tipperary) an only son and heir,
  JAMES ANDERSON of Grace Dieu, *m.* 1st, in 1756, Henrietta Boyd, and 2ndly, 1764, Susanna, youngest dau. of Christmas Paul, by Ellen his wife, dau. of Robert Carew, M.P., of Castle Boro, co. Wexford (*see* CAREW *of Ballinamona*), and had issue, by 2nd wife,
  1. JAMES, his heir.
  2. Paul, C.B., K.C.H., General and Colonel of the 78th Highlanders, A.D.C. to Sir John Moore, and some time Governor o Pendennis Castle, *b.* 29 March, 1767; *d.s.p.* at Bath, 1851.
  3. Alexander, Capt. in the Army; *d.s.p.* at Bath, 1833.
  4. Henry, R.N., *d.s.p.*
  5. Joshua (Rev.), heir to his brother.
  6. Robert, an officer in the 42nd Regt., who was killed at the Battle of Alexandria, *s.p.*
  1. Ellen, *d.s.p.*
The eldest son,
  JAMES ANDERSON, of Grace Dieu, *d.* in London, 1838, *s.p.*, and left his estates to his brother,
  THE REV. JOSHUA ANDERSON, M.A., of Grace Dieu, Rector of Myshall, co. Carlow, *b.* 8 Dec. 1770; *m.* 1 Oct. 1807, Anne, eldest dau. of Capt. William Perceval (*see* PERCEVAL *of Temple House*), and *d.* 6 April, 1859, leaving by her (who *d.* 24 March, 1854) issue
  1. JAMES, his heir.
  2. William *b.* Aug. 1812; *d.* 20 Nov. 1904; *m.* 24 Aug. 1859,

IRELAND. Andrews.

Elizabeth Paul (who d. 21 Dec. 1910), 3rd dau. of Samuel Wallis Adams, J.P., of Kilbree, co. Cork, and had issue,
1. Joshua Alexander, b. 19 Jan. 1867, Rector of Arborfield; m. Edith Constance, dau. of Henry Hainworth, of Blackheath.
2. William James, M.R.C.S., L.R.C.P., b. 2 March, 1869.
  1. Wilhelmina Elizabeth, m. Albert Alexander McCall, 76th Regt., and has issue.
3. Robert Carew, M.D., Deputy Inspector of Hospitals, formerly Surgeon-Major in the 13th Light Dragoons, m. 13 Oct. 1853, Jane Wallis, only dau. of the Rev. Henry Bolton, M.A., Vicar of Dysart, Enos, Queen's Co. (see BOLTON of Mount Bolton and Fatlock Castle), and had issue,
  1. Robert Henry, b. 17 Aug. 1854; d.s.p. 31 Dec. 1896.
  2. Charles Alexander, Major-Gen., C.B., Commanding the troops in South China from 1910 (Headquarters House, Hong Kong), b. 10 Feb. 1857; m. 11 Jan. 1893, Ellen Katherine, younger dau. of George Bevan Russell, M.D.
  3. William Paul, b. 16 June, 1858, Major Indian Army.
  4. Francis James, b. 17 Feb. 1860, Col. R.E., Assist. Director of Fortifications and Works, War Office.
  5. Joshua Perceval, b. 4 May, 1863; d.s.p. 9 Oct. 1905.
    1. Frances Anne Grace.
    2. Catherine Jane Henrietta, m. 28 Jan. 1902, Harry Mervyn Kemmis-Betty, Lieut. R.N., eldest son of Col. Joshua F. Kemmis-Betty, late R.A., of Hawkhurst, Kent.
4. Paul Christmas, of Prospect, co. Kilkenny, b. 1817; d.s.p. 24 Feb. 1907.
5. Alexander, R.N., Commander of H.M.S. Cressy, d. on board his ship in the Baltic, and was buried on the Island of Nargen, Aug. 1854.
  1. Anne, m. 4 Feb. 1845, Charles Newport Bolton, B.A., of Brook Lodge, co. Waterford. He d. 1884.
  2. Jane Ellen, d. 14 March, 1906.
  3. Ellen, m. 13 Dec. 1859, George Bevan Russell, M.D. He d. 9 Feb. 1902.
  4. Catherine, d. 18 Feb. 1855.
  5. Henrietta.   6. Susanna, d. 14 Sept. 1911.
The eldest son,
JAMES ANDERSON, of Grace Dieu, J.P., b. 4 Aug. 1810; m. 25 April, 1842, Margaret, youngest dau. of Thomas Carew, of Ballinamona Park, J.P., by his wife Jane, eldest dau. and co-heir of Sir John Alcock, Knt. of Waterford (see CAREW of Ballinamona). He d. 22 Oct. 1867, and by her (who d. 29 Feb. 1864) had issue,
1. James Paul, b. 21 Jan. 1850; d. 26 Sept. 1860.
2. THOMAS WILLIAM, his heir.
3. ALEXANDER CAREW, of Ballymountain, co. Kilkenny, J.P., b. 6 May, 1856; m. 24 Aug. 1880, Margaret Winifred Alicia, youngest dau. of Nicholas Alfred Power, of Belle Vue, co. Kilkenny (see POWER of Faithlegg), and has issue,
  Paul Alexander, b. 5 Jan. 1883.
  Muriel Louise.
1. Jane Margaret, m. 15 Dec. 1868, Lieut.-Col. Michael Clare Garsia, C.B., Inspector-Gen. of Military Prisons. He d. 20 April, 1903, leaving issue,
  1. Clare James.   2. Herbert.   3. Harry Carew.
Seat—Grace Dieu Lodge, Waterford. Club—Kildare Street, Dublin.

ANDREWS OF RATHENNY.

JOHN BOLTON ANDREWS, of Rathenny, King's Co., J.P., b. 9 March, 1874.

Lineage.—CORNET JOHN ANDREWS, of Rath, King's Co., to whom the Rathenny Estate was granted by Letters Patent dated 12 Feb. 1667-19, CHARLES II, d. about 1688. He m. Alice, dau. of Thomas Maunsell, of Derryvillane, co. Cork (see MAUNSELL of Limerick), and left issue,
1. JOHN, of whom presently.
2. Aphra, m. — Dixon.
The elder son,
JOHN ANDREWS, of Rathenny, m. 1682, Elizabeth, dau. of Sir Robert Cole, Kt., of Ballymackey, co. Tipperary, d. 1732, and had issue,
1. ROBERT, his heir, who d. 1743, having had issue an only child,
  Elizabeth, m. Richard Hawkshaw.
2. MAUNSELL (who s. to the estate on the death of his elder brother), and of whom presently.
3. Thomas, d.v.p.
1. Anna, m. — Allen.   2. Mary, m. — Allen.
3. Elizabeth, m. James Johnston.
4. Rebecka, m. — Cole.   5. Aphra, m. Joseph Smith.
The 2nd son,
MAUNSELL ANDREWS, of Rathenny, m. 1719, Elizabeth, dau. of Nicholas Toler, of Beechwood, co. Tipperary, d. 24 Feb. 1769, and had issue,
1. JOHN, of whom presently.   2. Robert.   3. Daniel.
4. Maunsell, m. 1774, Mary née Alley, widow of Samuel Gason.
1. Jane, m. 1759, George Jackson.
2. Eleanor, m. 1761, Richard Hawkshaw.
3. Catherine, m. 1759, George Pepper.
The eldest son,
JOHN ANDREWS, of Rathenny, m. 1st, 1753, Emilia, dau. of Christopher Nicholson, of Balrath, co. Meath (see that family), and by her had issue,
1. Elizabeth, m. 1787, Corker Wright, of Rutland, and had issue.
2. Eleanor, m. 1777, Capt. Simon Pepper.
3. Mary, m. George Lodge.
4. Amelia, m. 1806, Richard Lysaght.
He m. 2ndly, 1766, Ann, dau. of Humphrey Jones, of Mullinabro, co. Kilkenny (see that family), and by her had issue,
1. John, d.s.p.
2. MAUNSELL, who s. and of whom presently.
3. Humphrey, lost at sea s.p.   4. Christopher, d.s.p.
5. George, d.s.p.
1. Anna Maria, m. 1797, Vincent Lamb.
2. Sarah, m. 1801, Humphrey Denis.
3. Rebecca, m. 1804, Trevor Lloyd Blunden, of Ballyduggan.
The 2nd son,
MAUNSELL ANDREWS of Rathenny, High Sheriff of King's Co. 1806, b. 1769; m. 1st, 1792, Mary, dau. of Samuel Gason, of Knockinglass, and m. 2ndly, 1801, Mary, dau. of Rev. Ralph Hawtrey, Rector of Gaulskill, co. Kilkenny. He d. 2 July, 1864, and by his 2nd wife he had issue,
1. JOHN, of whom presently.
2. Maunsell Hawtrey, m. 1843, Ellen, dau. of John Saunders, and d.s.p. 21 Jan. 1888.
3. George, m. 1853, Elizabeth Lucy, dau. of Rev. Wm. Minchin, of Greenhills, King's Co., and widow of Johnston Stoney, of Emell Castle, d. 3 Feb. 1907, and left issue,
  Georgina, m. Robert Mulock Emerson, and has issue.
1. Sarah, d. unm. 1881.
2. Mary Anne, m. 1835, John Thwaites, M.D., of Ceylon, and had issue,
3. Catherine, d. unm. 26 Dec. 1881.
4. Charlotte Hawtrey, d. unm. 29 April, 1880.
5. Maria, m. 1833, Professor Charles Benson, M.D., President Royal College of Surgeons, Ireland, and d. 1887, having had issue.
6. Elizabeth.
The eldest son,
JOHN ANDREWS, of Rathenny, m. 1834, Elizabeth, dau. of Robert Hall, of Merton Hall, co. Tipperary, and d. 12 Dec. 1879, leaving issue,
1. MAUNSELL, of whom presently.
2. John Hall, M.D., m. 1880, Mary Letitia, dau. of Edward Saunders, of Ballinderry, co. Tipperary, and d. 19 June, 1890, leaving issue,
  Ida Ellen Amy, m. Henry Ward Bailey, and has issue.
1. Eliza (called Ida), m. 1858, John Wright Bowles, Archdeacon of Killaloe and Rector of Nenagh, and d. 21 Aug. 1898, having had issue.
2. Mary Hall, m. Major-Gen. John Hamilton Cox, C.B., and has issue.
3. Anne Hall, m. 1862, John Morton, and has issue.
4. Robina Hall, m. 1874, Joseph Charles Macraith, and has issue.
5. Sarah Georgina, m. (as his first wife) 24 Aug. 1864, Robert Jocelyn Waller, of Summerville, Nenagh, J.P., and d. 6 Aug. 1877, having had issue (see WALLER of Prior Park).
The eldest son,
MAUNSELL ANDREWS, of Rathenny, m. 1873, Kate Mary, dau. of John Bolton, of Altavilla, Queen's Co., and d. 2 Jan. 1890, having had issue,
1. JOHN BOLTON, now of Rathenny.
2. Maunsell Hawtrey, b. 27 Nov. 1876, d. 3 March, 1906.
Arms—Vert, a saltire or surmounted by another gu. Crest—Out of a coronet or, a blackamoor's head wreathed of the colours and collared gold. Motto—Virtute et valore.
Seat—Rathenny, King's Co.

ANDREWS OF ARDARA.

THE RIGHT HON. THOMAS ANDREWS, P.C., of Ardara, Comber, co. Down, D.L., Chairman of the Down County Council, a member of the Appeal Commission under the Local Government Act (Ireland) 1898, member of Arterial Drainage Commission (Ireland), 1905, President Ulster Liberal Unionist Association, and Chairman of the Belfast and co. Down Railway, was sworn of the Privy Council in Ireland on the occasion of the

Annesley.   THE LANDED GENTRY.   10

Royal Visit, 1903, *b.* 26 Feb. 1843; *m.* 15 Sept. 1870, Eliza, dau. of James Alexander Pirrie, of LittleClandeboye, co. Down, and Eliza Montgomery, his wife, and has issue,
 1. JOHN MILLER, *b.* 17 July, 1871; *m.* 10 Sept. 1902, Jessie, dau. of Joseph Ormrod.
 2. Thomas, *b.* 7 Feb. 1873; *m.* 24 June, 1908, Helen Reilly, dau. of late John D. Barbour, D.L. of Conway, Dunmurry.
 3. James, *b.* 3 Jan. 1877.
 4. William, *b.* 25 Aug. 1886.
 1. Eliza Montgomery (Nina), *m.* 26 April, 1906, Lawrence Arthur Hind, 3rd son of Jesse Hind, of Edwalton, Notts.

Lineage.—JAMES ANDREWS, of The Old House, Comber, co. Down, *b.* 6 Dec. 1762; *d.* 2 July, 1841, having *m.* Frances Glenny, by whom he had a son,
 JOHN ANDREWS, of Uraghmore, Comber, co. Down, J.P., High Sheriff co. Down 1857, *b.* 15 Nov. 1792; *m.* 25 Aug. 1826, Sarah, dau. of William Drennan, M.D., of Cabin Hill, co. Down, and Sarah Swanwick, his wife. She *d.* 13 Feb. 1902, aged 95. He *d.* 13 May, 1864, having had issue,
  1. James, J.P., *b.* 23 Nov. 1829; *m.* 21 March, 1863, Mary Catherine, dau. of Robert Andrews, LL.D., Q.C., and *d.* 7 Feb. 1882, having had issue,
   1. Herbert William.   2. Arthur Macdonald.
   3. Henry Percy.   4. Cecil Frank.
   1. Amy.   2. Eileen Lucy.
  2. William Drennan (Right Hon.), P.C. (Ireland), B.A., LL.D., Trin. Coll. Dublin, Justice of the King's Bench in Ireland, called to the Bar 1855, Q.C. 1872, raised to the Bench 1882, resigned 1910 (51, *Lower Leeson Street, Dublin*), *b.* 24 Jan. 1832; *m.* 20 Aug. 1857, Eliza, dau. of the late John Galloway, of Monkstown, co. Dublin. She *d.s.p.* 6 April, 1901.
  3. John, J.P., *b.* 27 Jan. 1838; *m.* 5 May, 1868, Annie, dau. of Isaac Andrews, and *d.* 28 March, 1903, having had issue,
   1. John Drennan.   2. William Lennox.
   1. Mary.   2. Eva.
   3. Ethel.
  4. THOMAS, of Ardara.
  1. Sarah, *d.* aged 2.
  2. Sarah, *d. unm.* 1845.
  3. Frances, *b.* 19 Feb. 1850; *m.* 3 April, 1878, Edmund W. Garrett.

Arms—Az., on a fesse or three mullets of the field. *Crest*—A dove holding in the bill an olive branch all ppr., charged on the breast with a mullet az. *Motto*—Always faithful.

Seat—Ardara, Comber, co. Down. *Club*—Ulster Reform, Belfast; Ulster Club, Belfast; County Club, Downpatrick.

ANNESLEY. *See* BURKE'S PEERAGE, **ANNESLEY, E.**

ARCHDALE OF CASTLE ARCHDALE.

EDWARD ARCHDALE, of Castle Archdale, co. Fermanagh, J.P. and D.L., High Sheriff 1902, High Sheriff co. Tyrone 1906, B.A., Keble Coll. Oxford, C.E., *b.* 22 March, 1850; *s.* his uncle, 1899; *m.* 22 Jan. 1908, Elizabeth, 2nd dau. of the late Nicholas Harwood, of H.M. Dockyard, Pembroke, and widow of Capt. W. Wingfield Clarke, Leicestershire Regt.

Lineage.—JOHN ARCHDALL, of Archdall, co. Fermanagh, High Sheriff 1616, formerly of Norsome Hall, co. Norfolk, went to Ireland *temp.* Queen ELIZABETH, and obtained a grant of lands in the co. Fermanagh, by patent, dated 13 July, 1612, to hold for ever as of the Castle of Dublin by fealty, which lands were erected into the Manor of Archdall, with 300 acres in demesne and power to hold a Court Baron. He *m.* Katherine, dau. of Sir William Temple, Knt., sometime Provost of Trinity College, Dublin. She *m.* 2ndly, Sir John Veel, Knt., and *d.* 23 Nov. 1642. John Archdall left issue,
 1. EDWARD, his heir, of whom hereafter.
 2. Martin (Ven.), Archdeacon of Ferns, 1629, *d.* before 1660.
 3. John (Ven.), B.D., Archdeacon of Killala, 1637, and of Achonry, 1638, *m.* the dau. of Donnellan, of co. Roscommon, and *d.* 1668, leaving a son,
  John (Rev.), Vicar of Lusk, co. Dublin, 1679, *m.* by licence, dated 1 April, 1679, Elizabeth, dau. of John Barnard, of Drumin, co. Louth. She *d.* Dec. 1731. He *d.* 1690, leaving with a dau. Frances, three sons,
   (1) John, of Drumin, whose will is dated 9 June, 1703. He *m.* Anne, dau. of Robert Clarke, and by her (who *m.* 2ndly, 1710, Francis Johnston, of Darrycholaught, co. Fermanagh) left a posthumous son,
    John, of Drumin, *d. unm.* 13 June, 1787.
   (2) William, of Dublin, in the Paymaster-General's Department, *m.* Henrietta, dau. of Rev. Henry Goone, Vicar Choral of the Cathedral of Tuam. Her will is dated 25 July, 1765. He *d.* 5 Sept. 1751, leaving three daus.: 1. Elizabeth; 2. Angel, *m.* 12 Jan. 1748-9, William Preston; 3. Katherine, *m.* — Dobson; and two sons,
    1. MERVYN (Rev.), Rector of Attanagh, co. Kilkenny, and afterwards of Slane, co. Meath, *b.* 22 April, 1732; *m.* 1st

by licence, dated 30 July, 1747, Sarah Colles, of Dublin, and had issue,
 MERVYN, of Dublin, Solicitor to the Commissioners of Customs, *m.* March, 1784, Maria Murray, of Dublin, and had, with a dau. Sarah, *m.* Francis Hervey, two sons,
  (*a*) HENRY MERVYN, *b.* 1792, Capt. 68th Regt., *d. unm.* Feb. 1868.
  (*b*) William Frederick, of Farmhill, co. Wexford, *b.* 1798; *m.* 13 June, 1822, Elizabeth (who *d.* 27 Jan. 1888), dau. of Henry Rowley Henry, and *d.* 7 March, 1865, leaving, with nine daus.: Sarah; Alicia; Maria; Elizabeth; Susan; Letitia, *m.* 30 June, 1863, Very Rev. Humphrey E. Ellison, Dean of Ferns, who *d.* 12 Feb. 1897; Martha; Mary; and Charlotte), two sons,
   1. MERVYN (Right Rev.), D.D., Bishop of Killaloe, Kilfenora, Clonfert, and Kilmacduagh (*Clarisford, Killaloe, co. Clare*). *b.* 16 Feb. 1831; *m.* 21 Jan. 1863, Henrietta, dau. of Eyre William Preston, of Clontarf, co. Dublin, and grand-dau. of William Preston, by Hon. Frances Dorothea Evans his wife, dau. and co-heir of John, 5th Lord Carbery, and by her (who *d.* 11 May, 1903) has issue,
    (1) MERVYN (Rev.), Acting Chaplain to the Forces, Belfast, B.A. Trin. Coll. Dublin, *b.* 27 Jan. 1868; *m.* 21 April, 1897, Alice Sheridan, dau. of Robert L. Hamilton, of Shankill, co. Monaghan, and Windsor, Belfast, and has issue,
     Alice Hamilton, *b.* 18 July, 1899.
    (2) Eyre William Preston (Rev), Canon of Killaloe, Rector of Killaloe Union, M.A. Trin. Coll. Dublin, *b.* 26 Feb. 1871; *m.* 28 June, 1905, Edith Gladys Jeanette, dau. of the late Robert de Ros Rose, of Ahabeg and Foxhall, co. Limerick, and has issue,
     Mervyn, *b.* 23 April, 1906.
    (3) William Frederick, *b.* 26 Feb. 1873.
    (1) Anne Angel, *b.* 11 March, 1866.
    (3) Elizabeth, *b.* 9 July, 1869.
   2. William Frederick (Rev.), Canon of Cork, M.A. Trin. Coll. Dublin, Rector of Rathcooney, co. Cork, *b.* 4 Feb. 1835; *m.* Constance Ryall Sarah (*d.* 23 July, 1910), dau. of James Ramsey Akers Smith, of Carrigbarrabane, co. Waterford, J.P., and has issue,
    (1) Ethel Katherine, *m.* 27 June, 1895, Major Harry Vaughan Gorle, D.S.O., youngest son of the late Capt. John Taylor Gorle, of Metherell Tower, co. Devon. She *d.* 23 Nov. 1904, leaving issue.
    (2) Henrietta Constance.
    (3) Grace Ramsay.
  Henrietta, *m.* 24 March (licence dated 16 March, 1772), Rev. John Dalton Harewood, of Clonmel, Rector of Attanagh.
 Rev. Mervyn Archdall, the well-known antiquary, author of the *Monasticon Hibernicum*, and Editor of the last edition of Lodge's *Peerage of Ireland*, *m.* 2ndly, Abigal Young, but had no further issue. He *d.* 6 Aug. 1791.
 2. Henry, *m.* 26 Feb. 1762, Anne Fuller, and had two sons, *a.* William (Rev.), Rector of Tintern, co. Wexford (father of Ven. John Charles Archdall, Archdeacon of Ferns, Antonia, *m.* 27 May, 1839, Hon. Frederick Saville, 5th son of John, 3rd Earl of Mexborough, and had issue). *b.* Henry, who had two sons.
   (3) Barnard, *m.* Mary, dau. of John Hathorne, of Drogheda, and had issue,
    1. John.   2. Thomas.
    1. Mary, *m.* — Clare.
 1. Lettice, *m.* Tobias Norris, of Dublin, and *d.* 28 Oct. 1642.
The elder son,
 EDWARD ARCHDALL, of Castle Archdall, *b.* 1604; *m.* Angel, dau. of Sir Paul Gore, 1st bart., of Manor Gore, by whom he had a son and successor,
 WILLIAM ARCHDALL, of Castle Archdall, High Sheriff co. Fermanagh 1667, *m.* Elizabeth, dau. of Henry Mervyn, of Trillick, co. Tyrone, and had issue,
  1. MERVYN, his heir.
  2. EDWARD, successor to his brother.
  1. ANGEL, *s.* to the estates on the death of her brother. Mr. Archdall, who was attainted 1689, by the Parliament of JAMES II, was *s.* by his eldest son,
  MERVYN ARCHDALL, of Castle Archdall, High Sheriff co. Fermanagh 1714, *d. unm.* 27 Dec. 1726, and was *s.* by his brother,
  EDWARD ARCHDALL, of Castle Archdall, High Sheriff co. Fermanagh 1722, *m.* 1st, Frances, dau. of Sir John Caldwell, Bart., of Castle Caldwell, co. Fermanagh; and 2ndly, Elizabeth, dau. of John Cole, of Florence Court, same co. (ancestor of the Earl of Enniskillen), but by her (who *m.* 2ndly, 7 Dec. 1731, Hon. Bysse Molesworth) had no issue. At his death *s.p.* the estates devolved upon his sister,
  ANGEL ARCHDALL, of Castle Archdall, who *m.* NICHOLAS MONTGOMERY, of Derrygonnelly, co. Fermanagh, M.P. Mr. Montgomery adopted the surname of ARCHDALE, and left by the heiress of Archdall (who *d.* about 1742 or 1747) an only son,
  MERVYN ARCHDALE, of Castle Archdale and Trillick, Col. in the Army, M.P. for co. Fermanagh, and High Sheriff 1773, *m.* by licence, dated 12 July, 1762, Hon. Mary Dawson, dau. of William Henry, Viscount Carlow, and sister of John, 1st Earl of Portarlington, and *d.* 1813, having by her had issue,
   1. MERVYN, his heir.   2. WILLIAM, *s.* his brother.

3. Edward, of Riversdale, co. Fermanagh, J.P. and D.L., High Sheriff 1813, *m.* 2 Oct. 1809, Matilda, 2nd dau. of William Humphrys, of Ballyhaise, co. Cavan, and *d.* 12 May, 1864, having had issue,
  1. MERVYN EDWARD, *s.* his uncle.
  2. WILLIAM HUMPHRYS, late of Castle Archdale.
  3. Edward, of Lisnaskea, co. Fermanagh, *b.* 1816, Lieut.-Col. in the Army, and Col. Fermanagh Militia, J.P. co. Fermanagh, High Sheriff 1872 ; *m.* 1st, 21 Nov. 1846, Caroline Anne, dau. of Charles Claude Clifton, of Tymawr, co. Brecon. He *m.* 2ndly, 9 Feb. 1875, Eleanor Jane (*d.* 23 July, 1907), youngest dau. of Robert Stewart, of Lisburn, and *d.* 1886.
  4. Henry Montgomery (Rev.), M.A., of Thornhill, co. Fermanagh, formerly incumbent of St. Michael's, *b.* 1818 ; *m.* 1848, Sarah Elizabeth, dau. of James Blackwood Price, of Saintfield, and *d.* 14 Feb. 1898, leaving issue by her (who *d.* 7 Aug. 1911),
    (1) EDWARD, now of Castle Archdale.
    (2) Henry Dawson, *b.* 1851.
    (3) James Blackwood, Maj. late R.A. and Army Ordnance Department, *b.* 17 July, 1853 ; *m.* Feb., 1886, Elizabeth, dau. of the late George May, of Cambridge, and has issue, Henry Blackwood, *b.* 15 March, 1887.
    (4) Audley Mervyn (44, *Shirley Avenue, Southampton*), *b.* 1 Oct. 1855 ; *m.* 17 Sept. 1895, Mary Scott, dau. of the late George Elphinstone, of Oakfield House, Streatham, and has issue,
      1. George Mervyn, *b.* 14 Aug. 1896.
      1. Margaret Helen, *b.* 1 Oct. 1897.
      2. Beatrice Mary, *b.* 13 April, 1901.
    (5) Montgomery, *b.* 1858.
    (6) George, of Dromard, Kesh, co. Fermanagh, High Sheriff 1904, late Capt. 5th Battal'on Royal Ir sh R flcs. *b.* 27 Jan. 1860 ; *m.* 28 Dec. 1894, Mary, dau. of the late John Graham, of Parade House, Cowes, and has issue,
      1. Mervyn Henry Dawson, *b.* 11 March, 1904.
      2. George Montgomery, *b.* 6 July, 1907.
      1. Helen Audley. 2. Mary Blackwood.
      3. Sarah Matilda. 4. Joan.
    (1) Elizabeth Price.
    (2) Sarah Blackwood, *m.* Nov. 1886, Rev. Edward Blanchard Ryan, Rector of Strangford, co. Down, and has issue.
    (3) Matilda Humphries. (4) Richmal Magnell.
  5. Nicholas Montgomery of Crock na Crieve, co. Fermanagh, J.P. for that co. and Longford, *b.* 18 Feb. 1820 ; *m.* 27 Jan. 1852, Adelaide Mary, 4th dau. of the Rev. John Grey Porter, of Kilskeery and Belleisle, co. Fermanagh, son of the Bishop of Clogher, and *d.* 2 Feb. 1877, suddenly, in the hunting field, leaving issue,
    (1) Edward Mervyn, of Crock na Crieve and Riversdale (*see* ARCHDALE *of Riversdale*).
    (2) John Porter PORTER, of Clonbalt, co. Longford (*see* PORTER *of Clonbalt*).
    (3) William Henry, *b.* 16 Nov. 1856 ; *d. unm.* 29 March, 1875.
    (4) Henry Butler, *b.* 4 Dec. 1857 ; *d. unm.* 22 Oct. 1858.
    (5) Nicholas Francis, *b.* 19 Feb. 1862 ; *m.* 19 April, 1887, Alice, eldest dau. of Philip Henry Egerton, of Gladwyn, Gresford. She *d.s.p.* 1889.
    (6) Theodore Montgomery, D.S.O., Major R.H.A., *b.* 24 Sept. 1873 ; *m.* 9 Oct. 1901, Helen Alexander, dau. of the late Alexander Russel, of St. Andrews, N.B., and has issue,
      1a. Nicholas Montgomery, *b.* 27 July, 1902.
      2a. Alexander Mervyn, *b.* 27 Nov. 1905.
      1a. Helen Elizabeth, *b.* 21 Aug. 1907.
    (1) Margaret Eleanor, *b.* 23 Feb. 1854.
    (2) Matilda Lavinia, *b.* 7 Dec. 1859 ; *d. unm.* 14 July, 1876.
    (3) Margaret Eleanor.
  6. John, in the 52nd Light Infantry, *d.* of yellow fever at Berbice, 1841.
  7. Hugh Montgomery, of Drumadravy, co. Fermanagh, Capt. 52nd Regt., *m.* 23 Sept. 1857, Lizzie, dau. of Sir Hugh Stewart, 2nd bart., of Ballygawley, and *d.* 1880, leaving issue,
    (1) Edward Hugh, *b.* 1861 ; *m.* 10 May, 1899, Dorothy Mary, only dau. of the late Albert Bolton, and had issue.
    (2) Henry St. George, *b.* 1862.
    (3) Alfred Montgomery, *b.* 1864.
    (4) William Stewart, *b.* 1870 ; *m.* 7 Sept. 1898, Emily Laura, dau. of Hugh Lyons Montgomery (*see* MONTGOMERY *of Belhavel*).
    (5) Lionel John Dawson, *b.* 1874.
    (6) Nicholas James Mervyn, *b.* 1878.
    (1) Minnie, *d.* 3 April, 1888, having *m.* Major Hugh James Archdale.
    (2) Henrietta Julia Maud. (3) Margaret Mathilda.
    (4) Emily Mary Hamilton.
  8. Audley Mervyn, of Underdown, co. Hereford, J.P., Capt. R.A., *b.* 1826 ; *m.* 1854, Sybilla Mary, 3rd dau. of Philip John Miles, of Liegh Court, Bristol, and *d.* 1893, having by her (who *d.* 1889) had, with other issue,
    Mervyn Edward, of The Retreat, co. Devon, Maj. late Gloucester Regt., *b.* 21 Dec. 1855 ; *m.* 12 April, 1887, Minna, eldest dau. of Fulbert Archer, of Timaru. New Zealand, and by her (who *d.* 1900) has a son, Edward Mervyn, *b.* 1888.
  9. James Mervyn, *d.* 1840.
  1. Mary.
  2. Letitia Jane, *m.* 1834, Rev. Butler Brooke, Rector of Aghavea, younger son of Sir Henry Brooke, 1st bart., of Colbrooke. He *d.s.p.*, 14 Nov. 1869. She *d.* 1899.
  3. Richmall Magnall. 4. Matilda, *d. unm.* 1852.

4. Henry, late Capt. 6th Dragoon Guards, *m.* Jane, dau. of Philip Doyne, which lady *d.s.p.*
1. Mary, *m.* Rt. Hon. Sir John Stewart, 1st bart., of Athenry, co. Tyrone, M.P., Attorney General for Ireland 1799, and *d.* 28 May, 1795, leaving issue (*see* BURKE's *Peerage*, STEWART *of Athenry* BART.).
2. Angel, *m.* John Richardson, of Rossfad House, co. Fermanagh.
3. Caroline. **4.** Anne.
5. Catharine.
6. Elizabeth, *m.* Dacre Hamilton, of Cornacassa, co. Monaghan.
7. Sidney, *m.* 10 May, 1800, Robert Hamilton, of the city of Dublin.
8. Wilhelmina Henrietta, *m.* Augustine Macnamara, of Dublin.
The eldest son,
MERVYN ARCHDALE, of Castle Archdale and Trillick, a Gen. in the Army, Lieut.-Gov. of the Isle of Wight, and M.P. in eleven Parl'aments for co. Fermanagh, *b.* 1763 ; *m.* Feb. 1806, Jane, dau. of Gustavus Rochfort, co. Westmeath, but *d.s.p.* 1839, when he was *s.* by his brother,
WILLIAM ARCHDALE, of Castle Archdale, Lieut.-Col. in the Army, High Sheriff co. Fermanagh 1845, *m.* Martha Hawley, dau. of James Clarke, of Castle Carey, Somerset, and dying *s.p.* 1863, was *s.* by his nephew,
MERVYN EDWARD ARCHDALE, of Castle Archdale, co. Fermanagh, and Trillick, co. Tyrone, *b.* 1812 ; J.P. and D.L. co. Fermanagh, High Sheriff 1879, and J.P. for cos. Donegal and Tyrone, late a Capt. 6th (Inniskilling) Dragoons, M.P. for Fermanagh 1834-74 ; *m.* Emma Inez, dau. of Jacob Goulding, of London and Kew. He *d.* 22 Dec. 1895. She *d.* 30 Aug. 1874. He was *s.* by his brother,
WILLIAM HUMPHRYS MERVYN ARCHDALE, of Castle Archdale, Fermanagh, J.P. and D.L. for that co., and High Sheriff 1845, J.P. co. Tyrone and High Sheriff 1861, M.P. co. Fermanagh 1874-85, B.A. Exeter Coll. Oxford, *b.* 1813 ; *m.* 1st, 15 April, 1845, Emily Mary Rebecca, eldest dau. of the late Hon. and Rev. John Charles Maude. She *d.* 1892. He *m.* 2ndly, 1894, Matilda (*Gortinore, Monkstown, co. Dublin*), dau. of William Alley, of Artane, co. Dublin. Mr. W. H. Archdale *s.* his brother 1895, and assumed by Royal Licence the additional surname of MERVYN in accordance with the will of his uncle Gen. Mervyn Archdale, and *d.s.p.* 23 June, 1899, when he was *s.* by his nephew EDWARD, now of Castle Archdale.

Seats—Castle Archdale, Irvinestown, co. Fermanagh, and Trillick Lodge, co. Tyrone.

ARCHDALE OF RIVERSDALE.

EDWARD MERVYN ARCHDALE, of Riversdale, co. Fermanagh, J.P. and D.L., High Sheriff, 1884, M.P. for North Fermanagh, 1898-1903, Lieut. ret. R.N., *b.* 26 Jan. 1853 ; *m.* 10 June, 1880, Alice Bland, youngest dau. of the late Quintin Fleming, of Chapelville, Dingle, Liverpool, and has issue,
  1. NICHOLAS EDWARD, Lieut. R.N., *b.* 11 June, 1881.
  2. William Porter Palgrave, *b.* 1 Dec. 1883.
  3. Audley Quintin, Lieut. R.F.A., *b.* 3 April, 1886.
  4. Dominick Mervyn, *b.* 4 April, 1892.
  5. Humphrys, Cadet R.N., *b.* 29 July, 1896.
  1. Angel, *b.* 10 Aug. 1882 ; *m.* 31 Aug. 1909, P. M. Loftus Tottenham, Inspector-General of Irrigation in Sudan, and has issue.

Mr. Archdale is the eldest son of Nicholas Montgomery Archdale, of Crock na Crieve, who *d.* 2 Feb. 1877, and Adelaide Mary, his wife, 4th dau. of the Rev. John Grey Porter, of Belleisle, co. Fermanagh (*see that family*), and grandson of Edward Archdale, D.L., of Riversdale, who *d.* 12 May, 1864.

Lineage.—*See* ARCHDALE, of Castle Archdale.
Seat—Riversdale, Ballinamallard, co. Fermanagh. *Club*—Kildare Street.

WRIGHT-ARMSTRONG OF KILLYLEA.

HENRY BRUCE WRIGHT ARMSTRONG, of Killylea, co. Armagh, J.P. and D.L., High Sheriff for that co. 1875, and High Sheriff for co. Longford 1894, M.A. Trin. Coll., Cambridge, called to the bar at the Inner Temple 1868, *b.* 27 July, 1844 ; *s.* 1872 ; *m.* 14 Nov. 1883, Margaret, dau. of William Leader, of Rosnalee, co. Cork, and has issue,
  1. WILLIAM FORTESCUE, Lieut. R.A., *b.* 13 Aug. 1885.
  2. Michael Richard Leader, *b.* 27 Nov. 1889.

Armstrong. THE LANDED GENTRY. 12

3. Henry Maxwell, *b.* 12 Feb. 1891.
4. James Robert Bargrave, *b.* 6 April, 1893.
5. Christopher Wyborne, *b.* 9 May, 1899.
1. Frances Margaret Alice.   2. Dorothea Gertrude.
3. Margaret Helen Elizabeth.

Lineage.—EDWARD ARMSTRONG, son of William Armstrong, by Jane Garver his wife, *m.* 1760, Grace Jones, and had two sons,
1. WILLIAM JONES.   2. Edward.
The elder,
REV. WILLIAM JONES ARMSTRONG, M.A., Rector of the Union of Termonfechan, co. Louth, *m.* Sept. 1786, Margaret, 3rd dau. of Alderman John Tew, Lord Mayor of Dublin (and Margaret Maxwell, his wife, grandniece of John, 1st Lord Farnham), and grand-dau. of Alderman David Tew, Lord Mayor of same city 1752, by whom he had issue,
1. WILLIAM JONES, his heir.
2. John Tew, *m.* Anne, only dau. of Ralph Tew, of Raddinstown co. Meath, and had issue,
  1. Maxwell.   2. John.
  3. Thomas Fortescue, *d.* 31 Jan. 1908.
  1. Anne.
3. Thomas Knox, of Fellowes Hall, J.P. co. Armagh, *m.* Catherine Frances, 2nd dau. of the late Wallop Brabazon, of Rath House, co. Louth, by Jane his 1st wife, dau. of Josias Dupré, of Wilton Park, Bucks, and *d.* at Rome, Jan. 1840, leaving issue,
  1. Jane Rebecca, *m.* 25 Nov. 1890, Acheson St. George, of Wood Park, co. Armagh. He *d.s.p.* 2 July, 1902 (*see that family*).
  2. Diana Lucinda, *d. unm.*
1. Helen, *m.* the Rev. John Kerr, Rector of the Union of Termonfechan.
2. Anne, *m.* Walter Newton, late of the 21st Light Dragoons.
3. Diana Jane, dec.
The eldest son,
WILLIAM JONES ARMSTRONG, of Killylea, J.P. and D.L., High Sheriff 1840, *b.* 22 May, 1794 ; *m.* 3 Feb. 1842, Frances Elizabeth, widow of Col. Sir Henry M'Creagh, C.B., K.C.H., &c., and only dau. of Capt. Christopher Wilson, of the 22nd Foot, and by her (who *d.* 1894) had issue,
1. WILLIAM FORTESCUE, *b.* 28 Jan. 1843, late 7th Hussars, *d. unm.* 2 May, 1871.
2. HENRY BRUCE, now of Killylea.
Mr. Armstrong assumed, by Royal Licence 20 Feb. 1868, the name and arms of WRIGHT under the will of Lady Frances E. Wright-Wilson, and *d.* 1872.

Arms—Quarterly : 1st and 4th, ARMSTRONG, per pale gu. and vert, three dexter armed arms, couped at the shoulders and embowed, the hands clenched, ppr. ; 2nd and 3rd, WRIGHT, arg. three bars gemel gu., on a chief az. three leopards' faces or, a canton erm. for distinction. Crests—1st, ARMSTRONG : Out of a mural coronet or, an armed arm embowed, the hand grasping an oak tree eradicated, ppr. ; 2nd, WRIGHT : Out of a mural crown, chequy, or and gu., a dragon's head vert, on the neck three leopards' faces as in the arms, between two bars gemel, a trefoil slipped or. Motto—Invictus maneo.

Seats—Killylea, co. Armagh and Dean's Hill, Armagh. Clubs—Carlton, S.W., and Kildare Street, Dublin.

HEATON-ARMSTRONG OF FARNEY CASTLE AND MOUNT HEATON.

WILLIAM CHARLES HEATON - ARMSTRONG (senior representative of the Armstrongs of Farney Castle and Mount Heaton), Lord of the Manor of Roscrea, King's Co., M.P. for Sudbury 1906-:o, *b.* 1 Sept. 1853 ; *m.* 7 Sept. 1885, at Veldes, Austria, the Baronesse Bertha Maxmiliana Zois-Edelstein, only surviving dau. of the 4th Baron Zois-Edelstein, of Austria, and has issue,

1. WILLIAM DUNCAN FRANCIS, *b.* at Veldes, Austria, 29 Sept. 1886.
2. John Dunamace, *b.* in Middlesex, 21 Feb. 1888.
1. Bertha Grace, *b.* in London, 2 Jan. 1893.

Mr. Heaton-Armstrong succeeded, at his father's death, 29 April, 1891, to the representation of the families of Armstrong, of Farney Castle and Mount Heaton, Mealiffe, &c. ; of MacDonnell, of New Hall ; and also of the family of Heaton, of Moorhouse, Yorkshire, whose representative (*temp.* Queen ELIZABETH) was Bishop of Ely. Mr. Heaton-Armstrong is 19th in descent from King EDWARD I of England and 14th from King JAMES II of Scotland (*see* BURKE's *Royal Descents*).

Lineage.—SIR THOMAS ARMSTRONG, Knt., M.P., *b.* at Nimeguen, in Holland. He obtained considerable grants of land in Ireland, among others the lands of Straffan, co. Kildare, and house property in the cities of Waterford, Limerick, and Leicester. He had been a great sufferer in the royal cause, and was very active for CHARLES II before the Restoration. His enterprising spirit excited the jealousy of Cromwell, who threw him into prison and even threatened his life. He was after the Restoration reappointed Quarter-Master Gen. of the Cavalry in Ireland, and *d.* Nov. 1662, leaving issue a son,
SIR THOMAS ARMSTRONG engaged with all the zeal that was natural to him in the service of the Duke of Monmouth. Finding himself obnoxious to the court he fled the kingdom and went to Holland, and his flight was soon followed by outlawry. He was seized abroad and sent to London where he was condemned for the Rye House Plot by Chief Justice Jeffries, and executed on the 20th June, 1684, without a trial, and with peculiar circumstances of rigour. (*See State Trials.*) He at his death denied having ever had any intention against his Majesty's life. The attainder was subsequently reversed in the Court of King's Bench, 6 WILLIAM III, and by Act of Parliament £6,000 and an annuity of £2,000 a year was granted to Lady Armstrong. Sir Thomas was gentleman of the horse to King CHARLES II, Capt. of the 1st troop of Royal Horse Guards, commission dated 30 Dec. 12 CHARLES II, and Lieut.-Col. of the 3rd troop of Horse Guards and served in Parliament for Stafford (1640) and for Leicestershire (1660). He *m.* Katherine, dau. of James Pollexfen, of Stansted Mont-Fitchet, co. Essex, and by her (who *d.* 1693) had three daus.,
1. Jane, *m.* the distinguished Admiral Mathew.
2. Mary, *m.* Mr. Pollexfen, the celebrated lawyer, who defended Lord William Russell in 1683.
3. Catherine, *d. unm.*
The only brother of Sir Thomas was CAPT. WILLIAM ARMSTRONG, founder of the family in Tipperary, who went over to Ireland and settled in the old castle at Farney Bridge (lease granted by Duke of Ormonde, 3 Nov. 1670), near Thurles, where he was followed by his brother's widow, Lady Armstrong. He obtained a grant under the Act of Settlement of Bohercarron and other lands in the county of Limerick dated 3 March, 1666.
WILLIAM ARMSTRONG was Capt. of the troop of horse attached to the Tipperary Militia in 1688. He *m.* Alice, dau. of Sir Thomas Deane, and by her had issue, two sons,
1. JOHN, his successor.
2. Thomas, of Mealiffe (*see that family*).
The elder son,
JOHN ARMSTRONG, M.P. of Farney Castle, *s.* his father, and *m.* in 1695, Juliana, 2nd dau. of Robert Carew, of Ballyboro, co. Wexford, ancestor of Lord Carew (by Anne, dau. of Andrew Lynn, of Ballynamona, co. Waterford). He purchased, in 1677, large estates including the abbey and lands of Holycross, Ballycahill, &c. He was one of the Poll Tax Commissioners in 1669. He *d.* 16 May, 1707 (adm. to his widow 26 Aug. 1717), leaving issue by his wife (who survived him, and *d.* 27 Nov. 1737, aged 61) four sons,
1. WILLIAM, his successor.   2. Robert, *d. unm.*
3. John, ancestor of the present Farney Castle branch. He *m.* in 1740, Anne, dau. of Anthony Blunt, of the co. Kilkenny, by whom he had issue, four sons and three daus.
4. James William, in holy orders, *m.* Sarah Nicholson.
The eldest son,
COL. WILLIAM ARMSTRONG, M.P., of Farney Castle and Mount Heaton, *b.* 1 June, 1688, as Col. of the Tipperary Militia, High Sheriff in 1738. He *m.* 6 March, 1731, Mary, 3rd dau. and co-heiress of Francis Heaton, of Mount Heaton, King's Co. (and formerly of Moorhouse in the co. York, where they were settled at the time of the Conquest) by Elizabeth, dau. of Robert Curtis, of Inane, M.P. The principal family residence was then changed to Mount Heaton (otherwise called Ballyskennagh), and Farney Castle was subsequently given over to his younger brother John. William (having survived his wife) *d.* intestate 1 Jan. 1767, leaving issue, a son and a dau.,
JOHN, of whom presently.
Mary, *m.* 12 Sept. 1755, the Very Rev. George Thomas, D.D., and *d.* 27 March, 1795, leaving issue.
The son and heir,
THE RIGHT HON. JOHN ARMSTRONG, M.P., P.C., of Farney Castle and Mount Heaton, *b.* in 1732 ; *s.* his father in 1767. He *m.* 17 July, 1770, Letitia (*b.* 1724), eldest dau. and co-heiress of Abraham Greene of Ballymacreece, co. Limerick (by Honoria his wife, dau. of William Piers, of Portarlington, Queen's Co., 4th son of Sir W. Piers, Bart,, of Tristernagh Abbey, by the Lady Honoria Fitzmaurice, dau. of the 20th Earl of Kerry). He served in several parliaments for the boroughs of Kilmallock and Fore, and was made a member of the King's Privy Council in Ireland on 9 Sept. 1789. At one time he raised a troop of horse for the King's service, and maintained them at his own cost, refusing all offers of reward for his services. In consideration of other important services he had done the country, he was twice urged by the Irish Government to take a baronetcy, which he declined. It was subsequently arranged that he was to be made a peer, under the title of Baron of Dunamace, in Ireland, and the patent was lodged at the Hanaper Office, when he *d.* suddenly before the patent had passed the Great Seal, at Mount Heaton, 12 Sept. 1791, aged 59. He was buried in the churchyard at Ballycahill, and left issue (by his wife, who *m.* 2ndly, the Very Rev. James Hobson, and *d.* at Sidmouth, 28 Jan. 1820, aged 75, and is buried there), one son and one dau.,

WILLIAM HENRY, his heir.
Elizabeth Mary, b. 20 Jan. 1773; d. (accidentally burned) in Dublin, 26 Feb. 1780, and is bur. at Ballycahill.
The son and heir,
WILLIAM HENRY ARMSTRONG, M.P., of Mount Heaton, b. at Toulouse in France, 21 June, 1774; m. 7 April, 1809, Bridget, only dau. and (in her issue) co-heiress of the late Col. Charles Macdonnell, M.P., of New Hall, co. Clare (by Bridget, dau. of John Bayly, of Debsborough, co. Tipperary). He voted against the union of England and Ireland, as mentioned by Sir J. Barrington in his memoirs. From the year 1816 he resided almost entirely on the Continent, and, not intending to return to Ireland, he sold, in 1817, Mount Heaton, and in 1834, his Fermanagh, and nearly all his Limerick, Tipperary and English estates, 133,460 acres. He d. at Passy, near Paris, 21 Sept. 1835, aged 61, and is buried in the Montmartre Cemetery at Paris. He had issue by his wife (who d. 20 Oct. 1860, aged 70) four sons and seven daus.,
1. JOHN, late representative of the family.
2. Charles William, b. at Abbeville, 19 April, 1819; d. there, 31 May, 1819.
3. William Edward ARMSTRONG-MACDONNELL, of New Hall, co. Clare, J.P. and D.L., High Sheriff 1853, Col. Com. Clare Militia ; took the additional surname and arms of MACDONNELL by Royal Licence in 1858 ; m. 20 July, 1858, Hon. Juliana Cecilia O'Brien, eldest dau. of Lucius, 13th Lord Inchiquin, and d. in Dublin, 11 Nov. 1883, leaving five sons and three daus. (see ARMSTRONG-MACDONNELL of New Hall).
4. Charles, late of Larch Hill, co. Clare (79, *George Street, Limerick*), b. at Florence, 7 May, 1830, assumed the additional name of HEATON in 1884 ; m. 29 March, 1856, Georgina Maria, eldest dau. of Richard John Stacpoole, of Eden Vale, co. Clare, J.P. and D.L., and d. 18 Feb. 1906, having had issue,
   1. Charles Richard Beauchamp, b. 3 Sept. 1858 ; m. 24 April, 1895, Ethel Maria Beatrice, dau. of Charles de la Cherois Purdon, M.D., and has issue,
      (1) Charles George William Stacpoole, b. 12 Feb. 1896.
      (2) Louis John, b. 26 April, 1905.
      (3) Robert Carew, b. 8 Dec. 1907.
   2. George William Bayly, b. 11 March, 1860 ; m. 9 Oct. 1895, Alice Jane, dau. of Frederick William Garron, of Ilford House, Essex.
   3. William Henry, b. 16 July, 1863 ; d. unm. 28 Oct. 1906.
   1. Elizabeth Letitia, m. 7 Aug. 1895, Col. Richard Arthur Milton Henn, commanding Limerick City Artillery, late R.A., and has issue (see HENN of *Paradise Hill*).
   2. Letitia Mary, b. at Mount Heaton, 11 Feb. 1810 ; d. there, 11 July, 1811.
   2. Letitia Charlotte, m. 1 June, 1841, Charles William Hamilton, J.P., of Hamwood, co. Meath, and d. 28 June, 1872, leaving issue. He d. 16 Feb. 1880.
   3. Catherine Gertrude, m. 17 Oct. 1839, John Bayly, of Debsborough, co. Tipperary, and d. 4 Oct. 1874, having by him (who d. 14 May, 1865) had issue (see *that family*).
   4. Bridget, m. 23 March, 1849, James Dobree, of Rock Lodge, co. Devon, and d. 4 April, 1880, leaving issue.
   5. Mary, m. 12 July, 1842, the Ven. Evans Johnston, D.D., B.A., Archdeacon of Ferns, and d. 8 March, 1885, leaving issue.
   6. Emily Dorothea, b. 21 Dec. 1817 ; d. unm. at Paris, 5 Feb. 1836, and is bur. near her father.
   7. Louisa, m. 21 Dec. 1861, Rev. Francis Henry Hall, incumbent of Holly Mount, co. Down (who d. 10 June, 1880). She d.s.p. 14 Nov. 1891.
The eldest son,
JOHN HEATON-ARMSTRONG, Lord of the Manor of Roscrea, was heir-male of the family of ARMSTRONG of *Farney Castle, Mount Heaton and Mealiffe*, as well as of the families of MACDONNELL of *New Hall* and HEATON of *Yorkshire*. In accordance with the terms of his grandfather's will, he assumed by Royal Licence the additional surname and arms of HEATON. He was b. at Mount Heaton 1 May, 1815 ; m. at H.B.M. Embassy, Vienna, 29 May, 1849, Josephine Thérèse Mayr, of Leoben, Styria, and by her (who d. in Jersey, 5 April, 1858, and is there buried) (see BARONS MAYR-MELNHOF in *the Peerage of Austria*) had issue,
1. John Childe, b. 1 Jan. 1850 ; m. 21 Nov. 1885, Lucy Ann, youngest dau. of Major Charles Henry Cobbe, 60th Regt., and d.s.p. in London, 30 March, 1886, and is bur. there.
2. WILLIAM CHARLES, present representative of the family.
1. Bids Louisa. 2. Lucy Emily.
Mr. Heaton-Armstrong served as Lieut. in the Austrian Cuirassiers and Walmoden Dragoons, and was offered to be created a Count of the Austrian Empire and a Chamberlain to the Emperor, but declined the honour. In later years, from 1839 to 1848, he was distinguished as a traveller in South America and Australia, in which latter country he made many valuable discoveries. He d. 29 April, 1891, at Goertz, and is there buried.
Arms—Quarterly : 1st and 4th (ARMSTRONG) gu., three dexter arms vambranced and embowed ppr. ; 2nd and 3rd (HEATON) vert, a lion rampant arg. Crests—1st (ARMSTRONG), a dexter arm vambranced and embowed, the hand grasping an armed leg couped at the thigh and bleeding, all ppr. ; 2nd (HEATON), a lion rampant ppr. ducally crowned, plain collared and chained or. Motto—Vi et armis.
Residence—30, Portland Place, London, W. Club—Union.

SAVAGE-ARMSTRONG OF CORRATINNER.

MARIE ELIZABETH SAVAGE-ARMSTRONG, of Corratinner, co. Cavan, younger dau. and co-heiress of the late Rev. John Wrixon, M.A., Vicar of Malone, co. Antrim, and his wife Anne Arabella, dau. and eventual co-heiress of the late Rear-Admiral J. Dawson, m. 24 April, 1879, GEORGE FRANCIS SAVAGE-ARMSTRONG, M.A. (*stip. con.*), Dub. Univ., D.Lit. (*honoris causâ*), R.U.I., Author of *The Tragedy of Israel, Stories of Wicklow, One of the Infinite, Ballads of Down*, and many other poetical works. Mr. Savage-Armstrong, b. 5 May, 1845, was the only surviving son of the late Edmund John Armstrong, who d. 1870, by his wife Jane (who d. 3 Jan. 1880), dau. and eventual heiress of the late Rev. Henry Savage, of Glastry, in the Ards, co. Down, B.A. and J.P., Incumbent of Ardkeen (see NUGENT-SAVAGE of *Portaferry*, and BURKE'S *Family Records*, SAVAGE). On the death of a maternal uncle, he assumed by deed poll, 29 Dec. 1890, as representative of his grandfather, the additional surname of SAVAGE, and d. 24 July, 1906, leaving issue,
1. FRANCIS SAVAGE NESBITT, Capt. 1st Batt. South Staffs Regt., educated at Shrewsbury and served in South African War 1899-1902 (Queen's medal with three clasps and King's medal with two clasps), b. 5 July, 1880.
2. John Raymond Savage, Capt. 4th Batt. Leinster Regt., educated at Shrewsbury and Trin. Coll. Dublin, b. 13 May, 1882.
1. Arabella Guendolen Savage.

Lineage.—THOMAS DAWSON, elder brother of Dr. Robert Dawson, consecrated Bishop of Clonfert 1627, went to Ireland 1601, it is stated, from Temple Sowerby, Westmorland, and purchased the lands of Castle Dawson, co. Londonderry. His son and successor,
THOMAS DAWSON, Commissary of the Musters of the Army in Ireland, d. 1683, and was s. by his son,
THOMAS DAWSON, of Castle Dawson, M.P. for Antrim, who m. Olivia Upton, of Castle Upton, co. Antrim, and was s. by his brother,
JOSHUA DAWSON, of Castle Dawson, M.P. for Wicklow, and Secretary for Ireland, *temp.* Queen ANNE. He m. Jan. 1695-96, Anne, dau. of Thomas Carr, son of Sir George Carr, Secretary for Ireland, and d. 1727, leaving, with other issue,
1. ARTHUR, his son and heir, a Baron of the Exchequer, ancestor of DAWSON of *Moyola Park*, co. Londonderry, now represented by LADY SPENCER CHICHESTER (see BURKE'S *Peerage*, DONEGALL, M.).
2. William, Surveyor-General of Munster, m. and had issue.
3. CHARLES, of whose line we treat.
1. Mary, m. to Right Hon. Henry Hamilton, M.P.
The youngest son,
CHARLES DAWSON, H.M. Inspector of Customs for Ireland, m. Sarah, dau. of John Downing, of Bellaghy and Rowesgift, co. Londonderry (b. 1700), eldest son of Col. Adam Downing (served with distinction at the siege of Derry and the Battle of the Boyne, b. 1666, d. 1719), and grandson of Henry Downing (b. 1630, younger brother of Sir George Downing, Bart., the eminent statesman, *temp.* CHARLES II ; *see* FULLERTON of *Ballintoy* and BEAUMONT-NESBITT of *Tubberdaly*), and by her had issue, two sons and three daus. The elder surviving son,
REAR ADMIRAL JOHN DAWSON, R.N., of Carrickfergus, and of co. Cavan, b. 1760, served in the war with America, &c., under Rodney and Howe ; m. his 1st cousin, Medicis, eldest dau. of the Rev. Alexander Clotworthy Downing, of Bellaghy and Rowesgift, co. Londonderry, Rector of Leckpatrick, co. Tyrone, and of Thamazine his wife, dau. and heiress of Albert Nesbitt, of Tubberdaly, King's Co., and by her had issue,
1. Charles, d. in infancy.
2. Alexander, Lieut. R.N., b. 18 Dec. 1800 ; m. Elizabeth, dau. of Richard Gresley (see BURKE'S *Peerage*, GRESLEY, Bart.), and d. 1841, s.p.
3. Andrew Hamond Snape, M.A., in Holy Orders, of Dunloskin, Carrickfergus, and of co. Cavan, m. Anne, dau. of Robert Haire, Q.C., of Ballagh House, co. Fermanagh, and d. 1873, s.p.
1. THAMAZINE, eventual co-heiress with her sister, Mrs. Wrixon, b. 1796, m. 1824, Rev. John Bradshaw, Incumbent of Lambeg, co. Antrim. She d. 1883, leaving an only child, Thamazine, m. to the Rev. T. G. Beaumont, M.A., whose eldest son, EDWARD DOWNING BEAUMONT-NESBITT, is now of Tubberdaly.
2. ANNE ARABELLA, of Corratinner, co. Cavan, co-heiress with her sister, Mrs. Bradshaw, m. 1847, the Rev. John Wrixon, M.A., Vicar of Malone, co. Antrim, youngest son of Capt. John Wrixon, 5th Dragoon Guards, by his wife, Maria, dau. of Col. Bentley, H.E.I.C.S., and grandson of Edward Wrixon, of Gurteenbaha, co. Cork (d. 1788), great-grandson of Henry Wrixon, of Blossomfort, co. Cork, and great-great-grandson of John Wrixon, of Blossomfort and Lissard, co. Cork, whose grandfather was Robert Wrixon, of co. Cork (living 1666). Mr. Wrixon d. 1876, leaving issue,
1. ANNA MEDICI, now of Dunloskin, Carrickfergus, and of co. Cavan, co-heiress with her sister, Mrs. SAVAGE-ARMSTRONG, m. 1870, to JOHN GODFREY ECHLIN, of Ardquin, and has issue (see ECHLIN of *Ardquin*).
2. MARIE ELIZABETH, now of Corratinner, co-heiress with her sister, Mrs. ECHLIN.

Residence—Strangford House, Strangford, co. Down.

ARMSTRONG OF MOYALIFFE AND CHAFFPOOL.

MARCUS BERESFORD ARMSTRONG, of Mealiffe, co. Tipperary, and Chaffpool, co. Sligo, J.P. and D.L. co. Tipperary, High Sheriff co. Tipperary 1905, and J.P. co. Sligo, late Capt. 8th Brig. N. Irish Div. R.A., *b.* 19 May, 1861, only son of William Armstrong of Chaffpool, who *d.* 1889, and Catherine his wife, dau. of Gen. Clark, *m.* 11 April, 1888, Rosalie Cornelia, 2nd dau. of Maurice Cecly Maude, of Lenaghan Park, Enniskillen (*see* BURKE'S *Peerage*, HAWARDEN, V.), and has issue.

1. WILLIAM MAURICE, Lieut. 10th Royal Hussars, *b.* 20 Aug. 1889.
1. Cornelia Ione Kathleen. 2. Rosalie Winona.
3. Lisalie Maude.

Mr. M. B. Armstrong had four sisters: 1. Elise Catherine *m.* Robert Gun, 2nd son of Sir R. G. Paul, Bart., Ballyglan, co. Waterford; 2. Eleanor Clara; 3. Mildred Alice; and 4. Grace *d.* 1905.

Lineage.—This is a younger branch of the family of ARMSTRONG *of Mount Heaton* (*whom see*). THOMAS ARMSTRONG, of Mealiffe, co. Tipperary, High Sheriff *temp.* ANNE, younger son of Capt. William Armstrong, and Alice his wife, dau. of Sir Thomas Deane. He was *b.* 1671, *m.* Mary, dau. of Robert Carew, of Castleboro', and *d.* 20 July, 1741, leaving seven sons and six daus. His descendant,

REV. WILLIAM CAREW ARMSTRONG, of Mealiffe, Chancellor of Cashel, *m.* 11 Nov. 1789, Hon. Katherine Elleanor Beresford, eldest dau. of the Most Rev. William, 1st Lord Decies, Archbishop of Tuam, and *d.* May, 1839, having by her (who *d.* 1837) had, with other issue, a son,

JOHN ARMSTRONG, of Mealiffe, J.P. and D.L., *m.* 1818, Catherine, dau. and heir of Thomas Somers, of Chaffpool, co. Sligo, and *d.* 2 Dec. 1846, having by her (who *d.* 21 April, 1868) had issue,
1. William, Capt. 47th Regt., *m.* Mathilde Rose, dau. of Count de la Brosse, and *d.* 7 March, 1849, having by her (who *m.* 2ndly, Thomas Armstrong) had a son,
   John, *d.* young.
2. Thomas Somers, Lieut. 60th Rifles, *d.* 7 June, 1847.
3. Marcus, *d.* young.
4. George de la Poer, of Mealiffe, *d. unm.* June, 1864.
5. James Wood, of Chaffpool, co. Sligo, Capt. R.N., J.P. and D.L., High Sheriff 1873, *b.* 21 Nov. 1827; *d. unm.*
6. EDWARD MARCUS, late of Mealiffe and Chaffpool.
7. Francis Henry, *b.* 1836, *d. unm.*
1. Elizabeth, *d. unm.* 2. Kathleen Eleanor, *d. unm.*

The 6th son,

EDWARD MARCUS ARMSTRONG, of Moyaliffe, Thurles, co. Tipperary, J.P. and D.L., High Sheriff 1884, late Capt. 55th Regt., *b.* 20 Sept. 1829; *m.* 19 Oct. 1863, Frances, youngest dau. of Walter Steele, of Moynalty, co. Monaghan, by his wife Mary Sophia Jocelyn, and *d.s.p.* 29 March, 1899, when he was *s.* by his cousin.

Seats—Moyaliffe, Thurles; and Chaffpool, Ballymote, co. Sligo. **Club**—Kildare Street, Dublin.

ARMSTRONG OF GARRY CASTLE.

THOMAS ST. GEORGE ARMSTRONG, of Garry Castle, King's Co., Gentleman-in-waiting to H.M. the King of Portugal, Knight Commander of the Royal and Military Order of the Conception of Christ of Portugal; Knight of St. John of Jerusalem (Malta); Knight of the Order of the Holy Sepulchre, &c., &c., *b.* 26 Nov. 1838; *m.* 14 June, 1886, Maria do Carmen de Portugal de Faria, dau. of Viscount Augusto de Faria, and Maria de Portugal, related to the Royal House of Paz and de Godoy of Spain, and has issue,

Maria Helena Justa, *b.* 9 April, 1887, *m.* Count Gouziaque d'Aymar de Chateaubriand.

Lineage.—ANDREW ARMSTRONG, *b.* 1732, 3rd son of ANDREW ARMSTRONG, Treasurer of the King's Co. (*see* BURKE'S *Peerage*, ARMSTRONG, Bt.), was an Officer in the 14th Regt., but being severely wounded at the siege of Louisberg, he retired from the army. He resided at Garry Castle, King's Co., and was County Treasurer and J.P. He *m.* 5 May, 1756, Elizabeth, only dau. of Capt. James Buchanan, of Craigavern and Dromakill, Scotland, of the family of that ilk, and by her (who *d.* 21 Sept. 1813, aged 72) had issue,
1. Archibald, *b.* 1 Nov. 1763, Capt. in the E.I.C.S., *d.s.p.*
2. Andrew, *b.* 20 Oct. 1764, Lieut. 54th Regt.; *m.* 14 Jan. 1793, Anne, dau. of Andrew Armstrong, of Gallen, and had issue,
   1. William Bigoe, *b.* 1801, dec. 2. John, *d.* 1855.
   1. Constancia Maria, *d. unm.*

2. Elizabeth, *m.* William Baillie Brett, and had issue.
3. THOMAS ST. GEORGE, of Garry Castle.
4. William Bigoe, of Bal Iver, King's Co., Treasurer of the co., *b.* 19 July, 1768; *m.* 1796, Jane Wilhelmina, only child of Gen. James Ferrier, R.E., and by her (who *d.* 16 April, 1829) had an only child,
   James Ferrier, of Bal Iver, Treasurer of the co., *m.* 14 Jan. 1836, Honoria, dau. of John Fleming, M.P. of Stoneham Park, Hants, and *d.* 13 April, 1866, leaving an only son,
      William Bigoe, of Bal Iver, Treasurer of the co., *m.* 4 April, 1866, Anna Maria de Courcy, 2nd dau. of James Freeman Hughes, of The Grove, Stillorgan, co. Dublin, and *d.s.p.* 1890.
5. James, *b.* 20 Aug. 1769, formerly Lieut. 46th Regt. and subsequently Paymaster 57th. He *m.* in the West Indies, and is deceased.
6. Edmund, *b.* 10 Jan. 1772, Maj. in the E.I.C.S.; *m.* Leonora Lucas, and *d.* in India 1809, having had one son and three daus.,
   1. Andrew Bigoe, in the E.I.C.S., *b.* 11 June, 1802; killed in action in Burmah.
   1. Leonora, *d. unm.* 2. Mary Elizabeth.
   3. Catherine Rebecca.
7. Bigoe Charles, *b.* 17 May, 1775, Capt. 57th Regt.: *d. unm.*
1. Catherine Rebecca, *m.* 27 Jan. 1784, Hugh Conrahy, and had issue,
2. Mary, *m.* 1792, Capt. William Grant, of the Clare Militia, son of James Grant, and had issue.
3. Elizabeth, *m.* 1794, John Armstrong, Lieut. Royal Irish Artillery, of co. Fermanagh, and had issue.

The 3rd son,

THOMAS ST. GEORGE ARMSTRONG, of Garry Castle House, King's Co., High Sheriff 1809, *b.* 14 Nov. 1765; *m.* 14 Feb. 1792, Elizabeth, dau. of Thomas Priaulx, of the Island of Guernsey, of an ancient Norman family, and *d.* 1844, leaving issue,
1. CARTERET ANDREW, of Garry Castle.
2. Thomas St. George, *b.* April, 1798; *m.* Donna Justa de Villanueva, dau. of Don Pedro de Villanueva, a Castillian of noble descent, settled in Buenos Ayres, and *d.* 9 June, 1875, having by her (who *d.* 18 Jan. 1876) had issue,
   1. THOMAS ST. GEORGE, now of Garry Castle (by purchase from his cousin, Maj. Carteret A. Armstrong, 16 May, 1890)..
   1. Isabel, *m.* Don Frederico de Elortondo (dec.), of Buenos Ayres, and has issue.
   2. Emma. 3. Justa, *d. unm.* 24 April, 1888.
   4. Dolores, *m.* Mons. Enrique Dosé, of Havre, and has issue.
3. William Bigoe, *b.* 13 April, 1800; *m.* 1st, Elizabeth Banko, and had by her three sons and two daus.,
   1. CARTERET ANDREW, late of Garry Castle, late Capt. 10th Regt., J.P. for King's Co. and Maj. (retired) 3rd Batt. East Lancashire Regt. *b.* 25 Nov. 1838; *m.* 3 Sept. 1863, Ellen, 2nd dau. of the late Hugh Dawson, of Leyland and West Cliff, co. Lancaster, and *d.* 1893. She *d.s.p.* 9 April, 1904.
   2. Thomas St. George, *b.* 5 Feb. 1845; *d.* 20 Jan. 1875.
   3. John Le Merchant, *b.* 5 Feb. 1845; *d.* 18 Oct. 1883.
   1. Elizabeth Priaulx, *m.* Col. James Crawford.
   2. Justa Honoria Villanueva, *m.* Thomas A. White, of Ballybrophy, Queen's Co. (*see* WHITE, *of Charleville*).
Mr. W. B. Armstrong *m.* 2ndly, Katherine Temple, and *d.* 2 Oct. 1866, leaving by her had two sons and one dau.,
   4. William Bigoe. 5. Osmond de Beauvoir Priaulx.
   3. Isabel Elortondo.
4. John Priaulx, of Claremont, *b.* 21 Jan. 1802, J.P. King's Co.; *m.* 20 Nov. 1827, his cousin Emma, 6th dau. of the late Thomas Priaulx, of Montville House, Island of Guernsey, and *d.* 1879, leaving issue,
   1. Thomas Priaulx St. George, of Claremont, Banagher, King's Co., J.P., *b.* 28 March, 1833, Knt. of the Legion of Honour, late Maj. 49th Regt., served in that Regt. throughout the Crimea; *m.* 31 Oct. 1860, Elizabeth Mary, dau. of the late Robert James Graves, F.R.S., of Cloghan Castle, King's Co., and by her (who *d.* 1892) has issue,
      (1) John Priaulx, late Ceylon Civil Service, Superintendent of Police (retired), *b.* 10 Dec. 1866.
      (2) Reginald Graves, J.P., co. Wicklow, F.R.S.I., *b.* 20 April, 1868.
      (3) James St. George Priaulx, Hon. Major in the Army, late Major Imp. Yeomanry, served in the Matabele War 1896 (medal), Mashonaland 1897 (clasp), Bechuanaland, &c. (medal and clasp), throughout South African War with the Imp. Yeomanry 1900-02 (Queen's medal, three clasps; King's medal, two clasps), mentioned in Despatches and granted Hon. rank of Major in the Army, *b.* 13 Oct. 1873.
      (1) Olivia Graves Priaulx.
      (2) Anna Louisa, who *d.* 1885.
   2. John Priaulx, *b.* 8 June, 1836; *d. unm.* 25 May, 1901.
   3. James St. George, Capt. 22nd Regt., *b.* 4 July, 1838; *d.* 28 July, 1872.
   4. Edmond Ireland (Rev.), *b.* 14 Aug. 1841; *m.* 1st, Miss Robinson, and 2ndly, Mary Ormsby, and by his 1st wife had a dau.,
      Emma.
   5. Andrew Carteret, *b.* 11 March, 1845.
   1. Anna Louisa, *b.* 1 Aug. 1829; *d.* 10 Aug. 1850.

The eldest son,

CARTERET ANDREW ARMSTRONG, of Garry Castle, Barrister-at-Law, *b.* 19 May, 1797; *d. unm.* 7 April, 1869, having devised his property to his nephew, MAJ. CARTERET ANDREW ARMSTRONG, who sold Garry Castle to his cousin, 16 May, 1890.

Seat—Garry Castle House, Banagher, King's Co. *Residence*—32, Rue de Monceau, Paris.

ARTHUR OF GLANOMERA.

CHARLES WILLIAM AUGUSTUS ARTHUR, of Glanomera, co. Clare, Capt. City of Limerick Art., *b.* 24 Sept. 1882 ; *s.* his father 1888 ; *m.* 1904, Rose Violet, 3rd dau. of the late John Joseph Roche-Kelly, of Rockstown Castle and Islandmore, co. Limerick, and has had issue,

Charles Augustus, *b.* 11 July ; *d.* 5 Aug. 1905.

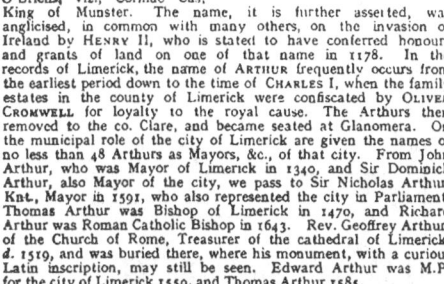

Lineage.—The ARTHURS are stated to have been originally "Artureighs," and to derive their descent from a common ancestor with the O'Briens, viz., Cormac Cas, King of Munster. The name, it is further asserted, was anglicised, in common with many others, on the invasion of Ireland by HENRY II, who is stated to have conferred honours and grants of land on one of that name in 1178. In the records of Limerick, the name of ARTHUR frequently occurs from the earliest period down to the time of CHARLES I, when the family estates in the county of Limerick were confiscated by OLIVER CROMWELL for loyalty to the royal cause. The Arthurs then removed to the co. Clare, and became seated at Glanomera. On the municipal role of the city of Limerick are given the names of no less than 48 Arthurs as Mayors, &c., of that city. From John Arthur, who was Mayor of Limerick in 1340, and Sir Dominick Arthur, also Mayor of the city, we pass to Sir Nicholas Arthur, Knt., Mayor in 1591, who also represented the city in Parliament. Thomas Arthur was Bishop of Limerick in 1470, and Richard Arthur was Roman Catholic Bishop in 1643. Rev. Geoffrey Arthur, of the Church of Rome, Treasurer of the cathedral of Limerick, *d.* 1519, and was buried there, where his monument, with a curious Latin inscription, may still be seen. Edward Arthur was M.P. for the city of Limerick 1559, and Thomas Arthur 1585.

THOMAS ARTHUR, of Glanomera, son of Piers Arthur, by Margaret his wife, dau. and heiress of Thomas Arthur, of Glanomera, representative of this ancient house, *m.* Elizabeth, dau. of Capt. John Butler, heiress of the BUTLERS *of Kilmoyler*, co. Tipperary, descended from Hon. Piers Butler, 7th son of James, 9th Earl of Ormonde, by his wife Joan, dau. and heiress of 11th Earl of Desmond, and was father of

THOMAS ARTHUR, of Glanomera, who *m.* Nov. 1766, Lucy, 4th dau. of Sir Edward O'Brien Bart., of Dromoland, and left by her at his decease, 1803 (with a dau. Mary, *m.* Richard Henn, of Paradise, co. Clare), an only son and successor,

THOMAS ARTHUR, of Glanomera, D.L., *b.* April, 1778 ; *m.* 10 April, 1803, Harriet 2nd dau. and co-heir (with her only sister, Charlotte, wife of Sir Edward O'Brien, Bart., of Dromoland) of William Smith, of Cabirmoyle, co. Limerick, and had (with nine daus. all deceased) seven sons,

1. THOMAS, his heir.
2. William Smith, *b.* 13 June, 1809 ; *m.* 1830, Caroline Sydney, eldest dau. of Frederick Saintbury Parker, of Saintbury, co. Dublin, and *d.s.p.* March, 1840.
3. LUCIUS (Rev.), heir to his brother.
4. EDWARD, Barrister-at-Law, *b.* 7 Jan. 1817 ; *d.s.p.* 6 Aug. 1853.
5. Richard Augustus, J.P. co. Clare, *b.* 27 Aug. 1819 ; *m.* 13 Aug. 1885, Augusta, eldest dau. of the late Lieut.-Gen. George Dean-Pitt, C.B., Keeper of the Crown Jewels. He *d.s.p.* 29 March, 1902.
6. Henry (Rev.), Canon of Ferns, Diocese of Ossory, *b.* 12 Nov. 1820 ; *m.* 13 April, 1847, Ellen, 2nd dau. of Henry Joy Tombe, and *d.s.p.*
7. Frederick Brian Boru (Rev.), *b.* 12 Sept. 1822 ; *d. unm.* 19 Jan. 1870.

Mr. Arthur *d.* 6 May, 1845, and was *s.* by his eldest son,

THOMAS ARTHUR, of Glanomera, *b.* 10 Sept. 1806 ; educated at Eton and Christ Church College, Oxford, who *d. unm.* 12 Sept. 1884, and was *s.* by his brother,

REV. LUCIUS ARTHUR, of Glanomera, educated at Harrow and Trin. Coll. Camb., *b.* 31 July, 1810 ; *m.* 21 April, 1840, Caroline Elizabeth, dau. and co-heir of John Havcock Jervis, of Moseley, co. Warwick, and Eliza, his wife, and *d.* 4 Jan. 1887, having by her (who *d.* 1 April, 1869) had issue,

1. THOMAS LUCIUS JERVIS, late of Glanomera.
2. Edward Henry Frederick, *d.* an infant.
3. Charles William Augustus. Capt. 65th Regt., *b.* 20 April, 1851 ; *d. unm.* at Morar, Bengal, 9 March, 1882.
1. Harriet Elizabeth Augusta, *m.* 26 April, 1871, Richard Perceval Fry, late H.M. Ind. Navy, who *d.s.p.* 6 Nov. 1892.
2. Ellen Lucy Julia, *m.* 2 Feb. 1893, George Stevenson, late of Tor House, Matlock.
3. Maria Anne Florence, *d. unm.* 31 July, 1878.
4. Charlotte Katherine Susan.
5. Grace Caroline Frances, *m.* 6 Nov. 1889, Rev. Frederick James Johnston-Smith, LL.D.

The eldest son,

THOMAS LUCIUS JERVIS ARTHUR, of Glanomera, J.P. co. Clare, formerly Lieut. Durham Fusiliers, and Capt. 6th R. V. Regt., *b.* 30 June, 1847 ; *m.* 28 April, 1881, Constance Helen, dau. of William Steele Studdert, of Clonboy, co. Clare, by Constance his wife, dau. of Robert George Massy (*see* BURKE'S *Peerage*, MASSY, B.), and *d.* 1888, having by her (who *m.* 2ndly, 1894, the late William Paumier Ball, Barrister-at-Law, son of Right Hon. J. T. Ball, P.C., and *d.* 17 June, 1902) had issue.

1. CHARLES WILLIAM AUGUSTUS, now of Glanomera.
2. Desmond Phelps Pery Lucius Studdert, *b.* 31 March, 1884.

Arms—Gu., a chevron arg. between three rests (or clarions) or, quartering BUTLER and FITZGERALD, Earls of Desmond, with numerous other quarterings. **Crest**—A falcon rising ppr. jessed and belled or. **Motto**—Impelle obstantia.

Seats—Glanomera, O'Brien's Bridge, and Corracloon-Arthur, co. Clare.

BERESFORD-ASH OF ASHBROOK.

COLONEL WILLIAM RANDAL HAMILTON BERESFORD - ASH, of Ashbrook, co. Londonderry, D.L., late Royal Welsh Fus., *b.* 19 July, 1859 ; *m.* 23 Oct. 1886, Lady Florence Marion Browne, dau. of 5th Marquis of Sligo (*see* BURKE'S *Peerage*), and has issue,

DOUGLAS, *b.* 8 Sept. 1887, Lieut. Royal Fusiliers.

Colonel Beresford-Ash is the eldest son of JOHN BARRÉ BERESFORD, of Learmount, co. Londonderry (who *d.* 30 Aug. 1895), by Caroline, his 2nd wife (who *d.* 13 Jan. 1901), only child of William Hamilton Ash, D.L., of Ashbrook, co. Londonderry (by Lady Elizabeth Emma Douglas, his wife, who *d.* 2 Feb. 1857, sister of 17th Earl of Morton) and granddau. of William Hamilton Ash, of Ashbrook (who assumed the name of ASH, and *d.* 29 May, 1821), son of William Hamilton and Jane, his wife, dau. of George Ash and sister and heir of George Ash, of Ashbrook. He assumed the additional name and arms of ASH by Royal Licence, 26 June, 1901. The late John Barré Beresford, of Learmount, was grandson of the Right Hon. John Beresford, 2nd son of Marcus 1st Earl of Tyrone (*see* BURKE'S *Peerage*, WATERFORD, M.).

Lineage.—*See* BURKE'S *Peerage*, WATERFORD, M.

Arms—Quarterly 1st and 4th arg. two chevronels gu. in the dexter chief a trefoil slipped vert (ASH) ; 2nd and 3rd quarterly 1 and 4 arg. crusily fitchée three fleurs-de-lys, a bordure engrailed sa. (BERESFORD) 2 and 3 arg. a chief indented sa. (DE LA POER) a crescent for difference. **Crests**—1. A squirrel sejant ppr., holding in its paws a trefoil slipped vert (ASH). 2. A dragon's head erased vert pierced through the neck with a broken tilting spear the point thrust through the lower jaw all ppr., a crescent or for difference (BERESFORD). **Motto**—Nil nisi cruce.

Seat—Ashbrook, Londonderry. **Club**—Naval and Military.

ATHY OF RENVILLE.

EDMOND JOSEPH PHILIP LYNCH-ATHY, of Renville, co. Galway, J.P., late Capt. Galway Artillery, High Sheriff for co. Galway 1904, *b.* 2 June, 1859 ; *m.* 26 Oct. 1881, Annette Frances, younger dau. of Richard Gradwell, of Dowth Hall, co. Meath, and Carlanstown, co. Westmeath, J.P. (*see that family*), and has issue,

MURIEL PAULINE ANNETTE.

Lineage.—EDMOND ATHY, of Galway, *m.* Margaret, dau. of Stephen Lynch, of Galway, and by her had a son,

Andrew Athy, of Beleek, co. Mayo, Capt. in the Army of James II, *m.* Anastacia, dau. of Dominick Joyce, of Galway, and Maude his wife, dau. of Marcus Lynch, of Galway. They had issue a son,
Edmond Athy, of Galway, *m.* Margaret, dau. and heir of Philip Lynch, of Renville, co. Galway (and Sarah his wife, dau. of Oliver Ormsby, of Castle Clough, co. Galway), and grand-dau. of Philip Lynch, of Renville, co. Galway, and Margaret, his wife, dau. of George Baynham, of Bristol. They had issue,
 1. Philip Lynch, his heir. 2. John.
 3. Oliver, *m.* a dau. of John Skerrett, of Ballinduff.
 4. Christopher. 5. Edmond.
 1. Sarah.
 2. Jane, *m.* John Moore, of Ashbrook, co. Mayo, and had issue (*see* Moore *of Moore Hall*).
The eldest son,
Philip Lynch Athy, of Renville, *m.* Eleanor French, of a family of one of the Tribes of Galway, and had issue,
 1. Edmond Lynch, his heir. 2. Andrew.
 1. Katherine. 2. Jane.
Mr. Athy, whose will is dated 21 June, 1774, was *s.* by his eldest son,
Edmond Lynch Athy, of Renville, *m.* 6 Feb. 1777, the dau. of Peter Nottingham, of Fairfield, co. Galway, and had,
Philip Edmond Lynch, his heir.
Eleanor, *m.* E. Taaffe.
Mr. Athy, whose will is dated 4 July, 1808, was *s.* by his son,
Philip Edmond Lynch Athy, of Renville, *m.* 16 Dec. 1809, Bridget, dau. of Randle MacDonnell, of Fairfield House, Dublin, and had (with other issue deceased),
 1. Randal Edmond Lynch, his heir.
 2. Myles (Rev.), a priest of the Order of St. Benedict, *d.* Oct. 1892.
 1. Katherine.
Mr. Athy *d.* 18 May, 1840, and was *s.* by his son,
Randal Edmond Lynch Athy, of Renville, *b.* 1814; *m.* 27 April, 1858, Margaret, dau. of William Hill Buckle, 14th Regt., of Chaceley, co. Worcester. She *d.* 31 March, 1891. He *d.* 10 April, 1875, leaving issue,
Edmond Joseph Philip Lynch, now of Renville.
Mary Elizabeth, *m.* 28 April, 1889, Frederick Hounsell, and has issue, Randle, *b.* 1 March, 1890.

Arms—Chequy gu. and arg., on a chevron of the 1st three estoiles or.
Seat—Renville, Oranmore co., Galway. Club—United Service.

ATKINSON OF CANGORT.

Guy Montague Atkinson, of Cangort, King's Co., *b.* 30 March, 1882; *s.* his father, 1890.

Lineage.—Lieut. Anthony Atkinson, of the Island of Kiltobrett, King's Co., who made his will 10 May, 1626, left issue by Mary, dau. of Thomas Bathe,
 1. William, of whom presently.
 2. John. 3. George.
 4. Thomas.
 1. Mary. 2. Frances.
 3. Elizabeth.
 4. Jane. 5. Margaret.
 6. Anne.
William Atkinson, of Cangort, *b.* 1613; *m.* Anne, dau. of Bartholomew Pelsley, of Punchestown, co. Kildare, who had interest in the lands of Kilbalyminkin, co. Tipperary, and by her has issue, one son and a dau.,
 1. Anthony, of whom next.
 1. A dau., *m.* Thomas Newcomen.
Anthony Atkinson, of Cangort, *m.* Anne, dau. of Sir Robert Newcomen and Anna Bullea his wife, and by her (who *m.* 2ndly 1664, Wm. Tynte (*see* Tynte *of Tynte Park*), and 3rdly, Wm. Digby, of Newtown, King's Co.), had issue,
 1. William, his heir.
 2. Newcomen, ancestor of Atkinson, of Millvale, whose descent is given below.
 3. Charles, *d. unm.* 1686.
 1. Frances, *m.* Thomas, son of Henry L'Estrange, of Moystown, King's Co.
The eldest son,
William Atkinson, of Cangort, *m.* Anne, dau. of William Hamilton, grand-dau. of Sir Francis Hamilton, Bart., of Killeshandra, co. Cavan. He *d.* 1684, having had issue by his wife (who *m.* 2ndly — Blake, and 3rdly Major Marcus French, of Rahassan),
 1. Anthony, his heir. 2. William.
The elder son,
Anthony Atkinson, of Cangort, M.P. for St. Johnstown 1711-13 and for Belfast 1713-14; *m.* 1709, Mary, dau. of Admiral John Guy, of Greenwich, Kent (celebrated for having relieved Derry by breaking the boom), and *d.* Dec. 1743, having had, with other ssue,
 1. William, Barrister-at-Law, *d.v.p.*

2. Guy, of whom next.
3. Anthony, of Headfield, King's Co., *d.s.p.*
4. Charles, *m.* Mary, dau. of Robert Saunderson, of Clover Hill, co. Cavan, and had a son (*see* Atkinson *of Ashley Park*).
5. Newcomen.
 1. Anne, *m.* Francis Saunderson, of Castle Saunderson, co. Cavan (*see that family*).
 2. Frances, *m.* (setts. dated 30 March, 1749) Nathaniel Robbins of Hymanstown, co. Tipperary, and had issue.
 3. Harriet, *m.* 2 Sept. 1749, Robert Saunderson.
 4. Jane, *m.* — Armstrong.
 5. Frances, *m.* 1749, Nathaniel Robbins, of Hymenstown, co. Tipperary.
 6. Catherine, *m.* George Fraser, of Cuba, King's Co.
 7. Harriet.
His eldest surviving son,
Rev. Guy Atkinson, of Cangort, Rector of Aghoghill, co. Antrim, and Vicar of Trim, who *m.* 1st, 1747, Jane, dau. of Charles Maule, and niece of Henry, Bishop of Meath, and had by her an only child, Anthony, who *d.s.p.* He *m.* 2ndly, Jane, dau. of Jackson Wray, of co. Donegal, and *d.* 1794, having had by her,
 1. Hugh, who *d.* in India.
 2. Guy, an Officer in the Navy, blown up by the explosion of a ship on fire.
 3. Jackson Wray, of whom presently.
 4. Charles (Rev.), Rector of Creggan, co. Armagh. *m.* Thomasine, dau. of the Rev. Samuel Downing, of co. Londonderry, and had a dau., who *m.* Arthur Hill Read, of Donnybrook, co. Tipperary, and had issue.
 5. George, *m.* Leonora, dau. of Jackson Wray, of Brentford, co. Antrim, and assumed, by Royal Licence, the surname and arms of Wray. Their 3rd son, George Cecil Gore Wray, of Monasterevan and Ardnamara, co. Donegal, *m.* 1844, Charlotte dau. of Col. Charles Douglas Waller, R.A.
 1. Maria, *m.* George R. Golding.
The 3rd son,
Jackson Wray Atkinson, of Cangort, Lieut.-Col. of the King's Co. Militia, High Sheriff King's Co. 1803, *b.* 1766; *m.* 1794, Sarah, dau. of Richard Caddell, of Downpatrick, and had issue,
 1. Guy, his heir.
 2. Henry, *b.* July, 1806; *m.* 9 April, 1839, Elizabeth Jane, eldest dau. of the Rev. William Brownlow Savage, Rector of Shinrone, King's Co., and had issue,
  1. Charles, *b.* 23 Dec. 1842.
  2. John Lavallin Savage, *b.* 4 March, 1846.
  3. Guy, *b.* 9 April, 1848; *d.* 14 April, 1852.
  4. William Henry, *b.* 4 Feb. 1850.
  5. William Brownlow Savage, *b.* 20 March, 1851; *d.* 20 March, 1872.
  1. Elizabeth Barbara, *m.* 13 Sept. 1859, Edward Kerry Supple.
  2. Sarah Anne. 3. Catherine Sophia.
  4. Caroline Frances Stewart. 5. Ida Anna Margaret.
 3. Charles, an Officer 10th Native Cavalry E.I.C.S., *d.* in India from the bite of a snake, 1840.
 4. Richard, of Gortmore, Dundrum, *b.* 6 Oct. 1818; *m.* 14 Oct 1840, Mary Jane Elisabeth, dau. of Capt. George R. Golding, of Lime Park, co. Tyrone, and Georgina his wife, dau. of Rev. Travers Hume, D.D., Vicar of Arden, and *d.* 18 July, 1871, having by her (who *d.* 18 June, 1886) had issue,
  1. Guy Travers, *b.* 18 June, *d.* 30 Oct. 1843.
  2. Richard Gustavus, *b.* 5 May, *d.* 10 Oct. 1850.
  3. Edward Dupré (Rev.), LL.B., of Gortmore, Dundrum, co. Dublin, Archdeacon of Dromore, and Rector of Donaghcloney, co. Dublin. *b.* 2 Feb. 1855; *m.* 10 Oct. 1878, Katherine Elisabeth, eldest dau. of Major-Gen. Edmund L'Estrange, of Kilcummin, King's Co., and Dora his wife, 3rd dau. of Rev. John Colthurst, Rector of Bovevagh, co. Derry, and has issue,
   (1) Richard Guy, *b.* 21 Aug. 1879.
   (2) Edward Arthur, *b.* 30 Nov. 1885.
   (1) Dora Georgiana, *b.* 28 March, 1882.
   (2) Mary Kathleen, *b.* 30 Nov. 1885.
   (3) Emily Saida, *b.* 3 July, 1888.
  1. Georgiana, *b.* 28 Sept. 1841.
  2. Sarah Maria, *b.* 31 Jan. 1845.
  3. Alicia Emily, *b.* 18 Feb. 1847; *d.* 4 Feb. 1848.
  4. Katherine Mabel, *b.* 25 Aug. 1857; *m.* 13 April, 1875, Rev. Robert Baker Stoney, D.D., Treasurer of Ch. Ch. Cathedral, Dublin, and Vicar of Holy Trinity, Killiney, and has issue (*see* Butler-Stoney *of Portland Park*).
  5. Emmeline Caroline, *b.* 18 Sept. 1859; *m.* 1896, Alfred St. George Hamilton, of Cluan na Greina, Foxrock, co. Dublin.
 6. Mary Jane, *b.* 10 Aug. 1861; *d.* 24 Oct. 1874.
 1. Sarah. 2. Maria.
 3. Mabella Jane.
 4. Caroline Steuart, *m.* William L'Estrange, of Kilcummin.
 5. Emily Rebecca. 6. Harriet Anne.
Col. Atkinson *d.* 14 Aug. 1846, and was *s.* by his eldest son,
Guy Atkinson, of Cangort, J.P., High Sheriff King's Co. 1846, *b.* 14 July, 1800; *m.* 24 Oct. 1839, Anne Margaret, 2nd dau. of William Trench, of Cangort Park, brother of the 1st Lord Ashtown, and had issue,
 1. Charles, *d.* an infant at Rome, 1841.
 2. Guy Newcomen, of Cangort.
 3. William Henry, *b.* 28 Aug. 1848; *m.* 1877, Anna, dau. of Lewis Moore, of Cremorgan, and has issue,
  Guy Hamilton, *m.* 18 Feb. 1909, Sybil Gertrude, dau. of Rev. Canon Homan.
 4. Richard Frederick, 67th Regt., *b.* 11 Dec. 1849.
 1. Sarah Harriet, *m.* 11 May, 1865, George Arthur Waller, eldest son of W.T. Waller, of Prior Park (*see that family*).
 2. Emily, *m.* 4 Oct. 1865, George A. Western.

3. **Caroline Sophia**, *m.* 14 Dec. 1869, Lieut.-Col. James Halifax Western, C.M.G., Royal Engineers, and has issue.

Mr. Atkinson *d.* 1859, and was *s.* by his eldest surviving son,

GUY NEWCOMEN ATKINSON, of Cangort, *b.* 4 Jan. 1847, J.P., Lieut.-Col. 85th Light Infantry; *m.* 19 July, 1877, Frances Elizabeth, only dau. of the Hon. Laurence Harman King-Harman, of Rockingham, co. Roscommon (see BURKE'S *Peerage*, KINGSTON, E.), and *d.* 10 Feb. 1890, having had issue,
1. **Guy Edward**, *b.* 10 Dec. 1878; *d.* 24 May, 1879.
2. **GUY MONTAGUE**, now of Cangort.
3. **Gerald Newcomen**, *b.* 10 March, 1884.
1. **Helen Mary**, *b.* 30 Sept. 1880; *m.* 5 Sept. 1908, Capt. Robert William Hare, D.S.O., Norfolk Regt., only son of Robert Dillon Hare, of Ballymore, co. Cork (see BURKE'S *Peerage*, LISTOWEL, E.).

Arms—Or, an eagle displayed, with two heads, az., beaked and legged gu.; in chief, a rose of the last, seeded gold between two martlets sa. **Crest**—An eagle displayed with two heads az., beaked and legged gu. *Motto*—Deo et regi fidelis.

Seat—Cangort, Shinrone, King's Co. *Residence*—Quarry House, Shrewsbury.

ATKINSON OF BALLYNEWRY.

The 2nd son of Anthony Atkinson, of Cangort, and Anne Newcomen (*see above*) was,

CAPT. NEWCOMEN ATKINSON *m.* — L'Estrange, and had issue.

GEORGE ATKINSON, of Dundalk, *b. circa* 1700; *d.* 1784; *m.* Margaret Foster, and had issue,
1. JAMES, of whom presently.
2. David, of Channon Rock, Mount Rush, and Corderry, co. Louth, J.P. and D.L. co. Louth, *b.* 1734; *d.* 24 March, 1816; *m.* Hannah (*b.* in 1731; *d.* 9 July, 1815), dau. of Dudley Trueman, and had issue,
   1. George, *m.* — Rogers.
   2. David, Capt. in the Louth Mil., *b.* 1769; *d.* at Mill Vale, 2 Aug. 1807; bur. at Dundalk; *m.* Anne, dau. of Benjamin Bell, of Ballynewry, Barrister-at-Law, and had issue,
      (1) Benjamin, of Ballynewry, *b. circa* 1790; *d.* 1876; *m.* 1st, ——— (*b.* 1798; *d.* 8 March, 1824), dau. of Byrne, of Lurgan, and by her had issue,
         1. David, *d.s.p.* in America.
         1. Anne Jane, *m.* 23 June, 1834, Thomas Ross.
         2. Eliza, *m.* 16 Sept. 1837, Robert Finlay.
         3. Mary, *m.* 5 Nov. 1836, John Fleming, of the Hill, Monaghan.
         4. Julia, *m.* Godfrey Ball.
      Benjamin *m.* 2ndly, Mary, dau. of John MacCormac, of Belfast, and by her had further issue,
         2. John, of Ballynewry, *b.* July, 1827; *d.* 31 Jan. 1888; *m.* 2 June, 1870, Mary, only dau. of Samuel McClintock, of Granshaw Lodge, Londonderry, and had issue,
            Ben, of Ballynewry, co. Armagh, Major R.H.A., *b.* 9 Jan. 1872; *m.* 1 Jan. 1903, Letitia Janet Emily, only dau. of E. K. Norman, of Mistley Lodge, Manningtree, and has issue,
               John Edward Acheson, *b.* 6 March, 1909.
               Rosalind Mary, *b.* 5 Nov. 1904.
         3. Henry, *d.s.p.* in America.
         4. George Grindall, Lieut. in the Armagh Mil., *d.s.p.*
         5. William MacCormac, Lieut. in the Armagh Mil., *d.s.p.*
         5. Hannah Trueman, *m.* 1st, 10 June, 1857, her cousin, William John Henry Upton, of Carrickfergus; 2ndly Martin Bourke, of Quinboro', co. Limerick.
         6. Dorothea, *d.s.p.* 7. Adelaide, *d.s.p.*
      (2) George Grindall, of Corderry, *b.* 1801; *d.* 15 Aug. 1855.
      (3) David, *d. unm.* (4) James, *d. unm.*
         (1) Hannah Julia, *m.* her cousin David Smith, of Clonooney, Clones, J.P. для co. Monaghan (*q.v.i.*), and has issue.
         (2) Elizabeth, *m.* 1st, Henry Upton, of Ballinabirna, co. Limerick, and had issue. She *m.* 2ndly, her cousin, James Robinson, of Burleigh Hall, co. Antrim.
   3. James, *b.* 1772; *d.* 1 Feb. 1832; *m.* Butler, and had with other issue,
      Hannah (eld. dau.), *m.* 31 Jan. 1828, Haden Smith, of Newry.
   4. Thomas.
      1. Mary, *m.* Henry Smith, of Channon Rock, and had issue, David, of Clonooney, Clones, J.P. for co. Monaghan, *m.* his 1st cousin, Hannah Julia Atkinson (*see above*).
   3. John, of Dundalk, *m.* Jane Eastwood, and had issue, Jane, *m.* 16 July, 1832, Robert Murphy, of Castletown.
   4. George, *b.* 1750; *d. unm.* 22 Dec. 1821.
   1. Elizabeth, *m.* John Foster (*d.* before 3 July, 1782), of Skyhill, and had issue.
   2. Margaret, *m.* George Twibill, and had issue.
   3. Anne, *m.* John Baillie. 4. Mary, *d. unm.* 1779.
   5. Dorothea, *d. unm.* 1803.

The eldest son,

JAMES ATKINSON, of Newry, and of Mill Vale, *b.* 1730; *d.* 3 Dec. 1815; *m.* 1 Feb. 1757, Alice (*d.* before 1804), youngest dau. of Robert Gordon, of Newry, and had issue,
1. GEORGE, of whom presently.
2. Robert, *b.* 1763; *d.* 4 Sept. 1766.
3. James, of Newry, *b.* 19 Aug. 1766; *d.* 1805; *m.* 11 May, 1791, Hannah, dau. of William Barrett (cousin of Lord Carlton), of Castle Blake, co. Tipperary, and Mary his wife, and had issue,
   1. Robert Gordon, Lieut. of Marines, *d.* 20 March, 1792; *d. unm.* 4 Dec. 1820, killed in action in the attack made on the North Fort of Mocha, in the Mediterranean.

I.L.G.

2. William, an officer in the Spanish Army, *b.* 16 May, 1793; *d. unm.*
3. John, of Benburb, *b.* 12 March, 1799; *d.* 22 March, 1834; *m.* 14 Dec. 1831, Isabella Eliza, dau. of Major Frood, of Dundalk, and had issue,
   (1) James, *b.* 3 Feb. 1833. (2) John, *b.* 28 March, 1834.
   Isabella Eliza Atkinson (otherwise Frood) *m.* 2ndly, her former husband's first cousin, Rev. Robert Gordon Atkinson (*see above*).
   1. Maria, *b.* 1795; *m.* 1st, James Wallace, of Liverpool, Merchant, and had issue, three daus.
   Maria Wallace (formerly Atkinson) *m.* 2ndly, William Brackenbury, of Aswardby, co. Lincoln, an officer in the 61st Foot, and by him had issue,
      (1) William, *d. unm.*
      (2) Richard, Capt. 61st Foot, *d. unm.*
      (3) Charles Booth, Major-Gen. R.A., *b.* 7 Nov. 1831; *d.* 20 June, 1890; *m.* 1854, Hilda, dau. of the Hon. Archibald Campbell and Agnes his wife, and had issue.
      (4) Sir Henry, Lieut.-Gen., K.C.B., K.C.S.I., R.A., *m.* Œmilia, relict of — Morley, dau. of Henry Halswell, of Kensington Gate, retired Judge of Zealand and J.P. for co. Middlesex.
      1. Catherine, *m.* William Nevin Wallace, of Downpatrick J.P. and D L., and *d.* leaving a dau., Maria Wallace.
      (2) Jemima, *d. unm.* (3) Hannah Maria.
      (4) Henrietta.
   2. Alicia, *b.* 14 April; *d.* 15 Sept. 1792.
   3. Alicia, *b.* 7 Sept. 1800; *d.* 10 Feb. 1879; *m.* 1822, David, eld. surv. son of James Bell, of Newry, and had issue,
      (1) James, *d. unm.* (2) James, *d. unm.* 29 Apr.l, 1863.
      (3) John Gordon, *d. unm.* 18 May. 1829.
      (4) Samuel, *d.* in 1887; *m.* Louisa Ruthven, and had issue, Ethel Alice Ruthven. Maude Mary Ruthven.
      (1) Anne. (2) Anne Gordon.
      (3) Catherine.
      (4) Fanny Johnston, *m.* 12 April, 1856, Ernest Randolph Mackesy, Major 97th Foot, and had issue.
      (5) Alicia Hannah Maria. (6) Mary Hervey.
      (7) Rebekah Hartford.
   4. Anne, *b.* 28 Feb. 1802.
   5. Sarah, *b.* 9 June, 1805; *m.* 5 Dec. 1826, Samuel Alexander of Dundalk.
   1. Alicia, of Newry, *b.* 21 Feb. 1761, *d. unm.* 20 March, 1836.
   2. Margaret, *b.* 9 Feb. 1765; *d. unm.* 27 April, 1777.

The eldest son,

GEORGE ATKINSON, J.P., of Mill Vale, *b.* 15 Nov. 1758, *d.* 17 May, 1820; *m.* 12 July, 1804, Anne Wallace (*d.* 6 Oct. 1827); dau. of Robert Baillie, and had issue,

Rev. Robert Gordon, *b.* 5 Feb. 1807; *d.* 12 July, 1865; *m.* 5 May, 1841, Isabella Eliza (*d.* 3 July, 1864), dau. of Major Frood, of Dundalk, and relict of John Atkinson, of Benburb, and had issue,
   1. George (St. *Lawrence Road, Clontarf*, co. *Dublin*), *b.* 1842.
   1. Isabella Eliza, *b.* 3 March, 1844; *d.* 27 March, 1890; *m.* 24 Aug. 1882, Rev. John Gaggin (*d.* 14 Dec. 1894), Rector of New Chapel, Clonmell, co. Tipperary, and had issue,
      Isabella Jane, *b.* 1883; *d. unm.* 29 July, 1901.
   2. Isabella, *b.* at Mill Vale, 1 June, 1808; *d.* 22 Jan. 1858; *m.* 4 Aug. 1832, Rev. Charles Crossle (*see above*).

BIGGS-ATKINSON OF ASHLEY PARK.

MRS. ALICE MARJORY BIGGS-ATKINSON, of Ashley Park, 2nd dau. of the late James Netterville Atkinson, of Ashley Park, *m.* 1903, Thomas Bateson Biggs, Solicitor, Capt. 3rd Batt. Royal Irish Regt. (*see below*), who adopted the additional surname of Atkinson by Deed Poll, 18 Nov. 1903.

Lineage.—CHARLES ATKINSON, younger son of Anthony Atkinson, of Cangort (*see that family*), *m.* Mary, dau. of Robert Saunderson, of Clover Hill, co. Cavan, and had a son,

ANTHONY ATKINSON, *m.* Catharine, dau. of Dominick Blake, of Castlegrove, co. Galway, by Frances his wife, dau. of Nicholas, 5th Viscount Netterville, and *d.* 1815, having had issue,
1. James. 2. Charles.
3. GEORGE GUY, of whom presently.
1. Charlotte, *d. unm.*

The 3rd son,

GEORGE GUY ATKINSON, of Ashley Park, J.P., *b.* 1799; *m.* Bridget, dau. of P. Murphy, Rahone, co. Tipperary, and *d.* 30 July, 1872, leaving issue,
1. JOHN, of Derryharan, King's Co., *m.* 1st, 1874, Anna, dau. of Rev. J. C. Walker, Rector of Ballinasloe, and by her (who *d.* 2 Dec. 1892) has issue,
   1. Guy Netterville.
   1. Anna. 2. Bridget, *d. unm.* 1901.
He *m.* 2ndly, 2 June, 1894, Ethel Maud, dau. of the late Richard Beasley, of Old Grange, co. Kildare. He *d.* 1901.
2. George, M.D., *d. unm.* in the Afghan War, 1880.
3. JAMES NETTERVILLE, late of Ashley Park.

The 3rd son,

JAMES NETTERVILLE ATKINSON, of Ashley Park, co. Tipperary, J.P., High Sheriff 1892, B.A. Trin. Coll. Dublin, 1863, *b.* 1 March, 1843; *m.* 30 Sept. 1875, Margaret Teresa, dau. of William B. Smithwick, J.P., of Youghal House, Nenagh, and *d.* 22 May, 1893, leaving three daus.,

B

1. GUSTAVA MARY.
2. ALICE MARJORY, now of Ashley Park.
3. KATHLEEN ANNA.

Seat—Ashley Park, near Nenagh.

FAMILY OF BIGGS.

GEORGE BIGGS, of Santa Cruz, co. Tipperary, and subsequently of Bellevue, who was of the same family as Richard Biggs, of Castle Biggs, High Sheriff of co. Tipperary 1777 (who *d.s.p.* 1795, having devised his estates to his nephew, Wm. Ledger, afterwards Biggs), had an only son,

THOMAS BIGGS, of Bellevue, co. Tipperary, J.P., *m.* his cousin Elizabeth Biggs, and *d.* 1795, leaving issue,
1. GEORGE WASHINGTON, his heir.   2. Benjamin.
3. Thomas.
1. Mary.

The eldest son,
GEORGE WASHINGTON BIGGS, of Bellevue, *b.* 1783; *m.* 1807, Anne, dau. of Samuel Dickson, of Ballinguile, co. Limerick, and *d.* 1844, having by her (who *d.* 1860) had issue,
1. THOMAS, who s. to Bellevue.
2. SAMUEL DICKSON, of whom hereafter.
3. George Washington, Rev., *d. unm.* 1908.
4. Stephen Dickson, *d.* 8 April, 1910.
1. Mary.   2. Elizabeth.
3. Catherine.   4. Anne.
5. Georgina.
6. Helena, *m.* John Parker, of Brookfield, co. Tipperary.

The eldest son,
THOMAS BIGGS, of Bellevue, *b.* 1815; *d. unm.* 1844, a few months after his father's decease, and was *s.* by his next brother,
SAMUEL DICKSON BIGGS, of Bellevue, *b.* 1817; *m.* 1870, Elizabeth Goodwin, step-dau. of William Johnston, and *d.* 1904, leaving issue,
1. GEORGE, now of Bellevue.   2. William Johnston.
3. Samuel Dickson.
4. Thomas Bateson, *m.* 1903, Alice Margery, dau. and co-heir of James Netterville Atkinson, of Ashley Park (*see above*).
1. Anne.
2. Avereena Maud, *m.* 1904, Thomas Hardman, eldest son of Col. Brereton, of Rathurles, co. Tipperary.

The eldest son,
GEORGE BIGGS, of Bellevue, *b.* 1872; *s.* his father 1904; *m.* Grace, dau. of Surg. Lieut.-Col. Robinson, R.A.M.C., and has issue,
1. Samuel.   2. Cecil Raymond.
3. Basil.
4. Zalie.

ATKINSON OF CAVANGARDEN.

THOMAS JOHN ATKINSON, of Cavangarden, co. Donegal, J.P. and D.L., High Sheriff 1893, *b.* 14 Feb. 1845; *m.* 20 April, 1880, Elizabeth, dau. of Arthur Magee Day, of Rathgar, Dublin, and has issue,
1. THOMAS JOHN DAY, J.P., B.A. Trin. Coll. Dublin, Barrister-at-Law, Lieut. Dub. Univ. Contingent, Officers Training Corps *b.* 4 March, 1882.
1. Charlotte Elizabeth.   2. Elizabeth Arthurina.
3. Mabel Angela Wray, *d. unm.* 15 April, 1911.
4. Arthurina Josephine.

Lineage.—CAPT. CHARLES ATKINSON, of an ancient Yorkshire family, settled in Ireland, *temp.* ELIZABETH, and left two sons, of whom one settled at Rebins, co. Mayo (and was ancestor of Atkinson, of Rehins), while the other,
WILLIAM ATKINSON, of Creevy, near Ballyshannon, owned large estates in Kilbarron, co. Donegal. He *d.* about 1660. His son and heir,
THOMAS ATKINSON, called "senior" in the Act of Attainder, Parliament of Dublin 1689, *temp.* JAMES II, *b.* about 1620, and *d.* about 1702, leaving a son,
THOMAS ATKINSON, called "junior" in the Act of Attainder. The property was restored *temp.* WILLIAM III. He was *b.* 1655, and *d.* 1738. His son,
JOHN ATKINSON, *b.* about 1682; *m.* 1711, Rebecca, dau. of William Wray, of Ards, co. Donegal, and *d.* 1748, leaving a son,
THOMAS ATKINSON, *b.* 1713; *m.* 16 Nov. 1752, Letitia, dau. of George Knox, of Rathmullen and Moneymore, co. Donegal, and *d.* 11 May, 1873, leaving a son,
JOHN ATKINSON, J.P., *b.* 1754; *m.* 20 March, 1776, Elizabeth, dau. of Andrew Hamilton, of Ballymadonnell, co. Donegal, High Sheriff 1800. He *d.* 15 May, 1833. His son,
THOMAS JOHN ATKINSON, of Cavangarden, Ballyshannon, co. Donegal, J.P., High Sheriff, 1817, *b.* May, 1781; *m.* 1808, Elizabeth, only dau. of Joseph White, Lieut. 17th Light Dragoons, of Cheltenham. He *d.* 25 March, 1881. His son,
JOHN ATKINSON, of Cavangarden, J.P., M.A., Trin. Coll. Dublin, Barrister-at-Law, *b.* Dec. 1817; *m.* May, 1842, Ellen, dau. of Robert Dean Mecredy, Q.C., M.A., of Carnew, co. Down. She *d.* 12 May, 1900. He *d.v.p.* 26 May, 1879, leaving issue,
1. THOMAS JOHN, now of Cavangarden.
2. John Robert, *b.* 1849; *d. unm.* Oct. 1865.
3. George Andrew, of Skea Hall, Enniskillen, *b.* 29 April, 1851; *m.* 22 March, 1880, Marion Anna Elizabeth, only dau. of Henry Berkeley Geraghty, B.A., Dublin, Barrister-at-Law (by Katherine his wife, dau. of Robert W. Fearon, Barrister-at-Law), and granddau. of James Geraghty, Q.C., and has issue,
  1. John, Lieut. 3rd Batt. Royal Inn. Fus., *b.* Aug. 1883; *m.* May, 1908, Wilhelmina Victoria, 2nd dau. of Petre Thürn.

2. Robert Henry Geraghty, *b.* Sept. 1884.
3. Andrew George, *b.* March, 1891.
4. William Claude Hamilton, *b.* June, 1895.
5. Norman James Charlton Fearon, *b.* Aug. 1897.
1. Elizabeth Maude.
2. Ethel Kathleen Jane, *m.* 23 Nov. 1910, H. Carl A. Thienne, B.Sc., Civil Engineer.
3. Olive Lindley Vivian Florence, *m.* Aug. 1907, Rev. James Alexander Wilson, M.A., Rector of Cleenish, co. Fermanagh, and has issue.
4. Angel Marion.   5. Eileen Letitia Charlotte.
6. Mary Myrtle Gwendoline.
4. James Law, M.D., *b.* May, 1856; *m.* Sept. 1889, but *d.s.p.* 17 March, 1897.
5. William White, *b.* 1863; *d. unm.* 1900.
6. Andrew Hamilton, *b.* 1865; *d. unm.* 1899.
1. Elizabeth Charlotte Jane, *b.* 1848.
2. Ellen Theodosia Adelaide, *b.* 1853; *m.* 24 May, 1874, Robert Mecredy, and has issue two sons and two daus.

Seat—Cavangarden, Ballyshannon, co. Donegal.

ATKINSON OF GLENWILLIAM.

THOMAS RICHARD DURBIN ATKINSON, of Glenwilliam Castle, Ballingarry, co. Limerick, and Skea House, co. Fermanagh, J.P. and D.L. co. Limerick, High Sheriff 1888, educated at Trinity Hall, Camb., *b.* 21 Jan. 1863; *m.* 28 Feb. 1884, Sophie Mary, dau. of Capt. Thomas Wilkinson, 30th Regt., of St. Oswald's, co. Limerick, J.P., and has issue,

1. Eileen Violet.   2. Sybil Maud.

Lineage.—THOMAS ATKINSON obtained a grant of land in co. Monaghan under the Act of Settlement 21 June, 1667. His descendant,
THOMAS ATKINSON, of Anaghabawn, co. Monaghan (son of Thomas Atkinson, of Anaghabawn, co. Monaghan, who *d.* 1824, aged 88), *b.* 1770, *m.* 1799, Sarah, dau. of Richard Philips, of Drumcall, and *d.* 1830, having by her (who *d.* 1848) had issue,
1. EDWARD, now of Glenwilliam Castle.
2. Thomas, *b.* 1805, *d.* 1892, leaving issue, two sons and four daus.
3. John, M.D., *b.* 1810, *d.s.p.* 1837.
4. Richard, *b.* 1814, *d.s.p.* 1856.
1. Eliza, *b.* 1800, *m.* Frances Finley.
2. Jane, *b.* 1803, *m.* Dr. John Wordsworth, and *d.* 1822.
3. Rebecca, *b.* 1807, *m.* Joseph Crawford, of Newbliss, co. Monaghan, and *d.* 1892.

The eldest son,
EDWARD ATKINSON, of Glenwilliam Castle, co. Limerick, and Skea House, Enniskillen, J.P. co. Limerick and Drogheda, High Sheriff, Drogheda, 1824, *b.* 1801, *m.* 1st, 1813, Rosetta, dau. of Capt. John Shaw McCulloch. She *d.* 1849, leaving issue,
1. John (Right Hon.), BARON ATKINSON, of Glenwilliam (cr. 19 Dec. 1905), a Lord of Appeal in Ordinary, P.C., K.C., Attorney-Gen. for Ireland 1892 and 1895–1905, M.P. for North Derry 1895–1905, Bencher of King's Inns, Dublin and of the Inner Temple (39, *Hyde Park Gate, W.*; 68, *Fitzwilliam Square, Dublin*; *Carlton Club*), *b.* 1844, *m.* 1873, Rowena (*d.* 17 Jan. 1911), dau. of Richard Chute, M.D., of Tralee, and has issue,
  1. Hon. Edward Chute, *b.* 1875, *d. unm.* 26 July, 1906.
  2. Hon. Cecil Thomas, B.A. Trin. Coll. Dublin, Barrister-at-Law, *b.* 1876, *m.* 6 Aug. 1903, Florence, dau. of Godfrey Lovelace Taylor, J.P., of Grangeville, co. Wexford, and has issue,
    (1) John Godfrey, *b.* 18 Jan. 1910.
    (1) Dorothea Emily Mary, *b.* 22 May, 1904.
    (2) Rowena Cecilia, *b.* 23 May, 1906.
  3. Hon. Hector John, Capt. Roy. Irish Fus., *b.* 3 June, 1879; *m.* 1910, Sybil, youngest dau. of late George Ievers, of Glenmair, co. Cork.
  4. Hon. Hubert Rowan, Capt. Connaught Rangers, *b.* 6 Oct. 1882; *m.* 30 Jan. 1907, Mabel Coralie, dau. of late George Gerard Tyrrell.
2. Edward, *b.* 1846, *m.* 1872, Lydia, dau. of William Rutherford, J.P. of Drum, co. Monaghan, and *d.* 1875, leaving issue,
  1. Edward William, Capt. Royal Inniskilling Fus., B.A. Trin. Coll. Dublin (*Army and Navy Club*), *b.* 12 Aug. 1873; *m.* 20 April, 1907, Louise H. S., 2nd dau. of John Power Oliver, I.M.S.
  2. Joseph Albert Nelson, B.A. Trin. Coll. Dublin, Barrister-at-Law (*Pretoria, Transvaal, S. Africa*), *b.* 19 Jan. 1875; *m.*

1907, Teresa Clare, dau. of J. Sheridan, Esq., of Galway, and has issue.
Edward Sheridan, b. 1909.
Doreen Lydia Claire, b. 1908.
1. Anna, m. 1st, 1859, Henry Warren, of Drummin House, Meath, who d. 1869, leaving issue. She m. 2ndly, Rev. Brabazon William Brunker, M.A., Vicar of Duleek, co. Meath, who d. 1877.
2. Rosetta, m. 1869, Joseph Williams, who d. 1876, leaving issue.
3. Sarah Rosetta, m. 1877. Brabazon Brunker, eld. son of Robert - Burrows Brunker, Solicitor, of Simmons Court House, Dublin, and has issue.
Mr. Edward Atkinson m. 2ndly, 1856, Emma, dau. of Maj. Durbin, 36th Regt., and Mary his wife, dau. of Henry Drax, of Charborough, Dorset, and d. 1876, having by her had issue,
3. Thomas Richard Durbin, now of Glenwilliam Castle.
4. Emma Anne, m. 1882, Deane Shelton, of Rossmore, co. Limerick, and has issue, six children.

Arms—Per pale gu. and arg., an eagle displayed with two heads counterchanged, on a chief engrailed erm., a rose ppr. between two martlets or. **Crest**—A falcon rising ppr. belled and jessed or, holding in its beak a fleur-de-lys per pale gu. and arg. **Motto**—Virtute et valore.
Seats—Glenwilliam Castle, Ballingarry, co. Limerick ; and Skea House, Enniskillen, co. Fermanagh.

ATKINSON OF CROWHILL.

Joseph Atkinson, of Crowhill, co. Armagh, late Lieut. 67th Regt., J.P. co. Armagh, Secretary to the Grand Jury and afterwards to the County Council, b. 1845 ; m. 1st, 1871, Annie Edith, dau. of John Jervais Broadwood, of Buchan Hill, Sussex, and by her had issue,
1. Joseph Jervais, b. 1873 ; m. 5 Nov. 1907, Beatrix Pearl, only dau. of E. J. Webb.
2. Walter Hope Johnston, b. 1875.
3. John Broadwood, b. 1894.
He m. 2ndly, 1898, Kathleen Mary, 4th dau. of the late Henry Blake Mahon, of Belleville, co. Galway, and by her has issue,
1. Judith Mary, b. 1900.
Lineage.—This family came to Ireland at the time of the Cromwellian settlement.
Joseph Atkinson, of Crowhill, co. Armagh, J.P., b. 1760 ; m. Sarah, dau. of Thomas Hope, of Crowhill, and d. 1835, having had issue a son,
Thomas Atkinson, of Crowhill, Capt. Armagh Militia, High Sheriff 1825, b. 1793 ; m. 1819, Elizabeth, 4th dau. of James Johnston, D.L., of Knappagh, co. Armagh, and Martha his wife, dau. of John Burges, of Parkanaur, co. Tyrone. She d. 1873, aged 75. He d. 1844, having had issue,
1. Joseph, late of Crowhill.
2. James Hope, Capt. 72nd Highlanders, b. 1825 ; m. 1858, Elfrida, dau. of — Abbott, of Smyrna, and d. 1865, having had two daus.,
  1. Annie, m. Count Mazza, Italian Consul in Canada.
  2. Elfrida, m. 1882, Count Victor de Revel, Italian Consul at Smyrna.
1. Martha, b. 1820 ; d. 1831.
The elder son,
Joseph Atkinson, of Crowhill, co. Armagh, J.P. and D.L., High Sheriff 1855, Chairman of the County Council ; b. 1822 ; m. 11 April, 1844, Judith Charlotte, dau. of Richard Barnsley and Sarah, his wife, dau. of John Smith of Ballyhaskin, Westmeath, and Judith his wife, dau. of Samuel De la Cherois, of Donaghadee, co. Down, and d. 10 Oct. 1903, having had issue,
1. Joseph, his heir.
2. James Johnston, B.A., T.C.D., b. 1847 ; d. 2 Jan. 1905.
3. Robert Richard, J.P., of Summer Island, Loughall, b. 1855 ; m. 31 July, 1907, Mary Frances Josephine, only dau. of Henry J. Nicholson, J.P., of Crannagael, co. Armagh (see that family).
4. Ynyr Henry, b. 1861 ; m. 1886, Rose, dau. of Edward McColdrick, of Dakota, U.S.A., and has issue,
Lionel Robert, b. 1887.   Eveleen, b. 1899.
1. Annie Johnston, b. 1851 ; m. 11 April, 1872, Richard James Harden, D.L., of Harrybrook, co. Armagh, and has issue (see that family).
Seat—Crowhill Loughall, co. Armagh.   **Residence**—Summer Island, Loughall.

AUCHENLECK OF CREVENAGH.

Daniel George Harold Auchenleck, of Crevenagh, co. Tyrone, b. 18 Sept. 1877, educated at Winchester and Trin. Coll. Oxford, Capt. Royal Inniskilling Fusiliers ; m. 1902, Charlotte Madaline, only dau. of the late Robert W. Scott, of Dungannon, co. Tyrone, and has had issue,
Robert Patrick, b. and d. 17 March, 1906.
Lineage.—Rev. James Auchenleck, Rector of Cleenish, co. Fermanagh, b. 1646 ; m. Margaret, a relative of President Keith, and by her (who d. 1680, aged 39) had, with other issue who d. young,
1. James, of whom presently.
2. William, who lived in Tyrone, m. 1708, Miss Maxwell.
3. Alexander, m. Miss Boggs.   4. Sydney.
1. Katherine, m. John Montgomery, of Croghan, co. Donegal.
2. Margaret.
3. Jean, m. Provost Gamble, of Strabane.
His will dated 17 Feb. 1684, was proved 6 April, 1685. The elder son,
James Auchenleck, sen., of Thomastown, m. circa 1698, Elisabeth, dau. of Col. James Corry, M.P., of Castle Coole, and d. 1746 having had, with other issue, who d. young,
1. James, his heir.   2. Alexander, bapt. 1706.
1. Rebecca, m. 1719, Andrew Leonard.
2. Margaret, m. 1721, Thomas Enery, of Prospect, co. Cavan.
3. Mary, m. — Noble.   4. Sarah, m. — Scott.
5. Elisabeth, m. John Dane, of Killyhevlin (see that family).
The elder son,
James Auchenleck, jun., of Thomastown, co. Fermanagh, b. 1704 ; m. 1734, Susanna, dau. of John Corry, of Lisanock. He d. 1752, having had issue,
1. Leslie, d. 1785, bur. at Derryvullan.
2. Armar, twin with his brother, Leslie, m. Mrs. McGregor, née Spear, and had issue,
  1. Alexander, m. and had issue,
    (1) Alexander, m. — Armstrong, of Drumlene, and had issue,
      1. John, d. 1899.   2. Alexander, d.s.p.
      3. Armar.
    (2) James, m. Mary, dau. of his uncle, William Auchenleck, and had issue,
      1. Armar, of Cuttiagh, d. unm. 1880.
      2. Daniel, d. unm. 1882.
        1. A dau., m. — Chartres, of Maguiresbridge.
        2. Alice, d. 1898.
    2. William, of Cuttiagh m. and had issue,
      Mary, m. her cousin, James Auchenleck.
3. James, M.D., R.N., d.s.p.
4. John, in the Civil Service, m. Miss Aynesworth, and had issue,
  1. Capt. James, m. Lucinda Magill, and had issue,
    (1) John, d. unm.
    (2) A dau., m. — Ward, of Piaustown, co. Down.
    (3) Anne, d. unm.
5. William, d. 1803, leaving issue,
  1. Mary.   2. Margaret.
6. George.   7. Corry.
8. Rev. Alexander, of whom presently.
9. Rev. Anketell, b. posthumous, Curate of Termonmaguirke, who had a son, Richard.
1. Elisabeth, d. unm. 1824.
2. Sarah, m. — Cluff, of Ratoran.
The Rev. Alexander Auchinleck, of Castle Lodge and Mullans, Fintona, co. Tyrone, Rector of Rossory, co. Fermanagh, b. 1749, m. 1784, Jane, dau. of James Lowry Eccles, of Shannock, co. Fermanagh, and d. 1833, having by her (who d. 1829) had issue,
1. James Eccles (Rev.), of Castle Lodge and Mullans, J.P., b. 1786, m. 1815, Caroline, dau. of Richard Fiddis, of Tullycreevy House, co. Fermanagh, and d. 1829, leaving issue,
  1. Alexander Eccles (Rev.), of Castle Lodge and Mullans, Fintona, co. Tyrone, Vicar of Car-Colston, Notts, b. 1825 ; m. 1st, 3 June, 1862, Fanny, dau. of John Crozier, J.P., of Gortra House, co. Fermanagh (see Burke's Family Records). She d.s.p. 15 Sept. 1864. He m. 2ndly, 21 Sept. 1870, Sidney, dau. of John Laurence Spear, J.P., of Glenally House, co. Tyrone. She d.s.p. 12 Aug. 1881.
    1. Jane Eccles, m. 15 Nov. 1836, William Crozier, 2nd son of John Crozier, J.P., of Gortra House (see Burke's Family Records).
    2. Susan Caroline, d. unm.
    3. Elizabeth Ward, m. P. G. Hippolite Marlet, Avocat of Semur, Burgundy, and has issue.
    4. Henrietta Margaret Enery, m. Rev. Thomas Lewis.
2. William, an Officer, d. in India, unm.
3. John (Rev.), Rector of Dunboyne, co. Meath, and Ballyhack, co. Wexford, b. 1796, m. 1825, Katherine, dau. of Rev. Thomas Johnston, and d. 20 June, 1870, having by her (who d. 28 Dec. 1892) had issue,
  1. John Claude Alexander, Lieut.-Col. R.A., m. 9 Nov. 1874, Mary Eleanor, dau. of John Eyre, D.L., of Eyrecourt (see that family), and d. 1892, having had issue,
    (1) Claude John Eyre, Indian Army, b. 21 June, 1884.
    (2) Armar Leslie, b. 1887.
    (1) Cerise Eleanor Gordon.   (2) Katherine Ruth Leighton.
  2. William Henry, Lieut.-Col. late R.A., b. 2 Aug. 1841 ; m. 28 June, 1898, Constance Mildred Spilsbury, youngest dau. of William Halford, of 30, Cambridge Square, W. He d. 16 Oct. 1901, leaving issue,
    William John Alexander Halford, b. 8 Aug. 1899.
  3. Daniel.
    1. Jane Katherine, d. unm. 8 July, 1883.
    2. Fanny.   3. Katherine.
4. Daniel Eccles, of whom presently.
1. Anna, m. 1809, Richard Dane, J.P., of Killyhevlin, co. Fermanagh.
The younger son,
Daniel Eccles Auchinleck, of Crevenagh, b. 1797 ; m. Nov. 1833, Elizabeth Dorothea, dau. of Rev. Thomas Lindsay Stack, J.P., Rector of Badony, and d. 1849, having by her (who d. 14 Sept. 1868) had issue,
1. Thomas, late of Crevenagh.
2. William Lowry, b. 1841, Col. 63rd Regt., Brig.-Gen. Calcutta ; d. 13 Feb. 1891.
3. Daniel, late Maj. Royal Scots Fusiliers, b. 1847 ; killed at Taindah, Burma, 15 Sept. 1886.

1. Margaret Jane, m. 1859, the Right Rev. Charles Maurice Stack, Lord Bishop of Clogher, J.P., D.D., and has issue.
2. Anna Mary, m. Brig.-Surg. Constantine Read, Army Medical Staff.

The eldest son,
THOMAS AUCHINLECK, of Crevenagh, co. Tyrone, and of Shannock Green, co. Fermanagh, b. 16 Jan. 1837, J.P. and D.L. co. Tyrone, High Sheriff, co. Tyrone, 1872, Hon. Maj. Royal Tyrone Fusiliers, formerly Lieut. 11th (North Devon) Regt.; m. 29 Sept. 1868, Jane, dau. of George H. Loxdale, of Grassendale, Liverpool, son of Joseph Loxdale, of Kingsland, co. Salop, and d. 1893, leaving issue,

1. DANIEL GEORGE HAROLD, now of Crevenagh.
1. Bessie Sarah, m. 7 Aug. 1907, Lieut.-Col. Thomas Francis Bushe, C.M.G., R.A.
2. Norah Lilian Loxdale, m. 29 July, 1896, Rev. James George Reginald Darling, Rector of Eyke, Suffolk, youngest son of the late Rev. James George Darling.

Seat—Crevenagh, Omagh, co. Tyrone.

AYLMER OF COURTOWN.

MAJOR JOHN ALGERNON AYLMER, of Courtown, Kilcock, co. Kildare, J.P. and D.L., High Sheriff 1896, Major late 4th Dragoon Guards, B.A. Trin. Coll. Cambridge, b. 22 Dec. 1853; m. 12 April, 1886, Blanche, 3rd dau. of John Eveleigh Wyndham, of Clearwell Court, Gloucestershire, and widow of Capt. George Montgomery, R.H.A., and by her (who d. 8 March, 1895) has issue,

JOHN WYNDHAM, Lieut. 4th Dragoon Gds. b. 9 March, 1889.
Stella Wyndham, m. 3 March, 1909, Capt. John M. Colchester-Wemyss (see COLCHESTER-WEMYSS of Westbury), and has issue.

Lineage.—RICHARD AYLMER, of Lyons, co. Kildare, living 1421, one of the Keepers of the Peace for the cos. of Dublin and Kildare 1432, Sovereign of the Borough of Tassagard, anno 10 HENRY VI, was direct ancestor of BARTHOLOMEW AYLMER, of Lyons, co. Kildare; m. Margaret, dau. of Sir Christopher Cheevers, Knt. of Macetown, and had issue,

1. RICHARD, his heir.
2. GERALD (Sir), ancestor of the LORDS AYLMER (see BURKE's Peerage).
1. Anne, m. Sir Thomas Luttrell, Knt., of Luttrellstown, Lord Chief Justice of Common Pleas.

The eldest son,
RICHARD AYLMER, of Lyons, appointed Chief Sergeant of the co. Kildare, 1 June, 27 HENRY VIII, A.D. 1535, m. Genet, dau. and heir of Alderman Thomas Tew, of Dublin, and was s. by his son,
RICHARD AYLMER, of Lyons, m. Elinor, dau. of George Fleming, 2nd son of James, Lord Slane, and had,

1. THOMAS, his heir.
2. George, of Cloncurrie, co. Kildare, m. Mary, dau. of Patrick Hussey, Baron of Galtrim.
3. Gerald (Sir), created a bart. (see BURKE's Peerage and Baronetage).
4. Edward, m. Katherine, dau. of Robert Fitzgerald, of Alloone.

The eldest son,
THOMAS AYLMER, of Lyons, s. his father, and had livery of his estate, 20 July, 1562. He m. Alison, dau. of Thomas Cusac, of Cussingtown, Lord Chancellor of Ireland, and by her (who d. Dec. 1623) had

1. BARTHOLOMEW, s. his father, and was ancestor of AYLMER of Lyons.
2. Richard, of Hartwell, who left four sons.
3. JOHN, ancestor of AYLMER of Courtown.

The 3rd son,
JOHN AYLMER, of Ballykennan, co. Kildare, m. Elinor, dau. of Hussey, of Moyle Hussey, and had (with three daus., Ellice, m. Gerald Dillon, of Kellynyon, co. Westmeath; Cicely; and Alison) five sons,

1. MATTHEW, his heir.   2. George.
3. Robert, m. Katherine, dau. of Piers Power, of Monalargie, by Lady Katherine his wife, dau. of Walter, 11th Earl of Ormonde and Ossory, and had,
JAMES, m. Esther, dau. of Thomas Luther, of Ballyboy, King's Co., and was father of
Robert, of Painstown, co. Kildare, m. Anne, dau. and heir of Patrick Wogan, of Richardstown, and grand-dau. of William Wogan, of Rathcoffey, and had issue,
Charles, of Painstown, m. 1st, Rose, dau. of James O'Reilly, of Roristown, co. Meath, and had an only dau.; Catherine Rose, m. 1786, Sir Robert Barnewall, 8th bart., of Crickstown, and d. 10 Feb. 1790. He m. 2ndly, Esmay, dau. of William Piers, of Castletown, and had Robert, of Painstown, d.s.p.; William, d.s.p. 1820; Gerald, d.s.p.; and Anne, m. 1793, Christopher Barnewall, of Meadstown.
4. Bartholomew.   5. Richard.

Mr. Aylmer d. 26 June, 1632, and was s. by his eldest son,
MATTHEW AYLMER, of Ballykennan, b. 1606; m. Elizabeth, dau. of — Wogan, of Rathcoffey, co. Kildare, and was s. by his son,
JOHN AYLMER, of Ballykennan, who d. 1702, leaving (with a dau., Alice, m. 1704, William Humphrey, of Hollywood, co. Wicklow, and three younger sons, Richard, Matthew, and Thomas) an elder son, his heir,
JOHN AYLMER, of Ballykennan, m. 1678, Mary, dau. of Thomas Breedon, of Bearecourt, and had, with six daus., as many sons,

1. JOHN, his heir, m. 1705, Mary, dau. of Thomas Whyte, of Pitchfordstown, co. Kildare, and d. 1708, leaving a dau., Martha, and an only son,
JOHN, of Ballykennan, d. unm. 26 July, 1712.
2. Thomas, d. in France.   3. CHARLES, of whom hereafter.
4. Andrew.   5. Matthew, m. and left issue.   6. James, d.s.p., m.

Mr. Aylmer's will is dated 22 March, 1704, and he d. soon after. His 3rd son,
CHARLES AYLMER, of Ballykennan, s. his nephew in 1712; m. the dau. of Gerrard Crosbie, and d. 5 May, 1754, leaving an only son,
CHARLES AYLMER, of Ballykennan, m. 11 Sept. 1749, the dau. of James Tyrrell, of Clonard, co. Kildare, and had issue,

1. MICHAEL, his heir.
2. Richard, Lieut. 17th Regt., m. Eliza, dau. of Admiral Richard Norris, R.N., and had two sons,
1. Charles, 54th Regt., b. 24 May, 1774; m. 15 Dec. 1806, Mary, dau. of Thomas Luther, of Clonmel. She d. 26 Sept. 1856. He d. 10 Dec. 1863, leaving issue,
(1) Fenton Richard, b. 16 April, 1808; d. unm. 1834.
(2) Charles Arthur, b. 28 Sept. 1814; m. 10 Aug. 1853, Hon. Sophia Mackay, dau. of Alexander, 8th Lord Reay. She d.s.p. 24 Sept. 1866. He d. 1884.
(3) Henry Gerald, b. 1 Aug. 1818; m. 17 June, 1854, Harriet Anna, dau. of Rev. John Scott, Rector of Little Kimble, Bucks. He d. 17 Dec. 1908. They had issue,
Henry Scott, b. 9 April, 1858; d. 8 March, 1877.
Mary Beatrice.
2. Richard, 17th Dragoons, d.s.p.

Mr. Aylmer was s. by his eldest son,
MICHAEL AYLMER, of Courtown and Ballykennan, Col. in the Army, m. March, 1777, Frances Amelia, dau. of Richard Hornidge, of Tulfarris, D.L. co. Wicklow, and had
JOHN, his successor.
Emily, m. 1799, Whitney Upton Gledstanes, of Fardross, co. Fermanagh.

Col. Aylmer was s. by his only son,
JOHN AYLMER, of Courtown, m. 29 Dec. 1828, Margaret Susan, dau. of Sir Fenton Aylmer, 8th bart., of Donadea Castle. and d. 5 March, 1857, having by her (who d. Dec. 1892) had issue,

1. MICHAEL, his heir.
1. Jane Grace, d. unm. 1896.
2. Margaret, m. 1856, Charles Michael Bury (formerly Wright), of Downings, co. Kildare. Both are deceased.
3. Emily, m. 8 Nov. 1859, the late Thomas Chapman.
4. Elizabeth, d. unm. 1900.
5. Cecilia.   6. Lucy Harriet, m. Louis Hack.

His eldest son,
MICHAEL AYLMER, of Courtown, J.P., b. 30 May, 1831; m. Feb. 1853, Charlotte, dau. of Hans Hendrick, of Kerdiffstown, co. Kildare. He d. 4 April, 1885. She d. Nov. 1893, leaving issue,

1. JOHN ALGERNON, his heir.
2. HANS HENDRICK (see HENDRICK-AYLMER of Kerdiffstown).
3. Algernon Ambrose Michael, of Rathmore, co. Kildare, B.A. Trin. Coll. Dublin (Kildare Street Club), b. 23 June, 1857; m. 10 June, 1886, Frances Sophia, dau. of Meade Caulfeild Dennis, of Fortgranite, co. Wicklow, and has issue,
Richard Michael, b. 5 Oct. 1887.
Theodora Margaret, b. 21 Feb. 1893.
1. Florence Mary, m. 1st, 21 March, 1882, Lieut.-Col. Walter Joseph Borrowes, youngest son of Sir Erasmus Borrowes, 8th bart., of Gilltown, and has issue (see BURKE's Peerage). He d. 11 Sept. 1893. She m. 2ndly, 1895, William Gore, and d. 1907.

Arms—Arg., a cross sa. between four Cornish choughs ppr.
Crest—A Cornish chough, rising out of a ducal coronet, all ppr.
Motto—Hallelujah.
Seat—Courtown, Kilcock, co. Kildare. Clubs—Naval and Military, Cavalry, and Kildare Street.

HENDRICK-AYLMER OF KERDIFFSTOWN.

HANS HENDRICK HENDRICK-AYLMER, of Kerdiffstown, co. Kildare, J.P., High Sheriff 1894, Barrister-at-Law, B.A. Trin. Coll. Dublin, b. 23 May, 1856; m. May, 1886, Florence, dau. of Alexander Edwards, of Ballyhire, co. Wexford, and has had issue,

1. CHARLES PERCY, b. 1887; d. 1 Dec. 1906.
2. Gerald Hans, b. 1897.
1. Muriel Charlotte.
2. Violet Lucy.

Mr. Hendrick-Aylmer assumed the additional surname and arms of HENDRICK by Royal Licence in 1889.

IRELAND. Bagot.

Lineage.—See AYLMER of Courtown.
Arms—1st and 4th, arg., a cross sa. between four Cornish choughs ppr. for AYLMER; 2nd and 3rd, az., three leopards' faces for HENDRICK. **Crests**—1st, AYLMER, out of a ducal coronet, a chough rising ppr.; 2nd, HENDRICK, out of a ducal coronet, a crescent gu. **Motto**—Hallelujah.
Seat—Kerdiffstown, near Naas.

TOLER-AYLWARD OF SHANKILL CASTLE.

HECTOR JAMES CHARLES TOLER-AYLWARD, of Shankill Castle, co. Kilkenny, and Bloomfield, co. Roscommon, J.P. and D.L. co. Kilkenny, High Sheriff 1886, b. 13 June, 1839, assumed by Royal Licence, dated 30 May, 1884, the additional surname and arms of AYLWARD, on succeeding his uncle. He m. April, 1894, Emily Mary Eliza, only child of James Butler, of Verona, Monkstown, co. Dublin, and has issue,

1. HECTOR JAMES, b. 9 March, 1895.
2. Victor George, b. 11 Oct. 1897.

Lineage.—This family is of antiquity in Ireland, and was settled in co. Waterford at a very early period, where for more than three centuries it was in the enjoyment of large possessions. The first on record is RICHARD AYLWARD, of Faithlegg, co. Waterford, from whom descended a family which became possessed of Glensillan, called from them Aylwardstown, and other lands in co. Kilkenny.
WILLIAM AYLWARD, of Aylwardstown, living 1562, d. about 1608, leaving a son
PETER (or Piers) AYLWARD, of Aylwardstown, High Constable of the barony of Ida, m. Ellen, dau. of Nicholas FitzGerald, of Gurteen, co. Kilkenny (see FITZGERALD of Turlough), and had issue,
NICHOLAS AYLWARD, of Aylwardstown, transplanted to co. Galway in 1653, m. Ellen, dau. of James Keally, of Gowran, co. Kilkenny, and had a son,
PETER AYLWARD, of Aylwardstown, and of Shankill, co. Kilkenny, m. Elizabeth, eldest dau. and eventual co-heir of Sir Richard Butler, Bart., of Polestown, co. Kilkenny, and by her (who d. 21 Oct. 1708) had a son and successor,
NICHOLAS AYLWARD, of Shankill, M.P. for Thomastown, Sheriff co. Kilkenny, 1742. He m. 5 Aug. 1719, Catherine, 2nd dau. of Maurice Keating, of Narraghmore, co. Kildare, and d. 1756, leaving two sons,
1. NICHOLAS, his heir. 2. Peter, who d. unm. 1801.
The elder son,
NICHOLAS AYLWARD, of Shankill, High Sheriff co. Kilkenny 1757; m. 1st, 14 July, 1756, Mary (d. Dec. 1767), dau. of Benjamin Kearney, by whom he had issue,
1. PETER, his heir. 2. Nicholas, d. unm.
1. Katherine.
He m. 2ndly, April, 1769, Susanna, widow of Edmund Waring (she m. 2ndly, Oct. 1772, Rev. Henry Candler and d. 4 Aug. 1775.) He was s. at his death, 1 Aug. 1772, by his elder son,
PETER AYLWARD, of Shankill, who m. Anne Kearney, of New Ross, co. Wexford, and d. 1792, having had a son and heir,
NICHOLAS JOHN PATRICK AYLWARD, of Shankill, bapt. 17 March, 1787; m. 1805, Elizabeth (d. 25 Feb. 1851), eldest dau. of James Kearney, of Blanchville, co. Kilkenny, and had issue,
1. JAMES KEARNEY, his heir. 2. Nicholas, d.s.p.
3. Peter Charles, d.s.p.
1. Mary Anne, m. 1835, Rev. Peter Toler, B.A., son of Rev. John Toler, Rector of Kenstown, co. Meath, J.P. co. Cork, and d. 1850, leaving by him (who d. May, 1883),
HECTOR JAMES CHARLES TOLER AYLWARD, now of Shankill.
Meriel Elizabeth, m. 1869, R. Devenish (deceased), and has two daus.
2. Elizabeth, m. Rev. Clopton Henry Keogh.
3. Susanna. 4. Waller.
5. Meriel, m. May, 1849, Robert Young, of Clonsingle, co. Tipperary.
Mr. Aylward d. 1832, and was s. by his eldest son,
JAMES KEARNEY AYLWARD, of Shankill, b. 1811, J.P. and D.L. co. Kilkenny, High Sheriff 1837, assumed by Royal Licence, 1876, the additional surname of Kearney upon succeeding to a moiety of the estates of his kinsman, JAMES CHARLES KEARNEY, of Blanchville, same co., m. 1853, Isabella, dau. of Lieut.-Col. Arthur Forbes, 32nd Regt., and widow of Beauchamp Newton, and d.s.p. 1 Feb. 1884, when he was s. by his nephew, HECTOR JAMES CHARLES TOLER, now TOLER-AYLWARD.

Arms—Quarterly: 1st and 4th, az., a fleur-de-lis between two estoiles of six points in bend dexter, and as many increscents in bend sinister, or, for AYLWARD; 2nd and 3rd, arg. on a cross gu between four oak leaves vert, a fleur-de-lis or, for TOLER. **Crests**—1st, AYLWARD, out of a ducal coronet or, an arm embowed, vested az., cuffed arg., the hand ppr. grasping an anchor gold; 2nd, TOLER, out of a mural crown ppr. a fleur-de-lis or, charged with an ermine spot, sa. **Motto**—Verus et fidelis semper.
Seat—Shankill Castle, Whitehall, co. Kilkenny.

BAGENAL OF BENEKERRY.

BEAUCHAMP FREDERICK BAGENAL, of Benekerry, co. Carlow, J.P. and D.L., formerly Lieut. 45th Regt., High Sheriff co. Carlow 1871, b. 10 Sept. 1846; m. 5 July, 1870, Ethel Constance Mary, dau. of the late Robert Westley Hall-Dare, of Newtownbarry, co. Wexford, and has issue,

1. BEAUCHAMP WALTER, b. 5 Jan. 1873; m. 14 May, 1903, Marion Cecile, only dau. of Robert Seymour, of Killanoolie, co. Galway.
2. Charles James, b. 22 March, 1877.
1. Mary Verena, b. 4 April, 1871; d. unm. 13 Feb. 1889.
2. Violet Ethel, b. 24 Aug. 1882.
3. Kathleen Prudence Eirene, b. 28 Dec. 1886; m. 6 April, 1907, Capt. William Steuart Burkett Blackett, Gren. Gds., only son of late Commander A. C. S. Blackett, and has issue (see BLACKETT of Wylaw).

Lineage.—PHILIP NEWTON, of Benekerry, b. 1796, High Sheriff co. Carlow 1833, 2nd son of Philip Newton, of Dunleckny (see that family), by Sarah Bagenal his wife, assumed by Royal Licence, dated 6 March, 1832, the surname and arms of BAGENAL only. He m. 1838, Georgiana Thomasina, dau. of Maj. James Boyd, King's Dragoon Guards, of Rosslare, co. Wexford, and Georgina his wife, 2nd dau. of Hon. George Jocelyn (see BURKE's Peerage, RODEN, E.), and d. 24 June, 1856, having by her (who d. 1 March, 1897) had issue,
1. WALTER PHILIP, his heir.
2. BEAUCHAMP FREDERICK, successor to his brother.
3. James Philip, Indian Telegraph Staff, b. 22 June, 1848; d. unm. at Allahabad, India, 4 June, 1869.
4. Philip Henry, B.A. Oxon, Barrister-at-Law, General Inspector of the Local Government Board (17, Clarence Drive, Harrogate), b. 18 June, 1850; m. 15 April, 1884, Harriot Jocelyn, dau. of Walter Hore, late of Linfield, co. Limerick, and Marion Jane his wife, dau. of Right Rev. H. Griffin, D.D., Bishop of Limerick, and has issue,
   1. Dudleigh John, b. 28 Sept. 1886; d. 18 March, 1887.
   2. Philip Hope Edward, b. 11 Feb. 1888.
   3. Nicholas Beauchamp, b. 5 July, 1891.
   1. Faith Marion Jane, b. 6 Sept. 1889.
   2. Georgina Charis Mabel, b. 1 Sept. 1894.
1. Georgina Elizabeth, b. 15 Jan. 1839; d. 17 Nov. 1910.
2. Lucy Isabel, b. 9 Dec. 1843; d. Feb. 1845.
3. Sarah Catherine, b. 9 Dec. 1844.

His eldest son,
CAPT. WALTER PHILIP BAGENAL, of Benekerry, b. 3 May, 1841, Capt. 16th Lancers; d. unm. at Bangalore, India, 24 Nov. 1869, and was s. by his brother.

Arms—Barry of four erm. and or, a lion ramp., az. **Crest**—An heraldic antelope, sejant, vert, attired, unguled, ducally gorged and chained or.
Seat—Benekerry, Carlow.

BAGOT OF AUGHRANE AND BALLYMOE.

MILO VICTOR NEVILLE-BAGOT, of Ballymoe, and of Aughrane Castle, co. Galway, b. March, 1880; m. Oct. 1908, Maria, only dau. of late Signor Boccacio, of Turin, Italy.

Lineage.—EDWARD BAGOT, of Harristown, King's Co., and of Walterstown, co. Kildare, b. 1620, was a Royal Commissioner for King's Co. 1663, and High Sheriff co. Kildare 1677, and King's Co. 1680. He m. 1659, Catherine, dau. of William Colborne, of Great Connell, Kildare, and d. 1711, aged 90, leaving

1. MILO, of whom presently.
2. Arthur, executor of his father's will.
3. Christopher, ancestor of the Nurney and Kilnoon branches.
4. Elizabeth, m. James Medlicott, of Dunmurry, co. Kildare.

The eldest son,
COL. MILO BAGOT, of Ard, Newtown, and Kilcoursey, b. 1660, m. 1770, Margaret, dau. of Edmond and sister of Col. Andrew Armstrong, of Mauristown, co. Kildare, and d. 1739, leaving
1. JOHN, of whom presently. 2. Michael, d.s p. 1744.
3. Charles, ancestor of BAGOT of Kilcoursey.
1. Elizabeth, m. W. Armstrong, of Ballycumber, King's Co.
2. Mary, d.s.p.

Col. Bagot settled Ard on his eldest son, by deed, dated 1 May, 1725, and Kilcoursey on his 3rd son, Charles, by deed 30 May, 1734. The eldest son,
JOHN BAGOT, of Ard, King's Co., b. 1702, m. 1728, Mary Herbert, of Durrow Abbey, King's Co., d. 1760, leaving issue, 1. Milo, d.s.p.; 2. William, d.s.p.; 3. Charles, d.s.p.; 4. JOHN LLOYD, who continued the family; 5. Thomas, d.s.p.; and two daus., 1. Mary, d.s.p.; 2. Margaret, m. Archibald Armstrong, of Garry Castle, King's Co. The 4th son,
JOHN LLOYD BAGOT, of Ard and Ballymoe, Capt. 37th Foot, and A.D.C. to Lord Cornwallis during the American War, m. 1775, Catherine Anne, dau. of Michael Cuffe, of Ballymoe, son of Capt. Francis Cuffe, and grandson (by his wife Mary, dau. of Thomas Caulfeild, of Donamon Castle, co. Roscommon) of Capt. Thomas Cuffe, brother of Sir James, grandfather of James Cuffe, Lord Tyrawley, and of Elizabeth Cuffe, alias Pakenham, created Countess of Longford. He d. 1718, leaving issue,
1. John Cuffe, d.s.p. 2. William, d.s.p.
3. THOMAS NEVILLE, of whom presently.
1. Cordelia. 2. Louisa.
3. Isabella. 4. Maria.

He was s. by his 3rd son,
THOMAS NEVILLE BAGOT, of Ard and Ballymoe, b. 1784; m. 1811, Ellen, dau. of John Fallon, of Runnimead, co. Roscommon, and Letitia his wife, dau. of John Lambert, of Milford (son of Walter Lambert, of Cregclare, by his second wife, Miss Martyn, of Tullyra Castle), by his wife Mary, dau. of Sir Henry Burke, Bart., of Glynsk Castle, co. Galway, by his wife Cisley Netterville, and d. 8 Feb. 1863, leaving issue,
1. JOHN LLOYD NEVILLE BAGOT, of Ballymoe and Aughrane.
2. Bernard William, of Carranure, co. Roscommon, Barrister-at-Law, J.P., b. 1818; m. 1st, 1850, Euphemia, dau. of the late Richard J. Hinds, of Rathgar, and by her (who d. 1855) had issue,
1. Richard John Hindes (Rev.), m. 1876, Emily Louisa, eldest dau. of H. L. Bean, and d. 1880, leaving issue,
Louisa Mary Frances.
He m. 2ndly, 1862, Josephine Isabella, dau. of Joseph A. Holmes, D.I., of Clogher, co. Sligo, and d. 22 Jan. 1899, leaving issue,
1. Frances Letitia, m. 31 Aug. 1889, Lieut.-Col. F. M. Giubb, R.E., D.S.O.
2. Isabella, m. 2 Jan. 1891, Maj. Frederic Pelham Abbot Hardy, Army Service Corps.
3. Charles Augustus, of Dublin, m. 1858, Fanny Louisa, dau. of A. S. Kerr, and d. 1877, having had issue,
1. George Hindes. 2. Bernard William.
3. William Sidney.
4. Christopher Neville, of Aughrane Castle, co. Galway, J.P., m. 8 Aug. 1875, Alice, dau. of Sir William Verner, 2nd bart., M.P. for co. Armagh, and d. 23 May, 1877, leaving a son,
William Hugh Neville, b. 22 Oct. 1875.
His widow m. 30 Oct. 1879, Reginald Wynne Roberts, and by him had issue. She d. 9 July, 1905.
1. Letitia Mary. 2. Ellen, d. unm. 26 July, 1866.
3. Catherine, m. Francis Meagher, of Ballinderry, co. Tipperary.

The eldest son,
JOHN LLOYD NEVILLE-BAGOT, of Ballymoe, J.P. cos. Galway, Clare, and Roscommon, b. Nov. 1814; m. 1846, Anna Georgina, only dau. of Edward Henry Kirwan, of Ballyturin Castle, co. Galway, and by her (who d. May, 1888) had issue,
1. EDWARD THOMAS LLOYD, of Ballymoe and Aughrane.
2. Edward Henry Kirwan, b. 1850, d. unm. 1882.
3. John Christopher, of Ballyturin House, Gort, co. Galway, J.P., b. 1856; m. 20 Oct. 1891, Anna Catherine, only dau. of Lieut.-Col. William Fleming, late 95th Regt., of Mayfield, Ashbourne, Derbyshire, and has issue,
1. Mary Eileen. 2. Kathleen Anna.
4. Charles Henry, of Curraghmore, Athleague, co. Roscommon, b. May, 1860; m. 10 Nov. 1891, Georgina Louisa, 4th dau. of John Osborne, M.D., of Lindville, co. Cork, and has issue,
1. Charles Edward Kirwan, b. 3 June, 1895.
1. Anna Georgina, b. 14 Sept. 1892.
2. Gwendolin Frances, b. 8 Dec. 1898.
1. Anna Isabella.
2. Ellen Georgina, m. 12 Dec. 1907, Harry, eld. son of Henry Huggins, of St. Anne's, Lancs.

Mr. Neville-Bagot d. 1890 and was s. by his eldest son,
EDWARD THOMAS LLOYD NEVILLE-BAGOT, of Ballymoe and Aughrane, co. Galway, b. 1848, m. 1876, Ellen, dau. of Francis Meagher, of Ballinderry, co. Tipperary, and d. Oct. 1890, leaving one son,
MILO VICTOR, now of Ballymoe and Aughrane, and of Turin, Italy.

Arms—Erm. two chevronels az. in the dexter chief point a trefoil, slipped, vert, quartering CUFF, of the family of Lord TYRAWLEY. Crest—Issuing from a ducal coronet of a goat's head ermines horned of the first. Motto—Antiquum obtinens.

Seat—Ballymoe, co. Galway, and Aughrane Castle, Ballygar, co. Galway.

BAGWELL OF MARLFIELD.

RICHARD BAGWELL, of Marlfield, co. Tipperary, J.P., D.L., High Sheriff 1869, and J.P. co. Waterford, b. 9 Dec. 1840, educated at Harrow and Christ Church, Oxford, M.A., called to the Bar at the Inner Temple 1866, late Capt. S. Tipperary Artillery; m. 9 Jan. 1873, Harriette Philippa, dau. of Philip Jocelyn Newton, of Dunleckney, co. Carlow, and has issue,

1. JOHN PHILIP (Chantry House, Melbourne, Derbyshire), b. 11 Aug. 1874; m. 23 Jan. 1901, Louisa, youngest dau. of the late Maj.-Gen. George Shaw, C.B., and has issue,
1. Richard, b. 21 Oct. 1901.
2. William, b. 1905.
1. Lilla Cecily, b. 26 Oct. 1902.
1. Emily Georgiana. 2. Margaret.
3. Lilla.

Lineage.—WILLIAM BAGWELL, M.P. for Clonmel (son of John Bagwell, of Clonmel and Burgagary, banker, and grandson of William Bagwell, of Ballylougbane, living in 1707); m. 1749, Jane, dau. and co-heir of John Harper, of Belgrove, co. Cork, and dying 1756, left, with three daus., a son and heir,
JOHN BAGWELL, M.P. for co. Tipperary, and Col. of the Militia, who purchased Marlfield, co. Tipperary. He m. 1774, Mary, dau. of Richard Hare, of Ennismore, and sister of William, 1st Earl of Listowel, by whom he had issue (with four daus., Margaret, m. John Kelly, of Strancally Castle; Jane, m. Lieut.-Gen. Sir Eyre Coote; Catherine, m. John Croker, of Ballinaguard; and Mary, m. Henry Langley, of Brittas Castle) two sons,
1. WILLIAM, his heir.
2. Richard (Rev.), Dean of Clogher, who m. 1808, Margaret, dau. of Edward Croker, of Ballinaguard, and had issue,
1. JOHN, successor to his uncle.
2. Edward Bagwell Purefoy, of Greenfield, co. Tipperary, formerly Capt. 4th Hussars, Hon. Col. Tipperary Artillery Militia, High Sheriff co. Tipperary 1856, and Vice-Lieut. of the co. (see PUREFOY of Greenfields); d. 2 July, 1883.
1. Margaret, m. Joseph Gore, of Derrymore, co. Clare.
2. Mary, m. George Gough, of Woodstown, co. Limerick.
3. Jane, m. Benjamin B. Frend.

Col. Bagwell was s. at his decease by his eldest son,
COL. THE RIGHT HON. WILLIAM BAGWELL, of Marlfield, M.P., a Privy Councillor and Muster-Master-General for Ireland, at whose decease, unm. 1825, the estates devolved on his nephew,
JOHN BAGWELL, of Marlfield, J.P. and D.L., High Sheriff co. Tipperary 1834, M.P. for Clonmel 1857-74, b. 3 April, 1811; m. 21 June, 1838, Hon. Frances Eliza Prittie, sister of Henry, 3rd Lord Dunalley, and d. 2 March, 1883, having by her (who d. 17 April, 1901) had issue,
1. RICHARD, now of Marlfield.
2. William, of East Grove, Queenstown, J.P. co. Cork, b. 5 March, 1849; m. 1881, Mary, dau. of C. Spring Rice, and has issue,
1. John, M.V.O., Lieut. Norf. Regt., b. 3 March, 1884.
1. Dorcas Bousfield, b. 1882.
2. Frances, b. 1886.
1. Elizabeth, d. unm. 1886.
2. Margaret, m. 1862, John Thornton Rogers, of River Hill, Kent.
3. Emily, m. 1873, J. Carrington Ley, one of H.M.'s Inspectors of Schools.
4. Fanny.

Seat—Marlfield, near Clonmel. Clubs—Athenæum, Oxford and Cambridge, S.W., and Kildare Street, Dublin.

BAGWELL-PUREFOY. See PUREFOY.

BAILIE OF RINGDUFFERIN.

The late MAJOR JAMES BAILIE, of Ringdufferin, co. Down, J.P., M.A. Trin. Coll. Dublin, Major (retired) 87th R.I. Fusiliers, formerly of the 60th Rifles, served ten years in India, and had the medal for the Indian Mutiny, b. 31 Jan. 1823; m. 15 May, 1850, his cousin Charlotte Jemima, eldest dau. of Capt. William Cossart Carleton, 4th son of Very Rev. Peter Carleton, Dean of St. Patrick's, and d. 28 Feb. 1896, bur. in Killyleigh Churchyard, having had issue,

1. Edward Robert, d. in infancy, 1855.
1. HARRIET LOUISA. 2. KATHLEEN.
3. LOUISA.

Lineage.—DAVID BAILLIE, of Lamington, the second son of SIR WILLIAM BAILLIE, of Lamington, and Marion his wife, dau. of Sir John Seaton, of Seaton (see BAILLIE of Dochfour), was father of
ALEXANDER BAILLIE, of Dunraget, b. about 1540, an Officer in the English Army, who purchased the lands of Innishargie, co. Down, and had a son,

ALEXANDER BAILIE, of Innishargie and Ringdufferin, co. Down, who altered the spelling of his surname, was *b*. 1587; *d*. 20 Aug. 1682, leaving issue,
1. John, of Innishargie, *b*. 1623, *m*. Catherine Cary, and *d*. 1687, leaving, with other issue, an eldest son,
James, of Innishargie House, *b*. 1653; *m*. Jane, dau. of Sir Francis Annesley, of Castle William, co. Down, and *d*. 1710, leaving, with other issue, a son,
John, of Innishargie House, co. Down, High Sheriff 1725, *b*. 1697; *m*. Jane, dau. of Mathew Forde, of Seaforde, co. Down, and *d*. 1759, leaving, with other issue, a dau. Anne Sarah, *m*. William Mercer, of Fair Hill, co. Louth, and a son,
James, of Innishargie House, which he sold, was High Sheriff 1767, M.P. for Hillsborough, *b*. 1724; *m*. Anne, dau. of Francis Hall, of Strangford, co. Down, and *d.s.p.* 1787.
2. EDWARD, of whom we treat.

The 2nd son,
EDWARD BAILIE, settled at Ringdufferin, *m*. Elizabeth, only dau. of James Dunbar, and was s. by his eldest son,
ALEXANDER BAILIE, who became the absolute purchaser of Ringdufferin in 1674. He was s. by his son,
EDWARD BAILIE, of Ringdufferin, High Sheriff co. Down in 1730, who *d*. 1774, at the age of 84. His 2nd son,
JAMES BAILIE, of Ringdufferin, *b*. 1735, J.P., Deputy-Governor of co. Down; *m*. 1793, Sophia Loudon; and, dying 1810, was s. by his eldest son,
JAMES BAILIE, of Ringdufferin, *b*. 1797, Barrister-at-Law, J.P. and D.L., *m*. 1st, 1821, Charlotte, dau. of Very Rev. Peter Carleton, Dean of St. Patrick's, Dublin, and by her (who *d*. 1825) had a son,
1. JAMES, his heir.
He *m*. 2ndly, 1829, Harriett Alice, dau. of Rev. Henry Mahon, and had by her three daus.,
1. Louisa Anne, *d. unm*. 23 Dec. 1898.
2. Sophia Emily, dec.
3. Harriet Alice Gertrude.
He *d*. June, 1863, when his only son, JAMES, s. him in the Ringdufferin and a small portion of the old Innishargie estate.

Seat—Ringdufferin, Toy, near Killyleigh.

BAINBRIDGE OF FRANKFIELD.

JOHN HUGH BAINBRIDGE, of Frankfield, co. Cork, and of Elfordleigh, Plympton, S. Devon, Lieut. R.N., *b*. 31 May, 1879; *m*. 23 July, 1907, Kathleen Irene, only dau. of the late Lewis Sparrow, of Strode, Ivybridge, Devon, and has issue,
Rose Marie Irène, *b*. 20 Feb., 1909.

Lineage—Bainbridge, originally Baynbrig, is a name of great antiquity in the north of England.
THOMAS BAINBRIDGE, of Croydon Lodge, Burslow, and Portnells, Surrey, and Queen's Square, London, *m*. Anne, dau. of Morgan Waters, of Tyfig, co. Glamorgan (by Grace his wife, dau. of Thomas Swan, of Great Coxwell, co. Berks), and widow of J. Rowlandson of Lancaster; and *d*. 8 Jan. 1830, leaving by her (who *d*. 21 Dec 1834) a son,
JOHN HUGH BAINBRIDGE, of Frankfield, near Douglas, co. Cork. *m*. Jan. 1839, Jane Anne, dau. of Henry Westropp, of Richmond, co. Limerick, by whom (who *d*. 9 Oct. 1859) he had,
1. JOHN HUGH, late of Frankfield.
2. Ernest, *b*. 27 Feb. 1848; *d*. 1 Dec. 1849.
3. Angelo Coutts, Indian Civil Service, *b*. 18 April, 1850; *d*. in India, 1876.
1. Eleanor Jane, *m*. 3 June, 1863, Robert Samuel Gregg, D.D., Bishop of Cork, Cloyne, and Ross 1878, and afterwards Primate of all Ireland, and *d*. 26 June, 1893. He *d*. 1896, leaving issue.
2. Jane Anne, *m*. July, 1886, Rev. Arthur John Spencer.
Mr. Bainbridge was accidentally drowned, 10 June, 1877. His eldest son,
REAR ADMIRAL JOHN HUGH BAINBRIDGE, of Frankfield, co. Cork, and Elfordleigh, Plympton, Devon, J.P. co. Cork, sometime A.D.C. to the Queen, *b*. 31 May, 1845; *m*. 14 Sept. 1875, Rose Catherine, dau. of Col. Edward Birch-Reynardson, C.B., of Rushington Manor, co. Southampton, by Emily his wife, dau. of Vere Fane, of Little Ponton Hall, co. Lincoln (*see* BURKE'S *Peerage*, WESTMORLAND, E.), and *d*. 10 Aug. 1901, having had issue,
1. JOHN HUGH, now of Frankfield.
1. Kathleen Grace Fane, *m*. 12 Sept. 1905, Lieut.-Col. Hugh Fortescue Coleridge, D.S.O., and has issue.
2. Gwendolen Eleanor, *m*. 4 June, 1901, Major A. B. Fox, Somersetshire L.I. (*Sandpits, Powick, Worcester*), and has had issue.
3. Dorothy Emily, *m*. Lieut. Bowles, R.A.

Seat—Frankfield, Cork. Residence—Elfordleigh, Plympton, South Devon.

BAKER OF LISMACUE.

ALLEN BAKER, of Lismacue, co. Tipperary, M.R.C.V.S., *b*. 24 July, 1881; *m*. 7 July, 1910, Frances Violet (now of Ballinard), eld. dau. of the late Lieut.-Col. William Cooper-Chadwick, of Ballinard, Tipperary (*see that family*).

Lineage.—THOMAS BAKER, the first of this family who settled at Lattinmore, co. Tipperary, went to Ireland with the Lord Deputy, Sussex. His widow, Anne Baker, who was living at Knockroid, Barony of Clanwilliam, 8 July, 1642, put in her claim, and that of her son, Walter, as sufferers, in 1641. This son,
WALTER BAKER, entered Trin. Coll. Dublin 30 Sept. 1640, aged 17, as 2nd son of Thomas Baker, of Lattinmore, *b*. at Ballincallagh. 1623. He got a re-grant from CHARLES II of the lands of Killenaliff, Lattinmore and Lattinbeg, Yorticord, and Kilpatrick, in co. Tipperary, containing 1,200 Irish acres. This patent was enrolled 5 May, 1677, and it states that the lands were in Thomas Baker's possession "long before the Great Rebellion" of 1641. He *m*. Martha Osborne, and left issue, three sons and two daus. The 2nd son,
RICHARD BAKER, of Lattinmore, co. Tipperary, s. his father. He *m*. and left issue, a son,
WILLIAM BAKER, s. his father in his estates, and purchased, 1700 (from Col. Blunt), the estate of Lismacue, and was High Sheriff co. Tipperary 1726. He *m*. 17 July, 1700, Margaret, eldest dau. of Hugh Massy, of Duntryleague, co. Limerick, and had issue, seven sons and four daus.,
1. HUGH, his heir.   2. Charles.
3. Thomas.   4. Richard.
5. William.   6. Walter.
7. Godfrey, of Cork, *m*. 1744, Elizabeth, dau. of Peter Cossart, of Cork, and had (with two daus., Elizabeth, *m*. Nicholas Wrixon, and Katherine, *m*. Thomas Pope) four sons,
1. Godfrey, *m*. Margaret, dau. of Hugh, 1st Lord Massy, and by her (who *m*. 2ndly, Capt. Wheeler, R.N., and was mother of Gen. Sir Hugh Wheeler, killed at Cawnpore) had issue,
Godfrey Hugh Massy, *m*. Elizabeth, only child of Marmaduke Grace, and had an only dau. and heiress,
Eleanor, *m*. 1848, Richard Rogers Coxwell Rogers, of Dowdeswell Court, co. Gloucester, and has issue.
2. Hugh, *m*. Miss Phipps, and had issue,
(1) Godfrey Phipps, Col. H.E.I.C.S.
(2) George, Capt. R.A., *m*. and had one dau., *m*. Capt. Monck, 22nd Regt.
(3) Hugh Cossart, Maj. H.E.I.C.S., *m*. Mary Popplewell, and had issue,
Hugh (Rev.), *d.s.p.*
Catherine, *m*. 1865, Augustin William Langdon, and has issue.
(3) Dorcas, *m*. Gen. Peter Stewart, R.A., who *d*. 1867, leaving issue.
3. Peter, *d.s.p.* 1813.
4. William Massy, Col. H.E.I.C.S., settled at Fort William, Glanmire, co. Cork; *m*. 19 Feb. 1807, Mary Towgood, only child of the Rev. Richard Davies, of Dawstown, co. Cork, and *d*. 12 Nov. 1829, leaving issue,
(1) GODFREY THOMAS, of Fort William, *b*. 18 April, 1810; *m*. 1841, Maria Elizabeth, 4th dau. of Charles Silver Oliver, of Inchera, co. Cork, M.P., and by her (who *d*. 14 June, 1901) left issue,
Godfrey William, *b*. 24 Oct. 1851; *d*. at Heidelberg, 11 Dec. 1865.
Maria Elizabeth Thomasine.
(2) William, Col. H.E.I.C.S., *m*. Frances Roupell, dau. of James Simpson, and *d*. 1877, leaving issue,
1. Godfrey Alexander, B.A. Cambridge.
2. William Savage, B.A., T.C.D., Lieut. 20th Regt.
(3) Richard Davies, Capt. 51st Light Infantry, *d.s.p.* 1873.
(4) Hugh Percy, Capt. Fusiliers, *d.s.p.* 12 Jan. 1846.
(5) James Swayne, Capt. R.E., *d.s.p.* 1871.
(1) Dorcas French, *m*. Capt. Francis J. Green, of Greenmount, co. Limerick, and *d.s.p.* 1830.
(2) Eleanor Davies, *m*. 3 Aug. 1843, Edward Hoare Garde, and has issue.
(3) Katherine Pope.
(4) Elizabeth, *m*. — Bolton.
(5) Margaret, *m*. her cousin, the Rev. Godfrey Massy, of Mount Sion.
(6) Alice, *m*. — Shepherd.   (7) Amy, *d. unm*.
The eldest son,
HUGH BAKER, of Lismacue, *m*. 1730, Catherine, dau. of Robert Ryves, of Ryves Castle, Ballyskiddane, co. Limerick, and *d*. 25 Jan. 1772, having had issue,
1. WILLIAM, his heir.
2. Thomas, *m*. May, 1771, Rose, dau. of Sir Nevil Hickman, Bt., had one son, dec.
3. Hugh, *m*. Sydney Coates, and had issue.
4. Walter, *d. unm*.   5. Edward, *d.* young.
6. Kilner, *m*. 1st, 9 Sept. 1783, Elizabeth, 2nd dau. and co-heir of the Rev. Robert Nettles, Rector of Ballinamona, co. Cork, and had issue, a son and two daus. He *m*. 2ndly, the dau. of Kilner Brasier, by whom he had no issue.
1. Elizabeth, *m*. May, 1759, her cousin, the Hon. John Massy, *d.s.p.*
2. Margaret, *m*. Kilner Brasier. 3. Catherine, *d. unm*.
The eldest son,
WILLIAM BAKER, of Lismacue, Col. Irish Volunteers, *m*. Elizabeth, 2nd dau. of the Very Rev. Charles Massy, of Doonass, Dean of Limerick, and sister of Sir Hugh Dillon Massy, 1st bart., of Doonass, and had issue,
1. WILLIAM, his heir.
2. Hugh, *m*. Anne, dau. of James Reardon, of Tipperary, and *d*. 1801, leaving issue,
1. HUGH, who s. his uncle at Lismacue.
2. William, Rector of Shronel, co. Tipperary, *m*. Sidney, dau. of John Scott Baker, and *d*. 1874 leaving issue,
Hugh Sidney (Rev.), Preacher of St. Patrick's Cathedral, Cashel, *d*. 1883.

Balfe. THE LANDED GENTRY. 24

1. Elizabeth, d. unm. 1867.
3. Charles Massy, Lieut.-Col. 14th Dragoons, d. unm.
4. Robert, m. Miss Collins.
1. Elizabeth, m. Henry Fry, of Frybrook, co. Roscommon.
2. Catherine, m. Johnstone Stoney, of Oakley Park, King's Co.
3. Grace, m. 1st, Richard Taylor; and 2ndly, Maj.-Gen. Robert Philott, R.A.
4. Margaret, d. unm.
Mr. Baker d. 1808, and was s. by his eldest son,
WILLIAM BAKER, of Lismacue, s. his father 1808; m. Elizabeth, dau. of Sir Thomas Roberts, 1st bart., of Brightfieldstown, co. Cork, but d.s.p.; he was murdered 27 Nov. 1815, when he was s. by his nephew,
HUGH BAKER, of Lismacue, b. 1 Aug. 1798; m. Marion, only child of Charles Conyers, of Castletown Conyers, co. Limerick, and left issue,
1. HUGH, his heir.
2. CHARLES CONYERS MASSY, late of Lismacue, which he purchased from his brother's heirs.
3. William, M.A.
4. Augustine Fitzgerald (Sir), M.A. Trin. Coll. Dublin, Pres. of Incorporated Law Society of Ireland 1903 (56, Merrion Square, Dublin), b. 1851.
1. Marion Elizabeth, m. George Cole Baker, J.P., who d. 1870.
2. Anne, m. Lieut.-Col. Morley Stratford Tynte Dennis, of Barraderry, co. Wicklow. She d. Jan. 1900. He d. 1902.
3. Elizabeth Henrietta, m. Robert B. Gordon.
4. Mary Rachel, m. John Twynam, of Soberton House, Hants.
Mr. Baker d. 5 Nov. 1868, and was s. by his eldest son,
HUGH BAKER, of Lismacue, b. 1845; m. 1 March, 1879, Frances Elizabeth, dau. of John Massy, of Kingswell, co. Tipperary, and d. 9 July, 1887, having by her (who m. 2ndly, 13 Sept. 1888, Ralph Hall Bunbury, of Noremount, co. Kilkenny) had issue,
HUGH, b. 1 March, 1880.
Alice Maud Massy, b. 21 Aug. 1883.
CHARLES CONYERS MASSY BAKER, of Lismacue, co. Tipperary, J.P., B.A. Worcester Coll. Oxford, Barrister-at-Law, b. 1847; m. 10 June, 1880, Harriet Booth, dau. of George Allen, of Oakdale, Surrey, and had issue,
1. ALLEN, now of Lismacue.
2. Conyers, m. Feb. 1911, Susan Dorothea Geraldine, 2nd dau. of Archdeacon Robert Jones Sylvester Devenish, Rector of Cahir (see DEVENISH of Mount Pleasant).
3. Massy. 4. Dennis.
1. Irene.
He d. 12 Jan. 1905.
Seat—Lismacue, Tipperary, co. Tipperary.

BALFE OF SOUTH PARK.

MICHAEL JOSEPH BALFE, of South Park, co. Roscommon, J.P. and D.L., High Sheriff 1875 and 1890, Capt. and Hon. Major 5th Batt. Connaught Rangers, b. 10 June, 1850; m. 29 July, 1885, Kathleen, 4th dau. of John O'Connell, D.L., and grand-dau. of Daniel O'Connell, of Derrynane Abbey, co. Kerry (see that family), and has issue,
1. MICHAEL EDWARD JOSEPH, b. 13 Oct. 1887; m. 27 June, 1911, Harriet, only dau. of Richard Galwey, of Ardsallagh, Cork.
2. Maurice O'Connell Francis, b. 3 Dec. 1888.
3. James Morgan, b. 8 Oct. 1889.
1. Alice Elizabeth Mary Angela. 2. Kathleen Mary.
Lineage.—WALTER BALFE, of Heathfield, co. Roscommon (son of Michael Balfe, by his wife, a dau. of — Foster, of Mount Foster, co. Galway, and grandson of Thomas Balfe), m. Jane, dau. of Nicholas French, of Frenchlawn, co. Roscommon, and by her had issue, two daus. (the elder m. John Irwin, of Oran, and the younger, m. 1st, — Taaffe, and 2ndly, — Scully) and ten sons,
1. MICHAEL, his heir.
2. John, of Lissadurn, co. Roscommon, m. a dau. of Thos. Smith, of Fort Castle, King's Co., and had two sons and one dau.
3. Nicholas, d. unm. 4. Patrick, d. unm.
5. Edmund, of Marlborough Street, Dublin, m. Elizabeth, youngest dau. of John Dolphin, of Turoe, co. Galway, and left issue,
1. Nicholas, m. Miss Dubourdieu, and had issue.
1. Eleanor Maria Theresa, m. 1853, Thomas Netterville, brother of Viscount Netterville, and d. 7 March, 1855.
2. Maria, m. Dr. Veitch.
6. Walter, an Officer in the Army, d. unm.
7. George, d. unm. 8. Richard, d. unm.
9. Christopher, m. Fanny, 3rd dau. of Thomas O'Conor, of New Gard'n, and left one son,
Walter, Lieut.-Col. late 11th Hussars, m. Miss Esmé Mary Fitzgibbon (d. 14 July, 1907), and d. 4 March, 1899, leaving issue, two daus., of whom the younger, Frances Esmé m. 30 Jan. 1904, Major Frederick Arthur Fryer, Inniskilling Dragoons, son of Sir Frederick Fryer, K.C.S.I.
10. James, of Runnymeade, co. Roscommon, m. Mary Anne, younger dau. of Edward Martyn, of Tullyra Castle, co. Galway, and left four daus., his co-heirs,
1. Mary, m. 1852, Col. Charles Raleigh Chichester, eldest son of Sir Charles Chichester, K.C.T., and d. 1871 (see CHICHESTER-CONSTABLE).

2. Ellen, m. 2 July, 1858, Charles Michael Berington, of Little Malvern Court, co. Worcester (see that family), and d. 18 Aug. 1868.
3. Jane, m. Capt. Newton Charles Chichester.
4. Catherine, m. Col. De Morelle, and d. leaving a dau.
The eldest son,
MICHAEL BALFE, of South Park, m. 1st, Sally, dau. of John Dolphin, of Turoe, co. Galway, and had by her an only child,
Maria, m. Jeremiah John Murphy, Q.C., late a Master in Chancery in Ireland, and d. leaving issue.
Mr. Balfe m. 2ndly, 1810, Alicia, dau. of Thomas Smith, of Fort Castle, Philipstown, King's Co., and widow of C. Taaffe, and by her (who d. 1834) had issue,
1. MICHAEL, his heir. 2. NICHOLAS, heir to his brother.
3. PATRICK JOSEPH, successor to his brother.
4. James, m. a dau. of Charles Hawkes, of Briarfield, co. Roscommon, and d. June, 1872, leaving two sons, Michael and James, and five daus., Caroline, Alice, Geraldine, Katie, and Mary Bella.
1. Anne, m. Patrick Breen, J.P., of Castlebridge, co. Wexford, and d. 1850.
2. Sarah, m. Thomas Blake, of Glenloe Abbey, co. Galway.
3. Kate Mary, m. Morgan O'Connell, formerly M.P. for co. Meath, 2nd son of Daniel O'Connell, of Derrynane Abbey, co. Kerry, M.P.
Mr. Balfe d. 1838, and was s. by his eldest son,
MICHAEL BALFE, of South Park, who m. 1st, Sarah, dau. of Thomas Redington, of Rye Hill, co. Galway, who d. 1833; and 2ndly, Catherine, eldest dau. of Bernard Mullins, J.P., of Ballycigan, King's Co., and of FitzWilliam Square, Dublin, but d.s.p. 1839, when he was s. by his brother,
NICHOLAS BALFE, of South Park, who m. Jane, dau. of Andrew Ennis, of Roebuck, near Dublin, and dying s.p. 1856, was s. by his brother,
PATRICK JOSEPH BALFE, of South Park, J.P., High Sheriff 1858, late Capt. 5th Batt. Connaught Rangers, b. Sept. 1819; m. 5 Nov. 1847, Anna Mary, 2nd dau. of William MacDermott, of Springfield, co. Galway, by Anna his wife, dau. of Maj. Bodkin, of Rahoon and Kilclooneg, co. Galway, and d. Dec. 1886, having by her (who d. 5 Sept. 1884) had issue,
1. MICHAEL JOSEPH, now of South Park.
2. Nicholas Dominick Joseph, b. 5 Aug. 1854; m. April, 1894, Margaret, dau. of the late Sir Patrick Hackett, Knt., and has issue, a dau.
3. Patrick Joseph, b. 1 June, 1857.
1. Annie Mary, m. 14 June, 1869, Charles Edward Hawkes, of Briarfield, co. Roscommon, J.P.
2. Katie Mary, m. 26 Feb. 1875, Cornelius Alexander Keogh, late of Birchfield, co. Clare, and Oakport, co. Roscommon, J.P.
3. Alice Mary Maude. 4. May Josephine Ignatius.
Seat—South Park, Castlerea, co. Roscommon.

BALFOUR OF TOWNLEY HALL.

BLAYNEY REYNELL TOWNLEY BALFOUR, of Townley Hall, co. Louth, J.P. cos. Louth, Meath and Drogheda, D.L. co. Louth, High Sheriff co. Louth, 1885 and 1908, M.A., Trin. Coll. Camb., b. 15 April, 1845; m. 24 Jan. 1906, Madeline Elizabeth, elder dau. of John Kells Ingram, LL.D., formerly Vice-Provost of Trin. Coll. Dublin.
Lineage.—SIR WILLIAM BALFOUR, of Pitcullo, co. Fife, Governor of the Tower under CHARLES I, and settled in Ireland on the purchase of an estate in the co. Fermanagh, from his uncle, Lord Balfour, of Clanawley (see BURKE's Extinct Peerages). He m. 1st, Helen, dau. of Archibald, Lord Napier, and had,
1. Alexander, Col. in the Dutch Army, m. Elizabeth Anne Bueuch.
2. William, served in the Netherlands, and d.s.p.
He m. 2ndly, Isabella, a Dutch lady, widow of Henry Moore, and by her had,
3. CHARLES, of whom presently.
2. Emilia, m. before 1657, Alexander, 4th Earl of Moray, K.T.
1. Isabella, m. 1649, John, 3rd Lord Balfour, of Burleigh.
3. Susanna, m. Hugh, Lord Hamilton, of Glenawley.
The younger son,
CHARLES BALFOUR, of Castle Balfour, m. 1665, Cicely, dau. and heir of Sir Robert Byron, of Colwick, Notts, and d. May, 1713, leaving issue,
1. WILLIAM, his heir.
1. Lucy, m. 1st, 1684, Hugh McGill, of Kirkestown, co. Down, and 2ndly, 1692, Blayney Townley, of Piedmont, co. Louth, and by him (who d. 22 Aug. 17 2) had, with other issue,
1. HARRY, s. his uncle. 2. BLAYNEY, of whom presently.
2. Another dau.
The only son,
WILLIAM BALFOUR, of Castle Balfour, attainted by JAMES II 1689; d. unm. 1738, and was s. by his nephew,
HARRY TOWNLEY, of Piedmont, co. Louth, who assumed the name of BALFOUR, under the will of his uncle, and s. to his estates in co. Fermanagh (afterwards sold to the Earl of Erne), b. 19 Dec. 1693; m. 1724, Anne, dau. of Col. Henry Percy, and d. July, 1741, leaving with a dau., Emelia, a son,
WILLIAM CHARLES TOWNLEY BALFOUR, of Castle Balfour, m. 1754, Mary, dau. of Major Thomas Aston, and d.s.p. 21 Nov. 1759, and was s. by his uncle,
BLAYNEY TOWNLEY BALFOUR, b. 1705; m. 30 Nov. 1734, his cousin, Mary, dau. and heiress of Hamilton Townley, of Townley

Hall, and relict of William Tenison, of Thomastown, co. Louth, and had,
1. Hamilton, *b.* 1742, *d.* 1746.
2. BLAYNEY TOWNLEY, High Sheriff co. Louth 1771, *b.* 1744; *m.* 20 Feb. 1768, Letitia, dau. of Francis Leigh, M.P. for Drogheda, by Anne his wife, dau. of Henry Bingham, of Newbrook, co. Mayo, and *d.v.p.* 8 Dec. 1771, leaving issue,
  1. BLAYNEY, successor to his grandfather.
  1. Anna Maria, *m.* 1793, Very Rev. Thomas Vesey Dawson, Dean of Clonmacnois, and nephew to Thomas, 1st Lord Cremorne. He *d.s.p.* 1811, and his widow *d.* 1820.
  2. Mary Frances, *d. unm.* 1820.
Mr. Balfour *d.* 1788, aged 84, and was *s.* by his grandson,
BLAYNEY BALFOUR, of Townley Hall, J.P. and D.L., *b.* 28 May, 1769; *m.* 17 Oct. 1797. Lady Florence Cole, dau. of William Willoughby, 1st Earl of Enniskillen, and by her (who *d.* 1 March, 1862) had issue,
  1. BLAYNEY, his heir.
  2. Willoughby William (Rev.), for forty years Rector of Aston Flamville-cum-Burbage, co. Leicester, *b.* 10 Oct. 1801; *d. unm.* 29 June, 1888.
  3. Francis Leigh, *b.* 22 Feb. 1805; *d.* at Honduras, 29 Oct. 1833, *unm.*
  4. Arthur Lowry, *b.* 3 Dec. 1809, Capt. 32nd Foot; *d.* in India, 13 July, 1850.
  5. Lowry Vesey, Secretary of the Order of St. Patrick, and Gentleman-at-Large to the Lord Lieut., *b.* 30 March, 1819; *d. unm.* 12 Feb. 1878.
  1. Anne Maria, *b.* 5 July, 1800; *d. unm.* 1892.
  2. Letitia Frances, *b.* 7 Nov. 1805; *d. unm.* 1885.
  3. Florence Henrietta, *b.* 28 July, 1808; *d. unm.* 23 July, 1881.
  4. Elizabeth Sarah, *d. unm.* 1838.
Mr. Balfour was Member of the Irish Parliament 1797-1800, for the borough of Belturbet, and was High Sheriff co. Louth 1792. He *d.* 22 Dec. 1856, and was *s.* by his eldest son,
BLAYNEY TOWNLEY BALFOUR, of Townley Hall, J.P., High Sheriff co. Louth, 1841, Lieut.-Governor of the Bahama Islands 1833, *b.* 2 July, 1799; *m.* 12 Jan. 1843. Elizabeth Catherine, dau. and heiress of Richard Molesworth Reynell, of Reynella, co. Westmeath (*see* REYNELL *of Killynon*), and *d.* 5 Sept. 1882, leaving issue,
  1. BLAYNEY REYNELL, his heir.
  2. Francis Richard (Right Rev.), M.A., Assistant Bishop of Bloemfontein, South Africa, *b.* 21 June, 1846.
  1. Catherine Florence Agnes, *b.* 17 Jan. 1858; *d. unm.* 13 Jan. 1912.
  2. Mary Henrietta, *b.* 23 Oct. 1860.
Seat—Townley Hall, near Drogheda, co. Louth. *Club*—Sackville Street, Dublin.

BAM. *See* **STEWART-BAM.**

BANNATYNE OF FANNINGSTOWN CASTLE.
See **BANNATYNE OF HALDON.**

BANON OF BROUGHALL CASTLE.

CHRISTOPHER JAMES PATRICK BANON, of Broughall Castle, King's Co., D.L., J.P., High Sheriff 1904, *b.* 17 March, 1863; *s.* his father 1873; *m.* 15 Sept. 1908, his cousin, Rose, only dau. of Valerio, Count Magawly Cerati de Calry (*see* BURKE'S *Peerage, Foreign Titles*).
Lineage.—JAMES O'BANON had issue,
  1. EDWARD, of whom next.
  2. James, Capt., who after the battle of the Boyne accompanied Sarsfield to France, where he left issue.
The elder son,
EDWARD BANON, of Rathcastle, co. Westmeath, *b.* 1636; *d.* 1705, being bur. at Templemavally Abbey. He *m.* a dau. of O'Molloy and left issue a son,
THOMAS BANON, of Rathcastle, and Mearescourt, co. Westmeath, will dated 4 Dec. 1765, proved 1767; *m.* Mary ——, who had issue,
  1. EDWARD.
  1. Anne.
The elder son,
EDWARD BANON, of Meares Court, co. Westmeath, and Rathcastle, *b.* 1730, and *d.*   (will proved 1804), having *m.* Catherine, dau. of Francis Lyons, of Irishtown, co. Westneath, by whom he had issue,

1. Thomas, of Irishtown House, *b.* 1772; *d.* 1856, having *m.*, 1807, Bridget Ellenor (*d.* 1858), dau. of George Davys, J.P., of Clonbonny, co. Longford, by whom he had issue,
  1. Edward, *b.* 1808; *m.* 1844, a dau. of —— Masters, of Cregan, co. Roscommon, and *d.* in Australia, leaving issue, a dau., Elizabeth Alice.
  2. Richard Davys, Insp.-Gen. of Hospitals, served in Sikh War and Indian Mutiny, *b.* 1812; *d.* 1870; having *m.* 1849, Adelaide, dau. of Thomas Penny White, M.A., Cambridge, by his marriage with Elizabeth Channing, of Fir Grove House, Droxford, Hants, and had issue,
    (1) Arthur, Capt. Indian Army (ret.), *b.* 1850.
    (2) Henry Charles, *b.* 1860.
    (3) Frederick Lionel, Col. late Shropshire L.I., A.A.G. War Office, served in Soudan Campaign 1885, and South African War 1899-1902, *b.* 2 June, 1862 (1, *Sloane Gardens, S.W.*); *m.* 11 Dec. 1890, Helen Mary, dau. of Robert McEwen McIlwraith, of 35, Hans Place, S.W., and has issue,
      Ronald Awly, *b.* 20 March, 1893.
    (4) Herbert, *b.* 1864; *d. unm.* 1887.
    (1) Mary.
  3. Christopher.
  1. Anne.   2. Frances.   3. Maria.
  2. Edward, *b.* 1776; *d.* 1790.
  3. Andrew, *b.* 1777.
  4. Christopher (Rev.), of Oldtown, *b.* 1778; *d.* 1847.
  5. JAMES, of whom next.
  1. Mary, *m.* John FitzGerald, of Redmondstown, and had issue.
The 5th son,
JAMES BANON, of Irishtown, co. Westmeath, *b.* 1781; *m.* 1808, Mary Bridget, 2nd dau. of Count Patrick Awly Magawly de Calry (*see* BURKE'S *Peerage, Foreign Titles*), of Temora, King's Co. He *d.* 1847, leaving by her (who *d.* 1833) issue,
  1. CHRISTOPHER, of whom next.
  2. Awly, M.D. (St. Andrews), Vice-Pres. Roy. Coll. Surg. (Ireland) 1866-67, *b.* 1812; *m.* 2 June, 1840, Jane (*d.* 11 Feb. 1874), dau. of Henry Lambert, of Carnagh (*see that family*). He *d.s.p.* 1867.
  3. EDWARD JOSEPH, who *s.* his brother Christopher.
  4. Andrew, of Irishtown, J.P., *b.* 1823; *m.* 1864, Annie, eldest dau. of Edward Beatagh, Q.C., and *d.* 1891, leaving issue,
    1. Awly Edward   2. Edward.
    3. Andrew.   4. James Arthur.
    5. Christopher.
    1. Mary Jeanette.   2. Lucie.
    3. Nannie.
  1. Jeanette.
  2. Mary Frances, *m.* 1856, Gilbert Nugent, of Jamestown Court, co. Westmeath, and *d.* 1887, leaving issue.
  3. Ellen, *d. unm.*
He was *s.* by his eldest son,
CHRISTOPHER BANON, of Irishtown, J.P., who also *s.* his cousin, Sir Nicholas FitzSimon, D.L., M.P., in the Broughall Castle Estates, 1849. He was *b.* 1810 and *d.s.p.* 24 May, 1863, having *m.* Marie, relict of William Sweetman, being *s.* by his brother,
EDWARD JOSEPH BANON of Broughall Castle, King's Co., J.P., D.L., R.M., co. Meath, served in the Crimean Campaign *b.*, ? *d.* 1873, having *m.* 1857, Ellen, eldest dau. of John FitzGerald, of Carrick, co. Tipperary, by whom he had issue,
  1. CHRISTOPHER JAMES PATRICK, now of Broughall Castle.
  2. Edward Magawly, *b.* 6 Aug. 1868; *m.* June, 1909, Agnes, dau. of J. B. Manning, of Riverside Drive, New York.
  1. Ellen Mary.
  2. Frances Patricia, *m.* Edward Hamilton Barry, M.D.
  3. Benedicta Magawly.   4. Josephine Mary.
Arms—Vert, an Irish wolfhound courant arg. between three trefoils slipped or. Crest—An arm in armour embowed, the hand grasping a sword entwined with a garland of trefoils, all ppr. Motto—Fidelis et constans.

Seat—Broughall Castle, Frankford, King's Co.

BARCROFT OF THE GLEN.

JOSEPH BARCROFT, of the Glen, Newry, co. Down, M.A. Camb., B.Sc. London and Fellow King's Coll. Camb., *b.* 1872; *s.* his father 18 Nov. 1905; *m.* 5 Aug. 1903, Mary Agnetta, younger dau. of Sir Robert S. Ball, and has issue,
  1. HENRY, *b.* 18 Oct. 1904.
  2. Robert Ball, *b.* 4 May, 1909.
Lineage. — AMBROSE BARCROFT, of the Haigh, near Foulridge, and afterwards of Foulridge Hall, Lancashire, son of THOMAS BARCROFT, of Foulridge Hall, son of HENRY BARCROFT, of Foulridge, younger son of WILLIAM BARCROFT, of Barcroft, Lancashire (who *d.* 1581). where his family was seated from the earliest times to which records extend, down to the middle of the 17th century

Barrett. THE LANDED GENTRY. 26

(see WHITAKER's *History of Whalley*). Barcroft passed by the marriage of one of the daus. and co-heirs of Thomas Barcroft, of Barcroft, last of his line, who *d.* 1668 (great-grandson of William Barcroft, above mentioned), to the Bradshaws, and afterwards by purchase to the Townleys. Ambrose Barcroft *m.* Mary, dau. of — Hartley, of Wellhead, near Colne. His will, dated 30 Sept. 1641, was proved at Chester 9 May, 1668. He had issue,
1. Thomas, of the Haigh, *m.* Alice, dau. of J. Hargreaves, of Heyroyd, co. Lancaster, and had a son, Ambrose.
2. Ambrose (Rev.), Incumbent of Cavan, went to Ireland with his brother. He left a dau. Ellen, *m.* — Burroughs, of Dublin.
3. WILLIAM, of whom presently.
4. John.
5. Paul, of York.
6. Robert, settled in Bedfordshire, and was ancestor of the BARCROFT family.
1. Mary, *d. unm. v.p.*
2. Janet, *m.* John Jackson, son of Christopher Jackson, of Westholme.

The 3rd son,
WILLIAM BARCROFT, went to Ireland and settled at Ballylaking, King's Co., *b.* at Noyna, near Colne, Lancashire, 4 Aug. 1612; *m.* 1st, Grace, dau. of Henry Rycroft, of Moss House, within Foulridge, and by her had five children, who were drowned with their mother when crossing to Ireland to join her husband. He *m.* 2ndly, Margaret, dau. of Daniel Bernard, of Allincot, Colne, co. Lancaster. She *d.* at Drumcooley, King's Co., 1700. He *d.* there 2 Feb. 1696, and was bur. at Rosenallis, 4 Feb. following. By his second wife he had issue,
1. AMBROSE, of whom presently.
2. Thomas, *d.s.p.*
3. John, a minister of the Society of Friends. *b.* 2 June, 1664; *m.* Elizabeth, dau. of Henry Tibbs. He *d.* 24 Nov. 1723, leaving issue, extinct in the male line. His will was dated 24 Jan. 1723. Her will, dated 9 March, 1739, was proved 26 Nov. 1740
1. Ellen, *d. unm.* 27 Aug. 1678.

The eldest son,
AMBROSE BARCROFT, of Drumcooley, King's Co., *b.* at Heigh, Thornton, Yorks, *m.* Jane, dau. of William Slade, of Athlone, and *d.* at Drumcooley, 4 May, 1687, having by her (who *m.* 2ndly, — Gribble) had issue,
1. Ambrose, *b.* 4 April, 1680; *d. unm.*
2. WILLIAM, of whom presently.
3. Thomas, *b.* 2 June, 1686, *d.* 18 Nov. 1709.
1. Ellen, *b.* 3 Nov. 1682; *m.* William Fayle.
2. Alice, *b.* 26 Aug. 1684; *m.* Joseph Medcalf.

The 2nd son,
WILLIAM BARCROFT, of Ballybritton, King's Co., *b.* 7 Feb. 1681; *m.* 24 May, 1705, Ellen, dau. of Joseph Inman, and *d.* at Ballybritton 5 June, 1709, having by her, who *m.* 2ndly, Daniel Bewley, had issue,
1. Joseph, of Dublin, *b.* 31 March, 1706; *m.* 1st, Molina, dau. of Alexander Jaffray, of Kingswell, near Aberdeen, and had issue, who *d. unm.* He *m.* 2ndly, 29 April, 1744, Hannah, dau. of Jonathan Thomas. His will, dated 3 May, 1784, was proved 23 Dec. 1784.
2. AMBROSE, of whom presently.
1. Elizabeth, *b.* 13 June, 1709; *d.* 2 Dec. 1709.

The younger son,
AMBROSE BARCROFT, of Dublin, *b.* 22 Aug. 1707, *m.* Abigail, dau. of Thomas Wilcocks. His will, dated 12 June, 1758, was proved 24 Dec. 1760. He had issue,
1. WILLIAM, of whom presently.
2. Thomas, *m.* Mary, dau. of Francis Penrose, of Waterford, and had, with a dau., two sons, Ambrose and Penrose.
3. Joseph. 4. Ambrose.
1. Elizabeth.

The eldest son,
WILLIAM BARCROFT, of Dublin, *b.* 11 Jan. 1734; *m.* 17 Feb. 1757, Mary, dau. of John Pim, of Lackagh, Queen's Co. She *d.* 23 April, 1782. He *d.* Dec. 1772, having had issue,
1. Joseph, *b.* 18 Dec. 1757; *m.* Anne, dau. of — Cartwright, and *d.* 1810, leaving two daus.,
  1. Mary, *m.* — Wright.
  2. Elizabeth, *m.* — Bell.
2. JOHN, of whom presently.
3. George, *b.* 28 May, 1700; *m.* Mary, dau. of — Hutchinson, of Waterford, and had issue,
  1. Joseph Inman.
  2. William, a sea captain, accidentally killed at Liverpool.
  3. John, ⎫
  1. Sarah, ⎬ went to America.
  2. Mary, ⎭
4. Ambrose, *d.* an infant.

The second son,
JOHN BARCROFT, of Lisburn, *b.* 30 Nov. 1758; *m.* Sarah, dau. of James Hogg, of Lisburn (uncle of Sir James Weir Hogg, Bart.). She *b.* 21 March, 1856, aged 82. He *d.* 30 July, 1815, having had issue,
1. JOSEPH, of whom presently.
2. William James, *m.* Hannah Wakefield, dau. of Dr. Hancock, and had issue,
  1. Marv. 2. Ruth.
3. John Pim. *m.* Anna, dau. of Thomas Malcomson, of Lurgan, and *d.* 18 Feb. 1867, having had issue,
  1. John, J.P. co. Armagh, *b.* 14 Dec. 1836; *d.* 7 Aug. 1907.
  2. Thomas Malcomson, J.P. co. Armagh, *b.* 17 March, 1838; *d.* 23 Nov. 1911, leaving issue,
    (1) John Pim (Rev.), M.A. Dub.
3. William, *b.* 16 Oct. 1839; *m.* Sarah, dau. of Joseph Barcroft.
4. William Greer, *b.* 8 May, 1841.
5. Jonathan Hogg, *b.* 1842. His widow, Margaret, *d.* 7 Sept. 1908.
6. Frederick.

The eldest son,
JOSEPH BARCROFT, of Lisburn, and afterwards of Stangmore Lodge, co. Tyrone, *b.* 1799; *m.* Mary, dau. of John Wandesford Wright, of New York, U.S.A. She *d.* 20 Jan. 1856. He *d.* 20 Nov. 1855, having had issue,
1. HENRY, late of the Glen.
1. Elizabeth, *m.* 1864, Sir Samuel Lee Anderson, Principal Crown Solicitor for Ireland. He *d.* 1886. She *d.* 25 Sept. 1909.
2. Sarah, of Stangmore Lodge, *m.* William Barcroft.

The eldest son,
HENRY BARCROFT, of the Glen, co. Armagh, D.L., High Sheriff 1890, *b.* 1839; *d.* 18 Nov. 1905; *m.* 1867, Anna (*The Glen, Newry*), dau. of David Malcomson, of Melview, co. Tipperary, and had issue,
1. JOSEPH, now of The Glen.
2. David Malcomson, *b.* 1875.
1. Sarah Richardson. 2. Mary.
3. Anna Henrietta.

Arms—Arg. a lion ramp. sa. in the dexter chief point a trefoil slipped vert. *Crest*—A demi bear rampant gu. muzzled and charged on the shoulder with a trefoil slipped or.
Seat—The Glen, Newry. *Club*—Cambridge University.

BARRETT-HAMILTON. See **HAMILTON.**

BARRINGTON-WHITE. See **WHITE.**

BARRINGTON.
See BURKE'S PEERAGE, **BARRINGTON**, Bart.

BARRY OF FIRVILLE.

FREDERICK FRANCIS BARRY, of Firville, co. Cork, *b.* 3 Aug. 1859; *m.* 15 July, 1889, Winifride Mary (*d.* 14 July, 1907), dau. of E. Ingress Bell, F.R.I.B.A., of St. Stephen's, Sutton, Surrey, and has issue,
1. Magdalen Phyllis, *b.* 24 April, 1890.
2. Helen Mary, *b.* 22 May, 1902.

Lineage.—MICHAEL BARRY, of Elm Park, Farran co. Cork, *b.* 1783; *m.* 21 Feb. 1804, Eliza (*b.* 1781), dau. of Valentine McSwiney, of Macroom, co. Cork, and had issue,
1. James, *b.* 1805.
2. Valentine. *b.* 1808; *m.* McSwiney, *d.s.p.*
3. Charles, *b.* 1809. 4. MICHAEL, of whom next.
5. Thomas, *b.* 1814; *m.* a dau. of Ellen Harding, dau. of Henry Harding, of Firville, Macroom, co. Cork, and had issue with a son who *d. unm.*
Michael of Firville, Macroom, which property he inherited from his mother, *d.s.p.* 1908.
Ellen.
1. Eliza, *b.* 1812; *d. unm.*,

The 4th son,
MICHAEL BARRY, M.R.I.A., Barrister-at-Law, Professor of Law, Queen's University, Ireland, *b.* 24 Sept. 1810; *d.* 24 June, 1869, *m.* 20 June, 1835, Helen, dau. of James Hardman, of Clough Hall, Kenyon, Lancs., and Devonshire Place, London, by whom he had issue,
1. MICHAEL THOMAS RICHARD, of whom next.
1. Sarah, *b.* 19 Aug. 1837; *m.* 1873, as his 2nd wife, James Fitzgerald Lombard (*see* LOMBARD *of South Hill*).
2. Helen, *b.* 3 May, 1839; *m.* as his 2nd wife, 25 Sept. 1883, M. J. Clery, J.P. co. Limerick, of Moorfield, co. Dublin, who *d.s.p.*
3. Anne, *b.* 11 April, 1842; *m.* 14 Sept. 1868, W. A. Craig, of Crotonstown House, co. Kildare, J.P., M.R.I.A., and has issue.
4. Henrietta, *b.* 30 June, 1843.
5. Celia, a nun, *b.* 22 May, 1845.

The only son,
THE HON. MICHAEL THOMAS RICHARD BARRY, Acting Chief Justice of Gold Coast, *b.* 16 April, 1836; *d.* 1866; *m.* 7 Oct. 1858, Laura Frances, dau. of John Rorke, of Tyrrelstown, co. Dublin, and by her had issue,
1. FREDERICK FRANCIS, now of Firville.
1. Mary Helen, *m.* as his 2nd wife, 2 Feb. 1886, Aime F. Pitel, of the Wintons, East Croydon, Surrey, and has issue.
2. Laura, *m.* A. de Massias, killed with all issue in the disaster at St. Pierre, Martinique.

Arms—Barry of six arg. and gu., on a chief vert, a ship between two trefoils slipped or. *Crest*—Out of a castle with two towers **or**, a wolf's head per pale arg. and gu., langued of the last.. *Motto*—Boutez en avant.
Seat—Firville, Macroom, co. Cork. *Residence*—St. Helen's, Wallington, Surrey.

BARRY OF LEAMLARA.

HENRY JOSEPH ARTHUR ROBERT BRUNO STANDISH BARRY, of Leamlara, co. Cork, J.P., *b.* 8 Nov. 1873; *m.* 18 April, 1899, Eleanor Lilian Heléne, dau. of Maj.-Gen. C. B. Lucie-Smith, M.S.C., and has issue,

1. CHARLES HENRY JOSEPH ROBERT GARRETT STANDISH, *b.* 9 Feb. 1900.
1. Marcella Standish.
2. Margaret Standish.

Lineage.—JOHN BARRY, of Leamlara, *temp.* CHARLES I, *m.* Isabel Nagle, of Moneanimie, and had a son, GARRETT, his heir. By a grant from CHARLES I, in the 12th year of his reign (1636), the family estates were confirmed to this proprietor. John Barry was *s.* by his son, GARRETT BARRY, of Leinlara, or Leamlara, who obtained from CHARLES II a confirmatory grant of Leamlara. He *m.* Ellen, dau. of Daniel Duff O'Cahill, by Ellen his wife, dau. of M'Cartie Reagh. He was *s.* at his decease by his son, DAVID BARRY, of Leamlara, who *m.* Catherine, dau. of Standish Grady, of Elton, co. Limerick, and was father of STANDISH BARRY, of Leamlara, who *m.* 1708, Eleanor, dau. of Thady Quin, of Adare, co. Limerick, and had issue, three sons, DAVID; GARRETT; and John, *d. unm.*; and six daus., Catherine, *m.* Joseph Anthony; Elizabeth, *m.* Patrick Lacy, of Miltown, co. Limerick, whose dau. was mother of Sir De Lacy Evans, K.C.B.; Margaret, *m.* John Stack; Mary; Eleanor; and Anne, *m.* Simon Haly, of Ballyhally. The eldest son, DAVID BARRY, of Leamlara, dying without issue, was *s.* by his brother, GARRETT BARRY, of Leamlara, who *m.* Mary Anne Hussey, dau. of the Baron of Galtrim, and, dying in 1786, left with two daus., Anne, wife of Timothy Deasy, and Eleanor, wife of Hatton Conron, a son, STANDISH BARRY, of Leamlara, who *m.* July, 1787, Margaret, dau. of Philip Roche, of Limerick (*see* ROCHE *of Grannagh Castle*), and had three sons and three daus.,

1. GARRETT STANDISH, his heir.   2. John, *d. unm.* 1833.
3. HENRY STANDISH, who *s.* his brother as male heir of the family, 1864.
1. Margaret, *m.* Thomas Butler, of Ballycarron.
2. PENELOPE, of Leamlara, who purchased the estate from her eldest brother, and is deceased.
3. Anne.

Mr. Barry *d.* April, 1821, and was *s.* by his eldest son, GARRETT STANDISH BARRY, of Leamlara, co. Cork, J.P. and D.L., High Sheriff 1830. Mr. Barry was the first Catholic Member of Parliament elected by the co. Cork, after the Act of Emancipation in 1829. He *d.* 26 Dec. 1864, and was *s.* in the representation of the family by his next surviving brother, HENRY STANDISH BARRY, of Leamlara, *m.*1836, Angelina, youngest dau. of William Brander, of Morden Hall, Surrey, and *d.* 31 Aug. 1870, leaving a son and successor, CHARLES STANDISH BARRY, of Leamlara, co. Cork, J.P., *b.* 1847; *m.* 5 Aug. 1869, Hon. Margaret Mary Southwell, dau. of Lieut.-Col. Hon. Arthur Francis Southwell, and sister of the 4th Viscount Southwell, K.P., and *d.* 10 Nov. 1897, leaving issue, HENRY JOSEPH ARTHUR ROPERT BRUNO STANDISH, now of Leamlara. Winifred Mary Standish, *d. unm.* 15 May, 1892.

Arms—Arg., three bars gemels, gu. Crest—A castle arg., from the top issuing a wolf's head sa. Motto—Boutez en avant.

Seat—Leamlara House, Carrigtuohill, co. Cork.

BARRY OF SANDVILLE.

JAMES GRENE BARRY, of Sandville, and of Bellevue, co. Limerick, J.P. and D.L., *b.* 20 April, 1841; *m.* 20 June, 1881, Mary Elizabeth, only dau. of Thomas Kane, M.D., J.P., of Whitehall, Limerick, and has issue,

1. JAMES THOMAS, B.A. and B.E. Trin. Coll. Dublin, *b.* 8 June, 1882.
2. Gerald, of Thurles, M.R.C.V.S., *b.* 18 Dec. 1883.
3. Donal, *b.* 29 Sept. 1885, Assist. Commissioner, Malay Fed. States Police.
4. William, *b.* 2 April, 1887.
5. John, *b.* 30 Dec. 1893.
1. Mary Nesta, *b.* 6 Dec. 1888.
2. Anna Maud, *b.* 5 Feb. 1892.

Lineage.—By an Inquisition taken at St. Francis' Abbey, Limerick, dated 12 March, 1623, DONAL BARRY, of Ballyguybeg, in the barony of Clanwilliam, co. Limerick (who *d.* 30 April, 1612), was found to have held in fee *ultra reprisas*, the lands of Ballyguybeg and Bohergar. By his wife, Sabina O'Hea (living 12 March, 1623), he had issue,

1. DONAL, his heir.
2. David, was father of MacDavid Barry, of Farnane, who was *b.* 1648; *d.* 6 July, 1736, having had issue, by his wife (who *d.* 1737),
   1. Michael, of Farnane, *d.s.p.* 1748.
   2. Thomas, of Rathwood.   3. Edmund.
   4. David.
   1. Mary, *m.* R. Hayes, of Killuragh.
3. Edmund.   4. Lewis.
1. Elizabeth.

The eldest son, DONAL BARRY, *b.* 1588, aged 24 years at his father's death; *m.* Joanna, dau. of John Bourke, of Brittas, co. Limerick, and *d.* 1633. There is an elaborate inscription on his tomb and his coat of arms, with the crescent, distinguishing his descent from a 2nd son; he is described as the "very noble" of the "ancient race of Barry" who had "served his country with liberality." Donal Barry had issue,

1. DONAL, who *s.*, *m.* Mary, dau. of O'Ryan, of Annagh, co. Limerick. Having joined the confederate Catholics in 1642, his property was confiscated, and he and his family transplanted across the Shannon (certificate of transplantation dated 19 Dec. 1653). This branch of the family became extinct on the death of James Barry in 1766.
2. DAVID, of whom next.   3. Edmund.
4. Thomas.

The 2nd son, DAVID BARRY, of Fryarstown, *m.* the dau. and co-heiress of William Ryan, of Clonkeen, and *d.* after 1655, leaving issue, JOHN, and Gerald (or Garrett). The elder son, JOHN BARRY, of Fryarstown, had issue, GARRETT, David, and Thomas. The eldest son, GARRETT BARRY, of Fryarstown, *m.* a dau. of Raleigh of Ballingoulagh, by whom he had JOHN, Garrett, and Daniel (or Donal). The eldest son, JOHN BARRY, of Fryarstown, *d.* 1761. By his wife Mary Burke, of Lodge, he had issue, a dau., Mary, and a son, JAMES BARRY, of Fryarstown, *b.* 4 Feb. 1749; *m.* 3 Nov. 1767, Anastatia, dau. of M. Bourke, of Askeaton, and *d.* 1 May, 1819, having had issue,

1. James, of Rockstown, *b.* 3 May, 1771; *m.* 10 Feb. 1812, Mary, dau. of John Molony, of Cragg, co. Clare (*see that family*), and *d.* 25f uly, 1828, leaving issue, three daus.,
   1. Dilliana, of Rockstown, *m.* 11 July, 1846, Ralph Westropp Brereton, of Ballyadams, Queen's Co., with has issue.
   2. Mary, *m.* S Jan. 1833, Henry Potter, of Ballynolan, co. Limerick.
   3. Alice, *m.* 10 Oct. 1841, Chartres Brew Molony, of Ennis, and left issue.
2. JOHN, of whom presently.
3. Thomas, *b.* 1783, *m.* Mary, dau. of Jasper Hartwell, of Bruff, *d.* 1837, and leaving issue.

The 2nd son, JOHN BARRY, of Fryarstown (now Sandville), *b.* 20 Feb. 1779; *m.* 13 Feb. 1804, Mary, dau. of R. O'Shaughnessy, of Friarstown Lodge, and by her (who *d.* 3 April, 1855) had issue,

1. JAMES, his heir.
2. Thomas, of Caherline, *b.* 1809; *m.* 26 Aug. 1835, Margaret, dau. of M. Bourke, of Ballyglass, and by her (who *d.* 14 Dec. 1860) had issue. He *d.* 22 March, 1866, and was bur. at Sandhurst, Australia.
3. John, of Sandville, *b.* 1824; *d.s.p.* 10 Nov. 1860.
1. Marianne, *m.* 27 Feb. 1843, John Ball (who *d.* 15 Feb. 1849), and *d.* 14 March, 1901, leaving issue.

Mr. Barry *d.* 29 Aug. 1839, and was *s.* by his son, JAMES BARRY, of Bellevue, Croom, co. Limerick, J.P., *b.* 17 Nov. 1805; *m.* 1st, 18 July, 1833, Christina, dau. of Daniel Cranchy, D.L., of Charleville. She *d.s.p.* 6 May, 1835. He *m.* 2ndly, 29 Nov. 1837, Maria Helena, dau. of John Grene, of Cappamurra, Cashel, of an ancient Kent family, and *d.* 3 Sept. 1856, having by her (who *d.* 2 June, 1878) had issue,

1. JAMES GRENE, his heir.
2. Albert (Rev.), C.S.S.R., of Mount St. Alphonsus, Limerick, *b.* 23 May, 1842; *d.s.p.* 3 June, 1909.
3. William, of Buenos Ayros, *b.* 21 Oct. 1850.
4. Nicholas, of Limerick, *b.* 5 Aug. 1853.
5. John, of Victoria, Australia, *b.* 27 Nov. 1856.
1. Annie, *b.* 14 June, 1844; *m.* 30 Nov. 1867, Thomas Butler, of Suirvale, Tipperary, and *d.* 14 Jan. 1898, leaving issue.
2. Mary, *b.* 29 April, 1855.

Arms—Arg. three bars gemel gu., a bordure and in chief a crescent az. for difference. Crest—Out of a castle arg. charged with a crescent as in the arms, a wolf's head sa. Motto—Boutez en avant.

Seat—Sandville House, Ballyneety; and Bellevue, Croom, co. Limerick. Club—County Club, Limerick.

BARRY OF CASTLE COR.

WILLIAM NORTON BARRY, of Castle Cor, co. Cork, J.P., *b.* 20 June, 1859; *m.* 1st, Feb. 1881, Constance Marianne, 3rd dau. of Frederick John Walker, of The

Priory, Bathwick. He m. 2ndly, 1 June, 1899, Adelaide Maude, 5th dau. of Sir John Wrixon Becher, 3rd bart.

Lineage.—RICHARD BARRY, m. 15 June, 1754, Mary Norton, and had issue,

RICHARD BARRY, 11th Hussars, m. Eliza, dau. of Darby O'Grady, of Rockbarton, co. Limerick, and sister of Standish, 1st Viscount Guillamore, purchased the estate of Castle Cor from the family of Deane Freeman, and had issue (with a dau., Frances, m. July, 1833, Dudley Persse, of Roxborough, see that family) a son and heir,

WILLIAM NORTON BARRY, of Castle Cor, J.P., Major 8th Hussars; b. 1820; m. 1st, 1845. Arabella, dau. of Col. Persse, by whom he had a dau. Elizabeth, m. Oct. 1868, John Short, of Bickham, co. Devon. He m. 2ndly, 19 Jan. 1856, Elizabeth, dau. of Sir William Wrixon-Becher, 1st bart. of Ballygiblin, and d. 1871, leaving by her (who d. 22 May, 1906), with a dau., Frances Norton, b. 1861; d. 1862, a son and heir, WILLIAM NORTON, now of Castle Cor.

Seat—Castle Cor, Kanturk, co. Cork; and Derry Keel, Gort, co. Galway. *Club*—Army and Navy.

BURY-BARRY OF BALLYCLOUGH.

JAMES ROBERT (BARRY) BURY-BARRY, of Ballyclough, co. Cork, J.P., High Sheriff 1910, b. 3 Jan. 1875; s. his great-uncle in 1888, when he assumed, by Royal Licence, 12 Jan. 1889, the additional name of BARRY; m. 3 Oct. 1906, Judith Isabel, only dau. of W. R. Ringrose-Voase, J.P., of Anlaby House, Yorks. (see that family), and has issue,

Nesta Anne.

Lineage.—REDMOND BARRY, of Lisnegar and Rathcormack, co. Cork, M'Adam Barry, m. 1st, Mary, dau. of John Boyle, of Castle Lyons, co. Cork, and had issue, a son and two daus.,
1. JAMES, his heir.
1. Anne. m. Samuel Hartwell, Capt. in the Army, slain at Landen, 1693.
2. Catherine, m. Alan Brodrick, 1st Viscount Midleton.

Mr. Barry m. 2ndly, 1666, Jane, eldest dau. of Sir Nicholas Purdon, Knt. of Ballyclough, co. Cork, M.P. for Baltimore, and had, with two daus., another son,

2. REDMOND, of Ballyclough, co. Cork, who m. 1700, the dau. of Samuel Crofts, of Velverstown, co. Cork, and by her had a son and heir,

REDMOND, of Ballyclough, High Sheriff co. Cork 1734, who m. Henrietta, 2nd dau. of William Dunscombe, of Mount Desart, co. Cork, and had issue,

JAMES, his heir, of whom hereafter, as successor to his cousin, Redmond Barry, of Rathcormack, as M'ADAM BARRY.

Mary, m. Richard Aldworth St. Leger, Viscount Doneraile.

Mr. Barry, whose will, dated 3 March, 1681, was proved 23 March, 1690, was s. by his elder son by his 1st wife,

JAMES BARRY, of Rathcormack, *M'Adam Barry*, Col. in the Army, who m. 1st, Mary, dau. of Abraham Anselm, of London, and had issue, two sons and a dau., viz.,
1. JAMES, his heir.
2. REDMOND, successor to his brother.
1. Mary, d. unm.

Col. Barry m. 2ndly, Susanna, dau. of John Townsend, of Timoleague, co. Cork, by Lady Katherine Barry his wife, dau. of Richard, Earl of Barrymore, and had issue, two sons, David, M.D., Patrick, M.D., both d.s.p.; and two daus., Elizabeth, m. Noblett Dunscombe, of Mount Desart, co. Cork; and Katharine, m. John Townsend, Col. Barry was s. by his elder son,

JAMES BARRY, of Rathcormack, *M'Adam Barry*, High Sheriff co. Cork 1721, who d. unm. and was s. by his next brother,

REDMOND BARRY, of Rathcormack, *M'Adam Barry*. He d.s.p. 1750, and was s. by his cousin,

JAMES BARRY, of Ballyclough, *M'Adam Barry*. He m. March, 1765, Elizabeth, dau. and co-heiress of Abraham Greene, of Ballymachree, co. Limerick, and d. 25 Oct. 1793, leaving an elder son and heir,

REDMOND BARRY, of Ballyclough, *M'Adam Barry*, d. unm. 10 Feb. 1812, when the representation devolved upon his brother,

HENRY GREENE BARRY, of Ballyclough, *M'Adam Barry*, Major-Gen. in the Army, High Sheriff co. Cork 1821, who m. 21 Sept. 1804,

Phœbe, dau. of John Armstrong Drought, of Lettybrook, King's Co., and d. 13 May, 1838, leaving issue,
1. JAMES, his heir, of Ballyclough.
2. Henry, Capt, E.I.C.S., killed in Burmah 1853, *unm*.
3. Redmond (Sir), LL.D. Trin. Coll. Dublin, Senior Puisne Judge of the Supreme Court of Victoria and Chancellor of the University of Melbourne. 4. ST. LEGER, of Ballyclough.
5. John Richard, Lieut. 86th Foot, d. in India, *unm*.
6. William Wigram, C.B., Maj.-Gen. R.A., d. 19 April, 1883.
1. Letitia, m. Rev. Robert Bury, of Carrigrenane, co. Cork, Prebendary of Coole, son of Phineas Bury, of Little Island (see that family), and grandson of Phineas Bury, of Little Island, 5th son of John Bury, of Shannon Grove (see BURY of Charleville). He d. 1853, having had issue,
 1. Robert, Capt. 7th Dragoon Guards, m. Anna Maria, dau. of Richard Hart, and by her (who m. 2ndly, 29 April, 1891, Capt. J. R. Broadley, R.N.) left issue, a son and a dau.,
 JAMES ROBERT BARRY, now of Ballyclough, s. his great-uncle 1888, and assumed the additional name of BARRY.
 Letitia Mary, m. 1896, Capt. Norman Layton, Royal Sussex Regt.
 2. John Thomas, Capt. R.A., A.D.C. to Major-Gen. Primrose.
 1. Phœbe Hester Jane, m. 4 May, 1861, Gen. Robert Pratt, C.B. (who d. 27 Dec. 1886).
 2. Letitia Elizabeth, m. Capt. Richard Pennefather Going, of Ballynonty House, co. Tipperary.
 3. Hester Beatrice, m. 1st, 1861, Capt. Francis Fox (who d. 1864), grandson of Col. and Lady Anne Fox, of Fox Hall, co. Longford (see that family), and 2ndly, 16 Feb. 1865, Major-Gen. George de la Poer Beresford, Madras S. Corps, and has issue (see BURKE's *Peerage and Baronetage*, DECIES. B.).
 4. Charlotte Mary, m. 8 Oct. 1864, Capt. Crofton Toler Vandeleur late 10th Hussars, and 7th Dragoon Guards (see VANDELEUR of *Kilrush*).
2. Eliza, m. Col. Murray Simpson.
3. Caroline, d. unm. 1 April, 1872.
4. Katherine, m. Col. Osborne Broadley, and d. 6 Feb. 1873, leaving issue. 5. Phœbe, d. *unm*.
6. Charlotte, m. John Carroll, J.P., Barrister. He d. 1875. She d. 1901.
7. Louisa, d. *unm*.

His eldest son,

JAMES BARRY, of Ballyclough, *M'Adam Barry*, J.P. and D.L., High Sheriff 1841, b. 28 July, 1805; Capt. in the Army; m. 2 March, 1841, Olivia Maria, dau. and sole heiress of Francis Drew, of Mocollop Castle, co. Waterford, and *d.s.p.* 30 April, 1881. His widow m. 2ndly, 1883, Lieut.-Col. George Edward Hillier, C.B., late Inspector-Gen. Roy. Irish Constabulary, and d. 1884. Mr. Barry was s. by his brother,

ST. LEGER BARRY, of Ballyclough, *M'Adam Barry*, J.P., late Capt. 65th Foot, b. 1835; m. 1883, Mary Caroline Theresa, dau. of George Carr, and d. 7 July, 1888, and was s. by his grand-nephew, as above.

Arms—Quarterly: 1st and 4th, Barry of six arg. and gu., for BARRY; 2nd and 3rd, vert, a cross-crosslet or, in chief a crescent arg. for difference, for BURY. **Crests**—1st, BARRY—Out of a castle arg. a wolf's head couped sa. langued gu.; 2nd, BURY—A boar's head couped at the neck or, tusked arg., langued gu., transfixed through the neck by a spear ppr., and charged with a crescent for difference gu. **Mottoes**—Under the arms—Boutez en avant; over the 2nd crest—Virtus sub cruce crescit.

Seat—Ballyclough, Kilworth, co. Cork.

BARRY OF SUMMER HILL.

JOHN EDMUND BARRY, of Summer Hill House, co. Wexford, J.P. and D.L., b. 1853; m. 1st, 1880, Minnie, only dau. of the late Richard Joseph Devereux, M.P., of Summer Hill, co. Wexford. She d. 1893, having had issue a son d. 1898. He m. 2ndly, 1898, Olivia Goodall, widow of Maj.-Gen. A. Loftus Steele, and dau. of the late Capt. George Pemberton Pigott, of Slevoy Castle (see that family), and by her has issue,

RAYMOND CHARLES DEVEREUX, b. 1899.

Lineage.—SIR JOHN EDMUND BARRY, Knt., of 12, Mountjoy Square, Dublin, President of the Dublin Chamber of Commerce 1897-9, member of the Dublin Port and Docks Board, 1867-97, and since 1899, Member of Board of Superintendence of Dublin Hospitals, and Governor Royal Hibernian Military School, Phœnix Park, since 1903, b. 6 Feb. 1828, eldest son of the late John Barry, merchant, of Dublin; m. 1 Sept. 1849, Teresa, dau. of the late John Keefe, of Ifterknock, co. Meath, and has, with other issue, an eldest son,

JOHN EDMUND, of Summer Hill.

Residences—Rocklands, Wexford, and Ballygeary. *Club*—Constitutional.

IRELAND. Barton.

SMITH-BARRY OF BALLY EDMOND.

ROBERT COURTENAY SMITH-BARRY, of Bally Edmond, co. Cork, J.P., b. 19 Feb. 1858.

Lineage.—JOHN COURTENAY, son of George Courtenay, m. Anne, dau. of — Browne, of Bally Edmond, co. Cork, and left with a younger son Thomas, an elder son,
GEORGE COURTENAY, of Bally Edmond, m. Anne, eldest dau. of Leonard Ashe, of Drisbane, co. Cork, and by her, who d. 1823, had with other issue, a son,
ROBERT COURTENAY, of Bally Edmond, J.P., m. by licence, 20 Sept. 1790, Catherine, 2nd dau. of John Nash, of Ballybeen, co. Cork (see NASH of Finnstown), and by her, who d. 1799, had issue,
1. George, of Dromadda, co. Cork, High Sheriff 1826, b. 1795; m. settlements dated 29 July, 1814, Caroline Augusta, eldest sister of John Smith Barry, of Marbury Hall, Cheshire and Fota, co. Cork (see BURKE's Peerage, BARRYMORE, B.). She d. 28 May, 1853. He d.v.p. 10 Dec. 1837, having had issue,
 1. GEORGE, s. his grandfather.
 2. John, b. 1824; d. 1843.
 1. Caroline Augusta, m. 1840, Mountiford Longfield, D.L., of Castle Mary, co. Cork, who d. 8 Nov. 1864, leaving issue (see that family).
2. JOHN, s. his nephew George.
1. Anne, m. 1811, Simon Dring, of Rockgrove, co. Cork, and d.s.p. 1812. He d. 13 Dec. 1833.
2. Eliza Mary, m. 21 April, 1814. John Smith Barry, of Marbury Hall, and Fota, and d. 16 April, 1828, having by him, who d. 26 Feb. 1837, had issue,
 1. John, b. 25 Sept. 1821; d. unm. March, 1834.
 2. James Hugh, father of the 1st BARON BARRYMORE (see BURKE's Peerage).
 3. Robert Hugh, Capt. 10th Hussars, b. 13 Jan. 1820; d. unm. 25 April, 1849.
 4. RICHARD HUGH, of whom presently.
 1. Anne, b. 14 March, 1817; d. unm. Nov. 1834.
 2. Catherine Mary, d. unm. 1813.

Mr. Robert Courtenay was s. by his grandson,
GEORGE COURTENAY, of Bally Edmond, b. 1822; d. unm. 1844, when he was s. by his uncle,
JOHN COURTENAY, of Bally Edmond and Ballymagooly, co. Cork, High Sheriff 1852, b. 1798, s. his nephew 1844, but d. unm. 1861, when he was s. by his nephew,
RICHARD HUGH SMITH BARRY, of Bally Edmond, J.P. and D.L., co. Cork, and J.P. Hants, Capt. (retired) 12th Lancers, and sometime Adm. Royal Cork Yacht Club, b. 21 Feb. 1823, 4th son of John Smith Barry, of Marbury and Fota, and Eliza Mary his wife, 2nd dau. of Robert Courtenay, of Bally Edmond (see above), s. his uncle 1861; m. 18 April, 1850, Georgina Charlotte, dau. of Col. J. Grey, of Backford Hall, Northumberland. She d. 9 Sept. 1893. He d. 23 Jan. 1894, leaving issue,
1. ROBERT COURTENAY, now of Bally Edmond.
2. Cecil'Arthur, b. 19 Oct. 1863; d. 21 Nov. 1908; m. the dau. of W. H. Barry, and had issue, two daus.
1. Nina Mary Georgina, b. 15 June, 1859; m. Sept. 1885, Maj. Thomas Henry Burton Forster, of Holt, Wilts. and has issue.
2. Aileen Emma, b. 25 April, 1861; m. 25 April, 1882, Godfrey Hugh Wheeler Coxwell-Rogers, of Ablington Manor and Dowdeswell Court, co. Gloucester, and has issue (see that family).
3. Kathleen Winifriede, b. 25 Oct. 1868.

Arms—Quarterly 1st and 4th arg. three bars gemel gu. (BARRY), 2nd and 3rd quarterly 1st and 4th gu., on a chevron or between three bezants as many crosses patée fitchée sa. (SMITH), 2nd and 3rd az. a fesse arg. between three porcupines or (HERIZ), the whole within a bordure compony erm. and of the second. Crest—A castle arg. issuing from the battlements thereof a wolf's head charged with a cross patée fitchée or. Motto—Boutez en avant.

Seat—Bally Edmond, Midleton, co. Cork.

SMITH-BARRY OF LOUTH.

JAMES HUGH SMITH-BARRY, of Louth, and of Stowell Park, Pewsey, Wilts., J.P. for that co. and High Sheriff for Louth 1870, late Lieut. Gren. Guards, b. 11 Jan. 1845; m. 1 Dec. 1874, Lady Charlotte Jane Cole, dau. of 3rd Earl of Enniskillen, and has issue,
ROBERT, b. 4 April, 1886.

Mr. J. H. Smith-Barry is the youngest son of the late James Hugh Smith Barry, D.L., of Fota, co. Cork, and Marbury, co. Chester (who d. 31 Dec. 1857), and only brother of Arthur Hugh, 1st Lord Barrymore (see BURKE's Peerage).

Arms—Quarterly 1st and 4th arg., three bars gemel gu. (BARRY), 2nd and 3rd quarterly 1st and 4th gu., on a chevron or between three bezants as many crosses patée fitchée sa. (SMITH), 2nd and 3rd az. a fesse arg. between three porcupines or (HERIZ), the whole within a bordure compony erm. and of the second. Crest—A castle arg. issuing from the battlements thereof a wolf's head charged with a cross patée fitchée or. Motto—Boutez en avant.

Seat—Stowell Park, Pewsey, Wilts.

SMITH-BARRY.

See BURKE's PEERAGE, **BARRYMORE, B.**

HAROLD-BARRY OF BALLYVONARE.

HAROLD PHILIP HAROLD-BARRY, of Ballyvonare, co. Cork, b. 19 Nov. 1865; m. 30 April, 1895, Helen Frances Mary, dau. of John Gerard Riddell, of Hermeston Hall, Rotherham, Yorks., and has issue,
1. JOHN GERARD, b. 28 Jan. 1896.
2. Charles William, b. 21 May, 1897.
3. Edward Basil, b. 1 Sept. 1901.
1. Hilda Mary Philomena, b. 25 May, 1900.

Lineage.—The family of HAROLD was long seated in the co. Dublin, where they possessed large estates at Harold's Cross. The immediate ancestor of this branch was RICHARD HAROLD, of Singland and Pennywell, co. Limerick, m. 1782, Mary, only child and heiress of John Barry, of Ballyvonare, co. Cork, and had a son,
JOHN HAROLD-BARRY, of Ballyvonare, co. Cork (who assumed the additional name of Barry on inheriting the Barry property) m. 1st, 1822, Eliza, dau. of Henry Harrison, of Castle Harrison, co. Cork, and had issue (with Richard, Henry, Margaret, who all d. young), a son,
JOHN, of whom presently.
Mr. Harold Barry m. 2ndly, 1843, Margaret, Hon. Chanoinesse of the Order of St. Anne of Bavaria, sister of the Right Hon. Sir Thomas Esmonde, Bart., P.C., of Ballynastragh, co. Wexford, and widow of Peter Locke, of Athgoe, co. Dublin. She d.s.p. 25 Dec. 1878. His son,
JOHN HAROLD-BARRY, of Ballyvonare, co. Cork, J.P. and D.L., High Sheriff 1880, b. Aug. 1823; m. Oct. 1860, Margaret Josephine, dau. of William Gibson, of Roebuck, co. Dublin, and Belvedere Place, Dublin, and d. 5 May, 1898, leaving issue,
1. John, b. 1863; d. 1864.
2. HAROLD PHILIP, now of Ballyvonare.
3. William John, b. Sept. 1869; d. at Krugersdorp, South Africa, 2 Feb. 1896, from wounds received in action.
4. Richard, b. and d. 1871.
5. Edward Daniel (Rev.), b. Aug. 1872.
6. Philip, b. March, 1874.
7. Henry Alan, b. April, 1876.
8. Thomas, b. and d. 1879. 9. John, b. Aug. 1884.
1. Marcella, m. Garrett Nagle, of Clogher, co. Cork, and has issue.
2. Eliza. 3. Margaret Josephine.
4. Anne, m. Thomas Leahy, of Woodfort, co. Cork, and has issue.
5. Isabella.

Arms—Gu., a pall flory arg. between three plates one and two, each charged with an estoile of six points of the field. Crest—A demi-angel vested gu. winged and crined or.

Seat—Ballyvonare, Buttevant, co. Cork. Club—Royal Yacht Club, Queenstown.

BARTON OF GREENFORT.

COL. BAPTIST JOHNSTON BARTON, of Greenfort and Portsalon, co. Donegal, late Col. 5th Batt. Royal Inniskilling Fusiliers, formerly Lieut. 33rd Regt., J.P. and D.L., High Sheriff co. Donegal 1877, A.D.C. to H.M. King Edward VII. 1905-10, and to King George since 1910; b. 15 July, 1848; m. 29 July, 1875, Isabel, youngest dau. of Robert McClintock, D.L., of Dunmore, co. Donegal, and has issue,

1. BAPTIST JOHNSTON, Capt. late West Riding Regt., b. 21 Oct. 1876; m. 26 Oct. 1908, Kathleen Maude, dau. of Egbert de Hamel, of Middleton Hall, Warwickshire, and has issue, Ernestine Isabel.
2. Gustavus, late Lieut. R.N. Reserve, b. 19 July, 1879; m. 910, Anne Farquharson, dau. of W. Duguid, of Ballater.
3. Ralph Edward, Lieut. R.G.A., b. 25 Oct. 1882; d. unm. 3 Nov. 1906.
4. Edward Humphrey, late 2nd Lieut. Donegal Art. Militia, b. 9 Jan. 1884; m. 22 Feb. 1911, Christina Letitia Aileen, only dau. of Henry Maturin Johnston, M.D.
5. Bertram, b. 31 July, 1885.
6. Charles Geoffrey, b. 28 Dec. 1889.
1. Margaret Isabel, m. 14 Jan. 1911, Herbert March, of Whittington Grange, Worcestershire.
2. Evelyn Mary Alice, m. 4 June, 1910, John Ingarsby Carver, eldest son of Fred. W. Carver, of Oakhurst, Knutsford, and has issue.

Lineage.—This family was established in Ireland by THOMAS BARTON, of Norwich, who is said to have accompanied the Earl of Essex's army to that kingdom. He was one of the first burgesses of Enniskillen (see Charter of Enniskillen, Cal. State Papers, 1611-14). In 1610 he obtained a grant of land comprising a district called Drumminshin and Neeairn, co. Fermanagh. Some of these lands were exchanged by him for others in the neighbourhood still in the possession of the elder branch of the family. He m. Margaret Lloyd, and had a son,
ANTHONY BARTON, who left issue a son,
WILLIAM BARTON, of Bowe Island and Curraghmore, co. Fermanagh, b. about 1630, m. Jane Hannah Forster, and d. 22 Feb. 1693, having had two sons,
1. EDWARD, of whom we treat.
2. WILLIAM, of Curraghmore, ancestor of BARTON of Grove.
The elder son,
EDWARD BARTON, of Bowe Island, co. Fermanagh, m. Mildrethe, sister of Robert Coonyngham, and d. 10 March, 1729, leaving issue,
1. WILLIAM, of whom we treat.
2. Edward, m. his cousin Elizabeth (Anna), dau. of William Barton, of Curraghmore, and had a son, John, of Bordeaux, who d. 10 April, 1816, leaving issue, and a dau., m. Robert Dickson.
3. James. 4. Michael.
5. Oliver. 6. Christopher.
7. Thomas.
The eldest son,
WILLIAM BARTON, left issue three sons and three daus.,
1. John, will dated 23 May, 1750.
2. Edward, of Spring Hill, co. Tyrone, High Sheriff, co. Fermanagh 1777, m. Mary, 2nd dau. of John Galbraith, of Roscavy, co. Tyrone (see that family). His will, dated 23 Feb. 1796, was proved 2 April, 1801.
3. GUSTAVUS, of whom we treat.
1. Lettice, m.— Cuthb.rson.
2. Frances, m. Thomas Rusborough, of Cloncarn and Cloontivern, co. Fermanagh, and d. 1816, leaving issue (see BURKE's Family Records).
3. Mary, m. — Conner.
The 3rd son,
GUSTAVUS BARTON, left issue by his first wife, four sons,
1. BAPTIST.
2. Edward (Ven.), Archdeacon of Ferns, m. Margaret Coleman, and d. 11 Aug. 1847, leaving issue,
 1. Edward, Capt. in the Army, d. unm.
 2. John, b. Dec. 1810; m. 1835, Mary, dau. of Molyneux Nicholson, M.D., of Westport, co. Mayo, and d. Dec. 1884, having had issue,
  (1) Edward, d. young.
  (2) Molyneux, of Grangebeg, co. Kildare, M.A., Barrister-at-Law, present representative of the family of BARTON (38, Upper Fitzwilliam Street, Dublin), b. 1 Nov. 1846; m. 10 Aug. 1882, Charlotte Frances Yates, dau. of the late Lieut.-Col. Edmund Yates Peel, 85th Regt., son of Lieut.-Gen. the Right Hon. Jonathan Peel, P.C. (see BURKE's Peerage PEEL, Bart.), and has issue,
   1. Cecil Molyneux.
   2. Henry John Chadwick.
   3. Ernest Ffoliott, d. 1909.
   4. Reginald Victor, R.N.
   1. Gwendolen Mary.
   2. Doris Adelaide.
   3. Miriam Charlotte.
  (3) Charles, d. young.
  (1) Elizabeth, m. Charles Place.
  (2) Jane, m. Arnold de Courcy Gildea.
 3. Charles, d. young.
 1. Margaret.
 2. Jane, d. 1832.
 3. Frances.
 4. Mary Anne.
3. John, who left three daus., who d. unm.
4. Charles.
Gustavus Barton m. 2ndly, about 1772, Harriett, sister and co-heiress of Baptist Johnston, of co. Monaghan, and with her acquired the estate of Drumsallogh in that co., and had issue,
5. BAPTIST JOHNSTON, of whom we treat.
6. James Murray, of Derryhallagh, J.P. co. Monaghan, m. circa 1803, Mary, dau. of Brabazon Brabazon, of Summer Hill, co. Dublin, and left a son, Freeman, who d. unm. 1899.
7. Freeman, left issue, Edward, d. unm.; and John, d. unm.
The 5th son,

MAJOR BAPTIST JOHNSTON BARTON, 64th Foot, of Drumsallogh, co. Monaghan, b. 1774; m. 1815, Catherine, dau. and eventually heiress of Ralph Babington, of Greenfort, and d. 1819, having by her, who d. 1865 (with two daus.), a son,
BAPTIST JOHNSTON BARTON, of Portsalon, co. Donegal, and Derryhaller, co. Monaghan, b. 30 Nov. 1816; m. June, 1842, Maria, only dau. of William McLaughlin, of Ramelton, and d. Aug. 1851, having by her (who d. Nov. 1875) had issue,
1. BAPTIST JOHNSTON, now of Greenfort.
1. Ellen Harriet, m. 4 Aug. 1864, Rev. Thomas T. Gray, F.T.C.D., and d. 14 Feb. 1880, leaving issue, three sons and four daus.
2. Katherine Sara.

Seats—Greenfort, Letterkenny, co. Donegal; Portsalon, co. Donegal.

BARTON OF GROVE.

MARY ELIZABETH BARTON, of Grove, co. Tipperary, only dau. of Major Thomas Frobisher, Bengal Army, of Cheltenham, J.P. and D.L., m. Dec. 1862, the late SAMUEL HENRY BARTON, J.P. and D.L., of Grove, co. Tipperary, and by him (who was b. 1817, and d. 27 Oct. 1891) has issue,
1. WILLIAM HENRY HUGH, b. Feb. 1871.
2. Charles Robert, b. March, 1877; m. Sept. 1904, Ethel, dau. of George Cobden, of Clonmel, co. Tipperary.
1. Rose Catherine Florence.

Lineage.—WILLIAM BARTON, of Curraghmore, second son of William Barton, of Bowe Island and Curraghmore, co. Fermanagh (see BARTON of Greenfort). He m. Elizabeth, dau. of John Dickson, of Ballyshannon, and d. 1695, having had issue,
1. THOMAS, his heir.
2. George, d. unm.
3. James, m. his cousin, the dau. of Col. Murray, of Antigua, and had a dau., m. Francis Warren Rossington.
1. Elizabeth (Anna), m. 1st, her cousin Edward Barton, and had issue, and 2ndly, David Johnston, and had issue.
2. Everina, m. James Boyd, and had issue.
The eldest son,
THOMAS BARTON, of Curraghmore, co. Fermanagh, b. 21 Dec. 1694, who established the house of business at Bordeaux 1725, and acquired a considerable fortune. He purchased the estate of Grove, co. Tipperary, 1752. He m. 1 Nov. 1722, his cousin Margaret, youngest dau. of Robert Delap, of Ballyshannon. She d. 27 Jan. 1775. He d. 18 Oct. 1780, leaving an only child,
WILLIAM BARTON, of Grove, co. Tipperary, b. 5 Aug. 1723; m. 1 Aug. 1754, Grace, eldest dau. of Very Rev. Charles Massy, of Doonas, co. Clare, Dean of Limerick, and sister of Sir Hugh Dillon Massy, 1st bart. of Doonas, and d. 1792, having had issue,
1. THOMAS, his heir.
2. William, of Clonelly, b. 20 Aug. 1758, succeeded to the estates of Clonelly, co. Fermanagh; m. 1796, Anne Isabella, dau. of Folliott Warren, of Lodge, co. Kilkenny, and d. 18 May, 1835, leaving by her (who d. 1810) issue,
 1. Folliott Warren, of Clonelly, J.P. and D.L., b. 15 Sept. 1798, High Sheriff co. Fermanagh 1834, d. unm.
 2. Edward Barton, Barrister-at-Law, d. unm. 3 Feb. 1837.
3. CHARLES (see BARTON of Waterfoot).
4. Hugh, of Straffan, co. Kildare (see that family).
5. Robert (Sir), K.C.H., a Lieut.-Gen. in the Army, b. 26 July, 1768; m. 1st, 1802, Maria, dau. and co-heir of John Paynter, and had issue,
 1. Hugh, a Lieut.-Col. in the Army, d. unm. Sept. 1877.
 1. Grace, m. Capt. Addison.   2. Maria, d. unm.
He m. 2ndly, Marion Colette, dau. of John Addison, and relict of Col. McPherson, and had by her a dau.,
 3. Alexandrine, m. Sir Henry Durrant, Bart.
6. DUNBAR, of Rochestown, co. Tipperary, at one time High Sheriff co. Tipperary, b. 7 Nov. 1769; m. 1798, Elizabeth, heiress of the Rochestown estate, dau. of Rev. Samuel Riall, Rector of Killenaule, and had issue,
 1. Samuel William, of Rochestown, co. Tipperary, b. 10 April, 1803; m. 13 July, 1831, Emma Maria, dau. of the Hon. Christopher Hely Hutchinson, M.P. for Cork, and by her (who d. 7 March, 1889) left issue,
  (1) CHRISTOPHER, of Rochestown, J.P., Lieut.-Col. 18th Hussars, b. 22 Feb. 1834.
  (2) Dunbar Henry, b. 16 Oct. 1841.
  (3) Crosbie, Col. 19th Regt., b. 29 June, 1845; m. 12 Dec. 1878, Mrs. Hamilton, eldest dau. of Richard Warburton of Garryhinch. He d. 1901.
  (4) William Archer, b. 29 May, 1847.
  (1) Elizabeth Mary, m. 11 July, 1872, Antoni Marcelli Szymanski.
  (2) Anna Grace, d. unm.   (3) Mary.
  (4) Evelyn Isabella.

IRELAND. Barton.

2. Dunbar Thomas, Lieut. 1st Royal Drag⁰⁰ⁿˢ, b. 1806; d. 1829.
3. Augustine Hugh, b. 1815; m. 12 Oct, 1853, Emily, widow of J. M'Calmont, of Abbeylands, and dau. of James Martin, of Ross, co. Galway. She d. 30 Nov. 1907. He d. 23 Oct. 1874, leaving two daus.,
(1) Emily Alma, m. 21 April, 1881, Sir George Frederick Brooke, Bart. of Somerton, co. Dublin, and d. 28 Sept. 1910, having had issue.
(2) Rose.
4. Thomas Henry, Dublin Metropolitan Police Magistrate, b. 1816; m. 6 Jan. 1853, Hon. Charlotte, dau. of John, 3rd Lord Plunket, and d. 1878, leaving issue,
(1) Dunbar Plunket, one of the Judges of the King's Bench Division of the High Court of Justice in Ireland; M.A. Oxford, M.P. for Mid-Armagh 1891-1900, Sol.-Gen. for Ireland 1897-1900, Judge of the High Court of Justice in Ireland 1900 (19, Clyde Road, Dublin), b. 1853; m. 5 Oct. 1900, Mary, dau. of Joseph Manly, of Dublin, and has issue,
Dunbar Patrick, b. 18 Aug. 1901.
(2) Augustine Frederick Palliser, Local Gov. Auditor of Berks and Oxfordshire Districts, M.A., T.C.D., b. 1854.
(3) Aubrey David Plunket, b. 1864; m. 1901, Kathryn Floding, of Virginia, U.S.A., and has issue, a dau.
(4) Ion Plunket, Lieut. and Commander R.N., b. 1871; d. 2 Oct. 1899.
(1) Sylvia Charlotte Elizabeth, m. 1881, Arthur G. K. Woodgate, and has issue (see WOODGATE of Pembury).
(2) Eleanor Constance. (3) Violet Grace Louisa.
Mr. Dunbar Barton d. 19 May, 1848; his widow d. 16 Oct. 1853.
1. Grace, b. 21 March, 1762; m. 1784, John Palliser, of Derryluskan, co. Tipperary, and d. 13 March, 1844, leaving issue.
2. Elizabeth, b. 25 July, 1764; m. Lieut.-Gen. Sir Augustine Fitzgerald, Bart., who d.s.p. 3 Dec. 1834.
3. Margaret Everina, b. 4 Nov. 1772; m. 2 March, 1792, Hugh, 3rd Lord Massy, and d. 14 Sept. 1820, leaving issue.
The eldest son,
THOMAS BARTON, of Grove, M.P. for Fethard before the Union, b. 26 Jan. 1757; m. Mary, dau. of Chambré Brabazon Ponsonby, of Ashgrove, and sister of Chambré Brabazon Ponsonby Barker, of Kilcooly Abbey, and d. 1820, leaving issue,
1. WILLIAM, of Grove.
2. Chambré Brabazon, Lieut.-Col. 2nd Life Guards, d. 1834.
3. Charles Robert, Maj. 14th Light Dragoons, d. unm.
1. Mary, m. 8 Sept. 1834, George FitzGerald, son of Lord Robert Fitzgerald; she d. 25 Jan. 1866.
2. Grace, m. 1st, Lieut.-Col. Pennefather, of Newpark, co. Tipperary, and 2ndly, Major Michael Angelo Galliazzi, of the Austrian Service, and had issue.
3. Catherine, m. Edmund Staples, of Dunmore, Queen's Co.
The eldest son,
WILLIAM BARTON, of Grove, J.P. and D.L., and High Sheriff 1825, b. 21 June, 1790; m. April, 1815, Catherine, dau. of Samuel Perry, of Woodroffe, by Deborah his wife, dau. of 1st Lord Dunalley, and d. 1837, having by her (who d. April, 1872) had issue,
1. THOMAS BARKER, late of Grove.
2. SAMUEL HENRY, heir to his brother.
3. William Hugh, b. 1820; m. Mary, dau. of Capt. Blakeney, and has issue, five sons and four daus.
1. Deborah, m. John Wade, 2nd son of William Blaney Wade, of Clonabrany, co. Meath, and left issue.
2. Mary Frances, m. 4 Oct. 1845, Charles Shaw, Q.C. She d. 17 March, 1865. He d. 9 Dec. 1870, leaving issue (see BURKE's Peerage, SHAW, Bart.).
3. Catherine Grace, m. 19 June, 1852, Sir Robert Shaw, Bart., and d. 15 Dec. 1902, leaving issue (see BURKE's Peerage).
4. Anne Margaret, m. George Gough, of Rathronan, co. Tipperary, who d.s.p. 18 April, 1889.
5. Emily Martha.
The eldest son,
THOMAS BARKER BARTON, of Grove, co. Tipperary, J.P., b. 1816; d. unm. 21 Feb. 1871, and was s. by his brother,
SAMUEL HENRY, late of Grove (see above).
Arms—Arg. a rose gu. seeded or and barbed vert between three boars' heads erased ppr. Crest—A boar's head erased ppr. Motto—Fide et fortitudine.
Seat—Grove, near Fethard, co. Tipperary. Residence—15, Lansdown Place, Cheltenham.

BARTON OF THE WATERFOOT.

CHARLES ROBERT BARTON, of The Waterfoot, co. Fermanagh, J.P. and D.L. cos. Fermanagh and Donegal, High Sheriff co. Fermanagh 1863, Capt. Fermanagh Militia, b. 15 Nov. 1832; m. 1 Aug. 1872, Henrietta Martha Mervyn, dau. of Henry Mervyn Richardson, of Rossfad, co. Fermanagh, D.L. (see that family), and has issue,
1. WILLIAM HUGH, Capt. Army Service Corps (late Scottish Rifles), b. 30 May, 1874.
2. Henry Charles Johnston, b. 12 Oct. 1876; m. 30 April, 1910, Ethel Maude, youngest dau. of William Bancroft Espeut, M.L.C., of Spring Garden, Jamaica.
3. Charles Nathaniel, b. 5 Jan. 1884.
4. Bertram James Richardson, b. 23 Feb. 1891.

1. Mary Jane Florence, m. 27 Oct. 1897, Henry Burnley Rathborne, of Dunsinea, co. Dublin, and has issue.
2. Everina Margaret. 3. Caroline Angel Charlotte.
4. Henrietta Emily Violet. m. 2 Oct. 1902, Frederick Lambart Staden, eldest son of Col. Joseph Sladen, of Ripple Court, Kent (see that family), by his 2nd wife Lady Sarah Sophia, dau. of 8th Earl of Cavan, and has issue.
5. Mildred Penelope Matilda. 6. Susannah Cecil Grace.
Lineage.—LIEUT.-GEN. CHARLES BARTON, Lieut.-Col. 2nd Life Guards, 3rd son of William Barton, of Grove, co. Tipperary, by Grace his wife, dau. of Very Rev. Charles Massey, of Doonas, Dean of Limerick, b. 20 April, 1760; m. Feb. 1800, Susannah, dau. of Nathaniel Weld Johnston, of Bordeaux, by his 1st wife, Anna Eleanor Stewart, and d. 1821, leaving issue,
1. HUGH WILLIAM, his heir.
2. Nathaniel Dunbar, Lieut.-Col. Bengal Cavalry, m. 1831, Honoria, sister of Sir Henry Lawrence.
3. Thomas Charles, of Bonn, b. 1 Dec. 1805; d. unm. 3 Feb. 1856.
4. Robert, of Sydney, Australia, J.P., b. 1807; m. 1840, Emily, eld. dau. of Maj. Darval, and had issue.
5. Albert Evelyn, b. 1812; d. unm. 1874.
1. Susannah, m. Rev. John Stirling.
2. Anna Eleanor, m. Rev. F. D. Maurice, Professor of English Literature, King's College.
His eldest son,
HUGH WILLIAM BARTON, of The Waterfoot, J.P., D.L., High Sheriff co. Fermanagh 1837, Lieut.-Col. of the 2nd Life Guards, b. 13 Dec. 1800; m. 9 Feb. 1832, Mary Caroline, eldest dau. of Robert Johnston, of Kinlough House, co. Leitrim. He d. 4 Dec. 1870. She d. 11 March, 1899, leaving issue,
1. CHARLES ROBERT, now of The Waterfoot.
2. James, late Capt. R.A., b. 13 Aug 1834; m. 23 Aug. 1859, Mary Barbara, dau. of Sir David Barclay, 10th bart. of Pierston, co. Ayr, and has issue,
1. Hugh Barclay, b. 11 July, 1865; d. unm.
2. James, b. 14 April, 1867; d. unm.
3. Charles, b. 20 March, 1873.
4. Sidney, b. 26 Nov. 1876.
1. Louisa. 2. May.
3. Harriet. 4. Irene.
3. Folliott, C.E., b. 23 May, 1838; m. 19 March, 1873, Florence Maude, 6th dau. of Hugh Lyons Montgomery, of Belhavel, and d. 1883, leaving issue, Ffolliott Cyril.
4. Hugh St. George, Capt. 60th Rifles, b. 19 Nov. 1839; d. 12 June, 1875.
5. Robert, R.N., b. 3 Nov. 1841; d. 3 April, 1869.
6. Thomas Lloyd, b. 2 Dec. 1855; m. Fanny Isaacs.
7. Nathaniel Albert Delap, Maj. 88th Regt., b. 29 Nov. 1857; m. 1888, Ellen, dau. of — Jordan, U.S.A., and had issue,
Thomas Hugh, b. 1 July, 1890.
1. Florence Anna, m. Gen. Dawson, late 18th Regt.
2. Mary Everina, m. 29 Jan. 1868, James M. Sinclair, D.L. of Holly Hill, co. Donegal, and has issue.
Arms, Crest and Motto—Same as BARTON of Grove.
Seat—The Waterfoot, Pettigo, co. Fermanagh.

BARTON OF STRAFFAN HOUSE.

BERTRAM HUGH BARTON, of Straffan House, co. Kildare, J.P., D.L., High Sheriff 1908, b. 24 Sept. 1858; s. his father 11 Sept. 1904; m. 26 July, 1899, Lilian Edith Laura, only dau. of Lieut.-Col. Sir Frederick Walter Carden, Bart (see BURKE's Peerage), and has issue,
1. FREDERICK BERTRAM, b. 19 June, 1900.
2. Hugh Ronald, b. 29 June, 1902.
1. Storeen Lily, b. 21 June, 1906.
Lineage.—HUGH BARTON (4th son of William Barton, of Grove, (see that family) byGrace Massy his wife,dau. of the Dean of Limerick), who,by his own energy, industry, and activity, acquired at Bordeaux a very large fortune, which he invested in the purchase of the Straffan estate and other lands in Ireland in 1831, and also in the purchase of the Château Langoa, and a portion of the adjacent property of Leoville, both in the parish of St. Julien Medoc, near Bordeaux. During the reign of terror, 1793-4, he was imprisoned as an alien, but by the connivance of his wife, daughter of a naturalised Frenchman of Scottish origin, he effected his escape to Ireland. During his absence the business in Bordeaux was managed by Daniel Guestier, with whom he entered into partnership 1802. This partnership has continued from father to son to the present time. In 1840 he served as High Sheriff of co. Kildare. He was b. 8 Jan. 1766; m. 17 Dec. 1791, Anne, dau. of Nathaniel Weld Johnston, of Bordeaux, and d. 25 May, 1854, having by her (who d. 3 Aug. 1842) had issue,
1. Hugh, b. 7 March, 1797; d. young.
2. NATHANIEL, late of Straffan.
3. THOMAS JOHNSTON, of Glendalough (see that family).
4. Daniel, late Capt. 7th Fusiliers, b. 21 Feb. 1806; m. Margaret Simpson, and had a son, Daniel, m. 10 Nov. 1887, Victoria Alexandrina Julia, dau. of Sir Robert Peel, 3rd bart
5. Hugh, b. 21 March, 1807; d. 8 Nov. 1860.
1. Susan, b. 33 March, 1793; d. 22 Dec. 1803.
2. Anna, b. 1798; d. 1811.
3. Grace, d. an infant.
4. Isabella, b. 20 June, 1804; d. unm. 28 March, 1897.

Barton. THE LANDED GENTRY. 32

5. Susan Elizabeth, m. 9 Sept. 1828, Eyre, 3rd Lord Clarina, and d. 14 Nov. 1886, leaving issue.
6. Charlotte, b. 1812; d. an infant.

His eldest son,
NATHANIEL BARTON, of Straffan House, co. Kildare, J.P. and D.L., High Sheriff in 1850-51, b. 7 Sept. 1799; m. 12 July, 1823, Mary Susanna, dau. of Harry Harmood Scott, Consul at Bordeaux, by Anne his wife, dau. of Rev. Newton Ogle, D.D., of Kirkley, Northumberland, and d. 29 Nov. 1867, having by her (who d. 18 March, 1867) had issue,
1. HUGH LYNEDOCH, late of Straffan.
2. Harry Fitzgerald, b. 21 Aug. 1826; d. 17 May, 1848.
3. BERTRAM FRANCIS, late of Straffan.
4. Charles Thomas Hugh, b. 23 Nov. 1834; m. 21 June, 1859, Clara Sophia, youngest dau. of Frank Cutler, R.N., of Upton Lodge, Brixham, Devon, and d. 11 Sept. 1871, having had issue,
  1. Francis Savile, b. 8 April, 1861, late Lieut. Queen's Bays and Scots Guards, m. 8 Jan. 1889, Mabel Mary, youngest dau. of Capt. Sayers, 23rd Regt. Royal Welsh Fusiliers, and has issue,
    (1) Charles Thomas Hugh, b. 18 Sept. 1889.
    (2) Arthur William, b. 2 Jan. 1892.
  2. Charles Scott, b. 12 Aug. 1865; m. 26 June, 1890, Ellen A. dau. of William Johnston, of Aiguesvives, Touraine, France, and has had issue,
    (1) Robert Francis Arthur, b. 7 Feb. 1902.
    (2) Violet Clara Isabella, b. 16 July, 1891.
    (3) Alice Charlotte, b. 6 Oct. 1902.
[5. Francis Savile, b. 23 Nov. 1836; d. 3 Jan. 1860.
1. Mary Esther Isabella, d. young, 11 Jan. 1844.
2. Anna Susan Frederica.
3. Isabel Charlotte.
4. Alice Catherine Harriet, d. unm. 17 April, 1867.

The eldest son,
HUGH LYNEDOCH BARTON, of Straffan House, co. Kildare, J.P. and D.L., High Sheriff 1861; late Major Kildare Rifles, formerly Lieut. 6th Inniskillings; b. 30 Aug. 1824; m. 18 April, 1855, Hon. Anna Emily Massey, eldest dau. of Eyre, 3rd Lord Clarina, and d.s.p. 23 Feb. 1890. He was s. by his brother,
BERTRAM FRANCIS BARTON, of Straffan House, co. Kildare, High Sheriff 1903, b. 19 March, 1830; d. 11 Sept. 1904; m. 27 Sept. 1855, Fannie Annie, eldest dau. of Frank Cutler, R.N., of Upton Lodge, Brixham, Devon, and by her (who d. 29 Nov. 1907) had issue,
1. BERTRAM HUGH, now of Straffan House.
2. Harry Scott, of Hewshott House, Liphook, b. 11 Jan. 1862; m. 18 June, 1893, Augusta Mary, dau. of Leedham White.
  1. Mary Fannie, m. 25 Oct. 1883, Thomas Edward Studdy, youngest son of Henry Studdy, of Waddeton Court, Brixham, Devon, J.P. and D.L., and has issue (see that family).
2. Isabel Eleanor.

Arms and Crest—Same as BARTON of Grove. Motto—Fide et fortitudine.

Seat—Straffan House, co. Kildare. Clubs—Junior Carlton, and Kildare Street, Dublin.

BARTON OF GLENDALOUGH HOUSE.

ROBERT CHILDERS BARTON, of Glendalough House, co. Wicklow, b. 14 March, 1881.

Lineage.—THOMAS JOHNSTON BARTON, of Glendalough, co. Wicklow, J.P. and D.L., b. Sept. 1802; 2nd son of Hugh Barton, of Straffan (see that family); m. 25 March, 1830, Frances, dau. of Edward Morris, Master in Chancery, by Hon. Mary Erskine his wife, dau. of Thomas, 1st Lord Erskine, and d. 4 Dec. 1864, having by her (who d. 4 Oct. 1867) had issue,
1. THOMAS ERSKINE, of whom presently.
2. Hugh Massey, 7th Foot, b. 10 Feb. 1834; d. 1880.
3. CHARLES WILLIAM, of Glendalough.
4. Robert Johnston, b. 20 Feb. 1839, Capt. Coldstream Guards. Killed in action in Zululand, 28 March, 1879.
  1. Frances Isabella, m. 1st, 19 May, 1859, James C. Hart, of Druincrosshall, N.B., late Capt. 16th Lancers, who d. 1876. She m. 2ndly, 1880, Fletcher Menzies, of Menzies.
  2. Georgiana Susanna Arabel, m. 1856, George Booth, and d. 1868, leaving issue.
  3. Anna Mary Henrietta, m. R. C. Childers (who d. 1876), eldest son of the Rev. Charles Childers, H.M. Chaplain at Nice; and d. 1884, leaving issue.
  4. Beatrice Louisa, m. 3 Dec. 1864, Hugh Francis Massy, Capt. 19th Regt., and d. 23 Jan. 1893, leaving issue (see Massy of Grantstown). He d. Feb. 1900.

His eldest son,
THOMAS ERSKINE BARTON, of Glendalough, b. 1830; d. unm. 1874, when he was s. by his brother,
CHARLES WILLIAM BARTON, of Glendalough House, J.P., High Sheriff 1882, b. 13 July, 1836; m. 26 Oct. 1876, Agnes, 4th dau. of the Rev. Charles Childers, H.M. Chaplain at Nice, and Canon of Gibraltar, and d. 3 Oct. 1890, leaving issue,
1. ROBERT CHILDERS, now of Glendalough House.
2. Charles Erskine, b. 7 Dec. 1882.
3. Thomas Eyre, b. 15 Aug. 1884.
  1. Frances, b. 21 Dec. 1877.
  2. Dulcibella, b. 25 Dec. 1879.

Arms, Crest and Motto—As BARTON of Grove.

Seat—Glendalough House, Annamoe, co. Wicklow.

BATEMAN, OF BEDFORD HOUSE.

FREDERICK REGINALD BATEMAN, of Bedford House, co. Kerry, J.P., b. 1848, High Sheriff 1897, s. to the estates at the decease of his uncle John Bateman.

Lineage.—MAJ. ROWLAND BATEMAN, son of Henry Bateman, by Elizabeth, dau. of John Wasbye, got a grant of the lands of Killeen, co Kerry, and served as High Sheriff in 1669. He m. Charity Wilson, and had issue two sons and two daus., viz.,
1. Francis, d.s.p. 1707.
2. JOHN, who s. to Killeen.
1. Belinda, m. Richard Yielding, of Tralee.
2. Margaret, m. — Morris.

His successor,
JOHN BATEMAN, of Killeen, otherwise Oak Park, m. 1st, Frances, dau. of William Trenchard, of Mt. Trenchard, co.
who d.s.p.; and 2ndly, Anne, dau. of Col. the Right Hon. George Evans, of Carass, co. Limerick, and d. 1719, leaving issue,
1. ROWLAND, of whom hereafter.
2. George, of Dromultin, co. Kerry, b. 1711; m. Sarah, dau. of Anthony Stoughton, of Rattoo, co. Kerry, by whom he had issue,
  1. John, of Dromultin, m. 1764, Elizabeth, dau. of William Meredith, of Annaghmore, co. Kerry, and had issue,
    (1) John, d.s.p.
    (1) Jane, m. 1st, 1779, Conway Blennerhassett; and 2ndly, Pierse Crosbie.
  2. George, of Hollypark, m. 1764, Elizabeth, dau. of William Meredith, of Dicksgrove, co. Kerry, and left a son, William, m. 1795, Catherine, dau. of George Lloyd.
    1. Dorothy, m. — Lloyd, of Cork.
    2. Frances, m. 1778, Mountiford Longfield, of Castle Mary, co. Cork, M.P.
  3. Thomas, of Mount Catherine, co. Limerick, m. 1st, 1735, Jane Delahoyde, of Cork; he m. 2ndly, 22 Jan. 1740, Alice, 2nd dau. of Thomas Sadleir, of Sopwell Hall, co. Tipperary, and d. 1756, having by her had a son,
    Francis Sadleir, d.s.p.
  4. John, of Alta Villa, co. Limerick, High Sheriff 1749; m. 1st, 1745, Elizabeth, elder dau. of Thomas Sadleir, of Sopwell Hall, co. Tipperary, by whom (who d. 1748) he had a dau.,
    1. Catherine.
  He m. 2ndly, 1756, Grace, dau. of Henry Brooke, of Colebrooke, co. Fermanagh, M.P., and d. 1792, having had further issue, viz.,
    1. John, of Altavilla, Barrister-at-Law, m. 1782, Mary, dau. and heiress of Thomas Bourke, of Anglingham, co. Galway, and from this marriage descended the BATEMANS, of Rosetown, co. Kildare.
    2. Henry (Rev.), d. 1822.
    3. George Brooke, Barrister-at-Law, d. unm. 1809.
    2. Letitia, m. 1778, Gerald Blennerhassett, of Riddlestown, co. Limerick.
    3. Frances, m. Rev. Thomas Lloyd.
  1. Mary. m. Francis Morris.
  2. Frances, m. Thomas Lloyd, of Fanstown, co. Limerick.

The eldest son,
ROWLAND BATEMAN, of Oak Park, b. 1705; m. 1727, Elizabeth, dau. of Nicholas Colthurst, of Ballyhaly, co. Cork, and d. 1754, having had issue,
1. Rowland, of Oak Park, J.P., High Sheriff 1758, M.P. for Kerry and for Tralee; m. 1758, Letitia, dau. and co-heir of Sir Thomas Denny, Knt., by whom he had issue,
  1. Rowland, of Oak Park, m. 1790, Arabella, dau. of Sir Barry Denny, Bart., and had issue,
    (1) John, of Oak Park, J.P., High Sheriff 1820, M.P. Tralee 1837, b. 1792; m. 1824, Frances, dau. of Nathaniel Bland, of Randall's Park, Surrey, and d. 1865, leaving a son, Roland, who d.s.p.
    (2) William, d. unm. (3) Thomas, d. under age.
    (1) Jane, d. young.
    (2) Letitia, m. 1831, Emanuel Hutchinson Orpen, of Mount Tallant, co. Kerry.
  2. Thomas, d. unm. 1783.
  1. Agnes, m. 1785, Richard Chute, of Chute Hall, co. Kerry.
  2. Elizabeth, m. 1785, Col. James Crosbie, M.P., of Ballybeige, co. Kerry.
2. COLTHURST, of whom presently.
3. John, J.P. co. Kerry, m. 1770, Olivia, Countess of Rosse, but d.s.p.
1. Elizabeth, m. 1748, Anthony Stoughton, of Rattoo, co. Kerry.
2. Anne, m. Francis Crosbie, of Rusheen, co. Kerry.
3. Penelope, m. 1756, Richard Smyth, of Ballinatray, co. Waterford.
4. Mary, m. Thomas FitzGerald, Knight of Glin.
5. Sarah, m. May, 1771, Rev. John Barry, D.D., Dean of Elphin.
6. Frances, m. Pierce Crosbie, of Ballyheigne, co. Kerry.
7. Jane, m. 1770, Richard Dunscombe.

The 2nd son,
COLTHURST BATEMAN, of Bedford House, co. Kerry, J.P., m. 1779, dau. of Robert Dobson, of Anngrove, co. Cork, and d. 1821, leaving issue,
1. COLTHURST, of whom hereafter.
2. Rowland (Rev.), m. Elizabeth, dau. of Maurice FitzMaurice, and widow of James Edington.
3. John, d. unm. 1819.
1. Jane, m. Capt. Robert Dobson, 5th Foot.
2. Anne, m. 1807 Patrick Maitland (grandfather of the Earl of Lauderdale).

3. Elizabeth.
4. Dorothea, *m.* 1st, George Augustus Sim...n'; and 2ndly, Admiral John Maitland.

The eldest son,
COLTHURST BATEMAN, of Bedford House, co. Kerry, and of Bartholey, Monmouth, J.P., High Sheriff of Monmouth 1839, *b.* 1780; *m.* 1809, Jane Sarah, dau. and heiress of John Kemeys Gardner-Kemeys, of Bartholey, co. Monmouth, and *d.* 1859, leaving issue,
1. JOHN, his heir.
2. George Colthurst, *b.* 1815; *d.* 1852 *unm.*
3. Rowland, R.N., *b.* 1816; *d. unm.* 1839.
4. Robert, J.P. Monmouth, *m.* and had issue,
   1. FREDERICK REGINALD, now of Bedford House.
   2. Robert William, *b.* 1850.   3. John Kemeys, *b.* 1855.
      1. Frances.   2. Mary.
5. Reginald, R.N., *b.* 1820   6. Thomas, *b.* 1823.
7. Frederick, *b.* 1825; *d. unm.* 1847.
1. Jane, *m.* 1836, John Gwalter Palairet.   2. Sarah.

The eldest son,
JOHN BATEMAN, of Bartholey and Bedford House, *b.* 1814, *d. unm.*, when the Irish estates devolved on his nephew, FREDERICK REGINALD BATEMAN aforesaid.

Seat—Bedford House, Listowel.   *Residence*—Rosbeigh, Glenbeigh, co. Kerry.

DE YARBURGH-BATESON.

See BURKE'S PEERAGE, **DERAMORE, B.**

BATT OF RATHMULLAN.

CHARLES LYONS BATT (jointly with his sisters, Alice and Mabel, of Rathmullan House, co. Donegal), *b.* 24 Oct. 1860.

Lineage.—This family, stated to have been originally from Cornwall, was founded in Ireland by SAMUEL BATT, of Osier Hill and New Ross, merchant, who acquired considerable property in the co. Wexford about 1650. He *d.* intestate, leaving by Alice his wife (who took out administration to him 6 June, 1702) a son,
SAMUEL BATT, of New Ross and Osier Hill, Merchant, whose will, dated 28 March, 1705, was proved in Jan. 1716. He left by Deborah, his 2nd wife, five sons,
1. THOMAS, of whom hereafter.
2. Narcissus (Rev.), *d.s.p.*; will proved 3 March, 1767.
3. Samuel, of Rathneddin, *d.s.p.*; will dated 13 June, 1772.
4. Joseph, of Grange; will proved 8 May, 1780, left issue.
5. Benjamin, of New Ross; will proved 3 June, 1780, left issue.

The eldest son,
THOMAS BATT, of Osier Hill, *m.* 1713, Jane, dau. of Thomas Devereux, and was *s.* by his eldest son,
SAMUEL BATT, father of Major Thomas Batt, who was killed in the American War, when the property devolved on his youngest brother,
ROBERT BATT, of Osier Hill, co. Wexford, Capt. 18th Regt., who *m.* 1765, Hannah, dau. of Samuel Hyde, of Belfast, and *d.* 1783, having had issue five sons,
1. NARCISSUS, of Purdysburn, co. Down, and Osier Hill, co. Wexford, High Sheriff 1835, *m.* 1793, Margaret, dau. of Thomas Greg, and *d.* 1840, having by her (who *d.* 1843) had issue,
   1. Robert, of Purdysburn and Osier Hill, J.P. and D.L., High Sheriff 1846, *b.* 1795; *m.* 1841, Charlotte, dau. of Samuel Wood, of Upton, Cheshire, and *d.* 24 July, 1864, having by her had, with four daus., a son,
      ROBERT NARCISSUS, of Purdysburn, co. Down, J.P. and D.L., High Sheriff 1870, *b.* 10 Nov. 1844; *m.* 6 March, 1866, Marion Emily, eldest dau. of Sir Edward Samuel Walker, of Berry Hill, Mansfield, Notts., and *d.* 20 Nov. 1891, having by her (who *d.* 1892) had issue,
         1. EVELEEN MAY, *b.* 1867; *m.* 1892, Capt. Charles Arthur Staniland, late Royal Scots Greys.
         2. NELLA LILIAN, *m.* 18 Dec. 1894, Frederick Knight Essell, of the Buffs.
   2. Thomas, of Strandmills, *b.* 1805; *d.s.p.* 1861.
      1. Elizabeth.   3. Mary, *m.* Thomas Greg.
      2. William.   3. Samuel.
   4. Robert.   5. THOMAS, of whom presently.

The youngest son,
THOMAS BATT, of Rathmullan, co. Donegal, *m.* 1st, Elizabeth, dau. of Robert Waddell, of Island Derry, co. Down, and by her had issue,
Thomas, of whom presently,
Elizabeth, *m.* Cæsar George Otway.
He *m.* 2ndly, Sarah, dau. of Samuel Lyle, of The Oaks, but she *d.s.p.* He *d.* 1857, and was *s.* by his only son,
THOMAS BATT, of Rathmullan, J.P. and D.L., High Sheriff 1844, M.A. Trin. Coll. Camb., *b.* 1816; *m.* 6 July, 1852, Charlotte,

dau. of Ven. Edmond Hesketh Dalrymple Knox, late Archdeacon of Killaloe (*see* BURKE'S *Peerage,* RANFURLY, E.), and *d.* 1897 leaving issue,
1. THOMAS EDMOND, late of Rathmullan.
2. Alfred Acheson, *b.* 15 May, 1856.
3. Edmond Hesketh, *b.* 6 Dec. 1857; *d.* 1882.
4. Arthur Robert, *b.* 27 April, 1859; *d.* 1891.
5. CHARLES LYONS, now jointly of Rathmullan.
6. Gerard Otway, *b.* 28 Feb. 1862.
7. Robert Devereux, *b.* 6 Nov. 1863.
8. Octavius, *b.* 16 April, 1865.
9. Frederick Shelley, *b.* 1869, *d.* 1876.
1. Agnes Charlotte, *m.* 23 Aug. 1877, Archibald H. Duthie (who *d.s.p.* 1883).
2. ALICE ELIZABETH, now jointly of Rathmullan.
3. MABEL MACKENZIE, now jointly of Rathmullan.

COL. THOMAS EDMOND BATT, of Rathmullan House, co. Donegal, J.P., late Lieut.-Col. Commanding Donegal Artillery, *b.* 14 Oct. 1854; *d.* 27 Dec. 1908, when he was *s.* jointly by his brother and sisters as above mentioned,

Arms—Arg. on a cross between four bats sa. three escallops in pale or. Crest—A crescent arg. charged with an escallop gu. Motto—Virtute et valore.

Seat—Rathmullan House, co. Donegal.

BATTERSBY OF LOUGHBAWN.

JOHN RADCLIFF BATTERSBY, of Loughbawn, co. Westmeath, J.P. for that co. and for Meath, of Lincoln's Inn, Barrister-at-Law, *b.* 30 Sept. 1839; *m.* 9 Aug. 1873, Augusta Helen, dau. of John Rynd, of Reynella, co. Westmeath, and has issue,
1. GEORGE, *b.* 11 Jan. 1877.
2. Augustus Wolfe (Rev.), *b.* 10 Feb. 1885.
3. John Radcliff, *b.* 26 Jan. 1886.
1. Edith Frances, *m.* 5 May, 1909, George Maxwell, of Corduff, co. Dublin (*see that family*).
2. Millie, *m.* 22 July, 1909, George Astley Rotheram (*see* ROTHERAM *of Crossdrum*).
3. Dorothy.   4. Rosalie.
5. Mona Phillippa.

Lineage.—WILLIAM BATTERSBY, of Smithstown, co. Meath, *m.* Mary, dau. of Ambrose Sherman, and had issue,
1. William, of Smithstown, *m.* Miss Grant, and *d.s.p.*
2. Robert, of Bobsville.
3. JOHN, of whom presently.

The 3rd son,
JOHN BATTERSBY, of Lakefield, co. Meath, J.P., *b.* 1722; *m.* 1st, Elizabeth Shields, of Monaghan, and by her had an only child,
1. WILLIAM, of Freffans, co. Meath, *b.* 16 Nov. 1764; *m.* Frances, dau. of Nathaniel Preston, of Swainstown (*see that family*), and *d.* 1848, having had issue,
   1. William, *d.s.p.*
   2. Nathaniel, *d.s.p.*
   3. John, *d.s.p.*
   4. Francis William, *d. unm.*
   5. Arthur, *m.* Eliza, dau. of Major Dillon, and *d.* leaving issue, a son and a dau.,
      William Arthur.
      Almeria Grace, *d. unm.*
   1. Georgina.
   2. Anne, *m.* Lambert Disney, and had issue.
   3. Frances Isabella, *m.* Chas. John Battersby, of Cromlyn, and has issue (*see below*).
John Battersby *m.* 2ndly, 7 Sept. 1765, Sarah, dau. of Rev. Henry Leslie, of Nutfield, co. Fermanagh, and by her had issue,
2. Leslie (Rev.), of Skreene, co. Sligo, *b.* 20 July, 1766; *m.* 5 July, 1796, Anna Maria, dau. of Patrick Palmer, Barrister-at-Law, F.T.C.D., and had issue,
   1. John Palmer, Capt. R.N., settled at Ancaster, Upper Canada; *m.* Maria Jones, and *d.* 1888, having had issue,
      (1) Leslie Charles, *b.* 27 April, 1836; *m.* Helen Maria Harding.
      (2) John Palmer, *b.* 30 Dec. 1837.
      (3) Charles, *b.* 2 Jan. 1840; *m.* Maria Jane Walker, had issue,
         1. John Palmer, *b.* 12 Nov. 1874; *d.* 11 Aug. 1896.
         2. Henry Chas. Pinckney, *b.* 4 July, 1876.
         3. Edwin Lee Campbell, *b.* 18 Aug. 1880; *m.* Nov. 1909.
         E. E. Trowbridge, and has issue, a dau.,
            Eleanor Beatrice, *b.* 26 Aug. 1910
         1. Edith Beatrice, *b.* 27 Aug. 1878; *d.* 31 Oct. 1900.

Battley. THE LANDED GENTRY. 34

(4) Arthur, *d. young*.
(5) Edwin, *b.* 1845; *d. young*.
(1) Eleanor Palmer, *b.* 12 Aug. 1842, *unm.*
(2) Maria, *b.* 1846; *d. young*.
2. Leslie Patrick, settled in Canada, Lieut.R.N.; *m.* Katherine Jones, and had issue,
  (1) Leslie Charles, *b.* March, 1841; *m.* 5 June, 1873, Annie Caroline, dau. of J. C. Benett, of Dorset, England; *d.* 21 Sept. 1888, had issue,
    1. Leslie Charles, *b.* 1 March, 1874.
    2. Jno. Bennett, *b.* 23 Oct. 1875.
    3. Arthur Henry Jones, *b.* 23 Feb. 1878.
    4. William Falconer, *b.* 16 Dec. 1879.
    5. George Philip, *b.* 4 Dec. 1884.
    1. Madeline Toonce, *b.* 18 March, 1882; *d.* 2 Jan. 1883.
  (1) Eleanor Toonic, *m.* 21 June, 1860, Craven Chadwick; *d.* 9 Jan. 1868, and had issue (*see* CHADWICK, *of Ballinrad*).
  (2) Anna Maria, *d. young*.
3. Joseph, *d.s.p.*
4. Edwin, of Dublin, *m.* Eleanor Jones, and had eleven children.
5. Arthur, *m.* S. E. Maskelyne.
6. George, of Dublin, *d.* 30 March, 1901.
7. William, *d. young*.   8. Henry, *d.s.p.*
9. William, settled at Hamilton, Upper Canada; *m.* Susanna Ryall, and *d.s.p.*
1. Catherine, *m.* — Harvey, *d.s.p.*
2. Sarah, *d. unm.*
3. Eleanor, *m.* — Griffith, and had issue, one dau.
4. Anna Maria, *d. unm.*
5. Lydia, *m.* — Bell, *d.s.p.*
6. Mary, *d. unm.*
3. THOMAS, of whom hereafter.
4. Francis, Col. 8th Foot, C.B., of Listoke House, Drogheda, *b.* 19 Sept. 1795; *m.* Eliza, 2nd dau. of George Rotherham, of Crossdrum, co. Meath, and had issue,
John Prevost, Major-Gen. late 60th Royal Rifles, formerly Assistant Director of Military Education (*Lyncroft, Portmore Park, Weybridge*), *b.* 16 Oct. 1826; *m.* 7 Sept. 1857, Louisa Wilhelmina, 2nd dau. of Sir William Dillon, 4th bart. (*see* BURKE's *Peerage and Baronetage*), and has issue,
  (1) Henry Francis, *b.* 10 Feb. 1862; *m.* 21 April, 1909, Frances Muriel (Pearl), elder dau. of Henry C. Saunders, of Weybridge.
  (2) Herbert Dillon, *b.* 14 Jan. 1872; *d.s.p.*
  (1) Helen Elizabeth.
  (2) Louisa Georgina, *m.* Rev. Wellesley Burnaby, and had issue.
  (3) Ethel, *d. unm.*
Frances, *m.* 1st, June, 1848, Mathew Coates, of Newton Prospect, co. Meath; and 2ndly, Dr. Wade, M.D., and had issue.
5. John, of Lakefield, *b.* 28 June, 1781, J.P. co. Meath; *m.* Frances, dau. of Robert Wade, of Clonabrany, co. Meath; and *d.* 1839, leaving issue,
1. John (Rev.), of Drumelton, co. Westmeath, *m.* Miss Maunsell, and *d.s.p.*
2. Robert, of Lakefield, *d.s.p.* 1898.
3. Thomas, *d.s.p.*
1. Marianne, *m.* — Daly.
6. Alexander, *b.* 10 Aug. 1783; *m.* 10 July, 1807, Eliza, dau. of James Cusac, of Lara, co. Kildare; and had a son,
John, of Miltown, co. Westmeath.
7. Henry Robert, Post-Capt. R.N., *m.* 10 May, 1810, the dau. of William Chapman, and niece of Sir Thomas Chapman, Bart., of Killua Castle, co. Westmeath, and *d.s.p.*
8. George, *b.* 20 April, 1788, Capt. 1st Dragoon Guards, fell returning from the last charge of the cavalry at Waterloo. Capt. Battersby *d. unm.*
1. Catherine, *m.* — Higinbotham, and had issue.
2. Penelope, *d. unm.*
John Battersby *d.* 1803. The 3rd son,
THOMAS BATTERSBY, *b.* 23 Oct. 1767; *m.* 16 Oct. 1799, Margaret Catharine, eldest dau. of George Rotherham, of Crossdrum, co. Meath, and *d.* 20 Feb. 1839, having by her (who *d.* 17 Dec. 1862) had issue,
1. GEORGE, his heir.
2. Thomas, of Newcastle House, Oldcastle, co. Meath, J.P. cos. Meath, Westmeath, and Cavan, *b.* 16 Oct. 1803; *m.* 17 May, 1837, Henrietta Mary Anne, dau. of John Rotton, of Bath, and granddau. of the late Right Hon. John Radcliff, P.C., LL.D., and *d.* Oct. 1887, having by her (who *d.* 1894) had issue,
  1. Edward, of Larkfield, co. Westmeath, J.P., late Capt. 9th Batt. Rifle Brigade, formerly Midshipman R.N. (17, *Herbert Place, Dublin*), *b.* 12 March, 1849; *m.* 3 Aug. 1899, Frances Anna (*d.* 20 Sept. 1909), only surviving dau. of David Ogden, of 17, Herbert Place, Dublin, and of Annesboro, co. Wexford, and *d.s.p.* 27 Oct. 1910.
  2. Thomas, of Newcastle House, co. Meath, J.P., *d. unm.* 25 Dec. 1885.
  3. Henry, *m.* 1st, Miss Kitson, and 2ndly, Miss Featherstonhaugh, and had a dau., Frances.
  4. John Albert, of Newcastle House, co. Meath, J.P., *m.* his cousin Feb.1890, Alice Isabella (*see below*), dau. of Charles J. Battersby, J.P., of Cromlyn, co. Westmeath, and has issue,
    (1) Thomas Charles, *d.* an infant.
    (1) Violet Frances.
    (2) Alice Christiana.
  5. Charles, *d. young*.
  1. Christiana Bettana.
  2. Henrietta Isabella, *m.* Robert Macready, and has issue.
3. Edward, Lieut. R.N., *b.* 3 May, 1805; *d. unm.* 4 Oct. 1839.

4. Henry, *b.* 1808; *m.* 1st, 13 Feb. 1846, Frances, dau. of T. Rutherford, of St. Doolagh's, co. Dublin (who *d.s.p.* 1854); and 2ndly, 1857, Annie, dau. of Lieut.-Col. Kelly; and *d.s.p.* 1868. His widow *d.* 18 Dec. 1910.
5. Francis, M.D., *b.* 10 Nov. 1812; *m.* 1st, 11 March, 1852, Elizabeth, dau. of Rev. Robert Stephenson Crooke, and by her (who *d.* 25 April, 1855) had an only child,
Thomas Stephenson Francis, K.C., *b.* 17 April, 1855; *m.* 25 July, 1883, Jeanie, dau. of Samuel Gerrard, and has issue,
  (1) Francis John Gerrard. *b.* 1894.
  (1) Elizabeth, *b.* 1884; *m.* 26 Sept. 1907, Timothy W. Bridge, I.C.S.
  (2) Violet Norah Jeanie, *b.* 1890.
  (3) Beryl Alice, *b.* 1895.
He *m.* 2ndly, June, 1862, Charlotte, dau. of John Brien, of Castletown, co. Fermanagh. He *d.* 1891. She *d.s.p.* May, 1879.
8. Frederick William, *b.* 15 May, 1819; *d.s.p.* 1847.
7. Charles John, of Cromlyn, Rathowen, co. Westmeath, *b.* 3 Feb. 1821; *m.* 1854, Frances Isabella, dau. of William Battersby, of Freffans (*see above*), and *d.* 22 May, 1897, having had issue,
  1. Thomas Preston, of Cromlyn, co. Westmeath, Brigadier-Gen., Inspector of Army Ordnance Services, *b.* 10 Aug. 1856; *m.* 9 Oct. 1884, Agnes Janet, dau. of John Evens, of The Haven, St. Stephen's, Canterbury, and has issue,
Charles Fremoult Preston, Lieut. R.F.A., *b.* 11 July, 1887.
    1. Frances Catherine, *m.* 1883, E. Hopkins, Ceylon C.S., and *d.* Oct. 1887, leaving issue.
    2. Alice Isabella, *m.* Feb. 1890, her cousin John Albert Battersby, of Newcastle House, co. Meath, and has issue (*see above*).
    3. Lucy Elizabeth.   4. Evangeline Henrietta.
    5. Caroline Maude, *m.* 30 Aug. 1910, Capt. W. Brown, A.S.C.
3. William Alexander (Rev.), *b.* 4 June, 1825; *d.s.p.*
1. Catherine, *m.* 16 Nov. 1846, William Smith Harman, of Crossdrum, and *d.* 1866, leaving issue.
2. Sarah, *m.* 29 Jan. 1841, Rev. Hugh Henry O'Neill, of Monter-Connaught, co. Cavan, and *d.* 1872, leaving issue.
3. Elizabeth Jane, *d. unm.*
4. Isabella, *d. unm.* 16 April, 1900.
5. Barbara, *m.* 1851, Thomas White, J.P., of Peppard's Castle, co. Wexford, and had issue.
The eldest son,
GEORGE BATTERSBY of Loughbawn, Q.C., LL.D., J.P., Judge of the Provincial Court of Dublin, *b.* 8 Sept. 1802; *m.* 10 Dec. 1830, Charlotte Sarah, dau. of the late Right Hon. John Radcliff, P.C. LL.D., Judge of the Prerogative Court in Ireland, of Mespil House, co. Dublin. by whom (who *d.* 17 Aug. 1876) he left at his death, 9 June, 1880,
1. Thomas George, LL.D., Barrister-at-Law, *b.* 9 Oct. 1832; *m.* 8 Dec. 1864, Georgina Maria Bessy, dau. of the late Col. William Middleton, 42nd Highlanders; and *d.* 11 Sept. 1871, leaving two dans.,
  1. Charlotte Middleton, *m.* 1889. Major A. D. Thorne, King's Own Royal Lancaster Regt., and *d.* 2 Nov. 1904, leaving issue.
  2. Ethel Middleton, *m.* Robert Cumming, Indian Army.
Mrs. Thomas George Battersby assumed by Royal Licence, 1875, the additional surname and arms of WYBRANTS, and *m.* 2ndly, Capt. Temple Leighton Phipson, who also assumed by Royal Licence, 1876, the additional surname of WYBRANTS, and *d.* 1883.   2. JOHN RADCLIFF, now of Loughbawn.
1. Betanna Catherine, *m.* 10 Jan. 1852, John Colley Pounden, of Ballywalter, J.P. co. Wexford, and has issue.

Arms—Or a saltire paly of twelve erm. and gu., a crescent in chief sa. **Crest**—A ram pass. erm. armed and unguled or. **Motto**—Ante honorem est humilitas.

Seat—Loughbawn, Collinstown, co. Westmeath.

BATTLEY OF BELVEDERE HALL.

LIEUT.-COL. D'OYLY CADE BATTLEY, of Belvedere Hall, co. Wicklow, Lieut.-Col. 3rd Batt. The Duke of Cambridge's Own (Middlesex) Regt., J.P. cos. Cork, Wicklow, and Dublin, High Sheriff co. Wicklow 1889, co. Dublin, 1911, D.L. co. Wicklow, has Coronation Medal, *b.* 1841; *m.* 1868, Annie Cecilia, dau. of William Henry Jackson, of Inane, co. Tipperary, by Cecilia his wife, dau. of John Westropp, of Attyflin (*see* WESTROPP *of Attyflin*), J.P. co. Limerick, and has had issue.

1. WILLIAM D'OYLY, Lieut.-Col. General Reserve of Officers, *b.* 1870.
2. Rochfort Cade, *b.* 23 March, 1873.
3. Louisa Cecilia, *m.* 12 Aug. 1903, Charles Gavin Pilkington Wilson, eldest son of the late John Wilson (13th Hussars), of Rooske, co. Meath, and has issue.
2. Mabel Margaretta Annie, *d.* 28 Oct. 1885.
3. Eveleen Charlotte Maud.

Lineage.—WILLIAM BATTLEY, whose ancestors were settled at Bury St. Edmunds, co. Suffolk, as appears from the will of his grandson, resident in co. Clare, *temp.* JAMES I; he had issue,
1. NICHOLAS, of whom hereafter.
2. William, settled in co. Cork, and had a son, Edmund, attainted by JAMES II 1689.
1. Sarah, *m.* Christopher Sexton, of co. Limerick.
The eldest son,

NICHOLAS BATTLEY, was *b*. in co. Clare, 1622, and entered Trin. Coll. Dublin, 20 May, 1638. By Anne his wife he had issue,
1. JOHN (Ven.), D.D., Fellow Trinity Coll. Cambridge, *b*. at Bury St. Edmunds, 1647, appointed Rector of Adesham, co. Kent, 1684, and Archdeacon of Canterbury 1688 ; *m*. Mary, dau. of Sir Henry Oxenden, 1st bart. of Dene ; *d.s.p.* 10 Oct. 1708, and was bur. at Canterbury Cathedral. His widow *d*. 25 Dec. 1741, aged 85.
2. Nicholas (Rev.), B.A. Trin. Coll. Cambridge 1668, M.A. 1672, Rector of Ivechurch, and Vicar of Bekesborne, co. Kent, 1685 ; *d*. 10 May, 1704, leaving by Anne his wife,
  1. Charles, *d.s.p.* June, 1714.
  2. JOHN (Rev.), entered Trinity Coll. Cambridge 1706, Rector of Wordwell, co. Suffolk, 1736, devisee of his uncle Samuel Battley ; *m*. 1714, Anne Sydney, dau. of his uncle Samuel's wife by her 1st husband, and had (with an elder son, John, who *d.s.p.*),
    (1) CHARLES (Rev.), *b*. 1709, Rector of Witherden, co. Suffolk, inherited the Bury St. Edmund's estates ; *d*. 8 March, 1731, leaving one son,
    WALDEGRAVE (Rev.), *b*. 1748, Curate of Shotteley, co. Suffolk. *d*. March, 1814.
  3. Oliver (Rev.), *b*. 1697, B.D. Christ Church Coll. Cambridge 1734, Rector of Iron Acton, co. Gloucester, 1736 ; *d*. 1763.
  4. Anne, living *unm*. 1714.
3. Samuel, obtained grants of lands in co. Cavan 1662, and co. Fermanagh 1667 ; also was possessed of lands in cos. Waterford and Wexford, all of which he eventually sold, and purchased estates in Suffolk ; *m*. Anne, widow of — Sydney, and *d.s.p.* 1714, having devised by his will, dated 6 April, 1712, a yearly payment to the sextons of St. Mary's Church, Bury St. Edmunds, for the keeping in repair the tomb of his ancestors.
4. THOMAS, of whom hereafter.
5. Charles, of Westminster, admitted to the Middle Temple 8 Dec. 1686, Receiver and Collector of the Rents of Westminster Abbey, Secretary in the Remembrancer's Office in the Exchequer, *m*. (licence 23 Aug. 1692) Elizabeth, dau. of John Needham, of Westminster ; and *d*. 1722, having had three sons, who *d*. young, and several daus. all baptized at Westminster ; of the latter Elizabeth, bapt. 2 Dec. 1713, *m*. James Brooker, of St. Bride's, London ; and Jane, bapt. 16 March, 1707, *m*. James Merest, Assistant Clerk of the House of Lords.
  1. Anne, living *unm*. 1712.
  2. Beata, *m*. — Morden.
Nicholas Battley *d*. at Bury St. Edmunds. His 4th son,
THOMAS BATTLEY, baptized at St. Mary's, Bury St. Edmunds, 16 May, 1651, was, with his wife, a legatee of his brother, Samuel Battley. He had two sons and one dau.,
  1. John, *b*. 1696, appointed Receiver, Solicitor, and Steward of the Courts of the Dean and Chapter of Westminster by patent dated 27 April, 1723 ; *d*. 10 June, 1729, leaving his wife Elizabeth his universal legatee.
  2. WILLIAM, of whom hereafter.
  1. Mary, devisee of her uncle Samuel.
The 2nd son,
WILLIAM BATTLEY, was admitted an Honorary Member of the King's Inns, Dublin. He *m*. the dau. of Thomas Cade, of Willbrook, Rathfarnham, co. Dublin, and heiress of her brother, Thomas Cade, and by her had issue,
  1. JOHN, of whom hereafter.
  2. William, whose will was proved in Dublin 2 Jan. 1773 ; *m*. and had issue.
  3. Edmund.
William Battley *d*. Jan. 1736. His eldest son,
JOHN BATTLEY, of Willbrook, was admitted a member of the King's Inns 1758, *s*. his maternal uncle 1783, *m*. Frances, sister of John Butler, and had issue,
  1. THOMAS CADE, his heir.
  2. William, Lieut.-Col. 60th Rifles, accidentally killed at Gibraltar.
  1. Elizabeth.
Mr. Battley *d*. 1808, and was *s*. by his eldest son,
THOMAS CADE BATTLEY, of Willbrook, *b*. 1771, entered Trin. Coll. Dublin 20 Nov. 1788, aged 17 ; B.A. 1794, called to the Bar Trinity Term 1794 ; *m*. Belinda, dau. of Rev. Richard Chappell Grange, of Sallymount, co. Wicklow, by Mary his wife, dau. and (with her sister Diana, *m*. 1780, Sir John Hadley D'Oyly, 6th bart. of Shottisham, co-heir of William Rochfort, of Clontarf (brother of Robert, 1st Earl of Belvedere), by Henrietta his wife, dau. of Col. John Ramsay and Mary, Lady Osborne his wife, widow of Sir Nicholas Osborne, 5th bart., of Ballintaylor, and dau. of Right Rev. Thomas Smyth, D.D., Bishop of Limerick, and *d*. 20 Sept. 1851, having by her (who *d*. 9 Nov. 1863, aged 95) had issue,
  1. Richard, Capt. 22nd Regt., *d*. *unm*.
  2. John Cade, entered T.C.D. 1817, aged 17, Capt. 30th Regt. ; *d. unm*. in India.
  3. D'OYLY WILLIAM, of whom hereafter.
  4. Thomas, Registrar of the Court of Bankruptcy, *m*. Marcella, dau. of John Connolly, of Newhaggard, co. Meath, and *d.s.p.* 1881.
  5. Charles Bushe (Rev.), *d*. 1881.
  6. Rochfort, *m*. Rose, dau. of — Field, and *d*. 1866, leaving a son, Rochfort Cade Lestock, Major Essex Regt., *b*. 6 Oct. 1864.
  1. Elizabeth, *m*. Major Larkins, R.H.A. ; *d*. in India.
  2. Harriet, *m*. William C. Browne, of Rochfort Lodge, Richmond, Surrey, and Cromwell Crescent, London ; *d*. 1882.
  3. Anna Maria, *m*. Alexander Edie, of Thorn Hill, co. Tyrone.
His eldest surviving son,
D'OYLY WILLIAM BATTLEY, of Belvedere Hall, Major (retired) 77th Regt., derived descent through his maternal grandmother, Mary Rochfort, from the Royal House of Plantagenet, *b*. Jan. 1808 ; *m*. 1839, Margaret, dau. of William Edie, of Thornhill, J.P. co. Tyrone, by Dorothy his wife, dau. of Nesbitt Downing, of Tubberdaly, J.P. King's Co., and *d*. 2 Nov. 1887, having by her (who *d*. 13 Jan. 1871) had issue,
1. D'OYLY CADE, now of Belvedere Hall.
2. Rochfort, *b*. 1844 ; *m*. 1871, Annie, dau. of Major John Graham Sadler, J.P., of Hymenstown, co. Tipperary, and *d*. 29 April, 1885, leaving issue, a son, John, and two daus.

Seat—Belvedere Hall, Bray, co. Wicklow. *Clubs*—United Service and Constitutional, S.W.

BAYLY OF DEBSBOROUGH.

CAPT. JOHN BAYLY, of Debsborough, co. Tipperary, J.P., High Sheriff 1894, late Capt. Suffolk Regt., educated at Eton, *b*. 10 July, 1858,

Lineage.—JOHN BAYLY, of Debsborough, co. Tipperary, to whom the farm grants were made in 1702, by the Duke of Ormonde, *m*. 1690, Elizabeth, dau. of Henry Prittie, of Kilboy, co. Tipperary, and *d*. 1709, having had issue, JOHN, his heir, Henry and Elizabeth. His widow *m*. 2ndly, Major John Foley. The elder son,
JOHN BAYLY, of Debsborough, *b*. 17 June, 1691 ; *m*. 7 July, 1702, Deborah, dau. and coheiress of Ven. Benjamin Neale, Archdeacon of Leighlin, by Hannah his wife, dau. of Jeffery Paul, of Bough, co. Carlow, and by her (who *m*. 2ndly, 1735, Henry Prittie, of Dunalley Castle, M.P., and *d*. 3 Nov. 1760) had issue,
  1. JOHN, of Debsborough.
  2. Benjamin Neale, Barrister, who *d*. leaving an only son, Benjamin Neale, *m*. Letitia, dau. of Henry Archer, of Ballyseskin, co. Wexford, and had issue.
  3. Neale.   4. Henry.
  5. Paul.
  6. Constantine, *m*. 1748, Charlotte, dau. of Richard Falkiner, of Mount Falcon (*see that family*).
  1. Hannah.   2. Elizabeth.
The eldest son,
JOHN BAYLY, of Debsborough, High Sheriff 1759, *b*. 4 Dec. 1724 ; *m*. Bridget, dau. of Robert Holmes, of Johnstown, co. Tipperary, and had issue, JOHN ; Henry ; Benjamin ; Peter ; William ; Deborah ; Lucinda ; Bridget, *m*. Charles M'Donell, of New Hall, M.P. for co. Clare ; and Charlotte. The eldest son,
JOHN BAYLY, of Debsborough, *b*. 1755 ; *d.v.p.* 1783, having *m*. 1776, Catherine, eldest dau. and coheir of Lancelot Crosbie, of Tubrid, co. Kerry, and by her, who inherited the estates of her uncle, John Gustavus Crosbie, M.P., was father of
JOHN BAYLY, of Debsborough, *b*. 15 Dec. 1777 ; *m*. 1 May, 1800, Mary Elizabeth Helena, only child and heir of Richard Uniacke of Mount Uniacke, co. Cork, and *d*. 8 March, 1800, having had issue,
1. JOHN, of Debsborough.
2. Richard Uniacke, of Ballyre, co. Cork, and Ballynaclogh, co. Tipperary, J.P., *b*. 1 Nov. 1806 ; *m*. 7 Feb. 1837, Harriet (who *d*. 1888), only dau. of Very Rev. John Head, Dean of Killaloe, and *d*. 1888, having had issue,
  1. Richard Uniacke, *b*. 15 Dec. 1838 ; *d*. 1860.
  2. John Prittie, of Ballyre and Ballynaclogh, Commander R.N. (retired), *b*. 14 July, 1842 ; *m*. 1886, Annie, dau. of John Warburton, of Cahervillahow, Golden, co. Tipperary and had issue,
    Richard William Uniacke, *b*. 1881.
  3. Edward Crosbie, of Killough Castle, Thurles, co. Tipperary, J.P. cos. Cork, Waterford and Tipperary, late Capt. Tipperary Militia, B.A. Trin. Coll. Dublin, *b*. 27 Jan. 1844 ; *m*. 15 Aug. 1878, Isabel, dau. of Charles Edward Davison, and has issue,
    (1) Edward Crofton Seton, *b*. 25 June, 1883.
    (2) Launcelot Myles, *b*. 1884.
    (3) Gerald Maurice Eyre, *b*. 1886.
    (4) Harold Crosbie, *b*. 1894.
    (5) Jasper Uniacke, *b*. 1895.
    (1) Isabel Harriet, *d*. young, 1897.
    (2) Ethel Iris, *m*. Arthur Lloyd.
    (3) Clementina Mary.
  4. George.   5. William.
  6. Henry, *d*. young, 1856.   7. Francis.
  1. Susan, *m*. 1876, N. White.
  2. Helena Harriet.
  3. Geraldine, *m*. Frank D. Hurst.
3. Lancelot Peter, *b*. 27 Sept. 1807 ; *m*. Oct. 1841, Lydia Catherine, only dau. of Very Rev. Gilbert Holmes, Dean of Ardfert, and *d*. Sept. 1855, leaving issue,
  Lancelot Gilbert Alexander, of Bayly's Farm, *b*. 27 Aug. 1842 ; *m*. 26 Jan. 1869, Frances Katharine (*d*. 25 June, 1905), 2nd dau. of Rev. Thomas Luby, D.D., Senior Fellow, Trin. Coll. Dublin, and *d*. 4 June, 1871, leaving issue, with one dau. (Edmée Lydia Henrietta, *b*. 28 Oct. 1871), a son,
    Lancelot Francis Saunderson, of Bayly's Farm, *b*. 16 Oct. 1869 ; *m*. 7 March, 1907, Kathleen Josephine, dau. of Major E. H. Drake, of Cliftou. She *d*. 2 April, 1911.
  Henrietta.
4. Henry Prittie, of Bally Keef, co. Limerick, *m*. Isabella Yelding, of Tralee, co. Kerry, and had issue,
  Letitia Harriet, *m*. 30 Jan. 1868, James Graham Vansittart, of Tillsonburg, Ontario (*see* VANSITTART-NEALE *of Bisham Abbey*), and *d*. 1879.
The eldest son,
JOHN BAYLY, of Debsborough, J.P. and D.L., High Sheriff 1845, *b*. 3 Sept. 1805 ; *m*. 1st, 13 May, 1829, Catherine, youngest

C 2

dau. of Thomas Yates, of Bury, Lancashire. She d. 22 Sept. 1833, leaving issue,
1. JOHN, of Debsborough.
He m. 2ndly, 17 Oct. 1839, Gertrude Catherine, 3rd dau. of the late William Henry Armstrong, of Mount Heaton, King's Co. She d. 4 Oct. 1874, having had issue,
2. Lancelot Peter, b. 9 Feb. 1842; d. 17 Aug. 1855.
He d. 14 May, 1865, and was s. by his only surviving son,
JOHN BAYLY, of Debsborough, J.P. and D.L., High Sheriff 1874, Capt. 1st Duke of Lancaster's Militia, b. 30 Nov. 1830; m. 3 Sept. 1857, Mary Anne Charlotte, youngest dau. of Daniel Barrington, 2nd son of Sir Joseph Barrington, 1st bart. She d. 31 July, 1870. He had issue,
1. JOHN, now of Debsborough,
2. Richard Edmond (*Debsborough, co. Tipperary*), b. 9 June, 1859; m. 9 Oct. 1909, Anna Selina, widow of Major William Arthur de Warrene Waller (see WALLER *of Prior Park*), and dau. of E. W. Waller, of Artona, by whom (who d. 4 Feb. 1911) he has issue.
3. William Yates, b. 19 Jan. 1864.
4. Lancelot, b. 19 Dec. 1869.
1. Catherine Charlotte, m. 2 Aug. 1887, John Beatty Barrington, of Ashroe, co. Limerick, and has issue (see BURKE'S *Peerage*, BARRINGTON, Bart.).
2. Mary Elizabeth, m. 4 Jan. 1899, James J. Maher, of Clonsilla, co. Dublin.
3. Helen Olivia, d. 1874.
4. Florence Jane, m. 7 Oct. 1890, Croker Barrington, of Barrington's Bridge, co. Limerick, and has issue (see BURKE'S *Peerage*, BARRINGTON, Bart.).

Seat—Debsborough, co. Tipperary.

BAYLY OF BALLYARTHUR.

EDWARD ARCHIBALD THEODORE BAYLY, of Ballyarthur, co. Wicklow, Capt. Royal Welsh Fus. (attached to Egyptian Army, 10th Sudanese Regt.), b. 19 June, 1877.

Lineage.—EDWARD SYMES BAYLY, D.L., of Ballyarthur (see BURKE'S *Peerage*, ANGLESEY, M.), b. 9 April, 1807; d. 26 Nov. 1884; m. 20 June, 1835, Catherine, dau. of the Right Hon. Maurice FitzGerald, Knight of Kerry (see BURKE'S *Peerage*, FITZGERALD, Bart.). She d. 1898, having had with other issue an eldest surviving son,
EDWARD RICHARD BAYLY, of Ballyarthur, co. Wicklow, J.P. and D.L., formerly Ensign 3rd Buffs, and Lieut.-Col. late Commanding 7th Brigade Irish Div. R.A., Assistant Land Commissioner, Ireland, b. 20 June, 1845; d. 11 Oct. 1907; m. 10 Aug. 1875, Adelaide Alicia, eldest dau. of Col. Charles Tottenham, of Woodstock, co. Wicklow, and Plas Berwyn, co. Denbigh (see BURKE'S *Peerage*, ELY, M.), by his wife, the Hon. Isabella Maude (see BURKE'S *Peerage*, DE MONTALT, E.), and has issue,
1. EDWARD ARCHIBALD THEODORE, now of Ballyarthur.
2. Charles John, b. 8 Sept. 1878.
1. Adela Maude, b. 27 Jan. 1880.
2. Kathleen Isabel, b. 6 March, 1882.

Arms—Quarterly, 1st gu., a chevron vair between three martlets or (BAYLY), 2nd Barry of four erm. and or, a lion rampant az. (BAGENAL), 3rd arg. crusilly az. three talbot's heads, erased sa. langued gu. (HALL), 4th gu., three cinquefoils. arg. (LAMBERT), 5th erminois three increscents az. (SYMES), 6th arg. on a fess between three wolf's heads sa. as many mullets of the field (CLIFFE). Crest—A boar's head erased ppr. charged with a mullet arg. Motto—Quid clarius astris.

Seat—Ballyarthur, Ovoca, co. Wicklow.

BAYLY-VANDELEUR. See VANDELEUR.

BEAMISH OF KILMALOODA.

SAMPSON THOMAS BEAMISH, of Kilmalooda, co. Cork, J.P., b. Nov. 1870; s. his grandfather 1881.

Lineage.—Amongst the list of English settlers in Ireland about the time of Queen ELIZABETH, appears the names of "Beamish" or "Beamis," and the lands granted to members of the family in co. Cork were confirmed to three brothers under Act of Settlement by Patent, dated 24 April, 20 CHARLES II. The mother of the three patentees, CATHERINE BEAMISH, of Ballymodan, widow, was living 1642 (her will was proved in Dio. Cork same year). She had issue, one dau. and four sons,

1. JOHN, of West Gully, Ballymodan, co. Cork, m. Elizabeth, dau. of Isaac Philpot, of Cloncaloo, co. Cork. His will is dated 18 Oct. 1668, and names four sons, John; Isaac; THOMAS; Francis; and six daus., Elizabeth; Mary; Catherine; Rebecca; Alice; Mabel. He d. 1669. His 3rd son, THOMAS, of West Gully, who was father of THOMAS, of Raheroon, left by Elizabeth his wife, a son and successor, THOMAS, of Raheroon, m. 1728, Jane, dau. of Richard Beamish, of Garranloughane, or Willsgrove, and had, with three daus. (Elizabeth, m. Vincent Austen; Mary, m. Stawell Webb; Catherine, m. 1763, Jonas Travers, of Butlerstown), an only son,
RICHARD, of Raheroon; m. Elizabeth, dau. of Arthur Bernard, of Palace Anne, co. Cork, by Mary his wife, dau. of Francis Adderley, of Innishannon, and has issue,
(1) Thomas, Major 33rd Regt., d.s.p.
(2) Arthur BEAMISH-BERNARD, of Palace Anne and Raheroon, took the additional surname of BERNARD. He d. unm. in 1854.
(3) Vincent, Lieut. 8th King's Regt., d.s.p. in the West Indies.
(4) George, Capt. 31st Regt., b. 1820; d. unm.
(5) Bernard, Lieut. 84th Regt., m. Dec. 1838, Elizabeth, dau. of John Beamish, of Cashel, co. Cork, and d.s.p.
(6) Samuel BEAMISH-BERNARD, Capt. 84th Regt., took the additional surname of BERNARD, m. Ellen, dau. of Godfrey Byrne, of Bow Park, near Dublin, and had (with three daus.) two sons,
1. Arthur, d.s.p.
2. Richard, killed at the battle of Antietam, U.S.A.
(7) Adderley BEAMISH-BERNARD, Capt. 31st Regt., of Kilcoleman House, co. Cork, and Byard's Lodge, co. York, d. at Mayence, 17 July, 1866. He m. 1st, Frances, dau. of Gen. George Bernard, of Heaton Lodge, Yorks, Col. 84th Regt., Usher of the Black Rod, and took the name of BERNARD, and by her had one child,
1. Mary Isabella, m. John Bowen, of Oak Grove, co. Cork, and d.s.p. 1864.
He m. 2ndly, 1843, Anna Catherine, 3rd dau. of Capt. George Walker, R.N., by whom (who d. 1882) he had two sons,
1. George Adderley Hale, b. 23 July, 1846; Rittmeister and Chef d'Escadron, 9th Pomeranian Lancers, Prussian service; served in Austro-Prussian war (medals); and in Franco-German war (1870-71), medal and the Order of the Iron Cross; m. 1886, Emily Louise Zehe, and has Hermann, b. 1888.
2. Richard M. H. Roger de la Poer, b. 20 Feb. 1852; Lieut. 9th Pomeranian Lancers, served in the Franco-German War (medals).
(8) Richard, d. unm.
(1) Elizabeth, m. her cousin Thomas Austen, of Sheaf, co. Cork.
(2) Mary, m. Maj. William Sullivan, 79th Regt.
(3) Jane, m. her cousin Francis Bernard, 4th son of Capt. Arthur Bernard, 84th Regt., 3rd son of Arthur Bernard, of Palace Anne, by Mary Adderley his wife.
(4) Anne, d. unm.
2. FRANCIS, ancestor of BEAMISH *of Kilmalooda*.
3. Thomas, Patentee of Lands under the Act of Settlement; Provost of Bandon 1655, 1665, and 1675. His will, dated 1681, was proved in Cork, and he left issue, with two daus.,
Daniel, Provost of Bandon 1687, m. 1688, Elizabeth Williams, of Kilbrogan, and is supposed to have d.s.p.
4. Richard, joint Patentee of Lands under the Act of Settlement, had a son,
Richard, d.s.p.
1. Katherine, m. William Wright.

The 2nd son,
FRANCIS BEAMISH, of Kilmalooda, garrisoned his residence in the rebellion of 1641; m. Catherine, dau. of Francis Bernard, of Castle Mahon (ancestor of the Earls of Bandon), and had issue (with three daus.),
1. FRANCIS, s. his father.
2. John, of Keelworrough, m. 1698, Jane Wood, of Kinneigh, and had issue,
1. FRANCIS, s. his cousin at Kilmalooda.
2. John, of Lisgibba, m. 1736, Mary Good, of Kilmeen, and was father of Richard Beamish, who settled in America, and left descendants.
3. Thomas, d.s.p.
4. Richard, of Cashelmore, m. 1730, Mary, dau. of Charles Vignoles, and had issue,
(1) John, of Cashelmore, m. 10 Aug. 1767, Eliza, dau. of Hewitt Poole, of Mayfield, and had issue,
1. John, of Cashelmore and Hare Hill, co. Cork, m. 1st, Jane, dau. of John Howe, of Glounavorrane, and by her had issue,
a. John Howe, d. unm.
b. Richard, d.s.p.
c. Thomas, of Hare Hill, and Cashelmore, m. Margaret Helene, only dau. of Richard Smyth, of Castle Downeen. She d. Aug. 1886. He d. March, 1886, aged 86, leaving issue,
(a) John, of Cashelmore, co. Cork, b. 1840; m. Elizabeth, dau. of James Edward Somerville, M.D. She d. 1882. He d. 28 Sept. 1908, leaving issue,
1. Thomas. 2. James.
3. John. 4. Edward.
5. Neville.
1. Eileen, m. 22 Feb. 1911, Robert de Stretton Berkeley Herrick, Lieut. I.M.S., 3rd son of Rev. George Herrick, Rector of Nohoval, co. Cork.

(b) Richard, of Hare Hill, Bandon, J.P., b. 24 Dec. 1855; m. Jan. 1889, Amy Oliver, dau. of William Smithwick.
(a) Barbara, m. 1st, A. Hannay, and 2ndly, Andrew Scott.
(b) Jane Howe, m. Henry Beamish, of Dunmore (see below).
(c) Elizabeth Mary, d. young.
(d) Mary Elizabeth, m. R. Stowards.
(e) Margaret, m. Michael French, J.P., of Westwood, Ross Carbery, and had issue.
(f) Katherine Hewitt, m. E. L. Bevis.
(g) Ellen, m. E. Pim, and d. Sept. 1907.
(h) Alice, d. unm.
a. Elizabeth, m. Dec. 1838, Bernard Beamish, Lieut. 84th Regt.
b. Mary.
He m. 2ndly, Catherine, dau. of Thomas Hewitt, and by her had,
c. Catherine, d. unm.
1. Mary, d. young.
2. Lydia, m. Sept. 1806, Andrew Poole, of Kilrush.
3. Elizabeth, d. Feb. 1849.
(2) George, of Clogheen, m. 1789, Catherine, dau. of Henry Baldwin, of Old Court, by Catherine his wife, dau. of Jonas Morris, of Dunkettle, and had issue,
1. Thomas (Rev.), of Beaumont House and of Reengarrigeen, B.A. Trin. Coll. Dublin, m. Eliza, dau. of Boyle Travers, of Ballymacowen, and d.s.p. 1855.
2. Richard, of Beaumont, J.P., b. 1799; m. 1829, Susan Becher (d. 14 Aug. 1903, aged 94), 2nd dau. of Richard Hungerford, of Cappoen, and d. 15 Nov. 1867, having had issue,
a. George (Rev.), B.A. Trin. Coll. Dublin, b. 1830; m. 1st, 1864, Elizabeth, dau. of Rev. William Chadwick Neligan. LL.D. She d. 1865, leaving issue,
(a) Elizabeth, m. Newton Price, and has issue.
He m. 2ndly, 1871, Henrietta, dau. of George Crofts, of Temple Hill, and d. 2 March, 1900, having by her had issue,
(a) Richard, b. 30 June, 1874.
(b) George Crofts, Capt. India Med. Service, d. unm. at Jhansi, India, 24 Sept. 1905.
(c) James Aylmer, M.B. (Roy. Univ. of Ireland), b. 16 Nov. 1881.
(b) Susan Becher.
(c) Jane Bredin, m. 6 June, 1906, Gerald Udal, 4th son of William Udal, of Olton Hall, Birmingham, and has issue.
(d) Henrietta O'Donoghue Martin, m. 20 Sept. 1910, J. Philip Ziervogel, M.D., F.R.C.S., 3rd son of C. F. Ziervogel, Resident Magistrate, of Arcadia, Pretoria.
b. Richard, m. Maria, dau. of William Bleazby, of Bleazby Hall, Ross Carbery.
c. Thomas, of Passage West, co. Cork, M.D., J.P., b. April, 1838; m. 1st, May, 1865, Harriet Sophia, dau. of Rev. Thomas Walker, Rector of Kilmalooda. She d.s.p. 1875. He m. 2ndly, 2 Aug. 1876, Anna Jane (she d. 13 Sept. 1905), youngest dau. of John William Topp, of Bellevue, co. Cork, by Eliza his wife, dau. of William Johnson, of Rockenham, Passage West, and has issue,
(a) Richard de Beaumont, Barrister-at-Law, Lincoln's Inn, Capt. Cork Art., B.A. Caius Coll. Camb., b. 2 Sept. 1877.
(b) St. John Hungerford (Rev.), B.A. Corpus Christi Coll. Camb., b. 17 Dec. 1878, Curate of Winslow, Bucks.
(c) Thomas Henry Baldwin, b. 1 Sept. 1880; d. 9 Sept. 1891.
(a) Eileen Elizabeth Susan Harriet, m. 15 Sept. 1909, Capt. Norcott d'Esterre Roberts, youngest son of Richard Roberts, J.P., of Ardmore, co. Cork (see that family).
d. Henry Baldwin, M.D.
e. John.   f. Becher Hungerford.
g. William Baldwin.
a. Jane Hungerford, m. 10 Nov. 1873, Henry Hungerford Whitney, J.P., of The Turrets, Nohoval, co. Cork, he d.s.p. 16 Feb. 1906.
b. Katherine Baldwin.
c. Susan Becher.
d. Mary Elizabeth, m. George Hungerford, and had issue. She d. 12 Oct. 1911.
e. Annie Maria, m. George Beamish, and d. 17 Jan. 1900, leaving issue.
f. Rhoda, m. William Slade Boake, and d. in Ceylon.
g. Charlotte Sophia, m. 1st, Thomas R. Whitney (who d. 27 Nov. 1887), and 2ndly, Boyle FitzHenry Travers.
3. George, M.D., m. 1830, Sophia, dau. of Samuel Orpen, of Woodville, Kerry, and had issue,
a. George, m. his cousin Annie Maria, dau. of Richard Beamish, J.P., of Beaumont, and by her (who d. 17 Jan. 1900) had issue.
b. Orpen, M.D., m. Susan Sarah, dau. of William Holmes, of Carrigmore, and has issue.
c. Richard.   c. Horace.
e. John, m. his cousin Anne, dau. of Henry Baldwin Beamish (see below).
a. Sophia, d. unm.
b. Elizabeth Henrietta, d. unm. 9 Dec. 1896 } twins.
c. Anne Maria, d. unm. 24 Dec. 1899
d. Kathleen Baldwin.

4. Henry Baldwin, of Dunmore, b 1800; m. 1st, 1825, Anne, dau. of Thomas Marmion, and had issue,
a. Henry George, of Dunmore, Clonakilty, Cork; m. Jane Howe, dau. of Thomas Beamish, of Cashelmore (see above), and d. 9 Jan. 1909, leaving issue,
(a) Alfred St. John.
(b) Arthur Livingstone, of Dunmore.
(a) Eleanor Mary Barbara.
b. Thomas, m. Harriet Grattan, and has issue, two sons and two daus.
c. Richard, m. Ena Leech, and has issue, a son.
d. George, has issue, a son and a dau.
e. Marmion, m. Grace Morris, and d.s.p. 19 Nov. 1900.
a. Gertrude Elizabeth, m. 1858, Henry Boyle Travers, J.P., of Ballymacowen, and d. 23 Dec. 1909, leaving issue.
b. Katherine, d.s.p.
c. Mary, m. Samuel Prosser, d.s.p.
d. Henrietta.
e. Anne, m. her cousin (see above) John Beamish.
He m. 2ndly, 1859, Sarah Elizabeth, dau. of John Sadleir Forster, of Cork, and d. 27 July, 1892, having by her had issue,
f. John Forster (Rev.), Vicar of Upperthong, Yorkshire, b. 23 Nov. 1867; m. 14 April, 1898, Emily, 4th dau. of Rev. William Mathew Plues, and has issue,
(a) Terence Forster Baldwin, b. 21 Nov. 1900.
(b) Brian Plues, b. 26 Aug. 1902.
(a) Kathleen Emily, b. 4 Feb. 1899.
g. William, b. May, 1869; m. Oct. 1896, Dora, dau. of Major Christie, Chief of the Punjab Police.
f. Frances May, m. April, 1885, Lieut.-Col. Thomas Robinson, I.M.S. (he d.s.p. 3 Oct. 1908).
g. Georgina, m. Sept. 1880, Arthur Sumner, and has issue.
h. Sarah, m. 10 May, 1905, George Frederick Welsford, M.B. Cantab, of Tiverton, Devonshire, and has issue, a dau.
i. Mary, m. 11 Jan. 1905, David Kingston Wren, of Dromovane House, Bandon.
j. Elizabeth.
5. John, of Maulbrack d. unm.
1. Katherine Morris, m. John Teulon, J.P., of Bandon, and had issue.
2. Eliza, m. Henry Austin, of Ring.
3. Mary, m. Richard Tonsou Evanson, of Four-mile-Water, and had issue.
4. Harriett, m. Thomas Morris, of Castle Salem, and had issue.
5. Anne, m. George Sweetman, and had issue.
3. RICHARD, of Garranloughane, ancestor of BEAMISH of Mountbeamish (see that family).
4. Thomas.
Mr. Beamish, of Kilmalooda, d. 1679, and was s. by his eldest son, FRANCIS BEAMISH, of Kilmalooda, m. 1677-8, Anne, dau. of John Freke, by whom (who m. 2ndly, John Smith) he had, with a dau., Anne, a son and successor,
FRANCIS BEAMISH, of Kilmalooda, m. 1726, Elizabeth, dau. of Joseph Jervois, of Brade, and widow of Percy Smyth, of Headborough, but d.s.p. He was s. by his cousin,
FRANCIS BEAMISH, of Kilmalooda (eldest son of John Beamish, of Keelworrough), m. 1727, Mary Warren, of Kilmichael, and had issue (with three daus.) an only son,
FRANCIS BEAMISH, of Kilmalooda, m. 1758, Elizabeth, dau. of John Sealy, of Richmount, co. Cork, and had issue,
1. FRANCIS, his heir.
2. SAMPSON, s. his nephew, Townsend.
3. John, of Killinear and Bandon, M.D., m. Maria, dau. of John Teulon, and had issue (with daus.) five sons,
1. Francis, of Killinear and Bandon, Barrister-at-Law.
2. Charles, Major-Gen. in the Army; late 35th Foot.
3. John (Rev.), m. 1842, Mary, 2nd dau. of William Allen, of Liscongill, co. Cork. She d. 29 July, 1906. He d. 1847, leaving issue.
4. Peter Teulon (Ven.), Archdeacon of Melbourne, D.D. and LL.D., m. Isabella Mary, dau. of Captain John Bews, 73rd Regt., and had issue,
(1) Francis, m. and has issue, a son,
Francis Teulon, b. 1890.
(1) Mary.   (2) Henrietta.
(3) Emma Cusack Russell.
5. George, Dean.
1. Eleanor, m. 1784, William Austin.
2. Elizabeth, m. Richard Gillman, of Gurteen.
3. A dau., m. Boyle Travers, of Ballymacowen.
The eldest son,
FRANCIS BEAMISH, of Kilmalooda, m. Mary, dau. of Francis Townsend, of Clogheen, co. Cork, and had three daus. and two sons.
The elder son,
TOWNSEND BEAMISH, of Kilmalooda, m. Mary, dau. of Walter Atkins, and had one child, who predeceased him. He was s. in the Kilmalooda estates by his uncle,
SAMPSON BEAMISH, of Kilmalooda, J.P., m. 1800, Catherine, dau. of the Rev. Thomas Waller Evans (nephew of George, 1st Lord Carbery), and had issue,
1. THOMAS, of Kilmalooda.   2. SAMPSON, of Kilmalooda.
1. Elizabeth, m. Francis Bennett, of Clonakilty.
Mr. Beamish was s. at his decease by his eldest son,
THOMAS BEAMISH, of Kilmalooda, J.P., m. 3 Jan. 1829, Lydia Maria, eldest dau. of Capt. Andrew Poole, of Kilrush; she d.s.p. 1860; he d.s.p. 4 April, 1874, and was s. by his brother,
SAMPSON BEAMISH, of Kilmalooda, J.P., m. 1836, Elizabeth, 2nd

dau. of Capt. Andrew Poole, of Kilrush. She d. 1898. He d. 4 Feb. 1881, having had issue,
1. THOMAS, J.P., b. 1840; m. Hannah, only child of Rev. John Madras, and d.v.p. 1878, leaving issue,
  1. SAMPSON THOMAS, present representative.
    1. Lydia Maria Poole, m. 1897, Spencer Eaton Travers, son of Robert Travers, of Timoleague Abbey, co. Cork, and has issue.
    2. Hannah Madras, m. 1904, William Verling Tayler, son of William Parker Tayler, R.N., of Glenbrook, co. Cork, and has issue.
2. Andrew Poole, d. unm. 1879.
3. Francis John, J.P., of Lettacollum, b. 1856; m. 1877, Alice, dau. of H. J. Hungerford, of Cahirmore, co. Cork, and d.s.p. 6 May, 1897.
1. Lydia Maria, d. unm. 1880.
2. Elizabeth Poole, m. Warren Crook, J.P., of Oldtown.
3. Mary Charlotte.

Seat—Kilmalooda House, Timoleague, co. Cork.

BEAMISH OF MOUNTBEAMISH.

COL. DAVID GREGORY BEAMISH, Col. in the Army, late Lieut.-Col. 5th Northumberland Fusiliers, b. 23 March, 1842; m. Nov. 1877, Mary, dau. of Thomas Hammond, and has issue,
1. Ella Wright, m. 11 Nov. 1903, Charles, 3rd son of Henry Evans, of the Bank of Ireland, and has issue.
2. Ellen Prudence Gregory.

Lineage.—RICHARD BEAMISH, of Upper Bolteen or Mountbeamish and Garranloughane, or Willsgrove, and other lands in co. Cork, was 3rd son of Francis Beamish, of Kilmalooda (see that family), by Catherine, dau. of Francis Bernard, M.P., of Castle Bernard. He m. 1695, Mary Townsend, of Clonakilty, by whom he had issue,
1. John (Rev.), of Maulbrack, co. Cork, M.A., b. 1697; m. 1740, Elizabeth, dau. of George Morris, J.P., of Benduffe, and d. 1777, having had issue,
  1. Francis, d.s.p.
  2. John (Rev.), Rector of Berehaven, m. Mary, dau. of William Purcell, of Park, co. Cork.
2. GEORGE, of whom hereafter.
3. WILLIAM, of Willsgrove, Capt. R.N.; m. 1750, Alice, (who d. 1773), dau. of Major William North Ludlow Bernard, of Castle Bernard, by Rose Echlin, co-heiress with her sister Hester, the mother of Thomas Knox, 1st Viscount Northland, and had issue (see BEAMISH of Comphull).
4. Thomas, m. 1738, Dorothy, dau. of Samuel Swete, of Kilglas, co. Cork, J.P., and d.s.p.
1. Jane, m. 1728, Thomas Beamish, of Raharoon.

The 2nd son,
GEORGE BEAMISH, of Mountbeamish, m. 1748, Frances, dau. of Henry Jones, J.P., of Drombeg, co. Cork, and by her had issue (besides a son, George, who m. Anne, sister of Major Beresford Gahan, and had issue, George, who m. a dau. of the Rev. W. Stewart of Kilgariff), an eldest son,
REV. SAMUEL BEAMISH, of Mountbeamish, J.P., Vicar of Kinsale; m. 1st, July, 1774, Mary, dau. of John Stamer, of Rock Castle, by whom he had issue,
1. George, in the Army, d.s.p.   2. Samuel, d.s.p.
3. JOHN SAMUEL, of Mountbeamish.
4. William, m. Sept. 1809, Harriet, dau. of Adam Newman, of Dromore, and sister of Very Rev. Horatio Townsend Newman, Dean of Cork. He had issue,
  1. Samuel George, Capt. 5th Regt.; m. 1834, Hannah, only child of John Slingsby, of Yorkshire, and had,
    (1) Henry Slingsby, late 14th Light Dragoons, dec.
    (2) George John Newman, late 14th Foot, dec.
    (1) Frances Susanna Charlotte.
  2. John Newman, of Queenstown, J.P., Barrister-at-Law; m. 1852, Ellen, widow of J. B. O'Sullivan, Barrister-at-Law, and d. 23 Oct. 1886.
  3. Adam Newman (Rev.), b. 1815; m. his cousin, the dau. of Adam Newman, of Dromore House, and had issue,
    William Henry, b. 1819; m. Aug. 1876, Mary Helena, dau. of Francis Jervis, of Brade, and has issue,
      Jervis William Newman.
      Helena Newman.
  4. William, m. 1st, dau. of Rev. J. Hingston, LL.B., Vicar-General of Cloyne, and by her (who d. 1868) had no issue. He m. 2ndly, 1871, Mary Webb, dau. of George Loane, Surgeon H.M.'s 48th and 49th Regt., and d. 1883, leaving an only son, William Henry, Lieut. 3rd Royal Dublin Fusiliers, d. unm. 19 April, 1900.
  1. Sarah, m. Major Edward Rogers, of the 3rd Buffs.
  2. Frances Annie, m. Gen. Nicholas Hamilton, K.H., of 5th Regt., Col. of H.M.'s 82nd Regt., and had issue.
Rev. S. Beamish, of Mountbeamish, m. 2ndly, 1791, Mary, dau. of Joshua Hamilton (by his wife, dau. of Sir Richard Cox, Bart., M.P.), brother of the Right Hon. Sackville Hamilton, M.P., Secretary of State for Ireland, and grandson of Gen. 1st Viscount Boyne, and by her had issue,
5. Henry Hamilton (Rev.), J.P., Vicar of Kinsale, Incumbent of Trinity Chapel, London, a distinguished preacher and controversialist, b. 3 Jan. 1796; m. 1st, 1820, Anne Isabella, only child of the Rev. Edward Spread, of Bride, Rector of Youghal, by Anne his wife, sister and co-heir of Percy Scott Smyth, of Headborough. She d. 17 May, 1847, leaving issue,
  1. Samuel Henry (Rev.), one of H.M.'s Chaplains in India, and Vicar of Lamorbey, Kent, b. 12 June, 1821; d. unm. 11 Jan. 1900.
  2. Edward Spread, of Halfway Street House, near Bexley, Kent, Lieut.-Col. R.A., J.P., m. 1st, Elizabeth, dau. of John Dougal, D.L., of Glenferness, Morayshire, and by her (who d. 1863) had a dau.,
    (1) Anne Isabella.
    He m. 2ndly, 1868, Diana Spencer, dau. of Frederick Mortimer Lewin, I.C.S., of Halfway Street, Kent. She d. 14 Nov. 1903. He d. 17 April, 1892, leaving issue,
    (1) Frederick Chaloner, of Halfway Street House, Kent, Cape Mounted Rifles, late Lieut. Queen's Own Royal West Kent Regt., b. 24 Nov. 1870; m. 17 Jan. 1905, Elizabeth, dau. of John Campbell Dick, and has issue,
      Lizette.
    (2) Edward Percy Fitzroy, b. 1873.
    (3) Charles Noel Bernard, B.A. Emm. Coll. Camb., b. 12 Feb. 1877.
    (2) Augusta Diana. b. 18 Jan. 1869.
    (3) Constance Elizabeth Noel, d. young, May, 1872.
    (4) Edith Spread, d. an infant, 1872.
    (5) Olive Mary, b. 28 Oct. 1875.
    (6) Cecilia Hamilton, b. 27 July, 1880.
  3. Henry Hamilton, C.B., Rear-Admiral, A.D.C. to the Queen, 1878-80, served with distinction in Burmah, Baltic, China (three medals with clasps). He was b. 16 April, 1829; m. 1st, Louisa, widow of Capt. Forman, Rifle Brigade, and eldest dau. of John and Lady Louisa Slater Harrison, of Shelswell Park, Oxon. She d. 1865, leaving a dau.,
    (1) Louisa Esther, d. young.
    He m. 2ndly, 1867, Blanche Georgina, younger dau. of Capt. W. Marjoribanks Hughes, 4th Dragoons, who had assumed by Royal Licence the names of LOFTUS OTWAY (see Barondage). He d. 18 July, 1901, having by her had issue,
    (1) Robert Otway Hamilton, late Lieut. R.N., b. Sept. 1868.
    (2) Sackville Edward Cecil Hamilton, Capt. West India Regt., b. 13 May, 1872.
    (3) Henry Hamilton.
    (4) Percy Tufton Hamilton, Commander R.N.
    (5) Gustavus W. Loftus Hamilton, d. young.
    (6) John Spread Hamilton.
    (2) Maud Louisa Hamilton, m. 15 Aug. 1893, Maj.-Gen. Sir W. Hope Meiklejohn, K.C.B., C.M.G. He d. 1 May, 1909.
    (3) Evelyn Frances Hamilton.
    (4) Margaret Esther Hamilton, m. 9 March, 1904, Capt. Horace Mackenzie Smith, D.S.O., 85th K.L.I., and has issue.
  4. John Bedell, d.s.p. 1854.
  5. Percy Smyth, of Casa Santa Croce, Alassio, late of the Admiralty, m. 1st, Ada Nuenberg, eldest dau. of Bright Smith, J.P.; she d. 1873, leaving issue, a dau.,
    Ethel Margaret Hamilton.
    He m. 2ndly, 1875, Frances Emily, widow of Col. Strange, C.B., R.H.A., and dau. of Major-Gen. Ormsby, Governor Royal Military Academy, Woolwich, by Emily Lavina, dau. of the Hon. and Right Rev. William Knox, Bishop of Derry. She d. 25 Nov. 1902. He d. 11 Dec. 1908.
    1. Isabella Anne, d. unm. 24 June, 1892.
    2. Mary Hamilton, m. 24 May, 1846, Rev. Charles Henry Ramsden, of Carlton, Notts., and d. July, 1902, leaving issue (see that family).
    3. Anne Elizabeth, d. unm. 13 Oct. 1899.
    4. Jane Anne Wilhelmina St. Maur, d. unm. 21 Aug. 1853.
    5. Esther Matilda Grace, d. unm. Dec. 1882.
    6. Frances Lucy Margaret, m. 29 Jan. 1903, Frederick Pering Jellard.
  The Rev. Henry Hamilton Beamish m. 2ndly, 1850, Frances, widow of John Dick, I.C.S., and dau. of John Udny, Judge of the Supreme Court of Calcutta, and d. 1872, leaving a dau.,
  7. Catherine Emily, m. 18 Jan. 1887, Rev. Joseph Blaydes Palmer, Vicar of South Stainley, Leeds.
  3. Mary Hamilton, m. Rev. Richard Webb.

The 3rd son,
JOHN SAMUEL BEAMISH, of Mountbeamish, m. 1 Sept. 1802, Arabella, dau. of Benjamin Swayne, of Aghada House, and d. 1853, leaving issue,
1. Samuel (Rev.), d. unm.
2. Benjamin Swayne, of Mountbeamish, m. Charity Margaret, dau. of Thomas Little, and d.s.p. 1879.
3. John, d.s.p.
4. George, of Mountbeamish, m. Nov. 1844, Lucy, dau. of S. Crosthwaite, and d.s.p. Dec. 1881.
5. WILLIAM, of whom presently.
1. Elizabeth, m. July, 1837, Henry Herrick.
2. Isabella, m. Feb. 1836, Henry Jones.
3. Harriet, m. 1854, Capt. William Hamilton, 37th Regt., and d. 1902.
4. Frances Anne, m. 1845, Frederick Caleb McCarthy, of Carignavar House, and d.s.p.

The youngest son,
WILLIAM BEAMISH, of Mountbeamish, Physician, m. May, 1840, Ellen, dau. of Lieut.-Col. David Gregory, 45th Regt., and d. 1887, having had issue,
1. DAVID GREGORY, present representative.
2. William, b. 1848; d. 1892.
3. Benjamin, b. Dec. 1860; m. 21 March, 1888, Florence, dau. of Thomas Vance, of Blackrock House, co. Dublin, and has issue,
  1. Desmond William, b. 13 May, 1891.
  2. Geoffrey Gordon Vance, b. 4 Jan. 1895.

IRELAND. Beamish.

1. Arabella, *m.* 1867, Surg.-Gen. Graham Auchinleck, who *d.* 4 July, 1902.
2. Ellen Katherine, *m.* 1870, F. T. D. Reid, 6th Inniskilling Dragoons, and *d.* 1868.
3. Elizabeth Henrietta, *m.* 1 Dec. 1900, Maj. Edward Charles William Gilborne, late 5th Lancers.
4. Charity Margaret, *m.* 1881, Capt. Creighton, 107th Regt., and *d.* 1903.
5. Emily, *d. unm.* 1883.
Residence—1, Eglinton Park, Kingstown.

BEAMISH OF COMPHULL.

WILLIAM ROBERT DELACOUR BEAMISH, of Comphull, co. Sligo, Lieut. R,E,, *b.* 29 Sept. 1879.

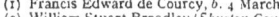

Lineage.—CAPT. WILLIAM BEAMISH, R.N., of Willsgrove (3rd son of Richard Beamish, of Mountbeamish (*see preceding article*), *m.* 1750, Alice, dau. of Major William North Ludlow Bernard, of Castle Bernard, and *d.* 1773, having by her (who *d.* 1792) had issue,
1. Francis Bernard, of Willsgrove, Barrister-at-Law, M.P. for Rathcormac, sold his paternal property to his kinsman, the Earl of Bandon, and *d. unm.* 1805.
2. Richard, *b.* 11 Feb. 1755; *d. unm.*
3. WILLIAM, of whom presently.
4. Charles (Rev.), *d.* at Pisa, 30 Sept. 1842, leaving issue, by Susannah his wife.
5. James, *d. unm.* 6. Isaac, *d. unm.*
1. Rose, *m.* William Cuthbert, of Bloomfield, co. Cork, and *d.* 1834.
2. Mary, *m.* Thomas Ware, J.P., of Woodford, and *d.* 1839, leaving issue.
The 3rd son,
WILLIAM BEAMISH, of Beaumont, entered the Royal Navy, exchanged into the Army and served in the American War as Adjt. of the 19th Regt., *b.* 13 May, 1760; *m.* 19 Sept. 1789, Anne Jane Margaret, dau. of Robert Delacour, of Mallow, Treasurer of co. Cork, and by her (who *d.* 8 Aug. 1852) had issue,
1. William, of Beaumont, *b.* 19 July, 1790; *m.* 15 Sept. 1814, Hon. Mary de Courcy, dau. of John, 26th Lord Kingsale, and *d.* 1 Oct. 1838, having by her (who *d.* 17 April, 1825) had issue,
  1. William, of Beaumont, M.A. (Cantab.), *b.* 27 Feb. 1821; *d. unm.* 1847.
  2. John de Courcy, of Beaumont, R.N., *b.* 1822; *d. unm.* 1848.
  1. Susan, *d. unm.* 1831.
  2. Anne Jane Margaret, *m.* May, 1846, Rev. William Hamilton Thompson, Rector of Stoke Dry, J.P. co. Rutland, and *d.* 18 Jan. 1892, leaving issue two daus.
2. ROBERT DELACOUR, of whom presently.
3. Charles, *d.* young. 4. Hugh, *d.* young.
5. North Ludlow, of Annemount, co. Cork, J.P., High Sheriff 1855, Knight of the Guelphic Order, Capt. 4th Dragoon Guards, Lieut.-Col., *à la suite*, in the Hanoverian Service, F.R.S., *b.* 29 Dec. 1796; *m.* 17 May, 1841, Aline Marie, dau. and co-heiress of Rev. John Eric Forsström, Dean of Munktorp, and *d.* 28 April, 1872, having by her (who *d.* 13 Feb. 1900) had issue,
  1. North Ludlow Axel, of Ashgrove, co. Cork, J.P., B.A. Trin. Coll. Dublin, *b.* 14 June, 1842; *m.* 16 Nov. 1869, his cousin, Edith Annie, dau. and co-heiress of Rev. William Hamilton Thompson, Rector of Stoke Dry (*see above*), and has issue,
    (1) Ludlow Hamilton, *b.* 26 Jan. 1871.
    (2) Harold Delacour, Capt. Leicester Regt., *b.* 23 June, 1874.
    (1) Ethel Hulda Frances, *d. unm.* 5 July, 1896.
  2. William Adolphe, late 31st Regt., *b.* 15 June, 1844.
  3. George Horace Townseand, *b.* 8 Dec. 1847.
  1. Aline Matilda Hulda. 2. Alice, *d.* young.
6. Richard, F.R.S. (*see* BEAMISH *of Ashbourne*).
7. Charles, of Delacour Villa, co. Cork, J.P., *b.* 1 Jan. 1801; *m.* Caroline, dau. of — Smith, and *d.* 18 Jan. 1867, having had (with daus.) a son,
  Charles, *d. unm.* Jan. 1878.
8. Francis Bernard, of Grenville House, J.P. and D.L. co. Cork, High Sheriff 1852, Mayor 1846, F.R.S. 1837-41, and 1857-65, *b.* 5 April, 1802; *m.* 3 May, 1837, Hon. Catherine Savery de Lisle de Courcy, dau. of Capt. the Hon. Michael de Courcy, R.N., and sister of John Stapleton, 28th Lord Kingsale; and *d.* 1 Feb. 1868, leaving by her (who *d.* 5 Feb. 1874) a son,
  Francis Bernard Servington, of Tuckton House, Christchurch, Hants, *b.* 31 Jan. 1839; *m.* 24 July, 1862, Kate Phœbe, dau. of Lieut.-Col. Edward Osburne Broadley, and by her (who *d.* 10 March, 1873) had issue,

(1) Francis Edward de Courcy, *b.* 4 March, 1866.
(2) William Stuart Broadley (*Shurton Court, near Bridgwater*), *b.* 1868; *m.* Zelic, only dau. of Capt. Sydney Smith, and has had issue, two sons and a dau., Daphne Alice Geraldine Dashwood, *d.* 22 Sept. 1907.
9. James Caulfield, of Plymouth, *b.* 1 May, 1803; *m.* Louisa Erskine, dau. of Lieut.-Col. Archibald Macdonald, C.B., Adjutant-Gen. of H.M. Forces in India. She *d.* 15 Sept. 1907. He *d.* 26 March, 1862, leaving issue,
  Caulfield Francis, Capt. 45th Regt., *b.* 1834; *d. unm.* 29 Sept. 1881.
  Louisa Kate, *m.* 1863, Morley Headlam, of Gilmonby Hall, co. York, and Whorlton Grange, co. Durham. She *d.* 15 April, 1910. He *d.* 18 Dec. 1884, leaving issue (*see that family*).
10. Godfrey Clarke, R.N., *d. unm.* 11. Arthur, *d.* young.
1. Dorcas, *m.* 1829, Maj.-Gen. Frederick Meade, of Belmont, co. Cork, and *d.s.p.* 17 April, 1873. He *d.* 12 Sept. 1865.
2. Alice, *d.* young.
Mr. Beamish *d.* 17 April, 1828. The 2nd son,
ROBERT DELACOUR BEAMISH, of Ditchley, co. Cork, High Sheriff 1841, M.A. Camb., Barrister-at-Law, *b.* 16 July, 1791; *m.* Maria Anne, dau. of Lieut.-Col. Archibald Macdonald, C.B. He *d.* 27 May, 1877, having had issue,
1. William Delacour, *b.* 16 Jan. 1841; *d. unm.* 21 Nov. 1872.
2. Archibald Macdonald, Capt. 37th Regt., *b.* 28 May, 1842; *d. unm.* 22 June, 1877.
3. JAMES CAULFIELD, of whom presently.
4. Grenville Pigott, *b.* 22 March, 1851.
The 3rd son,
JAMES CAULFIELD BEAMISH, of Ditchley, co. Cork, and Comphull, co. Sligo, J.P. for both cos., Senior Capt. 8th Brig. N. Irish Div. R.A. and Royal Cork Art. Mil., *b.* 1847; *m.* 1st, 1868, Lizzie, dau. of Richard Beare Tooker, and by her (div. 1877) had issue,
  1. Alice Maud. 2. Maria.
He *m.* 2ndly, 14 Dec. 1878, Elizabeth, dau. and heiress of Peter Niddrin, J.P., of Comphull, co. Sligo, and Over Howden, co. Berwick, and *d.* 18 May, 1896, leaving issue,
  1. WILLIAM ROBERT DELACOUR, now of Comphull.

Arms—Arg., a lion ramp. between three trefoils, slipped gu.
Crest—A demi lion ramp. gu. charged on the shoulder with a trefoil slipped or. Motto—Virtus insignit audentes.
Seat—Comphull, Dromore West, co. Sligo.

BEAMISH OF ASHBOURNE.

RICHARD HENRIK BEAMISH, of Ashbourne, co. Cork, High Sheriff of the City of Cork, 1907 and 1911, D.L., *b.* 16 June, 1861; *m.* 14 Oct. 1903, Violet, dau. of Col. W. Pitcairn Campbell, A.D.C., 3rd batt. King's Royal Rifle Corps, and has issue,

1. RICHARD PIGOTT, *b.* 14 June, 1909.
1. Huldine Violet, *b.* 17 June, 1906.
2. Noreen Violet, *b.*

Lineage.—RICHARD BEAMISH, F.R.S., sometime an officer Coldstream Guards, author of the *Life of Brunel* and other works, 6th son of William Beamish, of Beaumont (*see* BEAMISH *of Comphull*), *b.* 16 July, 1798; *m.* 1831, Theodosia Mary, only dau. and heiress of Lieut.-Col. Augustus George Charles Heise, C.B., K.H., by Theodosia his wife, dau. and co-heiress of Rev. William King, Rector of Mallow. She *d.* 23 April, 1874. He *d.* 20 Nov. 1873, leaving issue,
1. RICHARD PIGOTT, late of Ashbourne.
2. Alten Augustus William, Lieut.-Col. R.E., *b.* 24 Sept. 1841; *m.* 20 Dec. 1892, May Ross, dau. of Sir John Gillespie, and Margaret his wife, dau. of George Robertson. She *d.* 17 Nov. 1906. He *d.* 21 March, 1902, having had issue,
  1. Alten, *b.* 30 Aug., *d.* 6 Sept. 1893.
  2. Arthur John, *b.* 17 Nov. 1894.
  3. George Gillespie, *b.* 3 Jan. 1901.
1. Anne Theodosia, *m.* 2 Nov. 1880, the Hon. and Rev. Edward Plantagenet Airey Talbot, Vicar of Evercreech, Somerset (*see* BURKE'S *Peerage*, TALBOT DE MALAHIDE, B.). He *d.s.p.* 16 March, 1904. She *d.* 10 Jan. 1905.
2. Emily Isabella, *m.* 1884, Robert Emil Le Bauld de Nans, Col. Prussian Art., Knight of the Red Eagle and Prussian Crown.
The elder son,
RICHARD PIGOTT BEAMISH, of Ashbourne, co. Cork, J.P. and D.L., sometime Capt. W. Cork Art. Mil., *b.* 21 June, 1832; *m.* 20 May, 1858, Hulda Elizabeth Constance, only dau. and heir of Charles Gustavus Mosander, Knight of the North Star of Sweden, by Hulda Phillippina his wife, dau. and co-heiress of Rev. John Erik Forsström. She *d.* 24 Dec. 1892. He *d.* 7 June, 1899, having had issue,
1. RICHARD HENRIK, now of Ashbourne.
2. Gustaf William, *b.* 5 Jan. 1864.
1. Huldine, *m.* Baron Carl Alexander Fock, Capt. 1st Royal Swedish Foot Guards, Knight of the Sword of Sweden.

Arms—Arg. a lion ramp., betw. three trefoils slipped gu. **Crest**—A demi lion ramp. gu. charged on the shoulder with a trefoil slipped or. **Motto**—Virtus insignit audentes.
Seat—Ashbourne, Glounthaune, co. Cork.

BEAUMONT-NESBITT. See NESBITT.

WRIXON-BECHER OF CASTLE HYDE.

WILLIAM NICHOLAS WRIXON-BECHER, of Castle Hyde, co. Cork, D.L., M.A., late Lieut. 62nd Regt., *b.* 1831; *m.* 1888, Georgiana, dau. of Capt. W. Herrick, of Shippool, Innishannon, co. Cork. Mr. Wrixon-Becher is the youngest son of Sir William Wrixon-Becher, 1st bart. (who *d.* Oct. 1850), and Elizabeth his wife, dau. of John O'Neill.
Lineage, Arms, &c.—See BURKE's *Peerage*.
Seat—Castle Hyde, Fermoy, co. Cork.

WRIXON-BECHER.
See BURKE's PEERAGE, **WRIXON-BECHER**, Bart.

BELLEW. See BURKE'S PEERAGE, BELLEW, GRATTAN-BELLEW, Bart.

BELLINGHAM.
See BURKE's PEERAGE, **BELLINGHAM**, Bart.

BENCE-JONES. See JONES.

BENNETT OF CASTLE ROE.

REV. EDMUND THOMAS BENNETT, of Castle Roe, co. Londonderry, M.A. Oxford, Vicar of Littleton, Winchester, 1899-1901, *b.* 9 Aug. 1849; *m.* 24 Sept. 1872, Laura Maria, eld. dau. of the late Lieut.-Col. Thomas Edmonds Holmes, Oxfordshire L.I., and has issue,
1. LIONEL EDMUND ANSTEY, late Lieut. Oxfordshire L.I., served in S. Africa 1901 (severely wounded, medal with three clasps), *b.* 18 April, 1875; *m.* 19 April, 1898, Anna Constance Georgina (who *d.* 27 May, 1900), only child of Gen. the Hon. Charles Dawson Plunkett, son of the 11th Baron Louth (see BURKE's *Peerage*).
1. Eveline Anstey, *m.* 26 Feb. 1895, Francis Edward Drummond-Hay, M.V.O., British Consul at Christiania, and has issue (see BURKE's *Peerage*, KINNOULL, E.).
2. Muriel Grace Charlotte Anstey, *m.* 4 Jan. 1908, Thomas Erskine Lambert, eldest son of Cowley Lambert, J.P., of Little Tangley, near Guildford, and has issue.
Lineage.—THOMAS BENNETT, of Castle Roe, co. Londonderry, J.P., *m.* Jane, dau. of Major Ovens. She *d.* 4 May, 1858. He *d.* 11 Feb. 1873, having had issue,
1. THOMAS, of whom presently.
2. Stephen (Rev.), M.A. Oriel Coll. Oxon, late Rector of Uphill, Somerset (*Grantlands, Uppculme, Devon*), *b.* 1827, *m.* 1873, Emily, dau. of Henry D. Brown, H.E.I.C.S., formerly Judge at Poona, India, and grand-dau. of Sir Lionel Darell, Bart. (see BURKE's *Peerage*).
The elder son,
THOMAS BENNETT, of Christ's Coll. Camb., *m.* 8 Oct. 1848, Charlotte, dau. of John Anstey. She *d.* 7 Dec. 1891. He *d.v.p.* 15 Oct. 1856, leaving issue,
1. EDMUND THOMAS, now of Castle Roe.
2. Thomas John Filmer (Rev.), M.A. St. John's Coll. Camb., incumbent of Curzon Chapel, Mayfair, *m.* 1877, Alice (*d.* 4 June, 1908), 3rd dau. of W. Marsh, of Bath, and has issue,
   1. Maurice Filmer, Capt. R.M.L.I., *b.* 2 July, 1878; *m.* 11 Sept. 1906, Bianca Rosalie Russell, dau. of the late Rev. S. Russell Davies, Vicar of Lewisham, and has issue,
      John Russell Filmer, *b.* 16 Sept. 1909.
   2. Harold Filmer.
   1. Alice Filmer, *d.* 10 Dec. 1902.
3. John Anstey, Capt. Inniskilling Fus., *d. unm.*
Seat—Castle Roe, Coleraine, co. Londonderry. **Residence**—Woodlands, The King's Ride, Camberley.

BERESFORD OF LEARMOUNT.

RALPH HENRY BARRÉ DE LA POER BERESFORD, of Learmount Castle, co. Londonderry, *b.* 26 Nov. 1886; *s.* his grandfather, 1895, only son of MAJOR JOHN CLAUDIUS MONTGOMERY BERESFORD, R.E. (who *d.v.p.* 19 Sept. 1894), by Rosa Sophia Montgomery his wife, dau. of Ralph Smyth, of Greenhills, Drogheda, and grandson of JOHN BARRÉ BERESFORD, D.L., of Learmount and Ashbrook, co. Londonderry (who *d.* 30 Aug. 1895), who was grandson of the RIGHT HON. JOHN BERESFORD, 2nd son of MARCUS, 1st EARL OF TYRONE (see BURKE's *Peerage*, WATERFORD, M.).
Lineage.—See BURKE's *Peerage*, WATERFORD, M.
Arms—Quarterly: 1st and 4th, arg. crusilly fitchée three fleurs-de-lis a border engrailed sa., for BERESFORD; 2nd and 3rd, arg. a chief indented sa., for POWER. **Crest**—A dragon's head erased arg. pierced through the neck with a broken spear or, point arg., thrust through the upper jaw. **Motto**—Nil nisi cruce.
Seat—Learmount Castle, Park, co. Londonderry.

PACK-BERESFORD OF FENAGH.

DENIS ROBERT PACK-BERESFORD, of Fenagh House, co. Carlow, J.P. and D.L., High Sheriff 1890, *b.* 23 March, 1864, educated at Rugby, B.A. Ch. Ch. Oxford; *m.* 11 Aug. 1891, Alice Harriet Cromie, only dau. of the late James Acheson Lyle, of Portstewart House (see *that family*).

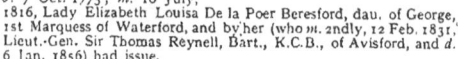

Lineage.—MAJOR-GEN. SIR DENIS PACK, K.C.B., son of the Very Rev. Thomas Pack, Dean of Ossory (see REYNELL-PACK *of Netherton*), *b.* 7 Oct. 1775; *m.* 10 July, 1816, Lady Elizabeth Louisa De la Poer Beresford, dau. of George, 1st Marquess of Waterford, and by her (who *m.* 2ndly, 12 Feb. 1831, Lieut.-Gen. Sir Thomas Reynell, Bart., K.C.B., of Avisford, and *d.* 6 Jan. 1856) had issue,
1. ARTHUR JOHN REYNELL, his heir (see REYNELL-PACK *of Netherton*).
2. DENIS WILLIAM, of whom hereafter.
1. Anne Elizabeth, *m.* 28 Sept. 1869, Rev. George J. Mapletoft. Paterson, Rector of Brome, Suffolk.
2. Elizabeth Catherine, *m.* 7 July, 1842, Sir John William Hamilton Hanson, Bart. He *d.* 2 Aug. 1873.
Sir Denis *d.* 24 July, 1823. His 2nd son,
DENIS WILLIAM PACK-BERESFORD, of Fenagh, J.P. and D.L., High Sheriff 1856, M.P. co. Carlow, Capt. R.A., *b.* 7 July, 1818; *m.* 12 Feb. 1863, Annette Caroline, only dau. of Robert Clayton Browne, of Browne's Hill, co. Carlow (see *that family*), and by her (who *d.* 11 Feb. 1892) had issue,
1. DENIS ROBERT, his heir.
2. Arthur William, Capt. and Brevet Major R.A., and Major S. African Const., served throughout S. African War 1899-1902 (twice mentioned in despatches), *b.* 23 April, 1868; *d.* on service, 4 March, 1902.
3. Charles George, Major Royal West Kent Regt., served in the Malakand and Bunei field force (medal with clasp), Punjaub frontier 1897-98, S. African War (medal with four clasps), mentioned in despatches Sept. 1900, *b.* 21 Nov. 1869.
4. Henry John, Capt. Highland L.I., served in the Malakand and Bunei field force (medal with clasp), Punjaub frontier 1897-98, *b.* 22 Aug. 1871; *m.* 28 July, 1904, Sybil Maud, youngest dau. of the late John Bell, of Rushpool Hall, Yorks, and has issue,
   1. Denis Johu, *b.* 27 Oct. 1905.
   2. Tristram Anthony, *b.* 8 May, 1907.
5. Reynell James, *b.* 21 Dec. 1872; *m.* 17 June, 1899, Florence, only dau. of Frederick Leith, of Walmer, Kent, and has issue,
   Arthur Reynell, *b.* 28 April, 1906.
   Joyce Annette, *b.* 27 July, 1900.
6. Hugh de la Poer, *b.* 11 July, 1874.
7. Algernon Dunbar, *b.* 25 July, 1875; *d.* 5 Dec. 1908.
1. Elizabeth Harriet.
2. Annette Louisa.
This gentleman assumed, by Royal Licence dated 6 March, 1854, the additional name and arms of BERESFORD, in compliance with the will of William Carr, Viscount Beresford, G.C.B. He *d.* 28 Dec. 1881.

Arms—Quarterly: 1st and 4th arg., crusilly fitchée, three fleurs-de-lis, sa.,within a bordure wavy pean (for BERESFORD); 2nd and 3rd quarterly sa. and erminois, in the first quarter a sword in bend sinister, arg., pomelled and hilted or, encircled by a wreath of the last, in the fourth a cinquefoil of the third, in the centre chief, pendent from a crimson riband bordered blue, a representation of a golden cross, and clasps, presented to Sir Denis Pack by GEORGE III (for PACK). *Crests*—1st, BERESFORD. Issuant from a mural crown or, a dragon's head per fess wavy az. and gu., the lower part of the neck transfixed by a broken spear, in the mouth the remaining part of the spear, the point upwards or. 2nd, PACK. A mural crown arg. issuing therefrom a lion's head gu., gorged with a wreath or. *Motto*—Nil nisi cruce.
Seat—Fenagh House, Bagnalstown, co. Carlow.

BERESFORD OF AWBAWN.

EDWARD BERESFORD, of Awbawn, co. Cavan, High Sheriff 1906, *b.* 11 Sept. 1863; *m.* 1st, 1886, Emily Constance Frederica, dau. of Henry Beilby Milner. She *d.* 30 Oct. 1889, leaving issue,
1. Mary, *m.* 8 Aug. 1907, Reginald Moreton, 4th son of Capt. Hon. Reynolds Moreton, R.N. (*see* BURKE's *Peerage*, DUCIE, E.).
2. Aline.

He *m.* 2ndly, 30 April, 1903, Florence Lilian, dau. of Capt. Hon. Reynolds Moreton, R.N., D.L. (*see* BURKE's *Peerage*, DUCIE, E.), and has issue,
1. George Henry William De la Poer, *b.* 23 July, 1904.

Lineage.—THE MOST REV. MARCUS GERVAIS BERESFORD, Archbishop of Armagh (who *d.* 26 Dec. 1885), and Mary his 1st wife (who *d.* 31 Dec. 1845), dau. of Henry Peisley L'Estrange, of Moystown, King's Co., and great-great-grandson of Marcus, 1st Earl of Tyrone (*see* BURKE's *Peerage*, WATERFORD, M.), had issue,
GEORGE DE LA POER BERESFORD, of Awbawn, co. Cavan, J.P. and D.L., High Sheriff 1867, and J.P. co. Armagh, High Sheriff 1887, M.P. for co. Armagh 1875-85, *b.* 22 April, 1831; *d.* 3 Aug. 1906; *m.* 24 April, 1860, Mary Annabella, dau. of Rev. William Vernon Harcourt (*see* BURKE's *Peerage*, VERNON, B.), and had issue,
1. Marcus William, Capt. Rifle Brigade, *b.* 8 May, 1862; *d. unm.* 7 Aug. 1900.
2. EDWARD, now of Awbawn.
1. Selina Mary Emily, *d. unm.* 10 Nov. 1880.
2. Kathleen.

Seat—Awbawn, Killeshandra, co. Cavan. *Clubs*—Boodles and Kildare Street.

BERESFORD OF WOODHOUSE.

JOHN GEORGE BERESFORD, of Woodhouse, co. Waterford, J.P. co. Wicklow, *b.* 10 June, 1847; *m.* 21 Feb. 1898, Emilie Eleanora, youngest dau. of Adrian Iselin, of New York, U.S.A.

Mr. Beresford is the second son of Col. George John Beresford, R.A. (who *d.* 1864), and Frances Constantia, his 2nd wife (who *d.* 29 Oct. 1867), dau. of Robert John Uniacke, D.L., of Woodhouse, co. Waterford, and great grandson of the Right Hon. John Beresford, 2nd son of Marcus, 1st Earl of Tyrone. He *s.* his elder brother, Robert Henry Beresford, D.L., of Woodhouse, who *d.s.p.* 30 Jan. 1903.

Lineage, Arms, &c.—*See* BURKE's *Peerage*, WATERFORD, M.
Seat—Woodhouse, Kilmacthomas, Waterford.

BERESFORD.
See BURKE's PEERAGE, **WATERFORD, M.**

BERESFORD-ASH. *See* ASH.

BERNARD OF CASTLE BERNARD.

The late THOMAS SCROPE WELLESLEY BERNARD, representing the family of Bernard, of Castle Bernard, J.P. King's Co., Capt. and Hon. Major (retired) 3rd Batt. South Lancashire Regt., formerly Capt. 44th Regt., *b.* 18 Oct. 1850; *m.* 1880,

Monica Gertrude (now of Castle Bernard), 6th dau. of W. H. Darby, of Leap Castle, Roscrea (*see that family*), and *d.* 1 Feb. 1905, leaving issue,
1. Marguerite Cecil Elizabeth, *m.* Oct. 1906, Charles J. Alexander.
2. Monica Charlotte Emily.
3. Kathrine Anne.   4. Maude Mary Gertrude.

Lineage.—THOMAS BERNARD, of Oldtown and Clonmulsh, co. Carlow, High Sheriff 1708; *m.* Deborah, dau. of Matthew Shepperd, of Killerick, co. Carlow, and sister of Jonathan Shepperd, of Killerick, co. Carlow, and widow of Edward Humfrey, of Clonagh, co. Carlow. She *d.* 1686. He *d.* 1720, leaving issue,
1. CHARLES, of Bernard's Grove, Queen's Co., High Sheriff of Carlow in 1718; *d.* 1728, leaving issue.
2. Franks, of Castletown, King's Co., *m.* and had issue.
3. JOSEPH, of whom we treat.

The 3rd son,
JOSEPH BERNARD, of Straw Hill, co. Carlow, and Castletown, King's Co., High Sheriff of the former in 1730, *b.* 1694; *m.* 1717, Mary, dau. of John Edwards, of Old Court, co. Wicklow, and had, with five daus., three sons,
1. THOMAS, his heir.
2. John, Capt. R.N., who *m.* his cousin Frances, dau. of Sir Gilbert Pickering, Bart., and left one son,
Joseph, of Frankfort, King's Co., *m.* Rebecca Margaret, dau. of Ralph Smyth, of Milford, co. Tipperary, and left issue.
3. William, of Straw Hill, co. Carlow, *m.* his cousin Mary Bernard, by whom he had,
Thomas, of Straw Hill, who *d.* 1807, leaving, besides daus., two sons.

Mr. Bernard *d.* 1764, and was *s.* by his eldest son,
THOMAS BERNARD, of Castletown, *m.* Jane, Mrs. Armstrong, eldest dau. and co-heiress (with her sisters, Mrs. Drought, of Whigsborough, and Mrs. Tarleton) of Adam Mitchell, of Ratbgibbon, and *d.* 1788, leaving, with daus., of whom, Grace, *m.* Philip Going, of Monaquil, Susannah, *m.* Bigoe Armstrong, and Barbara, *m.* Sept. 1749, Robert Lauder, of Moyclare, an only son,
THOMAS BERNARD, of Castle Bernard, *m.* 1st, April, 1768, Mary, dau. of Jonathan Willington, of Castle Willington, King's Co., and 2ndly, 1780, Margaret, dau. and co-heir of Nicholas Biddulph, of Rathrobin and Portal (*see that family*), and widow of Alexander Cornwall. She *d.s.p.* 31 March, 1811. By the former he left, at his decease in 1815 (with four daus., the eldest of whom, Mary, *m.* Sir Robert Waller, Bart.), one son,
THOMAS BERNARD, of Castle Bernard, Col. King's Co. Militia, and for more than thirty-two years M.P. for the co., *b.* 1769; *m.* 1st, 1800, Elizabeth, dau. of Henry, 1st Lord Dunalley, which lady *d.s.p.* 1802; and 2ndly, 29 July, 1814, Lady Catherine Henrietta Hely-Hutchinson, sister of John, 3rd Earl of Donoughmore, by whom (who *d.* 1844) he had four sons and two daus.,
1. THOMAS, his heir.
2. Francis, *b.* Dec. 1818; *d. unm.* Dec. 1847.
3. John Henry Scroope, *b.* May, 1820, Lieut. 18th (Royal Irish) Regt., subsequently Major in the Turkish Contingent in the Crimea; served in the first campaign in China; *m.* 30 May, 1849, Cecile, dau. of M. Racine, and *d.* Sept. 1856, leaving issue,
THOMAS SCROPE WELLESLEY.
Marguerite Adeline, *m.* 1875, Capt. Caulfeild French. 94th Regt., J.P. and D.L., of Castle Bernard, son of William John French (cousin of Lord de Freyne), by Harriet Anna his wife, only dau. of James Caulfeild, of Drumcairne (*see* FRENCH *of Castle Bernard*). She *d.* 18 July, 1910. He *d.* June, 1910.
4. Richard Wellesley, an officer in the army, present at the battles of Alma, Balaclava, and Inkerman, Lieut.-Col. King's Co. Militia, formerly in the Austrian service; Deputy Ranger of the Curragh of Kildare, Chamberlain at the Court of Dublin in the Vice-Royalties of the Dukes of Abercorn and Marlborough, *b.* March, 1822; *m.* 31 Aug. 1859, Ellen Georgina, widow of Col. the Hon. Henry Handcock, and dau. of Lieut.-Col. Henry Williams, R.A. He *d.s.p.* Sept. 1877. She *d.* 28 Jan. 1907.
1. Frances Margaret, *m.* 1846, S. H. Goold-Adams, and *d.* March, 1850, leaving issue (*see that family*).
2. Marguerite, *d.* 1842.

Col. Bernard *d.* 18 May, 1834, and was *s.* by his eldest son,
THOMAS BERNARD, of Castle Bernard, Lord-Lieutenant and Custos Rotulorum of that co., and High Sheriff 1837, Lieut.-Col. in the Army, 12th Lancers, Col. King's Co. Militia, *b.* Sept. 1816. Col. Bernard *d. unm.* Dec. 1882.

Residence—30, Saumarez Street, St. Peter Port, Guernsey. *Clubs*—Army and Navy and Kildare Street.

BERNARD OF CASTLE HACKET.

PERCY BRODRICK BERNARD, of Castle Hacket, co. Galway, J.P. and D.L., co. Galway, High Sheriff 1884, J.P. co. Cork, and M.P. for Bandon 1880, B.A. Oxford, son of the Hon. and Right Rev. Charles Brodrick, Lord Bishop of Tuam (by Jane Grace his wife, sister of George, 7th Baron Carbery), and nephew of Francis, 3rd Earl of Bandon (*see* BURKE's *Peerage*). Mr. Percy Bernard *m.* 1st, 11 April, 1872, Beatrice, dau. of John Newton Lane, of King's Bromley Manor, co. Stafford, which lady *d.* 1 May, 1876, leaving a son,

1. Ronald Percy Hamilton, Captain Rifle Brigade, b. 18 March, 1875.

Mr. Percy Bernard m. 2ndly, 6 Feb. 1880, Mary Lissey, sister and heir of John Thomas Macan Kirwan, of Castle Hacket, and by her (who d. 1 Aug. 1898) has issue,

2. DENIS JOHN CHARLES KIRWAN, Lieut. Rifle Brigade, b. 22 Oct. 1882.
3. Percy Arthur Erpald, b. 17 Feb. 1889.
1. Frances Mary, b. 18 Nov. 1880; m. 22 Feb. 1900, George Arthur Paley, of Langcliffe, co. York (see that family).
2. Mary Winifred, b. 27 Oct. 1886.

He m. 3rdly, 2 June, 1900, Eva, dau. of Henry Hoare, of Staplehurst (see that family), and by her has issue,

4. Murrogh Wyndham Percy, b. 5 Feb. 1902.

Lineage.—STEPHEN KIRWAN, 2nd son of Thomas Oge Kirwan (see KIRWAN of Cregg), had, with other issue, a son, RICHARD KIRWAN, father of STEPHEN KIRWAN, whose son, SIR JOHN KIRWAN, Knt., was Mayor of Galway in 1686, and representative in Parliament, left a son, SIMON KIRWAN, whose son, JOHN KIRWAN, of Castle Hacket, d. 1781, leaving by his wife, a Miss Daly, of Dalystown, co. Galway, three sons, JOHN, Denis, and James, of whom the eldest,

JOHN KIRWAN, of Castle Hacket, m. Mary, dau. of Henry Boyle Carter, of Castle Martin, co. Kildare, by Susanna his wife (m. 1750), dau. and co-heir of Sir Arthur Shaen, Bart., of Kilmore, and dying June, 1821, left, with a dau., two sons,
1. JOHN, his heir.
2. Henry, m. Miss Bingham, and had issue.

The elder son,
JOHN KIRWAN, of Castle Hacket, b. 1780; m. 1806, Penelope, eldest dau. of John Hardiman Burke, of St. Clerans, and by her (who d. 19 Nov. 1842) had issue,
1. John, of Castle Hacket, d. aged 20, 10 June, 1827, and was s. by his brother.
2. DENIS, of whom presently.
1. Elizabeth, m. 17 Sept 1839, Edward, 3rd Lord Cloncurry, who d. 4 April, 1869. She d. 8 May, 1895, leaving issue (see BURKE'S PEERAGE).

Mr. Kirwan d. 22 June, 1842. His 2nd son,
DENIS KIRWAN, of Castle Hacket, J.P. and D.L., High Sheriff 1844, b. 4 Sept. 1808; m. 11 April, 1844, Anne Margaret, only child of Major Thomas Macan, of Greenmount, co. Louth, and d. 19 Feb. 1872, leaving issue,
JOHN THOMAS MACAN, his heir.
MARY LISSEY, late of Castle Hacket.

The son,
JOHN THOMAS MACAN KIRWAN, of Castle Hacket, b. 23 Feb. 1851, Lieut. 7th Royal Fusiliers; d.s.p. 23 June, 1875, and was s. by his sister.

Arms of Bernard.—See BANDON, Earl of, BURKE'S Peerage and Baronetage.
Seat—Castle Hacket, near Tuam, co. Galway. Clubs—Carlton and Kildare Street, Dublin.

MORROGH-BERNARD OF FAHAGH COURT.

The late EDWARD JOSEPH BERNARD MORROGH-BERNARD, of Fahagh Court, co. Kerry, J.P., High Sheriff 1870, b. 18 Nov. 1843; m. 3 Feb. 1880, Matilda Anne Williams, eldest dau. of Samuel James Brown, of Loftus Hill, co. York, and d.s.p. 18 Nov. 1903.

Lineage.—EDMUND MORROGH, m. Mary Nagle, of co. Cork, and was father of
JAMES MORROGH, of the city of Cork, m. 1780, Jane Morrogh, of Lisbon, Portugal (of the Kilworth branch of the Morroghs), and by her (who d. 1817) left at his decease in 1804, five sons and four daus.,
1. EDWARD, of whom presently.
2. John, settled in New York, m. Mary, dau. of Francis Plowden, of Plowden, and had issue.
3. James, m. Helen, dau. of Alexander McCarthy, and d. 1868, having had issue.
4. Henry, m. Helena Power, and d. 1853, having had issue.
5. Andrew, d. unm.
1. Jane, m. Charles O'Donoghue, of the Glens, co. Kerry, and had issue.
2. Theresa, m. 1804, Patrick Russell, of Mount Russell, co. Cork, and d. 1835, leaving issue.

3. Eliza, m. — O'Shea, of co. Cork, and d.s.p.
4. Christina, d. unm.

The eldest son,
EDWARD MORROGH, of Glanmire House, co. Cork, J.P., b. 1785; m. 1st, 1809, Christian, dau. of Robert Joseph ffrench, of Rahasana, co. Galway, and by her (who d. 1812) had issue,
1. JAMES, his heir.

Mr. Edward Morrogh m. 2ndly, 1816, Martha, 2nd dau. and eventual heiress of John Bernard, of Ballynagare, co. Kerry, and by her (who d. 15 Aug. 1869) had issue. one son and three daus.,
2. John Morrogh, J.P. and D.L., High Sheriff co. Kerry 1864, who took the name of BERNARD, b. 19 March, 1819; m. 18 March, 1841, Frances Mary, only dau. and heiress of Joseph Blount, of Hurtsbourne Tarrant, Hants, and d. 22 Aug. 1866, having by her (who d. 27 April, 1888) had issue,
  1. EDWARD JOSEPH BERNARD, late of Fahagh Court.
  2. Bertram Francis, b. 14 Jan. 1846; m. 1888, Blanche Chichizola, and has issue,
    (1) John Francis.
    (2) Bertram Andrew.
    (1) Mary Agnes.
    (2) Alice Ulbandina.
    (3) Louisa.
  3. Cyril Charles, b. 5 Jan. 1852; m. 1884, and has three sons.
  4. Arthur Mary, b. 3 June, 1854.
  5. Alfred Francis Mary, b. 17 Feb. 1856.
  6. Eustace Mary, of Curraghmount, Buttevant, co. Cork, b. 30 March, 1858; m. 11 Dec. 1888, Mary Anne, dau. of Samuel James Brown, of Loftus Hill, co. York, and has issue,
    (1) John Alexander, b. 8 Dec. 1890.
    (2) Eustace Anthony, b. 3 Sept. 1893.
    (3) Francis, b. 12 June, 1896.
    (4) Joseph George, b. 26 March, 1898.
    (1) Mildred Mary Sophia Rose.
    (2) Mary Anne Matilda.
  7. Gilbert Mary, b. 22 Feb. 1864; m. 14 Feb. 1900, Catherine Reid, and has issue, Eileen Frances.
  1. Agnes Mary, a Sister of Charity, b. 24 Feb. 1842.
  2. Alice Gertrude, b. 23 Dec. 1848; m. 8 Jan. 1880, Michael Russell, of Glanmore, co. Cork, and has issue (see that family).
  3. Emily Mary, b. 7 Nov. 1860.
1. Jane, m. Patrick Shannon, of Corbally House, co. Limerick, and d. 1902, having had issue.
2. Mary, d. unm. 1845.
3. Martha, m. Richard Croker Smyth, and d.s.p. 1855.

The eldest son,
JAMES MORROGH, of Old Court, co. Cork, J.P., High Sheriff 1864, b. 17 Sept. 1810; m. 3 July, 1844, Christine, 2nd dau. of James D. Lyons, D.L., of Croome House, co. Limerick, and by her (who d. Oct. 1885) had issue,
Christian, b. and d. 1846.

Mr. Morrogh d. Feb. 1884, and was s. by his nephew.

Arms—Az., a harp or, stringed arg., between three escallops of the second. Crest—A staff ppr., with a flag attached az., charged with a harp, as in the arms. Motto—Virtus invicta.

Seat—Fahagh Court, Faha, Killarney, co. Kerry.

BERNARD. See BURKE'S PEERAGE, BANDON, E.

BERRIDGE OF BALLYNAHINCH CASTLE.

RICHARD BERRIDGE, of Ballynahinch Castle, co. Galway, J.P. and D.L., High Sheriff 1894, b. 1870, son of the late Richard Berridge, of Ballynahinch Castle (who d. 1887); m. 1905, Marie Eulalia, dau. of Robert W. Lesley, of Lesselyn Court, Haverford, Penn., U.S.A., and has issue,

1. Robert Lesley, b. 19 Sept. 1907.
2. Francis Richard, b. 21 Dec. 1910.
1. Anne Thomson, b. 13 Jan. 1906.
2. Eulalia Beatrice, b. 4 Jan. 1910.

Arms—Az., on a fesse between three dolphins naiant or, as many anchors erect sa. Crest—On an anchor fessewise sa., a dove rising ppr. Motto—Semper fidelis.

Seat—Ballynahinch Castle, Connemara, co. Galway.

BIDDULPH OF RATHROBIN.

LIEUT.-COL. MIDDLETON WESTENRA BIDDULPH, of Rathrobin, King's Co., J.P. and D.L., High Sheriff 1901, late 5th (Northumberland) Fus., b. 17 Aug. 1849; m. 21 Oct. 1891, Vera Josephine, dau. of the late Sir William Henry Flower, K.C.B., D.C.L., LL.D., F.R.S., Director of the Natural History Museum.

Lineage.—FRANCIS BYDDULPH, of Kilpatrick, co. Wexford, d. 1673, leaving issue, by his wife Alice, three sons,
1. Richard, of Kilpatrick, m. 1679, Martha, dau. of John Vivors, of Crosstown, co. Wexford, and by her (who m. 2ndly, Michael Jones, of Droghenure, King's Co.), had issue, two sons and two daus.,
   1. Rowland. 2. Richard.
   1. Elizabeth. 2. Susanna.
2. Thomas, of Wexford (nuncupative will, Ferns 1677), who m. 1674, Elizabeth Raby and d.s.p.
3. Nicholas, who settled at Rathrobin.

NICHOLAS BIDDULPH, got a lease of Rathrobin, renewable for ever, from Baron Shelbourne 25 Oct. 1694, and built a house near the old castle. He d. intestate 5 March, 1702, having by Charity his wife (who m. 2ndly, John Newcombe, of Aghanvilla, King's Co.), and d. 18 March, 1753) had issue,
1. FRANCIS, of Rathrobin and Fortal.
2. JOHN, of Stradbally, Queen's Co. (will dated 26 May, 1739, proved 29 April, 1741), left issue, four sons,
   1. Francis, of Vicarstown, Queen's Co., J.P., b. 21 June, 1727; m. 1765, Eliza Harrison (who d. 1827, aged 90). He d. 11 Sept. 1806, having had issue,
      (1) FRANCIS HARRISON, of whom presently.
      (2) Nicholas John, b. 23 Aug. 1778; d. 1779.
      (1) Eliza, b. 26 June, 1766; m. 20 Feb. 1788, Richard Grattan, of Drummin, co. Kildare.
      (2) Mary Anne, b. 9 July, 1769; m. William Scott, of Graiguenaskerry, Queen's Co.
      (3) Patience, b. March, 1771; d. June, 1772.
      (4) Frances Margaret Sarah, b. June, 1772; d. 1775.
      (5) Patience, b. Oct. 1773; m. 1801, Henry T. Warner.
      (6) Harriett, b. 1781; m. 26 Jan. 1799, Rev. Richard Clarke, Rector of Geashill, King's Co.
   2. Nicholas, of Glenkeen, near Borrisoleigh, co. Tipperary, b. 1737; m. 1st, by licence, 1759, Elizabeth, dau. of Charles Dempsey, of Dublin, and had issue,
      (1) Francis, of Mount Oliver, Queen's Co., b. 1770; m. Mary, dau. of Major Richard Steele, of Kyle, Queen's Co., and d. 1826, having had issue,
         1. Nicholas of Congor, co. Tipperary, and of Fortal, King's Co., b. 1803; m. 1st, 1833, Catherine, dau. of Rev. Edward Lucas, of Rathkenny, co. Cavan. She d. 1834, leaving issue,
            a. Francis Edward, of Fortal, Lieut.-Col. late 9th Regt., B.A. Trin. Coll. Dublin, J.P. King's Co. (Marie Lodge, Dalkey), b. 1834; m. 1861, Annabella, dau. of John Campbell Kennedy, of Ballyrainey House, co. Down, and has issue,
               (a) Nicholas Trafalgar, Major Durham L.I. (Northwood, Andover, Hants), b. 6 Dec. 1863; m. 1894, Marion Flora Campbell, dau. of Capt. Augustus Warburton, 15th Regt., and has issue,
                  Francis John, b. 1896.
                  Mary Eileen Frances.
               (b) Hugh Wray, Major 4th Batt. Connaught Rangers, b. 1866; m. Nov. 1903, Violet, 3rd dau. of John Gregory Martyn, J.P., and has issue,
                  1. Cecil. 2. Francis.
                  3. Sheelah.
               (c) Arthur Stuart, b. 1867; d. 1878.
               (d) Charles Thomas, Captain 3rd Batt. Leinster Regt.; d. in S. Africa, 1900.
               (a) Catherine Mary, d. at Bangalore, 1869.
               (b) Amy, m. 1st, 1896, Surg.-Capt. Walker (who d. 1898), and 2ndly, 1902, Wilfred FitzGerald, son of Capt. Crofton FitzGerald.
               (c) May Teresa, m. 1904, Lieut. Charles Pease, Loyal N. Lancs. Regt.
               (d) Beatrix Anne.
            He m. 2ndly, 1839, Isabella, dau. of James Digges La Touche, of Sans Souci, co. Dublin. She d. 19 Sept. 1888. He d. 5 April, 1888, leaving issue, by her
            b. James Digges La Touche, b. 1842; d. 1896.
            c. Robert Waller, Fleet Surgeon R.N., b. 1845; m. Caroline, dau. of Rev. F. T. Studdert, and has issue,
               Robert Nicholas William, Surgeon R.N.
               Caroline Isabella.
            d. William Nicholas, b. 1848.
            e. Richard Edmund, Dep. Surg.-Gen. R.N., b. 1852; m. Gertrude, dau. of Dr. Allen, and has issue three daus., Violet, Hyacinth, and Muriel.
            a. Isabella, m. 1860, William Henry Head, of Derrylahan, King's Co., D.L., and has issue (see that family).
            b. Mary. c. Anne, d. unm. 1901.
            d. Grace, d. unm. 1896. e. Ellen, d. unm.
         2. Richard, m. Catherine, dau. of Col. Bates, and d. 1888, leaving issue, settled in Canada.
         3. Francis Waller, m. Miss Shore.
         1. Anne, m. 1823, Capt. Hugh Boyd Wray, 40th Regt., and had issue.

(2) Thomas, Midshipman R.N., drowned on the Royal George when she went down in 1788.
(1) Elizabeth, m. 1st, 22 July, 1789, Jonathan Willington, of Castle Willington, and 2ndly, 1806, Sir Robert Waller, Bart., of Merton Hall, co. Tipperary. Lady Waller inherited by will of her cousin Margaret, Mrs. Bernard, a moiety of the Rathrobin and Fortal estates, and d.s.p. 1851.
Mr. Nicholas Biddulph m. 2ndly, 1776, Hannah, dau. of Joseph Cooke, of Currangreny, co. Tipperary, and d. 1799, having by her had issue,
(2) Hannah, m. John Grene, of Cappamurra, co. Tipperary.
3. Richard, m. 1755, Prudence Toukes, and d.s.p.
4. John, Lieut. in the Army, m. 30 Nov. 1769, Alice, dau. of Angel Scott, and widow of Nicholas Biddulph, of Fortal, and d.s.p.
1. Mary.
1. Alice, m. by licence, 29 Jan. 1701, Kildare Tarleton, of Geashill and Ballylevin, King's Co. (who d. 1711), and d.s.p.
2. Jane.

The elder son,

FRANCIS BIDDULPH, of Rathrobin and Fortal, King's Co., got a lease of Fortal for ever from Lord Shelbourne 1722, b. 1690; m. by licence, 7 Aug. 1712, Mary, dau. of Robert Jackson, of Knockinglass, co. Tipperary, and by her had a son,

NICHOLAS BIDDULPH, of Rathrobin and Fortal, J.P., High Sheriff 1741, m. 1st (settlement dated 26 April, 1736), Patience, eldest dau. of Thomas Colley, of Killurin, King's Co., and by her had issue,
1. Margaret, m. 1st, 1762, Alexander Coruwall, of Lismola, co. Limerick (who d. 1779), and 2ndly, 1780, Thomas Bernard, of Castletown, King's Co. (see BERNARD of Castle Bernard), and d.s.p. 31 March, 1811.
2. Sarah, m. 8 Feb. 1769, Gifford Nesbitt, of Tubberdaly, King's Co., and d.s.p. 1772, having bequeathed her moiety of the estate to her sister Margaret.

He m. 2ndly, 1754, Alice, eldest dau. of Angel Scott, of Caharacco. Clare, and by her (who m. 2ndly, John Biddulph) had a son,
1. Angel, d. a minor.
He d. 11 June, 1762. His cousin,

FRANCIS HARRISON BIDDULPH, of Vicarstown, Registrar of the Court of Exchequer (son of Francis Biddulph, of Vicarstown) had a protracted dispute 1811-24, in regard to the Rathrobin and Fortal estates with Sir Robert Waller on the death of his cousin Margaret, Mrs. Bernard (see above), and eventually s. by compromise to the Rathrobin portion, while Fortal went to his cousin Nicholas Biddulph, of Congor (see above). He was b. 26 Dec. 1774; m. 1797, Mary, eldest dau. of Francis Marsh, Barrister-at-Law (see that family). She d. 9 Aug. 1861, aged 88. He d. July, 1827, having had issue,
1. FRANCIS MARSH, of whom presently.
2. Nicholas, b. 20 Dec. 1805; m. Miss Steele, and d. 1900.
3. William Francis, b. 1 March, 1809; d. young.
4. Anne, b. 15 Sept. 1798; m. Captain Simon Biddulph, Regt., son of Sir Theophilus Biddulph, Bart., and had issue (see BURKE'S Peerage). He d. 25 April, 1823.
2. Elizabeth, b. 10 Nov. 1799; d. 10 June, 1893.
3. Mary, b. 10 March, 1801; d. 10 Sept. 1801.
4. Mary, b. 16 Sept. 1803; d. 2 April, 1863.
5. Frances.
6. Harriet, b. 8 Nov. 1810, went to America.
7. Jane, b. 8 May, 1812, went to America.
8. Sarah, b. 11 Dec. 1814, went to Australia.
9. Charlotte, b. 9 Dec. 1815. 10. Patience, b. March, 1817.
11. Caroline, b. 16 May, 1819; d. 28 May, 1874.

The eldest son,

FRANCIS MARSH BIDDULPH, of Rathrobin, b. April, 1802; m. 1845, Lucy, 2nd dau. of Robert Bickerstaffe, of Preston, Lancashire. She d. 29 Aug. 1896, aged 75. He d. 28 March, 1868, having had issue,
1. Francis, b. 14 Aug., d. 31 Aug. 1848.
2. MIDDLETON WESTENRA, now of Rathrobin.
3. Assheton, of Moneyguyneen, King's Co., b. 12 Oct. 1850; m 17 June, 1880, Florence Caroline, younger dau. of Rev. Cunningham Boothby, Vicar of Holwell, Oxfordshire, and has issue,
   1. Robert Assheton, b. 4 Aug. 1891.
      1. Kathleen Jane, b. 12 May, 1881; m. 22 Jan. 1906, Arthur Tilson Shaen Magan, and has issue (see MAGAN of Clonearl).
      2. Ierne Grace, b. 6 Jan. 1884.
   3. Norah Beatrice, b. 15 Nov. 1885.
   4. Ethne Patricia, b. 17 March, 1889.
4. Franc Digby, b. 22 April, 1853; m. 15 Sept. 1885, Louisa Colclough, dau. of John Thomas Rossborough-Colclough and heiress of Tintern Abbey, and assumed the additional name of COLCLOUGH. He d. 13 July, 1895, leaving issue (see COLCLOUGH of Tintern Abbey).
1. Annie Adela Waller, b. 25 March, 1847; m. 1866, Capt. Willcocks, of St. Lawrence, Chapelizod.
2. Gertrude Louisa, b. 22 Sept. 1856; m. 1st, 25 Feb. George Carpenter Anderson, and 2ndly, 1890, Dr. Nevil Pour Cadell.

Seat—Rathrobin, Tullamore. Club—Naval and Military.

BIDDULPH-COLCLOUGH. See COLCLOUGH.

BIGGS-ATKINSON. See ATKINSON.

BINGHAM OF BINGHAM CASTLE.

Denis George Broad Bingham, of Bingham Castle, co. Mayo, b. 27 Nov. 1875; s. his grandfather 1902; m. 2 June, 1909, Ina Mary, dau. of Capt. George Alexander Broad, M.V.O., R.N. (retired), commanding H.M. Yacht *Alberta*.

Lineage.—This family is a cadet branch of BINGHAM *of Melcombe Bingham (see that family)*, and descends from a common ancestor with the Earls of Lucan and the Lords Clanmorris.

George Bingham, Military Governor of Sligo 1596, *m.* 1569, Cicely, dau. of Robert Martin, and had issue,
1. Henry, ancestor of the Earls of Lucan.
2. John, of whom we treat.

The younger son,
John Bingham, resided at Foxford, co. Mayo. He was grandfather of
The Right Hon. Henry Bingham, of Newbrook, at one time one of the Lords Justices of Ireland, whose son,
John Bingham, of Newbrook, *m.* 1 June, 1738, Frances, eldest dau. and co-heir (with her sister Susannah, wife of Thomas Carter, Castle Martin, co. Kildare) of Sir Arthur Shaen, Bart., and was father of
Henry Bingham, of Newbrook, *m.* Oct. 1761, Letitia, dau. of Denis Daly, of Raford, co. Galway, by his wife, Lady Anne de Burgh, sister of John, 11th Earl of Clanricarde, and had issue,
1. John, of Newbrook, father of 1st Lord Clanmorris.
2. Henry, of whom presently.
3. Denis, of Bingham Castle, co. Mayo, whose eldest dau., Anne, *m.* her cousin Robert Augustus Bingham (*see below*).
1. Anne, *m.* 1778, Christopher French St. George, of Tyrone House, co. Galway. 2. Frances.
3. Letitia. 4. Charlotte.
5. Harriett. 6. Louisa.
d. 1790. The 2nd son,
Henry Bingham, *m.* 1795, Anne, dau. of Robert Bodkin, of gh. co. Galway, and had issue,

Henry, *d.s.p.* 2. Robert Augustus, his heir.
3. John Charles (Rev.), *m.* Sarah, dau. of Luke Higgins, of Castlebar.
1. Anne. 2. Maria.
3. Harriet, *m.* Benjamin Jenings.
The 2nd son,
Robert Augustus Bingham, *m.* 1817, his cousin Anne, eldest dau. of Major Denis Bingham, of Bingham Castle, co. Mayo, and *d.* 1828, leaving issue,
1. Denis, late of Bingham Castle.
2. Henry, of Annagh House, co. Mayo, *m.* 1st, Sept. 1846, Margaret F. McGrale, by whom he had, with other issue,
Robert Augustus, *b.* 11 June, 1848 ; *d.* 1884 ; *m.* 1879, Helen Halliday Little, by whom he had issue,
Henry Herbert Shaen, of Annagh, Belmullet, co. Mayo, J.P., *b.* 22 Feb. 1881 ; *m.* 6 June, 1906, Annie Frances, only dau. of late John Thompson, of Windsor Park, Belfast, and has issue,
1. Josephine Frances Doreen.
2. Sheila Mary Geraldine.
Mr. Henry Bingham *m.* 2ndly, 1876, Maria, 5th dau. of the late Benjamin Jenings, of Mount Jenings co. Mayo. He *d.* 27 March, 1894, leaving issue by both marriages.
3. Robert Augustus.
1. Anne, *d. unm.* 17 March, 1897.
2. Maria, *m.* George d'Arcy, of co. Westmeath, and had issue.
3. Letitia, *d. unm.*
The eldest son,
Denis Bingham, of Bingham Castle, co. Mayo, J.P., *b.* 8 Sept. 1818 ; *m.* 19 Feb. 1846, Elizabeth Elinor, only child and heiress of Arthur Nash, of Carne House, co. Mayo. She *d.* 11 Jan. 1894. He *d.* 4 Dec. 1902, having had issue,
Denis George Charles Arthur, *b.* 19 Nov. 1849 ; *m.* 1874, Maria Mary Hutchinson, eldest dau. of Capt. W. E. Broad, R.N. *d.* 19 April, 1881. He *d.v.p.* 1878, leaving issue,
Denis George Broad, now of Bingham Castle.
Charles Henry Arthur Shaen Richard, *b.* 9 April, 1877.
Gerald Henry, *b.* 6 July, 1855 ; *m.* 1877, Augusta Cecilia Morton, dau. of the late Rowland Agustus Griffith Davies, of Fick, Cornwall.
Hard Lionel Nash, *b.* 29 Oct. 1856, *d.* 1901.
Bert Milcombe, *b.* 31 Aug. 1858 ; *d.* 12 Feb. 1864.
Maide Elizabeth, *m.* 10 July, 1867, Henry Tilson, eldest heir of Thomas Shaen Carter, of Watlington Park, Oxon, *d.* 1884.
Constance Letitia Anne, *m.* 1873, Cochrane E. Palmer, eld. son of Robert Palmer, J.P., of Beckfield House, Queen's Co. th Clara, *d. unm.* 4. Frances Anne Shaen, *d. unm.*

5. Ernestine Elizabeth, *d. unm.*
6. Viola Alexandra, *m.* 1885, Arthur Shaen-Carter, Lieut. R.N.

Arms—Az., a bend, cotised between six crosses-pattée, or. *Crest*—A rock, thereon an eagle, rising, all ppr. *Motto*—Spes mea Christus.

Seat—Bingham Castle, Belmullet, co. Mayo.

BINGHAM. *See* Burke's Peerage, **CLANMORRIS, B.**

BINGHAM. *See* Burke's Peerage, **LUCAN, E.**

BLACKBURNE OF TANKARDSTOWN.

Francis William Blackburne, of Tankardstown, co. Meath, J.P., High Sheriff 1898, *b.* 7 March, 1851 ; *m.* 9 Dec. 1895, Olivia Beatrice Louisa, youngest dau. of Col. John Anstruther Thomson, of Charleton, Fife, N.B., and has had issue,
1. William John Anstruther, *b.* 30 Nov. 1904.
1. Mary Elizabeth Rosia St. Clair. *d.* 1904.
2. Elena Frances Margaret Anne.
3. Amabel Clementina Olive Georgina.

Lineage.—George Blackburne, of co. Meath, *d.* in March, 1769, leaving by Mary his wife, a dau., Mary, and three sons, Richard ; Edward, J.P. for Meath ; and Anthony, Barrister-at-Law, whose will was proved 1 June, 1804 ; he left issue, Anthony J.P., of Parsonstown, co. Meath, High Sheriff 1829, and three daus., of whom the eldest *m.* Anthony Crofton. The eldest son,
Richard Blackburne, of Great Foot'stown, co. Meath, *m.* (licence dated 1774) Elizabeth, dau. of Francis Hopkins, by Jane Foster his wife, and by her (who *d.* 1826) had issue,
1. Francis (Right Hon.), of Rathfarnham Castle.
1. Jane, *m.* William Webb, Deputy Commissary-General, and *d.* 1860.
2. Eliza. 3. Anna Maria.
Mr. Blackburne *d.* 1798. His son,
Right Hon. Francis Blackburne, of Rathfarnham Castle, co. Dublin, *b.* 11 Nov. 1782 ; *m.* 1809, Jane, dau. of William Martley, M.D., son of John Martley, of Ballyfallan, co. Meath. and by her (who *d.* Sept. 1872) had issue,
1. William Martley, his heir.
2. Francis, *b.* 1822 ; *d. unm.* 1863.
3. Edward, of Rathfarnham Castle, co. Dublin, J.P., LL.D., Q.C., *b.* 1823 ; *m.* 1857, Georgiana Arabella, dau. of Robert Graves, of Merrion Square, Dublin. He *d.* 7 Dec. 1902, leaving issue by her, who *d.* 18 Jan. 1911,
Francis, *b.* 1859.
Georgiana Beatrice.
4. Frederick John, J.P., of Renny House, co. Cork, and Keymer, Sussex, *b.* 1827 ; *m.* 1856, Annette, dau. of Eardley Hall, of Wilmington, Essex, and *d.* Oct. 1863, leaving a son,
Frederick John Eardley, *b.* 1858 ; *m.* 1885, Mary Elizabeth, 2nd dau. of Henry Dixon, of Watlington, Oxon.
5. John Henry, *b.* 1828 ; *m.* 1857, Elizabeth, dau. of Anthony Crofton, of Lincoln's Inn, Barrister-at-Law.
6. Anthony, *d. unm.* 1867.
1. Alicia Catherine, *m.* Capt. George Daniel, R.N., who *d.* 1856.
2. Jane Isabella, *m.* Thomas Rice Henn, Q.C., D.L., of Paradise Hill, co. Clare, Recorder of Galway, who *d.* 29 April, 1902, leaving issue (*see that family*).
3. Elizabeth, *m.* Thomas Percival Westby, of Roebuck Castle, co. Dublin, and *d.* 1863.
This distinguished lawyer, who held in Ireland the great legal appointments of Attorney-General, Master of the Rolls, Lord Chief Justice, Lord Justice of Appeal, and Lord High Chancellor, was educated at Trinity College (where he gained the gold medal), and was called to the Irish bar, 1805. In 1822 he became King's Counsel, and 1826 Sergeant-at-Law. He *d.* 17 Sept. 1867, and was bur. at Mount Jerome, co. Dublin. His eldest son,
William Martley Blackburne, of Tankardstown, co. Meath, *b.* 1821 ; *m.* 1847, Mary, dau. of the Rev. William Thorpe, D.D., and *d.* 8 May, 1868, leaving by her (who *m.* 2ndly, 10 Dec. 1869, George Lefroy, and *d.* Sept. 1889),
1. Francis William, his heir.
2. Augustus Edward William, *b.* 1860 ; *m.* 1891, Isabella Eyre, of Florence, Italy, and *d.* Feb. 1893, leaving issue,
Francis Currell, *b.* May, 1892.
1. Eva Amabel, *m.* July, 1890, Charles Currell Eyre, of Florence, Italy. She *d.* 15 June, 1909.

Seat—Tankardstown, Slane, co. Meath. *Clubs*—Oxford and Cambridge ; Kildare Street, Dublin.

BLACKER OF CARRICKBLACKER AND WOODBROOK.

REV. ROBERT SHAPLAND CAREW BLACKER, of Woodbrook, co. Wexford, and Carrickblacker, co. Armagh, J.P. cos. Wexford and Armagh, M.A. Trin. Coll. Dublin, formerly Rector of Marholm, co. Northampton, and Honorary Canon of Peterborough, b. 29 Jan. 1826; m. 9 Sept. 1858, Theodosia Charlotte Sophia, dau. of the late George Meara, of May Park, co. Waterford, and Sarah Catherine his wife, sister of Edward Southwell, 3rd Viscount Bangor. She d. 1890, having had issue,

1. William Robert George, b. 29 Feb. 1860; d. 13 March 1880.
2. EDWARD CAREW, J.P. and D.L. co. Wexford, High Sheriff 1908 b. 13 July, 1863.
3. Stewart Ward William, late Major R.F.A., J.P., for co. Armagh, b. 4 July, 1865; m. 6 Jan. 1903, Eva Mary Lucy St. John only child of Col. Edward Albert FitzRoy, of Hale Place, Farnham, Surrey (see BURKE'S *Peerage*, SOUTHAMPTON, B.), and has issue,
   1. William Desmond, b. 20 Sept. 1903.
   2. Robert Stewart, b. 21 Sept. 1909.
   3. Terence FitzRoy, b. 15 Oct. 1910.
   1. Betty Mary, b. 20 Dec. 1905.
   2. Joan Lucy, b. 28 July, 1908.

Lineage.—The first of the family who settled in Armagh, VALENTINE BLACKER, of Carrick, co. Armagh, Commandant of Horse and Foot, b. 1597, went from Poppleton, Yorks, to Ireland and purchased in 1660, from Sir Anthony Cope, of Loughgall, the manor of Carrowbrack, subsequently known as Carrickblacker. He m. Judith, dau. of Michael Harrison of Ballydargan, co. Down (who d. 27 March, 1664), and d. 17 Aug. 1677, leaving issue,
1. Ferdinando, "Capitaine-Leifftenante" in Sir John Savile's troop of Horse. Will proved P.C.C.
2. GEORGE, of whom next.
1. Violetta, m. — Gill.   2. Dora.
3. Maud.

GEORGE BLACKER, of Carrickblacker, a firm adherent of the royal house of Stuart, Lieut.-Col. in the Army, High Sheriff of Armagh 1684, m. Rose, dau. and heiress of William Latham, of Ballytroan, co. Tyrone, by Rosa his wife, dau. of Rowland Young, of Drakestown, who d. in 1689. He was s. by his son,
WILLIAM BLACKER, of Carrick and Ballytroan, a staunch supporter of WILLIAM III, fought at the Boyne; he m. 1st, about the year 1666, Elizabeth, dau. of Col. the Hon. Robert Stewart, of Irry and Stewart Hall, in the co. Tyrone, 3rd son of Andrew, 1st Lord Castlestewart, and by her (who d. 11 Jan. 1678) he had issue,
1. STEWART, his heir.
2. Robert, ancestor of BLACKER of *Drogheda and Meath*.
Mr. Blacker m. 2ndly, Hannah Lawrence, and 3rdly, Theodosia, dau. of Oliver St. John, of Tanderagee Castle, co. Armagh, and had issue,
3. Samuel, ancestor of BLACKER of *Elm Park and Tullahinel*.
Mr. Blacker d. 1732, and was s. by his eldest son,
STEWART BLACKER, of Carrickblacker, High Sheriff co. Tyrone 1706, b. in 1671; m. 1704, Barbara, dau. of the Rev. Henry Young, A.M., and niece and heiress of William Latham, of Brookend, co. Tyrone, and by her (will proved 1743) had issue,
1. WILLIAM, his heir.
2. Latham, b. 1711; m. Martha, dau. of Peter Beaver, of Drogheda, by whom (who d. Sept. 1802) he left issue (see BURKE'S *Family Records*).
3. Henry (Rev.), M.A., b. 10 July, 1713; m. Miss Martin, and had a dau.,
Frances, who d. unm. 1831.
4. George, of Hallsmill, co. Down, b. 26 Sept. 1718; m. 1st, 1744, Mary, only surviving dau. of Joseph Nicholson, LL.D.; and 2ndly, 1746, Alicia, only child of Edward Dowdall, of Mountown, co. Meath, and had with other issue, James Blacker, of Dublin, J.P., b. 14 Aug. 1759; m. Miss Mansergh, and had, *inter alios*, Rev. George Blacker, Chaplain to the city of Dublin, and Rector of Taghadoe, co. Kildare, who d.s.p. May, 1871.
1. Barbara, b. 23 Oct. 1706; m. James Twigg, of Roghan Castle, co. Tyrone.
Mr. Blacker d. 1751, aged 80, and was s. by his eldest son,
WILLIAM BLACKER, of Carrickblacker and Brookend, High Sheriff co. Armagh 1734, and co. Tyrone 1749, b. 12 Sept. 1709; m. 8 Aug. 1738, Letitia, eldest dau. of Henry Cary, of Dungiven Castle, M.P. for co. Londonderry, and had issue,

1. STEWART, his heir.
2. William, Capt. 105th Regt., served in the American War, m. 1784, Susan, dau. and heiress of Ven. Arthur Jacob, of Woodbrook, co. Wexford, Archdeacon of Armagh, and Rector of Killanne, and had issue,
   1. William, of Woodbrook, s. to his mother's estate, b. 1790; m. 1814, Elizabeth Anne, dau. of Robert Shapland Carew, of Castleboro, co. Wexford, and sister of Robert Shapland, 1st Lord Carew, Lieutenant of co. Wexford, and d. May, 1831, having by her (who d. 19 March, 1877) had issue,
      (1) William Jacob, of Woodbrook, J.P., D.L., High Sheriff 1852, Major Wexford Militia, b. 1823; m. 26 May, 1849, Elizabeth, dau. of Hervey Pratt de Montmorency, of Castlemorres, co. Kilkenny, by Rose Lloyd his wife, dau. of Right Rev. John Kearney, D.D., Bishop of Ossory, and d.s.p. 27 Dec. 1869, when he was s. by his only brother.
      (2) ROBERT SHAPLAND CAREW, heir to his brother, present representative of the family.
      (1) Anne, m. 16 Nov. 1848, Sir Robert Joshua Paul, 3rd bart. of Ballyglan, and d. May, 1858, leaving issue.
      (2) Susan, m. 8 Jan. 1840, Very Rev. Anthony La Touche Kirwan, Dean of Limerick, son of Very Rev. Walter Blake Kirwan, Dean of Killala. She d. 17 May, 1908.
      (3) Ellen Letitia, d. Feb. 1908.
      (4) Hannah Dorothea, m. 1 Oct. 1858, John Yeoman, of Milton, co. Northampton. She d. 7 Feb. 1910.
      (5) Jane Mary.
   2. Edward, d. unm.
   1. Letitia.   2. Jane.
   3. Hannah.   4. Susan.
3. Henry, Capt. 65th Regt., who served in the American War, and was wounded and taken prisoner with General Burgoyne, at Saratoga. He inherited from his maternal uncle, the Right Hon Edward Cary, the house and property of Milburn, co. Derry, and d. 1 Sept. 1827, leaving his estates to his nephew, the Rev Richard Olpherts.
4. George (Rev.), Vicar of Seagoe, d. 1 May, 1810, aged 46.
   1. Eliza, b. 1739; m. Sir William Dunkin, Judge of the Supreme Court of Judicature, Bengal.
   2. Barbara, m. Richard Olpherts, of Armagh, and had issue.
   3. Martha, d. unm. 1840.
   4. Alicia, m. 1772, General Sir James Stewart Denham, Bart G.C.H.   5. Jane, m. James Fleming, of Belleville. co. Cavan
   6. Letitia, m. Lieut.-Gen. the Hon Edward Stopford, 2nd son of James, 1st Earl of Courtown.   7. Lucinda, d. unm. 1843.
Mr. Blacker d. 1783, and was s. by his eldest son,
THE VERY REV. STEWART BLACKER, of Carrickblacker, Dean of Leighlin, Archdeacon of Dromore, Rector of Dumcree, Moyntaga, and Donagheloney, and Vicar of Seagoe, b. 1740; m. Eliza, dau. of Sir Hugh Hill, Bart., M.P. for Londonderry, by whom (who d. 27 Feb. 1797) he had four sons and five daus.,
1. WILLIAM, his heir.
2. George, Capt. F.I.C.S., b. 27 Dec. 1784; m. Anne, dau. of Capt. William Sloane, Royal Bengal Artillery, and had issue
   1. STEWART, of Carrickblacker, s. his uncle.
   1. Eliza Hill, m. 29 Feb. 1844, Thomas Eyre Hodder, son of Col. Hodder, of Hoddersfield, co. Cork.
   2. Hester Anne, m. 14 April, 1859, Frederick Ludwig von Stieglitz, of the Glen, co. Armagh, Baron von Stieglitz. She d.s.p. Jan. 1893.
   3. Sophia Mary, d. unm. 30 April, 1838.
Capt. George Blacker d. 31 Aug. 1815.
3. Stewart, Capt. R.N., d. unm. 25 April, 1826.
4. James Stewart (Rev.), A.M., Rector of Keady, co. Armagh, b. 16 Feb. 1795; m. 30 Nov. 1824, Eliza, eldest dau. of Conyngham Greg, of Ballymenoch, co. Down, and dying 1835, left issue,
   1. Stewart Beresford, b. Dec. 1826; d.s.p. 4 May, 1853.
   2. James Conyngham, b. April, 1832; d.s.p. 28 April, 1870.
   1. Eliza.   2. Sophia.
1. Letitia, m. George Studdert, of Bunratty Castle, co. Clare, and d. 8 April, 1831.
2. Sophia, m. 1st, Matthew Forde, of Seaforde, co. Down; and 2ndly, 1818, William Stewart Hamilton, of Brownhall, co. Donegal. She d. June, 1829.
3. Eliza, m. 1st, Hugh Lyons Montgomery, of Belhavel, co. Leitrim, and Lawrencetown, co. Down. He was killed by a fall from his horse, 26 April, 1826. She m. 2ndly, in France, 29 Sept 1830, Monsieur de Chompré, Royal Cuirassiers.
4. Louisa, m. John Rea, of St. Columbs, co. Derry (who d. 1830) she d. 1815.   5. Caroline, d. unm. 30 April, 1828.
Dean Blacker d. 1 Dec. 1826, aged 86, and was s. by his son,
LIEUT.-COL. WILLIAM BLACKER, of Carrickblacker, M.A., b. 1 Sept. 1777, Lieut.-Col. Armagh Militia, J.P. and D.L., High Sheriff 1811; m. Nov. 1810, Anne, eldest dau. of Sir Andrew Ferguson, Bart., M.P., but had no issue. Col. Blacker was appointed Vice-Treasurer of Ireland Jan. 1817, and held office until 1829, when he resigned. He d.s.p. 25 Nov. 1855, and was s. by his nephew,
STEWART BLACKER, of Carrickblacker, J.P., D.L., M.A., M.R.I.A., Barrister-at-Law, High Sheriff 1859, d. unm. 16 Dec. 1881, when Carrickblacker devolved on his sister, the Baroness Stieglitz, for her life, and the representation of the family reverted to his kinsman, REV. ROBERT SHAPLAND CAREW BLACKER, of Woodbrook.

Arms—Arg., on a mount vert, a warrior in complete armour in the act of advancing towards the right and brandishing in his dexter hand a battle-axe ppr., from his shoulder a mantle flowing gules. *Crest*—A dexter armed arm embowed ppr., the hand gauntletted and grasping a battle-axe ppr. *Motto*—Pro Deo et rege.

Seats—Woodbrook, Killanne, Enniscorthy, co. Wexford, and Carrickblacker, Portadown, co. Armagh. *Club*—Kildare Street.

Blacker. THE LANDED GENTRY. 46

BLACKER-DOUGLASS. See DOUGLASS.

BLACKWOOD. See BURKE'S PEERAGE, DUFFERIN, M.

BLACKWOOD-PRICE. See PRICE.

BLAKE OF RENVYLE.

EDGAR VALENTINE MYLES BLAKE, of Renvyle, co. Galway, b. 1 Dec. 1903; s. his father 20 May, 1910.

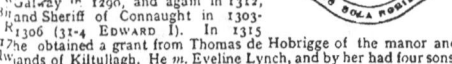

Lineage.—In 6 EDWARD I (1278), the castle and lands of Kiltorroge, and the castle and four quarters of Ballim'croe (now Carn(more) situate in the Barony of Dunkellin in the co. Galway, were granted to RICHARD CADDELL, who took the name of Niger or Blake, and was the common ancestor of all the families of Blake in Connaught. He was Portreeve of the town of Galway in 1290, and again in 1312, and Sheriff of Connaught in 1303-1306 (31-4 EDWARD I). In 1315 he obtained a grant from Thomas de Hobrigge of the manor and lands of Kiltullagh. He m. Eveline Lynch, and by her had four sons,
1. WALTER, of whom presently.
2. John, who m. Joanna Godsun, and had two sons, William and Edmund, whose will was proved at Athenry, 16 Oct. 1420.
3. Nicholas.   4. Valentine.

The eldest son,
WALTER BLAKE, Burgess of Galway, got a grant of the customs of Galway, 3 Dec. 1346. He made his will, March, 1357 (31 EDWARD III) granting all his lands to his elder son, Henry. He left issue, five sons,
1. Henry (senior), Burgess of Galway, got a lease, 4 Feb. 1383, for 20 years of the tithes of Doflyche, near Galway, from Dermot O'Conor, Abbott of Knockmoy (Collis Victoria). He was indicted for high treason for joining in the rebellion of Sir William (or Ulick) de Burgh, in 1388, but received pardon for this on returning to the king's allegiance in 1395. His will is dated 1421 (9 HENRY V), and by it he devises all his lands to his nephew, William Blake (son of his brother, Geoffrey Blake), and his heirs, with remainders to his other nephews, Walter (Oge) Blake (second son of his brother, John (Oge) Blake), and Henry Blake (son of his brother, Thomas (Niger) Blake). He left issue, one child only,
Silly (Cille or Gyllie), who on the 6 Oct. 1438 (17 HENRY VI), as dau. and heir of Henry Blake, deceased, granted by deed to her cousin german, Henry Blake, son and heir of John (Oge) Bakel, burgess of Athenry, all the messuages, lands and tenements that descended or might in future descend to her as heir of her father. In 1435 this Silly Blake joined with her cousins, Henry Blake, jun. (son of John Oge Blake); Walter Oge Blake; William (FitzGeoffrey) Blake; and Henry (FitzThomas Niger) Blake, in making a perpetual grant to the parish church of St. Nicholas in Galway.
2. JOHN (Oge), of whom presently.
3. Geoffrey, ancestor of the Blakes of Ballyglunin, of Ballinafad, and the Blakes, Lords Wallscourt.
4. Thomas (Niger), who left a son,
Henry, mentioned as remainder-man in the will of his uncle, Henry Blake, senior, dated 1421.
5. William, mentioned in the will of his brother, John Oge Blake dated 1420.

The 2nd son,
JOHN (OGE) BLAKE, Provost of Athenry in 1394, obtained in 1395 a grant of lands in Athenry from Philip, son of William Bermingham of Athenry. He m. Margaret, dau. of Philip le Brun and made his will 1420, leaving issue,
1. HENRY (junior), of whom presently.
2. Walter, a legatee under the will of his uncle, Henry Blake, senior (see above). In 1435 he joined with his brother Henry and his cousins in the grant of a sum of money in perpetuity to St. Nicholas' Church, Galway.

The eldest son,
HENRY BLAKE (junior), a burgess of Galway and of Athenry, mentioned in a deed of award, dated 1424. In 1435 he joined with his brother Walter (Oge) and his first cousins William FitzGeoffrey, Silly (dau. of Henry Blake, senior), and Henry (FitzThomas Niger), in the grant to St. Nicholas' Church, Galway; in 1438 he got the grant from his first cousin, Silly, already referred to. He m. Mary, dau. of Bermingham, of Athenry, and made his will 1457, in which he bequeathed certain houses and lands in the liberties of Athenry to his eldest son, and other lands to his four younger sons. He left issue,
1. JOHN, of whom presently.
2. Nicholas, mentioned in the will of his father, and in an award dated 1490, between him and his brother Richard.
3. Thomas, mentioned in his father's will, and d. without issue, as stated in the award of 1490.
4. Walter, mentioned in his father's will.
5. Richard, mentioned in his father's will, d.s.p.m. 1502.

The eldest son,
JOHN BLAKE, burgess of Galway, agreed in 1445 (together with his father, Henry) to refer to the arbitration of Willig Burke, Lord of Clanrickarde, and Sheriff of Connaught, and Master John, Friar-Gen. of the Friar Preachers, all disputes between himself and his cousin William FitzGeoffrey Blake concerning the division of the lands of Henry Blake, senior, deceased. He m. Juliana French, and made his will 14 March, 1468, in which he mentions his wife and children. He appointed John, son of William Blake, and Nicholas French, executors, and Peter Lynch and Robert French overseers. He left issue,
1. VALENTINE, of whom presently.
2. William, mentioned in his father's will, m. Katiline MacCurke, and made his will, 1488, appointing his brother Valentine the executor, and recommending to his care his son and daughters.
1. Eveline, mentioned in her father's will; m. Peter Lynch, 1st Mayor of Galway, in 1486.
2. Anorine, mentioned in her father's will.

The elder son,
VALENTINE (VADYN) BLAKE, mentioned in his father's will; m. 1st, Margaret Skerrett, and 2ndly, Eveline, dau. of Geoffrey Lynch, and made his will 12 July, 1499 (proved 26 July following), leaving issue,
1. JOHN (only son by the first wife), of whom presently.
2. Valentine (Oge), mentioned in the will, 1499, of his father, Valentine, d.s.p.
3. Thomas, ancestor of the BLAKES of Towerhill (see that family).
4. William, mentioned in his father's will 1499, d.s.p.
5. Francis.
1. Anastasia, living 1499, m. William Browne (FitzStephen).

The eldest son,
JOHN BLAKE, m. Eveline Skerret, and d. about 1503, leaving issue, a son and two daus.
1. NICHOLAS, of whom presently.
1. Julia, m. Ambrose Bodkin (FitzJohn), who was bailiff of Galway 1570.   2. Anstace, m. before 1543, John Niel, of Galway.

The only son,
NICHOLAS BLAKE, Mayor of Galway 1555. An award was made 6 July, 1542 (34 HENRY VIII), by Patrick Barnewall, Serjeant-at-Law, between this Nicholas Blake and his kinsman Richard Blake, son of Geoffrey (see BLAKE of Ballyglunin), to settle disputes between them as to the division of lands inherited from Henry Blake, sen. Nicholas Blake m. 1st, Ennes, dau. of Marcus French, and 2nd son of Geoffrey French, but she d.s.p. He m. 2ndly, in 1556, Cecilia, dau. of Walter Lynch, and made his will 18 Sept. 1564 (proved 28 Sept. 1568), having by her had issue,
JOHN, of whom presently.
Eveline, m. John Lynch (FitzRichard FitzSander).

The only son,
JOHN BLAKE, Burgess of Galway. On 6 March, 1571, a decree was made on the complaint of this John Blake, or Cadell, and of John FitzRichard Blake or Cadell (see BLAKE of Ballyglunin), by the Lord President and Council of Connaught, by which it was decreed that the lands belonging to the complainants in Kiltullagh, &c., should be held by them for ever, free from all charges to the Queen or any other charges. This decree was ratified and confirmed by a decree made 25 Oct. 1616, by the Lord Deputy and Commissioners appointed for settling the King's (JAMES I.) compositions. He mortgaged, 27 June, 1579 (22 ELIZABETH), a moiety of the lands of Morughe and Doulis in the franchises of Galway, to Julian Browne, wife of John Blake FitzRichard (see BLAKE of Ballyglunin), and this mortgage was redeemed in 1593. He m. Cecilia Skerret, and d. 20 April, 1581, having by her (who survived him) had issue, a son,
NICHOLAS BLAKE, of Galway, merchant, a minor at his father's death, was one of the parties to the decree of 25 Oct. 1616. He m. 1st, Catbaline Brown, by whom he had no issue. He m. 2ndly Juliana, dau. of Valentine ffrench, and d. intestate 28 Feb. 1621 (inq. p.m. 21 Oct. that year) leaving issue,
1. JOHN, of whom presently.
2. Martin, who d. before 1653, leaving two sons and a dau.,
1. Francis.   2. John.
1. Mary, m. John Lynch.
3. James, who had a son,
Patrick.
4. Nicholas (Oge).
1. Mary, m. Patrick Bodkin.

The eldest son,
JOHN BLAKE, Mayor of Galway 1646. In 1640, when the Lord Deputy, Sir Thomas Wentworth, Earl of Strafford, was carrying out his scheme for the Plantation of Connaught, this John Blake presented a petition to the Commissioners of the Plantation, accompanied by his pedigree and other ancient documents, upon which they certified that he was the lineal and eldest descendant of Richard Caddle, alias Blake, Sheriff of Connaught 1306, and awarded him

IRELAND.   Blake.

he claimed properties.* His ancestral estates were confiscated by he Cromwellian Commissioners in 1655, and he was transplanted o Mullaghmore, Tyaquin, co. Galway. He *m.* Mary French, and iad issue,
1. THOMAS, his successor.
2. Henry, emigrated to Montserrat in 1670, returned to Galway in Sept. 1676, and purchased the estates of Lehinch and Renvyle a 1677-8, and *d.* March, 1704 (will dated 26 Jan. 1702), having iad issue,
  1. Patrick, *d.v.p.* 1693, leaving a son,
    Henry, of Lehinch, *m.* 1721, Charity, dau. of Maurice Annesley, of Rath, co. Meath, and widow of Francis Palmer, and *d.* 1732, leaving a son,
      Henry, of Lehinch, who *d.s.p.* 1780 (will dated 5 May, 1779, proved 8 Nov. 1780), leaving his estates to his kinsman Valentine Blake, 2nd son of Mark Blake (*see below*).
  2. John, of Ballinakill, who left a son, Henry, of Ballinakill, *m.* 1735, Jane Browne, of Moyne, and had a dau., Catherine, *m.* Nicholas Lynch, of Barna.
  3. Nicholas.
    1. Katharine, *m.* Sir Robert Lynch, 4th bart., of Castlecarra, co. Mayo.
  3. John, purchased his brother Henry's estate at Montserrat, and *d.* 1692, leaving a dau., Catharine, *m.* Nicholas Lynch, of Antigua.
  4. Nicholas, will proved 1683. He left a dau., Anstas.
  1. Catherine, *m.* Francis Browne.
  2. Julliane. 3. Mary. 4. Sheila.
John Blake *d.* intestate at Mullaghmore 1680, and was *s.* by his eldest son,
THOMAS BLAKE, of Mullaghmore and of Galway, merchant, *m.* 1658, Mary, eldest dau. of Nicholas Blake, of Kiltullagh, and had issue,
  1. JOHN, of whom presently. 2. Nicholas.
  1. Catharine. 2. Juliana, *m.* 1684, Philip Butler.
  3. Mary, *m.* 1683, Bartholomew Lynch.
The elder son,
JOHN BLAKE, of Mullaghmore, of Windfield, which he purchased 1703, *m.* 28 Dec. 1695, Eveline Lynch, of Bellacurren, and *d.* 1720 (will dated 17 June, 1720, proved 20 April, 1725), leaving issue,
  1. THOMAS, his heir.
  2. Mark, *m.* 18 Sept. 1731, Joan, dau. of Ignatius French, of Carrowrea, son of Valentine French, and had issue (with several daus.),
    1. Ignatius (called Naty), *d. unm.* at Lima, 1794.
    2. VALENTINE, *s.* his kinsman Henry Blake, of Lehinch and Renvyle, in 1780 (*see below*).
    3. John, of Mullaghmore and Windfield, co. Galway, and The Heath, co. Mayo (*see* BLAKE *of Annefield*).
  3. Nicholas. 4. Patrick.
  1. Demphna.
  2. Margaret, *m.* 1st, about 1745, Mark Blake, of Ballinafad (who *d.s.p.* 1760). She *m.* 2ndly, 1765, Henry Lynch, of Clogher.
The eldest son,
THOMAS BLAKE, of Mullaghmore and Windfield, *m.* 1719, Anne, dau. of John Bodkin, of Annagh, co. Galway, and had issue,
  1. JOHN, his heir. 2. Martin, *d.s.p.*
  3. Marcus, *d.s.p.* 4. Nicholas, *d.s.p.*
  1. Ellen, *m.* James Kelly. 2. Bridget, *m.* Andrew Concannon.
  3. Catharine, *m.* McDermott.
  4. Mary, *m.* Michael Browne, of Moyne.
  5. Margaret, *m.* Thomas Fitzmaurice.
  6. Julia, *m.* — Birmingham.
Thomas Blake *d.* May, 1762 (will proved that year), and was *s.* by his eldest son,
JOHN BLAKE, of Mullaghmore and Windfield, *m.* 1751, Mary, dau. of Patrick Kirwan (senior), of Cregg, but *d.s.p.* By his will, dated 27 Feb. 1786, proved 21 Feb. 1788, he devised his estates to his cousin John Blake, 3rd son of Mark Blake (*see* BLAKE *of*

*To prove his ancestral title to the lands of Kiltorroge, Ballym'croe and Kiltollagh. The petition states that the petitioner's ancestors "did plant thereabouts, being an auncient English familye, and there continued without changde of languadge, manners, or habit, and without once matching with any Irish familye since the nynth yeare of King Edward the Second. . . . That the peticioner is the eleventh masculyn English descent lyneally descended from father to the sonn, in the offices of the peticioner of the sayd lands from Richard Caddle *dicto Nigro* . . . And that although the peticioner after soe long a tracte of tyme, he called Blake or *Niger*, yett in the offices taken *post mortem* of his auncestors, they were called Blake *alias* Caddle." The Commissioners reported "Wee doe fynd by auncient evidences some without date by the auncient characters whereof wee conceave the same to have ben made in the Raygne of King Edward the First, and some others bearinge date in the sixt yeare of the Raigne of King Edward the First, that the Mannor and lands of Kiltorroge . . . and the towne and lands of Ballym'croe . . . were then graunted unto Richard Caddle *dicto Nigro*, and his heirs . . . and that the Castle and Mannor of Kiltullagh were graunted unto the said Richard Caddle *dicto Nigro* and his heirs by deed dated the 9th yeare of King Edward the Second. . . . And wee further fynd that the peticioner the said John Blake *alias* Caddle did by a petegree produced before us and proved by severall matters of recorde and by divers and sundrie auncient wills and deeds made by his auncestors, prove himself to be heire male of the boddye of the said Richard Caddle *dicto Nigro*. . . . Uppon all which wee conceave . . . that the said John Blake *alias* Caddle . . . being of an auncient Englishe blood and surname, have and doth contynewe in the possessions by him held as aforesaid. . . . Given at his Majesties Inns the 5th of June, 1640, Richard Bolton, Chancellor; Garrat Lowther."

Annefield). He was *s.* eventually in the representation of his family by his cousin,
VALENTINE BLAKE, of Lehinch and Renvyle, High Sheriff of Mayo 1781, 2nd son of Mark Blake (*see above*). He *s.* his kinsman Henry Blake, of Lehinch, in 1780 in the Lehinch and Renvyle properties (*see above*). He *m.* 1788, Anna Maria, dau. of the Hon. and Rev. Richard Henry Roper, of Clones, son of Henry, 8th Lord Teynham, by Anne, Baroness Dacre, his wife; and by her (who *m.* 2ndly, James Shuttleworth, of Barton Lodge, co. Lancaster) had issue,
  1. HENRY, his successor. 2. Marcus, *d.* young.
  1. Jane Maria, *d. unm.* 1815. 2. Caroline, *d. unm.* 1812.
  3. Julia Frances, *m.* Rev. Henry Burke, a younger son of Michael Burke, of Ballydugan, co. Galway.
Mr. Blake *d.* 1800, and was *s.* by his elder son,
HENRY BLAKE, of Renvyle, J.P., *b.* 18 Nov. 1789; *m.* 22 Dec. 1810, Martha Louisa, dau. of Joseph Attersoll, of Portland Place, London, and by her (who *d.* June, 1853) had issue,
  1. EDGAR HENRY, his successor.
  2. Harold Henry, *b.* 1 July, 1817; *d. unm.* Nov. 1873.
  3. Ethelbert Henry, M.D., L.R.C.S., Deputy Inspector-Gen. of Hospitals, formerly Surgeon R.A., *b.* Dec. 1818; *m.* Oct. 1849. Jane Caroline, dau. of Dr. Hay, H.E.I.C.S. He *d.* 6 June, 1897. She *d.* 21 Nov. 1911, leaving issue,
    1. Henry, *b.* 14 June, 1852, M.B., Great Yarmouth; *m.* 28 April, 1881, Lucy Agnes, dau. of Thomas Mounsey, of Oakfield, Garstang, Lancashire, and has issue,
      (1) Valentine Henry, *b.* 29 Jan. 1882.
      (2) Harold Henry, *b.* 1 Aug. 1883.
      (3) Denis Henry, *b.* 29 April, 1889.
      (1) Gertrude Mary, *b.* 22 Sept. 1885.
    2. Arthur Henry, M.A. Camb., *b.* 22 Nov. 1857; *m.* 19 April, 1893, Dora Mabel, dau. of John Rogers of Rawdon House, Bedford, and has issue,
      (1) Roger Derrick Campbell, *b.* 8 March, 1895.
      (2) Arthur Shirley Ethelbert, *b.* 28 May, 1896.
    3. William Henry, M.D. Brussels, *b.* 12 Jan. 1863; *m.* 11 June, 1890, Caroline Spencer, dau. of Rev. J. C. Bradley, and has issue, John Churchill, *b.* 30 May, 1894.
      Rose Spencer, *b.* 15 May, 1891.
    4. Robert, *b.* at Gibraltar, 1865; *d.* young.
    1. Edith Mary, *d.* in 1851. 2. Emma.
    3. Caroline Maria.
    4. Emilie Susette, *d.* at Gibraltar, Sept. 1865. 5. Ethel Jane.
    6. Eleanor Martha, *m.* 27 Dec. 1899, Rev. Arthur Leigh Barker, Vicar of Sway, Hants.
  4. Egbert Henry, R.E., *b.* 15 Sept. 1821; lost in the wreck of the "Solway," 8 April, 1843.
  5. Ethelred Henry, *d.* 1838, aged 14.
  6. Ethelstane Henry, *b.* 3 April, 1826; *m.* Aug. 1866, Sophia Marguerite, dau. of Louis Gaudard, of Lausanne, Switzerland, and *d.* 8 June, 1884, leaving issue,
    1. Herbert Edgar, *b.* 24 May, 1873; *m.* 26 Nov. 1895, Maud, dau. of — Bumpus, and has issue,
      Ethelbert.
    2. Egbert Mabille, *b.* 4 Nov. 1874.
    1. Ellen Marguerite, *m.* 2 June, 1897, Thomas Eagleston Gordon, M.B., F.R.C.S.I., and has issue,
  7. Herbert Henry, *b.* 4 May, 1828; *d. unm.* 1855.
  1. Emelie Anna, *d. unm.* 1867.
  2. Eleanor Elizabeth, *d. unm.* 25 July, 1882.
Mr. Blake *d.* 6 May, 1856, and was *s.* by his eldest son,
EDGAR HENRY BLAKE, of Renvyle, Capt. R.N., J.P., *b.* 19 Dec. 1814; *m.* 2 March, 1861, Caroline Johanna, dau. of Rev. Henry A. Burke, a younger son of Michael Burke, of Ballydugan, co. Galway; and *d.* 25 Nov. 1872, leaving issue,
  1. HENRY EDGAR VALENTINE, late of Renvyle.
  2. Robert Attersoll (*Barkley, Guelo, S. Africa*), *b.* 17 Jan. 1867; *m.* 24 Jan. 1902, Jane Frances Mary, only dau. of the late Charles Carter Blake, D.Sc., elder son of Charles Ignatius Blake, of Quinfero, S. America.
  1. Julia Emilie Martha.
The elder son,
HENRY EDGAR VALENTINE BLAKE, of Renvyle, co. Galway, and Foil Tra. Howth, co. Dublin, J.P., L.R.C.P. and R.C.S.I., *b.* 20 Aug. 1864; *m.* 2 Oct. 1901, Elizabeth Josephine, only dau. of Surgeon Thomas William Myles, of Foil Tra, Howth, co. Dublin, and *d.* 20 May, 1910, having had issue,
  EDGAR VALENTINE MYLES, now of Renvyle.
  Joan Caroline Fanella, *b.* 1 Aug. 1902.

Arms—Arg. a fret gu. Crest—A mountain cat passant ppr. Motto—Virtus sola nobilitat.

Seat—Renvyle, Letterfrack, Connemara, co. Galway.

BLAKE OF ANNEFIELD.

ST. JOHN ROBERT BOWEN BLAKE, of Annefield, co. Mayo, *b.* May, 1867; *m.* Katherine, dau. of Rev. Powell Jones, Rector of Newton, St. Petrock, Devon.

Lineage.—JOHN BLAKE, of the Heath, co. Mayo, J.P., 3rd son of Mark Blake (2nd son of John Blake, of Mullaghmore and Windfield), and younger brother of Valentine Blake of Lehinch and Renvyle (*see that family*), *s.* to Mullaghmore and Windfield, co. Galway, the old family property, by devise of his cousin, John Blake in 1788. He *m.* Aug. 1787, Mary, dau. of Christopher Bowen of Hollymount, co. Mayo (*see that family*), and *d.* 1812, leaving issue,

Blake. THE LANDED GENTRY. 48

1. CHRISTOPHER JOHN, his heir.
2. HENRY MARTYN, s. his nephew.
1. Anna Maria, m. William Malachy Burke, of Ballyduggan, and had issue (see that family).
The elder son,
CHRISTOPHER JOHN BLAKE, of Windfield, m. Elizabeth, dau. of John Burke, of St. Clerans, and d. 14 March, 1820, leaving issue,
1. JOHN BOWEN, his heir.
1. Elizabeth.   2. Maria.
The only son,
JOHN BOWEN BLAKE, of Windfield, d. unm. 1823, and was s. by his uncle,
HENRY MARTYN BLAKE, of Windfield, co. Galway, and the Heath and Kilnock, co. Mayo, b. 1796, m. Anastasia Gaussen, and by her had a son,
1. JOHN HENRY, his heir.
He m. 2ndly, Nichola Frances Charlotte, dau. of Robert ffrench, of Monivea (see that family). She d. Jan. 1878. He d. Jan. 1857, leaving with several daus. (of whom Annie Maria, m. Acheson Sydney O'Brien ffrench, D.L., and has issue (see FFRENCH of Monivea), and Johanna Isabella, m. 1st, 1864, Croasdaile Molony, of Granahan, who d.s.p. 1872, and 2ndly, 1873, John Blakeney of Abbert, who d. 1901, leaving issue (see that family), two sons,
2. Robert ffrench (Rev.), of Kilnock, co. Mayo, Rector of Staple, Kent, B.A T.C.D., b. 18 June, 1838 ; m. 8 Nov. 1877, Mary Elizabeth, dau. of Arthur T. Hewitt, D.L. She d. 28 July, 1900. He d. 18 Oct. 1900, leaving issue,
1. Arthur O'Brien ffrench, of Kilnock, co. Mayo (The Mount, Uxbridge), Major Royal East Kent. Yeo., b. 22 Feb. 1879 ; m. Laura Iris, dau. of Harry Walker, of Cadogan Place.
2. Robert Charles Sydney ffrench, 2nd Lieut. The Buffs, b. 18 July, 1880, accidentally shot in S. Africa, 19 May, 1902.
3. St. John Lucius O'Brien Acheson ffrench, 2nd Lieut. 21st Lancers, b. 26 May, 1889.
4. Desmond O'Brien Evelyn ffrench, b. 30 June, 1900.
1. Nora Mary Nicola Rosamond ffrench, b. 12 Sept. 1886.
3. Lucius O'Brien, m. Cecilia, widow of Rev, Crole Windham, of Rutland Gate, and d.s.p. 28 Nov., 1901.
The eldest son,
JOHN HENRY BLAKE, of Annefield and the Heath, co. Mayo, J.P., Capt. 4th Lancashire Militia, b. 1819, m. 1865, Sarah Nassau, dau. of Rev. John MacGregor Grier, Vicar of Stourbridge, Staffordshire, and d. 1873, leaving issue,
1. Sr. JOHN ROBERT BOWEN, now of Annefield.
2. Lyoden Henry Edward, b. May, 1867 ; m. Millicent, dau. of Major Brady, and has issue, two sons.
1. Sarah Christina Maria, m. April, 1887, Cecil Cornthwaite Powell, of Westerham, Kent.
Arms—See BLAKE of Renvyle.
Seat—Annefield, co. Mayo.

BLAKE OF TOWER HILL.

COL. MAURICE CHARLES JOSEPH BLAKE, C.B., of Towerhill, co. Mayo, J.P., D.L., High Sheriff of Mayo 1864 ; late Col. 3rd Batt. Connaught Rangers, b. 20 July, 1837 ; m. 24 Nov. 1863, Jeannette, only surviving dau. of Surgeon Richard Pearce O'Reilly, of Sans Souci, co. Dublin (by his 2nd wife, Olivia, 3rd dau. of Nicholas Kenney, of Rocksavage, co. Monaghan), and has issue,
1. VALENTINE JOSEPH, late Capt. 3rd Batt. Connaught Rangers, b. 10 June, 1866.
2. Charles Joseph, b. 11 June, 1867.
1. Olivia.   2. Georgina.
3. Cecilia, d. 1886.   4. Margaret.
5. Frances, d. unm. 8 Sept. 1897.
Lineage.—This is a branch of BLAKE of Renvyle, but more immediately descending from the house of BLAKE of Menlo (Baronet).
THOMAS BLAKE, 3rd son of Valentine Blake (who d. 1499), by his wife, Eveline Lynch (see BLAKE of Renvyle), was Mayor of the town of Galway in 1545 and 1562. He had a son,
WALTER, m. Juliane Browne, and d. vita patris in 1573, leaving three sons,
1. VALENTINE (Sir), of whom hereafter.
2. JAMES (Capt.), m. Margery, dau. of Alderman Dominick Browne, of Galway, and d. at Galway, 20 Feb. 1635, leaving issue,
GEOFFREY, m. Juliane, dau. of Thomas Martin, of Galway, and had issue.
WALTER, who on 17 Aug. 1677, got a grant by patent of the lands of Drum, co. Galway, and is ancestor of the family of BLAKE of Drum, and afterwards of Gortnamona, co. Galway.
Jennet, m. 1st, John Browne, of Galway ; 2ndly, Rory O'Flaherty, of Killagh, co. Galway.
3. ROBERT (FitzWalter, FitzThomas), Mayor of the town of Galway, 1624, who had four sons,
(1) JOHN, who was Sheriff of the town of Galway during his father's mayoralty, 1624.   (2) Anthony.
(3) Dominick.
(4) Nicholas, m. the dau. of Stanton, and had a son, Robert, m. 4 March, 1639, Sarah, 3rd dau of Sir Francis Blake, Knt. of Ford, Durham, and Twisel. co. Northumberland and by her had a son, Francis (Sir), created a bart. 3 May, 1774, which title became extinct on the death of Sir Francis Blake, 3rd bart. of Twisel, who d. s.p.l. 1860.
Thomas Blake, who at his decease was seised in fee of a moiety of the castle and lands of Ballym'croe (now Carnmore), which had been granted in 1278 to his ancestor Richard Caddell, surnamed Blake, d. 20 Jan. 1574 (post mortem inq. dated 21 July, 1576), and was s. by his grandson and heir,
SIR VALENTINE BLAKE (FitzWalter, FitzThomas), b. 1560, Mayor of town of Galway in 1611, and again in 1630 ; got a grant 8 June, 1621, of the castle and lands of Muckiniss, co. Clare, and was created a baronet of Ireland on 10 July, 1622. He m. 1st, Margaret, dau. of Robuck French, by whom he had issue, two sons and three daus.,
1. THOMAS (Sir), of whom hereafter.
2. Francis, Mayor of Galway in 1640.
1. Juliane, m. Adam Font, of Galway.
2. Margaret, m. 1st, Sir Nicholas Arthur ; 2ndly, Theobald, Butler, of the family of Lord Caheir.
3. Anne, m. Richard Darcy.
Sir Valentine m. 2ndly, Annabel, dau. of James Lynch, but by her (who survived him) had no issue ; his will, dated 20 June, 1629 (with codicil dated 2 Jan. 1634), was proved in 1634. He d. 2 Jan. 1634 (inq. dated 23 April, 1636), and was bur. in St. Francis' Abbey, Galway, in the Chapel of " Our Lady of Loretto," erected by himself. He was s. by his eldest son,
SIR THOMAS BLAKE, of Menlo, co. Galway, 2nd bart. ; he was Mayor of Galway in 1637. In the Strafford Survey of Mayo, 1636, he is returned as the owner of the lands of Clonyne (now forming the estate of Towerhill) in the Barony of Carra, co. Mayo. Sir Thomas m. Juliane Browne, dau. of Geoffrey Browne, of Carrowbrowne, and had issue (with several daus., one of whom, Moggine, m. James Lynch, of Galway) four sons,
1. SIR VALENTINE, created a knight in the lifetime of his grandfather, Sir Valentine Blake, 1st bart.
2. Walter, first of Galway, but afterwards of Exning, Suffolk. On 22 Feb. 1668, he got a grant by patent, under the Acts of Settlement, of the lands of Menlo and of Ballym'croe, alias Carnmore, in co. Galway, and the lands of Clooneen, co. Mayo, part of the estate of his then deceased brother, Sir Valentine Blake, 3rd bart., which had been sequestrated by the Cromwellian Government ; and in 1669 he executed a deed of settlement of these lands into his four nephews (sons of his brother, Sir Valentine Blake, 3rd bart.), viz., Sir Thomas Blake, 4th bart., Henry Blake, Francis Blake, and John Blake, successively in tail male. This Walter Blake's will, in which he is described as " of Exning, Suffolk," is dated 21 Nov. 1672, and was proved in London 29 April, 1674. He d.s.p.
3. Geoffrey (Rev.), a priest in Holy Orders of the Roman Catholic Church.
4. John (Rev.), a priest in Holy Orders of the Roman Catholic Church.
Sir Thomas Blake d. in 1642, and was s. by his eldest son,
SIR VALENTINE BLAKE, of Menlo, 3rd bart., Mayor of Galway in 1643. He m. (marriage settlement 27 June, 1632) Ellinor, 2nd dau. of Sir Henry Lynch, of Galway, 1st bart. (see LYNCH-BLOSSE, Bart.), and by her (who survived him) left issue four sons and three daus., namely,
1. SIR THOMAS, his heir, 4th bart. of Menlo, whose descendants in the male line became extinct upon the death s.p. of his great grandson, Sir Ulick Blake, 8th bart., in 1766.
2. Henry, who had a son,
Thomas, of Breandrum, co. Galway, who d. 1764, leaving issue,
(1) Thomas (Sir), of Breandrum, who s. as 9th bart. in 1766, and d.s.p. masc. in 1787.
(2) Walter (Sir), who s. his brother as 10th bart., and is ancestor of the present Sir Valentine Blake, of Menlo, 14th bart.
3. Francis, supposed to have been a patentee of lands in the State of Carolina. He had a son,
Joseph, one of the " Lords Proprietors " of Carolina who surrendered their patent rights to the Crown in 1728. He d.s.p.
4. JOHN (ancestor of BLAKE of Towerhill), of whom hereafter.
1. Juliane, m. Alexander Kirwan, of Dalgan, co. Mayo.
2. Elizabeth, m. Andrew Blake, of Fartigar and Castle Grove, 7th son of Robert Blake, of Ardfry. From this marriage descend the Canadian families of Blake.
3. Annabel (Nell or Elena), m. Thomas Fleming, whom she survived, and whose will she proved in the Diocesan Court of Tuam on 4 April, 1689. She d. intestate in 1705.
Sir Valentine Blake, 3rd bart., d. 1652. His will, dated 1 June, 1651, was proved in Dublin, 12 April, 1654. The extensive estates of Sir Valentine in the cos. of Clare, Galway, and Mayo, and in the town of Galway, were, after the death of Sir Valentine, sequestrated by the Cromwellian Government ; but after King CHARLES II's restoration Sir Valentine's widow, Dame Ellinor Blake, obtained on 14 July, 1663, a decree of the Court of Claims, whereby she was restored as " an innocent Papist " to the castle and lands of Muckiniss and the castle and lands of Ballyally, both in co. Clare. Sir Valentine Blake's 4th son,
JOHN BLAKE, of Muckiniss, co. Clare, m. (marriage settlement dated 10 Jan. 1678) Mary, dau. of Isidore Lynch, of Drimcong, co. Galway, and upon his marriage certain portions of the lands of Muckiniss were settled on him for life, with remainder to his first and other sons in tail male. On 20 Feb. 1680 he obtained a grant by Patent (conjointly with Marcus French) of the castle and lands of Muckiniss and Ballyally in co. Clare, to hold to certain uses. He was one of the burgesses of the town of Galway under the new Charter of Incorporation granted in 1688 by King JAMES II. By his wife, Mary (who survived him) he had issue, two sons. namely,
1. ISIDORE, his heir, of whom hereafter.   2. Patrick.
In the Civil War in Ireland, 1689-91, he held a commission as Capt.

Col. Dominick Browne's regiment of infantry in King JAMES' ish Army, and was killed in action at the siege of Athlone in June, 1691. His eldest son (then an infant),

ISIDORE BLAKE, of Clooneen, co. Mayo, on 3 March, 1701, obtained decree from the trustees of Forfeited Estates declaring that he as entitled to the estate tail in the lands of Muckiniss limited to im under his father's marriage settlement of 1678. He subsequently obtained from his cousin Sir Walter Blake, 6th bart. of Menlo, lease for years of the lands of Clooneen, co. Mayo. He *m.* Mary, ster of Mark Blake, of Ballinafad, co. Mayo (whose will was proved i Tuam Diocese on 14 Sept. 1759), and of Walter Blake, of Ballinafad whose will was proved in Dublin on 8 June, 1758), and by her (who redeceased him) had issue, three sons and three daus., viz.,

1. MAURICE, his heir, of whom hereafter.
2. Patrick (Capt.), *m.* 21 Feb. 1761, Catharine, 2nd dau. of John Foster, of Higham Dikes, Northumberland, and had issue (with a son) two daus., viz.,
  1. Elizabeth, *m.* 11 Nov. 1780, Hyancinth Kirwan, of Cregg.
  2. Anne, *m.* James Darcy, Barrister-at-Law.
3. John, of Arran Quay, Dublin, Banker, who *m.* 1755, Mary, sister of Arthur Browne, of Ellistron, co. Mayo, and widow of Valentine Blake, of London, Merchant, 2nd son of Sir Walter Blake, of Menlo, 6th bart., and *d.* 1800, leaving issue, three sons and one dau., viz.,
  1. Isidore, *m.* Aug. 1781, Jane, only dau. of Henry Lynch, of Clogher, co. Mayo, by his 1st wife, Cecilia, dau. of Dominick Lynch, of Tuam, and *d.* 1822, having had issue, two sons, namely,
    (1) Henry (Major), of Fisher Hill, co. Mayo, *d.s.p.* Will dated 1832, proved 1844.
    (2) Robert, Lieut. 84th Regt., who had two sons, who *d.* young.
  2. Valentine, emigrated in 1795 to New York ; *d.* there in 1811.
  3. Maurice, of Abbey Street, Dublin, Merchant, *d. unm.* 3 Dec. 1831.
  1. Mary, *m.* 30 Nov. 1783, Richard Darcy, of Rockvale, co. Clare (see DARCY of *Newforest*).
4. Catharine (Catto), *m.* Frank Lynch.
5. Anstas (Nancy). 6. Bridget.

Isidore Blake, after the marriage of his eldest son, Maurice Blake (in 1741), went to reside in the town of Galway, and *d.* April, 1763, and was bur. in St. Francis' Abbey, in Galway. He was *s.* by his eldest son,

MAURICE BLAKE, first of the town of Galway, afterwards of Clooneen, co. Mayo. In 1753 he purchased the fee simple of the estate of Clooneen, co. Mayo, from Sir Ulick Blake, 8th bart. of Menlo. He *m.* (marriage article 25 Feb. 1741) Ann, eldest daus. of Walter Blake of the town of Galway, merchant (who *d.* 1776), and niece of Dr. Anthony Blake, of Carrobrowne, R.C. Archbishop of Armagh (who *d.* in 1787), and by her (who survived him) had issue surviving, two sons, namely,
1. ISIDORE, his heir.
2. Anthony, of Ross Lodge, co. Galway, *m.* Katharine, dau. of William Burke, of Keelogues, co. Mayo, and had issue, Maurice, of Ross Lodge.

Maurice Blake, of Clooneen, *d.* at Bath, in England, on 17 Jan. 1789, and was bur. in St. Francis' Abbey, in the town of Galway; his will, dated 20 June, 1786, was proved in Dublin on 25 June, 1790. He was *s.* by his eldest son,

ISIDORE BLAKE, first of Towerhill (Clooneen), co. Mayo, afterwards of Oldhead, Westport, co. Mayo ; J.P. for Mayo He was the first of this family who took up his residence at Towaghty (anglicised into Towerhill), near Clooneen, co. Mayo. He *m.* (marriage articles 6 July, 1767), Frances, 3rd dau. and one of the coheiresses of Thomas Ruttledge, of Cornfield, co. Mayo, by his wife, Mary, dau. of Thomas Reddington, of Cregana, co. Galway, and by her (who *d.* March 1824) had issue, six sons and four daus, viz.,
1. MAURICE, his heir.
2. Thomas, of Lakeview, co. Mayo, *m.* 1799, Margaret, dau. of Edward Dowell, and *d.* in 1822, having had issue by her (who survived him), four sons and two daus., viz.,
  1. Isidore, of Rockfield, *d.s.p.* 2. Thomas, *d.s.p.*
  3. Edward, first of Lakeview, afterwards of Brussels, Belgium. *m.* in 1844, Margaret, dau. of John Nolan, of Ballinderry, co. Galway ; and *d.* at Brussels, Sept. 1892 having had issue, Edward, *d.v.p., unm.*
  Mary, *d. unm.* 1900.
  4. Patrick, of Dublin, Solicitor, *d. unm.* 1865.
  1. Frances, *d.* young. 2. Eliza, *d. unm.* 1891.
3. John, of Woodbine Lodge, Portarlington (afterwards of Weston, Dublin), *m.* Charlotte, dau. of Patrick Blake, of Corbally, co. Galway, and *d.* 1853, having had (with other children) a son, Isidore John, Barrister-at-Law, of Gray's Inn (1834).
4. Peter, of Wilford Lodge, co. Mayo, *m.* 11 Oct. 1809, Mary, dau. of John McLoughlin, of Newfield, co. Mayo ; *d.* 1816, leaving issue, a son and two daus., viz.,
  1. Isidore Peter, of Belmullet, co. Mayo, *m.* and had issue.
  1. Mary, *m.* Walter Bourke, Q.C., of Carrowkeel, co. Mayo.
  2. Celia, *m.* Isidore Lynch, of Arrandale, co. Galway, 2nd son of Arthur Lynch, of Petersburgh Castle, co. Galway, *d.s.p.*
5. Anthony, of Dublin, Solicitor, and of St. Orans, near Galway, *m.* Rebecca, dau. of Skerrett, of the family of Skerrett, of Ballindooly, co. Galway, and widow of Col. Lines Fawcett, and *d.* 1840, having had issue,
  1. Isidore, *d. unm.*
  2. Joseph, of Tummeenaune and Carrick, co. Galway, *m.* his first cousin Fanny, dau. of Arthur Lynch, of Petersburgh Castle, co. Galway ; and *d.* in 1886, having had issue, by her (who *d.* Jan. 1894), three sons and two daus., viz.,
    (1) Anthony, Surgeon of Medicine, *m.* 21 Jan. 1902, Winifred, dau. of Michael Hopkins, and has issue, Joseph, *b.* 21 Dec. 1902.
    J.L.G.

(2) Arthur. (3) Fawcett.
(1) Mary, *d.* young.
(2) Frances, *m.* her cousin Charles Crean, M.D., of Windsor, Ballyhaunis, co. Mayo, and *d.* leaving issue.
1. Frances, *m.* — Hickson. of Dublin ; and *d.* in 1891, leaving issue.
2. Mary, *m.* James Valentine Browne, of Galway, eldest son of Alexander Browne, 51st Regt., and had issue.
6 Isidore, Capt. in 4th Dragoons, *m.* Anne Coleman, and by her had issue (with other children),
Anthony } who emigrated to Australia.
Isidore }

1. Maria, *m.* Marcus Lynch, of Cloghballymore, co. Galway (2nd son of Marcus Lynch, of Barna, co. Galway), and by him (who *d.* 1816) (will dated 8 Nov. 1815) had issue, five daus., the eldest of whom,
  Anne Lynch, *m.* her cousin Maurice Blake, of Ballinafad, co. Mayo (see BLAKE of *Ballinafad*).
2. Ann, *m.* (articles dated Jan. 1800) Joseph Bourke, of Carrowkeele, co. Mayo, and had issue, three sons and three daus. Her eldest son,
  Walter Bourke, Q.C., of Carrowkeel, *m.* his cousin Mary, dau. of Peter Blake, of Wilford Lodge (see *above*).
3. Frances, *m.* 1812, Arthur Lynch, of Petersburgh Castle, co. Galway, and had issue, two sons and a dau.,
  Fanny, who *m.* her 1st cousin Joseph Blake, 2nd son of Anthony Blake (*see above*).
4. Catharine, *m.* 7 Aug. 1807. Daniel Jones, of Banada, co. Sligo, and predeceased him, leaving issue, a dau.

Isidore Blake, of Towerhill, in 1803, went to reside at Oldhead, near Westport, co. Mayo, and *d.* 15 Dec. 1818, and was buried in St. Francis' Abbey, in Galway. Administration with his will (dated 23 Oct. 1815) annexed, was granted on 3 July, 1819. He was *s.* by his eldest son,

MAURICE BLAKE, of Towerhill, D.L., J.P. for Mayo ; Major in North Mayo Militia. He *m.* 4 Aug. 1803 (articles dated 3 Aug. 1803), Maria, only surviving dau. of Valentine O'Connor, of Dominick Street, Dublin, Merchant, by his wife Mary, eldest dau. of Edward Moore, of Mount Brown, co. Dublin. She *d.* July, 1810, having had issue,
1. Isidore, *b.* Oct. 1806 ; *d.* 1809.
2. VALENTINE O'CONNOR, his heir.
1. Mary, *m.* (marriage settlement dated 3 Aug. 1824) Denis O'Conor, eldest son of Owen O'Conor Don, of Clonalis, co. Roscommon (see *that family*). She *d.* 12 June, 1841.
2. Frances, *d.* an infant.
3. Honoria, *m.* 1835, Edward O'Conor, 2nd son of Owen O'Conor Don, of Clonalis, and had issue (see O'CONOR Don).

Major Maurice Blake, of Towerhill, *d.* 7 May, 1847 ; bur. at R.C. Parish Chapel of Carnacon, co. Mayo. He was *s.* by his eldest surviving son,

VALENTINE O'CONNOR BLAKE, of Towerhill, co. Mayo, and Bunowen Castle and Carnmore, co. Galway, D.L. and J.P. for cos. Galway and Mayo, High Sheriff Mayo 1839, *b.* 1 Jan. 1808 ; *m.* 7 Jan. 1836 (marriage settlement dated 22 Dec. 1835), Hon. Margaret, only dau. of Charles Austin, 3rd Baron Ffrench of Castle ffrench, co. Galway, by his wife, Maria, dau. of John Browne, of Moyne, co. Galway, and by her (who *d.* 16 July, 1869) had issue, seven sons and three daus., viz.,
1. MAURICE CHARLES JOSEPH, now of Tower Hill.
2. Charles Joseph, of Heath House, Queen's Co., and Bunowen Castle, co. Galway (*whom see*).
3. Valentine Joseph, J.P. for Mayo and Roscommon (9, *Fitzwilliam Square, Dublin*), *b.* 4 Oct. 1842, *m.* 1 Sept. 1880, Hon. Mary, only dau. of Charles, 3rd Baron De Freyne of French Park, co. Roscommon (see BURKE's *Peerage*), and has issue,
  1. Arthur. 2. Valentine.
  3. Isidore. 4. Lionel.
  5. Harold. 6. Gerald.
  1. Kathleen. 2. Gladys.
  3. Mary, dec. 21 Nov. 1904.
4. Robert Joseph, *b.* 3 Feb. 1847.
5. Thomas Joseph, Barrister-at-Law, *b.* 27 May, 1849.
6. Martin Joseph, Barrister-at-Law, of the Middle Temple (10, *Old Square, Lincoln's Inn*).
7. John Joseph, *d.* 25 May, 1866.
1. Mary, Mother Prioress of the Benedictine Convent of St. Mary of the Angels, Princethorpe, co. Warwick, *d.* 3 Dec. 1895.
2. Ellen Mary, *d.* in infancy.
3. Margaret Mary, *d. unm.* 4 May, 1891 ; bur. at Heath Chapel, Queen's Co.

Valentine O'Connor Blake *d.* at Bray, co. Wicklow, 9 Aug. 1879 (will proved Oct. 1879), and was *s.* by his eldest son.

Arms—Same as BLAKE of *Renvyle*.
Seat—Towerhill, co. Mayo.

BLAKE OF HEATH HOUSE.

CHARLES JOSEPH BLAKE, of Heath House, Queen's Co., and Bunowen Castle, co. Galway, J.P. for Queen's and Galway cos. ; High Sheriff of Queen's Co. 1895 ; B.A. of Dublin University, and Barrister-

D

at-Law. Mr. Blake is the 2nd son of the late Valentine O'Connor Blake, of Towerhill, co. Mayo (*see preceding memoir*).

Lineage.—See BLAKE *of Towerhill.*

Residences—Heath House, Queen's Co., and Bunowen Castle, Clifden, co. Galway. *Clubs*—Kildare Street, and Stephen's Green, Dublin; Raleigh, London.

BLAKE OF BALLYGLUNIN PARK.

ROBERT BLAKE, of Ballyglunin Park, co. Galway, High Sheriff of the town of Galway 1892, *s.* his brother 1891; *b.* 3 Dec. 1834.

Lineage.—This family of Blake springs from GEOFFREY BLAKE, 3rd son of Walter Blake (who got a grant of the customs of Galway in 1346), and grandson of RICHARD CADDELL (or Niger), ancestor of all the families of BLAKE in Connaught (*see* BLAKE *of Renvyle*). Geoffrey Blake left two sons,
1. WILLIAM, of whom presently.
2. Walter, who was probably the person named as executor in the will dated 1420, of John (Oge) Blake (*see* BLAKE *of Renvyle*).

The elder son,
WILLIAM BLAKE, Burgess of Galway, living 1453, was devisee under the will, dated 1421, of his uncle, Henry Blake, senior, and joined in the grant made in 1435 to the church of St. Nicholas. In 1445 an award was made between him and his cousins Henry (fitz John Oge Blake) and John (fitz Henry) Blake, to settle disputes between them as to the division of lands of Henry Blake, senior. He left issue, three sons,
1. JOHN, of whom presently.
2. Andrew. 3. Thomas.

The eldest son,
JOHN BLAKE, Mayor of Galway 1488, as appears by a deed of agreement made in this year between him, William de Burgo and Dominick Lynch (fitz John). He was appointed one of the executors of the will of John Blake (fitz Henry) dated 1468 (*see* BLAKE *of Renvyle*). He left issue, four sons,
1. Geoffrey, probably Bailiff of Galway in 1486. He left issue a son,
    Richard, Mayor of Galway 1533, who had various disputes as to his title to the lands of Kiltollagh, &c., inherited by him from his ancestor William as devisee of Henry Blake (fitz Walter) as is mentioned in a decree of the Irish Court of Chancery, *temp.* HENRY VIII, *circa* 1536, and in an award of 1542. He, with his son and heir, John, in 1558, confirmed his ancestors' gifts to the church of St. Nicholas. He appears to have *d.* in 1564, as in the following year his name disappears from the list of masters or ex-mayors in which it had appeared from 1534 to 1564 (both inclusive). He had issue, four sons,
    (1) Geoffrey, *d.* young, *v.p.*
    (2) John, Mayor of Galway 1578. On 6 March, 1571, he and his kinsman, John Fitz Nicholas Blake, obtained the decree of the Lord President and Council of Connaught (*see* BLAKE *of Renvyle*). He *m.* Julia Browne, and *d.* about 1586, having by her (who *m.* 2ndly, Anthony Kirwan) had issue, two sons, Arthur, and Walter, who was one of the parties to the decree of 1616, by which the decree of 1371 was ratified and confirmed.
    (3) Martin.   (4) Thomas.
2. Walter, Bishop of Clonmacnois in 1487, who was appointed in 1506 by King HENRY VII to the Archbishopric of Tuam, but this translation was not sanctioned by the Pope.
3. ANDREW, of whom presently.
4. Peter.

The 3rd son,
ANDREW BLAKE, living *temp.* HENRY VII, left issue, three sons, of whom the third was Walter, ancestor of the BLAKES *of Ballinafad* (*whom see*) and BLAKE *of Ardfry* (*see* BURKE'S *Peerage*, WALLSCOURT, B.).

ANDREW BLAKE, Alderman, of Galway, son of Patrick, who is believed to have been a descendant of the second son of Andrew above-mentioned, *m.* Juliane Martyn, and had issue,
1. WALTER, of Drunmacrina, co. Mayo, ancestor of Blake of that place, and of Oranmore, co. Galway.
2. MARTIN, ancestor of this line.
3. Andrew, of Galway, merchant, *m.* Christiana Martyn, and *d.* 1687 (will proved 22 Aug. that year) leaving issue, from whom descends the family of Blake of Furbough, now Daly of Raford (*see that family*).

Alderman Andrew Blake's will, dated 20 Dec. 1624, was proved 9 Feb. 1630. His 2nd son,
MARTIN BLAKE, of Cummer, Sheriff of the town of Galway 1648, had a grant of lands in co. Galway (barony of Clare) in 1677 (29 CHARLES II); he purchased in 1671, the estate of Ballyglunin, *alias* Kilmoylane, from the Cromwellian planter Charles Holcraft; he *m.* 1st, in 1640, Margaret Martyn, of Dangan, by whom he had issue,
1. PETER, his heir.

He *m.* 2ndly, Aug. 1652, Anne Joyes, widow of Patrick Bodkin, and *d.* 8 Aug. 1691, leaving issue by his 2nd wife,
2. Patrick, whose will, dated 12 Feb. 1676, was proved in France 21 March, 1677.
1. Margaret, *m.* 1672, Joseph Lynch, of Ballycurrin.
2. Gyles or Julia.

His eldest son,

PETER BLAKE, of Cummer and Ballyglunin, *m.* 1667, Sybilla Joyce, and *d.* 21 Sept. 1691, leaving issue, three sons and three daus.,
1. MARTIN, of whom presently.
2. Patrick, of St. Kitts, in West Indies, *m.* Mary Ann, dau. of Andrew Bodkin, of Montserrat, and *d.* 7 March, 1744 (will proved in Antigua in 1745) having had issue, two sons,
    1. Martin, of St. Kitts, West Indies, *m.* Sarah, dau. of Dominick Trant; and *d.s.p.* in his father's lifetime (will proved 25 Aug. 1743).
    2. Andrew, of St. Kitts and Montserrat, *m.* Marcella French; and *d.* in London (will proved 11 Nov. 1762), leaving issue,
    (1) Patrick (Sir), of Langham, Suffolk, created a Bart. 8 Oct. 1772; *d.* 1 July, 1784 (*see* BURKE'S *Peerage*, BLAKE *of Langham*, Bart.).
    (2) Christopher, *d. unm.* 1780.
    (3) Edward, *d. unm.* 1763.
    (4) Arthur, who had issue, Arthur Garland and Edward.
    (1) Frances Barbara, *m.* Thomas Hodges, and had issue.
    (2) Marianne, *m.* 1st, — Austerbat; and 2ndly, Thomas, Lord Montfort, who *d.* 24 Oct. 1799.
3. Nicholas, of the town of Galway, *d.* 1747, leaving three sons, Patrick, Peter, and Arthur; and two daus., Sibilla, and Mary, *m.* Valentine Browne, of Tuam.
1. Margaret, *m.* 1st, in 1686, Christopher Ffrench (son of Robuck Ffrench, of Cloghballymore, co. Galway), who *d.* 1688; she *m.* 2ndly, Patrick Lynch, of Galway, Doctor of Medicine.
2. Sibilla. 3. Anne.

The eldest son,
MARTIN BLAKE (FitzPeter) of Cummer and Ballyglunin, *m.* 28 Nov. 1691, Margaret, dau. of Edmond French, of Boyle Abbey, co. Roscommon, and *d.* 1737, leaving issue, two sons and three daus.,
1. EDMOND, of whom presently.
2. Martin (Major), of Antigua and St. Kitts, in West Indies, and of Sevenoaks, Kent, *m.* 24 Dec. 1735, Elizabeth, only dau. of John Burke, of Antigua, and had issue; will proved in London, 16 Oct. 1767.
1. Sibilla, *m.* 1723, Andrew Blake, of Castle Grove.
2. Mary, *m.* Alexander Bodkin, of Anbally, co. Galway.
3. A dau. (name unknown), a nun.

The elder son,
EDMOND BLAKE, of Ballyglunin, *m.* 14 Dec. 1724, Mary French, of Rahasane, and had four sons,
1. MARTIN, his heir.
2. John, *d.s.p.* his will is dated 24 Feb. 1774.
3. Robert. (Rev.), *d.s.p.*   4. Peter (Rev.), *d.s.p.*

Mr. Blake *d.* 1771, and was *s.* by his eldest son,
MARTIN BLAKE, of Ballyglunin, *m.* 1751, Bridget, dau. of Walter Joyce, of Galway, and *d.* 1777, leaving issue,
1. EDMOND, of Ballyglunin, *m.* 1780, Mary, dau. of Nugent Sylvester Aylward, of Ballinagar (which lady afterwards *m.* 1789, Col. John Blake, of Furbo), and *d.* 1782, having had one son,
    Martin Stephen, who *d. unm.* 1788.
2. WALTER, of whom presently.
3. Martin (Rev.), of the Order of St. Francis, *d.s.p.*
4. Pierce (Rev.).
5. John, of Tuam, *m.* 31 Dec. 1803, Olivia Ann, dau. of Christopher French, of Brook Lodge (of the family of French, of Tyrone, co. Galway), and *d.* 6 Oct. 1822, having had issue a son and a dau.,
    John Joseph, of Garbally, King's Co., *m.* 3 Oct. 1829, Elizabeth, dau. of John Bodkin, of Annagh, co. Galway, and had issue,
    (1) John St. George, *d.* in infancy.
    (1) Harriett, a nun.
    (2) Olivia, *m.* 1867, John Taaffe, of Smarmore Castle, co. Louth, and had issue (*see that family*).
    Julia Maria, *m.* 1835, Martin Kirwan Blake, 3rd son of Charles Blake, of Merlin Park, and *d.* 1877, leaving issue (*see* BLAKE DE BURGH, *of Coolcon*).

The 2nd son,
WALTER BLAKE, who succeeded to Ballyglunin in 1788, *m.* 1789, Mary Archdeacon, sister of the Rev. Nicholas Joseph Archdeacon, R.C. Bishop of Kilmacduagh, and had issue,
1. MARTIN JOSEPH, his heir.
2. Henry, *m.* June, 1827, Adelaide, eldest dau. of Robert French, of Monivea Castle, co. Galway, and *d.* 17 Oct. 1858, leaving issue,
    1. WALTER MARTIN, late of Ballyglunin Park.
    2. ROBERT, now of Ballyglunin Park.
    3. Henry, who emigrated to Australia.
    4. Martin Joseph, of Ballina, co. Galway.
    5. John William Smith O'Brien, late Lieut.-Col. Comm. 1st Batt. 10th (Lincolnshire) Regt., *m.* Christian, dau. of the late Sherrington Gilder, and widow of Arthur Frisby He *d.* 25 Jan. 1907, leaving issue,
        Nicola Patricia Mary.
    1. Adelaide.
    2. Elizabeth, *m.* 1892, Michael Den Keating, of Woodsgift, co. Kilkenny.
    3. Nichola, *m.* Andrew Veitch, of Galway, and *d.s.p.*
    4. Mary.   5. Bidilia.

Walter Blake *d.* 1802, and was *s.* by his eldest son,
MARTIN JOSEPH BLAKE, D.L., of Ballyglunin Park, *b.* 1790, was M.P. for borough of Galway for a long period; he *d. unm.* March, 1861, and was *s.* by his nephew,
WALTER MARTIN BLAKE, of Ballyglunin, *b.* 1828; High Sheriff of Galway Town 1885, *d. unm.* 25 Sept, 1891, and was *s.* by his brother.

Arms—Arg. a fret gu.   Crest—A mountain cat, passant guardant, ppr.   Motto—Virtus sola nobilitat.

Seat—Ballyglunin Park, Ballyglunin, co. Galway. *Clubs*—Kildare Street, Dublin; County Galway Club, Galway; Constitutional Club, London.

IRELAND.   Blakeney

BLAKE OF BALLINAFAD.

LIEUT.-COL. LLEWELLYN BLAKE, of Ballinafad, co. Mayo, and Cloghballymore, co. Galway, J.P. and D.L. for the former co., High Sheriff of Galway Town 1886, J.P. co. Galway, late 6th Batt. Connaught Rangers, b. 1842.

Lineage.—This family is descended from WALTER BLAKE, 3rd son of ANDREW FITZJOHN BLAKE (see BLAKE of Ballyglunin). He left, with other issue, two sons,
1. MARCUS, of whom presently.
2. ROBERT, ancestor of Lord Wallscourt (see BURKE'S Peerage).

The elder son,
MARCUS BLAKE, got grants of land in Galway and Mayo 18 June, 1618, and 27 March, 1619, and had issue,
1. WALTER, of whom presently.
2. Thomas, who had a son, Henry, of Culgad, co. Mayo, who d. 1675.

The elder son,
WALTER BLAKE, purchased other lands in co. Mayo, from David O'Kelly, of Dunamona. He m. Mary, dau. of Piers Kirwan, and d. 5 June, 1633, leaving issue,
1. MARCUS, of whom presently.
1. Jennet.   2. Mary.

The only son,
MARCUS OGE BLAKE (or Maurice Blake) who in 1681 obtained a re-grant by patent dated 30 June, 33 CHARLES II, of the lands of Gissiden and other lands in the barony of Carra, co. Mayo, which are now the estate of Ballinafad, and belonged to his father. He m. Anstace, dau. of John Darcy, of Kinloch, co. Mayo. and left issue,
1. MARK, of whom presently.
2. Walter, of Ballinafad, d. unm. (will dated 28 April, 1758), proved 3 June, 1758).   3. John.
1. Mary, m. Isidore Blake, of Clooneen, co. Mayo, and had issue (see BLAKE of Towerhill).
2. Anstas, m. — Lynch.   3. Margaret, m. — Carroll.

The eldest son,
MARK BLAKE, of Ballinafad, m. 25 Oct. 1712, Juliana, dau. of Edmund Kirwan, of Dalgin, and d. about 1759 (will dated 28 Aug. 1756, proved 14 Sept. 1759) leaving issue,
1. MAURICE, of whom presently.
2. Mark, of Knockmore, m. about 1745, Margaret, dau. of John Blake of Windfield (see BLAKE of Renvyle), and d.s.p. 29 May, 1760. His widow m. 26 June, 1765, Henry Lynch, of Clogher.
1. Anstas, m. 1742, Mark Lynch, of Barna (see that family), and had issue.

The elder son,
MAURICE BLAKE, of Ballinafad, m. 1733, Sibilla, dau. of Roebuck French, of Dooras, co. Galway, and d. about 1779, leaving issue,
1. MARK, of whom presently.
1. Julia, m. Francis Lynch.   2. Catharine.
3. Mary, m. her cousin Mark Blake, who d.s.p. 1783.
4. Anstase, d. unm.

The only son,
MARK BLAKE, of Ballinafad, m. Jan. 1777, Christian, only dau. of Martin Kirwan, of Blindwell, co. Galway, and d. about 1810, having had issue,
1. MAURICE.   2. Martin.
3. Mark.   4. Joseph.
1. Mary, m. 1815, Andrew Browne, of Moyvilla.

The eldest,
MAURICE BLAKE, of Ballinafad, High Sheriff co. Mayo 1838, m. Anne, dau. and heiress of Marcus Lynch, of Cloghballymore, co. Galway, by Maria his wife, eldest dau. of Isidore Blake, of Towerhill, and d. 1852, having had issue,
1. MARK, of Ballinafad.
2. Maurice, Capt. 19th Regt. (ret.), who had issue.
3. Martin, d.s.p.   4. JOSEPH, late of Ballinafad.
5. LLEWELLYN, now of Ballinafad.
1. Mary, m. George Henry Moore, of Moore Hall, M.P. for co. Mayo, who d. 1870.
2. Catherine, m. March, 1853, Arthur O'Conor, J.P., of The Palace, Elphin, co Roscommon, and had issue (see O'CONOR of Mount Druid).
3. Anna, m. William Murphy, of Mount Merrion, co. Dublin.
4. Julia, m. G. E. Browne, of Brownestown, co. Mayo.
5. Victoria, m. 1st, March, 1859, Thomas ffrench (nephew of Lord ffrench). He d.s.p. 30 May, 1859. She m. 2ndly, Lieut.-Gen. Andrew Browne, C.B., who d. 8 April, 1883, leaving issue.

The eldest son,
MARK BLAKE, of Ballinafad, J.P., M.P. for co. Mayo from 1840 to 1846, and High Sheriff 1855, b. 1818; d.s.p. June, 1886, and was s. by his brother,
JOSEPH BLAKE, of Ballinafad, who d. unm., and was s. by his brother.

Arms—Arg. a fret gu. **Crest**—A mountain cat, passant, ppr. **Motto**—Virtus sola nobilitat.

Seats—Ballinafad, co. Mayo; Cloghballymore, co. Galway.

BLAKE OF RATHVILLE. See DALY.

BLAKE. See BLAKE DE BURGH.

BLAKE. See BURKE'S PEERAGE, **WALLSCOURT, B.**

BLAKENEY OF CASTLE BLAKENEY.

ROBERT EDWARD BLAKENEY, of Abbert, Castle Blakeney, co. Galway, b. 1858; s. his brother 1905; m. 1897, Katherine Everleigh, dau. of William Batt, of Cackenfy, and widow of Frederick Howe Windham.

Lineage.— THOMAS BLAKENEY, by his 2nd wife, a Miss Hatton, had issue,
1. ROBERT of whom below.
2. William, of Mount Blakeney and Thomastown, co. Limerick. Lieut. in the Army, d. 31 March, 1664, and bur. in St. Peter's Kilmallock. He had issue,
1. William, of Mount Blakeney and Thomastown, M.P. for Kilmallock. Had a grant of lands in co. Limerick 11 Dec. 1666. Will dated 10 Nov. 1701, proved 22 April, 1718. He m. Elizabeth, dau. of Henry Bowerman, and had issue.
(1) WILLIAM (Sir), LORD BLAKENEY, of Mount Blakeney, co. Limerick (cr. 1757), K.B., Lieut.-Gen., M.P. for Kilmallock 1727-1756, Governor of Stirling Castle 1744, Lieut.-Gov. of Minorca 1747, Brig.-Gen. in Cartbagena Exped. 1741, defended Fort St. Philip against French Exped. under Duc de Richelieu 1756, b. 1670; d. unm. 20 Sept. 1761, bur. in Westminster Abbey.
(2) Charles, Lieut. Royal Regt. of Ireland.
(3) John, Lieut. Sir Harry Goring's Regt.
(4) Robert, of Mount Blakeuey and Thomastown, Major in the Army, d. 18 Nov. 1763, having m. Deborah (will proved 1775), dau. of Grice Smyth, of Ballynatray (see that family), by whom he had issue,
1. William, of Mount Blakeney and Thomastown, B.A. (Trin. Coll. Dublin), Barrister-at-Law, d. 15 Sept. 1811, having m. 1764, Gertrude, dau. of R'chard Smyth, of Ballynatray (see that family), by whom he had issue,
(1) Robert (Rev.), B.C.L. Oxon, Rector of Elm, co. Somerset, b. 6 June, 1792; d. unm. 13 Jan. 1825.
2. Grice, Gen. in the Army, Col. 4th (Blakeney's) Royal Veteran Batt., J.P. cos. Tipperary and Limerick, b. 1741; d. unm. 16 Nov. 1816.
1. Gertrude, m. 28 May, 1752, her cousin Col. Robert Blakeney, M.P. of Abbert, to whom refer.
(1) Margaret, m. R. Armstrong, of Cork.
(2) Mary, m. — Le Strange.
(3) Elizabeth, m. John Creed.
(4) Hatton (? Catherine), m. Lancelot (? Joseph) Gubbins, of Maidstone Castle, co. Limerick.
2. George, Lieut.-Col. of Sir Henry Goring's Regt. of Foot, served at Cadiz 1702, and at the taking of Vigo, at the siege of Toulon, 1707, and at the capture of Cagliari 1708. Will dated 10 June, 1726, proved 10 May, 1728.
3. John.   4. George.
5. Charles.   6. Henry.
1. Hatton, m. — Pepper, of Drogheda.
2. A dau., m — Lovelace.   3. A dau., m. — Gardner.

The eldest son,
ROBERT BLAKENEY, of Gallagh, co. Galway, Major in Sir Charles Coote's Regt. of Dragoons (will dated 10 Feb. 1638, proved 6 July, 1660), m. Susannah, dau. of Edward Ormsby, of Tobervaddy, co. Roscommon, High Sheriff for cos. Galway and Mayo, and by her (who d. 29 Sept. 1659)and was bur. in St. Michael's Church, Dublin, vide Fun. Entry), he had issue,
1. JOHN, of whom presently.
2. Charles.
3. Robert, of Chappel Finaghly, co. Galway, High Sheriff 1707, Capt. in Lord Meath's Regt. of Foot, wounded at the first siege of Limerick, 1690, Mayor of Galway 1715, d.s.p. 12 Oct. 1731 (will dated 9 Aug. 1731 proved 16 Oct. 1731), having m. Elizabeth, dau. of — Rogers, and widow of — McDonald.
4. Edward, of Gallagh, for whose descendants see below.
1. Mary, m. Robert Ormsby, of Cloghaus, co. Mayo.
2. Susannah, m. — Godwin, of Tuam.

The eldest son,
JOHN BLAKENEY, of Gallogh, b. 1649, entered Trin. Coll. Dublin, 18 June, 1666, B.A. 1671; m. 1671, Sarah, dau. of Dudley Persse, Dean of Kilmacduagh, and d. 1691 (Admon. 19 April, 1691), leaving issue,
1. ROBERT, of whom presently.
2. John, of Distington, Cumberland, Capt. Royal Regt. of Ireland, served at Blenheim and Malplaquet, and d.s.p. 21 May, 1749.

D 2

Blakeney.   THE LANDED GENTRY.   52

3. William.
1. Mary, *m.* Thomas Taylor.
The eldest son,
ROBERT BLAKENEY, of Abbert and Castle Blakeney, High Sheriff co. Galway 1709 and 1729, M.P. for Athenry, 1721-33; *m.* Sarah, dau. of Gilbert Ormsby, M.P. (*see* ORMSBY *of Gortner Abbey*). He *d.* 1733 (will dated 16 April, 1733, proved 5 Dec. 1733), having had, with four daus., three sons,
1. JOHN, of whom presently.
2. George, Capt. 27th Regt., *b.* 27 Jan. 1716; *d.* 25 Feb. 1779, having *m.* Mary, dau. of John Dixon, of Gilgarron, co. Cumberland, and by her (who *d.* 17 Sept. 1800) he had with other issue a dau., named Hatton, and a son,
  Robert, of Whitehaven, J.P. and D.L. co. Cumberland, *d.* 6 Nov. 1822, having *m.* Margaret (*d.* 14 Feb. 1828), dau. of Rev. Samuel de le Brouf Edwards, M.A., of Pentre Hall, Montgomery.
3. Gilbert.
The eldest son,
JOHN BLAKENEY, of Abbert, High Sheriff co. Galway 1727 and 1738, M.P. for Athenry 1727-47; *m.* Grace, dau. of Henry Persse, of Roxborough (*see that family*), and *d.* 21 Aug. 1747, having had issue,
1. ROBERT, of Abbert, Col. Galway Mil., High Sheriff 1754, M.P. for Athenry 1747-63; *m.* 28 May, 1752, Gertrude, dau. of Major Robert Blakeney, of Mount Blakeney, co. Limerick (*see below*), and *d.* Jan. 1763, having had issue,
  John, of Abbert, M.P. for Athenry 1776-89, *d. unm.* Aug. 1789.
  Grace, *m.* May, 1786, Thomas Lyon, of Watercastle, Queen's Co.
2. John, of Ashfield, Col. Galway Mil., High Sheriff 1768, M.P. for Athenry 1763-89, *d. unm.* July, 1789.
3. THEOPHILUS, of whom presently.
4. William, Lieut.-Col. Royal Welsh Fus., M.P. for Athenry 1781-3 and 1790-9, severely wounded at the Battle of Bunker's Hill, *d.* 9 Nov. 1804, having *m.* Sarah Shields, of Newcastle-on-Tyne, by whom he had issue (with three daus.),
  1. William Augustus, Major 87th Regt., *d.* 3 Sept. 1848, having *m.* Sarah O'Dell, by whom he had issue.
  2. John Theophilus, M.A. Camb., Barrister-at-Law, *d. unm.* 31 March, 1856.
  3. Hargrave.
  4. Thomas, Lieut.-Col. 66th Regt.
  5. Edward (Sir), G.C.B., G.C.H., K.T.S., Field Marshal, Col. in Chief of the Rifle Brigade, 17 years Commander of the Forces in Ireland, Governor of Chelsea Hospital, *b.* 26 March, 1778; *d.s.p.* 2 Aug. 1868; *m.* 5 March, 1814, Mary (*d.* 21 Jan. 1861), dau. of Col. Thomas Gardiner, H.E.I.C.S.
  6. Samuel, Capt. 6th Regt.
  7. Robert.
  8. Henry Persse, Major 66th Regt.
1. Sarah, *m.* 1750, William Persse, of Roxborough (*see that family*).
2. Mary, *m.* 19 June, 1759, Thomas Taylor.
The 3rd son,
THEOPHILUS BLAKENEY, of Abbert, and formerly of Mulpit, M.P. for Athenry 1769-76, for Carlingford 1776-83, and again for Athenry 1783-99, High Sheriff co. Galway 1773; *m.* Nov. 1782, Margaret, eldest dau. of John Stafford, of Gillstown, co. Roscommon, and had issue
1. JOHN HENRY, of Abbert.
1. Bridget, *m.* Sir Richard Bligh St. George, Bart. of Woodsgift, co. Kilkenny (*see* BURKE'S *Peerage*).
2. Margaret, *m.* John O'Dwyer, Barrister-at-Law.
3. Elizabeth, *m.* Capt. De Hugo, of the French National Guard.
4. Harriett, *m.* Arthur St. George, of Kilrush House.
Capt. Blakeney *d.* 22 Sept. 1813, and was *s.* by his eldest son,
JOHN HENRY BLAKENEY, of Abbert, J.P. and D.L., High Sheriff in 1810, *m.* 1 July, 1813, Charlotte, 3rd dau. of Sir Ross Mahon, 1st bart. of Castlegar, co. Galway (*see* BURKE'S *Peerage*), by Elizabeth his 1st wife, sister of John Denis, 1st Marquess of Sligo, and *d.* 17 Nov. 1858, having by her (who *d.* 2 Aug. 1865) had issue,
1. JOHN, late of Abbert.
2. Robert, late Major 48th Regt., served in Crimean Campaign and at Siege of Sebastopol, Queen's Foreign Service Messenger, *b.* 1848; *m.* 2 Oct. 1860, Hon. Mary Sophia, eldest dau. of Henry Jeffery, 5th Viscount Ashbrook (*see* BURKE'S *Peerage*). She *d.* 17 April, 1886. He *d.* 20 June, 1902, leaving issue,
  1. Henry Ross, *b.* 2 April, 1862.
  2. Frederick Robert, *b.* 16 May, 1863.
  3. Ernest Charles Cecil, *b.* 27 Jan. 1869.
  1. Frances Alice.
  2. Beatrice Maud, *d. unm.* 27 April, 1899.
3. William, Col. E.I.C.S.
4. Edward, *d.* 9 Nov. 1910, aged 79.
5. Henry, Col., served through Crimean War, *m.* 27 July, 1865, Louisa Jane, dau. of Francis C. Hutchinson M.D., of Carlisle.
1. Elizabeth Margaret, *m.* 24 April, 1834, Albemarle Cator, deceased, eldest son of John Cator, of Beckenham Place, Kent, and Woodbastwick Hall, Norfolk (*see that family*).
2. Sarah.   3. Mary.
4. Louisa.
5. Harriette Anne, *m.* William Henry Coussmaker, of Westwood, Surrey, and *d.* his widow, 6 March, 1903, aged 80.
6. Margaret Grace, *d. unm.* 7 Sept. 1911, aged 85.
7. Anna, *m.* 20 Dec. 1855, Charles Morgan Norwood, of Hull, M.P.
The eldest son,
JOHN BLAKENEY, of Abbert, Castle Blakeney, co. Galway, J.P. and D.L., High Sheriff 1873, late of the 23rd R. W. Fusiliers, *b.* Oct. 1826; *m.* 1st, 1854, Frances, dau. of James Hardiman Burke, of St. Cleran's, and by her (who *d.* 5 Aug. 1869) had issue,

1. JOHN THEOPHILUS, late of Abbert.
2. ROBERT EDWARD, now of Abbert.
1. Anne.   2. Mary, *m.* Rev. J. O. Coussmaker.
3. Fanny, *m.* 1895, Gilbert Mahon.
Mr. Blakeney *m.* 2ndly, 1873, Joanna, widow of Croasdaile Molony, of Kilneerandie and Granahan, co. Clare, and dau. of Henry Martyn Blake, of The Heath, co. Mayo, and Windfield, co. Galway, and niece of Robert ffrench, J.P., D.L., of Monivea Castle, co. Galway, and by her had issue,
3. Henry Robert William, *m.* 29 April, 1905, Aileen Mary, only dau. of George R. Armstrong.
4. Ethel Frances Charlotte, *m.* 1895, Lucien Jerome, H.B.M. Consular Service, *d.* at Havana 1898, during the Cuban war.
He *d.* 1901, and was *s.* by his eldest son,
JOHN THEOPHILUS BLAKENEY, of Abbert, Castle Blakeney, J.P. co. Galway, *b.* 31 Jan. 1855; *d. unm.* 16 Jan. 1905, when he was *s.* by his brother.

The 4th son of Major Robert Blakeney, of Gallagh, and Susannah Ormsby (*see above*).
EDWARD BLAKENEY, of Gallagh, co. Galway, *m.* Anne, dau. of Thomas Staunton, M.P. for Galway, had issue,
1. Robert, *m.* a sister of Simon Marshall, of Tuam, they had issue,
  1. Edward, *d. unm.*
  2. Simon (will dated 21 June, 1777), of Gortgariffe co. Galway; *m.* Marcella, his cousin, dau. of Thomas Blakeney, of Feigh, co. Galway (*see below*). They had issue,
    (1) Charles.   (2) Edward.
    (1) Isabella, *m.* 1787, James Beytagh, of Mannin, co. Mayo.
    (2) Sarah.
  3. Robert, of Gortgariffe, co. Galway, Lieut. 119th Foot, *d. unm.*
  1. A dau., *m.* Rev. A. Wadman.
2. THOMAS, of whom presently.
3. John, *m.* Miss Lovelace, of Roscommon, and had issue.
The 2nd son,
THOMAS BLAKENEY, of Feigh, co. Galway, *m.* Sarah, dau. of Robert Burke, of Tyaquin, co. Galway (she *d.* 15 Feb. 1753). His will dated 2 Oct. 1761, proved 15 July, 1762. He was bur. 27 May 1762, at Tuam Cathedral, and had issue,
1. Edward, of Newman's Street, London, W., His B.M. Consul at Nice 1757, Private Secretary to Gen. the Right Hon. Lord Blakeney, K.C.B., Lieut.-Governor of Minorca (*d. unm.*; will dated 15 March, 1799, proved 29 June, 1799.
2. Thomas, of Dublin, *m.* Margaret Wallace (who was bur. 6 April, 1795); will dated 30 Nov. 1787. He *d.s.p.* and was bur. 23 July, 1789.
3. Robert, Lieut. 27th Regt. of Foot, *d.* off the Havannas 1764.
4. George, *d. unm.*
5. CHARLES, of whom presently.
1. Elizabeth, *m.* Thomas Waldron, of Drumsna, co. Leitrim (*see* WALDRON-HAMILTON *of Ashfort House*).
2. Deborah, *m.* 1750, Andrew Kirwan, of Coraghan, co. Galway.
3. Marcella, *m.* her cousin Simon Blakeney, of Gortgariffe, co. Galway (*see above*).
4. Jane, *m.* James Nesbitt.
The 5th son,
CHARLES BLAKENEY, of Feigh, and Currenlarman, co. Galway, and of Cloncera, co. Roscommon, *b.* 1731; *d.* 1815; *m.* 6 March, 1761, Bridget (*d.* 15 Sept. 1776), dau. and heir of Barnaby Gunning, of Hollywell, co. Roscommon (*see* BURKE'S *Peerage*, GUNNING, BT.), and left issue,
1. JOHN EDWARD, of whom presently.
2. Thomas (Rev.), of Hollywell, B.A., T.C.D., Rector of Roscommon, *d.* 17 Jan. 1845; *m.* Aug. 1801, Alicia, dau. and heir of the Most Rev. William Newcome, D.D., Archbishop of Armagh and Primate of Ireland; they had issue,
  1. Charles William, of Hollywell, co. Roscommon, Barrister-at-Law, Judge of the High Court of Queensland 1836-1858, *b.* 2 Aug. 1802; *d.* 12 Jan. 1876; *m.* 1826, Ellen Frances, dau. of George C. Jeffreys, of Blarney Castle, co. Cork, and had issue, William Theophilus, Registrar-Gen. for Queenstown, *b.* 9 Sept. 1832; *m.* 31 March, 1853, Eliza Louise, dau. of Frederick Carr, of Tullamore, Inspector Royal Irish Constabulary (she *d.* 6 April, 1907). He *d.* 26 June, 1898, and had issue.
  2. Thomas.
  3. Edward, of Sallymount, co. Roscommon, *b.* 26 May, 1805; *d.* 27 March, 1857, having *m.* 10 Aug. 1842, Anne, dau. of Dermot Garvey, and had issue,
    (1) Edward Thomas, L.R.C.S.I., of Roscommon, *b.* 10 June, 1849, and *m.* 1881, Belinda, dau. of Andrew Irwin, of Ballymoe, co. Roscommon.
    (2) Richard Henry, *b.* 18 Sept. 1851, and *m.* 14 Feb. 1894, Henrietta Mary, dau. of Stephen Callisson-Smith, and has issue, two sons and a dau.
    (1) Alicia, *b.* 23 Oct. 1843, and *m.* 3 June, 1863, Henry de la Valle Smyth, of Hollywell, co. Roscommon, J.P. and R.M.
    (2) Francis.   (3) Anne.
    (4) Catherine Gunning, *b.* 3 March, 1854, and *m.* 6 Nov. 1876, Henry Mark Scott, L.R.C.S., M.R.C.P.I., of Castle Hollow, Inniscron, co. Sligo.
  4. Robert, of 3, Fitzwilliam Square, Dublin, M.A. (T.C.D.), Barrister-at-Law, *b.* 8 Nov. 1807; *m.* 1846, Rachel Ann Stewart, and had issue.
  5. George, of Moville, co. Donegal, Officer in the Irish Constabulary, *b.* 20 Aug. 1809 (will dated 21 Aug. 1846, proved 13 Sept. 1853)
    1. Anne.   2. Catherine.
  3. Robert, of Curraghmore, co. Roscommon, M.A., Barrister-at-Law 1799, *b.* 13 July, 1766 (will dated 15 Feb. 1840, proved

13 Feb. 1841); *m.* Margaret, dau. of Samuel L. Owens, of Dundermot, co. Roscommon, High Sheriff for co. Roscommon, and left issue,
Mary Anne, *m.* John H. Mitchell, of Coolmeen, co. Roscommon.
4. **William**, Lieut. 19th Regt. of Foot, killed in action at Kandy, Ceylon, 15 June, 1803.
1. **Anne**, *m.* 20 July, 1779, Lieut.-Col. the Hon. Richard St. Leger (see BURKE's *Peerage*, DONERAILE, VISCT.). She *d.* July, 1809.
2. **Bridget**, *m.* 1791, Thomas Henu, of Paradise, co. Clare (see that family).
The eldest son,
JOHN EDWARD BLAKENEY, of Greenhall, co. Roscommon, 1st Lieut. Royal Marine L.I., *b.* 7 June, 1763; *d.* 30 Oct. 1853; *m.* 1st, Frances, dau. of Thomas Bradley (she was bur. 25 April, 1820), and by her had issue,
1. **Richard**, of whom presently.
2. **John**, Capt. Russian Hussars, killed at Verdun.
3. **Thomas**, 1st Lieut. Royal Marine L.I., 5th Oct. 1808.
4. **Theophilus**, *b.* 10 Jan. 1803.
5. **Robert**, *b.* 5 June, 1805.
He *m.* 2ndly, 1822, Magdalen, dau. of de Courcy, Ireland, and widow of John Purdon, of Low Park, co. Roscommon, and had a dau.,
1. Mary Ann, *d.s.p.*
The eldest son,
RICHARD BLAKENEY, 1st Lieut. Royal Marine L.I., mentioned in despatches dated 10 Feb. 1809, from Capt. Sir George Scott, H.M.S. "Horatio," *d.* 26 Sept. 1840, having *m.* 21 Aug. 1816, Susan Maria, dau. of John Purdon, of Low Park, co. Roscommon, and had issue,
1. **Richard Paul**, of whom presently.
2. **John Edward**, D.D., M.A., Archdeacon and Vicar of Sheffield, Canon of York, Chaplain-in-Ordinary to Queen Victoria, *b.* 7 Dec. 1824; *d.* 12 Jan. 1895; *m.* 3 June, 1856, Martha, dau. of Benjamin Derbyshire, J.P., of Claughton, Cheshire. Had issue,
   1. Edward Purdon, M.A. Camb., Vicar of Wadsley, Yorkshire, *b.* 12 Oct. 1870; *m.* 20 June, 1899, Hilda Kate, eldest dau. of William Ernest Dring, M.D., and has issue, four sons.
   2. John St. Leger, M.A. Camb., Vicar of Anston, Yorkshire, *b.* 15 Dec. 1873.
      1. Martha Susan, *b.* 25 Dec. 1862; *m.* 21 Dec. 1880, Samuel Roberts, of Queen's Tower, Sheffield, M.A. Camb., Barrister-at-Law, J.P., D.L., M.P. for Ecclesall, Sheffield, and has issue.
3. **William Purdon**, *b.* 1834; *m.* Emily, dau. of Capt. R. Clegg, and *d.* 2 Jan. 1879, and had issue,
   William Purdon, *b.* 2 Feb. 1854, Vicar of Thorpe Salvin, Yorkshire; *m.* Elizabeth, dau. and co-heir of Dr. Wilson, of Cheltenham, and has issue,
   Leslie St. Leger, *b.* 13 April, 1890, Lieut. Lancs. Fus.
1. Eleanor Maria, *m.* Rev. William Clementson, M.A.
The eldest son,
RICHARD PAUL BLAKENEY, D.D. (Honoris Causâ) Edinburgh, LL.D. (Trin. Coll. Dublin), Canon and Prebend. of York, Rector and Rural Dean of Bridlington, Yorkshire, *b.* 3 June, 1820; *d.* 31 Dec. 1884; *m.* 1st, 1841, Anne, dau. and heir of Lieut. Richard O'Connor, R.N., and had issue,
Susan, *m.* 10 Oct. 1865, Rev. Albert Wade, M.A.
Canon Blakeney *m.* 2ndly, 2 Dec. 1856, Elizabeth, younger dau. and co-heir of Robert Bibby, of Liverpool, and had issue,
1. **Richard** (Rev.), M.A. Oxford, Hon. Canon of Peterborough, Vicar and Rural Dean of Melton Mowbray, *b.* 14 Oct. 1857; *m.* 16 April, 1884, Alice, eldest dau. and co-heir of Henry Unwin, J.P., of Broom Cross, Sheffield.
2. **Robert Bibby** (Rev.), M.A. St. Peter's Coll. Cambridge, Rector of Southport, Lancashire, *b.* 1 Feb. 1865; *m.* 19 July, 1894, Constance Eleanor, 2nd dau. of Col. Henry Zouch Darrah, B.S.C.
3. **John Edward Charles**, Major 3rd Essex Regt., Resident Northern Nigeria, *b.* 20 Dec. 1866; *m.* 27 Feb. 1899, Louise Margaret, eld. dau. of Lieut.-Col. Lorenzo Mosse, 67th South Hants Regt.
4. **Herbert de Courcy** (Rev.), Chaplain London County Asylums, *b.* 18 Dec. 1873; *m.* 2 Oct. 1895, Edith (div. 8 Feb. 1909), dau. of Thomas Bower, and has issue,
   1. Dorothy de Courcy, *b.* 17 Jan. 1901.
   2. Irene de Courcy, *b.* 24 Feb. 1902.
1. **Elizabeth Gunning**, *b.* 18 Nov. 1858. *m.* 14 July, 1881, Capt. Arthur Penry William, R.N., and *d.* 3 Feb. 1882.
2. **Ellen St. Leger**, *b.* 23 Nov. 1859; *m.* 28 July, 1887, Rev. John Howard Deazeley, M.A., Rector of Killybegs, co. Donegal.
3. **Florence Purdon**, *b.* 26 Dec. 1861; *d.* 20 Jan. 1900.
4. **Magdalen Amelia Ireland**, *b.* 2 Nov. 1868; *m.* 6 Jan. 1898, Rev. Lancelot Hicks Becher, M.A., Vicar of Banks, Lancashire, and has issue.
5. **Constance**, *b.* 8 Sept. 1870; *m.* 8 Dec. 1896, Maj. Walter de Sausmarez Cavley, Lieut.-Col. comdg. 1st Batt. 14th Prince of Wales Own (West York Regt.).

Arms—(as registered Ulster's Office, Fun. Entry, 1659)—Az., a chevron between three leopards' faces arg. **Crest**—Out of a ducal coronet or, an arm erect, couped at the elbow, vested gu. cuffed arg., in the hand a sword ppr., hilt and pommel gold. **Motto**—Auxilium meum ab alto (as registered College of Arms to Gen. Sir William Blakeney, K.B., afterwards Lord Blakeney, on obtaining a grant of supporters as K.B.) sable, a chevron ermine between three leopards' faces or. **Crest**—Out of clouds proper an arm erect, vested azure, the hand grasping a sword all ppr. *Motto*—as above.

Seats—Abbert, Ballyglunin, co. Galway; Benekerry Lodge, co. Carlow. **Club**—Kildare Street, Dublin.

BLAKISTON-HOUSTOUN. See **HOUSTOUN**.

BLAND, late OF DERRIQUIN.

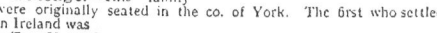

JAMES FRANKLIN BLAND, late of Derriquin Castle, co. Kerry, B.A. Trin. Coll. Dublin, *b.* 1850; *m.* 31 Dec. 1873, Agnes Margaret, eldest dau. of Samuel Wilson Block. 15. Talbot Square, Hyde Park, London, and has issue,
1. FRANCIS CHRISTOPHER CECIL *b.* 1875.
2. Archibald Franklin Wilson, *b.* 1885.
3. Godfrey Hamilton, *b.* 1889.
1. Agnes Emma.
2. Eveleen. 3. Ethel.

Lineage.—This family were originally seated in the co. of York. The first who settled in Ireland was
THE VERY REV. JAMES BLAND, Archdeacon of Limerick, and Dean of Ardfert. In a deed of sale registered in Wakefield, in 1717, he is described as of Killarney, co. Kerry, Ireland, and as disposing of his estates in Sedbergh, co. York, to Richard Willen. He was the son of John Bland, of Sedbergh, as proved by the records of St. John's College, Cambridge, where he was admitted on 3 May, 1684. He went to Ireland as Chaplain to Lord Deputy Sidney, in 1692. He *m.* Lucy, dau. of Sir Francis Brewster, Lord Mayor of Dublin 1674-75, and was father of the Rev. Francis Bland (whose great-grandson, the VEN. NATHANIEL BLAND, Archdeacon of Aghadoe, who *d.* 25 Feb. 1885, was the head of the family) and of
NATHANIEL BLAND, LL.D., Judge of the Prerogative Court of Dublin, and Vicar-General of the Diocese of Ardfert and Aghadoe. He *m.* 1st, Diana, only dau. and heiress of Nicholas Kemeys, and had by her a son,
1. JAMES, his heir.
He *m.* 2ndly, Lucy, dau. of Francis Heaton, by whom he had issue,
2. Francis, father, by Catherine Mahoney his wife, of Col. James Francis Bland, of Killarney, and of Frances, *m.* Rev. Robert Hewson.
3. Nathaniel, *m.* Mary Mead, but had no issue.
4. George, *m.* Hannah Westropp, but had no issue.
1. Lucy, *m.* George Orpen, a Military Officer, distinguished at Minden, 4th son of the Rev. Thomas Orpen, of Killowen, co. Kerry.
2. Hester, *m.* Robert Sinclair, Laird of Freswick, Caithness.
3. Dorothea, *m.* Francis Crumpe, and had, with other issue, Nathaniel Crumpe, of Randalls Park, in Surrey, who took the additional surname of BLAND.
Dr. Bland was *s.* by his eldest son,
THE REV. JAMES BLAND, of Derriquin Castle, who *m.* 1st, Elizabeth, dau. of Christopher Julian; and 2ndly, Barbara, dau. of — Nash, by the former of whom he had, with other issue, a dau., Letitia, *m.* Major Nathaniel Bland (father of the Ven. Nathaniel Bland, Archdeacon of Aghadoe, who *d.* 25 Feb. 1885), and a son and successor,
FRANCIS CHRISTOPHER BLAND, of Derriquin Castle, *m.* 15 March, 1798, Lucinda, dau. of Arthur Bastable Herbert (eldest son of Bastable Herbert), of Brewsterfield, near Killarney, by his wife Barbara, dau. of Maurice FitzGerald, Knt. of Kerry (son of John, FitzGerald, Knight of Kerry, by Hon. Honora O'Brien his wife dau. of Conor, 2nd Viscount Clare), and by her (who *d.* 1862) had,
1. JAMES FRANKLIN, late of Derriquin. 2. Arthur.
3. John, *d.* March, 1859. 4. Edward.
1. Elizabeth, *m.* Frederick Hyde.
2. Lucy, *m.* Capt. Thomas Stuart, R.N.
3. Frances Diana (*d.* 23 April, 1872), *m.* 1832, Thomas Harnett Fuller, of Glashnacree, co. Kerry (see that family), son of Capt. Edward Fuller, by Elizabeth his wife, dau. of Rev. John Blennerhassett, Rector of Tralee. The only son of this marriage is James Franklin Fuller, F.S.A., Fellow of the Royal Institute of British Architects.
4. Mary Matilda.
5. Christina Frances, *m.* Robert Acheson Thompson.
6. Clara Dalinda, *m.* William Allen.
Mr. Bland was *s.* by his eldest son,
JAMES FRANKLIN BLAND, of Derriquin Castle, J.P., High Sheriff 1835, *b.* 24 Jan. 1799; *m.* 27 Dec. 1825, Emma, dau. of Joseph Taylor, of Dunkerron Castle, co. Kerry, Major Bengal Artillery, and had issue,
1. FRANCIS CHRISTOPHER, late of Derriquin.
2. James Franklin, Capt. 57th Foot, *b.* 10 Jan. 1828; killed at the battle of Inkerman.
1. Alice Phillis, *m.* 20 Dec. 1853, Usher Williamson, eldest son of the Rev. Benjamin Williamson, of Old Dromore, co. Cork.
He *d.* 6 March, 1863. His elder son,
FRANCIS CHRISTOPHER BLAND, of Derriquin Castle, co. Kerry, J.P., *b.* 8 Oct. 1826; High Sheriff 1859; *s.* his father 1863; *m.* 23 June, 1819, Jane, dau. of the Rev. Archibald Robert Hamilton, of Cork, and *d.* 5 April, 1814, leaving issue,
1. JAMES FRANKLIN, his heir, who sold Derriquin.
2. Archibald Robert Hamilton, M.D., *m.* 20 Sept. 1884, Mary, widow of J. W. Jackson, and dau. of — Harris.

Bland. THE LANDED GENTRY. 54

3. Francis Christopher Earle.
4. Richard Townsend Herbert, *m.* 22 Dec. 1894, Katherine Annie Parr, 3rd dau. of William Monckton, of Portishead, co. Somerset, and *d.* 28 May, 1899.
1. Emma Alice. 2. Jane Hamilton.
3. Catherine Cotter, *m.* 21 July 1885, Augustus W. Addinsell.
4. Alice Phillis, *m.* 21 March, 1887, R. Wanless Smith, Scottish Rifles, eldest son of E. J. Smith, of Clonard, co. Dublin.
5. Mary Evelyn, *m.* 19 Oct. 1886, Sir Arthur Henry McMahon, K.C.I.E., C.S.I., Maj. Indian Army, son of Lieut.-Gen. C. A. McMahon, F.R.S., and has issue.

Arms—Erm. on a bend sa. three pheons or, in the sinister chief point a cinquefoil vert quartering KEMEYS. *Crest*—A cock ppr., charged on the breast with a pheon or. *Motto*—Eloquentia sagitta.
Residence—Hollywood, Kenmare.

BLAND OF BLANDSFORT.

HUMPHREY LOFTUS BLAND, of Blandsfort, Queen's Co., High Sheriff of Co. Wicklow, 1905, and Queen's Co., 1912, J.P., D.L., late Lieut. 5th Fus., *b.* 9 April, 1869; *s.* his father 3 Dec. 1908; *m.* 16 May, 1900, Muriel Elsie, dau. of the late John Scott, of Elmstead Grange, Chislehurst, and has issue,
WILLIAM, *b.* 8 Aug. 1901.
Alice Mary.

Lineage. — COL. JOHN BLAND purchased land in Queen's Co. 1699, and built Blandsfort, which was finished in 1715. He had two brothers, Humphrey and William, and three sisters: 1. Frances, *m.*—Lawless; 2. Anna, *d. unm.*; 3. Elizabeth, *d. unm.* By his will, dated 14 June, 1728, he devised Blandsfort to his brother Humphrey and his heirs, and in default to his brother William and the heir of his body lawfully begotten. He *d.s.p.* 1728, and was accordingly *s.* by his brother, GEN. HUMPHREY BLAND, of Blandsfort, Queen's Co., Quartermaster-General 1742, Maj.-Gen. at Culloden, Gov. of Gibraltar 1749, and Com.-in-Chief, Scotland, 1752-63, Col. 1st Dragoon Guards, *m.* Elizabeth, dau. of Lord Stair, but *d.s.p.* 8 May, 1763, and was *s.* by his nephew, JOHN, son of his brother, CAPT. WILLIAM BLAND, Capt. 8th Dragoons, *m.* 1st (setts. dated 14 Sept. 1720), Elizabeth Jones, *alias* Horseman, dau. of William Cock, and by her had a son,
1. JOHN, of Blandsfort.

He *m.* 2ndly (setts. dated 8 Nov. 1732, lic. 28 Nov. 1732), Letitia, dau. of Col. Hercules Davis, of the Battle-Axe Guards, and *d.* 1746, having by her had issue,
2. Humphry, Capt. 62nd Regt., *m.* 1763, Mary, dau. of Edward Matthews, and *d.* 1788, having had issue,
 1. Sarah Elizabeth. 2. Dorcas Letitia.
3. Jane Wilson, *m.* July, 1775, Thomas Sinclaire, of Belfast, and had issue a dau.
3. Thomas, General in the Army, Col. of the 5th or Bland's Dragoons, *d.s.p.* 1816.
4. Neville, Capt. in the Army, *m.* Charlotte, dau. of Smith, of Colbarey, co. Tipperary, and *d.* 1789, having had issue,
 1. Humphry Dalrymple, Lieut.-Col. 47th Regt., *m.* June, 1793, Mary Graham, and had a dau.,
  Ellen, *m.*—Easton.
 2. Loftus Otway, Post Capt. R.N., was promoted to that rank for the capture of the "Liguria" 7 Aug. 1798 (see JAMES'S *Naval History*), *m.* Sarah, dau. of Samuel Foote, of Demerara, and widow of —Ashbourner, and had issue,
  (1) Neville Loftus, of Bath.
  (1) Sarah Otway, *m.* Charles Clarke, of Graigneroe, co. Tipperary, and had issue (*see that family*).
  (2) Elizabeth, *m.* Charles Mansergh, of Clifford, co. Cork.
 3. William.
 1. Margaret, *m.*—Cole.

JOHN BLAND, of Blandsfort, *b.* 1723, *s.* his uncle General Humphrey, *m.* 1763, Sarah, dau. of Charles Birch, of Birchgrove, co. Wexford, and *d.* 1790, leaving issue,
1. JOHN, his heir.
2. Robert, Capt. 72nd Regt. 3. William.
1. Elizabeth, *m.* J. Crawford, of Balintober, Nenagh, co. Tipperary.
2. Anne, *m.* George Pringle, of Stradbally.
3. Catherine.
4. Hannah, *m.*—Nugent.

The eldest son,
JOHN BLAND, of Blandsfort, Ensign 15th Regt., *m.* 1790, Elizabeth, dau. of Robert Birch, M.P., of Turvey, co. Dublin, and by her (who *d.* 1836) left at his decease 1810, three sons and three daus., viz.,
1. JOHN THOMAS, his heir.
2. Robert Wintringham (Rev.), of Abbeyville, co. Antrim, J.P.,

b. 21 Feb. 1794; *m.* 14 July, 1826, Alicia, 3rd dau. of the Rev. Edward Evans, of Gortmerron, Dungannon, co. Tyrone. She *d.* 10 Oct. 1879. He *d.* 21 Dec. 1880, leaving issue,
 1. JOHN HUMPHRY, of Fernagh, Whiteabbey, co. Antrim, *b.* 20 May, 1828; *m.* 30 Oct. 1867, Emily Charlotte (*d.* 27 Dec. 1906), dau. of Rev. Wyndham Carlyon Madden, of Berg Apton, Norfolk, and has issue
  (1) Robert Wyndham Humphry Maciel, *b.* 27 Jan. 1872.
  (1) Eva Charlotte Alice, *b.* 10 Nov. 1868; *m.* 30 Nov. 1911, George Lucas Blackley Borton, elder son of late Capt. Henry Borton, R.H.A.
  (2) Lilian Emily, *b.* 28 Sept. 1878; *m.* her cousin 3 Oct. 1911, Charles Loftus Bland, late R.A. (*see below*).
 2. Edward Loftus, Maj.-Gen. late R.E., of White Abbey, co. Antrim, *b.* 10 Dec. 1829; *m.* 4 Jan. 1859, Emma Frances, dau. of Robert Fergusson Franks, of Jerpoint, co. Kilkenny, and by her (who *d.* 7 July, 1894) has issue,
  (1) Robert Norman, C.M.G., B.A. Trin. Coll. Dublin, Res. Councillor, Penang, 1907-10 (*White Abbey, co. Antrim*), *b.* 8 Oct. 1859; *m.* 18 Sept. 1895, Laura, dau. of late Thomas Shelford, C.M.G., of Singapore and Hythe, Kent, and has had issue,
   1. Thomas Edward, *b.* 24 Feb. 1903.
   2. Robert Lawrence St Colum, *b.* 1905; *d.* 26 Jan. 1907.
   1. A dau.
  (2) John Otway Percy (*The Clock House, Shepperton-on-Thames*), *b.* 15 Nov. 1863; *m.* 29 Nov. 1889, Louisa, dau. of William Dearborn, of San Francisco.
  (3) Edward Humphrey, Lieut.-Col. R.E., *b.* 3 May, 1866; *m.* 7 April, 1894, Bertha Mary, 3rd dau. of J. Fletcher Moore, D.L., of Manor Kilbride, co. Dublin (*see that family*), and has issue,
   1. Humphry Otway Carleton, *b.* 8 July, 1901.
   1. Angela Doreen Loftus, *b.* 5 April, 1898.
   2. Vivienne Rosalie, twin with her brother.
  (4) William St. Colum, Maj. R.A., *b.* 6 June, 1868; *m.* 5 Sept. 1903, Kathleen, youngest dau. of the late Edward D. S. Ogilvie, of Yulgibbar, N.S. Wales, and has issue,
   1. Kathleen Frances Theodosia, *b.* 19 Sept. 1904.
   2. Margaret Alice, *b.* 12 July, 1907.
  (5) Thomas Dundas, *b.* 7 Jan. 1876, murdered in Corea 15 Aug. 1900.
  (6) Charles Loftus, Lieut. late R.A. (*Quatsino, Vancouver Island*), *b.* 24 Oct. 1881; *m.* 3 Oct. 1911, his cousin, Lilian Emily, younger dau. of John Humphry Bland, of Fernagh (*see above*).
  (1) Mary.
  (2) Alice Rosalie Henrietta, *m.* Sept. 1899, Capt. Arthur Desborough, R.A. (3) Sydney Frances Josephine.
 3. Robert Henry, J.P., *b.* 4 Oct. 1834; *m.* Caroline, dau. of Charles H. Croker, of Montevideo.
  1. Marianne Sinclaire, *m.* Aug. 1855, Maj.-Gen. Conolly McCausland, R.E., and left issue two daus.
  2. Sarah Maria, *m.* 15 Dec. 1857, Gen. W. J. Smythe, R.A., F.R.S., who *d.* 1887.
  3. Alice Louisa Jane, *m.* 2 Oct. 1871, Edward Lawrenson, of Nurney, co. Kildare, and Sutton House, Howth, co. Dublin, and *d.* March, 1900, leaving issue.
 3. Charles Humphry, R.N., lost in the wreck of the St. George off coast of Denmark, Dec. 1811, aged 16.
 4. LOFTUS HENRY, late of Blandsfort.
  1. Catherine Jane, *m.* 1st, Capt. Richard Croker, R.N., of Thornbury, Queen's Co., and had issue; and 2ndly, Rev. Thomas Frere Bowerbank, Vicar of Chiswick, Middlesex, who *d.s.p.* 1867.
  2. Sarah Annie, *d. unm.* 1823.
  3. Georgina Elizabeth, *m.* James Franck Rolleston, of Franckfort Castle, King's Co., and had issue (*see that family*).

The eldest son,
JOHN THOMAS BLAND, of Blandsfort, Cornet 4th Q.O. Dragoons, *m.* Margaret Elizabeth, dau. of John Bond, of Bath, and dying *s.p.s.* 1849, devised Blandsfort to his brother,
LOFTUS HENRY BLAND, of Blandsfort, M.A., Q.C., M.P. for the King's Co., *b.* Aug. 1805; *m.* 1st, 20 Aug. 1840, Charlotte Elizabeth, 2nd dau. of Gen. the Hon. Arthur Grove Annesley, of Ann's Grove, co. Cork, and by her (who *d.* 26 March, 1842) had a son,
1. JOHN LOFTUS, late of Blandsfort.

He *m.* 2ndly, 2 Dec. 1843, Annie Jane, eldest dau. of the late John Prendergast Hackett, of Stratford Place, London, and by her (who *d.* 17 Jan. 1904) had issue,
2. Thomas Dalrymple, Lieut. 4th Hussars, *b.* 9 June, 1846; *d.* 1869.
1. Elizabeth Emily, *m.* March, 1878, the Very Rev. Dean Warburton. He *d.s.p.* 3 May, 1900. She *d.* 21 July, 1901 (*see* WARBURTON *of Garryhinch*).
2. Annie Sophia Alicia.

Mr. Loftus Bland, M.P. for King's Co. 1852-59, was appointed Chairman of Quarter Sessions, co. Cavan, 1862. He *d.* 21 Jan. 1872.
The elder son,
JOHN LOFTUS BLAND, of Blandsfort, Queen's Co., J.P., D.L., *b.* 2 June, 1841; *s.* his father 21 Jan. 1872, late Capt. 6th Inniskilling Dragoons; *m.* 1st, 2 July, 1868, Alice, 2nd dau. of George Hotham, late Capt. R.E. (*see* BURKE'S *Peerage,* HOTHAM, B.), and by her (who *d.* 31 Jan. 1898) had
HUMPHREY LOFTUS, now of Blandsfort.

Mr. J. L. Bland *m.* 2ndly, 27 July, 1899, Georgiana Augusta, dau. of George White West, of Ardenode, co. Kildare (*see* WEST *of White Park*), and *d.* 3 Dec. 1908.

Arms—Arg., on a bend sa., three pheons or, in the sinister chief point a crescent gu. *Crest*—Out of a ducal coronet a lion's head ppr., charged with a crescent gu. *Motto*—Quo fata vocant.
Seat—Blandsfort, Abbeyleix. *Club*—Kildare Street, Dublin.

BLENNERHASSETT OF BALLYSEEDY.

ARTHUR BLENNER-HASSETT, of Ballyseedy, co. Kerry, J.P. and D.L., High Sheriff 1878, late Major 4th Batt. R. Munster Fusiliers, b. 26 June, 1856; s. his father 1859; m. 6 June, 1882, Clara Nesta Richarda, only dau. of Desmond John Edmund FitzGerald, THE KNIGHT OF GLIN, and has,
1. Nesta Georgie. 2. Hilda. 3. Vera.

Lineage.—This family, which is of English origin, settled in Ireland, temp. Queen ELIZABETH, about 1580, and has, since that period, maintained the highest rank amongst the gentry of the co. Kerry, where the first settler, THOMAS BLENNERHASSETT, of Flimby, co. Cumberland, M.P. for Carlisle 1584-5, with his son, ROBERT, obtained grants of lands in co. Kerry. This
ROBERT BLENNERHASSETT was M.P. for Tralee 1613, and th[e] Provost of the town. He m. Elizabeth, dau. of Jenkin Conway, and had (with a dau., Elizabeth, m. Capt. George Norton, of Moyagh Castle, co. Clare) three sons,
1. JOHN, his heir.
2. Edward, High Sheriff co. Kerry 1642, m. Mary, dau. of Edward Vauclier.
3. Arthur, m. Mary FitzGerald, of Ballynard, and was ancestor of BLENNERHASSETT of Riddlestown.

The eldest son,
JOHN BLENNERHASSETT, of Ballyseedy, M.P. Kerry, High Sheriff co. Kerry 1641, m. Martha, dau. of George Lynn, of Southwick Hall, and had issue,
1. JOHN, his heir.
2. Robert, High Sheriff co. Kerry 1622, M.P. Tralee 1634; m. Avice, dau. and co-heir of Jenkin Conway, of Killorglin, co. Kerry, and was ancestor of BLENNERHASSETT, Bart. of Blennerville, and of BLENNERHASSETT of Kells, co. Kerry.
3. Thomas, m. Ellen Stoughton.
1. Mary, m. Capt. Thomas Wren, of Litter.
2. Alice, m. Edmund Conway.
3. Lucy, m. Lieut. John Walker.

The eldest son,
JOHN BLENNERHASSETT, of Ballyseedy, M.P. for co. Kerry, High Sheriff 1658; m. Elizabeth, dau. of Sir Edward Denny, Knt. of Tralee Castle, and Ruth, his wife, eldest dau. of Sir Thomas Roper, Viscount Ballinglass, by whom (who was b. 25 Feb. 1635) he had issue,
1. Arthur, m. a dau. of Sir Boyle Maynard, Knt. of Curryglass, and d. at Tralee Castle, 7 Jan. 1686.
2. JOHN, of whom presently.
1. Ruth, m. 1st, Thomas Browne, and 2ndly, Thomas Blennerhassett, of Riddlestown.

The 2nd son,
JOHN BLENNERHASSETT, of Ballyseedy, M.P. for co. Kerry, m. Margaret, dau. of Crosbie, of Tubrid, and had (with a dau., Agnes, m. Robert Rogers, of Ashgrove, co. Cork) five sons,
1. JOHN, his heir. 2. Arthur, d.s.p.
3. Thomas, m. Avice Spring, and bad issue.
4. Pierce, d.s.p.
5. William, of Elm Grove, m. Mary, dau. of Alderman John Morley, Mayor of Cork 1718, and had issue,
WILLIAM, who s. to the estates.
Agnes, m. William Godfrey, 1st bart. of Bushfield.
Mr. Blennerhassett d. 1709, and was s. by his eldest son,
JOHN BLENNERHASSETT, of Ballyseedy, M.P. for Tralee 1709, High Sheriff co. Kerry 1717; m. Jane, dau. of Edward Denny, co. Tralee, and had issue,
1. JOHN, his heir.
2. Arthur, b. 1709; m. Jane, dau. of Monsieur Girardot, and widow of Col. Hamilton, and had two daus., co-heirs,
1. Jane, m. 23 June, 1783, George, 1st Lord Headley.
2. Juliana, m. 15 April, 1779, Michael Tisdall, of Charlesfort (see that family).
1. Agnes, b. 1722; m. Sir Thomas Denny, Knt. of Tralee.
2. Arabella, b. 1726; m. 1st, Richard Ponsonby, of Crotto, and 2ndly, Arthur Blennerhassett. 3. Letitia, d.s.p.
4. Mary, m. Launcelot Crosbie, of Tubrid.

The eldest son,
JOHN BLENNERHASSETT, of Ballyseedy, b. 1715, High Sheriff co. Kerry 1740; m. 1st, Ann, dau. of William Crosbie, of Tubrid, and widow of John Leslie, by whom he had no issue; and 2ndly, Frances, dau. of Edward Herbert, of Kilcow, by whom he had issue,
1. John, d. unm. v.p. 2. Arthur, d. unm. v.p.
1. Frances, m. 1782, Rev. Jemmett Browne, of Riverstown, co. Cork.
Mr. Blennerhassett dying thus without surviving male issue, the entailed estates devolved on his cousin,
WILLIAM BLENNERHASSETT, of Ballyseedy, High Sheriff co. Kerry 1761; m. 1765, Catherine, eldest dau. and co-heir of Noble Johnson, and had two sons and three daus.,
1. JOHN, his heir. 2. ARTHUR, who s. his brother.
1. Catherine, m. 1st, John Gustavus Crosbie, and 2ndly, George Rowan, of Rathauny, co. Limerick.
2. Frances, m. 1st, Anthony Denny, and 2ndly, Col. Sir George Morris.
3. Mary, m. Nevinson de Courcy, Capt. R.N.
Mr. Blennerhassett, whose will is dated 19 Jan. 1797, was s. by his eldest son,
JOHN BLENNERHASSETT, of Ballyseedy, M.P. co. Kerry 1794; d. unm., and was s. by his brother,
ARTHUR BLENNERHASSETT, of Ballyseedy, High Sheriff co. Kerry 1821; m. Dorcas, dau. of George Twiss, of Anna, co. Kerry, by Honora his wife, dau. of William Mereditb, of Dicksgrove, and had issue,
1. ARTHUR, his heir.
2. William (Rev.), Vicar of Iwerne Minster, Dorset, m. Emma Sophia Houssemayne, eldest dau. of F. Houssemayne du Boulay, and has issue, 1. John, d. unm.; 2. William, of Netley Firs, Hants, m. 26 May, 1904, Isabella Sara, 2nd dau. of the late Maxwell Anckettill of Leatherhead, Surrey (see ANCKETILL of Anckétill's Grove); 3. Arthur, Capt. R.N.; 4. Francis. 1. Marianne; 2. Emma Sophia; 3. Agnes.
3. John (Rev.), M.A. Rector of Ryme Intrinsica, Dorset, m. Elizabeth, dau. of F. Houssemayne du Boulay, of Forest House, Essex, and had four daus.,
1. Georgina, m. 28 April, 1864, Sir Augustus Riversdale Warren, 5th bart. of Warren's Court, and d. 1893, having had issue (see BURKE'S Peerage).
2. Geraldine de Courcy, m. 10 Aug. 1869, William George Digby Wingfield Digby (see WINGFIELD-DIGBY of Sherborne).
3. Bessie Houssemayne, m. 31 Oct. 1867, Charles Mark Allanson, 4th Lord Headley, and has issue (see BURKE'S Peerage).
4. Ada, m. — Chapman.
4. Crosbie, d.s.p. 5. Thomas, of Shannavalla.
6. Barry, Lieut.-Col. 71st Regt., d.s.p.
7. Nevinson de Courcy, R.N., d. unm.
1. Georgina, m. her cousin Edward Denny.
2. Margaret, d. unm.

The eldest son,
ARTHUR BLENNERHASSETT, of Ballyseedy, High Sheriff 1821, and M.P. for Derry 1836; m. Frances Deane, dau. of Henry Deane Grady, and by her (who d. 1834) had issue,
1. HENRY DEANE, his heir.
2. CHARLES JOHN ALLANSON WINN, successor to his brother.
1. Dorcas, m. Robert Conway Hurly, and d.s.p.
2. Amelia, m. Hon. Chichester Skeffington, and d. 3 Aug. 1887.
3. Ada, m. Standish, 3rd Viscount Guillamore, and d. 1867.
4. Frances Annabella, m. 6 Dec. 1859, Sir John Richard Wolseley, 6th bart. of Mount Wolseley, who d. 20 June, 1874, leaving issue (see BURKE'S Peerage). She d. 30 May, 1907.
Mr. Blennerhassett d. 1843, and was s. by his son,
HENRY DEANE BLENNERHASSETT, of Ballyseedy, who d. unm., and was s. by his brother,
CHARLES JOHN ALLANSON WINN BLENNERHASSETT, of Ballyseedy, J.P., High Sheriff 1858, b. 1830; m. 26 Sept. 1855, Marianne, 4th dau. of John Hickson, of the Grove, Dingle, J.P. and D.L., by Barbara his wife, dau. of John Mahony, of Dromore, and by her (who m. 2ndly, 1862, William Walker, 2nd son of Richard Walker, M.P.) he left at his decease, 9 Dec. 1859, a son and successor, the present ARTHUR BLENNERHASSETT, and a dau., Barbara Georgina, d. unm. Jan. 1867.

Arms—Gu., a chevron erm., between three dolphins, embowed, arg. Crest—A wolf sejant, ppr. Motto—Fortes fortuna juvat.
Seat—Ballyseedy House, near Tralee. Clubs—Kildare Street, Royal St. George's Yacht Club.

BLENNERHASSETT OF KELLS.

ROWLAND PONSONBY BLENNERHASSETT, of Kells, co. Kerry, J.P., K.C., M.P. for Kerry 1872-85, b. 22 July, 1850; m. 21 Sept. 1876, Mary Beatrice, 3rd dau. of the late Walter Armstrong, of Ennismore Gardens, S.W., and has issue,
RICHARD FRANCIS PONSONBY, b. 29 June, 1879.

Mr. Blennerhassett is the only son of the late Richard Francis Blennerhassett, of Kells, who d.v.p. 16 Feb. 1854 (by Honoria his wife, who d. 1884, dau. of William Carrique Ponsonby of Crotto), and grandson of Rowland Blennerhassett of Kells, who d. 12 April, 1854, 4th son of Sir Rowland Blennerhassett, 1st bart., who d. 14 March, 1821.

Lineage.—See BURKE'S Peerage, BLENNERHASSETT, Bart.
Arms—Gu., a chevron erm., between three dolphins, embowed, arg. Crest—A wolf sejant, ppr. Motto—Fortes fortuna juvat.
Seat—Kells, co. Kerry. Town Residence—52, Hans Place, S.W. Clubs—Brooks's and St. James's.

BLENNERHASSETT. See BURKE'S PEERAGE, BLENNERHASSETT, Bart.

Bligh. THE LANDED GENTRY. 56

BLIGH OF BRITTAS.

CAPT. FREDERICK ARTHUR BLIGH, of Brittas, Nobber, co. Meath, J.P., High Sheriff 1904 late Capt. R.A., *b.* 3 July, 1861; *m.* 22 June 1898, Mary Wentworth, 2nd dau. of Lieut.-Gen. Wentworth Forbes, and has issue,

Gwendolen Mary, *b.* 19 Jan. 1905.

Lineage.—JOHN BLIGH, of Rathmore, co. Meath, M.P. for Rathmore 1660, Commissioner of Inland Excise 1665, went to Ireland as Agent of the Adventurers for the forfeited estates in 1641 (3rd son of William Bligh, of Plymouth), bapt. 22 Feb. 1616-17, *m.* Catherine sister of William Fuller, Bishop of Lincoln. She *d.* before 8 Dec. 1669. He *d.* 3 Nov. 1666, leaving an only son,

THE RIGHT HON. THOMAS BLIGH, P.C., of Rathmore, co. Meath, M.P. 1701, *b.* 1654; *m.* 9 Dec. 1682, Elizabeth, dau. of Col. James Naper, of Loughcrew, co. Meath. She *d.* 21 March, 1736-7. He *d.* 28 Aug. 1710, having had issue,

1. JOHN, created EARL OF DARNLEY (see BURKE'S *Peerage*).
2. Thomas, of Brittas, Lieut.-Gen. in the Army, M.P. for Athboy 1715, *b.* 14 Aug. 1693; *m.* 1st, 19 Aug. 1737, Elizabeth, sister of William Bury, of Shannon Grove, co. Limerick. She *d.* 23 March, 1759. He *m.* 2ndly, Oct. 1760, Frances, sister of Theophilus Jones. He *d.s.p.* Aug. 1775. 3. ROBERT, of whom presently.

The youngest son,

THE VERY REV. ROBERT BLIGH, Dean of Elphin, *m.* 1st, July, 1742, Catherine Elliot, widow of Charles Boyle, of Arraghlin Bridge, co. Cork. She *d.* 15 Jan. 1757. He *m.* 2ndly, 18 March, 1759, the dau. of — Winthrop, of London, and had issue,

1. THOMAS CHERBURGH, of whom presently.
2. Robert, *d.s.p.*
1. Frances Theodosia, *m.* 5 Feb. 1788, Robert, 2nd Earl of Roden, K.P. He *d.* 29 June, 1840. She *d.* 22 May, 1802, leaving issue.
2. Katherine, *m.* 20 Dec. 1798, Hon. Hugh Howard, who *d.* 3 Nov. 1840, leaving issue (see BURKE'S *Peerage*, WICKLOW, E.).

The elder son,

THOMAS CHERBURGH BLIGH, of Brittas, *m.* 3 Nov. 1790, his cousin, Lady Theodosia Bligh, dau. of John, 3rd Earl of Darnley. She *d.* 21 Jan. 1840. He *d.* 17 Sept. 1830, leaving issue,

1. Thomas, Capt. Coldstream Guards, *m.* Helena, dau. of Col. Thomas Paterson, and *d.v.p.s.p.* She *m.* 2ndly, 10 Nov. 1828, William, 4th Earl of Mornington. She *d.* 1 July, 1857. She *d.* 7 April, 1869, leaving issue (see BURKE's *Peerage*, WELLINGTON, D.).
2. EDWARD, of Brittas.
3. Charles, *b.* 15 Dec. 1808, *m.* 17 July, 1837, Fanny Catherine, dau. of Sir William George Parker, Bart. She *d.* 7 Jan. 1894. He *d.* 1892, having had issue,
 1. Charles Francis, *b.* 1 June, 1846; *d.* 20 Jan. 1872.
 2. William George.
 1. Elizabeth.
 2. Sophia Henrietta, *m.* 23 May, 1866, John Gillett Livesay, and has issue.
 3. Emily Rose, *m.* 1 May, 1878, Robert Vesey Stoney, of Rosturk Castle, co. Mayo.
 4. Georgina Theodosia, dec.
1. Frances, *m.* 23 March, 1830, George Vicessimus Wigram, who *d.s.p.* 1 Jan. 1879. 2. Sarah, *d. unm.*
3. Elizabeth, *m.* 1st, 1828, John Cuming, Barrister-at-Law, who *d.* 1 Aug. 1831, leaving issue an only dau. (Elizabeth, *m.* 1850, Edward Foley); and 2ndly, 10 May, 1838, John Fountain Elwin, F.R.C.P., and by him had issue.

The eldest surviving son,

EDWARD BLIGH, of Brittas, J.P. and D.L., *b.* 1779; *m.* 1827, Sophia, dau. of Charles Eversfield, of Denne Park, Sussex, and *d.* 11 April, 1872, having had issue a son and a dau.,

FREDERICK CHERBURGH, of Brittas.
Theodosia *m.* 1850, her cousin. Edward Tredcroft, of Horsham, Sussex, and had issue.

The only son,

FREDERICK CHERBURGH BLIGH, of Brittas, J.P. co. Meath, Maj. 41st Regt., *b.* 23 April, 1829; *m.* 14 Sept. 1858, Emily Matilda, dau. of Hinton East, and *d.* 30 Nov. 1901, having by her had issue,

1. FREDERICK ARTHUR, now of Brittas.
1. Eva Sophia. 2. Ada Theodosia. 3. Eldina Mary.

Arms.—Az. a griffin segreant or armed and langued gu. between three crescents arg. Crest—A griffin's head erased or. Motto—Finem respice.

Seat—Brittas, Nobber, co. Meath.

BLOOD, LATE OF CRANAGHER.

GEN. SIR BINDON BLOOD, G.C.B., lately of Cranagher, co. Clare, commanded the Forces in the Punjab from 1901 to 1906, *b.* 7 Nov. 1842; *m.* 12 July, 1883, Charlotte Elizabeth, dau. of Sir Auckland Colvin, K.C.S.I., &c., and has had issue,

1. Bindon Auckland William, *b.* April, *d.* May, 1888.
1. Mary Meta, *b.* July, 1884; *d.* 1 May, 1898.
2. Charlotte Carissima, *m.* 14 Sept. 1910, Capt. Richard Hugh Royds Brocklebank, 9th Queen's Royal Lancers.

Sir Bindon served in the Jowaki Exped. 1877, in the Zulu War 1879, in the Afghan War 1879-80, in the Egyptian Exped. 1882, in Chitral 1895, in command of Malakand and Buner Field Forces 1897-98, and in the S. African War 1901.

Lineage.—EDMUND BLOOD, of Kilnaboy Castle and Bohersallagh, co. Clare, an officer in the Army, went to Ireland about 1595. He was M.P. for Ennis 1613. He left issue,

1. NEPTUNE, of whom presently. 2. Edmund.
3. Thomas, who left issue, a son, Col. Thomas Blood, of Sarney, co. Meath, who attempted to carry off the Crown jewels. His estate in Ireland was forfeited, but he had a pardon and pension from the king, dated 8 Aug. 1671. He *m.* 1 June, 1650, Mary, dau. of Lieut.-Col. John Holcroft, of Holcroft, co. Lancaster. He *d.* 24 Aug. 1680, leaving issue,
 1. Thomas, bapt. 30 March, 1651; *m.* Miss Delafaye or Delabaye, and *d.v.p.*, leaving a son,
 Edmund, Capt. in the Army, of Albany, North America, where he was living with his wife and family in 1734.
 2. William, *a.s.p.*
 3. Holcroft, Major-Gen., Clerk of the Crown and Peace co. Clare 1676, served in the fleet during war with Holland 1672-3; afterwards cadet in Louis XIV's Guards, Capt. of Pioneers in JAMES II's Army, present at Athlone and Limerick, wounded at the siege of Cavan, distinguished himself as chief engineer at the siege of Venloo, commanded Artillery at Blenheim and Ramilies under Marlborough, *d.* 30 Aug. 1707, aged 50; *m.* Elizabeth (will dated 8 Feb. 1721-2, pr. in London 23 Dec. 1725).
 4. Edmund, Purser of H.M.S. "Jersey," *d.* 1679.
 5. Charles.
 1. Mary, *m.* — Corbett.
 2. Elizabeth, *m.* Edward Everard.
4. William, of Dunboyne, co. Meath; *m.* Margery Row, and left issue.

The eldest son,

REV. NEPTUNE BLOOD, D.D., *b.* about 1595 (so called because he was born at sea), ordained Priest 18 March, 1622-3, Dean of Kilfenora and Prebendary of Rath 27 Jan. 1663, J.P., and Vicar-Gen. of the diocese of Kilfenora, 27 April, 1676. He is said to have *m.* three times. One of his wives was Elizabeth, eldest dau. of Higgat Lone, Dean of Kilfenora. He left issue,

1. THOMAS, his heir.
2. Edmond, from whom the BLOODS *of Brickhill*, co. Clare, are descended.
3. Peregrine, of Knocknareeha, co. Clare, Commissioner for collecting poll tax 1695.
4. Neptune (Rev.), Dean of Kilfenora, 8 Dec. 1692; *m.* Isabella, dau. of Samuel Pullein, Archbishop of Tuam, and *d.* 30 March, 1716, leaving issue.
 1. Samuel, *m.* 1707, Laura, dau. of Rev. Richard Verling, of Glannamor, co. Cork, and left a son,
 William, of Ennis, an Officer in the Revenue.
 2. George, who left issue. 3. Vesey.
5. Henry.

The eldest son,

THOMAS BLOOD, of Bobersallagh, co. Clare, *m.* a dau. — Davis, and by her had issue, six sons and one dau.,

1. Neptune, of Bohersallagh, co. Clare, *m.* Alice Scott, but *d.s.p.* 25 Nov. 1744. 2. THOMAS, of whom presently.
3. Matthew, of Cragaunboy, ancestor of BLOOD of Ballykilty (*see that family*). 4. Edmund, who left issue.
5. Mark, *d.* 24 Dec. 1751, leaving issue from whom descend the BLOODS, of Ballysheen, co. Clare, and of Huntley Court, co. Gloucester.
6. William, from whom the BLOODS, of Fautore, co. Clare, now extinct.
1. Deborah, *m.* Edmund Blood.

The second son,

THOMAS BLOOD, of Cahirnemoher and Bohersallagh, co. Clare, *m.* Elizabeth. dau. of Capt. John Greene, of Old Abbey, co. Limerick, by Catherine his wife, dau. and coheir of Capt. Anthony Horsey, of Kilcroney, co. Kilkenny. He *d.* 12 July, 1730, having had issue,
1. Thomas, *d. unm.* July, 1741. 2. WILLIAM, of whom presently.
3. Anthony, *d.s.p.* 4. Edmund, *d.s.p.m.*
1. Anne, *m.* William Adams, of Ballygriffin, co. Clare.

The second son,
WILLIAM BLOOD, of Roxton, co. Clare, J.P., High Sheriff, 1750 ; *m.* 1747, Ann, dau. of William Chadwick, of Ballinard, co. Tipperary. He *d.* 1791, leaving issue,
1. WILLIAM, of whom presently.
2. Thomas, from whom descend the BLOODS of Essex.
3. Neptune, of Applevale, co. Clare, Ensign 61st Regt., *m.* Marianne, dau. of Thomas Davies, of Newcastle, co. Galway. She *d.* 1 Nov. 1837. He *d.* 9 Oct. 1797, aged 45, leaving issue. From him descended the BLOODS of Applevale.
4. Michael, of Baskin Hill, co. Dublin, J.P., *d.* 18 Oct. 1812, aged 56, leaving issue by his second wife, Cecilia Compton, a dau. Frances, *m.* James Tynions, of Baskin Hill, co. Dublin.
5. Frederick (Rev.), Rector of Kilnaboy, and Vicar of Kilkeedy, Prebendary of Dysert, co. Clare, *m.* Susan Powell.
6. Richard, of Bannvale, co. Down, *m.* Jane Maria, dau. of Capt. Thomas Shaw of the Lurgan Yeom., and left issue,
    1. Frederick, of Hermitage, co. Dublin, Lieut. R.N., *m.* Sarah Mary Morris, of Lurgan, but *d.s.p.*
    2. Randal, *d. unm.* 3. Thomas, *d. unm.* 4. Michael, *d. unm.*
    5. Clements, Maj.-Gen. Bombay Artillery, served with distinction in Afghanistan and Punjab, *d. unm.*
    6. Richard, of Dromoher, co. Clare, Maj.-Gen. Bombay N.I., *d. unm.* 8 July, 1877.
    1, Frances Anne, *m.* Lieut. Charles North, 50th Regt., and *d.* 1884, aged 93.
    2. Jane.
1. Jane, *m.* Edward William Burton, of Clifden, co. Clare, High Sheriff 1799, and had issue.

The eldest son,
WILLIAM BLOOD, of Roxton, co. Clare, J.P., High Sheriff 1774, Col. of the Ennis Volunteers, *m.* 1772, Elizabeth. dau of Nicholas Bindon, by Elizabeth, his second wife, dau. of Patrick French, of Monival, and *d.* 5 Nov. 1784, aged 35, having had issue, with a dau. Nicola, an only son,
BINDON BLOOD, of Cranagher, co. Clare, J.P. and D.L., High Sheriff 1819, *b.* 17 March, 1775 ; *m.* 1st, his cousin Anne, dau. of Edward William Burton, of Clifden, co. Clare, and Jane his wife (*see above*), and by her had issue,
1. Elizabeth, *d. unm.* 2. Jane, *d. unm.*
3. Anne, *m.* George Stoney, of Oakley Park, King's Co., and had issue.
4. Mary, *m.* 14 May, 1832, Aylward O'Conor, of Miltown, co. Roscommon, and had issue (*see* O'CONNOR (*or* O'CONOR) *of Rathnew*).
5. Fanny, *m.* William Hamilton, M.D., and *d.s.p.*
6. Nicola, *d. unm.*

He *m.* 2ndly, by licence, 27 Dec. 1809, Harriet, dau. of Christopher Bagot, of Nurney, co. Kildare, and by her had issue,
1. William, *d.s.p.* 2. Bindon, *d.* young.
3. Bagot, *d.* young. 4. WILLIAM BINDON, of whom presently.
7. Katherine, *m.* Charles M. Bagot, Barrister-at-Law.

He *m.* 3rdly, Maria, dau. of — Hinckley, of Tenterden, Kent, and by her had issue,
5. Bindon, of Dublin, *d.s.p.* 22 Jan. 1859.
6. Bagot, of Rockforest, co. Clare, J.P., High Sheriff 1883, *b.* 1845, *m.* Katherine Florence, dau. of Maj. Charles Washington Studdert, of Cragmoher, co. Clare, and *d.* 11 Feb. 1897, leaving issue,
    1. Bindon, Capt. 8th Cavalry I.A., served in S. African War 1901 ; *b.* 30 Dec. 1881.
    2. Charles Newman, *b.* 10 June, 1887.
    1. Katherine Nicola, *b.* 5 Oct. 1883 ; *m.* Major Francis Hyslop, King's Regt.
8. Mary Anne, *m.* Hugh Baker Stoney, M.B., of Abbeyleix, and had issue (*see* BUTLER-STONEY *of Portland Park*).
9. Frances, *d.s.p.* 10. Maria, *d.s.p.*

Mr. Bindon Blood *d.* 27 Jan. 1855. His 4th son,
WILLIAM BINDON BLOOD, of Cranagher, J.P., *b.* 20 Jan. 1817 ; *m.* 1st, Margaret, dau. of Robert Stewart, of Hawthornside, co. Roxburgh. and by her had issue,
1. BINDON (Sir), lately of Cranagher.
2. Bagot William, M.Inst.C.E., Lieut.-Col. 2nd Batt. Bombay, Baroda and Central India Vol. Rifles, late Chief Eng. Rajputana Malwa Railway (*Albert House, Dalkey*), *b.* 6 Nov. 1844 ; *d.* 4 Feb. 1910 ; *m.* 18 March, 1874, Mary Jane, dau. of Col. Thomas Biggs, Royal Bombay Art., of Alburys, Wrington, Somerset, and has issue,
    1. William Bindon, *b.* 1876, *d.* 1884.
    2. Bagot Neptune, *b.* 12 May, 1882.
    3. Robert Stewart, *b.* 1887, *d.* 1888.
    1. Katherine May, *b.* 1875.
    2. Meta Ethel, *b.* 1879, *d.* 1881.
    3. Charlotte Nicola, *b.* 1886.
    4. Hariott Eleanor, *b.* 1896.
3. Robert, M.D., Col. R.A.M.C., P.M.O. VIIth Division (*Primrose Hill, Kingstown, near Dublin*), *b.* 10 March, 1847 ; *m.* 9 Oct. 1879, Catherine Sarah, dau. of the late William Barker Drury, of Boden Park, co. Dublin.
1. Margaret, *m.* her cousin, Aylward Owen Blood O'Conor, LL.D., who *d.* 12 Oct. 1911, leaving issue (*see* O'CONNOR (*or* O'CONOR) *of Rathnew*).

He *m.* 2ndly, 1855, Maria Augusta, dau. of Robert Henry Persse, of Castle Boy, co. Galway (*see* PERSSE *of Roxborough*). She *d* 23 Jan. 1860, leaving issue,
4. William Persse, Col. D.A.A.G., War Office, formerly Maj. Royal Irish Fus., D.A.A.G., 2nd Army Corps, Salisbury, B.A. Trin. Coll. Dublin, served in Egypt Exped. 1882, Black Mountain Exped. 1888, and in Mohmund and Tirah Campaigns 1897, *b.* 26 Feb. 1857 ; *m.* 23 Jan. 1888, Marienne Frances, dau. of Capt. James William Robarts, 9th Lancers, of Belmore Hall, Kent, and has issue,
    1. William Edmund Robarts, *b.* 19 Feb. 1897.
    1. Wilhelmina Augusta, *b.* 11 April, 1890.
    2. Vera Hernione May, *b.* 20 Feb. 1893.

Mr. William Bindon Blood *d.* 31 Jan. 1894, and was s. by his eldest son.

Arms—Quarterly 1st and 4th Arg. a fesse indented gu. between six martlets sa. (BLOOD) 2nd and 3rd gu. three escallops arg. within a bordure engrailed or (BINDON). **Crest** —Issuant from waves of the sea a demi figure of Neptune all ppr. **Motto**—Honor virtutis præmium.

Residence—183, St. James's Court, S.W. *Clubs*—Naval and Military and the Marlborough.

BLOOD OF BALLYKILTY.

JOHN BLOOD, of Ballykilty, co. Clare, *b.* 9 June, 1849 ; *m.* 1st, 7 March, 1878, Jane, dau. of Thomas Studdert, of Ballyhannan, co. Clare, and by her (who *d.* 16 Jan. 1902) has issue,
1. CHARLES FITZGERALD, *b.* 2 April, 1879.
2. John Frederick, *b.* 10 Nov. 1880 ; *d.* 18 Dec. 1893.
3. William Holcroft, *b.* 29 May, 1887, Lieut. Q.O.C. of Guides.

He *m.* 2ndly, 21 Oct. 1908, the Hon. Geraldine Mary, eldest dau. of Edward Donough, 14th Baron Inchiquin, and widow of (*see* BURKE'S *Peerage*) Thomas George Stacpoole-Mahon, of Corbally, co. Clare (*see that family*).

Lineage. — MATTHEW BLOOD, of Cragaunboy, co. Clare, 3rd son of THOMAS BLOOD, eldest son of the Rev. NEPTUNE BLOOD (*see* BLOOD, *of Cranagher*), *m.* Elizabeth, dau. of Henry Lucas, and *d.* 29 Sept. 1760, aged 84, leaving issue,
1. JOHN, of whom presently.
2. George, *d.s.p.*
3. Matthew, of Cragaunboy, co. Clare, *m.* Caroline, dau. of Andrew Roe, of Grantstown and Roe's Green, co. Tipperary. She *d.* 1805. He *d.* Aug. 1794, leaving issue, from whom the BLOODS *of Dublin* are descended.
1. Abigail, *m.* Joseph Adams, Attorney-at-Law.
2. Hannah, *m.* 1st, John Constantine, and 2ndly, John Brampton

The eldest son,
JOHN BLOOD, of Castle Fergus and Ballykilty, co. Clare, *m.* Mary, dau. of Charles FitzGerald, of Shepperton, co. Clare. He *d.* 16 Jan. 1799, aged 78, leaving issue,
1. Matthew, of Castle Fergus, Ensign 22nd Foot, Lieut. 57th Regt., J.P., co. Clare ; *m.* 6 Feb. 1784, Dorothea Julia, dau. of the Rev. Jacques Ingram, and niece of Dr. Smyth, Archbishop of Dublin. He *d.* 20 Aug. 1820, and was ancestor of the BLOOD-SMYTHS *of Castle Fergus*.
2. NEPTUNE, of whom presently.
1. Hannah, *m.* George Studdert, of Kilkishen, co. Clare.
2. Jane, *m.* John Singleton, of Ballygoreen, co. Clare.
3. Alice, *m.* Robert Young, of co. Tipperary.

The 2nd son,
NEPTUNE BLOOD, of Ballykilty, co. Clare, Capt. Clare Militia, formerly 62nd Foot, *m.* (licence bond dated 18 May, 1798) Anne, dau. of Joseph Anthony, of Seafield, co. Waterford. He *d.* 29 May, 1815, leaving issue,
1. John, of Ballykilty, co. Clare, J.P., *b.* 4 Oct. 1803 ; *d. unm.* 4 April, 1861.
2. Joseph Mark Anthony, of Ballykilty, Surgeon, *b.* 19 June, 1806 ; *d. unm.* 13 Oct. 1838.
3. FITZGERALD, of whom we treat.
1. Alicia, bapt. 17 March 1805 ; *m.* 15 Oct. 1824, Francis John Castles, Surgeon, and had issue.
2. Jane, *b.* 13 July, 1810 ; *m.* 27 March, 1827, Thomas Jacob, of Thornbury, Queen's Co., Crown Solicitor for that co., and *d.* 21 March, 1880. He *d.* 17 July, 1865, leaving issue.

3. Kitty, b. 14 March, 1812 ; m. Capt. Thomas Blood, 6th Regt., of Fantore, co. Clare, who served in the Peninsular War (medal with nine clasps). She d. May 1872. He d.s.p. 30 Dec. 1856.
The 3rd son,
FITZGERALD BLOOD, of Ballykilty, J.P. co. Clare, b. about 1815 ; m. 5 Jan. 1848, Millicent Anne, dau. of Francis Morice, of Springfield, co. Clare, by Maria his wife, dau. of Capt. William Spaight, of Corbally, co. Clare. She d. 27 Jan. 1888. He d. 25 May, 1864, leaving issue,
1. JOHN, now of Ballykilty.
2. Joseph Fitzgerald, of 8, Lorne Road, Birkenhead, co. Chester, Surgeon-Maj. (ret.) 8th Bengal Cavalry, M.A., M.D. of Trin. Coll. Dublin, served in Afghan War 1878-9, b. 15 March, 1853 ; m. 20 July, 1887, Eliza, dau. of Henry James Dudgeon, J.P., of the Priory, Blackrock, co. Dublin, and has issue,
 1. Brian, educated at Winchester, B.A. New College, Oxford, b. 1 July, 1889.
 2. Morice, Cadet Royal Naval College, Osborne 1910, b. 30 April, 1897.
 1. Olive Millicent, b. 11 April, 1892.
 2. Barbara Florence, b. 14 April, 1894.
3. Francis, bapt. 28 May, 1854 ; d. 13 May, 1865.
4. Neptune Fitzgerald, of Vrede, Orange Free State, S. Africa, B.A., M.D. Trin. Coll. Dublin, b. 16 July, 1856 ; m. 19 Feb. 1884, Rebecca Sarah, dau. of Capt. Augustus Hartford, 59th Regt., of Rose Court, Portarlington, Queen's Co. She d. 26 July, 1898. He d.s.p. 6 Feb. 1902.
5. Charles Holcroft, of Willow Bank, Limerick, late of Johannesburg, Transvaal, S. Africa, M.A., M.D. Trin. Coll. Dublin, late Civil Surgeon with Natal Field Force in S. African War 1900-2 (Queen's and King's medals and clasps), b. 29 Dec. 1858 ; m. 26 Feb. 1908, Agnes, dau. of the Very Rev. James Hastings Allen, Dean of Killaloe.
6. Frederick William, of Johannesburg, S. Africa, b. 1 June, 1860 ; m. 27 Oct. 1892, Alice, dau. of Frederick Randolph Höhne, sometime Sec. of State of the Orange Free State, d.s.p. at Johannesburg, 28 March, 1910.
1. Maria Ann, b. 13 July, 1851 ; m. 14 Jan. 1874, Edmund Maghlin Russell, of Milford, co. Limerick, and has issue.
2. Millicent Amelia Charlotte, b. 18 Sept. 1862 ; m. 15 Nov. 1882, Capt. Harry Gordon Fellowes-Gordon, J.P. and D.L., 3rd Batt. Gordon Highlanders, late 76th Regt., of Knockespoch, co. Aberdeen, eldest son of Rear-Admiral William Abdy Fellowes-Gordon, of Knockespoch, Aberdeen, and has issue.

Arms—Arg. on a fess indented gu. between six martlets sa. two crescents or. Crest—Issuant from waves of the sea a demi-figure of Neptune all ppr. Motto—Honor virtutis præmium.
Seat—Ballykilty, co. Clare.

BLOOMFIELD OF CASTLE CALDWELL.

MEYNELL CALDWELL EGERTON RODNEY BLOOMFIELD, of Castle Caldwell, co. Fermanagh, b. 1882, s. his grandfather 1897.

Lineage.—BENJAMIN BLOOMFIELD, or BLUMFIELD, of Eyre Court, co. Galway, made his will 17 July, 1737, which was proved 13 Jan. following. By Dorothy his wife he left four sons and two daus.,
1. JOHN, of whom hereafter.
2. Joseph, b. 1710, entered Trin. Coll. Dublin, 14 Oct. 1726, aged 16 years, B.A. 1731.
3. Benjamin of Meelick, co. Galway, whose son,
  John, of Newport, co. Tipperary, m. Charlotte, dau. of Samuel Waller, and sister of Sir Robert Waller, 1st bart. of Newport, by whom (who d. 1 Feb. 1828) he had issue,
   (1) BENJAMIN, 1st Lord Bloomfield, G.C.B., G.C.H., b. 13 April, 1762 ; m. 7 Sept. 1797, Harriott, dau. of John Douglas, of Grantham, co. Lincoln. She d. 12 Sept. 1868. He d. 15 Aug. 1846, leaving issue,
     1. John Arthur Douglas, 2nd and last Baron Bloomfield, G.C.B., P.C., b. 12 Nov. 1802 ; m. 4 Sept. 1845, Hon. Georgiana Liddell, dau. of Thomas, 1st Lord Ravensworth. He d.s.p. 17 Aug. 1879.
     1. Harriott Anne, m. 5 June, 1833, Col. Thomas Henry Kingscote, of Kingscote. He d. 19 Dec. 1861, leaving issue (see that family). She d. 31 July, 1901.
     2. Georgiana Mary Emilia, m. 22 Oct. 1836, Henry Trench, of Cangort. He d. 7 March, 1881. She d. 13 Jan. 1893, leaving issue (see that family).
   (1) Anne, m. Thomas Ryder Pepper, of Loughton, co. Tipperary. She d.s.p. April, 1841.
   (2) Charlotte, m. 19 March, 1800, Very Rev. Thomas Bunbury Gough, Dean of Derry. She d. 14 Feb. 1862. He d. 8 May, 1860.
4. Richard.
1. Dorothy.   2. Anne.
Benjamin Bloomfield d. 1737. His eldest son,
JOHN BLOOMFIELD, of Redwood, co. Tipperary, High Sheriff, 1753, d. 7 March, 1771, having m. by licence, dated 28 Feb. 1742, Jane, dau. of Brig.-Gen. George Jocelyn, and had issue,
1. JOHN, his heir.
2. George, m. by licence, dated 5 Dec. 1789, Elizabeth Bayley, of Dublin, and d.s.p.
3. Jocelyn, d. intestate and s.p. ; administration 17 Aug. 1791.
4. Robert.
1. Dorothea, m. 20 Aug. 1775, George, 2nd Earl of Belvedere.
2. Jane.

3. Frances, m. July, 1779, Gustavus Rochfort-Hume, of Rochfort, M.P.
The eldest son,
JOHN BLOOMFIELD, of Redwood, m. Jane, dau. of Sir John Colpoys, and had issue,
JOHN COLPOYS, his successor.
Dorothea, m. by licence, dated 9 March, 1798, Thomas Hunt, of Dublin, merchant.
The son,
JOHN COLPOYS BLOOMFIELD, of Redwood, High Sheriff co. Fermanagh 1825, b. 1788 ; m. 11 June, 1817, Frances Arabella, eldest dau. and co-heir of Sir John Caldwell, 6th bart. of Castle Caldwell, and by her (who d. 1872) had issue,
1. JOHN CALDWELL, of Castle Caldwell.
2. Fitz-Maurice Gustavus, of New Park, Waterford, J.P. co. Waterford, formerly Capt. Bengal Artillery, b. 13 Feb. 1824 ; m. 21 June, 1848, Henrietta Sophia (d. 19 Feb. 1906), dau. of John Commerell, of Stroode Park, Sussex, and d. 1894, leaving issue,
 1. Fitz-Maurice Edmund, b. 1859 ; d. 15 Feb. 1871.
 2. Godfrey Herbert, of New Park, co. Waterford, b. 5 March, 1865 ; m. 16 Sept. 1896, Emmeline Louisa, dau. of Sir John Arnott, Bart. (see BURKE's Peerage and Baronetage), and has issue,
   (1) Fitzmaurice John Commerell, b. 1897.
   (2) Gustavus Herbert William, b. 2 March, 1899.
   (1) Kathleen Lily Ives, b. 21 March, 1901.
 1. Sophia Arabella Edith, m. 2 Feb. 1870, William Capel, Major 82nd Regt., of The Grove, Stroud, co. Gloucester, and has issue.
 2. Kathleen Mary.
 3. Charlotte Dorothea, m. 31 Aug. 1876, Joseph Mills, late Capt. 5th Dragoon Guards.
 4. Alice Eliza Helen, m. 1st, 2 June, 1874, Frederick Malcolmson, and by him has issue. She m. 2ndly, 26 Feb. 1880, Andrew Caldecott Caldwell, eldest son of Edward Caldecott Caldwell, 3rd Dragoon Guards.
 5. Henrietta Julia, m. 23 April, 1883, Lieut.-Col. Walter Lindsay, late Rifle Brigade, and has issue (see BURKE's Peerage, CRAWFORD, E.).
 6. Ethel Adelaide.
3. Godfrey Colpoys, Major in the Army, b. 6 April, 1826 ; m. 1st, 18 Oct. 1855, Juliana, dau. of Robert Lane, of Ryelands, co. Hereford ; and 2ndly, 8 May, 1862, Ellen, dau. of Thomas Charles Bridges, of The Lodge, Ludlow, and by her (who d. 29 Jan. 1901) has one son and two daus.
4. Alleyne FitzHerbert Fenton, Lieut.-Col. Indian Army (Retired), b. 1832 ; m. 2 Sept. 1864, Eleanor Loftus, dau. of Nicholas Loftus Tottenham, of Glenfarne Hall, co. Fermanagh, and has issue,
 1. FitzHerbert Wheatly, b. 31 Oct. 1870.
 2. Jocelyn, b. 14 March, 1877 ; d. 18 Oct. 1880.
 1. Constance Caldwell.   2. Evelyn Eleanor.
1. Frances, m. 1839, John Minchin Walcott.
Mr. Bloomfield d. Jan. 1881. His eldest son,
JOHN CALDWELL BLOOMFIELD, of Castle Caldwell, co. Fermanagh, J.P. and D.L., High Sheriff 1874, b. 5 Feb. 1823 ; m. 1st, 1846, Elizabeth, elder dau. of William d'Arcy (Irvine) d'Arcy, of Necarn Castle, co. Fermanagh, and by her (who d. 10 March, 1874) had issue,
Benjamin Francis Meynell, J.P., Capt. Fermanagh Militia, b. 1850 ; m. 12 Jan. 1875, Lydia Frances, dau. of Sir William Henry Marsham Style, Bart. He d.v.p. 26 Nov. 1886. She d. 23 June, 1900, leaving issue,
 1. MEYNELL CALDWELL EGERTON RODNEY, now of Castle Caldwell.
 1. Marian Blanche, m. 3 June, 1903, Rev. Benjamin T. du Boe, eldest son of the late J. N. du Boe, of Riverstown, co. Kildare.
 2. Grace Maria Louisa ; m. 6 Dec. 1898, Arthur Francis Forster, eldest son of William Stewart Forster, of Rumwood, Maidstone.
Blanche Caldwell, m. 30 June, 1879, Rev. Canon Charles Thornton Primrose Grierson, son of George A. Grierson, of Rathfarnham House, co. Dublin, and has issue.
Mr. Bloomfield m. 2ndly, 12 Aug. 1875, Adelaide Hannah Frances, dau. of Sir Josiah Hort, 2nd bart. He d. 27 Feb. 1897, and was s. by his grandson.

Seat—Castle Caldwell. Belleek, co. Fermanagh.

LYNCH-BLOSSE.   See BURKE's PEERAGE, LYNCH-BLOSSE, Bart.

BOLTON OF MOUNT BOLTON.

CHARLES PERCEVAL BOLTON, of Mount Bolton, co. Waterford, J.P., High Sheriff 1893, b. 18 Sept. 1849 ; s. his father 1884.

Lineage—The founder of this family in Ireland was CAPT. WILLIAM BOLTON, an officer of Dragoons in the Protector's Army, who stormed and took Fatlock Castle, Oct. 1649, and obtained a large grant of land in the co. of Waterford in 1667. He held the office of Mayor of Waterford in 1662. By Abigail his wife, dau. of Col. Prittie, he had several children ; from the eldest son, Cornelius, Capt. in Col. Collingwood's Regt., descends WILLIAM EDWARD BOLTON, an officer in 18th Hussars. Capt. William Bolton's brother,

THOMAS BOLTON, appointed to a company in Col. Fleetwood's Regt. 1652, Mayor of Waterford in 1671, d. 1682, leaving issue, The eldest son,
THOMAS BOLTON, b. 1654, was appointed Recorder of Waterford in place of Sir R. Stephens, 13 Jan. 1682. His son,
WILLIAM BOLTON, of Fatlock Castle, Capt. in Col. Edward May's troop of Dragoons, was left by will, dated 22 May, 1718, heir to the extensive estates of his cousin, Charles Bolton, brother of the Very Rev. Hugh Bolton, Dean of Waterford. He d. 12 March, 1750, leaving (with two daus, Mary, m. R. Lymbery, of Killcopp House, co. Waterford, and Eleanor, d. unm. in 1783) a son,
JOHN BOLTON, first of Fatlock Castle, and afterwards of Mount Bolton, m. 5 Dec. 1745, Anne Snow, of Snowhaven, co. Kilkenny, and d. 25 April, 1792, having had issue,
1. CHARLES, his heir.
2. Robert (Sir), Lieut.-Gen. G.C.H., of Swerford Park, Oxford shire, Aide-de-Camp to GEORGE III., and Equerry to GEORGE IV. He d. 15 March, 1836.
1. Hannah, m. 21 May, 1772, Maunsell Bowers, of Mount Prospect, co. Kilkenny, and had issue, three sons and six daus.
The son and heir,
CHARLES BOLTON, bapt. 18 April, 1759; m. 1st, Jane, dau. of the Ven. John Doyle, M.A., Archdeacon of Kilmacduagh, and sister of Lieut.-Gen. Doyle, of Waterford, by whom he had one son,
1. JOHN, his heir.
Mr. Bolton m. 2ndly, Ellen, eldest dau. of Harry Wallis, of Drishane Castle, co. Cork, and by her had issue,
2. Henry, A.M., Vicar of Dysart, Enos, and Kilteale, Queen's Co., b. 8 April, 1787; m. 19 Dec. 1814, Frances, 2nd dau. of Sir Simon Newport, Knt., by Jane his wife, younger dau. of the Ven. Archdeacon Alcock; and d. 8 Nov. 1854, having by her (who d. 14 Dec. 1880) had issue,
1. CHARLES NEWPORT, of Brook Lodge, co. Waterford, s. his cousin at Mount Bolton, 1878.
2. Robert Wallis, b. 2 May, 1819; d. 25 Feb. 1820.
1. Jane Wallis, m. 13 Oct. 1853, Robert Carew Anderson, M.D., Surgeon-Major, Dep.-Insp.-Gen., late of the 13th Hussars, 3rd son of the Rev. Joshua Anderson, Rector and Vicar of Myshall, co. Carlow. She left issue, five sons and two daus.
1. Elizabeth, m. 1823, Sir Simon Newport, Knt. of Waterford, but d.s.p. 1 Dec. 1844.
The eldest son,
JOHN BOLTON, of Mount Bolton, b. 1783; m. Eliza, 2nd dau. of Maunsell Bowers, and dying in 1807, aged 24, was s. by his son,
JOHN BOLTON, of Mount Bolton, Major 7th Dragoon Guards, b. 1807; d. suddenly in London, 1841, and was s. by his sister,
JANE BOLTON, of Mount Bolton, who d. unm. 16 June, 1878, and was s. by her cousin,
CHARLES NEWPORT BOLTON, of Mount Bolton, b. 15 March, 1816; m. 4 Feb. 1845, Anne, eldest dau. of the Rev. Joshua Anderson, M.A (Rector of Myshall, co. Carlow) of Grace Dieu, co. Waterford, by Anne his wife, eldest dau. of Capt. William Perceval, and by her (who d. 1 Sept. 1884) had issue,
1. HENRY ANDERSON, b. 7 March, 1848; m. 29 Sept. 1880.
2. CHARLES PERCEVAL, s. his father in the Mount Bolton property under the will of Miss Jane Bolton.
1. Anne Frances Ellen.
Mr. Bolton d. 25 April, 1884.
Seat—Mount Bolton, co. Waterford. Residence—Brook Lodge, Halfway House, Waterford.

BOLTON OF CASTLE RING.

JOHN MARSHALL BOLTON, of Castle Ring, co. Louth, and Donaghmoyne, co. Monaghan, J.P. for both cos., High Sheriff for the latter 1894, B.A., Trin, Coll. Dublin, b. Feb. 1858; m. 12 Dec. 1895, Florinda Julia, eldest dau. of the late Rev. James Robert ffolliott, M.A., Rector of Moira, co. Down, by Julia his wife, of Tierernane, Strand, and Upper Ballylehane, Queen's Co., dau. of Charles Warner Hovenden, of Ballylehane (see FFOLLIOTT of Tierernane).

Lineage.—The pedigree of this family is registered in Ulster's Office, Dublin.
JOHN BOLTON, of Great Fenton, in Staffordshire, son of ROGER BOLTON, descended from the family of BOLTON of Bolton, Lancashire, m. Margaret, dau. of Richard Ashe, of Ashe, Staffordshire, and by her, who d. in Dublin 11 Oct. 1620, had a son,
SIR RICHARD BOLTON, Knt., of Courtduff, LORD CHANCELLOR OF IRELAND, m. 1st, Frances, dau. of Richard Walter, of Stafford, and by her had issue,

1. Edward (Sir), Lord Chief Baron of the Exchequer, from whom descended the BOLTONS of Bective Abbey, co. Meath.
2. Richard.
3. John.
4. THOMAS, of whom presently.
1. Anne, m. Arthur Hill, M.P. of Hillsborough, and had issue (see BURKE'S Peerage, DOWNSHIRE, M.).
2. Mary, m. 1st, Patrick Nangle, of Navan, and 2ndly, Edward Bermingham.
He m. 2ndly, Margaret, dau. of Sir Patrick Barnewall, Kt. of Turvey. He made his will 1634. The fourth son,
THOMAS BOLTON, of Knock, co, Louth, m. Alice, dau. of — Knilton, and by her had issue a son,
NICHOLAS BOLTON, of Knock, co. Louth, m. Anne, dau. of Anthony Buckworth, of Dromore, by Sarah his wife, dau. of Edward Bermingham, of Ballagh, and had issue,
1. THOMAS, ancestor of BOLTON of Tullydonnell.
2. ANTHONY, of whom presently.
3. Theophilus (Most Rev.), D.D. P.C., Archbishop of Cashel, d.s.p. 31 Jan. 1744 will dated 27 July, 1743.
The second son,
ANTHONY BOLTON, of Grange, co. Louth, m. Martha, dau. of — Sheldon, and d. before 1754, leaving a son,
CHARLES BOLTON, of Castle Ring, co. Louth, m. setts. dated 26 Nov. 1771, his cousin Sidney, dau. of Richard Bolton, of Dromiskin and d. Aug. 1805, having by her had issue, a son,
RICHARD BOLTON, of Castle Ring, co. Louth, b. 20 Aug. 1772; m. 18 Feb. 1808, Marianne, only dau. of Gibbons Ruxton, of Blackcastle, co. Meath, and Ardee, co. Louth, and widow of W. Young, and d. 1850, having had issue,
1, Charles, Maj., of Ulimbah, Newcastle, N.S.W. b. 24 Nov. 1808; d. 1894, leaving a dau.,
Sidney Elizabeth, m. 1st, — Geary, and 2ndly, Ven. Archdeacon Bode.
2. John, b. 27 Dec. 1809; d. Aug. 1900.
3. RICHARD, of whom presently.
The third son,
RICHARD BOLTON, of Castle Ring, co. Louth, and Donaghmoyne, co. Monaghan, J.P., b. 21 Feb. 1811; m. 20 Jan. 1853, Mary Sophia Ward, dau. of Rev. Cornelius Marshall (see MARSHALL of Baronne Court), and d. 1872, having had issue,
1. JOHN MARSHALL, now of Castle Ring.
2. Archer Clive, Maj. Northants regt., b. 24 June, 1859.
3. Richard, b. 1861, m. Clare, dau. of — Barret, and d.s.p. 1893.
1. Anna Sophia, m. 22 June, 1876, Richard Baillie Henry, of Rathneston, co. Louth, and has issue
2. Sidney, d. unm.
3. Margaret Cornelia.
4. Elizabeth Gason Ruxton, m. Rev. Hugh Massy.
5. Josephine Florinda, m. 11 Sept. 1889, Rev. Charles Francis Bosvile Tottenham, and has issue (see TOTTENHAM of Ballycurry).
Arms—Or on a chevron gu three lions couchant of the field.
Crest—A hawk ppr. belled or.
Seats—Castle Ring, co. Louth, and Donaghmoyne, Carrickmacross, co. Monaghan.

BOLTON OF THE ISLAND.

WILLIAM BOLTON, of The Island, co. Wexford, b. 19 Jan. 1850; m. 12 Sept. 1872, Annie Douglas, dau. of John Rowe, D.L., of Ballycross, co. Wexford, and has issue,
1. William, b. 17 Aug. 1877.
1. Eva Susan, m. 5 Jan. 1904, Hon. Hamilton Robert Tilson Grogan Fitzmaurice Deane-Morgan, eldest son of Baron Muskerry. He d. in India 30 July, 1907, leaving issue (see BURKE'S Peerage). She m. 2ndly, 15 Feb. 1911, Godfrey William Edward Massy, of New Court, Bray, co. Wicklow (see MASSY of Grantstown Hall).
2. Anna Margaret, m. 12 Nov. 1902, Frederic Hughes, of Bally Cross, Bridgetown, co. Wexford, eldest son of the late Sir Frederic Hughes, D.L., of Rosslare Fort, co. Wexford, and has issue.
Lineage.—RICHARD BOLTON, of Ballyduff and Cold Harbour, son of Richard Bolton, of Ballyduff, co. Wexford, m. Ann Roberts, and had issue,
1. RICHARD, who had two sons,
1. Richard, father of Robert Bolton.
2. Edward, father of
(1) Richard, of Dublin, solicitor.
(2) Henry, of Ballinastraw, d.s.p. 21 Feb. 1884.
(3) Edward, of Dublin. (4) John, of Dublin.
(5) William, of Ballinastraw, Dublin.
2. John, of The Island, whose will, dated 10 Aug. 1758, was proved 10 Nov. following. He d.s.p., and bequeathed The Island and a considerable fortune to his brother William.
3. WILLIAM, of whom hereafter. 4. BENJAMIN.
5. Abraham, of Ballinvally, co. Wexford, m. Anne Eyres, and had a son,
Henry, of Monamolin, co. Wexford, went to New York 1772; m. Mary, dau. of Adam Sutton, of Bog and Warren, co. Wexford, and had a dau.,
Isabella, m. Joaquin Carrion, of Madrid, Councillor of State to the King of Spain.
6. Hugh. 7. Henry, m. and had issue.
8. Edward.
1. Elizabeth. m. William Perceval, of Ballytrammon, co. Wexford.

2. Mary. 3. Diana.
Mr. Bolton d. 1730; his will dated 8 Jan. that year was proved the 14th of the same month. His 3rd son,
WILLIAM BOLTON, a Commissioner for taking Affidavits in Wexford, inherited The Island under the will of his brother John Bolton. He m. 1st, Grace, 2nd dau. of Deiny Cuffe, of Sandhill, co. Carlow, and had three sons,
1. WILLIAM, his successor.
2. Henry Denny, m. (lic. 20 Aug.) 1776, Anna Maria, elder dau. of Jonah Wheeler, of Lyrath, co. Kilkenny, and had issue, William,
3. John.
He m. 2ndly, Miss Lyndon, and had issue,
4. Lyndon, of Dublin, m. by licence, dated 1 Nov. 1793, Jane Carpenter, also of Dublin, and had, with four daus., four sons.
  1. Richard.
  2. Lyndon Henry (Rev.), of Carrickmines, co. Dublin, and of Burren and Cooleague, co. Cavan, Rector of Drumcondra, co. Meath, b. 10 March, 1801; m. 26 Jan. 1826, Anna Maria, dau. of Walter Bourne, Clerk of the Crown to the Queen's Bench, and to the N.E. Circuit, Ireland, and d. 20 Nov. 1869, having by her (who d. 14 May, 1886) had with other issue,
    (1) Lyndon, b. 20 Nov. 1826; m. 15 Dec. 1858, Elizabeth Henrietta, dau. of Edward Creed, of Ballyclough House, co. Cork. She d. 17 Dec. 1893. He d. 4 April, 1900, leaving an only son,
      Lyndon, of Burren and Cooleague, co. Cavan, of the Patent Office, London (4, Shakespeare Road, Bedford), b. 31 May, 1860, m. 6 June, 1895, Gertrude Mary, eldest dau. of Joseph Hunt, J.P., of Canterbury, and has issue,
        a. Lyndon, b. 25 May, 1899.
        a. Joan Creed, b. 17 April, 1896.
        b. Rachel Gertrude, b. 16 July, 1902.
        c. Elizabeth Georgiana, b. 3 Sept. 1908.
    (2) Richard Knott (Rev.), of Carrickmines, co. Dublin, late Rector of Fenny Bentley, Ashbourne, Derbyshire, M.A., b. 1 May, 1830; m. 17 April, 1856, Josephine Ruth Susannie, dau. of Rev. James Taylor, Vicar of St. John's, Newcastle-on-Tyne, and d. 13 April, 1909, having had issue,
      1. Evelyn Mary, m. 3 Feb. 1881, Edmund Wilson Barnes, of Glapwell Hall, Derbyshire, and has issue (see BARNES of Ashgate).
      2. Josephine Anna, m. Rev. Ernest Edwin Morris, M.A., Vicar of Ashbourne, Derbyshire, and has issue, four sons and two daus.
  3. Abraham Irwin, M.D., d. 25 May, 1909. 4. William Gordon.
The eldest son,
WILLIAM BOLTON, of The Island, was High Sheriff, co. Wexford, 1789. He m. (licence dated 11 Oct. 1780) Dorothea, dau. of Sir John Blunden, 1st bart. of Castle Blunden, and had issue,
1. WILLIAM, his heir.
2. Philip, of Holly Lodge, Rathmines, co. Dublin, b. 1785; Major in the Army; d.s.p.
3. Overington, d.s.p. 4. John, of Ballynapierce, d. unm
1. Anne, m. Alexander Tovey, 20th Regt.; and d. 1821.
2. Lucy, m. David Ledwith, M.D.
3. Dorothea, m. Richard Ledwith.
The eldest son,
WILLIAM BOLTON, of The Island, High Sheriff 1816, m. Jane, dau. of Joshua Nunn, of St. Margaret's, co. Wexford, and d. 1853, leaving a son and heir,
WILLIAM BOLTON, of The Island, J.P. and D.L., High Sheriff 1856, b. 1815; m. 1843, Susan, dau. of Mountiford Westropp, of Limerick, and by her (who d. 1886) has issue,
1. WILLIAM, now of The Island.
2. Mountiford, d. unm. in S. America.
1. Jane, m. 15 July, 1869, William Henry West, of Farmley, J.P. co. Wexford, and has issue,

Seat—The Island, Kilmuckridge, Gorey, co. Wexford.

BOMFORD OF OAKLEY PARK.

GEORGE LYNDON BOMFORD, of Oakley Park, co. Meath, J.P., b. 29 Sept. 1867; m. 5 Aug. 1897, Helen Maude Mary, dau. of the Rev. Corbould Warren, J.P., of Tacolneston Old Hall, Norfolk, and has issue,
1. GEORGE WARREN, b. 25 April, 1900.
1. Elinor Louise, d. young. 2. Evelyn Maude.
3. Dorothea.

Lineage.—In 1692, LAURENCE BOMFORD, was living at Clonmahon, co. Meath; he d. 1720, at the advanced age of 103, having had issue by his wife Eleanor, four sons and four daus. His eldest son, THOMAS BOMFORD, of Rahinstown, co. Meath, Secretary of the Court of Claims, d.s.p. 4 Feb. 1740, and was s. by his brother, STEPHEN BOMFORD, of Gallow, co. Meath, who m. Anne Smith, of Violetstown, co. Westmeath, by whom he had issue, Thomas; STEPHEN; John; David, ancestor of John North Bomford, of Ferrans and Gallow; and Isaac; and four daus. He d. in 1756, and was s. by his eldest surviving son,
STEPHEN BOMFORD, J.P., of Rahinstown, m. April, 1745, Elizabeth, dau. of Stephen Sibthorpe, of Brownstown, co. Louth, by Margaret his wife, sister of the Right Hon. Anthony Foster, Chief Baron of the Exchequer in Ireland, and had with other issue,
1. ROBERT, his heir, of Rahinstown, m. 1792, Maria, dau. of the Hon. James Massy Dawson, 2nd son of Hugh, 1st Lord Massy, and had issue,

1. ROBERT GEORGE, of Rahinstown, b. 1802; High Sheriff of Meath 1832; m. 1826, Elizabeth, only child of James Traill Kennedy, of Annandale, co. Down, and d.s.p. 1846. His widow m. 2ndly, 6 June, 1850, Marcus Gervais Beresford, D.D., Archbishop of Armagh, and d. 1 July, 1870.
1. Annette, m. Sir Thomas H. Hesketh, Bart.
2. Jane Rosetta, m. 25 Feb. 1822, Richard Martin Southcote Mansergh, of Grenane, co. Tipperary.
3. Frances, m. Richard Bolton, of Bective Abbey.
4. Jemima, m. Richard Bolton, of Brook Lodge, co. Waterford.
5. Sarah Maria, m. 1831, the Hon. Frederick Tollemache.
6. Susan, m. 1826, the Rev. Charles Rudinge Martin, who d. 1847.
2. GEORGE, of Drumlargan.
The 2nd son,
GEORGE BOMFORD, of Drumlargan, m. 1809, Arabella, dau. of Samuel Winter, of Agher, and by her (who d. 11 Sept. 1815) had issue,
1. GEORGE, of Oakley Park.
2. Samuel, Major Royal North Gloucester Militia and of the 3rd Dragoon Guards, m. 11 July, 1839, Frances Jane, dau. of Samuel Pratt Winter, 3rd son of Samuel Winter, of Agher, and had issue,
  1. Rodon Charles, b. 1845. 2. Laurence George, b. 1847.
  3. Trevor, b. 1849.
  4. Gerald (Sir), K.C.I.E., M.D., late Director-Gen. Ind. Med. Service, formerly Principal of Med. Coll. Calcutta (Hillersdon House, Dover), b. 19 July, 1851; m. 1881, Mary Florence, dau. of Major-Gen. F. Eteson, late the Buffs.
  5. Victor Reginald (Rev.), Vicar of Wigginton, Staffordshire, b. 21 March, 1859; m. 3 July, 1883 Letitia Sarah, dau. of Rev. Francis Talbot Purcell (see PURCELL of Glannamore), and d. 24 Aug. 1900, leaving a dau.,
    Frances, b. 14 Feb. 1887.
  1. Caroline Frances, d. 1859.
Mr. Bomford d. Jan. 1814, and was s. by his elder son,
GEORGE BOMFORD, of Oakley Park, co. Meath, J.P., High Sheriff 1860, b. 11 April, 1811; m. 23 July, 1832, Arabella, dau. of John Pratt Winter, of Agher, and d. 1886, having had issue,
1. GEORGE WINTER, b. 12 Nov. 1834; m. 17 April, 1861, Flora Mary McVeagh, dau. of Rev. Francis R. Sadleir, D.D., and d. 22 June, 1884, leaving issue,
  GEORGE SADLEIR, b. 1 Dec. 1864; d. unm. 1 Dec. 1894.
  Arabella Anne, of Drumlargan.
2. JOHN FRANCIS, of Oakley Park.
3. Samuel Stephen, b. 18 April, 1841; d. 22 Aug. 1872.
4. Arthur Chichester, b. 27 July, 1851; d. 14 Oct. 1854.
5. Robert Laurence, b. 3 Sept. 1857.
1. Anne, d. unm. 8 Jan. 1912.
2. Arabella Anna, d. 19 Feb. 1910, m. 1863, George W. Ruxton, of Rahanna, co. Louth, and had issue (see RUXTON of Ardee). He d. 25 Dec. 1899.
3. Elizabeth. 4. Victoria Adela. 5. Margaret Winter.
The 2nd son,
JOHN FRANCIS BOMFORD, of Oakley Park, co. Meath, J.P., b. 22 Dec. 1837; m. 1866, Elinor, dau. of Rev. Lyndon H. Bolton, of Priorsland, co. Dublin, and d. 13 Sept. 1911, having had issue,
1. GEORGE LYNDON, now of Oakley Park.
2. John Stephen, b. 26 Dec. 1869; d. 9 Oct. 1891.
3. Lyndon Henry, b. 1 Feb. 1871; d. 3 Aug. 1907.
4. Samuel Richard, b. 15 Dec. 1873; d. 13 Feb. 1907.
5. Charles Francis, b. 13 March, 1878.
6. Trevor Broughton, b. 1 June, 1880; m. 18 Jan. 1911, Birdie, dau. of Claud Chaloner, J.P., of Kingsfort, co. Meath.
7. William Harold, b. 1 Jan. 1885.
1. Anna Arabella, m. 12 July, 1899, Rev. Claud Robert Longfield (d. 26 Sept. 1903), son of the Rev. Richard Longfield, Canon of Cloyne, and has issue, Richard Charles, b. 17 April, 1901.
2. Elinor May, m. 12 July, 1892, Hugh Golding Constable, son of Capt. Charles Golding Constable, H.M. Indian Navy, F.R.G.S., son of John Constable, R.A., and has issue, John Hugh, b. 28 Feb. 1896, and Winoa.
3. Gwendoline, m. 3 Oct. 1900, Rev. Leonard McNeill Shelford, and has issue, Leonard, John, Flora Elinor, and Gwendoline May.

Residence—Oakley Park, Kells, co. Meath.

BOMFORD OF GALLOW AND FERRANS.

JOHN GEORGE NORTH-BOMFORD, of Gallow, and Ferrans, co. Meath, Lieut. 7th Royal Fusiliers, b. 13 Oct. 1883; s. his mother (on her re-marriage) 16 Dec. 1908; m. 5 Oct. 1909, Hilda Frances, youngest dau. of the late George Shaw Munn, Rector of Madresfield, Malvern.

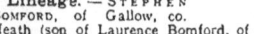

Lineage. — STEPHEN BOMFORD, of Gallow, co. Meath (son of Laurence Bomford, of Clonmahon, co. Meath, and brother of Thomas Bomford, of Rahinstown), m. Anne Smith, of

Violetstown, co. Westmeath, and had issue by her, 1. Thomas; 2. Stephen, ancestor of BOMFORD of *Oakley Park*; 3. John; 4. DAVID; and 5. Isaac. The 4th son,
DAVID BOMFORD, of Gallow, *m.* Dec. 1756, Sarah, dau. of David Burtchaell, of Brownstown, co. Kildare (*see* BURTCHAELL *of Brandondale*). Her will, dated 26 Aug. 1814, was proved 23 March, 1816. His will, dated 17 April, 1807, was proved 2 Feb. 1810. He had issue,
  1. Isaac, of Gallow, bapt. 31 March, 1766, *d.s.p.* Will dated 19 Dec. 1835.
  1. Jane, *m.* Aug. 1785, Duke Cooper, of Great Down, co. Westmeath.
  2. ANNE, *m.* July, 1786, JOHN NORTH, of Whitwell, co. Westmeath, and had issue three sons,
    1. David, *m.* Catherine, dau. of J. Pim, and had issue.
    2. ISAAC, of whom we treat.
    3. John, *m.* Ellen, dau. of Robert Barbour, of Tyrrells Pass, co. Westmeath, and had issue.
  3. Mary Elizabeth, bapt. 28 Sept. 1768, *d.* young.
  4. Sarah Frances, *m.* 1803, John Coates, of Coolcor, co. Westmeath.
The grandson,
ISAAC NORTH-BOMFORD, of Gallow, co. Meath (son of John North and Anne his wife, dau. of David Bomford), assumed the name and arms of BOMFORD; *m.* 8 Oct. 1830, Belinda Emily, dau. of Capt. Abraham John Pilkington, of Kilbride Castle, co. Westmeath, and *d.* 1866, having by her (who *d.* 1852) had issue,
  1. Isaac, Capt. 59th Regt., served in China, *b.* 6 June, 1834; *d. unm.* 6 April, 1861. 2. JOHN, late of Gallow Ferrans.
  3. David George, *b.* 5 Feb. 1840, M.D.; *m.* 1867, Mary, dau. of — Gubbins, Castle Troy, co. Limerick, and *d.* 13 Oct. 1869, leaving a dau., Annabella, *m.* 12 April, 1899, Thomas Robert Griffin, B.L., of Baggot Street, Dublin.
  4. Stephen Robert, *d.* young, 1856.
  5. Horatio, *b.* 16 Feb. 1847; *m.* Alice, dau. of Richard Summers, Tyrell's Pass, co. Westmeath, and has issue, with two daus., a son, Isaac John, *b.* 14 April, 1882.
  1. Mary Jane, *m.* John Emerson, of Clonshanny, King's Co., and has issue.
  2. Anna Bella, *m.* 12 April, 1860, Sir Benjamin Whitney, of Upper FitzWilliam Street, Dublin. She *d.* 16 Jan. 1899, leaving issue (*see* WHITNEY *of Brayfort*).
  3. Louisa Emily, *d.* young.
  4. Belinda Emily, *m.* Col. Edward Napoleon L'Estrange, 22nd Regt., and has issue.
JOHN NORTH-BOMFORD, of Gallow and Ferrans, co. Meath, J.P., late Capt. 20th Regt., served in Burmah and Bengal 1857; *b.* 17 July, 1838; *m.* 1st, 24 July, 1867, Charlotte, eldest dau. of John Devenish Meares, of Meares Court, co. Westmeath, D.L., but by her (who *d.* 1881) had no issue. He *m.* 2ndly, 5 Sept. 1882, Mary Wilhelmina Constance, eldest dau. of Sir William S. B. Kaye, C.B., Q.C., LL.D., Private Secretary to the Lord-Lieut. of Ireland, and had issue by her a son,
JOHN GEORGE, now of Gallow.
He *d.* 16 Oct. 1905. His widow re-*m.* 16 Dec. 1908, Lieut.-Col. Phineas Barrett Villiers-Tuthill (*see* TUTHILL *of Kilmore*).

Arms—Quarterly: 1st and 4th, az., on a fesse erm. three crosscrosslets fitchée gu., for BOMFORD; 2nd and 3rd, per pale or and az. a lion passant between three fleurs-de-lis counterchanged for NORTH. **Crests**—1st, for BOMFORD, a griffin segreant arg., charged on the shoulder with a cross-crosslet fitchée gu.; 2nd, for NORTH, a wyvern's head, erased vert, langued gu., collared and chained or. **Motto**—*Vir. tutus. et. fidelis.*
Seat—Gallow Ferrans, Kilcock, co. Meath—**Club**—Kildare Street, Dublin.

BOND OF FARRAGH.

JAMES WILLOUGHBY BOND, of Farragh, co. Longford, J.P. and D.L., High Sheriff 1870, *b.* 11 July, 1837; *m.* 22 Nov. 1864, Emma Georgiana Charlotte, dau. of William Hunter Little, D.L., of Llanvair Grange, co. Monmouth (*see that family*), and has issue,
  1. WILLOUGHBY JAMES, B.A. Camb., J.P. co. Longford, High Sheriff 1905, *b.* 10 June, 1867; *m.* 30 April, 1892, Mary Rosa Kerr, dau. of Capt. William Bond, of Newtown Bond, co. Longford, and has issue,
    1. Brian Willoughby, *b.* 15 Jan. 1894.
    2. Francis Willoughby, *b.* 3 Feb. 1901.
    1. Mary Hunter.   2. Kathleen Sidney.
  2. Wensley Hunter, *b.* 7 Dec. 1876.
  1. Georgiana Sidney, *m.* 20 Nov. 1895, Maj. R. Mac Geough-Bond, R.F.A. (*see that family*).
  2. Henrietta Letitia. 3. Alicia Mabel, *d. unm.* 27 Jan. 1886.
  4. Ethel Emma Louisa.

Lineage.—EPHRAIM BOND, came from Yorkshire and settled in Derry about 1650. He *m.* the dau. of — Dewin, and had two sons,
  1. WILLIAM, of whom presently.
  2. John, of Ballyclapham, co. Londonderry, who left issue.
The elder son,
WILLIAM BOND, of Glenlough, co. Londonderry, who left issue a son,
JAMES BOND, of Glenlough, *m.* the dau. of — Burns, and had issue, five sons,
  1. William.   2. JAMES, of whom presently.
  3. Oliver.   4. Thomas.   5. Saint.
The second son,

REV. JAMES BOND, Presbyterian Minister, of Corboy, co. Longford, *m.* Catherine, dau. of Rev. Thomas Wensley, of Lifford, co. Donegal, and had with four daus. as many sons,
  1. Wensley (Very Rev.), Dean of Ross 1773-1813, *b.* 1736; *m.* by licence 10 Aug. 1778, Rebecca, dau. of William Forward, of Fermoy, and niece of Right Hon. John Hely-Hutchinson, and *d.* 1820, having had with four daus. two sons,
    1. James Forward (Very Rev.), Dean of Ross 1813-29, *b.* 1779; *m.* 1st, 15 Feb. 1815, Sarah Hester, dau. of John Croker, and sister of the Right Hon. John Wilson Croker. She *d.s.p.* 1816. He *m.* 2ndly, 21 May, 1825, Christiana Margaretta, dau. of Rev. the Hon. Lorenzo Hely-Hutchinson, and had an only dau. The Dean *d.* Aug. 1829.
    2. Richard Wensley, *m.* Sophia, dau. of Rev. James Bond, of Lecarrow, co. Roscommon, and *d.* 3 Oct. 1860, having had with five daus. three sons, (1) Wensley, (2) James, and (3) Richard Thomas.
  2. James (Sir), Bart., of Coolamber, co. Longford, M.P. for Naas 1790-7, created a baronet 21 Jan. 1794, *m.* 27 July, 1770, Anne, widow of Richard Eyre and dau. of William Hornby, Governor of Bombay. She *d.* 1809. His son, Sir Thomas Bond, 2nd Bart., *d.s.p.* 3 March, 1823, when the baronetcy became extinct.
  3. WILLIAM, of whom presently.   4. Thomas, who left issue.
  1. Letitia, *m.* Simon Little.
The 3rd son,
WILLIAM BOND, of Edgworthstown, co. Longford, High Sheriff 1794, *m.* Elizabeth, dau. of Alexander Perry, and *d.* 1811, leaving issue,
  1. James Wensley, of Cartroncard, co. Longford, High Sheriff 1822, *d.* 8 Feb. 1843.
  2. Alexander Perry, of Ardglass, co. Westmeath, D.L., *m.* 15 Jan. 1836, Rosetta, dau. of Saville Dowling, and *d.* 1851, leaving issue.
  3. Thomas.
  4. WILLOUGHBY, of whom we treat.
The youngest son,
WILLOUGHBY BOND, of Farragh, co. Longford, J.P. and D.L., High Sheriff 1832, *b.* 1790; *m.* 2 June, 1829, Alicia Sidney, dau. of William Gosselin, of Abbey Derg, co. Longford. She *d.* Sept. 1882. He *d.* 5 Nov. 1875, having had issue,
  1. William Wensley, Lieut. 50th Regt., *b.* 2 Oct. 1834; *d. unm.* 8 Dec. 1854.
  2. JAMES WILLOUGHBY, now of Farragh.
  1. Sidney Margaret, *m.* 1st, 6 July, 1854, Thomas James Meredith, of Cloonamahon, co. Sligo, who *d.* 1860, and 2ndly, 2 June, 1870, John Henry Kincaid, of 78, Merrion Square, Dublin.

Seat—Farragh, Longford.

MACGEOUGH-BOND OF DRUMSILL.

WALTER WILLIAM ADRIAN MACGEOUGH-BOND, of Drumsill, co. Armagh, Vice-President of Court of Appeal at Cairo, Egypt, *b.* 1857; *m.* 26 Sept. 1901, Ada Marion, youngest dau. of the late Charles Nichols, of Dunedin, N.Z., and has issue,
WALTER ALBERT NEVILL, *b.* 27 June, 1908.

Lineage.—JOSHUA MACGEOUGH, of Drumsill, co. Armagh, made his will 23 June, 1755, which was proved 19 June, 1756. He *m.* Anne, only dau. and heir of Brig.-Gen. the Right Hon. William Graham, and had issue,
  1. WILLIAM, his heir.
  2. John, *d.s p.* 26 June, 1761.
  3. Samuel, of Derrycaw, co. Armagh, High Sheriff 1776; *m.* Elizabeth, dau. of William Smyth, and had with two daus., of whom Anne, *m.* July, 1777, Owen O'Malley, of Melcomb, co. Mayo, two sons,
    1. Joshua, of Greenwood Park, co. Tyrone, *m.* his cousin, Anne, dau. of William MacGeough, of Drumsill. His will was proved 1793. He left issue, William, Joshua, Henry, and Elizabeth.
    2. Samuel, *d.s.p.*
  1. Elizabeth, *m.* 9 Aug. 1732, William Houston (*see* BLAKISTON-HOUSTON *of Orangefield*).
  2. Mary, *m.* — Robinson.   3. Anne.
The eldest son,
WILLIAM MACGEOUGH, of Drumsill, *m.* 1st, Elizabeth, dau. and heir of Walter Bond, of Bondville, co. Armagh, and by her had a son,
  1. JOSHUA, his heir.
He *m.* 2ndly, the dau. of Joseph Boyd, and by her had three daus.,

1. Elizabeth, *m.* — Alfray.
2. Mary.
3. Anne, *m.* Joshua MacGeough, of Greenwood Park, co. Down (*see above*).

He *d.* about 1791 (will dated 2 Feb. 1778, proved 9 March, 1791). His only son,

JOSHUA MACGEOUGH, of Drumsill, co. Armagh, *m.* Anue, dau. of Joseph Johnstone, of Nappa, co. Armagh, and had two sons,
1. WILLIAM, his heir, of Drumsill, *d.s.p.*
2. WALTER, of whom we treat.

The younger son,

WALTER MACGEOUGH-BOND, of Drumsill, Silver Bridge, and the Argory, co. Armagh, High Sheriff 1819, Barrister-at-Law, assumed by Royal Licence, 5 Nov. 1824, the name and arms of BOND in addition to his own; *m.* 1830, Anne, 2nd dau. of Ralph Smyth, of Gaybrook, co. Westmeath. She *d.* 1892. He *d.* 17 March, 1866, having had with other issue,
1. JOSHUA WALTER, late of Drumsill.
2. Ralph MACGEOUGH-BOND-SHELTON, of the Argory, co. Armagh (*see that family*).
3. William, *m* 24 Nov. 1869, Mary Armit, 3rd dau. of William Armit Lees (*see* BURKE's *Peerage,* LEES, Bart.), and left issue. His widow *m.* 2ndly, 30 July, 1903, Col. Beauchamp John Colclough Doran, C.B.
4. Robert John MACGEOUGH, of Silver Bridge, co. Armagh, J.P., *b.* 22 Sept. 1838; *m.* 11 March, 1869, Alice, dau. of James Sivewright, of Brighton. She *d.* 1871. He *d.* 9 April, 1903, leaving an only child,
Alice, *m.* 9 Sept. 1891, Maxwell Vandeleur Blacker-Douglass, of Grace Hall, and has issue (*see that family*).
1. Mary Isabella, *m.* Robert Staples, of Dunmore, Queen's Co.
2. Anna Maria, *m.* 4 Oct. 1867, Randal, 13th Lord Louth. She *d.* 27 Oct. 1868. He *d.* 19 July, 1883, leaving issue (*see* BURKE's *Peerage*).

The eldest son,

JOSHUA WALTER MACGEOUGH-BOND, of Drumsill, co. Armagh, J.P. and D.L., High Sheriff 1872, M.P. for Armagh 1855-57 and 1859-65, late 49th Foot, *b.* 1831; *m.* 1856, Albertine Louise, dau. of Frederick Shanahan, Barrister-at-Law. He *d.* 29 Aug. 1905. She *d.* 18 Nov. 1902, leaving issue,
1. WALTER WILLIAM ADRIAN, now of Drumsill.
2. Ralph Xavier, late Major R.A., *m.* 20 Nov. 1895, Georgina, dau. of James Willoughby Bond, of Farragh (*see that family*), and has issue,
Ralph.
Mabel.
1. Angeline, *m.* Raoul Recorbet, of La Chaux, and has issue.
2. Anne, *m.* Henri Ayet, of La Forest. He *d.* 18 July, 1902.

Arms—Quarterly 1st and 4th, or on a chevron gu. three annulets arg. (BOND); 2nd and 3rd, Per bend sa. and or three leopard's faces two and one counterchanged (MACGEOUGH). **Crests**—1. BOND: A lion sejant arg. charged on the shoulder with an annulet sa. 2. MACGEOUGH: A naked dexter arm embowed, the hand grasping a scymitar in the act of striking, all ppr. **Motto**—*Nemo me impune lacessit.*

Seat—Drumsill, Armagh. **Club**—Travellers'.

BONHAM OF BALLINTAGGART.

COL. JOHN BONHAM, C.B., of Ballintaggart, co. Kildare, J.P. cos. Kildare and Wicklow, High Sheriff co. Carlow 1900, Col. R.H.A. (retired), *b.* July, 1834; *m.* 1870, Mary Anne, dau. of Philip Wroughton, of Woolley Park, Berks, and by her (who *d.* 1891) has had issue,
1. FRANCIS WARREN, *b.* 1871.
2. John Wroughton, *b.* 1875; *m.* 14 June, 1911, Lilian Mary, youngest dau. of Charles Robert Hamilton, of Hamwood (*see that family*).
1. Georgiana Maye, *m.* 21 April, 1909, Rev. Bernard Smith. She *d.* 16 June, 1910.
2. Mary Alice, *m.* H. F. Morris. She *d.* 11 June, 1909.
3. Margaret Leslie.

Lineage.—FRANCIS BONHAM, of Dublin, *b.* 1673; *m.* before 1716, Mary Shelley, and *d.* 1755, having had, with other issue,
1. JOHN, his heir.
2. Robert, of Dublin, *d.* 1760.

The elder son,

JOHN BONHAM, of Dublin, *b.* 1704; *m.* 1738, Susanna, dau. of Richard Warren, of Grangebeg, co. Kildare, and *d.* about 1780 (will dated 30 June, 1780, proved 26 Feb. 1781), having by her (who *d.* 1809) had issue,
1. FRANCIS WARREN, his heir.
2. Richard Paul, *b.* 1761; *d.* 1807.
1. Frances Anne, *m.* (licence 1778), Robert Johnstone.
2. Elizabeth, *m.* 1768, Joshua Paul Meredyth.
3. Mary, *m.* March, 1764, Sydenham Snow, and had issue.
4. Wilhelmina, *m.* 9 July, 1761, William Parsons Hoey, of Richmond, co. Dublin, and had issue, Hannah.

The son and heir,

FRANCIS WARREN BONHAM, *b.* 1740; *m.* 1st, March, 1767, Mary Ann, dau. of Dr. Leslie, Bishop of Limerick, and sister of Sir Edward Leslie, Bart., and by her had issue, JOHN, of whom presently, and Joyce, who *d. unm.* He *m.* 2ndly, Jan. 1777, Dorothea Herbert, and *d.* 1810, having had further issue, Francis Robert, *b.* 1785;

d. 1863 *unm.*; Susan, *b.* 1780, *d.* 1863, *unm.*; and others who *d.* young. The eldest son,

JOHN BONHAM, of Ballintaggart, J.P., *b.* 21 June, 1769; served as High Sheriff co. Kildare 1835. He *m.* 1796, Margaret, widow of Capt. Clifton, H.E.I.C.S., and dau. of — Jones, and by her (who *d.* 1848) left, at his decease, 1844, a son and heir,

REV. JOHN BONHAM, of Ballintaggart, M.A. Oxon, J.P. co. Kildare, *b.* 22 Feb. 1798; *d.* 1875; *m.* 30 Oct. 1827, Barbarina, 3rd dau. and co-heiress of John Norris, of Hughenden House, Bucks, and by her (who *d.* 1882) had issue,
1. FRANCIS, late of Ballintaggart.
2. JOHN, now of Ballintaggart.
1. Margaret Louisa, *m.* 1855, Arthur Wyatt, of Earlswood, co. Wexford, and has issue. 2. Mary, *d.* 1849.
3. Ann Blanche, *m.* 14 Nov. 1859, Col. Henry Hamilton Pratt, late 94th Regt., and has issue.
4. Agnes Jane Susan, *d.* 1906.

He *d.* 1875, and was s. by his elder son,

FRANCIS BONHAM, of Ballintaggart, Maj. 71st Highland Light Infantry, *b.* 5 Nov. 1831; *m.* 16 July, 1868, Emily Mary Georgiana, dau. of James Reid, of Millbank House, Fermoy, who *d.* 1889. He *d.* 1892.

Seat—Ballintaggart, Colbinstown, co. Kildare. **Clubs**—United Service, S.W.; Kildare Street, Dublin.

BONYNGE.

CHARLES WILLIAM BONYNGE, of 42, Prince's Gate, London, *b.* 5 Oct. 1838; *m.* 5 June, 1869, Rodie S. D., dau. of James M. Stephens (a planter in the Southern States), and descended on her mother's side from the family of U.S. Senator George Read, one of the signers of the Declaration of Independence (*see* BURKE's *Peerage*), and has issue,

Louise Selina, *m.* 8 Aug. 1892, Major-Gen. Sir John Grenfell Maxwell. K.C.B., C.V.O., C.M.G., D.S.O., late Royal Highlanders (Black Watth), and has issue one dau., Helene Philae, to whom H.R.H. Princess Christian stood sponsor.

Lineage.—FRANCIS BONYNGE, *m.* 1779, Miss Wickham, of co. Meath, and by her (who *d.* 6 Jan. 1835) had issue,
1. Francis. 2. John.
3. Thomas. 4. William.

Mr. Bonynge *d.* Jan. 1824. His son,

THOMAS BONYNGE, of Ranelagh, *m.* 22 Dec. 1834, Louisa Selena Taylor, of London, and *d.* Feb. 1892, having by her (who *d.* March, 1878) had issue,
1. CHARLES WILLIAM, of Prince's Gate.
2. Thomas.
3. Arthur (Rev.), M.A., D.D., R.D., Rector of Kilfarboy, co. Clare, *m.* 1st, Lydia Kennedy. He *m.* 2ndly, 5 June, 1895, Elenor Bonynge, 3rd dau. of the late John Frederick Knipe, M.D., F.R.C.S.I., &c., of Beneavin House, Glasnevin, co. Dublin. He *d.* 17 Nov. 1910, leaving issue,
 1. Arthur Francis, *b.* 24 Aug. 1896.
 2. Frederick Charles, *b.* 15 June, 1900.
4. Francis George, M.D., L.R.C.S.I., *d.* 1901.
5. Walter Alfred.
1. Isabella, *d.* 1906.

Arms—Arg., two bars gu., each charged with as many escallops or; on a chief indented az., an annulet of the third. **Crest**—An ostrich ppr., charged with an escallop sa., and holding in the beak a key of the same. **Motto**—*Virtute decoratus.*
Residence—42, Prince's Gate, S.W.

BORROWES. *See* BURKE'S PEERAGE, **BORROWES, Bart.**

BOURCHIER OF DROMLINE AND ARDINODE.

HERBERT FRANCIS BOURCHIER, of Dromline, Crosderry, Knockalough and Craherabeg, co. Clare, and of Ardinode and Loughbritogue, co. Kildare, B.A. Trin. Coll. Dublin, *b.* 7 Feb. 1868.

Lineage.—This branch of the Bourchier family went to Ireland in 1690. THOMAS BOURCHIER, of King's Sutton, Northants, an officer in King William's Dragoons, settled at Craig, co. Tipperary; *m.* Elizabeth, dau. of Lieut. James Maxwell, and had, with other issue, an elder son,

HENRY BOURCHIER, *m.* the dau. of — Watson, of Caherhenley, co. Clare, and had, with two other sons, William and Thomas, who both *d. unm.*, an eldest son,

WATSON BOURCHIER, who *m.* Miss McNamara, and had, with other issue, an eldest son,

JOHN BOURCHIER, of Elm Hill, Broadford, co. Clare, *m.* 1st, the dau. of Hugh Ingoldsby Massey, and by her had a son,

1. Hugh, *d.* young.

He *m.* 2ndly, Elizabeth, dau. of Terence McMahon, of Ballykilty, co. Clare, whose estates were forfeited, and by her had issue,

2. John, Maj.-Gen. R.A., commanded the Artillery at the taking of the French West India Islands of Martinique, St. Lucia and Les Saintes under Sir Charles Grey in 1793. He afterwards commanded the Cork District; *m.* Mary, dau. of Thomas Macnamara of Ardcloney, co. Clare, and had issue,

   1. Daniel Macnamara, Maj. R.A., served in the Peninsular War (despatches after Badajos) and at Waterloo; *m.* Mary, dau. and heiress of James Wilson, of Dunboyne Castle, co. Meath, and had issue.

   2. Thomas (Sir), K.C.B., Adm. R.N., Commandant of Chatham Dockyard, served in China 1841; *m.* Jane, dau. of Adm. Sir Edward Codrington, and had a son John, *d.* young.

   3. Plunket, Col. Royal Welsh Fus.

3. THOMAS, of whom we treat.

John Bourchier was killed in a duel at eighty years of age. His youngest son,

THOMAS BOURCHIER, of Killiney Castle, co. Dublin, Clerk of the Crown and Hanaper and Usher of the Black Rod in the Irish House of Commons, *m.* Dorothea, dau. of Rev. — Hadlock, and had issue,

1. JOHN, of whom presently.
1. Dorothea, *m.* Rev. J. R. Hodson, and had issue.
2. Lucy, *m.* Rev. Dr. Magrath, Bishop of Jamaica, and had issue.
3. Annie, *m.* Rev. P. Bolton.
4. Caroline, *m.* — FitzGerald, and had issue.
5. Mary, *d. unm.*   6. Elizabeth, *d. unm.*

The only son,

JOHN BOURCHIER, of Smithville, Nenagh, co. Tipperary, and Killiney Castle, co. Dublin, Barrister-at-Law, *m.* Mary, dau. of Richard Townshend Herbert, of Cahirnane, co. Kerry (*see that family*), and had issue,

1. THOMAS, of whom presently.
2. John, *d. unm.*   3. Herbert, *d. unm.*
1. Mary, *m.* Alexander Gordon, 1st Royal Regt., and had issue.
2. Annie, *m.* Deputy Surg.-Gen. Henry Day Fowler, Bengal Army, and had issue.
3. Jane, *m.* Capt. Mundell, and had issue.
4. Elizabeth, *m.* Henry Bayly, of Donnybrook, co. Tipperary, and had issue.
5. Lavinia, *m.* Henry Badcock, of Ballinware, co. Tipperary, and had issue.

The eldest son,

THOMAS BOURCHIER, of Crosthwaite Park, Kingstown, *b.* 29 Sept. 1826; *m.* 4 May, 1861, Henrietta Octavia, dau. of Rev. John Delmege, of Rathbranagh, co. Limerick (*see* DELMEGE *of Rathkeale*). He *d.* 19 Aug. 1895, having had issue,

1. John Herbert, *b.* 28 April, 1866.
2. HERBERT FRANCIS, his heir.
1. Maria Anna Herbert.   2. Edith Geraldine Herbert.

Residence—Dromline, Foxrock, co. Dublin.

BOURCHIER OF BAGGOTSTOWN.

HENRY JAMES BOURCHIER, of Baggotstown, co. Limerick, *b.* 14 Aug. 1842; *m.* 5 March, 1867, Nina Darley, eldest dau. of the Rev. John Leech, D.D., of Mitchelstown (*see* LEECH *of Cloonconra*), and has had issue,

1. John de Louvain, *b.* 6 Sept. 1868; *d.* an infant.
4. CLAUD JAMES HENRY ST. JOHN, *b.* 6 Aug. 1875; *m.* 10 Oct. 1911, Alice Renée, elder dau. of H. B. Rowan, late of Braiswick Lodge, Colchester.
3. Wilfrid la Rive, B.A. (Rev.), *b.* 22 March, 1884.
1. Florence Mary, *m.* Rev. Arthur Davis, B.D.
2. Harriet Nina, *m.* 16 Aug. 1899, Rev. Alexander Duff Moore (*see* MOORE *of Moore Lodge*).
3. Clare Farran.   4. Frances Chadwick.
5. Irene Sara.   6. Cicely Charlotte.

Lineage.—The estate of Baggotstown was acquired by JOHN BOURCHIER some time subsequent to the attainder of Thomas Baggot, of that place, in 1651.

JOHN BOURCHIER, of 1664, of Baggotstown and Kilcullane, co. Limerick, and Maidenhall, co. Cork, was possessed of several estates in those counties, which he divided between his sons. He *m.* Faith, dau. of O'Grady, of Kilballyowen, co. Limerick, by Frances his wife, dau. of John Anketell, and the Lady Lucy Anketell, dau. of Mervyn, 2nd Earl of Castlehaven and 12th Lord Audley, of Heleigh, and by her (who was maternally 10th in descent from the marriage of Sir William Bourchier, Count of Eu, with Anne Plantagenet, dau. and heir of Thomas of Woodstock, youngest son of EDWARD III) had issue,

1. Thomas, *d.s.p.*
2. James, of Kilcullane, on whom that estate was settled by will of his father, dated 1739, *m.* 1740, Mary, dau. of Michael Bevan, of Camas, and had issue,

James, of Kilcullane, *m.* 1769, Martha, dau. of William Gabbett, of Caherline, co. Limerick, High Sheriff 1775, and had issue,

  (1) William, of Kilcullane, *s.* 1808; *m.* Heloise, dau. of Col. Dillon, of co. Roscommon, and niece and adopted dau. of Sir Peter Nugent, Bart., and Lady Nugent, of Donore, co. Westmeath, by whom he had an only son, William, an officer in the Army, who joined with his father in the sale of the Kilcullane estate to the 1st Viscount Guillamore, 7 July, 1812, and *d. unm.*

  (2) Joseph Gabbett, a Capt. in the Army, *m.* 1st, Margaret, dau. of Thomas Franks, of Carrig, by whom he had an only dau., and 2ndly, a dau. of Capt. John Gabbett, of Shepperton, by whom he had issue, Joseph Gabbett (Rev.), of Ifield, Kent, who *d.* 13 Dec. 1898, having *m.* 16 Dec. 1851, Jane. Allen (22, *Marina, St. Leonards-on-Sea*), dau. of Daniel Sullivan, of Fermoy House, co. Cork, by whom he had issue, Joseph Gabbett, *b.* 30 April, 1854.

Mary Louise.

(3) Thomas, *m.* in India, a niece of Sir Theophilus Metcalf, and *d.s.p.* 1844.

(4) Henry, of Frankfort, co. Limerick.

(5) Richard, *m.* Catherine, dau. of James Bold, and had, with other issue,

  1. John.   2. Stanley.
  3. Thomas, *m.* Elizabeth, dau. of John Bourchier, of Baggotstown.
  1. Lucy, *m.* Lieut. Augustus Whymper, R.N.
  2. Elizabeth Mary, *m.* 9 Jan. 1851, Maj.-Gen. Sir Archibald Edward Harbord Anson, R.A., K.C.M.G., nephew of the 1st Viscount Anson. She *d.* 23 Sept. 1891, having had issue (*see* BURKE's *Peerage*, ANSON, Bart.).

3. JOHN, of whom presently.
1. Lucy, *m.* Richard Lane, of Kilderry.
2. Mary, *m.* her cousin Richard Anketell.

John Bourchier *d.* aged 80, in 1744. His 3rd son,

JOHN BOURCHIER, of Baggotstown, Oakfield, and Maidenhall, *s.* to those properties on his father's death 1744. He *m.* Arabella, dau. of James Mason, of Coolcen, co. Limerick, and had issue,

1. JAMES JOHN, his heir.
1. Arabella, *m.* John Boles Reeves, of Belfort, co. Cork, and was grandmother of William Reeves, Bishop of Down.
2. Faith, *m.* Henry Gabbett.

His will is dated 1 Oct. 1774. His son,

JAMES JOHN BOURCHIER, of Baggotstown, *m.* 30 Aug. 1766, Mary, dau. of Joseph Gubbins, of Kilfrush, co. Limerick, by whom he had issue,

1. JOHN, his heir.
2. James, B.A., who, after a distinguished University career, entered the Army, and *d.* whilst serving as senior Capt. of his Regt. (Royal York Fusiliers) in Jamaica.
3. Henry, Lieut.-Col. Royal Irish Artillery, *d. unm.*
4. Joseph Gubbins, *d. unm.*
1. Mary, *d.* young.   2. Anne, *d.* young.
3. Elizabeth, *m.* John Sherlock, of Ballydeigue.

He was *s.* by his eldest son,

JOHN BOURCHIER, of Baggotstown, Lieut. 58th Regt., *m.* 10 Aug. 1797, Charlotte, 4th dau. of William Chadwick, of Ballinard, by Christiana his wife, sister of Sir John Craven Carden, Bart., of Templemore Abbey, co. Tipperary, by whom he had issue,

1. JOHN, his heir.
2. John James Stephen, *d.* an infant.
1. Christiana, *m.* Richard Eaton, J.P., and had issue, Richard, J.P., co. Limerick, *m.* Clara, dau. of John Netterville Barron, J.P.
2. Marianne, *m.* Thomas, eldest son of Henry Grove Grady, of Bellwood, co. Tipperary, by Mary Margaret his wife, only dau. and heiress of Thomas Lidwill, of Clonmore (*see* LIDWILL *of Dromard*), and great-granddau. of Gerald, 24th Lord Kingsale.
3. Charlotte, *m.* her cousin William Chadwick, of Ballinard, and *d.s.p.* 17 Jan. 1874.   4. Sophia, *d. unm.*
5. Elizabeth, *m.* Thomas Bourchier, *d.s.p.*   6. Clarinda, *d. unm.*

Mr. Bourchier *d.* 1845. and was *s.* by his son,

JOHN BOURCHIER, of Baggotstown, co. Limerick, J.P., B.A. Trin. Coll. Dublin, *b.* 1811; *s.* 1845; *m.* 9 July, 1833, Sarah, eldest dau. and eventually co-heir of David Aher, of Castlecomer, co. Kilkenny, by Susan his wife, dau. and co-heir of Capt. W. C. Wilkinson, of Castlecomer, and niece of Sir Henry Wilkinson, K.C., of Corballis, co. Dublin, and had issue,

1. John, *d.* young.
2. HENRY JAMES, now of Baggotstown.
3. William, *d.* an infant.
4. Richard Eaton, late Lieut. 1st Royal Scots, *m.* 10 Aug. 1876, Geraldine Amelia Beamish (*d.* 24 July, 1909), dau. of Right Hon. and Most Rev. Thomas Stuart Townshend, D.D., Bishop of Meath, and has issue,

John Somerset Townshend, *b.* June, 1877.

5. James David, F.R.G.S., of La Rive, Castlecomer, co. Kilkenny, late of the Inner Temple, M.A. Camb. (King's Coll.), where he graduated as first class classic, 1876; is Grand Officer of the Order of Prince Danilo of Montenegro, Commander of the Order of the Saviour of Greece, and Officer of the Order of St. Alexander of Bulgaria (*Athenæum, St. James' and New University Clubs*).

6. William Chadwick (Rev.), M.A., Rector of Knockaney, co. Limerick, Chaplain to the Marquess Camden, and late Chaplain Royal Navy, *b.* 28 Feb. 1852; *m.* 23 March, 1889, Katharine Christian, dau. of Cathcart Thomson, J.P., of Pine Wood,

Halifax, N.S., and granddau. of the Hon. Joseph Howe, Lieut.-Governor of Nova Scotia, and has issue,
Cathcart Charles William, Lieut. R.N., b. 20 Jan. 1890.
1. Susan, d. young.
2. Charlotte Sophia, m. Aug. 1863, Richard Austin Cooper Chadwick, of Ballinard, co. Tipperary, 2nd son of Samuel Cooper, J.P., of Killenure Castle, in the same co. (see COOPER *of Killenure* and CHADWICK *of Ballinard*), who assumed the additional name and arms of CHADWICK by Royal Sign Manual, dated 15 Jan. 1855.
Mr. Bourchier d. 24 May, 1885.
Seat—Baggotstown House, Kilmallock, co. Limerick. *Residence*—Melbrooke, Clonmel, co. Tipperary.

BOURKE OF THORNFIELDS.

RICHARD VANDELEUR BOURKE, of Thornfields, co. Limerick, b. 1884; s. his father 17 May, 1910.

Lineage.—RICHARD BOURKE, of Dromsally, co. Limerick, d. in 1734, and was s. by his eldest son,
RICHARD BOURKE, of Dromsally, who was three times married, and d. 1761, leaving, by his first wife, Sarah, a son,
1. JOHN, of Shallee, co. Tipperary, who m. Lucia Parker, and d. leaving, with two daus., one son,
JOHN, of whom hereafter.
Mr. Richard Bourke m. 2ndly, Mary, dau. of James Donellan, of Johnstown, co. Meath, and had another son,
2. RICHARD (Sir), of Castle Connell, who assumed the original surname of DE BURGHO, and was created a Baronet of Ireland 16 June, 1785. Sir Richard m. 1st, 15 Jan. 1755, Frances, eldest dau. of Daniel Webb, of Meadstown, co. Limerick, by whom he had two daus.,
 1. Frances, m. John Blake, of Ross, co. Clare.
 2. Maria Theresa, m. John MacNamara, of Smithstown, in the same co.
Sir Richard m. 2ndly, 1781, Elizabeth, dau. of Anthony Dwyer, of Singleton, co. Limerick, and d. 1790, leaving two sons,
 1. SIR RICHARD, 2nd bart., d. unm. 1834.
 2. SIR JOHN ALLEN, 3rd bart., m. 1st, the sister of Gen. Gage John Hall, but by her had no issue; and 2ndly, in 1820, Anna Matilda, eldest dau. of Richard Waller, of Castle Waller, and d. 1839, leaving,
  (1) SIR RICHARD DONELLAN DE BURGHO, 4th bart., b. 1 April, 1821; m. 8 Aug. 1844, Catherine, dau. of Brooke Brasier, of Ballyellis, co. Cork, and d.s.p. 1873, when the title became extinct.
  3. William Henry Frederick Waller, d.s.p. 1848.
  1. Maria Theresa, d. 31 Oct. 1846.
  2. Elizabeth, d. 23 Dec. 1849.
  3. Frances.
  4. Isabella.
  5. Joanna Allen.
Mr. Bourke was s. by his grandson, the son of his eldest son by his 1st wife,
JOHN BOURKE, of Shallee, m. 1775, Anne, dau. of Edmund Ryan, of the city of Dublin, and of Boscobel, co. Tipperary, and by her (who d. 1837) had issue,
1. RICHARD, his heir.
2. Edmund, d. young.
3. John, d. young.
1. Frances Emma, m. Rev. Hencage Horsley, only son of the Right Rev. Samuel Horsley, D.D., Lord Bishop of St. Asaph. She d. 1821, leaving issue.
Mr. Bourke d. 1795. His eldest son,
LIEUT.-GEN. SIR RICHARD BOURKE, K.C.B., of Thornfields, co. Limerick, J.P., High Sheriff 1839, b. 4 May, 1777; m. 1 March, 1800, Elizabeth Jane, youngest dau. of the Land Tax for Middlesex (of the BOURKES *of Urey*), and by her (who d. 7 May, 1832) had issue,
1. JOHN, b. 11 Feb. 1803; d. 17 Nov. 1868.
2. RICHARD, of Thornfields.
1. Mary Jane, m. 1827, Dudley Montagu Perceval, C.B., 4th son of the Right Hon. Spencer Perceval, Chancellor of the Exchequer, and had issue.
2. Anne, m. 1833, Sir Edward Deas Thompson, Colonial Secretary in New South Wales, 2nd son of Sir John Thompson, K.C.H., formerly a Commissioner of the Navy, and had issue.
3. Frances, m. 1831, Rev. John Jebb, D.D., Rector of Peterstow, Ross, co. Hereford, eldest dau. of the Hon. Richard Jebb, a Justice of the King's Bench, Ireland, and d. 15 Jan. 1866.
4. Georgina, d. young.
5. Lucy, d. 1822, unm.
Sir Richard Bourke, a distinguished officer, was Lieutenant-Governor of the Cape of Good Hope from 1825 to 1828, and Governor-in-Chief of New South Wales and Van Diemen's Land from 1831 to Dec. 1837. He d. 12 Aug. 1855, and was s. by his 2nd son,
RICHARD BOURKE, of Thornfields, co. Limerick, J.P., D.L., b. 30 May, 1812, Barrister-at-Law, and Local Government Inspector; m. 10 Oct. 1844, Anne, dau. of O'Grady of Kilballyowen, co. Limerick, and d. 5 April, 1904, leaving by her (who d. 1878) issue, with three daus., four sons,
1. JOHN ULICK, late of Thornfields.
2. Richard, Local Government Auditor, b. 5 Feb. 1849; m. 1898, Helena Mary, only dau. of Daniel Cronin-Coltsman, of Glenflesk Castle (see that family).
3. Gerald, late Capt. Horse Artillery, b. 19 April, 1850; m. 1882, Blanche, dau. of Gen. Sir William Payn, K.C.B.
4. Edmund, Commr. Local Gov. Board (Ireland), b. 12 Feb. 1857.
1. Anne Elizabeth.
2. Alice Slaney, m. Commander John Warde Osborne, R.N.
3. Una Mary, m. 29 Sept. 1896, Rev. W. I. Adams, succentor of St. Mary's Cathedral, Limerick.
The eldest son,

JOHN ULICK BOURKE, of Thornfields, Barrister-at-Law, Res. Magistrate in Ireland, b. 8 July, 1845; m. 1876, Elizabeth Agnes, dau. of Col. John Vandeleur, late 10th Hussars, of Ballinacourty, co. Limerick, and d. 17 May, 1910, leaving issue,
1. RICHARD VANDELEUR, now of Thornfields.
2. Ulick Launcelot, b. 1888.
1. Slaney Agnes.
2. Aileen Anne.
Seat—Thornfields, Lisnagry, co. Limerick.

LEGGE-BOURKE OF HAYES.

NIGEL WALTER HENRY LEGGE-BOURKE, of Hayes, co. Meath, b. 13 Nov. 1889, Lieut. Coldstream Guards, a Page of Honour to H.M. King Edward VII 1902-06. Mr. Legge-Bourke, who is the only son of Hon. Sir Henry Charles Legge, K.C.V.O. (see BURKE'S *Peerage*, DARTMOUTH, E.), by Hon. Amy Gwendoline Lambart, dau. of Gustavus William Lambart, of Bean Parc, co. Meath (see that family), assumed the name and arms of BOURKE by Royal Licence, 26 April, 1911, on succeeding to the estate of the Hon. Henry Lorton Bourke, of Hayes, co. Meath (see BURKE'S *Peerage*, MAYO, E.).

Arms—Quarterly, 1st and 4th, per fess or and erm., a cross gu. in the 1st quarter a lion ramp., and in the 2nd a hand erect couped at the wrist, both sa., on a canton qu., three narcissi pierced arg. (for BOURKE); 2nd and 3rd, az., a stag's head cabossed arg. (for LEGGE). **Crests**—1st, a cat-a-mountain sejeant guardant ppr., collared gu., chained or (for BOURKE); 2nd, out of a ducal coronet a plume of six feathers alternately arg. and az. (for LEGGE). **Mottoes**—1st, A Cruce Salus (for BOURKE); 2nd, Gaudet tentamine virtus (for LEGGE).

Seat—Hayes, Beau Parc, co. Meath.

BOURKE. *See* BURKE'S PEERAGE, **MAYO, E.**

BOWEN OF BOWEN'S COURT.

HENRY CHARLES COLE BOWEN, of Bowen's Court, co. Cork, M.A. Trin. Coll. Dublin, Barrister-at-Law, b. 21 Jan. 1862; m. 10 April, 1890, Florence Isabella, 3rd dau. of the late Henry FitzGeorge Colley, of Mount Temple, co. Dublin (see BURKE'S *Peerage*, HARBERTON, V.), and has issue,
Elizabeth Dorothea Cole, b. 7 June, 1899.

Lineage.—This family is lineally descended from HARRY BOWEN, of Court House, in Ilston, co. Glamorgan (2nd son of THEODORE BOWEN AP HARRY BOWEN, of Court House, to MAENARCH, Lord of Brecknock, 14th in descent from CARADOC VRAICHVRAS), who d. in 1582, leaving with other issue, a son,
HENRY BOWEN, of Llanellan, co. Glamorgan, m. to Margaret, dau. of H. Holland, Rector of Cheriton. His son,

HENRY BOWEN, a Colonel in Cromwell's army, was the first of this family who settled in Ireland. He *m.* 1st, Anne, dau. and heir of Henry Mansell, by whom he had, with other issue,
JOHN, who *s.* him.
He *m.* 2ndly, Katherine, dau. of William Price, of Gellihir, and *d.* at Farrihy, co. Cork, 1658 (his will is dated 18 Dec. 1658, and proved 10 Feb. 1658-59), and was *s.* by his eldest son,
JOHN BOWEN, of Farrihy, *m.* 1660, Mary, dau. and heir of John Nicholls, of Kilbolane, co. Cork, Capt. in the Army, and had issue, three sons and two daus. He *d.* in the year 1718, and was *s.* by his eldest son,
JOHN BOWEN, of Kilbolane, *m.* 1st, 1691, Deborah, dau. of Arthur Hyde, of Castle Hyde, co. Cork, by whom he had no issue. He *m.* 2ndly, 1695, Catherine, dau. of Richard Stephens, of Newcastle, co. Limerick, and *d.* 1720, having by her had (with two daus.),
1. HENRY, of Kilbolane.
2. JOHN, of Carrigadrohid, co. Cork, *m.* 1724, Elizabeth, dau. of Rev. D. Chidley Coote, and had issue,
John, of Carrigadrohid Castle and Oak Grove, *m.* 1st, Katherine, dau. of Angel Scott, of Cahircon, co. Clare, and by her had issue,
(1) Katherine, *m.* James Barry.
(2) Jane, *m.* 1777, John Colthurst, of Dripsey Castle, and had issue (*see that family*).
(3) Margaret, *m.* 18 Dec. 1787, Robert Warren Gumbleton, of Fort William Park, co. Waterford, and Glanatore, co. Cork, and had issue.
He *m.* 2ndly, 1797, Anne, dau. of Benjamin White, of Bridepark, co. Cork, and *d.* 1824, having by her (who was bur. 15 Oct. 1850) had,
(1) John, of Carrigadrohid and Oak Grove, *b.* 15 Jan. 1798; *m.* 3 June, 1819, Mary, dau. and heir of William Honner, of Roundhill, co. Cork, and *d.* 9 May, 1870, having by her (who was bur. 12 March, 1862) had issue,
1. John, of Oak Grove, *b.* 27 May, 1824; *m.* 1st, by licence dated 20 May, 1847, Mary Isabella Beamish, dau. of Maj. Adderley Beamish-Bernard, of Palace Ann and Kilcoleman House, co. Cork. She *d.s.p.* March, 1865. He *m.* 2ndly, Dora Anne, dau. of Abraham Cross, of Cork, and *d.s.p.* 24 May, 1873.
2. William Honner, *b.* 16 July, 1827; *d. unm.* 17 July, 1864.
3. Edward Riggs White, *b.* 10 Aug. 1835; *d. unm.* Aug. 1873.
4. Robert Walter Travers, of Oak Grove, and Dripsey Castle, co. Cork, *b.* 16 March 1840, assumed by Royal Licence, 1882, the additional surname and arms of COLTHURST; *m.* 15 Aug. 1878, Georgina de Bellasis, dau. of Alfred Greer, of Dripsey House, by Peggy his wife, dau. of John Colthurst, of Dripsey Castle, and *d.* 16 Nov. 1896, leaving issue (*see* BOWEN-COLTHURST *of Dripsey*).
1. Wilhelmina Maria, *d. unm.* 15 Nov. 1890.
2. Anne White, *d. unm.* 17 April, 1889.
3. Eliza Travers, of Coolalta, co. Cork, *d. unm.* Nov. 1910.
4. Catherine Jane, *d.* an infant.
5. Mary, *d.* an infant.
6. Frances Mary, *m.* James Gartside, and has issue.
7. Mary Sarah, *d. unm.* 9 April, 1869.
8. Helena Jane Travers, *m.* 8 Aug. 1867, William Boyle Moore, of Borleigh, co. Cork.
3. Stephens.
The eldest son,
HENRY BOWEN, of Kilbolane, co. Cork, *m.* 1716, Jane, only child and heir of Robert Cole, of Ballymackey, co. Tipperary, and by her had issue, a dau., Catherine Bowen, and a son,
HENRY COLE BOWEN, of Bowen's Court, *m.* 6 Jan. 1760, his 1st cousin Margaret, dau. of Ralph Warter Wilson, and *d.* March, 1788, having had by her (who *d.* 1802) eight sons and six daus.,
1. HENRY COLE, of Bowen's Court.
2. John, *m.* Martha Randall, and *d.s.p.*
3. Ralph, *m.* 1804, Mary, dau. of Edmund Doherty, of Mount Bruis, co. Tipperary, and had issue,
1. Henry, *m.* Anne Jane, dau. of Hampden Ely, and had,
(1) Ralph, *d.s.p.* (2) Hampden, *d. unm.*
(3) Henry, *d. unm.*
(1) Anne, *m.* Francis B. Cole Metge, of Sion, co. Meath.
(2) Mary.
2 Edmond, *m.* Miss Lysaght, and had a son, Edmond.
3. Charles, *d.* 1889, leaving issue.
1. Jane. 2. Mary, *m.* Ven. Archdeacon Pryce Peacock.
3. Elizabeth, *m.* Col. H. E. F. B. Sidley.
4. Robert, *m.* 1 Feb. 1806, Elizabeth, dau. of William Galwey, and *d.* 10 May, 1827, having by her (who *d.* 1861) had issue,
1. HENRY COLE, of whom presently.
2. Robert Cole, Barrister-at-Law, *m.* Elizabeth, dau. of Joseph Mason, of Cooline, co. Limerick.
3. Edward, bapt. 30 Oct. 1817 ; *d.s.p.*
1. Elizabeth, bapt. 15 Oct. 1824 ; *m.* Matthew Braddell.
5. Nicholls, *m.* Brianna, dau. of Robert Travers, and had issue,
1. Henry ; 2. Robert ; 3. Nicholls ; 4. John ; and 1. Brianna ;
2. Mary ; 3. Catherine.
6. William, *d. unm.*
7. Stephens, *m.* and had two sons, 1. Henry ; 2. Stephens.
8. Edward, *d.s.p.*
1. Jane, *m.* Rev. William Berkley.
2. Thomasine, *m.* Hon. George Jocelyn (*see* BURKE'S *Peerage*, RODEN, E.). She *d.* 15 Oct. 1818. He *d.* leaving issue.
3. Catherine, *m.* John Wight.
4. Margaret, *m.* 1st, 1798, William Perry, and 2ndly, —Maunsell.
5. Henrietta, *m.* John Metge, M.P., of Athlumney, and had issue. (*see* METGE *of Athlumney*).

I.L.G

6. Isabella, *m.* 7 Jan. 1830, Edward Sheffield Cassan.
The eldest son,
HENRY COLE BOWEN, of Bowen's Court, *m.* 1789, Catherine, dau. of Henry Prittie (afterwards Lord Dunalley), and *d.s.p.* 1837, when he was *s.* by his nephew,
HENRY COLE BOWEN, of Bowen's Court, J.P., *b.* 28 Jan. 1808 ; *m.* 7 March, 1829, Eliza Wade (*d.* 18 May, 1868), dau. of St. John Galwey, M.D., of Mallow, and *d.* 15 Sept. 1841, having had issue,
1. ROBERT ST. JOHN COLE, late of Bowen's Court.
2. Henry Cole, Capt. R.A., *b.* 29 March, 1838 ; *d* 27 Sept. 1874.
1. Sarah Cole, *m.* 8 Feb. 1859, Rev. Brabazon T. Disney, M.A., who *d.* 1902.
2. Anne Cole.
3. Henrietta Cole, *m.* 15 Sept. 1863, her cousin, Arthur Gethin Creagh, and has issue.
The elder son,
ROBERT ST. JOHN COLE BOWEN, of Bowen's Court, J.P. cos. Cork and Tipperary, High Sheriff for the latter co. 1865, Capt. 87th South Cork Light Infantry, M.A. Trin. Coll. Dublin, *b.* 13 Aug. 1830 ; *m.* 1st, 3 Dec. 1860, Elizabeth Jane, 2nd dau. of Charles Clarke, D.I.., of Graiguenoe Park, co. Tipperary, and by her (who *d.* 20 Aug. 1881) had issue,
1. HENRY CHARLES COLE, now of Bowen's Court.
2. Robert Cole, *b.* 9 April, 1863 ; Capt. Essex Regt. ; *d.* 3 Aug. 1894.
3. Charles Otway Cole, D.S.O., Major R.E., served in S. African War 1899-1901 (despatches twice, D.S.O.), *b.* 30 Aug. 1867 ; *d. unm.* 18 March, 1910.
4. Edward Neville Cole, *b.* and *d.* 1870.
5. St. John Cole, Res. Magistrate O.R. Colony, *b.* 20 Sept. 1872 ; *m.* 1903, Winifred, dau. of Edward Rosslein, of Winburg, O.R. Colony, and has issue,
1. Robert Edward Cole, *b.* 1904.
2. Henry Cole, *b.* 1906.
6. Arthur Marshal Cole, *b.* 3 Dec. 1873 ; *d.* 17 Jan. 1874.
7. Mervyn William Cole, *b.* 4 March, 1875 ; *m.* March, 1901, Mary Florence, dau. of John Wild, of Rhyl, co. Flint.
8. William Walter Travers Cole, *b.* 24 Feb. and *d.* 29 May, 1877.
1. Sarah Frances Cole.
2. Elizabeth Harriet Mary Cole, *d.* 27 Oct. 1865.
3. Anne Marcella Cole. 4. Mary Elizabeth Cole.
5. Elizabeth Constance Cole.
He *m.* 2ndly, Nov. 1882, Georgiana Constance Antoinette (who *d.s.p.* 8 July, 1886), 4th dau. of Charles Carden Mansergh, of Clifford, co. Cork, and *d.* 28 July, 1888, when he was *s.* by his eldest son.

Arms—Az., a stag lodged arg., attired or, and vulned in the back, with an arrow *gu.* **Crest**—A hawk close ppr. **Motto**—Cautus a futuro.

Seat—Bowen's Court, Kildorrery, co. Cork.

BOWEN OF HOLLYMOUNT.

THE HON. AND REV. WILLIAM EDWARD BOWEN, of Hollymount, co. Mayo, M.A. Balliol Coll. Oxford, *b.* Nov. 1862 ; *m.* 1890, Catharine, dau. of the late Rev. Canon Morse, Vicar of St. Mary's, Nottingham.

Lineage.—WILLIAM BOWEN, of Hollymount, co. Mayo, *m.* Sarah Blake and had two sons,
1. CHRISTOPHER, his heir.
2. William, *m.* Ellen Burke, and *d.* 1786, leaving a son,
CHRISTOPHER, of whom hereafter.
The elder son,
CHRISTOPHER BOWEN, of Hollymount, *m.* Anne Allen, but by her had no male issue ; his dau. Anne, *m.* Anthony Elwood, of Annefield, co. Mayo, and had a son, Anthony Elwood, who assumed the surname of BOWEN.
Mr. Bowen *d.* 1812. His nephew,
CHRISTOPHER BOWEN, J.P., of Hollymount, *m.* 1800, Elizabeth, dau. of Croasdaile Miller, of Milford, and by her (who *d.* Jan. 1815) had issue,
1. CHRISTOPHER (Rev.), his heir.
2. Croasdaile of Milford, assumed by Royal Licence, dated 1 Feb. 1812, the surname and arms of MILLER (*see* MILLER *of Milford*).
3. Charles, *b.* 15 May, 1804 ; *m.* 19 Nov. 1829, Georgiana, dau. of Joseph Lambert, of Brookhill, co. Mayo, and *d.* 3 April, 1871, leaving issue (*see* BURKE'S *Colonial Gentry*). She *d.* 11 Aug. 1902, aged 100.
4. Robert, *m.* Jane, dau. of Edward R. Courtenay, of Drumsilk, co. Down, and *d.* 1882. She *d.* same year, leaving issue.
5. William, *d. unm.* 6. Edward George, *d. unm.* 1873.
1. Anne, *d. unm.* 1876. 2. Eliza Louisa, *d.* 1834.
Mr. Bowen *d.* Aug. 1828, and was *s.* by his eldest son,

F.

Rev. Christopher Bowen, M.A., of Hollymount, and Heatherwood, Isle of Wight, formerly Rector of St. Thomas, Winchester, *b.* 16 Oct. 1801 ; *m.* 17 Jan. 1834, Katherine Emily, dau. of Sir Richard Steele, 3rd bart. of Hampstead, and *d.* 1890, having by her (who *d.* 1 Feb. 1902) had issue,
1. Charles Synge Christopher, late of Hollymount.
2. Edward Ernest, M.A., late Fellow of Trin. Coll. Camb., and Senior Assistant Master of Harrow School, *b.* March, 1836 ; *d. unm.* 8 April, 1901.
3. Francis Robert Steele, B.A., Barrister-at-Law, took the additional name of Graves, on his marriage with Frances Elizabeth, dau. of Sir Maxwell Steele Graves, Bart. of Mickleton Manor, co. Gloucester, and *d.* 16 July, 1876.

The eldest son,
The Right Hon. Sir Charles Synge Christopher Bowen, Baron Bowen, of Hollymount, co. Mayo, and of Colwood, Sussex, *b.* 1 Jan. 1835, F.R.S., Hon. D.C.L. Oxford, and Visitor of Balliol Coll. ; called to the Bar at Lincoln's Inn 1861, appointed Recorder of Penzance 1872 ; a Judge of the Queen's Bench Division 1879, Lord Justice of Appeal 1882, and sworn a Privy Councillor same year. In 1893 he was made a Lord of Appeal in Ordinary, and was created a peer for life as Baron Bowen, of Colwood. He *m.* Feb. 1862, Emily Frances, dau. of James Meadows Rendel, F.R.S., and *d.* 11 April, 1894, leaving issue,
1. William Edward, now of Hollymount.
2. Maxwell Steele, late Lieut. 3rd Batt. Derbyshire Regt. (*Savile and Royal Automobile Clubs*), *b.* Oct. 1865.
1. Ethel Kate, *b.* Nov. 1870 ; *m.* 1894, Josiah Clement Wedgwood, of Moddershall, Stone, Staffs., M.P. for Newcastle-under-Lyne, son of the late Clement Francis Wedgwood, of Barlaston, and has issue.

Arms—Gu., a stag trippant arg., pierced in the back with an arrow and attired or. Crest—A falcon close ppr. belled or. Motto—Esse quam videri
Residences—119, Barkston Gardens, S.W., and Glenheadon, Totland, Isle of Wight. Club—Athenæum.

BOWEN OF MANTUA AND BURT HOUSE.

Edward Ferguson Bowen, of Mantua, co. Roscommon, and Burt House, co. Donegal, D.L. co. Roscommon, J.P. cos. Donegal, Roscommon and Wexford, High Sheriff co. Roscommon 1901, *b.* 1860 ; *m.* 6 Sept. 1887, Louisa Frances, elder dau. and co-heir of Richard Joseph Grace, of Bruff, co. Limerick, and niece of the late John Dowell FitzGerald Grace, of Mantua and Gracefield (*see below*). Mr. Bowen is the eldest son of the late John Gordon Bowen, J.P., of Burt House, co. Donegal (who *d.* 1891), by Emily Harriet his wife, dau. of Arthur Willoughby Cole-Hamilton, of Beltrim (*see that family*).

Lineage.—Oliver Grace, of Gracefield, *b.* 1661, eldest son of William Grace, of Ballylinch Castle, co. Kilkenny, by Ellinor, dau. of Pierce Butler (eldest son of 1st Viscount Galmoy), and of Margaret, dau. of Nicholas, 1st Viscount Netterville, *m.* Elizabeth, dau. of John Bryan, of Bawnmore, co. Kilkenny. He *d.* 8 June, 1708, and had issue,
Michael Grace, of Gracefield, inherited as coheir-at-law with his nephew Robert Grace, of Courtstown, the undevised estates of the Sheffield family in Sussex, Middlesex and York, *m.* Mary, dau. of John Galway, of Lota House, co. Cork, and Elizabeth, dau. of William Meade, and sister of Sir John Meade, ancestor of Earls of Clanwilliam, and had issue,
1. Oliver, of Gracefield, his heir.
2. John, *d.* 1777.
3. William, *m.* Mary, dau. of Richard Harford, of Marshfield, co. Dublin, and ancestor of Grace baronets (*see* Burke's *Peerage*).

Mr. Grace *d.* 19 Feb. 1760. His eldest son,
Oliver Grace, of Gracefield, *m.* Mary, dau. and heiress of John Dowell, of Montagh, now Mantua, co. Roscommon, and had issue,
1. Michael, of Gracefield, *d.* 9 Jan. 1797, having *m.* 17 Feb. 1760, Mary, dau. and coheir of Nicholas Plunket, of Dunsoghly, co. Dublin, and dying 25 Aug. 1785, aged 63, left an only child, Alicia Grace, of Gracefield, *m.* June, 1792, Morgan Kavanagh, 3rd son of Thomas Kavanagh, of Borris House (*see that family*).
2. John, of whom presently.

Mr. Grace *d.* 24 Aug. 1782, aged 77. The 2nd son,
John Grace, of Mantua, *b.* 1734, served several years in the Austrian Army ; *m.* 3 July, 1783, Mary Clare, 2nd dau. and coheiress of Patrick Hussey, of Ardmore, co. Kerry, by whom (who *d.* 7 Nov. 1819) he had one son and two daus.,
1. Oliver Dowell John, his heir.
1. Catherine Eliza, *m.* Aug. 1821, Rice Hussey, of Milltown, co. Kerry.
2. Maria, a nun, *d.* April, 1837.

Mr. Grace *d.* 25 April, 1811, at the age of 75. His only son,
Oliver Dowell John Grace, of Mantua, and of Gracefield, Queen's Co., chief of his house, and male representative of the ancient feudal Lords of Courtstown, late M.P. for co. Roscommon,

J.P. and D.L., High Sheriff 1831, *b.* 19 Oct. 1791 ; *m.* 3 Sept. 1819, Frances Mary, only dau. of the late Sir Richard Nagle, Bart. of Jamestown, co. Westmeath, by his 1st wife, Catherine FitzGerald, of Punchars Grange, co. Kildare, and by her (who *d.* 1 June, 1828) had issue,
1. John Dowell FitzGerald, late of Mantua.
2. Richard Joseph, R.M., of Bruff, co. Limerick, *b.* 8 March, 1824 ; *m.* 1st, Nov. 1848, Mary Jane, dau. of William Sweetman, of Raheny, co. Dublin, which lady *d.s.p.* 1 Sept. 1858. He *m.* 2ndly, Barbara, dau. of James Taaffe, of Loughboy, co. Mayo, and *d.* May 1864, leaving by her two daus. and coheirs,
1. Louisa Frances, *m.* (*as above*) 6 Sept. 1887, Edward Ferguson Bowen, of Burt House, Donegal.
2. Frances Mary, *m.* 5 Oct. 1886, Capt. Joseph Henry Lachlan White, D.L., late 5th (Northumberland) Fusiliers, of Bredfield House, Woodbridge, Suffolk (*see* White *of Gracefield*).
3. Raymond Joseph, *d.* 13 Oct. 1831.
1. Mary Clare, *m.* 6 March, 1848, Robert Archbold, of Davidstown, co. Kildare, who *d.* Feb. 1853. She *d.* 11 Aug. 1892.

Mr. Grace *d.* 1871. His eldest son,
John Dowell FitzGerald Grace, of Mantua House, co. Roscommon, and Gracefield, Queen's Co., J.P. co. Westmeath and Queen's Co., High Sheriff for the latter co. 1858, J.P. and D.L. co. Roscommon, High Sheriff 1847, *b.* 11 July, 1821 ; *m.* 1 Feb. 1855, Grace, dau. of Thomas Thistlethwayte, of Southwick Park, Hants, by Tryphena, his wife, youngest dau. of Dr. Henry Bathurst, Bishop of Norwich. She *d.* 1881. He *d.s.p.* 11 May, 1897, and was *s.* by his two nieces.

Seats—Mantua House, Castlerea, co. Roscommon, and Burt House, Londonderry. Club—Kildare Street.

BOWEN-COLTHURST. See COLTHURST.

BOWLES OF AHERN.

Spotswood Bowles, of Ahern, co. Cork, *b.* 7 Oct. 1854 ; *s.* his uncle, Major George Bowles, in 1886 ; *m.* 30 Nov. 1899, Grace Elizabeth, dau. of the late Sir Edward Hudson-Kinahan, Bart, (*see* Burke's *Peerage and Baronetage*).

Lineage.—Thomas Boles, *b.* 1608 ; who was settled at Liscarroll, co. Cork, prior to the Rebellion of 1641 ; is mentioned as Captain in the depositions of Col. Richard Townsend, of Col. John Gifforde, and of Capt. Peter Cary, taken in Cork 1654, by the State Commissioners, as one who did good service in securing the city for the English interest in 1649. He is styled Captain in a deposition made by himself in 1654, and also in his will, dated 16 Nov. 1682, proved 1683. He was admitted a freeman of Cork 1655. His brother Richard Boles, *b.* 1614, had a grant of lands confirmed to him as one of the officers who served before June 5, 1649, in the Barony of Orrery and Kilmore and co. Cork, *m.* 1645, Abigail, dau. of Ende of Cork, merchant, and made over his property by deed to his eldest son, Thomas, in his lifetime, reserving an annuity for himself and wife. He *d.* 1693, buried in the old church of Killybraher, where "The Tomb of the Boles's of Moyge" still remains. He was the direct ancestor of the Rev. James Thomas Boles, A.M., J.P. for Devon, sometime of Crowcombe Rectory, Somerset, who *s.* to Ryll Court, Devon, and an interest in Moyge, co. Cork on the death of his uncle, Lieut.-Gen. Thomas Boles, in 1850.
Capt. Thomas Boles had by Anne his wife (who was buried at Cloyne Cathedral) two sons,
1. John, of Kilbree, after of Inch, had no son, his property, which was very considerable, went by his will, dated 22 March, 1700, proved 8 May, 1702, between his three daus.,
1. Elizabeth, *m.* 1694, Samuel Hodder, of Fountainstown.
2. Anne, *m.* 1700, Randal Warner, of Liscremin.
3. Mary, of Kilbree, after of Inch, who *d. unm.* and intestate
2. Thomas, who carried on the family.

Capt. Thomas Boles *d.* 26 June, 1683. His 2nd son,
Thomas Boles, of Ballinacurra, *b.* 13 April, 1646 ; *m.* 1682, Elizabeth, dau. of John Downing, of Broomfield, Midleton, co. Cork, had, with other issue,
1. Thomas, who inherited the Kilbree and Carrig estates on the death of Mary Boles, his cousin. He left two daus.,
(1) Anne, *m.* Henry Bowles, of Glenaboy and Youghal.
(2) Mary, *m.* William Peard, of Peardmount.
2. John, of Woodstock, 1726, after of Carringnashinny, *m.* Margery, dau. of John Colborne, of Ballintubber, will dated 26 June, 1739, *d.* 1739, buried in Cloyne, ancestor of the branches who resided at Mogeely, Gortgreine, and Kilmountain, now extinct in the male line. 3. Robert, of whom presently.

Thomas Boles made his will 12 Nov. 1698. His youngest son,
Robert Boles, of Springfield, near Tallow, *m.* 1st, 1716, Elizabeth, dau. of John Croker, of Ballyanker, near Lismore, and left a son,
1. Jonathan, *d.s.p.m.*

IRELAND. Boyd.

le *m*. 2ndly, 1731, Katherine, dau. of Richard Benjer, of Springfield, and had by her two sons and a dau.,
2. Spotswood, Col. of the Bombay Artillery, who was killed by one of his own guns at the taking of a fort on the Malabar coast, *m*. and *d.s.p.*
3. GEORGE, of whom hereafter.
1. Anne, *m*. Charles Nixon Green, of Youghal.
Robert Boles *d*. 1746. His youngest son,
GEORGE BOLES, *afterwards* BOWLES, of Mountprospect, near Tallow, co. Cork (the name being so spelt in his military commission and continued by him and his descendants), J.P., *b*. 1739 ; was a Lieut. 7th Light Dragoons ; *m*. 1764, Dorothea, dau. of Henry Hunt, of Friarstown, co. Limerick, and by her (who *d*. 1838, aged 94) left issue,
1. Henry, J.P., of Glanaboy and Youghal, *m*. Ann, dau. of Thos. Boles, of Youghal, and *d.s.p.m.* 1824, when his estates went between his daus. and their issue.
2. George, of Mountprospect, Maj. 8th Regt. of Foot, served in Egypt under Sir Ralph Abercromby ; *m*. 1st, Elizabeth, dau. of John Nason, of Newtown, co. Cork ; she *d*. without surviving issue ; and 2ndly, Catherine Jones, dau. of William Hall, of Bath, and *d*. 1826, leaving issue, three sons,
  1. George, of Mountprospect, *d*. 15 May, 1879, leaving issue.
  2. Harry, Lieut. H.E.I.C.S., *d*. in India, 14 Sept. 1864, leaving issue.
  3. William, Lieut. 66th Regt., *d. unm*. 1879.
3. SPOTSWOOD, of whom hereafter.
1. Ann, *m*. Francis Woodley, of Leades, co. Cork, and had issue.
2. Catherine, *m*. Lieut.-Col. John Creighton, and had issue.
3. Dorothea, *m*. Lieut.-Gen. Sir Henry Oakes, 2nd bart., of Mitcham, Surrey, and had issue.
4. Margaret, *m*. Rev. Ralph Wartar Wilson, of Kilcummer, co. Cork, and had issue.
5. Charlotte, *m*. Lieut. Henry Palmer, 68th Regt., after 37th Regt.
6. Maria, *m*. 1st, Lieut.-Col. Browning ; 2ndly, Lieut.-Col. Bradish.
7. Sophia, *m*. 1st, Robert Corban ; 2ndly, John Benjamin Bloomfield.
8. Harriet, *m*. Major-Gen. James Alexander, and had issue.
9. Isabella de Vere, *m*. Wm. Woodley, Lieut. City of Cork Militia, and had issue.
George Bowles (whose will is dated 12 Feb. 1792) *d*. 1803, and was buried at Tallow. His 3rd son,
SPOTSWOOD BOWLES, of Ahern, co. Cork, J.P., sometime Lieut. 29th Regt., *b*. 1784 ; *m*. 1812, Jane (*d*. 24 Dec. 1885), eldest dau. of Thomas John, of Youghal, J.P., and *d*. 2 Feb. 1864, having had issue,
1. GEORGE, late of Ahern.
2. Thomas John, *b*. 5 Dec. 1814 ; Lieut. 99th Regt., *d*. 7 March, 1885.
3. Henry, *b*. 23 July, 1816 ; *d. unm* 1859
4. Spotswood, of Springfield, Castlemartyr, *b*. 3 April, 1818 ; *m*. 29 Nov. 1849, Anne Eliza Boles, eldest dau. of William Webb, of Castlenugent, J.P. co. Longford, *s*. to Springfield and Mogeely, near Castlemartyr, on the death of his relative, Rev. William Boles, 1855, and *d*. 1 Nov. 1893, having by her (who *d*. 10 Aug. 1892) had issue,
  1. WILLIAM, of Springfield, co. Cork, *b*. 8 Dec. 1850 ; *m*. 29 Jan. 1898, Elizabeth Wood (*d*. 9 May, 1904), eldest dau. of Francis Edward Rowland, J.P., of Kilboy House, Cloyne, co. Cork. He *d*. 19 Nov. 1911.
  2. SPOTSWOOD, now of Ahern.
  3. George Henry, now of Springfield, co. Cork, *b*. 6 Sept. 1856.
5. William John, *d. unm*. 1822.
6. John Wright (Rev.), *b*. 13 Oct. 1823, M.A., Incumbent of Nenagh and Archdeacon of Killaloe ; *m*. 1st, 24 June, 1852, Ann Charlotte, dau. of William Henry Gabbett, of Caherline, co. Limerick. She *d*. 17 April, 1853, leaving issue,
  1. Ann Charlotte, *m*. 11 Nov. 1875, Gen. Sir William Henry Seymour, K.C.B., Colonel, Queen's Bays.
Rev. J. W. Bowles *m*. 2ndly, 17 June, 1858, Eliza, dau. of John Andrews, of Ratheny, J.P. King's Co. She *d*. 21 Aug. 1898. He *d*. 24 Aug. 1888, having had further issue,
  1. Ludlow Tonson, *b*. 28 April, 1859 ; Maj. (retired) East Surrey Regt., *m*. 18 Jan. 1894, Rosa Elizabeth, dau. of the late the Right Hon. W. S. Baxter, M.P. for Montrose Burghs.
  2. Spotswood Robert, M.A., *b*. 24 July, 1861.
  3. John de Vere, Capt. R.F.A., *b*. 19 March, 1877 ; *m*. 2 Feb. 1905. Evelyn Grahame, dau. of William Walker Tennant, of Ballinard, Fethard, co. Tipperary.
  2. Eliza Rebecca, *d*. 14 Feb. 1865.
  3. Ida Jane.
7. William Robert, *b*. 19 Oct. 1827, of Liverpool, late Lieut. South Cork Militia, *m*. and *d*. 5 March, 1890, leaving issue.
8. Vere Hunt, of Rosanna, co. Cork, *b*. 6 April, 1829 ; Lieut.-Gen. in the Army, formerly Col. commanding 83rd Regimental District. Served with the 63rd Regt. throughout the Crimean Campaign 1854-5, which corps he commanded as Lieut.-Col. from Aug. 1867 till Dec. 1875, when he exchanged into the 37th Foot, and was appointed to the command of the 83rd Regimental District at Belfast, in 1877. Had the Crimean medal with four clasps for Alma, Balaklava, Inkerman, and Sebastopol, the 5th Class Order of the Medjidie and Turkish War Medal, *m*. 4 June, 1868, Ellen Anne (*d*. 2 Sept. 1911), dau. of Robert Hunt, of Cloughnadromin and Green Hills, J.P. co. Limerick. He *d*. 7 Jan. 1904.
1. Margaret Sarah Lydia, *d*. an infant, 1822.
2. Dorothea, *d*. 24 May, 1907, having *m*. Richard Nason, of Newtown, and had issue.

3. Margaret John, *m*. 27 Feb. 1862, James Matthew Green, Capt. 70th Regt., eldest son of Thomas Murdock Green, of Aghadoe, Killeagh, co. Cork, J.P., and had issue. She *d*. 14 Nov. 1896.
Mr. Bowles was *s*. by his eldest son,
GEORGE BOWLES, of Ahern, M.A., Major South Cork Militia, *b*. 8 Oct. 1813 ; *d*. 26 Feb. 1886, and was *s*. by his nephew.

Seat—Ahern, Conna, co. Cork.

BOYD OF BALLYMACOOL.

WILLIAM HENRY BOYD, of Ballymacool, co. Donegal, J.P. and D.L., High Sheriff 1892, *b*. 26 Aug. 1843 ; *s*. his uncle, 1891, and assumed by Royal Licence the name of BOYD, in lieu of his patronymic Porter ; *m*. 15 July, 1879, Charlotte Agnes, dau. of Col. James Henry Dopping, J.P. (*see that family*), and has issue,
1. JOHN DOPPING, *b*. 14 Feb. 1886, 2nd Lieut. Queen's Regt.
2. William Henry Ker Porter, *b*. 4 Feb. 1890.
3. Charles Knox Basil Boyd, R.N.R., *b*. 2 June, 1892.
1. Mary Rosalie, *b*. 8 June, 1880.
2. Helen, *b*. 17 April, 1882.
3. Agnes, *b*. 18 April, 1888 ; *m*. 2 June, 1910, Walter Newton Drew, of Raincliffe, Ecclesfield, Yorks, only son of late Major Edwin Drew, R.A.M.C.
4. Haidee, *b*. 4 June, 1891.

Lineage.—JOHN BOYD, of Letterkenny, son of JOHN BOYD, of Letterkenny, and grandson of JOHN BOYD, who built the family mansion of Letterkenny, 1672, claimed descent from a younger branch of the ancient Scottish family of Boyd, Earls of Kilmarnock, *m*. 1736, Ann, dau. of Alderman Gamble, of Derry, and had, with other issue,
1. JOHN, his heir.
2. Robert.
3. William Stewart, Lieut. Carbineers, killed in India.
4. Mossum, an officer of Customs, who left issue.
5. Archibald, of Derry (who *m*. Anne MacNeill, of the Colonsay family, and was father of the gallant Capt. JOHN MACNEILL BOYD, R.N., of the "Ajax," who perished at Kingstown, near Dublin, in the memorable storm of 9 Feb. 1861, and of Archibald Boyd, Dean of Exeter).
6. Alexander.
Mr. Doyd *d*. 1764, and was *s*. by his son,
JOHN BOYD, Major in the Donegal Militia, *b*. 1740 ; *m*. 1766, Martha, eldest dau. of Col. Stewart, Governor of Bahama Islands, and *d*. 1810, leaving a son,
JOHN BOYD, Barrister-at-Law, *b*. 20 Aug. 1769 ; *m*. 26 Jan. 1799, Frances, 2nd dau. of Sir Samuel Hayes, Bart. of Drumboe Castle, and *d*. 1836, leaving issue,
1. JOHN ROBERT, of Ballymacool.
2. William, Capt. in the 87th Royal Irish Fusiliers, afterwards Capt. and Brevet Major in the Scots Greys, *d. unm*. in the Crimea 1854.
1. Mary, *m*. Jan. 1835, William H. Porter, of Mildmay Park, London, son of Henry Porter. She *d*. 1886, having by him (who *d*. 1883) had issue,
  1. WILLIAM HENRY, now of Ballymacool.
  1. Mary, *d*. 1905.
  2. Rose, *d*. 1909, having *m*. 1871, Rev. James Colby, M.A.
  3. Anna Lighton.
2. Patty, *d. unm*.
3. Frances, *d. unm*.
4. Anna Maria, *m*. William Stewart Ross, of Sheep Hill, co. Derry, and is deceased.
5. Isabella, *m*. John Robinson, and is dec.
The elder son,
JOHN ROBERT BOYD, of Ballymacool, co. Donegal, J.P. and D.L., M.A. Trin. Coll. Dublin, Barrister-at-Law, High Sheriff 1846, *b*. 24 June, 1806 ; *m*. 6 Aug. 1851, Mary Louisa, eldest dau. of the Rev. William Knox, of Clonleigh, and *d*. 30 March, 1891. She *d*. 1 Sept. 1878. He was *s*. by his nephew, WILLIAM HENRY, now of Ballymacool.

Arms—Az., a fess chequy arg. and gu. in chief a trefoil or. Crest—A dexter hand, couped at the wrist, erect, pointing upwards with thumb and first two fingers ppr., the hand charged with a trefoil or. Motto—Confido.

Seat—Ballymacool, Letterkenny, co. Donegal.

BOYD-ROCHFORT. See ROCHFORT.

E 2

BOYLE OF LIMAVADY.

ALEXANDER BOYLE, of Bridge Hill, Limavady, co. Londonderry, J.P., B.A., Trin. Coll. Dublin 1868, called to the Bar at King's Inns, Dublin 1870, late Major Londonderry Artillery S. Div. R.A., member of the Town Commissioners and subsequently of the Urban Council of Limavady, b. 8 Aug. 1845; m. 8 Jan. 1873, Louisa, youngest dau. of Brudenell Plummer, C.I., R.I.C. (see PLUMMER), of Mount Plummer, co. Limerick, by Martha Thomas his wife, and has issue,

1. EDWARD MAURICE FITZ-GERALD, Solicitor (res. *Gorteen, Limavady*), b. 1 Nov. 1873; m. 29 June, 1898, Ethel Maude, eldest dau. of Capt. Robert Alexander Ogilby, D.L., of Pellipar House (*see that family*), and has issue,
   1. Alexander Robert, b. 25 June, 1899.
   2. Edward Ogilby, b. 11 Oct. 1902.
   1. Gladys Maude, b. 19 Feb. 1901.
2. Brudenell Plummer, M.I.E.E., b. 7 Aug. 1877; m. 1907, at the Cathedral, Singapore, Letitia Gwendoline Birney, only dau. of Edward Agnew Jones Stevenson, of Wellington, New Zealand, and has issue,
   Edward Brudenell Stevenson, b. 20 Nov. 1909.
   Alice Letitia Louisa, b. 1 Aug. 1908.
3. Alexander Frederick, F.R.C.A., b. 29 April, 1880.
4. Charles Edwin John, b. 13 Dec. 1884.
1. Geraldine Olive Martha, b. 21 Dec. 1875.
2. Louise Muriel, b. 9 April, 1883.

Lineage.—JAMES BOYLE, who settled at Limavady, and obtained a grant of lands from Phillips, was admitted and sworn a Freeman of the Corporation of Limavady 29 Oct. 1664, and elected a Burgess 12 Dec. 1674 (which Corporation was created by Charter from JAMES I, 31 March, 1613), and subsequently seven times Provost of Limavady from the year 1677 to 1702. He d. 1719, leaving two sons,
1. JOHN, his heir.
2. James, admitted Freeman of the Limavady Corporation 5 Oct. 1716.

His eldest son,
JOHN BOYLE, of Bridge Hill, Newtown-Limavady, was admitted Freeman of the Corporation 5 Oct. 1716, and was on the Vestry of the Parish of Drumachose from 1732 to 1746. The date stone in Bridge Hill House bears his name Anno 1732, with his Coat of Arms. He m. 1st, Miss Harr, who d.s.p. He m. 2ndly, 29 Dec. 1743, Ann, dau. of Alexander Ogilby (*see that family*), and by her (who m. 2ndly, Charles Harris, of London, and d. 28 Nov. 1773) had issue,
1. JAMES, his heir. 2. ALEXANDER, of whom presently.
1. Anne (Nancy), m. William Lane, and had issue.
2. Mary, m. (setts. dated 10 Jan. 1767) Nicholas Moore, eldest son of Charles Moore, of Kilkeel, co. Down, and had issue.

Mr. John Boyle was s. by his elder son,
JAMES BOYLE, of Bridge Hill, Col. of the Limavady Volunteers, was on the Vestry of the Parish of Drumachose 1765, b. 31 Oct. 1744; m. 1st, 4 May, 1/68, Elizabeth, eldest dau. of William Holmes, of Donaghmore, co. Tyrone, and Martha Stuart, and by her (who d. 1776) had issue,
1. John, b. 1 July, 1772; d.v.p. 1793.
2. William, b. 17 Dec. 1773; d.v.p., killed by the natives at the Island of Grenada, West Indies.
3. ROBERT, his heir.
1. Martha, d. young.
2. Mary Anne, b. 23 April, 1771; m. 12 Aug. 1791, James Parke, Lieut. Desertcreat Infantry, of Stewartstown, co. Tyrone, who d. 29 March, 1851, leaving issue. She d. 24 June, 1857.

Col. James Boyle m. 2ndly (setts. dated 18 May, 1779), Margaret Campbell. She d.s.p. He m. 3rdly (setts. dated 2 Jan. 1781), Elizabeth, dau. of Col. Thomas Boyle and Ann Torrens, and by her had further issue,
4. Thomas, d. young.
3. Elizabeth Torrens, m. 1803, Andrew Sutherland.
4. Nancy, d.s.p.

He m. 4thly, 1803, Margaret Ann, dau. of Capt. Parkinson, R.N. (she took out administration to her husband's estate), and by her (who d. 1848) had further issue,
5. James Parkinson, b. 1803, called to the Bar 1838; m. 1832, Mary Ann, dau. of George Overend. She d. 1862. He d. 1849, having had issue,
   1. James, b. 1835; m. Ellen Cox, and had issue.
   2. Abraham, d.s.p.
   3. William Henry, b. 1839; m. Sarah Davies, and had issue.
   1. Elizabeth Caroline,   2. Margaret, d.s.p.

6. Robert Alexander, d.s.p.
5. Margaret Ann, b. 26 Dec. 1805; m. 1832, Robert Macalister, 4th son of Dougal Macalister, of Dalchuirn, and had issue.

Col. Boyle d. 1810, and was s. by his 3rd son,
ROBERT BOYLE, of Bridge Hill, b. 14 Feb. 1775, sold portion of his father's property and Bridge Hill House to his uncle, Alexander Boyle. He emigrated to America and subsequently went to India, where he d.s.p., and was s. by his uncle,
ALEXANDER BOYLE, of Bridge Hill, Newton-Limavady, on vestry of Parish of Drumachose from 1774 to 1821, churchwarden 1775 and 1766, b. 1748; m. Elizabeth, 3rd dau. of Michael Ross, of Limavady. She d. 22 June, 1828, leaving issue,
1. JOHN, his heir.
2. EDWARD, of whom presently.
3. Michael, Lieut. 5th Native Infantry, Fort St. George, India, d. of fever at Tripassore, India, 30 Oct. 1804.
4. Alexander, b. 1788; d.s.p. 24 Oct. 1857.
1. Catherine, b. 20 Jan. 1782; d.s.p. 7 Sept. 1845.
2. Ann Eliza, m. her cousin, Rev. Robert Alexander Parke, and had issue.

Mr. Boyle d. 18 Feb. 1828, and was s. by his eldest son,
JOHN BOYLE, of Bridge Hill, Newtown-Limavady, b. 8 April, 1780, J.P. co. Londonderry, Freeman of the City of Londonderry (ad. 26 April, 1811), Member of the Council of Coleraine, Capt. commanding the Balteagh Corps of Infantry, Member of the County Londonderry Grand Jury, agent to the 2nd Marquis of Waterford, on the vestry of the Parish of Drumachose 1812-28, Churchwarden 1823. He d.s.p. 12 March, 1836, and was s. by his brother,
EDWARD BOYLE, of Bridge Hill, Newtown-Limavady, b. 1784. Solicitor, Law Agent to the Marquis of Waterford; m. 1st (setts. dated 7 Aug. 1837), Julia, dau. of James Stirling, of Walworth, and by her (who d. 1 Oct. 1840) had issue,
1. Georgina, b. 17 Oct. 1839; m. Hugh Pollen, and d. 1902, leaving issue.

He m. 2ndly (setts. dated 24 June, 1844), his cousin, Mary Anne, dau. of James Parke, of Stewartstown, co. Tyrone, and by her (who d. 5 Jan. 1890), had issue,
1. ALEXANDER, now of Bridge Hill.
2. John, b. 27 Feb. 1847, B.A., Dublin, Solicitor; d.s.p. 17 Jan. 1890.
3. Edward, b. 17 July, 1848; d.s.p. 20 May, 1864.
4. James, b. 8 Aug. 1849, B.A., Dublin, late Capt. Queen's Royal Antrim Rifles, served in the Zulu War, d.s.p. 14 May, 1906.
5. David Grainger, b. 5 July, 1853; d.s.p. 7 March, 1893.

Mr. Boyle d. 10 Aug. 1861, and was s. by his eldest son, Alexander Boyle, now of Bridge Hill.

Arms—Per chevron crenellée or and gu. three hart's horns erect counter-changed. Crest—A hart's head couped per chevron crenellée or and gu. Motto—Dominus Providebit.
Residence—Bridge Hill, Limavady, co. Londonderry.

BOYSE OF BANNOW.

HENRY THOMAS ARTHUR SHAPLAND BOYSE, of Bannow, co. Wexford, J.P., High Sheriff 1910, late Lieut. 1st Batt. R. Irish Regt., b. 5 Jan. 1878. m. 11 May, 1911, Elinor Mercy Claude, dau. of the late Claud Baggallay, K.C.

Lineage.—NATHANIEL BOYSE, son of John Boyse, of Mullaghterry, co. Tyrone, by Anne, his wife, who d. 1 May, 1664 (Nathaniel being then aged 24 and married), obtained a grant under the Act of Settlement, 3 Nov. 18 CHARLES II, of Bannow and was High Sheriff of the county Wexford 1677. He had, by Magdalen his wife, four sons and one dau.,
1. John, living 10 May, 1676.
2. NATHANIEL, of whom presently.
3. Jacob, Capt. in Lord Mountjoy's Regt., High Sheriff co. Wexford 1720, M.P. for Bannow 1715-24; whose will, dated 25 May, 1724, was proved 30th of the same month.
4. Benjamin, of Dublin. (Will dated 20 June, 1711, proved 17 Nov. 1712.)
1. Patience, m. — Vicary, of Wexford, and d. 1744.

Mr. Boyse d. 1678 (will dated 10 May, 1678, proved 30 Aug. foll.). His second son,
NATHANIEL BOYSE, of Bannow, M.P. for Bannow 1692-1714, who purchased in 1703, from the Commissioners for the sale of forfeited estates, lands in the co. Wexford, and the Queen's Co.; he m. Frances, dau. of Samuel Helsham, of Kilkenny, and had issue,
1. NATHANIEL, his successor.
2. Samuel, of Cullenstown, M.P. for Bannow 1725-30, whose will, dated 9 May, 1728, was proved 15 July, 1730. He m. Anne, dau. of Thomas Cooke, and had, with three daus., Frances, Elizabeth, and Anne, a son,
   THOMAS, of Bishop's Hall, co. Kilkenny, whose will, dated 12 Aug. 1785, was proved 1791. He m. Margaret (will proved 1775), dau. of Edmund Jackson, of Portnescully, co. Kilkenny, by whom he had issue,
     (1) SAMUEL, who eventually s. to Bannow.
     (1) Nina, m. John Greene, of Greenville, co. Kilkenny. She d. 30 Sept. 1780.
     (2) Mary Anne, m. Musgrave, of Myrtle Grove.
     (3) Frances, m. Robert Thomas Carew, of Ballinamona, co. Waterford.
     (4) Margaret, m. William Watts, of Dublin. (5) Jane, d. unm.

3. Jacob, bapt. at St. Bride's, Dublin, 25 Aug. 1704; d. 1729.
1. Frances, bapt. at same place, 9 March, 1699; m. (lic. 27 March, 1736) Nathaniel Radford, of Brideswell, co. Wexford.
2. Anne, bapt. at same place, 19 Aug. 1706; m. Thomas Cooke.
Mr. Boyse, whose will, dated 8 April, 1714, was proved 17 Dec. following, was s. by his eldest son,
NATHANIEL BOYSE, of Bannow, bapt. at St. Bride's, Dublin, 26 May, 1702; m. Elizabeth, dau. of Richard Rowe, of Ballyharty, co. Wexford. Her will, dated 22 Jan. 1759, was proved 26 July, 1759. They had issue,
1. RICHARD, his heir.
2. Nathaniel (Rev.), b. 1727, B.A. Trin. Coll. Dublin. Oct. 1751, Vicar of Newmarket, co. Cork, d. unm. 31 May, 1792. Will proved that year.
1. Elizabeth, m. as his 1st wife, John Glascott, of Aldertown, co. Wexford, and d.s p. 23 Feb. 1768. He d.s.p. 5 Dec. 1810.
2. Frances, m. as 2nd wife, Doctor Thomas Carr, of Waterford, and had a son, George Carr (who s. to the Bannow estates, and d.s.p.), and two daus., Elizabeth and Francis, who sold the estates to Samuel Boyse.
Mr. Boyse, whose will, dated 13 June, 1726, was proved 7 May, 1735, was s. by his eldest son,
RICHARD BOYSE, of Bannow, b. 1726, High Sheriff co. Wexford 1755; m. by licence dated 21 Feb. 1753, Margaret (who d. 22 Sept. 1808), dau. of Col. Philip Savage, of Kilgibbon, co. Wexford, and d.s.p. 23 Jan. 1793, when his estates passed to his nephew, George Carr, and upon his death s.p. they passed to George Carr's sisters as co-heirs, and were eventually purchased by their kinsman, the heir male of the family,
SAMUEL BOYSE, of Bannow and Bishop's Hall, who m. by licence dated to March, 1780, Dorothea, dau. of Robert Shapland Carew, of Castleboro', co. Wexford, by whom (who d. 29 Dec. 1835) he had issue,
1. THOMAS, his heir.
2. Shapland, C.B., Lieut.-Col. 13th Dragoons, d. unm. 1832.
3. RICHARD, s. his brother at Bannow.
1. Dorothea, d. unm.   2. Jane, d. unm.
3. Frances, d. unm.
4. Margaret, m. 24 Aug. 1808, Henry Holdsworth Hunt, of Waterford, and had, with two daus., three sons,
1. HENRY SAMUEL, late of Bannow.
2. William Boyse, b. 1811, d. unm.
3. Thomas, b. 1815, d. 1847.
4. Robert Shapland (Rev.), Vicar of Mark Beech, Kent, b. 1817, d. 1904.
5. Richard Arthur, b. 1819, d. 1863.
1. Dorothea, b. 1813; d. unm. Jan. 1902.
2. Jane Ellen, b. 1821, d. 1895.
5. Mary, d. unm.
Mr. Boyse d. 26 Dec. 1830, and was s. by his eldest son,
THOMAS BOYSE, of Bannow, D.L. and J.P., High Sheriff 1841, b. 25 Dec. 1785; m. Jane Stratford, dau. of John Kirwan, Barrister-at-Law, and widow of Cæsar Colcough, of Tintern Abbey, co. Wexford. Mr. Boyse d.s.p. 1853 (his widow survived until 4 May, 1878), and was s. by his brother,
REV. RICHARD BOYSE, of Bannow, m. Winifred Berners Plestow, of Watlington Hall, Norfolk, by whom (who d. 7 Jan. 1861) he had an only son,
Augustus Freeman, J.P. and D.L. co. Wexford, b. 26 Sept. 1822; m. Mrs. Josephine Smith, widow, and d.s.p. in his father's lifetime, Sept. 1859.
Mr. Boyse d. March, 1864, and was s. by his nephew,
HENRY SAMUEL HUNT BOYSE, of Bannow, J.P., D.L., Capt. R.N., b. 1809; m. 27 July, 1847, Emily, dau. of Col. Thomas Steele, Madras Native Infantry (see STEELE of Rathbride), and had issue,
1. HENRY ARTHUR, late of Bannow.
2. St. George Philip, b. 15 Aug. 1855.
3. William Shapland, b. 16 June, 1857.
4. Richard Thomas, b. 13 Nov. 1862.
1. Emily Thomasine Mary, m. 1872, Robert Tyndall, of Oaklands, co. Wexford.
2. Elizabeth Dorothea. m. 5 Dec. 1871, Alexander Frederick Stewart, of Ballyedmond, co. Down, Capt. 6th Inniskilling Dragoons.
3. Philippa Kate Grace, d. young, 22 Feb. 1855.
4. Augusta Jane, m. 1891, Rev. G. H. M. Hamilton, late Vicar of Tandridge, Surrey.
Capt. Boyse obtained his first commission R.N. 10 Dec. 1835, and was appointed successively Lieut. in the "Racer 18," North America and West Indian Station; "Clio, 16," "Orestes, 18," and "President, 50," all South American Station; and to the command of the "Basilisk, 50," in the Pacific; was appointed Commander 10 March, 1846, and Capt. 1 July, 1864. On the death of his uncle, 1864, be s. to the Bannow estate, and thereupon adopted the surname of BOYSE, and d. 23 Dec. 1880, aged 71, when he was s. by his eldest son,
HENRY ARTHUR HUNT BOYSE, of Bannow, J.P. and D.L., High Sheriff 1882, Col. 3rd Batt. Royal Irish Regt., b. 11 March, 1847; m. 2 May, 1872, Emily Clare, only dau. of Rev. Thomas Harvey, of Cowden, Edenbridge, Kent, and d. 17 Jan. 1902, leaving issue,
1. HENRY THOMAS ARTHUR SHAPLAND, now of Bannow.
1. Emily Dorothea Mary Clare, b. 7 Aug. 1873; m. 3 Feb. 1898, Capt. William Perry, 3rd Batt. Royal Irish Regt., of Woodrooff, co. Tipperary (see that family).
2. Vera Marguerite Mansel, b. 27 Jan. 1875; m. 8 July, 1896, Charles Edward Wogan-Browne, 2nd son of Major Francis Browne, of Castle Browne, co. Kildare (see that family).

Seat—Bannow, co. Wexford.   Club—Kildare Street, Dublin.

MOORE-BRABAZON OF TARA HOUSE.

WILLIAM LOCKHART CHAMBRE MOORE-BRABAZON, of Tara House, co. Meath, late Lieut. Coldstream Guards, b. 3 Jan. 1880; s. his father 11 Jan. 1908.

Lineage.—JOHN MOORE, of Dublin, acquired in 1721, certain lands in the Barony of Mellifont, co. Louth, under an Act of Parliament, passed for the sale of the estates of William Graham. He m. a sister of the Right Hon. Charles Campbell, M.P., of New Grange, co. Meath, and had issue, Charles, Barrister-at-Law, d.s.p.; Alice, m. Gen. Sir John Whiteford, Bart., and a younger son,
JOHN MOORE, of Tullyhallen, co. Meath, M.D., m. 26 Aug. 1752, Frideswide, dau. of Dixie Coddington, of Athlumney Castle, co. Meath, and had issue,
1. JOHN, his heir,
1. Alice, m. Thomas Achmuty, of Madeira.
2. Jane, m. July, 1799, Hon. and Very Rev. John Hewitt, Dean of Cloyne.
3. Frideswide, m. 1786, Col. Hon. Robert Henry Southwell.
Dr. Moore was shot at his own door by an unknown person in 1788, when he was s. by his son,
JOHN MOORE, of New Lodge, co. Herts, b. 20 Sept. 1763; m. 1st, 24 May, 1788, Barbara, dau. of Hon. William Brabazon (2nd son of Edward, 7th Earl of Meath), of Tara House, co. Meath, by Katherine his wife, only dau. of Arthur Gifford, of Aghern, co. Cork, and had issue,
1. WILLIAM JOHN, his heir.
2. Arthur John, Major, b. 24 Sept. 1791, an Officer in the Royal Navy, served under Admiral Blackwood; m. 31 July, 1827, Sophia, dau. of Col. Yates, and had issue.
1. JOHN ARTHUR HENRY, late of Tara House, who s. his uncle in 1866.
2. William Richard, B.C.S., Joint Magistrate at Mirzapore, killed in the Mutiny.
3. Charles William, B.C.S., who left issue.
4. Adolphus Warburton, India Office, d.
1. Frances Stewart, m. Capt. Richard Charles Acton Throckmorton, late 87th Foot, and d. 1895 (see BURKE'S Peerage and Baronetage).
3. Charles Henry, b. 21 March, 1798; d.
Mr. Moore m. 2ndly, 26 April, 1839, Charlotte, dau. of George Samuel Collyer, and d. April, 1842, when he was s. by his eldest son,
REV. WILLIAM JOHN MOORE-BRABAZON, of Tara House, b. 29 April, 1789, who having s. to his mother's family estates, assumed by Sign Manual in July, 1845, the additional name and arms of BRABAZON. He d.s.p. in 1866, when he was s. by his nephew,
JOHN ARTHUR HENRY MOORE-BRABAZON, of Tara House, co. Meath, and of Tallyallen, co. Louth, High Sheriff co. Louth 1872, Hon. Lieut.-Col. in the Army, late Major Bengal Staff Corps, b. 13 June, 1828; s. his uncle, the Rev. W. J. Moore-Brabazon, in 1866, when he adopted the additional name of BRABAZON; m. Feb. 1879, Emma Sophia, dau. of Alfred Richards, of Tewkesbury Lodge, Forest Hill, Kent. He d. 11 Jan. 1908, having had issue,
1. WILLIAM LOCKHART CHAMBRE, now of Tara House.
2. John Theodore Cuthbert, b. 1884; m. 27 Nov. 1906, Hilda Mary, only dau. of the late Charles Henry Krabbé, of Buenos Ayres.
1. Kathleen Barbara Sophia, m. 13 Sept. 1911, Sir Gustavus Francis William Lambart, 1st Bart. of Beau Parc, co. Meath (see BURKE'S Peerage).
2. Hebe Crystabel Frideswide.

Seat—Tara House, co. Meath.

BRABAZON.   See BURKE'S PEERAGE, MEATH, E.

BRASIER OF BALLYELLIS.

BROOKE RICHARD BRASIER, of Ballyellis, co. Cork, J.P. cos. Cork and Limerick, b. 1852.

Lineage.—PAUL BRASIER, of Coleraine, co. Londonderry, obtained extensive grants of land temp. CHARLES II, m. Sarah dau. of Sir Tristram Beresford, Bart. of Coleraine, and by her (who d. 15 Jan. 1673) had a son,
COL. KILNER BRASIER, of Bagnal, co. Donegal, M.P. successively for Dundalk, St. Johnstown, and Kilmallock. Col. Brasier m. Anne, 3rd dau. of Sir Henry Brooke, of Brookesborough, co. Fermanagh, Knt., by his 2nd wife, Anne, dau. of Sir George St. George, Knt., of Carrickdromrusk, co. Leitrim, and had a son,
KILNER BRASIER, m. 1st, Elizabeth, dau. of Dean Charles Massey; and 2ndly, Miss Ryves, of Castle Jane, co. Limerick. Mr. Brasier d. 1759, and by his 1st wife had a son,
BROOKE BRASIER, of Rivers, co. Limerick, m. 17 July, 1756, Elizabeth Johnson, dau. and co-heiress (with Amy, wife of Sir

Thomas Roberts, and Mary, wife of Ralph Westrop) of William Johnson, of Lizard, co. Limerick, and had an only son,
    KILNER BRASIER, High Sheriff co. Cork 1793, b. 1751 ; m. 1788, Mary, eldest dau. and coheiress of John Creagh, M.D., of Creagh Castle, co. Cork, by Judith Usher his wife, and had issue,
1. BROOKE, of whom presently.
2. JOHN, of Creagh Castle, assumed the name of CREAGH ; he m. 1801, Elizabeth, dau. and heiress of Charles Widenham, of Castle Widenham, co. Cork, and left at his decease an only child,
    PRISCILLA WIDENHAM, who s. to the Widenham estates, and m. 8 May, 1819, Henry Mitchell Smyth, 2nd son of Grice Smyth, of Ballynatray, co. Waterford (see SMYTH of Castle Widenham).
3. William Johnson, Capt. 27th Inniskillen Regt., d. unm.
4. Kilner, R.N., d. unm.
5. George Washington, ancestor of BRASIER-CREAGH, of Creagh Castle (see that family).
1. Catherine, m. Rev. Richard Bourne, Rector of Rathangan.
2. Judith, m. John Wilkinson, of Limerick, and is deceased.
3. Emma, m. James Griffin, of Foynes, co. Limerick.
4. Mary, m. Attiwell Wood, of Leeds, co. Cork.
5. Lucy, m. 1st, Charles Bell, and 2ndly, Bertie Jarvis, of Antigua, West Indies.
The eldest son,
    BROOKE BRASIER, of Bally Ellis, co. Cork, m. Ellen, dau. and co-heir of Henry Mitchell, of Mitchellsfort, co. Cork, and left issue,
1. KILNER, his heir.
2. Henry, of Mitchellsfort, who assumed the name of MITCHELL (see MITCHELL of Mitchellsfort).
3. Brooke, d. unm.
4. John Wellington, m. Barbara, dau. of John Smyth, of Temple Michael, co. Waterford, and had one son, Brooke.
5. Grice, who emigrated to Australia.
1. Ellen, m. William Quin, of Loughlougher Castle, co. Tipperary, who d. 1869.
2. Mary, m. John Smyth, of Temple Michael.
3. Catherine, m. 1844, Sir Richard de Burgho, Bart., who d.s.p. 1873.
The eldest son,
    KILNER BRASIER, of Ballyellis, J.P., m. Mary, dau. of James Griffin, of Foynes, co. Limerick, and d. 1874, leaving issue,
1. BROOKE RICHARD, now of Ballyellis.
2. Kilner.   3. Henry.   4. Charles.
    Arms—Quarterly per fess indented or and sa. four cinquefoils counterchanged. Crest—A demi lion rampant per pale and sa.
    Motto—Amor patriae.
    Seat—Ballyellis, Mallow, co. Cork.

BRASIER-CREAGH. See CREAGH.

BRASIER-MITCHELL. See MITCHELL.

BRERETON OF RATHURLESS, CO. TIPPERARY.

COL. THOMAS SADLEIR BRERETON, of Rathurless, b. 1834 ; m. 1862, Frances, dau. of Edward Townley Hardman, of Newbliss, co. Monaghan, M.D., and has issue surviving,
1. THOMAS HARDMAN, b. 1866 ; m. 1904, Avecena Maud, dau. of Samuel Dickson Biggs, of Bellevue, co. Tipperary (see BIGGS-ATKINSON of Ashley Park), and has issue,
    (1) Avereena Maud.   (2) Patricia Hardman.
2. Hardman John Ker, b. 1873 ; m. 1904, Florence, dau. of Robert Benjamin Heuston, of Ballyhisteen, co. Tipperary, and has one son and one dau.,
    1. John Hardman, b. 1907.
    1. Frances Vera Mary.   2. Nancy.
3. Franc Sadleir, b. 1880, Capt. 4th Batt. Royal Irish Fus., served in S. African War.
1. Maria, m. 1894, David England Young, of Ballygibbon, co. Tipperary, and Harding Grove, co. Galway.
2. Frances Gertrude.
3. Isabella m. Richard Vincent Johnston, of Llandudno.
4. Eileen.
    Lineage.—THOMAS BRERETON, of Clonanihy, co. Tipperary, m. Mary, dau. of James Carrol, of Ballycrenode, co. Tipperary, and by her (who d. 1783) had issue,
1. JOHN, his heir.
2. Daniel, of Tombricane, co. Tipperary, b. 1731 ; m. 1772, Mary, dau. of Rev. Meade Nesbitt, of Fort Nesbitt, co Tipperary, and d. 1818, leaving an only child,
    Anne, m. 1796, Thomas Brereton, of Kilmartin, Queen's Co.
3. Thomas, of Ash Park (now Riverston), co. Tipperary, b. 1742; m. Anne, dau. of Samuel Lawrence, of Ash Park, and Millmount, and d. 1776, from a fall while out hunting, having by her (who m. 2ndly, 1781, Saunders Young, of Nenagh) had issue,
    Thomas, of London, m. 1810, Maria, dau. of Thos. Brereton Watson, of Clonanihy, co. Tipperary, and had issue,
    (1) Henry.   (2) Robt. Lawrence.
    (3) Wm. Watson.
    (1) Caroline Catherine.

1. Mary, m. 1765, John Watson, of Brook Watson, co. Tipperary.
The eldest son,
    JOHN BRERETON, of Rathurless, co. Tipperary, b. 1729 ; m. 1767, Margaret, dau. of George Watson, of Garrykennedy, co. Tipperary, and d. 1813, having by her (who d. 1800, aged 51) had issue,
1. THOMAS, his successor.
2. John, of Old Court, co. Tipperary, b. 1787 ; m. Anne, dau. of Simpson Hackett, of Riverstown, co. Tipperary, and had issue,
    1. John Robert, Barrister-at-Law, b. 1817 ; m. Mary, dau. of Garrett O'Moore, of Cloghan Castle, King's Co., D.L., and d. 1871, leaving issue,
    (1) O'Moore.
    (1) Grace.   (2) Geraldine.
    (3) Mary, m. 1874, Sir Garrett O'Moore Creagh, V.C., and had issue (see CREAGH of Cahirbane).
    2. Simpson Hachett, of Clongowna, co. Tipperary, m. 1850, Mary Sophia Parker, and had issue,
    (1) John, M.D., d.s.p.   (2) Herbert, of Clongowna.
    (1) Maud.   (2) Sophia, d. unm. 1907.
    (3) Margaret, d. unm.
    (4) Georgina, m. Edward Justin McCarthy.
    1. Margaret Maria, d. unm. 1873.
    2. Sarah, m. 1842, John Bennett, of Grange, King's Co.
1. Dora, m. Robert Langford, of Rowell, co. Limerick (see that family).
2. Mary, m. 1818, Peter Watson, of Roscrea, and subsequently of Tasmania.
The eldest son,
    THOMAS BRERETON, of Rathurless, J.P., many years a Resident Magistrate, b. 20 Nov. 1785 ; m. 1 Dec. 1817, Maria, 2nd dau. of Capt. Thomas Sadleir, of Castletown, co. Tipperary, and d. 24 Aug. 1860, having by her (who d. 17 Dec. 1874) had issue,
1. Thomas Sadleir, now of Rathurless.
2. John Sadleir, Lieut.-Col. late 67 Foot, b. 1836 ; m. 1869, his cousin, Margaretta Watson, dau. of Edwin Sadleir, of Oak Wood, King's Co., and d. 1908, having had issue,
    Thomas Edwin, b. 1878.
    Myra, m. Ralph Peyton Sadler, Capt. Derby Regt.
3. Franc Sadleir, formerly Lieut. King's Royal Rifles, b. 1838 ; m. 1865, Isabella, dau. of Frederick Robert Beeston. He d. 4 Dec. 1911, having had issue,
    1. Thos. Bloomfield Sadleir, b. 1866 ; m. 1900, Maud, dau. of Edward Wilson, of Carshalton, Surrey, and has issue,
    Ralph Sadleir, b 1902.
    Eileen Sadleir.
    2. Franc Sadleir, of Blackfoot City, U.S.A., b. 1867.
    3. John Sadleir, of Ogden, U.S.A., b. 1870 ; m. Jane Branson, and has,
    Fredk. Sadleir, b. 1898.
    4. Frederick Sadleir, Capt. R.A.M.C. (ret.), of Southport, Lancs., b. 1872, author of "With Shield and Assegai" and numerous other works ; m. 1898, Ethel, dau. of Wm. James Lamb, and has issue,
    Allen Sadleir, b. 1899.
    Olive Sadleir, b. 1900.
1. Margaret, m. 1867, Maj.-Gen. Ernest Berger, late Lincolnshire Regt.
    Seat—Rathurless, Nenagh, co. Tipperary.

FRENCH - BREWSTER OF CLOONANARTMORE.

ROBERT ABRAHAM FRENCH-BREWSTER, of Cloonanartmore, co. Roscommon, Haroldstown, co. Carlow, and Grange, co. Wicklow, Capt. late Irish Guards (formerly Lieut. Royal Fusiliers), b. 30 July, 1877.
    Lineage.—SAMUEL and DANIEL BREWSTER had a grant of land in Tipperary under the Act of Settlement, temp. CHARLES II.
    HENRY BREWSTER, of Lebanty, co. Carlow, son of HENRY BREWSTER and Elizabeth, his wife, m. about 1699 Elizabeth Leybourne, and had issue.
The elder son,
    SAMUEL BREWSTER, of Ballywilliamroe, co. Carlow, b. 11 July, 1700, made his will 1 April, 1756, which was proved 1 June following. He left by Anne, his wife,
1. Henry, m. Anne, dau. of John Perkins of Ballintrain, co. Carlow, and had issue,
2. WILLIAM, of whom presently.
3. Samuel, m. Elizabeth Garrett, and had issue, a dau.
4. John d.s.p.
1. Elizabeth, m. Robert Twiss.
2. Anne.
The second son,
    WILLIAM BREWSTER, of Ballynulta, co. Wicklow, m. 1767, Mary, dau. of Edward Jones, of Tullow, co. Carlow, and sister of Abraham Jones, of Tullow, and had issue,

IRELAND. Brinkley.

1. WILLIAM BAGENAL, of whom presently.
2. Edward, *m.* Sarah, dau. of Robert Gray and *d.* June, 1836, leaving issue.
3. Henry, *d. unm.*
1. Mary, *m.* — Fitz-Henry, of Larkfield, co. Wicklow.

The eldest son,
WILLIAM BAGENAL BREWSTER, of Ballynulta, co. Wicklow, *m.* Anne, dau. of Thomas Bates, and had issue,
1. ABRAHAM, of whom presently.
2. William Thomas, *d.unm.* 1821.
3. Robert Jones (Rev.), *d. unm,* 1832.
1. Mary, *m.* 1819, Samuel Allen, of Higham Ferrers, Northants, and *d.* 1873.
2. Margaret, *m.* 1819, Archibald Montfort, of Killenure, co. Wicklow, and *d.* 1850.

The eldest son,
THE RIGHT HON. ABRAHAM BREWSTER, P.C., Lord Chancellor of Ireland, B.A. Trin. Coll., Dublin, 1817, Barrister-at-Law 1819, King's Counsel 1835, Sol.-Gen. for Ireland 1846, Attorney-Gen. 1853, P.C. 1853, Lord Justice of Appeal 1866, and Lord Chancellor 1867, *b.* 1796, *m.* 1819, Mary Ann, dau. of Robert Gray, of Upton House, co. Carlow. She *d.* 1862. He *d,* 26 July, 1874, having had issue,
1. William Bagenal, Capt. Rifle Brigade and Lieut.-Col. of the Inns of Court Volunteers, *b.* 1820, *m.* 1858, Georgiana, dau. of James Campbell, of Craigie Down, co. Ayr, and *d.s.p.* 1864, *vita patris.*
2. Elizabeth Mary, *m.* 21 June, 1850, as his second wife, Henry Sneyd French, of Clonsilla, co. Dublin (*see* FRENCH *of Castle Bernard*), 3rd son of Robert Henry French, of Dublin, merchant, (uncle of 1st Baron de Freyne), and grandson of Arthur French, M.P., of French Park, co. Roscommon (*see* BURKE'S *Peerage,* DE FREYNE, B.). Mr. Henry Sneyd French *d.* 20 Sept. 1850. She *d.v.p.* 10 Nov. 1868, leaving an only son,
ROBERT ABRAHAM BREWSTER, *s.* his maternal grandfather, 1874.

The grandson and heir,
ROBERT ABRAHAM BREWSTER FRENCH - BREWSTER, of Cloonanartmore, co. Roscommon, Haroldstown, co. Carlow, and Grange, co. Wicklow, High Sheriff co. Carlow 1882, sometime Lieut. King's Dragoon Guards, M.P. for Portarlington 1883-5, *b.* 4 April, 1851, assumed by Royal Licence 13 Aug. 1874, the additional name and arms of BREWSTER on succeeding his grandfather, the Right Hon. Abraham Brewster; *m.* 1st, 28 Sept. 1876, Geraldine (*St. Albans House,* 143, *Gloucester Road, S.W.*), dau. of Henry Ritchie Cooper, of Ballindalloch, co. Stirling, and by her (who divorced him 1 July, 1890) had issue,
1. ROBERT ABRAHAM, his heir.
2. Henry Gerald, 2nd Lieut. King's Royal Rifle Corps, *b.* 24 Sept. 1878, killed in action at Spion Kop, 24 Jan. 1900.
3. William Bagenal, *b.* 26 Aug. 1880; *d.* an infant.
4. Arthur Ord, late King's Royal Rifle Corps, *b.* 31 July, 1882. He *m.* 2ndly, 28 Jan. 1895, Annie Hodge, dau. of George Hodge, by whom he had no issue. He *d.* 20 May, 1901.

Arms—Quarterly 1st and 4th, az. on a chevron engrailed erm. between three estoiles arg. a trefoil slipped vert (BREWSTER) 2nd and 3rd erm. a chevron sa. a martlet for difference (FRENCH).
Crests—1. A leopard's head erased az. bezantée in the mouth a trefoil slipped vert (BREWSTER). 2. A dolphin naiant ppr. (FRENCH). Motto—Verité soyez ma garde.
Residence—St. Alban's House, 143, Gloucester Road, S.W.
Clubs—Guards; Army and Navy; Whites.

BRINKLEY OF FORTLAND.

JOHN LLOYD BRINKLEY, of Fortland, co. Sligo, J.P. and D.L., High Sheriff 1885, *b.* 8 June, 1852; *m.* 17 July, 1880, Annie Constance Isabel Worthington, 2nd dau. of the late Rowland Edward Cooper, and has issue,
1. JOHN ROWLAND LLOYD, Lieut. R.F.A., *b.* 17 Sept. 1882; *m.* 6 June, 1911, Dorothy Helen Agatha, younger dau. of Frederick Page, F.R.C.S., D.C.L., of Newcastle-on-Tyne.
2. Edward Graves, *b.* 23 Dec. 1883; *m.* 23 April, 1910, Nadine, younger dau. of Sir Reginald W. Proctor-Beauchamp, 5th Bart. (*see* BURKE'S *Peerage*).
3. George Yorke Lloyd, *b.* 30 July, 1896; *d.* 1907.
1. Mabel Fitzgerald, *m.* Feb. 1911, Charles H. Niven, 3rd son of Commander Oswald B. Niven, R.N.
2. Edith Sybil.
3. Annie Constance, *d.* young, 1889.
4. Ruth Minna Constance.

Lineage.—THE RIGHT REV. JOHN BRINKLEY, D.D., *b.* at Woodbridge, Suffolk, in 1766, entered Caius Coll. Cambridge, 29 Aug. 1783, became B.A. and Senior Wrangler in 1788, and M.A. 1791 was appointed Astronomer Royal in 1792, Archdeacon of Clogher 1808, President of the Royal Irish Academy 1822, and Bishop of Cloyne 8 Oct. 1826. His lordship *m.* 12 July, 1792, Esther, dau. of Matthew Weld, of Dublin, and had two sons and one dau.,
1. JOHN, of whom hereafter.
2. Matthew, of Parsonstown, co. Meath, *b.* 2 March, 1797, admitted a Vicar-Choral of Cloyne 31 March, 1831, J.P. co. Meath; *m.* 5 March, 1821, Henrietta, dau. of Very Rev. Richard Graves, Dean of Ardagh (*see* GRAVES *of Cloghan Castle*), and *d.* 27 April, 1855, having had issue by her (who also *d.* in 1855),
1. John, *d. unm.*
2. RICHARD GRAVES, of Fortland.
3. Matthew, Lieut. 97th Foot, Secretary to the Governor of Australia.
4. Hercules.   5. Francis.
1. Esther, *m.* John Alexander, of Milford, co. Carlow.
2. Eliza, *m.* William Henry Longfield, of Careystown, co. Cork.
3. Harriet, *m.* Richard Henry Farrer, of Dunamaise, Queen's Co.
4. Minna, *m.* G. A. Rotherham, of Kilbride Castle, co. Meath, 5. Anna, *m.* 1st, 25 Aug. 1860, James, 5th Earl of Kingston. He *d.s.p.* 8 Sept. 1869. She *m.* 2ndly, 29 July, 1873, William Downes Webber, of Kellavil, Queen's Co. She *d.s.p.* 29 Oct. 1909.   6. Arabella.
7. Jane, *m.* 27 March, 1861, Edward Vernon, eldest son of J. B. Venables Vernon, of Clontarf Castle, co. Dublin.
1. Sarah, *m.* Robert James Graves, M.D., and *d.s.p.*
The Bishop of Cloyne *d.* 14 Sept. 1835. His eldest son,
THE REV. JOHN BRINKLEY, Rector of Glanworth, Diocese of Cloyne, *b.* 1793. *m.* Anna, 2nd dau. and co-heir of Rev. Walter Stephens, of Hybla, co. Kildare, by Arabella his wife, dau. of Capt. William Glascott, 24th Foot, 3rd son of George Glascott, of Aldertown, and had issue,
1. John, 9th Lancers, *d. unm.* in India 1851.
2. WALTER STEPHENS, of Knockmaroon House.
1. Sarah.
Rev. John Brinkley *d.* 14 Feb. 1847, and was *s.* by his eldest son, JOHN, at whose decease, *unm.* the estate devolved on his brother, WALTER STEPHENS BRINKLEY, of Knockmaroon House, co. Dublin, J.P., sometime 11th Hussars, *b.* 12 Dec. 1826; *m.* 24 July, 1851, Susanna Caroline, dau. of Major Michael Turner, King's Dragoon Guards, of Ipswich, son of Nathaniel Turner, of Stoke Hall, Suffolk, and by her (who *d.* 2 March, 1908) had issue,
1. JOHN TURNER, Chief Constable of Warwickshire, late Capt. The Prince of Wales's North Staffordshire Regt. (*Wasperton House, near Warwick*), *b.* 23 Oct. 1855; *m.* 3 Nov. 1885, Mary, oldest dau. of the late Gen. H. A. Carleton, C.B., R.A. (*see* CARLETON *of Clare*), and has issue,
1. John Carleton, *d.* an infant.
2. John Patrick, *d.* an infant.
1. Sheila Mary.
2. Walter Frederick Brownlow (Rev.), Vicar of Abbotsleigh, Somersetshire, M.A. Camb., *b.* 29 July, 1859; *m.* 26 Jan. 1897, Emmeline Lydia (who *d.* 14 March, 1902), youngest dau. of the late Gen. J. C. Brooke, and widow of T. W. Miles P.W.D. India, of Caragh, co. Kerry, and has issue,
Kathleen Sophia.
3. Charles Michael Edgeworth, Major 4th Dragoon Guards, Chief Constable of Lincolnshire, *b.* 6 May, 1861; *m.* 3 March, 1892, Evelyn Everard, 2nd dau. of the late Maj. Thomas Everard Hutton, of Middleton Hall, Norfolk, late 4th Dragoons, and *d.* 31 July, 1903, leaving issue,
1. Walter Everard, *b.* 18 Sept. 1893.
1. Maud Agneta.   2. Violet Kathleen.
3. Norah Julia.
1. Julia Katherine, *d. unm.* 1911.
2. Anna Isabella, *m.* 3 Dec. 1884, Major Maurice Elrington Bisset, R.E., of Lessendrum, Huntly, N.B. He *d.* 15 June, 1909, leaving issue (*see that family*).
3. Susannah Kathleen, *d. unm.* 1896
Mr. Brinkley *d.* 31 March, 1884. His cousin,
RICHARD GRAVES BRINKLEY, of Fortland, *b.* 21 Sept. 1823; *m.* 20 Dec. 1845, Hester, only child of James Stuart Downs Dodd Lloyd, of Ardagh, co. Sligo (by Charlotte his wife, dau. of George Hepenstal), and grand-dau. of Owen Lloyd, of Croghan, co. Roscommon, and by her (who *d.* 31 July, 1906) had issue,
1. JOHN LLOYD, now of Fortland.
2. James William Arthur, *b.* 15 March, 1854; *b.* 1867.
3. Richard Henry Lee King, Capt. (ret.) 1st Batt. Royal Warwickshire Regt., *b.* 31 Oct. 1860.
1. Charlotte Ida Harriette, *d. unm.* 14 Aug. 1898.
2. Louisa Maria Susan, *m.* 19 Sept. 1868, Major-Gen. F. R. Crofton, late 2nd Batt. Royal Irish Rifles (86th Regt.), 2nd son of Sir Malby Crofton, 2nd bart. of Longford House, and has issue.
3. Harriette Adela, *m.* 24 March, 1872, Henry Skey, Lieut. 54th Foot, and had issue.
4. Alice Maud Elizabeth, *m.* 21 Dec. 1876, Thomas Weeding Weeding, J.P. co. Surrey, and has issue.
5. Anna Edith, *d. unm.* 1875.
Mr. R. G. Brinkley *d.* 15 May, 1890.

Arms—Az. a cross patonce engrailed and in chief three estoiles or. Crest—A cross patonce engrailed surmounted of an estoile, all or. Motto—Mutabimur.

Seat—Fortland, Easkey, co. Sligo. Residence—Allershaw, Folkestone.

Briscoe.   THE LANDED GENTRY.   72

BRISCOE OF RIVERDALE AND SCREGGAN.

EDWARD JOHN MARRIOTT BRISCOE, of Riverdale, co. Westmeath, and of Screggan Manor, King's Co., b. 28 Sept. 1862; s. his father 1 May, 1911, late Capt. 4th Brig. N. Irish Div. R.A., J.P. King's Co.; m. 22 Jan. 1891, Diana Louisa, only dau. of Col. Robert Wilson Hartley, of Beech Park, co. Dublin (see that family).

Lineage.—In 1720, RALPH BRISCOE acquired by purchase, the lordship and manor of Rathleen, King's Co. He m. Eleanor, sister of John Price, M.P. for Wicklow, and had by her, with other issue, an eldest son,
HENRY BRISCOE, Capt. Royal Horse Guards (Blue), who was father of
EDWARD BRISCOE, J.P., m. 5 June, 1752, Frances, dau. of Rev. Essex Edgeworth, of co. Longford, and had a dau. Eleanor, m. Andrew Armstrong, of Clara, J.P. His youngest brother,
WILLIAM BRISCOE, whose will, dated 27 July, 1772, was proved 8 Feb. 1775; m. 1st, 1761, Emily, dau. of James Nesbit, of Tubberdaly, which lady d.s.p.; and 2ndly, 1770, Ismena, dau. of James Nugent, of Clonlost, co. Westmeath, by whom he had,
1. EDWARD JOHN.
2. William Nugent, m. and left issue.
1. Eleanor Anne.

The elder son,
EDWARD JOHN BRISCOE, of Riverdale, co. Westmeath, and Screggan, King's Co., D.L., Col. Yeomanry Cavalry, b. 1770; s. to the entailed property of his uncle Edward, and served as High Sheriff of co. Westmeath 1800. He m. 1790, Frances, dau. of Thomas Fetherstonhaugh, of Bracklyn, co. Westmeath, and d. 1815, leaving issue,
1. WILLIAM THOMAS, his heir.
2. Edward, of Grangemore, co. Westmeath, b. 1799, served as High Sheriff 1833; m. 1829, Hester, youngest dau. of James Rynd, of Ryndville, co. Meath, and d. 1842, leaving issue,
 1. John Fetherstonhaugh, of Grangemore, and Lake House, co. Westmeath, J.P., b. Aug. 1830; m. April, 1852, Katherine Rebecca, dau. of William Peareth, of Usworth House, co. Durham, and d. 1882, leaving issue,
  (1) William John, b. 1856; lost at sea, 1875.
  (2) Algernon Thomas Fetherstonhaugh, of Lake House, and Curristown, co. Westmeath, J.P., b. 7 March, 1872; m. 1889, Mary Elizabeth, 2nd dau. of Rev. J. J. Moutray, of Favour Royal, co. Tyrone, and has issue,
   Mary Elizabeth.
  (1) Katherine Rebecca, m. 1884, John Nuttall, of Tittour, co. Wicklow.
  (2) Julia Isabella, m. 1884, Robert S. Hickey, of Taughmon, Mullingar, and d. in India 1886, leaving issue.
  (3) Cecilia Julia.
  (4) Isabella Frances, d. unm. 28 July, 1910.
  (5) Rosa Ellen, m. 1885, R. G. C. Flower, and has issue.
 2. James, b. 1832; d. 8 July, 1860.
 1. Maria Elizabeth, d. 1858.
 3. James, m. Harriet, dau. of Thomas Coates, of Staplestown, co. Kildare.
 4. Fetherston, m. Charlotte, dau. of John Phillips, and d. 1871, leaving three daus.,
  1. Frances, m. Rev. Richard Dowse, Dean of Clonmacnoise.
  2. Elizabeth.
  3. Charlotte Eleanor, m. 15 April, 1860, Freeman William Deane (see DEANE of Berkley).
 1. Jane, m. Humphrey Bor.
 2. Eleanor, m. James Johnston.   3. Anna Maria.

The eldest son,
WILLIAM THOMAS BRISCOE, J.P., of Riverdale, b. 1792; m. 1818, Maria Elizabeth, dau. of James Rynd, of Derryvolan, co. Fermanagh and Ryndville, co. Meath, and d. 1854, having by her (who d. 1874) had issue,
1. EDWARD JOHN, late of Riverdale.
2. James Rynd (Rev.), M.A. Trin. Coll. Dublin, Vicar of Ilminster, Somerset, b. Sept. 1821; m. 1845, Barbara, dau. of Benjamin Riky, of Ballylow, co. Carlow, and d. 5 Jan. 1898, having had issue,
 1. William Thomas (The Grange, Kington Langley, Chippenham, Wilts), b. 1840; m. 1875, Alice Agnes, dau. of Francis Spencer, of 10, Sydney Place, Bath, and has had issue,
  (1) Howard William, b. 1876, d. 1878.
  (2) John Fetherstonhaugh (Rev.), M.A. Oxon, Rector of Bagborough, Taunton, since 1904, b. 1877.
  (3) James Rynd, B.A. Cantab. (Achill, Chippenham, Wilts), b. 1879; m. 3 Oct. 1911, Margery Vera Ernle, dau. of Rev. Andrew Pope, Rector of Langley Burrell, Chippenham.
  (4) William Thomas, B.A. Cantab., M.R.C.S., L.R.C.P., b. 1880; m. 21 June, 1910, Nancy, younger dau. of Andrew Pringle, J.P., of Borgue, co. Kirkcudbright.
  (5) Alexander Angus Riky, b. 1886, d. 1887.
  (6) Ralph Angus Nugent, B.A. Cantab., b. 1888.
  (7) Arthur Francis Riky, b. 1895, d. 1899.
 2. Benjamin, b. 1852, m. 1882, Harriett Frances, dau. of Rev. Edward Cay Adams, Rector of Hawkchurch, and has issue,
  (1) Benjamin Ralph Cay, b. 1886.
  (1) Frances Mary.
  (2) Margaret Catherine.
 3. James Rynd, b. 1855, m. 1894, Linda Sybil, dau. of John R. Pine-Coffin, of Portledge, Devon (see that family), and has issue, Kathleen.
 4. Edward John Henry Havelock, b. 1858, d. 1878.

5. Francis Percival, b. 1862, d. 1887.
1. Barbara.   2. Maria Elizabeth.
3. Katherine.
4. Emily, d. 1864.
1. Hester Matilda, d. 1870.
2. Frances, d. unm. 1900.

The elder son,
EDWARD JOHN BRISCOE, of Riverdale, co. Westmeath, and of Screggan, King's Co., J.P. co. Westmeath, High Sheriff King's Co. 1860, b. 23 April, 1819; m. 23 Sept. 1852, Anna Rebecca, eldest dau. of Rev. Sir William M. Smith-Marriott, Bart., and d, 1 May, 1911, having had issue,
1. William Thomas, b 1855; d. 1859.
2. EDWARD JOHN MARRIOTT, now of Riverdale.
3. Robert Ralph, b. 25 Dec. 1867, B.A. Trin. Coll. Cambridge; d. unm. 29 April, 1896.
1. Julia Elizabeth.   2. Maria Elizabeth, d. 1870.

Seat—Riverdale. Killucan, Westmeath.

BROOKE OF SUMMERTON. See BURKE'S PEERAGE,
BROOKE, Bart.

BROOKE OF DROMAVANA.

MAJOR EARDLEY WILMOT BROOKE, of Dromavana, co. Cavan, Army Service Corps, late of the 60th Rifles, b. 2 Feb. 1870; m. 24 Nov. 1902, Beatrice Anna Caroline Isabella, eldest dau. of Clifford Lloyd, of Victoria Castle, Killiney, co. Dublin (see LLOYD of Lossett), and has issue,

GUY WILMOT, b. 3 Aug. 1904.

Lineage.—WILLIAM BROOKE, who purchased Dromavana from the Sanderson family 1685. Had three sons,
1. WILLIAM, of Runtavan House, co. Cavan, Scholar of Trinity College, Dublin, 1691, Rector of Killinkere, Mullagh, &c., m. Lettice, 2nd dau. of Simon Digby, D.D., Bishop of Elphin (see BURKE'S Peerage, DIGBY, B.), and had issue two sons,
 1. HENRY BROOKE, of Rantavan, Barrister-at-Law, author of Gustavus Vasa, Fool of Quality, Farmer's Letter, b. 1704; m. his cousin Catherine Meares, of Meares Court, co. Westmeath, and had twenty-two children, of whom survived, Arthur, in the Army, d. young.
  Charlotte, author of Translations from Irish Bards, d. 1792.
 2. Robert Brooke, m. his cousin Honor, dau. of Rev. Henry Brooke, Rector of Kinawley, co. Fermanagh, and had issue,
  (1) Henry, of Dublin, whose son was William Brooke, of Hastings, whose dau. was Mrs. Dolier, whose dau. m. Ven. Cadwallader Wolseley, Archdeacon of Glendalough, and is authoress of Villerois and many popular religious books.
  (2) Thomas Digby, m. and had issue,
   Thomas Henry, author of History of St. Helena, Secretary to the Council and Acting Governor of St. Helena, m. Miss Wright, and had issue, Thomas, of London, m. Miss Brabazon, and other issue.
  (3) Henry Daniel Digby, of Coolock House, m. Miss Lucinda Dobbyn, and had issue, 1. Joseph; 2. Henry; 3. Leonard (who m. Rhoda, dau. of J. Prentice, of Caledon, co. Tyrone, and has issue a. Henry, of Oxton, Birkenhead; b. Leonard, m. his cousin Sybil Diana, dau. of Rev. Stopford Brooke; and a. Rhoda Annie); 4. William; and five daus.
  (4) Digby, an Officer of Engineers, killed in India.
  (5) Robert, of Prosperous, co. Kildare, Col. in the Army, and Governor of St. Helena 1795, when he received the thanks of the King and Government through Mr. Dundas, for his relief of the Cape of Good Hope, by sending troops against the Dutch; and in 1799 Col. Brooke was presented by Marquess Wellesley, Governor of India, with a diamond-hilted sword, in full assembly. He m. Mrs. Wynne, née Mapletoft, and had issue,
   1. James, Major Bengal Horse Artillery, m. Miss Patton, dau. of Governor Robert Patton, and had issue, a son, Harold Kynnesman Mapletoft, m. Margaret Louisa Symonds, of Hinton Abbey, and d. 1867, leaving issue, (a) Ellen Louisa Symonds, m. 1870, Rev. Stephen Prust Jose, M.A., Vicar of Churchill, Somerset, and has issue; (b) Margaret Selina Patton, m. 1871, Peter Hugh Jekyll Lowes Rye, of Te Hill, N.Z., and has issue); and a dau. Anna, m. Rev. Thomas Spencer, A.M.
   2. Rev. John Michael, Rector of Ahenas, Cork, m. Louisa, dau. of Dean Holt Waring, of Waringstown, and had issue, Anna, m. — Ridley.

1. Elizabeth, *m.* H. A. Marshall, of Ceylon, and had issue, John A. B. Marshall, M.A., and Rev. Henry, of Bath, *m.* Miss Lucy Sadler, and has issue.
2. ALEXANDER, of Dromavana, of whom presently.
3. Henry (Rev.), Scholar of Trinity College, Dublin 1700, Rector of Kinawley, co. Fermanagh, *m.* Thomasine, dau. of Rev. Thomas Tucker, Rector of Moynalty, and had issue,
Henry, Governor of Madras, and afterwards of Rathcoffy, co. Kildare, *m.* and had, with other issue,
(1) Henry.
(2) William, Lieut.-Gen. and Col. 5th Dragoon Guards, *m.* Mary, dau. of Lieut.-Gen. Nicholls, and *d.* at Bath *s.p.*
(3) Robert, of Royal Crescent, Bath, *m.* 1st, Anne, dau. of Stephen Ram, of Ramsfort, co. Wexford, and Lady Charlotte Slopford his wife, dau. of James, 1st Earl of Courtown ; *m.* 2ndly, Miss Sill, dau. of the Rev. H. Sill, and has issue,
1. Henry, late of the 11th Hussars, *m.* the dau. of Myles Ponsonby, J.P., Hale Hall, Cumberland.
1. Sally. 2. Mary.
Honor, *m.* her cousin Robert Brooke, of Rantavan, and had issue as above.
The 2nd son,
ALEXANDER BROOKE, of Dromavana, *m.* July, 1713, Catherine, eldest dau. of Richard Young, J.P., of Drumgoon, co. Cavan, and had issue a son,
REV. WILLIAM BROOKE, D.D., of Dromavana and of Firmount, co. Longford, Scholar Trinity College Dublin, *b.* 1720 ; Rector of the Union of Granard for fifty years to whom honourable and interesting reference is made by Maria Edgeworth in the *Memoirs* of her father, vol. ii., p. 12. He *m.* his cousin Elizabeth, dau. of Mathew Young, of Lahard, co. Cavan, by his wife, Miss Nesbit, and had issue,
1. Richard (Rev.), of Dromavana, Rector of Ballyconnel, *d.s.p.* 1818.   2. WILLIAM.
1. Honor, *m.* Eyles Irwin, of Bellevue, Fermanagh, the Oriental traveller, and had issue.
The 2nd son,
WILLIAM BROOKE, M.D., of Dromavana, Dublin, and of Culmaine House, co. Monaghan, *b.* 1769 ; *m.* Angel, dau. of Capt. Edward Perry, co. Tyrone, and niece and heiress of Col. Richard Graham, co. Monaghan,* and had issue,
1. WILLIAM (Right Hon.), of Dromavana.
2. Edward Perry (Rev.), formerly Capt. 62nd Foot, Precentor and Canon of Dromore Cathedral, and Rector of Magheralin, co. Down, *b.* 1799 ; *m.* 1837, Lucy Catherine, dau. of Dr. James Saurin, Bishop of Dromore, and *d.* 1892, having by her (who *d.* 1887) had issue,
1. William Saurin, Col. Bengal Army, *b.* 26 June, 1838 ; *m.* Jane, dau. of J. McMaster. He *d.* 13 June, 1902, leaving issue,
(1) Edward William Saurin, Lieut. R.A., *b.* 25 March, 1873.
(2) John William.
(1) Mary, *m.* Capt. Grenville E. Temple, Sherwood Foresters.
(2) Marguerite.
2. James Mark Saurin (Rev.), late H.M. 17th Regt., Rector of St. Mary, Woolnoth, London ; *m.* Amy, only dau. and heiress of John R. Stanford, of Badingham, Suffolk, and has issue,
(1) John, dec.   (2) Edward James.
(1) Myrtle.   (2) Bryony.
(3) Avens.   (4) Orpine.
3. George Howard, *d.* young.
4. Loftus Edward, *m.* Rosamund, dau. of Rev. Meredith Brown.
1. Elizabeth Lucy, *m.* Edward Saunders, dec.
2. Cornelia Angelina, *m.* Augustus E. Brush, J.P., of Drumnabreeze, co. Down. She *d.* 3 May, 1907, having had issue.
3. Frances Charlotte, *m.* Lieut.-Col. W. B. Digby, of Balnacarra, co. Westmeath.
3. Richard Sinclair (Rev.), D.D., Rector of Wyton, Hunts, *b.* 1802 ; *m.* Anna Maria, dau. of the Rev. Dr. Joseph Stopford, of the Courtown family, Rector of Conwal, and ex-Fellow of Trin. College, Dublin. He *d.* 6 Aug. 1882. She *d.* 24 April, 1903, leaving issue,
1. Stopford Augustus (Rev.), *b.* 1832 ; *m.* March, 1858, Emma Diana, eldest dau. of T. Wentworth Beaumont, of Bretton Park, co. York, M.P. for Northumberland, and has issue,
(1) Stopford William Wentworth, *b.* 18 Jan. 1859 ; *m.* 1903, Helen T. Ellis, of Boston, U.S.A.
(2) Graham Vernon, dec.
(1) Honor.
(2) Maud, *m.* 8 Oct. 1897, Thomas William Rolleston, son of Charles Rolleston-Spunner, Q.C. (*see* ROLLESTON *of Franckfort Castle*), and has issue.   (3) Evelyn.
(4) Olive, *m.* Rev. L. Jacks, and has issue, five sons and a dau.
(5) Sybil, *m.* her cousin Leslie Brooke, and has issue.
(6) Verona, *m.* 28 Jan. 1908, Rev. Cecil Welland.

---

* Major Brooke, as the representative of the Grahams, formerly of Rahin, Queen's Co., who were a branch of the Netherby family, is in possession of a massive old ring (stated to have been a royal gift) worn by his lineal ancestor, Sir Richard Græme, and commemorative of an act of extraordinary chivalry at the fight of Aherlow, A.D. 1600. Here it was that Capt. Richard Græme, commanding a band of sixty horse, attacked and " rowted " the whole forces of the Sugan Earl of Desmond, consisting of 600 soldiers. In his third charge Græme penetrated to their camp, seizing their carriages, standards, &c. ; but in his fourth assault he charged so desperately that he " scattered their whole battalions," and that with such effect that Stafford says the Earl's forces were utterly broken and he was brought to a desperate " fortune," and never again could rally to a head, " but gat him into Ulster."— *See Pacata Hibernia, pp.* 149, 150.

2. William Graham, Barrister-at-Law, *d.* 27 April, 1907.
3. Edward Thomas, Maor-Gen. late Royal Engineers, *d.* 1910.
4. Arthur Sinclair (Rev.), Rector of Slingsby, co. York, *m.* Mary Ellen, dau. of R. P. Rodick, of Woodclose, Arnside, and has issue,
Roderick St. Clair.
Janet Honor.
1. Anna Stopford, *m.* Very Rev. T. J. Welland, Bishop of Down, and left issue.
2. Cecilia.   3. Elizabeth Honor.   4. Angel Stopford.
4. Irwin Alexander, drowned.
5. George Perry, Capt. 68th Native Infantry, *d.* in India, 1844.
1. Margaret, *m.* Thomas Atkinson, of co. Donegal, and *d.* 1880, leaving issue.
2. Elizabeth, *d.* 1890.   3. Catherine, *d.* 1819.
4. Frances, *d.* 1818.
The eldest son,
RIGHT HON. WILLIAM BROOKE, of Dromavana and Taney Hill House, co. Dublin, Q.C. and LL.D., Master in Chancery, and Commissioner of the Great Seal in Ireland, *b.* 22 July, 1796 ; *m.* 1st, 26 Aug. 1819, Emily Margaret, only dau. of Robert Rogers Wilmot, Deputy Recorder of Cork, and sister of Edward Wilmot-Chetwode (*see* CHETWODE *of Woodbrooke*), and by her (who *d.* 1850) had issue,
1. William Armitage, *b.* 3 July, 1823 ; *d.* 1903.
2. ROBERT WILMOT, of whom presently.
3. Henry Edward (Rev.), *b.* 20 May, 1829 ; *m.* Maria, dau. of Rev. J. A. Jetter, Vicar of Ironbridge, co. Salop, and *d.* 5 April, 1897, leaving issue,
1. William Montagu, *b.* 1861.
2. Charles Wilmot, twin with his brother, *d.* 1861.
3. Henry Sinclair (Rev.), Vicar of Pembury, Tunbridge Wells, *b.* 1865 ; *m.* 14 April, 1898, Georgina Louisa Margaret, eldest dau. of Capt. T. Stuart Russell, D.L., of St. John's, Wakefield, W.R. York, Chief Constable, by Louisa Charlotte Emily, dau. of the Rev. Sir Thomas Eardley Wilmot Blomefield, 3rd bart. She *d.* 16 Nov. 1906. He *m.* 2ndly, 28 April, 1909, Violet Wason, eldest dau. of the late James Wason, of Merton Hall, Newton Stewart, N.B., and had issue,
(1) Henry James Sinclair, *b.* 20 Feb. 1910.
(2) Rollo Sinclair, *b.* 22 Jan. 1911.
1. Margaret Graham, *b.* 1863, *m.* 1889, her cousin Graham Wilmot Brooke, who *d.* 5 March, 1892, leaving issue (*see above*).
4. Charles Francis, *b.* 21 May, 1835 ; Lieut. 40th Foot, fell in battle at Waitara, New Zealand, 27 June, 1860.
1. Caroline Hamilton, *m.* Sept. 1844, B. Clifford Lloyd, LL.D. and Q.C., and *d.* 1864, leaving issue.
Mr. Brooke *m.* 2ndly, Catherine A. D., dau. of Rev. William Bradford, Rector of Storrington, co. Sussex, but by her (who *d.* 1882) had no issue. He *d.* 19 Aug. 1881, and was *s.* by his 2nd son,
LIEUT.-COL. ROBERT WILMOT BROOKE, of Dromavana, and of Heathdene, Southborough, Tunbridge Wells, Lieut.-Col. (retired) 60th Rifles, *b.* 15 Dec. 1826 ; *m.* 1st, 9 April, 1863, Elizabeth Joanna Anne, only dau. of Gen. Sir Duncan MacGregor, K.C.B., by Elizabeth Douglas Trotter his wife, dau. of Sir William Dick, 4th bart. of Prestonfield, and by her (who *d.* 28 July, 1883) has had issue,
1. Graham Wilmot, of the Church Missionary Society, *b.* 23 Feb. 1865 ; *m.* 11 Dec. 1889, Margaret Graham, only dau. of Rev. H. E. Brooke, and *d.* at Lokija, River Niger, Africa, 5 March, 1892, leaving issue,
Duncan Graham Wilmot, *b.* 1 Nov. 1890 ; *d.* 28 July, 1897.
2. Douglas Wilmot, *b.* 27 April, 1867 ; *d.* 10 May, 1868.
3. EARDLEY WILMOT, now of Dromavana.
1. Lilian Elizabeth Emily, *b.* 20 Feb. 1864 ; *d.* 10 Feb. 1865.
Col. Brooke *m.* 2ndly, 1885, Bertha Alice, 5th dau. of the late Admiral Sir J. Crawford Caffin, K.C.B., and *d.* 8 April, 1898, leaving issue,
4. Robert Crawford Wilmot, *b.* 14 Oct. 1887.
5. James Morton Wilmot, *b.* 27 Oct. 1888.
Seat—Dromavana, co. Cavan.

BROOKE OF ARDEEN.

FRANCIS THEOPHILUS BROOKE, of Ardeen, co. Wicklow, J.P. and D.L., co. Fermanagh, J.P. co. Wicklow, late Lieut. R.N., *b.* 1851 ; *m.* 20 June, 1877, Alice Mary, dau. of Very Rev. W. Ogle Moore, Dean of Clogher ; she *d.* 16 April, 1909, having had issue,
1. GEORGE FRANK (*Donkerhock, Caledon, Cape Colony*), Capt. late Connaught Rangers, A.D.C. to Commander in Ch. Dublin, served in South African War (dangerously wounded at Colenso, medal), *b.* 30 Oct. 1878 ; *m.* 12 June, 1907, Theodora Olivia, dau. of Richard Meredith Jackson, of Natal, and has issue,
1. Frank Hastings, *b.* 18 March, 1909.
2. Oliver George, *b.* 3 July, 1911.
2. Henry Hastings, Lieut. 5th Batt. Connaught Rangers, served in South African War (medal), *b.* 28 April, 1884.
1. Alice Gertrude, *m.* 26 April, 1905, Dermot Henry Doyne, D.L., of St. Austin's, Follow, co. Carlow, younger son of Charles Mervyn Doyne, of Wells (*see that family*).
Mr. Brooke is the youngest son of George Augustus Frederick Brooke, D.L., of Ashbrooke, co. Fermanagh (who *d.* 20 Feb. 1874), and Lady Arabella

Brooke. THE LANDED GENTRY. 74

Georgiana Hastings his wife (who d. 29 Jan. 1899), dau. of Hans Francis, 11th Earl of Huntingdon, and grandson of Sir Henry Brooke, 1st Bart. of Colebrooke.

Lineage, Arms. &c.—See BURKE's *Peerage*, BROOKE, Bart.
Seat—Ardeen, Shillelagh, co. Wicklow. **Clubs**—Kildare Street and Bachelors'.

BROOKE. See BURKE's PEERAGE, **BROOKE, Bart.**

BROWN OF CLONBOY.

ERNEST GEORGE BROWN, of Clonboy, co. Clare, Lord of that Manor, and of Lisnagry, co. Limerick, J.P. co. Clare, b. 7 Aug. 1864 ; s. his father 20 Oct. 1907.

Lineage.—JOHN BROWN, of Maghlands, in Scotland, m. Jane, dau. of Sir Robert Gordon, of Lochinvar (by his wife, Lady Isabella Ruthven, dau. of the 1st Earl of Gowrie), and sister of 1st Viscount Kenmure. His son,
JOHN BROWN, marched into England with CHARLES II to Worcester ; he had a command in the Horse under the Duke of Hamilton ; after being severely wounded at Worcester he fled to Ireland and settled at Dungannon, co. Tyrone, where he d. temp. CHARLES II. By Alice his wife, he left a son,
WILLIAM BROWN, b. at Belfast, 1658, Lieut. and Adjutant of Col. St. John's Regt. of Foot, served with distinction at Derry, Aughrim, Boyne, and the siege of Limerick. He settled at Clonboy 1691, his grant being confirmed together with the tolls of Bridgetown fair in 1717, m. 20 Feb. 1676, Elizabeth, dau. of Edward Rock, of the Vale of Evesham, and d. 28 Feb. 1725-6, leaving by her a numerous family of which the eldest son,
THE VEN. JOHN BROWN, Archdeacon and Chancellor of Limerick, Rector of Rathkeale, J.P., b. 24 Jan. 1684 ; m. 6 Aug. 1717, Anne, eldest dau. of John Vincent, of Erina, co. Clare, Alderman of Limerick, and was s. by his son,
JOHN BROWN, of Danesford and Mount Brown, co. Limerick, b. 3 April, 1724 ; m. 12 Jan. 1751, Meliora, dau. and co-heir of Col. the Hon. Henry Southwell, 2nd son of Thomas, 1st Viscount Southwell, and had issue, two sons,
1. HENRY, his heir.
2. John Southwell, of Mount Brown, co. Limerick, b. 31 March, 1763 ; m. 11 March, 1794, Mary, dau. of Nathaniel Gordon, of Whitehill, co. Lanark, and by her (who d. 6 Dec. 1842) had issue,
  1. JOHN SOUTHWELL, of Mount Brown, an Officer in the 10th Hussars, b. 9 March, 1794 ; m. 22 July, 1817, Margaret Anne, 2nd dau. of Major-Gen. Agmondisham Vesey, of Hampton Court, Middlesex, and d. 1872, having by her (who d. 13 Jan. 1853) had issue,
    (1) EDWARD JOHN VESEY, of Mount Brown, co. Limerick, J.P., Lieut.-Col. late 60th Rifles, b. 6 Dec. 1818 ; m. 16 Sept. 1848, Rose Augusta, 4th dau. of Admiral Sir William Parker, Bart., G.C.B., and d.s.p. 19 Sept. 1894.
    (2) John, Lieut. 25th Bombay Native Infantry, b. 3 July, 1823, accidentally killed in India, July 1841.
    (3) Vesey Agmondisham, of Mount Brown, b. 3 June, 1824 ; m. 1855, Mary Edith, dau. of Rev. Edward Massingberd, and d. Sept. 1895, leaving issue, a dau.
    (4) Henry Francis, b. 3 Oct. 1824 ; m. 1848, Maria, dau. of Frederick Smith, of Moulmain, and by her (who d. 1853) has a dau.,
      Sophia.
    (5) Thomas Anthony Southwell, b. 2 Jan. 1826, Col. late 83rd Regt. ; m. 16 Jan. 1856, Laura Lysaght Mary, dau. of George Hewson, of Castle Hewson, co. Limerick, and has, with other issue,
      John Southwell, Major 2nd Batt. Royal Irish Rifles, b. 22 April, 1859.
    (6) Sidney Reynett, b. 22 July, 1831 ; m. 1st, April, 1858, Mary, dau. of William Cox, of Ballynoe, co. Limerick, and by her (who d. April, 1861) has issue,
      1. Alice Vesey, b. 1859.
    He m. 2ndly, March, 1868, Charlotte Gower, dau. of Charles R. Blandy, of Maderia, and d. Jan. 1903, leaving further issue,
      1. Charles Sidney Vesey, b. 1867. His wife, Mary Elizabeth, d. 13 May, 1902.
      2. Florence Vesey, b. 1869.
      3. Charlotte Mary Vesey, b. 1876.
      4. Rose Sidney Vesey, b. 1880.
      5. Helen Margaret Vesey, b. 1885.
    (1) Mary Gordon. (2) Augusta Margaret.
  2. Nathaniel Gordon, b. 22 April, 1795 ; d. 1796.
  3. Henry, b. 19 April, 1797.
  4. Vincent, b. 23 June, 1809 ; m. Mary Darley, dau. of — Coghlan.
    1. Laura, m. 1825, George Hewson, of Castle Hewson, co. Limerick.

  2. Meliora, m. 1826, Alexander Elliott, of Tanavaller.
  3. Mary Anne, m. 1825, Major Charles Carthew.
  4. Elizabeth Catherine. 5. Catherine, d. unm. 1822.
  1. Anne, m. Robert Peppard, of Cappagh, co. Limerick.
  2. Phœbe, m. 1st, John Finch, a younger son of William Finch, of Kilcolman, co. Tipperary ; and 2ndly, George Hewson.
  3. Frances, m. Michael Cantillon Heffernan, of co. Limerick.
The eldest son and heir,
HENRY BROWN, of Danesford, and of Clonboy, co. Clare, and at one period of Rich Hill, b. 26 Aug. 1754 ; m. 1782, Sarah, dau. and heiress of Richard Pierce, of Lisnagry, co. Limerick, (of a family originally from Wilts and Berkshire), by Mary his wife, dau. of Col. William Harrison, of Ballycarrane, co. Waterford, and had issue,
1. JOHN, of Clonboy.
2. Henry, m. the dau. of Col. Jones, of co. Galway, and had issue.
3. Edward, m. Miss Whelan, of co. Carlow, and had issue.
4. Pierce, m. Miss Bouchier, and had issue.
5. William, m. Miss Fitzgerald, of Limerick, and had issue.
6. Francis, of Mount Southwell, m. Anne, dau. of James Hill, of Graig, and had issue,
  Henry Southwell, d. unm.
  Mary, m. 6 Oct. 1837, James Hill, of Graig, co. Cork.
1. Meliora, m. Thomas Alexander Odell, of Odellville, co. Limerick, and had issue.
2. Sarah, m. — Sharman.
3. Anna, m. 1st, James Griffin ; and 2ndly, — Cassan.
4. Catherine, m. W. J. Lawrenson, and had issue.
Mr. Brown d. 1836. His eldest son,
JOHN BROWN, of Bridgetown (Clonboy), Capt. Limerick Militia, m. 1801, Constance (who d. 1860), 2nd dau. of Col. William Odell, of The Grove, co. Limerick (M.P. for co. Limerick for thirty years, and a Lord of the Treasury), by Aphra his wife, dau. of John Crone, of Byblow, co. Cork. Mr. Brown d.v.p. Jan. 1833, having had issue,
1. JOHN, late of Clonboy.
2. William, m. Mildred, dau. of Thomas Odell, and d. leaving one dau.,
  Mildred, m. 1856, Charles Sandes, of Carrigafoyle, co. Kerry.
3. Henry, m. Sarah, dau. of Major Thomas Odell, and d. leaving issue.
4. Thomas Anthony Southwell, m. 1836, Isma Cowley, 4th dau. of Thomas Lidwill, of Cloomore, and Cormackstown, co. Tipperary, by Mary his wife, eldest dau. of Robert Atkins, of Firville, and d. having had issue,
  1. John, M.D., m. 3 Jan. 1866, Nanny, dau. of John Peppard, of Cappagh.
  2. Thomas, m. Matilda, dau. of Robert Lidwill, and d. Jan. 1877.
  3. Robert Lidwill, b. 29 May, 1842 ; m. 10 Sept. 1866, Louisa Catherine, eldest dau. of the late James Stanley, of the Grange, Armagh, and has issue,
    (1) Thomas Anthony Stanley, b. 15 June, 1867.
    (2) Stanley, b. 3 Sept. 1868.
    (3) Robert William, b. 15 Jan. 1871.
    (1) Ismenia, b. 5 Jan. 1873.
    (2) Mildred, b. 8 Oct. 1874.
    (3) Maud Lidwill, b. 26 Nov. 1876.
5. Richard Pierce, dec.
1. Aphra, m. 1st, James Fisher ; and 2ndly, William Scanlan, Barrister-at-Law, and is dec.
2. Sarah, m. 1 March, 1834, Hugh Scanlan.
3. Frances, m. Rev. Richard Maunsell, of Milford, co. Limerick, dec.
4. Phœbe, m. William Odell, Surgeon-Major, Army Medical Department, dec.
5. Emily, m. Matthew Scanlan, both dec.
The eldest son,
JOHN BROWN, of Clonboy, co. Clare, J.P., s. his grandfather 1836. He was b. 23 Jan. 1802 ; m. 25 Aug. 1826, Mary Charlotte, eldest dau. of Thomas Lidwell, of Cloomore and Cormackstown, co. Tipperary, by Mary his wife, dau. of Robert Atkins, of Firville, co. Cork, and d. 6 Dec. 1870, having by her (who d. 26 Dec, 1878) had issue,
1. John, b. 19 Sept. 1827 ; m. 1855, Harriet Vereker, dau. of John Westropp.
2. ROBERT LIDWILL, late of Clonboy.
3. William Thomas, b. 13 Oct. 1839, dec.
4. George Arthur, b. 25 March, 1841.
1. Mary Atkins, m. 1860, Thomas Stannard McAdam.
2. Isma Helen, d. 1 July, 1911 ; m. 1855, Capt. Richard Cradock, 17th Regt.
3. Constance Margaret, m. 1860, Thomas George Mawe, 1st West Indian Regt.
The second son,
ROBERT LIDWILL BROWN, of Clonboy, co. Clare, and of Lisnagry, co. Limerick, J.P. cos. Clare and Limerick, b. 8 Aug. 1837 ; m. Jan. 1862, Margaret, dau. of Col. Sheldon Cradock, M.P., of Hartforth Hall, Richmond, Yorkshire, and d. 20 Oct. 1907, having had issue,
1. ERNEST GEORGE, now of Clonboy.
2. Richard Cradock, b. 3 Nov. 1868 ; d. 21 Nov. 1907.
3. Harry Lidwill, b. 16 Dec. 1873 ; d.s.p. 23 Sept. 1895.
1. Isma Frances Lidwill, m. Keith Ogilvie Baird Young, of Ascreavie, co. Forfar.
2. Constance Meta.
3. Esther Lisba Marion, m. Ronald Vickers, son of Col. T. B. Vickers, of Queen's Gate Gardens, S.W., and d. 5 Feb. 1909.
4. Jackaleen Maude, m. Aug. 1899, Henry Hay McKerrell-Brown, of 10, North Park Terrace, Edinburgh, and has issue.
5. Helen Cowly.
6. Mona Isobel, m. April, 1910, Capt. T. S. Skinner, P.O.W.P., son of Col. Skinner, R.E.
Seat—Clonboy, O'Brien's Bridge, co. Clare.

BROWNE OF NEW GROVE.

THOMAS HENRY BRADY BROWNE, of New Grove, co. Clare, J.P. co. Clare, High Sheriff 1907, Capt. R.F.A. (Special Reserve), formerly Lieut. 5th Lancers, *b.* 1882; *m.* 1907, Mabel Frances, dau. of Nathaniel Mayne, M.D., of Longford, and has issue,

1. THOMAS HENRY BRADY, *b.* 29 June, 1911.
1. Deborah Violet Brady.

Lineage—EDMOND BROWNE, of Ballyslattery, or New Grove, co. Clare, son of Edmond Browne, *m.* Bridget, dau. and co-heir of Thomas Blaney, of Furgonan, Montgomery, and had issue,
1. THOMAS, his heir.
2. Edmund.
3. Nevil.
1. Mary, *d. unm.*
2. Anne, *m.* John Miller, of Ballycasey co. Clare.

The eldest son,
THOMAS BROWNE, of New Grove, *b.* 1661; *d.* 17 Sept. 1717; *m.* 1694, Elizabeth, dau. of William Smith, of Dunagrogne, co. Clare. and had issue,
1. EDMUND, his heir.
2. Thomas, whose will dated 23 July, 1779, was proved 27 Aug. 1780, *d.s.p.*
3. George, *d.s.p.* 1768.
1. A dau. *m.* Richard Hart, of Ballyhenor, co. Clare.
2. Anne, *m.* William Miller, of Ballycasey.

The eldest son,
EDMUND BROWNE, of New Grove, *d.* 1768, High Sheriff co. Clare 1733 and 1745; *m.* Jan. 1726, Jane, dau. of Mountiford Westropp, of Attyflin, co. Limerick (*see that family*), and had issue,
1. THOMAS, his heir. 2. Mountiford.
3. William.
1. Jane, *m.* Thomas Westropp, of Ballysteen, co. Limerick (*see* WESTROPP *of Attyflin*).
2. Anne, *m.* 29 May, 1760, Vere Hunt, of Curragh, co. Limerick (*see* HUNT *of Cummer More*).
3. Gertrude, *m.* Robert Hunt, of Inchirourke, co. Limerick (*see* HUNT *of Cummer More*).
4. Letitia, *m.* Poole Hickman, of Kilmore, co. Clare.
5. Bridget, *m.* 12 Jan. 1764, William Henn, of Paradise, co. Clare (*see that family*).

The eldest son,
THOMAS BROWNE, of New Grove, *b.* 1726; *d.* 1779, High Sheriff co. Clare 1773, *m.* 1765, Mary, dau. of William Westby, of High Park, co. Wicklow (*see* WESTBY *of Roebuck Castle*), who had issue,
1. EDMUND, his heir. 2. William.
3. THOMAS, who s. his nephew.
1. Mary, *m.* Henry Brady, of Raheens, co. Clare, and had issue, LUKE BRADY, of Brookville, co. Clare, *d.* 25 Jan. 1864; *m.* Anne, dau. of Rev. Windham Magrath-FitzGerald, of Limerick, and had,
   (1) HENRY BRADY, *d.v.p., s.p.*
   (2) WINDHAM BRADY, who s. and assumed the name and arms of BROWNE, of whom hereafter.
   (3) THOMAS BROWNE BRADY, who s. his brother.
2. Jane, *m.* Francis Greene, of Kilranalagh, co. Wicklow.
3. Anne, *m.* Jeremiah Hayes, of Killaragh, co. Tipperary.
4. Matilda, *m.* 1st, John Harrison, of Garruragh, co. Clare; 2ndly, Nicholas Coyne, of Moyne, co. Clare.

The eldest son,
EDMUND BROWNE, of New Grove, *d.* Dec. 1801; *m.* 1798, Anne, dau. of Poole Hickman, of Kilmore, Collene, and left issue,
1. THOMAS, his heir.
1. Mary, *m.* 20 Dec. 1824, Francis Gore, of Tyredagh Castle, co. Clare (*see* HICKMAN *of Tyredagh Castle*).
2. Letitia.

The eldest son,
THOMAS BROWNE, of New Grove, *d.s.p.* March, 1813, and was s. by his uncle,
THOMAS BROWNE, of New Grove, *b.* March, 1774; *d.* 9 Feb. 1847, J.P., D.L., co. Clare, High Sheriff 1808, *m.* 7 Nov. 1814, Elizabeth, dau. of Laurence Comyn, of Moyne, co. Clare, *s.p.* On her death, 9 Sept. 1864, the estates passed to her husband's eldest surviving grand-nephew,
WINDHAM BROWNE, of New Grove, Ensign 17th Foot, *b.* April, 1844, who, by Royal Licence 3 Jan. 1866, assumed the name and arms of BROWNE in lieu of Brady. He *d.s.p.* and was *s.* by his brother,
THOMAS BROWNE BROWNE, of New Grove, *b.* 1847; *d.* 1901, assumed the name and arms of BROWNE in lieu of Brady by Royal Licence, 3 March, 1877. He *m.* 1875, Emily Ellen Josephine, dau. of John Perry, of Castle View, co. Clare, and had issue,
1. THOMAS HENRY BRADY, now of New Grove.
2. Windham Alexander, *b.* 1887.
3. Alfred Lucius, *b.* 1888.

Arms—Arg. on a bend engrailed between two plain double cottises sa., three eagles displayed with two heads of the first, in the sinister chief point a pellet. **Crest**—An eagle displayed with two heads or pale ar. and sa., the dexter wing charged with a pellet, the sinister with a plate. **Motto**—Nec timeo nec sperno.
Seats—New Grove, Tulla, co. Clare, and Cartron, Burrin co. Clare.

KNOX-BROWNE OF AUGHENTAINE CASTLE.

JOHN HERVEY KNOX-BROWNE, of Aughentaine Castle, co. Tyrone, J.P. and D.L., High Sheriff 1887, late Capt. 12th Lancers, and A.D.C. to his Grace the Duke of Abercorn, Lord-Lieut. of Ireland in 1866, and Lieut.-Col. 9th Brigade North Irish Division Royal Artillery, assumed the additional name and arms of Knox, by Royal sign-manual, dated 16 March, 1874; *b.* 1841; *m.* 19 Dec. 1867, Louisa Elizabeth, dau. of Sir Francis Arthur Knox-Gore, Bart. of Beleek Manor, co. Mayo, by Sarah his wife, dau. of Col. Charles Nesbitt Knox, of Castle Lacken, co. Mayo, and by her (who *d.* 22 May, 1903) has issue,

1. THOMAS ARTHUR HERVEY, late Capt. Mid Ulster Artillery, *b.* 29 May, 1870.
2. Mervyn William Charles Nesbitt, *b.* 21 April, 1880; *m.* 1 Aug. 1911, May, only dau. of late Barry George.
1. Sarah Hannah Madeline. 2. Augusta Caroline.
3. Eileen Hester Louisa, *m.* 22 March, 1911, Lieut. George Richard Colin Campbell, R.N., son of Rev. E. F. Campbell, M.A., Rector of Killyman, co. Tyrone.

Lineage.—JOHN HAMILTON BROWNE, of Comber House, co. Londonderry, and Aughentaine, co. Tyrone, son of THOMAS BROWNE, of co. Londonderry, by Elizabeth Hamilton his wife, niece of James Hamilton, Provost of Strabane about 1720, and grandson of GEORGE BROWNE, also of Londonderry, by his wife, Mary, dau. of Col. Hogg; *m.* 1795, Jane Matilda, dau. of William Lecky, of Castle Fin, co. Donegal, M.P. for Londonderry in the Irish House of Commons, by Hannah his wife, dau. of Conolly McCausland, D.L. of Drenagh, co. Derry, and *d.* 1848, having by her (who *d.* 1855) had issue.
1. Conolly William Lecky, of Comber House, *d. unm.* 1862.
2. THOMAS RICHARDSON, *s.* to Aughentaine.
3. GEORGE, of Comber House, J.P., D.L. co. Londonderry, formerly Major 44th Regt., *b.* 1816; *m.* 1844, Susan Mary, dau. of Thomas Hilton, of Ardwick, near Manchester, and *d.* 1887 having had issue,
   1. John Walter L'Estrange Hamilton, of the 9th Lancers, *b.* 1846; *d.s.p.d.* 1880.
   2. William Lecky Hamilton, Capt. R.N., of Comber House, *s.* his father 1887; *b.* 1848; *d. unm.* 12 Dec. 1900.
   3. Cecil Hamilton BROWNE-LECKY, now of Comber House, J.P., High Sheriff of co. Londonderry 1906, Lieut.-Col. 5th R.I. Fus., assumed the name of LECKY by Deed Poll 1898.
4. John Hamilton, *d. unm.*
1. Hannah Sidney.
2. Elizabeth, *m.* John Cole (*see* BURKE'S *Peerage*, ENNISKILLEN, E.).

The 2nd but eldest surviving son,
THOMAS RICHARDSON BROWNE, of Aughentaine, J.P. and D.L., High Sheriff of Tyrone in 1832; *b.* 1810; *m.* 1839, Sarah, 4th dau. of Hervey Pratt de Montmorency, of Castle Morres, co. Kilkenny, D.L., and by her (who *d.* 1 March, 1889) had issue,
1. JOHN HERVEY, his heir.
2. Raymond Saville, who assumed the additional name of LECKY after that of Browne, under royal sign-manual, dated 4 March, 1871, in compliance with the will of his great uncle, Conolly William M'Causland Lecky, of Londonderry, and *d. unm.* 20 Aug. 1837.
3. Conolly William Lecky Browne-Lecky, of Derry, High Sheriff city and co. Londonderry 1888, who assumed the additional name of LECKY under royal sign-manual, dated 12 May, 1874, in compliance with the will of his great-uncle, Conolly William M'Causland Lecky, of Londonderry; *s.* his brother 1873; *m.* 28 Nov. 1878, Annie Henrietta, eldest dau. of Charles Eccles, D.L., of Ecclesville, and has, with other issue,
Raymond S. C. De Montmorency, *b.* 1881.

1. Rose Sarah, *m.* Major J. D. Ellis, late 22nd Regt.
2. Caroline Frances, *m.* 23 May, 1871, John Stewart Eccles, of Ecclesville, D.L. co. Tyrone, and had issue (*see* McCLINTOCK *of Seskinore*).
3. Matilda Theodosia, *m.* 11 Dec. 1883, Capt. Charles Eccles, son of Charles Eccles, of Ecclesville (*see* McCLINTOCK *of Seskinore*).

Mr. Browne *d.* 29 May, 1882.

Arms—Quarterly, 1st and 4th erm., a chev. az. betw. two fleurs-de-lis in chief and a cinquefoil in base sa. for BROWNE, 2nd and 3rd gu. within a border engr. a falcon wings expanded or, charged on the breast with a pheon sa. on a canton of the second a fess chequy arg. and az. for KNOX. **Crests**—1st, BROWNE. An eagle displayed with two heads vert, charged on each wing with a fleur-de-lis or ; 2nd KNOX, a falcon on a perch close ppr. charged on the breast with a pheon sa. **Mottoes**—(Over) Moveo et proficio ; Suivez raison.

Seat—Aughentaine Castle, Five-Mile-Town, co. Tyrone. *Club* —Kildare Street.

BROWNE OF BROWNESTOWN.

GEORGE EAKINS BROWNE, of Brownestown, co. Mayo, J.P. and D.L., M.P. 1870-80, *b.* 1837 ; *m.* 1st, 1858, Julia, 4th dau. of the late Maurice Blake, of Ballinafad. She *d.* 1876, leaving issue,

1. George Maurice, *d. unm.* 1879.
2. LLEWELLYN MONTAGUE Major 5th Royal Dublin Fus.
   1. Anna, *m.* James Wilson.
   2. Mary, a nun.
   3. Gabriel, *d. inf.*
   4. Stella, *m.* 1st, Edward W. Keegan ; 2ndly, George Power-Lalor (*see that family*).

He *m.* 2ndly, 1879, Julia Mary, dau. of James Lynch, and had issue,

5. Kathleen, *m.* Bartholomew Hackett, M.D.

He *m.* 3rdly, 1883, Honoria Eleanor, dau. of Francis Murphy of Kilcairne, co. Meath.

Lineage.—ANDREW BROWNE, 4th son of Josias Browne, of the Neale (*see* BURKE's *Peerage*, KILMAINE, B.), by Joan his wife, dau. of Edward Bermingham, of Carrick, co. Kildare. He *m.* Catherine, dau. of Ulick Burke, of Castlehackett, and had issue,

1. VALENTINE, his heir,
2. Augustine, *m.* Anastasia, dau. of John Cormack, and had issue, 1. Andrew, 2. John, and 1. Margaret.
   1. Alice, *m.* Edmund Kelly.
   2. Joan, *m.* Arthur Lynch. 3. Margaret, *m.* Paul Daly.
   4. Bridget, *m.* Edward Brown.

The elder son,
VALENTINE BROWNE, of Liskellan, co. Mayo, *m.* Maud, dau. of Thomas Lovelock. His will, dated 20 May, 1701, was proved at Tuam, 5 Jan. 1704. He had issue,
1. GEORGE, his heir.
2. Andrew. 3. John.
1. Maud. 2. Bridget.

The eldest son,
GEORGE BROWNE, of Liskellan, *m.* Elizabeth, dau. of John Browne, of the Neale, and had, with an elder son, who *d.* young, a son and a dau.

JOHN, his heir.
Julia, whose will, dated 3 May, 1742, was proved 10 Oct. that year.

The only surviving son,
JOHN BROWNE, of Brownestown, co. Mayo, *m.* Catherine (*d.* May, 1778), dau. of Denis Daly, and *d.* May, 1762, leaving issue,
1. GEORGE, his heir.
2. Denis, *m.* Alice, dau. of James Mahon, of Oughterdowney, co. Galway.
1. Elizabeth, *m.* Dec. 1760, Hugh O'Donell, Jr., of Newport, co. Mayo.
2. Margaret, *m.* Henry Lynch, of Ballycurran, co. Mayo.

The elder son,
GEORGE BROWNE, of Brownestown, *m.* 12 Sept. 1762, Catherine, dau. of Maurice Blake, of Ballinafad. His will, dated 8 March, 1798, was proved 12 Dec. 1801. He left issue,
1. GEORGE, his heir.
2. John, *d. unm.* Nov. 1810. Will dated 3 Sept. 1810, proved 22 Nov. 1820.
3. Maurice. 4. Denis. 5. Andrew.
1. Maria, *d. unm.* 1829.
2. Elizabeth, *m.* George Martyn, of Gregan's Castle, co. Clare.
3. Frances, *m.* 1807, Hyacinth George Burke, of Slatefield, co. Galway.

The eldest son,
GEORGE BROWNE, of Brownestown, whose will, dated 14 Feb. 1823, was proved 10 Nov. 1829. By Catherine, dau. of — Stuart, his first wife, he had a son,
JOHN JOSEPH, *s.* his grandfather.

The son,
JOHN JOSEPH BROWNE, of Brownestown, *m.* Maria, dau. of Walter Eakins, and *d.* 1844 (will dated 17 Nov. 1843, proved 3 June, 1845), having had two sons, of whom,
1. GEORGE EAKINS, *s.* to Brownestown.
2. Walter J., *d. unm.*, will proved Oct. 1908.

Arms—Sa. three lions passant in bend between two double cotises arg. **Crest**—An eagle displayed vert. **Motto**—Suivez raison.

Seat—Brownestown, co. Mayo. *Residence*—14, Shanganagh Terrace, Killeney, co. Dublin. *Club*—Reform.

WOGAN-BROWNE OF CASTLE BROWNE.

COL. FRANCIS WILLIAM NICHOLAS WOGAN-BROWNE, of Castle Browne and Kerederu, co. Kildare, late commanding 3rd King's Own Hussars, *b.* 17 Feb. 1854 ; *m.* 11 Aug. 1879, Beda, 3rd dau. of James Costello, of Fox Hall, co. Dublin. He assumed by deed poll, 30 Jan. 1880, the additional name of WOGAN, which had been borne as a Christian name by the family for several generations. He has had issue.

1. Francis Thomas, 2nd Lieut. Scottish Rifles, *b.* 29 June, 1882 ; *d.* 4 Oct. 1902, drowned at Greystones, co. Wicklow.
2. Henry Edward, *b.* 21 Aug. 1883 ; *d.* 27 Oct. 1886.
3. JOHN HUBERT, *b.* 23 July, 1896.
4. Mary Charlotte Anna, *b.* 12 Sept. 1880 ; *m.* 12 July, 1905, Major Alfred Maitland Addison, son of the late Capt. C. Maitland Addison, 59th Foot.
2. Beatrice Judith, *b.* 9 April, 1886 ; *d.* 22 Oct. 1886.
3. Judith Helen, *b.* 18 Oct. 1887.
4. Dorothea, *b.* 15 Aug. 1890 ; *d. unm.* 31 Aug. 1910.
5. Claire Renée, *b.* 9 Aug. 1893.

Lineage.—JOHN BROWN, of Giggotstown, co. Kildare, whose will, dated 3 May, 1629, was proved 6 May following, *m.* Ellis Stoak, and by her had issue,
1. Christopher. 2. THOMAS, of whom we treat.

The younger son,
THOMAS BROWNE, of Dublin and Castle Browne, co. Kildare, admitted to the King's Inns as Attorney 27 May, 1639 ; *m.* 22 June, 1646, Begnet, dau. and heiress of Nicholas Stephens, of Dublin, and *d.* 2 April, 1693 (will dated 19 Oct. 1687, and proved 28 June, 1694), having by her (who *d.* 22 Dec. 1665) had issue (with three daus. : 1. Honora, *m.* 1 May, 1665, Col. James Dempsey ; 2. Mary, *m.* Patrick Alen, of St. Wolstan's, co. Kildare ; and 3. Ciceley) a son,
JOHN BROWNE, of Dublin and Castle Browne, co. Kildare, *m.* May, 1685, Hon. Mary, dau. of William, 3rd Viscount Fitzwilliam (*see* BURKE's *Extinct Peerage*), and *d.* 27 Jan. 1693, aged 42 (will dated 25 and proved 30 Jan. same year), having by her (who *d.* 19 May, 1693) had issue,
1. STEPHEN FITZWILLIAM, of whom presently.
2. Christopher, of Castle Browne, co. Kildare, *d. unm.* 23 Dec. 1736 (will dated 18 Dec. 1736, proved 3 Feb. 1736-7).
3. Bruno, administration granted 14 Nov. 1741, to his widow Elizabeth.
1. Alice, *m.* John Taylor.
2. Anne, *d.* 21 Dec. 1736 (will dated 21 Nov. 1736, proved 28 July, 1737).
3. Elizabeth.

The 2nd son,
STEPHEN FITZWILLIAM BROWNE, of Castle Browne, *m.* (1st), his cousin, dau. of Thomas, 4th Viscount FitzWilliam. She *d.* 23 July, 1722, and (2ndly), Judith, 2nd dau. of John Wogan, of Rathcoffey, co. Kildare, by Judith Moore, his wife, and *d.* 3 July, 1767, leaving issue,
1. John, *d.s.p.* 1777. 2. Thomas.
3. Nicholas. 4. MICHAEL, of whom presently.
5. Christopher.
6. Anthony, Col. in the Saxon Service, *m.* M. Saegrea, and had issue,
Anthony, *m.* Mary, dau. of Gen. Cuppage, and had issue,
Anthony, Major in the Army, *m.* M. Gildea, and has issue.
1. Rose, *d. unm.* 2. Elizabeth, *d. unm.*

The 4th son,

IRELAND. Browne.

MICHAEL BROWNE, of Castle Browne (sometimes called Clongoweswood), Col. in the French Service, m. his cousin Catherine, dau. of Col. Nicholas Wogan,* of Rathcoffey, and d. c. 1778, leaving issue,
1. Thomas, m. Sarah Pearson, a lady of considerable property in Westmorland, and d.s.p.
2. MICHAEL WOGAN, of whom presently.
1. Judith. 2. Eliza.
The youngest son,
MICHAEL WOGAN BROWNE, of Castle Browne, Gen. in the Saxon Service, and A.D.C. to the King of Saxony, by whom he was created a baron, was commander of the Guards and Governor of Dresden, he m. Augusta Frances, dau. of Col. Thomas Prescott, of the Guards, and grand-dau. of 1st Viscount Falmouth, by Charlotte his wife, niece of the great Duke of Marlborough, and had issue,
1. Thomas, Major in the Army, d.s.p. 1877.
2. Arthur, Capt. in the Austrian Service, d. unm.
3. FRANCIS, of whom we treat.
Lieut.-Gen. Michael Wogan Browne d. 1824. His youngest son, FRANCIS BROWNE, of Castle Browne, and Tours, France, Major 7th Hungarian Hussars, Austrian Service, b. 1809 ; m. 1849, Charlotte Rose, dau. of Gen. Baron de Keredern de Trobriaud, Chief of the Staff of Marechal Davoust, Duc D'Auerstadt, and by her (who d. 17 Dec. 1902) had issue,
1. FRANCIS WILLIAM NICHOLAS, now of Castle Browne.
2. Charles Michael Edward, of L'Hermitage, St. Cyre, Indre et Loire, Capt. 3rd Batt. Royal Irish Regt., b. 3 Oct. 1861 ; m. 8 July, 1896, Vera Marguerite Mansel, youngest dau. of the late Col. Hunt Boyse, J.P., of Bannow, co. Wexford (see that family).
1. Charlotte, b. 1851 ; m. Jan. 1878, Capt. Desiré Dupin des Vastines, 7e Chasseurs à cheval, and d.s.p. May, 1878.
2. Anne Regina, a nun, b. 1853.
Major F. Browne d. March, 1876.
Arms—Quarterly, 1st and 4th, sa. a chevron between three cranes arg. (for BROWNE), 2nd per pale ermine and gu., a saltire counterchanged (for STEPHENS), 3rd, or on a chief sa., three martlets of the field (for WOGAN). Crest—A tiger az. maned, tufted and armed or. Motto—Qui non ciconia tigris.
Residence—Keredern, Naas, co. Kildare.

BROWNE OF BREAGHWY.

DOMINICK SIDNEY BROWNE, of Breaghwy, co. Mayo, J.P., D.L., High Sheriff 1896, Capt. and Hon. Major late 3rd Batt. Royal Scots Fusiliers, b. 31 March, 1866 ; m. 20 June, 1895, Elizabeth Naomi, eldest dau. of Hon. R. R. Dobell, of Beauvoir Manor, Quebec, Canada, M.P. and P.C. Canadian Parliament, and has issue,
1. DOMINICK ANDREW SIDNEY, b. 29 Feb. 1904.
1. Naomi Frances Muriel, b. 5 Jan. 1897.
2. Noël Sidney, b. 23 Dec. 1899.
3. Moyra Rose, b. 1 Jan. 1903.
Lineage.—DOMINICK BROWNE, of Breaghwy, co. Mayo, Capt. in the Army (younger son of Sir John Browne, 1st bart., of the Neale, ancestor of the Lord Kilmaine), m. Barbara, dau. of Sir Henry Talbot, and niece of the Duke of Tyrconnell, and was father of
ANDREW BROWNE, of Breaghwy, m. Allinor, dau. of Alexander Kirwan, of Dalgin, and had a son,
DOMINICK BROWNE, of Breaghwy, b. 1701 ; m. 1st, Mabel, dau. of Sir John Browne, Bt. of the Neale, who d.s.p. ; 2ndly, Anne (d. Dec.

---

* Col. Nicholas Wogan of Rathcoffey, co. Kildare, was the son of John Wogan of Rathcoffey, and Judith Moore his wife, and a direct descendant of Sir John Wogan, Chief Governor of Ireland in 1295 and 1310. Col. Wogan's sister Judith, m. as in the text, Stephen Fitzwilliam Browne, of Castle Browne. Col. Wogan m. Rose, dau. and heir of Sir Neill O'Neill, Bart. His will, dated 5 Feb. 1757, was proved 19 Dec. 1770. He left issue,
1. John, of Rathcoffey, m. Hon. Hellen Browne (sister of Lord Kenmare), who d. 1784.
1. Frances, m. John Talbot, of Malahide, and was grandmother of Richard Wogan Talbot, 2nd Baron Talbot of Malahide.
2. Catherine, m. as in the text, her cousin, Col. Michael Browne, of Castle Browne.

1771), dau. of Martin D'Arcy, of Houndswood, co. Mayo, and d. 1776, leaving issue,
1. ANDREW NICHOLAS, his heir.
2. John Edmond (Sir), created a Bart. of Ireland in 1797.
The elder son,
ANDREW NICHOLAS BROWNE, of Breaghwy, a Deputy Governor for Mayo, m. Mary, dau. of E. Gilker, and d. 1796, having by her (who d. 1836) had issue,
1. DOMINICK, Major 88th Regt., d. unm. 1803.
2. Edmond, Lieut.-Col. 36th Regt., d. unm. 18 April, 1838.
3. JOHN, of whom we treat.
1. Ann. m. Charles Tyler, d.s.p.
2. Catherine, m. Capt. G. Cox, and d.s.p.
3. Dorothea, m. Capt. J. Hoey, and had issue.
4. Rose, m. J. Mullins.
5. Maria, m. James Howell, d.s.p.
6. Eliza, d. unm.
The 3rd son,
LIEUT.-COL. JOHN BROWNE, of Breaghwy, who served with distinction at Waterloo, and in several engagements in the Peninsular War, b. 1790; m. 2 Oct. 1823, Frances Jane, dau. of John Hawthorn, of Jamaica, and by her (who d. 14 Jan. 1891) had issue,
1. DOMINICK ANDREW, late of Breaghwy.
2. Montague, Col. late 24th Regt., m. 1st, Margaret Elizabeth only dau. of Charles Maurice Stack, and had two sons, who d. unm., 2ndly, Emily, dau. of Charles Hall Stack, of Mutloghmore, co. Tyrone. She d. 1897, and he m. 3rdly, Kate, dau. of Rev. J. Dixon, D.D.
3. Henry John, m. Constance Harding, and d. 1877, having had one son, who d. unm.
4. Frederick Augustus, d. unm.
5. Arthur Wellesley Wyndham, d. unm.
6. Edmond Charles, Col. commanding Royal Scots Fusiliers Regntl. District, b. 8 April, 1843; d. 7 Jan. 1910, having m. 1894, Catharine, only dau. of Patrick Ness, of Braco Castle, N.B.
7. Augustus Hawthorn.
1. Rose Mary Anne, m. John Mitchell, of Hawthorn Lodge, Ayr, N.B. He d. May, 1883. She d. Oct. 1899.
2. Sarah Jane, m. Henry Finch, of Ashurstwood, Sussex.
3. Mary Louisa, d. unm. 5 Nov. 1908.
Col. Browne d. 20 Nov. 1849, and was s. by his eldest son,
DOMINICK ANDREW BROWNE, of Breaghwy, co. Mayo, J.P., D.L., High Sheriff 1881, b. 30 June, 1824 ; educated at the R. M. College, Sandhurst ; m. 26 July, 1864, Emily Louisa (Breaghwy, Castlebar, and 32, Portland Court, W.), only dau. of John Sidney Hawkins, of Brompton, eldest son of Sir John Hawkins, Knt., Chairman of Quarter Sessions for Middlesex, and d. 9 Sept. 1902, leaving issue,
1. DOMINICK SIDNEY, now of Breaghwy.
2. Francis John Sidney, b. 23 Aug. 1867 ; d. 30 June, 1875.
Arms—Sa. three lions passant in bend between two double cotises arg. Crest—An eagle displayed vert. Motto—Suivez raison.
Seat—Breaghwy, Castlebar. Clubs—United University and Orleans, S.W., and Kildare Street, Dublin.

BROWNE OF RATHAIN.

DODWELL FRANCIS BROWNE, of Rathain, co. Mayo, M.A. and LL.B. Trinity College, Dublin, J.P. co. Mayo, Barrister-at-Law of the Irish Bar and Advocate of the Supreme Court of Ceylon, was appointed 15 Jan. 1893, District Judge of Colombo, and retired on pension April, 1903, b. 23 May, 1841 ; m. 9 Aug. 1871, Annabella, dau. of Samuel Glenny, of Liverpool (son of Isaac George Glenny, Seneschal of Newry, who was grandson of Isaac Glenny, of Glenville, co. Down), and has issue,
1. DODWELL, M.B. Trin. Coll. Dublin, b. 4 May, 1872, Medical Officer and Resident Magistrate, Port Hedland, West Australia ; m. 1903, Harriett Lilian Heppingstone, and has issue,
  1. Annabel Mary Dodwell. 2. Margaret Lilian Dodwell.
2. Keppel Glenny Dodwell, Barrister-at-Law Irel. and Adv. Ceylon, b. 15 Aug. 1873 ; d. 1 Oct. 1908.
3. O'Donel Henry Dodwell, M.D. Trin. Coll. Dub., Naas, b. 20 Sept. 1878 ; m. 1902, Grace Louisa Glover, and has issue, O'Donel Thornley Dodwell, b. 1903.
1. Norah Lucy Frances Dodwell.
Lineage.—DODWELL BROWNE, of Rathain or Rahins, co. Mayo, 3rd son of Sir John Browne, 5th bart. of the Neale, ancestor of the BARONS KILMAINE (see BURKE's Peerage) by Margaret, his 1st wife, dau. and co-heir of Henry Dodwell, of Athlone, m. April, 1762, Elizabeth, eldest dau. and co-heir of James Cuff, Lord Tyrawley, and d. about 1796, leaving a son,
DODWELL BROWNE, of Rathain, Lieut. R.N., m. 1797, Maria, dau. of Sir Neal O'Donol, Bart., of Newport, and it is supposed to have d. in Canada about 1819, having by her (who d. 1809) had issue,
1. HUGH JOHN HENRY, of whom presently.
2. NEAL O'DONEL, late of Rathain.
1. Mary Anne Moore, m. Peter Digges La Touche (see that family).
2. Margaret Elizabeth, m. 30 Aug. 1819, Hon. Henry Caulfield, of Hockley, co. Armagh, 3rd son of James, 4th Viscount Charlemont, and d. 20 Oct. 1878, leaving issue by him, who d. 4 March, 1862 (see BURKE's Peerage).
3. Matilda Dorcas, m. Alexander Richey.
4. Louisa Julia, m. Dr. Benjamin Guinness Darley.
5. Maria, m. Dr. Long.

Browne. THE LANDED GENTRY. 78

The elder son,
HUGH JOHN HENRY BROWNE, of Rathain, co. Mayo, b. 6 Feb. 1800; d. unm. 2 Oct. 1868, and was s. by his brother,
NEAL O'DONEL BROWNE, of Rathain, co. Mayo, Resident Magistrate, King's Co., 1839-48, co. Cork, 1848-67, b. 29 Dec. 1804; m. Sarah, dau. of Abel Labertouche, and by her (who d. 24 Aug. 1843) had issue, an only son,
DODWELL FRANCIS, now of Rathain.
Mr. N. O'D. Browne d. 15 March, 1874.

Arms—Sa. three lions passant in bend between two double cotises argent. Crest—An eagle displayed vert. Motto—Suivez raison.
Residence—Rathain, Castlebar, co. Mayo.

BROWNE OF RIVERSTOWN.

CHARLTON BASIL JEMMETT BROWNE, of Riverstown, co. Cork, b. 2 July, 1866; m. 22 Dec. 1898, Rosa Cicely, dau. of Edward Salter, and has issue,
WARHAM, b. 14 May, 1904.
Mary Cicely, b. 7 July, 1902.

Lineage.—THOMAS BROWNE used on his seal on deeds of the 17th century the arms of BROWNE, of Abbot's Roding, and South Weald Hall, Essex, with augmentation granted to Sir Wiston Browne, Gentleman of the Chamber to HENRY VIII, 1511. These arms were: Gu. a chevron between three lions' gambs erect and erased arg. within a bordure of the second on a chief of the last an eagle displayed sa. He settled in the city of Cork about the time of the Restoration, and m. 1st, 1663, Anne, dau. of Robert Vowell, who d. without issue; he m. 2ndly, in 1666, Helena, dau. of William Hovell, of Kinsale, co. Cork, and by her left issue,
1. EDWARD, of whom presently.
1. Helena, m. James Kingsmill.
2. Mary, m. Hugh Millerd.
The son,
EDWARD BROWNE, Mayor of Cork 1714, purchased Riverstown, co. Cork, b. 1676; m. 1699, Judith, dau. and heiress of Warham Jemmett, and had issue,
1. JEMMETT (Rev.), of whom presently.
2. Thomas, m. Judith, only child of Ambrose Jackson, and left issue.
3. Edward, d. unm. at Lisbon, 1769.
4. St. John (Rev.), D.D., m. Amelia, dau. of Edward St. George, and left issue. His younger son was Sir George Sackville Browne, K.C.B.
5. William Hovell.   6. John, d. 1782.
1. Mary, d. 1789.
2. Judith, m. Rev. John Kenney, son of William Kenney, by Catherine, dau. of Sir Peter Courthope, and left issue (see KENNEY-HERBERT).
The eldest son,
THE MOST REV. JEMMETT BROWNE, of Riverstown, was successively Dean of Ross 1733, Bishop of Killaloe 1743, of Cork 1745, and of Elphin 1772, and Archbishop of Tuam 1775. He m. 1723, Alice, dau. of Thomas Waterhouse, and d. 1782, having had issue,
1. EDWARD, of whom presently.
2. Thomas (Rev.), m. 1st, Feb. 1751, Anne, dau. of Rev. David Waterhouse, of Inchowleran, co. Kilkenny. He m. 2ndly, 29 April, 1758, — Waldron, and left issue by his 1st wife,
1. Alice, m. 25 Sept. 1775, Lieut.-Col. Roger Parke, of Dunalley, co. Sligo (see that family).
2. Lydia, m. Caleb Falkner, eldest son of Sir Riggs Falkner, 1st bart. of Anne Mount, co. Cork, and d.s.p.m.
3. Warham, bapt. 15 Nov. 1733, Ensign 35th Regt. 1758.
1. Elizabeth, m. Ven. Chambre Corker, Archdeacon of Ardagh.
His eldest son,
THE VEN. EDWARD BROWNE, Archdeacon of Ross, b. 1726; m. 1st, 1752, Anne, dau. of Christopher Earbery, of Shandangan, co. Cork, by whom he had issue,
1. JEMMETT (Rev.), of whom presently.
2. CHRISTOPHER (Rev.), d. unm. 1802.
1. Hannah, d. unm.
He m. 2ndly, Mary Gertrude, dau. of Richard Jenkins, of Bicton Hall, co. Salop (see JENKINS of Cuckton), and d. 1777, leaving issue,
3. Charlton (Rev.), d. unm.   4. Edward, R.N.
2. Mary Anne, d. unm.   3. Isabella, d. unm.
4. Emma, d. unm.
5. Harriott Gertrude, m. 20 April, Capt. Anthony Kynnersley, of Shrewsbury, co. Salop, and left issue (see that family).
The eldest son,
REV. JEMMETT BROWNE, of Riverstown, prebendary of Killaspugmillane, co. Cork, m. 1784, Frances, dau. and heiress of John, Blennerhassett, of Ballyseedy (see that family), and d. 3 March, 1797, having had issue,

1. JEMMETT, his successor.
1. JOHN, successor to his brother.
1. Frances, m. 1813, Rev. Francis Fox, of Fox Hall, co. Longford, and left issue (see Fox of Fox Hall).
2. Jane, d. unm.
3. Annabella, d. unm.
His elder son,
JEMMETT BROWNE, of Riverstown, High Sheriff co. Cork 1816, d. unm. 1850, and was s. by his brother,
REV. JOHN BROWNE, of Riverstown, LL.B., b. 1795; m. 1832, Maria Judith, dau. of Rev. James Hamilton (see HAMILTON of Cornacassa), and d. 25 July, 1857, having had issue,
1. JEMMETT, his heir.
2. John Christopher, scholar of Corpus Christi Coll. Oxford, d. 1857.
3. Edward Francis, Lieut.-Col. (retired) 35th Regt., b. 3 Dec. 1835; m. 9 Aug. 1877, Elizabeth Mary, eldest dau. of Augustin Robinson, of West Lavant House, Sussex, and has issue,
1. Wiston John, b. 23 Sept. 1878.
2. Anthony Edward, Capt. 1st Batt. Royal Sussex Regt., b. 26 Jan. 1882.
1. Dorothy Margaret.
1. Margaret, d. unm. 8 July, 1906.
2. Frances, d. in infancy.
3. Annabel, d. unm. 1866.   4. Grace, d. unm. 1863.
5. Caroline Maria.   6. Emma Isabella.
7. Selina.   8. Alice, d. young.
The eldest son,
JEMMETT BROWNE, of Riverstown, co. Cork, b. 6 Dec. 1832; m. 1st, 10 Aug. 1864, Frances Mary, dau. of Henry Miles Custance. She d. 15 March, 1875, having had issue,
1. CHARLTON BASIL JEMMETT, now of Riverstown.
2. Arthur Blennerhassett Jemmett, b. 29 May, 1869.
1. Ethel Georgiana Jemmett.
He m. 2ndly, 19 June, 1877, his cousin Frances Caroline Cecil, eldest dau. of Major William Walter Stephenson, Rifle Brigade, and Grace Mary his wife, dau. of Rev. Francis Fox, of Fox Hall. He d. 5 May, 1897, leaving issue by her,
3. William Kellerman Jemmett, b. 24 April, 1878.
2. Grace Muriel Jemmett.

Arms—Gu. a chevron between three lion's gambs erased and erect or, on a chief crenellée arg. an eagle displayed sa. Crest—On an eastern crown or an eagle displayed with two heads sa. Motto—Hoc age.

Seat—Riverstown, co. Cork. Residence—3, Wells Road, North Gate, Regent's Park, London, N.W.

BROWNE. See BURKE'S PEERAGE, KENMARE, E., KILMAINE, B., and SLIGO, M.

BROWNE-CLAYTON. See CLAYTON.

BROWNLOW. See BURKE'S PEERAGE, LURGAN, B.

BRUCE OF BENBURB.

JAMES BRUCE, of Benburb, co. Tyrone, J.P. and D.L., High Sheriff 1886, b. 13 April, 1835; m. 4 Jan. 1877, Mary Hogg, dau. of William Thompson, M.D., of Lisburn, and relict of George Mitchell. She d.s.p. 4 May, 1893.

Lineage.—THOMAS DE BRUYS, of Clackmannan, m. Marjorie Chatteris (who, as his relict, had, 1359-60, a tierce of the lands of Clackmannan), and d. before 1348, having had issue, a son,
ROBERT DE BRUYS, who had a charter of Clackmannan from King DAVID II as "dilecto consanguineo." He m. Isabel, dau.

of Sir Robert Stewart, of Durrisdeer and Innermeath, and *d.* before 1389, leaving issue,
1. ROBERT, his heir.
2. James, Bishop of Dunkeld and Glasgow, and Lord Chancellor of Scotland.
The elder son,
SIR ROBERT DE BRUS, *s.* his father in Clackmannan, *m.* the dau. of Sir John Scrimgeour, of Dudhope, Constable of Dundee, and had issue,
1. DAVID (Sir), his heir.
2. ALEXANDER, of Stanehouse and Airth, of whom we treat.
Sir Robert had also a natural son, Thomas, of Kennet. The 2nd son,
ALEXANDER DE BRUS, was first of the House of Airth. He is proved to have been a son of Sir Robert de Brus, of Clackmannan, by an original birth brief in the possession of the Comte de Bruce in France, in which he is mentioned as " Alexander Brussius Comarchus de Airth, qui quidem Alexander Brussius fuit filius legitimi domini Roberti Brussii Comarchi de Clakmanan Equitis Aurati." He had numerous charters from the Abbots of Holywood, and from Kings JAMES I and II., and died *ante* 1487, having *m.* 1st, Janet, dau. of the 1st Lord Livingston, by whom he had no issue. He *m.* 2ndly, Margaret, dau. of Sir Malcolm Forrester, of Torwoodhead, and by her had issue,
1. JOHN, of whom presently.
2. Alexander (Sir), of Brigham and Earlshall, male line believed to be extinct.
3. Edward, of Kinnaird, male line extinct.
4. Lucas, of Cultmalundie, male line extinct.
5. Robert, of Auchenbowie, ancestor of that family.
6. David.
The eldest son,
SIR JOHN DE BRUS, *m.* 1471, Elizabeth, dau. of Sir William Mentieth, of Karse, and was killed by the Menteiths, of Karse, 1483, *vit. pat.*, having had issue,
1. ROBERT, his heir.
2. Thomas, of Lethbertsheilles, ancestor of that branch and of the Comtes de Bruce in France.
3. James, of Mungowallis.
1. Helen, *m.* Mentieth, of Karse.
2. Janet, *m.* William Livingstone, of Kilsyth.
3. Elizabeth, *m.* Muir, of Skaithmure.
The eldest son,
SIR ROBERT BRUS, *s.* his grandfather in Airth ; *m.* Euphame, dau. of Alexander, 2nd Lord Montgomerie, and sister to Hugh, 1st Earl of Eglingtoun ; he was killed at Flodden 1513, having had issue.
1. ROBERT, his heir. 2. John.
1. Isabel, *m.* Andreas de Methven de eodem.
The eldest son,
SIR ROBERT BRUS, *s.* his father in Airth 1513 ; *m.* 1st, Elizabeth Mentieth, relict of — Erskine, by whom he had no issue ; *m.* 2ndly, Janet, dau. of Sir Walter Forrester, of Carden, by whom he had issue,
1. ALEXANDER, his heir. 2. John.
3. Capt. James, male line extinct.
4. William.
1. A dau., *m.* Drummond, of Medhope.
Sir Robert *m.* 3rdly, Marian, dau. of Sir David Bruce, 7th Baron of Clackmannon, and by her had issue,
5. Andrew, of Dysart and Nethermongal.
6. Robert, of Baldrig.
The eldest son,
SIR ALEXANDER BRUCE, *s.* his father in Airth, in which estate he was infefted 8 March, 1552 ; *m.* Janet, dau. of Alexander, 5th Lord Livingston, *d.* 16 March, 1600, having had issue,
1. WILLIAM, his heir.
2. Robert, of Kinnaird, male line extinct.
3. Sir John, of Kincavel, male line extinct.
4. Sir Alexander, of Bangour, male line extinct.
5. Robert, of Garvel.
1. Marion, *m.* William Mentieth, of Karse
2. A dau., *d s.p.*
The eldest son,
WILLIAM BRUCE, *m.* Jean, dau. of John, 5th Lord Fleming, and sister to John, 1st Earl of Wigton ; *d.* Feb. 1590, *vit. pat.*, having had issue,
1. JOHN (Sir), his heir, male line extinct.
2. William (Sir), of Stenhouse, created Bart of Nova Scotia, June, 1629 ; ancestor of that branch.
3. Alexander,⎫
4. Robert, ⎬ all *d.s.p.*
5. Alexander,⎭
6. PATRICK, of Newtoune, of whom we treat.
The youngest and 3rd surviving son,
PATRICK BRUCE, had the estate of Newtoune of Bothkenner, *m.* 1627, Janet, dau. of John Jacksoun, merchant in Edinburgh ; they had a charter of the lands of Newtoune 5 July, 1627, and had issue,
1. Patrick, *d.s.p. vit. pat.*
2. William, his heir, and ancestor of the Bruces, of Newtoune and Cowden, male line extinct.
3. MICHAEL, of whom we treat.
The youngest son,
MICHAEL BRUCE, was Minister of Killinchie, co. Down, *m.* Jean, dau. of Robert Bruce, of Kinnaird (and sister of Col. Robert Bruce, of Kinnaird, and of the Life Guards of CHARLES I, who *d.* of wounds received at Worcester) ; he suffered much persecution on religious grounds ; *d.* at Anworth, Wigtonshire, 1693, having had issue,
1. JAMES, his heir.

2. Robert, ⎫
3. Michael, ⎬ all *d.* young.
1. Anna, ⎭
The eldest son,
JAMES BRUCE, was Minister of Killyleagh, co. Down ; *m.* 25 Sept. 1685, Margaret, dau. of Lieut.-Col. James Traill, of Tolychin, co. Down. She *d.* 1706. His will is dated Feb. 1725. He left issue, ten children, of whom we have record of four sons and three daus.,
1. MICHAEL, his heir.
2. Patrick, Minister of Killyleagh, ancestor of Sir Henry Hervey Bruce, Bart., of Downhill co. Londonderry.
3. William, of Dublin and Ardagon, co. Down, *d. unm.* 1755.
4. Hans, *d. unm.*
1. Mary, *m.* Rev. James Fleming.
2. Eleanor, ⎫
3. Magdalen, ⎬ *d. unm.*
The eldest son,
MICHAEL BRUCE, *b.* 27 July, 1686, was Minister of Hollywood, co. Down ; *m.* Mary Ker ; *d.* Dec. 1735, having had issue,
1. JAMES, *m.* and left an only dau., Anne.
2. SAMUEL, of whom we treat.
3. William, *d.s.p.* 1764.
1. Eleanor, *d.s.p.*
The 2nd, but eldest surviving son,
SAMUEL BRUCE, *b.* 17 March, 1722, was Minister of the Presbyterian Church, Wood Street, Dublin ; *m.* March, 1751, Rose, dau. of Robert Rainey, of Magherafelt ; *d.* 12 Feb. 1767 (will proved 19 Feb. 1767), having left issue,
1. Michael, drowned at Carrickfergus, *s.p.* 1779.
2. WILLIAM, of whom presently.
3. Robert, of Frenchay, near Bristol, *m.* Mary, dau. of Joseph Edye, and had issue,
1. Robert, of Frenchay, *m.* Isabella, dau. of Arthur Palmer, and by her had issue,
(1) Robert, of Clifton, *m.* Rosa Boulton, by whom he had issue,
Robert Arthur, *m.* Alice Lucy, dau. of Edward Vaughan.
(2) Arthur William, *d.s.p.*
(1) Mary Anne Isabella.
2. William, Barrister-at-Law, *m.* Eliza Dovey, *d.s.p.* 31 Dec. 1877.
1. Anne, *m.* her cousin Haliday Bruce.
4. Samuel, of Dame Street and Dundrum, Dublin, *d.s.p.*
1. Elizabeth,⎫
2. Mary, ⎬ all *d. unm.*
3. Eleanor, ⎭
The eldest surviving son,
WILLIAM BRUCE, *b.* 30 July, 1757, was Minister of the 1st Presbyterian Church, Belfast ; *m.* Susannah, dau. of Robert Hutton ; *d.* 27 Feb. 1841, having had issue,
1. SAMUEL, of whom presently.
2. William, *b.* 16 Nov. 1790, was Minister of the 1st Presbyterian Church, Belfast ; *m.* Jane Elizabeth, dau. of William Smith, of Barbadoes ; *d.* 25 Oct. 1868, having left issue,
1. William, ⎫
2. Samuel, ⎬ who all *d. unm.*
3. Henry, ⎭
1. Margaret, *m.* Lucius O. Hutton.
2. Susannah. 3. Jane Elizabeth.
4. Eliza.
5. Maria, *m.* Herbert D. Derbishire.
6. Charlotte.
3. Haliday, of Glennageragh House, co. Dublin, *m.* Anne, dau. of Robert Bruce, of Frenchay ; *d.* 1856, having left issue,
1. Robert, *d.* young.
1. Eliza, *d.* young.
2. Eliza, *m.* Professor John Couch Adams, the distinguished astronomer.
3 Emily Rose, *d.* young.
4. Henry, of Demerara, afterwards of London : *m.* Mary, dau. of John Swanwick, and *d.* 31 Aug. 1864, having left issue,
1. Henry Michael. 2. Alexander, *d.s.p.*
3. William Wallace, V.D., Lieut.-Col. 20th Middlesex (Artists) Volunteers, *d.* 20 Oct. 1907 ; *m.* Agnes Mabel (9, *Airlie Gardens, Campden Hill, London, W.*), dau. of Thomas Fielding Johnson, J.P., of Leicester, and has issue,
(1) Marjorie. (2) Geraldine.
(3) Rosalind. (4) Eileen.
(5) Beatrix. (6) Elfreda.
1. Anna Maria. *d.s.p.* 2. Emily.
3. Mary Louisa. 4. Clara, *m.* Russell Swanwick.
5. Katherine.
1. Eliza, *m.* William Curry, M.P., Armagh, Master in Chancery, Ireland, and *d.s.p.*
2. Emily, *m.* John Strong Armstrong.
3. Maria, *m.* Edward Hutton, M.D.
4. Susannah, *d.s.p.*
The eldest son,
SAMUEL BRUCE, of Thorndale, co. Antrim, *b.* 1789 ; *m.* Annette, dau. of James Ferguson, of White Park, co. Antrim, and *d.* 4 May, 845, having had issue,
1. William Robert, of Rockford, co. Dublin, Master of the Queen's Bench, Ireland, *b.* 1 Oct. 1833 ; *m.* 11 Aug. 1870, Florence Helen, dau. of Alexander Osborne, and *d.* 25 June, 1902, leaving issue,
1. Nigel William, *d.* young.
2. Thomas Robert, heir male of the Bruces of Newtoune, *b.* 1 July, 1885.
3. Reginald James, *b.* 7 April, 1887.

1. Enid, *m.* 9 July, 1891, Thomas Stoker, C.S.I., B.A., son of Abraham Stoker and brother of Sir William Thornley Stoker, 1st Bart. (*see* BURKE'S *Peerage*).
2. Lilian Florence, *m.* Capt. Eugene Le Mesurier, who *d.* 29 May, 1906.
3. Louie Mary, *m.* 30 Aug. 1905, Major W. Hessey, Northumberland Fus., and has issue.
4. Mabel.
2. JAMES, of Benhurb.
3. Samuel, of Norton Hall, Campden, co. Gloster (*see* BRUCE *of Norton Hall*).
Arms—Or, a saltire and a chief gu. in the dexter chief a mullet arg. and in base a cinquefoil of the second. Crest—A horse's head couped arg. bridled gu. and charged on the neck with a cinquefoil as in the arms. Motto—Do well, doubt not.
Seat—The Manor House, Benhurb, co. Tyrone. Clubs—Carlton and Boodle's.

BRUCE OF MILTOWN CASTLE.

GEORGE EVANS BRUCE, of Miltown Castle, co. Cork, Major Norfolk Regt., *b.* 15 Nov. 1867.
Lineage.—This is a branch of the great Scottish house of BRUCE. ALEXANDER BRUCE, 2nd son of Sir Andrew Bruce, of Earlshall, co. Fife (who was lineally descended from Sir Robert Bruce, 1st Baron of Clackmannan), by Helen his wife, dau. of Patrick, 7th Lord Gray, took an active part as a Royalist in the cause of King CHARLES I. In 1651 he was made a prisoner at the battle of Worcester, and suffered two years' imprisonment. "As soon as this Alexander obtained his liberty" (we are quoting from Sir Robert Douglas's *Baronage of Scotland*), "he *m.* Mary, only dau. of Capt. Brooks, Commander of the *Swallow*, sloop of war, and niece of Jonathan Saul, an Irish gentleman, then residing in London, who had been very kind to him, both during his confinement and afterwards. In 1654, he retired to Ireland with his lady, and settled at Bandon in that kingdom, where he died some years thereafter, leaving issue, a son." This son,
SAUL BRUCE, was twice Provost of Bandon, and lived in great friendship and intimacy with Sir Richard Cox, Lord Chancellor of Ireland, Judge Bernard, &c. He *m.* Mary, dau. of Mr. Ryce, Burgess of Bandon, and had issue,
1. Saul, who *d. unm.*
2. JONATHAN, of whom presently.
3. Charles. 4. David.
The 2nd son,
THE VERY REV. JONATHAN BRUCE, Dean of Kilfenora, *m.* Mary, dau. of Rev. Lewis Prytherick, and had issue.
1. Lewis, D.D., Vicar of Rainham, in Essex, and Preacher of H.M.'s Chapel in Somerset House,
2. Saul, *d.s.p.*
3. Charles David, *d.s.p.* 4. GEORGE.
1. Mary, *m.* Capt. Samuel Hobson.
2. Catherine, Mrs. Delabide. 3. Sarah, Mrs. Roberts.
The youngest son,
GEORGE BRUCE, Barrister-at-Law, *m.* 1753, Mary, dau. of Thomas Evans, of Miltown Castle, co. Cork, M.P. (brother of George, 1st Lord Carbery), by Mary his wife, dau. of John Waller, of Castletown, co. Limerick, and by her (who *d.* Feb. 1799) left with other issue, a son,
THE REV. JONATHAN BRUCE, of Miltown, who *m.* 17 April, 1781, his cousin, Mary, dau. of Eyre Evans, of Miltown Castle, and by her (who *d.* 9 Feb. 1837) had issue,
1. GEORGE EVANS, of Miltown Castle.
2. Eyre Evans, Major-Gen. H.E.I.C.S., *m.* twice, and had issue, George Robert, and three daus.
3. Jonathan, *m.* Anne, dau. of Major Maxwell, and has, with five other sons and two daus., Richard Isaac, C.I.E., late Commr. in Punjab (*Quetta, Fairfax Road, Teddington*), *b.* 1840; *m.* 1871, Lilla, dau. of Rev. J. Beavor Webb, Rector of Dunderrow, Kinsale, co. Cork, and has with other issue,
1. Jonathan Maxwell, Capt. 37th Punjabis, *b.* 22 June, 1873, *m.* 14 Sept. 1905, Mabel Walrond, 3rd dau. of Henry Trengrouse, J.P., of Hampton Wick.
2. Charles Edward, Capt. Indian Army, *b.* 23 March, 1876, *m.* 1 Oct. 1908, Doris, youngest dau. of late John Wilding, of Preston.
1. Elizabeth Evans, *m.* Charles Conyers, of Castletown; she *d.s.p.* 1868.
2. Mary, *m.* Eyre Massy, of Glenville.
The eldest son,
GEORGE EVANS BRUCE, of Miltown Castle, J.P., *b.* 17 Jan. 1782; *m.* 4 Aug. 1818, Frances, 2nd dau. of Major Greene, H.E.I.C.S., of Lota, co. Cork, by the Hon. Jane Massy, his wife, dau. of Hugh, 2nd Lord Massy, and had issue,
1. JONATHAN, of Miltown Castle.
1. Jane Greene. 2. Mary.
3. Frances Catherine, *m.* her cousin Jonathan Massy, of Glenville.
4. Georgina, *m.* Robert Gibbings, of Woodville.
Mr. Bruce *d.* 27 Feb. 1868, and was *s.* by his only son,
JONATHAN BRUCE, of Miltown Castle, J.P. cos. Cork, Limerick, and Tipperary, *b.* 18 June, 1819; *m.* 27 July, 1865, Annie Sophia, dau. of Thomas Hussey de Burgh, late Capt. 61st Regt., and great-grand-dau. of the Chief Baron Hussey Burgh, and *d.* 9 Dec. 1884, leaving issue by his wife, who *d.* 21 May, 1906,
1. GEORGE EVANS, now of Miltown Castle.
1. Kate de Burgh.
2. Frances Eveleen, *m.* 9 April, 1901, Malcolm Cotter Cariston Seton, only son of Bertram William Seton (*see* SETON *of Treskerby*).
Seat—Miltown Castle, Charleville, co. Cork. Club—Army and Navy.

BRUCE OF BALLYSCULLION.
See BURKE'S PEERAGE, BRUCE, Bart.

BRUCE. See BURKE'S PEERAGE, BRUCE, Bart.

BRUCE-KINGSMILL. See KINGSMILL.

BRUEN OF OAK PARK AND COOLBAWN.

HENRY BRUEN, of Oak Park, co. Carlow, and Coolbawn, co. Wexford, late Lieut. R.A., High Sheriff co. Carlow 1886 and co. Wexford, 1909, *b.* 26 July, 1856; *m.* 17 Nov. 1886, Agnes Mary, youngest dau. of Right Hon. Arthur MacMurrough Kavanagh, P.C., of Borris, co. Carlow, and had issue,
HENRY ARTHUR, Lieut. 15th Hussars, *b.* Sept. 1887.
Lineage.—JAMES BRUEN (said to have been of Tarvin, co. Chester), went to Ireland in Cromwell's Army and settled at Abbeyboyle, co. Roscommon. He was administrator to his brother, Henry Bruen, of Dublin, 20 Nov. 1700.
MOSES BRUEN, of Boyle, co. Roscommon, who *d.* 1757 (will dated 8 July, 1750, proved 24 Sept. following), left issue,
1. Moses.
2. HENRY, of Oak Park.
1. Bridget, *m.* John Stafford, of Gillstown, co. Roscommon.
2. Mary, *m.* John Knott.
3. Elinor Catherine, *d. unm.* 1798.
4. Margaret, *m.* — Fleming. 5. Elizabeth.
The 2nd son,
COL. HENRY BRUEN, M.P., of Oak Park, co. Carlow removed, about the year 1775, to estates which he purchased in co. Carlow. He *m.* 16 Oct. 1787, Harriette Dorothea, dau. of Francis Knox, of Rappa Castle, co. Mayo, and *d.* 1795, leaving issue,
1. HENRY, his heir.
2. John, of Coolbawn, co. Wexford, *d.s.p.* 1828.
3. Francis, of Coolbawn, co. Wexford, J.P. and D.L., M.P. for Carlow, *b.* 1800; *m.* 1823, Lady Catherine Anne Nugent, 2nd dau. of George Frederick, 7th Earl of Westmeath, and *d.s.p.* 15 Dec. 1867.
1. Maria, *m.* R. Longfield.
2. Margaret, *m.* Rev. Francis Ruttledge, of Bloomfield, co. Mayo.
3. Harriett, *m.* Rev. George Edward Vernon, and *d.* 5 Feb. 1866. He *d.* 16 March, 1870, leaving issue (*see* VERNON *of Clontarf Castle*).
The son and heir,
COL. HENRY BRUEN, of Oak Park, M.P. co. Carlow, *m.* 1822, Anne Wandesforde, dau. of Thomas Kavanagh, M.P., of Borris House, co. Carlow, by the Lady Elizabeth his wife, dau. of John, 17th Earl of Ormonde, and *d.* 1852, leaving issue,
1. HENRY, of Oak Park.
1. Elizabeth, *d.* 1848.
2. Harriet, *m.* 1857, Lorenzo William Alexander, who *d.* 1867.
3. Anne, *m.* 27 April, 1854, Rev. Benjamin Burton, and *d.* Feb. 1871, leaving issue.
The son and heir,
THE RIGHT HON. HENRY BRUEN, of Oak Park, co. Carlow, and Coolbawn, co. Wexford, M.P. co. Carlow 1857 to 1880, J.P. and D.L. of that co., and High Sheriff 1853, J.P. co. Wexford, High Sheriff 1883; sworn a Privy Councillor for Ireland 1880; *b.* 16 June, 1828; *d.* 8 March, 1912; *m.* 6 June, 1854, Mary Margaret, 3rd dau. of Col. Edward M. Conolly, of Castletown, co. Kildare, M.P., and by her (who *d.* 13 May 1894) had issue,
1. HENRY, now of Oak Park.
2. Edward Francis, Capt. R.N.
3. John Richard, *d.* 30 Nov. 1874.
4. Arthur Thomas, *m.* 14 July, 1908, Lily, youngest dau. of F. Ruttledge, J.P., of Enniscorthy.
5. Charles, *d. unm.* 23 Feb. 1905.
1. Katherine Anne, *m.* 26 Feb. 1874, Thomas, 2nd Lord Rathdonnell (*see* BURKE'S *Peerage and Baronetage*, RATHDONNELL, B.).
2. Mary Susan.
3. Elizabeth, *m.* 16 Oct. 1894, Edward Ussher Roberts, of Gaultier-Woodstown, Waterford, only son of the late Arthur Ussher Roberts.
4. Eleanor.
5. Helen, *m.* 11 Aug. 1896, Major Charles W. Bishop, son of James Bishop, of Hamstead Park, Newbury.
6. Grace, *m.* 4 Aug. 1910, Sir Hunt Henry Allen Johnson-Walsh, 5th Bart. (*see* BURKE'S *Peerage*).
Seats—Oak Park, Carlow; Coolbawn, Enniscorthy. Club—Naval and Military.

BRYAN OF JENKINSTOWN.
See BURKE'S PEERAGE, BELLEW.

IRELAND. Buchanan.

BRYAN OF UPTON AND BORRMOUNT.

CAPT. LOFTUS ANTHONY BRYAN, of Upton, and Borrmount Manor, co. Wexford, J.P. and D.L., High Sheriff 1892, Capt. the Waterford Artillery, Southern Division, R.A.; *b.* 14 Feb. 1867; *m.* 1886, Annie, youngest dau. of the late M. R. Ryan, J.P., of Temple Mungret, co. Limerick, and has issue,

1. LOFTUS ANTHONY, *b.* 2 Oct. 1886.
2. William Jacob, *b.* 5 Oct. 1889.
3. John Donough Owen, *b.* 26 Oct. 1904.
1. Bertha Charlotte Georgina.
2. Annie Caitlin Elizabeth.

Lineage.—ABRAHAM BRYAN, of Dublin, Merchant, *temp.* Queen ANNE, had two sons,
1. JACOB, of whom hereafter.
2. Philip, of Norwich, Norfolk.

The elder son,
REV. JACOB BRYAN, Rector of Kilrush, in the diocese of Meath, *b.* in Dublin, 1708, entered Trin. Coll. Dublin, 17 July, 1728, aged 20 years, and was M.A. 1730. He *m.* 28 April, 1739, Mary, dau. of Isaac Dickinson, of Dublin, and of Streetgate, Cumberland, and had issue,
1. ISAAC, his successor.
2. Daniel, M.D., *b.* 20 June, 1757; *d. unm.*
1. Elinor, *b.* 24 Feb. 1748; *m.* Thomas Hacket.
2. Martha, *m.* 1813, Richard Swift, of Lynn, co. Westmeath, and had issue.

He *d.* 6 Oct. 1794. His elder son,
THE REV. ISAAC BRYAN, Rector of Horetown, co. Wexford, *b.* 13 May, 1746; *m.* 25 June, 1785, Mary, dau. of Maurice Howlin D'Arcy, of Coolure, co. Wexford, by Eleanor his wife, eldest dau. of Charles Tottenham, M.P., of Tottenham Green, co. Wexford, sister of Sir John Tottenham, 1st bart. of Tottenham Green, and aunt of Sir Charles Tottenham Loftus, 2nd bart., created EARL and MARQUESS OF ELY. By her (who *d.* 1803), Rev. Isaac Bryan left at his decease, 1796, two daus., who both *m.*, the youngest *m.* Mr. Jackson, President, U.S.A., and three sons,
1. Jacob Edward, *d.s.p.*
2. Meade Dennis, *b.* 23 Jan. 1790, *d.s.p.*
3. LOFTUS ANTHONY, of Upton.

The 3rd son,
LOFTUS ANTHONY BRYAN, of Upton, co. Wexford, High Sheriff of the city of Dublin 1836-7 (the Freedom of the City of Dublin was conferred on Mr. Loftus Bryan), *b.* 24 Aug. 1793; *m.* 13 Oct. 1832, Marian, dau. of William Izon, of The Lodge, West Bromwich, co. Stafford, and bad issue,
1. ISAAC WILLIAM, his heir.
2. Loftus Anthony, of Highfield, co. Dublin, B.A. Trin. Coll. Dublin, *b.* 15 April, 1837; *m.* 14 Nov. 1865, Georgina Percival, youngest dau. of Thomas M'Craith, son of Thomas M'Craith, of Loughloher, co. Tipperary, and *d.* 3 Oct. 1871, leaving by her (who *m.* 2ndly, 1886, Major-Gen. John Roe, formerly of Rockwell, co. Tipperary, and *d.* 3 Oct. 1808) an only surviving son,
LOFTUS ANTHONY, now of Upton and Borrmount Manor.
3. Jacob, *b.* 1840; *d. unm.* 31 March, 1866.
4. William Izon, late of Upton and Borrmount Manor.
1. Charlotte, *d.* 19 April, 1910, having *m.* the late Very Rev. Francis Swift, of Lynn Lodge, co. Westmeath, Dean of Clonmacnoise, and Rector of Mullingar, co. Westmeath.
2. Marian *m.* 30 June, 1868, George Gledstanes Richards, eldest son of John Richards, of Macmine Castle, co. Wexford, who *d.* 24 Feb. 1876, leaving issue (*see that family*).

Mr. Bryan *d.* 1865, and was *s.* by his eldest son,
ISAAC WILLIAM BRYAN, of Upton, J.P., co. Wexford, Barrister-at-Law, M.A., Trin. Coll. Dublin, *b.* 29 Nov. 1833; *d. unm.* 7 Dec. 1866, and devised Upton to his younger brother,
WILLIAM IZON BRYAN, of Upton and Borrmount Manor, co. Wexford, J.P., Barrister-at-Law, M.A., and LL.B. Trin. Coll. Dublin, *b.* 29 Aug. 1841; *d. unm.* 21 Jan. 1873, when he was *s.* by his nephew, the present proprietor.

Arms—Erm., a lion rampant gu. crowned or, between two cinquefoils in chief and a fleur-de-lis in base az., a canton of the second charged with three bars dancetté arg. Crest—On a mural crown ppr. a lion rampant gu. collared gemelle or and charged on the shoulder with a cinquefoil arg. Motto—Ferro mea recupero.
Seats—Upton, Kilmuckridge, Gorey, co. Wexford; Borrmount Manor, Enniscorthy; Kilribbon House, Enniscorthy, co. Wexford.

I.L.G.

BUCHANAN OF EDENFEL.

LIEUT.-COL. JOHN BLACKER BUCHANAN, of Edenfel, co. Tyrone, R.A.M.C., (retired) served in S. African War, *b.* 26 April, 1863; *m.* Oct. 1894. Mary, eldest dau. of Rev. A. Harland, of Harefield, Middlesex, and has issue.
1. Helena Margaret } twins, *b.* 13 July, 1898.
2. Evaleen Mary }
3. Mary Elizabeth, *b.* July, 1905.

Lineage.—THOMAS BUCHANAN, of Carbeth, was son of Thomas Buchanan (by Isabel, dau. of Murdoch Stuart, Duke of Albany), 3rd son of Sir Walter de Buchanan, 13th Laird of Buchanan (*see* BUCHANAN-HAMILTON). He *m.* 2ndly, his cousin, dau. of Buchanan of that ilk, and had issue,
JOHN BUCHANAN, of Gartincaber, parish of Buchanan, co. Stirling, *b.* 1545; *m.* and had issue,
GEORGE BUCHANAN, of Gartincaber, *b.* 1578; *m.* Elizabeth, dau. of Walter Leckie, of Dishcour, and had issue,
1. JOHN, of whom presently.
2. George (descendants in America).
3. Thomas, of Gartincaber.

The eldest son,
JOHN BUCHANAN, for whom his father purchased the lands of Blairluisk, co. Dumbarton, *b.* 1615; *m.* his cousin Jean, and had issue,
GEORGE BUCHANAN, of Blairluisk, *b.* 1648; sold Blairluisk 1674, to his brother William, and settled near Omagh, co. Tyrone; *m.* Elizabeth Mayne, and had issue,
JOHN BUCHANAN, *b.* 1676; *m.* 1703, Catherine Black, and had issue four sons, of whom,
1. JOHN, his heir.
2. Thomas, ancestor of James Buchanan, 15th President of the United States.

The son and heir,
JOHN BUCHANAN, *b.* 1704; *m.* 1st, 1735, Jane Nixon, and had issue,
JOHN BUCHANAN, of Omagh, *b.* 1736; *m.* 1st, Maria, dau. of Capt. Long, which lady *d.s.p.*; 2ndly, 1771, Sarah, dau. of Oliver Sproule, and *d.* 1820, leaving issue with several daus.,
1. James, *b.* 1772, was H.B.M. Consul General in America (1817 to 1844), where his descendants still remain.
2. JOHN, of whom presently. 3. George, *b.* 1782; *d.s.p.* 1869.
4. William, *b.* 1784; *d.* 1835.
5. Alexander, *b.* 1786; *d.s.p.* 1840.

The 2nd son,
JOHN BUCHANAN, of Omagh, *b.* 1779; purchased Lisnamallard from Sir Hugh Stewart, Bart. in 1828; *m.* 6 April, 1820, Mary Jane, dau. of the late James Blacker, a Divisional Magistrate of Dublin, High Sheriff 1803 (*see* BLACKER *of Woodbrook*). She *d.* Feb. 1857. He *d.* Jan. 1842, leaving issue,
1. John Blacker, *b.* Jan. 1821; *d.s.p.* Dec. 1860.
2. James Blacker, *b.* Dec. 1824; *d.s.p.* April, 1852.
3. George, of Keston Towers, Kent, *b.* May, 1827; *m.* 1860, Gertrude, dau. of George Armitage, D.L., of Nunthorpe, co. York (*see that family*). and *d.s.p.* June, 1897.
4. William Blacker, *b.* Jan. 1831; *d.s.p.* Feb. 1857.
5. Mansergh George, *b.* Oct. 1832; *d.s.p.* Oct. 1876.
6. Alexander Carlile, of The Oaks, Morden, Manitoba, *b.* Feb. 1834; *m.* 19 Nov. 1863, Anna Sophia, dau. of James Wilson, and *d.* Dec. 1897, leaving issue, settled in Canada.
7. LEWIS MANSERGH, late of Edenfel and Lisnamallard.
1. Jane Elizabeth, of Lisnamallard, co. Tyrone, *d. unm.* 3 Dec. 1910.
2. Sarah Caroline, *d. unm.* March, 1893.
3. Elizabeth Eleanor, of Lisnamallard, co. Tyrone, *d. unm.* April, 1906.

The 7th son,
COL. LEWIS MANSERGH BUCHANAN, C.B., F.R.G.S., of Edenfel and Lisnamallard, co. Tyrone, *b.* 31 Dec. 1836; Hon. Col. and late Lieut.-Col. commanding 4th Batt. Royal Inniskilling Fusiliers, formerly an Officer of the 88th Connaught Rangers, in which regt. he served through the Indian Mutiny. He *d.* 23 April, 1908, having *m.* 1st, 1862, Ebanor Margaret (*d.* 1877), dau. of the late William Whitla, of Lisburn (*see* WHITLA *of Ben Eaden*); and 2ndly, 1879, Wilhelmina (*d.* 1 April, 1908), dau. of George A. Molony, R.M.; and by his first wife had issue,
1. JOHN BLACKER, now of Edenfel.
2. Lewis Ernest, Capt. and Hon. Maj. 4th Batt. Royal Innis. Fus., served in S. African War, *b.* 4 Sept. 1868; *m.* 3 Dec. 1903, Constance Kate, dau. of Frederick S. Goulding, of Brockley, Kent, and has issue,
1. Joyce Elinor, *b.* 22 Aug. 1905.
2. Audrey Elizabeth, *b.* 26 March, 1907.
3. Constance Phyllis, *b.* 9 Oct. 1909.
3. Mansergh George Reginald, *b.* 7 Sept. 1872; *m.* 1896, Amy, dau. of John Hughes, of Blackburn.
4. Calvert James Stronge, served in S. African War, *b.* 10 July, 1874.
1. Ethel Elizabeth, *d.* 1 Nov. 1910, having *m.* Jan. 1889, William D. Grubb, of Bessbrook.
2. Mary Jane Eleanor, *m.* Sept. 1888, Effingham MacDowel F.R.C.S.I.
3. Alice Lilian, *m.* 30 Nov. 1898, Charles Stuart Hope, of Kylemere, Bickley, son of the late Rev. James Hope, Rector of Whalley Range, Manchester.
4. Eleanora Agnes, *m.* 3 Sept. 1902, Col. Mackenzie Churchill, of The Granleys, Cheltenham.

Seat—Edenfel, Omagh, co. Tyrone.

F

BUDGEN OF BALLINDONEY.

STEPHEN THEODORE JANSSEN EDMUND BUDGEN, of Ballindoney, co. Wexford, J.P., b. 16 Dec. 1875; m. 30 March, 1910, Elizabeth Siddons, elder dau. of the late Major-Gen. John Anstruther Angus, B.N.I.

Lineage.—JOHN BUDGEN, of Penshurst, Kent, son of WILLIAM BUDGEN, of Penshurst, Kent, who d. temp. HENRY VIII, left issue,
 1. OLIVER, of whom presently.
 2. William (Rev.), of Emanuel Coll. Camb.
 1. Susan, m. John Fry, of Mitchells, Spredburst.

The eldest son,
OLIVER BUDGEN, of Haesden, Leigh, near Tonbridge, Kent, b. 1555, d. 1625, leaving a son,
JOHN BUDGEN, of West Newdegate, Surrey, which he purchased 1636, was educated at Clare Coll. Camb., m. 1st, the dau. of Bennett, of Hastings, and by her had,
 1. John, d. 1652.
He m. 2ndly, Elizabeth, dau. of John Steere, of Ockley, and by her had issue,
 2. John, M.A., M.D., and Fell. of Trin. Coll. Camb.; d. unm. 1696.
 3. William, Fell. of Trin. Coll. Camb., d. 1661.
 4. Thomas, d. 1671.   5. Edward, d. 1716.
 6. JAMES, of whom presently.
 1. Elizabeth, m. — Bridger, and had issue.

The youngest son,
JAMES BUDGEN, of West Newdegate, Surrey; m. the widow of — Morton, and dau. of Rev. Mr. Lee, of Bucks, and had issue,
 1. John, M.A., M.D. Trin. Coll. Oxford, b. 1676; m. Mary, dau. of James Ede, of Cudworth. She d. 1768. He d.s.p. June, 1740.
 2. EDWARD, of whom presently.
 3. James, b. 1680, d. unm. 1707.

The second son,
EDWARD BUDGEN, of West Newdegate, and Shrub Hill, Dorking, Sheriff of Surrey 1698, b. 1677; m. Elizabeth, dau. of James Ede, of Cudworth, and d. Aug. 1719, leaving issue,
 1. Edward, m. Mary, dau. and heir of Peter Hussey, of Shire, and d.s.p. 12 Aug. 1728.
 2. John, d. young.   3. William, d. young.
 4. James, B.A., Trin. Coll. Oxford, 1702; m. Mary, dau. of J. Ede, of Cudworth, and d. 8 March, 1731. She m. 2ndly, Richard Morton and d. 1778.
 5. THOMAS, of whom presently.

The youngest son,
THOMAS BUDGEN, of West Newdegate, and Shrub Hill, Dorking, M.P. for Surrey in the last two Parliaments of GEORGE II. and the first of GEORGE III. who refused a baronetcy in both those reigns, m. Penelope, dau. of Daniel Smith, Governor of Nevis, and d. 3 March, 1772, leaving issue,
JOHN SMITH, his heir.
Penelope, m. William Hewson, and had issue.

The only son,
JOHN SMITH BUDGEN, of West Newdegate, and Dorking, M.A. Trin. Coll. Oxford, b. 28 June, 1741; m. Lucretia, dau. of Matthew Mills, of St. Christopher's. She d. 8 Nov. 1798. He d. 25 May, 1805, leaving with three daus., Lucretia, Cornelia, and Maria, an only son,
MAJOR THOMAS BUDGEN, of Holmesdale, Nutfield, Surrey, J.P. and D.L., Major Surrey Militia, who sold Newdegate Manor in 1807; m. 18 May, 1789, Lydia Sarah Genevera, dau. of Edward Nourse, of Stanstead, Essex, and d. May, 1852, having by her (who d. 8 Aug. 1818) had issue,
 1. JOHN ROBERT, of Ballindoney.
 2. Thomas, retired Major-Gen., late Col. Royal Engineers, b. 1 July, 1795; m. Fanny, dau. of Col. Maule, and left three sons and four daus. The eldest son, John, late of 95th Regt.; and the 2nd, William Thomas, Col. Royal Artillery, D.S.O., m. Olivia Georgiana, 2nd dau. of Gen. Jervois, R.A., and d. 28 July, 1894, leaving Temple, William, and Florence.
 1. Lucretia Mary, d. unm. 1808.   2. Lydia Martha.

The elder son,
JOHN ROBERT BUDGEN, of Richmond House, Twickenham, and of Ballindoney, co. Wexford, late Capt. Rifle Brigade, J.P. and D.L. for Surrey, and J.P. for co. Wexford, b. 1 Dec. 1791; m. 13 Jan. 1823, Williamza Caroline Mary, 3rd dau. of Col. Lorenzo Moore, of the Battleaxe Guards, by Henrietta, his wife, only dau. of Sir Stephen Theodore Janssen, Bart., Lord Mayor of London 1754, and by her (who d. 18 Nov. 1870) had issue,
 1. THOMAS JOHN, later of Ballindoney.
 1. Anne Williamza, b. 4 Oct. 1826.
 2. Maria Cornelia, d. unm. 11 April, 1879.

Capt. Budgen had the Waterloo medal and eight Peninsular clasps. He d. at Beaulieu, Jersey, 4 Dec. 1866. His only son,
THOMAS JOHN BUDGEN, of Ballindoney, co. Wexford, J.P., b. 16 Jan. 1824; d. 29 April, 1911; m. 18 July, 1872, Julia, dau. of Rev. Edmund Dewdney, Incumbent of St. John's, Porstea, and grand-dau. of Thomas Lindsey, of Hollymount, co. Mayo, and by her (who d. 5 Nov. 1888) had issue,
STEPHEN THEODORE JANSSEN EDMUND, now of Ballindoney.

Seat—Ballindoney, Ballywilliam, New Ross, co. Wexford. **Residence**—Richmond House, Twickenham. **Clubs**—Junior Conservative, and Conservative (Edinburgh).

DUNBAR-BULLER OF WOBURN.

CHARLES WILLIAM DUNBAR-BULLER, of Woburn, co. Down, and Tofts Monks, Norfolk, J.P. and D.L., co. Down, High Sheriff 1894, D.L. Norfolk, formerly Fellow and Sub-warden of All Souls' Coll. Oxford, b. 2 Oct. 1847; m. 22 July, 1890, Georgiana Anne Elizabeth, only surviving child of the late George Dunbar, D.L., sometime M.P. for Belfast. He assumed the additional name and arms of DUNBAR by Royal Licence 1891.

Lineage—(of DUNBAR)—JAMES DUNBAR, a cadet of the family of Dunbar, of Hempriggs, in Scotland, had a son,
GEORGE DUNBAR, of Belfast and afterwards of Dungannon, co. Tyrone. His will, dated 7 Jan. 1779, was proved 18 Nov. that year. He left issue,
 1. JOHN, of whom presently.
 1. A dau. m. Henry Joy.
 2. Eleanor.

The only son,
JOHN DUNBAR, of Dungannon, co. Tyrone, m. Wilfrida, dau. of John Gilmore, of Boghead, co. Antrim, and had issue,
 1. John Gilmore, of Woburn, co. Down, m. Mary, dau. of John Cunningham, of Belfast, and d.s.p.
 2. George, d.s.p.
 1. Sarah, m. Alexander Orr, of Landmore, co. Londonderry, and had issue,
  1. James Alexander ORR, m. Anne, dau. of William Johnston, of Belfast, and had a son, James.
  2. GEORGE DUNBAR, of whom presently.
  1. Elizabeth, m. Rev. John Paul, of Aghadowey, co. Londonderry.
  2. Anna Alexandra, m. Rev. Michael Dillon Pilkington, of Riverville, co. Galway.
 2. Eleanor, m. Rev. John Houghton, of Middleton, Lancashire.

The grandson,
GEORGE DUNBAR DUNBAR (formerly Orr), of Woburn, co. Down, Barrister-at-Law, D.L. co. Down, M.P. for Belfast 1835-7 and 1838-41, assumed by Royal Licence 18 March, 1833, the name and arms of DUNBAR in lieu of his patronymic ORR, b. 1800; m. 13 April, 1844, Harriet Susan Isabella, only dau. of Lord George Thomas Beresford (see BURKE's Peerage, WATERFORD, M.). She d. 18 April, 1859. He d. 12 Aug. 1875, having had issue,
John George Henry William, of Woburn, co. Down, Capt. 1st Life Guards, b. 13 June, 1848; d. 1884.
GEORGIANA ANNE ELIZABETH, m. as above, 22 July, 1890.
CHARLES WILLIAM BULLER, now DUNBAR-BULLER.

Lineage—(of BULLER)—JOHN BULLER, of East Looe, and Bake, co. Cornwall, M.P. for East Looe 1747-86 and a Lord of the Admiralty, b. 24 Jan. 1721, 3rd son of John Francis Buller, of Morval (see BULLER of Downes), and Rebecca his wife, dau. and co-heir of Sir Jonathan Trelawney, Bart., Bishop of Winchester. He m. 1st, 3 March, 1760, Mary, dau. of Sir John St. Aubyn, Bart., M.P. She d. 14 Aug. 1767, leaving issue, two sons,
 1. John, M.P. for East Looe, m. Augusta, dau. of R. Nixon, and d.s.p. 1807.
 2. Edward (Sir), Bart. of Trenant Park, Vice-Adm. of the Red, created a baronet 3 Oct. 1808, b. 24 Dec. 1764; m. 15 March, 1789, Gertrude, dau. of Col. Philip van Cortlands, and d. 15 April, 1824, when the title became extinct. He had issue,
  John St. Aubyn, d. young.
  Anna Maria, m. 25 Feb. 1824, Lieut.-Col. James Drummond Elphinstone, who assumed the name of BULLER. He d. 8 March, 1857. She d. 26 Feb. 1845, leaving issue (see BURKE's Peerage, ELPHINSTONE, B.).

Mr. John Buller m. 2ndly, 4 Nov. 1768, Elizabeth Caroline, dau. of John Hunter. She d. 17 Jan. 1798. He d. 26 July, 1786, having by her had issue, one son and a dau.,
 3. FREDERICK WILLIAM, of whom presently.
 1. Caroline, m. 18 May, 1791, her cousin, William Buller, of Whimple, Devon. He d. 22 April, 1817. She d. 1 June, 1860, leaving issue (see BULLER of Downes).

The only son by the second marriage,
LIEUT.-GEN. FREDERICK WILLIAM BULLER, of Pelynt, and Lanreath, co. Cornwall, M.P. for East Looe, 1798-1802, m. 6 April, 1795, Charlotte, dau. of George Tomkyns, and d. 5 Nov. 1855, having had issue,
 1. Frederick Thomas, of Pelynt, and Lanreath, Maj.-Gen. in the Army, b. 6 A... 797; m. 16 Aug. 1821, Lady Agnes Percy, dau. of ...ugh, Duke of Northumberland, K.G. She d. 4 June, 1856. He d.s.p. 5 June, 1860.
 2. WILLIAM, of whom presently.

3. George (Sir), G.C.B., Gen. in the Army, late Rifle Brigade, *b.* 30 May, 1800; *m.* 22 Oct. 1855, Henrietta, dau. of Gen. Sir John Macdonald, G.C.B. She *d.s.p.* 18 April, 1881. He *d.* Feb. 1884.
4. John, R.N., *b.* 28 Dec. 1802; *d. unm.*
1. Charlotte, *d. unm.*
2. Caroline, *m.* 16 March, 1836, George Warwick, 1st Lord Poltimore. He *d.* 19 Dec. 1858. She *d.* 29 May, 1863, leaving issue (*see* BURKE's *Peerage*).
3. Agnes, *d. unm.*
4. Georgiana Amelia, *m.* 3 March, 1836, Charles Hulse, of Stoke Park, Guildford. He *d.* 25 May, 1883. She *d.* 18 Dec. 1897, leaving issue (*see* BURKE's *Peerage*, HULSE, Bart.).

The second son,
THE REV. WILLIAM BULLER, of Pelynt and Lanreath, Cornwall, Rector of Hemington, Somerset, M.A., Worcester Coll. Oxford, *b.* 1 June, 1799; *s.* his brother 1860; *m.* 1st, 15 Sept. 1835, Leonora Sophia, dau. of John Bond, of Grange, Dorset. She *d.s.p.* 6 Jan. 1836. He *m.* 2ndly, 13 Aug. 1845, Eleanor, dau. of Rev. William Coney, of Cookham, Berks, and *d.* 31 May, 1862, having by her had issue,
1. CHARLES WILLIAM, now of Woburn.
2. Frederick George (Rev.), Rector of Birch, Manchester, *b.* 1855, *m.* 8 Sept. 1886, Margaret Mildred, dau. of Sir John W. H. Anson, 2nd Bart., and has issue,
  1. Hugh Algernon, *b.* 20 Aug. 1887.
  2. John Frederick, *b.* 27 March, 1889.
  3. Frederick Edwin, *b.* 14 July, 1892.
  1. Winifred Margaret, *b.* 9 July, 1897.
3. Warwick Augustus, *b.* 1857; *m.* Frances, dau. of Maj. H. A. Cubitt, of Earlham Lodge, Norwich (*see* CUBITT *of Honing*), and has issue,
  1. Francis Warwick, *b.* 16 Jan. 1903.
  1. Nora Dorothy. 2. Phillis Emily.
  3. Alice Irene. 4. Eleanor Violet.
1. Ellen Georgina, *d.* Aug. 1909.
2. Alice Lucy, *m.* 13 Dec. 1877, Capt. Samuel Francis Dashwood, who *d.s.p.* 2 May, 1897.
3. Caroline, *m.* 19 July, 1884, Rev. John Barrington Pelham, Vicar of Thundridge, Ware, 2nd son of the Hon. and Right Rev. J. T. Pelham, D.D. Bishop of Norwich (*see* BURKE's *Peerage*, CHICHESTER, E.).
4. Sophia Leonora, *d. unm.* 1883.

Arms—Quarterly 1st and 4th sa. on a cross quarterpierced arg. four eagles displayed of the field (BULLER) 2nd and 3rd per pale or and arg. three cushions, two and one within a double tressure flory counterflory gu. all within a bordure vair, and for distinction in the fess point a cross crosslet of the third (DUNBAR). **Crests**—
1. A Saracen's head affrontée couped at the shoulders ppr. (BULLER).
2. A demi lion or armed and holding in the dexter paw a rose gu. leaved and barbed vert, charged for distinction on the shoulder with a cross crosslet gu. (DUNBAR). **Motto**—Aquila non capit muscas.

Seats—Woburn, Donaghadee, co. Down; Trerissome, Flushing, Cornwall. *Town Residence*—15, Upper Grosvenor Street, W. *Clubs*—Brooks's, St. James', and United University, S.W.; Ulster, Belfast; and Devon and Exeter, Exeter.

BUNBURY OF CRANAVONANE.

HAMILTON JOSEPH BUNBURY, of Cranavonane, co. Carlow, Capt. 4th Batt. Highland L.I., formerly Capt. 2nd Vol. Batt. Royal Sussex Regt., *b.* 14 Feb. 1866.

Lineage.—SIR HENRY BUNBURY, Knt. of Stanney, co. Chester, descended from David de Bunbury, Lord of Bunbury, *temp.* EDWARD III, was knighted 1603. He *m.* 1st, Anne, dau. of Geoffrey Shakerley, of Shakerley, Lancashire, and by her was ancestor of the Bunburys, baronets of Stanney (*see* BURKE's *Peerage*). He *m.* 2ndly, Martha, dau. of Edward Norris, of Speke, Lancashire, and *d.* 1634, having by her had a son,
THOMAS BUNBURY, *m.* 1st, Eleanor, dau. of Henry Birkenhead, of Backford, and 2ndly, Margaret, dau. of William Willcox, and was bur. 9 Dec. 1668, aged 62, at Stoke, Cheshire, leaving issue. His third son,
BENJAMIN BUNBURY, of Killerig, co. Carlow, bapt. at Stoke, 13 Sept. 1642, settled in Ireland; *m.* Mary, widow of Matthew Sheppard, of Owles, co. Leicester. Her will was proved 1741. Their son,
THOMAS BUNBURY, of Cloghna and Cranavonane, *m.* about 1697, Rose Jackson. He *d.* 1743. She *d.* Feb. 1738, leaving two sons,

1. Thomas, of Cloghna, *d.s.p.* bur. at Tullow, co. Carlow. Will proved 1781.
2. BENJAMIN, *s.* his brother.

The younger son
BENJAMIN BUNBURY, of Cranavonane, *m.* Rose, dau. of Dean Mervyn, of co. Carlow, and by her (who *d.* 20 Oct. 1761), left (with a dau. *m.*—Norris) an only son,
THOMAS BUNBURY, of Cranavonane, High Sheriff 1761, Capt. in the Army, *m.* 1758, Mary, dau. of Jeremiah Milles, D.D., Dean of Exeter. His will was proved Jan. 1791. He left issue,
1. Benjamin, of Marlston House, Newbury, Berks., Major in the Army, *b.* 1760, *m.* Anne, dau. and coheir of Henry Cowling, of Richmond, Yorks., and left issue,
  Henry Mill, of Marlston House, Berks., and of Cranavonane, co. Carlow, *b.* 1809; *m.* 1st, 1813, his cousin Mary Diana, who *d.* 1864, only dau. of Col. Hamilton Welch Bunbury, of Cranavonane, and 2ndly, 13 Feb. 1866, Ellen Elizabeth, dau. of Right Hon. C. Tennyson d'Eyncourt, of Bayons Manor, Lincoln (*see that family*). He *d.s.p.* 1886. She *d.* 12 Feb. 1900.
  Anne, *b.* 1803, *m.* 1829, Maj. Louis Versturme, K.H. She *d.* 1881.
  Maj. Benjamin Bunbury *m.* 2ndly, Eliza Susannah, dau. of Benjamin Harenc, of Foot's Cray Place, Kent, and widow of Col. Taubman, but had no issue by her.
2. Harrison Charles, R.N., *b.* 1764, *d. unm.*
3. Hugh Mill, of whom presently.
4. Hamilton Welch, of Cranavonane, co. Carlow, Col. 3rd Buffs., *b.* 1772, *m.* 1810, Mary, dau. of Matthew Russell, of Brancepeth Castle, co. Durham, and *d.* 1833, leaving an only dau.,
  Mary Diana, *b.* 1811, *m.* 1833, her cousin, Henry Mill Bunbury, of Marlston House (*see above*). She *d.s.p.* 1864.
5. John Monseer, R.N., *b.* 1775, *d.s.p.* 1798.
6. Thomas, K.H., Lieut.-Gen. in the Army and Col. 60th Rifles, *b.* 1783, *m.* Jane, dau. and coheir of John Pearse, of Standon House, Wilts, and *d.* 1857, leaving issue,
  1. Thomas Charles, Lieut. 60th Rifles, *b.* 1812, *d.s.p.* 1894.
  2. Stonehouse George, Lieut.-Col. 67th Regt., *b.* 1818, *m.* Miss G. D. Vidal, and *d.s.p.* 1880.
  3. Harry, 60th Rifles, *b.* 1819, *d. unm.*
  1. Catherine, *b.* 1815, *d. unm.* 1838.

The third son,
HUGH MILL BUNBURY, of West Hill, Wandsworth, *b.* 11 Feb. 1766; *m.* 1st, 1791, Lydia Cox, and by her had a son and a dau.,
1. Hugh Mill, settled in Canada, *b.* 1800, *d.* 1866.
1. Lydia Jane, *b.* 1796, *m.* Count Alfred de Vigny, the Poet, Capt in the Red Mousquetaires of Louis XVIII, and *d.s.p.*
He *m.* 2ndly, 1822, Alicia, dau. of Philip Lillie, of Drumdoe Castle, co. Roscommon. She *d.* 13 Oct. 1863. He *d.* 2 Nov. 1838, having by her had issue,
2. PHILIP PETER MILL, of whom presently.
3. Henry Hugh, *b.* 1831, *d.s.p.* 1870.
4. Charles Thomas, Lieut.-Col. late 1st Batt. Rifle Brigade (*Cotswold House, Winchester*), *b.* 3 March, 1836; *m.* 7 April, 1875, Lady Harriot Emily, sister of the 1st Marquess of Zetland, and has issue,
  1. Charles Hamilton de St. Pierre, Capt. Yorkshire Regt., *b.* 23 Sept. 1877; *m.* 22 Nov. 1905, Dorothy Agnes, eldest dau. of Herbert Hughes, C.M.G., of Ashdell Grove, Sheffield, and has issue,
    Sylvia Dorothy Mary, 2 Nov. 1909.
  2. Wilfred Joseph, *b.* 1882; *m.* 24 Sept. 1908, Dorothy Beresford, dau. of Major A. J. Preston, of Aislaby Lodge, Yorkshire, and has issue, a dau., *b.* Nov. 1909.
  3. Bertram John, *b.* 1887.
  4. Evelyn James, *b.* 1888.
  1. Mary Beatrice Theresa, *b.* 1879.
  2. Cecilia Mary, *b.* 1891.
5. Francis Hamilton, *b.* 1839, *d.s.p.* 1858.
1. Alice Mary Delphine, *b.* 1823, *d. unm.* 1899.
2. Elizabeth Catherine, *b.* 1827, *m.* 1854, Count Constantine Jasienski.
3. Anne Maria, *b.* 1829, a Carmelite nun; *d.s.p.* 1906.
4. Alicia Belinda, *b.* 1833, *m.* Count Alexander Jasienski, and *d.* 1885, leaving a son.

The eldest son by the second marriage,
PHILIP PETER MILL BUNBURY, Capt. 7th Dragoon Guards, *b.* 23 March, 1824; *m.* 12 Jan. 1865, Georgina, dau. of Peter MacEvoy, of Wimbledon, Surrey, and Great Cumberland Place. She *d.* 30 May, 1885. He *d.* 25 July, 1894, having had issue,
HAMILTON JOSEPH, now of Cranavonane.
Mary Alicia, *b.* 1867, a nun of the Order of the Good Shepherds.

Arms—Arg. on a bend sa. three chess rooks of the field. **Crest**—Two swords saltirewise passing through the mouth of a leopard's face or, the blades ppr, hilts gold. *Motto*—Firmum in vita nihil.

Estate—Cranavonane, co. Carlow. *Residence*—Denham Lodge, Weston Underwood, Olney. *Clubs*—Boodle's and Wellington.

M'CLINTOCK-BUNBURY.
See **RATHDONNELL, B.**

BUNBURY-TIGHE. *See* TIGHE

BURDETT OF COOLFIN AND BALLYMANY.

ARTHUR HUGO DE BURDET BURDETT, of Ballymany, co. Kildare, and Coolfin, King's Co., J.P. and High Sheriff for the latter co. 1896, late Capt. 4th Batt. Royal Dublin Fusiliers, *b.* 27 March, 1863, educated at Eton; *m.* 23 July, 1884. Henrietta Maude, youngest dau. of the late Robert St. George, of Ivy Lodge, Ballinasloe, and grand-dau. of Sir Richard Bligh St. George, 2nd bart. of Woodsgift, co. Kilkenny (*see* BURKE'S *Peerage*) and has issue,

1. ARTHUR ST. GEORGE, *b.* 19 July, 1895, educated at Eton.
1. Grace Sophia, *b.* 21 Dec. 1885.
2. Maude, *b.* 8 Dec. 1889.

Lineage.—THE REV. GEORGE BURDETT, M.A., Dean of Leighlin 1668, *d.* 1671, administration of his goods being granted to his son, Thomas Burdett, of Garryhill, co. Carlow (father of Thomas Burdett, created a Baronet). Another and younger son,
SAMUEL BURDETT, settled at Lismalin, co. Tipperary. He *m.* Judith, dau. of Capt. Thomas Evatt, and left at his decease, 1664, two sons : the elder, George, of Lismalin, *d.s.p.* ; the younger,
THE VERY REV. JOHN BURDETT, Dean of Clonfert, *m.* Margaret, 5th dau. of Sir John Cole, Bart. of Newland, co. Dublin, and dying 1726, left, with other issue, a dau. Lettice, wife of Algernon Warren, of Kilkenny, and a son,
ARTHUR BURDETT, of Lismalin, who *m.* 1725, Grace, dau. of John Head, of Derry Castle, and had (with three daus., one of whom, Grace, *m.* Barry, 1st Earl of Farnham) two sons, Arthur Burdett, of Bellaville, High Sheriff co. Kildare 1791, who *d.* 1796, *s.p.*; and
GEORGE BURDETT, of the Heath House, Queen's Co., sometime Cornet and Lieut. in the "Black Horse," M.P. for Thomastown and Callan in the last Irish Parliament. He was *b.* 1735; *m.* Jane, 2nd dau. of John Frend, and *d.* 1817, leaving issue,
1. ARTHUR, of whom presently.
2. George, of Longtown House, co. Kildare, Capt. R.N., *m.* 1st, Mary Jane, dau. of the late Lieut.-Gen. Whitelock, and 2nd, Catherine Dorothea, only dau. and heiress of the late Col. William Browne, of Glengarry, co. Dublin, by whom he had issue,
 1. George, *m.* Harriet, dau. of William Willan, and *d.s.p.*
 1. Frances Elizabeth, *m.* Thomas Pery Knox, who *d.* 1893. She *d.* 1900.
 2. Catherine Jane, *m.* 1836, Richard Brouncker, of Boveridge, Dorset (*see that family*), and is dec.
3. JOHN (Rev.), of Cushcallow, King's Co., Vicar of Rynagh and Gallen, King's Co., and Rector of Ballygarth, co. Meath, *b.* 1775; *m.* 4 Dec. 1802, Margaret Anne, 6th dau. of Michael Head, D.L., of Derry Castle, co. Tipperary, by Margaret, his wife, 6th dau. of Henry Prittie, of Kilboy, in the same co., aunt to the 1st Lord Dunalley, and had issue,
 1. John Head, of Hunstanton, and Cushcallow, King's Co., J.P., Barrister-at-Law, *b.* 27 Oct. 1809; *m.* 20 July, 1842, his 1st cousin, Adelaide Louisa, youngest dau. of Arthur Burdett, of Ballymany, co. Kildare (*see infra*), and *d.s.p.* 4 March, 1870. His widow *d.* 20 Jan. 1905.
 2. Henry (Rev.), Rector of Ballybay co. Monaghan, *b.* 5 Dec. 1812; *m.* 23 June, 1842, Sybilla, dau. of Thomas Fleetwood, of Banagher. She *d.* 1907. He *d.* 1875, leaving issue,
  (1) Henry Plantagenet (Rev.) (5, Colleton Crescent, Exeter), Rector of St. Mary's Steps, Exeter, *b.* 1853; *m.* 1892, Maria Louisa, dau. of John Curry, of Farcham, Hants.
  (2) John Head (15, *Waldemar Avenue, Ealing*), *b.* 1855; *m.* 1882, Ada, dau. of the late Rev. Moses Leatham, and has had issue,
   1. John Head, L.R.C.P. and M.R.C.S.E., *b.* 1884, is Surgeon R.N.
   2. Henry Leatham, *b.* 1887.
   3. Charles Plantagenet, *b.* 1890.
   4. Cyril Trench, *b.* 1896.
   1. Katherine Adelaide, *b.* 1882 ; *d.* 1892.
   2. Sybil Mary, *b.* 1885.
  (1) Louisa Jane, *b.* 1860.
 3. Arthur Michael, *b.* 1815 ; *d. unm.* 1 Feb. 1847.
 4. George Prittie, *b.* 1817 ; *d. unm.* 21 June, 1893.
 5. Francis Robert, *b.* 1822 ; *d. unm.* 28 Nov. 1843.
 1. Margaret Anne, *d.* 1850, *unm.*
 2. Jane, *d.* 1883 *unm.*
 3. Grace, *m.* 2 Jan. 1834, John Eyre Trench, of Clonfert House, co. Galway (*see* TRENCH *of Clonfert*), and had issue. She *d.*
24 Jan. 1889. Her 3rd dau. Grace, *m.* 25 March, 1862, her cousin Arthur Burdett, Esq., late of Coolfin (*see below*), and *d.* 17 April, 1863, leaving issue an only son, the present ARTHUR HUGO BURDETT, of Coolfin.
 4. Maria, *d.* 1854.
 5. Louisa, *m.* Col. Dawes, Bengal Art., and *d.* in India 1857 leaving issue.
1. Grace, *m.* Col. Henry Peisley L'Estrange, of Moystown, King's Co., and is dec.
2. Jane, *m.* Francis Brooke, Lieut.-Col. 4th King's Own Regt. of Foot, and brother of the late Sir Henry Brooke, of Colebrook, Bart., and is dec.

The eldest son,
ARTHUR BURDETT, of Ballymany, and Ballywalter, who purchased the Coolfin Estate in 1836, *b.* 1770; *m.* 1810, Anna, only dau. of William Ripley, of Liverpool, and *d.* 1842, having by her (who *d.* 1859) had issue,
1. GEORGE, his heir.
2. ARTHUR, late representative.
1. Mary Jane, *b.* 1812 ; *m.* 1848, Lieut.-Col. Robert Brookes, 24th Regt., who was killed at the battle of Chilianwallah, 1849 ; she *d.* 29 July, 1895.
2. Anna, *b.* 1815 ; *m.* 1842, Edward John Collingwood, of Lilburn Tower, and Churton House, co. Northumberland (*see that family*), and *d.* 1879, leaving issue. He *d.* 1895.
3. Adelaide Louisa, *b.* 1817 ; *m.* 1842, her cousin, John Head Burdett, of Hunstanton, King's Co., who *d.* 4 March, 1870 (*see above*). She *d.* 20 Jan. 1905.

The eldest son,
GEORGE BURDETT, of Ballymany, and of Ballywalter, co. Tipperary, *b.* 25 Sept. 1813 ; *d.s.p.* in 1875, and was *s.* by his only brother.
ARTHUR BURDETT, of Ballymany, also of Ballywalter, co. Tipperary, and Coolfin, King's Co., *b.* 1 Sept. 1814, J.P. for King's Co., High Sheriff 1877, B.A. Trin. Coll. Dublin ; *m.* 1st, 25 March, 1862, his cousin, Grace Florinda, 3rd dau. of John Eyre Trench, of Clonfert House, co. Galway (*see that family*), by whom (who *d.* 17 April, 1863) he had issue,
ARTHUR HUGO DE BURDET, now of Ballymany and Coolfin.
He *m.* 2ndly, 18 Dec. 1875, Emma Wyke, youngest dau. of Major Francis Russell Eagar, 31st Regt. She *d.s.p.* 29 Sept. 1901. He *d.* 16 Jan. 1884, and was *s.* by his only son.

Arms—Paly of six arg. and az. on a bend gu. three martlets or.
Crest—On a tower arg. a martlet with wings displayed or.
Seat—Coolfin, near Banagher, King's Co. **Clubs**—Kildare Street, Dublin, Sports, S.W., and Royal St. George Yacht, Kingstown.

BURGES OF PARKANAUR.

YNYR ALFRED BURGES, of Parkanaur, co. Tyrone. *b.* 16 April, 1900 ; *s.* his grandfather 14 Aug. 1908.

Lineage.—SAMUEL BURCHES, *b.* 1645 ; *m.* 1684, Margaret Williams, of Llan Elian, in N. Wales, and had two sons,
1. David, *b.* 1685, who *m.* Elizabeth Cust, and was for some years Rector of St. Mark's Church, Dublin.
2. JOSEPH, of whom presently.

Both brothers eventually moved northwards to the city of Armagh during the primacy of Archbishop Lindsay, with whom they were connected. The younger son,
JOSEPH BURCHES, *b.* 1689, and bapt. next day (for the times were again troublous) at St. Michlan's Church, Dublin ; *m.* 1716, Elizabeth, dau. of Ynyr Lloyd, of East Ham, Essex (Deputy Secretary of the East India Company), and had (with two daus. Margaret, and Alice, wife of Francis Methold) three sons,
1. Joseph (Rev.), *d.* 1746. 2. JOHN, of whom hereafter.
3. YNYR, of East Ham, who held an influential post in the East India Company, and was offered the baronetcy subsequently conferred on his son-in-law. He was *b.* 1723 ; *m.* 1747, Margaret, dau. of Governor Browne, and *d.* 1792, leaving issue, a dau. and heir,
Margaret, *m.* 1st, 1771, Sir John Smith, Bart., who took the additional surname of BURGES, but *d.s.p.* 24 April, 1803 ; his widow *m.* 2ndly, 23 July, 1810, John, 4th Earl Poulett, of Hinton St. George, Somerset, but *d.s.p.* 27 May, 1838, when her kinsman, JOHN YNYR BURGES, *s.* her in her estates.

The 2nd son,
JOHN BURGES, *b.* 1722 ; *m.* 20 Nov. 1763, Martha, dau. of Robert Ford, and *d.* 1790, leaving issue (with two daus. Mary, *m.* 1784, George Perry, of Seskinore, co. Tyrone ; and Martha, *m.* 1787, James Johnston, of Knappagh, co. Armagh) a son,

JOHN HENRY BURGES, of Wood Park, co. Armagh, b. 15 July, 1766; m. 1794, Marianne, eldest dau. and eventually co-heir of Sir Richard Johnston, Bart., of Guildford, and had issue,
 1. JOHN YNYR, of Parkanaur and East Ham. 2. Richard, dec.
 1. Margaret Anne, m. July, 1815, Gen. Thomas Charretie, of the 2nd Life Guards, who d. Jan. 1866. She d. 1869.
 2. Matilda, d. Nov. 1805.
The only surviving son,
 JOHN YNYR BURGES, of Parkanaur, co. Tyrone and Thorpe Hall, and East Ham, Essex, J.P. and D.L., High Sheriff, co. Tyrone 1829, b. 31 Jan. 1708 ; m. 21 March, 1833, Lady Caroline Clements, youngest dau. of Nathaniel, 2nd Earl of Leitrim, K.P., and d. 20 April, 1889, having by her (who d. 12 Oct. 1869) had issue,
 1. YNYR HENRY, late of Parkanaur.
 2. Charles Skeffington, b. 19 Aug. 1835 ; d. 1845.
 3. Clements Keppel, d. March, 1840.
 4. John Richard Alexander Wamphray, b. 25 Aug. 1843 ; d. 1850,
 1. Mary Anne Margaret.
 2. Alice Caroline m. Col. Francis Brodigan, of Piltown House, Drogheda. He d. 8 March, 1910.
 COL. YNYR HENRY BURGES, of Parkanaur, co. Tyrone, J.P. and D.L., High Sheriff 1869 ; formerly Commanding 6th Brigade N.I. Div. R.A. ; b. 31 Jan. 1834 ; m. 1st, 7 Sept. 1859, Hon. Edith Bootle-Wilbraham, 3rd dau. of the late Hon. Richard Bootle-Wilbraham, and sister of 1st Earl of Lathom, and by her (who d. 2 Feb. 1894) had issue,
 1. YNYR RICHARD PATRICK, High Sheriff co. Tyrone 1898, b. 15 March, 1866 ; m. 23 Oct. 1895, Frederica Florence Elizabeth, eldest dau. of the late Alfred Gillett (see GILLETT of Banbury), and d.v.p. 20 Dec. 1905, having had issue,
  1. YNYR ALFRED, now of Parkanaur.
  2. Richard Ynyr, b. 21 Aug. 1901.
  3. Patrick Claud, b. 14 June, 1905.
  1. Winifred Edith, b. 12 Oct. 1896 ; d. 9 Jan. 1897.
  2. Margaret Elizabeth, b. 18 Sept. 1903.
 2. John Ynyr Wilbraham, b. 13 Feb. 1871 ; d.s.p. 8 Jan. 1895.
 1. Edith Alice, m. 16 Oct. 1895, Arthur Howard Frere, elder son of the late Philip Howard Frere, of Dungate and Paston House, Cambridge, and has issue (see BURKE's Family Records).
 2. Ethel Margaret, m. 7 Oct. 1885, Sir James Henry Stronge, Bart., and has issue (see BURKE's Peerage).
 3. Lilian Adela, b. 1864, d. 1870.
 4. Myrtle Constance, m. 22 Sept. 1900, John Marcus Poer O'Shee, and has issue (see O'SHEE of Gardenmorris).
 5. Beatrice Annette, b. and d. 1873.
 6. Irene Caroline, m. 9 Feb. 1898, Ernald Edward Richardson, who d. 7 July, 1900, leaving issue (see RICHARDSON of Glanbrydan).
Col. Burges m. 2ndly, 5 May, 1896, Mary, dau. of George Pearce, of Bishop's Lydeard, and d. 14 Aug. 1908, being s. by his grandson.
 Arms—Quarterly : 1st and 4th, or, a fess chequy arg. and az., in chief two cross-crosslets gu. and in base a covered cup of the last, for BURGES ; 2nd, paly of eight or and gu., all within a bordure of the first pelletée, for LLOYD ; 3rd, arg., a saltire sa., on a chief gu., three cushions or, for JOHNSTON. Crests—1. A dove rising arg., beaked and membered gu., in its beak a palm branch ppr., for BURGES ; 2. a lion rampant gu., langued az., in the dexter paw an annulet, enclosing a fleur-de-lis arg., for LLOYD. Motto—Tace aut face.
 Seat—Parkanaur, Castle Caulfeild, co. Tyrone.

BURKE OF BALLYDUGAN.

MICHAEL HENRY BURKE, of Ballydugan, co. Galway, J.P., b. 6 July, 1853 ; m. 1901, Ethel Maud, dau. of Robert Henry, of Toghermore (see HENRY of Lodge), and has issue,
 WILLIAM ST. GEORGE, b. 1902.

Lineage.—MICHAEL BURKE, of Ballintober, co. Roscommon, who purchased Ballydugan, 1726, from the Lynch family, was son of William Burke,* of the Clogheroge branch of the family, by his wife a dau. o. aly, of Cloncha. He m. 1st, Miss Flynn ; 2ndly, Miss Dillon, of Clonbrook ; and 3rdly, Mary, dau. of Burke, of Meelick. By the first two he had no issue, but by the 3rd, he was father of
 1. WILLIAM, his heir.
 1. Honora, m. Andrew Blake, of Furbough.
 2. Marcella, m. Malachy Daly, of Benmore.
Mr. Burke's will bears date 12 Jan. 1735. His son and heir,
 WILLIAM BURKE, of Ballintober, co. Roscommon and Ballydugan, co. Galway, m. Mabel, dau. of Malachy Donelan, of Bally Donelan, co. Galway, by Mary his wife, dau. of Thomas Power Daly, eldest son of the Right Hon. Denis Daly, of Carrownekelly, 2nd Justice of the Common Pleas, temp. JAMES II, and was father of
 MICHAEL BURKE, of Ballydugan, M.P. for Athenry, a Director of Inland Navigation and one of the Surveyors-General for Ireland, who served as High Sheriff of the co. of Galway 1780, and for the town of Galway 1796. He m. Sarah, only child of John Morgan, of Monksfield, co. Galway, by Sarah his wife, 3rd dau. of Francis Ormsby, of Willowbrook, co. Sligo, and by her (who d. 11 Oct. 1813) had issue,
 1. WILLIAM MALACHY, of Ballydugan.
 2. John (Rev.), Vicar of Kilcolgan, co. Galway, Provost of Kilmacduagh, and Prebendary of Kilconnell, m. Mary Anne, sister of Arthur Guinness, of Beaumont, near Dublin, and dying 1842, left,
  1. MICHAEL JOHN, of Canterbury, N.Z., Barrister-at-Law, d. 1869, leaving issue. 2. Arthur, d. in Australia.
  3. William, Barrister-at-Law, m. 6 April, 1858, Anne, eldest dau. of the late Stephen W. Creaghe, and d. 12 July, 1908 having had issue.
  4. Edward Frederick, of Gortmore, Dundrum, co. Dublin, m. Miss Nutting, of Clifton, and d. 2 Nov. 1887 (his widow m. 2ndly, 10 April, 1889, Henry Wyatt, Commander P. and O. Service).
  5. John, m. Miss Watson, and has issue.
  1. Elizabeth. 2. Mabel Maria, wife of Thomas Trouton.
  3. Louisa.
 3. Michael, Collector of Excise, and formerly a Magistrate for co. Galway, d. unm. 1846.
 4. Thomas, of Belvedere Place, Dublin, m. Louisa, relict of Thomas Burke, of Spring Garden, co. Galway, and dau. of Dominick Daly, by Johanna Larriet his wife, sister of the 1st Lord Wallscourt, and d.s.p.
 5. Henry (Rev.), m. Francis Juile, only dau. of Val. Blake, of Lehinch, co. Mayo, by Anna Maria his wife, dau. of the Hon. and Rev. Richard Henry Roper, son of Lord Teynham, and had Michael, George, and other issue.
 6. Denis, of Fortlands, co. Galway, m. Maria, dau. of the late Major Graham, and left issue,
 Michael Charles Christopher, of Ballinahone House, co. Armagh, who d. 13 Dec. 1901, having m. Amy Mary (d. 24 July, 1898), dau. of Rev. Robert Jervois, by whom he left issue,
  (1) Denis Charles, Capt. 3rd Batt. Roy. Irish Fus., b. 13 June, 1876 ; m. Merili, dau. of Peter Griffin, of Alta Villa, co. Limerick.
  (2) Robert Jervois, b. 28 Sept. 1879.
  (3) Charles James, Lieut. 18th Roy. Irish Regt., b. 9 March, 1882 ; m. 28 April, 1909, Beatrice Osborn, 3rd dau. of W. Shakspeare, of 42 Prince's Gardens, S.W., and of Yateley, Glos.
  (1) Amy Mary, b. 1 May, 1877 ; m. Charles Arthur Maunsell, of Finnettcrstown.
  (2) Charlotte Helen, b. 19 July, 1878 ; m. Lieut. Alexander R. Palmer, R.N.
  (3) Olive Edith, b. 1883 ; d. unm. 10 May, 1886.
 Frances, m. Dominick Burke of Cahernagarry, co. Galway.
 1. Sarah, d. unm. 1852.
 2. Mabel, m. 1832, Rev. James Temple Nansel, M.A., and has issue.
Mr. Burke, who sold, under an Act of Parliament, the fee simple estate of Ballintober, d. 1838, and was s. by his eldest son,
 WILLIAM MALACHY BURKE, of Ballydugan, Barrister-at-Law, High Sheriff of co. Galway 1822, b. 1784 ; m. Anna Maria, only dau. of John Blake, of Windfield, and by her (who d. 1847) left at his decease, Jan. 1853,
 1. MICHAEL, of Ballydugan.
 2. John William (Rev.), Chaplain to the Earl of Tankerville, B.A. Cambridge ; b. 1817 ; m. 1881, Croasdella, younger dau. of Croasdaile Bowen-Miller, of Milford, co. Mayo, J.P. He d. 16 Nov. 1901.
 3. William Malachy, M.D., of St. Stephen's Green, Dublin, F.R.C.P.I., Registrar-General for Ireland, Physician to Stephen's Hospital ; m. 1852, Harriet Isabella, only dau. of the Rev. Hugh Hamilton, of Churchill, co. Fermanagh, by Elizabeth his wife, sister of the late Sir Thomas Staples, Bart., and d. leaving issue, three sons,
  1. William Henry Marsh, Capt. King's Own L.I. South Yorkshire Regt., b. 9 April, 1850 ; d. at Belfast.
  2. John Albert, b. 18 Feb. 1862.
  3. Edmund, b. 5 March, 1865.
  1. Grace Elizabeth Anna Maria, m. 1877, Andrew Jameson, B.A. Cambridge, 2nd son of the late Andrew Jameson, of Alloa, N.B
 4. Thomas James (Rev.), Rector of Babeury, Somerset. m. 1856, Miss Fraser, and d. 24 May, 1897, leaving issue,
  1. William Henry, B.A., M.B., B.Ch., D.P.H. Trin. Coll. Dublin, Lieut.-Col. Indian Medical Service (ret.), b. 5 Nov. 1858 ; m. 17 April, 1890, Edith Louisa, dau. of the late Thomas Trouton, of Clouskeagh, co. Dublin, and has issue,
   (1) Reginald Valentine, 2nd Lieut. Connaught Rangers, b. 14 Feb. 1891.
   (2) Rudolph Edmund Maurice.
  1. Mabel Mary.
  2. Henrietta Louisa, m. 15 Sept. 1880, Brabazon Newcomen Casement, 2nd son of John Casement, of Magherintemple, co. Antrim, J.P., and d. Nov. 1881.
  3. Emily Florence.
 5. Edmund, Barrister-at-Law, A.B., ex-Scholar and Classical Moderator, Trin. Coll. Dublin, and Professor of History in the Elphinstone Coll. Bombay, d. on his way home, 1864.
  1. Mary, d. unm. 1891. 2. Sarah, d. unm. 1878.
  3. Caroline Frances, d. 1817.
The eldest son,
 REV. MICHAEL BURKE, A.M., of Ballydugan, co. Galway, formerly Incumbent of Castle Archdall, co. Fermanagh, m. 1848, Isabella, dau. of James Clarke, Capt. 12th Lancers, and niece of Mrs. Archdall, of Castle Archdall, and d. 29 Jan. 1886, leaving issue,
 1. William Malachy James, b. 14 March, 1851 ; d. 1864.
 2. MICHAEL HENRY, now of Ballydugan.
 3. John Hawley, Capt. West Yorkshire Regt., b. 28 June, 1854 ; m. 17 Feb. 1888, Mary Alice, eldest dau. of Col. Henry Vansittart Riddell, Divisional Judge, Lahore, and d. in India, 24 Oct. 1887, having had by her (who m. 2ndly, John Burke), with other issue, Noel Michael, b. 11 Dec. 1885.
 4. Thomas Edmund, Capt. King's Own Royal Lancashire Regt., b. 24 Aug. 1856.
 5. George Selwyn, b. 9 July, 1858.

---
* A brother of this William Burke, entered the Neapolitan service and attained high military rank at Naples.

Burke. THE LANDED GENTRY. 86

1. Eliza Martha.
2. Isabella Mary, *m.* to Edward Cripps Villiers, J.P., of Beech Hill, co. Galway
Seat—Ballydugan, near Lughrea.

URKE OF OWER (now TEELING).

MARGARET MARY, MRS. LUKE TEELING, of Ower, co. Galway, only child of the late WILLIAM JOSEPH BURKE, of Ower, *s.* her father 1895; *m.* 8 Sept. 1898, LUKE ALEXANDER TEELING, Accountant-General of the Supreme Court of Judicature, Ireland, J.P., cos. Galway and Mayo, and has issue,
LUKE WILLIAM BURKE, *b.* 5 Feb. 1903.

Mr. Teeling is the son of Charles George Teeling and the grandson of Charles Hamilton Teeling, who was the son of Luke Teeling, who took a prominent part in the political movements in Ireland in the 18th century.

Lineage.—SIR REDMOND DE BURGH, 2nd son of ULICK DE BURGH, and younger brother of RICKARD OGE, *MacWilliam Oughter*, Chief of all the Burkes, ancestor of the Marquess of Clanricarde (see BURKE's *Peerage*), had issue, a son,
JOHN BUY (The Yellow), of Castle Hacket, co. Galway, founded the powerful sept of John Buy McRedmond. His son,
MILES DE BURGH (or BURKE), of Castle Hacket, living there about 1480, left a son,
REDMOND DE BURGH, of Castle Hacket, who left issue, a son,
ULICK BURKE, of Castle Hacket, and Cahirmorris, and a great estate adjoining, *d.* 1571, as appears from an inquisition taken in Galway, 1586. His eldest son,
JOHN BURKE, of Castle Hacket, *m.* Margaret, dau. of Thady Kelly, of Mullaghmore, a descendant of the ancient Princes of Hymaine, and by her left a son,
ULICK BURKE, of Castle Hacket. *m.* Honora Bourke, dau. of Viscount Mayo, and grand-dau. of the celebrated Grana Uaile (Queen of the Owles), and had issue, JOHN, his heir; Catherine, *m.* Andrew Browne, of Brownestown; Isabella, *m.* The O Conor Don. Ulick Burke, after the massacre of Shruel, in which many Protestants were slain, harboured the Protestant Bishop of Killala and others, as appears by a letter from the Bishop to the Marquess of Clanricarde, dated from Castle Hacket. Ulick and his son are mentioned in Lord Clanricarde's memoirs as persons whose adhesion was important for the pacification of the county. The property of Castle Hacket was created by JAMES I. in 1619, the manor of Castle Hacket in favour of Ulick. The son and heir,
JOHN BURKE, of Castle Hacket, forfeited, during the confiscations, the greater portion of his estates, retaining, however, Ower, part of the ancient property. He *m.* Mary Bermingham, dau. of the 17th Lord Athenry, Premier Baron of Ireland, by whom he left at his death, 1684 or 1685,
1. ULICK, of whom presently.
2. Francis, *m.* Margaret, dau. of Darby Daly, of Killimore.
3. Thomas, *m.* Mary, dau. of Edward Hearne, of Hearnesbrook.
The son and successor,
ULICK BURKE, of Ower, *m.* Catherine, dau. of Stephen Lynch, of Doughiskea (descended from James Lynch FitzStephen, the Mayor of Galway 1493), by Ellinor, dau. of Sir John Browne, Bart., of The Neale, ancestor of Lord Kilmaine. By her he left at his death, in 1716,
1. John, *d.s.p.*, a Capt. in Gen. Dillon's Regt. in France.
2. MYLES, of whom presently.
3. Dominick, whose son, Myles, *m.* Catherine, dau. of Sir Walter Blake, Bart., of Menlo, and left issue,
  1. Myles, *m.* Catherine, grand-dau. of Dominick Blake, of Castle Grove, by his wife, dau. of Sir Joseph Hoare, Bart., and left issue (1) Myles ; (2) Walter ; (3) William; and (1) Eliza, *m.* Charles, son of Charles Peshall.
  2. Stephen, *m.* Julia, sister of the foregoing Catherine, and had issue, (1) Myles ; (2) Joseph ; (3) Walter ; (4) Stephen ; (1) Eliza ; (2) Catherine ; (3) Elly.
  1. Maria, *m.* Martin Kirwan, of Hillsbrook, co. Galway.
The 2nd son,
MYLES BURKE, of Ower, who *s.* his father, *m.* Mary, dau. of Stephen Lynch Fitz-Thomas, of Tubberoe, and niece of Sir Dominick Browne, and by her left issue,
1. John, a Franciscan friar.
2. Stephen, of Ower, *m.* Marcella, dau. of James Martin, of Ross, and left issue,
Barbara, *m.* 1785, Mark Lynch, by whom she had, Patrick Marcus Lynch, of Duras, and Renmore, co. Galway (*see that family*).
3. Dominick, *d.s.p.*   4. Francis, *d.s.p.*
5. WILLIAM, of whom presently.
1. Jane, *m.* Henry Jordan, of Rosslevin.
2. Barbara, *m.* 10 April, 1751, Sir Walter Blake, 10th Bart., of Menlo Castle, and had issue (see BURKE's *Peerage*).
The 5th son,
WILLIAM BURKE, of Ower, *s.* his brother, and *m.* 1775, Teresa Kirwan, of Hillsbrook, co. Galway, by whom (who *d.* 1791) he left at his death in 1801,
1. John, of Ower J.P. co. Galway, an officer of the 79th and 38th Regts., served in the Peninsular War ; *m.* Maria, eldest dau. of Oliver Martyn, M.D., of Galway, and *d.s.p.* 3 Oct. 1849.
2. JOSEPH, of whom presently.

3. Francis, the mathematician, *m.* Catherine, dau. of Ulick Jenings, of Ironpool (*see that family*), and left issue by her,
  1. William (Rev.), in the Church of Rome.
  2. Ulick.   3. John.
  1. Bessy.   2. Teresa.
4. Stephen, } both *d.* without issue.
5. William, }
1. Mary, *m.* James Garvey, of Tully, co. Mayo. She *m.* 2ndly, Major Allen, and left issue.
2. Julia, *m.* Francis Leigh, Surgeon in the 60th Rifles, and left issue.
3. Barbara, *m.* Bartholomew St. Leger, of Ballyheragh, co. Mayo, and had issue.
4. Bridget, a nun.
The 2nd son,
JOSEPH BURKE, of Ower, J.P., *b.* 8 July, 1781 ; *m.* 9 April, 1823, Margaret, 3rd dau. of Oliver Martyn, M.D., of Galway, of the family of the MARTYNS *of Tillyra*, and by her (who *d.* 1872) had issue,
1. WILLIAM JOSEPH, late of Ower.
2. Oliver, Barrister-at-Law, Knight of the Order of St. Gregory the Great, author of many works ; *d.* 1889.
3. John, M.D., of Manila ; *b.* 30 Nov. 1832 ; *m.* 6 Feb. 1869, Victoria, only dau. and heir of Benjamin Butler, of Manila, and *d.* 20 Sept. 1886, leaving issue,
  1. Joseph Butler, *b.* 8 Dec. 1869 ; *d.* 10 Sept. 1911.
  2. John Benjamin Butler, M.A., Fellow of Owens Coll. Manchester, author of various scientific papers, educated at Trin. Coll. Dublin, and Trin. Coll. Camb., *b.* 4 Nov. 1871.
  3. William Joseph Butler, of Manila, M.D. Trin. Coll. Dublin, *b.* 17 Feb. 1873.
    1. Mary, *m.* Fernand O. Desbarats, of Bordeaux, and has issue, Victoria Charlotte.
4. Richard, M.D., Knight of the Order of Isabella the Catholic, *d.s.p.* 28 Sept. 1883.
1. Elizabeth, *m.* Thomas O'Conor Donelan, J.P., of Sylan, and by him (who *d.* 1874) has issue (*see that family*).
2. Teresa, *d. unm.*
3. Maria, *d. unm.* 18 Sept. 1896.
Mr. Burke *s.* his brother, 3 Oct. 1849 ; and *d.* 14 May, 1861, and was *s.* by his eldest son,
WILLIAM JOSEPH BURKE, of Ower, co. Galway, J.P., Barrister-at-Law, *b.* 1 May, 1825 ; *m.* 10 June, 1858, Barbara Ellen, dau. of Thomas Blake Turner, of St. John's Abbey, co. Galway. She *d.* 26 Feb. 1891. He *d.* 2 Sept. 1895, having had issue, a dau.,
MARGARET MARY, now of Ower.

Arms (of BURKE)—Or, a cross gu. in the dexter canton a lion rampant sa. Crest—A chained cat sejant guardant ppr. Motto—Ung roy, ung foy, ung loy. Arms (of TEELING)—Or, two pallets dancettée gu. Crest—A fleur-de-lys per pale dancettée or and gu. Motto—Sola virtus invicta.

Seat—Ower, near Headford. co. Galway. Residence—Bartra, Eglinton Road, Dublin.

BURKE (now MAXWELL) OF ISSERCLERAN.

ANNE CELESTINE BURKE, of Issercleran, co. Galway, *m.* 1st, 4 Nov. 1856, Major Frances Horatio de Vere, R.E. (who *d.* 22 Aug. 1865), youngest son of Sir Aubrey de Vere, 2nd bart. of Curragh Chase, co. Limerick, and had three daus.,
1. Mary, *m.* 1st, 1879, Major William Utting Cole, 3rd Dragoon Guards, eldest son of W. H. Cole, of Westwoodhay House, co. Berks. He *d.* 1892. She *m.* 2ndly, 19 April, 1894, Major Herbert William Studd, D.S.O., Coldstream Guards, and bas issue.
2. Eleanor Hester, *m.* 9 July, 1885, Sir Frederick William Shaw, Bart, D.S.O., of Bushey Park, and has issue (*see* BURKE's *Peerage and Baronetage*).
3. Margaret, *m.* 1st, 1886, Francis F. Joyce, who *d.* May, 1899, leaving issue. She *m.* 2ndly, Oct. 1909, Major Cyril Prescott Decie, R.A.

Mrs. de Vere *m.* 2ndly, 20 Feb. 1873. Rev. Charleton Maxwell (who *d.* July, 1895), J.P., formerly Rector of Leckpatrick, co. Tyrone.

Lineage.—JOHN BURKE, of Issercleran co. Galway, *m.* Jane, dau. of Michael Burke, of Cloughanover, a descendant of the Burkes of Castle Hacket, and had,with a dau., Ellen, wife of John Dolphin, of Turoe, a son and successor,
JAMES BURKE, of Issercleran, *m.* Penelope, dau. of Robert Hardiman, of Loughrea, and had, with a dau., who *m.* — Browne, of Gloves, co. Galway, a son,
JOHN HARDIMAN BURKE, of Issercleran, *m.* 1783 or 1784, Elizabeth, dau. of Andrew Armstrong, of Clara House, King's Co., by whom he h. d issuc,
1. JAMES HARDIMAN, his heir.
2. Robert, dec.   3. John.
1. Penelope, *m.* John Kirwan, of Castle Hacket, co. Galway.
2. Elizabeth, *m.* Christopher John Blake, of Winfield, co. Galway.
Mr. Burke took the name of HARDIMAN in addition to that of BURKE, pursuant to the will of his maternal uncle, Robert Hardiman, whose estates and property he inherited upon that gentleman's death, 1800. He *d.* Dec. 1808, and was *s.* by his son,
JAMES HARDIMAN BURKE, of Issercleran, sometime an officer 7th Fus., *b.* 1788 ; *m.* Oct. 1817, Anne, dau. of Robert O'Hara, of Raheen, co. Galway, and by her (who *d.* 1844) had issue.

1. JOHN, late of Isserelcran.
2. ROBERT O'HARA, *b.* 1821; an Officer in the Austrian Service, and distinguished for his command of the expedition across Australia, in the course of which he perished, 1861.
3. James Thomas, *b.* 1828; an Officer R.E., fell gallantly in Turkey, 1854.
1. Fanny Maria, *m.* John Blakeny, of Abbert, co. Galway.
2. Elizabeth, *m.* 1846, Lieut.-Col. W. C. Menzies, R.E.
3. HESTER ALBINIA, of Isserelcran, *d.* 1866.
4. ANNE CELESTINE, now of Isserelcran.

Mr. Burke, who served the Office of Sheriff, *d.* 9 Jan. 1854, and was *s.* by his eldest son,
  JOHN HARDIMAN BURKE, of St. Clerans, Lieut.-Col. 3rd Buffs, and previously Capt. 88th Connaught Rangers and A.D.C. to Sir John Burgoyne, during the Crimean War; he *d.* 7 Aug. 1863, and was *s.* by his sister, HESTER ALBINIA, who *d.* 1866, and was *s.* by her sister, ANNE CELESTINE, now of St. Clerans.

Seat—Isserelcran, Craughwell.

BURKE OF SPRINGFIELD.

IVAN SHULDHAM BURKE, of Springfield, Dalkey, co. Dublin, *b.*   *s.* his grandfather 23 March, 1908; *m.* 12 Jan. 1909, Aimée Muriel, dau. of Rev. Canon MacLulich.

Lineage.—MARTIN BURKE, of Springfield, co. Tipperary (who *d.* 1863), left issue by Anne, his wife, dau. of late Edmond Burke, of Roscrea, an eldest son,
  JAMES MILO BURKE, of Springfield, Dalkey, co. Dublin, J.P., D.L., B.A. Trin. Coll. Dublin, Barrister-at-Law, *b.* 1814; *m.* 1st, 1844, Eliza, dau. of C. Eiffe. She *d.* 1865, leaving issue,
  Martin John, Q.C., B.A. Trin. Coll. Dublin, *b.* 1848; *m.* 1881, Elizabeth, only dau. of Capt. William Barron Stanton, 91st Regt., and *d.v.p.* 1893, leaving issue by her (who *m.* 2ndly, Joseph Wallace Boyce, M.D., aud *d.* 1903), with one dau., a son,
  IVAN SHULDHAM, now of Springfield.
He *m.* 2ndly, Kate (*d.* 1894), dau. of James Ferguson, and *s.* by his grandson, 23 March, 1908, being *s.* by his grandson.

Residence—Springfield, Dalkey, co. Dublin.

BURKE. *See* BURKE'S PEERAGE, BURKE, Bart.

BURROWES OF STRADONE HOUSE.

THOMAS JAMES BURROWES, of Stradone House, co. Cavan, J.P. and D.L., High Sheriff 1902, *b.* 13 May, 1880; *s.* his father, 1893.

Lineage.—This family was established in Ireland by ROBERT BOROWES, who settled at Dumlane, co. Cavan, on the settlement of Ulster by King JAMES I. His eldest son and heir, THOMAS BOROWES, became possessed of Stradone, of which estate he also received a patent of confirmation from King CHARLES I, 1638.
  THOMAS BURROWES, of Stradone House, High Sheriff co. Cavan 1743, *m.* Jane, dau. of Thomas Nesbitt, of Lismore House, co. Cavan, and had issue,
1. ROBERT, of Stradone.
2. Thomas, of Dangan Castle, co. Meath, Col. H.E.I.C.S., *m.* 1st, Miss Greenland, and had a son,
  1. Arnold Robinson, Major Scots Fusilier Guards, who served through the Peninsular War as A.D.C. to Field-Marshal Viscount Beresford, *m.* Harriet, dau. of Richard Beresford, of Fenny Bentley, co. Derby, and had issue, several sons and daus.
 Col. Thomas Burrowes *m.* 2ndly, Hon. Frances Beresford, 4th dau. of William, 1st Lord Decies, Archbishop of Tuam, and had issue,
  2. William Nesbitt, Lieut.-Col. 17th Lancers, *m.* Susanna Henrietta Bermingham, dau. of Thomas Bermingham Daly Henry Sewell, and had issue,
   (1) Augustus, dec.   (2) W. Arnold, dec.
   (3) Henry Adrian, of Dangan Castle, co. Meath, *b.* 12 Feb. 1837; *d.* 27 Jan. 1886, having *m.* 1st. 1870, Rose, dau. of Aylmer Porter, by whom he had issue,

1a. Henry Adrian.
2a. Robert Aylmer.
1a. Edith Aylmer, *m.* 7 July, 1904, Stuart Palmer.
2a. Grace Mary, who *m.* 25 March, 1903, Capt. Edward Charles Massy, R.A.
He *m.* 2ndly, 6 April, 1880, Rose (16, *Boulevarde Douville, St. Servan, Ille et Vilaine, France*), dau. of Major F. P. Drury, by whom he had further issue,
3a. Patrick William, *b.* 16 Jan. 1881, Lieut. 25th Cavalry Frontier Force.
4a. Arnold Francis, Lieut. R.N., *b.* 27 Aug. 1882.
  1. Elizabeth, *m.* the Baron de Cetto, Bavarian Minister to the Court of St. James.
3. Arnold (Rev.), *d. unm.*   4. Cosby, *d. unm.* in India.
1. Margery, *d. unm.*
2. Anne, *m.* the Rev. William Wade, Rector of Dromore, co. Tyrone.
3. Martha, *d. unm.*
4. Jane, *m.* James Purefoy, of Woodfield, co. Galway.

The eldest son,
  ROBERT BURROWES, of Stradone House, High Sheriff co. Cavan 1773, *m.* Sophia, dau. of the Ven. Joseph Story, Archdeacon of Kilmore, and by her had (with four daus.), Jane, *m.* Samuel Moore, of Moyne Hall, co. Cavan; and Sophia, *m.* Brabazon Noble; Anne, *m.* Hon. and Very Rev. George Gore, Dean of Kilala; Frances, *d. unm.*), a son and heir,
  THOMAS BURROWES, of Stradone House, High Sheriff co. Cavan 1803, Major in the Army, *m.* 1807, Susan, dau. of the Rev. Henry Seward, of Badsey, co. Worcester, and had issue,
1. ROBERT, of Stradone.
2. James Edward, *b.* Nov. 1820; *m.* 1854, Mary Anne, 2nd dau. of John Nesbitt, of Lismore, co. Cavan, and *d.* leaving a son,
  THOMAS COSBY, of Lismore, co. Cavan (*see* BURROWES *of Lismore*).
3. Henry, *d.* young.
4. Honora Seward, *m.* 1835, the Hon. Thomas Leslie.
Mr. Burrowes *d.* April, 1836, and was *s.* by his eldest son,
  ROBERT BURROWES, of Stradone House, J.P. and D.L., High Sheriff 1838, and M.P. for Cavan 1855 to 1857, *b.* 19 March, 1810; *m.* 16 Oct. 1838, Anne Frances, only dau. of John Carden, of Barnane, co. Tipperary, and by her (who *d.* 1902) had issue,
1. Thomas, *b.* 17 July, 1839; *d.* an infant.
2. ROBERT JAMES, his heir.
3. Arnold Henry, *b.* 22 Oct. 1846; *d.* 1848.
1. Frances Susan, *m.* 2 Dec. 1869, Sir John Olpherts, C.V.O., D.L., of Ballyconnell, and has issue.
2. Honora, *d.* Feb. 1856.
3. Mary Anne Cecilia, *d.* Sept. 1854.
Mr. Burrowes *d.* 30 Nov. 1881. His only surviving son,
  ROBERT JAMES BURROWES, of Stradone House, co. Cavan, J.P. and D.L., High Sheriff 1883, *b.* 9 Sept. 1844, formerly Capt. 1st Dragoon Guards; *m.* 1 June, 1876, Ella (44, *Thurloe Square, S.W.*), dau. of Commodore Magruder, U.S. Navy, and niece of Major-Gen. J. B. Magruder, and *d.* 18 Dec. 1893, leaving issue,
1. THOMAS JAMES, now of Stradone.
2. Robert Philip, Capt. Rifle Brigade, *b.* 10 March, 1882.
1. Helena Mary, *b.* 6 June, 1877; *d.* 2 Oct. 1878.
2. Kathleen Fanny, *b.* 8 Oct. 1880; *m.* 12 Feb. 1907, Thomas George Wills-Sandford, of Willsgrove, co. Roscommon, and has issue (*see that family*).

Arms—Or on a cross gu. five mullets arg. in each chief quarter a lion passant sa., ducally crowned and langued of the second. *Crest*—A lion sejant guardant sa., ducally crowned or, langued gu. *Motto*—Non vi sed virtute.

Seat—Stradone House, Cavan.   *Residence*—22, Lowndes Street, S.W.   *Club*—Bachelors'.

BURROWES OF LISMORE.

THOMAS COSBY BURROWES, of Lismore, co. Cavan, J.P., D.L., High Sheriff 1888, *b.* 1856; *s.* his uncle Alexander Nesbitt, of Lismore, 1886; *m.* 15 April, 1885, the Hon. Anna Frances Maxwell, younger dau. of Hon. Richard Thomas Maxwell, of Fortland, co. Cavan, and sister of Somerset, 10th Lord Farnham (*see* BURKE'S *Peerage*), and has issue,
1. Eleanor Mary Cosby.   2. Rosamund Charlotte Cosby.

Lineage.—ANDREW NESBITT, of Brenter (presumed to be son of Thomas Nesbitt, of Newbottle, and grandson of George Nesbitt, who *d.* 1590), assignee from the Earl of Annandale, of the estates of Brenter and Malmusock, co. Donegal, was father of
  ANDREW NESBITT, who served in the army of CHARLES I. in Ireland, *m.* Anne Lindsay, and *d.* 1692, leaving four sons,
1. THOMAS, of whom hereafter.
2 Albert, an eminent merchant in London, sat in Parliament for the boroughs of Huntingdon and St. Michael; *m.* 24 Nov. 1729, Elizabeth, dau. of John Gould, and *d.* 1753, leaving a dau., Rachael, who *m.* Richard Bard Harcourt, of Pendley, Herts, and carried into the Harcourt family the estates of Brentner and Melmusock, which estates Thomas Nesbitt, after his settlement in Cavan, sold to his said brother Albert.
3. Robert, *m.* Margaret, younger dau. of Arnold Cosby.
4. Alexander, *m.* the dau. of John Gould, and *d.* 1743.
The eldest son,
  THOMAS NESBITT, of Grangemore, co. Westmeath, High Sheriff

Burtchaell. THE LANDED GENTRY. 88

1720, and M.P. for borough of Cavan 1715-50, *m*. 1st, 1701, Susan Lyons, by whom he had one son,
1. Charles Robert, who *d. unm.*
He *m*. 2ndly, 1713, Jane, dau. and heir of Arnold Cosby, of Lismore, co. Cavan (son of William Cosby, grandson of Arnold Cosby, great-grandson of Alexander Cosby and Dorcas Sidney, his wife). By this marriage, Thomas Nesbitt came into possession of Lismore and other estates in Cavan. He *d*. 1750, having by her had issue (with seven daus.) three sons,
2. Cosby, of whom presently.
3. William, *m*. Mary Blackwood.
4. Arnold, a merchant in London, *m*. Miss Thrale, sister of Henry Thrale of Streatham. He represented Cricklade, and afterwards Winchelsea, in Parliament, and *d.s.p.* 1765.

The 2nd son,
Cosby Nesbitt, of Lismore, M.P. for Cavan 1750-67, High Sheriff 1764, *b.* 1718 ; *s.* to the Cavan estates on the death of his father ; *m.* (setts. dated 17 Sept. 1743) Anne, dau. of John Enery, of Bawnboy, by Frances, sister of George Nixon, of Nixon Hal', co. Fermanagh (*see* Burke's *Family Records*). His will, dated 28 Nov. 1777, was proved 27 July, 1791. He had issue,
1. Thomas, of whom presently.
2. John, merchant in London, M.P. for Winchelsea, *d. unm.*
3. Cosby.
4. Albert (Rev.), D.D., Chaplain to the Prince Regent, Vicar of Denn, J.P., co. Cavan, *d. unm.* 30 Jan. 1822.
1. Mary.
2. Frances, *m*. William Moore, of Tullyvin, co. Cavan, and *d.* 27 March, 1833.
3. Jane, *m*. James Young, of Lahard, co. Cavan.
Mr. Nesbitt was *s.* by his eldest son,
Thomas Nesbitt, of Lismore, Col. in the Army, M.P. for Cavan, 1768-99, High Sheriff 1769, *m.* Feb. 1768, Louisa, youngest dau. and co-heir of John Daniel De Gennes, of Portarlington, Col. in the British Service, and left issue,
1. Cosby, his heir.   2. John, *s.* his brother.
3. Thomas, who left by Anne his wife, two sons and a dau.,
    1. John Albert, of Fort Hill, co. Cavan, J.P., *b.* 1811 ; *d.* 31 Dec. 1886.
    2. Thomas.
    1. Louisa, *m*. Major Moore, of The Rocks, Crossdoney.
Col. Nesbitt *d.* 1820, and was *s.* by his eldest son,
Cosby Nesbitt, of Lismore, J.P. and D.L., High Sheriff 1798, Major Cavan Militia, *b.* 20 Nov. 1769 ; *m.* Elizabeth Hancox, but *d.s.p.* 19 July, 1837, when the estates devolved upon his brother,
John Nesbitt, of Lismore House, J.P. and D.L., High Sheriff 1840, *m.* Elizabeth, dau. of John Tatam, of Moulton, co. Lincoln, and *d.* 1 Jan. 1853, leaving issue,
1. Cosby Thomas, of Lismore House, J.P., D.L., M.A. Oxon., *d. unm.* 30 April, 1856.
2. Alexander, of Lismore.
1. Frances.   2. Mary Anne, *s.* her brother.

The 2nd son,
Alexander Nesbitt, of Lismore House, co. Cavan, and Old Lands, co. Sussex, D.L., High Sheriff co. Cavan 1862, *b.* 1817, *s.* his brother 1855 ; *m.* 1855, Cecilia, dau. of Frederick Franks, Capt. R.N. She *d.* 6 Nov. 1900. He *d.s.p.* 21 June, 1886, when he was *s.* by his sister,
Mary Anne, *m.* 4 July, 1854, James Edward Burrowes, 2nd son of Thomas Burrowes, of Stradone (*see that family*), and *d.* 12 March, 1857, leaving issue,
Thomas Cosby Burrowes, now of Lismore.

Arms—*See* Burrowes *of Stradone.*
Seat—Lismore House, Crossdoney, co. Cavan.

BURTCHAELL OF BRANDONDALE.

Sarah Caroline Margaret Burtchaell, of Brandondale, co. Kilkenny, youngest dau. of William Russell Farmar, of Bloomfield, co. Wexford, by his 2nd wife Henrietta, 2nd dau. of Harry Alcock, of Wilton Castle, co. Wexford (*see those families*) ; *m*. 23 April, 1878, Richard Rothe Burtchaell, of Brandondale, J.P. cos. Kilkenny and Carlow, who *d.s.p.* 23 Dec. 1903.

Lineage.—Michael Burtchaell of Burgagemore, co. Wicklow, *b.* circa 1648 ; *d.* 4 Oct. 1732. He *m.* three times. By his 1st wife he had,

1. Peter, of Kilteel, co. Kildare, *d.* March, 1744 ; *m.* 1st 1714, Faithful, dau. and co-heiress of Griffith Allen, of Kilteel ; *m.* 2ndly, Sarah, dau. of John Wilson, of Crookstown, co. Meath, and left issue.
He *m.* 2ndly, Elizabeth, dau. of Thomas Keyes, and by her, who *d.* May, 1699, had two sons and a dau.,
2. Thomas, of whom presently.
3. John, bapt. 27 March, 1696.
1. Elizabeth, bapt. at St. Mary's, Blessinton, 14 July, 1698.
He *m.* 3rdly 17 Sept. 1699, Patience, dau. of — Morgan, and had with other issue,
4. George, of Burgage, bapt. 4 July, 1702 ; *m.* (*lic* 5 May), 1731, Mary, dau. of — Burtonwood, and left issue.
5. David, of Brownstown, co. Kildare, *b.* 1707 ; *d.* 18 Sept., 1783 ; *m.* Jane, dau. of William Senior, of Drumnagh, co. Dublin, and had a son and two daus.,
    David, of Brownstown, Lieut. Naas Independent Light Dragoons, *b.* 1740 ; *d.* 2 Dec. 1834 ; *m.* July, 1771, Mary, dau. of Richard Senior, of Aughasan, Queen's Co., and had issue.
    Mary *m.* John Leedom.
    Sarah, *m.* Dec. 1756, David Bomford, of Gallow, co. Meath (*see that family*).
2. Sinai, bapt. 10 Nov. 1701 ; *m.* John Harper.

The 2nd son,
Thomas Burtchaell, of Moneen, and Lacken, co. Kilkenny, *b.* 1690 ; *d.* 21 Dec. 1769 ; *m.* 1st 1718, Anne, 2nd dau. of William Mainwaring, of Moneen, co. Kilkenny (which he purchased from the Trustees of Forfeited Estates 18th June, 1703), and sister and co-heir of Gayton Mainwaring, of Moneen, and had, with a dau. Elizabeth, three sons,
1. William, of Kilcaran, co. Kilkenny, *d.* Feb. 1786, having had a son Thomas, who *d.v.p.* leaving a dau. Anne.
2. Michael, *d.s.p.*   3. John, *d.s.p.*
He *m.* 2ndly, Anne, dau. of — Kehoe, and had two sons,
4. Thomas, *d.s.p.*   5. Edward, Purser R.N.
He *m.* 3rdly, 1743, Anne (*b.* 1711 ; *d.* 22 Sept. 1785), dau. of Francis Lee, of Wells, co. Carlow, and had two sons and two daus.
6. Peter, of whom presently.
7. David, of Lacken, *b.* 1745 ; *d.* 25 Sept. 1833 ; *m.* 1st. Feb. 1781, Anne, dau. of Robert Johnston, of Curraghboy, co. Kilkenny, and 2ndly (*lic.* 18 Jan.), 1798, Catherine (*d.* 13 Aug. 1849), dau. of — White, and left issue by both.
1. Catherine, *m.* Edward Bassett.
2. Anne *m.* William Johnston.

The 6th son,
Peter Burtchaell, of Coolroe, co. Kilkenny, *b.* 1744 ; *d.* 19 April, 1815, Sovereign of Thomastown and Portreeve of Gowran ; *m.* 1st (*lic.* 14 Feb.) 1784, Catherine, dau. of John Rothe, of Kilcullen, co. Kilkenny (*see* Rothe *late of Mount Rothe*). She, who was *b.* 1758, *d.* 5 Apr 1, 1789, leaving issue,
1. Thomas, *b.* 25 Dec., 1784 ; *d. unm.* 28 April, 1813.
2. David, his heir.
1. Mary, *b.* 9 June, 1786 ; *d.* 1813 ; *m.* Nov. 1807, Richard Divine of Ullard, co. Kilkenny.
He *m.* 2ndly, 28 Aug. 1791, Dorcas, dau. of Patrick Divine, of Graignamanagh, and had issue, with others that *d.* young,
3. Patrick, *b.* 4 Aug. 1793 ; *d.* 18 Sept. 1845 ; *m.* 12 May, 1816, Augusta (*d.* 18 June, 1867), dau. of James Byrn, of Park, co. Carlow, by Catherine his wife, eldest dau. of Nicholas Montgomery Archdall, M.P of Castle Archdall, co. Fermanagh, and left issue.
4. Richard, *b.* 13 March, 1796 ; *d.* 22 April, 1882 ; *m.* 1st, 27 July, 1824, Anne, dau. of Christopher Daly, of Derry, co. Galway, and left issue by her, who *d.* 7 Feb. 1869. He *m.* 2ndly, 1 Feb. 1872, Lucy, dau. of Henry Pilkington, of Park Lane House, Yorkshire (*see* Burke's *Landed entry*, 3rd edition), *s.p.*
5. George, *b.* 22 Dec. 1798 ; *d.* Dec. 1857, Mid. R.N., Chief Officer of Coast Guards ; *m.* 1831, Anne, dau. of Dowling Wall, of Leighlinbridge, co. Carlow, and left issue by her, who *d.* 20 Jan. 1885.
6. Edward, *b.* 25 Oct. 1802 ; *d.* in America ; *m.* 6 Oct. 1825, Sarah, dau. of Thomas Tunsted, of Old Leighlin, and left issue.
7. William, *b.* 14 Nov. 1803 ; *d.* 15 July, 1876 ; *m.* 3 Nov. 1824, Catherine, dau. of Christopher Daly, of Derry, co. Galway, and had with other issue,
    William Daly, *b.* 24 May, 1834, of Norcross, Georgia ; *m.* 17 Feb. 1859, Maria Mackay, dau. of John Lee Williams, and by her, who *d.* 24 Feb. 1897, had two sons and three daus.,
    (1) George Sarsfield, *b.* 19 April, 1861 ; *m.* 1886, George Virginia Blount, and has issue,
        1. John Blount, *b.* 2 June, 1892.
        2. George Daly, *b.* Oct. 1894.
        3. Joseph Grey, *b.* 26 Sept. 1898.
        4. William Daves, *b.* Sept. 1908.
        1. Louise, *m.* Oct. 1906, Charles Wilson.
        2. Nina Floy.
    (2) William Lee, *b.* 22 April, 1863 ; *m.* 1894, Dora Ambrose.
    (1) Mary Daly.   (2) Martha Agnes.
    (3) Louisa Brandon, *m.* Jan. 1891, Reps Hardaway Jones.
8. Samuel, *b.* 1 April, 1812 ; *d. unm.*
2. Elizabeth, *b.* 30 June, 1792 ; *d.* Jan. 1862 ; *m.* 9 Aug. 1812, Nicholas Byrn, of Carlow.
3. Rebecca, *b.* 2 Nov. 1794 ; *d.* 3 Jan. 1880 ; *m.* 29 Oct. 1822, Abraham Prim Cronyn.
4. Dorcas, *b.* 9 Jan. 1807 ; *m.* 12 Dec. 1825, Francis Flood.
5. Frances, *b.* 9 Dec. 1810 ; *d.* 2 March, 1873, *unm.*

The 2nd son,
David Burtchaell, of Brandondale, co. Kilkenny, *b.* 11 Jan. 1788 ; *d.* 7 July, 1865 ; J.P. cos. Kilkenny and Carlow, Sovereign of Thomastown and Portreeve of Gowran. On the death of his uncle, Richard Rothe, of Kilcullen, co. Kilkenny, *s.p.*, he became

the representative of that family. He m. 12 Dec. 1815, Jane, dau. of Gilmore Dames, of Dublin, and by her, who was b. 20 Jan. 1790, and d. 14 Jan. 1862, had issue, with a son who d. an infant,
1. Henry, of Coolroe, b. 5 Dec. 1816; d. 29 March, 1890; m. 1st, 25 Feb. 1842, Hannah, dau. of Rev. Edward Hunt, of Jerpoint, co. Kilkenny, and had no issue by her who d. 10 March, 1843. He m. 2ndly, 17 Sept. 1857, Emily, dau. of Joseph O'Brien, and had with other issue,
David, of Coolroe, b. 7 Sept. 1858; d. 19 Jan. 1907; m. 8 Sept. 1888, Jennie, dau. of John Jackson, of Talavera House, Templemore, co. Tipperary, and left issue,
David Henry Rothe, b. 10 Aug. 1890.
Dorothy Eleanor. Kathleen Muriel Brandon.
2. Peter b. 31 Oct. 1820; d. 21 June, 1894, C.E., Co. Surveyor of Carlow 1851-60, and of Kilkenny 1860-94; m. 3 Aug. 1852, Maria Isabella, eldest dau. of Lundy Edward Foot, 14, Upper Fitzwilliam Street, Dublin (see Foot, late of the Rower), and had by her, who d. 12 March, 1898, three sons and three daus.,
 1. George Dames, b. 12 June, 1853, M.A., LL.B. (Dub.), Barrister, King's Inns 1879. Athlone Pursuivant and Registrar of the Office of Arms, Ireland, 1908, Deputy Ulster King of Arms Nov. 1910 to Feb. 1911.
 2. David Edward, b. 9 Feb. 1859; d. 27 July, 1910, B.A.I. (Dub.); m. 23 Dec. 1904, Caroline Harriet Crosby, dau. of Thomas Boyd, of Chilcomb Lodge, co. Kilkenny, Clerk of the Crown and Peace, co. Tipperary; s.p.
 3. Charles Henry, b. 30 Aug. 1866, M.B., &c. (Dub.), Lieut.-Col. R.A. Medical Corps, Assistant Director General R.A. Medical Service, 1910; m. 6 June, 1903, Bertha Marcella, dau. of John George Aurel, of Johannesburg, and has issue,
  (1) Bertha Vivien.   (2) Mary Frances.
 1. Lelias Jane, d. 4 Sept. 1901, unm.   2. Mary Isabella.
 3. Elizabeth Emily.
3. George Dames, b. July, 1822; lost in the wreck of the "Solway," 7 April, 1843, Lieut. R. Engineers.
4. Gilmore, b. 17 Jan. 1829; d. 15 May, 1852; Lieut. R. Artillery.
5. Somerset Brafeild (Rev.), b. 30 Sept. 1832; d. 6 June, 1898, M.A. (Dub.); m. 20 Nov. 1866, Katherine Elizabeth, 2nd dau. of William Russell Farmar, of Bloomfield, co. Wexford (see that family), and left issue,
 1. Mary Elizabeth Constance, m. 21 May, 1898, William Knox Johnson, M.A. (Oxon), Professor of Literature R. College, Benares. He d. 19 June, 1906, s.p.
 2. Kathleen Jane, m. 21 Nov. 1910, James Laurence Mercer Tod-Mercer (see TOD-MERCER of Scotsbank).
6. RICHARD ROTHE, late of Brandondale.
1. Sarah, d. 5 June, 1887, unm.
2. Catherine Maunsell, d. 9 Oct. 1836, unm.
3. Mary, d. 24 Aug., 1894, unm.
4. Jane d. 15 Sept. 1840, unm.
The 6th son,
RICHARD ROTHE BURTCHAELL, of Brandondale, b. 28 July, 1831, J.P. cos. Kilkenny and Carlow; m. 23 April, 1878, Sarah Caroline Margaret (now of Brandondale), youngest dau. of William Russell Farmar, of Bloomfield, co. Wexford (see that family). He d.s.p. 23 Dec. 1903.

Arms.—1st and 4th: Per pale az. and gu. on a chevron between three cross-crosslets or, as many cinquefoils of the first (Burtchaell). 2nd and 3rd: Or, on a mount in base vert, a stag trippant arg., under an oak tree ppr. (Rothe). Crest—On a mount vert, a lion rampant sa. supporting on the sinister side an oak tree ppr. Motto—Quo Fata Vocant.
Seat—Brandondale, Graignamanagh, co. Kilkenny.

BURTON OF CARRIGAHOLT CASTLE.

WILLIAM CONYNGHAM VANDELEUR BURTON, of Carrigaholt Castle, co. Clare, J.P. and D.L., High Sheriff 1886, late an Officer 68th Regt., b. 19 Sept. 1846; m. 16 Jan. 1896, Lilias, dau. of Thomas Green, of Wilby and Athellington, Suffolk. Mr. Burton is the only surviving son of HENRY STUART BURTON, of Carrigaholt Castle, who d. 10 Feb. 1867, and grandson of the HON. SIR FRANCIS NATHANIEL BURTON, G.C.H., twin brother of Henry, 1st Marquess CONYNGHAM (see BURKE'S Peerage). He s. his brother 1883.

Lineage.—(See BURKE'S Peerage, CONYNGHAM, M.)
Seat—Carrigaholt Castle, Carrigaholt, co. Clare. Club—Kildare Street, Dublin.

BURTON OF BURTON HALL.

WILLIAM FITZ-WILLIAM BURTON, of Burton Hall, co. Carlow, and of Goltho Hall, Wragby, co. Lincoln, b. 30 April, 1849; s. his father 29 April, 1909; m. 12 April, 1877, Georgiana Spencer, 4th dau. of Capt. the Hon. William Henry George Wellesley, R.N., and grand-dau. of Henry, 1st Lord Cowley (see BURKE'S Peerage), and has issue,
1. WILLIAM MAINWARING, b. 11 July, 1881.
2. Benjamin Wellesley, b. 20 Sept. 1883.
3. Arthur Fitzwilliam, b. 27 Feb. 1889; d. 14 June, 1905.
4. Augustus Frederick, b. 9 April, 1891; d. 15 Nov. that year.
5. Alfred Henry Wellesley, b. 20 Aug. 1892.
6. Gerald John Lloyd, b. 9 Sept. 1893.
7. Edward Thomas Derrick, b. 8 Aug. 1895.
1. Georgiana Coralie, b. 29 Sept. 1879.
2. Lettice Amelia, b. 18 Aug. 1882.
3. Frances Mary Alicia, b. 7 March, 1885.
4. Charlotte Louisa Kathleen, b. 24 March, 1887.

Lineage.—SIR EDWARD BURTON, Knt. of Longner, representative of the family, "was with King EDWARD IV., successful in fourteen set battles between the Houses of York and Lancaster; and for his great loyalty and services, he was made knightbanneret, under the royal standard in the field," A.D. 1460. He was s. by his son,
SIR ROBERT BURTON, Knt. of Longner, knighted by EDWARD IV., 1478; got a grant of arms from Wryth, Norroy, dated 22 May, 1478, and was father of
SIR EDWARD BURTON, Knt. of Longner, Master of the Robes to HENRY VII., m. Jocosa, dau. of Thomas Cressett, of Upton Cressett, co. Salop, and d. 23 April, 1524, leaving, with 3 younger son, Thomas, an elder son, his successor,
JOHN BURTON, of Longner, m. Elizabeth, dau. of Thomas Poyner, of Boston, co. Salop, and had issue,
1. EDWARD, his successor.
2. Jane, m. Thomas Corbet, of Longner.
3. Eleanor, m. Randolph Bannister, of Lacon.
4. Ann, m. — Bostock, of Moreton Say, co. Salop.
5. Ankred, m. — Wright, of London.
6. Mary, m. — Barker, of Bridgnorth, co. Salop.
Sir Edward d. 22 Oct. 1543, and was s. by his only son,
EDWARD BURTON, of Longner, m. Ann, dau. and heir of Nicholas Madocks, of Wem and Cotton, co. Salop, and had issue,
1. THOMAS, his heir, ancestor of BURTON of Longner (see that family).
2. EDWARD, of whom next.
3. Humphrey.   4. Timothy.
1. Mary, m. Sir Richard Lloyd, Knt. of Ripton.
2. Dorothy, m. John Milton, of Weston, co. Stafford.
3. Katherine, m. George Corbet, of Hope, co. Salop.
Mr. Burton d. 1558, and was s. by his eldest son,
EDWARD BURTON had issue, two sons, who both settled in Ireland in 1610,
1. Francis, d.s.p.
2. THOMAS, of whom next.
The younger son,
THOMAS BURTON, of Buncraggy, co. Clare, whose will was proved 15 Feb. 1666, m. Ann, dau. of — Shepherd, of Baycote, co. Hereford, and had issue (with two daus., Martha, m. Rev. John Andrew, D.D., and Jane, m. Alan Swanwicke) an only son,
SAMUEL BURTON, of Buncraggy, co. Clare, m. Margery Harris, and d. 1712 (will proved 1 Dec. 1712), leaving, issue,
1. Francis, of Buncraggy, M.P., m. Alice, dau. of Thomas Tilson, and had issue,
Francis (Right Hon.), of Buncraggy, M.P., m. Mary, only dau. of Henry Conyngham, M.P., by whom he was ancestor of the MARQUESSES OF CONYNGHAM (see BURKE'S Peerage).
2. Charles, m. Mary, dau. of William Hickman, and d.s.p.
3. BENJAMIN, of whom next.
1. Dorothea, m. Samuel Bindon, of co. Clare.
The 3rd son,
BENJAMIN BURTON, becoming an eminent banker in Dublin, was Lord Mayor of that city in 1706, and represented it in Parliament from 1703-23; he m. 22 May, 1686, Grace, elder dau. of Robert Stratford, of Belan, co. Kildare, and by her (who d. in London, July, 1721) had six sons, with as many daus.,
1. SAMUEL, of whom below.

Bury. THE LANDED GENTRY. 90

2. Robert, of Hackettstown, co. Carlow, High Sheriff 1730, Capt. Battle-Axe Guards, *d.s.p.*, having *m.* Katherine, dau. of Thomas Ryves, of Rathangan, co. Wicklow.
3. Benjamin.   6. Edward.
5. Charles (Sir), M.P. for Dublin 1749-60, Lord Mayor 1752-53 He was knighted by the Viceroy 9 Jan. 1749-50, and was created a BARONET OF IRELAND, 2 Oct. 1758. He *d.* 6 June, 1775, having *m.* Sept. 1731, Margaret, eldest dau. of Richard Meredyth, of Shrowland, co. Kildare, by whom he had issue, with five daus., an only son.
Charles (Sir), 2nd Bart. of Pollerton, who *d.* 1812, having *m.* 11 Aug. 1778, Catherine, 3rd dau. of John (Cuffe), 2nd Lord Desart, by whom (who *d.* 1827) he had,
(1) Charles (Sir), 3rd Bart., High Sheriff co. Carlow 1820, who *m.* in 1807, Susannah, dau. of Joshua-Paul Meredyth, and *d.* 6 Jan. 1830, leaving a dau., Sophia, who *d.* in 1843, and a son, Sir CHARLES, 4th Bart., who *d. unm.* 21 May, 1842, and was *s.* by his cousin.
(2) John, a Capt. in the 17th Light Dragoons, *d.* in 1813.
(3) Benjamin, Lieut. in the 19th Lancers, High Sheriff co. Carlow 1816, *m.* Grace Ann, only child of William Roberts, of 91, Gloster Place, Portman Square, and *d.* in 1831, leaving issue,
  1. CHARLES WILLIAM CUFFE (Sir), 5th Bart., High Sheriff co. Carlow 1851, *b.* 13 Jan. 1823. late Lieut. 1st Dragoons ; *m.* 16 Dec. 1861, Georgiana Mary, only dau. of David Haliburton Dallas, and *d.s.p.* 2 Oct. 1902, when the baronetcy became extinct.
  2. Robert, *d.* in 1843.
  3. Adolphus William Desart, C.B., Col. late 7th Dragoon Guards, *b.* 1827 ; *m.* 11 June, 1863, Sophia Louis, dau. of Gen. Sir John Slade, Bart., G.C.H., and *d.* 11 Feb. 1882, leaving Grace Ellen, *m.* 16 Sept. 1890, Sir Francis Charles Edward Denys-Burton, 3rd Bart., and has had issue (see BURKE's *Peerage*), and Gertrude Mary.
  4. Augustus, *d.* an infant.
  1. Catherine Anne Galloway.
  2. Adelaide.
(4) William, *m.* in 1814, Mary, eldest dau. and co-heiress of Samuel Skey, of Spring Grove, near Bewdly, Worcestershire, and *d.* in 1826, leaving issue,
  1. William, a Lieut. in the Guards, and Aide-de-camp to the King of Bavaria, *b.* Aug. 1815 ; *d.* 17 July, 1859, *unm.*
  2. Samuel Skey, *b.* 1821 ; *m.* 30 Sept. 1861, Susan Bristowe Berridge, widow of Thomas Miller, of Leicester, and *d.* 1868, leaving a dau., Mary Katherine (*m.* 1880, George F. Stevenson, LL.B., and has issue).
  3. Charles James, *b.* 1824 ; *d. unm.* 1875.
  1. Mary Louisa, *d.* 1856.
  2. Catherine Sarah, *d.* 24 Sept. 1892.
  3. Lucy Caroline, *m.* to Alfred Carrington Dick, and *d.* 21 Jan. 1892.
(5) Richard, *d.* 22 Aug. 1871.
(6) George.
(7) Edward, *m.* to Miss Eustace, and *d.s.p.*
(1) Grace Anna, *m.* to Henry Faulkner, of Castleton, Carlow.
(2) Catherine, *d. unm.*   (3) Sophia, *d. unm.*
6. Francis, *m.* in 1738, Rachael, eldest dau. of Dr. Edward Smyth, Bishop of Down, and had (with a son, who *d. unm.*) a dau., Maria, *m.* to Richard Cox, of Castletown.
1. Mary, *m.* to Aug. 1701, Philip Doyne, of Wells, co. Wexford (see *that family*). She *d.* 10 July, 1705.
2. Grace, *m.* to Edward Hoare, of Dunkettle.
3. Elizabeth, *m.* to Richard Hoare.
4. Lettice, *m.* 29 March, 1711, Henry Brooke, M.P. of Colebrook, co. Fermanagh.
5. Abigail, *m.* 1st, to John Walsh, of Ballykilcaven, Queen's Co., and 2ndly, to Allen Johnson, of Kilternan.
6. Jane.

The eldest son of Benjamin Burton, of Dublin,

SAMUEL BURTON, of Burton Hall, M.P. for Sligo 1713, and for Dublin 1727, High Sheriff co. Carlow 1724 ; *m.* 1st, 17 June, 1708, Anne, dau. of Charles Campbell, of Dublin, and by her (who was killed by the fall of a scaffold at the coronation of GEORGE I, 20 Oct. 1714) had issue,
1. BENJAMIN, his heir.   2. Hughes, *b.* 20 Jan. 1710.
3. Samuel.
1. Katherine, *m.* 28 Feb. 1731, Nicholas, 5th Viscount Netterville.
Mr. Burton *m.* 2ndly, Mary Hinde, by whom he had another dau.,
2. Mary.
He was *s.* by his eldest son,

THE RIGHT HON. BENJAMIN BURTON, P.C. (Ireland), of Burton Hall, M.P. for Knocktopher 1741, and for Carlow 1761, High Sheriff co. Carlow 1736, Commissioner of the Revenue in Ireland, *b.* 10 Jan. 1709 ; *d.* intestate, administration of his goods being granted to his 2nd but eldest surviving son 17 Nov. 1763. He *m.* 9 Dec. 1734, Lady Anne Ponsonby, dau. of Brabazon, 1st Earl of Bessborough, and had issue, four sons and two daus.,
1. Benjamin, High Sheriff, co. Carlow, 1760, M.P. for co. Sligo 1757, and for Boyle 1761, *d. unm.* 1763.
2. WILLIAM, *s.* to the estates.
3. Campbell, *d.* young.   4. Ponsonby, *d.* young.
1. Sarah, *m.* 1763, John Hyde, of Castle Hyde, co. Cork.
2. Anna, *d. unm.* March, 1764.
His 2nd but eldest surviving son,

WILLIAM HENRY BURTON, of Burton Hall, *b.* 16 July, 1739 ; *m.* 12 Dec. 1765, Mary, only child of Henry Aston, of East Aston, co. Wicklow, and had issue,
1. BENJAMIN, of whom next.

2. William Henry, *b.* 15 Nov. 1767 ; *d. unm.* 31 Dec. 1799.
1. Martha, *d. unm.* 6 Sept. 1797.
Mr. Burton *d.* 7 Jan. 1818, and was *s.* by his grandson. His eldest son,

BENJAMIN BURTON, of Walcot House, Stamford, Lincs., *b.* 12 Sept. 1766 ; *m.* 15 Dec. 1794, Anne, dau. of Thomas Mainwaring, of Goltho, co. Lincoln, and had issue,
1. WILLIAM FITZWILLIAM, who *s.* his grandfather.
2. Benjamin, *b.* 10 July, 1799 ; *d. unm.* 6 Nov. 1853.
1. Mary Elizabeth, *m.* 19 Dec. 1819, Sir Richard Sutton, Bart., of Norwood Park, co. Notts ; *d.* 1 July, 1842.
2. Sophia Catherine, *m.* 5 Aug. 1824, Robert Thoroton, Col. Grenadier Guards.
Mr. Burton *d.v.p.* 26 April, 1808. His son,

WILLIAM FITZWILLIAM BURTON, of Burton Hall, *b.* 22 Sept. 1796 ; J.P., High Sheriff of Carlow 1822. He *s.* his grandfather 7 Jan. 1818 ; *m.* 1st, 18 July, 1825, Mary, dau. of Sir John Power, 1st bart., of Kilfane, co. Kilkenny, and by her (who *d.* 25 Jan. 1839), had issue,
1. WILLIAM FITZWILLIAM, late of Burton Hall.
2. Benjamin (Rev.), *b.* 17 Sept. 1829 ; *m.* 27 April, 1854, Anne, dau. of Col. Henry Bruen, M.P., of Oak Park, co. Carlow. He *d.* 15 Feb. 1856. She *d.* Feb. 1871, leaving issue,
  Benjamin, C.B., Major-Gen. R.A., served in S. African War 1899-1901 (despatches, C.B., medals, with five clasps), *b.* 10 March, 1855.
  Mary Elizabeth, *m.* 16 June, 1880, Col. the Hon. Edward Lawless, brother of 4th Baron Cloncurry.
3. John Power, *b.* 3 Sept. 1833 ; *d.* 10 April, 1869 ; *m.* 31 Dec. 1861, Adelaide Harriet, 4th dau. of Henry S. Close, of Newtown Park, co. Dublin, and had issue, four sons,
  1. John Henry, *b.* 7 Oct. 1862.
  2. Arthur Power, *b.* 15 March, 1865.
  3. Algernon, *b.* 25 Nov. 1866 ; *m.* 19 May, 1907, Edith Constance, dau. of Horace F. Tahourdin, and has issue, with one dau., a son,
    Edward, *b.* 23 April, 1909.
  4. Percy Charles, *b.* 19 May, 1868.
4. Charles, Capt. 99th Regt., *b.* 24 Oct. 1836 ; *m.* 25 April, 1871, Mary Edith, dau. of Rev. John Charles Davenport, Rector of Skeffington, co. Leicester. He *d.* 27 Feb. 1900, leaving issue, with a son, Charles Conyngham, *b.* 1881, and since dec., three daus.,
  1. Florence Helen, *dec.*   2. Mary Bertha.   3. Norah.
1. Harriet Anne, *m.* 29 July, 1851, Sir Richard Sutton, 4th bart. of Norwood. He *d.* 2 Oct. 1878. She *d.* 22 March, 1901, leaving issue (see BURKE's *Peerage*).
2. Mary Frances, *m.* 18 Nov. 1862, Rev. Thomas George Onslow Rector of Catmore, co. Berks. She *d.* 25 May, 1905. He *d.* 21 Aug. 1911, leaving issue (see BURKE's *Peerage*, ONSLOW, E. *of*).
3. Sophia Charlotte, *m.* 22 Jan. 1856, John Henry Edward Fock, Baron de Robeck, and *d.* 15 July, 1903, leaving issue (see *that family*).
4. Helen Mary, *d. unm.* 22 April, 1903.
Mr. Burton *m.* 2ndly, 5 Oct. 1840, Eleanor Mary, dau. of William Browne, of Browne's Hill, co. Carlow, which lady *d.s.p.* 5 Dec. 1870. He *d.* 15 Nov. 1844. The eldest son,

WILLIAM FITZWILLIAM BURTON, of Burton Hall, co. Carlow, J.P., High Sheriff 1849, formerly of the 4th Light Dragoons, *b.* 14 May, 1826 ; *m.* 1st, 17 June, 1848, Coralie Augusta Frederica, 3rd dau. of the late Henry Lloyd, of Farrinrory, co. Tipperary, by Harriet Amelia his wife, dau. of Sir John Craven Carden, 1st bart. (see BURKE's *Peerage*), and by her (who *d.* 11 Jan. 1862) had issue,
1. WILLIAM FITZWILLIAM, now of Burton Hall.
2. Alfred Henry, *b.* 29 March, 1853.
He *m.* 2ndly, 6 Jan. 1894, Clara Louisa, dau. of John Cayley, of Bickley, Kent (see BURKE's *Peerage*, CAYLEY, Bart.), and *d.* 29 April, 1909.

Arms—Per pale az. and purpure, a cross engrailed or, between four roses arg. **Crest**—On a ducal coronet a dexter gauntlet, the palm inwards ppr. **Motto**—Deus providebit.
Seat—Burton Hall, Carlow.

BURY OF CHARLEVILLE FOREST.

LADY EMILY ALFREDA JULIA HOWARD BURY, of Charleville Forest, King's Co., youngest dau. and eventually co-heir of Charles William, 3rd Earl of Charleville, *b.* 16 Oct. 1856 ; *m.* 20 Sept. 1881, Capt. Kenneth Howard, eldest son of Hon. James Kenneth Howard, 4th son of Thomas, 16th Earl of Suffolk. (*See* BURKE'S *Peerage*.)

Capt. Howard assumed by Royal Licence 14 Dec. 1881, the additional surname and arms of Bury, was High Sheriff of King's Co. 1884, and *d.* 24 Aug. 1885, leaving issue,

CHARLES KENNETH, *b.* 15 Aug. 1883.
Marjory Alfreda Beaujolois, *b.* 16 July, 1885; *d. unm.* 8 Dec. 1907.

Lineage.—PHINEAS BURY had a grant of lands in co. Limerick, 14 Nov 1666, and in the barony of Barrymore, co. Cork, 10 June, 1668. He was High Sheriff of the latter co. 1673. His 2nd son, JOHN BURY, of Shannon Grove, co. Limerick, took out administration to his elder brother Richard, 11 Jan. 1691. He *m.* Jane, only dau. of Rev. William Palliser, D.D., Archbishop of Cashel, and *d.* 1722, having had issue,

1. WILLIAM, of whom presently.
2. John, who assumed the name of PALLISER, and was ancestor of Palliser, of Derryluskan, co. Tipperary (*see that family*).
3. Richard, of Mount Pleasant, co. Clare, *m.* Anne, dau. of Mountiford Westropp, of Attyflin, co. Limerick. His will, dated 12 Dec. 1733, was proved 17 May, 1735. His widow *m.* 2ndly, William Spaight.
4. Thomas, of Curraghbridge, co. Limerick, *d.s.p.* Will dated 11 Sept. 1767, proved 19 April, 1774.
5. PHINEAS, ancestor of Bury, *of Little Island* (*see that family*), and BURY-BARRY, of *Ballyclough* (*see that family*).
1. Elizabeth, *m.* Mountiford Westropp, of Attyflin, co. Limerick.

The eldest son,
WILLIAM BURY, of Shannon Grove, High Sheriff co. Limerick 1726, *m.* 27 Jan. 1723, Jane, only dau. of Right Hon. John Moore, of Croghan, King's Co., 1st Lord Tullamore, and sister and heir of Charles, 1st Earl of Charleville, and had issue,

1. JOHN. 2. Charles.
3. William. 4. Richard. 5. Thomas.
1. Jane.
2. Georgiana, *m.* Richard, 4th Viscount Boyne.
3. Mary. 4. Elizabeth.

The eldest son,
JOHN BURY, of Shannon Grove and Charleville Forest, *b.* 1725; *s.* his uncle Charles, Earl of Charleville, in the Moore estates, 17 Feb. 1764. He *m.* 1761, Catharine, 2nd dau. and co-heir of Francis Sadleir, of Sopwell Hall, co. Tipperary, and by that lady (who *m.* 2ndly, June, 1766, Henry Prittie, afterwards Lord Dunalley *see* BURKE's *Peerage*), left at his decease, 4 Aug. 1764, an only son, CHARLES WILLIAM BURY, of Charleville Forest, in the King's Co., *b.* 30 June, 1764; who was raised to the peerage of Ireland as Baron *Tullamore*, 26 Nov. 1797; created *Viscount Charleville*, 29 Dec. 1800, and EARL OF CHARLEVILLE, 16 Feb. 1806. He *m.* 4 June, 1798, Catherine Maria, widow of James Tisdall, of Bawn, co. Louth, and dau. and sole heir of Thomas Townley Dawson, by whom he left at his decease, 31 Oct. 1835, an only son,
CHARLES WILLIAM, 2nd Earl of Charleville, *b.* 29 April, 1801, *m.* 26 Feb. 1821, Harriet Charlotte Beaujolois, 3rd dau. of Col. John Campbell, of Shawheld, and Lady Charlotte Susan Maria Campbell his wife, dau. of John, 5th Duke of Argyll, and by her (who. *d.* 1 Feb. 1848) had issue,

1. CHARLES WILLIAM GEORGE, 3rd Earl.
2. John JAMES, Capt. R.E., *b.* 22 Oct. 1827; *m.* 24 June, 1852, Charlotte Theresa (34, *Beaufort Road, Kingston-on-Thames*), only dau. of Thomas Austin, and *d.* 18 Jan. 1864, having by her (who *m.* 2ndly, 1868, Herbert O'Meara) had issue,
  1. Beaujolois Arabella Charlotte, *d.* 1 Nov. 1865.
  2. Georgina Florence, *m.* 24 June, 1879, Lieut.-Col. Edward Guy Selby Smyth, late Royal Irish Rifles, son of Gen. Sir Edward Selby Smyth, K.C.M.G., and has issue.
  3. Louisa Emily Austin, *d. unm.* 1881.
  4. Ada Pierce Tighe, *m.* 20 April, 1885, Col. Raymond Oliver de Montmorency, late Royal Irish Rifles, who *d.s.p.* 1894.
3. ALFRED, 5th Earl, *b.* 19 Feb. 1829; *m.* 20 June, 1854, Emily Frances, 3rd dau. of Gen. Sir William Wood, K.C.B., K.H., Col. of the 14th Foot. He *s.* his nephew 1874, and *d.s.p.* 28 June, 1875, when the earldom became extinct.
4. Beaujolois Eleanora Catherine, *m.* 30 June, 1853, Hastings Dent (who *d.* 7 June, 1864), son of John Dent, M.P., and has issue (*see* BURKE'S *Landed Gentry*).

His lordship *d.* 14 July, 1851, and was *s.* by his eldest son,
CHARLES WILLIAM GEORGE, 3rd Earl of Charleville, *b.* 8 March, 1822, Lieut. 43rd Foot; *m.* 7 March, 1850, Arabella Louisa, youngest dau. of the late Henry Case, of Shenston Moss. co. Stafford (who *d.* 8 July, 1857). He *d.* 19 Jan. 1850, leaving issue,

1. CHARLES WILLIAM FRANCIS, 4th Earl, *b.* 16 May, 1852; *d. unm.* 3 Nov. 1874, when he was *s.* by his uncle.
2. John William, *b.* 31 Aug. 1854; *d.* 20 Aug. 1872.
1. Katherine Arabella Beaujolois, *m.* 3 June, 1873, Col. Edmund Bacon Hutton, Royal Dragoons, and had issue. She *d.* 3 Feb. 1901.
2. Harriet Hugh Adelaide, accidentally killed by a fall, 3 April, 1861.
3. EMILY ALFREDA JULIA, now of Charleville.

Arms—Quarterly, 1st and 4th vert, a cross crosslet or (BURY); 2nd and 3rd gu., on a bend between six cross crosslets fitchée arg., an escutcheon or charged with a demi lion rampant pierced through the mouth by an arrow within a double tressure flory counterflory of the first, a crescent sa. for difference (HOWARD). **Crests**—1. A boar's head couped at the neck or, tusked arg., langued gu., transfixed through the neck by a spear ppr., charged for difference with a cross crosslet vert (BURY). 2. On a chapeau gu. turned up erm. a lion statant guardant tail extended or ducally gorged arg. charged on the body with a crescent of the first for difference (HOWARD). **Mottoes**—(under the arms), Virtus sub cruce crescit; and (over the second crest), Nous maintieudrons.

Seat—Charleville Forest, King's Co.

BURY OF LITTLE ISLAND AND CURRAGHBRIDGE.

WILLIAM PENNEFATHER ARTHUR FORBES PHINEAS BURY, of Curraghbridge, co. Limerick, and Carrigrenane, co. Cork, *b.* 26 Sept. 1868; *s.* his uncle, 1895; *m.* 1899, Catherine, dau. of Maurice Collins, of Shauntrade, co. Limerick, and has issue,

PHINEAS, *b.* 1902.
Iris Euphemia.

Lineage.—PHINEAS BURY, of Little Island, co. Cork, 5th son of JOHN BURY, of Shannon Grove, co. Limerick (*see* BURY *of Charleville*); *m.* by licence dated 25 Feb. 1734, Hester, dau. of Thomas Moland, and had, with a dau. Hester (wife of Edward Candler-Brown, of Prior Park, Somerset) a son and successor,
PHINEAS BURY, of Little Island, *m.* Jane, dau. of Boyle Aldworth, of Newmarket, co. Cork, and had issue,

1. PHINEAS, his heir.
2. Robert (Rev.), of Carrigrenane, co. Cork, Prebendary of Coole, co. Cork, *m.* Letitia, dau. of Gen. Henry Green Barry, of Ballyclough, co, Cork, and *d.* 1853, leaving issue (*see* BURY-BARRY *of Ballyclough*). 3. Richard. 4. Thomas, Commander, R.N.
1. Jane. 2. Hester.

The eldest son,
PHINEAS BURY, J.P., of Little Island, Capt. 57th Regt., and afterwards 7th Dragoon Guards, *m.* 1st, Miss Eliza Stuart, who *d.s.p.*; and 2ndly, Elizabeth, dau. of William Pennefather, son of Kingsmill Pennefather, M.P., and by her had issue,

1. PHINEAS, his heir, late of Little Island.
2. William Phineas, of Carrigrenane, co. Cork, *b.* 27 Nov. 1842; *m.* Harriet (*d.* 26 Dec. 1911), dau. of Arthur Forbes, of Newstone, co. Meath, and had issue,
  WILLIAM PENNEFATHER ARTHUR FORBES PHINEAS, now of Curraghbridge.
1. Frances Jane, *m.* C. T. Tuckey, Major 41st Regt., dec.

Mr. Bury *d.* 1853, and was *s.* by his eldest son,
PHINEAS BURY, of Little Island, co. Cork, and Curraghbridge, Adare, co. Limerick, J.P. for Cork, High Sheriff 1865, *b.* 7 March, 1841; formerly Capt. 15th (King's) Hussars, and late Capt. and Hon. Major East Kent Militia, and *d.s.p.* 9 May, 1895.

Arms—Vert, a cross-crosslet or, on a canton arg. an ermine spot. **Crest**—A boar's head or, couped at the shoulder, pierced through the neck with a spear imbrued ppr. **Motto**—Virtus sub cruce crescit.

Seats—Carrigrenane, Little Island, co. Cork; and Curraghbridge, Adare, co. Limerick. **Club**—Junior Constitutional.

BURY-BARRY. *See* BARRY.

BUSHE OF GLENCAIRN ABBEY.

FRANCES MARIA and AGNES CHARLOTTE BUSHE, of Glencairn Abbey, co. Waterford, daus. and co-heirs of the late Gervase Parker Bushe, of Glencairn Abbey, who *d.* 1879.

The elder dau., FRANCES MARIA, *m.* 22 Nov. 1884, Ambrose William Bushe Power, of Barrettstown, co. Tipperary, and Clonmoyle, co. Waterford, J.P., High Sheriff 1899, late Indian Civil Service, eldest son of the Ven. Ambrose Power, Archdeacon of Lismore, who *d.* 8 Nov. 1869, and Susan his 1st wife (who *d.* 7 Aug. 1854), dau.

of John Thacker, of Ballymelish, Queen's Co., and grandson of Sir John Power, 1st bart. of Kilfane (*see* BURKE'S *Peerage*). Mr. Ambrose W. B. Power *d.* 10 March, 1907, having had issue,

1. AMBROSE GRATTAN, *b.* 22 April, 1887; *m.* 21 July, 1908, Ada Mary, youngest dau. of Richard A. Cooper-Chadwick, of Ballinard, co. Tipperary (*see that family*).
1. Sylvia, *m.* 23 Nov. 1909, Walter Seton Cassels, I.C.S.
2. Irene Noel.

Lineage.—JOHN BUSHE had a grant of land in Kilfane, co. Kilkenny, 10 Dec. 1670. By Mary his wife, dau. and heir of John Grey, he left, with four daus., Elizabeth, *m.* Samuel Hobson, of Waterford; Ann, *m.* Joseph Harries; another, Mrs. Woodroffe; and another, Mrs. Berkeley; two sons,

1. AMYAS, his heir.
2. Arthur, of Dangen, co. Kilkenny, Secretary to the Commissioners of Revenue, *m.* 1st, Ann, dau. of Sir Thomas Worsop, Knt. of Dunshaughlin, co. Meath, and had issue,
    1. Worsop, of Dangen, *b.* 1692; entered Trin. Coll. Dublin, 20 May, 1711, aged 19; *d. unm.* His will, dated 3 Aug. 1738, was proved in 1760.
    Arthur Bushe *m.* 2ndly, 17 Oct. 1695, Mary, dau. of John Forth, by whom (who *d.* April, 1717) he had further issue,
    2. William, of Dublin, *b.* 1696; entered Trin. Coll. Dublin, 20 May, 1711, aged 15; whose will, dated 4 June, 1793, was proved 7 Feb. 1796; he *m.* Hannah, sister of Edmund Donelan, of Streamstown, co. Westmeath, and had a son, Worsop, who *d.s.p.*; and a dau. Anne, *m.* Rev. Henry Tilson, of Dublin.
    3. John, *b.* 1705; entered Trin. Coll. Dublin, 20 March, 1722, aged 17.   4. Thomas.
    1. Mary.   2. Letitia, *d. unm.* 1757.

Mr. Bushe was *s.* by his eldest son,
AMYAS BUSHE, of Kilfane, co. Kilkenny, High Sheriff co. Kilkenny 1706; *m.* Eleanor, dau. of Sir Christopher Wandesford, 1st bart. of Kirklington, and had issue by her (who *d.* 1706).

1. Christopher, who *d.v.p.*, leaving by Margaret his wife, an only son,
    AMYAS (or AMIAS), who *s.* his grandfather.
2. Arthur, of Kilmurry, High Sheriff co. Kilkenny, 1736, *b.* 1691; entered Trin. Coll. Dublin, 28 June, 1711, aged 20; his will, dated 4 Jan. 1761, was proved 25th of the next month. He *m.* Mary Martin, and left issue, three sons,
    1. Amias, *b.* 1716, entered Trin. Coll. Dublin, 20 April, 1734, aged 18; *d.* young.
    2. Thomas (Rev.), D.D., of Kilmurry, Rector of Gowran, co. Kilkenny, and Prebendary of Inniscarra, co. Cork, Chaplain of Kingston College, co. Cork, *b.* 1727; entered Trin. Coll. Dublin, 28 June, 1743, aged 16; B.A. 1747; *m.* Katherine, dau. of Charles Doyle, of Bramblestown, co. Kilkenny, and sister of Gen. Sir John Doyle, and *d.* Sept. 1795, having had issue,
        (1) CHARLES KENDAL (Right Hon.), *b.* 1767, one of the most distinguished Advocates and Orators of his time, appointed LORD CHIEF JUSTICE of Ireland in 1822, *m.* Dec. 1793, Anne, dau. of John Crampton, of Merrion Square, Dublin, and sister of Sir Philip Crampton, Bart., M.D. She *d.* 17 May, 1857. He *d.* 10 July, 1843, having had issue,
            1. John, *m.* 1817, Lady Louisa Hare, dau. of the 1st Earl of Listowel. She *d.* 18 April, 1855. He *d.s.p.* 1870.
            2. Charles (Rev.), Rector of Castlehaven, co. Cork, *b.* 30 March, 1800; *m.* 1st, Fanny Elizabeth, dau. of James Bury, of St. Leonards, Nazing, Essex (*see that family*). She *d.* 21 May, 1837, leaving issue,
                a. Charles Percy, Capt. R.N., J.P. Cinque Ports (*Leelands, Walmer, Kent, and United Service Club*), *b.* 16 Oct. 1835; *m.* 1st, 5 Oct. 1871, Louisa Eleanor, widow of Hugh Dale Mathie, of Arran Cottage, co. Wexford. She *d.* 18 March, 1883. He *m.* 2ndly, 18 July, 1887, Adelaide Charlotte Devereux, dau. of Rev. John Harris, Rector of Shercock, co. Cavan, and has issue,
                    Sylvia Louisa Kendal, *b.* 30 June, 1890.
                b. Horace Kendal, Maj.-Gen. Bombay Army, *b.* 18 Jan. 1837; *m.* 3 April, 1872, Mary, dau. of Col. John Caulfeild, of Bloomfield, co. Westmeath (*see* BURKE'S *Peerage*, CHARLEMONT, V.), and *d.s.p.* 24 Nov. 1898.
            He *m.* 2ndly, 27 Aug. 1839, Emmeline Katherine Egerton, dau. of Vice-Admiral Sir Josiah Coghill, 3rd Bart. She *d.* 26 Aug. 1879. He *d.* 25 Aug. 1866, having by her had issue,
                c. Cecil Josiah Lambton, M.B. Surg.-Maj. A.M.S., *b.* 25 March, 1840; *m.* 6 April, 1880, Ailleen Mary Beatrice, dau. of Rev. Arthur Hasmer, and *d.* 1898, leaving issue, three sons and two daus.
                d. Seymour Coghill Hort, K.C., J.P. co. Cork, Senior Crown Prosecutor for Dublin (*University Club, Dublin*), *b.* 5 April, 1853; *m.* 17 July, 1886, Lady Kathleen Maude, dau. of the Earl de Montalt.
                    a. Gertrude Egerton, *m.* 14 Dec. 1865, David John Copeland Jones.
                    b. Constance Theodosia Antoinette.
                    c. Sophia Caroline, *m.* 16 June, 1870, Vice-Admiral Arthur Cecil Henry Paget, late R.N., and has issue (*see* BURKE'S *Peerage*, ANGLESEY, M.).
                    d. Josephine Percy, *m.* 1 July, 1873, Capt. William McNeil Cairns, late 43rd L.I.
            3. Thomas, Secretary to the late Ecclesiastical Commissioners, *m.* Miss Phillips, and *d.* 1862, leaving issue,
                a. Charles Kendal KENDAL-BUSHE (which name he adopted 28 Oct. 1908), late Col. 59th Regt., of Bramhope, Old Charlton, *m.* 29 Sept. 1863, Henrietta Victoria Alexandria, 3rd dau. of Arthur French, of Clonsilla, co. Dublin (*see* LESLIE *of Ballibay*). He *d.* 29 Sept. 1911, having had issue,
                    (a) Charles Kendal, Capt. 2nd Dragoon Guards, *b.* 1865.
                    (b) Amyas Robert Leslie, Lieut. R.N., *b.* 1866; *d. unm.* 24 Feb. 1895.   (c) Charles Albert, *d.* 1895.
                    (a) Olivia Florence.
                b. John Phillips (Rev.), M.A. Trin. Coll. Dublin, late Rector of Castlehaven, *d.* 6 April, 1907, having *m.* Louisa Cameron.
                    a. Florence, *m.* Charles Mitford.
                    b. Maria Dorothea, *m.* 30 April, 1851, James Thomas Barlow.   *c.* Pauline.   *d.* Rosina.
                    e. Sylvia, *m.* Bolton Falkner.
            4. Arthur, Master of the Court of Queen's Bench, *m.* 1st, Miss Christian, and 2ndly, Miss Martin, and *d.* 1876, leaving issue by his 1st wife,
                a. Percy, *m.* Miss Atkinson.
                b. Hastings, *d.* 1863.   *c.* Arthur, *m.* Miss Keogh.
                d. George Douglas, *m.* Harriet Mary Augusta, dau. of Rev. John Dunne (*see* DUNNE *of Brittas*), and *d.* 16 Aug. 1901, leaving issue,
                    a. Mary, *m.* Henry Townshend, son of Judge Townshend.
                    b. Madeline, *m.* James Jackson, son of James Edward Jackson, Dean of Armagh.
                    c. Rosalie.   *d.* Kendal.   *e.* Zara.
                1. Anna Maria, *m.* 27 Jan. 1819, Adm. Sir Josiah Coghill, Bart., and *d.* 10 March, 1848. He *d.* 20 June, 1850, leaving issue.
                2. Katherine, *m.* Michael Charles Fox, son of Judge Fox.
                3. Charlotte, *m.* 5 April, 1824, John, 3rd Lord Plunket, who *d.* April, 1870.   4. Elizabeth, *d. unm.*
                5. Maria Belissa, *m.* Rev. John Harris, Rector of Shercock, co. Cavan, and *d.* his widow 8 Feb. 1908.
                6. Henrietta, *m.* 1833, Robert F. Franks, of Jerpoint.
            (2) Thomas (Rev.), *d. unm.*
            (1) Elizabeth, *m.* Rev. William Gorman.
            (2) Mary Martin, *m.* William Warren.
            (3) Katherine.   (4) Harriett, *m.* John Domville.
        3. Paul, Major in the Army. *d. unm.*
    3. Amias, *b.* 1706; entered Trin. Coll. Dublin, 14 June, 1721, aged 15; *d. unm.*
        1. Elinor, *m.* Christopher Hewetson, of Thomastown, co. Kilkenny.
        2. Elizabeth, *m.* Edward Deane, of Terenure, co. Dublin, M.P. for Inistioge.

Mr. Bushe *m.* 2ndly, Mrs. Drysdale, widow. His will, dated 29 Aug. 1724, was proved 2 March, 1730. He was *s.* by his grandson, AMYAS (or AMIAS) BUSHE, of Kilfane, High Sheriff co. Kilkenny 1733; *m.* 2 May, 1737, Elizabeth, dau. and heir of Gervase Parker, General of Horse, Governor of Cork and Kinsale, and Commander-in-Chief in Ireland; and *d.* 1773, leaving an only son and heir,

GERVASE PARKER BUSHE, of Kilfane, M.P., High Sheriff co. Kilkenny 1768; whose will, dated 30 June, 1792, was proved 30 Aug. 1793. He *m.* Feb. 1768, Mary, dau. of James Grattan, M.P., Recorder of Dublin, and sister of the Right Hon. Henry Grattan, M.P., and had issue,

1. HENRY AMYAS, his heir.
2. William (Rev.), of Templeport, co. Cavan, Rector of St. George's, Dublin; *m.* Letitia, dau. of Frederick Geale, and by her (who *d.* 1819) had issue,
    1. William, Lieut.-Col. 7th Hussars, *m.* but *d.s.p.*
    2. Gervase Henry, *m.* Isabella, eldest dau. of Arthur Ussher, of Ballysaggartmore. Lismore, and left one son,
        William Daxon, *d.* 14 June, 1906.
        1. Letitia, *m.* John Percy, of Garadice, co. Leitrim.
        2. Isabella. *m.* Henry Monck Mason, Barrister-at-Law and *d.* 26 Dec. 1873, aged 57.
3. Gervase Parker, of Kilfane, Barrister-at-Law, *m.* May, 1806, Eliza, dau. of John Latham, of Meldrum, co. Tipperary, and widow of Thomas Hacket, and had issue,
    1. Anna, *m.* 19 May, 1835, Hedworth Lambton, M.P., brother of 1st Earl of Durham (*see* BURKE'S *Peerage*), and *d.* 1843. He *d.* 16 Sept. 1876.
    2. Georgiana, *m.* Capt. the Hon. Francis Maude, R.N., 6th son of 1st Viscount Hawarden, and *d.* 2 July, 1882, leaving issue (*see* BURKE'S *Peerage*, DE MONTALT, E.).
4. Richard.
5. Robert, of Trinidad, whose son,
    John Scott, C.M.G., Colonial Sec. at St. Anne's, Trinidad, *b.* 1825, *m.* 1st, 1848, Martha, dau. of Ven. George Cummins, Archdeacon of Trinidad. She *d.* 1880, and he *m.* 2ndly, 1882, Louisa, dau. of Rev. E. P. Smith, and *d.* 24 Jan. 1887.
    1. Charlotte, *m.* Rev. Dean Scott.
2. Frances, *m.* 1794, Right Rev. George de la Poer Beresford, Bishop of Kilmore, and had issue (*see* BURKE'S *Peerage*, WATERFORD, M.).
3. Harriett, *m.* Sir John Power, 1st bart. of Kilfane, and had issue (*see* BURKE'S *Peerage*).
4. Maria.

Mr. Bushe, whose will, dated 30 Jan. 1792, was proved 30 Aug. 1793, was *s.* by his eldest son,

HENRY AMYAS BUSHE, of Glencairn Abbey, High Sheriff co. Waterford 1826; *m.* Lavinia, eldest dau. of Richard Gumbleton, of Castle Richard (now called Glencairn Abbey), co. Waterford, and *s.* by the bequest of his brother-in-law, Richard Edward Gumbleton, who *d.* 1819, to Glencairn Abbey, and was *s.* at his decease by his son.

GERVASE BUSHE, of Glencairn Abbey, J.P., D.L., High Sheriff 1837, Lieut.-Col. in the Army, formerly in the 15th and 7th Hussars, *b.* 2 April, 1806; *m.* 27 May, 1857, Georgina Agnes, dau. of Lieut. William Smart, R.N., and *d.* 1879, leaving issue, two daus.,

1. FRANCES MARIA.   2. AGNES CHARLOTTE.

Arms—Quarterly: 1st and 4th, az., a wolf rampant arg., collared a[nd] chained or; in chief three crosses pattée fitchée of the second (1st); 2nd and 3rd, barry of six, arg. and az., a bend compony o[f] and gu. (GREY). *Crest*—A goat's head couped arg., armed s[a]. *Motto*—Moderata durant.
Seat—Glencairn Abbey, Lismore, co. Waterford.

BUTLER OF KILMURRY.

LIEUT.-COL. SOMERSET JAMES BUTLER, of Kilmurry, co. Kilkenny, J.P. and D.L., High Sheriff 1893, late Royal Berkshire Regt., b. 2 Feb. 1849, Col. Butler is the eldest surviving son of Capt. Henry Butler, of Kilmurry (who d. 13 April, 1881), and Clara his wife (who d. 28 Dec. 1901), dau. of John Taylor, of Newark, co. Leicester, and grandson of Col. the Hon. Peirce Butler, M.P., of Kilmurry, 4th son of Edmund, 11th Viscount Mountgarret.

Lineage, Arms, &c.—See BURKE's *Peerage*, MOUNTGARRET, V.

Seat—Kilmurry, Thomastown, co. Kilkenny. **Clubs**—Jun. United Service and Kildare Street.

BUTLER OF BALLYCARRON.

THOMAS BUTLER, of Ballycarron, co. Tipperary, J.P. and D.L., High Sheriff 1880, b. 1826, 4th son of the late Thomas Butler, of Ballycarron, and Margaret his wife, dau. of Standish Barry, of Lemlara *(see that family)*.

Seat—Ballycarron, Golden, co. Tipperary.

BUTLER OF PRIESTOWN.

JAMES TOTTENHAM BUTLER, of Priestown, co. Meath, of Altameenagh, Laghey, co. Donegal, J.P. cos. Donegal and Meath, b. 4 June, 1868, Capt. 5th Batt. Leinster Regt.; m. 1906, Geraldine B. M., younger dau. of the late Henry St. George Osborne late Royal Dragoons, of Dardistown Castle, co. Meath.

Lineage.—THE REV. PIERCE BUTLER, Prebendary of Killanully, co. Cork, 1672, and Rector of Clanbehy, Kilmore, Dromodecaher, and Kilmane-prior, co. Kerry, 6 April, 1686, youngest son of Theobald Butler, of Killoskehan and Eleanor O'Meagher his wife and grandson of James, 2nd Baron of Dunboyne (see BURKE's *Peerage*), m. Margaret, dau. of Walter Blake, of co. Galway, and was bur. at Glanbeagh, co. Kerry, 1714, having had issue,
1. James, *d.s.p.* 2. THEOBALD, of whom we treat.

The younger son,
THEOBALD BUTLER, of Priestown, co. Meath, m. 1st, Maria O'Hara, who *d.s.p.*, and 2ndly, at Finglas, co. Dublin, 14 Aug. 1722, Mary, dau. of Sir Nathaniel Whitwell, Alderman of Dublin, and by her had issue,
2. JAMES, of whom presently.
2. Whitwell, ancestor of BUTLER of Waterville (*see that family*).
1. Ellen, m. Robert Beatty.

The elder son,
JAMES BUTLER, of Priestown, m. Dorothea, dau. of Sir Richard Steele, bart., by whom he left issue,
1. RICHARD, of whom hereafter.
2. James, Lieut.-Gen. and Governor of Sandhurst College, who m. 1st, Elizabeth Pitcairne, by whom he left issue, James Arthur, General in the Army; Alexander, Capt. in the Army; Jeannette; Elizabeth; Katherine; and Rosa. He m. 2ndly, Frances Glover, who *d.s.p.* in 1828; and 3rdly, Miss Bateman. He *d*. Aug. 1836.
3. Theobald, m. Lucy, dau. of — Richards.
4. Whitwell, *d.s.p.* 5. Pierce, *d.s.p.*
6. Nathaniel Edward, m. Anne, dau. of the Rev. Mr. Stone. *d.s.p.* 1842.
1. Rose, *d. unm.*

The eldest son,

THE REV. RICHARD BUTLER, D.D., Vicar of Burnchurch, co. Kilkenny, m. 1792, Martha, 2nd dau. of Richard Rothwell, of Rockfield and Berford, co. Meath (*see that family*), and had,
1. JAMES (Rev.), late of Priestown.
2. Richard (Very Rev.), Dean of Clonmacnoise and Vicar of Trim, b. 14 Oct. 1794; m. 14 Aug. 1826, Harriet, dau. of R. L. Edgeworth, of Edgeworthstown (*see that family*), and *d.s.p.* 17 July, 1862.
3. Thomas Lewin, Capt. 79th Highlanders, *d.s.p.* 1848.
4. Whitwell, of Staffordstown, co. Meath, J.P., b. 1799, m. 1833, Elizabeth, dau. of John Paine Garnett, of Arch Hall, co. Meath (*see that family*). She *d*. May, 1865. He *d*. 12 July, 1877, leaving issue,
   1. Whitwell, of Staffordstown, *d*. 16 Nov. 1881.
   2. Richard John, of Staffordstown, b. 1840; *d*. 14 Oct. 1908; m. 1870, Georgina Eleanor, dau. of Charles Rothwell, of Kells. She *d*. 1888, leaving, with other issue, a son,
      (1) Richard John, b. 1879; m. 1 Sept. 1909, Grace, dau. of George Ernest Rothwell.
      (1) Synolda, m. 5 Aug. 1903, Rev. Arthur Cowan Digby French, eldest son of the Rev. Robert Digby French, Vicar of Market Weighton, Yorks.
      (2) Ethel Georgina, m. 23 Oct. 1911, Edward Apsley Parker White, M.R.C.V.S.
      1. Mary. 2. Elizabeth.
   5. Edward (Rev.), m. 1st, 1830, Henrietta, dau. of Henry Skryne, of Warleigh, Somersetshire, by whom (who *d*. in 1832) he had a son,
      1. Bagot, *d.* an infant.
   He m. 2ndly, in 1853, Anne Elizabeth, dau. of William Woodville, by whom (who *d*. in 1845) he had a son,
      2. William Theobald, Lieut.-Col. in the Army, b. 1838, m. 1872, Anne Robina, dau. of Maj. Brickenden, and *d*. 1845.
   The Rev. E. Butler m. 3rdly, 1846, Blanche, dau. of Philip Perring, of Devon, by whom (who *d*. 1867) he had a son,
      3. Edward.
   He m. 4thly, Mary Elizabeth, dau. of Richard Rothwell, of Rockfield, co. Meath, by whom he had issue, a dau.,
      1. Dorothea.
   He *d*. Feb. 1877.
   6. John, of Maiden Hall, m. 11 Oct. 1854, Mary, dau. of Robert Barton, of Greenhill, co. Kilkenny, and *d*. 1890, having had issue,
      1. Richard, b. 1858; *d.* Aug. 1877.
      2. George, of Maiden Hall, co. Kilkenny, J.P., High Sheriff 1901; m. 25 Jan. 1898, Harriet Neville, dau. of Marshall Neville Clarke, of Graiguenoe Park, co. Tipperary, and has issue with a dau., a son,
         Hubert Michael, b. 1900.
      1. Florence Elizabeth. 2. Harriet.
   1. Mary, *d.* 1865, *unm.*
Dr. Butler *d*. in 1841, and was s. by his eldest son,
THE REV. JAMES BUTLER, of Priestown, b. 1793; m. 1818, Isabella, eldest dau. of Thomas Rothwell, of Rockfield, co. Meath, and by her (who *d*. 1876) had issue,
1. Richard, *d.* 1851.
2. THOMAS, his heir.
3. James, of Brownstown Park, co. Meath, b. 1823; m. 7 June, 1864, Mary Elizabeth, only dau. of Tottenham Alley, of Hill of Ward, Athboy, co. Meath, and *d*. 1891, having had issue,
   1. JAMES TOTTENHAM, now of Priestown.
   1. Frances Isabel, m. 1896, Ernest Pitman, 2nd son of the late Sir Isaac Pitman.
   2. Augusta Madalene.
1. Helena. 2. Matilda.
3. Isabella. 4. Augusta, *d.* young.
5. Emma, m. 3 Dec. 1889, Vincent Gernou, of Hammondstown, co. Louth, and *d.s.p.* 11 Nov. 1899.
Rev. James Butler *d*. 1872, and was s. by his son,
THOMAS BUTLER, of Priestown, co. Meath, b. 1822, *d. unm.*, and was s. by his nephew.

Arms—Or a chief indented az. three escallops in bend counterchanged. *Motto*—Timor Domini fons vitae.

Seats—Priestown, co. Meath, and Altameenagh, co. Donegal. **Club**—Sackville Street Dublin.

BUTLER OF WATERVILLE.

JAMES WHITWELL BUTLER, of Waterville House, co. Kerry, b. 19 Oct. 1807; s. his father 20 Nov. 1905.

Lineage.—WHITWELL BUTLER, of Waterville, co. Kerry, youngest son of Theobald Butler, of Priestown, co. Meath (*see that family*), m. Belinda Yielding, and had issue,
1. JAMES, his heir. 2. Whitwell.
1. Ellen;
The elder son,
JAMES BUTLER, of Waterville, co. Kerry, J.P. and D.L., m. 1817, Agnes, eldest dau. of the Rev. John Day, M.A., Rector of Kiltallagh, co. Kerry (by whom Arabella, his wife, dau. of Sir William Godfrey, Bart., of Bushfield (Kilcoleman), co. Kerry), grandson of Rev. John Day, M.A., Chancellor of Ardfert, by Lucy his wife, 6th dau. of Maurice FitzGerald, Knight of Kerry. She *d*. May, 1829. He *d*. June, 1863, leaving issue,
1. JAMES, his heir.
2. John, *d. unm.* July, 1854.
1. Arabella Agnes. 2. Belinda, *d. unm.*

The elder son,
JAMES BUTLER, of Waterville, J.P., b. 28 May, 1820; m. 28 Oct. 1847, Anne Margaret, only dau. of Roger Green Davis, of Killeagh,

co. Cork, son of William Davis, by Margaret his wife, dau. of Roger Green, of Youghal. She d. 30 March, 1903. He d. 26 Oct. 1887, having had issue,
1. JAMES EDWARD, late of Waterville.
2. Theobald, b. 8 Aug. 1857 ; m. 19 Oct. 1880, Elizabeth, dau. of Richard Bayley, of Green Park, Kilmallock, and has had issue,
 1. James Bayley, d. young.
 2. Theobald FitzWalter, b. 1894.
 1. Elizabeth Susan Aileen.
 2. Arabella Agnes Muriel.
 3. Gwenda Mary.   4. Synolda.
3. John Edward, b. 15 Nov. 1858 ; d. 2 Nov. 1880.
 1. Elizabeth Agnes.
 2. Belinda Beatty, m. 22 June, 1875, her cousin, Rev. William Spotswood Green, C.B. (1907) M.A., H.M.'s Inspector of Fisheries, Ireland, only son of Charles Green, of Youghal, co. Cork, J.P., and has issue.   3. Mary Pratt.
 4. Agnes Arabella, d. unm. 30 Jan. 1909.
 5. Margaret Mackenzie John.
The eldest son,
JAMES EDWARD BUTLER, of Waterville House, co. Kerry, J.P., High Sheriff 1892, b. 23 Jan. 1856 ; m. 24 Feb. 1897, Mary Goyne (Waterville House, co. Kerry), eldest dau. of William Goyne Stevens, and d. 20 Nov. 1905, leaving issue,
1. JAMES WHITWELL, now of Waterville.
2. John Hubert, b. 27 July, 1900.
3. Edward Vincent, b. 25 Jan. 1902.
1. Arabella Agnes.
2. Mary Rosellen,   } twins.
3. Belinda Yielding, }

Arms—See BUTLER of Priestown.

Seat—Waterville House, Waterville, co. Kerry.

BUTLER. See BURKE'S PEERAGE, **BUTLER, Bart., LANESBOROUGH, E., MOUNTGARRET, V., and ORMONDE, M.**

BUTLER-CREAGH. See **CREAGH.**

BUTLER-KEARNEY. See **KEARNEY.**

BUTLER-STONEY. See **STONEY.**

BUTLER. See **WOOLSEY-BUTLER.**

CARY-CADDELL OF HARBOURSTOWN.

AGNES MARY, MRS. CARY-CADDELL, of Harbourstown, co. Meath, only surviving dau. and co-heir of Admiral Arthur William Jerningham, and Sophia Mary Margaret his wife, of Harbourstown, sister and heir of Robert Caddell, of Harbourstown, b. 6 Jan. 1838 ; s. her mother, 18 Oct. 1899 ; m. 3 Oct. 1865, Stanley Edward George Cary, of Follaton, Devon, J.P. (see that family), and by him (who d. 10 July, 1902) has had issue,

1. GEORGE STANLEY, Lieut. Royal Irish Rifles, b. 19 Sept. 1867, m. 16 Dec. 1895, Lisette, 3rd dau. of Lord Fitzwarren Chichester, brother of the Marquess of Donegall (see BURKE'S Peerage), and d.s.p. 4 April, 1896.
2. Francis Joseph, b. 1 July, 1878.
1. Cecilia Mary, m. 24 April, 1893, Thomas Boylan, of Hilltown, co. Meath, and has issue.
2. Bertha Mary Winifred.

Mrs. Cary assumed by Royal Licence, 5 May, 1900, the additional name and arms of CADDELL.

Lineage.—JOHN CADDELL, of the Naule, made his will 29 Sept. 1581, proved 31 Jan. 1581-2, in which he mentions, " Richard Caddell, late of Harbourstown."

THOMAS CADDELL, of Harbourstown, co. Meath, mentions in his will, proved 25 Jan. 1588, his cousin Richard Caddell, of the Naule, his uncle Richard Caddell, and his late brother Edward Caddell

and Mary Cusack, his widow. He m. Ann, sister of Walter Brett, and had issue,
1. Robert, his heir, living 1588 and 1596 ; and dead before 1607.
2. John, living 1588 and 1596 ; and dead before 1607.
1. Margery, m. John Field. Both living 1588.

PATRICK CADDELL, of Harbourstown. His son,
RICHARD CADDELL, of Harbourstown, was a Capt. under Lord Gormanstown in 1641. He made a settlement of his Harbourstown estates, 14 CHARLES I (1639) on his grandsons Richard and his brother. He was still living 1663. He had a son,
Robert, who d.v.p. before 1639, leaving two sons,
 1. Richard, on whom his grandfather settled his estates in 1639. He was dead in 1663.
 2. JAMES, of whom presently.
His grandson,
JAMES CADDELL, of Timoolo, co. Meath, who was aged 7 at the Rebellion in 1641, the son of Robert Caddell, claimed the Harbourstown estates in the Court of Innocents, 6 Nov. 1663 (14 CHARLES II) but apparently did not get possession. He m. Aminetta, sister of James Barnewall, of Bremore. He d. 1678. His will dated 9 Sept. 1678, was proved 12 Nov. following. He had issue,
1. RICHARD, of whom presently.
2. John.   3. Robert.
4. Mathew.   5. Thomas.
The eldest son,
RICHARD CADDELL, of Harbourstown, co. Meath, m. Oct. 1693, Margery, dau. of Thomas Plunkett, of Tulchanoge, co. Meath. He d. 1742, leaving issue,
1. THOMAS, of whom presently.
2. Richard, m. Elinor, dau. of — Killikelly, but d.s p.
3. Robert, d. unm.
1. Mary, d. unm.
2. Frances, m. 3 June, 1744, Luke Plunkett, of Portmarnock.
3. Bridget, m. 26 April, 1735, William Plunkett.
The eldest son,
THOMAS CADDELL, of Harbourstown, m. about 1726, Celia, dau. of Iriel Farrell, of Cambo and Cluniquin, co. Roscommon, and Sarah his wife, dau. and heir of Ulick Burke, of Clare, co. Galway. She d. 19 April, 1748. He d. March 1765, leaving issue,
1. Richard, b. 1728. s. by devise to the estates in Sligo, Roscommon, and Galway of his uncle James Farrell, of Killmore, co. Roscommon, and assumed in consequence the name of FARRELL. He d. unm. 1811.
2. ROBERT, of whom presently.
1. Mary Ann, m. 1754, John Nugent, Count Nugent, Col. in the Austrian service, brother of Gen. Count James Nugent, Chamberlain to the Empress Maria Teresa. She d.s.p. 1794.
The younger son,
ROBERT CADDELL FARRELL, of Harbourstown, co. Meath, s. his brother 1811, and also assumed the name of FARRELL, b. Sept. 1729 ; m. 13 July, 1765, Ann, dau. of Walter Blake, of Oranmore, co. Galway, and Bridget, his wife, dau. of Denis Daly, of Raford, co. Galway. She d. 1791.   He d. 23 Feb. 1818, leaving issue,
1. RICHARD O'FERRALL, of whom presently.
1. Celia, m. 22 Mar. 1794, Charles Picault, of San Domingo, and d.s.p.
2. Bridget, m. 22 May, 1795, William Dardis, of Giggenstown, Westmeath, and had issue, two sons and three daus., all of whom d. unm.
3. Rose, m. 1798, William Macdonald, and had issue, a dau.
The only son,
RICHARD O'FERRALL CADDELL, of Harbourstown, co. Meath, b. 6 June, 1780 ; m. Sept. 1806, Hon. Paulina Southwell, dau. of Thomas Arthur, Viscount Southwell. She d. 5 May, 1856. He d. 3 Jan. same year, leaving issue,
1. ROBERT, his heir.
1. SOPHIA MARY MARGARET, late of Harbourstown.
2. Cecilia, b. 1812 ; d. unm. 1877.
3. Paulina, a nun, b. 1817.
The only son,
ROBERT CADDELL, of Harbourstown, co. Meath, High Sheriff 1873, b. 1810 ; d. unm. 1887, and was s. by his sister,
SOPHIA MARY MARGARET, MRS. JERNINGHAM, of Harbourstown, co. Meath, dau. of Richard O'Ferrall Caddell, of Harbourstown, and sister and heir of Robert Caddell, of Harbourstown, last male heir of his family. She was b. 23 May, 1809 ; m. 19 April, 1836, Admiral Arthur William Jerningham, son of William Charles Jerningham and nephew of George William, Baron Stafford (see BURKE'S Peerage). Admiral Jerningham d. 24 Nov. 1889. She d. 18 Oct. 1899, having had issue,
1. Paulina, a nun, at Newhall, b. 1837 ; d. 4 Feb. 1868.
2. AGNES MARY, now of Harbourstown.
3. Cecilia Mary, b. 1842 ; m. 30 April, 1862, Capt. Iltyd Thomas Mansel Nicholl, R.N., 2nd son of the Right Hon. John Nicholl, P.C., M.P. of Merthyr Mawr, co. Glamorgan. Capt. Nicholl d. 17 Dec. 1885. She d. 15 Feb. 1879, leaving issue (see that family).

Arms—Arg. on a bend sa. three roses of the field (CARY) ; on an escutcheon of pretence quarterly 1st and 4th arg. fretty gu. on a chief vert a lion rampant or (CADDELL) ; 2nd and 3rd arg. three lozenge-shaped arming-buckles tongues fesswise gu. (JERNINGHAM).

Seat—Harbourstown, Balbriggan, co. Meath. Residence—10, Manson Place, Queen's Gate, S.W.

ROPER-CALDBECK OF MOYLE PARK.

WILLIAM CALDBECK ROPER CALDBECK, of Moyle Park, co. Dublin, J.P., Major (retired) 5th Batt. Royal Dublin Fusiliers, B.A. Trinity Coll. Dublin, called to the bar of the Inner Temple 1896, served in S. African War, b. 28 Jan. 1855; m. 1 Dec. 1898, Alice Mary, youngest dau. of Jasper Young, of Carroch, New Galloway, N.B., and 74, Gloucester Road, S.W., and has issue,

1. WILLIAM NOEL, b. 19 Dec. 1902.
2. George Reginald, b. 3 May, 1904.
3. Arthur Terence, b. 16 June, 1906.
4. Harry Bertram, b. 15 May, 1911.
1. Julia Christian Dora, b. 21 Sept. 1900.

Lineage—(of ROPER).—WILLIAM ROPER, of Blitterlees, m. 23 Nov. 1727, Elizabeth Sealby, and had issue,
1. Thomas, bapt. 13 April, 1729; d. at Blitterlees, 14 Jan. 1799, aged 70.
2. JOHN, of whom presently.
3. Joseph, bapt. 1737.
1. Mary, bapt. 3 Feb. 1733.

The 2nd son,

JOHN ROPER, of Kingsidehill, bapt. 9 May, 1730, was bur. 10 Oct. 1788, aged 58, and left, by Frances his wife (who d. 24 Jan. 1815), with two sons, Thomas and John, who d. in infancy, a son, WILLIAM ROPER, of Kingsidehill, bapt. at Blitterlees, 11 June, 1777, and was bur. there 26 April, 1833, aged 56, and left by Catherine Penny his wife (who d. 24 Jan. 1815) a son,

THOMAS ROPER, of Moyle Park, Clondalkin, co. Dublin, J.P., b. 29 Aug. 1819; m. 29 Aug. 1850, Dora, dau. of Francis Cope Caldbeck, and d. 27 Aug. 1887, having by her (who d. 12 June, 1885) had issue,

WILLIAM CALDBECK, now of Moyle.
Annie Frances, m. 28 Jan. 1875, Major Cecil Murphy, R.A., and has issue, 1. Lionel; 2. Lewis; 3. Cecil; and 1. Dora.

Lineage—(of CALDBECK).—WILLIAM CALDBECK, of Clondalkin, and Larch Hill, Whitechurch, co. Dublin, King's Counsel, Col. of the Lawyers' Artillery Volunteers, at the time of the Rebellion, and Treasurer of King's Inns, m. Anne Keatinge, and d. 6 Sept. 1803, aged 70, and was bur. at Clondalkin, having by her (who d. 21 June, 1821, aged 76) had issue,
1. WILLIAM, of whom hereafter.
2. Frederick, m. Eliza Pearson, niece or grand-niece of Bishop Pearson, and had issue,
1. William, J.P. and D.L., High Sheriff, of Moyle Park, d. unm. leaving the property to his cousin WILLIAM CALDBECK ROPER-CALDBECK, now of Moyle Park.
2. Richard, d.s.p.
1. Fanny, d. unm.
3. Harry, went abroad and was not heard of again.

The eldest son,

WILLIAM CALDBECK, m. Dora, dau. of Francis Graham, of New Barns, West Malling, Kent, and sister of Anne, wife of Joseph Fulton (see below) and had issue,
1. William Eaton, of Lisburn, co. Antrim, b. 1787; m. 4 March, 1808, his first cousin, Amelia (or Emelia) Boyd, dau. of the late Joseph Fulton, of Lisburn. She d. 31 Jan. 1870, aged 82. He d. 25 Sept. 1858, leaving issue,
1. William Eaton, High Sheriff co. Dublin 1844, bapt. 18 Aug. 1815; d. 21 Sept. 1855.
2. Joseph Fulton, bapt. 4 June, 1819; d. 1 Aug. 1840.
3. Thomas Fulton, of Eaton Brae, co. Dublin, J.P., High Sheriff 1871, b. 1821; m. 1851, Charlotte, dau. of William Stewart, M.D., of Lisburn. She d. 2 Feb. 1897. He d. 1891, having had issue,
William Fulton, m. 1890, Sara, dau. of J. Watkins, and d. 1896, leaving issue,
1. Thomas Fulton, b. 9 Aug. 1894; d. 8 April, 1910.
2. William Eaton, b. 24 May, 1896.
1. Charlotte Hannah, b. 14 Sept. 1891.
2. Sarah Frances, b. 2 Sept. 1892.
1. Anne Fulton, bapt. 29 July, 1811; m. William Grieg, of Derryvolgie, Lisburn, who d.s.p. 23 March, 1839.
2. Dorothea, d. young, 21 April, 1837.
3. Emily, bapt. 18 Jan. 1823; d. 1909; m. 26 Feb. 1851, Lieut.-Col. Charles William Thompson, 58th Regt., of Ballyherin, co. Donegal, who d. 30 Dec. 1881, leaving issue,
(1) Charles, d. May, 1861.
(2) Evelyn, d. 18 March, 1868.
(1) Amy, m. 4 Aug. 1874, Hon. Walter C. Pepys, son of the Earl of Cottenham, and d. 7 July, 1908, having had issue (see BURKE'S Peerage).
4. Elizabeth, d. 7 April, 1835.
2. FRANCIS COPE, of whom we treat.

The younger son,

FRANCIS COPE CALDBECK, was given the freedom of the City of Dublin in 1799; m. Anne Curran, niece of the Right Hon. Sir John Philpot Curran, Master of the Rolls, and by her (who d. 27 Jan. 1867) had issue, a son and a dau.,
William Francis Cope, m. Annabelle, dau. of S. Hugo, and had issue,
1. William Cope, Lieut. 87th Regt., b. 15 Dec. 1867; d. 1895.
2. Francis Curran.
1. Florence, m. 1894, Surg.-Major Walter Stafford.
DORA, m. 29 Aug. 1850, THOMAS ROPER, of Moyle Park (see above), and had issue, WILLIAM CALDBECK ROPER CALDBECK, now of Moyle Park.

Seat—Moyle Park, Clondalkin, co. Dublin. Residence—Lenwade Lodge, Great Witchingham, Norfolk. Clubs—Junior United Service, S.W.; University, Dublin; and Norfolk (Norwich).

CALDWELL OF NEW GRANGE.

CHARLES HENRY BULWER CALDWELL, of New Grange, co. Meath, High Sheriff 1902, b. 3 June, 1863; s. his uncle 1896.

Lineage.—The family is of Scottish origin. ANDREW CALDWELL, b. 1683; m. 1706, Catherine, sister of the Right Hon. Charles Campbell, M.P., of New Grange, co. Meath, and d. 1731, leaving a son,

CHARLES CALDWELL, of Dublin, Solicitor to the Customs, b. 14 June, 1707; m. 1732, Elizabeth, dau. of Benjamin Heywood, of Liverpool, by Anne his wife, sister of General Arthur Graham, of Armagh, and by her (who d. 19 Nov. 1792) had, with other issue,
1. Andrew, of Cavendish Row, Rutland Square, Dublin, Barrister-at-Law, b. 19 Dec. 1733; d.s.p. 2 July, 1808.
2. Charles, of Liverpool, b. 1737; d. 10 Jan. 1814, leaving issue,
1. George (Rev.), Fellow of Jesus Coll. Cambridge; m. 4 Dec. 1817, Harriot, youngest dau. and, in her issue, co-heiress of Sir William Abdy, 4th bart. of Felix Hall, Capt. R.N., and had issue.
2. William, of Kingston, Jamaica, Member of the House of Assembly, d. 29 Jan. 1819.
1. Anne, m. George Dunbar, 2nd son of Sir George Dunbar, Bart.
2. Harriot.
3. BENJAMIN (Sir), of whom presently.
4. Ponsonby, b. 26 Nov. 1746; d. 7 Nov. 1819.
1. Amelia, m. 22 Jan. 1761, George Cockburn.
2. Catherine, m. Phineas Riall, of Heywood, co. Tipperary.
3. Mary Elizabeth, m. 26 Jan. 1768, Jacob Sankey, of Coolmore, co. Tipperary.

Mr. Caldwell d. 1776. The 3rd son,

ADMIRAL SIR BENJAMIN CALDWELL, G.C.B., b. 31 Jan. 1738-9; m. 7 June, 1784, Charlotte, dau. of Admiral Henry Osborn, Vice-Admiral of England (a younger son of Sir John Osborn, 1st bart. of Chicksands Priory, co. Bedford), and d. 1820, having by her (who d. 22 Sept. 1819) had a son,

CHARLES ANDREW CALDWELL, of New Grange, co. Meath, b. 25 March, 1785, who m. 1 Dec. 1808, Charlotte Ann, 2nd dau. and, in her issue, co-heiress of Sir William Abdy, 4th bart. of Felix Hall, Capt. R.N., and d. 11 Feb. 1859, having by her (who d. 29 March, 1858) had issue,
1. CHARLES BENJAMIN, late of New Grange.
2. James Thomas, Commander R.N., b. 28 Dec. 1810; d. at Paris, Aug. 1849.
3. William Charles, late Capt. 47th Regt., b. 1 May, 1812; d. 29 Oct. 1877.
4. Henry, Commodore R.N., C.B., A.D.C. to the Queen, m. 16 June, 1858, Mary Eleanor, youngest dau. of William Earle Lytton Bulwer, of Heydon Hall, Norfolk, and d. 7 April, 1868, leaving issue,
1. CHARLES HENRY BULWER, now of New Grange.
1. Mary Elizabeth Abdy, m. Capt. H. A. F. Merewether, and has a dau., Irene.
2. Emily Charlotte Ernestine, m. Col. H. Cooper, and has one son, Derek, and a dau., Barbara.
3. Henrica Eleanor, m. 28 June, 1899, Col. Edward Augustine Earle Bulwer, youngest son of Gen. Lytton Bulwer, C.B. (see that family).
1. Mary Catherine. 2. Charlotte Louisa.

The eldest son,

CHARLES BENJAMIN CALDWELL, of New Grange, co. Meath, late Capt. 91st Regt., b. 9 Oct. 1809; m. 13 Dec. 1868, Sophia Frances eldest dau. of Hon. Wm. Cust, Commissioner of Customs (see BURKE'S Peerage, BROWNLOW, E.). She d. 28 Jan. 1908. He d.s.p. 16 Jan. 1896.

Arms (H. Coll.)—Or, three piles sa. the centre one charged with a wreath of oak of the field, the others each with a fountain and in base four barrulets wavy alternately gu. and vert. Crest—Issuant from a naval crown or, a demi lion, the dexter paw grasping a scymitar ppr. pommel and hilt gold, the sinister resting on an anchor erect, also ppr. Motto—Ense libertatem petit inimico tyrannis.
Seat—New Grange, Slane, co. Meath; New Grange Lodge, Bray, co. Wicklow. Residence—The Cedars, Windlesham, Surrey.

CANNING OF ROSSTREVOR.

THE HON. ALBERT STRATFORD GEORGE CANNING, of The Lodge, Rosstrevor, co. Down, J.P. and D.L. Londonderry, J.P. co. Down, author of various prose works, b. 24 Aug. 1832. Mr. Canning is the younger son of George, 1st Baron Garvagh (who d. 20 Aug. 1840), and Rosabelle Charlotte Isabella his wife (who d. 23 Dec. 1891), dau. of Henry Bonham, M.P.

Lineage, Arms, &c.—See BURKE'S Peerage, GARVAGH, B. Residence—The Lodge, Rosstrevor, co. Down. Club—Carlton.

Canning. THE LANDED GENTRY. 96

CANNING. See BURKE'S PEERAGE, **GARVAGH, B.**

DE BURGH-CANNING. See BURKE'S PEERAGE, **CLANRICARDE, M.**

CARDEN OF BARNANE.

ANDREW MURRAY CARDEN, of Barnane, co. Tipperary, J.P., High Sheriff 1888, late Capt. Royal Horse Artillery, b. 4 Aug. 1853.

Lineage.—JOHN CARDEN, of Templemore, co. Tipperary, settled there about 1550, m. Priscilla, dau. of John Kent, of Poleran, co. Kilkenny, Collector of Waterford. She d. 1735 (will proved 9 Dec. 1735). He d. 1728, aged 105 (will proved 3 Sept. 1728), having had, with several daus.,—
1. JONATHAN, of Barnane.
2. JOHN, of Templemore, ancestor of the CARDENS, Baronets of Templemore, and the CARDENS of Fishmoyne (see that family).
3. William, of Lismore, Queen's Co , m. Gertrude, dau. of Richard Warburton, of Garryhinch, and d. 1760, leaving issue.

The eldest son,
JONATHAN CARDEN, of Barnane, co. Tipperary, which he acquired by indenture 17 June, 1701, from Stephen Moore, of Kilworth, co. Cork. He is mentioned as eldest son in an unproved will of John Carden, his father, dated 12 Feb. 1717. He d.v.p. 1703 (will proved 12 April, 1703) and left by Bridget his wife (who m. 2ndly, John Barry) a son,
JOHN CARDEN, of Barnane, J.P., who came of age 11 May, 1720, mentioned in the will 1717 of his grandfather. He m. (setts. dated 15 Jan. 1725) Anna Sophia, youngest dau. of Andrew Roe, of Roesgreen, co. Tipperary, and d. intestate, 6 June, 1771 (admon. 2 Aug. 1771) having had issue,
1. JOHN, of whom presently.
2. Frederick, d. before 1768.
3. Jonathan, d. before 1768.
4. Nicholas, living 1790, left issue.
5. Leonidas, living 1765.
1. Sophia, m. (setts. dated 30 Dec. 1783) William Chadwick, of Ballinard, and d. Sept. 1825, aged 82 (see that family).

The eldest son,
JOHN CARDEN, of Barnane, sometime Lieut. R.A., b. 1731 ; m. 16 April, 1765, Elizabeth, dau. of Moore Disney and d. 31 Aug. 1789, having had issue,
1. Andrew, b. 1768 ; d.v.p. 10 Oct. 1786, s.p.
2. JOHN, of whom presently.
3. Jonathan, d. unm.
4. Washington, Capt. 30th Regt., d. 31 Dec. 1844. leaving issue.
1. Elizabeth, m. William Jones.

The elder surviving son,
JOHN CARDEN, of Barnane, J.P. and D.L., High Sheriff 1796 ; m. 21 Nov. 1809, Ann, only dau. and heiress of Henry Rutter, of Lincoln, and d. 22 March, 1822. having had issue,
1. JOHN RUTTER, his heir.
2. Henry, b. 16 July, 1814 ; d. an infant.
3. ANDREW, of whom presently.
4. Lionel (Rev.), b. 22 April, 1817 ; m. 2 Sept. 1845, Lucy Lawrence, youngest dau. of William Young Ottley, F.R.S. She d. 22 May, 1907. He d. 20 Sept. 1851, leaving issue,
   1. Lionel Edward Gresley, Envoy Extraordinary and Minister Plenipo in 1st v in H.M.'s Diplomatic Service, b. 15 Sept. 1851 ; m. 15 Feb. 1881. Anne Eliza, dau. of John Lefferts, of Flatbush, Long Island, U.S.A.
      1. Edith, d. young.   2. Lucy Anne.
      3. Alice Maria Fraser.
5. Charles Wilson, Capt. 36th Herefordshire Regt., b. 9 Sept. 1818, m. Jane, dau. of Edward Bolton King, D.L., of Chadshunt, co. Warwick. She d. 5 Sept. 1903. He d. 24 Nov. 1894, having had issue,
   1. Charles Edward, b. 3 Aug. 1856 ; m. Eliza Wyrill, and has issue.
   2. Alfred, Lieut. 2nd W.I. Regt., b. 11 June, 1859, drowned at sea, 10 March, 1883.
   3. Eustace, b. 29 Dec. 1863 ; m. Lilias Markham, and was drowned at sea, 9 June, 1897, leaving issue
   4. John, C.M.G., Col. and Commandant Northern Rhodesian Police, b. 13 May, 1870 ; m. 25 Oct. 1900, Susan Ellen, dau. of late Drury Wake, of Pitsford House, Northampton (see BURKE's Peerage, WAKE, Bart.), and has issue,
      Andrew, b. 4 Aug. 1910.

1. Eveleen.   2. Georgiana Anne, d. young.
3. Bertha.
4. Maud, m. 13 July, 1897, William Thurnall, of Kettering, and has issue.
5. Catherine Octavia, m. 1st, 17 Oct. 1888, Capt. Charles Gustavus Whittaker Edward s, 58th Regt., of Sealvham, Pembrokeshire, who d.s.p. 7 May, 1902. She m. 2ndly, 4 Oct. 1905, Victor James Higgon, J.P., 2nd son of Capt. Higgon, R.A., of Scotton. and has issue.
6. James (Rev.), M.A. Oxford, b. 6 Oct. 1819 ; d. unm. 18 Feb. 1883.
1. Anna Frances, m. 13 Oct. 1838, Robert Burrowes, of Stradone, co. Cavan, and d. 1902, leaving issue (see that family). He d. 30 Nov. 1881.

The eldest son,
JOHN RUTTER CARDEN, of Barnane, J.P., D.L., b. 5 Feb. 1811 ; d. unm. 1866, when he was s. by his brother,
ANDREW CARDEN, of Barnane, J.P., D.L., High Sheriff 1873, Capt. 60th Rifles, b. 28 Sept. 1815 ; m. 4 Aug. 1847, Anne, eldest dau. of Lieut.-Gen. Sackville Hamilton Berkeley, and had issue,
1. William Berkeley, R.E., b. 25 Feb. 1852 ; d. unm. 16 March, 1873.
2. ANDREW MURRAY, now of Barnane.
3. Sackville Hamilton, Rear-Adml. R.N., b. 3 May, 1857 ; m. 1st, 1878, Maria Louisa, dau. of Loftus J. Nunn, late Capt. 99th Foot. He m. 2ndly, 8 May, 1909, Henrietta, eldest dau. of W. English Harrison.
4. Arnold Philip, County Inspector R.I.C., b. 9 Feb. 1859 ; m. Eva, dau. of Robert Hamilton, and has issue.
5. Louis Peile, Lieut.-Col. R.A., b. 10 Sept. 1860 ; m. Mary Elizabeth, dau. of James MacCarthy Monogh, of Innishbeg, co. Cork, and has issue, a dau., Eileen Annie, b. 21 June, 1899.
6. Lionel Berkeley, b. 17 May, 1863 ; m., and has issue, settled in U.S.A.
7. John Rutter, Major 15th Ludhiana Sikhs, b. 7 July, 1867.
1. Mary Rutter, m. April, 1875, Capt. James Ogilvie Dalgleish, 29th Regt., and has issue.
2. Florence Annie, m. 4 Oct. 1887, Rev. John Newman Lombard, M.A., Rector of Balrothey, co. Dublin.
3. Florence Maud, d. an infant.   4. Rosa, d. an infant.

Capt. Carden m. 2ndly, 21 June, 1876, Clara Maria (who d.s.p. 1902), dau. of Hon. Edward de Moleyns, and widow of R. J. Berkeley, Q.C., and d. 27 Nov. 1876, when he was s. by his son.

Arms—Arg., a lozenge gu., between three pheons sa. **Crest**—A pheon sa. *Motto*—Fide et amore.
Seat—Barnane, near Templemore, co. Tipperary. **Clubs**—Naval and Military and Kildare Street.

CARDEN OF FISHMOYNE.

RICHARD GEORGE CARDEN, of Fishmoyne, co. Tipperary, J.P. and D.L., b. 8 June, 1866 ; m. 24 Nov. 1897, Isabel Frances, only surviving child of the late John Toler, of 22, Lower Fitzwilliam Street, Dublin, and has issue,
RICHARD HENRY LOWRY, b. 1 Dec. 1900.
Isabel Hester Louise, b. 5 May, 1899.

Lineage.—JOHN CARDEN, of Templemore, 2nd son of John Carden and Priscilla Kent (see CARDEN of Barnane), who m. Rebecca, dau. of Paul Minchin, of Ballynakill, and had issue,
1. JOHN, ancestor of CARDEN, Bart., of Templemore Abbey (see BURKE'S Peerage and Baronetage).
2. MINCHIN, of whom hereafter.
3. Paul.

The 2nd son,
MINCHIN CARDEN, of Fishmoyne, m. 23 Feb. 1749, Lucy, dau. of Richard Lockwood, of Cashel, and had issue,
1. JOHN, his heir.   2. RICHARD, s. his brother.
1. Elizabeth, m. Hamilton Lowe, of Brookhill, co. Tipperary.

The elder son,
JOHN CARDEN, of Fishmoyne, m. 1st, 1785, Sydney, dau. of Arthur Graham ; and 2ndly, 1789, Eliza, dau. of Theophilus Bolton, but had no issue. He d. 19 July, 1794, and was s. by his brother,
RICHARD CARDEN, of Fishmoyne, an officer in the 12th Regt. of Dragoons, m. 6 May, 1785, Jane, dau. of Very Rev. Dixie Blundell, Dean of Kildare, and had a son,
RICHARD MINCHIN, his heir.
Mr. Carden d. Feb. 1812, and was s. by his son,
RICHARD MINCHIN CARDEN, of Fishmoyne, J.P. and D.L., b. 1 July, 1799 ; m. 2 Aug. 1821, Emily Henrietta, only dau. of Major Battier, 5th Fusiliers, and had issue,
1. Richard William Thomas, b. 1822 ; d.v.p. 1838.
2. John Batier, Barrister-at-Law, b. 1824 ; d.v.p. 1858.
3. HENRY ROBERT, late of Fishmoyne.
4. Edward Arthur, b. 1827 ; d. 1845.
5. Sydney, Lieut. Royal Artillery, b. 1828 ; d. 1851.
6. Minchin, b. 1829 ; d. 1847.
7. William Joseph, Chief Paymaster and Hon. Col. Army Pay Department, b. 17 March, 1833 ; m. 1st, 1859, Florence Marsh, who d. 1862, leaving a dau.,
   1. Florence.

He m. 2ndly, 1864, Anne, widow of Bulwer Headly, and by her (who d. 8 Jan. 1896) had issue,

IRELAND. Carleton.

1. Sydney Arthur, b. 9 June, 1865.
2. John Minchin (*Mildura, P.O., Murray River, Victoria, Australia*), b. Dec. 1866 ; *m.* 13 Dec. 1892, Alexandra Louisa, dau. of the Hon. R. J. Handcock, son of 3rd Baron Castlemaine, and has issue,
   Brian Craven, b. Aug. 1899.
2. Kathleen Lloyd.
He *m.* 3rdly, 3 April, 1897, Mabel Ellen, only dau. of Col. George W. Rippon, late Chief Paymaster Army Pay Department, and *d.* 18 May, 1904.
3. Harriette Emily, *m.* 10 March, 1863, Arthur William Knox-Gore, Lieut.-Col. North Mayo Militia (*d.* 31 Jan. 1885), 2nd son of Sir Arthur Knox-Gore, 1st bart. of Belleek Manor, co. Mayo.
2. Jane Rosetta, *a. unm.*
Mr. Carden *d.* 11 May, 1873, and was *s.* by his eldest surviving son,
HENRY ROBERT CARDEN, of Fishmoyne, J.P. and D.L., Lieut.-Col. in the Army, formerly 77th Regt., b. 28 June, 1826 ; *m.* 10 Aug. 1865, Louisa Harriet, 2nd dau. of Hans Hamilton Woods, of Milverton Hall and Whitestown House, co. Dublin, J.P. and D.L., and has issue,
1. RICHARD GEORGE, now of Fishmoyne.
2. Henry Hamilton Woods, b. 17 Aug. 1870.
3. John St. Leger Taylour, b. 31 March, 1872 ; *d.* 24 July, 1891.
1. Louisa Emily May.
2. Evelyn Frances, *m.* 17 Sept. 1904, Loftus Otway Clarke (*see* CLARKE *of Graiguenoe Park*).
Lieut.-Col. Carden served throughout the entire Crimean campaign. He received the Crimean medal and three clasps, was a Chevalier of the Order of the Legion of Honour, the Order of the Mejidie, and Turkish medals. He *d.* 15 Dec. 1880, and was *s.* by his eldest son.
Seat—Fishmoyne, Borrisoleigh, co. Tipperary. *Clubs*—Kildare Street, Dublin, and Piccadilly, London.

CARDEN. *See* BURKE'S PEERAGE, **CARDEN**, Bart.

CAREW OF BALLINAMONA PARK.

ROBERT THOMAS CAREW, of Ballinamona Park, co. Waterford, J.P. and D.L., High Sheriff 1891, Major and Hon. Lieut.-Col. Waterford Art. S. Div. R.A., late Capt. 6th Batt. Rifle Brigade, b. 22 May, 1860 ; *m.* 1st, 4 Aug. 1887, Constance Charlotte Mary, dau. of Major-Gen. William Creagh, Bombay Staff Corps, and grand-dau. of Gen. Sir Michael Creagh, K.H., and by her (who *d.* 15 Oct. 1900) has issue,
ROBERT JOHN HENRY, b. 7 June, 1888, Lieut. 1st Batt. Royal Dublin Fus.
He *m.* 2ndly, 30 Oct. 1905, Mary, dau. of late Major Purcell O'Gorman, 90th Light Infantry, and sometime M.P. for Waterford.
Lineage.—THOMAS CAREW, of Ballinamona, co. Waterford, 2nd surviving son of Robert Carew, of Castleborough, co. Wexford, and brother of Robert Carew, M.P. for Waterford 1740, who *d.s.p.*, and of Shapland Carew, of Castleboro, grandfather of Robert Shapland, 1st Lord Carew. He was M.P. for Dungarvan and High Sheriff of Waterford 1742, b. 11 Aug. 1708 ; *m.* 12 Nov. 1715, Eliza Rickarda, dau. of James May, of Mayfield, by Letitia his wife, dau. of William, 1st Viscount Duncannon, and had issue,
1. ROBERT THOMAS, his heir.
2. John Mutlow, *m.* Miss Jones, of Mullinabro.
3. Ponsonby, *m.* Miss Giles.
1. Elizabeth, *m.* Richard Chartres.
2. Letitia, *m.* Rev. John Kennedy, of Fethard Castle, co. Wexford.
The eldest son,
ROBERT THOMAS CAREW, of Ballinamona, M.P. Dungarvan, High Sheriff Waterford 1779, b. 22 May, 1747 ; *m.* 4 July, 1771, Frances, dau. of Thomas Boyse, of Bishop's Hall, co. Kilkenny, and had issue,
1. THOMAS, his heir.
2. Robert Shapland, b. 25 Aug. 1777 ; Capt. in the 18th Hussars, killed at Vittoria, June, 1813.
1. Margaret, *m.* Robert Hunt, of Sidbury House, Devon.
Mr. Carew *d.* 11 April, 1834, and was *s.* by his son,
THOMAS CAREW, of Ballinamona, J.P., D.L., b. 23 Aug. 1775 ; *m.* 8 April, 1807, Jane, eldest dau. and co-heir of Sir John Alcock, Knt., of Waterford, who *d.* 1867, and had issue (who *d.* 1857) had issue,
1. ROBERT THOMAS, his heir.
2. John Henry Alcock, Capt. 95th Regt., b. 2 Feb. 1819 ; *d.* 1869.
1. Jane. 2. Frances, *d.* 1883. 3. Marianne.
4. Henrietta, *m.* 24 Aug. 1842, Thomas Edward Ivens.
5. Margaret, *m.* 22 April, 1842, James Anderson, of Grace Dieu, Waterford, who *d.* 1867, and had issue (*see that family*).
Mr. Carew *d.* 4 Oct. 1853, and was *s.* by his eldest son,
ROBERT THOMAS CAREW, of Ballinamona, J.P. and D.L., High Sheriff 1866 ; *m.* 28 July, 1859, Henrietta, eldest dau. of Richard Clayton Browne-Clayton, J.P. and D.L., of Adlington Hall, co. Lan-

I.L.G.

caster, and Carrigbyrne, co. Wexford, and *d.* 20 Jan. 1886, having by her (who *d.* 8 June, 1884, aged 53) had,
1. ROBERT THOMAS, now of Ballinamona Park.
2. Richard Clayton, of Ballindud, Waterford, J.P. (*United Service Club*), Lieut. R.N. (retired list), Capt. late Reserve of Officers, b. 20 Aug. 1861 ; *m.* 14 April, 1891, Catherine, dau. of Capt. Edward Croker, 17th Leicestershire Regt., of Cheltenham, and has issue,
   Reginald Lionel Otho, b. 10 Jan. 1892.
   Catherine Henrietta Rosalie, b. 31 Dec. 1894.
3. Ponsonby May Lyon, b. 13 April, 1865 ; Major, late 20th Hussars and Royal Warwickshire Regt. (*Cavalry Club*) ; *m.* 1st, 9 June, 1894, Jane, dau. of Rev. Cyril Stacey, and by her (who *d.* 11 Aug. 1896) had issue,
   Mary Gladys, b. 11 Nov. 1895.
He *m.* 2ndly, 6 Jan. 1910, Vida Hope Carmichael, dau. of Lieut.-Col. Robert Story, of Bingfield, co. Cavan.
4. Bampfylde Leonard, b. 21 April, 1868 ; Major, late 4th Dragoon Guards, *m.* 18 Aug. 1909, Jeanne Ethel, dau. of Col. Frank Walker, of Turf Moor, New Brighton, Cheshire.
1. Catherine Jane, *m.* 1890, Charles Orby Shipley, and has issue (*see* SHIPLEY *of Twyford Moors*).
Seat—Ballinamona Park, Waterford.

CAREW. *See* BURKE'S PEERAGE, **CAREW**, B.

CARLETON OF CLARE.

COLONEL HENRY AUGUSTUS CARLETON, of Clare, co. Tipperary, and Greenfields, co. Cork, Major 12th Bengal Cavalry, b. 6 May, 1858 ; *m.* 29 Jan. 1895, Marguerite Sophia, dau. of the late Gabriel Eynard, of Les Genets, Canton de Vaud, Switzerland, and has issue,
HENRY, b. 1896.
Lineage.—FRANCIS CARLETON, of Cork, b. 1713 ; 3rd son of John Carleton, of Darling Hill, High Sheriff for Tipperary 1717 ; whose pedigree is registered in Ulster's Office, Dublin Castle ; *m.* 1737, Rebecca, dau. of Hugh Lawton, of Castle Jane, co. Cork, and by her (who *d.* Feb. 1797) he left issue at his decease, 1791,
1. HUGH, b. 11 Sept. 1739, who became Lord Chief Justice of the Court of Common Pleas, and was created BARON CARLETON of Anner, 1789, and VISCOUNT CARLETON of Clare, 1797. He *m.* 1st, 2 Aug. 1766, Elizabeth, only dau. of Richard Mercer, of Dublin ; she *d.s.p.* 27 May, 1794. He *m.* 2ndly, Mary Buckley, 2nd dau. of Abednego Matthew, M.P. ; she *d.s.p.* 13 March, 1810. Lord Carleton *d.* 1826.
2. Francis, of Green Park, co. Down, *m.* Dorcas, dau. of Roger Hall, of Narrow Water, and *d.s.p.* 1829.
3. JOHN, of whom presently.
1. Mary, *d.* 1769. 2. Isabella, *d.* 1771.
3. Rebecca, *m.* 18 Sept. 1779, Hugh Millerd ; *d.s.p.* July, 1804.
4. Sarah, *d.* 1766. 5. Grace, *m.* Sampson Jervois, and *d.s.p.*
The 3rd son,
JOHN CARLETON, of Dublin, *m.* Aug. 1776, Elizabeth, dau. and heir of Thomas Hodgson, of Dublin, and *d.* intestate 1781, leaving issue,
1. FRANCIS, of Clare. 1. Rebecca, *d. unm.*
2. Dorothea, *m.* Edward Reeves, of Ballyglissane, co. Cork. She *d.* 1855, and left issue.
The only son,
FRANCIS CARLETON, who *s.* to the estates of his uncle, Viscount Carleton, of Clare, was b. 6 Aug. 1780, and was formerly of the 10th Hussars ; he *m.* 9 Sept. 1809, Charlotte Molyneux (who *d.* Dec. 1874), eldest dau. of George Molyneux Montgomerie, of Garboldisham Hall, co. Norfolk, descended from Hugh, 1st Earl of Eglinton, and *d.* 26 Jan. 1870, having had issue,
1. HUGH FRANCIS, late of Clare.
2. HENRY ALEXANDER, late of Clare.
3. Frederick, b. 23 July, 1821 ; *d. unm.* 15 May, 1867.
4. Percival Augustus, b. 7 April, 1825 ; Capt. 1st Surrey Militia, served in the Anglo-Turkish Contingent ; *m.* 21 April, 1855, Susan Georgiana, dau. of Charles Hare, of Wormley, Herts, and *d.* 13 Dec. 1869, leaving a dau.,
   Frances Laura, *m.* 23 Feb. 1897, Major Arthur M. Connolly, Royal Marines.
1. Mary, *m.* 1838, Auguste de Mont Richer, of the Chateau de Lully, Morges, Switzerland, who *d.* 1861, leaving issue. She *d.* 2 July, 1898. 2. Sophia.

G

Carleton. THE LANDED GENTRY. 98

The eldest son,
HUGH FRANCIS CARLETON, of Clare, co. Tipperary, and Greenfields, co. Cork, b. 1810; m. 30 Nov. 1859, Lydia (who d. 1892), dau. of Ven. Henry Williams, Archdeacon of Wainate, New Zealand. He d.s.p. 14 July, 1890, and was s. by his brother,
GEN. HENRY ALEXANDER CARLETON, C.B., of Clare, co. Tipperary, and Greenfields, co. Cork, Gen. and Col. Commandant of the Royal Artillery, b. 28 Feb. 1814; s. to the family estates of his great-uncle Hugh, Viscount Carleton, of Clare, co. Tipperary, and Greenfields, co. Cork, by deed of conveyance from his father in 1867; m. 22 Dec. 1855, Elizabeth, dau. of Armor Boyle, of Dundrum, Ireland, and by her (who d. 1 Aug. 1878) had issue,
1. HENRY AUGUSTUS, now of Clare.
2. Montgomery Launcelot, b. 4 June, 1861, Col. Royal Artillery; m. 16 Dec. 1908, Marguerite Helen, 3rd dau. of Sir Lionel Edward Darell, 5th Bart. (see BURKE's Peerage), and has issue, Guy, b. 1909.
3. Hugh Dudley, D.S.O., b. 24 Dec. 1865, Maj. 2nd W. India Regt., m. 11 Aug. 1904, Lady Jane Edith Seymour (Ragley Hall, Alcester, Warwickshire), youngest dau. of Hugh de Grey, 6th, Marquess of Hertford (see BURKE'S Peerage). He d. 9 Aug. 1906, leaving issue, a son,
Henry Hugh Seymour, b. 26 May, 1906.
4. Frederic Montgomerie, D.S.O., late Maj. King's Own (4th Regt.), (15, Tite Street, Chelsea. Club—United Service), b. 21 July, 1867, m. 20 Nov. 1899, Emma Gwendolen Priscilla, eldest dau. of Sampson S. Lloyd (see LLOYD of Dolobran), and has issue,
1. Guy, b. 18 April, 1902.
2. John Dudley, b. 29 Aug. 1908.
1. Claire Emilia, b. 5 Dec. 1901.
1. Mary, m. 3 Nov. 1885, Capt. John Brinkley, N. Stafford Regt., Chief Constable of Warwickshire, and has issue (see BRINKLEY of Fortland).
2. Edith Charlotte.
3. Alice, m. 21 Oct. 1890, John Stratford Dugdale, K.C., and has issue.

Gen. Carleton served under Sir Colin Campbell (afterwards created Lord Clyde, against the frontier tribes at Peshawur in 1851, and afterwards in 1858, commanded the Bengal Artillery Division of the siege train at the siege and capture of Lucknow. He also commanded the Artillery at the action of Nawabgunge Barabunkee, in June, 1858. He d. 22 Feb. 1900, and was s. by his eldest son.

Arms—Arg., on a bend sa. three mascles of the field. *Crest*—Out of a ducal coronet or, a unicorn's head arg. the horn twisted, of the first and second. *Motto*—Nunquam non paratus.

Residence—Steeple Aston, Oxon. *Club*—Cavalry.

CARLETON-L'ESTRANGE. See L'ESTRANGE.

CARMICHAEL-FERRALL. See FERRALL.

CARR, FORMERLY OF ARNESTOWN.

EDWARD THOMAS WHITMORE CARR, of Camlin, co. Wexford, b. 1888.

Lineage.—WILLIAM CARR, of Stonehouse, co. Waterford, which he acquired by deeds dated 13 and 14 Oct. 1727, left a son,
GEORGE CARR, of Stonehouse, whose will was proved 25 April, 1748; m. Elizabeth, only dau. of Thomas Bowers, of Rathcurby, by Aphra, dau. of Boyle Maunsell, of Gallskill, co. Kilkenny, and had two sons,
1. William, disinherited by his father.
2. Thomas, his heir.
THOMAS CARR, of Stonehouse, whose will was proved 8 Nov. 1776, m. 1st, a dau. of Gen. Edward Whitmore, Governor of Long Island, and had a son,
1. EDWARD, his heir.
He m. 2ndly, Frances, dau. of Nathaniel Boyse, of Bannow, co. Wexford (see that family), and by her, who d. April, 1781, had a son and two daus.,
2. George, of Bannow, d.s.p. 9 Jan. 1824.
1. Frances Anne, d. unm. Jan. 1840.
2. Elizabeth, m. Oct. 1789, Simon Osborne, of Annefield, co. Kilkenny.
REV. EDWARD CARR, B.A. (Dub.) 1770, Rector of Kilmacow, co. Kilkenny, d. 2 Jan. 1815; m. Jan. 1773, Sarah, dau. of George Forster, of Thomastown, co. Kilkenny, and by her, who d. Oct. 1837, aged 85, had three sons and three daus.,
1. George Whitmore (Rev.), of Ardross, co. Wexford, d. 27 Jan. 1849; m. Charlotte, dau. of William Shaw, of Sandpitts, co. Kilkenny (see SHAW, Bart., 1821), and by her, who d. 6 July, 1848, a et 63, had three sons and six daus.,
1. George, C.B. Indian Col. Madras Army, b 1806; d. 1902; m. Cecilia Elizabeth, widow of Rev. Charles Fewtrill Wylde.
2. William Patrick, b. 1814, d. 1861; m. 1848, Elizabeth, dau. of John French, and had three sons and four daus.,
(1) George Whitmore, b. 1849; m. Emily Smithers, and has a son, George.
(2) Edward Charles, b. 1856.

(3) Henry Gregory Dunlop, b. 1858.
(1) Anna Hawthorne.
(2) Emily Charlotte, m. Frederick Pollen, I.C.S.
(3) Lizzie Hawthorne } twins.
(4) Mary Meredith }
3. Edward Charles, b. 1817, d. unm. 6 Oct. 1837.
1. Charlotte, d. 28 April, 1891; m. 16 Aug. 1830, Gen. Michael William Smith, C.B. (see CUSACK-SMITH, Bart.).
2. Sarah Drake, d. 15 March, 1895; m. 1833, Edward Carr, of Camlin (see below).
3. Emily Leslie, d. 13 Jan. 1886; m. Richard Lett, of Balloughton, co. Wexford.
4. Elizabeth Frances, d. 1863; m. Col. John Wilson.
5. Jane Catherine, d. 1862; m. Anthony Walsh, Lieut. 17th Regiment.
6. Eleanor Tottenham, d. 1854; m. 1848, Edward Kough, of New Ross.
2. EDWARD, of Arnestown, of whom presently.
3. Thomas, m. 24 June, 1805, Eleanor Colclough, and had one son and three daus.,
1. Edward (Rev.), LL.D. (Dub.), Rector of St. Helens, b. 1809, d. 1886; m. 1st, Anne, dau. of Rev. J. Cooper, Rector o' Kilaman, and had issue. He m. 2ndly, 8 Nov. 1876, Hon. Mary Louisa, sister of Samuel, 8th Viscount Molesworth, s.p. The issue of the 1st marriage was a son and a dau.,
George. Sarah, m. Dr. Long.
1. Maria, d. 4 Nov. 1884; m. 1st, John Hibbits; 2ndly, 27 April, 1848, Edward Warner, of Highams, Essex, M.P. for Norwich (see WARNER, Bart.).
2. Anne, m. Rev. J. Gallagher.
3. Frances, m. Rev. George Herriot, Vicar of St. Anne's, Newcastle-on-Tyne.
1. Anne, m. James Braddell.
2. Frances, d. 9 May, 1871; m. 1 April, 1801, Bernard Shaw (see SHAW, Bart., cr. 1821).
3. Sarah, m. John Carroll, M.D.

EDWARD CARR, of Arnestown, co. Wexford, d. 14 May, 1857; m. 20 Oct. 1808, Maria, dau. of Samuel Kough, of New Ross, and by her, who d. 22 April, 1874, had nine sons and two daus.,
1. EDWARD, his heir.
2. Thomas Kough, b. 1811; d. 23 Feb. 1869; m. 1837, Jane, dau. of George Kough, and had two sons and a dau.
1. Edward, b. 1838.
2. George Thomas, b. 1840.
1. Hanna Cornelia, m. Alphonse Perrin, of San Antonio.
3. George, b. 1814; d. 1886; m. 1848, Mary, dau. of Samuel Kough, and had with other issue d. young,
1. Howard, Lieut.-Col. R.A.M.C., b. 1863; m. 8 Jan. 1903, Harriet Constance, dau. of Thomas Kough, of Newtown Villa, Kilkenny, and has issue.
2. Hampden.
1. Alice, m. 1884, William Crooke, I.C.S.
4. William Wallis, b. 1861, d. 31 March, 1895; m. 1848, Arabella Susanna, dau. of William Clarke, and left issue.
5. Elliott Elmes (Rev.), M.A. (Dub.), b. 1818, d. 26 Jan. 1908, Rector o' Rathsaran; m. 1850, Sydney Anne Watson, and left issue,
1. Edward, b. 1855.
2. John Despard, b. 1865.
3. Percy, b. 1867.
1. Sophia Matilda.
2. Sydney Alice, m. 1898, C. Lett, of Enniscorthy.
3. Isabel Veiling.
4. Ella.
6. Jonas King, b. 1820, d. 1907, Surgeon-Major R.A., m. 1st, 24 Oct. 1850, Jeanette, dau. of John King, 32nd Light Infantry, and had issue,
1. Edward Elliott, C.B. (1900), Col. Comm. Royal Scots Fusiliers (The Spital, Paxton, Berwick-on-Tweed), b. 31 May, 1854; m. 18 Dec. 1883, Rosa Elizabeth, dau. of Rev. A. Hall, and has a son,
Percy Wykeham King, b. 18 Oct. 1884, Lieut. Seaforth Highlanders.
2. William Henry, b. 27 Jan. 1856; d. 11 April, 1856.
3. Arthur Nisbet, b. 23 April, 1859, Lieut.-Col. 3rd Bombay Cavalry.
4. Charles Ernest, b. 1 May, 1861, late Lieut. Yorkshire L.I.
5. Frederick Gifford, b. 26 Aug. 1862.
6. George Perceval, b. 10 March, 1864.
1. Maria Augusta, m. Capt. Edwin Harris.
2. Caroline Amelia.
3. Jeanette.
4. Mary Alice.
He m. 2ndly, Fanny Rebecca, dau. of Major Ben', 3rd Northumberland Fusiliers, and had a son,
6. Francis Oxenham, b. 17 April, 1872, late Lieut. R.A.
He m. 3rdly, Charlotte, dau. of J. Brown Leman Tarrant, widow of Lieut. Samuel Hamilton, R.N., and had two sons,
7. Harry Gardiner, b. 12 Feb. 1877, Capt. R.A.
8. Stanhope Mason, b. 3 Dec. 1878.
7. Nicholas Gifford, b. 1821, d.s.p. 26 April, 1903; m. 1st, 1867, Sophy Sarah (d. 1880), dau. of Col. Packe, 2ndly, 1885, Elizabeth, dau. of Christopher Vero.
8. Whitmore (Rev.), M.A. (Dub.), b. 1823, d. 1903; m. Emma Loftt, dau. of H. G. C. Blake, of Chichester, and had a son, Whitmore, and a dau.
9. Henry, b. 1825, d. 1867; m. Charlotte Shaw, dau. of Richard Lett, of Balloughton, co. Wexford. She d. 18 Oct. 1907.
1. Eliza, d. 1876; m. 1839, Rev. T. Uniacke Townsend, Rector of Inistioge (see TOWNSHEND of Myross Wood).

2. Sarah, d. 1855; m. 11 Nov. 1840, Capt. William George Beagin, 2nd Madras Native Infantry, and by him, who d. 24 Dec. 1852, had issue, with two daus.
 1. Edward George Daves Beagin, b. 10 Sept. 1841, Major Madras S.C.; m. 1875, Kate, dau. of J. B. Ward, d.s.p. 1 Jan. 1890.
 2. William Whitmore Beagin, b. 10 Oct. 1845, Lieut. 59th Re. iment, settled in New Zealand.
 3. Aribur Hav Beagin, b. 24 Jan. 1850; m. Anna, dau. of John Roe, of Norwich.
 4. Alfred Henry Beagin, b. 16 May, 1851; m. 31 May, 1906, Edith Mary, dau. of Charles Selby.
 EDWARD CARR, of Camlin, co. Wexford, b. 1809, d. 1 Nov. 1892; m. 1833, Sarah Drake, dau. of Rev. George Whitmore Carr, of Ardross, and had three sons and a dau.,
 1. Edward Michael, b. 19 Aug. 1843, d. 9 June, 1858.
 2. GEORGE WHITMORE, his heir.
 3. Elliott William Wilton, b. 1846, d. 3 April, 1899; m. 1878, Eleanor Isabell, dau. of Thomas Goff, of Wexford, and by her, who d. 4 March, 1890, had issue,
  Edward, b. 1879. Eunice Cecilia Hawkshaw.
 1. Charlotte Catherine, m. 1881, Arthur B. Cherry, of New Ross.
 GEORGE WHITMORE CARR, of Camlin, b. 1846, d. 26 July, 1908, B.A. (Dub.), Barrister, King's Inns, Michaelmas, 1880; m. 1880, Susan, dau. of Thomas MacDowell, of Armagh, and had issue,
 1. EDWARD THOMAS WHITMORE, present representative.
 1. Helen MacDowell, d. 14 Feb. 1883.
 2. Dorothy Sarah.
 Arms (confirmed to Col. Edward Elliott Carr, C.B., and his descendants only)—Per chevron gules and azure on a chevron between three pheons argent as many estoiles sable. Crest—A stag's head erased ppr. attired or, and gorged with three rings of the last. Motto—Est nulla fallacia.
 Residence—Camlin, New Ross.

CARROL OF LISSEN HALL AND TULLA HOUSE.

ALICE ISABEL CARROL, of Lissen Hall and Tulla House, co. Tipperary, jointly with her sisters, MAUDE ROSE (Mrs. G. M. Angas), and FLORENCE KATE (Mrs. P. C. Scott), s. their brother, 1897.

Lineage.—RICHARD CARROL left issue a son,
JAMES CARROL, of Tulla, co. Tipperary, m. Elizabeth, dau. of William Carrol, of Balliecrenode, and with her acquired the lands of Lissen or Kilkeary. His elder son,
JAMES CARROL, of Tulla, to whom the lands of Lishenaclouta, Garrynamony, and others in the barony of Upper Ormonde, co. Tipperary, were granted 4 July, 1712, by his cousin Anthony Carrol, of Emell Castle. His commission as Captain in the army is dated 1689. He d. intestate 1728 unm., and was s. by his brother,
WILLIAM CARROL, of Tulla, Lieut. in Viscount Mountjoy's Regiment 1697, and d. 1749, leaving a son,
WILLIAM CARROL, of Tulla, an officer in the Army, m. Ellen, dau. of — Dalton, and d. 1802, having had issue,
 1. WILLIAM, or whom presently.
 1. Margaret, m. — Nugent, and had issue a son, Pierce, whose will is dated 19 July, 1739.
 2. Dorothy, m. about 1773, W. Griffin.   3. Catherine, d. unm.
The only son,
WILLIAM CARROL, of Lissen Hall and of Tulla, co. Tipperary, m. 5 May, 1772, Susanna Parker, and d. 28 Feb. 1816, having had issue,
 1. WILLIAM PARKER (Sir), of whom presently.
 2. John, will dated 6 Dec. 1842.   3. Morgan.
 4. Richard, Lieut.-Col. in the Portuguese service, served in the Peninsular War. His wife's name was Mary.
The eldest son,
LIEUT.-GEN. SIR WILLIAM PARKER CARROL, K.C.H., C.B., of Lissen Hall and Tulla House. co. Tipperary, sometime of the 88th Connaught Rangers, Maj.-Gen. and Col. of the regiment of Hibernia in the Spanish service, Knight of the Order of Charles III of Spain, and many other orders, served with great distinction throughout the Peninsular War, and received the freedom of the city of Dublin, b. 27 Jan. 1776; m. 17 March, 1817, Emma Sophia, dau. of M. E. Sherwell, of Kew, Surrey. She d. July, 1819. He d. 2 July, 1842, having had issue,
 1. WILLIAM HUTCHINSON, his heir.
 2. John Egerton, b. 25 Jan. 1819; d. 30 May, 1852.
The elder son,
CAPT. WILLIAM HUTCHINSON CARROL, of Lissen Hall and Tulla House, co. Tipperary, J.P., Capt. 35th Regt. and Inniskilling Dragoons, b. 22 Dec. 1817; m. 10 Dec. 1862, Elizabeth Leslie, dau. of the late Capt. Charles W. G. Griffin, R.N. She d. 23 June, 1887. He d. 6 Sept. 1895, having had issue,
 1. Hutchinson, b. 2 Aug. 1869; d. unm. 19 Dec. 1887, v.p.
 2. EGERTON GRIFFIN, late of Lissen Hall.
 1. ALICE ISABEL, s. to Lissen Hall, jointly with her sisters 1897.
 2. MAUDE ROSE, m. 14 June, 1902, George Maxwell Angas, of the Manor, Wissendene, Rutland, and has issue,
  Rosaleen Maude, b. 15 March, 1903.
 3. FLORENCE KATE, m. 11 Nov. 1896, Philip Clement Scott, and has issue,
  Anthony Gerald O'Carrol, b. 22 June, 1899.
The only surviving son,

EGERTON GRIFFIN CARROL, of Lissen Hall and Tulla House, co. Tipperary, b. 6 July, 1871; m. 1 Oct. 1896, Alice Caroline Mary, 3rd dau. of Capt. William Gibson, D.L., of Rockforest, co. Tipperary (see that family), and d.s.p. 22 Feb. 1897, when he was s. by his sisters. His widow m. 17 Sept. 1898, Capt. Henry Godfrey Howorth, R.A, eldest son of Sir Henry Hoyle Howorth, K.C.I.E., F.R.S.

Seats—Lissen Hall, Nenagh, and Tulla House, both co. Tipperary.

CARROLL OF ASHFORD.

ALEXANDER ERNEST CARROLL, of Munduff, Ashford, co. Wicklow, b. 1870; m. 1897, Margaret, 3rd dau. of Thomas Henderson, by whom he had issue,
 Ellen Beatrice Mary, b. 1898.

Lineage.—ALEXANDER CARROLL, of Dublin, whose will, dated 9 May, 1768, was proved 28 June following, left by Anne his wife, sister of William Fairbrother, three sons, 1. GEORGE; 2. Coote; and 3. Alexander; and four daus., 1. Mary; 2. Anne, m. Philip Perceval; 3. Prudence; and 4. Sarah.
The eldest son,
GEORGE CARROLL, of Great Denmark Street, Dublin, J.P. and High Sheriff co. Wicklow 1772; m. 1769, Jane Irvine, and by her (who d. 1801) he had three sons,
 1. ALEXANDER, of Mountjoy Square, Dublin, J.P., High Sheriff co. Wicklow 1821; d.s.p. 1856.
 2. GEORGE, of Thorp Arch, co. York, and Munduff, co. Wicklow, b. 1774; m. 1806, Frances, only child of Richard Hodsden, of Woldingham, Surrey, and his wife, Dorothy Lister, of Woodhouse, near Halifax, who was directly descended, in the female line, from the ancient family of STERNE of Elvington and Woodhouse, of which were Richard Sterne, D.D., Archbishop of York in the time of CHARLES II, and the Rev. Laurence Sterne, M.A., author of The Sentimental Journey. She d. 1849. He d. 1848, leaving issue,
  1. COOTE ALEXANDER, of Ashford, Wicklow, b. Nov. 1812; educated at Eton; High Sheriff 1862, J.P. Wicklow and W.R. York; m. Nov. 1843, Elizabeth, dau. of William Tayler, of Torr, Devon, who d. June, 1863. He d.s.p. 1886.
  2. Richard Sterne of Tolston Lodge, Tadcaster, Major and West York Militia, J.P. for W.R. York, b. 1814; m. Dec. 1863, Louisa, youngest dau. of Sir Henry Boynton, 9th bart. of Barmston, co. York, and d.s.p. May, 1879.
  3. George Frederick, of Ashford, Wicklow, b. 1817; d.s.p. 1889.
  4. Francis Rawdon, b. 1821; d. Jan. 1868.
  3. STANFORD, of whom presently.
He d. 1816. The youngest son,
STANFORD CARROL, of Bellpark, co. Wicklow, and Vane Street, Bath, an officer 1st Dragoon Guards, m. 1st, Louisa, dau. of Sir Thomas Heathcote, of co. Stafford, by whom he had two sons, who d.s.p. He m. 2ndly, 1822, Catherine Maria, dau. of John Benett, LL.D., Rector of Donhead, St. Andrew, Wilts, and of Ower Moigne, co. Dorset, son of Thomas Benett, of Norton Bavant, and Pythouse, Wilts, and d. 1846, having by her (who d. 1869) had issue,
 1. FREDERICK (Rev.), late of Ashford.
 2. Alexander, d.s.p. 1855.
 1. Catherine Maria, b. 1823; d. unm. 1893.
The elder son,
REV. FREDERICK CARROLL, of Ashford and Munduff, co. Wicklow, and of Woodhouse, Halifax, co. York; M.A. (Cantab.), Vicar of Tallington, Linclon, 1861-94, b. 23 Dec. 1827; m. 1851, Ellen Charlotte, 4th dau. of Henry Sankey, R.N., of Preston House, Kent, and Green Park, Bath, and d. 15 May, 1899, having by her (who d. 1885) had issue,
 1. Stanford Henry, b. 1854; d. 1856.
 2. FREDERICK HARRY, of Munduff, Ashford, Wicklow, late Capt. Connaught Rangers, b. 1855; d. 2 June, 1908.
 3. Henry Arthur Edward, b. 1861; d. 1862.
 4. Raymond John Hereward Wake, b. 1867.
 5. ALEXANDER ERNEST, now of Munduff, Ashford, Wicklow.
 1. Ellen Frances Katharine, b. 1852; m. 1887, Hugh Hamilton, 3rd son of Col. Digby St. Vincent Hamilton, of Green Park, Bath.
 2. Ethel Lina Maude Mary, b. 1863; m. 27 Oct. 1891, Rev. J. D. Jones, Vicar of Saxilby, near Lincoln.

Arms—Per pale arg. and gu. two lions combatant counter-changed, supporting a sword erect in pale ppr. Crest—On a stump of a tree sprouting ppr., a falcon rising per pale arg. and gu. belled and jessed or. Motto—Flecti non frangi.
Residence—7, Appian Way, Leeson Park, Dublin.

CARSON OF SHANROE.

THOMAS CARSON, of Shanroe, co. Monaghan, late Capt. Royal Irish Rifles, J.P. co. Longford, B.A. Trin. Coll., Camb., *b.* 10 Jan. 1866; *m.* 15 March, 1900, Annette Maude, youngest dau. of Col. W. H. King Harman, of Newcastle (*see that family*), and has issue,

1. THOMAS WENTWORTH, *b.* 8 Sept. 1906.
1. Lilian Eleanor, *b.* 19 April, 1901.
2. Marjorie Maude, *b.* 13 Sept. 1903.

Lineage.—The family of Carson has been settled in the co. Monaghan since the middle of the 17th century. On 2 July, 1667, JOHN CARSON, of Shanroe, in that co., purchased from Thomas Coote, of Cootehill, co. Cavan, the estate of Shanroe, which has passed in unbroken male descent to the present representative (*vide* SHIRLEY's *Monaghan*, London; 1877, Part II., p. 221). Mr. Carson's only son,

THOMAS CARSON, of Feymore, co. Tyrone, who was the granting party in a settlement of 14 Nov. 1715, was then owner of Shanroe, amongst other lands thereby settled. On 25 June, 1706, he purchased from Richard Robinson, of Tullegoney, the lands of Silloo, co. Monaghan which still form part of the family estate. He endured the famous siege of Derry, and had issue,

1. THOMAS.
2. Joseph (Rev.), *b.* at Keilrunan, co. Tyrone, 1695; educated at Armagh under Mr. Martin, entered Trinity Coll. Dublin, 12 May, 1714, and was elected a scholar of the House in 1716. He was living in the co. Fermanagh in 1753, and 30 June, 1763, was collated to the Vicarage of Errigal Trough, Diocese of Clogher, where he *d.*

The eldest son,

REV. THOMAS CARSON, of Tyrone, was Curate of Errigal Trough, 1713, subsequently appointed Rector of Finner, co. Donegal. In 1724, he was granted premises in Ballyshannon by the Right Hon. William Conolly, which are still in the possession of his representative. He *m.* (marriage articles dated 13 Nov. 1715) Catherine Robinson, and had issue,

1. THOMAS (Rev.), his heir.
2. Joseph, party to a deed of 6 Feb. 1746; *d.* 7 Oct. 1786.
1. Elizabeth, living 2 April, 1734; *d.* 23 July, 1795.

The eldest son,

REV. THOMAS CARSON, of Ward House, co. Donegal, *m.* 7 Sept. 1762, Mary, only dau. of James Dawson, of Kilmore, co. Monaghan, by Catherine his wife, dau. of George Scott, of Roagh, co. Monaghan, High Sheriff 1704, by Jane his wife, dau. of Ralph Barlow. By her (who *m.* 2ndly, 21 March 1770, Matthew Burnside, of Corcreevy House, co. Tyrone) he had issue,

1. THOMAS (Rev.), his heir.
2. Joseph, of the City of Dublin, *b.* 1765; *m.* 1797, Anne, dau. of J. Caldbeck, of Kilmashogue and Clondalkin, co. Dublin; *d.* 11 April, 1802, leaving an only child,
Dorothea, *m.* 1823, Edward Moore, of The Bawn, co. Tyrone (who *d.* Jan. 1859), and had issue. She *d.* 18 Nov. 1878.

The eldest son,

REV. THOMAS CARSON, Rector of Kilmahon, Diocese of Cloyne, and Domestic Chaplain to Murrough, 5th Earl of Inchiquin (his opinion seems to have been highly valued by Bishop Bennet, of Cloyne, one of whose letters to him is printed in BRADY's *Clerical and Parochial Records of Cork, Cloyne, and Ross*, Dublin: 1863, Vol. II., p. 279), *b.* Nov. 1763; *m.* 16 Sept. 1802, Elizabeth, eldest dau. of Christopher Waggett, of Kitsborough, co. Cork, by Johanna his wife, dau. of Thomas Barkley, of Limerick, by Elizabeth his wife, dau. of Francis Fosberry, of Kilcooley, co. Limerick, co-heir with her sister Jane, wife of Parker Dunscombe, of her brother, William Waggett, Q.C., Recorder of Cork, by whom (who *d.* 14 Nov. 1824) he had issue,

1. THOMAS (Right Rev.), his heir.
2. Joseph (Rev.), D.D., Vice-Provost of Trinity College, Dublin, *b.* 5 May, 1815; *m.* 21 July, 1841, Harriett, only dau. of William Pitt Blunden, of Wellington, co. Kilkenny, by Harriett his wife, only dau. of Thomas Pope, of Popefield, Queen's Co., and sister to Sir John Blunden, 2nd bart. of Castle Blunden, co. Kilkenny, and *d.* 1 Feb. 1898, having by her (who *d.* 28 June, 1884) had issue,
  1. Thomas Henry, Scholar, M.A. Trin. Coll. Dublin, K.C. (6, *New Square, Lincoln's Inn, W.C.*), *b.* 24 Nov. 1844; *m.* 1st, 15 Aug. 1876, Mary Sophia, dau. of Rev. Comyns Tucker, of Beech Hill, Morchard-Bishop, Devon. She *d.* 9 May, 1879. He *m.* 2ndly, 12 April, 1887, Marie Louise Emma, dau. of the late Albert Bernouilli Barlow, formerly of Le Havre, and has issue, Joseph Baldwin.
    1. Harriett, *m.* 26 Oct. 1865, John Henville Hulbert (*d.* 8 May, 1908), of Aylwards, Middlesex, and had issue. She *d.* 14 Dec. 1884.
    2. Elizabeth Sophia, *m.* 4 Sept. 1873, Ven. Robert Walsh, M.A., Rector of Donnybrook and Archdeacon of Dublin, eldest son of Right Hon. John Edward Walsh, formerly Master of the Rolls in Ireland, and *d.* 28 Feb. 1893, leaving issue.
    3. Frances Anna.
    4. Maria Jane.
    5. Josephine Eleanor.
    6. Alice Olivia.
1. Maria, *d. unm.* Aug. 1830.
2. Elizabeth, *m.* 25 Nov. 1841, James Colthurst (*d.* 1898), only surviving son of James Colthurst, Capt. 3rd Buffs, by Hester his wife, dau. of Sir Augustus Warren, 2nd bart. of Warrenscourt (*see* BURKE's *Peerage*), and *d.* 4 March, 1873, leaving issue.
3. Anna, *m.* 3 Feb. 1844 Rev. William Allen Fisher (*d.* 7 Aug. 1880), Rector of Kilmoe, co. Cork, 2nd son of Joseph Devonshire Fisher, of Woodmount, co. Waterford, and *d.* 11 Jan. 1900, leaving issue.

Mr. Carson *d.* 30 Aug. 1816, and was *s.* by his eldest son,

RIGHT REV. THOMAS CARSON, LL.D., Bishop of Kilmore, Elphin, and Ardagh, *b.* 27 Aug. 1805, Vicar of Urney and Annageliffe 1838, Rector of Cloon and Vicar-General of Kilmore 1854, Dean of Kilmore 1860; consecrated at Armagh 2 Oct. 1870; *m.* 29 Sept. 1833, Eleanor Anne, eldest dau. of Robert Burton, of Dublin, by Elinor his 2nd wife, youngest dau. of William Williams, of Dublin, by Deborah Wilme his wife, by whom (who *d.* 3 Jan. 1859) he had issue,

1. THOMAS WILLIAM, of whom presently.
2. JOSEPH JOHN HENRY, of whom presently.
3. Robert Burton (Rev.), Vicar of Haynes, co. Bedford, ex-Scholar, M.A. Trinity Coll. Dublin, *b.* 18 Sept. 1845; *m.* 1st, 3 Nov. 1879, Elizabeth, eldest dau. of Rev. W. A. Fisher, and by her (who *d.* 12 Oct. 1882) had issue,
  1. Thomas Allen, *b.* 29 Sept. 1871; *m.* 31 July, 1900, Emily Florence, dau. of the Rev. W. E. Hallam, Rector of Barnadiston, Haverhill, Suffolk.
  2. William Robert (Rev.), *b.* 2 Aug. 1874; *d. unm.* 21 Nov. 1903.
  3. Robert Burton Coleridge (Rev.), M.A. Oxon., *b.* 5 Oct. 1882, Assistant Curate of St. John the Evangelist, Clevedon, Somerset.
Mr. Carson *m.* 2ndly, 14 June, 1887, Mary Catherine Eleanor, dau. of the late Rev. Brook Edward Bridges, by Louisa Ann his wife, dau. of Sir J. Osborn, of Chicksands Priory, Bart. He *d.* 19 June, 1899.
4. Henry Watters (Rev.), Rector of Santry, co. Dublin, ex-Scholar, B.D. Trinity Coll. Dublin, *b.* 13 July, 1847; *m.* 26 June, 1872, Isabel Jane, dau. of Hon. Henry Martley, Judge of the Landed Estates Court, Dublin, grandson of John Martley, of Ballyfallon, co. Meath, and *d.s.p.* 1 Sept. 1895.
1. Eleanor Isabella.
2. Elizabeth, *d. unm.* 27 May, 1865.
3. Isabella Deborah, *m.* 25 Oct. 1871, Herbert Baldwin Colthurst, M.A., Barrister-at-Law (*d.* 21 Dec. 1906), and has issue.
4. Harriet Anna Mary, *d. unm.* 4 Oct. 1874.

The Bishop *d.* 7 July, 1874, at Portrush, and was bur. within the walls of the ancient church of Ballywillan, near that place, and a stained glass window has been placed in the Bedell Memorial Cathedral, Kilmore, as a memorial of his episcopate. The eldest son,

REV. THOMAS WILLIAM CARSON, of Shanroe, ex-Scholar and M.A. Trin. Coll. Dublin, *b.* 20 Dec. 1834; became the representative of this family on the death of his father, Right Rev. Thomas Carson, Bishop of Kilmore, Elphin, and Ardagh, 1874. He *d.s.p.* 23 Nov. 1895, and was *s.* by his brother,

JOSEPH JOHN HENRY CARSON, J.P., co. Antrim, ex-Scholar M.A. Trin. Coll. Dublin, Governor of the Bank of Ireland, *b.* 24 July, 1837; *m.* 1 July, 1862, Maria Alice, youngest dau. of Henry George Johnston, of Fort Johnston, co. Monaghan, J.P. and High Sheriff 1859, by Maria his wife, dau. of Walter Young, of Monaghan, and *d.* 3 Dec. 1907, leaving issue,

1. THOMAS, his successor.
2. Henry Johnston, *b.* 26 Nov. 1867; *m.* 14 April, 1909, Mona Beatrix Hulton, eldest dau. of the Rev. G. F. Sams, Rector of Emberton, and Rural Dean, and has issue,
Beatrix Mary Johnston, *b.* 7 May, 1910.
8. William Burton, *b.* 5 May, 1872; *m.* 10 Sept. 1897, Alice, dau. of Thomas Plunkett Cairnes, of Stameen, co. Drogheda, and has issue,
  1. Thomas Alan Cairnes, *b.* 7 Feb. 1906.
  2. Charles Gaussen Joseph, *b.* 13 Dec. 1908.
1. Maria Elizabeth.
2. Eleanor Louisa, *d. unm.* 26 Dec. 1882.

Residence—Cloncallow, co. Longford.

CARTER OF SHAEN MANOR.

GEORGE TILSON SHAEN CARTER, of Shaen Manor, co. Mayo, J.P., *b.* 6 March, 1848, educated at St. John's Coll. Oxford; *m.* 15 April, 1878, Eva Augusta, dau. of William French, of Ardsallagh, co. Meath, and by her (who *d.* 15 July, 1891) has issue,

1. VICTOR TILSON ARTHUR SHAEN, (*Shaen Lodge, Belmullet, co. Mayo*), *b.* 3 June, 1879; *m.* 4 Sept. 1909, Wilfreda Christine, 2nd dau. of late Richard Davis, of Hove, Sussex, and has issue,
Barbara Grace, *b.* 10 Aug. 1910.
2. Ernest de Freyne Tilson Shaen, *b.* 5 Sept. 1883; *d.* Nov. 1883.
1. Muriel Una Shaen, *b.* 7 Aug. 1881; *m.* 25 April, 1906, Cecil C. H. Moriarty, D.I., R.I.C.

He *m.* 2ndly, 3 Oct. 1894, Grace, eldest dau. of Rev. D. Hughes, of Trinity House, Sudbury, Suffolk, late Vicar of Little Waldingfield. She *d.s.p.* 11 June, 1908.

Lineage.—THOMAS CARTER, of Robertstown, co. Meath, Sergeant-at-Arms, a gentleman whose services at the Revolution were very considerable, for he not only served King WILLIAM at the battle of the Boyne, but secured divers useful books and writings belonging to King JAMES and his secretaries; *m.* twice; by his 1st wife, Margaret Houghton, he was father of

THE RIGHT HON. THOMAS CARTER.

Mr. Carter *m.* 2ndly, 2 Aug. 1702, Isabella, dau. of Matthew, 2nd son of Sir Matthew Boynton, Bart., of Barmeston, co. York, and widow of Wentworth, 4th Earl of Roscommon (the Poet), but by her he had no issue. His son,

THE RIGHT HON. THOMAS CARTER, Master of the Rolls, Secretary of State and Privy Councillor, 1732, of Robertstown and Rathnally, co. Meath, *d.* 1763; *m.* 1719, Mary, dau. and co-heiress (with her sister Frances, *m.* 1st, the Earl of Rosse; 2ndly, Viscount Jocelyn, but who *d.s.p.*), of Thomas Claxton, of Dublin, and had issue,

1. THOMAS, M.P. for Old Leighlin, *m.* Anna Maria, sister of Sir George Armytage, Bart. of Kirkless, co. York, and by her (who *m.* 2ndly, 18 Sept. 1766, John Nicholson, of Balrath, co. Meath, and had issue, one dau., MARY, *m.* Skeffington Thompson, of co. Meath, and had issue (*see* THOMPSON *of Rathnally*).
2. HENRY BOYLE, of whom presently.
1. Francis, *m.* 1st, 27 Feb. 1749, the Right Rev. Philip Twysden, D.D., Bishop of Raphoe, by whom she had issue, on only dau., Frances, *m.* 4 March, 1770, George Bussey, 4th Earl of Jersey. Mrs. Twysden *m.* 2ndly, Gen. James Johnstone, Col. of the Scots Greys.
2. Susan, *m.* 21 April, 1743, Thomas Trotter, of Duleek, co. Louth, grandfather of Elizabeth, Marchioness of Thomond.
3. Mary, *d. unm.*

The 2nd son,

HENRY BOYLE CARTER, of Castle Martin, Capt. in Col. Irwin's Regt., *m.* 23 Feb. 1750, Susanna, dau. and co-heiress (with her sister, Frances, who *m.* 1 June, 1738, John Bingham, of Newbrook, grandfather of John Bingham, 1st Lord Clanmorris) of Sir Arthur Shaen, Bart., of Kilmore, co. Roscommon, and widow without issue of James Wynne, of Hazlewood, co. Sligo, and by her had issue,

1. THOMAS, his heir.
2. Arthur, Col. 14th Dragoons, *d. unm.*
3. Henry, Capt. Scots Greys, *d.s.p.*
1. Mary, *m.* John Kirwan, of Castle Hackett, co. Galway.

The eldest son,

THOMAS CARTER, of Castle Martin, *b.* 20 May, 1753; *m.* Jan. 1783, Catherine, dau. of Hon. John Butler, brother of Humphrey, 1st Earl of Lanesborough, and had issue,

1. WILLIAM HENRY, his heir.
2. John, Admiral R.N., *b.* 1785, *m.* 1833, Julia Adery, dau. of William Payne Georges. She *d.* 1868. He *d.* 1863, having had issue,
1. John Henry Stockmar, *b.* 30 March, 1834, killed in the trenches before Sebastopol, 2 May, 1855.
2. William Henry, Capt. 16th Foot, *b.* 17 May, 1836; *m.* 1861, Louisa, dau. of H. Le Mesurier, of Quebec, and has issue,
(1) Arthur Butler, *b.* 22 April, *d.* 18 July, 1872
(2) George Herbert, *b.* 21 Oct. 1873.
(3) William le Mesurier. (4) Basil Brooke.
(1) Julia Louisa Adery, *m.* Rev. Gustavus Nicholls, and has issue.
(2) Lucy Florence. (3) Edith.
(4) Ethel Maude, *d.* young. (5) Lilian May.
3. Thomas Tupper CARTER-CAMPBELL, Col. R.E., assumed the additional name of Campbell 1893, *b.* 8 Feb. 1838; *m.* 15 Sept. 1864, Emily Georgiana, of Possil, co. Lanark, and Ardrisbaig, co. Argyll, dau. of Gen. George Campbell, C.B., and *d.* 14 Jan. 1900, leaving issue (*see* CARTER-CAMPBELL *of Possil*).
4. Arthur Shaen, late Capt. 51st King's Own Yorkshire L.I., *b.* 2 July, 1840.
5. Albert Michael, late India Office, *b.* 16 April, 1842.
6. Georges Crofton Collingwood, Commander R.N., *b.* 26 May, 1845; *d.* 20 Oct. 1895.
7. Butler Julius Septimus Octavius, Lieut. (retired) R.N., *b.* 5 Oct. 1846; *m.* Katherine, dau. of Rev. F. Blaydes.
8. Augustus Cecil, *b.* 22 Aug. 1848; *m.* Mary, dau. of H. Jordan, and *d.* 17 July, 1894, leaving issue,
(1) Georges. (2) Charles. (3) William.
9. Charles Carré, Maj. R.E., *b.* 28 Oct. 1850; *m.* 1880, Ethel, dau. of J. Salter, and *d.* 18 Aug. 1888, leaving issue,
John Fillis Carré, Lieut. 35th Sikhs, Indian Army, *b.* 11 Jan. 1882.
1. Catherine Julia, *m.* William Mulcaster Freer, of Montreal, and has issue.
3. Thomas, Capt. R.A., *d.s.p.*
1. Margaret, *m.* James Hamilton, of Ballymacoll, co. Meath, leaving issue (*see that family*).

The eldest son,

WILLIAM HENRY CARTER, of Castle Martin, co. Kildare, J.P. and D.L., and High Sheriff 1817, *b.* 18 Dec. 1783, *m.* 1st, 23 June, 1809, Elizabeth, 3rd dau. of Francis Brooke, and sister of Sir Henry Brooke, Bart., of Colebrooke, co. Fermanagh, and by her (who *d.* 21 March, 1820) had issue,

THOMAS SHAEN CARTER, late of Watlington Park.
Susanna, *m.* 26 Oct. 1846, Hon. Francis Sadleir Prittie, brother of Henry, 3rd Lord Dunalley, and left issue.
Mr. Carter *m.* 2ndly, 10 June, 1846, Frances, sister of Robert, 5th Earl of Mayo, but by her, who predeceased him, had no issue. Mr. Carter *d.* 6 July, 1859. His only son,

THOMAS SHAEN CARTER, of Watlington Park, J.P., *b.* 10 Sept. 1813; *m.* 21 July, 1842, Maria Susan, only surviving child and heiress of Col. John Henry Tilson, of Watlington Park, descended from Henry Tilson, Bishop of Elphin, *temp.* CHARLES I, and by her (who *d.* 23 Aug. 1868) had issue,

1. HENRY TILSON SHAEN, of Watlington Park.
2. GEORGE TILSON SHAEN, now of Shaen Manor.
3. Thomas Tilson Shaen, *b.* 16 June, 1849; *m.* and *d.* in America 3 Nov. 1891.
4. Arthur Tilson Shaen, Lieut. R.N., *b.* 14 Sept. 1851; *m.* 6 June, 1885, Viola Alexandra, dau. of Denis Bingham, of Bingham Castle, and *d.* at Malta, 11 June, 1894, leaving issue, Claude.
5. Francis Tilson Shaen, *b.* 24 Sept. 1852, Lieut. R.A., killed near Fermoy when hunting.
6. Ernest Tilson Shaen, Lieut. Army Service Corps, killed by the Boers, *b.* 7 March, 1855.
7. Basil Tilson Shaen (Rev.), Vicar of Watlington, *b.* 2 Feb. 1858; *d.* 1895.
8. Gerald Tilson Shaen, *b.* 27 March, 1861.
9. Lionel Tilson Shaen, *b.* 6 Jan. 1864; *d.* 13 Oct. 1867.
1. Augusta Susanna Shaen, *m.* 11 Jan. 1866, George Milward, junr., J.P., of Lechlade Manor, co. Gloucester, and has issue.
2. Elizabeth Sophia Shaen, *m.* Hugh Hamersly, and has issue.
He *d.* 24 Oct. 1875, and was *s.* by his eldest son,

HENRY TILSON SHAEN CARTER, of Watlington Park, 17th Lancers, *b.* 21 June, 1846; *s.* 1875; *m.* 9 July, 1867, Adelaide Elizabeth, eldest dau. of Denis Bingham, of Bingham Castle, co. Mayo, J.P. He *d.s.p.* 5 March, 1882, and was *s.* by his brother.

Arms—Quarterly: 1st and 4th, arg., two lions combatant sa.; (CARTER); 2nd, vert a lion rampant or (SHAEN); 3rd, or on a bend plain cotised between two garbs az. a mitre of the field (TILSON).
Crest—A talbot passant arg, on a mural crown or, charged with three buckles az. **Motto**—Victrix patientia duri.

Seat—Shaen Manor, Belmullet, co. Mayo. *Residence*—44, Tisbury Road, Hove, Sussex.

CARY-CADDELL. *See* **CADDELL.**

CASEMENT OF MAGHERINTEMPLE.

ROGER CASEMENT, of Magherintemple, co. Antrim, *b.* 30 Nov. 1850; *m.* 8 Feb. 1877, Susanna, dau. of James Beatty, C.E., and has issue,

1. JOHN, Lieut. R.N., *b.* 19 March, 1880.
2. Francis, Capt. R.A.M.C.
3. Roger Hugh, P.W. Dept., India.
4. Robert James.
5. Edgar Reginald, P.W. Dept., India.

Lineage. — This family migrated to Ireland from Ramsey, Isle of Man, early in the 18th century, having originally been of French extraction.

HUGH CASEMENT, *m.* 1749, Elizabeth, dau. of George Higginson, of Magheragall. She *d.* 8 July, 1801, aged 80. He *d.* 10 July, 1797, aged 77, having had issue,

1. George, Surgeon R.N., *m.* 1st, Elizabeth Montgomery, and had two sons,
1. JOHN MONTGOMERY, *m.* Mary, dau. of John McGildowny, and *d.* 1839, leaving by her (who *d.* in 1843),
(1) EDMUND MCGILDOWNY CASEMENT, of Invermore, co. Antrim, J.P., *b.* 1812; *d. unm.* 1876.
(2) George, Lieut. R.E.
(1) Elizabeth, *m.* Capt. Gillespie, 15th Hussars.
(2) Mary, *m.* Henry Mills, and is dec.
(3) Matilda, *m.* John W. Fulton, Barrister-at-Law, and is dec.
(4) Jane, *d. unm.* (5) Grace, *d. unm.*
(6) Anne, *m.* General M'Cleverty.
2. William (Sir), K.C.B.
Surg. George Casement *m.* 2ndly, Matilda Montgomery, and by her had two sons,
3. George, Major in the Army. 4. Hugh, Lieut. in the Army.
2. ROGER, of whom presently.

The 2nd son,

ROGER CASEMENT, of Harryville, co. Antrim, *m.* 1st, 17—, Catherine, dau. of Julius Cosnahan, of Peel, Isle of Man, and by her (who *d.* 1803) had, with other issue,

1. THOMAS, his successor.
2. Robert (Rev.), of Harryville, Ballymena, *m.* and *d.* leaving one dau.,
Fanny Waring.
Mr. Casement *m.* 2ndly, 1819, Margaret, dau. of Andrew M'Quilty, and had by her (who *d.* Nov. 1877) further issue,
?. George, of Fenagh, co. Antrim, Barrister-at-Law, *d. unm.* 1882.
4. JOHN, late of Magherintemple.
5. Julius, of Cronroe, co. Wicklow, M.A. Trin. Coll. Dublin, J.P. cos. Antrim, Londonderry and Wicklow, High Sheriff 1877, *b.* 1830; *m.* 1863, Maria Clarke, dau. of Rev. J. Lacy-Barnard, Rector of Powerscourt, and has issue,
1. Roger, Major R.F.A., High Sheriff 1907, *b.* 24 Feb. 1864. *m.* 30 Aug. 1898, Catherine Isabelle, dau. of Col. Charles George Tottenham, of Ballycurry, co. Wicklow (*see that family*).

Cassan. THE LANDED GENTRY. 102

2. Joshua Bernard, Lieut. 2nd Durham Light Infantry, b. 16 Sept. 1868; d. 29 July, 1894.
3. Julius, Lieut. R.A., d.s.p. 3 Sept. 1896, aged 20.
4. John Moore, Commander R.N., b. 13 Sept. 1877; m. 6 Feb. 1905, Annie M., dau. of F. T. Gervers, of Collingham Road, S.W., and has issue, (1) a son, b. 30 July, 1907, and (2) a son, b. 16 Feb. 1910.
  1. Margaret, m. 25 April, 1900, Capt. Robert Mervyn Bermingham Otway-Ruthven (see that family).
  2. May.   3. Minie, d. unm. 11 March, 1901.
1. Elizabeth, m. 1854, Moore Smith.
2. Annie, m. 1st, Thomas Luscombe, of Dublin; 2ndly, Frederick H. Ross, County Inspector R.I.C., of Crowpark, Trim.

Mr. Casement d. 19 May, 1832. His eldest surviving son,
THOMAS CASEMENT, of Ballee House, co. Antrim, J.P., High Sheriff 1874, b. 19 March, 1799; m. 22 Sept. 1848, Dorinda Deborah, dau. of Thomas Abbot, J.P., of Mount Bellew, co. Galway, and d. 11 June, 1874, leaving an only dau. and heiress,
CATHERINE COSNAHAN, of Ballee House, m. 4 March, 1869, Col. Eldred Thomas Pottinger, R.A.

His half brother,
JOHN CASEMENT, of Magherintemple, co. Antrim, J.P., High Sheriff 1881, M.A. Trin. Coll. Dublin, b. 29 Nov. 1825; m. 1st, 6 Aug. 1849, Charlotte, dau. of Brabazon Newcomen, of Camla House, co. Roscommon, and by her (who d. May, 1857) had issue,
1. ROGER, now of Magherintemple.
2. Brabazon Newcomen, M.D., b. 19 Aug. 1852; d. Feb. 1910; m. 15 Sept. 1880, Henrietta Louisa, dau. of Rev. Thomas James Burke, Rector of Babcary, co. Somerset, and by her (who d. 1881) has a dau.,
  1. Charlotte Mary.
He m. 2ndly, 1884, Islet, dau. of — Scott, of Kempsey, New South Wales, and has issue,
1. Raymond.
2. Margery.
3. John, Rear-Admiral R.N., b. 22 July, 1854; m. Maria, dau. of the Right Hon. John Young. He d. 8 June, 1910, leaving issue, a dau.,
  Charlotte.
Mr. Casement m. 2ndly, 1859, Charlotte, dau. of Alexander Miller, of Ballycastle. He d. 13 Oct. 1902.

Arms—Erm., a lion rampant guardant ppr. charged with a mullet gu., and holding in the paws a sword erect also ppr. pomel and hilt gold, encircled round the point with a wreath vert, on a chief embattled gu. a tower arg. between two elephants' heads erased or. Crest—A mural crown gu. issuing therefrom a demi-tiger rampant guardant ppr., charged with a mullet of the first and crowned with an Eastern crown or holding in the paws a sword erect ppr. pommel and hilt gold, the point encircled with a wreath vert. Motto—Dum spiro spero.

Seat—Magherintemple, Ballycastle, co. Antrim.

CASSAN OF SHEFFIELD.

FLORA ADELAIDE CASSAN, of Sheffield House, Queen's Co., s. her father 14 Feb. 1905.

Lineage.—STEPHEN CASSAN, a native of Montpelier, b. 1659, sought refuge in Holland at the Revocation of the Edict of Nantes; and in 1689, being then an Officer in the Foreign Brigade, was engaged under the command of Schomberg, in Ireland, in which kingdom he eventually settled. He m. 1692, Elizabeth, dau. and sole heir of Gen. Joseph Sheffield, of Navestock, Essex, and Cappoly, Queen's Co., A.D.C. to the Duke of Buckingham, son of Sir Sampson Sheffield, of Seton, Rutland, and had an only son,
MATTHEW CASSAN, of Cappoly or Sheffield, b. 1693, who built the present mansion at Sheffield. Mr. Cassan m. 1st, Ann, dau. of Jonathan Baldwin, of Sumner Hill, Queen's Co., and had (besides two daus., Eliza, m. the Rev. George Cook; and Margaret, m. Aaron Crossley Seymour), two sons, STEPHEN, his heir; Richard Sheffield, Barrister-at-Law, b. 1729, m. Isabella, dau. of Alexander Hamilton, of Knock, co. Dublin, M.P., and left at his decease four daus., his co-heirs. Mr. Cassan m. 2ndly, Christian, dau. of John Walsh, of Jamaica, and had by her, Joseph (Rev.), of Stradbally, b. 1742, d. 1830, aged 88, leaving issue, John, a Capt. in the Army d. 1805, leaving issue; Christiana, b. 12 March, 1743, m. James Price, of Westfield, Queen's Co. The eldest son and heir,
STEPHEN CASSAN, of Sheffield, Barrister-at-Law, b. 22 May, 1724-5; High Sheriff Queen's Co. 1763; m. 9 Dec. 1750, Alicia, relict of Benjamin Hunt, and dau. of William Mercer, of Fair Hill. co. Louth. Mr. Cassan d. 26 April, 1773, aged 48. Mrs. Cassan d. 6 Feb. 1789. They had two sons and a dau.,
1. MATTHEW, his heir.
2. Stephen, Barrister-at-Law, b. 2 Jan. 1757; m. 4 March, 1786, Sarah, only dau. and eventual heir of Charles Mears, Capt. of the "Egmont"; and d. 26 Jan. 1794, leaving an only son,
  STEPHEN HYDE, M.A., F.S.A., Vicar of Bruton and of Wyke, Somerset; m. 27 Dec. 1820, Frances, 3rd dau. of the Rev. William Ireland, M.A., Vicar of Frome, and had at his decease, 19 July, 1841, one son and three daus.,
    (1) Algernon William, b. 18 July, 1822.
    (1) Gertrude Anne Caley.   (2) Frances Alicia.
    (3) Florence Georgina.
1. Alicia, m. Rev. George Howse, M.A., Rector of Inch.

Mr. Cassan was s. at his decease by his elder son,
MATTHEW CASSAN, of Sheffield, b. 1754, High Sheriff 1783; Major in the Queen's Co. Militia; m. 1st, 18 May, 1776, Sarah (who d. 1815), 3rd dau. of Col. Forde, of Seaforde, co. Down; and 2ndly, 15 Sept. 1819, Catherine, dau. of John Head, of Ashley Park, co. Tipperary, but left at his decease, 1 Nov. 1838, issue only by the 1st wife, one son,
STEPHEN SHEFFIELD CASSAN, of Sheffield, J.P., Barrister-at-Law, b. 18 Oct. 1777; m. Aug. 1809, Anne Elizabeth, dau. of Edward Laurenson, of Capponellan, co. Kilkenny, and by her (who d. 1858) had issue,
1. MATTHEW SHEFFIELD, late of Sheffield.
2. Stephen Sheffield, dec.   3. Edward, dec.
4. Arthur Moore 84th Regt., d. in India, 1847.
1. Sarah Elizabeth, dec.   2. Mary Ann, dec.
3. Alicia, dec.   4. Anne, dec.
5. Margaret, dec.

Mr. Cassan d. 1848. The eldest son,
MATTHEW SHEFFIELD CASSAN, of Sheffield House, Queen's Co., J.P., High Sheriff 1843, b. 23 Dec. 1815; m. 1 May, 1843, Phoebe Louisa Dawson-Damer (dau. of John, Earl of Portarlington), and d. 14 Feb. 1905, having by her (who d. 1886) had issue,
1. FRANCIS SEYMOUR STUART, b. 12 July, 1849.
2. Henry Erskine, b. 14 Sept. 1849; d. 12 July, 1907.
3. Stephen Sheffield, b. 29 Aug. 1851; dec.
4. Matthew Sheffield, b. 14 Sept. 1852; d. 20 April, 1910.
5. Edward Lawrenson, dec.   6. Reginald Sheffield, d. unm.
1. Emily Anne, m. 13 Feb. 1875, Lieut.-Col. J. Cecil Grove-Price, R.A., of Croydon, Surrey.
2. FLORA ADELAIDE, now of Sheffield.
3. Anne Elizabeth, d. 24 Nov. 1905, having m. William Alexander Robertson, who d. 1887.

Arms—Arg., three oaks, eradicated ppr. Crest—Issuant from an earl's coronet, a boar's head and neck or, langued gu. Motto—Arva parentum juvant.

Seat—Sheffield, near Maryborough.

CASSIDI OF GLENBROOK.

FRANCIS RICHARD CASSIDI, of Glenbrook, near Magherafelt, co. Derry, b. 8 Feb. 1858, M.A., M.D. Trin. Coll. Dublin; Associate of the Order of St. John of Jerusalem; m. 20 July, 1887, Marion Elizabeth, dau. of John Duncanson, M.D., of Alloa, N.B., and has issue,
1. FRANCIS LAIRD, b. 20 Dec. 1889.
2. Robert Alexander, b. 18 Nov. 1894.
1. Marjorie May, b. 11 May, 1888; d. 12 Oct. 1890.

Lineage.—HENRY O'CASSIDY, M.D., who had followed his ancestral pursuits in medicine, was of Greatwood, Mullaghbawn, and Drumkirk, co Louth, and of various estates in the co. Monaghan. He was b. circa 1650; m. and had issue, with others,
1. FERGUS, his heir.
2. Edmond, Scholar of Trinity Coll. Dublin in 1710.
1. Margaret, m. Eugene O' Docherty, of Newtown, co. Leitrim.

The elder son,
FERGUS O'CASSIDY, of Greatwood, co. Louth, and of "Derry," co. Monaghan, had two sons. The elder,
PATRICK CASSIDY, was of Derry, in the parish of Magheracloony near Carrickmacross. He m. Catherine Flood, and had issue. Mr. Cassidy's last will was dated 6 July, 1753, was proved 5 March, 1757. Among other directions he desired "to be buried in my tombe at Carrick McCross." His youngest son,
FRANCIS CASSIDY, b. circa 1747, was of Cashel, co. Tipperary. He m. Sarah Magee, a first cousin of William Magee, Archbishop of Dublin, and had issue,
1. MARK, his heir.
2. Francis Duff, Capt. 60th Rifles, Private Secretary to Lord Castlereagh, the Statesman. By Mary Anne his wife (who d. at Dudley, 24 Feb. 1877, aged 91) he had,
  1. Mark.
    1. Frances, m. Samuel Lazarus, son of the late Joshua George Lazarus, missionary to the Jews in Liverpool, and has issue,
      (1) Julius Samuel.
      (1) Mary Frances.   (2) Elizabeth Henrietta.
  2. Maria, Mrs. Henry Roper, of Dudley.
3. Francis, d. young.

He d. 1802. His eldest son was

THE REV. MARK CASSIDY, A.M., b. 1 Aug. 1777, Scholar of Trinity Coll. Dublin 1797. He m. 1808, Henrietta, dau. (by his wife, Marguerite Vateau, the only child and heiress of Paul Peter Isaac Vateau, the descendant of a Huguenot refugee, who had settled in Dublin) and co-heiress with her sister Esther, wife of Rev. Prebendary Cleland, of Samuel Jackson, of Stormount, near Belfast, a West Indian Planter (*see* CLELAND *of Stormont Castle*); and by her (who d. 14 Dec. 1858) he had issue,
1. Samuel, of Glenbrook, co. Derry, m. Esther Scott, but d.s.p. 27 Nov. 1843.
2. FRANCIS PETER, his heir.
3. Charles, d. unm. at Slingsby, Yorkshire, 2 March, 1857.
4. Frederick (Rev.), Vicar of Grindon, co. Durham, d. unm. 27 Aug. 1882.
6. Robert, LL.D., of Hackamore House, Belfast, m. Anne, dau. of Dr. Ardagh, and d. 11 Nov. 1873, leaving issue,
  Robert, K.C., m. 14 March, 1907, Adelaide, dau. of late Herman vor. Eber, of Winnipeg.
7. Loftus Tottenham, Lieut.-Col. 18th Hussars, m. Jane, dau. of Col. Barlow, and d. 1 March, 1887, leaving issue.
8. Alfred, m. Sarah Louisa, dau. of W. N. Bryett, of Birkdal , Southport, and d. 7 Oct. 1893, leaving issue.
1. Sarah, d. unm. 13 Oct. 1873.
2. Henrietta, m. Richard Wilson, J.P., of Carnlough, co. Antrim, and d. 22 June, 1880, leaving by him (who d. 19 May, 1879) a son, 1888, leaving issue.
3. Fanny, m. Col. Audain, late of 10th Infantry, and d. 13 Oct, 1888, leaving issue.
4. Emily, m. Rev. Samuel Hayman (see HAYMAN *of Myrtle Grove and South Abbey*), and d. 24 July, 1894, leaving issue.
The Rev. M. Cassidy was Chancellor of Kilfenora, and Incumbent of Newtownards, and d. 10 Dec. 1839, being s. by his 2nd son,
FRANCIS PETER CASSIDI, of Glenbrook, co. Derry, J.P., of the 34th Regt., retired Col. of the Army, m. 2 June, 1853, Maria Lucy Anne, 4th dau. of Matthew Hayman, of South Abbey, Youghal, and had issue,
1. FRANCIS RICHARD, now of Glenbrook.
1. Helen Hayman Henrietta.   2. Mary Mortimer.
Col. Cassidi served with his regiment during the Indian Mutiny, and was severely wounded at the battle of Cawnpore, 26 Nov. 1857. He d. 24 Sept. 1879.

Seat—Glenbrook, Magherafelt, co. Derry.

CAULFEILD OF DONAMON.

ALGERNON THOMAS ST. GEORGE CAULFEILD, of Donamon Castle, co. Roscommon, J.P. cos. Roscommon and Galway, High Sheriff for the former co. 1899, b. 31 July, 1869; s. his grandfather, 1896. Mr. Caulfeild is the only son of St. George Francis Robert Caulfeild, Capt. 1st Life Guards (who d.v.p. 9 March, 1875), by Louisa Ann (now Lady Rumbold) his wife, only dau. of Thomas Russell Crampton, C.E., and grandson of Francis St. George Caulfeild, late of Donamon Castle, son of St. George Caulfeild, of Donamon, son of Col. John Caulfeild, 4th son of the Hon. and Rev. Charles Caulfeild, 2nd son of William, 2nd Viscount Charlemont. The above-mentioned Col. John Caulfeild s. 1778 to the estates of his kinsman Chief Justice St. George Caulfeild, of Donamon, grandson of the Hon. Thomas Caulfeild, of Donamon, youngest son of William, 2nd Baron Charlemont.

Lineage.—*See* BURKE's *Peerage*, CHARLEMONT, V.

Arms—Barry of ten arg. and gu. on a canton of the second a lion passant guardant or. *Crest*—A dragon's head erased gu. gorged with a bar gemelle arg. *Motto*—Deo duce ferro comitante.

Seats—Donamon Castle, co. Roscommon, and Vicar's Hill, Lymington, Hants. *Clubs*—Carlton, Travellers', and R.Y.S.

CAULFEILD.

See BURKE's PEERAGE, CHARLEMONT, V.

CAVENDISH.

See BURKE's PEERAGE, DEVONSHIRE, D.

CHADWICK OF BALLINARD.

The late WILLIAM COOPER-CHADWICK, of Ballinard. co. Tipperary, Hon. Col. Tipperary Artillery, b. 14 Nov. 1855; m. Feb. 1886, ANNA MARIA ROBERTINA HEPHZIBAH, who d. 7 Nov. 1911, dau. of the late John Langley, J.P., of Knockanure, co. Tipperary, and d. 24 Nov. 1895, leaving two daus.,
1. FRANCES VIOLET, now of Ballinard, b. 8 April, 1887; m. 7 July, 1910, Allen Baker, of Lismacue, Bansha, co. Tipperary (*whom see*).
2. Kathleen Lilian, b. 15 Aug. 1893.

Lineage.—WILLIAM CHADWICK, of Ballinard, m. circa 1675, Elizabeth, dau. of William Gabbett, of Caherline, co. Limerick, and had (with a dau. Grace, m. Clement Sadleir) a son,
WILLIAM CHADWICK, of Ballinard and Gurthakilleen, temp. Queen ANNE, m. Jane Greene, and d. 1748, having by her (who d. Sept. 1779) had issue,
1. RICHARD, his heir.   2. William, living 1720. left issue.
3. Rodulph, living 1720.
4. Michael, living 1720, left issue.
1. Katherine, m. 1743, Vere Hunt, of Curragh, co. Limerick.
The eldest son,
RICHARD CHADWICK, of Ballinard, d. 14 Feb. 1771, possessed landed property of considerable extent, which he divided among his sons. He m. 1st, 1738, Rebecca, dau. of James Ellard, and by her had issue,
1. WILLIAM, of Ballinard.
2. Richard (Rev.), Rector of Doone, co. Tipperary, b. 1751, m. 1770, Margaret, dau. of Nicholas Sadleir, of Golden Garden, co. Tipperary, and d. May, 1817, having had issue,
  1. Richard, b. 1774; d. July, 1836, commanded a company of Volunteers in 1798, he had issue several sons and daus., of whom,
    (1) Richard, was murdered at Holy Cross, June, 1829.
    (2) John, an attorney in Dublin, left issue.
    (3) William, of Arravale, Tipperary, had issue,
      1. Edward, Lieut.-Col. (*Holly Grove, Fittleworth, Sussex*), formerly of 7th Dragoon Guards and (Major) 16th Lancers, served in S. Africa, Boer War, with Imperial Yeomanry.
      2. Charles.
    (1) James, of Cashel, High Constable of Tipperary, d. 1875.
    2. James, Major 59th East Lancashire Regt., b. 15 May, 1789; m. 1st, Josephine Chapuis, and had issue, one son, who d. young; and 2ndly, Mrs. Isabella, dau. of the Rev. George Markham, Dean of York, and grand-dau. of the Right Rev. William Markham, Archbishop of York 1777, and had issue,
      (1) Edward Frederick, b. 3 March 1829, Col. late 33rd (Duke of Wellington's) Regt., late of Chetnole, now of Westfield, Dorchester, Dorsetshire, m. in 1882, Amy, dau. of Rev. Charles Torkington (son of James Torkington), and Ellen Cookson, his wife, and has issue,
        1. Frederick James, b. 1883, Lieut. 104th Wellesley Rifles, Bombay.
        2. Edward William, b. 1884, Lieut. 101st Company R.G.A.
        3. Richard Markham, b. 1894.
        1. Josephine.   2. Ellen.
        3. Amy Margaret.   4. Norah Alicia.
      (2) Richard, m. Rachel ——, and had issue,
        1. James, Capt. Munster Fus., d. unm.
        2. Redmond Arthur, living U.S.A.
        1. Annie Isabella, m. Rev. Arthur Babington Cartwright, Archdeacon of Malta.
      (3) Isabella, d. unm.
      (4) Josephine Adelaide, unm.
      (5) Alicia, m. Rev. William Moyle Rogers, and has issue.
      (6) Margaret Emma, m. Philip Sheppard (dec.), and has had issue.
      (7) Ellen, m. Rev. George Hayton, d. leaving issue.
    3. Thomas, 18th Light Dragoons, b. 1752; m. 1 June, 1779, Sarah Lockwood, of Cashel, and d. July, 1812, leaving issue.
  4. James, who also left issue.
  5. Frederick, of Littleton, m. Sarah Minchin, and had issue.
    1. A dau., m. William Minchin, of Greenhills, and had issue.
He m. 2ndly, 1768, Jane, dau. of Nicholas Sadleir, of Golden Garden (who m. 2ndly, 1772, Rev. Anthony Armstrong), and by her had issue,
6. Nicholas, b. 1771; d. Jan. 1854, leaving issue.
7. Michael, of Jersey, who also left issue.
The eldest son,

WILLIAM CHADWICK, of Ballinard, b. 1741; m. 1st, 1768, Christiana, dau. of John Carden, of Templemore Abbey, and sister of Sir John Craven Carden, 1st bart. of Templemore Abbey, and by her (who d. Feb 1782) he had, with six daus., two sons.

1. Richard,* b. between 1769 and 1777, and probably d. before 1839, m. — Barclay, and had issue, besides a dau., one son, William Barclay, b. about 1790; d. in London 1861, was Capt. in 2nd Royal Surrey Militia; m. Abba Thule, dau. of Dr. Sharpe, and had issue, a dau., Fanny, who d. young, and one son,

Richard Weller, b. 1812; d. in London Nov. 1864, who was for some time an Officer in the Army, and afterwards served in the Spanish Army in the Carlist Rebellion, was Manager of the Eastern Counties Railway, and afterwards of the Eastern Bengal Railway in India; m. in 1851, Georgiana Ann, dau. of the Rev. Charles Spencer Bourchier, Rector of Great Hallingbury, co. Essex, and Vicar of Sandridge, co. Hertford, and had issue (besides a dau., Georgiana Ludee Frere, m. to Robert Balderston Mackay, son of James Mackay, of Blair Castle, but d.s.p. 12 April, 1891) one son,

John Barclay Bourchier (Hollywood, California), b. 5 Aug. 1853, late of the Civil Service and local Military Service in Jamaica, and is a Capt. in the Reserve of Officers of that island; m. 2 Sept. 1898, at Trinity Church, New York, Helen Sophia, dau. of James Porter, of Sarnia, Canada.

2. JOHN CRAVEN, of whom presently.

William Chadwick m. 2ndly, Sophia, dau. of John Golden Garden Carden, of Barnane (see that family). She d.s.p. Sept. 1825, aged 82. He d. March, 1825, and was s. by his son,

JOHN CRAVEN CHADWICK, of Ballinard, b. 1778; m. 1799, Elizabeth, dau. of Samuel Cooper, of Killenure Castle, co. Tipperary. She d. 3 April, 1831. By her he had issue,

1. WILLIAM, of whom presently.
2. Samuel Cooper, of Dunmore, co. Waterford, b. Jan. 1801; m. Letitia, dau. of Thomas Hall, and d.s.p. 15 June, 1890. She d. 1886.
3. Austin Cooper, of Damerville, co. Tipperary, m. Anne, dau. of Dr. Millet, of Cove, co. Cork, and had several sons and daus., who settled in Australia.
4. John Craven, b. 6 April, 1811, settled in Canada in 1836, at Cravendale, near Ancaster, co. Wentworth, and was subsequently of Guelph, co. Wellington. He m. 1st, 3 Jan. 1836, Louisa, dau. of Jonathan Bell, merchant in London; by Maria, dau. of Edward Vaux; and 2ndly, 15 Dec. 1847, Caroline, dau. of Joseph Eade, of Newington, Middlesex, and Hitchin, co. Hertford (by Eliza, dau. of Edward Vaux). She d.s.p. 5 Sept. 1874. He m. 3rdly, 4 May, 1876, Elizabeth, dau. of James Beatty, of Toronto. He d. 10 Nov. 1889, having by his 1st wife (who d. 1844) had issue,

1. John Craven, b. 12 Feb. 1837; m. 1st, 21 June, 1860, Eleanor Toonie, dau. of Leslie Battersby, Lieut. R.N., and grand-dau. of Rev. Leslie Battersby, of Skreene, co. Sligo, and by her (who d. 9 Jan. 1868) had surviving issue,
  (1) Craven Bell, b. 2 April, 1863; m. Flora Jennie, dau. of Ralph Hinds, and widow of Alexander Carroll, and has had issue,
    1. Alexander Joseph, b. 12 Nov. 1886; d. 30 Dec. 1887.
    2. William Francis, b. Jan. 1889.
  (2) Francis Henry, b. 11 Aug. 1866, of Lakeport, California, m. Rose Catherine, dau. of William Dwight Fiske, and has issue.

John Craven m. 2ndly, April, 1870, Sybella Annie, dau. of William Mockler, of Fermoy, co. Cork, and d. 8 April, 1890, having by her (who d. 22 Feb. 1891) had issue,
  (3) William Herbert Austin, b. 27 Jan. 1871; d. unm.
  (4) Richard Frederick, b. 18 April, 1874.
  (5) Ethelred James Mockler, b. 15 Oct. 1875.
  (6) Reginald Beatty Atkinson, b. 10 Dec. 1883.
  (1) Sybella Eade Nicola.
  (2) Norah Annie, m. Justus Roedding, of Ayton, Ontario.

2. Frederick Jasper, of Guelph, b. 19 Nov. 1838, Capt. in the Reserve Militia; m. 3 Sept. 1861, Elisabeth, dau. of Rev. Edward Michael Stewart, of Clooney, co. Derry, and of Killymoon, co. Donegal, grandson maternally of Edward Michael, 2nd Lord Longford, and d. 20 June, 1891, having by her (who d. 3 Aug. 1894) had issue,
  (1) Jasper William, b. 10 Nov. 1866; m. Alexandrina Agatha, dau. of Samuel John Cowley, and has issue,
    William Gustavus.
  (2) Frederick Austin Pakenham (Rev.), b. 9 June, 1873, in Holy Orders, Rector of St. Paul's, Vancouver, British Columbia; m. Alberta Louise, dau. of Samuel Dice, of Milton, Ontario (she d. 16 Jan. 1902), and has issue, two sons,
    1. John Pakenham Dice, b. 14 May, 1899.
    2. Frederick Stewart, b. 31 Aug. 1900.
  (1) Louisa Caroline Stewart, d. unm.
  (2) Charlotte Rose.
  (3) Kathleen Christiana Maria, m. William Henry Pepler, M.D., and has issue.

3. Edward Marion, of Toronto, Barrister-at-Law, K.C., Lay Canon and Treasurer of St. Alban's Cathedral, Toronto, a Major in the Active Militia, retired from 2nd Regt. the Queen's Own Rifles of Canada, b. 22 Sept. 1840; m. 1st, 28 June, 1864, Ellen Byrne, dau. of James Beatty, of Toronto, who d.s.p. 10 Feb. 1865; and 2ndly, 20 Feb. 1868, Maria Martha, dau. of Alexander Fisher, of Toronto, by whom he has issue,

---

* In a former edition of BURKE's Landed Gentry erroneously stated to have died unmarried.

(1) William Craven Vaux, b. 6 Dec. 1868, Lieut.-Col. Commanding 9th Mississauga Horse (Active Militia of Canada); m. 29 Dec. 1898, Jessie Dorothea, dau. of Robert Murray, of New York, and had issue,
  Patricia Katharine, who d. an infant.
(2) Edward Alister Eade, b. 13 Feb. 1871; m. 4 June, 1898, Florence Edith, dau. of Thomas Campbell Kemp, and has issue,
  1. Edward Norman Loud, b. 7 April, 1899.
  2. Austin Ralph, b. 10 July, 1901.
  1. Edith Marion, b. 16 Feb. 1906.
(3) George Darcy Austin, b. 22 Feb. 1880; m. 3 July, 1907, Bessie Carlisle, dau. of John Edward MacCorquodale.
(4) Richard Ellard Carden, b. 16 Feb. 1885.
(5) Bryan Damer Seymour, b. 24 June, 1888.
(1) Fanny Marion, m. 30 June, 1888, to James Grayson Smith, Barrister-at-Law, and d. 13 Jan. 1905, leaving issue.
(2) Louisa Mary Caroline.

4. Austin Cooper, of Guelph, Barrister-at-Law, Senior Judge for co. Wellington, b. 18 Nov. 1842; m. 19 Dec. 1867, Caroline Christie, dau. of Ralph Charles Nicholson, of Toronto, Canada, and of Lewes, Sussex, and has issue,
  Henry Austin, b. 15 April, 1883, of Perth, Ontario, Barrister-at-Law; m. 30 Sept. 1908, Mary Helena, dau. of George William Sandilands, and has issue.
  Caroline Gladys May.

5. Richard, bapt. 8 April, 1813; d. unm.
6. Frederick, bapt. 16 Feb. 1815; m. and had issue.
7. Edward Butler, bapt. 24 Oct. 1817; d. unm. 13 April, 1859.

1. Frances, m. Rev. John Seymour, of Clonloughlan, near Cloughjordan, son of Rev. John Seymour, Rector of Shronell, co. Tipperary, and d. 1879, leaving issue.
2. Christiana Rosetta, m. 30 June, 1832, Richard M. Forsayeth, M.D., of Templemore, and d. 1871, leaving issue.
3. Elizabeth, b. 3 July, 1827, Rev. William Bryan, of Gurteen, near Clonmel, and had issue.
4. Caroline Damer, m. Rev. Joseph Cooke Armstrong, of Ballyporeen, co. Tipperary, afterwards of Clonmel, and d.s.p. 1856.

John Craven Chadwick d. March, 1851, and was s. by his eldest son,

WILLIAM CHADWICK, of Ballinard, b. 1800; m. 1st, Wilhelmina, dau. of Rev. John Seymour, Rector of Shronell, co. Tipperary, and by her (who d. Dec. 1836) had issue,
1. KATHERINE, m. 6 Feb. 1855, Richard Austin Cooper, 2nd son of Samuel Cooper, of Killenure (see below).
2. Elizabeth, d. April, 1839, aged 5 years.
3. Fanny, d. unm.

Mr. Chadwick m. 2ndly, Charlotte (who d. 17 Jan. 1874), dau. of John Bourchier, of Bagotstown, co. Limerick; and d. 1876, when he was s. by his son-in-law,

RICHARD AUSTIN COOPER-CHADWICK, of Ballinard, co. Tipperary, m. 1st (as above), 6 Feb. 1855, Katherine, elder dau. and co-heir of William Chadwick, of Ballinard, having previously assumed by Royal sign-manual, dated 15 Jan. 1855, the additional name and arms of CHADWICK for himself and the issue of his marriage with the said Katherine Chadwick, and by her (who d. 12 Dec. 1855) had issue a son,
1. WILLIAM, late of Ballinard.

Mr. Cooper-Chadwick m. 2ndly, 1863, Charlotte Sophia, only dau. of John Bourchier (the younger), of Bagotstown, co. Limerick, and d. 19 Jan. 1893, leaving further issue,
2. John, of Fanningstown House, Piltown, co. Kilkenny, b. 13 May, 1864; m. 17 Oct. 1896, Wilhelmina, 2nd dau. of Samuel Heuston, J.P., of Barrowstown, co. Tipperary, and has issue,
  1. John Lionel, b. 16 Feb. 1899.
  2. Samuel Victor, b. 1 Nov. 1903.
3. Richard Austin.
4. Austin Samuel, m. 30 March, 1910, Florence Banks, dau. of Joseph Harris, of Richmond, Surrey.
1. Katherine Louisa.   2. Elizabeth Sarah.
3. Charlotte Sophia.
4. Frances Anna, m. 12 April, 1898, Sutherland Matterson, eldest son of Joseph Matterson, of Castle Troy, co. Limerick.
5. Ada Mary, m. 21 July, 1908, Ambrose Grattan Power, only son of late Ambrose William Bushe Power, D.L. (see BUSHE of Glencairn Abbey, and see BURKE's Peerage, POWER, Bart.).

Arms of COOPER-CHADWICK—Quarterly 1st and 4th, or, an inescutcheon gu. charged with a lily slipped and leaved ppr. within an orle of martlets sa., for CHADWICK; 2nd and 3rd, per pale indented arg. and sa. three bulls passant counterchanged a canton az., for COOPER. Crests—1st: A martlet, sa., charged on the breast with a crescent arg. holding in the bill a lily stemmed and slipped ppr., for CHADWICK. 2nd: On a mount vert a bull passant per pale arg. and sa. gorged with a collar dancetté, az., for COOPER. Mottoes—Stans cum rege; and over the crest, In candore decus. Arms of CHADWICK (borne by some other members of the family)—Party per pale gu. and sa. within an orle of eight martlets an inescutcheon arg., charged with a cross of the 1st and in the 1st quarter a crescent of the 2nd. Crest—A martlet arg., holding in his bill a white lily slipped and leaved ppr., borne fesseways, the flower to the sinister. Mottoes—Over crest, In candore decus; under arms, Toujours pret.

Seat—Ballinard, Tipperary.

CHAINE OF BALLYCRAIGY.

WILLIAM CHAINE, of Carnfunnock and Ballycraigy, co. Antrim, D.L., High Sheriff 1902, B.A. Trin. Coll. Camb., b. 1865. Mr. Chaine is son of the late James Chaine, D.L., of Ballycraigy, M.P. co. Antrim, 1874-85, High Sheriff 1873 (who d. 1885, aged 44), and Henrietta his wife, dau. of Charles A. Creery, and grandson of James Chaine, of Ballycraigy, by Maria his wife, dau. of Francis Whittle, of Muckomore, co. Antrim.

Seats—Carnfunnock, Larne, and Ballycraigy, Muckomore, both co. Antrim. *Club*—Carlton.

CHALONER OF KING'S FORT.

CLAUD CHALONER, of King's Fort, co. Meath, J.P. cos. Cavan and Meath, b. 20 Nov. 1838; m. 2 June, 1875, Henrietta Ann, eldest dau. of Alexander Montgomery, of Kilmer, co. Meath (*see that family*), and has issue,
1. Richard Alexander, Lieut. Royal Innis. Fus., b. 2 June, 1879; d. unm. 22 April, 1902, from wounds received at Rooival, Western Transvaal.
2. CLAUD WILLOUGHBY, Lieut. 3rd Batt. Royal Innis. Fus., b. Jan. 1882.
3. Shirley, b. 1886; d. 30 May, 1902.
4. John, b. 27 May, 1889.
1. Sophia Elizabeth, b. 22 Feb. 1877.
2. Emily, b. 21 May, 1878.
3. Henrietta Frances, b. Jan. 1881.
4. Nicola, b. 25 Nov. 1884; d. Jan. 1885.

Mr. Chaloner assumed the name of CHALONER in lieu of COLE HAMILTON on succeeding to King's Fort.

Lineage.—REV. JOHN CHALONER, of Shropshire, Chaplain of the "Royal Sovereign," had issue,
REV. JOHN CHALONER, of Rathanree, co. Meath, b. 1658, entered Trin. Coll. Dublin 7 July, 1675, Scholar 1676, B.A. 1679, M.A. 1682; m. a dau. of Rev. Laurence Clutterbuck, M.A. (Cantab.), of Derryloskan, co. Tipperary. His will, dated 23 Feb. 1733, was proved 30 April following. He left issue,
1. JOHN, his heir.
2. Laurence, M.A. (Dublin), b. 1705, who left issue, John and Mary.
3. Richard (Rev.), M.A. (Dublin), b. 1707, Archdeacon of Cashel; d. 28 Dec. 1746, his dau. Mary, m. Wray Palliser, of Derryloskan (*see* PALLISER *of Annestown*).
1. Mary, m. John Kellet.
The eldest son,
JOHN CHALONER, of Kingsfort, co. Meath, m. by licence 6 May, 1732, Charity, dau. of Robert Graham, of Drogheda. His will, dated 21 Sept. 1778, proved 14 Jan. 1779. He left issue,
1. RICHARD, his heir. 2. Laurence. 3. John.
4. Charles, m. 24 Jan. 1777, — Barrington (she d. May, 1778), and left issue.
1. A dau., m. 28 Aug. 1756, Rev. John Betty.
2. Letitia.
The eldest son,
RICHARD CHALONER, of Kingsfort, co. Meath, High Sheriff 1784; m. Nov. 1784, Frances Maria, dau. of Edward Herbert, M.P., by Nichola Sophia his wife, eldest dau. of John, Lord Desert, and left issue, five daus.,
1. NICHOLA SOPHIA, of whom presently.
2. Catherine, m. 1811, John Knox, of Mount Falcon (*see that family*).
3. Jane Thomasine, m. James Wemyss Pope, of Wellington (Cahirleske), co. Kilkenny.
4. Frances Maria, m. William Lindsay, of Wilford, co. Galway.
5. Charity, m. Abraham Whyte Baker, of Ballytobin, co. Kilkenny.
The eldest dau. and co-heir,
NICHOLA SOPHIA CHALONER, of Kingsfort, m. 1st, 10 Oct. 1805, Claud William Cole-Hamilton, of Beltrim (*see* BURKE's *Peerage*, ENNISKILLEN, E.), and by him (who d. 25 April, 1822) had issue,
1. Arthur Willoughby, of Beltrim, co. Tyrone, D.L., b. 23 Nov. 1806; m. 16 Dec. 1831, Emilia Katherine, dau. of Rev. Charles Cobbe Beresford (*see* BURKE's *Peerage*, WATERFORD, M.). She d. 19 Nov. 1869. He d. 16 Dec. 1891, having had, with an eldest son, William Claud, ancestor of COLE-HAMILTON, of Beltrim (*see that family*), and several younger sons, a second son,
CLAUD, now of King's Fort.
2. Richard, of whom presently.
She m. 2ndly, 25 Jan. 1826, Col. Joseph Pratt, of Cabra Castle (*see that family*). He d. 27 Aug. 1863. She was s. by her second son,
RICHARD CHALONER, of King's Fort, co. Meath, J.P., High Sheriff 1855, sometime Lieut. 12th Lancers, who assumed the name of CHALONER 1832. b. 25 April, 1810; m. Feb. 1835, Harriet, dau. of Charles Arthur Tisdall, of Charlesfort, co. Meath, and d.s.p. 29 Nov. 1879, and was s. by his nephew, CLAUD COLE-HAMILTON, now CHALONER of King's Fort.

Seat—King's Fort, Moynalty, co. Meath.

CHAMBERS OF FOSTERSTOWN.

RICHARD EDWARD ELLIOT CHAMBERS, of Fosterstown, Trim, co. Meath, and of Pill House, Barnstaple, Devonshire, b. 7 April, 1863; m. 11 Sept. 1894, Edith Frances, youngest surviving dau. of Henry Chandos-Pole-Gell, of Hopton Hall, Derbyshire, J.P. (*see that family*), and has issue,

1. EDWARD CHANDOS ELLIOT, b. 4 April, 1896.
1. Auriel Hermione Dorothy.
2. Gwendoline Margaret Elliot.

Lineage.—JOSEPH CHAMBERS, of Taylorstown, co. Wexford, b. about 1655-60, held property in the baronies of Shelburne, Bargy and Bantry, including land outside the Bewley Gate, within and without the Liberties of New Ross, where a townland is still called "Chambersland," and also held property in Shelmaliere barony and in the town of Wexford. He was living at Taylorstown Castle, in Shelburne barony in 7 QUEEN ANNE (1708-09) till his death. In his will (dated 31 May, 1726, proved 29 November, 1726) he desired to be buried in Clongeen Churchyard. He left a widow, Sarah, four sons (another son, Francis, having d. before 1724) and four daus. The three elder children were,
1. ROBERT, of whom presently.
2. Joseph, who had some property in and near Wexford.
1. Mary, eld. dau., m. 18 April, 1722, Arthur Meadows, of Wexford and had issue (*see that family*).
The eldest son,
ROBERT CHAMBERS, of Arklow, in Shelburne barony, and of New Ross, co. Wexford, b. about 1694, was made a Freeman of New Ross, 28 Nov. 1715, and admitted to that Freedom 30 Aug. 1721. He m. about 1715-20, Mary, sister and co-heir of Alan Cox, of New Ross, and of Ballyvadden, co. Wexford, High Sheriff of co. Wexford 1747. She was and dau. of the Rev. Jasper Cox (b. 1653; d. 1712), M.A. (Dublin), Prebendary of Coolstuffe and Kilrush (Ferns). She predeceased her husband 1756-57. Their son,
JOSEPH CHAMBERS, of Trim, co. Meath, b. about 1716-20. He m. 1st, about 1740, Mary, b. 1715, eldest dau. of the Rev. Stafford Lightburne, of Trim, Rector of Churchtown, co. Westmeath, 1733-47, and Vicar of Rathgraffe or Castlepollard, co. Westmeath 1747-51 (by Hannah, eldest dau. of Willoughby Swift, of Hereford, *see* SWIFTE *of Swiftsheath*). Of this marriage there was issue,
1. William, of Trim, co. Meath, d.v.p. unm. 1767.
1. Dorothea, m. George Carter, of Annaghkeene, co. Galway, and had issue.
2. Elizabeth, d. unm. 1766-7.
He m. 2ndly, Sept. 1764, Dorothea, dau. of John Carshore, of Trim. He d. 4 Oct. 1773, having had issue by his 2nd wife (who d. 5 May, 1793),
2. EDWARD ELLIOT, of whom presently.
3. Elizabeth Maria, d. young.
4. Anne, m. Stewart Osborne, of Trim, and had issue.
5. Mary d. unm. May, 1844.
The eldest son,
EDWARD ELLIOT CHAMBERS, of Crow Park, Trim, co. Meath, and of 8, Fitzwilliam Place, Dublin, and later of Fosterstown, Westbury-on-Trym, b. 4 Aug. 1772; m. 1st, 1801, Elizabeth, only surviving dau. and heir of William Carshore, of Fosterstown and Trim, Lieut. Trim Yeomanry Corps 1800 (d. 1823). She d. June, 1836. He became Capt. Commandant of the Trim Yeomanry Corps, succeeding in the active command its first Captain, his maternal uncle, Adam Carshore, of Kilcooley, co. Meath, jointly with whom, in 1796, he had raised that corps which took part in the suppression of the Rebellion of 1798 and was disbanded in 1814. He m. 2ndly, 17 Dec. 1840, Louisa, 4th dau. of Nevill Barry, 2nd son of Charles Barry (d. 1 Feb. 1826), of Kilcarne, co. Meath. He d. 25 Jan. 1857. By his 2nd wife, who long survived him, he had no issue. By his 1st wife he had six sons and three daus.,
1. Adam Carshore, b. 5 Sept. 1804, entered Trin. Coll. Dublin, 5 Nov. 1821; d. while an undergraduate about 1824.
2. William Joseph, b. 1806; d. May, 1806.
3. EDWARD ELLIOT, his successor, of whom presently.
4. William, b. 1816, B.A. (Dublin) 1838, L.R.C.S.I. 1840, M.A. 1842; d. unm. 13 Nov. 1843.
5. Joseph (Rev.), B.A. (Dublin), b. 10 Aug. 1819; d. 20 Jan. 1905, Vicar of Cury-with-Gunwalloe, Cornwall; m. 26 May, 1845, Harriet, youngest dau. of Nevill Barry, by whom (who predeceased him 16 Feb. 1902) he had issue,
1. Edward Eliot (Rev.), B.A. (Dublin), Vicar of West Lyttelton and Chaplain to seamen in the Port of Lyttelton, New Zealand from 1885, acting Chaplain R.N., Australian Squadron

from 1892, Col. Chaplain, Royal Artillery of New Zealand and V.D. 1905-06, b. 6 Jan. 1850; m. 16 June, 1877, Annie (d. 16 May, 1908). 4th dau. of John Hewitt, of St. Andrew Gate, York.
2. Joseph William, b. 24 Oct. 1858, entered Trin. Coll. Dublin 1880.
3. Richard Wellesey Benjamin, Capt. Q.M. 9th New Zealand Contingent 1902, S. African War and afterwards Staff Capt. in Defence Office, New Zealand; b. 11 May, 1861. Killed by accident at Allumbah, Queensland, Australia, 15 Sept., 1908; m. 1st, 1 Dec. 1881, Jane Grant (d. 20 Dec. 1896), dau. of Andrew Munro, and widow of Philip Ross, by whom he left a dau., Violet Forth Barry. He m. 2ndly, 16 May, 1899, Imelda, dau. of Maj-Gen. T. E. Britten, Bo.S.C., and left issue, a dau., Kathleen Ladysmith.
1. Anna Harriet, b. 18 Jan. 1862; d. 14 Dec. 1889.
2. Louisa Sophia.
6. Richard Wellesley, Maj.-Gen. Bengal Staff Corps, b. 10 Feb. 1823, served with 11th Native Infantry, Bengal, in the Bundelkund campaign 1842-43, in the force under Brig.-Gen. F. Young, and was present in the action of Bhagaura 7 Dec. 1842. Served with the regt. in the Army of the Sutlej in the campaign of 1845-46 (medal), and was present at the surrender of "Kot-Kanera" 1846. As adjutant of his regt. was present at Meerut on the outbreak of the Mutiny, and proceeded with the force under Brig.-Gen. A. Wilson on 27 May, as Orderly Officer to Lieut.-Col. Custance, 6th Dragoon Guards (Carabineers) to Delhi. He was present at the two actions on the Hindun, near Ghaziuddin-nagar on 30 and 31 May, 1857; in the action of Badli-ki-Serai, 8 June, 1857; at the siege of Delhi, 15 June, to 12 Sept. (mentioned in despatches); present at siege and capture of Lucknow, March, 1858; mutiny clasps for "Delhi" and "Lucknow"; m. 12 Aug. 1854, Charlotte, dau. of Thos. Britten, and sister of Maj.-Gen. Thos. Ernest Britten, Bo.S.C. She was killed at Meerut, 10 May, 1857, on the outbreak of the Indian Mutiny, having had a son, d. an infant. He m. 2ndly, 25 March, 1860, Elizabeth Louisa Mary Jane, dau. of the Rev. William Marston, Vicar of Llangarren, Ross, Herefordshire, by whom he had a son, b. 1872, d. young, and a dau., Irene Constance Gwendoline, b. 1873. Maj.-Gen. Chambers d. 25 Oct. 1905.
1. Jane, b. 1802-03; d. July, 1810.
2. Elizabeth Mary, b. 1807; m. about 1826, Thomas Browning Haslam, M.D., twice Mayor of Carnarvon 1841-43. He d. 18 Nov. 1848, aged 45. She d. 2 Jan. 1844, leaving four daus.
3. Aine, b. 19 May, 1811, d. unm. 1 Aug. 1827.
The eldest surviving son and heir,
EDWARD ELLIOT CHAMBERS, of Southmead, Westbury-on-Trym, Gloucestershire, and who s. to the estate in Ireland; b. 16 Oct. 1812, M.A. Oxford, Barrister-at-Law. He d. 23 Nov. 1865, having m., 29 May, 1857, Elizabeth, dau. of James Narroway, and by her (who d. 5 June, 1889) he had issue,
1. RICHARD EDWARD ELLIOT, his successor, now of Fosterstown.
1. Frances Emma Annie, m. 23 Oct. 1888, George Brodie MacFarlan Port, grandson of the last John Port, of Ilam Hall, Staffs., and has issue.
2. Charlotte Penelope, b. 9 May, 1859; d. 4 Feb. 1888.
3. Euphemia Dorothea Sophia, m. 17 May, 1890, Cecil Charles Ridley Sumner (d. 13 Aug. 1900), 3rd surviving son of Charles Sumner, of Harescombe Grange, Stroud, Gloucestershire, J.P., M.A. Balliol Coll. Oxford, and Judge of County Courts, Gloucestershire, and has issue.
4. Edith Elliot, m. Oct. 1900, James Wright Grant, M.B., C.M.

Arms—Sa., a cross couped, engrailed and quarter-pierced erm, between four martlets rising or. Crest—Out of a ducal crestcoronet or, charged with a cross humettée gu., a demi-eagle displayed of the last, winged and collared of the first. Motto—Non prœda sed victoria.

Seat—Fosterstown, Trim. Residence—Pill House, Barnstaple, Devonshire.

CHAMBRÉ OF DUNGANNON.

HUNT WALSH CHAMBRÉ, of Dungannon House, co. Tyrone, J.P., b. 22 Sept. 1831; m. 9 Aug. 1860, Mary Anne Brunette, d. 8 Feb. 1912, elder dau. of John Brett Johnston, of Ballykilbeg, co. Down (see that family), and has issue,
1. HUNT WALSH ALAN, b. 29 June, 1861; m. 7 Oct. 1893, Charlotte Harriett, 4th dau. of William Tiptind Woods, of Quebec.
2. John Brett Johnstone Meredith, b. 8 Sept. 1864; m. 29 Nov. 1894, Adeline Sophia, 3rd dau. of George McQuestion, of Ashbrook, Leeson Park, Dublin, and has issue,
1. Hunt Walsh Albert, b. 14 June, 1901; d. 28 Oct. 1904.
1. Olive Mainie Brunette.
2. Kathleen Obré.

3. William Thomas Meredith, b. 24 March; d. Dec. 1867.
4. Charles Barclay Macpherson, b. 3 Aug. 1870; m. 4 Sept. 1904, Nina Lisa Francis Ochiltree, 4th dau. of Rev. Alexander George Stuart, of Bogay House, co. Donegal, and has issue,
Alan Stuart Hunt, b. 7 Jan. 1908.
5. John, b. 19 April, 1879; m. 3 July, 1909, Florence Kathleen, eldest dau. of Rev. Thomas R. Conway, of Drummully Rectory, Clones, and has issue,
William Richard Hunt Walsh.
6. William Henry Calcott, b. 15 Dec. 1880; m. 25 Feb. 1904, Frances Jane, eldest dau. of R. Davies, of Dublin, and has issue,
Hunt John Francis William, b. 18 Oct. 1904.
Mainie Frances b. 26 Dec. 1906.
1. Thomasina Elizabeth Crochley.
2. Rebecca Mary Brunette.
3. Olivia Isabella Kathleen, d. young, 5 March, 1873.
4. Jane Henry Wray Young Mabel.
5. Kathleen Georgiana Evelyn.

Lineage.—This family descends from JOHN DE LA CHAMBRÉ, who settled in Denbighshire, under Henry Lacy, Earl of Lincoln, in 1275 (see CHAMBRÉS of Pentre). He is stated (in a very ancient pedigree in Norman French, now in the possession of Edward Chambré Vaughan, of Burlton Hall, Salop) to have been descended from "Johan de la Chambré, a nobelle Normanne, who entered Englande in ye traine of King William ye Conqueraure." He m. Mawith, dau. of Blethyn Vaughan, and had a son,
HENRY CHAMBRÉ, of Llewenni, living 1236; m. Katherine, dau. of Edmond Chariton, and had a son,
JOSHUA CHAMBRÉ, of Llewenni; m. Margaret, dau. of Ludowick de la More, and had a son,
MORGAN CHAMBRÉ, of Llewenni; m. Anne, dau. of Peter le Cnive, and had a son,
SAMUEL CHAMBRÉ, of Llewenni; m. Mary, dau. of William Lloyd (or Rosendale), and had a son,
JOHN CHAMBRÉ, of Llewenni; m. Jane, dau. of John Conway, and had a son,
HUGH CHAMBRÉ, of Llewenni; m. Martha, dau. of William Ravenscroft, of Denbigh, and had three sons. The third son,
WILLIAM CHAMBRÉ, of Llewenni; m. Katherine, dau. and co-heir of Jenkin Pigott, of Denbigh, and had issue. The eldest son, HENRY, was ancestor of the family of CHAMBRÉS of Pentre (see that family), while the second son,
ROBERT CHAMBRÉ, m. Elizabeth Peake, and had, with a dau., a son,
JENKIN CHAMBRÉ, m. the dau. of —Kynaston, and had a son,
RICHARD CHAMBRÉ, Lord of the Manor of Petton, Salop, m. Mary, dau. of John Hill, of Court of Hill, Ludlow, Shropshire, and d. 1563, leaving a 2nd son,
GEORGE CHAMBRÉ, of Petton, Salop, m. Judith, dau. and co-heir of Walter Calcott, of Willingscot, co. Oxford, and had issue, with a dau. and three sons, all named Calcott,
1. Calcott, d.s.p.
2. Calcott, of Carnowe and Shelala, m. 1st, Lucy, dau. of Goburt, of Coventry, but by her had no issue. He m. 2ndly, Mary (b. 1584), dau. of Edward Villiers, of Howthorpe. His will is dated 8 Oct. 1628, and proved 30 Dec. 1635. He d. 29 Oct. 1635, having had issue,
1. Calcott, of Carnowe, Lord of the Manor of Shelala, gave by deed dated Jan. 1636, from his woods at Shelala, two hundred tons of oak squared towards the building of portion of Trinity College, Dublin, m. Mary, dau. of Ralph Leicester, of Toft, Cheshire, and d. 17 Sept. 1638, having had issue,
(1) Calcott, d. young.
(1) Mary, m. Alexander Temple, of Ballinderry, co. Cork, son of Col. John Temple, and had an only child, Mary, m. 1st, Nov. 1676, Abraham Yarner, and by him had three daus. She m. 2ndly, Hugh Eccles, of Dublin, but by him had no issue. In her will, dated 8 June, 1706, she enjoined her descendants to take the name of CHAMBRÉ.
(2) Jane, d.s.p.
1. Elizabeth, m. Francis Sandford, of Sandford, Cheshire.
2. Mary, m. 1632, Edward Brabazon, 2nd Earl of Meath, who was drowned 25 March, 1675. She was bur. in Dublin 14 Sept. 1685, leaving issue.
3. CALCOTT, of whom we treat.
1. Hester, m. Richard Willis.
The youngest son,
CALCOTT CHAMBRÉ, of Moynmore, co. Wicklow, of which he obtained a grant, but conveyed it in 1638 to his nephew, Calcott, of Carnowe. He m. Edith, dau. of John Ward (see BLAKEWAY, M.S. Bodleian Library), and by her had issue,
1. George, of Ballymurrough, co. Wexford, d. intestate. (Admon. to his brother 26 March, 1722.)
2. CALCOTT, of whom presently.
1. A dau., m. Robert Sunderland.
The younger son,
CALCOTT CHAMBRÉ, of Coolatrundle, co. Wexford, b. 1602, who left issue, two sons,
1. Calcott, m. before 1722, Elizabeth Sunderland, niece of Robert Sunderland above mentioned.
2. CALCOTT, of Carnowe.
The younger son,
CAPT. CALCOTT CHAMBRÉ, of Carnowe, co. Wicklow, m. Mary, dau. of Oliver Walsh, of Dollardstown, co. Kildare, and Ballykilcaven, Queen's Co., by Edith his wife, sister of Raphael Hunt. She administered to his will 2 March, 1723, and d. 17 Aug. 1753, having had a son,
HUNT CALCOTT CHAMBRÉ, of Carnowe Castle, co. Wicklow, m. 4 June, 1735, Anna Maria, eldest dau. and co-heir of William Meredith, and d. 1782, having had (with other children, who

IRELAND. Chamney.

d. unm.), three daus., Elinor, *m.* George Daker, of Atby, co. Kildare ; Anne, *m.* Lieut.-Col. William Conolly, 18th Foot ; and Henrietta, *m.* William Madden) a son and successor,
MEREDITH CALCOTT CHAMBRÉ, of Hawthorn Hill (otherwise Killeavy), co. Armagh, an officer in the army, *b.* 1742 ; *m.* 30 July, 1785, Margaret, dau. and co-heir of George Faulkner, of Dublin, and by her (who *d.* 31 March, 1837) had issue,
1. HUNT WALSH, heir to his father.
2. William, Major-Gen. in the Army, late 11th Foot, *d. unm.* 24 Oct. 1876.
1. Maria, *m.* Rev. Robert Henry, Rector of Jonesborough, co. Armagh.

Mr. Chambré *d.* 8 Feb. 1812, and was s. by his eldest son,
HUNT WALSH CHAMBRÉ, of Hawthorn Hill, co. Armagh, Capt. Mullaglass Yeomanry, J.P. and High Sheriff 1829, *b.* 9 Dec. 1787 ; *m.* 15 May, 1813, Rebecca, only dau. of William Upton, of Ballynabearney, co. Limerick. She *d.* 11 Aug. 1871. He *d.* 3 March, 1848, leaving issue,
1. MEREDITH, of Hawthorn Hill, J.P., *b.* 15 May, 1814 ; *m.* 4 April, 1843, Mabella, only dau. of Kenrick Morres Hamilton Jones, of Moneyglass House, co. Antrim, and *d.* 10 Dec. 1879. having had issue by her (who *d.* 14 March, 1911),
  1. Hunt Walsh, *b.* 16 Feb. 1844 ; *d. unm.* 1 March, 1871.
  2. Kenrick Hamilton, *b.* 10 April, 1845 ; *d. unm.* 7 July, 1866.
  3. Thomas Morris Hamilton Jones, *b.* 30 April, 1847.
  1. Rebecca, *b.* 6 July, 1849 ; *d. unm.* 17 Dec. 1881.
  2. Mabella, *b.* 12 June, 1850 ; *d. unm.*
2. William, *b.* 1 May, 1825 ; *m.* 1st, Mary, dau. of — Searight, and 2ndly, 25 July, 1857, Fanny Diana, dau. of Joseph Booth, of Darver Castle, co. Louth, and *d.* 19 July, 1865, having had two sons and five daus.
3. HUNT WALSH, now of Dungannon House.
4. JOHN, of Hawthorn Hill (*see next article*).
1. Catherine, *b.* 1 Jan. 1816 ; *m.* 28 Jan. 1846, George William Leech, of the Abbey, Rathkeale.
2. Anna Maria, *b.* 23 Dec. 1817 ; *m.* 19 Aug. 1840, Charles Leech, K.C., and *d.* 26 Sept. 1899, leaving issue (see LEECH *of Cloonconra*).
3. Rebecca, *b.* 16 Oct. 1819.
4. Margaret Elizabeth, *b.* 13 Sept. 1821 ; *m.* 6 Oct. 1848, Townley William Hardman, of Dalkey, and *d.* 4 May, 1897.
5. Olivia Henrietta Agnes, *b.* 26 June, 1823 ; *m.* Robert Crokshank, of Coleraine, and *d.* 10 May, 1891.
6. Mary Frances, *b.* 18 May, 1827.
7. Jane Hunt, *b.* 15 June, 1829 ; *m.* Rev. Henry Wray Young, Rector of Donaghendry, co. Tyrone, and *d.* 31 Jan. 1882.

Arms—Quarterly of eight, 1st az., a dexter armed arm embowed or the hand grasping the stalk of a red rose slipped and leaved ppr. (CHAMBRÉ) ; 2nd, arg. a fesse counter compony or and az., between three lion's heads erased sa. a burdure gu. charged with eight escallops of the first (CHAMBRÉ) : 3rd, erm. three lozenges conjoined in fess sa. a bordure engrailed of the last (PIGOTT) ; 4th, per pale or and gu. on a chief arg. three ducks close sa. beaked and membered of the second (CALCOTT) ; 5th, az. a lion ramp. or (MEREDITH) ; 6th, per fess. arg. and sa. a lion rump. counter-changed (POWELL) ; 7th, az. a fess engrailed between three lions rampant or (SYMONDS) ; and 8th, gu. three talbot's heads erased or, on a chief argent gutty de sang a lion passant sa (WHITCHURCH). Crest—A greyhound's head erased arg. collared az. therefrom a cord knotted and terminated by a ring or. Motto—Tutamen pulchris.

Seat—Dungannon House, co. Tyrone.

CHAMBRE, OF HAWTHORN HILL.

JOHN CHAMBRÉ, of Hawthorn Hill, co. Armagh, and Mespil House, Dublin, *b.* 30 Jan. 1834, 4th son of Hunt Walsh Chambré, J.P., of Hawthorn Hill (who *d.* 3 March, 1848), and Rebecca his wife (who *d.* 11 Aug. 1871), only dau. of William Upton of Ballynabearney, co. Limerick.

Lineage, Arms, &c. *See preceding article.*

Seats—Hawthorn Hill, Newry, co. Armagh, and Mespil House, Dublin.

CHAPMAN. *See* BURKE'S PEERAGE, CHAPMAN, Bart.

CHAMNEY OF SCHOMBERG.

WILLIAM CHAMNEY, of Schonberg, co. Wicklow, *b.* Oct. 1855, J.P. co. Wicklow.

Lineage.—JOHN CHAMNEY, of Shillelagh Forge, and Bullard, co. Wicklow, and Ballynellot, co. Wexford, *b.* 1650 ; *d.* 11 April, 1733 ; *m.* 3 April, 1686, Jane, dau. of Thomas Bacon. Her will dated 2 Dec. 1744, was proved 24 Oct. 1746. Issue,
1. THOMAS, his heir.
2. Edward, of Knocklow, co. Wicklow, High Sheriff 1743, *d.* 22 Aug. 1747 ; *m.* Oct. 1727,Catherine White, and had,
  1. Thomas, of Knocklow, *d.s.p.* Aug. 1798.
  2. John, *d.s.p.*
  1. Catherine, *m.* 1748, John Ferrall, M.D., and had an only dau., Catherine, *m.* Maj.-Gen. Hugh Lyle Carmichael (see CARMICHAEL-FERRALL *of Augher Castle*).
  2. Jane, *m.* Thomas Walters.
3. John, of Ballyforge, co. Wexford, *d.* 1761 ; *m.* 12 Jan. 1744-5, Anne, dau. of Henry Cope, State Physician, and had,
  1. John, of Castletown, co. Wexford, *d.* 1767 ; *m.* 31 Dec. 1761, Jane, dau. of William Johnson, of Arklow, and by her (who *m.* 2ndly, Dec. 1773, Benjamin Garstin (see GARSTIN *of Bragantown*) and *d.* 1823) had an only dau.,
    Dorothea, *m.* April, 1792, Rev. John Barker, and *d.s.p.* 1836.
  2. Joseph, of Ballyrahine, co. Wicklow, *b.* 1747, Capt. Coollattin Yeomanry, killed 2 July, 1798.
  3. Henry, *b.* 1748 ; *d. unm.* 1786.
  4. Thomas, of Ballyrahine, co. Wicklow, *b.* 1754 ; *d.* 1808 ; *m.* 7 Nov. 1774, Mary Geoghegan, and left issue,
    Henry, of Ballyrahine, *b.* 1786 ; *d.* 1828 ; *m.* 29 Nov. 1811, Elizabeth, dau. of James Symes, of Coolboy, and left issue.
    1. Elizabeth, *m.* — Bagge.
    2. Catherine, *m.* — Scriven.
4. Joseph, of Forge, Shillelagh, High Sheriff co. Wicklow 1738 ; *d. unm.* 27 Sept. 1741.
1. Elizabeth, *d.* 6 Feb. 1721 ; *m.* Percival Hunt (see HUNT *of Danesfort*).
2. Susanna, *m.* 1712, Thomas Cole.
3. Anne, *d.* Nov. 1743 ; *m.* John Archer, of Mount John, co. Wicklow.
4. Catherine, *d.* 1712 ; *m.* 26 Nov. 1706, John Swan, of Baldwinstown, co. Wexford.

The eldest son,
THOMAS CHAMNEY, of Platten, co. Meath, and Ballyshanogue, co. Wexford, *d.* 11 July, 1735 ; *m.* 24 Jan. 1715, Margaret, dau. of Francis Graves, of Drogheda, and by her (who *d.* Oct. 1734) had,
1. John, *d.* young.
2. Graves, of Platten, *b.* 3 June, 1723 ; *d. unm.* 16 Oct. 1794.
3. JOHN, of whom presently.
1. Elizabeth, *b.* 4 March, 1717 ; *d.* Dec. 1777 ; *m.* 1746, Edward Archer, of Mount John.
2. Jane, *b.* 3 June, 1718 ; *m.* 1738, William Aickin.
3. Esther, *b.* 14 July, 1719 ; *d.* 8 Sept. 1787 ; *m.* 13 June, 1748, Henry Cusack, of Moyaugher and Girley, co. Meath (see CUSACK *of Gerardstown*).
4. Frances, *b.* 13 Dec. 1720 ; *m.* 1744, Thomas Jones.
5. Catherine, *b.* 29 Nov. 1726 ; *d.* 1809 ; *m.* 1754, Joseph Swan, of Tombrean, co. Wicklow.
6. Susanna, *b.* 23 July, 1727 ; *m.* 1748, John Blacker.

The 3rd son,
JOHN CHAMNEY, of Drogheda, *b.* 29 July, 1724 ; *d.* Nov. 1792 ; *m.* 3 June, 1749, Sarah, dau. of Bartholomew Partinton-Van Homrigh, of Drogheda, and had,
1. Thomas, *m.* Katherine Frances, dau. of Samuel Forster, of Kilmurry, co. Meath, and *d.s.p.* She *m.* 2ndly, Athanasius Cusack, of Laragh, co. Kildare (see CUSACK *of Gerardstown*).
2. WILLIAM GRAVES, of whom presently.
3. John Van Homrigh, *b.* 1758 ; *d.* 1796, Capt. 25th Foot.
4. Bartholomew, of Rathmullen, co. Meath, *d.* 1 July, 1804.
1. Elizabeth, *b.* 1717 ; *m.* Rev. Joseph Irwin.
2. Margaret, *m.* John Coulter.
3. Sarah, *m.* Patrick Ewing.
4. Ethelinda, *m.* John Warren.
5. Frances, *m.* 11 April, 1795, John Johnston Fullerton.
6. Juliet, *m.* 4 June, 1796, Richard Plunkett, of Ardkern, co. Roscommon
7. Susan, *m.* — Blacker.
8. Mary Anne, *m.* Edward Ball, of Dunover, co. Meath.

The 2nd son,
WILLIAM GRAVES CHAMNEY, *m.* Hester Mansall, and had issue,
1. Graves, *b.* 1784 ; *m.* Eliza Massey, and had issue, all *d.s.p.*
2. Robert Mascall, *b.* 23 April, 1787 ; *d.* 26 Feb. 1865 ; *m.* 9 May, 1816, Mary Elizabeth, dau. of John Richard Mascall, of Ashford, Kent, Capt. R.N., and by her (who *d.* 31 Dec. 1872) had,
  1. Robert Mascall (Rev.), M.A. (Cantab), *b.* 7 Oct. 1821 ; *d.* 5 Dec. 1894 ; *m.* 1st, 25 Aug. 1850, Sophia Catherine, dau. of Rev. William H. Cole, and by her (who *d.* 6 March, 1852) had,
    Paul Martin (Rev.), *b.* 4 March, 1852, M.A. (Oxon), Vicar of St. Luke's, Richmond, Surrey ; *m.* 15 July, 1884, Leonora

Charley. THE LANDED GENTRY. 108

Marian Ellen, eldest dau. of Henry Charles Greenwood, of The Towers, Market Drayton, and has issue surviving, Ronald Martin, *b.* 25 July, 1887.
Norman Paul, *b.* 15 March, 1891.
The Rev. Robert Mascall Chamney *m.* 2ndly, 27 Dec. 1854 Sarah Bennett, only dau. of William Bateman, of Folkestone. She *d.s.p.* 28 June, 1885. He *m.* 3rdly, 15 July, 1886, Isabella Louisa, eldest dau. of Thomas Reynolds Reynolds, of Burford, Oxfordshire. She *d.s.p.* 30 March, 1892.
1. Mary Greenhill, *d.* 27 Dec. 1831.
2. Caroline, *d.* 15 Dec. 1904.
3. Elizabeth, *d.* 5 Feb. 1897; *m.* 24 Aug. 1859, George Frederick Hodgson, M.R.C.S.
3. John, *b.* 8 May, 1794; *d.* 14 April, 1867; *m.* 25 May, 1819, Melinda, dau. of John Edward Fogarty, of Cashel, and had with others who *d.* young,
 1. John Edward, *b.* 23 May, 1820; *d.* 31 Dec. 1857; *m.* 10 Feb. 1853, Mary, dau. of George Taylor, of Lessonfield, co. Dublin, and had,
  (1) George Taylor, *b.* 18 Oct. 1855.
   (1) Mary.
   (2) Sophia, *d.* 9 Jan. 1900; *m.* 29 April, 1897, Albert Grumpelt, of Barkley West, S.A.
 2. WILLIAM GRAVES, of whom presently.
 3. Robert Mascall, *b.* 29 Nov. 1822; *d.* 13 July, 1877; *m.* 1852, Ellen, dau. of Edward Beere, of Bushfield Avenue, Dublin, and had with other issue,
  (1) Albert Edward, *b.* 6 July, 1853; *d.* 18 Feb. 1885: *m.* 19 Aug. 1880, Margaret Maria, dau. of Miles Stirling, of Thomastown, co. Kilkenny, and had,
   Robert Mascall, *b.* 11 July, 1881.
   Margaret Stirling.
  (2) John Edward, *b.* 23 Dec. 1863; *m.* 9 Jan., 1892, Kathleen, dau. of Michael Howard, and has,
   1. Robert Mascall, *b.* 5 Aug. 1893.
   2. William Joseph, *b.* 5 Feb. 1895.
   3. John Edward, *b.* 29 May, 1898.
  (1) Melinda, *m.* 6 Sept. 1887, Walter Joseph Corcoran, of Ballyhaye, co. Wexford.
 4. Arthur Taylor, *b.* 23 March, 1841; *m.* 24 Oct. 1870, Emily, dau. of Loftus Bateman, of Dublin, and has,
   Arthur Loftus, *b.* 8 Oct. 1874.
   Melinda.
 1. Melinda Louisa, *d.* 25 June, 1874; *m.* 29 July, 1846, George Heron, of Liverpool, who *d.* 25 March, 1863.
 2. Mary Anne, *d.* 14 May, 1884; *m.* 1 May, 1858, William H. Tyrrell, of Dublin, who *d.* 30 Dec. 1861.
 3. Elizabeth, *d.* 12 March, 1886; *m.* 4 Aug. 1859, William Lawrence Stroud, of Liverpool, who *d.* 12 April, 1902.
1. Sarah, *m.* Adam Ledwich.
2. Frances, *m.* Charles Hughes.

WILLIAM GRAVES CHAMNEY, *b.* 29 May, 1821; *d.* 8 Dec. 1869, called to the Bar at the King's Inns, Easter 1848; *m.* 29 Aug. 1851, Harriett Bulkeley, dau. and sole heir of Joseph Bulkeley-Johnson, of Mortlake House, Congleton, Cheshire, by Sophia, dau. and heir of Holland Watson, and by her (who *d.* 28 Feb. 1866) had issue,
1. Bulkeley, *b.* 24 June, 1852; *d.* 30 Jan. 1853.
2. WILLIAM, now of Schonberg.
1. Harriett Louisa Mary, *d.* 15 Feb. 1856.
2. Sophia Watson, *d.* 10 Aug. 1908.
3. Harriett Frances, *d.* 4 Dec. 1896.

Arms.—Quarterly 1st and 4th, gu. a chevron engrailed arg. between in chief two esquire's helmets, and in base a garb, all ppr. on a canton of the 2nd an oak tree eradicated and fructed of the 3 d (CHAMNEY); 2nd quarterly 1st and 4th, per pale sa. and az. on a saltire arg., between three towers of the last in flames ppr., one in chief and two in fess, and in base two tilting spears in saltire of the last five game cocks gu. (JOHNSON); 2nd and 3rd, sa. a chevron between three bulls' heads cabossed arg. (BULKELEY); 3rd, arg., on a chevron engrailed az. between three martlets sa., as many crescents or (WATSON). **Crest**—A garb or, banded gu., enclosing two hatchets in saltire ppr. **Motto**—Ceres juncta marte.
Residences—Schonberg, Bray, co. Wicklow; 15, Elgin Road, Dublin.

CHARLEY OF SEYMOUR HILL.

EDWARD JOHNSON CHARLEY, of Seymour Hill, co. Antrim, J.P., *b.* 10 Dec. 1859.

Lineage.—The family of Charley, or Chorley, passing over from the north of England, settled in Ulster in the 17th century, at first at Belfast, where they were owners of house property for two hundred years, and afterwards at Finaghy, co. Antrim, where RALPH CHARLEY, of Finaghy House, *b.* 1664; *d.* 1746, aged 82. His son,
JOHN CHARLEY, of Finaghy, *b.* 1712; *d.* 1793, aged 81, leaving a son and successor,
JOHN CHARLEY, of Finaghy House, *b.* 1744; *m.* 1763, Anne Jane, dau. of Richard Wolfenden, of Harmony Hill, co. Down, and *d.* 26 Jan. 1812, aged 68, having by her (who *d.* 3 Feb. 1818) had issue,

1. JOHN, of Finaghy House, *b.* 1784; *d. unm.* 1844.
2. MATTHEW, of Finaghy House, *b.* 1788; *m.* 1819, Mary Anne, dau. of Walter Roberts, of Colin House; and *d.* 1846, leaving issue.
 1. JOHN STOUPPE, of Finaghy House, co. Antrim, and Island of Arranmore, co. Donegal, J.P. cos. Donegal, Antrim, and Borough of Belfast, High Sheriff co. Donegal 1875-6, *b.* 1825; *m.* 1851, Mary Stewart, dau. of Francis Forster, J.P., of Roshine Lodge, co. Donegal, and *d.* 14 April, 1878, having had issue,
  (1) JOHN FRANCIS WILLIAM, Major (2nd in command) 1st Batt. Royal Inniskilling Fusiliers, Commandant of Messourie, North West Provinces of India; *b.* 14 May, 1857; fell mortally wounded while leading his regt. at the battle of Colenso, 12 Dec. 1899.
  (2) WALTER ROBERTS MATTHEW, J.P., heir male of the family, *b.* 1859; is *m.* and settled at Pine Lake, Alberta, Canada.
  (1) Mary Grace Leader. (2) Constance Stewart.
  (3) Charlotte Elizabeth.
 2. Matthew, *b.* 1827, *m.* 1856, Isabel Irvine, and *d.* 1870, having had issue,
  (1) Edith, *m.* Rev. W. H. Winn, Rector of Dunsfold, Godalming, Surrey, and has issue two sons.
  (2) Isabel.
 3. William Thomas (Sir), K.C., D.C.L. Oxford, Common Serjeant of London 1878-92, Member of Court of Lieutenancy of London, M.P. for Salford 1868 to 1880, Past Master of the Lorimers' Co., and Hon. Col. 3rd Vol. Batt. Royal Fusiliers (V.D.), *b.* 5 March. 1833; *m.* 11 Feb. 1890, Clara dau. of the late F. G. Harbord, of Kirby Park, Cheshire, and *d.* 1904, having had issue,
  (1) Clara Noel.
  (2) Estelle Dumergue.
 1. Annie, *d.* 1871.
 2. Susan, *m.* the Rev. H. N. Dupont, and *d.* 1 May, 1897.
 3. Letitia, *m.* 1851, Maj. William Mackay Mackenzie, and has issue, one son and four daus.
 3. WILLIAM, of Seymour Hill.
The 3rd son,
WILLIAM CHARLEY, of Seymour Hill, Dunmurry, *m.* 1817, Isabella, eldest dau. of William Hunter, J.P., of Dunmurry, and *d.* 20 Feb. 1838, aged 37, having had issue,
1. JOHN, of Seymour Hill.
2. WILLIAM, s. his brother.
3. Edward, of Conway House, Lisburn, *m.* 1st, Mary, dau. of A. Caldecott, of Woodford Hall, Essex, and had a dau., *m.* to Capt. Poe, R.N.; and 2ndly, Catherine Jane, dau. of J. Richardson, J.P., of Lambeg House, Lisburn, and *d.* Nov. 1868, leaving issue,
 1. Edward (Rev.), Rector of Rossett, Denbighshire, *b.* 20 March, 1860; *m.* Eva, dau. of Alfred Thomas, J.P., of Frodsham, Cheshire.
 1. Edith Margaret, *b.* 5 June, 1857; *m.* Rev. W. Paige Cox, Rector of Alderley Edge, Cheshire, and has two daus.
 2. Kathleen Isabel Airth, *b.* 3 March, 1864.
1. Mary, *d.* 1887.
2. Anne Jane, *d.* 2 Nov. 1904, having *m.* William Stevenson, jun., of Belfast.
3. Eliza, *m.* Andrew Caldecott, J.P., of Pishobury Park, Sawbridgeworth, co. Hertford. and has issue.
4. Isabella, *m.* the Rev. R. Leslie Scott, Rector of Little Parndon, Essex.
5. Emily.
The eldest son,
JOHN CHARLEY, of Seymour Hill, co. Antrim, *d. unm.* 17 Dec. 1843, aged 25, and was *s.* by his brother,
WILLIAM CHARLEY, of Seymour Hill, co. Antrim, J.P., D.L., *b.* 11 April, 1826; *m.* 1 Oct. 1856, Ellen Anna Matilda, dau. of Edward Johnson. J.P., of Ballymacash, near Lisburn, and grand-dau. of Rev. Philip Johnson, J.P. and D.L., and *d.* 30 Sept. 1890, having by her (who *d.* Feb. 1890) had issue,
1. WILLIAM, *b.* 24 Nov. 1857; *d. unm.* 30 June, 1904.
2. EDWARD JOHNSON, now of Seymour Hill.
3. John George Stewart, *b.* 19 Dec. 1863; *d.* 22 May, 1886.
4. Thomas Henry FitzWilliam, *b.* 27 Jan. 1866; *d.* 28 March, 1885.
5. Arthur Frederick, of Mossvale, co. Down, *b.* 25 Sept. 1870.
6. Harold Richard, Capt. 1st Batt. Royal Irish Rifles, *b.* 4 April, 1875.
1. Ellen Frances Isabella, *m.* 6 April, 1893. Charles Howard Duffin, of Roselands, near Belfast, and has issue.
2. Elizabeth Mary Florence.
3. Emily Constance Jane, *m.* 29 April, 1903, James Stewart Reade, eldest son of James T. Reade, of Ardara, Belfast.
4. Wilhelmina Maud Isabel.

Arms—Arg., on a chevron gu. between three corn bluebottles slipped ppr. a mullet or. **Crest**—On a chapeau gu. turned up erm, a falcon's head erased arg. charged with a cinquefoil of the first, in the beak a corn bluebottle as in the arms. **Motto**—Justus esto et non metue.

Seats—Seymour Hill, Dunmurry, co. Antrim; and Mossvale, co. Down. **Club**—Ulster, Belfast.

CHARTERIS OF CAHIR.

RICHARD BUTLER CHARTERIS, of Cahir Lodge, co. Tipperary, Major and Hon. Lieut.-Col. Warwickshire Yeomanry. Staff Officer Inspector General of Cavalry, served in S. Africa 1900-1, *b.* 12 Oct.

IRELAND. Chetwode.

1866; *m*. 8 Aug. 1890, Pamela, dau. of Robert Dyer, of Layham, Ipswich.
 Lineage.—RICHARD BUTLER, 2nd Earl of Glengall, a representative peer, *b.* in May, 1794; *m.* 20 Feb. 1834, Margaret Lauretta, younger dau. and co-heir of William Mellish, of Woodford, Essex, and by her (who *d.* 1863) had issue,
 1. MARGARET, who *s.* to the estates.
 2. MATILDA, *b.* 20 Aug. 1836; *d. unm.* 18 March, 1861.
Lord Glengall *d.* 22 June, 1858, when the Earldom of Glengall and Viscounty of Cahir became EXTINCT. He was *s.* in his estates by his eldest dau.,
 LADY MARGARET BUTLER, of Cahir Lodge, co. Tipperary, *b.* 27 Nov. 1834; *m.* 2 Aug. 1858, Lieut.-Col. Hon. RICHARD CHARTERIS, 2nd son of Francis, 8th Earl of Wemyss and March, by whom (who *d.* 16 March, 1874) she has issue,
 1. RICHARD, now of Cahir Lodge.
 2. Edmund Butler, late Lieut. Royal Horse Guards, *b.* 28 Sept. 1870.
 1. Elinor Margaret, *b.* 1 Sept. 1859; *m.* 12 July, 1888, Col. Inigo Richmond Jones, of Kelston Park, co. Somerset, and has issue (*see that family*).
 2. Maud Emily, *b.* 27 Aug. 1860; *m.* 29 Oct. 1889, Lieut.-Col. Charles Arthur Wynne-Finch, of Voelas, co. Denbigh, and has issue (*see that family*).
 Seat—Cahir Lodge, Tipperary. *Town Residence*—27, Curzon Street, Mayfair. *Clubs*—Turf, White's, and Royal Yacht Squadron.

CHEARNLEY OF SALTERBRIDGE.

HENRY PHILIP CHEARNLEY, of Salterbridge, co. Waterford, J.P., D.L., High Sheriff 1882, Major Waterford Artillery Militia, *b.* 2 Jan. 1852; *m.* 16 Sept. 1879, Anne Elizabeth, dau. of John Palmer, of Tralee, and has had issue,
 1. Anthony Richard, *b.* July, 1880; *d.* 12 May, 1881.
 2. HENRY JOHN, Capt. Supplementary List R.F.A., *b.* 4 Sept. 1882; *m.* 1910, Dora, 2nd dau. of late Henry Lamont, of Gribton, Dumfriesshire.
 3. Charles Leopold, *b.* 12 Oct. 1883.
 4. Cecil Philip, *b.* 29 March, 1885.
 1. Aileen, *b.* 22 June, 1886.
 Lineage.—SAMUEL CHEARNLEY (son of Anthony Chearnley, of Kilgrogy), *m.* Mary, dau. of Phill Moore (who *d.* 28 Jan. 1724-5), and *d.* 31 Aug. 1741, having by her (who was *b.* at Bandon Bridge, co. Cork, 25 Oct. 1681, and *d.* 21 June, 1756) had issue,
 1. ANTHONY, of whom presently.
 2. Samuel, *d.* at Birr, 12 March, 1746, aged 29.
The son and heir,
 ANTHONY CHEARNLEY, of Spring Park, Affane, co. Waterford, whose will (dated 10 July, 1785) was proved 26 March, 1877, *m.* 1st, Anna Gervais, who *d.* 28 March, 1755, and by her had a son, Thomas. He *m.* 2ndly, Janet, dau. and co-heir of Richard Musgrave, of Salterbridge, co. Waterford, by whom he had issue,
 1. Samuel, *b.* 27 Sept. 1756.
 2. RICHARD, of whom hereafter.
 3. ANTHONY, *s.* his brother Richard.
 4. Christopher, *b.* 1 Feb. 1763; *d.* an infant.
 5. Joseph, *b.* 16 April, 1764; *d.* 14 Dec. 1827.
 6. John, *b.* 4 March, 1772.
 7. Christopher Musgrave, *b.* 17 Feb. 1769; *d.* March, 1816.
 1. Jannet, *b.* 24 July, 1759; *m.* 22 Sept. 1785, Capt. W. Hale, of Rockfield.
 2. Mary, *b.* 8 Sept. 1765; *m.* 27 Jan. 1791, John Grove White, of Kilburne, co. Cork, and *d.* 1836, leaving issue (*see* WHITE *of Kilbyrne*).
 3. Elizabeth Musgrave, *b.* 25 Feb. 1767; *m.* Charles Elliott, of Woodville, co. Wexford.
The eldest son of the 2nd wife,
 RICHARD CHEARNLEY, of Salterbridge, *s.* to his mother's property. 23 Nov. 1760, and *d.s.p.* 1 Sept. 1791, when he was *s.* by his brother,
 ANTHONY CHEARNLEY, of Salterbridge, High Sheriff of co. Waterford 1809, *b.* 1 Dec. 1761; *m.* 1st, Aug. 1796, Julia Browne, of Gallstown, co. Meath; and 2ndly, Isabella, dau. of William Newcome, D.D., Archbishop of Armagh, by whom he had issue,
 1. Anthony, *b.* 19 Nov. 1806; *d. unm.*
 2. RICHARD, of whom presently.
 3. William, Capt. 8th King's Regt., formerly Col. Commandant Volunteers at Halifax, Nova Scotia, *b.* 18 Jan. 1809; *d.* 9 July, 1871, leaving by Mary his wife, a dau.,
 Edith Musgrave, *m.* 15 June, 1898, W. Lambe, B.C.S., 3rd son of the late W. Lambe, M.A. Dublin.
 4. Edward, *b.* 6 Jan. 1810; *d.* same year.
 5. Philip Armitage, *b.* 6 Jan. 1811; *d.* same year.
 6. Philip, *b.* 15 Sept. 1814; *d. unm.* 21 Oct. 1507.
 7. John, *b.* 15 May, 1817; *d. unm.* 28 March, 1867.
The 2nd son,
 RICHARD CHEARNLEY, of Salterbridge, J.P. and D.L., High Sheriff co. Waterford 1842, *b.* 13 Dec. 1807; *m.* Mary, dau. of Ven. Henry Cotton, LL.D., Archdeacon of Cashel, and by her (who *d.* 28 April, 1877) had issue,
 1. RICHARD ANTHONY, his successor.
 2. HENRY PHILIP, successor to his brother.
 3. William John, *b.* 31 Dec. 1854; *d. unm.* 1 June, 1888.
 4. Walter Cecil, *b.* 11 May, 1859.
 1. Isabella Mary, *m.* 20 Oct. 1874, William John Perceval-Maxwell, of Moore Hill, co. Waterford, and had issue (*see* PERCEVAL-MAXWELL *of Finnebrogue*).

 2. Frances Jane, *d. unm.* 24 April, 1911.
 3. Mary.
Mr. Chearnley *d.* 4 Jan. 1863, and was *s.* by his eldest son,
 RICHARD ANTHONY CHEARNLEY, of Salterbridge, *b.* 10 May, 1850, J.P., D.L., High Sheriff co. Waterford 1850; *d.s.p.* 27 Dec. 1879, when he was *s.* by his brother.
 Seat—Salterbridge, Cappoquin, co. Waterford. *Clubs*—Constitutional, Kildare Street, and County Cork.

CHEROIS. *See* DE LA CHEROIS.

WILMOT-CHETWODE OF WOODBROOK.

ALICE MARGARET AGNES WILMOT CHETWODE, of Woodbrook, Queen's Co.
 Lineage.—SIR NICHOLAS WILMOT, of Osmaston (*see* BURKE'S *Peerage*, EARDLEY-WILMOT *of Berkswell*), *d.* 28 Dec. 1682, leaving issue by his wife, Dorothy, dau. of Sir Henry Harper, of Calke, an eldest son,
 ROBERT WILMOT, M.P. for Derby, *d.* 1722, who by his wife, Elizabeth, dau. and sole heir of Edward Eardley, of Eardley, Staffs, other issue (*see* BURKE'S *Peerage*), a 2nd son,
 JOHN WILMOT, *m.* Frances, dau. of Francis Barker, and had issue,
 1. ROBERT, his heir.
 1. Elizabeth.
 2. Alice, *m.* John Ryder, D.D., Archbishop of Tuam.
 ROBERT WILMOT, *m.* Mary, dau. of Joseph Hall, of Nettleton, Notts, and has issue,
 1. Robert, *m.* and left issue.
 2. EDWARD, of whom presently.
 1. Alice, *m.* Thomas Copley, of Nether Hall, Doncaster.
The 2nd son,
 EDWARD WILMOT, of Drogheda and Cork, *d.* 1815; *m.* Martha, dau. and co-heir of Rev. Charles Moore, Rector of Innishannon (*see* MOORE *of Cremorgan*), and had issue,
 1. ROBERT ROGERS, his heir.
 2. Edward Eardley, Lieut.-Col. R.A., *m.* Mary Anne, dau. of Daniel Conner, of Ballybricken (*see that family*), and had issue.
 3. Charles, R.N., *d.* aged 19.
 1. Catherine.
 2. Martha, *m.* Rev. William Bradford, Rector of Storrington, Sussex.
 3. Alicia.
 4. Harriett, *m.* James Garnier, of Barbadoes.
 5. Dorothea, *m.* Roger Eaton, of Pvrglas, Wales.
 6. Anna Maria, *m.* Rev. John Hardy.
 ROBERT ROGERS WILMOT, Deputy Recorder of Cork, *m.* Eliza, dau. of Rev. John Chetwood, Rector of Rathcooney (*see* CHETWOOD-AIKEN). They had issue,
 EDWARD, of whom next.
 Emily Margaret, *m.* 26 Aug. 1819, Right Hon. William Brooke, of Dromovana, co. Cavan, Master-in-Chancery, and had issue (*see that family*).
 EDWARD WILMOT-CHETWODE, of Woodbrook, *s.* to the estates of Jonathan Chetwood, of Woodbrook (*see* CHETWOOD-AIKEN), and assumed by Royal licence, dated 18 Sept. 1839, the additional surname and arms of CHETWODE. He was *b.* 4 Feb. 1801, and *d.* 9 May, 1874. He *m.* Lady Jean Janet Erskine, dau. of John Thomas, Earl of Mar. She *d.* 16 May, 1861, having had issue,
 1. Knightley Jonathan, of Woodbrook, *b.* 31 May, 1831; *d.* 12 Jan. 1887; *m.* 20 Nov. 1872, Henriette, widow of Count Kalling, of Swerting, Sweden, and dau. of late Marcchal de la Cour Charles Uggla, of Stora Djülo, Sweden.
 2. Edward Robert Erskine, *b.* 24 Sept. 1852; *d.* 1880; *m.* 1 Sept. 1875, Gertrude, dau. of Rev. Alfred Hamilton, of Taney, co. Dublin, and had issue,
 1. Edward Erskine, *b.* 11 June, 1878; *d.* 1900.
 1. Gertrude Florence Evelyn.
 2. Kathleen Rita, *b.* 9 Nov. 1879.
 1. ALICE MARGARET AGNES, now of Woodbrook.
 2. Fanny Elizabeth Isabella, *d.* 1895.
 3. Janet Philadelphia, *d.* 1880, having *m.* T. O'Donoghue.
 Arms—Quarterly, 1st, quarterly arg. and gu., four crosses formée counterchanged, an annulet az. for difference (CHETWODE); 2nd, or, three crescents gu. (DE WAHULL); 3rd, sa. on a fess or between three eagles' heads erased arg., as many escallops gu., a mullet for difference (WILMOT); 4th, vert, a lion rampant and in chief three estoiles or (O'MORE).
 Seat—Woodbrook, Portarlington.

THE LANDED GENTRY.

CHEVERS OF KILLYAN.

JOHN JOSEPH CHEVERS, of Killyan House, co. Galway, J.P. and D.L., High Sheriff of Galway Town 1893-4, b. 28 Nov. 1866, late Capt. 4th Batt. Connaught Rangers; m. 23 Jan. 1894, Frederica Sophia Elizabeth Mary, younger dau. of Henry Owen Lewis, D.L., of Inniskeen, co. Monaghan (see *that family*), and has issue,

1. NORMAN MICHAEL JOSEPH HENRY, b. 16 July, 1898.
2. Michael John Joseph, b. 27 Aug. 1902.
3. John Aloysius Joseph, b. 19 May, 1909.
4. Hyacinth Edward Joseph, b. 1 June, 1910.
1. Frederica Annie.
2. Annie Mary Frances.
3. Ellis. 4. Frances.

Lineage—WALTER CHEVERS, of Ballyhaly, co. Wexford, chief of his name according to a funeral entry in Ulster's Office, was Commissioner, co. Meath, 3 EDWARD IV, 1483. He m. Ellen, dau. of Sir William Wells, Lord Chancellor of Ireland, and by her had, with a dau. Margaret, m. Bartholomew Aylmer, of Lyons, a son and heir,

NICHOLAS CHEVERS, of Ballyhaly, m. Alice, dau. of Robert Fitzsimons, and sister of Walter Fitzsimons, Archbishop of Dublin, and by her (who m. 2ndly, Nicholas, Lord Howth. and 3rdly, — Plunket, of Loughcrew) had, with a dau. Joan, m. William Hore, of Harperstown, co. Wexford, a son and heir,

SIR WALTER CHEVERS, of Ballyhaly, m. Elena, dau. of Nicholas, Lord Howth, and by her had, with two younger sons, John and Thomas, a son and heir,

SIR CHRISTOPHER CHEVERS, of Ballyhaly and Ballycullen, co. Wexford, m. 1st, Maude, dau. of Walter Kelly, Alderman of Dublin, and by her had issue,

1. JOHN, his heir.
2. Nicholas, of Donnacarny, co. Meath, whose dau. Katherine, m. William Locke, of Colmanstown, co. Dublin.
3. Patrick. d. unm. 1585. 6. Walter. 5. Thomas.
1. A dau., m. — Golding.
2. Margaret, m. Robert Kent.
3. Katherine, m. Patrick Talbot, of Malahide.

He m. 2ndly, Anne Plunkett, an heiress, by whom he acquired Macetown, co. Meath, Rathmore, co. Wicklow and large estates in cos. Kildare and Carlow. Her will is dated 1583. Sir Christopher d. 20 March, 1581 (will dated 18 March, 1550, proved 1581), having by her had issue,

4. Elenor. 5. Ellis.
6. Janet. 7. Margaret.

His eldest son,

JOHN CHEVERS, of Macetown, co. Meath, b. 1549; m. 1st, Katherine, dau. and co-heir of Henry Travers, of Monkstown, co. Dublin, and by her had issue,

1. CHRISTOPHER, his heir.
2. Henry, of Monkstown, m. Katherine, dau. of Richard Fitzwilliam, of Merrion, co. Dublin, and sister of Thomas Fitzwilliam, 1st Viscount Fitzwilliam, and had issue.
3. Richard.
1. Jennett. 2. Frances.
3. Elinor m. Thomas Luttrell, of Luttrellstown, co. Dublin.

He m. 2ndly, Elinor Segrave, and d. 30 April, 1599 (will dated 20 April, 1595). His eldest son,

CHRISTOPHER CHEVERS, of Macetown, to whom the dignity of a baronet was given by JAMES I, but no patent appears to have followed. He m. 1st, Eleanor, dau. of Christopher, 14th Lord Delvin, and sister of Richard, 1st Earl of Westmeath, and by her had issue,

1. JOHN, his heir. 2. Christopher.
3. Garrett, m. Katherine Anne, dau. of Hamon Chevers, of Killiane, co. Wexford.
4. Anthony. 5. Richard. 6. Peter.
1. Mary, m. Edward Dalton.
2. Bridget. 3. Anne.

He m. 2ndly, Jane, dau. of Jerome Bath, of Edickstown, co. Meath, and d. 7 Nov. 1640, having by her had issue,

7. William.
8. Jerome, of Drogheda, merchant, Sheriff of that town 1671, who left issue by Katherine his wife.

The eldest son,

JOHN CHEVERS, of Macetown, was transplanted to Connaught by Cromwell, and obtained a grant of Killyan, co. Galway, 1667, from CHARLES II. m. 1st, Mary, dau. of Sir Henry Bealing, of Killisk, co. Kildare, and 2ndly, Joan, dau. of Edward Sutton, and left three sons,

1. Edward, VISCOUNT MOUNT LEINSTER, and Baron Bannow, so created by JAMES II, 23 Aug. 1689. He was present at the battle of the Boyne with the King, was included in the articles of Limerick, but relinquished the benefits of the capitulation and accompanied his dethroned sovereign into exile and was attainted. He m. Ann, dau. of Patrick Sarsfield, of Lucan, and sister of Patrick, Earl of Lucan. He d. abroad 1709, and his male issue became extinct.
2. Andrew, of Cregan, co. Galway, who had an only son, Hyacinth of Cregan, who d.s.p. Will dated 29 July, 1757, proved 14 Nov. 1758.
3. JOHN, of whom presently.

The third son,

JOHN CHEVERS, of Killyan, co. Galway, m. Ellis, dau. of Edward Geoghegan, of Castletown, co. Westmeath, and had issue.

1. MICHAEL, his heir.
2. Edward, of Leckafin, m. Bridget Telberton, and had issue.
3. Christopher, m. Barbara, dau. of John Smyth, and eventual co-heir of her brother Valentine Smyth, of Dama, co. Kilkenny, and had a dau., Barbara, m. 24 Sept. 1771, Lawrence Coyne Nugent, of Finnoe.
4. Mathias, Knt. of St. Jago, Governor of Fuentarabia, d.s.p. Oct. 1771.
5. Augustin (Most Rev.), Bishop of Meath, d. 18 Aug. 1778.
6. Hyacinth, who left an only dau., m. 10 Feb. 1759, John Fallon, of Cloonagh, co. Roscommon.
1. Margaret, m. Richard Burke, of Glinsk.
2. A dau., m. Hugh O'Connor.

The eldest son,

MICHAEL CHEVERS, of Killyan, co. Galway, m. Margaret, dau. of O'Flyn, of Turlough, co. Galway, by whom (whose will, dated 31 March, 1780, was proved 21 July following) he had, with a dau., m. Michael Blake, of Kiltulla Castle, co. Galway, and another son, John, who d.s.p., two sons,

1. Christopher, m. Nov. 1769, Hon. Frances Nugent, dau. of William Nugent, of Pallas, Lord Riverston, and d.s.p.
2. HYACINTH, who carried on the line.

Mr. Chevers made his will 2 July, 1776, which was proved 16 Oct. 1779, and his elder son dying s.p., the family estate and representation eventually devolved on the 2nd son,

HYACINTH CHEVERS, of Killyan, m. about 1782, Mary, dau. of Patrick Lynch, of Cottage, co. Galway, and had issue,

1. JOHN, his heir. 2. Christopher.
3. Patrick, m. Eleanor, dau. of — Cashell, and bad issue,
 1. Hyacinth.
 2. George, m. Louisa, widow of Richard D'Arcy, of New Forest.
 1. Grace.
1. Mary, m. Michael R. Plunkett, an Officer in the Army.
2. Eliza, m. James D'Arcy, of New Forest, co. Galway, and Rockvale, co. Clare.

The eldest son,

JOHN CHEVERS, of Killyan, J.P. and D.L., High Sheriff 1836-7, b. 16 May, 1790; m. 20 Dec. 1822, Eleanor, eldest dau. of John MacDonnell, of Caranacon, co. Mayo, and d. 7 April, 1857, having had issue,

1. MICHAEL JOSEPH, of Killyan.
2. Christopher, of Lincoln's Inn, Barrister-at-Law, who adopted the additional surname of MACDONNELL, and is dec.
3. Joseph, who adopted the additional surname of MACDONNELL, pursuant to his maternal uncle's will, and is dec.
4. Patrick Edward, d. unm.
1. Maria.

The eldest son,

MICHAEL JOSEPH CHEVERS, of Killyan, J.P. and D.L., b. Oct. 1827, High Sheriff 1860-61; m. 10 July, 1865, Annie, 2nd dau. of Hon. Martin ffrench, of Ballinamore Park, co. Galway (see BURKE's *Peerage*, FFRENCH. B.). She d. 3 Oct. 1898, leaving issue.

1. JOHN JOSEPH, now of Killyan.
2. Martin Joseph, b. 30 Nov. 1867.
3. Michael Joseph. 4. Rufus Joseph.
5. Henry Joseph.
1. Margaret, m. 19 April, 1899, John Felix O'Neill, M.A., son of Hugh O'Neill, of Dalkey.
2. Nina.
3. Evelyn.
4. Josephine, m. 8 June, 1904, James Hayes.

Mr. Chevers d. 10 April, 1889.

Arms—Gu., three goats salient arg. **Crest**—A demi-goat arg. as in the arms collared gu., horned and unguled or. **Motto**—En Dieu es ma foi.

Seat—Killyan House, Ballinasloe, co. Galway.

CHICHESTER OF MOYOLA PARK.

LIEUT.-COL. ROBERT PEEL DAWSON SPENCER CHICHESTER, of Moyola Park, co. Londonderry, and Dooish, co. Donegal, J.P. and D.L. co. Londonderry, and J.P. cos. Antrim and Donegal, High Sheriff co. Londonderry 1907, High Sheriff co. Antrim 1911, Lieut.-Col. commanding 6th Batt. D.C.O. Middlesex Regt., late Capt. 1st Batt. Irish Guards, served in British Central Africa 1897-1900 (medal and clasp), and in S. African War (medal and clasp), b. 13 Aug. 1873; m. 11 Dec. 1901, Dehra, only child of the late James

III   IRELAND.   Chute.

Kerr-Fisher, of the Manor House, Kilrea, co. Antrim, and Castlerock, co. Londonderry, and has issue,
   ROBERT JAMES SPENCER, b. 30 Sept. 1902.
   Marion Caroline Dehra, b. 16 May, 1904.

Col. Chichester is the eldest son of the late Lord Adolphus John Spencer Churchill Chichester, D.L., of Moyola (who d. 5 March, 1901), and Mary his wife, only child of Col. Robert Peel Dawson, M.P., of Moyola Park, and grandson of Edward, 4th Marquess of Donegall (who d. 20 Jan. 1889).

   Lineage, Arms, &c.—*See* BURKE's *Peerage*, DONEGALL, M.
   Seats—Moyola Park, Castledawson, co. Londonderry, and Dooish, co. Donegal. *Residence*—76, The Drive, Hove, Sussex; Eden Lodge, Dungiven, co. Londonderry. *Clubs*—Guards, White's, Junior United Service, Ulster (Belfast), and Union (Brighton).

CHICHESTER.
See BURKE'S PEERAGE, **TEMPLEMORE, B.**

CHUTE OF CHUTE HALL.

CAPT. RICHARD AREMBERG BLENNERHASSETT CHUTE, of Chute Hall, co. Kerry, Capt. Manchester Regt., late F. Surrey Regt., b. 24 June, 1870.

   Lineage.—GEORGE CHUTE, a military Officer, went into Ireland during the rebellion of Desmond and obtained grants of land near Dingle, which were soon, however, alienated. He m. Miss Evans, of co. Cork, and had a son,
   DANIEL CHUTE, who acquired in marriage with a dau. of McElligott, the lands of Tulligaron (subsequently called Chute Hall), which were afterwards, with others since disposed of, confirmed by patent 1630, under which they are now held. He left (with a dau., m. to — Crosbie) a son and successor,
   RICHARD CHUTE, of Tulligaron, co. Kerry, afterwards of Chute Hall, High Sheriff co. Kerry 1664, elected M.P. for co. Kerry 1661 but unseated; m. Agnes, sister of Sir Thomas Crosbie, of Ardfert (*see that family*), and dau. of Col. David Crosbie, M.P. for Ardfert 1639, and was s. by his son,
   EUSEBIUS CHUTE, of Tulligaron, High Sheriff co. Kerry 1697, m. Mary, sister of Mr. Justice Bernard, of the Court of Common Pleas in Ireland, ancestor of the Earls of Bandon, and had issue,
1. RICHARD, his heir.
2. Francis, Collector of Tralee, J.P. co. Kerry in 1736; m. Rebecca, aunt of Sir John Allen Johnson, Bart., and sister of Very Rev. Ralph Walsh, Dean of Dromore. He d.s.p. His will was proved 11 May, 1753, and his widow's 9 Aug. 1800.
3. Pierce, ancestor of the CHUTES *of Tralee*.
4. Arthur (Rev.), b. at Tullygarron, entered Trin. Coll. Dublin 16 June, 1717, aged 18, B.A. 1721, M.A. 1724, Faculty to hold parishes of Mollahiffe (Aghado), Kilboriane, &c., 1741; d. unm.
5. Thomas.

The eldest son,
   RICHARD CHUTE, of Tulligaron, m. Charity, dau. of Arthur Herbert, of Currens, co. Kerry (*see that family*), and had issue,
1. FRANCIS, his heir.
2. Richard, of Roxborough, co. Kerry.
1. Margaret, m. George Rowan, of Rathanny, and had issue.
2. Agnes, m. John Sealy, of Maglass, and had issue.
3. Catherine, m. Cornelius MGillicuddy (M' Gillicuddy of The Reeks) and had issue.

Mr. Chute was s. by his eldest son,
   FRANCIS CHUTE, of Tulligaron, or Chute Hall, Kerry, High Sheriff 1757, m. 8 Aug. 1761, Ruth, dau. of Sir Riggs Falkiner, Bart., of Anne Mount, co. Cork, and had issue,
1. RICHARD, his heir.
2. Falkiner, Capt. 22nd Light Dragoons, m. Anne, dau. of Capt. Goddard, of Queen's Co., and left at his decease, an only dau., Catherine, m. William Cooke, of Retreat, near Athlone, and had issue.
3. Caleb, Capt. 69th Foot, m. Elizabeth, dau. of Theophilus Yielding, of Cahir Anne, co. Kerry, and d. Nov. 1851. She d. 14 March, 1851.
4. Francis Bernard, m. Jane, dau. of John Rowan, of Castle Gregory, and has issue,
   Francis Bernard, m. — Rae, and had issue.
   Elizabeth, m. Thomas Sandes, of Sallowglen.
5. Arthur, m. Frances, dau. of John Lindsay, of Lindville, Cork, and d. 8 March, 1863, having had issue,
1. Francis (Rev.), d. 12 Sept. 1839.
2. John Lindsay (Rev.), Rector of Dingle, co Kerry, b. 1800; m. 1st, 1832, Jane Lucinda, dau. of William Dobbs Burleigh, of Burleigh Hill, Carrickfergus, and by her (who d. 1855) had issue,
   (1) Arthur, b 1836; m. 12 Jan. 1864, Helena, 3rd dau. of Henry Ridgeway, of Riverview House, Waterford. She d. 1875. He d. 31 Dec. 1899, leaving issue,
      1. John Henry Challoner, b. 1868.
      2. Arthur Francis, b. 1873; d. 1902.
      1. Jane Lucy Burleigh, b. 1866; m. 1897, Henry D'Esterre Strevens, of Castle Coote, co. Roscommon.

(2) William Burleigh, b. 1837.
(3) Francis John, b. 1839; m. 1st, 1860, Juliana Elizabeth Haase Bird, and 2ndly, 1900, Edith Allen, but has no issue.
(4) John (Rev.), M.A. T.C.D., Vicar of St. Jude's, Hunslet, Leeds, b. 1841; m. 1883, Emily Marian, dau. of Rev. Thomas Heury Flynn, Vicar of Holy Trinity, Lowmoor, and has issue,
   1. Reginald Arthur John (Rev.), B.A. Oxon b. 1884.
   2. Cecil Burleigh (Rev.), B.A. Oxon, b. 1887.
   1. Muriel Constance, b. 1885; d. Oct. 1904.
   2. Irene Mabel, b. 1891.
(5) Henry George, b. 1843; m. 1875, the dau. of Major Lockhart, of Melbourne, Australia, and has issue.
   (1) Annie, b. 1833.
   (2) Frances Wills, b. 1834; m. 1862, William McLoughlin, of Castle Coote, co. Roscommon.
   (3) Ruth, b. 1845.
He m. 2ndly, Josephine, dau. of Charles Haines. He d. 6 Jan. 1871. She d. 21 March, 1895, leaving issue,
   (3) Charles George Falkiner, M.A., Barrister-at-Law; m. 4 Sept. 1895, his cousin Katherine Agnes, eldest dau., of Robert V. Haines, and has issue.
   1. Frances, d. unm. Sept. 1874.
   2. Ruth, d. unm. Sept. 1875.
   3. Anne, m. 28 Oct. 1841, Rev. Samuel Bell Leonard, Rector of Drumtarriff, co. Cork, and had issue, an only dau., Margaret Frances, m. 22 Feb. 1872, Rev. Henry Swanzy, M.A., Rector of Castle Magner, co. Cork, only son of Canon Swanzy, of Newberry, co. Cork (see BURKE'S *Family Records*).
1. Margaret, m. Thomas William Sandes, of Sallowglen, co. Kerry, and had issue.
2. Ruth, m. Thomas Elliot, of Garrynthenavally, Kerry, and had issue, a son, d. Sept. 1875.
Mr. Chute d. 1782, and was s. by his eldest son,
   RICHARD CHUTE, of Chute Hall, b. 1763; High Sheriff 1786; m. 1st, 1785, Agnes, dau. of Rowland Bateman, of Oak Park, M.P for co. Kerry, and had by her,
1. FRANCIS, his heir.
2. Rowland, of Lee Brook, near Tralee, Capt. 58th Regt., m. Frances, dau. of Col. James Crosbie, of Ballyheigue Castle, M.P. for co. Kerry, and had, with another son, who d. unm.,
   1. Richard Rowland, of Lee Brook, J.P., Capt. late Cameronians, b. 26 July, 1829; m. 1861, Margaret, only dau. of the late James Eidingtoun, D.L., of Gargunnock, and Elizabeth his wife, eld. dau. of Maurice FitzMaurice, J.P., of Duagh, Kerry, and has issue,
      (1) Rowland Eidington, b. 1863; m. 16 July, 1891, Margaret Urquhart, dau. of the Rev. Charles Tyner, Rector of Kilcoleman, co. Kerry.
      (2) FitzJames, m. 4 Jan. 1899, Edith Gertrude, dau. of the late W. Lyle Thomson, and has issue,
         Rowland FitzMaurice Eidington.
      (3) Richard Crosbie.
      (1) Eliza Bateman.   (2) Frances Ethel.
      (3) Rosamond Margaret.
   1. Elizabeth Crosbie.
   2. Agnes Bateman, m. Rev. William D. Wade, Treasurer of Ardfert, and d. 3 July, 1897, aged 70, leaving issue.
1. Lætitia, m. William Raymond, of Dromin, co. Kerry, and had issue.
2. Ruth, m. William Cooke, of Retreat, near Athlone, d. 20 Nov. 1862.
3. Agnes, m. Richard Mason, of Cappanhame, co. Limerick, and had issue.
Mr. Chute m. 2ndly, 1798, Elizabeth, dau. of the Rev. William Maunsell, D.D., of Limerick, and had issue,
3. William Maunsell, m. Sarah, dau. of the Rev. Edward Nash, of Ballycarthy, near Tralee, and d. 17 March, 1850, leaving a son, Richard, Lieut. R.A., d. 1 May, 1862, and a dau., Clementina Fergusson, m. 1807, Sir Raymond West, K.C.I.E., and d. 10 May, 1896, leaving issue.
4. Richard, M.D., of Tralee, m. Elizabeth, dau. of George Rowan, of Rathanny, and d. 14 Sept. 1856, leaving,
   1. Richard, late an Ensign, 8th Foot.
   2. George.
   1. Rowena, m. 1st. Arthur Crisp, which marriage was dissolved; and 2ndly, 1873, Right Hon. Lord Atkinson, P.C., and has issue (*see* ATKINSON *of Glenwilliam*).
4. Elizabeth, m. Rev. Robert Wade, of Tralee; d. 10 Nov. 1862.
5. Dorothea, m. 29 Dec. 1824, William Neligan, of Tralee, and had issue.
6. Margaret, d. Sept. 1883.
The eldest son,
   FRANCIS CHUTE, of Chute Hall, m. 1st, 13 Feb. 1810, Mary Anne, dau. of Trevor Bomford, of Dublin, and by her (who d. 1815) had issue,
1. RICHARD, of Chute Hall.
2. Trevor (Sir), K.C.B., Gen. in the Army, m. 1868, Ellen, eldest dau. of Samuel Browning, of Auckland, New Zealand, and d. 12 March, 1886. She m. 2ndly, 1890, Lieut.-Col. George Tennant Carre, late R.A.
3. Rowland, d. Aug. 1851.
1. Mary, m. William Harnett, and has issue.
Mr. Chute m. 2ndly, Arabella, dau. of the Rev. Maynard Denny, of Churchill, brother of Sir Barry Denny, Bart., of Tralee, M.P. for co. Kerry, and by that lady had,
4. Francis, Lieut. 70th Regt., d. 1853.
5. Arthur, Lieut. 94th Regt., d. Feb. 1890.
2. Arabella.   3. Penelope, d. 28 Nov. 1863.
Mr. Chute m. 3rdly, Penelope Antonia, 4th dau. of Richard Town-

Clark THE LANDED GENTRY.

send Herbert, of Cahirnane, M.P. for Kerry. She d. 7 May, 1870. He d. 12 Aug. 1849, and was s. by his eldest son,
RICHARD CHUTE, of Chute Hall, J.P. and D.L., b. 22 May, 1811; m. 1st, 18 Oct. 1836, Theodora, dau. and heir of Arthur Blennerhassett, of Blennerville, by Helen Jane his wife, dau. of Thomas Lord Ventry, and grand-dau. of Sir Rowland Blennerhassett, Bart. of Blennerville, and by her (who d. 25 July, 1845) had issue,
1. FRANCIS BLENNERHASSETT, late of Chute Hall.
2. Arthur Rowland, 90th Regt., b. 20 Dec. 1838; d. 23 Feb. 1858, at Calcutta.
3. Trevor Bomford, d. July, 1846.
1. Melicent Agnes, m. 30 April, 1867, Robert Leslie, J.P. and D.L., of Tarbet House, co. Kerry, and has issue.
2. Helena Jane, m. 30 Nov. 1875, Capt. Francis Ogilvie Fuller, of the 101st Regt. He d.s.p. 19 Sept. 1876.

Mr. Chute m. 2ndly, 3 March, 1847, Hon. Rose de Moleyns, 2nd dau. of Thomas Townsend Aremberg, 3rd Lord Ventry, and by her (who d. 21 April, 1898) had issue,
4. Thomas Aremberg, b. 14 Oct. 1853.
5. Richard Trevor, b. 17 July, 1856; Lieut. 66th Regt., killed in the battle of Miawand, Afghan War, 20 July, 1880.
6. Mary Anne, m. Nov. 1879, Milhem Shakoor Bey, of Ainzahalta, the Lebanon and Ministry of War, Egypt, and has issue, Trevor Monsoor, b. 1880; Luceya Rose.
4. Theodora Eliza.
5. Rosa, m. 28 Sept. 1889, Henry Dudgeon, of the Priory, Stillorgan, co. Dublin, and has issue, Cyril Henry, b. 1890; Dorothy, Rose (twin), Florence (twin), and Lilian Mary.
6. Frances Ruth, d. 10 Aug. 1871.
7. Arabella Emily.

He d. 13 Sept. 1862, and was s. by his eldest son,
FRANCIS BLENNERHASSETT CHUTE, of Chute Hall, co. Kerry, J.P., High Sheriff 1865, late Lieut. Kerry Militia, b. 18 Sept. 1837; s. his father 1862; m. 6 Feb. 1869, Cherubina Herbert D'Esterre, eldest dau. of the late Norcott D'Esterre Roberts (see ROBERTS of Ardmore), and d. 1902, having issue,
1. RICHARD AREMBERG BLENNERHASSETT, now of Chute Hall.
2. Arthur Torrens, b. 5 Oct. 1871.
3. Challoner Francis Trevor, b. 2 April, 1885; m. 29 June, 1911, Maud E. St. Clair, dau. of late Edward O'Brien Hobson, of Myler's Park, Wexford.
1. Theodora Evelyn.   2. Cherry Herbert Ada.

Seats—Chute Hall, Tralee; Blennerville, co. Kerry.

CLARK OF LARGANTOGHER.

JAMES JACKSON CLARK, of Largantogher, co. Londonderry, J.P., D.L., High Sheriff 1875, Hon. Lieut.-Col. 9th Brigade North Irish Div. R.A., b. 6 April, 1845; m. 16 Nov. 1883, Mary, eldest dau. of Col. Sir William Lenox Conyngham, K.C.B., Springhill, Moneymore, and has issue,
1. JAMES JACKSON LENOX CONYNGHAM, R.N., b. 1884.
2. Francis Hartley Hall (Rev.)
3. Roland Arbuthnot, Lieut. R.N.
1. Elleanor Laura.

Lineage.—This family, originally from Salford, settled in co. Londonderry, 1690.
JOHN CLARK, of Maghera, co. Londonderry, m. about 1695, Jane White, of Belfast. He d. 1707, leaving issue by her,
1. JACKSON, of whom presently.
2. John, b. 1697; d. unm. 1721.

The elder son,
JACKSON CLARK, of Maghera, b. about 1698; m. 1720 (will bears date 20 Nov. 1754), and left issue,
1. John, who was adopted by his uncle, John, and s. to his estate, left issue, one son and six daus.
2. ALEXANDER, of whom presently.
3. Arthur, settled in America.
4. William, also in America.
1. Sarah, m. Dr. James Ferguson, of Belfast.
2. A dau., m. Gilbert Ledlie.
3. Jane.   4. Margaret.

The 2nd son,
ALEXANDER CLARK, b. 1723; m. 1757, Elizabeth, dau. of William Stevenson, of Knockan. She d. 7 July, 1813. He d. 1806, having had issue,
1. ALEXANDER, his heir.
2. Jackson, m. 1785, Jane, dau. of Gen. Patterson, of Maghera, and had issue.
3. William, d. unm. 1827.
1. Margaret, m. 1794, William Stevenson, of Ashpark.

The eldest son,
ALEXANDER CLARK, of Maghera, b. 1767; m. 6 May, 1805, Margaret, dau. of James Johnston, of Sommerhill, co. Donegal (she d. 31 Oct. 1838). Mr. Clark d. 1 March, 1842, having had issue,
1. Alexander Jackson, b. 12 June, 1807, J.P. co. Londonderry; d. unm. 7 July, 1834.
2. JAMES JOHNSTON, of Largantogher House.
1. Rebecca Lucinda, m. 9 April, 1834, John Stevenson, Fort William, J.P. and D.L.; issue two daus., both dec.
2. Elizabeth, d. unm. 22 Dec. 1835.

The 2nd son,
JAMES JOHNSTON CLARK, of Largantogher House, J.P. and D.L., High Sheriff 1849, b. 9 Jan. 1809; m. 28 April, 1837, Frances, 4th dau. of Robert Hall, of Merton Hall, co. Tipperary, and had issue,
1. Alexander Jackson, an Officer in the Army, b. 8 Jan. 1840; d. unm. 10 Feb. 1863.
2. JAMES JACKSON, now of Largantogher House.
3. John, who on the death of his uncle assumed the name of HALL, b. 17 Dec. 1816; appointed Registrar General of Shipping and Seamen; m. 1878, Dorothea, dau. of Col. Keown, of Knockbracen, co. Down, and has issue. He d. 13 April, 1902.
4. William Owens (Sir), late Chief Justice of Chief Court, Punjab, b. 14 Jan. 1849; called to the English Bar 1881; knighted 1903; m. 1885, Florence, dau. of R. Lawrie, and has issue. His only dau., Lillian Florence, m. 20 Sept. 1900, Evelyn R. Abbott, son of the late Samuel Abbott, of Argentina.
1. Elizabeth Hall, m. 21 Feb. 1867, Thomas Spotswood Ash, of Knockcloughram, J.P. co. Londonderry.
2. Margaret Johnston, m. 23 July, 1862, John Kells Ingram, LL.D., F.T.C.D., Vice Provost of Trinity College.
3. Fanny Florence Emily.
4. Rebecca Edith Lucinda.

Mr. Clark was elected Member of Parliament for co. Londonderry, on the resignation of Sir Thomas Bateson, and again at the General Election in 1857. He d. 1891.

Arms—Gu., three swords, erect in pale, ppr. hilts and pommels, or, a canton arg. charged with a trefoil, vert. Crest—Out of a mural crown an arm, embowed in armour, holding a dagger all ppr., the arm charged with a trefoil, vert. Motto—Virtute et labore.

Seat—Largantogher, Maghera, co. Londonderry. Club—Kildare Street, Dublin.

CLARKE OF GRAIGUENOE PARK.

CHARLES NEVILLE CLARKE, of Graiguenoe Park, co. Tipperary, J.P. and D.L., High Sheriff 1891, B.A. Pembroke Coll. Camb. 1887, b. 19 Jan. 1866; m. 5 Feb. 1896, Bertha, dau. of the late John Kynaston Cross, of Fernclough, Bolton, Lancashire, M.P. for Bolton and sometime Under Sec. of State for India, and has issue,
1. MARSHAL NEVILLE, b. 10 Jan. 1897.
2. Edward Neville, b. 14 Jan. 1900.
3. John Vernon Carlton, b. 13 June, 1907.

Lineage.—REV. MARSHAL CLARKE. Rector and Vicar of Sbronell, Diocese of Emly, m. Elizabeth, dau. of Rev. Patrick Hare, and d. 1833, having had issue seven sons,
1. Patrick, b. 1786; d. 1847, having m. 1st, Catherine, dau. of Wray Palliser Hickman; 2ndly, the widow of Walsh, and 3rdly, the widow of French. He had issue,
1. Wray, d.s.p.
1. Catherine, m. John Vincent, son of Rev. George Vincent.
2. Eliza, m. William Roe, of Rockwell, co. Tipperary.
3. Mary.
2. John (Sir), K.C.B., Col. 5th Dragoons, served in the Peninsular War, for some time General in Spanish Army, b. 1787; d. unm. 1854.
3. Marshal, Major H.E.I.C.S., Madras Army, b. 1789; d. unm. 1833.
4. Samuel, Capt. 87th Regt., served in Peninsular War, d. in Spain 1813 unm.
5. CHARLES, of Graiguenoe Park, of whom presently.
6. Robert, of Bansha, co. Tipperary, J.P., b. 1804; m. 1st, Sarah Jane, dau. of Rev. Holford Banner, Rector of Dideot, Berks. She d. 1833, having had issue. He m. 2ndly, Anne, dau. of Capt. Richard Butler, of Castle Comer, 27th Regt., and d. 1868, having had issue,
1. Robert Vaughan, of Three Castles, co. Kilkenny, m. 1873, Mary Anne, dau. of John Vincent.
2. Marshal   3. Benjamin.
4. Charles Eldon, of Newtown House, Holy Cross, co. Tipperary, m. Elia, dau. of James Butler, of Drom, co. Tipperary, and has issue,
(1) Charles Lionel.
(2) Cecil Cholmondeley (*The Hermitage, Holycross, co. Tipperary*; 66, *Cheyne Court, Chelsea, S.W.*), m. 22 April, 1911, Fanny Ethel, elder dau. of Major Edward Augustus Carter (*see Peerage*, HEMPHILL, Baron).
(1) Blanche Elia Catherine, m. 1905, Arthur Gordon Wyatt Cooke (*Newtown House, Thurles, co. Tipperary*), 2nd son of Sir William Cooke, Bart., of Wheatley Hall, Doncaster (see BURKE's *Peerage*), and has issue.
1. Mary Jane, m. Feb. 1863, Godwin Meade Pratt Swifte, of Swittesheath, co. Kilkenny (*see that family*).

2. Elizabeth, *m.* 1867, Capt. Jerome O'Brien, late 28th Regt., and has issue (see O'BRIEN *of Ballynalacken Castle*).
3. Anne, *m.* 8 Aug. 1867, Lord O'Brien, Lord Chief Justice of Ireland, and has issue (see BURKE's *Peerage*).
4. Katherine, *m.* Thomas Maunsell, of Deer Park, co. Clare.
5. Georgina Hannah, *m.* 5 June, 1873, Col. Charles James Butler-Kearney, of Drom, co. Tipperary, and has issue (*see that family*).
7. Mark (Rev.), Rector and Vicar of Shronell, *m.* 6 April, 1837, Maria, dau. of William Hill, of Donnybrook, Doneraile, co. Cork, and *d.* 6 Sept. 1848, leaving issue,
1. Marshal James (Sir), K.C.M.G., late R.A., Resident Commissioner in Southern Rhodesia, *b.* 24 Oct. 1841; *m.* 1880, Annie Stacy (*The Lodge, Enniskerry, co. Wicklow*), dau. of Major-Gen. Bannastre Lloyd, B.C.S. (see BURKE's *Peerage*, MOSTYN, B.), and *d.* April, 1909, leaving issue,
  (1) Marshal Llewellyn, Lieut. R.N.
  (2) Brian Lloyd, Lieut. Indian Army.
  (1) Elizabeth.
2. William, *d. unm.* 1900.
1. Eliza, *m.* 5 March, 1861, Edward Falconer Litton, Judge of the Supreme Court in Ireland (who *d.* 27 Nov. 1890). She *d.* Jan. 1871, leaving issue (see LITTON *of Ardavilling*).
2. Maria, *m.* Rev. Robert Going.
3. Jane. 4. Anne.
The 5th son,
CHARLES CLARKE, of Graiguenoe Park, co. Tipperary, J.P. and D.L., High Sheriff 1862, *b.* 1803; *m.* Sarah Otway, dau. of Capt. Loftus Otway Bland, R.N., and *d.* Aug. 1879, leaving issue,
1. MARSHAL NEVILLE, his heir.
1. Sarah Elizabeth, *d. unm.* 20 April, 1905.
2. Elizabeth, *m.* 3 Dec. 1860, Robert Cole Bowen, of Bowen's Court, co. Cork (*see that family*).
The only son,
MARSHAL NEVILLE CLARKE, of Graiguenoe Park, co. Tipperary, J.P., M.A. Trin. Coll. Dublin, Barrister-at-Law, *b.* 1828; *m.* 1864, Mary, dau. of Col. Charles Pearson, 61st Regt., of Cheltenham, and *d.* 10 May, 1884, leaving issue,
1. CHARLES NEVILLE, now of Graiguenoe Park.
2. Loftus Otway, Deputy Commissioner Indian Civil Service, B.A. Christ Church, Oxford, *b.* 1871; *m.* 17 Feb. 1904, Evelyn Frances, youngest dau. of late Lieut.-Col. Richard Carden, of Fishmoyne, co. Tipperary (*see that family*), and has issue,
  George Henry Vernon, *b.* 1908.
3. George Vernon, Capt. R.F.A., *b.* 2 Sept. 1873; *d. unm.*, killed in South African War, 8 April, 1902.
4. Marshal Falconer, Capt. Cheshire Regt., *b.* 3 Feb. 1876; *m.* 12 April, 1910, Olive Sydney, dau. of Rev. Canon Lionel Garnett, B.A., Rector of Christleton, Cheshire (see GARNETT *of Wyreside*).
1. Harriet Neville, *m.* 25 Jan. 1898, George Butler, of Maiden Hall, co. Kilkenny, and has issue (see BUTLER *of Priestown*).
2. Marion Sarah Neville, *m.* 18 Sept. 1907, Capt. Johnson A. Busfield, Cheshire Regt.

Seat—Graiguenoe Park, Holy Cross, Thurles, co. Tipperary. *Clubs*—Oxford and Cambridge, Wellington, and Kildare Street.

BROWNE-CLAYTON OF BROWNE'S HILL.

ROBERT CLAYTON BROWNE-CLAYTON, of Browne's Hill, co. Carlow, late Major 5th Lancers, *b.* 24 Feb. 1870; *s.* his father 13 Jan. 1907; *m.* 16 Nov. 1905, Mary Magdalene, 3rd dau. of Edward Wienholt, of Jondaryan, Queensland, and has issue,
WILLIAM PATRICK, *b.* 27 Sept. 1906.
Annette Mary, *b.* 28 April, 1908.

Lineage.—ROBERT BROWNE, of Carlow, whose will (dated 10 Feb. 1677) was proved 27 May, 1678, left by Jane his wife, three sons,
1. JOHN. 2. William.
3. Robert.
The eldest son,
JOHN BROWNE, of Carlow, *m.* about 1680, Mary, dau. of Robert Jennings, of Kilkea Castle, co. Kildare, of the family of JENNINGS *of Selden*, co. York. Their son and successor,
WILLIAM BROWNE, of Browne's Hill, *m.* Elizabeth, dau. of John Clayton, Dean of Kildare, and sister to the learned Robert Clayton, Bishop of Clogher. By this lady, who descended from the family of that name, of Adlington Hall, co. Lancaster, he had,
1. JOHN, *d. unm.* 23 April, 1765.
2. ROBERT, successor to his father.
1. Anne, *m.* 20 July, 1758, Right Rev. Thomas Bernard, D.D., Bishop of Limerick.
2. Catherine, *m.* Rev. Abraham Symes, D.D.
3. Mary, *m.* Peter Gale, of Ashfield, Queen's Co.
4. Juliana, *m.* Thomas Cooper, of Newton, co. Carlow.
Mr. Browne *d.* 1772, aged 88, and was *s.* by his eldest son,
ROBERT BROWNE, of Browne's Hill, *m.* 27 March, 1762, Eleanor, dau. of Redmond Morres, M.P. for Dublin, and had issue,
1. WILLIAM, his heir.
2. Robert, Lieut.-Gen. in the Army, *b.* 10 March, 1845; *m.* 1 Dec. 1803, Henrietta, only dau. and heir of Sir Richard Clayton, Bart., of Adlington, co. Lancaster, and assumed the name and arms of CLAYTON by Royal licence 6 April, 1829, and had issue by her (who *d.* 8 Sept. 1858) a son and a dau.,

Richard-Clayton, *b.* 12 Nov. 1807; *d.* 1886; of Adlington Hall, Lanes., and Carrigbyrne, co. Wexford; *m.* 5 Jan. 1830, Catherine Jane, only dau. of Rev. J. Dobson, and had one son and four daus. by her (who *d.* 1889),
  (1) Robert John, *d.s.p.* of wounds received at Sebastopol, 18 June, 1854, aged 20.
  (1) Henrietta, *m.* 28 July, 1859, Robert Thomas Carew, of Ballinamona, co. Waterford (*see that family*).
  (2) Katherine Annette, *m.* 16 April, 1857, Col. Philip Savage Alcock (see ALCOCK *of Wilton*).
  (3) Emma.
  (4) Mary Edith, *m.* 15 Jan. 1885, Major Thomas Edwards Harman, of Palace, co. Wexford (*see that family*).
3. Redmond, Col. in the Army, *d. unm.*
4. John (Rev.).
1. Elizabeth, *d. unm.* 2. Anne, *d. unm.*
Mr. Browne *d.* Jan. 1816, aged 87, and was *s.* by his eldest son,
WILLIAM BROWNE, of Browne's Hill, J.P. and Custos Rotulorum, co. Carlow, M.P. for Portarlington, *b.* Jan. 1763; *m.* 1st, 1793, Lady Charlotte Bourke, dau. of Joseph Deane, 3rd Earl of Mayo, Archbishop of Tuam (see BURKE's *Peerage*), and by her (who *d.* 1806) had issue,
1. ROBERT CLAYTON, his heir.
2. Joseph Deane, Capt. Carabineers, *m.* Miss Thursby, and *d.* 1 Jan. 1878.
1. Elizabeth, *m.* Sir Jonah Denny Wheeler-Cuffe, 1st bart. of Lyrath, co. Kilkenny, and *d.* 15 Jan. 1871 (see BURKE's *Peerage*).
2. Eleanor Mary, *m.* William FitzWilliam Burton, of Burton Hall, co. Carlow, who *d.* 1844 (*see that family*).
3. Charlotte, *m.* William Brownlow, of Knapton, Queen's Co.
4. Annette, *m.* 1826, Hon. and Ven. Henry Scott Stopford, Archdeacon of Leighlin, and *d.* March, 1842 (see BURKE's *Peerage*, COURTOWN).
He *m.* 2ndly, 1815, the Lady Letitia Toler, dau. of John, 1st Earl of Norbury (see BURKE's *Peerage*), Lord Chief Justice of the Common Pleas in Ireland, by his wife Grace Graham, Baroness Norwood, and by this lady had issue,
3. John Toler.
4. William Raymond, late Capt. 7th Fusiliers, *d.* 1 Oct. 1907, having *m.* and had issue. His eldest dau., Letitia Grace, *m.* 23 Nov. 1887, Sir William Henry Hornby, Bart., M.P. of Whinfield, Blackburn (see BURKE's *Peerage*).
5. Hector Graham, *m.* 1878, Gertrude Sophia, eldest dau. of John Horrocks Ainsworth, of Moss Bank (see AINSWORTH *of Smithell's Hall*).
5. Grace Isabella, *m.* 26 June, 1852, Richard Godfrey Bosanquet, of Benham Park, Berks, and had issue (see BOSANQUET *of Cleddon*).
Mr. Browne, High Sheriff co. Carlow 1794, *d.* 1 April, 1840, and was *s.* by his eldest son,
ROBERT CLAYTON BROWNE, M.A. of Browne's Hill, co. Carlow, J.P. and D.L., High Sheriff 1831, *b.* 28 Jan. 1799; *m.* 28 Oct. 1834, Harriette Augusta, 3rd dau. of Hans Hamilton, many years M.P. for co. Dublin, and had issue,
1. WILLIAM CLAYTON, late of Browne's Hill.
2. Charles Henry, *b.* 13 Nov. 1836; Col. in the Army, *d. unm.* 1889.
3. Robert Clayton, *b.* 3 May, 1839; *d. unm.* 14 Dec. 1906.
1. Annette Caroline, *m.* 12 Feb. 1863, Denis William Pack-Beresford, of Fenagh Lodge, M.P. for co. Carlow. She *d.* 1892. He *d.* 1881, leaving issue (*see that family*).
Mr. Browne *d.* 22 July, 1888. The eldest son,
WILLIAM CLAYTON BROWNE-CLAYTON, of Browne's Hill, co. Carlow, J.P. and D.L., High Sheriff 1859, *b.* 20 Nov. 1835; *m.* 10 Jan. 1867, Caroline, 5th dau. of John Watson Barton, of Stapleton Park, near Pontefract, co. York (*see that family*), and had issue,
1. ROBERT CLAYTON, now of Browne's Hill.
2. William Clayton, 2nd Lieut. Royal West Kent Regt., *b.* 29 July, 1873, killed in action at Agrah Malakan, 30 Sept. 1897.
3. Lionel Denis, *b.* 1874.
1. Mary Caroline, *m.* 6 Oct. 1898, Thomas Henry Bruen Ruttledge, of Bloomfield, co. Mayo (*see that family*).
2. Annette Constance. 3. Margaret Frances.
4. Florence Hope, *m.* 28 April, 1904, Lieut.-Col. Horace James Johnston, D.S.O., younger son of Francis Johnston, of Dunsdale, co. Kent, and has issue
5. Kathleen Louisa Octavia. 6. Madeline Emma.
7. Lucy Victoria, *m.* 12 Dec. 1901, Claud Edward Pease, 3rd son of the late Arthur Pease, M.P., of Marske-by-the-Sea, Yorks (see BURKE's *Peerage*, PEASE, Bart.).
8. Julia Harriet Vere.
9. Caroline Zöe, *m.* 14 Dec. 1905, Capt. Hubert Chase Hall, late 5th Fusiliers, only son of Major Hall, of Denbie, Lockerbie, N.B.
Mr. Browne-Clayton assumed the additional name of CLAYTON, by Royal Licence, 1889, and *d.* 13 Jan. 1907.

Seat—Browne's Hall, co. Carlow. *Clubs*—Cavalry and Kildare Street.

CLELAND OF RATH-GAEL.

The late RICHARD ROSE-CLELAND, of Rath-Gael House, co. Down, *b.* 1 May, 1836; *s.* his brother 10 May, 1856; *m.* 30 Sept. 1861, Elizabeth Wilhelmina, eldest dau. of Robert Kennedy, of Lisburn, co. Antrim, and *d.* 15 Feb. 1892, having by her (who *d.* 15 Sept. 1893) had issue,

1. James Dowsett, b. 13 Oct. 1862.
2. Robert Kennedy, b. 9 Oct. 1863.
3. Richard, b. 11 Nov. 1864; d. 7 July, 1865.
4. Charles Arthur, b. 18 Sept. 1876.
1. Elizabeth Helen Louisa.
2. Mary Isabella Eveline.
3. Edith Adelaide.
4. Maude Ethel.
5. Florence May.
6. Alice Gertrude.
7. Catherine Mabel.
8. Harriet Ella.

Rath-Gael now belongs to the youngest son and the seven youngest daus.

Lineage.—JOHN CLELAND, of Whithorn, co. Wigton, Scotland, appointed factor to James, 5th Earl of Galloway, m. 1731, Margaret Murdoch, only child of — Murdoch, Provost of Whithorn; and d. 10 Aug. 1747, leaving issue by her,
JAMES, of whom hereafter.
Agnes, b. 4 Sept. 1740; m. 1st, 5 June, 1766, Lieut. Richard Rose, H.E.I.C.S., who d. at Trichinopoly, 7 June, 1768, of wounds received at the siege of Ahtoor, by whom she had an only child,
JAMES DOWSETT ROSE-CLELAND, of whom presently.
She m. 2ndly, 1774, William Nicholson, of Ballow House, but by him had no issue; she d. 11 July, 1775.
The son and successor,
JAMES CLELAND, of Newtownards, co. Down, b. 4 May, 1736; m. 1770, Sarah, only child of Capt. Patrick Baird (brother of William Baird, of Newbyth, and James Baird, of London, and uncle to General Sir David Baird), and d. 14 May, 1777, s.p. Mr. Cleland was s. by his nephew,
JAMES DOWSETT ROSE-CLELAND, of Rath-Gael, b. 24 March, 1767; J.P. and D.L., High Sheriff 1805. He m. 1st, 14 Aug. 1790, Sarah, only child of William Eaton Andrews, of London, and by that lady (who d. 2 Oct. 1830) had a son and dau.,
1. WILLIAM NICHOLSON, b. 18 June, 1794; d. 20 Nov. 1794.
1. Elizabeth Hawkins, m. 3 Sept. 1829, Fortescue Gregg, of Knockearn, co. Antrim.
He m. 2ndly, 10 Dec. 1832, Elizabeth, eldest dau. of William Nicholson Steele Nicholson, of Ballow House, by Isabella Handcock his wife (see that family), and by her had issue,
2. JAMES BLACKWOOD, heir to his father.
3. RICHARD, successor to his brother.
4. Edward Allen, b. 21 Jan. 1840.
5. Henry Somerville, b. 4 Nov. 1843.
2. Agnes Elizabeth.
3. Isabel Hamilton, m. 20 Oct. 1874, Robert Steele Nicholson, and has issue.
4. Margaret Sabina, m. 19 June, 1877, Arthur Wellington Garner, of Garnerville, near Belfast.
Mr. Rose-Cleland d. 25 Sept. 1852, and was s. by his son,
JAMES BLACKWOOD ROSE-CLELAND, of Rath-Gael House, co. Down, b. 30 Jan. 1835; who d. at Constantinople, 10 May, 1856, and was s. by his brother, the late RICHARD ROSE-CLELAND, of Rath-Gael House.

Seat—Rath-Gael House, Bangor, co. Down.

CLELAND OF STORMONT CASTLE.

ARTHUR CHARLES STEWART CLELAND, of Stormont Castle, co. Down, late Lieut. 3rd Batt. P. W. Leinster Regt., b. 25 July, 1865; m. 1890, Mabel Sophia, only dau. of Lieut.-Col. D'Aguilar, late Grenadier Guards.

Lineage.—THE REV. JOHN CLELAND, Prebendary of Armagh, b. 1755; m. 7 Sept. 1805, Esther, dau. and co-heiress of Samuel Jackson, of Stormont, by his wife Margaret Vateau, only child and heiress of Paul Peter Isaac Vateau, the descendant of a French Huguenot family, and d. 25 June, 1834, having had issue,
1. SAMUEL JACKSON, of Stormont Castle, co. Down, b. 1808; m. 3 Nov. 1834, Elizabeth, dau. of James Joyce, of Thornhill; d. 20 May, 1842, leaving,
1. JOHN, late of Stormont Castle.
2. James Vance, of Ennismore, co. Armagh, J.P., b. 7 May, 1838, late Capt. 3rd Hussars; m. 4 Nov. 1862, Emily Catherine, only dau. of Sir George Molyneux, Bart., of Castle Dillon, and d. 1886, leaving issue,
(1) Samuel, b. 1864. (2) George Molyneux.
3. Robert Stewart, b. 17 June, 1840, Col. 9th Lancers; d. at Murree, 7 Aug. 1881, from wounds received in the action before Cabul, 11 Dec. 1880.
4. Samuel Frederick Stewart, late Scots Greys, b. 24 Aug. 1842; d. 16 Jan. 1902.
1. Margaret.
2. Robert Stewart, b. 1810; d. under age.
1. Sarah Frances, m. 6 July, 1831, Robert Richard Tighe, of Woodstock, and d.s.p. 24 March, 1832. (He m. 2ndly, Louisa Joan, widow of Hon. Edward Wingfield.)
His grandson,
JOHN CLELAND, of Stormont Castle, co. Down, J.P. and D.L., High Sheriff 1866, b. 22 Sept. 1836; m. 7 May, 1859, Thérèse Maria, only dau. of Capt. Thomas Leyland, of Haggerston Castle, Northumberland, and Hyde Park House, London, and d. 1893, having by her (who m. 2ndly, George T. Taylor, of Tredenham House, Farnborough, Hants, and d. 8 June, 1903) had issue,
1. ARTHUR CHARLES STEWART, now of Stormont Castle.
2. Andrew Leyland Hillyar, b. 5 Sept. 1868.
1. Florence Rachel Thérèse Laura, d. 12 Aug. 1894, having m. 9 Aug. 1879, Edward Umfreville Blackett, of Wylam, Northumberland, and Barnacrothy, co. Tipperary, Lieut. R.A. (see that family).

Seat—Stormont Castle, Dundonald, co. Down.

CLEMENTS OF KILLADOON, CO. KILDARE.

HENRY JOHN BERESFORD CLEMENTS, of Killadoon, co. Kildare, and of Lough Rynn, co. Leitrim, High Sheriff of Cavan 1891, J.P. and D.L. co. Leitrim, and High Sheriff 1893, J.P. co. Kildare, b. 22 Oct. 1869; m. 31 Oct. 1893, Eléonore, youngest dau. of William Wickham, M.P., of Binsted Wyck (see that family), and has issue.
1. HENRY THEOPHILUS WICKHAM, b. 12 Nov. 1898.
2. Charles Marcus Lefevre, b. 4 Nov. 1904.
3. Robert Nathaniel b. 7 July, 1910.
1. Eléonore Mary Sophia, b. 24 March, 1895.
2. Cecily Catharine, b. 12 Jan. 1900.
3. Violet Gertrude, b. 2 Sept. 1902.

Lineage.—THE RIGHT HON. HENRY THEOPHILUS CLEMENTS, P.C., Lieut.-Col. 69th Regt., M.P. for co. Leitrim, 2nd son of Right Hon. Nathaniel Clements, M.P., and brother of Robert, 1st Earl of Leitrim; m. 1st, 2 June, 1770, Mary, dau. and heir of Gen. Webb, by whom he had issue,
1. Harriett, m. William Moore Hodder.
2. Maria, m. Very Rev. Dean Keatinge.
He m. 2ndly, 7 Aug. 1778, Catharine, dau. of Right Hon. John Beresford (by Anne, dau. of Gen. Count de Ligondés), and d. 26 Oct. 1795, having by her (who d. 7 Jan. 1836) had issue,
1. HENRY JOHN, his heir.
2. John Marcus, of Glenboy, M.P. co. Leitrim, Lieut.-Col. 18th Hussars, b. 4 May, 1789; m. 27 July, 1822, Catherine Frances, dau. of Godfrey Wentworth, of Wolley Park, co. York (see that family). She d. 1838. He d. 1833, leaving issue,
1. A son, who d. young.
2. John Marcus, of Glenboy, High Sheriff co. Leitrim 1868, b. 27 July, 1826; m. 2 Nov. 1854, Victoria Isabella, dau. of James Robert White, of White Hall, co. Antrim. He d. 1896. She d. 26 May, 1902, having had issue,
(1) John Marcus, late I.S.C., b. 9 Dec. 1856; d.s.p.
(2) James Robert, b. 23 Nov. 1858; d. 23 April, 1896.
(3) George Stewart, b. 15 July, 1860.
(4) Charles Henry, b. 7 Sept. 1861; m. 1886, Julia, dau. of Col. Watson, and d. 1903, leaving issue, two daus.
(5) Henry Victor, b. 16 Oct. 1866.
(1) Catherine Frances.
(2) Selina Mary Louisa, m. 1st, 1890, Hugh White, who d. 1902; and 2ndly, 1904, Frank Brown, youngest son of Charles Brown, of Eridge House, Croydon.
3. Henry George John (Rev.), M.A., Vicar of Sidmouth, Devon, b. 3 Nov. 1829; m. 31 Oct. 1855, his cousin Selina (d. 31 July, 1892), dau. of Col. Henry John Clements.
3. Anna Barbara, b. 1779; d. young.
4. Selina, b. 17 Aug. 1780; m. 13 July, 1803, Sir William Mordaunt Sturt Milner, 4th bart., and d. 28 May, 1805. He d. 25 March, 1855, leaving issue.
His eldest son,
HENRY JOHN CLEMENTS, Col. in the Leitrim Militia, and M.P. for co. Leitrim from 1805 to 1818 and for co. Cavan from 1840 till his death, 1843; b. 16 July, 1781; m. 11 Dec. 1811, Louisa, 2nd dau. of James Stewart, M.P. of Killymoon (by his wife Hon. Elizabeth Molesworth, dau. of Richard, 3rd Viscount Molesworth), and by her (who d. 27 April, 1850) had issue,
1. HENRY THEOPHILUS, late of Ashfield Lodge.
1. Elizabeth Henrietta Catherine, d. young, 21 Jan. 1827.
2. Selina, m. 31 Oct. 1855, Rev. Henry G. J. Clements, Vicar of Sidmouth, Devon, and d. 31 July, 1892.
3. Louisa, d. unm. 17 March, 1879.
4. Mary Isabella, d. unm. 6 Aug. 1890.
5. Catherine, d. young, Sept. 1830.
Col. Clements d. 7 Jan. 1843. His son,
HENRY THEOPHILUS CLEMENTS, of Ashfield Lodge, co. Cavan, late Col. Leitrim Rifles, J.P. and D.L. co. Cavan, and J.P. co.

Leitrim, High Sheriff co. Cavan 1849, and co. Leitrim 1870, b. 24 July, 1820; m. 3 Dec. 1868, Gertrude Caroline Lucy, dau. of Rev. David F. Markham, Rector of Great Horkesley, Essex, and Canon of Windsor. He d. 7 Jan. 1904, having had issue,
1. HENRY JOHN BERESFORD, now of Killadoon and Lough Rynn.
2. Alfred William, b. 29 Jan. 1871; d. 3 Feb. 1876.
3. Robert Markham, b. 6 Nov. 1876; d. 13 Dec. 1876.
4. Marcus Louis Stewart, of Ashfield Lodge, co. Cavan, Lieut. King's Royal Rifle Corps, b. 29 Sept. 1879.
1. Gertrude Mary Catharine.   2. Selina Margaret Maud.

Arms—Arg., two bendlets wavy sa. on a chief gu. three bezants.
Crest—A hawk statant ppr.   *Motto*—Patriis virtutibus.
Seats—Killadoon, Celbridge; and Lough Rynn, co. Leitrim.
Clubs—Carlton, and Kildare Street (Dublin).

LUCAS-CLEMENTS OF RATHKENNY.

THEOPHILUS EDWARD LUCAS-CLEMENTS, of Rathkenny, co. Cavan, J.P., High Sheriff 1905, b. 3 Jan. 1864; m. 9 July, 1907, Lalage Emily, 4th dau. of the late Henry West, Q.C., of Loughlinstown House, co. Dublin (see WEST of White Park).

Lineage.—ROBERT CLEMENTS, son of DANIEL CLEMENTS, of Rathkenny, co. Cavan, was M.P. for Carrickfergus 1692, and possessed large estates in Down and Cavan. In 1689 he was attainted, but on the accession of WILLIAM III was restored to his estates in Cavan, and appointed Deputy Treasurer in Ireland. He m. Miss Sandford, of the Castlerea family, and had issue,
1. Theophilus (the Right Hon.), M.P. for Cavan, m. Elizabeth, dau. of Francis Burton, of Bancraggy, but d.s.p.
2. ROBERT, of whom presently.
3. NATHANIEL, father of the 1st Lord Leitrim.
1. Mary, m. 1715, Robert Tighe, of Mitchelstown, co. Westmeath (see that family).

The 2nd son,
ROBERT CLEMENTS, M.P. for Newry 1715; d. 1723, leaving a son,
THEOPHILUS CLEMENTS, of Rathkenny, co. Cavan, whose dau. and heiress,
ELIZABETH ANNE, m. REV. EDWARD LUCAS, of Cootehill, a younger son of Edward Lucas, of Castle Shane, co. Monaghan, and had with three daus. 1. Catherine, m. 1833, Nicholas Biddulph; 2. Elizabeth, m. 1823, Rev. James Leslie Montgomery Scott; and 3. Anne, m. 1827, Thomas Scott, of Willsboro, co. Derry, a son and heir,
THEOPHILUS EDWARD LUCAS-CLEMENTS, of Rathkenny, who assumed the surname and arms of CLEMENTS, under Royal Licence, 2 July, 1823. He m. 22 Sept. 1829, Elizabeth Beatrice, dau. of the Rev. Shuckburgh Whitney Upton, and d. 1852, leaving issue,
1. THEOPHILUS, of whom presently.
2. Henry Upton, d. unm. 10 July, 1872.
3. Charles John Fulk, d. 1873.
1. Isabella Margaret, m. Robert Alloway, of the Derries, Queen's Co., and dying 1876, left issue.
2. Olivia Beatrice, d. unm. 1861.

The only surviving son,
THEOPHILUS LUCAS-CLEMENTS, of Rathkenny, co. Cavan, J.P. and D.L., High Sheriff 1857, b. 15 Oct. 1830; m. 5 Feb. 1861, Emily Caroline, dau. of William Magill, of Lyttleton, co. Westmeath, and by her (who d. March, 1870) had issue,
1. THEOPHILUS EDWARD, now of Rathkenny.
2. Caroline Mabel Harriet, m. 24 Sept. 1907, Rev. Edward Aubrey Forster.

He m. 2ndly, 1874, Agnes Jane, 3rd dau. of James Stirling, J.P., of Ballawley Park, co. Dublin, and d. 7 April, 1898, having by her had issue,
1. Arthur Upton, b. 1876; d. 1877.
3. Shuckburg Upton Lucas.
3. Alice May Gwendoline.
4. Agnes Laura Elfrida, m. 25 Oct. 1906, Frances Lucas Clements Scott, eldest son of Rev. F. M. Scott, Vicar of Poulton Fairford, co. Gloucester.

Arms—Quarterly: 1st and 4th, arg., two bendlets wavy sa. on a chief gu. three bezants, for CLEMENTS; 2nd and 3rd, arg., a fesse between six annulets gu., for LUCAS. *Crests*—1st, a hawk close ppr. belled and jessed or; 2nd, a demi-griffin arg. beaked and membered, or. *Motto*—Patriis virtutibus.
Seat—Rathkenny, near Cootehill, co. Cavan.

CLIBBORN OF MOATE.

GEORGE HOLMES CLIBBORN, of the Castle, Moate, co. Westmeath.

Lineage.—JOHN CLIBBORN, b. 1623, came from Cliburn, co. Westmorland, with the Army of the Parliament, and settled at Moate, co. Westmeath. He m. Dinah English, and was father of JOSHUA CLIBBORN, of Moate, b. 1665; whose will, dated 21 Feb. 1727-8, was proved same year; by Sarah his wife he left issue,
1. JOHN, his successor.
2. Abraham, of Dublin, Merchant, m. Anne, dau. of John Coppeck, and d. 1762, having by her (whose will, dated 9 May, 1756, was proved 9 May, 1770) had issue,
   1. Sarah.   2. Jane.
   3. Elizabeth.
3. Joshua.   4. George.
5. Robert, of Whelan Grove, co. Kildare (whose will, dated 23 April, 1785, was proved 23 June, 1786), m. Annie Martin, and had two sons and a dau.,
   1. Joshua, m. 8 April, 1752, Lydia, dau. of William Cooper, of Cooper Hill, Queen's Co., and had a son,
      Robert, of co. Dublin, Merchant, m. Elizabeth Morris, and d. 1798, leaving
      1. Joshua.
      1. Mary.   2. Lydia.
   2. Henry, to whom his father left Whelan Grove.
   1. Sarah, m. 23 Aug. 1754, Edward Cooper, of Cooper Hill.
6. James, of Moate (whose will, dated 9 Sept. 1780, was proved 23 April, 1783); by Experience Barclay his wife, he left issue, Barclay, to whom his father left the lands of Raheens, m. Sarah, dau. of William Cooper, of Cooper Hill, in the Queen's Co., by Experience his wife, dau. of Abel Strettel, of Dublin, and had issue,
   (1) James.   (2) William Cooper.
   (3) Joshua.   (4) John Barclay.
   (5) Edward, m. his cousin Mary, dau. of George Clibborn, of Moate.
   (6) Thomas.   (7) Robert.
   (1) Lydia, m. 1843, Jonathan Goodbody, of Charlestown House, King's Co., who d. 1889, leaving issue (see that family).
   (2) Sarah.
   (3) Anne, m. 1783, John Johnston Darragh. She d. 13 April, 1847.
   (4) Eliza.   (5) Sophia.
1. Mary (Mrs. Jackson).   2. Dinah (Mrs. Wilson).
3. Sarah.   4. Jane.

Mr. Clibborn d. 1728. His eldest son,
JOHN CLIBBORN, of Moate Castle, b. 1695; m. Sarah, dau. of Hoop, of Hoop Hill, near Lurgan, co. Armagh, by whom (whose will, dated 2 Aug. 1770, was proved 25 Feb. 1774) he had issue,
1. Joshua, m. Hannah, dau. of Jacob Goff, of Dublin, and sister of Jacob Goff, of Horetown, co. Wexford, by whom (who m. 2ndly, William Pigott, of Slevoy, same co.) he had an only dau. Mary Goff.
2. GEORGE, of whom hereafter.
3. Abraham, of Aghernergil, co. Westmeath, d. 1762.
4. Robert.
1. Elizabeth (Mrs. Sutton).   2. Ruth
3. Sarah, m. John Pim.   4. Jane.
5. Ann (Mrs.) Pim.   6. Abigail.

Mr. Clibborn's will, dated 3 July, 1754, was proved 14 June, 1764. His 2nd son,
GEORGE CLIBBORN, of Moate, m. 1st, Elizabeth Strettel, of co. Dublin, by whom he had issue,
1. JOHN, his successor.   2. Thomas Strettel, d. unm.
3. Joshua, d.s.p.; will dated 6 March, 1793, proved next year.
1. Sarah, m. Joseph Fade Goff, of Newtown Park, co. Dublin.

Mr. Clibborn m. 2ndly, June, 1777, Anne, dau. of George Homan, of Shurock, co. Westmeath, by whom he had further issue,
4. William, m. Miss Bailey.   5. George.
2. Anne, m. John White.   3. Abigail.
4. Jane.   5. Mary, m. Edward Clibborn.
6. Ruth.

Mr. Clibborn was s. by his eldest son,
JOHN CLIBBORN, of Moate Castle, m. Elizabeth, widow of Richard Fetherstonhaugh, and had surviving issue,
1. CUTHBERT JOHN, his successor.
1. Mary, m. her cousin William Goff.
2. Sarah.   3. Abigail.

Mr. Clibborn was s. by his only surviving son,
CUTHBERT JOHN CLIBBORN, of Moate, J.P., b. 1803; m. Feb. 1836, Jane, dau. of George Arbuthnot Holmes, of Moorock, in the King's Co. (see HOLMES of Moycashel), and d. 1847, having had by her (who d. 2 March, 1876) four sons and one dau.,
1. THOMAS STRETTELL, of Moate Castle.
2. George Holmes, b. 23 Aug. 1840; d. March, 1853.
3. Cuthbert John, of Belfast, Inspector Local Government Board, J.P. co. Wicklow, M.B., M. Ch., b. 10 Jan. 1846; m. 1st, Nov. 1871, Mary Graves, dau. of Graves Cathrew, Barrister-at-Law, and has issue,
   1. Graves Cathrew, b. 1875, d. 1892.
   2. Cuthbert John, b. 1877.
   1. Jane Holmes, b. 1872, d. 1894.
   2. Georgina, b. 1874, d. 1891.   3. Muriel, b. 1879.
He m. 2ndly, 15 Dec. 1910, Edith Frances, 3rd dau. of William Fetherstonhaugh, of Grouse Lodge, widow of John J. Nugent, of Rosemount.
4. John, C.I.E., of Moorock House, Ballycumber, King's Co., B.A. and C.E. T.C.D., Lieut.-Col. Indian Staff Corps; Pres. of Com-

mittee of Industrial Education, India, 1901-2, late Principal of the Thomasom Coll. of Engineering, Roorkee, India (11. *Nevern Square, S. Kensington*). *b.* 8 Dec. 1847; *m.* 8 Nov. 1881, Anne Léonie Macpherson Frith, dau. of Surg.-Gen. John Butler Hamilton, Army Medical Staff, and grand-dau. of Major Charles Pratt Hamilton, nephew of Lieut.-Gen. Sir Charles Pratt, K.C.B., and has issue,
 1. Cuthbert John Hamilton, Lieut. R.F.A., *b.* at Mussourie, Nov. 1883.
 2. Cecil Hamilton, *b.* at Aligarh, 19 Feb. 1886.
  1. Léonie Annie Holmes, *b.* at Naini Tal, 16 Sept. 1882 ; *m.* 30 March, 1909, Claud Quarry, eldest son of W. Quarry, of Bedford.
  2. Violet Louise, *b.* at Aligarh, 29 Jan. 1885 ; *m.* 4 Oct. 1911, Capt. Richard Eyre, of Prospect, King's Co.
 1. Jane Moore, *b.* 8 Aug. 1838 ; *d.* 13 Aug. 1853.

The eldest son,
THOMAS STRETTELL CLIBBORN, of the Castle, Moate, co. Westmeath, and of Holmesby, Elizabeth Bay, Sydney, New South Wales, Australia, late Secretary of the Australian Jockey Club, Sydney, *b.* 4 Feb. 1837 ; *m.* Oct. 1868, Clarinda Mary, dau. of Richard Magan, of Rockfield, co. Westmeath (*see* MAGAN *of Emoe*), and *d.* 31 Dec. 1910, having had issue,
 1. GEORGE HOLMES, now of Moate.
 1. Ethel Mary, *b.* at Ballarat, Victoria, Australia, 1871.
 2. Adelaide Beryl, *b.* at Sydney, New South Wales, Sept. 1873 ; *d.* Jan. 1874.

Seat—The Castle, Moate, co. Westmeath. *Residence*—Holmesby, Elizabeth Bay, Sydney, New South Wales, Australia.

CLIFFE OF BELLEVUE.

ANTHONY LOFTUS CLIFFE, of Bellevue, co. Wexford, J.P. and D.L., High Sheriff 1897, late Capt. 3rd Batt. Royal Irish Regt., *b.* 4 June, 1861 ; *s.* his father 1894 ; *m.* 23 July, 1904, Frances Emma, dau. of Capt. Segrave, of Cabra (*see that family*), and widow of Sir John Talbot Power, 3rd Bart. (*see* BURKE'S *Peerage*).

Lineage.—JOHN CLIFFE, of Westminster (son of Anthony Cliffe of Westminster), went to Ireland as Secretary-at-War of the Army sent by the Parliament under the command of CROMWELL 1649, and acquired grants of land in the cos. of Wexford and Meath. He *m.* Eleanor, 5th dau. of Nicholas Loftus, of Fethard, co. Wexford, grandfather of the 1st Lord Loftus, of Loftus Hall, and by her (who was *b.* 1 Dec. 1641, and *d.* 3 Sept. 1700) had issue. Mr. Cliffe was M.P. for Taghmon 1661, and High Sheriff co. Wexford 1680. His eldest son,
JOHN CLIFFE, of Mulrancan Hall, Duogulph Castle and New Ross, *b.* 3 May, 1661 ; *m.* 1694, Barbara, eldest dau. and eventual heir of William Carr, of the city of Cork, and had issue,
 1. JOHN, his heir.
 2. William, of New Ross, *b.* 5 April, 1701 ; *m.* his cousin Eleanor dau. of Richard Vigors, of Old Leighlin, co. Carlow, and had issue seven sons, who all *d. unm.* except the
    Rev. John Cliffe, of New Ross, *b.* 1736, who *m.* Sarah, dau. and co-heir of Richard Wilson, and dying there 14 Feb. 1816, left issue, one son and two daus.,
     (1) John, who was lost in his passage from Bristol to Waterford 1817, *unm.*
     (1) Sarah, *m.* March, 1803, Henry Loftus Tottenham, of Macmurrough co. Wexford, and *d.* 12 Dec. 1830.
     (2) Anne, *m.* Sept. 1810, the Rev. Thomas Mercer Vigors, of Burbage, co. Carlow.
 3. Anthony, *b.* 30 March, 1703, a Major in the Army.
 4. Edward, *b.* 26 Aug. 1705.
 5. George, *b.* 27 May, 1707.
 6. Edward, *b.* 30 July, 1709.
 7. Loftus, *b.* Dec. 1710, Major in the Army, *d.* 1766. He *m.* Anne, dau. of William Hore, of Harperstown, co. Wexford, and *d.* March, 1814, aged 83, having had issue, one son and three daus.,
  1 Walter, Lieut.-Gen. in the Army, *b.* 4 Feb. 1757 ; *m.* Harriet,

dau. of Gen. Sir Anthony Farrington, Bart., and *d.* July, 1816, leaving an only child,
     Loftus Anthony (Rev.), of Osborne Place, Wilton, Taunton, Somersetshire, *b.* 12 Sept. 1795 ; *m.* 1 Aug. 1821, Salome, dau. of John Capon, of Taunton, and *d.* 12 Aug. 1877, having had an only dau.,
      Harriet Salome, *m.* July, 1844, Arthur Kinglake, of Taunton.
  1. Dorothy, *b.* 2 Jan. 1756; *m.* John Harvey, of Killiane Castle, co. Wexford, and *d.* 1813.
  2. Barbara, *b.* 6 Dec. 1762 ; *m.* 22 Oct. 1784, John Stanford, of Born, co. Cavan.
  3. Anne, *b.* 2 Feb. 1764 ; *m.* 1 May, 1783, Rev. Roger Owen, Rector of Camolia, co. Wexford.
 8. Henry, *b.* 17 March, 1711 ; supposed to have *d.* a child.
 9. Henry, *b.* 16 Dec. 1714.
 1. Barbara, *b.* 16 July, 1695 ; *m.* Charles Tottenham, of Tottenham Green.
 2. Barbara, *b.* 27 Oct. 1697 ; *m.* Arthur Gifford, of Aherne, co. Cork, and had issue, an only child, Catherine, *m.* 10 May, 1764, the Hon. William Brabazon, 2nd son of Edward, 7th Earl of Meath, and had issue.
 3. Anne, *b.* 11 Jan. 1698. 4. Elizabeth, *b.* 27 Feb. 1699.
 5. Mary, *b.* May, 1704 ; *m.* John Leigh, of Rosegarland, co. Wexford, and had a son and dau. (*see that family*).

Mr. Cliffe was one of the Commissioners for raising money by loan for WILLIAM III, in the co. Wexford 1695 and 1698, and was M.P. for Bannow from 1692 to 1715. He was *s.* by his eldest son,
JOHN CLIFFE, of New Ross, *b.* Aug. 1696 ; *m.* 9 Jan. 1727-8, Jane, eldest dau. of his cousin, Henry Cliffe, of Sutton, Surrey, and had issue,
 1. JOHN, his heir.
 2. ANTHONY, who *s.* his brother John.
 3. Edward Lard, *d.s.p.*
 1. Barbara, *b.* 13 Jan. 1728-9 ; *d. unm.*
 2. Jane, *b.* 19 Oct. 1730 ; *m.* 1st, the Rev. Joshua Tench, of Bryanstown, and had issue. She *m.* 2ndly, Charles Tottenham, of New Ross, but had no issue by him. She *d.* 11 Jan. 1797.
 3. Mary, *b.* 2 Feb. 1740 ; *d. unm.* 1834, at Bath.
 4. Henrietta, *b.* July, 1748 ; *d. unm.* 1821, at Bath.

The eldest son,
JOHN CLIFFE, of New Ross, of which he was Recorder, *b.* 31 Aug. 1733 ; *d. unm.* 1795, and was *s.* by his brother,
ANTHONY CLIFFE, of Abbeybraney, New Ross, *b.* 11 Oct. 1734, Capt. 4th Horse, 1 Oct. 1766, Major 4th Dragoon Guards ; *m.* 1795, Frances, eldest dau. of Col. Joseph Deane, of Terenure, co. Dublin, and left at his decease, 1803 (with two daus., Jane Catherine, *m.* Robert Shapland, late of Castle Boro, co. Wexford ; and Cecilia Frances, *m.* Robert Daniel, of New Forest, co. Westmeath), an only son,
ANTHONY CLIFFE, of Bellevue, High Sheriff 1823, *b.* 10 March, 1800 ; *m.* 23 June, 1821, his cousin Isabella Frances, dau. of Col. Charles Powell Leslie, of Glasslough, co. Monaghan, M.P., and by her (who *d.* 17 Oct. 1873) had issue,
 1. ANTHONY JOHN, late of Bellevue.
 2. Charles Henry, Capt. 58th Foot, *b.* June, 1826 ; *m.* 4 Nov. 1857, Marie Josephine, 5th dau. of Charles Adams, of Mytton Hall, Shropshire, and *d.* Sept. 1866, leaving,
    Francis Henry, *b.* 16 Jan. 1862.
 3. Edward, late Capt. 52nd Regt., *b.* April, 1830.
 1. Marianne Jane Place.
 2. Frances Harriett, *d.* 1870. 3. Isabella Catherine.
 4. Emily Cecilia, *d. unm.* July, 1863.
 5. Jane Elizabeth, *m.* 8 Sept. 1858, Thomas Redington Roche, only son of Stephen Roche, J.P., of Rye Hill, co. Galway, and Moyvanines, and Clounties, co. Limerick.
 6. Eleanor Barbara.

Mr. Cliffe *d.* 27 Aug. 1878. His eldest son,
ANTHONY JOHN CLIFFE, of Bellevue, co. Wexford, J.P., D.L., *b.* Oct. 1822 ; *m.* 8 Sept. 1858, Amy, 2nd dau. of Sir John Howley, 1st Serjeant-at-Law in Ireland, and *d.* 25 Jan. 1894, having by her (who *d.* 7 Nov. 1906) had issue,
 1. ANTHONY LOFTUS, now of Bellevue.
 2. John Edward, *b.* 10 Oct. 1862.
 3. Henry Cecil, *b.* 28 Feb. 1864, late Capt. 3rd King's Own Hussars, *d.s.p.* 23 Nov. 1892.
 1. Isabella Sarah Mary, *d.* in infancy.
 2. Amy Mary Paulina, *m.* 3 June, 1891, 11th Earl of Galloway (*see* BURKE'S *Peerage*)

Arms—Erm., on a fess between three wolves' heads, erased sa. a trefoil between two mullets or. *Crest*—A wolf's head erased quarterly per pale indented or and sa. *Motto*—In cruce glorior.

Seat—Bellevue, Wexford. *Clubs*—White's, Wellington, and Sackville Street, Dublin.

CLIVE OF BALLYCROY. *See* CLIVE OF PERRYSTONE.

CLOSE OF DRUMBANAGHER.

MAJ. MAXWELL ARCHIBALD CLOSE, of Drumbanagher, co. Armagh, High Sheriff 1908, Major late 11th and 13th Hussars, b. 5 Oct. 1853; m. 2 June, 1891, Lady Muriel Albany, eldest dau. of the 5th Earl of Castlestuart, and has issue,
1. MAXWELL STUART, b. 1 Feb. 1892.
2. Archibald Maxwell, b. 1 Oct. 1903.
1. Lilias Augusta Muriel.
2. Agatha Katharine Rose.

Lineage.—RICHARD CLOSE, the first of the family who settled in Ireland, was the younger son of a Yorkshire family then residing at Easby, near Richmond, Yorks, and held a commission in the army sent from England in the reign of CHARLES I, 1640. He acquired property in co. Monaghan, but after the Restoration fixed himself at Lisnegarvey (now Lisburn) co. Antrim. There he lived and died, leaving a son and heir,

RICHARD CLOSE, who inherited the Monaghan estates. He m. Mary, sister of Samuel Waring, of Waringstown, co. Down, M.P. for Hillsborough, and left at his decease, five sons and three daus. The eldest son, Richard Close, m. 1708, Rose, dau. of Roger Hall, of Mount Hall, Narrow Water, co. Down, and had issue, now extinct. The 2nd son,

THE REV. SAMUEL CLOSE, Rector of Donaghenry, Stewardstown, co. Tyrone, b. 1683, entered Trin. Coll. Dublin, 26 April, 1700; m. Catherine, dau. of Capt. James Butler, of Bramblestown, co. Kilkenny, by Dame Margaret Maxwell, of Mullatinny (Elm Park), co. Armagh, relict of Sir Robert Maxwell, Bart. of Ballycastle, co. Derry, and dau. and heiress of Henry Maxwell, of Mullatinny, and had (with four daus., **1.** Margaret, m. Capt. Charles Woolly, and had issue; **2.** Mary, d. unm.; **3.** Catherine, d. unm.; and **4.** Elizabeth, m. 24 March, 1763, to Peter Gervais) a son and successor,

MAXWELL CLOSE, who s. his grandmother, Lady Maxwell (who d. 1758) in the possession of Elm Park, and the lands settled upon him. He was High Sheriff co. Armagh 1780. He m. 6 July, 1748, Mary, eldest dau. of Capt. Robert Maxwell, of Fellows Hall, co. Armagh, brother of John, 1st Lord Farnham (see BURKE'S *Peerage*), and had issue,
1. Samuel, his heir.
2. Robert, d. unm.
3. Barry (Sir), b. Dec. 1756, a Major-Gen. H.E.I.C.S., who was created a Baronet 1812. This highly distinguished officer d.s.p. April, 1813, when the title expired.
4. Farnham, d. in the Island of Guadaloupe, 1794, Lieut.-Col. 65th Regt., unm.
1. Grace, b. Jan. 1750; m. the Rev. Dr. St. John Blacker.
2. Catherine, b. Nov. 1753; m. Arthur Noble.
3. Margaret. 4. Mary. 5. Elizabeth.

Mr. Close d. 1793, and was s. by his eldest son,

THE REV. SAMUEL CLOSE, of Elm Park, Rector of Keady, co. Armagh, and of Drakestown, Meath, b. Sept. 1749; m. 25 April, 1782, Deborah, dau. of the Very Rev. Arthur de Robillard Champagné, Dean of Clonmacnoise, son of Major Josias de Robillard Champagné, by the Lady Jane Forbes his wife, dau. of Arthur, 2nd Earl of Granard (see BURKE'S *Peerage*), and by her (who d. 1815) had four sons and three daus.,
1. MAXWELL, his heir.
2. Robert, Col. H.E.I.S., m. 21 July, 1827, Caroline Sophia, sister of the late Sir Thomas Palmer, Bart. of Northamptonshire, and has had issue,
 1. Barry Maxwell, d. 1873. 2. Vere Henry, d. 1911.
 1. Sophia, m. 23 Dec. 1856, Henry Orlando Bridgeman, who d.s.p. 14 June, 1879 (see BURKE'S *Peerage*, BRADFORD, E.).
 2. Emily, d. 1870.
3. Henry Samuel, of Newtown Park, co. Dublin, m. 1821, Jane, dau. of the Very Rev. Holt Waring, of Waringstown, co. Down, Dean of Dromore, and had issue,
 1. Maxwell Henry (Rev.), M.A., M.R.I.A., b. 1822; d. 12 Sept. 1903.
 2. Robert Barry, b. 1825; d. 24 April, 1908, m. Augusta, dau. of Rev. J. Vaughan, of Gotham, Notts. She d. 26 Nov. 1902.
 3. Samuel Holt, d. July, 1897, aged 71.
 4. Henry Walter, m. 1879, Mary Acton, dau. of Rev. Botry Pigott, and d. Oct. 1890.
 5. George Champagné, Major 45th Regt., d. Feb. 1879.
 6. Arthur Richard, Capt. 43rd Light Infantry, killed in New Zealand War, 1865.
 7. William John, m. Lucy, dau. of Rev. Botry Pigott.
 8. Farnham Chidley, m. 16 Sept. 1890, Mary Amelia, eldest dau. of the late Hon. William H. G. Wellesley (see BURKE'S *Peerage*, COWLEY, E.). He d. 13 Jan. 1901.
 1. Catherine Deborah Agnes, m. 23 Nov. 1852, her cousin M. C. Close, D.L., of Drumbanagher, who d. 25 Jan. 1903, leaving issue (see below).
 2. Emily Jane, m. J. C. Scriven, and d. 1860.
 3. Adelaide Harriet, m. John Burton, of Burton Hall, Carlow

4. John Forbes (Rev.), Rector of Mourne, co. Down; d. 1883; m. 1st, 1822, Mary Sophia, youngest dau. of Charles Brownlow of Lurgan, and sister of Charles, 1st Lord Lurgan, and had issue,
 1. Caroline, m. Gen. Sir Arthur Borton, G.C.B., and had issue. She d. 24 April, 1908.
 He m. 2ndly, 4 June, 1852, Marie Esther, widow of Col. Steinbelt, and dau. of Rev. J. Fullagar; and 3rdly, Adelaide, dau. o Edmund Gilling Hallewell, and had issue,
 1. John Forbes, m. Emily Mary, dau. of Rev. Duncan Macfarlane, and d. 22 Feb. 1894, leaving issue,
  Duncan Forbes, b. 15 Sept. 1889.
  Janet Marjorie, b. 19 Jan. 1893.
 2. Charles Barry, Major 9th Norfolk Regt., b. 16 Feb. 1862; m. 2 Oct. 1897. Hazel Mary, dau. of Col. Henry Wood, C.B., late Rifle Brigade. He d. 17 March, 1908, leaving issue,
  Violet, b. 4 July, 1905.
 2. Ellen Augusta, m. 1890, Rev. Samuel Smartt, M.A., Vicar of Newry, and has issue, two daus.
 3. Adelaide Victoria.
1. Mary, m. May, 1812, Sir Justinian Isham, 8th bart. of Lamport, co. Northampton, and d. 1878.
2. Jane, m. 8 May, 1827, Col. Chidley Coote, brother of Sir Charles Henry Coote, Bart. of Ballyfin, and had issue.
3. Harriet, m. 1825, Rev. Ralph Coote, Lynally, King's Co., youngest brother of Sir C. H. Coote, Bart.

Mr. Close d. 1817, and was s. by his son,
MAXWELL CLOSE, of Drumbanagher, J.P. and D.L., High Sheriff 1818, Col. in the Army, b. 14 March, 1783; m. 14 March, 1820, Anna Elizabeth, sister of Charles, 1st Lord Lurgan, and by her (who d. 2 Jan. 1863) had issue,
1. MAXWELL CHARLES, late of Drumbanagher.
2. Barry b. 22 June, 1833.

Mr. Close d. 16 Dec. 1867. His elder son,
MAXWELL CHARLES CLOSE, of Drumbanagher, co. Armagh, M.A., J.P. and D.L., High Sheriff 1854, M.P. co. Armagh 1857 to 1864, and 1874 to 1885, b. 25 June, 1827; m. 23 Nov. 1852, Catherine Deborah Agnes, dau. of Henry Samuel Close, of Newtown Park, co. Dublin, and d. 25 Jan. 1903, having had issue,
1. MAXWELL ARCHIBALD, now of Drumbanagher.
2. Henry Samuel, b. 12 Nov. 1863; m. 4 Sept. 1890, Edith Dorothy Blanche, 3rd dau. of Capt. Henry Segrave, 12th Foot, of Kiltymon, co. Wicklow, and has issue,
 Barry Maxwell, b. 27 Sept. 1897.
 1. Edith, d. Aug. 1869. 2. Emily Beatrice.
 3. Mary Geraldine. 4. Flora Lucy.
 5. Kate Violet, d. 30 Dec. 1889. 6. Grace Wilmina.
 7. Alice Evelyn, m. 7 June, 1899, Rev. John Thomas Waller, Rector of St. Laurence, Limerick (see WALLER *of Castletown*).

Arms—Quarterly, 1st and 4th: Az., on a chevron arg. between three mullets, or, a fetterlock sa. between two bugle horns ppr., garnished of the 3rd stringed gu. 2nd quarterly, 1st and 4th: Or, a chief indented az., 2nd and 3rd gu. three covered cups or, over all a cross moline sa., and all within a bordure arg. (for BUTLER). 3rd Arg., a saltire sa.; a chief paly of six of the 1st and 2nd (for MAXWELL). On an escutcheon of pretence, quarterly, 1st and 4th,: Or, a fess per saltire gu. and erm., between in chief a bull's head couped, and in base a galley sa. (for RICHARDSON). 2nd and 3rd, quarterly, 1st: Or, a lion rampant, with a double tressure flory counter flory gu. 2nd: Or, a fess chequy arg. and az., in chief a label of three points gu.; 3rd Arg., a saltire engrailed between four roses gu. 4th: Az., a lion rampant arg., the whole within a bordure compony arg. and az. (for STUART). **Crest**—Out of an eastern crown a demi-lion vert holding a battleaxe ppr. *Motto*—Fortis et fidelis.

Seats—Drumbanagher, near Newry; Drum Manor, Cookstown co. Tyrone.

COATES OF RATHMORE.

The late VICTOR COATES, of Rathmore, co. Antrim, and of Glentoran, co. Down, J.P. and D.L. co. Antrim, High Sheriff 1893, b. 1826; m. 26 May, 1863, Margaret Airth (now of Rathmore), dau. of Jonathan Richardson, of Lambeg, and had with other issue,
1. WILLIAM, b. 1864.
4. Victor H. (*Wood End, Crowhurst, Sussex*), b. 1866; m. 1896, Kathleen Jane Marshall, dau. of Clement Cotterill Redfern, of the Inner Temple, Barrister-at-Law, and has issue,
 Victor, b. 1897.
 Margaret Helen, b. 1899.

Mr. Coates, who d. 27 July, 1910, was son of the late William Coates, J.P., of Glentoran, High Sheriff 1869 (who d. 1878), by Mary his wife, dau. of Maurice Lindsay, of Ashfield.

Seat—Rathmore, co. Antrim.

COBBE OF NEWBRIDGE HOUSE.

Thomas Maberly Cobbe, of Newbridge House, co. Dublin, b. 1884; m. 6 April, 1905, Eleanor Colville, 2nd dau. of Col. Colville Frankland.

Lineage.—William Cobbe, of Steventon, co. Southampton, b. circa 1450, was father of John Cobbe, of Swaraton (The Grange), who m. Army Barnes, and had a son, Thomas Cobbe, of Swaraton, b. circa 1510, living at the time of the Visitation of Hampshire 1575, when he received from Robert Cooke (Clarenceux) a ratification of the "armes and chriests of his ancestors." By his 2nd wife, Agnes, dau. of John Hunt, Thomas Cobbe was father of Richard, B.D., Fellow and Vice-President of Corpus Christi College, Oxon, and one of its earliest benefactors; also of two other sons, joint possessors of the estate of Northington, adjoining Swaraton. By his 1st wife, Margaret, dau. of Edward Beronshaw, Thomas Cobbe had, with other issue,

Michael Cobbe, of Swaraton, b. 1547; d. 40 Elizabeth. He m. Joan. eldest dau. and heiress of George Welborne, of Allington, Dorset, and had issue. The eldest son,

Thomas Cobbe, of Swaraton, 1575, Capt. of a foot company 1634; m. Catherine, dau. of the Ven. Owen Owen, Archdeacon of Anglesey, and Rector of Burton-Latymer, sister of John Owen, Bishop of St. Asaph. By her he had, Michael, who m. Anne, dau. of Bishop Broomfield, of Titchfield, M.P., and had issue, Arthur; Lucy; and

Richard Cobbe, b. 1607; returned Knight of the Shire for Hants, 1656; m. Honor, dau. of Sir Richard Norton, of Rotherfield, 2nd bart., and had issue,

Thomas Cobbe, Governor of the Isle of Man, m. Veriana, dau. of James Chaloner, M.P. during the Long Parliament, by his wife Ursula, dau. of Sir Philip Fairfax, of Steeton, and had issue,
1. Richard Chaloner, Col. of Militia, m. Mary dau. of F. Godolphin, Governor of Scilly, and was father of Richard, D.D., Rector of Finglas, father of Richard Chaloner Cobbe, D.D., Rector of Little Marlow, Bucks, father (with other children) of Frances, m. to Hans Francis, 11th Earl of Huntingdon.
2. William, Capt., d.s.p. 1749.   3. Charles.

The youngest son,
Charles Cobbe, D.D., b. 1686; successively Bishop of Killala, Dromore, and Kildare, and Archbishop of Dublin; m. Dorothea, dau. of the Right Hon. Sir Richard Levinge, Bart., Speaker of the House of Commons, and Chief Justice of Common Pleas in Ireland, widow of Sir John Rawdon, Bart. of Moira. The Archbishop built Newbridge House about 1737, and d. 14 April, 1765, leaving one surviving son,

Thomas Cobbe, of Newbridge, M.P., Col. of Militia, b. 1733, m. 1751, Lady Eliza Beresford, dau. of Marcus, 1st Earl of Tyrone, and sister of George, Marquess of Waterford. By her he had issue two daus., Catherine, m. Hon. Henry Pelham (and had issue, Catherine, and Frances, m. Capt. Murray); and Elizabeth Dorothea, m. Sir Henry Tuite, Bart., but d.s.p. 1850; and one son,

Charles Cobbe, of Newbridge, M.P., b. 1756; m. Anne Power Trench, sister of William, 1st Earl of Clancarty, and by her (who d. 1835) left at his decease v.p. 1798, five sons,
1. Charles, his heir, of Newbridge.
2. George, General R.A., b. 1782; m. Amelia, dau. of the Rev. Royston Barton, and dying 9 March, 1865, left issue,
    1. Charles Henry, Major H.E.I.C.S. (dec.), m. and had issue.
    2. Thomas Monck, m. 16 Aug. 1839, Sophia, dau. of Burton Tandy, of Mornington House, co. Meath.
        1. Frances, m. Dawson Littledale, and by him (who d. 1884) had issue.
        2. Anna.
        3. Linda, m. Thomas Thompson, D.L., of Hollywood Rath, co. Dublin, and has issue.
3. Henry, Vicar of Templeton, d.s.p. 1823.
4. Thomas Alexander, Col. H.E.I.C.S., b. 1788; d. 1836; m. Nuzzeer Begum, dau. of Azeeze Khan, of Cashmere, and had issue,
    1. Henry Clermont, Col. C.B., Commanding 4th Regt., killed at Sebastopol 1855, s.p.
    2. Charles Augustus, Lieut.-Col., of Springfield, Great Romans Road, Southsea, D.L. for W.R. Yorks, b. 1817; m. and d. 18 March, 1901, leaving issue. His widow, Sarah Anne, d. 15 March, 1908.
    3. William, d.s.p.
    4. Francis Hastings, Lieut.-Col. R. A.
    5. Alexander Hugh (Sir), K.C.B., Lieut.-Gen., late Col. Commanding 17th Regt., b. 1825; m. 1863, Emily Barbara, dau. of Capt. G. Stanhope Jones, 59th Regt., and d. 13 Sept. 1899 having by her (who d. 1886) had, with other issue,
        (1) Henry Hercules, D.S.O., b. 26 Feb. 1860; m. 15 April, 1907, Jeanne, dau. of Col. H. W. B. Boyd, I.M.S., Bombay.
        (2) Alexander Stanhope, V.C., D.S.O., Major and Bt.-Col. Indian Army, b. 5 Jan. 1870; m. 1 Oct. 1910, Winifred, dau. of A. E. Bowen, of Colworth, Beds.
    1. Azélie.
    2. Florence (dec.), m. 1st, John Ensor, of Rolesby, and had issue; 2ndly, Chardin Wroughton.
3. Laura, m. John Locke, M.P., and has issue.
4. Sophia.   5. Eliza.
5. William Power, Capt. R.N., b. 1790; m. Elizabeth Bridget, dau. of Richard Fortescue Starkey, M.P., and dying 8 April, 1831, left issue,
    1. Charles Power, Capt. 13th Light Infantry, d.s.p.
    2. William Power (Rev.), M.A., m. Jane Selina (16, Codwyne Road, Dover), dau. of Col. George John Beresford, R.A., of Woodhouse, co. Waterford, and d. 18 April, 1889, having had issue,
        Charles William Beresford (Rev.) (16, Codwyne Road, Dover), b. 20 July, 1875.
    1. Jane Power, d. unm. 18 Nov. 1887.
    2. Flora Power, d. unm. 15 March, 1875.
    3. Elizabeth Dorothea Power, d. unm. 3 Dec. 1902.

The eldest son,
Charles Cobbe, of Newbridge, co. Dublin, J.P. and D.L., High Sheriff 1821, b. 1781; m. 1809, Frances, only dau. of Capt. Thomas Conway, of Morden Park, Surrey, and by her (who d. 1847) had,
1. Charles, late of Newbridge.
2. Thomas, Barrister-at-Law, b. 1813; m. Janet Finlay, dau. of Thomas Grahame, and d. 13 May, 1882, leaving by her (who d. 22 Aug. 1884) issue,
    1. Leuric Charles, late of Newbridge.
    2. Hervic Nugent Grahame.
    1. Helen Louise.   2. Frances Conway.
3. William, b. 1816; m. Clara, dau. of J. Nottidge, of Rose Hill, Suffolk.
4. Henry (Rev.), M.A., Rector of Maulden. Beds., b. 1817; m. and has issue,
    1. Mabel.   2. Winifred.
    3. Amy Beresford.
1. Frances Power, d. unm. 5 April, 1904.

Mr. Cobbe d. 11 Nov. 1857, and was s. by his eldest son,
Charles Cobbe, of Newbridge House, M.A., J.P., D.L., High Sheriff co. Dublin 1841, and co. Louth 1867, b. 17 Aug. 1811; m. 1st, May, 1839, Louisa Caroline, dau. of George Frederick Brooke, of Summerton, co. Dublin (she d. 2 June, 1882); 2ndly, June, 1883, Charlotte, dau. of Rev. Henry Moore, of Julianstown Rectory, co. Meath, and d. 5 July, 1886. She d. 26 Oct. 1901. He was s. by his nephew,

Leuric Charles Cobbe, of Newbridge House, b.   m.   , and had with other issue,

Thomas Maberly, now of Newbridge.

Arms—Gu. a fess arg., in chief two swans of the last. Crest—Out of a ducal coronet gu. a pelican's head and neck vulning itself ppr. Mottoes—Moriens cano; over the crest: In sanguine vita.

Seat—Newbridge House, Donabate, co. Dublin.

COCHRANE OF RED CASTLE.

Richard Francis Ernest Cochrane, of Red Castle, co. Donegal, Capt. and Hon. Major 5th Batt. Innis. Fus., High Sheriff 1908, J.P. co. Donegal, b. 18 Sept. 1873.

Lineage.— (see Burke's Peerage).—Thomas, 10th Earl of Dundonald, G.C.B., the great Admiral (who d. 31 Oct. 1860), and Katherine Frances Corbet, his wife (who d. 25 Jan. 1865), dau. of Thomas Barnes, of Romford. Essex, had a youngest son,

Capt. the Hon. Ernest Grey Lambton Cochrane, of Red Castle, co. Donegal, J.P. and D.L., High Sheriff 1879, Capt. R.N. (retired), b. 4 June, 1834; m. 1st, 15 Sept. 1864, Adelaide, only dau. of Col. Samuel W. Blackall, Governor of Sierra Leone, and afterwards of Queensland. She d. 3 Oct. following. He m. 2ndly, 16 Oct. 1866, Elizabeth Frances Maria, only child of Richard Doherty, of Red Castle, co. Donegal. He d. 26 Feb. 1911, having had issue,
1. Thomas Alfred Dundonald O'Dogherty, b. 23 Sept. 1868; d. unm.
2. Richard Francis Ernest, now of Red Castle.
3. Ernest Algernon, b. 11 May, 1877.
4. Horace Cochrane Egerton, b. 1883.
1. Elizabeth Rosetta Stewart, b. 19 Oct. 1867.
2. Adelaide Maria, b. 19 Oct. 1874.
3. Frances Katherine, b. 8 Nov. 1875.
4. Blanch Edith, b. 4 Oct. 1879.
5. Mabel Alice Marie, b. 6 March, 1884.

Arms, &c.—See Burke's Peerage, Dundonald, E.

Seats—Red Castle, near Londonderry, Mintiaghs Lodge, Buncrana, co. Donegal. Club—United Service.

CODDINGTON OF OLDBRIDGE.

JOHN NICHOLAS CODDINGTON, of Oldbridge, co. Meath, J.P. and D.L., formerly Major and Hon. Lieut.-Col. Royal Meath Regt. of Militia, *b.* 24 June, 1828 ; *m.* 1st, 1870, Lelia Jane, elder dau. of the late James Lennox William Naper, of Loughcrew, co. Meath, and by her (who *d.* 1 Feb. 1879) has issue,

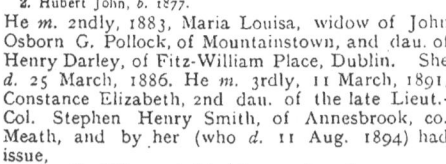

1. ARTHUR FRANCIS, *b.* 1873 ; *m.* 9 Oct. 1908, Dorothie Rhoda, dau. of Francis C. Osborne, of Smithstown, Drogheda, and had issue,
   DIXIE HENRY, *b.* 9 Nov. 1909.
2. Hubert John, *b.* 1877.

He *m.* 2ndly, 1883, Maria Louisa, widow of John Osborn G. Pollock, of Mountainstown, and dau. of Henry Darley, of Fitz-William Place, Dublin. She *d.* 25 March, 1886. He *m.* 3rdly, 11 March, 1891, Constance Elizabeth, 2nd dau. of the late Lieut.-Col. Stephen Henry Smith, of Annesbrook, co. Meath, and by her (who *d.* 11 Aug. 1894) had issue,
  Audrey Muriel Raymond, *d.* in infancy, 21 Aug. 1895.

Lineage.—WILLIAM CODDINGTON, of Holm Patrick, co. Dublin, High Sheriff co. Wicklow 1656 ; *m.* Thomasine Calton, and by her had three sons and seven daus. He *d.* 1657, aged 50. His son and heir,

CAPT. NICHOLAS CODDINGTON, of Holm Patrick, *d.* July, 1685, leaving by his 2nd wife, Anne, who survived him, three sons and one dau. (his 1st wife Elizabeth, dau. of William Aston, *d.s.p.* 1657). The eldest son,

CAPT. DIXIE CODDINGTON, of Holm Patrick, *b.* 1665, High Sheriff co. Dublin 1695, served on WILLIAM III's staff at the battle of the Boyne. He *m.* 1686, his cousin Anne, dau. and heiress of his uncle, John Cuddington, of Clonerry, King's Co., by whom (who *d.* 1736) he left at his death, 22 July, 1728, six sons and three daus.,

1. JOHN, his heir.
2. Nicholas, of Drogheda, *m.* 14 July, 1722, Mary, dau. of Henry Tennison, of Dillonstown. co. Louth, and *d.* Nov. 1737, leaving by her (who *d.* 1785) a son,
   DIXIE, heir to his uncle in 1740.
3. Dixie, of Athlumney Castle, co. Meath, principal Serjeant-at-Arms from 1768 to his death in August, 1777. He *m.* 27 June 1753, Hannah, dau. of Thomas Knox.
4. Henry, of Tankardstown, co. Meath, Barrister, *d.s.p.*
5. William, Vicar of Carrickmacross, co. Monaghan.
6. Robert.
  1. Anne. 2. Elizabeth, *m.* John Lyster, of Rocksavage.
  3. Jane, *b.* 1700 ; *m.* 15 July, 1723, Ralph Blundel, of Dublin ; and *d.* 2 Aug. 1742.

The eldest son,
JOHN CODDINGTON, of Oldbridge, co. Meath, *m.* 1710, Frances, dau. and co-heir of Capt. John Osborn, of Balgeen, by whom (who *d.* 1747) he had one son,
  John, drowned in the Boyne the day he came of age, 1736.
Mr. Coddington *d.* 1740, and was *s.* by his nephew,
  DIXIE CODDINGTON, of Oldbridge. He *m.* 1754, Catherine, dau. of Thomas Burgh, of Bert, and had seven sons, who all *d.* young. He *d.* in Dublin 1794, and was *s.* by his brother,
  HENRY CODDINGTON, of Oldbridge, *b.* 1728. After the death of his cousin, Dixie Coddington, 1791, he became Deputy Serjeant-at Arms, and was so at the Union, 1800, at which time he was also patron of one of the seats for the borough of Dunleer. He *m.* 1762, Elizabeth, dau. of Latham Blacker, of Rathescar, co. Louth, and had issue,

1. NICHOLAS, his heir.
2. Henry, *m.* Eleanor Hamilton, of Browne Hall, co. Donegal, and *d.* leaving three daus., one of whom *m.* the Rev. Thomas Lindesay, Rector of Upper Cumber, co. Londonderry.
3. Latham (Rev.), M.A., Rector of Timolin, co. Kildare, *m.* Anne, dau. of Col. Bellingham, of Ardagh, co. Louth, and had with other issue, Henry (Rev.), and John George, of Ravensdale, co. Louth.
4. Thomas, *d. unm.*
1. Martha, *m.* Philip Pendleton, of Moortown, co. Meath, and left issue.
2. Elizabeth, *m.* — Winder, and has issue.
3. Anne, *m.* Edward Augustus Waller (*see* WALLER *of Rockvale*), and *d.* leaving issue.
4. Mary Jane, *m.* George Lendrum, of Jamestown, co. Fermanagh, and *d.* leaving issue.

Mr. Coddington *d.* 21 Dec. 1816, and was *s.* by his son,
  NICHOLAS CODDINGTON, of Oldbridge, *m.* July, 1793, Letitia, dau. of Gaynor Barry, of Beau, co. Dublin, and had issue,
1. HENRY BARRY, of Oldbridge.

2. Joshua William, Capt. R.E., *m.* 1840, Agnes, dau. of Gen. Emmett, R.E., and *d.* 1853, leaving issue,
  1. Charles Edward. 2. Edward Fitzherbert.
3. Fitzherbert Nicholas, Major in the Army, *m.* 1841, Jane, dau. of Col. Trelawny, R.A., Governor of St. Helena, and *d.* 1853, leaving issue,
  1. Fitzherbert Henry. 2. Charles Hamlyn.
  1. Blanche Martha.
1. Anna Elizabeth, *m.* 1826, John Fitzherbert Ruxton, of Ardee House, co. Louth, and *d.* leaving issue (*see that family*).
2. Letitia Mary, *d.* 15 Oct. 1879.

Upon the decease of Mr. Coddington, 31 Aug. 1837, aged 72, he was *s.* by his eldest son,
HENRY BARRY CODDINGTON, of Oldbridge, co. Meath, J.P., High Sheriff 1843, *b.* 22 May, 1802 ; *m.* 26 Sept. 1827, Maria, eldest dau. of William Sharman Crawford, of Crawfordsburn, co. Down, and *d.* 23 March, 1888, having by her (who *d.* 23 March, 1845) had issue,
1. JOHN NICHOLAS, now of Oldbridge.
2. William Henry, *b.* 19 June, 1833 ; *m.* 21 March, 1866, Rose, dau. of Nathan Cairns.
3. Henry Joshua, *b.* 21 Aug. 1836 ; *d.* Sept. 1866.
4. Fitzherbert, Col. Bengal S.C., *b.* 2 May, 1838 ; *m.* 20 Aug. 1863, Julia, only dau. of Richard de Vahuency, and *d.* 25 April, 1889, leaving issue,
  Herbert Adolphe, D.S.O., Lieut.-Col. late Royal Irish Fusiliers (*Old Manor House, Chilworth, Surrey*), *b.* 19 Sept. 1864 ; *m.* 25 Feb. 1905, Bertha Violet Mary, only dau. of the late G. C. Kempthorne Bennett, of Maldivia, Wynberg, Capetown.
5. Arthur Blayney, Col. R.E., *b.* 20 Feb. 1840 ; *m.* 27 June, 1872, Ellen Bertha, 2nd dau. of Oswald Bloxsome, of The Grove, Ryde, Isle of Wight, and *d.* 15 Dec. 1888. She *d.* 17 Oct. 1880, leaving issue. Their eldst dau. Irene Spencer, *m.* 5 Oct. 1899, Maj. Christopher Robert Ingram Brooke, Yorkshire L.I. (*see* BURKE's *Peerage*, BROOKE, Bart.). Their youngest dau., Gladys Beryl, *m.* 22 Feb. 1902, Capt. Charles Bonham Carter, son of Henry Bonham Carter, of Hyde Park Square, W.
6. Dixie Latham, *b.* 23 March, 1845 ; *d. unm.* 6 Jan. 1897.
1. Letitia Mabella, *m.* 30 Sept. 1857, Robert Fowler, of Rahinstown, co. Meath, and *d.* 25 Jan. 1879, leaving issue (*see that family*).
2. Maria Anna, *d.* Oct. 1891.

Arms—Gu., a cross or, fretty az. between four trefoils slipped of the 2nd. *Crest*—A wolf's head erased or, charged with a trefoil slipped ppr. *Mottoes*—Nil desperandum ; or, Nec metuas nec optes.

Seat—Oldbridge, near Drogheda.

COGHILL. *See* BURKE's PEERAGE, COGHILL, Bart.

COLCLOUGH OF TINTERN ABBEY.

The late LOUISA MARIA SUSANNA COLCLOUGH BIDDULPH-COLCLOUGH, *s.* her mother, 3 Nov. 1884 ; *m.* 15 Sept. 1885, Franc Digby Biddulph, Capt.' 3rd Middlesex Militia (who assumed the surname and arms of COLCLOUGH, by Royal Letters Patent in 1886), youngest son of Francis Wellesley Marsh Biddulph, of Rathrobin (*see that family*). She *d.* 29 Jan. 1912, having by him (who *d.* 13 July, 1895) had issue,
  Cæsar Thomas Bickerstaffe Plantagenet, *b.* 15 Sept. 1886 *d.* 6 July, 1888.
  Lucy Wilmot Maria Susanna Biddulph, *b.* 2 June, 1890.

Lineage.—The very ancient descent of Colclough is very fully set forth in the Visitation of Staffordshire, 1583 ; Visitation, co. Wexford, 1618 ; Visitation City of London, 1634, and the registries in Ulster's Office, Dublin Castle. The Visitation of Staffordshire commences with

RICHARD COLCLOUGH, of Bluerton, co. Stafford, 1367, who was ancestor of
SIR ANTHONY COLCLOUGH, Knt. of Tintern Abbey, co. Wexford, and Bluerton and Woolstanton, co. Stafford, who went to Ireland 34 HENRY VIII, and was afterwards Captain of Queen Elizabeth's Band of Pensioners. He had a commission, dated 21 March, 1559, to execute Martial Law throughout the co. Wexford, except in O'Morchoe's county. On 10 Oct. 1565, Queen ELIZABETH addressed a letter to Sir Henry Sidney, the Lord Deputy, ordering a lease in reversion to be made to Sir Anthony of the dissolved monastery and lands of Tintern, co. Wexford, upon the expiration of a lease formerly made to Sir James Crofts, Knt. of Crofts, co. Hereford, the interest of which Sir Anthony had purchased 18 May, 1557, and by Patent, dated 27 Aug. 1575, the Queen granted the said monastery and lands to Sir Anthony and his heirs in fee. He *m.* Clare, dau. of Francis Agard, of Foston, co. Derby, a Privy Councillor in Ireland, and Governor of the co. Wexford, by whom (who *m.* 2ndly, Sir Thomas Williams, Knt., and *d.* 1590) he had issue, seven sons and five daus. Sir Anthony Colclough was knighted in 1582. He *d.* 9 Dec. 1584, and was bur. at Tintern, where his monument and epitaph are still to be seen. He was *s.* by his son,
SIR THOMAS COLCLOUGH, Knt. of Tintern Abbey, J.P., who was *b.* 1 April, 1564. He *m.* 1st, Martha, dau. of Adam Loftus Arch-

Colclough. THE LANDED GENTRY. 120

bishop of Armagh, Lord Chancellor, by whom (who *d.* 19 March, 1609) he had issue, six sons and five daus.,
1. Thomas, *d.s.p.* before March, 1609.
2. ADAM (Sir), his heir.
3. John, of Pouldarrig, living 1642; *m.* Katherine, dau. of Sir William Synnott, Knt. of Rosegarland, co. Wexford, by whom he had two sons; 1. Adam, *a.s.p.* 1652; 2. Anthony, *d.* young, before 1649; and four daus.: 1. Mary, *m.* James Butler, of Cloughnagieragh, co. Wexford; 2. Martha, *m.* Thomas Cullen, of Cullenstown, co. Wexford; 3. Clara, a nun; 4. Katherine, *d. unm.*
4. Richard, living 1624, *d.s.p.*
5. Leonard, *d.s.p.*
6. Anthony, *d.s.p.*
1. Anne, *m.* 1st, Nicholas Bagenal, of Dunleckney, co. Carlow, and 2ndly, Sir Thomas Butler, Bart. of Garryhundon, same co.
2. Jane, *m.* John Wogan, of Woxton Hall, co. Pembroke.
3. Martha, *m.* John Pigott, of Dysart, Queen's Co.
4. Eleanor, *m.* Brian Kavanagh, of Poulmonty, co. Wexford, and Borris, co. Carlow.
5. Mary, *m.* Sir Nicholas Walshe, Knt. of Ballycarrigmore, co. Wexford.

Sir Thomas *m.* 2ndly, 1612, Eleanor, dau. of Dudley Bagenal, of Dunleckney, co. Carlow, by whom (who *m.* 2ndly, Luke, 1st Earl of Fingall, and *d.* 1632) he had further issue, with a dau. Mabal, *d. unm.*, two sons,
7. Dudley, of Monart, co. Wexford, *b.* 1613; *m.* 1st, Katherine, dau. of Patrick Esmonde, of the House of Johnstown, and 2ndly, Mary, dau. of Sir Patrick Barnewall, Bart. of Crickstown, and *d.* in France, 1663, having had by his first wife with two younger sons, Lawrence and Thomas, who *d.s.p.*, an elder son,

Patrick, of Duffrey Hall, D.L., co. Wexford, High Sheriff 1688, M.P. for Enniscorthy 1689; *m.* Katherine, dau. of Col. Walter Bagenal, of Dunleckney, co. Callow. and by her (who *d.* 6 Nov. 1700) he left at his decease, 1691, four sons and two daus.,
(1) Dudley, of Duffrey Hall, *m.* Nov. 1691, Mary, dau. of Hon. Francis Barnewall, of Begstown 4th son of Nicholas, 1st Viscount Kingsland, by whom (who subsequently *m.* Benjamin Flaherty, of Dublin, and *d.* Dec. 1725) he left at his decease, 12 July, 1712, six sons and two daus.,
1. CÆSAR, of whom hereafter, as successor to Tintern Abbey.
2. Francis, in the Irish Brigade in France *d.s.p.*
3. Thomas, *m.* Frances, dau. of Cæsar Colclough, of Rosegarland, and had an only son, Adam, "English Adam," *d. unm.* 1759.
4. John, ancestor of COLCLOUGH, of Ballytiege, extinct in the male line.
5. HENRY, of Kildavin, co. Carlow, the ancestor of Lieut.-Col. COLCLOUGH, the heir male of the family.
6. Dudley, *d. unm.* 1739.
1. Margaret, *m.* Charles Byrne, of Kilmocar, co. Kilkenny.
2. Mary Anne, *m.* 29 Nov. 1717, John Byrne, of Cabinteely, co. Dublin.
(2) Adam, of Boley, co. Wexford, *m.* 1st, 1701, Margaret, dau. of Richard Masterton, of Moneyseed, co. Wexford, by whom he had two sons: 1. Patrick, of Dunmain, *m.* Katherine Harper, and *d.s.p.* 29 April, 1770; 2. Richard, *d.s.p.* 1736; and three daus.: 1. Catherine; 2. Frances; 3. Thomasina. He *m.* 2ndly, 1720, Mary, dau. of Andrew Forde, of Ballyfad, co. Wexford, and *d.* March, 1734, having had issue by her, four sons and two daus.: 3. Anthony; 4. Cæsar; 5. Adam. 6. Thomas; 4. Elinor, *d.* young; 5. Mary, *m.* Samuel Turner, of Wexford.
(3) Thomas, *d.s.p.*, killed in a duel in Wexford, 1690.
(4) Patrick, *d.s.p.*, accidentally killed by his gun.
(1) Elizabeth, *m.* John Nugent, of Castle Nugent, co. Longford.
(2) Katherine, *d. unm.*

8. Anthony, of Rathlin, *m.* Mary, dau. of William Esmonde, of Johnstown, co. Wexford, M.P. for Wexford 1634, and had (with a dau. *m.* James Butler, of Ballinleg) two sons,
1. Adam, of Gray's Inn, London, *m.* Mary, dau. of Col. Thomas Blague, Groom of the Chamber to CHARLES II, Maid of Honour to Anne, Duchess of York, celebrated by Count de Grammont, as " Ses paupières blondes," by whom he had a son,
William, of Gray's Inn, *d.s.p.*
2. Cæsar, of Rosegarland, M.P. for Taghmon 1719, whose will, dated 24 April, 1724, was proved in 1726. He *m.* by licence, dated 11 March, 1686, Mary, dau. of William Ivory, of New Ross, co. Wexford, by whom (who *d.* 1697) he had issue, one son, Anthony, of Ballysop, who *m.* Elizabeth, dau. of William Fitzgerald, of the Little Island, co. Waterford, and *d.s.p.* 1728 ; and six daus.: 1. Frances, *m.* her cousin Thomas Colclough; 2. Margaret, *d. unm.* 1697; 3. Eleanor Maria, *m.* William Sutton, of Longraige, co. Wexford; 4. Mary, *d. unm.*; 5. Mabel, *d. unm.*; 6. Anne, *d. unm.*

Sir Thomas Colclough, who was knighted 24 Oct. 1591, *d.* 23 Aug. 1624, and was buried at Tintern. His eldest son to survive was

SIR ADAM COLCLOUGH, 1st bart. of Tintern Abbey, *b.* 1600, High Sheriff co. Wexford 1630; created a bart. 21 July, 1628. He *m.* (settlements dated 26 March, 1623) Alice, dau. of Sir Robert Rich, Knt., Master in Chancery in England, and *d.* 4 April, 1637, when he was *s.* by his only son,

SIR CÆSAR COLCLOUGH, 2nd bart. of Tintern Abbey, *b.* 1642; *m.* Frances, dau. of Sir William Clarke, Bart. of Thame. co. Oxford, and *d.* 22 June, 1614, leaving a dau., MARGARET, of whom hereafter, and one son, his successor,

SIR CÆSAR COLCLOUGH, 3rd bart. of Tintern Abbey, *d.s.p.* 22 Sept. 1687, when the title became extinct, and the estates devolved on his only sister,

MARGARET COLCLOUGH, *m.* 1st, Oct. 1673, Robert Leigh, of Rosegarland, who thereupon assumed the surname of COLCLOUGH; and 2ndly, 1696, John Pigott, of Kinfinney, co. Limerick, who also assumed the surname of COLCLOUGH, and *d.* 8 May, 1717. She *d.s.p.* 23 April, 1723, when she was *s.* at Tintern by her kinsman and heir male,

CÆSAR COLCLOUGH, of Tintern Abbey, eldest son of Dudley Colclough, of Duffrey Hall, *b.* 1696, Col. Wexford Militia, M.P. for Wexford 1727; *m.* 1st, by licence, dated 20 Jan. 1717, Frances Muschamp, dau. of Sir Thomas Vesey, 1st bart. of Knapton, Bishop of Ossory, by whom (who *d.* 1719) he had an only dau., Margaret, who *d.* young. He *m.* 2ndly, 18 July, 1721, Henrietta, dau. of Agmondisham Vesey, of Lucan, co. Dublin, by whom (who *d.* 7 Dec. 1771), he had issue,
1. Cæsar, *b.* 1722, *d.s.p.v.p.*
2. Vesey, *b.* 1724, *m.* Mary, dau. of Sir John Bingham, Bart. of Castlebar, and widow of Hugh Montgomery (who *d.* 6 Feb. 1745); he *d.* 1 Feb. 1745, and was father of a posthumous son,
VESEY, who *s.* his grandfather.
3. Dudley, *d.s.p.v.p.*
4. Agmondisham Vesey, Capt. in the Army, killed in a duel, *unm.* 1758.
5. Adam, of Duffrey Hall, J.P. co. Wexford, High Sheriff 1769; *m.* by licence, dated 31 Jan. 1753, Mary Ann, dau. of John Byrne, of Cabinteely, co. Dublin (his will dated 17 Nov. 1793, was proved 9 Jan. 1800), he *d.* 1799, leaving issue,
1. Cæsar, Barrister-at-Law, Chief Justice of Prince Edward's Island and Newfoundland, *b.* 1754; *m.* 27 Oct. 1804, Susan, dau. of James Leech, of St. James's, Westminster, and *d.* 10 Feb. 1822, having by her (who *d.* 4 Nov. 1851) had issue,
(1) Edward, *b.* in Newfoundland, 1807, *d.* an infant.
(2) Louisa Ponsonby, *b.* 13 July, 1809; *d. unm.* 25 May, 1833.
(3) MARY GREY WENTWORTH, of Tintern Abbey, *s.* as heir general of the family at the death of her kinsman, Cæsar Colclough, of Tintern Abbey, in 1842.
2. Agmondisham, *d.s.p.v.p.*
3. Dudley (Rev.), of Enniscorthy Castle, co. Wexford, *b.* 1766; *m.* by licence (d. 1 March, 1802), Mary, dau. of Luke Gavan, of Dublin, and *d.* Aug. 1830, having had issue,
(1) Cæsar Dudley, *d. unm.* Feb. 1833,
(2) Luke Gavan, *d. unm.* April, 1833.
(3) Agmondisham Vesey, of Newtown Barry, co. Wexford, *m.* 1836, Matilda Barker, dau. of John Jackson, Liverpool, and *d.* 1840, leaving by her (who *m.* 2ndly, Rev. William Sherrard, Rector of Castle Lyons, co. Cork) a son, Cæsar Dudley, *b.* 6. March, 1840, *d.* May, 1841, and two daus., Mary Louisa, *d.* young; and Matilda Mary, *m.* 15 July, 1875, John George Nason of Terramount, J.P. co. Cork.
(1) Mary Louisa, *d. unm.* Nov. 1832.
4. John, *d. unm.* in Portugal, 1792.
5. SARSFIELD, who became heir male of the family on the death of his kinsman, Cæsar Colclough, of Tintern Abbey.
6. Adam, Capt. Royal Artillery, *d. unm.* 1795.
6. Thomas (Rev.), D.D., of Kilmagee, co. Kildare, *m.* 17 July, 1759, Florence, dau. of Hon. Bysse Molesworth, by whom he had, 1. Cæsar, of 36th Regt., *d.s.p.* Administration granted 19 Jan. 1792.
1. Florence, *d. unm.*
2. Harriett, *m.* Col. Jonas Watson, who was killed by the rebels on the Three Rock Mountain, co. Wexford, May, 1798.
Rev. Dr. Colclough *m.* 2ndly, 1769, Charlotte Hartstronge, and had further issue. three daus..
3. Charlotte Maria, *m.* William Burroughs, of Dublin, solicitor.
4. Mary Anne, *m.* Arthur Thomas, of Newton, co. Kildare.
5. Sarah, *m.* May, 1793, Thomas M'Glathry, of Holyhead, Merchant.
7. Richard, Capt. 7th Dragoons, Town Major of Galway; *m.* 1771, Mary, sister of Rev. Thomas Moore O'Meara, of Ballyandra, co. Tipperary, and had issue, four sons, who *d.s.p.*, and three daus.,
1. Frances, *m.* Joseph Johnstone, M.D.
2. Anne, *m.* Cæsar Colclough, of Athy, co. Kildare, and Portobello, co. Wexford.
3. Harriett, *m.* 15 July, 1766, William Thomas, of Brookville, co. Kilkenny.
4. Mary, *d. unm.*
5. Margaret, *d. unm.*
6. Lora, *d. unm.*

Col. Colclough *d.* 15 April, 1766, and was *s.* by his grandson,

VESEY COLCLOUGH, of Tintern Abbey, M.P. co. Wexford, High Sheriff 1767, *b.* 1 July, 1745; *m.* 2 Aug. 1765, Katherine, dau. of John Grogan, of Johnstown, co. Wexford, by whom (who *d.* 25 April, 1783) he had issue,
1. CÆSAR, his heir.
2. John, M.P., co. Wexford, *b.* 3 Dec. 1767; *d. unm.*, shot in a duel, by William Congreve Alcock, of Wilton, 30 May, 1807.
3. Vesey, *b.* 1769; *d.* 1770.

Mr. Colclough (who was known in the co. Wexford as "Sir Vesey") *d.* 8 July, 1794, and was *s.* by his eldest son,

CÆSAR COLCLOUGH, of Tintern Abbey, M.P. co. Wexford, *b.* 8 May, 1766; *m.* 30 Nov. 1818, Jane Stratford, dau. of John Kirwan, Barrister, and by her (who *m.* 2ndly, Thomas Boyse, of Bannow, and *d.* 4 May, 1878) had no issue. He *d.* 23 Aug. 1824, when Tintern Abbey and the estates descended to (and after some litigation on the part of his widow), were settled on his second cousin and heiress at law,

MARY GREY WENTWORTH ROSSBOROUGH-COLCLOUGH, of Tintern Abbey, co. Wexford, only surviving dau. and heiress of Cæsar Colclough, of Duffrey Hall; *s.* her father, 1822, and her kinsman 1842; *b.* 9 July, 1811; *m.* 12 Jan. 1848, JOHN THOMAS ROSSBOROUGH, of Mullinagood, co. Longford, eldest son of John Rossborough, of Nicholson's Court and Clancaulfield House, co. Longford, and

grandson of Hugh Rossborough, of Mullingoan, co. Fermanagh, by Margaret, his 1st wife, dau. of John Nicholson, of Nicholson's Court and Clancaulfield House (*see* BURKE'S *Family Records*, CROZIER). He was a J.P., D.L., co. Wexford, and High Sheriff 1860, and assumed by Royal Licence, dated 3 June, 1853, the additional surname and arms of COLCLOUGH, and *d.* 11 Aug. 1869. Mrs. Colclough *d.* 3 Nov. 1884, leaving,
1. LOUISE MARIA SUSANNA COLCLOUGH, now of Tintern Abbey.
2. Susanna Frances Julia, *m.* 14 Nov. 1872, John Lloyd, of Gloster, D.L. King's Co., who *d.* 26 Jan. 1883, leaving issue. Mrs. Lloyd *d.* 1886.
3. Mary Grey Wentworth Fanning.
4. Belinda Powell Leech Trumble.

Arms—Quarterly: 1st and 4th arg., five eaglets displayed in cross sa. (for COLCLOUGH); 2nd and 3rd per pale vert and az. an eagle displayed erm. armed and beaked between four trefoils, slipped or (for BIDDULPH). *Crests*—1st, COLCLOUGH: A demi-eagle displayed sa. ducally gorged or; 2nd, BIDDULPH: A wolf rampant arg. guttê de sang, gorged with a bar gemel az., and charged with a trefoil slipped ppr. *Motto*—His calcabo gentes.

Seat—Tintern Abbey, Ballycullane, New Ross, co. Wexford.

COLE OF WOODVIEW.

THOMAS WILLOUGHBY COLE, of Woodview, Innishannon, co. Cork, M.B., Trin. Coll. Dub., *b.* 23 April, 1862.

Lineage.—JOHN COLE, went to Ireland about 1614, and settled at Ballishannon, co. Donegal, and was father of
WILLIAM COLE, an Officer in OLIVER CROMWELL'S Army, who was father of
JOHN COLE, *b.* about 1650, whose son,
WILLIAM COLE, Captain in the Army, was living at Mallow, co. Cork, in 1730. He *m.* Ann, dau. and heir of Col. Bartholomew Purdon, of Ballyclough, co. Cork, M.P. for Doneraile, and widow of Robert Coote, of Ballyclough, brother of Sir George Coote, and had a son,
JOHN COLE, of Cork, *m.* 1st, Ann, dau. of Ringrose Atkins, of Firville, co. Cork, by whom he had one son,
1. John Atkins, who *d. unm.*
He *m.* 2ndly, Mary Fisher, of Charleville, same co., and had issue,
2. Alexander, *b.* 16 July, 1756; *d.* young.
3. JOHN, of whom hereafter.
4. Charles, of Cork, *b.* 6 Oct. 1765; *m.* 1786, Sarah, dau. of John Harding, of Ballingohig, co. Cork, and *d.* 26 Oct. 1813, having had issue,
 1. John, *d.* young.
  1. Katherine, *d.* 5 July, 1844.
  2. Louisa, *d.* 24 Aug. 1872.
  3. Harriett, *d. unm.* 10 Nov. 1879.
  4. Eliza, *d.* 1829.   5. Caroline, *d.* 3 Aug. 1876.
5. Christopher, of Cheltenham, Capt. North Cork Rifles (Militia), High Sheriff of Cork City 1803, *b.* 8 Dec. 1767; *m.* June, 1790, Elizabeth, dau. of Samuel Allin, of Youghal, and *d.* 24 Aug. 1850, having had two sons, both of whom *d.* young. She *d.* 23 Aug. 1831.
6. Thomas (Rev.), A.M., *b.* 8 Oct. 1769; *m.* 1794, Louisa, dau. of Rev. John Blennerhassett, Rector of Tralee, and *d.s.p.* Sept. 1830.
7. William, Surveyor of the Customs at Cork, *b.* 16 Jan. 1776; *m.* Jane, dau. of John Young, of Bantry, and sister of General P. Young, distinguished at the siege of Seringapatam. He had, with two sons who *d.* young,
 1. Phillis Jane, *m.* 21 Nov. 1826, Rev. Thomas Lloyd Coghlan, D.D., Vicar of Ballyspillane, in the Diocese of Ross, and had issue.
 2. Mary.
1. Grace, *b.* 6 Dec. 1754; *d.* young.
2. Mary, *b.* 2 Feb. 1758; *m.* Thomas Gonnell, of Cork.
3. Grace, *b.* 11 Dec. 1761.
4. Ann, *b.* 15 Feb. 1764; *m.* Thomas Harding, of Ballingohig, Mayor of Cork 1808, who *d.s.p.* 1824.
5. Susan, *b.* 6 Jan. 1772; *m.* William Smith, of Cork.
The eldest surviving son,
JOHN COLE, of Oldwood, co. Cork, *b.* 4 Feb. 1760; *m.* Margaret, dau. of Samuel Allin, of Youghal, and had issue,
1. John, *d. unm.*   2. Samuel Allin, *d. unm.*
3. Charles, R.N., a gallant naval officer, *d. unm.*
4. Christopher, *d.* young.
5. THOMAS CHRISTOPHER, of whom hereafter.
1. Sarah Grace, *m.* Dec. 1838, Capt. Hugh Forbes, 45th Regt., and *d.* 22 Oct. 1874.
2. Eliza, *d. unm.* 16 July, 1850.
3. Anne Margaretta, *m.* 25 Nov. 1828, Walter Williams Harris, M.D., 6th son of James Harris, B.A., of Barry's Hall, co. Cork, and *d.* 27 Feb. 1830.
Mr. Cole *d.* 1826. His only surviving son,
THOMAS CHRISTOPHER COLE, of Woodview, Innishannon, co. Cork, J.P., *b.* 14 Feb. 1807; *m.* 1830, Harriett Jane, only dau. of Charles Bodrick Garde, of Ballindiniss, co. Cork, by Harriet his wife, eldest dau. of Maj. Henry Croker, of Quartertown House, Mallow, and by her (who *d.* 21 March, 1892) had issue,
1. JOHN HARDING (Rev.), of whom next.
2. Charles Christopher, Capt. 80th Regt., *b.* 15 May, 1844; *d.* (by accident, while Government Agent in Queensland) 26 Aug. 1888.
3. Christopher Dillon Croker, M.D., *b.* 17 June, 1846.
1. Harriette Mary.

2. Eliza Sarah Emily, *m.* 8 Aug. 1882, the Very Rev. Thomas Brisbane Warren, A.M., Dean of York, and Rector of St. Fin Barr's, formerly Rector of St. Peter's and Precentor of Cork, eldest son of Brisbane Warren, of Woodview, Union Hall, co. Cork. He *d.* 8 Jan. 1894.
Mr. Cole *d.* 20 Jan. 1877. The eldest son,
REV. JOHN HARDING COLE, of Woodview, Innishannon, co. Cork, A.B., T.C.D., Rector and Vicar of Leighmoney, Diocese of Cork, formerly Lieut. South Cork Light Infantry, *b.* 18 Sept. 1831; *m.* 1st, 19 July, 1859, Adelaide Ann, dau. of George Culloden Frend, of Rutha, co. Limerick, and Rosetta, co. Cork (*see* FREND *of Roolcagh*), and by her (who *d.* 17 June, 1892) has issue,
1. THOMAS WILLOUGHBY, now of Woodview.
2. George Frend, *b.* 14 June, 1867; *d.* 5 April, 1881.
1. Letitia Victoria, *m.* 27 April, 1886, Dr. Quintin Richard Darling, son of Richard Sisson Darling, of Trinidad.
2. Hariette Mary Adelaide, *m.* 10 Aug. 1899, Harry James Neill, son of H. J. Neill, of Rockport, co. Down.
The Rev. J. H. Cole *m.* 2ndly, 11 Jan. 1900, Dorothea Emily Morton, youngest dau. of Rev. Thomas Olden, D.D., Vicar of Ballyclough, Mallow, co. Cork, and *d.* 15 May, 1909.

Seat—Woodview, Innishannon, co. Cork.

COLE. *See* BURKE'S PEERAGE, **ENNISKILLEN**, E.

COLE-HAMILTON. *See* **HAMILTON.**

COLHOUN OF CARRICKBALDOEY.

LIEUT.-COL. CHARLES KING COLHOUN, of Carrickbaldoey, co. Donegal, late Maj. (84th) York and Lancaster Regt., *b.* 12 Oct. 1858; *m.* 11 Oct. 1900, Flora, eldest dau. of Col. E. P. Mainwaring, Indian Army, by Florentia Ann, his wife, eldest dau. of Brig.-Gen. F. Brind, C.B., Bengal Horse Artillery, and has issue, a son, *b.* 3 Nov. 1909.

Lineage.—The Laird of Luss (Alexander Colquhoun) on the Plantation of Ulster had a grant in the co. of Doneal of 1,000 acres called Corkagh. He appears to have been accompanied to Ireland by several members of his clan. He was made a denizen of Ireland by the name of Sir Alexander Colquhoun, of Corkagh, in the co. Donegal, Knt. by Patent, dated 20 May 15 JAC I, which also includes the name of Daniel Colquhoun of Corkie, co. Donegal. In the same year the Laird of Luss was succeeded by his son, Sir John Colquhoun of Luss, created a baronet in 1625. By Patent dated 14 July, 1630, another member of the family, Robert Colquhoune (probably Robert Colquhoun, afterwards of Camstradden) was granted letters of denization together with Corkagh, which was then created the Manor of Corkagh, with the usual manorial rights. Part of the lands were subsequently acquired by Humphrey and Robert Galbraith, who by deed dated 1 May, 1654, conveyed, among other denominations of land, the quarter of Corkagh and Lebindish, and the town and lands of Carrickballydown, *alias* Carrickballyduff to Sir John Calhowne, Junior, Knt. and Bart. (of Luss). The last-mentioned lands have been for over a century in the possession of the King family, ancestors of the present Colhoun family, who would appear to descend from some of the junior branches who settled in Ireland.
JOHN COLHOUN, of Carrickballydine, 1718, son of — Colhoun and Susanna Leslie (?) his wife, left issue, a son,
CHARLES COLHOUN, of Letterkenny, admon. granted to his son 12 Jan. 1761, *m.* Mary, dau. of Charles King, of Letterkenny (will dated 17 May, 1736), and sister of John King, of Brownstown, co. Kildare (will dated 16 Nov. 1761, proved 19 March, 1779), and of Rev. Andrew King, of Dublin (will dated 23 May, 1786). They had issue a son,
CHARLES COLHOUN, of Letterkenny, co. Donegal, *b.* 20 Nov. 1738; *m.* 1st (setts. dated 4 April, 1766), Jane, dau. of David Richardson, of Oaklands, co. Tyrone, and by her (who *d.* 2 Jan. 1774) had issue,
1. Margaret, *m.* Brooke Chambers, of Rockhill, co. Donegal.
2. Jane Mary, *m.* Sir John Magennis, Mayor of Londonderry, knighted by GEORGE IV., 30 Aug. 1821.
He *m.* 2ndly, Mary, dau. of Thomas Grove, of Castlegrove. By her he had a son,
1. CHARLES, his heir.
The only son,

CHARLES COLHOUN, b. 10 March, 1780; m. 22 July, 1806, Anne (b. 23 Oct. 1785), eldest dau. of Rev. Dr. John Ellison, Rector of Cleenish (see ELLISON-MACARTNEY of *Mountjoy Grange*), by Anne his wife, dau. of John Olphert (see OLPHERT of *Ballyconnell*) and Letitia his wife, dau. of Rev. Andrew Hamilton, D.D., and Sarah his wife, only dau. and heiress of Henry Conyngham, of Castle Conyngham, co. Derry. Charles Colhoun d. about 1817 (will dated 25 May, 1804, proved 18 May, 1817). By her (who d. 22 May, 1833) he left issue,
1. CHARLES KING, of whom presently.
1. Anne, b. 15 Aug. 1807; m. (setts. 17 Oct. 1835) John Chambers, of Foxhall, who d. 1865, leaving issue.
2. Mary, b. 10 Sept. 1808, m. Henry Maunsell, M.D., and d. 6 June, 1835, leaving issue.
3. Margaret, b. 20 Feb. 1812; m. John Macartney, Barrister-at-Law, and had issue.
4. Henrietta, b. 12 Dec. 1813; m. Robert Little, M.D., and had issue.
The only son,
CHARLES KING COLHOUN, of Carrickballydoey, b. 30 Jan. 1811; m. 15 Oct. 1833, Ellen (b. 12 July, 1813), dau. of G. Alcock and Sophia Jane his wife, dau. of George Lowther, of Kilcrue (see LOWTHER of *Shrigley Park*). He d. 13 Sept. 1836 (will dated 17 Oct. 1835, proved 9 May, 1837). She d. 28 Nov. 1888, leaving issue an only child,
CHARLES KING COLHOUN, of Carrickballydoey, co. Donegal. sometime Capt. and Hon. Maj. Royal Tyrone Fusiliers, b. 2 Sept. 1834; m. 22 July, 1856, Lydia, dau. of Rev. G. N. Tredennick, of Kildoney and Woodhill Ardara, co. Donegal, by Lydia his wife, dau. of the Most Rev. William Magee, Archbishop of Dublin. He d. 19 Dec. 1880, leaving issue,
1. CHARLES KING, his heir.
1. Alice Lydia Sophia Tredennick.
2. Edith Wilhelmina.

Arms—Per pale arg. and sa. a saltire between four mullets counterchanged. **Crest**—A buck's head erased per pale vert and arg. charged with two mullets in pale counterchanged. *Motto*—Viget sub cruce.
Club—Naval and Military.

COLLINS (now ALDWORTH) OF ARDNALEE.

MRS. LENA STEPHANIE ALDWORTH, of Ardnalee, co. Cork, elder dau. and co-heir of John Stephen Collins (see below), s. her father 15 Feb. 1906; m. 27 Aug. 1901, Major John Oliver Aldworth, of Newmarket Court, co. Cork (see *that family*).

Lineage.—The first member of this family who appears to have settled and obtained lands in Ireland was
JOHN COLLINS, one of the '49 Officers (*i.e.* an Officer of the Protestant Army of CHARLES I, disbanded in 1649), who obtained lands, in satisfaction of arrears of pay, a grant of lands in the co. and city of Limerick, under the Patent, dated 22 March, 1666, made to the Earls of Roscommon and Orrery, in trust for him and other officers. He was s. by
JOHN COLLINS, of Ballynoe, co. Limerick, afterwards of Rathcoole, co. Cork, who made his will 22 July, 1708. He obtained the lands of Rathcoole the following year, and was s. by his son,
STEPHEN COLLINS, of Rathcoole, who m. Jane Purdin, and d. before 1763, leaving a son and heir,
JAMES COLLINS, of Rathcoole, who m. 4 Feb. 1758, Diana, dau. and heiress of Abraham Coakley, by whom he acquired lands in the co. Wexford, which had been granted to her ancestor, Capt. Thomas Coakley, 28 June, 22 CHARLES II. He made his will, 20 July, 1770, which was proved in 1772, and was s. by his son,
JOHN COLLINS, of Gurteenard, co. Cork, b. 1761; m. 1795, Mary, eldest dau. of William Allen, of Greenfield, co. Cork, by Anne his wife, dau. and co-heir of William Philpot, of Dromaghly, same co., and d. 28 July, 1808, leaving by her (who d. 1816) a son and successor,
STEPHEN COLLINS, of Merrion Square, Dublin, Barrister-at-Law, Q.C., b. 10 June, 1799; m. Jan. 1831, Francis, dau. of William Henn, Master in Chancery, by Susanna his wife, sister of Sir Jonathan Lovett, Bart., of Liscombe, Bucks, and d. 13 Sept. 1843, leaving by her (who d. 31 Jan. 1842),
1. JOHN STEPHEN, of Ardnalee.
2. William Henry, Maj. R.E.; m. Alice, dau. of E. B. Bradley, of Cromwell Road, S.W., and d. 1880, leaving issue.
Alice Margaret.

3. Richard Henn (The Right Hon. Sir), BARON COLLINS, of Kensington (created 6 March, 1907) a Life Peer and a Lord of Appeal in Ordinary 1907-1910, P.C. (1897), Fellow of Downing Coll, Camb. 1865, M.A. 1898, Hon. Fellow 1880, Hon. LL.D. 1902, Barrister-at-Law 1867, Q.C. 1883, Bencher 1885, Judge of the High Court, Queen's Bench Division 1891, Lord Justice of the Court of Appeal 1897, and Master of the Rolls 1901-1907, Member of the Venezuela Arbitration Tribunal 1898, b. 1842; m. 1868, Jane (3, *Bramham Gardens, S.W.*), dau. of Very Rev. Ogle William Moore, Dean of Clogher, and d. 3 Jan. 1911, leaving issue,
1. Richard Henn (Hon.), D.S.O., Capt. Royal Berks Regt., served in S. African War 1899-1902 (despatches, Queen's medal with three clasps and King's medal with two clasps) (*Army and Navy Club*), b. 2 April, 1873; m. 17 June, 1909, May Eveline, youngest dau. of late Herbert Glendinning Bambridge, of Solihull, co. Warwick, and has issue,
Richard Henn, b. 20 April, 1911.
2. Stephen Ogle Henn (Hon.) (28, *Beaufort Gardens, S.W.*; 4, *Brick Court, Temple, E.C.*), m. 14 Dec. 1899, Agnes Julia, dau. of Frederick Lambert, of Garratts Hall, Banstead (see *that family*), and has issue,
(1) John Stephen, b. 21 May, 1903.
(1) Mary Pamela, b. 1901.
(2) Agnes Patience, b. 1907.
(3) Barbara Margaret, b. 1910.
1. Frances Helen (Hon.), m. 1 Nov. 1905, Rev. Henry Henn, M.A. (*Reedley Lodge, Burnley*), Bishop Suffragan of Burnley, and Hon. Canon of Manchester, youngest son of late Thomas Rice Henn, of Paradise Hill, co. Clare, J.P., D.L. (see *that family*).
2. Hilda Jane (Hon.), m. 30 Jan. 1906, Rev. John Arthur Garton, M.A., Vicar of St. Paul's, Mill Hill (*The Vicarage, Mill Hill, N.W.*), and has issue.
3. Mary Brenda Nepenthe (Hon.), m. 7 Dec. 1905, William Claude Frederick Vaudrey-Barker-Mill, of Mottisfont Abbey Hants, and has issue.
1. Susan Henn, m. 1861, George Alexander, of Milford, co. Carlow, and d. July, 1895, leaving issue.
2. Frances Ellinor. *d.s.p.*
The eldest son,
JOHN STEPHEN COLLINS, of Ardnalee, co. Cork, J.P., b. 14 March, 1834, called to the Bar 1858; m. 16 April, 1873, Henrietta Cecil (*Dhu Corrig, Ardmore, Youghal*), dau. of Henry William Wray, and grand-dau. of John James Wray, of Castle Wray, co. Donegal, and d. 15 Feb. 1906, having had issue,
1. LENA STEPHANIE, now of Ardnalee.
2. Olive Susan, m. 28 April, 1903, Thomas Somerville Reeves, of Glandore House, co. Cork, and of Dromore House, Douglas, Cork.

Arms—Arg. two lions combatant ppr., on a chief az. a pelican of the first, vulning herself gu. **Crest**—A pelican as in the arms, gorged with a plain collar az. *Motto*—Dant vulnera vitam.
Seat—Ardnalee, Carrigrohane, co. Cork.

COOKE-COLLIS OF CASTLE COOKE.

COL. WILLIAM COOKE-COLLIS, C.M.G., of Castle Cooke, co. Cork, J.P. and D.L., High Sheriff, co. Cork 1907, Lieut.-Col. late Royal Irish Rifles, formerly Lieut.-Col. and Hon. Col. Commanding 9th Batt. King's Royal Rifle Corps (North Cork Militia), served in the Afghan War 1879-80 (despatches, medal), Soudan Campaign 1885 (despatches, medal with clasp, bronze star), and in South African War 1899-1901 (despatches, medal with four clasps, C. M. G.), Aide-de-Camp to the King, b. 1 Aug. 1847; m. 6 Nov. 1875, Katherine Maria, dau. of Col. James Oliphant, R.E., of Worlington Hall, Suffolk, and by her (who d. 27 Jan. 1891) has issue,
1. WILLIAM JAMES NORMAN, Capt. Royal Irish Rifles, served in South Africa and wounded at Dewetsdorp 1900 (despatches), b. 7 May, 1876; m. 1905, Cleonice, dau. of Major G. F. Gamble, and has issue, a dau., b. 10 March, 1907.
2. Maurice Talbot, b. 5 July, 1879.
1. Nora, m. 31 Oct. 1906, Major Arthur Johnston Allardyce, The

Lancashire Fusiliers, son. of Col. Allardyce, of Culquoich, Aberdeenshire.
2. Katherine Sophia, m. 25 Jan. 1905, Thomas St. John Grant, of Kilmurav, co. Cork.
3. Geraldine, m. 18 Aug. 1904, Capt. James S. FitzGerald, The Royal Irish Regt.

Col. Cooke - Collis m. 2ndly, 4 Sept. 1894, Elizabeth Marian Shrubsole, eldest dau. of the late Edward Cunliffe, of 66, The Drive, Brighton, and by her has issue,
3. Edward Cunliffe, b. 27 Oct. 1902.
4. Philip William, b. 3 July, 1900.
4. Elizabeth Susan.
5. Mary Doreen.
6. Diana Florence, b. 20 Nov. 1904.

Lineage.—PETER COOKE was resident in co. Cork before the war of 1641. By Margaret his wife he had several sons, all young when the war broke out, viz.,
1. THOMAS, of whom presently.
2. Robert, Capt., had issue,
  1. Robert, known for his eccentricity, and by the appellation of " Linen Cooke."
  2. William, of Youghal, who was a merchant.
3. Edward, ancestor of the COOKES of Kiltynan Castle, co. Tipperary.
4. Peter, resided at Tallagh, in the co. Waterford, and from him are descended the family of COOKE of Cordangan, co. Tipperary, and that of COOKE of Fort William, in the same co.

The eldest son,
THOMAS COOKE, an Officer in Lord Brogbill's Cavalry, left issue, three sons and a dau.,
1. THOMAS, of whom presently. 2. Peter.
3. Zachary.
1. Anne.

The eldest,
THOMAS COOKE, a very wealthy merchant in the city of Cork, and a member of the Society of Quakers, m. 29 Sept. 1661, Joan Harwood, and had issue. By his will he directed that he should be interred in the Quaker's burial ground of Cork ; but having gone to London during the wars, he m. 2ndly, Beatrix Datchelor, and was buried with her at St. Andrew-under-Shaft, 1706, where his monument is still preserved. Dungallane, on which was situated an old castle, was subsequently denominated Castle Cooke. He was attainted by the Parliament held under JAMES II, at Dublin, 7 May, 1689. He bequeathed his estates to his only son,
PETER COOKE, of Castle Cooke, co. Cork, m. 23 April, 1696, Elizabeth Mitchell, and had two sons and one dau.,
1. THOMAS, his heir.
2. ZACHARY, who s. his brother Thomas.
1. Elizabeth, m. John Collis, of Cork, eldest surviving son of William Collis (see COLLIS of Tieraclea), by Mary his wife, eldest dau. of the Rev. Benjamin Cross, D.D., and had issue,
  WILLIAM (Rev.), m. his cousin Martha, heiress of Castle Cooke, as hereafter.

The eldest son,
THOMAS COOKE, of Ahada and Castle Cooke, m. Dorothy, dau. of Robert Sheilds, of Wainstown, co. Meath, niece of Clotworthy Sheilds alias Wade, of Clonabrany, and by her left three daus.,
1. Elizabeth, m. Sir Thomas Blackall, and d.s.p.
2. Martha, eventual heiress, m. 22 Nov. 1750, her cousin the Rev. William Collis.
3. Anne, m. W. Cosgrave.

Thomas Cooke was s. by his brother,
ZACHARY COOKE, of Castle Cooke, who, dying unm., was s. by his niece,
MARTHA COOKE, m. her cousin the Rev. William Collis, Rector of Church Hill, and Kilgobben, co. Kerry (who d. 25 May, 1754), son of John Collis, of co. Cork (see COLLIS of Tieraclea), by Elizabeth his wife, only dau. of Peter Cooke, of Castle Cooke (see above), and had issue,
1. ZACHARY, of whom presently.
2. William COLLIS, of Richmond, co. Waterford, and Mountford Lodge, Fermoy, co. Cork, Barrister-at-Law, m. Jane, eldest dau. of Peter Carey, of Careysville, co. Cork, and d. 22 April, 1839, leaving issue,
  1. John, Lieut. 61st Regt., present at Talavera and Salamanca, in which battle he had both eyes shot out ; d. unm. 31 Oct. 1840.
  2. Peter, of Mountford Lodge, Fermoy, Capt. 95th Regt., b. 4 July, 1793 ; m. 19 June, 1843, Elizabeth Mitchell, dau. of John Carey, of South Creg, Fermoy. She d. Dec. 1884. He d. 28 Jan. 1871, having had issue,
    (1) William Gun, of Barrymore Lodge, Castle Lyons, co. Cork, Lieut.-Col. (retired) the Queen's Royal West Surrey Regt., b. 16 April, 1845 ; m. 4 Dec. 1890, Mabel Katherine, dau. of Capt. G. Ll. Robson, 5th Dragoon Guards, of Altwood, Berks, and has issue,
      1. William Henry, b. 4 June, 1892.
      2. John George, b. 2 March, 1895.
      1. Marjorie, b. 21 Dec. 1893.
    (2) John George, b. 4 March, 1847 ; d. unm. 26 Oct. 1879.
    (3) Edward Peter, b. 13 April, 1849 ; d. unm. 1887.
    (1) Elizabeth Martha, b. 13 April, 1844 ; d. unm. 24 Nov. 1893.
  3. George Gun (Rev.), d. unm.
  4. Richard, Lieut. 99th Regt., m. Mary Large, and was father of Surg.-Gen. William Collis, who d.s.p.
  5. Zachary, Lieut. South Cork Militia, d. unm.

1. Martha, m. William Large.
1. Martha, d. unm.

The elder son,
THE REV. ZACHARY COOKE-COLLIS, Archdeacon of Cloyne, s. to the Castle Cooke estate, and assumed the additional surname of COOKE. He m. 1782, Jane, dau. of Charles Leslie, M.D., of the city of Cork, by Anne his wife, dau. of Alderman Lawton, of the same city, and had issue,
1. WILLIAM, of Castle Cooke.
1. Annie Leslie, m. Thomas Perrott, of Upland, co. Cork.
2. Mary Peacock, m. David Barry, M.D., of Fermoy.
3. Sarah Hyde, m. John Perrott, of Limerick.

He was s. by his only son,
WILLIAM COOKE-COLLIS, of Castle Cooke, co. Cork, J.P., Capt. 62nd Regt. and in the North Cork Militia, b. 30 Jan. 1783 ; m. 28 June, 1808, Elizabeth Geraldine De Courcy, eldest dau. of Maurice Uniacke Atkin, of Leadington, co. Cork, and had issue,
1. William, J.P., b. 18 May, 1809 ; m. 11 April, 1836, Sarah, eldest surviving dau. of John Hyde, of Castle Hyde, co. Cork, D.L., and sister and co-heir of John Hyde, formerly of Castle Hyde, and afterwards of Creg, and d. 18 Oct. 1842, leaving three daus., his co-heiresses,
  1. SARAH, m. 20 Sept. 1859, Richard Edward Beck, late Capt. 89th Regt., and of Derwyn, co. Monmouth, who d. 26 Oct. 1887. His widow assumed by Royal Licence dated 22 Dec. 1888, for herself and her issue, the surname and arms of HYDE in lieu of Beck, in compliance with the will of her uncle, John Hyde, of Creg.
  2. Mary Matilda, m. Col. E. D. Smith, Assist. Quartermaster-General, Dublin District, and d. 29 Jan. 1881.
  3. Elizabeth Geraldine, m. 1st, Maj. John McDonald Cuppage, 89th Foot ; and 2ndly, 4 Aug. 1868, Capt. Arthur W. Spens, 71st Regt., 3rd son of Archibald Spens, of Lathallan Park, co. Stirling, and d. 27 Jan. 1896.
2. MAURICE ATKIN (Rev.), s. to Castle Cooke.
3. John Thomas, b. 29 Oct. 1818 ; d. 13 July, 1891.
1. Elizabeth Margaret, m. 1 Sept. 1826, Edward Keily Carey, of Careysville, co. Cork, and d. 13 Sept. 1881, leaving issue.
2. Jane Leslie, m. 22 Oct. 1839, Rev. Jasper Alexander Grant, of Templenoe, Rector of Castle Hyde, and d. 7. Nov. 1892, leaving issue.

Mr. Cooke-Collis d. 22 March, 1867, and was s. by his son,
REV. MAURICE ATKIN COOKE-COLLIS, D.D., of Castle Cooke, co. Cork. Rector of Queenstown, b. 24 March, 1812 ; m. 27 June, 1839, Anne, eldest dau. of the Rev. John Talbot, of Ardfert Abbey, M.A. Camb., 2nd son of William Talbot, of Mount Talbot, co. Roscommon, by his wife, Lady Anne Crosbie, eldest dau. of William, 1st Earl of Glandore, and by her (who d. 10 Dec. 1896) had issue,
1. WILLIAM, his heir.
2. John Talbot, b. 30 May, 1849, B.A. Pem. Coll. Cambridge ; m. 2 April, 1891, Amalie Elizabeth, dau. of John Conrad Reuss, of Upper Long Ditton, Surrey.
3. Maurice Crosbie, Col. (retired) Indian Army, served in Afghan Frontier and China Campaigns (medals), b. 9 Oct. 1850.
  1. Jane Lloyd, m. 1st, 11 Dec. 1866, Nathaniel Cox Barton, R.N., who d. May, 1868 ; and 2ndly, 23 Jan. 1877, James Erskine Oliphant, Bombay Civil Service. He d. 21 Dec. 1909.
  2. Geraldine de Courcy, m. 9 Feb. 1869, Augustus P. Barton, and d. at Bundaberg, Queensland, 6 Jan. 1885.
  3. Annie Talbot Crosbie. 4. Emma Theodosia.

Mr. Cooke Collis d. 8. Dec. 1882.

Arms—Quarterly : 1st and 4th arg. on a chevron engrailed sa. bezantée between three lions' heads erased gu. four barrulets or (COLLIS) ; 2nd and 3rd arg. on a chevron embattled counter-embattled gu. between three tigers' heads erased sa. each charged on the neck with a bar gemel or, three cinquefoils of the last (COOKE). Crest—A cormorant sa. bezantée collared or wings endorsed and inverted preying on a fish ppr. Motto—Mens conscia recti.

Seat—Castle Cooke, Kilworth, co. Cork.

COLLIS OF TIERACLEA.

STEPHEN EDWARD COLLIS, of Tieraclea, co. Kerry, b. 6 Oct. 1872.

Lineage.—WILLIAM COLLIS, an officer in Heriome Sankey's Regt. of Horse, in Cromwell's army, left a son,
JOHN COLLIS, m. Mary, dau. of Philip Corridon, of Kilmacaha, and had a son,
WILLIAM COLLIS, of Lisedoge, co. Kerry, m. 1685, Martha, 2nd dau. of Col. Frederick Mullins, of Ballingobbin (now Burnham), near Dingle, by his wife Jane, 4th dau. of Dean John Eveleigh, by Mildred Caldwell his wife, and had a son,
1. WILLIAM, of whom presently.

He m. 2ndly, 1693, Mary, 2nd dau. of Rev. Dr. Benjamin Cross, Rector of Christ Church, Cork, by Anne his wife, 2nd dau. of Dean John Eveleigh, before mentioned, and had issue,
2. JOHN, m. Elizabeth, dau. of Peter Cooke, and was ancestor of the Castle Cooke branch.
3. Thomas (Rev.), Vicar of Dingle, m. Avis Blennerhassett, of the Ballyseedy family, and left issue, a dau.,
Jane, m. Frederick Mullins, eldest brother of Thomas, 1st Lord Ventry.

Collis. THE LANDED GENTRY. 124

4. Edward, s. his half-brother; m. Ellen, dau of Christopher Hilliard, of Ballygarron, and had issue. He was ancestor of the family of COLLIS of Lismore, co. Kerry.
5. ROBERT, of whom hereafter.
The son of the 1st marriage,
REV. WILLIAM COLLIS, Vicar-General of the Diocese of Ardfert, m. Isabella Galwey (d. 23 Nov. 1771), of the family of GALWEY of Carbery, and d.s.p. 25 May, 1754, leaving all his estates to his half-brother Edward.
ROBERT COLLIS, 5th son of William Collis, by Mary his 2nd wife, m. 1st, Elizabeth Day, dau. of Edward Day, of Tralee; and 2ndly, in 1743, Mary, dau. of Maurice Fitzgerald, Knight of Kerry, by Elizabeth, sister of Maurice Crosbie, 1st Lord Brandon. By his 2nd wife (who m. 2ndly, Thomas Rice, grandfather of Thomas, 1st Lord Mounteagle) he had issue,
1. MAURICE (Rev.), Rector of Kilsallaghan, co. Dublin, m. Anne, dau. of Ambrose Wilson, of Cahirconlish House, co. Limerick, and d.s.p.
2. Thomas, m. 1784, Eliza, 3rd dau. of Thomas Chaytor, of Charlemont Place, Dublin, and d. 17 Aug. 1795, leaving issue,
    1. Thomas (Rev.), d. unm.
    2. William, Lieut. Royal Marines, b. 21 April, 1788; m. Eliza, dau. of William Allan, Barrister-at-Law, and d.s.p. 10 Feb. 1866.
    3. Maurice Fitzgerald, Capt. H.E.I.C.S., b. 18 April, 1790; d. unm. 7 Feb. 1824.
    4. STEPHEN EDWARD, eventually of Tieraclea.
1. Mary, m. 1st, Rev. Samuel Despard, Rector of Tyrrellpass, Westmeath; and 2ndly, Rev. William Drought, Rector of Cloghlane, and d.s.p. 3 Nov. 1869.
3. John Fitzgerald, Deputy Keeper of the Records in Ireland, m. Margaret, dau. of John Day, and by her (who m. 2ndly, 1795, Robert Staveley) left issue,
    1. John Day, d.s.p.
    2. Robert FitzGerald (Rev.), Prebendary of Kilconnel, co. Galway, b. 12 Aug. 1790; m. 24 May, 1815, Maria, dau. of Edward Bourke, of Nun's Island, co. Galway. She d. 27 Jan. 1876. He d. 6 May, 1863, leaving issue,
        (1) John Day (Rev.), D.D., Vicar of Stratford-on-Avon, Fellow of Worcester Coll. Oxford, b. 24 Feb. 1816; m. 1st, 18 June, 1846, Josephine Martha (who d. 16 Oct. 1868), dau. of J. C. Tyler, and 2ndly, 11 Aug. 1871, Elizabeth, widow of Rear-Admiral Douglas Curry, and dau. of Edward Castleman, D.L., of Chettle Manor, Dorset, and d.s.p. 1 April, 1879.
        (2) Robert Denny, b. 16 Jan. 1819; m. 1855, Sophia Frost, of Montreal. She d. 1 Sept. 1866. He d. 8 Oct. 1864, leaving issue,
            1. William Robert FitzGerald, b. 16 Oct. 1857; m. Constance, dau. of — de Winton.
                1. Caroline Amy, d. young.
                2. Evaleen.
        (3) Edward George, b. 11 Aug. 1821; d. 25 March, 1822.
        (4) Maurice Henry, M.D., F.R.C.S.I., b. 15 Oct. 1824; m. 10 Aug. 1852, Sarah Marcella Lyster, dau. of William Jameson, M.D., and d. 28 March, 1869, leaving issue,
            1. Robert William, F.R.C.S.I., b. 8 Aug. 1854; m. Kate, dau. of — Greer, of Ballyoonan, co. Louth.
            2. Maurice Henry FitzGerald (Rev.), B.D., Vicar of Antrim, b. 3 June, 1859; m. 1stly, July, 1889, Constance, dau. of Henry Mitchell, of Drumreaske, co. Monaghan. She d. 28 March, 1902, having had issue,
                a. Maurice Fitzgerald, b. 18 March, 1898.
                a. Lucy Helena.   b. Edith Sara.
                c. Constance Blanche Mary. d. Geraldine Maud.
                e. Kathleen Margaret.   f. Honora Frances.
            He m. 2ndly, 19 April, 1910, Ida Kathleen, dau. of Wakefield Dixon, of Dunowen, Belfast, and has issue,
                b. Robert Desmond Fitzgerald, b. 14 Sept. 1911.
        3. William Stewart, B.A. Trin. Coll. Dublin, b. 27 Sept. 1860; m. 20 Aug. 1886, Edith, dau. of J. K. Barton, M.D., of Dublin, and has issue.
            1. Lucy Elizabeth Jean, m. 14 Sept. 1880, George Abraham Grierson, C.I.E., I.C.S.
            2. Maria Louisa, m. 31 Jan. 1900, Capt. Ernest Gordon Farquharson. R.E., 3rd son of Col. M. H. Farquharson, R.M.L.I. He d. 1902.
            3. Sarah Henrietta, m. H. R. Spackman, M.D., of Penn Fields, Staffordshire, and has issue.
            4. Jessie Margaret.
        (5) Richard, b. 13 Jan. 1826; d. unm. 16 Sept. 1855.
        (6) William Bourke, b. 25 June, 1827; d. unm. 30 Jan. 1845.
        (7) Edward, b. 25 March, 1829; d. unm. 12 Aug. 1870.
        (8) Stewart, b. 22 Nov. 1831; d. unm. 22 Sept. 1869.
        (1) Elizabeth Anne, m. 29 Oct. 1840, Ambrose Rush, who d. 12 Feb. 1864.
        (2) Margaret.
        (3) Maria Adelaide, m. 22 Jan. 1862, Rev. John Beatty, and had issue, one son, d. in infancy.
    3. Maurice, an eminent surgeon of Dublin, m. 1821, Frances, sister of Rev. Edward Herbert, of Kilpeacon, co. Limerick. She d s.p. 1850.
Mr. Collis was eventually s. by his grandson,
STEPHEN EDWARD COLLIS, of Tieraclea, co. Kerry, J P. cos. Kerry and Limerick, b. 31 July, 1794; m. 29 July, 1829, Margaret, eldest dau. of Thomas William Sandes, D.L., of Sallow Glen, co. Kerry, and by her (who d. 25 Aug. 1868) had issue,
1 STEPHEN EDWARD, his heir.
2. Thomas William Sandes (Rev.), First Vicar of St. Bartholomew's, Brighton, b. 3 Nov. 1835; d. 6 Jan. 1905.
3. Maurice Fitzgerald, b. 3 May, 1837; d. 16 March, 1838.

4. Francis William, C.B. (1890), Maj.-Gen. retired, Indian Army, Col. 21st Punjabis, b. 8 July, 1839; m. 2 March, 1878, Charlotte Mary Debnam (New Brighton, Emsworth, Hants), dau. of Col. Anthony Stewart, B.S.C. (see STEWART of Ardvorlich). He d. 22 Dec. 1905, leaving issue,
1. Margaret, m. 19 July, 1911, Ronald Charles Kindersley, son of Capt. H. W. S. Kindersley, 29th Regt.
2. Frances Alice Debnam, m. 30 July, 1908, Capt. William Murray Stewart, Cameron Highlanders (see STEWART of Ardvorlich).
5. William James Fitzgerald, b. 10 Dec. 1842; m. 21 Oct. 1881, Amy, dau. of Berkeley B. Talbot, of Byrne, South Africa.
6. Falkiner Sandes COLLIS-SANDES, of Oak Park, co. Kerry (see COLLIS-SANDES of Oak Park).
1. Mary and 2. Anna, twins, d. in infancy, 24 Dec. 1833.
3. Margaret Elizabeth, d. unm. 31 Oct. 1861.
4. Anna Ruth, d. unm. 21 Aug. 1866.
5. Elizabeth, d. 18 Sept. 1909, having m. 29 Sept. 1859, Rev. Thomas Williamson Peile, Rector of Ashmore, Dorset. He d. April, 1904.
6. Mary, d. unm. 31 Jan. 1904.
7. Frances, m. 20 Oct. 1880, the Rev. G. McCutchan, B.D., Rector of Kenmare, co. Kerry, and has issue, a dau.
8. Gertrude Kathleen.
Mr. Collis d. 7 Jan. 1880, and was s. by his eldest son,
STEPHEN EDWARD COLLIS, of Tieraclea, co. Kerry, J.P. cos. Kerry and Limerick, High Sheriff of Kerry 1884, b. 7 July, 1831; m. 1st, 25 Jan. 1865, Sophie Thompson, younger dau. of Rev. Francis W. Grant, M.A., of Banff, N.B., and had issue,
STEPHEN EDWARD, now of Tieraclea.
He m. 2ndly. 23 April, 1906, Lilian Veronica L'Estrange, youngest dau. of the late Daniel Reardon, M.D., R.N., by whom he had issue, Stephanie Edna, b. 17 Oct. 1907.
He d. 16 May, 1912, being s. by his son.
Seat—Tieraclea, Tarbert, co. Kerry.

COLLIS-SANDES. See SANDES.

COLLUM OF BELLEVUE.

The late ARTHUR PERCIVAL TOD COLLUM, of Bellevue, co. Fermanagh and Loughan House, co. Cavan, D.L. and J.P. co. Fermanagh, High Sheriff 1890, Barrister-at-Law, late Capt. 3rd Batt. Innis. Fus., b. 26 Feb. 1866, d. 28 Jan. 1911.

Lineage.—WILLIAM COLLUM, of Bellevue, co. Fermanagh, and Loughan House, co. Cavan, J.P. and D.L. co. Fermanagh, High Sheriff 1878, sometime Capt. 94th Regt., son of John Collum, of Bellevue, b. 1837; m. 1865, Mary, dau. of the late Robert Nixon, of Loughan House, co. Cavan, and widow of John G. Hamilton Brown. He d. 1898, leaving issue,
1. ARTHUR PERCIVAL TOD, late of Bellevue.
2. JOHN ERNEST FRANCIS, now of Bellevue, High Sheriff co. Fermanagh 1908, s. his brother; m. 1899, dau. of ——
3. Harold Alexander Lloyd.
1. Evelyne, m. 1896, Capt. E. S. White, of Coomhola Lodge, Bantry, co. Cork.

Seats—Bellevue, Tamlaght, Enniskillen, and Loughan House, Blacklion, co. Cavan. Clubs—Junior United Service, S.W.

COLOMB OF DROMQUINNA AND DUNKERRON.

RUPERT PALMER COLOMB, of Dromquinna and Dunkerron, co. Kerry, b. 6 March, 1891; s. his father 28 May, 1909; m. 10 Nov. 1904, Mabel Louisa, elder dau. of John Murray Mordaunt, J.P., D.L. (see BURKE's Peerage, MORDAUNT, Bart., and has issue, a dau.,

Caragh, b. 31 July, 1906.

Lineage.—GEN. GEORGE THOMAS COLOMB, Col. 97th Regt. (son of Philip Colomb, who d. 1795), m. 31 Aug. 1820, Mary, 3rd dau. of Sir Abrabam Bradley King, Bart. (see BURKE's Peerage, KING of Corrard, Bart.), and by her (who d. 25 Feb. 1866) had issue,
1. George Hatton, Col. late R.A., d. unm. 30 May, 1910.
2. Wellington, late Inspector-Gen. R.I.C., d. unm. 7 May, 1895.
3. Philip Howard, Vice-Admiral R.N., of Steeple Court, Botley, Hants, b. 1831; m. 1857, Eleanor, dau. of the late Capt. Hooke, of the 34th Regt. He d. 14 Oct. 1899, leaving issue, with three daus.,
    1. Richard Pasley, Lieut.-Col., b. 23 June, 1858; m. 1 May, 1890, Hermione, dau. of late Dr. Chitty, of Deadham, Suffolk.
    2. Francis Cracroft, Col., b. 24 March, 1861; m. 27 Sept. 1890, Mary, dau. of J. H. Hilliard, J.P., of Cahirslee, Tralee.

3. George Henry Cooper, Lieut.-Col... *b.* 8 Dec. 1862; *m.* 13 Jan. 1891, Helen, dau. of Col. Russell Skinner, Indian Army.
4. P—— H——, Capt. R.N., *b.* 13 Dec. 1867; *m.* 18 Feb. 1908, Kathleen Charlotte, eldest dau. of Col. Edmund Bacon Hutton, of Blidworth Dale, Nottingham (*see* HUTTON *of Gate Burton*).
5. H—— W——, Commander R.N., *b.* 18 Sept. 1871; *m.* 7 June, 1903, Anne Coatalen, dau. of A. Davis.
6. Kenneth M——, *b.* 29 Jan. 1874.
4. JOHN CHARLES READY (Sir), of Dromquinna.
1. Elizabeth Ann, *d. unm.* 8 Jan. 1900.
2. Mary, *m.* to Col. K. D. Mackenzie, C.B., who is dec.
3. Harriet Olivia.
Gen. Colomb *d.* 20 March, 1874. The 4th son,
THE RIGHT HON. SIR JOHN CHARLES READY COLOMB, P.C., K.C.M.G., of Dromquinna, and Dunkerron, co. Kerry, J.P. and D.L., High Sheriff 1895, late M.P. for Tower Hamlets (Bow and Bromley Div.) 1886-92 ; ; M.P. for Great Yarmouth 1895-1900, formerly Capt. Royal Marine Artillery, was sworn of the Privy Council in Ireland on the occasion of the Royal Visit, 1903 ; *b.* 1 May, 1838. He *d.* 27, May, 1909, having *m.* 1 Jan. 1866, Emily Anna, dau. of Robert Samuel Palmer, and widow of Charles Augustus Paget, Lieut. R.N. (*see* BURKE'S *Peerage*, ANGLESEA, M.). She *d.* 16 June, 1907, leaving issue,
1. RUPERT PALMER, now of Dromquinna.
1. Laura Olivia, *m.* 28 March, 1894, Ruthven Frederic Ruthven Smith, of Bramcote, Notts, and has issue (*see* SMITH *of Bramcote*).
2. Gwendaline Rose Emily, *m.* 25 July, 1900, Thomas Mordaunt Snagge, eldest son of His Honour Judge Sir Thomas Snagge, D.L. for Oxfordshire, and has issue, Thomas Geoffrey, *b.* 11 Jan. 1902, and John Derrick, *b.* 8 May, 1904.

Seat—Dromquinna, Kenmare, co. Kerry. *Town Residence*—75, Belgrave Road, S.W.

BOWEN-COLTHURST OF DRIPSEY.

The late ROBERT WALTER TRAVERS BOWEN-COLTHURST, of Oakgrove and Dripsey Castle, co. Cork, J.P., *b.* 16 March, 1840 ; *m.* 15 Aug. 1878, GEORGINA DE BELLASIS (now of Dripsey), only dau. of Alfred Greer, of Dripsey House, co. Cork, J.P. (*see that family*), by his 2nd wife Peggy, only dau. of Major John Bowen Colthurst, of Dripsey Castle, co. Cork (*see* BURKE'S *Peerage and Baronetage*, COLTHURST, Bart.), and *d.* 16 Nov. 1896, leaving issue,
1. JOHN COLTHURST, Capt. Royal Irish Rifles, *b.* 12 Aug. 1880 ; *m.* 2 April, 1910, Hon. Rosalinda Laetitia Butler, youngest dau. of Robert, 25th Baron of Dunboyne (*see* BURKE'S *Peerage*), and has issue,
Robert St. John.
2. Robert MacGregor, Vice-Chamberlain to H.E. the Lord Lieutenant of Ireland since 1908, *b.* 15 Sept. 1883 ; *m.* 5 Dec. 1907, Winifred, dau. of Rev. Charles Frederick Cumber West, Vicar of Charlbury, Oxford, and has issue,
1. Peggy. 2. Honor Georgina.
1. Beatrice Clotilde, *m.* 7 Jan. 1909, Major E. R. Cottingham, M.V.O., late Royal Marine Artillery, and has issue (*see* COTTINGHAM).
2. Peggy de Billinghurst Frieda.

Mr. Bowen-Colthurst and his wife assumed, by Royal Licence dated 9 Dec. 1882, the additional surname and arms of COLTHURST in compliance with the testamentary injunction contained in the will of Joseph Colthurst, of Dripsey Castle. Mr. Bowen-Colthurst was the youngest son of the late John Bowen, of Carrigadrohid Castle and Oakgrove, co. Cork (*see* BOWEN *of Bowen's Court*).

Lineage.—JAMES COLTHURST, of Dripsey Castle, co. Cork, High Sheriff 1747 (brother of Sir John Conway Colthurst, 1st bart. (*see* BURKE'S *Peerage*)), *m.* Elizabeth, dau. of Col. Christopher Russell, 17th Regt., of Pemsey, co. Cork, Governor of Majorca and Minorca, and great-grand-dau. of Dr. Hook, Bishop of Worcester, and by her (who *m.* 2ndly, 7 Aug. 1763, Joseph Oates, of Kilnahone, co. Cork, and *d.* 1775) had issue,
1. JOHN, his heir.
2. James, Capt. in the Army. *m.* Susan, dau. of Christopher Carr, of Ballymenty-beg, co. Limerick, and *d.* Feb. 1837, having bad issue, two sons and two daus.,
1. James Robert Conway, Col. in the Army ; *m.* Corinna Vracciliotti. She *d.* 6 April, 1842. He *d.* 2 Feb. 1871, having had issue,

(1) James Nicholas, Col. 83rd and 6th Regt., *b.* 7 March, 1833.
(2) Corinna Susan, *m.* 20 Nov. 1855, Rev. John Blake Whitley, Prebendary of Ross, and Vicar of Templebryan, co. Cork, and has issue.
(2) Emily, *m.* 8 May, 1866, Thomas Herbert, son of Rev. Arthur Herbert (*see* HERBERT *of Cahirnane*), and has issue.
(3) Harriet, *d. unm.* 3 June, 1878.
(4) Charlotte, *m.* 20 Nov. 1861, Richard Griffith.
2. Nicholas, Major in the Army, *m.* Elizabeth Brabazon, of Dromisken, and *d.* 16 Dec. 1857, having bad issue,
(1) Louisa, *m.* John Ryan.
(2) Helena, *m.* Major Lake.
1. Elizabeth. 2. Susan.
3. Nicholas, an Officer in the Army, *d. unm.* ; was Town Major of the city of Cork.
4. Wallis, *d. unm.*
1. Mehetable, *m.* Robert Travers, of the city of Cork, and had issue.
James Colthurst *d.* 1757, and was *s.* by his eldest son,
JOHN COLTHURST, of Dripsey Castle, *m.* 1777, Jane, dau. of John Bowen, of Carrigadrohid Castle and Oakgrove House co. Cork (*see* BOWEN *of Bowen's Court*), and Katherine, his first wife, dau. of Bindon Scott, of Cahircon, co. Clare, and had (with other issue who *d.* young),
1. JOHN BOWEN, his heir.
2. James, Capt. 3rd Buffs ; *m.* 30 July, 1808, Esther, sister of Sir Augustus Warren, Bart., and by her (who *d.* 22 July, 1872) had issue, two sons,
1. Augustus Warren (Rev.), *d. unm.* 1841.
2. James, LL.D., *b.* 1814 ; *m.* 25 Nov. 1841, Elizabeth, dau. of Rev. Thomas Carson (*see* CARSON *of Shanroe*). She *d.* 4 March, 1873, having had issue,
(1) Herbert Baldwin, M.A., Barrister-at-Law, *b.* 20 March, 1845 ; *d.* 21 Dec. 1906 ; *m.* 25 Oct. 1871, Isabella Deborah, dau. of Right Rev. Thomas Carson, LL.D., Bishop of Kilmore (*see* CARSON *of Shanroc*), and had issue,
1. Joseph Riversdale (Rev.), M.A. Camb., *b.* 30 March, 1874 ; *m.* 1 June, 1910, Georgina Hickson, dau. of Alexander Nixon-Montgomery, F.R.C.P.I., and grand-dau. of George Montgomery, M.D. (*see* MONTGOMERY *of Beaulieu*).
1. Elizabeth Carson, *d. unm.* 14 March, 1873.
2. Elleanor Anne Mary.
(2) Ludlow Tonson, M.D. Edin., Surg. R.N., *b.* 21 Oct. 1853 ; *m.* 9 Feb. 1887, Lillie, dau. of John Davis.
(1) Eliza Anna Waggett Webb, *m.* 28 Dec. 1872, Col. Isaac Hoysted, R.A.M.C., and *d.* 12 Feb. 1879, leaving issue.
(2) Rose, *d. unm.* 2 June, 1859.
3. Nicholas, Capt. R.N., *m.* twice, but had no issue.
4. Charles, of Clonmoyle House, co. Cork, *m.* 1820, Lavinia, dau. of Robert Gumbleton, of Castleview, co. Waterford, and had issue,
1. Charles William, of Clonmoyle, *m.* the dau. of — Patterson.
1. Kate. 2. Lavinia.
3. Meta, *d. unm.* 4. Charlotte.
1. Jane, *m.* William Busteed, of Riversdale, House, co. Cork.
2. Catherine, *m.* John Pyne, of Clonmoyle Cottage, co. Cork.
John Colthurst *d.* Jan. 1815, and was *s.* by his eldest son,
JOHN BOWEN COLTHURST, of Dripsey Castle, Major in the Army, *b.* 4 June, 1779 ; *m.* 6 Jan. 1806, Peggy, dau. of the Rev. William Billinghurst, of Mitchen Hall, Firgrove, and Poyle Park, Surrey, and great-grand-dau. of George Woodroffe, of Poyle Park, and by her (who *d.* 2 April, 1865) had issue,
1. JOHN HENRY, his heir. 2. Richardson, *d.* in India, 1838.
3. GEORGE CHARLES EDWARD, of Carhue House, co. Cork, *b.* 16 May, 1811.
4. JOSEPH, heir to his brother.
1. Peggy, *m.* 19 Nov. 1853, Alfred Greer, of Dripsey House, co. Cork (son of Thomas Greer, of Rhone Hill, co. Tyrone). He *d.* 29 Dec. 1891. She *d.* 7 Feb. 1880, leaving an only dau. and heiress, GEORGINA DE BELLASIS GREER, now of Dripsey, *m.* as above stated, 15 Aug. 1878, ROBERT WALTER TRAVERS BOWEN-COLTHURST (*see above*).
Major Colthurst *d.* 10 May, 1848, and was *s.* by his son,
JOHN HENRY COLTHURST, of Dripsey Castle, *b.* 3 May, 1808 ; who *d. unm.* 15 Oct. 1865, and was *s.* by his brother,
JOSEPH COLTHURST, of Dripsey Castle, co. Cork, *b.* 7 Aug. 1812 ; *d. unm.* 4 Oct. 1882, when he was *s.* according to the provisions of his will, dated 10 Oct. 1873, by his niece,
GEORGINA DE BELLASIS, now Mrs. Bowen-Colthurst, of Dripsey Castle.

Arms—Quarterly : 1st and 4th, arg., on a fess between three colts courant sa. as many trefoils slipped or a crescent for difference, for COLTHURST ; 2nd and 3rd, per pale, az. and gu., a stag trippant arg., pierced in the back with an arrow and attired or, for BOWEN. **Crests**—1st, COLTHURST, a colt courant sa. charged on the shoulder with a crescent or ; 2nd, BOWEN, on a mount vert, a falcon, close ppr. belled or. **Motto**—Justum et tenacem.
Seats—Oakgrove, Killinardrish, and Dripsey Castle, Coachford, co. Cork.

COLTHURST.
See BURKE'S PEERAGE, **COLTHURST**, Bart.

COLTHURST-VESEY. *See* VESEY.

CRONIN-COLTSMANN OF GLENFLESK CASTLE.

DANIEL JOHN CRONIN-COLTSMANN, of Glenflesk Castle, Killarney, J.P. cos. Cork and Kerry, D.L. and High Sheriff for the latter co. 1899; b. 21 May, 1855; m. 1st, 1879, Mary Margaret, dau. of John Nicholas Murphy, of Clifton, co. Cork, and by her (who d. 1895) has issue,

1. DANIEL FRANCIS, b. 1885.
1. Alice.   2. Lissa Margaret.

He m. 2ndly, 1896, Lissa, dau. of Kinard Baghot de la Bere, of Burbage Hall (see that family), and has issue.

Lineage.—DANIEL DUGGAN, son of Denis Duggan, by Frances his wife, dau. of Michael Galwey, of Enniskeane, co. Cork, and Mary his wife, sister of DANIEL CRONIN, of Park, co. Kerry, became possessed of Park at the death of his grand-uncle, Daniel Cronin, in 1786, and adopted the surname of CRONIN. He m. June, 1786, Mary Ann, dau. of James Lombard, of Cork, and was father of

DANIEL CRONIN, of Park, Killarney, m. 1814, Christina, dau. and heiress of John Coltsmann, of Glenflesk Castle, and by her (who d. 1822) left at his decease, 1857, two sons and one dau.,
1. DANIEL CRONIN COLTSMANN, of whom presently.
2. John L. Cronin, m. Minnie MacDonnell, and had issue, five sons and two daus.
1. Christina, m. Dennis Duggan (dec.), and had one son and three daus.
2. Mary Anne, m. Francis Dennehy, both dec.

The elder son,
DANIEL CRONIN-COLTSMANN, of Glenflesk Castle, co. Kerry, J.P. and D.L., High Sheriff 1847, b. 1816; m. 1854, Helena, dau. of John Lyons, of Saunders' Park, co. Cork, descended from the family of Lyons of Croome, co. Limerick, and d. 1894, leaving issue,
1. DANIEL JOHN COLTSMANN, now of Glenflesk Castle.
2. John Lewis, b. 1856.   3. Dennis Coltsmann.
4. Francis Coltsmanu.
1. Helena Mary, m. 1898, Richard Bourke, Local Government Auditor, of Halton, Helen's Bay, co. Down, 2nd son of Richard Bourke, of Thornfields (see that family).
Seat—Glenflesk Castle, Killarney.   Club—Union.

COMYN OF WOODSTOCK AND KILCORNEY.

DAVID CHARLES EDWARD FFRENCH COMYN, b. 2 April, 1876, late Lieut. in the Black Watch, late Major Egyptian Army and acting Governor of Halfa Province (Sudan), served in S. African War 1900-2, and has two medals with five clasps, F.R.G.S., Author of "Service and Sport in the Sudan."

Lineage.—EDMUND COMYN, of Inchybeg, co. Tipperary, left a son and heir,
DAVID COMYN, of Inchybeg, who was s. by his eldest son,
EDMUND COMYN, of Inchybeg, who signed the roll of Confederated Catholics, m. Jennett Sarsfield, and had issue (all named in a deed of feoffment, dated 4 March, 1608).
1. William, d.s.p.   2. GEORGE, of whom presently.   3. John.
The eldest surviving son,
GEORGE COMYN, of Inchybeg, who represented Munster at the Council of Kilkenny (see Gilbert's Hist. of the Confederates), m. Margaret Berkeley, and had issue, an only son,
JOHN COMYN, of Kilcorney, co. Clare, m. Margaret, dau. and co-heir of Thomas Comyn, of Park, by his wife Joan Fanning, of Limerick. She claimed as "an innocent Papist," and was transplanted to Kilcorney, 1641. He was Mayor of Limerick 1661. They had issue,
1. DAVID, of whom presently.   2. Stephen.
3. William.
The eldest son,
DAVID COMYN, of Kilcorney, m. 14 Feb. 1693, Elizabeth, dau. of James Davoren, of Lisdoonvarna Castle, co. Clare, and d. 11 May, 1710, leaving issue,
1. LAWRENCE, of whom presently.
2. George, M.D., Physician to Louis XIV, King of France.
3. Nicholas,   4. William.
1. Elizabeth, m. Francis Fitzgerald, of Kilcarragh.
The eldest son,
LAURENCE COMYN, of Kilcorney, m. 28 Nov. 1734, Julian, dau. of Peter Martyn, of Coole, co. Galway, and d. 10 April, 1785, leaving issue,
1. DAVID, of whom presently.
2. George, of Hollywell, co. Clare (see COMYN of Holywell).
The elder son,
DAVID COMYN, of Kilcorney, m. 8 Feb. 1762, Dorothea, dau. of William Macnamara, of Doolen, co. Clare, by Catherine his wife, dau. and heir of Francis Sarsfield, and d. 20 Dec. 1776, leaving issue,
1. LAURENCE, of whom presently.
2. Nicholas, m. and had issue.

3. William, Capt. R.N., m. Annabella, dau of Hugh Campbell of Balquherrie and Sombeg, and had issue.
The eldest son,
LAURENCE COMYN, of Woodstock and Kilcorney, m. 24 March, 1800, Jane, eldest dau. of Nicholas Lynch, of Barna, co. Galway, by Catherine, his wife, only child of Henry Blake, of Ballinahill, co. Galway, and d. 28 June, 1819, leaving issue,
1. FRANCIS, of whom presently.
2. John Sarsfield, d.s.p. 30 May, 1835.
3. Sarsfield Peter, D.L., d.s.p. 24 June, 1866.
1. Catherine, m. Cornelius, Baron Von Stenz Von Hagen.
2. Harriett, d. unm.
The eldest son,
FRANCIS COMYN, of Woodstock and Kilcorney, b. 3 Oct. 1801; m. 28 April, 1834, Honoria, only dau. of Edward James Beytagh, of Cappagh, co. Galway, by Sarah his wife, dau. of Thomas Lord Ffrench, and d. 9 June, 1873, having by her had issue,
1. FRANCIS, of Woodstock and Kilcorney.
2. John Sarsfield, Surg.-Gen. in the Army, M.D., M.A., b. 6 Feb. 1837; m. Sophia, dau. of Gen. Owen, and has issue,
Francis, m. a dau. of Rev. — Bailey.
Sophia, m. H. Ussher, R.N.R.
3. Charles, b. 2 April, 1844, Capt. in the Emperor (of Mexico) Maximilian's Body Guard and a Knt. of Guadelupe.
4. William, b. 25 Jan. 1846.
5. George, M.D., b. 17 March, 1848.
6. Harry Edward, M.D., b. 1 Oct. 1850.
1. Rose Selina, m. Conte Cavaliere Carlo Strozzi, of Florence. He d. 8 Dec. 1907.
2. Laura, m. Robert Beytagh, of Manin, co. Mayo, and d.s.p.
The eldest son,
FRANCIS COMYN, of Woodstock, Galway, and Kilcorney, co. Clare, J.P. for cos. Clare, Galway and Mayo, and Galway Borough, High Sheriff Galway 1868, late Lieut. Galway Militia, b. 12 Nov. 1835; m. 4 Sept. 1865, Cecilia Gertrude, only child and heir of Walter Bourke, Q.C., of Carrowkeele, co. Mayo, by Mary, dau. of Peter Blake, of Towerhill, co. Mayo, and d. 13 Sept. 1903, having had issue,
1. Walter Bourke, b. 10 Oct. 1868, an officer in the service of the Foreign Office, East Africa Protectorate; d. unm. 24 May, 1900.
2. John Sarsfield, Lieut. Royal West Kent Regt., served in Lepai Expedition (medal and clasp), b. 15 Sept. 1870; d. unm. on service 14 June, 1898.
3. DAVID CHARLES EDWARD FFRENCH, his heir.
4. Kenneth Henry Dolphin, served in S. African War (medal with clasps), b. 1 Oct. 1879; d. unm. on service, 3 June, 1900.
1. Mary.   2. Aimée.
3. Eva, m. H. Reaney and has issue.
4. Ethel, d. young.   5. Dorothea.
Residence—Woodstock, Galway.

COMYN OF HOLYWELL.

CHARLES JAMES COMYN, of Lisdooney, co. Clare, J.P. King's County, m. Marion, eldest dau. of Bernard Daly, of Tullamore and Hazlebrook, Terenure, and has had issue,

BERNARD DALY.
Clarinda, d. in infancy.
Lineage.—GEORGE COMYN, of Holywell (see COMYN of Woodstock), m. Margaret Lysaght, of Bally Keale Court, co. Clare, and had issue,
1. Peter, d. unm.
2. Thomas, m. Margaret, eldest dau. of Major Skerrett, of Finavara (see that family), and had issue, with two daus.,
George, d. unm. in Australia.
3. GEORGE, of whom presently.
1. Maria, m. Michael Kenny.
2. Matilda, m. Charles Mahon, of New Park.
3. Juliana, m. James Blake Butler.
4. Margaret, m. John McNamara.
The 3rd son,
GEORGE COMYN, m. 1837, Clarinda, dau. of Major Skerrett, of Finavara (see that family). She d. 1892, and had issue,
1. George, d. in infancy.
2. William Skerrett, d. unm. in Australia 1885.
3. CHARLES JAMES, now of Lisdoonie.
Residence—Lisdoonie, Barrow-in-Furness.

COMYN OF BALLINDERRY AND RYEFIELD.

ANDREW NUGENT COMYN, of Ballinderry, co. Galway, and Ryefield, co. Roscommon, J.P. co. Galway, b. 25 Oct. 1831; m. 26 Nov. 1867, Mary (d. 6 Feb. 1910), 2nd dau. of John O'Connell, M.P., and granddau. of Daniel O'Connell, of Derrynane Abbey (see that family), and has issue,

1. NICHOLAS O'CONNELL, b. 19 June, 1869; m. 14 Oct. 1911, Cecil, eldest dau. of Francis W. Mahony, of St. Helen's, Blarney, co. Cork.
2. Andrew Daniel, b. 23 Sept. 1872.
3. Lewis James, b. 13 March, 1878.
1. Elizabeth Mary, m. 20 Sept. 1898, Edmund Ronayne Mahony, of Marysboro, co. Cork, and has issue (see MAHONY of Lota Beg).
2. Geraldine Mary, m. 29 Jan. 1901, Austin M. King, of Bath.
3. Eily Mary, m. 4 Sept. 1900, Blake Kelly, of Rock Hill, co. Galway.

Lineage.—ANDREW COMYN, of Ryefield, co. Roscommon, m. 1786, the sister and heir of Lewis Ward, of Ballymacward and Ballinderry, co. Galway (who m. Jane, dau. of Stephen Donelan, of Jamaica, and d.s.p.), and by her had an eldest son,
NICHOLAS COMYN, of Ballinderry and Ryefield, b. 1787; m. 1830, Sabina, dau. of John Joyes, of Woodquay, co. Galway, and d. 1843, having had issue,
1. ANDREW NUGENT, now of Ballinderry and Ryefield.
2. John Ward, b. 25 July, 1835.
1. Mary Ellen, d. young. 2. Sabina, d. young.
3. Lizzie, d. young.

Seats—Ballinderry, Ballinasloe, co. Galway and Ryefield Elphin, co. Roscommon.

CONGREVE OF MOUNT CONGREVE.

JOHN CONGREVE, of Mount Congreve, co. Waterford, J.P., D.L., High Sheriff 1906, served as Capt. in Border Regt. in S. African War 1900-1, b. 9 Feb. 1872; m. 26 July, 1904, Lady Helena Blanche Irene Ponsonby, 2nd dau. of Edward, 8th Earl of Bessborough (see BURKE's Peerage), and has issue,
AMBROSE CHRISTIAN, b. 4 April, 1907.

Lineage.—REV. JOHN CONGREVE, of Kilmacow, co. Kilkenny, b. 1654, son of John Congreve, of the co. Cork; m. Rebecca, dau. of Lieut.-Col. Oliver Jones, and sister and co-heir of Ambrose Jones, and had issue,
1. AMBROSE, his heir.
1. Mary, 2nd wife of James Ussher, of Ballintaylor, co. Waterford.
2. Elizabeth, m. John Power, ancestor of the Powers, Barts. of Kilfane (see BURKE's Peerage).
3. Jane, m. Edward Saunders.
The Rev. John Congreve, whose will, dated 12 May, 1710, was proved 14 June, 1710, was s. by his son,
AMBROSE CONGREVE, of Waterford, b. 1698; m. 1725, Elinor, dau. of John Lapp, and widow of — Roche, and by her (who m. 3rdly, John Whitcomb, D.D., Archbishop of Cashel) left at his decease Aug. 1741, a son and successor,
JOHN CONGREVE, of Mount Congreve, High Sheriff co. Waterford 1755, m. April, 1758, Mary, dau. of Beverley Ussher, of Kilmeadon (see USSHER of Eastwell), by his 1st wife Mary, dau. of Nicholas Lysaght, and sister of the 1st Lord Lisle (see BURKE's Peerage), and had two sons,
1. JOHN, of Landscape, High Sheriff co. Waterford 1792, who d.s.p. 1801.
2. AMBROSE.
The 2nd son,
AMBROSE USSHER CONGREVE, of Mount Congreve, whose will, dated 21 Oct. 1801, was proved 18 July, 1809, m. Anne, dau. of John Jenkins, and by her (who m. 2ndly, Major Arthur Fleming, R.H.A.) had issue,
1. JOHN, late of Mount Congreve.
2. Ambrose, b. 1801, appointed Cornet 14th Light Dragoons 1823, d. unm. 1839.
1. Jane, m. 31 Oct. 1823, John Cooke, of Kiltinane Castle, co. Tipperary (see that family).
His eldest son,
JOHN CONGREVE, of Mount Congreve, D.L., b. 1800, High Sheriff 1823; m. Nov. 1827, Hon. Louisa Harriet Dillon, dau. of Luke, 2nd Lord Clonbrock (see BURKE's Peerage), and by her (who d. 4 Aug. 1881) had issue,
1. AMBROSE, late of Mount Congreve.
1. Louisa Anne, d. unm. 12 Jan. 1910.
2. Augusta Mary.
3. Jane, m. 28 Sept. 1876, Admiral Baron von Oesterreicher.
He d. 2 June, 1863. His only son,
AMBROSE CONGREVE, of Mount Congreve, co. Waterford, J.P. and D.L., High Sheriff 1871, b. 16 Jan. 1832; formerly Lieut. 2nd Life Guards; m. 26 July, 1866, his cousin Alice Elizabeth Dillon, 6th dau. of Robert, 3rd Lord Clonbrock (see BURKE's Peerage), and d. 15 March, 1901, having by her (who d. 18 Dec. 1878) had issue,
1. JOHN, now of Mount Congreve.
2. Ambrose, b. 30 Nov. 1875; m. 5 June, 1901, Aileen Allison, 3rd dau. of William Johnston, of Woodslee, Cheshire.
3. Leopold Hugh, b. 10 Sept. 1877; m. Dec. 1909, Anne Vincent, of Minneapolis, U.S.A.
1. Caroline Mabel, d. unm. 1895.
2. Eleanor Augusta. 3. Violet Jane.

Seat—Mount Congreve, Kilmeadon, Waterford.

PHILLIPS-CONN OF BELTURBET AND MOUNT IDA.

HIGHGATE HENRY PHILLIPS-CONN, of Belturbet, co. Cavan and Mount Ida, co. Kilkenny, J.P., M.A. and M.D. Dublin University, formerly Surgeon - Captain, R.A.M.C. and 44th (East Essex) Regt. b. 1841; m. 1870, Fanny, only dau. of the late Henry Meredith, of Edgbaston, and has issue,
1. THOMAS HARRY MEREDITH, b. 1881.
1. Mabel Constance.
2. Violet Frances.

Mr. H. H. Phillips-Conn s. to the Mount Ida estates in 1893, on the death of his uncle by marriage, the late John Lambly Conn, and, in accordance with his will, assumed by Royal Licence 4 July, 1894, the additional surname and arms of CONN. He also s. to the Glenview estates on the death s.p. of his elder brother Rev. T. G. J. Phillips, 3 April, 1898.

Lineage.—(of PHILIPS)—THOMAS PHILLIPS, Provost of Belturbet 1662, m. 1661, Jane, dau. of Thomas Richardson, of Dublin. He d. 1700 (will dated 5 Feb. 1699), leaving three sons,
1. JAMES, his heir.
2. William, who left a dau., m. Valentine Swords.
3. Thomas, of Belturbet, co. Cavan, d. intestate (administration granted to his brother James, 14 July, 1692).
The eldest son,
JAMES PHILLIPS, m. 1702, Margaret Haynes, of Lislin, co. Cavan, and with her acquired estates in that co. He was s. by his only son,
THOMAS PHILLIPS, m. Mary Anne, dau. of John Wade, of Clonebrany, co. Meath, and d. intestate (administration granted 24 Dec. 1730), leaving an only son and heir,
MICHAEL PHILLIPS, of Edorgole, b. 1730, who obtained under the will of his maternal uncle, John Wade, the lands of Coolcot or Ashgreen, co. Meath. He m. 1771, Mabel, dau. of Stearne Tighe, of Dublin (2nd son of Robert Tighe, of co. Westmeath), and by her was father of
THOMAS PHILLIPS, of Ashgreen, co. Meath, m. 1st, Anne, dau. of John Tandy, of Johnsbrook, co. Meath, and by her had issue,
1. MICHAEL, his heir.
2. Thomas, M.D., who settled in Canada, and left issue.
1. Mabel, d. unm. 2. Marion, m. Robert Miller.
Mr. Phillips m. 2ndly, Helen, dau. of Joshua Nunn, of St. Margaret's, co. Wexford, and by her had issue,
3. Joshua, m. his cousin Anne Phillips, and had an only son, Frederick William, of Dublin.
4. Frances, m. B. A. Leonard.
5. Jane, m. Stearne Phillips.
6. Marianne, m. Dr. J. Taylor.
7. Elfrida, m. William Miller.
His eldest son,
MICHAEL PHILLIPS, of Glenview, Major in the Cavan Militia, J.P. co. Cavan, b. 1796; m. 1832, Mary Anne, dau. of Highgate Tench, of Ballyhealy, co. Wexford, by Frances his wife, eldest dau. of Joshua Nunn, of St. Margaret's, and d. 23 Dec. 1876, leaving two sons,
1. THOMAS GEORGE JOHNSTON, late of Glenview.
2. HIGHGATE HENRY, now of Belturbet and Mount Ida.
The elder son,
REV. THOMAS GEORGE JOHNSTON PHILLIPS, of Glenview, co. Cavan, M.A., Rector of Fenagh, co. Carlow; b. 1834; m. 1860, Charlotte Maria, dau. of Edward Lewis, of Violetstown, co. Westmeath, and d.s.p. 3 April, 1898, when he was s. by his only brother.

Lineage.—(of CONN).
JOHN CONN, m. Mary, dau. of John Underwood, C.E., and niece of the Rev. William Lambly, Rector of Rower, co. Kilkenny, and by her had issue,
1. BENJAMIN.
2. Joseph, who m. Mary Gleeson, and by her had a dau., Sarah, m. Saunders Rogers, of Tramore.
The elder son,
BENJAMIN CONN, of Mount Ida, m. 1811, Elizabeth, dau. of Capt. Peter Dalton, of Glenfield, co. Tipperary, and d. 1862, having by her (who d. 1858) had issue,
1. JOHN LAMBLY, of Mount Ida.
1. Kate Elizabeth, d. unm.
2. Marianne, m. 26 April, 1853, Martin Costelloe, and had issue.
The only son,
JOHN LAMBLY CONN, of Mount Ida, co. Kilkenny, b. 8 Aug. 1812; m. 16 July, 1844, Frances, eldest dau. of the late Highgate Tench,

Connellan. THE LANDED GENTRY. 128

of Ballyhealy House, co. Wexford, and grand-dau. of the late Col. Joshua Nunn, of St. Margaret's, in the same co., and d. 1893, having had issue,
1. Benjamin Higatt, b. 1846; d. unm. 7 Aug. 1861.
2. John Nunn, b. 1847; d. 1849.

Mr. Conn devised his estates to his wife's nephew, Highgate Henry Phillips, who has assumed by Royal Licence the additional name and arms of CONN.

Arms—Quarterly: 1st and 4th, vert, a bend engrailed plain cotised arg. for CONN; 2nd and 3rd, az., a chevron engrailed between three falcons arg. belled or, for PHILLIPS. *Crest*—A falcon's head, erased ppr. armed or holding in its beak a lure gu. *Motto*—Vincit qui patitur.

Seat—Mount Ida, Ferrybank, near Waterford.

CONNELLAN OF COOLMORE.

JAMES HERCULES FITZWALTER HENRY CONNELLAN, of Coolmore, co. Kilkenny, J.P. and D.L., High Sheriff 1890, Hon. Col. (ret.) 5th Royal Irish Regt., and Capt. Hampshire Regt., b. 20 Aug. 1849; m. 5 April, 1881, Laura Elizabeth, youngest dau. of Richard Ussher Roberts, and by her (who d. 24 Feb. 1899) has issue,

PETER MARTIN, b. 19 Feb. 1882, Capt. Hampshire Regt. m. 18 Oct. 1911, Winifred, 3rd dau. of the late Arthur Niblett, of Haresfield Court, Gloucestershire.
Marguerite Elizabeth, b. 23 Oct. 1884.

Lineage.—MARTIN CONNELLAN, d. 1788, m. Miss Butler, had six sons, all of whom d. without legitimate male issue, except the youngest.

PETER CONNELLAN, b. 1745; m. Miss Marguerite Galhie, a lady of French extraction, and by her (who d. 1796) had issue,

PETER, b. 7 July, 1782; m. March, 1805, Harriett, dau. of James Corry, Clerk of the Journals of the Irish House of Commons, and Secretary to the Irish Linen Board, and predeceasing his father, 11 Nov. 1806, left two sons,
1. PETER, successor to his grandfather.
2. James Corry (posthumous), b. 15 Jan. 1807, M.A. of Oriel Coll. Oxford, Barrister-at-Law, and formerly one of the Inspectors-General of Prisons in Ireland. He d. 1885.

Anne, m. Pierce Blake, of Holly Park, co. Galway, brother of the Right Hon. Anthony Richard Blake, Chief Remembrancer of Ireland.

Mr. Connellan d. 1820, aged 75, and was s. by his grandson,

PETER CONNELLAN, J.P. and D.L., of Coolmore, b. 3 Feb. 1806, educated at Winchester Coll. and Oriel Coll. Oxon; High Sheriff 1836; m. 25 July, 1844, Anne Maria, 2nd dau. of the Rev. Sir Hercules Richard Langrishe, 3rd bart. of Knocktopher Abbey, co. Kilkenny, by whom (who d. 19 Sept. 1899) he had,
1. JAMES HERCULES FITZWALTER HENRY, now of Coolmore.
2. Corry Langrishe, late Capt. the Buffs, b. 22 Dec. 1857; m. 29 April, 1905, Geraldine Mary Georgiana, 2nd dau. of Sir Charles Fairlie Cuninghame, Bart (see BURKE's *Peerage*), and has issue, a dau., b. 14 March, 1906.
3. Richard Sherrard, b. 20 July, 1860; d. 16 May, 1875.
1. Maria Isabella. m. Oct. 1870, Capt. George Gethin, of Earlsfield, co. Sligo, and has issue.
2. Harriet Charlotte, m. 15 Sept. 1874, Capt. William Law, R.A., who d. 1881.
3. Fanny Rose, m. 17 July, 1875, Sir Owen Randal Slacke, C.B., late 10th Hussars. He d. 27 April, 1910, leaving issue (*see* SLACKE, *late of Ashleigh*).
4. Georgina Jane, m. 29 Oct. 1878, Jenico, 14th Viscount Gormanston, G.C.M.G. (who d. 29 Oct., 1907) leaving issue (*see* BURKE's *Peerage*).
5. Eliza Mary, d. 7 Dec. 1892.
6. Annie Louisa, m. 3 July, 1894, Col. the Hon. F. W. Shore, R.A.
7. Cecilia, m. 6 Oct. 1887, W. J. O'Hara, youngest son of Rev. James Dunn O'Hara, of The Castle, Portstewart, and had issue (*see* O'HARA, *late of O'Hara Brook*).

Mr. Connellan d. 11 Aug. 1885.

Arms—Per fess az. and vert a fesse or, between a pelican arg. vulned gu. in chief, and a land tortoise passant of the third in base. *Crest*—An owl perched on the stump of an oak tree ppr. *Motto*—Inter utrumque.

Seat—Coolmore, Thomastown, co. Kilkenny. *Club*—Army and Navy.

CONNER OF MANCH.

HENRY DANIEL CONNER, of Manch House, co. Cork, K.C., M.A. Trin. Coll. Dublin, b. 3 Oct. 1859; m. 24 Aug. 1881, Anne, dau. of Rev. Goodwin Purcell, Vicar of Charlesworth, co. Derby (see PURCELL *of Glannanore*), and Sarah his wife, dau. of Joseph Lea, of Bostock, Cheshire, and has issue,
1. DANIEL GOODWIN, b. 2 Dec. 1884.
2. Henry Longfield, b. 7 Nov. 1887.
1. Alice Mary.

Lineage.—CORNELIUS CONNER, the first of the family who settled in co. Cork, m. 1670, Mrs. Joane Splane. His name and that of his son Daniel appear in the Jacobite Corporation of Bandon in 1690. His will bears date 1 Sept. 1719. His son,

DANIEL CONNER, of Bandon, merchant, purchased estates principally situate in co. Cork. He d. Feb. 1761, having m. 1698, Margaret Slone, and had issue,
1. Daniel, of Bandon, merchant, d. 1737, leaving one son, who d. in infancy.
2. WILLIAM, of whom hereafter.
3. GEORGE, of Ballybricken, who left a dau., Mary Anne, m. 1778, John Lysaght, 2nd Lord Lisle; and a son, DANIEL, m. 6 Feb. 1779, Mary, dau. of Kingsmill Pennefather, M.P., and was father of
   DANIEL CONNER, J.P. of Ballybricken, co. Cork. He m. his cousin Anna, dau. of William Pennefather, and had a son,
   RICHARD, of Ballybricken, Capt. R.N., m. 1833, Elizabeth Perrott, and by her (who d. 1853) had issue,
   1. DANIEL, of Ballybricken, co. Cork, J.P., b. 27 Sept. 1835; m. 14 June, 1866, Emily, dau. of Henry Steigen Berger, of 30, Cleveland Square, Hyde Park, and d. 31 Dec. 1899, leaving issue,
      (1) DANIEL HENRY, of Ballybricken, co. Cork (*Lines End, Winchelsea*), b. 5 April, 1867; m. 14 Jan. 1902, Florence Jane, dau. of Capt. Horace Townshend, 99th Regt.
      (2) Richard, b. 29 Dec. 1868.
      (3) Henry, } twins, b. 17 Sept. 1872.
      (4) Samuel,
      (1) Emily, b. 13 May, 1870.
      (2) Kathleen Louisa, b. 30 May, 1877.
   2. William, M.D., m. 6 June, 1872, Ellen Lawrence, dau. of William Colbourne, of Monkstown, co. Cork.
   3. George, late Col. commanding 28th Regt., d. 14 Feb. 1905, aged 59.
   1. Elizabeth Mary, m. 28 April, 1870, Samuel Willy Perrott.

Mr. Conner d. in 1862, and was s. by his eldest son.
4. Henry (Rev.).
1. Jane, m. 1720, John Lapp, of Cork, merchant.
2. Mary, m. Rev. Bartholomew Thomas, of Everton, co. Carlow.
3. Hannah, m. 1731, William Delahoyde.
4. Elizabeth, m. 1743, Richard Gumbleton, of Castle Richard, co. Waterford.

The 2nd son,

WILLIAM CONNER, of Connerville, co. Cork, M.P. for Bandon 1765, m. Oct. 1721, Anne, dau. of Roger Bernard, of Palace Anne, co. Cork, and had two sons,
1. ROGER, his heir.   2. William.

His elder son,

ROGER CONNER, of Connerville, m. 26 Feb. 1753. Anne Longfield, sister of Richard, Viscount Longueville, and had issue,
1. DANIEL, his heir.
2. William, Lieut.-Col. Cork Militia, m. July, 1777, Mary, dau. of Thomas Grant, of Kilmurry, and left, with other issue,
   1. William, d.s.p.
   2. Richard Longfield (Rev.), of Downdaniel, co. Cork, m. Frances Gertrude, dau. of William Honnor, and had two sons,
      (1) William Robert, of Milton, near Bandon, co. Cork, b. 1820; m. 1854, Frances Oldham, eldest dau. of Richard Warren, M.D., and d.s.p.
      (2) Richard Mountifort (Rev.), of Downdaniel, co. Cork, S.F.T.C.D., m. 1851, his cousin Grace, dau. of Daniel Conner, of Manch (*see below*), and has issue,
         William Daniel, Col. late R.E., b. 28 Jan. 1854.
3. Robert Longfield, of Fort Robert, co. Cork, m. Miss Madras, and left issue, three daus.
4. Roger, of Connerville, b. 8 March, 1763; m. 1st, Louisa Anna, dau. of Col. Strachan, of the 32nd Regt., by whom he had issue,
   1. Roderick, settled in Van Diemen's Land.
   1. Louisa, who d. unm.

He m. 2ndly, 1788, Wilhelmina, dau. of Nicholas Bowen, of Bowenscourt, co. Cork, by whom he had issue,
   2. Arthur, who m. his cousin Mary Conner, of Fort Robert.
   3. Feargus Edward, b. 1796, M.P. for Cork 1832, and for Nottingham 1847; d. 31 Aug. 1854.
   4. Francis Burdett, an Officer in the Bolivian Army.
   5. George Roger, m. his cousin Elizabeth Conner, of Fort Robert.
5. Arthur, b. 1765; representative in the Irish Parliament for the borough of Philipstown; m. 1807, Elisa de Caritat de Condorcet, only child of Marie Jean Antoine Nicholas, Marquis de Condorcet, by Sophia de Grouchy his wife, sister of the famous Marshal Grouchy, and was subsequently known as General Condorcet O'Connor, of the French Service. He d. 23 April, 1852, at the Chateau de Bignon, Loiret, leaving issue.

The eldest son,

DANIEL CONNER, of Orme Square, Bayswater, London, b. 1754; m. 5 Feb. 1789, Mary Elizabeth, dau. of Rev. Arthur Hyde, (see HYDE of Castle Hyde). He d. 1848, leaving issue,
1. DANIEL, his heir.
1. Mary, m. 18 March, 1819, Jonathan Henry Christie, Barrister-at-Law, and d. 16 Nov. 1875, leaving issue.
2. Sophia, d.s.p.
3. Sarah, m. 29 May, 1829, Rev. Thomas Lathbury, of Bath, and left issue.
4. Charlotte, d. unm.
5. Ann, m. Thomas King.
6. Louisa, m. Rev. Daniel Wheeler, of Blagden, Somerset.

The only son,
DANIEL CONNER, of Manch House, b. 13 Feb. 1798; m. 4 June, 1822, Elizabeth, dau. of the Rev. Mountifort Longfield, of Church Hill, co. Cork; and d. Feb. 1880, leaving,
1. DANIEL, of whom presently.
2. Mountifort Longfield, b. 18 Sept. 1824; m. 4 Dec. 1849, Anna, dau. of Rev. Godfrey Smith, but d.s.p. 1880.
1. Grace, m. 1851, her cousin Rev. Richard Mountifort Conner, of Downdaniel, co. Cork, S.F.T.C.D. (see above).
2. Mary, m. 1852, Rev. Edward Lysaght, who d. 1853.
3. Elizabeth, m. 1857, William Lysaght.
4. Louisa, m. June, 1859, Adam Newman Meade, who d. 1878, leaving issue (see MEADE of Ballymartle).
5. Charlotte Alicia.

The eldest son,
DANIEL CONNER, of Manch House, co. Cork, J.P., b. 25 Feb. 1823; m. 6 Jan. 1848, Patience, dau. of Henry Longfield, of Waterloo co. Cork, and Mary his wife, dau. of John Powell, of Seacourt, co. Cork, and d. 19 Dec. 1896, leaving issue,
1. HENRY DANIEL, now of Manch.
1. Patience Alicia. 2. Mary Elizabeth.
3. Elizabeth Anna, m. Dec. 1894, Major George O'Connor, 6th Dragoons, of Illane Roe, Rochestown, co. Cork.
4. Henrietta Louisa.

Seat—Manch House, Ballineen, co. Cork. Residence—16, Fitzwilliam Place, Dublin.

CONOLLY OF CASTLETOWN.

CAPT. EDWARD MICHAEL CONOLLY, of Castletown, co. Kildare, late Capt. R.A., b. 20 Feb. 1874.

Lineage.—RIGHT HON. WILLIAM CONOLLY, of Castletown, co. Kildare, and Stratton Hall, co. Stafford, was nephew of the Right Hon. WILLIAM CONOLLY, of Castletown, Speaker of the House of Commons in Ireland, who m. Catherine Conyngham (d. 23 Sept. 1752), and d.s.p. 1729. He m. (settlements dated 28 April, 1733) Lady Anne Wentworth, dau. of Thomas, 3rd Earl of Strafford, and sister and co-heir of William, 4th Earl of Strafford, and had issue,
1. THOMAS, his heir.
1. Katherine, m. 23 Feb. 1754, Ralph, Earl of Ross, and d.s.p. 3 May, 1771.
2. Anne, m. 5 March, 1761, George Byng, and was mother of Sir John Byng, G.C.B., created 1847, Earl of Strafford.
3. Harriet, d. May, 1771; m. June, 1764, Right Hon. John Staples, of Lyssan, co. Tyrone, a Privy Councillor in Ireland, and had issue,
1. William Conolly Staples, m. Anne, dau. of Sir James Stewart 7th bart. of Fort Stewart, by whom (who d. 30 March, 1867) he had no issue. He d. 30 March, 1798.
1. Louisa Staples, m. 24 June, 1783, Admiral Hon. Sir Thomas Pakenham, 2nd son of Thomas, Lord Longford, and Elizabeth his wife, Countess of Longford, in her own right. Sir Thomas d. 2 Feb. 1836, leaving an elder son,
EDWARD MICHAEL PAKENHAM, of whom hereafter, as successor to the Conolly estates.
2. Harriett Margaret Staples, m. 9 Feb. 1796, Richard, 1st Earl of Clancarty, and d. 30 Dec. 1847, leaving issue (see BURKE's Peerage).
4. Frances, m. William, 5th Viscount Howe, and d.s.p.
5. Caroline, m. 7 Dec. 1770, John, 2nd Earl of Buckinghamshire, and d. 26 Jan. 1817, leaving issue (see BURKE's Peerage).
6. Lucy, b. 10 June, 1740.
7. Jane, m. 10 Feb. 1770, George Robert FitzGerald, of Turlough, and d. 1780, leaving a dau.

Right Hon. William Conolly d. 3 Jan. 1754, and was s. by his eldest son,
RIGHT HON. THOMAS CONOLLY, of Castletown, a Privy Councillor in Ireland, m. 30 Dec. 1758, Lady Louisa Augusta Lennox, dau. of Charles, 2nd Duke of Richmond and Lennox, K.G., and d.s.p. By his will, proved 1808, he devised his estates to his widow for life, and at her death, which occurred in 1821, they devolved on his grand-nephew, who, thereupon assuming the surname and arms of CONOLLY by Royal Licence 27 Aug. 1821, became
EDWARD MICHAEL CONOLLY, of Castletown and Cliff, Lieut.-Col. Donegal Militia, and M.P. for co. Donegal, b. 24 Aug. 1786. He m. 20 May, 1819, Catherine Jane, dau. of Chambré Brabazon Ponsonby-Barker, by the Lady Henrietta Taylour his wife, dau. of Thomas, Earl of Bective, and had issue,
1. THOMAS, his heir.
2. Chambré Brabazon, d. 1835.
3. Frederick William Edward, b. 1826.
4. Arthur Wellesley, Capt. 30th Foot, b. 1828; killed at Inkerman, 5 Nov. 1854.
5. John Augustus, V.C., Lieut.-Col. in the Army, late Coldstream Guards, gallantly distinguished himself in the Crimea, b. 1829; m. 4 Aug. 1864, Ida Charlotte, youngest dau. of Edwyn Burnaby, of Baggrave Hall, co. Leicester, and d. 28 Jan. 1889, having by her (who d. 1886) had issue,
1. John Richard Arthur, b. 1869.
1. Aileen Geta Katherine, m. 10 Nov. 1891, Eustace Abel Smith, of Longhills, Lincoln, and has issue.
2. Oonagh Edwina, m. 22 Jan. 1891, John McNeill, Coldstream Guards, and has issue.
3. Louisa Augusta.
4. Irene Beatrice.
6. Richard, Sec. of Legation at Pekin, d. 28 Aug. 1870.
1. Louisa Augusta, m. 28 July, 1846, Clotworthy Wellington William Robert, 3rd Lord Langford, and was accidentally drowned, 5 Nov. 1853.
2. Henrietta, m. 29 May, 1880, Rev. Edward Montgomery Moore.
3. Mary Margaret, m. 6 June, 1854, Henry Bruen, of Oak Park, co. Carlow, M.P. (see that family).
4. Frances Catherine, d. 10 Jan. 1874.

Mr. Conolly d. 1848, and was s. by his eldest son,
THOMAS CONOLLY, of Castletown and Cliff, J.P. and D.L., High Sheriff 1848, and M.P. co. Donegal, b. 23 Feb. 1823; m. 1 Sept. 1868, Sarah Elizabeth, dau. of Joseph Shaw, of Temple House, Celbridge, co. Kildare, and had issue,
1. THOMAS, his heir.
2. William, b. 29 Oct. 1872; d. 17 June, 1895.
3. EDWARD MICHAEL, now of Castletown.
1. Catherine, b. 20 Oct. 1871; m. 21 April, 1904, Gerald Shapland Carew, only son of late Hon. Shapland F. Carew (see BURKE's Peerage, CAREW, B.).

Mr. Conolly d. 1876, and was s. by his eldest son,
THOMAS CONOLLY, of Castletown, co. Kildare, and Cliff, co. Donegal, Lieut. Scots Greys, b. 1 Sept. 1870, killed in action at Nitral's Nek, S. Africa, 11 July, 1900.

Arms—Arg., on a saltire engr. sa. five escallops of the field.
Crest—An arm couped below the elbow in pale ppr. vested az. cuffed arg. holding in the hand a chaplet or. Motto—Fiat Dei voluntas.

Seat—Castletown, Celbridge.

CONSIDINE OF DERK.

HEFFERNAN JAMES CONSIDINE, of Derk, co. Limerick, and of Farm Hill, in the same co., b. 3 Oct. 1883; s. his father, 12 Feb. 1912.

Lineage.—HEFFERNAN CONSIDINE, of Derk, co. Limerick, J.P. and D.L., High Sheriff 1859, son of Heffernan Considine D.L., of Derk, co. Limerick, who s. his maternal uncle William Heffernan, of Derk, in 1808, and d. 1833, aged 74, b. 1816; m. 1845, Mary, dau. of John MacMahon, J.P., of Firgrove, co. Clare. She d. 1885. He d. 1895, leaving issue,
1. HEFFERNAN JAMES FRITZ JOSEPH JOHN, of Derk.
2. Daniel (Rev.), S.J., b. 1849.
3. Percy (Shefford, Beds), b. 1861; m. 1st. 1896, Frances, dau. of F. Challenger Kelly, J.P. She d. 1897, leaving a son, Percy, b. 1897.
He m. 2ndly, 1900, Carmen, dau. of F. Challenger Kelly, J.P., and has issue.
4. St. John, b. 1862, Auditor, Local Government Board.
5. Patrick, b. 1867; m. 1901, Mary, dau. of John Smithwick, D.L., of Kilcreene, co. Kilkenny.
6. Thomas Ivor, b. 1868, F.R.C.S.I., Inspector of Lunatic Asylums.
1. Anna, m. 1880, Col. William White, late 15th Hussars, son of John White, D.L., of Nantenan, co. Limerick. He d. 1909.
2. Elizabeth.
3. Mary, m. 2 July, 1878, Lieut.-Col. William McCarthy O'Leary, S. Lancashire Regt., son of John McCarthy O'Leary, D.L., of Coomelagan, co. Cork. He was killed in South Africa, 27 Feb. 1900, leaving issue (see that family).
4. Helena.
5. Francis, a nun of the Ursuline Order.
6. Emily, m. 23 July, 1896, John Hyacinth Talbot, D.L., of Castle Talbot (see that family).
7. Mary Angela. d. unm. 1886.

The eldest son,
SIR HEFFERNAN JAMES FRITZ JOSEPH JOHN CONSIDINE, Knt. Bachelor (1908), C.B., M.V.O., of Derk, co. Limerick, and of Farm Hill, co. Dublin, D.L., co. Limerick High Sheriff 1881, Deputy Inspector-General Royal Irish Constab. 1900-11, B.A. Lincoln Coll. Oxford, formerly Resident Magistrate in Ireland 1882-1900, b. 24 Oct. 1846; m. 8 Jan. 1880, Emily Mary, dau. of John Hyacinth Talbot, D.L., of Castle Talbot, and Ballytrent, co.

Constable. THE LANDED GENTRY. 130

Wexford, sometime M.P. for New Ross, and Elizabeth his wife, dau. of Sir John Power, 1st bart., and d. 12 Feb. 1912, and by her (who d. 1903) had issue,
1. HEFFERNAN JAMES, now of Derk.
2. Talbot John, b. 30 Nov. 1884.
3. Christopher Daniel, b. 21 Dec. 1887.
4. Francis Augustus Reginald, b. 7 Feb. 1892.
5. St. John Power, b. 23 July, 1893.
1. Elizabeth Mary.   2. Mary.
3. Matilda Mary.   4. Anne Eliza Frances Mary.
Seat—Derk, Pallas Green, co. Limerick. *Residence*—Farm Hill, Dundrum.

CHICHESTER-CONSTABLE OF RUNNAMOAT.
See **CHICHESTER-CONSTABLE OF BURTON CONSTABLE, YORKS.**

LENOX-CONYNGHAM OF SPRING HILL.

WILLIAM ARBUTHNOT LENOX-CONYNGHAM, of Spring Hill, co. Londonderry, J.P., High Sheriff, 1909, late Major Worcestershire Regt., served in S. Africa 1900-1 (medal, three clasps), b. 8 Sept. 1857; m. 9 Aug. 1899, Mina Ethel, younger dau. and co-heir of James Corry Jones Lowry, D.L., of Rockdale, co. Tyrone (*see that family*), and has issue,
1. WILLIAM LOWRY, b. 20 Nov. 1903.
2. James Desmond, b. 20 May, 1905.
1. Wilhelmina Diana, b. 10 May, 1902.

Lineage.—WILLIAM CUNNINGHAM, a Scottish Protestant, was settled in the townland of Ballindrum, in which Spring Hill is situated, in 1609. Spring Hill was conveyed by the Salter's Company to the Conyngham family in 1657. The family of Lenox was settled in Londonderry, *temp.* JAMES I.
GEORGE CONYNGHAM, of Spring Hill, who m. 3 Aug. 1721, Anne, dau. of Dr. Peacock, of Cultra, and had issue,
1. WILLIAM, his heir.
2. DAVID, successor to his brother.
3. John, d. *unm.* 1775.
1. Anne, m. 13 June, 1745, Clotworthy Lenox, of the city of Londonderry (2nd son of John Lenox, by Rebecca Upton his wife, and grandson of James Lenox, M.P. for Derry, who was distinguished at the siege of that city), and had issue,
    1. John
    2. GEORGE, of whom hereafter.
    3. Clotworthy.
    1. Rebecca.
Mr. Conyngham d. 1765, and was s. by his eldest son,
WILLIAM CONYNGHAM, of Spring Hill, b. 29 April, 1723; in early life he entered the Army, and served with great distinction with his regiment, the 4th Horse, on the Continent, but on the death of his father he returned. He m. 3 Aug. 1775, Jane, only dau. of James Hamilton, of Brown Hall, co. Donegal, and relict of John Hamilton, of Castlefin, in the same co. Mr. Conyngham, who sat in Parliament for the Borough of Dundalk, d. without issue in 1784, and was s. by his brother,
DAVID CONYNGHAM, who also d. without issue, when according to the will of WILLIAM CONYNGHAM, the estates devolved upon his nephew,
GEORGE LENOX, who adopted the surname of CONYNGHAM. He m. 1st, 11 April, 1779, Jane, eldest dau. of Jane Conyngham, by her 1st marriage with John Hamilton, of Castlefin, and by her (who d. 20 Feb. 1793) had an only son,
1. WILLIAM LENOX, of Spring Hill.
Mr. Lenox Conyngham m. 2ndly, 5 April, 1794, Olivia, 4th dau. of William Irvine, of Castle Irvine, co. Fermanagh, and by her had issue,
2. George, Chief Clerk in the Secretary for State's Office for Foreign Affairs, m. Elizabeth, only child of Robert Holmes, of Dublin, Barrister-at-Law, and had issue, one son and one dau., Mary Ann Grace Louisa, m. 20 Aug. 1851, Hayes, 4th Viscount Doneraile, who d. 26 Aug. 1887, leaving issue (*see* BURKE's *Peerage*). She d. 24 Feb. 1907.
1. Sophia, m. the Hon. A. G. Stuart, of co. Tyrone.
2. Anna, m. C. A. Nicholson, of Balrath, co. Meath.
3. Harriett, m. Capt. Joseph Portlock, R.E.   4. Eliza.
The only son by the first marriage,
WILLIAM LENOX CONYNGHAM, of Spring Hill, J.P. and D.L., High Sheriff of Tyrone 1818, b. 9 Jan. 1702; m. 7 June, 1819, Charlotte Melosina, dau. of the Right Hon. John Staples, of Lissan, and by her (who d. 1847) had issue,
1. WILLIAM FITZWILLIAM (Sir), of Spring Hill.
2. John Staples Molesworth, b. 9 Jan. 1831; d. 17 Feb. 1851.
1. Harriett Rebecca Frances, m. 31 Jan. 1854, Marcus M'Causland Gage, of Streeve Hill.
2. Jane Hamilton, d. *unm.* 25 Nov. 1843.

3. Charlotte Melosina, m. 3 Oct. 1868, Major James David Beresford, 76th Foot (*see* BURKE's *Peerage*, WATERFORD, M.). She d. 17 Aug. 1880. He d.s.p. 27 Oct. 1878.
The eldest son,
SIR WILLIAM FITZWILLIAM LENOX-CONYNGHAM, K.C.B., of Spring Hill, co. Londonderry, J.P., D.L., High Sheriff 1859, and High Sheriff co. Tyrone 1868, Hon. Col. of the Londonderry Militia, formerly in the 88th Regt., b. 25 April, 1824; m. 5 Aug. 1856, Laura Calvert, dau. of George Arbuthnot, of Elderslie, Surrey, and d. 4 Dec. 1906, leaving issue,
1. WILLIAM ARBUTHNOT, now of Spring Hill.
2. George Hugh, b. 1 April, 1859; m. 13 April, 1898, Barbara Josephine, dau. of Capt. E. H. Turton, of Upshall Castle, Yorks (*see that family*).
3. John Staples Molesworth, Maj. Connaught Rangers, b. 23 Nov. 1861; m. 17 Dec. 1891, Violet, 2nd dau. of the late Henry Beveridge Donaldson, of Melbourne.
4. Arthur Beresford, b. 31 Aug. 1864; m. Feb. 1892, Emmeline Constance, dau. of H. Dowsett, of Port Elizabeth.
5. Gerald Ponsonby, Major R.E. b. 21 Aug. 1866; m. 15 Nov. 1890, Elsie Margaret, dau. of Surg.-Gen. Bradshaw, C.B.
6. Edward Fraser, b. 17 Dec. 1867; m. 10 Jan. 1899, Elizabeth Madeline, 2nd dau. of the late William Alexander Gunning, of Cookstown, co. Tyrone.
7. Hubert Maxwell, A.V.D., b. 18 Oct. 1869; m. 19 Oct. 1909, Eva, dau. of Edmund Sanders Darley, of Fern Hill, co. Dublin.
1. Elizabeth Mary, m. Nov. 1883, Lieut.-Col. J. Jackson Clark, of Largantoghor, co. Derry.
2. Charlotte Melosina.
3. Laura Eleanor, m. 28 Dec. 1895, James D. Duff, Fellow of Trinity College, Camb., 3rd son of Col. Duff, of Knockleith, cc. Aberdeen.
4. Harriet Alice Katherine.
Seat—Spring Hill, Moneymore, co. Londonderry.

COOKE OF KILTINANE.

ROBERT JOSEPH COOKE, of Kiltinane Castle, co. Tipperary, J.P., D.L., High Sheriff 1911, Lieut.-Col. (ret. pay), late comdg. 2nd Batt. Cheshire Regt., b. 1861; m. 1890, Henrietta, younger dau. of the late Louis Schloss, of Crumpsall Lodge, Crumpsall, Manchester.

Lineage.—EDWARD COOKE, son of Peter Cooke, and brother of Thomas Cooke, ancestor of the Castle Cooke family (*see* COOKE-COLLIS), had a grant of 1,300 acres in the cos. of Tipperary and Limerick. He m. and left issue,
1. JOHN, of Kiltinane Castle.
2. Peter (Rev.), Rector of Wells, co. Carlow.
The elder son,
JOHN COOKE, was one of the Commissioners named on the statutes of 9 WILLIAM III, c. 8, and 10 WILLIAM III, c. 3, for assessing the land and poll-taxes in co. Tipperary. His son and heir,
ROBERT COOKE, of Kiltinane Castle, was father, by his wife Christina, sister of Field-Marshal Wade, of
EDWARD COOKE, of Kiltinane Castle, m. 12 Oct. 1757, Abygail, dau. of John Greene, of Greenville, co. Kilkenny (*see that family*), and had issue, with a dau. Frances, m. Lieut.-Col. John Jackson Glover, 11th Infantry, a son and heir,
ROBERT COOKE, of Kiltinane Castle, J.P., m. Dec. 1791, Hannah, dau. of Sir Richard Wheeler Cuffe, Kt. of Leyrath, and had issue,
1. JOHN, of whom presently.   2. Robert.
1. Abigail, m. Rev. John Galwey, eldest son of Ven. William Galwey, Archdeacon of Cashel.
2. Anne Rosetta, d. *unm.* 1894.
He d. at Kiltinane Castle, 22 Feb.1849, aged 88 years, having survived his elder son,
JOHN COOKE, m. 31 Oct. 1823, Jane, dau. of Ambrose Ussher Congreve, of Mount Congreve, co. Waterford (*see that family*), and d.v.p. Oct. 1843, leaving by her (who d. 2 June, 1880) issue,
1. ROBERT, late of Kiltinane Castle.
2. Ambrose (Rev.), A.M., Vicar of Clane, co. Kildare, m. 1857, Maria, dau. of Rev. Joseph Chapman, and d. June, 1888, leaving issue, two sons and one dau., of whom,
    ROBERT JOSEPH s. his uncle and is now of Kiltinane.
3. Edward, d. 1905.   4. Frederick.
5. John, Major late 3rd Hussars, d. 1904.
6. Wheeler.
1. Anne, d. *unm.* 20 Feb. 1906.
2. Louisa, d. *unm.* 1889.
The eledst son,
ROBERT COOKE, of Kiltinane Castle, co. Tipperary, J.P., D.L., b. 1825; m. 1864, Henrietta, dau. of the late John Cornwall, of Brownstown House, co. Meath, and Rutland Square, Dublin. She d. 13 June, 1888. He d.s.p. 5 March, 1908, and was s. by his nephew.
Seat—Kiltinane Castle, Fethard, co. Tipperary.

COOKE-COLLIS. *See* COLLIS.

COOKE-CROSS. *See* CROSS.

COOKMAN OF MONART.

NATHANIEL EDWARD ROGERS COOKMAN, of Monart, co. Wexford, b. 1894; s. his grandfather 17 March, 1908.

Lineage.—EDWARD COOKMAN, of Enniscorthy, co. Wexford, J.P., High Sheriff 1763, m. 1752, Elizabeth Bayly, and d. 1774, having by her (who m. 2ndly, 1775, Joseph Bayley) had issue,
NATHANIEL COOKMAN, of Tomadilly, and Asherove, J.P., m. 1783, Elizabeth, eldest dau. and co-heir of Edward Rogers, of Monart, co. Wexford, by whom he had, with other issue, a son,
EDWARD ROGERS COOKMAN, of Monart, J.P., Barrister-at-Law, m. 1st, 1816, Mary Elizabeth, dau. of Col. Narcissus Huson, of Mt. Anna; and 2ndly, 1859, Isabella Stein, dau. of Andrew Jameson. Mr. Cookman d. 1865, having by his 1st wife had issue,
1. Charles Cassar, m. 1848, Charlotte, dau. of John Johnes, of Dolancothy, co. Carmarthen, Record and County Court Judge; d.v.p. 1859.
2. Edward Rogers, d. unm.
3. NATHANIEL NARCISSUS, of whom below.
4. William, of Kiltrea, co. Wexford, M.D., J.P., b. 1830; m. 16 April, 1868, Elizabeth, only dau. of William Bonville, of Bryn Towy, co. Carmarthen, and d. 19 Nov. 1911, having had issue,
   William Henry Elydyr, b. 3 June, 1870.
1. Alicia, d.v.p.
2. Mary, m. 1845, Samuel Tench.
The 3rd son,
NATHANIEL NARCISSUS COOKMAN, of Monart, J.P. and D.L., b. 1827; m. 1st, 1859, Laura Emma, dau. of Frederick J. Walter, of London. She d. 1861, leaving issue,
1. Edward Rogers Frederick, b. 12 Feb. 1861; m. 1892, Sarah, dau. of A. G. Davis, of Fairfield, co. Wexford, and d.v.p. 24 Nov. 1907, leaving issue,
   1. NATHANIEL EDWARD ROGERS, b. 1894, now of Monart.
   2. Charles Sydney.
Mr. Cookman m. 2ndly, 28 Nov. 1864, Sarah Porter, dau. of James Thornton, of Theobalds, Herts, and widow of George Putland Newbury, of Verona, co. Wexford, by whom he had further issue, viz.,
2. Nathaniel George.   3. Henry.
1. Mary, m. 23 Jan. 1908, Hugh Aylmer Thornton, I.C.S., 3rd son of T. Thoruton, of Swaffham, Norfolk.
He d. 17 March, 1908, when he was s. at Monart by his grandson, as above.

Seat—Monart, Enniscorthy, co. Wexford.

COOPER OF MARKREE CASTLE.

BRYAN RICCO COOPER, of Markree Castle, co. Sligo, J.P., D.L., High Sheriff 1908, b. 17 June, 1884, educated at Eton and R.M.A., Woolwich, Lieut. R.F.A. 1904, Capt. Special Reserve R.F.A. 1908, late Capt. Sligo Artill., M.P. for Dublin County (S.) Jan. to Dec. 1910; s. his grandfather 26 Feb. 1902; m. 19 March, 1910, Marion Dorothy, elder dau. of Edward Stanley Handcock, of Fulmer, Bucks. (see BURKE'S *Peerage*, CASTLEMAINE, B.), and has issue,

Ursula Rose, b. 17 May, 1911.

Lineage.—EDWARD COOPER, a Cornet in Richard, Lord Coloney's regiment of Dragoons, settling in Ireland, became possessed of a great estate in that kingdom. His will, dated 20 Dec. 1679, was proved 5 Jan. 1680. By Margaret his wife, dau. of Nicholas Mahon, of Ballinamulty, co. Roscommon, he had issue,
1. Edward, d.s.p.   2. ARTHUR, his heir.
3. Richard, to whom his father gave his lands in the counties of Limerick and Kerry.
1. Mary, m. George Ormsby, of Lough Mask.
2. Margaret, m. Gustavus Hamilton.
The 2nd son,
ARTHUR COOPER, of Markree, co. Sligo, heir to his brother Edward, m. (art. dated 18 May, 1693) Mary, dau. of Sir Joshua Allen, Knt., father of John, 1st Viscount Allen, and had issue.
1. JOSHUA, his heir.
2. Richard, d.s.p.
1. Mary, m. Robert Folliott, of Hollybrook.
2. Elizabeth.   3. Anne, m. John Perceval.
4. Eleanor, d. unm.   5. Margaret.
The eldest son,

JOSHUA COOPER, of Markree (whose will, dated 3 Aug. 1757), was proved 17 Jan. 1758), m. (art. dated 5 May, 1729) Mary, dau. of Richard Bingham, of Newbrook, co. Mayo, and left two sons; the younger, Richard, of Bath, m. Miss Leigh, but d.s.p. The elder,
THE RIGHT HON. JOSHUA COOPER, of Markree, M.P. co. Sligo, and of the Privy Council in Ireland, m. (art. dated 10 May, 1788) Alicia, only dau. and heir of Edward Synge, D.D., Bishop of Elphin, and had issue,
1. JOSHUA, of Markree, m. Elizabeth, dau. of Robert Lindsay, and d. 1837, s.p.
2. Edward Synge, m. Anne, dau. of Harry Verelst, Governor of Bengal, and d. 1830, leaving issue,
   1. EDWARD JOSHUA, late of Markree.
   2. Joshua Harry, d.s.p.
   3. Richard Wordsworth, b. 1801; m. 1826, Hon. Emilia Eleanor de Montmorency, dau. of Lodge Evans, 1st Viscount Frankfort de Montmorency, and d. March, 1850, leaving issue,
      (1) EDWARD HENRY, late of Markree Castle.
      (2) Joshua Harry, of Dunboden, co. Westmeath, J.P., High Sheriff 1875, Col. (retired) late Lieut.-Col. 7th Fusiliers, b. 1831; m. June, 1857, Helen Malet, dau. of Capt. Haydon, R.N. He d. 19 July, 1901, leaving issue,
         1. Edward Joshua, of Dunboden, C.B., M.V.O., D.S.O., Lieut.-Col. Royal Fusiliers, b. 21 April, 1858; m. 1894, Effie, only dau. of James Forrest Balmain, of Dalvreck, co. Perth.
         2. Richard Wordsworth, b. 1860.
         3. Myles Henry, Lieut. R.N., b. 1862, killed in action 1888, d. unm.
            1. Constance Emily, m. 1881, W. Jackson, of Rugby.
      (3) Richard Augustus, of Kiteloonagh, co. Tipperary, J.P. co. Warwick, Lieut.-Col. and Hon. Col. 4th Batt. R. Irish Regt. formerly Capt. Scots Fusilier Guards, b. 1833; m. 1866, his cousin Cecily Florence, youngest dau. of Edward J. Cooper, of Markree, and d. 1890.
      (4) William Synge Cooper, b. 1843.
         (1) Emelia Ann, m. 1850, Charles Hartpole Bowen, of Courtwood, Queen's Co.
         (2) Catherine Elizabeth, m. N. R. Sykes, 4th son of Joseph Sykes, of Rawell.
         (3) Frances Louisa.
   2. Richard, d.s.p.
   1. Jane, d. unm.
His grandson,
EDWARD JOSHUA COOPER, of Markree, M.P. for that co., m. 1st, Sophia, 3rd dau. of Henry Peisley L'Estrange, of Moyestown, King's Co., which lady d.s.p.; and 2ndly, Sarah Frances, dau. of the late Owen Wynne, of Haslewood, co. Sligo, by whom he had issue,
1. Laura Frances, m. 7 Feb. 1860, Dudley Warre, Commander late R.N., 2nd son of J. A. Warre, M.P. She d. 15 March, 1893, leaving issue (see that family).
2. Charlotte Sophie.
3. Emma Marie, m. 8 Sept. 1870, Henry Eastwood.
4. Selina Elizabeth.
5. Cicely Florence, m. 8 May, 1866, Richard Augustus Cooper, Capt. Scots Fusilier Guards, 3rd son of Richard W. Cooper.
Mr. Cooper d. 23 April, 1863, and was s. by his nephew,
THE RIGHT HON. LIEUT.-COL. EDWARD HENRY COOPER, P.C., of Markree Castle, co. Sligo, Lieut. of that co., J.P., High Sheriff 1871, late Lieut.-Col. Grenadier Guards, M.P. co. Sligo 1865-8, b. 9 July, 1827; m. Aug. 1858, Charlotte Maria, only child of Edward Wheler Mills, youngest son of William Mills, of Bisterne, Hants, and d. 26 Feb. 1902, leaving issue,
1. Francis Edward, Major R.F.A., b. 12 May, 1859; m. Sept. 1883, Ella, eldest dau. of Col. Mark Prendergast, B.S.C., and d.v.p. 26 May, 1900, leaving issue,
   1. BRYAN RICCO, now of Markree.
   2. Guy Edward, b. 27 Nov. 1891.
   1. Beatrice Kathleen, b. July, 1886; m. 31 July, 1907, Frederick Rowland Williams-Wynn, youngest son of the late Charles Watkin Williams-Wynn, M.P., Recorder of Oswestry, and has issue (see BURKE's *Peerage*, WYNN, Bart.).
   2. Helen Mary, b. March, 1895.
   3. Cicely Frances Anne, b. July, 1897.
2. Richard Joshua, C.V.O. (1900), M.V.O. (1902), of Blackwell Hall, Bucks, Col. Irish Guards 1906; Brev.-Col. 1904; served with Egyptian Expedition, 1882, present at action of Mahuta and at battle of Tel-el-Kebir (medal with clasp, bronze star), and in S. Africa, 1900, as Railway Staff Officer; was Private Sec. to Lord-Lieut. (Earl of Dudley) 1904-5 (3, *Grosvenor Gardens*, S.W.), b. 18 July, 1860, Col. late Grenadier and Irish Guards; m. 17 Dec. 1904, Constance Mary, dau. of the late Alexander William Grant Thorold, of Cosgrove Hall, Northants (see that family).
3. Arthur Charles, b. May, 1864.
1. Kathleen Emily, b. 1861.
2. Florence Lucy, twin with Arthur Charles.
3. Venetia Helen.

Arms—Quarterly: 1st az., on a chevron, between three cinque; foils or, two lions passant respecting each other sa.; 2nd, arg. a chevron engrailed between three martlets az.; 3rd, az., three millstones ppr.; 4th, arg., an eagle displayed with two heads sa. beaked and legged gu. **Crest**—A demi-man affrontée, habited per pale arg. and sa., in the dexter hand ppr. a covered cup or, on the head wreathed round the temples arg. and az. a cap gu. **Motto**—Deo, patria, rege.

Seat—Markree Castle, Collooney, co. Sligo. *Clubs*—Carlton, Kildare Street, Dublin.

Cooper. THE LANDED GENTRY. 132

COOPER OF COOPER'S HILL.

WILLIAM AUGUSTUS COOPER, of Cooper's Hill, Queen's Co., J.P., b. 24 Oct. 1839, M.A. Trin. Coll. Dublin, 1874.

Lineage.—EDWARD COOPER fought in the Battle of the Boyne in King WILLIAM'S Army, and was granted lands in co. Carlow.

THOMAS COOPER, of Newtown, co. Carlow, sold his estate in co. Carlow and purchased the Sragh estate in Queen's Co. He joined the Society of Friends, and d. 23 June, 1714, and was bur. at New Garden, co. Carlow. He had two sons, William, who d. 7 Nov. 1713, and

EDWARD COOPER, of Sragh (now Cooper's Hill), Queen's Co., m. 26 May, 1697, Ann, dau. of John Inglefield, of Dublin, and had issue,
1. Thomas, b. 22 Jan. 1699; d. 16 Feb. following.
2. Thomas, b. 29 Sept. 1703; d. 17 July, 1711.
3. Edward, b. 3 April, 1705. 4. John, b. 6 Aug. 1706.
5. WILLIAM, of whom hereafter.
1. Elizabeth, b. 1 Aug. 1700; d. 12 March, 1702.
2. Sarah, b. 25 Sept. 1702; m. Abel Strettell, of Dublin, and d. 9 Aug. 1719.
3. Anne, b. 7 Sept. 1713; m. 12 Aug. 1733, John Penrose, of Waterford, son of William Penrose.

Edward Cooper's will is dated 29 Oct. 1739. He had the lands of Cranemore, co. Carlow, and Aghnacross, and Knockardigur, Queen's Co. His youngest son,

WILLIAM COOPER, of Cooper's Hill, alias Sragh, b. 7 Aug. 1709; m. 31 Jan. 1730, Experience, dau. of Abel Strettell, of Dublin, merchant, by whom (who d. 13 May, 1773, will dated 18 Sept. 1769, proved 1771) he had issue,
1. EDWARD, his heir.
2. Abel, b. 17 Oct. 1734.
3. Thomas, of Mullimast, co. Kildare, b. 3 Jan. 1736, whose dau. and heiress, Juliana, m. 6 Aug. 1789, Richard, 2nd Lord Waterpark, and d. 11 Oct. 1847.
1. Lydia, m. Robert Clibborn, son of Joshua Clibborn, of Whylam Grove, co. Kildare.
2. Anne Clibborn, b. 29 April, 1738.
3. Sarah Clibborn, b. 5 May, 1739; m. Barclay Clibborn, of Moate Castle, co. Westmeath.

William Cooper's will is dated 1760, and was proved 20 Jan. 1761. He d. 28 Dec. 1760, and was s. by his eldest son,

EDWARD COOPER, of Cooper's Hill, b. 1 May, 1733; m. 23 May, 1754, Sarah, dau. of Robert Clibborn, of Whylam Grove, co. Kildare, and had issue,
1. WILLIAM, his heir.
2. Edward, b. 13 March, 1767.
1. Ann, b. 14 Oct. 1755; d. unm. 1834.

Mr. Cooper d. 17 Feb. 1797, and was s. by his eldest son,

WILLIAM COOPER, of Cooper's Hill, b. 7 Feb. 1757, High Sheriff co. Carlow 1793; m. by licence, dated 28 April, 1789, Susan, dau. of William Cope, of Merrion Square, Dublin (see BURKE's Peerage, COPE, Bart.), by whom (who was b. 27 Aug. 1766, and d. 1826) he had issue,
1. WILLIAM COPE, his heir.
2. Edward, b. 1800; d. unm. 1826.
3. ROBERT, of Cooper's Hill, heir to his brother.
4. Henry, b. 1809; a Gen. in the Army, Col. in the 45th "Sherwood" Foresters, was for many years at the Cape and in Natal and Acting Governor of that colony in the absence of the Civil Governor; m. 1843, Jane, dau. of — Boughton, and d. 1878, having had issue,
Henry, b. 1845; d. 1878.
1. Elizabeth, m. 1825, Joseph Fishbourne (d. 1826), of Straw Hall, co. Carlow, and d. 1876, leaving a dau., Sarah, m. Rev. F. J. Durbin, Vicar of Harston, Cambridgeshire.
2. Sarah, b. 1793; d. 1825. 3. Susan, b. 1794; d. 1875.
4. Anne, b. 1798; d. unm. 1893.
5. Charlotte, m. Rev. R. Hamilton, and d. 1882.
6. Alicia, d. unm. 1894.
7. Maria Theresa, d. unm. 14 March, 1897.

Mr. Cooper d. June, 1830, and was s. by his eldest son,

WILLIAM COPE COOPER, of Cooper's Hill, J.P., D.L., High Sheriff for Queen's Co. 1831, b. 1795; d. unm. 1874, when he was s. by his next surviving brother,

REV. ROBERT COOPER, of Cooper's Hill, M.A. Trin. Coll. Dublin, Incumbent of Aghade and Gilbertstown, co. Carlow, b. 15 Aug. 1802; d. 20 Oct. 1870; m. 1838, Alicia Maria (Isabella), dau. of William Augustus Le Hunte, of Artramont, co. Wexford, and by her (who d. 16 Sept. 1883) had issue,
1. WILLIAM AUGUSTUS, his heir.
2. Edward George, b. 1842, M.A. T.C.D. 1874; d. unm. March, 1879.
3. Robert Thomas, b. 1844, M.A., M.D. T.C.D.; m. 1870, Mary Amelia, dau. of Maj.-Gen. John Byng, C.B., Madras Cavalry. He d. 14 Sept. 1903, leaving issue,
1. Robert Montagu Le Hunte, M.D., Capt. R.A.M.C., and Surgeon attached 2nd Batt. Grenadier Guards, b. 30 March, 1872.
1. Edith Clara Byng. 2. Eveline Gladys Graeme.
4. Charles Hamlet, C.E., Surveyor Urban District Council, Wimbledon, b. 1854.
1. Susan Cope, d. 15 Aug. 1904.

Seat—Cooper's Hill, Carlow.

COOPER OF COOPER HILL.

ROBERT COOPER, of Cooper Hill, co. Limerick, J.P., Lieut. late R. Indian Marine, and a Younger Brother of Trinity House, b. 1866; m. 1901, Etheldred Louisa Hamilton, dau. of Frederick George Hilton Price, F.S.A., and has issue, two daus.

Lineage. — CHRISTOPHER TUTHILL, Lieut. R.N., m. Grace, dau. of Robert Reeves, of Platten, co. Meath, and had with other issue, an eldest son,
JAMES COOPER.

JAMES COOPER COOPER (formerly Tuthill), of Cooper Hill, co. Limerick, J.P., on succeeding to the estate of Cooper Hill, under the will of his relative Honora, relict of James Cooper, of Cooper Hill, assumed by Royal Licence, 1844, in compliance therewith the name and arms of COOPER. He d. 1906, having had by his 1st wife Mary (d. 1877), dau. of the late Charles Pickering, of Roebuck, co. Dublin, with other issue,
1. James, b. 1865.
2. ROBERT, now of Cooper Hill.

Arms—Sa., a fesse wavy erm. between three lions rampant or. Crest—A demi-lion rampant or. Motto—Noli irritare leonem.
Seat—Cooper Hill, Clarina, co. Limerick. Club—Junior Naval and Military.

COOPER OF KILLENURE.

AUSTIN SAMUEL COOPER, of Killenure Castle, co. Tipperary, J.P., Capt. 2nd Cheshire Regt., served with 2nd Cheshire Regt. in S. African War 1900-02 (Queen's medal with three clasps, King's medal with two clasps), (ret. pay) 1905, joined 3rd Batt. Cheshire Regt. 1905, Hon. Major 1906, retired 1910, b. 8 Nov. 1870; m. 16 Jan. 1907, Evelyn Ethel, elder dau. of John R. Leahy, of South Pasadena, California (see LEAHY of Carriglea), and has issue,
1. AUSTIN FRANCIS, b. 20 Jan. 1909.
2. Astley John, b. 25 Sept. 1911.
1. Doreen Eleanora Anna, b. 14 Nov. 1907.

Lineage.—AUSTIN COOPER (whose father held an appointment in the Court of CHARLES I), though a supporter of the royal cause, subsequently purchased a tract of land from Hammond, a soldier of CROMWELL's on the restoration of CHARLES II. He was obliged to forfeit, whereupon he sold all his possessions in England, and retired to Ireland 1661, before the Act of Oblivion was passed. He m. at Hampton Court, Mary, dau. of Henry Dodson, of Kingston-on-Thames, and niece to Erasmus Smith, who left large estates for the endowment of schools in Ireland; by her he had issue, six sons and three daus. The 2nd son,

AUSTIN COOPER, b. at Hampton Court, 1653, fixed his residence at Beamore, near Drogheda, co. Meath. He m. 15 July, 1683, Susanna, dau. of William Ransford, and dying 17 Oct. 1743, left with other issue,
1. SAMUEL, his heir.
2. Joseph, of Barn Hall, co. Kildare, m. 29 March, 1748, Hannah, dau. of Henry Delamain, and d. 2 July, 1786, leaving issue.

The eldest son,

SAMUEL COOPER, of Beamore, b. 1686; m. Dorothea, dau. of William Harrison, of Carlisle, and dying 26 Dec. 1761, left, with other issue,
1. Samuel, of Beamore. 2. WILLIAM, of whom hereafter.
3. John, of Cooperhill, co. Meath, m. 18 Sept. 1753, Mary, dau. and co-heiress of Thomas Paget, and dying in 1808, left, with other issue,
Nathaniel, of Cooperhill, Capt. 68th Regt., m. 1795, Elizabeth, dau. of Hugh Lyons Montgomery, and dying 1818, left, with other issue, Nathaniel, of Cooperhill, m. Anne, dau. of Henry Irwin, of Streamtown, co. Sligo, and dying 1852, left, with other issue, Henry Alexander Cooper, now of Cooperhill.

The 2nd son,

WILLIAM COOPER, b. 1721, becoming Registrar of the Diocese of Cashel, fixed his residence at Killenure 1746. He m. May, 1747, Jane, dau. of Henry Wayland, of Kilmore House, co. Tipperary, and by her had, with several daus.,
1. SAMUEL, of whom presently.
2. AUSTIN, b. 1759, F.S.A. and M.R.S.A., of Merrion Square, Abbeyville House, and Kinnealy, co. Dublin. This gentleman held places of high trust and emolument under the Irish Government, and was a devoted antiquary and lover of literature. He m. 17 July, 1786, Sarah MacWilliam, dau. of Timothy Turner, and dying 30 Aug. 1830, left, with other issue, a son,

Rev. Austin Cooper, of Kinnealy, who *m.* Margaret, dau. of James Armstrong, and dying 1871, left, with othe. issue, a son, Austin Damer Cooper, of Drumnigh and Kinnealy, *b.* 2 Jan. 1831.

Mr. Cooper *d.* 15 Nov. 1769, and was *s.* by his eldest son,

SAMUEL COOPER, of Killenure, *b.* 14 June, 1750 ; *m.* 1769, Frances, dau. of David Butler, of Garranleagh, co. Tipperary, and dying 1831, was *s.* by his only surviving son,

WILLIAM COOPER, of Killenure, J.P., *b.* 19 July, 1772 ; *m.* 27 April, 1798, Rebecca, dau. of Rev. Richard Chadwick, of Perryville, co. Tipperary, and dying 9 April, 1850, left issue, a son and a dau., Eleanor, wife of Richard William Ralph Sadleir, of Sadleir's Wells, co. Tipperary, and was *s.* by his only surviving son,

SAMUEL COOPER, of Killenure, J.P., an Officer 2nd or Queen's Regt., *b.* April, 1800 ; *m.* March, 1829, Louisa Salisbury, dau. of Richard Long, of Longfield, co. Tipperary ; and dying Jan. 1861, left issue,

1. SAMUEL, of Killenure.
2. RICHARD AUSTIN, *m.* 1855, Katherine, eldest dau. of William Chadwick, of Ballinard, co. Tipperary, and assumed by Royal Licence, the name and arms of CHADWICK in addition to those of COOPER (*see* COOPER-CHADWICK *of Ballinard*). Mr. Cooper-Chadwick *m.* 2ndly, 1863, Charlotte Sophia, eldest dau. of John Bourchier, J.P., of Baggotstown, co. Limerick, and *d.* 19 Jan. 1893, leaving issue.
3. William, *d.* in Australia.   4. AUSTIN, late of Killenure.
5. Edward, Capt. Mercantile Marine, *d.* at sea.
6. Astley, Commander R.N. (medals for China and Abyssinia) ; *d.* 1872.
1. Charity, *m.* 1854, John Battersby, of Bobsville, co. Meath.
2. Maria Louisa, *m.* 1866, Edward Rotheram, of Sallymount, co. Westmeath.

The eldest son,

SAMUEL COOPER, of Killenure Castle, *b.* 1829, an Officer in the 44th Regt., with which he served in the Eastern Expedition 1854 ; *d.* 21 July, 1877, *unm.*, and was *s.* by his brother,

AUSTIN COOPER, of Killenure Castle, co. Tipperary, J.P. and High Sheriff 1893, Lieut. R.N., Reserve, *b.* 1835 ; *m.* 1st, Sept. 1868, Anna Wilhelmina, dau. of Very Rev. Ogle William Moore, Dean of Clogher and formerly Dean of Cashel, and by her (who *d.* Nov. 1870) had issue,

AUSTIN SAMUEL, now of Killenure.

He *m.* 2ndly, 14 Aug. 1878, Emma Harriet, 2nd dau. of Major-Gen. W. Armstrong, 22nd Regt., and *d.* 1897, and was *s.* by his only son. His widow *m.* 15 Aug. 1911, Cecil V. Barrington.

Seat—Killenure, Dundrum, co. Tipperary. *Club*—Kildare Street, Dublin.

ASHLEY-COOPER.

[*See* BURKE'S PEERAGE, **SHAFTESBURY, E.**

COOPER-CHADWICK. *See* **CHADWICK.**

COOTE OF BALLYCLOUGH CASTLE AND BEARFOREST.

CHARLES ROBERT PURDON COOTE, of Ballyclough Castle and Bearforest, co. Cork, *b.* 23 Jan. 1875, only son of the late Charles Purdon-Coote, D.L. of Ballyclough Castle, and Bearforest, co. Cork, who *d.* 20 Sept. 1893, and Harriette Louisa, his wife, dau. of Robert Perceval Maxwell, D.L. of Finnebrogue, and great-grandson of Robert Carr Coote, next brother of Sir Charles Henry Coote, 9th bart.

Lineage Arms, &c.—*See* BURKE'S *Peerage*, COOTE, Bart.
Seats—Ballyclough Castle, and Bearforest, Mallow, co. Cork. *Club*—Kildare Street, Dublin.

COOTE OF MOUNT COOTE.

CHARLES JAMES COOTE, of Mount Coote, co. Limerick, late Capt. 1st Batt. 18th Royal Irish Regt., *b.* 19 Aug. 1837 ; *s.* his uncle 1897 ; *m.* 6 June, 1867, Emily, youngest dau. of the Hon. and Rev. Henry Pakenham, D.D., Dean of St. Patrick's (*see* BURKE'S *Peerage*, LONGFORD, E.). She *d.s.p.* 23 May, 1896.

Mr. Coote is the only surviving son of the late Lieut.-Col. Charles James Coote, 18th Regt., who *d.* 24 May, 1853, and Anne his wife, dau. of Thomas Stewart, and nephew of Charles John Aldworth Coote, of Mount Coote, who *d.s.p.* 20 Jan. 1897, and 6th in descent, from Sir Philips Coote, Knt. of Mount Coote, grandson of Sir Charles Coote, 1st bart.

Lineage, Arms, &c.—*See* BURKE'S *Peerage*, COOTE.
Seat—Mount Coote, Kilmallock, co. Limerick. *Residence*—10, Somerset Place, Bath. *Clubs*—Union and Windham.

COOTE OF CARROWROE PARK.

STANLEY VICTOR COOTE, of Carrowroe Park, co. Roscommon, J.P., High Sheriff 1900, M.A. Oxford, *b.* 30 May, 1862 ; *m.* 26 Oct. 1889, Louisa, dau. of Ven. Frederick Bathurst, Archdeacon of Bedford, and has had issue,

1. Margaret Stanley, *b.* 24 Oct. 1893 ; *d.* 21 June, 1894.
2. Honor Dorothea, *b.* 18 Nov. 1896.

Mr. Coote is the only son of the late Adm. Robert Coote, C.B., who *d.* 17 March, 1898, and Lucy his wife, of Tahlee, Beckenham, dau. of Adm. Sir William E. Parry, K.C.B., and grandson of Sir Charles Henry Coote, 9th Bart., of Ballyfin.

Lineage, Arms, &c.—*See* BURKE'S *Peerage*, COOTE, Bart.
Seat—Carrowroe Park, Roscommon. *Residence*—Burley Manor, Ringwood. *Clubs*—Union, Automobile.

COOTE. *See* BURKE'S PEERAGE, **COOTE, Bart.**

COPE OF DRUMMILLY.

JOHN GARLAND COPE, of Drummilly, co. Armagh, J.P. and D.L., *b.* 25 July, 1850 ; *m.* 1st, 23 April, 1878, Theresa Charlotte, dau. of Ralph S. Obré, of Clantilew, co. Armagh, and by her (who *d.* 15 Dec. 1880) has issue,

JOHN RALPH OBRÉ, *b.* 6 May, 1879.

He *m.* 2ndly, 27 Jan. 1900, Mary Edith, dau. of Col. Lonsdale A. Hale, R.E.

Lineage. — WALTER COPE, of Drummilly, co. Armagh, eldest son of Richard Cope (3rd son of Sir Anthony Cope, 1st bart. of Hanwell, (*see* BURKE'S *Peerage and Baronetage*), by Anne his wife, sister of Sir William Walter, left at his decease (his will was dated 1658), by Abigail his 1st wife, dau. of Thomas Moigne, Bishop of Kilmore, a son and heir,

WALTER COPE, of Drummilly, *m.* Jane, dau. of Very Rev. James Downham, Dean of Armagh, and by her (who *d.* April, 1688) left a son,

WALTER COPE, of Drummilly, *m.* Sarah, dau. of Thomas Tippling, and *d.* 1724, leaving a son, WALTER, of whom presently, and five daus., all of whom *d. unm.*, except the youngest, Abigail who *m.* May, 1758, Archdeacon Samuel Meade, and had one dau., SARAH ARABELLA ABIGAIL, of whom hereafter. Mr. Cope was *s.* by his son,

THE RIGHT REV. DR. WALTER COPE, of Drummilly, Bishop of Ferns and Leighlin, *m.* Anne, dau. of Sir Arthur Acheson, Bart. of Gosford, co. Armagh, but *d.s.p.* 31 July, 1787, and was *s.* by his niece,

SARAH ARABELLA ABIGAIL MEADE, who assumed the surname of COPE. She *m.* Nicholas Archdale, of Castle Archdale, co. Fermanagh, and had issue (besides one dau. ANNA, who *s.* her brother) three sons, Walter, *d. unm.* ; Samuel Walter, *d. unm.* ; and

ARTHUR WALTER COPE, of Drummilly, who *m.* Caroline Lester, and had one dau., Caroline Arabella Archdale (*d.* 20 April, 1906), who *m.* Francis Wilson Heath, of New Grove, Lisburn. Mr. Cope *d.* 8 Nov. 1846, and was *s.* under the will of his grand-uncle, Dr. Walter Cope, by his sister

Cope.   THE LANDED GENTRY.   134

ANNA, of Drummilly, *m.* 3 March, 1814, Nathaniel Garland, of Michaelstowe (*see that family*). He *d.* 3 Jan. 1845. Mrs. Garland on *s.* to Drummilly, assumed the name of COPE, under Royal Licence, and *d.* 4 May, 1867, having by will devised her estates to her 3rd dau.,

GEORGINA CATHERINE, of Drummilly, who *m.* 16 May, 1848, JOHN ALEXANDER MAINLEY PINNIGER. They assumed by Royal Licence 10 Aug. 1867, the name and arms of COPE. He was J.P. and High Sheriff co. Armagh 1868, and *d.* 21 March, 1892, aged 68, having had issue,

1. Edgar Broome, *b.* 26 March, 1849 ; *d. unm.* July, 1891.
2. JOHN GARLAND, now of Drummilly.
3. Arthur Mainley, *b.* 27 April, 1854.
4. George Cope, *b.* 12 July, 1855 ; *m.* 5 July, 1906, Marie Catherine, widow of late Richard Christian, of Radlett, Herts, and dau. of late Thomas John Pittar.
5. Frederick Lorance, *b.* 26 Feb. 1857.
1. Amy.
2. Anna Martha Georgina, *m.* to James Prinsep Beadle.
3. Mary Constance, *m.* Charles Stewart Lovell.

Mrs. Cope *d.* 19 April, 1895, and was *s.* by her eldest surviving son.

Arms—Arg., on a chevron az. between three roses gu. slipped and leaved ppr. as many fleurs-de-lis, or. Crest—Out of a fleur-de-lis or, a dragon's head issuing gu. Motto—Æquo adeste animo.

Seat—Drummilly, Loughgall, co. Armagh. Residence—28, Burton Court, Chelsea, S.W. Club—Constitutional.

COPE OF LOUGHGALL MANOR.

FRANCIS ROBERT COPE, of The Manor, Loughgall, co. Armagh, D.L., *b.* 21 Nov. 1853.

Lineage. — ANTHONY COPE, of Portadown, co. Armagh, younger brother of Walter Cope, of Drummilly (*see that family*), and grandson of Sir Anthony Cope, 1st bart., of Hanwell (*see* BURKE'S *Peerage and Baronetage*), *m.* Jane, dau. of Thomas Moigne, Bishop of Kilmore, by whom (who *d.* 31 Dec. 1640) he had an only son,

VERY REV. ANTHONY COPE, LL.D., Dean of Elphin, *m.* his 2nd cousin, Elizabeth, dau. and eventual heiress of Henry Cope, of Loughgall, and grand-dau. of Anthony Cope, of Armagh, who was 2nd son of Sir Anthony Cope, 1st bart. of Bramshill, and *d.* Feb. 1705, leaving, with other issue, a son and heir,

ROBERT COPE, of Loughgall, M.P. for Armagh, *m.* 1st, Sept. 1707, Letitia, dau. of Arthur Brownlow, of Lurgan, who *d.s.p.* ; and 2ndly, 6 March, 1701, Elizabeth, dau. of Sir William Fownes, Bart. of Woodstock, by whom (who *d.* 4 Dec. 1748) he had with other issue (of whom Elizabeth, *m.* 7 June, 1740, Thomas Morris Jones, of Moneyglass, and had issue, *see that family*),

1. ANTHONY (Very Rev.), *s.* his father in the Manor of Mount Norris, appointed Dean of Armagh 1753, *d.s.p.* 26 April, 1764. His widow *m.* Charles Jackson, Bishop of Kildare.
2. ARTHUR, of whom hereafter.

Mr. Cope *d.* 17 March, 1753. His younger son,

ARTHUR COPE, of Loughgall, *m.* Jan. 1761, Ellen Osborne, and had issue,

1. ROBERT CAMDEN, his heir.
2. Kendrick, Lieut.-Col , *d. unm.* Aug. 1827.
1. Emma.   2. Elizabeth.
3. MARY, *m.* COL. RICHARD DOOLAN, E.I.C.S., and had two sons,
   1. ROBERT WRIGHT COPE DOOLAN, who assumed the surname of COPE on succeeding to the estates of his cousin.
   2. Kenrick Hugh Doolan, *m.* Sept. 1831, Mary Leigh, and *d.* 1848.

The elder son,

ROBERT CAMDEN COPE, of Loughgall, M.P. for Armagh, Lieut.-Col. Armagh Militia, *m.* Mary, dau. of Samuel Elliott, Governor of Antigua, and had an only son,

ARTHUR COPE, of Loughgall, *b.* 1814 ; *d.s.p.* 1844, and bequeathed his estates to his cousin,

ROBERT WRIGHT COPE DOOLAN, of Loughgall Manor, J.P. and D.L., *b.* 2 Feb. 1810 ; who assumed the surname and the additional arms of COPE by Royal Licence 30 May, 1844, *m.* 6 June, 1848, Cecilia Philippa, dau. of Capt. Shawe Taylor, of Castle Taylor, co. Galway, and *d.* 1858, having had issue,

1. FRANCIS ROBERT, now of Loughgall Manor.
1. Albinia Elizabeth, *m.* 1876, Rev. Francis Arthur Powys, 4th son of Henry Philip Powys, of Hardwick House, Berks.
2. Emma Sophia.
3. Helen Gertrude, *m.* 1877, The Ven. Francis Briggs Sowter, Archdeacon of Dorset.

Arms—Quarterly : 1st and 4th, COPE, arg., on a chevron az. between three roses gu. stalked and leaved vert, as many fleurs-de-lis or, a mullet of the second for difference ; 2nd and 3rd, DOOLAN, arg., three crescents in pale az. between two pellets in fess. Crests—1st, COPE, out of a fleur-de-lis az, charged with a mullet gu. a dragon's head of the second ; 2nd, DOOLAN, on a chapeau az. turned up erm. a crescent or, therefrom issuant a trefoil slipped vert. Motto—Æquo adeste animo.

Seat—The Manor, Loughgall.

COPLEN-LANGFORD. *See* LANGFORD.

COPPINGER OF ROSSMORE (formerly of Ballyvolane).

JAMES COPPINGER, of Rossmore House, co. Cork, *b.* 1863 ; *m.* Delia, dau. of Thomas McDonnell, of the city of Cork.

Lineage.—STEPHEN COPPINGER, chief of the name, Alderman and sometime Mayor of Cork, M.P. for the city of Cork in the first year of Queen ELIZABETH, 1559, *d.* 2 July, 1600, and was *s.* by his eldest son,

WILLIAM COPPINGER, aged 30 years at the time of his father's death. He *d.s.p.* 1 Dec. 1606, and was *s.* by his next brother,

THOMAS COPPINGER, aged 28 years at the time of his brother's death. He *m.* Catherine, eldest dau. of Alderman John Coppinger, the eldest son of the John Coppinger, who was ancestor of the Coppingers or Copingers of Crosshaven, of Glenville, of Carhue, of Cloghane, and of Coolnapishy or Peafield, all in the co. Cork, by his 1st wife Johan, dau. of Justice John Meagh, Judge of the Munster Presidency Court. He *d.* 24 Dec. 1635, leaving issue,
1. STEPHEN, his successor.   2. John, *unm.* in 1636.
1. Catherine, *m.* Francis Roche, High Sheriff of Cork, 1641, ancestor of Lord Fermoy (*see* BURKE'S *Peerage*).
2. Joan.

The eldest son,

STEPHEN COPPINGER, of Ballyvolane, *b.* 1610 ; *m.* Ellice, dau. of Henry Gould, of Cork, Alderman, and *d.* 28 July, 1681, having by her (who *d.* 1688) had issue,
1. THOMAS, his successor.
2. William, High Sheriff of Cork 1687, outlawed for high treason, and was the ancestor of the Coppingers of Bordeaux.
3. Henry, also outlawed for his loyalty ; was a Capt. in the service of King JAMES II. (Carroll Dragoons), and was ancestor of the Coppingers of Ballynoe, co. Cork, and Rock Abbey, co. Tipperary.
4. Matthew, outlawed as a Jacobite.

The eldest son,

THOMAS COPPINGER, of Ballyvolane, was attainted and outlawed for his loyalty to King JAMES II. (*see* inquisition enrolled in Chancery, taken at the Guildhall, Cork, upon his attainder, and dated 31 March, 1693) and retired to France. From a letter of his son, Stephen, dated 7 July, 1729, he appears to have been then still living. He *m.* Jan. 1669, Hellen, dau. of Edward Galway, of Lotabeg, co. Cork, who *d.* 1684. They had issue, four sons and two daus.,
1. STEPHEN, his successor.
2. Edward, predeceased his father. He is said to have been a Capt. in the service of King JAMES II., and to have been mortally wounded in the celebrated engagement at Bottlehill, near Mallow, co. Cork, 1 April, 1691. In the petition of his brother John to the Court of Claims, Chichester House, he is stated to have *d. unm.* in 1696.
3. John, of Granacloyne, in the barony of Barrymore, co. Cork, ancestor of Coppingers of Midleton (*see that family*).
4. Edmond, obtained a decree of the Court of Claims, Chichester House, establishing his right of succession to Ballyvolane, and the other settled lands of his father upon failure of issue of his brothers, Stephen and John. Nothing further is now known of him.
1. Joan, *m.* Nov. 1706, Conor O'Brien, of Kilcor, co. Cork.
2. Katherine, *m.* Nov. 1706, Joseph Ronayne, of Cork.

He was *s.* by his eldest son,

STEPHEN COPPINGER, of Ballyvolane, described in the minute of his marriage contract (registered at Rochelle, in France, 18 Oct. 1700) as " Seigneur de Villetoreau " ; *m.* his cousin Johanna, dau. of Stephen Gould, of Cork (her sister subsequently *m.* his brother John). He had issue,
1. JOHN, his heir.   2. WILLIAM, eventual inheritor.
3. Joseph, *m.* 1743, Mary Arthur, and had issue, six sons and three daus.
1. Mary, *m.* 2 Feb. 1732, Patrick Rochfort, and *d.* 17 Aug. 1736.
2. Teresa, *m.* Patrick Sarsfield, of Johnstown, co. Cork.

Mr. Coppinger was *s.* by his eldest son,

JOHN COPPINGER, of Ballyvolane, *m.* 1st, 1729, Mary, eldest dau. and co-heiress of Nicholas Blundell, of Crosby, by Frances, dau. of Marmaduke, Lord Langdale and by her (who *d.* 6 Aug. 1734) had issue, one son, viz., Stephen Coppinger, who *d.* young, 1745. He *m.* 2ndly, 1736, Elizabeth, dau. and co-heiress of Michael Moore, of Drogheda, and by her (who *d.* 1770) had issue, one dau., Marianne, who *m.* 27 July, 1767, Charles Howard, 11th Duke of Norfolk (*see* BURKE'S *Peerage*), and *d.* 22 May, 1769, in giving birth to a still-born son.

Mr. Coppinger, of Ballyvolane, *d.* about 1747, and was *s.* by his next brother,

WILLIAM COPPINGER, of Ballyvolane and Barryscourt, *m.* 1737, his cousin Elizabeth, dau. of John Galwey, of Luota, co. Cork, and g[ra]d-dau. of Colonel John Butler, of Westcourt, co. Kilkenny, 2nd son of the Hon. Richard Butler, of Kilcash, General of the Confederate Catholics, and brother of the 1st Duke of Ormond. He had issue (besides four daus., viz., 1. Mary, who *m.* Feb. 1770, Cornelius O'Brien, of Kilcor, co. Cork, and had issue; 2. Catherine, who *m.* Oct. 1779, John Callanan, M.D. of Cork; 3. Elizabeth, a nun; and 4. Teresa, *m.* Nov. 1789, Pierce Power, of Clonmult, co. Cork, and had issue) seven sons,
1. Stephen, who predeceased his father, dying in boyhood, in the co. Kilkenny.
2. WILLIAM, his successor. 3. John, *d. unm.*
4. THOMAS, of Rossmore, co. Cork, of whom later.
5. Richard, an Officer in the Austrian service, *d. unm.* at Prague.
6. Joseph, of Ballydaniel, co. Cork, *m.* his cousin, Alicia, dau. of John Coppinger, of Granacloyne, and had issue, one son, William Joseph, *m.* his cousin, Margaret, sister of Cornelius O'Brien, of Kilcor, co. Cork, and had issue (besides three daus., viz., Alice; Mary, a nun; and Margaret) two sons,
(1) John Joseph, of Omaha, Neb., Brig.-Gen. U.S. Army, is next in remainder to Ballyvolane and other Coppinger estates in co. Cork upon failure of the issue of the present proprietor, under the will of the late William Coppinger, of Ballyvolane and Barryscourt, Colonel Coppinger, *b.* 1835; *m.* 6 Feb. 1883, Alice Stanwood, dau. of Senator Blane (Republican candidate for the Presidency of the United States of America), and has issue, one son,
Blaine Coppinger, *b.* 6 Nov. 1883.
(2) Henry.
7. James, *m.* his cousin Alicia, sister of his cousin Stephen William Coppinger, of Midleton, and had issue (besides four daus., 1. Eliza, *d. unm.* 1868; 2. Jane, *d. unm.* 1847; 3. Mary, an Ursuline nun, *d.* 1876; and 4. Alicia, a Presentation nun, *d.* 1878) six sons,
1. John, *d.s.p.* about 1818.
2. William, *m.* 1st, Ellen, dau. of Richard Moylan, and by her had issue one son,
(1) James, R.C. priest (who *d.* 1849).
He *m.* 2ndly, Harriet, dau. of the Rev. James Sanders, and by her had issue a son and dau.,
(2) William, Professor in the Lycée National, Paris.
(1) Harriet.
3. James, *d. unm.* 1847.
4. Stephen, *d.* 1831. He *m.* Louisa, only dau. of James Usborne, of Trinidad, and had issue one son, Hiliary, *d. unm.* 1852, and three daus.,
(1) Mary, *m.* Michael Lennon, of Trinidad, and had issue.
(2) Louisa.   (3) Jane.
5. Thomas Stephen, Commander R.N., *m.* 1827, Rosanna, dau. of William Duncan, and dying 1878, left issue,
(1) Albert William Duncan Coppinger, M.D., of Bath, *b.* 1848.
(1) Alicia Mary, *d.* 1854.   (2) Mary Jane, *d.* 1856.
(3) Victoria.
6. Richard, *d. unm.* 1853.
Mr. Coppinger, of Ballyvolane and Barryscourt, *d.* about 1775, and was *s.* by his eldest surviving son,
WILLIAM COPPINGER, *b.* about 1740; *m.* Nov. 1777, his third cousin, Jane (who *d.* 31 Jan. 1833), sister and heiress of Donat McMahon, of Clenagh, co. Clare, and *d.* 15 July, 1816, having had issue, two sons and two daus.,
1. WILLIAM, of Barryscourt, co. Cork and Ballylean Lodge, co. Clare, representative of the Coppingers, of Ballyvolane, and the McMahons, of Clenagh, co. Clare, *b.* 9 Dec. 1778; *d. unm.* 6 Nov. 1862. At his death the Coppinger family estates (including Ballyvolane, Barryscourt, Granacloyne, &c.) passed, by devise, to his nephew.
2. John McMahon, 13th Dragoons, *d. unm.* 1830.
1. Elizabeth, *m.* Feb. 1806, John O'Connell, of Grenagh, co. Kerry, brother of Daniel O'Connell, M.P. (*see* O'CONNELL *of Darrynane*) and *d.* 21 Dec. 1863, having had issue, two sons and two daus.,
1. MORGAN JOHN O'CONNELL, heir to his uncle, of Barryscourt, co. Cork, and Ballylean, co. Clare, Barrister-at-Law, M.P. for co. Kerry (1635-1652), *b.* 27 Aug. 1811; *m.* 21 Feb. 1865, Mary Anne, dau. and heiress of Charles Bianconi, D.L. of Longfield, co. Tipperary. She *d.* 28 Jan. 1908. He *d.* 2 July, 1875, having had issue (*see* O'CONNELL *of Darrynane*).
2. John Dominick Patrick, a R.C. priest, *b.* 25 March, 1828; *d.* 1873.
1. Jane Frances, *m.* 1st, Charles, The O'Donoghoe, of the Glens, and by him had issue one son, viz., Daniel, the late "O'Donoghue, of the Glens," M.P.; she *m.* 2ndly, John McCarthy O'Leary, D.L., of Coomlagane, co. Cork, and by him had issue, four sons and four daus.
2. Catherine Mary, *m.* Samuel Vines, and has issue, three sons.
2. Mary, *m.* her cousin, James Blackney, eldest son of Walter Blackney, M.P. for co. Carlow, *d.s.p.* Sept. 1833.
We now return to
THOMAS COPPINGER, of Rossmore, co. Cork, 4th son of William Coppinger, of Ballyvolane and Barryscourt, and Elizabeth Galwey. He *m.* his cousin Dorinda, dau. of Edmond Barry, of Dundellerick, and Rocklodge, co. Cork, by Johanna Coppinger, of Granacloyne, and had issue (besides four daus., 1. Johanna, who *m.* her cousin, Stephen William Coppinger, of Midleton, and had issue; 2. Dorinda, who *m.* her cousin, Luke Shea, of the Rennies, co. Cork; 3. Mary, who *m.* Michael Cronin, of Cork; and 4. Teresa, who *m.* James Fitzgerald, of Carrigacrump, co. Cork), four sons,
1. EDMOND, of Rossmore.
2. William, *m.* 1st, Mary, dau. and co-heiress of John Power, of Brooklodge, co. Waterford, and *m.* 2ndly, Elizabeth, dau. of John Hickson, of the co. tKerry, and *d.* March, 1837. By his 1st marriage he had issue one son and one dau.,
Thomas Power Coppinger, an Officer in the service of ISABELLA II. of Spain; *b.* 1808, *m.* 1845, Marian, dau. of Capt. W. Crotty, R.N., and *d.* 1864, having had issue.
Mary, *m.* Pearce Power, of Clonmult, eldest son of Teresa Coppinger, of Barry's Court.
3. John, *d. unm.* 1850.   4. Joseph, *d. unm.* 1854.
The eldest son,
EDMOND COPPINGER, of Rossmore, *m.* Alice, dau. of Luke Shea, by his wife Catherine Coppinger, of Granacloyne, and had issue (besides a dau. Catherine, who *m.* her cousin, Cornelius O'Brien, J.P., of Kilcor), one son,
THOMAS FITZEDMUND COPPINGER, of Rossmore, *b.* 1808; *m.* 1st, his cousin, Marcella, sister of the late Major-General Sir Michael Galwey. She *d.* 1847, having had issue (besides a dau., Marcella, who *m.* John Hartnett, J.P., of Carrigeen, co. Cork) two sons,
1. Edmond, *b.* 1843; *d.v.p.*
2. THOMAS, of Rossmore, of whom below.
Mr. Coppinger, of Rossmore, *m.* 2ndly, his first cousin, Elizabeth Fitzgerald, dau. of James FitzGerald, by his wife Teresa Coppinger, and *d.* 1881, having by her had issue, four sons and three daus.,
3. William, *d.* young.   4. John, *d.* young.
5. James, now of Rossmore, *b.* 1863.
6. Edward (*Melbourne, Victoria*), *b.* 1865.
1. Teresa.   2. Alicia.
3. Dora.
The 2nd son,
THOMAS COPPINGER, of Rossmore, *b.* 1844; *d. unm.* 1897, when he was *s.* by his half-brother as above.

Seat—Rossmore, Carrigtwohill, co. Cork.

COPPINGER OF MIDLETON.

THOMAS STEPHEN COPPINGER, of Midleton, co. Cork, J.P., *b.* 1 July, 1843; *s.* his brother 1862; *m.* 4 March, 1878, Martha, eldest dau. and co-heiress of Edward Murphy, of Cahirelly, co. Limerick, and has issue,
1. Bertram Edward, *b.* 11 Aug. 1880; *d.* 1893.
2. THOMAS STEPHEN, *b.* 8 Oct. 1885.
1. Elizabeth Mary.   2. Hilda Marta.
3. Violet.   4. Mary Annette.
5. Rose Cecilia.

Lineage.—JOHN COPPINGER, of Granacloyne, co. Cork, 3rd son of Thomas Coppinger, of Ballyvolane (*see* COPPINGER *of Rossmore*), *m.* Nov. 1711, Mary Gould, sister of the wife of his eldest brother, Stephen, of Ballyvolane, and had issue (besides a dau. Johanna, who *m.* Edmond Barry, of Dundellerick and Rocklodge, co. Cork, and had issue, amongst other children, Dorinda, who *m.* her cousin Thomas, of Rossmore, son of William Coppinger, of Barryvolane, whose issue have since become the senior surviving branch of the Ballyvolane Coppingers) two sons, namely,
1. John, who *m.* Alice, dau. of John Lonergan, of The Wilderness, co. Tipperary, and had issue three sons, 1. John, 2. William, and 3. Morgan, who all *d.* young and *unm.*, and four daus., namely, 1. Catherine, *m.* Luke Shea, of Britfieldstown, co. Cork, and was mother of Alice, wife of Edmond Coppinger, of Rossmore (*see* COPPINGER O'CONNELL); 2. Mary, *m.* Robert Wigstrum, and had issue; 3. Alicia, who *m.* her cousin Joseph, son of William Coppinger, of Ballyvolane; and 4. Hanna, who *m.* Luke Gardiner, of Cork.
2. WILLIAM, of whom presently.
The 2nd son,
WILLIAM COPPINGER, of Granacloyne, *b.* 1720; *m.* April, 1755, Mary, dau. of — Gould, of Cork, and *d.* Oct. 1787, leaving issue (besides three daus., namely, 1. Alicia, *m.* her cousin James, son of William Coppinger, of Ballyvolane, and had issue; 2. Charlotte, *m.* Maurice Fitzgerald, representative of the seneschal of Imokilly; and 3. Anne, *m.* 1794, Garrett Barry, representative of the Barrys of Rahinisky and Robertstown, and *d.s.p.*), one son, namely,
STEPHEN WILLIAM COPPINGER, of Midleton, co. Cork, *b.* 17 May, 1761; *m.* his cousin, Johanna, dau. of the above-mentioned Thomas Coppinger, of Rossmore, and had issue (besides two daus., viz., 1. Dorinda, *m.* John Mussen Ashlin, of Rushhill, co. Surrey, and Carrigrennan, co. Cork, and dying 6 July, 1884, left issue; and 2. Mary) six sons, namely,
1. THOMAS STEPHEN, his successor.
2. Stephen William, in holy orders of the Church of Rome, *d.* 1851.
3. Joseph William, M.A., Solicitor, of Farmley, Dundrum, co. Dublin, and of East Clonmult, co. Cork, *b.* 8 Sept. 1807; *m.* 11 June 1835, Agnes Mary, only dau. of William Labor Cooke, of Fortwilliam, co. Tipperary, representative of the Cookes of Gurranegreney; and *d.* 28 July, 1883, having had issue,
1. Stephen William, *b.* 1864, Margaret, dau. of Joseph Hanly, of Ardavon, co. Dublin. He *d.* 23 Jan. 1899. She *d.* 6 June, 1878, leaving issue, four sons and two daus.,
(1) Joseph, *b.* 1867.
(2) John, *b.* 1868; *m.* Feb. 1904, Ellen Agnes Lynch.
(3) Stephen, *b.* 1873.   (4) Richard, *b.* 1876.
(1) Agnes.
(2) Nannie, *m.* 21 Jan. 1903, William Hewson Carroll, and has issue.

Corbally. THE LANDED GENTRY.

2. Valentine John, Barrister-at-Law (8, *Morehampton Road, Dublin*), b. 14 Feb. 1841; m. 12 Aug. 1872, Katherine, eldest dau. of Sir Robert Kane, of Fortlands, co. Dublin, and Glendree, co. Clare, and had issue, four sons,
  (1) Walter Valentine, M.D., F.R.C.S.I., Capt. I.M.S. (Bengal), b. 1 March, 1875; m. 30 June, 1909, Rita, only dau. of William Henry O'Kelly, of Sion House, Glenageary, co. Dublin, and has issue.
  (2) Robert Henry, Commander R.N., b. 5 March, 1877; m. 27 Sept. 1909, Georgiana Katherine Grace, 3rd dau. of late G. Bousfield Long, J.P., of The Chipping House, Wotton-under-Edge, and has issue,
    Robert Patrick, b. 3 Aug. 1910.
  (3) Charles Joseph, Capt. R.A.M.C., b. 5 Nov. 1880; m. 16 Sept. 1908, Aimée Louise, dau. of late G. T. Jackson, Advocate, High Court, Lucknow, and has issue,
    Marguerite.
  (4) Francis Romney, Capt. I.M.S., b. 10 May, 1883.
3. Charles Philip, of Ballyrearta, co. Cork, M.D., F.R.C.S.I., Fellow of the Royal University, d. unm. 22 Dec. 1908.
4. Richard William, M.D., Inspector-Gen. of Hospitals and Fleets, R.N., the well known author, naturalist, and explorer, m. 8 Jan. 1884, Tillie, elder dau. of Harvey Browne, of New South Wales and Queensland. He d. 2 April, 1910, having had issue,
  (1) Richard Vernon, b. 3 Nov. 1884; d. 11 Oct. 1888.
  (2) Brendan, Lieut. R.N., b. 15 May, 1886.
  (3) Cuthbert, R.N., b. 28 April, 1890.
  (1) Eily Frances, b. 30 Sept. 1887.
5. John Joseph.
6. William, d. young.
1. Susan, d. young.
2. Agnes, d. unm. 23 April, 1898.
4. William, of Ballyrearta, co. Cork, d. unm. 16 Jan. 1885.
5. Richard, of Midleton House, d. unm. 1847.
6. Edmond Stephen, of Glenturkin, co. Cork, m. Maria, only dau. of Thomas Brenan, and d. 2 Aug. 1881, having had issue, six sons and two daus.,
  1. Thomas Edmond. 2. Richard.
  3. Joseph. 4. Edmond, d.s.p. Sept. 1881;
  5. William. 6. John.
  1. Alicia, a nun.
  2. Annette, m. 1909, James Kearney, of Cairo.
Mr. Coppinger, of Midleton, d. 23 Oct. 1820, and was s. by his eldest son,
THOMAS STEPHEN COPPINGER, of Midleton, J.P., b. 6 Jan. 1800; m. 13 Feb. 1840, Annette, dau. of Sir John Power, Bart., of Edermine, co. Wexford, and d. 13 Aug. 1861, having by her (who d. 1889) had issue, three sons,
1. JOHN, of Midleton, co. Cork, b. 1841; d. unm. 16 June, 1862.
2. THOMAS STEPHEN, the present representative.
3. Stephen Power, Capt. 3rd Batt. Royal Munster Fusiliers, b. 1847; m. 1873, his cousin Ada, dau. of Thomas Power, M.D., of Clonmult, co. Cork, and d. 29 May, 1900, having had issue,
  1. Thomas Power, b. 1 Oct. 1879.
  1. Annette Mary Adeline, d. 1884.
  2. Emily Mary Jane, m. 9 Sept. 1899, Eric Severne, son of Edwin Severne, of Warwick.
  3. Ada Elizabeth, m. 4 Feb. 1907, Col. E. S. Bridger, late Gren. Gds.

Seat—Midleton Lodge, Midleton, co. Cork.

CORBALLY OF RATHBEALE.

ELIAS MARY BENEDICT CORBALLY, of Rathbeale Hall, co. Dublin, J.P. co. Dublin, M.A. Trin. Coll. Dublin, b. 1868; m. 26 Nov. 1910, Lady Mary Pepys, dau. of the 3rd Earl of Cottenham (see BURKE's *Peerage*), and has issue,

MATTHEW CHARLES MARY PEPYS, b. 8 Nov. 1911.

Lineage.—MATTHEW CORBALLY, of Rathbeale Hall, co. Dublin, b. 1751, m. 1785, his first cousin Mary, dau. of Edward Dease, by Alice his wife, dau. of Elias Corbally, of Rathregan, co. Meath, and had issue a son,
ELIAS CORBALLY, of Rathbeale Hall, co. Dublin, m. 1835, Margaret, dau. of James Murphy, of Rosemount, co. Dublin. She d. 1866. He d. Sept. 1846, leaving an only son,
MATTHEW JAMES CORBALLY, of Rathbeale Hall, co. Dublin, J.P. and D.L., b. 18 Aug. 1837; m. 7 Feb. 1865, Sara Louisa, dau. and co-heir of Thomas O'Kelly, of Bridge House, co. Kerry, and d. 30 April, 1907, having had issue,
1. ELIAS MARY BENEDICT, now of Rathbeale.
2. Matthew, b. 1872.
3. Louis William, b. 1876; m. 26 April, 1906, Nancy, dau. of John J. Whyte, D.L., of Loughbrickland (see *that family*)
4. Cyril. 5. Herbert.
1. Mary Margaret, m. 1 Sept. 1902, Charles Austin, 6th Baron ffrench, and has had issue (see BURKE's *Peerage*).
2. Angela Mary, m. 24 Feb. 1903, Commander Reginald Yorke Tyrwhitt, R.N., youngest son of the late Rev. R. St. John Tyrwhitt, of Christ Church, Oxford.
3. Edith Mary. 4. Josephine Mary.
5. Frances Mary.

Seat—Rathbeale Hall, Swords, Dublin. Club—Windham.

CORCOR OF COR CASTLE.

MRS. SOPHIA CORCOR, of Cor Castle, co. Cork, dau. of late John Tonson Rye, of Rye Court, m. 1840 the late James Richard Moore Corcor, of Cor Castle, who d. 1872, leaving issue (see *below*), and s. her last surviving son 1873.

Lineage.—ROBERT CORKER, of Manchester, bur. there 24 Oct. 1648, had issue,
1. THOMAS, bapt. at Manchester 2 Dec. 1638, of whom below.
2. John, bapt. at Manchester 24 Jan. 1640-1, bur. 5 Feb. 1640-1.
3. John, b. 1643, matric. Trin. Coll. Dublin 10 May, 1659, aged 16.
4. Francis, bapt. 12 Jan. 1644-5; bur. 21 April, 1646.
5. Francis, bapt. 26 July, 1646.
6. Benjamin, bur. 18 March, 1648-9.
The eldest son,
THOMAS CORKER, bapt. at Manchester 2 Dec. 1638, Merchant, of Dublin; m. (lic. 28 Feb.) 1662, Abigail, dau. of Robert Chambre, of Dublin, and d. 19 March, 1716, aged 78; bur. at Churchtown, co. Louth. Issue,
1. Edward, of Ballymaloe, co. Cork, Lieut.-Col., will dated 14 Oct. 1725, proved 1733; m. 1701, Margaret, dau. of Peter Wallis, of Shangarry, co. Cork; s.p.
2. CHAMBRE, of whom below.
3. Thomas, bur. at St. John's, Dublin, 8 Nov. 1666.
4. Thomas, will proved 1737; m. 1715, Ruth, dau. of Richard Falkiner; s.p. Her will proved 1772.
1. Mary, bur. at St. John's 3 Nov. 1666.
2. Anne, m. — Wright.
3. Elizabeth, m. Edward Bolton.
4. Margaret.
5. Sarah, m. — Morton.
6. Mary, m. — Ruddock.
The 2nd son,
CHAMBRE CORKER, of Falmouth and afterwards of Dublin, Mayor of Falmouth 1716, 1717 and 1723, d. in Dublin 12 June, 1747, will proved 1748; m. Honour, dau. of William Methuish. Issue,
1. Robert (Rev.), b. at Falmouth 1704, matric. Trin. Coll. Dublin 23 May, 1722, B.A. 1727, Rector of St. Buryan, Cornwall, will proved 1765; m. 1737, Hannah, dau. and co-heir of James Tresilian, of Tresider. Issue,
  1. Chambre, d. unm. 1740.
  2. Robert, b. 1743; d. unm. 1770, will.
  3. Edward, b. 1744.
  4. James Chambre, b. 1747; d. unm. 1789.
  5. Joseph, b. 1752; d. unm. 1771.
  1. Martha, b. 1738; d. unm. 1780.
  2. Rebecca, b. 1739; m. Richard Dennis.
  3. Hannah, b. 1741.
  4. Elizabeth, b. 1745; m. John Vigurs.
2. THOMAS, of whom next.
3. Edward, b. 1713. 4. William, b. 1717.
5. Chambre, b. 1719; m. (?) dau. of Rendel Heron, and had issue, Thomas.
1. Rebecca, b. 1709; d. unm. 1739.
2. Abigail, b. 1712; m. Patrick Briscoe.
3. Martha, b. 1715; d. unm. 1790.
4. Anne, b. 1716.
The 2nd son,
THOMAS CORKER, b. 1707, purchased property near Innishannon from the Earl of Cork and Burlington, and built Firgrove, where he resided. He m. 20 April, 1738, Hannah, dau. of Rev. John Moore, and had issue,
1. John. 2. Thomas.
3. CHAMBRE of whom next.
The 3rd son,
CHAMBRE CORKER, of Upper Lola, Cork, Archdeacon of Ardagh (will proved 1790), m. Elizabeth, dau. of Dr. Jemmett Brown, Archbishop of Tuam, by whom he had issue,
CHAMBRE CORKER, of Dowdaniel and Cor Castle, Innishannon, who served in the Royal Navy and was afterwards Capt. 87th South Cork L.I., b. 1773; d. 1845, having m. 1st, Caroline (d. 6 Aug. 1825), dau. of Richard Badham Thornhill, of Thornhill Lawn, by whom he had issue,
1. Chambré, b. 1802; m. — Victoire, dau. of Gen. Greaves, of Frankfort, Innishannon, and had issue,
  1. Chambré, b. 6 Oct. 1834, entered the Army, and d. in India.
  1. Carolin Victoire, b. 10 Feb. 1827.
  2. Victoire Emily, b. 6 Nov. 1830.
2. JAMES RICHARD MOORE, late of Cor Castle.
1. Eliza, b. 1800; m. Henry Baldwin, of Mount Pleasant, Bandon, and d. 14 Dec. 1833, having had issue.
2. Caroline, b. 1805; d. unm. 11 June, 1838.
3. Anna Sophia, b. 1810; m. 22 June, 1848, Capt. William Henry Herrick, late 51st Regt. (see HERRICK of *Shippool*), and had issue.
He m. 2ndly, — Ellen Gertrude Mann, by whom he had further issue,
3. Anthony, d. young.
4. Gertrude Caroline. 5. Elizabeth Anna Mann.
6. Louisa, d. young. 7. Katherine, m.
The 2nd son,
JAMES RICHARD MOORE CORCOR, of Cor Castle, b. 1814; d. 1872, having m. 14 March, 1840, Sophia, eldest dau. of late John Tonson Rye of Rye Court (see *that family*), and had issue,

1. Chambré, *d. unm.* 17 Jan. 1867.
2. RICHARD RYE, of whom next.
3. Eliza Katherine, *m.* Henry Slorach, M.D., Surgeon, South Cork L.I.
2. Caroline Georgina Sophia, *m.* Henry Stillington Grey Stephenson, of Lympsham Manor, Somerset, and has issue.
3. Georgina Alice, *m.* Col. T. Herbert Brock, Royal West Kent Regt., and *d.* 1890, having had issue.

Is 2nd son,
RICHARD RYE CORCOR, of Cor Castle, Lieut. and Adjt. 24th Regt., *d. unm.* at Gibraltar 6 March, 1873, when he was *s.* by his brother, now of Cor Castle.

Seat—Cor Castle, co. Cork.

CORNOCK OF CROMWELLSFORT.

JOHN HAWKES CORNOCK, of Cromwellsfort, co. Wexford, J.P., *b.* 9 Nov. 1841; assumed by Royal Licence, dated 1 March, 1883, the additional surname and arms of CORNOCK, on succeeding to Cromwellsfort. He *m.* 4 Feb. 1875, Mary Charlotte, only child and heir of Richard Hughes, of Wrexham, co. Denbigh, and Emma Edisbury his wife, and has issue,

1. JOHN, Capt. 3rd Royal Irish Regt. (*Little Clonard, Wexford*), *b.* 16 July, 1876; *m.* 21 Feb. 1906, Elsa, eldest dau. of Col. Burrows, of Budleigh Salterton, Devon.
2. Zack Edisbury, *b.* 5 Nov. 1880.
3. Richard, *b.* 13 May, 1886; *d.* 31 May, 1899.
1. Henrietta Emma, *b.* 18 March, 1883; *m.* 2 Aug. 1906, Harry Hall Irvine.

Lineage.—LIEUT.-COL. JACOB CORNOCK commanded a brigade at the battle of Naseby, after which he went to Ireland, and got a grant of Banemore, Upper Clarragh and Cloghskreggy, co. Kilkenny, by patent dated 3 Dec. 1668. His will is dated 9 Nov. 1671, and he left, by his wife, whose surname was Evans, two sons,
1. ISAAC, his successor.
2. Zachariah, of Kilkenny, merchant, *a.* intestate. Administration granted 16 July, 1691.

The elder son,
ISAAC CORNOCK, of Cork, *m.* 22 June, 1686, Hannah, only child of Lieut.-Col. Corbett, of Ferns, co. Wexford, and had, with two daus., Melior and Hannah, one son. His will, dated 20 March, 1689, was proved 12 Jan. 1691. His only son,
ISAAC CORNOCK, of Cork, *b.* 1687; *m.* 23 Sept. 1708, Mary, dau. of George Jervois, of Brade, co. Cork, and *d.* Aug. 1732, leaving an only son,
ZACHARIAH CORNOCK, of Kilcasson, *m.* 1709; *m.* Frances, dau. of the Rev. Bartholomew Thomas, Rector of Ferns; and *d.* 31 Dec. 1740, leaving with three daus., Mary (*d.* April, 1749), Frances Hannah (*d.* June, 1749), and Elizabeth (*d.* June, 1749), an only son,
ISAAC CORNOCK, of Kilcasson, *b.* Aug. 1739; *m.* 10 Oct. 1764, Sarah, dau. of Francis Wheeler, of Motabeg, co. Wexford, great-grandson of Col. Francis Wheeler, of Cromwell's Army, and by her (who *d.* 2 Aug. 1779) had issue,
1. ZACHARIAH, his successor.
1. Frances, *d. unm.* 26 March, 1783.
2. Mary, *m.* 5 March, 1789, John Hawkes, of Grange, co. Cork, J.P., and *d.* 13 June, 1848, having by him (who *d.* 2 July, 1832) three sons and three daus.,
  1. John. 2. Isaac Cornock.
  3. ZACHARIAH CORNOCK HAWKES, of Moneens House, co. Cork, *m.* 1840, Henrietta Margaret, dau. of John Long, of Westfield, and *d.* 27 May, 1874, leaving issue,
    (1) JOHN HAWKES, now of Cromwellsfort.
    (2) Zachariah Cornock Hawkes, *m.* 1872, and left issue three sons and three daus.
    (3) Richard Henry Hawkes.
    (4) Isaac Cornock Hawkes, *m.* 1881, and left issue.
    (5) William Hawkes, *m.* 1880, and has three sons and one dau.
    (1) Henrietta, *d. unm.*
    (2) Frances Mary Hawkes, *m.* 1877, and has one son and two daus.
  1. Mary Anne. 2. Frances.
  3. Sarah.

He *d.* 30 Nov. 1804, and was *s.* by his only son,
THE REV. ZACHARIAH CORNOCK, of Cromwellsfort, J.P., *b.* 3 March, 1770; *m.* 17 Feb. 1815, Charlotte dau. of Thomas Burgh, of Bert, co. Kildare, and sister of Ulysses, 2nd Lord Downes, and by her (who *d.* 1 Sept. 1827) had issue,
1. ISAAC, his heir.
2. Thomas Burgh, *d. unm.* 2 June, 1829.
3. Zachariah Burch, *m.* 1858, Elizabeth Alicia, only dau. of Capt. William Huson, of Springfield, and *d.* 1874, leaving an only son,
  ZACHARIAH CHARLES, late of Cromwellsfort.

Rev. Zachariah Cornock *d.* 1858, and was *s.* by his eldest son,
ISAAC CORNOCK, of Cromwellsfort, J.P., served in 14th Light Dragoons, *b.* 1815; *d. unm.* 5 Oct. 1874, when he was *s.* by his nephew,
ZACHARIAH CHARLES CORNOCK, of Cromwellsfort, *b.* May, 1860; *d. unm.* at Bournemouth, co. Southampton, 12 Dec. 1882, and was *s.* by his kinsman JOHN HAWKES CORNOCK, now of Cromwellsfort.

Arms—Quarterly: 1st and 4th, per fess gu and az., a dexter cubit arm issuing from the sinister, grasping in the hand a sword, all ppr., in chief two crescents or, for CORNOCK; 2nd and 3rd, arg. a pale gu., three hawks' heads erased two and one, counterchanged, in the centre chief point a cross pattée or, for HAWKES. **Crests**—1st, CORNOCK: a dexter cubit arm fesswise, the hand grasping a sword erect, all ppr., the arm charged with two crescents in fess az.; 2nd, HAWKES: On a branch oak sprouting lying fesswise, a hawk rising, all ppr., jessed and belled or (with motto over, Virtute non vi). **Motto**—Animo et fide.

Seat—Cromwellsfort, Wexford.

CORRY. *See* BURKE'S PEERAGE, **BELMORE, E.**

COSBY OF STRADBALLY.

ROBERT ASHWORTH GODOLPHIN COSBY, of Stradbally Hall, Queen's Co., Vice-Lieutenant, J.P., High Sheriff 1863, Col. 3rd Leinster Regt., late Lieut. Inniskilling Dragoons, *b.* 7 April, 1837; *m.* 1st, 18 Oct. 1859, Alice Sophia Elizabeth, only dau. of Sir George Edward Pocock, Bart., of The Priory, Christchurch, Hampshire, and by her (who *d.* 1878) has had issue,

1. DUDLEY SYDNEY ASHWORTH, *b.* 12 Jan. 1862, late Lieut. Rifle Brigade and Capt. 3rd Scottish Rifles (*West Cliff Lodge, West Bournemouth, Hants, and Naval and Military Club*); *m.* 30 April, 1895, Emily Mabel, only dau. and heir of Lieut.-Gen. James Gubbins, C.B., and has issue,
  1. Errold Ashworth Sydney, *b.* 15 Dec. 1898.
  2. Eric James Dudley, *b.* 20 Feb. 1901.
  3. Ivan Robert Sydney, *b.* 19 May, 1910.
  1. Irene Mabel Alys, *b.* 9 March, 1897.
  2. Dulcie Iris Violet, *b.* 3 Feb. 1903.
2. Sydney George Coventry, Lieut. Rifle Brigade, *b.* 23 July, 1864; *d. unm.* 1891.
1. Edith Augusta Emily, *m.* 10 Aug. 1887, Col. Hon. Henry Edward Maxwell, D.S.O., Black Watch, brother of Lord Farnham, and son of Hon. Richard Maxwell, and has issue (*see* BURKE'S *Peerage*).
2. Mary Powlett, *m.* 17 May, 1893, William H. Persse, eldest son of Henry Persse, of Glenarde, co. Galway, and has issue (*see* PERSSE *of Moyode*).
3. Aline Islay.
4. Lilian Alice.
5. Violet Grace, *m.* 11 Jan. 1894, Frederick Oliver, Baron Ashtown, and has issue (*see* BURKE'S *Peerage*).

Col. Cosby *m.* 2ndly, 22 Jan. 1885, Eliza, dau. of Rev. Capel Molyneux, Vicar of St. Paul's, Onslow Square, and widow of Sir Charles Goring, 9th bart. of Highden, Sussex.

Lineage.—FRANCIS COSBIE, who settled in Ireland *temp.* Queen MARY (Carew MSS.), an active defender of the Pale, *b.* 1510, was appointed by patent 14 Feb. 1558, General of the Kerne, and granted, 1562, the site of the suppressed Abbey of Stradbally; he *m.* Elizabeth Palmes, and had issue,
1. ALEXANDER, his heir.
2. Henry, *d.* in his father's lifetime.
3. Arnold, who served under Robert, Earl of Leicester, in the Low Countries, executed in England for killing Richard Burke, of Castleconnell in a duel 1590.

Cosby. THE LANDED GENTRY.

Francis Cosbie fell at the battle of Glendelough 1580. (*Annals of the Four Masters* and *Camden Annals*.) He was s. by his eldest son,

ALEXANDER COSBIE, of Stradbally Abbey, who also obtained very extensive grants of land in the Queen's Co. (*Records of the Rolls*.) He m. Dorcas, dau. of William Sydney, of Otford, Kent, Maid of Honour to Queen ELIZABETH, and by her (who m. 2ndly, Sir Thomas Cooch, Knt., of Donnybarrie, co. Donegal, and d. 1606, had issue,

1. FRANCIS, of Stradbally, Captain of the Kerne, m. Helen, dau. of Robert Harpole, of Shrule, Queen's Co., and fell immediately after his father at the battle of Stradbally Bridge, 19 May, 1596, leaving by her (who m. 2ndly, Sir Thomas Loftus, of Killyan, King's Co.), an infant child,
   WILLIAM, who s. him.
2. RICHARD, s. to his nephew.
3. Charles, b. 12 Sept. 1585; m. a dau. of the Loftus family, who d. 23 Nov. 1632.
4. Arnold, of Drumaragh, b. 20 June, 1594, settled in the co. Cavan, and planted a branch of the family there.
   1. Mabel, m. George Harpoole, of Shrule, in the Queen's Co., and d. 1632. He d. same year.
   2. Rose, b. 2 Nov. 1582; m. Hon. Richard St. Lawrence, who d. 21 March, 1659.

Alexander Cosbie, slain at the battle of Stradbally Bridge with the O'Mores, 19 May, 1596 (*Annals of the Four Masters*), was s., although for a few minutes only, by his eldest son,

FRANCIS COSBIE, of Stradbally Hall, who being slain as stated above, never enjoyed the inheritance, but was s. by his infant child.

WILLIAM COSBY, of Stradbally Hall, b. 16 March, 1596, who d. June that year, when the estates reverted to his uncle,

RICHARD COSBY, of Stradbally Hall, Captain of the Kerne, who gained the battle of Dunamase over the O'Mores, 1606; he had livery of his lands 2 Dec. 1608. He m. Elizabeth,* dau. of Sir Robert Pigott, Knt. of Dysert, by whom (who m. 2ndly, Barnaby O'Dunn, of Brittas, and d. 1669) he had issue,

1. ALEXANDER, his heir.
2. FRANCIS, who s. his nephew at Stradbally.
3. Sydney, b. 2 Oct. 1613; m. Miss Segar, who d. 11 July, 1663.
4. William, Capt. in the Army, m. Jane Stafford, and d. 13 Sept. 1683, leaving issue, which became extinct in the male line.
   1. Dorcas, m. Adam Loftus, of Ballymanus.

Richard Cosby d. 5 Dec. 1631, and was s. by his eldest son,

ALEXANDER COSBY, of Stradbally Hall, b. 8 Feb. 1610; had livery of his lands 18 May, 1632; m. Anne, dau. of Sir Francis Slingsby, Knt. of Kilmore, co. Cork; and dying 6 Aug. 1636, was s. by his son,

FRANCIS COSBY, of Stradbally Hall, who d.s.p. before 8 Feb. 1638, when he was s. by his uncle,

FRANCIS COSBY, of Stradbally Hall, M.P. for Carysfort, b. 5 July, 1612, had livery of his nephew's lands, 8 Feb. 1638; m. Ann, dau. of Sir Thomas Loftus, Knt. of Killyan, by whom (who d. 1673) he had issue,

1. ALEXANDER, his heir.
2. Thomas, of Vicarstown, m. Elizabeth, dau. of William Smith, and d. 1713, leaving a son,
   Francis, of Vicarstown, m. Ann, dau. of John Pigott, of Kilfinny, and had a son,
   (1) THOMAS, of Vicarstown, b. 1742, of whom hereafter, as successor to Stradbally.
   (2) Francis Seymour, d.s.p.
   (1) Frances.
   (2) Anne, m. 1st, March, 1764, John Ward, Lieut. 9th Regt.
   (3) Ellinor, m. 15 April, 1774, Bernard Ward.
3. Sydney, of Ballymanus, m. Sarah Harding, and d. 1716, leaving issue, now extinct.

The eldest son,

ALEXANDER COSBY, of Stradbally Hall, m. Elizabeth, dau. of Henry L'Estrange, of Moystown, King's Co., by whom (who d. 1692) he had issue,

1. DUDLEY, his heir.
2. Henry, b. 1675, Capt. of Foot, m. Charity, dau. of John Higgins, and d. in Spain, 1705, leaving a son, Alexander, d.s.p. 3 May, 1733, and three daus.
3. Thomas, Major of Foot, m. Jane, widow of Thomas Maunsell, of Gallskill, co. Kilkenny, and dau. of Henry Loftus, and sister of Nicholas, Viscount Loftus, of Ely, which lady d. 3 March, 1734. He d. 15 May, 1735, leaving two daus.,
   1. Anne, m. Charles Davies, Lieut. of Foot.   2. Jane.
4. Loftus, Capt. of Foot, d. at Marseilles, 3 Jan. 1726.
5. Alexander, Lieut.-Col. and Lieut.-Governor of Nova Scotia, m. Anne, dau. of Alexander Winnard, of Annapolis, and had two sons and two daus.,

* Through this lady, the family of Cosby of Stradbally descends from EDWARD I, King of England. ELIZABETH was the dau. of Sir ROBERT PIGOTT, by THOMZIN, his wife, dau. and co-heir of CHRISTOPHER PEYTON, grandson of FRANCIS PAYTON, by ELIZABETH, his wife, dau. of REGINALD BROOKE, of Aspall, Suffolk, son of Sir THOMAS BROOKE, Knt., jure uxoris, Baron Cobham, and JOANE, his wife, only dau. and heir of Sir REGINALD BRAYBROOKE, Knt., and JOANE, Baroness Cobham, his wife, dau. and heir of Sir JOHN DELAPOOLE, Knt., and JOANE, his wife, dau. and heir of JOHN DE COBHAM, Baron de Cobham, and MARGARET his wife, dau. of HUGH DE COURTENAY, 2nd Earl of Devon, and MARGARET, his wife, dau. of HUMPHREY DE BOHUN, Earl of Hereford, and Essex, and ELIZABETH, his wife, 7th dau. of EDWARD I of England, by ELEANOR, his 1st wife, dau. of FERDINAND III, King of Castile and Leon.

1. William, a Capt. in the Army, d.s.p. 1748.
2. PHILLIPS, of whom hereafter, as successor to Stradbally.
   1. Elizabeth, m. Capt. Foye.
   2. Mary, m. Capt. Charles Cotterell.
6. William, Brigadier-Gen., Col. of the Royal Irish Regt., Governor of New York and the Jerseys, m. 1711, Grace, sister George Montagu, Earl of Halifax, K.B., and left by that lady (who d. 25 Dec. 1767), at his decease, 10 March, 1736, the following issue,
   1. William, an Officer in the Army.
   2. Henry, Capt. R.N., d. 1753.
   1. Elizabeth, m. 1st, Lord Augustus Fitzroy, 2nd son of Charles 2nd Duke of Grafton. He d. 24 May, 1741, leaving issue. S m. 2ndly, James Jeffreys.
   2. Grace, m. — Murray, of New York.
7. Arnold.
   1. Anne, b. 10 March, 1667; m. 14 March, 1690, James Wall, Coolnamuck, co. Waterford.
   2. Elizabeth, b. 2 May, 1669; m. 4 Jan. 1691, Lieut.-Gen. Richard Phillips, Governor of Nova Scotia, and d. 24 Jan. 1739. He d. 1752.
   3. Jane, b. 1670.
   4. Dorcas, b. 30 April, 1683; m. 1st, 1705, Magrath; 2ndly, Robert Forbes.
   5. Isabella.
   6. Celia, m. Robert Weldon, of Rosscumro.
   7. Dorothy.

Alexander Cosby d. 1694, and was s. by his eldest son,

DUDLEY COSBY, of Stradbally Hall, b. 2 May, 1662, Lieut.-Col., M.P. for Queen's Co. He m. 1st, Ann, dau. and heir of Sir Andrew Owen, Knt., which lady d.s.p. 21 Aug. 1698; and 2ndly, Sarah, dau. of Periam Pole, of Ballyfin, by whom he had

POLE, his heir.
Sarah, m. 2 March, 1730, Robert Meredyth, of Shrowland, Kildare, and d. Sept. 1755.

Col. Cosby d. 24 May, 1729, and was s. by his son,

POLE COSBY, of Stradbally Hall, m. Mary, dau. and co-heir of Henry Dodwell, of Manor Dodwell, co. Roscommon, and by her (who d. 9 Jan. 1742) left at his decease, 20 May, 1766 (with a dau. Sarah, b. 1730, m. 1st, the Right Hon. Arthur Upton, of Castle Upton; and 2ndly, Robert, Earl of Farnham), a son and successor,

DUDLEY ALEXANDER SYDNEY COSBY, BARON SYDNEY, of Leix, in the Peerage of Ireland, so created 14 July, 1768. His Lordship was Minister Plenipotentiary to the Court of Denmark. He m. c. 1773, Lady Isabella St. Lawrence (who d. 28 Oct. 1836), dau. of Thomas, 1st Earl of Howth, but d. in the ensuing month, 17 Jan. 1774, without issue. His peerage became extinct, while the inheritance reverted to his Lordship's cousin,

PHILLIPS COSBY, of Stradbally Hall, Admiral of the White. He m. Aug. 1792, Eliza, dau. of William Gunthorpe, and sister of William Gunthorpe, of Southampton, but having no issue, was s. at his decease by his kinsman,

THOMAS COSBY, of Vicarstown, and afterwards of Stradbally, b. 1742; m. 1st, Frances Booker, and by her (who d. June, 1770) had two sons, d. young. He m. 2ndly (settlements dated 14 Aug. 1779), Grace, dau. and co-heir of George Johnstone, of Glaslough, co. Monaghan, and had issue,

1. Dudley, accidentally drowned 3 July, 1789, s.p.
2. Francis, drowned at Cork, 25 Aug. 1791, s.p.
3. THOMAS, his heir.

He d. 10 Dec. 1798, and was s. by his only surviving son,

THOMAS COSBY, of Stradbally Hall, Governor of Queen's Co.; High Sheriff 1809; m. 25 Aug. 1802, Charlotte Elizabeth, dau. of the Right Hon. Thomas Kelly, Lord Chief Justice of the Court of Common Pleas, Ireland, and by her (who d. 1863) had issue,

1. THOMAS PHILLIPS, of Stradbally.
2. William (Rev.), m. Dora, dau. of Lorenzo Jephson, of Wilmar, co. Tipperary, by Hon. Martha Prittie, his wife, dau. of Henry Sadlier, 1st Lord Dunalley, and d. 1 Dec. 1872, having had issue,
   1. THOMAS PRITTIE, Col. 14th Regt., m. Annie, dau. of Rev. Charles Fife.
   1. Martha.   2. Frances.
3. Sydney, m. 1 Nov. 1831, Emily, elder dau. and co-heir of Capt. Robert Ashworth, of Shirley House, Twickenham, Middlesex. She d. 23 Aug. 1863. He d. 7 Aug. 1840, leaving issue,
   1. ROBERT ASHWORTH GODOLPHIN, now of Stradbally Hall.
   1. Margaret Mary Pole, m. 1st, 12 Dec. 1855, John Chidley Coote, Capt. 43rd Light Infantry, 2nd son of Sir Charles Coote, of Ballyfin (who d. 26 April, 1879), and 2ndly, 14 July, 1880, Sir Charles Pigott, 3rd bart. of Knapton.
   2. Charlotte Emily, m. 22 Aug. 1866, Lieut.-Gen. James Gubbins C.B., Assist.-Adjt.-Gen. at Malta, and has issue, one dau., Mabel.
4. Wellesley Pole, m. 1841, Marie, 2nd dau. and co-heir of Robert Ashworth, of Shirley House, and d.s.p. 1842.
1. Frances Elizabeth, m. 1837, Horace Rochfort, of Clogrenane Castle, co. Carlow; and d. 1841, leaving issue.
2. Harriet Georgiana, m. 29 Aug. 1831, Frederick, Lord Ashtown, and had issue (see BURKE's *Peerage*).

Mr. Cosby, High Sheriff of Queen's Co., d. 22 Jan. 1832, and was s. by his son,

THOMAS PHILLIPS COSBY, of Stradbally Hall, J.P. and D.L., b. 20 Sept. 1803, High Sheriff 1834, Capt. Royal Regt. Horse Guards, and d.s.p. 1851, when the property devolved on his nephew.

Arms—Quarterly: 1st and 4th, arg., a chevron between three leopards' faces sa., on a canton or, a saltire vert between a crosscrosslet in chief gu. a lizard erect in the dexter, and a salmon in the sinister, fess-point of the fourth and a dexter hand couped in base of the fifth: 2nd and 3rd, az., three shackles or, on a canton arg. a ltire gu. between a sinister hand couped in chief of the last two ilmons in fess and one in base vert. *Crest*—A griffin segreant, is wings e cct gu. supporting a broken spear or, headed arg. *otto*—Audaces fortuna uvat.

Seat—Stradbally Hall. Queen's Co. *Clubs*—Wellington and my and Navy.

COTTINGHAM.

MAJOR EDWARD ODEN COTTINGHAM, V.O., R.M.A. (retired 1907), b. 6 Sept 1866; m. 7 Jan. 1909, Mary Beatrice Clotilde, eldest dau. of the late Robert W. T. Bowen-Colthurst, of Oak Grove, Killinardrish, co. Cork (*see that family*). He served in the S. African War, 1900, as Special Service Officer, Instructor of Naval Gunnery to R.M.A. 1904-7. Has issue,

1. EDWARD BOWEN, } twins, b. 17 Sept. 1909.
2. JAMES HENRY, }

Lineage.—THE REV. GEORGE COTTINGHAM, Rector of Monaghan 1633, B.A. Trin. Coll. Dublin 1624, Fellow 1627, ordained 1629, sometime Chaplain to Henry Power, Viscount of Valentia, was descended from the family of COTTINGHAM, seated at Wrenbury, Cheshire, and previously at Cottingham, near Kingston-upon-Hull, Yorks. He d. about 1661, having had issue,
1. John, who seems to have d.s.p.
2. JAMES, of whom presently.
3. Henry (Ven.), B.A. Trin. Coll. Dublin 1660, Dean of Clonmacnoise 1668, Archdeacon of Meath 1681, m. by licence 18 Nov. 1667, Margaret, dau. of Capt. Thomas Price, and d. 20 Feb. 1697-8, leaving issue (will proved 1698),
  1. Henry, M.A. Trin. Coll. Dublin 1695, b. 1671.
  2. James, who m. Susannah, dau. of Sir H. Piers, Bt.
4. Charles, who had a son, George. Charles d. in London, 1690-91.

The second son,
CAPT. JAMES COTTINGHAM, of Dublin, banker and goldsmith, m. 1st, 28 Jan. 1674-5, Elizabeth, dau. of Alderman Lewis Des Mynières, by Elizabeth Hill his wife. He m. 2ndly, Elizabeth Edwards, his cousin, who d.s.p. 1706. Will proved 1707. He fled to Chester in 1688, when JAMES II landed in Ireland, and his 1st wife d. there in 1690 and was bur. at St. Bridget's Church. He was admitted to the Freedom of the City Dec. 1668. He was bur. 13 Feb. 1702-3. His will was proved 2 April, 1703. He had issue,
1. JAMES, of whom presently.
2. Charles, bur. 26 Jan. 1683-4.
1. Mary, bur. 3 Feb. 1681-2.
2. Elizabeth, m. David Wilson.

His son and heir,
REV. JAMES COTTINGHAM, of Ballyhaise, co. Cavan, b. 1677; d. Nov. 1753; M.A. Trin. Coll. Dublin 1702, Vicar of Lavey 1721; m. Mary, dau. of Rev. William Greene, of Dresternan, co. Fermanagh, Rector of Killesher. She d. 8 Feb., was bur. 11 Feb. 1762 (will proved that year), having had issue,
1. William, d.s.p.; will proved 1752.
2. Henry, of Whaley Abbey, co. Wicklow, m. by licence, 31 March, 1749, Judith Walter. His will was proved 1784. He d.s.p.
3. George, whose dau. Judith, m. Edward Druitt.
4. JAMES, of whom presently.
1. Elizabeth, m. 23 Sept. 1731, Charles King, of Corrard, co. Fermanagh, and had issue (see BURKE's *Peerage*, KING, Bart.).
2. Mary, m. 1750, Thos. Tweedy, of Dublin.

The youngest son,
REV. JAMES COTTINGHAM, D.D., Vicar of Cavan 1745-1804, and Head Master of Cavan Royal School, m. 20 April, 1751, Rose, dau. of Capt. Charles Wardlaw. She was bur. 21 May, 1813, aged 84. He d. 20 March, 1804 (will proved that year), having had issue,
1. JAMES HENRY, of whom presently.
1. Catherine, m Charles Johnstone, of Drum, co. Monaghan, and had issue.
2. Mary, m. Alexander Lecky, and had issue.
3. Elizabeth, m. Dr. Armstrong, of Cavan, and d.s.p.

The only son,
JAMES HENRY COTTINGHAM, of Summerville, co. Cavan, Barrister-at-Law, Capt. of Cavan Cavalry. He commanded a small force of 200 men and defeated a body of Insurgents 6,000 strong at Granard 5° ept. 1798, for which service he was admitted to the Freedom of the City of Dublin 12 Nov. 1798; b. 1762; m. 1st, 31 May, 1788, at St. Michael's Church, Cornhill, London, Frances Barnett, dau. of Edward Woolery, of St. Andrew, Jamaica. Edward Woollery m. at Isleworth, Middlesex, 18 Sept. 1760, Frances Shettlewood Barnett. His will dated 25 Sept. 1797, was proved 20 Nov. following. She was bur. 6 June, 1809, leaving issue,
1. James Courtney, of Dublin, b. 1788; d. 1875; m. 1816 Hannah, dau. of Rev. Christopher Robinson, Rector of Granard, and had issue,
  1. James Barrister-at-Law, of Manchester, b. 25 Dec. 1817; d. 1906; m. 1893, Sophia Rebecca, dau. of Wm. Hy. Pope.
  2. Christopher John, Barrister-at-Law, b. 1819; d. 1882; m. 1849, Margaret Clare ("*Collingwood*," *Parkstone, near Bournemouth*), dau. of Lieut. Arthur Walsh, R.N., Judge at Kingstown, Jamaica, and had issue,
    (1) St. John James, b. 1854; m. Jessica Webb.
    (2) Arthur St. Lawrence, b. 1855; d. 1879.
    (3) Christopher Courtney, b. 1865; d. 1886.
    (4) Wilbraham (71, *Strand Road, Sandymount, Dublin*), b. 1868; m. Feb. 1901, Louise Adelaide, only dau. of late Charles Macdona, of Dublin, and has had issue,
      1. Hector Courtney Dillon, b. Nov. 1901.
      2. Ronald Clifford Douglas, b. Jan. 1904; d. Aug. 1904.
      1. Eileen Marion, b. 1902.
      2. Margaret Lenore Adelaide, b. 1905.
      3. Olivia Kathleen Seymour, b. 1907.
    (1) Clare, dec.
    (2) Edith, m. Digby Seymour, youngest son of William Digby Seymour, Q.C., and is dec.
    (3) Agnes, m. Commander A. S. Montagu, R.N.
    (4) Maud, m. 1st, Charles Honau; 2ndly, David Hume M.R.C.S., and is dec.
    (5) Alice Preston, d. unm. 17 Feb. 1909.
    (6) Frances Edwina.
    (7) Helen Cordelia, m. Alfred Deighton.
  1. Elizabeth, m. 1st, Evelyn Ashley, who d.s.p. 1858, and 2ndly, 1861, Thomas Langlois Lefroy. She d.s.p. 1900.
  2. Frances, m. 1844, Hugh Fleming, who d. 1859, leaving issue.
  3. Anne, m. 1848, Arthur Hill Griffith, brother of Sir Richard Griffith, 1st bart., and d. 1882, leaving issue.
  4. Maria, m. John Bleakley.   5. Jane, d. unm.
  6. Lucy, m. George Griffith, another brother of Sir Richard Griffith.
2. Edward, of whom presently.
3. Henry (Rev.), M.A. Trin. Coll. Dublin, Rector of Ballymachugh, d.s.p. 1870; m. 1st, 15 Oct. 1810, Mary, dau. of Jason Hassard, of Carden Hill, co. Fermanagh, High Sheriff 1771; 2ndly, 1853, Mary, dau. of J. W. Freeman.
  1. Maria, m. 15 Nov. 1817, Rev. Sir Hercules Richard Langrishe 3rd bart. She d. 5 Oct. 1870. He d. 13 Jan. 1862, leaving issue (see BURKE's *Peerage*).
  2. Frances, m. 1822, John Dopping, of Derryeassan, co. Longford. She d. Dec. 1867. He d. 3 April, 1855, leaving issue (see DOPPING-HEPENSTAL of *Derryvassan*).
  3. Rose, d. unm. 1869.   4. Elizabeth, d. young.
Mr. J. H. Cottingham m. 2ndly, 1814, Maria, dau. of Roger Wilbraham, of Darford, and widow of Christopher Palles, of Mount Palles, co. Cavan. She d.s.p. 1845. He d. 21 May, 1819 (will proved that year). His second son,
MAJOR EDWARD COTTINGHAM, of Belfield, co. Dublin, Inspector-Gen. of Prisons, served with the 28th and 85th Regts. in the Peninsular War, and was severely wounded at the Battle of Albuera, b. 1790; m. 1826, Frances, dau. of Richardson Williams, of Clontarf, co. Dublin. She d. 2 July, 1889. He d. 3 Jan. 1848, having had issue,
1. Henry Maxwell, d. young, 1833.
2. EDWARD RODEN, of whom presently.
3. George Alexander Hamilton, d. young, 15 June, 1842.
4. James William, d. young, 8 April, 1845.
1. Elizabeth Maria, d. unm. 26 April, 1907.
2. Frances Hamilton, m. Robert Tritton, and had issue, one son, Edward, who d. unm.
3. Adelaide Louisa, d. unm. 1846.
4. Emily Rose, d. unm. 1865.
5. Catherine Edith, d. young, 1845.

The only surviving son,
COL. EDWARD RODEN COTTINGHAM, R.A., of Hermits Hill, Burghfield, Berks, served in the Indian Mutiny, the Egyptian War and the Bechuanaland Expedition, b. 11 Aug. 1834; m. 16 Oct. 1862, Eliza Anne, only dau. of Charles Johnson, M.D. She d. 27 May, 1900. He d. 17 Aug. 1901 (will proved that year), having had issue,
1. EDWARD RODEN, his heir.
2. Charles Scarborough, Capt. Manchester Regt., b. 3 July, 1868; d. unm. on active service in the Sudan, 18 Oct. 1898.
3. Henry Langrishe, Capt. R.F.A., b. 2 Oct. 1871.
1. Rosa Minna, d. unm. 1889.   2. Florence.
3. Rosabel Emily.

Arms—(Confirmed to the descendants of Major Edward Cottingham)—Sa. between two bars or as many hinds counter-trippant arg. *Crest*—Between two scimitars a Saracen's head couped at the shoulders ppr., wreathed round the temples arg. and az. *Motto*—Cadere non cedere possum.

Residence—2, Pennsylvania Park, Exeter. *Club*—United Service, Pall Mall, S.W.

Cramer. THE LANDED GENTRY.

CRAMER OF BALLINDINISK.

The late JOHN THOMAS CRAMER, of Ballindinisk House, co. Cork, Capt. Tipperary Artillery, Assistant District Commissioner, Sierra Leone Protectorate, b. 1 Dec. 1858; m. 11 April, 1890, Adelaide, eld. dau. of Col. Edward Napoleon L'Estrange, (see that family) and d. Feb. 1907, having had issue,

1. JOHN THOMAS, b. 6 March, 1892.
2. George L'Estrange, b. 5 Nov. 1896.
1. Marjorie Gwendolin, b. 17 Jan. 1891.

Lineage.—The founder of the family in Ireland was TOBIAS VON CRAMER or KRAMER, of Lower Germany; in the reign of JAMES I. he settled in Ireland, and was made a free denizen 28 May, 1639. He was father of BALTHAZAR CRAMER, who left issue two sons, TOBIAS and John, and two daus. The eldest son,

TOBIAS CRAMER, had assigned to him for his services under CROMWELL, the lands of Ballyfoile, which were afterwards confirmed by patent under the Act of Settlement. He was Sheriff of Dublin 1653, and High Sheriff co. Kilkenny 1669. By Mary his wife, he had two sons and two daus.,
1. BALTHAZAR, of whom presently.
2. Tobias.
1. Hester, the wife of Sir John Coghill, Bart.
2. Deborah, wife of Arthur Webb.

The elder son,
BALTHAZAR CRAMER, of Ballyfoil, co. Kilkenny, b. in Dublin 1644, High Sheriff co. Kilkenny 1683; m. 1st, Elizabeth, widow of Dr. Hugh Drysdale, who d.s.p.; and 2ndly, Sarah, dau. of Lieut.-Col. Oliver Jones, and by her had issue,
1. OLIVER, m. Hester, dau. of Sir John Coghill, and by her was ancestor of the baronets COGHILL and CRAMER ROBERTS of Sallymount.
2. AMBROSE, of whom presently.
1. Jane, wife of Philip Savage, of Rock Savage.

The 2nd son,
AMBROSE CRAMER, was Sheriff of Cork 1723, and Mayor 1725. His eldest son, by Ursula Browne, his wife,
BALTHAZAR CRAMER, of Coolcower, co. Cork, m. Elizabeth, dau. of William Stephens, of Chilcomb, co. Kilkenny, M.D., and had issue, a son,
MARMADUKE CRAMER, of Rathmore, co. Cork, who m. Jan. 1781, Sarah, dau. of Richard Gumbleton, of Castle Richard, co. Waterford; and d. 1817, having had issue. The eldest son,
JOHN THOMAS CRAMER, of Rathmore, co. Cork, J.P., m. 1814, Barbara Mary Anne Mileburn, dau. of the Rev. Dr. Thomas, and by her (who d. 20 March, 1857) he left at his decease, 5 Nov. 1845, two sons,
1. MARMADUKE COGHILL, late of Rathmore.
2. John Thomas, of Ballindinisk House, co. Cork, J.P., B.A., Barrister-at-Law, formerly Lieut. 7th Dragoon Guards, b. 20 March, 1820; m. 22 Dec. 1875, Mary Augusta, dau. of the Rev. Henry Richard Rogers, of Killeagh, co. Cork, by Augusta Lyster his wife, and d. 1873, leaving issue,
JOHN THOMAS, now of Ballindinisk.
Edith Barbara.

The elder son,
MARMADUKE COGHILL CRAMER, of Rathmore, co. Cork, J.P. and D.L., High Sheriff 1881, Barrister-at-Law, b. 23 Nov. 1817; m. 17 July, 1851, Caroline Elizabeth, only dau. and heir of Robert Honner, J.P. of Clancool, co. Cork, and d. 1896, leaving issue,
1. Mary Barbara, m. 1873, Henry Bonnor Maurice, of Bodynfoel, co. Montgomery, by whom (who d. 14 Jan. 1879) she had no issue. She d. 1877.
2. Caroline Elizabeth, m. 22 Oct. 1887, James O'Grady Delmege, D.L., of Castlepark, co. Limerick, and has issue (see that family).
3. Wilhelmina Idonea, m. 2 Dec. 1884, Capt. William Stopford, 9th Batt. the King's Royal Rifle Corps, eldest son of Rev. Joseph Stopford, of Ferney (see BURKE's Peerage, COURTOWN, E.).

Arms—Per fesse dancetty az. and or, in chief two fleurs-de-lys of the last a canton erm. Crest—A fleur-de-lys or between a pair of wings expanded or penned arg. Mottoes—"Inevitabile fatum," and (over the crest) "Mors ultima linea verum."

Seat—Cramers Court, Kinsale. co. Cork.

CRAMER-ROBERTS. See ROBERTS.

CRAMSIE OF O'HARABROOK.

ROBERT ALEXANDER CRAMSIE, of O'Harabrook, co. Antrim, b. 23 May, 1888; s. his father 29 Jan. 1903; m. 3 Aug. 1910, Florence Eugenia, youngest dau. of Lieut.-Col. Hezlet, R.A., of Bovagh House, Aghadowey, co. Londonderry.

Lineage.—ROGER CRAMSIE, settled at Ballymoney, co. Antrim, about 1709. He left two sons,
1. John, who left issue, a son, John, who m. Mary, dau. of — Macaulay, and had a son, James, who m. 1st, the widow of Daniel Maxwell. She d.s.p. He m. 2ndly, Elizabeth, dau. of Roland McQuillan, and had a son, John, m. 1892, Anne, dau. of McKeown, and had a son, John, b. 1843; m. 1876, Marguerite Helène, dau. of MacHenry, of Paris, and has a dau. Marguerite Marie.
2. PATRICK, of whom presently.

The younger son,
PATRICK CRAMSIE, of Ballymoney, co. Antrim, m. the dau. of — Moon, and had three sons and one dau.,
1. JAMES, of whom presently.
2. William, who left issue.
3. John, who went to Jamaica in 1769.
1. Rose, m. John Doherty, of Ballybrake.

The eldest son,
JAMES CRAMSIE, of Ballymoney, m. the dau. of — Todd, and had with three daus. three sons,
1. John, of Cross.
2. JAMES, of whom presently.
3. William, m. the dau. of — Boyd, and left issue.

The 2nd son,
JAMES CRAMSIE, of Ballymoney, b. 1786, m. 1816, the dau. of — Thomson, and d. 1855, having had two sons,
1. Adam, d. in India v.p. 1843.
2. JAMES, of whom presently.

The younger son,
JAMES CRAMSIE, of Ballymoney, Solicitor, b. 2 April, 1818; m. 1847, Eliza, dau. of Alexander Murray, R.N. of Drumadown. She d. 13 April, 1896. He d. 17 April, 1873, having had issue,
1. JAMES SINCLAIR, late of O'Harabrook.
2. Alexander Murray, R.N., b. 1850, d. unm. 1881.
3. Robert, Barrister-at-Law, b. 1852.
4. Richard Lyle, b. 1855, d. 1872.
1. Jane Thomson, m. 1875, Edward William Bailey, R.I.C.

The eldest son,
CAPT. JAMES SINCLAIR CRAMSIE, of O'Harabrook, co. Antrim, J.P., High Sheriff 1889, Capt. 5th Northumberland Fus., M.A. Trin. Coll. Dublin, b. 8 March, 1858; m. 5 Sept. 1882, Laura Mary, dau. of the late Capt. Antoine Sloet Butler, C.B., 7th Dragoon Guards, and grand-dau. of Sir Thomas Butler, 8th bart. (see BURKE's Peerage), and d. 29 Jan. 1903, having had issue,
1. James Antoine, b. 13 Nov. 1884; d. 1891.
2. ROBERT ALEXANDER, now of O'Harabrook.
3. James Randal Beresford, b. 22 July, 1892.
4. Arthur Butler, b. 23 March, 1894.
5. Charles Murray, b. 2 Nov. 1897.
6. John Moore, b. 27 Sept. 1902.
1. Netta Elizabeth Laura, b. 26 Aug. 1886.

Arms—Az. on a fesse or between three lions rampant arg. as many trefoils vert. Crest—A stag's head couped pierced through the neck with an arrow embrued ppr. and charged with a trefoil vert. Motto—Labor omnia vincit.

Seat—O'Harabrook, Ballymoney, co. Antrim.

SHARMAN-CRAWFORD OF CRAWFORDS-BURN.

ROBERT GORDON SHARMAN-CRAWFORD, M.A., of Crawfordsburn, co. Down, J.P and D.L., High Sheriff 1895, Lieut.-Col. and Col. late commanding 3rd Batt. Royal Irish Rifles, 15th Hussars and 16th Lancers, *b.* 10 Sept. 1853 ; *m.* 12 Sept. 1882, Annie Helen, eldest dau. of Ernest Arbouin, of Brighton, and has issue,

TERENCE, *b.* 31 Aug. 1892.
Helen Mary, *m.* 31 March, 1910, Hugh Carver, 2nd son of F. Carver, of Oakhurst, Knutsford.

Lineage.—WILLIAM CRAWFORD, purchased the estate of Crawfordsburn, co. Down, from Lord Clanbrassil about 1670, was s. therein by his son,

JOHN CRAWFORD, of Crawfordsburn, *m.* Jane, dau. of Crawford of Ballysavage, co. Antrim, and was father of

JAMES CRAWFORD, of Crawfordsburn, *d.* April, 1777 ; *m.* Mabel, dau. of Hugh Johnson, of Rademon, co. Down, and sister and heiress of Arthur Johnson, of Rademon, M.P. for Killyleagh, and had issue,

1. JOHN, his heir.
2. Arthur, *m.* 1794, Theodosia, dau. of James Waddell, of Springfield, and had issue,
   1. James, *m.* Ellen, dau. of John S. Ferguson, of Ballysillan, and *d.* 1860, leaving issue,
      (1) Arthur, left issue, one dau.
      (2) James, *d.s.p.*
      (3) William, *b.* 1829 ; *m.* Annie Alicia, dau. of Robert Thomson, of Castleton. She *d.* 1867. He *d.* 1907. They had issue,
         1. William Goldon, *b.* 2 Aug. 1863 ; *m.* Florence Jane, dau. of Thomas Montgomery, of Ballydrain, and has issue,
            (1) Kenneth Arthur, *b.* 26 Jan. 1898.
            (2) Cecil Hugh, *b.* 3 April, 1904.
         2. Robert James, *b.* 26 Jan. 1865 ; *m.* Julia, dau. of H. J. Neill, of Rockport, and has issue,
            Kathleen Maude.
         3. Arthur Henry, *b.* 4 Dec. 1867.
         1. Alice Maude.
      (4) John, *d.s.p.*
      (5) Thomas Douglas, *b.* 1831 ; *m.* 11 June, 1863, Eleanor Fridiswide, dau. of William Sharman-Crawford. She *d.* Oct. 1909, leaving issue,
         1. James William, *b.* 8 April, 1864.
         2. Charles Frederick Ernest, *b.* 2 June, 1865.
         3. Alfred Douglas, *b.* 10 June, 1868.
         1. Eleanor Fridiswide Mary, *m.* 21 Dec. 1903, William Bigoe White, and has issue (*see* WHITE *of Charleville*).
         2. Emily Theodosia, *m.* Major Frank Allfrey, late Dorset Regt. now 3rd Royal Suffolk Regt., and has issue.
      (6) Henry.   (7) George.
      (8) Charles, *d.s.p.*
      (1) Ellen, *m.* Samuel Brewin, of Culland Hall, Derby, and *d.s.p.* 1908.
      (2) Theodosia.   (3) Emily.
   2. William, *m.* Jane, dau. of William Cairns, of Parkmount, and *d.s.p.* 1872.
   3. John, of New Orleans, *m.* — Mackintosh, and had issue.
3. James, whose dau. Jane, *m.* 1795, Francis Savage, of Hollymount, co. Down, M.P.
4. William, of Lakelands, co. Cork, *m.* 1st, Miss Cooke, and had issue (with three other daus., who *d. unm.*),
   1. William, of Lakelands, *m.* 1813, Dulcibella, dau. of Abraham Morris, of Dunkettle, co. Cork, M.P., and *d.* 1840, leaving issue,
      William Horatio, of Lakelands, who *d. unm.* 1888.
      Tomasine, *m.* Rev. James Gordon-Oswald.
   2. George, *d. unm.* 1864.
      1. Jane, *m.* 1807, Jonas Morris, of Dunkettle, co. Cork, D.L.
He *m.* 2ndly, 1799, Mary, dau. of James Uniacke, of Castletown, co. Cork, and by her had issue,
   3. Robert, *d. unm.* 1875.
   4. Henry, Capt. 89th Regt., *d. unm.* 1890.
   2. Mary, *m.* 1825, Robert Gordon, of Florida Manor, co. Down, D.L.
   3. Catherine.   4. Frances.
   5. Emily.
   6. Louisa, *m.* 1846, Arthur Johnston Sharman-Crawford, of Crawfordsburn.
1. Jane, *d. unm.* 1836.
2. Anne, *m.* 1774, James Alexander, 1st Earl of Caledon.
3. Mary, *m.* 1789, David Gordon, of Florida Manor, co. Down.

The eldest son,

JOHN CRAWFORD, of Crawfordsburn, J.P., *m.* Jan. 1774, Maria, u. of Hugh Kennedy, of Cultra co. Down, (*see that family*), and *d.* ill 1827), having had issue,

Arthur Johnston, of Rademon, J.P., Barrister-at-Law, High Sheriff, co. Down, 1818, *b.* 1786 ; *d.v.p. unm.*
MABEL FRIDESWEDE, eventually sole heiress, *m.* 5 Dec. 1805, WILLIAM SHARMAN, of Moira Castle, co. Down.
MABEL FRIDISWID CRAWFORD, of Crawfordsburn, *m.* 5 Dec. 1805, WILLIAM SHARMAN, who took the additional surname and arms of CRAWFORD, and *d.* 21 Dec. 1844, baving by him had issue,

1. JOHN, his heir.
2. ARTHUR JOHNSTON, heir to his brother.
3. James, of Rademon House, near Crossgar, co. Down, M.P. for co. Down 1874-8, *b.* 24 Aug. 1812 ; *d.s.p.* 27 April. 1878.
4. Frederick, *b.* 15 July, 1814 ; *d.s.p.* 18 April, 1851.
5. Charles, *b.* 21 April, 1816 ; *d.s.p.* 4 March, 1903.
6. William, *b.* 1823. *m.* 27 June, 1854, Emily, dau. of Robert Macaulay, of Larne, co. Antrim. He *d.* 19 July, 1879. She *d.* 30 March, 1899.
7. Henry, of Dublin, *b.* 11 July, 1825 ; *m.* Ellen, dau. of the late William Goddard, of The Lodge, near Belfast, and has issue.
   1. Herbert.   2. Henry Francis.
   1. Ida Florence.
1. Maria, *m.* 26 Sept. 1827, Henry Barry Coddington, of Oldbridge, co. Meath, who *d.* 23 March, 1888. She *d.* 23 March, 1845, leaving issue (*see that family*).
2. Arminella, *b.* 11 May, 1818 ; *d. unm.* 16 June, 1865.
3. Mabel.
4. Eleanor Tridiswide, *m.* 11 June, 1863, Thomas Douglas Crawford, of Portbreda, co. Down, and *d.* Oct. 1909, leaving issue (*see above*).

Mr. William Sharman-Crawford assumed the latter surname, in addition to his paternal one of SHARMAN, by Royal Licence 1827, in compliance with the will of the late John Crawford. He was J.P. and D.L. and served as High Sheriff 1811, was M.P. for the borough of Dundalk from 1834, till the dissolution 1837 and subsequently sat for Rochdale. He was the eldest son of William Sharman, of Moira Castle, co. Down, Col. Union Regt. of Volunteers (who *d.* 1803) by Arminella his wife, dau. of Hill Willson, of Purdysburn, co. Down. He was *b.* 3 Sept. 1780 ; and *d.* 17 Oct. 1861, and was s. by his eldest son,

JOHN SHARMAN-CRAWFORD, of Crawfordsburn, J.P. and D.L., Major of the North Down Militia, High Sheriff co. Down 1839, *b.* 12 Oct. 1809 ; *d. unm.* 16 June, 1884, and was s. by his brother,

ARTHUR JOHNSTON SHARMAN-CRAWFORD, of Crawfordsburn, J.P., and D.L., High Sheriff 1888, M.A., Barrister-at-Law, a Director of the Belfast Banking Company, *b.* 8 March, 1811 ; *m.* 31 March, 1846, Louisa Alicia, dau. of William Crawford, of Lakelands, co. Cork. She *d.* 31 July, 1887, leaving issue,

1. William Henry, *b.* 10 Jan. 1847 ; *m.* 8 Jan. 1874, Elizabeth Maraquita, eldest dau. of Lieut.-Col. James W. Graves, late of the 18th Royal Irish Brigade, and *d.s.p.* 22 Dec. 1890. She *m.* 2ndly, 29 Nov. 1890, Warren Edward Rowland Jackson, of Ahavesk, co. Cork (who *d.* 22 Nov. 1893).
2. Arthur Johnston, *b.* 5 Nov. 1850 ; *d.* 27 July, 1862.
3. ROBERT GORDON, now of Crawfordsburn.
4. Arthur Frederick, of Lota Lodge, Glanmire, co. Cork, *b.* 29 Sept. 1862 ; *m.* 6 Nov. 1890, Ida Florence, 3rd dau. of the late W. J. Perry, of Ardlui, Blackrock, co. Dublin, and has issue,
   Gerald Arthur, *b.* 30 July, 1891.   Aileen.
1. Mary Elizabeth, *d.* young, 3 Dec. 1860.
2. Louisa Mabel, *d.* young, 11 Nov. 1868.
3. Alice Aimée, *m.* 6 Jan. 1879, Robert Francis Gordon, 2nd son of Rev. John F. Gordon, Rector of Annahilt, co. Down. She *d.* 14 Aug. 1883, leaving issue, one dau. (*see* GORDON *of Florida Manor*).

Mr. Sharman-Crawford *d.* 5 Sept. 1891.

LINEAGE OF SHARMAN.

JOHN SHARMAN, of Grange, co. Antrim (elder brother of Capt. William Sharman, M.P. for Randalstown 1749-60, who *m.* 1740, Anne, dau. of John O'Neill, of Shane's Castle, and *d.s.p.* 1775), had issue, two sons and three daus.,

1. WILLIAM, of whom hereafter.
2. Richard.
1. Letitia, *m.* Roger Moore, of Clover Hill, co. Antrim.
2. Anne, *m.* Isaac Heron.
3. Sarah, *m.* 1775, Stafford Gorman, of Broom Mount, co. Antrim.

The eldest son,

WILLIAM SHARMAN, of Moira Castle, co. Down, Barrister-at-Law, Col. of the Union Volunteers, M.P. for Lisburn, *m* 1773, Arminella, dau. of Hill Willson, of Purdysburn, co. Down, and *d.* 1803, leaving issue,

1. WILLIAM, who assumed the name of CRAWFORD, as above stated.
2. John Hill.
1. Eleanor, *m.* 1804, Hill Willson, of Rosebrook, co. Antrim.

Arms—Quarterly : 1st and 4th, gu. on a fess erm. between three mullets arg., two crescents interlaced or, for CRAWFORD, 2nd, or, a dove rising, holding in the beak a laurel sprig ppr. ; 3rd, gu., a lion rampant arg. *Crest*—1st, A dove close ppr. ; 2nd, A dove, as in the arms. *Motto*—Durum patientia frango.

Seats—Crawfordsburn, Belfast ; and Rademon, Crossgar, co. Down.

CRAWFORD OF STONEWOLD.

ROBERT CRAWFORD, of Stonewold, co. Donegal, J.P. and D.L., High Sheriff 1894, M.A. Dublin, and Cantab. (*ad eundem*), Master in Engineering, *honoris causâ*, Dublin 1883, M.R.I.A., M.Inst. C.E., Professor of Civil Engineering Dublin University 1882–7, *b.* 2 June, 1831; *m.* 1st, 9 Dec. 1856, Emily Sarah, dau. of James Crawford, M.D., of Montreal, and by her (who *d.* 18 May, 1870) has had issue,

1. James Samuel, *b.* 20 Jan. ; *d.* 6 Dec. 1858.
2. ROBERT KARL, *b.* 27 Sept. 1850 ; B.A. (1st Class Classical Tripos Part I. 1882), M.A. 1891, Ex-Sch. and Prizeman of Emmanuel Coll. Camb., M.A. Dublin (*ad eundum*) ; *m.* 20 June, 1891, Dora Minnie Helen, only child of Frederic Otté, and has issue,
   Robert Frederick, *b.* 13 July, 1895.
3. Ernest Caldwell, B.A. (Ex-Sch. 1st Honour and Prizeman Trin. Coll., and Graduate in Honours, Dublin University) 1885, *b.* 26 Jan. 1861 ; *m.* 25 June, 1902, Kathleen Mary, dau. of John Kinsella.
4. Duncan John, *b.* 24 Aug. 1862 ; *d.* 17 Feb. 1864.
5. William Saunders (Rev.), B.A (First Sen. Moderator and Gold Medallist in Classics) Dublin University 1886, Vice-Chancellor's Prizeman Greek Verse 1888, B.D. 1889, D.D. 1901, Ex-Sch. Trin. Coll. Dublin, *b.* 12 July, 1864 ; *m.* 26 Oct. 1898, Annie Harriet, dau. of the Rev. George Mather, of Huntley Hall, Staffordshire and widow of Llewellyn S. Lloyd, and has issue,
   Donald Robert George, *b.* 18 June, 1901.
   Ursula Mary.
6. Henry Arthur, C.B., served in the Imperial Yeomanry in S. African War 1900-1 (medal with three clasps), *b.* 11 May, 1870.
1. Alice Emily.
2. Emma Mary, *m.* 17 Sept. 1902, Francis Thomas Rountree, youngest son of G. A. Rountree, M.D.

He *m.* 2ndly, 1 June, 1876, Anna, dau. of Thomas Troubridge Stubbs, of Ballyshannon, co. Donegal, and by her (who *d.* 11 Dec. 1880) has had further issue,

7. Thomas Troubridge, *b.* 19 April, 1877 ; *d. unm.* 11 Dec. 1900.
8. Alfred, 1st Honour and Prizeman Trin. Coll. Dublin, and Graduate in honours, B.A. Dublin 1901 ; *b.* 1 Aug. 1878 ; *m.* Emily, dau. of Peter Clark, of Klipsdam, S. Africa, and has issue.
9. Edward, } twins, *b.* 23 Nov. 1880.
10. Frederick, }

Lineage.—ALEXANDER CRAWFURD, of the Point, near Killybegs, younger son of Malcolm Crawfurd, of Kilbirny, by his wife, Margaret, dau. of John Cunninghame, Laird of Glengarnock, *m.* Miss Crichton. He settled in Donegal among the Scotch Colonists from Ayrshire early in the 17th century. His son,
   ROBERT CRAWFORD, of Lifford, co. Donegal, mentioned as joint executor (with Capt. John Hamilton, of the same parish) in the will (dated 20 March, 1653, proved 12 July, 1661) of his brother, John Crawford, who left an only son, John. Robert Crawford was either father or grandfather of
   ROBERT CRAWFORD, of the parish of Killymard, co. Donegal, *b.* about 1660-5. His will (dated 13 May, 1735) was proved 26 July, 1737. The executors were Edward Crichton, his son, Hugh Crawford, and his son-in-law, Robert Hewet. He left issue by his 1st marriage,
1. HUGH, his heir.
1. Margaret, *m.* Robert Hewet.
By his second wife he had issue,
2. Robert, of Killymard. 3. James, of Donegal.
The eldest son,
   HUGH CRAWFORD, of Drumark, was *b.* about 1690 or 1695. His will is dated 28 Feb. 1760. He had three sons and four daus.,
1. JAMES, of whom presently.
2. Hugh, of Drumark ; *m.* Miss Crawford, and had issue.
3. Robert, *d.v.p.* leaving a dau., Bell.
1. Catherine, *m.* Zacchcus Cochrane, of Edenmore, and had issue.
2. Isabella, *m.* George Knight, and had issue.
3. Jane, *m.* — Purviance. 4. Mary, *d. unm.*
The eldest son,
   JAMES CRAWFORD, of Donegal, was *b.* at Drumark about 1725. He afterwards removed to Donegal, Drumark being left to his younger brother by his father's will. He *m.* Mary, dau. of James Makelwaine, of Ballyshannon, and niece of the Rev. John Makelwaine, of Gregstown, near Donegal. His will, dated 18 Nov. 1801, was proved 19 Dec. 1809. He had issue,
1. James, of Donegal, *m.* Sarah Purviance, and had issue,
   1. James, of Garvagh, afterwards of Farmhill, *m.* Miss Stephenson, and had issue.
   2. David, of Shrewsbury, *m.* Miss Bailey of that town, and had issue.
   3. Alexander, *s.p.* 4. Andrew, *s.p.*
   1. Mary Jane, *m.* the Rev. — Niblock.
2. DAVID, of Ballyshannon, of whom presently.
3. Andrew, *m.* Fanny Kincaid, and had issue,

1. James, *s.p.* 2. David.
3. Joseph, of Dublin.
4. Andrew, of Tennessee, U.S.A.
1. Mary.
1. Jane, *m.* Nathaniel Nilson, and had issue.
2. Mary, *m.* James Cochrane, of Edenmore, and had issue.

The 2nd son,
DAVID CRAWFORD, of Ballyshannon, M.D., J.P., sometime Surgeon R.N., *b.* in Donegal, 1759 ; *m.* 18 Aug. 1791, Sarah, dau. and heiress of the Rev. Robert Caldwell, and a descendant in the 6th generation from Allan Dunlop of Irvine, co. Ayr, by his wife, *née* Montgomery. She *d.* 18 Feb. 1853. He *d.* 8 Nov. 1825, having had issue ten sons and four daus.,
1. Robert, of Ballyshannon, *b.* 6 Oct. 1792 ; *m.* 29 Sept. 1823, Frances, dau. of James Forbes, of Danby, Ballyshannon. He *d.* 26 Oct. 1824, leaving an only child,
   Sarah Frances, bapt. 22 Aug. 1824 ; *m.* Rev. Robert Ellis, and had issue, four sons and one dau.
2. James, M.D. of Montreal, Canada, sometime Assistant Surg. 24th and 68th Regt., *b.* 20 Feb. 1794 ; *m.* Emma Matilda, dau. of John Platt, of Montreal. He *d.* 28 Dec. 1855, leaving issue,
   1. James David, Lieut.-Col. of the Royal Scotch Regt. of Volunteers of Montreal, *m.* Annie R., dau. of John Smith, of Montreal, and had issue, John and James, twins, *d.* infants ; Frederick Lindsay, *m.* Henrietta Penfold ; Arthur Lewis ; Clara, twin with Frederick Lindsay, *m.* William L. S. Jackson ; and Evelyn Isabel Godhilda, *m.* 1898, Francis Charles Annesley.
   2. William, a civil engineer.
   3. Henry, *m.* Kate, dau. of the Rev. — Boyle, of West Frampton, Province of Quebec, Canada, and has issue,
      Emily Caroline.
   1. Emma Georgina Elizabeth, *d. unm.*
   2. Emily Sarah, *m.* Robert Crawford, and *d.* 1870.
   3. Henrietta Mary. 4. Eugenia Margaret.
   5. Selina Jane, *m.* Henry Atkinson, of Etchemin, Quebec. and has issue.
3. SAMUEL, of whom presently.
4. David, *b.* 2 June, 1797 ; *d. unm.* 3 Oct. 1820.
5. John, *b.* 29 May, 1798 ; *d.* 29 March, 1799.
6. John, of Cartron Abbey, J.P. co. Longford, and Chief Magistrate ("Sovereign") of the town of Longford, *b.* 6 Jan. 1800 ; *m.* Jane, dau. of Rev. George Crawford, Vicar-General of Ardagh, He *d.* 10 March, 1860, leaving issue,
   1. David. 2. John George, *d. unm.* In New Zealand.
   3. William Robert. 4. James Travers.
   5. Robert Caldwell. 6. Thomas Pakenham.
   1. Margaret, *m.* — Harding, C.E, and left issue.
   2. Sarah, *m.* 7 July, 1875, Edward Waller Stoney, and has issue (*see* BUTLER-STONEY *of Portland Park*).
   3. Mary.
7. William, M.D., of Bicton House, Shrewsbury, *b.* 1 May, 1801 ; *m.* Elizabeth Hunt (*née* Morris), He *d.* 6 Oct. 1855, *s.p.* She *d.* 21 May, 1867.
8. Andrew, solicitor, *b.* 1 May, 1802 ; *m.* Mary Emma Coyne, and *d.* 4 Feb. 1873, having had issue,
   1. David James, *m.* Edith Mary, dau. of James Wilson, and had issue,
      Geraldine Frances Emma.
   2. John James Legbey, *m.* Frances Maria, dau. of Frank Ermatinger, of Montreal, and had issue,
      (1) Reginald.
      (1) Kate. (2) Emily.
      (3) Harriet Garewood.
   1. Sarah Caldwell.
9. Hugh, *b.* 26 Dec. 1809 ; *d.* 19 March, 1810.
10. Hugh, *b.* 21 March, and *d.* 16 June, 1815.
1. Margaret, *b.* 5 Nov. 1803, and *d.* 28 Feb. 1865, having *m.* 26 Aug. 1829, James Cochrane, of Edenmore, Clerk of the Peace for co. Donegal, by whom she had three sons and four daus.
2. Mary, *b.* 13 Sept. 1805 ; *m.* 26 May, 1824, Rev. Robert Warren, of Crookstown House, co. Cork, who *d.* 7 May, 1879, leaving issue, six sons and five daus.
3. Sarah, *b.* 28 Nov. 1807 ; *d.* 1817.
4. Elizabeth, *b.* 12 Feb. 1811 ; *d. unm.* 11 Jan. 1885.

The 3rd son,
SAMUEL CRAWFORD, of Ballyshannon, Solicitor, *b.* 6 April, 1795, was for many years coroner of the Southern Division of co. Donega, and Seneschal of the Manors of Ballyshannon and Kilmacrenan, and for forty-five years (up to the time of his death) Local Director of the Branch of the Provincial Bank of Ireland at Ballyshannon. He *m.* 8 July, 1823, Margaret, younger dau. of John Duncan, of 6, Granby Row, Dublin. She *d.* 20 June, 1876. He *d.* 28 March, 1881, having had issue,
1. John Duncan of Lanode, Drumsala, India, Surgeon-Major in the Indian Army, B.A., B.M. Dublin, M.R.C.S I., *b.* 20 April, 1824, received the medal for the Indian Mutiny (1857-8) as well as that for the war on the north-west frontier. He *d. unm.* 10 May, 1871.
2. David, *b.* 17 July, 1827 ; *d.* 17 Dec. 1903 ; *m.* 18 July, 1862, Anne Martha, dau. of John Montgomery, of Dunmucrum, Ballyshannon, by whom (who *d.* 31 Dec. 1883) he had two sons and two daus.
   1. Robert Montgomery, M.V.O., Commissioner Cape Mounted Police, served in Bechuanaland Exped. 1884–5, Bechuanaland Rebellion 1896–7 (medal and clasp), and S. African War 1899 1902 (despatches, medals and clasps), *b.* 12 May, 1863 ; *m.* 1906, Jane Smyth, dau. of Capt. Edward Fiddes, J.P., of Holywood, co. Monaghan, and has issue (*see* CRAWFORD *of Dunmucrum*).
   2. John Lindsay, *b.* 20 July, 1865 ; *m.* Jean Milne, and has issue (*see* CRAWFORD *of Dunmucrum*).

IRELAND. Creagh.

1. Mary Elizabeth.
2. Helen Lindsay, twin with John.
3. ROBERT, now of Stonewold.
4. Sarah Emily, m. 18 March, 1851, Rev. Walter Riky, Perpetual Curate of Queenborough, Kent, who was lost at sea 1865 on the voyage from Australia, the ship in which he sailed having been burned. She d. 21 July, 1883, having had issue, two sons and one dau.

Arms—Gu., a fess ermine, between three crosses pattée arg. **Crest**—An ermine pass. ppr., charged on the shoulder with a trefoil, slipped, or. **Motto**—Sine labe nota.
Seat—Stonewold, Ballyshannon, co. Donegal.

CRAWFORD OF DUNMUCRUM.

ROBERT MONTGOMERY CRAWFORD, of Dunmucrum, M.V.O., Commissioner of the Cape Mounted Police. Served in the Bechuanaland Expedition 1884-85, Bechuanaland Rebellion 1896-97 (medal and clasp), Anglo-Boer War 1899-1902 (Queen and King's medals and clasps, mentioned in despatches), b. 12 May, 1863; m. 20 Sept. 1906, Jane Smyth, dau. of Capt. Edward Fiddes, J.P., of Holywood, co. Monaghan, late 2nd Batt. 12th Regt., and has issue,

1. EDWARD FIDDES, b. 15 June, 1907.
2. Robert Montgomery, b. 14 Nov. 1910.

Lineage.—ALEXANDER MONTGOMERY came from Ayrshire about 1610 and settled in Dunmucrum, near Ballyshannon, co. Donegal. He m. Elinor, youngest dau. of Hugh Dunlop, of Sligo, a son of Allan Dunlop, of Irvine, by his wife, A. Montgomery. This marriage, his residence and the birth of his son, Hugh Montgomery, of Dunmucrum, are mentioned in the account of the DELAP family written in 1723 by Samuel Delap, of Raan (see DELAP of Monellan).

HUGH MONTGOMERY, of Dunmucrum, son of Alexander, had a son,

JOHN MONTGOMERY, of Dunmucrum and Carrickboy. He is mentioned in King JAMES' Act of Attainder, 1689. His son,

JOHN MONTGOMERY, of Dunmucrum, purchased (deeds dated 1724) from the Right Hon. William Conolly the lands of Dunmucrum which his family had occupied as tenants since coming to Ireland under Lord Folliot and his successors.

HUGH MONTGOMERY, of Dunmucrum, son of foregoing John, m. Jane, dau. of Baptist Gamble, of Rosorry, co. Fermanagh, and had issue,

1. JOHN, of whom next.
1. Magdalen, m. Rev. John Galt of Coleraine, and left issue (see GALT of Ballysally).
2. Anne, m. Rev. William Dinnen, d.s.p.
3. Harriet, m. Rev. Moses Paul, issue extinct.
4. Jane, m. Mr. Hansbro.
5. Medea, m. Lieut. Nichols, R.N.

JOHN MONTGOMERY, of Dunmucrum, m. Mary Ann, dau. of the Rev. James Fiddes, of Holywood, co. Monaghan, Rector of Drumsnat. He d. 1848, leaving issue,

1. Jane, m. Henry Coane, of Higginstown, near Ballyshannon, Barrister-at-Law, and had issue.
2. Anne Martha, m. 18 July, 1862, David Crawford (who d. 17 Dec. 1903), son of Samuel Crawford, of Ballyshannon (see CRAWFORD of Stonewold). This dau., Anne, inherited all her father's landed property which at her death, 31 Dec. 1883, she left to her children.

DAVID CRAWFORD, of Dunmucrum, and his wife, Anne Montgomery (above mentioned), had two sons and two daus.,

1. ROBERT MONTGOMERY, see above.
2. John Lindsay, served in Matabele Rebellion 1896 (medal), Bechuanaland Expedition 1884-85, b. 1865; m. Jean, dau. of James Milne, and has issue,
   1. John Montgomery, b. 1907.   1. Grace, b. 1905.
   2. Mary, b. 1909.
1. Mary Elizabeth.
2. Helen Lindsay, twin with John.

Arms—(of CRAWFORD)—Gu., a fesse erm. between three crosses patée arg. **Crest**—An ermine passant ppr., charged on the shoulder with a trefoil slipped or. **Motto**—Sine labe nota.
Seat—Dunmucrum, Ballyshannon, Ireland. **Residence**—Nooitgedacht, Cape Town, South Africa.

CREAGH OF BALLY ANDREW.

MAJOR - GEN. ARTHUR GETHIN CREAGH, C.B., of Bally Andrew and of Creagh House, Doneraile, Major - Gen. R.A., commanded the 6th (Poona) Div. in India 1905, and the troops in Mauritius 1907-09, sometime A.D.C. to Viscount Wolseley, b. 12 Feb. 1855; m. 9 Sept. 1889, Beatrice Carlota, dau. of John Granville Grenfell, and has issue,

1. Elma Gethin.
2. Moriel Elsie Maxwell, m. 4 April, 1910, Lieut. Raymond Theodore Pelly, Adjutant 2nd Batt. Loyal N. Lancs. Regt., younger son of Rev. Canon Raymond Pelly (see BURKE's Peerage, PELLY, Bart.).

Lineage.—CHRISTOPHER CREAGH, b. 1486 or 1487, was Mayor of Cork 1541, and a man of great influence and power amongst the native Irish. He m. Mary, dau. of Dominick Roche, and was s. by his son,

JOHN CREAGH, m. 1557, Mary, dau. of Michael Waters, and d. about 1601, having had issue,
1. Christopher, who d. before his father.   2. JOHN.

The 2nd son,
JOHN CREAGH, b. 1561; m. Margaret, dau. of George Archdeken, and dying 2 May, 1614, left issue,
1. Christopher, d.s.p.
2. WILLIAM, of whom presently.
3. Michael, m. the dau. of O'Driscoll, and had issue, one son, Michael (Sir), Lord Mayor of Dublin 1688, and Col. in the service of JAMES II.
4. John, of Ballyvolane, co. Clare, Col. in the Army of the Confederated Catholics 1641, m. dau. of Lysaght and left issue a dau., Christian, m. Philip Stacpoole, of Mountcashell, and had issue.

The 2nd son,
WILLIAM CREAGH, d. 1594; m. Ellen, dau. of Roche FitzRichard, of Poulnalong Castle, and d. before 1670, having had issue,
1. JOHN, of whom next.
2. Pierce, m. Mary Price, and had issue,
   Christopher, m. Jane Galwey, and had issue,
   (1) John, of Ballybunnion, co. Kerry.
   (2) William, d.s.p.
   (3) Patrick, m. Elizabeth Cooke, and left issue,
       1. Anne, m. Denis Moylan, of Cork, and had issue.
       2. Elizabeth, m. 1786, Major Daniel Mahony, of Dunlogh Castle, co. Kerry.

Their eldest son,
JOHN CREAGH, b. 1631; m. Julia, dau. of Giles Verdon, and left issue, four sons.
1. JOHN, of whom presently.
2. William (ancestor of WILLIAM CREAGH, of Ballygarrett, co. Cork).
3. Stephen, d.s.p.
4. Dominick (ancestor of JOHN CREAGH, of Dromarten, co. Kerry).

The eldest son,
JOHN CREAGH, of Kilowen, co. Cork, b. 1667; m. 1695, Elinor, dau. of Col. John Barret, of Castlemore. By her he had issue,
1. RICHARD, m. 1746, Gertrude Armstead, and left issue,
   William, m. 1786, Rebecca Morris, co-heiress of Daniel Theophilus Morris, of Ballingown, co. Kerry, and left one dau., Sarah, m. to Ezekiel Tydd Abbott.
   Sarah, m. 1774, Right Hon. John Philpot Curran, Master of the Rolls in Ireland, and d. 18 Nov. 1841, aged 89.
2. John, of Creagh Castle, co. Cork, m. 1st, 1756, Rachel Ruddock, of Wallstown, near Doneraile, and had issue,
   1. Catherine, m. to William Stawell, of Kilbrack, and d.s.p. Mr. Creagh m. 2ndly, Judith, dau. of Beverley Ussher, of Carpagh, co. Waterford, and widow of Edmond Shuldham, of Dunmanway, and left a dau.,
   2. Mary, m. 1770, Kilner Brasier, of Lizard, co. Limerick, and by him was mother of GEORGE WASHINGTON BRASIER-CREAGH, of Creagh Castle (see that family).
3. Stephen, of Kilowen, m. Ellen Leyne; d.s.p.
4. William, an officer in the Austrian Service; d. abroad
5. James, d.s.p.
6. MICHAEL, of whom hereafter.
1. Catherine, m. James Stackpoole, of the Austrian Service, both d.s.p.

The 6th son,
MICHAEL CREACH, of Laurentinum, co. Cork, b. 1706; m. 1741, Catharine Parker, of the family of Inchiquin, and by her had one son, John, d. young. Mr. Creagh m. 2ndly, 1745, Mary Gethin, sister and heiress of Capt. Richard Gethin, by whom he had issue, and dying 11 Nov. 1781, was s. by his son,

Creagh. THE LANDED GENTRY. 144

ARTHUR GETHIN CREAGH, of Laurentinum, b. Nov. 1746; m. 27 March, 1770, Isabella, dau. of William Bagwell, M.P., of Clonmel, co. Tipperary, and d. 13 May, 1833, having had issue,
1. MICHAEL, of Laurentinum, b. 25 March, 1771; m. June, 1796, Sarah Dobson, dau. of Shapland Carew, of Castleboro', and left at his decease, 17 Oct. 1845, an only child,
 Isabella Carew, m. John Singleton, of Quinville, co. Clare, and had issue.
2. JOHN BAGWELL, of whom presently.
3. Arthur Gethin, of Doneraile, b. 1780; m. 1840, Eliza, only dau. of Admiral Henry Evans, of Oldtown, Doneraile, but had no issue.
4. William, Lieut. Cavalry, E.I.C.S., b. 1782; d. of fatigue, after a series of engagements with the forces under Holkar.
5. Benjamin Bousfield, of Doneraile, b. 1784; m. Margaret Morris, and d. 12 May, 1846, leaving issue,
 1. Arthur Gethin. 2. Benjamin.
 3. John Merrick.
 1. Isabella. 2. Dorcas.
1. Jane, m. Capt. Taylor, and had issue.
2. Isabella, m. Matthew Shawe, late Lieut.-Col. 87th Foot, and had issue.
3. Mary, m. Thady McNamara, of Ayle, co. Clare, who d.s.p.
4. Dorcas, m. James Norcott, of Springfield, and had issue.
5. Emily, m. Ion Studdert, of Elm Hill, co. Limerick, and had issue.
The 2nd son,
 THE REV. JOHN BAGWELL CREAGH, of Bally Andrew, co. Cork, Vicar of Carrig and Rector of Rincurran, b. 26 Dec. 1772; m. 28 July, 1797, Gertrude, dau. of John Miller, of Toonaghmore, co. Clare, and by her (who d. 11 March, 1844, aged 63) had issue, seven sons and five daus.,
1. ARTHUR GETHIN, his heir.
2. John, b. 1802; m. 1830, Mary, dau. of St. John Galwey, of Mallow, co. Cork, and d. 9 March, 1841, leaving a son,
 Arthur Gethin, of Mount Ruby, Mallow, co. Cork b. 1836; m. Sept. 1863, Henrietta Cole, dau. of the late Henry Cole Bowen, of Bowen's Court (see that family), and had issue,
  (1) John (Ardcrasib, Mallow, co. Cork), J.P. co. Cork, Capt. and Hon. Major North Cork Militia, also served in Lincoln Regt. and served in Boer War 1899-1901 (medal, three clasps), b. 26 Nov. 1866; m. 22 Nov. 1906, Mona, dau. of late Major Philip Quirk, 67th Regt.
  (2) Arthur Gethin, b. 18 June, 1873; d. 1896.
  (3) Henry St. John, b. 23 July, 1875.
  (4) William Galwey, b. 1880; d. 1885.
  (5) James Galwey, b. 1887.
  (1) Eliza, d. 1874. (2) Mary Galwey.
3. Thomas Miller, b. 1803; Lieut. and Paymaster of the 52nd Foot; m. 1843, Eliza Hewitt, of Glancoole, co. Cork.
4. Michael, b. July, 1811; m. 24 May, 1843, Louisa Emma, dau. of James Dominick Bourke, of Becan, co. Mayo, Surgeon R.N., by his wife, Louisa Collingwood, and has issue,
 1. John, b. 23 Feb. 1844; d.s.p.
 2. Michael Clayton, b. 25 May, 1845; d.s.p.
 3. Randolph Gethin, b. 25 March, 1847; d.s.p.
 4. Arthur Gethin, b. 31 July, 1850.
 1. Gertrude Olivia. 2. Louisa, dec.
5. Richard Gethin, b. June, 1813; m. 1842, Isabella Mellifont, and has issue,
 1. John, b. 1843. 2. Richard Gethin, b. 1845.
 1. Gertrude Miller. 2. Isabella Gethin.
6. Benjamin Bousfield, b. 27 Dec. 1839, in Doneraile. He m. at South Melbourne, 6 Sept. 1865, Elizabeth Trenwith, dau. of W. H. Trenwith, of Cork. She was b. 25 Nov. 1840, and bapt. at Frankfield Church. He d. 15 April, 1905, at Port Napier, N.Z., leaving issue,
 1. Arthur Trenwith, b. at South Melbourne, 25 Feb. 1867; m. 23 April, 1902, to Florence Rolls, of Napier, N.Z., and has issue, a dau., Norma Gethin, b. 16 Feb. 1905.
 2. Benjamin Bousfield, b. 10 May, 1874, at Wellington, N.Z.; m. at Napier, 25 April, 1898, Elizabeth Jane Williams, of Napier, N.Z., and has issue,
  (1) John Brasier, b. 9 Aug. 1900.
  (2) Arthur Trenwith, b. 30 June, 1903.
 3. George Brasier, b. 13 Jan. 1877, at Wellington, N.Z.
 4. Norman Shaw, b. 10 May, 1884.
 1. Edith Maud Mary, b. 5 Jan. 1869; m. 2 April, 1891, Thomas Barry, of Napier, and has issue.
 2. Ethel Bousfield, b. 14 Feb. 1871; m. 17 Sept. 1891, Hugh Wilson, of Christchurch, N.Z., and has issue.
 3. Constance Elizabeth, b. 5 Jan. 1879; m. 28 Aug. 1900, John Fraser, of Napier, N.Z.
 4. Kathleen, b. 26 March, 1881; m. 30 Oct. 1906, William John Magill, of Napier, N.Z.
 1. Isabella Gethin, m. William Davis, M.D.
 2. Rebecca, m. 20 Feb. 1834, Arthur MacMurrogh Murphy, The O'Morchoe, of Oulartleigh, co. Wexford (see that family).
 3. Eliza, m. John Stevens, M.D., of St. Kiverne, Cornwall.
The Rev. J. B. Creagh d. 12 Feb. 1846, and was s. by his son,
 ARTHUR GETHIN CREAGH, of Bally Andrew, b. 1799; m. 1827, his cousin, Mary, only dau. and heir of James McGhee, of Carrahane, co. Clare, and by her (who d. 1851) had
1. JOHN BAGWELL, now of Bally Andrew.
2. Arthur Gethin, of Carrahane, co. Clare, J.P., b. 22 Feb. 1830; d. 4 Nov. 1911.
3. Thomas Miller, b. 1833, d. unm.
4. Michael, d. unm.
1. Rebecca Victoria.
Mr. Creagh d. 25 Feb. 1849. His eldest son,

JOHN BAGWELL CREAGH, of Bally Andrew, co. Cork, b. 31 Aug. 1828; m. 23 Feb. 1854, Matilda Emily Victoria, eldest dau. of Major Grant Wolseley, 25th Regt., and sister of Viscount Wolseley, K.P., G.C.B., and d. 9 Oct. 1906, having had issue,
1. ARTHUR GETHIN, now of Bally Andrew.
2. Erle Wolseley, b. 1 May, 1859.
1. Moriet Frances, m. 8 July, 1884. Lieut-Col. Frederick John Evelegh, Comg. 1st Batt. Royal Garrison Regt., late Oxfordshire Light Infantry, and has issue. He d. March, 1907.

Arms—Arg., a chevron gu. between three laurel branches vert, on a chief az. as many bezants. Crest—A horse's head erased argent, caparisoned gu. in the headstall of the bridle a laurel branch vert. Motto—Virtute et numine.

Seats—Hermitage, Bally Andrew, near Doneraile, co. Cork, and Creagh House, Doneraile. Club—Army and Navy.

CREAGH late of BALLYGARRETT.

PIERCE NAGLE CREAGH, L.R.C.P.I., L.R.C.S.I., and L.M., b. 1877; m. Magda, dau. of Hamar Grisewood, D.L., of Foxcole House, Shipston-on-Stour.

Lineage.—JOHN CREAGH (see CREAGH of Bally Andrew), b. 1631; m. Julia, dau. of Giles Verdon. He was one of those denominated ancient Irish inhabitants, and as such was expelled from the city of Cork, to which he never returned. He was bur. at Clonfert, near Newmarket, co. Cork. He left issue,
1. JOHN, ancestor of the Creaghs of Laurentinum and of Ballyandrew, the senior branch of the family (see that family).
2. William Creagh, m. Catherine Rice, of co. Kerry, and left, MICHAEL, of whom presently.
3. Stephen, d.s.p.
4. Dominick, ancestor of Creagh of Dromartin, co. Kerry.
 MICHAEL CREAGH, m. Johanna, dau. of Charles McCarthy, of Stonefield, co. Cork. His will is dated 28 Feb. 1764. He left to his widow, in addition to the provision made for her by her articles of marriage, his household goods, plate, jewels, his chaise and pair of horses. He was s. by his only child,
 WILLIAM CREAGH, of Old Town, near Shanballymore, co. Cork, who m. 1770, Sarah Nagle, of Annakissy (near Doneraile), a niece of the celebrated Nano Nagle, who introduced the Ursuline Order of Nuns from France in to Ireland, and who founded the Presentation Order of Nuns. On 2 June, 1770, one Samuel Windis, a Protestant informer, filed his Bill in the Court of Exchequer in Ireland against the said William Creagh and Michael Creagh, of Laurentinum, alleging that a certain conveyance executed by him to Michael Creagh, of Laurentinum, a Protestant, was intended as a cover for the said Michael Creagh, who had been all his life, to quote the said Bill, "a Papist or person professing the Popish religion." A decree was pronounced, 15 May, 1771, and duly enrolled. William Creagh, by his marriage with Sarah Nagle, had issue, with two daus. (of whom one, styled the beautiful Jane Creagh, m. 26 Nov. 1791, William Hickie, of Killelton, she d. 1829 (see that family); another m. Murtogh O'Conour, of Ahanagran, co. Kerry) three sons,
1. Michael, d.s.p.
2. Pierce, m. 1803, Isabella Leeson, and d. leaving (with one dau. Sarah, m.— Barry, of Dundulerick) one son,
 William, of Ballygarrett, m. 1845, his 1st cousin, Helena, dau. of James Creagh and Mary Anne Barry, his wife. He d. 1878, leaving with two daus. (of whom Helena, m. Martin Cormac, and d. 1901, and Minnie, d. unm. 1907), three sons,
 (1) Pierce, a Capt. in the 16th Regt., who d.s.p.
 (2) James Nagle, Surgeon-Col. 9th K.R.R.C. (North Cork Militia), in South Africa of disease contracted whilst serving with his regt. in the S. African War against the Boers. He m. 18—, Jeanie Keegan, and left issue,
  1. PIERCE NAGLE. present representative.
  2. Richard, b. 1878.
  3. Peter Herbert, b. 17 Aug. 1882, Lieut. 1st Batt. Leicestershire Regt.
 (3) William, m. 1879, his cousin, Emma, dau. of Gerard Barry, R.M., of Ballinahina, nr. Fermoy, and d. at sea in 1891, leaving issue,
  1. William, b. 1881.
  2. Mary Helen (Mollie), b. Oct. 1882; m. 5 June, 1907, Capt. T. G. Gibson, Inniskilling Dragoons, son of T. G. Gibson, of Newcastle-on-Tyne, and Lesbury, Northumberland.
3. James Creagh, of Ballygriffin, Killavullen, co. Cork, m. Mary Anne, only dau. of Philip Barry, of Ballinahina, co. Cork. He d. 1846, having had with other issue,
 1. Philip William, b. 1817; m. 1860, his cousin, Anna Maria, eldest dau. of James W. Barry, of Dundulerick, and d. 8 April, 1901, leaving issue,
  (1) James William, late Capt. 9th Batt. K.R.R.C. (North Cork Militia), who has assumed the name of BARRY, and has inherited the estate of Dundulerick, and who m. in 1900 Mignon Glazebrook, and has issue,
   1. Marie Danielle. 2. Sarah.
   3. Joan. 4. Phyllis.
  (2) Philip W., of Corrinville, Fermoy, m. 1895, Sarah, dau. of C. O'Callaghan, of Chairduggan, co. Cork, and has issue,
   1. Edward, b. 29 Feb. 1896.
   2. Pierce, b. 14 Jan. 1902.

IRELAND. Creagh.

1. Sarah, *m.* 1836, Francis Henry Downing, Solicitor, Killarney, and *d.* 12 Nov. 1887, having had issue, five daus. and four sons.
2. Helena, who *m.* her cousin, William Creagh, as above mentioned.

Arms—*See* CREAGH *of Ballyandrew*. *Residence*—"Gleugarriff," Walker Road, Cardiff.

CREAGH OF CAHIRBANE.

CHARLES VANDELEUR CREAGH, C.M.G., of Cahirbane, co. Clare, C.M.G., Barrister-at-Law, late Governor of British North Borneo and Labuan, *b.* 1842; *s.* his elder brother 12 April, 1910; *m.* 6 June, 1882, Blanche Frances, dau. of the late Capt. Edwardes, 30th Regt., of Rhydygors, co. Carmarthen, and has issue,

1. James Vandeleur, Lieut. R.N., *b.* 30 Aug. 1883; *m.* 12 Nov. 1908, Adela May, eldest dau. of Philip C. Cork, C.M.G., Colonial Sec. of Jamaica, and has issue,
   James Philip Vandeleur, *b.* 14 Sept. 1909.
2. O'Moore Charles, *b.* 7 Dec. 1896.
1. Dorothy Vandeleur, *b.* 25 April, 1885

Lineage.—CHARLES CREAGH, of Lisduff, co. Clare, moved to Cahirbane in 1710, *m.* Ann, dau. of George Matthews, brother of the Earl of Llandaff, and was father of

ANDREW CREAGH, of Cahirbane, *m.* 28 April, 1752, Elizabeth, dau. of James FitzGerald, of Carrigoran, co. Clare, and has issue, an only dau., Anne, *m.* William Massey, of Glenville, co. Limerick, and an only son,

JAMES CREAGH, of Cahirbane, J.P., and Major co. Clare Yeomanry; *m.* 1776, his first cousin, Anne, only dau. of Giles Vandeleur, of Ralahine, co. Clare (by his wife, dau. of Edward FitzGerald, of Carrigoran), sister of Col. Boyle Vandeleur, of Ralahine, who commanded the Clare Militia at the battle of Ross during the rebellion. By her (who *d.* 1832) he had issue,

1. CHARLES, of Carrigerry, co. Clare, J.P., *b.* 12 Aug. 1777, Lieut. 12th Light Dragoons, also Major of the Clare Militia; *m.* 11 June, 1811, Louisa, dau. of Charles Costello, D.L., J.P., of Edmonstown, co. Mayo, and left issue,
   1. Mary, *d. unm.* 1860.
   2. Margaret, *m.* 1st, John Bonynge, of Rathorpe, co. Clare; and 2ndly, Henry Butler, of Castle Crine, co. Clare, and had issue by the first marriage, an only dau., Louisa.
   3. Anne, *m.* John FitzWilliam Scott, of Knoppogue Castle, co. Clare, and *d.* 1867, having had issue.
   4. Diana, *m.* Thomas Gabbett, of Corbally, co. Clare, and has issue, an only dau.
   5. Eliza, *m.* Richard Langford, of Kilcosgriffe, co. Limerick.
2. Andrew, Lieut. 8th Royal Irish Light Dragoons, *d. unm.* 1823.
3. Boyle Vandeleur, Lieut. R.A., *d. unm.* 1826; Aide-de-Camp to the Marquess of Anglesey, when Lord-Lieut. of Ireland.
4. James, of Cahirbane, Newmarket-on-Fergus, co. Clare, Capt. R.N., *m.* Grace Emily (who *d.* 1891), 2nd dau. of O'Moore, of Cloghan Castle, King's Co., D.L., J.P., by his wife Mary, dau. of Col. Bateman, of Alta Villa, co. Limerick, and *d.* 22 March, 1857, having had issue, nine sons and two daus.,
   1. JAMES, late of Cahirbane.
   2. O'Moore, *b.* 1837; *d.* 1850.
   3. CHARLES VANDELEUR, now of Cahirbane.
   4. Boyle Purdon, of Rathorpe, co. Clare, J.P., D.L., High Sheriff 1902, late Capt. Indian Marine and Port Officer and Hon. Presidency Magistrate, Calcutta, *b.* March, 1844; *m.* 8 Oct. 1889, Margaret Louisa, dau. of John North Bonynge, of Ballintubber, co. Longford, and Rathorpe, co. Clare. He *d.s.p.* 15 March, 1905.
   5. Garrett O'Moore (Sir), G.C.B., V.C., General Commander-in-Chief in India, commanded Field Force, China, 1901-3 (*Naval and Military Club*); *b.* 2 April, 1848; *m.* 1st, May, 1874, Mary, dau. of John Brereton, by Mary, his wife, dau. of The O'Moore, of Cloghan Castle. She *d.* Sept. 1876, leaving a dau.,
      May Geraldine, *b.* 16 May, 1876.
   He *m.* 2ndly, April, 1890, Elizabeth (Lilla), dau. of the late E. Read, of Kelverton, Bucks., and by her has issue,
      Duncan Vandeleur, Lieut. 7th Hussars, *b.* 16 May, 1892.
   6. Hubert, *d. unm.* 1857.
   7. Edward Fitzgerald, Sub-Lieut. R.N., retired, *m.* 4 Nov. 1891, Charlotte Duncan, dau. of John Julius Pringle, U.S.N., of Charlestown, South Carolina, and *d.s.p.* 25 Oct. 1902. His widow *m.* 2ndly, 7 Aug. 1906, Frank Carew Radcliffe, 2nd son of late Walter Coplestone Radcliffe.
   8. Arthur Richard, Lieut. R.N., killed in the destruction of H.M.S. *Doterell*, April, 1881; *d. unm.*
   9. Augustine, Assistant Commissary-General, *m.* Bessie, dau. of Crofton Hamilton FitzGerald, and *d.* 1887, leaving issue, one dau., Joan.
   1. Jane Vandeleur, *d. unm.* 1858.
   2. Mary Emily, *m.* 1st, George Spaight, and by him had issue, a dau. She *m.* 2ndly, 1872, Theodorovitch Antonovitch, Baron von Holdt, Knight of St. Anne and Knight of the Vladimir Cross, of Riga, Councillor of State and Knight Commander of the Orders of St. Stanislas, St. Vladimir Danuebroc and Star of Abyssinia, and by him had issue. She *d.* 17 Aug. 1910.
5. Giles Vandeleur, Col. 81st Regt., *m.* Elizabeth, eldest dau. of O'Moore, D.L., J.P., of Cloghan Castle, King's Co., and *d.* 1871, leaving by her (who *d.* 23 May, 1854), two sons and six daus.,

I I G

1. Charles Augustine FitzGerald, Maj.-Gen. late South Staffordshire Regt., *b.* 10 June, 1835; *m.* 1st, Mary Aune, eldest dau. of Richard Dodd, of Elm Bank, co. Hertford, and niece of Sir Fairfax Moresby, Admiral of the Fleet, and by her (who *d.* July, 1881) had a son,
   Charles Hamilton Vandeleur.
He *m.* 2ndly, 16 May, 1882, Louisa Beatrice Gerard, dau. of Col. Gerard Elrington, late Scots Guards, and by her had issue a dau., and *d.* 29 Nov. 1902. His widow *m.* 2ndly, 20 Jan. 1904, Henry Grierson, son of late George Grierson, of Rathfarlane House, co. Dublin.
2. Giles Vandeleur, of Fitzroy, near Taunton, and of Wilby and Athelington, Suffolk, *b.* 11 Dec. 1849; Lieut. Royal Buckinghamshire King's Own Militia; *m.* 25 July, 1882, Georgiana Juliana, eldest dau. and co-heiress of Thomas Green, of Wilby and Athelington Hall, co. Suffolk, Lieut. 93rd Highlanders, and by her (who *m.* 2ndly, Dec. 1903, George Wilmot Lindsay, eldest son of late John Lindsay, of Dumfries, N.B.), left issue, a son,
   Giles Desmond Vandeleur, *b.* 3 July, 1884.
   1. Ellen, *m.* her cousin, Crofton Hamilton FitzGerald, Capt. Clare Militia, eldest son of Crofton Vandeleur FitzGerald, by his wife, dau. of Rowen Hamilton, Lieut. R.N., C.B., of Killyleagh Castle, co. Down, and grand-dau. of Gen. Sir George Cockburn, nephew of Gen. Sir Augustine FitzGerald, Bart., of Carrigoran, for many years M.P. for the co. Clare, and has issue a son, Wilfred, and three daus., 1. Bessie Diana; 2. Geraldine; 3. Ellen Creagh, *m.* 1stly, 1888, her cousin, Sir George Cumming FitzGerald, 5th and last Bart. He *d.s.p.* 10 May, 1908. She *m.* 2ndly, 21 April, 1909, Richard Donne Lee James, of 3, Temple Gardens, Temple.
   2. Emily Jane, *m.* 1860, Robert Law, of Newpark, co. Kildare, eldest son of M. Law, by his wife Sarah, dau. of Crofton Vandeleur FitzGerald.
   3. Mary Letitia Longfield, *m.* Hon. William Rodolph Wigley, of Glenelg.
   4. Bessie Augusta Ness, *m.* Edward Picton Philipps, of Kilbarth, co. Pembroke. She *d.* 18 Nov. 1907.
   5. Geraldine O'Moore, *m.* Dudley Phillips, of Dunston Grove, co. Pembroke.
   6. Isabella Diana, *m.* Richard Hart Harvey, of Hermons Hill, and Slade, co. Pembroke.
1. Anne, *m.* Oliver Isdell, J.P., Capt. Longford Militia, of Collinstown, co. Westmeath, and *d.* 1876, leaving issue.
2. Eliza, *m.* John Scott, of Cahircon and Crevagh, co. Clare, and had issue, a son and has heir, John Creagh Scott, and two daus.
3. Diana, *m.* Charles Costello, D.L., J.P., of Edmondstown, co. Mayo, and *d.s.p.*
4. Ellen FitzGerald, *d.* 1876.

The eldest son,
JAMES CREAGH, of Cahirbane, late Capt. 1st Royals, served in the Crimea, *b.* 1836; *s.* his father 22 March, 1857; *m.* 1886, Marion, dau. of J. Wardell, of Leicester, and *d.* 12 April, 1910, when he was *s.* by his brother.

Seat—Cahirbane, co. Clare. *Residence*—32, Charlton Road, Blackheath, S.E.

CREAGH OF DANGAN.

MRS. OLIVIA MCMAHON-CREAGH, of Dangan, co. Clare, sister of the late Richard Creagh, of Dangan *m.* 4 Sept. 1884, Hugh Michell Macnamara MacMahon, Capt. and Hon. Major 7th Brigade S. Irish Division R.A., who assumed by Royal Licence 19 Sept. 1885, the additional name and the arms of CREAGH. He *d.* 5 June, 1889, having had issue,

A son, *b.* 9 Dec. 1885; *d.* 18 Nov. 1896.
Olivia Mary, *b.* 8 May, 1888.

Lineage.—PIERSE CREAGH, of Adare, Mayor of Limerick 1651, son and heir of Pierse Creagh, of Adare, M.P. for the city of Limerick 1639, *m.* in that year M. MacNamara, of Creattalough, co. Clare, and *d.* 1670, at his castle of Dangan. He was *s.* by his son,

SIMON CREAGH, of Dangan, *m.* Mary MacMahon, of the Castle of Clenagh, and was father of

PIERSE CREAGH, of Dangan, *d.* 28 Oct. 1753; *m.* Elizabeth, dau. of George Mathew, of Thomastown, co. Tipperary, half sister of James, 1st Marquess of Ormonde, and aunt to the 1st Lord Landaff, and had issue, a son and dau.,

PIERSE, his heir.
Elizabeth, *m.* Daveren, of Lisdoonvarna.

Mr. Pierse Creagh was *s.* by his son,
PIERSE CREAGH, of Dangan, *d.* Sept. 1779, having *m.* 1st, 1738, Catherine, dau. of Valentine Quin, of Adare, and aunt to the 1st Earl of Dunraven and Mountearl, but had no surviving issue; 2ndly, 1755, Gertrude Maghlia, of Brickhill, and by her had a son,
1. ROBERT, his heir, of whom presently.
And 3rdly 11 Sept., 1759, Lavinia, dau. of Richard Pennefather, of Newpark, and aunt of Lord Chief Justice Pennefather and Baron Pennefather, and by this lady had two sons and a dau.,
2. Richard, of Dangan, *m.* Christiana O'Callaghan, of Maryfort, and *d.* 1836, leaving three sons, Pierse and RICHARD (both *d. unm.*), and CORNELIUS, of Dangan; and two daus., Olivia and Lavinia.
3. Simon, *m.* his cousin Dora, dau. of B. MacNamara, by Elizabeth his wife, dau. of Daveron, Lisdoonvarna, and *d.* 1815, leaving four sons,

Creagh. THE LANDED GENTRY. 146

1. Pierse, m. 1836, Belinda (d. 9 March, 1908), dau. of Walter Butler, of Walterstown, co. Clare. She d. 9 March, 1908. He d. 1870, leaving issue,
(1) Simon, of Bryan's Castle, near Quin, co. Clare, J.P., b. May, 1842: m. 1871, Helena, dau. of J. O'Donnell.
(2) Walter.
(1) Henrietta, m. 1st, Edward Browne, of Cooloe, co. Galway ; and 2ndly, 1890, Lieut.-Gen. Sir Richard Hieram Sankey, K.C.B. (see SANKEY of Coolmore). He d. 11 Nov. 1908, leaving issue.
(2) Belinda Olivia, m. 1st, John Murphy, of Mount Loftus, co. Kilkenny ; and 2ndly, Maurice Lindsay Coates, of Springfield, Belfast.
2. Simon Macnamara, m. Charlotte, dau. of Capt. William Leader, of Ashgrove, Macroom, co. Cork, and had issue,
Isabel, m. 17 Oct. 1877, Lieut.-Col. Ulick Albert Jenings, Army Medical Service, of Ironpool, co. Galway (see that family), and had issue.
3. MacNamara, dec.
4. Richard.
1. Charity, m. Gerald Carrick.
Mr. Creagh d. Sept. 1779, when he was s. by his eldest son,
ROBERT CREAGH, of Dangan, m. Miss Kean. He d.s.p. 1842, when the representation devolved upon his nephew, RICHARD, to whom s. his brother,
CORNELIUS CREAGH, of Dangan, b. 1812 ; m. 1843, and by Mary his wife (who d. 1864) had issue,
1. RICHARD, of Dangan, b. 24 Aug. 1845 ; d.s.p. 19 July, 1881.
2. Cornelius, d.s.p. 20 Oct. 1879.
1. Agnes Mary, m. 1864, Peter Blake, J.P., of Cromlin, co. Galway, and d. 29 Aug. 1872.
2. Christina, m. 1st, 1865, John Galwey, of Doon, who d. 1867. She m. 2ndly, about 1869, Dr. James Eaton Turner, of Tuam.
3. OLIVIA, now of Dangan.
4. Elizabeth Clara, m. 13 Nov. 1888, Major Walter Blake Butler-Creagh, 51st Yorks. Light Infantry, of Walterstown, co. Clare, and has issue (see that family).

Arms—Arg., a chevron gu. between three laurel branches vert, on a chief az. as many besants. Crest—A horse's head erased arg., caparisoned gu., in the headstall of the bridle a laurel branch vert. Motto —Vive Deo ut vivas.

Seat—Dangan Kilkishen, Dangan Cross, co. Clare.

BUTLER-CREAGH OF WALTERSTOWN.

LIEUT.-COL. WALTER BLAKE BUTLER, of Walterstown, co. Clare, Lieut.-Col. late Yorkshire L.I. (51st L.I.), served in Afghan War 1878-1880 (medal), Zhob Valley Exped. 1890, S. African War 1899-1901 (medal, three clasps), b. 25 Jan. 1858 ; m. 13 Nov. 1888, Elizabeth Clara, youngest dau. and co-heir of Cornelius Creagh, of Dangan, co. Clare (see that family), and has issue,

RICHARD, b. 10 May, 1890.
Mary Gertrude, b. 10 Jan. 1892.

Major Butler assumed by Royal Licence 1 Aug. 1889, the additional surname and arms of CREAGH, after that of BUTLER, but has himself discontinued the use of the surname of CREAGH, which, however, is retained by his wife and children.

Lineage.—WILLIAM BUTLER, of Doone, co. Clare, m. Belinda, dau. of Francis Butler, of Cregg, and had issue,
1. Peter, of Bunahow, d.s.p.
2. William, of Bunahow, m. Anne, dau. of Robert Blake Forster, and had issue.
3. WALTER, of whom presently.
1. Elizabeth, m. Anthony Colpoys.
The 3rd son,
WALTER BUTLER, of Walterstown, m. Teresa, dau. of Michael Blake, of Frenchfort, co. Galway, and d. 1831, leaving issue,
1. Michael, of Walterstown, d.s.p.
2. Walter is dec.
3. Anthony (Rev.), late Capt. 87th Roy. Irish Fus., and R.C. Bishop of Demerara.
4. NICHOLAS, of whom presently.
5. Michael,
1. Rebecca Victoria.
Mr. Creagh d. 25 Feb. 1849. His eldest son,

1. Belinda, m. 1806, Pierse Creagh, who d. 1870, leaving issue (see CREAGH of Dangan).
The 4th son,
NICHOLAS BUTLER, of Walterstown, co. Clare, J.P., b. 17 March, 1827 ; m. 18 Dec. 1856, Anna, dau. of William Butler, of Bunabow, co. Clare. He d. 25 Sept. 1892, leaving issue,
1. WALTER BLAKE, now of Walterstown.
2. Francis, b. 23 Sept. 1862.

Arms—Quarterly 1st and 4th arg., a chevron gu. between three laurel branches vert, on a chief az. as many bezants, a fleur-de-lys sa. for distinction (CREAGH) ; 2nd and 3rd or, a crescent sa. on a chief dove-tailed gu., three covered cups arg. (BUTLER.) Crests—1. A horse's head erased arg. caparisoned gu. in the headstall of the bridle a laurel branch vert, and charged on the neck for distinction with a fleur-de-lys sa. (CREAGH). 2. A plume of five ostrich feathers arg., charged with a covered cup gu. therefrom issuant a falcon rising ppr. (BUTLER). Mottoes—1. Virtute et numine (CREAGH) ; 2. Comme je trouve (BUTLER).

Seat—Walterstown, Crusheen, co. Clare. Clubs—Junior Army and Navy ; United Service, Dublin ; County, Clare.

BRASIER-CREAGH OF CREAGH CASTLE.

JOHN WASHINGTON BRASIER-CREAGH, of Creagh Castle, co. Cork, J.P., Capt. 9th Batt. King's Royal Rifle Corps, b. 24 Dec. 1864.

Lineage.—KILNER BRASIER, only son of Brooke Brasier, of Rivers, co. Limerick (see BRASIER of Ballyellis), b. 1751, m. 1788, Mary, eldest dau. & co-heiress of John Creagh, M.D., of Creagh Castle (see CREAGH of Ballyandrew), and had issue, with five daus.,
1. Brooke, ancestor of BRASIER, of Ballyellis.
2. JOHN, of Creagh Castle.
3. William Johnson, Capt. 27th Regt., d. unm.
4. Kilner, R.N., d. unm.
5. GEORGE WASHINGTON, of whom presently.
The second son,
JOHN BRASIER-CREAGH, of Creagh Castle, assumed the name of CREAGH, m. 1801, Elizabeth, dau. and heiress of Charles Widenham, of Castle Widenham, and left an only child,
Priscilla Widenham, of Castle Widenham, m. 8 May, 1819, Henry Mitchell Smyth, and had issue (see SMYTH of Castle Widenham).
His youngest brother,
GEORGE WASHINGTON BRASIER-CREAGH, of Creagh Castle, J.P., b. 12 April, 1797 ; m. 1st, 31 July, 1822, Anne Catherine, dau. of Rev. Bartholomew Pack, Rector of Ettagh, King's Co., and by her (who d. 23 May, 1866) had issue,
1. WILLIAM, b. 26 March, 1826 ; m. 9 Jan. 1862, Isabella Anne Caroline, youngest dau. of the late Thomas Hungerford, R.N., and d.v.p. 6 April, 1866, leaving two sons,
1. JOHN WASHINGTON, now of Creagh Castle.
2. William Hungerford, b. 7 Dec. 1866, settled in New York.
1. Anne Catherine, d. 1 Oct. 1881.
2. John, R.N., b. 12 Aug. 1830 ; m. July, 1859, Kate Frances, dau. of the late F. Holmes, J.P., of Beechmount, Queenstown, co. Cork, and had issue two sons,
1. George Percy, Capt. 9th Bengal Lancers, A.D.C. to the Marquis of Lansdowne, Viceroy of India, b. 4 Sept. 1864 ; m. 12 Nov. 1898, Margorie Cecil Rachel, dau. of Richard Battye, of Crosland Hill and Skelton Hall (see that family). She d. 28 Dec. 1899. Capt. Brasier-Creagh d. 27 April, 1900, from wounds received in action in South Africa while commanding Robert's Horse, leaving a son,
Brian Richmond, b. 12 Sept. 1899.
2. Sydney John, m. the dau. of Major Warren, of Ballyglisane House, co. Cork, and had issue.
1. Catherine, m. C. S. Langley, and has a dau.
2. Gertrude, d. unm.
3. George Washington, b. 31 July, 1832 ; m. Averina, dau. and heiress of Capt. William Sherlock, late 69th Regt., and d. 27 May, 1900, leaving issue,
1. William Harrington Sherlock, of Stream Hill, Doneraile, J.P. co. Cork (who uses the names of Langley-Brasier-Creagh), b. 14 April, 1857 ; m. 1st, 14 April, 1887, Jane, dau. and heir of Henry Langley, of Byblox, Doneraile, co. Cork. She d.s.p. 4 May, 1889. He m. 2ndly, 27 Feb. 1902, Ella May, 4th dau. of E. M. Denny, of Bryanston Square, London.
2. George Washington, C.M.G., Lieut.-Col. R.A.M.C. (Raleigh Club), b. 20 June, 1858 ; m. 20 Oct. 1909, Amie Lambton (widow of Major Younghusband, 14th Bengal Lancers), dau. and heir of — Hooper, of Cheltenham, Gloucestershire.
3. Henry Beresford, b. 2 April, 1862, late R.N., m. 19 Dec. 1893, Eliza, dau. of the Rev. Edmond Rambaut, and has issue,
Edmond Beresford, b. 4 Nov. 1895.
4. Richard Sherlock, late Major 9th Batt. King's Royal Rifle Corps, now of 3rd Batt. Royal Munster Fus.
5. Kilner Charles, late Capt. Imp. Light Horse, now of the R.F.A. (3rd North Midland Brigade), b. 26 April, 1869 ; m 7 Feb. 1907, Agnes Fanny Marland, youngest dau. of the late Edward M. Denny, of 11, Bryanston Square, London, and has issue,
(1) George Edward Brian, b. 25 Feb. 1908.
(2) Kilner Rupert, b. 12 Dec. 1909.
(3) Neville Henry Sherlock, b. 1911.
6. Sherlock (Woodville, Buttevant, co. Cork), b. 9 June, 1874.

1. Averina, *m.* William Humphreys, of Broomfield, Middleton, and has issue.
2. Constance, *m.* William Oliver, and has issue.
3. Lily, *m.* 1 Aug. 1903, Stephen Redington Roche, of Ryehill, co. Galway (*see that family*).
4. Richard Brooke Bartholomew, late Mate R.N., *b.* 1834.
5. Kilner Augustus Arthur, *b.* 9 March, 1839, J.P., Lieut.-Col. 4th Batt. Prince Albert's Light Infantry, formerly in the Military Train; *m.* 3 Sept. 1869, Catherine Hermione, dau. of Henry Crawshay, of Oaklands Park, co. Gloucester, and Llanylan Castle, Glamorgan. He *d.* at Abbotswood, co. Gloucester, 24 Nov. 1890.
1. Catherine, *m.* 1852, Capt. R. Beecher Stowards, 8th Regt.
2. Lucy Susan.   3. Anna Frances.
Mr. G. W. Brasier-Creagh *m.* 2ndly, 10 Aug. 1868, Mary Grace Jessie, youngest dau. of R. J. R. Cotter, of Donoughmore, by whom he had a dau.,
4. Mary Josephine.
He *d.* 3 June, 1876.

Seat—Creagh Castle, Doneraile, co. Cork.

CRICHTON OF MULLABODEN.

LIEUT.-COL. THE HON. CHARLES FREDERICK CRICHTON, of Mullaboden, co. Kildare, J.P. and D.L., High Sheriff 1886, Lieut.-Col. (retired) Gren. Guards, B.A. Exeter Coll. Oxford, *b.* 5 Nov. 1841; *m.* 2 Jan. 1873, Lady Madeline Olivia Susan Taylour, eld. dau. of Thomas, 3rd Marquess of Headfort. She *d.* 27 Jan. 1876, leaving issue,

HUBERT FRANCIS, Major Irish Guards, served in Nile Expedition 1898, and in South Africa 1902, *b.* 17 Dec. 1874; *m.* 14 July, 1903, Esther Eliza, dau. of Llewellyn Traherne Bassett Saunderson, of Dromkeen, co. Cavan, and has issue.
1. Doris Madeline, *b.* 29 May, 1904.
2. Enid Irene Adelaide, *b.* 27 Feb. 1907.
Amelia, *b.* 6 Dec. 1900, Capt. Sir John P. Milbanke, 10th bart., V.C., 10th Hussars, and has issue (*see* BURKE'S *Peerage*).
Col. Crichton is 2nd son of John, 3rd Earl of Erne, who *d.* 3 Oct. 1885, by Selina Griselda his wife, who *d.* 6 Sept. 1884, dau. of the Rev. Charles Cobb Beresford.

Lineage, Arms, &c.—*See* BURKE'S *Peerage*, ERNE, E.

Seat—Mullaboden, Naas, co. Kildare. *Clubs*—Bachelors' and Kildare Street.

CRICHTON OF DERK LODGE.

ALEXANDER JOSEPH CRICHTON, of Carrowgarry, co. Sligo, J.P., High Sheriff 1892, *b.* 30 March, 1861; *m.* 11 July, 1884, Olga Bestyeff, dau. of Johannes and Louisa Bienemann, and has issue,

1. ALEXANDER GODFREY, *b.* 26 May, 1886.
2. Brian Dodwell, *b.* 2 Aug. 1887.
3. Eric Cuthbert, *b.* 18 Sept. 1888.
1. Olga Margaret, *b.* 15 April, 1893.

Lineage.—On the death of EDWARD DODWELL, author of *A Tour in Greece*, &c., Frances Dodwell, Lady Crichton, became the heiress of the family property. SIR ALEXANDER CRICHTON, Knight Grand Cross of St. Anne and St. Vladimir, Knight of the Red Eagle of Prussia, *b.* 2 Dec. 1763; *m.* 27 Sept. 1800, Frances Dodwell, and *d.* 4 June, 1856, leaving by her (who *d.* 21 Jan. 1858) a son,
ALEXANDER CRICHTON, *b.* 24 Sept. 1811; *m.* 11 July, 1860, Annette Octavia Bockchanin, and *d.* 11 Jan. 1888, having had issue,
1. ALEXANDER JOSEPH, now of Carrowgarry.
2. Edward Dodwell, *b.* 26 March, 1862.
3. Henry Maximilian Richard, *b.* 3 Nov. 1863.
1. Dora Annette, *b.* 16 Nov. 1875.

Seat—Carrowgarry (or Tanrago West), Ballysodare, co. Sligo.

CRICHTON. *See* BURKE'S PEERAGE, ERNE, E.

CROASDAILE OF RYNN.

MAJOR LANCELOT CROASDAILE, of Rynn, Queen's Co., J.P. and D.L., late Capt. and Hon. Major 4th Batt. Leinster Regt., formerly Capt. Beds. Regt., *b.* 9 Nov. 1858; *m.* 13 Dec. 1887, Mary Josephine (*d.* 1905), dau. of Alexander Bryn O'Hara O'Rourke, of Brooklyn, co. Down, and The Drift, Belfast, and Catharine his wife, dau. of Cornelius Kelly, R.N., and has issue,

1. LANCELOT HENRY BENEDICT, *b.* 9 Oct. 1888.
1. Mary Carmel, *b.* 14 Oct. 1889.
2. Honor Mary Imelda, *b.* 15 May, 1892.

Lineage.—THOMAS CROASDAILE, *m.* the dau. and co-heir of Sir Henry Waddington, Knt., of Cloghstoken, co. Galway, High Sheriff 1672, M.P. for Athenry 1661, and had issue,
1. Thomas, of Cloghstoken, co. Galway, Ballinroan, co. Leitrim, and Rynn, Queen's Co., *m.* Mary, dau. of Col. Richard Ringrose, of Moynoe, co. Clare. His will dated 15 Sept. was proved 17 Nov. 1709, in which he left his landed estates to his brothers. He had six daus.,
1. Alice, *m.* R. Shaw, of Woodstock, co. Galway.
2. Elizabeth, *m.* 1st, Maj. Morgan Ryan, of Derryjasfil, co. Clare, and 2ndly, 1715, James Molony, of Kiltanon, and had issue.
3. Letitia, *d. unm.*
4. Jane, *m.* R. Miller, of Milford, co. Mayo.
5. Agnes, *d. unm.*
6. Ann, *m.* S. Ormsby, of Springhill, co. Mayo.
2. HENRY, of whom presently.
3. Richard, left issue by Jane his wife, a son,
Thomas, Col. in the Army, *s.* to Rynn, Queen's Co., on the death of his uncle. He left by Mary, his wife, dau. of Col. Samuel Eyre, a son,
Pierson, *b.* 1711; *d.s.p.* 1785.
4. John, of Frisnure, co. Galway, left issue by Ellen his wife,
1. Richard, of Rynn, Queen's Co., and Frisnure, co. Galway, *d.s.p.*, will dated 1748.
2. John, left issue by Mary his wife, Richard of Mountmellick.
1. Alice, *m.* F. Moore.
1. Elizabeth, *m.* W. Despard.
The second son,
HENRY CROASDAILE, of Cloghstoken, Ballinroan, and Woodford, living 1699, left issue by Alice his wife, three sons.
1. THOMAS, of whom presently.   2. Henry.
3. Richard.
The eldest son,
THOMAS CROASDAILE, of Ballinroan and Woodford, co. Galway, High Sheriff 1721, *m.* 1705, Elizabeth, dau. of Richard Pilkington, of Torre, co. Westmeath, and had issue,
1. HENRY, of whom presently.
2. Pilkington, of Liskeard, near Gort, *m.* Elizabeth, dau. of S. Tuncker, Chief Justice of Barbados, and *d.* 1783, leaving issue,
1. Letitia, *m.* P. Despard, of Laurel Hill, Queen's Co.
2. Elizabeth, *m.* Arundel Madden.
3. John (Rev.), left issue.
4. Richard, Col. in the Army, *m.* 24 Nov. 1774, Margaret Dunn, and had issue,
Richard, who had eight sons, of whom (1) Edward; (2) Despard, of Golden Square, London, *d.s.p.* 1819.
5. William, *d.s.p.*
The eldest son,
HENRY CROASDAILE, of Woodford, High Sheriff co. Galway 1744, *b.* 1708; *m.* Mary, dau. of K. Despard, of Crannagh. She *d.* 1779. He *d.* 1778, leaving, with a younger son, Henry, who *d.s.p.*, an elder son,
COL. RICHARD CROASDAILE, of Woodford, co. Galway (which he sold), and of Rynn, Queen's Co. (which he had inherited), High Sheriff Queen's Co. 1772, and co. Galway 1775, *m.* 10 Sept. 1775, Elizabeth, dau. of Lancelot Sandes, of Kilcaven, Queen's Co., and had issue,
1. LANCELOT, of Rynn.
2. Thomas, R.N., *d.s.p.* 1836.
3. Henry, Major in the Army, *d.* 1828.
4. George, *m.* Mary, dau. of J. Henderson, and had issue, 1. Richard, 2. George, 3. Henry, 1. Margaret, and 2. Mary.
5. Edward, *d.s.p.*
1. Mary, *m.* Rev. Thomas Pigott, of Knapton, and had issue.
2. Elizabeth, *m.* Gen. Vandeleur.
3. Catherine, *m.* Thomas Trench, of Millicent, co. Kildare, and had issue.
The eldest son,
LANCELOT CROASDAILE, of Rynn, Queen's Co., High Sheriff 1811; *m.* Susan, dau. of F. Brownrigg, of Edenderry, and had issue,
1. Richard *d.* young, 1834.   2. JOHN, of whom presently.
1. Elizabeth Anne, *m.* 8 Dec. 1843, Rev. John Essex Edward Edgeworth, of Kilshrewly, co. Longford. She *d.* his widow 15 June, 1906, leaving issue (*see that family*).
The only surviving son,
JOHN CROASDAILE, of Rynn, Queen's Co., J.P., High Sheriff 1855, Capt. Queen's Co. Rifles, *b.* 1830; *m.* 1853, Anna Jane, dau. of Richard Townshend, of Myrosswood, co. Cork, and *d.* 1889, leaving issue,
1. LANCELOT, now of Rynn.
2. Richard, *b.* 1861; *m.* 1897, Emma Estella, dau. of — Hurst, of U.S.A., and has issue,
1. Richard Edward, *b.* 1898.
2. Cameron, *b.* 1902.
3. Henry Frederick, *b.* 1863; *m.* 10 March, 1891, Mary Ellen, dau. of John Lloyd, of Liverpool, and has issue,
1. John Lloyd, *b.* 1894.   2. Lancelot, *b.* 1898.
1. Violet, *b.* 1902.
4. John Ernest, *b.* 1867; *m.* 17 July, 1907, Una Fetherstonhaugh, dau. of Lindsey Bucknall Barker, of Glenard, Belfast.
5. Frederick George, *b.* 1870; *d.* 1889.
1. Helen, *m.* 1898, Edward R. Wade, Barrister-at-Law, and has issue.

Seat—Rynn, Rosenallis, Queen's Co.

CROFTON OF LAKEFIELD.

CAPT. DUKE ARTHUR CROFTON, R.N., of Lakefield, co. Leitrim. J.P., D.L., High Sheriff 1906, *b.* 18 Dec. 1850; *m.* 13 Nov. 1883, Augusta Maude, dau. of Gen. Sir J. H. Lefroy, K.C.M.G., C.B., R.A., and has issue,

1. Hugh Lefroy, *b.* 10 Sept. 1884, Lieut. R. Inniskilling Fus.
2. Philip Duke, *b.* 12 April, 1886, Lieut. R.N.
3. John Henry, *b.* 8 Dec. 1889, Lieut. Roy. Irish Regt.
4. Richard Marsh, *b.* 6 April, 1891.
5. Patrick George, *b.* 12 Dec. 1899.
1. Amy Dundas, *b.* 30 Jun. 1893.
2. Hilda Frances, *b.* 9 July, 1894.

Lineage. — MICHAEL CROFTON, of Harristown and Park, co. Meath, descended from JOHN CROFTON, of Ballymurray, Auditor-Gen. *temp.* ELIZABETH, *m.* Ann, dau. of George Webb, and *d.* 1721, having had issue,

1. George, *m.* Ann Slack, and *d.* 1736, having had issue,
   1. Ann, *d.* an infant.
   2. Mary, *m.* her cousin Duke Crofton, of Lakefield (*see below*).
2. DUKE, of whom presently.
1. Elizabeth, *m.* — Brereton.
2. Ann, *m.* — McCartney.

The 2nd son,

DUKE CROFTON, of Park and Lurga, *m.* Honour (*d.* April, 1779), dau. of Caleb Warren, of Trim, and had issue,

1. Edward, *d.* young.
2. John, *m.* Ann Whitelaw, and *d.s.p.*
3. DUKE, of whom presently.
1. Ann, *m.* 20 Oct. 1754, Randal Slack, of Lakefield, and *d.s.p.* 1801.
2. Jane, *m.* T. Cooper, of The Downs.

The only surviving son,

DUKE CROFTON, of Lakefield, co. Leitrim, *s.* to that property 1801, by will of his uncle Randal Slack, *m.* his first cousin Mary, dau. of George Crofton (*see above*). She *d.* 1779, leaving issue. He *m.* 2ndly, Maria, youngest dau. of the late James Webster of Longford, and left with a dau., Susanna, *m.* 1791, the Rev. Henry Crofton, and son of Sir Morgan Crofton, Bart., a son,

DUKE CROFTON, of Lakefield, J.P. and D.L., High Sheriff 1800, Capt. in the Mohill Yeomanry, *b.* 13 Nov. 1768 ; *m.* 18 Aug. 1808, Alicia (*d.* 1866), eldest dau. of William Jones, of Belleville, co. Westmeath, by whom he had issue,

1. DUKE, of Lakefield.
2. WILLIAM, late of Lakefield.
3. John (Rev.), *m.* 1 July, 1843, Anne Newcomen, youngest dau. of Berry Norris, of Mohill, co. Leitrim. He *d.* Dec. 1868. She *d.* 28 Nov. 1902, having had issue,
   1. Duke Fraser, *d.* an infant.
   2. William Jones, M.B., Trin. Coll. Dublin, Capt. retired, A.M.S., *b.* 23 Nov. 1862 ; *m.* Nov. 1887, Kate Dunbar, 2nd dau. of Charles R. C. Tichborne, LL.D., Ph.D., L.R.C.S., M.R.I.A., and *d.* Dec. 1905, having had issue,
      (1) Kathleea Tichborne.
      (2) Nora Norris.
      (3) Eileen Constance Vera.
      (4) Violet Mabel Ruby.
   1. Dorcas Alice.
   2. Elizabeth Anna, *m.* 1878, Berry Norris, of U.S.A., and *d.* 1879.
   3. Helen Augusta.
   4. Henrietta Dorothea.
4. Richard Henry, Major-Gen. R.A., *m.* 22 June, 1848, Frances Mary (*d.* 19 Feb. 1906), 2nd dau. of Arthur Cuthbert Marsh, of Eastbury, Herts, and *d.* 23 March, 1897, leaving issue.
   1. DUKE ARTHUR, Capt. R.N., now of Lakefield.
   2. Richard Martin, Maj. R.H.A., *b.* 8 Nov. 1854 ; *m.* Marion Emma, widow of Maj. Alfred Fox Cotton, Indian S.C. (*see* BURKE's *Peerage*, COMBERMERE, V.), and dau. of Adm. Sir L. G. Heath, K.C.B., and *d.s.p.* 24 Jan. 1899.
   3. Caldwell Henry, Maj. late R.A. (*Heathyfield, Farnham, Surrey*) ; *b.* Oct. 1856 ; *m.* 9 April, 1890, Helen Rose Anne, 3rd dau. of the late Sir William Milman, 3rd bart., and has issue,
      Richard Cecil Milman, *b.* 25 Aug. 1895.
   1. Amy, *m.* John Swinton Isaac, D.L., of Boughton Park, Worcester, and has issue.
5. Henry Robert, Lieut. R.N., *m.* 13 April, 1850, Bessie, dau. of Dr. Singer, Bishop of Meath, and *d.* 1857, leaving issue,
   Joseph Singer.
6. Travers, Capt. 52nd Madras Native Infantry, *m.* 7 April, 1850, Annie E., eldest dau. of James Singer, and *d.* 1861, leaving an only child,
   Jane Singer, *m.* 6 April, 1876, Henry Willoughby Stewart Lyons Montgomery, of Bellbavel (*see that family*).
7. Gustavus St. John, Capt. R.E ; fell at Sebastopol, 1855.
1. Mary, *m.* 30 Sept. 1846, Charles Stanhope Crofton, youngest son of Rev. Henry Crofton, and has issue.
2. Alicia Maria, *d. unm.* 1859..

He *d.* 1845. His eldest son,

DUKE CROFTON, of Lakefield, *d. unm.* Nov. 1873, and was *s.* by his next brother.

WILLIAM CROFTON, of Lakefield, M.D., J.P., *m.* 30 March, 1848, Frances Emelia (who *d.* 23 Oct. 1910), only dau. of Capt. N. J. C. Dunn, R.N., of Montagu Villa, Cheltenham, and *d.s.p.* 1886.

Arms—Per pale dancettée or and az., a lion passant-guardant counterchanged. **Crest**—Seven ears of wheat on one stalk, ppr. **Motto**—Dat Deus incrementum.

Seat—Lakefield, Mohill, co. Leitrim. **Residence**—Montagu Villa, Cheltenham.

CROFTON. See BURKE's PEERAGE, **CROFTON, B.** and **CROFTON, Bart.**

CROFTS OF VELVETSTOWN.

CHRISTOPHER CROFTS, of Velvetstown and Castle Wrixon, co. Cork, *b.* 14 Feb, 1826 ; *s.* his uncle 1868 ; *m.* 14 March, 1861, Sarah, 2nd dau. of William Lysagh , of Hazlewood, co. Cork, by Frances his wife, dau. and co-heir of William Atkins, of Fountainville, and has had issue,

1. CHRISTOPHER GEORGE, *b.* 27 Jan. 1866.
2. William Herbert, *b.* 15 June, 1867.
3. Thomas Harry, *b.* 4 Feb. 1869.
4. Sidney Edward, *b.* 11 June, 1875.
1. Frances Catherine, *d.* 1875.
2. Alice Marian.
3. Emily Grace.
4. Elizabeth Mary.
5. Florence Ellen.
6. Kathleen Anne.

Lineage.—GEORGE CROFTS, of Velvetstown, J.P. for co. Kerry in 1678, who fled to England in 1689 with his wife and ten children. He *m.* Mary, dau. of — Freeman, of Cahirmee House, co. Cork, and had nineteen children, ten sons and nine daus., of whom a younger son, Capt. James Crofts, of Cahircella, co. Clare. left issue by his 1st wife, an only child named Catherine, *m.* Augustine Fitzgerald, of co. Clare ; and three daus., Elizabeth, *m.* 14 Dec. 1703, Jacob, Ringrose ; Anne, *m.* George Redman, of co. Kerry, and Susannah.

His eldest son and heir,

CHRISTOPHER CROFTS, of Velvetstown, *b.* 1694 ; *m.* 1st, Mary, dau. of Peter Graham, of Dromore, and of Conveymore, both in co. Cork, and had issue,

1. GEORGE, of Stream Hill, co. Cork, *b.* 1722 ; *m.* Mary, dau. of Cornelius Holmes, of Shinnanah, in the same co., and *d.* 1801, leaving, *inter alios*, Susan, wife of Robert Philpot, of Newmarket, co. Cork ; Mary, wife of Roger Atkins, of Rossagh ; a son and heir,

   CHRISTOPHER, of Stream Hill, *b.* 1737 ; *m.* 1st, Christian, dau. of Charles Creed, of Ballynanty, co. Limerick, and by her had, *inter alios*,
      Mary, *m.* Henry Lee, of Barna, co. Tipperary.
   He *m.* 2ndly, Anne, dau. of Richard Crone, of Ballydineen, co. Cork, and *d.* 10 Nov. 1837, aged 90, leaving by this latter lady, with other children, a son and heir,
      George, of Stream Hill, *m.* 1815, Anne, eldest dau. of Thomas H. Forrest, J.P. of Broom Hill, co. Cork, by Anne his wife, dau. of Rev. John Aldwell, Rector of Newchapel, Cahir, co. Tipperary, and had, with other issue,
         1. Christopher, *b.* 1822, *m.* Harriette Mary, only dau. of Capt. James Atkin, 61st Foot, of Leadington, co. Cork, and Margaret his wife, dau. of George Robbins, of Hymenstown, co. Tipperary, and the Hon. Rebecca Massy his wife. He had issue,
            a. George, *d.* young.
            b. Christopher.
            a. Margaret Robbins Atkin.
            b. Harriette Mary, *m.* Fred. Falls.
            c. Anne.
            d. Elizabeth Uniacke FitzGerald.
            e. Louisa Atkin, *d. unm.*
            f. Georgina Henrietta.
         2. Thomas, *m.* Mary, dau. of Harry Wallis (*see* WALLIS *of Drishane*), and *d.s.p.*
         3. George.
2. WILLIAM, of Velvetstown, of whom presently.
3. Christopher, *d.s.p.*
1. Mary, *m.* John Bond, of Ballynahalisk, co. Cork.
2. Catherine, *m.* John Wilkisson, of Johnstown, co. Cork.

Mr. Crofts *m.* 2ndly, Mary, dau. of William Austen, of Lislevaune, co. Cork, and by her had one dau., who *d.* young. He *d.* 9 July, 1757. His 2nd son,

WILLIAM CROFTS, of Velvetstown, b. 1726; m. 1754, Elizabeth, dau. of John Bere, of Gurteen, co. Cork, and by her (who d. 1813, aged 86) left at his decease, 1784, seven sons and four daus., of whom were,
1. CHRISTOPHER, his heir.
2. George, b. 23 Oct. 1763; m. and left issue by his 2nd wife an only child, m. William Prittie Harris, of Lakeview, co. Cork.
3. William, of Danesfort, co. Cork, b. 1 Aug. 1765; m. Catherine Anne, dau. of Bartholomew Gibbings, of Gibbings Grove, and d. 20 Dec. 1801, having had four daus., co-heiresses,
  1. Elizabeth, m. the Rev. John Beasley.
  2. Anne, m. the Rev. Arthur Bernard Baldwin, Vicar of Raghan, co. Cork.
  3. Jane, m. George Sackville Cotter, Capt. 69th Regt.
  4. Wilhelmina, m. John Wrixon, jun., of Somerville, co. Cork.
4. James, b. 31 July, 1766; m. Jane, dau. of Aylmer Allen, of Woodview, co. Cork, and had issue.
5. Richard, b. 7 June, 1767; m. Sarah, sister of Carden Terry, and d. 5 June, 1823, leaving (with other issue),
  William, m. Marian, eldest dau. of Richard Giffard Campion, of Bushey Park, and had issue, five daus.
6. Robert, b. 10 March, 1769; m. 1807, Mary, dau. of Thomas Nash, of Rockfield, co. Cork and d. 21 May, 1818, having had issue,
7. Charles, b. 18 April, 1770; d. unm.
1. Ruth, m. Michael Busteed, Mayor of Cork, 1801.
2. Mary, m. her cousin, William Fitzgerald, of co. Clare.
3. Catherine, m. Charles O'Keefe, of Mount Keefe, co. Cork.
4. Elizabeth, m. Robert Keene, of Hermitage, co. Clare.

The eldest son and heir,
CHRISTOPHER CROFTS, of Velvetstown, b. 5 March, 1755; m. 1782, Mary, dau. of Thomas Lucas, of Richfordstown, co. Cork; and by her (who d. 1 June, 1838, aged 80) had issue,
1. THOMAS LUCAS, of whom hereafter.
2. WILLIAM, heir to his brother.
3. Christopher, of F llyhowra, co. Cork, b. 3 Nov. 1792; m. 1824, Alice, dau. of Richard Nason, of Ballyhowra Lodge, co. Cork, and d. 17 March, 1861, having by her (who d. Jan. 1866) had issue,
  1. CHRISTOPHER, now of Velvetstown.
  2. Richard Nason, of Ballyhowra Lodge, co. Cork, J.P., b. 19 March, 1834; m. 1869, Bessie, dau. of Rev. William H. Nason. She d. his widow 20 Nov. 1911, having had issue,
    (1) Christopher, b. 1877.
    (2) Richard.
    (1) Alice.
    (2) Maud.
  1. Catherine Nason.
1. Dorah, m. Henry Langley, of Ballyellis, co. Cork.
2. Elizabeth, m. 28 Sept. 1809, John Nash, of Rockfield, co. Cork, and had issue.
3. Ruth, m. her cousin, Carden T. Crofts.

Mr. Christopher Crofts d. 21 June, 1811. His eldest son,
THOMAS LUCAS CROFTS, of Velvetstown, b. 2 June, 1790; d. unm. 1851, when he was s. by his next brother,
REV. WILLIAM CROFTS, of Velvetstown, b. 19 Aug. 1791; d. unm. 31 July, 1869, and was s. by his nephew.

Seat—Velvetstown House, near Buttevant, co. Cork.

CROKER OF BALLYNAGARDE.

COURTENAY LE POER TRENCH CROKER, of Ballynagarde and Blackwater, co. Limerick, J.P. and D.L., Auditor Local Government Board since 1882, b. 27 Feb. 1853; m. 29 July, 1882, Mary, youngest dau. of the late Ven. Charles Hare, Archdeacon of Limerick.

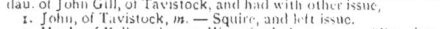

Lineage.—This is a branch of the house of CROKER (or CROCKER) of Lincham, Devon, a family so ancient that an old proverbial distich records that,
  "Croker, Crewys and Coplestone
  When the conqueror came, were at home."

SIR JOHN CROKER, of Lineham, Devon, Knt., d. 14 March, 1508; m. Elizabeth, dau. of Sir Richard Fortescue, of Punsbourne, Herts, and had issue,
JOHN CROKER, of Lineham, d. 1520; m. Elizabeth, dau. of Sir Lewis Pollard, and by her (who m. 2ndly, Sir Hugh Trevanyon, K.B., and d. 21 May, 1531), had issue,
JOHN CROKER, of Lineham, living 1548; m. Elizabeth, dau. of Richard Strode, of Newnham, Devon, and had with other issue,
1. JOHN, of Lineham, d. 18 Nov. 1612; m. Agnes, dau. and heir of John Scrivington, of Tavistock, Devon, and left issue.

2. Thomas, of St. Agnes, Cornwall, d. before 1620; m. Margery, dau. of John Gill, of Tavistock, and had with other issue,
  1. John, of Tavistock, m. — Squire, and left issue.
  2. Hugh, of Ballyander, co. Waterford, d. 1644; m. Alice, dau. of — Taylor, and left issue.
  3. EDWARD, of whom next.

EDWARD CROKER, of Rawleighstown, co Limerick, 3rd son of Thomas Croker, of St. Agnes, Cornwall, m. Catherine, dau. of John Downing, and was murdered 1641. His son and heir,
JOHN CROKER, of Rawleighstown, b. circa 1624; m. 1st, Arabella dau. of Sir Thomas Browne, and had issue. Mr. Croker d. 12 July, 1717, in his 93rd year. His son and heir,
EDWARD CROKER, of Rawleighstown, b. 1653, High Sheriff 1709; m. 10 Dec. 1679, Mary Bucknor, and by her (who d. 15 April, 1728, aged 68) left at his decease, 1732, a son,
JOHN CROKER, of Ballynagarde, co. Limerick, J.P. temp. GEORGE I, who d. 6 Nov. 1751, leaving by Anne, dau. of Andrew Richards, his wife,
1. EDWARD, his heir.
2. Andrew, m. Elizabeth, dau. of Walter Taylor, of Raheens, co. Galway.
3. Abraham, Surveyor of Revenue.
4. Richard.
5. John, of Dublin, whose 3rd son, Thomas, m. Anne, dau. of William Ryves, and d. 13 April, 1800, leaving an only child, Anne, who m. Sir Edward Crofton, Bart., and was created BARONESS CROFTON.
6. Walter, m. twice.

The eldest son,
EDWARD CROKER, of Ballynagarde, High Sheriff 1735, m. 1726, Elizabeth, dau. of Henry Prittie, of Kilboy, and had, with three daus., three sons, JOHN, Henry, and Edward, of whom the eldest,
JOHN CROKER, of Ballynagarde, High Sheriff 1755, m. 18 April, 1753, Sarah, dau. of Richard Pennefather, M.P., and had issue,
1. EDWARD, his heir.
2. Richard (Rev.), B.A., Rector of Croom, m. Mary, dau. of James Guthrie, of Carass Park, co. Galway.
3. John, General in the Army, m. Honora, dau. of John O'Grady, of Cahir Guillamore, co. Limerick.
4. William, Solicitor, m. Margaret, dau. of Col. Edward O'Brien, of Ennistymon, co. Clare.
5. Henry, of Quartertown, co. Cork, ancestor of CROKER, of Glencairn (see that family).
1. Sarah, m. April, 1786, Launcelot Charles Sandys, of Kilcoran, Queen's Co., and Carrigafoyle, co. Kerry.
2. Charity, m. 1789, John O'Grady, of Cahir Guillamore, co. Limerick (see BURKE'S Peerage, GUILLAMORE, V.).
3. Elizabeth, m. Edward Croker, of Grange Hill, co. Limerick.

The eldest son,
EDWARD CROKER, of Ballynagarde, m. 1783, Margaret Anne, youngest dau. of Richard Hare, and sister to William, 1st Earl of Listowel, and had issue,
1. JOHN, of whom presently.
2. Richard Hare, Col. late 18th Hussars, m. Emilia, dau. of Joseph Haigh, of Whitwell Hall, co. York, and d. 15 Jan. 1854, having by her (who d. 6 May, 1887) had issue. His son, Capt. Arthur Charles Croker, 77th Regt., d. 3 Nov. 1899.
3. Edward (Rev.), m. Miss Lascelles, and has issue.
4. William (Col.), C.B., 17th Regt., m. the dau. of Charles Stokes, Bengal Civil Service, and d. 11 Aug. 1852, leaving issue,
  Edward, late Capt. 17th Regt.
5. Henry, 5th son of Edward of Ballynagarde, m. Miss O'Grady, of Linfield, co. Limerick and had issue.
  Henry Braddell Croker, of Beanfield, co. Wexford, J.P., Capt. 57th Regt., m. 1st, Mary, dau. of Col. Vicq; and 2ndly, Ellen, dau. of Thos. O'Grady, of Aghamarta, co. Cork. Capt. Croker d. 1880, having by his 1st wife had issue,
    (1) Capt. Wm. Henry Croker, now of Beanfield, b. 1852; m. 1879, Frances, dau. of Vicomte de Vahner.
    (1) Anne, m. E. Abbott.
    (2) Blanche, m. Chas. Tottenham Reade, of Donishall, co. Wexford.
6. Charles, Capt. R.N., m. Miss Crone, and d. 23 Dec. 1877, leaving issue.
7. Robert, m. Miss O'Grady, of The Grange, and d. May, 1848, leaving issue.
8. Thomas (Rev.), m. Miss E. Hugh, of Whitwell and has issue.
1. Margaret, m. the Very Rev. Richard Bagwell, of Marfield, Dean of Clogher.
2. Sarah, m. Major George Gough, eldest son of Col. Gough, of Woodstown, co. Limerick, and brother of Gen. Lord Gough G.C.B.

The eldest son,
JOHN CROKER, of Ballynagarde and Raleighstown, J.P., High Sheriff 1832, b. 4 Oct. 1784; m. 14 Sept. 1807, Catherine Adeline, youngest dau. of Col. Bagwell, of Marlfield, co. Tipperary, M.P., and had issue,
1. EDWARD, his heir.
1. Marianne Margaret.
2. Margaret Anne.
3. Catherine Adeline Bagwell, d. young.
4. Henrietta, m. Frederick John Partridge, R N., son of John Partridge, of Bishop Wood, co. Hereford.
5. Janet, m. Francis Walsh, son of George Walsh, of Lisbon.

Mr. Croker d. 3 March, 1858. His son,
EDWARD CROKER, of Ballynagarde and Raleighstown, co. Limerick, J.P. and D.L., Capt. 17th Lancers, b. 31 Aug. 1812; m. 17 May, 1841, Lady Georgiana Ellen Monck, 9th dau. of Henry Stanley Earl of Rathdowne, and by her (who d. 20 March, 1857) had issue,
1. John, b. 16 March, 1842; m. Oct. 1864, Harriet Donaldson, and d.v.p. 19 Feb. 1867, leaving an only son,

JOHN MONCK, of Ballynagarde, b. 18 Sept. 1866; d. unm. 6 Oct. 1889.
2. HENRY STANLEY MONCK, of Ballynagarde, co. Limerick, J.P. and D.L., b. 26 March, 1846; d. unm. 22 June, 1897.
3. FREDERICK EDWARD ALBERT, of Ballynagarde, co. Limerick, J.P. and D.L., formerly R.N., b. 4 May, 1847; m. Emily Adelaide, 2nd dau. of the late Capt. W. Clune, 5th Royal Fusiliers, and d. 14 Aug. 1900, s.p.
4. Edward William Dunlo, b. 14 Sept. 1849, Capt. 93rd Highlanders; m. 5 Jan. 1875, Florence Elizabeth (who m. 2ndly, 14 Aug. 1902, Right Hon. H. E. Chatterton, P.C., Vice-Chancellor of Ireland, who d. 30 Aug. 1910), dau. of Major Charles Gore 72nd Highlanders (see HICKMAN of Tyredagh Castle), and d. 10 May, 1893, leaving issue. His youngest dau., Constance Evelyn Naneye, m. 9 Dec. 1909, Robert Sheffield Stuart, 2nd son of A. J. Stewart, Madras C. S. (see BURKE'S Peerage, CASTLE STEWART, E.).
5. COURTENAY LE POER TRENCH, now of Ballynagarde.
6. Charles de la Poer Beresford, b. 28 Nov. 1856; m. 11 Oct. 1884, Edith Elizabeth, dau. of Alfred Adams. She d. 24 March, 1886. He d. 7 March, 1891, leaving an only son,
Alfred Edward Beresford, b. 19 March, 1886.
1. Frances Mary, d. Feb. 1902, having m. March, 1880, Edward John de la Poer, and had issue.
2. Alice Georgiana.
3. Georgiana Ellen Monck, m. 9 Feb. 1882, Richard Powell Rees, of The Firs, co. Hereford, late Capt. 7th Dragoon Guards, and d. 3 June, 1885.
4. Alma Louisa Geraldine Isabella, m. Nov. 1874, Arthur Hamilton, of Hollybrook, Foxrock, co. Dublin, son of Charles Hamilton, of Hamwood, and has issue.
Capt. Croker d. 1869, and was s. by his grandson.

Arms—Arg., a chevron engrailed gu. between three ravens ppr. Crest—A two-handled drinking cup or, above it three fleurs-de-lys arg. Motto—Deus alit eos.
Seat—Ballynagarde, co. Limerick. Club—Limerick County.

CROKER OF GLENCAIRN.

RICHARD WELSTED CROKER, of Glencairn, co. Dublin, b. 1841; m. Nov. 1873, Elizabeth, dau. of Samuel Fraser, of New York, and has surviving issue.
1. Howard, b. 5 April, 1886.
1. Florence Geneveve. 2. Ethel.
Lineage.—HENRY CROKER, youngest son of John Croker, of Ballynagarde, co. Limerick (see that family), b. 1758; d. 23 May, 1836. Maj. in the Army; m. 1793, Harriet, only dau. and heir of John Dillon, of Quartertown, co. Cork, and had issue,
1. John Dillon, of Quartertown, m. 28 May, 1811, Elizabeth, dau. of William Roberts, of Union Island, co. Cork, and left issue.
2. Richard, m. — Devonshire. 3. Edward.
4. William Roberts, b. 10 July, 1816; d. 18 May, 1850; m. 1839, Catherine Margaret, dau. of William Croker, of Dublin, Solicitor, and left,
1. Henry William, b. 10 March, 1843; d. 19 June, 1902; m. 19 June, 1873, Charlotte, dau. of Blakeney Gubbins, of Fort Louis, co. Sligo, and left,
William Henry, Blakeney, Richard, Arthur, Kathleen Emily, Florence Margaret and Charlotte Elizabeth.
2. James O'Brien, b. 16 April, 1847; m. 7 Oct. 1880, Henrietta Emily, dau. of William Odlum, of Meelick, Queen's Co., and has,
(1) Edward James O'Brien, b. 3 July, 1881, R.N.
(2) George Fitzgerald, b. 20 Oct. 1885, R.N.
(3) Crofton, b. 4 Jan. 1888.
(4) William Penuefather, b. 6 Oct. 1889.
(5) Reginald, b. 27 April, 1891.
(6) Launcelot Hungerford, b. 20 Jan. 1895.
(1) Elizabeth Brought. (2) Emma Wilhelmina.
1. Isabella Florence, m. 8 April, 1880, Rev. George FitzGerald Russell, M.A.
5. Eyre Coote, b. 1 May, 1800; d. 1883; m. Nov. 1827, Florence, dau. of John Welsted, of Ballywalter, co. Cork (see that family), and left,
1. Henry.
2. Edward, m. Adelaide, dau. of — Franklin, and had,
Edward Frank, Richard and Adelaide.
3. RICHARD WELSTED, now of Glencairn.
1. Eliza Roberts m. 1880, William J. Jenkins, of Virginia.
2. Henrietta Victoria, m. 6 Nov. 1857, Samuel Warren, of Blackrock, co. Dublin. She d. 1901. He d. 1902, leaving issue one son and four daus.
Arms.—See CROKER of Ballynagarde, quartering DILLON.
Residence—Glencairn, Sandyford, co. Dublin.

CROKER OF THE GRANGE.

HELEN MARIA (Lady Dyer) and MISS CAROLINE CROKER, sisters and co-heirs of Edward Croker, D.L., of The Grange, co. Limerick, s. their brother, 1896.

Lineage.—This family is maternally a branch of the O'GRADY of Killballyowen family.
NICHOLAS GRADY, of The Grange, d. 12 March, 1772 (whose will was proved 13 May, 1773), m. Helen, dau. of John Morony, of co Clare, and had issue,
1. Henry, d. 1784.
2. Thomas, m. Henrietta, dau. of Sir George Armytage, Bart. and d. 1788.
3. STANDISH, of whom presently.
1. Margaret, m. John Monsell.
2. Mary, m. 1788, Viscount Harberton.
3. Helen, m. Thomas Lee, Groom of the Bedchamber to H.R.H. the late Duke of Gloucester.
The youngest son,
STANDISH GRADY, of The Grange, m. Margaret Morony, and d. 1816, having had issue,
1. Henry, d. Dec. 1853.
2. THOMAS, late of The Grange.
3. Standish, dec.
1. Helen, dec.
2. Maria, m. John Crone, of Byblox, co. Cork, and d. June, 1867.
3. Margaret, m. the Rev. Robert Croker, and d. 1874, having had issue,
1. EDWARD, late of The Grange.
1. HELEN MARIA, of The Grange (The Knoll, Ascot, Berks), m. 29 July, 1858, Sir Swinnerton Halliday Dyer, 12th bart. of Tottenham, who d. 16 March, 1882, leaving issue (see BURKE'S Peerage and Baronetage).
2. CAROLINE, of The Grange.
The 2nd son,
THOMAS O'GRADY, of The Grange, co. Limerick, J.P., d. unm. July, 1861, and was s. by his nephew,
EDWARD CROKER, of The Grange, co. Limerick, J.P. and D.L., late Capt. 47th Regt., High Sheriff 1868, b. 1836, s. 1861; and d.s.p. 1 June, 1896.

Seat—The Grange, Limerick.

DE LA CHEROIS-CROMMELIN OF CARROWDORE CASTLE.

MARIA HENRIETTA and EVELYN ANGÉLIQUE DE LA CHEROIS-CROMMELIN, of Carrowdore Castle, co. Down, s. (jointly with their late sister Mrs. Shaw) their brother, 15 June, 1902.

Lineage. — The Crommelins, though established in France and possessed of considerable property at Armandcourt in Picardy, for more than a century before the Revocation of the Edict of Nantes, came originally from the Low Countries. ARMAND CROMMELIN resided on his estate, near Courtrai, in the reign of CHARLES V; but in consequence of the persecutions of the Protestants by Alva, in the reign of PHILIP II, his family left, and his son, JEAN, settled at St. Quuetin, and became Seigneur de Camas, through his marriage with Marie, dau. of Jacques de Semery. "Ce marriage fut célébré à Follembourg château royal entre Chauny et Coucy, le 17 Déc. 1595, honoré de la présence de Madame Catherine de France, sœur du roi HENRI IV, qui y tenoit sa cœur." Of this marriage were three sons,
1. PIERRE, "naquit au Château de Mony St. Phar le 28 Nov. 1596, et eut pour marraine Madame Catherine de France," and m. Marie Desormeaux de Cambray, and left a son, Samuel, who m. Madeleine Testard de St. Quentin, and at the Revocation, took refuge at Haarlem, where he d. 1687, leaving (with other children, whose descendants still remain in Holland) a dau., Anne, who m. her cousin, Louis Crommelin, who settled in Ireland 1698.
2. JEAN, of whom presently. 3. Adrien.
Two of Jean de Camas's grandsons, named Jaques and Adrien, received patents of letters of nobility from LOUIS XIV.; and others became Seigneurs de Mézières, Senandcourt, Armandcourt, and de Bersy. A grand-dau. of the latter m. the Comte de Stolberg, in Prussia, 1733. The 2nd son of Jean de Camas,
JEAN CROMMELIN, b. 1603; m. Rachel Jaquelet du Castlet, and d. at St. Qunetin 1650, leaving several children, of whom the eldest.
LOUIS CROMMELIN, b. at St. Qunetin 1625; m. 1648, Marie Metayer, and had issue eight children. At the Revocation, almost all this family fled to Holland; but the following eventually settled in Ireland,
1. LOUIS, who founded the linen trade in Ireland. In 1698, Louis with two brothers and three sisters, and several cousins and members of his family, "was induced" by King WILLIAM III of England, to go over to Ireland, where they settled at Lisburn, co. Antrim, bringing with them a number of tradesmen and a capital of £20,000 with which they established the linen manufacture, which was adopted by the natives, and has flourished ever since. In consideration of Louis having spent £10,000 on its establishment, King WILLIAM, who was most interested in its success, conferred on him a pension of £200 a year for the life of his son, on whose early death, it was discontinued. He was

b. 1650; m. 1680, his cousin Anne, dau. of Samuel Crommelin; left France in 1685, and settling first at Amsterdam, came to Lisburn in 1698; he had issue, one son and one dau.,
Louis, who d. at Lisburn 1711, *unm.*, aged 28.
Magdaleine, m. Capt. de Bernière d'Alençon.
2. **Samuel**, m. 1st, Judith Truffet de Laon, and 2ndly, Mdlle. de Belcastel, sister of Lieut.-Gen. Belcastel, and left four sons, of whom all male issue has now become extinct.
3. **William**, m. Miss Butler, of the Ormonde family, and had a son, Louis, who d. *unm.*, and a dau.
1. Jeane, m. Abraham Gillot, whose dau. m. the elder son of the Samuel mentioned above.
2. Anne, m. 1st, Isaac Cousin de Meaux; and 2ndly, Daniel de la Cherois, by whom she had an only dau.,
Marie Angélique Madeleine, d. at Donaghdee 22 Aug. 1771, who m. Thomas Montgomery, last Earl of Mount Alexander, by whom, having no children, she was left all his property, and on her death she left it to be divided between her cousins, Samuel de la Cherois and Nicholas Crommelin.
3. **Marie**, of whom we treat.
The youngest dau.,
Marie Crommelin, m. 1st, Isaac Testard de Blois; and 2ndly, Nicholas de la Cherois, Major, and afterwards Lieut.-Col. in the Regt. of the Comte de Marton, under **William III**, who d. 1706, leaving two children,
Samuel, of whom presently.
Madeleine, m. her cousin Daniel Crommelin.
The only son,
Samuel de la Cherois, b. 1700; m. 1731, Mdlle. Sarah Cormière, and d. 1784. Their 3rd son,
Samuel de la Cherois, b. 1744, assumed, in compliance with the will of his cousin, Nicholas Crommelin, of Lisburn, the additional surname of Crommelin. He m. 16 April, 1776, Maria, only dau. of Rev. Dr. Thomas Dobbs, of Trin. Coll. Dublin (brother of Conway Dobbs, of Castle Dobbs, co. Antrim, Governor of North Carolina), by Mary his wife, dau. of J. Young, and had, besides other issue,
Nicholas de la Cherois-Crommelin, of Carrowdore Castle, J.P. and D.L., High Sheriff of Down 1821, and of Antrim 1830, b. 10 June, 1783; m. 17 Dec. 1810, Elizabeth, 2nd dau. of William, 2nd Lord Ventry, and had by her three sons and four daus.,
1. **Samuel Arthur Hill**, his heir.
2. Nicholas, of Rockport, Cushenden, Larne, b. 7 March, 1819; m. 8 Jan. 1851, Annie, 2nd dau. of Andrew Mulholland, of Springvale, co. Down, and d. 16 March, 1900, leaving issue,
 1. Thomas William, b. 30 Nov. 1852; d. *unm.* 1870.
 2. **Nicholas Andrew**, of The Caves, Cushenden, J.P. co. Antrim and co. Down, late Capt. 5th Batt. Royal Irish Rifles, heir male of the family, b. 8 Jan. 1861; m. 1st, 19 Sept. 1900, Blanche Marjorie, 4th dau. of Thomas Montgomery, of Ballydrain, co. Antrim (*see that family*). She d. 1 Feb. 1909. He m. 2ndly, 7 April, 1910, Katharine Dalbiac, youngest dau. of James Charles Cleghorn, of Brachenside, Woburn Sands, Beds. (*see* Tancred *of Weens*).
 3. Andrew Claude, b. 6 Feb. 1865; m. 1897, Letitia, only dau. of the late Rev.—Noble, and has two children.
  1. Elizabeth, m. 1883, Rev. John Gordon Holmes, who d. 1890, leaving issue.   2. Mary.
  3. Andrina, m. 1891, Rev. William Bell, son of Col. Bell.
  4. Clara.
  5. Constance, m. 23 July, 1903, John Masefield, 2nd son of the late G. E. Masefield.
3. William Thomas (Rev.), b. 14 Feb. 1820; m. 23 Oct. 1855, Matilda, dau. of William Cairnes, and by her (who d. 29 Oct. 1856) had a dau.,
Matilda Helen.
1. Anna Sarah, m. 1856, Rev. Frederick Flood, and d. 1889.
2. Maria Matilda, d. *unm.* 1872.
3. Clara Suzanne, d. young.
4. Elizabeth Emily, m. 12 July, 1840, John Robert Irwin, of Carnagh, co. Armagh, leaving issue (*see* Irwin *of Mount Irwin*).
He d. 29 March, 1863, and was s. by his eldest son,
Samuel Arthur Hill de la Cherois-Crommelin, of Carrowdore Castle, J.P. and D.L., High Sheriff co. Down 1852, b. 25 Dec. 1817; m. 30 Oct. 1845, Maria Maria, only dau. of John Graves Thompson, of co. Tyrone, and by her (who d. 4 Feb. 1884) had issue,
1. Louis Nicholas, b. 15 Aug. 1846; d. Dec. 1869.
2. Arthur Claude, b. 11 June, 1856; d. Aug. 1869.
3. **Frederic Armand**, late of Carrowdore Castle.
1. Lucy Marguerite, d. Aug. 1881.
2. Maria Henrietta, now of Carrowdore Castle.
3. Caroline Anna, m. Dec. 1895, Robert Barton Shaw (*see* Burke's *Peerage and Baronetage*). She *d.s.p.* 1 Feb. 1910.
4. Florence Frances, m. 1886, Rhys Goring-Thomas, of Plas Llannon, Llanelly, S. Wales, and d. 1895.
5. Evelyn Angélique, now of Carrowdore Castle.
Mr. De la Cherois-Crommelin d. 24 Feb. 1885. His only surviving son,
Frederick Armand De La Cherois-Crommelin, of Carrowdore Castle, J.P., b. 7 Nov. 1861; m. 16 Dec. 1891, Nina, youngest dau. of late Rev. Calvert R. Jones, of Heathfield, Swansea, and *d.s.p.* 15 June, 1902. He was s. by his sisters as above.

Arms—Quarterly: 1st and 4th, az., on a chevron between three martlets arg., those in chief respecting each other, a trefoil slipped vert, for Crommelin; 2nd and 3rd, gu. a chevron between three mullets in chief, one or and in base an anchor arg, for De la Cherois. **Crests**—Crommelin: Out of a ducal coronet or, a swan rising ppr.; De la Cherois: An anchor az. **Motto**—Fac et spera.

Seat—Carrowdore Castle, Donaghadee, co. Down.

CRONIN-COLTSMAN. *See* **COLTSMAN.**

CROSBIE OF BALLYHEIGUE.

James Dayrolles Crosbie, of Ballyheigue Castle, co. Kerry, J.P. and D.L., High Sheriff 1894, late Lieut. Royal Welsh Fusiliers, b. 19 Aug. 1865; m. 28 July, 1894, Maria Caroline, dau. of the late Major James Leith, V.C., Scots Greys, and granddau. of Sir Alexander Leith, of Glenkindie, and has issue,

Oonah Mary.

Lineage.—This is a branch of the Crosbies of Ardfert, extinct Earls of Glandore (*see* Burke's *Extinct Peerage*), themselves scions of a family long settled in the Queen's Co. and in co. Kerry, and now represented by Crosbie, Bart. of Maryborough. The common ancestor of the Baronet's family and the two branches of Ardfert and Ballyheigue was
Right Rev. John Crosbie, Bishop of Ardfert, appointed to that see by patent dated 15 Dec. 1601. The Queen's letter to the Lord Deputy, Lord Mountjoy, dated from the Manor of Oatland, 2 Oct. 1600, directing his appointment, describes him as "A graduate in schools, of English race, skilled in the English tongue, and well disposed in religion." He was previously Prebendary of Disert, in the Diocese of Limerick. He m. Winifred, dau. of O'Lalor, of the Queen's Co., and had, with four daus, six sons,
1. **Walter** (Sir), 1st bart., of Maryborough in the Queen's Co., m. Mabel, dau. of Sir Nicholas Browne, Knt. of Molahiffe (ancestor of the Earl of Kenmare), and was created a bart. 1630. He left issue (*see* Burke's *Peerage*).
2. **David**, of whom presently.
3. John (Sir), of Tullyglass, co. Down, knighted 16 Aug. 1628; m. 23 July, 1638, Mary, widow of Richard Fowler, and dau. of Edward Boughton, of Causton, Warwick, and d. 14 Jan. 1639.
4. Patrick, admitted to Gray's Inn, 7 May, 1619.
5. William, living 1658.
6. Richard, admitted to Lincoln's Inn, 12 Jan. 1622.
The Bishop of Ardfert d. Sept. 1621. His 2nd son,
David Crosbie, of Ardfert, Col. in the Army, and Governor co. Kerry 1641, stood a siege in the Castle of Ballingarry for more than twelve months. He was afterwards Governor of Kinsale for **Charles I**; in 1646 he inherited a portion of the estate of his cousin Sir Pierce Crosbie, Bart., son of Patrick Crosbie, who had been granted a large portion of The O'More's estate in Leix. He m. a dau. of Right Rev. John Steere, Bishop of Ardfert, and had, with four daus., two sons,
1. **Thomas** (Sir), his heir.
2. Patrick, of Tubrid, co. Kerry, m. Agnes, dau. of Arthur Freke of Cork (and sister of Percy Freke, of Bilney, co. Norfolk, whose son Ralph was created a bart. 4 June, 1713), and had, with other issue,
Arthur, b. 1688, entered Trin. Coll. Dublin, 8 April, 1705.
Col. Crosbie, whose will, dated 31 Dec. 1657, was proved 3 May, 1658, was s. by his eldest son,
Sir Thomas Crosbie, Knt. of Ardfert, High Sheriff co. Kerry 1668, knighted by the Duke of Ormonde, in consideration of the loyalty of his family during Oliver Cromwell's rebellion. He was M.P. co. Kerry in the Parliament held in Dublin by James II. in 1688, and refused to take the oath of allegiance to William III. Sir Thomas m. 1st, Bridget, dau. of Robert Tynte, co. Cork, and had issue,
1. **David**, of Ardfert, his successor, High Sheriff co. Kerry 1683, m. 1680, Jane, dau. and co-heir of William Hamilton, of Liscloony, King's Co., was father of
Maurice, 1st Lord Brandon, so created 1758, whose son, William, 2nd Lord Brandon, was created Earl of Glandore (*see* Burke's *Extinct Peerage*, and Talbot-Crosbie *of Ardfert*).
2. William, Major in the Army.
3. Patrick (Rev.), b. 1664, entered Trin. Coll. Dublin 7 May, 1680, B.A. 1684, *d.s.p.*
4. Walter, b. 1666, entered Trin. Coll. Dublin 23 June, 1682, and *d.s.p.*
1. Sarah, m. Henry Stoughton, of Rattoo, co. Kerry.
2. Bridget, m. Philip Morgel, *d.s.p.*
Sir Thomas m. 2ndly, Ellen, dau. of Garrett FitzGerald, of Ballynard, co. Limerick, and widow of Sir Ralph Wilson, by whom he had no issue; and 3rdly, 1680, Elizabeth, dau. and co-heir of William Hamilton, of Liscloony, King's Co., by whom he had a dau., Ann, living 1694, and four sons,
5. **Thomas**, of whom hereafter.
6. John, Major in the Army, lost an arm in action, was present at the battles of Dettingen and Culloden. He was living in co.

Wicklow in 1752; made his will 9 April, 1742, which was proved 25 March, 1762, and left by Mary his wife, two daus.,
  1. Elizabeth. 2. Anne.
7. Pierce, of Rusheen, co. Kerry, Barrister-at-Law, b. 1684; d. April, 1761, entered Trin. Coll. Dublin 13 March, 1701; m. Margaret, dau. of William Sandes, of Carrigfoyle (see SANDES of Sallow Glen). His will, dated 10 Sept. 1757, was proved in 1767. He left,
  1. Francis, High Sheriff co. Kerry 1757, m. Ann, dau. of Rowland Bateman, of Oak Park, co. Kerry, and d.s.p.
    1. Mary, m. James Crosbie, of Ballyheigue.
    2. Ann, m. Christopher Hilliard.
8. Charles, Col. in the Army, served in Flanders under the Duke of Marlborough, m. 1st, the dau. of Thomas Warburton, of Winnington, co. Chester, and sister of Jane, Duchess of John, 2nd Duke of Argyll, by whom he had two sons and as many daus. He m. 2ndly, Deborah, dau. and co-heir of Henry Birkenhead, and widow of William Glegg, of Caldy Grange, co. Chester.
  1. Ann, m. 1st, Richard Malone, of Ballynahown, in the King's Co.; 2ndly, William L'Estrange, of Tuitstown, co. Westmeath, and 3rdly, Peter Holmes, of Johnstown.
Sir Thomas made his will 20 July, 1694, which was proved 7 Feb. 1695. By a very peculiar, probably unique, settlement, executed on the marriages of Sir Thomas Crosbie and his eldest son respectively, to the two sisters, *on the same day* (A.D. 1680), a new settlement and redistribution of all the familly estates was made, by which those of Ballyheigue were appointed to the issue of the last marriage. Under this settlement Ballyheigue passed to the eldest son of his 3rd marriage,
  THOMAS CROSBIE, of Ballyheigue, M.P. for Kerry 1709, High Sheriff 1712 and 1714, m. 1711, Lady Margaret Barry, dau. of Richard, 2nd Earl of Ballymore, and had issue,
  1. JAMES, his heir.
    1. Anne Dorothy, m. William Carrigue, of Glandine, co. Clare.
    2. Harriet Jane, m. Lancelot Crosbie, of Tubrid.
Mr. Crosbie, whose will, dated 18 Aug. 1724, was proved 12 May, 1731, was s. by his son and heir,
  JAMES CROSBIE, of Ballyheigue, High Sheriff co. Kerry, 1751; m. Mary, dau. of Pierse Crosbie, of Rusheen, and d. March, 1761, leaving issue,
  1. PIERSE, his heir.   2. James, d.s.p.
  1. Catherine, d.s.p.   2. Henrietta, d.s.p.
Mr. Crosbie d. March, 1761, and was s. by his eldest son,
  PIERSE CROSBIE, of Ballyheigue, High Sheriff co. Kerry 1797, m. Frances, dau. of Rowland Bateman, of Oak Park, and had issue,
  1. JAMES, his heir.
  2. Pierse, m. Jane Bateman, widow of Conway Blennerhassett, and had issue,
    1. Francis.   2. James.
    3. Pierse.
    1. Mary, m. Hon. William Massey.
    2. Frances Anne, m. Robert Leslie, of Tarbert House.
  1. Elizabeth, m. General John Michel.
The elder son,
  JAMES CROSBIE, of Ballyheigue, Col. of the Militia, M.P. and Custos Rotulorum for co. Kerry, High Sheriff 1792, m. 1785, his cousin, Elizabeth, dau. of Rowland Bateman, of Oak Park; and by her (who d. 20 Aug. 1836) had issue,
  1. PIERSE, his heir.   2. James, d.s.p.
  3. Francis, m. Maria Harte, of Coolrus, co. Limerick, and d.s.p.
  4. Thomas.
    1. Letitia, m. Capt. W. M. Twiss.
    2. Frances, m. Capt. Rowland Chute, of Leebrook.
Col. Crosbie d. 20 Sept. 1736, and was s. by his son,
  PIERSE CROSBIE, of Ballyheigue, High Sheriff 1815; m. 1st, Elizabeth, dau. of Gen. John Mitchell. She d.s.p. He m. 2ndly, July, 1831, Elizabeth, dau. of Thomas William Sandes, D.L. of Sallow Glen, co. Kerry, by whom (who d. 25 May, 1835) he had issue,
  1. JAMES, late of Ballyheigue.
    1. Margaret Catherine, m. 4 Jan. 1859, Meade Caulfeild Dennis, of Fort Granite, co. Wicklow, and d. 1886.
Mr. Crosbie m. 3rdly, Margaret, dau. of Leslie Wren, of Littur, co. Kerry, and had further issue,
  2. William Wren, d. unm. 18 April, 1875.
  3. Pierse, late Lieut. 7th Royal Fusiliers, m. 22 Aug. 1875, Lissie, dau. of Thomas McClelland, of Greencastle, co. Donegal. He d. 4 March, 1907, having had issue,
    Walter McClelland, Roy. Munster Fus., m. 2 June, 1909, Honor Alice, dau. of Very Rev. Lucius H. O'Brien, Dean of Limerick.
  4. Leslie Wren, m. Agnes, dau. of Rowland Bateman.
  5. George Wren, d. unm. 20 Dec. 1884.
  6. Francis, m. 19 Dec. 1876, Henrietta Anne, dau. of Thomas Smith, of Woodford, Listowel, County Inspector R.I.C., co. Kerry, and has
    1. Margaret Henrietta, b. 28 Nov. 1877.
    2. Maria Alice, b. 2 Sept. 1887.
  2. Elizabeth Margaret, m. Capt. Lawrence Mathew Malet, R.N.
  3. Alice Julia, m. Rev. William Blunt, and d. 31 Dec. 1873.
He d. 13 May, 1849, and was s. by his eldest son,
  JAMES CROSBIE, of Ballyheigue Castle, co. Kerry, J.P. and D.L., late Col. Commanding Kerry Militia, High Sheriff 1862, b. 11 Dec. 1832; m. 7 Feb. 1860, Rosa, dau. of Sir John Lister Lister-Kaye, 2nd bart. of Denby Grange, co. York, and d. 5 Sept. 1879, having had issue,
  1. PIERS LISTER, b. 24 Dec. 1860; d. at Harrow, 10 April, 1878.
  2. JAMES DAVROLLES, now of Ballyheigue.
  1. Kathleen Matilda, m. 31 Oct. 1883, John Hamlyn Borrer, of Angeston, co. Gloucester.
  2. Rosa Marguerite, m. 10 Nov. 1887, John Alan G. Bengough, of The Ridge, Wotton-under-Edge, co. Gloucester. He d. 24 Nov. 1899.

3. Marcia Ellen, m. 2 June, 1886, Ernest Akroyd Kinnear, of Glenorleigh, Kingswear, South Devon. He d. 20 April, 1910.

Arms—Arg., a lion rampant sa. in chief two dexter hands couped and erect gu. Crest—Three swords, two in saltire, the points downwards, the third in pale, point upwards, environed with a snake, all ppr. Motto—Indignante invidia florebit justus.
Seat—Ballyheigue Castle, Tralee, co. Kerry. Clubs—Naval and Military, Carlton, Junior Constitutional, and Kildare Street, Dublin.

TALBOT-CROSBIE OF ARDFERT ABBEY.

LINDSEY BERTIE TALBOT-CROSBIE, of Ardfert Abbey, co. Kerry, J.P. and D.L., High Sheriff 1903, Lieut. R.N. (retired). b. 11 Aug. 1844; m. 29 March, 1871, Anne, dau. of the late Col. E. T. Coke, of Trusley, Derby (see that family), and by her has had issue,
  1. Hugh, b. 8 Feb. 1872; d. of wounds received in action in S. Africa 27 July, 1901.
  2. JOHN BURRELL, b. 8 July, 1873; m. 3 May, 1910, Mary, dau. of Gilbert Leitch.
  3. Edward Wynne, b. 30 Aug. 1874.
  4. William Hamilton, b. 2 Feb. 1875; m. 7 Dec. 1905, Augusta, 4th dau. of Rev. A. D. Morton, D.D., and has issue,
    1. Lindrey Morton, b. 31 Dec. 1906.
    1. Priscilla Eileen, b. 26 July, 1908.
    2. Sheila Anne, b. 5 Feb. 1911.
  5. Malcolm Bertie, b. 15 June, 1879; d. 6 July following.
  6. Maurice Bertie, Lieut. R.A., B.A. (Trin. Coll. Dublin) (Addiston, Seymour Park, Plymouth), m. 14 Nov. 1907, Olga Agneta, dau. of Frederick Lincoln Bevan, J.P. co. Kent, of Chipstead Place, Sevenoaks (see BEVAN of Trent Park), and has issue,
    Darnley John Coke, b. 10 Dec. 1910.
    Lesbia Violet, b. 15 Dec. 1908.
  7. David Bligh, b. 25 Oct. 1881.
  1. Susan Angele Phœbe Anne, m. 5 Aug. 1909, Herbert Henniker Heaton, son of John Henniker Heaton, M.P., and has issue, John Lindsey Patrick, b. 5 July, 1910.
  2. Diana Patience Linda Mary.

Mr. Talbot-Crosbie is the heir-general of the Earls of Glandore.

Lineage.—Sir THOMAS CROSBIE, Knt. of Ardfert (see CROSBIE of Ballyheigue), High Sheriff co. Kerry 1668, knighted by the Duke of Ormonde, in consideration of the loyalty of his family during Oliver Cromwell's rebellion. He was M.P. for co. Kerry in the Parliament held in Dublin by JAMES II in 1688, and refused to take the oath of allegiance to WILLIAM III. Sir Thomas m. 1st, Bridget, dau. of Robert Tynte, co. Cork, and had issue,
  1. DAVID, his successor.
  2. William, Major in the Army, d.s.p.
  3. Patrick (Rev.), b. 1664, d.s.p.
  4. Walter, b. 1666, d.s.p.
  1. Sarah, m. Henry Stoughton, of Rattoo, co. Kerry.
  2. Bridget, m. Philip Morgel.
Sir Thomas m. 2ndly, Ellen, dau. of Garrett FitzGerald, of Ballynard, co. Limerick, and widow of Sir Ralph Wilson, by whom he had no issue, and 3rdly, 1680, Elizabeth, dau. and co-heir of William Hamilton, of Liscloony, King's Co., by whom he had with other issue,
  5. THOMAS, ancestor of CROSBIE, of Ballyheigue.
Sir Thomas d. 1694, and was s. by his eldest son,
  DAVID CROSBIE, of Ardfert, High Sheriff co. Kerry 1683, m. 1680, Jane, dau. and co-heir of William Hamilton, of Liscloony, King's Co., and d. 1717, leaving a son,
  SIR MAURICE CROSBIE, Knt. of Ardfert, M.P. co. Kerry 1713, created 16 Sept. 1758, BARON BRANDEN of Branden, co. Kerry. He m. Dec. 1712, Lady Elizabeth Anne FitzMaurice, dau. of Thomas, 1st Earl of Kerry, and by her (who d. 17 Dec. 1757) had, with four daus.,
  1. WILLIAM, 2nd Baron.
  2. John, m. Elizabeth Fisher, and d.s.p. May, 1755.
  3. Maurice (Rev.), Dean of Limerick, m. 1st, 22 March, 1762, Elizabeth, dau. of William Gun, of Kilmary, co. Kerry, and by her (who d. 14 April, 1767) had an only dau.,
    Elizabeth, m. Edward Moore, of Mooresfort, co. Tipperary.
    He m. 2ndly, 13 Aug. 1768, Pyne, dau. of Sir Henry Cavendish, 1st bart. of Doveridge, and had by her, with three daus., one son,
    WILLIAM, 4TH BARON BRANDEN, D.D. Rector of Castle Island, co. Kerry, b. 1 Nov. 1771; s. his cousin 1815; m. 3 May, 1815, Elizabeth, dau. of Col. David La Touche, of Marlay, and d. without male issue, 3 May, 1832, when the barony of Brandon became extinct. She d. 1 April, 1862.
Lord Brandon d. 20 Jan. 1762, and was s. by his eldest son,

WILLIAM CROSBIE, 2nd Baron Brandon, created 30 Nov. 1771, Viscount Crosbie, and 22 July, 1776, EARL OF GLANDORE. He m. 1st, Nov. 1745, Lady Theodosia Bligh, dau. of John, 1st Earl of Darnley, and by her (who d. 20 May, 1777) had,
1. Maurice, b. 17 Feb. 1749; d. young.
2. JOHN, 2ND EARL OF GLANDORE, P.C., F.R.S., M.A., b. 25 May, 1753; m. 26 Nov 1777, Hon. Diana Sackville. dau. of George, 1st Viscount Sackville, and d.s.p. 23 Oct. 1815, when his Viscounty and Earldom became extinct. She d. 29 Aug. 1814.
1. ANNE, of whom hereafter.
2. Theodosia, d. unm. 3 June, 1782.
3. Arabella, m. 27 Feb. 1783, Hon. Edward Ward.

The Earl m. 2ndly, 1 Nov. 1777, Jane, dau. of Edward Vesey, and widow of John Ward, but had no further issue. He d. 11 April, 1781. His eldest dau.,
LADY ANNE CROSBIE, b. 1 Dec. 1754; m. May, 1775, William John Talbot, of Mount Talbot, co. Roscommon (see that family), and had, with other issue,
THE REV. JOHN TALBOT, of Ardfert, who assumed by Royal Licence, dated 14 Feb. 1816, the name and arms of CROSBIE in lieu of that of TALBOT, pursuant to the will of his uncle, John, last Earl of Glandore. He was M.P. for the Borough of Ardfert previous to his taking holy orders. He m. Sept. 1811, Jane, dau. of Thomas Lloyd, by whom he had issue,
1. WILLIAM, late of Ardfert Abbey.
2. John, of Mount Talbot, co. Roscommon (see TALBOT of Mount Talbot).
1. Anne, m. 27 June, 1839, Rev. Maurice Atkin Cooke-Collis, D.D., of Castle Cooke, co. Cork, and had issue (see that family).
2. Diana, m. 6 Aug. 1835, Edward Thomas Coke, of Debdale, Hall, Notts, 3rd son of D'Ewes Coke, of Brook Hill, co. Derby, and had issue (see that family).

The Rev. John Crosbie d. Jan. 1818. The elder son,
WILLIAM TALBOT TALBOT-CROSBIE, of Ardfert Abbey, co. Kerry, J.P., D.L., High Sheriff 1848, b. 19 March, 1817; m. 1st, 29 July, 1839, Susan Anne, dau. of the Hon. Lindsey Merrik Peter Burrell, 2nd son of Peter, 1st Lord Gwydyr, and brother of Peter Robert, 19th Lord Willoughby d'Eresby. She d. 16 Aug. 1850, leaving issue,
1. JOHN TALBOT DARNLEY, of whom presently.
2. LINDSEY BERTIE, now of Ardfert Abbey.
3. William David, b. 17 June, 1849; m. 3 Oct. 1874, his cousin, Kathleen Sophia, dau. of Col. E. T. Coke, of Trusley (see that family).
1. Emily Jane Georgiana.
2. Emma Anne, m. 9 July, 1885, James Gordon Oswald, of Scotstown, co. Renfrew, who d. 3 Jan. 1897.
3. Susan Elizabeth, m. 22 Nov. 1866, Owen Phibbs, of Lisheen, co. Sligo, and has issue (see that family).
4. Frances Charlotte, m. 25 May, 1868, George Frederic Trench, of Abbeylands, Ardfert. She d. 13 Jan. 1907, leaving issue (see ASHTOWN, B.).

He m. 2ndly, 4 Nov. 1868, Mary Jane, eldest dau. of Maj.-Gen. Sir Henry Torrens, K.C.B., and widow of Sir Ralph Abercrombie Anstruther, 4th bart. of Balcaskie. She d. 26 Aug. 1886. Mr. Talbot-Crosbie assumed by Royal Licence, 11 Nov. 1880, the additional surname of Talbot, and d. 4 Sept. 1899. His eldest son,
LIEUT.-COL. JOHN TALBOT DARNLEY TALBOT-CROSBIE, of Ardfert Abbey, J.P., sometime Lieut.-Col. King's Royal Rifles, b. 1 May, 1843; m. 30 Oct. 1884, Margaret, dau. of Henry Farquharson, of St. Leonards, Dorset, and widow of Capt. John Paynter, Scots Guards (see PAYNTER of Gate House). She d. 2 Dec. 1891. He d.s.p. 2 Nov. 1899, and was s. by his brother.

Arms—Quarterly: 1st and 4th, arg. a lion rampant sa., in chief two dexter hands couped at the wrist gu. (CROSBIE): 2nd and 3rd gu. three cinquefoils two and one erm. (HAMILTON). Crest—Three swords two in saltire, pommels upwards, and one erect, pommel downwards, ppr. hilted or, enwrapped by a snake also ppr. Motto—Indignante invidia florebit justus.
Seat—Ardfert Abbey, Ardfert, co. Kerry. Club—Kildare Street, Dublin.

INNES-CROSS OF DROMANTINE.

ARTHUR CHARLES WOLSELEY INNES-CROSS, of Dromantine, co. Down, b. 8 June, 1888.

Lineage.—This family claims descent from that of INNES of Leuchars, a younger branch of the ancient house of Innes, proprietors of the lands of that name in the year 1160; when by a crown charter of King MALCOLM IV, Berowald, styled "of Flanders," became first feudal baron or lord of Innes. His lineal descendant, JAMES, 16th feudal Baron of Innes, held the appointment of "Esquire" to King JAMES III; and among the family papers is still preserved a charter of some lands granted to him by that monarch, "for faithful service to us of our beloved Esquire, James Innes of that Ilk."

JAMES INNES, Laird of Innes, who in 1490 had the honour of entertaining King JAMES IV, and many distinguished personages of his court, at his mansion of Innes, m. Janet Gordon, dau. of Alexander, 1st Earl of Huntly, and had two sons, Alexander, whose line subsequently failed, and
ROBERT INNES, of Cromy and Rathmackenzie, m. the dau. of William Meldrum, Baron of Fyvie, and had issue,
1. JAMES, of Cromy (who fell at the battle of Pinkie), was ancestor of a long line of Lairds of Innes, now represented by their lineal descendant, the Duke of Roxburghe.
2. ALEXANDER, of whom we treat.

The 2nd son,
ALEXANDER, of Blackhills, was ancestor of the family of INNES of Leuchars, co. Fife. His grandson,
ALEXANDER INNES, of Cotts, and afterwards on the death of his half-brother in 1619, of Leuchars, and Baillie of the Regality and Constable of the Castle of Spynie, known in the family by the quaint soubriquet of "Craig-in-Peril" (see BURKE's Romance of the Aristocracy), m. his cousin, Marjory Gordon, eldest dau. of William Gordon, Baron of Gight, great-great-grandson of George, 2nd Earl of Huntly, and his Countess, the Princess Annabella Stewart, youngest dau. of King JAMES I of Scotland. Alexander Innes d. in 1634, leaving with other issue,
1. JOHN, of whom presently.
2. Alexander, m. Mary, dau. and heiress of Sir Robert Jacob, Knt. Solicitor-General for Ireland, and d. 1646, leaving issue, with two daus.,
  1. Charles.   2. Gordon.
3. Robert, Quartermaster-General.
4. James, Major in the Army, imprisoned by the Parliament in 1643.

The eldest son,
JOHN INNES, of Leuchars, Baillie of the Regality and Constable of the Castle of Spynie (offices confirmed to him by Act of Parliament, 1641), had joined in 1625 the Scots Guards in the service of the King of France. He m. 1622, Elizabeth, only dau. of Archibald Douglas, of Pittendreich, and d. 1645, leaving issue,
1. JOHN, of Leuchars, imprisoned by the Covenanters, and his estate sequestered until the Restoration.
2. Robert, killed by the Covenanters at Leuchars.
3. ALEXANDER.

The last named,
ALEXANDER INNES, is called by some the 2nd, and by others, the 5th son, of John Innes. He is said to have gone to Ireland at the Restoration, and from him is traced the Irish branch of the family. He m. the dau. of Rev. Edward Brice, Minister of Ballycarry, co. Antrim, and by her had issue,
1. Brice, of Dromalig, co. Down.
2. John, of Dublin, living 1691.
3. Robert, Capt. in Lord Charlemont's Regt., d. 1699.
4. WILLIAM.

The youngest son,
WILLIAM INNES, of Belfast and Dublin, m. his cousin, Jane, dau. of Robert Brice, of Castle Chichester, co. Antrim, and had, with two daus, five sons,
1. Joseph, merchant and shipowner at Belfast, d. 1736.
2. John.   3. Alexander.
4. WILLIAM, of whom presently.
5. Robert, b. in Dublin, 1695, d. young.

The 4th son,
REV. WILLIAM INNES, b. in Dublin, 1691; m. Isabella, dau. of Lieut.-Col. James Simpson, and d. 1735, having had, with five daus., three sons,
1. WILLIAM, of whom presently.   2. John.
3. James, Lieut.-Col. in the Army, served in Flanders, m. Jane, dau. of — Mussenden, of Larchfield, co. Down, and d. 1762.

The eldest son,
WILLIAM INNES, of Glen Manor, now Dromantine, co. Down, m. 1744, Dorothea, dau. of Charles Brice, of Castle Chichester, co. Antrim. She d. 1785. He d. 1785, having had issue,
1. CHARLES, his heir.
2. Edward, d. unm.
3. ARTHUR, s. his brother.
1. Dorothea, d. unm.
2. Rose, m. Thomas Blake, 2nd son of Sir Walter Blake, Bart., of Menlo.

The eldest son,
CHARLES BRICE INNES, of Dromantine, High Sheriff of Down in 1775, d. unm. 1804, and was s. by his brother,
ARTHUR INNES, of Dromantine, Capt. 9th Dragoons, High Sheriff of Down in 1814, m. 1796, Anne, dau. of Edward Crow, of Tullamore, King's Co., Major 9th Dragoons, and had issue,
1. Charles, d. an infant, 1799.
2. ARTHUR, his successor.
3. William George, b. 1810; d. 1829.
1. Margaret, m. Charles O'Hara, of O'Hara's Brook, co. Antrim, and d. 31 March, 1884.
2. Dorothea Elizabeth, m. 1829, William Edmonds, 6th Dragoons, of the Leasowes, Salop, and d. 21 March, 1891.

The son and heir,
ARTHUR INNES, of Dromantine, J.P. and D.L., High Sheriff 1832, Lieut. 3rd Dragoon Guards, m. 15 May, 1829, Mary Jervis, dau. and heir of William Wolseley, Admiral of the Red. She d. 24 Jan. 1886. He d. 1835, leaving issue,
1. ARTHUR CHARLES, late of Dromantine.
1. Mary Catherine.
2. Anne Northesk, m. Col. James Loftus Winniett Nunn, late 80th Regt. She d. 1 March, 1887. He d. 16 May, 1899.
3. Emma Jean, d. unm. 23 Oct. 1868.

The only son and heir,

Arthur Charles Innes-Cross, of Dromantine, co. Down, J.P. and D.L., M.P. for Newry 1865 to 1868, b. 25 Nov. 1834; m. 1st, 16 July, 1858, Louisa Letitia Henrietta, 2nd dau. of the late James Brabazon, of Mornington House, co. Meath, and by her (who d. 27 Jan. 1886) had issue, a dau.,
1. Edith Clara Brabazon, d. young, 1866.
He m. 2ndly, 21 Sept. 1887, Jane Beauchamp Cross, now of Dartan, dau. of the late Col. Cross, D.L., of Dartan, co Armagh (see that family), whose name he assumed by Royal Licence, and d. 14 April, 1902, having had further issue,
1. Arthur Charles Wolseley Innes, now of Dromantine.
2. Sydney Maxwell, b. 29 April, 1894.
2. Marian Dorothea.
His widow m. 2ndly, 18 March, 1907, Herbert Martin Cooke, eldest son of the late Mason Cooke, of Ely, who assumed by Royal Licence, 14 March, 1908, the name and arms of Cross.

Arms—Quarterly: 1st and 4th, quarterly gu. and or, in the 1st and 4th quarters a cross potent arg., in the 2nd and 3rd quarters, a rose of the first, seeded of the second, barbed vert, for Cross; 2nd and 3rd, arg., three estoiles az. a border engrailed of the last, charged alternately with eight bezants, and as many trefoils or, for Innes. Crest—1st, Cross—A stork ppr., holding in the beak a cross potent fitchée arg., and resting the dexter claw on a rose gu. seeded or, barbed vert,; 2nd, Innes—An estoile az. Mottoes—*Under the Arms*, Certavi et vici; *over the second crest*, Be traiste.

Seat—Dromantine, Newry, co. Down.

COOKE-CROSS OF DARTAN.

The late Mrs. Sarah Jane Beauchamp Cooke-Cross, of Dartan, co. Armagh, only surviving child of the late William Cross, of Dartan, s. her brother 1 Aug. 1906; m. 1st (as his 2nd wife), 21 Sept. 1887, Arthur Charles Innes, of Dromantine, who assumed by Royal Licence the additional surname and arms of Cross, and had issue,
1. Arthur Charles Wolseley Innes-Cross, now of Dromantine (see that family).
2. Sydney Maxwell, b. 29 April, 1894.
1. Marian Dorothea.
Arthur Charles Innes-Cross d. 14 April, 1902. Mrs. Innes-Cross m. 2ndly, 18 March, 1907, Herbert Martin Cooke (eld. son of the late Mason Cooke, of Ely), who assumed by Royal Licence, 14 March, 1908, the additional name and the arms of Cross. She d. 16 Nov. 1911.

Lineage.—This Lancashire family settled in Ireland at the Plantation of Ulster, 1611, in the parish of Tynan, co. Armagh. From a tombstone in Tynan churchyard it appears that James Cross was buried there 28 Feb. 16-8 (the third figure is indecipherable and the church books for a lengthened period are not forthcoming). Two of his sons, John and William, were amongst the defenders of Derry, who signed the address to King William III and Queen Mary on the relief of that city in 1689, when they returned to co. Armagh, where the descendants of John have resided ever since. William d. unm. (date not known). John Cross d. Feb. 1742, having had issue by his wife Jane, five sons and three daus. The eldest son,
Richard Cross, of Dartan, s. his father, and d. 13 July, 1776, having had issue by his wife Margaret two sons and four daus. The 2nd son and successor,
William Cross, of Dartan, m. 24 Aug. 1743, Mrs. Mary Stratford, of Dartan (née Irwin), and had issue,
1. Richard, b. 1 Sept. 1783; d.s.p.
2. William Irwin, b. 18 Sept. 1785; d. 22 July, 1809
3. John, of whom presently.
4. Maxwell, b. 26 July, 1790; d. 11 July, 1863.
1. Mary, b. 24 Sept. 1788; d. 1809, m. James Burroughs, of Prospect, co. Dublin.
William Cross was appointed a Deputy-Governor of co. Armagh, 10 May, 1793. He d. 12 Jan. 1812, and was s. by his 3rd son,
John Cross, of Dartan, b. 17 Jan. 1787, an Officer in the Army, who saw much service in the 52nd Light Infantry during the Peninsular War. He accompanied the expedition to Sweden in 1807, and proceeded thence to Portugal, 1808. He took part in the battle of Corunna, the actions preceding it, and all the subsequent campaigns with the 52nd Regt.; battle of Waterloo, and occupation of Paris; three times wounded; received the war medal with ten clasps, also the Waterloo Medal; subsequently commanded the 68th Light Infantry, from which Regt. he retired in 1843. Col. Cross was a member of the Royal Hanoverian Guelphic Order, Lieut.-Governor commanding the forces in the island of Jamaica; commission dated 26 July, 1838. He d. 27 Sept. 1850, and was s. by his brother,
Maxwell Cross, of Dartan, D.L. and J.P. co. Armagh, High Sheriff 1847; m. Sarah, dau. of William Hardy, J.P. co. Armagh. He d. 11 July, 1863, and was s. by his only son,
William Cross, of Dartan, J.P. and D.L., High Sheriff 1860, formerly Capt. and Adjutant 68th Light Infantry and Col.-Commandant of the Armagh Light Infantry Militia, b. 9 June, 1815; m. 15 Feb. 1844, Frances Jane, only dau. of Major-Gen. Pennell Cole, Royal Engineers. She d. 2 July, 1896. He d. 1 Aug. 1882, having had issue,
1. Maxwell, b. 4 Jan. 1845; d. unm. 24 April, 1869.
2. William Pennell, late of Dartan.
1. Sarah Jane Beauchamp, now of Dartan.
The 2nd son,
William Pennell Cross, of Dartan, co. Armagh, J.P., Barrister-at-Law, LL.B., b. 8 Dec. 1 49; m. 6 Nov. 1883, Beatrice Lucinda. dau. of Rev. Dominick Augustus Browne, M.A., and d.s.p. 1 Aug. 1906, when he was s. by his only sister.

Arms—Quarterly, gu. and or, in the 1st and 4th quarters a cross potent arg.; in the 2nd and 3rd quarters, a rose of the first, seeded of the second, barbed vert, a canton of the third for distinction. Crest—A stork ppr. holding in the beak a cross potent fitchée arg., and resting the dexter claw on a rose gu. seeded or, barbed vert, charged on the breast with a cross potent fitchée az. for distinction.

Seat—Dartan, Killylea, co. Armagh.

CROWE OF DROMORE HOUSE.

Thomas Crowe, of Dromore House, co. Clare, J.P. and D.L., High Sheriff 1877, late Lieut. 17th Lancers, b. 30 Sept. 1844; m. 1890, Lily Violet, dau. of Thomas Flavin, of Passage East, co. Waterford, and has, with other issue,
Thomas, b. 1892.

Lineage.—
Thomas Crowe, of Ennis, son of Robert Crowe, son of Thomas Crowe, 2nd son of Robert Crowe, of Nutfield, m. Miss Wainwright, of Dublin, and had issue, four sons and five daus. The only son to leave issue,
Thomas Crowe, of The Abbey, Ennis, J.P., m. 1799, Ellen, eldest dau. of John Tymons, of Ballyket, co. Clare, and had issue,
1. Thomas, of Dromore House.
2. John, Capt. 93rd Highlanders, m. 18 Aug. 1829, Frances Elizabeth, dau. of the Hon. E. Stather, Legislative Council of Nevis, West Indies. He left issue,
   1. Thomas Carlisle, Major-Gen. late Royal Horse Artillery, b. 1830; m. 1859, Ellen Maynard, dau. of the late Rev. William B. Clarke, F.R.S., and has issue,
      (1) Mordaunt Abingdon Carlisle, Major R.A., b. 7 Nov. 1867; m. 19 April, 1899, Ethel Clara, dau. of Frederick Tankard, of Afton Manor, Freshwater, I. of Wight, and has issue, Sheila Kathleen Carlisle, b. 28 July, 1901.
      (2) William Maynard Carlisle, Capt. late Royal Warwickshire Regt., b. 11 Sept. 1870; m. 5 Nov. 1904, Elizabeth, widow of Cecil Archer and dau. of Robert Pearce, of Loperwood Manor, Hants.
      (1) Eleanor Louisa Carlisle.
      (2) Agnes Dolores Carlisle.
   2. Robert, Capt. late 60th Rifles, b. 1833; d. 21 Aug. 1902.
   3. William Mordaunt.   4. James Daniell.
   5. George Wyndham.   6. John Wainwright.
   1. Ellen.   2. Anne Stather.
   3. Frances.
3. James, d. unm.   4. William, d. unm.
5. Robert, H.E.I.C.S. (mil.), d. unm.
6. Wainwright, of Cahircalla, Ennis, J.P., High Sheriff, co. Clare, 1860, b. 29 Dec. 1817; m. 29 April, 1857, Annie Millicent, only dau. of Rev. George Spaight, of Corbally, and by her had issue,
   1. Thomas George, b. 3 June, 1858; d. 1864.
   2. Wainwright Francis, of Cahircalla, J.P., b. 1862, m. 1883,

Ellen Mary, dau. of Thomas Delahunty, of Le Mans, Iowa, U.S.A., and has issue,
(1) Muriel Frances, b. 1888. (2) Milicent, b. 1894.
3. William, d. 1900.
4. Henry, Barrister-at-Law, m. 25 July, 1894, Constance Kate younger dau. of Alexander West, of Balhall, co. Forfar (see WEST of White Park).
5. Robert. 6. Edmund.
1. Mary Gertrude, m. her 1st cousin, son of the late Thomas Crowe, of Dromore.
2. Edith Millicent, m. 10 Nov. 1887, Wyndham Harry Galwey, younger son of Sir William Payne Galwey, Bart.
3. Nellie. 4. Annie.
1. Eliza, m. William Keane, of Ennis.
2. Ellen, m. Joseph Tabuteau, R.M., Cork (see TABUTEAU-HERRICK of Shippool).
3. Anne, m. Thomas Keane, J.P., of Ennis.
4. Matilda, m. James Johnston, of Kincardine Castle, co. Perth, N.B.

The eldest son,
THOMAS CROWE, of Dromore House, J.P. and D.L., High Sheriff 1838, Barrister-at-Law, b. 1803; m. 1838, Isabella (d. 7 Sept. 1907), eldest dau. of William Hoare Hume, of Humewood, co. Wicklow, M.P., and had issue,
1. THOMAS, now of Dromore House, } twins, b. 30 Sept. 1844.
2. William,
3. Robert Hume, J.P. co. Clare, b. 25 March, 1846; d. 14 June, 1907, having m. 14 Nov. 1872, Geraldine Sophia (now of Moyriesk), dau. of the late J. Foster Vesey Fitzgerald, of Moyriesk, and has issue,
Thomas FitzGerald Hume, late Lieut. R.F.A., b. 1878; m. 1909, Madelon Violet Jean, 3rd dau. of Right Rev. William Cyprian Pinkham, D.D., Bishop of Calgary, Canada.
Geraldine Isabella Norah, m. 19 July, 1894, Richard John Stacpoole, D.L., of Eden Vale (whom see), and has issue.
4. George, b. 18 April, 1853.
1. Charlotte,
2. Ellen, m. 1868, Lieut.-Col. William FitzHenry Spaight, R.E.
3. Isabella. 4. Eliza.
Mr. Crowe d. 1877.

Arms—Arg., on a mount vert an oak tree ppr., a canton gu. charged with an antique Irish crown or. **Crest**—On a mount vert an Irish wolf-hound arg. collared gu. **Motto**—Skagh Mac-en-chroe.
Seat—Dromore House, Ruan, co. Clare. **Club**—Kildare Street.

CUFFE. See BURKE'S PEERAGE, DESART, E.

WHEELER-CUFFE.
See BURKE'S PEERAGE, **WHEELER-CUFFE, Bart.**

CULLEN OF CORRY.

HENRY CHARLES CULLEN, of Corry, co. Leitrim, and Thorn Hill, co. Cavan, J.P. for the former co., b. 1 May, 1840; m. 29 April, 1869, Jane, dau. of William Nixon, J.P., of Thornhill, co. Cavan, and has issue,
1. Francis Nisbett, b. 12 Feb. 1872; d. unm. 22 March, 1899.
2. WILLIAM NIXON, b. 18 Aug. 1873.
3. Harold Willoughby, b. 17 Sept. 1875.
4. Henry Charles Richard, b. 9 April, 1879.
1. Jane Macartney. 2. Maude Adams.

Lineage.—This family, which claims to be derived from the old Irish race of O'Cuilleans, is stated to have migrated for a time to Scotland, but to have obtained by patent considerable grants of land in the co. Leitrim.
CHARLES I., but to have obtained by patent considerable grants of land in the co. Leitrim.
PATRICK CULLEN, of Skreeny, Manor Hamilton, co. Leitrim, m. Isabella, dau. of Cairncross Nisbett, of Aughamore, co. Roscommon, and had issue,
1 John, m. Hon. Katherine Bermingham, dau. of Francis, 21st Lord Athenry, and widow of Patrick Wemyss, of Danesfort, M.P. co. Kilkenny.
2. James, d.v.p. 3. PATRICK, who carried on the line.
1. Margaret (Mrs. Carter). 2. Grissell (Mrs. Nixon).
3. Mary (Mrs. Dundas).
Mr. Cullen d. 1774. His 3rd son,
PATRICK CULLEN, of Skreeny, m. Judith, dau. of Owen Wynne, of Haslewood, co. Sligo, and had issue,
1. Patrick, m. (licence 10 March, 1747) Margaret Nesbitt, of Mohill, co. Longford.
2. CAIRNCROSS (Rev.), Rector of Manor Hamilton, m. Elizabeth, dau. and co-heir of James Soden, of Grange, co. Sligo, and had issue,
1. CAIRNCROSS, of Skreeny, m. 10 April, 1800, Hester, dau. of Major Dickson, of Woodville, co. Leitrim, M.P. for Ballyshannon, and dying 1801, left by her (who m. 2ndly, the Rev. Herbert Mandeville Nash) an only son,
CAIRNCROSS THOMAS, of Glenade, co. Leitrim, J.P. and D.L., High Sheriff 1835, b. 20 Jan. 1802; m. 13 Feb. 1832,

Jane Eleanor, 3rd dau. of Henry Palmer, of Shriff, co. Leitrim, by Catherine his wife, eldest dau. of the Rev. Cairncross Cullen, of Skreeny, Rector of Manor Hamilton, and d. 16 March, 1878, having had issue,
1. CAIRNCROSS PALMER, b. 22 March, 1835; d. 12 April 1878.
2. Henry John James, b. 23 June, 1836; d. Oct. 1836.
1. Hester Jane.
2. Kate Susannah, m. 15 Sept. 1865; d. 6 Feb. 1873.
3. Minnie Victoria, m. 30 April, 1857, Rev. J. Hamilton, Rector of Manor Hamilton.
4. Ethel Henrietta, d. 23 Sept. 1857.
5. Constance Elizabeth, d. 3 March, 1862.
6. Gertrude Marion.
2. John, of Skreeny, J.P., Lieut.-Col. of the Leitrim Militia, m. (licence 22 Dec. 1810) Bridget, dau. of Daniel Finucane, of Stamer Park, co. Clare.
3. Henry Francis, m. Hester, dau. of John Dickson, of Woodville, co. Leitrim, Barrister-at-Law.
1. Catherine, m. Henry Palmer, Capt. in the Prince of Wales Fencibles.
2. Jane Elizabeth, m. George Gledstanes, of co. Tryone.
3. Eliza Melvina, m. 1st, Major Jones, 25th Light Dragoons; and 2ndly, Lieut.-Col. Campbell, 9th Royal Lancers.
3. John. 4. Francis, Major Carbineers, d. unm.
5. JAMES, of whom hereafter.
6. Henry, Capt. Leitrim Militia, d. unm.
1. Judith Anne.
2. Margaret, m. Rev. Whitwell Sneyd.
3. Elizabeth, m. John L'Estrange, of Keolstown, co. Westmeath.
4. Isabella, m. Aug. 1777, Francis Isdell, of Rockbrook, co. Westmeath.
Mr. Cullen d. 1775. His 5th son,
JAMES CULLEN, of Skreeny, Col. in the Army, m. 10 Dec. 1788, Anna, dau. of Col. Samuel Adams, D.L., of Mine Hall, co. Cavan, and had issue,
FRANCIS NISBETT, his heir.
Anna, m. Capt. Richard Patton, son of Major James Patton, D.L., of Clatto, co. Fife, and the Priory, Lichfield, co. Stafford. She d. 14 June, 1869, leaving issue (see PATTON-BETHUNE of Clayton Priory).
Col. Cullen d. 10 Aug. 1808. His son,
FRANCIS NISBETT CULLEN, of Corry, J.P. cos. Leitrim, Sligo, and Cavan, High Sheriff 1836; b. May, 1804; m. 16 May, 1838, Marianne Louisa, dau. of Capt. Henry Palmer, of Shriff, co. Leitrim, and d. 1 June, 1864, leaving issue,
1. Edmond Willoughby, Capt. in the Army, b. 9 March, 1839; d.s.p. 18 Sept. 1894.
2. HENRY CHARLES, of Corry.
3. Richard Francis, Capt. in the Army, b. 20 Aug. 1843; d.s.p. 11 April, 1886.
4. Francis James, Capt. in the Army, b. 1846; killed in action at Maiwand, July, 1880.
5. William Adams, b. 1848; d.s.p. Aug. 1894.
6. Arthur Patrick, b. 1852; d.s.p. 7 Sept. 1882.
1. Elizabeth Catherine, d. unm. 1892.
2. Anna Louisa, d. unm. 1891.

Seats—Corry, Drumkeeran, co. Leitrim; and Thorn Hill House, Black Lion, co. Cavan.

GUN-CUNINGHAME OF MOUNT KENNEDY.

CORNWALLIS ROBERT DUCAREL GUN-CUNINGHAME, of Mount Kennedy, co. Wicklow, J.P. and D.L., High Sheriff 1886, late Capt. and Hon. Major 7th Brigade N. Irish Div. R.A., b. 9 June, 1857; m. 1st, 27 Sept. 1886, Isabella, youngest dau. of the late Richard Wingfield, and by her (who d. 30 June, 1902) has issue,
1. ROBERT GEORGE ARTHUR, b. 4 Jan. 1896.
2. Henry Maurice Benedict, b. 2 March, 1897.
1. Dorothy Isabella, b. 11 April, 1888; m. 6 Jan. 1910, Edward Trafford Martin, eldest surviving son of Rev. Canon Henry Martin.
2. May, b. 16 May, 1890. 3. Mary Winifred, b. 17 Aug. 1892.

He m. 2ndly, 27 April, 1904, Constance Evelyn, youngest dau. of the late Edwin Joseph Vipan.

Cuppage.

Lineage.—The pedigree of this family with alliances is fully set out in NISBET's *Heraldry*, with authorities down to 1800. SIR ROBERT DE CUNINGHAME Lord of Kilmaurs, living in 1350, had two sons, Sir William, ancestor of the Cunninghames, Earls of Glencairn, and SIR ANDREW DE CUNINGHAME, of Polmaise, ancestor of Drumquhasle, to whom DAVID II gave a grant of the lands of Pitkelendy, and whose descendant in the 3rd generation,

ALEXANDER CUNINGHAME, Laird of Drumquhasle, *m.* Margaret, dau. and co-heir of Willam Park, of that ilk, by Margaret his wife, dau. of Allan, Lord Cathcart, and left issue,

ALEXANDER CUNINGHAME, Lord of Drumquhasle, *m.* the Hon. Mary Erskine, dau. of Robert, Lord Erskine, by Elizabeth, his wife, dau. of Sir George Campbell, Knt., of Loudoun, and had a son and heir,

JOHN CUNINGHAME, Laird of Drumquhasle, Master of the Household to JAMES VI, called the "Regent's Right Hand," as being the chief adviser of the Earl of Lennox ; *m.* Janet, eldest dau. and co-heir of James Cuninghame, of Polmaise, and had issue,
1. John, of Drumquhasle, *m.* Margaret, dau. of Robert, Lord Elphinston.
2. James, *d.s.p.*
3. ROBERT, of whom presently.
1. Janet, *m.* Malcolm Douglas, of Mains.
2. Margaret, *m.* Peter Napier, of Kilmahow.

The 3rd son,
ROBERT CUNINGHAME, of Drumbeg, *m.* Elspeth, dau. of William Buchanan, of Ross and Portnellan, and left two sons,
1. John. 2. WILLIAM.

The 2nd,
WILLIAM CUNINGHAME, of Drumbeg, was served heir to his brother 1644 ; *m.* Alice, dau. of John Buchanan, of Arnprior, and was father of

JOHN CUNINGHAME, of Bandalloch, *m.* Jean, dau. of William Weir, of the family of Blackwood, and had issue, six sons. The youngest,

DAVID CUNINGHAME, of Seabegs, Col. in the Army, Fort-Major of Stirling Castle, 1745, *m.* Margaret, dau. of J. Callander, of Craigforth. and had issue,
1. ROBERT, created Baron Rossmore, of whom presently.
2. James, Lieut.-Gen. in the Army, Governor of Barbados, 1780, one of those selected to escort Queen CHARLOTTE to England, *d. unm.* 1788.
1. Jean, *m.* — Munro, *d.s.p.*
2. Elizabeth, *m.* Campbell, of Ardkinglass, and left issue, two sons, both *d.s.p.*
3. Anne (co-heir with her sisters), *m.* Com.-Gen. Robert Gordon, of New Grove, son of John Gordon, of Kevenborough, by Anne, dau. and co-heir of Sir Nicholas Loftus, and by him (who *d.* 1781) had four surviving daus., co-heirs,
  1. Elizabeth, *m.* — Crooke, of co. Cork.
  2. Margaret, *m.* W. Warren, son of Sir Robert Warren, Bart.
  3. Harriet, *m.* 1st, Lieut. Norcott, and had issue ; and 2ndly, James N. Taylor, of Borton, and left issue.
  4. Jean, heir to her uncle, Lord Rossmore, *m.* GEORGE GUN, of whom presently.

The elder son,
ROBERT CUNINGHAME, of Mount Kennedy, Gen. in the Army, was elevated to the peerage of Ireland, 19 Oct. 1796, in the dignity of BARON ROSSMORE, *of Monaghan* : and as he had no issue by his wife, Elizabeth, dau. of John Murray, and co-heir of her mother, Mary, Dowager Lady Blayney, dau. and heir of Sir Alexander Cairnes, Bart , the patent of creation contained a reversionary clause limiting the barony, at his lordship's decease, without male issue, to his wife's family, 1st, to Henry Alexander Nathaniel Jones, and the heirs male of his body ; 2ndly, to Warner William Westenra, and the heirs male of his body ; and 3rdly, to Henry Westenra, and the heirs male of his body. Mr. Jones and the Messrs. Westenra were grandsons of the aforesaid Mary, Dowager Lady Blayney. Lord Rossmore *d.* 6 Aug. 1801, and Henry Alexander Nathaniel Jones having predeceased him *unm.*, the title devolved upon WARNER WILLIAM WESTENRA, as 2nd Baron (*see* BURKE's *Peerage*), and his Wicklow estates, at the death of his widow, 25 Dec. 1825, on his niece, Jean Gordon, wife of George Gun, of Kilmorna, co. Kerry (*see* GUN *of Rattoo*), who having assumed the name and arms of CUNINGHAME by Royal Licence, dated 3 March, 1826, became

GEORGE GUN-CUNINGHAME, of Mount Kennedy. By Jean Gordon his wife (who *d.* 30 Nov. 1831) he had,
1. ROBERT, his heir.
1. Anne, *d. unm.* 2. Matilda, *d. unm.*
3. Eliza, *m.* 1 Feb. 1812, Arthur Henry, of Lodge Park, Straffan, co. Kildare, and *d.* 28 July, 1853, leaving issue (*see that family*).
4. Henrietta, *d. unm.*
5. Jane, *m.* 7 March, 1814, Francis Jack, 2nd Earl of Kilmorey, and left issue (*see* BURKE's *Peerage*).
6. Georgiana Frances, *m.* 25 Oct. 1815, Sir Simeon Henry Stuart, 5th bart. of Harteley Mauduit, and had issue (*see* BURKE's *Peerage*).

Mr. Gun-Cuninghame *d.* 15 Feb. 1827, and was *s.* by his only son,
ROBERT GUN-CUNINGHAME, of Mount Kennedy, D.L., *b.* 4 Sept. 1792 ; *m.* 1st, 21 July, 1817, Elizabeth Foulkes, of Birchamp House, co. Gloucester, only child and heir of Archibald Hamilton Foulkes, of Coolawinna, co. Wicklow, by Elizabeth, dau. and co-heir of Gerard Ducarel, Marquis Ducarel, of Château Mulds, and by her (who *d.* 14 July, 1829) had issue,
1. ROBERT GEORGE ARCHIBALD HAMILTON, his heir.
2. George Philip Henry, *d.* young.
3. Philip Henry, *d.* an infant.
1. Elizabeth Jane, *b.* 31 March, 1819 ; *d. unm.* 12 May, 1839.
2. Adolphina Frederica, for whom H.R.H. Adolphus Frederick,

Duke of Cambridge, stood sponsor, *b.* 10 Sept. 1820 ; *m.* 30 April, 1860, her cousin Frederick Hugh Henry, of Lodge Park, Straffan, co. Kildare, J.P., and left issue (*see that family*).
3. Jane, *b.* 14 Sept. 1821 ; *m.* 1st, 15 Nov. 1839, Peirce K. Mahony, of Kilmorna, co. Kerry, and left issue (*see that family*). She *m.* 2ndly, 8 April, 1856, Col. W. H. Vicars, 61st Regt., and *d.* 12 Nov. 1873, having by him (who *d.* 4 April, 1869) had issue,
  1. William Henry, Maj. Reserve of Officers, late Lieut. 90th L.I., *b.* 14 June, 1858.
  2. Frederick George, M.D., *b.* 4 Aug. 1860 ; *m.* 1st, 2 Sept. 1884, Dorothea Ida, elder dau. of Mons. Adolf Janasz, of Plochocin, near Warsaw, and by her (who *d.* 23 June, 1885) had issue, Dora, *b.* 14 June, 1885. He *m.* 2ndly, 10 Jan. 1894, Eugenie Matilde, 4th dau. of Capt. Haskett Smith, of Hyde, Weston, Bath.
  3. Arthur Edward (Sir), K.C.V.O., Ulster King of Arms from 1893 to 1908, F.S.A., a trustee of the National Library of Ireland, *b.* 27 July, 1864.
    1. Edith J. M., *m.* 27 Sept. 1884, Mons. D. J. Janasz, of Wolica, near Warsaw, Poland, and has issue, two sons and a dau.
  4. Mary Julia, *b.* 8 May, 1825 ; *d.* 16 Jan. 1826.

Mr. Gun-Cuninghame *m.* 2ndly, 11 Sept. 1832, Hon. Annabel Erina Pery, eldest dau. of Viscount Glentworth, eldest son of the 1st Earl of Limerick, and *d.* 7 June, 1877, having by her (who *d.* 25 April, 1841) had issue,
4. Edmund. 5. Albert Glentworth.
6. Cecil.
7. Glencairn Dunsmere Stuart, *b.* 12 Feb. 1841.
5. Nina Augusta Erina, *b.* 28 June, 1836 ; *d.* 1869, having *m.* John Wilson Moore, and had issue.
6. Eva Adelaide, *b.* 14 Dec. 1838 ; *d.* about 1880, having *m.* J. M. Muldary, and had issue.

His eldest son,
ROBERT GEORGE ARCHIBALD HAMILTON GUN-CUNINGHAME, of Mount Kennedy and Coolawinna, Col. Wicklow Artillery, D.L., *b.* 3 May, 1818 ; *m.* 23 July, 1844, Isabella (who *d.* 5 Aug. 1904), only dau. of Right Rev. Lord Robert Ponsonby Tottenham, Bishop of Clogher (2nd son of the 1st Marquis of Ely), by Hon. Alicia Maude his wife, dau. of Cornwallis, 1st Viscount Hawarden, and *d.* 12 May, 1880, having had issue,
1. CORNWALLIS ROBERT DUCAREL, now of Mount Kennedy.
1. Alicia, *d. unm.* 12 Dec. 1883.
2. Elizabeth, *d.* an infant. 3. Anne, *d.* an infant.
4. Isabella, *d.* an infant.
5. Emily Eleanor, *m.* 23 Aug. 1884, Robert, son of R. F. Ellis, of Seapark, co. Wicklow. She *d.* 25 Aug. 1910. He *d.s.p.* 25 Sept. 1903.
6. Mary Isabella, *m.* 15 Nov. 1877, Lieut.-Col. W. Stewart Hamilton, late 90th L.I., and by him (who *d.* 6 June, 1893) has issue,
  1. Archibald Hans Blackwood, *b.* 19 Sept. 1879.
  2. William Stewart, *b.* 5 April, 1882.
7. Lucy Phillippa, *d.* an infant.
8. Augusta, *d. unm.* 26 Oct. 1910.
9. Beatrice Elizabeth, *m.* 23 March, 1884, James Hamilton, M.D., She *d.* 9 Dec. 1898. He *d.* 29 Aug. 1899, leaving issue,
  1. Charles Robert, *b.* 16 June, 1888.
  2. Albert, *b.* 8 June, 1890.
  3. Douglas, *b.* 18 Feb. 1893.
  4. Eric, *b.* 21 March, 1896.
  1. Beatrice Maude, *b.* 30 Dec. 1886.

Arms—Quarterly : 1st and 4th, arg., a shakefork sa. betw. three roses gu. barbed and seeded vert, for CUNINGHAME ; 2nd and 3rd az., a chevron ermine, between three cannon barrels fesswise or, for GUN. *Crest*—The stump of an oak tree fructed with a single acorn ppr. (*motto over*: Tandem). *Motto*—Over, fork, over.

Seat—Mount Kennedy, co. Wicklow.

CUPPAGE OF MOUNT EDWARDS.

GRANVILLE WILLIAM VERNON CUPPAGE, of Mount Edwards, co. Antrim, *s.* his brother 1908, Deputy Commissioner of Lands and Works, Victoria, B.C., *b.* 30 June, 1867 ; *m.* 1st, 18 May, 1898, Marion Gwendoline, dau. of Lieut.-Col. A. J. G. Kane, U.S.A. He *m.* 2ndly, 25 Dec. 1909, Edith Madeleine, only dau. of Frederick Murray Reade (*see* READE *of Ipsden*).

Lineage.—The family of CUPPAIDGE came originally from Germany, and the first member of it on record is

FAUSTUS CUPPAIDGE, who removed from England to Ireland in 1604, and after the settlement, obtained the estate near Coleraine. He had, with other issue,
1. STEPHEN, of whom presently.
2. Faustus, *m.* Miss Haddock, of Garnerabane, and had three sons, of whom the eldest,
  Faustus served as a Cornet in Lord Conway's troop during the rebellion, and then got his debenture at Cuppaidge's Bridge (formerly Ballytrasna) ; he *m.* Miss Low, of Newton, co. Wicklow, and had three sons,
    (1) George, who *m.* and had three daus.
    (2) Richard, of Ballybrodie, co. Westmeath, who *d.* of wounds inflicted by the Irish rebels.

(3) John (Rev.), Rector of Magberline, Dio. of Dromore, *m.* 1693, Elizabeth, dau. of William Waring, of Waringston, co. Down, and *d.* 1725, leaving two sons, of whom the younger, John, of Killowning, co. Tipperary, Capt. in the Army, *m.* — dau. of James Otway, and grand-dau. of John Otway, of Castle Otway, co. Tipperary; his eldest son, John Loftus, *m.* 17 Dec. 1768, Dorothy, dau. of Dean Handcock, father of the 1st Lord Castlemaine, and *d.* 15 April, 1797, leaving three sons, 1. Richard, *m.* but had no issue; 2. William, *d. unm.*; 3. George, *m.* Elizabeth, youngest dau. of Adam Cuppage, of Lurgan, and had issue.

The elder son,
STEPHEN CUPPAIDGE, represented the borough of Coleraine in Parliament 1641. His grandson,
VERY REV. GEORGE CUPPAIDGE, Dean of Connor, accompanied Admiral Vernon on the celebrated expedition to Portobello in 1730, as private chaplain, and was rewarded for his services by the City of London, with the presentation of the living of Coleraine. He *m.* Miss Burke, great-aunt of the celebrated Edmund Burke, and had a son,
REV. BURKE CUPPAIDGE, Rector of Coleraine, who *m.* Miss Kirkpatrick, and was father of
GEN. WILLIAM CUPPAGE, of Shooter's Hill, who *m.* Mrs. Cairnes (*née* Nicholls), and had a son,
LIEUT.-GEN. SIR BURKE CUPPAGE, K.C.B., R.A., *m.* Miss McLeod, dau. of Gen. and Lady Emily McLeod, and *d.* 1877, having had issue,
1. Robert, killed in the Indian Mutiny.
2. Burke, 21st Hussars, *d.* July, 1864.
1. Emily, } both of Hampton Court Palace.
2. Jane,

JOHN CUPPAGE, of Clough Castle, a younger son of the above-mentioned Stephen Cuppaidge, M.P., acquired a fortune and purchased an estate in co. Antrim. He *d.* 1700, and part of his property called Garden Hill (now Leslie Hill) was sold by his son,
REV. ALEXANDER CUPPAGE, who *m.* Miss Boyd, sister of Col. Boyd, M.P. for co. Antrim. Mr. Cuppage was drowned between Ballycastle and Rathlin Island, and was *s.* in the possession of the remaining portion of his property by Elizabeth, the dau. of his eldest son, who *m.* her second cousin John Cuppage, and was mother of Adam Cuppage, of Glenbank, co. Antrum. Rev. Alexander Cuppage's younger son,
GEN. ALEXANDER CUPPAGE, *m.* Clarinda, sister of Sir Charles Bruce, K.C.B., and *d.* 1847, leaving a son,
EDMOND FLOYD CUPPAGE, of Mount Edwards, co. Antrim, and Clare Grove, co. Dublin, *b.* 27 Oct. 1809; *m.* 1st, 1832, Louisa Elizabeth, dau. of George Thompson, of Clonskeagh Castle, co. Dublin, and by her (who *d.* 1843) had issue,
1. ALEXANDER, of Mount Edwards.
2. George William, of Riverston, co. Meath, J.P. for that co. and co. Dublin, *b.* 11 Nov. 1836; *m.* 2 June, 1863, Louisa Emily (*d.* 2 Jan. 1908), only dau. of J. E. V. Vernon, of Clontarf Castle, co. Dublin, J.P. and D.L., and *d.* 7 Aug. 1908, having had issue,
  1. EDMOND VERNON, of Clare Hall and Mount Edwards.
  2. GRANVILLE WILLIAM VERNON, now of Mount Edwards.
  3. Louis Robert Vernon, *b.* 23 March, 1871,
  4. GEORGE EDWARD VERNON, now of Clare Hall, *b.* 17 Jan. 1875; *m.* 15 June, 1910, Stella, dau. of Bernard Kearney, of Clooncoore House, co. Roscommon.
  1. Florence, *d.* 25 Nov. 1868.
  2. Eleanor Maud Vernon, *m.* July, 1890, Richard Scott Lamb, youngest son of R. W. Lamb, D.L. of West Denton, Northumberland. He *d.* 31 Jan. 1903, leaving one son and four daus.
  3. Louisa Catherine Lindsay.
3. Edmond, *b.* Nov. 1838; *d.* 20 Jan. 1842.
4. Hamlet Wade, Capt. 43rd Light Infantry, *b.* 17 Aug. 1841; *m.* 1st, 27 June, 1866, Hannah, dau. of D. Thompson; she *d.s.p.*; 2ndly, 1 Aug. 1872, Alice Kenah, third dau. of Thomas Exham, of Monkstown, co. Cork, nephew of Gen. Sir Thomas Kenah, K.C.B., and *d.* 6 July, 1889, leaving issue,
  1. Thomas Wade.   2. Alexander Henry.
  3. George.   4. Burke.
  1. Alice Frances Mary.   2. Ellen Sophia.
  3. Ethel.
1. Ellen Sophia, *b.* 27 July, 1840; *d.* 11 Nov. 1858.

Mr. Cuppage *m.* 2ndly, Susan, dau. of Henry Garnett, of Green Park, co. Meath, and widow of Hans Hamilton Johnstone, and by her (who *d.* 1883) had further issue,
5. Edmond Francis Floyd, *b.* 12 Feb. 1850; drowned in the Red Sea, Sept. 1869.
2. Alice Clarinda, *m.* 1st, 12 Jan. 1864, Henry W. White, 11th Hussars (*see* WHITE *of Cloone Grange*), who *d.s.p.* Dec. 1882; 2ndly, 16 Jan. 1884, Alfred Crofton French, late Capt. 43rd Light Infantry, who *d.* 4 March, 1907 (*see* FRENCH *of Castle Bernard*).

Mr. Cuppage *d.* 23 May, 1864, and was *s.* by his eldest son,
ALEXANDER CUPPAGE, of Mount Edwards, formerly Lieut. 4th Dragoon Guards, *b.* 16 Nov. 1833; *d. unm.* 7 Feb. 1907. His nephew,
EDMOND VERNON CUPPAGE, of Clare Hall, co. Dublin, and of Mount Edwards, Major S. Staffs. Regt., *b.* 4 May, 1866; *d. unm.* 26 Dec. 1908, and was *s.* by his brother as above.

Seat—Mount Edwards, Cushendall, co. Antrim. *Residence*—Mount Edwards, Victoria, British Columbia.

CUPPAGE OF CLARE HALL.

GEORGE EDWARD VERNON CUPPAGE, of Clare Hall, co. Dublin, and of Clifford, Castletownroche, co. Cork, J.P., *b.* 17 Jan. 1875; *m.* 15 June, 1910, Stella Mary, dau. of the late Bernard Kearney, *s.* his elder brother, Major Edmond Vernon Cuppage, of Mount Edwards and Clare Hall, in the Clare Hall Estates 26 Dec. 1908. He is the 4th son of the late George William Cuppage, of Riverson, co. Meath, by Louisa Emily, only dau. of J. E. V. Vernon, of Clontarf Castle, co. Dublin, J.P., D.L.

Lineage.—*See* CUPPAGE *of Mount Edwards*.

Seat—Clare Hall, Raheny, co. Dublin. *Residence*—Clifford, Castletownroche, co. Cork.

CUSACK OF GERARDSTOWN.

JAMES WILLIAM HENRY CLAUD CUSACK, of Abbeville House, co. Dublin, J.P., High Sheriff 1900, Maj. (ret.) 1st Batt. Royal Irish Fusiliers, *b.* at Lucca, Italy, 29 Aug. 1856; *m.* 15 Nov. 1887, his cousin Mary, youngest dau. of Sir Ralph Smith Cusack, D.L., of Furry Park, co. Dublin.

Lineage. — ATHANASIUS CUSACK, of Clonard, who made his will 1679, leaving issue, by Bridget his wife, dau. and heir of Patrick, son of Francis Barnewell, of Beggstown, son of Nicholas, Lord Kingsland, a son and successor,
JAMES CUSACK, of Clonard, *b.* 1656, an Officer in King James II's Army at the battle of the Boyne. He *d.* 13 Aug. 1722, having made his will 1720, leaving issue, by Catherine his wife, dau. and eventual heir of Robert Cusack, of Staffordstown,
1. ATHANASIUS, his heir.
2. HENRY, who had Clonard (*see* BARKER *of Clonboy*).
1. Mararey, *m.* 1st, Christopher Wilson, of Moyaugher; and 2ndly, to John Martley.

The elder son,
ATHANASIUS CUSACK, inherited his father's lease of Moyaugher. He *m.* 3 July, 1707, Catherine, dau. of Roger Lloyd, by Alice his wife, sister of John Martley of Ballyfallan, co. Meath, and left, with several daus., two sons,
1. James, who *d.s.p.* 1776.
2. HENRY, of whom presently.

The younger son,
HENRY CUSACK, of Moyaugher and Girley, *m.* Esther, dau. of Thomas Chamney, of Platten, and *d.* 6 May, 1792, leaving issue six sons and three daus. The eldest son,
ATHANASIUS CUSACK, of Laragh, co. Kildare, Moyaugher, and Girley, *b.* 11 May, 1749; *d.* 1813, aged 64, and was bur. in St. Thomas's, Dublin. He *m.* 1st, 1778, Mary Ann, only dau. of Edward Rotherham, of Crossdrum, and by her had issue,
1. HENRY, of Girley, *m.* Anne, dau. of Richard Rothwell, of Birford, co. Meath, by his wife Anne, a dau. and co-heir with her sister, Lady Chapman, of George Lowther, of Hurlestown, and *d.* 1817, leaving issue, two daus.,
  1. Mary, *m.* 1836, Charles Cutliffe Drake, of Ashford, Devon.
  2. Anne.
2. Edward (Rev.), *m.* 1809, Alicia Wolfe, of co. Kildare, but had no issue.
3. JAMES WILLIAM, his heir.
4. George, of Moyaugher, J.P. for Meath, *b.* 6 May, 1790.
1. Elizabeth, *m.* Alexander Battersby.

Mr. Cusack *m.* 2ndly, 1794, Katherine Frances, dau. of Samuel Forster, of Kilmurry, co. Meath, and relict of Thomas Chamney, and had issue by her,
5. Samuel, M.D., *m.* Sarah, dau. of Johnston Stoney, of Oakley Park, co. Tipperary, and left issue,
  Samuel.
  Margaret, *d. unm.* 5 June, 1899.
2. Frances, *m.* Capt. John Kelly.
3. Alicia, *m.* Robert Warren, of Killiney Castle, co. Dublin.

The 3rd son,

Daly. THE LANDED GENTRY. 158

James William Cusack, M.D., of Abbeville, co. Dublin, and Cussington, co. Meath. Surgeon in Ordinary to the Queen in Ireland, m. April, 1818, Elizabeth Frances, eldest dau. and co-heir of Joseph Bernard, of Greenhills, King's Co., and by her (who d. 4 Sept. 1837) had issue,

1. Henry Thomas, of Abbeville House, Barrister-at-Law, Lieut. R. North Devon Mounted Rifles, b. 20 Oct. 1820; m. 1854, Sophia Anne, dau. of the late William Tanner, of Blacklands House, Wilts, and d. 1865, leaving issue by her (who d. 1877),
   1. Athanasius F. W. G. de Geneville, of Abbeville House, J.P., High Sheriff co. Dublin 1881, b. at Florence, 17 Feb. 1855; d. unm. 5 Jan. 1887.
   2. James William Henry Claud, now of Abbeville House.
2. Ralph Smith (Sir), Knt., M.A., of Furry Park, Raheny, co. Dublin, Barrister-at-Law, J.P. and D.L., Chairman of the Midland Great Western Railway, b. 16 Nov. 1821; d. 3 March, 1910; m. 23 April, 1850, Elizabeth, 2nd dau. of Richard Barker, of Sterling, co. Dublin. She d. 22 Feb. 1902, leaving issue,
   1. James William, b. 6 Dec. 1851; m. 1874, Elizabeth, dau. of R. Morrisson, of Cork, and d. 1886, leaving issue,
      Ralph, b. 1876; m. 17 June, 1905, Mabel, eldest dau. of John Arthur Cooper Ormsby.
   2. Ralph Smith, b. 4 July, 1856.
   3. Richard Charles Massey, b. 29 Oct. 1860; d. 6 Aug. 1907.
   4. Henry Edward, b. 6 Nov. 1865; m. 12 July, 1892, Louisa Constance, dau. of Edward Venables Vernon of Clontarf Castle (see that family).
   1. Mary Alice.   2. Elizabeth Frances.
   3. Mary, m. 15 Nov. 1887, her cousin Maj. James W. H. C. Cusack, of Abbeville House.
3. James William, M.D., b. 6 Aug. 1824; m. 12 July, 1849, Sarah, 3rd dau. of the late William Tanner, of Blacklands House, and d. 1868, leaving issue.
4. Thomas Bernard, b. 11 Dec. 1831; m. Ellen, eldest dau. of William Tanner, of Lockridge, Wilts, and d. 1864. She d. 26 Dec. 1900, leaving issue.
1. Mary Anne, m. 7 May, 1845, Robert H. Tilly, of Tolerton Park, Carlow.
2. Elizabeth Jane, m. 7 May, 1850, Samuel George Wilmot, M.D., of Dublin.

Mr. Cusack m. 2ndly, 10 Sept. 1838, Frances, relict of Richard Rothwell, of Hurlestown, co. Meath, and dau. of Rev. S. Radcliffe, and d. 25 Sept. 1861.

Arms—Per pale or and az. a fess counterchanged. *Crest*—A mermaid sa. holding in the dexter hand a sword, sinister, a sceptre. *Mottoes*—" Ave Maria, plena gratia ! " and " En Dieu est mon espoir."

Seat—Abbeville House, Malahide, co. Dublin.

DALY OF RAFORD.

John Archer Daly, of Raford, and Furbough, co. Galway, J.P., D.L., High Sheriff 1866, Col. Commanding 4th Batt. Connaught Rangers (assumed the surname and arms of Daly in lieu of his patronymic Blake by Royal Licence, dated 24 April, 1837, in compliance with the testamentary injunction of his maternal great-uncle, Hyacinth Daly, of Raford), b. 11 Jan. 1835; m. 30 April, 1864, Lady Anne Elizabeth Charlotte Nugent, dau. of Anthony Francis, 9th Earl of Westmeath, and by her (who d. Dec. 1906) had issue,

Denis Andrew Malachy, Lieut. in the Army, b. 27 Sept. 1865; m. 3 June, 1899, Kathleen Mary, only dau. of Richard Lynch, of Petersburgh, co. Galway. He d.v.p. Nov. 1899, having had posthumous issue, a son and a dau.,
  Denis, b. March, d. Aug. 1900.
  Denise (twin with her brother).
Anne Christian, b. 6 Sept. 1866; d. unm. 1897.

Lineage.—The House of Daly, of Raford, is a branch of the very ancient Irish sept of O'Daly, now represented by Lord Dunsandle and Clanconal.

James Daly, of Raford, younger son of James Daly, of Carrownakelly, co. Galway, and brother of Denis Daly, the great-grandfather of Denis, 1st Lord Dunsandle and Clanconal, was s. by his son,

Denis Daly, of Raford, who m. Anastasia, dau. of Hyacinth D'Arcy, of Kiltulla, co. Galway, and had, with four daus. (Anstace; Catherine, m. John Browne; Margaret, m. John Kirwan, of Castle Hacket; and Bridget, m. Walter Blake, of Dunmacrina and Oranmore), two sons,

1. Denis, his heir.
2. Hyacinth, of Dalystown, co. Galway, d. June, 1782, whose will dated 1 Sept. 1775, was proved 26 July, 1782. He m. April, 1740, Rose, sister and heiress of Thomas Coghlan (styled *The Maw*), chief of the ancient sept of MacCoghlan, Dynasts of Lower Delvin, by whom he had a son and a dau.,

The Right Hon. Denis Bowes Daly, of Dalystown, M.P. co. Galway, and a Privy Councillor in Ireland, m. by licence, dated 26 Aug. 1780, Mary Charlotte (d. 26 Aug. 1781), dau. of Right Hon. John Ponsonby, sister of William, 1st Lord Ponsonby, of Imokilly, and grand-dau. of Brabazon, 1st Earl of Bessborough, and d. 17 Dec. 1821, aged 76.
Margaret, m. by licence, dated 19 Nov. 1782, Right Hon. Sir Skeffington Smyth, Bart.

3. Charles, d. 4 Jan. 1758, having m. 17 March, 1756, Jane, widow of John Tew and dau. of — Hill.

Mr. Daly, d. 21 June, 1759, and whose will, dated 5 Feb. 1759, was proved 11 Aug. 1759, was s. by his elder son,

Denis Daly, of Raford, m. 1735, Lady Anne Burke (d. Jan. 1794), dau. of Michael, 10th Earl of Clanricarde, and had issue,

1. Denis, his heir.
2. Michael, of Loughrea and Mount Pleasant, co. Galway, and Tokay Lodge, co. Dublin, m. Feb. 1766, Lady Johanna Gore, dau. of Arthur, 1st Earl of Arran, and widow of Philip Doyne, of Wells, co. Wexford, and d. 23 Oct. 1808, aged 64, having had issue,
   1. Denis, Lieut. Galway Militia, d.v.p., leaving one dau., Katherine.
   2. Arthur Henry, b. 26 June, 1768; m. three times, and d. June, 1826, leaving issue.
   3. Hyacinth Richard, of Mount Pleasant, Col. in the Army, had by his 1st wife Mary, an only son, Denis, who d. young; and by his 2nd wife Honoria Keogh (with two younger sons, Anthony and James, d.s.p.), a son,
      Richard Gore, of Woodview, Eyre Court, co. Galway, m. May, 1840, Annie Jane, dau. of Col. Arthur Disney, of Ballysax, co. Kildare, and d. at Melbourne, Australia, 31 Dec. 1859, leaving by her (who d. 10 May, 1882) a dau., Annie Evelyn, b. 20 March, 1859), and four sons,
      1. Hyacinth, of Melbourne, b. 20 Feb. 1842; m. 1868, Bolinda Gordon, dau. of Thomas Picton Reede, of Dublin, and d. 24 Jan. 1901, leaving issue,
         (1) Richard Picton Gore, b. 7 July, 1870; m. 20 Jan. 1896, Louisa Harriet, 4th dau. of Richard Tudor Davies, of Melbourne, and has issue,
            1. Louisa Bolinda, b. 31 Dec. 1896.
            2. Elinor, b. 15 April, 1899.
            3. Doreen Disney, b. 5 May, 1904.
         (1) Mary Annie Harriet, b. 28 May, 1869.
         (2) Elinor Thomasina, b. 1 April, 1872.
      2. Arthur Disney Joseph, of Albert Park, Melbourne, b. 20 Aug. 1845; m. 1876, Laura, dau. of J. B. Pritchard, Melbourne, and d. 5 Oct. 1904, leaving two sons and a dau.
      3. William Disney John Eyre, of Onitchambo, Melbourne, b. 11 May, 1847; m. 27 April, 1882, Florence Eleanore (*Fairview, Burwood, Melbourne*), dau. of Gustave Becks, Consul-General for Belgium in Australia, and d. 20 May, 1902, having had issue, William Constant Becks, b. 19 Dec. 1883; Richard Strahan, b. 19 June, 1885; Clarance Wells Didier, b. 5 May, 1890; Gustav Anthony Disney, b. 1895; Eleanor Margaretta, b. 8 July, 1887; and Anastasia, b. 1892.
      4. Anthony, b. 20 May, 1850; d. 1894.
   1. Anne, m. Sept. 1791, Gyles Eyre, of Eyre Court, co. Galway.
   1. Anastasia, m. 12 Oct. 1761, Sir George Browne, 6th bart. of the Neale.
   2. Letitia, m. 1st, 28 Oct. 1761, Henry Bingham, of Newbrook, and 2ndly, March, 1794, Walter Blake, younger son of Sir Walter Blake, 10th bart. of Menlo, but by him had no issue.
   3. Margaret, m. 1st, 3 May, 1762, Charles Blake, of Merlin Park, and 2ndly, John D'Arcy, and 3rdly, June, 1792, Stephen Blake, of Woodstock, younger son of Sir Walter Blake, 10th bart. of Menlo, and d. 1825.

Mr. Daly d. 14 March, 1791, aged 91, and was s. by his son,

Denis Daly, of Raford, m. Ann, dau. of Malachy Donellan, of Ballydonellan, co. Galway, and had three sons,
1. Denis, of Raford, m. by licence, dated 9 Oct. 1799, Anna Maria Harrison, of Dublin, and d.s.p. 1807.
2. Malachy, of Raford, m. June, 1797, Julia, dau. of Sir Thomas Burke, 1st bart. of Marble Hill, and had two daus.,
   1. Anne, m. 3 Oct. 1829, Anthony Francis, 5th Earl of Westmeath, and d. 27 Sept. 1871, having had issue (see Burke's *Peerage*).
   2. Maria Julia, of whom presently.
3. Hyacinth, of Raford.

The 3rd son,

Hyacinth Daly, of Raford, eventually succeeded, and dying without surviving issue, 5 Nov. 1836, bequeathed his estates to his grand-nephew, the elder son of

Maria Julia Daly, 2nd dau. of his brother Malachy. She m.

22 Sept. 1832, Andrew William Blake,* of Furbough, co. Galway, and had issue,
1. JOHN ARCHER, heir to his grand-uncle, assumed the surname of DALY, and is now of Raford.
2. Malachy Joseph, Clerk of the Peace, co. Galway, *b.* 5 July, 1836; *d. unm.* 12 May, 1902.
3. Andrew William, *b.* 2 June, 1842.
  1. Julia Maria, *d. unm.* 2 June, 1854.
  2. Elizabeth Ann.
3. Emily Margaret, *m.* 24 July, 1866, William, 10th Earl of Westmeath, and *d.* 7 July, 1906, leaving issue (*see* BURKE'S *Peerage*). He *d.* 31 May, 1883.
4. Charlotte Frances, *m.* 29 Oct. 1863, John Smyth, of Masonbrook, co. Galway, who *d.* 3 March, 1905, leaving issue (*see that family*).
Mr. Blake *d.* 1868.

Arms—Per fess arg. and or, a lion rampant, per fess sa. and gu. in chief two dexter hands couped at the wrists of the last. *Crest*—In front of an oak tree ppr. fructed or, a greyhound courant sa. collared gold. *Motto*—Deo fidelis et regi.

Seats—Raford, Athenry; and Furbough, Galway.

DALY OF DUNSANDLE.

The late WILLIAM DALY, of Dunsandle Galway, and of Thomastown Castle, co. Tipperary, J.P. and D.L. co. Galway, High Sheriff 1901, *b.* 1850; *m.* 16 Aug. 1893, Julia Catherine Anne, elder dau. of the late Sir Thomas Burke, Bart., of Marble Hill, and Lady Mary his wife, dau. of the Earl of Westmeath, and *d.* 27 Dec. 1910, having had issue,

1. DENIS WILLIAM, *b.* 1894. 2. William Cecil, *b.* 1897.
3. James Henry, *b.* 1899.
1. Mary Frances, *b.* 1895.

Mr. Daly's brother,
CAPT. DENIS ST. GEORGE DALY, of Dunsandle, co. Galway, late 18th Hussars (*Over Norton Park, Chipping Norton, co. Oxford*), *b.* 5 Sept. 1862; *m.* 2 May, 1896, Rose Zara, dau. of Albert Brassey, M.P., of Heythrop, co. Oxford, and has issue,

*ANDREW BLAKE, of Galway, 3rd son of Andrew FitzPatrick Blake (*see* BLAKE *of Ballyglunin*), *m.* Christian Martyn, and *d.* 1687 (will dated 20 Oct. 1681, proved 22 Aug. 1687), leaving issue,
1. FRANCIS, of whom presently.
2. Nicholas. 3. Patrick.
4. Martin. 5. Dominick.
6. Walter. 7. Augustin.
1. Anne. 2. Katherine.
The eldest son,
FRANCIS BLAKE, of Furbough, co. Galway, *m.* Jane Martyn, and by her had issue,
1. THOMAS, of whom presently.
2. John, of Ballymanagh, co. Galway, *m.* Sarah, dau. of — French, of Aggard, co. Galway, and *d.* 26 Nov. 1763, leaving issue, Andrew, of Ballymanagh, *m.* (art. dated 4 Feb. 1760) Honoria, eld. dau. of Michael Burke, of Ballydugan, co. Galway, and *d.* about 1781 (will dated 22 Sept. 1763, proved 25 April, 1781), leaving issue,
  (1) JOHN, of whom presently, *s.* his cousin Thomas.
  (2) Andrew, Capt. 88th Regt., killed at Talavera, 28 July, 1809.
  (1) Sarah.
The elder son,
THOMAS BLAKE, of Furbough, who left issue two sons,
1. FRANCIS, his heir. 2. Jasper.
The elder son,
FRANCIS BLAKE, of Furbough, living 1748, had issue, an only son,
THOMAS BLAKE, of Furbough, living 1760, who *d.s.p.*, when he was *s.* by his cousin,
LIEUT.-COL. JOHN BLAKE, of Furbough, Mayor of Galway 1830; *m.* 1st, March, 1789, Mary, dau. of Nugent Sylvester Aylward, of Ballinagar, co. Galway, and widow of Edmond Blake, of Ballyglunin (*see that family*), but by her had no issue. He *m.* 2ndly, 1797, Maria, second dau. of Edmond Galway, of Cork, and by her had issue,
1. ANDREW WILLIAM, of Furbough, co. Galway, J.P. and D.L., High Sheriff 1841, *b.* 22 Aug. 1798; *m.* as above, 22 Sept. 1832, Maria Julia, dau. of Malachy Daly, of Raford.
2. Edmond, last Mayor of Galway 1836-41, *b.* 1803; *m.* 24 Nov. 1870, Anne, dau. of Christopher St. George, of Tyrone, co. Galway, and *d.* 1895, leaving a dau.,
Anne.
3. John Henry, of Rathville, co. Galway, J.P.; *m.* Harriet, dau. of Francis J. Lynch, M.D., of Mount Pleasant, co. Galway, and *d.* 1882, leaving issue,
  1. Edmund Martin, of Rathville, co. Galway, J.P. (*Rathville, Kiltulla, near Athenry*), *b.* 1876.
  2. Henry Francis.
Col. Blake *d.* 18 Oct. 1836, and was *s.* by his eldest son.

1. DENIS BOWES, *b.* 6 Jan. 1900.
2. Dermot Ralph, *b.* 4 Aug. 1908.
1. Rosie Eileen May, *b.* 11 Sept. 1898.
2. Denise Violet, *b.* 11 Aug. 1902.
3. Lilah Maude, *b.* 6 Oct. 1906.

Mr. William Daly and his brother Capt. Denis St. George Daly *s.* jointly to all the estates of Denis St. George, 2nd Baron Dunsandle, who *d.* 11 Jan. 1893.

Seat—Dunsandle, Athenry, co. Galway.

DALY OF CASTLE DALY.

JAMES (JOSEPH) DERMOT DALY, of Castle Daly, co. Galway, J.P., M.A. Royal University, called to the Irish Bar 1897, *b.* 11 May, 1868; *s.* his father 12 April, 1910; *m.* 3 Aug. 1898, Mary, 2nd dau. of Thomas Aliaga Kelly, of 64, Upper Leeson Street, Dublin, and has had issue,
1. DERMOT JOSEPH, *b.* 2 July, 1900.
2. James Francis, *b.* 11 Jan. 1902.
3. Hugh Tadhg, *b.* 4 Feb.; *d.* 11 April, 1903.
4. Godfrey Peter Thomas, *b.* 19 Sept. 1909.
1. Mary Margaret Paula, *b.* 28 June, 1899.
2. Christina Mary Angela, *b.* 13 Oct. 1904.
3. Mabel Mary Magdalene, *b.* 25 July, 1906.
4. Marion Honour Josephine, *b.* 8 March, 1908.

Lineage.—DERMOT O'DALY, who built the house of Killimer, co. Galway, and had a grant, 21 June, 1578, of the Manor of Larha in that county, *d.* 10 Nov. 1614, leaving five sons,
1. Teige, or Thady, of Killimer, *m.* Cisly, dau. of Connor O'Kelly, and had four sons,
  1. Denis, of Killimer, *m.* Margaret, dau. of John Donnellan, of Ballydonelan, and left issue.
  2. Dermot. 3. Teige.
  4. John, who left issue.
2. Dermot, of Clonbrooke, left three sons, Teige, Charles, and Dermot.
3. Donogh, of Larha, left two sons,
  1. James, of Carrownekelly, ancestor of LORD DUNSANDLE (*see* BURKE'S *Peerage*).
  2. Dermot.
4. Ferdinando, of Oughtercluny, left two sons, Oliver and John.
5. Godfrey, of Newcastle.
The 5th son,
GODFREY O'DALY, of Newcastle, co. Galway, 5th son of Dermot O'Daly, of Killimer, was father of
DERMOT, or DARBY O'DALY, who held three cartrons and a half of land in Newcastle called Corrobane in 1640, which were forfeited in 1653, and he was transplanted to Cloonbanniv, near Ahascragh, afterwards called Daly's Grove, 10 July, 1656; he was *s.* by
DARBY DALY, of Daly's Grove, *b.* 1721; *d.* 1777; *m.* Teresa, dau. of James O'Flanagan, of Boulauna, and by her (who *d.* 1817) had two sons and two daus.,
1. Francis, of Ballylee Castle, *m.* 1 Nov. 1786, Elinor, dau. of — Foster; 2ndly, — Staunton, and left, with daus. and other sons,
  1. Francis Dermot, Lieut.-Col. 4th Light Dragoons, *d.* 1857; *m.* 1st, Mary McIntosh; 2ndly, Sarah Bidgood, and with a dau. left two sons,
    (1) Francis Dermot, *d. unm.*
    (2) Henry Dermot (Sir), G.C.B., C.I.E., General, *b.* 25 Oct. 1823; *d.* 21 July, 1895; *m.* 1st, 21 Oct. 1852, Susan Ely Ellen, dau. of Edward Kirkpatrick, who *d.* and left with three daus., five sons,
      1. Edward Dermot Hamilton, Lieut. Ben. S.C., *m.*
      2. Henry Laurence, 15th Hussars, *m.*
      3. George Kirkpatrick, Indian S.C., *d. unm.* 1866.
      4. Hugh, C.S.I., C.I.E., (*Buckland Grange, Ryde, Isle of Wight*), *b.* 29 May, 1860, Lieut.-Col. Indian Army, *m.* 16 July, 1891, Diana Maria, dau. of Charles Denison of Pennsylvania, U.S.A.
      5. Arthur Crawford, *m.*
    Sir Henry *m.* 2ndly, 1882, Charlotte Claudine Georgina, widow of A. C. Stirling Murray-Dunlop, dau. of James Coape, and had a son,
      6. Victor, *b.* 1890.

2. Richard, m. and left four sons,
(1) Daniel O'Connor, d. unm. 1892.
(2) Francis, m.
(3) William, m.
(4) Richard, m.
2. PETER, of Castle Daly, of whom presently.
1. Anne, m. Thomas Jackson Cocking, Major 56th Regt. Foot.
2. Elizabeth, m. Andrew Nowlan, of Prospect.

The 2nd son,
PETER DALY, of Castle Daly, and Daly's Grove, co. Galway, also of Daly's Grove, Jamaica, who d. 1846, m. Bridget Louisa (d. 1843), dau. of Christopher McEvoy, of Santa Cruz, and of Portman Square, London, and had issue,
1. JAMES PETER, his heir.
2. Peter Paul, of Daly's Grove, co. Galway, who d. 1881, having m. Anne, dau. of Hubert Thomas Dolphin, of Turoe, co. Galway, and left issue,
1. Peter Joseph, of Daly's Grove, who d. 3 Feb. 1910, having m. 1884, Marie Jeanne Françoise (*Daly's Grove, Ahascragh, co. Galway*), 2nd dau. of Albert Moutens d'Oosterwyck, of Château de Loenhout, Anvers, Belgium, and had issue, with three daus., a son,
Albert Peter Vincent, b. 1891.
2. Hubert, S.J. 3. Oliver, S.J.
4. James, S.J. 5. Francis, S.J., d. 1907.
6. Albert, dec.
1. Mary, a nun.
2. Louisa, d. 1910, having m. Baron de Coppin de Grinchamp, of Château de Florifloux, Namur, Belgium.
3. Anne Marie, m. 29 Aug. 1882, Matthew John Purcell, of Burton Park, co. Cork (*see that family*).

The elder son,
JAMES PETER DALY, of Castle Daly, J.P. and D.L., High Sheriff 1853, b. March, 1808; m. Jan. 1830, Margaret, eldest dau. of Hubert Thomas Dolphin, of Turoe, co. Galway (*see that family*), and by her (who d. April, 1879) had issue,
1. Peter Hubert, Lieut. 3rd Light Dragoons, b. Nov. 1838; d. April, 1861.
2. JAMES DERMOT, his heir.
3. Mary, m. James Johnston, J.P. and D.L., of Carrickbreda, co. Armagh, and had issue.
2. Louisa, m. Walter Joyce, J.P., of Corgary House, co. Galway, and had issue.
3. Teresa, m. Festus, eldest son of Cornelius J. O'Kelly, of Gallagh, co. Galway, and had issue.
4. Anne, m. Jan. 1883, Henry W. Devlin, Surgeon-Major 44th Regt.
5. Christina. m. 1860, Matthew D'Arcy, J.P and D.L., of Dublin and Kilcroney House, Bray, co. Wicklow, M.P. co. Wexford 1868 to 1874, and had issue.
6. Helen, d. unm. 1885.

Mr. Daly d. April, 1881, and was s. by his eldest surviving son,
JAMES DERMOT DALY, of Castle Daly, co. Glaway, J.P., b. 22 Dec. 1840; d. 12 April, 1910; m. 20 Nov. 1865, Christina Gertrude (d. 26 Jan. 1905), youngest dau. of Cornelius Joseph O'Kelly, of Gallagh, co. Galway, and had issue, a son,
JAMES (JOSEPH) DERMOT, now of Castle Daly.

Arms—Per fess arg. and or a lion rampant per fesse sa. and gu., in chief two dexter hands couped at the wrist of the last. Crest—In front of an oak tree ppr., a greyhound courant sa. collared or. Motto—Deo et regi fidelis.

Seat—Castle Daly, Loughrea.

DALY OF TULLAMORE.

BERNARD DALY, of Dunboy, co. Dublin, and Old Hall, Tullamore, King's Co., J.P. for that co., High Sheriff 1897, M.A. Trin. Coll. Dublin, late Capt. Army Reserve, and formerly 6th Batt. Royal Irish Rifles, b. Sept. 1861; m. 24 July, 1897, Maud, 3rd dau. of the late Capt. St. George Gray, 1st Royal Scots, and has issue,
1. BERNARD BRIAN ST. GEORGE, b. 18 April, 1909.
1. Beryl, b. 1899.
2. Hazel, b. 1903.

Capt. Daly is the only son of the late Bernard Daly, of Hazlebrook, co. Dublin, and Tullamore, King's Co., High Sheriff 1871, who d. 1887, and Mary Ann his wife, only dau. of John Willcocks, R.N., son of Sir John Willcocks.

Seat—Old Hall, Tullamore, King's Co. Residence—23, Highfield Road, Dublin.

LONGWORTH-DAMES OF GREENHILL.

THOMAS DUDLEY LONGWORTH-DAMES, of Greenhill, King's Co., b. 28 April, 1897; s. his grandfather 25 Feb. 1911.

Lineage.—THOMAS LONGWORTH-DAMES, of Greenhill, J.P., King's Co., 3rd son of Francis Longworth, of Creggan Castle, co. Westmeath, by Elizabeth his wife, dau. and co-heir (with her sister Mary, wife of James Middleton Berry) of Thomas Dames, of Rathmoyle, King's Co. (eldest son of John Dames, of Rathmoyle, and grandson of John Dames, who d. intestate 1732), adopted the additional surname of DAMES, as heir of his maternal grandfather Thomas Dames, of Rathmoyle. He was b. 1768; m. 1788, Jane, youngest dau. of Mansel Burke, son of Anthony Burke, of Springheld, co. Galway. She d. 29 May, 1841. He d. 5 Sept. 1825, leaving issue,
1. FRANCIS, his heir.
2. Mansel John, b. Dec. 1792; m. Julia, dau. of Edward Ombler, of Camerton, co. York. He d.s.p. 5 Sept. 1880. She d. 26 Sept. 1881.
3. Thomas, Capt. 1st Dragoon Guards, b. Sept. 1794; d. unm. 3 July, 1845.
4. John, of South Molton, Devon, bapt. 1 Jan. 1803; d.s.p. 11 April, 1881.
5. Arthur (Rev.), M.A., Vicar of Kenton, Devon, b. 29 Feb. 1804; m. 15 Oct. 1844, Susanna Emma, dau. of Thomas Brown, of Horton House, Wilts, and d. 20 Jan. 1887, leaving issue.
6. William, Lieut.-Gen. late 37th Regt., and Hon. Col. 5th Fusiliers; bapt. 2 March, 1806; m. 6 Nov. 1834, Christian Elizabeth, dau. of Peter Smith, of Toronto, Canada, and d. 20 Feb. 1868, leaving issue, one son and two daus.
7. George, late Capt. 66th Regt., bapt. 7 Aug. 1808; m. 1st, 20 Dec. 1836, Emma, dau. of William Kemble, of Quebec, and had by her (who d. 4 March, 1845) a son,
1. George Francis, d. unm. 15 April, 1860.
He m. 2ndly, 13 March, 1847, Caroline Amelia Brunswick, 5th dau. of Thomas Northmore, of Cleve House, Devon, by his 2nd wife, Emmeline, dau. of Sir John Eden, 4th bart. of Windlestone Park, Durham, and had issue,
2. Mansel, Indian Civil Service, b. 12 Jan. 1850; m. 1878, Mary Ann, dau. of — Ivens, and has issue,
Norah Carew, m. 14 April, 1909, Francis William Bolton Smith, of The Charterhouse, Godalming.
3. Francis William, b. 28 Jan. 1856.
4. Henry Northmore, b. 21 Feb. 1857.
1. Amy Northmore, m. 8 Jan. 1873, John Edward Wharton Rotton.
2. Caroline Charlotte, m. Aug. 1873, Major Walter Augustus Parker, R.A.M.C., M.R.C.S., L.R.C.P.
3. Elfrida Gertrude.
Capt. G. L. Dames d. 20 March, 1860.
1. Jane, m. Hugh Hamill, of Hartfield, co. Dublin, who d. 16 May, 1835, leaving issue : she d. 12 June, 1863.
2. Eliza, d. unm. 16 Dec. 1835.
3. Maria, m. 24 Nov. 1851, Robert Fleetwood Rynd, of Ryndville, co. Meath. He d. 10 March, 1875. She d. 1 Dec. 1893, leaving issue (*see that family*).

The eldest son,
FRANCIS LONGWORTH DAMES, of Greenhill, King's Co., J.P. and D.L., High Sheriff 1832, b. 25 Dec. 1789; m. 1st, 5 June, 1830, Anna, youngest dau. of the Rev. Travers Hume, D.D., by Elizabeth Balaguier his wife, niece and heiress of George, Earl Macartney, and by her (who d. 21 Sept. 1835) had issue,
1. THOMAS, of Greenhill.
2. FRANCIS TRAVERS DAMES LONGWORTH, of Glynwood (*see that family*).
1. Elizabeth D. an infant, 1835.
He m. 2ndly, 13 Aug. 1839, Elizabeth Selina, youngest dau. of Ralph Smyth, of Gaybrook, co. Westmeath, by Hannah Maria his wife, 2nd dau. of Sir Robert Staples, Bart. of Durrow, Queen's Co., and by her (who d. 13 June, 1885) had issue,
3. Ralph, b. June, 1840; d. 15 Feb. 1841.
4. Robert Staples, of 21 Herbert Street, Dublin, Barrister-at-Law, b. 9 Oct. 1841; m. 8 Aug. 1876, Mary Anne Alice, eldest dau. of James Jameson, of Delvin, co. Dublin, and has issue,
Francis James Nesbitt, b. 20 May, 1879; m. 14 April, 1905, Mary, 2nd dau. of Lieut.-Col. Francis McFarland, of Claremont, Chichester Park, Belfast, and has issue.
2. Mary Jane, b. 29 May, 1843; m. 4 April, 1866, Charles Colley Palmer, of Rahan, co. Kildare, and has issue (*see that family*).
He d. 6 Oct. 1863. His eldest son,
THOMAS LONGWORTH-DAMES, of Greenhill, King's Co., J.P. and D.L., High Sheriff 1869, late First Capt. R.A., b. 12 March, 1831; m. 29 April, 1858, Eunice Jane, 2nd dau. of Samuel Talbot Hassell, of Hull, Yorkshire, and d. 25 Feb. 1911, having by her had issue,
1. Francis Talbot, Capt. R.A., b. 16 June, 1860; d. unm. 30 Jan. 1888.
2. Gustavus Montagu, b. 17 April, 1862; d. unm. 2 April, 1901.
3. Thomas Mansel, of Ballybrittain, Edenderry, King's Co., J.P., b. 16 Feb. 1869; m. 3 June, 1896, Mabel Elizabeth, only dau. of Charles Colley Palmer, D.L., of Rahan (*see that family*), and d.v.p. 8 Jan. 1909, having had issue,
1. THOMAS DUDLEY, now of Greenhill.
2. Desmond Charles, b. 10 Oct. 1901.
1. Gertrude Anna, b. 14 Feb. 1859; d. 9 April, 1868.
2. Eunice Mary, b. 9 Nov. 1864; m. 12 April, 1888, Maj. George Westley Richards, late Royal Berkshire Regt., only son of George Seale Richards, of Worcester. She d. 8 Oct. 1903, leaving issue.
3. Katherine Edith, b. 11 Feb. 1868; d. 13 March, 1868.
4. Ethel, b. 10 Feb. 1872; m. 13 Dec. 1899, Robert Rivington Pilkington, Barrister-at-Law, Western Australia, son of Henry Mulock Pilkington, of Tore, co. Westmeath, and has issue (*see that family*).
5. Kathleen Thomasine, b. 7 July, 1875.

Seat—Greenhill, Edenderry, King's Co.

DAMES-LONGWORTH. See LONGWORTH.

DANE, late OF KILLYHEVLIN.

JAMES WHITESIDE DANE, of Castle Warden, co. Kildare, and Bonnybrook, co. Fermanagh, D.L. for the latter co. and Clerk of the Crown and Peace for co. Kildare, b. 22 June, 1856.

Lineage.—JOHN DANE emigrated from England and was settled at Enniskillen in 1667-8, where he was Churchwarden. He d. Feb. 1678, leaving issue by Mary, his wife, dau. of Peter Weldon,
1. PAUL, of whom hereafter.
2. Richard, m. 22 Oct. 1672, Debora Cole.
1. Elizabeth, m. 13 Oct. 1673. John Clarke.
2. Anne, m. 13 April, 1678, John Stewart.

The eldest son,
PAUL DANE, of Killyhevlin, b. 1646, Provost of Enniskillen 1687-9. He was present at the Battle of the Boyne. KING WILLIAM III gave him the two pictures of himself and QUEEN MARY now in Enniskillen Town Hall. He d. 8 Jan. 1745, having been m. twice. He m. 1st, — Martin, and had issue,
1. JOHN, of whom hereafter.

He m. 2ndly, 18 Sept. 1680, Elisa Story, leaving issue,
2. Christopher, bapt. 1684; d. 1727; m. circa 1708, Mary, eld. dau. of Governor Gustavus Hamilton, of Monea Castle, and had with other issue,
  1. Paul, bapt. 1709; d. circa 1787.
    1. Jane, bapt. 1711-12. 2. Elisabeth, bapt. 1716.
    3. Martha, bapt. 1718.
  3. Martin (Rev.), b. 1699, entered Trin. Coll. Dublin 1717; m. and had issue.
4. William, in the Army, killed in action.
5. Paul, in the Army, bur. in Enniskillen 1707.
6. Richard, bur. 1707.
7. Thomas (Rev.), in Holy Orders, Curate of Tynan (?), m. and had issue.
1. Mary, bapt. 1681; m. — O'Neill.
2. Margaret, bapt. 1683; m. 1707, James Ball.
3. Catherine, d.u.p., having m. Paul Moore.
4. Wilhelmina.   5. Elisabeth.
6. Jane.   7. Eleanor.

The eldest son,
JOHN DANE, of Killyhevlin, b. circa 1679, served in Brig. Wolseley's Regt. of Horse, and subsequently abroad under the Duke of Marlborough, who gave him a jewelled sword; m. 1734, Elisabeth, dau. of James Auchenleck, of Thomastown, co. Fermanagh (see that family), by Elisabeth, dau. of Col. James Corry, of Castlecoole (see BURKE's Peerage, BELMORE, E.). She d. 1772. He d. 1742, leaving issue,
1. PAUL, of whom hereafter.
1. Elisabeth.   2. Sarah, b. 1734.

The only son,
PAUL DANE, of Killyhevlin, m. circa 1769, Margaret Swords (who remarried after his decease). He d. 1800, leaving issue,
1. RICHARD, of whom presently.
2. William, Capt. 13th Regt. of Foot 1794, formerly in 101st Foot and in Capt. Cowan's Company, d. at Wexford during the rebellion.
3. James, of Dromard, m. a dau. of James Armstrong, of Enniskillen, and had issue,
  1. Paul, Clerk of Enniskillen Union, m. and had issue,
    (1) Paul, m. Margaret Dunne,
    (2) Somerset, m. ————. Both he and his brother emigrated.
  2. William, a Dispensary Doctor and Barony Constable, d. unm.
  3. John, of Glasmullagh, m. Ann Dunne, and d.s.p.
  4. Christopher, Inniskilling Dragoons, d. unm.
  5. Richard, of Glasmullagh and Dromard, emigrated to Canada, formerly enlisted in 6th Inniskilling Dragoons, and a Barony Constable, m. Ann Smith, and d. 1867, leaving with other issue who d. young,
    (1) Armar, bapt. 1827; d. young.
    (2) Paul.   (3) John Both, of Michigan, U.S.A.
  6. Alexander, of Dromard, drowned 1857.
  1. A dau., m. — Lloyd.
4. John, Capt. 98th Regt of Foot, formerly in 6th Foot and in the New Independant Company 1794, A.D.C. to H.R.H. the Duke of Gloucester, served during Irish Rebellion and American War; d. before 1817; m. a dau. of Maj. Humphries, 6th Foot, and had issue,
  1. John, Capt. in the Army, afterwards Gold Commissioner in Victoria, m. ———, and had issue,
    (1) John, d. 1860.
    (1) Juliana, m. — Cropper, of Hawthorn, Victoria.
    (2) Another dau.
  2. Martin, Lieut. 4th Foot, m. ————.
5. Paul, Ensign in Tyrone Militia.
6. Christopher, of Enniskillen, d. unm.
7. Alexander, d. young.
1. Catherine, m. Dr. Trimble.
2. Elsabeth, m. Capt. George Willis.

The eldest son,
RICHARD MARTIN DANE, of Killyhevlin, J.P., D.L., High Sheriff 1816, many years Provost of Belturbet, b. 1770; m. 12 Aug. 1809, Anna, dau. of Rev. Alexander Auchinleck, of Lisgoole Abbey, Rector of Rossory, co. Fermanagh, and d. 29 Jan. 1842, having had issue,
1. Paul, of Killyhevlin, b. 5 July, 1810; m. Georgina Saunderson, of Ballyconnor, who d. circa 1889-90. He d.s.p. 23 Oct. 1873.
2. Somerset, Doctor in the Army, b. 1811; d. 1842.
3. Richard Martin, M.D., C.B., b. 4 April, 1813, Inspector-Gen. of Hospitals; m. 1844, Sophia, dau. of Col. Charles Griffiths, and d. 27 March, 1901, leaving with other issue, who d. young,

I. L. G.

1. Edward Adrian, b. 25 May, 1846, emigrated to Australia.
2. Arthur Henry Cole, M.D., Col. I.M.S., b. 23 March, 1852; m. Isabella Campbell Yates; d. 1903.
3. Sir Richard Morris, K.C.I.E. (1909), I.C.S. from 1872, Inspector-Gen. of Excise and Salt for India since 1907, b 21 May, 1854; m. 1880, Emily, 3rd dau. of Sir Edward Leeds 3rd bart. (see BURKE's Peerage, LEEDS, BART.), from whom he obtained a divorce, 1901, and has issue living.
4. Sir Louis William, G.C.I.E. (1912), K.C.I.E. (1905), C.S.I., I.C.S. from 1876, Lieut.-Governor of the Punjaub since 1908, R.M. co. Kerry 1900-1, b. 21 March, 1856; m. 1882, Edith, 3rd dau. of the late Lieut.-Gen. Sir Francis Booth Norman, K.C.B., and has issue, two sons and three daus.
4. WILLIAM AUCHINLECK, of whom presently.
5. Alexander, d. young.
6. Armar Lowry-Corry, b. 1825; d. 1826.
7. Daniel Elden, b. 1828; d. 1833.
8. John, b. 1831; d. 1833.
1. Juliana, b. 1814; m. William Acheson O'Brien, of Drumsilla, co. Leitrim; d. 1895.
2. Anna Maria, b. 1819; d. 1859 s.p.; m. John Charles Doveton Coane.
3. Eva, d. in infancy.
4. Henrietta, b. 1828; m. William Macartney (see ELLISON-MACARTNEY of Mountjoy Grange).
5. Margaret, b. 1827; m. George Lowe O'Keefe, and has issue.

The 4th son,
WILLIAM AUCHINLECK DANE, of Killyreagh, co. Fermanagh, and 37, Rutland Square, Dublin, Solicitor, b. 1816; m. 28 Jan. 1846, Sarah, youngest dau. of Benjamin Friel Foster, 46th Regt., of Drumloo, co. Monaghan, and Elisabeth, his wife, dau. of James Moorhead, of Annagh-ma-Kerrig. She d. 2 June, 1885. He d. 27 April, 1873, leaving issue,
1. Paul, Clerk of the Crown and Peace for co. Wicklow, b. 15 Mar. 1847; m. 1st, 1877, Charlotte Elisabeth, dau. of Thomas Dodson Palmer, and had issue,
  1. William Auchinleck, b. 1878; d. 1881.
  2. Thomas Spunner Palmer, b. 1881; m. 1901, Sarah Williams Paul Dane, m. 2ndly, 19 June, 1884, Frances Georgina, dau. of John Hubert Moore, of Ballymorris, Queen's Co. He d. 9 Dec. 1886. She remarried Dr. McLeod.
2. Rev. Benjamin Friel Foster, M.A., Trin. Coll. Dublin, b. 15 Mar. 1850.
3. Richard Martin, K.C., County Court Judge, co. Mayo 1898-1903, J.P. cos. Fermanagh and Meath, M.A. Trin. Coll Dublin, 1873, called to the Bar 1877, J.C. 1896, M.P. North Fermanagh 1892-98, b. 4 Nov. 1852; m. 1st, Kate, dau. of Rev. Frederick Eldon Barnes, Rector of Kilmaley, co. Clare. She d. April 1889, leaving,
  1. James Auchinleck, late Lieut. R.F.A., b. 18 May, 1883; m. 9 Oct. 1909, Elgiva Mary Rathorn, dau. and heiress of the Hon. Wm. Thomas Wentworth Fitzwilliam, of Alwalton Hall, Peterborough (see BURKE's Peerage, FITZWILLIAM, E.), and has issue,
    Richard Auchinleck, b. 20 Sept. 1911.
Richard Martin Dane m. 2ndly, Annie Eleanor, only dau. of William Thompson, of Rathnally, and Ross, co. Meath (see that family). He d. 22 Mar. 1903, leaving issue by her (who m. 2ndly, 3 Sept. 1908, her cousin, Francis D'Arcy Thompson, see that family),
Dorothy Anne.
4. James Whiteside, now of Castle Warden.
1. Elisabeth, b. 1848; d. 1851.
2. Florence, b. 24 June, 1850; d. unm. 19 July, 1873.
3. Anna, b. 29 July, 1854; d. unm. 1874.
4. Sarah Gertrude, b. 18 March, 1860; d. 21 Oct. 1908; m. 1st, 8 Aug. 1884, Robert A. Ross Todd, Solicitor; and 2ndly, Thomas R. Bradshaw, and had issue.

Seats—Castle Warden, Naas, co. Kildare, and Bonnybrook, Enniskillen, co. Fermanagh. **Club**—Hibernian United Service.

DANIELL OF NEW FOREST.

JOHN JOSEPH DANIELL, of New Forest, co. Westmeath, b. 20 March, 1868. s. his father 1911.

Lineage.—BRIDGES DANIELL, of Dublin, whose will is dated 31 July, 1740, and was proved 18 Feb. 1740-1, m. Catherine, dau. of Henry Wade, of Clonebraney, co. Meath, and sister and co-heir of John Wade, of Clonebraney, and had issue, with three daus., three sons,
1. Richard, d.v.p.
2. John, of Clonebraney, who assumed the name of WADE; he m. Hester, dau. of Robert Shields, of Wainstown, and had issue (see WADE of Clonebraney).
3. MICHAEL.

The 3rd son,

MICHAEL DANIELL, *m.* 22 Feb. 1765, Margaret, dau. of Samuel Woodward of Woodville, co. Meath, and had two sons, John Daniell, of Bellevue, co. Meath, Capt. 17th Lancers, who *d.* 15 May, 1840 ; and
HENRY DANIELL, of New Forest, J.P. for the cos. of Meath and Westmeath, who served as High Sheriff of the latter, 1803. He was *b.* Sept. 1767 ; *m.* 15 Aug. 1794, Isabella (*d.* 13 Oct. 1814), 2nd dau. of Robert Tighe, of South Hill, co. Westmeath, M.P. for Carrick, by Isabella, his wife, sister of Sir Gilbert King, Bart. of Charleston, co. Roscommon, and had issue,

1. Robert Benjamin, J.P. and D.L., *b.* 27 Sept. 1796 ; *m.* 31 July, 1827, Cecilia Frances, youngest dau. of Major Anthony Cliffe, of Bellevue, co. Wexford, and by her (who *d.* 18 May, 1863) left at his decease, 6 Aug. 1841,
   1. ROBERT GEORGE, of New Forest.
   2. Anthony John, *b.* 16 March, 1833.
      1. Frances ; *d. unm.*
      2. Isabella Jane.
      3. Henrietta Cecilia, *m.* 1859, Patrick Segrave, J.P. (*see* SEGRAVE *of Cabra*).
2. George, Capt. R.N., J.P., *b.* 31 Aug. 1797 ; *m.* 23 June, 1842, Alicia Katherine, eldest dau. of the Right Hon. Francis Blackburne, and dying 2 Nov. 1856, left a son,
   Francis Henry Blackburne, *m.* 21 May 1877. Caroline Sophia, eldest dau. of William Bence Jones, of Lisselan, co. Cork, and has issue.
3. Henry (Rev.), Rector of Portnashangan, co. Westmeath, *b.* 28 July, 1801 ; *d. unm.* 29 March, 1836.
4. John Michael, Lieut. 26th Regt., *b.* 19 Oct. 1815 ; *d. unm.* at Chusan, 27 Nov. 1840.
   1. Isabella Margaret, *m.* 3 May, 1821, William Hamilton Smyth, of Drum House, co. Down, son, by his 2nd marriage, of William Smyth, of Drumcree, M.P. for Westmeath, and *d.* 1889, leaving issue (*see that family*).
   2. Frances Louisa, *d. unm.* 24 Feb. 1826.

Mr. Daniel *d.* 30 July, 1843.
ROBERT GEORGE DANIELL, of New Forest, co. Westmeath, J.P., *b.* 12 June, 1831 ; *m.* 19 Aug. 1864, Ellen (who *d.* 20 Jan. 1908), 2nd dau. of John O'Brien, of Edeu Vale, co. Clare, M.P. for Limerick. He *d.* 15 Dec. 1911, having left issue,
1. JOHN JOSEPH, now of New Forest.
2. Robert George, *b.* 2 July, 1870.
3. Henry, *b.* 20 Dec. 1872 ; *d. unm.*
1. Cecilia.   2. Ellen.

Arms—Arg., a pale fusilly sa., in dexter chief point a crescent gu. *Crest*—An unicorn's head, erased arg., armed and crined, or, charged with a crescent gu. *Motto*—Pro fide et patria.

Seat—New Forest, Tyrellspass, Westmeath.

DARBY OF LEAP CASTLE.

JONATHAN CHARLES DARBY, of Leap Castle, King's Co., J.P. and D.L., High Sheriff 1883, and J.P. co. Tipperary, *b.* 28 April, 1855 ; *m.* 7 Nov. 1889, Mildred Henrietta Gordon, younger dau. of Richard Dill, M.D., of Burgess Hill, Sussex, and Brighton, and has issue,
1. Jonathan, *b.* 2 April, *d.* 30 April, 1892.
2. HORATIO GORDON, *b.* 19 Oct. 1898.
1. Augusta Diana O'Carroll, *b.* July, 1893.
2. Cicely Mildred O'Carroll, *b.* 27 Jan. 1895.
3. Florence Patricia O'Carroll, *b.* 4 Jan. 1904.

Lineage.—JONATHAN DARBY, of Leap, King's Co., High Sheriff 1674, will dated 6 March, 1685, left issue, by Deborah, his wife,
1. JONATHAN, his heir.
2. George.   3. John.
4. William.
1. Mary.

The eldest son,
JONATHAN DARBY, of Leap, living 25 Dec. 1708, left issue, one son and two daus.,
1. JONATHAN, his heir.
1. Sarah, *m.* — Atkinson.   2. Mary, *m.* — Gray.
The only son,

JONATHAN DARBY, of Leap, J.P., living 25 Dec. 1708. His wife, Anna Maria, dau. of Benjamin Frend, of Boskell, co. Limerick, was living 1744. His will, dated 13 Dec. 1742, was proved 22 Feb. 1743-4. He left issue, three sons and three daus., of whom,
1. JONATHAN, s. his father.
2. Damer, of Dublin, *m.* 1st, Letitia, dau. of Robert Lovett, by whom he had issue an ony dau.,
   Sarah, *m.* 1st, 1773, Lieut. Thomas Eyre (who *d.* 1775) and 2ndly, 1776, Thomas Tydd.
He *m.* 2ndly, 1776, Mrs. Sarah Eccles, and *d.* 1791.
3. Japhet, *m.* 1751, Sophia West.
1. Anne, *m.* (setts. dated 16 and 17 July, 1736) Rev. Isaac Weld.
2. Anne, *m.* 1745, Samuel Laban, of Dublin.
3. Lucy.

The eldest son,
JONATHAN DARBY, of Leap, *b.* 1713 ; *m.* (setts. dated 10 and 11 May, 1745) Susanna, dau. of Jonathan Lovett, of Dromoyle, King's Co., and *d.* 1776, having had issue,
1. JONATHAN, of Leap, High Sheriff King's Co. 1787, *m.* his cousin, Eleanor, dau. of Jonathan Lovett, of Kingsmill, co. Tipperary, and left an only child,
   Eleanor.
2. Robert, *b.* 1747, *d.* 1764.
3. HENRY D'ESTERRE (Sir), K.C.B., of Leap Castle, Adm. R.N., distinguished for his gallant conduct in command of H.M.S. "Bellerophon" at the Battle of the Nile, *b.* 1749, *d. unm.* 1823.
4. JOHN, of whom presently.
5. William Lovett, *b.* 1753 ; *m.* Elizabeth, dau. of John Hawkshaw, and *d.* 1804, having had a son,
   Jonathan Lovett (Rev.), *m.* Anne Johns, and *d.* 1858.
6. Verney, of Dublin, and of Annvilla, King's Co., High Sheriff King's Co. 1799, M.P. for Gowran, *b.* 1754 ; *m.* 11 Nov. 1778, Anna Maria, dau. of George Maquay, and *d.* 1818, having had issue,
   1. William, who left issue.
   1. Maria.
   2. Jane, *m.* Surg. Burke, Rifle Brigade.
7. Christopher, Gen. in the Army, *b.* 1758 ; *m.* Ruth, dau. of George Wharton, Lieut.-Gov. of Rhode Island, America, and *d.s.p.* 1832.
8. Edward Hawke, *m.* Ruth Cumberland, and had one son and two daus.,
   1. Jonathan, Capt. 54th Regt., *d.* in Jamaica.
   1. Susanna, *m.* 1815, Very Rev. John Head, Dean of Killaloe, and had issue.
   2. Harriet.
1. Sarah, *m.* her cousin, Sir Jonathan Lovett, Bart., of Liscombe, Bucks, who *d.s.p.m.s.* 12 Jan. 1812. She was bur. 14 May, 1836.

The 4th son,
JOHN DARBY, of Marklye, Sussex, and afterwards of Leap Castle, King's Co., *b.* 1751 ; *m.* 1784, Anne, dau. of Samuel Vaughan. She *d.* 1847. He *d.* 1834, leaving issue,
1. Jonathan, B.A., Ch. Ch. Oxford, *b.* 1787 ; *d. unm.*
2. WILLIAM HENRY, his heir.
3. Christopher Lovett (Rev.), of Kells Priory, co. Kilkenny, M.A. Ch. Ch. Oxford, *b.* 1792 ; *m.* 1817, Mary. dau. of Alexander Boyle and Grace his wife, dau. of Richard Vicars. She *d.* 1869.
He *d.* 1874, leaving issue,
   1. Jonathan, *b.* 1820 ; *d. unm.* 1856.
   2. Christopher Lovett, *b.* 1825 ; *d.* 1884.
   3. John Lionel (Very Rev.), D.D., T.C.D., Dean of Chester, *b.* 20 Nov. 1831 ; *m.* 4 May, 1871, Cecilia Catharine, dau. of the late Rev. Canon Frank George Hopwood, by Lady Ellinor Mary his wife, dau. of the 13th Earl of Derby, and has issue,
      (1) Lionel Frank Christopher, Barrister-at-Law, *b.* 29 April, 1873.
      (2) Arthur John Lovett, *b.* 9 Jan. 1876.
      (3) Edward Henry d'Esterre, *b.* 7 March, 1880.
      (1) Mary Cecilia, *b.* 15 March, 1872.
      (2) Constance Ellinor Katharine, *b.* 22 May, 1882.
   1. Anne, *b.* 1818 ; *d. unm.* 1887.
   2. Mary, *b.* 1823 ; *m.* 1868, the late Rev. George Edward Haviland, of Warbleton, Sussex. He *d.* 1889. She *d.* 1893, leaving issue.
   3. Elizabeth La Touche, *b.* 1826 ; *d. unm.* 1851.
   4. Catharine Frances, *b.* 1828 ; *d. unm.* 1874.
4. George, of Marklye, Sussex, M.P. for E. Sussex 1837-46, Barrister-at-Law, M.A., *b.* 1796, *m.* 1827, Maria, dau. of Samuel Homfray, M.P., and *d.* 1878, having had issue,
   1. Jonathan George Norton, M.A. Ch. Ch. Oxford, Barrister-at-Law, *b.* 1829, *m.* 1869, Susan, dau. of Nathan Wetherell, and *d.s.p.* 1870.
   2. John Ciere Scott (Rev.), M.A. Ch. Ch. Oxford, Rector of Machen, co. Monmouth, *b.* 1830 ; *m.* 1st, 3 June, 1863, Mary Lewis, dau. of Charles John Bigge, of Linden, Northumberland. She *d.* 1889, leaving issue,
      (1) John Charles Homfray, *b.* 1864.
      (2) Walter George, *b.* 1865 ; *m.* 1900, Violet, dau. of Richard Beeston, and has issue, Mary Dolla.
      (3) Selby Lovett, *b.* 1868, *d.* 1899.
      (4) Henry d'Esterre, *b.* 1868.
      (5) George Scott, *b.* 1870.
      (6) Herbert Milford, *b.* 1872 ; *m.* 1901, Ursula Taylor.
      (7) Frederic Milman, *b.* 1875.
   He *m.* 2ndly, 1892, Emily Mary, dau. of John Potter, of Machen. He *d.* 1900, having by her had issue,
      (8) William Edward Clere Augustus, *b.* 1893.

3. Edward George, b. 1837; m. 1870, Mary, dau. of Salisbury Everard, and has issue,
  (1) Harrie Edward, b. 1871.
  (2) Greville Lewis, b. 1872, d. same year.
  (3) Charles, b. 1874.
  (4) Francis William, b. 1876.
  (5) Jonathan George Salisbury, b. 1879; d. unm. 23 Feb. 1909.
  (6) Frederick John d'Esterre, b. 1880.
  (7) Robert Walter Homfray, b. 1884; d. unm. 25 Sept. 1906.
  (8) Richard John Purefoy, b. 1885; d. unm. 10 May, 1907.
  (1) Ann Gertrude Sarah, b. 1873.
  (2) Maria Katherine Letitia, b. 1877.
  (3) Charlotte Laura, b. 1878, d. 1881.
  (4) Mary, b. and d. 1881.
4. William Homfray Fuller, b. 1846, d. 1890.
1. Maria Jane, b. 1828; m. 1855, Rev. George Edward Haviland. He d. 1889, leaving issue.
2. Letitia Lovett, b. 1833, d. 1861.
3. Eleanor Anne, b. 1834; d. unm. 16 June, 1910.
4. Katherine Maria, b. 1836, d. 1860.
5. Mary, b. 1840, d. 1891.
6. Anne Rodney, b. 1842.
7. Frances St. Quinton, b. 1844.
8. Clara Elizabeth, b. 1848, d. 1892.
5. Horatio d'Esterre, b. 1798; d. unm. 1885.
6. John Nelson, b. 1800, d. unm. 1882.
1. Susannah, b. 1785; m. 6 Jan. 1806, Right Hon. Edward Pennefather, Lord Chief Justice of Ireland, and d. 6 April, 1862, leaving by him (who d. 6 Sept. 1847) issue (see PENNEFATHER of *Rathsallagh*).
2. Sarah, b. 1794, d. unm. 1877.
3. Letitia Lovett, b. 1802.

The eldest surviving son,
WILLIAM HENRY DARBY, of Leap Castle, M.A. Ch. Ch. Oxford, b. 1790; m. 1st, Laura Charlotte, dau. of Edward Jeremiah Curteis, of Windmill Hill, Sussex. She d. 27 March, 1846, leaving issue,
1. Jonathan, J.P. King's Co., b. 25 June, 1828; m. 7 Sept. 1853, his cousin, Caroline Curteis, dau. of John Graham, of the Elms, Sussex, and d.v.p. 19 Sept. 1872, having had issue,
  1. Jonathan, b. 1 July, 1854; d. an infant.
  2. JONATHAN CHARLES, s. his grandfather.
  3. Horatio Graham, b. 5 July, 1856; m. Christine Adami, and d. Feb. 1895. She d.s.p.
  4. William Reginald, b. 18 Dec. 1865.
  1. Laura Caroline, b. 25 Jan. 1858; m. 29 Aug. 1887, Joseph Michael Plunkett, who adopted the name of MAC FADDEN, and has issue.
  2. Florence Anne, b. 13 Feb. 1860; d. unm. 3 Nov. 1895.
  3. Mary Georgiana (Lily), b. 3 Feb. 1862; m. 1886, Federingo Sartory, and d. 2 May, 1902.
  4. Charlotte Curteis, b. 18 Aug. 1867.
1. Mary Charlotte, m. William Johns, and d. having had issue.
He m. 2ndly, 28 Jan. 1848, Elizabeth, dau. of William Drought. She d. Dec. 1882, leaving issue,
2. William Henry, Col. R.A. (*Naval and Military Club*), b. 8 March, 1855; m. 19 July, 1887, Gertrude, dau. of the late John Charlesworth Dodgson Charlesworth, of Chapelthorpe Hall, Yorks. and has issue,
William Henry D'Esterre, b. 27 July, 1888, B.A. Ch. Ch. Oxford.
3. John Nelson, b. 1864.
2. Elizabeth Henrietta, m. 5 Aug. 1869, W. P. H. Lloyd Vaughan, of Golden Grove (*see that family*).
3. Wilhelmina Katharine Anne, m. 6 Dec. 1878, Major Ivar MacIvor, C.I.E. Indian Army, son of the Rev. James MacIvor, D.D., and has issue. He d. 1897.
4. Laura Susan Eleanor, m. 1890, Rev. Owen Charles Carr (*see* CARR-ELLISON).
5. Theodora Lovett, m. 11 Nov. 1879, Col. Frederick Mackenzie Fraser, of Castle Fraser, who d.s.p. 19 May, 1897 (*see that family*).
6. Laura Caroline, m. 25 July, 1878, John Tyndall, of Glenlock, Ceylon, and had issue. He d. 1897. She d. 1907.
7. Monica Gertrude, m. 1880, Major T. S. Wellesley Bernard, late 44th Regt. (d. 1 Feb. 1905), and has issue, four daus. (*see* BERNARD *of Castle Bernard*).
8. Maude Mary, m. 17 Feb. 1887, Col. Robert Chambers Hellard C.B., R.E., son of the late Charles Bettesworth Hellard, of Portsmouth.
9. Anne Vaughan, m. 27 Nov. 1896, Col. William Rice Edwards C.M.G., M.D., Indian Med. Service (*see* EDWARDS *of Nouington*).
Mr. W. H. Darby d. 20 Feb. 1880, and was s. by his grandson.

Arms—Az. on a chevron arg. between three garbs or a naval coronet of the first between two anchors sa., in the centre chief pendent from a riband of the second fimbriated of the field a representation of the gold medal conferred on Adm. Sir Henry d'Esterre Darby, K.C.B., beneath the medal the word "Nile" in gold letters on the field. **Crest**—A garb or banded with a naval crown az. in front of an anchor in bend sinister sa. **Motto**—Spero meliora.

Seat—Leap Castle, Roscrea, King's Co. **Club**—Kildare Street.

D'ARCY OF CORBETSTOWN.

FRANCIS MEAGER D'ARCY, of The Leasowes, Penn, co. Staffs, b. 28 Nov. 1864; present representative and heir male of D'Arcy of Corbetstown; m. 12 Oct. 1895, Rose Patrice, dau. of the late S. J. Fellows, of Wolverhampton, and has issue,
1. JOHN LESLIE FELLOWS, b. 23 Dec. 1896.
2. Frank Geoffrey, b. 13 Dec. 1899.
1. Joan, b. 2 Oct. 1902.
2. Frances Margret, b. 24 May, 1904.

Lineage.—This family descends from the great Irish branch of the Anglo-Norman family of D'Arcy, descended from Sir JOHN D'ARCY, Lord Deputy of Ireland A.D. 1323. Corbetstown, the residence of this line, was for centuries the estate of D'ARCY of Plattyn, the senior line of the family. NICHOLAS D'ARCY, of Platten, who was the owner of Corbetstown, Ballyeighter, &c., forfeited after 1641. He m. twice, 1st, Catherine, dau. of James Purcell, of Loughmore, by whom he had
1. George, who d.v.p. leaving a son,
  NICHOLAS, of Plattyn, heir to his grandfather.
He m. 2ndly, Frances, widow of Sir Christopher Bellew, Knt. of Castleton, by whom he had
2. Edward.
3. Christopher.
4. Thomas.
5. Arthur
6. Nicholas.
On all of these children he made settlements, charging his lands of Ballyeighter, &c. The grandson,
NICHOLAS D'ARCY, of Plattyn, s. his grandfather, and was declared an "Innocent Papist" in 1666, when he was restored to his lands, but he forfeited after 1690, and Corbetstown was sold by the Commissioners of Forfeited Estates, 1703, to James Young. This James Young demised Corbetstown to
CHRISTOPHER D'ARCY, for the lives of his wife Mary and his eldest son, with a clause for perpetual renewal. In 1702 he lodge with the Chichester Honor Commissioners a claim on the lands of Ballyeighter, created by Nicholas D'Arcy, of Plattyn, under deed of 23 April, 1683. He and his wife were both dead in 1738, when his eldest son and heir,
FRANCIS D'ARCY, of Corbetstown, obtained a renewal of the lease of that family, 1 Feb. that year. He d. intestate, leaving, by Margaret his wife, two sons, Thomas, who s. him and d.s.p., and JOHN D'ARCY, of Corbetstown, who s. his brother and administered to his father, 13 Oct. 1756. He m. Elizabeth Fetherston, of the House of Bracklyn, and had issue,
1. FRANCIS, his heir.
2. Judge Thomas, Capt. 80th Regt., and Brevet-Major 4th Royal Veteran Batt., b. 8 Sept. 1773; m. 16 May, 1799, Elizabeth, dau. of William Sheppard, of Wolverhampton, co. Stafford, and had issue, Thomas Edward Whitehall, of Wolverhampton, father, by Mary Anne his wife, dau. of Edward Willcox, of Wolverhampton, of JOHN SHEPPARD D'ARCY, late representative and heir male of D'ARCY of Corbetstown.
3. John Fetherston.

The eldest son,
FRANCIS D'ARCY, of Corbetstown, s. his father, m. Eleanor Briscoe, and d. 1830, when he was by his only son,
JOHN D'ARCY, of Corbetstown, who d. unm., when the representation of the family devolved on his kinsman, the heir male of his uncle, Judge Thomas D'Arcy, whose grandson,
JOHN SHEPPARD D'ARCY, of Finchfield, near Wolverhampton, b. 29 July, 1840; m. 16 Feb. 1864, Emily, dau. of William Meager, of Swansea, and d. 27 Dec. 1885, having had issue,
1. FRANCIS MEAGER, present representative.
2. Cuthbert Edward, b. 14 March, 1872.
3. Basil Norman, b. 16 Oct. 1874.
4. Lionel John Montague, b. 12 Oct. 1877.
5. Gerald Claude Randolph, b. 7 Feb. 1882.
1. Louise Madeline, m. Charles Whitney.
2. Blanche Emily, m. Herbert Daniel Northwood.

Arms—Az. semée of cross-crosslets and three cinquefoils arg. **Crest**—On a chapeau gu. turned up erm. a bull sa. armed or. **Motto**—Un Dieu un roi.

Residence—The Leasowes, near Wolverhampton.

D'ARCY OF NEW FOREST.

HYACINTH D'ARCY, of New Forest, co. Galway, Fisher Hill, co. Mayo, and Rockvale, co. Clare, b. 26 Feb. 1830; J.P. and D.L. co. Galway, and High Sheriff 1877; s. his brother 1869; m. 13 June, 1878, Louisa Alicia, dau. of Samuel James Brown, J.P. and D.L., of Loftus Hill, co. York, and has issue,

1. JAMES, b. 29 March, 1880.
2. Richard, b. 10 April, 1881.
3. Isidore, b. 26 June, 1882.
4. Hyacinth, b. 13 Nov. 1883.
5. Lionel George, b. 2 Feb. 1888.
1. Mary L. E.
2. Sophia J. M.
3. Teresa M.
4. Maud.

Lineage.—MARTIN D'ARCY, High Sheriff co. Galway, was 2nd son of James D'Arcy, of Kiltullagh, Vice-President of Connaught temp. Queen ELIZABETH. He was descended, according to Hardiman and the pedigree recorded at Ulster's Office in 1770, from the Anglo-Norman family of D'ARCY; but according to O'Donovan, on the authority of the Irish genealogist, MacFerbis, he was descended from Walter Riabhach O'Dorchaidhe, the first man of the family who came to Galway. Martin D'Arcy suffered much persecution from Thomas Wentworth, Earl of Strafford, and d. 3 Jan. 1636. His arms "Arg., a cross between four crosses patée sa." are recorded in Ulster's Office. He m. Christian, dau. of Richard Martin, Alderman of Galway, and had a son and heir,

RICHARD D'ARCY, m. Mary, dau. of Nicholas Browne, of Galway, and was father of

MARTIN D'ARCY, of Clonuane, co. Clare, m. 20 May, 1653, Catherine, dau. of Sir Richard Blake, Bart. of Ardfry, and d. 17 Oct. 1690, leaving issue,

RICHARD D'ARCY, of Clonuane, m. Catherine, dau. of Major Peter Blake, of Corbally, and d. 16 Dec. 1727, leaving a son,

DOMINICK D'ARCY, of Rockvale, co. Clare, m. Elizabeth, dau. of James Butler, of Doon, in the same county, and d. 26 Dec. 1727, leaving three sons, Richard, d.s.p.; James, d.s.p. 19 Aug. 1772; and DOMINICK; and a dau. m. M. Hogan, of Cross. The youngest son,

DOMINICK D'ARCY, of Clonuane, near Rockvale, m. Bridget, dau. of Stephen Blake, of Moorfield, co. Galway, and had issue,
1. RICHARD, his heir.
2. James, Barrister-at-Law, d. unm. 1790.
1. Mary Anne, m. Christopher O'Brien, of Ennistymon, co. Clare, and d. 1804.

The elder son and heir,

RICHARD D'ARCY, of Rockvale, Deputy-Governor co. Galway, Capt. Yeomanry Cavalry, m. 30 Nov. 1783, Mary, dau. of John Blake, of the city of Dublin (a younger brother of Maurice Blake, of Tower Hill, co. Mayo), and by her had six sons, and d. 8 July, 1832.

1. Dominick, b. 1784, Capt. 47th Regt.; d.s.p. 1811.
2. John, d.s.p. 1822.
3. JAMES, of whom presently.
4. Richard, d.s.p.
5. Isidore, b. 1789, an Officer 56th Regt.; d.s.p. 8 Dec. 1850.
6. Martin, of Wellfort, co. Galway, b. 1791; m. 17 June, 1817, Henrietta, dau. of Dominick Beytagh, of Cappagh House, and dying 1844, left issue,
   1. Richard.   2. Dominick.
   3. John.   4. James.
   1. Mary.

The 3rd son,

JAMES D'ARCY, of New Forest, J.P., b. 10 Feb. 1787; m. 20 Sept. 1827, Elizabeth, dau. of Hyacinth Chevers, of Killyan, and d. 8 April, 1851, leaving issue,

1. RICHARD, of New Forest, J.P. and D.L., b. 20 April, 1829; High Sheriff co. Galway, 1863; m. 30 Dec. 1868, Louisa Margaret, eldest dau. of William Murphy, by Margaret O'Conor his wife, niece of O'Conor Don, and d.s.p. 23 Sept. 1869.
2. HYACINTH, now of New Forest.
1. Mary.   2. Elizabeth.

Arms—Az. semée of cross-crosslets and three cinquefoils arg. Crest—On a chapeau gu. turned up erm. a bull sa. armed or. Motto—Un Dieu un roi.

Seats—New Forest, Ballinasloe, co. Galway; Fisher Hill, Castlebar, Rockvale, Gort.

D'ARCY OF HYDE PARK.

REV. GEORGE JAMES AUDOMAR D'ARCY, of Hyde Park, co. Westmeath, Vicar of Worksop, Notts., and Rural Dean, M.A. Oxon, b. 11 Oct. 1861.

Lineage.—JOHN D'ARCY, 1ST LORD D'ARCY DE KNAYTH (see BURKE's Peerage), governed Ireland as justiciary for many years. He fought against Scotland on many occasions with distinction especially at the Battle of Halidon Hill (1333). He was Constable of the Tower of London during the preparations for the war with France (1346), and was one of the principal bannerets at Crecy, flying the banner of the D'Arcy's of Noeton. He left the Siege of Calais to take charge of David Bruce. He m. 1st, Emmeline, dau. and heir of Walter Heron, and by her had issue,

John, whose heirs general have been the LORDS D'ARCY DE KNAYTH (see BURKE's Peerage, D'ARCY DE KNAYTH, B.).

He m. 2ndly, 3 July, 1329, Joan, widow of Thomas FitzGerald, Earl of Kildare, dau. of Richard de Burgh, Earl of Ulster, by whom he had issue (with three sons, who all d.s.p.),

WILLIAM, of whom we treat.

Elizabeth, who m. James Butler, Earl of Ormonde.

Lord D'Arcy d. 30 May, 1347. His son,

SIR WILLIAM D'ARCY, was present at Crecy and was the founder of the house of D'Arcy of Plattyn, co. Meath. He inherited lands granted by EDWARD III to his father and mother and to their heirs male for the good services rendered by his father to EDWARD II. Hyde Park, co. Westmeath, is a part of the land comprised in the grant. He was b. at Maynooth 1330; m. Catherine, dau. of Robert Fitzgerald, of Allen, co. Kildare, and had issue,

SIR JOHN D'ARCY of Plattyn a minor and heir to his grandmother in the manor of Martyr, co. Kildare 1362. He was Sheriff of Meath 1404 and 1415, and m. Jane Pettit, by whom he had issue,

WILLIAM D'ARCY, of Plattyn, who m. Anne Barnewall, of Crickstown, co. Westmeath, and by her had issue,

JOHN D'ARCY, of Plattyn, who m. Margaret Fleming, dau. of Lord Slane, by whom he had issue,

1. WILLIAM, of whom next.
2. Nicholas, ancestor of D'Arcy of Gorteen (see D'ARCY of Stanmore).

The elder son,

SIR WILLIAM D'ARCY, of Plattyn, who was living 1477, m. Isabel (or Elizabeth), dau. of Christopher Plunkett, of Killeen, by whom he had issue,

SIR WILLIAM D'ARCY, of Plattyn, Vice-Treasurer of Ireland seized of the manors of Rathwire and Lynn, co. Westmeath, 1. HENRY VIII. He m. Margaret, dau. of Nicholas St. Lawrence Baron Howth, and d. 1540, having had issue,

GEORGE D'ARCY, of Plattyn. He m. Jane, dau. and heir of Tuite M'Riccard, of Sonagh, and by her had issue,

1. William (Sir), of Plattyn, the ancestor of the subsequent D'Arcys of Plattyn. The estates were forfeited temp. Commonwealth, and the male issue of this branch is now extinct.
2. THOMAS, of whom next.

The younger son,

THOMAS D'ARCY, of Dunmow, co. Meath, m. Margaret, dau. of Richard Kiltole, and was father of JOHN D'ARCY, of Dunmow, whose son and heir, WILLIAM D'ARCY, of Dunmow, m. Margaret Brandon, niece of Thomas Brandon, of Dundalk, and had a son, THOMAS D'ARCY, of Dunmow, aged 28 in 1630, m. Alicia Nugent, of New Haggard, and was father of GEORGE D'ARCY, of Dunmow, declared an innocent Papist 20 Aug. 1663, who, by Alice his wife, dau. of Thomas Nugent, of Clonlost, co. Westmeath, had a son, THOMAS, of Lisnabin, co. Westmeath, who predeceased his father, leaving by Jane his wife, dau. of Bellew, of Bellewstown, co. Meath, a son and successor to his grandfather, viz.,

JOHN D'ARCY, of Dunmow, m. 1727, Elizabeth, dau. and coheiress of Thomas Judge, of Grangebeg, co. Westmeath, and by her (who d. 1773) had

1. JUDGE, of Dunmow and Grangebeg, d. 1766, leaving by Elizabeth Nugent his wife, an only dau. and heiress,
   ELIZA, m. 31 March, 1788, Col. George's Marcus Irvine, of Castle Irvine, co. Fermanagh, and d. 1829, leaving issue (see that family).
2. JAMES, of whom we treat.

The younger son,

JAMES D'ARCY, of Hyde Park, co. Westmeath, b. 1740; m. 1766, Martha, dau. of William Grierson, of Deanstown, co. Dublin, and heiress of Joshua Palin, and by her (who d. 1782) had issue,

1. JOHN, his heir.
2. Joshua (Rev.), Rector of Killalon, Diocese of Meath, m. 1811, Sarah, dau. of Capt. Fleming, co. Kildare, and had issue, six sons and three daus, of whom the eldest,
   JOHN SAMUEL D'ARCY, of Bagatelle, co. Westmeath, m. 1834, Louisa, only dau. of William Handcock, by Anne his wife, dau. of John Henry, of Carrintrilly, co. Galway, and d. 1849, having had issue two sons and two daus.

8. Thomas (dec.), Major in the Army, and at his death Inspector-General of Police in Ulster. He m. Eliza, dau. of Captain Buchanan, and has left two sons and three daus. ; the eldest son, William James, who was at the Irish Bar, d.s.p. 1846.
1. Eliza, m. Major Henry Charles Sirr, of the City of Dublin, and had two sons, Joseph D'Arcy Sirr, Rector of Kilcoman ; Henry Charles Sirr, at the English Bar ; and two daus.
2. Alice.   3. Martha, m. F. Handy.
4. Frances, m. Joseph Fox, of Doolistown, co. Meath, and had issue three daus.
5. Harriet, m. James Fox, of Galtrim, co. Meath, and had issue three sons and three daus.

Mr. D'Arcy d. 1803, and was s. by his eldest son,
JOHN D'ARCY, of Hyde Park, b. 1767, J.P. ; m. 1st, 1803, Emily, dau. of Thomas Purdon, of Huntingdon, co. Westmeath, which lady d.s.p. 1803, and 2ndly, 8 Oct. 1817, Mary Anne, dau. and co-heir of Thomas Cary, of Dublin, and by her (who d. 1856) had issue,
1. GEORGE JAMES NORMAN, of Hyde Park.
2. Thomas Lavallin, of Ginnet's Park, co. Meath, b. 14 March, 1821 ; m. 1st, 27 March, 1845, Maria Louisa, youngest dau. of James Fox, of Galtrim, co. Meath, and by her (who d. 1871) had issue,
    1. John Bertram (Rev.), b. 27 Dec. 1845.
    2. Lavallin Cary, b. 6 May, 1847.
    1. Hariotte Alicia, d. unm.   2. Frances Marianne, d. unm.
    3. Maria Louisa, d. unm.
He m. 2ndly, 1872, Catherine Grace, dau. of Rev. James Crawford, and d. 1886.
3. John Charles, of Mount Tallant, co. Dublin, b. 26 March, 1828 ; m. 22 Jan. 1852, Henrietta Anna, eldest dau. of Thomas Brierly, of Dublin, and d. 30 Sept. 1902, leaving issue,
    1. Charles Frederick (Right Rev.), M.A., D.D., Bishop of Down and Connor and Dromore, late of Ossory, Ferns, and Leighlin, and previously of Clogher, formerly Vicar and Dean of Belfast 1900–03, and Canon of St. Patrick's, Dublin (Culloden, Craigavad, co. Down), b. 2 Jan. 1859 ; m. 12 June, 1889, Harriet Le Bertt, eldest dau. of the late Richard Lewis, of Comrie, co. Down, and has issue,
       (1) John Conyers, b. 12 Feb. 1894.
       (1) Ellinor Marian.   (2) Henrietta Grace Lewis.
       (3) Dorothy Frances.
    1. Henrietta, dec.   2. Marion.
    3. Louisa Frances.
4. Anthony Ralph (Rev.), Rector of Nympsfield, co. Gloucester, b. 19 May, 1832 ; m. 19 Jan. 1860, Caroline, youngest dau. of Thomas Brierley, of Dublin, and d. 17 Sept. 1894, leaving issue,
    1. Ralph Francis, of Beach House, Kessingland, Suffolk, M.A. Cantab., b. 1864 ; m. 12 June, 1900, Dorothy Isabel Munro, eldest dau. of Edgell E. Westmacott, of Richmond, Surrey.
    2. Thomas Anthony.   3. Arthur.
    1. Marietta.   2. Adelaide
    1. Martha Emily.   2. Frances Louisa, d. 1903.
8. Phœbe Sophia, d. 1865.

Mr. D'Arcy d. 1846. The eldest son,
GEORGE JAMES NORMAN D'ARCY, of Hyde Park, co. Westmeath, J.P. cos. Meath and Westmeath, B.A. T.C.D., Barrister-at-Law b. 3 March, 1820, m. 1st, 30 Jan. 1856, Antoinette Jane, 2nd dau. of Anthony John Dopping, D.L., of Calmolvn, co. Meath, and by her (who d. Nov. 1877) had issue,
1. Norman John, b. 22 Nov. 1856 ; drowned in Lake Qu'Appelle, Canada, 5 May, 1882.
2. GEORGE JAMES AUDOMAR (Rev.), now of Hyde Park.
1. Annie, d. 1874.   2. May Cary.
3. Adela Maud Eliza.
Mr. D'Arcy m. 2ndly, Oct. 1882, Annie Ouseley, eldest dau. of Rev. Jeremiah Lane, Rector of Kilashee, Diocese of Kildare, and d. 1904, having by her had further issue,
4. Grace Ellinor Edith.   5. Florence Phœbe Gertrude.

Arms—1st and 4th : Az. semée of cross-crosslets and three cinquefoils, arg., for D'ARCY ; 2nd and 3rd : Quarterly gu. and arg., for TUITE. Crest—On a chapeau, or cap of maintenance, erm. turned up gu. a bull sa. armed or. Motto—Un Dieu, un roi.
Seat—Hyde Park, Killucan, co. Westmeath. Residence—The Vicarage, Worksop, Notts.

HALL-DARE OF NEWTOWNBARRY.

ROBERT WESTLEY HALL-DARE, of Newtownbarry House, co. Wexford, and East Hall, Wennington, Essex, J.P. and D.L. co. Wexford, J.P. co. Carlow, High Sheriff of Wexford 1891, and of Carlow 1896, late Capt. 9th Brig. N. Irish Div. R.A., b. 14 Oct. 1866 ; s. his father 1876; m. 6 April, 1896, Helen, 2nd dau. of the late John Taylor Gordon, of Nethermuir, Aberdeenshire, and Blackhouse, co. Ayr, and has issue,

1. ROBERT WESTLEY, b. 12 Aug. 1899.
2. Charles Grafton, b. 12 March. 1902.
1. Audrey, b. 11 May, 1897.
2. Daphne, b. 10 Sept. 1906.

Lineage.—ELIZABETH EATON, eldest dau. and co-heir of Henry Eaton, of North Lodge, Essex, by Elizabeth, his wife, last surviving child of George Mildmay, of Corbett's Stye, Essex, m. 1st, 1779, JOHN DARE, of Bentry Heath, Essex, and by him (who d. 1781) she had an only child,
John Hopkins-Dare, of Theydon Bois, Essex, who d. unm. 9 Jan. 1805.
Mrs. Dare m. 2ndly, 7 May, 1791, JOHN MARMADUKE GRAFTON, of Cranbrook House (only son of John Marmaduke Grafton, of Romford), who took the surname of DARE, in addition to that of GRAFTON, by Royal Sign Manual, dated 12 Dec. 1805, and d. 22 Nov. 1810. Mrs. Dare d. 24 March, 1823, leaving by her 2nd husband an only child,
ELIZABETH GRAFTON-DARE, b. 7 May, 1793 ; m. 8 Nov. 1815, ROBERT WESTLEY HALL, of Wyefield, and of Cranbrook, High Sheriff of Essex 1821, and M.P. for South Essex, who took by Royal Sign Manual, dated 25 April, 1823, the surname and arms of DARE in addition to those of HALL. Mr. Hall-Dare and his sister, Elizabeth Catherine (wife of Thomas Harper King, of Hay Hill, co. Gloucester), were the children of Robert Westley Hall, of Ilford Lodge and FitzWalters, Essex, by Maria Elizabeth his wife (m. 1785), widow of Abraham de Codyn, of Demerara, and dau. of Cornelius Brower, of the same place and grandchildren of the Rev. Westley Hall, who d. in London, circa 1770. The Rev. Westley Hall was son of one of the Halls of Hillsborough, Kent, m. the sister of Sir Robert Westley, Lord Mayor of London. Mr. Hall-Dare d. 20 May, 1836, and by his said wife, Elizabeth Grafton-Dare (who d. 18 Nov. 1858), left issue,
1. ROBERT WESTLEY, his heir.
2. John Grafton, b. 31 July, 1818 ; d. 25 Feb. 1819.
3. Henry, b. 8 Feb. 1825, formerly Capt. 23rd Royal Welsh Fusiliers, and late Under Treasurer of the Inner Temple ; m. 1st, 22 April, 1851, Agatha, dau. of S. T. Kekewich, M.P., and by her (who d. 12 Feb. 1878, aged 53) left issue,
    Henry Arthur Kekewich, Barrister-at-Law, b. 29 May, 1854 ; d 27 Nov. 1880.
    Blanche, m. 17 Nov. 1880, John Lee Warner, of the Indian Civil Service, and has issue.
Mr. Henry Hall-Dare m. 2ndly, 24 May, 1882, Alice Mary, dau. of Daniel Tupper, of Melrose, Guernsey.
4. Arthur Charles, b. 1836 ; d. an infant.
5. Francis Marmaduke, late 23rd Royal Welsh Fusiliers, b. 28 Feb. 1830 ; d May, 1867.
1. Mary Elizabeth, d. unm. 1 April, 1908.
2. Emma Burton, m. Thomas Hilton Bothamley, d. 24 Jan. 1877, leaving issue.
3. Anne Mildmay, d. 10 Oct. 1823.   4. Agnes, dec.
5. Elizabeth, m. Rev J. T. R, Fussell, and d. 11 April, 1882, leaving issue.

The eldest son,
ROBERT WESTLEY HALL-DARE, of FitzWalters, Essex, b. 21 Jan. 1817 ; m. 18 April, 1839, Frances Anna Catherine, dau. of Gustavus Lambart, of Beauparc, co. Meath, and by her (who d. 2 Sept. 1862) had issue,
1. ROBERT WESTLEY, his heir.
2. Charles, d. 31 Jan. 1876, aged 15.
1. Olivia Frances Grafton, m. July, 1883, Rev. Richard Johnston, of Kilmore, co. Armagh, and d. Nov. 1906.
2. Mabel Virginia Anna, m. Aug. 1877, J. Theodore Bent.
3. Ethel Constance Mary, m. 5 July, 1870, Beachamp Frederick Bageanal, of Benekerry, co. Carlow.
4. Frances Maria, m. 11 June, 1891, Rev. Edward Waller Hobson, of Colnan, co. Tipperary, Canon of St. Patrick's Cathedral, Armagh, and Rector of Portadown.
Mr. Hall-Dare d. 23 April, 1866. His elder son,
ROBERT WESTLEY HALL-DARE, of Newtonbarry House, co. Wexford and Theydon Bois, Essex, J.P. and D.L., co. Wexford (High Sheriff 1872), and J.P. co. Carlow, High Sheriff 1868, b. 8 June, 1840 ; m. 27 Oct. 1863, Caroline Susan Henrietta, 2nd dau. of Henry Newton, of Mount Leinster Lodge, co. Carlow, by Elizabeth Doyne his wife, and had issue,
1. John Marmaduke, b. 13 Sept. 1865 ; d. an infant.
2. ROBERT WESTLEY, now of Newtonbarry.
3. Arthur Mildmay, b. 11 Oct. 1867 ; m. 8 July, 1897, Edith Clare, eld. dau. of Henry C. FitzHerbert, of Abbeyleix, Queen's Co. (see FITZHERBERT of Black Castle), and has issue,
    1. Francis Miles, b. 14 Jan., d. 15 Feb. 1900.
    2. Derrick Arthur, b. 4 Dec. 1900.
    1. Irene Clare, b. 3 Aug. 1898.
1. Elizabeth Frances, m. 7 July, 1886, John Olphert Adair, and has issue.
2. Hilda Mary, m. 30 Dec. 1890, James Erskine Wise Booth, and has issue.
3. Evelyn Una, m. 30 April, 1896, Richard Bankes Barron, 2nd son of Richard Bankes Barron, of Roxbury, Chertsey, and has issue.
He d. 18 March, 1876, aged 35.

Arms—Quarterly : 1st and 4th, az., a lion rampant arg. between three lozenges each charged with an increscent gu., in chief a cross-crosslet gold, for DARE ; 2nd and 3rd, sa., on a chevron engrailed between three battle-axes erect or, as many eagles displayed of the field, for HALL. Crests—For DARE : A demi-lion rampant az., bezantée, charged on the shoulder with a cross-crosslet or, and holding between the paws a lozenge charged with an increscent gu. in the arms ; for HALL : A horse's head couped sa.

Daunt. THE LANDED GENTRY. 166

semée of mullets or, armed ppr., bridled arg., on the head two ostrich feathers of the first and third, and holding in the mouth a battle-axe or. *Motto*—Loyauté sans tache.
Seat—Newtownbarry House, Newtownbarry, co. Wexford, and East Hall, Wennington, Essex. *Clubs*—Carlton and Kildare Street.

DAUNT OF TRACTON ABBEY.

REV. ACHILLES DAUNT, of Tracton Abbey, co. Cork, M.A. Oxon, Rector of Broome, co. Norfolk, 1892-6, Curate of Wimborne, Dorset, 1896 to 1898, and Curate of Sherborne, 1899, Rector of Charlton, Horethorne, Dorset, 1906, *b.* 1867; *s.* his father 17 June, 1878 ; *m.* 1st, 27 July, 1892, Ida, dau. of the late Sir Godfrey Carey, of Rozel, Guernsey, Bailiff, and has issue,

1. ACHILLES, *b.* 26 Oct. 1894.

He *m.* 2ndly, 4 Feb. 1902, Georgina Græme, dau. of Rev. Lawrence Græme Allan Roberts, Rector of Lillington, Dorset, formerly Commander R.N., and has further issue,

2. Leslie Henry Græme, *b.* 19 Jan. 1904.

Lineage.—SIMON DAUNT, living in co. Gloucester *circa* 1380 was *s.* at his decease by his eldest son,

NICHOLAS DAUNT, who *m.* Alice, dau. of Sir John de Tracy, Knt. of Sudely and Toddington, co. Gloucester, ancestor of Lord Sudeley of Toddington, and by her had a son,

NICHOLAS DAUNT, who was living in 1446. He *m.* Alice, dau. and co-heiress of Sir Walter Jordan, Knt. of Kamme, co. Dorset, by whom he had issue, Nicholas and JOHN. Of Nicholas we have no further record. The 2nd son,

JOHN DAUNT, *m.* Anne, dau. of Sir Robert Stawell, Knt. of Cotherston, Somerset, ancestor of the Lords Stawell, of Somerton, Having espoused the Lancastrian side in the wars of the Roses, he was called on by Prince Edward, son of King HENRY VI, and Margaret of Anjou, to aid the House of Lancaster in resisting EDWARD IV. The following is a copy of the Prince's letter to John Daunt :—

"Trusty and well beloved, Wee greet yowe well ; acquaint yowe that this day wee be arrived at Waymoth in safety, blessed be our Lorde, and at our landing wee have knowledge that the King's great rebell Edward, Earl of March, approacheth in armes towards the King's highness ; which Edward wee propose, with God's grace, to encounter with all haste possible. Wherefore wee hartely pray yowe, and in the King's name charge yowe, that yowe incontinent after the sighte hereof, come to us wheresoever wee be, with all such fellowship as yowe can make in your most defensible aray, as our trust is that yowe will do.

" Written at Waymoth aforesaid, the xiii day of April, [1471].

" Moreover wee will that yowe charge the Bayliffe of *mer rân Ption* to make all the people there come in their beste aray to us, in all haste, and that the said Bayliffe bring with him the rent for our Lady Day last past, and hee nor the tenants fayle not, as hee intends to have our favour.

EDWARD.

" To our trusty and well beloved John Daunt."

The eldest son and heir,

JOHN DAUNT, *m.* Margery, dau. and sole heiress of Robert Owlpen, Lord of the Manor of Owlpen, co. Gloucester, and became possessed of that manor in right of his wife, by whom he had

1. CHRISTOPHER. 2. John.
3. George. 4. Robert.
5. William.
1. Jane. 2. Alice.

He *d.* 1522, and was *s.* by his eldest son,

CHRISTOPHER DAUNT, of Owlpen, who *m.* Anne, dau. of Giles Basset, of Yewley, co. Gloucester, by whom he had issue,

1. THOMAS, of whom presently.
2. William. 3. Giles.
1. Alice, *m.* John Rogers, gent.

His eldest son,

THOMAS DAUNT, of Owlpen, who *m.* Alice, dau. of William Throckmorton, of Tortworth, co. Gloucester, and aunt of Sir William Throckmorton, Bart., and *d.* 29 Nov. 1574, leaving issue,

1. Henry, of Owlpen, *m.* a dau. of Giles Hussey, of Moxcombe, Somerset, and *d.s.p.m.*
2. Thomas, of Owlpen, co. Gloucester, of Tracton Abbey, and of Gortigrenane, co. Cork, *m.* Mary, dau. of Bryan Jones, of Glamorgan, and *d.* 1620, having by her (who *d.* 1631) had issue,
   Thomas, of Owlpen and Gortigrenane, *m.* Catherine, dau. of John Clayton, of Chesters, and *d.* 1670, leaving issue,
   (1) Thomas, *m.* Eliza, dau. of Sir Gabriel Lowe, Knight of Newark, but *d.s.p.m.*

(2) Achilles, of Owlpen, *d. unm.*
(3) John, *d.* young.
(4) George, of Nohoval and Gortigrenane, *m.* Martha, dau. of Major Turner, of Bandonbridge, co. Cork, and *d.* 1697, leaving issue,
  1. Thomas, of Owlpen and Gortigrenane, *m.* 1697, Elizabeth, dau. of the Rev. George Synge, and *d.* 1745, leaving issue, twin sons,
     a. Thomas, of Owlpen, *d.s.p.*
     b. Achiles, of Owlpen, and Gortigrenane, *m.* 1742, his cousin, Anne, dau. of Henry Daunt, of Knocknamara, and left issue, a son,
       Thomas, of Owlpen and Gortigrenane, *b.* 1755 ; *m.* Mary, dau. of George Baker, of co. Cork, and *d.* 1803, leaving an only dau. and heiress,
       Mary, *m.* 1815, Thomas Anthony Stoughton, of Ballymorgan (*see that family*).
  2. Henry, of Knocknamara, *m.* 1706, Ann, dau. of Thomas Knolles, of Killeighty, co. Cork, and had, with other issue,
     a. Thomas (Rev.), of Fahalea, co. Cork, *b.* 1707 ; *m.* 1755, Lettice, dau. of John Digby, of Ladenstown, and had, with other issue, a son,
       Thomas, of Fahalea, *m.* June, 1779, his cousin, Frances, dau. of Rev. Achilles Daunt, of Newborough, and had issue,
         (a) Thomas Achiles, *b.* 1780 ; *m.* 31 Aug. 1806, Mary, dau. of John Coghlan, of Courtmacsherry, and had issue,
           (1) Thomas, of Killenure and Grange, *b.* 1807 ; *m.* 1828, Amelia, dau. of Major John Warren, 84th Regt., and had issue.
           (2) Henry, of Fahalea, *b.* 1812 ; *m.* 1832, Frances, dau. of Henry Busteed, and had issue.
         (b) George Digby, *b.* 1782, had issue.
         (c) Henry.
     b. Hungerford, *m.* Joyce, dau. of Jonas Travers, of Butlerstown, co. Cork, and had issue,
       George, M.D., of Cork, *b.* 1775 ; *m.* his cousin Mary, dau. of Thomas Daunt, of Fahalea, and had issue.
       Ann, *d. unm.*
  (1) Frances, *m.* Henry Tyre, of Hardwicke, co. Gloucester.
  (2) Catherine, *m.* Sir Peter Courthorpe, of Courtstown, M.P. for Cork 1661.
  Margaret, *m.* Barachias Baker, of Carrigroham Castle, co. Cork.
3. Giles.
4. WILLIAM, of whom presently.
1. Elizabeth, *m.* Christopher Kingscote, of Kingscote.
2. Mary, *m.* Robert Thorne.
3. Joyce, *m.* Humphrey Thorne.

The youngest son,

WILLIAM DAUNT, *m.* Mary, dau. of Thomas Hutton, of Hutton, co. York, by whom he had issue,
  1. WILLIAM. 2. Thomas, who *m.* Susan Curle.

He was *s.* by his elder son,

WILLIAM DAUNT, *m.* Mary, dau. of Isham Nowell. At this time we find in the MS. depositions preserved in Trinity Coll. Dublin, a claim made on the Government, in 1642, by James Daunt, described as " late of Tracton Abbey," for £622, on account of losses sustained in the Civil war of the preceding year. This James had been High Sheriff of co. Cork 1627. He was *s.* in the Tracton Abbey by

WILLIAM DAUNT, of Tracton Abbey, *m.* Jane, dau. of John Dolbear, of Cork, and *d.* 1676, leaving, with other issue, two sons,
  1. ACHILLES, his successor in Tracton.
  2. FRANCIS (*see DAUNT of Kilcascan*).

His elder son,

ACHILLES DAUNT, of Tracton Abbey, *m.* 1st, 1667, Elizabeth, dau. of Thomas Hungerford, of Inchidony, co. Cork, by whom he had issue,
  1. Thomas, *m.* 1692, Jane Saunders, and to him his father gave the lands of Kilpatrick, co. Cork.
  2. WILLIAM.
  1. Margaret. 2. Susanna.
  3. Angel.

He *m.* 2ndly, Margaret, dau. of — Shuler, and widow of Thomas Herrick, of Shippool, co. Cork, by whom he had issue,
  3. Francis. 4. John.
  5. Richard.

He *d.* 1711, and was *s.* in Tracton Abbey by his 2nd son,

WILLIAM DAUNT, of Tracton Abbey, *m.* 1st, 1700, Mary, dau. of William Bayly, by whom he had issue, 1. ACHILLES ; 2. William, *m.* 1739, Barbara Busteed ; 2. Bayly ; 4. George ; 5. James ; and 6. Swithin ; besides daus. He was *s.* by his eldest son,

ACHILLES DAUNT, of Tracton Abbey, *m.* 1727, Elizabeth, dau. of Edward Bullen, of Oldhead, near Kinsale, by whom he had issue,
  1. WILLIAM. 2. Edward.

He was *s.* by his elder son,

WILLIAM DAUNT, of Tracton Abbey, *m.* 1753, Anne, dau. of Thomas Austin, of Inskinny, co. Cork, by whom he had (with other issue) a son,

ACHILLES DAUNT, of Tracton Abbey, *m.* June, 1785, Mary, dau. of John Gillman, of Curraheen, co. Cork, and *d.* 1831, and was *s.* by his eldest son,

ACHILLES DAUNT, of Tracton Abbey, *m.* 3 Jan. 1831, Mary, 3rd dau. of John Isaac Heard, M.P. for Kinsale (*see that family*), and in 1839 High Sheriff of co. Cork, and *d.* 1871, having had issue,
  1. ACHILLES, of whom presently.
  2. John, Lieut. 39th Regt., *d.* 1856.

3. Robert, R.N., *d.* 1861.
4. William (Ven.), Rector of Queenstown, Archdeacon of Cloyne, co. Cork, *m.* 1877, Rosamond Anne, dau. of Sir Gilbert King, Bart. of Charlestown, co. Roscommon.
5. Edward Stephen (Rev.), Rector of Greystones, co. Wicklow, *m.* 10 July, 1873, Sarah Gertrude, eldest dau. of the Rev. Robert William Whelan, Canon St. Patrick's, Dublin, and grand-dau. of James Pratt, of Kinsale, co. Cork, and has issue,
  1. Edward Achilles, late Lieut. Norfolk Regt., *b.* 11 June, 1874.
  2. Robert Henry, *b.* 4 June, 1875; *d.* 19 April, 1893.
  3. Reginald Hope, *b.* 18 Nov. 1879; *d.* 18 July, 1881.
  4. William Percy, *b.* 25 Oct. 1883.
  5. Hugh Maurice, *b.* 14 Feb. 1893.
  1. Violet Mary Frances, *b.* 15 March, 1895.
4. Henry, *m.* Ethel, dau. of R. L. Warren.
1. Frances, *m.* George Newman Dunn, M.D.
2. Mary.   3. Martha Anne, *d.*
4. Eleanor H.

His eldest son,
Very Rev. Achilles Daunt, D.D., of Tracton Abbey, Dean of Cork, who *m.* 24 Feb. 1863, Catherine Mary, eldest dau. of Rev. John Leslie, of Castlemartyr, and *d.* 17 June, 1878, leaving issue,
  1. Achilles, now of Tracton Abbey.
  1. Mary Leslie, *b.* 7 Nov. 1865.
  2. Emily Gertrude, *b.* 20 Jan. 1867.

Arms—Quarterly: 1st and 4th arg., a chevron sa., between three choughs' heads ppr. (Daunt); 2nd and 3rd, sa. a chevron arg. between three owls (Owlepen). *Crest*—A bugle horn or, stringed sa. *Motto*—Vigilo et spero.

Seat—Tracton Abbey, Kinsale, co. Cork. *Residence*—Charlton Horethorne, Sherborne, Dorset.

DAUNT OF KILCASCAN.

Achilles Thomas Daunt, of Kilcascan Castle, co. Cork, J.P., *b.* 9 Oct. 1849; *m.* 15 May, 1877, Anna Maria, dau. of Bartholomew Corballis, of Berwick, and niece of John Corballis, Q.C., of Rosemount, co. Dublin, and has issue,
1. Achilles Henry Wilson Joseph Corballis, *b.* 20 July, 1879; *d.* 6 Sept. same year.
2. Achilles Thomas Wilson O'Neill, *b.* 15 Aug. 1880; *m.* 1909, Elizabeth, dau. of George Dey, of Moose Creek, Ontario, and has issue,
  Mary Dorothea, *b.* 1910.
3. Reginald Nigel, *b.* 31 Jan. 1889.
1. Mary Margaret Alicia, *b.* 8 July, 1878; *d.* Feb. 1879.
2. Mary Henrietta Frances Louisa O'Neill, *b.* 2 June, 1882; *m.* 3 March, 1906, F. Goring Wilmer, only son of the late Henry Chudleigh Wilmer, 85th Regt.
3. Mary Lucy Dorothea O'Neill, *b.* 9 Sept. 1883.

Lineage.—William Daunt, of Tracton Abbey (*see preceding family*), *d.* 1676, leaving a 2nd son,
Francis Daunt, of Knockatour, co. Cork, *m.* 1667, Mary, dau. of George Wood, Gent., of Ballymony, same co., by whom he had issue, 1. George, of Knockatour, *m.* 1692, Dorothy, dau. of Thomas Knolles, of Killeighy, co. Cork, by whom he had issue; 2. William, of whom presently; 3. Francis, *m.* 1700, Mary, dau. of — Austin, by whom he had, with other issue, Samuel Daunt, of Knocknasillagh, High Sheriff co. Cork 1749. The 2nd son,
William Daunt, of Kilcascan, *m.* 1697, Rachael, dau. of Thomas Knolles, of Killeighy, by whom he had (besides other issue),
  1. Joseph.
  2. Francis, who *d.s.p.*
He acquired Kilcascan 1712, and dying 1760, was s. by his eldest son,
Joseph Daunt, of Kilcascan, *b.* 1702. He *m.* 1729, Sarah, dau. of John Rashleigh, of Cleoncoose and Ballinadee, co. Cork, and *d.* 1783, having had (besides dans.) an only son.
William Daunt, of Kilcascan, *b.* 1750; *m.* May, 1775, Jane, dau. of Richard Gumbleton, of Castle Richard, co. Waterford, High Sheriff co. Waterford 1772, and niece maternally of William Conner of Connerville, co. Cork, M.P. for Bandon 1761, and *d.* 1809, having by her (who *d.* 1830) had issue,
1. Joseph.
2. Richard Gumbleton, Capt. 90th Regt., *m.* 1st, Anne, dau. of Rev. John Dixon, Vicar of Humbleton, co. York, by whom he had issue, Richard Gumbleton, Harold, and Anna Theresa (*m.* John Lloyd, of Patrick's Hill, and had issue). He *m.* 2ndly, his cousin Margaret, dau. of Robert Warren Gumbleton, of Glanatore, co. Cork.
3. Robert Gumbleton, Lieut. 62nd Regt., *m.* Miss Harris, of Cork, by whom he had issue.

His eldest son,
Joseph Daunt, of Kilcascan, *b.* 1779; *m.* 1st, June, 1806, Jane, dau. of Rev. Thomas Wilson, D.D., S.F.T.C.D., Rector of Ard-straw, co. Tyrone, and niece of John Wilson, Governor of Minorca, by whom (who *d.* 10 Feb. 1816) he had issue,
1. William Joseph O'Neill, late of Kilcascan.
2. Thomas Wilson, *b.* 20 Aug. 1808; *d. unm.* 2 July, 1854.
3. Henry, who *d.* in infancy.
1. Catherine Elizabeth.
2. Lavinia Jane Isabella.

He *m.* 2ndly, 1822, his cousin Jane, dau. of Robert Warren Gumbleton, of Glanatore, co. Cork, and *d.* 1826, having by her (who *d.* Jan. 1867) had issue, a dau.,
3. Margaret Alice, *b.* 1826.

His eldest son,
William Joseph O'Neill Daunt, of Kilcascan, co. Cork, M.P. for Mallow 1832-3, *b.* 28 April, 1807; *m.* July, 1839, Ellen, dau. of Daniel Hickey. He *d.* 29 June, 1894. She *d.* 9 June, 1897, leaving issue,
Achilles Thomas, now of Kilcascan.
Alice Ismene.

Arms, **Crest**, and **Motto**—Same as Daunt of Tracton Abbey.
Seat—Kilcascan, Ballyneen, co. Cork.

WESTROPP-DAWSON OF CHARLESFORT.

Francis Walter Westropp-Dawson, of Charlesfort, co. Wexford, J.P., High Sheriff 1899; High Sheriff co. Carlow 1911; *b.* 9 Dec. 1859, late Lieut. 4th Batt. the East Surrey Regt. and Capt. 3rd Batt. Royal Irish Regt.; *m.* 1889, Charlotte, only surviving child of the late John Crichton Gray, J.P., of Upton, co. Carlow, and has issue,
1. Walter Henry Mountiford, *b.* 1893.
2. Robert Gray.
1. Laura Frances.

Lineage.—Thomas Dawson, of Termonmaguirk, co. Armagh (2nd son of Walter Dawson, of Armagh, and brother of Walter Dawson, grandfather of Thomas, 1st Lord Dartrey (*see* Burke's Peerage, Dartrey E.), s. to the lands of Termonmaguirk in 1704 under his father's will. By Mary his wife, he left three sons and four daus., viz.,
1. Chapell, of Dublin, *b.* 1699; *m.* June, 1731, Hannah Maria, dau. of Thomas Townley, of Dromroosk, co. Cavan, and had, with four daus. (1. Jane, *b.* 15 May, 1733; 2. Mary, *b.* 29 June, 1734; 3. Charity, *b.* 28 March, 1736; 4. Hannah, *m.* Archibald Richardson), an only son,
  Thomas Townley, of Kinsealy, co. Dublin, *m.* 21 Nov. 1759, Joanna, dau. of Anderson Saunders, of Newtown Saunders, co. Wicklow, and had an only dau.,
    Katherine Marie, *m.* 1st, James Tisdall, and 2ndly, 4 June, 1798, Charles William, 1st Earl of Charleville.
2. Walter, of whom presently.
3. Edward.
1. Elizabeth, *d. unm.* 1775.
2. Charity, *m.* John Lyndon, of Glasnevin, co. Dublin.
3. Margaret.
4. Mary, Mrs. Fulton.

Mr. Thomas Dawson *d.* 1728. His 2nd son,
Walter Dawson, of Clare Castle, co. Armagh, *b.* 1700, *m.* 1st, (marr. setts. 30 Dec. 1731), Elizabeth, dau. and heiress of Rev. Edmund Newton, of Umrigar, co. Wicklow; 2ndly, June, 1741, dau. of Henry Grattan; and 3rdly, Elizabeth, widow of — Bennett, and dau. of — Fenton, of co. Lancaster, and had issue,
1. Thomas, of Clare Castle, M.P. co. Armagh, *m.* Sarah Miles, and had one dau.,
  Charlotte Eliza, *m.* 1st, Rev. Charles Dawson, and 2ndly, Ven. John Charles Archdall, Archdeacon of Ferns.
2. James, of Forkhill, Assistant Barrister, co. Armagh, *m.* 3 June, 1798, Lydia Daly, and had issue,
  1. Richard, *d.s.p.* 1866.
  2. Vesey Thomas, *d.* leaving issue.
3. Charles, of whom presently.

Mr. Dawson obtained the co. Wexford estates through his 1st wife. He *d.* 1756. His 3rd son,
Charles Dawson, of Charlesfort, *b.* 1745; *m.* Deborah, dau. of John Bury, *alias* Palliser, of Comragh, co. Waterford, and had issue,
1. Walter, his heir.
2. Charles (Rev.), *m.* his cousin Charlotte Eliza, dau. of Thomas Dawson, of Clare Castle, and was murdered 1834, leaving by her (who *m.* 2ndly, Ven. John Charles Archdall, Archdeacon of Ferns) an only dau., Deborah.

Dawson. THE LANDED GENTRY. 168

3. RICHARD, of Bunratty, co. Clare, m. Ellen Studdert, and d. 1817, leaving a posthumous son,
  RICHARD DAWSON, J.P. of Bunratty, m. 1854, Geraldine Fitzgerald A. V. Lloyd, and left four sons and three daus.,
  (1) Richard, b. 1855; m. Isabel, dau. of Patrick Fletcher, of Jura, N.B., and has issue,
    Geraldine Patricia.
  (2) William, b. 1858; d. 1900.
  (3) Palliser, b. 1860; m. Elizabeth Geraldine F. S., dau. of John Prouquall Pierce, of Oakville, Ontario, and has issue,
    1. Richard John Palliser, b. 1887.
    2. Walter Henry Palliser, b. 1890; d. 1900.
    3. William Charles Palliser, b. 1896.
    4. George Bury Palliser, b. 1899; d. 1900.
    1. Anna Geraldine Elizabeth, b. 1898; d. 1898.
  (4) George Ussher.
  (1) Annie, b. 1856; m. 30 Dec. 1884, Francis Morice, of Springfield, co. Clare, who d. 29 April, 1897, leaving an only child, Francis William, b. 8 April, 1887; d. 27 Sept. 1901.
  (2) Ellen Geraldine Louisa.
  (3) Geraldine Elizabeth, m. William Bleaden Croft, M.A., Winchester College, and has issue.
1. Eliza, m. 1815, Clement Milward, of Tullogher, co. Kilkenny, Adm. R.N., and had issue (see MILWARD of Alice Holt).
2. Jane, m. 1813, Montiford Westropp, of Mellon, co. Limerick, and had, with other issue (see WESTROPP of Mellon).
  WALTER MONTIFORD WESTROPP-DAWSON, of Charlesfort, of whom presently.
3. Anna, m. Henry Butler, of Castle Crine, co. Clare, and had issue (see BUTLER of Castle Crine).
Mr. Dawson d. 1833, and was s. by his eldest son,
  WALTER DAWSON, of Charlesfort, J.P., who d. unm. 1859, having by deed dated 14 April, 1857, settled his estates on his nephew, WALTER MONTIFORD WESTROPP, who thereupon assumed by Royal Licence, dated 14 Oct. 1859, the additional surname and arms of DAWSON. This gentleman,
  WALTER MONTIFORD WESTROPP-DAWSON, of Charlesfort, co. Wexford, late Capt. 19th Regt., J.P. and D.L. for co Wexford, b. 26 Sept. 1826; m. 22 Feb. 1859, Laura Felicia Susan, youngest dau. of Sir William Clay, M.P., 1st bart. of Fulwell. She d. 19 Feb. 1901. He d. 17 April, 1896, leaving issue,
    1. FRANCIS WALTER, now of Charlesfort.
    2 Arthur Temple, b. 4 Sept. 1865; m. Agnes Mary, dau. of William Latham, of Lincoln's Inn. She d. 1 July, 1894.
    3. Horace Montiford, b. 24 April, 1877; m. 9 Nov. 1908, Leila Louisa, Bidie, eldest dau. of Sir David Monro, of Allan, Rossshire.
    1. Laura Jane, b. 26 March, 1862; m. 26 Sept. 1883, Sir Edmund Charles Simeon, 5th bart. of Grazeley, and has issue (see BURKE's Peerage).
    2. Marian Elizabeth, b. 60 April, 1869.
Arms—Quarterly: 1st and 4th, az., on a bend between two estoiles or, three claws sa., for DAWSON; 2nd and 3rd, sa., a lion rampant arg., ducally crowned or, in the dexter chief point an annulet of the last, for WESTROPP. Crests—1st, On clouds ppr., an estoile as in the arms, an escroll above with the motto, Toujours propice, for DAWSON; 2nd, An eagle's head couped ern., charged with an annulet gu., for WESTROPP. Motto—Tourne vers l'occident.
Seat—Upton, Bagenalstown, co. Carlow. Residence—Charlesfort, Ferns, co. Wexford. Club—Carlton.

MASSY-DAWSON OF BALLYNACOURTE.

GEORGE HENRY EDWARD MASSY-DAWSON, of Ballynacourte, co. Tipperary, J.P., b. 8 Oct. 1864; m. 25 Sept. 1894, Rosalie Margaretta, dau. of Jean Hunziker. Mr. Massy-Dawson is the only surviving son of the late George Staunton King Massy-Dawson, D.L., of Ballynacourte, who d. 14 Nov. 1897, by Grace Elizabeth his 1st wife, who d. 9 Nov. 1865, dau. of Sir William Leeson and grandson of James Hewitt Massy-Dawson, of Ballynacourte, eldest son of Hon. James Massy-Dawson, of Ballynacourte, 2nd son of Hugh, 1st Baron Massy, by Mary his wife, dau. and heir of James Dawson, of Ballynacourte.
Lineage.—See BURKE's Peerage, MASSY, B.
Arms—Arg., a chevron between three lozenges sa. (MASSY). Crest—Out of a ducal coronet or, a bull's head gu. armed sa. (MASSY).
Seat—Ballynacourte, Tipperary.

DAWSON. See BURKE's PEERAGE. DARTREY, E.

DAY.

THE RIGHT REV. MAURICE DAY, D.D., Bishop of Clogher, b. 1843, educated at Trin. Coll. Dublin (B.A. 1865, M.A. 1872, Hon. D.D. 1908); Incumbent of Greystones 1873-6, of Killiney 1876-94, and of St. Matthias, Dublin 1894-1905; Canon of Ch. Ch. Cathedral, Dublin 1901-5, and Incumbent of St. Mary's, Kilkenny, and Dean of Ossory 1905-7; consecrated Bishop of Clogher 1908; m. 1873, Charlotte Francis Mary Forbes, dau. of Herbert Taylor Ottley, York Terrace, Regent's Park, and has issue,
1. JOHN GODFREY FITZ MAURICE (Rev.), M.A. Camb., b. 1874.
2. Herbert Taylor Ottley, B.A. (T.C.D.), b. 1875.
3. Maurice Fitzmaurice, Lieut. King's Own Yorkshire L.I., b. 1878.
1. Kathleen Mary Agnes.

Lineage.—The first of the family settled in Kerry appears to have been EDWARD DAY, of Tralee (son of — Day, by Ellen Quarry, of Cork), who by his wife Catherine, dau. of William Fuller and his wife Ellinor (dau. of Thos. Hodder, of Ballea Castle, co. Cork) had issue, two sons and two daus., viz.,
1. JOHN, of whom hereafter.
2. Edward (Rev.), m. Mary, dau. of John Rowan, of Castle Gregory, granddau. of Dean John Leslie, famed for his loyal services in 1688, and left issue,
  1. James (Rev.), Rector of Tralee, and Vicar-General of the diocese of Ardfert and Aghadoe, m. Margaret, dau. of M'Gillycuddy, of The Reeks, and left issue,
    (1) Edward (Rev.), Rector of Kilgobbin, who m. Deborah, dau. of John Curry, and had issue, James; John, Lieut. H.E.I.Co.'s service; Richard; Edward; Robert; Leslie; Margaret; Deborah, m. to James John Hickson, of Hilville; Betsey; Agnes; Lucy; and Sarah.
    Richard.
    (2) John Sealy, Capt. 87th Regt.
    (3) James Leslie, Major in the Bengal Army.
    (1) Agnes.
    (2) Sarah, m. to John James Hickson.
    (3) Alicia, m. to James Morphy.
    (4) Lucy.
  2. Edward, in Holy Orders, d. unm.
  1. Sarah, m. to John Rae, of Derrymore.
1. Ellen, m. Giles Rae, of Derrymore, co. Kerry, and had issue.
2. Elizabeth, m. to Robert Collis.
The eldest son,
The REV. JOHN DAY, m. 1737, Lucy Fitzgerald, dau. of Maurice Knight, of Kerry, by Elizabeth Crosbie, sister of Maurice, 1st Lord Brandon, and had issue,
1. EDWARD, Archdeacon of Ardfert and Aghadoe, who m. Barbara Forward, and had,
  Edward, of Beaufort (Rev.), m. April, 1802, Harriett, eldest dau. and co-heir of John Rowan, of Castle Gregory, co. Kerry, and had,
  (1) EDWARD (Rev.), Rector of St. John's, Sligo, m. Anne, dau. of Richd. Holmes, of Dublin, and had five sons and four daus.
  (2) Robert, of Loghercannon, Kerry, Barrister-at-Law, m. July, 1808, Christian, dau. of William Marshall, of Dublin, and had issue, William, who m. Mary, dau. of Alexander Elliott, of Killscrim, Kerry.
  (3) Margaret, m. Oct. 1796, John Mahony, of Dromore Castle, and by him left issue (see that family).
  (2) Lucy, m. 1796, Rev. William Godfrey, Rector of Kenmare, and brother of Sir John Godfrey, Bart., and had issue (see BURKE's Peerage).
  (3) Barbara, d. unm.
2. John, Mayor of Cork 1806, m. Margaret Hewson, and left issue,
  1. John (Rev.), Rector of Kiltallagh, co. Kerry, m. Arabella, dau. of Sir William Godfrey, Bart., and had issue,
    (1) John Godfrey (Very Rev.), Rector of Valentia, Dean of Ardfert, m. 1834 his cousin, Eleanor, dau. of Sir John Godfrey, Bart. (see BURKE's Peerage), and had issue,
      1. MAURICE, now Bishop of Clogher.
      2. James. 3. Edward.
      1. Eleanor Frances. 2. Agnes Arabella.
    (2) Edward, in the H.E.I.Co.'s service.
    (3) Robert, m. Alicia Thompson, of Dublin.
    (4) William (Rev.), d.s.p.

(5) Maurice (Right Rev.), late Bishop of Cashel, *m.* 1852, Jane, dau. of J. Gabbett (*see* GABBETT *of Caherline*), and had issue,
    Maurice William (Very Rev.), present Dean of Cashel, *m.* 1887, Katherine L. F. Garfit, and has issue,
      a. Maurice Charles.   *b.* Geoffrey William.
      c. John Edward.   *d.* Charles Lionel.
      a. Mary Katherine.
(1) Agnes, *m.* 1817, James Butler, of Waterville, in Kerry, and *d.* 1829. He *d.* June, 1863, leaving issue.
(2) Margaret, *m.* Capt. Roderick Mackenzie, brother of Sir Francis Mackenzie, 5th Bart., of Gairloch, N.B. (*see* BURKE'S *Peerage*).
(3) Ellen.   (4) Arabella.
2. Edward, Lieut.-Col. in the H.E.I.Co.'s service, *m.* Mary, dau. of Patrick Trant, of Dingle, and has issue.
  1. Elizabeth, *m.* Oliver Stokes.
  2. Margaret, *m.* John Fitzgerald Collis.
  3. Lucy, *d. unm.*
  4. Catherine, *d. unm.*
3. Robert, M.P. for Ardfert, in the Irish Parliament, and one of the Justices of the Court of King's Bench, in Ireland, *m.* Aug. 1774, Mary Potts, of London. Judge Day *d.* at an advanced age, in 1841, having had one dau.,
  ELIZABETH, *m.* 26 May, 1795, Sir Edward Denny, Bart., of Tralee, and left issue (*see* BURKE'S *Peerage*).
1. Catherine, *m.* Thomas Frauks, and left issue.

Arms—Per chevron, arg. and az., three mullets, counterchanged. *Crest*—Two dexter hands clasped together ppr., each from a wing expanded quarterly or and az. counterchanged. *Motto*—Sic itur ad astra.

Residence—Bishops' Court, Clones. *Club*—University, Dublin.

DEANE late OF GLENDARAGH.

BERKELEY ST. GEORGE DEANE, formerly of Glendaragh, co. Wicklow, J.P., Commander R.N., *b.* 17 Nov. 1844; *m.* 5 July, 1880, Emily Jane, dau. of Nelson Houghton, of Ashley Lodge, Ryde, Isle of Wight, and has issue,
  Olive Isabel, *b.* 23 July, 1887.

Lineage.—WILLIAM DEANE, of The Woodhouse in Farmcote, parish of Guyting, co. Gloucester, *temp.* Queen ELIZABETH, *m.* Anne, dau. of Sir Edward Wykeham, Knt. of Swalcliffe, co. Oxford [ancestor of SOPHIA, *Baroness Wenman* (*see* BURKE'S *Extinct Peerage*), and of Wykeham of Thame Park], and by her (who was bur. at Guyting, 3 June, 1602) had six sons, viz.,
1. John.
2. Anthony, grandfather of Sir Anthony Deane, Chief Commissioner of the Navy *temp.* CHARLES II.
3. William.   4. Richard.
5. Bartholomew.
6. EDWARD, of whom we treat.

The youngest son,
EDWARD DEANE, of Pinnock, co. Gloucester, *m.* 1st, Joan Colet, and by her (who was bur. at Guyting 1608) had,
1. George.   2. Robert, *b.* 1606.
1. Margaret, *b.* and *d.* 1596.   2. Elizabeth Anne, *b.* 1599.
8. Edward, *b.* 1604.
He *m.* 2ndly, 1609, Anne Wase, and by her (who was bur. at Buckingham 1670) had,
1. Richard, the Republican General-at-Sea, bapt. at Guyting 8 July, 1610; one of the Commissioners on the trial of CHARLES I; signed the order for the murder of the King; killed in an engagement with the Dutch, 2 June, 1653, and was bur. in HENRY VII. Chapel, Westminster Abbey, but after the Restoration his body, with those of several other regicides, was exhumed, under Royal warrant of 9 Sept. 1661, and bur. in a common pit in the churchyard. He *m.* at the Temple Church, London, 21 May, 1647, Mary, dau. of John Grimditch, of Knottingley, co. York, and had two daus., 1. Hannah; 2. Mary.
2. Samuel, *d.* young.   3. Nathaniel, *d.s.p.*
4. JOSEPH, of whom hereafter.
1. Naomi, *b.* 1613.   2. Hannah.
3. Jane, *m.* 1st, Dru Sparrow, Secretary to the Generals-at-Sea, under OLIVER CROMWELL, who was killed in action at sea 18 Feb. 1652. She *m.* 2ndly, — Monteage, an attorney.

The youngest son,
JOSEPH DEANE, of Crumlin, co. Dublin, *b.* at Pinnock, 2 Feb. 1624, petitioned by his kinsman, Humphry Wykeham, for admission as one of the Founders kin to Winchester College 1635, and was afterwards Cornet in Rainsborough's Regiment of Horse, volunteered for service in Ireland under OLIVER CROMWELL, and attained the rank of Major. He was granted by patents of 16 Jan. 1666, and 22 June, 1670, 9, 313 acres, statute, in the counties of Dublin, Meath, Kildenny, and Down, and by deed of 12 March, 1670, purchased from Richard Talbot (afterwards Earl and Duke of Tyrconnel) the manor of Terenure, co. Dublin, for £4,000 and was High Sheriff co. Dublin 1677. By his 1st wife Anne he had,
1. JOSEPH, of Crumlin, his successor, *b.* at Ravensthorpe, co. Northampton, 6 Jan. 1649, entered Trin. Coll. Dublin, 2 June, 1664; *m.* 1673, Elizabeth, dau. of Most Rev. John Parker, D.D., Archbishop of Dublin, and *d.* 8 Dec. 1698, leaving, with two daus., Elizabeth and Anne, one son,
JOSEPH, of Crumlin, *b.* in Dublin, 1675, entered Trin. Coll. Dublin 29 July, 1699, Barrister-at-Law, appointed Lord Chief Baron of the Exchequer, 14 Oct. 1714. He *m.*, by licence, 26 Sept. 1699, Margaret, dau. of Hon. Henry Boyle, of Castle Martyr, co. Cork, 2nd son of Roger, 1st Earl of Orrery, and *d.* 4 May, 1715, leaving by her (who *d.* July, 1717), five daus., his co-heirs,
(1) Elizabeth, *m.* by licence of 30 April, 1722, Hayes, 4th Viscount Doneraile.
(2) Anne, *m.* by licence of 8 Feb. 1724, Arthur, 1st Viscount Dungannon.
(3) Mary, *m.* by licence of 12 May, 1725, John, 1st Earl of Mayo.
(4) Katherine, *m.* by licence of 6 Dec. 1725, John, 1st Viscount Lisle.
(5) Margaret, *m.* 12 April, 1732, John FitzGerald, Knight of Kerry.
1. Anne, *m.* by licence of 4 May, 1673, Godwin Swifte, Attorney-General to the Duke of Ormonde.
2. Elizabeth, *m.* 1st, by licence of 17 May, 1672, Capt. Henry Grey, who *d.* 16 Oct. 1675; and 2ndly, July, 1677, Donough O'Brien, of Lemenagh, co. Clare. She *d.* 16 Jan. 1684.
Major Deane *m.* 2ndly, 1679, Elizabeth, dau. of Maurice Cuffe, of Quin, co. Clare, and had by her (who *d.* 3 April, 1698) further issue,
2. EDWARD, of whom hereafter.
3. Dorothy, *m.* Maurice Berkeley, of Glasnevin, co. Dublin. Her will dated 18 Aug. 1724, was proved 14 Jan. 1728. She left a son, Maurice Berkeley, of Scark, co. Wexford, *b.* 1687.
Major Deane *d.* 21 Dec. 1699. His son by his 2nd wife,
EDWARD DEANE, of Terenure, obtained this estate from his father, and got a confirmation 21 Dec. 1700, from the Commissioners of Forfeited Estates (the Duke of Tyrconnel having been attainted) of the purchase of the estate made by his father. He was M.P. for Inistioge 1692, for co. Dublin 1695, and again for Inistioge 1703, which he represented till his death; High Sheriff co. Dublin 1692, and co. Kilkenny 1710. He *m.* (settlements dated 30 Aug. 1678) Anne, dau. of William Bulkeley, of the Isle of Wight, and had issue,
1. EDWARD, his heir.
2. Stephen, *b.* 1687, entered Trin. Coll. Dublin, 28 Oct. 1703. M.P. for Inistioge, 12 Sept. 1717; *m.* Mary, dau. of Rev. Samuel Price, Vicar of Straffan, and sister of Most Rev. Arthur Price, D.D., Archbishop of Cashel, and had issue,
  1. Edward, of Dangan, co. Kilkenny.   2. Stephen, *d.s.p.*
  1. Anne, *d. unm.* 1747.
  2. Hannah, *m.* by licence of 30 June, 1727, Rev. Alexander Bradford.
  3. Frances, *m.* 1732, Very Rev. Bartholomew Vigors, Dean of Leighlin.
3. Joseph, Portrieve of Inistioge, *temp.* GEORGE I.
Mr. Deane *d.* intestate. Administration was granted 17 Sept. 1717, to his eldest son,
EDWARD DEANE, of Terenure, *b.* at Lymington, co. Southampton, 1682, entered Trin. Coll. Dublin, 24 Feb. 1699, M.P. for Inistioge from 1715 till his death, High Sheriff co. Kilkenny, 1718; *m.* Elizabeth, dau. of Amias Bushe, of Kilfane, co. Kilkenny, and had issue,
1. EDWARD, his heir, entered Trin. Coll. Dublin, 9 March, 1732, admitted a member of the King's Inns, Michaelmas, 1741, M.P. for Inistioge, 16 Oct. 1745; *s.* his father at Terenure 1748, and was shot by Maj.-Gen. Thomas Pigott, of Knapton, Queen's Co., in a duel 1751. He *d. unm.*, and was *s.* by his brother
2. Amias, entered Trin. Coll. Dublin, 29 May, 1735; *d. unm.*
3. JOSEPH, who carried on the family.
1. Frances, *m.* by licence of 18 Feb. 1752 Standish Grady, of Ballyvolane, co. Limerick.
2. Wilhelmina, *m.* by licence of 28 Nov. 1748, Nicholas Bowen, of Bowen's Court, co. Cork.
3. Elizabeth, *m.* 1750, Standish O'Grady, 5th son of The O'Grady of Killballyneen, co. Limerick.
Mr. Deane *d.* Dec. 1748. His youngest son,
JOSEPH DEANE, of Terenure, and of Dangan, co. Kilkenny, *s.* his eldest brother in 1751, was M.P. for Inistioge 1762, for co. Kilkenny 1768, for co. Dublin 1769, and Col. of the co. Dublin Volunteers. He *m.* 1st, 26 June, 1754, Jane, only dau. of William Freeman, of Castle Cor, co. Cork and heiress of her brother, Matthew Freeman, and by her (who *d.* March, 1764) had an only son,
1. EDWARD, of Castle Cor, *b.* 9 Jan. 1760, entered Christ Church Coll. Oxford 1777, High Sheriff co. Cork, 1797, inherited the estates of his mother's family under the will of her brother, Matthew Freeman, 1775, when he adopted the additional surname of FREEMAN. He *m.* 1781, Mary, dau. of Richard Plummer, of Mount Plummer, co. Limerick, and *d.* 25 March, 1826, leaving, with other issue,
JOSEPH, of Castle Cor, J.P., D.L., *b.* 28 Oct. 1783, Esquire to Henry, 3rd Earl of Shannon, at his installation as Knight of St. Patrick, 28 June, 1809, High Sheriff co. Cork, 1811. He *m.* 24 Aug. 1811, Elizabeth, dau. of Robert McCarthy, of Carrignavar, co. Cork (*see* MAC'ARTIE *of Carrignavar*), and *d.* 24 Jan. 1840, leaving, with other issue,

EDWARD, of Castle Cor, J.P., D.L., who sold his co. Cork estates. He m. 28 Oct. 1841, Charlotte Flora Jemima, dau. of John Lee Allen, of Errol Park, co. Perth, and was father of JOSEPH EDWARD DEANE FREEMAN, b. 29 Aug. 1842, who d. at Coolgardie, West Australia, 2 Sept. 1906.
Col. Deane m. 2ndly, by licence of 14 Aug. 1764, Mrs. Jane Daly, widow, dau. of Rowley Hill, of Walworth, co. Londonderry, and sister of Sir Hugh Hill, 1st bart. of Brooke Hall, but by her had no issue. He m. 3rdly, Katherine, dau. of John Greene, of Greene-ville, co. Kilkenny, and had by her,

2. JOHN BERKELEY, of whom hereafter.
3. Joseph, m. 11 Sept. 1810, Sarah, dau. of John Drake, of Coolback, co. Wexford, and sister and heiress of George Drake, of Stokestown, same co., and by her (who d. 24 July, 1854) had issue,
   1. JOHN, s. to Stokestown, and assumed by Royal Licence dated 6 April, 1853, the additional surname and arms of DRAKE (see DRAKE of Stokestown).
   2. Joseph William, of Longraige, co. Wexford, bapt. 13 May, 1815, called to the bar Trinity Term, 1838; d. 24 Dec. 1908; m. 1865, Julia, dau. of Strangman Davis Goff, of Horetown, same co., and had issue,
     (1) William Joseph, b. 29 Dec. 1867; m. 16 Feb. 1911, Eileen Violet, dau. of Henry William Weldon, of Bantry.
     (1) Sarah Drake.
     (2) Julia.
   1. Sarah, m. Henry Roe, of Knockmullen, co. Wexford, and had issue.
   2. Katherine Elizabeth, m. 18 Jan. 1855, Abraham Alcock, New Ross, M.D.
   3. Juliana Frances.
4. William, d. unm.
5. Amias, Capt. 96th Regt., m. Mary, widow of Thomas Whelan, and dau. of — White, his wife, and d.s.p. 4 March, 1856.
1. Frances, m. 1st, Major Anthony Cliffe, of New Ross; and 2ndly, Frances Corbet Singleton, of Aclare, co. Meath, and Corbet Hill, co. Wexford.
2. Katherine, d. unm.
3. Eliza, m. Dec. 1800, Rev. Allan Cliffe, co. Hereford.
4. Wilhelmina, m. John Lloyd Edwards, of Robuck, co. Dublin, and Camolin Park, co. Wexford, J.P., and d. 1872, having by him (who d. 1842) had issue.
5. Lydia, m. Abraham Brush, J.P. co. Cavan.

Col. Deane d. 1801. His eldest son by his 3rd wife,
JOHN BERKELEY DEANE, of Berkeley, co. Wexford, s. to that estate under the will of his cousin, Maurice Berkeley; m. 1800, Cecilia, dau. of Gen. Knudson, E.I.C., and had issue,
1. JOHN ST. GEORGE, his heir.
2. William Christian, bapt. 27 Sept. 1807, Lieut. R.N.; m. 13 April, 1844, Caroline Hoskins, younger dau. of George Arundel Nixon, of Brownsbarn, co. Kilkenny, and d.s.p. 1845.
3. GEORGE KNUDSON, of Orchardstown, co. Dublin, J.P., Barrister-at-Law, bapt. 12 Nov. 1811; m. 1 June, 1840, Isabella, dau. of John Wise, of Bahernagore, co. Limerick, by Henrietta his wife, dau. of Sir James Lawrence Cotter, 2nd bart. of Rockforest, M.P., and d. 9 April, 1887, having had issue,
   1. BERKELEY ST. GEORGE, recently of Glendaragh.
   2. George Knudson, Lieut. 4th Hussars, b. 1847; d. unm. 20 Dec. 1875.
   3. Freeman William, b. 1849; m. Charlotte Eleanor, dau. of Featherstonhaugh Briscoe, of Riverdale, co. Westmeath.
   1. Henrietta Frances, m. 26 Nov. 1874, Joseph Abbott, son of John Moore Abbott, Gardner Street, Dublin, and has issue.
   2. Cecilia Katherine, m. 24 July, 1878, Henry Joseph Deane Roe, of Knockmullen, co. Wexford, and has issue.
1. Cecilia, of Glendaragh, co. Wicklow, m. 27 Oct. 1858, Rev. Lambert Watson Hepenstal, of Altadore, co. Wicklow, who d. 1859 (see DOPPING-HEPENSTAL of Derrycassan).
2. Frances, d. unm. 21 Feb. 1900.
3. Elizabeth, m. May, 1847, James Lawrence Wise, and has issue.

Mr. John Berkeley Deane d. 1837, and was s. by his eldest son,
JOHN ST. GEORGE DEANE, of Berkeley, J.P., D.L., b. 1803; m. 1st, 1847, Grace Waudesford, dau. of Thomas Kavanagh, of Borris, co. Carlow, by his 1st wife, Lady Elizabeth Butler, dau. of John, 17th Earl of Ormonde and Ossory; and 2ndly, 1850, Katherine, dau. of John Gordon, of Aikenhead, co. Lanark, and d. 1 June, 1879, leaving by his 2nd wife (who d. 9 July, 1899) an only dau. and heiress,
KATHERINE CECILIA, m. 1892, Albert Henry Tyndall, of Ballyanne, co. Wexford, 4th son of Robert Tyndall, of Oaklands, co. Wexford (see that family).

Arms—Arg., on a chevron gu. between three cornish choughs sa. beaked and legged of the second, as many crosses-pattées of the field. Crest—A tortoise displayed ppr. Motto—Ferendo non feriendo.

Residence—Beech Hurst, Bray, co. Wicklow.

DEANE-DRAKE. See DRAKE.

DEASE OF TURBOTSTON.

MAJOR GERALD DEASE, of Turbotston, co. Westmeath, Major late Royal Fusiliers, J.P. and D.L. for cos. Westmeath (High Sheriff 1909) and Cavan (High Sheriff 1899), Commissioner of National Education in Ireland, b. 8 Aug. 1854; m. 3 June, 1896, Florence Helen, 2nd dau. of the late George Marley, of Gaunless House, Bishop Auckland.

Lineage.—The family of Dease (formerly spelt Deece) is one of the oldest in Westmeath. The list of Forfeited Estates in that county shows that the Deases are one of the few families who held property in 1641. in the district where they still reside. An old undated manuscript in the possession of the family states that " in 1272 in EDWARD the First of England reign," Edmond Dease purchased Turbotstown, and was s. by Garret, Edmond, Garret, Richard, James, Richard, James, William, Richard, Oliver Garret, James, Garret. In a roll of the gentry of the Liberty of Trim 1436, appears the name of James Dease, of Turbotstown. In a manuscript temp. HENRY VIII. occurs among the gentry of Meath the name of " Richard Dees of Turbottstown."

RICHARD DEASE, of Turbotston, s. about 1568. He was appointed a Commissioner for Musters for the co. Westmeath, 12 May, 1583, and 4 July, 1584; m. Elizabeth Nugent, of Carlanstown, and had issue,
1. JAMES, his heir.
2. Thomas, Bishop of Meath, b. 1568; d. 1652.
3. Lawrence, d. 1649, leaving issue, all mentioned in the will of their uncle the bishop,
   1. Oliver, Vicar-Gen. of Diocese of Meath.
   2. Richard.   3. Garret.
   4. Watt.   5. Laurence.

The eldest son,
JAMES DEASE, of Turbotston, was included in a pardon 9 June, 1602. His will, dated 5 Jan. 1628-9, was proved 10 March following. He m. Margaret Leicester, and had issue,
1. RICHARD, his heir.   2. Gerald.
3. William.
1. Catherine.   2. Margaret.
3. Mary.   4. Anne.

The eldest son,
RICHARD DEASE, of Turbotston, b. 1603; m. Mary Brown. He was deprived of his estates after the Rebellion of 1641, but these were bought back from the Pakenhams with the proceeds of the Cavan property, which had been held in trust for them by the Pollards of Castle Pollard. He made over his possessions, such as they were, to his son James, and d. 1650, leaving issue, with three daus.,
1. JAMES.   2. William.
3. Oliver.   4. Michael.

The eldest son,
JAMES DEASE, of Turbotston, was living 1637. He d. 1707, having m. as his 2nd wife, Mary Nugent, by whom he had issue,
1. Richard, d.v.p. in France.
2. WILLIAM, who s. his father.

The 2nd son,
WILLIAM DEASE, of Turbotston, s. his father; m. 4 May, 1704, Eleanor Nangle, and had issue,
1. RICHARD, his heir.
2. JOHN, successor to his brother Oliver.
3. OLIVER, s. his brother Richard.
4. GARRETT, who eventually s. to the estates.
5. Patrick, who had three sons, 1. Richard; 2. John; 3. Oliver.
1. Eleanor, m. 24 Jan. 1750-1, Patrick Cruise, of Rahood, co. Meath.
2. Katherine.   3. Ann.

Mr. Dease d. Jan. 1750-1, and was s. by his eldest son,
RICHARD DEASE, of Turbotston, and of the Middle Temple, London, d.s.p. 24 April, 1759, and was s. by his brother,
JOHN DEASE, of Turbotston, who was killed by a fall from his horse. He d. unm. 27 March, 1672, and intestate. Administration was granted 28 July, 1762, and he was s. by his next brother,
OLIVER DEASE, of Turbotston, m. Mary, sister of Philip Tuite, of Newcastle, and d.s.p. 1771, when he was s. by his brother,
GARRETT DEASE, of Turbotston, who m. 1740, Susan, dau. and co-heir of Oliver Plunkett, of Rathmore Castle, co. Meath, and d. 1790, was father of
JAMES DEASE, of Turbotston, b. 1793; m. 1788, Lady Theresa Plunkett, only dau. of Arthur James, 7th Earl of Fingall, and by her had issue,
1. GERALD, his heir.
2. William Henry, of Rath House, Queen's Co., m. Frances, only dau. and co-heir of H. de Friese, and d.s.p. 1856.
1. Mary, d. 1851.   2. Theresa, d. 1852.
3. Charlotte, d. 1868.

The elder son,
GERALD DEASE, of Turbotston, b. 1790; m. 1820, Elizabeth, dau. (and co-heir with her sisters, Bridget, who m. 1809, Thomas O'Reilly, and d. 1851; Ellen, wife of J. J. Bagot, of Castle Bagot;

IRELAND.   De Burgh.

Marcella, a nun; and Catherine, Countess of Kenmare) of Edmund O'Callaghan, of Kilgory, co. Clare, and by her (who d. 1846) had issue,
  1. JAMES ARTHUR, his heir.
  2. Edmund Gerald, of Rath House (see DEASE of Rath House).
  3. Gerald Richard (Sir), K.C.V.O., of Celbridge Abbey, co. Kildare, b. 1831, Hon. Col., late Lieut.-Col. of Cavan Regt. (4th Batt. R.I. Fusiliers), Chamberlain to H. E. the Lord Lieutenant of Ireland, J.P. cos. Kildare and Meath, m. 25 Nov. 1863, Emily, dau. of Sir Robert Throckmorton, 8th bart. He d. 18 Oct. 1903, leaving issue,
    1. William Gerald, b. 1867; m. 28 July, 1897, Gertrude, dau. of Col. W. R. Lascelles, of Norley, Cheshire (see BURKE'S Peerage, HAREWOOD, E.), and has issue,
      Ernest Joseph, b. 1899.
      Cynthia Mary, b. 1902.
    2. Arthur Joseph, lately Page of Honor Viceregal Court, b. 1871.
    1. Eveline Mary, m. 1901, F. Léoni, of Rome.
Mr. Dease d. 1854, and was s. by his eldest son,
JAMES ARTHUR DEASE, of Turbotston, J.P. and D.L., Vice-Lieut. of Cavan, b. 30 May, 1826; m. 11 Aug. 1853, Charlotte (d. 30 March, 1905), eldest dau. of Edmund William Jerningham (nephew of George William, Lord Stafford), by Matilda Waterton, his wife, and d. 5 Sept. 1874, leaving issue,
  1. GERALD, his heir.
  2. Edmund Fitzlaurence, of Culmullen, Drumree, co. Meath, J.P., b. 20 Dec. 1856; m. 15 Nov. 1888, Katherine, dau. of the late Maurice Murray, of Beech Hill, Cork, J.P., D.L., and has issue,
    Maurice James, 2nd Lieut. Roy. Fus., b. 28 Sept. 1889.
    Maud Mary, b. 15 Sept. 1890.
  1. Mary Elizabeth, m. 2 Feb. 1880, Charles William, 3rd Earl of Gainsborough (see BURKE'S Peerage).
  2. Maude Mary, m. 15 April, 1884, Right Hon. John Naish, Lord High Chancellor of Ireland 1885, and has issue.
  3. Ida Mary, a Franciscan nun.   4. Teresa Mary.
  5. Elizabeth Mary, a nun.
  6. Mabel Mary, a sister of charity.
  7. Madeline Mary, m. 1884, Charles Liddell, of Warwick Hall, Carlisle, and has issue.
  8. Kathleen Mary, a sister of charity.
  9. Anna Maria, d. 1872.   10. Alice Mary Frances.
Arms—Arg., a lion rampant gu. Crest—A lion rampant gu. holding a sword ppr. Motto—Toujours prêt.
Seat—Turbotston, Coole. Clubs—Naval and Military and Kildare Street.

DEASE OF RATH.

EDMUND JAMES DEASE, of Rath House, Queen's Co., J.P. and D.L. for Queen's Co. Resident Magistrate for co. Tipperary, late Major 4th Batt. Royal Fus., b. Oct. 1861; m. 1896, Mabel, eld. dau. of Ambrose More O'Ferrall, J.P., D.L., of Balyna, co. Kildare, and Glenmonnow, Herefordshire (see that family), and has issue,
  RICHARD EDMUND ANTHONY, b. 1897.
  Marion.
Lineage.—GERALD DEASE, of Turbotston, b. 1790; d. 1854; m. 1820, Elizabeth, dau. and co-heir of Edmund O'Callaghan, of Kilgory, co. Clare, and by her (who d. 1846) had with other issue (see DEASE of Turbotstown), a 2nd son,
EDMUND GERALD DEASE, of Rath House, Queen's Co., J.P. and D.L., High Sheriff 1859, M.P. for Queen's Co. 1870-80, a Commissioner of National Education in Ireland, and a Member of the Senate of the Royal University, b. 6 Sept. 1829; d. 17 July, 1904; m. 21 June, 1859, Mary (Rath House, Ballybrittas), 4th dau. of the late Henry Grattan, of Celbridge Abbey, co. Kildare, M.P. for Meath, and grand-dau. of the Right Hon. Henry Grattan, and had issue,
  1. EDMUND JAMES CHARLES, now of Rath.
  2. Louis George, b. 1867.
  1. Teresa Mary, m. 1894, John Mulhall, J.P. co. Sligo, Vice-Chairman General Prisons Board, Ireland (14, Earlsfort Terrace, Dublin).
  2. Mary.   3. Charlotte.
Lineage. Arms, &c.—See DEASE of Turbotston.
Seat—Rath House, Ballybrittas. Residence—Newtown, Nenagh, co. Tipperary.

DE BATHE. See BURKE'S PEERAGE, DE BATHE, Bart.

DE BURGH OF OLDTOWN.

LIEUT.-COL. THOMAS JOHN DE BURGH, of Oldtown, co. Kildare, J.P. and D.L., High Sheriff 1884, commanded 17th Batt. Imperial Yeomanry in S. Africa 1900-1, late Lieut. 57th Regt. and 5th Dragoon Guards, b. 1 Nov. 1851; m. 23 April, 1878, Emily Anne, eldest dau. of Henry John, Baron de Robeck (see BURKE'S Peerage, Foreign Titles), of Gowran Grange, co. Kildare, and has issue,

  1. HUBERT HENRY, Lieut. R.N., b. 16 Feb. 1879.
  2. Eric, Lieut. 9th Hodson's Horse, b. 10 May, 1881.
  3. Maurice Ulick, b. 15 Oct. 1882.
  4. Charles, Lieut. R.N., b. 17 July, 1886; m. 1 Feb. 1910, Isabel Caroline Berkeley, dau. of Rev. E. F. Campbell, M.A.
  5. Thomas, 2nd Lieut. 31st (Duke of Connaught's) Lancers, Indian Army, b. 10 Sept. 1888.
  1. Coralie Helen.   2. Zoë.
  3. Una, d. young, 1890.
Lineage.—WILLIAM DE BURGH, brother of Hubert de Burgh, Earl of Kent, received a grant of lands in Ireland about 1185. William de Burgh m. a dau. of Donnell Mor O'Brien, King of Thomond, and d. in 1204, leaving a son,
RICHARD DE BURGH (" the elder "), m. Una, (or Hodierna) de Gernon, grand-dau. of O'Connor, King of Connaught (son of Cahill Croodery, or the Red Hand). He d. 1243, leaving two sons,
  1. Walter, Lord of Connaught, EARL OF ULSTER, m. Avelina, sister and co-heir of Richard, Lord Fitz John, and d. 1271. His son,
    Richard, 2ND EARL OF ULSTER, known as the Red Earl, m. in or before Feb. 1281, Margaret, dau. of Sir John de Burgh, of Lanvalay, and d. 1326, having had issue, a son,
    Sir John de Burgh, m. about 1306, Elizabeth de Clare, foundress in 1346 of Clare College, Cambridge, dau. of Gilbert, Earl of Gloucester and Hertford (by Joan, dau. of King EDWARD I). She d. 4 Nov. 1360, but Sir John d.v.p. 18 June, 1313. Their son,
    William, 3RD EARL OF ULSTER, m. Maud, dau. of Henry, Earl of Lancaster, grandson of KING HENRY III, and left an only child,
      Lady Elizabeth de Burgh, suo jure COUNTESS OF ULSTER, who m. 9 Sept. 1352, Lionel of Antwerp, Duke of Clarence, son of EDWARD III. Through this marriage all the hereditary rights, originally granted to William Fitz Adlemde Burgh, reverted to the Kings of England.
  2. WILLIAM OGE, of whom we treat.
The younger son,
WILLIAM OGE DE BURGH, surnamed "Athankip," served with his father in France, with HENRY III in 1215, in Scotland, invaded Desmond and slew Cormac, Lord of Desmond, and was put to death at Athankip in 1270, while a hostage to the King of Connaught. His son,
SIR WILLIAM DE BURGH, surnamed "Liath," m. a dau. of Mac-Jordan, and was custos of Ireland in 1308, and won the battle of Athenry in 1316. He d. in 1324, and had with other issue,
  1. Sir William Ulick de Burgh, who d. about 1353, and was ancestor of the Earls and Marquesses of Clanricarde.
  2. SIR EDMOND BOURKE, of whom we treat.
The younger son,
SIR EDMOND BOURKE, surnamed "Albanach," d. 1375, leaving a son,
SIR THOMAS BOURKE, Justice of Connaught. He m. 1397, a dau. of the O'Conor, and d. in 1402, leaving five sons, of whom four s. each other in the "Lordship of the MacWilliam Bourkes." The 4th son, John, was ancestor of the Earls of Mayo. The eldest son,
WALTER DE BURGH or BOURKE, of Shruel, was for 20 years Lord of the MacWilliam Bourkes. He was b. about 1360; m. Sabia, dau. of O'Brien, Lord of Thomond, and d. 1440, and was s. by his eldest son,
JOHN DE BURGH or BOURK, of Shruel, m. a sister of the O'Brien, whom he had overthrown, and acquired by exchange in 1420 the property of Dromkeen, and settled there at Dromkeen in co. Limerick. His eldest son,
WILLIAM, of Dromkeen, surnamed "Dhue" (or Black), was s. by his son, MEYLER, of Dromkeen, surnamed "Sleaght-Meyler," who was s. by his son, RICHARD, of Dromkeen, who was s. by his son, RICHARD, "Oge," of Dromkeen, who was s. by his son, MEYLER, of Dromkeen, who was s. by his son, ULICK, or Ulysses, of Dromkeen, whose son, Richard, of Dromkeen, in Holy Orders, was s. by his son,
RIGHT REV. ULYSSES BURGH, of Dromkeen, LORD BISHOP OF ARDAGH, appointed by patent, dated 8 Sept. 1692, and consecrated 11th of the same month. He m. 1683, Mary, dau. of Col. William Kingsmill, of Ballyowen, co. Tipperary, and had issue,
  1. RICKARD (Rev.), of Dromkeen, Prebendary of Kilbragh, b. 1666, m. 25 Feb. 1699, Elizabeth Griffin, and by her (who d. 1716) left at his decease,
    1. Michael, d. unm. 1716.
    2. THOMAS BURGH, of Dromkeen, whose will (dated 6 Dec. 1734) was proved in 1747. He m. 1726, his cousin Mary Burgh, of Oldtown, and had with a son, RICHARD, of Dromkeen (who d.s.p. 1762, and left Dromkeen to his maternal cousin, the Right Hon. Walter Hussey, who then assumed the name of BURGH, and d. 1783), a dau., Mary, m. 1753, Philpot Wolfe, of Forenaghts, co. Kildare.
    3. Richard (Rev.), of Mount Bruis, co. Tipperary, who, dying 1778, left issue,
      (1) Richard Ulysses.   (2) Thomas.
      (1) Mary, m. William Byam, of Byams, Antigua, and Woodborough, co. Somerset, a Capt. 68th Regt.
    4. William, d. unm. 1735.
    1. Elizabeth, m. John Gabbett, of Rathjordan.
    2. Anne, m. 1731, William Monsell, of Tervoe.
    3. Mary, m. Thomas Lloyd, of Tower Hill.
    4. Dorothea, m. William Gabbett, of Caherlane.
  2. WILLIAM, of Bert, Comptroller and Accountant-General, m. 1693, Margaret, dau. of Thomas Parnell, of Congleton, Cheshire, and d. 1744, leaving issue,
    1. Thomas, of Bert, M.P., for Lanesborough, m. 1731, Anne,

De Burgh. THE LANDED GENTRY. 172

dau. of Right Rev. Dives Downes, Bishop of Cork, and Ross, and had issue,
  (1) William, m. Margaret, dau. of George Warburton, of Firmount, and d.s.p. 1808 (bur. in York Minster). He was associated politically with Horace Walpole.
  (2) Thomas, M.P., Accountant-General, m. 1775, Anne, dau. of David Aigion, and d. 1810, having by her (who d. 1831) had issue,
    1. Ulysses, 2nd Lord Downes, G.C.B., K.T.S., Gen. in the Army, b. 15 Aug. 1788; s. his cousin William, 1st Lord Downes, m. 1st, 20 June, 1815, Maria, only dau. and heir of Walter Bagenal, of Bagenalstown, and by her (who d. 20 Aug. 1842) had issue, two daus., Anne, m. 27 April, 1838, John Henry, Earl of Clonmell; and Charlotte, m. 12 Feb. 1851, James, Lord Seaton. He m. 2ndly, 4 Aug. 1846, Christopheria, widow of John Willis Fleming, of Stoneham, and dan. of James Buchanan, but by her (who d. 18 Oct. 1860) he had no issue. Lord Downes d.s.p.m. 26 July, 1864 (see BURKE's Extinct Peerage).
    1. Anne, m. Nathaniel Sneyd, M.P.
    2. Mary, m. John Staunton Rochfort, of Clogrennan.
    3. Charlotte, m. 17 Feb. 1815, Rev. Zachariah Cornock, and d. 1827.
  (3) Robert, H.E.I.C.S., m. Anne, dau. of Hugh Hickman, of Fenloe, co. Clare, and had issue,
    1. Mary, m. 31 July, 1800, her cousin Rev. John Hussey Burgh, of Dromkeen, and had issue (see HUSSEY-DE-BURGH of Dromkeen).
    2. Catherine, m. Alexander Hamilton, son of George Hamilton, of Hampton, Baron of The Exchequer.
    (1) Margaretta Amelia, created Baroness Oriel 5 June, 1790, Viscountess Ferrard 1797, and m. 14 Dec. 1764, John Foster, created Baron Oriel 1821, and had issue (see BURKE's Peerage, MASSEREENE, V.).
    (2) Anne, m. 4 July, 1767, Right Hon. Walter Hussey-Burgh, and d. 1782, leaving issue (see HUSSEY-DE BURGH of Dromkeen).
    (3) Dorothea, m. 1760, John Rochfort, of Clogrennan (see that family).
    (4) Catherine, m. 1754, Dixie Coddington, of Oldbridge (see that family).
    (5) Maria, m. Dec. 1762, Michael Keating, of Castle Mey.
  1. Elizabeth, m. 1736, the Right Hon. Anthony Foster, Lord Chief Baron, and had, with other issue, a son, John, created Lord Oriel (see BURKE's Peerage, MASSEREENE, V.).
3. THOMAS, of Oldtown, of whom presently.
4. John, of Troy House, co. Monmouth, b. 1673; d. 1743, leaving two sons,
  1. Henry (Rev.), whose only dau. and heir, Maria, m. Thomas Johnes, of Hafod.
  2. Ashburnham, of Stanley Park, co. Gloucester, and had issue, Henry.
5. Charles, d. unm. (admon. 6 May, 1693).
1. Margaret, m. — Shepheard.
2. Elizabeth, m. 1687, Boyle, son of Sir R. Aldworth.
3. Dorothea, m. Right Rev. Thomas Smyth, Bishop of Limerick, ancestor of Viscounts Gort (see BURKE's Peerage).

THOMAS BURGH, of Oldtown, 3rd son of the Bishop of Ardagh, b. 1670, M.P. for Naas 1713, Engineer and Surveyor-General for Ireland; m. Mary, dau. of Right Rev. William Smyth, Bishop of Kilmore (see SMYTH of Gaybrook), by whom (who d. 23 Oct. 1753) he had issue,
1. THOMAS, his heir.
2. Theobald, b. 1709; d. 1727.
3. Ulysses, d. unm. 1742.
4. John (Rev.), Vicar of Donaghmore, co. Monaghan, m. 1763, Anna Maria Walden, and d. 1767.
5. Richard, d. after 1769.
1. Elizabeth, m. Ignatius Hussey, of Donore, co. Kildare, and was mother of RIGHT HON. WALTER HUSSEY-BURGH, Lord Chief Baron of the Exchequer in Ireland (see HUSSEY-DE-BURGH of Donore and Dromkeen).
2. Mary, m. 1726, her cousin Thomas Burgh, of Dromkeen.
3. Dorothea, m. 1749 (as his 2nd wife), Right Hon. Anthony Foster, Lord Chief Baron of the Exchequer in Ireland and d.s.p.
4. Catherine, m. Very Rev. John Alcock, D.D., Dean of Ferns, and d. 1797.

Mr. Burgh d. 10 Dec. 1730, and was s. by his eldest son,
THOMAS BURGH, of Oldtown, M.P. for Lanesborough, and for Naas, b. 1707; m. 1st, by licence, dated 19 Dec. 1734, Margaret, dau. and co-heir of William Sprigg, of Clonevoe, by whom (who d. 30 Dec. 1744) he had issue,
1. Alice, m. J. Fox, 24th Regt.

He m. 2ndly, June, 1752, Katherine, dau. of Sir Richard Wolseley, 1st bart. of Mount Wolseley, by whom he had,
1. THOMAS, his heir.   2. Richard.
2. Mary, b. 1759; d. 1811.
3. Catherine, m. 1765, James Caulfield, of Castle Stewart, co. Tyrone.

Mr. Burgh d. 23 June, 1759, and was s. by his eldest son,
THOMAS BURGH, of Oldtown, M.P. successively for Harristown and Fore, b. 23 Jan. 1754; m. 10 Aug. 1784, Florinda, dau. of Right Hon. Charles Gardiner, M.P. and sister of Luke, 1st Viscount Mountjoy by whom (who d. 1830) he had issue,
1. THOMAS JOHN, his heir, Dean of Cloyne.
2. Charles, drowned, 1793.
3. Walter (Rev.), Vicar of Naas, m. 1839, Elizabeth Langrishe, and d.s.p. 1858.
4. Luke, R.N., b. 1791, killed in action at sea, 1809.

5. Arthur, R.N., b. 1792; d. unm. 1835.
6. Charles, b. 1795; drowned 1822.
7. John, Major 93rd Highlanders, b. 1799; m. Emma Maria Hunt, and d. 1875, leaving a son,
  Hubert John, b. 1845; d. unm. 1877.
8. William (Rev.), D.D., Rector of Ardboe, and of St. John's Church, Sandymount, Dublin, b. 1801; m. 1st, Feb. 1827, Anne, dau. of Rev. John Copinger, and by her (who d. 1850) had issue. He m. 2ndly, Janet Macartney, and d. 1866. He left issue,
  1. Maurice Thomas (Ven.) M.A. Dublin, Archdeacon of Kildare and Vicar of Naas, b. 29 Dec. 1827; m. 3 July, 1861, Henrietta, dau. of Edward John Barry Beauman, of Furness. She d. 31 Dec. 1893. He d. 31 Oct. 1894, leaving issue,
    (1) William Edward (Rev.), B.A., T.C.D., Chaplain to the Troops in S. Africa during the war, b. 4 July, 1863; d. unm. 4 Sept. 1902, at Woodstock, Cape Colony, of disease contracted on active service.
    (2) Edward Joseph, of Loggadowden, Ballymore-Eustace, co. Kildare, J.P., b. 1 Nov. 1864; m. 1st, Oct. 1886, Oliveria Cromwell Frankland, dau. of Adm. Frankland. She d. 26 Oct. 1886. He m. 2ndly, 9 June, 1891, Aimée Florence, youngest dau. of George Frederick Truscott, and by her has issue,
      John Maurice Truscott, b. 23 Jan. 1895.
      Nancy Olive, b. 9 May, 1892.
    (1) Elizabeth Anne, b. 1 Nov. 1864; d. unm. 1889.
    (2) Mary Florinda, b. 15 July, 1867; m. 15 Sept. 1903, Arthur Walter Lempriere Hanbury, only son of Walter G. Hanbury, of Worcester Park, Surrey.
    (3) Charlotte Josephine, b. 14 July, 1869.
  2. William, b. 1820; m. 1864, Hannah, dau. of Thomas Monck Mason, Capt. R.N.; and d. 1878, leaving one son,
    William.
  3. Hubert, in Holy Orders of the Church of Rome, b. 1830; d. 24 April, 1901.
  4. John, b. 1831; d. 1833.
  5. Walter, b. 1834; m. 1862, May Mayne, and d. that year.
  6. Alfred Charles, b. 1857; m. 25 Feb. 1880, Clemina Elizabeth, dau. of the Hon. Henry Martley, Q.C., Judge of the Landed Estates Court, Ireland (see that family), and had issue, a dau.
  7. Ernest Macartney, b. 1863; m. 1888, Constance Yeo, and has issue.
  1. Letitia, d. 1841.
  2. Sarah Anne, m. 1858, Lieut.-Col. Edward Codrington, and has issue.
  3. Maria, m. 1860, Rev. A. Labatt, and had issue.
  4. Theodosia Isabella, m. 2 Sept. 1858, Hon. Edward Ogilvie, of Yulgilbar, Clarence River, New South Wales, and has issue.
  5. Emma Sophia, m. 1861, Col. Robert French.
  6. Anne Charlotte, d. 1891.   7. Cecilia.
  8. Edith, m. 1879, Thomas Rolleston, and has issue.
  9. Florence, d. 1886.
  10. Agatha, m. 1890, Rev. George Tombe.
  11. Maud, d. 1882.
1. Florinda, d. unm. 1869.
2. Dorothea, m. Capt. Thomas Monck Mason, R.N., and has issue.
3. Maria, d. 1803.
4. Anna Maria, m. Ernest Augustus Belford, and d. 1863, leaving issue.

Mr. Burgh d. 1832, and was s. by his eldest son,
VERY REV. THOMAS JOHN BURGH,* of Oldtown, Dean of Cloyne, m. 4 May, 1811, the Lady Anna Louisa Hely-Hutchinson, dau. of the Right Hon. Francis Hely-Hutchinson, M.P., and sister of John, 3rd Earl of Donoughmore. (Her sister, the Lady Charlotte, m. Richard Wolfe, of Forenaghts, the last descendant of Mary Burgh, of Dromkeen (vide ante), and d.s.p. 1870). Lady Anna, who d. 27 Dec. 1857, had issue,
1. Thomas John, b. and d. 1812.   2. THOMAS, of Oldtown.
3. Francis, Lieut.-Col. Dublin City Artillery, d.s.p. 1892.
4. Henry, LL.D., m. 17 Aug. 1848, Elizabeth Louisa, dau. of Hans Hendrick of Kerdiffstown, co. Kildare, and d. 1876, s.p.
5. Ulysses, b. 1820; d. 1827.
6. Hubert, b. 1821; d. 1827.
7. Robert, of Caversham, Guildford, W. Australia, b. 23 June, 1822; m. 1846, Clara, dau. of R. Wellerton, and d. 1884, leaving issue, Henry, Clara, Fanny, and Louisa.
8. George, of Millbanke House, co. Kildare, m. 1850, Constance, dau. of Wellesley Mathews, and d. 6 March, 1855, leaving issue, Edward Odo, d. unm. 1880.
  Violet Flora, m. 7 Oct. 1875, Andrew Alexander Watt, D.L., of Thornhill, and has issue (see that family).
9. John, b. 1830; d. 1837.
1. Frances Louisa, m. Nov. 1852, Samuel Hamilton Goold-Adams (see that family). She d. 13 Sept. 1905.
2. Florinda (twin with her sister, Charlotte), m. 26 Oct. 1861, Thomas Hutchinson Tristram, D.C.L., Chancellor of the Diocese of London, and has issue.
3. Charlotte, m. Oct. 1857. Lieut.-Col. James Stuart Tighe, of Rossanagh, co. Wicklow. He d. 3 July, 1904, leaving issue (see TIGHE of Woodstock).

The Dean of Cloyne d. 4 Sept. 1845, and was s. by his eldest surviving son,

---

* Extract from a Patent dated 6 March, 1848, Office of Arms, Dublin Castle (Sir William Betham, Ulster). " . . . . having traced the descent of the Right Hon. Ulysses Lord Baron Downes, and THOMAS BURGH of Oldtown, and finding them, from sufficient evidence, to be descended legitimately from the ancient and noble family of DE BURGH, of which there were Earls of Cornwall, Kent, and Ulster, they have fully established their right to re-assume their ancient name of DE BURGH."

THOMAS DE BURGH, of Oldtown, b. 2 June, 1813; m. 15 April, 1848, Jane, only child of Major Thomas Campbell-Graham, 1st Royal Scots, of Scarva House, co. Monaghan, and d. 15 July, 1872, leaving issue,
1. THOMAS JOHN, now of Oldtown.
2. Ulick George Campbell, C.B., of Scarva, Col. in the Army, late Deputy Inspector Gen. of Remounts at Headquarters, late 3rd and 7th Dragoon Guards, B.A. Trin. Coll. Dublin, b. 19 July, 1855; m. 22 Nov. 1883, Anna Blanche Constance, only child of Charles Augustus Francis, 3rd son of Lord William Paget (see BURKE's *Peerage*, ANGLESEY, M.), and has issue,
  1. Geoffrey Henry Paget, b. and d. 1884.
  2. Desmond Herlouin, b. 5 Aug. 1897.
3. Hugo Henry Patrick, of Ballinapearce, co. Wexford, b. 8 June, 1868; m. 7 Oct. 1893, Mabel, dau. of J. Beaumont, of Tarnley Lodge, St. Albans. He was killed in action 11 April, 1900, at Jammersburg Drift, near Wepener, Orange River Colony. He left issue,
  1. Hugo Graham, b. 16 Oct. 1894.
  2. Ulric Campbell, b. 29 July, 1898.
  1. Marguerita, b. 27 March, 1897.
1. Anna Louisa Margaret, m. 22 Oct. 1874, Commander Dashwood Goldie Tandy, R.N., who d. 3 Oct. 1883, leaving issue,
  Reginald Dashwood, of Johnsbrook, Kells, co. Meath, late Lieut. Lancashire Fus., b. 25 May, 1883; m. 9 May, 1906, Valerie Olivia Wellesley, dau. of Arthur George Henry Wellesley (see BURKE's *Peerage*, WELLINGTON, D.), and has issue,
    (1) Reginald Napper, b. 15 June, 1909.
    (2) Cyril Edward, b. 17 Oct. 1911.
2. Una, b. and d. 1859.

Arms—Or a cross gu. *Crest*—A cat-a-mountain sejant guardant ppr., collared and chained or. *Motto*—A cruce salus.

Seat—Oldtown, Naas, co. Kildare. *Clubs*—Carlton and Kildare Street.

DE BURGH OF DROMKEEN AND DONORE.

JOHN DIGBY TOWNSEND HUSSEY DE BURGH, of Dromkeen House, co. Limerick, J.P., b. 16 Sept. 1870: s. his grandfather, 1887; m. 7 Sept. 1897, Elizabeth Mary Madara, dau. of the late Rev. Francis Cooper, B.A., Rector of Cahir, co. Tipperary, and has issue,
1. ULICK FRANCIS, b. 9 Nov. 1900.
2. Hubert Walter Digby Townsend, b. 28 Oct. 1907.
1. Evelyn Mary Louisa, b. June, 1898.
2. Elizabeth Emily, b. June, 1903.

Lineage.—IGNATIUS HUSSEY, of Donore, co. Kildare, b. before 1690, 3rd son of Walter Hussey, of Donore, and grandson of Edward Hussey, of Mulhussey (see HUSSEY-WALSH of *Mulhussey*) conformed to the Protestant Religion 10 Aug. 1718, entered Gray's Inn as a student 3 March, 1704, and called to the Bar M.T. 27 Nov. 1719; m. 9 Oct. 1724, 1st, a dau. of William Bursey; and 2ndly, 13 July, 1740, Elizabeth (b. 7 June, 1705; d. 22 Oct. 1757; made will 21 Aug. 1746, proved 4 Nov. 1757), dau. of Thomas de Burgh, of Oldtown, in same co., M.P. for Naas. He made will 4 Sept. 1741, proved 3 March, 1743. He d. 13 Jan. 1743-4, being the father of
THE RIGHT HON. WALTER HUSSEY-BURGH, distinguished as one of the most eloquent advocates at the Irish Bar. He became afterwards Lord Chief Baron of the Court of Exchequer in Ireland. Mr. Hussey-Burgh became possessed of one-half of the property of Dromkeen, on the death of his cousin Richard Burgh, and adopted the name of BURGH, in accordance with that gentleman's will (see DE BURGH *of Oldtown*). He was b. 23 Aug. 1742; m. 4 July, 1767, Anne, dau. of Thomas Burgh, of Bert, co. Kildare, by Anne his wife, dau. of Right Rev. Dive Downes, Bishop of Cork and Ross, and by her (who d. 1782) had issue,
1. JOHN, of whom presently.
1. Eliza, m. 4 Feb. 1797, Archdeacon Hill.
2. Catherine, m. as his second wife, 4 Nov. 1794, Sir John Macartney, Bart. (who d. 29 May, 1812). She d. 10 Sept. 1840.
3. Mary, m. 24 Feb. 1793, Richard Griffith, M.P. of Millicent, co. Kildare; d. 10 Sept. 1820.
4. Anne, b. 2 June, 1814; m. 19 May, 1798, Bucknell M'Carthy.
Chief Baron Hussey-Burgh d. 29 Oct. 1783, and was s. by his son,
THE REV. JOHN HUSSEY-BURGH, of Dromkeen, b. 1768; m. 31 July, 1800, Mary, dau. of Robert Burgh, 3rd son of Thomas Burgh, of Bert, ancestor of Lord Downes, and had issue,
1. WALTER, his heir.
2. Robert (Rev.), b. 1 Sept. 1803; m. Louisa, dau. of James Fitzgerald, of Shepperton, co. Clare.
3. Edward, b. 30 Nov. 1811; m. about 1854, Ellen, dau. of — Meares, and had Edward, and other issue; he d. March, 1865.
4. Thomas, b. 30 Nov. 1816; Capt. 61st Regt.; m. 8 May, 1840, Georgina Maria (b. 1820; d. 12 July, 1881), dau. of Thomas Kearney, C.B., of Sunville, co. Limerick, and d. 1848, having had, with two daus. (1. Anne Sophia, m. 27 July, 1865, Jonathan Bruce, of Miltown Castle, co. Cork, and has issue (*see that family*); and 2. Kate), a son,
  Thomas Francis, of Sunville, J.P., Lieut.-Col. late Leicestershire Regt., b. 9 Sept. 1845; m. 6 Feb. 1882, Lilias McDowall, dau. of late Maj.-Gen. Stockley.

1. Anne, b. 2 June, 1814; m. Dr. Reardon, of Limerick, and d. 1902, leaving issue.
Mr. Hussey-Burgh d. 7 May, 1830, and was s. by his eldest son,
WALTER HUSSEY DE BURGH, of Donore House, co. Kildare, of Dromkeen House, co. Limerick, and Cae Llenar, co. Carnarvon, J.P., High Sheriff of Kildare 1839-40, b. 27 June, 1801; m. 1st, 18 May, 1820, Elizabeth Jane, dau of James Fitzgerald, of Shepperton. co. Clare, and had issue,
1. JOHN HAMILTON, of Dromkeen.
1. Mary Adelaide, d. 10 Feb. 1908.
2. Elizabeth Jane, bapt. 31 Oct. 1824.
3. Louisa Catherine, bapt. 13 Jan. 1826; m. 20 Oct. 1863, Francis Hamilton, of Rowleston, co. Dublin, who d. 1868.
4. Charlotte Elizabeth, m. — Townsend.
5. Harriett, b. 3, bapt. 6 March, 1827.
6. Anna Maria, m. William Ker, of Killingworth River, Goulbourne, Australia, and has issue. 7. Flora.
He m. 2ndly, 11 Feb. 1840, Hessie, dau. of Rev. Alexander M'Clintock, 2nd son of the late John M'Clintock, of Drumcar, co. Louth (see MCCLINTOCK of *Rathvinden*), and by her (who d. 27 June, 1858) had issue,
2. Albert Edward Walter, b. 20 Feb. 1842; d. 23 April, 1861.
3. ULYSSES HUBERT, of Donore, b. 25 May, 1850.
4. Alexander Averil, b. 15 Sept. 1854.
8. Victoria Dorothea, m. 22 Jan. 1863, George Wilmot, of The Mount, Shoreham, Kent, and has issue. 9. Fanny.
10. Hessie Emily, m. 13 May, 1896, Rev. William Joseph Edwards, Rector of Llandow and Vicar of Colwinstone, S. Wales.
11. Gertrude Florence Ann. 12. Gwenellen Georgina Caroline.
13. Helena Louisa.
He d. 19 Oct. 1862, and was s. in Dromkeen by his eldest son, JOHN HAMILTON; and in Donore House, by his 2nd surviving son, ULYSSES HUBERT. The eldest son,
JOHN HAMILTON HUSSEY DE BURGH, of Dromkeen House, and Kilfinnan Castle, co. Cork, J.P. co. Limerick, b. 10 June, 1822; m. 1 May, 1844, Louisa, dau. of Jonas M. Townsend, of Shepperton, co. Cork, and d. May, 1887, having had issue,
1. WALTER JOHN, b. 1845; m. 12 Nov. 1860, Emily Florence, dau. of Thomas Sherlock, and d.v.p. 1874, leaving issue,
  1. JOHN DIGBY TOWNSHEND, now of Dromkeen House.
  2. Hubert. b. 1873, d. an infant.
  1. Mary Emily, b. 31 May, 1872.
2. Maurice, b. 1848; m. 1891, dau. of — Sm'th, of Nenagh, widow of Major Whitty, and d. 1 May, 1890.
3. John, b. 1850; d. 17 Aug. 1896; m. Wilhelmina, dau. of — Hungerford.
4. Ulysses, b. 1858.   5. Hubert.
1. Jane Adeliza Clementina, b. 1845; m. 1st, 29 Sept., 1864, Henry John Stephens Townshend, of Castle Townshend, co. Cork, who d. 7 Sept. 1869, leaving issue (*see that family*); 2ndly, Arthur Cave, of Schull.
2. Louisa, b. 1849; m. John Hamilton Bryan, of Dunmanway.

Seats—Dromkeen, Pallas Green, Limerick, and Kilfinnan Castle, Glandore, co. Cork.

BLAKE DE BURGH OF COOLCON.

CHARLES ORMSBY BLAKE DE BURGH, of Coolcon, co. Mayo, and of Rath O'Nora, co. Sligo, b. 29 March, 1840; m. 29 July, 1868, his cousin Honora Mabel Angela, only child and heiress of Walter Blake Lawrence of Lisreaghan, Capt. 41st Regt. and Knight of Malta, and by her (who d. 1873) has issue,

Violet Olivia, b. 17 July, 1869.

Mr. C. O. Blake has assumed by Royal Licence, dated 23 Oct. 1896, the additional surname of DE BURGH.

Lineage.—Richard Caddell (or Niger), of Kiltorrogue, co. Galway, the common ancestor of all the families of Blake, in Connaught, was living 1277, 1290, 1312, and 1315. He left, with other issue, a son,
WALTER BLAKE, Burgess of Galway, living 1346, who left, with other issue, a 3rd son,
GEOFFREY BLAKE, who left, with other issue, an eldest son,
WILLIAM BLAKE, Burgess of Galway, living 1421, 1424, 1445, and 1453. He left, with other issue, an eldest son,
JOHN BLAKE, Mayor of Galway 1488, m. Amabel de Burgh, who left, with other issue, a 3rd son,
ANDREW BLAKE, who left three sons, of whom the third,
WALTER BLAKE, left issue, two sons,

De la Cherois.

1. Marcus, from whom the family of BLAKE of Ballinafad is descended.
2. ROBERT, of whom we treat.

The 2nd son,
ROBERT BLAKE, of Ballincourt and Ardfry, co. Galway, *m.* Katherine, dau. of Richard D'Arcy, and *d.* 1615, leaving, with other issue, two sons,
1. Richard, the eldest son, who was ancestor of Lord Wallscourt (see BURKE's *Peerage*).
2. JOHN, of whom we treat.

The younger son,
JOHN BLAKE, of Coolcon, co. Mayo, purchased in 1632, from the Right Hon. Lord Lambert two quarters of land called Cloonebanane, and two quarters called Carnehely, both in the barony of Kilmaine, co. Mayo; and in 1634, he obtained by way of mortgage from John McJoyne, the Castle of Coolcon, and two quarters of land adjoining it, in the same barony and co.; in 1636, he was the owner of the moiety of the four quarters of Ballyglass, and sometime prior to that year he obtained by way of mortgage from Redmond McRuddery, of Castlereagh, one cartron of Carrowenkilleen, and half a quarter in Carroweveline, being all situate in the barony of Claremorris, and co. Mayo. He was one of the forfeiting proprietors of 1641, when these properties as well as his house in Galway, were confiscated by the Cromwellian Government. He was *s.* by his eldest son and heir,
FRANCIS BLAKE, of Moyne Castle, co. Mayo, J.P. co. Galway, to whom the castle of Coolcon, and the other forfeited estates of his father were restored by letters patent, dated 17 May (enrolled 26 July), 1677, by CHARLES II. He and his son Martin, in common with the rest of the Irish Roman Catholics, fought on the side of King JAMES in 1691, and were attainted for high treason, but were pardoned in 1698 by WILLIAM III. His will was proved at Tuam in 1716. His son and heir,
MARTIN BLAKE, of Coolcon, became a Protestant, 8 June, 1709 (Protestant Converts, Rolls Office). He *m.* Mabel, dau. of Sir George Browne, 2nd bart. of the Neale, by whom he had issue,
1. FRANCIS, of whom presently.
2. Jane, *m.* Edmund Dillon, of Hollywell, co. Mayo.
3. Alice, *m.* Kirwan, of Blindwell, co. Mayo.

The only son,
FRANCIS BLAKE, of Coolcon, *m.* 13 June, 1721, Frances, dau. and eventually co-heiress of Charles Daly, of Callow, by Anne his wife, dau. of Hyacinth D'Arcy, of Kiltullagh, and by her (who *m.* 2ndly, John D'Arcy, of Ballykine, co. Mayo) had issue,
1. CHARLES, of whom presently.
2. John, Major of Galway Volunteers 1779.
3. Anthony of Shruel House, *m.* Margaret, dau. of Martin Kirwan, of Dalgin Park, co. Mayo and *d.s.p.* His will was proved 3 Jan. 1806.
4. Martin, *d. unm.* 1805.
1. Mabel, *d. unm.* 1797. 2. Anne, *d. unm.*

The eldest son,
CHARLES BLAKE, of Coolcon and Moyne, *m.* 17 April, 1762, Margaret, dau. of Denis Daly, of Raford, by Lady Anne Burke his wife, dau. of Michael, 10th Earl of Clanricarde, and *d.* 1769, having by her (who *m.* 2ndly, John D'Arcy, of Ballykine, and 3rdly, Stephen Blake, 4th son of Sir Walter Blake, 10th bart. of Menlo) had issue,
1. CHARLES, of whom presently.
2. Denis John, Capt. 89th Regt. was mortally wounded at the battle of Alexandria, on the staff of Sir Ralph Abercrombie. His will was proved in Dublin 1803.
1. Frances, *m.* John D'Arcy, of Houndswood, and had issue.

The elder son,
CHARLES BLAKE, of Coolcon, Moyne, and Merlin Park, J.P. and D.L., *m.* 3 Aug. 1790, his cousin Georgina, dau. and co-heir of Sir George Browne, 6th bart., of the Neale, and niece of John, 1st Lord Kilmaine, and by her (who *d.* 24 Nov. 1840) had issue,
1. CHARLES KILMAINE, his heir.
2. Denis John, *m.* April, 1831, Anna, dau. of Samuel Poer, of Belleville Park, co. Waterford, and had issue.
3. Martin Kirwan, *m.* 1835, Julia Maria, dau. of John Blake, of Tuam (see BLAKE *of Ballyglunin*), and had issue,
  1. Charles, *d.s.p.* 2. John. 3. Martin.
4. George Francis, J.P., Registrar of the Royal College of Surgeons, Dublin.
1. Olivia. 2. Georgina.
3. Julia.
1. Georgiana, *m.* 1 March, 1813, Walter Lawrence, of Lisreaghan, co. Galway, High Sheriff 1820, and had issue (*see that family*).
2. Margaret, *m.* George Kirwan, of Dalgin Park, co. Mayo, and *d.s.p.* 1875. 3. Frances Augusta.

The eldest son,
CHARLES KILMAINE BLAKE, of Coolcon and Merlin Park, J.P. and D.L. co. Mayo, High Sheriff co. Galway 1844, *m.* 7 May, 1839, Dorothea Stewart, last surviving child and heir of Thomas Gore Ormsby, of Comyn, co. Sligo, and *d.* 1867, leaving issue,
1. CHARLES ORMSBY, now of Coolcon.
2. Francis Thomas, *b.* 1843.

Arms—Quarterly; 1st and 4th arg, a fret gu. (BLAKE); 2nd and 3rd, or a cross gu. in the first canton a lion rampant sa. (DE BURGH). **Crests**—1. A cat-a-mountain passant guardant ppr. (BLAKE); 2. A cat-a-mountain sejant guardant ppr., collared and chained or (DE BURGH). **Motto**—Virtus sola nobilitat.

Seat—Coolcon, co. Mayo.

DE LA CHEROIS OF DONAGHADEE.

GEORGE LESLIE DE LA CHEROIS, of the Manor House, Donaghadee, co. Down, *b.* 1866.

Lineage.—The family of De la Cherois descends from the younger branch of an ancient and noble house in France, formerly resident at Cheroy or Cherois, a small town near Sens, in the province of Champagne, whence the family name is derived.

The Revocation of the Edict of Nantes, in the year 1685, compelled the De la Cherois, being Protestants, to leave their native country. In the year 1641,
CAPT. SAMUEL DE LA CHEROIS (ancestor of the family settled in Ireland) served in the war undertaken by Cardinal Richelieu against the House of Austria. He left three sons,
1. NICHOLAS, of whom presently.
2. Daniel, Capt., fled to Holland with his brothers, 1685, and was afterwards Capt. in William's Army.
3. Bourjonval, Lieut. in the Army, killed at Dungannon, *d. unm.*

The eldest son,
NICHOLAS DE LA CHEROIS, embraced the military profession and was made a Capt. of Fusiliers by Louis XIV, 1677. In the year 1685 he fled with his brothers to Holland, where they were received with great kindness by the Statholder, into whose service they entered, obtaining commissions in the Dutch Army of the same rank as those they had held in that of France. In 1689, WILLIAM, Prince of Orange, being called to the throne of Great Britain, formed several regiments of French Huguenots, in one of which Nicholas de la Cherois was appointed Major, Daniel, Captain, and Bourjonval, Lieutenant. They accompanied King WILLIAM to Ireland 1690, and finally settled there. Major de la Cherois distinguished himself at the battle of the Boyne, and afterwards performed a very gallant action, making fifteen hundred men lay down their arms with only a subaltern's guard, for which he was presented by the Government with fifteen hundred crowns and a Lieutenant-Colonelcy. He *m.* Marie, sister of Louis Crommelin, of St. Quentin, Picardy, France, and left a dau., Madeleine, *m.* Daniel Crommelin, of Lisburn, and an only son,
SAMUEL DE LA CHEROIS, *b.* 1700; *m.* 1731, Mademoiselle Sarah Cormière, and had issue,
1. DANIEL, his heir. 2. Nicholas, Capt. 9th Foot, *d.s.p.* 1829.
3. Samuel, who assumed the name of CROMMELIN (*see* CROMMELIN *of Carrowdore*).
1. Judith, *m.* John Smyth.

The eldest son,
DANIEL DE LA CHEROIS, of Donaghadee, *m.* 13 Feb. 1782, Mary, dau. of Alexander Crommelin, and had issue,
1. DANIEL, of Donaghadee, *b.* 1 Dec. 1783; J.P. and D.L., High Sheriff co. Down 1829; *d.s.p.* 1850.
2. Samuel Louis, J.P. and D.L., *m.* 1820, Mary, dau. of John Roland, and *d.* 1836, having had issue,
  1. Nicholas, J.P., of Ballywilliam, *m.* 16 July, 1864, Annie Tenant, who *d.* 18 Nov. 1895. He *d.s.p.* 15 Jan. 1874.
  2. DANIEL, of The Manor House, Donaghadee.
  3. Samuel, of Ballywilliam, Donaghadee, *d.* 5 Dec. 1908; *m.* 26 Sept. 1854, Catherine O'Donell (who *d.* 26 Dec. 1909), only dau. of Rev. William Young, of Ballywilliam, and left with other issue,
    Samuel George, *b.* 1856.
  4. Louis, Lieut. R.N., dec. 5. Alexander, dec.
  1. Jane, *m.* 3 Feb. 1856, Capt. William Young McDowel, and *d.s.p.* 21 Nov. 1866. He *m.* 2ndly, 4 Feb. 1867, Mary, dau. of James Moore, and *d.* June, 1880, leaving issue.
3. Nicholas, Ensign 47th Regt., killed in Spain, at Barossa, 1811.
1. Mary, *d.* 1854.

The 2nd son,
DANIEL DE LA CHEROIS, of the Manor House, Donaghadee, co. Down, J.P. and D.L., High Sheriff 1863, M.A. Trin. Coll. Dublin, Barrister-at-Law (1849), *b.* 1825, and *d.* 8 April, 1905, having *m.* 1854, Ellen, dau. of George Leslie, and by her (who *d.* 4 Dec. 1891) had issue,
1. DANIEL LOUIS, who *s.* his father.
2. Edmund Bourjonval, M.D., *m.* Jan. 1893, the widow of C. Fisher, of Brighton, and *d.* 1901.
3. GEORGE LESLIE, now of The Manor House, Donaghadee.
4. Charles Hutcheson, M.R.C.V.S.
1. Elizabeth Mary Angelica, *d. unm.* 29 March, 1910.
2. Helen Vaughan, *m.* 10 Sept. 1891, Edwin Hamilton, M.A., Barrister, and has issue (*see* HAMILTON *of Hampton Hall*).
3. Mary Louise, *m.* Sept. 1892, E. N. Leslie, of Donaghadee.
4. Edith Madeline.

The eldest son,
DANIEL LOUIS DE LA CHEROIS, of The Manor House, Donaghadee, Major and Hon. Lieut.-Col. 3rd Batt. Royal Irish Rifles, late Lieut. 4th Hussars, J.P. co. Down, *b.* 1855, and *d. unm.* 26 Nov. 1909, being *s.* by his brother.

IRELAND. Delmege.

Arms—Gu., a chevron between three mullets in chief one and two or, and an anchor arg. in base. *Crest*—An anchor erect az. *Motto*—Fac et spera.
Seat—The Manor House, Donaghadee, co. Down. *Club*—Ulster, Belfast.

DE LA CHEROIS—CROMMELIN. *See* CROMMELIN.

DELAP OF MONELLAN.

JAMES BOGLE DELAP, of Monellan, co. Donegal, and The Manor House, Lillingstone Lovel, Bucks, J.P. for Bucks, High Sheriff co. Donegal 1874, late Hon. Major Royal Bucks Hussars, *b.* 8 Jan. 1847; *m.* 7 Feb. 1872, Marion, dau. of Protheroe Smith, M.D., and has issue,

JAMES ONSLOW KINGSMILL, *b.* 12 July, 1881; *m.* 27 Jan. 1904, Dorothy Audrey, only dau. of Duncan Davison, of Bedford, and has issue,
  Hugh Alan, *b.* 8 May, 1906.
  Isabella Singleton.

Lineage.—ALLAN DUNLOP, who resided at Irving, co. Ayr, *m.* Miss Montgomery, and had six daus. and one son, HUGH DUNLOP, who is stated to have left Scotland and settled in Sligo, Ireland, about the year 1600. He *m.* Miss Aiken, and left three sons, one of whom, ROBERT DUNLOP, of Sligo, Merchant, removed to Ballyshannon, and *m.* Jane Murray, and was father of

ROBERT DELAP, of Ballyshannon, Merchant, living 1681, who *m.* Anna, dau. of Rev. Robert Lindsey, of Killybegs, co. Donegal, and by her (who was living in 1724) had issue. The 2nd, but eldest surviving son,

REV. SAMUEL DELAP, of Rawn or Raan, co. Donegal, Minister of Letterkenny, whose will, dated 10 Aug. 1762, was proved in the Diocese of Armagh, 6 Jan. 1763, had, by Sarah his wife, with five daus., five sons, of whom the youngest,

SAMUEL DELAP, of Ramelton, co. Donegal, Treasurer of that co., *m.* Anne, eldest dau. of Rev. Seth Drummond, and *d.* 1781, leaving a dau., Sarah, *m.* Joseph Storey, of Bingfield; and a son,

ROBERT DELAP, of Monellan, Barrister-at-Law, *m.* about 1776, Mary Ann, only child of James Bogle, of Monellan, and *d.* 1782, having had issue,
1. SAMUEL FRANCIS, his heir.
2. James Bogle, of Stoke Park, Surrey, J.P. and D.L., Lieut.-Col. 1st Regt. Surrey Militia, *b.* 24 June, 1779; *m.* 6 May, 1809, Harriet, eldest dau. and co-heiress (with her sister, Susan Eliza, *m.* Col. Hon. Thomas Cranley Onslow, 2nd son of the Earl of Onslow) of Nathaniel Hillier, of Stoke Park, and *d.s.p.* Nov. 1850, his widow surviving until 1859.
3. William Drummond Dunlop, of Monasterboyce, co. Louth, *b.* 3 July, 1760, resumed by Royal Licence, 24 Jan. 1861, his family's original surname of DUNLOP. He *m.* 1st, 5 Sept. 1795, Catherine, eldest dau. of Right Rev. William Foster, D.D., Bishop of Clogher, and by her (who *d.* 5 Sept. 1842) had issue,
  1. ROBERT FOSTER, of Monasterboice, J.P., High Sheriff 1873, *b.* 10 April, 1809; *m.* 15 March, 1836, Hon. Anne Elizabeth Skeffington, sister of John, Viscount Massereene and Ferrard, K.P., and *d.* Nov. 1875, having had issue,
    (1) William James Skeffington, Lieut. R.E., *b.* at Geneva, 24 Nov. 1847; *d.* Sept. 1871.
    (1) Harriett Catherine.
    (2) Annette Elizabeth, *m.* 1870, Sir Leopold M'Clintock.
    (3) Blanche Louisa, *m.* 1881, Charles E. M'Clintock.
    (4) Helen Mary, *m.* 1874, Rev. H. West.
    (5) Dorothea Roberta, *m.* 1880, Richard Quin.
    (6) Mary Rachael.
  1. Catherine Letitia Drummond, *d. unm.* 1827.
  2. Mary Anne Sarah, *m.* David Ross, of Bladensburg, and *d.* 1841.
  3. Henrietta Jemima, *d. unm.* 1831.

He *m.* 2ndly, Mary, 2nd dau. of Col. Henry Gore Sankey, of Fort Frederick, co. Cavan, and *d.* 1875.

The eldest son,

SAMUEL FRANCIS DELAP, of Monellan, J.P. and D.L., *b.* 31 Dec. 1776; *m.* 1800, Susan, youngest dau. of the Hon. John Bennett, Judge of the Queen's Bench in Ireland, and by her (who *d.* 1825) had issue,
1. ROBERT, of Monellan.
2. John (Rev.), *m.* Marianne Sarah, only dau. of Robert Saunderson, of Dromkeen, co. Cavan, but *d.s.p.* 1841; his widow *m.* 8 March, 1853, the Hon. and Rev. George de la Poer Beresford, grandson of the 1st Lord Decies, and *d.* 14 Feb. 1884.
  1. Jane, *d.* 1864.
  2. Mary Anne, *m.* 31 May, 1864, Somerset Richard, 8th Lord Farnham, and *d.* 1 Nov. 1873. Lord Farnham *d.* 4 June, 1884.

The elder son,

THE REV. ROBERT DELAP, of Monellan, co. Donegal, *b.* 1 June, 1802; *m.* 16 Nov. 1835, Isabella, youngest dau. and co-heir of Sir James Galbraith, Bart., and *d.* 28 July, 1885, having by her (who *d.* 1870) had issue,
JAMES BOGLE, now of Monellan.
Susan Dorothea.

Arms—Quarterly: 1st and 4th, gu. on a pile arg. an eagle with two heads displayed of the field, armed or, between in base two roses of the second, barbed and seeded ppr. for DELAP; 2nd and 3rd, per pale az., and gu., a trefoil slipped arg. between three boars'

heads erased or, for GALBRAITH. *Crest*—A dexter arm in armour, grasping a sword combined with an arm sinister holding a rose sprig and bud ppr. Motto over, Merito. *Motto*—E spinis.
Seat—Monellan, Killygordon, co. Donegal Manor House, Lillingstone, Lovel, Bucks. *Club*—Carlton.

DE LA POER. *See* POWER.

DELMEGE or DOLMAGE OF RATHKEALE.

AUSTIN JONAS DOLMAGE, of Rathkeale, co. Limerick, *b.* July, 1838; *m.* Sept. 1864, Frances Millicent, only child of Goodrich Shedden, of Efford, Hants, late Capt. 8th Hussars (*see* SHEDDEN *of Paulerspury*), and has issue,
1. JOHN SHEDDEN, *b.* 1866.
2. Cecil Goodrich Julius, M.A., LL.D., Barrister-at-Law, *b.* 1870, *d.* 1 Nov. 1908.
3. Francis Alfred Emilio, Capt. 4th Batt. Connaught Rangers, *b.* 1875.

Mr. Dolmage was for several years an officer in the 49th and 22nd Regiments, and in the 87th Royal Irish Fusiliers. He also served in the Italian Army in the campaign of 1860-1, and is a Knight of SS. Maurice and Lazarre, and the Crown of Italy.

Lineage. The family of DOLMAGE, or DELMEGE (as the name is also written), is of Alsatian origin, and descends from ADAM DOLMAGE, who settled in the co. Limerick, *temp.* Louis XIV, being compelled, as were many other Protestants, to seek refuge in Ireland. He had a younger brother, Julius, who at the same time settled in the Island of Jamaica, where he and his descendants became possessed of considerable property. The last of this line, Adam Dolmage, *d.* in 1835, and his estates of Charlottenburg, Hopewell, and Union Hall, passed to his only child, a dau.

ADAM JOHN DOLMAGE, of Rathkeale, co. Limerick, whose grandfather quitted France on the Revocation of the Edict of Nantes, was a Capt. Loyal German Fusiliers in 1778. He *m.* Eliza Powell, and had issue,
1. JULIUS, his successor.
2. Tobias, of Court Lodge, co. Limerick; *m.* Arabella Collis, of the Kerry family of that name, and had issue,
  1. Collis Christopher John, Surg.-Major, served in the Kaffir war with the 27th Regt., and on the Staff during the Crimean campaign and Indian Mutiny. He *m.* Susan Maria, dau. of A. Chiappini, and *d.* 1861, having by her (who *d.* 8 April, 1902; had issue,
    (1) Edward Toby, of Ceylon, and Whitehall Court, S.W., *m.* Agnes Jessie, eldest dau. of John Scott. She *d.* 1875, having had issue, a son,
      Robert John, *b.* Feb. 1875.
    (2) Anthony Ansdell, of Ceylon, and Ashley Gardens, S.W., *m.* Edith, dau. of William Allan Geddes, and has issue,
      1. Edward, *d.* 1894.
      2. Cartrae Hamilton, Capt. 21st Lancers, *b.* 14 Jan. 1880; *m.* 19 Dec. 1906, Rose Isabel de Montmorency, 2nd dau. of John Stewart Eccles, of Ecclesville, co. Tyrone (*see* MCCLINTOCK *of Seskinore*), and has issue,
        Anthony Charles Stuart, *b.* 1 Dec. 1910.
      (1) Antoinette. (2) Clarissa.
    (3) Frances, *m.* Archibald Forsyth.
    (4) Caroline, *m.* James Forbes.
  2. Robert, *m.* Maria, dau. of Rev. Arthur Smith Adamson, Rector of Grange Gorman, Dublin.
  3. Tobias, Barrister-at-Law, *d.* 1847.
    1. Margaret, *m.* Rev. Arthur S. Adamson.   2. Anne.
3. Christopher, of Castle Park (*see* DELMEGE *of Castle Park*).
4. James, an Officer 23rd Fusiliers, settled in Canada, *m.* and had issue.
5. John (Rev.), of Rathbranagh, co. Limerick, Rector of Youghalarra, and Prebendary of Droughter and Island Eddy, *m.* 21 July, 1825, Maria Anna, dau. of Col. Thomas Barry, of Leighsbrook, co. Meath, and grand-dau. and co-heiress of John, 5th Lord Carbery, and *d.* 19 April, 1874, having had issue,
  1. John Evans, of Mountgraigue, near Croom, co. Limerick, J.P., M.A., *b.* 1830; *m.* Dec. 1865, Constance, eldest dau. of Richard Studdert, of Fort House, co. Clare, and Frances his wife, dau. of Hon. George Massy, and *d.* 1892, leaving issue,
    John Richard, of Mountgraigue, Croom, co. Limerick, *b.* 12 Aug. 1870.
    Frances Maria Constance.
  2. Adam William Stafford, J.P., Barrister-at-Law, of Ballywire, co. Tipperary, *m.* June, 1871, Jane, only surviving dau. of Rev. Barry Denny, Rector of Caherciveen and Churchill,

Delmege. THE LANDED GENTRY. 176

co. Kerry, and of Upper Fitzwilliam Street, Dublin, who d. 1884. He m. 2ndly, Frances Catherine, youngest dau. of James William Butler Scott, of Annsgrove Abbey, Queen's Co., and has issue,
(1) Eyre Bolton Massy.
(2) Hugh Barry Evans, b. 25 March, 1891.
3. Julius James John, d. 5 March, 1907.
1. Maria Juliana Evans, d. 30 Sept. 1909.
2. Emily Jane Barry, m. 17 July, 1861, her cousin, Col. Francis Hugh Massy Wheeler, brother of General Sir Hugh Massy Wheeler, K.C.B., who was killed in Cawnpore in the Indian Mutiny.
3. Margaret Isabella Johanna.
4. Henrietta Octavia, m. 4 May, 1861, Thomas Bourchier, eldest son of John Bourchier, and has issue (see BOURCHIER of Dromline and Ardinode).
5. Eveline Ida Anna Johanna.
The eldest son,
JULIUS DOLMAGE, of Rathkeale, Capt. 4th King's Own Regt., was b. 1772; s. his father, and m. 1799, Susanne, only dau. of Gédéon Philippes de Gorrequer, of St. Brelades, Jersey, and grand-dau. of Jacques Guillaume Philippes, Sieur de Gorrequer, of the Province of Brittany. Mr. Dolmage d. 1849, leaving issue,
1. JULIUS, his successor.
2. Gideon Gorrequer, Deputy-Inspector-Gen. of Hospitals, late 8th Hussars and 7th Dragoon Guards, m. Julia, dau. of Mark Browne, of Mount Hazel, co. Galway, and d. 1866, having had a son,
Julius Albert, Lieut. Bengal Military Police, who d. 1878.
1. Margaret, m. Rev. James Griffith.
2. Julia, m. George Blake Hickson, Q.C.
3. Rebecca, m. John Benn, of Dromore House, co. Tipperary.
The elder son,
JULIUS DELMEGE, of Rathkeale, b. 1800; s. his father, and m. 1833, Belinda, dau. of Samuel Leake, of Riverlawn, co. Limerick, and d. 1868, having had issue,
1. Julius de Gorrequer, an Officer 23rd Fusiliers and afterwards Col. in the Persian Army, and Knt. of the Lion and Sun, d. unm.
2. AUSTIN JONAS, now of Rathkeale.
3. John Phillipes, an Officer in the Army, d. unm. at Dinapore, 1865.
4. Alfred Gideon, M.V.O., Hon. Surgeon to the King., Dep. Inspector-Gen. of Hospitals and Fleets, R.N., b. 1846; m. 1884, Mary Elizabeth, dau. of Right Hon. James Anthony Lawson, Judge of the High Court, and has issue,
1. Julius de Gorrequer. 2. James Anthony.
3. Claude Philippe.
5. William Henry.
6. Arthur James, M.A., Barrister-at-Law.
7. Louis Edward, m. Rosalie, dau. of Rev. W. Croskerry, and has issue, a son,
Julius.
1. Susan, m. David Ferguson, of Smithfield House, co. Limerick.
2. Mary, m. Gillespie O'Dwyer, of San Guillermo, Entre Rios, Argentine Republic.
3. Julia, m. Rev. S. Payne, LL.D., Rector of Delamere, Cheshire, Chaplain (retired) R.N.
4. Belinda, m. Rev. C. Benson, M.A., Rector of Lucan, Dublin.
5. Emily Blanche, m. Sept. 1880, Arthur Edward James Barker, Professor of Surgery, University Coll. London, of Harley Street, Cavendish Square, W.

Arms—Per chevron arg. and az. in chief two crescents of the last, issuant therefrom as many fleurs-de-lis gu., and in base a crescent or, issuant therefrom a fleur-de-lis of the first, in the centre chief point a spear's head ppr. gutté de sang. *Crest*—A boar's head erased and erect per pale gu. and sa. langued az., armed or. *Motto*—Inveniam aut faciam.

Seat—Rathkeale, co. Limerick. *Town Residence*—243, Cromwell Road, S.W. *Club*—Union.

DELMEGE OF CASTLE PARK.

JAMES O'GRADY DELMEGE, of Castle Park, co. Limerick, J.P. and D.L., High Sheriff 1893, J.P. co. Clare, B.A. Trin. Coll. Dublin, Capt. South of Ireland Imp. Yeom., also Capt. South Irish Horse, b. 1848; m. 22 Oct. 1887, Caroline, dau. and co-heir of Marmaduke Coghill Cramer, D.L., of Rathmore, Kinsale (see CRAMER of Ballindrinish), and has issue,
1. MARMADUKE COGHILL CRAMER, b. 1889.
2. James O'Grady, b. 18 March, 1891.
3. John Christopher Royse, b. 1894.
4. Hugh Jocelyn, b. 1898.
1. Caroline Marie.

Lineage.—CHRISTOPHER DELMEGE, of Castle Park, co. Limerick, J.P., b. 1785, 3rd son of Adam John Delmege or Dulmage of Rathkeale (see that family), and Eliza Powell his wife; m. Martha Forde Royse, dau. of John Yielding, Barrister-at-Law, and d. 1859, leaving issue,
1. JOHN CHRISTOPHER, of whom presently.
1. Isabella, m. Robert Atkins Lidwill, of Clonmore, co. Tipperary.
2. Martha, m. Samuel Caswell, of Blackwater, co. Clare, and had issue.
3. Eliza, m. 21 June, 1858, Daniel Meares Maunsell, of Ballywilliam, co. Limerick.
4. Annabella.
The only son,
JOHN CHRISTOPHER DELMEGE, of Castle Park, J.P. cos. Limerick, Clare and Cork, High Sheriff co. Limerick 1880, m. 1845, Katherine, dau. of James O'Grady, of Raheen, co. Limerick, and niece of Viscount Guillamore. She d. 1869. He d. 1893, having had issue,
1. Christopher John, 48th Regt., b. 1847; d. 1883.
2. JAMES O'GRADY, now of Castle Park.
1. Maria Julia, d. unm.
2. Mathilda, m. Rev. Canon O'Grady, of Bantry.
3. Kathleen.   4. Amy Ellen.

Arms—Per chevron arg. and az. in chief two crescents of the last issuant from each a fleur-de-lys gu. and in base a crescent or issuant therefrom a fleur-de-lys of the first; in the centre chief point a spear's head ppr. gutté de sang. *Crest*—A boar's head erased and erect per pale gu. and sa. langued az, armed or. *Motto*—Inveniam aut faciam.

Seat—Castle Park, Limerick.

EVELEIGH DE MOLEYNS. *See* BURKE'S PEERAGE, VENTRY, B.

DE MONTMORENCY OF CASTLE MORRES.

VEN. WALLER DE MONTMORENCY, of Castle Morres, co. Kilkenny, M.A. Trin. Coll. Cambridge, J.P., Archdeacon of Ossory, formerly Vicar of Kilsheelan, Diocese of Lismore, and rural dean of Ossory, b. Sept. 1841; m. Nov. 1872, Mary, dau. of Right Rev. James Thomas O'Brien, Bishop of Ossory, Ferns, and Leighlin, and has issue,
1. JOHN PRATT, Capt. (retired) R.N., b. Aug. 1873; m. 22 April, 1908, Margaret Elinor, eldest dau. of late Col. Pym, R.A.
2. Geoffrey Fitz-Harvey, I.C.S., Assistant Commissioner Punjab, late Scholar Pemb. Coll. Camb., b. Aug. 1876.

Lineage.—MAJOR HARVEY RANDALL SAVILLE PRATT DE MONTMORENCY, b. Sept. 1782, 3rd son of Rev. Joseph Pratt, of Cabra Castle, co. Cavan, by Hon. Sarah De Montmorency his wife, dau. of Harvey, Viscount Mountmorres, of Castle Morres; s. to the estates of his mother's family, and assumed the surname and arms of DE MONTMORENCY by Royal Licence, 27 Sept. 1831. He m. July, 1811, Rose Lloyd, dau. of John Kearney, Bishop of Ossory, and by her (who d. Jan. 1874) had issue,
1. JOHN, late of Castle Morres.
2. Joseph, Capt. 59th Regt.
3. Harvey Mervyn, of Kilcoran, Callan, co. Kilkenny, m. 24 Aug. 1853, Louisa, 2nd dau. of William Morris Reade, of Rossenara, co. Kilkenny, and d. 22 Sept. 1899, leaving issue. His eldest son, Harvey William, d. 31 Aug. 1887.
4. Raymond.
1. Anne Sarah, m. John Congreve Fleming, and had issue.
2. Letitia, m. John Armstrong, of Graigaverne, Queen's Co., and had issue.   3. Rose, d. unm.
4. Elizabeth, m. William Jacob Blacker, of Woodbrook, co. Wexford, D.L., who d.s.p. 27 Dec. 1869.
5. Sarah, m. Thomas R. Browne, of Augbentaine, co. Tyrone, and has issue.
6. Fanny, m. Capt. Thomas Le Poer Bookey, of Doninga, co. Kilkenny.
Mr. de Montmorency d. 20 Sept. 1859, and was s. by his eldest son,
JOHN PRATT DE MONTMORENCY, of Castle Morres, co. Kilkenny, b. 1 May, 1815; m. 28 June, 1838, Hon. Henrietta O'Grady, dau. of Standish, 1st Viscount Guillamore. She d. 9 Feb. 1891, having had issue,
1. HARVEY JOHN, his heir.
2. WALLER, successor to his brother, now of Castle Morres.
3. Mervyn Standish, Barrister-at-Law, B.A. Oxon., b. 29 June, 1844; m. 19 June, 1883, Annie, widow of Gustaf Baron de Geer, of Zeist, Holland

IRELAND. Dennis.

4. Raymond Oliver, Col. late 2nd Batt. Royal Irish Rifles, b. 11 Oct. 1845; m. 20 April, 1885, Ada Pierce Tighe, dau. and co-heir of Hon. John James Bury, son of the 2nd Earl of Charleville, and d.s.p. 1894.
1. Katherine Maria.
2. Rose Emily, m. 15 July, 1873, Capt. Frederic Arthur Bertie, son of Hon. and Rev. Frederick Bertie and Lady Georgina Bertie, of Weston Manor, co. Oxford, who d. 20 Sept. 1885, leaving issue (see BURKE'S *Peerage*, ABINGDON, E.).
He d. 6 May, 1868, and was s. by his eldest son,
HARVEY JOHN DE MONTMORENCY, of Castle Morres, co. Kilkenny, J.P., High Sheriff, late 2nd Dragoon Guards, b. May, 1840; m. 12 Nov. 1867, Grace, dau. of Sir Thomas Fraser Grove, Bart., of Ferne, Wilts, and d. 20 Jan. 1873, leaving issue, a dau.,
Henrietta Kathleen.
Arms—Or, a cross gu. between four eagles displayed az.
Crest—On a ducal crown or, a peacock in his pride ppr. *Motto*—Dieu ayde.
Seat—Castle Morres, Knocktopher, co. Kilkenny.

DENNEHY OF BROOK LODGE.

MAJ.-GEN. SIR THOMAS DENNEHY, K.C.I.E., of Brook Lodge, co. Cork, J.P. and D.L., High Sheriff 1897, J.P. co. Kerry, Maj.-Gen. retired, Bengal Army, Extra Groom in Waiting to the King, and formerly to Queen Victoria, sometime Political Resident in Rajputana, b. 1829; m. 1859, Elisabeth, dau. of Thomas Moriarty, of Dingle, co. Kerry, and has issue,
Lachlan, b. 1863, d. 1897.
A dau., m. John O'Halloran, of Fermoy.
Lineage.—THOMAS DENNEHY, of Belleview, Fermoy, co. Cork, J.P., left issue,
1. JOHN, of whom presently.
2. Richard, of Prospect House, Innishannon, co. Cork, m. Eliza, beth, and dau. of Michael Galwey of Kilkeran House, co. Cork, and had issue,
    1. Michael, of Prospect House, co. Cork, J.P., acted as Resident Magistrate co. Galway, 1880-3, b. 4 May, 1839.
    1. Frances, b. 20 Aug. 1840.   2. Elizabeth, b. 4 May, 1847.
The elder son,
JOHN DENNEHY, of Brooklodge, co. Cork, m. Maria, dau. of Patrick Moriarty, of Castledrum, and Glencar, co. Kerry, and d. 1857, leaving, with other issue, an eldest son, MAJ.-GEN. SIR THOMAS DENNEHY, K.C.I.E.
Seat—Brooklodge, Fermoy, co. Cork. *Town Residence*—89, Jermyn Street, S.W. *Club*—Junior United Service, S.W.

DENNIS OF FORT GRANITE.

MAJOR MEADE JAMES CROSBIE DENNIS, of Fort Granite, co. Wicklow, and Ballybunnion, co. Kerry, J.P., Major R.A., b. 25 March, 1865; m. 12 Oct. 1892, Hon. Alice Handcock, youngest dau. of Richard, 4th Baron Castlemaine, and has issue,
1. MEADE EDWARD, b. 6 Aug. 1893.
2. Stratford Hercules, b. 1899.
1. Margaret Delia.
Lineage.—This family is a branch of the House of SWIFT, of Swiftsheath, co. Kilkenny, and Lionsden, co. Meath, descended more immediately from SWIFT, of Lynn, co. Westmeath.
THOMAS SWIFT, of Lynnbury, co. Westmeath, 2nd son of Meade Swift, of Lynn (*see that family*), m. Frances, only dau. of John Dennis, of Kilsale, co. Cork, by Anne Bullen his wife, and sister of Right Hon. James Dennis, Lord Chief Baron of the Exchequer in Ireland (who was created by patent, 13 Dec. 1780, Lord Tracton, of Tracton Abbey, co. Cork), and had issue,
1. MEADE (Rev.), of whom presently.
2. John, Barrister-at-Law, who, with his elder brother, adopted the surname of DENNIS. He m. Emily, dau. of Robert Hamilton, and d. at Sidmouth 1830, leaving issue,
    1. James, Barrister-at-Law, d.s.p.
    2. Robert, Capt. E.I.C.S., m. Louisa, dau. of Gen. Rumley, E.I.C.S., and d. 1849, having had issue,
        Robert, of Laracor, Old Bath Road, Cheltenham, late Lieut. 20th Regt., m. 30 Oct. 1872, Catherine Jane, dau. of the late R. J. Browne, of Newry, and has issue,
        1. Richard Jebb, of West Demars, Arrow Lakes, British Columbia, b. 30 March, 1876.
        2. John Tracton, 2nd Lieut. Royal Dublin Fusiliers, b. 7 Feb. 1878, wounded at Hart's Hill, S. Africa, Feb. 1900, and d. of enteric fever at Aliwal North, 2 May, 1900.
        3. Cecil, Solicitor, b. 8 March, 1880.
        4. Randal Hamilton, C.E., Bengal and N.W. Railway Company, b. 17 June, 1881.
        Emily, m. Lieut.-Col. Richard Green, late 49th Regt.
    1. Mary.
Lord Tracton d.s.p. 1782, when the title expired. His estates in Kerry he bequeathed to his eldest nephew and heir-at-law, Rev.
I.L.G.

Meade Swift; and those in the cos. of Cork and Dublin to his other nephew, John Swift, subject to a jointure of £1,800 per annum to Lady Tracton, and on condition that they and their heirs should take the name and arms of DENNIS. Mr. Thomas Swift's elder son,
REV. MEADE SWIFT, s. accordingly to the co. Kerry estates of his maternal uncle, Lord Tracton, and adopted the surname of DENNIS. He m. Delia Sophia, 2nd dau. of Morley Saunders, of Saunders Grove, co. Wicklow, by Lady Martha Stratford his wife, dau. of John, 1st Earl of Aldborough, and by her had issue,
1. THOMAS STRATFORD, his heir.
2. Meade Paul (Rev.), m. Mary Anne Coane, co. Fermanagh, and d. 1867, having had issue,
    1. FitzMeade Tynte, d. unm. v.p.
    1. Delia, d. unm. v.p.
    2. Jemima Henrietta, of Lynnbury, d. unm. 1907.
3. James Aldborough, m. Caroline Wynne, dau. and co-heir of Col. Topp, and d.s.p.
4. John, M.D., m. Elizabeth Manders, and left one son, Aldborough, and two daus.,
    1. Isabella, m. Edgar Flower.   2. Ellen.
5. George Morley (Rev.), M.A. T.C.D., Rector of Enniscoffey and Kilbride, co. Westmeath, b. 1803; m. 1832, Elizabeth Sophia, elder dau. and co-heiress of Capt. Joseph McGuire, J.P. of Cavan (see McGUIRE *of Clonca*), and by her (who d. 23 March, 1879) had issue,
    1. Joseph Morley Swifte-Dennis (Rev.), M.D., Rector of Edermine, co. Wexford, formerly Rector of Ballinaclough and Kilkeary, co. Tipperary, b. 8 March, 1833; d. 29 Sept. 1908; assumed additional name of SWIFTE, 10 April, 1885; m. 18 June, 1856, Alicia Mary, 2nd dau. of John Devereux Byrne, of Leighlinbridge, co. Carlow, by Alicia his wife, dau. of Henry Rogers, of Killala, and had issue,
        (1) Morley Saunders Meade, b. 19 March, 1863, Capt. 5th Batt. 18th Royal Irish Regt., m. 25 June, 1889, Jessie, dau. of the late Dr. Thomas G. Proctor, of Liverpool.
        (2) Harloven Devereux Aldborough, Lieut. 5th Batt. Royal Irish Regt., b. 7 July, 1866; d. unm. 13 May, 1885.
        (1) Frances Josephine Alicia, m. 1883, Major Robert Fetherston Devereux (see DEVEREUX *of Ballyrankin*), and has issue.
        (2) Charlotte Elizabeth Sophia, d. unm. 5 Dec. 1869.
    2. Charles Stratford, of Lake View, Waterford, b. 1834; m. 1869, Emily Sophia, dau. of Rev. Richard Allott Tighe Gregory.
    3. Meade Robson, b. 1841; m. 1868, Clara, dau. of Robert Hobbes, of Stratford-on-Avon, and d. 2 Jan. 1877, leaving issue, two sons.
    4. Morley, b. 1848; d. unm. May, 1860.
    5. Adolphus Lambert, b. 1850, Lieut. 62nd Regt.; d. unm. in India, 26 Nov. 1876.
    6. Ffolliott Reginald, b. 1852, L.R.C.P. and C.S., Edinburgh. His wife Mary d. his widow, 10 Aug. 1901.
    7. Albert Lewis Edward, b. 1854; d. 15 Sept. 1909.
    7. Albert Lewis Edward, b. 1854.
    1. Henrietta, m. 1857, Robert J. Reamsbotham, Co. Inspector R.I.C., Armagh, and d. 11 Aug. 1888, leaving issue.
    2. Marion, m. 1865, William Albert Hobbes, of Stratford-on-Avon, and had issue.
    3. Sophia Elizabeth, m. 2 Jan. 1868, Frederick Agar, of Ponder's End, Middlesex, M.D.
    4. Elizabeth Adelaide, d. unm. 27 Dec. 1854.
    5. Caroline Helena, m. 5 Oct. 1870, William Mallet, of 63, Burlington Street, Manchester, M.D.
1. Martha Sophia, d. unm.
2. Frances Maria, m. Capt. William Harrison, 69th Regt.
3. Anne, m. Thomas Heron.   4. Louisa, m. John Gibbs.
5. Eliza, m. Richard Cane.
The eldest son,
THOMAS STRATFORD DENNIS, of Fort Granite, J.P., b. 12 June, 1781; m. 30 Jan. 1810, his cousin, Katherine Martha Maria, eldest dau. of Morley Saunders, of Saunders Grove, co. Wicklow, by his wife Ellen Katherine, dau. of James Glascock, of Music Hall, co. Dublin, and by her (who d. 15 July, 1825) had issue,
1. MEADE CAULFIELD, of Fort Granite.
2. Morley Stratford Tynte, A.M., J.P., of Barraderry House, Kiltegan, Baltinglass, b. 1811, Lieut.-Col. late 76th Foot; m. 9 May, 1866, Anne, 2nd dau. of Hugh Baker, of Lismacue, co. Tipperary.
3. John FitzThomas, b. 1816, Major, late 95th Foot; m. 24 May, 1854, Jane, only dau. of Jebb Brown, M.D., Staff Surgeon, and has issue,
    1. Thomas Stratford, b. 1861; d. unm. 9 Aug. 1888, accidentally killed.
    1. Katherine Martha Mary.
    2. Ellen Louisa.   3. Mary Sophia.
    4. Charlotte Jane, m. 22 July, 1899, Rowland Henry Rochfort Wade, and has issue (see WADE *of Carrowmore*).
4. James Benjamin, b. 1817, Major-Gen. R.A.; m. 1st, 9 June, 1859, Eily, eldest dau. of William Barker Drury, of Boden Park, Rathfarnham, Barrister-at-Law (who d. 19 April, 1861); 2ndly, 28 June, 1866, Emma, 3rd dau. of Col. William Broome Salmon, Bombay Staff Corps, and has issue,
    1. Emmeline Maude, m. Capt. W. E. Benson, Essex Regt.
    2. Kathleen Louisa Rose, m. 19 Sept. 1894, Lieut. Gerald C. A. Marescaux, 2nd son of Laurence M. Marescaux, and has issue, Geoffrey Dennis St. Quintin, and Lawrence Mortimer Tracton.
    3. Ethel Mary, m. Capt. Lindesay Knox, and has issue, Esme Rosalie and Daphne Emmeline (twins), and Barbara Elizabeth.
    4. Rosalie Margaret.

M

5. Robert William, Barrister-at-Law, b. 1821; d. unm. 15 Dec. 1874.
6. Edward Albert, of Eadestown, J.P. cos. Wicklow and Carlow, b. 1823; d. 1899; m. 19 May, 1858, Mary Frances, 2nd dau. of Rev. John Nunn Woodroffe, Prebendary of Cahirlac, co. Cork.
1. Katherine Sophia, d. 1907; m. 18 Sept. 1848, Rev. Solomon Donovan, Rector of Horetown, Precentor of the Diocese of Ferns (see Donovan of Ballymore), who d.s.p. 7 June, 1882.
2. Ellen Louisa, m. 8 Jan. 1857, Maurice Fitzgerald Sandes, of Oak Park, Tralee, co. Kerry, J.P., M.A., Registrar-General of Bengal, and d.s.p. 16 March, 1894. He d. 4 March, 1879.
Mr. Dennis d. 21 Dec. 1870, and was s. by his eldest son,
MEADE CAULFEILD DENNIS, of Fort Granite and Ballybunnion, J.P. for cos. of Wicklow, Kerry, and Carlow, M.A. Trin. Coll. Dublin, High Sheriff co. Wicklow 1873, b. 1810; m. 4 Jan. 1855, Margaret Katherine, dau. of Major Pierce Crosbie, of Ballyheigue Castle, co. Kerry (see that family), and by her (who d. 6 Feb. 1886) had issue,
1. Stratford Thomas Crosbie, Lieut. R.H.A., b. 1862; d. unm. 1889.
2. MEADE JAMES CROSBIE, now of Fort Granite.
3. Maurice Falkiner, Lieut. Seaforth Highlanders, High Sheriff, co. Wicklow, 1910.
1. Anne Elizabeth Emily.
2. Ellen Katherine Charlotte, m. 22 June, 1876, Francis Metcalfe, of Metcalfe Park, co. Kildare.
3. Elizabeth Margaret.
4. Frances Sophia, m. 1886, Algernon A. Aylmer, of Rathmore, co. Kildare.
Mr. Dennis d. 6 Dec. 1891.
Seat—Fort Granite, Baltinglass, co. Wicklow.

DENNY OF MOORSTOWN AND DRUMLONE.

REV. EDWARD DENNY, M.A., of Moorstown, co. Tipperary, and Drumlone, co. Fermanagh, Vicar of St. Peter's, Vauxhall, formerly Vicar of Kempley, b. 4 Aug. 1853; m. 1 July, 1875, Alma Mary, eldest dau. of Charles John Chesshyre, of Bennington, Cheltenham, co. Gloucester, and has issue,
1. Anthony, b. 13 July, 1879; d. 21 Feb. 1880.
2. EDWARD MAYNARD CONINGSBY, b. 4 March, 1883.
3. Barry Maynard Rynd, b. 2 Jan. 1885.
4. John Maynard, b. 3 Sept. 1886.
5. Maynard Henry Blennerhassett, b. 6 June, 1888; d. unm. 10 Jan. 1907.
6. Mowbray Charles Maynard, b. 20 May, 1891.
7. Michael Maynard, b. 3 Oct. 1895.
1. Alma Margaret Mary, b. 20 July, 1876.
2. Muriel Mary, b. 9 Jan. 1878.
3. Clare Innocentia Mary, b. 28 Dec. 1880.
4. Joan Champernown Mary, b. 5 Feb. 1890.
5. Katherine Mary Monica, b. 25 Aug. 1893.
6. Doris Mary Georgina, b. 15 Dec. 1894.

Lineage.—This is a branch of DENNY, Bart. of Tralee.
EDWARD DENNY, a Col. of Carabineers, M.P. for Tralee, brother of Sir Barry Denny, 1st bart. of Tralee (see BURKE's Peerage and Baronetage), s. under the will of his elder brother Arthur, to the Tipperary estate of his uncle, Sir Thomas Denny, Knt., of Tralee, co. Kerry, m. 1769, Mary, dau. and heiress of David Rynd, of Derryvullan and Drumlone, co. Fermanagh, and d. Feb. 1775, having by her (who d. 1774) had two sons,
1. Edward, an Officer in 6th Regt. of Dragoons, b. 1771; d. unm. 18 Aug. 1798.
2. ANTHONY, of whom below.
His 2nd son,
ANTHONY DENNY, of Moorstown, b. 1773; m. 1799, Frances Anne Wilhelmina, 2nd dau. of William Blennerhassett, of Ballyseedy, co. Kerry, and by her (who m. 2ndly, Sir George Morris, 3rd Buffs, Usher of the Black Rod of the Order of St. Patrick) had two sons and a dau.,
1. EDWARD, of whom below.
2. William, Col. 71st Regt., m. Ewretta, dau. of Hon. J. Richardson, of Montreal, and d.s.p. 6 Oct. 1886.
1. Mary, m. 1824, Charles O'Malley, of Hawthorn Lodge, co. Mayo, and d. 1883, leaving an only son, William.
Mr. Denny d. 1806. His elder son,
EDWARD DENNY, of Moorstown, b. 1800, an Officer in 3rd Buffs, High Sheriff co. Fermanagh, 1823; m. 1823, his cousin Georgina, eldest dau. of Arthur Blennerhassett, of Ballyseedy, co. Kerry, and d. at Rome, 11 Nov. 1838, leaving by her (who d. 1826) an only son,
ANTHONY DENNY, of Moorstown, b. 11 Oct. 1823, an Officer in 71st Regt., m. 21 Sept. 1852, Sarah Jane, eldest dau. of Rev. G. P. Lockwood, M.A., Rector of South Hackney, Middlesex, and d. 5 April, 1857, having by her (who d. 3 Oct. 1902) had three sons,
1. EDWARD, his heir.
2. Anthony, b. 30 July, 1854; m. 22 Nov. 1882, Clara, dau. of Charles Richardson, of Springfield, co. Down, and d. 17 Jan. 1893, leaving issue,
Anthony, b. 23 Dec. 1883.
3. Arthur Lockwood (Rev.) (Hatfield House, Lowestoft), b. 16 March, 1856.

Arms—Gu. a saltire arg. between twelve cross-crosslets or. Crest—A cubit arm vested az. turned up arg. holding five wheatears or. Motto—Et mea messis erit.
Residence—St. Peter's Vicarage, Vauxhall.

DE ROBECK OF GOWRAN GRANGE.

HENRY EDWARD WILLIAM FOCK, BARON DE ROBECK, of Gowran Grange, co. Kildare, a Baron in the Kingdom of Sweden, J.P., D.L. co. Kildare, Capt. late R.A., afterwards Lieut.-Col. Wicklow Artillery, b. 2 March, 1859; m. 21 Dec. 1886, Anne, youngest dau. of Lorenzo William Alexander, of Straw Hall, co. Carlow, and has issue,
1. John Henry Edward, b. 10 April, 1895.
2. Bernard Lorenzo, b. 24 June, 1898.
3. Michael, b. 27 Sept. 1903.
1. Dorothy Zoe, m. 8 Oct. 1910, Digby Robert Peel, R.F.A., son of William Felton Peel, of Alexandria, Egypt.
2. Olave Harriet. 3. Muriel Elizabeth.

Lineage. Arms. &c.—See BURKE's Peerage, Foreign Titles.
JOHN HENRY EDWARD FOCK, BARON DE ROBECK, of Gowran Grange, co. Kildare, a baron in the kingdom of Sweden, Ranger of the Curragh, J.P. cos. Kildare and Wicklow, D.L. co. Kildare, High Sheriff for that co. 1859 and for co. Wicklow 1884, late Capt. 8th Foot and Maj. Kildare Militia, b. 28 Nov. 1823; m. 22 Jan. 1856, Sophia Charlotte, 3rd dau. of the late William Fitzwilliam Burton, of Burton Hall, co. Carlow, and d. 23 Aug. 1904, having by her (who d. 15 July, 1903) had issue.
1. HENRY EDWARD WILLIAM, now BARON DE ROBECK.
2. John Michael, Capt. R.N., b. 10 June, 1862.
3. Richard FitzPatrick, b. 28 Feb. 1864; d. 28 Oct. 1865.
4. William, b. 2 Jan. 1868; deceased.
5. Charles Richard, Capt. 3rd Roy. Dublin Fus., b. 27 March, 1871; m. 7 Nov. 1894, Louisa Emily Isabella, 2nd dau. of Major William Andros Warren, R.A.
4. Bernard Edward, b. 31 Dec. 1876; d. Feb. 1877.
1. Emily Anne, m. 23 April, 1878, Thomas De Burgh, of Old Town, co. Kildare, and has issue (see that family).
2. Gertrude Elizabeth Mary.
3. Coralie Annetta Helen Georgina, d. 5 Nov. 1879.
4. Zoe Anna Judith, m. 19 Aug. 1890, Capt. William Francis Tremayne, late 4th Dragoon Guards, eldest son of Col. Tremayne, of Carclew, Cornwall.

Seat—Gowran Grange, Naas, co. Kildare. Clubs—Army and Navy and Kildare Street.

DE SALIS OF LOUGHGUR.

JOHN FRANCIS CHARLES FANE DE SALIS, C.V.O., C.M.G., of Loughgur, co. Limerick, a Count of the Germanic or Holy Roman Empire, Envoy Extraordinary and Min. Plen. at Cettinje from 1911, formerly Councillor of H.M. Embassy at Berlin, J.P. and D.L. co. Limerick, J.P. co. Armagh, b. 19 July, 1864; m. 1890, Hélène Marie de Riquet, dau. of Prince Eugène de Caraman-Chimay, and by her (who d. 31 May, 1902) has issue,
1. JEAN EUGÈNE, b. 4 Oct. 1891.
2. Antoine Rodolphe, b. 2 Jan. 1893.
3. Pierre François, b. 18 May, 1902.

Count de Salis is the eldest son of John Francis William, Count de Salis, who d. 7 Aug. 1871, and Amelia Frances Harriet his wife, who d. 8 Jan. 1885, dau. of Christopher Tower, of Huntsmore, Bucks.

Lineage, Arms, &c.—See BURKE's Peerage, Foreign Titles.
Seats—Loughgur, Kilmallock, co. Limerick, and Bondo, Grisons, Switzerland. Clubs—Travellers', White's, and Marlborough.

IRELAND.   Devenish.

DE STACPOOLE OF MOUNT HAZEL AND TOBERTYNAN.

GEORGE DE STACPOOLE, of Mount Hazel, co. Galway, and Tobertynan, co. Meath, Duke and Marquis de Stacpoole in the Papal States, and Count and Viscount de Stacpoole in the kingdom of France, J.P. co. Galway, late Lieut. 3rd Batt. Yorks Regt., *b.* 21 June, 1860 ; *m.* 1 Dec. 1883, Pauline, only child and heiress of the late Edward MacEvoy, of Tobertynan, co. Meath, sometime M.P. for that co., and Eliza his wife, only child and heiress of Andrew Browne, of Mount Hazel, co. Galway, and has issue,

1. GEORGE MARY EDWARD JOSEPH PATRICK, Lieut. 3rd Batt. Royal Irish Fusiliers, *b.* 8 March, 1886.
2. Edward Hubert Michael, Lieut. Leinster Regt., *b.* 29 Sept. 1888.
3. Francis Gustave Mary, *b.* 26 Oct. 1890.
4. Robert Andrew, Lieut. Connaught Raugers, *b.* 25 May, 1892.
5. Roderick Algernon, *b.* 11 Aug. 1895.
1. Gertrude Mary Pauline, *b.* 7 Oct. 1884 ; *m.* 16 Sept. 1907, Major Harry McMicking, D.S.O., and has issue (*see* MCMICKING *of Miltonise*).

The Duke de Stacpoole is the only son of George Stanislaus, 3rd Duke de Stacpoole, who *d.* 16 March, 1896 (*see* BURKE'S *Peerage, Foreign Titles*), and Maria his wife, dau. of Thomas Dunn, of Bath House, Northumberland.

Lineage.—FRANCIS MACEVOY, of Tobertynan, one of the most distinguished surgeons of his time, was son of Edward MacEvoy, of Dring, co. Longford, and grandson (by Anne D'Arcy his wife) of Christopher MacEvoy, whose younger brother was of Santa Cruz, and had a son, Christopher MacEvoy, of Wimbledon, Surrey, *m.* Anne, dau. of Thomas Fetherstonhaugh, of Bracklyn Castle, co. Westmeath (*see that family*), and had a son, Edward, who *d.* before him *unm.* He *d.* himself 1808, and was *s.* by his brother, JAMES MACEVOY, of Tobertynan, co. Meath, and Frankford, co. Longford, *m.* 1824, Theresa, youngest dau. and co-heir of Sir Joshua Colles Meredyth, Bart., by Maria his wife, dau. and heir of Laurence Coyne Nugent, of Finea, co. Cavan, and *d.* 1834, having by her (who *d.* 24 Oct. 1896, aged 96) had issue,
1. EDWARD FRANCIS, late of Tobertynan.
2. Joshua James, J.P., formerly R.N., and afterwards an officer in the Dublin Artillery, *b.* 1829 ; *m.* 22 Nov. 1860, the Hon. Mary Netterville, only surviving dau. and heir of James, 7th Viscount Netterville, and assumed by Royal Licence, dated 7 April, 1865, the surname and arms of NETTERVILLE only, and has issue,
 1. Mary Eliza Theresa.   2. Theresa Reddis.
 3. Eliza Theodora, a Nun, *d.* 30 May, 1904.
 4. Rose Emily, *m.* 1 Sept. 1892, Edward Alexander O'Byrne, eldest son of Count O'Byrne, of Corville, co. Tipperary, and has issue (*whom see*).
 5. Barbara, *m.* 16 July, 1891, Nicholas Synnott, Barrister-at-Law, eldest son of the late Thomas Synnott, of Innismore, co. Dublin, and has issue.
 6. Victoria.   7. Pauline.
 1. Maria Theresa, *m.* 13 April, 1852, Richard Gradwell, J.P., of Dowth Hall, co. Meath, and by him (who *d.* 28 Oct. 1884) has issue (*see* GRADWELL *of Dowth Hall*).
 2. Barbara Frances, *m.* 8 Jan. 1856, Sir Bernard Burke, C.B., LL.D., Ulster King-of-Arms (who *d.* 12 Dec. 1892), and *d.* 15 Jan. 1887, leaving issue (*see* BURKE *of Aubries*).

The elder dau. EDWARD FRANCIS MACEVOY, of Tobertynan, co. Meath, Mount Hazel, co. Galway, and Frankford, co. Longford, J.P., M.P. co. Meath 1855 to 1874, formerly Lieut. in the 6th Dragoon Guards (Carabineers), educated at Cambridge, *b.* 5 Sept. 1826 ; *m.* 24 Oct. 1850, Eliza Teresa, dau. and heiress of Andrew Browne, of Mount Hazel, co. Galway, son of Nicholas Browne, of Mount Hazel, by Eleanor his wife (afterwards Viscountess Strangford), youngest dau. of Sir Thomas Burke, 1st bart. He *d.* 10 Feb. 1899. She *d.* 30 March, 1904, leaving an only child.
PAULINE, *m.* (*as above*), GEORGE, 4TH DUKE DE STACPOOLE, now of Mount Hazel and Tobertynan.

Arms—Arg. a lion rampant gu. collared or holding in the forepaws a sword ppr., a canton erm. thereon a fleur de lys gold.
Crest—A pelican in her piety ppr. collared or, pendent therefrom a shield arg. charged with a lion rampant gu. **Mottoes**—(over the crest) I die for those I love. (Under the arms) Pro deo et rege, pro patria et lege.
Seat—Mount Hazel, Ballymacward, co. Galway, and Tobertynan, Enfield, co. Meath. *Town Residence*—14, Cadogan Square, S.W. *Club*—St. James's.

DEVENISH OF MOUNT PLEASANT.

REV. WILLIAM DEVENISH, of Mount Pleasant, co. Roscommon, B.A. Trin. Coll. Dublin, late Rector of Abbeylara, co. Longford, *b.* 24 Oct. 1840 ; *m.* 7 April, 1891, Christian Rebecca, only dau. of Henry Murray, M.D. of Belfast.

Lineage.—CHRISTOPHER DEVENISH, of Carrowclowgher, co. Roscommon, *m.* Susan, dau. of John Hinde, of Castlemine, by Mary his wife, dau. of Judge Jones, of Athlone, and had issue,
WILLIAM DEVENISH, eldest son and heir, *m.* Deborah Blackburne, and had issue,
1. WILLIAM, of whom presently.
2. Christopher.
3. George.
1. Elizabeth, *m.* John Homan.   2. Susannah, *m.* Peter Cooper.
His eldest son,
WILLIAM DEVENISH, of Rush Hill, co. Roscommon, *m.* Anne, dau. of Francis Fetherston, of Whiterock, co. Longford, and had issue,
1. GEORGE, his heir.
2. Christopher.
3. John.
1. Susan, *m.* 1786, Robert Jones Lloyd, of Ardnagoyan, co. Roscommon.
The eldest son,
GEORGE DEVENISH, of Mount Pleasant, *m.* 1772, Sarah, dau. of Godfrey Hemsworth, of co. Tipperary, and *d.* 1829, leaving issue (with several daus.),
1. WILLIAM, of whom presently.
2. Godfrey, R.A.   3. George.
4. John.
5. Robert, J.P., of Rush Hill, co. Roscommon, *b.* 12 Dec. 1785 ; *m.* 21 Feb. 1816, Theodosia, youngest dau. of Rev. Luke Mahon, of Strokestown House, and *d.* 18 March, 1864, leaving issue,
 1. George, *b.* 2 Dec. 1822 ; *m.* the dau. of Major Jones, and *d.* March, 1893, leaving three daus. and one son.
 2. John, of Rush Hill and Jamestown, co. Leitrim, J.P., *b.* 4 Feb. 1833 ; *d.* 13 Aug. 1905 ; *m.* 18 June, 1854, Elizabeth Frances, dau. of Thomas Jones, of Drumard, and had issue,
  (1) Robert, *b.* 1859 ; *m.* 9 Nov. 1882, Kate, dau. of Thomas Russell, of Tully House, co. Roscommon, and has issue,
   1. John, *b.* 18 Nov. 1883 ; *m.* 6 June, 1910, Amy, dau. of W. R. Lewis, Cape Colony.
   2. Robert, *b.* 8 Sept. 1885.
   3. Thomas Samuel, *b.* 4 Sept. 1891.
   1. Elizabeth Frances, *b.* 7 May, 1887 ; *m.* 12 Jan. 1911, William Jocelyn de Warrenne Waller, J.P., son of George Arthur Waller, of Prior Park, co. Tipperary (*see that family*).
  (2) William Percy *b.* 14 April, 1861 ; *d.* April, 1897, leaving issue.
   (1) Theodosia Olivia, *b.* 4 March, 1868.
  1. Sarah, *m.* 6 Dec. 1837, Thomas Morton, of Ruaun, and left issue three sons and three daus.
  2. Anne, *m.* 19 Dec. 1849, William Ll[oyd], D.L., of Rockville, and left issue, six daus. and one son.
  3. Mary, *b.* 1829.
 6. Christopher.
The eldest son,
WILLIAM DEVENISH, of Mount Pleasant, co. Roscommon, *b.* 1780 ; *m.* Hannah, dau. of John Lloyd, M.D., of Dublin, and of Cloonfinlough House, co. Roscommon, and had issue,
1. JOHN, his heir.   2. William.
3. Robert, of Cloonfinlough House, *m.* 1869, Mereal Elizabeth, only dau. of Rev. Peter Toler, A.B. of Bloomfield, and *d.* June, 1880, leaving two daus., Lillie and Hannah.
 1. Anna.
 2. Sarah, *m.* William Lloyd O'Brien, of Mount Francis, co. Roscommon.
 3. Hannah.
 4. Jane, *m.* William Mahon, 2nd son of Bartholomew Mahon, of Clonfree.
 5. Susan.
Mr. Devenish *d.* Nov. 1838, and was *s.* by his eldest son,
JOHN DEVENISH, of Mount Pleasant, J.P., *b.* 21 June, 1814 ; *m.* 20 Sept. 1838, Susan, dau. of Michael Fox, of Stephen's Green, Dublin, by Susan his wife, dau. of Robert Jones Lloyd, and had issue,
1. WILLIAM (Rev.), now of Mount Pleasant.
2. Michael Fox, *b.* 24 Feb. 1842 ; *d.* 16 April, 1866.
3. John Lloyd, of Kilglas House, Strokestown, co. Roscommon, *b.* 2 Dec. 1848 ; *m.* 19 June, 1884, Mary Arthur Kate, eldest dau. of Robert Jones Fox, Clerk of the Peace, co. Roscommon, and has issue, Susan.
4. Robert Jones Sylvester (Rev.), Archdeacon of Waterford, M.A., T.C.D., Canon of St. Patrick's Cathedral, Waterford, and Vicar of Cahir, co. Tipperary, *b.* 6 Dec. 1850 ; *m.* 5 Feb. 1877, Rosamond Kate, only dau. of Rev. W. J. Price, LL.D., of Waterford, and has issue,
 1. John Graham, Capt. late Inniskilling Fus.
 2. William Roberts.
 3. Robert Cecil Sylvester, B.A.
 1. Rosamund Esther, *m.* 7 June, 1910, Rev. John Going, M.A.
 2. Geraldine Susan Dorothea, *m.* Feb. 1911, Conyers Baker, Solicitor (*see* BAKER *of Lismacue*).
1. Susan Emma, *d.* 8 July, 1867.
2. Jane Sophia Moore.
3. Anne Sarah Fetherstone H., *m.* 17 Oct. 1883, John James

Devenish. THE LANDED GENTRY. 180

Goodlatte Murray, Physician and Surgeon, eldest son of Henry Murray, M.D., Belfast.
4. Eliza Rebecca Geraldina, *m.* Major-Gen. A. Anderson, 3rd Madras L.I.
5. Hannah Lucinda, *m.* 20 April, 1884, Rev. Joseph Tramplesure, of Birkenhead.
6. Arabella Margaret.
Mr. Devenish *d.* 2 Feb. 1878, and was *s.* by his eldest son.
Seat—Mount Pleasant, Strokestown, co. Roscommon. *Residence*—Claremont, Cypress Avenue, Bloomfield, Belfast.

DEVENISH-MEARES. *See* MEARES.

DE VERE OF CURRAGH CHASE.

ROBERT STEPHEN VERE DE VERE, of Curragh Chase, co. Limerick, J.P., LL.B. Camb., Barrister-at-Law, Attorney-Gen. Seychelles Islands since 1907, *b.* 23 July, 1872. Mr. de Vere is the only son of the late Major Aubrey Stephen Vere O'Brien, 60th Rifles, who *d.* 18 Dec. 1898, and Lucy Harriette his wife, now Mrs. de Vere, only dau. of Major-Gen. Wynne, R.E., and grandson of the Hon. Robert O'Brien (brother of Lucius, 13th Lord Inchiquin), and Ellinor Jane Alicia Lucy, his wife, who *d.* 5 March, 1889, eldest dau. of Sir Aubrey de Vere, 2nd bart., and sister of Sir Stephen Edward de Vere, 4th bart. Mr. de Vere *s,* in 1898 to Curragh Chase on the death of his father to whom that estate had been conveyed by his uncles, Sir Stephen Edward de Vere, 4th Bart. and Aubrey de Vere (who died *unm.* 20 Jan. 1902). Mr. de Vere, together with his mother, assumed the name of DE VERE in lieu of his patronymic O'BRIEN, 9 April, 1899. He *m.* 26 Sept. 1906, Isabel Catherine, only surv. child of Rt. Rev. Handley Carr Glynne Moule, D.D., Bishop of Durham.

Lineage.—*See* HUNT *of Cumnor More and* BURKE'S *Peerage.* INCHIQUIN, B.

Arms—Quarterly: 1st and 4th quarterly gu. and or in the dexter chief quarter a mullet arg. (DE VERE): 2nd and 3rd quarterly 1st and 4th gu. three lions passant guardant in pale per pale or and arg.: 2nd arg. three piles issuing from the chief and meeting in point gu.: and 3rd or a pheon az. (O'BRIEN). *Crest*—On a cap of dignity az. lined erm. a boar passant az. armed, bristled, and unguled or. *Motto*—Vero nihil verius.

Seat—Curragh Chase, co. Limerick. *Residence*—Victoria, Seychelles Islands. *Club*—Wellington.

DEVEREUX OF BALLYRANKIN.

THE REV. NICHOLAS JESSOP DEVEREUX, of Ballyrankin House, co. Wexford, M.A., T.C.D., Vicar of St. Mary's, Hoxton, and Private Chaplain to the Duke of Portland, *b.* 12 Sept. 1841; *m.* 1887, Florence Sarah, eldest dau. of Ferdinand Greatrex, of Uxbridge, co. Middlesex.

Lineage.—NICHOLAS DEVEREUX, of Ballybarna, otherwise Kilrush, co. Wexford (descended from the ancient family of DEVEREUX *of Ballmagir*, in the same co., which settled there in the reign of King JOHN), made his will 27 Nov. 1698, and it was proved at Ferns 28 Dec. following. He had two sons, JAMES, of Kilrush, who *d.s.p.*, and

JOHN DEVEREUX, of Ballybarna, or Kilrush, *m.* Mary Clare, and by her had issue,
1. NICHOLAS, of whom presently.
2. Matthew, of Ballybarna and Ballyrankin, *m.* 1754, a dau. of Bartholomew Murphy, of Enniscorthy, and *d.s.p.*
3. Thomas.
4. Ignatius, in Holy Orders of the Church of Rome.
1. Clare, *m.* Patrick Sutton, of Enniscorthy.
The eldest son,
NICHOLAS DEVEREUX, of Bunclody, co. Wexford, whose will bears date 20 Jan. 1762, *m.* Mary, dau. of Gerald Kavanagh, of Ballybranah, co. Carlow, a branch of the Borris family, and by her had issue,
1. JOHN, of whom presently.
1. Mary, *m.* 1760, James, son of Edmund Fitzpatrick, of Clonleigh, co. Wexford.
2. Clare, *m.* 1771, Rev. Ulysses Jacob, of Siggingtown, co. Wexford.
3. Frances, *m.* Col. John Bayley; and 2ndly, Edward Fitzgerald, M.D.
The only son,
JOHN DEVEREUX, of Kilrush, and afterwards of Newtown Barry, High Sheriff, J.P., co. Wexford 1764, *b.* 1726; *m.* 1757, Charlotte, dau. of Walter Chapland Bayley, of Gowran, co. Kilkenny, and had issue,
1. Thomas, of Ballyrankin House, *d. unm.*
2. JOHN, of whom presently.
1. Elizabeth. 2. Elinor.
3. Mary, *m.* Robert Clifford, co. Wexford, *d.s.p.*
4. Charlotte, *m.* Joseph Marshall, of Birr, King's Co.
The younger son,
JOHN DEVEREUX, of Ballyrankin House, *b.* 1768, Major of the Wexford Militia 27 July, 1801; *m.* 1796, Anastacia, dau. and heir of Hyacinth Daly, of Killimur Castle, Mayor of Galway, by Anne his wife, dau. and co-heir of Dermot Daly, of Kilimur, and had issue,
1. NICHOLAS, of whom presently.
2. Hyacinth, B.A. Trin. Coll. Dublin, *b.* 11 June, 1803; *d.s.p.* 1824.
1. Charlotte, *m.* James Douglas Johnstone, of Snow Hill, co. Fermanagh, and *d.* 1843, leaving issue.
2. Maria, *m.* Richard Hall, of Innismore Hall, co. Fermanagh, and had issue.
Major Devereux *d.* 1841, and was *s.* by his elder son,
REV. NICHOLAS DEVEREUX, D.D., of Ballyrankin House, co. Wexford, and Killimur Castle, co. Galway, Rector and Prebendary of the parish of Kilrush, *b.* 17 Sept. 1799; *m.* 10 April, 1833, Maria, 2nd dau. of John Harward Jessop, of Doory Hall, co. Longford, and York Place, Portman Square, London, by Frances his wife, only dau. and heiress of Sir Frederick Flood, Bart., of Newtown-Ormonde, M.P. co. Wexford, and *d.* 12 Sept. 1867, having had issue,
1. JOHN DALY, late of Ballyrankin House.
2. Frederick Flood, late Lieut. 87th Royal Irish Fusiliers, *b.* 29 April, 1836, of Farm Hill House, co. Kildare; *m.* 15 Aug. 1868, Elizabeth, widow of W. Fleetwood, and *d.s.p.* 6 Feb. 1869.
3. NICHOLAS JESSOP (Rev.), now of Ballyrankin House.
4. Hyacinth Daly, *b.* 3 Jan. 1846, now of Texas, U.S.A., formerly Lieut. 87th Royal Irish Fusiliers; *m.* 16 Jan. 1890, Miss Nichol.
5. Robert Fetherston, *b.* 25 May, 1847, Major (retired) 2nd West India Regt.; *m.* 29 Aug. 1883, Frances Josephine Alicia, only dau. of Rev. Morley Swifte-Dennis, A.M., M.D., Rector of Eldermine, co. Wexford, and has, with other issue,
John Nicholas, *b.* 1885.
A dau., *b.* 1 June, 1899.
1. Frances, *m.* 23 July, 1856, Rev. John Harward Jessop Handcock, Incumbent of Woodlands, Kent, grandson of Richard, 2nd Lord Castlemaine, and *d.* 4 Feb. 1864, leaving issue.
2. Maria, *m.* 20 April, 1865, Alfred Henry Wynne, of Collon House, Collon, J.P. co. Louth, 2nd son of Capt. George Wynne, late Scots Greys, who was grandson of Right Hon. Owen Wynne, of Hazelwood, co. Sligo, and has issue.
3. Anna Statira, *m.* 3 Nov. 1877, Dacre Ives Barrett-Leonard, son of the Rev. Dacre Barrett-Leonard, 1st bart. of Belhus, and *d.* 18 Jan. 1892.
Rev. Nicholas-Devereux sold Killimur in 1860 to Lord Dunsandle, and *d.* 1867. He was *s.* by his eldest son,
JOHN DALY DEVEREUX, of Ballyrankin House, co. Wexford, B.A., J.P., *b.* 12 June, 1834, Barrister-at-Law, late Capt. Wexford Militia; *m.* 29 July, 1882, his cousin, Saminina Maria, only surviving child of Col. James Douglas Johnstone, of Snowhill, co. Fermanagb, and widow of William Wainwright Braddell, of Ballingate, co. Wicklow, J.P., and *d.* 18 May, 1898.

Arms—Quarterly: 1st and 4th erm., a fess gu. in chief three torteaux; 2nd and 3rd, per fess arg. and or, a lion rampant per fess sa. and gu. in chief two open dexter hands of the last. *Crest*—A buck trippant ppr. *Motto*—Per angusta ad augusta.

Seat—Ballyrankin House, Ferns, co. Wexford. *Residence*—St. Mary's Vicarage, Provost Street, Hoxton, N.

HUME (now DICK) OF CO. WICKLOW.

QUINTIN DICK DICK, of co. Wicklow, and of Carantrila Park, co. Galway, High Sheriff 1898, late Capt. Derbyshire Y.C. and Royal Antrim Rifles, D.L. co. Wicklow, b. 13 April, 1847; s. his uncle, The Right Hon. W. W. F. Dick 1892, under the will of his grand-uncle, Quintin Dick, M.P. for Malden. Mr. Quintin Dick assumed by Royal Licence 23 Nov. 1892, the surname and arms of DICK. He m. 27 Oct. 1908, Lorna Katherine, dau. of Major Ernest Charles Penn Curzon (son of Col. the Hon. Ernest George Curzon), late 18th Hussars (see BURKE'S *Peerage*, HOWE, E.), by his wife Edith, dau. of Charles Henry Bassett, of Watermouth Castle, Devon (see that family).

Lineage.—ANDREW HUME (son and successor of Gavain Hume), " Captain of Tantallon," distinguished in the French Service, and grandson of Alexander Hume, 3rd Baron of Polwarth) returned to Scotland and purchased the estate of the Rhodes near to the lands of the 1st Sir John Hume, of North Berwick. He m. Mosea Seaton, dau. of Seaton of Barnes, and niece to the Earl of Winton, by whom he had (with a dau., m. George Hume, of Pinkerton) four sons, 1. ROBERT, his heir; 2. Thomas; 3. John; 4. William. Andrew Hume d. 1594 or 1595.

SIR THOMAS HUME, of the City of Dublin, Knt., in the household of the Duke of Ormonde, Lord-Lieutenant of Ireland, received from His Excellency, in 1641, a grant of extensive lands in co. Tipperary, and in 1665, a further grant of estates in the same co., " on account of his sufferings for the King and for King CHARLES I." He was shortly afterwards knighted by the Lord-Lieut, in Dublin, and d.s.p. 3 July, 1668. He m. Anne, dau. of — Trench. She m. 2ndly, 1688, Capt. George Mathew, of Thomastown, co. Tipperary, who d. Oct. 1689. She d. March, 1702. Sir Thomas's nephew,

THOMAS HUME, of Bawn, co. Cavan, and afterwards of St. Johnstown, co. Longford, was one of the executors to his aunt, Dame Anne Hume, otherwise Mathew, in 1702, at which date he was living in Dublin. Mr. Hume was twice m., and by his 1st wife had with other issue,
1. WILLIAM, his heir.
2. Robert, ancestor of the HUMES of Lisanure or Lisnober, co. Cavan.
1. Catherine, m. Rev. Hugh Skellern, Rector of Killeshandra, co. Cavan 1705-29.

He m. 2ndly, Elizabeth Lewis, of London, widow of Hugh Galbraith, of St. Johnstown, but she d.s.p. in her husband's lifetime, 1723. Mr. Hume was s. by his eldest son,

WILLIAM HUME, of Humewood, m. Anna, dau. of John Denison, of Dublin, and had two sons (of whom the 2nd son, Denison Hume m. Feb. 1769, a dau. of Robert Hume, of co. Cavan) and five daus. He d. 26 May, 1752, and was s. by his eldest son,

GEORGE HUME, of Humewood, m. 1744, Anna, dau. of Thomas Butler, of Newcastle, co. Wicklow, and d. Aug. 1765, having had issue,
1. WILLIAM, of whom presently.
2. George, d.s.p. 1776.
3. John Latouche, m. the dau. of — Constable, and d. about 1826, having had issue,
    1. Clement, d. unm.
    2. William, d. unm.
    3. Robert, Ensign in the Army, m. Miss Pentland, but d.s.p. She m. 2ndly, Capt. Childers, and left issue.
    4. Henry, m. the dau. of — Gallwey, and d.s.p. 31 Dec. 1884. He devised his lands near Mallow to his cousin, William Charles Hume.
    5. Joseph, d. unm.
    1. Isabella.
    2. Maria, d. unm.
1. Anna, m. Benjamin Wills, and left a dau.
2. Margaret, d. unm. 17 Nov. 1775.
3. Isabella.

The eldest son,
WILLIAM HUME, of Humewood, M.P. co. Wicklow, b. 1774; shot by a party of rebels in the Wicklow Mountains, 8 Oct. 1798. He m. Catherine, eldest dau. of Sir Joseph Hoare, Bart., M.P., of Annabella, co. Cork, and had two sons and four daus.,
1. WILLIAM HOARE, his heir.
2. Joseph Samuel, b. 15 June, 1774; m. Eliza, dau. of Rev. Charles Smyth, of Smythfield, co. Limerick, Rector of Croagh, and left issue,

1. William Charles, of Ballinvollo, co. Wicklow, J.P., b. 1805; m. 1837, Charlotte, dau. of Henry William Thompson, of Stonebrook, co. Kildare, and d. 4 Nov. 1890, leaving issue,
    (1) Joseph Samuel, of Ballinvollo, co. Wicklow, and Ashgrove, co. Cork, served as District Inspector Royal Irish Constabulary 1859-98 b. 22 Nov. 1837; m. 13 Sept. 1864, Eda Eveline, dau. of James Porter, M.D., of Carlow, and has issue,
        1. William Charles Porter, b. 6 May, 1869.
        2. Richard Henry, b. 15 April, 1873; d. 8 Nov. 1896.
        3. George Ponsonby, b. 21 Nov. 1875.
        1. Eliza Ethel, d. young.
        2. Eda Dorcas.
    (2) Henry Harrington, b. 22 Feb. 1838; d. of wounds received in the American Civil War.
    (3) Charles Thompson, d. an infant.
    (4) George Skeffington Conner, b. 18 Oct. 1843; settled in Australia.
    (5) William Hume Blake, b. 27 April, 1847; went to New Zealand.
    (6) Arthur Lee Guinness, b. 13 Jan. 1849; settled in New Zealand.
    (7) Benjamin Lee Guinness, killed at Maiwand.
    (8) Charles Thompson.
    (9) John James Nugent.
    (1) Eliza, d. young.
    (2) Margaret Bruce.
1. Catherine, m. her cousin, William Hume Blake, successively Solicitor-Gen., Chancellor and President of the High Court of Appeal, Canada, and had issue.
2. Eliza Rebecca Guinness, b. 1806, m. 1830 George Skeffington Conner, Puisne Judge in Canada. She d.s.p. Nov. 1883.
3. Anne Honora, m. John Small, and had issue.
1. Catherine, b. 26 April, 1773; m. William Franks, of Carrig, co. Cork.
2. Anna, b. 4 June, 1775; m. Rev. Dominick Edward Blake, and had issue.
3. Jane, b. 10 July, 1780; m. the Hon. and Rev. Maurice Mahon, afterwards Lord Hartland, and d.s.p. 12 Dec. 1838.
4. Grace, b. 1 Sept. 1783; d. unm.

The elder son,
WILLIAM HOARE HUME, of Humewood, M.P. for Wicklow, b. 3 Feb. 1772; m. 1804, Charlotte Anna, only dau. of Samuel Dick, of Dublin (vide infra), and by her (who d. 11 May, 1864) had issue,
1. WILLIAM WENTWORTH FITZWILLIAM (Right Hon.), of whom presently.
2. Quintin Dick (Rev.), b. 23 Nov. 1806; m. 5 May, 1830, his cousin, Anna, dau. of William Richardson, of Athy, and d. 25 Nov. 1871, having by her (who d. 10 Sept. 1886) had issue,
    1. William Hoare, an Officer in the 51st Regt., b. 6 Jan. 1840; d. unm. 26 Oct. 1873.
    2. QUINTIN DICK, heir male of the HUMES of Humewood.
    3. Charles Joseph, b. Sept. 1849; d. unm. 2/ June, 1883.
    1. Isabella, m. 10 Sept. 1863, Capt. George Archibald Warden, 66th Regt., and d. Aug. 1871, leaving issue.
    2. Anna Maria, m. Aug. 1867, Major John Leslie, J.P., of Kiltibegs, co. Monaghan, and d. March, 1877, leaving issue.
    3. Charlotte, d. unm. 1861.
3. George Ponsonby, Lieut.-Col. 58th Regt., d. unm. 14 Oct. 1866.
1. Charlotte Isabella Forster, m. Thomas Crowe, of Dromore Castle, co. Clare, J.P., D.L., High Sheriff co. Clare 1838, and by him (who d. 1877) has issue.
2. Charlotte Jane, m. her cousin, the late Sir George Forster, Bart. of Tullaghan, co. Monaghan, M.P. She d.s.p. 9 Aug. 1889.

Mr. Hume d. 5 Nov. 1815, and was s. by his son,
THE RIGHT HON. WILLIAM WENTWORTH FITZWILLIAM DICK (formerly William Wentworth Fitzwilliam Hume), of Humewood, co. Wicklow, D.L., J.P., High Sheriff 1844, M.P. for co. Wicklow 1852 to 1880, b. 28 Oct. 1805; m. 8 June, 1829, Margaret Bruce, eldest dau. of Robert Chaloner, M.P. of Guisboro', co. York, by the Hon. Frances Laura Dundas, his wife, dau. of the last Lord Dundas, and by her (who d. 13 June, 1837) had issue,
1. William Hoare, d. 28 Nov. 1841, aged 7.
2. William Chaloner, d. in infancy.
1. Frances Laura.
2. Charlotte Anna, m. 4 Oct. 1853, Richard P. Long, of Rood Ashton, Wilts, J.P., and D.L., M.P. for that co., and by him (who d. 16 Feb. 1875) had issue (see LONG of Rood Ashton). She d. 18 Dec. 1899.

The Rt. Hon. W. W. F. Hume, who assumed the surname and arms of Dick only, by Royal Licence, 17 June, 1864, d. 15 Sept. 1892, and was s. by his nephew,
QUINTIN DICK HUME (the present head of the family), who thereupon assumed the surname of DICK.

FAMILY OF DICK.

ROBERT DICK, of a Scotch family, obtained a grant of the lands of Dunovarnan, co. Antrim, from Randall, Earl of Antrim, prior to 1635, and was s. by his son or grandson,
ROBERT DICK, of Garry, co. Antrim, b. about 1650, who was s. by his son,
JOHN DICK, of Dublin, who m. Anne, dau. of William Adair, and had with other issue, a son,
QUINTIN DICK, of Nenagh, co. Tipperary, m. Anne, sister of Hugh Ker, of Dublin, and d. 1768, leaving three sons and two daus. His eldest son,
SAMUEL DICK, of Dublin, m. Charlotte, dau. of Nicholas Forster, of Tullaghan, co. Monaghan, and had issue,
1. Quintin, formerly M.P. for Malden, who resided at 20, Curzon Street, Mayfair, London, and d. unm. 26 March, 1858.

2. Hugh, *d. unm.* 3. William Forster, *d. unm.*
1. CHARLOTTE ANNA, *m.* William Hoare Hume, of Humewood, co. Wicklow, M.P. for that co. and *d.* 11 May, 1864, leaving issue (*see* HUME *family*).

Arms—Quarterly 1st and 4th, gu. a sword in pale, point upwards, ppr. hilted and pommelled or, between two mullets in chief of the last (DICK), 2nd vert a lion rampant arg. (HUME), 3rd arg. three popinjays vert, beaked and collared gu. (PEPDIE). *Crest*—A leopard sejant ppr. *Motto*—Semper fidelis.

Seat—Carintrila, Park, co. Galway. *Residence*—12 Grosvenor Crescent, Belgrave Square, S.W. *Clubs*—Carlton, Arthur's, Junior United Service, Bachelors' and Kildare Street, Dublin.

DICKSON OF WOODVILLE.

The late JOHN WILLIAM DICKSON, of Woodville, and Dungarberry, co. Leitrim, J.P. cos. Donegal and Leitrim, *b.* 19 Nov. 1842, late Lieut.-Col. 4th Batt. Durham L.I., and formerly Lieut. 71st Highland L.I. ; *m.* 30 April, 1885, Marian Devereux, 2nd dau. of Mark Lambert, of Whitley Hall, Northumberland, J.P. He *d.s.p.* 7 Nov. 1899.

Lineage.—JOHN DICKSON, of Ballyshannon, co. Donegal, *b.* 1718, *m.* 1740, Frances, dau. of Daniel Eccles, of Castletown, co. Tyrone, J.P., High Sheriff 1720, by Mary, dau. of Robert Lowry ; and *d.* 1774, having by her (who *d.* 1776) had issue,
THOMAS, of Woodville.
Ann, *m.* 28 Feb. 1773, her cousin, Daniel Eccles, of Ecclesville, J.P., D.L., High Sheriff 1772, and *d.* 11 March, 1819, having by him (who *d.* 31 July, 1808) had a son,
John Dickson Eccles, of Ecclesville (*see* MCCLINTOCK *of Seskinore*).

His son,
THOMAS DICKSON, of Woodville, co. Leitrim, M.P. for Ballyshannon, *b.* 1741 ; *m.* 14 Dec. 1775, Hester, dau. of Rev. James Lowry, by his wife Hester, dau. of John Richardson of Richbill, co. Armagh (James Lowry was brother to Galbraith Lowry, father of Armar, 1st Earl Belmore), and *d.* 7 July, 1817, having by her (who *d.* 16 Jan. 1793) had issue,
1. JOHN, of Woodville.
2. James Lowry (Rev.), *b.* 19 Aug. 1783 ; *m.* 3 March, 1810, his cousin, Mary, dau. of Daniel Eccles, of Ecclesville (*see* MCCLINTOCK *of Seskinore*), and *d.* 23 Nov. 1861, having by her (who *d.* 17 March, 1858) had issue,
  1. Thomas, *b.* 15 July, 1813 ; *d.* 22 July, 1885.
  2. Daniel Eccles (Rev.), *b.* 2 March, 1824.
   1. Anna Maria, *d.* 27 Sept. 1884.
   2. Jemima Anne Eccles, *d.* 28 July, 1879.
   3. Hester, *m.* 1852, Rev. John Harris Morell, and *d.* 5 Nov. 1865.
3. Thomas, in the Army, *b.* 9 Nov. 1784 ; *d.* abroad 2 Sept. 1807.
4. Robert Lowry, *b.* 3 Nov. 1789 ; *m.* 1815, Alicia, dau. of the Rev. Daniel Lucas, and *d.* April, 1848, having had issue,
  1. Thomas, in the Army.
  2. Daniel Lucas (Rev.), *m.* Lizzie Cullen.
   1. Nannie, *m.* her cousin, Rev. Robert Gilbert Eccles, Rector of Kilbrogan.
   2. Hester.
   3. Frances.
5. William, R.N., *b.* 9 July, 1791 ; *m.* 1817, his cousin, Hester, dau. of Daniel Eccles (*see* MCCLINTOCK *of Seskinore*), and *d.* 10 July, 1854, having had issue,
  Thomas William, of Rochfort Lodge.
  Anna Eliza, *m.* Robert William Newburgh Jenkins, Capt. 8th (King's Royal Irish) Hussars.
  1. Hester, *m.* 1st, 1800, Cairncross Cullen, of Screeny, co. Leitrim, and 2ndly, Rev. Herbert Mandeville Nash.
  2. Frances, *m.* Thomas Llewellyn Nash, Barrister-at-Law, and had issue.
  3. Jemima, *m.* 30 Oct. 1810, her cousin, John Dickson Eccles, of Ecclesville, J.P., D.L. (*see* MCCLINTOCK *of Seskinore*), and *d.* 8 April, 1829, having by him (who *d.* 1830) had issue.
The eldest son,
JOHN DICKSON, of Woodville, *b.* 13 Aug. 1781 ; *m.* 10 Nov. 1803, Mary Louisa, dau. of J. Bodkin, of Thomastown, co. Galway, and *d.* 4 Jan. 1822, leaving by her (who *d.* 17 March, 1819) issue,
1. Thomas, *b.* 8 Aug. 1804 ; *d.* 1825.
2. James, *b.* 1805 ; *d. unm.*
3. JOHN REYNOLDS, of Woodville.
4. Hyacinth, *b.* 15 Feb. 1809 ; *d. unm.* 1878.
5. Robert, *b.* 24 May, 1810, *m.* 1859, Anna, dau. of J. Pentland, and widow of Capt. Green, and has issue,
  1. John, *b.* 1865.
  1. Anna, *m.* 19 March, 1889, Rev. Frederick Beavan, eldest son of John Beavan, of Elton Hall and Camus, co. Limerick.
  2. Harriette.
6. William, *b.* Aug. 1811 ; *d.* young.
7. Terence, *b.* 1813 ; *d.* young.
8. Alexander, Barrister-at-Law, *b.* 23 Feb. 1817 ; *m.* Harriet Louisa Carey, and *d.s.p.* 1877.
9. Joseph William (Rev.), *b.* 5 March, 1819 ; *m.* Louisa, dau. of Rev. William Frazer, Vicar of Shawrahan and Temple Terry, by Louisa his wife, dau. of Rev. William Archdall.

1. Hester Jane, *m.* Henry Francis, 3rd son of Rev. Cairncross Cullen, of Manorhamilton, and *d.* 3 March, 1884.
2. Belinda Mary, *m.* R. Herdman, M.D.
3. Mary Belinda, *m.* her cousin William Newcombe.

Mr. Dickson was *s.* by his son,
JOHN REYNOLDS DICKSON, of Woodville and Dungarberry, J.P., *b.* 11 Aug. 1807 ; *m.* 29 April, 1837, Clara, dau. of Capt. John Skene, R.N., C.B., of Lethenty, co. Aberdeen, and *d.* 7 June, 1880, having by her (who *d.* 15 May, 1879) had issue,
1. JOHN WILLIAM, his heir.
2. Thomas Hyacinth, retired Commander R.N., *b.* 11 Sept. 1844 ; *d.* 12 Sept. 1888.
1. Ida Frances, *m.* 1st, 1865, James Nias Croke, retired Commander, R.N., and by him (who *d.* 1879) had Ida Clara Mary, *m.* 1889, John Marpot Piercy, Capt. Dorset Regt. Mrs. Croke *m.* 2ndly, 14 July, 1884, John Croke, of Studeley Priory, co. Oxford.
2. Mary Elizabeth, *d.* 1854.
3. Clara Hester, *m.* Jan. 1871, Frances Laurence Gore Little, Major R.A., 7th son of John Little, of Stewartstown, co. Tyrone, and has issue (*see that family*).
4. Edythe Grace, *m.* 1873, Robert Edgeworth Johnstone, only son of James Johnstone, of Magheramena, co. Fermanagh, J.P., D.L., and *d.* 14 Jan. 1887, having by him (who *d.* Aug. 1882 had issue.
5. Audley Harriette, *m.* 1875, William Henry White (who *d.* May, 1892), of Cloone Grange, co. Leitrim, J.P. and D.L., High Sheriff, 1879, and *d.* 6 May, 1887, leaving issue (*see that family*).

Mr. Dickson *d.* 1880, and was *s.* by his eldest son.

Seats—Woodville, Tullaghan, co. Leitrim ; Tullaghan House, by Sligo.

DICKSON OF KILDIMO.

COL. WILLIAM DICKSON DICKSON, of Kildimo House, co. Limerick, J.P., High Sheriff 1890, late commanding Limerick City Artillery, S. Division, R.G.A., B.A. Trin. Coll, Dublin, *b.* 27 April, 1853 ; *m.* 17 Feb. 1897, his cousin, Frances Louisa, elder dau. of the late Rev. Lewis Montagu Maunsell, Rector of Kilskyre, co. Meath, and Mary his wife, dau. of Rev. Richard Bell Booth, of Kilskyre, co. Meath, and has issue,
1. Elizabeth Rebecca Frances.
2. Norah Constance.
3. Ruth Caroline.

Col. Dickson is the only child of the late Rev. William Francis Maunsell, Rector of Kildimo, who *d.* 10 June, 1895, and Rebecca Caroline his wife, who *d.* 27 April, 1853, elder dau. of Rev. Richard Dickson, of Vermont, Clarina, co. Limerick, and Anne his wife, dau. of Sir James Chatterton, 1st Bart., and sister of the late Samuel Frederick Dickson, D.L., of Mulcair. Col. Dickson *s.* his uncle the late S. F. Dickson, D.L., and assumed by Royal Licence 27 Dec. 1900, the name and arms of DICKSON.

Lineage.—*See* MAUNSELL *of Spa Hill.*

Lineage (of DICKSON).—STEPHEN DICKSON, son of Richard Dickson, of Ballybonogue, co. Limerick, *m.* Mary Lane and by her had issue,
1. Richard, who inherited the family estates, *m.* and *d.* leaving a son,
  1. Stephen, of Clonshire and Ballynaguile, *d.s.p.l.*
2. John, of Liverpool, merchant, *m.* and left issue an only surviving dau.,
  1. Honora, *m.* James Cooper, of Cooper Hill, co. Limerick, and *d.s.p.*
3. Stephen, Barrister-at-Law, *m.* and left with other issue,
  1. Arthur, Capt., *m.* a dau. of Marshall MacDonald, Duke of Tarrento, and had issue,
   (1) Eleanor Sophia MacDonald Dickson, *d. unm.*
  2. James Thomas, Barrister-at-Law, *m.* Alicia, dau. of George Lee, of Barna, co. Tipperary, and had issue,
   (1) Stephen, *d.s.p.*
   (1) Alicia, heiress of her uncle, Capt. Arthur Dickson, *m.* William Lee, of Bettyville, co. Limerick (*see* LEE *of Barna*), and had issue.

4. Patrick, d.s.p.
5. Daniel, merchant in Limerick, d., leaving issue by Anne, his wife, in 1794.
　1. Daniel.
　　1. Isabella, m. 1795, Richard Peppard.
　　2. Prudence, m. before 1794, — Bennett.
　　3. Honora.　　4. Belinda.
6. Samuel, of whom we treat.

The youngest son,
Samuel Dickson, of Ballynaguile, m. 1st, Miss Farrell, of co. Limerick, and by her had issue, a dau., who m. Richard Power, of Muiroe, co. Tipperary, and had issue. He m. 2ndly, 1775, Mary, dau. of John Norris, of the city of Limerick and by her had issue,
1. Stephen, J.P., D.L., Barrister-at-Law, and Commissioner of Bankrupts, High Sheriff co. Limerick 1809, d. unm. 1839, leaving large estates.
2. John, b. June, 1778, J.P., D.L. of Clonshire, co. Limerick, Lieut.-Col. Co. Limerick Militia.
3. Samuel, J.P. for co. and city of Limerick, High Sheriff of the former 1828, contested Limerick City 1830 and 1832, M.P. co. Limerick 1849-50, d. 1850.
4. Richard, Rev., of whom hereafter.
5. William, C.B., of Beenham House, Berks., a Major-Gen. in the E.I.C.S., m. Harriet, eld. dau. of Maj.-Gen. Sir Thos. Dallas, K.C.B. (see Dallas-Yorke of Walmersgate), and d. before 1860, leaving issue,
　1. Samuel Auchmuty, b. 1817, of Croon Castle, near Limerick J.P., D.L. for co. Limerick, Lieut.-Col. commanding Royal Limerick Militia, formerly Capt. 13th Light Dragoons, M.P. co. Limerick 1859; m. 1847, Maria Teresa, dau. of N. Saunders, and d.s.p. 1870.
　2. William Thomas, b. 9 Jan. 1830, Maj.-Gen. and Hon. Lieut. Gen. and Col. 16th Lancers; d. 19 Aug. 1909, unm.
　1. A dau.
　2. Eliza Harriet, m. 25 Aug. 1845, Sir John Neeld, Bart., and had issue (see Burke's Peerage, Neeld, Bt.).
　3. Fanny Charlotte, m. 14 Jan. 1847, as his 1st wife, Hon. Mortimer Sackville-West, afterwards created Baron Sackville, and she d.s.p. 19 Jan. 1870 (see Burke's Peerage, Sackville, Baron).
1. Mary m. 1819, Right Rev. Stephen Creagh Sandes, Bishop of Cashel Emly, Waterford, and Lismore, and d. 16 July, 1866, having had issue (see Sandes of Sallow Glen).
2. Anne, m. George Washington Biggs, of Bellevue, co. Tipperary, and had issue.
3. Catherine, m. 27 April, 1811, Sir Robert Bateson, Bt., of Belvoir Park, co. Down, and had issue (see Burke's Peerage, Deramore, B.), and d. 21 Jan. 1874. He d. 21 April, 1863.
4. Elisa.
The 4th son,
Rev. Richard Dickson, Rector of Kilkeedy, of Vermont, co. Limerick, m. Anna (who d. 1835), dau. and heiress of Sir James Chatterton, Bart., of Castle Mahan, co. Cork, d. circa 1860, having had issue,
1. Samuel Frederick, of whom presently.
2. William, Rev.
　1. Rebecca Caroline, d. 27 April, 1853; m. 14 Sept. 1847, Rev. William Francis Maunsell, Rector of Kildimo (see Maunsell of Spa Hill), who d. 1895, and had issue,
　　William Dickson Maunsell, now Dickson, now of Kildimo House, and Mulcair, co. Limerick.
　2. Maria Frances, m. William Peters Smith, of Bellmont, Raheny who, in 1874, assumed the names and arms of Chatterton by Royal licence.
The elder son,
Samuel Frederick Dickson, D.L., of Mulcair co. Limerick, and of West Croeves, co. Limerick, b. 1811, J.P. and D.L. co. Limerick, High Sheriff 1849; d. 1900, when he was s. by his nephew, Col. William Dickson Maunsell, now of Mulcair and Kildimo, who has assumed the surname and arms of Dickson (see ante).

Arms—Quarterly 1st and 4th, az. a crescent between three mullets arg. on a chief or as many pallets gu. (Dickson); 2nd and 3rd arg. a chevron between three maunches sa. (Maunsell). Crest—Out of battlements a naked arm embowed holding a sword all ppr. Motto—Fortes fortuna juvat.
Seats—Kildimo House and Mulcair, co. Limerick, and Southill, Dean Park, Bournemouth. Clubs—Union, S.W., and County, Limerick.

DILLON. See Burke's Peerage, CLONBROCK, B. and DILLON, Bart.

DIXON. See Burke's Peerage, DIXON, Bart.

DOBBIN OF ARMAGH.

George Miller Dobbin, of Drummulla House, co. Louth, J.P. cos. Armagh and Louth, High Sheriff co. Armagh 1884, Lieut.-Col. (retired) Royal Artillery, b. 25 Jan. 1833; m. 9 April, 1868, Elizabeth Jane (who d. 1 Dec. 1905), dau. of Col. George Turnbull Marshall, of Bengal Army, and has issue,

1. Leonard George William, Capt. Northampton Regt., b. 31 March, 1871.
2. Herbert Thomas, Capt. 1st Batt. Duke of Cornwall's L.I., b. 27 May, 1878.
3. George Henry, b. 28 Aug. 1881; d. 2 April, 1892.
4. Arthur William, Lieut. R.A., b. 24 March, 1883.
1. Rhoda Margaret Elizabeth.
2. Mary Marshall.
3. Annie, m. 1 Nov. 1902, Capt. J. H. M. Beasley, R.A.

Lineage.—The family of Dobbin is of ancient standing in the North of Ireland. About the period of the Revolution, viz., in 1690, two brothers of this family removed from Carrickfergus to Armagh, viz., Thomas Dobbin and Robert Dobbin. The younger brother,
Robert Dobbin, settled at Ternescobe, co. Armagh. He made his will 14 Jan. 1734-5, and it was proved in the Diocesan Court of Armagh, 22 July, 1735, in which year he died, leaving issue six sons. The youngest son,
Leonard Dobbin of Armagh, m. Mary, dau. of Thomas Oates, and niece of General Murray distinguished at the siege of Derry (of the family of Murray of Philiphaugh), and had issue,
1. Thomas, his heir.
2. Leonard, of Armagh, D L., for many years M.P. for Armagh, b. 29 Sept. 1762; d. unm. 20 Feb. 1844.
3. John, M.D., d. unm. 22 Oct. 1820.
1. Anne, b. 1741; m. William Curry, of Auchnacloy, co. Tyrone, and d. June, 1820, leaving a dau. Mrs. Maziere, and one son, William Curry, Serjeant-at-Law, and M.P. for Armagh, afterwards a Master in Chancery, m. 1816, Miss Bruce, and d.s.p. 1824.
2. Jane d. unm.　　3. Mary, d. unm. March, 1802.

The eldest son,
Thomas Dobbin, of Armagh, b. 1754; m. 26 May, 1787, Rhoda, dau. of Robert Brown, of Kiltown, co. Donegal, by his wife Lucinda Parke, of Dunalley, co. Sligo, and d. 12 Aug. 1801, having had issue,
1. Leonard, his heir.
2. Robert Brown, Lieut. 66th Regt., b. 6 Sept. 1790; killed at Anhao, France, 10 Sept. 1813, having been previously wounded at the battle of Orthes.
3. Thomas, J.P. Armagh, b. 3 Aug. 1795; m. 3 Oct. 1827, Lucy, dau. of John Donnelly, and sister of William Donnelly, C.B., LL.D., Registrar-General, which lady d.s.p. 30 Sept. 1831; he d. 24 May, 1871.
4. Alexander John, of Armagh, b. 29 March, 1797; d. 18 May, 1877.
1. Lucinda, m. 1809, Henry D. Brooke, of Prosperous, co. Kildare, and d. his widow, Dec. 1860.
2. Mary, m. Rev. William Hamilton Maxwell, Prebendary of Balla, who d. 29 Dec. 1850.
3. Jane, d. 11 May, 1875.
4. Anne, m. 2 Oct. 1828, Henry Leslie Prentice, of Caledon, J.P., and d. Oct. 1863.
5. Rhoda, m. William Hanna, Barrister-at-Law; and d. 17 June, 1847.

The eldest son,
Leonard Dobbin, of the City of Armagh, of Wood Park, co. Armagh, and of Templeport, co. Cavan, Clerk of the Peace for the co. of Armagh, b. 29 April, 1789; m. 12 Sept. 1822, Mary, 4th dau. of Rev. George Miller, D.D., Fellow of Trin. Coll. Dublin, and Rector of Derryvolan, co. Fermanagh, and by her (who d. 24 Jan. 1848) had issue,
1. Leonard, of the Inner Temple, London, b. 8 March, 1825; d. unm. 8 Nov. 1848.
2. Thomas, Solicitor in Chancery, b. 6 Jan. 1831; d. unm. 26 March, 1865.
3. George Miller, now of Drummulla.
4. Robert Alexander, 6th Regt. European Foot, Bengal, b. 17 March, 1835; m. Louisa, dau. of William Walker, and d. 5 Sept. 1875, leaving issue, four sons and two daus.
5. William, Clerk of the Crown for the co. Armagh, b. 24 May, 1837; m. 12 Aug. 1868, Katharine Lydia Emily, 2nd dau. of James Bell, of Ardcarne, Ballinasloe, and d. 27 Aug. 1875, leaving by her (who d. 16 June, 1876) issue, one son and three daus.
6. Alexander John (Rev.), M.A. Trin. Coll. Dublin, b. 23 June, 1840; d. unm. 7 July, 1880.
7. Henry Brooke, M.A., LL.D. Trin. Coll. Dublin, b. 21 March, 1842; m. 3 July, 1867, Elizabeth, eldest dau. of John Hart, of Glanville Hall, South Australia, and d. 22 July, 1873, leaving issue, two sons and two daus. His eldest son, Leonard, m. 5 Sept. 1905, Marie Cooper.
8. Charles Edward, M.A. Trin. Coll. Dublin, Solicitor in Chancery, b. 11 April, 1846; d. unm. 14 June, 1879.

1. Elizabeth, d. March, 1910; m. Hall Stirling, son of the Rev. John B. Stirling, Rector of Inniskeen, co. Armagh.
2. Rhoda Mary, m. Thomas Hanna, of Gardiner's Place, Dublin; and d. 24 Oct. 1860, leaving issue, William Leonard and Elizabeth, m. 1 Aug. 1895, Rev. Alexander Nixon Montgomery, Rector of Aughnamullen, co. Monaghan.

Mr. Dobbin, who was nephew and heir-at-law of Leonard Dobbin, of Armagh, a Deputy-Lieut. for the co., and for many years M.P. for his native city of Armagh, d. 5 May, 1881, and was s. by his eldest surviving son.

Arms—Gu., between two flaunches chequy arg. and sa. five mullets of six points, two, one and two, or, a crescent of the last for difference. *Crest*—Out of a mural crown ppr., charged with a crescent or, an oak branch acorned also ppr. *Motto*—Re e merito.

Seat—Drummulla House, Omeath, Newry.

DOBBS OF CASTLE DOBBS.

ARCHIBALD EDWARD DOBBS, of Castle Dobbs, co. Antrim, J.P., High Sheriff, 1909, M.A., Balliol Coll., Oxford, Barrister-at-Law, b. 29 June 1838; m. 4 May, 1875, Edith Mary, 2nd dau. of Sir James Timmins Chance, 1st Bart. (see BURKE'S *Peerage*), and has issue,

1. ARTHUR FREDERICK, B.A. King's Coll. Camb., Capt. Antrim R.G. Reserve Art., b. 31 March, 1876.
2. Francis Wellesley, M.A. Trin. Coll. Camb. (twin), b. 31 March, 1876.
3. Archibald Edward, M.A. and Fellow King's Coll. Camb., b. 27 Aug. 1882.

Lineage.—This family was established in Ireland by JOHN DOBBS, who accompanied Sir Henry Dockwra to that country in 1596, and was subsequently his deputy as Treasurer for Ulster. This John Dobbs m. 1603, Margaret (who d. 6 Nov. 1620—Funeral entry), only child of John Dalway of Ballyhill, and by her had two sons, Foulk, who was lost, with his father, in returning from England; and HERCULES DOBBS, who s. to his father's property; he m. Magdalen West, of Ballydugan, co. Down, and left an only son,

RICHARD DOBBS, High Sheriff co. Antrim, 1664, who m. 1655, Dorothy, dau. and co-heir of Bryan Willans, of Clints Hall, Richmond, Yorks, and had by her (with three daus). two sons. Mr. Dobbs, d. 1701. leaving his estate to his younger son,

RICHARD DOBBS, of Castletown, b. 1660; who m. 1st, Mary, dau. of Archibald Stewart, of Ballintoy, and had (with two daus., Jane, m. Edward Brice, of Kilroot; and Elizabeth, d. unm.) three sons,
1. ARTHUR, his heir.
2. Richard, who served in the Navy, afterwards a Fellow of Trin. Coll. Dublin, and Rector of Lisburn, m. Mrs. Lambert, and had three sons,
1. Richard (Rev.), Dean of Connor, ancestor of DOBBS *of Glenariffe Lodge (whom see)*.
2. Francis, Barrister-at-Law, M.P. for Charlemont in Grattan's Parliament.
3. William, R.N., fell in action at Belfast Lough
3. Marmaduke.

He m. 2ndly, Margaret Clugston, of Belfast, and by her had three daus. He was High Sheriff co. Antrim 1694, and d. 1711. His eldest son and heir,

ARTHUR DOBBS, b. 2 April, 1689, High Sheriff co. Antrim 1720, and for many years M.P. for Carrickfergus; m. Anne, dau. and heir of Capt. Osborne, of Timahoe, co. Kildare, and relict of Capt. Norbury, by whom he had issue. Mr. Dobbs, who was appointed Engineer and Surveyor-General of Ireland, by Sir Robert Walpole, was, 1753, sent out as Governor of North Carolina, where he acquired large possessions. He was s. by his eldest son,

CONWAY RICHARD DOBBS, of Castle Dobbs, M.P. for Carrickfergus, and High Sheriff co. Antrim 1752, who m. 1st, Anne, dau. of Alexander Stewart of Ballintoy, and by her (who d. 19 Feb. 1765) had issue,
1. RICHARD, his heir.

He m. 2ndly, Charity, widow of Stephen Rice, of Mount Rice, co. Kildare, and dau. of Robert Borrowes of Kildare, by Mary, his wife, dau. of John O'Neill, of Shanes Castle, co. Antrim, and by her had issue,
2. Edward Brice, Capt. in the Army, and twice Mayor of Carrickfergus, d. at Castle Dobbs, Feb. 1803.
3. Robert Conway (Rev.), m. 1798, Wilhelmina Josepha, dau. of the Rev. William Bristow, Vicar of Belfast, and d. 9 Dec. 1809, aged 38, leaving issue,
1. William Cary Dobbs, of Ashurst, Killiney, co. Dublin, Q.C., M.P. for Carrickfergus, and subsequently one of the Judges of the Landed Estates Court in Ireland, b. 4 April, 1806; m. May, 1836, Eleanor Jones, eldest dau of Henry Westropp, of Richmond, co. Limerick. She d. 18 April, 1900. He d. 17 April, 1869, leaving issue.
(1) Robert Conway, of Camphire, Cappoquin, co. Waterford, and Ashurst, Killiney, co. Dublin, M.A. Camb., Barrister-at-Law, Lincoln's Inn, b. 26 Dec. 1842; m. 28 Sept. 1869, Edith Julianna, dau. of Henry Fowler Broadwood, of Lyne, Horsham, Surrey; and has issue,
1. William Cary, b. 14 Oct., 1870.
2. Henry Robert Conway, C.I.E., I.C.S. (Res.—Quetta, Baluchistan, India), b. 26 Aug. 1871; m. 4 March, 1907, Esmé, dau. of George Rivaz, of Canterbury, and has issue.
3. Arthur Conway, b. 1 Nov. 1874; m. 17 April, 1906; Elinor Augusta, dau. of late Otto Christian von Schönberg,

1. Mildred Elinor. 2. Edith Sybil. 3. Alison Charity.
(1) Elinor, d. unm. 25 Aug. 1892.
(2) Charity Frances, m. May, 1875, Christian Otto Ven Schönberg, of the House of Bornitz, Saxony, and d. 10 Aug. 1893, leaving issue, Elinor Augusta and Frieda Hildegarde.
1. Rose, m. William Maunsell Reeves, of Vosterberg, co. Cork.
2. Charity, m. John M'Donnell, M.D., of Dublin.
3. Frances Ann, m. Richard Ellis, eldest son of the late Richard Ellis, Master in Chancery.
4. Mary, m. Richard Reeves, of Fitzwilliam Place, Dublin.
1. Frances, m. Edward Gayer.

Mr. Dobbs d. 11 April, 1811, and was s. by his son,
RICHARD DOBBS, of Castle Dobbs, who m. 1792, Nichola, dau. of Michael Obins, of Portadown, by Nichola his wife, 2nd dau. of Richard, 1st Viscount Gosford, and by her had issue,
1. CONWAY RICHARD, of Castle Dobbs.
2. Archibald Edward, M.A. Trin. Coll. Dublin, Barrister-at-Law, Master of Supreme Court, Calcutta, m. in India, Elizabeth Catherine, dau. of George Chapman, and d. April, 1838, leaving one son,
ARCHIBALD EDWARD, now of Castle Dobbs.
3. Acheson, dec.
1. Nichola, dec. Frances, dec.
3. Olivia, also dec.

Mr. Dobbs d. 24 Jan. 1840, and was s. by his eldest son,
CONWAY RICHARD DOBBS, of Castle Dobbs, J.P. and D.L., High Sheriff co. Antrim 1841, and M.P. for Carrickfergus 1832, b. 1796; m. 1st, 26 Aug. 1826, Charlotte Maria, dau. and co-heiress of William Sinclair, of Fort William, co. Antrim, and had issue,
1. Richard Archibald Conway, b. 2 Oct. 1842; d. 24 Feb. 1853.
2. MONTAGU WILLIAM EDWARD, of Castle Dobbs.
1. Olivia Nichola, m. 11 Nov. 1854, Sir James Macaulay Higginson, K.C.B., Governor of Mauritius. She d. Oct. 1906.
2. Frances Millicent, m. 11 Nov. 1856, Major-Gen. Hugh Boyd.
3. Charlotte Louisa Mary, d. 28 March, 1860.
4. Alicia Hester Caroline, m. 6 April, 1853, Sir Gerald George Aylmer, 9th bart. of Donadea Castle, co. Kildare, who d. 25 June, 1883.
5. Harriet Sydney, m. 1st, 28 Aug. 1850, George, Duke of Manchester. He d. 18 Aug. 1855, leaving issue (see BURKE's *Peerage*). She m. 2ndly, 16 Dec. 1858, Sir Arthur Stevenson Blackwood K.C.B., grandson of Admiral Hon. Sir Henry Blackwood, Bart. (see BURKE's *Peerage*). He d. 2 Oct. 1893, leaving issue. She d. 30 May, 1907.
6. Nichola Susan, d. 19 June, 1857.
7. Milicent Georgina Montagu, m. 10 Nov. 1864, G. W. Bulkeley Hughes, Capt. 62nd Regt.

He m. 2ndly, 1875, Winifred Susannah, youngest dau. of Benjamin Morris, of Lewes, Sussex, and d. 28 Feb. 1886. His eldest son,
MONTAGU WILLIAM EDWARD DOBBS, of Castle Dobbs, co. Antrim, J.P. and D.L., High Sheriff for co. Kildare 1871, and for co. Antrim 1888, M.A. Trin. Coll. Cambridge, Barrister-at-Law, b. 28 Sept. 1844, and d. 7 April, 1906, being s. by his cousin.

Arms—Quarterly; 1st and 4th, per pale sa. and arg. a chevron engrailed between three unicorns' heads erased all counterchanged, for DOBBS; 2nd and 3rd sa. three lions' passant guardant (the two in chief rencontrant) arg., for DALWAY. *Crest*—A unicorn's head erased arg. *Motto*—Amor Dei et proximi summa beatitudo.

Seat—Castle Dobbs, Carrickfergus, co. Antrim. *Club*—Sackville Street.

DOBBS OF GLENARIFFE LODGE.

CONWAY RICHARD DOBBS, of Glenariffe Lodge, co. Antrim, Major R.E., b. 2 Dec. 1867; m. April, 1895, Jane Constance, dau. of N. Carleton Atkinson, of Belgrave Square, Monkstown, co. Dublin, and has issue,
1. CONWAY EDWARD, b. 1898.
2. Nithsdale Conway, b. 1900.

Lineage.—CONWAY EDWARD DOBBS, 4th son of the Very Rev. Richard Dobbs, Dean of Connor (see DOBBS *of Castle Dobbs*), m. in 1806, and d. 1870, leaving by Maria Sophia his wife, who d. in 1869, three sons and five daus.,
1. Richard Conway, m. Lucretia Burleigh, and d. 1862.
2. Francis William, m. Maria Graham, and d. 1901.
3. CONWAY EDWARD, of whom presently.
1. Jane Eliza, m. Col. Lawe, and d. 1860.
2. Harriet, m. Rev. R. Cartwright, and d. 1870 (see BURKE's *Colonial Gentry*).
3. Maria, m. Judge Waters, and d. 1850.
4. Madeline Mary, d. unm. 1902.
5. Catherine Josephine, m. Rev. F. Hill, and d. 1902.

The youngest son,
CONWAY EDWARD DOBBS, of Glenariffe Lodge, co. Antrim, and Dalguise, co. Dublin, J.P. for co. Antrim, High Sheriff for Carrickfergus 1875, and co. Louth, 1882, b. 22 Aug. 1818; m. 14 March, 1865, Sarah, dau. of St. Clair Kelburn Mulholland, of Eglantine, Hillsboro', co. Down, and d. 18 April, 1898, leaving issue,
1. CONWAY RICHARD, now of Glenariffe Lodge.
2. St. Clair Mulholland, D.L. for co. Antrim, b. 29 Jan. 1870.
3. Henry Hugh, b. 19 Feb. 1875.
1. Margaret Emmeline, b. 29 Nov. 1873.

Arms—See DOBBS *of Castle Dobbs*.
Seat—Glenariffe Lodge, Parkmore, co. Antrim.

DOHERTY OF OAKLANDS.

RICHARD WHEELER DOHERTY, of Oaklands, co. Cork, J.P., b. 20 Oct. 1857; m. 9 Feb. 1881, Elizabeth Anna Maria, dau. of Jacob Biggs, and has issue,

RICHARD EDWARD ERNEST BIGGS, M.A. Trin. Coll. Dublin, Lieut. 3rd Batt. Royal Munster Fus., b. 16 April, 1882.
Jessica Florence, b. 14 July, 1883; m. 30 March, 1910, Frank Gascoigne Heath, son of William Henry Heath, of Woodlands, Croydon, and has issue, Jessica Aileen and Nancy Jenifer.

Lineage.—The name DOHERTY or O'DOCHARTY is derived from Dochartach, Lord of Inishowen, co. Donegal, son and heir of Maongal of Inishowen, and grandson of Fianan, Lord of Inishowen, who was 3rd son of Cean Fagla, Prince of Tireconnell (now the county of Donegal) and 12th in descent from Conal Gulban, 7th son of Niall of the Nine Hostages. The descendant and representative of the chiefs of Inishowen,

SIR JOHN MOR O'DOCHERTY, of Inishowen, submitted to the English, and was knighted 3 Dec. 1541, by Sir Anthony St. Leger, the Lord Deputy. He m. Rosa, dau. of Manus O'Donnell, Lord of Tireconnell, and d. 1566, leaving an eldest son,

SIR JOHN OGE O'DOCHERTY, Knt., Lord of Inishowen, knighted May, 1585, m. Rose, dau. of Shane O'Neill, Prince of Tyrone, and had issue,

1. Cahir (Sir) Knt., of Inishowen, m. Mary, dau. of Christopher 4th Lord Gormanston and was defeated and slain by the English 1610. He d.s.p.
2. JOHN, of whom presently.
3. Roric.
1. Rose, m. 1st, Caffar O'Donnell, of Caffarsconce, co. Donegal, nephew of the 1st Earl of Tyrconnell, and 2ndly, Eugene O'Neill, Commander-in-Chief of the Irish Army, 1641.
2. Margaret, m. Hugh O'Hanlon.
3. Eleanor, m. before 1615, Sir William Brownlow (who d. 2 Jan. 1660-1), ancestor of Lord Lurgan (see BURKE'S *Peerage*).

The second son,
JOHN O'DOCHERTY, of Londonderry, d. 1638; m. Elizabeth, eldest dau. of Patrick O'Cahane, of Londonderry, and had issue,
1. John of Londonderry.
2. Eugene (or Owen), m. 1638, Mary, dau. of Con O'Rourke, of Cloncorrick, co. Leitrim, and d. 1642, leaving issue from whom descended the family of O'Docherty, of Baillieborough, co. Cavan, and the family of Doherty of Dublin, both now extinct.
3. WILLIAM, of whom we treat.

The third son,
WILLIAM O'DOCHERTY, of Inishowen, m. Mary, 2nd dau. of Hugh Oge O'Hanlon, and left issue an only son,
JOHN O'DOHERTY, of Inishowen, who settled in co. Tipperary, m. Bridget, dau. of William Lathum, of New Place, co. Donegal (and sister of Barbara, wife of Edward Synge, Bishop of Cork, Cloyne, and Ross). He d. 1679, having had issue,
1. John (Rev.), M.A., Precentor of the Cathedral of Cashel, d. unm. Will dated 5 May, 1714, was proved 26 July, 1715.
2. Latham, of Dublin, m. Jane, dau. of Archibald Richardson, and had, with other issue, an eldest son, Richard, d. unm.
3. JAMES, of whom presently.
4. Samuel, who was married.
5. Dick Synge.
1. Bridget, m. Rev. Andrew Symes, Rector of Ballymoney, co. Cork, and had issue.
2. Barbara, m. James Hawkins, who d. before 1714, leaving issue.
3. Anne, m. Wilson, and had issue.
4. Sydney.

The third son,
JAMES DOHERTY, m. Frances, dau. of — Symes, and had issue, three sons and two daus.
1. Edward, whose widow m. Richard Fenwith.
2. JAMES, of whom presently.
3. George.
1. Bridget, m. John Doherty, and had issue.
2. Frances, m. Samuel Lane.

The second son,
REV. JAMES DOHERTY, of Palmershill, M.A., Rector of Myross, co. Cork, 1752-9, m. (bond 23 Nov. 1732) Elizabeth, dau. of Robert Travers, of Roundhill House, Bandon. His will, dated 6 Feb., was proved 23 June, 1759. He left surviving issue,
1. SAMUEL, of whom presently.
1. Catherine.
2. Elizabeth.
3. Mary.

The only son,
SAMUEL DOHERTY, of Coolnaconnaught, co. Cork, m. 30 Oct. 1757, Jane, dau. of William Hagartie, and buried by her (who m. 2ndly, Edward Gillman, and d. Dec. 1789) had issue,
1. William, d. unm.
2. JAMES, of whom presently.
1. Elizabeth, m. Andrew Burke, and had issue.

The second son,
JAMES DOHERTY, m. 1781, Mary, dau. of Edward Gillman, of Rockhouse, Innishannon, co. Cork, and d. 3 Oct. 1801, leaving issue,
1. Samuel, b. 29 Feb. 1782; d. 24 May, 1812, leaving issue, James, d. 17 May, 1818.
2. James, b. 2 Aug., d. 3 Sept. 1783.
3. William, b. 14 Nov., d. 28 Nov. 1785.
4. William, b. 4 June, 1787; m. Jane Bayler.
5. EDWARD, of whom presently.
6. James, b. 19 May, 1790; d. 2 Feb. 1802.
7. George, b. 4 Dec. 1791; d. 12 June, 1796.
8. John Gillman, b. 15 Jan. 1794; d. 16 April, 1866.
9. Henry, b. 23 March, 1796; d. 1797.
1. Elizabeth, b. 22 Nov. 1784; d. 12 Nov. 1785.
2. Mary, b. 1 April, 1799; m. 29 Feb. 1848, William Swanton, of Sunville, co. Cork, and d. March, 1875.

The fifth son,
EDWARD DOHERTY, of Kilbrogan Place, Bandon, co. Cork, Provost of Bandon, 1839, b. 31 March, 1789; m. 31 Dec. 1812, Sarah, dau. of Thomas Wheeler, of Bandon, and d. 12 Dec. 1870, leaving issue,
1. Edward James, who left issue.
2. John Wheeler, d. unm.
3. RICHARD WHEELER, of whom presently.
4. Thomas, d. unm.
5. John, d. unm.
1. Sarah Anne, d. unm.
2. Maria Wheeler, d. unm.
3. Dora, d. unm.
4. Harriet, d. unm.

The third son,
RICHARD WHEELER DOHERTY, m. 19 April, 1848, Martha, dau. of Richard Wheeler; and d. 10 May, 1883, leaving issue,
1. Edward, d. unm.
2. RICHARD WHEELER, of Oaklands.
1. Sarah Mary, d. unm.
2. Charlotte Wheeler, d. unm.

Residence—Oaklands, Bandon, co. Cork.

DOLLING OF MAGHERALIN.

CALEDON JOSIAS RADCLYFFE DOLLING, of Magheralin, co. Down, b. 17 May, 1857; m. 30 Jan. 1883, Harriette Amabel (d. 31 July, 1909), dau. of John Gregory Crace, of Springfield, Dulwich, and has issue,
1. CALEDON ROBERT JOHN, b. 10 Aug. 1886.
2. Harry Holbiche, b. 9 Jan. 1893.
1. Ulrica Margaret.
2. Mary Noel.
3. Dorothea Cecil.

Lineage.—This family is of ancient French extraction. About the year 1580, a younger son of the Count Dolling, of the village of Dolling, near Toulouse, having embraced Huguenot opinions, fled to England, and settled in the Isle of Purbeck, where he was living in 1613. His descendant,

ROBERT DOLLING, left the Isle of Purbeck, and established himself in London. By Mary his wife he had an only son,
JAMES DOLLING, of London, b. 1708; m. 1741, Mary, only child and heiress of the Hon. J. Radclyffe, of Stockport, co. Chester, and Hatton Garden, London, cousin-german of the ill-fated Earl of Derwentwater, and left, with one dau., Mary Radclyffe, an only son,
REV. ROBERT RADCLYFFE DOLLING, Rector of Tilsey, Surrey, Vicar of Aldenham, Herts, and Rector of Bolnhurst, co. Bedford, J.P. for Herts, b. 1745; m. 1780, Mary, dau. of Paul Saunders (which lady m. 2ndly, 1815, Sir R. Dundas, a Swedish nobleman), and had issue,
1. BOUGHEY WILLIAM.
2. John, d. at Westminster College.
3. James Adams, Capt. 58th Foot, killed in Egypt, leaving by his wife Frances, dau. of Rev. Dr. Bond, a son,
Robert James, in Holy Orders.
1. Mary, m. Thomas Tomkins, and had issue.

The eldest son,
REV. BOUGHEY WILLIAM DOLLING, of Magheralin, co. Down, Fellow of Exeter Coll. Oxford, Rector of Magheralin, and Precentor of Dromore, b. 3 June, 1782; m. 28 July, 1806, Mary, dau. of John Short, of Solihull, co. Warwick, and had issue,
1. ROBERT HOLBECHE, his heir.
1. Mary Radclyffe, m. James Thomas Bolton, of The Elms, Warwickshire.
2. Emily Jane Saunders, m. the Rev. Thomas Hassard Montgomery, of Springfield, co. Down, eldest son of Alexander Montgomery, of Kilmur, and had issue.

He d. 13 Jan. 1853, having been Rector of Magheralin for upwards of 46 years, and was s. by his eldest son,
ROBERT HOLBECHE DOLLING, of Magheralin, J.P. Down and Monaghan, and J.P. and D.L. Londonderry, High Sheriff 1865, Barrister-at-Law, b. 13 Feb. 1809; m. 21 Jan. 1842, Eliza, 3rd dau. of Josias Du Pré Alexander, M.P., nephew of James, 1st Earl of Caledon, and d. 22 Sept. 1878, having by her (who d. 1870) had issue,

Dolmage. THE LANDED GENTRY. 186

1. ROBERT WILLIAM RADCLYFFE (Rev.), late of Magheralin.
2. CALEDON JOSIAS RADCLYFFE, now of Magheralin.
   1. Mary Emma Radclyffe, d. 15 Sept. 1910; m. 4 Aug. 1883, James Head Staples, 2nd son of Sir N. A. Staples, Bart.
   2. Elise Ann Radclyffe.
   3. Adelaide Harriette Radclyffe.
   4. Geraldine Bouverie Radclyffe.
   5. Nina Caroline Radclyffe. 6. Josephine Maud Radclyffe.
   7. Ulrica Douglass Radclyffe, d. 17 April, 1872.

The eldest son,
REV. ROBERT WILLIAM RADCLYFFE DOLLING, of Magheralin, co. Down, b. 13 Feb. 1851; educated at Harrow and Cambridge, Curate of St. Agatha's Mission, Landport, Portsea, Hants, 1888-96, d. unm. 15 May, 1902.

Arms—Per fess arg. and az. in fess dancettée per fess dancettée sa. and of the first. Crest—A buck's head, ppr. attired or, gorget with two bars dancettée arg. Motto—Spero.

Seat—Edenmore, Magheralin, co. Down.

DOLMAGE. See DELMEGE.

DOLPHIN OF TUROE.

SHEELAH DOLPHIN, of Turoe, co. Galway, b. 20 July, 1904; s. her father 21 Aug. 1907.

Lineage.—HUBERT DOLPHIN, living at Goulbully 1691, preferred remaining in his native country in the hope of preserving some of the property. He m. 1st, Sarah M. Burke, of Derryhale; and 2ndly, Miss Deane, by both of whom he had issue. The eldest son of the 1st marriage,

JOHN DOLPHIN, of Goulbully and Turoe, m. Mary Geohegan, of Westmeath, and had issue. The eldest son,

HUBERT DOLPHIN, m. Helen, dau. of Martin, of Raheen, of the Tullyra family, and had issue,
1. JOHN, his heir.
2. Oliver, of Loughrea, m. 1770, Margaret Helen, dau. of Lewis Collin, of Dublin, and d. 1805, leaving four sons,
   1. HUBERT THOMAS, heir to his uncle.
   2. Anthony, d. unm.
   3. Paul, of Loughrea, m. Miss Burke, of Spring Gardens.
   4. Henry, of Loughrea, m. 1st, a dau. of Pierce Blake, of Holly Park, co. Galway; and 2ndly, Miss Skerrett, of the Ballinduff family. By the former he had issue,
      (1) Pierce, his heir. (2) Anthony.
      (1) Anne.
3. Henry, d. unm.
4. Thomas, in the Spanish service, m. a Mexican lady.
1. Margaret, m. Dominick Burke, of Killymor.

The eldest son,
JOHN DOLPHIN, of Turoe, m. Eleanor, dau. of John Burke, of St. Cleraus, and had daus. only,
1. Jane, a nun in the convent of Loughrea.
2. Margaret, m. 1790, John Browne, of Moyne, and had issue.
3. Anne, a nun in the convent of Loughrea.
4. Celia, m. John McDonnell, of Carnacon, and had issue.
5. Eleanor, m. Thomas Reddington, of Ryehill, and had issue.
6. Sally, m. Michael Balfe, of South Park, and had an only child.
7. Elizabeth, m. Edmund Balfe, of Marlborough Street.

Mr. Dolphin dying s.p.m. was s. by his nephew,
HUBERT THOMAS DOLPHIN, of Turoe, m. 1804, Mary, dau. of Peter Grehan, of Dublin, by his wife Mary, dau. of Stephen Roche, of Limerick, and of Granagh Castle, co. Kilkenny, and had issue,
1. OLIVER, his heir.
2. Peter Hubert, of Danesfort, Loughrea, co. Galway, J.P., b. 1816, m. 1852, Antoinette, dau. of Peter McEvoy, of Great Cumberland Place, and Wimbledon, Surrey, and d. 1898, having had issue,
   1. Marie Antoinette, m. 29 April, 1875, Thomas Tighe, of The Heath, Claremorris, J.P., D.L., High Sheriff co. Mayo 1879, M.P. co. Mayo, 1874, and by him has issue (see that family).
   2. Georgina. 3. Anna.
   4. Teresa.
1. Margaret, m. Jan. 1830, James Peter Daly, of Castle Daly, co. Galway (see that family).
2. Anastatia, } both nuns in the Carmelite Convent of Loughrea.
3. Lucy,   }
4. Ann, m. Peter Daly, of Daly's Grove, co. Galway, J.P., brother to James Daly, of Castle Daly.
5. Helen, a nun in Westport. 6. Lucy, a nun.
7. Monica, d. unm. 1896.

Mr. Dolphin d. 1829, and was s. by his eldest son,
OLIVER DOLPHIN, of Turoe, Barrister-at-Law, b. 1805; m. 13 April, 1842, Mary, dau. of Andrew Browne, of Movilla, co. Galway, by Mary his wife, sister of Maurice Blake, of Ballinafad, co. Mayo, and had issue,
1. ANDREW, of Turoe, b. 1846; d. Oct. 1891.
2. Oliver, b. 1850; d. 1890.
3. HUBERT PETER, of Turoe.
1. Mary, m. 1863, Andrew Martyn, of Spiddell, co. Galway, 2nd son of Edward Martyn, of Tillyra, co. Galway.
2. Monica, m. 1st, 1867, Thomas Kirwan, D.L., of Blindwell, co. Galway, who d.s.p. 1881. She m. 2ndly, 1890, Ormsby Bowen Miller, D.L. (see MILLER of Milford).

3. Henrietta, d. 1865. 4. Katherine, d. 1867.
5. Anne,
Mr. Dolphin d. 1882. The 3rd son,
HUBERT PETER DOLPHIN, of Turoe, co. Galway, b. 1853; s. his brother; m. 28 June, 1899, Mabel Agnes, dau. of Henry de Blaquiere, of Fiddane House, co. Galway, and d. 21 Aug. 1907, having had issue,
SHEELAH, now of Turoe.

Seat—Turoe, Loughrea, co. Galway.

DOMVILE OF LOUGHLINSTOWN.

CHARLES BARRY DOMVILE, of Loughlinstown House, co. Dublin, b. 22 July, 1894; s. his grandfather 6 Feb. 1910.

Lineage.—THE REV. HENRY BARRY DOMVILE, M.A. Oxford, Rector of Pencombe, Hereford, 2nd son of CHARLES POCKLINGTON (afterward DOMVILE) by Margaret his wife, dau. of Thomas Sheppard, and younger brother of Sir Compton Domvile, 1st bart. (see BURKE'S Peerage), m. Mary, dau. and heir of William Russell, of Powick Court, co. Worcester (see BURKE'S Peerage, HAMPTON, B.), by Mary his wife, dau. and co-heir of Joseph Cocks, brother of Charles, Lord Somers. He d. 2 Jan. 1856, having had issue,
1. Henry Barry, Barrister-at-Law, Clerk of the Peace, co. Worcester, b. 1813; m. 27 Sept. 1838, Frances, eldest dau. of Rev. Edward Winnington-Ingram, Prebendary of Worcester (see BURKE'S Peerage, WINNINGTON, Bart.). She d. 8 July 1884. He d.v.p. 24 Aug. 1843, leaving issue,
   1. HERBERT WINNINGTON, of Loughlinstown.
   2. Compton Edward (Sir), G.C.B. (1904), G.C.V.O. (1903), Adm. R.N. (ret. 1907), Commander-in-Chief Mediterranean Squadron 1902-5, A.D.C. to Queen Victoria, 1888-91, is Knight Grand Cross of the Order of the Saviour of Greece and has 1st Class in Brilliants of the Medjidie (The Chantry House, Hurstpierpoint, Sussex; United Service Club), b. 10 Oct. 1842, m. 3 Aug. 1876, Isabella, dau. of Edmund Yates Peel, Res. Magistrate at Letterkenny, and has issue,
      (1) Barry Edward, Lieut. R.N., b. 1878.
      (2) Archibald Compton Winnington, b. 1884.
      (1) Adelaide Mary, b. 1877.
      (2) Georgina Isabella Frances, b. 1888.
      (3) May Louise, b. 3 April, 1893.
   3. Barry Francis, Lieut.-Col. late R.A., b. 11 Dec. 1844; m. Annie, dau. of Gen. C. F. Smith, B.S.C.; 25 Jan. 1894, having by her (who m. 2ndly, 1 June, 1895, Frederick William Capron) had issue,
      Aileen Frances, b. 2 Jan. 1877; m. 24 July, 1907, Herbert Gall, eldest son of Capt. Herbert Reay Gall, late Northumberland Fus.
   1. Frances Mary, b. 12 Aug. 1841; m. 1st, 5 April, 1866, Henry Stewart Oldnall Russell, of Sion House, Kidderminster. He d. 22 July, 1872, leaving issue (see RUSSELL-OLDNALL). She m. 2ndly, 8 Sept. 1877, Gen. Sir John Frederick Crease, K.C.B., and has issue,
2. William, Maj. in the Army, d. unm.
3. Charles (Rev.), Rector of Nettleton Wilts, b. 1816, m. 1851, Augusta Pratt, dau. of Sir William Oldnall Russell (see RUSSELL-OLDNALL), and widow of Lieut.-Col. Archibald Erskine, 45th Regt. She d. 25 April, 1890. He d. 16 May, 1898, leaving issue,
   1. John Russell Compton, Capt. I.S.C., b. 17 July, 1856; m. 10 Oct. 1889, Constance Julia, dau. of Sir Howard W. Elphinston, 3rd bart.; and d. 1 July, 1893, leaving issue,
      Evelyn Constance, b. 19 Jan. 1891.
   2. Charles William Barry, R.N., b. 1861; d. unm. 5 June, 1880.
   3. Henry Lloyd Erskine, d. young, 25 Oct. 1869.
   4. Beauchamp Victor Santry, Capt. 3rd Batt. Roy. Munster Fus., served in S. Africa 1900-2 (despatches, Queen's medal with three clasps, King's medal with two clasps) (Jun. Naval and Military and Constitutional Clubs), b. 8 Jan. 1864; m. Harriet Matilda, only dau. of Rev. R. Croly, M.A., Vicar of Dunkeswell, Devon.
   5. Edwin Arthur, b. 1 Dec. 1865.
   1. Louisa Alberta.
   2. Emma Florence, m. 10 Sept. 1878, Walter Jarvis.
   3. Rosa Mary, m. 22 Feb. 1886, Maj. George E. Rogers, late King's Dragoon Guards.
   4. Henrietta Emily, m. Rev. Arthur Vaughan Davies, and has issue.
   5. Eva Kathleen, b. 1 Feb. 1868; d. unm. 13 Sept. 1897.

4. John Russell, Capt. R.A., *m.* Aug. 1842, his cousin Augusta, dau. of Rev. William Domvile, Rector of Winforton, co. Hereford. She *d.* 26 Nov. 1866. He *d.* 1 May, 1852, leaving issue,
 Henry William Russell, *b.* 7 Oct. 1848; *m.* 28 Sept. 1876, Florence, dau. of Rev. William Montgomery Beresford, Vicar of Gortin (*see* BURKE'S *Peerage*, WATERFORD, M.), and has issue,
  (1) Claude Henry, *b.* 3 Aug. 1878.
  (2) Eileen Augusta, *b.* 22 Jan. 1877.
 Mary Augusta, *d. unm.* 5 Jan. 1878.
1. Mary Ann.

The grandson,
MAJ. HERBERT WINNINGTON DOMVILE, of Loughlinstown House, co. Dublin, J.P. and D.L., High Sheriff 1901, J.P. Worcestershire, late Maj. 4th Batt. Worcestershire Regt., Knight of Grace of the Order of St. John of Jerusalem, formerly Assistant Secretary to the First Lord of the Admiralty, and afterwards Secretary to the First Commissioner of Works, *b.* 11 July, 1840; *m.* 1st, 5 Dec. 1868, Marie Elizabeth, eldest dau. of John Koozen, of Weesenstein and Dresden, Saxony. She *d.* 2 Nov. 1876, leaving issue,
 1. COMPTON CHARLES, *b.* 21 Nov. 1868; *m.* 25 June, 1892, Eleanor Maria Isabel, eldest dau. of Thomas Richardson, of Kirklevington, Yorks, and *d.v.p.* 1906, having had issue, a son,
  CHARLES BARRY, now of Loughlinstown.
 2. Henry Koozen, *b.* 29 May, 1872.
He *m.* 2ndly, 23 Sept. 1880, Rose, 2nd dau. of Adm. of the Fleet Sir George Sartorius, G.C.B., and widow of Capt. John Winnington, and by her had issue,
 1. Rose Margaret, *b.* 21 Nov. 1882.
 2. Grace Frances, *b.* 19 July, 1885; *m.* 25 Jan. 1911, Philip Robert Bald, son of the late Col. Reinhold Bald.
He *m.* 3rdly, 3 Nov. 1906, Harriet Sarah, eldest dau. of Rev. William Montgomery Beresford, Rector of Lower Baldoney, co. Tyrone (*see* BURKE'S *Peerage*, WATERFORD, M.), and *d.* 6 Feb. 1910.

Arms—Quarterly indented of four, 1st az. a lion rampant arg. collared gu. on a canton sa. a lion of England between three esquire's helmets, arg.; 2nd barry of six arg. and gu. a bend counterchanged; 3rd barry of six arg. and gu. and 4th az. a lion rampant arg. collared gu. *Crest*—A lion's head erased arg. ducally crowned or. *Motto*—Qui stat caveat ne cadat.

Seat—Loughlinstown House, co. Dublin. *Residence*—The Lakes, Kidderminster, Worcestershire.

DONELAN OF SYLANMORE.

DERMOT O'CONOR DONELAN, of Sylanmore, Tuam, co. Galway, J.P., *b.* 6 March, 1853.

Lineage. — The family of DONELAN, one of the most ancient in Ireland, claims descent from Domhnalleu, great-grandson of Domhnall, son of Bresal, founder of Clan Bresal, who was son of Dluthach, Prince of Hymany, who *d.* 738. A descendant, Tully O'Donelan, re-built the castle of Ballydonelan in 1412, which had been destroyed by fire in 1407. The original Black Castle, as it was known, is alleged to have been built in 936, and traces of it still remain. Tully O'Donelan's great-grandson, Loughlin Donelan, of Ballydonelan, *m.* Cicely, dau. of William O'Kelly of Calla, and *d.* 1548, leaving a son,
THE MOST REV. NEHEMIAH DONELAN, Archbishop of Tuam, was educated at Cambridge, consecrated in 1595, and resigned in 1609. He *m.* Elizabeth, dau. of Nicholas O'Donel, of Tyrconnell, and *d.* in 1609, shortly after his resignation, leaving issue,
1. JOHN, of whom presently.
2. Edmond (Ven.), Archdeacon of Cashel, M.A. and Fellow of Trin. Coll. Dublin, *m.* Margaret, dau. of Rev. Luke Ussher, Archdeacon of Armagh, and *d.* 1640, leaving issue.
3. James (Sir), Fellow of Trin. Coll. Dublin, represented Dublin University in Parliament 1634, was Lord Chief Justice of the Common Pleas, and knighted 1661. He *m.* 1st, Ann, dau. of Alderman Richard Barry, of Dublin, and sister of James, 1st Lord Santry, and by her had four sons and two daus. He *m.* 2ndly, Sarah, 4th dau. of Dr. Jonas Wheeler, Bishop of Ossory, and widow of Matthew Tyrrell, of Dublin, and *d.* 1665, having by her had a son,
 Nehemiah, Lord Chief Baron 1703, who *d.* 1705, leaving issue, from whom were descended the Nixon Donelans, formerly of Artane Castle, co. Dublin, and Ravensdale, co. Kildare.

4. William (Rev.), M.A. Dublin, *m.* Jane, dau. of Ralph Golborne, and *d.* 30 Oct. 1634.
5. Teige (Thadeus) (Rev.), M.A. Dublin, *m.* Elizabeth, dau. of Right Rev. William Golborne, Bishop of Kildare.
6. Mortogh or Nicholas (Rev.), Lector in the Augustinian Convent at Vienna in 1647.

The eldest son,
JOHN DONELAN, of Ballydonelan, High Sheriff co. Galway 1612, *m.* Dorothy, dau. of William Mostyn, Governor of Athlone. She *d.* 1666. He *d.* April, 1655, having had issue,
1. MELAUGHLIN or LOUGHLIN.
2. William, of Leitrim, co. Galway, High Sheriff 1641, *m.* Cecilia, dau. of William Reogh Kelly, of Knockcroghery, co. Roscommon, and left issue.
3. Edmund, of Killaghmore, ancestor of the family of Killagh (*whom see*).
4. James. 5. Loughlin.
6. Nicholas (Rev.). 7. Murtogh (Rev.).
8. Eugene (Rev.).

The eldest son,
LOUGHLIN, or MELAGHLIN DONELAN, of Ballydonelan, *m.* Christian, dau. of Robert Blake, of Ardfry. He *d.* Aug. 1673 (will dated 3 May, 1673), having had three sons,
1. John, of Ballydonelan, ancestor of the families of Ballydonelan, Nutgrove and Hillswood. From the Nutgrove branch descends Capt. A. J. C. Donelan, M.P., of Ballymona, co. Cork.
2. NICHOLAS, of whom presently.
3. Richard, of Ballyeighter, ancestor of the family of that place.

The 2nd son,
NICHOLAS DONELAN, of Rabally, co. Galway, *m.* 1st, Elizabeth, dau. of John French, of Aggard, and by her had issue,
 1. John, of Rabally.
 1. Mary, *m.* Thomas Kirwan, of Galway.
He *m.* 2ndly, Rebecca, dau. of Walter Taylor, of Castle Taylor, and *d.* 1718, having by her had,
 2. NEHEMIAH, of whom presently.

The younger son,
NEHEMIAH DONELAN, of Caheroyan and Peterswell, *m.* 1739, Marcia, eldest dau. of Robert Shaw, of Newford, and Alice, his wife, dau. and co-heiress of Thomas Croasdaile, of Clostoken, co. Galway, and *d.* Jan. 1771, leaving issue,
1. Nicholas, *m.* 23 Aug. 1772, Catherine, dau. of William Doolan, of Caddisburne, and had issue,
 1. Nehemiah, *d.s.p.* 1840.
 2. John, Lieut. 66th Regt., *d.s.p.* 1832.
 3. William *d.s.p.* 1839.
 2. Robert, *d.s.p.* 1805.
 3. THOMAS, of whom presently.
 4. John, *d.s.p.* 1810.
 1. Alice, *m.* 4 Aug. 1770, Patrick Burke.
 2. Rebecca, *m.* Nov. 1770, Thomas Kirwan, of Blindwell.

The 3rd son,
THOMAS DONELAN, of Peterswell, co. Galway, *m.* 2 July, 1771, Mabel,* dau. of Dermot O'Conor, of Sylan, and sister and heir of the Most Rev. Thomas O'Conor, D.D., Bishop of Achonry, and *d.* 1816, leaving issue,
1. DERMOT, of whom presently.
1. Marcia, *m.* John Joyce, of Oxford, co. Mayo.
2. Belinda, a nun. 3. Alice.
4. Margaret.

The only son,
DERMOT DONELAN, of Sylan, and Peterswell, co. Galway, *s.* to the former in right of his mother, and to the latter estate in 1840 on the death *s.p.* of his cousin, Nehemiah. He was *b.* 1781; *m.* 11 Nov. 1811, Maria, 2nd dau. of William Keary, of Clough, and sister of Rev. William Keary, Vicar of Mornington (sometime Capt. 5th Dragoon Guards), and *d.* 11 April, 1852, leaving issue,
1. THOMAS O'CONOR, of whom presently.
2. William, *d.s.p.* 1877.
1. Belinda, *m.* Charles Lynch, Capt. East York Militia, and *d.* 1862.
2. Elizabeth.

The elder son,
THOMAS O'CONOR DONELAN, of Sylanmore and Peterswell, *b.* 1812; *m.* 27 Oct. 1851, Elizabeth, eldest dau. of Joseph Burke, of Ower, co. Galway (*see that family*). She *d.* 6 Sept. 1906. He *d.* 18 Aug. 1874, leaving issue,
1. DERMOT O'CONOR, now of Sylanmore and Peterswell.
2. Joseph O'Conor, of San Miguel, Manila (*Thatched House Club, S.W.*), *b.* 24 Aug. 1856.
3. John O'Conor, M.D. (*St. Dymphna's, North Circular Road, Dublin, and Stephen's Green Club, Dublin*), *b.* 14 Aug. 1866; *m.* 12 Jan. 1910, Margaret, dau. of late Andrew Moore, of Ashton, co. Dublin.
4. Thomas O'Conor, M.R.C.S., late Lieut. 4th Batt. Connaught Rangers, *b.* 1 July, 1872.
1. Mary, a nun.
2. Margaret, *d.* an infant.

O'Conor of Sylan.

This branch of the O'Connors Sligo, was represented in 1641 by MALACHY, or LOUGHLIN O'CONNOR, of Tuam, subsequently Kilcluney and Sylan, who *m.* Mabel Atrea, the dau. of O'Rourke, of Brefni, and *d.* July, 1680, will made 14 July, 1680, proved 20 April, 1681, leaving a son,
DERMOT O'CONNOR, of Sylan, Capt. in Col. Dominick Browne's Regt. in the Irish Army of JAMES II. *m.* (setts. dated 4 Jan. 1677) Alice, dau. of Isidore Lynch, of Drimcong, and was killed at the second siege of Limerick, 1691, leaving issue,

Donelan. THE LANDED GENTRY. 188

1. Laughlin O'Conor, of Sylan, Lieut. in Col. Dominick Browne's Regt. in the Irish Army of JAMES II, d. Nov. 1703.
2. Matthias, killed in war between 1689-1701.
3. Turlough, Lieut. in Col. Dominick Browne's Regt., killed in war between 1689-1701.
4. Hugh, m. 1st, 1709, Jane, dau. of Valentine Browne, of Galway, and had issue,
Dermot, of Sylan, J.P. co. Galway, b. 1710; m. before 1746, Mabel, 2nd dau. of Edmund O'Flynn, of Turlough. She d. 3 Oct. 1757; he d. 12 Dec. 1793, leaving issue,
(1) Edmund, Capt. in the Green Horse (now 5th Dragoon Guards), d.s.p. 1787.
(2) Thomas (Most Rev.), D.D., consecrated Bishop of Achonry 9 Dec. 1787, titular Archbishop of Tuam 1803, d. 18 Feb. 1803.
(1) Mary, m. John Melville.
(2) MABEL, m. at Tuam, 2 July, 1771, THOMAS DONELAN, of Peterswell, co. Galway, and d. 19 May, 1820 (see above).
Hugh O'Conor m. 2ndly, 1718 (setts. dated 12 April), Agnes (will dated 21 March, proved 26 April, 1763), widow of James Tully, of Girrah, and dau. of — Browne, by whom he had issue, Andrew.
He d. 1736; his widow (will dated 21 March, proved 26 April, 1763).
5. Michael, d. before 1700.
6. Mark, living 1700.
7. Bryan, m. the dau. of Michael Browne, of Tuam, and had issue,
1. Hugh, first of Galway and then of Douglas, Isle of Man, m. Feb. 1742, Honoria, dau. of Valentine Browne, of Galway, She d. Dec. 1771. He d. 1783 (bur. at St. James' Church, Dublin, 10 May, 1783), leaving issue,
(1) Valentine, of Oakley Park, Blackrock, co. Dublin, b. 1744, m. 10 June, 1775, Mary (d. 3 May, 1783), dau. of Edmund Moore, of Mount Browne, and d. 19 Jan. 1814, leaving issue,
1. Hugh, bapt. 30 July, 1781, d.s.p. at Oxford, March, 1815.
1. Mary, m. 4 Aug. 1803, Maurice Blake, of Towerhill.
2. Honora, bapt. 4 Nov. 1779.
(2) Malachy, b. 1753; m. 27 Oct. 1803, Lydia (b. 14 March, 1775; d. 20 Feb. 1863), widow of Bryan Blake and dau. of Alexander Brodie, of Windyhills, Antigua, and d. at Bath, 2 Jan. 1831, leaving issue,
Honoria, b. 26 Aug. 1804; d. 9 Nov. 1859; m. 27 July, 1831, John Sweetman, of Drumbaragh, co. Meath.
(1) Monica, m. 22 Dec. 1765, Hugh O'Connor, of London and Dublin, and d. 1814, leaving issue (see O'CONNOR-HENCHY of Stonebrook).
(2) Mary, m. 5 Dec. 1772, Christopher Sherlock. He d. 29 Oct. 1785. Her will proved 24 Dec. 1807.
(3) Julia.
1. Arabella. (2) Margaret.
3. Celia, m. Henry Blake.
8. Gyles, m. 1650, Andrew Merrick, of Kilbenane, 2nd son of William Merrick, of Tully, co. Mayo.

Arms (of DONELAN)—Arg. an oak tree eradicated vert. Crest— On a mount vert a lion rampant or. Motto—Omni violentia major.
Seat—Sylanmore, Tuam, co. Galway. Club—County Galway.

DONELAN OF KILLAGH.

RICHARD DONELAN, of Killagh, co. Galway, b. 23 June, 1867; s. his uncle 1910; m. 9 Sept. 1896, Mary, a dau. of Edwin Rickard, and has issue,
1. NORMAN, b. 6 Dec. 1904.
1. Ida Florence, b. 20 April, 1899.
2. Doris Constance, b. 19 Oct. 1900.
3. Verna, b. 31 Jan. 1908.

Lineage.—EDMUND DONELAN, of Killaghmore, co. Galway, 3rd son of John Donelan, of Ballydonelan (see DONELAN of Sylanmore), and Dorothy his wife, dau. of William Mostyn. He d. 1679, leaving an only son and heir,
WILLIAM DONELAN, who claimed Killaghmore before the Trustees of forfeited estates at Chichester House in 1700. He left issue,
1. JOSEPH, his heir.
2. Peter, Bishop of Clonfert, b. 1678; d. at Killagh, May, 1778.
The elder son,
JOSEPH DONELAN, of Killagh, m. 1st, Margaret, dau. and co-heir of Ulick Burke, of Kilcarrunan, and by her had an only dau.,
1. Honora.
He m. 2ndly, Margaret, dau. of Laghlin Daly, of Benmore, and had two sons,
1. STEPHEN, his heir. 2. Hyacinth.
His will is dated 16 July, 1736. The elder son,
STEPHEN DONELAN, of Killagh, m. Feb. 1752, Elizabeth, dau. of Edmund Kelly, of Ballyforan, and d. 1794, leaving a son,
JOSEPH DONELAN, of Killagh, m. April, 1780, Ellis, dau. of Charles Lambert, of Creg Clare. She d. Aug. 1823. He d. 1798, leaving issue,
1. STEPHEN JOSEPH, his heir.
1. Eliza, m. 8 Aug. 1803, Sir Valentine John Blake, 12th Bart., of Menlo, M.P. He d. Jan. 1847. She d. 8 May, 1836, leaving issue (see BURKE's Peerage).
2. Ellis, d. unm.
The only son,

STEPHEN JOSEPH DONELAN, of Killagh, J.P., b. 6 March, 1789; m. 1 Dec. 1826, Evelyne Wilhelmina Catherine, youngest dau. of Robert French, of Monivea Castle (see FFRENCH of Monivea). She d. Oct. 1880. He d. Oct. 1866, leaving issue,
1. STEPHEN JOSEPH ROBERT, of Killagh.
2. Joseph Arthur, b. 1833.
3. Robert, of Donsford, Karabeal, Victoria, Australia, b. 8 Dec. 1834; d. 26 July, 1900, having m. B. Lally, by whom (who d. 9 Sept. 1909) he had issue,
4. Richard, b. 1837. 5. Charles, b. 1839.
1. Eliza Ellis, m. Alexander Kirkpatrick Wilson.
2. Evelyne. 3. Mary Ellis.
4. Nicola Maria. 5. Arabella Catherine.
The eldest son,
STEPHEN JOSEPH ROBERT DONELAN, of Killagh, co. Galway, b. 26 April, 1830, and d. 15 Dec. 1910, being s. by his nephew.

Arms—See DONELAN of Sylanmore.
Seat—Killagh, co. Galway.

DONOVAN OF BALLYMORE.

RICHARD DONOVAN, of Ballymore, co. Wexford, and Corrolanty, King's Co., J.P. and D.L. Wexford, High Sheriff 1888, L.L.B. Trin. Coll. Camb., b. 25 Nov. 1858; s. his father 24 June, 1884; m. 1 Nov. 1888, Constance Eleanor, 2nd dau. of Alfred Lillingstone, of Southwold, Suffolk, and has issue,
1. RICKARD CHARLIE, b. 28 April, 1898.
1. Constance Agnes Bright, b. 13 Feb. 1893.
2. Barbara, b. 15 Nov. 1900.
3. Phoebe, b. 23 Feb. 1902.

Lineage.—DONEL OGE NA CARTAN O'DONOVAN, of Clogbatradbally Castle, co. Cork, Chief of Clan Lochlin temp. JAMES I, made a surrender of his estates to the King 28 June, 1615, and received a regrant of the same by patent 29 Jan. 1616.
He had three sons,
1. Moriertagh McDonel oge, s. as Chief of Clan Lochlin, and was s. by his son, Donel McMoriertagh, who was attainted 1641, and d.s.p.
2. Dermot, who had, with a younger son, Daniel, two sons,
1. Jeremiah, who s. his cousin as Chief of Clan Lochlin, and whose line failed with his sons.
2. Cornelius, of Kilmacabea, whose descendant became Chief of Clan Lochlin, now represented by
REV. JEREMIAH ALEXANDER O'DONOVAN, Chief of Clan Lochlin, b. 1849; m. 1877, Esther Bell, dau. of Rev. John O'Callaghan, and has a son and heir,
RICHARD BARTHOLOMEW, b. 15 June, 1878.
3. RICKARD, ancestor of DONOVAN of Ballymore.
Donel oge na Cartan O'Donovan d. 24 Jan. 1629. His 3rd son,
RICKARD NA CARTAN O'DONOVAN, was father of
MORTOGH O'DONOVAN, who removed from the co. Cork, and resided in Dublin with his cousin Jeremiah O'Donovan, afterwards Chief of Clan Lochlin. He was father of
RICKARD DONOVAN, of Clonmore, co. Wexford, the first of this family who settled in co. Wexford. He m. Mary, sister and co-heir of Alderman Thomas Kieran, Sheriff of Dublin, 1687, and had five sons and three daus.,
1. RICKARD, d.v.p. 2. MORTOGH, his heir.
3. Cornelius, of Clonmore, m. 1st, Bridget, dau. of Abraham Hughes, of Ballytrent, co. Wexford, and had issue,
1. Abraham, a Physician in Enniscorthy, d.s.p.
2. Rickard, of Clonmore, m. Winifred, dau. of Henry Milward, of Ballyharron, co. Wexford, and d. 1781, leaving five daus.,
(1) Eliza, m. Aug. 1763, Cadwallader Edwards, of Ballyhire, co. Wexford.
(2) Sarah, m. June, 1773, John Cox, of Coolcliffe, co. Wexford.
(3) Winifred, m. Rev. Joseph Miller, of New Ross, as his second wife.
(4) Lucy, m. 18 July, 1769, John Glascott, of Aldertown, co. Wexford.

(5) Julia, *m.* June, 1776, Richard Newton King, of Macmine, co. Wexford.
Cornelius Donovan *m.* 2ndly, Mary, dau. of John Harvey, of Killiane Casle, same co., and had issue,
3. John, *d. unm.*   4. Cornelius.
1. Elizabeth.
2. Juliana, *m.* Cornelius Fitzpatrick, Ensign in the Wexford Militia.
Cornelius Donovan's will, dated 20 Oct. 1735, was proved in the Diocese of Ferns, 18 July, 1739.
4. Rickard, of Camolin, co. Wexford, *m.* the dau. of Richard Nixon, of Newtown, co. Wexford, and had issue,
1. George.
2. Cornelius, a Capt. of Dragoons. He resided at Newtown Barry, and left a son, William, and two daus., Juliana, *m.* 1st, Oct. 1756, Joshua Thomas, of Bolacreen, and 2ndly, Oct. 1763, John Henry Edkins ; Mary, *m.* Robert Blaney, of Camolin.
3. Rickard, *d.s.p.*
4. Rickard, who had by Constance, his wife, two sons and one dau.,
(1) George, of Kilmuckridge.
(2) Rickard, of Crowneyhorn.
(1) Mary, *m.* Jan. 1765, Thomas Philips, of Kilscoran.
5. Nixon, *d. unm.* 25 Nov. 1741.
1. Juliana, *m.* 1st, 15 Sept. 1741, Richard, 6th Earl of Anglesey ; 2ndly, Matthew Talbot, of Castle Talbot, co. Wexford, and *d.* 20 Nov. 1776.
5. Thomas, left a son Mortogh.
1. Mary, *m.* Clement Clough, of Ballyorley, co. Wexford.
2. Ann, *m.* Jeremiah King, of Machmine, co. Wexford.
3. Elizabeth, *m.* July, 1701, Rev. Michael Mosse, Rector of White Church, co. Wexford.
Mr. Donovan *d.* 1707, and was *s.* by his 2nd son,
MORTOGH DONOVAN, of Ballymore, J.P., High Sheriff co. Wexford 1704, *b.* 20 May, 1667 ; *m.* 1st, 13 Aug. 1696, Lucy, dau. of Henry Archer, of Ballyhoge, co. Wexford, and had two sons,
1. RICKARD, his heir.
2. Henry, *d.* Dec. 1737, having had, by Elizabeth his wife, Elizabeth, *d.* Feb. 1726, and Lucy, *d.* Jan. 1731.
He *m.* 2ndly (settlements dated 23 May, 1704), Anna, dau. of Robert Carew, of Castleboro, co. Wexford, by whom (who *d.* 1713) he had further issue,
3. Robert, of Bride Street, Dublin, Alderman of the City, and High Sheriff 1750 ; *m.* Katherine, dau. of Francis Toplady (High Sheriff co. Wexford 1715), and *d.* May, 1755, leaving
1. Francis, *d.* Oct. 1773, leaving two sons,
(1) Richard, of Tibberton, co. Gloucester, *b.* 1766 ; *d.* 1815, having had an only dau., who predeceased him in Jan. 1814.
(2) Francis of Tipperton, *d.* June, 1819.
1. Elizabeth, bapt. 11 Oct. 1737 ; *d. unm.,* bur. 21 July, 1761.
2. Katherine, bapt. 16 March, 1744 ; *m.* by licence, dated 9 Dec. 1769, Rev. Samuel Hayden, Rector of Ferns, and Prebendary of Clone, who was murdered at Enniscorthy by the Rebels, 23 May, 1798.
4. Richard.
1. Elizabeth.
2. Juliana, *m.* by licence, dated 20 May, 1729, Andrew Lynn, of Waterford, Gent.
Mr. Donovan *d.* 1712, and was *s.* by his eldest son,
RICKARD DONOVAN, of Ballymore, High Sheriff co. Wexford 1724, a Captain of Horse, *b.* 20 May, 1697, who *m.* Elizabeth, dau. of Edward Rogers, of Bessmount, co. Wexford, by whom (who *d.* 2 July, 1778) he had issue,
1. EDWARD, his heir.
1. Lucy, *m.* by licence, dated 17 Oct. 1752, Gilfred Lawson, eldest son of Rev. Wilfred Lawson.
2. Mary, *d. unm.* 1805.
3. Frances, *m.* by licence, dated 26 June, 1751, Charles Hill, of St. John's, co. Wexford, and *d.* 1758.
Mr. Donovan *d.* 15 July, 1768, and was *s.* by his son,
EDWARD DONOVAN, of Ballymore, Barrister-at-Law, who *m.* 7 Oct. 1747, Mary, dau. and heir of Capt. John Broughton, of Maidstone, Kent, by Mary his wife, only dau. of Samuel Ogle, M.P. for Berwick, by his 1st wife, Elizabeth Dawson, and had by her (who *d.* May, 1794) issue,
1. RICHARD, his heir.
2. Edward (Rev.), Rector of Ballymore, co. Westmeath, *b.* 16 June, 1754 ; *d. unm.* 27 May, 1827.
3. George, *b.* 12 Feb. 1758, went to America ; *m.* Mary, dau. of James Devereux, co. Wexford, and had issue, two daus.,
1. Phœbe, *m.*
2. Mary, *m.* James McCabe.
4. Robert, of Peter Street, Dublin, Solicitor, *b.* 3 Jan. 1760 ; *d.s.p.* Aug. 1828.
5. William, Lieut. R.N., *b.* 12 June, 1763 ; *d. unm.* 1814.
6. John, bapt. 27 Feb. 1769, Attorney-General at Sierra Leone, *d. unm.* 1817.
1. Mary, *b.* 7 July, 1748 ; *d. unm.* 22 Sept. 1824.
2. Eliza, *b.* 29 Nov. 1750 ; *d. unm.* 22 July, 1831.
3. Lucy, *b.* 3 May, 1753 ; *m.* James Barker, of Great Britain Street, Dublin, and *d.* 2 Sept. 1839.
4. Harriet, *b.* 17 July, 1755 ; *d. unm.* May, 1788.
5. Frances, bapt. 22 Sept. 1756 ; *d. unm.* May, 1772.
6. Charlotte, *b.* 31 Jan. 1759 ; *m.* Rev. Josiah Jehoiada Richards, and *d.* 1818.
7. Julia, *b.* 14 April, 1762 ; *m.* Robert Verner, of Golden Lane, Dublin, and *d.* March, 1840.
8. Caroline, *b.* 4 Jan. 1762 ; *d. unm.* 1844.
Mr. Donovan *d.* 16 April, 1773, and was *s.* by his eldest son,

RICHARD DONOVAN, of Ballymore, J.P., *b.* 27 Jan. 1752 ; *m.* 28 June, 1780, Anne, dau. of Goddard Richards, of Grange, co. Wexford, by whom (who *d.* 12 July, 1831) he had,
1. RICHARD, his heir.
2. Goddard Edward, *b.* April, 1784, Capt. 83rd Regt. ; *d. unm.,* murdered at Orange River, South Africa, 1803.
3. Robert, of Gourtduff, co. Dublin, M.A., *b.* 17 Oct. 1785 ; *m.* 12 Dec. 1812, Mary, dau. of Major Joseph Taylor, H E.I.C.S., and *d.* 23 Aug. 1860, leaving issue,
1. Richard Edward.   2. Robert.
3. Henry, *d.* 17 July, 1876, leaving issue.
4. Edwin, *m.* and has issue.
5. Albert William.
1. Harriet Ann, *m.* 1st, 26 July, 1837, James M'Kenny, of Dublin, who *d.* 1852, and 2ndly, 1858, Anthony Smith.
2. Laura.   3. Mary Medora.
4. John, Solicitor, bapt. 9 July, 1787 ; *d. unm.* 1 May, 1825.
5. George (Rev.), bapt. 9 April, 1789 ; *m.* 28 Jan. 1828, and *d.* 7 July, 1848, leaving issue, of whom survive,
1. Richard Archer Hewetson, *b.* 18 July, 1830 ; *m.* Josephine, dau. of Samuel White.
2. Solomon Ogle Richards, *b.* 18 March, 1838 ; *m.* 3 April, 1871, Mary Jane, dau. of John Francis Watson, and has
(1) George, *b.* 20 Feb. 1877.
(1) Mary Harriett.   (2) Lucy Frances.
(3) Kathleen Caroline.   (4) Anne.
3. William John Henry, *b.* 2 Oct. 1844.
1. Katherine Anne.   2. Julia Maria Frances.
6. William, of Enniscorthy, Solicitor, bapt. 19 Oct. 1792 ; *m.* 1st, 6 Oct. 1829, Elizabeth, dau. and in her issue sole heir of Capt. John Dallas, of the 46th Regt., and by her (who *d.* 14 Jan. 1834) had an only son,
WILLIAM JOHN O'DONNOVAN, LL.D., *b.* 9 June, 1832 ; *d.* 1903 ; *m.* 10 Oct. 1872, his first cousin, Ann Beata, dau. of John Glascott, of Killowen.
He *m.* 2ndly, 28 Sept. 1854, Elizabeth, dau. of Rev. Solomon Richards, of Solsboro', and *d.* 7 Jan. 1863.
7. Henry, Lieut. R.N., *b.* 6 Dec. 1795 ; *d. unm.* 28 April, 1824.
8. Soloman (Rev.), M.A., Rector of Horetown, Precentor of the Diocese of Ferns, *b.* Oct. 1801 ; *m.* 18 Sept. 1848, Katherine Sophia, dau. of Thomas Stratford Dennis, of Fort Granite, and *d.s.p.* 7 June, 1882.   She *d.* 7 March, 1907.
9. Arthur, bapt. 6 July, 1806 ; *d.* young.
1. Anne, *m.* 3 Aug. 1803, Solomon Speer, of Granitefield, and *d.* 10 Dec. 1865.
2. Katherine, *d. unm.* 24 Jan. 1837.
3. Mary, *m.* 9 Dec. 1829, John Glascott, of Killowen, and *d.* 24 July, 1867, leaving issue.
4. Eliza, *m.* 9 Dec. 1829, William Russell Parmar, of Bloomfield, and *d.* 23 Nov. 1844.
5. Sarah Caroline, *d. unm.* 15 May, 1880.
Mr. Donovan *d.* 9 Jan. 1816, and was *s.* by his eldest son,
RICHARD DONOVAN, of Ballymore, *b.* 21 April, 1781 ; High Sheriff co. Wexford, 1819 ; *m.* 18 Oct. 1816, Frances, eldest dau. of Edward Westby, of High Park, co. Wicklow, Master in Chancery, and by her (who *d.* 29 March, 1853) had issue,
1. RICHARD, his heir.
2. Edward Westby, Gen. (retired), Col. E. Yorkshire Regt., formerly Lieut.-Col. 33rd Regt., and 100th Regts., Chevalier of the Legion of Honour, had the Crimean Medals, and the Order of the Medjidie, *b.* 6 Sept. 1821 ; *m.* 26 July, 1870 ; Louisa Jane, 3rd dau. of Lieut.-Col. Vernon, late Coldstream Guards, and *d.* Jan. 1897, having had issue,
Edward Herbert, *b.* 8 Oct. 1874, Midshipman R.N.
3. Henry George, Lieut. 33rd Regt., *b.* 2 Feb. 1826 ; killed at the storming of the Redan 18 Sept. 1855.
4. Robert, *b.* 5 April, 1829 ; *d. unm.*
1. Phœbe, *d. unm.* 3 March, 1883.
2. Frances.   3. Annie, *d. unm.* 2 Sept. 1847.
Mr. Donovan *d.* 7 April, 1849, and was *s.* by his eldest son,
RICHARD DONOVAN, of Ballymore, J.P. and D.L., High Sheriff 1859, and sometime Capt. in the Wexford Militia, *b.* 17 Oct. 1819 ; *m.* 9 Jan. 1856, Elizabeth Agnes, dau. of Rev. Henry Wynne, Rector of Ardcolm, and by her (who *d.* 7 Feb. 1901) had issue,
1. RICHARD, his heir.
2. Charles Henry Wynne, *b.* 26 June, 1860, Major Army Service Corps, formerly 4th Dragoon Guards, *d. unm.* 17 April, 1898, killed on service in Sierra Leone.
3. Edward Wynne, *b.* 2n Aug. 1862 ; *m.* 1 Feb. 1893 ; Cicely Mary, dau. of the late Alfred Ellis, of the Brand, Loughborough. She *d.* Nov. 1893, leaving issue,
Richard Brian, *b.* Nov. 1893.
4. Albert Francis, *b.* 30 Sept. 1868 ; *d.* 20 Jan. 1869.
1. Madeline Annie.   2. Agnes Adelaide.
3. Frances Louisa Alice.
Mr. Donovan *d.* 24 June, 1884, and was *s.* by his eldest son.

Arms—Arg., a dexter arm couped above the wrist vested gu., cuffed of the first, the hand grasping a sword in pale, the blade entwined with a serpent descending, all ppr. **Crest**—An eagle rising or.

Seat—Ballymore, Camolin, co. Wexford ; and Corolanty, Shinrone, King's Co.

Donovan. THE LANDED GENTRY. 190

DONOVAN OF SEAFIELD.

ST. JOHN HENRY DONOVAN, of Seafield, co. Kerry, J.P., High Sheriff 1909, Chairman of Kerry County Council 1899-1901, b. 29 Oct. 1863; m. 22 June, 1886, Susan Josephine, dau. of Daniel Donovan, of Ballyard, co. Kerry, by Agnes his wife, dau. of Edmund Purcell, of Tralee. She d. 1891, leaving issue,

1. HENRY JOSEPH BRENDAN, b. 15 May, 1887.
1. Mirian Agnes.
2. Kathleen Mary.
3. Agnes Mary Aloysia.

He m. 2ndly, 11 Feb. 1909, Eileen, eldest dau. of Thomas O'Connor, of Ballyseedy Tralee, and has issue,

2. John Aloysias Mary.
3. Thomas Joseph Anthony, twins, b. 4 July, 1910.

Lineage.—JOHN DONOVAN, of Frogmore Spa, Tralee, and the Square, Tralee, co. Kerry, m. Katherine, dau. of James Galwey of Skibbereen, co. Cork, and had issue. His 5th son, SIR HENRY DONOVAN, of Clogher's House, Seafield, Tralee, co. Kerry, J.P., High Sheriff 1873, Chairman of Town Commissioners of Tralee, b. 4 Dec. 1822; m. 16 June, 1853, Kathleen, dau. of the Hon. Patrick Morris, of St. John's, Newfoundland, and Frances Mary his wife, dau. of Dr. William Bullen, of Cork, and d. 16 July, 1886, having had issue,
ST. JOHN HENRY, now of Seafield.
Frances Mary Philippa.

Arms—Arg. issuing from the sinister a dexter cubit arm vested gu., cuffed az., the hand grasping an old Irish sword, the blade entwined with a serpent all ppr., in the dexter chief point a cross crosslet fitchée of the second. *Crest*—A falcon alighting ppr. holding in the beak a cross crosslet fitchée gu. *Motto*—Adjuvante Deo in hostes.
Seat—Seafield Spa, Tralee.

DOPPING-HEPENSTAL. See HEPENSTAL.

BLACKER-DOUGLASS OF GRACE HALL.

MAXWELL VANDELEUR BLACKER-DOUGLASS, of Grace Hall, co. Down, Elm Park, co. Armagh, J.P., D.L., High Sheriff co. Kerry 1905, High Sheriff co. Dublin 1909, late Lieut. 4th Batt. Royal Inniskilling Fusiliers, b. 1859; m. 9 Sept. 1891, Alice, only child of the late Robert MacGeough, of Silver Bridge, co. Armagh (see MACGEOUGH-BOND of Drumsill), and has issue,

1. ROBERT ST. JOHN, b. 30 Nov. 1892.
2. Charles Maxwell, b. 19 Feb. 1900.
1. Alice Florence, b. 20 Jan. 1895.

Lineage—(of DOUGLASS).—This family is of Scottish descent. ROBERT DOUGLASS, b. 1655, son of Robert Douglass, of co. Down, by Elizabeth Henderson his wife, was Lieut. in the Army of King WILLIAM III at the Battle of the Boyne. He was thrice married, 1st, to Miss Elliot; 2ndly, to Miss Whitney; and 3rdly, to Miss Usher; and d. Jan. 1733, when he was s. by his son,
CHARLES DOUGLASS, High Sheriff co. Down 1760; m. 1st, Grace, dau. of Richard Warring, of Waringstown, co. Down, but had no issue. He m. 2ndly, 1758, Theodosia, dau. of George St. George, of Woodsgift, co. Kilkenny, who was created a baronet 1766, and by her had issue,
1. THOMAS. 2. George.
3. Robert.

1. Elizabeth. 2. Ellen.
The eldest son,
THOMAS DOUGLASS, of Grace Hall, m. 1786, Elizabeth, dau. of Mathew Forde, of Seaforde, co. Down and Coolgreaney, co. Wexford, by Elizabeth his wife, sister of Thomas, 1st Viscount Northland, and had issue,
1. CHARLES MATHEW, his successor.
1. Elizabeth, m. the Rev. Samuel Blacker, of Elm Park, co. Armagh (see BLACKER family), and had, with other issue,
ST. JOHN THOMAS BLACKER-DOUGLASS, heir to his uncle.
2. Theodosia, m. the Rev. William Brownlow Forde, of Seaforde, co. Down.
The only son,
CHARLES MATHEW DOUGLASS, of Grace Hall, J.P. and D.L., High Sheriff co. Down 1836, b. 1793; d.s.p. 1880, and was s. under the provisions of his will, dated 10 Feb. 1865, and proved 31 March, 1860, by his nephew, ST. JOHN THOMAS BLACKER-DOUGLASS, of Grace Hall, &c.

Lineage—(of BLACKER).—SAMUEL BLACKER, of Tanderagee, co. Armagh, Barrister-at-Law, 3rd son of William Blacker, of Carrick Blacker, by Theodosia his 2nd wife, dau. of Sir Oliver St. John, Knt. of Tanderagee Castle, m. 29 April, 1734, Mary, dau. of Isaiah Corry, of Rock Corry, co. Monaghan, and had by her (who d. 30 Oct. 1771) a son,
REV. ST. JOHN BLACKER, M.R.I.A., Rector of Moira, co. Down, and Prebendary of Inver, co. Donegal, b. 28 Sept. 1743; m. 1st, 1767, Grace, dau. of Maxwell Close, of Elm Park, co. Armagh, by whom he had five sons and four daus.,
1. SAMUEL (Rev.), his heir.
2. Maxwell, of Dublin, Q.C., Chairman of Kilmainham, b. 14 March, 1773; d.s.p. 1843.
3. William, b. 1776; M.R.I.A.; d.s.p. 20 Oct. 1850.
4. Valentine, C.B., Lieut.-Col. E.I.C.S., Quartermaster-General of the Madras Army, Surveyor-General of India, &c., b. 1778; m. 22 Dec. 1813, Emma, dau. of Robert Johnson, of Elm Grove, Lancaster, and had three sons, Rev. Valentine Samuel Barry Blacker, Vicar of East and West Reedham, Norfolk, d. 10 Sept. 1858; Rev. Maxwell Julius, who left issue; and Murray Macgregor, of Claremont, co. Mayo, J.P. and D.L., b. 1824; m. 1851, his cousin Frances Elizabeth, dau. of the Rev. Samuel Blacker, LL.D., Rector of Mullabrack, and by her (who d. 1 July, 1905) has issue; and one dau., Emma Louisa Rosa. He d. 1823.
5. St. John, Lieut.-Col. in the Madras Army, and at one time Envoy to the Court of Persia, b. 14 March, 1786; m. 1828, Anne Hammond, only child of Sir Charles Morgan, and d. 1842, leaving two sons, St. John Maxwell, Lieut. 21st Fusiliers, d. 1852; William, and two daus., Charlotte and Isabella Louisa, m. 1854, Ferdinand, Baron de Wydenbruck.
1. Mary, d. unm. 27 July, 1857.
2. Catherine, m. 1st, Jan. 1804, Rev. Charles Barker, Canon of Wells; 2ndly, Rev. Robert Ball.
3. Grace, m. 6 May, 1809, Robert Alexander, of Gloucester Place, London, representative of the elder branch of the CALEDON family, and d. 1835.
4. Charlotte, m. 8 Dec. 1809, Gen. Munro, of Teaninich.
Rev. St. John Blacker m. 2ndly, Susan, dau. of Dr. Messiter, of London, but had no further issue. His eldest son,
REV. SAMUEL BLACKER, LL.D., Prebendary of Mullabrack, co. Armagh, b. 1771; m. Elizabeth, dau. of Thomas Douglass, of Grace Hall, co. Down, and had issue,
1. ST. JOHN THOMAS, his heir.
2. Thomas Samuel, of Castle Martin, co. Kildare; m. 9 Dec. 1852, Frances Mary Anne, dau. of Thomas A. Forde, of Seaforde, co. Down, and d. 1857, leaving issue,
   1. WILLIAM BLACKER, of Castle Martin, J.P., High Sheriff co. Kildare 1878, Capt. 3rd Batt. R. Dublin Fusiliers, b. 29 Sept. 1853; m. 28 April, 1877, Hon. Mary Lawless, dau. of Edward, 3rd Lord Cloncurry. He d. 21 Nov. 1907. She d. 20 June, 1885, leaving issue,
      (1) Cecil William, b. 27 Dec. 1877; d. 3 Feb. 1885.
      (2) Frederick St. John, Capt. Rifle Brigade, b. 6 March, 1881.
      (1) Marjorie Mary, m. 2 April, 1908, Major Arthur Alex Goschen, D.S.O., R.H.A. (see BURKE'S *Peerage*, GOSCHEN, V.).
   He m. 2ndly, 1892, Eva Harriett Cator, dau. of Edward Beauman, of Furness, co. Kildare, and d. 21 Nov. 1907, having by her had issue,
      (2) Alice
   2. Frederick Henry, b. 1854, formerly Capt. 4th Queen's Own Hussars, and late Major Notts Y.C.; m. 25 Nov. 1884, Anna, dau. of Sir Joseph Bazalgette, Knt., of St. Mary's, Wimbledon, C.B., and has issue,
      (1) William Frederick, Lieut. Roy. Irish Fus.
      (2) Francis, b. 1889. (3) Cecil, b. 1889.
      (1) Theresa.
   1. Louisa Elizabeth.
1. Theodosia, d. unm. 1847.
2. Frances Elizabeth, m. 1851, her cousin Murray Macgregor Blacker, of Claremont, co. Mayo. She d. 1 July, 1905.
3. Isabella, m. 1855, Rev. Arthur W. Boycott.
Rev. Samuel Blacker d. 1849, and was s. by his eldest son,
ST. JOHN THOMAS BLACKER-DOUGLASS, of Grace Hall, co. Down, Elm Park, co. Armagh and Tullahinnel, co. Kerry, J.P. cos. Kerry and Armagh, D.L. co. Kerry, High Sheriff co. Armagh 1861, and co. Kerry 1865, b. 1822; m. 1855, Elizabeth, dau. of Col. Crofton Moore Vandeleur, of Kilrush, co. Clare, M.P., by Lady Grace Toler his wife, dau. of Hector John, 2nd Earl of Norbury, and d. 26 Sept. 1900, leaving issue,
1. MAXWELL VANDELEUR, now of Grace Hall.
2. St. John Douglass Stewart, b. 16 Feb. 1871; m. 9 Nov. 1897, Isabel, only dau. of Major Pulteney, late 52nd Regt.

1. Grace Elizabeth, *d. unm.* 1878.
2. Georgiana Frances, *d. unm.* 1889.
3. Emily Theodosia, *m.* 1886, Capt. Thomas Graves Lowry Herbert Armstrong, Northumberland Fusiliers, of Kilclare, King's Co.

Mr. Blacker-Douglass assumed by Royal Licence, dated 10 June, 1880, the additional surname and arms of DOUGLASS, on s. to the estate of his uncle, Charles Matthew Douglass.

Arms—Quarterly: 1st and 4th, per pale arg. and or, a human heart gu. on a chief az. a trefoil slipped between two estoiles of the second, for DOUGLASS; 2nd and 3rd, arg. on a mount vert a warrior in complete armour in the act of advancing towards the right, and brandishing in his dexter hand a battle-axe ppr. from his shoulder a mantle flowing gu., for BLACKER. **Crests**—1st, DOUGLASS: A cubit arm erect ppr., the hand grasping a human heart as in the arms, and charged with a trefoil slipped vert; 2nd, BLACKER: A dexter arm embowed armed ppr. the hand gauntleted grasping a battle-axe, as in the arms. **Mottoes**—DOUGLASS, Forward; BLACKER, Pro Deo et rege.

Seat—Elm Park, Armagh. **Residence**—2, Bellevue Park, Killiney, co. Dublin.

DOWDALL FORMERLY OF MOUNTTOWN.

REV. LAUNCELOT JOHN GEORGE DOWNING DOWDALL, M.A., LL.B. (Dublin), M.A., B.D. (Oxon).

Lineage.—WALTER DOVEDALE, of Palmerston, co. Meath, living in 1318, was father of,
WALTER DOVEDALE, of co. Meath, Sheriff of co. Louth 1312, living 1335; *m.* Agnes, dau. of — Fleming, having by her had issue,
1. Nicholas, of Termonfechan, co. Louth, *m.* Isabella, dau. of —— and *d.s.p.*
2. WILLIAM, of whom next.

The 2nd son,
WILLIAM DOVEDALE was father of,
1. William, *d.s.p.*
2. WALTER, of whom next.

The 2nd son,
WALTER DOWDALL, of Drogheda, co. Louth, living 1382, was father of,
1. JOHN, of whom presently.
2. Robert.   3. Thomas.

The eldest son,
SIR JOHN DOWDALL, Knight, Sheriff of co. Louth, murdered at Dunleer *v.p.* 1364, father of,
SIR JOHN DOWDALL, of Newtown and Termonfechan, Knight, *m.* Anne, dau. of and heir of John Batome, having by her had issue,
1. Henry, of Termonfechan, Newtown, &c., living 1473; *m.* Janet, dau. of Robert, son of Sir Luke Dowdall, and had with other issue,
   1. Stephen, of Newtown, from whom descended the Newtown branch.
   2. Edward, of the town of Drogheda, 2nd son, who was father of,
      (1) George Dowdall, D.D., Lord Archbishop of Armagh and Primate of all Ireland, *b.* in Drogheda 1487, consecrated to Armagh 11 Dec. 1543; *d. unm.* in London 15 Aug. 1588.
2. LAURENCE, of whom presently.

The 2nd son,
LAURENCE DOWDALL, of Glasspistol, co. Louth, *m.* Isabella, dau. and sole heir of Richard FitzRichard, of Glasspistol, &c., and had issue,
JOHN DOWDALL, of Glasspistol, &c., *m.* Elinor, dau. of Marward, Baron of Skriae, co. Meath, having by her (who *m.* 2ndly, Robert Walsh) had issue,
1. Edward, of Glasspistol, *m.* Elinor, dau. and heir of Walter Galtrim, of Dundalk, co. Louth, and *d.* 6 March, 1590, having by her had issue,
   1. John, of Glasspistol, *m.* Anne, dau. of Sir Thomas Cusack, of Cushington, co. Meath, Knt., and was ancestor of the family of Dowdall of Athlumney, co. Meath, of whom Sir Luke Dowdall was created a Baronet of Ireland, 24 Nov. 1663; attainted 6 April, 1691; extinct 9 Dec. 1742.
2. WILLIAM, of whom presently.
3. Anne, *m.* Richard Moore, of Barmeath, co. Louth.

The 2nd son,
WILLIAM DOWDALL, of Mounttown, co. Meath, *m.* Catherine, dau. of Sir Nicholas Cusack, of Gerardstown, Knt., having by her had with other issue,
1. John.   2. LAWRENCE, of whom next.

The 2nd son,
LAWRENCE DOWDALL, of Mounttown, *m.* Matilda, dau. of Walter Newman, of Dublin, and *d.* Nov. 1617 (Funeral entry), having by her had issue,
1. EDWARD, of whom presently.
2. Nicholas, of Brownstown, co. Meath, ancestor of that family.

The eldest son,
EDWARD DOWDALL, of Mounttown, Registrar of the Court of Chancery in Ireland, *m.* Margaret, dau. of Sir Henry Piers, of Tristernagh, co. Westmeath, Bart., and *d.* 1 Dec. 1665, having by her had with other issue,
LAURENCE DOWDALL, of Mounttown, *m.* 1st, Honora, dau. and co-heir of Sir John Dowdall, of Kilfinny, co. Limerick, Knt., and by her (who *d.* 2 Oct. 1658) had issue,
1. Edward, *d.s.p.*   2. Elizabeth.
1. Margaret, *d.s.p.*

He *m.* 2ndly, Letitia, eld. dau. of Rt. Rev. Anthony Martin, D.D., Lord Bishop of Meath, and by her had issue,
2. LAUNCELOT, of whom presently.   3. John.
3. Catherine, *m.* Jerome Cheevers.

The 2nd son,
LAUNCELOT DOWDALL, of Mounttown, High Sheriff for co. Meath 1686, *m.* 1st, Mary, 2nd dau. of Ven. William Bulkeley, M.A., Archdeacon of Dublin, and by her had issue,
1. Bulkeley, *d.s.p.*
2. Laurence, *m.* Lavinia, dau. of John Phillips, of Newtownlimavady, co. Londonderry, and *d.s.p.*

He *m.* 2ndly, Jane, dau. of Richard Hanway, Alderman of Dublin, widow of Roger Jones, of Dollanstown, co. Meath, and by her had issue,
3. Edward, will 22 March, 1735; proved 30 Aug. 1739; *m.* Mary, dau. and co-heir of George Houghton, of Bormount, co. Wexford, and had four daus.,
   1. Rose, *m.* —. Galbraith.
   2. Jane, *m.* James Houghton.
   3. Letitia, *m.* — Edgar.
   4. Henrietta, *m.* Thomas Phillips.
4. LAUNCELOT, of whom presently.
1. Letitia, *m.* — Tunks.   2. Jane, *m.* Scott.

The 4th son,
REV. LAUNCELOT DOWDALL, *b.* 1689, entered Trin. Coll. Dublin, 1706, M.A. 1714; *m.* dau. of — Blacker, and by her had issue,
1. Laurence.
2. LAUNCELOT, of whom presently.

The 2nd son,
LAUNCELOT DOWDALL, *m.* 1769, Anne, dau. of Rev. John Gibson, by Elizabeth his wife, dau. of Rev. Anthony Raymond, D.D., Vice-Provost of Trin. Coll., Dublin, and by her had issue,
1. LAUNCELOT, of whom presently.
2. John, *d. unm.* 1834.
1. Elizabeth, *m.* William Studdert.

The eldest son,
REV. LAUNCELOT DOWDALL, D.D. (Dublin), *m.* Hannah Cassandra, dau. of Richard Eaton, and by her had issue,
1. LAUNCELOT, of whom presently.
2. John (Rev.), B.A., *d. unm.* 1844.
1. Lydia Anne.
2. Hanna Maria Cassandra, *d. unm.* 1847.

The eldest son,
REV. LAUNCELOT DOWDALL, M.A. (Dublin), *m.* April, 1846, Maria, dau. of John Downing, Judge of the Kandian Provinces (*see* FULLERTON *of Ballintoy*), and by her had issue,
1. LAUNCELOT JOHN GEORGE DOWNING, present representative.
2. Laurence Charles Edward Downing, C.B. 1901, M.A. (Dublin), Head of Administrative Department, Chief Secretary's Office, Dublin, *b.* 25 Sept. 1852.
3. Raymond Alexander Granville Fullerton, M.D. (Dublin).
1. Fanny Amy Elizabeth.   2. Jessie Maria Louisa.

Arms—Gu., a fess between five martlets arg. (Funeral entry of Laurence Dowdall, 1617: Gu., a fess between five doves arg.) **Crest**—A martlet arg. crowned or. **Motto**—Nec male notus Eques. **Residence**—West Lodge, Sackville Road, Hove, Brighton.

DOYNE OF WELLS.

CHARLES MERVYN DOYNE, of Wells, co. Wexford, J.P. and D.L., High Sheriff co. Wexford 1873, and co. Carlow 1875; M.A. Magdalene Coll. Cambridge; *b.* 27 Sept. 1839; *m.* 18 Nov. 1867, Lady Frances Mary Wentworth Fitzwilliam, eldest dau. of William Thomas Spencer, 6th Earl Fitzwilliam, K.G., and by her (who *d.* 28 Sept. 1903) has issue,

1. ROBERT WENTWORTH, late Capt. 4th Batt. Oxfordshire L.I., J.P., D.L. co. Wexford, *b.* 30 Dec. 1868; *m.* 30 April, 1898, Lady Mary Diana Lascelles, youngest dau. of the 4th Earl of Harewood (*see* BURKE's *Peerage*), and has issue, Robert Harry, *b.* 30 Jan. 1899.

Doyne. THE LANDED GENTRY.

2. Dermot Henry, of St. Austin's Abbey, Tullow, co. Carlow, J.P., D.L., High Sheriff 1902, b. 21 Nov. 1871; m. 26 April, 1905, Alice Gertrude, only dau. of Frank T. Brooke, of Ardeen, co. Wicklow (see that family), and has issue,
   1. Charles Hastings, b. 27 Dec. 1906.
   2. Francis Mervyn, b. 16 March, 1909.
1. Kathleen, b. 29 Sept. 1870.
2. Eveleen Margaret, b. 26 Jan. 1876.
3. Bridget Frances, b. 5 Oct. 1879.

Lineage.—This is an ancient Irish sept, whose chieftains formerly ruled over Hy-Regain, a territory comprised in the present Queen's Co. They were of the same race as O'Conor Failghe, O'More, and O'Dempsey, and Irish genealogists derived their descent from Cathair Mor, Monarch of Ireland.

RORY O'DOINN, Chief of Hy-Regain, d. according to the Annals of the Four Masters, A.D. 1427. The descent of the various branches of this sept, O'DUINNE, DOYNE, and DUNNE, was preserved in a pedigree deposited in the library of St. Isidore, Rome, by a member of the family who was a clergyman of the Church of Rome, in the early part of the 17th century, which is now among the Archives of the Franciscan Convent, Merchant's Quay, Dublin. The son of this chieftain,

LEYNAGH O'DUINNE, Chief of Hy-Regain, built Castlebrack, in the Queen's Co., to defray the expense of which he imposed a tribute on his sept, which his successors continued to extort down to the time of JAMES I. He m. a dau. of O'Neill of Ulster, and was s. by his son,

TEIG O'DUINNE, Chief of Hy-Regain, m. Ellen, dau. of Lord Power, of Curraghmore, co. Waterford, and was s. by his son,

TEIG O'DUINNE, Chief of Hy-Regain, m. Gormley, dau. of O'Conor Failghe, and had, with other issue, three sons,
1. TEIG, his successor.
2. Terence, of Kilcavan, ancestor of DUNNE, of Ards and Kilcooney, in the Queen's Co. (see DUNNE of Brittas).
3. Owen, of Park, ancestor of DOYNE, of Park, in the Queen's Co.

The eldest son,
TEIG O'DUINNE, Chief of Hy-Regain, s. his father as O'DOINN, and m. Elizabeth, dau. of James Fitz-Piers Fitz-Gerald, of Ballysonan and Cloncurry, co. Kildare, and had, with other issue, four sons,
1. TEIG-OGE, his heir.
2. Cormack, of Tyrtin Shine, and Rosboyne, m. twice, and had four sons, all mentioned in Deeds of Settlement of the estate,
   1. Donald.
   2. Donough.
   3. Art.
   4. Owney.
3. Barnaby, alias Brian, ancestor of DUNNE of Brittas.
4. Cahir or Charles, Master in Chancery, M.P. Trinity Coll. Dublin, got a grant of the greater portion of the Hy-Regain estate, by a fiat dated 29 June, 6 JAMES I, 1608, and d. unm., having bequeathed all his estates, by will dated 2 April, 1617, to his nephew, Brien Oge O'Duinne or Dunn, son of his brother Barnaby. O'Duinne made a settlement of his estates on his sons, with remainders to the descendants of his brothers Terence and Owen, by three several deeds, dated 20 July, 1590, 17 April, 1591, and 28 April, 1593. He was a very old man and blind in 1593, and was s. by his eldest son,

TEIG-OGE O'DUINNE, b. 1557. He surrendered his estates to JAMES I, and got a fiat for a patent for the same, which never passed, owing to the opposition of his younger brother, who having become a Protestant, obtained the estates for himself. He m. 1st, Margaret, dau. of Shane a Diamus O'Neill, and had a son, TEIG-REAGH, who got none of the estates. Teig-Oge was divorced from his wife (she m. 2ndly, Cuconach McGuire, Chief of McGuire), and m. 2ndly, Ellis, dau. of Redmond FitzGerald, of Barrowhill and Clonboyle, co. Kildare, and had several other sons. His eldest son,

TEIG REAGH O'DUINNE, who settled in Dublin, and got some property there. He m. Maud, dau. of James Byrne, and made his will 29 March, 1625, which was proved 8 June, 1626. He had, with several younger sons, an elder son, Henry, who s. to his father's lands and houses in Dublin, but d.s.p., and a second son,

MICHAEL DOYNE, of Knockirney, co. Antrim, who s. on the death, s.p., of his elder brother, to the Dublin lands and premises. He obtained lands in Antrim from Hugh Mergagh O'Neill, by deeds, dated 4 Nov. 1627, and 5 July, 1622, and obtained a pardon for the alienation of some of those lands, dated 28 Nov. 1631, 12 CHARLES I. He had four sons,
1. Derby, m. Sarah, sister of Stephen and Charles Dowdall, of co. Louth. On his marriage, his father, by deed dated 24 Aug. 1641, settled the lands in Antrim on him and his issue, and in default on his next brother. He d.s.p. same year.
2. MICHAEL, of whom presently.
3. James, d. unm. and intestate; administration granted to his nephew, Robert Doyne, 1666.
4. Dionysius, of Carrickfergus, co. Antrim, d. intestate; administration granted 1661.

The 2nd son,
MICHAEL DOYNE, s. on the death of his elder brother, s.p. to the Antrim and Dublin lands and premises, but was ousted therefrom by OLIVER CROMWELL; he d. soon after 1654, leaving by Bridget his wife, an infant son ROBERT. His widow m. 2ndly, Philip Harris, of Dublin, Gent., and jointly with her husband, lodged a petition in the Court of Claims, 6 Nov. 1661, 14 CHARLES II, and obtained a Decree of Innocence, 14 July, 1662 (Roll. V. Memb. 48), by which all the lands subject to her dowry were restored to her only son,

ROBERT DOYNE, Lord Chief Justice of Common Pleas in Ireland, b. in Dublin, 1651; entered Trinity Coll. Dublin, 28 Nov. 1667, called to the Bar Trinity Term, 1677; appointed Lord Chief Baron, 1 June, 1695, and Chief Justice of Common Pleas 1 Feb. 1703. He m. by licence, dated 8 Jan. 1684, Jane, dau. of Henry Whitfield, of Dublin, by whom (who d. Feb. 1711) he had issue,
1. PHILIP, his heir.
2. Whitfield, of Balygriffin, co. Dublin, bapt. 28 March, 1686; d.s.p. Jan. 1744.
3. Michael, Capt. in Brigadier Hargreave's Regt., d. unm.
4. Robert, bapt. 20 March, 1688; d. Nov. 1695.
1. Hester, d. unm.
2. Elizabeth.

Chief Justice Doyne d. 28 Feb. 1733, and was s. by his eldest son,

PHILIP DOYNE, of Wells, co. Wexford, b. 1685; m. 1st, 10 Aug. 1704, Mary, dau. of Benjamin Burton, of Dublin, Alderman of that city, by whom (who d. in childbed, 10 July, 1705) he had an only son,
1. ROBERT, his heir.

He m. 2ndly, 22 Feb. 1709, Frances South, by whom (who d. 13 Feb. 1712) he had issue,
2. John, Lieut. in the Army, b. 22 Feb. 1710; m. Jane, dau. of Robert Ross, of Rosstrevor, co. Down, and had a dau., Jane, bapt. 13 July, 1735.
3. Charles (Very Rev.), D.D., Dean of Leighlin, b. 3 Feb. 1711; m. 1st, 2 July, 1743, Anna Maria Bury, by whom (who d. Dec. 1762) he had issue,
   1. Bury, d. unm., will dated 12 Dec. 1772, and proved 1773.
   2. Philip, m. Jane, dau. of John Vigors, of Old Leighlin, co. Carlow, and had issue,
     (1) Philip, of Merrion Square, Dublin, d. unm. 11 Feb. 1858.
     (2) Richard, of Hermitage, co. Dublin, Major in the Army, m. Susanna, dau. of Thomas Kavanagh, of Borris, co. Carlow, and had issue,
       1. Philip Kavanagh, Lieut.-Col. late 4th Dragoon Guards, b. 11 April, 1848; m. 2 April, 1884, Florence Audrey, dau. of Maj.-Gen. Charles Edward Astell, of West Lodge, co. Dorset (see ASTELL of Woodbury). He d.s.p. 17 June, 1900. His widow m. 2ndly, 23 June, 1901, John Bertram Russell, eldest son of the late John Russell, of Pebblecombe, Surrey.
       2. Richard, of Ballygriffin, co. Dublin, m. 1896.
       1. Elizabeth Jane, m. 1 Sept. 1877, Thomas de Courcy, The O'Grady of Kilballyowen.
     (3) John (Rev.), of Old Leighlin, co. Carlow, b. 3 April, 1791; m. 29 Oct. 1819, Ellen, dau. of Thomas Armstrong, of Farney Castle, co. Tipperary, and d. 1841, having had issue,
       1. Philip John, of Fox Hall, co. Donegal, J.P., b. 3 Aug. 1820.
       2. Thomas William, b. 18 July, 1821; d. 6 Feb. 1823.
       3. William Thomas, b. 15 April, 1823.
       4. Richard Vigors, b. 19 Oct. 1824, called to the Bar 1850, of Ballygrange, Calcutta; m. at Calcutta, 1861, Anna Maria, dau. of William Henry Daniel, of Auburn, co. Westmeath (she was b. 29 March, 1842), and has issue, Mordaunt Berners, b. 16 Dec. 1864, Capt. 5th Lancers; Winifred, b. 1862.
       5. Charles Armstrong, b. 18 Feb. 1826; d. unm.
       6. Henry Archdall, J.P., Hon. Major and late Adjutant Donegal Artillery Militia, formerly Capt. R.A., b. 25 Oct. 1833; m. 1859, Lydia Clarke, dau. of George Hawks, of Redheugh Hall, Newcastle, and by her (who d. 26 June, 1911) has issue, John, b. 1860.
       1. Sophia Anne.
       2. Jean Eleanor, d. unm. 25 March, 1837.
       3. Frances Elizabeth.
       4. Anne, d. unm.
       5. Jane, m. Henry Archdall, Capt. late 6th Dragoon Guards.
   3. Charles Powlett, of Portarlington, m. 1785, Eliza Jane, dau. of William Vicars, of Ballynakillbeg, co. Carlow, and had issue,
     (1) Charles William (Rev.), Rector of Fethard, m. Charlotte, dau. of Thomas Stannus, of Portarlington, by whom (who d. 5 Jan. 1865) he had issue,
       1. Philip Walter (Rev.), m. 25 April, 1849, Emily Sophia, dau. of John Goddard Richards, of Ardemine (see that family). She d. 31 Dec. 1907. He d. 23 Oct. 1861, leaving issue,
         1a. Charles Goddard (Rev.), b. 26 Oct. 1852, M.A. Cantab, late Vicar of All Saints', Bournemouth.
         2a. Robert Walter, b. 15 May, 1857; m. 7 July, 1885, Gertrude Irene Hope, dau. of John Hollings, of the Watchetts, co. Surrey.
         3a. Philip Valentine, b. 14 Feb. 1859.
         4a. Herbert William, b. 12 Jan. 1861.
         1a. Anne Katherine, m. Rev. Willoughby Carter, curate of Hawarden, co. Flint.
         2a. Emily Elizabeth.
         3a. Charlotte Sophia Mary.
       2. Charles, d. unm. 1853.
       3. Vicars, d. unm. 1843.
       1. Elizabeth, m. Henry Newton, of Mount Leinster, co. Carlow.
       2. Charlotte, m. Very Rev. John Cotter McDonnell, Dean of Cashel.
       3. Henrietta Frances, m. 13 March, 1847, John Stuart Maconchy.
       4. Sophia, m. 13 Jan. 1857, Thomas Mercer Vigors, M.I.C.E., and has issue (see VIGORS of Burgage).
       5. Caroline, d. unm. 1871.

(2) Philip Paulet, *m.* Catherine Botham, co. Berks, and had one dau.,
    Frances.
(3) Bury, of Waltham Grove, co. Berks, *b.* 1794, J.P. and D.L. ; *m.* 1828, Caroline Mary Anne, dau. and co-heir of Col. Kearney, of White Waltham, co. Berks.
(4) Robert, of Borris, co. Carlow, *m.* Bella Mira, dau. of Valentine Munbee, Major in the Army, and had an only child,
    Jane Elizabeth, *m.* 6 Jan. 1855, Robert McIntire Renwick.
(1) Anne, *m.* Robert White, of Old Park, Rathdowney, in the Queen's Co.
(2) Elizabeth.
(3) Henrietta, *m.* 1824, William Hamilton, of Mountrath.
(4) Frances, *d. unm.*
(5) Georgina, *d. unm.*

The Very Rev. Charles Doyne *m.* 2ndly, 7 March, 1763, Mary, dau. of the Rev. Nicholas Milley, D.D., and relict of Wesley Harman, but had no further issue. He *d.* June, 1777.
    1. Henrietta, *b.* 3 Dec. 1709.

Mr. Doyne *m.* 3rdly, Elizabeth, dau. of James Stopford, of Courtown, and sister of James, 1st Earl of Courtown, and had further issue.
    4. James, *b.* 7 June, 1716 ; *m.* Elizabeth, dau. of Edward Pratt, and *d.s.p.* 1763.
    5. Whitfield, Examiner in the Court of Chancery, *b.* 1 May, 1719 ; *d.* 9 Dec. 1769.
    2. Frances, *m.* July, 1756, Rev. Francis Thompson, Rector of Druncree.
    3. Elizabeth.
    4. Susan, *m.* Mark White, of Cranacrower, co. Wexford.

Mr. Doyne *d.* 23 Jan. 1753, and was *s.* by his eldest son,
ROBERT DOYNE, of Wells, co. Wexford, *b.* 2 Jan. 1705, High Sheriff co. Wexford 1741, M.P. for the town of Wexford ; *m.* 1 July, 1731, Deborah, dau. of Francis Annesley, of Ballysonnan, co. Kildare, and had issue,
    1. PHILIP, his successor.
    2. ROBERT, successor to his brother.
    3. Benjamin Burton, of Altamont, co. Carlow, High Sheriff 1775 ; *m.* 23 Feb. 1768, Miss Stepney, and *d.s.p.* His will, dated 12 Dec. 1771, was proved 20 May, 1787.

Mr. Doyne *d.* 19 Aug. 1754, and was *s.* by his eldest son,
PHILIP DOYNE, of Wells, *b.* 20 March, 1733 ; *m.* 29 Aug. 1757, Lady Joanna Gore, dau. of Arthur, 1st Earl of Arran ; but *d.s.p.* 11 March, 1765, and his widow *m.* 2ndly, 21 Feb. 1766, Michael Daly, of Mount Pleasant, co. Galway. He was *s.* by his next brother,
ROBERT DOYNE, of Wells, *b.* 11 Nov. 1738 ; High Sheriff Co. Wexford 1777 ; *m.* 1777, Mary, dau. of Humphrey Ram, of Ramsfort, co. Wexford, by whom (who *d.* 1826) he had issue,
    1. ROBERT, his successor.
    1. Mary, *b.* 1779, *d. unm.* 1823.
    2. Jane, *b.* 1781, *d. unm.* 1829.
    3. Elizabeth, *b.* 1783, *m.* by licence, dated 17 April, 1806, Robert Dwyer, of Dublin.
    4. Georgina.
    5. Frances, *b.* 1787, *m.* 1827, St. George Irvine, of Ballynahown, co. Wexford, Major in the Army.

Mr. Doyne, whose will, dated 3 Sept. 1784, was proved 2 Feb. 1791, was *s.* by his only son,
ROBERT DOYNE, of Wells, J.P. and D.L., High Sheriff co. Wexford 1825, *b.* 2 March, 1782 ; *m.* 2 July, 1805, Annette Constantia, dau. of the Right Hon. John Beresford, grand-dau. of Marcus, 1st Earl of Tyrone, and relict of Robert Uniacke, of Woodhouse, co. Waterford, by whom (who *d.* 8 Aug. 1836) he had issue,
    1. ROBERT STEPHEN, his successor.
    2. Charles Henry, of St. Austin's Abbey, co. Carlow, J.P., Lieut. 87th Regt., *b.* Aug. 1809 ; *m.* 1845, Georgina Louisa, dau. of Capt. John Kennedy, of Dunbrody, co. Wexford, and *d.s.p.* March, 1867. Mrs. C. H. Doyne *d.* 23 March, 1893.
    1. Mary Annette, *d. unm.* March, 1869.
    2. Annette Constantia, *d. unm.* Sept. 1819.

Mr. Doyne *d.* Dec. 1850, and was *s.* by his eldest son,
ROBERT STEPHEN DOYNE, of Wells, J.P., D.L., High Sheriff co. Wexford 1835, and Carlow 1845, *b.* 23 Feb. 1806 ; *m.* 12 July, 1834, Sarah Emily Tynte, dau. of Col. Joseph Pratt, of Cabra, co. Cavan (*see that family*), by whom (who *d.* Dec. 1871) he had issue,
    1. Robert Tynte, *b.* 28 Dec. 1835 ; *d.* 10 Oct. 1836.
    2. Robert Scott, *b.* 13 July, 1838 ; *d.* 13 Sept. following.
    3. CHARLES MERVYN, now of Wells.
    4. Wardlaw Fitzherbert, *b.* 27 Dec. 1843 ; *d.* 14 Dec. 1850.
    5. James Walter Chaloner, of St. Austin's Abbey, co. Carlow, J.P. co. Wicklow, High Sheriff co. Carlow 1881, *b.* 25 April, 1851 ; *d. unm.* 22 March, 1898.
    6. Henry Arthur Beresford, *b.* 9 Oct. 1853 ; *d.* 27 Jan. 1854.
    1. Jemima, *b.* 1836 ; *d.* an infant.
    2. Jemima Elizabeth Tynte.
    3. Annette Louisa.
    4. Roberta Frances Mary.

Mr. Doyne *d.* 24 May, 1870.

Arms—Quarterly : 1st and 4th, gu., a fess dancettée, between three escallops, arg., for DOYNE ; 2nd and 3rd, az., an eagle displayed or, for O'DUINNE. **Crest**—A demi-eagle rising ppr., for DOYNE : A hollybusb ppr., in front thereof a lizard passant, or, for O'DUINNE. **Motto**—" Mullac a boo," the war cry of the sept of O'Duinne.

Seat—Wells, Gorey, co. Wexford. **Clubs**—Carlton and Kildare Street.

I.L.G.

DRAKE OF STOKESTOWN.

JOSEPH EDWARD DEANE-DRAKE, of Stokestown, co. Wexford, J.P. and D.L., High Sheriff 1905, *b.* 5 Nov. 1845 ; *s.* his father 20 Dec. 1855 ; *m.* 29 June, 1882, Dora Venables, only dau. of Richard Venables-Kyrke, J.P., of Nant-y-Frith, co. Flint, and by her (who *d.* 20 Aug. 1904) had,
    CECIL JOHN VENABLES, *b.* 30 March, 1887.
    Emily Frances, *m.* 2 June, 1900, Arthur Isaac Tyndall, youngest son of late Robert Tyndall, of Oaklands (*see that family*).

Lineage.—ROGER DRAKE, of Stokestown, co. Wexford, went to Ireland as Agent for the Victuallers of the Navy, was Commissioner for the Assessment for the co. Wexford, and got a grant of Stokestown and other property in co. Wexford. He *m.* Hannah, dau. and co-heiress of Major Samuel Sheppard, and had issue,
    1. JOHN, his heir.   2. Roger.
    1. Mary.   2. Charity.
    3. Margaret.   4. Patiens.

His will, dated 23 Oct. 1677, was proved 14 March, 1678, and he was *s.* by his elder son,
JOHN DRAKE, of Stokestown, who *m.* Mercy, " sister's dau." to William Bayne of Clocane, co. Kilkenny, and had issue,
    1. JOHN, *d. unm.*, bur. 17 Dec. 1729.
    3. DARIUS, his heir.
    2. Samuel, *d. unm.*, bur. 26 Sept. 1729.
    4. George, of Coolback, co. Wexford, bapt. 21 Jan. 1720 ; *m.* 1st, Elizabeth, dau. of John Allen, of Allen's Grove, co. Kilkenny, and had a son,
        1. John, of Coolback, *b.* 1745 ; *d.* 24 May, 1836 ; *m.* Sarah, dau. of Col. John Hanfield, by whom (who *d.* 12 July, 1828) he had (with two other daus., who *d.s.p.*) issue,
        (1) GEORGE, who *s.* to Stokestown.
        (2) John Handfield, bapt. 9 Feb. 1799 ; *d. unm.*
        (1) Sara, who *s.* her brother at Stokestown, *m.* 11 Sept. 1810, Joseph Deane, younger son of John Deane, M.P. of Terenure. He *d.* 1850. She *d.* 24 July, 1854, leaving issue,
        1. JOHN, assumed the name of DRAKE, and *s.* to Stokestown.
        1. Joseph William, of Longerage, *b.* 1803, Fulham, co. Wexford, and has Strangman Davis Goff, of Horetown, co. Wexford, had William Joseph, and other issue (*see* DEANE *of Berkeley*).
        1. Sarah, *m.* Henry Roe, of Knockmullen, co. Wexford.
        2. Katherine Elizabeth, *m.* 18 Jan. 1855, Abraham Alcock, M.D., and *d.* 1859.
        3. Juliana Frances.

George Drake *m.* 2ndly, 1763, Mrs. Mary Jones, widow, and had further issue,
    2. Darius, bapt. 13 April, 1767 ; bur. 17 April, 1779.
    1. Elizabeth, bapt. 9 March, 1764.
    2. Hannah, bapt. 10 June, 1765.
    1. Juliana, bapt. 17 Sept. 1721.   2. Ann.

Mr. Drake, whose will, dated 17 April, 1730, was proved 1740, was *s.* by his eldest surviving son,
DARIUS DRAKE, of Stokestown, *b.* 1711 ; *m.* Jane, dau. of Alexander Boyd, of Crook, co. Waterford (settlements dated 28 and 29 Oct. 1742), by whom (who *d.* 25 Aug. 1751, aged 28) he had issue,
    1. JOHN, his heir.
    1. Anne, *b.* 1750 ; *d. unm.* 9 Aug. 1808.
    2. Urith, *m.* by licence, dated 2 Jan. 1775, Robert Paul, of Johnshill, co. Waterford.

Mr. Drake *d.* 12 April, 1777, and was *s.* by his only son,
JOHN DRAKE, of Stokestown, High Sheriff of co. Wexford 1778, *b.* 1743 ; *d. unm.* 20 Dec. 1809, when the property devolved on his only surviving sister, Mrs. Paul, who devised it to her cousin, the heir male of the family,
GEORGE DRAKE, of Stokestown, *b.* 1776 ; *d. unm.* Sept. 1852, when Stokestown devolved, under Mrs. Paul's will, on his only sister, Mrs. Deane, and at her death, on his nephew, her son,
JOHN DEANE-DRAKE, of Stokestown, J.P. co. Wexford, *b.* 6 May, 1813 who, on the death of his uncle, assumed by Royal Licence in 1854, the additional name and arms of DRAKE. He *m.* 1843, Emily Letitia, dau. of Thomas Henry Watson, of Lumclone, co. Carlow, and by her (who *d.* 6 Jan. 1893) had issue,
    1. JOSEPH EDWARD, now of Stokestown.
    2. Henry Thomas, late Lieut. 56th Regt., *b.* 21 June, 1848.
    3. John Handfield, *b.* 5 March, 1852 ; *d. unm.* 2 May, 1897.
    4. Cosby Francis, *b.* 28 Oct. 1854.
    1. Annette Georgina, *b.* 3 June, 1844.
    2. Sarah Cecilia, *b.* 10 Oct. 1849 ; *m.* 10 Jan. 1872, Lieut.-Col. William Price Llewellyn Lewes, late 51st Regt., of Llysnewydd, co. Carmarthen.

Mr. Deane Drake *d.* 20 Dec. 1855.

Drew. THE LANDED GENTRY. 194

Arms—Quarterly; 1st and 4th, sa., a fess wavy arg. between two stars of six points or, for DRAKE; 2nd and 3rd, arg., on a chevron gu. between three Cornish choughs ppr., three crosses pattée of the field, for DEANE. Crests—1st, DRAKE: A dexter arm embowed in armour, the hand grasping a pole-axe all ppr. 2nd, DEANE: A tortoise displayed ppr. Motto—Sic parvis magna.
Seat—Stokestown, New Ross, co. Wexford.

DREW OF DREWSCOURT.

CLENNELL FRANK MASSY DREW, of Drewscourt, Charleville, co. Cork, J.P. co. Limerick, High Sheriff 1903, b. 27 Jan. 1877; m. 12 June, 1907, Gladys, younger dau. of late Major H. C. Wilkinson, 82nd Regt., and has issue,

ANTHONY FRANCIS CLENNELL, b. 27 May, 1911.

Lineage.—FRANCIS DREW, of Kilwinny, co. Waterford, and of Meanus, co. Kerry, went to Ireland, a Capt. in the Army of Queen ELIZABETH, 1598. He m. 1st, a dau. of Capt. Hart, of co. Limerick, and had with other issue, JOHN, of Kilwinny and Meanus, of whom there are numerous descendants; and 2ndly, Susanna, dau. of Leonard Knoyle, of Ballygaly, co. Waterford, and by the latter (who m. 2ndly, Col. J. Johnson) had, with other issue, a son, BARRY. The eldest son of the 2nd marriage,
BARRY DREW, of Ballyduff, co. Waterford, and of Drew's Court, co. Limerick, receiver to the estates of the Earl of Cork and Burlington, emp. JAMES II, m. 1st, a dau. of Sir Francis Foulkes, Knt. of Camphire, but by her had no issue; and 2ndly, Ruth, dau. of William Nettles, of Touraine, co. Waterford, by Mary his wife, sister of the celebrated Valentine Greatrakes, and had two sons,
1. FRANCIS, his heir.
2. John, of Ballyduff House, co. Waterford (see DREW of Mocollop).

The elder son,
FRANCIS DREW, of Drew's Court, co. Limerick, High Sheriff 1718, m. Margaret, 2nd dau. and co-heir (by Avarina his wife, dau. and co-heir of Capt. Gilbert Purdon, of Ballycahill, co. Tipperary) of John Ringrose, of Moynoe House, co. Clare, and had issue,
1. FRANCIS, of Drew's Court, d.s.p. 1759; m. April, 1757, Susanna, dau. of Richard Bourke, of Drumsallagh, co. Limerick.
2. JOHN, successor to his brother, d.s.p.
3. Bally, of Drew's Court, m. Mary, dau. of Odell Conyers, of Castletown Conyers, co. Limerick, and had one son and one dau., FRANCIS, of Drew's Court, m. Sarah, dau. and co-heir of Lloyd Langford, of co. Kerry, and d.s p.
MARGARET, of Drew's Court, heiress to her brother, m. John Cuffe Kelly, who d.s.p. She d. 15 March, 1845.
4. RINGROSE, of whom presently.
5. George Purdon, of Hyde Park, co. Dublin, one of the six Clerks in Chancery 1757; m. Letitia, sister of Sir William Godfrey, Bart., of Bushfield, co. Kerry, and d. 1785, aged 45, leaving issue,
  1. John Godfrey, Lieut.-Col. in the Army.
  2. George Purdon, Major 45th Regt.
  3. Barry, Capt. 45th Regt.   4. Francis, Capt. 45th Regt.
1. Alice, m. Charles O'Neill, M.P. for Cloghnakilty.
2. Jane, m. 1775, Rev. Robert Nettles.
3. Ruth, m. Joseph Hall, of Dublin.
4. Margaret, m. — Nash, of Brinny, co. Cork.

The 4th son,
RINGROSE DREW, of Skally, Coolrea, and of Drewsboro', m. 1st, Elizabeth, dau. of John Benn, of Rahine, co. Limerick, and had a son, Ringrose; 2ndly, 6 Oct. 1750, his cousin, Jane, only dau. of James Molony, of Kiltanon, co. Clare, and had issue, a son and heir,
FRANCIS DREW, of Drewsboro', High Sheriff co. Clare 1788, m. 1782, Frances, dau. of John Odell, of Bealduroghy, co. Limerick, and has issue two sons, RINGROSE, his heir; Francis, d.s.p.; and two daus., of whom one m. — Hulcatt; the other, Hugh Brady, of Raheen, co. Clare. The elder son,
RINGROSE DREW, of Drewsboro', m. Alicia, dau. of John Willington, of Killoskeane, co. Tipperary, and d. 1 Feb. 1835, leaving issue,
1. FRANCIS, of Drew's Court.
  1. Frances, m. John Tully, R.N.
  2. Alicia Willington, m. 23 July, 1836, Rev. Robert William Nesbit, M.A., and is dec.
  3. Eliza, m. Kivas Tully.

The only son,
FRANCIS DREW, of Drewscourt, b. 21 Oct. 1812; m. 17 July, 1833, Hon. Margaret Everina Massy, dau of Hugh, 3rd Lord Massy, and had issue,
1. FRANCIS MASSY, late of Drew's Court.
2. Ringrose, m. 8 Jan. 1881, Anna Alicia Susanna, dau. of William Ryan, of Ballymackeough, co. Tipperary (see that family), and d. 23 Dec. 1895, leaving issue,
  1. Francis William Massy.   2. Ringrose Charles Willington.
  1. Alicia Jeannette.   2. Anna Everina Margaret.
1. Margaret Everina, m. 7 Dec. 1872, Charles Convers, of Castletown, Conyers, co. Limerick.
2. Alicia.

He d. 17 June, 1875. The elder son,
COL. FRANCIS MASSY DREW, of Drewscourt, co. Limerick, Col. late 7th Hussars, Assistant-Inspector of Remounts, J.P. co. Limerick, b. 17 March, 1838; m. 2 June, 1874, Mary Anne, elder dau. of the late Anthony Wilkinson, of Coxhoe Hall, co. Durham, and d. 15 Oct. 1895, having by her (who d. Feb. 1877) had issue,
CLENNELL FRANK MASSY, now of Drewscourt.
Everina Mary Massy, b. 28 Sept. 1875; m. 6 Aug. 1897, Major Beresford Johnstone, Indian Army; d. 7 April, 1904.

Arms—Erm., a lion passant gu. Motto—Drogo nomen et vitus arma dedit.
Seat—Drewscourt, Charleville.

DREW OF MOCOLLOP.

HENRY WILLIAM DREW, of Mocollop Castle, co. Waterford, J.P., b, 14 March, 1848; m. 15 April, 1873, Cherry Geraldine, only dau. of Bolton S. Honeylorne, and has issue,
1. HENRY WILLIAM, b. 26 Jan. 1874.
2. Francis Charles, b. 1 April, 1875.
3. Cecil Bolton, b. 12 Sept. 1879.
4. Desmond, b. 16 Aug. 1886.
1. Kathleen Maud.   2. Violet Mary.

Lineage.—JOHN DREW, of Ballyduff House, co. Waterford, younger son of Barry Drew, of Drew's Court (see that family), m. 8 Jan. 1713, his cousin, Margaret, dau. and heiress of Francis Drew, of Kilwinny and Meanus, and by her had issue. The eldest son and heir,
FRANCIS DREW, M.D., of Meanus, Listry, and Rockfield, co. Kerry, and Ballyduff House, Waterpark, and Mocollop Castle, co. Waterford, m. 1752, Arabella, dau. and co-heiress of Col. William Godfrey, of Bushfield (now Kilcoleman Abbey), co. Kerry, by Elizabeth his wife, dau. and co-heir of the Rev. Richard Downing, of Knockgrafton, co. Tipperary. By her Dr. Drew had issue,
1. JOHN, of Listry and Rockfield, co. Kerry, and of Frogmore, near Youghal, co. Cork, m. 1786, Alicia, eldest dau. of Pierce Power, of Affane, co. Waterford, and d. 14 Dec. 1813, leaving by her (who d. 6 Dec. 1842) issue,
  1. Francis, of Meanus, co. Kerry, and Frogmore, near Youghal, m. Jane, dau. of Thomas Garde, of Ballindinis, co. Cork, and d. Dec. 1839, having had issue,
    (1) Francis.   (2) John.
    (1) Elizabeth.   (2) Deborah, dec.
    (3) Rebecca.   (4) Louisa.
  2. John, of Rockfield, co. Kerry, m. Helen, eldest dau. of John Elmore, and had,
    (1) John, dec.   (2) John Henry.
    (1) Helena.   (2) Alicia.
    (3) Catherine, m. Adam Newman Perry, of the City of Cork.
  3. Samuel Browning (Rev.), m. 1st, Mary, dau. of Col. Foot, of Millfort, co. Cork; and 2ndly, Anne, dau. of Richard Townsend Herbert, of Cahirnane, co. Kerry, and by the former had Browning, an Officer in the 14th Regt. of Foot, and Mary.
  4. Pierce William (Rev.), B.A., of Knockaverry Villa, The Strand, Youghal, co. Cork, Rector of Youghal, b. 13 March, 1799; m. 15 Sept. 1821, Eliazbeth, only dau. and heir of Thomas Oliver, of Wellington Place, Cork, and had issue,
    (1) PIERCE WILLIAM.   (2) Thomas.
    (1) Matilda Rowena, m. the Rev. David Henry Elrington, Vicar of Swords, co. Dublin (dec.).
    (2) Elizabeth Mona Brougham, m. 1st, the Rev. Henry Bickerstaff (dec.), 2ndly, Charles Brent.
    (3) Elizabeth Oliver, m. Rev. Henry Alexander.
    (4) Catherine Henrietta (twin with Elizabeth Oliver), m. David H. Lambert, of Mersey Villa, Rockferry, Cheshire.
    (5) Alice le Poer.
    (6) Christina Rebecca Pomeroy, m. 28 April, 1866, William Thomas, 3rd son of Standish Henry Harrison, of Castle Harrison, co. Cork, and had issue (see that family).
    (7) Agnes Margaret Naylor, m. 15 Aug. 1861, Edward Henry Meredyth. He d.s.p.m.s. 8 Oct. 1904.
  1. Arabella, m. Walter Atkin, of Atkinville, co. Cork.
  2. Elizabeth, d. unm.   3. Catherine, d. an infant.
  4. Alicia, m. Henry Lindsay, of Hayfield, co. Cork.
2. FRANCIS, of whom presently.
3. Barry, of Flower Hill, co. Waterford, m. Julia, dau. of Rev. James Hewson, and had a son, Barry, who m. Jane, dau. of Arthur Baker, of Balhery, co. Dublin.
4. William, d. unm.   5. Pascal Paoli, M.D.
1. Arabella, m. 1784, Peard Harrison-Peard, of Carrigeen, co. Cork.
2. Margaret, m. Edward Heard, of Ballintober, co. Cork, Major in the Army.
3. Deborah, m. Rev. Pierce Power, of Affane, co. Waterford, and d. 25 Feb. 1844.

Dr. Drew d. 3 Sept. 1787, aged 79. His 2nd son,
FRANCIS DREW, of Mocollop Castle, Lismore, co. Waterford, b. 1756, and m. Amy, dau. of Higatt Boyd, of Rosslare, co. Wexford and Amy Phillips his wife, and by her had issue,

1. Francis, of Mocollop, *d.* Sept. 1840; *m.* Anna Maria, dau. of T. Ross, and widow of T. Evans, and had issue, a son and a dau., Francis, an Officer in the Scots Greys, *d. unm.* 1839.
Olivia Maria, of Mocollop, *m.* 1st, 2 March, 1841, James Barry, of Ballyclough, co. York, who *d.s.p.* 30 April, 1881. She *m.* 2ndly, 1883, Lieut.-Col. George Edward Hillier, C.B., and *d.s.p.* 1884.
2. Tankerville, *m.* Jane, dau. of John Elmore, and left issue, Francis and Helen.
3. John, *d.s.p.*   4. Samuel, *d.s.p.*
5. James, *d.s.p.*   6. HENRY, of whom presently.
1. Lucinda, *m.* R. G. Campion, and had issue.
2. Emelia, *d. unm.*   3. Arabella, *d. unm.*
The youngest son,
HENRY DREW, of Wynberg, South Africa, *b.* 1810; *m.* 1841, Gertrude, dau. of — Allertyn, and widow of — Williams, and *d.* 1860, having by her (who *d.* 1875) had issue,
HENRY WILLIAM, now of Mocollop.
Elizabeth Anna Maria, *m.* 1866, the late Baron George von Ludwig, and has four daus.

Arms—*See* DREW *of Drewscourt.*
Seat—Mocollop Castle, Ballyduff, S.O., co. Waterford.

DRING OF TOWER HILL AND ROCKGROVE.

Lineage.—SIMON DRING, of Cork, whose will is dated 3 March, 1719-20, and proved 27 Oct. 1721; *m.* Temperance, dau. of William Morris, of Castle Selem, and by her had issue. The only son and heir,
ROBERT DRING, of Cork, *m.* 1718, Jane, eldest dau. of John Lapp, of Bandon, and was father of
SIMON DRING, of Cork, *d.* 1782; *m.* July, 1746, Mary, dau. of James Lombard, of Lombardstown, co. Cork, by Mary Uniacke his wife, and had issue,
1. Robert (Rev.), *m.* Eleanor, dau. of Robert Uniacke-Fitzgerald, of Corkbeg, co. Cork (*see that family*), by his 2nd wife, Frances, dau. of John Judkin, of Greenhills, co. Tipperary, and had issue,
1. Robert, *d.s.p.*
1. Frances Dorothea, *m.* 1803, Adam Newman, of Dromore, co. Cork, and had issue (*see* NEWMAN *of Newberry*).
2. Mary, *m.* Rev. J. Jervois, of Bandon, co. Cork, and had issue.
3. Clotilda Elizabeth, *m.* 2 Sept. 1806, Savage French, of Cuskinny, co. Cork, and had issue (*see that family*).
4. Eleanor, *m.* Thomas O'Grady, brother of the 1st Viscount Guillamore, and had issue (*see* O'GRADY *of Landscape*).
2. SIMON, of Rockgrove, of whom next.
1. Elizabeth Uniacke, *m.* Feb. 1774, James Uniacke, of Castletown, co. Cork, and had issue (*see* UNIACKE *of Castletown*).
2. Mary Anne Uniacke, *d.s.p.*
His 2nd son,
SIMON DRING, of Rockgrove, *m.* 6 July, 1786, Mary, dau. of Norman Uniacke, of Castletown, by Alicia, his wife, dau. of Bartholomew Purdon, Esq., of Garrane, and by her (who *d.* 2 Nov. 1820) had issue,
1. SIMON, his heir.
1. Catherine, *m.* Francis Savage, of Ballymodan.
2. Alicia, *m.* James Uniacke, of Glengarra.
Mr. Dring *d.* 23 April, 1811, and was *s.* by his son,
SIMON DRING, of Rockgrove, High Sheriff co. Cork 1827, *m.* 1st, Anne, dau. of Robert Courtney, of Bally Edmond, co. Cork, by whom he had no child; and 2ndly, 27 Nov. 1813, Clementina, dau. of Robert Harding, of Cork, by whom he had issue,
1. SIMON, his heir.
2. Robert Harding, *d.* 7 Feb. 1908; *m.* Catherine Georgina (*d.* 31 Jan. 1908), dau. of Francis Savage, of Ballymodan, co. Meath, and had issue, two sons and one dau. The younger but only surviving son,
SIMON, *s.* his cousin, 1889.
3. James, *d.* young.   4. William Henry, *d. unm.* 1886.
1. Clementina, *m.* M. C. Hendley, of Mount Rivers, Fermoy, and *d.* July, 1867, leaving issue, one son and six daus.
2. Mary Uniacke, *d. unm.* 1901.   3. Katherine, deceased.
4. Emily, deceased.
5. Elizabeth, *m.* 1850, Rev. Joseph Stopford, of Ferney, near Cork, who *d.* 9 June, 1801, leaving issue,
Mr. Dring *d.* 13 Dec. 1833, and was *s.* by his eldest son,
SIMON DRING, of Rockgrove, J.P., High Sheriff 1862, *b.* 22 Jan. 1818; *m.* 10 April, 1855, Henrietta (who *d.* 7 Oct. 1911), dau. of Joseph Gubbins, of Kilfrush, and *d.* 1879, leaving issue,
1. SIMON CROFTON, his heir.
2. HENRY STAMER, *s.* his brother.
1. Maria Josephine, *d.* young, 3 April, 1863.
The elder son,
SIMON CROFTON DRING, of Rockgrove, *b.* 18 Nov. 1860; *d.* 1886, and was *s.* by his brother,
HENRY STAMER DRING, of Rockgrove, co. Cork, *b.* 18 July, 1866; *d. unm.* 1889, and was *s.* by his 1st cousin, SIMON, late of Tower Hill.
SIMON DRING, of Tower Hill and Rockgrove, co. Cork, J.P., *b.* 20 March, 1854; *m.* 29 April, 1893, Mary Louise (*Tower Hill, Glanmire*), eldest dau. of John Finch, of Tullamore Park, co. Tipperary (*see that family*), and *d.* 13 Jan. 1900, having had issue,
1. SIMON HARDING, of Tower Hill, *b.* 7 March, 1894.
2. Robert Harding, *b.* 30 June, 1896.
1. Lena Mary.

Seat—Tower Hill, Glanmire and Rockgrove, both co. Cork.

DROUGHT OF LETTYBROOK.

THOMAS ARMSTRONG DROUGHT, of Lettybrook, King's Co., J.P. and D.L., High Sheriff 1889, late Capt. 28th Regt., *b.* 30 June, 1857; *s.* his father 1876; *m.* 6 Nov. 1884, Mary Letitia, dau. of Lieut.-Col. Edward Osborne Broadley, 32nd L.I., and has issue,
1. JOHN VICTOR, B.A. Oxford, Lieut. 124th Baluchistan Inf., Indian Army, *b.* 9 Jan. 1887.
2. Francis Gerald, *b.* 8 May, 1888.
3. Thomas David Broadley, *b.* 15 Nov. 1900.
1. Doris Marjorie.

Lineage.—About the year 1600, a rather numerous family of the name of Drought were settled in the co. Carlow, from which they spread into the co. Kildare, and the Queen's and King's Counties.
RICHARD DROUGHT, who settled at Cappogolan, King's Co., *m.* a dau. of John Baldwin, and had issue,
1. JOHN.   2. Arthur.
3. Richard.   4. Robert.
5. Thomas.
The eldest son,
JOHN DROUGHT, of Cappogolan, *m.* Mary, dau. of Euseby Beasly, and had issue. The eldest son,
JOHN DROUGHT, of The Heath, King's Co., *m.* Alice (*d.* 7 Jan 1778), dau. of Nathaniel Low, of Lowville, co. Galway, and had,
1. THOMAS, of whom presently.
2. John, of Whigsboro' (*see* DROUGHT *of Whigsboro'*).
3. Euseby, of Lettybrook, *m.* Dorothy Elliot, and had two sons and two daus.
4. William Beasley, Capt. 2nd Dragoons.
The eldest son,
THOMAS DROUGHT, of the Heath, otherwise Droughtville, *m.* 2 April, 1752, Caroline, dau. of Warneford Armstrong, of Clara, King's Co., and had, with three daus., Alice, Caroline, and Mary, two sons,
1. Thomas, of Droughtville, *b.* 1758; *m.* Frances Maria, dau. of Col. the Hon. Thomas Wallon, President of the Council of Jamaica, and had issue,
1. John, *b.* Nov. 1780.   2. James.
1. Jane, *m.* Capt. Henry Pigot.
2. Eliza, *m.* William Hawkins, eldest son of the Bishop of Raphoe.
2. JOHN ARMSTRONG, of whom presently.
The younger son,
JOHN ARMSTRONG DROUGHT, of Lettybrook, *b.* about 1762; *m.* 1784, Letitia, dau. of John Head, of Ashley Park, co. Tipperary, by Phœbe, his wife, sister of John, 1st Earl of Norbury, and had issue,
1. JOHN HEAD, of Lettybrook.
2. Michael Head, of Harristown, Queen's Co., Barrister-at-Law, *m.* Anna, dau. of William Hutchinson, of Timoney Hall, co. Tipperary, and *d.s.p.* Nov. 1850.
3. Thomas Armstrong, Gen. in the Army, Col. of the 15th Regt., *m.* 1847, Mary Isabel, dau. of Frederick Lock, son of Vice-Admiral Lock, and by her (who *d.* 28 Nov. 1906) had a son and five daus.,
1. John Armstrong Head, *m.* 1883, Annie Gertrude Turner.
1. Mary, *m.* C. Bischoff; *d.* 1883.
2. Letitia, *m.* J. Maunsell Reeves.
3. Kate, *m.* C. Waugh Tanqueray.   4. Emily.
5. Alice, *m.* 1884, C. Thorne, of Castle, co. Somerset.
1. Phœbe, *m.* Major-Gen. Barry.
2. Caroline, *m.* Richard Milett, of Kyle, co. Tipperary.
3. Letitia, *m.* James B. Elliott, of South Lodge, co. Tipperary, and *d.* 1839.
4. Maria Catherine, *d.* Nov. 1853.
5. Eliza Barbara, *d.* young.
Mr. Drought *d.* April, 1839. The eldest son,
JOHN HEAD DROUGHT, of Lettybrook, Lieut.-Col. in the Army, *b.* 20 Aug. 1790, J.P. and D.L., High Sheriff 1821, formerly in the 13th Light Dragoons; served in the Peninsula to the end of the war, at Waterloo, and at the capture of Paris, *m.* 20 July, 1853, Frances Jane, dau. of Henry Spunner, of Corolanty, and by her (who *d.* Nov. 1874) had issue,
1. THOMAS ARMSTRONG, now of Lettybrook.
2. John Head, *b.* 3 July, 1860.
1. Elizabeth Alice.
2. Letitia, *m.* 5 Jan. 1884, Francis Fletcher Barker, and has issue.
Col. Drought *d.* 29 April, 1876.

Arms—Or, a chevron vert between three wolves' heads erased gu. **Crest**—A rainbow issuant from clouds ppr. **Motto**—Semper sitiens.

Seat—Lettybrook, Kinnitty, King's Co.

DROUGHT OF WHIGSBORO'.

THOMAS HENRY DROUGHT, of Whigsboro', King's Co., J.P., b. 1855; m. 1888, Madeline Kyra, eldest dau. of Capt. E. C. McMurdo, late 79th Highlanders, and has issue,

1. ALEXANDER CHARLES, b. 8 Aug. 1899.
2. GEORGE EDWARD, b. 15 May, 1910.
3. Madeline Mary, b. 13 Aug. 1889.
4. Helen Iris, b. 24 April, 1891; d. 7 June, 1897.
5. Violet Caroline, b. 12 Oct. 1897.

Lineage.—JOHN DROUGHT, of Whigsboro', b. 1725, 2nd son of John Drought, of the Heath, by Alice Low his wife (*see* DROUGHT *of Lettybrook*); *m.* 1747 Susanna (Mrs. Clarke), dau. of Adam Mitchell, of Ratheibbon, King's Co., and had an only son,

JOHN DROUGHT, of Whigsboro', b. 1751; *m.* 27 May, 1772, Isabella, dau. and co-heir of George Meares, of Dublin, and by her (who d. 1805) left at his decease, 1814,

1. JOHN THOMAS, his heir.
2. George Meares John, of Glencarrig (*see* DROUGHT *of Glencarrig*).
3. Francis.
1. Isabella, *m.* June, 1794, Robert James Enraght-Moony, of the Doon (*see that family*).
2. Susan, *m.* Robert Lawder, of Moyclare.
3. Elizabeth, *m.* Henry Spunner, of Corolanty.

The eldest son,

JOHN THOMAS DROUGHT, of Whigsboro', b. 4 April, 1782; *m.* Oct. 1805, Anne Carleton, sister of Col. Alexander Perceval, of Temple House, co. Sligo, and by her (who d. 5 May, 1841) had issue,

1. JOHN ALEXANDER, his heir.
2. Philip Francis, *m.* Miss Graves, of Limerick.
3. George Perceval, H.M. 62nd Regt., *m.* Miss Rathborne.
4. Francis Perceval, H.M. 53rd Regt.
5. Isabella Meares, *m.* Major L'Estrange.

Mr. Drought d. 30 Nov. 1851, and was s. by his son,

JOHN ALEXANDER DROUGHT, of Whigsboro', b. 19 Jan. 1808. Capt. King's Co. Militia, formerly Capt. in the Army; *m.* 16 Jan 1836, Caroline Susanna, dau. of Lieut.-Col. John White, of the 18th Regt., and d. 1859, leaving issue,

1. JOHN WILLIAM, of Whigsboro'.
2. THOMAS HENRY, s. his brother.
1. Caroline Jane Isabella, dec.
2. Annie Perceval, *m.* 1st, the late — Jones, and 2ndly, 14 Oct. 1879, Sir William John Menzies, of Edinburgh, who d. 14 Oct. 1905.
3. Alice Elizabeth, *m.* Major Locke, late 15th Regt.
4. Mary Frances, *m.* Deputy Surg.-Gen. Andrew Acres Stoney, late Scots Greys.
5. Georgiana Letitia, *m.* Col. W. Rogerson, late 53rd Shropshire L.I.
6. Charlotte Sarah Carr.
7. Heloïse Wilhelmina.

The elder son,

JOHN WILLIAM DROUGHT, of Whigsboro', J.P., formerly Capt. King's Co. Militia, b. 25 Sept. 1847; d. 1887, and was s. by his brother.

Arms, &c.—*See* DROUGHT *of Lettybrook*.

Seat—Whigsboro', Birr.

DROUGHT OF GLENCARRIG.

MAJOR JOHN THOMAS ACTON DROUGHT, of Glencarrig, co. Wicklow, Major (ret.), 4th Regt., b. 6 May, 1849; s. his brother 5 Nov. 1906.

Lineage.—GEORGE MEARES JOHN DROUGHT, of Glencarrig, J.P., 2nd son of John Drought, of Whigsboro' (*see that family*), by Isabella, dau. of George Meares, of Mearscourt, his wife, inherited the property of his grand-uncle, Major Fairbrother, *m.* Jane, dau. of Thomas Acton, of West Aston, co. Wicklow, and had (with six daus., who all d. unm.) three sons,

1. JOHN, of Glencarrig.
2. Thomas Acton (Rev.), Vicar of Clonoulty, co. Tipperary, and Canon of Cashel, *m.* 1845, Elizabeth Dorcas (d. 1852), dau. of Richard Reynell, of Killynon (*see that family*), and d. 13 Dec. 1892, leaving issue,
  1. George Meares (Rev.), Incumbent of St. Matthew's, Newtown, Mt. Kennedy, Canon of Ch. Ch. Cathedral 1905, b. 1846; *m.* 8 Feb. 1877, Beatrice, dau. of James Scott Robertson, C.B. She d. 25 Jan. 1893. He d. 30 June, 1909, leaving issue,
    George Thomas Acton, Capt. R.F.A., b. 2 Aug. 1880; *m.* 22 Sept. 1909, Louise Lockhart, elder dau. of Capt. Donald Fowler, late Argyll and Sutherland Highlanders, and has issue,
    George Richard Smerger, b. 4 Aug. 1910.
    Helen Elizabeth.
  1. Elizabeth Dorcas.
  2. Jane Harriett.
3. George Warburton, of Cargins, Roscommon, J.P., late Capt. 51st Light Infantry, b. 1823; *m.* 9 April, 1861, Anna Sophia, dau. of Rev. Thomas Acton, and d. 1880. His widow d. 3 Sept. 1911.
1. Caroline, d. unm.

Mr. Drought d. 4 March, 1844, and was s. by his eldest son,

REV. JOHN WILLIAM FAIRBROTHER DROUGHT, of Glencarrig, co. Wicklow, A.B. Trin. Coll. Dublin, b. 20 Sept. 1809; *m.* 1st, 28 May, 1837, Anna Maria, dau. of Richard Reynell, of Killynon, co. Westmeath, and by her (who d. 28 May, 1867) had issue,

1. George William Fairbrother, Capt. King's Co. Militia, b. 29 March, 1838; d. unm. 11 Feb. 1868.
2. RICHARD REYNELL, late of Glencarrig.
3. JOHN THOMAS ACTON, Major, now of Glencarrig.
1. Eliza Harriette, b. 21 March, 1845; d. unm. 5 March, 1874.

He *m.* 2ndly, 10 Nov. 1869, Caroline, dau. of the Rev. Theobald Butler, of Drom, co. Tipperary. He d. 23 Feb. 1891. She d. 9 May, 1899. The 2nd son,

RICHARD REYNELL DROUGHT, of Glencarrig, co. Wicklow, J.P., D.L., High Sheriff 1901, C.C. (co-opted), late Capt. Westmeath and Wicklow Militias, formerly Lieut. King's Own Yorkshire Light Infantry, b. 2 July, 1840; *m.* 26 June, 1869, Isabella Euphemia Anne, only child of the late Col. John James Nugent, D.L., of Clonlost, and d. 15 Nov. 1906, having had issue,

Kathleen, b. 1 Sept. and d. 4 Sept. 1886.

He was s. by his brother.

Arms, Crest, and Motto—As DROUGHT *of Lettybrook*.

Seat—Glencarrig and Ballinacoola, Glenealy, co. Wicklow.

DUCKETT OF DUCKETT'S GROVE.

The late WILLIAM DUCKETT, of Duckett's Grove, co. Carlow, and Newtown, co. Kildare, J.P. and D.L. co. Carlow, and J.P. co. Kildare, High Sheriff for co. Carlow 1854, and for the Queen's Co. 1881, b. 14 April, 1822; *m.* 1st, 16 Jan. 1868, Anna Maria, 3rd dau. of the late Thomas Harrison Morony, J.P., of Milltown House, Miltown Malbay, co. Clare. She d.s.p. 12 May, 1894. He *m.* 2ndly, 19 Nov. 1895, Marie Georgina (*now of Duckett's Grove and Newtown*), eldest dau. of the late Capt. Robert Gordon Cumming, 56th Regt. (who was present at Moodkee, Feroyestah, and Sobraon, and served in the Crimea), and widow of Theophilus Thompson, J.P., of Ford Lodge, co. Cavan. He d. 22 June, 1908.

Lineage of DUCKETT *see* EUSTACE-DUCKETT.

Seats—Duckett's Grove, Palatine, co. Carlow; and Newtown, co. Kildare. *Residence*—De Wyndesore, Raglan Road, Dublin; 46, Merrion Square, Dublin. *Clubs*—Conservative, S.W.; Kildare Street, Dublin; and Royal St. George Yacht, Kingstown.

EUSTACE-DUCKETT OF CASTLEMORE.

COL. JOHN JAMES HARDY ROWLAND EUSTACE-DUCKETT, of Castlemore and Hardymount, co. Carlow, J.P. and High Sheriff 1895, Col. 8th Batt. King's Royal Rifle Corps, b. 19 Sept. 1859; s. his father 1895; *m.* 5 Sept. 1895, Gertrude Amelia, dau. of Algernon Charles Heber Percy, of Hodnet Hall, Salop, and Airmyn Hall, Yorks (*see that family*), and has issue,

1. Hardy Rowland Algernon, b. 6 July, 1896; d. 19 July, 1897.
2. OLIVER HARDY, b. 29 April, 1899.
3. Rowland Hugh, b. 8 Oct. 1902.
1. Elisabeth Gertrude.
2. Doris Anna.
3. Diana, b. March, 1905.

Col. J. J. H. R. Eustace-Duckett, under will of William Duckett, dated 29 Feb. 1904, of Duckett's Grove, co. Carlow, who d. on 22 June, 1908, assumed the additional surname and arms of DUCKETT by Royal Licence dated 26 March, 1909.

Lineage.—OLIVER EUSTACE, M.P. for Carlow, *temp.* CHARLES I, 1639, settled his estate in co. Carlow (by deed 1639) on his grandson, Francis Eustace, living 1675 (son of ROWLAND EUSTACE). This Francis was father of

OLIVER EUSTACE, who *m.* (articles dated 9 Feb. 1682) Elinor, dau. of Robert Nugent, of Donore, co. Westmeath, and their son,
EDWARD EUSTACE, of Castlemore, *m.* (settlement dated 16 Feb. 1712) Bridget, dau. of Robert Longfield, of Kilbride, and had,
 1. JAMES, his heir.
 2. Robert, Col., who *m.* Feb. 1754, Catherine Whelan, and was ancestor of EUSTACE *of Newstown (see that family)*.
 3. William, *m.* Alethea, dau. of Robert Meredyth, of Greenhills, and had five daus., the youngest of whom,
   Grace Anne, *m.* Rev. Edward Martin, a Prebendary of St. Patrick's Cathedral, by whom (who *d.* 1839) she had issue.
 4. Thomas.
 1. Maria, *m.* Nathaniel Evans. 2. Anne, *m.* Jacob Warren.
 3. Bridget, Mrs. M'Carthy.
The eldest son and successor,
JAMES EUSTACE, of Castlemore, *m.* 1743, Elizabeth, only child and heir of John Hardy, of Kilballyhue, co. Carlow, and *d.* 1746, having had issue,
 1. EDWARD, his successor.
 2. Hardy, of Kilballyhue, co. Carlow, Major 1st Regt. of Horse, *m.* 1st, 25 Jan. 1770, Kitty, dau. of Philip Bernard; and 2ndly, Oct. 1773, Susanna, dau. of Franks Bernard; and *d.* 22 Aug. 1820, having had by her (who survived till 1835) issue,
   1. Hardy, *d.s.p.* 2. Thomas, *d.* 9 June, 1819.
   3. JAMES HARDY, s. his cousin in the Castlemore estates.
   1. Frances, *m.* Oliver Moore; *d.* 13 Jan. 1836.
   2. Catherine, *m.* 1st, Francis Willet Hopkins; and 2ndly, Anthony Brabazon, of Mornington; *d.* 18 May, 1852.
   3. Elizabeth, *m.* 16 March, 1803, James Eustace, J.P., and *d.* April, 1861, leaving issue *(see EUSTACE of Newstown)*.
   4. Bridget Longfield, *m.* Edward Burton, and *d.* 6 Feb. 1864. He *d.* 19 Dec. 1853.
   5. Anne (twin with Bridget), *d. unm.* 1860.
   6. Susannah, *m.* 16 Aug. 1841, Major William Edmond Fitzgerald, 82nd Regt., and *d.* 5 Feb. 1864.
   1. Elizabeth, *m.* J. Vine, of Dublin.
The elder son and heir,
EDWARD EUSTACE, of Castlemore, *m.* 1765, Eleanor, dau. of Sir Richard Butler, Bart., of Ballintemple, co. Carlow, and by her had issue,
 1. JAMES, his heir.
 2. Richard, Capt. in the 16th Regt., *d.* in India *unm.*
 3. Nicholas, Lieut.-Geo. of the 12th Regt., *d. unm.* in India, 1815.
 1. Henrietta, *m.* Rev. John Digby, of Landenstown, co. Kildare.
 2. Eleanor, *m.* Rev. J. McGhee. 3. Dorothea.
 4. Catherine, *m.* Capt. William McPherson.
 5. Alicia, *d. unm.* 1850. 6. Melecina, *m.* Thomas Talbot.
He *d.* 18 Oct. 1808, and was *s.* by his son,
MAJOR JAMES EUSTACE, of Castlemore, J.P., Major of the Roscommon Militia, and High Sheriff co. Carlow 1813, *b.* 1767; *m.* 23 July, 1792, Margaret, dau. of J. Thewles, of Rookwood, co. Galway, and by her (who *d.* 5 May, 1841) had issue,
 1. Edward, *d. unm.* 23 Oct. 1820.
 2. Harriette, *d. unm.* 26 Dec. 1846.
He *d.* 9 April, 1848, and, leaving no surviving issue, was *s.* by his cousin,
JAMES HARDY EUSTACE, of Hardymount and Castlemore, co. Carlow, J.P., High Sheriff 1835, and formerly Capt. 8th Regt., with a medal and clasp for services, *b.* 1783; *m.* March, 1826, Elizabeth, only surviving child of Arthur Reed, of Carlow; *d.* 6 Feb. 1859, and was *s.* by his only son and heir,
HARDY EUSTACE, of Castlemore and Hardymount, co. Carlow, J.P., High Sheriff 1862, *b.* 23 Jan. 1827; *m.* 11 Sept. 1856, Anna, 2nd dau. of John Dawson Duckett, of Duckett's Grove *(see that family)*, and *d.* 22 Feb. 1895, having by her (who *d.* 26 Oct. 1892) had issue,
 1. JOHN JAMES HARDY ROWLAND, now of Castlemore.
 2. Joseph William Duckett Francis, *b.* 8 Feb. 1861; *d.* 5 Nov. 1861.
 3. Frederic Adolphus Dawson Oliver, Major 5th Dragoon Guards, *b.* 4 Aug. 1866.
 1. Johanna Frederica Eugenia Gundreda, *m.* 28 Nov. 1891, Lieut.-Col. Reginald Joseline Heber Percy, late Rifle Brigade, 2nd son of A. C. Heber Percy, of Hodnet, and Airmyn *(see that family)*.
 2. Alexandrina Sabina Sara Anna, *m.* 12 Jan. 1888, William Edward Grogan, of Slaney Park, co. Wicklow, and has issue.
 3. Grace Isabella Florence Josephine, *m.* 3 Feb. 1906, Philip David Scott-Moncrieff, eldest son of W. D. Scott-Moncrieff.

Lineage *of* DUCKETT *of Duckett's Grove.*—THOMAS DUCKETT, who first settled in Ireland, and purchased, 1695, Kneestown, and other estates in the co. of Carlow, from Thomas Crosthwaite, of Cockermouth, is stated by Sir William Betham, Ulster, to have been the son of JAMES DUCKETT, of Grayrigg, co. Westmorland, by his 3rd wife, Elizabeth, dau. of Christopher Walker, of Workington, Cumberland. James Duckett, of Grayrigg, was 10th in descent from JOHN DUCKETT, of Grayrigg, *temp.* RICHARD II. (1377), who obtained that estate by his marriage with Margaret, dau. and heir of William de Windesore, Lord of the Manor of Grayrigg, in Westmorland *(see* BURKE'S *Dormant and Extinct Peerage)*. John Duckett, of Grayrigg, was son of HUGH DUCKETT, of Fillingham, Lincolnshire, who was great-grandson of RICHARD DUCKETT, of Fillingham, *temp.* JOHN and HENRY III. This descent is elaborately given in a pedigree certified by Sir William Betham, Ulster King of Arms, 12 March, 1842. The first settler in Ireland,
THOMAS DUCKETT, of Kneestown, co. Carlow, *m.* Judith, dau. and heir of Pierce Power, of Killowen, co. Waterford, and left a son,
THOMAS DUCKETT, of Phillipstown, which he purchased from the Earl of Ormonde, *m.* 8 July, 1687, Jane, dau. of John Bunce, of Goosey, Berks. She *d.* 2 Aug. 1698, and was bur. at New Garden, co. Waterford. His will, dated 18 Jan. 1732, was proved 13 May, 1735. He left with other issue, a son,
JOHN DUCKETT, of Philipstown and Newton, co. Kildare, *m.* Jane, dau. of Thomas Devonsher, by Sarah his wife, sister of Abraham Morris, of Cork, and had issue. His will, dated 13 April, 1733, was proved 17 May, 1738. The 4th son,
JONAS DUCKETT, of Duckett's Grove, co. Carlow, whose will, dated 7 July, 1796, was proved 21 Dec. 1797, *b.* 17 May, 1720; *m.* Hannah, dau. of William Alloway, of Dublin, and *d.* 8 Oct. 1797, having by her (who *d.* 29 Feb. 1796) had issue,
 1. WILLIAM, his heir.
 2. John, *b.* 6 March, 1764; *m.* Sarah, dau. of Samuel Stephens, and *d.s.p.*
 3. Thomas, *b.* 31 Sept. 1765; *m.* Catherine, dau. of Arundel Madden, of Dublin, and had an only dau.,
   Hannah Thomasine, *m.* 1st, the Rev. Samuel Madden; and 2ndly, Edward MacDonnell, of New Hall, co. Clare.
 4. Jonas, of Bellevue, co. Kildare, *d.s.p.* 3 June, 1849.
 5. Frederick, *b.* 4 Dec. 1768; *d.s.p.*
 1. Mary Alloway, *m.* her cousin, Thomas Fuller, and had issue.
 2. Hannah, *m.* Thomas Boake, of Boake Field, co. Kildare, and had issue.
 3. Jane, *m.* James Hart, of Dublin.
The eldest son,
WILLIAM DUCKETT, of Duckett's Grove, *b.* 7 Nov. 1761; *m.* 10 Sept. 1790, Elizabeth, dau. and co-heir of John Dawson Coates, of Dawson Court, co. Dublin, Banker in Dublin, and had issue,
 1. JOHN DAWSON, his heir.
 2. William, late of Russellstown Park, co. Carlow, J.P., High Sheriff 1825, *b.* 3 Jan. 1796; *m.* 18 Jan. 1843, Harriet Isabella Anne, only dau. of the late Lieut.-Col. Charles Edward Gordon, R.A., son of Charles Edward Gordon, of Wardhouse and Kildrummie, co. Aberdeen, and *d.* 10 Jan. 1868, having by her (who *d.* 27 Nov. 1852) had issue,
   1. William Gordon, *b.* 19 Nov. 1845; *d.* Dec. 1857.
   2. Steuart James Charles, of Russellstown Park, co. Carlow, J.P. and D.L., High Sheriff 1873, formerly Lieut. 13th Hussars, *b.* 10 Oct. 1847; *m.* 2 Aug. 1871, Catherine Seaton, youngest dau. of the late Sir John Dick-Lauder, Bart., and has issue,
     John Steuart, *b.* 1 June, 1876.
     Amy Anne Charlotte, *m.* 6 Oct. 1909, Louis Murray Philpotts, D.S.O., Major R.F.A., 2nd son of Rev. H. J. and Mrs. Philpotts, Walkern Rectory, Stevenage, Herts., and has issue.
   3. Charles Edward Henry Duckett-Steuart, of Rutland Lodge, co. Carlow, J.P., High Sheriff 1879, Capt. 8th Batt. K.R.R. Corps, *b.* 14 March, 1853; assumed the additional surname and arms of STEUART by Royal Licence, 1894; *d.* 1904; *m.* 21 Aug. 1873, Annie, youngest dau. of the Hon. B. Seymour (Senator), of Port Hope, Ontario, Canada, and has issue,
     William Steuart, *b.* 27 June, 1874.
     Aileene Seymour, *b.* 1 July, 1877; *m.* C. H. Dickinson, 3rd son of Dean Dickinson, of The Chapel Royal, Dublin.
   1. Harriet Elinor Alston, *m.* 20 May, 1869, the late Charles S. Elliott, 20th Regt. (who *d.* 12 Sept. 1890), younger son of T. Elliott, of Johnstown House, co. Carlow.
   3. Joseph Fade, *b.* 14 Dec. 1796; *d.* 2 June, 1875.
   4. Thomas Jonas, *b.* 26 March, 1799; *d. unm.*
   1. Elizabeth, *d.* young.
   2. Elizabeth Dawson, *m.* 18 June, 1843, William Richard Steuart, of Stewart's Lodge, co. Carlow, High Sheriff 1820, and *d.* 4 March, 1893.
The eldest son,
JOHN DAWSON DUCKETT, of Duckett's Grove, co. Carlow, and Newtown, co. Kildare, High Sheriff 1819, *b.* 10 Aug. 1791; *m.* 16 March, 1819, Sarah Summers, dau. of William Hutchinson, of Timoney, co. Tipperary, and by her (who *d.* 14 Feb. 1879) had issue,
 1. WILLIAM, late of Duckett's Grove.
 2. John Dawson, *d.* young, 2 June, 1841.
 1. Eliza Dawson, *d. unm.* 1 Feb. 1839.
 2. Anne, *m.* 11 Sept. 1856, HARDY EUSTACE (*d.* 22 Feb. 1895), only child of the late James Hardy Eustace, of Castlemore and Hardymount, co. Carlow *(see that family above)*, and had issue, JOHN JAMES HARDY ROWLAND EUSTACE-DUCKETT, of Castlemore *(see above)*, *b.* 19 Sept. 1859; and Johanna Frederica Eugenia Gundreda; and *d.* 26 Oct. 1892.
 3. Sarah, *d.* 12 March, 1879.
 4. Victoria Henrietta Josephine, *m.* 10 Oct. 1863, Capt. Arthur Nassau Bolton, formerly 56th Regt. and 14th Hussars, who *d.* 4 Feb. 1867. She *d.* 3 Sept. 1880, leaving issue,
   1. Richard Arthur Lennox Massy, *b.* 21 July, 1866, Capt. 13th Hussars.
   1. Aida Georgina Grace Josephine, *m.* 2 Feb. 1888, Samuel Murray Power, son of Capt. John W. Power, and has issue.
   2. Francis Gertrude Wilhelmina Arthurena Nassau, *m.* 30 April, 1896, Major F. I. Evans, Derbyshire Regt., of Dungar Park, King's Co., who *d.* same year.
Mr. John Dawson Duckett *d.* 27 Sept. 1866, and was *s.* by his son WILLIAM, late of Duckett's Grove. This WILLIAM DUCKETT, of Duckett's Grove, co. Carlow, and Newtown, co. Kildare, J.P. and D.L., co. Carlow, and J.P. co. Kildare, High Sheriff for co. Carlow 1854, and for the Queen's Co. 1881, *b.* 14 April, 1822; *m.* 1st, 16 Jan. 1868, Anna Maria, 3rd dau. of the late Thomas Harrison Morony, J.P. of Milltown House, Milltown Malbay, co. Clare. She *d.s.p.* 12 May, 1894. He *m.* 2ndly, 19 Nov. 1895, Marie Georgina *(now of Duckett's Grove and Newtown)*, eldest dau. of the late Capt. Robert Gordon Cumming, 56th Regt. (who was present at Moodkee, Ferovestah, and Sobraon, and served in the Crimea), and widow of Theophilus Thompson, J.P., of Ford Lodge, co. Cavan. He *d.s.p.* 22 June, 1908, and by his will, dated 29 Feb. 1904, he directed that

his nephew Col. John James Hardy Rowland Eustace should assume the additional surname and arms of DUCKETT.
Arms—Quarterly, 1st and 4th, sa., a saltire arg. (DUCKETT); 2nd and 3rd, gu., a saltire or (EUSTACE). *Crests*—1. Out of a coronet or, a plume of five ostrich feathers arg. (DUCKETT). 2. A stag's head cabossed, between the attires a crucifix all ppr. (EUSTACE). *Mottoes*—Spectemur agendo ; Soli Deo gloria.
Seats—Castlemore and Hardymount, Tullow, co. Carlow. *Clubs*—Junior Carlton, S.W. ; Kildare Street, Dublin, and Royal St. George Yacht Club, Kingstown.

DUKE OF NEWPARK.

THE REV. ROGER PHILIP DUKE, of Newpark, co. Sligo, B.A. (1897), ordained 1900, b. 1874 ; s. his father 1896.
Lineage.—By a deed dated 14 April. 1662, the lands of Kincreevin, co. Sligo, were granted by Richard Coote, Baron of Collooney, on behalf of the Crown, to,
JOHN DUKE, who was one of the Cromwellian *tituladoes*. He d. before 1679, and was s. by his eldest son,
ROBERT DUKE, who d. after 1731, being s. by his eldest surviving son,
JOHN DUKE, who m. 1731, Hatton, dau. of George Taaffe. He d. after 1756, and was s. by his eldest son,
ROBERT DUKE, b. 1732 ; m. 1756, Lucinda, dau. of William Parke, of Dunsmore and Dunally, co. Sligo, and d. 1792, leaving, with other issue,
1. John, d. unm.
2. William (Rev.), of Kincreevin, Rector of Collooney, and afterwards of Sligo, b. 1762 ; m. 1st, 1797, Anne, dau. of George Jones, of Fortland, co. Sligo ; and 2ndly, 1807, Mary, dau. of Thomas Palmer, of Summer Hill, co. Mayo, and d. 1834, having had issue,
    1. William Webber, d.s.p.
    2. Another son, d. an infant.
    1. Lucinda, m. Rev. Samuel Simpson, and had issue.
    2. MARY, who s. her father ; m. 26 Feb. 1836, her cousin, Jemmett Duke, son of Robert King Duke, of Newpark, and had issue (*see below*).
3. Alexander, of Duke House, Leamington, Major 8th Regt., m. and d.s.p.
4. ROBERT KING, of whom presently.
The 4th son,
ROBERT KING DUKE, of Newpark, J.P. and Deputy-Governor of Sligo, built Newpark, b. 1770 ; m. 1797, Anne, dau. of Lieut.-Col. Roger Parke, of Dunally, co. Sligo, and had issue,
1. Robert, b. 1798 ; killed in the hunting field 1829, s.p.
2. ROGER, of whom presently.
3. John, b. 1800 ; m. Mira, dau. of John Irwin, of Camlin, co. Roscommon, and d.s.p. 1854.
4. Jemmett, b. 5 June, 1801 ; m. (as above) 26 Feb. 1836, Mary, dau. and eventual heiress of Rev. William Duke, of Kincreevin, and d. 3 Dec. 1880, leaving issue by her (who d. 30 June, 1879),
    1. Robert Alexander, of Kincreevin, J.P. and D.L., High Sheriff 1880, B.A., L.C.E., b. 23 Dec. 1836 ; m. 26 Aug. 1885, Katharine, dau. of Major Patrick Laurence Oliphant, of Kinneddar, co. Fife. He d. 22 March, 1910.
    2. Jemmett Charles, of Kilmorgan, co. Sligo, Lieut.-Col. late 16th and 17th Lancers, b. 3 July, 1841 ; m. Oct. 1886, Alice Neville, dau. of John Dalton, of Sleningford Park, co. York, and Fillingam Castle, co. Lincoln, and has issue,
        Muriel Mary Georgiana, b. 1887.
    1. Lucinda Jane, d. unm. 1881.
    2. Sophia Elizabeth, m. 1886, Rev. T. G. Walker.
5. Alexander, b. 1805 ; m. Catherine Tighe ; d. 1876, leaving issue,
    1. Alexander, F.R.C.P.
    2. John Charles, Lieut.-Col. late Staff and 33rd Regt.
    1. Louisa, m. Rev. E. St. A. Duke.
Mr. Robert King Duke d. 1836, and was s. by his eldest surviving son,
ROGER DUKE, of Newpark, Sandhurst Cadet 1812-5, served with the 91st Regt. ; m. 1st, 1825, Eliza, dau. of Laurence Oliphant, of Kinneddar, co. Fife, by whom he had issue,
1. ROBERT, late of Newpark.
2. LAURENCE PATRICK, of whom presently.
He m. 2ndly, 1833, Margaret, dau. of John Cuninghame, of Craigends, co. Renfrew, by whom he had further issue,
3. Roger, b. 1835 ; m. 1867, Mary Jessie, dau. of Major Maurice Cely-Trevilian, of Midelney Place, co. Somerset. She d. 4 Sept. 1903.
4. Charles Johnstone Parke, b. 1847.
1. Margaret Cuninghame, b. 1837 ; d. unm. 22 March, 1910.
2. Anne, b. 1838 ; m. 1878, Rev. James Samuel William Durham, D.D., Rector of Ladbroke, Warwickshire, only son of James Andrew Durham, of Elm Lodge, Hampton-on-Thames, Director of the London and County Bank. She d. 20 March, 1911, leaving issue, James Andrew Durham (*Club—Marlborough, S.W.*), m. 1903, Lady Agnes Elizabeth Andrey Townshend (*see* BURKE's *Peerage*, TOWNSHEND, M.), and Margaret, m. as his 2nd wife, 25 April, 1908, Cyril Duncombe FitzRoy (*see* BURKE's *Peerage*, GRAFTON, D.).
3. Alice Browne, b. 1840 ; d. unm. 1893.
Mr. Roger Duke d. 1866, and was s. by his eldest son,

ROBERT DUKE, of Newpark, b. 1826 ; m. 1868, Amelia Charlotte Cromartie (who d. 11 March, 1900). He d.s.p. 1871, and was s. by his brother,
LAURENCE PATRICK DUKE, of Newpark, co. Sligo, b. 1830 ; m. 1873, Frances Helena, d. Dec. 1910, dau. of Rev. Philip Homan, M.A. and Scholar, T.C.D., of Ballylanigan, co. Tipperary, and d. 7 Sept. 1896, having had issue,
1. ROGER PHILIP, now of Newpark.
2. Francis Robert, b. 1876.
Seat—Newpark, Ballymote.

DUNBAR-BULLER. *See* BULLER.

DUNDAS OF CLOBEMON HALL.

JANE ANNA MARIA, MRS. L. G. DUNDAS, of Clobemon Hall, co. Wexford, widow of Lawrence George Dundas, J.P., who d. 1897, leaving issue (*see below*), and only child and heiress of Thomas Grimston, M.D., of Ripon, Yorks, by Anna Maria his wife, dau. of Rev. Charles Fynes Clinton.
Lineage.—MAJOR LAURENCE DUNDAS, of the 13th and 26th Light Dragoons, m. Ellen, eldest dau. of Michael Green, of Greenmount, Middleton, co. Cork, which lady d. in 1832. Major Dundas d. 1 March, 1796, on board H.M.S. *Dictator*, off the coast of Malabar, on the passage to St. Domingo. He had issue, with three daus.,
1. Michael Henry, Lieut. 80th Foot, killed by savages in New Zealand.
2. LAURENCE, of whom presently.
3. Thomas, Commander, R.N., b. 1791 ; m. Margaret Christian, dau. of J. P. Johnston, M.D., Caithness Highlanders, and d. 1845, having by her (who d. 1832) had issue, with a dau. Florence Eliza, d. in infancy, two sons,
    1. George Laurence, b. 1827 ; d. 1845.
    2. James Brown Johnston, of Kirkcaldy, N.B., b. 1833 ; d. 24 Dec. 1910 ; m. 1854, Mary Susanna, 2nd dau. of S. W. Hardy, M.D., and has issue,
        (1) Thomas Laurence, b. 1858 ; m. and has issue.
        (1) Clarissa Eliza, b. 1855 ; m. 1879, W. G. Davy.
        (2) Mary Florence, b. 1857 ; d. an infant.
The 2nd son,
MAJOR LAURENCE DUNDAS, 5th Fusiliers, of Blackrock, co. Dublin, served in the Peninsular War as A.D.C. to the Duke of Wellington (medal and four clasps), b. 1787 ; m. Sept. 1812, Charlotte Maria, only child of George Slator, of Swiftbrooke, co. Dublin, and d. 1866, having by her (who d. 1871) had issue,
1. LAURENCE GEORGE, of whom presently.
2. George Charles (Rev.), Vicar of St. Matthew's, Nottingham, b. 10 May, 1814 ; m. 1842, Constance, youngest dau. of C. Stevenson, of Hennor House, Leominster, and d. 16 April, 1883, having by her (who d. 4 Jan. 1858) had issue,
    1. Henry Laurence, Col. formerly A.A.G. Gibraltar, late 15th East York Regt., b. 1 Aug. 1843 ; m. 4 Aug. 1875, Ida Constance, only dau. of Rev. T. Burrowes, of co. Longford. He d. Nov. 1908, having had issue,
        (1) Laurence Evelyn, b. 29 May, 1876.
        (1) Ivy Muriel, b. 10 Oct. 1878 ; m. 21 July, 1906, Right Hon. (Joseph) Austen Chamberlain, P.C., M.P. (9, *Egerton Place, S.W.*), and has issue.
        (2) Ida Marguerite, b. 15 Oct. 1883.
    2. Frederick George, Capt. R.N., b. June, 1845 ; m. Feb. 1866, Eliza (95, *Comeragh Road, West Kensington*), dau. of C. Beck, and d. 5 March, 1899, having had issue,
        (1) Frederick Charles, Capt. Argyll and Sutherland Highlanders, b. 16 Jan. 1868 ; m. 1905, Elizabeth Drummond, eldest dau. of James Thomson, of Glenpark, Midlothian.
        (2) Laurence Leopold, Commander R.N., b. April, 1874 ; m. 11 April, 1908, Lilias, widow of George Ozilvie, I.C.S.
        (3) Harold Victor, Lieut. R.N., b. 10 Feb. 1877 ; m. 9 April, 1898, Sybil Alexa, dau. of Leopold Kate, of Sydney, N.S.W., and has issue, Frederick Victor Leopold, b. 3 May, 1901.
    3. Charles Leslie (Ven.), M.A. Jesus Coll. Oxon., Archdeacon of Dorset, Canon of Salisbury, and Vicar of Charminster, Dorset, formerly Dean of Hobart, Tasmania, b. 1 Nov. 1847 ; m. 1st, Helen, dau. of Rev. W. Cobb, who d.s.p. 2ndly, 16 May, 1874, his cousin, Fanny Maria, dau. of Rev. Thomas Henry Dundas, and has issue,
        (1) Charles Percival Dijring, b. 25 May, 1877 ; m. Aug. 1906, Helen, dau. of T. Nuttall, of Victoria, B.C., and has issue, Lawrence Charles Percival, b. 5 Sept. 1908.
        (2) Alan Charlesworth, Lieut. 1st Batt. 17th Middx. Regt., b. 10 May, 1880 ; m. 15 April, 1909, Clara Beatrice Risdon, only dau. of W. G. Davy, of King's Hill, Newport, Mon.
        (3) Frank Leslie, b. 18 Aug. 1882.
        (4) Henry Raymond (twin with his brother Frank Leslie).
    4. George Albert, Surgeon-Major late India Med. Dep., m. 1873, Essie Jemima, dau. of V. Hutton, of Nottingham, and d. in India of cholera, Oct. 1887, leaving issue, a son and a dau., Leslie, Capt. 3rd Gurkhas, Indian Army, m. 1906, his cousin Constance, dau. of Rev. T. J. Rider.

Constance, *m.* 28 April, 1900, Paul Irven, Lieut. R.N., son of John Dowler Irven, of Dutton Lodge, Preston Brook, Cheshire.
5. Sydney, *d.* young.
1. Margaret, *m.* 1877, Rev. Thomas John Rider, Vicar of Baschurch, co. Salop, formerly of Carrington, Notts., and has issue.
3. Thomas Henry (Rev.), *m.* 1st, Frances Diana, dau. of John Cummings, of Chester, who *d.* Dec. 1882, leaving issue, two daus., of whom the elder, Ada, *m.* 1871, Major Von Düring, of Osnabruck, Hanover, A.D.C. to George, King of Hanover, and has issue. Rev. H. Dundas *m.* 2ndly, 1884, Agnes, eldest dau. of Rev. Gilbert Beresford, Canon of Peterborough, and Rector of Hoby, co. Leicester, and *d.* (without further issue) at Cannes, 18 April, 1890. His widow *m.* 2ndly, 5 April, 1902, Gen. Sir J. Luther Vaughan, K.C.B., Indian Army.
4. William John (Rev.), D.D., late Rector of Moynalty, *b.* 8 July, 1820; *m.* 1st, Caroline, dau. of George Roe, of Farmley, Queen's Co. (by Caroline his wife, sister of Sir R. King, Bart., of Charlestown), and by her (who *d.* in 1872) had issue,
1. William John, *b.* 16 March, 1845; *d. unm.* 1864.
2. George, M.D., *b.* 12 July, 1847; *m.* Ellen, dau. of Arthur Perkins, of Ballybroney House, co. Mayo, and *d.s.p.* Aug. 1888.
3. Henry Arthur Laurence, of Calgary, Canada, *b.* 22 July, 1850; *m.* 1886; *d.s.p.* 21 May, 1889.
4. Lawrence Charles, D.S.O., Major late Liverpool Regt., *b.* 3 Feb. 1857; served in Afghan and Burmese wars, late Governor of Maidstone Prison, *m.* 2 March, 1898, Lady Mary Bertie, 2nd dau. of 11th Earl of Lindsey. He *d.s.p.* 9 June, 1903.
1. Caroline.
2. Ada, *d.* Aug. 1869.
1. Sarah Georgiana, *b.* 1819; *m.* 3 June, 1839, John Dooner, of Barton Lodge, Rathfarnham, co. Dublin, who *d.* 24 Jan. 1879, having had issue, three sons and three daus., She *d.* 28 Jan. 1900.
2. Adelaide Maria, *d.* 13 Oct. 1908; *m.* 7 June, 1853, James White Minchin, Major A.P.D. formerly Capt. 62nd foot, who *d.* June, 1886, having had issue, four sons and three daus.

The eldest son,
LAWRENCE (LORENZO) GEORGE DUNDAS, of Clobemon Hall, co. Wexford, J.P. for that co. and for the co. of Westmeath, *b.* 21 June, 1813; *m.* 1st, 1835, Ellen, eldest dau. of Rev. Richard Eyre, Rector of Eyre Court, co. Galway, and widow of Joseph Callanan, of Tullywood, by whom he had a son.
1. LORENZO GEORGE (Sir), K.C.B., Col. late commanding 6th Batt. Royal Fusiliers, formerly Capt. 62nd Foot, served in the Crimea at the storming of the Redan, 8 Sept. 1855 (medal) (*Gloucester Lodge, East Molesey*), *b.* 6 April, 1837; *m.* 1868, Lily, 4th dau. of Robert Adams, of 6, Kensington Park Gardens, and has issue,
1. Lorenzo Frank, *b.* 14 Feb. 1872.
2. Robert Claude, *b.* 30 June, 1874.
3. Frederic Eyre, *b.* 1 Oct. 1883.
1. Helen Mabel, *m.* May, 1899, Rev Alfred Flux, Rector of Carlton, Notts, and has issue, two sons and two daus.
2. Lilly Londina, *m.* 1909, Thomas Greer, and has issue, one son and two daus.

Mr. Dundas *m.* 2ndly, 3 Aug. 1854, JANE ANNA MARIA, of Clobemon Hall, only child and heiress of Thomas Grimston, M.D. of Ripon, co. York (by his wife Anna Maria, dau. of Rev. Charles Fynes Clinton), and *d.* 1897, leaving issue,
2. Thomas Fynes Clinton, Comm. R.N. (ret.), *b.* 24 Feb. 1859; served in Witu Campaign, E. Africa (despatches, medal with clasp), and in Egypt and the Soudan (medal, clasp, and bronze star). He *d. unm.* 2 Aug. 1910.
3. Sidney Lawrence, of Tacoma, Washington, U.S.A., *b.* 19 July, 1863; *m.* 1st, 1889, Nellie Curtis (who *d.* 25 March, 1905). He *m.* 2ndly, 21 May, 1906, Mary Ellen Hurley (1109, *South 4 Street, Tacoma, Washington, U.S.A.*), of Halifax, N.S., and *d.* 26 June, 1907, leaving issue,
Sidney Lorenzo James, *b.* 26 Feb. 1907.
4. Charles George, *b.* 1 Oct. 1866.
5. Henry James, *b.* 10 Aug. 1868; *d.* at Moss Vale, N.S.W., Sept. 1890.
6. John Ernest Frederick, *b.* 10 Dec. 1876.
1. Annie Frances, *m.* 1883, Reginald Graham Wordsworth, of Duffcarrig, co. Wexford, and the Stepping Stones, Ambleside, eldest son of the late W. Wordsworth, and grandson of the poet. She *d.* 24 May, 1887, leaving issue, a son and two daus.
2. Emma Florence, *m.* 1st, 3 Aug. 1880, Lionel Albert Vaillant of Weybridge, Surrey, who *d.s.p.* Feb. 1884; 2ndly, 2 Feb. 1887, George Langshaw Merriman, of Reigate, and has issue, two sons and two daus.
3. Caroline Anna Maria, *m.* Feb. 1892, Edward Crawford Bolton, of Koppa, Mysore, Madras Pres., eldest son of Maj.-Gen. Robert Henry Bolton, Madras Army, and has issue.
4. Ellen Marian, *m.* 23 March, 1889, Maj.-Gen. Eberhardt Rudolph Philipp Münch, of the German Army, and has issue, one son and one dau.
5. Ida Alexandra.
6. Constance Lily, *m.* 12 Oct. 1891, Henry Charles Quin, of Coolnagloose, co. Wexford, and has issue, three daus.
7. Ethel Alice, *m.* 12 July, 1894, Edward King, of Aston, Cheshire. He *d.s.p.* 23 Feb. 1903. She *d.* 13 Oct. 1905.
8. Eva Mary, *m.* 12 April, 1894, John George Gibbon, M.D., of Lakeview, Mullingar, co. Westmeath (*see* GIBBON *of Sleedagh*).
9. Norah Beatrice.
10. Hilda Gwendoline, *d.* 7 March, 1885.

Seat—Clobemon Hall, Ferns, co. Wexford. *Residence*—Wechylstone, Speldhurst, Tunbridge Wells.

DUNNE OF BRITTAS.

Lineage.— RORY O'DOINN, Chief of I-Regan, *d.*, according to the *Annals of the Four Masters*, A.D. 1427. He left a son,
LENAGH O'DOINN, Chief of I-Regan, built Castlebrack, in the Queen's Co. He *m.* a dau. of O'Nellan, and had two sons,
1. TEIG, his heir.
2. Falie.
The elder son,
TEIG O'DOINN, Chief of Iregan, *m.* 1st, Ellen, dau. of "Lord" Power' and had three sons,
1. TEIG (OGE), his heir.
2. Rory.
3. Edmundboy, father of Donogh Mac Edmundboy, living 1569.
He *m.* 2ndly, a dau. of the Earl of Kildare, and had two sons, Shane and Cahir. His eldest son,
TEIG (OGE) O'DOINN, Chief of Iregan, *m.* 1st, Gormla, dau. of O'Connor Faile, and had four sons,
1. Brien, *d.s.p.*
2. TEIGH (REOGH), his successor.
3. Edmund, of Park, had four sons,
1. Owen, of Park, living 1581, left two sons,
(1) Mortagh, living 1601.
(2) Dermot, living 1601, having then a son, Rory.
2. Lenagh, living 1581, father of Cahir, living in 1601.
3. Edmund reogh, living 1581.
4. Shane, father of Shane oge, living 1593.
4. Dermot.
He *m.* 2ndly, Giles, dau. of MacGillepatrick, of Upper Ossory, and had four sons,
5. Donogh, father of Murtogh, of Cowlebohelaine, living 1601, with six sons then living, Donogh, Brian, Shane, Rory, Dermot, Lisagh.
6. Cormac. 7. Cahir. 8. Dermot.
The 2nd son,
TEIGH (REOGH) or THADY O'DOINN, of Iregan, had a grant of English liberty for himself and his issue by Patent, 25 Oct. 1551. He *m.* a dau. of McMorrish, and had four sons and a dau.,
1. THADY or TEIG (OGE), his successor.
2. Torlogh or Terence, of Kilcavan, living in 1601, ancestor of DUNNE *of Kilcoony* (*see that family*).
3. Donagh, of Gurtin and Balliglass, living 1570.
4. Phelim.
1. Finola, granted English liberty 1568, *m.* Con O'Connor.
The eldest son,
THADY (or TEIG OGE) O'DOINN, of Tenchinch and Castlebrack, appointed Capt. of Iregan by Patent, 4 June, 1558, made settlements of his estates in 1590, 1591 and 1593, and was living in 1601; *m.* Elizabeth, dau. of James FitzGerald, of Ballysonan, co. Kildare, and had five sons,
1. TEIG (LOGHA), or TEIG OGE, or THADY, his heir.
2. Cormac, of Balleskenagh and Lisnarode, *m.* 1st, dau. of O'Molloy, and had a son, Donal. He *m.* 2ndly, Johanna, dau. of Sir William O'Carroll, whose marriage with John Bourke, Baron of Leitrim, was decreed void 9 Nov. 1585, and had a son, Cormac oge, who *m.* — Purcell, and a dau., Ellis.
3. Brian or Barnaby, got one-fourth of Iregan from his father, *m.* Margaret, dau. of Ferganainm O'Molloy, and *d.* 23 Dec. 1614, leaving issue,
1. BRIAN OGE, of whom hereafter. 2. Donogh.
3. Art Failie. 4. Phelim.
5. George. 6. Daniel.
7. Garrett.
1. Margaret. 2. Katherine.
3. Ellen. 4. Elizabeth.
4. CAHIR or CHARLES, of whom presently.
5. Murtogh.
1. Grany, *m.* Brian FitzPatrick, son of Florence Baron, of Upper Ossory.
2. A dau., *m.* Calvagh O'Molloy.
3. A dau., *m.* Mulrony O'Carroll.
The eldest son,
TEIGH (LOGHA) or THADY O'DOYNE, of Castlebrack, surrendered his estate 6 Jan. 1611, and had a regrant of the greater portion by Patent, 7 March, 1611. He *d.* 28 Oct. 1637 (*Inq. pm.*). He *m.* 1st, Margaret, dau. of Shane O'Neill, who left him and *m.* Cuconaght Maguire, and had by her a son,
1. Teigh reogh or Thady, *d.s.p.* before 1635.
He *m.* 2ndly, Ellis, dau. of Redmond FitzGerald, of Clonbolg, co. Kildare, and had seven sons, who survived infancy,
2. Edmund or Edward, *d.s.p.* before 1635.
3. John, *d.s.p.* before 1635.
4. William, of Park, by the death of three of his elder brethren without issue, eldest son and heir apparent, *d.v.p.* Dec. 1635 (Funeral Entry), *m.* Mary, dau. of Walter FitzGerald, of Glassealy, co. Kildare, and left four sons and three daus.,
1. Edward, *b.* Aug. 1619, found next of kin and heir to his grandfather, *Inq. pm.*
2. James. 3. William. 4. Oliver.
1. Bridget. 2. Mary. 3. Anne.
5. Richard, priest, Vicar-General of Kildare.
6. James.
7. Rory or Roger, certified his brother's death 1635.
8. Torlogh.

We now return to

CAHIR O'DOINN, *alias* CHARLES DUNN, LL.D., 4th son of Thady O'Doinn, Capt. of Iregan, Fellow of Trin. Coll. Dublin 1593, M.A. 1601, Master in Chancery 20 Sept. 1602, M.P. for the University 1613-14, Vice-Chancellor 1614; *d. unm.* 17 May, 1617 (Funeral Entry). He petitioned against the regrant of Iregan to his brother and got a grant to himself of Brittas and portion of the Iregan estates, which he bequeathed by his will dated 2 April, 1617, to his nephew,

BARNABY or BRIAN OGE DUNN, of Brittas, High Sheriff Queen's Co. 1623, *b.* 1590. He obtained from CHARLES I, a patent for a large estate in the barony of Tinnehinche, to hold to him and his heirs for ever in soccage, provided he did not take the name, style, or title of O'DOINN, and that he should drop that same and call himself BRIAN DUNN. He *m.* Sybella (who *d.* 1660), dau. of Sir Robert Piggott, Knt. of Dysart, and widow of Richard Cosby, of Stradbally, both in the Queen's Co., and *d.* 7 Nov. 1661, when he was *s.* by his son,

CAHIR or CHARLES DUNNE, of Brittas, who *m.* Margaret, sister of John Coghlan, of Birr, who *d.* July, 1696. He *d.* 1680, leaving issue,
1. TERENCE, his heir. 2. Edward, *d.s.p.*
3. Barnaby.
4. John, Capt. in the Army of JAMES II.
5. Charles, of Ballynakill; his will, dated 8 Feb. 1680, was proved 30 April, 1681.
6. Daniel.
1. Mary, *m.* 1683, Philip Molloy, King's Co.
2. Peggy. 3. Polly.
4. Clare, *m.* Owen Carroll, of Kilmannan, Queen's Co.

He was *s.* by his eldest son,

TERENCE DUNNE, of Brittas, Capt. in Moore's Regt. of Infantry, who fought for JAMES II, and fell at Aughrim 1691. He *m.* 1676, Margaret (who *d.* 1722), dau. of Daniel Byrne, and sister of Sir Gregory Byrne, 1st bart. of Timogue, M.P. for Ballnakill, and had issue,

1. DANIEL, of Brittas, *b.* 1678; *m.* 1703, Margaret, dau. and co-heir of Major-Gen. the Hon. William Nugent, M.P., 6th son of Richard, 2nd Earl of Westmeath, and *d.* 1738, leaving two daus., his co-heirs.
    1. Mary, *m.* John Hussey (*see* HUSSEY-WALSH *of Cranagh*).
    2. Alice, *m.* 1720, Nicholas Plunkett, of Dunsoghly, and was mother of MARGARET PLUNKETT, who *m.* her cousin, Francis Dunne, of Brittas.
2. Charles, *b.* 1679; *d.s.p.*
3. Barnaby of Rathleen, King's Co., *m.* Mary Molloy, and *d.* 1723, leaving two daus.,
    1. Mary. 2. Margaret.
4. EDWARD, of whom presently.
1. Dorothy, *m.* Arthur Molloy, of Gurtacor, King's Co.

The 4th son,

EDWARD DUNNE, of Brittas, *m.* 1730, Margaret, dau. of Francis Wyse, of the Manor of St. John, co. Waterford, by Mary his wife, dau. of Thomas Masterson, of Castletown, co. Wexford, and dying 26 July, 1765, left issue,
1. FRANCIS, his heir.
2. Barnaby, *d.s.p.*
1. Anastatia, *m.* 24 Dec. 1751, Charles Whyte, of Leixlip (*see* WHYTE *of Loughbrickland*).
2. Juliana, *m.* O'Carroll. 3. Margaret.
4. Mary.

The elder son,

FRANCIS DUNNE, of Brittas, *m.* 10 Aug. 1760, his cousin, Margaret, dau. and co-heir of Nicholas Plunkett, of Dunsoghly Castle, co. Dublin, by Alice his wife, dau. and co-heir of Daniel Dunne, (*see above*), and had issue,
1. EDWARD, his heir.
2. Francis, Col. 7th Dragoon Gds., *d.s.p.* 1844.
3. Nicholas, of the Austrian Service, killed in the storming of Fort du Rhin, during the French Revolutionary War.
1. M. at Brussels, Aug. 1782, Henry Osborn, of Dardistown Castle, co. Meath.
2. Frances, *d. unm.* 3. Katherine, *d. unm.*
4. Margaret, *m.* 1811, Ambrose O'Ferrall, of Balyna, co. Kildare, and *d.* 1826 (*see* MORI-O'FERRALL *of Balyna*).

Mr. Dunne *d.* 20 Aug. 1771 and was *s.* by his son,

EDWARD DUNNE, of Brittas, Gen. in the Army, Dep. Gov. and High Sheriff (1790) of Queen's Co., J.P. King's and Queen's Cos., M.P. for Maryborough. He took an active part in suppressing the Irish Rebellion of 1798, at which time he commanded the Pembrokeshire Fencible Cavalry, *b.* 21 Oct. 1771; *m.* 28 July, 1801, Frances, dau. of Simon White, of Bantry House, sister to Richard, 1st Earl of Bantry, and *d.* 24 Oct. 1844, having by her (who *d.* 2 Dec. 1856) had issue,
1. FRANCIS PLUNKETT, his heir.
2. EDWARD MEADOWS, *s.* to his brother.
3. Robert Hedges (Rev.), M.A. (Trin. Coll. Dublin), Rector of Churchtown 1839-61, and Kilnegarenagh 1864 to 1883, *b.* 12 July, 1804; *m.* 26 Sept. 1843, Martha, dau. of John Robinson, and niece of Adm. Hercules Robinson, of Rosmead, co. Westmeath, and *d.* 24 Oct. 1883, having by her (who *d.* March, 1882) had issue,
    1. Nicholas Plunkett, Lieut. 21st Regt., *d. unm.* 20 Dec. 1869.
    2. Edward O'Connor Plunkett, *b.* 16 Sept. 1848; *d.* 14 Feb. 1850.
    3. CHARLES HENRY PLUNKETT (*Killart, Clonaslee, Queen's Co.*), present male representative of the family of DUNNE of Brittas, J.P. King's and Queen's Cos., late 20th Regt. Lancs. Fus.
    3. Edward Eyre, *b.* 7 Nov. 1854; *d. unm.* 14 July, 1897, in Northern Rhodesia.
    4. ROBERT HEDGES PLUNKETT, of Brittas, Queen's Co., Ballycumber House, King's Co., and Dunsoghly Castle, co. Dublin,

J.P. for Queen's Co. and King's Co., *b.* 21 Dec. 1856. In 1898 he purchased the estate of Brittas from the daus. and co-heirs of the late Francis Plunkett Dunne, of Brittas (*see below*). He *d. unm.* 13 Jan. 1901.
5. Francis Plunkett, of Bal Iver, King's Co., J.P., *b.* 1838; *d. unm.* 25 Feb. 1901.
6. Richard, *b.* 26 Aug. 1870; *d. unm.* in Assam 1878.
1. Alice Plunkett, *b.* 2 Sept. 1844; *m.* 12 Jan. 1860, Major Arthur Shuckburgh Upton, of Coolatore, co. Westmeath, and *d.* 11 March, 1870, leaving issue (*see that family*).
2. Frances Jane, *b.* 17 Oct. 1850; *m.* 1st, 22 Oct. 1873, her cousin Francis Plunkett Dunne, of Brittas, and has issue (*see below*). She *m.* 2ndly, 20 Jan. 1887, Col. George H. A. Kinloch, Col. Somersetshire L.I. (only son of J. J. Kinloch, of Kair, Kincardineshire, D.L.), and by him has a dau., Grace Theodosia Farquhar.
3. Helen Lucy, *b.* 29 Sept. 1857; *m.* Dec. 1878, Col. Henry Thomas Finlay, of Corkagh House, Clondalkin, and *d.* 9 March, 1902, leaving issue (*see that family*).
4. Richard, Major 18th Royal Irish, *b.* 22 Nov. 1805; *d. unm.* 7 Dec. 1875.
5. Charles, of Ballycumber House, King's Co., J.P., Capt. 18th Royal Irish, *b.* 25 Nov. 1806; *d. unm.* March, 1890.
1. Frances Jane, *b.* 24 Nov. 1807; *d. unm.* 1892.

Gen. Dunne *d.* 12 Nov. 1844, and was *s.* by his eldest son,

RIGHT HON. FRANCIS PLUNKETT DUNNE, M.A., of Brittas and Dunsoghly Castle, co. Dublin. He was a Privy Councillor in Ireland, a Maj.-Gen. in the Army, and Lieut.-Col. Queen's Co. Militia, J.P. and D.L., M.P. for Portarlington from 1847 to 1857, and for the Queen's Co. from 1859 to 1868. Gen. Dunne held office as Clerk of the Ordnance 1852, and was Private Secretary to the Lord Lieutenant of Ireland from 1858 to 1859. He was *b.* 1802; *d. unm.* 6 July, 1874, and was *s.* by his brother,

EDWARD MEADOWS DUNNE, of Brittas, J.P., Barrister-at-Law, *b.* 1803; *m.* 12 Sept. 1835, Marianne, dau. of Langford Rowley Heyland, of Glendaragh, co. Antrim, and Tamlaght, Lieut.-Col. Derry Militia, and had by her (who *d.* 29 Aug. 1860) issue,
1. Edward Eyre, *b.* 1836; *d. unm.* 12 Sept. 1848.
2. Alexander Dupré, *b.* 1838; *d. unm.* 9 Oct. 1855.
3. FRANCIS PLUNKETT, his heir.

Mr. Dunne *d.* 19 Sept. 1875, and was *s.* by his only surviving son,

FRANCIS PLUNKETT DUNNE, of Brittas, J.P., High Sheriff 1878, *b.* 22 April, 1844; *m.* 22 Oct. 1873, his cousin, Frances Jane, dau. of Rev. Robert Hedges Dunne, Rector of Lemanaghan, in the King's Co., and by her (who *m.* 2ndly, 20 Jan. 1887, Col. George Hibbert Anchitel Kinloch, late Somersetshire L.I.) had issue,
1. Francis Plunkett, *d.* young.
1. ALICE MAUDE, now of Brittas, *b.* 26 Aug. 1874.
2. KATHLEEN PLUNKETT, now of Brittas, *b.* 22 July, 1875.

Mr. Dunne *d.* 2 Oct. 1878, leaving his estates to be equally divided between his two surviving daus., ALICE MAUDE and KATHLEEN PLUNKETT, who sold the estate of Brittas in 1898 to their uncle, Robert Hedges Plunkett Dunne (*see above*), on whose death, 1901, these ladies *s.* again to Brittas and Dunsoghly Castle. Mr. F. P. Dunne was *s.* in the male representation of his family by his cousin Charles Henry Plunkett Dunne.

Arms—Az., an eagle displayed or. **Crest**—On a mount an oak tree in front thereof a newt all ppr. **Motto**—Mullaher a boo.
Seats—Brittas, Clonaslee, Queen's Co.

DUNNE late OF KILCOONY.

TERENCE JOHN BOCKETT DUNNE, of Toutley Hall, Wokingham, Berks, B.A. (Dub.), late Major R. W. Surrey Regt., *b.* 17 April, 1846; *m.* 26 Oct. 1882, Alice Isabell, dau. of Philip Butler, of Tickford Abbey, Bucks.

Lineage.—TOLOGH or TERENCE O'DOINN, of Kilcavan, Queen's Co., 2nd son of Teig reogh O'Doinn, of Iregan, living 1601, (*see* DUNNE *of* BRITTAS) left a son

JOHN DOYNE, of Kilcavan, *d.* 18 Dec. 1636 (Funeral Entry); *m.* 1st, Margaret, dau. of Lisagh Dempsey, of Deskert, Queen's Co., and had three sons and three daus.,
1. TERENCE, his heir. 2. Antony.
3. John.
1. Eleanor, *m.* Christopher Hussey, of Hutton, Queen's Co.
2. Sarah, *m.* Lisagh Molloy. 3. Ellen.

He *m.* 2ndly, Helena, dau. of Capt. Hugh MacDonnell, of Tonekill, Queen's Co., and had two sons and two daus.,
4. Edmund. 5. Thomas.
4. Margaret, *m.* William Stephens, of Queen's Co.
5. Mary.

The eldest son,

TERENCE DUNNE, of Kilcavan, sold it to Col. Richard Grace, and lived at Ard, Queen's Co.; *m.* Margaret, dau. of Byrne. He *d.* intestate 1680, leaving a son,

JOHN DUNNE, of Ard, *d.* 1726, was father of

TERENCE DUNNE, of Ard, *d.* 1774, *m.* Jane, dau. of Laurence Esmonde, of Ballynastragh, co. Wexford (*see* ESMONDE, Bart.), and had two sons, Terence, of Ard, who *d.s.p.*, and LAURENCE, who *s.* his brother.

LAURENCE DUNNE, of Ard, *d.* 1804, *m.* Mary (who *d.* 1806), dau. of Patrick Kennan, of Ballinamoney, King's Co., and had three sons and three daus.,
1. JAMES, his heir.
2. John, *b.* 1768, *m.* dau. of Lawtin of Kilkenny, and left issue, two sons, James and John.
3. Laurence Esmonde, *b.* 1782, Major 22nd Regt., *m.* Sophia, dau. of James Disney, and had issue,

1. Arthur Disney, Barr.-at-law, b. 1826, d. 1872; m. Charlotte A. (who d. 16 Aug. 1873), dau. of Richard Clarke Bell. of Fethard, co. Wexford, and dau. of Muddenderry, Bengal, and had issue,
  (1) Arthur Mountjoy (of Highlands, Colne, Wilts), Barr.-at-law (Chambers: 10 King's Bench Walk, Temple, E.C.), b. 20 Oct. 1859; m. Alice Sidney, dau. of Sir John Lambert, K.C.I.E., late Commissioner of Police, Calcutta, and has issue,
    1. Arthur Sidney, b. 10 June, 1892.
    2. Laurence Rivers, b. 4 Oct. 1893.
  (2) Frank Prendergast, P.W.D. India, b. 4 April, 1864, d.s.p. 1903.
  (1) Alice Theresa Disney, m. 1889, Rivers Grenfell, 8th son of Sir Fred. Currie, 1st Bart., and has issue (see BURKE'S Peerage).
  (2) Charlotte Frances Beaufort, m. 1892, Lt.-Col. John Shakespear, C.I.E., D.S.O.
  (3) Eva, m. — Barkley, C.E., of Shanghai.
2. Fowns James Disney, b. 1827, d. 1903; m. Charlotte, dau. of George Clarke, and had issue, two daus.
3. Lawrence St. John, b. 1829, d. 1854.
4. Alexander, b. 1834, d. 1857
5. Richard, b. 1837, d. 1898; m. widow of Capt. H. Bowen, and had issue, five sons.
  1. Caroline, m. Dr. Clarke, of Mountmelliak.
  2. Sophia Louisa.
1. Jane, b. 1773, m. — Tarlton.
2. Mary, b. 1777, m. — Kelly.
3. Catherine, b. 1779, m. — Fitzgerald.
The eldest son,
JAMES DUNNE, of Ard and Bellview, last Sovereign of Portarlington, b. 1766, d. 1842; m. 1stly, Catherine (b. 1769, d. 1825), dau. of Marie Mosell; 2ndly, Lucy, dau. of — Hodgson, and by his first wife had issue, one son and seven daus.,
1. JOHN HENRY, his heir.
2. Isabella, b. 1792, d. 1848; m. Henry Cary, Commander R.N., and had issue.
2. Letetia, b. 1794; d. 1873.
3. Catherine, b. 1800; m. Rev. George Hare, Chaplain, Royal Hospital, Dublin, and had issue, three sons and five daus.
4. Mary Eliza, b. 1806; d. 1891.
5. Alice Anne Margaret, b. 1807; d. 1883.
6. Jane, b. 1808; d. 1886.   7. Charlotte, b. 1810; d. 1888.
The only son,
REV. JOHN HENRY DUNNE, Rector of Dunshanglin, co. Meath, b. 1790; d. 27 Aug. 1863; m. Augusta, dau. of John Bockett, and by her (who d. 7 Jan. 1862) had issue,
2. TERENCE JOHN BOCKETT, present representative.
2. Francis William Bradney (Rev.), B.A., LL.D., Dublin, Vicar of Goldington, Beds., sometime Barrister-at-Law, b. 11 June, 1850; m. 8 July, 1870, Henrietta, dau. of Henry Bradshaw, M.R.C.S., and has issue,
  1. Terence Francis Kilcavan, Lieut. R.A., B.A. Trin. Coll. Dublin, b. 15 July, 1879; m. 15 Oct. 1907, Sybil Louise, dau. of late John Patrick McNeill, M.D., T.C.D., of Knockmore House, Ballymore, co. Antrim.
  2. Francis John Newton, Lieut., Militia, b. 1887.
  1. Alice Augusta Jane Esmonde, b. 1877.
  2. Evelyn Russell, m. 22 July, 1903, John Cochrane Brady, Barrister-at-Law (who d. 25 March, 1912), son of the late John C. Brady, of Johnstown Park, co. Fermanagh.
1. Alice Sarah Bradney, b. 1844, m. Capt. Thompson, 78th Highlanders, and has issue. He d. 1905, aged 71.
2. Harriet Mary Augusta, b. 1847, m. George D. Bushe, R.N., and has issue. He d. 15 Aug. 1901.
Seat—Toutley Hall, Wokingham, Berks.

DUNSCOMBE OF MOUNT DESERT.

GEORGE DUNSCOMBE, of Mount Desert, co. Cork, J.P., B.A. Camb., b. 10 June, 1878.

Lineage.—NOBLETT DUNSCOMBE, b. 1626, was Mayor of Cork 1665. He m. 1652, Mary, niece of Sir William Hull, Knt. to Lemcon, co. Cork, and dau. of Henry Hull, of Clonakilty, co. Cork, and d. June, 1695, leaving one son, WILLIAM, of whom presently; and three daus., Elizabeth. m. 1673, Robert Rogers, M.P. for Cork; Mary, m. 1st, 1676, James Harlowyne, of Cork, and 2ndly, 1680, John Hull, of The Little Island; and Sarah, m. 1687, John Spread. The only son,
WILLIAM DUNSCOMBE, b. 1660; m. 1st, Oct. 1682, Catherine, sister to Sir John Meade, Bart., and by her (who d. Jan. 1692) he had (with four daus.) one son.
1. MEADE, b. 1691; m. Nov. 1720, Elizabeth, eldest dau. of Dillon Newman, of Cork, and d. 1729, leaving (with two daus., Mary and Catherine) two sons, William, b. 1721, and Richard, b. 1723, of whom there are many descendants.
William Dunscombe m. 2ndly, 1695, Mary, dau. of Alderman William Roberts, of Cork, and d. Sept. 1720, leaving issue two sons and two daus.,
2. Noblett, of Mount Desert, b. 1690, High Sheriff 1730, and M.P. for Lismore from 1727 to 1744, m. Elizabeth, dau. of James Barry, of Rathcormac, and d.s.p. May, 1745.
5. GEORGE, of whom presently.
6. Helena, who m. Stephen Mazicke.
4. Henrietta, who m. Redmond Barry, of Ballyclough.
Mr. Dunscombe purchased Mount Desert 1703. His 3rd son,
COL. GEORGE DUNSCOMBE, of Mount Desert, b. May, 1712; s. his brother 1745. He m. Feb. 1738, Penelope, 2nd dau. of Col. Nicholas Colthurst, of Ballyandly, co. Cork, by Penelope his wife, the only child of Sir John Topham, Knt. of Dublin, one of the Masters in Chancery, and d. Jan. 1752, leaving (with four daus., Penelope, m. 1760, John Carleton, of Woodside, co. Cork; Mary, m. July, 1769, Walter Atkin, of Leadington, co. Cork; Harriett, and Elizabeth, who both d. unm.) an only son and heir,
NICHOLAS DUNSCOMBE, of Mount Desert, b. 1741, High Sheriff 1765; m. May, 1764, Mary, only child of Thomas Parker, of Inchigagin, near Cork, by Mary his wife, the eldest dau. of Swithin White, of Cork, and had issue,
1. GEORGE, of whom presently.
2. Robert Parker, who assumed the name and arms of PARKER, in lieu of his patronymic, on succeeding to his mother's property. He m. 20 April, 1788, his cousin, Helen, one of the daus. of Richard Dunscombe, by Jane Bateman his wife, and d. July, 1815, leaving several sons and three daus.
3. William, Lieut. 12th Light Dragoons, b. Feb. 1827.
4. Thomas, an Alderman of Cork, m. Feb. 1798, Mary, eldest dau. of Alderman Shaw, of the City of Cork, and d. Dec. 1833, leaving issue,
  1. Nicholas (Rev.), Chancellor of the diocese of Cork, and Rector of St. Nicholas, Cork, b. 25 Dec. 1798; m. 3 Feb. 1844, his cousin, Penelope, youngest dau. of George Dunscombe, of Mount Desert.
  2. John Shaw, b. July, 1806; m. 1 Sept. 1830, Lucy, only child of Henry Orpen, of co. Kerry, d. 30 May, 1854.
  3. Thomas Shaw, b. 18 Feb. 1811; m. 24 July, 1850, Jane, the eldest dau. of William Gillespie.
  1. Isabella.
5. Nicholas, Rector of Kilcully, d. Aug. 1838, unm.
6. Rowland, formerly a Lieut. in the Army, d. April, 1835.
7. Parker, b. 30 Nov. 1781; m. 6 Jan. 1803, Jane, the 3rd and youngest sister of William Waggett, Recorder of Cork, and dau. of Christopher Waggett, of Kitsboro', and d. 4 June, 1829, leaving issue,
  1. NICHOLAS, of King William's Town House, co. Cork, J.P. and F.G.H.S., b. 20 Oct. 1804; m. 23 July, 1830, Anna Matilda, eldest dau. of Thomas Johnston, of Fort Johnston, near Glasslough, co. Monaghan (see that family), by Martha his 1st wife, eldest dau. of the Rev. James Hingston, LL.D., Vicar-General of the Diocese of Cloyne, and d. 1882, leaving by her (who d. 24 Oct. 1865),
    (1) PARKER, b. 7 Feb. 1834; m. 27 March, 1865, Elizabeth, eldest dau. of Abraham Ruddock, of co. Down, d. 1902, and has surviving issue,
    NICHOLAS, 25 March, 1867.
    (2) Nicholas, b. 18 Jan. 1835; m. 26 Oct. 1868, Helen Style, 3rd dau. of Lieut. Arthur Barrow, of the 30th Regt., and grand-dau. of Lieut.-Col. Barrow, of same Regt.; d. 6 Jan. 1870, leaving issue, Nicholas Blake, Major 128th Pioneer Regt., Indian Army, b. 22 July, 1869. He was senior Capt. in the 2nd East Kent, Nicholas's Royals, served in the 46th Regt. at Sebastopol, and obtained his company before that Russian stronghold, got medal and clasp for it, also the Sardinian and Turkish medals.
    (3) William Waggett, b. 27 April, 1837; wrecked on the Mucka Rocks, Palliser Bay, New Zealand, 14 Sept. 1869; was unm.
    (4) Henry, b. 5 June, 1839.
    (5) George, b. 6 Dec. 1843.
    (6) Clement, now of King Williamstown, M.A. and L.C.E. (Trin. Coll. Dublin), M.Inst C.E., formerly City Engineer of Liverpool and elected (1889) Chief Engineer, London County Council, b. 1856; m. 1805, Gertrude Hannah, 2nd dau. by his 1st wife of Alfred Clark, of Wood Dalling, Norfolk, and has issue,
      1. Clement, b. 1897.   2. Nicholas, b. 1898.
    (1) Martha, m. 24 Dec. 1851, Rev. Walter Johnston, eldest son of Henry George Johnston, of Fort Johnston, co. Monaghan, and d. 6 Feb. 1855, leaving an only dau.,
      Martha Dunscombe, m. 17 June, 1884, Thomas Herbert Knowles Duff, eldest son of Thomas Duff, D.L., of Aberlour, Banffshire, who d. May, 1900, leaving issue.
    (2) Jane Ellen Waggett, d. unm. 25 April, 1867.
  2. Christopher Waggett, b. 27 April, 1808; m. 6 July, 1830, Maria, only dau. of Rev. Edward Batchelor, of Dublin, and d. 5 Feb. 1839, leaving issue.
    (1) Parker, b. 26 Aug. 1831; m. 15 Sept. 1863, Anne Baldwin, youngest dau. of Rev. Thomas Waggett, Rector of Rathclarence, co. Cork, and has issue, one son and two daus.
      (2) Edward.   (3) Christopher.
      (1) Elizabeth.   (2) Jane.
    1. Johanna Waggett, m. 23 Dec. 1834, Rev. Dr. John Webb, LL.D. of The Hill, near Cork. He d. 9 Sept. 1842, leaving two sons,
      (1) John M'Donnell, Capt. 4th Royal Irish Dragoon Guards, b. Nov. 1825; m. 27 Nov. 1862, Cornelia Marcha, relict of William Haslett, and d. May, 1886, leaving an only dau.
      (2) Randal, b. Oct. 1832; m. 5 April, 1865, Mary Hunlis, only dau. of Robert Disom, of Verron Hall, Liverpool, and d. 8 July, 1894, leaving no surviving issue.
  1. Mary, d. unm. July, 1827.   2. Penelope, d. unm. 1816.
  3. Elizabeth, m. 1800, Abraham Lane, of the City of Cork, and Sheriff of the same 1798.
Mr. Dunscombe d. 15 March, 1793, and was s. by his eldest son,
GEORGE DUNSCOMBE, of Mount Desert, b. 17 March, 1765, High Sheriff 1789; m. 25 Sept. 1806, Lydia, the 2nd dau. of Charles Denroche, of Cork, by Anne Dorman his wife, and had issue,
1. NICHOLAS, late of Mount Desert.
1. Anne Dorman, m. 25 July, 1837, Benjamin Swete, of Greenville.   2. Mary Parker.
3. Lydia, m. 6 May, 1845, Rev. Henry Gillman.

4. Penelope, *m*. 3 Feb. 1844, to her cousin, Rev. Nicholas Dunscombe.

He *d*. 3 March, 1835, and was *s*. by his only son,

NICHOLAS DUNSCOMBE, of Mount Desert, J.P., D.L., and High Sheriff for co. Cork, 1860, *b*. 23 Aug. 1807; *m*. 2 April, 1839, Jane, 4th dau. of Robert Carr, of Cork, and *d*. 25 April, 1876, having had issue,

1. George, *b*. March, 1840; *m*. July, 1868, Mary, elder dau. and co-heir of the late Jasper Pyne, of Ballyrolane and Castle Masters, and *d*. 2 Aug. 1869, leaving an only child,
   Georgina Violet Mary Masters, *m*. 13 Dec. 1890, John Hopkinson Phillips, and has issue (*see* PHILLIPS *of Gaile*).
   His widow *m*. 2ndly, Aug. 1871, George Brown.
2. ROBERT, now of Mount Desert.
3. Noble Reginald, *d*. *unm*. 2 Aug. 1875.
1. Jane, *m*. Capt. Thomas Clarke, of the Royal Horse Artillery.

The 2nd son,

ROBERT DUNSCOMBE, of Mount Desert, co. Cork, J.P. co. Cork, D.L. for the City of Cork; was formerly in the 2nd Queen's Regt; *b*. 5 April, 1841; *m*. 28 Aug. 1876, Harriet Frances Beresford, younger dau. of the Rev. Arthur John Preston, M.A., Canon of Kildare, Rector of Kilmeage, Vicar of Rathernon and Prebendary of Lulliamore, co. Kildare, by Harriet Hickman his wife, eldest dau. of James Fitzgerald Massy, of Stoneville and Cloughnarold, co. Limerick, and *d*. 12 April, 1906, having had issue,

GEORGE WILLIAM, now of Mount Desert.
Araninta Lydia, *b*. 11 Aug. 1897; *m*. 2 Dec. 1908, Capt Desmond James Lambart Hartley, 3rd son of late Col. R. W. Hartley, of Beech Park, co. Dublin, and has issue (*see that family*).

Seat—Mount Desert, Cork.

DUNVILLE OF REDBURN.

The late ROBERT GRIMSHAW DUNVILLE, of Redburn, co. Down and Sion, co. Meath, J.P. and D.L. co. Down, High Sheriff 1886, and J.P. co. Meath, High Sheriff 1882, *b*. 1838; *m*. 1865, Jeanie (*now of Redburn*), dau. of William Chaine, of Moylena, and *d*. 17 Aug. 1910, having had issue,

JOHN DUNVILLE, of Sion, co. Meath, M.A. Trin. Coll. Camb., late Lieut. 5th Batt. Leinster Regt., Private Secretary to the Duke of Devonshire (46, *Portland Place, W*.), *b*. 20 Oct. 1866; *m*. 7 Jan. 1892, Violet Anne Blanche, 5th dau. of the late Gustavus William Lambart, D.L., of Beau Parc, co. Meath (*see* BURKE'S *Peerage*, CAVAN, E.), and has issue,

1. Robert Lambart, *b*. 18 Feb. 1893.
2. John Spencer, *b*. 7 May, 1896.
3. William Gustavus, *b*. 13 June, 1900.
1. Una, *b*. 22 Feb. 1903.

Mr. Dunville is the only son of the late John Dunville, by Mary, his wife, dau. of Robert Grimshaw, D.L., of Longwood, co. Antrim.

Seats—Redburn, Holywood, co. Down and Sion, Navan, co. Meath. *Clubs*—Turf, W., and Ulster, Belfast.

ECCLES OF ECCLESVILLE. *See* McCLINTOCK OF SESKINORE.

ECHLIN OF ARDQUIN.

JOHN GODFREY ECHLIN, of Ardquin, co. Down, *b*. 5 April, 1843; *m*. 1870, Anna Medici (*d*. 25 July, 1910), elder dau. and co-heir (with her sister, Mrs. Savage-Armstrong) of Rev. John Wrixon, M.A., Vicar of Malone, co. Antrim, youngest son of Capt. John Wrixon, 5th Dragoon Guards, by his wife Anne Arabella, dau. and co-heiress of Rear-Admiral John Dawson, R.N., of Carrickfergus, and has issue,

1. JOHN STAFFORD, *b*. 23 Feb. 1872; *m*. Feb. 1906, Georgina Hedwig Ida, dau. of John Albert Faller, of Crefeldt, Germany, and widow of the late Charles James Heddon, of Aldbourne, Wilts.
2. Godfry Cecil, Lieut. R.N., *b*. 12 Aug. 1874; *m*. Jan. 1906, Dorothy, dau. of Francis Leybourne Popham, of Littlecote, Wilts.
3. Bertram Wrixon, R.N.R., *b*. Nov. 1879; *m*. Oct. 1911, Hilda, dau. of William Keen, of Hove, Sussex.

Lineage.—RIGHT REV. ROBERT ECHLIN, 4th or 5th son of Henry Echlin of Pittadro, in the co. of Fife, was appointed Bishop of Down and Conor, by Patent dated 4 March, 1613, and made a free denizen of Ireland 18 May following. On the death *s.p*. of his nephew, Capt. Henry Echlin, Bishop Echlin became the head and representative of the Echlin family. He *m*. Jane, dau. of James Seton, of Latrisk, in Scotland, and had issue,

1. JOHN, his heir.
2. Hugh, *m*. Magdalen, dau. of Robert Cowell, co. Armagh.
1. Margaret, *m*. Ven. Robert Maxwell, Archdeacon of Down, afterwards Bishop of Kilmore, ancestor of the Earls of Farnham.
2. Isabel, *m*. Archibald Stewart, of Ballintoy, co. Antrim.
3. Jane, *m*. 1st, Henry Maxwell, of Finnebrogue, co. Down, and had issue (*see* MAXWELL *of Ballyrolly*). She *m*. 2ndly, the Ven. William Fullerton, Archdeacon of Armagh.
4. Euphemia.

The Bishop of Down *d*. at Ardquin, co. Down, 17 July, 1635, and was buried in the parish church of Templecrany, *alias* Ballyphilip, in the same co. His eldest son,

JOHN ECHLIN, of Ardquin, was made a free denizen of Ireland 9 Aug. 1633. He *m*. Mary, dau. of Sir Francis Stafford, Knt. of Mount Stafford, co. Antrim, and had issue,

1. ROBERT, his heir.
2. Francis, of Clonowen, co. Antrim, inherited the estate of his uncle, Sir Edmond Stafford, Knt. of Mount Stafford, and assumed that surname. He *m*. Sarah Macdonnell, of the family of the Earls of Antrim, and had issue.
1. Jane, *m*. James Leslie.
2. Elizabeth, *m*. Francis Hamilton, of Tullybrack, co. Armagh.
3. Mary, *m*. Capt. William Leslie, of Prospect, co. Antrim (*see* LESLIE *of Ballibay*).

The elder son,

ROBERT ECHLIN, of Ardquin, co. Down, *b*. 1628; *m*. Mary, dau. of Dr. Henry Leslie, Bishop of Meath, formerly of Down and Connor, and *d*. 25 April, 1657, having by her (who *m*. 2ndly, Sir Robert Ward, created a bart. 1682) had issue,

1. JOHN, his heir.
2. Henry (Sir), created a Baronet 1721, a Baron of the Court of Exchequer in Ireland, ancestor of ECHLIN, Bart. of Clonagh (*see* BURKE'S *Peerage, &c*.).
3. Robert, a Lieut.-Gen. in the Army, and Col. of the Inniskilling Dragoons, *m*. Anne Petty, dau. of Sir Francis Blundel, Bart., and *d.s.p*.
1. Jane, *m*. William Conyngham.

His eldest son,

JOHN ECHLIN, of Ardquin, *m*. 1673, Hester, dau. and heir of William Godfrey, of Coleraine, and had, with other issue,

1. CHARLES, his heir.
2. Robert (Rev.), *s*. his brother.
3. Godfrey, of Marlfield, *m*. Anne, dau. of JOHN SAVAGE, of Ballyvarley, co. Down, grandson of ROWLAND SAVAGE, of Portaferry, who was representative of the Portaferry branch of the ancient Anglo-Norman family of SAVAGE *of the Ards*, and ancestor of the SAVAGES (now NUGENTS) *of Portaferry*, and had issue,
   1. Godfrey, of Marlfield, *m*. 1756, Letitia, eldest dau. of George Macartney, of Lissanoure Castle, co. Antrim, and sister of George, Earl Macartney, Ambassador Extraordinary to China, but left no issue. 2. Rowland, *d*. *unm*.
   1. Anne, *m*. Henry Tisdall.
   2. Hester, *m*. to her cousin JOHN, son of the REV. ROBERT ECHLIN, of whom hereafter.
4. James, of Echlinville, *m*. 1738, Mary Ann Sampson, of Dublin, and *d.s.p*. 1757. She *re-m*. 1762, Stratford Eyre (*see* EYRE *of Eyrecourt*).
1. Mary. 2. Jane.
3. Hester, *m*. Thomas Knox, of Ballycruly, co. Down, and had a son, Thomas Knox, created, 1791, Viscount Northland, whose son, Thomas, 2nd Viscount, was created, 1831, Earl of Ranfurly.
4. Elizabeth, *m*. George Hamilton, of Tyrella, co. Down.
5. Rose, *m*. 1728, Major North Ludlow Bernard, and had a son, James Bernard, M.P., whose son, Francis Bernard, was created, in 1800, Earl of Bandon.

The eldest son,

CHARLES ECHLIN, of Ardquin, *m*. 1709, Ann, dau. of Thomas Knox, of Dungannon, and had an only son,

Thomas, who *d.s.p*.

Mr. Echlin *d*. 10 April, 1754, and was *s*. by his brother,

REV. ROBERT ECHLIN, of Ardquin, Incumbent of Newtownards, co. Down. He *m*. 1722, Jane, one of the daus. and co-heirs of James Manson, of Tynan, co. Armagh, and had issue,

1. JOHN, his heir. 2. Charles, *d*, *unm*.
1. Hester, *m*. James Donaldson, of Castle Dillon, co. Armagh.

Mr. Echlin, whose will, dated 1 Feb. 1756, was proved in 1761, was *s*. by his eldest son,

JOHN ECHLIN, of Thomastown, High Sheriff of the co. Down 1758, *b*. 1723; *m*. his first cousin Hester, dau. of Godfrey Echlin, of Marlfield (*see above*), and had issue,

1. CHARLES, his heir. 2. ROBERT, *d*. *unm*. 1770.
3. Godfrey, *d*. in infancy.
4. JOHN, of whom presently, as successor to his brother CHARLES.
5. James, *d*. *unm*.
1. Jane, *m*. George Matthews, of Springvale (now Ballywalter Park), co. Down, and *d*. 1803, leaving issue.

Mr. Echlin *d*. 4 March 1789, and was *s*. by his eldest son,

CHARLES ECHLIN, of Echlinville (Rhubane), co. Down, which latter place he inherited from his great-uncle, James Echlin. Mr. Echlin was High Sheriff of co. Down 1777. He *m*. 1st, Miss Anne Newburgh, of Ballyhaise House, co. Cavan, by whom he had issue, a dau., Letitia, who *d*. *unm*.; and 2ndly, Miss Anne Graham, by whom he had issue, a son, CHARLES GRAHAM, *d*. in infancy, and three daus., *d*. *unm*. Mr. Echlin *d*. 22 Feb. 1817, and was *s*. by his bro.

JOHN ECHLIN, of Thomastown, bapt. 23 March, 1757. He *m*. 8 Nov. 1786, Thomasine Hannah, dau. of George Fleming, of Dublin (of the family of the Barons of Slane), had a son, JOHN, his heir, and a dau., Thomasine, *m*. Thomas R. Moore, co. Cavan, and dying 25 Jan. 1825, he was *s*. by his only son,

JOHN ECHLIN, of Echlinville, Rhubane, D.L. and J.P., High Sheriff of co. Down 1827, *b.* 4 Oct. 1787; *m.* 3 Feb. 1809, his cousin, Thomasine, Margaret, dau. of John Armstrong, J.P., of Dublin, of the family of Armstrong of Mangerton, and *d.* 14 April, 1842, leaving issue,
1. JOHN ROBERT, his heir.
2. George Fleming, *b.* 27 June, 1812; *m.* 15 Aug. 1842, Harriet Georgina, only dau. of Col. Johnston, of the 8th Hussars, of Westfield, co. Dublin, and The Lodge, co. Donegal, and *d.* 23 Jan. 1869, leaving issue.
3. Charles, who *m.* and *d.* 3 Oct. 1903, leaving issue.
1. Elizabeth, *m.* Rev. James Gerahty, Rector of Donaghendry, co. Tyrone, and *d.* 1877, leaving issue.
2. Hester Jane, *m.* Rev. Charles Ward, M.A., Rector of Kilwaughter, co. Antrim, and *d.* 1877, leaving issue.
3. Thomasine Margaret, *m.* John Auchinleck Ward, and *d.* 1879, leaving issue.
4. Jane, *m.* the Rev. John Going, Rector of Hawkchurch, Devon, and *d.* leaving issue.
5. Margaretta Watson Jane Coville, *m.* Alex Cranston, and *d.s.p.* 1849.
6. Harriet, *m.* Henry Perceval, and has issue.
The elder son,
REV. JOHN ROBERT ECHLIN, M.A., J.P., of Echlinville (Rhubane) and Ardquin, co. Down, formerly Incumbent of Bronington, near Whitchurch, Salop, *b.* 15 July, 1811; *m.* 1st, 27 Sept. 1836, Jane, 3rd dau. of James Pedder, of Ashton Lodge (now Ashton Park), co. Lancaster, and by her (who *d.* 8 March, 1838) had issue,
1. John Pedder, *b.* 28 Nov. 1837; *d.* 16 Sept. 1838.
Mr. Echlin *m.* 2ndly, 26 Oct. 1841, Mary Anne, 2nd dau. of Ford North, of The Oaks, Ambleside, co. Westmorland, and by her (who *d.* 23 Dec. 1871) had issue,
2. JOHN GODFREY, now of Ardquin.
3. Frederick, Capt. R.N., *b.* 14 March, 1844; *m.* 1885, Lilias, dau. of Thomas Kerr, C.M.G., late Governor of the Falkland Islands, and *d.* 21 Dec. 1906, having had issue,
Frederick St. John Ford North, *b.* 17 Feb. 1889.
Annie Lilias.
4. Alfred Ford (Rev.), *b.* 27 Sept. 1849; *m.* Isabelle Grace, dau. of John Barrat; *d.* Jan. 1886, leaving issue,
Alfred John, *b.* 26 Sept. 1877.
1. Edith Althea, *m.* Rev. H. Joy, D.D., and has issue.
2. Thomasine Mary, *m.* Rev. George Read, M.A., who *d.* leaving no surviving issue.
Mr. Echlin *m.* 3rdly, 4 July, 1878, Henriette Wilhelmine Louise Margareth, eldest dau. of Richard Von Oertzen, of Crobnitz, Upper Lusatia, Germany, and by her (who *d.* 30 Dec. 1893) had no issue. The Rev. J. R. Echlin *d.* 15 Sept. 1891.

Arms—Quarterly: 1st and 4th or, an antique galley with sails furled sa., a forked pennon gu.; 2nd and 3rd gu., a fesse chequy arg. and az., on a chief over all arg., a stag pursued by a greyhound sa. **Crest**—A talbot passant ppr. **Motto**—Non sine præda.

Seat—Dunloskin, Carrickfergus. **Club**—Junior Constitutional, Piccadilly.

EDGE OF CLONBROCK.

RIGHT HON. SIR JOHN EDGE, P.C. (1908), of Clonbrock, Queen's Co., Member of Judicial Committee of Privy Council. Sir John was silver medalist (Ethics, Logics, and Metaphysics), B.A. and LL.B. Trin. Coll. Dublin 1861, Hon. LL.D., Allahabad University, 1894, Barrister-at-Law, King's Inn, Dublin, 1864, Middle Temple, London, 1866; Q.C. England 1886; Chief Justice of the North-Western Provinces, India, 1886-1898, member of Council of India 1898-1908, was Lieut.-Col. (Hon. Col.) Allahabad Rifle Corps and Commandant 3rd Ad. Batt. N.W.P. Volunteers, and Hon. A.D.C. to the Viceroy of India, Vice-Chancellor of the Allahabad University 1887 to 1893, Member of Royal Commission on War in S. Africa. He was *b.* 28 July, 1841; *m.* 18 Sept. 1867, Laura, youngest dau. of Thomas Loughborough, of Selwood Lodge, Tulse Hill, Surrey, by Frances Cornelia Lawrence, his 2nd wife, and has had issue,
1. JOHN, *b.* 7 Aug. 1873; *d. unm.* 14 Aug. 1896.
1. Esther Frances, *b.* 1868, *d.* 1872.
2. Ethel Laura, *m.* 15 March, 1893, Major Stuart George Knox,

C.I.E., of the Indian Army, eldest son of the Hon. Sir George Edward Knox, N.P., India, and has issue,
1. Stuart George Edge Inman, *b.* 27 Dec. 1896.
2. John, *b.* 2 Sept. 1904.
3. Kathleen Mary, *m.* 15 July, 1903, Lieut.-Col. Charles Trevor Caulfeild, R.A., 3rd son of Col. Robert Caulfeild, of Camolin House, co. Wexford, and has issue (*see* BURKE's *Peerage*, CHARLEMONT, V.).
4. Helga Violet.

Lineage.—The pedigree of this family is duly recorded at the Heralds' College.
ADAM DE EGGE had a grant of lands at Horton, co. Stafford, in 1338; his son,
ADAM DEL EGGE, obtained more lands at Horton in 1376. His son,
WILLIAM DEL EGGE, of Horton, *m.* 1376, Ellen, dau. of Robert de Bedulph. They had a son,
ROGER DEL EGGE, of Horton, who *m.* before 1420, Margaret, dau. of Richard de Rudyerd. Their son,
RICHARD EGGE, of Horton, had issue, by Alice his wife,
1. ROGER. 2. WILLIAM, of whom presently. 3. Hugh.
Richard Egge *d.* 1480. The 2nd son,
WILLIAM EGGE, of Horton, *m.* Dowce, dau. of Sir John Savage, knighted at Agincourt, and had issue,
1. CHRISTOPHER, of whom presently.
2. Peter. 3. William. 4. John.
William Egge was living in 1515; his eldest son,
CHRISTOPHER EGGE, of Horton, left issue, by Parnel Brereton his wife, three sons,
1. RICHARD, of whom presently. 2. William.
3. Christopher.
He *d.* 1541. His eldest son,
RICHARD EGGE, of Horton, *m.* Maude, dau. of William Bowyer, of Knypersley, and had issue, with four daus.,
1. CHRISTOPHER.
2. Ralph, from whom the Edges of Strelley, Notts.
3. William. 4. Richard.
5. Thomas, *m.* Elizabeth Cowell.
Richard Egge *d.* 1592. His eldest son,
CHRISTOPHER EGGE, of Horton, *m.* Joan, dau. of Lawrence Swetenham, of Somerford Booths, and had an only son, RICHARD.
Christopher Edge *d.* 1578. His son,
RICHARD EGGE, of Horton, *m.* Dorothy, dau. of Thomas Malkin, of Longsdon, and had issue, with four daus.,
1. Richard, *m.* Mary, dau. of Thomas Johnson, of Haselwood, co. Derby.
2. JOHN, of whom presently. 3. Walter.
4. Timothy, a Parliamentarian Commissioner.
Richard Edge *d.* 1647. His 2nd son,
JOHN EDGE, of Bishop's Offlow, co. Stafford, a Royalist whose estate was sequestrated by the Parliament, left issue, by Sarah his wife,
1. Richard. 2. William.
3. JOHN, of whom presently.
1. Elizabeth, *m.* Henry Terry.
2. Mary, *m.* Rev. William Ford, vicar of Eccleshall.
John Edge *d.* 1651. His 3rd son,
JOHN EDGE, *m.* Mary Bourne. He settled in Ireland, and was included in the Act of Attainder of 1689, of King JAMES'S Irish Parliament, as John Edge, Gent., of Dublin. He was bur. in Rathdrum, 2 Nov. 1714, having had (with five daus.),
1. William. 2. John.
3. Joseph. 4. Israel.
5. Richard. 6. DAVID, of whom presently.
The youngest son,
DAVID EDGE, *b.* in 1692; *m.* Margaret (who *d.* 1797), widow of John Gough, and dau. of Thomas Wybrants, and had issue,
1. JOHN, of whom presently.
2. Elias. 3. David. 4. Samuel.
1. Mary. 2. Elizabeth.
David Edge *d.* 28 May, 1773, and was bur. in Rathdrum. His eldest son,
JOHN EDGE, *b.* in 1732; *m.* Sarah (who *d.* 1825, aged 84), dau. of George Ougan, and Sarah his wife, and had the following issue,
1. David. 2. George. 3. Elias.
4. JOHN, of whom presently. 5. Samuel.
6. Isaiah; and seven daus.
John Edge *d.* Nov. 1790. His 4th son,
JOHN EDGE, was a Civil Engineer to the River Shannon Navigation and to the River Barrow Navigation, and later was a lessee of coal mines in the Queen's Co., of which co. he was J.P., *b.* 29 July, 1767; *m.* 31 Aug. 1800, Letitia, dau. of Charles Dallas, of Killashee, co. Longford, by Jane, his wife, dau. of — Hamilton, of co. Cavan, by his wife Rhoda, dau. of — Little, and by her (who *d.* 3 Feb. 1847) had issue,
1. John Dallas, Barrister-at-Law, *b.* 7 Jan. 1806; *m.* 17 Sept. 1835, Anne, 2nd dau. of Thomas Maunsell, of Dublin, and *d.* 11 Aug. 1842, leaving a surviving son,
John Henry, of Farnans, Queen's Co. Barrister-at-Law, King's Inn, Dublin, 1866, Q.C., J.P., Silver Medallist (English Literature and History), B.A. 1861, and M.A. Trin. Coll. Dublin, *b.* 11 June, 1841; *m.* 23 June, 1870, Georgina, dau. of William Munck Gibbon, LL.D. (*see* GIBBON *of Sleedagh*).
2. BENJAMIN BOOKER, of whom presently.
1. Sarah Jane, *m.* 1827, her cousin John Edge (who *d.* 22 Jan. 1862), and *d.* 3 Dec. 1885, leaving surviving issue,
1. John Dallas, Lieut.-Col. 1st Batt. Royal Irish Regiment, *b.* 13 Sept. 1842; *d.* 16 Dec. 1894.
2. Joseph Samuel, First Gold Medallist (Ethics, Logics, and Metaphysics), and B.A. Trin. Coll. Dublin 1871, Barrister-at-

Edgeworth. THE LANDED GENTRY. 204

Law, Middle Temple, London, 1874; King's Inn, Dublin, 1881, J.P. Queen's Co., b. 11 July, 1848.
1. Letitia, m. Rev. James Barnier, LL.D., Rector of Clomantagh. 2. Sarah.
Mr. Edge lived at Clonbrock House, Queen's Co. He d. 2 April, 1856, aged 88. The 2nd son,
BENJAMIN BOOKER EDGE, of Clonbrock, J.P., b. 12 April, 1810; m. 10 March, 1840, Esther Anne, only child of Thomas Allen, of the Park, co. Wicklow, by Elizabeth Dowzard, his 1st wife, and d. 28 April, 1887, leaving by her (who d. 3 March, 1879) an only child,
JOHN (Sir), now of Clonbrock.
Arms—(On record at College of Arms): Per fesse sa. and gu., an eagle displayed arg.; (on record in Ulster's Office): Per fess sa. and gu., an eagle displayed arg. on a chief or, a cinquefoil between two annulets of the second. *Crest*—A reindeer's head couped ppr. collared and chained or, and holding in its mouth a trevoil vert. *Motto*—Semper fidelis.
Residence—The Banks, Robertsbridge, Sussex. *Club*—Junior Carlton.

EDGEWORTH OF EDGEWORTHSTOWN.

FRANCIS YSIDRO EDGEWORTH, of Edgeworthstown, co. Longford, M.A. Oxon, D.C.L. Durham, Fellow of King's College, London, F.B.A., Barrister-at-Law, Fellow of All Souls, Oxford, Professor of Political Economy at Oxford, b. 8 Feb. 1845.

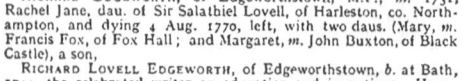

Lineage.—In the reign of ELIZABETH, about the year 563, two brothers, EDWARD and FRANCIS EDGEWORTH, went to Ireland, probably under the patronage of Essex and Cecil, as those names have since continued in the family. The elder son,
THE RIGHT REV. EDWARD EDGEWORTH, who was beneficed by Queen ELIZABETH, became Bishop of Down and Connor in 1593. He d. without issue, and was s. by his brother,
FRANCIS EDGEWORTH, Clerk of the Hanaper in 1610, m. Jane, dau. of Edward Tuite, and sister of Sir Edmond Tuite, and d. 10 March, 1625, having had by her (who founded an Irish Convent at St. Germain's, near Paris) a son and three daus.,
1. JOHN, his heir.
1. Anne, m. 1622, George Synge, Bishop of Cloyne.
2. Mary, m. Pierce Moore, of Raheenduff, Queen's Co. (see MOORE of Cremorgan).
3. Margaret, m. 1st, John King; 2ndly, John Bysse, Lord Chief Baron.
CAPT. JOHN EDGEWORTH, of Cranallagh Castle, in the co. of Longford, High Sheriff 1646, M.P. 1646-49, m. 1st, Anne, dau. of Sir Hugh Cullum, of Cloghouter Castle, co. Cavan, by whom he had a son, JOHN, his heir; and 2ndly, Mrs. Bridgman, widow of Edward Bridgman, brother to Sir Orlando Bridgman, the Lord Keeper. He was s. by his only son,
SIR JOHN EDGEWORTH, knighted by CHARLES II, 21 July, 1672, m. 1st, Mary, only dau. and heir of Edward Bridgman, and acquired with her an estate in Lancashire, besides a considerable fortune in money, and had by her six sons. By his 2nd wife Anne, he had three sons and two daus. Among his issue were,
1. FRANCIS, his heir.
2. Robert, ancestor of EDGEWORTH of *Kilshrewly* (see that family).
3. Henry, of Lissard, left a second son Essex, of Pallasmore, who left by Sarah Whyte his wife, a son, Francis Whyte Edgeworth, of Pallasmore, m. 1778, Susannah, dau. of Very Rev. Richard Handcock, Dean of Achonry, and sister of 1st Viscount Castlemaine, and had an only son, Rev. Francis Whyte Edgeworth, Chaplain of Christ Church, who m. Unity Matthews, of Kilmachan, and left one son, Essex Munroe Edgeworth, who d.s.p. 1867.
4. Essex (Rev.), of Templemichael, eldest son by the second marriage, who was grandfather of the celebrated Abbé Edgeworth, called from the estate his branch of the family possessed, Monsieur de Fermont.
The eldest son,
COL. FRANCIS EDGEWORTH, of Edgeworthstown, raised a regiment for WILLIAM III. He m. 1st, Dorothy, dau. of Hugh Cullum, of Lisnamain, co. Cavan, by whom he had a son, Francis, d. unm. He m. 2ndly, Dorothy, dau. of Sir Charles Hamilton, Bart., of Castle Hamilton, co. Cavan, and had a son, John, d.s.p., and a dau., Franceliza. He m. 3rdly, Mary, widow of John Bradstone (whose dau. Margaret Bradstone, m. Thomas Pakenham, of Pakenham Hall, father of the 1st Lord Longford), by whom he had a son and successor,

RICHARD EDGEWORTH, of Edgeworthstown, M.P., m. 1731, Rachel Jane, dau. of Sir Salathiel Lovell, of Harleston, co. Northampton, and dying 4 Aug. 1770, left, with two daus. (Mary, m. Francis Fox, of Fox Hall; and Margaret, m. John Buxton, of Black Castle), a son,
RICHARD LOVELL EDGEWORTH, of Edgeworthstown, b. at Bath, 1744, the celebrated writer on education and inventions. He m. 1st, Anna Maria, dau. of Paul Elers, of Black Bourton, co. Oxford, and had by her one son and three daus.,
1. Richard, b. May, 1765; d. 1796.
1. MARIA, the Authoress, b. 1 Jan. 1767; d. unm. 21 May, 1849.
2. Emmeline, m. 1802, John King, of Clifton, Bristol, and had issue.
3. Anna Maria, m. 1794, Dr. Beddoes, and d. 1824, leaving issue.
He m. 2ndly, 1773, Honora, dau. of Edward Sneyd, of Lichfield, youngest son of Ralph Sneyd, of Bishton, co. Stafford, and by her had a son,
2. LOVELL, who s. to the estates.
He m. 3rdly, 25 Dec. 1780, Elizabeth, dau. of Edward Sneyd, of Lichfield, and had by her (who d. Nov. 1797) five sons and four daus.,
3. Henry, b. 15 Sept. 1782; d. 1830.
4. CHARLES SNEYD, of whom presently.
5. William, b. 28 April, 1788; d. 1790.
6. Thomas Day, b. 25 Oct. 1789; d. 1792.
7. William, b. 27 Jan. 1794; d.s.p. 1829.
4. Elizabeth, d. 1800. 5. Charlotte, d. 1807.
5. Sophia, d. 1785.
7. Honora, m. 8 Nov. 1831, Admiral Sir Francis Beaufort, K.C.B., and d. his widow, 13 Feb. 1858.
He m. 4thly, 31 May, 1798, Frances Anne, dau. of the Rev. Daniel Augustus Beaufort, and had by her (who d. 10 Feb. 1865) two sons and four daus., viz.,
8. Francis Beaufort, b. 5 Oct. 1809; m. 1831, Rosa Florentina, dau. of Don. Antonio Eroles, of Catalonia, in Spain, and d. 12 Oct. 1846, leaving issue by her (who d. 18 June, 1864),
1. WILLIAM, Capt. 3rd Dragoon Guards, b. 1835; d. unm. 28 June, 1863.
2. ANTONIO EROLES, late of Edgeworthstown.
3. David Reid, J.P., b. 14 April, 1843; d. unm. 14 Oct. 1871.
4. Richard Lestock, b. 5 June, 1843; d. unm. at Naples, 8 May, 1869.
5. FRANCIS YSIDRO, now of Edgeworthstown.
1. Maria, m. 11 April, 1871, Rev. John Sanderson, M.A., Rector of Winchfield, Hants, and d. 1893, leaving issue.
9. Michael Pakenham, b. 24 May, 1812; m. Feb. 1846, Christina, dau. of Dr. Hugh Macpherson, of Aberdeen, and d. July, 1881, having had issue,
1. Christina Frances Edith, d. an infant, 1848.
2. Harriet Jessie, m. 4 April, 1877, Rev. Arthur Grey Butler, and has issue.
8. Frances Maria, m. 1829, Lestock P. Wilson, of London, and d. 5 Feb. 1848. Mr. Wilson d. 17 July, 1869.
9. Harriet, m. 1826, the Very Rev. Richard Butler, Dean of Clonmacnoise, who d. 17 July, 1862. She d. Feb. 1889.
10. Sophia, m. 1824, Barry Fox, of Annaghmore, King's Co. (who d. 1863), and d. 1 March, 1837, leaving issue (see *Fox of Fox Hall*).
11. Lucy Jane, m. June, 1843, Rev. Thomas Romney Robinson, D.D., who d. 28 Feb. 1882. She d. Jan. 1897.
Mr. Edgeworth d. 13 June, 1817, and was s. by his son,
LOVELL EDGEWORTH, of Edgeworthstown, J.P. and D.L., High Sheriff co. Longford 1819; b. 30 June, 1776. He d. unm. Dec. 1841, and was s. by his half brother,
CHARLES SNEYD EDGEWORTH, of Edgeworthstown, D.L., b. 30 Oct. 1786; m. 2 Sept. 1813, Henrica, dau. of John Broadhurst, of Foston Hall, co. Derby, which lady d. 30 Sept. 1846. He d.s.p. 31 March, 1864, and was s. by his nephew,
ANTONIO EROLES EDGEWORTH, of Edgeworthstown, co. Longford, M.A., ex-Scholar T.C.D., J.P. and D.L. co. Longford, High Sheriff 1890, b. 19 March, 1842; m. 1874, Françoise, dau. of Col. Delcher, of the French Service, and d.s.p. 24 April, 1911.

Arms—Per chevron gu. and or, three martlets counterchanged. *Crest*—On a ducal coronet a pelican vulning herself or. *Motto*—Constans contraria spernit.
Seat—Edgeworthstown House, co. Longford. *Clubs*—Alpine, Athenæum, and Savile.

EDGEWORTH OF KILSHREWLY.

THOMAS NEWCOMEN EDGEWORTH, of Kilshrewly, co. Longford, D.L. co. Longford, M.A. Trin. Coll. Dublin, b. 24 Dec. 1850; m. 22 Oct. 1878, Elizabeth du Pré, eldest dau. of John Wilson, of Daramona, co. Westmeath, and has issue,
1. KENNETH ESSEX, Capt. R.E., b. 26 Feb. 1880.
2. John Agnew, Lieut. R.E., b. 30 Jan. 1884.
1. Ethel Marian.

Lineage.—ROBERT EDGEWORTH, 2nd son of Sir John Edgeworth, Knt. (see EDGEWORTH of *Edgeworthstown*). He m. 1692, Catherine, only child of Sir Edward Tyrrell, Bart., of Lynn, co. Westmeath, and had issue, EDWARD; Pakington; and other children. The eldest son,
EDWARD EDGEWORTH, of Kilshrewly, m. 1717, Mary, dau. of John Hussey, of Courtown, co. Kildare, and had two sons, Robert, d.s.p. 22 June, 1774, and NEWCOMEN. The younger son,
NEWCOMEN EDGEWORTH, of Kilshrewly, m. 1st, Elizabeth, dau. of Col. Henry Edgeworth, of Lissard, co. Longford, which lady

d.s.p.; and 2ndly, 1774, Mary, only dau. of Laurence Connell, of St. Johnstown, same co., by Mary his wife, dau. of Capt. John Agnew, 7th son of Sir Stair Agnew, Bart., by whom (who *m.* 2ndly, 3 Dec. 1797, Capt. Francis Douglas, R.N.) he had issue. The eldest son,

ESSEX AGNEW EDGEWORTH, of Kilshrewly, a Lieut. 78th Regt., *d. unm.* 1795, and was *s.* by his brother,

THOMAS NEWCOMEN EDGEWORTH, of Kilshrewly, co. Longford, D.L., High Sheriff 1814-15, and Major Royal Limerick County Militia, *b.* 30 April, 1778; *m.* 1st, 1 Jan. 1806, Marian, only child of John Steele, of Carricklane, co. Armagh, by Catherine his wife, dau. of Robert Stuart, of Hanslong; 2ndly, 14 April, 1834, Mary, dau. of Thomas Montgomery, of Dublin. Mr. Edgeworth *d.* March, 1857. By the former (who *d.* 1832) he had surviving issue,

1. JOHN ESSEX EDWARD, of Kilshrewly.
2. George Thomas Henry, *b.* 4 Aug. 1816; *m.* 20 April, 1852, Amelia, only dau. of Gen. James Considine, 10th Regt., and *d.* 8 March, 1882, leaving one child,
   Amelia, who *d.* 8 July, 1883.
3. James Bridgeman, *b.* 9 July, 1823; *d.* May, 1861
1. Catherine Jemima, *m.* 1835, Rev. Francis de Montmorency St. George, Rector of St. Anne's, Shandon, Cork, and had issue.
2. Cecilia, *m.* 1835, James Johnston, of Magheremena, co. Fermanagh, D.L.   3. Elizabeth, *d.* March, 1887.

The eldest son,
THE REV. JOHN ESSEX EDWARD EDGEWORTH, of Kilshrewly, co. Longford, and Longwood, co. Meath, B.A. Trin. Coll. Dublin, *b.* 25 Sept. 1814; *m.* 8 Dec. 1843, Elizabeth Anne (*d.* 15 June, 1906), only dau. of the late Launcelot Croasdaile, of Rynn, Queen's Co.) (*see that family*), and *d.* 13 Aug. 1904, having had issue,

1. THOMAS NEWCOMEN, now of Kilshrewly.
2. Lancelot Croasdaile Agnew (Rev.), B.A. Trin. Coll. Dublin, *b.* 5 March, 1852; *m.* 29 May, 1893, Eliza, 2nd dau. of Joseph S. Cragg, of Longbridge, Hayes, Staffordshire.
3. Henry Essex, *b.* 25 Oct. 1855; *d.s.p.* 22 Oct. 1895.
4. Cecil Roger, *b.* 18 May, 1860; *m.* 23 July, 1891, Alice, dau. of the late H. J. Knox, of Durban, Natal, and *d.* 28 Jan. 1896, leaving a son,
   Roger Lovell, *b.* 10 Aug. 1892.
1. Edith Susan Marian, *m.* 20 Jan. 1886, Capt. Maxwell Fox, late R.N., of Annaghmore, King's Co., D.L.
2. Lucy Frances
3. Anna Rose Elizabeth, *d.* 30 May, 1889.

Arms—*See* EDGEWORTH *of Edgeworthstown.*
Seat—Cherbury, Boolerstown, co. Dublin.

KING-EDWARDS OF DARTANS HOUSE.

WILLIAM KING-EDWARDS, of Dartans House, co. Tyrone, J.P. and D.L., High Sheriff 1892, *b.* 1843; *m.* 1st, 1867, Sarah Esther, 4th dau. of William Ramsay, of Strabane, co. Tyrone, by Jane his wife, 2nd dau. of Dr. Loney, of Strabane, and has issue,

1. John Edward Edwards, *b.* 1871; *d. unm.* 1901.
2. William Bether, *b.* 1872; *d. unm.* 1895.
3. THOMAS RAMSAY, *b.* Aug. 1874; *m.* 1908, Annie Blanch, 2nd dau. of the late Rev. Thomas Lindsay Stack, D.D., Canon of Derry and has issue,
   Esther Olivia Maybelle.
1. Jane Elizabeth, *b.* June, 1869; *m.* 1896, Ralph Hall Reid, of Ballyshannon, and has issue.

He *m.* 2ndly, 1908, Anna Benigna, 4th dau. of Isaac Peyton Warren, of Warren Point, Clontarf. Mr. King-Edwards is the only child of the late Bether King, of Dartans House, co. Tyrone, who *d.* 1844, and Elizabeth his wife, who *d.* 1895, only dau. of Nehemiah Edwards, of Kilcroagh, co. Tyrone, and grandson of William King, of Dartans House, and Coleraine. Mr. King-Edwards assumed the additional name of EDWARDS, 1885.

Seat—Dartans House, Castlederg, co. Tyrone.

LESLIE-ELLIS OF MAGHERYMORE.

LIEUT.-COL. HENRY LESLIE-ELLIS, of Magherymore (Sea Park), co. Wicklow, J.P. and D.L., High Sheriff 1902, Lieut.-Col. late Royal Bucks Hussars, late Major Inniskilling Dragoons, F.S.A., F.R.G.S., *b.* 10 Feb. 1852; *m.* 7 April, 1894, Margaret, dau. of the late Rev. Septimus Rolleston, Rector of St. Minver, Cornwall, and has issue,

1. FRANCIS ROLLESTON LESLIE, *b.* 14 Jan. 1895.
2. John Lancelot, *b.* 4 March, 1902.
3. Charles Stanhope, *b.* 28 Nov. 1904.
1. Joan Leslie, *b.* 26 Feb. 1898.

Lineage.—THOMAS ELLIS, of Monaghan, eldest son of John Ellis (stated to have been fifth son of Sir Thomas Ellis, of Wyham), settled in Ireland in the latter part of the reign of CHARLES II. His name appears in the celebrated Act of Attainder of the following reign, as "Thomas Ellis, of Monaghan, Gentleman." He was *b. circa* 1650; *m.* twice, and had numerous issue by both marriages. His second wife was Elizabeth, dau. of John Harpur, and widow of — White. Thomas Ellis *d.* 9 Aug. 1714 (will proved 12 Oct. 1714). By his first wife, he had with other issue (*see* ELLIS *of Abbeyfeale*) a second son,

FRANCIS ELLIS, of Monaghan, *b.* 1683; *m.* 28 Aug. 1715, Joan Maxwell, and *d.* 15 June, 1773 (will dated 18 April, 1770, proved 4 Sept. 1773), having by her (who *d.* 27 March, 1729) had, among other issue,

1. Henry, Governor of Georgia and Nova Scotia, and Vice-Admiral, High Sheriff, and Provost Marshal of Grenada, Tobago, St. Vincent and Dominica, F.R.S., *b.* 29 Aug. 1721; *d. unm.* 21 Jan. 1806, at Naples.
2. ROBERT, of whom presently.

The 2nd son,
ROBERT ELLIS, of Draper Hill, Lisnaskea, co. Fermanagh, *b.* 11 Jan. 1726; *m.* Penelope, dau. of Rev. Alexander Leslie, of Aghnaloo, co. Fermanagh,* and *d.* 1782 (will dated 4 March, proved 5 April, 1782), having by her (who *d.* July, 1823) had issue,

1. Francis, of The Royal Crescent, Bath, *b.* 1772; *m.* Mary, dau. of William Kilbee, and *d.* 1842, having had issue,
   1. Henry William, 60th Regt., *b.* 1809; *d. unm.* 1841.
   2. Francis, 75th Regt., *b.* 1812; *m.* Maria, dau. of J. Ford, and *d.s.p.* 27 Aug. 1843.
   3. Robert Leslie, of Anstey Hall, Cambs., Fellow of Trinity College, Cambridge, a distinguished scholar and mathematician, *b.* 1817; *d. unm.* 12 May, 1859.
      1. Everina Frances, *m.* 1st, 20 Dec. 1834, Sir Gilbert Affleck, Bart. He *d.s.p.* Nov. 1854. She *m.* 2ndly, 1 July, 1858, Rev. William Whewell, D.D., Master of Trinity College, Cambridge. She *d.* 1 April, 1865. He *d.* 6 March, 1866.
      2. Penelope Sarah, *m.* Edward Wilberforce Unwin, and *d.* 1856.
      3. Mary Jane, *d.* young, 1831.
2. HENRY, of Mount Stewart.
3. Robert, *b.* 1775; *d. unm.* 1799.
4. Alexander, Lieut. 4th Regt., *b.* 1776; *d. unm.* 1796.
1. Jane, *m.* Rev. William Maxwell, D.D., of Falkland, co. Monaghan, and *d.* 1847.
2. Sarah, *d. unm.* 1809.
3. Isabella, *m.* William Mayne, of Freame Mount, co. Monaghan. She *d.* 1 Nov. 1799. He *d.* 25 Nov. 1817, leaving issue.
4. Penelope, *m.* 29 April, 1818, Rev. Francis Lawrence Gore, D.D., and *d.* 17 March, 1848.

The 2nd son,
HENRY ELLIS, of Mount Stewart, co. Dublin, *b.* 9 May, 1774; *m.* 12 Dec. 1810, Elizabeth, dau. of Thomas Cupples, M.D., of Lisburn, co. Antrim, and *d.* 27 April, 1848, having by her (who *d.* 10 June, 1879) had issue,

1. HENRY, *b.* 1812; *d. unm.* 22 May, 1835.
2. ROBERT FRANCIS, of whom presently.
3. Alexander Leslie, *b.* 9 Feb. 1825; *d.* 22 Oct. 1837.
4. Thomas Cupples, of St. Austin's, co. Wexford, J.P., *b.* 13 Feb. 1829; *m.* 21 June, 1860, Augusta Catherine, dau. of Rev. Thomas Burne Lancaster, Rector of Grittleton, Wilts. She *d.* 1 Nov. 1899. He *d.* 20 Aug. 1885, having had issue,
   1. Henry Herbert Maxwell, *b.* 31 May, 1861; *m.* July, 1885, Louise Van Metres, and has issue,
      (1) Henry Augustus Emilius, *b.* 18 Oct. 1888.
      (1) Catherine Inez.
      (2) Violet.
   2. Richard Hume Lancaster, *b.* 19 June, 1862; *d.* 10 Nov. 1875.
   3. Ernest Francis Leslie, of St. Austin's, co. Wexford, J.P., F.S.I., *b.* 22 Oct. 1867; *m.* 4 July, 1894, Harriett Eva, dau. of the late Matthew Johnson-Smyth, of Ingram, Lisburn, co. Antrim, and has issue,
      Eva Augusta Elizabeth, *b.* 25 April, 1899.
   4. Arnold Claud Lancaster, Lieut. R.N.R., *b.* 8 June, 1869; *m.* 17 Oct. 1899, Georgina Alice, dau. of Rev. James Sullivan, Rector of Askeaton, co. Limerick, and has issue,
      (1) Henry Thomas Cupples, *b.* 8 April, 1903; *d.* 3 March, 1904.
      (2) Arnold George, *b.* 24 Feb. 1905.
      (1) Florence Claudia Helena, *b.* 15 June, 1901.
   1. Emily Augusta Laura, *m.* 2 Aug. 1804, Frederick Adolphus Brabazon Turner, of Clonattin, co. Wexford.
   2. Violet Clara, *m.* 30 April, 1908, Rev. Ernest V. O'Connor.
5. Theophilus, *b.* 6 Dec. 1831; *d.* young, 18 Oct. 1837.
1. Jane, *m.* 21 Feb. 1831, Rev. Isaac Ashe, Rector of Kildress, co. Tyrone. He *d.* 22 March, 1888, leaving issue.

---

* THE REV. ALEXANDER LESLIE, of Aghnaloo (whose will, dated 10 April, 1758, was proved 28 Jan. 1762) was the son of the REV. WILLIAM LESLIE, of Glebhill, co. Fermanagh, Rector of Aghavea for fifty years (will dated 23 April, 1760, proved 4 March, 1762), son of ALEXANDER LESLIE, of Pitcaple, *b.* 6 Jan. 1657, son of ALEXANDER LESLIE, of Pitcaple, son of JOHN LESLIE, of Pitcaple, son of JOHN LESLIE, of Pitcaple, son of DUNCAN LESLIE, of Pitcaple, son of WILLIAM LESLIE, who *d.v.p.*, son of ALEXANDER LESLIE, 4th Baron of Pitcaple, living 1568, descended from Malcolm, son of Bertolf (living 12th century), *vide* SCOT's *Peerage, sub* ROTHES.

2. Penelope, *m.* 10 June, 1841, Rev. Richard Christie, Rector of Castlecombe, co. Wilts. He *d.* 8 Dec. 1888, leaving issue. She *d.* 17 Dec. 1908.
3. Elizabeth, *m.* 22 April, 1846, John Adams, Rear-Admiral of the White, Governor of Ascension Island. He *d.* 17 Dec. 1866. She *d.* 11 May, 1891, leaving issue.
4. Sarah Maria, *d.* young, 24 Oct. 1837.

His 2nd son,
ROBERT FRANCIS ELLIS, of Sea Park (now called Magherymore), co Wicklow, M.A. Trin. Coll. Dublin, J.P., High Sheriff of co. Monaghan 1867, and of co. Wicklow 1868, *b.* 22 Oct. 1822 ; *m.* 25 March, 1851, Elizabeth Mary, dau. of James Hawkins, of St. Fenton's, co. Dublin. She *d.* 28 March, 1883. He *d.* 12 Jan. 1899, having had issue,
1. HENRY, now of Magherymore.
2. Robert Leslie, *b.* 10 Sept. 1853 ; *m.* 23 Aug. 1884, Emily Eleanor, dau. of Col. R. Gun-Cuninghame, of Mount Kennedy, co. Wicklow. He *d.s.p.* 25 Sept. 1903. She *d.* 25 Aug. 1910.
3. Francis Leslie, *b.* 18 Oct. 1855 ; *d. unm.* 22 Dec. 1878.
4. Alexander Leslie, *b.* 6 Nov. 1856.
5. William Whewell Leslie, *b.* 2 May, 1859 ; *d. unm.* 10 June, 1906.
1. Isabella Frances Leslie, *d.* young, 6 Jan. 1857.
2. Emily Elizabeth Leslie, *b.* 15 Sept. 1864 ; *m.* 6 Jan. 1897, R. Middleton Hill, Chief Constable of co. Cornwall.

Arms—Quarterly 1st and 4th, Gu., on a fess arg. between three crescents or, as many escallops az., on a canton of the third a garb vert (ELLIS); 2nd and 3rd, Arg. on a bend az. between two spur rowels gu. three buckles or (LESLIE). *Crests*—1. ELLIS: A dolphin naiant embowed arg. charged with an escallop as in the arms. 2. LESLIE: A griffin's head erased with wings addorsed ppr. (motto over Grip fast). *Motto*—Non sine jure.

Seat—Magherymore, Wicklow. *Clubs*—Army and Navy, Wellington and Kildare Street.

ELLIS OF ABBEYFEALE.

The late RICHARD ELLIS, of Glenasrone, Abbeyfeale, co. Limerick, J.P., *b.* 15 June, 1858 ; *m.* 16 Sept. 1896, Edith Kate, dau. of Maj. Walter Edward Wood, of Dennis Coatham, Redcar, Yorks, and *d.* 22 Jan. 1908, leaving issue,
1. THOMAS, *b.* 21 June, 1899.
1. Dymphna Mary, *b.* 28 July, 1897.
2. Elizabeth Joyce, *b.* 21 April, 1901.

Lineage.—THOMAS ELLIS, of the town of Monaghan, and Dromlang and Dromskett, co. Monaghan, attainted *temp.* JAMES II, had issue (named in the order in which they are mentioned in his will) by his first wife,
1. Robert, of Monaghan, *m.* 20 Oct. 1733, Elizabeth Ireland, widow of — Moutray, and *d.s.p.* 1748.
2. Francis, ancestor of LESLIE-ELLIS of Magherymore (*see that family*).
3. RICHARD, of whom presently. 4. William, living 1714.
5. John, a minor in 1714. 6. Thomas, a minor in 1714.
7. Henry, a minor in 1714.
1. Elizabeth, *m.* — Spear.

He *m.* 2ndly, Elizabeth, dau. of John Harpur, and widow of — White, and *d.* 20 Aug. 1714 (will proved 12 Oct. that year), having by her (who *m.* 3rdly, 25 Feb. 1717, John Thompson, of Killehandrick, co. Cavan, who *d.* Oct. 1727, and *d.* 1738) had further issue,
8. Usher, *d.* young 1725.
9. Edward, of Dublin, *m.* 1726, Maria, dau. of Thomas White, of Redhills, co. Cavan, and *d.* 1773. He was ancestor of ELLIS of Rocklands, co. Dublin.
10. Samuel, *b.* 16 March, 1713 ; *d. unm.* 17 April, 1735.
2. Rebecca, *b.* 1711, *m.* (art. dated 22 April, 1729) Arnold Cosbie, son of Edward Cosbie, of Skea, co. Cavan (*see* COSBY *of Stradbally*).

The above-mentioned son,
RICHARD ELLIS, of Monaghan, and Drumnalee, co. Cavan, described in an Exchequer Bill, 31 May, 1742, as "eldest son and heir," *d.* 1774, leaving issue,
1. Thomas, of Dublin and Drumnalee, M.D., *m.* 1756, Mary Jones, and *d.s.p.* 1790.
2. RICHARD, of whom presently.
3. Dawson, of Monaghan and Dublin, *m.* 1st, 1771, Elizabeth Forster, and 2ndly, 1780, Jane Webb, and *d.* 1807 leaving issue by both marriages.
4. William (Rev.), who also left issue.
1. Dorcas, *d. unm.* 1809.

The 2nd son,
MAJOR RICHARD ELLIS, of Abbeyfeale, co. Limerick, and Drumnalee, co. Cavan, Major 66th Regt., *b.* 1738 ; *m.* Nov. 1770, Mary, dau. of Robert Hilliard, co. Kerry, and *d.* 1814, having had issue,
1. THOMAS, of whom presently.
2. William, *d. unm.*
3. Conyngham, Maj. 40th Regt., *b.* 1783, *d.* 1815 from wounds received at Waterloo, bur. in Brussels.
4. Henry, Capt. R.N., *b.* 1784, *m.* Mary Simpson, and *d.* 16 Nov. 1857, leaving issue, two sons, Thomas and Edward.
1. Barbara, *m.* 1791, William Turton, 61st Regt., and *d.* 1854.
2. Mary, *m.* John Busteed, and *d.* 1839.
3. Catherine, *m.* John Bagge, of Mallow, and *d.* 1852, leaving issue.
4. Anne, *d. unm.* 1851.

5. Harriet, *m.* 22 Feb. 1814, Col. Robert Clerke Wallace, K.H., King's Dragoon Guards, and had issue.
6. Louisa, *m.* Lieut.-Col. William James, and *d.* 1847.

The eldest son,
THOMAS ELLIS, Master in Chancery in Ireland, M.P. for Dublin, *b.* 1774 ; *m.* 3 Dec. 1804, Dymphna, dau. of Col. William Thomas Monsell, of Tervoe, co. Limerick (*see* BURKE'S *Peerage*, EMLY, B.), and *d.* 1832, having had issue,
1. RICHARD, of whom presently.
2. Conyngham (Rev.), Vicar of Cranbourne, Berks., *m.* 1st, his cousin, Diana, dau. of Ven. Thomas Bewley Monsell, Archdeacon of Derry (*see* BURKE'S *Peerage*, EMLY, B.), and by her (who *d.* 1851) had issue, a dau.,
  1. Jane Anne Hannah, *d.* 1909.
He *m.* 2ndly, Sophia, dau. of Mathew Babington, of Rothley Temple (*see that family*), and *d.* 4 Sept. 1891, having by her (who *d.* 15 Sept. 1903) had issue,
  1. Conyngham Richard Cecil, D.S.O., Major late Scottish Rifles, served in S. Africa 1899-1900, *b.* 28 March, 1863.
  2. Francis Henry Babington, *b.* 23 Sept. 1865 ; *m.* 25 Feb. 1909, Edith, widow of Robert Alexander McEwen and dau. of late John Newnham Winter, of Brighton.
  2. Dymphna. 3. Mary, *d. unm.* 1869.
  4. Bertha, *d. unm.* 1907. 5. Katharine.
  6. Margaret, *d. unm.* 1889.
3. Francis, Barrister-at-Law, Col. Commanding Tyrone Fus., *b.* 1819 ; *m.* 21 Sept. 1841, Louisa, dau. of Right Hon. Sir Thomas McMahon, Bart., Master of the Rolls. He *d.* 24 Oct. 1881. She *d.* 28 Sept. 1889, having had issue,
  1. Thomas (*Penticton, British Columbia*), *b.* 26 April, 1844 ; *m.* 1872, Mina Wade, and has issue.
  2. Francis Robert, *b.* 5 May, 1849.
  3. Charles Conyngham, C.B., Col. R.E., *b.* 2 March, 1852.
  4. Henry Augustus, *b.* 21 July, 1861.
  5. William Montague, Major R.E., *b.* 15 Oct. 1862.
  1. Charlotte Anne, *m.* 5 Sept. 1872, Major Burleigh Stuart, Tyrone Fus., and has issue (*see* BURKE'S *Peerage*, CASTLE-STEWART, E.).
  2. Frances Hannah. 3. Louisa Dymphna.
  4. Diana, *m.* 1877, Edward C. Thompson, M.P., and *d.* 1887, leaving issue.
4. Frederick, Capt. 9th Lancers, *b.* 1826, *m.* 1860, Elizabeth, eldest dau. of John Bonfoy Rooper, of Abbot's Ripton, Hunts. (*see that family*). She *d.* 1893. He *d.s.p.* 6 March, 1906.

The eldest son,
RICHARD ELLIS, of Abbeyfeale, co. Limerick, J.P. and D.L., *b.* 1805, *m.* 1st, 1829, Anne Frances, dau. of Rev. Robert Conway Dobbs, youngest son of Conway Richard Dobbs, M.P. (*see that family*), and by her (who *d.* 1851) had issue,
1. THOMAS, of whom presently.
2. Robert Conway Dobbs, sometime Capt. 22nd Regt., and Major Tyrone Fus., *b.* 1832, *m.* 1st, 1866, Josephine Maria, dau. of Peter Bancroft, of Norbiton Park, Kingston-on-Thames, and widow of Thomas Pakenham, of Glenoak, co. Antrim, and by her (who *d.* 1889) had issue,
  1. Charles Conway Dobbs, *b.* 20 Nov. 1869 ; *d.* 1 May, 1909.
  2. William Spencer Hamilton, *d.* young.
  3. George Royle Chappell, *b.* 12 Oct. 1873 ; *d. unm.* 29 Jan. 1901.
  4. Peter Bancroft, *b.* 3 Dec. 1874.
  5. Richard Ruthven, *b.* 1876, *d.* young.
  1. Frances Hester Mary, *m.* 1892, Rev. Daniel Davies, Vicar and Rural Dean of Wrexham and Canon Residentiary of St. Asaph, and has issue.
Major Ellis *m.* 2ndly, 28 Nov. 1891, Rose Sarah (*d.* 23 March, 1911), eldest dau. of Thomas Richardson Browne, D.L. of Aughentaine Castle, co. Tyrone (*see* KNOX-BROWNE *of Aughentaine*).
1. Dymphna.

Mr. Richard Ellis *m.* 2ndly, 1852, Mary, dau. of Henry Chandler, of Buckingham, and by her had issue,
3. Richard Henry Whateley, of Glenasrone, *b.* 1853 ; *m.* 1878, Thomasina Anne (*d.* 17 Nov. 1910), dau. of Robert Thompson, and has issue,
  1. Mary Bertha, *d.* 1910.
  2. Lurline, *m.* 8 Sept. 1910, John Hely Owen, of Ballyhorgan, co. Kerry.
2. Elizabeth Mary Dymphna, *m.* 21 April, 1903, Rev. W. E. Bentley, Rector of Brosna, co. Kerry.
He *m.* 3rdly, 1869, Louisa Theodora Blennerhasset, 3rd dau. of Edward Agar. She *d.s.p.* He *d.* 1879. His eldest son,
REV. THOMAS ELLIS, of Glenasrone, co. Limerick, Rector of Killylea, co. Armagh, *b.* 8 Oct. 1830 ; *m.* 1854, Louisa Jane, dau. of Lieut.-Col. Echlin Matthews, and *d.* 12 June, 1888, having had issue,
1. RICHARD, now of Abbeyfeale.
2. William Cary Dobbs (Rev.), *b.* 5 June, 1865 ; *d. unm.* 22 Dec. 1891.
1. Sarah Maria, *b.* July, 1855 ; *d. unm.* 20 Sept. 1884.
2. Frances Anne, *b.* 1 March, 1857.
3. Eleanor Jones, *b.* 18 June, 1860; *m.* 28 June, 1888, William Henry Kisbey, K.C., M.A., of Stramore House, Gilford, co. Down. County Court Judge for Louth and Armagh.

Seat—Glenasrone, Abbeyfeale, co. Limerick.

ELLISON-MACARTNEY. *See* **MACARTNEY.**

ENRAGHT-MOONY. *See* **MOONY.**

EUSTACE. *See* **EUSTACE-DUCKETT.**

ROBERTSON-EUSTACE OF ROBERTSTOWN.

ROBERT WILLIAM BARRINGTON ROBERTSON-EUSTACE, of Robertstown, co. Kildare, and Ballydale, co. Cork, Capt. Auxiliary Reserve and late 4th Batt. South Staffs Regt. He served in S. African War 1900–2, and is now Supt. Police British East Africa Protectorate, b. 1870, assumed by Royal Licence, 31 March, 1909, the arms of EUSTACE quarterly with those of ROBERTSON.

Lineage.—The family of Eustace, of ancient Norman descent, was established in Ireland by one of the companions in Arms of HENRY II, by whom he was appointed a Governor of co. Kildare.

SIR ROWLAND FITZ-EUSTACE, Knt., Lord of Kilcullen, Lord Deputy to the Duke of Clarence, and Lord High Treasurer of Ireland, which latter high post he held for thirty-eight years, was created by patent 5 March, 1462, for his many services, Lord Baron Portlester. This Sir Rowland, who was son and heir of Edward Fitz-Eustace (Rot. Pat. 1 EDWARD IV, Cau. Dub.), *m.* Margaret, dau. and heir of Jenico Dartas (Mem. Rot. 22 HENRY VII, 12 Ch. R. Off.), and widow of John, son of Sir John Dowdall, and had, with other issue, a dau. and co-heir,

ALISON, who *m.* Gerald, 8th Earl of Kildare, surnamed "the Great," and by him, was mother of Gerald, 9th Earl of Kildare, ancestor of the ducal House of Leinster. Alison Eustace, Countess of Kildare, *d.* in 1480, and was bur. in the new chapel of Kilcullen.

Sir Rowland, Lord Portlester, *d.* 14 Dec. 1496, and was bur. in the convent of Minors Friars, at Kilcullen (New Abbey), which he and his wife, Margaret, had founded and built.

SIR THOMAS EUSTACE (who became male heir of the great house of Eustace), created Baron of Kilcullen, co. Kildare, in 1541, and Viscount of Baltinglass, co. Wicklow, in 1542. His Lordship made a settlement of all his estates upon the marriage of his son, Sir Rowland Eustace, 2nd Viscount, with Joan, dau. of James, Lord Dunboyne. The 1st Viscount Baltinglass *m.* Margaret, dau. of Peter Talbot, of Malahide Castle, co. Dublin, by Catherine his wife, dau. of Gerald, Earl of Kildare, and had issue,
1. ROWLAND, of whom presently.
2. Richard.
1. Anne, *m.* O'Toole, of Magnelle.
2. Janet, *m.* Bryan McCahir, Cavanagh.
3. Margaret, *m.* George Burnell.

The eldest son,

SIR ROWLAND EUSTACE, Knt., 2nd Viscount Baltinglass, Baron Kilcullen, aged thirty-five in 1540, had livery of his estates 16 Nov. 1549. He *m.* Joan, dau. of James Butler, Lord Dunboyne, by the Lady Joan Butler his wife, dau. of Peter, 8th Earl of Ormonde, and had issue,
1. JAMES, of whom presently.
2. Edmund, of Tubber, who fled, being attainted in 1585. He *m.* Frances, dau. of Robert Pipho.
3. William, of Naas, of whom hereafter, as ancestor of the present representative of the family. 4. Thomas.
5. Walter, executed in Dublin 1583.
6. Richard, fled from Ireland.

The eldest son,

JAMES EUSTACE, 3rd VISCOUNT BALTINGLASS, joined the Earl of Desmond in arms, in the hope of placing Queen MARY of Scotland upon the throne, but the attempt proved abortive, and Baltinglass had to escape to Spain in 1583, where he soon after *d.* of grief. In two years after his death in 1585, an Act of Parliament was passed against the family, called the "statute of Baltinglass" which made estates tail forfeitable for treason. By these post facto laws, the family of Eustace was deprived of their estates and titles. He *m.* Mary, dau. and co-heir of Henry Travers, of Monkstown Castle, co. Dublin, by Genet Preston his wife, but *d.s.p.* His brother and eventual heir.

THE HON. WILLIAM EUSTACE, who was slain in rebellion 21 April, 1581, and his head taken to Dublin. He *m.* Margaret, dau. of Ashe, of Great Forenass, co. Kildare, and had (with a dau., Jane, wife of Capt. Archbold) an only son,

ROWLAND EUSTACE, *m.* Elizabeth Bigland, a Yorkshire lady, dau. of Mary Strickland, of Sizergh. By her he had two sons, of whom the elder, James, an Officer in the Army, died in early youth of the plague. The younger,

RICHARD EUSTACE, became representative of the family. He served as a sovereign of Naas, and inherited the property of Ashe's Castle there, derived from his grandmother, Margaret Ashe. He *m.* Mary, dau. of William Forster, and had issue,

1. JOHN, *d. unm.* at a very advanced age.
2. CHARLES, of whom presently.
3. William, *d.* very old and *unm.*
1. Elizabeth. 2. Avis, *m.* 1638, Alexander Graydon.
3. Mary.

Richard Eustace's will was dated 21 Aug. 1702, and proved 10 Sept. in the same year. His 2nd son,

CHARLES EUSTACE, *m.* Elizabeth, dau. of Capt. Borrowes, of Ardenode, co. Kildare, and had issue,
1. Richard, of Naas, whose line is extinct.
2. JOHN, of whom hereafter.
3. William, *d.s.p.*
4. Borrowes, *d.* young.
5. Alexander, in holy orders, *d. unm.*; will proved in 1779, probate to his nephew, Charles, son of his brother John.
6. Thomas, *d.* young.
1. Mary, and 2. Elizabeth, both *d.* young.

The will of Charles Eustace was dated 28 April, 1732, and proved 2 Feb. following. His 2nd son (whose descendants became eventually representatives of the family),

JOHN EUSTACE, of Naas, *m.* Elizabeth, dau. of Robert Graydon, of Russelstown (marriage licence dated 7 Dec. 1736), and, dying 16 Nov. 1769, was *s.* by his only son,

CHARLES EUSTACE, of Robertstown, co. Kildare, and of Corbally, Queen's Co., Lieut.-Gen. in the Army, and Member in the Irish Parliament, *m.* 9 Jan. 1763, Alicia, dau. of Oliver McCausland, of Stranorlar, M.P. for Strabane, and had issue,
1. CHARLES, his heir.
2. Oliver, Cornet of Horse, *d. unm.*
3. Henry, of Corbally, Queen's Co., Lieut.-Gen. in the Army, *m.* 1819, Henrietta, dau. of Peter Count Dalton, of Grenanstown, and *d.* 5 Oct. 1844, leaving issue,
 1. Henry, of Corbally, Queen's Co., and Grenanstown, Nenagh, co. Tipperary, J.P. and D.L., *b.* 1822; *m.* 9 Oct. 1861, Albertine, widow of Count Foschi, and youngest dau. of the late Gen. Marquis Paulucci, Governor-Gen. of Genoa. He *d.* 12 Aug. 1898. She *d.* 7 June, 1899, leaving a dau.,
  Henrietta (97, *Quai du Midi, Nice*), *b.* Oct. 1862.
 2. CHARLES EDWARD, present male representative of the family, late Lieut. 46th Regt., of 2 Rue de la Pleine, Geneva.
 3. John Roland, *d.s.p.* June, 1885.
 1. Henrietta, *d.* young.
 2. Rosalie, *m.* 15 Aug. 1853, the Marquis Ricci Parraciani, of Rome and Montepulciano, Tuscany. She *d.* 17 Dec. 1909.
4. William Cornwallis (Sir), Gen. in the Army, K.C.H., C.B., of Sandford Hall, Essex, *m.* 1st, 9 May, 1809, Catherine Frances, dau. of Lord Talbot, of Malahide, by whom (who *d.* 10 Dec. 1816) he had issue,
 1. Alexander Talbot Eustace Malpas, *m.* 12 June, 1845, Georgiana Charlotte, dau. of John Drummond, and *d.* 1870, leaving issue,
  (1) FRANCIS JOHN WILLIAM EUSTACE, C.B., Major-General (ret.), late R.A. (*Barton End, Nailsworth, Gloucestershire*). (*Travellers' and Naval and Military Clubs*), *b.* 17 Sept. 1849; *m.* 13 Feb. 1882, Marina Annie, 2nd dau. of Field-Marshal Sir Donald Martin Stewart, 1st bart., G.C.B., and has issue, Frank Rowland, *b.* 30 June, 1891.
  (2) Alexander Rowland, Capt. The Buffs, *b.* 8 Aug. 1859; killed in action at Driefontein in South African War, 10 March, 1900.
 1. Frances Catherine Elizabeth, *m.* 1st, 1841, Robert King, of Grosvenor Place; and 2ndly, to the Rev. Samuel Lloyd.
 2. Alicia Margaret Maria, *d. unm.* 1840.

Sir William *m.* 2ndly, Caroline Margaret, dau. of John King, Under Secretary of State, and by her had two sons,
 2. John Thomas. 3. Robert Henry.

He *m.* 3rdly, Emma, 2nd dau. and co-heir of Admiral Sir Eliab Harvey, of Chigwell, and had further issue, one dau.,
 3. Emma Louisa, *m.* 1854, Miles Lonsdale Formby, late of the Carabineers.

Sir William *d.* 9 Feb. 1855.
5. Alexander, Capt. of Dragoons, killed at Vimiera.
6. John Rowland (Sir), K.H., of Baltraney, co. Kildare, Lieut.-Gen. in the Army, High Sheriff co. Kildare 1848, *d. unm.* (*see* EUSTACE *of Kilcock*).
1. Elizabeth, *m.* the Rev. Henry Johnson.
2. Alicia, *m.* 1st, Nicholas Barnewell, 14th Lord Trimelstown; and 2ndly, Lieut.-Gen. Sir Evan Lloyd, by whom she left a son and two daus.
3. Mary Anne, *m.* Robert Shearman, of Grange, co. Kilkenny.

Lieut.-Gen. Eustace *d.* 1803, and was *s.* by his son,

REV. CHARLES EUSTACE, of Robertstown, who having become male representative of the family petitioned the Crown that his right to the VISCOUNTY OF BALTINGLASS might be acknowledged. His petition was referred to the Attorney-General of Ireland, who, having investigated the case, made a report thereon to Government, concluding thus : " I am of opinion that the petitioner has shown sufficient evidence of his right to the dignity of Viscount of Baltinglass, in case the attainder of James, the 3rd Viscount, created by the Act of Queen ELIZABETH, were reversed." The Rev. Charles Eustace *m.* 1805, Cassandra, dau. and co-heir of John Stannard, of Ballydoyle, co. Cork, by whom he had,
1. CHARLES STANNARD, of Robertstown.
1. ALICIA CATHERINE, *m.* 1827, Robert Robertson, Advocate, Sheriff Substitute of Stirlingshire, and *d.* 1878, having had issue,
 1. ROBERT JAMESON EUSTACE ROBERTSON EUSTACE, Col. in the Army, late 60th Rifles, who took by Royal Licence, dated 25 April, 1875, the surname of EUSTACE. He *m.* 9 April, 1863, Lady Katharine Legge (*Montague House, Wokingham*), dau. of

William, 4th Earl of Dartmouth (*see* BURKE's *Peerage*), and *d.* 1 April, 1889, leaving issue,
  (1) CHARLES LEGGE EUSTACE, late of Robertstown
  (2) ROBERT WILLIAM BARRINGTON, now of Robertstown.
  (3) Seton George Legge, *b.* 1871.
  (1) Alicia Katherine.   (2) Adelaide Mary.
  (3) Violet Theresa.
2. Charles Constance, *d.* young, 1857.
  1. Alice Trimleston, *m.* 1849, James Jameson, of Airfield, co. Dublin, and had issue.
  2. Helen Margaret, *d.* young.
2. Elizabeth, *m.* Henry Leader, of Mount Leader.
3. Catherine, *m.* Adm. Sir Alexander D. Y. Arbuthnot, who *d.* 8 May, 1871.
4. Jane, *m.* William H. Connor, R.N., brother of Daniel Connor, of Ballybricken, co. Cork.
The son and successor,
CHARLES STANNARD EUSTACE, of Robertstown, co. Kildare, and Ballydoyle, co. Cork, a Capt. in the Army, *m.* 1st, 8 April, 1843, Laura, dau. of Christopher Thomas Tower, of Weald Hall, Essex, and by her (who *d.* 1844) had one son, who *d.* in infancy. He *m.* 2ndly, 1864, Rosetta Philippa, dau. of the late Col. Cameron, of Danygraig, co. Glamorgan, but *d.s.p.* 1875. His widow *m.* 2ndly, 14 Feb. 1888, Percy Armytage, M.V.O., son of Col. Henry Armytage (*see* BURKE's *Peerage*, ARMYTAGE, Bart.). She *d.s.p.* 31 Dec. 1902. Capt. C. S. Eustace was *s.* in his estates at the death of his widow by his great nephew, CAPT. CHARLES LEGGE EUSTACE, D.S.O., now of Robertstown. His nephew,
CAPT. CHARLES LEGGE ROBERTSON-EUSTACE, D.S.O., of Robertstown, co. Kildare, and Ballydoyle, co. Cork, Capt. King's Royal Rifle Corps, served in Manipur Exped. 1891, in Burma 1891-2, in Mashonaland 1896, and in S. African War 1899-1902, *b.* 26 July, 1867 ; *s.* his maternal uncle, Capt. Charles Stannard Eustace, of Robertstown, at the death of his widow 1902, and assumd by Royal Licence, 30 Dec. 1903, the arms of EUSTACE quarterly with those of ROBERTSON. He *m.* 23 June, 1906, Marjory Edith, younger dau. of Major Thomas Leith, of Petinathen, co. Aberdeen (*see* LEITH *of Glenknady*), and *d.s.p.* 4 Oct. 1908, being *s.* by his brother.

Arms—Quarterly, 1st and 4th, or, a saltire gu. (EUSTACE) ; 2nd and 3rd gu., a chevron or between three wolf's heads erased arg. in the centre chief point a crescent of the last (ROBERTSON). Crest—A stag at gaze ppr., between the attires or, a crucifix arg. Motto—Cur me persequeris.

Seat—Robertstown, co. Kildare. Residence—Montague House, Wokingham, Berks. Club—Sports.

EUSTACE OF KILCOCK.

JOHN GEORGE EUSTACE, of Kilcock and Kinneagh, co. Kildare, late Oxfordshire Yeomanry, *b.* 11 Jan. 1857.

Lineage.—LIEUT.-GEN. SIR JOHN ROWLAND EUSTACE, K.H., of Baltrasney, co. Kildare, High Sheriff co. Kildare, *d. unm.* (*see* EUSTACE *of Robertstown*), and was *s.* by,
REV. WILLIAM GEORGE EUSTACE, of Kilcock and Kinneagh M.A. (formerly Arthurs), for many years Vicar of Stradbally, Queen's Co. He assumed by Royal Licence, 1 Oct. 1864, the surname and arms of EUSTACE. He was *b.* 2 July, 1824, and *d.* 4 Feb. 1890, having *m.* 1847, Helen (*d.* 19 Aug. 1898), 3rd dau. of the late John Waldron Wright, Magistrate of British Honduras (son of the late Thomas Nisbett Wright, of Foulksrath Castle, co. Kilkenny), by Ann, dau. of Capt. John Young, of Belize. They had issue,
1. William FitzEustace (Rev.), M.A. Camb., Vicar of Bishop's Lydeard, Somerset, R.D., *b.* 1848 ; *m.* 1890, Ethel, eldest dau. of Rev. Stafford Torliffe, of Staplegrove, Taunton, and has issue, Rowland.
  Alice.
2. JOHN GEORGE, now of Kilcock.
3. Herbert Rowland, B.A. Camb., *b.* 1859 ; *d. unm.* 28 May, 1885.
1. Helen Rosa, *b.* 20 Dec. 1849.
2. Mary Jane, *b.* 27 Feb. 1851.
3. Elizabeth Alice, *b.* 10 Sept. 1852 ; *d. unm.* 11 June, 1871.
4. Ada Ann, *b.* 22 Dec. 1853.

Arms—Or, a saltire gu., a bordure wavy az. in the centre chief point a fleur-de-lis of the 2nd. Crest—A stag at gaze ppr., charged with a fleur-de-lis and a saltire wavy couped in fesse gu. between the attires a crucifix arg. Motto—Cur me persequeris.
Residence—Fern Bank, Stow-on-the-Wold, Glos.

EUSTACE OF NEWSTOWN.

MAURICE JAMES EUSTACE, of Newstown, co. Carlow, *b.* 25 July, 1867 ; *m.* 28 April, 1909, Violet Mary, youngest dau. of J. A. Rossiter.

Lineage.—JAMES EUSTACE, J.P. (son of Col. Robert Eustace, by Catherine Whelan his wife, and grandson of Edward Eustace, of Castlemore (*see that family*), *m.* 16 March, 1803, Elizabeth, 3rd dau. of the late Major Eustace, J.P. of Castlemore, co. Carlow, and had issue,
1. HARDY, of Newstown.
2. Robert, dec.
1. Susanna, *m.* Alexander Brenan, R.N.
2. Catherine, *m.* the Rev. A. A. L. D. Nickson.
3. Sarah.
Mr. Eustace *d.* 13 June, 1831, and was *s.* by his elder son,
HARDY EUSTACE, of Newstown, J.P. and D.L., *b.* 12 Feb. 1812 ; *m.* 17 Aug. 1838, Bridget Anne, only dau. of James Brown, of Knocklow, co. Wicklow, Major in the 103rd Regt., and by her (who *d.* 1893) had issue,
1. JAMES, late of Newstown.   2. Robert, *b.* 17 July, 1840.
3. Edward, M.D., of Underwood, Cheltenham, Lieut.-Col. (retired) late R.A.M.C. ; *b.* 23 Dec. 1841 ; *m.* 1st, 12 Sept. 1878, Georgina Elizabeth Lucy, only surviving dau. of Col. Walter S. Stace, R.E., and grand-dau. of Admiral Sir Thomas Sabine Pasley, Bart., K.C.B., and by her (who *d.* 1893) had issue,
  1. Emmeline Georgina.   2. Dorothea.
  3. Katharine Sabine.
He *m.* 2ndly, 21 July, 1894, Mary Adelaide, 3rd dau. of Maj.-Gen. J. S. Rawlins, B.S.C., and *d.* 16 Feb. 1903, having by her had issue,
  1. Rowland, *b.* 11 Aug. 1895.
  2. Edward Arthur Rawlins, *b.* 18 Nov. 1899.
  3. Norman, *b.* 27 May, 1901.
4. Hardy, *b.* 2 Oct. 1843.
5. Thomas Swan, *b.* 6 Jan. 1855.
6. Joseph Swan, *b.* 27 March, 1859.
1. Catherine Elizabeth.   2. Elizabeth Frances.
3. Susanna.   4. Bridget Anne.
5. Margaret Sarah.
Mr. Eustace *d.* May, 1862. The eldest son,
JAMES EUSTACE, of Newstown, co. Carlow, High Sheriff 1874, *b.* 22 June, 1839 ; *m.* 28 June, 1865, Emily Catharine, youngest dau. of Gen. Sir Maurice Stack, K.C.B., by Cecilia his wife, dau. of Hugh Spottiswoode, of Spottiswoode, co. Berwick, and *d.* 10 Sept. 1905, having had issue,
1. MAURICE JAMES, now of Newstown.
2. John Spottiswoode, *b.* 1868.
3. Cecil Robert, *b.* 1876.   4. Roland Charles, *b.* 1880.
1. Emily Alison.

Arms—Gu., a saltire or. Crest—A stag's head cabossed between the attires a crucifix all ppr. Motto—Soli Deo gloria.
Seat—Newstown, near Tullow, co. Carlow.

EVANS OF CARKER.

JOHN WESTROP GREEN EVANS, of Carker House, co. Cork, J.P., *b.* 4 May, 1831 ; *s.* his father 1864 ; *m.* 1863, Anne (she *d.* Dec. 1904), dau. of M. O'Connor, of Newfield, co. Cork, and has issue,
1. RALPH, *b.* 1867.
2. Alfred, *b.* 1868 ; *m.* 1901, Margaret Gertrude, dau. of P. Kiley, of Red Hill, N.S.W., and has issue,
  Elystan Bernard, *b.* Aug. 1902.
3. Roberts Walter, B.L., LL.B., *b.* 1873 ; *m.* Oct. 1903, Bridget, dau. of William J. Murphy, of Oakley Square, London, and has issue.
1. Anne.
2. Henrietta Thomasina, *m.* 1901, Oliver Macgillicudy Graham, and has issue.
3. Georgina Elizabeth, *m.* 29 April, 1899, Bertram Percival, and has issue.
4. Mary.   5. Julia Christiana.
6. Gertrude Emmeline, *d. unm.* 18 July, 1894.

Lineage.—NATHANIEL EVANS, of Griston and Castle Roberts, co. Limerick, the first settler of this family in Ireland, had an only son,
NATHANIEL EVANS, of Carker House, co. Cork, who *m.* Bridget, eldest dau. and co-heir of Nicholas Green, of Carker, and had issue, two sons and one dau. The eldest son,
NICHOLAS GREEN EVANS, of Carker House, *m.* Hannah, dau. of Randal Roberts, of Britfieldstown, co. Cork, and had issue (with three sons and three daus. *d. unm.*),

1. NICHOLAS GREEN, of whom presently.
2. Nathaniel, *m.* a dau. of George Parker, and sister of Admiral Sir George Parker, and had a dau. *m.* Charles Vernon, of Lower Mount Street, Dublin.
3. Roberts, Major-Gen. Royal Artillery, *d.* 1835; *m.* Mary Martha, eldest dau. of Gen. Stephens, Royal Artillery, and had issue, one son and four daus.,
   1. Francis Roberts, Major E.I.C.S., *m.* Mary, dau. of William Eccles, of Eccles Street, Dublin.
   1. Amelia, *m.* Capt. William Lemoine, R.A.
   2. Eliza, *m.* George Ferris, Surgeon-Major R.A.
   3. Gertrude, *m.* Sir Henry Singer Keating, Knt., Justice of Common Pleas.
   4. Mary Martha, *m.* Orlando Saul Donnell, Inspector-General of Hospitals, A.M.D.
4. Henry, Vice-Admiral R.N., M.P. for Wexford, *m.* 1st, May, 1801, Elizabeth, eldest dau. and co-heir of Andrew Nash, of Rossnalee, co. Cork ; and 2ndly, 1812, Marianne, sister of Peter Holmes, of Peterfield, co. Tipperary, and dau. of Gilbert Holmes, of Belmont. He *d.* 16 Sept. 1842, having had issue by his 1st wife, with a dau., Elizabeth, *m.* Arthur Gethin Creagh, of Doneraile, co. Cork (*see* CREAGH *of Ballyandrew*), a son,
   Nicholas, of Newtown, co. Cork, J.P., Commander R.N., *b.* 2 Oct 1806 ; *m* 12 May, 1843, Catherine Alicia Gervais, dau. of Rev. Francis Gervais, of Cecil, Augher, co. Tyrone, and has issue,
      (1) Henry, *b.* 16 May, 1844.
      (2) Francis Nicholas, Barrister-at-Law, *b.* 14 Jun. 1846 ; *m.* 16 Feb. 1891, Emily Maynard Palmer, dau. of Col. Charles Christopher Oldfield, Bombay Cavalry, and had issue,
         1. Cosmo Francis, *b.* 1 June, 1894 ; *d.* 16 Nov. 1894.
         1. Sybil Nina, *b.* 14 Aug. 1896.
         2. Ione Grace, *b.* 4 Feb. 1892.
      (3) Hamilton Archibald, *b.* 7 Dec. 1847 ; *d.* 3 March, 1863.
      (4) Pierre Gervais, *b.* 14 Sept. 1849, Lieut. R.N., *d.* 10 Aug. 1877.
      (1) Julia Elizabeth, *m.* 21 Dec. 1876, Capt. Roberts Anderson, Imperial Austrian Army. She *d.s.p.* May, 1879. He *d.* July, 1878.
1. Martha, *m.* Thomas Newenham, of Lehena, co. Cork.

The eldest son,
NICHOLAS GREEN EVANS, of Carker House, Doneraile ; *m.* Nov. 1790, Anne, 4th dau. of Ralph Westropp, of Attyflin, co. Limerick (*see that family*), and had issue,
1. RALPH WESTROPP, of whom presently.
2. Nicholas, dec.
3. John, dec.
4. Roberts, dec.
5. Walter, dec.
1. Hannah, *m.* George Newenham, and is dec.
2. Mary, *m.* Arthur Norcott, and is dec.
3. Eliza, *d. unm.*
4. Emma, *d. unm.* 13 Jan. 1909, aged 100 years and 24 days.
5. Ellen, *d. unm.*

The eldest son,
RALPH WESTROPP EVANS, of Carker, served in 62nd Regt. in Peninsular War and received medal and clasps, *b.* 1794 ; *m.* 1818 his cousin, Henrietta Louisa, dau. of Ralph Westropp, by Harriet his wife, sister of Charles, 2nd Viscount Gort, and had issue,
1. Nicholas Green, *b.* 1820 ; *d. unm.* 1856.
2. JOHN WESTROP GREEN, now of Carker.
3. Ralph Westrop, *b.* 1833 ; *d.* an infant.
1. Harriette Eliza, *m.* 1854, Capt. Napoleon Herroquelle Berthier, 65th Regt., French Army, and *d.* 2 March, 1870.
2. Juliana, *d. unm.* 1833.
3. Mary, *d. unm.* 1832.
4. Thomasina Julia, *m.* 31 March, 1841, George Westrop, 2nd son of John Westrop, of Attyflin, co. Limerick, and *d.* 1855, leaving issue (*see that family*).
5. Anne Newnham, *d. unm.*
6. Georgiana, *d. unm.* 1834.
Mr. Evans *d.* 1864.

Seat—Carker House, near Doneraile.

EVANS OF GORTMERRON HOUSE.

GEORGE EDWARD AUGUSTINE EVANS, of Gortmerron House, co. Tyrone, Barrister in Canada, *b.* 13 April, 1860 ; *m.* 1897, Maude, 2nd dau. of Lieut.-Col. Henry Herbert Skill, late 11th Regt., and has issue,
1. GEORGE, *b.* 1899.
2. Patrick FitzGerald, *b.* 1901.
3. Arthur Armitage, *b.* 1908.

Lineage.—THOMAS EVANS was Capt. of a troop of horse in the English Army *temp.* CHARLES I. He served in Ireland in the Civil War, and obtained grants of land in co. Kilkenny, where he eventually settled, having also obtained estates in Queen's Co. He became an alderman of the city of Kilkenny, and served as Mayor in 1660 and 1666-69. He *m.* Katherine Weldon, and had issue, an only dau., Ellen, and an only son,

I. L. G.

WILLIAM EVANS, of Kilcreene, Kilkenny, created a bart. by patent dated 19 Feb. 1682, *m.* Jane, dau. and co-heir of Hon. Richard Coote, son of Charles, 2nd Earl of Mountrath, by his 2nd wife, Jane, dau. of Sir Robert Hannay, Bart. His dau. and eventual heiress, Catherine, *m.* Francis Morres, of Castle Morres.
EDWARD EVANS, brother of the above Thomas Evans, Sheriff of Kilkenny 25 July, 1665, commanded a troop in the Earl of Arran's Horse at the Battle of the Boyne. He *m.* and had issue,
1. Henry, of Belevans, co. Kilkenny, whose only son and heir, Joseph, of Belevans, was father of Joseph, of Belevans, who *d. unm.*, and left his large landed estates to found a charitable institution, now designated " Evans' Charity."
2. EDWARD, of whom we treat.

This
EDWARD EVANS, Mayor of Kilkenny 1732, *d.* Sept. 1738 ; *m.* 1st, Sarah Butler, and had one son, Ambrose. He *m.* 2ndly, Susanna Turvan *alias* Loidell, and had issue,
REV. GEORGE EVANS, Rector of Donaghmore, co. Tyrone, *m.* Priscilla, dau. of Robert Armitage, of Liverpool, and had,
1. Robert (Rev.), *m.* Emilia, dau. of Rev. J. Forbes, and had by her a dau., Rebecca Emilia, *m.* Euseby Stratford Kirwan, of Monkstown, co. Dublin, and *d.s.p.*
2. EDWARD, of whom presently.
1. Mary, *m.* Rev. Alexander George Stuart, of Tullynisken Glebe, co. Tyrone.

The 2nd son,
EDWARD EVANS, of Gortmerron House, co. Tyrone, J.P., *b.* 31 May, 1762 ; *m.* 1789, Sarah Maria, 2nd dau. of Thomas Kelly, of Dawson's Grove, co. Armagh, J.P., and *d.* 17 Aug. 1857, leaving issue,
1. George (Rev.), *m.* Elizabeth, dau. of William Murray, J.P., and *d.* in Canada, 19 May, 1878, having had issue,
   1. GEORGE, of Gortmerron.
   1. Frances.
   2. Sarah Maria.
   He emigrated with his family to Canada 1851, and resided at Gortmerron House, Oak Ville, Toronto.
2. Thomas Kelly, J.P., of Vesey Place, Kingstown, co. Dublin, *b.* June, 1795 ; *m.* Elizabeth, dau. of Capt. John Winder, Royal Artillery, and *d.* 13 Nov. 1873, having by her (who *d.* 22 July, 1888) had issue,
   1. Edward.
   2. John W.
   3. Dawson Kelly.
   4. Arthur Kelly, *b.* 18 June, 1842 ; *m.* Jimima Isabel, dau. of Alexander McCausland, of Drumnakilly, co. Tyrone, and *d.* 22 Oct. 1893, leaving issue,
      (1) Thomas Kelly.
      (2) Edward.
      (3) Arthur Kelly, Lieut. Royal Marines.
      (1) Louisa Kelly.
      (2) Maud Ethel, dec.
      (3) Elizabeth Widner, *m.* 1stly, Major A. F. G. Fullerton, 1st Leinster Regt., who *d.* in the S. African War. She *m.* 2ndly, Calverley J. Lyster of Bonraven, Birr, King's Co.
      (4) Norah Kathleen, *m.* Mervyn R. Wilson.
      (5) Alice Lyle, *m.* William Langford.
      (6) Ida Constance.
   1. Elizabeth Jane.
   2. Sarah Maria.
   3. Mary Anne.
   4. Alicia Campbell.
   5. Letitia Kelly.
   6. Jane Waring.
   7. Lucy Alexandrina.
3. ROBERT, of Gortmerron.
4. EDWARD, late of Gortmerron.
1. Louisa Jane, *m.* Capt. A. Stuart, 90th Regt. ; dec.
2. Priscilla, *m.* D. H. Sherrard, of Thorndale, co. Dublin ; dec.
3. Alicia, *m.* Rev. R. W. Bland, of Abbeville, Belfast.
4. Sarah Maria, *m.* John Echlin Matthews, of White Abbey, co. Antrim, Lieut.-Col. co. Down Militia ; dec.

The 3rd son,
ROBERT EVANS, of Gortmerron, J.P., *b.* 1799 ; *m.* 1829, Eleanor, dau. of Surgeon-Gen. George Stuart, of Dublin, and *d.* 21 July, 1876, when he was *s.* by his only surviving brother,
EDWARD EVANS, of Gortmerron, who *d.* 3 Feb. 1889, and was *s.* by his nephew,
GEORGE EVANS, of Gortmerron House, co. Tyrone, *b.* 1828 ; *s.* his uncle 1889 ; *m.* 13 Nov. 1858, Jane, dau. of the late Major Fitzgerald, Military Secretary and Aide-de-Camp to the Gov. General of Canada, and *d.* 23 Sept. 1905, having had issue,
1. GEORGE EDWARD AUGUSTINE, now of Gortmerron.
2. Arthur Thomas Kelly, *b.* 4 March, 1862.
1. Mary Eliza, *m.* 3 Jan. 1888, W. H. F. Lyons, of Brookhill, Lisburn.
2. Mabel Sara, *m.* 17 Dec. 1890, Algernon William, 6th and last Viscount Avonmore, who *d.* 3 Sept. 1910, leaving issue.
3. Louisa Evelyn.

Arms—Erm., three boars' heads couped sa. langued gu. *Crest*—A demi-lion rampant, reguardant erminois, holding between his paws a boar's head as in the arms. *Motto*—Libertas.
Seat—Gortmerron House, Dungannon, co. Tyrone. *Residence*—Holme House, Rusholme Road, Toronto, Canada.

EVANS OF ROCKFIELD.

USHER WILLIAMSON EVANS, of Rockfield, co. Westmeath, M.D., *b.* 5 Feb. 1823 ; late Deputy Inspector-General of Army Hospitals, served with distinction in the Crimean War, and has the medal and four clasps and Turkish medal ; *m.* 15 July, 1859, Caroline Fanny (*d.* 24 Sept. 1905), 3rd dau. of the late Capt. Boyle Travers, Rifle Brigade, and has issue,

O

Evans. THE LANDED GENTRY. 210

6. Francis Henry, late Lieut. 3rd Batt. Gloucestershire Regt.; b. 18 May, 1860.
7. Usher Williamson, Lieut.-Col. R.E., served in Chin-Lushai Exped. 1889-90 (medal with clasp), in Tirah Exped. (despatches, medal with two clasps), b. 26 June, 1864; m. 21 Sept. 1907, Julia Gertrude, 2nd dau. of the Rev. William Smith Davis.
3. William, D.S.O., Major R.F.A., served in S. Africa 1899-1901 (despatches, D.S.O., medal with five clasps), b. 11 Feb. 1871; m. 22 July, 1908, Dora Rosamund, dau. of James Young, of Bangalore, and grand-dau. of late Major-Gen. Francis Young, Madras I.C.
4. John, Capt. 1st Batt. Royal Inniskilling Fusiliers, served in S. Africa 1899-1902 (wounded, Queen's medal with four clasps, King's medal), b. 15 July, 1873.
5. Henry, b. 26 July, 1876.
1. Mary.   2. Caroline.

Lineage.—Hugh Evans, of Ballinrobe, co. Mayo, descended from Robert Evans, of the same family as the noble house of Carbery, made his will 24 Feb. 1718. He m. Catherine, sister of Samuel Burrowes (her will, dated 30 June, 1729, was proved in Dublin, 13 Aug. of that year); they had issue,
1. Michael, of Ballinrobe, m. Catherine Gilbert, and d. before 1729, leaving an only son,
   Hugh, of Dublin, who d. in his minority.
2. Hugh, of Ballinrobe, who d.s.p.
3. Francis, eventual heir.
1. Honora (d. before 1729), m. William Forster.
2. Ann, d. unm.

The 3rd son,
Francis Evans, of Dublin, m. 1st, 10 June, 1738, Martha, elder dau. and eventual co-heir of Joseph Sherwood, of Prior's Wood; and 2ndly (1779), Mrs. Christian Warren, widow (née Ogle). He d. 2 June, 1780, æt. 72; bur. at St. George's, Dublin, leaving issue by his first wife, who d. 16 April, 1774, æt. 54,
1. Nicholas, his heir.
2. Francis, Col. of Volunteers, 1782, m. Alicia, eldest dau. and eventually co-heir of William Ogle, of Fotham Park, co. Down, and d. Oct. 1811, leaving an only child,
   Francis, b. 15 Dec. 1784; m. 1st, Harriet, dau. of John Locke, of Walthamstowe (she d. 1821), and 2ndly, Hannah Anne, 2nd dau. of John Gardiner, of Farm Hill, co. Mayo (she d. 1879). He d. Feb. 1860, leaving issue,
      (1) Francis Locke, b. 23 Dec. 1802; m. 14 July, 1840, Anna Maria, 3rd dau. of Thomas Stuart, and d.s.p. 11 Feb. 1861.
      (2) John Ogle, of Belgarriff House, co. Mayo, b. 23 July, 1814; m. 1st, 2 Sept. 1837, Emily Jane, eldest dau. of Thomas Stuart, and by her has issue,
         1. Francis John, b. 13 July, 1838; d. Jan. 1851.
         2 Robert Locke, b. 5 Aug. 1839, M.D.; m. Frances, widow of J. Hamilton, of Belfast.
         3. Henry Francis Dobree, b. 8 Oct. 1840; d. Aug. 1843.
         4. Francis John, b. 20 Nov. 1841; d. Aug. 1844.
         5. John Sisson, b. 23 Oct. 1845, d. unm.
         6. Edmund, b. Sept. 1849; d. April, 1854.
         7. William Arthur, b. Feb. 1852; m. Helen, dau. of John Bentley.
         8. Arthur Locke, b. Nov. 1853; m. 1880, Eugenie, dau. of T. Bentley, and has a son, John William Washington, b. July, 1881.
         9. Charles Pownall, b. Oct. 1854; d. 1870.
         10. Francis, b. 1858.
         1. Emily Alicia Harriet, m. July, 1867, Standish O'Grady McDermott, J.P. of Clongee, co. Mayo, and has issue.
         2. Annie Louisa, d. unm. 18 Nov. 1911.
         3. Mary Olivia Nantes.
         4. Louisa Charlotte, m. and has issue.
         5. Harriet Francis, m. 1892, John Roper.
      He m. 2ndly, 7 Jan. 1891, Eliza, dau. of James Cullen.
      (3) William Octavus, b. Nov. 1815; d. 17 April, 1816.
      (1) Mary, m. July, 1850, William James Gwynne, of Antrim, and d. leaving issue.
      (2) Alicia Harriet, d. unm. 30 Jan. 1899.
      (3) Harriet.   (4) Elizabeth, d. an infant.

The elder son,
Nicholas Evans, of Baymount and Prior's Wood, co. Dublin, Capt. 47th Regt., m. Mary Anne, eldest dau. of Vigors Thomas, of Limerick, Capt. R.N. (by Mary his wife, eldest dau. and co-heir of Richard Gabbett, of Killonan, co. Limerick, and Ann his wife, dau. of Robert Cox, of the family of Ballynoe, in the same co.). He d. 7 June, 1803, having by her (who d. 31 March, 1814) had issue,
1. Francis, his heir.
2. Nicholas, Lieut. 41st Regt., d. unm. in the West Indies, circa 1796.
3. William, of Will, and Bowden, co. Devon, and Cheltenham, Lieut.-Col. 41st Regt., b. 23 Dec. 1779; m. 20 Feb. 1819, Ann Sarah, eldest dau. of William Sloane, of Armagh and Tobago, and d. 12 June, 1843, leaving issue by her (who d. 29 June, 1830, æt. 35).
   1. Charles Bidgood, b. 14 Feb. 1820; d. unm. in India, 1848.
   2. William Sloane Sloane-Evans (Rev.), B.A. Trinity Coll. Cambridge, adopted the name of Sloane, in addition to and before Evans, in 1849, Vicar of Egloskerry and Tremaine, Cornwall, and formerly Incumbent of Holy Trinity, Barnstaple, b. 21 Aug. 1823; m. 21 Aug. 1847, Selina, 2nd dau. of the late William Branscombe, of Devon. She d. 1896. He d. 4 March, 1899, leaving issue,
      (1) Helena Gertrude Vigors Spenser.
      (2) Lucy Georgina Sherwood.
      (3) Edith Fitzmaurice.
   (4) Emily Standish, d. an infant 5 Nov. 1856.
   (5) Clara Selina Valenscourt.
3. Henry Hill, b. 7 Feb. 1825; d. unm. 4 July, 1850.
1. Annie Sloane, m. 12 Nov. 1842, Rev. Philip Thomas Drayton, B.A., Oxford, and d. 18 Aug. 1878, leaving issue.
1. Martha, m. 1791, Thomas Smith, M.D., of Maiden Hall, co. Kilkenny, and d. leaving issue.
2. Mary Anne, m. 1832, John Francis Lane, of St. Anne's, Enniscorthy, J.P. for co. Wexford, and d.s.p. 9 Dec. 1870; he d. 7 Aug. 1861.

The eldest son,
Francis Evans, of Prior's Wood, co. Dublin, and Robinstown co. Westmeath, Barrister-at-Law, m. 1st, 5 Nov. 1793, Anna, dau. of William Hickey, of Violetstown, who d. 21 May, 1815; and 2ndly, 1821, Francis, eldest dau. of Monsieur François Berthomé de-la-Mothe, of Nantes, who d. without issue 1833. He d. 20 May, 1834, leaving issue by his first wife,
1. Nicholas, of Lough Park, his heir.
2. Francis (Rev.), D.C.L., Rector of St. John's, Woodhouse, and Incumbent of Simcoe, Canada West, b. 1 Jan. 1800; m. July, 1825, Maria Sophia, 2nd dau. of Rev. Thomas Frye Lewis, of Taunton, Somerset; and d. 6 Sept. 1858, having by her (who d. 29 July, 1881) had issue,
   1. George Mountain, M.A. of King's College, Toronto, Barrister-at-Law, b. 1 Feb. 1828; m. 21 Dec. 1870, Alice Louisa, dau. of Rev. Thomas Scales Ellerby, and d. 23 May, 1891, having had surviving issue,
      (1) Charles Francis Evans-Lewis, Barrister-at-Law, adopted the additional name of Lewis in accordance with the will of Rev. J. B. Lewis, 1874, b. 24 Nov. 1871.
      (2) Frederick Percival, b. 1 Jan. 1875; m. 3 June, 1903, Charlotte Mary, dau. of Henry Langtry Smyth, and has issue,
         George Langtry, b. 19 March, 1904.
         Mary Katherine Louisa, b. 1 Dec. 1908.
      (3) Vernon Lewis, b. 24 Dec. 1878; m. 6 June, 1906, Ferissa Gertrude, dau. of P. J. Brown, and has issue,
         Ferissa Alice Myrtle, b. 2 April, 1907.
   2. Francis, Barrister-at-Law, b. 23 Nov. 1829; m. 28 Jan. 1869, Cornelia E., dau. of John Thompson, R.N., and d. 1 Aug. 1895, leaving issue,
      (1) Francis George, b. 18 Jan. 1870; m. 15 June, 1904, Adelaide, dau. of John Langrill, M.D., and has issue,
         Francis John Lewis, b. 15 Feb. 1907.
         Marion Margaret, b. 19 July, 1905.
      (2) Reginald Bertram, b. 5 March, 1874.
      (1) Jessie Marion, b. 24 Jan. 1876.
      (2) Mabel Elizabeth, b. 5 March, 1879.
      (3) Maria Sophia Lewis, b. 14 Oct. 1881.
   3. William Berthomé (Rev.), Rector of St. John's Church, Woodhouse, Ontario, b. 24 Aug. 1835; m. Elizabeth Letitia, dau. of Capt. Minty, R.N., and d. 5 Dec. 1884, having had issue,
      (1) William Minty, b. 25 Feb. 1865; d. unm. 31 July, 1906.
      (2) Charles Hamilton Lewis, b. 15 March, 1870.
      (1) Marianne Frances, b. 18 April, 1865; m. 9 Dec. 1885, Francis Henry Kent, of Woodhouse.
      (2) Kathleen Louisa Huron, b. 22 Aug. 1868.
      (3) Maud Drayton, b. 21 Aug. 1875.
      (4) Edith Alice Georgina, b. 25 Nov. 1878.
   4. Henry James (Rev.), Rector of All Saints' Church, Montreal, and Hon. Canon of Christ's Church Cathedral, M.A., Trin. Coll. Toronto, b. 15 March, 1837; m. 13 July, 1865, Cara, dau. of William Rutherford Fitzwilliam Berford, of Riverview and Rideau, Perth, Ontario, Canada, and d. 22 May, 1903, leaving issue,
      Berthomé Willoughby, b. 10 Dec. 1875.
      Cara Blanche Berford, m. 14 Sept. 1898, David Gilbert Yates, M.D., of New York, U.S.A.
   5. Lewis Hamilton, of Toronto, Physician, b. 5 Sept. 1841; m. 6 Aug. 1871, Blanche, dau. of Capt. John Robert Arnold, and has issue,
      (1) Arthur Stuart, Capt. R.E., served in Somaliland Exped. (medal and clasp), b. 7 Sept. 1874; m. 7 Feb. 1900, Annie Amelia, dau. of Richard Nash, and has issue,
         Winifred Margery Stuart, b. 10 April, 1906.
      (1) Madeline Maud, b. 31 Jan. 1877.
      (2) Edith Grace, Jacqueline, b. 11 March, 1879.
      (3) Mary Frances Winifred, b. 5 June, 1883; m. 10 March, 1908, Arthur Keble Mussen.
   6. Thomas Frye Lewis (Very Rev.), D.D., D.C.L. Trin. Coll. Toronto, Dean of Montreal and Rector of St. Stephen's, b. 17 Dec. 1845; m. 1st, 30 Dec. 1873, Maria Stewart, dau. of Strachan Bethune, K.C., and Maria Phillips his wife, and by her (who d. 16 Oct. 1903) has had issue,
      (1) Harry Basil Ashton, b. 13 Dec. 1874; m. 6 Oct. 1906, May Muriel Ross, only dau. of Henry Harcourt Curtis, and has issue,
         Katharine Maye, b. 2 July, 1909.
      (2) Trevor Ainslie, b. 31 Dec. 1878.
      (3) Cyril Lewis, b. 12 Aug. 1882; d. young.
      (1) Muriel Maye, b. 12 April, 1877; m. Adam Cairns Hudspeth, and has issue,
      (2) Ruby Bethune, b. 1 Dec. 1885.
   He m. 2ndly, 11 June, 1908, Emily Elizabeth, 2nd dau. of Robert Henry Bethune, Banker, of Toronto, and by her has issue,
      (4) Robert Lewis, b. 7 May, 1911.
   1. Anna Sophia, b. 23 May, 1826.
   2. Charlotte Georgina, b. 13 March, 1831.

3. Maria Augusta, b. 5 Sept. 1833.
4. Rosamund Matilda, b. 25 June, 1839; m. William J. Marsh.
5. Frances Flora Georgina, b. 2 July, 1843; m. Rev. John P. Hincks, Canon of St. Paul's Cathedral, London, Ontario, and Rector of All Saints, Windsor, Ontario.
6. Jessie Margaret, b. 30 Nov. 1848; m. Rev. George Keyes, and d. 1 Nov. 1908, leaving issue.
3. William, Lieut. 41st Regt., d. unm. 1831.
4. Mary Anne, d. unm. Sept. 1871.

The eldest son,

NICHOLAS EVANS, of Lough Park, co. Westmeath, J.P. for co. Westmeath, b. Oct. 1795; m. 1819, Mary Anne, dau. of Usher Philpott Williamson, of Dromore, co. Cork, by his wife Anne, dau. of J. Lloyd, of Beechmount, and d. 23 Dec. 1879, having had issue by her (who d. 17 Sept. 1859),
1. Francis Hugh, of Trin. Coll. Dublin, late 1st Royal Regt., b. 10 Sept. 1821; d. unm. 21 Nov. 1856.
2. USHER WILLIAMSON, present representative.
3. Nicholas, b. 7 April, 1824; m. 1851, Louisa Holder, eldest dau. of Rev. Edward Batty, of Ballyhealey, co. Westmeath; d.s.p. 1882. She d. 2 Aug. 1895.
4. William, of Gillardstown House, Killucan, b. 12 April, 1829; m. 1st, 22 Feb. 1859, Mary Caroline, dau. of Thomas Montgomerie Webb, of Gilliardstown, co. Westmeath, J.P., and by her (who d. 10 April, 1890) has issue,
  1. Annie Charlotte Montgomerie, m. 18 Nov. 1902, Tenison Robbins, who d. 21 Feb. 1909.
  2. Constance Alexandra, d. 23 April, 1887.
  3. Mary Violet, m. Feb. 1895, William Hardy, of Ceylon.
He m. 2ndly, Feb. 1895, Agnes, dau. of Peter Smithwick, of Tullamore Park, co. Tipperary, and d. 16 Aug. 1907.
5. Benjamin Williamson, b. Oct. 1832; d. in infancy.
1. Anne, d. 24 March, 1886.
2. Frances Jane, d. unm. 6 June, 1864.
3. Maria, m. 1866, Barbon Flynn, who d.s.p. 8 Feb. 1882. She d. 31 Jan. 1899.
4. Sophia, d. in infancy.
5. Mary Anne Williamson, d. in infancy.
6. Ellen, d. in infancy.
7. Mary Anne Williamson.
8. Ellen, d. unm. 14 July, 1856.
9. Catherine.

Seat—Rockfield, co. Westmeath, Ireland. Residence—20, Apsley Road, Clifton, Bristol.

EVANS OF CHURCHLANDS.

MAJOR FISHER HENRY FREKE EVANS, D.S.O. (1902), B.A. Camb., of Churchlands, co. Donegal, J.P., D.L., High Sheriff 1911, Major late 4th Batt. King's Own (Royal Lancaster) Regt., served in S. African War 1900-1 (medal, three clasps, D.S.O.), b. 21 April, 1868; m. 1902, Marie Louise, eldest dau. of Major Arthur Kyle Haslett, R.E., of Carrownaffe House, Moville co., Donegal (by his wife Marie Louise de Kochler), and has issue,
1. FISHER ARTHUR HASLETT FREKE, b. 3 Aug. 1895.
2. Patrick Harry Freke, b. 5 June, 1905.

Lineage.—ROBERT MENDHAM EVANS, of Fatherwell Hall, Kent, had issue,
CAPT. RICHARD FISHER EVANS, of Eaton Rise, Ealing, b. 1815; m. 1866, Mary Helen Campbell, 3rd dau. of George von Dadelszen, of Altona, by his wife Margaret, dau. of Capt. Mackenzie, R.N., l. 1893, having had issue,
1. FISHER HENRY FREKE, now of Churchlands.
1. Matilda Helen Freke, m. 1901, Randall Sacheverall Bradburne, of Eversley, Northwood, Middlesex.
2. Margaret Christine Freke, m. 1893, Reginald Bernard Pearce (10, Campden Hill Court, W.), and has issue.
3. Amy Maud, m. 1896, Edward Gerald Ingham, of Cranberry, New South Wales, and has issue.

Residence—Carnagarve, Moville, co. Donegal.

EVATT OF MOUNT LOUISE.

GEORGE FORSTER EVATT, of Mount Louise, co. Monaghan, J.P. and D.L., High Sheriff 1897, b. 27 June, 1847; s. his father, 1894.

Lineage.—THE VERY REV. JOHN EVATT, Dean of Elphin 1613, m. 1st, Joan, dau. of Roger Badger, of Knockvicar, co. Roscommon, and by her had issue, now extinct. He m. 2ndly, Blanche, dau. of Edward Mervyn, of Petersfield, Hants, and by her, whose will was proved in Dublin in 1655, had three sons and two daus. The Dean d. 1634. His youngest son,

HUMPHREY EVATT, of Maghera, co. Tyrone, who was living 1661, left issue, a son,

HENRY EVATT, High Sheriff co. Monaghan 1698, m. Jane, dau. of — Walkinshaw, and had with a younger son Henry, a son,

HUMPHREY EVATT, of Mount Louise, co. Monaghan, High Sheriff 1740, m. Louisa, dau. of John Forster, of Tullaghan, co. Monaghan. His will is dated 18 Feb. 1752. He had issue four sons and five daus. The eldest son,

CHARLES EVATT, of Mount Louise, High Sheriff 1760; d. 30 March, 1771; m. Bettana, dau. of John Slacke, of Tyrafferty, co. Monaghan, and had issue,
1. HUMPHREY, his heir.
1. Louisa, m. Charles Lucas, of Castle Shane.
2. Mary.
3. Anne.

The only son,

HUMPHREY EVATT, of Mount Louise, High Sheriff 1796, d. 30 March, 1771; m. April, 1768, Elizabeth, only dau. of Rev. Samuel Bayley, and d. 1830, having had issue,
1. George, High Sheriff 1812.
2. SAMUEL ROBERT BAYLEY, of whom presently.
3. Charles (Rev.), Rector of Monaghan, d. 13 April, 1840; m. 1810, Sophia, dau. of Capt. John Bayley, and had, with four daus., three sons, 1. Charles Robert; 2. Evelyn; and 3. Clayton Bayley.
4. Evelyn, M.D., m. 1839, Berri, 3rd dau. of Capt. John Bayley and d.s.p. His widow m. 2ndly, 1843, John Hannon.
1. Elizabeth, m. 1834, William Pace Geoghegan.
2. Francess, m. 19 March, 1834, Henry Flood, M.D.

The second son,

SAMUEL ROBERT BAYLEY EVATT, of Mount Louise, co. Monaghan, J.P. and D.L., M.A. Trin. Coll. Dublin, b. 23 July, 1805; m. 15 Oct. 1838, Jane Sinclair, dau. of Rev. William Henry Pratt, and Maria Pollock his wife. She d. 8 March, 1862. He d. 30 Dec. 1894, having had issue,
1. Humphry, Colonial Surveyor at Sierra Leone, b. 9 July, 1839; d. unm. 19 Sept. 1865.
2. Robert, b. 1840; d. 1841.
3. Henry Oliver Ponsonby, b. 24 Sept. 1845; d. 1865.
4. GEORGE FORSTER, now of Mount Louise.
5. Edward Pratt, b. 17 March, 1853; m. Elizabeth, dau. of — Myllan, and left issue.
6. Robert Bayley, m. 1890, Margaret, dau. of — Wrigley and by her (who d. 1891) has issue,
  Robert Humphry, b. 1891.
7. William Henry Pratt, d. 12 Sept. 1910, having had issue two daus.
8. Evelyn John Charles, d. an infant.
1. Charlotte Elizabeth, b. 10 Sept. 1841; m. Rev. Stanley Treanor, and d. 1865, leaving a dau.
2. Louise Olivia Victoria, b. 1843; d. 1857.
3. Maria Ann, b. 1844; m. Alfred Gurner Salter, and has five sons and two daus.
4. Geraldine Almeria Jordon, b. 1848; d. 1858.
5. Frances Cordelia, b. 10 March, 1850; m. Philip Hoffe, and d. 30 April, 1893, leaving seven sons and one dau.
6. Jane Sinclair Agnes, b. 1851; d. 1862.
7. Ann Cordelia, b. 1856; d. 1858.
8. Louisa Geraldine Victoria, b. 1857; d. 1878.

Seat—Mount Louise, Smithborough, co. Monaghan.

EYRE OF EYRECOURT.

WILLIAM HENRY GREGORY EYRE, of Eyrecourt Castle, co. Galway, J.P., Assistant Land Commissioner in Ireland, b. 27 April, 1860; m. 5 Oct. 1901, Louisa Butler, 2nd dau. of Lewis Gower-Stewart, of Mount Pleasant, Ilfracombe, co. Devon, and has issue,
1. JOHN STEWART, b. 28 Dec. 1909.
1. Mary Victoria, b. 13 Sept. 1902.
2. Eleanor Margaret, b. 20 May, 1904.
3. Cerise Winifred, b. 20 Sept. 1908.

Lineage.—GILES EYRE, of Brickworth, Wilts, Sheriff 1640, who sat, with three of his sons, in the Council of Oliver Cromwell, was 2nd son of THOMAS EYRE, of New Sarum (see EYRE of Warrens), bapt. 27 Feb. 1572; m. 1603, Jane, dau. and heiress of Ambrose Snelgrove, of Redlynch, Wilts. He d. Jan. 1655, having had, with other issue,
1. Giles, of Brickworth, M.P. for Downton 1660, bapt. 10 Feb. 1607; m. Anne, dau. of Sir Richard Norton, Bart., of Rotherfield, and had issue. He was ancestor of the EYRES of Brickworth and Landford, Wilts., and of Botleigh Grange, Hants.
2. Ambrose, of Newhouse (purchased in 1633 and sold in 1660), m. Frances, widow of William Tooker, and had two sons and two daus.
3. William (Rev.), Rector of St. Edmunds, Sarum, author of Vindiciae Justificationis, b. 1613; bur. 30 Jan. 1669.

4. Robert, bapt. 19 Aug. 1618, supposed to have d. in infancy.
5. JOHN, of whom presently.
6. Thomas, M.P. for Wilts 1658, bapt. 1625.
7. Edward, High Sheriff co. Galway 1680, M.P., bapt. 23 Jan. 1626, settled in Galway; *m.* Jane, 2nd dau. of Lord Maynard, and by her was ancestor of the family of HEDGES-EYRE, of Macroom Castle.
8. Henry, Bencher of Lincoln's Inn, Recorder of Sarum and M.P. for Sarum 1658, bapt. 23 Oct. 1628, *m.* Dorothy, dau. of George Hastings, of Woodlands, Dorset. He *d.* 18 July, 1678.
The 5th son,
COL. THE RIGHT HON. JOHN EYRE, of Eyre Court Castle, co. Galway (which he built), sometime M.P. for Galway, High Sheriff co. Galway 1681, accompanied Gen. Ludlow to Ireland, and acquired large estates in cos. Galway, Tipperary, and Clare and in King's Co. By patent dated 1662, he was granted the Manor of Eyre Court with powers to empark; bapt. 22 Feb. 1623; *m.* Mary, dau. and heiress of Philip Bigoe, of Newtown, High Sheriff King's Co. 1662. Col. John Eyre *d.* 22 April, 1685 (will dated 13 March, 1685, proved 8 June following), having had issue,
1. JOHN, of whom presently.
2. Samuel, of Eyreville, co. Galway, Col. in the Army before Limerick 1690, M.P. for Galway 1713, High Sheriff 1696; *b.* 1651; *m.* 1st, his cousin, Jane, dau. of Edward Eyre, of Galway (*see above*), and by her had issue, one son,
 1. John, of Woodfield, Capt. in the Army, *m.* Mary, dau. of Thomas Willington. He was bur. 4 Oct. 1741, leaving issue,
  (1) Samuel, of Eyreville, *m.* 30 Dec. 1741, Charity, only child of Sir Thomas Dancer, Bart., of Modreeny, co. Tipperary. He *d.* 1789, having had issue,
   1a. Thomas Dancer, of Eyreville, Capt. 4th Dragoon Guards, *b.* 1751; *m.* 6 Jan. 1788, Letitia, dau. of Rev. Henry Cole, brother of John, 1st Lord Mountflorence (*see* BURKE's *Peerage*, ENNISKILLEN, E.), and widow of Major Burton Johnson, and *d.* 1799, leaving issue,
    Thomas Stratford, of Eyreville, co. Galway, J.P. *b.* 8 Dec. 1788; *m.* Feb. 1822, Grace Lynar, dau. of Rev. William Lynar Fawcett. She *d.* 27 June, 1834. He *d.* 28 Feb. 1877, having had issue,
     1c. Thomas Stratford, *b.* 30 Oct. 1822; *m.* 13 March, 1860, Marion Dallas, youngest dau. of Alexander Campbell, of Edinburgh. He *d.* Feb. 1898, having had issue,
      1d. Stratford, *b.* 30 Jan. 1862; *d.* 9 Feb. 1893.
      2d. Lionel Hedges, *b.* 27 May, 1863.
      3d. Willoughby Cole, *b.* 20 June, 1865; *m.* Minnie Heywood, and has issue,
       Arthur Lowry Cole.
      1d. Marian Letitia Eleanor, *m.* 10 Sept. 1901, Frederick Hayden Horsey, who *d. unm.* 28 Sept. 1909.
      2d. Grace Geraldine, *m.* 13 Aug. 1890, William Ingram WORTHINGTON-EYRE, of Eyreville, Kiltormer, Ballinasloe, co. Galway (12, *Tivoli Terrace, South Kingstown, co. Dublin*), who assumed by Royal Licence 12 April, 1902, the additional name of Eyre and the arms of Eyre only, and has with other issue, a son, William Stratford Eyre Worthington-Eyre, of Eyreville.
       3d. Olive Kathleen.
     2c. Robert Hedges, *d.s.p.*
     3c. William, *d.* 1869.
     4c. Alfred, *d.* before 1834.
     5c. Edward, *d.* before 1860.
     6c. Letitia.   2c. Grace Elizabeth.
     7c. Anchoretta, *m.* William T. Callanan, of Skycur, and *d.* 1870.
     4c. Florence, *d.* before 1834.
     5c. Amelia, *m.* Capt. Phayre, 24th Regt.
    Elizabeth Florence, *m.* Rev. Prebendary Hartigan, and had issue.
    2a. Chichester, *d.s.p.* 17 July, 1804.
    1a. Anchoretta, *m.* 13 Jan. 1764, her kinsman, Richard Eyre, and had issue (*see below*).
    2a. Mary, *m.* 20 Jan. 1771, Charles Groome.
    3a. Elizabeth, *m.* 24 Sept. 1771, Laughlin Madden.
   (2) Edward, *m.* Mary, dau. of — Blake, and *d.s.p.*
   (3) Thomas.
   (1) Mary, *m.* George Studdert, of Crea, King's Co.
   (2) Jane.   (3) Catherine.
   (4) Elizabeth, *m.* 1740, John Willington, of Killoskehane Castle, co. Tipperary, and had issue.
Col. Samuel Eyre *m.* 2ndly, Nov. 1696, Anne, dau. of Robert Stratford, M.P., of Baltinglass, and aunt of the 1st Earl of Aldborough, and *d.* 10 Aug. 1728, having by her had issue,
 2. Stratford, Governor of Galway, High Sheriff 1731, and Vice-Admiral of Munster, *m.* 1st, 29 Oct. 1735, Mary, dau. of Charles Dartiquenave; and 2ndly, 6 Aug. 1762, Mary Ann, widow of James Echlin, of Echlinville, co. Down (*see* ECHLIN *of Ardquin*). He had issue,
   Stratford, Lieut. in the Army, *d.s.p.* at Kilkenny.
   Marianne, *d.s.p.*
 3. Thomas, Col. in the Army, Master of the Ordnance in Ireland, M.P. for Fore and Thomastown, Westmeath, *m.* Anne, dau. of Col. Cook, and *d.* 1772.
  1. Anne, *m.* 1717, Robert Powell, only son of Richard Powell, of New Garden, co. Limerick, and had issue.
  2. Mary, *m.* Thomas Croasdaile.
  3. Frances, *m.* Willington Duffield.
  4. Barbara, *m.* John Hawkes.

1. Mary, *m.* 1679, Right Hon. George Evans, father of 1st Baron Carbery (*see* BURKE's *Peerage*).
2. Anne, *m.* 1686, Col. Richard St. George, M.P., and *d.s.p.* Nov. 1719.
The elder son,
JOHN EYRE, M.P., of Eyrecourt (known as proud Eyre), *b.* at Clonfert 1659; *m.* 1st, 7 Feb. 1677, Margery, dau. of Sir George Preston, of Craigmillar, and by her had issue. He *m.* 2ndly, 26 Feb. 1693-4, Anne, dau. of William Hamilton, of Liscloony, and widow of Matthew, Lord Louth. He *d.* 1709, having by his first wife had issue,
1. GEORGE, of whom presently.
2. JOHN, *s.* his brother George.
3. GILES (Very Rev.), *s.* his brother John.
1. Mary, *m.* Thomas Baldwin, of Corolanty, King's Co.
2. Elizabeth, *m.* Frederick Trench, of Garbally, M.P., ancestor of the Earl of Clancarty (*see* BURKE's *Peerage*).
3. Emilia, *m.* 1st, Rev. W. Wilson, of Shingles, co. Westmeath, and 2ndly, 24 May, 1746, John Rochfort, of Clogrenane, co. Carlow, and had issue.
4. Margery, *m.* Shuckburgh Whitney, of New Pass, co. Westmeath, Lieut.-Col. 13th Light Dragoons, killed at Falkirk 1746 *s.p.*
5. Jane, *d. unm.*
The eldest son,
GEORGE EYRE, of Eyrecourt, High Sheriff 1706; *b.* 1680; *m.* Lady Barbara Coningsby, dau. and co-heir of Thomas, Earl of Coningsby, and *d.* 1710, having had an only child,
Frances, *m.* 1729, William Jackson, of Coleraine, and had issue.
He was *s.* by his brother,
JOHN EYRE, of Eyrecourt, High Sheriff 1724, M.P.; *m.* 23 June, 1711, Hon. Rose Plunkett, dau. of Matthew, Lord Louth, by Anne, dau. of William Hamilton, of Liscloony, King's Co. She *d.s.p.* Aug. 1741. He *m.* 2ndly, 28 May, 1742, Jane, dau. of Robert Waller, of Rookwood, but *d.s.p.* Oct. 1745. His only surviving brother,
THE VERY REV. GILES EYRE, of Eyrecourt, Dean of Killaloe, matriculated at Trin. Coll. Dublin, 13 July, 1705, aged 16, M.A. 1712; *m.* 30 Dec. 1717, Mary, dau. of Richard Cox, eldest son of Sir Richard Cox, Bart., Lord Chancellor of Ireland. She *d.* Aug. 1760. He *d.* 17 Jan. 1750, having had issue, three sons,
1. JOHN, created BARON EYRE.
2. Richard, High Sheriff co. Galway 1749; *m.* 1st, 21 June, 1752, Emilia, dau. of Col. Trench, of Garbally, and by her had a dau.,
  1. Elizabeth, living 1773.
 He *m.* 2ndly, 13 Jan. 1764, his kinswoman Anchoretta, dau. of Samuel Eyre, of Eyreville (*see above*), and *d.* 30 March, 1780, having had issue,
  1. GILES, *s.* his uncle John, Lord Eyre.
  2. John, Capt. in the Army, bapt. 2 Nov. 1767; *m.* Jane, eldest dau. of James Purefoy, of Purefoy Place, King's Co., and had issue an only son,
   Richard, of Woodview, co. Galway, *m.* Eleanor, dau. of Capt. Baldwin, of Clancgown, King's Co., and by her had issue,
    1a. Richard FitzRichard, Lieut. 44th Foot, *d.* of cholera in the Crimea.
    2a. Philip Homan, Lieut.-Col. 38th Foot, served in the Crimea, the Indian Mutiny, the Egyptian War, and the Nile Expedition, *b.* 15 Aug. 1832; *m.* 14 Aug. 1873, Lucy Catherine Louisa, only dau. of the late William Clarke, of Clifton, and was killed in command of his regt. at Kirkekan, 10 Feb. 1885, leaving issue,
     1b. Gloster Richard James Philip, *d.* young, 26 April, 1876.
     2b. Hastings Elles John, late Lieut. 1st Batt. S. Staffordshire Regt., *b.* 29 Oct. 1877; *m.* Joan, youngest dau. of late John Baker White, of Street End, Canterbury, Kent.
     1b. Florence Louie Stewart.
    3a. Henry Baldwin, Lieut. 25th Foot (*Crumlin, Ontario, Canada*).
    4a. Thomas Stratford, in the Merchant Navy, *d. unm.*
    5a. Falkiner, *m.* Isabella, dau. of Dr. Quin, of Nenagh, and *d.s.p.*
    6a. Gerald Dillon, of Prospect, Ballycumber, King's Co., J.P., *m.* Fannie Elizabeth (*d.* 3 June, 1909), dau. of Rev. Francis Heaton Thomas, of Burnane, Tipperary, *d.* 21 Nov. 1910, having had issue,
     Richard Gerald, Lieut. Connaught Rangers, served throughout S. African war, *b.* 3 Feb. 1878.
    7a. Edmund, *d.s.p.*
     1a. Anne Grattan, *m.* Lieut.-Col. E. D'Heillemer Fairtlough, 48th Foot, and *d.s.p.*
  3. Richard (Rev.), of Hassop Park, Rector of Eyrecourt, LL.D. and M.A., Trin. Coll. Dublin, *b.* 20 Nov. 1768; *m.* Anne, dau. of Capt. the Hon. Paul Gore (*see* BURKE's *Peerage*, ARRAN, E). She *d.* 21 Aug. 1847. He *d.* 25 Nov. 1831, leaving issue,
   (1) Richard Booth (Rev.), M.A., Trin. Coll. Dublin, Rector of Eyrecourt, Prebend. of Clonfert, *b.* 30 Oct. 1798; *m.* 1st, 18 Aug. 1829, Sarah, dau. of Robert Persse, of Roxborough, co. Galway. She *d.* 13 Nov. 1841, leaving issue,
    1a. Richard Annesley, Capt. 53rd L.I., *m.* Dora Churton, and *d.s.p.* in New Zealand, 2 April, 1876.
    2a. Robert Dudley, of Auckland, New Zealand, *b.* 23 March, 1841; *m.* 16 June, 1866, Matilda, dau. of John William Sheppard Norton, and has issue,
     1b. Richard Booth Dudley, *b.* 1 May, 1867; *m.* and has issue.
     2b. Sydney Seymour, *b.* 19 July, 1875; *m.* 1904, Millicent Hallowell, and has issue.
     3b. Egmont Annesley, *b.* 7 May, 1877; *m.*
      1a. Maria Helena, *m.* Capt. Henry Albert Matthew Drought, Ind. Navy, and *d.* 1906, having had issue.

IRELAND. Eyre.

2a. Anne, m. her cousin Col. Thomas Eyre, 3rd Bombay Cavalry (see below).
3a. Catherine Frances, m. Donald MacDonnell, Bombay Gren., and had issue, a dau. Frances, d. young.
4a. Sara, m. 31 July, 1867, Augustus George West, of White Park, co. Fermanagh, late 76th Foot, and has issue (see that family).
5a. Elizabeth Jane, m. Jan. 1858, Col. Maurice Griffin Dennis, C.B., 60th Rifles. He d.s.p. 8 Dec. 1863. She d. 19 Oct. 1897.
Canon R. B. Eyre m. 2ndly, Honora Louisa Madeline, 4th dau. of Ven. James Strange Butson, Archdeacon of Clonfert. He d. 26 July, 1884, having by her had surviving issue,
3a. Hastings Augustus, Lieut.-Col. Army Pay Department, late 9th Foot (164, Dora Road, Wimbledon Park, S.W.), b. 2 Oct. 1854 ; m. 3 June, 1882, Kathleen Frances Walsh, and has had issue,
   1b. John Lionel, Lieut. Dorset Regt., b. 3 May, 1883 ; drowned in India 1907.
   2b. Richard Philip Hastings, b. 2 Nov. 1888.
   1b. Nora Kathleen.
6a. Madeline Esther, m. John Hope, of Kilpoole House, co. Wicklow, and has issue.
7a. Florence Geraldine, m. Alfred Loraine Persse, and has issue (see PERSSE of Roxborough).
(2) Giles (Rev.), M.A., b. 30 Oct. 1798 (twin with Richard) ; m. Dorinda Seymour, of Somerset, co. Galway, and d.s.p.
(3) John, of Hassop Park, co. Galway, J.P., m. Sara Mahon, and had issue,
   1a. Richard, Capt. 48th Foot, m. Monimia Mary, dau. of Maj. Butler, 45th Foot, and d. May, 1866, leaving issue,
      1b. John Richard.   2b. Annesley.
      3b. Richard.   4b. Robert.
   2a. Annesley, Capt. 90th L.I., d. unm.
   3a. Thomas, d. unm.
   4a. Robert, Lieut. W. India Regt., d. unm.
   5a. John Monsell.   6a. Giles, d. young.
   1a. Marian, m. Daniel Hubert Killikelly, and d. 3 July, 1902, having had issue.
(4) Robert Hedges, of Earlstone, Portumna, co. Galway, m. 1845, Jane Elizabeth Smythe, and d. 1897, leaving issue,
   1a. Richard John.   2a. Annesley, d. unm. v.p.
   3a. Robert Smythe, L.R.C.S.I., L.R.C.P.I., d. unm. 5 Dec. 1909.
(5) Annesley, Capt. 74th Highlanders and Adjutant Galway Militia, d.s.p.
   (1) Eleanor, m. 1st, Joseph Callanan, of Tullywood, and had issue ; and 2ndly, 1835, Lorenzo Dundas, of Clobemon Hall, and had issue (see that family).
   (2) Anne, d. unm.
   (3) Barbara, m. 1847, her cousin Robert Giles Montgomery, Surg.-Major 66th Foot, and d.s.p. 1897.
   (4) Eliza, m. 1st, Thomas Gisborne Burke, of Greenfield, who d.s.p. She m. 2ndly, Capt. Thomas Hay Nembhard, 16th Foot, and d.s.p.
4 Samuel, bapt. 10 Aug. 1772 ; d. Aug. 1808.
5. Robert, Capt. in the Army, bapt. 10 Oct. 1773, m. and had issue,
   Sophia.
6. Thomas, sometime Capt, 51st Foot and afterwards Brig.-Gen. in the S. American Forces in the War of Independence, bapt. 28 Dec. 1774 ; m. Elizabeth Russell. She d. 1820. He was killed at Rio de la Hache 11 Oct. 1819, having had with other issue who d. young, a son,
   Thomas, Col. 3rd Bombay Cavalry, b. 10 July, 1809 ; m. 1st, 1841, Emma, dau. of John Evans, of Stony Down, Essex. She d.s.p. 8 July, 1842. He m. 2ndly, 1845, Maria Euphemia, dau. of John Ross, Inverness, and by her (who d. 4 March, 1853) had issue,
      1b. Mary Charlotte Page.
      2b. Maria Euphemia Ross, m. 1896, Rev. Alfred Brook, Canon of Inverness, and d.s.p. 1904.
   He m. 3rdly, 12 April, 1854, his cousin Anne, dau. of Rev. Canon R. B. Eyre (see above), and had issue,
      1b. Thomas Arthur Page, b. 20 July, 1859 ; d. unm. in Rhodesia, 9 March, 1899.
      2b. Herbert Hedges, b. 28 Dec. 1867 ; killed in Mashonaland, 21 June, 1896.
      3b. Dudley Richard, b. 21 Nov. 1868 ; d. unm. 3 Dec. 1889.
      3b. Agnes, Persse, d. young, 1870.
      4b. Emma MacDonnell, m. Lieut.-Col. P. Murray, late 109th Foot, who d.s.p. 4 May, 1908.
      5b. Sarah Persse.
      6b. Frances MacDonnell, m. Toler Roberts Garvey, son of Toler R. Garvey, of Thornvale, King's Co., and has issue.
      7b. Laura Page, m. Capt. Hervey Beauchamp Welman, Shropshire L.I., and has issue.
1. Charity, bapt. 12 May, 1765.
2. Jane, m. Peter Blake, of Lismoe Castle, co. Galway, and had issue.
3. Mary, m. 1st, — Shewbridge, and 2ndly, 6 Nov. 1806, Lieut. John Montgomery, Galway L.I., and by him had issue.
3. Robert, Capt., m. Elizabeth Giffard, and d. March, 1792.
1. Mary, m. Edward Dalton, of Derrysack, co. Clare, and had issue.
The eldest son,
JOHN, BARON EYRE, of Eyrecourt, co. Galway, so created 16 July, 1768, Col. in the Army, matriculated at Trin. Coll. Dublin, 15 July, 1738, aged 18, LL.D. honoris causâ 1754 ; m. 1746, Eleanor, dau. of James Staunton, of Galway, and by her had issue, John, bapt. June, 1747, bur. 4 July, 1747.
Mary, m. Hon. Francis Caulfeild, younger son of James, Viscount Charlemont, and had issue.
Lord Eyre d. 30 Sept. 1781, when the peerage became extinct, but the family estates passed to his nephew,
GILES EYRE, of Evrecourt Castle, co. Galway, Col. of the Galway Militia, High Sheriff 1798 (eldest son of Richard Eyre, next brother of Lord Eyre), bapt. 19 July, 1766 ; m. 1st, 28 Sept. 1792, Anne, dau. of Michael Daly, of Mount Pleasant, and widow of Philip Doyne, of Wells, co. Wexford, and 2ndly, 1821, Sophia, dau. of Jonathan Walsh, of Walsh Park, co. Tipperary. Col. Eyre d. 1830, having by his 1st wife had issue,
1. JOHN, of whom presently.   2. Richard.
1. Anne, m. 21 Oct. 1817, Walter Lambert, of Castle Lambert, co. Galway, and had issue.
2. Anchoretta, m. Burton Persse, of Moyode, co. Galway.
3. Jane, m. Rev. Samuel Roberts, of Coote Hill, co. Cavan, and had issue.
4. Eleanor Anne, m. 1st, Col. Arthur Disney, H.E.I.C.S., and had issue ; and 2ndly, 1843, George Mahood.
The elder son,
JOHN EYRE, of Eyre Court, J.P., b. 15 May, 1794 ; m. 21 Aug. 1818, May, dau. of William Armit, of Dublin. He was killed in the hunting field 18 Feb. 1856, having had issue,
1. JOHN, of whom presently.
2. William Armit, Capt. 47th Regt., m. Maria Josephine, dau. of Adm. Ballingall, and by her, who m. 2ndly, Capt. Martley, had issue,
   1. William Armit, d.
   2. John, m. Clara K. Dunham, and has issue.
   3. George Henry Lewis, who also has issue.
   1. Mary Josephine.
3. Marmaduke, m. Eliza Jane Johnston, of Friarstown, co. Sligo, and d. 15 Aug. 1892, having had issue,
   1. Henry, d. young.   2. James, d.s.p.
   1. Elizabeth, m. 1st, Maj. Stewart Masters, Indian S.C., and by him has issue. She m. 2ndly, 3 June, 1903, James Hugh Moore Garrett, of Corrie Wood, Castlewellan (see GARRETT of Kilgaran).
   2. Ellen, d. 31 Jan. 1906.
1. Anastasia, m. Lieut.-Col. Henshaw Russell, 97th and 60th Foot, and had issue.
2. Charity (Cerise), m. 7 June, 1848, Lieut.-Gen. Sir Thomas Lionel John Gallwey, K.C.M.G., R.E., and d.s.p. 1849. He m. 2ndly, 1 Oct. 1851, Alice Dora, dau. of Maj. Peter MacDougall, and by her had issue.
3. Georgina, m. Henry Paul Samuel Eyre, of Liverpool, son of Rev. James Eyre, and has issue.
4. Eleanor, m. Capt. James Pitcairn Campbell, of Burton Hall, Cheshire, son of Rev. Augustus Campbell, Rector of Liverpool, and has issue.
5. Diana, m. 1st, Henry Howard Barbour, 17th Lancers, and by him had issue. She m. 2ndly, Dr. Hawkesley, who d.s.p.
6. Nannie (Nance). m. Capt. Butler Dunboyne Moore, 89th Regt., of Shannon Grove, King's Co., and d. 11 Jan. 1902, leaving issue.
7. Charlotte, d. unm.
8. Mary, m. her cousin John S. Armit, of Castle Jordan, co. Meath, and had issue.
9. Bessie Armit, m. George Hale, of Knowsley, Lancashire; and left issue.
The eldest son,
JOHN EYRE, of Eyre Court, J.P. and D.L., b. 12 April, 1820 ; m. 23 Oct. 1846, Eleanor Maria, eldest dau. of Hubert Butler Moore, of Shannon Grove, co. Galway. He d. 12 April, 1890, having had issue,
1. John, b. 27 Dec. 1851 ; d. unm. 9 Sept. 1881.
2. Hubert Butler Moore, Asst.-Commiss. of Police in Assam, b. 1857 ; d. unm. 10 May, 1878.
3. WILLIAM HENRY GREGORY, now of Eyre Court.
1. Alice Maude, m. 1st, 1873, Capt. John Blair Miller, 8th Hussars, of Pitcrivie, Forfarshire, who d. Oct. 1889, leaving issue. She m. 2ndly, 5 Jan. 1898, Thomas Henry Goodwin Newton, of Barrells Park, Warwickshire, who d. 22 March, 1907.
2. Mary Eleanor, m. 9 Nov. 1874, Lieut.-Col. John Claud Alexander Auchinleck, R.H.A., who d. 1892, leaving issue (see that family).
3. Constance, m. 1880, Rev. Samuel Peshall, Rector of Oldberrow, Warwickshire, and has issue.
4. Edith.
5. Cerise, m. 1889, Hugh Edward Campbell Beaver, of Bryn Glas, co. Montgomery, who d. 1892, leaving issue.
6. Beatrice Jane, m. 28 Aug. 1886, Capt. Edward William Forester Leighton, late 9th Foot, and has issue (see BURKE's Peerage, LEIGHTON, Bart.).
7. Bessie Caroline.

Arms—Arg. on a chevron sa. three quatrefoils or. *Crest*—A leg in armour couped at the thigh ppr., garnished and spurred or. *Motto*—Pro rege sæpe, pro patriâ semper.
Seat—Eyre Court Castle, co. Galway.

EYRE OF UPPERCOURT.

STANISLAS THOMAS EYRE, of Uppercourt, co. Kilkenny, J.P., D.L., High Sheriff 1910, b. 16 June, 1867 ; m. 29 Nov. 1900, Gertrude Mary Theresa, elder dau. of Anthony Norris, and has issue,

Fagan. THE LANDED GENTRY. 214

1. WILLIAM FRANCIS THOMAS PHILIP, b. 2 Sept. 1901.
2. Violet Mary Marguerite, b. 17 Aug. 1902.
3. Dorothy Mary Olive, b. 15 Aug. 1903.
4. Winefrede Mary Gertrude, b. 13 Aug. 1907.
5. Gertrude Mary Barbara, b. 14 Nov. 1911.

Mr. S. T. Eyre s. to Uppercourt on the death of his cousin Thomas Joseph Eyre, of Uppercourt, in Jan. 1902.

Lineage.—WILLIAM FRANCIS EYRE, b. 14 July, 1793, 5th son of VINCENT EYRE, of Highfield and Newbold (*see* EYRE *of Lindley*), m. 1st, 27 Aug. 1834, Victoria Eleanor Longhay, who d.s.p. 23 April, 1861. He m. 2ndly, 7 Jan. 1864, Ellen Josephine, dau. of William Witham, and had issue,
1. Oswald William, b. 5 March, 1865; d. unm. 31 Dec. 1897.
2. STANISLAS THOMAS, now of Uppercourt.
3. Francis Robert, b. 5 June, 1871; m. and d. 15 Jan. 1910, leaving issue, a dau.

Arms, &c.—*See* EYRE *of Lindley*.

Seat—Uppercourt, Freshford, co. Kilkenny. *Town House*—60, Ennismore Gardens, S.W. *Clubs*—Reform and Hurlingham.

FAGAN, FORMERLY OF FELTRIM.

WILLIAM CHARLES (TRANT) FAGAN, present male representative of the family of Fagan of Feltrim, b. 3 Jan. 1877.

Lineage.—The pedigree entered in the *Visitation of Dublin*, 1605, by Daniel Molyneux, Ulster King of Arms, commences with THOMAS FAGAN, of Dublin, m. 1524, Amy Nangle, dau. of the Baron of Navan, and by her acquired large estates in Dublin and elsewhere. He left issue, two sons,
1. Christopher, Mayor of Dublin 1573, High Sheriff 1565, m. Joan, dau. of Sir James FitzSimons, Mayor of Dublin, and had, with seven daus., an only son, Thomas, of Castle Fagan and Palmerston, co. Dublin (wi l 10 July, 1599), who left an only child Elinor, m. her cousin Richard Fagan, of Feltrim.
2. RICHARD, of whom we treat.

The 2nd son,
RICHARD FAGAN, of Feltrim and Bloike, co. Dublin, High Sheriff 1575, Mayor of Dublin 1587, m. Cecily Holmes, of Manchester. She d. 5 May, 1608. He d. 30 March, 1610, having had issue,
1. JOHN, his heir.
1. Ann, d. unm.
2. Mary, m. 1st, John Eustace, of Confey, co. Kildare, and 2ndly, Edward Wellesley, 3rd son of Garret Wellesley, of Dangan.

The only son,
JOHN FAGAN, of Feltrim, who received a regrant of his estates 27 Feb. 1611, m. 1st, Alice, dau. of Walter Segrave, Mayor of Dublin, and 2ndly, Alicia, dau. of Richard Finglass, of Westpalston, co. Dublin, and widow of Francis Plunkett. By his first wife only he had issue,
1. Richard, m. his cousin Elinor, only child of Thomas Fagan, of Castle Fagan (*see above*), and d.v.p. 6 Aug. 1622, leaving an only surviving son, Christopher, of Feltrim and Castle Fagan, m. May, 1636, Ann, dau. of Sir Nicholas White, Knt. of Leixlip, and had an elder son, Richard, his heir, who forfeited all his inheritance in the cause of JAMES II. He m. Elinor, dau. of Thomas Aylmer, of Lyons, and left three daus.
1. Ann, d. unm.
2. Helen, m. John Taylor, of Swords.
3. Mary, m. John Eustace.
2. Thomas, d. unm. v.p. 21 Oct. 1620.
3. George, d. unm. v.p. 1615.
4. JOHN, of whom we treat.
1. Mary, d. unm.
2. Anne, m. Christopher Dowdall, of Castle Dowdall, co. Louth.

The youngest and only surviving son,
JOHN FAGAN, who d. 1683, having had issue, three sons and one dau.,
1. William, who lost his fortune in the service of JAMES II. He d.s.p.
2. CHRISTOPHER, of whom presently.
3. James, Lieut.-Col. in Hamal's Regt. in the Spanish service settled in Spain.
1. Ellen, m. Dominick Rice, of Ballymacdoyle, and had issue.

The 2nd son,
CHRISTOPHER FAGAN, Capt. in Browne of Kenmare's Regt. of Infantry in the service of JAMES II, was comprised in the Capitulation of Limerick, and settled afterwards in Kerry. He m. Mary, dau. of Patrick Nagle, of Ballinamona Castle, co. Cork. His son,
PATRICK FAGAN, of Killarney, m. 1732, Christiana, dau. of Thomas Fitzmaurice, of Cossfoyle, Kerry, and had issue,
1. Christopher, in the French service, a Chevalier of the Order of St. Louis, b. 1733; m. Catharine, dau. of Joseph de Cortes, and d. 6 Jan. 1816, leaving issue, settled in France.
2. STEPHEN, of whom presently.
3. Robert, of Philadelphia, left issue, three sons and a dau., of whom
1. Christopher, b. 14 July, 1776; d. 18 March, 1845, Major-Gen. and Adj.-Gen. Bengal Army 1828, H.E.I.C.S.; m. 1st, Mary Eliza (d.s.p. 10 Nov. 1805), dau. of John Fagan, of Kiltallagh; m. 2ndly, Eliza Lawtie, of Calcutta (who d. 4 Jan. 1824); and 3rdly, 22 Feb. 1833, Maria, dau. of Rev. Charles Gibbon, by whom he had issue a dau., dau. of Rev. 2nd wife had issue, with three daus., three sons,
(1) Christopher Weston, Judge, Bengal C.S., m. 1st, Margaret Laird Galbraith, and had a dau., Margaret, m. Rev. James Hunter Monahan, D.D., of Dublin. He m. 2ndly, Henrietta Emily Williamson, and by her (who d. 28 Nov. 1904), had,
Christopher Weston, B.A. (Cantab), d. unm. 10 April, 1890.
Eleanor Anne, m. 24 Aug. 1881, Thomas Henry Gibbon Pearson, only son of Canon Pearson, J.P.
(2) Peter, Bombay Cavalry, d. 1842.
(3) George Smoult, b. 1824; d. 6 May, 1875, Judge of Small Cause Court, Calcutta, m. 7 Feb. 1855, Eliza Caroline (d. 27 Feb. 1900), dau. of Hon. Richard St. Leger (*see* DONERAILE, Viscount), and had with two daus.,
1. St. Leger Peterson Ricketts, b. 5 Feb. 1856; m. 1886, Kate Boswell.
2. Hans Richard St. Leger, b. 19 Aug. 1857.
3. George Lawtie St. Leger, Barrister-at-Law, b. 27 Nov. 1858; d. 13 Aug. 1885.
4. Arthur Roberts St. Leger, b. 24 Nov. 1862; m. 1901, Rose Topham, and has issue, with three daus.,
George St. Leger, b. 7 May, 1902.
4. Patrick, M.D., of New Ross, co. Wexford, m. Catherine Harper, of Ballingby.
5. Andrew, an Officer H.E.I.C.S.
6. John, of Kiltallagh, co. Kerry, m. 1772, Elizabeth, only child of George Hickson (*see* HICKSON *of Fermoyle*), and had (by other children who d. young,
1. George Hickson, b. 3 Nov. 1778; d. 25 May, 1821, Adjutant-Gen. Bengal Army; m. Harriet Lawtie, of Calcutta, and had, with four daus.,
(1) Christopher George, b. 1811; d. 1861, Col. 8th Bengal Cav., m. 1838, Louisa Williamson, and had, with daus., four sons, by her, who d. 13 July, 1885,
1. George H. W., b. 1841; d. 1899, Lieut.-Gen. Bombay Army; m. 1865, Helen, 2nd dau. of Major A. Rait, B.S.C., and had, with three daus.,
a. Denis Feltrim, b. 1871.
b. Francis William Feltrim, b. 1874.
c. Henry Feltrim, b. 1876.
d. Christopher George Feltrim, b. 1878; killed in S. Africa, 5 Sept. 1900.
2. James Lawtie, b. 4 Feb. 1843, Major-Gen. Bombay Army; m. 1866, Eliza Makgill, dau. of Capt. A. Ogilvy Dalgleish, 18th Foot, and has had,
a. Arthur Newton Dalgleish, b. 26 Dec. 1870; d. unm. 23 Dec. 1900, Lieut. and Adjutant 1st Lancers, Hyderabad.
b. John Lawtie, b. 1873, Indian Police; m. Phyllis, dau. of Col. Jackson.
a. Edith, m. 20 Feb. 1889, Sir George Washington Baxter (*see* BAXTER *of Kincaldrum*).
b. Mary Maude, m. 1893, Major Robert John Spurrell, of Glandyfi Castle, Cardiganshire.
3. Christopher Ramsay, b. 1853; d. unm. 1878.
4. Edward Rivaz (Rev.), b. 22 Feb. 1856, M.A. (Oxon), Rector of Wold Newton; m. 1881, Mary Flette Mitchell, dau. of Henry Larking, and has issue,
a. Edward Feltrim (Rev.), b. 28 April, 1882, B.A. (Oxon).
(2) George Hickson Urquhart (Rev.), Prebendary of Combs, Vicar of Rodney Stoke, b. 21 April, 1822; d. 1875; m. Rose, dau. of Sir Hardinge Giffard, Sup. Judge, Ceylon. She d.s.p. 17 Feb. 1899.
2. Patrick Charles, b. 17 March, 1780; d. 26 Oct. 1808, Lieut. H.E.I.C.S.; m. Maria, dau. of Rev. Dr. Sleator, St. David's, Naas. She d. 13 June, 1859, having had issue,
Eliza, m. George Franco, Bengal C.S.
3. Christopher Sullivan, b. 22 March, 1781; d. 26 May, 1843, C.B., Major-Gen. H.E.I.C.S.; m. 1st, 24 July, 1809, Agnes, dau. of Christopher Baldock, of New Malton, Yorks, and by her (who d. 19 April, 1826) had
(1) George Hickson, b. 18 Aug. 1810; d. 23 Nov. 1876, Lieut.-Col. Bengal Engineers; m. 1st, 28 Feb. 1839, Frances Brand, dau. of Francis Hedger, of Prior Lodge, Bath, and Garston Hall, Surrey, and by her (who d. 13 April, 1847) had issue surviving,
1. Christopher Sullivan Feltrim, b. 19 May, 1845, Gen. in the Army (retired) (*Feltrim, Exeter*); m. Alice, dau. of Thomas Green, of Badby, Northamptonshire, and has surviving issue,
a. Richard William Feltrim, b. 26 Feb. 1896.
a. Christine Alice Feltrim, b. 14 April, 1891.
b. Katherine Muriel Feltrim, b. 18 May, 1893.

1. Agnes Sarah Feltrim, b. 2 Aug. 1840; d. unm. 1881.
2. Christine Josephine, b. 17 March, 1842.

He m. 2ndly, 27 Nov. 1849, Mary, dau. of Capt. Thomas Pickering Clarke, R.N., and had,
2. George Hickson Feltrim (Rev.), b. 18 Oct. 1851, M.A. Oxon, Vicar of King's Kerswell, S. Devon.
3. William Feltrim (Rev.), b. 25 June, 1853; d. 19 Feb. 1909, M.A. (Oxon), Vicar of Hersham; m. 24 Oct. 1889, Ellen, dau. of Henry Brooks, of Hersham Lodge and left,
   a. Arthur William, b. 10 Dec. 1890.
   a. Kathleen Mary Feltrim, b. 12 Dec. 1897.
   b. Eileen Hilda de Lacy Feltrim, b. 29 May, 1905.
2. Frances Mary Feltrim, m. 27 Sept. 1872, Reginald Orne Brenton Carey Brenton, Lieut. R.N., and has issue.
3. Elizabeth Kathleen Feltrim, d. 30 Nov. 1882; m. 2 July, 1879, Rev. Alfred Vyvyan Cox, M.A., Vicar of Stockland, and has issue.
4. Geraldine Feltrim, b. 2 July, 1859.
5. Mabel Feltrim, b. 23 Sept. 1860.

(2) Christopher, b. 5 Nov. 1812; d. 13 April, 1842, of Calcutta; m. 27 Aug. 1841, Frederica Josephine, dau. of Joseph Buckley, and had issue, a dau., Christina, b. 26 Nov. 1842; m. 26 Sept. 1860, Lieut. W. B. Pauli, R.N., and d.s.p. 29 Dec. 1886.
(3) John, b. 29 Oct. 1815; d. 16 July, 1851, Capt. H.E.I.C.S., unm.
(4) Robert Charles Henry Baines, b. 14 May, 1823; killed at Delhi 12 April, 1857, Capt. Bengal Art.; m. 8 July, 1846, Sarah Humphrey (d. 21 July, 1909), dau. of Thomas William Bart, M.D., and has issue,
1. Charles Christopher Thomas (Rev.), b. 17 May, 1847; d. 21 Jan. 1890, M.A. (Cantab); m. dau. of Rev. Charles Felton Smith, M.A., of Crediton, Devon.
2. Robert Sidney Feltrim, b. 16 Feb. 1854; d. 21 Dec. 1903, Woods and Forests Dept., India; m. 28 April, 1887, Norah, dau. of Horace Christopher Fagan. She m. 2ndly, 4 Feb. 1905, Major Walter Merewether.
3. William Claude Horace, b. 2 May, 1857.
1. Harriet Agnes Georgina, m. Rev. Edward Sutton Dodd, of Godalming, Surrey.
2. Mary Catherine Annarkhalee, m. 11 Nov. 1875, H. Baxter.
(1) Eliza, b. 23 Sept. 1811; m. 4 Feb. 1831, Major-Gen. Sir James Wallace Sleigh, K.C.B., of Hanworth House, Middlesex, and left issue. He d. 5 Feb. 1865. She d. 2 Dec. 1868.
(2) Mary, b. 11 Jan. 1817; m. 27 Jan. 1836, James Erskine, Bombay C.S. She d. 26 June, 1843. He d. 1843, leaving issue.
(3) Catherine Baldock, b. 8 Sept. 1819; m. 4 Sept. 1843, Samuel Wauchope, Bombay C.S., and d. July, 1879, leaving issue.
(4) Agnes Cecilia Adelaide, b. 11 Aug. 1821; d. 21 June, 1865; m. 8 Sept. 1842, Charles Arthur Nicholson, Lieut. 25th Bombay N.I., and had issue.
(5) Caroline, m. 30 July, 1844, George Percival Leycester, Bombay C.S., who d. 1877. She d. 1858, leaving issue.

Major-Gen. Christopher Sullivan Fagan, C.B., m. 2ndly, 29 March, 1828, Elizabeth Jane, dau. of George Moule, of Melksham, and by her (who d. 17 Oct. 1882) had,
(5) William Turton, b. 5 July, 1831; d. 25 April, 1890, Major-Gen.; m. 3 March, 1862, Emily Rowe, dau. of James Stafford Livermore, and by her (who d. 2 Dec. 1897) left,
1. Patrick James, b. 3 July, 1865, B.A. (Cantab), I.C.S.; m. 19 July, 1890, Emily Frances, dau. of M. A. Robinson, and has,
   a. Bryan Walter, b. 13 Feb. 1893.
   b. Neil, b. 26 Feb. 1896.
   a. Aileen, b. 21 Feb. 1895.
2. Bryan Noel, b. 24 Dec. 1869.
3. Hugh William Farquharson (Rev.), b. 2 Oct. 1872, B.A. (Cantab); m. 30 Nov. 1911, Eustasia Violet, dau. of Rev. H. S. Alison.
1. Beatrice, b. 25 Aug. 1871; m. James Morton, of Darval, Ayrshire.
2. Theodora Mary, b. 26 Jan. 1878.
(6) Frederick Christopher (Rev.), b. 29 March, 1836; d. unm. 27 April, 1865, B.A. (Oxon).
(7) Feltrim Christopher (Rev.), b. 25 Aug. 1838; d. 22 Aug. 1872, M.A. (Oxon); m. Emily Helen (d.s.p. 17 May, 1899), dau. of Rev. Charles Brereton, B.C.L.
(8) Horace Christopher, b. 21 April, 1840; d. 18 Dec. 1878, Bengal N.I.; m. 4 Oct. 1866, Caroline, dau. of Rev. Edmund Phillott, and by her (who d. 12 April, 1903) had,
1. Frederick Christopher, b. 25 March, 1870; d. 12 May, 1894, Asst. Inspector Gen. Railway Police.
2. Edward Arthur, b. 25 Nov. 1871, Major Jacob's Horse, Scinde; m. 27 June, 1906, Mary Daubeney, dau. of Rev. R. E. Follett, of Winscombe Court, Somerset.
1. Norah Fanny, b. 15 April, 1869; m. 1st, 28 April, 1887, Robert Sidney Feltrim Fagan; m. 2ndly, 4 Feb. 1905, Major Walter Merewether, Indian Army.
2. Brydget Horatia, b. 28 Dec. 1878; m. 19 Jan. 1905, Major F. Wadeson, 37th Bengal Lancers, and has issue.
(6) Ellen Georgina, b. 17 Feb. 1829, m. Rev. Arthur Hosmer, M.A., who d. 1896, leaving issue.
(7) Salleen Christian Anne, b. 12 Nov. 1832; m. Rev. F. Phillott.
(8) Clementina Maria, b. 10 July, 1834; m. 5 July, 1856, Rev. Robert Duckworth. He d. 1888, leaving issue.

(9) Christine Penelope Eliza, b. 9 Dec. 1842; m. 9 April, 1866, Capt. Charles Albert Dodd, I.C.S. She d. 4 Oct. 1872.
4. James Patrick, b. 17 March, 1788; d. 1863, Major Bengal Army, m. Stephanie le Mere, and by her (who d. 16 Jan. 1873) had,
(1) George, settled in U.S.A., m. and left issue.
(2) James Langdale, killed at Mhow July, 1857, Capt. and Adj. 23rd N.I.
(3) John, dec.
(4) Christopher Sullivan, d. 24 Aug. 1867, Comm. 1st Regt. Hyderabad Contingent; m. 24 April, 1855, Ellen Denny (d. 7 Jan. 1907), and had,
1. Christopher George Forbes, b. 15 March, 1856, Lieut.-Col. 10th Bengal Lancers; m. Florence Evelyn Jessie, dau. of Surgeon-Major J. W. R. Amesbury, I.M.S., and has issue,
   a. Christopher Frederick Feltrim, b. 29 Aug. 1888.
   b. Richard Feltrim, b. 5 Feb. 1891.
   a. Evelyn Feltrim, b. 7 Dec. 1885.
2. Henry Horace Frederick, b. 9 April, 1858, Major Bengal Lancers; m. 10 Aug. 1893, Adela Beatrice, dau. of E. M. Denny, and has,
   a. Henry Patrick Feltrim, b. 6 March, 1900.
   b. Frederick Christopher Feltrim, b. 23 April, 1903.
   a. Muriel Beatrice, b. 11 July, 1894.
   b. Phyllis Marjorie, b. 16 Dec. 1897.
3. Hugh Rollo, b. 4 Aug. 1865, Major 55th Coke's Rifles; m. 6 Dec. 1906, Louisa Constance, dau. of Capt. A. W. Cobham, of Shinford Manor, Berks.
1. Ethel Maude, b. 26 July, 1862; m. 14 May, 1886, J. H. Meadows Bishop, Punjab Police. She d. 7 Oct. 1887.
2. Mabel Geraldine, b. 22 July, 1864; m. 2 July, 1887, Arthur Meredith, B.C.S., and has issue.
(1) Eliza Henrietta, b. 1812; m. Capt. W. O. Young, Bengal Art. She d. 1893, leaving issue.
(2) Stephanie, m. — Rochfort.
(3) Mary, m. Anthony Nugent, of Grenan, Thomastown, co. Kilkenny, and had issue.
1. Mary Eliza, b. 12 Feb. 1774; m. Major-Gen. Christopher Fagan (see above). She d.s.p. 10 Nov. 1805.
2. Christina, Abbess of Ursuline Convent, Cork, b. 13 Sept. 1776.
3. Eliza Mary, b. 5 April, 1782; m. Major-Gen. John Lowther Richardson, H.E.I.C.S.
4. Ellen, b. 1785; m. William Francis Leslie Fran, Bengal Art.
5. Catherine, b. 13 May, 1792; m. James Langdale.
6. Frances, b. 1794; d. Oct. 1801.
7. James, of high rank in the French and afterwards in the British service, d. 1 Oct. 1801.
8. William, d. unm.
1. Mary, m. — Sheehy.
2. Elizabeth, m. Christopher Sullivan.
3. Frances, m. Matthew Moriarty, M.D. of Tralee.
4. Ellen, d. unm.

The 2nd son,
STEPHEN FAGAN, of Cork, merchant, m. Helena, dau. of James Trant, of Castle Island, Kerry, and had issue,
1. JAMES, his heir.
2. Patrick, m. the dau. of — Hussey, of Dingle, and had issue three sons and one dau.
1. Eliza, m. Alexander McCarthy, of Cork.

The elder son,
JAMES FAGAN, m. Ellen, dau. of Ignatius Trant, of Cork, and by her had issue,
1. WILLIAM, of whom presently.
2. Charles.
1. Eliza.   2. Susan.

The elder son,
WILLIAM TRANT FAGAN, of Cork, J.P. and D.L., co. Cork, sometime M.P. for the city of Cork, m. 1827, Mary, dau. of Charles Addis, of Westminster, and had issue,
1. CHARLES ADDIS, late representative.
2. William Addis, Capt. 12th Lancers, M.P. for Carlow 1869-75, b. 15 Dec. 1832; m. 16 Nov. 1871, Frances, dau. of Daniel Mahony, of Dunloe Castle, Killarney. He d. 14 March, 1890 having by her (who m. 2ndly, 2 June, 1891, Maj.-Gen. Cecil Mangles, C.B., of Kitcombe, Alton, Hants) had issue,
WILLIAM CHARLES, present representative.
Maureen Elizabeth, m. 31 Aug. 1905, Major H. G. Levinge, o Knockdrinn Castle, co. Westmeath.
3. Hornby, an officer, H.E.I.C.S., killed in the massacre at Cawnpore, July, 1857, d. unm.
1. Mary, m. 23 Feb. 1858, Daniel Francis Leahy, of Shanakill, Cork, and d.s.p. about 1888.

The eldest son,
CHARLES ADDIS FAGAN, b. 1829; d. unm. 9 May, 1903, and was s. in the representation of his family by his nephew.

Arms—Per chevron gu. and erm. in chief three covered cups or. Crest—A griffin arg., winged and tufted or supporting in the talons an olive branch vert, fructed gold. Motto—Deo patriaeque fidelis.
Club—Bath.

———————

FALKINER OF MOUNT FALCON.

The late RICHARD HENRY FITZ-RICHARD FALKINER, of Mount Falcon, co. Tipperary, J.P., High Sheriff 1903, b. 1827; m. 1st, 28 Oct. 1859, Georgina, dau. of Thomas Sadleir, of Castletown (*see that family*), and by her, who d. had issue,

1. Richard Francis Octavius, b. 1866, d. unm. 1881.
2. FREDERICK RICHARD SAUNDERS, d.v.p. unm.
1. Tempe, b. 1860, d. unm. 1899.
2. Elmina Nina, b. 1861, m. 1881, Henry Whitmore Babbage, R.I.C.
3. Clara Georgina, b. 1864.   4. Mabel Robina, b. 1870.

He m. 2ndly, 18 Feb. 1898, Ellen Jane (*now of Mount Falcon*), eldest dau. of Edward Saunders, J.P., of Largy, co. Cavan, and Caroline his wife, dau. of John W. Knollys, of Reading, Berks, and d. 10 Oct. 1907.

Lineage.—MICHAEL FALKINER, of Brigart, Leeds, Yorks, m. at Leeds by licence 6 Aug. 1639, Susan, dau. of Christopher Jackson, of Hunslet, near Leeds. They had issue,
1. Michael, b. 2 March, 1640, will proved 1714. His male issue became extinct 1727.
2. Daniel, of Dublin, b. 16 Dec. 1641, ancestor of FALKINER, Bart. (*see* BURKE's *Peerage*).
3. John, b. 16 July, 1645; d. before his brothers.
4. RICHARD, of whom presently.
1. Sussanna, b. 23 Dec. 1644; m. William Booker.
2. Hannah, b. 1650, m. — Wymersley.

The youngest son,
RICHARD FALKINER, of Dublin, b. 1655, m. 1683, Mary, dau. of — Mason. His will was dated 3 Nov. 1698. He d. Dec. same year, having by her (who m. 2ndly, Joseph Kane, Lord Mayor of Dublin 1726) had issue,
RICHARD, his heir.
Ruth, m. Thomas Corker, but d.s.p. Will dated 8 Nov. 1760, proved 1772.

The only son,
RICHARD FALKINER, of Mount Falcon, which he built 1720, J.P. co. Tipperary, b. 1691; m. 1720, Maria, dau. of Daniel Rogers, of Ballynavin, co. Tipperary. He d. 1733 (will dated 25 Dec. that year), having had issue,
1. RICHARD, his heir.
2. Daniel, m. Catherine, dau. of J. Frend, and had issue.
3. Thomas, m. 1762, Mary, dau. of William Woodward, of Cloughprior, and d.s.p.
1. Mary, m. Samuel Barry, of Ballycreggam.
2. Charlotte, m. John Bayly (*see* BAVLY *of Debsborough*).

The eldest son,
RICHARD FALKINER, of Mount Falcon, co. Tipperary, Barrister-at-Law, b. 1721; m. Mary Anne, sister of Christopher Smart, the Poet, Fell. of Pembroke Coll. Cambridge. His will dated 3 Nov. 1785, was proved 1786. He left issue,
1. RICHARD DANIEL, his heir.
2. Thomas, Capt. in the Army, d. unm.
3. John, d. young.
4. Frederick, of Congor, Clerk of the Crown for co. Tipperary, b. 1760; m. 1795, Louisa, dau. of George David Fraser, of Park, King's Co., High Sheriff 1752, and by her (who d. 27 April, 1817) had a dau.,
Judith, m. Rev. John Rotheram Tarleton, Rector of Tyholland, and had issue.
1. Ruth, m. Thomas Stoney, of Arran Hill and Portland, and had issue (*see that family*).
2. Mary, d. unm.
3. Charlotte, d. unm.

The eldest son,
REV. RICHARD DANIEL FALKINER, of Mount Falcon, co. Tipperary, b. 1755; m. (setts. dated 16 Aug. 1777) Maria, dau. of Nathaniel Robbins, of Hymanstown, co. Tipperary, and Frances his wife, dau. of Anthony Atkinson, of Cangort, King's Co., by Mary his wife, dau. of Adm. John Guy. He d. 31 Dec. 1825, having had issue,
1. RICHARD, his heir.
2. Samuel, of Congor House, d. unm. 16 Oct. 1816.
3. Thomas, d. unm. Nov. 1797.
4. George, in the Army, d. unm. Oct. 1804.
5. Frederick, in the Army, b. 1786; d. unm. 18 March, 1813.
6. Daniel, of Beechwood, co. Tipperary, b. 2 Feb. 1787; m. 2 Oct. 1818, Rebecca, dau. of Thomas Sadleir, of Castletown (*see that family*). She d. 13 Sept. 1878. He d. 23 Feb. 1853, having had issue,
1. Franc Sadleir, of Boonoke, Conargo, N.S.W., b. 23 Oct. 1833; m. Emily Bazley, and has issue,
(1) Franc Brereton Sadleir.   (2) Norman Fraser.
(3) Otway Rothwell.   (4) Ralph Sadleir.
(5) Leigh Sadleir.
(1) Rebecca Sadleir.   (2) Alice Metford.
(3) Emilie Adelaide.   (4) Louise Fraser.
(5) Ethel Beatrice.
2. Daniel, b. 14 March, 1836.
1. Maria, m. 1 Jan. 1852, Laurence Metford, 6th Regt.
2. Louisa, m. 3 Feb. 1851, Capt. Webb, of Ballyhay, co. Down.
7. John, of Willsborough, b. 8 March, 1789; m. Dora, dau. of William Hemsworth, and had issue,
1. Richard (Rev.), b. 18 July, 1818; m. Isabella, dau. of — Wright, of Monaghan, and left issue.
2. Frederick, F.R.C.S I., b. 16 Oct. 1820; d.s.p.
8. Joseph, of Rodeen, m. Ann, dau. of Robert Fraser, and d. 11 Aug. 1857, having had issue,
1. Richard, b. 1820, m. Caroline, dau. of Eyre Coote Baldwin, of Bellpark, co. Tipperary, and Belfast.
2. Robert, b. 1825, m. Miss French, of Carney.
1. Jane, m. — Molloy.   2. Maria.
9. Arthur, d. unm.
10. Nathaniel, d. young.
11. Nathaniel, of Ballyrickard, b. Nov. 1797; m. 1st (setts. dated 4 Feb. 1824), Mary Ann, dau. of Philip Homan Baldwin, of Cloneygowan, Queen's Co., Capt. H.E.I.C.S. He m. 2ndly, Rebecca, dau. of Richard Litton. He d. 21 Nov. 1841, having by his first wife had issue,
1. Richard Baldwin, b. 26 April, 1825; m. Anne, dau. of N. B. M'Intire, and d. 3 Sept. 1898, leaving issue.
2. Frederick Baldwin, b. 2 June, 1832; d. 24 Aug. 1909; m. Mary, dau. of N. B. M'Intire.
3. Nathaniel Baldwin, b. 12 June, 1838; m. Elizabeth, dau. of Hon. E. Murray, of Ontario, and has issue.

The eldest son,
RICHARD FALKINER, of Mount Falcon, served in the Peninsular War in the 4th Dragoon Guards, b. 13 June, 1778; m. 17 Aug. 1825, Tempe, dau. of Richard Litton. She d. Jan. 1888, aged 92. He d. 25 April, 1833, having had issue,
1. RICHARD HENRY, his heir.
2. Travers Hartley, C.E., b. 1829.
3. Frederick Richard (Sir), Recorder of Dublin, K.C., M.A., Trin. Coll. Dublin, Bencher of the King's Inns, b. 19 Jan. 1831; m. 1st, April, 1861, Adelaide, dau. of Thomas Sadleir, of Castletown. She d. 2 June, 1877, leaving issue,
1. Frederick Richard, Lieut. R.H.A., b. 26 Jan. 1862; d. in India.
2. Cæsar Litton, Barrister-at-Law, Assistant Land Commissioner, b. 26 Sept. 1863; d. 5 Aug. 1908; m. 4 Aug. 1892, Henrietta Mary, dau. of the late Sir Thomas N. Deane, and had issue,
(1) Dorothy Cecil, b. 3 Feb. 1894.
(2) Irene Kathleen, b. 17 March, 1897.
3. Travers Hartley (Rev.), late Capt. Connaught Rangers, b. 13 May, 1871; m. 5 July, 1910, Annie, dau. of late Eustace Powhatan Sabine, of Adelaide, S. Australia, and widow of Sydney Oliver, of Sydney, N.S.W.
1. Tempe Eleanor Mary, m. 1st, 1890, Gen. William Charles Forrest, C.B., late 11th Hussars, who d. 1 April, 1902. She m. 2ndly, 24 Feb. 1906, Major George N. Munro, late Worcestershire Regt.
2. Adelaide Elmina, m. 27 Aug. 1903, Edward Francis Fetherstonhaugh (*see* FETHERSTONHAUGH *of Carrick*).
3. Robina.   4. Mary.
Sir Frederick m. 2ndly, Sept. 1878, Robina Hall, dau. of N. B. M'Intire, of Clover Hill, Dublin. She d.s.p. 1895. He d. 23 March, 1908.
4. Robert George, b. 1832; m. 1870, Lydia, dau. of Robert Murdock. He d.s.p. 1872.
1. Rebecca, d. young, 1837.

Arms—Or three falcons close ppr. in the centre chief point a mullet gu. Crest—A falcon's lure ppr. charged with a mullet gu. between two wings az. Motto—Fortuna favente.

Seat—Mount Falcon, Borrisokane, co. Tipperary.

FALLON OF NETTERVILLE LODGE.

BERNARD NETTERVILLE FALLON, of Netterville Lodge, co. Galway, J.P., M.I.C.E., educated at Trin. Coll. Dublin, b. 8 Jan. 1867.

Lineage.—REDMUND FALLON, Chief of the O'Fallon's country, whose mother was Jane, dau. of Richard More Rutledge, m. Jane O'Malone, of Balanahown, and had, with other issue, a son,
JOHN FALLON, of Runnimead, co. Roscommon, Capt. in the service of JAMES II, m. Catherine, dau. of Roger O'Flyn, of co. Roscommon, and was s. by his eldest son,
BRYAN FALLON, of Runnimead, m. 1703, Mary, dau. of Christopher, and grand-dau. of Alexander Irwin, of Oran, co. Roscommon, and had issue. The eldest son,
JOHN FALLON, of Runnimead, m. 1738, Margaret, dau. of Patrick Netterville, of Longford and Lecarrow, co. Galway, by Cecilia his wife, dau. of Sir Redmund Burke, of Glynsk, Bart. (Patrick Netterville's father, Nicholas, was son of Patrick, who was transplanted to co. Mayo, by order of CROMWELL, and grandson of Luke, 1st Viscount Netterville, of Dowth). They had issue, CHRISTOPHER and Henry. The elder son,
CHRISTOPHER FALLON, of Runnimead, m. Feb. 1761, Ellen, dau. of Anthony Fox, of Cloatanny, King's Co., by Jane his wife, only child of Veale Dillon, of Rath. Veale Dillon was a direct descendant of the Earls of Roscommon, and his male descendant would have been entitled to the Earldom. Christopher Fallon, by his wife Ellen Fox, had issue,
1. JOHN, his heir. 2. Anthony Fox, b. 12 Nov. 1771.
3. Henry, b. 9 Jan. 1774, who settled in Spain.
1. Jane, m. Count Magawley, of the King's Co.
2. Margaret, Mary Teresa, a Carmelite nun, Loughrea.
Christopher Fallon d. 29 Oct. 1795, and was s. by his son,
JOHN FALLON, of Runnimead, J.P. and D.L., b. 6 April, 1767; m. 6 Oct. 1784, Letitia, dau. of John Lambert, of Milford, by Mary his wife, dau. of Sir Henry Burke, Bart. of Glinsk, by Cisley Netterville his wife, and has issue,
1. BERNARD, his heir.
1. Maria, m. James Walter Sydney.
2. Cecilia, m. Thomas Costello, Barrister-at-Law.
3. Ellen, m. Thomas Neville Bagot, of Ballymoe.
4. Jane, m. H. Kelly, of Scregg, co. Roscommon.
The only son,
BERNARD FALLON, of Runnimead, m. 25 Feb. 1829, Mary, eldest dau. of Christopher French, J.P., of Frenchlawn, co. Roscommon, by Harriet his wife, dau. of Joseph McDonnell, of Caranacon, co. Mayo, and d. 6 Jan. 1840, leaving by her (who d. 4 Nov. 1864) issue,
1. John, late of Netterville Lodge.
1. Letitia, a Sister of Mercy, late Superior of the Sisters of Mercy, Newtownforbes.
2. Jane, a nun at Loretto Abbey, Rathfarnham (late Superior General of the Institute of Loretto in Ireland), d. 8 July, 1888.
3. Mary, an Ursuline nun in Rome.
4. Harriet, a Sister of Mercy, Superior of the Sisters of Mercy, Geelong, Australia.
The only son,
JOHN FALLON, of Netterville Lodge, co. Galway, J.P., B.A. Trin. Coll. Dublin, Barrister-at-Law, b. 9 Oct. 1835; m. 10 July, 1865, Cecilia, only dau. of Thomas Lynch, J.P. of Lavally, co. Galway (by Rosina his wife, dau. of Thomas Tighe, of Newford, co. Galway, and grand-dau. of Richard Tighe, of Laragh, co. Roscommon), and d. 8 Dec. 1891, having had issue,
1. BERNARD NETTERVILLE, now of Netterville Lodge.
2. John Christopher Joseph, 2nd Lieut. R.E., b. 10 March, 1868; drowned at Malta, June, 1893.
3. Christopher, b. 4 Sept. 1871; lost in the *Drummond Castle*, in 1896.
4. Anthony, b. 14 Dec. 1873.
1. Mary Rosina Harriet, a Sister of Mercy at Newtownforbes.

Arms,—Argent, two greyhounds rampant az. supporting a sword between them ppr. pommelled and hilted gu., quartering NETTERVILLE, FOX, and DILLON. Crest—A hawk rising jessed and belted or. Motto—Fortiter et fideliter.

Seat—Netterville Lodge, Toomard, Ballinasloe.

FARMAR OF BLOOMFIELD.

WILLIAM CECIL RUSSELL FARMAR, of Bloomfield, Major R.A., b. 25 Aug. 1869; m. 1899, Elfrida Louise, youngest dau. of Col. Montgomery Williams, Royal Canadian Regt.

Lineage.—JASPER FARMAR, a Major in the Army, took a prominent part in the settlement of Ireland 1653-58, m. the eldest dau. of Anthony Gamble, of co. Cork, and d. 1683-4, having had,
1. RICHARD, his heir.
2. Jasper, of Garrankenny Grange, co. Cork, left issue, settled in North America.
3. John, ancestor of FARMER, Bart. of Mount Pleasant, Sussex (*see* BURKE's *Peerage*).
4. Samuel, Major in the Army, who purchased several valuable estates in Virginia, left descendants in North America.
Major Farmar d. 1683-4. His eldest son,
RICHARD FARMAR, of Arderrack, co. Cork, m. 1675, Elizabeth, eldest dau. of Lieut.-Col. Robert Phaire, Governor of Cork under CROMWELL, 1650, and had three sons,
1. JASPER, of Kirconway, co. Cork, b. 1676, m. in 1701, Elizabeth, dau. of George Rogers, of Ashgrove, co. Cork, and had a son, RICHARD, d. unm. 1730.
2. ROBERT, who carried on the family.
3. John, M.D., b. in 1678, m. Lucy, second dau. of Cuthbert Wilkinson, and had (with one dau., Lucy) an only son, Jasper, m. 1st, Mrs. Lasier; and 2ndly, in 1774, Grace, 2nd dau. of Hovell Farmar, M.D., and had three children,
(1) Richard, an Officer in the 58th Regt., drowned at sea with his detachment in 1814.
(2) Jasper, Capt. Royal Marines, of Sunnybank, co. Hereford, J.P. and D.L., m. 1819, Meliora, widow of Peter Rickards, Mynors, of Treago, which lady d. 1829.
(1) Dora, d. unm. 1831.
The 2nd son,
ROBERT FARMAR, of Fergus, co. Cork, and of Thurles Beg, co. Tipperary, b. 1677, Major in the Army; m. 1700, Grace, 2nd dau. and co-heir of William Hovell, of Mount Hovell, co. Cork, by whom (who d. 1763, aged 80) he left at his decease, 1743,
1. HOVELL, of whom presently.
2. Edward, Capt. Royal Marines, b. 1710, m. 1st, 1738, Katherine, dau. of Poole St. Barbe, of Bittern, Hants, and widow of Lieut. Oates, R.N., by whom he had three children,
1. Edward, M.D., d.s.p. 1802.
2. Robert Hill, of Barnhill, co. Cork, Gen. of Marines, b. 1775, m. thrice; by his 2nd wife, Mildred, eldest dau. of Rev. Richard Farmar, he had four children,
(1) Robert Herring, b. 1794, an Officer 77th Regt.; m. 1817, Mary, only dau. of Armigher Sealey, of Cork, and d. 22 Aug. 1843, leaving issue,
1. Charles Lewis Atterbury, Major Royal Marines, b. 23 Jan. 1831, who had an only son, Charles Edward, d. 24 July, 1908.
1. Frances Georgiana.
2. Juliana Priscilla, m. 24 March, 1849, Thomas Osborne Stock, M.P. for Carlow.
(2) Edward Sterling, Gen. in the Army, b. 1798; m. 1836, Jane, only dau. of James Cunningham, Capt. R.N., and had issue,
1. Edward James Cunningham, b. 1845.
1. Jane Cunningham Mildred.
2. Georgiana Marianne.
3. Florence Lucinda Caroline.
4. Helen Theresa Unity Gordon.
(1) Elizabeth. (2) Marianne, d. 1824.
Gen. Farmar m. 3rdly, 1809, Elizabeth, eldest dau. of Dr. Mallet, a Physician, and relict of Thomas Symonds, Capt. R.N., and d. 2 Jan, 1839.
1. Katherine, d. 1824.
Capt. Edward Farmar m. 2ndly, 1772, Frances, eldest dau. of Edward Roberts, of Clover Hill, co. Cavan, and d. 1784, having had another son and a dau.,
3. Richard Hugh Hovell Sterling, of Castle Treasure, co. Cork, b. 1782, Capt. Royal Marines; m. 1818, Ann (who d. 1853), 3rd dau. of Thomas Grazebrook, of Stroud, co. Gloucester, and dying 1840, left issue,
(1) Richard, Capt. Royal Marines, b. 9 June, 1819; m. 15 Feb. 1854, Eleanor, youngest dau. of John Simpson, of Stoke, Devonport. She d. March, 1895. He d. 1 Jan. 1879, leaving issue,
Charles Richard Wylde, Cape Mounted Rifles, b. 1 Jan. 1858; m. 22 Dec. 1902, Katherine Anne, youngest dau. of George Dowling, of Carlton Colville, Suffolk, and has issue, Eleanor Anne, b. 4 Dec. 1904.
Katherine Anne Simpson.
(2) William Edward, Lieut.-Col. R.M.L.I. (retired), of Dorset Lodge, Bournemouth, Hants, b. 27 April, 1824; m. 17 Sept. 1850, Mary Dorset, youngest dau. of William Lawrance, of Fletton Tower, co. Huntingdon, and niece of Major J. D. Bringhurst, King's Dragoon Guards; killed at Waterloo, 18 June, 1815. He d. 6 Sept. 1910, having had issue,
1. Edward Dorset, Major late R.A.M.C., F.R.C.S. F.R.G.S., (*Glenlee, Staines, Middlesex*), served in Egypt with Cavalry Brigade in 1882, in Zululand 1888, in Upper Burmah in 1891, and on Malabar Coast in 1895, b. 2 Sept. 1854; adopted the additional surname of BRINGHURST, by Deed Poll, dated 6 Sept. 1884; m. 1st, 3 April, 1886, Grace Marion Letitia, eldest dau. of R. C. Alexander, Chief of the Police, S. Africa, and by her (who d. 29 May, 1888) had a dau., Hermione Beatrice Patience, b. 31 Jan. 1887. He m. 2ndly, 24 June, 1889, Ella, widow of Col. W. H. Christie, and dau. of Col. Blurton, and Queen's Regt. She d. 28 Aug. 1903; he m. 3rdly, 28 Jan. 1904, Claire (Dolly), 3rd dau. of J. Norton White, late of Wolverton, Bucks. She d. 28 April, 1910.
2. William Lawrance, Major R.A., b. 10 June, 1863; m. 10 May, 1893, Constance Jane Mary, eldest dau. of Maj.-Gen. W. J. Finch, late R.A., and has issue,
Frederick Walter, b. 8 May, 1894.
Mary Olive, b. 16 Aug. 1895.
1. Mary Lawrance, b. 29 Sept. 1857.
2. Dorset Ann Fraser, b. 12 March, 1867.

Farrell. THE LANDED GENTRY. 218

(1) Caroline, b. 11 Sept. 1822; d. unm. 12 July, 1900.
(2) Ann Grazebrook, b. 24 Aug. 1830; d. unm. 1 Jan. 1889.
6. Helen, d. unm. 1821.
8. Richard (Rev.), of Barnhill, co. Cork, Rector of Dunmanway and Timoleague, m. 1759, Elizabeth, dau. of Robert Freeman, of Ballinguile, and had two daus., of whom Mildred, the elder, m. her cousin, Gen. Robert Hill Farmar; and Mary Anne, m. — Herring, E.I.C.S.
1. Grace, m. 1726, her cousin, Hon. Richard Hill, of Beare, Forest, co. Cork, one of H.M. Council for South Carolina.
2. Elizabeth, m. John Beare, of Cork, and d. 1786.
3. Jane, m. William Wakeham, of Spring Hill, co. Cork.
4. Hannah, m. William Keyes; d. 1798, aged 84.
The eldest son,
HOVELL FARMAR, M.D., of Mount Hovell, co. Cork, b. 1701; m. 1739, Katherine Dorothea, eldest dau. of Christopher Russell, Col. 17th Regt., and Governor of Minorca, where he d. 1729, aged 59. By her (who d. 1778) Mr. Farmar had issue,
1. HUGH HOVELL, his heir.
2. Robert, Capt. in the 50th Regt., m. Jane, dau. of William Wakeham, and d.s.p.
1. Elizabeth, m. Joseph Oates, of Kilnabone, co. Cork, and d. in 1810.
2. Grace, m. Jasper Farmar.
Mr. Farmar d. 1770, and was s. by his elder son,
HUGH HOVELL FARMAR, of Dunsinane, co. Wexford, called to the Bar 1768. He m. 21 Oct. 1780, Jane, 2nd dau. of Michael Roberts, of Kilmony, co. Cork, by whom (who d. 25 March, 1838) he had issue,
1. HUGH HOVELL, of Dunsinane, J.P., b. 15 Jan. 1782; m. 12 Jan. 1815, Meliora Rickards, only dau. of Peter Rickards Mynors, of Treago, co. Hereford, and by her (who d. 11 Nov. 1854) left at his decease, 1828,
1. HUGH HOVELL BASKERVILLE (Rev.), d.s.p. 17 Jan. 1890.
2. WILLIAM ROBERTS, of Bedford House, Southampton, Major-Gen. in the Army, late Assistant-Commandant Royal Victoria Hospital, Netley, b. 14 March, 1825, served in the 50th Regt., and was severely wounded at the battle of Aliwal, served throughout the Indian Mutiny of 1857-8 in the 82nd Regt.; m. 1st, 20 May, 1851, Alicia Mary, only child of Edward Stone Cotgrave, Capt. R.N., and by her (who d. 10 April, 1861) had issue,
(1) RICHARD DE MALPAS COTGRAVE, b. 2 Dec. 1853; assumed the surname of COTGRAVE, in lieu of Farmar, in 1882, in accordance with the terms of the will of his grandfather, the late Capt. E. S. Cotgrave, R.N.; m. 6 Dec. 1877, Amelia, 3rd surviving dau. of the late Capt. William Walsingham Morison, M.S., and has issue,
1. Hugh Hovell Farmar, b. 10 June, 1882.
2. Reginald Walsingham Farmar, b. 20 July, 1883.
3. Christopher Russell Farmar, b. 23 Dec. 1891.
4. Montague Lewis Farmar, b. 28 Dec. 1892.
1. Aline Mary Farmar, b. 5 Jan. 1885; d. in Cyprus, 23 Nov. 1889.
2. Ella Grace Farmar, b. 4 June, 1886.
3. Beatrice Maud Farmar, b. 9 July, 1889.
4. Dorothy Evelyn Farmar, b. 1896.
(1) Alicia Mildred Cotgrave, d. 14 Nov. 1864
(2) Meliora Alianor Cotgrave, m. 2 Aug 1884, Francis Harper Treherne, Surgeon, A.M.D, and d. 1 Feb. 1891.
(3) Grace Ursula Cotgrave (Bonville, Park Road, Winchester), m. 5 Dec. 1883, Arthur E. Niblett, of Haresfield Court, co. Gloucester, J.P. (who d. 1904), and has surviving issue,
1. Alice Mildred, m. 1907, Evan Christopher Prichard.
2. Dora Winifred Gladys.
3. Winifred, m. 18 Oct. 1911, Capt. Peter Martin Connellan, Hampshire Regt.
Gen. Farmar m. 2ndly, 11 June, 1863, Ellenor Louisa (Bedford House, Southampton) eldest dau. of Rev. William Lewis Girardot, of Hinton Charterhousel and d. 26 July, 1896, leaving issue,
(2) Hugh Henry Foxcroft, Lieut. King's Royal Rifle Corps, b. 21 Aug. 1870, d.v.p. July, 1896.
(3) George Jaspar, Major Worcestershire Regt., Brigade Major 12th Infantry Brigade, b. 20 July, 1872.
(4) Harold Mynors, Capt. Lancashire Fusiliers, b. 15 June, 1878; m. 31 July, 1907, Violet, dau. of Sir William Dalby, and has issue,
Hugh William, b. 6 June, 1908.
Hyacinth Susan.
(4) Beatrice Emily.
(5) Cecily Eleanor, d. 17 May, 1871.
(6) Juliet Mary, m. April, 1892, Alfred Adams, Barrister-at-Law, son of Rev. H. C. Adams, Vicar of Old Shoreham, Sussex, and has issue.
(7) Ella Katherine.
(8) Rose Dorothea, m. June, 1898, Frederick Colpoys Keane, youngest son of Marcus Keane, of Beech Park, co. Clare (see that family).
(9) Violet Eleanor.
1. Meliora Mynors, m. 29 Jan. 1861, Hon. K. Edmund Augustus Blundell, Governor of Singapore, Malacca, and Prince of Wales' Island, who d. 12 Oct. 1868. She d. Dec. 1885.
2. Anna Catherina Rickards, m. 12 June, 1855, Rev. William Hirzel Le Marchant, D.D., Vicar of Haresfield, co. Gloucester.
3. Jane Philippa Baskerville, m. 9 Dec. 1852, John Whitehead, 67, Inverness Terrace, W., Barrister-at-Law.
2. Michael Roberts, an Officer in the Army, killed in action at Cuba, 1807.
8. WILLIAM RUSSELL, of whom presently.

1. Mary, m. Charles Hill, of St. John's, co. Wexford, M.D.
2. Katherine Dorothea, m. Richard Hill, of Urrinsfort, co. Wexford.
Mr. Farmar d. 12 Feb. 1812. His 3rd son,
WILLIAM RUSSELL FARMAR, of Bloomfield, J.P. co. Wexford, b. 1802; m. 1st, 9 Dec. 1829, Eliza, dau. of Richard Donovan, of Ballymore, by whom (who d. 23 Nov. 1844) he had issue,
1. WILLIAM HENRY, late of Bloomfield.
2. Hugh Jasper, b. 1833; d. young.
3. Richard Donovan, b. July, 1841; d. 5 April, 1844.
1. Anne Jane. 2. Mary Caroline, d. young.
3. Katherine Elizabeth, m. 20 Nov. 1866, Rev. Somerset Brafield Burtchaell (see that family).
4. Elizabeth Mary.
Mr. W. R. Farmar m. 2ndly, 29 Nov. 1853, Henrietta, dau. of Harry Alcock, of Wilton Castle, co. Wexford, and d. 20 Oct. 1871, leaving by her a dau.,
5. Sarah Caroline Margaret, m. 23 April, 1878, Richard Rothe Burtchaell, of Brandondale, co. Kilkenny (see that family).
The eldest son,
WILLIAM HENRY FARMAR, of Bloomfield, J.P., Capt. Wexford Militia, b. 21 April, 1831; m. 16 June, 1868, Frances Anastasia, dau. of Winston Newell Barron, of Kingbill House, co. Down and FitzWilliam Place, Dublin, Chairman of Quarter Sessions, co. Monaghan, grand-dau. of Capt. Newell, R.N., of Kinghill Hill, and niece of Sir Winston Barron, Bart., M.P. co. Waterford, and d. 9 Sept. 1876, leaving issue,
1. WILLIAM CECIL RUSSELL, now of Bloomfield.
2. Ralph Jasper Newell, b. 7 July, 1871.
3. Fitzhugh Hovell, Arthur, b. 22 March, 1874; d. unm. 24 April, 1906.
4. Henry Capel Donovan, b. 6 June, 1876.
1. Irene Frances Elizabeth, b. 13 Oct. 1872; m. 10 Oct. 1901, Rev. Duncan Canney (259, London Road, Thornton Heath), 4th son of the late Edward Henry Canney, of the Admiralty, and has issue, Duncan Edward Farmar, b. 29 Jan. 1911, and Irene Dorothea Elizabeth Donovan, b. 6 Aug. 1902.
2. Edith Emily Marian, b. 30 April, 1875.

Seat—Bloomfield, Enniscorthy, co. Wexford.

FARRELL OF MOYNALTY.

JOHN EDWARD JOSEPH FARRELL, of Moynalty, co. Meath, J.P., D.L., High Sheriff 1907, late Lieut. 1st Batt. Royal Warwickshire Regt.; b. 9 May, 1861; m. 12 May, 1884, Harriet, dau. of late Joseph Webb J. Nicolas, late 21st Regt., and has issue,
1. CECIL JOSEPH, Lieut. 5th Batt. Leinster Regt., b. 1885.
2. Valentine Joseph, b. 1888.
3. John Arthur Joseph, Lieut. 5th Batt. Leinster Regt., b. 1890.
4. Gerald Edward Joseph, b. 1895.
1. Mary Lucretia Margaret, b. 1891.
2. Monica Paulina Mary, b. 1893.
3. Margaret Georgina Mary, b. 1896.
4. Gertrude Florence Patricia Mary, b. 1898.
5. Helen Frances Mary, b. 1900.
6. Patricia Catherine Teresa Mary, b. 1904.

Lineage.—JOHN FARRELL, of Fingal, co. Dublin, b. 1710; m. circa 1737, Anne, dau. of Christopher Malone, of co. Westmeath, and d. 1767, leaving issue, a son,
JAMES FARRELL, b. 1748, of Moynalty and Robertstown, co. Meath, and of Merrion Square, Dublin; m. 1772, Eleanor, 2nd dau. of Thomas Laffan, of Johnstone, co. Kilkenny, and d. 20 May, 1823, having had issue,
1. JOHN, late of Moynalty.
2. Thomas, of Merrion Square, Dublin, and Robertstown, co. Meath, b. 1790; m. 13 April, 1819, Margaret Elizabeth (who d. 9 Oct. 1867), 2nd dau. of John Mears Grainger, of Causestown House, co. Meath, and d. 18 Nov. 1852, having had issue,
1. James, m. 16 Dec. 1861, Gabrielle Geneviève Emile Georgine, dau. of the late Camille Henri Melchior, Comte de Polignac, formerly Governor of the Chateau of Fontainebleau, France, younger brother of Prince de Polignac, Minister of CHARLES X of France, and d. 8 Oct. 1881. She d. 1888.
2. John, d. 31 March, 1842.
3. Thomas Arthur, of 37, Merrion Square, Dublin, M.A., Barrister-at-Law, late Capt. West Kent Militia, of Robertstown, J.P. co. Meath, m. 20 Aug. 1884, Hon. Randalina Anna Maria Louisa Plunkett, 2nd dau. of 12th Lord Louth. He d.s.p. 29 Dec. 1898. She m. 2ndly, 21 Feb. 1900, Francis Arthur Farrell (see below).
4. Edward Walter, of Robertstown, co. Meath, and 37, Merrion Square, Dublin, m. 20 Dec. 1870, Anna Maria Teresa, eldest dau. of the late John Thomas Selby (see SELBY of Biddlestone). She d. 10 June, 1872. He d. 24 April, 1903, leaving a dau., Flavia.
1. Jeannette Mary, d. young 10 Nov. 1838.
2. Eleonore, d. unm. 1902.
3. Mary Catherine, d. 1910, m. 20 Feb. 1851, Monsieur Jules Gengoult de Clairville, of the Chatelet, Coulandon, Allier, France, and by him (who d. 1895) has issue, a dau., Cecile Marguerite.
4. Margaret Adelaide.
1. Mary, m. Richard Dease, of Firmond, co. Kildare, who d. 1837.

2. Marsella, *m.* Matthew James Plunkett, of St. Margaret's, Dublin, and left, with four daus., one son, Oliver, who *m.* Anne, dau. of J. Brittain, and left a dau., Olivia, *m.* Charles O'C. Cosslett.
3. Anne, *m.* Joseph Brittain, Chief Justice of Demerara, and had two daus.
4. Jane, *m.* Thomas Laffan Kelly, Deputy-Governor Bank of Ireland, and *d.* 3 Oct. 1865, having had issue two sons and two daus., of whom Ellen, *m.* J. J. Whyte, of Loughbrickland, co. Down, and *d.* 1857, leaving one dau., Mary Ellen, *m.* 1892, Major Blount.

The elder son,
JOHN FARRELL, of Moynalty, co. Meath, J.P. and D.L., High Sheriff 1843, *b.* 1784; *m.* Jan. 1820, Elizabeth Emily, dau. of Francis Valentine Bennett, of Thomastown, King's Co., and *d.* 2 April, 1870, having had issue,
1. JOHN ARTHUR, of Moynalty.
2. Francis Arthur, *b.* June, 1828; late of the 7th Hussars, *m.* 21 Feb. 1900, Randalina Anna Maria Louisa, 2nd dau. of 12th Lord Louth and widow of Thomas Arthur Farrell, of Robertstown (*see above*).
3. Albert Charles Frederick, *b.* 1840; *d.* 1852.
1. Elizabeth Emily, *m.* June, 1851, James Farrell (who *d.* 1858), eldest son of Richard Farrell, Q.C., of North Great George's Street, and Newlawn, co. Dublin, and *d.* 1891, leaving issue,
1. Richard, J.P. cos. Wicklow and Dublin, *b.* Jan. 1854; *d.* 1893.
2. John Charles, Major Royal Sussex Regt., *m.* 1889, Mary Teresa, dau. of Charles Leslie, D.L., of Slindon and Fettercear, and *d.* 22 March, 1911, having had issue,
Cecil James Francis, *b.* 20 Aug. 1890, accidentaly drowned 12 Sept. 1910.
1. Agnes Mary Emily, *m.* the late Major Alfred Power, King's Own Yorks L.I., 2nd son of Nicholas Power, of Bellevue House, co. Waterford, and has issue (*see that family*).

The eldest son,
JOHN ARTHUR FARRELL, of Moynalty, co. Meath, J.P. and D.L. co. Meath, High Sheriff 1857, J.P. co. Cavan, and late Capt. Royal Meath Militia, *b.* 1825; *m.* 19 July, 1860, Hon Lucretia Pauline Mary Preston, 2nd dau. of Edward, 13th Viscount Gormanston, and *d.* 27 Nov. 1904, having had issue,
1. JOHN EDWARD JOSPEH, now of Moynalty.
2. Edward Francis Jenico Joseph, of Walterstown, Moynalty, co. Meath, Lieut.-Col. 5th Batt. Leinster Regt., J.P. co. Meath, *b.* Jan. 1863.
3. Jenico James Valentine Joseph (*Park House, Cary Park, Babbicombe, S. Devon*), *b.* May, 1864; *m.* 24 Jan. 1900, Helen Agatha, only dau. of Vernon Benbow, of Kempsford, Gloucester, and has issue,
1. Francis Vernon Joseph, *b.* 29 Feb. 1908.
1. Blanche Helen Mary, *b.* 26 Dec. 1901.
2. Madelaine Mary Agnes, *b.* 28 March, 1910.
4. Francis Henry Arthur Joseph, *b.* Feb., 1836.
5. Arthur William Patrick Joseph, *b.* March, 1867; *m.* 31 Jan. 1900, Harriett Mary, eldest dau. of the late Lieut.-Col. Harry Peisley L'Estrange, of Moystown, King's Co.
6. Charles Laurence Bennett Joseph, *b.* Aug. 1872.
1. Mary Lucretia Phillippa Josephine, *m.* 30 April, 1902, M. Kenneth Angelo, of Culachy, Fort Augustus, N.B.

Seat—Moynalty House, Kells, co. Meath. Clubs—Kildare Street, Dublin.

FAY OF FAYBROOK.

THOMAS ALLEN FAY, of Faybrook, co. Cavan, *b.* 1870; *m.* 21 July, 1908, Marie Therèse, dau. of James Charles Fisher, of Manchester and Lytham.

Lineage.—The family of DE FAY or DE LA FAY is traceable in the Records of the Pale since the reign of King JOHN, when lived Sir Richard de Fay, Knt., Chamberlain to de Lacy, Lord Palatine of Meath. There are pedigrees of three branches of the family recorded in the Book of Lecan and from that seated at Dernegara Castle, Westmeath, descends the Fay of Faybrook family.

GEORGE DE FAY, of Dernegara, son of Sir Mayne the Ritter (Knight), was seized 1300 of premises in Kilmer, Donore, and Glackmorne in right of his wife, Isabell, dau. of 5th Baron Delvin. His second son,
WALTER FITZGEORGE DE FAY had a suit in 1339 with his grandmother, Eglantina, widow of Lord Delvin, in which he was unsuccessful (*see* PLEA ROLL, 13 Edward III). His son,

ROGER FITZWALTER DE FAY inherited lands in the Baronies of Fore and Moyashel, and was seized of Dernegara, Comerstown, Ballindrinan, and Bartonstown.

These lands remained in the possession of the family until the time of Cromwell, when they were confiscated. A portion of them was restored at the Restoration by a Decree of Innocence, March 1663, to GARRET FAY and his three surviving brothers: 1. Meyler of Comerstown and Dublin, *m.* Alice Plunket, and *d.s.p.* Her will 1682. 2. Stephen (Rev.), a priest of Gartlandstown (will 1688), and 3. THOMAS, of whom presently. The above-mentioned,
GARRET FAY, of Dernegara Castle, *m.* 1665, Alice, dau. of Sir Thomas Nugent, Bart. of Moyrath, and *d.* April, 1686, leaving issue,
1. George of Dernegara, and Gartlandstown, *m.* Eliza, sister of Luke Cashel, of Down, Westmeath, and by her (who *m.* 2ndly, Richard Chope) had two daus.,
1. Mary, *m.* Richard Kennedy, and had issue.
2. Alison, *m.* Peter Lesack, and had issue.
He was Capt. in the Army of JAMES II, was attainted 1691, but was included in the articles of Limerick and thus saved his estate. Gartlandstown, etc., was in the possession of the descendants of his daus. in 1747.
2. John, attainted 1691, appears to have *d.s.p.*
1. Mary, *m.* Luke Cashell, of Down, co. Westmeath.
2. Ann, *m.* 1st, Capt. Stafford, and 2ndly, Counsellor Read, of Dunboyne, and *d.* 1737, leaving issue.
His brother, the above-mentioned,
THOMAS FAY, of Togher, was attainted 1691, and was plaintiff in Chancery bills 1706 and 1709, *m.* Anne Blake of Castletown House, Westmeath, and *d.* 1718, leaving issue,
1. MARTIN, his heir.
2. John More, of Damaelstown.
3. Thomas MacThomas.
1. Frances, *m.* Thomas Johnson of Smithtown, ancestor of Sir William Johnson, Bart., of New York. Her arms are given in the Johnson pedigree registered in Ulster's Office, 21 May, 1772.

The eldest son,
MARTIN FAY, of Damaelstown, and Corboggy, co. Meath, *m.* 1709, Katherine, dau. of — Malone, of Possextown, by Anne his wife, dau. of — Plunket, of Possextown and Gibstown, and *d.* 1765, aged 93, leaving issue,
1. THOMAS, his heir.
2. Patrick, of Corboggy, *d.* 1803.
3. John, of Trohanny, *d.* 1791.

The eldest son,
THOMAS FAY, of Annesbrook, and Maio House (Mount Williams), co. Meath, and Drumkirk, co. Cavan, *b.* 1710; *m.* Katherine, dau. of Thomas Murray of Tullawal and Shancor. She *d.* 21 May, 1772. He *d.* 31 Jan. 1796 (will dated 26 Jan. that year), having had issue,
1. Patrick, whose issue is extinct in Ireland.
2. JOHN, of Ballyhaise.

The second son,
JOHN FAY, of Ballyhaise, co. Cavan, *b.* 1760; *m.* 1st, 1788, Mary, dau. of Thadeus O'Dowda, of Clifferna, and by her had a son,
1. THOMAS, of Faybrook and Cootehill.
He *m.* 2ndly, 1796, Mary, dau. of James Brady, of Kilnacreiva, and by her had, with three younger sons who *d.* unm., an eldest son,
2. James, of Moyne Hall, *b.* 1800; *m.* Susan, dau. of James Maccabe, of Cavan, and *d.* 1866, leaving issue,
1. John, of Moyne Hall, co. Cavan, J.P. and D.L., High Sheriff 1873; *d.* 13 March, 1911.
2. Thomas Maccabe, of Heath Lodge and Fitzgibbon Street, Dublin, Barrister-at-Law, *d.s.p.* 23 April, 1879.
1. Annie, *m.* her cousin, Patrick Maccabe Fay, who *d.* 1892, leaving two daus. (*see below*).
2. Marie, *m.* Edward Howley, Barrister-at-Law, eldest son of P. C. Howley, J.P. of Cooga Manor, co. Sligo.
3. Susan, *m.* her cousin, Charles Joseph Fay, M.P., of Granite Lodge, who *d.* 1895, leaving issue (*see below*).
4. Kattie, *m.* B. T. Neary, M.D.
Mr. John Fay *d.* 31 Jan. 1836. The eldest son,
THOMAS FAY, of Faybrook, and Cootehill, co. Cavan, *b.* 1792, *m.* Oct. 1824, Mary, only dau. of Patrick Maccabe of Ballybay, co. Monaghan, and widow of Patrick Harris Herbert. She *d.* June, 1868. He *d.* 4 Sept. 1878, having had issue,
1. Patrick Maccabe, *b.* 1825; *m.* his cousin Annie, dau. of James Fay, of Moyne Hall (*see above*), and *d.* 1892, having had issue,
1. Marie Teresa.
2. Annie.
2. John Rowland, an officer in the French service, *d.s.p.*
3. Thomas Francis, of Faybrook, co. Cavan, late of Fosterstown House, co. Meath, *b.* 1833; *m.* 31 July, 1865, Mary, dau. of Michael Allen, of Trim, and has issue,
1. THOMAS ALLEN, now of Faybrook.
2. John Michael, *b.* 1877.
1. Madeline. 2. Agnes Jane.
4. JAMES HENRY, late of Faybrook.
5. Michael Edmund, *d.s.p.* 1869.
6. Charles Joseph, of Granite Lodge, co. Dublin, J.P., M.P. for Cavan, 1874-85, *b.* 1842; *m.* his cousin Susan, dau. of James Fay, of Moyne Hall (*see above*), and *d.* Oct. 1895, having had issue,
1. Jeffrey James, Barrister-at-Law.
2. Gerald.
1. Susan Henrietta, *m.* Louis C. P. Smith.
1. Marianne Frances, *m.* 1855, Philip Smith, J.P. of Artina, co. Cavan, and Colmanstown House, co. Galway. She *d.* 1901.
2. Eleanor Gertrude, *m.* 1863, John MacCarrick, of Cloonbarry House, co. Sligo. She *d.* 1875.

3. Gretta St. Clare, *m.* 1860, Francis O'Farrell, of Dublin. She *d.* 14 Nov. 1911.
The 4th son,
JAMES HENRY FAY, of Faybrook, co. Cavan, J.P., High Sheriff 1881, *b.* 20 May, 1838, and *d. unm.* 10 April, 1907, being *s.* by his nephew.

Arms—Vert two arms issuant from the dexter and sinister respectively vested or, cuffed arg. the hands ppr. grasping a sword erect of the third pomel and hilt of the second, the blade thrust through a dragon's head couped also gold. Crest—A dragon's head couped or. *Motto*—Toujours fidéle.

Seat—Faybrook, Cootehill, co. Cavan.

CARMICHAEL-FERRALL OF AUGHER CASTLE.

JOHN CARMICHAEL-FERRALL, of Augher Castle, co. Tyrone, B.A., Barrister-at-Law, J.P., D.L. co. Tyrone, High Sheriff 1907, *b.* 8 Nov. 1855; *m.* 28 Sept. 1899, Elizabeth Emily, 3rd dau. of the late Rev. David Henry Elrington, Vicar of swords, Dublin, and Matilda Rowena, his wife, dau. of Rev. Pierce William Drew, of the Strand House, Youghal.

Lineage.—HIS EXCELLENCY MAJOR-GEN. HUGH LYLE CARMICHAEL, Governor of Demerara, by Catherine his wife, last surviving child and heiress of John Ferrall, M.D., of Dublin, had issue,
LIEUT.-COL. JOHN O'FERRALL CARMICHAEL, 18th Regt. and 6th Dragoon Guards, of Duncroft House, Staines, Middlesex (who *d.* 13 July, 1836), *m.* Elizabeth, dau. of John Porter, D.D., Bishop of Clogher, and had issue,
1. JOHN JERVIS O'FERRALL, of Augher Castle.
1. Mary Anne, *m.* 1846, to Ven. Charles Burney (*d.* 1904), Archdeacon of Kingston-on-Thames, and Vicar of St. Mark's, Surbiton, Surrey.
JOHN JERVIS O'FERRALL CARMICHAEL-FERRALL, of Augher Castle, co. Tyrone, J.P. cos. Tyrone and Longford, Commander R.N., served under Sir C. Napier off the coast of Syria, and has the British and Turkish medals, *b.* 17 Oct. 1820; *m.* 13 June, 1850, Margaret, dau. of the late Sir John Nugent Humble, 1st bart. of Cloncoskoran, co. Waterford, and by her (who *d.* 25 July, 1898) had issue, a son,
JOHN, now of Augher Castle.
Capt. Carmichael-Ferrall, assumed the additional surname and arms of FERRALL by Royal Licence dated 20 July, 1852, and *d.* 1904, being *s.* by his only son.

Arms—Quarterly: 1st and 4th, FERRALL, vert, a lion rampant or; 2nd and 3rd, CARMICHAEL, arg., a fess wreathed gu. and az. in chief a trefoil vert. *Crests*—1st, FERRALL: Out of a ducal coronet or, a dexter hand gu.; 2nd, CARMICHAEL: An arm embowed in armour grasping a broken lance, all ppr. charged with a trefoil or. *Mottoes*—CARMICHAEL: Toujours prest. FERRALL: Loyauté sans tache.

Seat—Augher Castle, Augher, co. Tyrone.

FETHERSTONHAUGH OF BRACKLYN CASTLE.

CECIL HOWARD DIGBY FETHERSTONHAUGH, of Bracklyn Castle, co. Westmeath, J.P. and D.L., High Sheriff 1890, *b.* 22 Feb. 1857, late Capt. 1st Dragoons; *s.* his father 15 April, 1868; *m.* 8 Aug. 1885, Meriel Gertrude, eldest dau. of Edward Wilmot Williams, of Herringston, Dorset, and has issue,
ASHLEY ELLIOT HERBERT, Lieut. 14th Hussars, *b.* 3 July, 1886.
Meriel Eleanor, *b.* 12 Feb. 1897.

Lineage.—CUTHBERT FETHERSTONHAUGH, was the first of the name who settled in the co. of Westmeath. His eldest son was, CUTHBERT FETHERSTONHAUGH, who *m.* and had three sons,
1. CUTHBERT, his heir.
2. Thomas, ancestor of FETHERSTONHAUGH *of Carrick*, and FETHERSTON, Bart. *of Ardagh*.
3. Francis, ancestor of FETHERSTON *of Whitrock, co. Longford*.
The eldest son,
CUTHBERT FETHERSTONHAUGH, fixed his residence at Dardistown, 1726, *m.* Mary, dau. of Richard Magan (ancestor of Magan of Emoe), and left four sons,
1. JOHN, *m.* 1741, Anne, dau. of Morgan Magan, of Killeenbrack, and *d.* 1766, leaving a son and heir,
CUTHBERT, of Mosstown, High Sheriff 1781; *m.* 1770, Mary, dau. of Theobald Wolfe, and *d.* 1817, leaving issue,
(1) THEOBALD, of Mosstown, High Sheriff 1805, *m.* 1797, Mary, dau. of Jonathan Harding, of Harding Grove, co. Galway, and *d.* 17 Oct. 1844, leaving,
1. CUTHBERT, of Mosstown, High Sheriff 1841; *m.* 1827, Susan, dau. of William Curtis, of Annamore, and left issue, with several daus.,
   a. Theobald.   b. Cuthbert.
2. Theobald, of Newtown, Westmeath, *b.* 29 Nov. 1808; *m.* 26 July, 1849, Jane Maria, dau. of John Barlow, and left issue,
   a. Theobald, *b.* 6 March, 1855.
   b. William, *b.* 29 Dec. 1859.
   a. Charlotte Helena.
3. WILLIAM, of Grouse Lodge, Westmeath, J.P., *b.* 30 July, 1813; *m.* 13 May, 1845, Frances, dau. of Rev. Cuthbert Fetherstonhaugh, and *d.* 13 July, 1887, having had issue,
   a. THEOBALD, of Grouse Lodge, J.P., *b.* 12 Feb. 1846; *m.* 8 Feb. 1888, Kate Olivia, youngest dau. of Richard Bond, of Fairy Hall, co. Westmeath, and has issue,
      (a) William Ernest, *b.* 12 Nov. 1888.
      (b) Lewis Holmes, *b.* 27 June, 1894.
      (a) Theodora Eleanor Frances.
   b. Charles, *b.* 5 Jan. 1852.   c. Arthur, *b.* 29 April, 1857.
   a. Ann Holmes, *m.* 13 June, 1877, Lieut.-Col. Robert Vandeleur Kelly, C.B., M.D., N.S. Wales Army Med. Corps, 2nd son of the late Robert Hume Kelly, of Glencara, co. Westmeath, and has issue (*see that family*).
   b. Mary, *d.* 14 Dec. 1873.
   c. Margaret.
   d. Theodora Frances, *m.* 17 June, 1880, C. J. Coffy.
4. Harding, of Lissaugh Hill, Westmeath, who left issue.
1. Hanna, *m.* 1831, John Hubert Kelly, of Lynestown, co. Westmeath.
(2) Edward, of Grouse Lodge, *m.* Mary, dau. of Richard Magan, of Newtown, and had issue,
Cuthbert.
Mary, *m.* Richard Magan, of Rockfield.
2. THOMAS, of whom presently.
3. Richard.   4. William.
1. Margaret.
2. Frances, *m.* Joseph Daly, of Castle Daly, co. Westmeath.
The 2nd son,
THOMAS FETHERSTONHAUGH, of Bracklyn, co. Westmeath (whose will, dated 22 Nov., was proved 20 Dec. 1776), *m.* Mary, only child and heiress of Oliver Nugent, of Derrymore, and had issue,
1. JAMES, his heir.   2. John.
1. Anne, *m.* Francis MacEvoy, of Tobertynan, co. Meath, who *d.* 1808, without surviving issue.
2. Ismay.
3. Mary, *m.* 31 March, 1772, Samuel Lea Owen.
The eldest son,
JAMES FETHERSTONHAUGH, of Bracklyn, High Sheriff 1784, *m.* 1788, Margaret, 2nd dau. of Sir Richard Steele, 1st bart. of Hampstead, co. Dublin, and had issue,
1. THOMAS JAMES, his heir.
2. Richard Steele, ancestor of FETHERSTONHAUGH *of Rockview*.
3. John (Rev.), of Griffinstown, co. Westmeath, *b.* 1796, *m.* 27 March, 1821, Hon. Susan Maria Massy, dau. of Hugh, 3rd Lord Massy, and *d.* in 1874, leaving issue,
Harriet, *m.* 15 April, 1874, Robert Harding Massy, who *d.* 20 Dec. 1886, leaving issue.
1. Charlotte, *m.* Major Robert Tighe, M.P. of South Hill, co. Westmeath.
2. Margaret Anne, *m.* 1808, Sir Thomas Chapman, 2nd bart. of Killua Castle, and *d.* 21 Jan. 1871. He *d.* 23 Dec. 1837, leaving issue.
3. Harriet.
Mr. Fetherstonhaugh *d.* 1822, and was *s.* by his eldest son,
THOMAS JAMES FETHERSTONHAUGH, of Bracklyn Castle, J.P. and D.L., High Sheriff of Westmeath, *b.* 19 March, 1790; *m.* 18 Dec. 1816, Lady Eleanor Howard, 2nd dau. of William, 3rd Earl of Wicklow, and *d.* 13 Dec. 1853, having by her (who *m.* 2ndly, 15 April, 1856, Lieut.-Col. William Frederick Johnston, Grenadier Guards, and *d.* 24 Feb. 1885) had issue,
1. HOWARD, his heir.
1. Eleanor Margaret, *m.* 18 Aug. 1841, John Vignoles, eldest son of Very Rev. Charles Augustus Vignoles, Dean of Ossory. He *d.* 22 March, 1843, leaving issue.
2. Catherine Mary, *m.* 1845, Col. Thomas Arthur, 3rd Dragoon Guards, of Desborough, Northants, and *d.* 1891, leaving issue.
3. Frances Alicia, *m.* Capt. John Rodon, 3rd Dragoon Guards, and *d.* 23 Nov. 1898, leaving issue.
4. Emily Elizabeth, *b.* 11 Dec. 1834; *d.* 4 March, 1909.
His only son,
HOWARD FETHERSTONHAUGH, of Bracklyn Castle, Capt. 11th Regt., *b.* 23 May, 1819; *m.* 16 Aug. 1854, Lucy Emily, dau. of

William Wingfield, of Orsett Hall, Essex, and *d.* 15 April, 1868, having had issue,
1. CECIL HOWARD DIGBY, now of Bracklyn.
2. Frederick Howard, late Capt. The Cameronians, *b.* 3 Sept. 1858; *m.* 11 Oct. 1888, Beatrix Ellerie, youngest dau. of Hon. St. Leger Richard Glyn (*see* BURKE'S *Peerage*, WOLVERTON, B.), and has issue, two daus.
3. Herbert Howard, M.V.O., *b.* 9 Oct. 1860, late Lieut. 4th Batt. North Staffordshire Regt., and Gentleman-in-Waiting to the Lord Lieut. of Ireland.
4. Howard Steele Caulfeild, *b.* 16 April, 1862, *d.* in S. America 16 Dec. 1908.
5. Ernest Montague, *b.* 8 Nov. 1863; *m.* 1888, Rebecca, dau. of W. Stansfield, *d.s.p.* 13 Feb. 1906.
6. James, *b.* 1868.
1. Constance Lucy, *d.* Oct. 1860.
2. Florence Lucy, *m.* 1887, William Gore Lambarde, son of Multon Lambarde, of Beechmont, Kent, and has issue, a dau.,
Aurla.

Seat—Bracklyn Castle, Killucan.

FETHERSTONHAUGH late OF ROCKVIEW.

MAJ.-GEN. RICHARD STEELE RUPERT FETHERSTONHAUGH, C.B., formerly of Killulagh and Milltown, co. Westmeath, and now of Gwydyr House, Isle of Wight, Col. late King's Royal Rifles, served in Zulu Campaign 1879, and in Soudan 1885, and in S. African War 1899–1901 (C.B.); *b.* 20 Oct. 1848; *m.* 7 Oct. 1886, Florence, youngest dau. of the late Capt. George Collingwood Dickson, 23rd Madras L.I. (*see* BURKE'S *Peerage*, ISLINGTON, B.), and has issue,
1. RICHARD COLLINGWOOD, *b.* 3 March, 1893.
2. George Robert Alexander, *b.* 15 Nov. 1894.
1. Kathleen Florence.

Lineage.—RICHARD STEELE FETHERSTONHAUGH, of Rockview, co. Westmeath, 2nd son of JAMES FETHERSTON, of Bracklyn (*see that family*), and Margaret his wife, 2nd dau. of Sir Richard Steele, Bart., *b.* 24 Sept. 1795; *m.* 1820, Dorothea, dau. of Hon. Denis George, Baron of the Irish Court of Exchequer, and niece of Sir Rupert George, Bart. She *d.* 1 Aug. 1842. He *d.* 30 Aug. 1834, leaving issue,
1. RICHARD STEELE, of whom presently.
2. George Edward, Lieut. 3rd Dragoons, *b.* 19 Jan. 1825; *d.s.p.* 1846.
3. Rupert Pennefather, who assumed the name and arms of FRAMPTON (*see* FETHERSTONHAUGH-FRAMPTON *of Moreton*).
1. Maria, *m.* 22 July, 1849, Sir Benjamin James Chapman, 4th Bart. of Killua, and has issue (*see* BURKE'S *Peerage and Baronetage*).
2. Adelaide, *d. unm.* 1852.

The eldest son,
RICHARD STEELE FETHERSTONHAUGH, of Rockview, co. Westmeath, J.P. and D.L., High Sheriff 1847, *b.* 12 April, 1823; *m.* 13 Sept. 1846, Rosetta, eldest dau. of Sir David Roche, Bart. of Carass, co. Limerick, and *d.* 6 Oct. 1896, having by her (who *d.* 14 March, 1903) had issue,
1. RICHARD STEELE RUPERT, his heir.
2. John David, of Rockview House, Killucan, co. Westmeath, J.P. and D.L., High Sheriff 1905, Col. in the Army, late Lieut.-Col. Argyll and Sutherland Highlanders, served in N.W. Frontier Campaign, *b.* 20 Feb. 1850; *m.* 1 Sept. 1891, Margaret, 3rd dau. of Maj.-Gen. T. G. A. Oakes, C.B., and Frances his wife, dau. of J. Kincaid Lennox, D.L., of Lennox Castle, co. Stirling. He has issue,
John Lennox, *b.* 27 Aug. 1892.
Barbara Rosetta Frances, *b.* 20 Nov. 1898.
3. Albany Valentine, *b.* 14 Feb. 1852; *d. unm.* 18 Feb. 1873.
1. Frances Dorothea, *m.* July, 1889, John Rooke Rawlence, only son of John Rawlence, of Wilton, Wilts.

Residence—Gwydyr House, Ryde, Isle of Wight. *Club*—Naval and Military.

FETHERSTONHAUGH OF CARRICK.

FRANCIS BRYAN FETHERSTONHAUGH, of Carrick, co. Westmeath, *b.* 1892.

Lineage.—THOMAS FETHERSTONHAUGH, 2nd son of Cuthbert Fetherstonhaugh, and brother of Cuthbert Fetherstonhaugh, of Dardistown, settled at Carrick, co. Westmeath, *m.* Mary Sherlock, of Irishtown, and had four sons,
1. John (Very Rev.), Dean of Raphoe, *d. unm.* 1764.
2. WILLIAM, who carried on the line.
3. Francis, *m.* Mary Birch, and had issue,
Thomas, Lieut.-Col. H.E.I.C.S.; *m.* 10 Feb. 1814, Elizabeth, dau. of Sir Thomas Fetherston, 2nd Bart., and had issue,
(1) Georgina Eleanor.
(2) Caroline Emily, *m.* 10 April, 1860, George Schoales.
Mary, *m.* William Sherlock, of Irishtown, co. Kildare.

4. Ralph (Sir), created a bart. 26 June, 1776, ancestor of FETHERSTON, Bart. of Ardagh.
The 2nd son,
WILLIAM FETHERSTONHAUGH, of Carrick, *m.* Lydia, dau. of William Sherlock, of co. Kildare, and *d.* 1770, having had two sons,
1. Thomas, High Sheriff, co. Westmeath 1771, *m.* 16 Nov. 1771, his cousin Elizabeth, dau. of Sir Ralph Fetherston, 1st bart. of Ardagh, and *d.* before 1773, leaving an only child, who *d.* shortly after his father.
2. WILLIAM, who carried on the line.
The 2nd son,
WILLIAM FETHERSTONHAUGH, of Carrick, High Sheriff 1782, *b.* 1760; *m.* 1782, Susanna, dau. of Godfrey Wills, of Willsgrove, co. Roscommon. She *d.* 1823. He *d.* 1800, having had issue,
1. WILLIAM, his heir.
2. Godfrey, of North Great George's Street, Dublin, and Glenmore, Crossmolina, co. Mayo, *b.* 7 Sept. 1793; *m.* 7 Sept. 1824, Matilda, dau. of Rev. Stephen Radcliff, Incumbent of Skryne, co. Meath. She *d.* 13 April, 1875. He *d.* 1869, leaving issue,
1. William, of Glenmore, co. Mayo, J.P., M.A., Barrister-at-Law, *b.* 17 Sept. 1828; *m.* 6 Sept. 1854, his cousin Jane, dau. of William Fetherstonhaugh, of Carrick (*see below*), and by her (who *d.* 1903) has issue,
Elizabeth, *m.* 24 June, 1874, Oswald Birchall, of Ilkley, Yorks, and has issue.
2. Stephen Radcliff, of Rokeby, Howth, and 17, Eccles Street, Dublin, *b.* 10 Feb. 1830; *m.* 2 July, 1857, Jane, dau. of Joseph Boyce, D.L. She *d.* 1897. He *d.* 1895, leaving issue,
(1) Godfrey Fetherstonhaugh, K.C., of 5, Herbert Street, Dublin, and of Glenmore, Crossmolina, co. Mayo, J.P. cos. Westmeath, Mayo and Fermanagh, M.A. Trin. Coll. Dublin, Barrister Middle Temple, Member of Senate of Dublin University, M.P. North Fermanagh since 1906, *b.* 11 April, 1859.
(2) Alfred Joseph, *b.* 19 Oct. 1863; *m.* 1 May, 1888, Mary Isabel O'Bryen, and *d.* 1894, leaving a dau., Corinne.
(3) Albany, *b.* 14 Oct. 1865; *m.* Sept. 1907, his cousin, Frances Berry Fetherstonhaugh (*see below*), and has issue, one son.
(4) Edwyn, Major Royal Dublin Fus., *b.* 2 Nov. 1867.
(1) Violet, *m.* 15 Dec. 1900, George Scriven, M.D. and has issue, a son and a dau.
(2) Mary Adelaide, *d.* 18 Aug. 1882.
(3) Constance Martha, *m.* 9 Oct. 1907, Reginald S. Radcliffe, and has issue.
(4) Jane Emily, *m.* 1899, R. H. Ryland, and has issue.
(5) Alice Kathleen, *m.* 18 June, 1904, Lieut. William Peebles, M.V.O., R.N., 4th son of William Bellingham Peebles, B.A., M.B., J.P.
3. Godfrey, of Wyattville, co. Dublin, *b.* 31 Aug. 1831; *m.* 15 Sept. 1859, Susanna, dau. of the late Francis Berry, of Tullamore, King's Co., and had issue,
(1) Edward Francis, *b.* 16 May, 1874; *m.* 27 Aug. 1903, Adelaide Elmina, and dau. of Right Hon. Sir Frederick Falkiner, K.C. (*see* FALKINER *of Mount Falcon*).
(2) Godfrey Charles, *b.* 1880; *m.* 7 July, 1909, Maude Ada dau. of Rev. R. Peck.
(1) Frances Berry, *m.* Sept. 1907, her cousin, Albany Fetherstonhaugh (*see above*).
(2) Lilian Isabel.
4. Edward, *b.* 4 Jan. 1833, *m.* 20 March, 1866, Helena, dau. of Capt. Brotchie, and has issue,
Kate, *m.* 1897, Maj. S. G. Radcliff, Indian Army, and *d.* 1899, leaving a son.
1. Matilda.
1. Sarah, *m.* Rev. Robert Nixon.
2. Lydia, *m.* John Perkins, of Ballybroony, co. Mayo.
3. Anna Maria.
4. Elizabeth, *m.* 1st, Capt. James Given; and 2ndly, Rev. Stephen Radcliff.
Mr. Fetherstonhaugh *d.* 1800, and was *s.* by his eldest son,
WILLIAM FETHERSTONHAUGH, of Carrick, *b.* 15 July, 1783; *m.* 6 Oct. 1806, Elizabeth, 2nd dau. of William Orme, of Abbeytown, co. Mayo, and by her (who *d.* 1 June, 1830) had issue,
1. WILLIAM, of Carrick.
2. Thomas Orme (Rev.), of Moyne Glebe, Rathdrum, *b.* 4 July, 1809; *m.* 27 March, 1856, Henrietta Lucretia, dau. of Capt. Richardson, R.N., and *d.* 19 June, 1873, leaving issue.
1. Godfrey Arthur, late R.N., *b.* 13 Aug. 1860; *d.* 1880.
2. Edward, *b.* 21 May, 1863; *d.* 1884.
1. Henrietta Louisa, *m.* 26 July, 1892, Arthur Ernest Hobart Hampden, of Mayfield, Sydenham, and has issue (*see* BURKE'S *Peerage*, BUCKINGHAMSHIRE, E.).
3. John, *d. unm.* 1841.
4. Godfrey, of Ballinderry, Mullingar, *b.* 19 Dec. 1811; *m.* Aug. 1850, Hester, dau. of John Ebbs, and *d.* 5 April, 1868, having had issue. His eldest son, William, L.R.C.S.I., *d.* on West Coast of Africa, Feb. 1887.
5. Francis, *b.* 27 April, 1821; *m.* 1 Nov. 1845, Jane, dau. of Richard Swift, of Lynn Lodge, co. Westmeath, and has issue,
1. Francis Charles, *b.* 27 April, 1850; *m.* Marion, dau. of George Clarke.
2. Richard Swift, *b.* 18 April, 1855.
1. Jane Elizabeth, *m.* Richard Gilmour, of Toronto, Canada, and has two daus.
2. Maude Emily.
6. Henry, of Carrick Lodge, Mullingar, Governor of Tullamore Gaol, late Capt. Westmeath Rifles, *b.* 27 March, 1826; *m.* 19 Jan. 1869, Frances Augusta, dau. of Rev. Francis Hewson. She *d.* 5 Nov. 1875. He *d.* Aug. 1898, leaving issue,

Fetherstonhaugh. THE LANDED GENTRY. 222

1. Henry Hewson, b. 10 Jan. 1874; m. 25 Jan. 1899, Edith Margaret, dau. of Major George Lidwell, of Dromard (*see that family*), and has issue.
2. Rupert John, b. 9 July, 1875; m. 5 Aug. 1902, Charlotte Lucia Eileene, only dau. of the late William Neale, M.D., of Mountmellick, and has issue, a dau.
   1. Emily Cecilia, m. 4 Jan. 1899, Rev. Robert Stewart Craig, Rector of Tullamore, and has issue, a son.
   2. Laura Hardy.
1. Susanna, m. 22 Sept. 1836, Francis Berry, of Eglish Castle, and d. July, 1876.
2. Elizabeth, m. 1st, 1837, Samuel Handy, of Bracca Castle, who d.s.p. 1851; and 2ndly, Rear-Admiral F. L. Barnard.
3. Jane, m. 6 Sept. 1854, her cousin, William Fetherstonhaugh, of Glenmore, eldest son of Godfrey Fetherstonhaugh, of North Great George's Street, Dublin (*see above*) and had issue. She d. 1903.

Mr. Fetherstonhaugh d. 21 April, 1851, and was s. by his eldest son, WILLIAM FETHERSTONHAUGH, of Carrick, J.P., B.A. Dublin, b. 14 Dec. 1807; m. 20 Feb. 1834, Alicia, only surviving dau. of Francis Berry, of Eglish Castle, King's Co., and by her (who d. 17 May, 1883) had issue, with one son and three daus., who all d. unbaptised,

1. William, b. 13 Aug. 1836; d. 4 March, 1838.
2. FRANCIS BERRY, b. 7 Oct. 1837; m. Elizabeth, eldest dau. of George James Hornidge, of Calverston, co. Westmeath. She d. 28 Feb. 1894. He d.v.p. 29 Feb. 1878, having had issue,
   1. William Robert, b. 1866; d. 8 Aug. 1877.
   2. FRANCIS BERRY, late of Carrick.
      1. Sara Elizabeth, d. unm. 9 Nov. 1890.
      2. Mabel, m. — Godfrey.
3. William, b. 21 Oct. 1838; d. inf.
4. William, b. 27 Feb. 1840; m. 6 Oct. 1868, Frances, dau. of Wm. Reynolds, of Wood Park, Dublin, and has had issue,
   1. William Reynolds, b. 4 Feb. 1871.
   2. Francis John, b. 18 May, 1872; d. 28 March, 1876.
   3. Robert, b. 9 Aug. 1874.
   4. George, b. 20 Dec. 1876.
   5. Francis, b. 28 Oct. 1881; m. 9 Feb. 1907, Gertrude Joyce, 2nd dau. of Wollerstan Tordiffe, of Long Sutton Lodge, Langport, Somerset. He d. 6 Feb. 1912, having had issue,
      (1) Francis Edward, b. 22 May, 1908.
   1. Mary Alice, d. 17 March, 1876.
   2. Frances (Lily).
5. Thomas Orme, b. 15 Feb., d. 26 Feb. 1842.
6. Thomas Orme, b. 16 April, 1843; d. unm. 21 April, 1878.
1. Alicia Frances, m. 5 June, 1860, Arthur Gambell, of Washbrook, co. Westmeath, and d. 28 Dec. 1866, leaving issue, two sons and two daus.
2. Louisa Mary Jane (Bessie), d. unm.
3. Susan, m. 1st, George Roe Boyce, of Robinstown, co. Westmeath; and 2ndly, Capt. George Fredk. Harris, late 20th Regt.
4. Frances Maria Jane, m. 6 April, 1880, Frank Kirkman Loyd, late Capt. Royal Innis. Fus., and Hon. Lieut.-Col. 3rd Batt. Cheshire Regt. 1889–1897, J.P. Sussex, of Lealand's House, Groombridge, Sussex, 4th son of late T. K. Loyd, Bengal C.S. and has issue, Alfred W. Kirkman, Royal Sussex Regt., and Francis Fetherstonhaugh, 2nd Batt. Sherwood Foresters.
5. Anna Maria.

He d. 1 Aug. 1879, aged 72, and was s. by his grandson,
FRANCIS BARRY FETHERSTONHAUGH, of Carrick, Capt. 5th Batt. Royal Innis. Fus., b. 1868; m. 5 Oct. 1891, Martha Augusta Young, only dau. of William Faris, of Lurgan, and by her (who m. 2ndly, 26 Sept. 1900, Vere Richard Trench Gregory [Coole Park family]) had issue,
FRANCIS BRYAN, now of Carrick.
A dau.
Francis Berry Fetherstonhaugh d. 7 Jan. 1898, aged 29.
Seat—Carrick, Mullingar.

FETHERSTONHAUGH-WHITNEY.
See **WHITNEY.**

FFOLLIOTT OF HOLLYBROOK HOUSE.

MARGARET ZAIDA and MARIA HENRIETTA, daus. and co-heirs of the late John Ffolliott, of Hollybrook, s. (with their sister, Agnes Louisa, now dec.) their father 1894.

Lineage.—JOHN FFOLLIOTT, of Ballyshannon, co. Donegal, d. intestate, and administration was granted to his widow, Johanna, dau. of Edward Synge, D.D., Bishop of Cork, June, 1682. Their issue were several sons and one dau., wife of the Rev. John Moor. Of the sons, the eldest, Col. John Ffolliott, of Ballymacward, m. Lucy Wynne, of Hazlewood, and d. 1697; and the 2nd, FRANCIS, was ancestor of the present family of Hollybrook; and the 3rd was grandfather to Robert Ffolliott, of Hollybrook, who m. Mary, sister of Joshua Cooper, and d. 1746, leaving an only dau. Mary, wife of John Harloe. The 2nd son,
FRANCIS FFOLLIOTT, of Ballyshannon, m. 17 Dec. 1695, Letitia, dau. of Sir James Cuffe, and d. 1701, leaving a son,
JOHN FFOLLIOTT, of Lickhill, co. Worcester, who m. Frances Goodwin, and d. about 1765, leaving several children. The eldest son,
FRANCIS FFOLLIOTT, m. Barbara Allen, and was father of

JOHN FFOLLIOTT, of Hollybrook House, co. Sligo, who m. 2 Feb. 1793, Francis, sister of Sir William Jackson Homan, Bart., of Surrock, co. Westmeath, and had issue.
1. JOHN, of Hollybrook House.
2. Francis (Rev.), m. Fanny Maria, dau. of William Raymond, of Cockerham, Devon.
3. Philip Homan, R.N., d. unm.
1. Marianne, m. George Young, of Culdaff House, co. Donegal.
2. Frances, m. George Marmaduke Forster.
3. Barbara, m. Admiral Charles Frederick Payne, R.N.
4. Elizabeth, m. Thomas Bradshaw.
5. Henrietta, m. Rev. George Nesbitt Knox.
6. Lydia, m. William Eliot.
7. Georgiana, m. Rev. James Robert Pears, of Woodcote House, Surrey.
8. Susan, d. unm.

The eldest son,
JOHN FFOLLIOTT, of Hollybrook House, and Lickhill, b. 28 Dec. 1798; m. 17 Dec. 1821, Maria Lucy, dau. of Herbert Rawson Stepney, of Durrow, King's Co., by Alicia Vincentia his wife, dau. of H. P. L'Estrange, of Moystown, in the same co., and by her (who d. 12 June, 1877) had issue,
JOHN, late of Hollybrook House.
Zaida Maria, m. 15 June, 1847, Sir Thomas Erskine, Bart. of Cambo.

Mr. Ffolliott d. 11 Feb. 1868. The only son,
JOHN FFOLLIOTT, of Hollybrook House, co. Sligo, and Lickhill, co. Worcester, J.P. and D.L., co. Sligo, High Sheriff of Sligo 1851, and Leitrim 1882, late Hon. Col. Sligo Militia, b. 21 Nov. 1824; s. his father 1868; m. 20 March, 1856, Grace Charlotte (d. 2 Nov. 1909), dau. of Col. Philips, of Rhual, co. Flint, by Margaret Jane his wife, sister of Col. Palliser, of Comragh, co. Waterford, and d. 29 Dec. 1894, leaving issue,
1. MARGARET ZAIDI.
2. AGNES LOUISA, d. unm. 25 May, 1911.
3. MARIA HENRIETTA.   4. Anna Letitia, d. 1889.

Seat—Hollybrook House, Boyle, co. Sligo.

FFOLLIOTT OF TIERERNANE.

JULIA, MRS. FFOLLIOTT, of Tierernane Lodge, Ballickmoyler, Queen's Co., m. 4 Dec. 1867, Rev. James Robert Ffolliott, M.A., Rector of Moira, co. Down, who d. 1 April, 1874, leaving issue,
1. WILLIAM HOVENDEN, Capt. Londonderry R.G.A. (Militia), J.P. Queen's Co., High Sheriff 1909, b. 1872.
1. Florinda Julia, m. 12 Dec. 1895, John Marshall Bolton, of Castle Ring, co. Louth (*see that family*).
2. Ethel Maude, d. an infant, 26 Feb. 1871.
3. Catherine Henrietta.

Mrs. Ffolliott is dau. of CHARLES WARNER HOVENDEN, by Anne his wife, dau. of Arthur Aylmer Hovenden, J.P., D.L., of Ashfield Hall, Queen's Co. She s. to Ballylehane, and The Strand, Upper Ballickmoyler, Queen's Co., by the will of her cousin FLORINDA MARIA (who d. unm. 10 May, 1884), dau. of HENRY HOVENDEN. Miss Florinda Hovenden had s. her half-sister, ANNE (widow 1st, of Thomas Gregory, and 2ndly, of James Jackson Marshall), at her death s.p. 24 March, 1863. She had s. her brother, FRANCIS HOVENDEN, who d.s.p. 6 Feb. 1824. He had s. his maternal uncle, WILLIAM HOVENDEN, who d. 24 Sept. 1804, only son and heir of PIERS HOVENDEN, of Ballickmoyler, who d. 10 June, 1800, 2nd son of THOMAS HOVENDEN, of Towlerton Park, who d. 31 Aug. 1744. Mrs. Ffolliott s, also to Tierernane under the will of her uncle, William Hovenden, of Tierernane, who d.s.p. 26 Nov. 1892, who s. his eldest brother, John Moore Hovenden, of Tierernane, who d. unm. 1849, son and heir of Moore Hovenden, of Tierernane, and Julia, his wife, dau. of Charles Warren.

Lineage (*of* HOVENDEN).—*See that family.*
Seat—Tierernane Lodge, Ballickmoyler, Queen's Co.

FFORDE OF RAUGHLAN.

FRANCIS CRESWELL FFORDE, of Raughlan, co. Armagh, C.E., b. 22 June, 1873; m. 9 July, 1907, Cicely Agnes, dau. of Col. E. W. Creswell, late R.E., and has issue,
JAMES EDMUND, b. 26 June, 1908.
Mita Patricia, b. 3 June, 1909.

Lineage.—The Rev. Arthur Fforde (or Forde), Rector of Lurgan, 3rd son of Mathew Forde of Seaforde, M.P.,who *d.* 1729 (*see that family*), and Anne, his wife, dau. of William Brownlow, *m.* Alice Baillie, and *d.* 1767, leaving with other issue,

James Fforde, *m.* 10 Nov. 1759, his cousin Elizabeth, youngest dau. of Mathew Forde, of Seaforde, and *d.* 1803, leaving a son,

Capt. James Fforde, of Raughlan, co. Armagh, and of Dundalk, Capt. in the Army, *m.* March, 1797, Sarah Anne, dau. of John Page, and *d.* 1837, leaving issue,
1. James (Rev.), *d. unm.*
2. John, *m.* Miss Fetherstonhaugh, and *d.* 1846.
3. Robert, of whom we treat.
4. Arthur, *d.* in India.
5. Francis, of Raughlan, co. Armagh, *d. unm.* and was *s.* by his nephew, James, late of Raughlan.
1. Elizabeth, *m.* James Tipping, of Lisnawilly, co. Louth.

The third son,
Rev. Robert Fforde, Rector of Annaclone, co. Down, *b.* 1802, *m.* 1835, Mary Margaret, dau. of William Archer of Wexford, by Mary his wife, sister of Very Rev. Holt Waring, of Waringstown, Dean of Dromore (*see that family*). She *d.* 1876. He *d.* 1875, leaving issue,
1. James, of Raughlan.
2. Arthur, *d. unm.* 1865.
3. William, *d. unm.* 1862.
4. Robert, *d. unm.* 1861.
1. Mary Archer.
2. Anne Elizabeth, *m.* 15 April, 1879, James Cobourg Tipping, son of James Tipping, of Lisnawilly, co. Louth.
3. Frances, *d. unm.* 1875.

The eldest son,
James Fforde, of Raughlan, co. Armagh, J.P. cos. Armagh and Down, *b.* 26 Dec. 1836; *m.* 30 Jan. 1872, Martha Harriett, dau. of Thomas Creswell, of Lisbon, and *d.* 16 Oct. 1907, having had issue,
1. Francis Creswell, now of Raughlan.
2. Robert James, *b.* 15 Nov. 1875.
3. Arthur William Ronald, *b.* 30 March, 1877; *d.* 15 May, 1878.
4. Thomas Roderick, Lieut. R.N., *b.* 18 May, 1882.
5. Charles Holt, Lieut. R.N., *b.* 17 Feb. 1884.
6. Eric Harold, *b.* 30 Aug. 1887.
1. Aimée Mary Martha.
2. Eveleen Annie Archer, *m.* 12 July, 1910, Neville Ward Jackson, 2nd son of Col. Jackson, R.E.
3. Mabel Kathleen.

Seat—Raughlan, Lurgan, co. Armagh.

FFRENCH OF MONIVEA.

Kathleen Emily Alexandra Ffrench, of Monivea Castle, co. Galway, *b.* 20 June, 1864; *s.* 1896, her father, Robert Percy ffrench, of Monivea.

Lineage.—Robert ffrench, of the town of Galway, left issue, a son,

Patrick Begg Ffrench, who was seized in fee of the castle of Monvvea and other lands in the barony of Tiaquin, co. Galway, before 1619, according to a Chancery Inquisition (*post mortem*) taken at Loughrea 30 April, 1631. His will is dated 8 Feb. 1618. He executed a settlement of the said lands 1 Nov. 1622, and *d.* 6 Feb. 1630, when his son and heir, Robert, was of full age, and married Chanc. Inq.). By Mary Kirwan his wife he had five sons and four daus.,
1. Robert, his heir.
2. Andrew.
3. John.
4. James.
5. Marcus.
1. Margaret.
2. Jullianc.
3. Kate.
4. Anstace.

The eldest son and heir,
Robert Ffrench, of Monivea Castle, co. Galway, was dispossessed of the castle and lands in 1655 by the Cromwellian Commissioners, who allotted them to Mathias, 8th Lord Trimlestown, upon his transplantation from Meath into Connaught. Robert ffrench *m.* Elizabeth, dau. of Walter Taylor, of Ballymacragh, co. Galway, and by her had issue,
1. Patrick, of whom presently.
1. Evelyn.
2. Mary.

The son and heir,
Patrick Ffrench, of Monivea Castle, re-purchased the estates from John, 11th Lord Trimlestown. He conformed Protestant 22 Dec. 1709 and was M.P. for co. Galway 1713-15. He *m.* Jane, 5th dau. of Simon Digby, Bishop of Elphin (*see* Burke's *Peerage*, Digby, B.), and had issue,

1. Robert, his heir.
2. Digby, of Derrydonnell, *d.s.p.*
1. Jane, *m.* Rev. Jeremy Marsb, Rector of Athenry, and was grandmother of Sir Henry Marsh, Bart., M.D.
2. Elizabeth, *m.* Nicholas Bindon.
3. Mary.   4. Letitia, *d. unm.*

Mr. ffrench *d.* 3 June, 1744, and was *s.* by his elder son,
Robert Ffrench, of Monivea, M.P. for co. Galway 1753-61, and for the town of Galway 1768-76, *m.* April, 1746, Nichola, 2nd dau. of Sir Arthur Acheson, 5th bart. of Gosford, and sister of Archibald, 1st Viscount Gosford, and had issue,
1. Acheson, his heir.   2. Thomas.
3. Patrick.
4. Jeremiah, *m.* Lucinda, relict of Thomas St. George, and 4th dau. of Archibald, 1st Viscount Gosford.
1. Anne, *m.* May, 1768, Sir Lucius O'Brien, 3rd bart. of Dromoland.

Mr. ffrench, whose will, dated 14 Feb. 1778, was proved next year, was *s.* by his eldest son,
Acheson Ffrench, of Monivea, *m.* 1775, Mary, only dau. of Admiral Miller, of the Isle of Wight, and *d.* 1779, aged 22, leaving an only son,

Robert Ffrench, of Monivea Castle, J.P., educated at Oxford, and entered the Life Guards, High Sheriff co. Galway, *b.* 1 Jan. 1776; *m.* 1 Jan. 1799, Nichola Maria, eldest dau. of Sir Lucius O'Brien, 3rd bart. of Dromoland, by Anne French his wife, and by her (who *d.* 1848) had issue,
1. Robert, his heir.
2. Richard (twin with Robert), Lieut. R.A., *d.* 1832.
3. Lucius John, *b.* 1801, Capt. 9th Lancers, *d.* in India, 1842.
4. Edward Hyde, of Hyde Park, co. Galway, *b.* 1802; *d.* 16 Sept. 1851.
5. Patrick Digby, *b.* 1818.
6. Acheson Jeremy Sidney, *b.* 1810, of Monivea, Hamilton, Victoria; *m.* 8 Feb. 1842, Anna, 2nd dau. of Dr. John Walton, of London, and *d.* 29 Jan. 1870, leaving six sons and six daus.,
    1. Acheson Evelyn, of Bland, New South Wales, *b.* 9 Feb. 1849; *m.* 12 Nov. 1874, Marion (131, *Cromwell Road, S. Kensington*), dau. of Alexander Wilson, of Mount Emu, Victoria, and *d.* 15 March, 1896, leaving issue, a son and a dau.,
        Evelyn, *b.* 21 June, 1878.
        Valentine.
    2. Edward Victor, *b.* 15 Dec. 1850.
    3. Lucius, *b.* 9 July, 1852.
    4. John Ludlow, *b.* 18 Feb. 1860.
    5. Henry Albert, *b.* 6 March, 1862; *m.* 16 Dec. 1890, Winifred, 3rd dau. of Major James Legh Thursby (*see* Burke's *Peerage*, Thursby, Bart.), and has issue,
        Rollo Adrien Vlademir Thursby Marie Altieri ffrench, *b.* 30 July, 1892.
    6. Robert, *b.* 23 May, 1864.
    1. Amy.   2. Nichola Frances.
    3. Harriett Maria.   4. Marianne.
    5. Alice.   6. Annie.
1. Adelaide, *m.* June, 1827, Henry Blake, only brother of Martin Joseph Blake, of Ballyglunin (*see that family*).
2. Mary.
3. Nichola, *m.* 1830, Henry Martin Blake, of Windfield (*see* Blake *of Renvyle*).
4. Louisa, *m.* 1836, William Traill, of Ballylough, co. Antrim.
5. Eveline Wilhelmina Catherine, *m.* 1 Dec. 1826, Stephen Donelan, of Killagh, co. Galway. She *d.* Oct. 1880. He *d.* Oct. 1866, leaving issue (*see that family*).

Mr. ffrench *d.* Jan. 1851, and was *s.* by his eldest son,
Robert Ffrench, of Monivea, J.P. and D.L., High Sheriff 1824, formerly an Officer in the 63rd Regt., *b.* 6 Dec. 1799; *m.* 5 July, 1830, Katherine Eleanor, only dau. of Nicholas Browne, of Mount Hazel, co. Galway, by Ellen his wife, youngest dau. of Sir Thomas Burke, Bart. of Marble Hill (who *m.* 2ndly, Percy, Viscount Strangford), and by her (who *d.* May, 1843) had issue,
1. Robert Percy, his heir.
2. Acheson Sydney O'Brien, J.P. and D.L. co. Galway, *b.* 8 May, 1843; *m.* Annie, dau. of Henry Martin Blake, of Windfield (*see* Blake *of Renvyle*), and by her (who *d.* 4 Nov. 1906) had two daus.,
    1. Rosamond Nichola.
    2. Annie Christine Cecilia, *m.* Feb. 1909, Charles Fortescue Uniacke, 5th son of Capt. H. T. Uniacke, and has issue (*see* Uniacke *of Mount Uniacke*).

He was *s.* at his decease, Nov. 1876, by his eldest son,
Robert Percy Ffrench, of Monivea Castle, co. Galway, a Knight of the Sovereign Order of St. John of Jerusalem. He was educated at Rugby College, and served in the Diplomatic Service from 1852 to 1878, Secretary of Legation at Berne 1868, Acting Chargé d'Affaires Madrid in 1869, Secretary of Embassy St. Petersburg 1872, and at Vienna 1873, retired when Chargé d'Affaires at Vienna 1878, *b.* 9 Oct. 1832; *m.* April, 1863, Sophie, only child of Alexander de Kindiakoff, a Russian Noble, and *d.* at Naples, 22 April, 1896, leaving an only child,
Kathleen Emily Alexandra, now of Monivea.

Arms—Erm., a chevron sa. **Crest**—A dolphin naiant embowed ppr. **Motto**—Malo mori quam foedari.

Seat—Monivea Castle, co. Galway. *Town House*—3, Lower Grosvenor Place, S.W.

FFRENCH. *See* Burke's Peerage, **DE FREYNE, B.**

FILGATE OF LISSRENNY.

WILLIAM DE SALIS FILGATE, of Lissrenny, co. Louth, J.P. and D.L., High Sheriff 1879, late Capt. Louth Rifles, M.F.H. since 1860, b. 2 Dec. 1834; s. his father 23 Nov. 1875; m. 4 Oct. 1870, Georgiana Harriet, eldest dau. of the late William John French, of Ardsallagh, co. Meath, and has two daus.,

1. Violet Evelyn Sophia.
2. Eileen Georgina, m. 6 Aug. 1902, Richard Alexander Baillie Henry, of Rathnestin, Ardee, co. Louth, and has issue, two sons, William Rodolph, b. 18 Dec. 1905, and Townley Alexander Richard, b. 18 Dec. 1906.

Lineage.—From a genealogy in the possession of the family it appears that

WILLIAM FILGATE, said to have been a Cromwellian officer, who settled at Lisrenny, on a grant from CROMWELL, m. Anne Storey, of Lancashire, and had issue,
1. WILLIAM, whose line we follow.
2. Alexander, m. Jane Townley, and d. 18 Jan. 1725, leaving,
  1. William, who d. 20 Aug. 1775. He m. Martha, dau. of — Barron, by Margaret Patten his wife, and by her (who d. 1793) had issue,
    (1) Joseph, of (Little) Lisrenny, d.s.p. and intestate 1798.
    (2) Alexander, d.s.p.
    (1) Mary (Mrs. Sillery), d. 27 May, 1775.
    (2) Elizabeth, d. 1794.
    (3) Margaret, m. (licence dated 14 June, 1772) Randal Booth, of Dublin, and d. May, 1787, leaving issue,
      1. John;   2. Joseph, of Darver.
    (4) Martha, d.s.p.   (5) Jane (Mrs. Walsh), d. 1776.
2. Faithful,
3. John, d. 1793,   all of Little Lisrenny, which branch is
4. Alexander,   extinct.

The last named, Alexander, a Barrister, m. Dorcas, dau. of Alderman William Patten, of Drogheda, and had
  (1) Alexander.   (2) Townley Patten.
  (1) Eleanor.
  (2) Margaret, m. James Woodside, and had a son,
James, who was enjoined to take the name of PATTEN.

The elder son,
WILLIAM FILGATE, m. 1665, Anne, dau. of William Peppard, to which W. Peppard were confirmed by patent of CHARLES II. (1666), in trust for his son-in-law, Filgate, the lands granted as above stated. They had a son,
WILLIAM FILGATE, of Lisrenny, b. 1666; m. about 1694, Mary Smart, and d. 1721, aged 55 (will dated 23 Nov. 1721), having had issue,
1. John, b. 18 Feb. 1698; d. before his father.
2. ALEXANDER, of whom presently, as heir to his father.
3. Thomas, of Ardee, co. Louth, b. 21 June, 1704; m. 1734, Anne Sweetlove, of Dowdstown, and d. 18 Jan. 1785 (will, Dublin). Besides a dau., Anne, m. 1770, her cousin William Filgate, of Lissrenny, they had a son,
William, of Dublin, and Examinator in Chancery, m. (settlement dated 18 Aug. 1759) Mrs. Alice Robinson, and d. intestate Aug. 1766, leaving,
  (1) Alexander.
  (2) Thomas William, of Arthurstown, co. Louth, High Sheriff 1791, m. 1st, Emily, dau. of Ross Mahon, of Castlegar (and sister of Sir Ross Mahon, 1st bart.), by Anne his wife, dau. of John, 1st Earl of Altamont, and had issue,
    1. William (Rev.), m. his cousin Louisa, dau. of Rev. Henry Mahon, Rector of Tissauran, and by her (who d. 1843) had issue, a dau., Louisa.
    2. Charles, J.P., b. 1799; d. 1892.
He m. 2ndly, 1817, his cousin Mary Anne Margaret, youngest dau. of William Filgate, of Lissrenny, and d. 1846, having by her (who d. 1845) had issue,
    3. Thomas William, d. 1868.
    4. Louis Alexander, d. 1840.
    5. Townley, M.A. Trin. Coll. Dublin, b. 1825; d. 4 May, 1888; m. 1852, Martha Ellen, dau. of George Macartney, M.P., D.L. of Lissanoure, having by her (who d. 27 Feb. 1886) had issue,
      a. TOWNLEY RICHARD, now of Arthurstown, b. 1854; m. 1881, Helen, 3rd dau. of Rev. John Milne, and has issue,
        (a) Richard John, Norfolk Regt., b. 21 Jan. 1882; m. 28 Feb. 1911, Christine, 5th dau. of John McNairn, of Edinburgh.
        (b) Thomas William, Royal Munster Fus., b. 27 Feb. 1888.
        (a) Emily Margaret, b. 16 May, 1884; m. 7 Sept. 1909, Capt. George Alexander Stewart Gordon, Bengal Cavalry.
      a. Elizabeth (6, Hatch Street, Dublin).
      b. Anna Georgina, m. 28 Jan. 1893, George Brooke Young, and has issue.
    6. Richard, d. 1850.
      1. Louisa.
      2. Anne, m. Rev. Denis Browne, and had issue.
      3. Emily, d. unm. 1882.
        (1) Elizabeth, m. Samuel Adams.   (2) Anne, d. unm.
4. William, b. 23 Dec. 1706; d.v.p.s.p.
5. Stephen, of Ardee, co. Louth, b. 25 Dec. 1714; m. Margaret McMahon, and d. 1787 (will dated 5 Sept. 1786; proved 17 July, 1787) leaving an only child (except two sons d. young),

Mary, m. Rev. Joseph Wright, from whom descend the WRIGHTS of Killincome, co. Louth.
6. Richard, b. 21 March, 1716; d. 2 April, 1750, aged 34.
1. Anne, b. 5 Aug. 1695.
2. Thomasin, b. 29 Aug. 1696; m. (licence dated 5 Oct. 1716) Theophilus Taaffe, of Manfieldstown, co. Louth; d. 1765, and had a son,
Richard, whose posterity is extinct.
3. Frances, b. 16 March, 1709; d. unm.
4. Mary, b. 15 Aug. 1711; m. Robert Craig, the original proprietor of Arthurstown, after Viscount Taaffe's forfeiture.
5. Eleanor, b. 15 Nov. 1713.

Mr. Filgate was s. by his eldest surviving son,
ALEXANDER FILGATE, of Lissrenny, b. 30 April, 1702; d. 21 Oct. 1771; m. 1739, Elinor, dau. of — Byrne, of Seven Churches, co. Wicklow, who survived him to 18 Dec. 1799. By her he had issue,
1. WILLIAM, b. 22 July, 1740, his successor.
2. Francis,
3. John,   d. infants, 1745-50.
4. Richard,
5. TOWNLEY PATTEN, of Lowther Lodge, co. Dublin, and Drumgoolstown, co. Louth. He was called to the Bar 1776, and m. 1st, 1788, Miss Maxwell; 2ndly, 1797, Martha, widow of Alderman George Wrightson, of Dublin. His only surviving child and heiress,
Ellen, m. 1828, George Macartney, J.P. and D.L., M.P., and had issue, of whom her younger son assumed, by Royal Licence 1862, the surname of FILGATE (see FILGATE of Lowtherstone).
1. Dorcas, b. 11 Aug. 1741; m. Capt. Ruxton, and d.s.p.
2. Mary Anne, b. 28 Feb. 1742.
3. Margaret, b. 18 March, 1745; d. unm. 1828.
4. Eleanor, b. 20 May, 1747; d. 1799.
5. Thomasin, b. 12 Aug. 1748; m. 1782, Pierce Worthington, of Dublin marriage licence dated 9 Jan. 1782), and d.s.p.
6. Hannah, b. 11 Feb. 1753; d.v.p.
7. Frances, m. Cadwallader Lee, and had issue.

Mr. Filgate d. 21 Oct. 1771, and was s. by his eldest son,
WILLIAM FILGATE, of Lissrenny, b. 22 July, 1740; m. 2 Dec. 1770, his cousin, Anne, dau. of Thomas Filgate, of Ardee, and by her (who d. July, 1804) had issue,
1. ALEXANDER,
2. THOMAS,   who successively became of Lissrenny.
3. WILLIAM,
4. Townley, b. 1784; Vicar of Charlestown, co. Louth; m. Oct. 1809, Isabella, eldest dau. of William Ruxton, of Ardee House, M.P. (see that family). He d. 28 Dec. 1822, having by her (who d. Nov. 1855) had issue,
  1. William Henry, Barrister-at-Law, sometime Secretary to the Lord Chancellor of Ireland, b. 23 Aug. 1810; d. unm. 7 Jan. 1898.
  2. Samuel Fitzherbert, J.P. for cos. Down and Antrim, b. 2 March, 1815; m. 1852, Katherine Anne d. 25 Jan. 1906, dau. of the Right Hon. Edward Lucas, of Castle Shane, co. Monaghan (see that family), and d. 22 Sept. 1896.
    1. Anna, d. unm. Oct. 1886.
    2. Ellen, d. unm. 2 May, 1903.
  3. Richard, b. 1787; a Capt. in the Louth Regt.; d. unm. 1842.
  1. Eleanor, b. 1777; d. unm. 14 Sept. 1807.
  2. Anne, b. 1780; d. Dec. 1850.
  3. Mary Anne Margaret, b. 1790; m. 1817, Thomas William Filgate, of Arthurstown, co. Louth, High Sheriff of the co. 1791, and d. 1845, leaving issue (see above).

Mr. Filgate survived till 14 Dec. 1816, when he was s. by his eldest son,
ALEXANDER FILGATE, of Lissrenny, b. 1771, Lieut.-Col. of the Louth Militia, who dying unm. 1827, was s. by his brother,
THOMAS FILGATE, of Lissrenny, b. 1773, Barrister-at-Law, and Treasurer of the co. Louth, who dying unm. 1830, was s. by his brother,
WILLIAM FILGATE, of Lissrenny, J.P. for the cos. Louth and Monaghan, Treasurer for the co. Louth, and in 1832 High Sheriff of that co., b. 22 July, 1781; m. 27 Oct. 1831, Sophia Juliana Penelope, eldest dau. of Jerome, Count de Salis (see Foreign Titles, BURKE's Peerage), and by her (who d. 5 July, 1886) had issue,
1. WILLIAM DE SALIS, now of Lissrenny.
2. Alexander Jerome, Col. late R.E., b. 29 Aug. 1837; d. 9 Feb. 1909.
3. Rodolph Townley Richard, b. 18 Dec. 1839, H.M.'s Court of Probate, Ireland; d. 15 Dec. 1904.
4. Leopold George Plantagenet, J.P. co. Antrim, b. 20 Aug. 1843; d. 1 May, 1906.
5. Townley Fane, b. 26 Jan. 1846; Secretary, County Council, co. Louth.
6. Charles Roden (The Terrace, Matlock Bank, Derbyshire), Barrister-at-Law, b. 16 Oct. 1849; m. 27 Feb. 1906, Clare, 6th dau. of the late William Cooper, of Coventry, and has issue,
  William Alexander Jerome, b. 12 April, 1908.
  Margaret Penelope, b. 21 Jan. 1910.
1. Anne Harriett Penelope Eleanor, m. Sept. 1857, Thomas William Filgate, J.P., of Tullykeel, co. Louth, who d. 20 Feb. 1868.
Mr. Filgate d. 23 Nov. 1875.

Seat—Lissrenny, near Ardee, co. Louth. *Club*—Sackville Street (Dublin).

MACARTNEY-FILGATE OF LOWTHERSTONE.

WILLIAM TOWNLEY GEORGE SEYMOUR MACARTNEY-FILGATE, of Lowtherstone,co.Dublin, J.P., Knight of Grace of the Order of St. John of Jerusalem, Inspector for Industries, Dept. of Agriculture and Technical Instruction, Ireland, was Secretary of the Irish Committee of the Royal Commission, Paris Exhibition, 1898-9, Director, Irish Section, Glasgow Exhibition 1901 and Director Departmental Section, Cork Exhibition 1902, and officially represented Ireland at St. Louis Exhibition 1904, Dublin Exhibition 1907 and Franco-British Exhibition 1908. b. 28 Jan. 1864.

Lineage.—GEORGE MACARTNEY, of Lissanoure (see that family), J.P., D.L., M.P. co. Antrim (son of the Rev. Travers Hume and his wife Elizabeth Blaquier, niece of Earl Macartney), assumed by Royal Licence, 1814, the surname and arms of MACARTNEY, only under the will of his maternal grand-uncle above-mentioned. He was b. Oct. 1793, and d. 20 Oct. 1869, having m. May, 1828, Ellen, only surviving child and heir of Townley Patten Filgate, of Lowtherstone, co. Dublin, and Dromgoolstown, co. Meath (see FILGATE of Lisrenny), and by her (who d. 1847) he had with other issue (see MACARTNEY of Lissanoure), a 2nd son,

TOWNLEY PATTON HUME MACARTNEY-FILGATE, of Lowtherstone, co. Dublin, J.P., late Capt. 18th Hussars and Scots Greys, and Inspector-General of Jails and Registration, Bombay Presidency; he assumed by Royal Licence, 4 June, 1862, the additional surname and the arms of FILGATE, under the will of his maternal grandfather; b. Jan. 1841; m. 1862, Tryphena, eldest dau. of the Right Hon. Sir W. R. Seymour Fitzgerald, G.C.S.I., Governor of Bombay, and d. 30 Dec. 1906, having had issue,
1. WILLIAM TOWNLEY GEORGE SEYMOUR, now of Lowtherstone.
2. Edward John Patrick FitzGerald, Col. commanding 3rd Batt. Royal Irish Rifles (Hillbrook, Castleknock, co. Dublin and Kildare Street Club), b. 17 March, 1865; m. Jan. 1892, Bertha Eugenie, dau. of the late John Lomax, of Springfield, Bury, Lancashire, and has issue,
   John Victor Openshaw, b. 20 May, 1897.
   Mona Geraldine, b. 1 Feb. 1894.
3. Clement Henry Ross, b. 4 June, 1867; m. 29 Jan. 1910, Lucy Matilda, eldest dau. of late Robert Tunstall Tunstall-Moore, of Stedalt, co. Dublin.
4. Charles Alexander Hume, b. 11 March, 1869; m. Feb. 1893, Mary Stuart, dau. of the late Rev. J. Griffiths, of Braich-y-Aleyll, co. Carnarvon, and d. at sea 21 Nov. 1909, leaving issue,
   1. Arthur Melvin John, b. Oct. 1893.
   2. Terence Townley Constance Stuart, b. 19 Jan. 1898.
   3. Desmond Maurice Ulick Charles, b. 11 Oct. 1899.
   4. Clement David Harnaye, b. 19 Aug. 1904.
5. Arthur Robert Patten (Anavernia, Ravensdale, co. Louth), Capt. 3rd Batt. Royal Welsh Fusiliers, b. 3 Aug. 1870; m. 17 Oct. 1905, Georgina Honora (d. 27 Jan. 1907), dau. of late Capt. W. M. Douglas, and widow of Major C. L. Cotton, 3rd P.O.W Dragoon Gds.
6. Clare Campbell Graham, b. March, 1872.
7. Dermot Lowther Noel, b. 25 Dec. 1880.
1. Mabel Margaret Tryphena, b. 28 April, 1866; m. 20 Aug. 1890, Carthenae George Macartney, of Lissanoure (whom see).
2. Aileen Frances Beatrice, b. 8 Oct. 1877.

Arms—Az. two bars arg., between six mullets, three, two, and one or. **Crest**—A griffin sejant salient arg. pierced through the breast with a broken spear or holding the point in its beak. **Motto**—Virescit vulnere virtus.
Seat—Lowtherstone, Balbriggan, co. Dublin. **Clubs**—Kildare Street, Dublin; Royal St. George's Yacht, Kingstown.

FINCH OF TULLAMORE PARK.

JOHN FINCH, of Tullamore Park, co. Tipperary, J.P., late Devonshire Regt., b. 1828; s. his cousin 1870; m. 1871, Maria Elizabeth, dau. of Richard Russell, of Ballinacarriga, co. Limerick, J.P., and has issue, two daus.,
1. Mary Louise, m. 29 April, 1893, Simon Dring, of Glen Garra, co. Cork, and has issue (see that family).
2. Ethel.

I. L. G.

Lineage.—RALPH FINCH, of Watford (youngest son of John Finch, of Watford, and grandson of William Finch). He m. 27 Jan. 1606, Emma, dau. of George Baldwyn, of Watford, and dying 1622, was s. by his eldest son,
WILLIAM FINCH, of Watford, bapt. 23 July, 1612; m. twice, but had issue only by his first wife, Jane,
1. Ralph, of Chester, bapt. 2 Oct. 1632, who became by the will of his uncle (his father's younger brother), Col. Simon Finch, sole heir of all that gentleman's lands in Northamptonshire and in Ireland. He m. Elizabeth, dau. of Col. William Lunyel, of Chester, and d. 1685, having had issue, an only child, Mary, m. John Earle, of Liverpool, and had (with, a dau., Sarah, wife of the Hon. and Rev. John Stanley, Rector of Winwick, bro her of the 11th Earl of Derby) four sons, of whom the eldest surviving, RALPH EARLE, assumed the surname and arms of WILLIS (see WILLIS of Halsnead).
2. EDWARD, of whom presently.
3. William. 4. Walter.
5. Simon.

The 2nd son,
EDWARD FINCH, of Kilcoleman, co. Tipperary, m. Margaret, dau. of George Purdon, of Tinnerana, co. Clare, and had issue,
1. SIMON, his heir.
2. William, of Cork, m. Anne, dau. of William Massy, of Glenville, co. Limerick, and had issue,
   1. EDWARD, heir to his uncle, of whom hereafter.
   2. William, of Maryville, co. Limerick, m. Mary, dau. of Godfrey Massey, of Duntrileague, co. Limerick, but d.s.p.
   3. Frederick, d. unm. 4. Hugh, d. unm.
   5. George, of Kilcoleman, m. Amelia, dau. of Anthony Parker, of Castlelough, co. Tipperary, and d.s.p.
   6. John, of the Abbey, co. Limerick, m. Phœbe, dau. of John Brown, of Clonboy, co. Limerick, and had issue,
     (1) WILLIAM FINCH, of Kilcoleman, co. Tipperary, J.P., m. 1st, Marcella, dau. of Edward D'Alton Singleton, of Quinville, co. Clare, and relict of Henry Vereker D'Esterre; and 2ndly, 1869, Catherine Doyle, 2nd dau. of the late Rev. Freeman Wills Crofts, of Churchtown, and widow of Richard Gason, of Richmond, co. Tipperary. By his 1st wife he had issue,
       1. John, m. Mrs. Neligan, née Jessop, of Mount Jessop, and d. 18 Feb. 1879.
       2. Hugh, m. Lucinda, dau. of Rev. Mr. Greene, and d. 14 April, 1909, having had issue,
         a. William Heneage, Capt. 3rd Batt. Manchester Regt., m. 1 Oct. 1898, Cecil Harriet Beatrice Bermingham, dau. of W. C. B. Otway-Ruthven (see that family), and has issue,
           Margaret Patricia Rose.
         a. Lucinda, m. 1910, John Rolleston Wolfe, of Rockford, Nenagh, Hon. Lieut.-Col. 3rd Batt. Royal Irish Regt. (see WOLFE of Forenaghts).
       3. Charles Singleton of Kilcoleman, Nenagh, co. Tipperary, J.P., b. 1876; m. April, 1839, Anna Maria, dau. of Thomas Boyce, of Tivoli, co. Cork, and has issue,
         a. William Charles, b. March, 1862.
         a. Emily Marcella, m. Feb. 1890, Henry Cochrane, son of Thomas Cochrane, of co. Limerick.
         b. Marcella Singleton.
     (2) John Brown, of Cloomaken, co. Limerick, and Creagh Castle, co. Cork, m. Maria, dau. of Edward D'Alton Singleton, of Quinville, co. Clare, and had issue, a son,
       George Massy, of Bloomfield, Newport, co. Limerick, J.P. co. Tipperary, b. 19 Aug. 1839; m. Margaret Franks, dau. of Joseph Bevan, of Glenbevan, co. Limerick, and d. 27 Aug. 1895, leaving issue,
         a. John, of Bloomfield, Newport, co. Limerick, J.P. co. Tipperary, late Capt. 5th Batt. Royal Irish Regt., b. 29 May, 1864; m. 5 April, 1899, Anna Elizabeth, youngest dau. of Rev. William F. Seymour, 2nd son of Rev. Joseph John Seymour, Rector of Ballymacquord, co. Galway.
         b. Edward Bevan, b. 16 Feb. 1869.
     (3) HUGH FREDERICK, of Maryville, co. Limerick, late 6th Carabineers, m. 1st, Barbara, dau. of Capt. Hugh Brady, of Moynoe, co. Clare, by whom he had issue,
       1. JOHN, successor to his cousin, now of Tullamore Park.
       1. Elizabeth, d. unm. May, 1901. 2. Phœbe Frances.
       3. Barbara, d. 1908, m. George Williamson.
       He m. 2ndly, Mary, dau. of George Sexton, of Coonagh, co. Limerick, and had by her further issue,
         2. George William, of Maryville, J.P., Hon. Col. Limerick County Militia, d. 24 Sept. 1907; m. 1869, Maria Frances, dau. of John Francis Eyre Fitzgerald, Knt. of Glin, and has issue,
           a. Hugh Heneage, of Maryville, Capt. R.F.R.A., served in Ashanti and Northern Nigeria 1900-1901, b. 1871; m. 1906, Amy Margaret, younger dau. of Thomas William Sandes, of Sallow Glen, co. Kerry (see that family).
           b. George.
           c. Otho (Rock Hill, Horsham Road, Sussex), m. 1900, Florence Hilda, 3rd dau. of Joseph Lucas, J.P., of Fox Hunt Manor, Sussex, and has issue,
             Desmond Otho FitzGerald, b. 1910.
           d. Harry. c. William, d. 1900.
           f. Frederick.
         3. Frederick Thomas, m. 1882, Alice, eldest dau. of Rev. Thomas Westropp, Rector of Ardcanny, co. Limerick. She d. 24 May, 1898. He d. Nov. 1901.
         (1) George, m. Miss Langford, and has a dau.
           1. Anne. 2. Catherine.

1. Eleanor, *m.* Anthony Hickman, of Ballyket, co. Clare.
2. Alice.

The elder son and heir,
SIMON FINCH, of Kilcoleman, *d.s.p.* (his will is dated 10 April, 1744, and proved 15 Dec. 1758), and was s. by his nephew,
EDWARD FINCH, of Tullamore Park, *m.* Anna, dau. of Daniel O'Dwyer, of Tullaheady, co. Tipperary, and had issue,
1. WILLIAM, his heir, of Tullamore Park, *m.* Frances, dau. of Philip Coales, of Bath, and *d.s.p.* 17 April, 1864.
2. DANIEL, of Tullamore Park, *d.s.p.* 11 July, 1864.
3. EDWARD, late of Tullamore Park.   4. John.
1. Eliza.   2. Anne.

Mr. Finch *d.* Aug. 1843. His 3rd son,
EDWARD FINCH, of Tullamore Park, Capt. in the Life Guards, *m.* Jane, dau. of R. B. Wylde Browne, of Caughley, Salop, and dying in 1870, was *s.* by his cousin, the present
JOHN FINCH, of Tullamore Park.

Family Seats—Kilcoleman, Clareena, and Tullamore Park, Nenagh, co. Tipperary.

FINDLATER OF FERNSIDE.

MARION, LADY FINDLATER, of Fernside, co. Dublin, dau. of Lieut.-Col. Archibald Park, *m.* as his 2nd wife Sir William Huffington Findlater, who *d.* 16 April, 1906, having had issue (see below).

Lineage.—WILLIAM FINDLATER, of Londonderry, son of John Findlater of Greenock, N.B., *b.* 28 May, 1792; *m.* 6 June, 1822, Sophia, dau. of William Huffington, of Londonderry, and Fahan, co. Donegal. She *d.* 9 Feb. 1831, having had issue,
1. WILLIAM HUFFINGTON (Sir), of Fernside.
1. Janet (Jessie), *m.* 1859, Joseph Taylor. She *d.* 1890.
2. Sophia, *m.* 1st, 25 June, 1852, Henry Geoghegan, who *d.* Nov. 1856; 2ndly, Aug. 1861, Henry Porson Morse, who *d.* 15 Aug. 1874; and 3rdly, 31 July, 1877, Francis Johnston, who *d.* 26 Sept. 1896.
3. Margaret, *m.* 23 June, 1852, John Lloyd Blood, who *d.* 24 June, 1894.

SIR WILLIAM HUFFINGTON FINDLATER, Knt., of Fernside, co. Dublin, J.P. and D.L., M.P. for co. Monaghan 1880-5, unsuccessfully contested South Londonderry in 1885, President of the Incorporated Law Society of Ireland 1878-96, President of the Statistical Society of Ireland 1893-4, admitted a Solicitor 1846, founded law scholarships in 1877 and in 1900, *b.* 1 Jan. 1824; *m.* 1st, 1 Sept. 1853, Mary Jane, dau. of John Wolfe, of Dublin. She *d.s.p.* 31 May, 1877. He *m.* 2ndly, 26 Feb. 1878, Marion (now of *Fernside*), dau. of Lieut.-Col. Archibald Park, 24th Bengal N.I. (son of Mungo Park, the great African Explorer), and widow of T. A. Hodges, and *d.* 16 April, 1906, having by her had issue,
1. WILLIAM ALEXANDER VICTOR, 2nd Lieut. 2nd Batt. The Royal Irish Fus., *b.* 19 March, 1880.
2. Percival St. George, *b.* 24 March, 1882.
1. Muriel Dempster, *b.* 24 June, 1884; *d.* 2 Nov. 1896.

Arms—Az. a chevron between three estoiles in chief or and an eagle reguardant wings displayed in base ppr. **Crest**—On a rock an eagle reguardant wings displayed all ppr. the breast and each wing charged with an estoile or. **Motto**—Sit mihi libertas.

Residences—Fernside, Killiney, co. Dublin, and 22, Fitzwilliam Square, Dublin.

FINLAY OF CORKAGH.

HENRY THOMAS FINLAY, of Corkagh House, Clondalkin, co. Dublin, J.P. and D.L., formerly Royal Warwickshire Regt., Col. late Commanding 5th Batt. Royal Dublin Fusiliers, *b.* 15 Feb. 1847; *m.* 1st, 4 Dec. 1877, Helen Lucy, dau. of the Rev. Robert Hedges Dunne (*see* DUNNE *of Brittas*), and by her (who *d.* 9 March, 1902) has issue,
1. Francis Henry John, 2nd Lieut. Leinster Regt., *b.* 8 Jan. 1879; *d.* on service in S. Africa, 11 Dec. 1900.
2. GEORGE GUY, *b.* 1889.   3. Robert Alexander, *b.* 1893.
1. Edith Maud Olivia, *m.* 20 Jan. 1909, George Pomeroy Arthur Colley, of Faunagh, Rathgar, eldest son of late Henry FitzGeorge, of Mount Temple (*see* BURKE'S *Peerage*, HARBERTON, V).
2. Alice Caroline, *m.* 25 July, 1910, Major Gordon Travers Birdwood, I.M.S.

He *m.* 2ndly, 18 July, 1906, Emily Octavia, widow of James A. Lyle, of Glandore Lodge, co. Antrim (*see* LYLE *of Knocktarna*), and dau. of Hon. and Rev. Henry Ward, Rector of Killinchy, co. Down (*see* BURKE'S *Peerage*, BANGOR, V.).

Lineage.—JOHN FINLAY, *m.* Mary Savage, of Portaferry, co. Antrim. His eldest son,
ABRAHAM FINLAY, *d.* 1722, leaving a son,
THOMAS FINLAY, of Corkagh, *m.* Feb. 1735, Deborah, dau. of Lawrence Steele, of Rathbride, co. Kildare, and *d.* 7 Dec. 1771, leaving two sons, William Henry, *m.* the sister of his brother's wife, and had a dau. Elizabeth, *m.* Hans, 3rd Baron Dufferin, and an elder son,

COL. JOHN FINLAY, of Corkagh, sometime M.P. for co. Dublin, *m.* Elizabeth Stear, an heiress, of co. Bedford, and *d.* 1823, leaving issue,
THOMAS FINLAY, of Corkagh, Lieut.-Col. co. Dublin Light Infantry, *m.* 1804, Ursula, dau. of John Cromie, of Cromore, Portstewart, and by her (who *d.* 1868) he left at his decease, 1837,
1. JOHN WILLIAM, of Corkagh, of whom presently.
2. Thomas, *m.* Charlotte Mitford, and *d.* leaving one dau.
3. George.   4. Robert, *d.s.p.*
1. Anne Winifred, *m.* 1843, Edward James, of Swarland Park, Northumberland, and *d.* in 1872, leaving issue.
2. Ellen, *d. unm*   3. Selina, *d.s.p.*
4. Mary, *m.* Rev. T. Cooper.

The eldest son,
REV. JOHN WILLIAM FINLAY, of Corkagh, M.A., *b.* 1805; *m.* 1st, 1837, Henrietta Isabella, dau. of Major Henry Cole, of Twickenham, by whom (who *d.* 1847) he had issue,
1. HENRY THOMAS, now of Corkagh.
1. Elizabeth Owen, *m.* 1866, Richard John Ussher, of Cappagh, co. Waterford, and has issue.
2. Henrietta Ellen.   3. Selina Frances, *d.* 1860.
4. Olivia Anna, *m.* 1879, Capt. Ernest Foley, Middlesex Regt., and has issue.

Mr. Finlay *m.* 2ndly, 1849, Caroline Elizabeth, 3rd dau. of Charles Hamilton, of Hamwood (*see that family*), and Caroline, his wife, dau. of William Tighe, of Woodstock. He *d.* 1879. She *d.* 31 May, 1909.

Seat—Corkagh House, Clondalkin. **Club**—Kildare Street.

FINNY OF LEIXLIP.

HENRY LESLIE FINNY, of Ellesmere Port, near Chester, and Leixlip, co. Kildare, and Rathfinny, near Alfriston, Sussex, L.R.C.P., L.R.C.S., *b.* 9 May, 1862; *m.* 23 April, 1891, Eleanor Margaret (who in 1888 adopted the name of AKERMAN-FREASE), dau. of William Akerman, of Montreal, Canada, and has issue,
1 Henry Leslie, *b.* 5 May, 1894; *d.* 26 June, 1899.
2. JOHN WILLIAM MAGEE, *b.* 1 June, 1896.
3. Gerald Henry Maturin, *b.* 27 May, 1900.
1. Agnes Eleanor Ursula.
2. Eileen Margaret Anita.

Lineage.—THOMAS FINNY, of Westminster, *b.* 1689; was bur. in Dark Cloister, Westminster Abbey, 25 Jan. 1770, having by Elizabeth his wife (who *d.* 19 Jan. 1770, aged 86, and was also bur. in Westminster Abbey) had issue,
1. Daniel, left issue, two sons, James and John, of Castlebrack, Queen's Co.
2. Dennis, had two sons,
(1) James, of Ballyavil, King's Co., and had issue,
James.
(2) Michael.
3. James, of Ballevin, co. Kildare, whose will dated 3 June, was proved Consist. Ct., Kildare, 13 Sept. 1769; *m.* Mary, dau. of John Quatermants, and *d.s.p.*
4. John, who had issue,
1. Bryan.   2. James.
1. Bridget.   2. Margaret, *m.* — Hogan.
3. Elizabeth, *m.* — Hogan.
5. WILLIAM, of whom next.
1. Bridget, *m.* John Long, and had issue.

WILLIAM FINNY, who settled in Dublin about 1742 (will proved 14 July, 1762), left by Rosa his wife a son,
THOMAS FINNY, of Dublin, *d.* 21 Aug., and will proved 4 Sept. 1807, left, by Mary his wife (bur. at Clontarf 9 Nov. 1803),
1. WILLIAM, of whom presently.
2. James, of Dublin, *m.* Bridget (who *re-m.* 2ndly, 1805, William Clarke, of Dublin) and *d.* 1802, having had issue, with a dau., Elizabeth,
1. Thomas.
2. Robert, of Belfast, *m.* Jane, dau. of Alexander McAlister, of Belfast, and had issue, one son,
James, *d.* at Newry, 1881, aged 67, having *m.* Jane Campbell, by whom he had issue,
1. William, of New Zealand.
2. James, Artist, of Red Lion Street, London, *m.* Matilda Hayes (*d.* 1901), leaving issue,
a. James, *b.* 27 Jan. 1893.
b. William.
a. Matilda.
3. Lucius, R.N., and of Dublin Military Account Board, *d.* 1811, leaving with three daus., Charlotte (*d.s.p.*), Mary and Margaret (who *m.* 1825, Capt. Dennis Gladwell), an only son,

Thomas, of Dublin, b. 1792 ; m. 1st, Mary Evelyn, of Dublin ; and 2ndly, Mrs. Catherine Bradley, who survived him. He d. 4 Aug. 1874, leaving issue by his 1st marriage,
(1) Lucius, of Dublin, d. unm.
 (1) Anne, d. unm. (2) Margaret, d. unm.
 (3) Nannie, d. unm. (4) Martha, d. unm.
 (5) Charlotte, d. unm.
 (6) Mary Anne, m. John Horton, of Australia.
 (7) Susannah, m. James Johnston, L.D.S., Dublin.
The eldest son,
WILLIAM FINNY, of Dublin, served in the Royal Navy as a Midshipman under Nelson, commissioned 2nd Lieut. Marine Forces, 5 May, 1796, and retired wounded, and afterwards in the Indian Commissariat Dept., Commissioner Ass. Dep. Commissary-Gen. for Ireland, 25 June, 1802, and Dep. Commissary-Gen., 25 Sept. 1803 ; b. 1765 ; m. 21 March, 1787, Elizabeth, dau. and heiress of George Warner, of Dublin, Leixlip, Athy, and Kildare (by his 2nd wife Susaunah, dau. of Edward Turvey, of Dublin), and d. 21 June, 1815, having by her (who d. 1840) had issue, with a dau., Susannah Maria, a son,
REV. THOMAS HENRY COTTER FINNY, of Freechurch, co. Cork, afterwards Clondulane, B.A., T.C.D., b. 5 Jan. 1799 ; m. 1st, 30 March. 1826. Elizabeth, dau. of Rev. Henry Maturin, and by her (who d. 10 Jan. 1833) had,
1. HENRY MATURIN (Rev.), of whom presently.
He m. 2ndly, 1839, Frances, dau. of the Most Rev. William Magee, D.D., Archbishop of Dublin, and by her (who d. 1843) had issue,
2. William Magee (Rev.), B.A., Curate of St. Jude's, Liverpool, d. unm. 24 April, 1863.
3. John Magee, M.D., F.R.C.P., of 36. Merrion Square, Dublin, Prof. of Medicine Triu. Coll. Dublin, Ex-President of the Royal College of Physicians, b. 9 Feb. 1841 ; m. 24 July, 1873, Agnes Anne, dau. of William Watsou, of Dublin, and has issue,
 1. William Watson, M.A., Barrister-at-Law (Hamilton Lodge, Surbiton), b. 22 April, 1876 ; m. 8 Nov. 1904, Phyllis Rose, dau. of Philip Augustus Champion de Crespigny (see BURKE's Peerage, DE CRESPIGNY, Bart.), and has issue,
  (1) Edmund John Champion, b. 5 Aug. 1905.
  (2) Arthur William Magee, b. 29 Aug. 1909.
 2. Cecil Edward, M.D. (19, Herne Hill, S.E.), b. 30 July, 1877; m. 15 Dec. 1904, Isabel Norah, dau. of Richard Marriott, of Handsworth Wood, Stafford, and has issue,
  (1) Desmond Marriott, b. 12 Sept. 1906.
  (2) Richard Jeffery, b. 30 Jan. 1910.
 3. Arthur John, B.A., Inspector of Education, b. 29 Oct. 1884.
 4. Charles Morgan, b. 9 July, 1886, M.B., B.Ch., R.A.M.C.
 1. Alice Maye.
 2. Edith Constance, ⎫ twins.
 3. Mabel Florence, ⎭
1. Elizabeth Moulson, m. Rev. George Nesbitt Tredennick, B.A., and had issue (see TREDENNICK of Camlin).
He m. 3rdly, 1846, Mary Louisa, dau. of John Morris, of Marston, Somerset, and d. 18 Jan. 1872, having by her (who d. 19 April, 1878) had issue,
4. Thomas George Roecastle, Commander Royal Indian Marine, and Presidency Port Officer, Madras, b. 27 Oct. 1851 ; m. 4 Jan. 1899, Anita, dau. of John Russell Cameron, great grandson of John Cameron, of Lochiel, and d. 20 Feb. 1910, leaving issue,
 1. William David Cameron, b. 13 Nov. 1904.
 1. Agnes Cameron, b. 18 Nov. 1899.
 2. Violet Grace.
5. Arthur Benjamin, L.R.C.S., L.R.C.P., d. unm. 18 March, 1874.
2. Frances Susannah, m. 15 April, 1879, John Kendrick, of Leicester, and has issue.
3. Mary Kathleen (69, The Avenue, Bedford).
4. Emily Charlotte Henrietta, (69, Waldeck Avenue, Bedford).
The eldest son,
REV. HENRY MATURIN FINNY, of Gotham, co. Derby, B.A. T.C.D., b. 14 June, 1830 ; m. 13 Jan. 1859, Agnes Amelia, dau. of Rev. Edward Leslie, B.D. Oxon (see BURKE's Peerage and Baronetage, LESLIE, Bart.), he wife Margaret Higginson (see HIGGINSON of Carnalea), and d. 17 Feb. 1865, having by her (who m. 2ndly, 14 May, 1874, Rev. George Nesbitt Tredennick, who d. 7 July, 1876) had issue,
1. HENRY LESLIE, now of Leixlip.
2. William Evelyn St. Lawrence, M.B., M.Ch., L.R.C.P., of Tamesa, Kingston Hill, Surrey, J.P., Alderman and Mayor of Kingston-upon-Thames 1898-9, 1901-2 (King Edward VII Coronation Medal) and 1908-9, Hon. Associate, Order of St. John of Jerusalem 1911, b. 1 Sept. 1864 ; m. 19 Oct. 1898, Rosa, youngest dau. of the late William Clements, formerly of Cream Hall, Highbury and Woodside, Redhill, Surrey, and East Cowes, I. of Wight, and has issue,
 Thomas Clements Leslie Maturin, b. 1 Aug. 1900.
1. Violet Geraldine (La Maisonette, Kingston Hill, Surrey).

Arms—Quarterly: 1st and 4th, az. on a chevron between two trefoils slipped in chief, and a lion rampant in base or, three escallops gu. (for FINNY) ; 2nd and 3rd, erm. on a cross engrailed or five mullets vert (for WARNER). Crest—A demi-lion rampant gu., holding in the dexter paw a fleam and gorged with an antique crown or. Motto—" Spes mea Deus."

Seats—Ellesmere Port, near Chester. Residence—Leixlip, co. Kildare ; Rathfinny, near Alfriston, Sussex.

FITZ-GERALD.
The Knight of Glin.

DESMOND FITZ-JOHN LLOYD FITZ-GERALD, THE KNIGHT OF GLIN, of Glin Castle, co. Limerick, J.P. and D.L., High Sheriff 1904, late Capt. 3rd Batt. Royal Dublin Fusiliers, and late Capt. South Irish Horse, b. 1862 ; s. his father 1895 ; m. 28 Oct. 1897, Lady Rachel Wyndham Quin, 2nd dau. of the Earl of Dunraven, and by her (who d. 30 Jan. 1901) has issue,

DESMOND WINDHAM OTHO, b. 20 Jan. 1901.

Lineage.—GILBERT FITZ-JOHN, ancestor of the WHITE KNIGHT ; SIR JOHN FITZ-JOHN, ancestor of the KNIGHT OF GLIN ; MAURICE FITZ-JOHN, ancestor of the KNIGHT OF KERRY ; and THOMAS FITZ-JOHN, ancestor of the FITZGERALDS of the Island of Kerry, were brothers, whom John Fitz-Thomas Fitzgerald, Lord of Decies and Desmond, by virtue of his royal seigniory as a Count Palatine, created Knights, and their descendants have been so styled in patents under the Great Seal and other legal documents up to the present time.

SIR JOHN FITZ-JOHN, Knt., to whom his father gave the castles of Glyncorbury and Beagh, co. Limerick, was the 1st Knight of Glyn, and left issue,
1. JOHN FITZ-JOHN, his successor.
2. Gerald Fitz-John, ancestor of the family of FITZGERALD, of Clenfish and Castle Ishen, co. Cork, Barts.
Sir John Fitz-John was s. by his eldest son,
SIR JOHN FITZ-JOHN del Glyn, Knt., from whom descended,
THOMAS FITZ-GERALD, who was attainted with his father, and executed 11 Queen ELIZABETH, leaving a dau., Ellen, m. Sir Edmond Fitz-Harris, Knt. ; and a son, his successor,
EDMOND FITZ-GERALD, Knight of Glin, pardoned and restored to his estates, 13 June, 30 ELIZABETH. He m. Honora, dau. of Owen M'Carthy Reagh, and was s. by his son,
THOMAS FITZ-GERALD, Knight of Glin, who had livery of his lands 18 Dec. 1628. He surrendered those estates, and had them re-granted 22 June, 1635. He m. Joan, dau. of James, Lord Dunboyne, widow of Edmond Fitz-Gibbon, son of Edmond Fitz-Gibbon, the White Knight, and was s. by his son,
GERALD FITZ-GERALD, Knight of Glin, who made a deed of settlement of his estates, 5 Dec. 1672. He m. Joan O'Brien, and dying before 1700 (will dated July, 1687, Inq. at Limerick 25 July, 1696), left issue,
1. THOMAS, his successor. 2. John.
1. Mary, m. Cornelius Mahony (see MAHONY of Kilmorna).
2. Honora, m. Henry Fitz-Gerald, of Bremore, co. Kerry.
3. Helen. 4. Jane.
5. Ellen, m. John White.
His eldest son,
THOMAS FITZ-GERALD, Knight of Glin, seized of an estate in tail under the deed of settlement, in 1672, m. Mary, dau. of Edmond Fitz-Gerald, and had, with a dau., Catherine, m. Robert Fitz-Gerald, of Dublin, three sons, successively inheritors. The eldest,
EDMOND FITZ-GERALD, Knight of Glin, d.s.p., and was s. by his brother,
RICHARD FITZ-GERALD, Knight of Glin, who was s. by his brother,
THOMAS FITZ-GERALD, Knight of Glin, m. 6 Jan. 1755, Mary, dau. of John Bateman, of Oak Park, co. Kerry, and had issue,
1. JOHN, his heir.
1. Elizabeth, m. Rev. Thomas Lloyd, of Castle Lloyd, co. Tipperary.
2. Frances, m. Brudenell Plummer, of Mount Pleasant, co. Limerick, J.P., High Sheriff.
3. Ellen, m. Gustavus Matthias Hippislev.
4. Catharine, m. Maurice O'Connor, of co. Kerry.
5. Jane, m. Joseph Sargeant, of co. Limerick.
Thomas Fitz-Gerald, whose will is dated 17 Sept. 1781, and was proved 18 Feb. 1801, was s. by his eldest son,
JOHN FITZ-GERALD, Knight of Glin, m. Margaretta Maria, dau. of John Frauncies Gwynn, of Ford Abbey, Devon, and was s. by his only son,
JOHN FRAUNCEIS FITZ-GERALD, Knight of Glin, M.A., J.P. and D.L., High Sheriff co. Limerick 1830, b. 28 June, 1791 ; m. 28 July, 1812, Bridgetta, 5th dau. of Rev. Joseph Eyre, of Westerham, Kent, and had issue,
1. JOHN FRAUNCEIS EYRE, late Knight of Glin.
2. Edmond Urmston McLeod.
1. Geraldine Anne. 2. Margaretta Sophia.
The eldest son,
JOHN FRAUNCEIS EYRE FITZ-GERALD, Knight of Glin, b. 1813 ; m. 1835, Clara Anne, only dau. of Gérald Blennerhasset, of Riddlestown, co. Limerick, and had issue,

1. DESMOND JOHN EDMUND, of whom presently.
2. Gerald B., m. Georgiana Fitzgerald.
3. William Urmston, d. unm. 4. John F. E., m.
5. Thomas Otho, d. unm.
6. George W. M., d. unm. 25 April, 1872.
1. Geraldine Elizabeth Blennerhassett, m. 13 Dec. 1863, Thomas H. Greer, Capt. R.A., son of the late Major Greer, of The Grange.
2. Florence Sophia.
3. Margaretta, m. 1869, Col. George Finch, of Maryville, co. Limerick.

The Knight of Glin d. 25 Nov. 1866. The eldest son,
DESMOND JOHN EDMUND FITZ-GERALD, KNIGHT OF GLIN, of Glin Castle, co. Limerick, J.P. and D.L., High Sheriff 1870 and 1871, b. 1840; m. 1861, Isabella Lloyd, 2nd dau. of Rev. Michael Lloyd Apjohn, of Linfield, co. Limerick, and d. 17 Aug. 1895, leaving issue,
1. DESMOND FITZ-JOHN LLOYD, the present KNIGHT OF GLIN.
2. Urmston Fitz-Otho, Lieut. Royal Irish Fusiliers, b. 1864; d. unm. July, 1886, at Cherat, India.
3. Louis de Rottenburgh, b. 1867.
1. Clara Nesta Richarda, m. 6 June, 1882, Arthur Blennerhasset, D.L., of Ballyseedy, co. Kerry (see that family).

Arms—Erm., a saltier gu. Crest—A boar passant gu. bristled and armed or. Motto—Shanet a boo.

Seat—Glin Castle, co. Limerick. Clubs—Kildare Street, Dublin; County, Limerick; Cavalry, S.W.; Raleigh, S.W.; and St. George Yacht, Kingstown.

FITZGERALD OF TURLOUGH.

DESMOND GERALD FITZGERALD, of Turlough Park, co. Mayo. J.P., D.L., High Sheriff 1909, b. 25 May, 1863; s. his cousin, Charles Lionel Wingfield, 7 Jan. 1905; m. 23 Jan. 1912, Hilda Claire Willoughby, younger dau. of Lieut.-Col. Alfred G. W. Hemans, late Madras Cavalry, I.S.C., of Eagle Tower, Southsea.

Lineage.—This family descends traditionally from THOMAS FITZGERALD (3rd son of Maurice, Knight of Kerry), who m. the dau. and heir of O'Dae, or O'Dea, Chief of Ida, in Kilkenny, and assumed in consequence the name of O'Dea, by which the family was known till the end of the 16th century, when they resumed the name of FitzGerald. According to the registered pedigrees, Thomas, great-grandson of the above mentioned Thomas FitzGerald, or O'Dea, sat in the Parliament held before Thomas, Earl of Desmond, in 1465. Thomas, said to be his son, was member of the Parliament held at Trim, before Gerald, Earl of Kildare, in 1490. "Thomas O'Dea, of Gurtyns, co. Kilkenny, Gent.," was pardoned 6 July, 1549. "Thomas FitzGarrolde, alias Adaye, of Grutchins, co. Kilkenny, Gent.," was pardoned 24 May, 1566. "Thomas O'Da, of Gurtines, Gent.," was pardoned 24 Dec. 1571. About this time the name of O'Dea disappears altogether from public records, but Nicholas FitzGerald, of Gurtins, is frequently mentioned on juries in the reign of ELIZABETH.

An inquisition was taken 21 July, 1607, to ascertain the title of Nicholas FitzGerald, of "Le Gurteens," to his lands in the barony of Ida, co. Kilkenny, and the jury found that he was seized of them by hereditary descent. Nicholas then surrendered his entire estates to the Crown, 8 Dec. 1607, and received a new grant of them on the 17th Dec. following. He was the son of Thomas FitzGerald, and m. Helena, dau. of Piers Bourke, alias Gall, of Gallstown, and d. 29 Sept. 1617, and was bur. at Rathpatrick (M.I.), leaving a son and heir,

PATRICK FITZGERALD, of Gurtines, aged 50, in 1617, who left issue, a son,

THOMAS FITZGERALD, of Gurtines, m. Cicely, dau. of Thomas Archer, and by her (who m. 2ndly, Anthony Harrison) had a son,

JOHN FITZGERALD, of Gurtines, co. Kilkenny, was ordered, 21 Dec. 1653, to remove to Connaught, and was "planted" in the parish of Turlough, co. Mayo, where he was assigned half of the estates of Walter Bourke, which was confirmed to him under the Act of Settlement, 1677. He m. (settlement dated 19 June, 1660) Elizabeth, youngest dau. of Sir John Browne, bart., of the Neale, co. Mayo. His will, dated 23 July, 1717, was proved 21 Jan, 1720. He d. at Mohena, in Turlough, leaving issue,

1. THOMAS, of whom presently.
2. Edmond, living 1717, who had a son, John.
3. Patrick, of Kilnecarra, and of Galway, Merchant, living 1717, m. 1st (licence dated 20 Dec. 1706), Sicilia, dau. of Peter Darcy, of Galway, and by her (who d. 1719) had issue,

1. John, living 1717.
1. Elizabeth, who was deaf and dumb.

He m. 2ndly, 1721, Margaret, widow of John Leonard, of Carragh, and dau. of — Aylward, of Ballinagar, co. Galway, and d. 1738 (will dated 20 March, 1737-8, proved 30 May, 1738), having by her had issue,
2. PATRICK, ancestor of Hon. Nicholas FitzGerald, of Melbourne, who d. Aug. 1908, and of Sir Gerald FitzGerald, K.C.M.G. (see BURKE'S Family Records).
3. Francis, d. unm.
2. Mary, m. Charles Higgins, and had issue.
3. Jane, m. Alexander McDonnell, and had issue.
4. Catherine, m. John Mullarky, and had issue.
4. John, who d.v.p. (will dated 6 Sept. 1716, proved 7 Sept. 1717), leaving by Elizabeth his wife, three sons and a dau., 1. Nicholas of Copperinar, aged 18 in 1725; 2. Talbot; 3. Augustine; and 4. Cecilia.
5. George, living 1717.
6. Sylvester, living 1717, went abroad.
1. Mary, m. Henry Baccach McDermott Roe, of Kilronan, co. Roscommon, and had issue (see MACDERMOTT of Alderford).
2. Sisily, m. Richard Cormick.
3. Katherine, m. (licence dated 8 July, 1714) Francis Bourke, of Balluchyne, Cong, co Mayo, and had a son, John, living 1717.
4. Pegy, d. at School in Galway before 1717.

The eldest son,
THOMAS FITZGERALD, of Turlough, who conformed in 1717, m. 1st, Elizabeth Ferron (mother of Ralph Jenison, Master of the Buckhounds to GEORGE II). He m. 2ndly, Henrietta, dau. of John Browne, of the Neale, and d. 15 July, 1747 (M.I. at Turlough), having by her (who d. 8 Dec. 1774) had issue,
1. John, d.v.p. 2. GEORGE, of whom presently.
3. Nicholas, of Greensborough, co. Kilkenny, m. 16 April, 1754, Margaret, dau. and co-heir (with her sisters, Dorcas, m. Sir John Blackwood, and Anne, m. June, 1768, Sir William Hawkins, Ulster King of Arms) of James Stevenson, and Anne his wife, dau. of Gen. Nicholas Price, of Holywood, co. Down. His will dated 20 June, 1761, was proved 30 June, 1761. His widow m. 2ndly, Hon. Robert Moore. Nicholas d. 1761, leaving issue,
1. Thomas, of Kilfar, co. Roscommon, Lieut.-Col. in the Army, d. unm. (will dated 31 Oct. 1831, proved 14 Feb. 1833).
1. Anne, m. 1773, Walter Bermingham, of Dublin.
2. Henrietta, m. Dec. 1782, Henry Grattan, M.P., and had issue.
3. Elizabeth, m. 1 April, 1780, Rev. William Elliott, Vicar of Trim, sometime an Officer in the Army, and had issue. His will, dated 17 Feb. 1817, was proved 14 Feb. 1818.
4. Henry, d. 1775. 5. Edward, d. before 1747.
6. Michael, living 1747.
1. Elizabeth, d. before 1747.
2. Julia, m. 29 Feb. 1747-8, Lewis Butler, of Dublin.
3. Mary, m. the Marquess d'Arezzo, Governor of Naples.
4. Ciscilia, living 1747.
5. Bridget, under age 1747, m. 1743, Thomas Lyster, and had issue (see LYSTER of Grange).

The eldest surviving son,
GEORGE FITZGERALD, of Turlough, sometime a Capt. in the Austrian Service, m. 31 Oct. 1745, Lady Mary Hervey, sister of Frederick, 4th Earl of Bristol, Bishop of Derry, and d. 23 June, 1782. She was living in 1815, was burnt to death at a great age whilst saying her prayers. By her he had issue,
1. George Robert, m. 1st (settlements dated to Feb. 1770), Jane, dau. of the Right Hon. William Conolly, of Castletown, and by her (who d. 1780) had a dau., Mary Anne, who d. unm. April, 1794. He m. 2ndly, 1782, Sidney, dau. of Matthew Vaughan, of Carrowmore, co. Mayo, but by her had no issue.
2. CHARLES LIONEL, of whom we treat.

The younger son,
CHARLES LIONEL FITZGERALD, of Turlough Park, Lieut.-Col. of the North Mayo Militia, m. Sept. 1777, Dorothea, eldest dau. of Sir Thomas Butler, Bart., of Ballintemple, co. Carlow, and d. 29 April, 1805, having by her (who d. 11 April, 1829) had issue,
1. THOMAS GEORGE, of whom presently.
2. Edward Thomas, Lieut.-Col. in the Army, served as Assistant Quarter-Master-General with the Guards at Waterloo and other battles, b. 22 Dec. 1784; m. 20 Nov. 1811, Emma, youngest dau. of Edmond Green, of Medham, in the Isle of Wight, and d. 1845, leaving issue,
1. Lionel Charles Henry William, served in Portugal under Dom Pedro, from 1832 to the establishment of Donna Maria on the Throne in 1834, an Officer in the 2nd W. I. Regt., received the Orders of the Golden Fleece and Tower and Sword, b. 9 Sept. 1812; m. 31 Jan. 1839, Sarah Caroline, dau. of the Hon. Patrick Brown, of Nassau, N.P., and had issue,
(1) Desmond, C.E., of Brookline, Boston, Mass., U.S.A., b. 20 May, 1846; m. 21 June, 1870, Elizabeth Parker-Clarke, dau. of Stephen Salisbury, M.D., of Brookline, U.S., and has issue,
1. Harold, b. 19 May, 1877; m. 3 Oct. 1903, Eleanora, dau. of General Lewis Fitzgerald, of New York, and has issue,
Desmond, b. 16 June, 1910.
Eleanora, b. 7 May, 1906.
2. Stephen Salisbury, b. 19 Sept. 1878; m. 9 Sept. 1906, Agnes, dau. of Francis Blake, of Weston, Mass.
1. Caroline Elizabeth, m. 12 Dec. 1899, Charles Augustus Van Rensselaer, of New York, and has issue.
2. Harriot, m. 18 Nov. 1897, Robert Jones Clark, of Boston, Mass., and has issue.
(2) Lionel Gerard, b. 22 Jan.; d. 19 March, 1848.
(3) Ormond Edward, b. 6 July, 1849.

(1) Harriet Emma, *d.* 10 Dec. 1889.
(2) Geraldine Augusta, *d.* 3 Sept. 1847.
2. Edward Thomas, *b.* 19 Sept. 1817; *m.* 1856, Annie ffarington, dau. of Leonard S. Cox and Frances ffarington his wife, and had issue,
Edward Leonard, *b.* 17 June, 1859; *m.* 3 Aug. 1882, Florence Elizabeth Sophia, dau. of Robert J. Hunter, and has issue,
 1. Edward Walter, *b.* 19 Jan. 1885
 2. Desmond Gerald, *b.* 1 Sept. 1893.
  1. Florence.   2. Marjorie.
  3. Dorothy.   4. Audry.
Anne.
3. Henry Augustus Robert, Lieut. R.A., *b.* 8 Dec. 1824; *d.s.p.* 1845.
4. DESMOND GERALD, whose son s. to Turlough.
1. Louisa, *m.* 1836, Rev. Edward Powell.
2. Emma Mary, *m.* 1847, Rev. W. C. Townsend, Dean of Tuam.
3. Catherine Dorothea, *m.* 1848, Frederick Barry.
4. Dorothea Frances, *m.* 1847, Peter Burke.
5. Frances Anne, *d. unm.* 1909.
3. Charles Lionel, Lieut.-Col. in Army, of Grenadier Gds., attached to the Spanish Legion 1837, British Consul in the Balearic Islands, Ca.thageua, and at Mobile, Alabama, where he *d.* 1 Jan. 1845; *m.* 28 Dec. 1811, Marianne (*d.* 24 June, 1855), dau. of Lieut.-Col. Breedon, R.M., at St. Heliers, and had issue,
1. Charles Lionel Kirwan, Lieut.-Col. R.A., *b.* 2 Aug. 1814; *m.* 1st, Louisa, dau. of Lieut.-Col. Petty, R.A., and by her had issue,
 (1) Charles Lionel, killed in Roumania.
 (2) Desmond, in Canada.
 (3) Hervey, dec.
 (4) Alfred, in Canada.
 (5) Ormonde, in Canada.
 (1) Olivia.
He *m.* 2ndly, and *d.* in Ontario.
2. William Hervey, Major 68th Regt., *b.* 14 Sept. 1815; *m.* Maria, dau. of — Hamilton, of Hamilton, Canada, and had issue,
 (1) Duncan, settled in Canada.
 (2) Hervey, *m.* and settled in Brisbane, Australia.
3. Thomas, *b.* 23 Oct. 1816; *d.* young.
4. Henry, *b.* 5 March, 1820; *m.* Caroline H., dau. of Dr. Nott. of Castlebar, co. Mayo, and *d.* in Brookstead, Hobart Town, Tasmania, having had issue,
 (1) William.   (2) Ormonde.
 (3) Henry.   (4) Charles.
 (1) Ruth.
5. Alfred John, *b.* 7 Oct. 1821, Col. 60th Rifles; *m.* 1st, Mary Ellen, dau. of — Davis, of Parsons Town, King's Co.; and 2ndly, 1898, Isabel, dau. of Col. Hamilton, of Tunbridge Wells.
6. Ormonde, Capt. 87th Royal Irish Fus., *b.* 4 Nov. 1823; *m.* Catherine (*d.* 1894), dau. of — Dunne, of co. Wexford, and *d.* June, 1891, leaving issue,
 (1) Charles Thomas Edward, *b.* 1860; *d.* 1881.
 (2) Henry George, Deputy Insp.-Gen. Indian Police (4), *Cromwell Houses, Queen's Gate, S.W.*), *b.* 13 Nov. 1866.
 (3) Frederick Alfred, *b.* 10 Dec. 1868.
 (4) Ormonde Edward, *b.* 8 March, 1872.
 (5) Desmond, *b.* 26 June, 1877.
 (1) Augusta Marianne Louisa, *b.* 20 Aug. 1863; *m.* 1886, Arthur Oswald Wood, son of Oswald Wood, Deputy Commissioner in the Punjab.
 (2) Mary Ellen, *b.* 19 Aug. 1870; *d.* Nov. 1897.
7. Augustus Harry, *b.* 15 Sept. 1825; *m.* Annie, dau. of — Saunders, and *d.* having had issue,
 (1) Desmond Frederick Augustus, living in Auckland.
 (2) Alfred Hervey, *m.* 1902, Florence, 2nd dau. of Justice Martineau, of Fairlight, Sussex.
 (1) Florence Mary.   (2) Gertrude Annie Edith.
1. Jane Elizabeth Mary, *b.* 28 Sept. 1812; *m.* — Smith and *d.* in America.
2. Dorothea Mary, *b.* 4 March, 1818.
3. Mary Louisa, *b.* 14 Nov. 1827.
1. Dorothea Mary, *m.* 1808, Patrick Kirwan, of Dalgin Park, co. Mayo, and by him (who *d.* 1854) had issue (*see* MAITLAND-KIRWAN *of Gelston Castle*).
The eldest son,
THOMAS GEORGE FITZGERALD, of Turlough Park, co. Mayo, and Maperton House, Somerset, Lieut.-Col. in the Army, D.L., *b.* 5 June, 1778; *m.* 1st, 6 Sept. 1806, Delia, youngest dau. of Joshua Field, of Heaton co. York, and by her had issue,
1. CHARLES LIONEL WILLIAM, of whom presently.
 1. Elizabeth, *d.* young.   2. Sophia, *d.* young.
He *m.* 2ndly, 29 April, 1819, Elizabeth, only dau. of James Crowther, M.D., of Bolshay Hall, co. York, and by her (who *d.* 15 Sept. 1838) had issue,
2. Henry Thomas George, of Maperton House, Wincanton, Somerset, J.P., Major 1st W. York Rifles, and formerly an Officer 1st Life Guards, *b.* 5 March, 1820; *m.* 23 May, 1839, Elizabeth Harriott, eldest dau. of Rev. Samuel Wildman Yates, Vicar of St. Mary's, Reading. She *d.* 1886. He *d.* 1890, having had issue,
 1. George Wildman Yates, *b.* 29 March, 1840; *m.* Frances, dau. of Dr. Sprott Boyd, and *d.* at sea leaving a dau.
 2. CHARLES LIONEL WINGFIELD, who s. to Turlough.
 3. Edward Gerald, *b.* 26 March 1846; *m.* 23 April, 1873, Elizabeth Mary Regis, dau. of Henry Raymond Arundell, nephew of James Everard, 9th Lord Arundell, of Wardour, and *d.s.p.* 1891. She *d.* 18 Jan. 1902.
 1. Charlotte Elizabeth Harriott, *m.* 14 Nov. 1867, Col. John Talbot Coke, of Debdale Hall, Notts, and has issue.

2. Frances Geraldine, *m.* 30 April, 1868, Sir Richard Glyn, Bart., of Gaunts House, Dorset, and has issue.
3. Elizabeth Geraldine, *m.* John Eveleigh Wyndham, and has issue.
4. Mary Dorothea, *m.* Rev. Edward Newton Dickenson, and has issue.
The eldest son,
CHARLES LIONEL WILLIAM FITZGERALD, of Turlough Park, *m.* Dorothea Julia, 2nd dau. of Patrick Kirwan, of Dalgin Park, co. Mayo (*see that family*), and *d.* 9 Nov. 1834, leaving issue. His son,
CHARLES LIONEL FITZGERALD, of Turlough Park, J.P. and D.L., High Sheriff 1876, *b.* 24 Aug. 1833; *m.* 1st, 3 Dec. 1859, Emily, 2nd dau. of Michael Dungan. She *d.s.p.* 6 July, 1872. He *m.* 2ndly, 22 Oct. 1873, Isabella Emily, and dau. of Rev. Robert J. Serjeantson, Vicar of Snaith, co. York. She *d.s.p.* 21 Feb. 1900. He *m.* 3rdly, 25 April, 1901, Kathleen Mary, eldest dau. of Middleton O'Malley Knott, M.D. He *d.s.p.* 28 Dec. 1902, and was s. by his cousin.
CHARLES LIONEL WINGFIELD FITZGERALD, of Turlough Park, co. Mayo, *b.* 26 Dec. 1841; *s.* his cousin, 1902; *m.* 1893, Adolphine Caroline Annie Helena Marie, 2nd dau. of Capt. Schmitz, of the Imperial German Army, and *d.s.p.* 7 Jan. 1905, being *s.* by his cousin, Desmond Gerald FitzGerald (*now of Turlough*). His widow (*Winterton Hall, Hythe, near Southampton*) *m.* 2ndly, 24 July, 1906, Lester Guy Humphery, 5th son of the late George Francis Humphery, of Clapham Common.
DESMOND GERALD FITZGERALD (*see above*), *b.* 28 Dec. 1834; *m.* 20 May, 1862, Louisa, 2nd dau. of Matthew Crawford, of Crumlin, co. Westmeath, and *d.* 5 Jan. 1908, having by her (who *d.* 30 Nov. 1906) had issue,
1. DESMOND GERALD, now of Turlough.
2. Ormond Edward, *b.* 1 March, 1865; *m.* 16 June, 1900, Rebecca Susanna, 2nd dau. of Becher Lionel Fleming, of Newcourt, co. Cork, and *d.* 11 Feb. 1911, having had issue, Gerald.
Elizabeth Cicely.
3. Cecil Henry, C.E., *b.* 5 Jan. 1871; *m.* Mary, dau. of — Ruiter, of Leydenburg, Transvaal, and has issue,
Cecil.
Sheelah Nesta.
1. Emma Louisa Hope, *m.* Duncan Archibald McLeod, 2nd son of Rev. John McLeod, D.D., Minister of Govan. He *d.* 9 Dec. 1907, having had issue.
2. Ruby Gwendoline.

Arms—Erm. on a saltire gu. a mullet arg. *Crest*—On a mount ppr. a boar passant or. *Motto*—Honor probataque virtus.

Seat—Turlough Park, Castlebar co. Mayo. *Club*—Kildare Street.

FITZGERALD OF MOYVANE.

JOHN VESEY VESEY FITZGERALD, of Moyvane, co. Kerry, J.P. Warwickshire, Kerry, and Clare, K.C., *b.* 25 Feb. 1848; *m.* 1st, 14 Jan. 1891, Annie, dau. of John Ross, of Quebec, and by her (who *d.* Sept. 1896) has issue,

Theodora Frances.

He *m.* 2ndly, 15 May, 1899, Mabel Edith, dau. of Robert Charles Leslie, of Ballybay, co. Monaghan (*see that family*), and has issue,

WILLIAM PATRICK DESMOND, *b.* 17 March, 1900.

Lineage.—GARRETT FITZJOHN FITZGIBBON, of Coolcam Castle, in the Barony of Clangibbon, co. Cork (a branch of the FITZGIBBONS, the White Knights), *d.* 1637, leaving a son.

MAURICE FITZGIBBON, who *m.* Mary O'Keefe, as appears by inquisition taken at Mallow, 1638. He *d.* in the lifetime of his father, leaving a son and heir,

GERALD FITZMAURICE FITZGIBBON, heir to his grandfather, forfeited Coolcam in 1641, and settled in the co. of Clare. His son,

GERALD FITZGERALD FITZGIBBON, *m.* Margaret, only child and heiress of Moses Ashe, of Ballyline, co. Clare, Capt. in Cromwell's Army, and had issue,

MAURICE FITZGERALD, who dropped the surname of FITZGIBBON, which was never afterwards used by his descendants. He *m.* Penelope Barrett, of Hillsborough, co. Clare, by whom he had issue several sons and daus. He *d.* 1736. His 2nd son,

WILLIAM FITZGERALD, *b.* 1714; *m.* Eliza,* eldest dau. and co-

---

* She was 5th in female descent from Daniel O'Brien, 1st Viscount Clare (son of Connor, 3rd Earl of Thomond) and Catharine his wife, dau. of Gerald FitzGerald, 15th Earl of Desmond, *The Rebel Earl*, who was attainted 15 Nov. 1582, when his vast estates, the largest in Ireland, were forfeited. Daniel 3rd Viscount Clare, was attainted 1691. The Viscounty of Clare became extinct with the Earldom of Thomond 29 Dec. 1774.

heiress of Pierce Lynch, of Rathfiladown, co. Galway, by Ellen his wife, dau. of Theobald Butler, of Cregg and Ballygegan, and had issue several sons and daus., among whom Barbara, *m.* Richard Gregg, of Cappa, co. Clare, father of the Right Rev. John Gregg, D.D., Bishop of Cork, Cloyne, and Ross. The eldest son,

RIGHT HON. JAMES FITZGERALD, was called to the Bar of Ireland in 1769, and became Prime Serjeant of Ireland and a Privy Councillor. He *m.* Catherine, dau. and co-heiress of Rev. Henry Vesey, Warden of Galway, and great-granddau. of Most Rev. John Vesey, D.D., Archbishop of Tuam (ancestor of the Viscounts de Vesci). She was created in 1826 BARONESS FITZGERALD and VESCI, in the Peerage of Ireland, with remainder to her issue male by her husband, Right Hon. James Fitzgerald. There were surviving children of this marriage,

1. WILLIAM, 2nd Lord FITZGERALD and VESCI, who, having filled the office of Chancellor of the Exchequer in Ireland, was made President of the Board of Trade in the Duke of Wellington's Cabinet, but having in 1828 lost his seat for the co. of Clare, after a contest with Daniel O'Connell, and succeeding to the title of his mother, he was created Baron Fitzgerald of Desmond, and of Clangibbon, in the co. of Cork, in the Peerage of the United Kingdom. He afterwards was President of the Board of Control in Sir Robert Peel's Cabinet, and *d.s.p.* in 1843.
2. HENRY, 3rd Lord FITZGERALD and VESCI (Very Rev.), Dean of Kilmore, *m.* Elizabeth, dau. of Standish Grady, of Elton, in the co. of Limerick, and had issue, several daus. He *s.* his brother William in the Irish honours of the family, but dying in 1860, without issue male, the title became extinct.
1. Mary, *m.* Sir Ross Mahon, Bart., of Castlegar, co. Galway (*see* BURKE'S *Peerage and Baronetage*).
2. Letitia, *m.* JOHN LESLIE FOSTER, as hereafter.
3. Catherine, *d. unm.*

FAMILY OF FOSTER.

JOHN FOSTER, of Dunleer, co. Louth, for many years M.P. for that borough, *b.* 1665; *m.* in 1704, Mary, dau. of Col. William Fortescue, of Newrath, in the same co. (by Margaret his wife, only dau. of Nicholas Gernon, of Miltown, co. Louth, by Elizabeth Plunkett, dau. of Matthew, Lord Louth),† and grand-dau. of Sir Faithful Fortescue, Knt. of Dromiskee, ancestor of the Lords Clermont (*ext.*) and Carlingford, and had, with other issue,
1. ANTHONY, of whom presently.
2. Thomas (Rev.), ancestor of Foster, Bart., of Glyde Court (*see* BURKE'S *Peerage*).
3. William, M.P. for Dunleer, ancestor of Foster of Ballynascanlon (*see that family*).
1. Charlotte, *m.* Nicholas Forster, of Tullaghan, ancestor of Forster, Bart., of Coolderry.

The eldest son,
RIGHT HON. ANTHONY FOSTER, Lord Chief Baron of the Court of Exchequer in Ireland, *b.* 1705; *m.* Elizabeth, dau. of William Burgh, of Bert, co. Kildare, and had issue,
1. JOHN (RIGHT HON.), LORD ORIEL, Chancellor of the Exchequer, and last Speaker of the House of Commons in Ireland; created 1821, Baron Oriel. He *m.* Margaret, dau. of Thomas Burgh, M.P., of Bert, co. Kildare, by whom (who was created a Peeress of Ireland, 1790, as Baroness Oriel, and 1797, Viscountess Ferrard) his lordship had issue (*see* BURKE'S *Peerage*, MASSEREENE *and* FERRARD, V.).
2. WILLIAM, of whom presently.
1. Margaret, *m.* Most Rev. Henry Maxwell, Bishop of Meath, grandfather of Lord Farnham, and *d.* 1792.
The Chief Baron *d.* 1778. His 2nd son,
RIGHT REV. WILLIAM FOSTER, D.D., was consecrated 14 June, 1789, Bshop of Cork and Ross; translated to Kilmore 1790, and to Clogher 1796. He *m.* Catherine Letitia, dau. of Rev. Henry Leslie, D.D., of Ballybay, co. Monaghan (*see that family*) by whom (who *d.* 1814) he had (with other daus.) issue,
1. JOHN LESLIE, of whom presently.
2. WILLIAM (Rev.), Rector of Loughgilly, co. Armagh, *m.* Catherine, dau. of James Hamilton, of Brownhall, co. Donegal, and had issue.
1. Catherine, *m.* 1805, William Drummond Delap.
2. Anna, *m.* Jonas Stawell.
3. Henrietta, *m.* Jerome Fane, Count de Salis, and *d.* 1856, leaving issue.
4. Elizabeth, *m.* Rev. James MacCreight.
5. Letitia, *m.* John Henry North, Q.C., M.P.
The Bishop of Clogher *d.* 1797. His eldest son,
JOHN LESLIE FOSTER, M.P. co. Louth and for the University of Dublin, was one of the Barons of the Court of Exchequer in Ireland, *m.* 1814, Hon. LETITIA VESEY FITZGERALD, as before mentioned, and had issue,
1. WILLIAM LESLIE FOSTER-VESEY-FITZGERALD, late of Moyvane.
2. JOHN FOSTER VESEY FITZGERALD (Hon.), formerly Colonial Secretary of Victoria, Australia, Privy Councillor and Acting Governor of that Colony, *b.* 1818; *m.* 1850, Emily, dau. of Rev. John Joseph Fletcher, D.D., of Dunran, co. Wicklow, and *d.* 3 Jan. 1900, having by her (who *d.* 27 Nov. 1898) had issue,
 1. JOHN, now of Moyvane (*see that family*).
 1. Emily Geraldine Foster, *d. unm.* 27 Sept. 1903.
 2. Henrietta. 3. Louisa.
 4. Anna.

† Through this marriage the descent has been established of the Foster family, the Earls and Viscounts Clermont, and Lord Rathdonnell, from Roger de Gernon, who accompanied STRONGBOW, and settled in Louth. The Gernons were conspicuous in Louth throughout mediæval history, especially by reason of their share in the success attained over Edward Bruce at the Battle of Dundalk, for which they were largely rewarded by grants of land.

3. JAMES, late of Moyriesk, D.L. co. Clare, J.P. cos. Galway and Clare, High Sheriff of Clare 1868, *b.* 8 May, 1821; *m.* 4 Dec. 1845, Henrietta Louisa, dau. of Sir Ross Mahon, Bart., of Castlegar, co. Galway, by his wife, the Hon. Mary Geraldine FitzGerald and *d.* 10 Dec. 1893, having survived his wife (who *d.* on the same day), and by her had issue,
 1. JAMES, of Moyriesk, co. Clare, J.P., B.A. Trin. Coll. Dublin, K.C., *b.* 15 Nov. 1846, called to the Bar of Ireland, 1871; *d. unm.* 6 April, 1907.
 2. John George, *b.* 1849; *d. unm.* 1892.
 1. Henrietta Mary Emily, *m.* 1870, Capt. George Barrington Godbold, late 27th Regt., and *d.* 24 Dec. 1877, having by him (who *d.* 1 June, 1886) had issue.
 2. Geraldine Sophia, now of Moyriesk., *m.* 14 Nov. 1872, Robert Hume Crowe, of Toonagh, co. Clare, J.P. (*see* CROWE *of Dromore*), and has issue.
 1. Letitia, *d. unm.* 1908.

Baron Foster *d.* 1842. His widow, upon the death in 1860 of her brother Henry, 3rd Lord FitzGerald and Vesci, in accordance with the will of her brother William, 2nd Lord FitzGerald and Vesci, assumed for herself and her issue, by Sign Manual, the surnames and arms of VESEY-FITZGERALD after that of FOSTER. She *d.* 1864. The elder son,

WILLIAM LESLIE FOSTER-VESEY-FITZGERALD, of Moyvane, co. Kerry, Kilmurry MacMahon, co. Clare, and Mullacloe, co. Louth, J.P., *b.* 12 July, 1815; *m.* 27 April, 1847, Sarah Anne, only child of Henry Quilter, of Monken Hadley, Middlesex. She *d.* 1899. He *d.* 7 April, 1895, leaving issue,
1. JOHN VESEY VESEY FITZGERALD, now of Moyvane.
2. Gerald William Vesey FitzGerald, *b.* 20 March, 1850; *m.* 1885, Emma, dau. of Robert Leslie Vickers, of Emerson, Canada, and has issue,
 1. Gerald Arthur, *b.* 1886. 2. William Herbert Leslie, *b.* 1889.
 1. Nora, *d.* 1911.
3. Henry Martin, *b.* 1 April, 1852; *m.* 28 March, 1894, Frances Ella, dau. of the late John Ross, of Quebec.

Arms—Quarterly: 1st and 4th, grand quarters quarterly: 1st and 4th, erm., a saltire gu., for FITZGERALD; 2nd and 3rd, or, a cross sa. charged with a patriarchal cross of the field, for VESEY; 2nd and 3rd, grand quarters: arg., a chevron vert between three bugle horns sa. stringed gu., for FOSTER. Crests—On a ducal coronet or, a wild boar passant gu., charged with three annulets arg., for FITZGERALD; 2nd, a hand in armour holding a laurel branch, all ppr., for VESEY; 3rd, a stag trippant ppr., for FOSTER. Motto—Shanet a boo.

Seat—Moyvane, Newtown Sandes, co. Kerry. Residence—9, Campden Hill Road, W. Clubs—Athenæum and Union.

FITZGERALD OF MOYRHEA.

JOHN FOSTER-VESEY-FITZGERALD, of Moyrhea, co. Clare, M.A. Oxon., Barrister-at-Law, *b.* 1864; *m.* 20 Nov. 1900, Mary Edith, elder dau. of Col. Farquhar Glennie, Commandant Royal Mil. School of Music, Kneller Hall, and has issue,

LESLIE DESMOND EDWARD, *b.* 7 June, 1909.
Pamela Moira, *b.* 18 Dec. 1903.

He is the only son of the late Colonial Secretary of Victoria, Australia and Privy Councillor and sometime Acting Governor of that Colony, who *d.* 3 Jan. 1900.

Lineage and Arms—*See* FITZGERALD *of Moyvane.*

Seat—Moyrhea, co. Clare. Residence—11, Wilton Place, Knightsbridge, S.W. Chambers—1, Garden Court, Temple, E.C. Club—Carlton.

FITZGERALD OF COOLANOWLE.

GERALD RICHARD FREDERICK FITZGERALD, of Coolanowle, and Moate, Queen's Co., 2nd Lieut. R.E.M. Submarine Miners, *b.* 14 Dec. 1877; *s.* his father, 1898; *m.* 20 July, 1901, Alice Florence (who *d.* 1902), eldest dau. of the late Frank Campion, of The Mount, Derby.

Lineage.—GERALD FITZGERALD, of Moret, son of Gerald, 11th Earl of Kildare, by Grany ny Molloy, *m.* Margaret (who *d.* 1637), dau. of Robert Bowen, of Ballyadams, and *d.* 1601, having had, with three daus., a son,

GERALD FITZGERALD, of Tymogue and Moret and Loughcurran, High Sheriff, Queen's Co. 1637; *m.* Hon. Anne O'Dempsie (who *d.*

1 April, 1633), dau. of Terence, 1st Viscount Clanmalier, and d. 667, having had issue,
1. Thomas, of Tymogue and Moret, m. Sibella, dau. of John Pigott, of Dysart, Queen's Co. His will dated 5 March, 1666, was proved Dec. foll. He had a son.
Stephen, of Tymogue and Moret, b. 1662; m. Martha, dau. of Henry Gilbert, of Kilminchy. She d. 26 Dec. 1713. He d. 2 June, 1716, leaving a son,
Thomas, of Tymogue and Moret, m. a dau. of Sir Gregory Byrne. This line became extinct on the death of Hamilton FitzGerald, who m. Lady Charlotte Rawdon, dau. of the 1st Earl of Moira and sister of the 1st Marquis of Hastings.
2. GEORGE, of whom we treat.

The younger son,
GEORGE FITZGERALD, m. the dau. of — Hartpole, of Shrule, and left issue, a son,
GERALD FITZGERALD, of Coolanowle, Queen's Co., High Sheriff 1704; m. Mary, dau. of Sir Robert Hartpole, of Shrule Castle, and of Coolanowle, Queen's Co., and d. 1743, having by her (who d. 1772) had issue,
1. Robert, of Coolanowle, d.s.p. 1788.
2. Thomas, d.s.p.   3. William, d.s.p.
4. George, d.s.p.
5. RICHARD, of whom presently.
6. Gerald, d.s.p.   7. Alexander, d.s.p.
8. James, m. Mary, dau. of Robert Evance, and by her had issue, Robert Evance, m. Charlotte, dau. of M. Colombiers, and by her (who m. 2ndly, 1786. Gen. Milner, and d. 1844) had issue,
(1) Robert (Sir), K.C.H., Vice-Adm. R.N., b. 17 Jan. 1776; m. 1800, Jane, dau. of Richard Welsh, Chief Justice of Jamaica, and d. 1844, leaving, with other issue, who d.s.p.,
1. Charles Robert, b. 1803; d.s.p. 1880.
2. Gerald Stephen (Rev.), Rector of Wanstead, b. 1810; m. 1842, Susan Anne (who d. 27 Dec. 1881), dau. of Hon. and Rev. George Beresford (see BURKE's Peerage, DECIES, B.), and widow of M. O'Reilly, of Thomastown, and d. 1879, leaving with three other daughters,
a. Gerald Beresford, F.S.A., a novelist, b. 1849; m. 1881, Lucy, dau. of Francis Wickham, of North Hill, and has issue,
(a) Charles Robert Lewis, Lieut. Northumberland Fus., b. 17 May, 1883.
(b) George de la Poer Beresford, b. 1888.
(a) Mary Susan Beresford.
(b) Geraldine Elizabeth de Tessier.
(c) Mabel Henrietta Alicia.
b. Susan Jane, m. 1856, Right Rev. Charles John Ridgeway, D.D., Bishop of Chichester. She d. 1894, leaving issue.
3. Augustus Otway (Ven.), Archdeacon of Wells, b. 23 March, 1813; m. 1st, 1839, Sarah, dau. of Rev. Richard Proctor. She d.s.p. He m. 2ndly, 1843, Teresa, dau. of Rev. J. G. Thring, of Alford House (see BURKE's Peerage, THRING, B.). She d. 1867. He d. 1897, leaving issue,
a. Gerald Augustus, m. Alice, dau. of H. D. Skrine, of Warleigh Manor, and has issue,
(a) Maurice Henry.
(b) Robert Geoffrey.
b. Maurice Otto.
c. James Richard, Bombay C.S.
a. Mabel.
(2) James, Lieut.-Col. 3rd Foot Guards, A.D.C. to H.R.H. the Duke of York, d.s.p. 1802.

The 5th son,
COL. RICHARD FITZGERALD, of Moate and Kilminchy, Queen's Co., M.P. for Boyle, m. 1st, Margaret, dau. and heiress of James, 4th and last Lord Kingston, of Mitchelstown Castle, and by her (who d. 29 Jan. 1763) had a dau.,
1. Caroline, m. 5 Dec. 1769, her kinsman Robert, Lord Kingsborough, son of the Earl of Kingston, of Rockingham, co. Roscommon, and d. 13 Jan. 1823, having had issue (see BURKE's Peerage, KINGSTON, E.).
He m. 2ndly, 1766, Mary, dau. and heir of Fairfax Mercer, of Fair Hill, Louth, and d. 1776, having by her (who d. Jan. 1830) had issue,
1. GERALD, of whom presently.
2. Maria, d. unm. 1837.   3. Harriot, d. unm. 1839.
4. Margaret, m. 1795, the Hon. John Jocelyn, brother of 2nd Earl of Roden, who d. 1828, leaving issue (see BURKE's Peerage).

The only son,
GERALD FITZGERALD, of Coolanowle and Moate, Queen's Co., b. 28 Sept. 1772; m. 1st, 1794, Isabella, dau. of Sir Robert Staples Bart., of Dunmore, Queen's Co., and by her (who was b. 1778, and d. 1803) had issue,
1. Gerald, of Coolanowle and Moate, Queen's Co., and The Firs, Berks., J.P. and D.L., b. 18 Sept. 1801; m. 1827, Charlotte, sister of Lord Talbot de Malahide, and widow of Lieut.-Col. John Mervyn Cutcliffe, C.B., K.H., and d.s.p. 15 Dec. 1873. She d. 9 Nov. 1863.
1. Isabella, b. 30 Jan. 1796; d. unm. 1864.
2. Mary, b. 12 April, 1798; m. 1829, Rev. James Beesly, who d. 1855, leaving issue.
He m. 2ndly, 1813, Catherine, dau. of the Right Hon. Sir Lucius O'Brien, P.C., 3rd bart., M.P. of Dromoland, co. Clare, and by her (who d. 1819) had issue,
2. RICHARD (Rev.), of whom presently.
3. Lucius Henry, of The Firs, Berks, Barrister-at-Law, b. 1 Dec. 1815; m. 10 Sept. 1856, Mary Katharine, dau. of Admiral the Hon. Sir John Talbot, G.C.B., 3rd son of Richard Talbot, of Malahide, by Margaret his wife, Baroness Talbot, of Malahide, in her own right. She d. 27 Feb. 1897. He d. 9 Dec. 1891, having had issue,
1. Lucius, formerly Lieut. 3rd Batt. Duke of Edinburgh's (Wiltshire) Regt., b. 12 Jan. 1859.
2. Gerald Lucius, b. 16 June, 1868; m. 31 Oct. 1910, Katherine Agnes, dau. of late George Gaviller Styles, of Greenhithe, Kent.
3. Robert Lucius (Esuch, Paignton, Devon), b. 4 Oct. 1869; m. 1904, Amy Beatrice, eldest dau. of late Alfred Muir, of Rockswood, Broughton Park, Manchester, and has issue,
(1) Katheraine Constance Mary Maud, b. 17 May, 1905.
(2) Norah Beatrice, b. 26 June, 1910.
1. Mary Katharine Josephine.
2. Mary Charlotte Isabella, a nun.
3. Mary Julia Rose, a nun.
4. Lettice Mary Maude.
5. Mary Laura Theresa, a nun.
4. Robert, Capt. 12th Bombay N.I. and Commandant 5th Punjab Cav., b. 1817, d. unm. 1853.
5. James Edward, C.M.G. Auditor-Gen. and Comptroller of New Zealand, 1866-96, first Premier of New Zealand, b. 4 March, 1818; m. Aug. 1850, Francis Erskine, dau. of G. Draper, and d. 1896, leaving issue,
1. William, b. 12 Oct. 1853; m. Fanny, dau. of Dr. Featherston, Superintendent of Wellington, N.Z., and d. 4 June, 1888, leaving issue,
(1) Thomas.
(1) Katherine.   (2) Bessie.
2. Robert, b. 7 June, 1855; d. 15 July, 1878.
3. Gerald, b. 6 June, 1857; m. Ettie, dau. of — Budge, and has issue,
(1) Maurice.
(1) Oonagh.   (2) Moya.   (3) Elice.
4. Lyttelton (Rev.), b. 1 June, 1859; m. Dec. 1901, Georgiana, widow of Frank Campion, of The Mount, Derby.
5. Maurice, b. 18 April, 1861; d. 10 July, 1886.
6. Selwyn, b. 15 Jan. 1865; d. 16 May, 1880.
7. Otho (Rev.), b. 16 Sept. 1868.
8. Edward, b. 14 Aug. 1873.
1. Amy, b. 19 Feb. 1852; m. 20 May, 1876, William Hort Levin, of Wellington, N.Z., who d. Sept. 1893, leaving issue.
2. Evangeline, b. 9 Feb. 1863; m. James Brandon, and has issue.
3. Katharine, b. 6 Oct. 1866; d. 29 June, 1880.
4. Geraldine, b. 16 Sept. 1870.
5. Mabel, b. Feb. 1876; d. 21 Aug. 1880.
Mr Gerald FitzGerald m. 3rdly, 9 Nov. 1820, Emily, dau. of Robert Gibbons, younger brother of Sir William Gibbons, 3rd bart. of Stanwell Place, and d. 8 April, 1845, having by her (who was b. 25 April, 1799, and d. 23 Oct. 1884) had issue,
6. Frederick Charles, late R.N., b. 28 Nov. 1828; m. 2 June, 1853, Lilla Francisca, dau. of William Roberts, Clerk of the Pells in the Exchequer, and by her (who d. 25 Jan. 1903) has issue,
1. Frederick Richard, b. 17 July, 1869.
1. Lilla, m. Feb. 1897 (as below), her cousin Gerald Richard FitzGerald, of Coolanowle, and has issue.
2. Geraldine.   3. Edith, d. unm. 1 Sept. 1885.
4. Constance Emily, d. unm. 24 Aug. 1890.
7. John (Rev.), b. 24 July, 1830; m. Dec. 1853, Clare, dau. of Rev. George Musgrave, of Shillingdon Manor, Beds, and d. 30 Aug. 1896, having had two sons who d. young.
8. Gerard George, M.H.R., New Zealand, b. 10 Oct. 1833; m. Jane McKey, who d.s.p. 1886.
9. Arthur, of Berridon Hall, Bradworthy, Col. late 17th Punjab Native Infantry, b. Dec. 1835; d. unm. 7 Oct. 1907.
10. Henry Gibbons, R.N., b. 26 April, 1840; d.s.p. 30 June, 1890.
3. Emily Ann, d. young.
4. Caroline Mary, b. 1825; d. 26 April, 1845.
5. Emily, b. 12 Oct. 1822; d. unm. 23 Dec. 1870.
6. Lucia, d. unm. 20 Jan. 1905.
7. Margaret, m. 24 March, 1859, William Marriott, M.D., F.L.S., of Mentone, late 102nd Royal Madras Fusiliers, and has issue (see MARRIOTT of Avonbank). He d. 1 Feb. 1902.
8. Geraldine.

The 2nd son,
REV. RICHARD FITZGERALD, of Coolanowle and Moate, Queen's Co., Rector of Winslade, near Basingstoke, b. 18 July, 1814; m. 1838, Katherine Anne, dau. of R. E. N. Lee, and d. 6 June, 1895, having by her (who d. 1873) had issue,
GERALD RICHARD, late of Coolanowle.
Katherine Elizabeth, d. unm. 1870.

The only son,
GERALD RICHARD FITZGERALD, of Coolanowle and Moate, Queen's Co., b. 28 Jan. 1848; m. 13 Feb. 1877, his cousin Lilla, dau. of Frederick Charles FitzGerald, late R.N. (see above), and d. 17 April, 1898, leaving issue,
1. GERALD RICHARD FREDERICK, now of Coolanowle and Moate.
2. Robert O'Brien, b. 16 June, 1879; m. 1905, Constance Violet, younger dau. of late Frank Campion, Barrister-at-Law, of the Mount, Derby.
3. Arthur Stanley, 2nd Lieut. Royal Warwickshire Regt., b. 28 Jan. 1881.
4. Maurice Frederick, b. 22 Dec. 1883; d. 21 March, 1888
1. Geraldine Edith, b. 11 April, 1882; m. 6 Oct. 1903, William Montagu Alford, eldest son of the late William Alford, of Clifton, Bristol.

Arms—Arg. a saltire gu. a bordure az.
Seats—Coolanowle and Moate, Queen's Co.

FITZGERALD OF CARRIGORAN.

WILLIAM WALTER AUGUSTINE FITZGERALD, of Carrigoran. co. Clare, J.P. and D.L., High Sheriff 1897, b. 24 Nov. 1852; m. 30 Oct. 1894, Clara Emma, 2nd dau. of James Whitaker, of Huddersfield, Yorks., and widow of his 1st cousin, Lieut.-Col. Sir Augustine FitzGerald, 4th Bart., of Carrigoran (see BURKE'S *Peerage*).

Lineage. — FIELD MARSHAL SIR JOHN FORSTER FITZGERALD, G.C.B., Col. 18th Foot, M.P. for Clare, 1852-7, brother of Sir William Fitz-Gerald, 2nd bart. (see BURKE'S *Peerage*, FITZGERALD, Bart. of *Newmarket*), and 6th son of Col. Edward FitzGerald, M.P., of Carrigoran, and Anne Catherine, his second wife, dau. and co-heir of Maj. Thomas Burton, by Dorothy, his wife, dau. of Right Hon. John Forster, Chief Justice of the Common Pleas. Sir John was b. 1784; m. 1st, 1805, Charlotte, dau. of the Hon. Robert Hazen, of St. John's, New Brunswick, and by her had issue,
1. John Forster, Capt. 14th Hussars, mortally wounded in the Sikh War.
1. Charlotte, m. Otto, Baron von Ende.
2. Anne, m. 20 March, 1828, Sir Robert Keith Arbuthnot, 2nd Bart. He d. 4 March, 1873. She d. 6 March, 1882, leaving issue (see BURKE'S *Peerage*).
3. Dora, d. young.

Sir John m. 2ndly, 19 Dec. 1839, Jean, dau. of the Hon. Donald Ogilvy, of Clova, M.P., brother of the 6th Earl of Airlie. She d. 24 Sept. 1863. Sir John d. 24 March, 1877, the senior officer of the Army at the time of his death. By her he had issue,
2. Ferdinand, 18th Regt., d. in India.
3. WILLIAM WALTER AUGUSTINE, now of Carrigoran.
4. Geraldine, m. 27 Dec. 1876, M. E. Ogier de Pégot. She d. May, 1902.

Arms—Erm. a saltire gu. **Crest**—A knight in complete armour mounted on a horse at full speed, his sword drawn and beaver up all ppr. **Motto**—Fortis et fidelis.

Seat—Carrigoran, Newmarket on Fergus, co. Clare. **Clubs**—Carlton, S.W.; and Kildare Street, Dublin.

PURCELL-FITZGERALD OF THE LITTLE ISLAND.

GERALD PURCELL-FITZGERALD, of the Island, co. Waterford, formerly Lieut. 3rd Batt. Leicester Regt., b. 5 May, 1865; s. his uncle 1879; m. 1st, 28 Sept. 1892, Alice, dau. of Very Rev. Anthony La Touche Kirwan, D.D., Dean of Limerick. She d.s.p. 23 March, 1898. He m. 2ndly, 1 March, 1899, Eleanor, dau. of John Niccolls, of Uniontown, Pennsylvania, U.S.A., and by her has issue,

1. JOHN, b. 24 Sept. 1899.
2. Gerald } twins, b. 25 Oct. 1900.
3. Edward Maurice }
1. Mary Augusta Lisle, b. 6 Dec. 1908.

Lineage.—EDWARD FITZGERALD (son of John FitzGerald, Sheriff of Waterford 1639, son of Edward FitzGerald, of Waterford), m. 1st, Joan FitzGerald, and 2ndly, Joan Luttrell, and had issue by both. His third son,
JOHN FITZGERALD, left issue by Joan, his wife, a son and heir.
JOHN FITZGERALD, m. Maria Woodlock, and by her had issue, a son,

RICHARD FITZGERALD, Sheriff of Waterford 1687, m. 1st, Maria, Browne, and by her had issue. He m. 2ndly, Francisca Xaveria, dau. of Nicholas Wyse, of St. John's Priory, co. Waterford, and by her had numerous issue. His youngest son,
EDWARD FITZGERALD, of Waterford, m. 1st, Margaret, dau. of C. Browne, by whom he had issue. He m. 2ndly, Elizabeth Rochfort, and by her had issue. He m. 3rdly, Mary, dau. of Thomas Power of Clashmore, co. Waterford. She d.s.p. He d. 1736. His only son by his first wife,
JOHN FITZGERALD, of Williamstown, co. Waterford, m. 29 Aug. 1757, Anne, dau. of John Kennedy. She d. 1798. He d. 17 Jan. 1784, having had issue,
1. JOHN, his heir.
2. Charles, b. 1765, d. 1783.
3. George, b. 1768; d. unm. 1796.
1. Eleanor, m. 29 Sept. 1774, John Purcell, of Dublin, and had issue, a son,
JOHN, m. 16 May, 1801, his cousin Mary Frances, dau. and heir of John FitzGerald (see below).
2. Mary Anne, m. 1st, John Cologhan, of Teneriffe, and by him had two daus. She m. 2ndly, Mons. Bacheville, an officer in the French King's Guard, by whom she had no issue.

The eldest son,
JOHN FITZGERALD, of Williamstown, co. Waterford, High Sheriff of that co. and for Flints, b. 12 Oct. 1760; m. May, 1779, Mary, only dau. of Keane FitzGerald, of Totteridge, Herts. and d. 6 Sept. 1818, having had issue,
John Charles, b. 1781, m. Louisa Danvers, and d.s.p. Sept. 1807, vitâ patris.
MARY FRANCES, s. her father.

The only dau. and heir,
MARY FRANCES FITZGERALD, m. 16 May, 1801, her first cousin, JOHN PURCELL, M.D. of Kilkenny, eldest son of John Purcell, of Dublin, by Eleanor his wife, eldest dau. of John FitzGerald, of Williamstown (see above). Mr. Purcell assumed by Royal Licence 23 Sept. 1818, the name and arms of FITZGERALD only. He was M.P. for Seaford 1826-32, D.L. for Suffolk, High Sheriff for that co. 1824, and for Waterford 1838, and Lieut.-Col. 2nd East Suffolk Volunteers. He d. 18 March, 1852. She d. 30 Jan. 1855, having had issue,
1. JOHN, of whom presently.
2. Peter Slingsby, Capt. 2nd Regt. Lancashire Militia and 60th Rifles, m. Honoria, dau. of Valentine O'Connor, of Rockfield (see O'CONNOR-HENCHY of *Stonebrook*).
3. Edward, Author of *Omar Khayyam*, b. 31 March, 1809; m. Lucy, dau. of B. Barton.
1. Frances, d. 1820.
2. Mary Eleanor, m. 26 Dec. 1826, John Kerrich, of Geldeston Hall, Norfolk.
3. Jane Theresa, m. 29 May, 1832, Rev. John Brewster Wilkinson, Rector of Holbrook, Suffolk.
4. Isabella, m. 18 Oct. 1843, Gaetana Francesco Vignati, of Lodi.
5. Andalusia, m. Rev. Francis de Soyres.

The eldest son,
JOHN PURCELL-FITZGERALD, of the Little Island, co. Waterford, and of Boulge Hall, Suffolk, J.P., b. 29 June, 1803, assumed by Royal Licence Jan. 1858, the additional name and arms of PURCELL, b. 29 Jan. 1803; s. his mother 1855; m. 1st, 18 Nov. 1832, Augusta Jane Lisle, only dau. of Charles March Phillipps, M.P. of Garendon Park, and Grace Dieu Manor, co. Leicester. She d. 30 July, 1835, leaving issue,
1. GERALD CHARLES, his heir.
2. Maurice Noel Ryder, b. 22 Dec. 1835; m. 25 Jan. 1860, Annie, dau. of James Lawrie, and d. 17 Dec. 1878, having had issue,
1. Maurice, b. 4 Oct. 1862; d. 18 March, 1867.
2. GERALD, now of the Island.
3. Otho, b. 22 July, 1866; d. 4 June, 1888.
1. Mary Frances Geraldine, m. 15 May, 1880, Claude W. de Lacey, J.P. co. Waterford, who resumed the prefix de 1880, son of William Lacey, of Bestwall, Wareham, Dorset, and has issue. one surviving dau.
2. Geraldine, b. Oct. 1867; d. Aug. 1868.
3. Nesta, m. 3 June, 1891, John Digby Gordon, Barrister-at-Law, of Agra, Southbourne Road, Boscombe, son of Capt. John Gordon, Bombay S.C., and has issue, two daus.
1. Olivia Mary Frances, d. young, 2 May, 1838.

He m. 2ndly, 1843, Hester, dau. of William Haddon. She d.s.p. 9 Jan. 1888. He d. 1879. His elder son,
GERALD CHARLES PURCELL FITZGERALD, of Little Island, co. Waterford, J.P., Lieut. Waterford Art. M.A., b. 1 Sept. 1833; d. 3 June, 1879, and was s. by his nephew, GERALD, now of the Island.

Arms—Quarterly 1st and 4th Arg. a saltire gu. a mullet on a crescent for difference (FITZGERALD) 2nd and 3rd Arg. a saltire between four boar's heads couped sa. (PURCELL), **Crests**—1. A monkey ppr. environed about the middle and chained or, a mullet on a crescent for difference (FITZGERALD). 2. A cubit arm holding a sword ppr. pommel and hilt or pierced through the jaw of a boar's head couped sa. vulned and distilling drops of blood, the sleeve az. turned up arg. (PURCELL). **Motto**—(Over the first crest) Crom a boo.

Seat—Little Island, Waterford. **Residence**—Mount Olivet, Duarte, California.

WILSON-FITZGERALD OF CHALCOMBE AND INCHOVEAGH.

WILLIAM HENRY WILSON - FITZGERALD, of Inchoveagh, co. Clare, and Chalcombe House, co. Northampton, J.P. and D.L. co. Clare, and High Sheriff 1882, J.P. for Northamptonshire, B.A. University Coll. Oxford, Barrister of the Inner Temple (1867), assumed by Royal Licence, in 1872, the additional surname and arms of FITZGERALD,
in compliance with the testamentary injunctions of his maternal grandfather, William Fitzgerald, of Adelphi, *b.* 22 April, 1844; *m.* 21 Nov. 1885, Isabella Olave, only dau. of the late Russell C. Stanhope, of Parsonstown Manor, co. Meath (see BURKE's *Peerage*, HARRINGTON, E.), and has issue,

FRANCIS WILLIAM, Lieut. 1st Royal Dragoons, *b.* 8 Dec. 1886.
Olave Clare, *b.* 11 Feb. 1888.

Lineage.—THEOBALD FITZGERALD an Officer in the Irish Brigade, *m.* Miss McDonough, of the co. Clare, and had a son,
GERALD FITZGERALD, of Kilcarragh, co. Clare, *m.* 1st, Anne Perreau, of Cork, by whom (who *d.* 1734) he had issue,
1. Theobald, *m.* Miss Comyn, and had an only dau., who *m.* L. O'Brien.
2. FRANCIS, of whom hereafter.
3. Maurice, *d.s.p.*
4. Garrett, *m.* Juliana, dau. of Patrick Kerin, and had four sons and three daus. From him descended Francis Alexander FitzGerald, Baron of the Exchequer in Ireland, and Right Rev. William FitzGerald, Bishop of Killaloe.

Mr. Fitzgerald *m.* 2ndly, Anne Grady, by whom he had no issue. He *d.* 1762, and was bur. in the Cathedral of Kilfenora. His 2nd son,
FRANCIS FITZGERALD, of Kilcarragh, *m.* Elizabeth, dau. of David Comyn, of Kilcoursey, and had issue,
1. WILLIAM, his heir.
2. George, *m.* Miss Foster, co. Galway, and left a son and two daus.
3. John, *d. unm.*
1. Elizabeth, *m.* William Eames.

The eldest son,
WILLIAM FITZGERALD, of Kilcarragh, J.P., *m.* 1783, Anne, dau. of John Powell, of Cloverville, co. Limerick, and grand-dau. of Robert Powell, of Newgarden, same co., by Anne his wife, dau. of Col. Samuel Eyre, M.P. for Galway, and Anne his wife, dau. of Robert Stratford, of Baltinglass, M.P., the grandfather of John, 1st Earl of Aldborough, by whom he had two sons,
1. FRANCIS JOHN, his heir.
2. WILLIAM, successor to his brother.

Mr. Fitzgerald *d.* 1789, and was *s.* by his eldest son,
FRANCIS JOHN FITZGERALD, of Adelphi, co. Clare, *b.* 27 Dec. 1785; *d. unm.* 1854, and was *s.* by his brother,
WILLIAM FITZGERALD, of Adelphi, J.P., High Sheriff, co. Clare, 1842, *b.* 1789; *m.* 8 May, 1817, Juliana Cecilia, dau. of Maurice Fitzgerald, of Lifford, by whom (who *d.* 23 June, 1823) he had issue,
1. Mary, *m.* 21 Feb. 1837, Lucius, 13th Baron Inchiquin, and *d.* 26 May, 1852, leaving issue (see BURKE's *Peerage*).
2. Anne, *m.* 5 Dec. 1836, Richard Bassett Wilson, of Cliffe Hall, co. York (see WILSON *of Cliffe Hall*), and *d.* 11 July, 1877, leaving by him (who *d.* 23 March, 1867), with other issue (see WILSON *of Cliff Hall*), a 2nd son,
WILLIAM HENRY, *s.* his grandfather, and assumed the name and arms of FITZGERALD.

Mr. Fitzgerald *d.* 17 Feb. 1872, and bequeathed Inchoveagh to his grandson, the 2nd son of his dau. Anne, upon condition of his assuming the additional surname of FITZGERALD.

Arms—Quarterly: 1st and 4th erm. on a saltire gu. a boar's head couped or, for FITZGERALD; 2nd and 3rd, per pale arg. and az. on a fess cotised three lion's gambs fesswise all counterchanged, for WILSON. **Crest**—1st, FITZGERALD: a boar pass. gu. bristled and armed or, charged with a saltire couped of the last; 2nd, WILSON: On a mount vert in front of a lion's head erminois a lion's gamb erased arg. **Motto**—Shannet a boo.

Seat—Chalcombe House, near Banbury. **Clubs**—New University and Kildare Street (Dublin).

FITZGERALD-KENNEY. *See* KENNEY.

FITZGERALD-LOMBARD. *See* KENNEY.

FITZGERALD.

See BURKE's PEERAGE, LEINSTER, D., FITZGERALD, Bart., and DE ROS, B.

FITZGERALD OF RATHGAR. *See* ROPER.

PENROSE-FITZGERALD. *See* BURKE's PEERAGE
PENROSE-FITZGERALD, Bart.

FITZGIBBON OF CROHANA.

MARY, MRS. FITZGIBBON, of Crohana, co. Kilkenny, 2nd dau. of John Rhind, of Elgin, N.B.; *m.* 1875, as his 2nd wife, Maurice FitzGibbon, of Crohana (who *d.* 1881), and has issue (*see below*).

Lineage.—DAVID FITZGIBBON, alias *Mac an tShen Ridire*, or the son of the old Knight, so mentioned in an inq. post mort. 39 Queen ELIZABETH, was descended from the line of THE WHITE KNIGHT. He had two sons, GERALD, and MAURICE, of Ballynahinch, co. Limerick. The elder, GERALD FITZGIBBON, alias *Mac an tShen Ridire*, so designated in an inq. post mort. *temp.* JAMES I, was possessed of Knocklong, Hamonstown, and Ballyscaddan, co. Limerick. He was dead *s.p.* in 1582, when he was *s.* by his brother, MAURICE FITZGIBBON, alias *Mac an tShen Ridire*, of Ballynahinch, who, not having joined in Desmond's rebellion, was allowed to inherit his brother's lands, some of which he mortgaged to Maurice Hurley, 17 Jan. 1600. He *m.* Sheela, dau. of John Burke, of Killenane, co. Limerick, and had two sons,
1. GIBBON, who *s.* him.
2. Gerald, who was enfeoffed in the lands of Ballyscaddan by his brother, 24 April, 1615; by Ellen his wife (who survived him, and was transplanted by Oliver Cromwell at 55 years of age) he had a son,
John, of Ballyscaddan, *b.* about 1623, who was transplanted by Oliver Cromwell, Dec. 1653, having, by Catherine his wife, also transplanted, one son, Garrett, *b.* about 1648, and six daus., all of whom were transplanted with their father, being under 12 years of age.

Maurice FitzGibbon *d.* 1 Oct. 1601, and was *s.* by his elder son,
GIBBON FITZGIBBON, alias *Mac an tShen Ridire*, of Ballynahinch, so designated in an inq. 19 Sept. 1616; *m.* Margaret, dau. of O'Grady, by his wife, a dau. of McCann, and had with five daus. (1st, *m.* John Burgh, of Dromkeen; 2nd, *m.* O'Heyn, of Cahirass; 3rd, *m.* O'Quirk, of Muskry O'Quirks; 4th, *m.* Thomas Butler, of Derryclooney; and 5th, *m.* William Roche, of the House of Viscount Fermoy), two sons,
1. Maurice, of Ballynahinch, who *s.* his father, and *m.* 1st, Onora, dau. of Maurice Hurley, of Knocklong, who *d.s.p.*, and 2ndly, Helen, dau. of Burgate, of Castle Burgate, co. Limerick, and sister of Most Rev. William Burgate, D.D., Catholic Archbishop of Cashel, by whom he had a son,
GIBSON, who *s.* him, *m.* Mary, dau. of John MacNamara, of Ralaghee, co. Clare, and had one son,
GERALD, who *m.* Ellinor, dau. of Mortogh Brien, of Aghaross, and had, with two daus., one son,
GERALD, an Officer in the service of the King of France, who was killed at the siege of Philipsburgh, 1734, *unm.*
2. DAVID, of Neddans, of whom hereafter.

Gibbon FitzGibbon, who built the Castle of Ballynahinch, was *s.* (as above) by his elder son, whose male line failed 1734, when the representation of this line devolved on the descendants of the 2nd son as follows,

DAVID FITZGIBBON, of Neddans, co. Tipperary, who was Capt. of a troop of Horse in Col. Grady's regiment, and in Col. William O'Brien's regiment, by Commission 1640, and Governor of Ardfinnan Castle, co. Tipperary, when Oliver Cromwell took Clonmel; being besieged by Ireton, he was compelled to surrender, but on honourable terms. He *m.* Joanna, dau. of Theobald Butler, of Ruscagh, co. Tipperary, by Elizabeth his wife, dau. of "The Great Commerford of Bally Birr," co. Kilkenny, and had issue,
1. MAURICE, of whom hereafter.
2. JOHN, *m.* Cecilia, dau. of James Hackett, of Orchardstown, co. Tipperary, and *d.* 3 Sept. 1731.
3. THOMAS, followed JAMES II abroad, and served under the King of France.
1. Ellen, *m.* Morgan Ryan, of Silvergrove, co. Clare, Town Major of Limerick, appointed for life by Commission from WILLIAM III.
2. Katherine, *m.* Henry Power, of Tickencor, co. Waterford.
3. Margaret, *d. unm.*

David FitzGibbon lived to a great age, and was remembered by persons living in 1751, as "Old Captain FitzGibbon." His eldest son,

FitzHerbert. THE LANDED GENTRY. 234

MAURICE FITZGIBBON, of Clashmore, was a Capt. of Foot under JAMES II, and his father, on his marriage, 1693, settled his lands on him. He m. Ellen, dau. of Philip McCraith, called "The Heir of Sleivoge," by Katherine his wife, dau. of Walter Butler, and had two sons,
1. GIBBON, of Clashmore, b. 1694; m. March, 1731, Anastacia, dau. of Philip Ronayne, of Ronayne's Court (by Grace his wife, sister of Sir Thomas Osborne of Tickencor, 4th bart. of Ballintaylor), and widow of James Uniacke, of Cornaveagh, and had issue,
  1. MAURICE, an officer in the Revenue *temp.* GEORGE II.
  2. John, a merchant at Lisbon, Portugal, had one son, David.
  3. David, for whom a memorial and genealogy of his family was drawn up by his cousin, Gerald FitzGibbon.
    1. Katherine, m. Pierce FitzGerald, of Ballykennelly, co. Cork.
    2. Ellen. 3. Margaret.
2. PHILIP, who eventually carried on the family.

Maurice FitzGibbon was killed, *vita patris*, by his cousin, Capt. Darby O'Grady, of Elton. His 2nd son,
PHILIP FITZGIBBON, of Castle Grace, served for many years in foreign military service, m. Aphra, dau. and co-heir of Robert Sargent, of Castle Grace, and had issue,
1. ROBERT, who s. his father at Castle Grace, and d. unm.
2. MAURICE, s. his brother at Castle Grace, and d. unm. 19 Dec. 1793.
3. John, of Youghal, who had two sons, Robert and Philip, and a dau. Ellen, m. Henry Miles.
4. GERALD, of whom hereafter.
1. Ellen, m. — Prendergast.
2. Alice, m. 1st, — Kelso, and 2ndly, John Allen.

Philip FitzGibbon, whose will is dated 26 Jan. 1734. was s. at Castle Grace by his eldest son (*as above*), which place eventually devolved on the 4th son,
GERALD FITZGIBBON, of Castle Grace, to which place he s. under the will of his brother Maurice. He m. Elizabeth, dau. of Rev. Buckworth Dowding, Rector of Kilworth, co. Cork, and had issue,
1. Maurice, of Castle Grace, m. Sarah O'Dell, of Limerick, and d. 1817, having had (with three daus., Mary Anne; Katherine; and Sarah, m. — Louch, of Molesworth Street, Dublin) four sons,
  1. Richmond Allen, Capt. Madras Army, m. three times, and d.s.p. 31 July, 1871.
  2. Maurice, b. 1808; went to sea when a boy and has never been heard of since.
  3. Philip, d.s.p. 4. Gerald, d.s.p.
2. PHILIP, of whom hereafter.
3. Robert, Capt. 3rd Regt. (the Buffs), d. unm. 1832.
4. William, Capt. 83rd Regt., d. unm. 14 Feb. 1868.
5. Gerald, Capt. 23rd Regt. (Fusiliers), m. Sarah Alcock, and d. 7 April, 1844, having had, 1. Richmond; 2. John; 3. William; 4. Gerald, Lieut. 59th Regt.; and 1. Mary; all of whom d. unm.
6. Thomas, of Rosscarbery, co. Cork; m. 1st, 1825, Maria, dau. of Rev. John Richard Smyth, of Downeen, co. Cork, by whom (who d. 1841) he had issue,
  1. Gerald, b. 17 Nov. 1826. 2. Thomas, b. 23 Nov. 1828.
  3. John Richard, b. 2 Aug. 1832. 4. Richard.
  1. Elizabeth Thomasina, b. 25 April, 1830.
  2. Maria, b. 2 May, 1836. 3. Dora.
He m. 2ndly, 10 Feb. 1844, Henrietta, dau. of John Stricker, of Frangenborg, in India, Major in the Danish Army, and d. 14 July, 1868, leaving by her,
  5. Frederick, b. 9 Nov. 1845.
  6. Philip, b. 11 March, 1853.
  4. Marianne, b. 1 March, 1848.
  5. Fanny, b. 20 Feb. 1850. 6. Henrietta, b. 19 April, 1851.
1. Mary Anne, m. Walter Payne, of Kilworth, co. Cork.

Gerald FitzGibbon d. 16 May, 1791. His 2nd son,
PHILIP FITZGIBBON, of Mount Eagle, near Kilworth, co. Cork, an Officer in the Navy, served for several years in the East Indian Seas, and under Lord Exmouth in the Mediterranean, A.D. 1810, and was 2nd Lieut. on board the *Ceylon* (36) at the blockade of St. Louis, Mauritius, when his ship had to surrender to the French frigate *Venus* (44), and a corvette (6). He m. Elizabeth, dau. of Abraham Coates, of Killinure, co. Wicklow, by Elizabeth his wife, dau. of Valentine Greatrakes, of Affane, co. Waterford, and had,
1. MAURICE, his heir.
2. Abraham, C.E., of The Rookery, Great Stanmore, co. Middlesex, and of Moorside, Bushey Heath, Herts, b. 23 Jan. 1823; m. 31 March. 1853, Isabelle, dau. of Cornelius Stovin, of Chestnut Grove, Kingston-on-Thames, co. Surrey, and d. 4 April, 1887, having had issue,
  1. Maurice, b. 1 Jan. 1854; d. 21 Sept. following.
  2. Gerald, b. 27 June, 1857; m. 3 Aug. 1887, Marguerite, dau. of Thomas Matthews, of Holderness, Yorks., and has issue,
    (1) Allen Fitz-Gerald, b. 14 Aug. 1888.
    (2) Desmond Fitz-Gerald, b. 1 Nov. 1890.
    (3) Marguerite Clare. (4) Geraldine.
  3. Robert, b. 27 Aug. 1859; m. Edith Rose, of Montreal, Canada, and has issue, two daus.
  1. Constance, b. 11 July, 1855; m. 1 July, 1880, James Grove White, of Kilbyrne, near Doneraile, co. Cork, Col. Middlesex Regt. (*see* WHITE *of Kilbyrne*).
  2. Florence, b. 19 Dec. 1865; m. 20 May, 1891, Lieut.-Col. B. E. Ward, 1st Batt. Middlesex Regt., elder son of Major Edmond Ward, 107th Regt.
1. Elizabeth, d. unm. 15 Sept. 1825.
2. Mary Anne, m. Samuel Dudgeon, of Dublin.

Mr. FitzGibbon d. 1826, and was s. by his elder son,

MAURICE FITZGIBBON, of Crohana, co. Kilkenny, b. 16 April, 1818; m. 1st, 16 Feb. 1858, Isabella, dau. of Rev. John Stronach, by whom (who d. 12 Nov. 1874) he had issue,
1. PHILIP JOHN, of Poona, Bombay, b. 2 Dec. 1859; m. 26 Aug. 1884, Ruth Mary, dau. of M. Hearn, co. Cork, and has issue,
  1. Maurice Desmond, b. 23 May, 1895.
  1. Isabella Marion.
  2. Norah Ruth, d. in infancy.
  3. Irene Fraser. 4. Sybil Clare.
  5. Esme.
2. Maurice Coates, b. 31 Jan. 1862.
3. Arthur, b. 4 May, 1864.
4. Richmond, b. 30 June, 1869; d. 1887.
1. Elizabeth Anne, b. 27 May, 1860.
2. Blanche, b. 10 April, 1866.
3. Edith Jessie, b. 16 July, 1867.
4. Isabelle Geraldine, b. 1 Aug. 1870.
5. Ellen, b. 17 March, 1872.

Mr. FitzGibbon m. 2ndly, 4 Dec. 1875, MARY, now of Crohana, dau. of John Rhind, of Elgin, N.B., and by her had issue,
5. John Brenton, b. 22 Nov. 1876; m. 9 June, 1909, Elsie Elizabeth, only dau. of G. Montillon, of Fort Erie, Ontario, Canada, and has issue,
  John Ord, b. 30 June, 1910.
6. Archibald Coates, b. 29 Dec. 1878.

Mr. FitzGibbon d. 25 Feb. 1881, and was s. by his widow.

Arms—Erm., a saltire gu., on a chief arg., three annulets of the second. **Crest**—A boar pass. gu. charged with three annulets, in fess arg. **Motto**—Honore integro contemno fortunam.

Seat—Crohana, near Stonyford, co. Kilkenny.

FITZHERBERT OF BLACK CASTLE.

RICHARD RUXTON FITZHERBERT, of Shantonagh, co. Monaghan, and of Black Castle, co. Meath, J.P. co. Meath, D.L. co. Monaghan, High Sheriff 1880, b. 13 Sept. 1841; m. 3 Oct. 1865, Elizabeth Sophia, eldest dau. of the late Hugh Lyons Montgomery, of Belhavel, co. Leitrim, and has issue,
1. RICHARD RUXTON WALTER, Major 4th Batt. Leinster Regt., J.P. co. Meath, b. 9 Sept. 1866; m. 9 Dec. 1897, Violet Caroline, twin-dau. of James Moffat, D.L., of Elm Lodge, Windsor.
2. Bertram Richard Edward, b. 12 Jan. 1871.
1. Gladys Lilian Ruxton.

Lineage.—WILLIAM FITZHERBERT, of Shercock, co. Cavan, 2nd son of William FitzHerbert, 3rd Lord of Swynnerton (*see* FITZHERBERT *of Swynnerton*), by Anne, dau. of Sir Basil Brooke, Knt. of Madeley, co. Stafford, m. the only child of Henry Pierce, of Pierce Court, or Shercock, co. Cavan and had issue,
WILLIAM FITZHERBERT, of Shercock, who m. (settlements dated 2 Nov. 1703) Anne, dau. of Ven. Archdeacon Andrew Carleton, of Kilmore, and had issue, three sons, William, Andrew, and Arthur, who all d.s.p.; and five daus., Frances, m. Rev. Richard Richards; Anne, m. Robert Ker; Amelia, d. unm.; Mary, m. Rev. William Whittingham; and
LETITIA, m. JOHN RUXTON, M.P., of Ardree, co. Louth, and by him (who d. 14 Sept. 1785) had three sons and two daus.,
1. WILLIAM RUXTON, of Ardee House, co. Louth, and Shercock, co. Cavan (*see* RUXTON *of Ardee*).
2. JOHN, of Black Castle, co. Meath, m. 1770, Margaret, dau. of Richard Edgeworth, of Edgeworthstown, co. Longford, and d. July, 1825, aged 80, having had issue,
  1. Fitzherbert, Capt. 63rd Regt., d. 1799.
  2. RICHARD, who assumed the name of FITZHERBERT, of Black Castle, co. Meath, b. 3 Aug. 1775; m. 10 Jan. 1807, Elizabeth Selina, 3rd dau. of Sir Robert Staples, Bart., of Dunmore, Queen's Co., by the Hon. Jane Vesey, sister of Thomas, 2nd Viscount de Vesci.
    1. Sophia, who assumed the name of FITZHERBERT.
    2. Margaret.
  3. Samuel, of Swynnerton, co. Meath, who assumed the surname of FITZHERBERT, and d.s.p. 1826.
  1. Mary, m. James Corry, of Shantonaugh, co. Monaghan, and had a dau., LETITIA CORRY, who m. 23 Jan. 1810, THOMAS ROTHWELL, of Rockfield, co. Meath (*see* ROTHWELL), and was mother of Thomas Fitzherbert, of Black Castle.
  2. Anne.

The late
THOMAS FITZHERBERT, of Black Castle and Shantonagh, J.P. and D.L., High Sheriff co. Monaghan 1841 (son of Thomas Rothwell

and L itia Corry his wife as above), assumed, by Royal Licence, 19 Sep. . 1863, the surname and arms of FITZHERBERT in lieu of those of ROTHWELL. He was b. 18 Sept. 1814; m. 3 May, 1838, Frances Sydney, dau. of the Hon. and Rev. Arthur Vesey, Rector of Abbey Leix, Queen's Co., 2nd son of Thomas, 1st Viscount de Vesci, and by her (who d. 20 Sept. 1908) had issue,
1. RICHARD RUXTON, his heir.
2. Sidney Arthur, b. 12 Aug. 1843; d. 1900.
3. Arthur Vesey, b. 10 June, 1845; m. 19 March, 1873, Eveline Clemina Lyons, 4th dau. of Hugh Lyons Montgomery, of Belhavel, and has, with other issue,
   1. Arthur Hugh Francis, b. 5 Feb. 1874.
   2. Lambert De Winton Beresford William, b. 1 June, 1877.
   1. Alda Ethel Constance, b. 16 Sept. 1875.
4. Henry Corry, of Millbrook, Abbey, Leix, Queen's Co., J.P. co. Monaghan, b. 1 May, 1847; m. 19 Jan. 1876, Mary Emily, dau. of Col. Vansittart, Cordstream Guards, and has, with other issue, Arnold Vesey, b. 18 March, 1878.
   Edith Clare, b. 3 Feb. 1877; m. 8 July, 1897, Arthur Mildmay Hall-Dare, 2nd son of the late R. W. Hall-Dare, of Newtownbarry, and has issue (*see that family*).
5. William Nugent, b. 29 May, 1849; d. 19 May, 1851.
6. Edward George Corry, b. 27 June, 1856; d. 30 June, 1870.
7. Hubert Vesey, b. 19 July, 1862; d. *unm.* 11 Feb. 1888.
1. Selina Letitia.
2. Edith Emily Marguerite, m. 7 Oct. 1896, Clifford Lloyd, of Victoria Castle, Killiney.
Mr. Fitzherbert d. 29 April, 1879.

Arms—Arg., a chief vair or and gu., over all a bend sa. charged with a crescent of the field. *Crest*—A dexter cubit arm erect the hand clenched armed and gauntleted all ppr. charged with a crescent gu. *Motto*—Ung je serviray.

Seat—Black Castle, Navan; Shantonagh, Castle Blayney.

LINDSEY-FITZPATRICK OF HOLLYMOUNT.

HEREMON JOHN FRANCIS HEADFORD LINDSEY-FITZPATRICK, of Hollymount, co. Mayo, J.P. and D.L., High Sheriff 1889, who adopted the additional surname of LINDSEY, b. 1860; m. 1st, 1885, Mary Georgiana Cecilia Katherine, dau. and heir of Thomas Spencer LINDSEY, of Hollymount. She d. 5 Nov. 1895. He m. 2ndly, 25 July, 1908, Grace Agnes, widow of Col. Henry L'Estrange Malone (*see* MALONE *of Baronston*), and dau. of Francis Brooke, of Summerton (see BURKE's *Peerage*, BROOKE, Bart.). He is 3rd son of Rev. Frederick and Lady Olivia Fitzpatrick, of Bert, co. Kildare (see BURKE's *Peerage*, HEADFORT, M.).

Lineage.—THOMAS LINDSEY, a younger son of Thomas Lindsey, of Turin Catle, co. Mayo, and a descendant of the great Scottish House of Lindsay, m. 1757, Frances Muschamp Vesey, grand-dau. of Dr. John Vesey, Archbishop of Tuam, and had an only son,
THOMAS LINDSEY, of Hollymount, m. 1784, Lady Margaret Eleanor Bingham, dau. of Charles, 1st Earl of Lucan, and by her (who d. 27 May, 1839) had issue,
1. THOMAS SPENCER, of Hollymount.
2. Charles Richard, R.N., who was lost in the *Blenheim* 1807, with Sir Thomas Trowbridge.
3. William Henry Bingham, Lieut. 10th Hussars, at Waterloo, d. in India 1822.
1. Margaret Louisa, m. the Rev. J. G. Porter, eldest son of John Porter, D.D., Bishop of Clogher.
2. Anne, m. the Hon. and Rev. J. G. Browne, brother of Lord Oranmore.
3. Eleanor, m. James Reed, and d. 1840.
4. Emily, m. the Rev. Edmund Dowdney, and d. 1855, leaving issue.
5. Louisa.
The eldest son,
THOMAS SPENCER LINDSEY, of Hollymount, J.P. and D.L., High Sheriff 1822, b. 31 July, 1799; m. 11 May, 1818, Margaret Hester, only dau. of Richard Alexander Oswald, of Auchencruive, co. Ayr, and by her (who d. 1855) had issue,
1. Richard Alexander, an Officer in the Army, b. 15 March, 1823, dec.
2. THOMAS SPENCER, late of Hollymount.
1. Lucy, m. 26 June, 1851, George Ramsay Campbell.
2. Anne Eleanor Matilda Nina, m. 4 Nov. 1841, Baron Godefroy de Blonay, of Vernaud, in the Canton de Vaud, Switzerland. She d. 1871.
3. Hester Elizabeth Frances, m. 1864, Francis Ruttledge, son of the late Francis Ruttledge, of Bloomfield, co. Mayo.
4. Lillias Margaret Jane.   5. Katharine Mary, d. 1872.
Mr. Lindsey d. 21 Dec. 1867, and was s. by his 2nd son,
THOMAS SPENCER LINDSEY, of Hollymount, J.P. and D.L., Major South Mayo Rifles, b. 7 May, 1828; m. 6 April, 1864, Mary Catherine Caroline, 2nd dau. of George Hayward Lindsay, of Glasnevin, co. Dublin, and by her (who d. 8 Feb. 1881) had issue, MARY GEORGIANA CECILIA KATHERINE, his heir.
Mr. Lindsey d. 14 July, 1874.

Seat—Hollymount House, Hollymount, co. Mayo.

FITZPATRICK.
See BURKE's PEERAGE, **CASTLETOWN, B.**

WENTWORTH-FITZWILLIAM.
See BURKE's PEERAGE, **FITZWILLIAM, E.**

FLANAGAN OF RATHFUDAGH.

JOHN WOULFE FLANAGAN, of Rathfudagh, co. Roscommon, B.A., Barrister-at-Law, J.P. co. Sligo, High Sheriff co. Roscommon 1881, b. 6 April, 1852; m. 29 April, 1880, Maria Emily, 2nd dau. of the late Sir Justin Sheil, K.C.B., and by her (who d. 9 Jan. 1888) has issue,
JOHN HENRY, b. 10 Nov. 1881.
Jane Mary, b. 21 Dec. 1883.

Lineage.—TERENCE FLANAGAN, of St. Catherine's Park, Leixlip, son of John Flanagan, of Clogher, co. Roscommon, by Winifred Coyne his wife, m. May, 1813, Johanna, dau. of Stephen Woulfe, of Tiernaclane, co. Clare, and sister of the Lord Chief Baron Woulfe, and by her (who d. Jan. 1837) left at his decease, Jan. 1846, three sons
1. JOHN WOULFE, his heir.
2. STEPHEN WOULFE, of whom presently.
3. Terence Woulfe, m. 1848, Jane Hembden, and d. Dec. 1859.
The eldest son,
JOHN WOULFE FLANAGAN of Drumdoe, J.P. and D.L., High Sheriff 1851, b. 21 Aug. 1815; m. 14 Sept. 1848, Susan, 2nd dau. of Right Hon. Sir Michael O'Loghlen, Bart., Master of the Rolls in Ireland, and d.s.p. 28 Sept. 1869. His brother,
THE RIGHT HON. STEPHEN WOULFE FLANAGAN, M.A., J.P., a Bencher of King's Inns, b. 1817; m. Feb. 1851, Mary Deborah, dau. of John R. Corballis, LL.D., Q.C., and by her (who d. 8 Jan. 1886) had issue,
1. JOHN WOULFE, his heir.
2. Stephen Woulfe, J.P. co. Sligo (*Lecarrow, Boyle*), b. 14 Feb. 1854; m. 19 Oct. 1898, Eleanor Emily Gertrude, youngest dau. of Hugh MacTernan, J.P. and D.L., of Heapstown, co. Sligo (*see that family*), and has issue,
   1. Stephen Hugh James, b. 9 Feb. 1900.
   2. Henry Richard Joseph, b. 24 March, 1903.
   1. Frances Mary.
3. Terence, m. 17 Nov. 1892, Margaret Hester Wentworth, only dau. of Rev. William J. Loftie, and has issue,
   Barbara, b. 28 Feb. 1896.
4. James.   5. Richard.
6. Edward.
1. Johanna.   2. Jane.
3. Mary.   4. Frances, d. *unm.* 4 July, 1898.
5. Elizabeth.
This distinguished judge was called to the Irish Bar in 1838, made Q.C. 1859, appointed Judge of the Landed Estates Court in 1869, and sworn of the Privy Council of Ireland in 1876, and of Great Britain in 1885. He d. 6 Dec. 1891.

Residence—21, Tedworth Square, Chelsea.

SOLLY-FLOOD OF BALLYNASLANEY HOUSE.

MAJOR ARTHUR SOLLY-FLOOD, D.S.O., of Ballynaslaney House, co. Wexford, Major 4th Dragoon Guards, b. 28 Jan. 1871; s. his father 25 Nov. 1909.

Lineage.—FRANCIS FLOOD, of Burnchurch, M.P. for Callan 1703-5 and 1713-27, b. about 1660; m. June, 1692, Anne, only dau. and heir of John Warden, of Burnchurch, by Ann, his wife, dau. of Sir John Otway, Knt., of Ingmire Hall, Westmorland, and d. 1730, having had issue,
1. WARDEN, his successor.
2. John, of Farmley, co. Kilkenny, M.P., m. Jane, only dau. and heir of — Crompton, co. Wexford, and d. 16 Sept. 1774, leaving issue,

Flood. THE LANDED GENTRY. 236

1. JOHN, of Flood Hall, of whom presently.
2. FREDERICK (Sir), of Newton Ormond, co. Kilkenny, and Banna Lodge, co. Wexford, King's Counsel, Custos Rotulorum, and M.P. for co. Wexford, created a Baronet, 3 June, 1780. He m. 1st, 31 May, 1765, Lady Juliana Annesley, dau. of Richard, 6th Earl of Anglesey, who d.s.p. 1774 ; and 2ndly, May, 1769, Frances, dau. of Sir Henry Cavendish, 1st bart. of Doveridge, and d. 1 Feb. 1824, having by her had an only surviving dau., FRANCES, m. 1st, Sept. 1799, Richard Solly, of Walthamstow, and York Place, London, by whom (who d. 1803) she had issue,

   1. FREDERICK, her heir, of Ballynaslaney House, co. Wexford, J.P., M.A., Barrister-at-Law, who assumed, by Royal Licence, dated 14 Oct. 1818, the additional surname and arms of FLOOD, b. 7 Aug. 1801 ; m. 21 Aug. 1824, Mary, dau. of Rev. Thomas Willamson, Rector of Stoke Dameral, Devonport, and grand-dau. of Sir Hedworth Williamson, Bart., of Whitburn Hall, co. Durham, and d. 13 May, 1838, having by her (who d. 1864) had issue,
     a. EDWARD THOMAS SOLLY-FLOOD, of Ballynaslaney House, co. Wexford, J.P., b. 3 April, 1827 ; m. 28 May, 1853, Marianne, youngest dau. of Capt. James Harvey, of Kyle, and d. 1897, having by her (who d. 1896) had issue,
       (a) Frances Mary, m. 27 June, 1877, Philip Vandeleur Beatty, only son of David V. Beatty, of Borodale, co. Wexford, J.P., by Charlotte his wife, dau. of H. Alcock, of Wilton Castle, co. Wexford, J.P. and D.I..
       (b) Julia Anne Adelaide.
       (c) Kate, m. Willoughby H. Ross, H.M.C.S.,Melbourne, Australia.
       (d) Florence Mary.   (e) Ethel Dora.
     b. FREDERICK RICHARD (Sir), of Ballynaslaney House.
     c. Ferdinand Henry, Lieut. R.N., d. unm. 23 Feb. 1862.
     d. James Douglas Musgrave, d. unm.
      a. Frances Henrietta, m. John George Cockburn Curtis, and d. 8 Oct. 1896.
      b. Mary Frederica, m. 1st, Alfred Hohenlohe Patterson, son of Francis William Patterson, of Leamington Priors ; 2ndly, Frederick Brewster, d. 1906.
      c. Julia Anne Adelaide.
   1. Frances Elizabeth, m. 22 Oct. 1821, Sir George Ralph Fetherston, 3rd bart. of Ardagh, and d. 24 March, 1864.
   2. Caroline Jane, m. 8 Sept. 1821, Samuel Bradstreet Hore, of Lamberton, co. Wicklow, Capt. R.N., son of William Hore, of Harperstown, co. Wexford.

Mrs. Solly m. 2ndly, 1806, John Harward Jessop, of Doory Hall, co. Longford, and had further issue (see JESSOP of Doory Hall).

   1. Elizabeth, m. William Walsh.
   2. Sarah, m. Oct. 1760, Christopher Hewetson, and d. 1769.
   3. Catherine, m. 1st, Rev. James Myhill ; 2ndly, Aug. 1761, John Murray-Prior.

3. Francis, of Paulstown Castle, co. Kilkenny, J.P., High Sheriff, m. by licence dated 6 Sept. 1734, Frances, dau. of Col. Henry Hatton, of Great Clonard, co. Wexford, M.P., and had, with a dau., Frances, m. Aug. 1774, Monsieur Jacques Bethome de la Mothe, six sons,
   1. WARDEN, LL.D., M.P., Judge of the High Court of Admiralty, Ireland, from 1790 to 1794 ; m. 21 Aug. 1761, Anne, dau. of Morgan Donovan, of Ballincalleh, co. Cork (whose grandson Rev. Morgan Donovan, became O'DONOVAN in 1829), and had issue,
     (1) Warden, who predeceased his father, unm.
     (2) Francis, a Capt. in the Army, d. unm.
     (3) HENRY, of Paulstown Castle, b. 1769 ; m. 2 Sept. 1815, Anna Maria, dau. of Henry Lennon, and dying Nov. 1840, left issue,
       1. WILLIAM, of Paulstown Castle, J.P., b. 7 April, 1818 ; d. 1855.
       2. Charles, d. 12 July, 1848.
       1. Henrietta, of View Mount, Whitehall, Kilkenny, and of Paulstown Castle, d. unm. 15 Nov. 1901.
       2. Isabella, m. 26 Sept. 1853, Henry Flood, of Rutland Square, Dublin, who d. 1877, leaving issue. She d. 8 Dec. 1895.
     (4) O'Donovan, an Officer in the Army, served in Flanders under the Duke of York, at the sieges of Gibraltar and Minorca, m. Dec. 1800, Mademoiselle Anne Vignau, niece of the Comtesse de la Motte, Maid of Honour to MARIE ANTOINETTE, and left issue,
     WARDEN HATTON, an Officer in the Army, m. 21 April, 1835, Mary Grove, eldest dau. of Lieut.-Gen. the Hon. Arthur Grove Annesley, and niece of Earl Annesley, and d.s.p. in 1882.
     Marianne, m. Henry Oswald Smithe, E.I.C.S.
     (1) Marianne, m. Rev. Stuart Hamilton, of Tyrone, brother to Gen. Sir John Hamilton, Bart.
   2. Hatton, Col. 1st Dragoon Guards, d. unm.
   3. Henry, of View Mount, a Major in the Army, m. 15 March, 1770, a dau. of John Perkins, of Ballenshaine, co. Carlow, and had, with two daus., Frances and Mary, a son and heir,
     John, of Viewmount, Clerk of the Peace, co. Kilkenny, d. 12 Feb. 1850 ; m. by licence dated 7 March, 1797, Joanna, dau. of James Brushe, by Barbara Mitchell, his wife, and had issue surviving,
       1. John, Barrister-at-Law, m. 16 Dec. 1845, Jane, dau. of Thomas Clarke, and had issue.
       2. Henry, of Rutland Square, Dublin, m. 26 Sept. 1853, his cousin Isabella, dau. of Henry Flood, of Paulstown,

and d. 1877, having had issue, Henry, b. 1857, d. 1867 ; Frances Maud, m. 4 July, 1877, John Edward Hasell, of Dalemain. She d. his widow, 23 Dec. 1911.
   1. Elizabeth, m. 1829, Major John Stoyte, of the 24th Regt.
   2. Anne Augusta, m. John Galway Holmes, Barrister-at-Law.
4. Francis, m. 22 Feb. 1762, Dorothy, dau. of — Armstrong and had a son, Henry, who m. by licence, dated 26 Nov. 1780, Katherine Barton, of Kells, co. Kilkenny, and left issue.
   5. John (Rev.).   6. Charles.
4. Charles, of Ballymack, co. Kilkenny, d. unm., will dated 11 Oct. and proved 4 Nov. 1770.
5. Henry (Rev.), m. by licence, dated 2 July, 1773, Ann Baxter, co. Kilkenny, and d.s.p.
6. George (Rev.), D.D., Rector of Rathdowny, Queen's Co., d. 12 Sept. 1771 ; m. 1st, 1735, Anne Candler ; and 2ndly, by licence, dated 11 Feb. 1744, Frances Heydon, and had issue (his will is dated 5 Nov. 1770),
   1. Francis Warden (Rev.), Vicar of Inistioge, d. 28 Oct. 1817 ; m. Miss Palmer, and had an only child, Mary, m. 20 Oct. 1792, Richard Rothe, of Cappagh, and had a son, George Rothe-Flood.
   2. Richard.   3. William.
   1. Isabella.   2. Jane.
   3. Mary, m. 25 April, 1772, William Palmer, of Sragh, Queen's Co.
7. Richard, d. unm.   8. William, d. unm.
1. Anne, m. Ven. Henry Candler, Archdeacon of Ossory, and Rector of Callan.

The eldest son,

THE RIGHT HON. WARDEN FLOOD, of Flood Hall, a very distinguished lawyer, was Chief Justice of the Court of King's Bench of Ireland. He m. Miss Isabella Whiteside, by whom (who d. 13 Nov. 1778, aged 80) he had issue,
   1. HENRY, his heir.
   2. Warden Jocelyn, M.P. for Callan, d. unm. 1767.
   1. Isabella.

He d. 1764, and was s. by his son,

THE RIGHT HON. HENRY FLOOD, of Farmley, co. Kilkenny, This eminent person was b. 1732, and d. Dec. 1795, leaving behind him the character of one of the first statesmen of the age in which he lived. He m. 13 April, 1762, the Lady Frances Maria Beresford, dau. of Marcus, 1st Earl of Tyrone, but d.s.p. He devised his extensive estates to Dublin College for the encouragement of the Irish language, but those estates, after procrastinated litigation, reverted to his cousin and heir-at-law,

JOHN FLOOD, of Flood Hall, co. Kilkenny, son of John Flood, M.P., of Farnley (see above). He m. 31 Oct. 1770, Elizabeth, dau. of Boyle Aldworth, of Newmarket, co. Cork (see that family), by Jane his 1st wife, dau. of Robert Oliver, of Cloughnodfoy, and had issue,
   1. JOHN, his heir.   2. Robert, of Farnley, d. unm.
   1. Elizabeth.

Mr. Flood was s. at his decease by his elder son,

JOHN FLOOD, of Flood Hall, J.P. and D.L. for co. Kilkenny, who m. by licence, dated 30 Jan. 1811, Sarah, eldest dau. of the Right Hon. William Saurin, Attorney-General for Ireland, but d. without issue.

We now return to

MAJ.-GEN. SIR FREDERICK RICHARD SOLLY-FLOOD, K.C.B., of Ballynaslaney House, co. Wexford, Chief of the Staff in Egypt 1885-6, formerly Commandant Royal Military College, Sandurst, b. 19 March, 1829 ; m. 7 April, 1863, Constance Eliza (Porthmawr, Crickhowell, Breconshire), elder dau. of the late W. E. Frere, C.M.G., and d. 25 Nov. 1909, having had issue,
   1. Frederick Frere, b. 1867 ; d. 20 July, 1906.
   2. ARTHUR, now of Ballynaslaney.
   3. Richard Elles, Capt. Rifle Brigade.
   1. Constance Mary.

Arms—Quarterly : 1st and 4th, vert, a chevron, between three wolves' heads erased arg., for FLOOD ; 2nd and 3rd, arg. a chevron gu. between three sole fishes hauriant ppr. within a border engrailed sa., for SOLLY. Crest—A wolf's head erased arg. Motto—Vis unita fortior.

Seat—Ballynaslaney House, Kyle, co. Wexford. Residence—Porthmawr, Crickhowell, Breconshire. Club—Army and Navy.

HANFORD-FLOOD. See HANFORD.

FLOWER. See BURKE'S PEERAGE, ASHBROOK, V.

FOOT, formerly OF THE ROWER.

EDWARD GEORGE FOOT, of The Rower, co. Kilkenny, b. 24 Sept. 1870; m. 18 July, 1901, (Annie Emilie) Irene, dau. of Rev. Lundy Edward William Foote, Vicar of St. Peter's, Harrogate.

Lineage.— JOHN FOOT, son of Samuel Foot, b. in Devonshire 1668, came to Ireland in Lord Drogheda's Regiment, and was at the Battle of the Boyne. He left three sons,
1. JEFFERY, of whom presently.
2. James, of Limerick, d. March, 1770, leaving an only child, Jeffery, who d.s.p. April, 1827.
3. Robert.

The eldest son,
JEFFERY FOOT, of Dublin, b. 1704; m. 1st, 13 April, 1732, Jane, dau. and heir of James Lundy, of Ringsend (who d. 14 Aug. 1750, aged 106). She d. 2 Nov. 1745, having had, with other issue, who d. young,
1. James, b. 18 May, 1734; d. young.
2. LUNDY, of whom presently.
3. Stephen, b. 15 Dec. 1738; m. twice, and d. Oct. 1778, leaving issue,
  1. Stephen, d.s.p. 22 Aug. 1814.
    1. Christian, m. Feb. 1802, Mark Kerr.
    2. Elizabeth, m. Edward Clarke.
4. Simon, Lieut.-Col. 23rd Fus., Major 73rd Foot, b. 1740, d. unm. at Port-au-Prince, St. Domingo, 1795.
  1. Christian, m. July, 1769, Bernard Russell.

He d. 3 March, 1773, having married a second time. His eldest surviving son,
LUNDY FOOT, of Dublin, and afterwards of The Rower, co. Kilkenny, Darver, co. Louth, Salestown, co. Meath, and Orlagh, co. Dublin, which estates he purchased. He was Alderman of Dublin, and was fined for Sheriff, b. 16 April, 1735; m. 3 June, 1758, Catherine, dau. of Thomas Williams. She d. 26 March, 1810. He d. 2 Jan. 1805, leaving four sons and five daus.,
1. Jeffery, of Holly Park, co. Dublin, Alderman of Dublin, m. 1 Jan. 1791, Jane, dau. of James Williams, of Trammount, co. Meath. She d. 5 April, 1865. He d. 2 Sept. 1824, leaving six sons and four daus.,
  1. Lundy (Rev.), M.A. Dublin, Rector of Longbredy and Prebendary of Netherbury in Terra, Salisbury, m. 1st, 7 Nov. 1817, Elizabeth, dau. of Thomas Vicars, of Brownsford, co. Kilkenny. She d. 17 March, 1825, leaving three sons,
    (1) Jeffery Robert (Rev.), M.A. Camb., Vicar of Hanbury, m. 25 June, 1850, Louisa Maria, only dau. of Charles Montague Williams. She d. 22 Nov. 1874. He d.s.p. 1893.
    (2) Thomas Vicars, m. 10 March, 1845, Mary, dau. of John Paterson, Surgeon R.N., and d. 1889, leaving issue,
      1. Jeffery Vicars, d. young.
      2. Thomas Vicars, m. 1878, Jessie, dau. of — Cussons, and has issue, with four daus., two sons,
        a. Hedley Vicars, b. 1883.
        b. Rupert Vicars, b. 1887.
      3. Richard Vicars, m. 1875, Jane, dau. of — Robinson, and has issue, three sons and five daus.
    (3) Richard Gorges (Rev.), M.A. Dublin, Rector of Horton, m. 1850, Maria Louisa, dau. of John Samuel Swire, and d. 22 Nov. 1874, leaving a son,
      John Vicars (Rev.), M.A. Oxon, m. 18 Jan. 1888, Margaret Ada, dau. of William Hallam Elton, Commander R.N., and has issue, with three daus., a son,
        Richard Christopher Gorges, b. 22 Aug. 1894.

The Rev. Lundy Foot m. 2ndly, 28 Nov. 1827, Harriet, eldest dau. of Rev. John William Cunningham, Vicar of Harrow. He d. 5 Jan. 1873, having by her had issue,
  (4) Cunningham Noel (Rev.), B.A. Camb., Rector of Dogmersfield, m. 15 Jan. 1861, Sophia Maria, dau. of Rev. Richard Fayle, and has issue, six sons and a dau.
    (1) Sophia Elizabeth, m. 23 July, 1857, Montague Williams, of Woodland, Dorset, and is dec.
    (2) Ellen, dec.
    (3) Jane Olivia, d. unm. 8 Jan. 1908.
    (4) Louisa, dec.
2. James, M.A. Dublin, m. Letitia, dau. of Edward Barclay Glascock, and d. 2 Oct. 1866, leaving issue.
3. Simon, M.A. Dublin, J.P. co. Dublin, m. Aug. 1827, Mary Anne, dau. of Edward Barclay Glascock, and d. 1 Nov. 1873, leaving issue.
4. Jeffery, B.A. Dublin, d. unm.
5. Frederick (Rev.), M.A. Dublin, Rector of Fethard, co. Tipperary, m. 15 July, 1831, Sophia, dau. of Joseph Pemberton, and d. 23 Nov. 1871, leaving issue.
6. William, J.P. co. Kildare, m. 17 Dec. 1836, Margaret Esther, only dau. of John Revell, of Sea Park, co. Wicklow, and d. 19 March, 1902, leaving issue.

  1. Letitia, m. 1831, Rev. John Magee.
  2. Catherine Elizabeth, m. 7 Nov. 1827, Rev. William Magee.
  3. Louisa, m. 23 June, 1831, Rev. Joseph Callwell, Archdeacon of Clogher.
  4. Cecilia Eleanor, d. unm. 3 Oct. 1873.
2. LUNDY, of whom presently.
3. James, of Banville, co. Down, J.P., m. Nov. 1795, Sophia Isaac, dau. of Jeremiah D'Olier, of Collenges, co. Dublin, and d. 24 Sept. 1836, leaving issue.
4. Randal, Capt. 6th Dragoon Guards, who d. 15 Jan. 1841, having had issue, a son,
  Randal, Lieut. 5th Northumberland Fus., m. 17 Sept. 1835, Emily Florence, dau. of Lieut.-Col. Allen, R.A. She d. 12 Feb. 1902. He d. April, 1885, having had, with other issue,
    Lundy Edward William (Rev.), Vicar of St. Peter, Harrogate, Yorks, m. 25 Dec. 1867, Ann, dau. of Sir John Barran, Bart., and has issue,
      1. Harold (Rev.), b. 1870.
      2. Douglas, b. 1872.
      3. Charles Llewellyn, b. 1873; d. 1904.
      4. William Leslie, b. 1875; d. 1911.
      5. Trevor Mawdesley, b. 1877.
      6. Courtenay, b. 1878.
      1. Annie Lilian, m. 1898, John Bates Dester.
      2. Annie Emilie Irene, m. 18 July, 1901, her cousin, Edward George Foot, of The Rower (see above).
1. Elizabeth, m. 9 March, 1805, Rev. John Webb.
2. Jane, m. 14 May, 1791, Joseph Dickinson.
3. Martha.
4. Christian, m. 3 May, 1806, William Henry Maunsell.
5. Amelia, m. 26 Oct. 1796, George Darley.

The 2nd son,
LUNDY FOOT, of Rosbercon Castle and the Rower, co. Kilkenny, and Orlagh, co. Dublin, J.P. for both cos., B.A. Dublin, called to the Bar, King's Inns, 1788; b. 24 Oct. 1764; m. 29 Oct. 1790, Anne, dau. of William Gilbert, of Dublin. She d. 1 March, 1844. He was murdered at Rosbercon, 2 Jan. 1835, having had issue,
1. LUNDY EDWARD, of whom presently.
2. Simon Charles (Rev.), M.A. Dublin, Rector and Vicar of Knocktopher and Prebendary of Aghour, b. 8 June, 1808; m. 1st, 12 Jan. 1836, Matilda Frances, dau. of Robert James Enraght-Moony, of The Doon, King's Co. (see that family). She d. 23 Sept. 1838, leaving an only child,
  1. Robert James Matilda, b. Sept. 1838; m. 1st, 15 July, 1861, Elizabeth, dau. of John Hutchinson, of Kiltorkan, co. Kilkenny. She d.s.p. 18 Dec. 1861. He m. 2ndly, 24 Sept. 1863, Harriet, dau. of George Rideout, of Toronto, Canada, and d. 23 Nov. 1868, leaving three daus.

The Rev. S. C. Foot m. 2ndly, 29 Oct. 1840, Maria, dau. of Lieut.-Gen. Charles Turner. She d. 30 Nov. 1887. He d. 3 June, 1885, having by her had, with three daus., who d. unm., three sons,
  2. Charles Edward, Capt. R.N., b. 24 July, 1841, m. 5 Nov. 1873, Fanny Anne Jones, dau. of George Hammond Whalley, M.P. for Peterborough, and d. 16 Aug. 1884, having had issue,
    (1) Edward Hammond Whalley, b. 23 June, 1881.
    (2) Charles Laurence John Kirk, b. 14 Aug. 1884.
    (1) Lois, m. 31 March, 1910, Bertram F. Buck.
    (2) Anne Claudia Whalley, m. 8 Dec. 1909, Hon. Kenneth Robert Dundas, 4th son of 6th Viscount Melville (see BURKE'S Peerage).
  3. George Portlock, b. 10 Dec. 1850; d. unm. 25 July, 1874.
  4. Frederick Robert, b. 28 Nov. 1853; m. Nov. 1883, Kate, dau. of Robert Bramble, and has issue,
    (1) Harold Frederick Charles, Assist. Paymaster R.N., b. 1886.
    (2) Robert George Marmaduke, b. 29 Sept. 1887.
    (1) Georgina Maria, m. 19 July, 1911, Harold Bishop Mylchreest.
1. Catherine, m. 22 Dec. 1829, Francis Moony Enraght-Moony, of The Doon, and d. 19 Oct. 1877, leaving issue (see that family).

The eldest son,
LUNDY EDWARD FOOT, of The Rower, co. Kilkenny, and Fitzwilliam Street Dublin, B.A. Dublin, called to the Bar, King's Inns, 1817, m. 22 Aug. 1791; m. 22 Feb. 1819, Lelias, dau. of Nathaniel Callwell, of Fitzwilliam Square, Dublin, and Toneen, co. Longford. She d. 25 Aug. 1852. He d. 18 Aug. 1863, having had issue, with others who d. young,
1. Charles Henry, Scholar Trin. Coll. Dublin, B.A. 1855, called to the Bar, King's Inns 1856, b. 2 Oct. 1831; d. unm. 19 Dec. 1870.
2. Arthur Wynne, M.D. Dublin, F.K.Q.C.P.I., L.R.C.S.I., b. 22 Jan. 1838; m. 7 Aug. 1866, Hannah Georgina (who d. 27 Aug. 1911), dau. of Edward Hunt, of Belmore, co. Kilkenny, and d.s.p. 1 Sept. 1900
3. ALFRED GEORGE, of whom presently.
1. Maria Isabella, m. 3 Aug. 1852, Peter Burtchaell, of Kilkenny (see BURTCHAELL of Brandondale). She d. 18 March, 1898. He d. 21 June, 1894, leaving issue three sons and three daus.
2. Lelia Margaret, d. unm. 16 June, 1862.
3. Elizabeth Charlotte, d. unm 4 June, 1904.
4. Emily Jane, d. unm. 6 April, 1908.

The 3rd son,
ALFRED GEORGE FOOT, of The Rower, Lieut. R.E., b. 12 Jan. 1840; m. 1st, 7 Sept. 1865, Jessie Sykes, dau. of William Senhouse Gaitskell. She d. 9 Oct. 1873, having had issue,
1. Charles Alfred, b. 30 Dec. 1867; d. 27 May, 1868.
2. EDWARD GEORGE, now of The Rower.
1. Edith Mary Sykes, m. 12 May, 1905, Capt. Thomas H. Heming, R.N.

Foott. THE LANDED GENTRY.

He *m.* 2ndly, 7 Oct. 1882, Emily, dau. of John Porter. He *d.* 6 Dec. 1900, and was *s.* by his only surviving son.
Arms—Per chevron arg. and or three martlets az. *Crest*—A martlet az. charged on the breast with a cross humettée or. *Motto*—Spes mea Deus.
Residence—

FOOTT OF CARRIGACUNNA CASTLE.

GEORGE CARLETON FOOTT, of Carrigacunna Castle, co. Cork, J.P., *m.* 16 July, 1891, Elizabeth Alexandra Louise (who *d.s.p.* 18 July, 1910), dau. of Thomas O'Grady, J.P.
Lineage.—GEORGE FOOTT, of Milford, co. Cork, living *temp.* WILLIAM III, *m.* Deborah Wade, of Athy, co. Kildare, and had issue,
1. RICHARD, of Millford, his heir.
2. Thomas, of Springfort, *m.* 1734, Miss Pedder, and had issue,
   1. George, of Springfort, *d.s.p.*
      1. Thomasine, *d. unm.* 2. Deborah, *d. unm.*
   3. Ann, *m.* her cousin James Foott.
   4. Martha, *m.* 1778, J. H. Spratt, of Ballybeg.
3. Wade, *m.* Olivia, dau. of Capt. Calcott Chambre (*see* CHAMBRE *of Dungannon*), and had issue,
   1. George, *m.* Miss Dunscombe, and had, (1) Wade; and (2) Richard.
   2. Wade, *m.* Margaret, dau. of Edmund Nash, of Ballyteige, co. Limerick, and had a son, Wade, *m.* Ann, dau. of Michael Scanlan, and had issue.
   3. James, *m.* 1782, his cousin Ann, dau. of Thomas Foott, of Springfort, and *d.* 1838, aged 89, having had a son,
      Thomas Wade, of Baltidaniel, bapt. 1784; *m.* Mary, dau. of Walter Atkins, of Atkinville, and had issue,
      1. James, of Springfort, co. Cork, *m.* 28 June, 1842, Henrietta Ann, dau. of Henry Lumsden, of Auchindric, co. Aberdeen, and *d.* at Sydney, New South Wales, March, 1873, leaving issue.
         a. Thomas Wade, residing in Buntre, New South Wales, *b.* at Springfort, 13 June, 1843; *m.* 1st, Oct. 1874, Mary Hannay, eldest dau. of James Black, of Vynzala, South Brighton, Victoria, Australia, and *d.* 2 Feb. 1884, leaving issue,
         (a) CECIL HENRY, Capt. Royal Australian Eng. (*Lytton, Queensland*), *b.* 16 Jan. 1876; *m.* 15 Oct. 1901, Isabel Agnes, eldest dau. of G. T. McDonald, of Rocklea, Queensland, and has issue,
            a. Thomas Allan Brudenell, *b.* 14 May, 1904.
            b. Celia Mary Lumsden, *b.* 19 Oct. 1902.
         b. Sydney, *b.* 22 July, 1908.
         (b) Arthur Patrick, *b.* 29 March, 1879.
      b. Henry Lumsden,
         a. Katherine Tower. *b.* Mary Elizabeth.
         c. Henrietta Ann. *d.* Roberta Margaret Rolleston.
   2. Walter, *d. unm.* 3. Thomas, *d. unm.*
   4. John, Lieut.-Col. in the Army, *m.* Eliza Anne, dau. of George Thompson, Capt. 16th Lancers.
   5. William, *m.* and left issue.
      1. Catherine, *m.* 1834, Capt. Thomas Herrick, of Coolkerkey (*see* TABUTEAU-HERRICK *of Shippool*).
      2. Ann, *d. unm.* 3. Mary, *d. unm.*
      4. Susan, *d. unm.*
The eldest son,
RICHARD FOOTT, of Millford, *m.* Julet, dau. of Cornelius O'Callaghan, and had issue, a son and heir,
RICHARD FOOTT, of Millford, co. Cork, Col. of North Cork Militia, *m.* Oct. 1771, Mary, dau. of Henry Baldwin, of Curryvody and Mount Pleasant, co. Cork, by Alice his wife, sister of Sir Robert Warren, and by her (who *d.* 1841) left issue,
1. GEORGE, of Millford, bapt. 1772; *d.* 1814.
2. HENRY BALDWIN, late of Carrigacunna Castle.
3. Edward, of Gortmore, bapt. 1787; *m.* Ellen Charlotte, dau. of Cornelius O'Callaghan, of Cork, and has issue.
   1. Edward, *b.* 17 Feb. 1827, M.D., *m.* 1862, his cousin Mary, dau. of Richard O'Callaghan, of Killeenleigh, co. Cork, and *d.* 1874, having had issue.
   2. Richard Leslie, *b.* 11 March, 1829; *d.* Jan. 1860.
   1. Frances O'Callaghan.
   2. Ellen O'Callaghan, now of Gortmore.
   3. Mary Baldwin, *m.* Joseph Verling Carpenter, of Eden Hill.
1. Barbara, *m.* 1814, Thomas Edward Spratt, of Pencil Hill, and *d.* 1858, leaving issue (*see* SPRATT *of Pencil Hill*). He *d.* 21 Oct. 1833.
2. Mary Anne, bapt. 1787; *m.* Rev. Browning Drew, and *d.* 1822, leaving issue.
3. Alicia, *d. unm.* 1823.
Mr. Foott *d.* 1820, and was *s.* by his son,
HENRY BALDWIN FOOTT, of Carrigacunna Castle, co. Cork, bapt. 1778, J.P., *m.* Jane, eldest dau. of Rev. Edward Mitchell Carleton, of Woodside, co. Cork, by Elizabeth his wife, only child and heiress of William Withers, and by her (who *d.* 17 Dec. 1873) had issue,
1. Henry, *d.* 9 Jan. 1862, aged 25.
2. Carleton, *d.* 2 July, 1856, aged 15.
3. GEORGE CARLETON, now of Carrigacunna Castle.
1. Eliza Louisa, *m.* 13 July, 1854, her cousin Richard Spratt, of Pencil Hill, and has issue (*see that family*). He *d.* 1885, and she *d.* 26 Sept. 1893.
2. Mary Georgina.
3. Penelope Jane, *d.* 1 Oct. 1852, aged 17.
4. Henrietta Victoria, *d.* 29 Aug. 1864.
5. Emily, *m.* Edward Carleton Warren, only son of Edward Townsend Warren, 90th Regt.
6. Lucinda Harriette, *m.* Major Arthur Cook, 14th Regt.
Seat—Carrigacunna Castle, Killavullen, co. Cork.

FORBES. *See* BURKE'S PEERAGE, **GRANARD, E.**

FORDE OF SEAFORDE.

MAJ. WILLIAM GEORGE FORDE, of Seaforde, co. Down, J.P. and D.L., High Sheriff 1909, late Major 5th Batt. Royal Irish Rifles, served in S. Africa 1901-2, *b.* 7 March, 1868; *s.* his uncle 1902; *m.* 16 April, 1898, Sylvia Dorothea, only dau. of late Major A. F. Stewart, Inniskilling Dragoons, and has had issue,
1. THOMAS WILLIAM, *b.* 11 Feb. 1899.
2. Desmond Charles, *b.* 26 Feb. 1906.
1. Sylvia, *b.* and *d.* 20 Feb. 1904.
2. Cynthea Dorothea, *b.* 15 March, 1907.
Lineage.—NICHOLAS FORDE, of Coolgreany, co. Wexford, claiming Welsh extraction, *b.* 1605, leaving by his wife, Catherine White, five sons, of whom the 2nd,
MATHEW FORDE of Dublin, M.P., *s.* to the estates. He *d.* before the year 1657, leaving his only son,
NICHOLAS FORDE, of Killyleagh, co. Down, *m.* Elizabeth, dau. of Sir Adam Loftus, Knt. of Rathfarnham, and left an only son,
MATHEW FORDE, of Coolgreany, M.P. for co. Wexford, *m.* Margaret, dau. of Sir George Hamilton, Bart. (4th son of James, 1st Earl of Abercorn), by Mary Butler his wife, dau. of Thomas, Lord Thurles, and sister of James, 1st Duke of Ormonde. Mr. Forde left at his decease, 1709 (with two daus., the eldest of whom, Lucy, *m.* 1695, Sir Laurence Esmonde, Bart. of Ballynestra; and the younger, Jane, *m.* John Walsh, of Shanganah) an only son,
MATHEW FORDE, of Seaforde, M.P. for Downpatrick, *m.* 1698, Anne, dau. of William Brownlow, of Lurgan, and had,
1. MATHEW, his heir.
2. Francis, of Johnstown, co. Meath, Col. in the Army, distinguished in Lord Clive's wars in India, *m.* 1748, Margaret, dau. of Thomas Bowerbank, of Culgaita, Cumberland, and left issue.
3. Arthur, Rector of Lurgan, *m.* Alice Baillie, and *d.* 1767, leaving with other issue,
   1. James, ancestor of Fforde, of Raughlan (*whom see*).
   2. Matthew, merchant of Liverpool, who *m.* Frances Barton, and *d.* 1767, leaving one son, Arthur Brownlow (Rev.), M.A., Rector of Maghull, who left issue, a son, Arthur William, C.E., *m.* 5 Nov. 1846, Ada Emelia, dau. of Rev. Andrew O'Beirne, LL.D. She *d.* 31 Aug. 1873, leaving issue, Arthur Brownlow, *b.* 25 Sept. 1847; (*m.* 10 March, 1869, Mary Carver, dau. of Rev. G. U. Pope, D.D., and has issue.
1. Jane, *m.* John Baillie, of Inishargie.
2. Letitia, *m.* Mr. Nash. 3. Margaret, *d. unm.* 1773.
Mr. Forde *d.* 1729, and was *s.* by his eldest son,
MATHEW FORDE, of Seaforde and Coolgreany, M.P. for Bangor. He *m.* 1st, 1724, Christian, dau. of John Graham, of Platten, co. Meath, by whom he had issue; and 2ndly, Jane, relict of Sir Timothy Allen. He *d.* 1780, and was *s.* by his eldest son,
MATHEW FORDE, of Seaforde and Coolgreany, M.P. for Downpatrick, *m.* 1750, Elizabeth, dau. of Thomas Knox, of Dungannon, and sister of Thomas, 1st Viscount Northland, and had issue,
1. MATHEW, his heir.
1. Anne, *d. unm.*
2. Elizabeth, *m.* 1785, Thomas Douglass, of Grace Hall, co. Down, and *d.* 1840.
3. Jane, *m.* 1796, John Christopher Beauman, of Hyde Park, co. Wexford.
4. Charity, *m.* 1795, William Brownlow, of Lurgan, M.P. for co. Armagh; *d.* 1843.
Mr. Forde *d.* 1796, and was *s.* by his only son,
MATHEW FORDE, of Seaforde and Coolgreany, High Sheriff co. Down 1803, *m.* 1782, Catherine, eldest dau. of the Right Hon. William Brownlow, of Lurgan, M.P. for co. Armagh, and by her (who *d.* 1808) had issue,
1. MATHEW, his heir.
2. WILLIAM BROWNLOW, *s.* to his brother.
3. Thomas Arthur, Assistant Barrister, cos. Down and Roscommon, *m.* 1814, Louisa, 9th dau. of Michael Head, of Derry, co. Tipperary, and *d.* April, 1840, having had issue,
   1. Thomas Head, *d.s.p.*
   2. Mathew Bligh, Gen. R.A., *d.s.p.*
   3. Henry Charles, *d.* 1897. 4. John Vesey.
   5. Arthur Knox, Commander R.N., *b.* 1830; *d.* 7 June, 1906.
   6. Francis Clayton Octavius, *d.s.p.*
   7. Frederick Augustus Prittle, *d.s.p.*
   1. Catherine Margaret, *d.s.p.*
   2. Frances Mary Anne, *m.* 1835, Thomas Blacker, and *d.* 1863.

4. Arthur, *m.* Selina, dau. of William Blundell, and *d.* in India, 1828, leaving issue, now all dec.
  1. Mathew, *d.s.p.* 2. William.
  3. Arthur, *d.s.p.*
5. Francis Charles, late Capt. Royal Scots Greys, *m.* Letitia Jane, youngest dau. of O. Jones, of Woodhall, co. Norfolk; *d.* 1864.
  1. Anne, *m.* 1st, 1816, Francis Hoey, of Dunganstown, co. Wicklow, and by him (who *d.* 1818) had issue; and 2ndly, 1825, Capt. George King, R.N., and *d.* 1859, having had further issue.
  2. Isabella Jane Octavia, *m.* 1821, Clayton Bailey, of Norelands, co. Kilkenny, and *d.* 1865.

Mr. Forde *m.* 2ndly, 1811, Sophia, dau. of the Very Rev. Stewart Blacker, of Carrick, Dean of Leighlin, but by her (who *m.* 2ndly, 1818, William Stewart Hamilton, of Brown Hall, and *d.* 1829) he had no issue. He *d.* 1812, and was *s.* by his eldest son,

MATHEW FORDE, of Seaforde and Coolgreany, *b.* 1785, J.P. and D.L. for co. Down, Col. of the Royal North Down Militia, High Sheriff 1820, and M.P. for co. Down from 1821 to 1826. Col. Forde *m.* 1st, 1814, Mary Anne, only child of Francis Savage, of Hollymount, and Ardkeen, co. Down; and 2ndly, 1829, Lady Harriet Savage, 3rd dau. of Henry Thomas Butler, 2nd Earl of Carrick, and widow of Francis Savage; she *d.* 25 July, 1865. H *d.s.p.* 5 Aug. 1837, and was *s.* by his brother,

THE REV. WILLIAM BROWNLOW FORDE, of Seaforde, *b.* 1785; *m.* 7 Oct 1812, Theodosia Helena, dau. of Thomas Douglass, of Grace Hall, and by her (who *d.* 1875) had issue,
  1. Matthew Thomas, *b.* 17 May, 1816, an Officer in the Army, High Sheriff of Downshire 1840; *d.* May, 1847.
  2. WILLIAM BROWNLOW (Right Hon.), late of Seaforde.
  3. Francis Savage, *d.* 6 July, 1859.
  4. Charles Arthur, *b.* 24 June, 1828, Major Royal South Down Militia; *d.* 1872.
  5. Thomas Douglass, late Major 46th Regt., *b.* 10 Dec. 1830; *m.* 6 July, 1858, Georgina (*d.* 20 June, 1887), dau. of Capt. G. King, of St. Brendan's, co. Dublin. She *d.* 1887. He *d.* 27 July, 1897, leaving issue,
    1. WILLIAM GEORGE, now of Seaforde.
    1. Annie Helena Kathleen Elizabeth, *m.* 26 Oct. 1892, Lieut.-Col. Cameron Deane Shute, Rifle Brigade, and has issue, a dau. Noel Georgina Deane.
    2. Adeline Frances, *m.* 30 April, 1907, Capt. Raymond Andrew Nugent, R.N., son of the late Gen. Charles Nugent.
  1. Selina Charity, *m.* 24 Feb. 1857, the Rev. J. H. Freke, Rector of the parish of Saul, co. Down; *d.* 1870.
  2. Elizabeth Theodosia Catherine, *m.* 16 Dec. 1863, Capt. William Hall, R.A., of Narrow Water, co. Down, and *d.* 18 May, 1866, leaving issue (*see that family*).
  3. Harriette Anna, *m.* 8 March, 1859, Sir John Allen Johnston Walsh, Bart.

Mr. Forde *d.* 11 March, 1856, and was *s.* by his 2nd son,

THE RIGHT HON. WILLIAM BROWNLOW FORDE, of Seaforde, co. Down, P.C., Lieut.-Col. of the Royal South Down Militia from Nov. 1854 until 1881, when he was appointed Hon. Col. of the Regt. now the 5th Batt. Royal Irish Rifles, J.P. and D.L., High Sheriff 1853; M.P. for co. Down from 1857 to 1874; *b.* 5 Nov. 1823; *m.* 25 Oct. 1855, Adelaide, dau. of Gen. the Hon. Robert Meade, 2nd son of the 1st Earl of Clanwilliam. She *d.s.p.* 5 Sept. 1901. He *d.* 8 Feb. 1902.

Seat—Seaforde, Clough, co. Down. *Club*—Carlton.

FORSTER OF SWORDS.

COL. JAMES FITZEUSTACE FORSTER, of Swords, co. Dublin, J.P. and D.L., late Duke of Cornwall's L.I., *b.* 27 Sept. 1834, served in Egyptian Expedition 1882, Souakim Exped. 1884, and in Nile Exped. 1884-5. Col. Forster is the only son of the late Josiah M. Forster, of St. Croix, West Indies, by Jane Elizabeth his wife, dau. of Christopher Taylor, of Swords House, co. Dublin.

Seat—Swords House, co. Dublin.

FORSTER. *See* BURKE'S PEERAGE, **FORSTER**, Bart.

FORTESCUE OF STEPHENSTOWN.

MATTHEW CHARLES EDWARD FORTESCUE, of Stephenstown, co. Louth, J.P. and D.L., High Sheriff 1903, late Major 6th Batt. Royal Irish Rifles, *b.* 6 July, 1861; *m.* 1894, Edith Magdalen, eldest dau. of Sir Charles Arthur Fairlie - Cuninghame, 10th Bart. (*see* BURKE'S *Peerage*).

Lineage.—This is a cadet branch of the FORTESCUES *of Dromiskin* (from whom descended the EARLS of CLERMONT, and the late LORD CLERMONT AND CARLINGFORD).

WILLIAM FORTESCUE, of Newragh, co. Louth, younger son of SIR THOMAS FORTESCUE, of Dromisken (*see* BURKE'S *Peerage*, CARLINGFORD, B.), *m.* Margaret, dau. and heiress of Nicholas Gernon, of Miltown, co. Louth, and *d.* 1734, leaving with other issue, a 3rd son,

CAPT. MATTHEW FORTESCUE, R.N., who *m.* 14 Jan. 1757, Catherine Doogh, and had (with a dau. Catherine, *m.* Rev. John Fortescue) a son,

MATHEW FORTESCUE, of Stephenstown, *m.* 1 Jan. 1787, Mary Anne, eldest dau. of John McClintock, of Drumcar, M.P. (*see* BURKE'S *Peerage*, RATHDONNELL, B.), and had issue,
  1. MATHEW, his heir.
  1. Anna Maria, *m.* 1817, Sir George Forster, Bart., D.L., M.P. (*see* BURKE'S *Peerage*). 2. Harriet, *d.* young.
  3. Emily, *b.* 1797; *m.* 11 Nov. 1818, J. Harvey Thursby, of Abbington Abbey, co. Northampton, and *d.* 1870, leaving issue by him, who *d.* 1860 (*see* BURKE'S *Peerage*, THURSBY, Bart.).

The only son,

MATHEW FORTESCUE, of Stephenstown, D.L., *b.* 3 Sept. 1791; *m.* 1811, Catherine Eglantine, eldest dau. of Col. Blair, of Blair, M.P., and had issue,
  1. Mathew Charles, *d.* in infancy.
  2. JOHN CHARLES WILLIAM, his heir.
  3. Frederick Richard Norman, *b.* 11 July, 1823, Major Bengal S.C.; *m.* 6 Nov. 1860, Marion Jane, eldest dau. of Gen. Garstin, Comm. R.E., Bengal, and *d.* 14 Sept. 1867, leaving by her (who *d.* 13 June, 1901) issue,
    1. MATTHEW CHARLES EDWARD, now of Stephenstown.
    2. Frederick Richard Norman, *d.* in infancy.
    1. Kathleen Mary Geraldine, *m.* 1894, Eastwood J. J. Biggar, jun., of Falmore Hall, Louth.
  4. William Hamilton, *b.* 17 Dec. 1824; *d.* unm. 1858.
  5. Clermont Mathew Augustus, *b.* 22 March, 1829; *d.* 1834.

Mr. Mathew Fortescue *d.* 22 Jan. 1845, and was *s.* by his son,

JOHN CHARLES WILLIAM FORTESCUE, of Stephenstown and Corderry, Lieut.-Col. R.A., J.P. and D.L. co. Louth, High Sheriff 1861, Vice-Lieut. of Louth 1868-79, *b.* 17 April, 1822; *m.* 1857, Geraldine Olivia Mary Anne (who *d.* 1883), dau. of Rev. Frederick Pare, by the Hon. Geraldine de Rose his wife (*see* BURKE'S *Peerage*, DE ROS, B.), and *d.s.p.* 1891, when he was *s.* by his nephew,

Arms—Az., a bend engr. arg. cotised or. **Crest**—An heraldic tiger, ppr., supporting with his fore-paw, a plain shield arg. *Motto* —Forte scutum, salus ducum.

Seats—Stephenstown, Dundalk, co. Louth, and The Cottage, Wymondham, Oakham.

FOSBERY OF CLORANE.

GEORGE RALPH FOSBERY, of Kilgobbin, co. Limerick, J.P., *b.* 25 Sept. 1854; *m.* 19 April, 1888, Clara Elizabeth (who *d.* 1904), dau. of G. Urmston Blennerhasset, of Riddestown Park, co. Limerick.

Lineage.—FRANCIS FOSBERY, of Kilcooly, co. Limerick, whose will is dated 20 May, 1700, left issue by Mary his wife,
  1. FRANCIS, his heir; 2. William; and 1 Sarah. The elder son,

FRANCIS FOSBERY, of Clorane, co. Limerick, whose will is dated 18 June, 1717, left by Bridget his wife, four sons, and five daus. The 3rd son,

WILLIAM FOSBERY, of Kildimo, co. Limerick, *m.* Jane, dau. of Frank Evans, and had issue, three sons and three daus.,
  1. GEORGE, of whom presently.
  2. Francis, of Curraghbridge, co. Limerick; *m.* 16 March, 1773,

Fosbery. THE LANDED GENTRY. 240

Philippa, dau. of John Godfrey, of Bushfield, and sister of Sir William Godfrey, 1st bart., and d. 4 March, 1810, leaving issue,
1. George, of Curraghbridge, co. Limerick, b. 24 Dec. 1774; m. 12 May, 1812, Caroline, dau. of Richard Yielding of Clogher, co. Kerry, and had issue,
  (1) Francis George, of Blennerville, co. Kerry, and of Curraghbridge, co. Limerick, b. 9 March, 1813; m. 1st, 1841, Sarah Eleanor Wilhelmina (d. 5 July, 1861), only dau. of William Humphrey Smith, of St. Cronans, co. Tipperary, and had issue, nine daus.,
    1. Eleanor Josephine, m. 1st, 26 Aug. 1866, Robert Henry Eyton; 2ndly, Robert Nightingale.
    2. Frances Caroline.
    3. Laura Adela, dec., m. Frank Ronalds, New Zealand.
    4. Florence Emily, d. 1886; m. John B. Miley.
    5. Mary Augusta, m. Henry Widenham Maunsell, M.D.
    6. Philippa Anna, m. Richard Nancarrow.
    7. Sarah Gertrude, m. 1888, Sir James Mills, K.C.M.G.
    8. Eva Constance, m. George Michael Nation.
    9. Emma Clarence, m. Charles Cargill Kettle, Co. Court Judge, New Zealand.
  He m. 2ndly, Margaret Anna, dau. of Langer Carey, M.D., of Chinfield, Newport, co. Tipperary, and had three sons and a dau.,
    1. George Francis William, b. 9 June, 1869; m. Vivian de Burgh Lewis, and has three sons,
      a. Frank George Widenham.
      b. Gordon Widenham.
      c. Norman Widenham.
    2. Francis Yielding, dec., m. Helen Cox.
    3. Henry Percival.
    10. Ethel Mary, m. Samuel Turner, d.
  (2) Richard, b. 22 Nov. 1818; d. unm.
    (1) Catharine, a nun.
    (2) Anna Philippa, m. Oliver William Mason, of Aghamore.
    (3) Caroline Elizabeth
    (4) Jane Agnes, m. Joseph Smith, of St. Cronans, co. Tipperary, and had issue.
    (5) Elizabeth Barbara, m. Col. Charles P. Taylor, H.E.I.C.S., son of Lieut.-Gen. Henry Taylor, C.B., and had issue.
  2. William, b. 22 July, 1781; m. 1807, Elizabeth, dau. of — Goff, of Carrigfoy, co. Kerry, and d. 1851, having had issue, William, m. Jane Scott, and d.s.p.
  3. Francis, b. 9 Nov. 1784; m. 1808, Elizabeth, widow of John Creagh, and dau. of Charles Widenham, of Castle Widenham, and d. 28 Nov. 1859, having had issue,
    (1) Charles Widenham, of Castle Grey, co. Limerick, m. Elizabeth, dau. of — Wybrants, and had issue,
      1. Widenham Francis, of Mosstown, Westmeath, b. 13 Jan. 1837; m. 26 Nov. 1863, his cousin Mary, 2nd dau. of William Charles Fosbery (see below). She d. 5 May, 1902. He d. 5 Feb. 1889, having had issue,
        a. Charles Widenham (Dalewood, Micklcham, Dorking), b. 20 May, 1867; m. 27 Nov. 1902, Lucie Gwendaline, eld. dau. of the late David Evans, of Dalewood, Dorking.
        b. Arthur Champagné Widenham, b. 12 June, 1868; m. Feb. 1899, Ethel, dau. of the late Col. Thomson, Indian Staff Corps, and has issue,
          Charles Champagné Widenham, b. 1 July, 1900.
        c. Widenham Francis Widenham, C.M.G., b. 4 Oct. 1869; m. 20 Sept. 1898, Alice Martha, dau. of the late Surg.-Gen. Lamprey, and has issue,
          Francis Charles Widenham, b. 24 July, 1899.
        d. Gustavus Widenham, d. young.
        e. William Charles Widenham, b. 16 Sept. 1873; m. 23 Jan. 1908, Lily, 2nd dau. of W. A. Doyle, of Beulah Manitoba, and has issue,
          Phyllis Mary Carroll, b. 15 Jan. 1909.
        f. Forbes George Stephen Wybrants Widenham, b. 15 Dec. 1874.
        g. George Frederick Widenham, b. 2 Dec. 1882.
          a. Beatrice Widenham.
          b. Lilian Mary Widenham.
          c. Hilda Mary Widenham.
      1. Mary Letitia, m. 26 Aug. 1866, S. Scott.
      2. Augusta, m. Aug. 1877, Capt. J. C. Grant.
      (1) Frances, m. F. Parsons.
      (2) Mary Anne, m. Dr. Evans, of Limerick, and had issue.
      (3) Elizabeth, m.
  4. Henry in the Army, b. 11 Jan. 1789; m. 1820, Jane, dau. of — Westropp, and d.s.p.
  5. Godfrey, Capt. R.N., b. 24 Sept. 1791; m. 21 Aug. 1823, Catherine Lyons, dau. of John Walcott, of Croagh, co. Limerick, and had issue,
    (1) Francis Godfrey, d. unm.
    (2) John Walcott, m. Isabel, dau. of — Lightfoot, and had issue,
      1. Godfrey Montague, b. 1866.
      2. Edmund Walcott.   3. John Leslie.
      1. Muriel Isabel.   2. Edith Kate.
      3. Lilian Ethel.
    (3) Matthew Deane, m. Julia, dau. of Joseph Swannell.
    (4) George William (Rev.), Rector of Collingham, Notts, M.A. Camb., b. 23 June, 1832; m. 20 Aug. 1863, Frances, dau. of Charles Sanderson Sanderson, and has issue,
      1. Charles Sanderson, b. 1865.
      2. Gerald Walcott, b. 1867; m. 30 June, 1897, Alice Georgina Eveleigh, dau. of George Plater, of Riversfield, Erith, and has issue, a son and two daus.,
      3. Francis George, b. 1870; m. 4 March, 1897, Laura, dau.

of Alick Osborne, of Moss Vale, N.S.W., and has issue, a dau.
    4. Godfrey Lyons, b. 1874.
    5. Cyril Vincent, b. 1878; m. 23 July, 1907, Gertrude Charlotte, dau. of William Tritton, of Caistor, Lincs.
    6. George William b. 1881.
      1. Catherine Sanderson.
      2. Elizabeth Simpson.
      3. Mabel.
      4. Susannah Kathleen.
    (5) Edmund Walcott, C.M.G., Inspector-Gen. of Police, New South Wales (Sydney, Australia), b. 6 Feb. 1834; m. 26 Aug. 1856, Harriette, dau. of — Lightfoot, and has issue,
      1. Godfrey Walcott, d. unm.
      2. Eustace Edmund, b. 1859.
      3. Vincent Frank, b. Feb. 1866.
      1. Dora Ellen. m. W. A. Gordon, and has issue.
      2. Ada Kate, m. Richard Ernest Horsfall.
      3. Mabel Lucy, m. Consett Davis.
    (6) Edward Godfrey, m. Ann Melicent, dau. of — Bennet.
    (7) Charles Godfrey, d. an infant.
      (1) Dorothy Mary, m. Joseph Swannell.
      (2) Catherine Philippa, d. unm.
      (3) Susanna Lyons, d. unm.
      (4) Elizabeth Henrietta, d. an infant.
    1. Barbara, b. 24 Feb. 1776; m. 8 April, 1795, her cousin, Richard Parsons, and d. 1850, having had issue.
    2. Jane, b. 22 Feb. 1777; m. George Langford, of Marino, Kenmare.
    3. Letitia, b. 24 May, 1778; m. David Jameson, and d. 1854.
    4. Elizabeth, b. 4 June, 1780; m. 4 May, 1809, her cousin George Fosbery, of Clorane (see below).
    5. Philippa, b. 31 Oct. 1786; m. — Champagné.
    6. Anne, b. 20 April, 1790.
  3. William, b. 29 Sept. 1753; m. 1st, 29 April, 1779, Margaret, dau. of Richard Hoops, and by her (who d. 1801) had issue,
    1. William, b. 29 Oct. 1782; m. Maria, dau. of W. Ingleby, and had issue,
      (1) William Charles, of Everton, Liverpool, b. 1808; m. 1837, Mary Louisa, dau. of — Chawner, and had issue,
        1. Maria Louisa, m. Charles Mervyn Richardson, and had issue.
        2. Mary, m. 26 Nov. 1863, her cousin Widenham Francis Fosbery, of Mosstown (see above).
        3. Alice Margaret, m. 3 Feb. 1898, Rev. Joseph Cullen, M.A., Vicar of St. Matthew, Upper Clapton.
      (2) George Langford, of Pentremawr, co. Denbigh, b. 19 April, 1818; m. 1st, 1850, Eliza, dau. of — Butcher, and by her had issue,
        1. William George, b. 31 Aug. 1852; d. young.
        2. Norman, b. 3 Aug. 1859.
      Mr. G. L. Fosbery m. 2ndly, 31 March, 1864, Mary Anna Maria, dau. of James Wilson, of Brincliffe Tower, Sheffield, and d. 28 March, 1879, having by her had issue,
        3. Henry James Wilson, b. 24 Feb. 1867.
        4. Francis Langford, b. 29 April, 1870.
        5. Charles Leslie, b. 8 June, 1873.
        6. William Ingleby (Rev.), b. 28 Aug. 1874; d. unm. 21 Oct. 1903.
          1. Agnes Janette, b. 5 Jan. 1865; m. 18 May, 1892, A. E. Gerard.
          2. Elizabeth Maria, d. young.
          3. Ada Margaret, b. 4 May, 1868.
          4. Georgina Mary, b. 18 Nov. 1871.
      (1) Margaret, m. 1851, M. J. McCreight.
      (2) Emma, m. 1833, W. D. Wheeler, and has issue.
      (3) Annie, d. unm.
      (4) Maria, m. 1835, Samuel Butcher, of Endcliffe, Sheffield, and d. 1893, leaving issue.
      (5) Frances, m. 1843, J. C. Ferguson, M.D., of Liverpool, and had issue,
      (6) Agnes, m. 1856, George Pim.
    2. Alexander, b. 9 Nov. 1783; d. young.
    3. George, b. 12 Sept. 1787; d. unm.
    4. Francis, b. 7 Nov. 1791; m. Meliora, dau. of Rev. William Rose, of Adare, and had issue,
      (1) Francis, d. unm.
      (2) William, m. 1st, Esther, dau. of — Biss, and had issue,
        1. William Hubert Sayle, M.D., m. 7 June, 1898, Norah Mary Close.
      He m. 2ndly, Rebe, dau. of — Davies, and left further issue,
        2. Francis Clifford, M. D.
        1. Meliora Georgina, m. 1895, Dr. John Jarvis.
      (3) Frederick Richard.
        (1) Emily.
        (2) Maria.
    5. Henry, b. 25 July, 1793; m. Sarah Girdlestone, and d.s.p.
    6. Richard, d. young.
      1. Margaret, b. 24 Jan. 1780; d. young.
      2. Jane, b. 27 May, 1781; d. young.
      3. Alice, d. young.
      4. Anne, b. 8 March, 1789; m. 1st, John Boles Reeves, of Belfort, Charleville, co. Cork; 2ndly, Major Langton, and 3rdly, William Raymond, and had issue.
    Mr. William Fosbery, sen., m. 2ndly, 5 Nov. 1806, Anne, widow of Meredith Monsell, and dau. of Exham Vincent, and by her had issue,
  7. Thomas Vincent (Rev.), Vicar of Christ Church, Reading, b. 1 Oct. 1807; m. 24 May, 1831, Emily Sarah, dau. of George Gooch, by Amelia, his wife, dau. of John Kerrich, and d. 1875, leaving issue,

IRELAND. Fowler.

(1) George Vincent, V.C., Lieut.-Col. late Bengal S.C., *m.* Emmeline, dau. of Capt. Percy Hall, R.N. He *d.* 8 May, 1907, having had issue,
  1. Percy, *m.* Marion, dau. of — Chamberlin.
  2. George.
  3. Cecil.
  1. Cecilia, *m.* Baron de la Hitte, and has issue.
  2. Beatrice.
  3. Maude, *m.* Rev. Joseph Pyper, and had issue.
  4. Gertrude.
  5. Alice.
(2) William Thomas Exham, Major late 77th Regt. (*Thelton, Crossbush, Arundel*), *b.* 9 June, 1835; *m.* 1874, Jane Charlotte, dau. of Rev. Cunningham Boothby, and has issue,
  1. William Nigel, *b.* 1882; *m.* 20 Feb. 1908, Winifred Mary, younger dau. of Rev. Frederick Barker, of Folkestone
    1. Isabel, *d.* young.
    2. Eva, *d.* young.
  3. Lilian, *m.* 24 Oct. 1901, Charles Standish Paulet, of Staple Hill, co. Warwick (*see* BURKE'S *Peerage*, WINCHESTER, M.).
(3) Henry Thomas, *m.* Charlotte, dau. of — Hall, and had issue,
  1. Harry.
  2. Arthur.
  3. Ernest.
  4. Lionel.
  1. Ivy.
(4) Vincent, *d.* young.
(5) Clement Charles, *d.* young.
(6) Leonard Arthur, *m.* Edith, dau. of — Jones, and had with other issue,
  1. Gertrude.
  2. Olive.
(7) Charles.
(8) Edward Henry, late 66th Regt., *m.* Georgiana, dau. of Robert Fowler, and has issue,
  Georgiana.
  (1) Emily Georgiana, *m.* Rev. Edward Holmes, and has issue.
  (2) Gertrude, *m.* Rev. Arthur Clutterbuck, and has issue.
  (3) Georgiana, *d.* 1865, aged 19.
  (4) Mary, *m.* Rev. Alfred Begbie, and has issue.
5. Hannah, *b.* 1 Nov. 1811; *d.* young.
6. Georgiana, *b.* 16 May, 1813; *m.* 16 June, 1835, Hon. and Rev. Musgrave A. Harris, who *d.s.p.* 16 Aug. 1836 (*see* BURKE'S *Peerage*, HARRIS, B.).
7. Jane, *b.* 10 May, 1815; *d.* young.
1. Anna, *m.* John Langford, of Manns, co. Limerick.
2. Jane, *m.* John Langford, of Kilcoogriff, co. Limerick.
3. Elizabeth, *m.* Richard Parsons, of Craighbeg, co. Limerick.
The eldest son,
GEORGE FOSBERY, of Kildimo, *m.* 20 Oct. 1782, Christina Mary, only dau. of Thomas Rice, of Mount Trenchard, co. Limerick (ancestor of Lord Monteagle) by Mary his wife, dau. of Gerard FitzGerald, Knight of Kerry. She *d.* 1843. He *d.* 1791, having had issue,
1. GEORGE, of whom presently.
2. William, *d.* young.
3. Thomas Rice (Rev.), *b.* 3 Feb. 1788; *m.* Althea Maria, dau. of J. Smythe, of Barbavilla, co. Westmeath, and *d.s.p.* 4 Feb. 1828.
4. John Francis, Barrister-at-Law, *b.* Nov. 1790; *d. unm.* 10 Dec. 1871.
1. Mary Rice, *b.* 7 Nov. 1784; *m.* 15 April, 1809, William Henn, Master in Chancery. He *d.* 9 March, 1857. She *d.* 15 July, 1867, leaving issue (*see that family*).
2. Jane, *b.* 25 Dec. 1785; *m.* 1808, Col. Anthony Lyster, of Lysterfield. He *d.* May, 1819, Col. C. P. Leslie, M.P., of Glaslough, co. Monaghan. He *d.* 15 Nov. 1831. She *d.* 24 April, 1869, leaving issue (*see that family*).
The eldest son,
GEORGE FOSBERY, of Clorane and Curraghbridge, co. Limerick, J.P., *b.* 23 Oct. 1783; *m.* 4 May, 1805, his cousin Elizabeth Christina, dau. of Francis Fosbery, of Curraghbridge (*see above*). She *d.* 19 Sept. 1868. He *d.* July, 1847, leaving issue,
1. George, of Clorane, co. Limerick, J.P., *b.* 23 March, 1806; *m.* 1st, 29 Nov. 1829, Catherine, dau. of Thomas Leland, of Fitzwilliam Square, Dublin. She *d.* 1848, having had an only son, George, *b.* 30 Dec. 1830; *m.* 18 June, 1855, Sophia, 5th dau. of Rev. Edward Herbert, of Kilpeacon Glebe. She *d.* Jan. 1876. He *d.v.p.* 1 Dec. 1858, leaving issue, two daus.,
  (1) Alice Herbert, } both killed with their mother in the railway accident at Abbots Ripton, 1876.
  (2) Katherine, }
Mr. George Fosbery *m.* 2ndly, 10 July, 1851, Eliza, dau. of John Scott, of Firgrove, co. Clare. She *d.s.p.* Jan. 1893. He *d.* 28 Aug. 1875, and was *s.* by his brother, Thomas.
2. Francis, of Kilgobbin, *b.* 18 June, 1807; *d. unm.* 28 March, 1859.
3. THOMAS, of whom presently.
1. Elizabeth Philippa, *m.* 10 Dec. 1846, Sir John Nugent Humble, Bart., of Cloncoscoran. She *d.* 27 Sept. 1886. He *d.* 11 June, 1886, leaving issue (*see* BURKE'S *Peerage*, NUGENT, Bart.).
The youngest son,
THOMAS FOSBERY, of Kilgobbin, and Clorane, co. Limerick, *b.* 1 May, 1820; *m.* 25 March, 1852, Georgina, dau. of St. George Smith, of Greenbills, near Drogheda, and *d.* 1 April, 1893, leaving issue,
1. GEORGE RALPH, of Kilgobbin and Clorane.
2. Frank Robert, *b.* 1 Sept. 1857; *m.* 22 Nov. 1894, Rhoda Anne, eld. dau. of Surg. Major-Gen. G. L. Hinde, C.B., and has issue,

I.I.G.

1. Thomas Frank, *b.* 14 April, 1896; *d.* 26 May, 1897.
2. Frank Sidney Thomas, *b.* 21 Oct. 1897.
3. Robt. George Widenham, *b.* 17 April, 1899.
4. Standish John Langford, *b.* 27 Feb. 1902; *d.* 12 May, 1902.
5. Harry Tudor Raynor, *b.* 21 Dec. 1904.
6. William Edmond Vincent, *b.* 8 April, 1906.
1. Hildegarde Georgina Kathleen, *b.* 15 Sept. 1900.
2. Rhoda Amy, *b.* 6 June, 1903.
1. Mary Elizabeth, *m.* 19 Oct. 1879, Heffernan John Cantillon, of Manister House, Croom, co. Limerick, who *d.* 4 May, 1884, leaving a son and a dau.
2. Catherine Matilda, *m.* 5 Aug. 1874, John Stewart Handyside, of Akitio, Wellington, New Zealand, and has issue.
3. Jane Philippa.
4. Georgina Charlotte.

Seat—Kilgobbin, Patrickswell, co. Limerick.

FOSTER. *See* BURKE'S PEERAGE, **FOSTER, Bart.**

FOWLER OF RAHINSTON.

CAPT. ROBERT HENRY FOWLER, of Rahinston, and Rathmolyon, co. Meath, J.P. and D.L., High Sheriff co. Meath 1899, late Capt 85th King's Light Infantry, *b.* 28 June, 1857; *m.* 2 June, 1890, Mabel, dau. and co-heir of the late Hon. St. Leger R. Glyn (*see* BURKE'S *Peerage*, WOLVERTON, B.), and has issue,

1. ROBERT ST. LEGER, *b.* 7 April, 1891.
2. George Glyn, *b.* 21 Jan. 1896.

Lineage. — STEPHEN FOWLER (younger son of Richard Fowler, by Margaret, the dau. of Richard, Lord Newport), *m.* Elizabeth, dau. and heir of John Cock, of Skendleby Thorpe, of co. Lincoln, and had issue. His only surviving son,

GEORGE FOWLER, *m.* Mary, dau. and co-heir of Robert Hurst, and had,
1. George, *d. unm.*
2. Hurst, left a dau.
3. ROBERT, Archbishop of Dublin.
1. (?) Mary.

ROBERT FOWLER, D.D., who was educated at Westminster School, and at Trin. Coll. Cambridge, was one of the Chaplains to King GEORGE II, and Prebend. at Westminster. In 1771, he was consecrated Bishop of Killaloe and Kilfenora in Ireland, and 1773. was translated to the archiepiscopal see of Dublin. His Grace was subsequently sworn of the Privy Council, and became, at the institution of the Order of St. Patrick, 1783, its first Chancellor. The Archbishop *m.* Mildred, eldest dau. (and co-heir of her brother) of William Dealtry, of Gainsborough, co. Lincoln, and had a son, ROBERT; and two daus., Mildred, *m.* 1793, Edmund Butler, Earl of Kilkenny, and *d.* 1830; and Frances, *m.* 1795, Hon. and Rev. Richard Bourke, afterwards Bishop of Waterford (*see* BURKE'S *Peerage*, MAYO, E.). His Grace *d.* 10 Oct. 1801. The only son,
THE RIGHT REV. ROBERT FOWLER, educated at Westminster School and Christ Church, Oxford, was appointed Dean of St. Patrick's, became Archdeacon of Dublin, and was afterwards consecrated Bishop of Ossory and Ferns. He *m.* 30 Jan. 1796, Hon. Louisa Gardiner, eldest dau. of Luke, Viscount Mountjoy, and sister of Charles John, Earl of Blessington, and *d.* 31 Dec. 1841, aged 74, having had by her (who *d.* 1848) the following issue,
1. ROBERT, late of Rahinston House.
2. Luke, of Wellbrook (Rev.), Rector of Aghour, Freshford, co. Kilkenny, *b.* 18 Oct. 1799; *m.* 1st, 10 Feb. 1825, Elizabeth, 3rd dau. of Owen Wynne, of Hazelwood, co. Sligo. She *d.* 1855. He *m.* 2ndly, 15 Oct. 1864, Dorothea Dora, dau. of Thomas Jefferson, and widow of Thomas Mountjoy Vignoles, son of the Dean of Ossory. He *d.* 1 March, 1876, having by his first wife had issue,
  1. Charles John, Major-Gen. Royal Engineers, *b.* 2 Dec. 1826; *m.* 1862, Gertrude Sara, dau. of Capt. Taylor, and *d.* 3 Dec. 1896, having had issue,
    (1) Francis Charles, of Ashby Manor, Spilsby, Lincs, Maj. R.A. (80, *Redcliffe Square, S.W.*), *b.* 27 July, 1864; *m.* 12 July, 1910, Alice Evelyn, dau. of Capt. George Robert Elwes, late 14th Hussars, of "Bossington," Bournemouth.
    (2) Cole Cortlandt, Capt. R.N., Chevalier of Legion of Honour (*Josselyns, Little Horkesley, Colchester*), *b.* 7 Aug.

Q

1866; *m.* 12 Jan. 1905, Inez Gertrude Paget, 5th dau. of Berkeley Paget, D.L. (*see* BURKE'S *Peerage*, ANGLESEY, M.), and has issue,
 1. Florinda Gertrude, *b.* 12 Jan. 1906.
 2. Kathleen Adelaide, *b.* 27 Nov. 1908.
 (3) Arthur Robert Willoughby, B.A. Camb., *b.* 21 Jan. 1869; *m.* 26 Oct. 1907, Edith Mary, dau. of George Francis Marx, Capt. 68 Regt., and has issue,
  1. George Charles Willoughby, *b.* 3 Sept. 1908.
  2. Edward Cote Willoughby, *b.* 9 March, 1910.
 (1) Florence Emily Bontine, *b.* 4 July, 1863.
 (2) Edith Gertrude, *m.* May, 1905, Ernest Hanson, of Vancouver Island.
 (3) Mary Elizabeth, *m.* June, 1905, Edward Gates, M.D., of Florence.
 (4) May Irene, *d. unm.* 28 Aug. 1908.
 2. Arthur Robert, *b.* 1829, was a Capt. in H.M. 41st Regt.; *d.* March, 1867.
 3. Edward Willoughby, of Rosslare, co. Sligo, J.P., *b.* 6 Aug. 1831; *m.* 24 Aug. 1871, Kate Mary Barrett, only child of Michael Obins Seeley Jones, and grand-dau. of Michael Jones, of Lisgoole Abbey, co. Fermanagh, and *d.* 17 Jan. 1900, leaving issue,
  (1) Willoughby Jones, Capt. R.A., *b.* 25 Feb. 1873; *m.* 20 July, 1904, Gwendolen Ada, dau. of Col. W. B. Wade, C.B., of Eastwood, Bagenalstown, co. Carlow, and has issue, Kathleen Muriel, *b.* 10 Jan. 1908.
  (2) Cecil Arthur, *b.* 6 Feb. 1876.
  (3) Edward Gardiner, Capt. R.A., *b.* 2 Dec. 1879.
  (4) Charles Knox, *b.* 28 April, 1882.
  (1) Mildred Eleanor, *b.* 13 May, 1874; *d.* 13 June, 1874.
  (2) Elizabeth Kate, *b.* 25 July, 1878.
 1. Louisa Frances Florence, *m.* 9 Dec. 1866, Otway, 2nd son of Sir Jonah Wheeler Cuffe, Bart. of Leyrath, co. Kilkenny, and has issue (*see* BURKE'S *Peerage*).
The elder son,
 ROBERT FOWLER, of Rahinston and Rathmolyon, co. Meath, J.P. and D.L., *b.* 15 June, 1797; *m.* 1st, 20 Aug. 1820, Jane Anne, eldest dau. of Hon. John Crichton, and sister of John, 3rd Earl Erne, and by her (who *d.* 19 May, 1828) had issue,
 1. Robert, late of Rahinston.
 2. John Richard, *b.* 8 Oct. 1826; *m.* 23 May, 1877, Elizabeth, eldest dau. of Samuel Law, of Kilbarrack House, co. Dublin, and has issue,
  Richard Samuel Gardiner, *b.* 1 Aug. 1881.
  Charlotte Sarah.
 1. Jane, Margaret, *m.* 20 March, 1844, Gartside Tipping, eldest son of Thomas Tipping, of Crumsal Hall, co. Lancaster, and dying 13 March, 1857, left issue.
 2. Louisa Catherine, *m.* 26 Nov. 1846, James Henry Sclater, only son of James Henry Sclater, of Newick Park, Sussex, by Cecil his wife, dau. of Francis Saunderson, of Castle Saunderson, and dying 18 Aug. 1883, left issue.
Mr. Fowler *m.* 2ndly, 16 May, 1831, Lady Harriet Eleanor Wandesforde-Butler, eldest dau. of James, 2nd Marquess of Ormonde, and by her (who *d.* 28 Sept. 1885) had issue,
 8. James Haddington, *b.* 28 April, 1835; *d.* 19 Jan. following.
 2. Grace Louisa. 3. Harriet Selina, *d.* 31 March, 1888.
 4. Anne Mildred, *m.* 19 July, 1860, James Edward Bateman Dashwood, son of Admiral Dashwood, and has issue.
 5. Mary. 6. Emily.
He *d.* 6 Feb. 1868. His eldest son,
 ROBERT FOWLER, of Rahinston and Rathmolyon, co. Meath, M.A., J.P. and D.L., High Sheriff 1871, called to the Irish Bar 1850, *b.* 15 March, 1824; *s.* his father, 1868; *m.* 30 Sept. 1856, Letitia Mabel, dau. of Henry Barry Coddington, of Oldbridge, and *d.* 23 Oct. 1897, having by her (who *d.* 25 Jan. 1879) had issue,
 1. ROBERT HENRY, now of Rahinston.
 2. John Sharman, D.S.O., Maj. Royal Engineers, *b.* 29 July, 1864; *m.* 10 Aug. 1904, Mary Olivia Henrietta, dau. of John Monck Brooke, of Elm Grove, co. Dublin (*see* BURKE'S *Peerage*, BROOKE, Bart.), and has issue,
  Letitia Louisa Grace, *b.* 30 June, 1909.
 3. George Hurst, of Eureka, Kells, Meath, J.P., *b.* 6 April, 1866; *m.* 24 June, 1896, Mabel, 4th dau. of John Blakiston-Houston, of Orangefield, co. Down (*see that family*), and has issue,
  1. Frank, *b.* 28 May, 1897.
  2. Bryan John, *b.* 18 Aug. 1898.
 4. Francis Fitzherbert, *b.* 21 June, 1867; *d.* Feb. 1879.
 1. Louisa Marion, *m.* 17 Sept. 1898, Brig.-Gen. Alexander John Godley, Irish Guards (*see* BURKE'S *Peerage*, KILBRACKEN, B.).
 2. Florence Mary.
 3. Eleanor Katherine.

Arms—Quarterly: 1st and 4th az., on a chevron arg., between three lions passant guardant or, as many crosses patée sa.; 2nd and 3rd erm., on a canton gu. a horned owl arg. *Crest*—Out of a ducal coronet or, a demi-horned owl, wings expanded ppr. *Motto*—Este pernox.

Seat—Rahinston House, Enfield, co. Meath.

FOX OF KILCOURSEY.

JAMES GEORGE HUBERT FOX, of Galtrim House, co. Meath, J.P. co. Tipperary, late Lieut. 5th Royal Irish Lancers, *b.* 1 Jan. 1842, styled THE FOX, as chief of his name; *m.* 1st, 14 Nov. 1865, Elizabeth Amelia Lilian, dau. of Rev. J. B. Grant, Rector of Rathconrath, Westmeath, and by her (who *d.* May, 1875) has issue,
 1. BRABAZON HUBERT MAINE, Major (ret.), late Royal Irish Rifles, *b.* 6 Nov. 1868; *m.* 14 March, 1896, Florence Emily Clara, eldest dau. of Col. W. A. Le Mottée, late 18th Regt., of Templenoe, Fermoy, co. Cork, and has issue,
  Nial Arthur Hubert, *b.* 13 Sept. 1897.
 2. Arthur James, late Capt. 3rd Batt. Royal Irish Regt., *b.* 1 June, 1871; *m.* 7 Feb. 1912, at Colombo, Ceylon, Adelaide Sarah, dau. of late Henry Harte Barry, of Kanturk, co. Cork.
 1. Eleanor Frances, *d.* 1872.

He *m.* 2ndly, 30 May, 1877, Georgiana Frances, eldest dau. of Rev. C. Elrington McKay, Vicar of Laracor and Galtrim, and grand-dau. of George Ogle Moore, M.P. for the City of Dublin, and by her (who *d.* 30 Jan. 1879) has a dau.,
 2. Georgiana Frances, *b.* 21 April, 1878; *m.* 6 Sept. 1906, Edward John French, M.A. (Trin. Coll. Dublin), eldest son of John Alexander French, of St. Anne's, Donnybrook, co. Dublin, and has issue.

Lineage.—The name of this family is derived from Teige, chief of his sept, who was surnamed Sionnach, the Irish for Fox, and from him the family was ever after styled Sionnach, translated by the English to Fox, and the chief or head, by way of eminence, was called The Fox. They possessed the whole barony of Kilcoursey, in the King's Co., which was surrendered to Queen ELIZABETH by HUBERT FOX (The Fox), of Lehinchie, in the Barony of Kilcoursey, by deed dated 1 March, 1599, and was regranted 29 Jan. following to him and his heirs male to be held by knight's service *in capite*. The estates were confiscated during the Irish Rebellion, 1641-2, and the greater part conferred on the 1st Earl of Cavan.
 BRASSIL FOX, of Kilcoursey, King's Co., son of Art or Arthur Fox, who *d.* before 1600, *s.* his uncle, the above-mentioned Hubert Fox (The Fox) on his death *s.p.* 16 June, 1600. His long line of illustrious ancestors is given in the Funeral Entries at Ulster's Office, and in Sir William Betham's pedigree of the family. Brassil was great great-grandson of Carbery Fox, of Kilcoursey, slain 1500, sixth in descent from Rory Fox, The Fox, Lord of Kilcoursey, who *d.* 1287, 25th in descent (*see* O'FERRALL'S *Linea Antiqua*) from Neill Niagallagh, Monarch of All Ireland, called Niall of the Nine Hostages, ancestor through his eldest son of the Royal House of O'Neill. Brassil Fox *m.* Mary, dau. of Hugh Macgeoghegan, of Castletown, co. Westmeath, and dying 7 April, 1639, left, with other issue, an elder son,
 HUBERT FOX, of Kilcoursey, *m.* Mary, dau. of Lisagh or Lewis, O'Connor, of Leixlip, Kildare, and had a son,
 BRASSIL FOX, of Kilcoursey, who *m.* a dau. of the house of Magawley. He *d.s.p.* His brother,
 JAMES FOX, of Ballagh, co. Westmeath, who *m.* Jane Stone, had issue,
 1. ANTHONY, his heir.
 1. Jane, *m.* Anthony Coffy, of Kilglas, co. Kildare.
 2. Catherine, *d. unm.*
 3. Elizabeth, *d. unm.*
 ANTHONY FOX, of Ballagh, co. Westmeath, *m.* the dau. of Charles Kelly, of Castle Kelly, co. Galway, and *d.* 1751, leaving issue three sons, the eldest of whom,
 JAMES FOX, of Suntown, co. Westmeath, *b.* 1717; *m.* 1743, Millicent, dau. of Capt. Mathew Palin, of Hyde Park, co. Westmeath, and *d.* 1796, leaving a son and heir,
 MATHEW FOX, of Foxbrooke, *b.* 1745; *m.* Elizabeth, dau. of John Grierson, of Doolistown, co. Meath, and *d.* 15 May, 1808, leaving issue,
 1. JAMES, of whom presently.
 2. John, of Dublin, *b.* about 1774, *m.* Sarah, eldest dau. of Alexander Kingstone, of Mosstown, and had issue,
  1. Alexander Kingstone, County Inspector of Constabulary for Londonderry, *m.* Miss Paterson, and had issue.
  2. Mathew, Barrister-at-Law, *m.* 27 April, 1832, Charlotte, dau. of Robert Paterson, of Gracefield, and sister of the late Gen. Paterson, and *d.* 4 Dec. 1859, leaving by her (who *d.* 9 May, 1864),
   (1) John Joseph Paterson, Capt. 56th Pompadours, *b.* 28 April, 1833; *d.* May, 1910; *m.* 28 April, 1870, Kate Crofton, only child of Sir James Murray, M.D., of Dublin, by Mary

Allen, his 2nd wife, niece of Charles M'Garel, of Belgrave Square, London. She d. 1 March, 1908, having had issue,
Charles James, b. 14 April, 1871.
Kathleen Mary.
(2) Robert Paterson, Major la e 11th Hussars, b. 26 Jan. 1835 ; m. 28 Sept. 1864, Marion, dau. of Alfred Jee, of Oxford Square, and d. 22 Dec. 1878.
(1) Jane Paterson, d. 13 May, 1838.
(1) Charlotte Elizabeth, ⎱ twins, b. 19 July, 1842 ; the latter
(3) Joseph,   ⎰ d. young.
(3) Sarah Frances, d. March, 1845.
3. Joseph, of Doolistown, co. Meath, b. about 1778 ; m. 1807, Frances, 4th dau. of James D'Arcy, of Hyde Park (see that family), and d 1855, having by her (who d. 1840) had issue,
1. Elizabeth D'Arcy, d. 1890.
2. Dorothea Martha, m. 12 Feb. 1833, to the Rev. Joseph Brabazon Grant, A.B., Rector of Rathconrath, co. Westmeath, son of Joseph Grant, Barrister-at-Law, of the house of Grant of Rothicmurchus, co. Inverness. She d. 1889.
3. Emelie Anne, m. 1836, the Rev. Hugh Samuel Hamilton, Vicar-General of Dromore, who d.s.p. 1857.
4. William, of Dublin, b. about 1785 ; m. Ellen, eldest dau. of Adam Loftus Lynn, of Newport Lodge, co. Waterford, and by her (who d. 1844) left at his decease, 1859, several sons and daus. all settled in Wisconsin, United States, America.
1. Amelia, m. Robert Johnstone, of Goschen, co. Longford; d. 1844.
2. Anne, m. the Rev. Nicholas Gosselin, Rector of Tashinny, co. Longford, and is dec.
3. Maria, m. the Rev. Charles Johnstone, of co. Longford, and d. in America.
4. Eliza, m. William Fletcher, of Newry, co. Down.
5. Matilda, m. Robert Creighton, of Rice Hill, co. Cavan.
The eldest son,
JAMES FOX, of Foxbrooke and Galtrim House, co. Meath, b. 1773 ; m. 1st, Harriet, dau. of James D'Arcy, of Hyde Park, co. Westmeath, and by her (who d. about 1848) had issue,
1. MATHEW, of whom presently.
2. Henry Charles, M.D., d. unm.
3. James D'Arcy, of Foxbrooke, m. Sarah, dau. of James Tarrant, of Mallow, co. Cork, and had issue, Brazil Ellen, Maria, d.s.p., Harriett and Eliza, and settled in Australia.
1. Frances Eliza, m. 1st, April, 1830, J. M. Morton, of Hacketstown, co. Carlow, and had issue, one dau. ; and 2ndly, Dr. Thompson Brough, of Kiltegan, co. Carlow, and had issue, three sons and one dau.
2. Harriet, d. unm. 1856.
3. Maria, m. Thomas Lavallin D'Arcy, of the Hyde Park family. He m. 2ndly, 31 Jan. 1849, Margaret, dau. of John Crozier, of Gortra, co. Fermanagh (see BURKE'S Family Records), and d. 1850. She d.s.p. 24 April, 1872. His eldest son,
THE REV. MATHEW MAINE FOX, Rector of Galtrim, co. Meath, b. 1804 ; m. 1st, Anna, eldest dau. and co-heir of William Boyce, of Moyallen, co. Down. She d.s.p. He m. 2ndly, Ellen Anne, dau. of Andrew Armstrong, of Kilclare, King's Co., and by her (who d. 1845) he left at his decease, May, 1844, an only child.
JAMES GEORGE HUBERT FOX, the present representative of the family.

Arms—Arg. a lion rampant and in chief two dexter hands couped at the wrist gu. Crest—An arm embowed in armour holding a sword all ppr. Motto—Sionnach aboo.
Seat—Galtrim House, Summerhill, co. Meath.

FOX OF FOX HALL.

ADELINE FRANCES MARY Fox, of Fox Hall, co. Longford, s. her father 1885.

Lineage.—This family (anciently O'Caharny, afterwards changed to O'Sionach, anglicised Fox) have their descent from MAINE, 1st King of Teffia, 4th son of NIALL, the Nine of Hostages.

SIR PATRICK FOX, of Moyvore, co. Westmeath, Clerk of the Council, and Interpreter of Irish to the State, b. prior to 1560, purchased back from the O'Farrells the lands and castle of Rathreogh. He m. 1st, Janet, dau. of Walter Newman ; 2ndly, Catherine, dau. of Sir Gerald Aylmer, of Donadea, co. Meath. Sir Patrick d. 1618, and was s. by his eldest son,

NATHANIEL FOX, of Rathreogh, now Fox Hall, b. 1588, m. Elizabeth, dau. of Walter Hussey, of Moy Hussey, co. Meath. He d. 1634, leaving eight sons and three daus. He was s. by his eldest son,
PATRICK FOX, of Fox Hall, b. 1614 ; m. Barbara, dau. of Patrick, 7th Baron Dunsany, by Jane, dau. of Sir Thomas Heneage, of Hainton, and had issue. The 2nd, but eldest surviving son,
CHARLES FOX, of Fox Hall, b. 1636, had, by Elizabeth his 1st wife, four sons and two daus.,

1. PATRICK, of Fox Hall, m. Frances, dau. and heiress of Sir Edward Herbert, Bart., of Durrow, by Lady Hester Lambart, dau. of the Earl of Cavan, but d.s.p. 1735.
2. CHARLES, of whom presently.
3. Peyton, who settled at Port Mahon, near Newport, on the Inny. He was engaged in the wars and participated with Gen. Stanhope in the reduction of Minorca ; he attained the rank of Lieut.-Col. and m. Marthabetta Maria, dau. of Col. Henry Piers, of Tristernagh, and d. 1750.
4. Robert, d. unm. 1748, Grand Chamberlain and Eschaetor-General.
1. Alice, m. William Persse, of Spring Hill, co. Galway.
2. Jane, m. Anthony Hickman, of Ballyket, co. Clare.
Mr. Fox m. 2ndly, Thomazine, dau. of Col. Prime Iron Rochfort, of Beltranner, by whom he had one dau. He d. 1726. His 2nd son,
CHARLES FOX, eventually of Fox Hall, as heir to his elder brother, m. Jane, dau. of Col. Thomas Whitney, of Newpass, by his wife Maria Boleyn, and d. 1747, having had one son,
CHARLES FOX, m. 1725, his cousin Jane, dau. of Francis West, of Ringownie, co. Longford, and d.v.p. 27 Oct., 1746, leaving three sons and two daus. The eldest son,
FRANCIS FOX, of Fox Hall, b. 1727 ; m. 30 March, 1759, Mary, dau. of Richard Edgeworth, of Edgeworthstown, by Rachel his wife, dau. and heiress of Samuel Lovell, of Harleston, co. Northampton, by whom he left at his decease, 1779, one son,
RICHARD FOX, of Fox Hall, Col. of Militia, b. 1760 ; m. Dec. 1787, Lady Anne Maxwell, dau. of Barry, Earl of Farnham, and by her (who d. 1801) had issue five sons and five daus.,
1. FRANCIS, his heir.
2. Barry, J.P., b. 1789 ; entered the Army in 1807, attained the rank of Brevet-Major 1837, served in the Expedition to Walcheren, was at Corunna, Fuentes d'Honor, and in America. He m. 1824, Sophia, dau. of Richard Lovell Edgworth, and d. 1863, leaving issue,
1. Maxwell, Capt. R.N. (retired), of Annaghmore, King's Co., J.P. and D.L. for King's Co., High Sheriff 1868, and High Sheriff co. Longford 1885, b. 1824 ; m. 1st, 8 May, 1865, Florence Jane (who d.s.p. 17 Aug. 1882), eldest dau. of Right Hon. Sir Andrew Buchanan, Bart., K.C.B. ; 2ndly, 1886, Edith Susan Marian, eldest dau. of Rev. Essex Edgworth, of Kilshrewly, co. Longford, and d. 14 Sept. 1899, leaving, with other issue, Essex Barry, b. 1888.
2. William Waller, late Capt. 60th Rifles, m. 1871, his cousin, Emma Louisa, eldest dau. of the late Richard Maxwell Fox, of Fox Hall.
1. Mary Anne, d. unm. 5 July, 1906.
2. Charlotte, m. 21 June, 1865, Rev. Maxwell Coote, son of Col. Chidley Coote.
3. Charles, of Keady, co. Armagh, D.L., Barrister-at-Law, at one time M.P. for co. Longford, b. 1791 ; d. 1862.
4. John James (Rev.), b. 1792 ; m. 1825, Harriet Louisa, dau. of the late Rev. Charles Cobbe Beresford ; and d. March, 1879, having had issue,
1. Willoughby George, b. 1826 ; m. 1853, Eliza Anne Jane, dau. of Capt. William John Ottley, 2nd Bombay Cavalry, and has issue.
2. Charles Maxwell, D.D., m. Wilhelmina Banks, and has two sons and one dau.
3. Henry John.
4. Francis, m. 1861, Hester, dau. of the late Rev. Robert Bury, of Carrigrenane, co. Cork, and d. in 1884 ; she m. 2ndly, 16 Feb. 1865, Major-Gen. G. De la Poer Beresford, and has issue.
5. Frederic.   6. Barry John George.
1. Emily Grace, m. 1861, John E. Thompson, of Clonfin, co. Longford.
2. Charlotte Silvia, m. 1867, John Wynne, of Holywell, co. Sligo ; and d. 1874.
3. Harriett Elizabeth, m. Hercules Knox, of Rosslare, co. Sligo.
5. Richard, b. 1795 ; d. 1864 ; m. Jane Campbell, dau. of James Buchanan, of Blair Vadock, by Lady Janet, dau. of Earl of Caithness, and had issue,
1. Maxwell Sinclair, d. 1854.
2. Charles de Bassyn, of Cregg, co. Sligo, J.P., b. 1831 , m. 1871, Emma Penelope, dau. of Edmund Packe, and d. 1894, leaving, with other issue,
Charles Edmund, b. 1872 ; m. 30 Nov. 1905, Helen Beatrice Mowbray, dau. of Rev. — Mowbray, of East Thorpe, Essex.
Kathleen Edith Maude, m. 22 Dec. 1903, Capt. H. Darell Brown, Oxfordshire Lt. Inf., son of the late Rev. Lionel Darell Brown.
3. Henry, R.N., b. 1877 ; m. 1872, Georgina, dau. of Lieut.-Col. Halsted.
4. Eric Stanhope, Lieut.-Col. B.S.C., d. 1895.
5. Cecil, d. 1865.   6. Edward, d. 1894.
1. Selina Matilda, m. 1868, Charles Packe, of Stretton Hall, co. Leicester.
1. Margaret Grace, d. unm. 1819.
2. Mary Anne, d. unm. 1818.
3. Henrietta, d. unm. 1868.
4. Selina Judith, m. 1820, James Saunderson, 4th son of Francis Saunderson, of Castle Saunderson, co. Cavan, M.P., and had three daus.,
1. Grace, d. unm.
2. Selina Laura, m. 1st, 1853, Broke Turnor ; and 2ndly, Major W. Longstaffe.
3. Lydia Cecil, d. unm. 1882.
5. Elizabeth, d. unm.
Col. Fox d. 1833, and was s. by his eldest son,
THE REV. FRANCIS FOX, of Fox Hall, b. 1788 ; m. 1813, Frances, dau. of Rev. Jemmett Browne, D.D., of Riverstown, co. Cork

France. THE LANDED GENTRY. 244

(*see that family*), by Frances, his wife, dau. of Arthur Blennerhassett, of Balyseedy, co. Kerry, and had issue,
1. RICHARD MAXWELL, his heir. 2. John James Barry, dec.
3. Jemmett George, *b.* 1826 ; *m.* 1856, Dora Jane, dau. of John Francis West, M.D., of Rath, co. Westmeath, and had issue, two sons (of whom the elder, Francis George, Major R.A., *d.* 27 Feb. 1902) and three daus. ; he *d.* 1 Nov. 1868.
1. Fanny Arabella, *m.* Dr. Francis Robinson.
2. Grace Margaret, *m.* 1846, Major W. W. Stephenson.
3. Anne. *d. unm.* 1835.
4. Selina Mary, *m.* 1844, Hon. Bryon C. P. Cary, 3rd son of Viscount Falkland, and *d.* 1868.
5. Henrietta, *m.* Humphry Grylls, of Cornwall.
Mr. Fox was s., 1834, by his son,
RICHARD MAXWELL FOX, of Fox Hall, late M.P. and D.L. co. Longford, *b.* 1816 ; *m.* 1835, Susan Amelia, dau. of Admiral Sir L. W. Halsted, G.C.B., by Emma, his wife, dau. of Admiral Viscount Exmouth, and by her (who *d.* 10 Dec. 1868) had issue,
1. Francis William, *b.* 1836 ; *d.* 1855.
2. RICHARD EDWARD, late of Fox Hall.
1. Emma Louisa, *m.* 1871, to her cousin, Capt. William Waller Fox.
2. Frances Amelia.
3. Annie Elizabeth, *m.* 1867, Lieut.-Col. Ralph Dopping Hepenstal, D.L., of Derry Cassan, co. Longford, and *d.* 1878.
4. Susan Henrietta, *d.* 1883.
The eldest surviving son,
RICHARD EDWARD FOX, of Fox Hall, J.P., High Sheriff 1872, *b.* 28 Nov. 1846 ; *m.* 1870, Emily, younger dau. of the late Lieut.-Col. Godley, H.E.I.C.S., and *d.* 1885, having had issue,
1. Richard Niall Maxwell Barry, *b.* 11 Sept. 1877; *d.* 22 Aug. 1880.
1. ADELINE FRANCES MARY, now of Fox Hall.
2. Florence, *d.* 1873. 3. Evelyn Marian Emily.
Arms—Az., a sceptre in bend between two crowns or, a chief of the last. **Crest**—A sceptre or, in front of two wings conjoined and expanded gu. **Motto**—Nec elatus nec dejectus.

Seat—Fox Hall, Lenamore, co. Longford.

FRANCE-LUSHINGTON-TULLOCH.
See **TULLOCH.**

FRANKS OF CARRIG.

WILLIAM WHITMORE FRANKS, of Carrig Park, co. Cork, *b.* 1868.

Lineage.—DAVID FRANKS, of Garriarthur, co. Limerick, living there 28 Feb. 1718, was father of two sons,
1. THOMAS, his heir.
2. Mathew, of Moorestown, co. Limerick (*see* FRANKS *of Westfield, and* FRANKS *of Ballyscaddane*).
The elder son,
THOMAS FRANKS, of Garriarthur, co. Limerick, *b.* about 1700, *m.* Miss Hart, of co. Clare, and was father of (with William, *d.s.p.*, and a dau., *m.* to — Walsh),
THOMAS FRANKS, of Carrig, co. Cork, J.P., *m.* Margery, eldest dau. and co-heir of Richard Harte, of Grange, co. Limerick, and *d.* 1780, leaving issue,
1. DAVID, his heir.
2. WILLIAM, successor to his brother.
3. Thomas.
1. Catherine, *m.* as his 1st wife, her cousin, Sir John Franks (*see* FRANKS *of Ballyscaddane*) and *d.* 1872.
2. Margaret, *m.* 1st, 1796, Ralph Lawrenson, 1st Fencible Dragoons ; and 2ndly, Capt. Joseph Gabett Bourchier (*see* BOURCHIER *of Baggotstown*).
The elder son,
DAVID FRANKS, of Carrig, J.P., *m.* 1794, Maria Cecilia, dau. of James Nash, of Bellevue, co. Cork, and by her (who *m.* 2ndly, Major-Gen. Sir Thomas Browne, Col. 8th Hussars, and *d.* 1847) left no issue, and was *s.* by his brother,
WILLIAM FRANKS, of Carrig, J.P., *m.* 1792, Catherine, eldest dau. of William Hume, of Humewood, co. Wicklow, M.P., and had issue,
1. WILLIAM, of Carrig.
2. Thomas Harte (Sir), K.C.B., Major-Gen. in the Army, served with great distinction through the mutinies in India, *m.* 1st, Matilda, dau. of Richard Kay, and widow of the Rev. W. Fletcher ; and 2ndly, 1 March, 1859, Rebecca Constantina Elizabeth, widow of the late Samuel Brewis, of Langley House, Prestwich, Lancashire, and *d.s.p.* 5 Feb. 1862.
3. David Brudenell, *m.* 1837, Catherine, dau. of H. Thompson, and had issue. His dau., Louisa, *m.* her kinsman, Col. Robert Franks, R.A., who *d.s.p.* 1887.
1. Catherine Cecilia Jane, *m.* 1821, Sir Denham O. Jephson Norreys, Bart., M.P. She *d.* 14 Dec. 1853, leaving issue (*see* BURKE'S *Peerage*). He *d.* 10 July, 1888.
2. Margaret.
His eldest son,
WILLIAM HUME FRANKS, of Carrig, J.P., *m.* 1827, Eliza Savage, dau. of Adam Newman, of Dromore, co. Cork (*see* NEWMAN *of Newbury*), and *d.* 1870, having had issue,
1. THOMAS, of Carrig.
2. Adam Newman, bapt. 1833.
3. William Hume, bapt. 1837.
4. John David, bapt. 1838.
5. John Newman, bapt. 1840.

1. Frances Dora, bapt. 1832.
2. Catherine Maria, bapt. 1835.
The eldest son,
THOMAS FRANKS, of Carrig Park, J.P., *b.* 1828, *m.* 21 Oct. 1865, his cousin, Eleanor Marion, dau. of John Franks, of Ballyscaddane, co. Limerick (*see that family*), and had, with other issue,
1. WILLIAM WHITMORE, now of Carrig.
2. Thomas Denham, *b.* 1870 ; *d.* 1885.
1. Eleanor Margaret Elizabeth, *m.* 23 Oct. 1901, Alfred Edye Manning Foster, youngest son of Thomas Gregory Foster, of the Temple, Barrister-at-Law.

Seat—Carrig Park, co. Cork.

FRANKS OF WESTFIELD.

MATTHEW HENRY FRANKS, of Westfield Queen's Co., and of Garrettstown and Dromrahane, co. Cork, J.P. and D.L. Queen's Co., High Sheriff, 1902, J.P. co. Cork, *b.* 31 May, 1835 ; *m.* 9 Jan. 1869, Gertrude Priscilla (who *d.* 25 Aug. 1911), youngest dau. of the late Capt. George Despard, late 53rd Regt., of Rathmolyon, co. Meath, Resident Magistrate for that county, and has issue,

1. MATTHEW HENRY, of Woodbrook, Mountrath, Queen's Co., J.P., B.A. Dublin, F.S.I., *b.* 17 July, 1871 ; *m.* 2 Oct. 1895, Sarah, eldest dau. of Sir Robert Gardner, J.P., of Ashley House, Clyde Road, Dublin, and has issue,
  1. Henry Cecil, *b.* 29 June, 1899.
  2. Robert George Vandeleur, *b.* 12 April, *d.* 30 July, 1902.
2. George Despard, Major 19th Hussars, late A.D.C. to Gen. Commanding 7th Division, 3rd Army Corps, served in S. African War, including defence of Ladysmith, mentioned in despatches, medal, four clasps (*Hale House, Farnham, Surrey ; Cavalry Club*), *b.* 9 Jan. 1873 ; *m.* 6 June, 1908, May Geraldine, eldest dau. of late Lieut.-Gen. Sir Gerald de Courcy Morton, K.C.I.E., C.V.O., C.B., and has issue,
  Bryan Morton Forster, *b.* 12 Sept. 1910.
3. Thomas Fitzherbert, *b.* 26 April, 1874 ; *m.* Dec. 1895, Inez Ethel Mary, youngest dau. of the late Joseph Wilson, D.L., of Clonmore, Stillorgan, co. Dublin, and has issue,
  1. Henry George Stanley, *b.* 5 Nov. 1896.
  2. Archibald Fitzherbert, *b.* 5 Nov. 1897.
1. Gertrude Lucy Maria.

Lineage.—MATTHEW FRANKS, of Moorestown, co. Limerick, 2nd son of David Franks, of Garriarthur (*see* FRANKS *of Carrig*), *b.* about 1702 ; *m.* 1738, Una Upham, of co. Limerick, and had issue,
1. Henry, of Moorestown, co. Limerick, and of Maidstown, co. Cork, *b.* 1739 ; *m.* 5 Oct. 1763, Elizabeth, 3rd dau. of Robert Atkins, of Fountainville, co. Cork, and had issue,
  1. ROBERT, of Maidstone, *b.* 1767 ; *m.* Rebecca, dau. of Robert Molloy, of Streamstown, King's Co., and *d.* 26 Oct. 1843, leaving issue. His eldest son, HENRY, of Maidstown, and afterwards of Gortnavidera, co. Tipperary, *m.* Elizabeth, dau. of Ringrose Atkins, of Prospect Hill, co. Cork. She *d.s.p.* 1852.
  2. Thomas, *m.* Margaret, dau. of John Maunsell, of Ballybrood, co. Limerick, and had one son,
    Thomas, *d. unm.*
  3. Henry, *m.* and had issue.
  4. Charles, *m.* and had issue, Rev. James S. Franks, and others.
2. THOMAS, of whom we treat.
3. Welstead, of Kiffinnan, co. Limerick, *m.* 1776, Frances, dau. of William Chapman, of Mallow ; and had a son, Thomas, of Mallow ; *d.s.p.* 1805.
  1. Margaret, *m.* Noble Seyward, of Kilcannaway, co. Cork.
  2. Mary, *m.* Thomas Heffernan, of co. Limerick.
  3. Gertrude, *m.* Sir John Purcell, Knt., of High Fort, co. Cork.
  4. Ellen.
The 2nd son,
THOMAS FRANKS, of Ballymagooly, co. Cork, *m.* Catherine, dau. of Rev. John Day, and *d.* 1787, leaving issue,
1. MATTHEW, of whom presently.
2. JOHN (Sir), ancestor of FRANKS *of Ballyscaddane*.
3. William, an officer R.N., *d.s.p.*
4. Robert, of Leeson Street, Dublin, *d. unm.* 1850.
1. Lucy, *m.* 9 April, 1791, Thomas Cuthbert, who assumed the name of KEARNEY. She *d.* 26 July, 1853. He *d.* 12 Aug. 1837, leaving issue.
2. Catherine, *m.* Thomas Leland, of Fitzwilliam Square, Dublin, and had issue.

3. Anne, *m.* 5 May, 1802, Hickman Kearney. He *d.* 21 April, 1851. She *d.* 25 Feb. 1845, leaving issue.
4. Mary, *m.* 1801, George Palmer, and had a dau.

The eldest son,

MATTHEW FRANKS, of Jerpoint, co. Kilkenny, and 28, Merrion Square, Dublin, *b.* 1768 ; *m.* 31 Oct. 1803, Mary, dau. of Robert Fergusson. She *d.* 11 Oct. 1856. He *d.* 25 March, 1853, having had issue,
1. THOMAS, of whom presently.
2. Robert Fergusson, of Jerpoint, and Upper Mount Street, Dublin, Barrister-at-Law, *b.* 22 March, 1807 ; *m.* 24 Feb. 1834, Henrietta, dau. of the Right Hon. Charles Kendal Bushe, Lord Chief Justice of Ireland, and had issue,
1. Norman, C.I.E., Capt. late the Buffs, East Kent Regt., (65, *Onslow Square, S.W., and Army and Navy Club*), *b.* 18 Feb. 1843 ; *m.* 26 Aug. 1875, Frances Mary Jane, dau. of the late Charles Yorke Lucas-Calcraft, D.L., of Ancaster Hall, Lincoln (*see that family*), and has issue,
(1) Norman Robert, *b.* Oct. 1885 ; *d.* May, 1893.
(2) John Fergusson, Lieut. 60th Rifles, *b.* 12 Nov. 1888.
(1) Mary Henrietta, *m.* 17 Dec. 1911, Capt. Denis D. Wilson, 17th Cavalry, son of the late Col. Wilson, C.B., of Cliffe Hall (*see that family*).
2. Cecil, *b.* 25 Sept. 1846.
3. John Hamilton (Sir), C.B., J.P. Dublin, Secretary to the Irish Land Commission (*Dalriada, Blackrock, co. Dublin, and University Club, Dublin*), *b.* 10 May, 1848 ; *m.* 8 Dec. 1874, Catherine, 2nd dau. of Harry Lumsden, of Auchindoir, co. Aberdeen, and has issue,
(1) James Gordon (*Roseneath, Malahide, co. Dublin*), *b.* 10 Sept. 1875 ; *m.* 30 April, 1904, Margaret, 4th dau. of Right Hon. Gerald FitzGibbon, P.C., LL.D.
(2) Robert Fergusson, *b.* 5 June, 1887.
(1) Rosalie Henrietta. (2) Anne Eleanor.
(3) Kathleen Elizabeth, m. 11 Oct. 1911, Henry Stokes, M.D.
(4) Dorothea Mary, *m.* 3 April, 1907, Henry H. Dixon, D.Sc.
4. Kendal Matthew St. John (Sir), C.B., M.D., F.R.C.S.I. (*Kilmurry, Johannesburg, S.A.*), Past Vice-President of the Royal College of Surgeons in Ireland, Consulting Surgeon to the Forces in South Africa 1902 (*Kildare Street Club, Dublin*), *b.* 8 Feb. 1851 ; *m.* 1st, 3 Sept. 1879, Charlotte Selina, who *d.* 12 Oct. 1883, eld. dau. of Richard Jonas Greene, and Louisa Lilias his wife, dau. of John, 3rd Lord Plunket. He *m.* 2ndly, 1885, Gertrude Jane, who *d.* 1896, 4th dau. of Lieut.-Col. T. Bromhead Butt, 79th Highlanders, and has issue,
(1) Kendal Fergusson, Lieut. 117th Mahratta Regt., *b.* 1 Sept. 1886.
(2) Philip Hamilton, *b.* 22 April, 1890.
(3) Ivan Bromhead, Midshipman R.N., *b.* 1896.
(1) Geraldine Jane.
5. Charles Kendal Bushe, *b.* 18 Dec. 1852 ; *d.* 1895.
1. Emma, *m.* 4 Jan. 1859, Major-Gen. Edward Loftus Bland, and *d.* 7 July, 1894, leaving issue (*see* BLAND, *of Blandsfort*).
2. Henrietta, *m.* 15 Aug. 1863, Col. Bruce Brine, R.E., and has issue (*see* BURKE's *Family Records*).
3. Mary, *d. unm.* 4. Sydney.
5. Rosalie, *d. unm.*, killed at Abergele, 1868.
6. Florence, *d. unm.*
7. Josephine, *d. unm.*
3. Matthew, *d. unm.* 4. John, *d. unm.*
1. Catherine, *m.* 1843, Rev. Denis Mahony, of Dromore Castle, co. Kerry, who *d.* 21 April, 1851, leaving issue (*see that family*).
2. Mary, *m.* 12 July, 1833, John Waller, of Shannon Grove, Pallaskenry, co. Limerick, who *d.* 25 Oct. 1846, leaving issue (*see* WALLER *of Castletown*).
3. Ellen, *m.* 16 July, 1834, Josiah Smyly, M.D., Vice President, Royal College of Surgeons, Ireland, and had issue. He *d.* 19 Jan. 1864.

The eldest son,

THOMAS FRANKS, of Dromrahane, Mallow, co. Cork, and 21, Lower Fitzwilliam Street, Dublin, *b.* 7 Jan. 1805 ; *m.* 17 Oct. 1834, Mary Anne Cuthbert, dau. of Thomas Cuthbert Kearney, of Mountfieldsown and Garrettstown, co. Cork. She *d.* 9 Nov. 1900. He *d.* 1 Jan. 1875, having had issue,
1. MATTHEW HENRY, now of Westfield.
2. Thomas Cuthbert, *b.* 29 Jan. 1839 ; *m.* 24 Oct. 1876, Isabella Mary, dau. of the late William Digges La Touche, and has issue,
1. Thomas William, *b.* 2 Dec. 1880.
2. Clement La Touche, *b.* 28 Dec. 1882.
3. Sidney Forster, *b.* 9 Jan. 1890 ; *d.* 8 Dec. 1899.
1. Alice Louisa.
2. Mary Emily, *d.* 27 July, 1879.
3. Grace Kathleen, *d.* young, 6 May, 1886.
4. Beatrice Nora.
He *m.* 2ndly, 18 Aug. 1908, Elizabeth, dau. of Henry Colclough Stephens.
3. Clement John, *b.* 11 Nov. 1840 ; *d.* 11 July, 1845.
1. Lucy Catherine, *d.* young, 10 March, 1852.
2. Mary Ellen, *d. unm.* 7 June, 1896.

Arms—Vert, on a saltire or, a griffin's head erased gu. in the centre chief point a mullet of the second. *Crest*—Out of a mural crown or a griffin's head gu. between two wings erminois, each charged with a mullet sa. *Motto*—Sic vos non vobis.

Seats—Westfield, Mountrath, Queen's Co., Garrettstown, Kinsale, and Dromrahane, Mallow, both co. Cork.

FRANKS OF BALLYSCADDANE.

THOMAS JOHN FRANKS, of Ballyscaddane, co. Limerick, J.P. for co. Limerick, High Sheriff 1883, *b.* 17 Nov. 1831 ; *m.* 1st, 25 April, 1865, Clara, only dau. of George Mackenzie Kettle, of Dallicott House, Shropshire, and by her (who *d.* 1878) has issue,
1. GEORGE MACKENZIE, Major R.A., *b.* 16 Oct. 1868 *m.* 20 June, 1901, Paula Rodriguez, dau. of Manuel Garcia, and has issue,
1. Raynald Arthur MacKenzie, *b.* 7 April, 1904.
1. Beata Cynthia McKenzie, *b.* 20 April, 1902.
2. Noel Honor MacKenzie, *b.* 31 Dec. 1905.
2. Henry Grazebrook, *b.* 28 Feb. 1873 ; *d. unm.* 6 Nov. 1894.
1. Rhoda Mary Whitmore, *b.* 26 Jan. 1870 ; *m.* 23 Aug. 1906, Hamilton Townsend, I.C.S., and has issue.

He *m.* 2ndly, 29 April, 1886, Eleanor Agnes, youngest dau. of the late Rev. S. Marindin, of Chesterton, Bridgnorth (*see that family*).

Lineage.—SIR JOHN FRANKS, Q.C., Judge of the Supreme Court, Bengal, 2nd son of Thomas Franks, of Ballymagooly, co. Cork (*see* FRANKS *of Westfield*), *b.* 1769 ; *m.* 1st, his cousin Catherine (who *d.* 1812), dau. of Thomas Franks, of Carrig, co. Cork ; 2ndly, Jane, dau. of John Marshall, and widow of George Sandes, of Kilcavan ; and 3rdly, 1849, Sarah Wollaston, dau. and co-heir of William O'Regan, Barrister-at-Law, and had issue by his 1st wife only,
1. JOHN, his heir.
2. Matthew, 11th Dragoons, *b.* 1807 ; *m.* 20 May, 1830, Louisa, dau. of Capt. Robert Roche, E.I.C.S. She *d.* 11 April, 1879. He *d.* 1836, leaving issue,
1. John, *b.* 22 Aug. 1831 ; *m.* 7 Feb. 1861, Margaret, 4th dau. of Thomas Brown, D.L., of Ebbw Vale Park, co. Monmouth, and *d.s.p.* 1892.
2. Robert, Col. R.A., *b.* 27 Feb. 1835 ; *m.* his kinswoman, Louisa, dau. of David Brudenell Franks (*see* FRANKS *of Carrig*), and *d.s.p.*
1. Margaret, *m.* 9 Jan. 1826, the Ven. John Hawtayne, Archdeacon of Bombay, and had issue. She *d.* 14 Oct. 1828.
2. Catherine, *m.* Thomas Montgomery, of Killee Castle, and *d.s.p.* 28 Feb. 1828.
3. Lucy, *m.* 8 Dec. 1831, Henry Holroyd, son of Sir George S. Holroyd, Judge of the Court of King's Bench in England, and had issue. He *d.* 29 Sept. 1859.

Sir John Franks *d.* 11 Jan. 1852, and was s. by his son,

JOHN FRANKS, of Ballyscaddane, J.P. and D.L. Essex, and J.P. cos. Limerick and Tipperary, *b.* 1803 ; *m.* 30 Dec. 1828, Elenora, dau. of William Whitmore, of Dudmastone Hall, Salop, and by her (who *d.* 1888) had issue,
1. THOMAS JOHN, now of Ballyscaddane.
2. Henry Whitmore, Lieut.-Col. 107th Regt., *b.* 9 Aug. 1840 ; *m.* 20 July, 1876, Elizabeth, dau. of John Watts, of Norton Court, co. Gloucester, and *d.* 6 Oct. 1895, having had issue,
1. Hugh Whitmore.
1. Lizzie. 2. Mary.
1. Mary, *m.* 1855, Thomas Wise Gubbins, of Kilfrush, and *d.* same year.
2. Eleanor Marion, *m.* 21 Oct. 1865, Thomas Franks, of Carrig Park, co. Cork (*see that family*).

Mr. Franks *d.* 25 April, 1881.

Arms—Vert, on a saltire or, a griffin's head erased gu. ; in the centre chief point a mullet of the second. *Crest*—Out of a mural crown or, a griffin's head gu. between two wings erminois, each charged with a mullet sa. *Motto*—Sic vos non vobis.

Seat—Ballyscaddane, Knocklong, co. Limerick.

FRENCH. *See* FFRENCH.

FRENCH OF CLOONYQUIN.

MAJOR ARTHUR JOHN ST. GEORGE FRENCH, of Cloonyquin, co. Roscommon, J.P., High Sheriff 1902, Major Prince of Wales' (N. Staffordshire) Regt., served in operations in Zululand 1887-8, *b.* 24 Feb. 1853 ; *m.* 27 Jan. 1898, Pauline Anna, dau. of the Rev. Edward Haddock, Rector of Harlington, Middlesex, and has issue,
1. Christopher Edward Geoffrey, *b.* 1 Dec. 1898 ; *d.* 2 May, 1900.
2. HARRY ARTHUR ST. GEORGE, *b.* 10 May, 1900.

French. THE LANDED GENTRY. 246

1. Maeve Pauline Alberti, b. 22 Aug. 1902.
2. Daphne Annette Emily, b. 13 Oct. 1905.

Lineage.—CHRISTOPHER FRENCH, of Tyrone, Dunkellin, co. Galway (son of Jeffrey French, of Mulpitt, co. Galway, d. 1610), settled his estate 20 May, 1675, and d. intestate, 30 July, 1676, leaving issue by Jane his wife (all mentioned in a certificate dated 6 April, 1677, confirming their title to the lands of Tyrone, etc., *Connaught Certificates, Roll* IV, p. 46); 1. ARTHUR, his heir; 2 Jeffry, who had a grant by letters patent 10 Aug. 1677, enrolled 10 Jan. 1678, of the lands of Tyrone, iu Tiaquin, and of Mulrooge in Dunkellin, co. Galway, and 3. Robert, who had a numerous family.

The eldest son,
ARTHUR FRENCH, of Tyrone, co. Galway, Mayor of Galway 1691, m. 1st, 1675, Mary Kirwan, who d. 1689, leaving issue,
1. Christopher, of Tyrone, conformed 1704, m. about 27 Jan. 1699, Margery, 3rd dau. of Iriel Farrell, of Cloonyquin, co. Roscommon, by Sarah (*see below*) his wife, dau. of Ulick Burke, of Clare, co. Galway. He made his will 31 July, 1718, which was proved 1720. He was ancestor of the family of FRENCH (afterwards ST. GEORGE) of Tyrone (*see* ST. GEORGE *of Tyrone*). His widow Margery m. James Browne, of Galway, who d. 1760. Her will, dated 27 June, 1757. was proved 24 May, 1760, by her son, Arthur French, of Tyrone.
1. Juliane, m. 1700. Simon Kirwan, eldest son of Sir John Kirwan, of Castlehacket. She d.s.p.

Arthur French m. 2ndly, 2 May, 1691, Sarah, only dau. of Ulick Burke, of Clare, co. Galway, and widow of Iriel Farrell, of Cloonyquin, co. Roscommon. She d. 1730, having by him had issue,
2. ARTHUR, of whom presently.
3. Simon Arthur Hyacinth. His dau. Jane, m. 1774, Joseph Burke, and had issue (*see* BURKE *of Auberies*).
4. Jeffery, of the Middle Temple, and Jamaica, M.P. for Tavistock. Will dated 24 Feb. 1754, codicil 14 May, 1754, proved 20 May same year.
5. Patrick. 6. Christopher.
7. Edmund.
2. Ellen, m. — Proby.
3. Jane, m. Richard Murphy.
4. Mary, m. Arthur Plunket, and had issue.

Mr. Arthur French d. intestate 1712 (admon. to his widow 13 Jan. 1712-13). The eldest son by the second marriage,
ARTHUR FRENCH, of Cloonyquin, m. 7 Dec. 1715, Judith, dau. of Henry Davis, of Carrickfergus. His will dated 24 May, 1729, was proved 16 July, 1729, in which one of the executors appointed is " my cozen Arthur French, of French Park." His widow m. Laurence Paine, of Meath. Her will, dated 19 Nov. 1757, was proved 15 April, 1761. Mr. Arthur French left issue,
1. ARTHUR, his heir.
2. John, of the Middle Temple, d. unm., will dated 1 Aug. 1753, proved 1754.
3. Henry, who left issue, a son,
HENRY WALTER. S. his uncle.
4. Christopher, Lieut.-Col. 52nd Regt. served with distinction in the wars in America and the West Indies, b. about 1725, m. 1748, Margarita Alberti, of Minorca, and d. 1797, having had issue,
1. Arthur, b. 1752, killed in the American war at an early age.
2. JOHN, s. his cousin.

The eldest son,
ARTHUR FRENCH, of Cloonyquin and of Croydon, d. unm. 20 Feb. 1789, and was s. by his nephew,
HENRY WALTER FRENCH, of Cloonyquin, b. 21 April, 1749; m. Eleanor Plunkett. He made his will 30 April, 1817, with codicil dated 18 Feb. 1820. He d.s.p. and was s. by his cousin,
COL. JOHN FRENCH, Quartermaster-General under Sir G. Murray, who served in Holland during the war. He was b. 22 June, 1764; m. June, 1789, Anna, dau. of the Ven. Joseph Story, Archdeacon of Kilmore, and d. 1823, leaving with other issue, who d. young,
1. WILLIAM CHRISTOPHER ST. GEORGE, his heir.
1. Frances Arabella, b. 11 March, 1800; m. Rev. Thomas T. La Nauze, and d.s.p.
2. Emily Olivia, b. 8 Jan. 1806; m. Commander James Caulfeild, R.N., and d.s.p. 1891.

The only son,
WILLIAM CHRISTOPHER ST. GEORGE FRENCH, of Cloonyquin, Lieut. in the Carabineers, and A.D.C. to Sir John Hope, b. 24 July, 1790; m. 31 Jan. 1819, Dorothea Helen, dau. of Michael Harris, of Upper Merrion Street, Dublin, and d. 17 Feb. 1852, having by her (who d. Oct. 1840) had issue.
1. CHRISTOPHER, late of Cloonyquin.
2. William, Gen., C.B., R.A., b. 1 Feb. 1829; m. 5 May, 1863, Frederica Laura, 2nd dau. of Adolphe de Marescaux, of Saint Omer, France, and d. Oct. 1909, leaving issue,
1. Fanny Emily, m. May, 1901. Henri Des Champs de la Revière.
2. Evelyn Laura, m. 1909, Hay Marescaux.
3. St. George (Rev.), b. 10 April, 1831; m. Annie, dau. of Henry Roe, of Fitzwilliam Square, Dublin. She d. 1888. He d. 1889, leaving a dau., Ada.
1. Mary Anne, m. 23 Oct. 1851, John Richardson, LL.D., Q.C., eldest son of the Rev. John Richardson, of Summerhill, co. Fermanagh, and has issue.
2. Dorothea Jane, m. 8 June, 1847, Col. William Montgomerie Stewart Caulfeild, and has issue (*see* CHARLEMONT, V.).
3. Emily, d. unm. 14 June, 1907.

The eldest son,
CHRISTOPHER FRENCH, of Cloonyquin, co. Roscommon, J.P. and D.L., High Sheriff 1852, B.A. Oxon, b. 15 June, 1821; m. 12 Feb. 1851, Susan Emma, dau. of the Rev. William A. Percy, Rector of Carrick-on-Shannon, and d. 8 May, 1897, leaving issue,
1. ARTHUR JOHN ST. GEORGE, now of Cloonyquin.

2. William Percy (27, *Clifton Hill, St. John's Wood*, N.W.), b. 1 May, 1854; m. 1st, 28 June, 1890, Ethel Kathleen, dau. of the late William Armytage Moore, of Arnmore, co. Cavan. She d. 29 June, 1891, s.p.s. He m. 2ndly, 24 Jan. 1894, Helen May Cunningham, dau. of John Sheldon, and by her has issue,
1. Ettie Gwendoline, b. 4 Nov. 1894.
2. Molly Helen, b. 13 March, 1896.
3. Joan Phyllis, b. 26 April, 1903.
3. Harry Percy, b. 6 Sept. 1863; m. July, 1904, Henrietta Scott, and has issue,
Phyllis Hamilton, b. April, 1905.
4. Christopher St. George, late Lieut. 5th Batt. Royal Irish Fus., b. 13 April, 1872; m. 25 Aug. 1902, Helène, dau. of Wilhelm Espersson, of Kristianstad, Sweden.
1. Elizabeth Jane, d. 3 Dec. 1906.
2. Dorothea Emma.
3. Alice Kathleen, m. 30 July, 1884, Sir Alfred Macdonald Bulteel Irwin, C.S.I., Puisne Judge and officiating Chief Judge, Lower Burma (49, *Aylesbury Road, Dublin*). She d. 18 April, 1899, leaving issue.
4. Emily Lucy, m. Oct. 1890, Charles de Burgh Daly, M.D., and has issue.
5. Christine Laura Sophia.

Arms—Erm., a chevron sa. **Crest**—A dolphin naiant, ppr.
Seat—Cloonyquin, co. Roscommon.

FRENCH.

GEN. SIR JOHN DENTON PINKSTAN FRENCH, G.C.B. (1909), G.C.V.O. (1905), K.C.M.G. (1902), formerly a midshipman R.N., Gen., Col. 19th Hussars, which regiment he formerly commanded, Hon. Col. 1st Batt. Cambridgeshire Regt., Hon. LL.D. (Camb.) 1903, Hon. D.C.L. (Oxford) 1904, Grand Officer of the Legion of Honour, commanded 1st Cav. Brigade, Aldershot, 1899, and the Cav. in S. Africa 1899-1901, and was Gen. Officer and Com.-in-Chief the Aldershot Command 1901-7, appointed Insp.-Gen. of the Forces 1907, he served in the Nile Exped. 1884-5, at Abu Klea and Metammeh, S. African War 1889-1902, has the Orders of the Red Eagle of Prussia, 1st class, the Iron Crown of Austria, St. Alexander Nevski of Russia and the Spanish Order of Military Merit, Legion of Honour, and Dannebrog of Denmark; b. 1852; m. 1880, Eleonora Anna, 2nd dau. of the late Richard William Selby Lowndes, J.P., of Elmers, Bletchley, and has issue,
1. JOHN RICHARD LOWNDES, b. 1881.
2. Edward Gerald Fleming, b. 1883.
1. Essex Eleanora, b. 1886.

Lineage.—STEPHEN FRENCH, of the town of Galway, living at the end of the 16th century, was father of
PATRICK FRENCH, b. 1583, who was a Burgess of the town of Galway, and before 1636 had acquired as mortgagee and by purchase extensive landed property in cos. Sligo and Roscommon. He was deprived of a considerable portion in 1636 by Sir Thomas Wentworth (Earl of Strafford), then Lord Deputy of Ireland, but in 1656-7 he was, by decrees of the Cromwellian Commissioners, allotted 6,000 acres in co. Roscommon. His will, dated 1 Aug. 1659, was proved 1671. He d. 1669, at his mansion house of Dungar (now called French Park), built by himself, and was bur. in the Dominican Abbey of Clonshanville, near French Park, in a vault near the belfry, on which are engraved the arms of his family and this inscription : " Pray for the soule of Patrick French fitz Stephen, of Galway, Burgess, who lived in this world eighty-six years." He had issue, six sons, 1. Patrick; 2. DOMINICK, of whom presently; 3. Edmond; 4. Robert; 5. Francis; and 6. Anthony. The 2nd son,
DOMINICK FRENCH, of French Park, and of Boyle, co. Roscommon, to whom his father had by deed conveyed all his real estate, secured a grant of a considerable portion by patent from the Crown under the Acts of Settlement, 22 March, 1666 (19 CHARLES II.). He was appointed, conjointly with Sir Robert King, Governor and Conservator of the Peace in the counties of Roscommon and Sligo. He m. Anne, dau. of Right Rev. Dr. Edward King, Bishop of Elphin (*see* BURKE's *Peerage*, KING, Bart.), and had by her three sons and four daus., viz, 1. JOHN, his heir; 2. Dominick; 3. Patrick; 1. Mary, m. Edward Ormsby, M.P. for Galway in 1715 : 2. Margaret, m. J. ffolliott, of the co. of Sligo ; 3. Sarah ; 4. Anne. Dominick French, whose will bears date 3 May, and was proved 20 Sept. 1670, was bur. in the Cathedral of Elphin, where his monument is still to be seen. He was s. by his eldest son,
JOHN FRENCH, of French Park, called "Tierna More," or the great landowner, fought in the army of King WILLIAM, and commanded a troop in the Enniskillen Dragoons at the Battle of Aughrim, having been attainted on account of his Whig principles by the Parliament held by JAMES II. at Dublin, in 1690. In 1703, he acquired by purchase from the Trustees of the Forfeited Estates

IRELAND. French.

the greater part of the estate forfeited by Major Owen O'Conor, of Ballinagar. He represented Carrick-on-Shannon in Parliament in 1695 (WILLIAM III), became Knight of the shire for Galway in 1703, and again in 1710, and was elected for Tulsk, of which borough he was patron, in 1715 and 1722. He *m.* Anne, dau. of Sir Arthur Gore, Bart. of Newtown, ancestor of the Earl of Arran, and by her whose will, dated 8 May, 1734, was proved 22 June, 1756 (GEORGE II.) had issue,
1. ARTHUR, his heir, ancestor of Lord de Freyne (*see* BURKE's *Peerage*, DE FREYNE, B.).
2. Robert, M.P. for Jamestown, *s.* his uncleGore, as Judge of the Common Pleas in Ireland, *m.* Frances Hull, and *d.* 29 May, 1772, aged 82, bur. at St. Michan's, Dublin.
3. JOHN, of whom next.
4. William (Rev.), Dean of Ardagh, of Abbey Boyle and Oak Port in Roscommon. He *m.* Arabella Frances, dau. of the Very Rev. Jeremy Marsh, Dean of Kilmore, on of Francis, Archbishop of Dublin, by Mary, his wife, dau. and co-heir of Jeremy Taylor, D.D., Bishop of Down and Connor, and had issue.
1. Mary, *m.* Francis Ormsby, of Willybrooke, co. Sligo, and had issue.
2. Olivia, *m.* Rev. William Digby, of Lackan, co. Roscommon, son of the Bishop of Elphin, and cousin of Robert, 1st Lord Digby.
3. Catherine, *m.* 14 Sept. 1728, John Crofton, of Lissaderra.
4. Sarah, *m.* Gilbert King.

John French *d.* at an advanced age in 1754, leaving £1,000 (a very large sum in those days) to be expended on his funeral; his body was laid in state in the park for three days and nights and the county were feasted round it. He was *s.* by his eldest son. His 3rd son,
JOHN FRENCH, of High Lalle, co. Roscommon, whose will dated 14 April, 1733, was proved 1756; *m.* his cousin Judith, dau. of Gilbert King of Charlestown (*see* BURKE's *Peerage*, KING, Bart.), and by her (who *m.* 2ndly, Rev. Rees Saunders, of Whitchurch, Salop) had issue,
1. JOHN, of whom next.
2. Arthur, *d. unm.*
1. Anne, *d. unm.*
The elder son,
JOHN FRENCH, *b.* about 1714 ; *m.* Eleanora, dau. of Col. Pinkstan, by Lady Jean Fleming his wife, dau. of the Earl of Wigton, and had issue,
1. Hugh.
2. FLEMING, of whom next.
The younger son,
FLEMING FRENCH, of Ripple Vale, co. Kent, *m.* 1st, Sarah Denton, and 2ndly, Helen, dau. of Edward Pakenham, of Ripple Vale, and had issue by his 1st wife a son,
JOHN DENTON PINKSTAN FRENCH, *b.* 1777 ; *d.* at Calais 16 July, 1833, aged 56. He *m.* Charlotte Isaacson, and by her (who *d.* at Nelson Square, 11 Sept. 1848, aged 74) had issue, a son,
JOHN TRACY WILLIAM FRENCH, of Ripple Vale, Kent, J.P., D.L., Commander R.N. 1847, who owned estate of Pinkstan, otherwise Susielienbiog, *b.* 1808. His will dated Jan. 1846, with two codicils dated 1854, was proved April, 1855. He *d.* at Nice, 10 Feb. 1855, having *m.* (marriage contract 10 May, 1842) Margaret, dau. of William Eccles, of Glasgow, Merchant (son of James Eccles), and by her had issue,
1. JOHN DENTON PINKSTAN (SIR), *see above*.
1. Mary Ramody. 2. Charlotte.
3. Margaret. 4. Caroline Pinkstan.
5. Sarah Eleanor.

Arms—Erm., a chevron sa. *Crest*—A dolphin naiant ppr. *Residences*—The Manor House, Waltham Cross, Herts ; 22, North Audley Street. *Clubs*—Army and Navy, Marlborough, Bath, Cavalry.

FRENCH OF CUSKINNY.

SAVAGE FRENCH, of Cuskinny, co. Cork, J.P. and D.L., educated at Westminster and Ch. Ch. Oxon., *b.* 25 June, 1840 ; *m.* 29 April, 1869, Frances Maria, dau. of George Gough, of Rathronan House, Clonmel, co. Tipperary, and has issue,
1. Sampson Gough, Capt. Royal Irish Regt., *b.* 23 Jan. 1870, killed in action in S. Africa, 12 Feb. 1900, *d. unm.*
2. HUGH, *b.* 30 July, 1871.
3. Charles Newenham, Capt. Hampshire Regt., *b.* 13 July, 1875.
4. Wilfred Frankland, Lieut. R.N., *b.* 9 Nov. 1880.
1 Mary Charlotte.
2. Dorothy Melian, *m.* 19 Dec. 1911, Francis H. W. Goolden, Lieut. R.N., eld. son of E. R. Goolden, of Cookham Grove, Cookham.
3. Marjorie Harriette.

Lineage.—This family descends from RICHARD FRENCH, who *d.* in 1651, leaving a bequest to the poor of St. Finn Barr's parish, in the city of Cork, which is still paid from property belonging to the family. The said Richard French had issue by his wife, Elizabeth, five sons and four daus.,
1. Edmond, *m.* and had issue.
2. Bate, Sheriff of Cork, 1688, *m.* and had issue.
3. Richard.
4. Matthews, J.P. co. Cork, *m.* and had issue.
5. JAMES, of whom presently.
1. Elizabeth, *m.* William French.
2. Sarah, *m.* Richard Newman, ancestor of Newman, of Dromore, co. Cork.

3. Martha, *m.* Thomas Frankland, ancestor of the Franklands of Ashgrove, Great Island, co. Cork. 4. Anne French.
The 5th son,
JAMES FRENCH, J.P., was Mayor of Cork in 1696. His will, dated 10 Oct. 1705, was proved 15 Nov. 1711. He *m.* Elizabeth Savage, sister of Captains Philip and Edward Diamond, and had issue, six sons and four daus.,
1. Richard. 2. James.
3. Philip, Sheriff of Cork 1712.
4. Abraham, Mayor of Cork 1717.
5. SAVAGE, of whom presently. 6. Edward.
1. Susanna, *m.* Richard Cox, eldest son of Sir Richard Cox, Bart., Lord Chancellor of Ireland. 2. Frances.
The 5th son,
SAVAGE FRENCH, of Marino, J.P. co. Cork, whose will, dated 15 June, 1769, was proved 31 Jan. 1770, *m.* Mary, dau. and ultimate heir of George Towgood, by Catherine his wife, dau. and eventually co-heir of Alderman Christopher Crofts, of Cork, and had issue,
1. Sampson Towgood, *d.s.p.* 2. SAVAGE, of whom presently.
3. Richard Temple. 4. Matthew Dean Towgood.
1. Elizabeth Savage. 2. Catherine, *m.* Michael Becher.
3. Melian Towgood, *m.* 1766, Morgan Donovan, of Cork, and *d.* 1813, leaving a son, Rev. Morgan William Donovan, who became O'DONOVAN, on the death of his kinsman, in 1829 (*see* O'DONOVAN *of Clan Cathal*).
4. Dorcas.
The 2nd son,
SAVAGE FRENCH, of Marino, *m.* 29 Sept. 1770, Mary, dau. of Rev. Thomas Millerd, and had issue,
1. SAVAGE, his heir.
2. THOMAS GEORGE, of Marino, *b.* 8 Aug. 1780 ; *d.* 22 Sept. 1866 ; *m.* 16 May, 1811, Charlotte Granville, dau. of Pascoe Grenfell, M.P., of Taplow House, Bucks (*see* BURKE's *Peerage*, DESBOROUGH, B.), and by her (who *d.* 27 March, 1845) had issue,
1. PASCOE SAVAGE, of Marino, J.P., *b.* 1 Dec. 1815 ; *d.* 24 Sept. 1893.
1. Georgiana Hill, *d.* 18 March, 1904.
2. Emily Grenfell, dec.
3. Louisa Augusta, *m.* 9 Jan. 1840, the Hon. Robert Hare. She *d.* 9 Oct. 1853. He *d.* 8 July, 1865, leaving issue (*see* BURKE's *Peerage*, LISLOWELL, E.).
4. Henrietta Caroline, *d.*
5. Eleanor Dorcas, *m.* 12 Jan. 1859, Major-Gen. William James Stuart, R.E., and had issue (*see* STUART-FRENCH *of Marino*).
3. Sampson Towgood, *d. unm.* 1831.
The eldest son,
SAVAGE FRENCH, of Cuskinny, *m.* 2 Sept. 1806, Clotilda Elizabeth, dau. of the Rev. Robert Dring, of Rock Grove, co. Cork, and by her (who *d.* 9 Aug. 1832) left issue (at his decease, 28 Nov. 1834) five sons and nine daus.,
1. SAMPSON TOWGOOD WYNNE, his heir.
2. Robert Dring, R.N., *b.* 2 Oct. 1808 ; *d.* 24 March, 1838.
3. Thomas Fitzgerald (Ven.), Archdeacon of Killaloe, *b.* 25 Jan. 1825 ; *d.* 30 Dec. 1884 ; *m.* 28 June, 1859, Harriett Selina, 2nd dau. of James Molony, D.L., of Kiltanon, co. Clare, by Lucy his wife, sister of Sir Trevor Wheler, 8th bart. of Leamington, co. Warwick, and had issue,
1. Fitzgerald Charles, *b.* 1 May, 1861.
2. Riversdale Sampson, M.B., *b.* 28 Dec. 1862, *m.* 5 Aug. 1903, Lilian Elizabeth, dau. of late Henry Morgan Earberry Crofton, of Inchnappa, Ashford, co. Wicklow (*see* BURKE's *Peerage*).
3. Deane, *b.* 28 May, 1864.
4. Arthur James Pascoe, *b.* 3 Oct. 1865.
5. Raymond William, *b.* 11 May, 1867 ; *m.* 11 Feb. 1903, Sophie, widow of Francis R. Wolfe, and dau. of The O'Morchoe, of Foxrock, co. Dublin (*see* MACMURROGH-MURPHY).
6. Frederick Beresford, *b.* 18 Nov. 1869 ; *d.* 6 Dec. 1875.
7. Henry O'Donovan, *b.* 12 April, 1872.
1. Lucy Selina, *b.* 10 April, 1860.
2. Agnes Melian, *b.* 21 Oct. 1868.
4. Matthew Deane Towgood, R.N., *d.* at Tahiti, 16 Dec. 1843, on board H.M.S. *Basilisk*.
5. William Temple, *b.* 26 July, 1831 ; *d.* 9 Sept. 1851.
1. Elinor Elizabeth, *d. unm.* 2 April, 1885.
2. Maria Clotilda, *d. unm.* 27 Feb. 1828.
3. Elizabeth Frances, *d. unm.* 3 Aug. 1830.
4. Frances Melian, *d. unm.* 24 Feb. 1830.
5. Helen Louisa, *d. unm.* 11 Feb. 1892.
6. Henrietta Catherine, *d. unm.* 5 April, 1829.
7. Charlotte Georgina, *d. unm.* 30 Dec. 1884.
8. Georgina Wilhelmina Temple, *d. unm.* 27 Jan. 1903.
9. Melian Dorothea, *d. unm.* 4 Dec. 1905.
The son and successor,
SAMPSON TOWGOOD WYNNE FRENCH, of Cuskinny, co. Cork, J.P., *b.* 19 July, 1807 ; *m.* 12 Sept. 1837, Phebe Maria, youngest dau. of Samuel Perry, of Woodrooff, co. Tipperary, by the Hon. Deborah Prittie his wife, dau. of the 1st Lord Dunalley (*see* BURKE's *Peerage*), and by her (who *d.* 7 Sept. 1893) had issue,
1. SAVAGE, now of Cuskinny.
2. Sampson Towgood, } twins, *b.* 17 March, 1842 ; *d.* same
3. Henry Thomas, } month.
4. Sampson Towgood Samuel, *b.* 28 June, 1843 ; *d.* 22 Feb. 1847.
1. Deborah, *d. unm.* 26 Aug. 1858.
2. Elizabeth Anne, *d. unm.* Sept. 1871.
3. Caroline Mary, *m.* 1 Nov. 1864, Joseph Sladen, Capt. R.A., of Ripple Court, Kent, and *d.* 6 April, 1873, leaving issue (*see that family*).
4. Phœbe Maria Catherine.
He *d.* 12 Nov. 1878.

Seat—Cuskinny, Queenstown.

French.   THE LANDED GENTRY.   248

FRENCH OF MARINO.

MAJOR CLAUDE HOUSTON STUART-FRENCH, of Marino, co. Cork, b. 6 March, 1867, Major (ret.) 5th Dragoon Guards; m.
s. his brother 29 July, 1911; assumed the name and arms of FRENCH on succeeding to the estate by Royal Licence.

Lineage — THOMAS GEORGE FRENCH, of Marino (2nd son of Savage French, of Marino, see FRENCH of Cuskinny), b. 8 Aug. 1780; d. 22 Sept. 1866; m. 16 May, 1811, Charlotte Granville, dau. of Pascoe Grenfell, M.P., of Taplow House, Bucks (see BURKE's *Peerage*, DESBOROUGH, B.), and by her (who d. 27 March, 1845) had one son and five daus.,
1. Pascoe Savage, his heir.
1. Georgina Hill.   2. Emily Grenfell, d. unm.
3. Louisa Augusta, d. 9 Oct. 1853; m. 9 Jan. 1840, Hon. Robert Hare.
4. Henrietta Caroline, d. unm.
5. Eleanor Dorcas, m. 12 Jan. 1859, Major-Gen. William James Stuart, R.E., and had issue, four sons and two daus.,
    1. Hamilton, b. 27 March, 1860; d. unm. 11 May, 1882, Lieut. Essex Regt.
    2. Thomas George, who s. his uncle.
    3. Claude Houston, now of Marino.
    4. Pascoe Grenfell, b. 5 Oct. 1868; m.
    1. Charlotte Granville, m. Sept. 1884, Lieut.-Col. Robert F. M. F. M. Synge, late Highland L.I.
    2. Wilhelmina, m. Lieut.-Col. Mansell, R.A.

PASCOE SAVAGE FRENCH, of Marino, J.P. co. Cork, b. 1 Dec. 1815; d. 24 Sept. 1893, having devised his estate to his nephews successively on condition of assuming the name and arms of FRENCH,
THOMAS GEORGE STUART-FRENCH, of Marino, assumed the name and arms of FRENCH by Royal Licence 20 Oct. 1894, b. 2 Dec. 1862; d. unm. 29 July, 1911.

Arms—Quarterly 1st and 4th, sa., a bend between two dolphins naiant bendways arg., in the dexter chief point a crescent of the field (FRENCH). 2nd and 3rd quarterly (i) or, a lion rampant, within a double tressure flory counterflory gu.; (ii) or, a fesse chequy arg. and az. in chief a label of three points gu.; (iii) arg. a saltire engrailed between four roses gu.; (iv) az., a lion rampant arg., the whole within a bordure compony az. and arg., over all in the fesse point a crescent for difference (STUART). Crests—1. A dolphin naiant arg. charged with a crescent sa. (FRENCH); 2. a unicorn's head couped arg. armed crined and tufted or charged with a crescent gu. for difference (STUART). Motto—Veritas.

Seat—Marino, co. Cork.

FRENCH, sometime OF ARDSALLAGH.

The late CAPT. CAULFEILD FRENCH, of Castle Bernard, King's Co., J.P. and D.L., High Sheriff 1887, late Capt. 94th Regt., b. 27 Dec. 1839; m. 15 June, 1875, Margaret Adeline, dau. of the late Maj. John Henry Scroope Bernard, and grand-dau. of Col. Thomas Bernard, of Castle Bernard, M.P. (see that family), and Lady Catherine Henrietta Hely-Hutchinson, his wife, sister of John, 3rd Earl of Donoughmore. He d. 7 June, 1910. She d. 17 July, 1910, when the estate of Castle Bernard devolved equally upon the daus. of Thomas Scrope Wellesley Bernard, of Castle Bernard (see that family).

Lineage.—ROBERT HENRY FRENCH of Dublin, 5th son of Arthur French, M.P., of French Park (see BURKE's *Peerage*, DE FREYNE, B.), and Alicia his wife, dau. of Richard Magennis, of Dublin, m. 1798, Charlotte, dau. of John Reynell, of Castle Reynell, co. Westmeath. She d. Sept. 1853. He d. 28 Nov. 1847, leaving issue,
1. Arthur, of Dublin, m. 1 Feb. 1828, Emily Eleanor Wilhelmina, only surviving child of Charles Albert Leslie, of Ballibay, co. Monaghan, and d. 6 March, 1843, having had issue,
    1. Robert Charles LESLIE, of Ballibay, D.L., assumed by Royal Licence, 1885, the name and arms of LESLIE, b. 30 Nov. 1828; m. 5 Jan. 1867, Charlotte Philippa Mary, dau. of Capt. Edward Kelso, of Kelsoland and Horkesley (see that family), and has issue (see LESLIE of Ballibuy).

---

2. Charles Albert Leslie Attila, Col. late 2nd Dragoon Guards, b. 5 Oct. 1842; m. 19 June, 1873, Agnes, dau. of Samuel Laing, M.P., and has issue,
    (1) Charles Albert, b. 1877.
    (2) Cecil, b. 7 March, 1879.
1. Helena Charlotte, m. 12 Aug. 1851, James Blake, of Cregg Castle, co. Galway, and has issue.
2. Albertina Caroline, m. James Ryan.
3. Henrietta Victoria Alexandra, m. 29 Sept. 1863, Col. Charles Kendal Bushe, late 59th Regt., of Bramhope, Old Charlton, and has issue.
2. Richard Barton, Major-Gen. late 52nd L.I., m. 1836, Henrietta, dau. of Hamilton Gorges of Kilbrew. She d. 21 Oct. 1878. He d.s.p. 10 Nov. 1861.
3. Henry Sneyd, of Clonsilla, co. Dublin, High Sheriff of Dublin 1848, m. 1st, 15 Feb. 1843, Catherine, dau. of Piers Geale, and by her had issue,
    Selina Harriett, m. 5 June, 1866, Major-Gen. Townsend Aremberg de Moleyns, R.A., and has issue (see VENTRY. B.).
He m. 2ndly, 21 June, 1850, Elizabeth Mary, dau. of the Right Hon. Abraham Brewster, Lord Chancellor of Ireland. She d. 10 Nov. 1868. He d. 20 Sept. 1850, having by her had issue (see FRENCH-BREWSTER, of Cloonanartmore).
4. WILLIAM JOHN, of whom presently.
1. Louisa, m. 1816, Lieut.-Col. Raymond Pelly, C.B. She d. 20 April, 1882. He d. 20 Dec. 1845, leaving issue.
2. Elizabeth Alicia, m. 16 Feb. 1833, Hon. George Handcock. She d. 1 April, 1890. He d. 20 Oct. 1867, leaving issue (see BURKE's *Peerage*, CASTLEMAINE, B.).

The youngest son,
WILLIAM JOHN FRENCH, of Ardsallagh, co. Meath, High Sheriff of Dublin 1862, b. 28 Dec. 1812; m. 24 June, 1837, Harriett Anna, only dau. of James Caulfeild, of Drumcairne (see BURKE's *Peerage*, CHARLEMONT, V.). She d. 27 Feb. 1890. He d. 24 Dec. 1876, having had issue,
1. CAULFIELD, late of Castle Bernard.
2. Arthur Robert, b. 2 March, 1843; drowned 3 Aug. 1876.
3. Peregrine Maitland, late Capt. 69th Regt., b. 4 May, 1844; m. 6 June, 1889, Margaret Fleming, dau. of Robert Stewart Dykes.
4. Alfred Crofton, of Ballyglass, co. Roscommon, late Capt. 43rd L.I., b. 21 March, 1845; d. 4 March, 1908; m. 16 Jan. 1884, Alice Clarinda, widow of Henry White, 11th Hussars (see WHITE of *Cloone Grange*), and dau. of Edmund Floyd Cuppage, of Claregrove, co. Dublin.
5. Henry Richard, b. 2 Nov. 1850; d. 4 Nov. 1855.
6. William Algernon, b. 2 Nov. 1851; d. unm. 3 April, 1894.
7. Houston, late Capt. 2nd Life Guards, Clerk of the Cheque and Adjutant of the King's Body Guard, of the Yeomen of the Guard (59, Hans Road, S.W.), b. 27 March, 1853; m. 10 March, 1883, Ilene, dau. of Col. Ross.
1. Georgiana Harriett, m. 4 Oct. 1870, William de Salis Filgate of Lissrenny, co. Louth, and has issue (see that family).
2. Louisa, d. unm. 3 Dec. 1888.   8. Adela.
4. Ida Charlotte, m. 23 July, 1884, Rev. Henry Wray Young, Rector of Stewartstown, co. Tyrone.
5. Florence Clara.
6. Eva Augusta, m. 15 April, 1878, George Tilson Shaen-Carter, of Shaen Manor, co. Mayo, and d. 15 July, 1891, leaving issue (see that family).

Arms—Erm. a chevron sa.   Crest—A dolphin embowed ppr.
Motto—Malo mori quam foedari.

FRENCH-BREWSTER. See BREWSTER.

FREND OF ROOTIAGH.

GEORGE FREND, of Rootiagh, co. Limerick, and Silver Hills, King's Co., J.P. for King's Co. and Tipperary, b. 16 Feb. 1850; m. 25 April, 1877, Lucy Fanny, eldest dau. of Capt. Edward A. Blackett, R.N., of Wylam, Northumberland, and has issue,
1. GEORGE ALGERNON, b. 2 April, 1879.
2. Lionel William, b. 28 June, 1880; d. 9 July that year.
3. Edward Montagu, b. 30 Sept. 1881.
4. John Roberts, b. 7 Feb. 1883.
5. Henry Christopher Blackett, b. 22 June, 1891.
1. Lucy Georgiana, m. 17 July, 1907, Rev. F. R. Laurence, Rector of Templeharry.

Lineage.—JOHN FREND, a Capt. of a troop of horse, got a grant of 3,187 acres of land in co. Limerick (amongst other, Boskell); and was High Sheriff 1659-60. By Jane his wife, he had, with four daus., as many sons,
1. Samuel, of Carrickareely, co. Limerick.
2. Jonathan, of Kilmurry, co. Kilkenny.
3. John, Capt. in the Army.
4. BENJAMIN, of whom presently.

The youngest son,
BENJAMIN FREND, of Boskell, Temple Michael, and Knockanna,

and of Ballyreehy, King's Co., *m.* a dau. of the Rev. John Padfield, of Ballintemple, King's Co., Prebendary of Dysart, and had issue. The only surviving son,

BENJAMIN FREND, of Boskell, co. Limerick, and of Ballyreehy, King's Co., High Sheriff 1717, *m.* Bridget, dau. of Edward Kynaston, of London, and niece of Robert Colepeper, who left her half his estate, and had issue. The son and heir,

JOHN FREND, of Boskell, co. Limerick, Ballyreehy, King's Co., and of Dollinstown, co. Meath, High Sheriff 1740; *m.* 1st, 1728, Margaret, dau. of Col. Josias Campbell, of Mount Campbell, Drumsna, and by her (who *d.* 1734) had issue,
1. Letitia, *d. unm.*
2. Jane, *m.* 1766, George Burdett, of Heath House, King's Co., M.P. for Thomastown.
3. Margaret, *m.* Ormsby, of the co. Sligo.

He *m.* 2ndly, 1738, Jane, dau. of Henry Vereker, of Roxborough, co. Limerick, and had by her (who *d.* 1739) a son and heir,
1. BENJAMIN, of whom presently.

He *m.* 3rdly, Elizabeth, sister of John Ward, and had issue,
2. John, Capt. in the King's Co. Militia.   3. William.
4. Eliza.   5. Anne.   6. Caroline.

Mr. Frend *d.* 1749 and was *s.* by his son,

BENJAMIN FREND, of Boskell, co. Limerick, and of Cloneen, King's Co., High Sheriff 1782, *b.* 1739; *m.* 3 Nov. 1773, Arabella, dau. of George Purdon, of Tinnerana, co. Clare, M.P. (*see that family*), by Arabella Mary his wife, 3rd dau. and co-heir of Col. William Causabon, M.P. for Carrig, co. Cork, by Arabella his wife, 2nd dau. and co-heir of the Right Hon. Sir John Rogerson, Lord Chief Justice of the King's Bench, and had issue,
1. John, *d. unm.*, aged 22.
2. GEORGE CULLODEN, *s.* his father.
3. BENJAMIN, of Boskell, *b.* 1779, J.P. co. Limerick; *m.* 1810, Eliza, 2nd dau. of Gough Gough, of Woodstown, same co., and sister of Hugh, 1st Viscount Gough (*see* BURKE's *Peerage*), and *d.* Jan. 1858, leaving issue,
  1. BENJAMIN BUNBURY FREND, of Boskell, *m.* 13 Nov. 1842, Jane, dau. of Very Rev. Richard Bagwell, of Marfield, co. Tipperary, Dean of Clogher (*see* BAGWELL *of Marlfield*), and *d.* 1875, having by her (who *d.* 1891) had issue,
    (1) BENJAMIN, of Boskell, Major 60th Rifles, *b.* Oct. 1844; *d. unm.* in India 1883.
    (1) EDITH MARGARET, of Boskell, *m.* 15 June, 1876, George John Minchin, of Busherstown, King's Co. (*see that family*). He *d.s.p.* 16 Aug. 1897.
    (2) AGNES ELIZA, of Boskell, *m.* 1873, Robert de Ros Rose, of Ahabeg, co. Limerick. He *d.* April, 1900, leaving issue (*see that family*).
  2. George, Col., *m.* 14 April, 1853, Emily Hester Mary, dau. of the late Lieut.-Gen. Sir Robert Gardiner, K.C.B., R.A. She *d.* his widow 14 Jan. 1906, leaving issue,
    (1) George, Lieut.-Col. Northumberland Fusiliers, *b.* 3 April, 1857.
    (2) Robert Benjamin, *b.* 13 March, 1864; *d.* 15 July, 1907.
    (1) Caroline.   (2) Louisa.
  3. John William, *m.* 27 Dec. 1851, Elizabeth Crosbie, 2nd dau. and co-heir of Rev. Mathew Moore, and grand-dau. of Edward Moore, of Mooresfort, co. Tipperary, by Elizabeth his wife, dau. of Hon. and Very Rev. Maurice Crosbie, Dean of Limerick, and sister of William, 4th Lord Brandon (*see* TALBOT-CROSBIE *of Ardfert*), and had a dau.,
    Ada.
  4. William Causabon, *d.* young.
  1. Letitia, *m.* Rev. Benjamin B. Gough.
  2. Arabella, *d. unm.*
  3. Jane Eliza, *n..* Oct. 1841, William Going, of Ballyphilip, co. Tipperary (*see that family*). He *d.* 1879. She *d.* 2 Oct. 1892, leaving issue.
  4. Eliza, *m.* Rev. J. Byrne.   5. Sarah.
  6. Mary Isabella.
4. William (Rev.), *m.* Elizabeth, dau. of — Briscoe, of Tinvane, and by her (who *m.* 2ndly, Capt. Thomas Coppinger) had issue,
  1. Benjamin B.
  1. Mary, *d. unm.*   2. Eliza, *m.* Thomas Gough.
1. Arabella, *m.* 22 May, 1804, the Rev. Christopher Tuthill (*see that family*).
2. Georgina Harriet.   3. Adelaide Anne.
4. Martha Amelia.

Mr. Frend *d.* 23 Jan. 1809. He barred the entail of his estates, which he bequeathed to his 2nd surviving son, while the representation of his family devolved on to his eldest surviving son,

GEORGE CULLODEN FREND, of Limerick, *b.* 16 April, 1777; *m.* May, 1816, Letitia Jane, dau. of William Roberts, of Mount Rivers, co. Cork, by Eliza his wife, dau. of Joseph Poulter, of Dunkitt, co. Kilkenny, and Letitia his wife, dau. of Stratford Canning, of Garvagh, co. Londonderry, and aunt of Right Hon. George Canning, First Lord of the Treasury, by whom, who *d.* 25 April, 1873, he had issue,
1. John, *b.* 16 March, 1820; *d.* 24 July, 1826.
2. WILLIAM CAUSABON, of whom presently.
3. George Purdon, *d.* 4 Oct. 1842.
4. Benjamin, *m.* Emma, dau. of N. Grüt, of London, and has issue a son, Purdon, and a dau., Henrietta Elizabeth.
1. Elizabeth, *m.* Rev. George Burrowes, Prebendary of Carrigrobanmore, Ross, only son of Very Rev. Robert Burrowes, D.D., Dean of Cork.
2. Arabella Mary, *d.* 10 Nov. 1893.
3. Letitia Jane, *d.* 20 May, 1889.
4. Mary, *d.* 23 Feb. 1859.
5. Georgiana Harriett, *d.* 11 Nov. 1892.
6. Martha Amelia.

7. Adelaide Anne, *m.* 19 July, 1859, Rev. John Harding Cole, of Woodview, Innishannon, Rector of Leighmoney, co. Cork. She *d.* 17 June, 1892, leaving issue (*see that family*). He *d.* 15 May, 1909.

Mr. Frend *d.* 8 Feb. 1851, and was *s.* by his eldest son,

WILLIAM CAUSABON FREND, of Rootiagh, Lieut.-Col. H.M. 73rd Regt., *b.* 17 Sept. 1821; *m.* 3 Jan. 1849, Harriott Georgiana, 3rd dau. of Captain Garvey, R.N., of Thornvale, King's Co., and *d.* 29 March, 1886, having had issue,
1. GEORGE, now of Rootiagh and Silver Hills.
2. Causabon William, *b.* 18 June, 1851; *m.* 1 Sept. 1897, Stella Frances Eliza, eldest dau. of Rev. Eckersall Nixon, Canon of Killaloe (*see* BURKE's *Family Records*) and grand-dau. of Sir Andrew Armstrong, Bart., and has issue,
  1. Benjamin Archie Nixon Causabon, *b.* 12 Jan. 1908.
  1. Stella Constantia Harriet Causabon.
  2. Clara Causabon.
3. Henry, *b.* 17 Feb. 1853; *m.* 3 June, 1884, Mary Annie Johnstone, only child of Andrew Macnair Urquhart, and grand-dau. of John Urquhart, of Fair Hill, co. Lanark.
4. Frederick Roberts, *b.* 31 Jan. 1855; *d.* 25 May, 1857.
1. Jane, *m.* 22 Nov. 1877, Frederick Coore Mein, Lieut. 53rd Regt., and had issue. She *d.* 28 March, 1884.
2. Mary.

Seats—Rootiagh, co. Limerick, and Silver Hills, King's Co.

FULLER OF GLASHNACREE.

JAMES FRANKLIN FULLER, of Glashnacree, co. Kerry, F.S.A., *b.* 1835; *m.* 1860, Helen, dau. of John Prospére Guivion, and grand-dau. of Marshal (St. Cyr) Guivion, one of Napoleon's Generals, and has had,
1. Franklin Bland, Cadet R.M.A., 14 Jan. 1879, Lieut. R.A., 1880, *b.* 1 Jan. 1863; *d.* 13 June, 1882.
2. HARNETT JOHN, C.E., T.C.D., *b.* 14 Dec. 1866; *m.* 10 April, 1894, Augusta Hobart, 2nd dau. of the late John Hurly, J.P., of Fenit House, Tralee (*see* HURLY *of Glendutfe*), and has issue,
  Franklin Bland, *b.* 2 Nov. 1897.
1. May Florence, *m.* 1889, Sir Gabriel Stokes, K.C.S.I., son of Henry Stokes, of Askive, co. Kerry, and *d.* 15 Jan. 1897, leaving issue, Terence, Lieut., Indian Army; Adrian, R.N.; and Herbert.
2. Adela Bessie, *b.* 1868; *d.* 1886.   3. Evelyn Melicent.

Lineage.—This family was one of great respectability and opulence in the co. Kerry, possessing property in the neighbourhood of Dingle, the Samphires, Ballybunion, &c., long before the English settlers, under the "Plantation Scheme," established themselves in the locality. The first of whom there is any record was

JOHN FULLER, who is mentioned in the "Desmond Survey," A.D. 1583, as possessed of the townland of Bowlerstown (Ballybowler) and "certain lands in Ballybeg." He mortgaged Bowlerstown to Stephen Rice 1610. According to an Inquisition taken at Killarney, he and Maurice Fuller (probably his son) were seized in fee of the townlands of Ballyristin or Ballyristeenig and Ballytobin or Ballytobeenig, and conveyed them in 1635, to Teige Moriarty. That John Fuller was a man of mark at this period appears by an Inquisition taken at Killarney, 18 Aug. 1635 (Inq. No. 59 CHARLES I, co. Kerry, Chancery, calendered by the Record Commissioners 1818), which found that he held his lands "de Dno Rege in capite p. service militar," *i.e.* by Knight's service. He was pardoned, 1st of JAMES I, being then of Rahinane. Barbara Fuller, who *m.* Richard Alkins, of Firvile, was of the same family.

JOHN FULLER and WILLIAM FULLER signed as grand jurors at Tralee 1709, the presentment regarding outlaws (No. 617, co. Kerry, cart. 62 Record Office). The latter *m.* at Cloyne, 31 Jan. 1679, Elizabeth, dau. of John Whiting, of Kilbrin, co. Cork. We pass to

WILLIAM FULLER, *m.* 1713, Elinor, dau. and co-heir of Thomas Hodder, of Ballea Castle, Barrister-at-Law, High Sheriff of Cork 1697, and had, with two daus., Elinor (*m.* John Sealy, of Richmount, and Catherine (*m.* Edward Day, of Loghercannon), two sons,
1. WILLIAM, of whom presently.
2. George, High Sheriff Cork 1740, *m.* Catherine Austin, and had issue.
3. Thomas, of Fuller Park, Freeman of Cork 1718; *m.* 1711, Lydia, dau. of William Green, High Sheriff of Cork 1690, by Mary Hayes, his wife, and *d.* 1759, leaving, with other issue,
  1. William, *m.* Frances Grey,
  2. Richard, who *m.* Jane Roe, and was father of Major Thomas Richard Fuller, who *m.* as his 2nd wife, Mary, dau. of Capt. England, and was father of THE RIGHT REV. THOMAS BROCK FULLER, D.D., Bishop of Niagara, from whom the Canadian branch descends (*see* BURKE's *Colonial Gentry*).

The eldest brother,

WILLIAM FULLER, of West Kerries, near Tralee, obtained from Col. Denny, by lease, dated 25 Sept. 1733, for lives renewable for ever, 195 plantation acres of those lands, " as then held and enjoyed." He *m.* Jane, dau. of William Harnett, of Ballyhenry, by his wife, sister of Rev. William Pellican, Rector of Obrenan, by whom (who *d.* 1741) he had issue,

1. WILLIAM, whose will dated March, 1765, was proved 1765. He was ancestor of CAPT. JOHN CROSBIE-FULLER-HARNETT, who *d.s.p.*
2. THOMAS, of whom hereafter.
3. George, *m.* and had issue.
4. Robert, who *m.* Mary, dau. of Frederick and grand-dau. of Whittall Brown, and had issue.
1. Jane, *m.* William Payne, of Tralee, and had issue.
2. Ann, who is mentioned in the *Gentleman's Magazine*, July, 1790, as " authoress of several interesting and ingenious novels," *d. unm.*
3. A dau., *m.* — Bernard, of Sheheree.
4. Ellen, *m.* — Hilliard.
5. Elizabeth.

The 2nd son,

THOMAS FULLER, of Leemount, Treasurer of co. Cork, *m.* (Mar. Lic. 16 June, 1767), Ann, 3rd dau. of John Purcell, of Gurtinard, co. Cork, by Mary, his wife, dau. of Henry Leader, of Mount Leader, same co., and had issue,

1. James, who took the additional surname of HARNETT, *m.* 1783, Elizabeth, dau. of Townsend Gun, of Rattoo, co. Kerry, by Sarah his wife, dau. of Anthony Stoughton, of Ballyhorgan, in the same co., and by her (who *m.* 2ndly, William Carique Ponsonby, of Crotto, same co.) had issue,
Thomas, *d.s.p.*
Sarah, *m.* Capt. Oliver Guyon, R.N., who was lost in the Black Sea, and *d.s.p.*
2. JOHN, of Leemount, co. Cork, who also took the additional surname of HARNETT, *m.* Mary, dau. of Noblett Rogers, of Lota, in the same co., by Mary his wife, dau. of Ven. Michael Davies, Archdeacon of Cloyne, and had one son,
Thomas Noblett, *m.* Frances, dau. of Edmund L'Estrange, of Hunstanton, King's Co., by Henrietta his wife, sister of Col. Henry Piesley L'Estrange, of Moystown, same co., and *d.s.p.* She *d.* 1872.
3. EDWARD, of whom hereafter.

Mr. Fuller made his will, 4 Feb. 1790, which was proved 12 April, 1791. His youngest son,

EDWARD FULLER, of Beechmount and Sackville, co. Kerry, Capt. in the " Old Kerry " Militia, *m.* 1791, Elizabeth (*b.* 1772), dau. of Rev. John Blennerhassett, Rector of Tralee, by Louisa his wife, dau. and only surviving child of Capt. Thomas Goddard, of the Earl of Rothes' Regt., and Mary his wife (eldest dau. of William Mullins, of Burnham, co. Kerry, and sister of Thomas, 1st Lord Ventry), by whom he had issue,

1. THOMAS HARNETT, his successor.
2. Edward Goddard, *d.s.p.* 3. John Blennerhassett, *d.s.p.*
1. Louisa, *d. unm.*
2. Ann, *m.* Ven. Nathaniel Bland, Archdeacon of Aghadoe, and *d.s.p.*
3. Bessie, *m.* the late Sir Arthur Helps, K.C.B., D.C.L., and had issue,
1. Charles Leonard (Rev.), *m.* 1868, Emily, dau. of the late James Theobald, of the Hyde Abbey, Winchester, of Grays, Thurrock, Essex, and of Nunney, Somerset, J.P. and D.L. Hants and Essex. He *d.* 6 Aug. 1909, having had issue,
Arthur Leonard (Rev.), M.A., Vicar of Puddletown, co. Dorset, was Acting Chaplain in the S. African War (medal with five clasps), *b.* 1872.
2. Edmond, *m.* Mary Alice, dau. of A. J. Tapson, and has, issue,
Edmund, *b.* 4 April, 1888.
1. Alice Plucknett. 2. Rose. 3. Lucy.
4. Melicent, *m.* William Stone, of Lea Park, near Havant, late M.P. for Portsmouth, and has issue.

THOMAS HARNETT FULLER, of Glashnacree, co. Kerry, *b.* 1806; *m.* 1st, 3 Dec. 1832, Frances Diana, 3rd dau. of Francis Christopher Bland, of Derryquin Castle, same co. (*see that family*), J.P., D.L., by Lucinda his wife, dau. of Arthur Bastable Herbert, of Brewsterfield, same co. (son of Bastable Herbert, by Barbara, dau. of the Knight of Kerry), and by her (who *d.* 1872) had issue,

1. JAMES FRANKLIN, now of Glashnacree.
1. Louisa, *m.* 1862, Arthur Hyde, eldest son of Frederick Hyde, of Hollywood, J.P. co. Kerry (of the family of Hyde, of Castle Hyde) and has issue,
1. Arthur. 2. Thomas, *d.* 1895. 1. Frances.
2. Bessie, *m.* Michael Walsh, of Boston, and had issue.

Mr. Fuller *m.* 2ndly, Eliza, dau. of Richard Harris Purcell of Annabella Park, near Mallow, co. Cork, by Louisa, his wife, dau. of William Leader, of Mount Leader, in same co., and *d.* Dec. 1886, having had no issue by his second wife.

Arms—Arg., three bars gu. on a canton of the second a mullet or. **Crest**—A horse passant ppr. charged on the shoulder with a mullet or. **Motto**—Fortiter et recte.

Seat—Glashnacree, Kenmare, co. Kerry. *Residence*—Lassatier, Eglinton Road, Dublin.

FULLERTON OF BALLINTOY.

GEORGE FREDERICK DOWNING FULLERTON, of Ballintoy, co. Antrim, and of Alveston, co. Gloucester, and of Purley Park, Berks, late Capt. 4th Batt. Royal Irish Rifles, *b.* 4 April, 1857; *m.* 15 Jan. 1889, Leila Minna Gertrude, only child of Major A. M. Storer, of Purley Park, Berks (*see that family*), and has issue,

1. GEORGE CECIL, *b.* 7 May, 1891.
2. Richard Alexis, *b.* 12 Oct. 1893.
1. Ivy Leila, *b.* 4 Oct. 1889.
2. Myra Aida Violet, *b.* 30 June, 1896.

Lineage.—NICHOLAS DOWNING, of Drummond, co. Londonderry, made his will 18 Feb. 1698, and in it made bequests to his nephews, ADAM, John, George, and Daniel. He *d.s.p.* and was *s.* by his nephew,

COL. ADAM DOWNING, *b.* 1666. He was present at the siege of Derry, and at the Battle of the Boyne. He received the appointments of Deputy Governor of co. Derry, Col. of the Militia, and one of the Commissioners of Array; and also acquired a large tract of land in co. Derry, still possessed by his descendant. He *m.* Margaret, dau. of Thomas Jackson, of Coleraine (ancestor of Sir George Jackson, Bart.), by Margaret Beresford, and had issue,
1. Henry, *d.* in his minority. 2. JOHN.
Col. Adam Downing *d.* 1719, and was bur. at Bellaghy. The inscription on his monument mentions his descent from the Devonshire family. His son and successor,

JOHN DOWNING, of Bellaghy and Rowesgift, *b.* 1700, raised, at considerable expense, a body of men during the rising of 1745. He *m.* Anne, dau. and heir of the Rev. J. Roe, D.D., descended from an old Devonshire family, and had three sons,
1. Clotworthy, father of John and Giffard; the latter, a Military Officer, was severely wounded at Corunna.
2. DAWSON, of whom presently.
3. John, an Officer in the Army, who served in the Seven Years' War, and *d.s.p.* 1792.

The 2nd son,

DAWSON DOWNING, of Bellaghy and Rowesgift, co. Londonderry, *b.* 1739, inherited the ancient mansion, and resided in it till his death. He *m.* 1st, Catherine, only child of George Fullerton, and niece and heiress of Alexander Fullerton, of Ballintoy Castle, co. Antrim, descended from a branch of the ancient Scottish family of that name. The first of the family of Fullerton who settled in Ireland was Fergus Fullarton, in the reign of JAMES I. By her he had one son,
1. GEORGE, of whom presently.
Mr. Dawson Downing *m.* 2ndly, Sarah Catherine, dau. of Hugh Boyd, of Ballycastle, and by her had (with six daus., of whom Anne, *m.* Robert Magee; Martha, *m.* 1st, Arthur Handcock, and 2ndly, Rear-Admiral the Hon. William La Poer Trench; and Catherine, *m.* — Turnley) four sons,
2. John, of Rowesgift, Judge of the Supreme Court of the Canadian Provinces, *m.* and had issue three sons, George; Charles, of Bonne Conlan, co. Mayo; and John, Judge of the Supreme Court of the Kandian Provinces, who left issue six daus., Amy; Louisa; Maria, *m.* April, 1846, Rev. Launcelot Dowdall, M.A., and had issue (*see that family*); Jessie; Elizabeth; and Fanny.
3. Ezekiel. 4. William, an Officer in the Army.
5. David, a Major-General, *m.* 1st. Margaret Jean Ward; and 2ndly, Frances Anne Hamilton, dau. of Levitt Broadley Parkyns, of Notts, and by her had issue,
1. Arthur Edward, an Officer in the Army.
2. Cameron Macartney Harwood. 3. Charles Palmer.
4. De la Poer. 5. David Fitz-Gerald.
1. Margaret.

Mr. Downing's son by his 1st wife,

GEORGE ALEXANDER DOWNING, having inherited a considerable property from his great uncle, assumed by Royal Licence, 6 Dec. 1794, in compliance with that gentleman's testamentary injunction, the surname and arms of FULLERTON, and became of Tockington Manor and Gallintoy. He was *b.* 30 Nov. 1775; *m.* Mary Anne, dau. of James Peacock, and *d.* 1847, leaving three sons and five daus.
1. ALEXANDER GEORGE, his heir.
2. George, a Military Officer, dec.
3. David, of Pennington House, Lymington, Hants, J.P., *b.* 1820; *m.* 1847, Susannah Jane, dau. of Henry Mott, and *d.* 1892, leaving with five other daus.,
1. GEORGE FREDERICK, now of Ballintoy.
1. Alice Le Poer, *m.* 30 April, 1895, Edmund Trevor Lloyd Williams, 4th son of the late David Williams, M.P., of Deudreath Castle, co. Merioneth (*see* BURKE's *Peerage*, WILLIAMS, Bart.).
2. Mary Ellen Mildmay, *m.* 13 Jan. 1875, Col. Arthur Henry Courtenay, C.B., Master of the King's Bench in Ireland.
1. Catherine, dec.

2. Susan, *m.* John Maxwell, dec.
3. Frances, *m.* 1 Jan. 1835, Sir Andrew Armstrong, Bart., and *d.* 19 March, 1890, leaving issue (*see* BURKE'S *Peerage*).
4. Mary Anne, *m.* Rev. Canon Howman, and is dec.

The eldest son,
ALEXANDER GEORGE FULLERTON, of Ballintoy Castle, co. Antrim, Brevet-Major and formerly Capt. Royal Horse Guards (Blue) and an Attaché to the Embassy at Paris, *b.* 8 Aug. 1808 ; *m.* at Paris, July, 1833, Lady Georgiana Leveson-Gower, 2nd dau. of the late Earl Granville, G.C.B., and *d.* 12 May, 1907, having by her (who *d.* 19 Jan. 1885) had a son and heir,
WILLIAM GRANVILLE, *b.* at the British Embassy, Paris, 15 July, 1834 ; *d.v.p.* 1855.

Arms—(H. Coll.) Per fesse wavy or and sa., three otter's heads counterchanged. *Crest*—A camel's head couped per pale wavy or and sa., in the mouth a sugar cane ppr. *Motto*—Lux in tenebris.

Seats—Ballintoy, co. Antrim; Alveston, Gloucester; Purley Park, near Reading. *Clubs*—Boodle's, S.W.; Junior United Service, S.W.

FULTON OF BRAIDUJLE.

SIR EDMUND MCGILDOWNEY HOPE FULTON, Knt. Bachelor, C.S.I., of Braidujle, co. Antrim, *b.* 6 July, 1848; *s.* his father 1872, educated at Rugby, entered Bombay C.S. 1869, Judicial Commissioner, Lower Burmah 1891, Puisne Judge of the High Court of Bombay 1897, and Member of Council, Bombay, 1902 (retired 1907); *m.* 25 Nov. 1879, Cornelia Emily, only dau. of the late Sir Michael Westropp, Chief Justice of the High Court of Bombay (*see* BURKE'S *Family Records*), and by her (who *d.* 14 Aug. 1900) has issue,

1. JOHN HENRY WESTROPP, Barrister-at-Law, B.A. Camb. 1902, *b.* 2 Oct. 1880 ; *m.* 6 July, 1905, Violet Elise, dau. of Dep. Surgeon-Gen. Landale of Cheltenham.
2. Lionel Edmund, *b.* and *d.* 1884.
3. Edmund James, *b.* 8 Feb. 1895.
1. Bessie Maud, *b.* 29 Sept. 1882.
2. Evelyn Grace, *b.* and *d.* 1887.
3. Esme Mary, *b.* 17 Jan. 1892.

Lineage.—JOHN FULTON, *b.* about 1623, held in 1678, from Viscount Conway, a lease for three lives of the estate of Belsize, then already in his possession, which was situated close to the town of Lisburn, but within the limits of the parish of Derriaghy. The names of himself and Richard his brother and of their sons and kinsmen occur in the vestry books of those places as churchwardens or otherwise. His son,

JOHN FULTON, of Belsize, *b.* about 1653 ; *m.* 1691, Margaret, dau. of Thomas Camac, of Kilfallert, co. Down, and by her had issue,
1. James, of Lisburn, bapt. 26 May, 1692 ; *m.* about 1720, Ann Coulson, and *d.* about 1776, leaving issue,
 1. Robert Coulson, of Lisburn and Ballymacash, held lands and houses in Lisburn, and the estate of Ballymacash under the Earl of Hertford. He was *b.* 1723 ; *m.* 1752, Ann Forrest, and *d.* 1762, having by her (who *d.* 1767) had issue,
  (1) Richard, *b.* 1753, a prosperous linen merchant and financier, *m.* 3 March, 1774, Elizabeth, dau. of Andrew Shanks, of Lisburn, and *d.* 9 April, 1823, having by her (who *d.* 1812, aged 60) had issue,
   1. Robert, *b.* 1777 ; *d.* 1833, leaving by Jane his wife (who *d.* 1831, aged 63), 1, Joseph, *d.* 1831, aged 36 ; 2, James ; 3, Robert, *b.* 1807 ; and 1, Elizabeth Ann, *b.* 1805.
   2. Andrew, *b.* 1779 ; *m.* Isabella Wightman ; and *d.* 1822 ; having by her (who *d.* 1850, aged 70) had issue, 1, Richard, *d.* an infant ; 2, Andrew, *d.* an infant ; 3, William, *b.* 1806 ; *m.* Sophia Matilda Bolton (who *d.* 1879, aged 78), and *d.s.p.*, 1881 ; 1, Eliza, *m.* John Barbour, of Lisburn, who *d.* 1831, leaving issue ; and 2, Isabella, *d. unm.*
   3. James Forrest, Knight of the Guelphic Order 1838, Ensign Northampton Fencibles 1798, and 38th Foot 1801, A.D.C. to Sir George Prevost, Gov.-Gen. of Canada, and twice mentioned by him in despatches, Major 92nd Foot, Brevet Lieut.-Col. 1815, retired 1824, and settled in Belgium. He was *b.* 30 Sept. 1780 ; *m.* 1st, 24 Aug. 1807, Penelope Frances, only dau. of Richard Bowyer (who took the name of Atkins on *s.* Sir Richard Atkins as Lord of the Manor of Clapham), and by her (who *d.* 1836) had issue,
    a. George James, Lieut. 77th and 62nd Regts., drowned when landing in Burma 1840, *b.* 1817 ; *d. unm.*
    b. William Cornelius Bowyer, Lieut. R.E. 1836, *b.* 1818 ; *d. unm.* 1838.
    c. Henry Seymour Moore Donnelly, Capt. 49th Regt., *b.* 1822 ; *d. unm.* 1853.
    d. Richard Robert, of Parsonstown, King's Co., late 44th Regt., afterwards Royal Irish Constabulary, *b.* 7 May, 1823 ; *m.* 10 Nov. 1857, Margaret Ormsby, dau. of Robert Twiss, of Birdhill (*see that family*), and *d.* 1906, having by her (who *d.* 1909) had issue,
     (a) Edith Atkins Bowyer, *d.* 1868, aged 9.
     (b) Elizabeth Frances, *m.* 10 Jan. 1883, Capt. John Edward Maxwell Pilkington, 28th Regt., who *d.* 12 July, 1898. She *d.* 1907, leaving issue. Dick Wetherall, *b.* 7 May, 1898, and Eileen Mary, *b.* 7 Nov. 1883 ; *m.* 1904, F. O'Brien Horsford, and has issue.
     (c) May Ormsby, *m.* 21 June, 1888, Lieut.-Col. Alfred Ruttledge, 14th Regt., and has, John Forrest, *b.* 1 Aug. 1894 ; Richard Theodore, *b.* 14 Dec. 1897 ; Eric Peter Knox, *b.* 24 Aug. 1899.
    a. Eliza Ellen, *d. unm.* 1834, aged 17.
    Lieut.-Col. J. F. Fulton *m.* 2ndly, 7 Nov. 1838, Fanny Goodrich, 3rd dau. of John Sympson Jessopp, F.S.A., J.P., Barrister-at-Law, of Albury Place, Cheshunt, Herts, and Eliza Bridger, his wife, dau. of the Hon. Bridger Goodrich, sometime Governor of Bermuda, *d.* Dec. 1854, having by her (who *d.* 11 March, 1882, aged 70) had issue,
     e. James Forrest (Sir), K.C., B.A., LL.B., of The Cottage, Sheringham, and Guildhall, E.C., Recorder of the City of London since 1900, Common Serjeant of London, 1892 to 1900, sometime Recorder of Maidstone, formerly Senior Counsel to the Post Office, and to the Treasury at the Central Criminal Court, M.P. for West Ham, North, 1886-92, *b.* 12 July, 1846 ; *m.* 12 Aug. 1875, Sophia Browne, eldest dau. of John B. Nicholson, of Clare Lodge, Haxey, Rotherham, and has issue,
      (a) Forrest, Barrister-at-Law 1899, *b.* 6 June, 1876.
      (b) Leonard Jessopp, M.A. Oxon, B.C.L., Solicitor, Legal Adviser to the Public Trustee, *b.* 8 Jan. 1879 ; *m.* 27 July, 1909, Mabel Helen, youngest dau. of late Rev. H. A. M. Wilcox, Vicar of Wolston, Warwickshire (*see that family*), and has had issue,
       1. Janet, *b.* 2 June, 1910 ; *d.* 14 June, 1910.
       2. Mary Hermione, *b.* 17 Nov. 1911.
      (c) Eustace Cecil, M.A. Camb., Barrister-at-Law, *b.* 17 May, 1880.
      (d) Grenville Richard, *b.* 23 Oct. 1883, Solicitor, 3rd Clerk of Arraigns, Central Criminal Court.
      (a) Clare Sophia Margaret Goodrich, *b.* 21 Oct. 1886 ; *m.* 21 Oct. 1909, Hugh Robert Edward Harrison, eldest son of late Col. Harrison, of Caerhowel, Montgomeryshire (*see that family*). She *d.s.p.* 15 April, 1911.
     b. Fanny Goodrich, *b.* 1840 ; *m.* 1869, Rev. T. F. Buxton Scriven, Vicar of Luttons Ambo, Yorks, and *d.s.p.* 1894.
     c. Laura, *b.* 1841 ; *d.* 1844.
   4. Richard, Capt. 12th Royal Lancers, *b.* 1788 ; *d.s.p.* 1827.
   5. John Forrest, *b.* and *d.* 1790.
   1. Margaret, *b.* 1775 ; *m.* 1803, James Wightman ; and *d.* 1819, leaving issue.
   2. Ann (Fanny), *b.* 1776 ; *d. unm.* 1799.
   3. Eliza, *b.* 1778 ; *m.* 1802, James Ward, of Lisburn, and *d.* 1805, leaving a son, Thomas.
   4. Jane, *b.* 1782 ; *m.* 1805, Francis Abbot Thompson, and *d.* 1840, leaving issue.
   5. Mary Ann, *b.* 1783 ; *d. unm.*
   6. Grace, *b.* 1784 ; *d. unm.* 1865.
   7. Sarah, *b.* 1785 ; *d. unm.* 1802.
   8. Ellen, *b.* 1787 ; *d. unm.* 1864.
  (1) Jane, *d. unm.* 1791, aged 33.
 2. John, *b.* 1730.
 1. Elinor, *b.* 1725 ; *m.* 1748, William Bryson.
2. JOHN, of whom presently.
1. Elizabeth, *m.* about 1711, Thomas Tomson, and had issue.
2. Margaret, *m.* 29 Oct. 1745, Alexander M'Aulay, and left four daus.
3. Mary Ann, *m.* James Kenley.

The youngest son,
JOHN FULTON, of Lisburn and Calcutta, *b.* 1716, Merchant and Landowner, purchased property in Lisburn from his brother James, and his nephew Robert, and the Ballymacash estate from his great-nephew Richard. In 1780 he was appointed Assistant Registrar of the High Court of Calcutta, but, owing to shipwreck, he was eighteen months in reaching Calcutta, and found the post filled up. He then followed mercantile pursuits, and made a large fortune. He *m.* 1751, Anne, dau. of Thomas Wade, of Clonabrany, co. Westmeath, and Lurgan, and *d.* at sea, 26 July, 1803, on his homeward voyage, having by her (who *d.* 1799) had issue,
1. Joseph, of Lisburn, *b.* 1752 ; *m.* 1777, Ann, dau. of Francis Graham, of Lisburn, and sister of James Graham, of West Malling, Kent, and *d.* 1823, having by her (who *d.* 1833) had issue,
 1. Francis, of Calcutta, Merchant, *b.* 1778, lost at sea on his homeward voyage 1809, *d.s.p.*
 2. Thomas, *b.* 1780, Ensign 92nd Highlanders, afterwards Lieut. 78th Regt., and Major Armagh Militia, J.P. cos. Armagh and Antrim. He *m.* 1799, Lydia Johnson (*d.* 1843) but *d.s.p.* 1849.

3. Nicholas Graham, b. 1782, Ensign York Fencibles 1798, Cadet Bengal Army 1799, Lieut. 1800, killed in action 1804.
4. Henry, M.D., b. 3 April, 1793; m. 1st, 14 June, 1816, Jane, dau. of Dr. Finlay, of Belfast, and by her (who d. 1818) had a son, who d. 1819. He entered the Bengal Medical Service in 1828, but retired in 1829, and settled at Clonmore, Stillorgan, co. Dublin. He m. 2ndly, 2 Sept. 1830, Anne, dau. of John Miller, a lawyer, of Dublin, and d. 1859, having by her (who d. 1875) had issue,
  (1) Joseph, of Firmount, L.R.C.S.I., b. 22 May, 1844; m. 26 Jan. 1870, Florence Mary Walsh, of Dublin, and d. 21 June, 1878, having had issue (with two daus., Annie, b. 1870, and Elizabeth, b. 1873, who both d. in infancy) one son,
   Henry, of Lisburn, Sevenoaks, Kent, M.R.C.S., L.R.C.P., L.S.A., M.D. (Brussels), Hon. Lieut. in the Army and Capt. Royal Monmouthshire Royal Reserve Engineers, served in S. African War 1900 (medal with four clasps), b. 25 Dec. 1871; m. 21 Aug. 1894, Mary, dau. of Capt. James Barton, late R.H.A., of Blackheath, formerly of Mauritius, and has issue, Joseph Henry Caldbeck, b. 7 Oct. 1896, Theodore Stephen Miller, b. 24 Sept. 1899, and Marie Josephine, b. 24 Sept. 1895.
  (1) Catherine, b. 26 Oct. 1832; d. unm. 18 March, 1850.
  (2) Hannah Anne, b. 10 May, 1834; d. unm. 18 Jan. 1851.
  (3) Sara Jones, of Dublin, d. unm. 2 Sept. 1905.
  (4) Elizabeth, of Lisburn, Sevenoaks, b. 30 Dec. 1838; d. unm. 20 Feb. 1903.
  (5) Josephine, of the same place, b. 3 April, 1842; d. unm. 6 Feb. 1911.
1. Ann, b. 1776; m. 1799, Christopher Henry Barry Meade, Lieut. 64th Regt. of Limerick, and d. 1862, having by him, who d. 1814, had issue.
2 Elizabeth, b. 1783; m. 1817, John Cuppage Douglas, M.D., of Rutland Square, Dublin, and d.s.p.
3. Amelia (Emily) Boyd, b. 1787, m. 1808, her 1st cousin, William Eaton Caldbeck, son of William Caldbeck, of Clondalkin, and Dora Graham his wife, sister of Mrs. Joseph Fulton, above-mentioned (see ROPER-CALDBECK of Moyle).

2. James, of Lisburn, b. 1755; m. 1783, Anne, dau. of Henry Bell, of Lambeg, and d. 26 July, 1817, having by her (who d. 5 Jan. 1834, aged 75) had issue,
  1. John, Capt. 2nd Bengal European Regt., b. 1784; d. unm. at Lisburn, 1829.
  2. Robert Bell, Major Bengal Artillery, b. 1788; m. at Gretna Green, 30 Oct. and at Hillsboro', 9 Dec. 1817, Elizabeth Jane, dau. of George Stephenson, of Hillsboro', and d. 11 May, 1836, M.I., Lisburn Cathedral, having by her (who d. in New Zealand 1863, aged 64) had issue
    (1) James, b. 1824; d. in India, 1828.
    (2) George William Wright, Capt. Bengal Engineers, b. 1825; m. 1848, Isabella Sophia, dau. of Major R. Wroughton, grandson of Sir Philip Wroughton, and was killed 1857, during the defence of Lucknow, in which he greatly distinguished himself, having by her (who d. 1879) had issue,
      1. John Charles, of Marton, N.Z., b. 1849; d. 29 Oct. 1908.
      2. Frederick of Napier, N.Z., b. 1850.
      3. Robert, Lieut.-Col. I.S.C. 1st Goorkha Rifles (Sikhim medal with clasp, and clasp for Waziristan), b. 12 July, 1852; m. 1894, Blanche, dau. of Col. D. W. Martin, 8th King's Regt., and has issue, John Oswald, b. 1897, and Gwendoline, b. 1896.
      4. William Wright, of Marton, N.Z., b. 1854; m. Helen, dau. of R. Bett, of Marton, N.Z., and has issue,
        a. Howard, b. 9 Aug. 1880.
        b. Norman, b. 23 March, 1883; m. 1911, Florence Oakden.
        c. Frederick Robert, b. 2 June, 1890.
        d. George William Wright, b. 7 Feb. 1901.
      5. George Sibley, J.P., of Wakatipu, N.Z., b. 1857.
      1. Ellen Charlotte, b. 1856; m. 1881, Charles William Wallace, and has issue.
    (3) John, Lieut.-Gen. R.A., of The Downs, Outram, Dunedin, N.Z., J.P., entered the army 1845, served in the Punjab Campaign 1848-9 (medal), Indian Mutiny, including the siege of Delhi, mentioned in despatches (medal with clasp), and retired in 1883; Hon. Col. of the New Zealand Volunteers, b. 1827; m. 1858, Ellen, dau. of Major R. Wroughton, Dep. Surveyor-Gen. of India, and d. at Christ Church, N.Z., 14 July, 1899, having by her (who d. 1887) had issue,
      1. Sydney Wroughton, of Melbourne, b. 1859; m. 1894, Elsie Maud, dau. of J. S. Armstrong, Barrister-at-Law, and has issue, Sheila Alice Wroughton, b. 1895; Eileen Maud Wroughton, b. 1896; and Lorna Hope Wroughton, b. 1899.
      2. Percival James, of Warrnambool, Victoria, b. 1860.
      3. Charles Ross, b. 1864; d. 1866.
      4. Walter Menzies, Mining Engineer in Johannesburg, b. 1866; m. 1896, Gwendoline Adèle, dau. of Horace Baker, of Napier, N.Z.
      5. Onslow H. Crofton, b. 1868.
      6. Harry Townsend, D.S.O., Major Indian Army, 2nd P.W.O. Gurkhas (Malakand, Tirah, and S. African medals), b. 15 Aug. 1869; m. 3 March, 1905, Ada Hermina, 2nd dau. of John James Dixon, of Auckland, N.Z.
      7. Bertram Sproull, b. 1871; m. Dec. 1902, Lillian V. M., dau. of Col. Loveday, and has issue, Hylma, b. 1907.
      2. Agnes Selina Fanny, b. 1862; d. 1863.
      1. Ethel Anne, b. 1861.
      3. Hilda Caroline, b. 1875; m. 15 Sept. 1908, Capt.

Richard Woodroofe Bohm, son of the late William Bohm, of Bexhill, and has issue.
    (4) James (Hon.), of Ravenscliffe, West Taieri, N.Z., M.L.C., J.P., emigrated to New Zealand in 1848, held various important offices, elected to the House of Representatives for Dunedin 1879, and called to the Upper House 1890, b. 1830; m. 1852, Catherine Henrietta Elliott, dau. of William Henry Valpy, Judge in H.E.I.C.S., and d. 20 Nov. 1891, leaving issue,
      1. Arthur Robert William, M.I.C.E., M.I.M.E., b. 1853; m. 1883, Linda Marie, dau. of C. H. Weber, C.E., of Napier, N.Z., and d. 1889, leaving three sons, Hermann Weber, Civil Engineer in Shanghai, b. 1884; Guy Leslie, b. 1885; m. 1910, Emily Bulkley; and Arthur Clive, b. 1887.
      2. James Edward, M.I.C.E., b. 1854; m. 1885, Charlotte Fredericka, dau. of Major F. E. Budd, R.M.L.I., and has a dau., Jessie Marion Vera, b. 1887; m. 18 July, 1911, Frank Horton, M.A., Fellow of St. John's Coll. Camb.
      3. Francis John, b. 1857; d. 1874.
      4. Herbert Valpy, of Ravenscliffe, b. 1860; m. 1894, Emily Zoe, dau. of Julius S. Jeffreys, of Sandown, I. of Wight, and has Julius Herbert, b. 1901, Ngaio Zoe, b. 1899, and Ethne Owen, b. 1903.
      5. Robert Valpy, of Dunedin, M.D., C.M. Edin., b. 1865; m. 1890, Lillias Augusta, dau. of Henry C. Hertslet, of Hawkesbury, N.Z., and niece of the late Sir E. Hertslet, K.C.B., and has issue, Roland Arthur Hertslet, b. 1891; James Robert Bell Hertslet, b. 1892; d. 25 Dec. 1909; Noel Edward Hertslet, b. 1895; John Richard Hertslet, b. 1900; Enid Fanny Hertslet, b. 1893; and Gwenyth Lillian Hertslet, twin, b. 1900.
      1. Caroline Arabella, b. 1859.
      2. Catherine Juliet, b. 1862; m. 1893, Rev. R. R. M. Sutherland, of Kaikorai, N.Z., and has six sons and two daus.
      3. Mabel Violet, b. 1866; m. 1892 Professor Louis Edward Barnett, F.R.C.S., and has issue, three sons and two daus.
    (5) Robert, b. 1832, went to New Zealand, 1848, lost at sea in the Lord Raglan, 1863, when returning from England
    (6) Francis Crossley, J.P., of Hawke's Bay, N.Z., b. 1836; m. 1858, Fanny Fidela, dau. of E. S. Hall, of Sydney. He d. 1 May, 1901, leaving issue,
      1. Eustace Henry, b. 1860; m. 1891, Jane, dau. of Charles Peacock, of Hawke's Bay, and has issue, Eric Bronte, b. 1892; Kenneth, b. 1907; Sylvia Fidela Dora, b. 1891; and Norma, b. 1902.
      1. Alicia Charlotte, b. 1861; m. D. Reid, Barrister-at-Law, and has issue, three sons and a dau.
      2. Lina Eliza, b. 1863; m. 1889, W. J. Tabuteau, of Hawke's Bay. She d.s.p. 1908.
      3. Florence Dora, b. 1864. 4. Rosa Fidela, b. 1866; d. 1867.
      5. Iris Fidela, b. 1868; m. G. R. King, of Hawke's Bay, and has issue, a son and a dau.
    (1) Anne, b. 1819; m. 1847, James Dewar Bourdillon, Madras C.S., who d. 1883, leaving issue, three sons and three daus. The eldest son, Sir James Austin Bourdillon, K.C.S.I. (1904), V.D., I.C.S. Bengal (ret. 1905), late Resident at Mysore, was officiating Lieut.-Gov. Bengal 1902-3.
    (2) Jane, b. 1819; m. 1839, W. H. Sproull, of Belfast, and d. 1845, leaving a son and a dau.
    (3) Alicia Charlotte, b. 1822; d. unm. 1852.
    (4) Mary, b. and d. 1829.
  3. James Bell, b. 1791; m. 1816, Anne, dau. of Henry Stephenson, of York, and d. 1817, leaving an only dau.,
    Anne Bell, m. Dr. William Dalla Husband, Lord Mayor of York, and d. 1866, having by him (who d. 1892) had, with other issue, a son,
      James, who was lost in the Lord Raglan with Robert Fulton.
  4. Henry Stewart, b. 1795; killed out hunting, 1813, d.s.p.
  1. Mary, b. 1786; m. 1831, John McIntyre, of Belfast, and d.s.p. 1869.
  2. Ellen, b. 1787; m. 1806, Thomas Walker, Solicitor in Dublin, went to Mississippi, and had issue.
  3. Anna Bell, b. 1791; d. unm. 1879.
  4. Eliza, b. 1793; m. 1823, Thomas Reid, M.D., Surgeon R.N., and d.s.p. 1829.
  5. Jane, b. 1801; d. unm. 1887.
3. JOHN WILLIAMSON, of whom presently.
1. Eleanor, b. 1754; d. unm. 1835. 2. Ann, d. unm. 1814.
3. Eliza Overend, b. 1771; d. unm. 1818.

The youngest son,

JOHN WILLIAMSON FULTON, of Calcutta, and 4. Upper Harley Street, London, followed his father to Calcutta 1787, and was for many years an eminent Merchant there, and founder of the firm of Mackintosh, Fulton and McClintock, High Sheriff 1816, b. 1765; m. 1 Feb. 1806, Ann, widow of Capt. John Hunt, Bengal Army, and dau. and co-heir (with her sister Eleanor Sophia, wife of Lachlan Mackintosh, of Calcutta, and Raigmore, co. Inverness) of Robert Robertson, of Calcutta, of the Scotch family of Robertson of Insbes. He settled in London in 1820, and d. 22 Jan. 1830, having by her (who d. 27 May, 1845, aged 65) had issue,
1. JOHN WILLIAMSON, of whom presently.
2. Joseph Hennessey, Lieut. 5th Bengal N.I., acting Assistant Political Agent at Dorunda, Chutia Nagpore, b. 1816; d. 1843.
1. Eleanor Sophia, b. 1806; d. unm. 1849.
2. Anne, b. 1808; d. 1809.
3. Anne, b. 7 Sept. 1809; m. 10 March, 1831, James Hope, of Lower Seymour Street, London, M.D., F.R.S., Physician of St. George's Hospital (for notices of both, see Dict. of Nat. Biog., vol. xxxvii), who was descended from Henry, elder brother of Sir Thomas Hope, 1st bart. of Craighall. She d. 12 Feb. 1887. He d. 1841, leaving a son,

IRELAND. Gabbett.

Sir Theodore Cracraft Hope, K.C.S.I., C.I.E., who *m.* 16 Aug. 1866, his first cousin, Josephine Mary McGildowney, dau. of John Williamson Fulton, of Braidujle (*see below*).
4. Mary Charron, *b.* 4 Nov. 1811 ; *m.* 27 April, 1842, William Toller, late H.E.I.C.S., and *d.* 7 Nov. 1844, having by him (who *d.* 1885) had issue,
1. Caroline Hope, *b.* 1843 ; *m.* 1868, Comm. W. F. Johnson, R.N., brother of Sir Charles Brooke, G.C.M.G., present Raja of Sarawak, and *d.* 1899, leaving issue,
(1) Charles Hope Willes, *b.* 1871 ; *m.* 1897, Blanche, dau. of Lieut.-Col. Everett, and has issue.
(2) Henry Carslake Brooke, *b.* 1873.
(3) William Stuart Northcote, *b.* 1880
(1) Mary Emma, *b.* 1869; *m.* 1899, Dep. Insp.-Gen. E. R. H. Pollard, of Rostrevor (who *d.* 1906), and has issue.
2. Ellen Fulton (*Oakland, Sidmouth*), *b.* 1844.
5. Charlotte Hayes, *b.* 29 Aug. 1813 ; *m.* 10 Feb. 1832, George Mackintosh, of Geddes, convener of Nairnshire, and *d.* 10 Dec. 1883, having by him (who *d.* 1872) had issue,
1. William Alfred Bruce, *b.* 1837 ; *d. unm.* 1868.
1. Anne Agnew, *b.* 1832 ; *s.* to Geddes in 1872, and assumed the name of MACKINTOSH-WALKER, having *m.* 1859, John Walker, of Broughton, Cumberland (who *d.* 1907), and *d.* 1902, having had issue,
(1) Thomas Charles Bruce, *b.* 1862 ; *m.* 1893, Ellen Marianne, dau. of Rev. J. C. Gardiner, and has Charlie Algernon, *b.* 1894, John Ronald, *b.* 1898, Eileen Margaret, *b.* 1896, Beryl Marjorie, *b.* 1900, and Violet, *b.* 1908.
(1) Amy Florence, *b.* 1860 ; *m.* 13 Dec. 1897, Alexander M. Mackintosh, of The Hermitage, Nairn.
(2) Annie Elma, *b.* 1867 ; *m.* 1st, 8 Dec. 1891, Campbell Keir-Mackintosh, who *d.s.p.* 1897; and 2ndly, 19 April, 1899, Lieut.-Col. H. E. Dauncey, 6th Inniskilling Dragoons, and has issue.
2. Henrietta, *b* 1834 ; *d. unm.* 1854.
3. Eleanor Amy Matilda (*White Lodge, Farnham*), *b.* 1846.
The eldest son,
JOHN WILLIAMSON FULTON, of Braidujle, co. Antrim, and Braidujle House, co. Down, Barrister-at-Law, M.A., J.P. cos. Antrim and Down, *b.* 23 Dec. 1814 ; *m.* 25 June, 1840, Matilda, dau. of John Montgomery Casement, of Invermore, Larne, co. Antrim (by Mary, his wife, dau. of John McGildowney, of Clare Park, co. Antrim), and niece of Major Gen. Sir William Casement, K.C.B., and *d.* 10 Nov. 1872, having by her (who *d.* 27 Feb. 1894) had issue,
1. John Williamson Casement, *b.* 1841 ; *d.* 1855.
2. Edmund Casement Pollard, *b.* 1843 ; *d.* 1844.
3. EDMUND MCGILDOWNEY HOPE, now of Braidujle.
4. George Wade Robertson, Col. R.A., *b.* 15 Nov. 1853 ; *m.* 5 Oct. 1880, Alice Elizabeth, dau. of Major-Gen. W. Roberts, and has issue,
1. Maud Elizabeth Amy, *b.* 1881.
2. Eileen Hope, *b.* 1886.
1. Josephine Mary McGildowney, *b.* 19 March, 1845 ; *m.* 16 Aug. 1866, her first cousin, Sir Theodore Cracraft Hope, K.C.S.I. C.I.E., of Boothstown, Lancashire, and 21, Elvaston Place, London, only son of James Hope, M.D., F.R.S., and Anne, his wife, 3rd dau. of John Williamson Fulton, of Calcutta (*see above*). Sir Theodore was *b.* 9 Dec. 1831, entered the Bombay Civil Service 1853, Barrister-at-Law, 1866, held various appointments in the Revenue and Political Departments, member of Legislative Council of Gov.-Gen. of India 1875-80, and member of the Executive Council Gov.-Gen. 1882-7.

Arms.—Arg., a lion rampant az. debruised by a bend gobony erm. and gu. Crest—A cubit arm erect grasping a broken javelin, point to the sinister all ppr. Motto—Vi et virtute.
Estate—Braidujle, co. Antrim. Residence—Elmhurst, Cheltenham. Club—East India United Service.

GABBETT OF CAHERLINE.

The late RICHARD JOSEPH GABBETT, of Caherline, co. Limerick, J.P., *b.* Jan. 1828 ; *m.* 1863, Elizabeth Agnes (*now of Caherline*), eldest dau. of John Minchin, of Busherston, King's Co. (*see that family*), and is dec.

Lineage.—WILLIAM GABBETT, of Caherline and Rathjordan, co. Limerick (whose will was proved 1691), left, by Alicia his wife, dau. of Richard England, of Lifford, co. Clare, three daus. (Elizabeth, *m.* William Chadwick, of Ballinard ; Alice, *m.* Richard Sadlier, of Sopwell ; and Margaret, *m.* John Hamersley) and two sons,
1. John, of Rathjordan, Lieut. in the Army, 1695, and Commissioner for raising the Revenue 1695, 1696, and 1697 ; *m.* Mary, dau. and co-heiress of John Woods, and *d.* 1707, leaving a dau., Eleanor, wife of Ambrose Lane, and a son,
JOHN, of Rathjordan, High Sheriff co. Limerick 1713, *b.* 1686, *m.* Elizabeth, dau. of Rev. Rickard Burgh, of Dromkeen, and *d.s.p.*
2. WILLIAM, who carried on the line.
Mr. Gabbett *d.* 1686. His 2nd son,
WILLIAM GABBETT, of Caherline, *b.* 1658 ; *m.* Mary, dau. of William Carpenter, of Ardstragh, co. Limerick, and had issue,
1. WILLIAM, his heir.
2. Joseph, of High Park, *m.* Sarah, dau. of Rev. Zachary Ormsby, of Athlacan, co. Limerick, and *d.s.p.* 1741.
3. John, *m.* 1713, Mary, dau. of William Apjohn, of Kilduff, and had, with other issue,

WILLIAM, of Mount Minnett, *d.* 1779, leaving by his wife (a dau. of Rev. William Cudmore) a son,
WILLIAM, of Mount Minnett, who *m.* Margaret, dau. of Capt. George O'Brien, and *d.* 1824, leaving a son,
WILLIAM, of Mount Minnett, *m.* Elizabeth, dau. of Michael Furnell, of Cahirelly, and left issue, 1. WILLIAM, *b.* 22 Sept. 1830 ; *m.* Sarah, dau. of Cosmo Richardson, M.D., of Savannah ; 2. Joseph, *m.* Anne, dau. of Laurence Marshall, and has a son, Joseph ; 1, Mary, *m.* Capt. Thomas Little, R.M. ; 2, Elizabeth, *m.* Laureuce Marshall, of Toomaline, co. Limerick ; 3, Emma, *m.* Thomas Stewart Brodie, of Lethen ; 4, Charlotte Stackpoole, *m.* Charles Courtney, M.D. ; 5, Jane Anne, *m.* Rev. William Arthy.
4. Richard, *m.* Anne, dau. of Richard Cox, of Ballynoe, co. Limerick.
1. Elizabeth (Mrs. Parker).
2. Mercy, *m.* Warr Gough, son of William Gough, of Doonas, co. Clare.
Mr. Gabbett *d.* 27 Aug. 1713, and was *s.* by his eldest son,
WILLIAM GABBETT, of Caherline, *b.* 1680 ; *m.* 1st, Mary, dau. of Thomas Spiers, of Baggotstown, and by her (who *d.* 22 Nov. 1717) had,
1. WILLIAM, his heir.
2. Thomas Spiers, of Baggotstown, co. Cork, *m.* 1st, Eleanor, dau. of Gerald Blennerhassett, of Riddlestown, co. Limerick ; and 2ndly, Mary, dau. of Boyle Davies, of Bonnybrook, co. Cork, and had issue.
3. John, of Anaglin, co. Cork, *m.* Margaret, dau. of Sampson Cox, of Ballynoe, co. Limerick, and was father of
Thomas Gabbett, of Castle Lake, co. Clare, Mayor of Limerick, *m.* Mary, dau. of Poole Westropp, of Fort Anna, co. Clare (*see* WESTROPP *of Attyflin*), and had issue,
(1) Robert (Rev.), LL.D., Rector of Castletown, and Vicar-General of Killaloe, *m.* Mary, dau. of Thomas Studdert, of Bunratty, co. Clare (*see that family*), and *d.* 1836, having had issue,
1. John Studdert, of Castle Lake, J.P. for cos. Clare and Tipperary, *b.* 1805 ; *m.* 1839, Millicent, dau. of Thomas Studdert, of Bunratty (*see that family*), and by her (who *d.* 1883) had a son, Robert Studdert, J.P., *b.* 1841, *d.* 1873.
2. Thomas, Barrister-at-Law, *d.s.p.*
3. Robert, of Gary Kennedy, co. Tipperary, J.P., *b.* 1818 ; *m.* Gustave, dau. of John Brown, of Coulstoun, New South Wales.
1. Anna, *m.* 1827, William Bleasby Smithwick, of Youghal House, co. Tipperary, and had issue (*see that family*).
2. Elizabeth, *m.* 1837, Thomas Spaight, of Ardnataggle (*see* SPAIGHT *of Derry Castle*).
3. Mary, *m.* Peter Smithwick, of Youghal House, Shanbally, co. Tipperary (*see* SMITHWICK *of Youghal*). He *d.* 1894.
4. Constance, *m.* 1838, Henry Spaight, of Corbally (*see* SPAIGHT *of Derry Castle*).
5. Margaret, *m.* Rev. Standish Parker, of Castle Lough.
(2) Poole, of Corbally House, J.P. co. Clare, Treasurer co. Limerick, *m.* Marianne, dau. of Edmund FitzGerald, of Shannon Grove, and had issue, with four daus., Abigail, *m.* John Westropp, of Colreagh ; Marianne, *m.* Gen. Franklyn, R.E.; Marcella, *m.* Rev. Richard Moore, and Emily, *m.* Gen. Meares, R.A., four sons,
1. Thomas, *m.* 1st, Diana, dau. of Major Charles Creagh, of Cahirbane (*see that family*), and by her had a dau., Diana, *m.* Thomas Studdert, of Ballyshannon, co. Clare, and 2ndly, Margaret Agnes, dau. of Rev. Gerald Beere, and has by her a dau., Florence Elizabeth.
2. Edmund, Mayor of Limerick, 1858, *m.* Frances Mary, dau. of Capt. Rich, R.A., and had issue, 1, Poole, *m.* 1st, Charlotte Maria, dau. of Capt. Gosselin, 49th Regt., and has issue, Charlotte Louise ; he *m.* 2ndly, Marv Lysatt ; 2, Edmund Rich, *m.* his cousin Annie Eva May, dau. of Capt. Poole Gabbett, 31st Regt. (*see below*), and has issue two sons, Edmond Poole and Noel Lawrence ; 3. Henry Whitfield, *m.* Mabel Fauny, dau. of Henry Bond ; 1, Fanny Mary, *m.* Col. Granville Brown, R.A.; 2, Elizabeth Helen, *m.* Col. Ashton Shuttleworth, R.A., and has issue.
3. Poole, Capt. 31st Regt., served through the Sutlej Campaign, and was severely wounded at Sobraomo, *m.* Annie, dau. of Thomas Somerville, and *d.* 8 Dec. 1863, leaving 1. Poole Lawrence Arthur, *b.* 1858 ; 2, Thomas Somerville. *b.* 1859 ; *m.* Edith Kate, dau. of William Goodson ; 3, Gerald, *b.* 1863 ; 1, Eva, *m.* her cousin Edmund Rich Gabbett (*see above*).
4. Robert, Major R.A., *m.* Anna Maria, dau. of Capt. John Gabbett, of Shepperton, and by her (who *d.* 2 Oct. 1894) had issue, 1, Poole Robert, R.A.M.C., *b.* 20 Sept. 1848 ; *m.* Edith, dau. of Col. William Stewart Richardson, C.B., 46th Regt., and *d.* 27 Feb. 1899 ; 2, John Norcliffe, *b.* 11 Feb. 1851 ; *m.* Auriol, dau. and heir of Edward Lintott ; 3, Robert Poole, Assistant Commissary, *b.* 8 Dec. 1853 ; *m.* Mabel, dau. of Admiral Sir James Plumridge, K.C.B.; 1, Fanny Amelia, *m.* Capt. Charles Rich, R.A.
(3) John, of Shepperton, co. Clare, J.P., Capt. 88th Regt., *m.* Frances, dau. of Capt. Hallam, and had issue,
1. Thomas, Lieut. 61st Regt., killed at Delhi, 25 Aug, 1857.
2. John, *d.s.p.* 3. George Robert, *d.s.p.* 4. James, *d.s.p.*
1. Bessie, *m.* William Westropp, M.D.
2. Anna Maria, *m.* Major Robert Poole Gabbett, R.A.
3. Frances, *m.* Major Thomas Norcliffe Dalton, killed at Inkerman, son of John Dalton, of Sleningford Park, co. York. 4. Louisa. *m.* John Mahon.
5. Jane. 6. Amanda. 7. Margaret.

Mr. W. Gabbett *m.* 2ndly, 2 March, 1719, Anne, dau. of Benjamin Frend, of Boskell; and 3rdly, 29 Aug. 1721, Mary, dau. of William Freeman, of Castle Cor, and by the latter (who *m.* 2ndly, Col. Ludovic Peterson) had a son,
4. Joseph, Gen. in the Army, Col. 16th Regt., *m.* Alethea, dau. and heiress of Seymour Richmond, of Sparsholt, Berks, and *d.s.p.*, leaving his estate of Sparsholt, &c., to his brother William's son, Joseph, of High Park.

Mr. Gabbett *d.* 1727, and was *s.* by his eldest son,
  William Gabbett, of Caberline, *b.* 1706, J.P. co. Limerick; *m.* May, 1730, Dorothea, dau. of the Rev. Richard Burgh, of Dromkeen, co. Limerick, and had, beside a dau., Elizabeth, *m.* Bryan Mansergh, three sons,
1. William, his heir.
2. Richard, *d. unm.*
3. Joseph, of High Park, co. Limerick, and Sparsholt, Berks, Major 16th Regt., *s.* to the estates of his uncle, Lieut.-Gen. Gabbett, and of his great-uncle, Joseph Gabbett, of High Park. He *m.* 22 Aug. 1771, Mary, dau. of the Rev. Rickard Lloyd, of Castle Lloyd, and *d.* 16 July, 1818, aged 79, having by her (who *d.* 18 Jan. 1830) had issue,
  1. Joseph, of High Park, J.P., *b.* 16 May, 1776; *m.* Lucy, dau. of the Ven. William Maunsell, of Thorpe Malsor, Archdeacon of Kildare, and *d.* Dec. 1865, having had issue,
    (1) Joseph (Rev.), A.M., of High Park, and Rector of Pagham, Sussex, *b.* 1806; *m.* 1834, Harriet, eldest dau. of Charles Dudley Madden, of Spring Grove, co. Fermanagh, and had issue,
      1. Joseph, C.B., Col. Madras Staff Corps, *b.* 25 Nov. 1835; *m.* Catherine Mary, dau. of John Dalzell, and left issue,
        a. Pulteney Charles, Major I.M.S., *b.* 19 Oct. 1868; *m.* 25 Nov. 1901, Kate May, elder dau. of Henry Gask, of Bromley, Kent.
        b. Alexander Cecil, Major 95th Regt. (Sherwood Foresters), *b.* 10 Aug. 1871.
          a. Sydney Constance.   *b.* Mary Catherine.
          c. Mary Catherine.   *d.* Constance Josephine.
      2. Charles Edward Dudley, of Lanes Park, co. Tipperary, J.P., Major North Cork Rifles, *b.* 25 Oct. 1839; *d.* 5 Nov. 1889.
      3. Edward Cecil.
      1. Lucy Harriett.   2. Emily Catherine.
      3. Mary Sydney, *m.* Capt. George Hodgson, Madras Staff Corps.
      4. Caroline Flora.
    (2) William, Major-Gen. Madras Artillery, Aide-de-Camp to Lord Gough, at Goojerat, *m.* Ellen, dau. of Matthew Lauder, of Lauderdale, co. Leitrim, and *d.* 1857, having had,
      1. Hugh William, *b.* 29 March, 1859.
      1. Lucy Georgina.   2. Ellen Anne.   3. Alice Kate.
    (3) Robert (Rev.), Vicar of Foynes, co. Limerick, *d.* 5 Nov. 1889.
      (1) Lucy Caroline. *m.* 19 Sept. 1832, William Smith O'Brien, of Cahirmoyle, M.P. He *d.* 18 Jan. 1864. She *d.* 13 June, 1861, leaving issue (see Burke's *Peerage*, Inchiquin, B.).
      (2) Alice, *m.* John Surtees Stockley, R.A.
  2. William, of Ballyvornane, *b.* 5 July, 1782; *d.s.p.* 10 Dec. 1857.
  3. Thomas, *b.* 4 Aug. 1785; *d.s.p.* 18 April, 1857.
  1. Mary, *m.* Rev. George Studdert, Rector of Kilpeacon.
  2. Dorothea, *m.* 29 April, 1868, Robert Webb, son of Patrick Webb, and had issue (see Webb of *Webbsborough*).
  3. Alice.
1. Elizabeth, *m.* Bryan Mansergh.

Mr. Gabbett *d.* 1769, and was *s.* by his eldest son,
  William Gabbett, of Caberline, *b.* 1731; High Sheriff co. Limerick, as well as Mayor of Limerick, in 1775; *m.* Jane, dau. of Richard Maunsell, of Ballywilliam, and had besides a dau. (who *m.* W. Faulkner Minchin, of Annagh, co. Tipperary), three sons,
1. William, his heir.
2. Joseph, Barrister-at-Law, *m.* Mary, dau. of Edward Little, 37th Regt., and had issue,
  1. William (Rev.), Rector of Inniscarra, co. Cork, *m.* Mary, dau. of the Most Rev. Joseph Henderson Singer, Bishop of Meath, and had three sons,
    (1) Joseph, *d.s.p.*
    (2) William Edward, M.A. Oxford, *d.* 12 Aug. 1883.
    (3) Henry Singer, M.D.
  2. Matthew Richard, of Ballybrood, *m.* Angel, dau. of Thomas Atkinson, of Kilnantouge, King's Co., and had issue,
    (1) Joseph Edward, Indian Civil Service.
    (1) Mary.   (2) Margaret.
  3. Joseph (Rev.), *d.s.p.*
  4. Edward (Rev.), Rector of Croom, Archdeacon of Limerick, and Chancellor of Limerick Cathedral, *m.* 1st, Ellen, dau. of Rev. Cecil Smyly (see *that family*), Vicar of Carlingford, by whom he had a son,
    Edward, Indian Civil Service, *m.* 1902, the dau. of Lieut.-Col. Robert John Knox, of Ballytobin, co. Kilkenny.
  The Rev. E. Gabbett *m.* 2ndly, 22 Nov. 1871, Emily, dau. of Hugh Massy, of Riversdale, and has further issue,
    Mary, *m.* 1903, Richard Lloyd Pennefather, J.P., of Marlow, co. Tipperary.
    1. Charlotte.
    2. Jane, *m.* 1852, Right Rev. Maurice Day, Bishop of Cashel, and had issue (see *that family*).
    3. Mary.   4. Dorothea Maria.   5. Vescina.
  6. Hannah, *m.* Rev. John Caillard Erck, Vicar of Merton, co. Surrey.
3. Daniel, of Strand House, *m.* Oct. 1795, Alicia, dau. of John FitzGerald, son of James FitzGerald, of Carrigoran, and had issue,
  1. William, of Strand House, High Sheriff co. Limerick 1852; *m.* Georgiana, dau. of Richard Going, and *d.s.p.*

2. John, *m.* Anastasia, dau. of John Magrath Fitzgerald, of Ballinard, and had issue,
  (1) Daniel FitzGerald, 12th Light Dragoons, *d s.p.*
  (1) Alicia, *m.* Capt. William Tuthill, 1st Dragoon Guards.
  (2) Catherine, *m.* William Bredington Bredin, son of Gen. Bredin, R.A.
3. Daniel, of Bellefield, co. Limerick, *m.* Susanna, dau. of Rev. Windham Magrath FitzGerald, of Ballinard, and *d.* 20 Oct. 1857, leaving,
  (1) Daniel FitzGerald, of Cahirconlish House, co. Limerick, J.P., M.P. for Limerick 1879 to 1885, formerly Lieut. 2nd Life Guards and 10th Hussars, *b.* 7 Nov. 1841; *m.* 1894, Augusta Janey, elder dau. of E. Butler Thornton, of Sherton, co. Lancaster, and widow of James Parkin, of The Leathes, co. Cumberland. He *d.* 4 Aug. 1898.
  (2) Windham, of Mount Rivers, co. Tipperary, J.P., late Lieut. Clare Militia, *b.* 1 Sept. 1844; *m.* 1867, Fanny, dau. and co-heiress of Richard Phillips, of Mount Rivers, and had,
    1. William Hampden, *b.* 27 Feb. 1868, Lieut. Pembroke Yeomanry.
    2. Richard Edward Phillips, *b.* 14 April, 1869, Major Royal Welsh Fusiliers.
    1. Ida.
  (3) William Hampden, Lieut. R.N., *b.* 26 Jan. 1846; *d.* 29 Dec. 1862.
4. Richard, *m.* Deborah, dau. of Rev. Windham Magrath FitzGerald, and had issue,
  (1) Deborah Anne, *m.* Rev. Henry Peacock, M.A.
  (2) Alice, *m.* 1st, Oliver Fitzmaurice, of Duagh, co. Kerry; and 2ndly, Matthew Blood Smyth, of Castle Fergus, co. Clare.
  (3) Richarda, *m.* William Pryce Maunsell, of Fanstown, co. Limerick.
5. Joseph (Rev.), M.A., of Ardvullen, co. Limerick, Chancellor of Limerick and Prebendary of Effin, *b.* 26 Dec. 1806; *m.* 1839, Margaret, dau. of John Tuthill, of Kilmore, and had an only child.
  Margaret Elizabeth, *m.* 1866, Thomas Atcherley Massy Dicken, of Loppington House, Salop, and *d.* 4 Sept. 1883.
6. Robert, M.D., of Shelbourne House, *m.* Sarah, dau. of Capt. Browne, and *d.s.p.*
  1. Mary, *m.* Rev. John Wallace.
  2. Jane, *m.* Admiral Sir Burton Macnamara.
  3. Helena, *m.* Rev. Thomas Westropp, of Ardcanny.

Mr. Gabbett *d.* 1789, and was *s.* by his eldest son,
  William Gabbett, of Caherline, High Sheriff co. Limerick 1813, *m.* 1791, Jane, dau. of Richard Waller, of Castle Waller, co. Tipperary, and had issue,
1. William Henry, his heir.
  1. Anne, *d.* 1873.   2. Jane, *d.* 1850.

Mr. Gabbett *d.* 1828, aged 63, and was *s.* by his son,
  William Henry Gabbett, of Caherline, *b.* 10 Jan. 1795; *m.* 1st, Jan. 1822, Rebecca Anne, only dau. of Humphrey Jones, of Mullinabro, co. Kilkenny (see *that family*), and by her (who *d.* 1828) had issue,
1. Richard Joseph, late of Caherline.
1. Anne Charlotte, *m.* Rev. John Vere Bowles.

Mr. Gabbett *m.* 2ndly, Sept. 1829, Frances Margaret, dau. of Thomas Richard Going, of Erina, co. Clare, and had by her,
2. Henry Francis, *b.* 1839; *d.* 27 Oct. 1908.
3. Thomas Richard, *b.* 1831; *d.* 5 Jan. 1910.
2. Mary Caroline, *d. unm.* 3 April, 1911.
3. Wilhelmina Jane.

Seat—Caherline House, Lisnagry, co. Limerick.

GAGE OF RATHLIN ISLAND.

The late Gen. Ezekiel Gage, of Rathlin Island, co. Antrim, Gen. (retired) Madras Staff Corps, *b.* 28 July, 1819; *m.* 16 May, 1848, Maria, dau. of John Dobbs, of Waterford, and *d.* 3 May, 1906, having had issue,

1. Robert Charles, *m.* Georgina, dau. of William Braddell, and *d.* 1888, leaving a son, Robert Harvey, who is married and has issue one son and one dau.
2. Richard Stewart, of Rathlin Island, Capt. Roy. Dublin Fus., *b.* ; *m.* Norah Lilian (*The Manor House, Rathlin Island, co. Antrim*), dau. of O'Donnell Grimshaw, and *d.* 30 Oct. 1909, leaving issue,
  1. Ezekiel Hugh, of Rathlin Island, *b.* 12 Oct. 1896.
  2. Richard Francis O'Donnell.
3. Francis, M.D., *b.* ; *m.* Kate Moore, and *d.*, leaving issue,
  1. Francis, of Rathlin Island.
  2. John.   3. Ezekiel.
  4. Sinclair.
4. Alexander Hugh (Rev.), of Rathlin Island, M.A. Trin. Coll. Dublin, Chaplain R.N., *m.* 3 Feb. 1909, Violet Agnes Evangeline Courtenay, only child of Col. C. J. Blake, late R.A.

He devised Rathlin Island between his four sons.

Lineage.—The Rev. Robert Gage, Chaplain to Queen Anne, and to Lionel, Duke of Dorset, Lord-Lieut. of Ireland. He was for many years Prebendary of Aghadoey, in the Diocese of Derry, and in which he was *s.* by his son,
  The Rev. John Gage. Prebendary of Aghadoey, *m.* 26 Feb. 1733, Susan, dau. of the Rev. John Johnston, Rector of Clondevadogue, in the Diocese of Raphoe, and *d.* 28 Jan. 1763. His son,

ROBERT GAGE, High Sheriff co. Antrim 1787, *b.* 5 Oct. 1739 ; *m.* 25 Dec. 1776, Barbara, dau. of John Richardson, of Somerset, near Coleraine, co. Londonderry, and by her (who *d.* 1823) had issue,
1. John, *d. unm.* 2. Frederick, R.N., *d. unm.*
3. ROBERT, of whom presently.
1. Barbara ; *m.* Robert Harvey, of Malinhall, co. Donegal.
2. Susan, *d. unm.* 3. Mary Anne, *m.* Marcus Richardson.

Mr. Gage *d.* 11 Sept. 1801. His 3rd son,
THE REV. ROBERT GAGE, of Rathlin Island, J.P., *b.* 20 Oct. 1790 ; *m.* 12 Aug. 1812, Catherine, eldest dau. of Ezekiel Davis Boyd, of Ballycastle, co. Antrim, and by her (who *d.* 22 Oct. 1852) had issue,
1. ROBERT, of whom presently.
2. EZEKIEL, late of Rathlin.
3. John, *b.* 19 June, 1823 ; *d.* 21 Feb. 1829.
4. John, *b.* 1829, *d.* 25 Feb. 1850.
1. Catherine, *d.* 15 Feb. 1892. 2. Barbara, *d. unm.*
3. Rosetta, *m.* Gardiner Harvey, and is dec.
4. Amelia, dec.   5. Susan, dec.
6. Elizabeth (dec.) ; *m.* Robert H. Wallace Dunlop.
7. Adelaide.
8. Dorothea, *m.* 2 June, 1864, His Serene Highness Albrecht Prince of Waldeck and Pyrmont, Prussia, and *d.* at Heidelberg, in Germany, 11 Dec. 1883, leaving three sons and two daus.

Mr. Gage *d.* 29 Sept. 1862, and was *s.* by his eldest son,
ROBERT GAGE, of Rathlin Island, J.P., M.A. Trin. Coll. Dublin, *b.* 30 July, 1813 ; *d.s.p.* 1 March, 1891, and was *s.* by his brother, EZEKIEL, now of Rathlin Island.

Seat—Rathlin Island, Ballycastle, co. Antrim.

GAISFORD-ST. LAWRENCE.
See ST. LAWRENCE.

GALBRAITH OF CLANABOGAN.

SAMUEL HAROLD LYLE GALBRAITH, of Clanabogan, co. Tyrone, Capt. Royal Irish Regt., *b.* 31 Aug, 1876.

Lineage.—JOHN GALBRAITH settled at Roscavy, co. Tyrone, and *d.* 25 May, 1668, leaving a son and successor,
CAPT. JAMES GALBRAITH, of Roscavy, *m.* Mary, widow of Capt. James Gledstanes, of Fardross, co. Tyrone, and left an only son,
JOHN GALBRAITH, of Roscavy, *m.* Anne Maria, eldest dau. of Rev. Richard Forbes, of Gilberistown and Cookstown, co. Louth, Rector of Ballinderry, and *d.* 26 Jan. 1742, aged 72, having had issue.

JOHN GALBRAITH, of Roscavy, Barrister-at-Law, *m.* Katherine, dau. of Samuel Perry, of Mullaghmore, and had issue,
1. JAMES, his heir.   2. George (Rev.), *d. unm.*
3. John Forbes, *m.* the dau. of John Buchanan.
4. Samuel, of Greenmount and Omagh, J.P., High Sheriff co. Tyrone 1791, *m.* Margaret Vicentia, dau. of James Maxwell, and *d.* 7 April, 1812, aged 72, having had (with six daus.) three sons,
1. John, J.P. for Longford and Tyrone, *d.* 1808.
2. James, *m.* Hannah Elizabeth, only child of John Porter, of Waterford, and *d.s.p.* 1812.
3. Arthur Lowry, of Lisanally, co. Tyrone, J.P., *m.* 1st, Sarah, only child of James Glasco ; and 2ndly, Martha, dau. of James Johnston, of Knappagh, co. Armagh, and had a dau. and heiress, Jane. He served as High Sheriff of Tyrone 1816, and *d.* 1819, aged 38.
1. Katherine, *m.* Robert Pooler, of Tyross.
2. Mary, *m.* Edward Barton, of Spring Hill.
3. Anne, *m.* Montgomery Small.

John Galbraith *d.* Jan. 1751, aged 40, and was *s.* by his son,
JAMES GALBRAITH, of Roscavy, J.P., and a Deputy-Governor, co. Tyrone, and High Sheriff elect at the time of his death, 1768. He *m.* June, 1762, Mary, 3rd dau. of Brabazon Noble, of Donaghmoine, co. Monaghan, and had issue, two sons and five daus., who all *d. unm.* except the 2nd son,
JOHN GALBRAITH of Roscavy, who *s.* his father. He *m.* his cousin Katherine, dau. and eventually heiress of Samuel Galbraith, of Greenmount and Omagh, and *d.* Feb. 1800, leaving issue,
1. James, *d. unm.*
2. John, of Greenmount and Roscavy, J.P., *m.* his cousin, Jane, heiress of the unentailed estates of her father, Arthur Lowry Galbraith, by whom (who *d.* 28 March, 1865) he had issue,
1. John Arthur.   2. Arthur Lowry, *d. unm.*
3. James, Capt. Royal Tyrone Fusiliers, *d.* aged 22.
1. Sarah, *m.* Thomas Andrew Young, eldest son of Andrew Knight Young, of Monaghan.
3. George, an Officer 82nd Regt., *d.* 1816, aged 17.
4. SAMUEL, of whom we treat.

The youngest son,
SAMUEL GALBRAITH, of Clanabogan and Riverstown, co. Tyrone, and of Crowdrumin, co. Longford, *s.* to the entailed estates of his uncle, Arthur Lowry Galbraith, in 1819, and to those of his mother in 1832 ; *m.* 1824, Susanna Jane, 2nd dau. of the Rev. Robert Handcock, D.D., and had issue,
1. JOHN SAMUEL, of Clanabogan.
2. Robert, *d. unm.*
3. Samuel, Major Madras Staff Corps, *d. unm.*
4. GEORGE (Very Rev.), of Clanabogan.
5. James, Col. of the Berkshire Regt. (66th), killed at Maiwand, 27 July, 1880.
6. William Arthur, late Lieut. 54th Regt.
1. Jane.

2. Katherine, *m.* Nov. 1874, Rev. W. H. Scott, youngest son of the Rev. J. Scott, Rector of Portaferry, co. Down.

Mr. Galbraith was a Magistrate of Tyrone, and served the office of High Sheriff for that co. 1833, and for the co. of Longford 1840. He *d.* 15 Sept. 1864. The eldest son,
JOHN SAMUEL GALBRAITH, B.A., of Clanabogan and Riverstown, co. Tyrone, and of Crowdrumin, co. Longford, J.P. for both cos., D.L. for co. Tyrone, High Sheriff of Longford 1874, and of Tyrone 1875, *b.* 1828 ; *d. unm.* 16 Aug. 1903.

THE VERY REV. GEORGE GALBRAITH, of Clanabogan, co. Tyrone, M.A., Dean of Derry, late Rector of the United Parishes of Drumachose and Aghanloo, and Rural Dean, *b.* 1829 ; *m.* 4 Aug. 1874, Florence, youngest dau. of Acheson Lyle, of The Oaks, Lieut. of the co. of Londonderry (*see that family*), and *d.* 3 Oct. 1911, leaving issue,
1. SAMUEL HAROLD LYLE, now of Clanabogan.
2. James Ponsonby, Capt. R.E., *b.* 27 March, 1881.
1. Eleanor Georgina Susannah, *m.* 31 May, 1904, Rev. Walter Benson, eldest son of Rev. Canon Benson.

Seat—Clanabogan, near Omagh.

GALT OF BALLYSALLY.

WILLIAM HOWARD CURTIS GALT, of Ballysally, Coleraine, co. Londonderry, late Lieut. Antrim Rifles, Solicitor, *b.* 9 June, 1870 ; *m.* 27 Dec. 1902, Josephine, dau. of Sylvain Larbalestre, of Thollet, Vienne, France, and has issue,
HAMILTON CURTIS, *b.* 1904.

Lineage.—This family has been settled in co. Londonderry for many generations.
JOHN GALT, Mayor of Coleraine, *b.* 1621 ; *m.* Mary Hazlett, and *d.* (will dated 5 Feb. 1699, proved 2 Oct. 1700), having by her (who *d.* 27 June, 1697) had issue,
1. JOHN, of whom presently.
2. Lennox.   3. Chalmers.
1. Eleanor.   2. Mary, *m.* Gilbert Hall.

The eldest son,
JOHN GALT, of Coleraine, *b.* 1660 ; *m.* 1st, Eliza Martin (who *d.* 13 Oct. 1696) ; and 2ndly, Sarah Moore, and made his will 17 June, 1715, proved 1733, having by her had issue,
1. John, of Coleraine, *m.* Jane —, and *d.* (will dated 4 July, 1765, proved 13 Dec. 1766).
2. WILLIAM, of whom we treat.

The younger son,
WILLIAM GALT, of Edendrave, *m.* Elizabeth, dau. of — Dunlop, and *d.* (will dated 10 Nov. 1757, proved 4 Jan. 1776) leaving issue,
1. ROBERT, of Edendrave, co. Antrim, *m.* June, 1772, Elizabeth, dau. of John Thompson, of Muckamore, co. Antrim.
2. CHARLES, of whom presently.
1. Sarah, *m.* Rowley Heyland, of Longford Lodge, and Glenoak, co. Antrim, and *d.* 5 Feb. 1775.
2. Ann.   3. Ellinor.

The younger son,
CHARLES GALT, of Coleraine, *b.* 13 Sept. 1738 ; *m.* 16 Jan. 1765, Elizabeth Allen, and *d.* 16 June, 1801, having by her (who *d.* 14 April, 1788) had issue,
1. John (Rev.), *b.* 16 July, 1767 ; *m.* 22 Jan. 1800, Magdalen Montgomery, and *d.* 1845, having by her (who *d.* 30 March, 1824) had issue,
1. Charles, *b.* 13 Jan. 1801 ; *d.* 6 June, 1829.
2. John, *b.* 15 Aug. 1802 ; *d.* 31 March, 1820.
3. Hugh, Capt. 26th Regt., *b.* 12 July, 1805 ; *d.* in India, 1836.
4. Samuel Gamble, *b.* 2 March, 1807.
5. William, a celebrated Railroad Engineer, author of "Railway Reform," and other works ; *b.* 2 Aug. 1809 ; *d.* 18 Jan. 1892.
6. Samuel, *b.* 2 April, 1812.
7. Montgomery James Allen, *b.* 8 March, 1819.
2. Robert, an Officer in the Army, *b.* 25 May, 1774 ; *d. unm.* May, 1806.
3. Charles, of Ballyboggy House, co. Antrim, *b.* 30 Dec. 1775 ; *m.* Aug. 1801, Clementina Cox, of Dublin, and had issue,
1. Eliza, *m.* George Henderson, of Glasgow.
2. Jane Clementina, *d. unm.*
3. Ann, *m.* Robert Fisher, of Londonderry.
4. Mary, *m.* Dr. Thompson.
4. WILLIAM, of whom presently.
5. James, *b.* 25 Nov. 1783.
1. Mary, *b.* 25 Jan. 1766.   2. Jane, *b.* 10 Nov. 1768.
3. Elizabeth, *b.* 16 Aug. 1770.
4. Ann, *b.* 6 May, 1773 ; *m.* James Little, of Kilrea and Dungevin, and *d.* 1 Dec. 1811.
5. Helen, *b.* 22 May, 1778 ; *m.* Oct. 1801, Robert Miller, of Dublin.   6. Sally, *b.* 27 Aug. 1785.

The 4th son,
WILLIAM GALT, of Ballysally House, co. Antrim, *b.* 28 Oct. 1782 ; *m.* 1811, Elizabeth, dau. and co-heir of Griffin Curtis, of Ballysally, and of Dominica, W. Indies, and *d.* 23 Sept. 1838, having by her (who *d.* 30 June, 1824) had issue,

1. Griffin Curtis, of Ballysally House, Capt. Ceylon Rifles, *b.* 30 April, 1816; *d. unm.* 6 May, 1868, and was *s.* by his brother.
2. WILLIAM HOWARD, of whom presently.
1. Eliza Curtis, *b.* 17 June, 1813; *d. unm.*
2. Hellen, *b.* 27 Jan. 1822; *d. unm.*
3. Mary Anne, *b.* 30 Oct. 1824.
4. Louisa, *b.* 24 Sept. 1826.

The younger son,

WILLIAM HOWARD CURTIS, of Ballysally House, co. Londonderry, *b.* Dec. 1819; *m.* 7 Sept. 1869, Sarah Ann, dau. of George Moore, of Tullans, and *d.* 1 Aug. 1885, having by her (who *d.* 27 April, 1911) had issue,
1. WILLIAM HOWARD CURTIS, now of Ballysally.
2. George Moore, *b.* 2 June, 1871; *m.* 23 June, 1904, Lida Janette Batcheldar, of Nashua, U.S.A.
3. Charles John, *b.* 17 Jan. 1873; *m.* 1906, Maggie Mary, dau. of Digory Sargent Pearse, of Temuka, N.Z.
4. Griffin Curtis, *b.* May, 1881.
1. Mary Barklie, dec. 2. Sarah Jane, dec.

Arms—Az. on a chevron between three garbs or, banded gu., a man's head in profile couped below the shoulders ppr., wreathed az. Crest—On a garb fessways or, banded gu., a man's head as in the arms. Motto—Nihil melius virtute.

Seat—Ballysally House, Coleraine. Residence—Fort View, Coleraine. Club—St. George's, W.

GAMBLE OF KILLOOLY HALL.

ANDREW WILLIAM GAMBLE, of Killooly Hall, and Derrinboy House, King's Co., J.P., late Hon. Lieut.-Col. 3rd Batt. (P.O.W. Royal Canadians) Leinster Regt., late Major 2nd Royal Garrison Regt., late Capt. Northamptonshire Regt., *b.* 1853; *m.* 1895, Kate, dau. of Rev. Thomas Wilson, Rector of Stirling, and has had issue,

Richard Bowes, *d.* 1898.   Queenie Muriel.

Lineage.—ANNE HALLAM, of Newark, co. Leicester, widow, the sister and heiress of Edward Smith, an Alderman of London, who *d.* in 1686, gave by her will, 11 Jan. 1635, her properties of Seagrave, co. Leicester, and Little Clayton, co. Essex, and her property in the King's Co. among her three grandsons, EDWARD, JOHN, and SAMUEL GAMBLE, children of her dau., Susannah, then all minors. Edward, the eldest, lived at Seagrave, co. Leicester. He *m.* and had issue, John Elizabeth, and Susannah.

SAMUEL GAMBLE, the youngest, was ancestor of this family, bought his brother's shares of the Irish property, and lived at Carrick, co. Westmeath. He *m.* 1711, Catherine, dau. of Richard Pilkington, of Rathgarrett, Westmeath, and had by her one only child,

JOHN GAMBLE, *b. circa* 1713, in the Commission of the Peace, 1762; *m.* 1743, Elizabeth, dau. of Nicholas Ogle, of Grennastown, Westmeath, by whom he had issue,
1. NICHOLAS, of whom hereafter.
2. Nathaniel, a merchant in Dublin, *d.s.p.* 1784.
3. William Henry, Lieut. in the Line, *d.s.p.*
1. Catherine, *m.* 1778, John Blakeney, M.D., and *d.* 1814, leaving one child,
   John, an Officer in the 33rd Foot, *d.s.p.* in India, 1812.
2. Sophia, *d. unm.* 3. Mary Anne, *d. unm.* 1808.

Mr. Gamble *d.* 1784, and was *s.* by his eldest son,

NICHOLAS GAMBLE, J.P., Deputy-Governor of the King's Co., 1793; *m.* 1780, Rebecca, youngest dau. of Andrew Armstrong, of Castle Armstrong (*see* ARMSTRONG *of Garry Castle*), and had issue,
1. John, J.P., *d. unm.* 1827.
2. ANDREW WILLIAM, of whom hereafter.
3. Thomas Matcham, *d. unm.* 4. William, *d.s.p.* 1805.
1. Mary, *m.* Wm. Henry Steele, and *d.s.p.* 1806.
2. Eliza, *m.* Geo. Delany, *d.s.p.*
3. Sophia, *m.* Col. Nathaniel Carlton Maw, *d.s.p.*
4. Harriett, *d. unm.*
5. Charlotte, *m.* Robert Weldon Tarleton, of Newtown House, King's Co., who *d.* 1885, aged 90, and had issue.

Mr. Gamble *d.* 1816. His 2nd son,

ANDREW WILLIAM GAMBLE, carried the colours of the 20th Regt. at Talavera, and was wounded and made prisoner there. He was afterwards Capt. in 31st Regt.; he *m.* Jan. 1821, Elizabeth, dau. of Frederick Wilson, of Forest Hall, Newcastle-on-Tyne, and had issue,
1. Andrew William, *b.* Nov. 1821, *d. unm.* 1853.
2. RICHARD WILSON, of whom presently.
3. John Edward, *d. unm.* 1897.
1. Hannah Dent, *d. unm.* 1905.
2. Elizabeth, *d. unm.*
3. Sophia, *d. unm.* 1904.

The 2nd son,

HIS HONOUR RICHARD WILSON GAMBLE, of Killooly Hall, King's Co., and 51, Fitzwilliam Square, Dublin, J.P., County Court Judge for Armagh and Louth. He was Member of the Diocesan Synods of Dublin and Meath, a Member of the General Synod from its commencement, and contested the Parliamentary Borough of Rochdale in 1874 and 1880, and Halifax in 1876. His Honour Judge Gamble was *b.* 1823; *m.* Charlotte Rebecca, dau. of Martin Keene, of Dublin, and *d.* 19 April, 1887, having had issue,
1. ANDREW WILLIAM, now of Killooly.

2. Richard Keene, B.A. Trin. Coll. Dublin, Barrister-at-Law, J.P. (51, *Fitzwilliam Square, Dublin; Carriglea, Greystones, co. Wicklow*), *m.* 1892, Hannah Maria, dau. of Maurice Brooks, J.P. and D.L. of Oaklawn, co. Dublin, and has issue,
   1. Richard Maurice, *b.* 1893.
   2. George Sidney, *b.* Oct. 1898.
   1. Annie Alma.
1. Elizabeth Jane, *m.* 1887, Frederick Barrett, son of Thomas Barrett, of Kingsdene, Norwood, and has issue,
   1. Frederick, *b.* 6 June, 1887.
   1. Gladys Eileen.   2. Vera Florence.
2. Louisa, *m.* Edward M. Hill, Solicitor, London, and *d.s.p.*
3. Alexandra Sophia, *m.* 1901, Rev. Joseph Worthington Atkin, of St. Peter's, Cork, and has issue.

Seat—Killooly Hall, King's Co. Residence—Derrinboy House, Kilcormack, King's Co.

GARNETT OF WILLIAMSTON.

WILLIAM STAWELL GARNETT, of Williamston, co. Meath, J.P., High Sheriff 1864, *b.* 14 Aug. 1838; *m.* 27 Aug. 1859, Sally, dau. of Hamlet Garnett, of Teltown, J.P. co. Meath, and has issue,
1. GEORGE WILLIAM, *b.* 8 April, 1863.
2. Henry Reid, *b.* 24 March, 1865.
3. Stawell William Wade, *b.* 27 July, 1871.
1. Sally, *b.* 8 May, 1877.

Lineage.—GEORGE GARNETT, of Drogheda, *m.* Barbara Fleming, and *d.s.p.* By his will, dated 26 April, 1653, and proved 6 Feb. following, he settled his lands on his nephews, John, George, and Marks Garnett.

JOHN GARNETT, of Balgeeth, co. Meath, *temp.* Queen ANNE, *m.* Anne, dau. of Samuel Hatch, co. Meath, and had issue,
1. JOHN (Rev.), his successor.
2. George, of Huntstown, *m.* Anne Thompson, and had issue.
3. SAMUEL, ancestor of GARNETT *of Summerseat* (*see that family*).
4. Henry, ancestor of GARNETT *of Green Park*.
1. Elizabeth, *m.* 1739, Henry Kinkead.
2. Mary, *m.* 1738, William Battersby.

Mr. Garnett, whose will, dated 15 Jan. 1774, was proved 20 May following, was *s.* by his eldest son,

REV. JOHN GARNETT, who resided at Rathaldron Castle, *m.* 2 July, 1755, a dau. of Gibbons, Rector of Mellifont, co. Louth, and had, with two daus. (Margaret Jane, *m.* George Armstrong; and Elizabeth, *m.* Maurice Neligan) a son,

REV. GEORGE CHARLES GARNETT, of Williamston, co. Meath, *m.* Margaret, eldest dau. of Alan Wade, of Bachelor's Lodge, near Navan, by Anne Shenton his wife, and had issue,
1. HAMLET, of Teltown, co. Meath, *m.* 1832, Louisa, dau. of Col. Hamlet Wade, Rifle Brigade (by Mary his wife, dau. of Rev. Dr. William Langford, Canon of Windsor, and Private Chaplain to King GEORGE IV), and *d.* 1850, leaving issue, a son, George Charles, and a dau., Sally, *m.* 1859, her cousin W. S. GARNETT, of Williamston (*see above*).
2. GEORGE, of Williamston.
3. William, of Dunorver House, co. Meath, *m.* Julian, dau. of John Boyce, of Limerick.
1. Elinor, *m.* 1818, John Radcliffe.
2. Elizabeth, *m.* 1812, Owen Armstrong, of Belview.
3. Letitia, *m.* 1830, Thomas Gerrard, of Gibstown (*see that family*).
4. Margaret, *m.* 1828, William Tatlow.
5. Frances, *m.* 1818, Henry Reid.

The 2nd son,

GEORGE GARNETT, of Williamston, J.P., *m.* 1828, Catherine Anna, dau. of Jonas Stawell, J.P., of Oldcourt, co. Cork, and had issue,
1. WILLIAM STAWELL, now of Williamston.
2. Charles Leslie (Rev.), M.A., Rector of Ardtrea, co. Tyrone, *m.* 1st, 2 March, 1875, Lady Ella Sophia Stuart, dau. of Charles Knox, 4th Earl of Castle Stewart. She *d.* 2 May, 1900, leaving issue,
   1. Charles Leslie Stuart, *b.* 1879.
   2. Claude D'Estaville, *b.* 1884.
   1. Ella Dorothea Violet.   2. Marjory Patience Maud.
   3. Catherine Charlotte Winifred.
   4. Annette Blanche Lilian.   5. Rosamond.
   He *m.* 2ndly, 1902, Anne Elizabeth, dau. of the late Robert Quin Alexander, of Acton House, co. Armagh.
3. Wade Shenton, Barrister-at-Law.
1. Anna Letitia.

Mr. Garnett *d.* Oct. 1856.

Seat—Williamston, Kells, co. Meath.

GARNETT OF SUMMERSEAT.

RICHARD GARNETT, of Summerseat and Rosmeen, co. Meath, *b.* 22 Feb. 1879; *m.* 26 June, 1901, Bessie Ella, dau. of George Greer, of Dungannon, co. Tyrone.

Lineage.—SAMUEL GARNETT, of Summerseat, co. Meath, 3rd son of John Garnett, of Balgeeth (*see preceding Memoir*), *m.* 1772, Mary, dau. of John Rothwell, of Cannonstown, co. Meath (*see* ROTHWELL *of Rockfield*), and by her (who *d.* 1817) had two sons,

IRELAND. Garrett.

1. SAMUEL, of whom presently.
2. John Paine, of Arch Hall, High Sheriff 1821, m. 20 Aug. 1799, Mary, 'au. of William Cope, Dublin, and d. 9 Jan. 1846, having by her (who d. 1 June, 1846) had issue,
  1. SAMUEL, of Arch Hall, J.P., High Sheriff 1858, b. 1805 ; m. 1841, Marianne, dau. and co-heir of George Tandy, of Balrath, co. Meath, and d. 25 June, 1883, having by her (who d. 13 Oct. 1883) had issue,
    (1) JOHN PAINE, b. 1842 ; m. 12 July, 1864, Edith Charlotte, 3rd dau. of Henry Corbet Singleton, J.P. and D.L., of Aclare, co. Meath (*see that family*), and by her (who m. 2ndly, 1884, Cecil Gilliat) left issue at his death, Jan. 1872, an only son, JOHN PAINE, of Arch Hall, J.P., b. 22 Feb. 1866 ; d. unm. 1894.
    (2) Samuel, formerly of the 6th Dragoon Guards (Carabiniers), b. 1845 ; m. 1872, Charlotte Josephine, dau. of John Stanley Howard, of Friar's Hill, co. Wicklow, and d. 1892. She m. 2ndly, 23 Feb. 1892, Henry William Montagu, 16th Marquis of Winchester,
    (1) Mary.
  s William, of Caulton, co. Meath, d. unm.
  1. Charlotte, m. Rev. William Roper, and d. 23 Dec. 1880.
  2. Elizabeth, m. 1833, Whitwell Bulter, of Staffordstown, co. Meath.
Mr. Samuel Garnett d. 1803, and was s. by his elder son,
SAMUEL GARNETT, of Summerseat, J.P., b. 10 Nov. 1775 ; m. 1st, 26 Feb. 1805, Alice, dau. of Andrew Ellard, of Newton, co. Limerick, and by her had issue,
  1. SAMUEL, his heir.
  1. Anne, m. Sept. 1833, Rev. Richard Radcliff, Rector of Skyrne, co. Meath.
He m. 2ndly, 7 Dec. 1818, Mary Anne, dau. of Thomas Rothwell, of Rockfield, co. Meath, and had issue.
  2. RICHARD, successor to his elder brother.
  3. William, b. 29 June, 1820. 2. Helena. 3. Marianne.
  4. Isabella, m. 1850, Thomas Henry Johnson, of Carnaghlis, co. Antrim.
Mr. Garnett d. 20 Dec. 1862. His eldest son,
SAMUEL GARNETT, of Summerseat and Rosmeen, co. Meath, J.P., b. 3 Nov. 1806 ; m. May, 1831, Martha, dau. of the Rev. George O'Connor, of Ardlunnan, co. Meath, Rector of Castleknock ; and d.s.p. 19 May, 1874, when he was s. by his half brother,
RICHARD GARNETT, of Summerseat and Rosmeen, J.P. co. Meath, b. 13 Oct. 1821 ; m. 22 July, 1869, Louisa Hawkes, dau. of George Knox, J.P., and by her (who m. 2ndly, 1883, Trevor Blackwood Hamilton, of Vessington, and d. 1899) had issue,
  1. RICHARD, now of Summerseat.
  1. Mary. 2. Lousia, d. unm. 4 March, 1890.
Mr. Garnett d. 5 Feb. 1881.
Seats—Summerseat, Clonee ; and Rosmeen, near Kells, co. Meath.

GARRETT OF KILGARAN.

WILLIAM RAYMOND GARRETT, of Kilgaran, co. Carlow, b. 11 Aug. 1840 ; m. 24 Jan. 1867, Anna Barbara, dau. of the late William Eliot, of Radipole, Weymouth, D.L. and J.P. for Dorset, by Lydia his wife, dau. of John ffolliott, late M.P. for Sligo, and has issue,
1. JAMES HUGH ELIOT, b. 13 Nov. 1867, Indian Civil Service ; m. 2 July, 1889, Edith Geraldine, dau. of the late J. McNamara, of Arrah, Bengal, and co. Clare, and has issue,
  1. Lilian Margaret.
  2. Dorothy, m. 26 Dec. 1911, Noel Graham Dunbar.
  3. Winifred Raymond.
2. John Raymond, Major Royal Marine L.I., b. 7 June, 1869.
3. Arthur ffolliott, Capt. R.E., b. 27 April, 1875 ; m. 18 Dec. 1900, Ida, dau. of the late Rev. J. F. A. Gavin, Chaplain Bengal Establishment.

Lineage.—CAPT. JOHN GARRETT (one of five brothers serving in Oliver Cromwell's Army), had a grant of land in the Queen's Co., in pursuance of the Act of Settlement 23 Nov. 1666. He was father of
JAMES GARRETT, of Kilgaran and Clonferta, co. Carlow, b. 1676 ; m. Mary, dau. of Col. Blake, of Mayo, and d. circa 1760, having had by her (who d. 7 July, 1727) two sons, 1. THOMAS, his heir ; and 2. William, of Clonferta, who d. unm. ; will proved 1760. The former,

THOMAS GARRETT, of Kilgaran, otherwise Janeville, b. 1711 ; m. Anne, dau. of John Cole, residing at that time in the co. Wexford, and had issue,
1. JAMES, his heir.
1. Sarah, m. William Meredith.
2. Elizabeth, m. Samuel Brewster. 3. Lydia, m. J. Waters.
Mr. Garrett, whose will is dated 13 Aug. 1759, and proved 16 Nov. following, was s. by his son,
JAMES GARRETT, of Kilgaran, otherwise Janeville, b. 10 Oct. 1740, High Sheriff co. Carlow 1776 ; m. June, 1772, Jane, dau. and co-heir of John Perkins, of Ballintrane Castle, co. Carlow, and by her (who d. 7 June, 1788) had issue,
1. JOHN, of Janeville, d. unm.
2. WILLIAM, of Janeville.
1. Anne, m. Gilbert Pickering Rudkin, of Wells, co. Carlow, Capt. in the Army, High Sheriff co. Carlow 1808, and had issue, 1. Jane, m. Thomas Tench Vigors, of Erindale ; and 2. Maria, m. Henry Shaw Jones, of Randalstown.
2. Mary, m. John Watson, of Ballydarton, co. Carlow, High Sheriff 1834, and had, 1. John ; 2. William ; 1. Jane ; and 2. Diana.
3. Priscilla, d. unm.
Mr. Garrett d. 17 July, 1818. His 2nd son,
WILLIAM GARRETT, of Janeville, or Kilgaran, J.P., b. 10 Oct. 1783, High Sheriff co. Carlow 1806, Capt. 1st Carlow Yeomanry Cavalry ; m. 16 Nov. 1809, Margaret, dau. of Samuel Raymond, of Riversdale, co. Kerry, by Catherine his wife, dau. of Alexander Odell, of Oddlville, co. Limerick, and by her (who d. 25 May, 1857) had issue,
1. JAMES PERKINS, of Kilgaran.
2. Samuel Raymond, b. 1812 ; d. unm. 1876.
3. William Thomas (Rev.), of the Hall, Crakehall, co. York, M.A. and J.P., b. 1820 ; m. 1850, Anne (who d. 23 Oct. 1894), only dau. of John G. Horsfall, J.P., of Bolton Rhoyd, co. York, and by him (who d. 1884) had issue,
  1. Thomas Horsfall Heaton, of Crakehall, Bedale, b. 1851, Lieut.-Col. late 16th Lancers ; d. unm. Dec. 1900.
  2. William Perkins, d. 1860.
  3. John Raymond, b. 1858 ; Lieut. 60th Rifles, special service Zulu War, 1879, killed in action, battle of Ingogo, South Africa, 1881.
  1. Mary, m. 1875, John Michell, J.P. (who d. 1878), eldest son of John Michell, J.P. and D.L., of Forcett Park, co. York, and Glassel, co. Kincardine, N.B.
1. Catherine Georgiana Augusta, d. unm. June, 1855.
2. Jane, d. unm. 4 June, 1845.
3. Anna Maria, m. William Blackman Robertson, and d. June, 1865, leaving issue.
The eldest son,
REV. JAMES PERKINS GARRETT, of Kilgaran, co. Carlow, Rector of Killistown, in that co., b. 10 Oct. 1810 ; m. 5 Nov. 1834, Caroline Anne Elizabeth, dau. of Hugh Moore, Capt. 5th Dragoon Guards, of Eglantine House, and Mount Panther, co. Down, by Priscilla Cecilia his wife, dau. of William Armitage, of Moraston, co. Hereford, and widow of William Shaw, of Terenure, co. Dublin, and by her (who d. 10 Oct. 1887) had issue,
1. WILLIAM RAYMOND, now of Kilgaran.
2. James Hugh Moore, of Corrie Wood, Castlewellan, co. Down, b. 1842, Barrister-at-Law, J.P. cos. Cavan and Down ; m. 1st, 4 June, 1884, Amie, Baroness de Poelnitz, dau. of Baron and the Hon. Baroness de Poelnitz, of Bregenz, Austria, and grand-dau. of the 17th Lord Forbes, of Castle Forbes. She d. 24 Oct. 1891. He m. 2ndly, 11 April, 1894, Isabel, eldest dau. of the late Hon. Richard Maxwell. She d. 15 May, 1902 (*see* BURKE'S *Peerage*, FARNHAM, B.). He m. 3rdly, 3 June, 1903, Elizabeth, widow of Maj. Stenart Masters, I.S.C., and dau. of the late Marmaduke Eyre (*see* EYRE of *Eyrecourt*).
3. Annesley John, b. 1846, Lieut.-Col. and Military Secretary, Hyderabad, E.I., Bengal Staff Corps ; m. 6 Oct. 1887, Edith le Blanc, dau. of J. Grant Morris, J.P., of Allerton Priory, near Liverpool.
1. Priscilla Cecilia, m. 1854, John Winter Humphrys, J.P., of Ballyhaise House, co. Cavan, and d. 19 July, 1884, leaving issue (*see* HUMPHRYS of *Ballyhaise*).
2. Margaret Clarissa, m. 1862, Vesey Edmund Knox, J.P., of Shimnah, co. Down, 52nd Light Infantry, grandson of the Hon. Vesey Knox, 3rd son of the 1st Earl of Ranfurly, d. 1879, leaving issue (*see* BURKE'S *Peerage*).
3. Sydney Elizabeth Jane, m. 1st, 1874, Joseph Spender Clay, of Ford Manor, Surrey, and Stapinhill House, co. Stafford, son of Henry Clay, of Piercefield Park, co. Monmouth, by Elizabeth his wife, dau. of John Leigh, of Upton and Sandilands, co. Lancaster, and Luton Hoo Park, Beds, who d. 3 Nov. 1885, leaving issue, Herbert Henry, b. 1875.
Violet Sylvia Blanche, m. 30 Nov. 1896, Lord Bingham, eldest son of the Earl of Lucan (*see* BURKE'S *Peerage*).
She m. 2ndly, Beresford V. Melville, M.P., 2nd son of Rev. David Melville, Canon of Worcester.
4. Jane Harriette, m. 6 June, 1883, Sir Joseph Thomas Firbank, J.P. and D.L., of St. Julian's, co. Monmouth, and has issue. He d. 7 Oct. 1910, leaving issue (*see that family*).
5. Sylvia Christina Armitage, m. 26 June, 1878, Alexander Innes, 3rd Buffs, of Raemoir, Cowie and Dunnottar, co. Kincardine, J.P. and D.L. (who d. 13 Nov. 1882), and d. 1887, leaving issue (*see that family*).
Rev. J. P. Garrett d. 18 Oct. 1879.

Arms—Erm. on a fess az., a lion passant or. Crest—A lion passant az. langued gu. resting the sinister paw on a trefoil vert. Motto—Semper fidelis.

Seat—Kilgaran, co. Carlow. Club—Junior Constitutional, W.

GARSTIN OF BRAGANSTOWN.

JOHN RIBTON GARSTIN, of Braganstown, co. Louth, *b.* 27 Dec. 1836; *m.* 3 May, 1864, Mary Martha Toone, only dau. of James A. Durham, of Elm Lodge, Hampton-on-Thames (sometime Chairman of the London and County Bank), and by her (who *d.* 29 Dec. 1910, aged 64) had issue,

1. WILLIAM FORTESCUE COLBORNE, J.P., Major, late Royal Irish Rifles, *b.* 1 Jan. 1875, served through the war in South Africa (medal, &c.].
1. Helena Coruelia, *m.* 15 Nov. 1894, Rev. John Harvie Douglas, M.A., of Dagmar House, Canterbury, late Rector of Otterden, Kent, and has issue, one son and four daus.
2. Adeline Frances.
3. Rosamond Alethea.

Mr. Garstin is M.A. of Trin. Coll. Dublin (*ad eund.* Oxon.), and LL.B. and B.D. of Dublin (being the first layman to obtain the latter degree there); he is J.P. and D.L. co. Louth, High Sheriff 1880, J.P. co. Dublin, F.S.A., ex-President of the Royal Society of Antiquaries of Ireland, and Vice-President of the Royal Irish Academy (formerly Treasurer), a Visitor of the National Museum, Dublin, and Governor of Armagh Library and Observatory, &c. He purchased the Braganstown estate, after the death of the Rev. Anthony Garstin, head of the family originally seated there (*see succeeding genealogy*).

Lineage.—MAJOR JAMES GARSTIN, *b.* about 1593. was in Ireland before 1649, and served with CROMWELL'S Army. On 3 Aug. 1660, he was appointed by Gen. Monk (Duke of Albemarle), the Commander-in-Chief under CHARLES II, Provost-Marshal-General of the forces in Ireland, and in consideration of his services and money "adventured" by him, he was granted extensive lands in co. Meath, and Braganstown, co. Louth (an estate forfeited by the Taaffes, and which enjoyed manorial rights). These grants were confirmed by letters patent of CHARLES II, 5 Feb. 1666, the original of which is in the possession of the present Mr. Garstin, of Braganstown. Maj. Garstin was High Sheriff of Louth 1668. By his will (proved in Dublin 20 Jan. 1676-7) he left Braganstown to his grand-nephew, Norman, son of his nephew,

CAPT. SYMON GARSTIN, to whom the lands of Leragh and Ballykerrin, co. Westmeath, with the Castle of Leragh (still standing) were granted. After serving throughout the war, and subsequently aiding Sir William Petty in his surveying, he settled at Drogheda, and *d.* there 1660. By his wife Alice, who survived him (as did also his mother Katharine), he had issue,

1. WILLIAM, to whom Leragh Castle and the lands granted to his father were confirmed by royal patent, 5 Feb. 1666. He *m.* Martha, dau. of Thomas Ball, of Glasdromon, co. Armagh (sister of Abraham Ball, of Darver Castle, Louth), and *d.* 1685. leaving by her, who survived him, an only son, WILLIAM, who *d.* 1701, bequeathing his estate in co. Westmeath to his uncle John; and a dau., Norminda, *m.* (licence dated 24 Dec. 1729) to her cousin Rev. John Ball.
2. JOHN, of Leragh Castle, &c., who *s.* accordingly. His line we now follow, being that from which descends the present Braganstown family.
3. NORMAN, adopted by his grand-uncle, Maj. James Garstin, of Braganstown. His line, that of the family formerly seated at Braganstown, shall be taken up further on.
1. Katherine, to whom her father left by his will land at Ballymullen, near Dundalk, and " all the arrears that is due to me for my service in Ireland, from the beginning of the world to the date hereof." She *m.* William Goodwin, of Dundalk, 1661-2.
2. Anne, *m.* 1684-5. to Richard Smith.

The 2nd son,

JOHN GARSTIN, of Leragh Castle, and Ballykerrin, co. Westmeath, and of Tatestown, co. Meath, heir of his nephew, William, purchased, 1703, Mullaghard, co. Meath. He afterwards purchased Kilmore and Rahin, co. Kildare, where he resided. He *m.* Oct. 1686, Maria, only dau. of Enoch Reader, Alderman and Lord Mayor of Dublin. On the death of her brothers, Richard, Dean of Kilmore, and Enoch, Dean of Emly, and of William, Archdeacon of Cork, son of the latter, the representation of the Reader family vested in her grandson, as heir-at-law. She *d.* Nov. 1720. John Garstin was admitted a Freeman of Dunleer, of Ardee, 1701, and of Drogheda, 1702, and *d.* in Sept. 1733, leaving issue,

1. JAMES, his heir, *b.* about 1690.
1. Anne, *m.* 30 Aug. 1716, Thomas Fortescue, of Dromisken, co. Louth, ancestor of Lords Clermont and Carlingford (*see Peerage*).
2. Mary, living in 1752, *d. unm.*

The son,

JAMES GARSTIN, of Leragh Castle, and Kilmore (now called Woodlands), High Sheriff for co. Kildare 1729, and for Meath 1730, sold his Meath estate to Dean Swift to endow his hospital. He *m.* Maria, dau. of Benjamin Fish, of Tubberogan (now Castle Fish), co. Kildare, and *d.* about 1737, leaving,

1. JOHN, the ancestor of the English branch, of which presently.
2. BENJAMIN, whose line we now follow.
1. Mary, *m.* about 1750, Rev. Thomas Agmond Vesey, Rector of Dromglass, &c., grandson of Archbishop Vesey (*see* VESEY). He *d.* 1797, aged 74. She *d.* 1803, aged 79.
2. Cordelia, *m.* Ven. John Jackson, Archdeacon of Clogher, J.P., who *d.s.p.* 1787.
3. Elizabeth, *m.* (Rev.) Dr. Jacob.
4. Alicia, *m.* Mr. Robinson (of Armagh ?).

The 2nd son,

BENJAMIN GARSTIN, of Dublin, *m.* 17 May, 1748, Henrietta, youngest dau. of John Minchin, of Shanagary Castle, co. Tipperary, and by her (who *d.* 4 April, 1769) had issue,

1. JOHN, of whom presently.
2. William, *d.* young.
1. Elizabeth, *b.* 1750; *m.* 1773, Thomas Snagg, and *d.* 29. April, 1774, leaving an only child, Thomas (*see below*).
2. Anne Monica, *b.* 1751; *m.* 7 Aug. 1775, William, eldest son of Rev. Dr. Fergusson, and *d.* 31 May, 1835, leaving issue by him, who *d.* 23 Nov. 1799.
3. Cordelia, *b.* 1754; *m.* 1774, Capt. Henry Gudgeon, of Penzance, Cornwall, and *d.* 1841. He *d.* 1837, aged 81.
4. Alethea, Mrs. Allen.
5. Henrietta, *b.* 1759; *m.* 1779, Henry McAlister, of Fethard, who *d.* the year following, leaving a dau., Harriet; and 2ndly, 1784, Major Henry Bowen, 2nd Royal Veteran Battalion, and D.-J.-A.-G. at Malta, who *d.* 6 Feb. 1843, leaving issue. Mrs. Bowen survived to 4 July, 1853.

Mr. Garstin *m.* 2ndly, Dec. 1773, Jane, widow of John Chamney, of Castletown, co. Wicklow, and dau. of William Johnston, of Arklow. She *d.* 1823. He *d.* 4 April, 1779. His eldest son,

JOHN GARSTIN, of Molesworth Street, Dublin, *b.* Jan. 1753; *m.* 1st, 22 Jan. 1774, Juditha Eagar, who *d.* 31 Dec. 1790, leaving surviving issue,

1. JONATHAN HAYTER (" John"), 88th Regt. Connaught Rangers, *b.* 19 April, 1790; *m.* 14 Jan. 1815, Louisa Anne, eldest dau. of Thomas Gillanders, of Calcutta, and *d.* 27 Aug. 1828, leaving issue,
   1. JOHN FRANCIS, *b.* 28 Dec. 1819, Capt. 66th Bengal N.I.; *m.* 14 March, 1849, Eleanor, eldest surviving dau. of Rev. Christophilus Garstin, Rector of Ballyroney (*see succeeding Article*), and dying 7 Nov. 1858, left by her (who *d.* Feb. following) two sons, *d.* young, and one dau.,
      Eleanor Grace, *m.* 1st, 24 June, 1885, C. P. R. Cotter; 2ndly, Isaac Wolfe; and 3rdly, 1909, John Fleming, of Helston, Cornwall.
   2. William Thomas, *b.* 1823; Major Bengal N.I., *d. unm.*
   3. Marcus Augustus, *b.* 12 May, 1825, Capt. 73rd Bengal N.I., and Turkish Contingent; *m.* 28 June, 1860, and *d.s.p.* 23 Sept. 1863.
   1. Louisa, *m.* 5 May, 1831, John, eldest son of Sir Claudius Stephen Hunter, Bart., D.C.L., and *d.s.p.* 1884.
   2. Harriet Caroline, *m.* 2 Aug. 1837, Lieut.-Col. Robert McNair, Commanding 17th Bengal N.I., who *d.* of fatigue during the Indian Mutiny, 20 July, 1857, leaving issue.
   3. Sophia Frances, *m.* 23 March, 1843, Major-Gen. Augustus Abbott, C.B., Commanding Royal Artillery (Bengal), Hon. A.D.C. to the Hon. the Governor-General of India, and to Queen Victoria, Principal Commissary and Inspector General of the Ordnance Commissariat Department. He *d.* 25 Feb. 1867, leaving seven children.
   4. Emily, *m.* 31 Dec. 1844, Major George Holroyd, grandson of Sir George Holroyd, Chief Justice of the King's Bench, and had issue.
1. Henrietta Minchin, *b.* 24 Dec. 1774; *m.* 1805, her cousin Thomas Snagg (*see above*), who *d.* 1821. She *d.* 10 April, 1839, leaving issue.
2. Elizabeth Longfield, *b.* 8 Feb. 1784; *m.* 23 Oct. 1811, John Zinck, who *d.* 26 Nov. 1848. She *d.* at Hamburgh, 5 Nov. 1864, leaving one child, Elizabeth Garstin.

Mr. Garstin was made a Freeman (Honorary) of Dublin, 1777, and Waterford 1782. He *m.* 2ndly, 23 June, 1792, Mary, elder dau. of Richard Harman, of Brighton, Sussex, and *d.* 29 Sept. 1808, leaving by her (who *d.* 23 July, 1831) two sons,

2. WILLIAM, of Dublin, *b.* 27 Feb. 1794; *m.* 15 Jan. 1819, Anne, eldest dau. of William Walker, of High Park, co. Dublin, Red Castle, co. Derry, and Mountjoy Square, Dublin, by Jane Marsh, his wife (*see* MARSH *of Springmount*), and *d.* 25 Aug. 1875, having had issue by her (who predeceased him, 15 Jan. 1838), with two daus., who *d.* young, an only son,
   JOHN RIBTON, now of Braganstown.
3. Marcus Somerville, *b.* 1 Oct. 1797, Scholar of Trinity Hall, Cambridge, Barrister-at-Law of the Middle Temple; *m.* 27 Aug. 1822, Jane, only dau. of Lancelot Rainforth, of Dishfort, co. York, and *d.s.p.* 5 July, 1828, his widow surviving to 31 July, 1830.

Arms—Arg., on a pale sa. a lucy's head, couped, or, in the dexter chief point a fleur-de-lis gu. Crest—On a ducal coronet or, a dexter arm in armour embowed, in the hand a dagger, all ppr., the arm charged with a fleur-de-lis gu. Motto—Gladio et virtute.
Seat—Braganstown, Castle Bellingham.

ENGLISH BRANCH.

This, the senior branch, now extinct in the male line, descends from the eldest son of James Garstin, of Leragh Castle.

IRELAND. Garstin.

JOHN GARSTIN, of Leragh Castle and Ballykerrin, co. Westmeath, *m.* 1st, 19 Nov. 1741, Alethea, niece of Dr. John Farrell, of Carralaragh, co. Longford, and after purchasing a small property at Santry, co. Dublin (which passed into the possession of Lord Seaton), and leasing the estate of Tinnehinch, co. Wicklow, removed to London 1750, where he received a Government appointment, and lived at Whitehall. In 1761 he appears on a mission to one of the German Courts; and in 1766 he describes himself as having travelled "thro' all Europe and great part of Turkey in Asia on the King's business." His 1st wife *d.* 1772. His 2nd wife, Anne, survived him till 1805. He *d.* 1780, having by the former (besides John, *b.* 1747, from whom it is supposed families of the name in India and London descend; and Fortescue William, *b.* 1748, Lieut. H.E.I.C.S., *d. unm.* 1770) had issue,
1. Chichester Fortescue, Capt. 17th Dragoons, and Major Hampshire Militia, *b.* 1743; *m.* 1st, Catherine, dau. and co-heiress of Sir Henry Parker, Bart., and great-aunt of the celebrated Admiral Sir Hyde Parker. By her he had an only child, JOHN, *b.* 10 July, 1772, Capt. 41st Regt.; *d. unm.* at Montreal, 1799.
Major Garstin *m.* 2ndly, Alicia Caroline, dau. of Sir Charles Sheffield, Bart.. of St. Albans, where, dying 21 Jan. 1818, aged 63, she was bur. with her husband, who *d.* 5 March 1815.
2. ROBERT, *b.* 1744, served in all quarters of the globe in the Royal Artillery, and went on a mission to the Emperor of Morocco. He *m.* 1st, 30 Aug. 1764, Anna Elizabetha, sole dau. and heiress of Major Simon Bradstreet (nephew of the 1st bart. of that name); and brother of Gen. John Bradstreet, Governor of Newfoundland. By this lady, *b.* 1745, *d.* 1789, he had (with a dau. Anna Elizabetha, *d. unm.* 1789, aged 18) a son, JOHN BRADSTREET. He had also a son, Robert Longmore, Royal Artillery, Lieut.-Gen., *d. unm.* 1874. Col. Garstin *m.* 2ndly, 1792, Mary Lees, and became of Harold House, co. Bedford, in which co. he was appointed D.L. He became Lieut.-Col., and held a command in the Bedfordshire Militia. In 1809 he served as High Sheriff for Bedfordshire, in which year his wife died, whom he survived till 26 July, 1815. His son,
JOHN BRADSTREET, of Wakering Hall, Essex, *b.* 23 June, 1766, was Major 65th Regt., with which he saw much service. In 1792 he *m.* Mary, dau. of J. Ketchum, of New Brunswick, N.A., and *d.* 1821, leaving issue by her, who survived to 29 May, 1849.
(1) ROBERT, *b.* 28 Aug. 1799, Lieut.-Col. 3rd Madras Cavalry, and Commandant 4th Regt. of Nizam's Cavalry, A.D.C. to the Marquess of Tweeddale (Governor-General of India) and Government Commissioner to the Nabob of the Carnatic. He *d. unm.* at Pisa, 19 April, 1863.
(1) Mary, *m.* 13 May, 1816, William Hay, of Dunse Castle, co. Berwick, D.L., and Convenor of that co., and *d.* 10 June, 1863; leaving issue (*see* HAY *of Dunse*).
(2) Cordelia, of Exeter, *d. unm.* 3 April, 1867, aged 68.
1. Cordelia Ann, bapt. 26 July, 1751; *m.* 1st, 20 Oct. 1774, to Samuel Colborne, of Lymington, Hants, and by him had a son and a dau.,
(1) JOHN, created LORD SEATON, a Field-Marshal in the Army. G.C.B., G.C.H., G.C.M.G., K.M.T., K.S.G., K.T.S., Col. 2nd Life Guards, Governor-Gen. of Canada, Commander of the Forces in Ireland, &c., *b.* 16 Feb. 1778.
(1) Cordelia Ann, bapt. 5 Sept. 1575; *m.* 14 May, 1806, Rev. Duke Yonge, Vicar, of Antony, Cornwall, and *d.* 20 July, 1856, leaving issue (*see* YONGE *of Puslinch*).
Mrs. Colborne *m.* 2ndly, 1787, Rev. Thomas Bargus, vicar of Barkway, Herts, and Rector of Treford, Sussex. He *d.* 27 March, 1809, leaving by her, who had predeceased him, 15 March, 1791, a dau. and co-heiress,
(2) Alethea Henrietta, *b.* 7 June, 1780; *m.* Rev. John Yonge, head of the family seated at Puslinch, co. Devon (*see* YONGE *of Puslinch*).

BRANCH ORIGINALLY SEATED AT BRAGGANSTOWN.

The youngest son of Capt. Symon Garstin, mentioned in the preceding genealogy,
NORMAN GARSTIN, of Bragganstown, *s.* his grand-uncle, the original patentee, Jan. 1677, and, in the following June, *m.* Miss Anne Jones, of Tulleniskea, co. Monaghan (niece and devisee of Welbore Ellis, Bishop of Meath, and cousin of Lords Mendip, Clifden, and Normanton). He served as High Sheriff for Louth 1686, was one of the first four Justices appointed for that co. after the battle of the Boyne (sworn 16 July, 1690), and was one of the Commissioners appointed by the statute of 3 WILLIAM III. In 1698, he purchased from Godart, Earl of Athlone, the lands of Coolderry, co. Monaghan, the estate of Christopher, Lord Slane, attainted. He *d.* intestate 1719, leaving (with daus., of whom Alice, *m.* Rev. Boyle Travers, Vicar of Stabannon; and Abigail, *m.* 1710, Thos. Sweetlove, of Dowdstown) a son and heir,
THE REV. JAMES GARSTIN, of Bragganstown and Coolderry, and of Piercetown, co. Meath, Rector of Moyglare, in the same co. He *m.* (settlement dated 1 March, 1727) Elizabeth, dau. and heir of Capt. Anthony Brabazon, of Calliaghstown (great-nephew of the 1st Earl of Meath), and by his cousin James Brabazon, and by her (who *d.* 20 Oct. 1734) left,
1. Norman, *b.* 1729; *d.v.p.* 26 May, 1755, intestate.
2. ANTHONY, who succeeded. 3. James, *b.* 1732.
1. Mary, *b.* 1728; *m.* Brabazon Eccleston, of co. Louth, and had issue, Norminda and Elizabeth, who both married.
2. Anne, *m.* 1776, Rev. John Gifford, Rector of Boveva, co. Derry, and by him (who *d.* 9 Feb. 1782) had issue.
3. Dorcas, of Londonderry, *d. unm.* 1820, aged 88.
The Rev. Mr. Garstin *m.* again, and had issue (supposed to have *d.* young). He was *s.* by his son and heir,

ANTHONY GARSTIN, of Bragganstown, Coolderry and Piercetown, J.P., *b.* Sept. 1730. He was High Sheriff of the co. 1763, and on 4 June of that year, *m.* Anne, dau. of Christophilus Jenney, of The Park, co. Louth, and had.
1. CHRISTOPHILUS, his heir.
2. William, Louth Militia, afterwards Major 26th Regt. (Cameronians), *m.* 1805, Anne, dau. of Christophilus Clinch, of Peamount, co. Kildare, and was drowned while serving in Holland. His widow *d.s.p.* 1821.
3. Norman (Rev.), M.A., successively Chaplain to the Duke of Richmond, Lord Lieutenant of Ireland, and to the Royal Military School, Phœnix Park, Dublin; Prebendary of Kilpeacon, Limerick, and senior Colonial Chaplain in the Island of Ceylon, where he *d.* 1830, having had issue (by his wife Elizabeth, sister of Major Boyd, who *d.* 1826),
1. Norman, D.D., late Chaplain to the Forces in Ceylon, *m.* 16 Jan. 1847, Mary Anne, only dau. of Walter Wilson, of Bath and Frenchay, co. Gloucester, and had issue,
(1) Norman, *b.* 1849.
(2) Patrick Arthur, *b.* 1858.
(3) William, *b.* 1862.
(1) Louisa Charlotte.
Dr. Garstin assumed in 1864 the name of DE GARSTON, in lieu of his patronymic.
2. Anthony (Rev.), Chaplain Bengal Establishment 1841-68, Rector of Redmile, Lincoln, *b.* 1808; *m.* 1st, 15 Dec. 1836, Rebecca, dau. of Mr. Judge (Secretary to Mr. Spencer Percival), and by her (who *d.* 16 Dec. 1863) had issue surviving infancy,
(1) Norman Anthony, *b.* 1838, Indian C.S., retired; *m.* 1891, Elizabeth, widow of Charles Chapman and dau. of Gen. Tulloch.
(2) Harold Edward, *b.* 1848; killed at polo; *d. unm.* 1876.
(3) George Lindsay, Col. 9th Bengal Lancers, *b.* 1851, *m.* 1883, Mary Constance, eldest dau. of Rev. W. D. Walk, Rector of Rustall, Wilts, and has issue,
Horace Anthony, *b.* 1888.
(4) Frederick Clement, *b.* 1856, Cape C.S.; *m.* 1890, Ella, dau. of George Leslie, and has issue.
(1) Elizabeth Eleanor, *m.* 1856, David B. Lindsay.
(2) Lucy Anna, *m.* 1863, Major Dayrell, of Shudy Champs Park, Cambridge (*see that family*).
(3) Rebecca Caroline, *m.* 26 July, 1893, Maj. Horatio A. Yorke, R.E., Board of Trade Inspector of Railways, nephew of the Earl of Hardwicke.
(4) Alice Mary Boscawen.
(5) Emily Florence, *m.* 1879, Rev. J. W. Gamul Edwards, of Freckenham, Suffolk.
(6) Edith Laura, *m.* 1892, Rev. Wm. Andrews, Rector of Carlton-Scroope.
The Rev. A. Garstin *m.* 2ndly, 1871, Frances, dau. of Rev. R. Baker, and grand-dau. of Sir Richard Baker, and *d.* 31 Oct. 1899, having by her had a dau.,
(7) Fanny.
3. William, Lieut.-Col. 83rd Regt., *m.* 11 Oct. 1846, Mary Hastings, elder dau. and co-heiress of the Rev. Matthew Moore, Vicar of Cabirconlish (brother of Crosbie Moore, of Mooresfort), and *d.* May, 1861, leaving by her (who survived to 28 Feb. 1871) an only child,
Norman, *b.* 28 Aug. 1847; *m.* 1886, Louisa, dau. of Alfred Jones, of Bedford.
4. Christophilus, Capt. in the Army, *m.* E. J. J. Douglas, of a Canadian family, and *d.* leaving one son and two daus.
1. Eleanor Anne, *m.* 1825, John William Huskisson, Ceylon C.S. (nephew of Mr. Huskisson, M.P. for Liverpool), and *d.* 29 Dec. 1880, æt. 77, leaving issue.
2. Lucy, *m.* 1825, Major-Gen. Botet Tyrdell, 83rd Regt., who *d.s.p.* Jan. 1864. She survived to June, 1885.
3. Louisa, *d. unm.* 1883.
4. Anna, *m.* 1833, to William Lucas, M.D., Deputy Inspector-Gen. of Hospitals, and *d.* 2 Oct. 1859. Dr. Lucas *d.* suddenly 1868, leaving four children.
5. Elizabeth, *m.* 1831, Henry Whiting, Ceylon C.S., and has issue.
6. Caroline, *m.* 5 April, 1847, at Calcutta Cathedral, Edward Stanhope Pearson (son of the Very Rev. Hugh Nicholas Pearson, D.D., Dean of Salisbury, and Domestic Chaplain to GEORGE IV), and left two sons.
7. Sophia, *b.* 1821; *m.* David Baird Lindsay, of Calcutta, and *d.* in Ceylon, 1845, leaving a dau. Sophia.
4. James, Lieut. Louth Militia, and afterwards of 15th Regt., *b.* 11 Oct. 1772; *m.* 1821, Agnes, eldest dau. of John Stephenson, Penrith, Cumberland, and *d.s.p.* 1883.
1. Elizabeth, *m.* Capt. Waddell Cuninghame Douglas, of Dromore, co. Down, Royal Irish Artillery, and had issue.
2. Anne, *d. unm.* in London, 12 March, 1849, aged 80.
3. Maria, *m.* George Wade, co. Meath, who *d.s.p.* 1849. She *d.* 5 Dec. 1863.
Mr. Garstin *d.* 16 May, 1782 (his widow surviving till 1808, when she *d.*, aged 72), and was *s.* by his eldest son,
CHRISTOPHILUS GARSTIN, of Bragganstown, Coolderry, and Piercetown, *b.* 1766; sometime an officer in the 55th Regt., J.P., Deputy Governor and D.L. co. Louth, for which co. he was appointed High Sheriff. He *m.* 30 Oct. 1791, Elizabeth, eldest dau. of Andrew Thompson, of Newry, by whom he had issue,
1. ANTHONY, his heir.
2. Christophilus, sometime a Lieut. in the Louth Militia; ordained 1822, and presented by the Crown to the living of Cahir, and thence promoted to the Rectory of Drumballyroney, co. Down, *b.* 5 June, 1795; *m.* 1st, 26 July, 1818, Sarah, 2nd dau. of the

R 2

Rev. George Vesey, D.D., of Derrabard House, co. Tyrone (*see that family*), by whom (who d. 26 Aug. 1842) he had, besides children who d. young,
1. CHRISTOPHILUS, b. 2 Jan. 1825, heir to his uncle; *m*. but d.s.p. 1878.
2. Anthony, b. 6 Oct. 1832; *m*. and settled in New Zealand.
1. Eleanor, b. 12 Aug. 1826; *m*. 14 March, 1849, John Garstin, Capt. 66th Bengal N.I. (*see preceding pedigree*).

He *m*. 2ndly, 19 Feb. 1845, Harriet Frances, eldest dau. of Capt. Joseph Neynoe, of Castle Neynoe, co. Sligo, and by her (d. 9 Nov. 1860) left at his death, 17 Aug. 1864,
3. Charles Henry Neynoe, b. 20 Jan. 1849; *m*. Jane Bronte, and d. 14 April, 1899, leaving a son, Bertram.
4. John Joseph, b. 13 March. 1850; d. *unm*. 1870.
5. William Fitzroy, b. 19 March, 1855, Rector of Couwall (Letterkenny) since 1905; *m*. 4 Jan. 1881, Catherine Emily, dau. of the Ven. E. J. Hamilton, Archdeacon of Derry, and has had issue,
 (1) Edward James Hamilton, Surgeon R.N., b. 21 Nov. 1881, twin.
 (2) William Fitzroy Hamilton (Rev.), B.A. (Trin. Coll. Dublin), Chaplain Calcutta Cathedral, b. 21 Nov. 1881, twin; *m*. 31 Jan. 1910, Frances Dalziel, eldest dau. of late Col. Maitland, Indian Medical Service.
 (3) George Christophilus, b. 21 Sept. 1883.
 (4) John, b. 1885, Lieut. Connaught Rangers and A.S.C.
 (5) Richard, b. 1886, Lieut. Royal India Marines.
 (6) Charles Herbert, b. 1891; d. 8 Dec. 1900.
 (7) Norman Elliott, b. 22 Sept. 1893.
 (1) Catherine Georgiana May, b. 30 May, 1889.
 (2) Charlotte Emily Antoinetta, b. 7 July, 1892; d. 25 Dec. 1896.
6. Loftus Marcus, b. 7 Nov. 1858; d. *unm*. in India, 1879.
2. Harriet Jane, *m*. 20 Sept. 1876, Edmund R. Macnaghten, first cousin of Lord Macnaghten, and has two daus.
3. Caroline Matilda, *m*. Dec. 1878, Stewart Macnaghten, elder brother of her brother-in-law, and has issue two sons (*see* BURKE'S *Peerage*),
4. Emily Antoinette, d. *unm*. 1910.
5. Clara, *m*. Clarges Ruxton (*see* RUXTON *of Ardee*).

3. Norman, b. 7 Feb. 1804; *m*. 1854, Elizabeth Mary Dalton, and d. 23 Sept. 1879, having by her (who d. 17 Oct. 1900) had issue,
 1. Norman, b. 1861.
 2. Herbert (California, U.S.A.), b. 1863, *m*. 1892, Maud, dau. of Hon. V. Knudson, Hawaian Islands, and has issue,
  (1) Dalton, b. 1893. (2) Kenneth, b. 1895.
 3. Walter, b. 1866. 4. Christophilus, b. 1868.
 1. Elizabeth, *m*. 1890, Benjamin Halmeman.
 2. Madeleine.
1. Martha, b. 1792 (Mrs. Douglas).
2. Elizabeth, *m*. 4 June, 1819, Digby Marsh, of co. Longford, son of Francis Marsh, of The Abbey, Queen's Co. (*see* MARSH *of Springmount*). She d. 1891, aged 95, leaving two daus.
3. Charlotte, d. *unm*. 1869.
4. Frances Delia, d. *unm*. 1884.
5. Mary, d. *unm*. 1869. 6. Anne, d. *unm*. 1873.

Mr. Garstin d. 26 Jan. 1821 (his widow surviving until 19 Nov. 1857, when she d. at the age of 95), and was s. by his eldest son,
THE REV. ANTHONY GARSTIN, of Bragganstown and Coolderry, J.P., M.A., Rector of Mansfieldstown, b. 12 Nov. 1793; d. *unm*. 10 July, 1873, when the Bragganstown estate passed, as entailed, to his nephew, CAPT. CHRISTOPHILUS GARSTIN, nearest kinsman of the name to the present JOHN RIETON GARSTIN, by whom it was acquired in 1877.

GARTSIDE-SPAIGHT. *See* SPAIGHT.

TRENCH-GASCOIGNE OF KILFINANE.
See TRENCH-GASCOIGNE OF PARLINGTON, YORKS.

GASON OF RICHMOND.

RICHARD WILLS GASON, of Richmond, co. Tipperary, b. 21 July, 1846; *m*. 1871, Kate Hamley, 3rd dau. of Henry Turle, and has issue,

1. RICHARD, b. 12 July, 1872; *m*. 17 Jan. 1907, Frederica Louisa, dau. of Col. Arthur John Reynell Pack, C.B. (*see* REYNELL PACK *of Netherton*).
1. Kate Marion, b. 9 Aug. 1873.
2. Maria Lilian, b. 21 Jan. 1875.

Lineage.—JOHN GASON got a grant of Killeen, co. Tipperary, under the Act of Settlement. He d. prior to 1697, having by his wife, Rachel, had issue, two sons,
1. JOSEPH, his heir. 2. Charles.
The elder son,
JOSEPH GASON, of Ballycumine, co. Tipperary, *m*. Dorothy, dau. of Richard Waller, of Cully, co. Tipperary (*see* WALLER *of Rockvale*), and d. (will dated 1712), leaving issue, five sons and five daus.,
1. RICHARD, his heir. 2. Edward, d. 1749.
3. John, b. 1700. 4. Waller, d. 1741.
5. Joseph, of Nenagh, *m*. 1751, Elizabeth, widow of — Dawson, and dau. of Oliver Leake (by Sarah, dau. of Sir Loftus Dancer, 3rd Bart., *see* BURKE'S *Peerage*), and d. 1776 having had issue,

1. John, b. 1752; d. young.
2. Richard. 3. Loftus.
4. Amirald Dancer, in the Army, b. 1758; *m*. 1st, 1782, Sarah, dau. of Richard Poe, of Beleen, co. Tipperary; and 2ndly, 1799, Isabella, dau. of — Compton.
5. Joseph Waller, b. 1765; *m*. 1791, Catherine Poe.
1. Elizabeth. 2. Rachel.
3. Blanche, *m*. 1748, John Nicholson, of Capanugerane, co. Tipperary.
4. Dorothy, *m*. 1743, George Watson, of Garrykennedy, co. Tipperary.
5. Mary, *m*. James Cowan, of Ballinruan, co. Galway.

The eldest son,
RICHARD GASON, of Killashalloe (now Richmond), J.P., *m*. 1737, Elizabeth, widow of — Matthews, and dau. of Rev. Peter Wybrants, Rector of Ballymachey. He d. 1772, leaving four sons and four daus.,
1. John, *m*. 1757, Araminta Williams, and d.v.p. 1759, leaving an only son,
 John, of Shanbally, co. Tipperary, b. 1758; *m*. 1781, Amy, dau. of — Minchin; and 2ndly, Elizabeth, dau. of
 He d. 1818, leaving numerous issue, nine of whom d. young.
2. RICHARD, who s. to Richmond.
3. Thomas.
4. Samuel, of Arran Hill, co. Tipperary, *m*. 1763, Mary Alley, and d. 1772, having by her (who *m*. 2ndly, 1774, Maunsell Andrews, Lieut. 83rd Foot) had a dau.,
 Mary, *m*. 1792, Maunsell Andrews, of Firmount, King's Co.
1. Sarah.
2. Anne, *m*. 1760, Gilbert Toler, Cornet Royal Irish Regt.
3. Elizabeth, *m*. 1770, Gibbons Ruxton (*see* RUXTON *of Ardee, co. Louth*).
4. Mary, *m*. 1784, Wills Crofts, of Riverston, co. Tipperary.

The 2nd son,
RICHARD GASON, of Richmond, J.P., b. 1743; *m*. 1770, Alicia, dau. of Wills Crofts, of Churchtown, co. Cork (by his wife Eleanor Freeman, of Ballinguile), and d. 1829, having had issue,
1 RICHARD WILLS, of whom next.
1. Anna Maria, *m*. Thos. Richrad Houghton, of Kilmannock, co. Wexford.
2. Ellen, *m*. Cunningham Greg, of Ballymenoch, co. Down.
RICHARD WILLS GASON, of Richmond, J.P. and D.L., High Sheriff co. Tipperary 1842; *m*. 15 Nov. 1811, Anne, dau. of Charles Henry Leslie, of Wilton, co. Cork, and Lucia Izod his wife, and by her had issue,
1. RICHARD, of Richmond.
2. WILLS CROFTS, of Kilteelagh (*see next Memoir*).
3. Charles Henry, drowned with part of his regiment, the 62nd, in crossing the Ganges, 6 Sept. 1842.
1. Lucia, *m*. Hewitt Poole, of Mayfield.
2. Alicia Ellen Christina, *m*. 7 June, 1856, Pierce Purcell, of Altamira. She d. 7 July, 1909.
3. Catherine Mary Elizabeth.

The eldest son,
RICHARD GASON, of Richmond, J.P., *m*. Oct. 1845, Catherine Doyle, 2nd dau. of Rev. Freeman Willis Crofts, of Clogheen, and d. 1861, leaving issue,
1. RICHARD WILLS. now of Richmond.
2. Freeman Wills Crofts (Rev.), Rector of Maynooth, co. Kildare, b. 21 Dec. 1848; *m*. 1st, 1879, Elizabeth McCartie, eldest dau. of Freeman Crofts, J.P. of Clogheen, co. Cork, and has issue,
 1. Freeman Wills Crofts.
 1. Eileen Elizabeth, d. 19 Sept. 1910.
 2. Muriel Mary.
He *m*. 2ndly, 7 Nov. 1901, Deborah, youngest dau. of the late Charles Caulfeild Tuckey, of Kew, Surrey.

Seat—Richmond, near Nenagh, co. Tipperary.

GASON OF KILTEELAGH.

RICHARD WILLS GASON, of Kilteelagh, co. Tipperary, b. 16 Jan. 1865.

Lineage.—WILLS CROFTS GASON, of Kilteelagh, co. Tipperary, J.P., Late Lieut-Col. South Tipperary Militia, 2nd son of Richard Wills Gason, D.L., of Richmond (*see preceding article*); *m*. Oct. 1862, Agnes Julia, dau. of Capt. John S. Rich, R.H.A., of Port Stewart House, co. Antrim, and Woodlands, Castleconnell, co. Limerick, and widow of the Hon. and Rev. Charles Douglas, Rector of Donagheady (*see* BURKE'S *Peerage*, MORTON, E.), and d. 3 Nov. 1887, leaving issue,
1. RICHARD WILLS, now of Kilteelagh.
2. Charles Henry, b. 3 April, 1866; d. 19 Oct. 1896.
3. George Houghton, late Major 3rd Batt. Royal Dublin Fusiliers, b. 4 June. 1867.
4. Otho Francis (*St. Leonard's Road, Surbiton*), b. 28 Sept. 1869; *m*. 19 April, 1899, Ethel Gordon Steele, younger dau. of Edward Aubrey Hart, of Athol House, Surbiton.
1. Anne Leslie, *m*. 27 Aug. 1895, Capt. Prior Spunner Palmer, Ceylon Mounted Infantry, of Liskillen, Ceylon, youngest son of Thomas Spunner Palmer, M.D. of Merriou Square, Dublin. He d. 6 March, 1909.

Seat—Kilteelagh, Nenagh, co. Tipperary.

GAUSSEN OF SHANEMULLAGH.

PERCEVAL DAVID WILLIAM CAMPBELL GAUSSEN, of Shanemullagh House, co. Londonderry (Sen. Mod. T.C.D.), K.C., b. 2 July, 1862; m. 19 May, 1908, Letitia Elizabeth, dau. of Rev. James Wilson, of Tyholland Rectory, Monaghan, and has issue,

Anita Elizabeth Othwell Ash, b. 2 Jan. 1910.

Lineage.—This family derives from a French Huguenot Protestant, who, on the Revocation of the Edict of Nantes, escaped from his native country, and settled at Newry, in the North of Ireland. His name was DAVID GAUSSEN, and his wish, it is handed down, was to settle in England; but the vessel in which he sailed was obliged by a storm to run into Carlingford Bay for shelter. By Dorothy Fortescue his wife, dau. of the then Vicar of Dundalk, he left at his decease, 6 Oct. 1751, aged 87, three daus. and one son ; one of the former m. George Atkinson, of Dundalk, and another Rev. William Lucas, Vicar of Newry. The only son,
  DAVID GAUSSEN, also of Newry, left by Margaret his wife (who d. 10 Jan. 1810), at his decease, 4 July, 1802, with a dau. Elizabeth, d. 20 Feb. 1863, aged 109. a son,
  DAVID GAUSSEN, who resided for some years at Newry, and afterwards settled and d. at Ballyronan House, on the borders of Lough Neagh, co. Londonderry. He m. 1778. Elizabeth, dau. of James Campbell, of Drumban, co. Derry, and by her (who d. in 1816) left at his decease, 25 Jan. 1832, aged 78, with other issue,
1. DAVID, of whom presently.
2. Charles, of Greystones, co. Wicklow, b. 11 June, 1796 ; m. 21 March, 1827, Eliza, dau. of Robert Hardy, and d. 11 June, 1887, having by her (who d. 24 Nov. 1874) had issue,
  1. David, of Broughton Hall, Lechlade, and Gardiner's Place, Dublin, b. 3 Jan. 1834 ; m. 12 Sept. 1865, Elizabeth Sarah Apcar, and d. 2 Aug. 1899, having had issue,
    (1) Charles Louis, Capt. 18th Hussars, 3rd Bengal Cavalry, and Reserve of Officers, b. 26 Sept. 1869, killed at Tafel Kop, 20 Dec. 1901, d. unm.
    (2) James Robert, D.S.O., Capt. Indian Army (3rd Bengal Cav.) served in China 1900-1, of Duncote, Towcester, Northants ; b. 20 March, 1871 ; m. 5 Feb. 1894, Hilda Bertha, dau. of Major Douglas Cowslade Hennessey, late I.S.C., and has issue,
      1. Francis David Darley, b. 3 Sept. 1898.
      1. Grace Frances Elizabeth, b. 25 Sept. 1894.
      2. Hilda Evelyn, b. 24 Dec. 1896.
    (3) Arratoon William David, Capt. Highland L.I., b. 24 July, 1875.
    (1) Ella Sophia Seth Apcar, b. 4 Sept. 1866 ; m. 28 March, 1896, Capt. Frederick Hugh Gordon Cunliffe, Seaforth Highlanders and Royal Inniskilling Fusiliers, son of Cecil George Cunliffe, I.C.S.
    (2) Catherine Mary, b. 27 Jan. 1868 ; d. 13 April, 1869.
    (3) Nannie Isabella, b. 19 March, 1873 ; m. 16 Nov. 1895, Harold Anthony Smith, son of Charles Royds Smith.
    (4) Nina Alice, b. 19 March, 1873 ; m. 26 Jan. 1901, Marcus Stamer Beresford Gubbins, late Queen's Bays (see GUBBINS of Kilfrush).
  2. William Hardy, of Newtown Villa, Kilcullen, co. Kildare, b. 8 Nov. 1836 ; m. 28 June, 1866, Eliza, dau. of Rev. Richard Waddy Elgee, Rector of Wexford. He d. 13 Nov. 1910, and has issue,
    (1) Charles Richard, b. 23 Feb. 1869 ; d. unm. 19 Oct. 1884.
    (2) William Hardy, M.A., LL.B. Trin. Col. Dublin (14, Canning Road, Croydon) ; b. 25 Oct. 1870 ; m. 20 June, 1901, Helen, dau. of Henry Sadleir Ridings, and has issue,
      1. Hardy Sadleir, b. 25 April, 1903.
      2. Patrick Charles, b. 15 Sept. 1904.
      3. Louis Grant, b. 21 Sept. 1906.
      1. Helen Elizabeth, b. 23 Feb. 1910.
  3. James Robert, b. 9 Feb. 1838, m. Alicia Bayly, and d.s.p., 1870.
  1. Sarah, m. 1850, John Samuel Gaussen.
  2. Sophia, m. 1855, Thomas Plunket Cairnes, of Stameen, Drogheda.
  3. Annie Isabella, m. 23 Jan. 1877, Rev. William Edward Burroughes, eldest son of E. H. Burroughes, Q.C.

The elder son,
  DAVID GAUSSEN, of Lakeview House, co. Derry, J.P., m. 22 March, 1847, Anne, dau. of John Ash, of Magherafelt, and by her (who d. 31 March, 1848) had issue,
  1. DAVID CAMPBELL, late of Shanemullagh House.
  2. Charles John, d. 9 Oct. 1848.
  3. Thomas Lovette, Post Capt. R.N., highly distinguished in the war with Russia, as Lieut. of H.M.S. *Agamemnon*; d. 12 Oct. 1865.
  4. Edmund James (Rev.), m. Bessie, relict of Francis Thomas Scott, and dau. of John Kingsbury Elgee, Judge of the Supreme Court, U.S.A., and had issue,
    Edmund Stewart Lovette Ledoux, d. 5 Nov. 1869, aged 3.
  5. William Ash, of Ballyronan, m. 1st, 29 April, 1859, Margaret, dau. of Charles Hamilton, M.D., late 54th Regt., and had an only son,
    Arthur David Ash, of Ballyronan, co. Londonderry, J.P., High Sheriff 1901 ; m. 8 Nov. 1893, Letitia Frances, dau. of John George Donaldson, and grand-dau. of Hugh Rosborough Swanzy, of Commerney, co. Monaghan (see BURKE's *Family Records*), and has issue (with a dau., Madeline Frances),
      (1) William Ash, b. 24 Aug. 1894.
      (2) John George Ash, b. 14 March, d. 1 May, 1896.
      (1) Madeline Frances Ash, b. 18 July, 1899.

Mr. W. A. Gaussen m. 2ndly, 1 April, 1878, Caroline Jane, only dau. of William M. Gaussen, of Lake Lodge, co. Derry, and d. 19 May, 1890. She m. 2ndly, 25 Oct. 1893, Capt. Alexander Moore Armstrong, 63rd Regt., of Colmore House, co. Derry.
1. Helena, m. William Magill, M.D.
2. Jane, m. Charles Gaussen.
3. Isabella, m. 18 Oct. 1855, William Magill Gaussen.
4. Annie, m. 3 Sept. 1860, Robert L. Hamilton, son of Capt. Hamilton, 46th Regt.
5. Emily Mary, b. 24 Sept. 1888.

Mr. Gaussen d. 6 Nov. 1853, and was s. by his eldest son,
  DAVID CAMPBELL GAUSSEN, of Shanemullagh House, co. Londonderry, J.P., B.A., Barrister-at-Law, b. 5 Jan. 1815 ; m. 10 Oct. 1861, Annie Catherine, widow of Capt. Henry Robe Saunders, R.A., and dau. of Wm. Ottiwell, of Dublin, and d. 2 April, 1900, leaving issue,
1. PERCEVAL DAVID WILLIAM CAMPBELL, now of Shanemullagh House.
2. Thomas Ash, b. 30 March, d. 23 April, 1864.
3. Stenart MacNaghten Pennefather Ash, Barrister-at-Law and Resident Magistrate ; b. 4 July, 1866 ; m. 21 Feb. 1890, Gertrude Alice, 2nd dau. of E. Walter Last, of Finthorpe, Almondbury, Yorks. He d. 13 March, 1903, leaving,
  Christian Edward Spencer Perceval, b. 12 April, 1902.
1. Anita Kathleen Ottiwell, d. 22 Oct. 1905.

Seat—Shanemullagh House, Castle Dawson. *Residence*—17, Herbert Street, Dublin.

GENTLEMAN OF BALLYHORGAN.

ROBERT GEORGE GOODMAN GENTLEMAN, of Ballyhorgan and Mountcoal, co. Kerry, b. 22 July, 1846 ; m. Dec. 1873, Elizabeth, 2nd dau. of Arthur Vincent, of Shanagolden House, co. Limerick, and has issue,

1. GOODMAN GEORGE, b. 27 Oct. 1879.
2. Arthur Vincent, b. 8 Nov. 1887.
3. Robert John Kittson, b. 18 Aug. 1890.
1. Sarah Margaret Roberta.
2. Ethel Maude.

Lineage.—The first of this family of whom there is positive information was
  GEORGE GENTLEMAN, who resided at Lixnaw. He m. a Miss Mary Fitzmaurice, and had three sons and one dau., of whom the eldest son was,
  FRANCIS GENTLEMAN, of Ballyhorgan, who m. 1st, Anne, dau. of Robert Beazley, of Ballyhorgan North ; and 2ndly, Mary, dau. of Thomas Pierce, of Beenegahane. He had issue by his first wife only,
1. ROBERT, of whom presently.
1. Mary, m. John Blakeny Kittson, of Derry, co. Kerry.
2. Anne, m. Thomas Ivers, of Banmore.
3. Frances, m. Capt. William Davidson, of Dublin.
4. Elizabeth, m. Mr. Sheehy, of Nantenane, co. Limerick.

The only son,
  ROBERT GENTLEMAN, of Ballyhorgan, b. 1787 ; m. 1st, 25 May, 1815, Margaret, 2nd dau. and co-heiress of Major George Goodman, of Smith Park, co. Clare, and by her (who d. 6 July, 1825) he left three sons and one dau.,
1. GOODMAN, his heir. 2. Francis, b. 1820.
3. Robert, b. 1823 ; d. 22 Oct. 1845, aged 21.
1. Anne, m. 1st, 27 Oct. 1836, Lorenzo Frederick Shaw, of Dublin, who d. 26 Nov. 1838, leaving one son,
  1. Lorenzo Frederick Gentleman.
She m. 2ndly, Frederick John Eager, of Ballymullen, Tralee, and has by him two sons and one dau.,
  2. John Frederick.   3. Frederick George Leslie.
  1. Sarah Anne.

Mr. Gentleman m. 2ndly, 20 June, 1826, Letitia, eldest dau. of George Chatres, M.D., of Dublin, but by her (who d. 1857) he had no issue. He d. 21 April, 1846, and was s. by his son,
  GOODMAN GENTLEMAN, of Ballyhorgan and Mountcoal, co. Kerry, J.P., b. 12 May, 1818 ; m. 17 Feb. 1841, his cousin, Anne (d. 4 Feb. 1910), 2nd dau. of John Blakeny Kittson, of Derry, co. Kerry, and had surviving issue,
1. ROBERT GEORGE, now of Ballyhorgan.
2. John Kittson, M.D., b. 5 May, 1848.
1. Maria, m. Henry Amyrald Owen, of Foyle House, co. Kilkenny.
2. Frances, m. Anthony Allen, of Great Fredlane, co. Meath.
3. Annie Clifford.

Arms—Erm., two eagles displayed each with two heads in chief sa. and an esquire's helmet in base ppr. a chief indented gu.
Crest—A demi-eagle displayed with two heads sa. on each wing a trefoil or. *Motto*—Truth, honour, and courtesy.

Seat—Ballyhorgan, near Listowel.

GERNON OF ATHCARNE CASTLE.

The late HENRY CHESTER GERNON, of Athcarne Castle, co. Meath, J.P., Lieut.-Col. 5th Batt. Royal Dublin Fusiliers, b. 27 March, 1847; m. 11 Oct. 1871, Alice Louisa (*now of Athcarne Castle*), 2nd dau. of the late Lieut.-Col. Augustus F. Braham, and d. 1 April, 1908, having by her had issue,

1. JAMES ROBERT AUGUSTUS, b. 15 May, 1875.
2. Reginald Henry John, b. 29 Oct. 1882; m. 27 April, 1911, Jean, only dau. of late William H. Winchester, of Westfield, Mass. U.S.A.
3. Ward John, b. 31 Aug. 1884.
4. Cyril Louis Michael, b. 29 Sept. 1886; d. 7 Feb. 1912.
1. Evelyn Georgina Elizabeth, a Nun.
2. Margery Frances Mary, m. 17 July, 1907, Matthew McCann, of Ballinacad, Drogheda.
3. Alice Maude Emily, m. 8 Dec. 1904, J. Clibborn Hill.
4. Helen Elizabeth Mary. 5. Constance Susan Mary.

Lineage.—Few families can establish so long a line of distinguished ancestry as that of Gernon, their pedigree being deducible, link by link, from ROBERT DE GERNON, who accompanied WILLIAM THE CONQUEROR from Normandy, down to the present possessor of Athcarne.

RALPH DE GERNON (*temp.* HENRY II), son of Matthew de Gernon, and grandson of Robert Gernon, the Norman; m. and had two sons,
1. RALPH, of Pratwell, co. Derby.
2. ROGER, of whose line we treat. This Roger de Gernon went with Strongbow to Ireland. From him derived descent the distinguished family of GERNON of *Killincoole*, co. Louth, a 2nd son of which,

RICHARD GERNON of Gernonstown, m. Anne, dau. of Richard Plunket, of Loughcrew, and was father of

RICHARD GERNON, and of WILLIAM GERNON, of Drogheda, who m. Anne, dau. of John Warren, of Warrenstown, and by her was father of

CHRISTOPHER GERNON, of Drogheda, who m. Alicia Keating, and had a son,

WILLIAM GERNON, of Drogheda, who m. Mary, dau. of Peter Durham, of co. Meath, and was father of

CHRISTOPHER GERNON, of Drogheda, who m. Frances, dau. of Charles Wade, of Baiscaddon, and had,
1. RICHARD, of Dublin, living 1738, the first of the family who settled at Bordeaux in France; invested there, by command of King LOUIS XV. with the honorary title of King's Secretary. He d. at Bordeaux about the year 1770. He m. Mary, dau. of Martin Quody, by Lucy Petit his wife, dau. of Christopher Petit, of Cullen, co. Meath, by Mary his wife, dau. of Thomas Pilsworth, son of Christopher Petyt, by Mary his wife, dau. of John Hope of Mullingar. He had issue,
  1. CHRISTOPHER GERNON, of Bordeaux, ancestor of the GERNONS *of Paris*.
  2. John, Chevalier of the Order of St. Louis, and Senior Capt. of the Regiment of Lally, d. unm. 1813.
  1. Mary, wife of John O'Byrne, of Bordeaux.
2. William, d. unm. 3. THOMAS, of whom we treat.

The 3rd son,
THOMAS GERNON, of Darver, co. Louth, m. Miss Rose Kelly, and was father of

PATRICK GERNON, Deputy Governor of Drogheda by Warrant 17 Oct. 1803, b. at Darver, co. Louth, 1752; m. Mary, dau. of James Doran, of Drogheda, and had sixteen children, all of whom d. in youth, or unm., except Marianne, who m. John Bryne, of Saggard, and is deceased; Elizabeth, who m. Thomas Coleman, of Drogheda, and is also deceased; Judith, a nun, d. at Clan Convent, co. Kildare, Dec. 1853; and a son,

JAMES GERNON, of Athcarne Castle, J.P., High Sheriff of Drogheda, 1846, b. 14 Feb. 1780; m. 26 Oct. 1807, Marianne, 2nd dau. of James O'Reilly, Higginstown House, co. Longford, J.P., by Susan Dease his wife, and d. 7 July, 1863, having by her (who d. 28 Sept. 1865) had issue,
1. JAMES, of Athcarne Castle.
2. Patrick, b. March, 1813; d. 7 Feb. 1873.
3. Thomas, b. May, 1814; d. 20 Sept. 1863.
4. William, Barrister-at-Law, A.M. Trin. Coll. Dublin, High Sheriff, Drogheda, 1861, Joint Secretary to the Board of Charitable Donations and Bequests for Ireland, b. Sept. 1820; m. 1st, 20 Oct. 1846, Marianne, eldest dau. of Patrick Curtis, J.P., of Fitzwilliam Square, Dublin. She d. May, 1873. He d. 2 Nov. 1903, having had issue,
  1. William, m. 1869, and d. 11 Nov. 1890.
  2. James, d. 4 May, 1889. 3. Arthur, d. 11 Aug. 1890.
  4. Vincent of Hanmondstown, co. Louth, and 19, Clarinda Park, Kingstown, co. Dublin, m. 1st, 3 Dec. 1889, Emma, youngest dau. of Rev. James Butler, of Priestown, co. Meath.

She d. 11 Nov. 1899. He m. 2ndly, Eliza Mary, eldest dau. of Andrew P. Monaghan, J.P., of Drumlargan, co. Meath, and widow of Laurence Byrne O'Reilly, J.P., of Ballinlough, Kells, co. Meath.
  1. Louisa Hodierna. 2. Mary Margaret, d. 7 April, 1872.
Mr. William Gernon m. 2ndly, 15 Dec. 1874, Anne Mary Lavallin, youngest dau. of Timothy O'Donovan, J.P., of O'Donovan's Cove, Durrus, co. Cork, and relict of David FitzJames Barry, of Royal City of Cork Artillery. She d. his widow 9 Nov. 1911.
  1. Judith. 2. Helen.
  3. Susan, m. Sept. 1852, Stephen Stafford, of Ballymore, co. Wexford. 4. Louisa, a nun.

His eldest son,
JAMES GERNON, of Athcarne Castle, and Hammondstown, co. Louth, J.P., b. 2 Jan. 1811; m. 1st, 1 Oct. 1839, Marianne, dau. of George Gradwell, of Preston, co. Lancashire (*see* GRADWELL *of Dowth Hall*), and by her (who d. 1848) had issue,
1. James George, d. 12 Feb. 1859.
2. HENRY CHESTER, now of Athcarne.
1. Georgina Mary, m. 28 Nov. 1865, Francis Edward Joseph MacDonnell, J.P., eldest surviving son of Sir Francis MacDonnell, of Dunfierth, co. Kildare, High Sheriff 1863, and d. July, 1874. 2. Anna Maria, d. 5 May, 1858.

He m. 2ndly, Aug. 1849, Margaret, dau. of Edmund O'Reilly, of Sylvan Lodge, Rathgar, co. Dublin, and d. 2 Aug. 1870.

Arms—Arg., an eagle displayed with two heads sa. gorged with a chaplet and armed or. *Crest*—A horse passant arg. hoofed or. *Motto*—Parva contemnimus.

Seat—Athcarne Castle, Duleek, co. Meath.

GERRARD OF GIBBSTOWN.

THOMAS GERRARD, of Gibbstown and Boyne Hill, co. Meath, J.P. and D.L., High Sheriff 1863, and High Sheriff co. Cavan 1893, b. 10 Aug. 1834; s. his uncle Nov. 1838.

Lineage.—THOMAS GERRARD, of Gibbstown, co. Meath, b. 1643, will dated 10 Feb. 1716, and proved 15 March, 1719, had, by Elizabeth his wife, three sons and a dau.,
1. JOHN, his heir.
2. Thomas, of Liscarton, co. Meath, whose will, dated 3 Oct. 1763, was proved 4 Dec. same year. He m. by licence, dated 25 April, 1713, Miss Catherine Cooper, of co. Westmeath, and had issue.
3. Samuel, of Clonghill, co. Meath, the friend of Swift and Pope, d.s.p. 14 May, 1750. His will, dated 18 Oct., 1749, was proved 26 May, 1750.
1. Dorothy, m. Thomas Welsh.

Mr. Gerrard d. 14 Feb. 1719, and was s. by his eldest son,
JOHN GERRARD, of Gibbstown, m. by licence, dated 23 July, 1709, Margaret Flood, of Castlenock, co. Dublin, and had an only son,

THOMAS GERRARD, of Gibbstown, b. 1715; m. 23 Feb. 1771, Miss Elinor Carroll, and had issue,
1. JOHN, his heir.
2. Samuel, b. 6 July, 1777; d. unm. Sept. 1818.
3. Thomas, of Boyne Hill, Lieut.-Col. 23rd Light Dragoons, b. 9 Dec. 1779; m. 18 March, 1830, Letitia, dau. of Rev. George Charles Garnett, of Williamston, co. Meath (*see that family*), and d. 7 April, 1836, leaving issue,
  1. THOMAS, now of Gibbstown.
  1. Eleanor, m. 14 Oct. 1861, Joseph Clark Collins, only son of Robert Collins, of Garvarey Lodge, co. Fermanagh, and had issue.
  2. Elizabeth Mary, m. April, 1867, Col. H. T. Johnston, eldest son of Rev. Henry Johnston, Rector of Ratoath, co. Meath. She d. Feb. 1909, having had issue.
  3. Letitia Catherine, m. June, 1870, Arthur Le Champion Möller, late Capt. 40th Regt., son of Capt. Möller, and has issue.
4. William, b. 2 March, 1783; d. unm. April, 1811.
1. Rachel, m. 1797, Lieut. John Knipe, 51st Regt., and d. 1818, leaving issue.
2. Margaret, d. 18 April, 1805.
3. Eleanor, d. 15 March, 1782.

Mr. Gerrard d. 11 Sept. 1784, and was s. by his eldest son,
JOHN GERRARD, of Gibbstown, m. Marcella, dau. and eventual heiress of Frederick Netterville, of Longford, co. Galway, and Glasnevin, co. Dublin, representatives of the Netterville's of Lecarrow, the 2nd branch of the noble House of Netterville, by whom (who d. Nov. 1865) he had no issue. He d.s.p. Nov. 1838, and was s. by his nephew, THOMAS GERRARD, now of Gibbstown.

Seat—Gibbstown, Navan, co. Meath. *Clubs*—Kildare Street and Sackville Street.

GERVAIS OF CECIL.

FRANCIS PETER GERVAIS, of Cecil Manor, co. Tyrone, B.A., J.P. and D.L., High Sheriff 1902, Barrister-at-Law, *b.* 12 Dec. 1858; *m.* 17 April, 1884, Georgina Frances Dalrymple, only dau. of the late James Gilmour, of Warren Hill, co. Londonderry, and has issue,

Dorothy, *b.* 6 May, 1885.

Lineage.—JEAN GERVAIS, of Tournon, Guienne, France, *m.* Anne Fabre, and had two sons, PIERRE, *b.* 1677; and Daniel, *b.* 1679, both of whom, after their parents' death, and while still children, fled with an uncle at the Revocation of the Edict of Nantes, and settled in England. In 1710, DANIEL, the younger, was naturalized, and subsequently became a Capt. in the British Army, and Gentleman Usher to Queen ANNE. He *m.* Pauline Belagnier, dau. of the Minister of the French Protestant Church, Dublin, but *d.s.p.* His brother, elder son of Jean Jervais, PIERRE GERVAIS, *m.* 1717, Marie Françoise Girard, and *d.* 1730, having had three sons. The eldest,

PETER GERVAIS, Collector of Revenue, Armagh, *b.* 1722; *m.* 20 March, 1763, Elizabeth, 4th dau. of the Rev. Samuel Close, of Elm Park, co. Armagh (*see* CLOSE *of Drumbanagher*). They both *d.* Sept. 1809, leaving a son, FRANCIS; and two daus., Mary Anne, *m.* Rev. D. Kelly; and Elizabeth, *m.* John Winder, Capt. R.A. The son,

THE REV. FRANCIS GERVAIS, of Cecil, *m.* 16 March, 1807, Katherine Jane, dau. of Michael Tisdall, of Charlesfort, co. Meath, and *d.* 6 Oct. 1849, leaving a son and three daus.,

1. FRANCIS JOHN, late of Cecil.
1. Elizabeth, *m.* 7 July, 1829, the Hon. and Rev. John Pratt Hewitt.
2. Catherine, *m.* 9 May, 1842, Nicholas Evans, Capt. R.N., of Newton, co. Cork.
3. Juliana Henrietta, *d.* 25 March, 1896.

The only son,

FRANCIS JOHN GERVAIS, of Cecil, M.A., J.P. and D.L., High Sheriff 1846, *b.* 21 Aug. 1819; *m.* 16 Dec. 1852, Annie Catherine, eldest dau. of the Rev. John Richardson Young, of Kilmarron Rectory, co. Monaghan, and had issue,

1. FRANCIS PETER, now of Cecil Manor.
1. Katherine Mary. 2. Frances Elizabeth Haton.

Mr. Gervais *d.* 8 July, 1882.

Arms—Az., a chevron or between two lions rampant respectant arg. in chief and a white rose leaved and slipped ppr. in base, in the centre chief point a crescent of the third. *Crest*—A lion's head erased arg., charged with a fleur-de-lis az. *Motto*—Sic sustenta crescit.

Seat—Cecil Manor, Augher, co. Tyrone.

GIBBINGS OF GIBBINGS GROVE.

THE REV. RICHARD GIBBINGS, of Gibbings Grove, co. Cork, D.D., M.A. Trin. Coll. Dublin, Rector of Llanmerewig, Abermule, co. Montgomery, *b.* 16 April, 1835; *m.* 14 Jan. 1864, Elizabeth Rebecca, dau. of William Ware, Clerk of the Peace, co. Cork.

Lineage.—This family settled in Ireland *temp.* ELIZABETH at Shanagolden, co. Limerick.

THE REV. BARTHOLEMEW GIBBINGS, Rector of Kilcornan, in the Diocese of Limerick, from 1613, M.A. Trin. Coll. Dublin 1617, had three sons, officers in the Parliamentary Army, who received grants of land in lieu of pay from Cromwell, afterwards confirmed under the Act of Settlement 1661. His three sons,

1. Symon, who obtained a grant of Tourmore (afterwards Gibbings Grove), near Charleville, co. Cork, and with his son purchased other lands. He was *s.* by his son, John, of Gibbings Grove, who left an only dau. and heir, who *m.* her cousin, Bartholemew Gibbings (*see below*).

2. John, who obtained a grant of Cooline and other lands near Charleville, co. Cork, and was bur. there 23 Dec. 1678, leaving an only dau., Elizabeth, *m.* 1683, Col. Henry Bowerman.

3. BARTHOLEMEW, of Miltown.

The third son,

BARTHOLEMEW GIBBINGS, obtained a grant of Miltown, also near Charleville, co. Cork, which was afterwards sold to Col. Evans, of Ashhill, co. Limerick. His son,

BARTHOLEMEW GIBBINGS, Collector of Youghal, *m.* Jane, dau. of William Rice, of Kellestry, co. Clare, and left an eldest son,

BARTHOLEMEW GIBBINGS, *jure uxoris*, of Gibbings Grove (Tourmore), *m.* his cousin, the only child of John Gibbings, of Gibbings Groove (*see above*). He was *s.* by his son,

THOMAS GIBBINGS, of Gibbings Grove, co. Cork, *m.* 27 Oct. 1716, Anne, dau. of Robert Conron, of Walshtown, co. Cork. He *d.* 20 April, 1742. His will, dated 12 Feb. 1736, was proved 5 June, 1742. His eldest son,

BARTHOLEMEW GIBBINGS, of Gibbings Grove, *b.* 8 Nov. 1720; *m.* 1744, Elizabeth, dau. of the Ven. Richard Wight, Archdeacon of Limerick. His will, dated 16 Sept. 1773, was proved 24 Dec. 1781. He had issue,

1. Thomas, *b.* 6 Jan. 1745; *d.* 13 March, 1748.
2. RICHARD, his heir. 3. Thomas, *b.* 21 April, 1750.
4. Bartholemew, R.N., *b.* 9 June, 1751; *m.* Aug. 1791, Elizabeth, dau. and co-heir of John Armstead. He *d.s.p.* She *m.* 2ndly, George Wade.
5. Edward, Lieut.-Col. H.E.I.C.S., *b.* 27 June, 1754; *d. unm.*
6. Robert, *b.* 23 Dec. 1756; *m.* Barbara Woolley. She *d.* Nov. 1839. He *d.* 26 Jan. 1844, leaving issue, an only child, Mary Wooley, *m.* as his third wife, 2 Oct. 1838, Field-Marshal Viscount Combermere, G.C.B. He *d.* 21 Feb. 1865, leaving issue (*see* BURKE's *Peerage*). She *d.s.p.* 31 Aug. 1890.
7. Arthur, Lieut.-Col. H.E.I.C.S., *b.* 22 June, 1758; *m.* 1806, Catharine, dau. of John Cuthbert, and had issue,
  1. John Thomas Cuthbert, M.A. Trin. Coll. Dublin, Barrister-at-Law, *b.* 1807; *m.* 25 Jan. 1844, Jane, dau. of Capt. Amos Freeman Westropp, R.N. (*see* WESTROPP *of Attyflin*). He *d.* 23 Aug. 1858. She *d.* 21 Oct. 1907, having had issue,
    (1) Arthur, Major, King's Dragoon Guards, *d.* in India 27 Oct. 1881.
    (2) Amos Westropp, *d.s.p.*
    (3) John, Commander R.N. retired.
    (1) Catharine Cuthbert.
    (2) Jane, *m.* 4 Feb. 1890, R. Ottiwell Gifford Bennet, M.D., of Buxton. She *d.* his widow 21 Aug. 1906.
  1. Jane, *m.* 18 Jan. 1845, Rev. John Bleakley, Vicar of Ballymodan, co. Cork, and *d.s.p.*
  2. Margaret, *d. unm.*
8. William, *b.* 18, *d.* 10 June, 1759.
1. Jane, *d.* 31 May, 1754.
2. Mary, *m.* William Yielding, of Belle Isle, co. Limerick.
3. Catherine, *m.* William Crofts, of Danesfort, co. Cork, and had issue.
4. Elizabeth, *m.* Gen. Roberts, H.E.I.C.S., and *d.s.p.*

The son and heir,

REV. RICHARD GIBBINGS, of Gibbings Grove, co. Cork, *b.* 15 Feb. 1746; *m.* 1st, the dau. of Arthur Hyde, M.P., of Castle Hyde. She *d.s.p.* He *m.* 2ndly, Catherine, dau. of John Odell, and sister of Col. William Odell, M.P., of the Grove, and by her had issue,

1. BARTHOLEMEW, his heir.
2. Thomas (Rev.), Treasurer of Cloyne, *b.* 1788; *m.* 1st, 1812, Agnes, dau. of Capt. Bruce Roberts, of Charleville, co. Cork, and by her had issue. He *m.* 2ndly, 1853, Alicia, only dau. of Samuel Allin, of Youghal. He *d.* 1861, leaving issue,
  1. Richard (Rev.), D.D., Professor of Ecclesiastical History in Trin. Coll. Dublin, Hon. Canon of Kildare, *m.* 1846, Caroline, dau. of Rev. John Lovell Salvador, Student of Christ Church, Oxford, and had four children, of whom John Thomas, B.A., of Carrickmacross, *b.* 1852; *d.s.p.* 1908, having *m.* 27 Nov. 1907, Helen Rose, dau. of late John Edward Vernon, of Erne Hill, Belturbet, co. Cavan (*see that family*).
  2. Jonathan, *d. unm.*   3. Thomas, *d. unm.*
  4. William, *d. unm.*
  5. Robert (Rev.), M.A., Vicar of Radley, Berks, *b.* 1819; *m.* 5 May, 1859, Caroline, widow of Rev. Septimus Steekdale, and dau. of Hon. P. A. Irby (*see* BURKE's *Peerage*, BOSTON, B.). She *d.* 29 Jan. 1894. He *d.* 3 Jan. 1865, leaving three daus.,
    (1) Agnes Fanny, (2) Caroline Mary, and (3) Emma Louisa.
  6. Arthur, Capt. Bengal Cavalry, killed during the Mutiny at Sultanpore, 1857.
  1. Mary, *m.* Rev. George Burrowes, and is dead.
  2. Agnes, *m.* 1st, Thomas Cuthbert, of Garretstown, co. Cork, and 2ndly, Maj. Horsey, R.M.A.
  3. Sarah Oliver, *m.* Rev. A. W. M. Stewart.
1. Jane, *m.* Lieut.-Col. Edmund Odell (afterwards Westropp), of Ballysteen, co. Limerick, and had issue.

The elder son,

BARTHOLEMEW GIBBINGS, of Gibbings Grove, co. Cork, *b.* 1786; *m.* 1809, Anna Maria, dau. of Richard Smyth, of Ballylin, co. Limerick, and had issue,

1. RICHARD, his heir.
2. William, Barrister-at-Law, *m.* Sarah, dau. of G. Sandes, of Sallowglen, and *d.* 1881, leaving issue, 1. Thomas (Rev.), 2. Edward, and 1. Cherrie.
3. Thomas, *m.* Margaret, sister of the Hon. Baron Hughes, and *d.s.p.* She *m.* 2ndly, David FitzGerald, of Merrion Square, Dublin.
4. Robert Edward, of Woodville, co. Cork, J.P., *b.* 1824; *m.* 1854, Georgina Evans, dau. of George Bruce, J.P., of Milltown

Castle, co. Cork, and had issue, who have assumed the additional name of BRUCE and have settled in Argentina.
1. Catherine, m. Pierce Goold.
2. Mary, m. T. Prater.
3. Jane, m. J. P. Edgar, M.D.

The eldest son,
RICHARD GIBBINGS, of Gibbings Grove, co. Cork, b. 1 Jan. 1813; m. 1st, May, 1834, Octavia, dau. of Rev. Matthew Purcell, of Burton House, co. Cork, son of Sir J. Purcell, of Highfort (see *that family*), and by her (who d. Oct. 1836) had issue,
  1. RICHARD, now of Gibbings Grove.
  1. Octavia Purcell, m. 1859, J. W. Cronin, M.D., Fleet Surgeon R.N., and d. 1883.

He m. 2ndly, 1837, Elizabeth, dau. of John Gray, of Upton House. co. Carlow, and d. 1 Aug. 1876, having by her had a son,
2. Robert Philip, b. 1838.

Arms—Arg. on a bend between three fleurs-de-lys, two in chief and one in base az. a crescent or. *Crest*—A demi lion ppr. holding in his paws a fleur-de-lys az.

Seat—Gibbings Grove, Charleville, co. Cork. Residence—Llanmerewig, Abermule, co. Montgomery.

GIBBON OF SLEEDAGH.

EDWARD ACTON GIBBON, of Sleedagh, co. Wexford, J.P., M.A. Trin. Coll. Dublin, Brigade Surgeon (retired), A.M.D., b. 19 June, 1835; m. 4 March, 1875, Eliza Rebecca, 2nd dau. of Thomas Taylor, of the Chief Secretary's Office, Ireland, and had issue,
1. Edward Acton, b. 16 March, 1876; d. an infant.
2. CHARLES MONK, Capt. Royal Irish Fusiliers (*Bushlands, Sandhurst, Berks*), b. 1 Nov. 1877; m. 9 July, 1910, Margaret, youngest dau. of Alfred Crampton, of London, and has issue,
  Mary Crampton, b. 27 May, 1911.
3. Thomas Holroyd, Capt. R.A.M.C., b. 29 March, 1879; m. 11 Jan. 1910, Elizabeth M. Cooper, dau. of H. Cooper, of Omagh, Wexford.
4. Edward, Capt. R.A.M.C., b. 20 Dec. 1881.
1. Elizabeth Mary, b. 5 Nov. 1885; m. 4 Jan. 1912, Capt. Hugh St. John Jefferies, Worcs. Regt.

Lineage.—The family of Gibbons has been resident in the parish of Sedgley since the reign of HENRY VIII. William Gibbons was possessed of lands at Sedgley, in the year 1522, as appears by an extant deed, and was, as it is presumed, father of John Gibbons, of Sedgley, Churchwarden of that parish from 1567 to 1577, whose son, Thomas Gibbons, was bapt. at Sedgley 25 Feb. 1570. His son, Thomas Gibbons, of Ettingshall, was bapt. 26 March, 1596, and m. 7 Nov. 1622, Anne, dau. of — Pershouse, and had, with other issue, a son,
WILLIAM GIBBONS, of Ettingshall, Gent., bapt. 24 Jan. 1631, and d. 22 Aug. 1683, leaving by Anne his wife a son,
JOHN GIBBONS, of Sedgley, co. Stafford, b. 1662, m. at Ettingshall, 1690, Judith, dau. of Edward Bennett, and dying 9 Sept. 1727, left issue by her (who was bur. 25 Oct. 1716),
1. RICHARD, b. 1692, living 1730.
2. Edward, b. 1693; m. his cousin, Mary Gibbons, and had a dau., Anne; he is mentioned in the will of his brother John, 1743.
3. Tobias, b. 1695; m. 1720, Mary Evans: he was living 1730, and had a son, William, remainder man in the will of his uncle John, 1743; and two daus., Mary and Anne.
4. JOHN, of whom we treat.

The youngest son,
JOHN GIBBONS, formerly of Sedgley, co. Stafford, and afterwards of The Marsh, Church Stretton, Salop, b. 1701, settled at Kindlestown, co. Wicklow; m. circa 1732, Mary, dau. of Thomas Lloyd, of Merionethshire, North Wales, and had issue, two sons,
1. Thomas. 2. JOHN, of whom presently.

John Gibbons (the father) made his will 6 Dec. 1743, which was proved in the Court of Prerogative, Dublin, 4 Feb. 1749-50, and by it he devised his English estates at Sedgley and King's Swinford to his eldest son, Thomas, and his Irish estates to his 2nd son, John, with remainders over in both. He cropped the final "s" to his name. After his death his widow, Mary, m. the Rev. William Holroyd, uncle to the first Lord Sheffield, and had two daus., Sarah, wife of the Rev. Moore Smyth, and Mary, wife of the Rev. Jerome Alley. The younger son of John Gibbon and Mary Lloyd,
JOHN GIBBON, of Coldross, co. Wicklow, commonly called "Capt. Gibbon," having been Capt. of a corps of Yeomanry, b. 1736-7; m. at Delgany, 8 Aug. 1768, Mary, dau. and co-heir of Edward Whitten, of Dublin, and by her (who d. 20 Jan. 1820, aged 80 years) left at his decease, 12 Jan. 1819, amongst others, a third son,
EDWARD ACTON GIBBON, of Sandymount, co. Dublin; b. 31 Oct. 1771; m. at Neston Church, 29 April, 1802, Elizabeth, dau. of William Monk, of Neston, and by her (who d. 24 Jan. 1838) had a numerous family, who all d.s.p. in his lifetime, except his eldest son whom he left at his decease, 31 Dec. 1864, surviving him,
WILLIAM MONK GIBBON, LL.D., of Sandymount, co. Dublin, and the Parks, Neston, co. Chester, Barrister-at-Law, b. 4 March, 1804; m. 17 Oct. 1832, Anne, dau. of John Boxwell, of Sarshill, co. Wexford. She d. 29 Aug. 1886. He d. 29 Sept. 1882, having had issue,
1. EDWARD ACTON, now of Sleedagh.

2. John George, LL.D., Barrister-at-Law, b. 5 Aug. 1837; d. 10 Feb. 1909; m. 19 Aug. 1863, Mary Elinor, eldest dau. of Thomas Taylor, of The Castle, Dublin, and had issue.
  1. William Monk (Rev.), M.A., Trin. Coll. Dublin, b. 11 July, 1864; m. 15 Feb. 1894, Isabella Agnes, dau. of William Rice Meredith, and has issue,
    (1) William Monk, b. 15 Dec. 1896.
    (1) Georgina Marjorie. (2) Mary Eleanor.
  2. John George, M.D., M.Ch., T.C.D., of Lakeview, Mullingar, co. Westmeath, b. 23 Jan. 1868; m. 12 April, 1894, Eva Mary, dau. of Lorenzo Dundas, of Clobemon Hall, co. Wexford (see that family).
    1. Mary, m. 14 May, 1890, William Cotter Stubbs, M.A., Barrister-at-Law, Crown Prosecutor for cos. Monaghan and Louth, only son of Rev. John William Stubbs, D.D., of Fort William, and has issue.
    2. Anne, m. 8 April, 1891, Rev. Thomas Arthur O'Morchoe, M.A., eldest son of The O'Morchoe, and has issue (see that family).
    3. Nessie.
3. William Monk, A.M., J.P., of Templeshelin, co. Wexford, b. 14 Dec. 1838; m. 14 Nov. 1872, Margaret Usher, eldest dau. of Strangman Davis-Goff, J.P., of Horetown, co. Wexford, and has issue,
  Edward Acton, b. 28 Dec. 1873; m. 2 Feb. 1898, Eleanora, eldest dau. of Lieut.-Col. Nathaniel Alcock, A.M.D.
1. Mary, b. 4 Aug. 1833; d. unm. 3 Dec. 1855.
2. Georgina, b. 31 Dec. 1841; m. 23 June, 1870, John Henry Edge, A.M., K.C., Barrister-at-Law, and J.P. of Farnans, in the Queen's Co. (see EDGE of *Clonbrock*).

Seat—Sleedagh, co. Wexford.

GIBSON OF ROCKFOREST.

WILLIAM GIBSON, of Rockforest, co. Tipperary, J.P. and D.L. for that co., High Sheriff 1879, J.P., Queen's Co., M.A. Trin. Coll. Dublin, late Cap., 40th Regt., b. 4 Feb. 1836; m. 1st, 6 Feb. 1868, Emily Rachel, youngest dau. of Adm. Jervis Tucker, of Trematon Castle, Cornwall, and Sabine his wife, dau. of Adm. Young, of Barton End, co. Gloucester, and by her (who d. 13 Nov. 1909) had issue,
1. WILLIAM, Capt. 1st Batt. Durham L.I., b. 1 Sept. 1874; m. 4 July, 1906, Evelyn Rose Ethel, only dau. of Percy C. Reid, of Feering Bury, Kelvedon, Essex.
1. Sabine Lizzie, m. 7 Jan. 1895, Capt. Theophilus Frederick Walter Ricketts, late Leinster Regt.
2. Emily Charlotte, m. 2 Aug. 1893, Major Frederick Lord Aldersey Packman, East Surrey Regt.
3. Alice Caroline Mary, m. 1st, 1 Oct. 1896, Egerton G. Carrol, of Lissen Hall, co. Tipperary (see that family). He d s.p. 22 Feb. 1897. She m. 2ndly, 17 Sept. 1898, Capt. Henry Godfrey Howorth, R.A., eldest son of Sir Henry Hoyle Howorth, K.C.I.E.
4. Mary Albina, m. M. W. Whitridge, South Africa.
5. Lilian May.

He m. 2ndly, 10 Sept. 1910, Sophia, dau. of Henry White, D.L., of Charleville, Queen's Co. (see that family).

Lineage.—WILLIAM GIBSON, of Rockforest, co. Tipperary, and of 22, Merrion Square, Dublin, J.P. co. Tipperary, son of William Gibson of Lodge Park, co. Meath, b. 15 Feb. 1808; m. 1st, 27 Oct. 1831, Louisa, dau. of Joseph Grant, of Dublin, Barrister-at-Law. She d. 4 Dec. 1853, having had issue,
1. WILLIAM, now of Rockforest.
2. Edward, created BARON ASHBOURNE (see BURKE'S *Peerage*).
3. William Augustus, b. 16 April, 1839.
4. Charles, b. 2 Feb. 1844; d. Aug. 1897.
5. John George (Right Hon.), P.C., Justice of the King's Bench Division High Court of Justice in Ireland, M.A. Trin. Coll. Dublin, M.P. for Walton Division of Liverpool 1886-8 (38, Fitzwilliam Place, Dublin, Carlton and Athenæum Clubs, S.W., and *Dublin University Club*), b. 13 Feb. 1846; m. 8 Aug. 1871, Ann Sophia Mathilda, only dau. of Rev. John Hare, M.A. of Tullycorbet, co. Monaghan, and has issue,
  1. John William Pennefather, b. 31 July, 1872.
  2. William George, b. 13 Feb. 1874.
  1. Anna Elizabeth.
  2. Charlotte Mary Hare.
1. Elizabeth, m. 22 Oct. 1853, Francis Blackburne Martley, late of Ballyfallon, co Meath (6, *Prince Edward Mansions, Bayswater, W.*), and d. 23 Sept. 1908, leaving issue (see that family). He d. 24 Aug. 1894.

He m. 2ndly, 24 April, 1856, Charlotte (d. 3 June, 1900), only dau of John Hare, of Fitzwilliam Street, Dublin, and Deer Park, co. Tipperary and by her had a dau.,
2. Fanny Elizabeth.

Mr. William Gibson d. 20 Feb. 1872, and was s. by his eldest son.

Seat—Rockforest, Roscrea, co. Tipperary. Club—Kildare Street, Dublin.

GIFFORD late OF WESTBROOK.

FRANCIS HENRY GIFFORD, late of Westbrook, co. Wicklow, *m.* June, 1885, Florence Sydney, dau. of Henry Gerald Fletcher, and by her (who *d.* 25 Feb. 1910) had issue,

NICHOLAS FLETCHER, *b.* 4 Aug. 1889.
Florence Sophia, *b.* 7 July, 1887.

Lineage.—JOHN GIFFORD, of Itchell, co. Southampton, High Sheriff 2 HENRY VI, *d.* 10 June, 1444, and was *s.* by his son,
WILLIAM GIFFORD, of Itchell, who was father of
JOHN GIFFORD, of Itchell, who had two sons,
1. William (Sir), of Itchell, whose will is dated 15 June, 1549, *m.* Eleanor, dau. of Sir John Paulett, Knt. of Basing, sister of William, 1st Marquess of Winchester, and had a son,
John, of Itchell, *m.* Joan, dau. of Henry Bruges, Berks, and had two sons,
(1) JOHN, ancestor of GIFFORD *of Itchell.*
(2) RICHARD, ancestor of GIFFORD *of Castle Jordan*, co. Meath.
2. JOHN of whom hereafter.

The 2nd son,
JOHN GIFFORD, of Northall, Middlesex, had two sons, William (who had two daus.) and
JOHN GIFFORD, of Northall. *m.* Susan Wadley, by whom (who was *b.* 1530, and *d.* in childbed of her twelfth child) he was father of
WILLIAM GIFFORD, of Northall, *m.* Audry, dau. of Richard Lyon, of West Twyford, Middlesex, and had
1. WILLIAM, his heir.
2. Richard.
1. Eleanor, *m.* Francis Randolph, of Wood Babington, co. Warwick.
2. Susan, *d. unm.* April, 1631.
3. Isabella, *m.* George Gillingham, of Dorset.

The elder son,
WILLIAM GIFFORD, of London, living 1630, *m.* Dorothy, dau. of Jasper Scowles, of Wantage, Berks, and had, with other issue,
1. John, Col. in the A.my, *b.* 1622, got grants of Aghern and other lands in co. Cork, by patent dated 28 Sept 1666. He was a free Burgess of the Borough of New Ross, co. Wexford, and was ancestor of the GIFFORDS of *Aghern.*
2. JASPER, who settled in co. Wexford.
3. Charles.   4. Lyon.   5. William.

The second son,
JASPER GIFFORD, of Polemaloe, co. Wexford, removed to Dublin, and purchased by deed, dated 20 July, 1661, the lands of Polemaloe (now called Pilltown), Whitechurch, and Ballykelly, co. Wexford. He *m.* Anne Ravenscroft, by whom (who *m.* 2ndly, as 2nd wife, Thomas Compton) he had, with other issue,
1. WILLIAM, of Polemaloe, who sold his estate to his son-in-law, George Glascott. He *m.* Dec. 1699, Margaret, dau. of Clement Milward, Ballyharron, co. Wexford, by whom (who *d.* 4 May, 1718) he left, at his decease (his will, dated 17 June, 1743, was proved 4 Aug. 1753) three sons and four daus.
2. RAVENSCROFT, of whom presently.
3. Henry, of New Ross, *m.* Oct. 1606, Elizabeth, dau. of John Napper, of Kilscanlon, co. Wexford, and had issue, two sons and five daus.
1. Dorothy, bapt. at St. Bride's Church, Dublin, 21 Feb 1660, and bur. in the chancel of the same church 4 March following.
2. Elizabeth, *m.* 1st, William Dodd, of The Great Island; and 2ndly, 12 May, 1718, Richard Cross, of Ballybrazil, both in co. Wexford.

Mr. Gifford *d.* 1670. His 2nd son,
RAVENSCROFT GIFFORD, of Ballysop, J.P. co. Wexford, a Capt. in the Army, *m.* 1st, in March, 1693, Lettice, dau. of Roger Greenwell, of Ballynaclash, same co., by whom he had an only dau.,
1. Joan, who *d. unm.* Nov. 1727.
He *m.* 2ndly, Anne, dau. of Thomas Crompton, of Pilltown, in same co., and had issue,
1. NICHOLAS, his heir.
2. Thomas, of New Ross, had, by Sarah his wife (who *m.* 2ndly, Sept. 1741, Anthony Blunt, Alderman of Kilkenny, and *d.* Jan. 1769), a dau., 1. Mary Anne, *m.* 1761, Rev. Edward Groome, and two sons,
1. Ravenscroft, *b.* 1726; *d. unm.*
2. Thomas, of New Ross, *m.* 30 June, 1766, Jane, dau. of Sheppard French, of same place, Merchant, and had four daus.,
(1) Margaret, *b.* Feb. 1770; *d.* young.
(2) Ann, *b.* 1772; *d. unm.* 8 May, 1832.
(3) Jane, *m.* 25 April, 1793, Rev. John Jacob, Rector of Kilscoran, co. Wexford.
(4) Sarah, *m.* 10 March, 1799, Adam Glascott, of Portobello, and *d.* 28 Nov. 1837.
3. Ravenscroft, an Officer in the Spanish Army, *d.s.p.*

Capt. Gifford, whose will, dated 10 May, 1733, was proved 3 Nov. 1736, was *s.* by his eldest son,
NICHOLAS GIFFORD, of Ballysop, *b.* 1707; *m.* Jan. 1737, Katherine, dau. of William Sweeny, of Ballyteige, co. Wexford, and by her had two sons,
1. WILLIAM, his heir.
2. Ravenscroft, *b.* 1774; *d. unm.*; bur. at St. Werburgh, 10 Dec. 1762; admon. 16 May, 1766.

Mr. Gifford, whose will, dated 23 July, 1763, was proved 10 April, 1770, was *s.* by his eldest son,
WILLIAM GIFFORD, of Ballysop, *b.* 1740; *m.* 5 March, 1764, Margaret, dau. of George Glascott, of Aldertown, co. Wexford, and *d.* 1779, having by her (who *d.* March, 1791, aged 56) had an only son,

NICHOLAS GIFFORD, of Ballysop, *b.* 30 April, 1766; *m.* April 1791, Margaret, dau. of Mitchelbourne Symes, of Coolboy, co. Wicklow, by whom (who *d.* March, 1827) he had issue,
1. WILLIAM (Rev.), M.A., of Ballysop, Rector of Mageesha, co Cork, *b.* 5 Nov. 1795; *m.* 10 May, 1824, Arabella, eldest dau, o Rev. Walter Stephens, of Hybla, co. Kildare, and co-heir of he brother, Walter Stephens, of same place, and *d.* 26 Oct. 1866 having had issue,
1. WALTER STEPHENS, of Ballysop, J.P., *b.* 24 May, 1825; *d unm.* 8 Jan. 1872.
2. NICHOLAS, of Ballysop, *b.* 28 Feb. 1833; *d. unm.* 31 March 1896.
3. William James Brownlow, *d. unm.* 30 Aug. 1872.
1. Anna, *m.* 26 April, 1865, Edward Bridges, Capt. 48th Regt. 2nd son of Charles T. Bridges, of The Lodge, Ludlow, Salop and *d.* 26 March, 1870.
2. Arabella.
3. Margaret, *m.* 30 Oct. 1871, Capt. Edward Bridges, 2nd sor of Charles T. Bridges, of The Lodge, Ludlow, Salop, and ha issue.
4. Lucy Stephens, *m.* 26 Oct. 1864, Rev. Charles Bridges Rector of Bridenbury, co. Hereford, eldest son of Charles T Bridges, of the Lodge, Ludlow, Salop, and has issue.
5. Georgina, *d. unm.* 29 Aug. 1898.
6. Elizabeth, *d. unm.* May, 1900.
7. Wilhelmina.
2. NICHOLAS, of whom presently.
3. Charles Symes, *m.* Anne, dau. of Glascott Symes, and *d.* July 1861, having had issue,
1. Nicholas (went to Toronto, 1884), *b.* 15 July, 1829; *m.* 2 July, 1853, Tamzion Katherine Croker, dau. of Alexande Grant, of Clonakilty, co. Cork, and by her (who *d.* Sept. 1882 had,
(1) Charles Alexander, *d.* young.
(2) Charles Alexander, *b.* 1864.
(1) Florence, *d.* young.
(2) Edith Anne Symes, *d.* young.
(3) Tamzion Mary.
(4) Ida Grace.
(5) Alice Dawson.
2. Charles Symes, *b.* 1 June, 1836; *m.* 1st, 15 Dec. 1864 Susan Maria, dau. of Peter Blake, Royal Irish Constabulary by whom (who *d.* 28 April, 1871) he has had issue,
(1) Charles, *b.* 30 Aug. 1865.
(2) Henry Peter, *b.* 1866.
(3) William, *b.* 1 July, 1868, *d.* young.
(1) Annie Elizabeth, *d.* young.
He *m.* 2ndly, 10 Sept. 1874, Margaret, dau. of Nichola Gifford, of Rathcovle, co. Wicklow, and has further issue,
(4) John William, *b.* 12 Jan. 1877.
(5) George.
(6) Morton.
(2) Nicholina Sophia.
(3) Mary Elizabeth Edmonds.
(4) Alice Frances.
3. Glascott, *d. unm.* 1857.
4. John, *b.* 29 March, 1840; *m.* 26 April, 1877, Anna, dau. o Campbell Stewart, of Belfast.
5. George. *m.* Prudentia, dau. of Robert Murdoch, of Leesor Street, Dublin, and *d s.p.* Nov. 1875.
6. William Edward, *m.* 9 Feb. 1875, Martha, dau. of Willian Roycroft, of Danesfort, Carrick-on-Shannon, and *d.* 31 July 1875.
7. James Richard, *b.* 18 Jan. 1848; *m.* 11 Nov. 1875, Harriett Frances, eldest dau. of Robert Edwards.
1. Alicia, *m.* 1856, William Ardagh, and *d.* 12 Dec. 1886.
2. Margaret Anne.
3. Emma, *m.* 2 Feb. 1869, Robert Bourke Monsarratt, and *d.* t Feb. 1885, aged 41.
4. John Symes, Major E.I.Co., *b.* Jan. 1803; *m.* 12 April, 1845 Beata, dau. of John Glascott, of Killowen, co. Wexford, and *d.s.p.* 27 Aug. 1867.
5. George Glascott, *b.* Feb. 1804; *d. unm.* Sept. 1841.
6. Thomas, *b.* Nov. 1807; *d. unm.* in India.
7. James, Major E.I.Co., *b.* Aug. 1810, lost an arm during the Sikh War; *d. unm.* 17 May, 1853.
8. Henry, *b.* March, 1812; *d. unm.*
1. Mary Anne, *m.* 24 May, 1826, Henry Benjamin Archer Barrister-at-Law.
2. Eliza, *d. unm.* 28 Oct. 1884.

Mr. Gifford *d.* 13 Sept. 1830. His 2nd son,
NICHOLAS GIFFORD, of Rathcovle, co. Wicklow. *m.* Sophia, dau of Francis Henry Morton, of Fort Town, co. Wicklow, and *d.* Oct. 1871, having by her (who *d.* 1894) had issue,
1. Nicholas, *d. unm.*   2. FRANCIS, late of Westbrook.
1. Mary Elizabeth, *m.* William Edmonds, and *d.* Sept. 1877.
2. Margaret. *m.* 10 Sept. 1874, Charles Symes Gifford (*see above*)
3. Frances Anne, *m.* Frederick Jones, and *d.* Nov. 1881.
4. Georgina, *m.* Michael Thomas Mills.

Residence—18, Ormond Road, Rathmines, Dublin.

GILDEA OF CLOONCORMACK.

ARTHUR KNOX GILDEA, of Clooncormack, co. Mayo, J.P. and D.L., High Sheriff 1891; *b.* 18 Nov. 1858; *s.* his uncle 1888; *m.* 7 Feb. 1891, Jane, only dau. of the late Thomas Ruttledge, D.L., of Cornfield, co. Mayo, and has issue,

JOHN ARTHUR K.OX, *b.* 23 Nov. 1891.
Jane, *b.* 18 Feb. 1902.

Lineage.—According to the pedigree drawn up in 1718, the head of this family was JAMES GILDEA, of Gallagh and Port Royal, J.P. co. Mayo, High Sheriff *circa* 1723, *m.* Oct. 1728, Mary Stewart, of Summer Hill, and by her had (with three daus., Elenor; Anne, *m.* 4 Aug. 1777, Christopher Baynes; and Mary, and a younger son, Robert) an elder son,

JAMES GILDEA, of Port Royal, who *m.* 19 Jan. 1755, Mary Ruttledge, of Cornfield, and by her (who *d.* 27 Feb. 1788) had issue,
1. James, *b.* 19 Feb. 1756; *d.* 1787.
2. Andrew, Lieut. Royal Irish Regt. of Artillery, and A.D.C. to the Duke of Rutland; *d.v.p.* in London, 16 Feb. 1787.
3. ANTHONY, of whom presently.
4. William Mills, *b.* 3 June, 1761, Ensign 62nd Regt.; *d.* 5 Dec. 1787.
5. George, *b.* 30 Sept. 1762, High Sheriff 1808; *m.* Miss McManus, of Bartley Hill, and *d.* July, 1811.
6. Robert, *b.* 18 Jan. 1765.
7. Thomas, of Castlebar, and Ballinrobe, co. Mayo, *b.* 3 Oct. 1770; *m.* Feb. 1798, Susanna, dau. of Courtney Kenney, of Roxboro', co. Mayo, and had issue,
 1. James, *m.* Maria, dau. of Anthony Gildea, and is dec.
 2. George Robert (Very Rev.), Provost of Tuam, Rector of Moylough, and Rural Dean, *b.* 1 Dec. 1803; *m.* 29 Nov. 1826, Esther, only dau. and heir of Thomas Green, of Greenmount, co. Wexford. She *d.* 18 Jan. 1894. He *d.* 2 June, 1887, having had issue,
  (1) George Frederick, Major-Gen., C.B., late Royal Scots Fusiliers, J.P. co. Dumbarton, *b.* 10 Nov. 1831; *m.* 1st, 23 April, 1863, Frances Elizabeth Power, 2nd dau. of Major Henry Ireland Gascoyne, of Mackney, Ballinasloe, and by her (who *d.* Oct. 1872) had issue,
   1. Elizabeth Frances, *m.* 1897, Lionel Lyde, and has issue.
   2. Alleine Frederica, *m.* 1898, James Murray, and has issue.
  He *m.* 2ndly, 18 Aug. 1874, Eliza (who received the Order of the Royal Red Cross for her services at Pretoria), dau. of James Campbell, J.P. and D.L. of Tullichewan Castle, co. Dumbarton, and *d.* 2 April, 1898, leaving issue,
   1. George Frederick Campbell, 2nd Lieut. Royal Scots Fusiliers, *b.* 12 April, 1876; *d. unm.* on service in S. Africa, 18 April, 1901.
  (2) William (Rev.), Canon of Salisbury, Prebendary of Stratton, Rector of Upwey, Dorset, and Rural Dean, *b.* 4 Dec. 1833; *m.* 22 Oct. 1862, Sarah Caroline, dau. of Nathaniel Phillips Simes, and has issue,
   1. George Stanhope Simes, *b.* 17 June, 1864; *m.* 10 Dec. 1895, Mary Louisa Bourne, and has issue,
    a. Cecil, *b.* 1897.
    b. Stanhope, *b.* 1900.
    c. Eric, *b.* 1903.
    d. Ethel, *b.* 1896.
   2. John William Simes, *b.* 5 March, 1866; *m.* 1905, Maud Trew, and has issue,
    John, *b.* 1905.
    Maud Margaret, *b.* 1910.
   3. Robert Anthony Simes, *b.* 19 March, 1867; *d. unm.* 23 May, 1902.
   4. Harry Percival Simes, *b.* 29 Oct. 1872; *d. unm.* 18 Oct. 1896.
   5. James Frederick Simes, *b.* 7 July, 1884; *m.* 7 Sept. 1911, Evelyn Muriel Mutch, dau. of William Shenton.
    1. Ethel Angelina, *b.* 13 Feb. 1869; *m.* 14 Sept. 1896, David Lindsay Crawford. She *d.s.p.* 25 March, 1909.
    2. Esther Theodora, *b.* 6 Dec. 1870; *m.* 14 March, 1899, Arthur Franklin Guillemard, 2nd son of the Rev. James Guillemard, late Vicar of Kirklington.
    3. Gertrude Marian, *b.* 14 June, 1874; *m.* 1905, Rev. Frank Erle Trotman, and has issue.
    4. Wilhelmina Phillippa Caroline, *b.* 27 Sept. 1875.
  (3) James (Sir), K.C.V.O., C.B., Knight of Justice of St. John of Jerusalem, of Holme Bury, Watford, Herts, and 11, Hogarth Road, S.W., Hon. Col. 4th Batt. Royal Warwickshire Regt., has Jubilee and Coronation medals, *b.* 24 June, 1838; *m.* 24 Aug. 1864, Rachel Caroline, Lady of Justice of St. John of Jerusalem, dau. of Arthur Kett Barclay, D.L., of Bury Hill, Surrey. She *d.* 4 June, 1888, leaving issue,
   1. James Barclay, *b.* and *d.* 1868.
   2. George Arthur, *b.* 4 Dec. 1870, Esquire of St. John of Jerusalem, Major late 4th Batt. Lanc. Fus., served in the Matabele War 1893 (medal), and in S. African war (medal with two clasps); *m.* 11 Jan. 1900, Annie, dau. of J. Morgan-Thomas, of Glygarth, S. Wales, J.P. co. Brecon, and has issue,
    Gaynor Marie, *b.* 13 May, 1904.
   3. Edward, *b.* and *d.* 1879.
    1. Kathleen, a Lady of Grace of St. John of Jerusalem, *b.* 14 July, 1866; *m.* 1895, Capt. George Edward Wickham Legg, M.V.O., Knight of Grace of St. John of Jerusalem, late 80th S. Staffs. Regt., of 14, Pembroke Gardens, Kensington, W., and has issue,
     George Patrick Wickham, *b.* 1 Aug. 1899.
    2. Christian Helena, *b.* 5 June, 1885.
  (4) Thomas Stanhope, Col. Comm. 75th Regimental District, late 1st Batt. Gordon Highlanders, served in Afghan War 1879 (medal), *b.* 13 March, 1843; *m.* 31 Dec. 1890, Edith Louise, dau. of R. Bagge-Scott. He *d.s.p.* 10 June, 1899.
  (1) Mary, *b.* 27 Nov. 1827; *m.* 1853, Edward Maberly. He *d.* 1868. She *d.* 2 April, 1898.
  (2) Esther Maria. (3) Emma.
  (4) Susan Anne, *b.* 14 Sept. 1840; *d.* 24 Sept. 1860.
 3. Thomas Ruttledge, *m.* Anne, dau. of Charles Vigoyne, of Wicklow, and *d.s.p.* 4. William Andrew, *d. unm.*
 5. Stanhope Mason, 25th Regt., Lieut.-Col. (retired), *d. unm.*
  1. Eleanor Mary, *m.* Charles James Martin, and had issue.
  2. Barbara Anne, *d. unm.*
  3. Maria Eliabeth, *m.* Richard Everard Blake, Lieut. 10th Hussars, and had issue.
8. Robert, *b.* 19 April, 1776; *d.* 1822.
9. John, *b.* 24 June, 1779, Lieut. 17th Light Dragoons; *d.* in Jamaica.
 1. Mary, *d. unm.*
 2. Barbara, *m.* Capt. Walter Bourke, J.P., of Heathfield, and had issue. 3. Margaret. 4. Elenor.
 5. Anne, *m.* 13 Jan. 1790, John Gardiner, of Farnhill, and had issue.
 6. Margaret, *m.* Thomas Kirkwood, of Killerdaff, Ballycastle.

Mr. James Gildea *d.* at Cloonigashill, 8 Aug. 1790. His 3rd son, ANTHONY GILDEA, of Port Royal, J.P. and High Sheriff 1793, *m.* 14 Nov. 1803, Anne, 5th dau. of Francis Knox, of Rappa Castle, co. Mayo, and *d.* 1823, having had issue,
1. JAMES KNOX, of Clooncormack, High Sheriff 1835, *b.* 24 Sept. 1804; *d. unm.* 1870.
2. ANTHONY KNOX, of Clooncormack, *s.* his brother, J.P. and D.L. co. Mayo, Barrister-at-Law; *b.* 1810; *d. unm.* 5 Feb. 1888.
3. Robert, *d. unm.*
4. John Arthur, Major-Gen. 81st Regt., *m.* 1857, Elizabeth, youngest dau. of the late Robert Rickart-Hepburn, of Rickarton, co. Kincardine. She *d.* 25 Feb. 1909. He *d.* 7 Dec. 1873, leaving issue,
 1. ARTHUR KNOX, now of Clooncormack.
 2. Robert Hepburn, dec.
 3. Charles Bruce, *b.* 28 June, 1866; *m.* 24 May, 1890, Alice May Curtler. 4. William Ernest, *b.* 28 June, 1868.
 5. Reginald Anthony, *b.* 13 Nov. 1871; *d. unm.* 23 May, 1898.
 6. James Francis, *b.* 18 Feb. 1873; *d. unm.* 28 March, 1893.
  1. Robina Elizabeth, *m.* 23 March, 1898, Dr. Charles James Martin, and has issue. 2. Eleanor Minetta, *d. unm.*
5. Francis, 2nd Queen's Royals. *d. unm.*
1. Maria, *m.* James Gildea, and *d.* leaving issue.
2. Anne, *m.* 1848, Xaverius Blake, dec.
3. Harriet, *m.* 1847, John Knox, of Broadlands, and *d.* leaving issue. 4. Elizabeth, *d. unm.* 5. Louisa, *d. unm.*
6. Caroline, *m.* 1846, Lucius Deering, and left issue.
7. Charlotte, *m.* Feb. 1845, Major Charles O'Hara, 4th Bengal Lancers, and left issue.

Arms—Arg., on a mount vert a stag statant under an oak tree ppr., in the dexter chief point a cross crosslet fitchée gu. **Crest**—A wolf's head erased ppr. langued gu., charged on the neck with a cross crosslet as in the arms. **Motto**—Vincit qui patitur.
Seat—Clooncormack House, Hollymount, co. Mayo.

GILFOYLE OF CARROWCULLEN.

ANTHONY THOMAS GILFOYLE, of Carrowcullen House, co. Sligo, J.P. and D.L., High Sheriff 1897, M.A. Trin. Coll. Dublin, *b.* 1858; *m.* 1893, May, dau. of Simon Cullen, of Thornhill House, co. Sligo. High Sheriff 1894. Mr. Gilfoyle is the only surviving son of the late Thomas Gilfoyle, of Carrowcullen, co. Sligo, J.P. (who *d.* 1859), and Anne his wife, dau. of James Madden, of Camphill, co. Sligo.

Seat—Carrowcullen, Skreen, co. Sligo. **Club**—Stephen's Green, Dublin.

GILLMAN OF CLONTEADMORE.

HERBERT FRANCIS WEBB GILLMAN, of Clonteadmore, co. Cork, J.P., I.C.S., educated at Emmanuel Coll., Cambridge, *b.* 7 June, 1867; *m.* 9 Jan. 1904. Frances Mary, only child of Hon. C. J. Weir, Member of Madras Council of Fort St. George, Madras, and has issue, a dau.,
Ursula Mary.

Lineage.—JOHN GUYLEMYN, of London, and formerly of Anglesey, N. Wales (son of Richard Guylemyn, of Anglesey), Keeper of Bristol Castle, 1509, afterwards Usher of the King's Chamber, and subsequently Harbinger to Queen MARY. He obtained a grant of arms 1 Nov. 1553; by Anne Legh his 1st wife he had issue,
1. JOHN, Gentleman Usher 1524.
1. Anne, *m.* Richard Warren.

He *m.* 2ndly, Sussanna, dau. of Gerard Hornbolte, of Ghent, the painter, and widow of John Parker, and by her had issue,
2. HENRY, of whom presently.
2. Anne, *m.* Richard Waver, of Coventry.

He *m.* 3rdly, 7 July, 1554, Ellen, dau. of — Chatfield, and widow of — Poulset. She *m.* 3rdly, 1560, Cornelius de Vasse. John Guylemyn made his will 18 Oct. 1557, which was proved 18 June, 1558. His son,

HENRY GUYLEMYN, of Twickenham, Middlesex, *m.* Isabel, dau. of Thomas West, and was bur. 22 Feb. 1592-3, leaving, with a dau., Susan, *m.* 16 Jan. 1593-4, George Walkers, a son,

JOHN GILLMAN, of Curraheen, co. Cork, who went to Ireland in the Army of the Earl of Essex 1599, and settled there. He *m.* Eleanor, dau. of Conneghor O'Callaghan, of Clonmeen Castle, co. Cork, and *d.* 1644 (will dated 7 Jan., proved 27 Feb. that year), leaving issue,
1. Stephen, of Curraheen, *b.* 8 March, 1678, leaving by Ursula his wife,
 1. John, of Curraheen, bapt. 20 Jan. 1644-5; *m.* 28 June, 1679, Mary, dau. of Col. Hayward St. Leger, of Hayward's Hill, co. Cork, and *d.* 12 Feb. 1724-5. She *d.* 25 April, 1718. Their descendants became extinct in the male line on the death of Sir John St. Leger Gillman, Bart., in 1817.
 2. Robert, of Cloghines, co. Cork, *m.* 18 May, 1695, Susanna, widow of — Griffith, and *d.* without surviving issue, Aug. 1726.
 3. Stephen, of Clashmartle, bapt. 6 April, 1647; *d.s.p.* (will dated 8 March, 1709, proved 25 April, 1710).
 4. Sylvester, of Clashmartel, administration granted 31 July, 1724. He *d.s.p.*
 5. Henry, of Kilnagleary, co. Cork, *m.* 19 April, 1686, Letitia, dau. of Richard Clarke, and widow of Ralph Woodley, and *d.* 18 March, 1723-4, leaving issue,
 Phillip, of Kilnagleary, *d. unm.* 4 Sept. 1724.
 Ursula, *m.* 27 April, 1700, Edward Porter, of Tullig.
 1. Ellen, *d. unm.*, administration granted 21 June, 1692.
 2. Elizabeth, *m.* 19 Aug. 1684, John Jermyn, of Tullaneskv.
 2. HENRY, of whom presently.
 1. Alice, *m.* Philip Darville.
 2. Ellen, *m.* Epenetus Cross, of Crosshaven, co. Cork, and had issue.

The younger son,
HENRY GILLMAN, of Carrigrohane, co. Cork, *m.* 1st, Maude, dau. of Capt. James Elwill, of Bandon, co. Cork, and by her (who *d.* 1643) had issue,
1. Henry, living 1657; *d.s.p.*
2. RICHARD, of whom presently.
3. John, living 1657 and 1724. 4. Thomas, living 1657.
1. Ursula, *m.* William Barnes.
2. Magdalen, bapt. 20 Feb. 1645.

He *m.* 2ndly, Maud, sister of Theophilus Carey, of Carrigrohane, and *d.* Sept. 1657. His 2nd son,

RICHARD GILLMAN, of West Gurteen, and Old Park, co. Cork, *m.* Mary, only child of Walter Baldwin, of Mossgrove, and *d.* before 25 June, 1716, leaving issue,
1. HERBERT, of whom presently.
1. Elizabeth, *m.* 22 Nov. 1701, Martin Newman, of Kilnacloona, and had issue.
2. Mary, *m.* 20 Sept. 1698, Francis Brettridge, of Moyallow, co. Cork.
3. Barbara, *m.* 4 Oct. 1706, Cornelius O'Callaghan, of Derryalla.
4. Ellen, *m.* 14 Oct. 1713, Roger Callaghan, of Lismyleconnig.

The only son,
HERBERT GILLMAN, of Finnis, and Old Park, co. Cork, *m.* 1st, 11 April, 1724, Jane, 3rd dau. of John Webb, of Cloheenmilcon, co. Cork, and by her had issue,
1. Richard, *d.* 13 May, 1731, aged 5.
2. JOHN, of whom presently.

He *m.* 2ndly, 4 May, 1732, Sarah, dau. of Corlis Baldwin, of Lisnagat, and by her had issue,

3. Herbert, of Old Park, living 1770; *m.* 1st, 26 June, 1765 Ellinor, dau. of — Stors, and 2ndly, 22 July, 1767, Catherine only child of John Hawkes, of Monteen Castle, and had issue.

He *m.* 3rdly, 23 Feb. 1744, Penelope, dau. of Phillip French, o Rath, Mayor of Cork, and by her had issue,
1. Penelope French, *m.* 16 March, 1768, Jonas Barnard, o Carbue.
2. Mary, living 1757.

He made his will 31 Dec. 1757, which was proved Feb. 1765. Hi eldest surviving son,

JOHN GILLMAN, of Gurteen, *m.* 23 Oct. 1751, Sarah, dau. o Ralph Clear, Provost of Bandon, and *d.* 1770 (will dated 8 Apri: proved 7 Aug. that year), having by her (who was bur. 29 May 1766) had issue,
1. Richard, of Bandon and Gurteen, *m.* 1787, Elizabeth, dau. o Francis Beamish, of Kilmalooda, and *d.* Jan. 1796, having by he (who *d.* Aug. 1822) had issue,
 1. Mary Ann, *m.* 15 Nov. 1817, Major John Howard, 96tl Regt. who *d.* 1821. She *d.* 1858.
 2. Elizabeth, *m.* 5 Jan. 1815, Lieut.-Col. Isaac Henry Hewitt of Clancoole, who *d.* 1828. She *d.* 1856.
 3. Jane, *m.* 21 Sept. 1820, Simon Davies Crooke, of Oldtown who *d.* 7 June, 1862. She *d.* 8 Dec. 1881.
2. Herbert, of Rushfield, *m.* Mary, dau. of — Coghlan, and *d.s.p* She was bur. 23 Dec. 1820.
3. WEBB, of whom presently.
1. Mary, *m.* 3 March, 1785, John Hawkes, who *d.* 3 June, 1804 She *d.* 3 Sept. 1822, leaving issue.

The 3rd son,
WEBB GILLMAN, of Lakefield, co. Cork, *b.* 1756; *m.* 26 Jan. 1786 Catherine, 3rd dau. of William Crooke, of Derreen, and *d.* 3 Jan 1821, having by her (who *d.* 17 Jan. 1854) had issue,
1. HERBERT, of whom presently.
2. Webb, of Lakefield, *b.* 2 July, 1795; *m.* 11 Sept. 1844, Eliza beth, dau. of Thomas Gardiner, of Scart, co. Cork, and *d.* June, 1857, having by her (who *d.* 26 March, 1890) had issue,
 1. Webb, *b.* 5 Dec. 1845; *d. unm.* 2 April, 1864.
 2. Thomas Herbert, *b.* 20 Sept. 1847; *m.* 12 Oct. 1893, Mari: Catherine Beecher, dau. of Winthrop Baldwin Sealy, of Gort nahorna, and has issue, a dau.,
 Ursula May Sealy.
 1. Catherine Crooke, *d. unm.* 13 Feb. 1852.
 2. Elizabeth Jane, *m.* 30 July, 1885, Richard Hayes Barter, o Annsgrove, co. Cork, and has issue.
3. Richard, of Riverstown, co. Cork, bapt. 17 June, 1799; *d unm.* 25 Jan. 1850.
1. Elizabeth Mary, *d.* 16 March, 1819, William Hammond, o Pepper Hill, co. Cork, who *d.* 8 Feb. 1857. She *d.* 1858, leavin; issue.
2. Alice, *m.* 11 July, 1825, Thomas Borlster, of Dromaneen, cc Cork, who *d.* 3 Feb. 1871. She *d.* Aug. 1826, leaving issue.
3. Mary, *m.* 1st, 11 Feb. 1823, William Wiseman, of Desertmore who *d.s.p.* She *m.* 2ndly, 14 Jan. 1831, William Allen, of Glen ville, who *d.* 2 Aug. 1837, having issue. She *d.* 28 Sept. 1880

The eldest son,
HERBERT GILLMAN, of Clonteadmore, bapt. 16 Dec. 1791; *m.* 1st 5 May, 1830, Esther, 3rd dau. of John Barter Bennett of Cork Surgeon, and by her (who *d.* 3 Jan. 1842) had issue,
1. HERBERT WEBB, of whom presently.
1. Margaret, *m.* 26 June, 1856, Edward Henry Ruby, of Curragh co. Cork, who *d.* 18 May, 1895, leaving issue.
2. Catherine Crooke, *d.* an infant 27 Nov. 1835.
3. Susan Weekes, *m.* 1 June, 1871, William Howe Hennis, an *d.s.p.* 11 Jan. 1873.
4. Elizabeth Bennett, *m.* 28 Dec. 1871, Robert Conner Madras M.D., of Dripsey, co. Cork, who *d.s.p.* 7 July, 1884. She *d* 17 Jan. 1906.

He *m.* 2ndly, 12 Oct. 1847, Sarah Honeywood Pollock Skottowe dau. of Richard Neville Parker, of Waterview, co. Cork. She *d.s.p* 2 April, 1878. He *d.* 2 Dec. 1877. His eldest son,

HERBERT WEBB GILLMAN, of Clonteadmore, co. Cork, J.P., B.A Dublin, Barrister-at-Law of Lincoln's Inn, formerly District Judg, and sometime Treasurer in Ceylon, *b.* 28 May, 1832; *m.* 30 Aug 1866, Annie, 2nd dau. of Francis Mackwood, of Avon House, Yorks and Galboda, Ceylon, and *d.* 23 July, 1898, leaving issue,
1. HERBERT FRANCIS WEBB, now of Clonteadmore.
2. Webb, D.S.O., Major R.F.A., served in S. African War and ii Aro Expedition, W. Africa, General Staff Officer Portsmoutl Service 1910, *b.* 26 Oct. 1870; *m.* 8 Feb. 1911, Caroline Grac Elizabeth, only dau. of Charles Rube, of 17, Hill Street, W.
 1. Frances Hetty Webb, *m.* 11 Sept. 1902, Eyre Herbert Ievers, o Mount Ievers, co. Clare, and Glanduff Castle, co. Limerick, onl: son of James Butler Ievers, of Mount Ievers, and has issue (*se that family*).

Arms—Quarterly: 1st, arg. a man's leg sa. couped at the thigh gu. and gartered or; 2nd, arg. a two-headed eagle displayed sa ducally gorged or; 3rd, arg. three firebrands raguly and fired ppr. 4th, or, a chevron gu. between three martlets sa. on an escutcheor over all of the last, a cross moline between four crescents arg **Crest**—An eagle's head couped holding in the beak a firebrand so fired at both ends ppr. *Motto*—Non cantu sed actu.

Seat—Clonteadmore, co. Cork. *Club*—East India United Service S.W.

GILLMAN OF CLONAKILTY.

JOHN ST. LEGER GILLMAN, of the Retreat, Clonakilty, co. Cork, J.P., *b.* 11 July, 1870; *m.* 29 July, 1891, Jane Rolt, youngest dau. of the late Thomas Sherlock, Solicitor, of Devonshire Square, Bandon, co. Cork, and has issue,

1. Muriel Dorothy Elizabeth St. Leger.
2. Ivy Nevelle Mary St. Leger.
3. Claire Estelle Rolt St. Leger.
4. Lorraine Wigmore Jennie St. Leger.

Lineage.—JAMES GILLMAN, of Baltenlrack, co. Cork, descended, it is said, from an officer who settled in Ireland in 1690. *m.* 15 March, 1754, Eliza Clarke. She *d.* 10 Feb. 1810. He *d.* 12 March, 1801, having had, with another son James, ancestor of GILLMAN *of Oakmount, co. Cork*, a younger son.

HERBERT GILLMAN, of Bennett's Grove, Clonakilty, co. Cork, J.P., *m.* 1808, Elizabeth Davies, dau. of Frances Bennett, of Bennett's Grove, by Anne his wife, dau. of Westropp Watkins, of Old Court, Doneraile, and *d.* 14 March, 1840, having had issue,

1. James Francis, M.D., of Woodlands, Enniskean, co. Cork, J.P., *b.* 14 May, 1810; *m.* 1842, Susan Townshend, dau. of Samuel Bennett, of Tellinlana, Blackrock, co. Cork, and *d.* 5 Aug. 1858, having had issue, one son and three daus.
2. BENNETT WATKINS, late of the Retreat.
1. Elizabeth Sarah, *m.* 3 March, 1842, her cousin, James Gillman, of Oakmount, co. Cork, J.P., who *d.* 1858, leaving issue.

The younger son,

MAJ. BENNETT WATKINS GILLMAN, of the Retreat, Clonakilty, co. Cork, Major 12th Foot, *b.* 7 May, 1814; *m.* 25 May, 1859, Sarah Beamish, dau. of Francis Bennett, of Clonakilty, by Elizabeth his wife, only dau. of the late Sampson Beamish, of Kilmalooda, and *d.* 2 Feb. 1880, having had issue,

1. Bennett Watkins, *d.* young, 5 Nov. 1861.
2. JOHN ST. LEGER, now of the Retreat.
1. Elizabeth Davies Watkins.
2. Annie St. Leger.
3. Lucy.

Arms—Sa. a dexter leg couped above the knee or, in the dexter chief point an annulet of the last. *Crest*—A griffin's head erased sa. charged with an annulet or, holding in the beak a bear's paw of the last. *Motto*—Non cantu sed actu.

Seat—The Retreat, Clonakilty, co. Cork.

GLASCOTT OF ALDERTON.

WILLIAM GLASCOTT, of Alderton, co. Wexford, J.P. and D.L., High Sheriff 1902, late Capt. 30th foot, educated at Rugby, *b.* 29 June, 1837; *m.* 1st, 23 Aug. 1866, Mary, dau. of Hon. William Cayley, of Toronto (*see* BURKE'S *Colonial Gentry*), and by her (who *d.* 14 Aug. 1890) had issue,

1. William, *b.* 20 June, 1869; *d.v.p.* 6 May, 1904.
2. FRANCIS JAMES, *b.* 27 Jan. 1871; *d.* 19 May, 1893
3. PHILIP JOCELYN, *b.* 27 Aug. 1873.
4. Arthur Moberley, *b.* 8 Jan. 1876.
1. Ethel, *d.* 22 July, 1909.   2. Amy.
3. Eva Sophia.   4. Rose, *d.* 18 Oct. 1874
5. Elizabeth Emma Mary, *d.* 5 April, 1900.
6. Helen.   7. Hilda, *d.* 26 Oct. 1911.

He *m.* 2ndly, 3 Sept. 1891, Fanny Isabella, widow of John William Harris, Barrister-at-Law.

Lineage.—FRANCIS GLASCOTT, of Pilltown, on whom were settled by deed, dated 24 April, 1754, the house and demesne of Pilltown, and the town and lands of Whitechurch, *m.* by licence dated 18 March, 1754, Sarah, dau. of William Stephens, of Chilcombe, co. Kilkenny, M.D., and by her had issue,

1. George Stephens (Rev.), *b.* 1755, B.A. Trin. Coll. Dublin 1777, Rector of Killesk, and St. James, Dunbrody; wrecked in the Bristol Channel 1787; *d. unm.*
2. WILLIAM (Rev.), of whom hereafter.
3. John, of Creacon, co. Wexford, *m.* Susan, dau. of Francis Tree, of Boston, North America, and was bur. at Whitechurch, 13 April, 1817, having had issue by her (who was bur. at the same place, 13 June, 1818).
1. Margaret, *m.* 1st, Hibbert Newton, who *d.* Oct. 1795; and 2ndly, Rev. Theobald Brownrigg, Rector of Kells Grange, co. Kilkenny, who *d.* 1805.
2. Elizabeth, *m.* 13 Nov. 1794, John Rogers, of New Ross, who *d.* 18 Jan. 1799.
3. Frances, *d. unm.*, bur. 1 July, 1791.

Mr. Francis Glascott *d.* 1798. His 2nd son,

REV. WILLIAM GLASCOTT, of Pilltown, J.P., *b.* 1756; B.A. T.C.D. 1779, Rector of Killesk, and St. James, Dunbrody; *m.* (licence 10 Oct. 1787) Elizabeth, dau. of Rev. Samuel Madden, LL.D., Rector of Kells and Fiddown, co. Kilkenny, and by her (who *d.* 22 May, 1851) had,

1. JOHN, bapt. 29 Dec. 1793, bur. at Whitechurch, 12 April, 1794.
2. WILLIAM MADDEN, of whom presently.
1. Elizabeth, *m.* 29 March, 1815, Rev. James Morgan Stubbs, Rector of Rosdroit, co. Wexford, and *d.* 1847.
2. Lucy, *m.* 11 Jan. 1811, John Usher, of Landscape, co. Wexford, and *d.* 30 March, 1863.
3. Sarah, *d. unm.* 22 July, 1829.
4. Cassandra, *m.* 7 Nov. 1828, Richard Wybrants Atkinson, of Coldblow, co. Dublin, and *d.* June, 1862.
5. Wilhelmina, *d. unm.* 31 Oct. 1871, aged 74.
6. Margaret, *d. unm.* 7 Aug. 1817, aged 15.
7. Arabella, *d. unm.* 30 Nov. 1828, aged 24.

Rev. William Glascott *d.* 29 Nov. 1829. The 2nd son,

WILLIAM MADDEN GLASCOTT, of Pilltown, co. Wexford, J.P., High Sheriff 1834, *b.* 4 Sept. 1806, B.A. Trin. Coll. Dublin 1827; s. his father at Pilltown 1829, which had been remodelled, enlarged, and latterly named Alderton; *m.* 20 May, 1836, Elizabeth Harriet Lucy, dau. of Major James Boyd, of Rossclare, co. Wexford, and *d.* 15 Feb. 1895, having by her (who *d.* 21 March, 1877, aged 59) had issue,

1. WILLIAM, now of Alderton.
2. James Jocelyn, Major late the Manchester Regt., *b.* 17 April, 1845; *m.* 1st, 2 Dec. 1868, Anna Margaret Sophia, dau. of John Richards, of Macmine Castle, co. Wexford. She *d.* 13 Nov. 1909. He *m.* 2ndly, 27 Aug. 1910, Lily Elizabeth, dau. of late Edward Bear Ridges.
1. Georgina Elizabeth.
2. Bessie Dorothea, *m.* 30 Jan. 1869, Capt. Harry Philip Dawson 75th Regt.   3. Lucy Sophia.
4. Mary Isabel.   5. Amy Sarah.

Seat—Alderton House, New Ross, co. Wexford.

GLEDSTANES OF FARDROSS.

MOUTRAY GLEDSTANES, of Fardross, co. Tyrone, J.P. cos. Tyrone and Fermanagh, late Capt. Royal Tyrone Fusiliers, formerly 57th Regt., *b.* 28 April, 1845; *m.* 15 Jan. 1874, Helen Catherine, dau. of John James Verschoyle, of Tassagart, co. Dublin, by Catherine Helen his wife, dau. of Rev. W. H. Foster, and grand-dau. of Right Rev. W. Foster, D.D., Bishop of Clogher, and has issue,

1. AMBROSE UPTON, Capt. 30th Lancers, Gordon's Horse, *b.* 6 July, 1876; *m.* 18 Aug. 1900, Adelaide Isabella, dau. of late Major Robert Tankerville Webber (Welsh Fus.) (*see* WEBBER *of Lakefield*), and Isabella his wife, dau. of Hon. and Rev. W. Wingfield, Rector of Abbeyliers, Queen's Co. (*see* BURKE'S *Peerage*, POWERSCOURT, V.).
1. Helen Margaret Catherine.
2. Sophia Cecilia Marion.

Lineage.—This family, of Scotch extraction, has long been settled at Fardross. In 1688, CAPT. JAMES GLEDSTANES, equipped at his own expense a body of Yeomen, and led them to the relief of Derry, for which he received a certificate, and the thanks of Governor Walker. His eldest son,

JAMES GLEDSTANES, of Fardross, *m.* Miss Graham, of Hockley, near Armagh, and left issue,

1. Thomas, *d. unm.*
1. Anne, *m.* Matthew Jacob, of St. Johnstown, and Mobarnane, co. Tipperary.
2. Mary, *m.* 1755, Arthur Johnston, of Rademon, co. Down, M.P. for Killyleagh.
3. MARGARET, of whom presently.
4. Katherine, *m.* Charles King, M.P. of St. Angelo, co. Fermanagh,

The third dau. and eventually co-heir,

MARGARET GLEDSTANES, *m.* 1767, AMBROSE UPTON, Major 13th Dragoons, of Hermitage, co. Dublin. They both *d.* 1804, leaving a son and dau.,

WHITNEY UPTON, who took the name of GLEDSTANES. He *m.* 1st, 1795, Isabella, dau. of Rev. Anketell Moutray, of Favour Royal, co. Tyrone. She *d.s.p.* He *m.* 2ndly, 1799, Emily, dau. of

Michael Aylmer, of Courtown, co. Kildare, and by her (who *d*. 1811) had, besides a dau., Frances, who *d*. 1818, an only surviving son, AMBROSE, of whom presently.

MARY ANNE CATHERINE, *m*. 27 April, 1793, John Corry Moutray, D.L., of Favour Royal, co. Tyrone, who *d*. 26 April, 1859, leaving issue, six sons and three daus. (*see that family*). His youngest dau., Sophia, *m*. 14 Dec. 1838, Robert Hornidge, of Twickenham, King's Co., who assumed by Royal Licence, 1871, the name and arms of GLEDSTANES. He was 2nd son of Richard Hornidge, D.L., of Tulfarris, co. Wicklow (*see that family*). She *d*. 1848, leaving issue,
(1) MOUTRAY, now of Fardross.
(2) Robert, *b*. 1848.
(1) Cecilia, *d. unm.* 1867.
(2) Marion, *d. unm.* 1868.

He *m*. 2ndly, 1855, Mary, dau. of Mervyn Stewart, of Martray, co. Tyrone, by whom he had issue. He *d*. 1876.

The only surviving son of Mr. Upton Gledstanes,

AMBROSE UPTON GLEDSTANES, J.P., High Sheriff 1829, *b*. 22 Feb. 1802 ; *m*. 2 Oct. 1828, Cecilia, dau. of Richard Hornidge, D.L. of Tulfarris, co. Wicklow, and Elizabeth, his wife, dau. of Hugh Henry, of Lodge Park, co. Kildare, but by her (who *d*. 27 June, 1861) had no issue. He *d*. 1871, and was *s*. by his cousin.

Arms—Quarterly : 1st and 4th, per pale or and arg. within an orle of martlets sa. a savage's head couped, distilling drops of blood and wearing a bonnet composed of bay and holly leaves all ppr., for GLEDSTANES ; 2nd and 3rd, arg., on a chevron engrailed between three bugle horns stringed gu. a trefoil slipped or, for HORNIDGE. **Crest**—1st, GLEDSTANES : A demi-griffin sa. holding s spear ppr. transfixing a savage's head couped distilling drops of blood, and wearing a bonnet composed of bay and holly leaves as in the arms ; 2nd, HORNIDGE : Out of park palings ppr. a demi-huntsman affrontée, habited gu., belt and cap sa. winding a horn or; motto over, *Virtutis laus actio*. **Motto**—Under the arms : *Fide et virtute*.

Seat—Fardross, Clogher.

GOFF OF CARROWROE PARK.

THOMAS CLARENCE EDWARD GOFF, of Carrowroe Park, co. Roscommon, J.P. and D.L., High Sheriff 1891, Capt. 3rd Batt. Royal Scots Regt., *b*. 28 May, 1867 ; *m*. 15 April, 1896, Lady Cecilie Heathcote Drummond-Willoughby, 4th dau. of the Earl of Ancaster, and has issue,

THOMAS ROBERT CHARLES, *b*. 16 July, 1898.
Elizabeth Moyra, *b*. 30 May, 1897.

Lineage.—THE REV. THOMAS GOFF, M.A., of Eccles Street, Dublin, and of Carriglea, near Kingstown, co. Dublin, son of Robert Goff, by his wife, Sarah French, *m*. 1826, Anne, dau. of Capt. Caulfeild, R.N., by Theodosia Talbot his wife, granddau. of the Earl of Glandore, and *d*. Oct. 1844, leaving issue,
1. THOMAS WILLIAM, of whom presently.
2. Robert, late Capt. 16th Lancers, *b*. 10 April, 1831 ; *d*. Dec. 1881.
3. Charles Talbot, *b*. 22 July, 1837 ; *d*. 1870.
4. James Caulfeild, *b*. 14 Nov. 1838 ; *m*. 1876, Grace, dau. of W. B. Stoker, and has issue,
James, *b*. 1877. Grace, *b*. 1880.
5. John Crosbie, *b*. 6 Sept. 1840 ; *d*. 30 Nov. 1904 ; *m*. 1877, Theodosia, dau. of W. B. Stoker, and had issue, three sons and a dau.
6. William, *b*. 9 Feb. 1841.
1. Theodosia, *d*. young, 1854.

The eldest son,

THOMAS WILLIAM GOFF, of Oakport, co. Roscommon, D.L., Capt. 7th Dragoon Guards, *b*. 6 July, 1829, M.P. for that co. 1859 ; High Sheriff 1858 ; *m*. 17 March, 1863, Dorothea, eldest dau. of the late Rev. Lord Augustus Fitz Clarence, and by her (who *d*. 15 May, 1870) had issue,
1. THOMAS CLARENCE EDWARD, his heir.
1. Ethel Anne, *m*. 23 Dec. 1885, Henry de Courcy Agnew, 2nd son of the late Sir Andrew Agnew, Bart., of Lochnaw, and has issue (*see* BURKE's *Peerage and Baronetage*).
2. Muriel Helen.

Capt. Goff *d*. June, 1876.

Arms—Az., on a chevron between two fleurs-de-lis in chief and a demi-lion rampant, couped in base or, an annulet gu. *Crest*—A squirrel sejant holding a nut leaved all ppr. and charged on the shoulder with a fleur-de-lis or. *Motto*—Honestas optima politia.

Seat—Carrowroe, co. Roscommon. *Town Residence*—46, Pont Street, S.W. *Clubs*—St. James's, White's, and Kildare Street, Dublin.

GOING formerly OF TRAVERSTON.

ROBERT EDWARD GOING, late of Traverston, co. Tipperary, J.P., *b*. 13 Dec. 1861 ; *m*. 4 July, 1889, Edith Hamilton, dau. of Thomas Worthington, and has issue,

JOHN, *b*. 14 April, 1890.
Edith Mary, *b*. 1 May, 1891.

Lineage.—ROBERT GOING, of Cranagh, co. Tipperary, whose will was proved 1732, left, with three daus, three sons,
1. ROBERT, his heir.
2. JAMES, of Ballyphilip.
3. Philip, of Knockayne.

The eldest son,

ROBERT GOING, of Tullymoylan, co. Tipperary, *m*. Jane Johnstone, of co. Cork, a co-heiress, and had issue,
1. John, *d. unm.*
2. ROBERT, heir to his father, of whom presently.
3. James, of Belleisle, co. Clare, *m*. Miss Marcella Walsh, of Newtown, co. Limerick, and had, with other issue,
1. Robert, of Cragg, co. Tipperary, *b*. 1766 ; *m*. 1804, Anne, dau. of John Dwyer, and *d*. 1838, leaving issue,
JOHN, of Cragg, J.P., *b*. 1 Oct. 1812 ; *m*. 15 Jan. 1857, Eliza, dau. of Rev. Charles Mayne, A.M., Vicar-General of Cashel, and *d*. 16 Dec. 1880, having by her (who *d*. 22 May, 1902) had issue,
1. ROBERT EDWARD, now of Traverston.
2. Charles Mayne, of Cragg, co. Tipperary, J.P., D.L., *b*. 14 Aug. 1864.
3. John, Capt. S. Wales Borderers, *b*. 13 March, 1866 ; *m*. 3 Oct. 1894, Ethel Mary, dau. of — Bridger, and has issue,
Joan Mary Mayne, *b*. 1895.
1. Susan Ellen.
2. James, of Violet Hill, co. Clare, *m*. Jane, dau. of Marcus Paterson, by Mary his wife, 2nd dau. of Wyndham Quin, of Adare, M.P. for Kilmallock, and sister of Valentine Richard, 1st Earl of Dunraven, and had issue, five sons and two daus.,
(1) James. (2) Marcus.
(3) Wyndham Quin. (4) Robert.
(5) Richard.
(1) Mary. (2) Marcella.
4. Thomas, of Coolbea, co. Cork, *d.s.p.* 1793-4.
5. Richard, of Bird Hill, co. Tipperary, J.P., *m*. Anne, dau. of Henry White, of New Ross, same co., and had issue, four sons and four daus.,
1. John, Rector of Mealiffe, co. Tipperary, who was murdered, 1829, aged 60. He *m*. Frances Anne, eldest dau. of Rev. Walter Shirley, brother of the 4th, 5th, and 6th Earl Ferrers, and left by her (who *d*. 1838), with other issue,
(1) Richard, who *m*. a sister of the Rev. Peter Roe.
(2) Henry. (3) Thomas.
(4) Charles Waller, of Cranna House, near Nenagh, *m*. his cousin, Letitia, dau. of Thomas Johnson Stoney, of Oakley Park, and had issue,
John Charles, of Cranna House, near Nenagh.
(1) Frances, *m*. Rev. William Stoney, Rector of Castlebar.
2. Richard, Barrister-at-Law and Police Magistrate, of Bird Hill, *m*. and had issue ; murdered 1821.
3. Henry, *m*. his cousin, Sarah, dau. of Richard White, of Greenhall, co. Tipperary.
1. Letitia, *m*. 1st, S. J. Stoney, of Oakley Park ; and 2ndly, to Finch White.
2. Jane, *m*. Edward Butler, of Carlow, and is dec.
3. Rebecca, *m*. 1st, her cousin, Thomas Going, of Santa Cruz ; and 2ndly, Capt. Goodwin.
4. Eliza, *m*. Thomas J. Stoney, of Harvest Lodge, co. Tipperary.
6. Philip, of Monaquil, co. Tipperary, J.P., *m*. 1767, Grace, dau. of Thomas Bernard, and sister to Thomas Bernard, of Castle Bernard, King's Co., M.P. ; and *d*. 24 April, 1820, having had by his wife, who survived him until 1836, one son and three daus ,
1. Thomas, of Santa Cruz, co. Tipperary, *m*. Rebecca, 3rd dau. of his uncle, Richard Going, of Bird Hill, and predeceased his father, *s.p.*
1. MARY, co-heir, *m*. 1794, her cousin John Bennett, of Ballyloughane, co. Carlow, afterwards of Viewmount, in the same co. He *d.s.p.* 1827.
2. CHARLOTTE, co-heir, *m*. 31 Dec. 1798, Robert Atkins, eldest son of Major Robert Atkins, of Firville, co. Cork, and had, with other issue,
Rev. Philip Going Atkins-Going, of Firville, co. Cork, and of Monaquil, co. Tipperary, to which property he *s*. by the will of his maternal grandfather, and assumed the surname of GOING in addition to ATKINS.
3. JEMIMA MATILDA, co-heir, *m*. 12 April, 1804, Sir Amyrald Dancer, Bart. of Modreny and Cloughjordan, co. Tipperary.

Mr. Robert Going, of Traverston, *d*. July, 1779, and was *s*. by his eldest son,

ROBERT GOING, of Traverston, *m*. 20 Jan. 1764, Margaret, 2nd dau. of Thomas Maunsell, of Plassy, M.P. co. Limerick, by Dorothy his wife, dau. of Richard Waller, of Castle Waller, co. Limerick, and had, with two daus. (Jane, *m*. John Willington, of Castle Willington ; and Margaret, *m*. 1789, Edward Birch, of Roscrea), one son,

THOMAS GOING, of Traverston, High Sheriff for co. Tipperary 1803, *m*. Frances, dau. of Caleb Powell, of Clonshavoy, co. Limerick, and *d*. 12 Feb. 1841, aged 74, leaving issue,
1. ROBERT, of Traverston, 2. CALEB, of Traverston.
1. Margaret, *m*. 1837, William Walsh, of Fruagh, co. Limerick.
2. Frances.

3. Jane, *m.* 1845, Joseph Fishbourne, of Hermitage, co. Carlow.
4. Sarah, *m.* 1846, Paul Molloy.   5. Dorah.
The elder son,
ROBERT GOING, of Traverston, *d. unm.* 1863, and was *s.* by his brother,
CALEB GOING, of Traverston, J.P., *m.* Miss White, and *d.*, and was *s.* by his cousin,
ROBERT EDWARD GOING (refer to descendants of James Going, of Belleisle).
Seat—Traverston, Nenagh.

GOING OF BALLYPHILIP.

MABEL ANNA (Mrs. Threlfall, *Whixley Hall, York*) and BENA GOING, of Ballyphilip, *s.* their brother, 1897.

Lineage.—JAMES GOING, of Ballyphilip, son of Robert Going, of Cranagh (*see* GOING *of Traverston*), *d.* (will proved 1761), leaving a son,
AMBROSE GOING, of Ballyphilip, *b.* 1719; *d.* 1780; *m.* Bridget Hunt, and was father of
WILLIAM GOING, of Ballyphilip, *b.* 1745; *m.* 1784, Mary, eldest dau. of Newport White, of Kilmoylan, co. Limerick, and *d.* 1844, leaving a son and heir,
AMBROSE GOING, of Ballyphilip, co. Tipperary, *b.* Oct. 1785; *m.* Feb. 1811, Margaret, 4th dau. of Col. Richard Pennefather, of New Park, co. Tipperary, and had issue,
  1. WILLIAM, his heir.
  2. Richard Pennefather, J.P., *b.* 1821; *m.* 1862, Letitia Elizabeth, dau. of Rev. Robert Bury, of Killora, co. Cork, and *d.* 1872.
  3. John, of Wilford, co. Tipperary, *b.* Aug. 1822; *d.* 1873.
  1. Anna, *m.* 1835, Rev. Anthony Armstrong, Rector of Killoskully, and *d.* 1865.
  2. Margaret Isabella, *m.* 1841, Christopher F. Tuthill, M.D., of Dublin, and *d.* 12 June, 1858, leaving issue (*see* TUTHILL, *formerly of Kilmore*).
  3. Elizabeth Frances, *m.* 1846, John Harvey Adams, of Northlands, co. Cavan, and *d.* 1867.
  4. Dorothea, *m.* May, 1848, Samuel Murray Going, of Liskaveen House, co. Tipperary, and *d.* 1873.
Mr. Ambrose Going *d.* Aug. 1857, and was *s.* by his eldest son,
WILLIAM GOING, of Ballyphilip, J.P. and D.L., *b.* May, 1815; *m.* Oct. 1841, Jane Eliza, 2nd dau. of Benjamin Frend, of Rocklow, co. Tipperary, and Bosdill, co. Limerick (*see* FREND *of Rootiagh*), and by her (who *d.* 2 Oct. 1892) had issue,
  1. Ambrose, *b.* July, 1842; *d.* July, 1871.
  2. BENJAMIN FREND, his heir.
  1. Eliza, *m.* 1873, Major Alexander William Bailey, Fermanagh Light Infantry.
  2. Margaret, *m.* 1875, Owen Lloyd Mansergh, of Heathview, Tipperary, and afterwards of Liskeveen, Thurles (*see* MANSERGH *of Grenane*), and *d.* 1882.   3. Arabella Jane.
Mr. William Going *d.* 1879, and was *s.* by his eldest surviving son,
BENJAMIN FREND GOING, of Ballyphilip, co. Tipperary, J.P. and D.L., High Sheriff 1883; *b.* April, 1851; *m.* 1879, Florence T. A., 2nd dau. of Richard Fitzroy Creagh, of Millbrooke and Athassel, in the same co., and *d.* 7 March, 1883, the year he was High Sheriff, leaving issue,
  1. WILLIAM AMBROSE, of Ballyphilip, *b.* 31 Oct. 1881; *d.s.p.* 7 March, 1897.
  1. MABEL ANNA, of Ballyphilip, *m.* 25 Jan. 1908, Capt. Charles Morris Threlfall, late 8th Hussars, only son of Charles Threlfall of Tilstone Lodge, Tarforley, and had issue,
    Charles Reginald Morris, *b.* 15 Dec. 1908.
  2. Bena, of Ballyphilip.
Seat—Ballyphilip, Killenaule, co. Tipperary.

GOODBODY OF INCHMORE.

JAMES PERRY GOODBODY, of Inchmore, King's Co., J.P. and D.L., High Sheriff, 1894, *b.* 1853; *m.* 1875, Sophia, eld. dau. of Joseph Richardson, of Springfield, co. Down, and had issue,
  1. JAMES PERRY, *b.* 22 March, 1877; *m.* 26 April, 1905, Jane Frances, youngest dau. of Rev. William Henry Bond, M.A., of Petersfield.
  2. Joseph Harold (*Upton, Clara, Queen's Co.*), *b.* 1880; *m.* 16 April, 1903, Mary, youngest dau. of the late Lewis MacLellan, of Glasgow, and has issue,
    Harold Perry, *b.* 4 March, 1904,
    A dau., *b.* Dec. 1906.
  3. Reginald Marcus, *b.*   ; *m.* 21 Sept. 1910, Florence Edith, dau. of Charles Clarance.
Lineage.—ROBERT GOODBODY, of Charlestown House, King's Co., left with other issue two sons,
  1. Marcus, of whom presently.
  2. Jonathan, of Charlestown House, King's Co., *b.* 1812, *m.* 1843, Lydia, dau. of Barclay Clibborn, of Raheens (*see* CLIBBORN *of Moate*). He *d.* 1889, having had issue,
    1. Richard, of Clara House, King's Co., *b.* 1845; *m.* 11 April, 1872, Elizabeth, dau. of Ebenezer Pike, of Cork.
    2. Robert, of Charlestown House, King's Co., *b.* 1850; *d.* 13 April, 1911; *m.* 1875, Eliza, dau. of Sir John Barrington, D.L. of Killiney, co. Dublin, and had an only dau.,
      Margaret Jane Evelyn (Rita), *m.* 7 July, 1903, Norman Fritz Thompson, eldest son of the late S. W. Thompson, of Clairville, Reigate.
The elder son,
MARCUS GOODBODY, of Inchmore, King's Co., J.P., High Sheriff 1876, *b.* 1810; *m.* 1848, Hannah, dau. of James Perry, and *d.* 1885, having had issue,
  1. Robert, of Haldon, Pattison, New Jersey, U.S., M.A. Trin. Coll. Dublin, *b.* 25 July, 1850; *m.* 1872, Isabella Dora, dau. of Thomas Pim, of Kingstown, co. Dublin, and has issue.
  2. JAMES PERRY, now of Inchmore.
Seat—Inchmore, Clara, King's Co.   Club—University, Dublin.

GOOLD-ADAMS. *See* ADAMS.

GOOLD-VERSCHOYLE. *See* VERSCHOYLE.

GORDON OF DELAMONT.

CAPT. ALEXANDER ROBERT GISBORNE GORDON, of Delamont, co. Down, Capt. Royal Irish Regt., *b.* 28 July, 1882.

Lineage.—ROBERT GORDON, of Ballinteggart, co. Down, *m.* 1689, a dau. of George Ross, of Portabo, and sister of Robert Ross, of Rosstrevor (*see that family*), in the same co., ancestor of General Ross, who fell at the Battle of Bladensburgh, and had issue,
  1. JOHN, his heir.   2. Robert (Rev.).
Mr. Gordon *d.* 1720, and was *s.* by his son,
JOHN GORDON, of Ballinteggart, *b.* 1690, who *m.* 1st, 1720, his cousin Jane, dau. of Hugh Hamilton, of Ballytrenagh, and by her (who *d.* 1726) had issue,
  1. ROBERT, his heir.
  1. Jane, *m.* 1757, David Johnston.
Mr. Gordon *m.* 2ndly, Grace, dau. of Thomas Knox, of Dungannon, co. Tyrone, and had by her,
  2. Thomas Knox, of Loyalty Lodge, Ballinteggart, Barrister-at-Law, *b.* 1728, appointed 1771, Chief Justice of South Carolina, and *d.* 1796, leaving issue,
    1. Wills Hill.
    2. John, Major 50th Regt., *d. unm.*
    3. Arthur, Capt. 3rd Regt. (Buffs), *d. unm.*
    4. Thomas.
    1. Grace, *d. unm.*
  3. John, Lieut.-Col. 50th Regt., *b.* 1730; *m.* 7 Jan. 1780, Elizabeth, dau. of Sir Richard Warwick Bampfylde, 4th bart. of Poltimore, co. Devon, and *d.s.p.* 1782.
  2. Margery, *m.* William Haven.
  3. Elizabeth, *m.* Joseph Wallace.
Mr. Gordon *d.* Feb. 1771, leaving his estate at Ballinteggart to Thomas Knox Gordon, his eldest son by his second marriage. His eldest son by his first wife,
ROBERT GORDON, of Florida Manor, *b.* 1722; *m.* March, 1755, Alice, widow of Thomas Whyte, and only dau. of James Arbuckle, by Anne his wife, dau. of John Crawford, and niece and heir-at-law of David Crawford, of Florida, co. Down, and had issue,
  1. JOHN CRAWFORD, his heir.
  2. DAVID, of Delamount, successor to his brother.
  3. Robert, *m.* in 1804, Catherine Anne, dau. of John Clarke, of Belfast, and had issue,
    Robert Alexander, of Summerfield, *b.* 1811; *d.s.p.* 1894.
    Catherine, *d. unm.* 1900.
  4. Alexander, of Castle Place, Belfast, *b.* 1762; *m.* 23 Dec. 1799, Dorothea, dau. and co-heir of Gen. James Gisborne, Commander-in-Chief in Ireland, Governor of Charlemont and M.P. for Lismore, and *d.* 15 July, 1829, leaving issue,
    1. ROBERT FRANCIS, of Florida Manor.
    2. James Gisborne, Lieut. H.E.I.C.S. 30th Regt. N.I., *d. unm.* 1826.
    3. John Frederick (Rev.), Rector of Anahilt, co. Down, *b.* 17 March, 1807; *m.* 10 Dec. 1839, Dorothea Josepha, dau. of Alexander Miller, of Downpatrick, and *d.* 24 Sept. 1875, leaving issue by her (who *d.* 27 Aug. 1862),
      (1) ALEXANDER HAMILTON MILLER HAVEN, late of Delamont.
      (2) Robert Francis, of Conyngham Lodge, Curragh, *b.* 9 Feb. 1847; *d.* 12 May, 1911; *m.* 16 Jan. 1879, Alice Aimée (who *d.* 14 Aug. 1883), dau. of Arthur J. Sharman Crawford, of Crawfordsburn, co. Down, and had a dau.,
        Alice Mary Dorothea, *b.* 14 Jan. 1880.
      (3) John Frederick George, *b.* 29 Feb. 1850.
      (4) Thomas Gisborne, of Knocknagarne, Ballysax, Curragh, co. Kildare, *b.* 15 Dec. 1851; *m.* 7 Jan. 1890, Marie Louise, 2nd dau. of Ogilvie Blair Graham, of Larchfield, co. Down, and has issue,
        Thomas Gisborne, *b.* 31 Aug. 1899.
        Helen Ogilvie, *b.* 12 July, 1891.
      (1) Dorothea Josephine Gisborne, *b.* 25 Dec. 1840; *m.* 7 Jan. 1873, James Edward Scott, M.D., Dep. Surgeon-Gen. (*see* SCOTT *of Willsboro'*).
      (2) Frances Margaret, *b.* 20 April, 1844.
      (3) Marion Alice, *b.* 5 Nov. 1845; *d. unm.* 13 March, 1893.
      (4) Mary Augusta, *b.* 5 Oct. 1848; *m.* 7 Jan. 1879, Capt. William Somerset Ward, and has issue (*see* BURKE'S *Peerage*, BANGOR, V.).
      (5) Anne Catherine, *b.* 15 Feb. 1853; *m.* 1893, Ernest Radcliffe Crump.

IRELAND. Gore.

4. Alexander Thomas, *b.* 1811; *m.* 1st, 20 Nov. 1844, Miss Augusta Whitaker, by whom (who *d.* 1847) he had a son,
(1) Henry Pottinger, *b.* 1846; *d. unm.* 1879.
He *m.* 2ndly, 19 July, 1849, Rosina Frances, dau. and heir of Anderson McCausland of Culmore House, co. Derry, and *d.* 1871, leaving a son and dau.,
(2) ALEXANDER FREDERICK ST. JOHN, of Florida Manor, J.P., *b.* 30 Oct. 1852; *d.* 12 April, 1886, and was *s.* by his cousin, ALEXANDER HAMILTON MILLER HAVEN GORDON, of Delamont.
(1) Julia Elizabeth.
5. David, *b.* 1817; *d. unm.*
1. Marianne, *m.* Morts. Trucci, and *d.s.p.*
2. Alice Dorothea, *m.* Rev. George Robbins, and has issue.
1. Alice, *d. unm.*
2. Anne, *m.* Jan. 1799, Eldred Pottinger, of Mount Pottinger, co. Down, and had issue.
Mr. Gordon *d.* 1793, and was *s.* by his son,
JOHN CRAWFORD GORDON, of Florida, J.P. co. Down, Capt. 50th Regt., *d. unm.* Nov. 1797, and was *s.* by his brother, DAVID, of Delamont. This
DAVID GORDON, of Florida Manor, and Delamont, J.P. and D.L. co. Down, High Sheriff 1812, *b.* 1 June, 1759; *m.* 11 Sept. 1789, Mary, youngest dau. of James Crawford, of Crawfordsburn, and sister of Anne, Countess of James, 1st Earl of Caledon, by whom he had issue,
1. ROBERT, his heir to Florida Manor.
2. JAMES CRAWFORD, *s.* to Delamont.
1. Jane Maria, *d. unm.* 1864.
Mr. Gordon *d.* 2 March, 1837, and was *s.* by his son,
ROBERT GORGON, of Florida, J.P., D.L. co. Down, High Sheriff 1833, and for co. Tyrone 1843, *b.* 8 Sept. 1791; *m.* 25 Aug. 1825, Mary, dau. of William Crawford, of Lakelands, co. Cork; *d.s.p.* 1864, and was *s.* by his brother,
REV. JAMES CRAWFORD GORDON, of Florida Manor, and Delamont, M.A., Precentor of St. Patrick's Cathedral, co. Down, 1828-47, *b.* 28 April, 1796; *m.* Geraldine, dau. of James Penrose, of Woodhill, co. Cork (she *d.* Jan. 1881). He *d.s.p.* 12 Nov. 1867, and was *s.* by his cousin,
ROBERT FRANCIS GORDON, of Florida Manor, and Delamont House, co. Down, J.P. and D.L., High Sheriff co. Down 1873, *b.* 2 July, 1802; *d.s.p.* 7 Jan. 1883, and was *s.* at Delamont by his nephew, ALEXANDER HAMILTON MILLER HAVEN, father of the present possessor, and at Florida Manor by his nephew,
ALEXANDER FREDERICK ST. JOHN GORDON, of Florida Manor, J.P., *b.* 30 Oct. 1852; *d.s.p.* 12 April, 1886, and was *s.* by his cousin,
ALEXANDER HAMILTON MILLER HAVEN GORDON, of Florida Manor and Delamont, co. Down, J.P. and D.L., *b.* 6 Jan. 1842; *m.* 15 Sept. 1881, Ada Austen, eldest dau. of John Edward Eyre, Governor of Jamaica, of the Grange, Staple Aston, co. Oxford, and had issue,
1. ALEXANDER ROBERT GISBORNE, now of Delamont.
2. Eyre, Scholar Queen's Coll. Oxon., India Civil Service, *b.* 28 Feb. 1884.
3. John de la Hay, Lieut. 67th Punjabis, *b.* 30 March, 1887.
4. Edward Ormond, *b.* 1 March, 1888.
5. Henry Gisborne, Lieut. R.A., *b.* 29 Aug. 1889.
6. Eldred Pottinger, *b.* 24 May, 1891.
1. Ivy Dorothy Catherine, *b.* 1 Feb. 1886.
2. Margerie Frances, *b.* 18 Nov. 1893.
3. Honor, *b.* 13 April, 1896.
4. Marion Alice, *b.* 8 Dec. 1900.
Mr. Gordon *d.* 5 July, 1910, and was *s.* by his eldest son.
Seat—Delamont, Killyleigh, co. Down.

GORE OF DERRYMORE.

LIEUT.-GEN. EDWARD ARTHUR GORE of Derrymore, co. Clare, J.P. and D.L., Lieut.-Gen. (ret.), Assistant Adjutant-General, Northern District 1887-9, and in North Western District, Chester, 1889-92. Insp.-General of Remounts 1894-8, was Lieut.-Col. commanding Inniskilling Dragoons 1878-83, *b.* 1 Aug. 1839; *m.* 1877, Anna Josephine, eldest dau. of late William Cochrane, of Dublin. and has issue,

1. REGINALD EDWARD, Lieut. R.N. (*Broomer's House, Pulborough, Sussex*), *b.* 1880; *m.* 19 Dec. 1907, Lady Nellie Viola Castalia Florence Chetwynd-Talbot, only dau. of Charles Henry John, 20th Earl of Shrewsbury.

Lineage.—JOSEPH GORE, of Derrymore, co. Clare, 2nd son of Francis Gore, of Derrymore (*see* HICKMAN *of Tyredagh*), and Christiana Emma his wife, dau. of Sir Joseph Peacoke, Bart. of Baratin, co. Clare. He *m.* 1837, Margaret, dau. of Very Rev. Richard Bagwell, of Marlfield, Dean of Clogher, and *d.* 1847, having by her (who *d.* 1884) had issue,
EDWARD ARTHUR, now of Derrymore.
Margaret, *m.* Capt. Arthur Henley, 52nd L.I., of Eastwood, Bagnalstown, co. Carlow, and has issue.

Arms—Gu. on a fess between three crosses crosslets fitchée or, a trefoil slipped vert. Crest—An heraldic tiger rampant arg., collared gu, and charged on the shoulder with a trefoil as in the arms. Motto—In hoc signo vinces.

Seat—Derrymore, O'Callaghan's Mills, co. Clare. Clubs—Army and Navy, United Service, Windham, and Kildare Street, Dublin.

SAUNDERS-KNOX-GORE OF BELLEEK.

COL. WILLIAM ARTHUR GORE SAUNDERS-KNOX-GORE, of Belleek Manor, co. Mayo, J.P. and D.L. for that co. and High Sheriff 1899, J.P. co. Sligo, Lieut.-Col. and Hon. Col. late Reserve of Officers, previously commanding Donegal Royal Garrison Artillery Militia and formerly Major R.A., educated at Wellington and Royal Mil. Academy, Woolwich, served in Royal Artillery 1873-91, *b.* 5 Dec. 1854; *m.* 3 Aug. 1887, Maria Becher, eldest dau. of John Sampson Prince, and has issue,

WILLIAM ARTHUR CECIL, Lieut. King's Royal Rifle Corps, educated at Harrow and Sandhurst, *b.* 26 May, 1888.

Lineage.—JAMES KNOX-GORE, of Broadlands, co. Mayo Deputy Governor of that county, M.P. for Taghmon, co. Wexford, in the last Irish Parliament, and Ranger of the Curragh of Kildare, *b.* 25 March, 1774, 3rd son of Francis Knox, of Rappa Castle (*see that family*), and Mary his wife, dau. and co-heir of Paul Annesley Gore, M.P. of Belleek, co. Mayo, brother of Arthur, 1st Earl of Arran (*see* BURKE's *Peerage*), assumed by sign manual, 23 April, 1813, the additional name and arms of GORE, in compliance with the will of his maternal grandfather. He *m.* 19 Jan. 1800, his cousin Lady Maria Louisa Gore, eldest dau. of Arthur Saunders, and Earl of Arran. She *d.* 6 March, 1827. He *d.* 21 Oct. 1818, having had issue,
1. FRANCIS ARTHUR (Sir), of whom presently.
2. James, J.P, co. Mayo, *b.* 23 April, 1808, *m.* 8 April, 1833; Henrietta, dau. of Annesley Gore Knox, of Rappa (*see that family*), and left issue.
3. Henry William, Major in the Army, *b.* 1815; *d. unm.* 22 Jan. 1846.
4. Annesley, Lieut.-Gen. Madras Army, *m.* Ann Magdalen Louisa, dau. of Capt. Burns, and *d.* 12 Jan 1881, leaving issue.
5. George Edward, Capt. R.N., late of Gore Lodge, Glengeary, co. Dublin, *m.* 1876, Anne Jane, dau. of Andrew Irvine, of Irvinestown, co. Fermanagh.
1. Anna Maria, *m.* 28 Jan. 1819, John Frederick Knox, of Mount Falcon, co. Mayo, and *d.* 7 Jan. 1887. He *d.* 20 Sept. 1871, leaving issue (*see that family*).
2. Anna Maria, *m.* Lieut.-Col. Cuff, of Deal Castle, co. Mayo.
3. Eleanor Adelaide, *m.* 1832, Maj. John Gardiner, of Farm Hill, co. Mayo.
4. Charlotte Catherine, *m.* 12 July, 1836, Col. Ernest Knox, of Castlerea, and had issue. He *d.* 8 Sept. 1883.
The eldest son,
SIR FRANCIS ARTHUR KNOX-GORE, 1st bart., of Belleek Manor, co. Mayo, H.M. Lieutenant for co. Sligo, Col. Sligo Militia, High Sheriff 1840, *b.* 23 June, 1803, was created a baronet 5 Dec. 1868. He *m.* 4 Aug. 1829, Sarah, dau. of Charles Nesbit Knox, of Scurmore, co. Sligo, and Castle Lacken, co. Mayo (*see* KNOX *of Creagh*). She *d.* 8 May, 1888. He *d.* 21 May, 1873, having had issue,
1. Charles James (Sir), 2nd and last bart. of Belleek Manor, co. Mayo, J.P. co. Mayo, High Sheriff 1877, D.L. co. Sligo, High Sheriff 1888, Col. Sligo Militia, late Capt. 66th Regt. *b.* 20 Sept. 1831; *d. unm.* 1890, when the baronetcy became extinct.
2. Arthur William, of Ballina House, co. Mayo, J.P., High Sheriff 1878, Capt. 60th Rifles, *b.* 28 Oct. 1838; *m.* 10 March, 1863, Henrietta Emily, dau. of Richard M. Carden, of Fishmoyne, co. Tipperary. He *d.s.p.* 31 Jan. 1885.
1. Jane Louisa, *d.* young, 16 July, 1835.
2. MATHILDA, of whom presently.
3. Sarah Jane, *m.* 19 Dec. 1860, Edmund Henry Cockayne Pery-Knox-Gore, of Coolcoonan House, Foxford, co. Mayo, who *d.* 3 March, 1900, leaving issue (*see that family*).

Gore. THE LANDED GENTRY.

4. Louisa Elizabeth, *m.* 15 Dec. 1867, Lieut.-Col. John Harvey Knox-Browne, late 12th Lancers, of Aughentaine, co. Tyrone, and *d.* 22 May, 1903, having had issue (*see that family*).
5. Augusta Gertrude.
6. Agnes Frances Nina, *m.* 16 Aug. 1875, Utred Augustus Knox, of Mount Falcon, co. Mayo, and has issue (*see that family*).
7. Octavia Catherine, *m.* 11 Feb. 1873, Sir William W. R. Onslow, Bart., and has issue (*see* BURKE's *Peerage*).

The eldest surviving dau.,
MATHILDA KNOX-GORE, of Belleek Manor, co. Mayo, *m.* 27 March, 1854, MAJ.-GEN. WILLIAM BOYD SAUNDERS-KNOX-GORE, late R.A., of Ardmore, Torquay, High Sheriff co. Mayo 1895, who assumed by Royal Licence, 1891, the additional names and arms of KNOX-GORE. He was the son of Major William Saunders, R.H.A., and *d.* 29 March, 1902, having had issue,
1. WILLIAM ARTHUR of Belleek Manor.
2. Charles George Boyd, 2nd Lieut. 10th Hussars, *b.* 5 Nov. 1859; *d.* in India 1880.
3. Cecil Henry, Capt. 6th Dragoons and 2nd Dragoon Guards, *b.* 8 Feb. 1862; killed at Spion Kop Jan. 1900.
4. Arthur Harold Ward, Capt. Loyal N. Lancs. Regt., *b.* 5 Dec. 1870.
1. Georgina Sarah Eliza Frances.
2. Alice Maude, *m.* 27 April, 1905, Capt. Richard Jones Sankey, D.L., of Fort Frederic, co. Cavan, late 5th Dragoon Gds., only son of late John Sankey, of Merrion Square, Dublin, (*see* SANKEY *of Fort Frederic*).
3. Laura Elizabeth Mabel.
4. Sybil Katherine Octavia.

Arms—Quarterly 1st and 4th, grand quarters quarterly 1st and 4th gu. a fesse between three cross crosslets fitchée or all within a bordure arg. (GORE); 2nd and 3rd gu., a falcon rising or within an orle waved on the outer side and engrailed on the inner arg. a crescent for difference (KNOX); 2nd and 3rd, sa. on a chevron engrailed erm. a crescent az. between three bull's heads caboshed arg. (SAUNDERS). Crests—1. A wolf rampant or (GORE). 2. A falcon close perched on a rest ppr. (KNOX). 3. Out of a mural crown ppr. a bull's head gu. charged with a crescent or (SAUNDERS). Motto—In hoc signo vinces.

Seat—Belleek Manor, Ballina, co. Mayo. Clubs—Naval and Military and Kildare Street.

PERY-KNOX-GORE OF COOLCRONAN HOUSE.

EDMOND ARTHUR GORE PERY - KNOX-GORE, of Coolcronan House, co. Mayo, High Sheriff co. Mayo 1900, late Lieut. 6th Batt. Connaught Rangers, *b.* 3 July, 1861; *m.* 9 Nov. 1898, Amy, youngest dau. of Rev. Francis Gordon Sandys Lumsdaine (*see that family*), and has issue,

EDMOND MYLES, *b.* 30 July, 1904.
Sara Frances, *b.* 21 Aug. 1900.

Mr. Pery-Knox-Gore is the eldest son of Edmond Henry Cockayne Pery-Knox-Gore, D.L., High Sheriff 1880, of Coolcronan, and Bury House, Northants (who *d.* 3 March, 1900), by Sarah Jane his wife, now of Bury House, Northants, 3rd dau. and eventual co-heir of Sir Francis Arthur Knox-Gore, 1st bart. (*see* SAUNDERS-KNOX GORE *of Belleek*), and grandson of the Hon. Edmund Sexton Pery, of Bury House, 4th son of Edmond Henry, 1st Earl of Limerick. The late Mr. Pery-Knox-Gore assumed the additional name and arms of KNOX-GORE by Royal Licence, 1891.

Lineage.—*See* BURKE's *Peerage*, LIMERICK, E.

Arms—Quarterly 1st and 4th grand quarters quarterly 1 and 4 gu. a fess between three cross crosslets fitchée or, all within a bordure arg. (GORE); 2 and 3 gu. a falcon rising within an orle waved on the outer side and engrailed on the inner arg. a crescent for difference (KNOX); 2nd and 3rd grand quarters quarterly 1st and 4th quarterly gu. and or on a bend arg. three lions passant sa. (PERY) 2 and 3 per chevron engrailed or and sa. three pellets in chief and a stag passant in base of the first (HARTSTONGE). Crests—1. A wolf ramp. or (GORE); 2. A falcon close perched on a rest ppr. (KNOX); 3. A hind's head erased ppr. (PERY). Motto—In hoc signo vinces.

Seats—Coolcronan House, Ballina, co. Mayo, and the Bury House, Cottingham, Northants.

HUME-GORE OF DERRYLUSKAN.

ELLEN CAROLINE, LADY HUME-GORE, of Derryluskan, co. Tipperary, elder dau. and eventually co-heir of the late Mrs. Vernon-Gore, of Derryluskan, *m.* 18 July, 1857, Lieut.-Col. Sir Gustavus Hume, Lieut. of the Hon. Corps of Gentlemen-at-Arms, and late of the 38th Regt., son of the late Rev. Robert Hume, of Dublin (MACARTNEY *of Lissanoure*), and by him (who *d.* 16 June, 1891) has issue,

1. George Robert Vernon, Capt. Seaforth Highlanders, *b.* 26 July, 1859; *m.* 6 Oct. 1887, Mary, 2nd dau. of Robert Hathorn Johnston Stewart, D.L., of Physgill and Glasserton, co. Wigtown (*see that family*). He *d.* 3 Sept. 1901, leaving issue,
    1. GAVIN ROBERT VERNON, *b.* 23 July, 1888.
    2. Gustavus, *b.* 4 March, 1897.
    1. Gladys Ada.
2. Charles Vernon HUME, M.V.O., D.S.O., Col. R.F.A., late Military Attaché to the Court of Japan, A.D.C. to Field-Marshal Lord Roberts when Commander-in-Chief, East Indies, 1885-92, and A.A.G. to his Lordship during the war in S. Africa, *b.* 12 July, 1860; *m.* 30 Sept. 1897, Ursula Wilhelmina, dau. of Reginald Dykes Marshall, of Castlerigg Manor, Keswick, and has issue,
    1. Reginald Vernon, *b.* 7 Sept. 1898.
    1. Gillian Ursula.
    2. Rosemary Ethel, *b.* 2 April, 1907.
3. Gustavus Parker Vernon HUME, *b.* 2 July 1861, *d.* 21 March 1886.
4. Arthur Sinclair Vernon Hume, *b.* 6 July, 1865; *m.* Aug. 1893, Blanche, only dau. of T. J. Wyburn, of Melbourne, and has issue,
    1. Eileen. 2. Olive.
    3. Ursula.
5. Walter Vernon HUME, *b.* 27 April, 1875; *m.* Nov. 1904, Alice de Courcey, dau. of late William Thomas Harrison (*see* HARRISON *of Castle Harrison*).
1. Ada Mary, *m.* 8 June, 1886, Comm. Arthur Hill Ommanney-Peter Hill-Lowe, R.N., of Court of Hill, co. Salop, and *d.* 17 Dec. 1889, leaving issue a dau. (*see that family*).
2. Georgina Vernon, *m.* 5 Feb. 1885, Lieut.-Col. Robert Ireland Blackburne, D.L., of Hale Hall, Lancashire, only son of the late Col. John Ireland Blackburne, D.L., of Hale Hall, and has issue (*see that family*).

Lady Hume-Gore *s.* her mother, Mrs. Vernon-Gore, 1895, and together with her eldest son assumed by Royal Licence the additional name of GORE in that year.

Lineage.—REV. FRANCIS GORE, 2nd son of BRIGADIER-GEN. FRANCIS GORE, of Clonroad (*see* HICKMAN *of Tyredagh Castle*), by Catherine his wife, dau. of Sir Arthur Gore, Bart., of Newtown Gore, *m.* 1st, Frances, dau. of Sir Robert Gore, of Newtown, and relict of Charles Ingoldsby, by whom (who *d.* 1715) he left a son, Francis Lawrence, who *d. unm.* He *m.* 2ndly, 1717, a dau. of Edward Croker, of Ballinagard, co. Limerick, by whom he had a son, who *d. unm.* He *m.* 3rdly, Nov. 1740, Ellinor, youngest dau. of Col. Kingsmill Pennefather, of New Park, co. Tipperary, M.P., by whom (who *m.* 2ndly, 13 Jan. 1752, George Roberts, an Officer in the Army) he left issue,
1. GEORGE, of whom presently.
2. John, Capt. 5th Regt., killed at the battle of White Plains, 1776; *d. unm.*
    1. Katherine, *b.* 1744; *m.* George Parker, son of Rear-Admiral Sir Christopher Parker, and had issue,
        George (Sir), K.C.B., Admiral R.N., *b.* 1767; *m.* Arabella, dau. of Peter Butt, and *d.s.p.* 1847.
        Ellen, *m.* Nathaniel Evans, of Oldtown, co. Cork, and left an only child,
            GEORGINA KATHERINE, of whom presently, as heir to her cousin.

The elder son,
CAPT. GEORGE GORE, of Lawnsdown, Queen's Co., late 12th Light Dragoons, *m.* May, 1774, Catherine, eldest dau. and co-heiress of Lawrence Clutterbuck, of Derryluskan, by his wife Margaret, dau. of Henry Prittie, of Dunally Castle, co. Tipperary, and *d.* 1818, leaving issue,
1. Francis Lawrence (Rev.), *b.* 27 March, 1776; *m.* 9 April, 1818, Penelope, dau. of Francis Ellis, by whom he had a dau., Penelope Margaretta, *d. unm.* in her father's lifetime. Mr. Gore *d.* 20 Sept. 1848, and was *s.* by his brother.
2. George, Lieut.-Col. 9th Lancers, *b.* Jan. 1780; *m.* Lydia Smyth, and *d.s.p.* 23 July, 1862, having by his will devised all his estates on the decease of his surviving brother and sisters to his cousin, GEORGINA KATHERINE, only child of Nathaniel Evans (*see above*).
3. John (Rear-Admiral), *b.* May, 1784; *m.* Anne Tucker Gilbert, and *d.s.p.* 9 Dec. 1869.
    1. Margaret, *b.* Feb. 1775; *d. unm.* 18 April, 1855.
    2. Lavinia, *b.* Feb. 1781; *d. unm.* 2 March, 1873.
    3. Catherine, *b.* Nov. 1785; *d. unm.* 8 Nov. 1875.

His grand-niece,
GEORGINA KATHERINE (MRS. VERNON-GORE), of Derryluskan, co. Tipperary, only child of Nathaniel Evans, of Oldtown, co. Cork (*see above*), *m.* 14 Aug. 1828, Charles Vernon, elder son of Lieut.-Col. Brabazon Deanes Vernon (*see* VERNON *of Clontarf Castle*), and by him (who *d.* 13 April, 1874) had issue,
1. Charles Parker Venables, *b.* 1 July, 1829; *d. unm.* 10 July, 1879.
2. George Harcourt Venables, *b.* 1835; *d.* young, 7 Feb. 1852.

1. ELLEN CAROLINE, now of Derryluskan.
2. Caroline Diana, *m.* 15 July, 1854, William Ruxton, J.P. and D.L., of Ardee House, co. Louth, and by him (who *d.* 10 April, 1895) had issue (*see that family*).

Mrs. Vernon assumed, by Royal Licence, 1876, the additional name and arms of GORE, in accordance with the will of her cousin, Lieut.-Col. George Gore, of Derryluskan, and *d.* 28 April, 1895, and was *s.* by her elder dau. and co-heir, Ellen Caroline, now LADY HUME-GORE, of Derryluskan.

Lineage.—(*of* HUME).—GUSTAVUS HUME, of Dublin, State Surgeon, had issue,

REV. TRAVERS HUME, who was bur. 1757, having *m.* 1785, Elizabeth (*d.* 1805), only dau. of John Blaquier, Major of Dragoons, by Elizabeth his wife, dau. of George Macartney, and sister of Earl Macartney. They had issue,

1. GEORGE, who assumed the surname and arms of MACARTNEY (*see* MACARTNEY *of Lissanoure*).
2. Gustavus Thomas, *b.* 1794, served in the R.A. at the battle of Waterloo, and was afterwards in the 15th Hussars and 6th Dragoon Guards; *d. unm.* 1846.
3. John, *b.* Oct. 1795; *m.* 1st, Anna Waller, dau. of John Parker, by whom he had one son, Arthur, late 79th Highlanders, *b.* 21 June, 1840, and two daus., Mary, *m.* Capt. Hickey, 1st Bengal Lancers, and Elizabeth. He *m.* 2ndly, Elizabeth, dau. of Major Stewart, of the Rifles, by whom he had one son, John Stewart, *b.* Aug. 1856, Capt. South Staffordshire Regt. He *d.* 1859.
4. ROBERT, of whom presently.
1. Elizabeth, *m.* 1806, Henry Brooke, and *d.* 1823.
2. Georgiana, *m.* 1808, George Richard Golding, Capt. 4th Dragoon Guards, dec.
3. Alicia, *m.* 1823, Major-Gen. Oldfield, K.H., dec.
4. Anna, *m.* 1830, Francis Longworth Dames, of Greenhill, King's Co. and *d.* 1835 (*see that family*).

The youngest son,

REV. ROBERT HUME, *m.* 2 June, 1823, Mary, 3rd dau. of Michael Harris, and by her (who *d.* 1862) had issue,

1. ARTHUR, of Dawson Street, Dublin, *b.* 17 Aug. 1824; *m.* 14 June, 1854, Elizabeth, 2nd dau. of Robert F. Rynd, of Ryndville, co. Meath, and has,
   (1) Arthur Robert, Capt. Duke of Wellington's West Riding Regt., *b.* 21 Nov. 1856; *m.* 16 Jan. 1888, Violet Margaret Isabel, only dau. of Major-Gen. Hugh Rowlands, C.B., V.C., of Plastirion, co. Carnarvon.
   (1) Mary.   (2) Florence Elizabeth.
2. GUSTAVUS, of whom presently.
3. Robert (Sir), K.C.B., Lieut.-Gen., Knt. Legion of Honour, *b.* 23 Nov. 1828; *m.* 1872, Jane, dau. of R. Brown, and widow of Capt. Harris, of Indian Army. He *d.* 1909.
4. John Richard, Major-Gen. (retired), Knt. Legion of Honour.
5. Walter, Capt. late 38th Regt.
1. Elizabeth, *m.* G. D. Pakenham, late Capt. 4th Bengal Light Cavalry.

The 2nd son,

LIEUT.-COL. SIR GUSTAVUS HUME, Knt. of the Legion of Honour, Lieut. of Hon. Corps Gentlemen-at-Arms, *b.* 1826; *d.* 16 June, 1891; *m.* 18 July, 1857, Ellen Caroline (now Lady Hume-Gore) elder dau. and eventually co-heir of Charles Vernon and his wife Mrs. Vernon-Gore, and had issue (*see above*).

Seat—Derryluskan, co. Tipperary.   **Residence**—21, Royal York Crescent, Clifton, Bristol.

GORE OF FEDNEY.

WILLIAM CRAMPTON CRAWFORD GORE, of Fedney, co. Down, *b.* 24 Oct. 1871.

Lineage.—WILLIAM GORE, of Goremount, *b.* 1765; *m.* 1st, 1809, Mary Crawford, by whom (who *d.* 1813) he had a son,
WILLIAM, his heir.

He *m.* 2ndly, 8 Oct. 1816, Anna Sinclair Pollock, by whom he had further issue. His eldest son,

WILLIAM GORE, of Fedney, *b.* 12 May, 1812; *m.* 1837, Elizabeth Crawford, and *d.* March, 1848, leaving issue,
1. WILLIAM, of Fedney.
2. Crawford, *b.* 1824, dec.
1. Henriette Agnes, *m.* Thomas Moriarty, only son of Henry Moriarty, of Abbeytown, co. Roscommon, and has issue.

The elder son,

WILLIAM GORE, of Fedney, J.P. for co. Fermanagh, formerly Lieut. 13th Hussars, *b.* 22 March, 1838; *m.* 13 Sept. 1860, Dorothea Henrietta Waller (*d.* 7 May, 1907), dau. of Rev. Josiah Crampton, late Rector of Killesher, co. Fermanagh, and grand-dau. of the late Sir Philip Crampton, M.D., 1st bart., and had issue,

1. WILLIAM CRAMPTON CRAWFORD, his heir.
1. Elizabeth Dorothea, *m.* R. H. Darling, Rector of Kilpeacon, near Limerick.
2. Alice Florence, *m.* Edmund D'Olier, of Knocklinn, Bray, co. Wicklow.
3. Marion.

Mr. Gore *d.* 18 May, 1886.

Residence—Glenbrook, Enniskerry, co. Wicklow.

GORE. *See* BURKE'S PEERAGE, **ARRAN, E.**
ORMSBY-GORE. *See* BURKE'S PEERAGE, **HARLECH, B.**

GRACE. *See* BURKE'S PEERAGE, **GRACE, Bart.**

GRACE OF MANTUA. *See* **BOWEN OF MANTUA.**

GRADWELL OF PLATTEN HALL.

GEORGE FITZGERALD GRADWELL, of Platten Hall, co. Meath, J.P., *b.* 14 April, 1852; *m.* 25 Nov. 1896, Sarah, dau. of Francis William Leland, of Littlegrange, co. Louth, J.P., and has issue,
1. GEORGE FRANCIS, *b.* 29 Nov. 1898.
2. John Augustine, *b.* 2 June, 1900.
3. Francis William Edward, *b.* 21 June, 1902.

Lineage.—ROBERT GRADWELL, of Clifton, co. Lancs., *m.* Alice Holden, had a dau., Ann, who *m.*—Graystock; and a son,

RICHARD GRADWELL, of Clifton, *b.* 1701, who *m.* Ann Holden, and had issue,
1. Robert, who *d.* at the age of 21.
2 JOHN, of whose descendants we treat.
1. Helen, *m.* William Brown, and had issue, George Brown, D.D., first Catholic Bishop of Liverpool; Richard Brown; and Helen.
2. Dorothy.   3. Alice.

Richard Gradwell *d.* 1751. His 2nd son,

JOHN GRADWELL, of Clifton, *b.* 1749; *m.* 12 Oct. 1774, Margaret, dau. and heiress of John Gregson, of Balderstone, co. Lancaster, and by her (who *d.* 25 July, 1827) had issue,
1. Richard, of Clifton, *b.* 4 Aug. 1775; *m.* 1798. Jane Marsh, of Hindley, and *d.* 28 Oct. 1843, leaving an only child and heiress, Margaret, who inherited the Clifton and Balderstone property, and *m.* Richard Carr, of Preston; she *d.* 13 Sept. 1831.
2. John, who *d. unm.*
3. Robert, a Bishop in the Catholic Church, dec.
4. GEORGE, of whom presently.
5. Henry, Vicar-General Catholic Church, dec.
1. Ann, *d.* 1869.

Mr. Gradwell *d.* 21 April, 1829. His 4th son,

GEORGE GRADWELL, of Preston, co. Lancaster, Director of a bank there, Col. of Volunteers, and J.P., *b.* at Clifton, 6 Feb. 1779; *m.* 29 June, 1819, Mary, dau. of Richard Ashhurst, of Puddington, co. Chester, by Helen his wife, dau. of Richard Blundell, whose father was Richard Blundell, of Carside. By her (who *d.* 9 April, 1848) he had issue,
1. JOHN JOSEPH of whom next.
2. RICHARD, ancestor of Gradwell of Dowth Hall (*see that family*).
3. Robert (Right Rev.), Monsignor, Private Chaplain to H.H. the Pope, *b.* 1825; *d.* 16 May, 1906.
4. George (Rev.), *b.* 8 June, 1827; *d.* 1855.
5. Henry Joseph, *b.* 5 Nov., 1830; *d.* 1 Jan., 1831.
1. Mary Ann, *m.* 1 Oct. 1839, James Gernon, of Athcarne Castle, co. Meath, and *d.* 1848 (*see that family*).

Mr. Gradwell *d.* 1 Dec. 1849. The eldest son,

JOHN JOSEPH GRADWELL, of Platten Hall, co. Meath, J.P., High Sheriff of Drogheda, 1855, *b.* 22 April, 1822; *m.* 17 June, 1851, Ellen Mary, dau. of Peter Nugent Fitzgerald, of Soho, co. Westmeath. She *d.* 19 March, 1900. He *d.* 27 July, 1873. leaving issue,
1. GEORGE FITZGERALD, now of Platten Hall, co. Meath, J.P.
2. John Stephen, *b.* 1862.
3. Gerald Peter, *b.* 1866; *m.* 14 June, 1904, Ada, only dau. of late Joseph Alexander, of Enniskillen.
   1. Ellen Mary.   2. Cecilia.
   3. Mary Margaret.   4. Henrietta Maria.

Arms—*See* GRADWELL *of Dowth Hall*.
Seat—Platten Hall, Drogheda, co. Meath.

GRADWELL OF DOWTH HALL.

ROBERT BERNARD GEORGE ASHHURST GRADWELL, of Dowth Hall, co. Meath, and Carlanstown, co. Westmeath, J.P., late Capt. and Hon. Major 5th Batt. Leinster Regt. (Royal Meath Militia), High Sheriff co. Meath 1892; *b.* 2 July, 1858; *m.* 21 April, 1884, Lady Henrietta Maria Plunkett, younger dau. of Arthur James, 10th Earl of Fingall.

Lineage. — RICHARD GRADWELL, of Dowth Hall, co. Meath, and Carlanstown, co. Westmeath, J.P., 2nd son of George Gradwell, of Preston, Lancs. (*see* GRADWELL *of Platten Hall*), *b.* 29 April, 1824; *m.* 13 April, 1852, Maria Theresa, elder

Graham. THE LANDED GENTRY. 274

dau. of James MacEvoy, of Tobertynan, co. Meath, by Theresa his wife, youngest dau. and co-heir of Sir Joshua Colles Meredyth, Bart., and had issue,
1. ROBERT BERNARD GEORGE ASHHURST, now of Dowth Hall.
1. Theresa Henrietta, *m.* 20 Dec. 1877, Hon. Richard Anthony Nugent, of Stacumney, co. Kildare, and Ballymacoll, co. Meath, youngest son of Anthony Francis, 9th Earl of Westmeath, and has issue (*see* BURKE'S *Peerage*).
2. Annette Mary, *m.* 26 Oct. 1881, Edmund Lynch Athy, of Renville, co. Galway, and has issue (*see that family*).
Mr. Gradwell *d.* 28 Oct. 1884.

Arms—Or two foxes courant in pale ppr. in the centre chief point a rose gu. **Crest**—A stag trippant ppr. collared and chained or, charged with a rose gu. **Motto**—Nil desperandum.
Seat—Dowth Hall, Slane, co. Meath.

GRAHAM late OF DRUMGOON.

HECTOR ROBERT LUSHINGTON GRAHAM, of Ballinakill, Letterfrack co. Galway, *b.* 12 May, 1888; *m.* 1909, Ellen Violet Maudsley, only dau. of late Charles Francis Silcock.

Lineage.—ROBERT GRAHAM *m.* Elizabeth, dau. of Robert Armstrong, of Drumrallagh, co. Fermanagh, and had issue, a son.
FRANCIS GRAHAM, of Drumgoon; he aided in raising, and commanded as Capt. a troop of Yeomanry Cavalry in the Rebellion of 1798; *m.* Edessa, dau. of John Boyd, of co. Tyrone, and dying 1826, left issue,
1. ROBERT, of Drumgoon.
2. William, Col. in the Army, *m.* Maria, dau. of — French.
1. Eliza, *m.* Robert Brownrigg, of Norrismount, co. Wexford.
The elder son,
ROBERT GRAHAM, of Drumgoon, and of Ballinakill, co. Galway, *b.* May, 1786; *m.* 1st, Elizabeth, dau. of John Davis, of Summerhill, co. Kilkenny. She *d.* Feb. 1815, leaving issue. He *m.* 2ndly, Jane, dau. and heiress of John Speer, of Desert Creight, co. Tyrone, and *d.* Nov. 1865, having by his first wife had a son,
FRANCIS JOHN GRAHAM, of Drumgoon, co. Fermanagh, J.P. cos. Fermanagh and Galway, D.L. co. Fermanagh, High Sheriff co. Tyrone 1856, co. Fermanagh 1858 and 1887, and for co. Galway, 1893; *b.* 14 Feb. 1815; *m.* 3 April, 1879, Minna, 2nd dau. of the late Charles Hugh Lushington, of Rodmersham, co. Kent, and *d.* 21 Dec. 1902, leaving issue,
HECTOR ROBERT LUSHINGTON, his heir.

Arms—Or, a rose gu. barbed and seeded ppr., on a chief sa., three escallops of the first. **Crest**—An arm embowed vested az. cuffed arg., the hand ppr., grasping a staff raguly gu. **Motto**—Ratio mihi sufficit.
Seat—Ballinakill Lodge, Letterfrack, co. Galway.

GRAHAM OF LARCHFIELD.

OGILVIE BLAIR GRAHAM, of Larchfield, co. Down, late Capt, 5th Batt. Royal Irish Rifles, *b.* 3 July, 1865; *m.* 25 July, 1890, Grace Cottenham, dau. of the Right Hon. John Young, of Galgorn Castle, co. Antrim, and has issue,
1. OGILVIE BLAIR, *b.* 8 July, 1891.
2. Quintin Dick, *b.* 4 July, 1895.
3. Patrick Charles.

Lineage. — JOHN GRAHAM, settled in the co. Derry, near Magherafelt, 1768. He *m.* 1771, Mary, eldest dau. of Quintin Dick, of the Garry, near Ballymena, co. Antrim, and niece of John Campbell, of Donegal Palace, Belfast, Banker, and Ardfechan, Shankhill, and by her had four sons and two daus.,
1. John, *m.* 1800, his cousin, Mary Dick, and *d.* 1806. She *d.* 1808.
2. Hugh, in the Navy.
3. Quintin, *d.* aged 26.
4. CAMPBELL, of whom presently.
1. Mary, *m.* Andrew McLean.
2. Elizabeth (Mrs. Caird).
The fourth son,
CAMPBELL GRAHAM, of Belfast, *m.* 1806, Helen Jemima, dau. of James Blair Ogilvie,* of Ballyloran, co. Antrim, R.N., and by her (who *d.* 1851) had issue,
1. John, of Parade House, Cowes, I. of W., *b.* 1807; *d.* 1880; *m.* 1st, Agnes Russell, 2nd dau. of John Russell, of Edenderry, co. Down, by whom he had two children, who *d.* infants; 2ndly, Georgina Hawthorne, dau. of late Col. Hawthorne, of Belcamp, co. Dublin, and by her (who *d.* 1861) had no issue. He *m.* 3rdly, 16 March, 1866, Annie Maria, dau. of Frederick Evill, of Bath, and had issue,
1. John Ogilvie, Lieut. R.N., *b.* 1 April, 1871.
2. Campbell Frederick, C.M. Rifles, *b.* 17 June, 1872; *m.* 31 Dec. 1906, Frances Elizabeth, dau. of H. G. Cheesman, and has issue,
(1) Campbell Norwood, *b.* 8 Aug. 1908.
(2) Henry Rudolph, *b.* 29 March, 1910.
3. Hugh Hawthorn, *b.* 23 Aug. 1874; *d.* Sept. 1879.
1. Mary, *m.* 28 Dec. 1894, George Archdale, of Dromard, and has issue (*see* ARCHDALE *of Castle Archdale*).
2. Margaret Sarah, *d.* 1888.
3. Helen Ogilvie.
2. OGILVIE BLAIR, late of Larchfield.
3. Campbell, in the Army, *b.* 1823; *d.* *unm.*
1. Margaret Jane, *d.* *unm.*
2. Maria, *m.* Rev. Francis Dobbs, and has issue.
3. Elizabeth, *d.* 4. Dorothea, *d.*
5. Dorothea, *d.* 6. Helen Jemima.
7. Dorothea, *d.*
Mr. Graham *d.* 30 June, 1834. His 2nd son,
OGILVIE BLAIR GRAHAM, of Larchfield, co. Down, J.P. and D.L., High Sheriff for Antrim 1883, and for Down 1884, *b.* 12 Feb. 1820; *m.* 11 Dec. 1861, Louise Sara, dau. of Ambrose Lanfear, of New Orleans, U.S., by Mary Hills, his wife, and great-grand-dau. of Capt. Hayes, R.N. She *d.* 3 Feb. 1907. He *d.* 5 Aug. 1897, leaving issue,
1. OGILVIE BLAIR, now of Larchfield.
2. Charles Lanfear, Major 4th Hussars, and late Adj. Beds. Imp. Yeom., *b.* 10 Sept. 1866; *m.* 3 Dec. 1892, Constance Dennistown, dau. of David P. Sellar, of 68, Prince's Gate, London, and Dudbrook, co. Essex, and has issue,
1. Charles Gordon Norrie, Cadet R.N., *b.* 6 Sept. 1893.
2. John Rowan, *b.* 15 July, 1895; *d.* 6 Oct. 1895.
3. Charles Plenderleath, *b.* 26 July, 1898.
1. Constance Mary Lanfear, 17 Dec. 1899.
1. Helen Gertrude, *m.* 1 June, 1893, Hugh Gerald Brenan, Lieut. Royal Irish Rifles, son of the late Gerald Brenan.
2. Marie Louise, *m.* 7 Jan. 1890, Thomas Gisborne Gordon, and has issue (*see* GORDON *of Florida Manor*).
3. Emily Gwendolyn, *m.* 16 June, 1898, Major H. B. Lynch, Dorset Regt., only son of Lieut.-Gen. Lynch, K.L.I., of Partry, co. Mayo (*see that family*).

Seat—Larchfield, Lisburn, co. Down.

GRANT OF KILMURRY.

THOMAS ST. JOHN GRANT, of Kilmurry, co. Cork, District Magistrate, Orange River Colony, *b.* 1 Dec. 1874; *m.* 25 Jan. 1905, Katherine Sophia, dau. of Col. W. Cooke-Collis, D.L., of Castle Cooke (*see that family*).

Lineage.—The first of this family of whom any documentary accounts are handed down, was CAPT. JASPER GRANT, R.N., who obtained, 1667, an assignment of a mortgage of the lands of Grantstown, or Ballygraunt (therein then so called), and in the following year, 1668, had a conveyance in fee of the same from William Dobbyn. In this document he is described as Capt. Jasper Grant, of the City of Waterford. Capt. Jasper Grant, R.N., of Grantstown, *m.* some time about 1667, Gillian Hely, of Kinsale, sister of Francis Hely, afterwards of the City of Cork, and had a son,
JASPER GRANT, *m.* Annabella Fitzgerald, and was father of
JASPER GRANT, of Kilmurry, co. Cork, *m.* James Vaughan, of the family of Golden Grove, but left no issue, and was s. by his brother,
THOMAS GRANT, of Kilmurry, *m.* 29 July, 1719, Anne, dau. of James Usher, of Taylorstown, co. Waterford. Their son,
THOMAS GRANT, of Kilmurry, *m.* 11 Oct. 1748, Elizabeth, dau. of Thomas Campion, of Leitrim, and was father of
THOMAS GRANT, of Kilmurry, *m.* 28 Nov. 1792, Sarah, sister of Sir Richard Musgrave, Bart. of Tourin, co. Waterford, and was s. by his son,
THOMAS JOHN GRANT, of Kilmurry, *m.* Sept. 1821, his cousin Anna Esther, dau. of the Rev. Alexander Grant, Vicar of Clondu-

---

* His grandfather,
REV. WILLIAM OGILVIE, who was descended from the Airlie family, came from Scotland about 1700, *m.* Jane, dau. of Patrick Agnew, of Kilwaughter Castle, co. Antrim, and had a son,
WILLIAM OGILVIE, *m.* Elizabeth, 6th dau. of Major James Blair, of Blairmount (who defended the Bishop's Gate at the siege of Derry in 1688), and had a son,
JAMES BLAIR OGILVIE, of Ballyloran, co. Antrim, *m.* his first cousin, Margaret, dau. of William Shaw, of Doagh, and Dorothy his wife, 9th dau. of Major James Blair, of Blairmount, and had issue,
1. HELEN JEMIMA, *m.* as above CAMPBELL GRAHAM, of Belfast.
2. Elizabeth, of Doagh (or Merville), near Belfast.
3. Dorothea, *m.* 1st, 1802, her cousin, James Blair, of Blairmount (son of Major James Blair above-mentioned). He *d.s.p.* 14 Nov. 1817. She *m.* 2ndly, Major Rowan, of Mount Davys, co. Antrim.

Jane, and d. 17 Jan. 1832. leaving, with three daus. (Sarah, m. Samuel Morton Tuckey, of Killindonnell, co. Cork ; Anna ; and Susan Mary, m. Monsieur François Jules Turquet, Judge of the Cour Impériale, Angers, France), a son and heir,
  THOMAS ST. JOHN GRANT, of Kilmurry, J.P. and D.L., High Sheriff co. Waterford, 1852. and co. Cork, 1858, b. 20 Sept. 1822 ; m. 15 Aug. 1849, Eliza Anna Louisa, yongest dau. of the Rev. Thomas Hoare, of Glenamore, by Mary Anne, dau. of Henry Jesse Lloyd, of Lloydsboro' co. Tipperary, and grand-dau. of Sir Edward Hoare, Bart. of Annabella, and d. 18 Sept. 1868, leaving issue.
  1. THOMAS ST. JOHN, of Kilmurry.
  2. Edward Hoare, b. 4 May, 1859 ; m. June, 1888, Lena Colliachoune, and has issue,
  Lena Clotilda, b. June, 1889.
The elder son,
  THOMAS ST. JOHN GRANT, of Kilmurry, co. Cork, J.P., b. 25 Sept. 1852 ; d. 7 July, 1899 ; m. 4 Feb. 1874, Margaret Anna, 2nd dau. and co-heir of Edward Keily Carey, of Careysville, co. Cork, by his wife Margaret, eldest dau. of the late Capt. Cooke-Collis, of Castle Cooke (see that family), and had issue,
  1. THOMAS ST. JOHN, now of Kilmurry.
  2. Edward Keily Carey, b. 29 Aug. 1877.
  Seat—Kilmurry House, Kilworth, co. Cork.

GRAVES OF CLOGHAN CASTLE.

ROBERT KENNEDY GROGAN GRAVES, of Cloghan Castle, King's Co., M.R.C.S., L.R.C.P., b. 1 Jan. 1878; m. 16 Oct. 1906. Kathleen Gladys Mary, dau. of late George William, of Buckley Hall, Rochdale.

Lineage.—JOHN GRAVES, Burgess of the City of Limerick, temp. Queen ANNE, was Sheriff of that city 1719. He left by Anny his wife, two sons and a dau.,
  1. JAMES (Rev.), of whom hereafter.
  2. Richard, Sheriff of the city of Limerick 1735; m. Miss Jane Meggs, and had a son,
  Harry Meggs, Rector of Templemore, co. Tipperary.
  1. Abigail.
The elder son,
  REV. JAMES GRAVES, Rector of Gilfinnan and Darragh, co. Limerick, b. 18 Nov. 1713 ; m. 8 March, 1744, Jane, dau. of Rev. Thomas Ryder, Rector of Mitchelstown, co. Cork, and had issue,
  1. THOMAS (Very Rev.), Scholar of Trin. Coll. Dublin, 1763, appointed Dean of Ardfert 1802, and of Connor 1811, b. 3 March, 1745 ; m. 21 Nov. 1771, Ann, dau. of John Dunlevie, and by her (who d. 17 June, 1814, aged 63) he left at his decease, 30 Sept. 1828,
    1. JAMES WILLIAM, Major-Gen. in the Army and Col. Commanding 18th Royal Irish, b. 1774 ; m. at Trinidad 1802, Miss Marie Victoire Black, and d. 1845, having had issue,
      (1) Thomas Cockburn, Lieut. 18th Royal Irish, d. 1835.
      (2) James William, Lieut.-Col. in the Army and Staff Officer of Pensioners, m. 1849, Katherine Anne, 4th dau. of James Wood Wright, Gola, co. Monaghan, and d. 5 Oct. 1894.
      (3) John Crosbie, Col. 3rd Bombay Cavalry, m. Miss Mary Montgomery.
      (4) William Henry, Major 18th Royal Irish, m. Antoinetta, dau. of George Deane, of Harwich. She d. his widow 23 March, 1900.
      (5) Robert Stannus, Lieut. 66th Bengal Native Infantry, m. 1854, Miss A. J. King.
      (6) Alexander Hope, 18th Royal Irish, m. Marianna, dau. of George Deane, of Harwich.
      (1) Clotilda Bona, m. Major Robert Stannus, 29th Regt.
      (2) Anna Victoria, m. 1st, C. Croker, of Downdaniel, co. Cork ; and 2ndly, Lieut. H. Ainslie, R.N.
      (3) Emily Georgiana, d. unm. 1871.
      (4) Frances Charlotte, d. unm. 1871.
      (5) Mary Arabella.
      (6) Annabella, m. 1st, 1842, Capt. H. W. Magee, 45th Regt. ; and 2ndly, J. Rudge, who d. 1856.
      (7) Josephine Lacoste, m. 1848, Capt. George G. Bowring.
    2. John Crosbie, b. 2 July, 1776 ; m. 1806, Helena, eldest dau. and consecrated Bishop of Limerick 29 June, 1866 ; b. 6 Dec. 1812 ; m. 15 Sept. 1840, Selina, dau. of John Cheyne, M.D., Physician-General to the Forces in Ireland. She d. 15 Nov. 1873. He d. 17 July, 1899, leaving issue,

  1. John Cheyne, Indian Civil Service, b. 16 Nov. 1841 ; d. 9 Sept. 1868.
  2. Alfred Perceval, of Red Branch House, Wimbledon, and Erinfa, Harlech, M.A., late H.M. Inspector of Schools, b. 22 July, 1846 ; m. 1st, 29 Dec. 1874, Jane, dau. of James Cooper, of Cooper Hill, and by her (who d. 24 March, 1886) has,
    a. Philip Perceval, b. 25 Feb. 1876.
    b. Richard Massie, b. 14 Sept. 1880.
    c. Alfred Perceval, b. 14 Dec. 1881.
    a. Mary, m. 3 Sept. 1903, Arthur S. Preston, of Alexandria.
    b. Susan Winthrop Savatier, m. 12 July, 1910, Kenneth Macaulay, of Alexandria, son of late William Morison Macaulay, of Horsham.
  He m. 2ndly, 30 Dec. 1891, Amalie Elisabeth Sophie, eldest dau. of Professor Henrich von Ranke, of Munich, and has further issue,
    d. Robert Ranke, b. 24 July, 1895.
    e. Charles Patrick Ranke, b. 1 Dec. 1899.
    f. John Tiarks Ranke, b. 24 Feb. 1903.
    c. Clarissa Janie.   d. Rosaleen Louise.
  3. Arnold Felix, M.A., Barrister-at-Law, one of the Secretaries of Charitable Donations and Bequests, Ireland, b. 17 Nov. 1847; m. Constance Weatherley, and had Lionel Perceval, Arnold, Eric, Algernon and Geraldine.
  4. Charles Larcom, b. 15 Dec. 1856 ; m. 30 July, 1889, Alice Emma, eldest dau. of Lieut.-Col. George Henry Grey (see BURKE'S Peerage and Baronetage), and has issue,
    Cecil, b. 4 March, 1892.
    Adrian, b. 1896.
  5. Robert Wyndham, C.M.G., H.M. Consul-Gen. for Macedonia, at Salonika, b. 6 July, 1858 ; m. 1895, Elizabeth Catherine, dau. of the late J. Remmer Thomson, of Constantinople. She d. 20 March, 1902, leaving issue,
    Gerald Graham Gordon, b. 19 March, 1899.
  1. Helena Cecilia, m. 7 Aug. 1869, Lieut.-Col. Henry Littleton Powys (see BURKE'S Peerage, LILFORD, B.), and d. 27 June, 1886.
  2. Rosamund Selina, m. 3 July, 1877, Rear-Admiral Sir Richard Massie Blomfield, K.C.M.G., and has issue.
  3. Augusta Caroline.
  4. Ida Margaret, m. 14 Sept. 1885, Rear-Adm. Sir Richard Poore, 4th bart. of Rushall, and has issue (see BURKE'S Peerage).
  (1) Helena Clarissa, m. 1843, Leopold von Ranke, of Berlin, the Historian, and d. 1871, leaving issue.
  (2) Caroline, b. 1819, d. 1855.
  3. Thomas Ryder, b. 1784 ; had a son, Thomas William.
  4. William Henry, Capt. 18th Royal Irish, b. 1794 ; m. Julia Blosome.
    1. Arabella, b. 1773, d. 1850.   2. Anne, b. 1787.
  2. James William, R.N., b. 1747 ; m. 1st, Miss Fawson, by whom he had two sons, James and Thomas, and a dau. Elizabeth, m. Dr. O'Flaherty. He m. 2ndly, Miss Hilliard, by whom he had a son, Robert, and two daus., Jane, m. Mr. Roche, and Harriet, m. her cousin, Thomas Ryder Graves.
  3. John (Rev.), Rector of Ballingarry, m. 1st, Miss Ryves, by whom he had a son, 1. James William, who m. and had twenty-one children. He m. 2ndly, Miss Baker, by whom he had,
    2. John Baker, of Fortwilliam, co. Wexford, J.P., a Judge in Ceylon, m. 1st, Louisa, 2nd dau. of Robert Bellew, of Castle Martyr (see BURKE'S Extinct Peerage), and had issue,
      (1) John Bellew.
      (1) Frances Sarah, m. 1st, 6 March, 1839, Mumford Campbell, of Sutton Place, Sutton, Kent, and 2ndly, 17 April, 1856, Thomas Horn Fleet, of Darenth Grange. He d. 19 April, 1897, leaving issue (see that family). She d. 8 April, 1910.
      (2) Sydney.
    He m. 2ndly, 1827, Anne, dau. of James Howlin, of Ballycronegan (see that family).
    3. Hugh Ryves, m. Miss Marshall.
    4. Thomas Ryder, m. his cousin, Harriet, dau. of James William Graves.
    5. Harry Meggs, Major-Gen. Indian Army, m. and had issue.
    6. Richard.   7. William.
    1. Mabella, m. Rev. John Croker.   2. Jane.
    3. Sydney, m. Frederick Elderton.
    4. Katherine.   5. Sybella.
    6. Margaret, m. — Drought.   7. Bessie.
  4. RICHARD (Very Rev.), of whom hereafter.
  1. Patty, d. unm.   2. Anne, d. unm.
The Rev. James Graves d. Nov. 1783. His 4th son,
  VERY REV. RICHARD GRAVES, D.D., Dean of Ardagh, Fellow of Trin. Coll. Dublin, Regius Professor of Divinity, author of celebrated Theological Works, b. Oct. 1763 ; m. Eliza Mary, dau. of Rev. Dr. Drought, Professor of Divinity, and had issue,
    1. James, d. 1794.
    2. Richard Hastings (Rev.), D.D., Rector of Brigown, co. Cork, d. unm. 1877.
    3. Hercules Henry, d. unm.
    4. ROBERT JAMES, of whom hereafter.
    1. Eliza, m. 1st, Dr. Meredyth, F.T.C.D. ; and 2ndly, — Burton.
    2. Jane, m. Rev. Richard McDonnell, D.D., Provost of Trin. Coll. Dublin.
    3. Ann, m. 1st, Edward Johnson, of Bollynacash, and 2ndly, John Mayne.
    4. Harriet, m. 5 March, 1821. Matthew Brinkley, son of Bishop Brinkley, and had issue (see BRINKLEY of Fortland).
    5. Arabella, d. unm.
The Dean d. 31 March, 1829. His 4th son,

S 2

ROBERT JAMES GRAVES, of Merrion Square, Dublin, M.D., F.R.S., *m.* 1st, Miss Jane Eustace; 2ndly, Sarah, dau. of Right Rev. John Brinkley, D.D., Bishop of Cloyne, and 3rdly, Anna, dau. of Rev. William Grogan, of Slaney Park. He *d.* 1853, leaving issue by his 3rd wife,

1. Richard Drought (Rev.), *m.* 1856, Henrietta Katharine, dau. of Henry Mussenden Leathes, of Herringfleet Hall, Suffolk, and had issue,
   1. Robert de Mussenden, *b.* 27 Aug. 1859; *d.* same year.
   2. Richard Henry de Mussenden, twin with Robert, *d.* 1860.
   1. Georgina Mary, *m.* 1887, Alexander Hamilton Synge (*see* SYNGE *of Glanmore*).
2. WILLIAM GROGAN, of Cloghan Castle.
   1. Georgina Arabella, *m.* 25 Aug. 1857, Edward Blackburne, of Rathfarnham Castle, co. Dublin, Q.C., J.P.
   2. Eliza Mary, *m.* Thomas P. St. George Armstrong, J.P.
   3. Olivia Drew, *m.* J. Cassie Hatton, of Montreal, Q.C.
   4. Florence Belinda, *m.* 15 Jan. 1880, Maj.-Gen. Lawrence Worthington Parsons, C.B., R.A..

The 2nd son,
COLONEL WILLIAM GROGAN GRAVES, of Cloghan Castle, J.P. and D.L., High Sheriff, Lieut.-Col. Comm. 82nd (South Lancashire) Regt., *b.* 14 Feb. 1836; *m.* 1877, Georgina, 2nd dau. of Rev. Joseph Marshall, R.N., J.P., of Baronne Court, co. Tipperary, Baron de Prigny de Quérieux, in France, by Sophia his wife, dau. of Hugh Kennedy, of Cultra, co. Down, and by her (who *m.* 2ndly, 17 Oct. 1891, James Kingston Barton, J.P., of Green Hill, co. Kilkenny, by whom she has a son, Michael Kennedy Barton, *b.* 3 Oct. 1895) left two sons,

1. ROBERT KENNEDY GROGAN, now of Cloghan Castle.
2. William Geoffrey Plantagenet, Lieut. R.N., *b.* 22 May, 1881, drowned from H.M.S. *Gladiator* in collision in Solent, 25 April, 1908, *unm.*

Seat—Cloghan Castle, Banagher, King's Co.

GRAY, late OF GRAYMOUNT.

HAROLD WILLIAM STANNUS GRAY, formerly of Graymount, co. Antrim, J.P., High Sheriff 1895, *b.* 1867; *m.* 11 Jan. 1894, his cousin Rowena Elizabeth Dorothea, dau. of Thomas Robert Stannus, of Maghraleave, Lisburn, co. Antrim, J.P. (*see* STANNUS *of Carlingford*), and has issue,

TERENCE JAMES STANNUS, *b.* 14 Sept. 1895.

Lineage.—GEORGE GRAY, of Graymount, co. Antrim, was father of
WILLIAM GRAY, of Graymount, *m.* Mary Ann, dau. of James Harden, of Harrybrooke, D.L. co. Armagh, and was *s.* by his son,
GEORGE GRAY, of Graymount, co. Antrim, J.P. and D.L., High Sheriff in 1859, late Major Antrim Militia Artillery, *b.* 1816; *m.* 8 Feb. 1866, Elizabeth Emily Sophia, dau. of Very Rev. James Stannus, Dean of Ross (*see* STANNUS *of Carlingford*), and had issue,
1. HAROLD WILLIAM STANNUS, now of Graymount.
1. Millicent Georgina Mabel.
2. Beatrice Caroline Geraldine.

He *d.* 14 March, 1879.

Seats—Gog Magog Hills, Cambridgeshire, and Glenada House, Newcastle, co. Down.

GRAY late OF ENAGH.

ROBERT GRAY, late of Enagh, co. Armagh, J.P., F.R.C.P.I., *b.* 18 Oct. 1845; *m.* 10 July, 1867, Harriet Ann, dau. of Hampton Atkinson, and has issue,

1. HAMPTON ATKINSON, M.D. Trin. Coll. Dublin, *b.* 16 Aug. 1868.
2. Robert Alexander, Major Royal Irish Fusiliers *b.* 21 Dec. 1869.
3. Francis Audwbon, L.R.C.P. and S. Edin., *b.* 2 Jan. 1874.
1. Harriet Alice, *m.* 6 Jan. 1904, Major Henry J. R. St. G. Richardson, of Summer Hill, Clones, J.P., D.L.
2. Margaret Edith, *m.* 2 Sept. 1908, Rev. William Bagot Stack, M.A., youngest son of Right Rev. Bishop Stack, D.D.

Lineage—FRANCIS GRAY, of Enagh, Markethill, co. Armagh, descended from John Gray, who acquired the townlands of Enagh and Edenkennedy in 1698, *d.* 22 March, 1845, aged 95, leaving a son,
ROBERT GRAY, of Enagh, co Armagh, *b.* 13 April, 1808; *m.* 25 Jan. 1844, Margaret Gray, dau. of William Patterson and Margaret Pepper, his wife. She *d.* 31 Jan. 1890. He *d.* 18 March, 1867 leaving a son,
ROBERT, his heir.

Arms—Gu. a lion rampant arg. holding in the dexter paw a fleam or, on a canton of the last a harp az. *Crest*—An anchor in pale az. timbered ppr. and fluked or. *Motto*—Anchor fast anchor.
Residence—4, Charlemont Place, The Mall, Armagh. *Club*—Armagh County.

GREENE, late OF GREENVILLE.

The late LIEUT.-COL. JOHN JOSEPH GREENE, M.B., of Scart, co. Limerick, and of Drumgorey and Knockacoola, co. Waterford, Lieut.-Col. R.A.M.C., served in Afghanistan in 1880 (medal), and in the Soudan 1884-5 (medal with clasp and Khedive's star), present at the operations on the Egyptian frontier in 1886; *b.* 10 Oct. 1848; *d. unm.* 18 Aug. 1899.

Lineage.—CAPTAIN GODFREY GREENE, a "49 officer" (*vide* adjudication in his favour, 1649 officers, Roll I, 22 March, 1666) obtained a patent 23 July, 1678, of Moorestown Castle, co. Tipperary. On 13 Nov. 1662 he acquired from the Earl of Orrery a lease of Old Abbey, co. Limerick. Lord Cork in his diary states that on 3 April, 1633, he purchased Old Abbey from Sir Charles Coote, the "inheritance of which is in lease to one John Greene." This was probably the father of Godfrey Greene above mentioned. He *m.* 1st, 1645, Frances, dau. of Robert Cox, of Bruff, co. Limerick, and by her (who *d.* before 1678) had issue,

1. JOHN, of whom presently.
2. Godfrey, of Moorestown Castle, co. Tipperary, *m.* 17 Nov. 1683, Lydia, dau. of Phanuel Cook, of Garrvngubban, co. Tipperary, and widow of Mathew Jacob, of St. Johnstown, co. Tipperary, and *d.* 9 Jan. 1688, leaving issue,
   1. Godfrey, of Moorestown, *b.* 1686, who was killed at Clonmel, 23 Aug. 1735, in a duel by Baron Keating, *d. unm.* By his will, dated 19 Aug. 1735, he left Moorestown, co. Tipperary, Scart, co. Limerick, and Drumgorey, co. Waterford, to his uncle, JOHN GREENE, of Old Abbey, and his heirs.
      1. Frances, *m.* 14 Feb. 1703, John Cooksey, of Kilkenny, and had issue.
      2. Lydia, *m.* 1st, 16 Jan. 1705, John Nicholson, of Richardstown, co. Tipperary, and had issue. She *m.* 2ndly, Rev. Simon Fortin, of Tubrid, co. Tipperary, and *d.* 1724.
1. Mary, *m.* April, 1671, John Pennefather, of Kilcree, co. Kilkenny, and *d.* 1678, leaving issue.
2. Frances, *m.* Henry Chearnly.

By his 2nd wife (who *d.* Nov. 1681) he had further issue,
3. Thomas, of Low Grange, co. Kilkenny, *m.* 1st, Oct. 1696, Mary, dau. of Anthony Henthorne, of Dublin, and had issue,
   1. Godfrey.   2. Samuel.
   3. Anthony.   4. Thomas.
   1. Elizabeth.   2. Anne.

He *m.* 2ndly, 1709, Susanna, dau. of Richard Nuttall, of Dublin, and *d.* 22 Dec. 1753, leaving issue,
5. Nuttall, of Low Grange, *m.* 6 Jan. 1738, Elizabeth, dau. of Michael Rothe, of Butler's Grove, co. Kilkenny (*see* ROTHE *late of Mount Rothe*), and had an only dau. and heir,
   Letitia, *m.* 1st, 16 Oct. 1764, William Greene, of Kilmanahan Castle, co. Waterford, and 2ndly, 9 March, 1782, John Greene, of Greenville, co. Kilkenny, and *d.* 10 July, 1813, leaving issue,
Joseph, Barrister-at-Law, *d.s.p.* 1777.
Susanna, *m.* William Stotesbury.
4. Rodolphus, of Kilmanahan, co. Waterford, High Sheriff 1717, *m.* Mary, only dau. and heir of Michael Carey, of Ballymackee, co. Waterford, and had issue, with four daus.,
   1. Michael, of Kilnemack, co. Waterford, was *m.* three times, and *d.* Nov. 1756, leaving issue.
   2. Thomas, of Clonmel, *m.* Penelope, dau. of Jeffrey Prendergast, of Croane, co. Tipperary.
   3. Rodolphus, of Kilmanahan, High Sheriff 1744, *m.* 1 May, 1739, Catherine, dau. of Col. William Disney, of Churchtown, co. Waterford, and *d.* 1759, leaving, with other issue, an eldest son,
      William, of Kilmanahan, High Sheriff 1763, *b.* May, 1740; *m.* 16 Oct. 1764, his cousin, Letitia, dau. and heir of Nuttall Greene, of Low Grange (*see above*), and *d.* 24 Nov. 1780, leaving an eldest son,
      Lieut.-Col. Nuttall Greene, of Kilmanahan Castle, D.L., High Sheriff 1810, *b.* 18 Oct. 1769; *m.* 14 Nov. 1806, Charlotte Anne, dau. of William Parsons, of Dublin, and *d.* 15 Oct. 1847, leaving issue, five sons, who *d. unm.*, and nine daus.
5. Robert.   6. Richard.
7. Gilbert, of Ballymackee, co. Waterford, *b.* 1672.
8. Samuel, of Garryduff, co. Tipperary.
3. Susanna.   4. Hannah.
5. Bridget.   6. Deborah.

He *m.* 3rdly, Feb. 1681-2, Elizabeth Gough, and *d.* 13 May, 1682, having had issue.
9. Benjamin, of Dungarvan, co. Waterford, High Sheriff 1721, *b.* 17 Nov. 1682 ; *m.* 17 Nov. 1709, Mary, only dau. of Col. James Roch, of Glynn, co. Waterford (*see* ROCH *of Woodbine Hill*), and *d.* Sept. 1733, having by her (who *d.* 9 Dec. 1727) had issue,
  1. James Roch, of Dungarvan.
  2. Benjamin, of Tallow.
  3. William.
  1. Elizabeth, *m.* Peregrine Butler.

The eldest son,
JOHN GREENE, of Old Abbey, co. Limerick (whose will was proved 10 July, 1746) ; *m.* Catherine, dau. and heiress of Capt. Anthony Horsey, of Kilcroney, co. Kilkenny, and *d.* 5 May, 1745, aged 90, having by her (who *d.* 18 Feb. 1718) had issue,
  1. Pierce, *b.* 1679. killed 12 Nov. 1703 ; *d. unm.*
  2. GODFREY, of whom presently.
  3. George, of Old Abbey, High Sheriff 1732, *m.* 1st, 1723, Elizabeth, dau. of William Waller, of Cully, co. Tipperary. She *d.s.p.* He *m.* 2ndly, 1731, Margaret, dau. of David Crosbie, and widow of Lancelot Sandys, and *d.* 5 March, 1759, having by her (who *d.* 9 Feb. 1759) had, with a dau., Frances, *m.* 6 Dec. 1752, Richard Meredyth, of Rathnalough, co. Kerry, a son,
    John, of Old Abbey, *m.* 30 June, 1758, Catherine (who *d.* 8 Oct. 1798), dau. of Daniel Toler, of Beechwood, co. Tipperary, and sister to John, 1st Earl Norbury, and *d.* 2 March, 1784, leaving a dau.,
      Letitia, *b.* 1761; *m.* 1st, 29 Jan. 1776, Robert Dillon, 1st Baron Clonbrock, and 2ndly, May, 1802, Clement Archer, Pres. R.C.S.I., and *d.* 28 May, 1844.
  4. Richard.
  1. Catherine, *m.* April, 1725, Charles Minchin, eldest son of John Minchin, of Castle Inch.
  2. Elizabeth, *m.* Thomas Blood, of Bohersallagh, co. Clare.
  3. Frances, *m.* — Sweet.

The eldest surviving son,
GODFREY GREENE, of Greenville (formerly Kilcroney), *m.* 4 Oct. 1710, Abigail, eldest dau. of Chichester Phillips, M.P., of Drumcondra Castle, co. Dublin, and *d.* 3 March, 1736, having by her (who *d.* May, 1754) had issue,
  1. JOHN, of whom presently.
  2. William Nassau, of Carlow, afterwards of Kilkea, co. Kildare, *b.* 1714 ; *m.* 1st, 11 Aug. 1739, Amy, dau. of William Westland, of Dublin, and by her (who *d.* 22 Jan. 1761) had four sons,
    1. Godfrey, of Bachelors' Walk, Dublin, *d.s.p.* 31 May, 1768.
    2. William Nassau, *d.* in Calcutta, 1787.
    3. Robert, of Dublin, *m.* 1st, 28 Feb. 1766, Juliana, dau. of — Judge, and had issue, two sons and one dau. He *m.* 2ndly, 6 Jan. 1776, Mary, dau. of William Phillips (who was grandson of Chichester Phillips above mentioned), and had issue, five daus., of whom
      Amy, *b.* 1786 ; *m.* 11 Nov. 1807, her cousin, John Greene, of Millbrook (*see below*).
    4 John, of Millbrook, co. Kildare, High Sheriff 1801, *b.* 1749 ; *m.* 12 June, 1779, Mary Anne, only dau of John Cooper, of Cooper's Hill (*see that family*), and *d.* 28 July, 1819, having by her (who *d.* 24 Aug. 1822) had issue, an eldest surviving son,
      John, of Millbrook, *b.* 1782 ; *m.* 11 Nov. 1807, his cousin Amy, dau. of Robert Greene (*see above*), and *d.* 24 Dec. 1851, having by her (who *d.* 19 Aug. 1818) had issue, an eldest son,
        John, of Milbrook, *b.* 10 Feb. 1810 ; *m.* 21 April, 1836, Anne, dau. of Rev. Thomas Morgan, and *d.* 30 Aug. 1890, having by her (who *d.* 13 Aug. 1845) had an eldest surviving son,
          Thomas, of Millbrook, LL.D., T.C.D., J.P., High Sheriff 1895, *b.* 4 May, 1845 ; *m.* 1st, 15 April, 1863, Editha, dau. of John Bonfield Francis, and by her (who *d.* 2 Aug. 1876) had issue,
            (*a*) John Francis, *b.* 21 Feb. 1867 ; *d. unm.* 12 June, 1889.
            (*b*) Thomas Westland, *b.* 16 Dec. 1870.
            (*c*) Arthur, M.A., M.D. T.C.D., *b.* 3 Jan. 1876; *m.* 22 April, 1903, Wilhelmina Webb, 3rd dau. of Dr. William Wade Winslow, of Sunnyside, Gowna, co. Cavan, and has issue, John and Elizabeth.
            (*a*) Editha, *b.* 13 Jan. 1869.
          He *m.* 2ndly, 28 Aug. 1884, Ida Isabel, dau. of Christopher Carter Foottit. He *d.* 3 Nov. 1901.

Mr. W. N. Greene *m.* 2ndly, by licence, 27 Sept. 1762, Mary Bigg, who *d.* 22 Jan. 1777, having had a dau. who *d.* an infant, March, 1773, bur. at New Abbey. He *d.* 24 Feb. 1781.
  3. Robert.
  1. Catherine, *m.* 11 June, 1736, Humphrey Minchin, of Bushertown, King's Co.   2. Abigail.
  3. Susannah, *m.* 10 April, 1748, William Phillips (*see above*).

The eldest son,
JOHN GREENE, of Greenville, High Sheriff co. Kilkenny 1766, *m.* 1st, 3 Dec. 1737, Frances, dau. of Joseph Nicholson, of Richardstown, co. Tipperary, and widow of — Reynett, and by her (who *d.* 12 Nov. 1756) had issue,
  1. Godfrey, Barrister-at-Law, M.P. for Dungarvan 1778-90, sometime Accountant-Gen. to the Chancery, and Receiver-Gen. of the Stamp Duties, *b.* 6 May, 1742 ; *d. unm.* 16 April, 1793.
  2. JOHN, of whom presently.
  3. Joseph, of Shandon, and of Newtown House, co. Waterford Capt. 40th Regt. and Major in the Army, *b.* 22 Sept. 1746; *m.* 1st, Hannah Townsend, and by her (who *d.* 7 May, 1797) had issue,
    1. William, Lieut.-Col. R.A. ; *d. unm.* Nov. 1834.

    2. Joseph, Lieut. 25th Bengal N.I., *b.* 1789 ; *d. unm.* 21 Aug. 1814.
    3. Godfrey, Lieut. 34th Regt., *b.* 20 May, 1789 ; *d. unm.* 29 Nov. 1803.
    4. John, of Straw Hall, co. Carlow, Capt. 85th Regt., *b.* 1796 ; *m.* Eliza, dau. of John Philipps-Lougharne, of Orlandon, co. Pembroke, and *d.* 4 Sept. 1840, having by her (who *d.* 21 April, 1867) had issue.
    5. Thomas, Capt. R.N., *b.* 1799 ; *m.* 29 Jan. 1842, Elizabeth Anne, dau. of Denis MacCarthy, of Mosgrove, co. Cork, and *d.s.p.* 18 Aug. 1875. She *d.* 28 March, 1889.
    1. Frances, *m.* 24 Aug. 1820, Sir Edmund Skottowe.
    2. Catherine, *d. unm.* 3 June, 1814.
    3. Martha, *m.* 13 June, 1811, Rev. Edward Hunt, Rector of Dunkitt.
    4. Emma, *m.* 5 March, 1817, Rev. R. Jones Hobson, Archdeacon of Waterford.
    5. Hannah, *d. unm.* 16 June, 1813.

He *m.* 2ndly, Catherine, dau. of Jeremiah Foley, of Dungarvan, and *d.* 23 Nov. 1830, having by her (who *d.* 9 Jan. 1822) had issue,
  6. Joseph George, *b.* 29 Sept. 1806 ; *m.* 5 Oct. 1828, Maria, dau. and co-heir of William McKenzie, and *d.* 26 March, 1877, having by her had issue,
    (1) George, M.D. Edin., *b.* 29 Oct. 1837 ; *d.* Aug. 1874, leaving issue.
    (2) Richard, of Mont de la Rocque, St. Aubins, Jersey, C.I., *b.* 28 June, 1843 ; *m.* 10 March, 1877, Emma, dau. of James Rhodes, of Bradford, and widow of Edward Dickin, of Shipley, Yorks, and has issue.
      George Watters, M.A., M.D. Camb. (*Sidwell, Gerrard's Cross, Bucks*), *b.* 3 May, 1878 ; *m.* 24 April, 1906. Priscilla Mabel, dau. of A. H. Clapbam, of Thureby, Woodford Bridge, Essex, and has issue.
      John Richard, *b.* 6 March, 1911.
      Dorothy Norah Hilda, *b.* 4 April, 1907.
      Alice Norah Gertrude, *b.* 15 Oct. 1879.
  7. Richard Francis (Rev.), *b.* 1807 ; *d. unm.* 14 Feb. 1839.
  6. Mary Anne, *b.* 1803.
  7. Jane, *b.* 1805, a nun ; *d.* 11 Sept. 1845.

  4. William, of Lota, co. Cork, and of Janeville, co. Waterford, Major H.E.I.C.S., High Sheriff co. Kilkenny 1823, M.P. for Dungarvan 1802-6, *b.* 17 Jan. 1748 ; *m.* Oct. 1789, Jane, dau. of Hugh, 2nd Lord Massy, and *d.* 3 June 1829, having by her (who *d.* 4 Jan. 1848) had issue,
    1. William Hastings, of Lota, co. Cork, *b.* 1795 ; *m.* 22 March, 1822, Mary, only dau. of Dominick Sarsfield, of Doughclovne, co. Cork, and *d.* 9 June, 1881, having by her (who *d.* 5 Jan. 1875) had issue,
      (1) William Warren Hastings, *b.* April, 1825 ; *m.* 22 March, 1850, Frances Jane, dau. of William Hoare ; and *d.* 28 Jan. 1890, having by her (who *d.* 19 Jan. 1895) had issue,
        1. William Warren Hastings, *b.* 14 May, 1857.
        2. Sarsfield, *b.* 8 Feb. 1861.
        1. Frances, *b.* Nov. 1850.
        2. Minnie, *b.* 30 April, 1852.
        3. Catherine, *b.* 14 March, 1855.
        4. Frances Jane, *b.* 28 Jan. 1859.
      (2) Dominick Sarsfield, C.B., Maj.-Gen. R.A., *b.* 1826 ; *m* twice, and *d.s.p.* 11 Jan. 1892.
      (1) Jane, *b.* 1823.
    2. John, of Glenville, co. Waterford, *b.* 1801 ; *m.* 27 June, 1839, Emma, eldest dau. of Rev. Richard Jones Hobson, Archdeacon of Waterford ; and *d.* 31 Oct. 1870, having by her (who *d.* 19 Nov. 1863) had issue,
      (1) Richard Massy, *b.* 13 Jan. 1843.
      (2) Hugh, *b.* 1845 ; *d. unm.* 24 Aug. 1871.
      (3) John, *b.* 1851 ; *m.* 9 Oct. 1872, Julia Earner, dau. of Gen. Robert Sandeman, and had issue.
      (1) Emma, *b.* 11 March, 1841 ; *d.* 1855.
  3. Hugh Godfrey, of Rockview, co. Kilkenny, *b.* March, 1804 ; *d. unm.* 22 Aug. 1889.
  4. Godfrey, of Rockview, co. Kilkenny, Lieut. 48th B.N.I., *b.* 1806 ; *d. unm.* 13 Aug. 1857.
    1. Catherine, *m.* 31 Dec. 1812, George Tuthill, of Faba, co. Limerick, and *d.* Aug. 1845.
    2. Frances, *m.* 4 Aug. 1818, George Bruce, of Milltown Castle, co. Cork.
    3. Jane, *m.* Aug. 1815. John Bolton Massy, of Ballywire, co. Tipperary. She *d.* 21 Feb. 1879.
    4. Mary Anne, *m.* 1 Feb. 1842, Col. F. H. Massy Wheeler.
  5. Thomas (Rev.), Rector of Glankeen, co. Tipperary, *b.* 10 April, 1755 ; *d. unm.* Jan. 1807.
    1. Abigail, *m.* 12 Oct. 1757, Edward Cooke, of Kiltinane Castle, co. Tipperary.
    2. Lydia, *m.* 25 Feb. 1760, John Hobson.
    3. Frances, *d. unm.* 6 May, 1824.
    4. Catherine, *m.* 10 June, 1767, Joseph Deane, M.P., of Terenure, co. Dublin, and Dangan, co. Kilkenny.

He *m.* 2ndly, 20 Sept. 1760, Olympia, dau. of Robert Langrish (*see* BURKE's *Peerage and Baronetage*), and widow of George Birch, and by her (who *d.* 22 April, 1769) had issue,
  6. Robert, Lieut.-Col. 16th B.N.I., *b.* 19 Sept. 1761 ; *m.* 17 Aug. 1788, Lucy Evance, and *d.* 5 April, 1818, having by her had issue, Louisa, *m.* 30 Oct. 1819, Nicholas Willard, D.L. Sussex, and *d.* 22 May, 1866.
  7. Anthony, Major Bengal Artillery, *b.* 8 Sept. 1765 ; *m.* 29 Sept. 1795, Catharine, dau. of Francis Daniel, and *d.* 31 Jan. 1814, having by her (who *d.* 20 Jan. 1811) had issue,
    1. Anthony Sheppey, *b.* 5 Jan. 1800, *m.* 1st, Lilla, dau. of Capt.

Adam Callendar, and widow of Rev. Charles L. Chambers, and by her (who d. June, 1835) had,
  Lilla, b. 22 March, 1830; m. 1st, 26 Jan. 1848, William Foster Smithe, who d. 16 Jan. 1868. She m. 2ndly, 3 Feb. 1868, J. Stewart Roupell, of Richmond, Surrey, who d. 27 June, 1893. She d. 7 Feb. 1899, leaving issue.
He m. 2ndly, Anne, dau. of Sir John Bateman, and widow of Gen. Butler. She d.s.p. 11 March, 1863.
2. James Richard, Lieut. Bengal Artillery, b. 18 April, 1805; d. unm. 5 Oct. 1825.
3. Godfrey Thomas, C.B., of Kirby Cane Hall, Norfolk, Col. R.E., b. 1 Jan. 1807; m. 8 Aug. 1831, Harriett Elliot, dau. of William Wickham Cowell, and d. 27 Dec. 1866, having by her (who d. 5 June, 1894) had issue,
  (1) Catherine Rosalie, m. 1st, 17 Jan. 1854, Rev. Harry Dupuis, who d. 3 June, 1867, leaving issue. She m. 2ndly, 2 April, 1869, Sir Charles Jasper Selwyn, Lord Justice of Appeal, who d. 11 April, 1869. She m. 3rdly, 21 Feb. 1871, Francis Charles Hughes Hallett, and d. 6 July, 1875.
  (2) Amelia Harriet, m. 24 April, 1857, Henry Smithe, of Ellingham Hall, and d. 1869, leaving issue.
  (3) Ellen Margaret, m. 6 Aug. 1866, Lieut.-Gen. Sir Alfred Wilde, K.C.B., A.D.C., who d. 7 Feb. 1878, leaving issue.
  (4) Alice Olympia, d. young, 11 April, 1848.
  (5) Edith Josephine, m. 15 Sept. 1894, Thomas Henry Crowther.
1. Catherine Harriet, d. an infant, 28 April, 1798.
2. Olympia, d. an infant, 21 March, 1800.
3. Catherine Dundas, d. unm. 5 Sept. 1880.
4. Rosalie, m. 4 May, 1831, Rev. John Read Munn, Vicar of Ashburnham, and d. 12 Jan. 1876, leaving issue.
He m. 3rdly, Jane Storey, and d. Oct. 1798, having by her (who d. 1828) had further issue,
8. Richard, M.D., of Cork, afterwards of Dunkitt House, co. Kilkenny, b. 1784; m. 1st, 8 Sept. 1835, Henrietta, dau. of Sir Edmund Skottowe, and by her (who d. 17 Nov. 1836) had issue,
  1. Margaret Anne, b. Sept. 1839; d. 1 March, 1837.
He m. 2ndly, 16 Feb. 1838, Louisa, dau. of Major Henry Clinton Martin, M.A., and d. 2 March, 1859, having by her (who d. 26 Oct. 1869) had issue,
  1. John Clinton, Capt. R.A., b. Jan. 1839; m. 28 Dec. 1875, Elizabeth Jane, only dau. of John W. Blennerhassett Coulson, of Carlisle, and were both drowned 17 Feb. 1876.
  2. Charles Newton, b 5 Feb. 1847, drowned 19 Feb. 1880; d. unm.
The 2nd son,
JOHN GREENE, of Greenville, High Sheriff co. Kilkenny 1792, Capt. 8th Dragoons, b. 30 June, 1744; m. 1st, 10 June, 1775, Mira, widow of Christopher Musgrave, and dau. of Thomas Boyse, of Bishops Hall, co. Kilkenny, and by her (who d. 30 Sept. 1780) had issue,
1. John, of Greenville, b. 1776; m. 17 Jan. 1807, Anne Coote, only dau. of John Knox Grogan, of Johnstown, co. Wexford, and d. 23 Oct. 1810, leaving issue,
  John, of Greenville, b. 11 Oct. 1807, M.P. co. Kilkenny, 1847-65; d. unm. 16 June, 1883.
  Anne Coote, b. 27 May, 1810; m. 1st, April, 1833, George Powell Houghton, of Kilmannock House, co. Wexford, by whom she had issue. She m. 2ndly, Joseph Fade Goff, of Raheenduff House, co. Wicklow.
2. GODFREY, of whom presently.
1. Margaret, who d. 15 Feb. 1810, having m. 1 Jan. 1809, Rev. Edward Hunt, Rector of Dunkitt, and had issue.
He m. 2ndly, 9 March, 1782, Letitia, only child of Nuttall Greene, of Low Grange (see above), and widow of William Greene, of Kilmanahan Castle, by whom (who d. 10 July, 1813) he had an only son,
3. Joseph, of Low Grange, and Lake View, co. Kilkenny, Mayor 1824-5; High Sheriff 1808, Resident Magistrate 1831-58, b. 4 May, 1783; m. 17 Nov. 1804, Jane, dau. of William Newport, and niece of Sir John Newport, Bart., and d. 28 Feb. 1858, having by her (who d. 14 Nov. 1857) had issue,
  1. John Newport, of Newtown House, Kilkenny, b. 23 Oct. 1805; m. 3 Sept. 1839, Elizabeth, dau. of Capt. Samuel McGuire, R.N., of Clonea Castle, co. Waterford, and d. March, 1870, having by her (who d. 20 March, 1878) had issue,
    (1) John Newport, of Glen Conway, Norfolk, U.S.A., b. 27 June, 1843; m. 28 Aug. 1870, Cloe Tyler, dau. of Conway Whittle, of Norfolk, U.S.A., and d. 28 Jan. 1902, leaving issue, Urith Mary Newport, b. 27 Oct. 1879.
    (2) Joseph William, of Princess Anne, Vancouver, U.S.A., b. 13 Jan. 1848; d. unm. 22 March, 1899
    (1) Mary Eliza Newport, m. 6 May, 1873, William Hastings Greene (see below), and d.s.p. 19 March, 1874.
  2. William (Rev.), Vicar of Antrim, b. 4 Feb. 1807; m. 17 Sept. 1838, Fanny, dau. of Francis Whittle, of Muckamore, co. Antrim, and d. 29 July, 1885, having by her (who d. 27 Aug. 1897, had issue,
    (1) FRANCIS, of Augusta, Virginia, heir male of the family, b. 12 March, 1842; m. 28 July, 1890, Laura Isabel, dau. of Thomas Lovelock, and has issue,
      Ernest William Skeffington, b. 24 March, 1893.
      Viola Patricia, b. 29 June, 1891.
    (2) William Hastings, b. 9 April, 1853; m. 1st, 6 May, 1875, his cousin, Mary Eliza Newport, dau. of John Newport Greene (see above). She d.s.p. 19 March, 1874. He m. 2ndly, 13 April, 1878, Cornelia, dau. of H. Peyton, and has issue,
      1. Peyton William, b. 14 Dec. 1884.
      2. George Newport, b. 24 Nov. 1887.
    (3) James, b. 10 Oct. 1844; m. 5 Dec. 1876, Susan, dau. of W. H. Hollingsworth, and has issue,
      1. James Hollingsworth, b. 17 Sept. 1877.
      2. Francis Whittle, b. 29 June, 1879.
      1. Julia Ellen, b. 28 Aug. 1881.
    (4) Joseph Skeffington, b. 16 Oct. 1847.
    (5) Reginald Latimer Wellington, of Tregara House, Stratford-on-Avon, Surgeon, Mayor of Stratford 1891-4, b. 18 Dec. 1852; m. 29 April, 1882, Ethel, dau. of Richard Izod Downes, and has issue,
      Reginald Downes Latimer, b. 6 Feb. 1883.
      Beryl Latimer, b. 20 March, 1886.
    (6) Augustus Newport, b. 19 Sept. 1854; m. 2 Oct. 1880, Elena More, dau. of J. Mitchell, and d. 3 Feb. 1890, leaving issue,
      1. Joseph Campbell, b. 19 April, 1883.
      1. Frances Whittle, b. 25 Oct. 1881.
      2. Mary Newport, b. 23 Aug. 1886.
    (7) Walter Godfrey, b. 19 Nov. 1857; d. 15 Nov. 1865.
    (8) Henry Sarsfield, b. 25 July, 1861; m. 30 April, 1889, Florence Louisa, dau. of Henry Lamb, and has issue,
      1. Francis Augustus Henry, b. 30 July, 1890.
      2. John Newport, b. 3 Sept. 1891.
      3. George William Reynolds, b. 3 Dec. 1893.
    (1) Jane Ellen, b. 5 Aug. 1840.
    (2) Georgina Fanny, b. 17 Feb. 1851; m. 29 April, 1876, Rev. Alfred William Anson, and d. 4 Nov. 1892. He m. 2ndly, 1 Feb. 1894, Elena More, widow of Augustus Newport Greene (see above).
  3. Joseph, of Newtown House, b. 14 July, 1808; d. unm. 24 Jan. 1890.
  4. George Nuttall, Lieut.-Col. H.E.I.C.S., of Newtown House, b. 11 July, 1812; d. unm. 2 Aug. 1893.
  5. Reginald, b. 6 March, 1814; d. unm. 3 May, 1868.
    1. Sarah Jane, b. 2 Oct. 1809; m. 8 Dec. 1842, John Waring, of Springfield, co. Kilkenny, and d.s.p. 31 Oct. 1867.
    2. Ellen Elizabeth, d. an infant 11 Sept. 1811.
    3. Ellen Priscilla, d. an infant 25 Nov. 1818.
    4. Priscilla, b. 6 Dec. 1818; m. 12 Sept. 1843, Charles Newport, son of Rev. Francis Newport, and d. 6 March, 1860, leaving issue.
2. Eliza, d. unm. 22 March, 1808.
Mr. John Greene d. May, 1803. His 2nd son,
GODFREY GREENE, of Greenmount, co. Kilkenny, Lieut. 6th and 48th Regts., b. 1777; m. 13 Feb. 1806, Margaret, 2nd dau. and co-heiress of Rev. Joseph Poulter, Rector of Dunkitt, co. Kilkenny, and by her (who d. 13 Feb. 1848) had issue,
1. Joseph Poulter, b. 29 Oct. 1808; d. unm. 22 April, 1838.
2. JOHN, of whom presently.
1. Miranda, b. 12 Oct. 1807; m. 30 June, 1842, Owen O'Callaghan Tegart, and d. 4 April, 1872, leaving issue. He d. 10 Feb. 1865.
2. Eliza Letitia, b. 31 Jan. 1810; d. unm. 14 Jan. 1876.
3. Mary Anne, b. 29 Jan. 1811; d. an infant.
4. Letitia, b. 30 April, 1814; d. unm. 26 April, 1858.
Mr. Greene d. 4 May, 1859, aged 83. His one son,
JOHN GREENE, b. 1 June, 1813; m. 27 Feb. 1848, Charlotte, only child of Samuel Perry, of Manchester. He d. 20 Oct. 1889. She d. 15 June, 1903, having had issue,
1. JOHN JOSEPH, late representative.
2. Godfrey, b. 7 April, 1852; d. unm. 21 June, 1892.
3. William Hastings, b. 9 June, 1853; d. an infant.
1. Charlotte Letitia, b. 10 Nov. 1850, a Dominican nun.

Arms—Vert three bucks trippant or, each gorged with a ducal coronet gu. *Crest*—Out of a ducal coronet gu. a buck's head or. *Motto*—Nec timeo, nec sperno.

GREER OF TULLYLAGAN.

THOMAS GREER, of Tullylagan, co. Tyrone, J.P., b. 24 April, 1875; m. 1907, Constance Clara Annie, 2nd dau. of late Edward Cochrane Palmer, of Beckfield House, Queen's Co.

Lineage.—HENRY GRIER, of Rock Hall, and afterwards of Redford, near Grange, co. Tyrone, came to Ireland 1653. He m. 1652, Mary, dau. of Robert Turner, of Turnestead, Northumberland, and d. about 1675, having by her (who d. 1691) had issue,
1. JAMES.
2. Robert.
3. Thomas.

The eldest son,
JAMES GREER, of Lisacurran, co. Armagh, b. at Newton, Northumberland, 1653; m. 21 June, 1678, Eleanor, dau. and co-heir of John Rea, of Lisacurran, and left issue,
1. HENRY, ancestor of the GREERS of Grange, co. Tyrone.
2. JOHN, b. 1688, ancestor of the GREERS of Tullylagan and Seapark.

3. **Thomas**, of Clonrole, Lurgan, *b.* 1 Dec. 1690; *m.* Ann Henderson.
4. **James**, of Lisacurran, Lurgan, *b.* 18 June, 1693; *d.* 1761.
1. Mary, *b.* 7 Dec. 1685; *m.* William Douglas.

The 2nd son,
JOHN GREER, of Grace Hall, co. Armagh, and of Tullyanaghan, near Lurgan, *m.* 3 July, 1717, Mary, dau. of Jeremiah Hanks, of Birr, and widow of John Chambers, of Dublin, and *d.* 1741, having had several children, of whom the 2nd son,
THOMAS GREER, of Rhone Hill, became, on the extinction of the male line of his elder brother John, the head of the 2nd house of Irish Greers. He was *b.* 14 Nov. 1724; *m.* 2 April, 1746, Sarah, dau. of Thomas Greer, of Redford, his second cousin, and *d.* at Rhone Hill, 5 April, 1803, leaving issue,
1. Thomas, his heir.
2. Robert, *b.* 16 Nov. 1766; *d. unm.* in America, 1808.
1. Eleanor, *m.* Thomas Boardman, of Jonestown, Edenderry, King's Co.
2. Mary, *m.* Richard, son of Joseph Jacob, of Waterford.
3. Jane, *m.* James, son of Barclay Clibborn, of Moate, co. Westmeath.
4. Sarah, *m.* John, son of John Hancock, of Lurgan, Armagh.
5. Ann, *m.* James Nicholson.

The elder son,
THOMAS GREER, of Rhone Hill, *b.* 5 Sept. 1761; *m.* 14 Aug. 1787, Elizabeth, only child of William Jackson (descended from Richard Jackson, of Killingwold Grove, near Beverley, co. York. To this family the late Gen. Andrew Jackson, President of the United States, and the late " Stonewall " Jackson, the celebrated Confederate General, belonged). Thomas Greer *d.* 26 Feb. 1840, leaving issue,
1. Thomas, of Tullylagan.
2. William Jackson, of Rhone Hill, J.P., *b.* 8 June, 1797; *m.* 30 June, 1827, Margaret, dau. of Arthur Ussher, J.P., of Camphire, co. Waterford (a sister of William Mina, wife of Thomas Greer, of Tullylagan). She *d.* 2 Oct. 1873. He *d.* 17 Feb. 1841, leaving issue,
1. THOMAS FERGUS, of Rhone Hill, late 46th Regt., *b.* 29 Jan. 1829; *m.* 16 July, 1861, Elizabeth Sarah, eldest dau. of Major Sampson Carter, of Barmeen, co. Dublin, and *d.* 10 Aug. 1901, having had issue,
(1) Fergus William (Rev.), Rector of St. George's, Dublin, M.A., University Coll. Durham, *b.* 7 June, 1863; *m.* 3 July, 1890, Matilda, dau. of the late John Morriss, of Headford, co. Galway, and has issue,
1. Fergus Ussher Morriss, *b.* 20 May, 1891.
2. Kenneth MacGregor, } twins, *b.* 30 March, 1893.
3. Eric Roberts,
4. Roderick Denis, *b.* 19 May, 1896.
1. Ursula Margaret Jane Elizabeth, *b.* 23 Feb. 1903.
(2) Charles Edward, *b.* 16 May, 1866; *d. unm.* 30 July, 1887.
(1) Lucy Matilda, *m.* 27 July, 1897, George Greer of Bernagh, co. Tyrone.
(2) Helen MacGregor, *m.* 6 Aug. 1891, Hugh Harris, and has issue.
2. Arthur Jackson, of Thornton Lodge, Northallerton, late Surgeon Royal Scots Fusiliers, latterly Surgeon-Major 17th Lancers; retired Deputy Inspector-General, half pay, 1877; Crimean medal and four clasps, 5th Class of the Imperial Order of Medjidie, and Turkish medal; most honourably mentioned for services during the attack on the Redan, 18 June, 1855; *b.* 25 April, 1831; *m.* 17 Jan. 1866, Emma, eldest dau. of the late William Horsfall, of Hornby Grange, co. York, J.P., and by her (who *d.* 25 Feb. 1902) had issue,
Alured Ussher, *b.* 9 Nov. 1870.
Ada Horsfall.
3. William Henry (Rev.), Rector of Kilcolmane, co. Mayo, *b.* 11 May, 1835; *m.* 5 Sept. 1867, Charlotte, dau. of Richard Pike, of Beachgrove, co. Tyrone. He *d.* 1 March, 1872, leaving issue,
(1) Richard Ussher (Rev.), Rector of Banbridge, co. Down, M.A., *m.* 28 April, 1898, Elizabeth Lindsay, eld. dau. of Frederick Greer, of Tullylagan, and has issue,
1. Ussher McGregor, *b.* 8 June, 1899.
2. William Derrick Lindsey, *b.* 28 Feb. 1902.
1. Margaret Cecilia *b.* 21 March, 1905.
2. Monica Elizabeth, *b.* 27 Feb. 1907.
(1) Edith Sophia. (2) Marion MacGregor.
4. Edwin, M.A., Trin. Coll. Dublin, *b.* 10 Feb. 1839; *m.* Maria Theodosia, dau. of Richard Grainger, of Newcastle, and widow of Edward Hunt, of Jerpoint, co. Kilkenny.
1. Sophia Louisa, *m.* 14 June, 1859, Robert Butler Staveley, J.P., of Glanduff Castle, co. Limerick, and *d.* 21 March, 1872, leaving issue.
2. Lucy Ussher, *m.* 1st, 11 April, 1857, Henry Davis, of Waterford; 2ndly, 22 Jan. 1868, Col. Hampden Acton, J.P., son of Rev. Thomas Acton, of Dunganstown, co. Wicklow, and by him had issue. She *d.* 16 July, 1894.
3. John Robert, *b.* 11 Sept. 1800; *m.* 10 Sept. 1829, Sarah Diana, dau. of John Strangman, of Waterford. She *d.* 2 May, 1891. He *d.* 27 March, 1873, leaving issue,
1. John Robert (Rev.), *b.* 16 Aug. 1830; *m.* 1858, Rosalie, dau. of Nicholas Mansfield. She *d.* 13 June, 1869. He *d.* 10 March, 1871, leaving issue,
(1) John Robert, *d.* an infant, 5 April, 1863.
(2) Kenneth Mansfield, of Perth, W.A., *b.* 17 Feb. 1867.
(1) Margarite Eugenie, *m.* 19 April, 1883, Vaughan Benjamin Wintle, and has issue.
(2) Gabrielle.
(3) Rosalie Clare, *d.* young, 25 May, 1866.
2. Thomas Augustus, late 1st Sub-Inspector Royal Irish Constabulary, *b.* 6 July, 1838; *m.* 10 Oct. 1867, Selina Margaret,

3rd dau. of Thomas Hughes, of Ystrad Hall, co. Denbigh, J.P. and D.L. cos. Denbigh and Flint, and has issue,
(1) Frederick Augustus, *b.* 20 Feb. 1871, Major Royal Irish Fus. (87th Regt.).
(2) Hugh Conrad, D.I. Roy. I. Constab., *b.* 19 Aug. 1873.
(1) Amy Margaret.
3. George Newsom Strangman, *b.* 6 Dec. 1840; *d. unm.* 7 Jan. 1867.
1. Elizabeth Amelia, *m.* 27 July, 1864, Anthony Mann Hawkes, and has issue.
2. Priscilla Sophia, *d. unm.* 18 Aug. 1860.
4. ALFRED, of Dripsey House, co. Cork, J.P. (*see* GREER *of Sea Park*).
1. Sarah, *m.* 20 May, 1818, Hugh White, of Dublin, and *d.* 23 Dec. 1860, leaving issue.
2. Mary Jackson, *m.* 17 Nov. 1817, Thomas Winslow Manly, of Dublin, and *d.* 26 Dec. 1830, leaving issue.
3. Elizabeth, *m.* 16 Feb. 1831, George Thomas, of Eagle House, Brislington, formerly of Prior Park, Bath. She *d.s.p.* 16 Nov. 1893.
4. Caroline, *m.* 20 May, 1828, William Ridgway, of Bristol. She *d.* 18 June, 1893, leaving issue.
5. Louisa Jane, *m.* 26 April, 1837, Joseph Rake, of Bristol. She *d.* 16 Feb. 1896, leaving issue.
6. Priscilla Sophia, *d. unm.* 11 March, 1832.

The eldest son,
THOMAS GREER, of Tullylagan, J.P., *b.* 21 April, 1791; *m.* 17 April, 1826, William Mina, dau. of Arthur Ussher, of Camphire, co. Waterford, J.P. (*see* USSHER *of Eastwell*). She *d.* 21 Oct. 1879. Mr. Greer *d.* 4 June, 1870, leaving issue,
1. FREDERICK of Tullylagan.
2. Usher, *b.* 27 Feb. 1831; *d.* 9 Dec. 1851, when a student in Trin. Coll. Dublin, where he gained 1st place at his entrance in 1848.
1. Martha Ussher, *m.* 6 Dec. 1848, John Harding Ridge, eldest son of Rev. Jones Ridge, D.D., Rector of Cahir, co. Tipperary, brother of Col. Ridge, 5th Fusiliers, who was killed at the storming of Badajos; and has issue.
2. Elizabeth Jackson, *m.* 1st, 1 April, 1856, Rev. Thomas Francis Bushe, Vicar of Rathowen and Russah, co. Westmeath, son of Robert Bushe, and grandson of Gervais Parker Bushe, of Kilfane, and had issue (*see* BUSHE *of Glencairne*). She *m.* 2ndly, 20 Oct. 1863, James Corry Jones Lowry, Capt. R.A., Col. Donegal Artillery, eldest son of late James Corry Lowry, Q.C., of Rockdale, co. Tyrone, and has issue (*see* LOWRY *of Rockdale*). She *d.* 25 Nov. 1888.
3. Wilhelmina Sophia Priscilla.

The eldest son,
FREDERICK GREER, of Tullylagan, co. Tyrone, J.P., late R.N. *b.* 17 Feb. 1829; *m.* 30 June, 1874, Cecilia, eldest dau. of Sir Nathaniel Alexander Staples, Bart., of Lissan, co. Tyrone, by Elizabeth Lindsay his wife, only child of James Head and Cecilia his wife, 3rd dau. of the Hon. Robert Lindsay, of Balcarres, and *d.* 1908, having by her (who *d.* 13 July, 1891) had issue,
1. THOMAS, now of Tullylagan.
2. Nathaniel Alexander Staples, *b.* 13 Nov. 1876.
1. Elizabeth Lindsay, *m.* 28 April, 1898, Rev. Richard Ussher Greer, M.A., Rector of Banbridge, co. Down.
2. Mary Cosme, *m.* 24 April, 1903, Thomas Staples, 2nd son of the late Maj.-Gen. Thomas Molesworth Staples, Indian Staff Corps (*see* BURKE's *Peerage*).

Arms—Az., a lion rampant or, armed and langued gu., between three antique crowns of the second, on a canton arg. an oak tree eradicated, surmounted by a sword in bend sinister, ensigned on the point with a royal crown, all ppr. **Crest**—An eagle displayed ppr., charged on the breast with a quadrangular lock, arg. **Motto**—Memor esto.

Seat — Tullylagan, Dungannon. **Residence** — Curglasson, Stewartstown.

GREER OF THE GRANGE.

JOSEPH HENRY GREER, of Grange, Moy, co. Tyrone, Capt. late Highland Light Infantry, High Sheriff co. Kildare 1910, *b.* 9 Feb. 1855, *s.* his father in 1886; *m.* 9 Dec. 1886, Olivia Mary, eldest dau. of Major-Gen. George de la Poer Beresford (*see* BURKE's *Peerage*, DECIES, B.), by Hester Beatrice his wife, dau. of Robert Bury, of Clogrenane, and has issue,
1. ERIC BERESFORD, *b.* April, 1892.
2. Francis St. Leger, *b.* 13 July, 1894.

Lineage.—JAMES GRIER, of The Rock (from which the Irish branch springs), was settled there in 1633. James Grier and Mary his wife, of The Rock, Cumberland, had, *inter alios*, a son, Henry, and a dau., Anne, who *m.* Thomas Turner, of Turnerstown, Northumberland. The son,
HENRY GREER, *m.* 1652, Mary, sister of the above-named Thomas Turner, and removed in 1663 to Ireland, and settled at Redford, near Grange, co. Tyrone. He *d.* about 1675, leaving issue, three sons, James, Robert, and Thomas; the latter was shot in his mother's house at Redford in 1689, by the Rapparees. The eldest son,
JAMES GREER, of Lisacurran, co. Armagh, *b.* 1653; *m.* 21 Aug. 1678, Eleanor, dau. and co-heir of John Rea, of Lisacurran and left issue,
1. HENRY, of whom presently,

2. John, of Tullyanaghan, b. 1688 (ancestor of the GREERS of *Tullylagan and Sea Park, which see*).
3. Thomas, of Clonrole, Lurgan, b. 1 Dec. 1690 ; m. Anne Henderson.
4. James, of Lisacurran, Lurgan, b. 18 June, 1693 ; d. 1761.
1. Maty, b. 7 Dec. 1685 ; m. William Douglas.
The eldest son and heir,
HENRY GREER, b. 1681 ; m. 1704, Sarah Henderson, of Duncaldy, co. Londonderry, and d. July, 1756, leaving a son,
HENRY GREER, b. 1716 ; m. 3 June, 1741, Elizabeth, dau. of John Turner (grandson of Thomas Turner and Ann Greer his wife), and d. Dec. 1776, leaving (with three daus.,Ann, Henrietta, and Elizabeth, all of whom m. and left issue) a son and heir,
JOHN GREER, of the Grange, J.P., b. 1742 ; m. 17 Dec. 1762, Catherine, dau. of John Cuppage, of Garden Hill, co. Antrim, and had issue,
1. HENRY, b. 20 Nov. 1763 ; m. 1782, Jane, dau. and only child of John Lynam, of Dublin, and d.s.p. 2 Aug. 1814, having had issue,
  1. JOSEPH, successor to his grandfather.
  2. Richard (Rev.), b. 10 June, 1796 ; d. unm. 7 June, 1825.
    1. Jane.   2. Ann.
    3. Sophia.   4. Sarah.
2. John Turner, b. 18 May, 1766 ; d. 1786.
3. Thomas, b. 15 Nov. 1767, J.P. and Deputy Governor ; m. but d.s.p. 7 April, 1837.
4. James, b. 31 Jan. 1775, J.P. and Deputy Governor ; d.s.p. 7 Aug. 1842.
5. John Miers, b. 4 April, 1778, Commander R.N.
6. George, b. 17 May, 1779, J.P. for Armagh.
7. Alexander, b. 20 June, 1880, half-pay of the Army.
1. Elizabeth, m. John Malcolmson, of Clonmel, and d.s.p.
2. Mary.
3. Jane, m. John Lindsay, late H.M.'s Life Guards.
4. Catherine.
5. Sarah Mildred, m. 1st, Major Overend, E.I.C.S. ; and 2ndly, Rev. John O. Oldfield, Archdeacon of Elphin. She d.s.p. 18 Jan. 1823.
Mr. John Greer, who was a Deputy-Governor of the cos. of Armagh and Tyrone for upwards of 50 years, d. 6 Oct. 1818, and was s. by his grandson,
JOSEPH GREER, of The Grange, Major Commanding Royal Tyrone Militia Artillery, J.P. and D.L., b. 17 April, 1795 ; m. 5 June, 1816, Mary, dau. of Thomas Harpur, of Moy, by his wife Mary, dau. of James Richardson, of Brackaville, by his wife Mary, dau. of Edward Clements, of Bloomhill, all in co. Tyrone, and had issue,
1. HENRY HARPUR, of The Grange.
2. Thomas, R.N., b. 5 April, 1828 ; m. 13 Dec. 1863, Geraldine Elizabeth, eldest dau. of the late Knight of Glin.
1. Emily, m. 15 June, 1835, James Lowry, of Rochdale, and d. 22 April, 1851.
2. Jane, m. 6 Oct. 1842, Major Armar Lowry, late 30th Regt.
3. Maria, m. 1st, Thos. Hutton, M.D. ; 2ndly, General Crawley.
4. Anna, m. Darnton Hutton.
He d. 22 Nov. 1862, and was s. by his elder son,
HENRY HARPUR GREER, of The Grange, D.L., Gen. in the Army, Lieut.-Col. 68th Foot, C.B., b. 24 Feb. 1821 ; m. 14 Feb. 1850, Agnes Isabella, dau. of the Ven. Edmond Knox, Archdeacon of Killaloe, son of the Hon. and Right Rev. Edmond Knox, Bishop of Limerick, and grandson of Thomas, Viscount Northland, and had issue,
1. JOSEPH HENRY, now of The Grange.
1. Agnes Mary.
2. Emily Charlotte, m. 30 April, 1888, Rear-Admiral Reginald Geoffrey Otway Tupper, R.N., son of the late Capt. Charles William Tupper, 7th Royal Fusiliers, and grandson of the late Sir J. D. Wheeler-Cuffe, Bart. of Leyrath, co. Kilkenny (see BURKE's *Peerage*) and has issue (see *TUPPER of Guernsey*).
General Greer d. 26 March, 1886, and was s. by his only son.
Seat—The Grange, Moy, co. Tyrone. *Residence*—Curragh Grange, The Curragh, Co. Kildare. *Clubs*—Turf ; Army and Navy ; Naval and Military.

GREER OF SEA PARK.

The late THOMAS GREER, F.R.G.S., M.R.I.A., of Sea Park, co. Antrim and Carrickfergus, High Sheriff for Carrickfergus 1870, and co. Tyrone 1876, M.P. for Carrickfergus 1880-5, b. 4 April, 1837 ; m. 28 July, 1864, Margaret (now of Sea Park), only child and heiress of John Owden, of Sea Park, Belfast, and Brooklands, co. Antrim, by his wife Jane, dau. of John Greeves, of Bernagh, co. Tyrone. He d. 20 Sept. 1905, having had issue,

1. THOMAS MACGREGOR, educated at Eton, and Trinity Hall, Cambridge, J.P. co. Tyrone, b. 16 April, 1869 ; m. 1 March, 1892, Dorinda Florence, elder dau. of James Corry Jones Lowry, D.L. of Rockdale, co. Tyrone, Vice-Lieut. for that co., and has issue,
  1. Gladys Sylvia MacGregor, b. 10 July, 1896.
  2. Margaret Elizabeth MacGregor, b. 22 Oct. 1897 ; d. 28 May, 1909.
1. Helena MacGregor, m. 12 Dec. 1893, Robert Swinburne Lowry, Capt. R.N., eldest son of Lieut.-Gen. Lowry, C.B., and has issue.
2. Georgina Beatrice.   3. Eva Mildred.
Lineage.—ALFRED GREER, of Dripsey House, co. Cork, J.P., 4th surviving son of Thomas Greer, of Tullylagan (*see that family*) b. 2 Sept. 1805 ; m. 1st, 19 May, 1836, Helena, eldest dau. of Joshua Carroll, of St. Patrick's Place, Cork, and by her (who d. 9 June, 1849) had issue,
1. THOMAS, late of Sea Park.
2. Joshua Carroll, b. 20 May, 1838 ; d. unm. 4 Oct. 1855.
3. Alfred, of Dripsey, b. 14 June, 1839 ; d. unm. 9 Sept. 1907.
4. George Thomas, M.D., b. 5 April, 1843 ; m. 24 Dec. 1865, Elizabeth Mary, dau. of John Boileau, of Dublin.
5. MacGregor, Capt. Royal Engineers, b. 16 July, 1844 ; d. unm. 20 Jan. 1903.
Mr. Greer m. 2ndly, 19 Nov. 1853, Peggy, only dau. of Major John Bowen-Colthurst, of Dripsey Castle, co. Cork (see COLTHURST *of Dripsey and Ardrum*). She d. 7 Feb. 1880, leaving issue,
1. Georgina de Bellasis, m. 15 Aug. 1878, Robert Walter Travers Bowen-Colthurst, J.P., of Oakgrove and Dripsey Castle, co. Cork, and has issue (see *that family*). b. 16 Nov. 1896.
Mr. Greer d. 29 Dec. 1891, and was s. by his eldest son.

Arms—Az., a lion rampant or, armed and langued gu., between three antique crowns of the second, on a canton arg. an oak tree eradicated surmounted by a sword in bend sinister ensigned on the point with a royal crown all pp. *Crest*—An eagle displayed pp. charged on the breast with a quadrangle lock, arg. *Motto*—Memor esto.

Seat—Sea Park, Carrickfergus.

GREGORY OF COOLE PARK.

WILLIAM ROBERT GREGORY, of Coole Park, co. Galway, b. 1881 ; s. his father 1892, m. 26 Sept. 1907, Lily Margaret, youngest dau. of late Graham Graham Parry, of Colham, Virginia, U.S.A., and has issue,
RICHARD GRAHAM b. 6 Jan. 1909.
Lineage.—ROBERT GREGORY, many years Chairman of East India Company till 1783, and M.P. for Rochester in 1744 ; his two elder sons d. without issue. He d. 1810, and was s. by
RIGHT HON. WILLIAM GREGORY, Under-Secretary to the Lord Lieutenant of Ireland 1813-32, m. 1789, Lady Anne Trench, dau. of William Power Keating, 1st Earl of Clancarty. She d. 21 Nov. 1833. He d. 13 April, 1840, leaving issue,
1. ROBERT, his heir.
2. William (Rev.), Rector of Fiddown, co. Kilkenny, b. 24 June, 1792 ; m. 18 Aug. 1817, Anne, 2nd dau. of the late Sir Charles Levinge, 5th bart., of Knockdrin Castle, Westmeath, and d. 22 Dec. 1874, leaving issue,
Henry Charles, of West Court, Callan, co. Kilkenny, b. 10 Aug. 1827 ; m. 1st, 18 July, 1861, Charlotte Anne, youngest dau. of Rev. Charles Butler Stevenson, Rector of Callan. She d. 5 June, 1879, leaving issue,
  (1) Reginald Graham, b. 2 Dec. 1864.
  (2) Charles Levinge, b. 22 Aug. 1870 ; m. 30 Oct. 1900, Irma, dau. of the late Major Harran, 4th Dragoon Guards.
  (3) Vere Richard Trench, b. 16 Oct. 1871 ; m. 26 Sept. 1900, Martha Augusta Young, only dau. of William Farls, of Lurgan, and widow of Francis Berry Fetherstonhaugh, of Carrick (see *that family*).
  (4) Ernest Frederick, b. 12 July, 1874.
  (5) Godfrey Levinge, b. 3 Nov. 1875.
  (1) Hilda Mary, m. 1 Nov. 1907, David Ruttledge.
  (2) Annie Frances Maria.
  (3) Grace Ursula Levinge, d. unm. 16 Jan. 1908.
He m. 2ndly, 8 Dec. 1884, Alicia Fanny, 2nd dau. of Arthur Gambell, of Washbrook, Westmeath, and by her has issue,
  (6) Harry William, b. 6 Jan. 1886.
  (7) William Robert Fetherstonhaugh, b. 12 July, 1892.
  (4) Vera May.
The elder son,
ROBERT GREGORY, of Coole Park, m. 1815, Elizabeth O'Hara, of Raheen, co. Galway, and by her (who was b. 1799, and d. 1875) left at his decease, 1847, an only son,
RIGHT HON. SIR WILLIAM HENRY GREGORY, K.C.M.G., F.R.S., of Coole Park, co. Galway, a Privy Councillor of Ireland, J.P. and D.L., High Sheriff 1849, M.P. for Dublin from 1842 to 1847, and for the co. Galway 1857 to 1872, Governor of Ceylon 1872 to 1877, b. 13 June, 1817 ; m. 1st, Jan. 1872, Elizabeth, 3rd dau. of Sir William Clay, Bart., and widow of James Temple Bowdoin, late 4th Dragoon Guards, which lady d. 1873. He m. 2ndly, March, 1880, Isabella

Augusta, youngest dau. of Dudley Persse, of Roxborough, co. Galway, and had one son,
WILLIAM ROBERT, now of Coole Park.
Sir W. H. Gregory d. 6 March, 1892.

Seat—Coole Park, near Gort, co. Galway.

GREHAN OF CLONMEEN.

STEPHEN GREHAN, of Clonmeen, co. Cork, J.P. and D.L., High Sheriff 1883, b. 1858; m. 1883, Esther, dau. of Col. Charles Raleigh Chichester, of Runnamoat, co. Roscommon (see CHICHESTER-CONSTABLE of Burton-Constable, Yorks.). She d. 11 April, 1900, having had issue,

1. George, d. an infant, 1892.
2. STEPHEN ARTHUR, b. 1896.
1. Mary. 2. Magda.
3. Kathleen, m. 18 Aug. 1910, Richard, only surviving son of George Edward Ryan, of Inch, co. Tipperary (see that family).
4. Aileen.

Lineage.—THADY GREHAN, of Dublin, d. 1792, leaving, with a dau. Mary, who m. John Roche, three sons,
1. PETER, of whom below.
2. Andrew, m. dau. of Patrick White.
3. Patrick, m. Jane Moore, of Mount Browne, and had a son, Patrick, m. Catherine, dau. of George Mecham, and had, Patrick, m. 1842, Frances, dau. of John Pitchford, and left issue.

The eldest son,
PETER GREHAN, m. Mary, dau. of Stephen Roche, of Limerick (see ROCHE of Granagh Castle), and had issue, two sons and five daus.,
1. Thady.
2. STEPHEN, of whom next.
1. Margaret, m. John Joyce.
2. Anne, m. Jan. 1800, Thomas Segrave, of Dublin, who d. 1817, having had issue (see SEGRAVE of Cabra).
3. Mary, m. 1804, Hubert Thomas Dolphin, of Turoe, co. Galway, and had issue (see that family). He d. 1829.
4. Helen, m. Alexander Sherlock.
5. Lucy, m. Christopher Gallwey.

The 2nd son,
STEPHEN GREHAN, of 19, Rutland Square, Dublin, m. May, 1809, Margaret, dau. of George Ryan, of Inch, co. Tipperary (see that family), and had issue, a son,
GEORGE GREHAN, of Clonmeen, Banteer, co. Cork, High Sheriff 1859, b. 1811, m. 1855, Mary, dau. of Philip O'Reilly, of Colamber, co. Westmeath (see that family). She d. 1859. He d. 1886, leaving issue, an only child,
STEPHEN, now of Clonmeen.

Seat—Clonmeen, Banteer, co. Cork. Clubs—Windham and Kildare Street.

GREVILLE. See BURKE'S PEERAGE, GREVILLE, B.

GROVE OF CASTLE GROVE.

JOHN MONTGOMERY CHARLES GROVE, of Castle Grove, co. Donegal, J.P., b. 1847; m. 17 Aug. 1886, Lucy Georgina, dau. of Major - Gen. William Maunsell Gabbett, East India Co.'s Artillery, and has issue,

JAMES ROBERT WOOD, 2nd Lieut. Royal Dublin Fus., b. 18 March, 1888.
Lucy Dorothea Montgomery, b. 4 Sept. 1892; d. 17 Feb. 1908.

Lineage.—THOMAS GROVE, of Castle Shanahan, co. Donegal (son of Thomas Grove), living there 1666-77, Commissioner of Assessments for the county 1655, Collector of Customs in Londonderry 1643-74, Sheriff of Donegal 1664, m. Margaret, only dau. of Peter Benson, of Elagh, Alderman of Londonderry, and Margaret his wife and d. 17 Dec. 1681. Fun. Entry, Ulster's Office), having by her (who d. before 20 Feb. 1677-8) had issue,
1. WILLIAM, his heir.

---

1. Frances, m. 1687, John Buchanan.
2. Elizabeth, m. 1690, Robert Sherrard, merchant, of Dublin.
3. Helen, m. 1st, James Nugent; 2ndly, Samuel Hatchett.
4. Margaret, m. 1st, Rev. Richard Eaton, and 2ndly, Aug. 1697, William Vaughan.
5. Ann, m. 1st, Rev. John Walrond, and 2ndly, — Jerman.
6. Prudentia, m. 1st, Capt. Matthew Cockin, and 2ndly, Capt. James Nesbit, of Tullydonnel, co. Donegal, and had issue by both.

The only son,
WILLIAM GROVE, of Castle Shanahan, served through the siege of Derry 1688, purchased the Manor of Kingston 1684, from the Kingsmills, b. 1662; m. 1st, Sept. 1684, Constance, dau. of Maj. John Kingsmill, of Andover, Hants. (see KINGSMILL of Hermitage Park). She d. 1687, aged 22. He m. 2ndly, 1688, Elizabeth, eldest dau. of Sir James Leigh, Knt., of Cullinmore, co. Westmeath. She m. 2ndly, Col. John Mitchelbourne, of Glendermot. Mr. Grove was murdered by rebels 1697, leaving issue,
1. Thomas, of Castle Shanaghan, High Sheriff co. Donegal 1724. d.s.p. 1724.
2. WILLIAM, of whom presently.
3. James, of Grovehall, Sheriff co. Donegal 1737, m. Catherine, dau. of Rev. Matthew Leslie, Rector of Kilmacrenan, co. Donegal, and by her (who d. 10 June, 1778, aged 61) had issue,
  1. Thomas, of Grovehall, d. May, 1788.
  2. Leslie, of Grovehall (which he sold 1790), m. Sarah, dau. of Samuel Mercer, of Crosby Square, London. She d. Sept. 1819.
He d. Dec. 1794, having had issue,
  (1) Leslie Ralph, Capt. Bengal Art., killed at Dieg, 1804, d.s.p.
  (2) Samuel, Capt. R.N., d.s.p. June, 1817.
  (3) Henry Jones, Maj. 80th Foot, K.H., b. 1783; m. 1st, Sarah Northover Watts Pitt, and by her had issue,
    1. Henry Leslie, Major-Gen. Madras Staff Corps (62, West Cromwell Road, Earl's Court), b. 22 May, 1829; m. 1862, Elizabeth Donaldson, dau. of Charles Herbert Scott, of Montrose. She d. 13 June, 1879, having had issue,
      a. Henry Montgomery, H.B.M. Consul at Moscow, late Lieut. 1st Regt. Bengal Cavalry, b. 27 Feb. 1 67; m. 29 May, 1906, Lilian Mabel, dau. of Rev. Canon Alleyne Hall Hall, Rector of Chevening, Kent, and has issue,
        (a) Cecil James   ⎱twins, b. 21 July,
        (b) Patrick Montgomery ⎰ 1907.
        (c) Anthony Alleyne, b. 15 Nov. 1908.
      b. James Scott, Lieut. 1st Regt. Bengal Cavalry, b. 30 May, 1868; d. unm. Aug. 1895.
        a. Ethel Jane, b. 1863; d. 1869.
        b. Norah Matilda Mary, b. June, 1865; m. George Samuel Pollard.
        c. Mabel Robertson, b. Feb. 1874; m. Rev. W. E. Dixon.
        d. Bessie Marion Beaman, b. 1870.
        e. Katherine White, b. 1872, d. 1884.
        f. Eleanor Sinclair, b. 1875.
        g. Edith Leslie, b. 1878, m. 4 Sept. 1906, Francis John Heywood, son of Col. J. M. Heywood, late R.E., and has issue.
    1. Isabella Frances, b. 1818; m. Rev. James Wilson, M.A., and d. 1889.
    2. Marianne Maria, b. 1820; m. W. McKenzie, and d. 1900.
    3. Henrietta, m. 1849, James Powell, and d.
    4. Louisa, m. Cornelius Burges, and d.
Maj. H. J. Grove m. 2ndly, Mary Anne, dau. of Capt. Sinclair, R.N. She d. 31 Jan. 1857. He d. March, 1847, having by her had issue,
    2. Robert Welch, b. 3 Jan. 1839; m. Caroline, dau. of Major Woodward, Madras Army, and d. 24 Feb. 1898, having had issue,
      a. Sinclair Alexander Leslie, b. 4 Dec. 1874.
      b. Robert Norman Charles, b. 23 Feb. 1880.
      a. Emily Harriet, b. 29 June, 1863; m. 1885, Philip Lindlay Dacre Beaver, and has issue.
      b. Annie Caroline, b. 31 July, 1865; m. Major Arthur Gordon Hayne, 15th Madras Infantry, and has issue.
      c. Mary Eliza, b. 21 May, 1873; m. 1896, Herbert Henry Stanes.
      d. Selina Montgomery, b. 13 May, 1877.
    3. Alexander Sinclair, D.S.O., Col. on the Staff, Madras, b. 2 April, 1840; m. Kitty, 2nd dau. of Maj.-Gen. Ezekiel Gage. He d. 1897, having had issue,
      a. Catherine Sinclair, b. 25 June, 1874; m. 1894, Major Frederick William Bagshawe, Indian Army, and has issue.
      b. Mary Grace Montgomery, b. 12 July, 1876; m. 1897, Major Alan James Campbell, Indian Army, and has issue.
      c. Amy Leslie, b. 21 June, 1878; m. 1905, George Denman Partridge, I.C.S.
      d. Bessie Frances, b. 23 June, 1879.
      e. Annie Harvey, b. 17 Sept. 1881; m. 17 Jan. 1901, Charles Brent Neville Pelly, Supt. Madras Police, and has issue (see BURKE'S Peerage, PELLY, Bart.).
      f. Elma Wallace, b. 5 Feb. 1883.
      g. Dorothy Pelly, b. 18 Dec. 1884.
      h. Adelaide Winifred, b. 19 Dec. 1888.
  5. Mary Grav, m. Right Rev. John Martindale Speechly, D.D., Bishop of Travancore, S. India. He d. 22 Jan. 1898.
  5. Sarah, m. Col. C. M. White, Madras Staff Corps, and d. 1892.
  7. Charlotte, d. unm. 1850.
  8. Emily, d. unm. 1861.

(4) Frederick, Capt. 13th Dragoons, b. 1788; m. 1826, Frances Selina, eldest dau. of Col. Gregory, of Styvechale Park, Coventry. Both d.s.p. 1827.
(1) Isabella, m. Capt. Benjamin Chapman, 18th Royal Irish Regt., who d. about 1859.
(2) A dau., m. Capt. Fortnum.
(3) Sarah Mercer, b. 1782 ; m. 21 June, 1800, Col. Sir H. C. Montgomery, 1st bart., H.E.I.C.S. She d. 8 Dec. 1854. He d. 21 Jan. 1830, leaving issue.
3. Henry, Member of Council, Dominica, b. 1749; m. Isabelle, dau. of Thomas Wilson, of Pontefract, Yorks, Chief Judge of Dominica. She d. 1853. He d. 1788, having had issue,
(1) Henry Leslie, R.N., m. 1795, Polly, dau. of Edward Dunsterville, of Penryn, Cornwall. She d. 1843. He d. 1868, leaving issue,
  1. Henry Leslie, d. unm. 1825.
  2. John Colpoys, d. unm. 1829.
  3. George Wilson, m. 1832, Maria, dau. of J. W. Dunsterville, and had issue.
  4. Charles Bullen, d. young, 1815.
  5. Edward Elias Dunsterville, d. 1856.
(1) Isabella, d. unm. 1871. (2) Sarah, d. unm.
1. Elizabeth, m. Ven. Charles Leslie, D.D., Archdeacon of Raphoe. He d. 1781. She d. 1818.
2. Catherine. 3. Dorothy.
1. Constance, m. A. Slater.

The 2nd son,
WILLIAM GROVE, of Castle Grove, which he built 1730, High Sheriff co. Donegal 1727-8, m. Susanna, dau. of Philip Barry, of Kilcarra, co. Meath. He d. 1742-3, having by her (who d. 1780, aged 80) had issue,
1. Thomas, of Castle Grove, b. 1719 ; d.s.p. 1792.
2. James, of Castle Grove, b. 1725 ; m. Rose Vaughan, dau. of Basil Brooke, and d. 1793, having by her (who d. 1809, aged 74) had issue,
  1. Thomas, of Castle Grove, High Sheriff co. Donegal, assumed the name of BROOKE 1808, m. 1794, his cousin Mary Susanna, dau. of Rev. Charles Grove (see below), and d.s.p. 1830. She d. 1863.
  1. Jane, m. 1794, Thomas Young, of Logheske, co. Donegal.
  2. Mary Susanna, m. 1806, Col. William Richardson, of Richardstown, co. Louth, Capt. of the Irish Battleaxe Guards.
3. William, b. 1734 ; d. 1783.
4. Richard, m. Susanna Grier, of North Carolina, and d. 1766, leaving a son, William Barry.
5. Humphrey, of Letterkenny, co. Donegal, M.D., b. 1741 ; m. Barbara, dau. of — Delap. She d. 1809, aged 71. He d. 1784.
6. CHARLES, of whom presently.
1. Judith, d.s.p. 1812. 2. Elizabeth, d.s.p. 1810.

The youngest son,
REV. CHARLES GROVE, Vicar of Kilmacshalgan and Templeboy, co. Sligo, B.A., T.C.D., b. 1742 ; m. Mary Gilmour, and d. 1818, leaving issue,
1. William (Rev.), Vicar of Kilmacshalgan and Templeboy, co. Sligo, B.A. T.C.D., b. 1768 ; m. 1803, Elizabeth Dorothea, dau. of William Knox, of Ballybofey, co. Donegal, and d.s.p. 1857.
1. Mary Susannah, b. 1778 ; m. 1794, her cousin Thomas Grove, of Castle Grove, who took the name of BROOKE (see above), and d.s.p. 1863.
2. DOROTHY, of whom presently. 3. Helen Elizabeth.

The younger dau.,
DOROTHY GROVE, m. 1802, John Wood, of 9th Light Dragoons, son of James Wood, of Woodville, co. Sligo, by Maria his wife, dau. of James Leech, of Castle Conner, and by him (who d. Oct. 1816) had issue (with a dau., Mary, m. Henry Godfrey, and had issue), a son,
JAMES GROVE WOOD GROVE, of Castle Grove, co. Donegal, J.P. and D.L., High Sheriff 1855, B.A., Barrister-at-Law, adopted the name of GROVE in 1863 on succeeding to the Castle Grove Estate, b. 1803 ; m. 1843, Frances Judith, dau. of Robert Montgomery, of Convoy House, co. Donegal, by Maria Frances Stewart his wife, niece of Robert, 1st Marquess of Londonderry, and grand-dau. of the 1st Marquis of Drogheda. She d. Feb. 1896. He d. 1891, having had issue,
1. JOHN MONTGOMERY CHARLES, now of Castle Grove.
2. Robert Thomas Wood, Capt. R.N., b. 1850.
3. Charles William, b. 1853 ; m. about 1896, Emily, dau. of — Harris, and has issue,
  1. Charles. 1. Godfrey.
1. Mary Susanna Frances, b. June, 1846 ; d. March, 1850.
2. Dorothea Alice, m. 1871, Rev. Canon Charles William Boyton, M.A., of Londonderry, and has issue.
3. Frances Mary Ellen, m. Sept. 1896, William Leckie Ewing.

Arms (of GROVE)—Arg., on a chevron engrailed gu. three escallops of the field.

Seat—Castle Grove, Letterkenny, co. Donegal.

GROVE. See **WHITE.**

GRUBB OF ARDMAYLE.

LOUIS HENRY GRUBB, of Ardmayle, co. Tipperary, J.P., D.L., High Sheriff 1897, b. 17 July, 1865, B.A. Brasenose Coll. Oxon. 1888, M.A. 1897 ; m. 18 Jan. 1899, Sara Mary Watkins, dau. of Lieut.-Col. Alexander Grubb, late R.A., of Elsfield, Kent (see below), and has issue,
1. HENRY CECIL, b. 1899.
2. Cedric Alexander, b. 1902.
3. Samuel Louis, b. 1905.
1. Dorothy May Petrohell.

Lineage.—ISHMAEL GRUBB, of Ravensthorp, Northamptonshire, b. 1594 ; d. 1676, was father of,
JOHN GRUBB, of Ravensthorp, settled at Waterford in 1656 and was afterwards of Annaghs, co. Kilkenny, and Meyler's Park, co. Tipperary. He m. twice. 1st Mary, dau. of — Towers, and had issue,
1. Samuel, of Annaghs, co. Kilkenny, m. Rebecca, dau. of William Trasher, and left issue, now extinct.
1. Margaret, m. William Hughes.
2. Elizabeth, m. John Chamery, of London.
3. Frances, m. 1st James Cannam, 2ndly Joseph Hawkins.

By his 2nd wife, Elizabeth, he had a son,
JOHN GRUBB, of Meyler's Park and Woodhouse, co. Tipperary, d. 22 Feb. 1731 ; m. 4 Jan. 1707-8, Anne, only dau. of William Willan, and by her, who d. 13 Aug. 1765, had with other issue,
1. JOSEPH, his heir.
2. John, b. 1712 ; d. 1799 ; m. Mary Jones, and left issue.
3. William, b. 1714 ; m. Margaret Boles, who d. 1780, and left issue.
4. Benjamin, b. 1727 ; d. 1802 ; m. 1758, Susanna Malone, and left issue by her, who d. 1806,
1. Elizabeth, b. 1713 ; d. 1755 ; m. Gideon Taylor.
2. Anne, b. 1727 ; m. Simmons Sparrow.

The eldest son,
JOSEPH GRUBB, of Clonmel, b. 1709 ; d. 1782 ; m. Jan. 1736, Sarah Greer (b. 1716 ; d. 1788), and had twelve children of whom the following survived,
1. Thomas, b. 1736 ; d. 1809 ; m. 1764, Hannah Allen, and left issue by her, who d. 1801.
2. John, b. 1737 ; d. 1784 ; m. 1778, Sarah Pim, and left issue five daus. by her, who d. 1812.
3. Joseph, b. 1739 ; d. 1790 ; m. 1775, Sarah Ridgway, and left issue by her, who d. 1811.
4. SAMUEL, of whom presently.
1. Sarah, b. 1747 ; d. 1772 ; m. Jacob Handcock.
2. Rebecca, b. 1786, Joseph Strangman.

The 4th son,
SAMUEL GRUBB, of Clonmel, b. 1750 ; d. March, 1815 ; m. 17 April, 1776, Margaret Shackleton, and had eleven children, of whom survived,
1. Abraham, b. 1777 ; d. 1840 ; m. 1800, Susanna Banfield, and left issue by her, who d. 1834, four daus.
  1. Anne, m. 1824, Thomas Murray, d. 1881.
  2. Margaret, m. William Bell.
  3. Elizabeth, m. William Davis.
  4. Rebecca, d. 1880 ; m. 1st Sydney Brown, 2ndly Rev. John J. Sargint.
2. Richard, b. 1780 ; d. 1859 ; m. 1807, Susan, dau. of John Barcroft Haughton, and had issue,
  1. Samuel, b. 1809 ; d. 1843 ; m. 1834, Anna Watson (d. 1874), and had surviving issue,
    (1) Richard, b. 1835 ; m. 1876, Frances Field Castles (d. 1902), and had,
      Francis Lecky Watson, b. 1879.
    (2) Samuel Seymour, b. 1842 ; m. 1902, Mary Louisa Clarkson.
  2. Barcroft Haughton, b. 1811 ; d. 1879 ; m. 1834, Eliza Ridgway (d. 1892), and left surviving,
    Samuel, b. 1845 ; m. 1883, Anne Vennell.
  3. Richard, of Cahir Abbey, co. Tipperary, b. 1812 ; d. 1886 ; m. 1837, Mary, dau. of Richard Garratt, of Granite Hall, co. Dublin (d. 1870), and left,
    (1) Richard Cambridge, of Cahir Abbey, co. Tipperary, and Killeaton, co. Antrim, b. 1841 ; m. 1870, Hannah, dau. of Jonathan Richardson, and has,
      Richard, b. 1873.
      Lilian Margaret, m. 1892, Robert Henry Metge, of Athlumny, co. Meath, and had issue (see that family).
    (2) Alexander, of Elsfield House, Hollingbourne, Kent, b. 1842, late Lieut.-Col. R.A. ; m. 1871, Sarah Mary, dau. of Rev. Henry George Watkins, and has issue,
      1. Alexander Henry Watkins, b. 1873 ; Capt. R.E., D.S.O. ; m. 1898, Frances Marie, dau. of James Brent Cox, of Kentucky, U.S.A., and has,
        Alexander James Watkins, b. 1909.
      2. Herbert Watkins, b. 1875 ; m. 1909, Noel Mears.

3. Ernest Watkins (Rev.), M.A. (Oxon), b. 1877; m. 1907, Mary Pauline Bevan, and has issue,
Geoffrey Bevan Watkins, b. 1908.
4. Walter Bousfield Watkins, b. 1879.
5. Reginald Watkins, b. 1883; m. 1908, Zoe Kathleen Gwynne, and has,
Yvonne Watkins.
1. Sara Mary Watkins, m. 18 Jan. 1899, LOUIS HENRY GRUBB, now of Ardmayle (see above).
2. Elsie Maria Watkins, m. 1911, Dryden Donkin.
(3) Frederic Ernest, b. 1844; m. Edith Gonig (d. 1905), and had,
1. Frederick Ernest, b. 1878; m. 1906, Hilda Margaret McClintock, and has,
Robert McClintock, b. 1906.
2. Richard, b. 1880.   3. Reginald, b. 1882.
4. George Cambridge, b. 1888.
1. Maria Ganett, m. 1904, William Armfield.
2. Edith, m. 1908, Herbert Stansfield.
3. Matilda Harding, m. 1898, John Holdcroft.
4. Ethel Ernestine, m. 1905, Alfred Stansfield.
5. Olive Muriel.   6. Florence Claudia.
(4) Harry Percy (Rev.), M.A. (Dublin), Vicar of Holy Trinity, Macclesfield, b. 1848; m. 7 May, 1892, Margaret Adelaide, dau. of Herbert Crichton-Stuart, D.L. (see BUTE MARQUESS or), and has,
1. Harold Crichton Stuart, b. 1893.
2. Norman Percy, b. 1895.
3. Kenneth George, b. 1900.
1. Violet Margaret.
(5) William Pike, b. 1850; m. Jan. 1889, Ethel Elizabeth, dau. of Col. Lewis Mansergh Buchanan, C.B., of Edenfell, co. Tyrone (see that family), and has,
1. Lewis William Richardson, b. 1896.
2. Richard Cambridge Whitla, b. 1899.
1. Ethel Helena.
(6) Charles Alfred, b. 1851; m. Alice, dau. of — Britton, of St. Ives, Sydney, N.S.W.
(7) George Carleton, b. 1856; m. 1906, Ethel Wemyss Disney.
(1) Isabella, m. Stephen Daniel.
(2) Susanna, m. 1863, Alexander Airth Richardson, of Aberdeelvy, co. Antrim.
(3) Helena.
4. Frederic, b. 1815; d. 1891; m. 1842, Anne Haughton d. 1894), and left two daus.,
(1) Rose Frederica.
(2) Helena Christiania, m. 1st, 1890, William Sutherland (d. 1901); 2ndly, 7 June, 1910, Rev. Arthur B. Graham.
5. Augustus, b. 1824; d. 1878; m. 1852, Maria Elizabeth Hill, and left,
(1) Augustus Hill, b. 1853; d. unm. 1888.
(2) Ernest Pelham, b. 1854; m. 1888, E. M. Lawrence, and has,
Lawrence Ernest, b. 1892.
(3) Raglan Somerset, b. 1856; m. 1901, M. A. Hughes.
(4) Beaufort Somerset, b. 1862; m. 1890, E. F. Lowe.
(1) Juliana Carleton, m. 1884, Surg.-Maj. Thomas Holmstead.
(2) Clara Augusta, m. 1890, Joseph Meredith.
1. Sarah, d. 1878; m. 1833, Henry Ridgway.
2. Helena, m. 1834, John Grubb Richardson, of Bessbrook, co. Armagh.
3. Susan Eliza, m. 1st, 1843, William Carroll, 2ndly, 1860, William Hall Graham.
3. SAMUEL, of whom presently.
4. Robert, b. 1790; d. 1882; m. 1812, Anna Greer Fayle, and left issue.
5. Thomas Samuel, b. 1792; d. 1885; m. 1819, Elizabeth, dau. of John Barcroft Haughton (d. 1839), and left, with other issue,
1. Samuel Thomas, of Tower Hill, co. Waterford, b. 1821, J.P. cos. Kilkeny and Waterford, High Sheriff City of Waterfo d 1863; m. 1845, Eliza, only child of Rev. Alexander Alcock. She d. 1903, issue,
(1) Thomas Alcock Cambridge, b. 1846; m. 1880, Clementina, dau. of — Lange, and has,
Alcock George Francis, b. 1883; m. 1904, Berthe, dau. of John Frank, of Newcastle-on-Tyne.
(2) Alexander Newcomen Alcock, b. 1855.
2. Thomas Cambridge, b. 1824; d. 1903; m. 1st 1846, Jane Haughton, 2ndly Mary Ryan.
1. Margaret, m. 1851, Richard Davis Grubb, of Castle Grace, co. Tipperary.
1. Anne, m. Robert Fayle.   2. Sarah, m. Francis Davis.
3. Margaret, m. Thomas Fayle.
The 3rd son,
SAMUEL GRUBB, of Clogheen, co. Tipperary, b. 1787; d. 1859; m. 1819, Deborah Davis, and left issue,
1. Richard Davis, of Castle Grace, co. Tipperary, b. 1820; d. 1865; m. 1851, Margaret, dau. of Thomas Samuel Grubb, of Clonmel, and left,
Samuel Richard, of Castle Grace, b. 1855, J.P. co. Tipperary; m. 1885, Alice Hannah, dau. of Edward W. Binney, of Ravenscliffe, Isle of Man, and has,
Richard Raymond de Cruce, b. 1886, Lieut. 3rd Hussars.
Joan Mary.
Margaret, m. 1895, John Russell Mecham.
2. HENRY SAMUEL, of whom presently.
3. Arthur b. 1827; d. unm. 1882.
4. Robert, b. 1830; d. unm. 1864.
5. Edward, b. 1838; d. unm. 1878.
1. Sarah, m. 1865, Thomas Andrews.

2. Elizabeth, m. 1864, Edwin Taylor.
3. Louisa, m. 1860, Charles Barrington.
The 2nd son,
HENRY SAMUEL GRUBB, of Clogheen, co. Tipperary, b. 1825; d. 14 Oct. 1891; m. 1864, Martha Elizabeth, dau. of Thomas Hughes, of Ystrad, Denbigh, and left an only child,
LOUIS HENRY, now of Ardmayle.

Arms—Per chevron, erm. and gu., in base a harp or, stringed arg. on a chief crenellée of the last three roses ppr. Crest—A gryphon's head erased per chevron crenellée sa. and arg. charged with two roses in pale ppr. Motto—Bonne et assez belle.

Seat—Ardmayle, Cashel, co. Tipperary. Club—Kildare Street, Dublin.

GUBBINS OF KILFRUSH.

FRANCIS JOSEPH BERESFORD GUBBINS, of Kilfrush, co. Limerick, late Lieut. R.E., J.P. co. Limerick, High Sheriff 1906, b. 11 Dec. 1865; m. 14 June, 1893, Mary, eldest dau. of Alexander Ward, of White Mills, Dunleer, co. Louth.

Lineage.—JOSEPH GUBBINS, of Knocklong, co. Limerick, whose will, dated 1693, mentions his daus. and his two sons. The elder son,
JOSEPH GUBBINS, of Kilfrush, co. Limerick, who d. Jan. 1737, leaving, with a dau., Mary, m. 1713, Capt. John Miunitt, of Knygh Castle, co. Tipperary, a son,
JOSEPH GUBBINS, of Kilfrush, who entered Trinity College, Dublin, aged 18, 24 May, 1717. He m. (settlement dated 1 Jan. 1728) Anne, dau. of Stephen Grant, of Cork, and had issue,
1. JOSEPH, his heir.
2. JAMES, of Kenmare Castle, co. Limerick, m. 1st, June, 1772, Bridget, dau. of B. Wrixon, of co. Cork, and by her had issue,
1. JOSEPH, of Kenmare Castle. co. Limerick, High Sheriff 1806, m. 14 April, 1805, Annie, dau. of William Henn, of Paradise Hill, co. Clare, and by her (who d. 18 March, 1848) had issue,
(1) JAMES, of Kenmare Castle, J.P., b. 1 June, 1810; m. 18 Dec. 1845, Jane Hare, youngest dau. of Rev. Marshall Clarke, and d. 1858, having had issue,
Joseph Marshall, b. 10 Sept. 1846, dec.
Elizabeth Anne.
(2) William.
(3) Poole, Lieut. R.N., d. on board the Scylla at Port Royal, Jamaica, 25 April, 1843.
(1) Bridget, m. 22 April, 1843, Augustus Pentland, who d. 18 July, 1854, s.p.
1. Sarah, m. 1st, John Lysaght, of co. Cork; and 2ndly, John Wrixon, of Summerville, co. York.
He m. 2ndly, Letitia, dau. of Henry Sheares, of Cork, M.P. for Clonakilty, by Jane Anne his wife, dau. of Robert Bettesworth, of Whiterock, co. Cork, and had issue,
2. Henry (Rev.), Rector of Ballycahane, co. Limerick, and Garrison Chaplain of Limerick; m. 3 Nov. 1810, Avarina, sole surviving child of Capt. Robert Atkins, of Fountainville, co. York, by Jane Purdon his wife, 3rd dau. of Richard Ringrose Bowerman, of Moynoe House, co. Clare, and by her (who d. 21 May, 1827) had issue,
(1) Robert Atkins, Lieut. 62nd Regt., killed at Sutledge, 24 Dec. 1845, unm.   (2) Henry (Rev.), dec.
(1) Sarah, m. 1848, Roger O'Callaghan, son of Roger O'Callaghan.   (2) Avarina.   (3) Letitia.
3. William.
1. Anne, m. 1761, Charles Massy, of Griston, co. Limerick, brother of Hugh Massy, 1st Lord Massy.
2. Elizabeth, m. 18 July, 1761, Michael Bevan, eldest son of Henry Bevan, of Camas, co. Limerick.
3. Mary, m. 20 Aug. 1766, James John Bourchier, of Baggotstown.
4. Esther, m. Robert Lidwill, 2nd son of George Lidwill, of Dromard, co. Tipperary.
5. Margaret.   6. Dorothea.
The eldest son,
JOSEPH GUBBINS, of Kilfrush, whose will was dated 24 March, 1776, m. March, 1767, Mary, dau. of George Stamer, of Cahirnelly, co. Clare, and had issue,
1. GEORGE STAMER, his heir.
2. Joseph, Maj.-Gen. in the Army, m. 18 July, 1803, Charlotte, dau. of John Bathoe, of Bath. She d. 29 March, 1824. He d. 23 April, 1832, leaving issue,
1. John Panton, of The Oaks, Leamington, formerly H.E.I.C.S., D.L. co. Flint, and J.P. Anglesey and Warwickshire, b. 14 Sept. 1806; m. 1st, 1831, Emma Rhoda, dau. of Sir Robert Cuniffe, Bart., and had no issue. He m. 2ndly, 11 April, 1839, Mary Eyles, 2nd dau. of William Egerton, of Gresford Lodge, and had issue,
(1) John Egerton, Maj. R.A. (retired), b. 8 May, 1840; m. 23 Dec. 1877, Charlote Lyon.
(2) George William, Lieut. R.N., b. 24 Aug. 1854.
(3) Robert, Lieut. R.N., b. 7 Nov. 1857.
(4) Philip, Maj. R.E., b. 11 March, 1859; d. 25 Dec. 1901.
(1) Mary Elizabeth, m. Oct. 1877, Thomas Brock, son of the Dean of Guernsey.
2. Charles, Bengal Civil Service, m. the dau. of Joseph Hume, M.P.; he d. 1866.
3. Martin Richard, Bengal Civil Service, m. 3 Aug. 1841, Harriet Louisa, dau. of Frederick Nepean, of Calcutta, 2nd son of Sir Evan Nepean, 1st bart., Governor of Bombay (see BURKE'S Peerage, NEPEAN, Bart.). She d. 1895. He d. 1863, leaving issue,

Guinness. THE LANDED GENTRY. 284

(1) Martin Nepean, d. 1872.
(2) William Henry Bebb, d. 1883.
(3) Charles Edgeworth, Maj. late Bengal S.C., 3rd Hyderabad Cav., one of H.M.'s Corps of Gentlemen-at-Arms, b. 18 July, 1849; m. 12 Aug. 1875, Ellen Anna, dau. of the late Major-Gen. Edmund David Russell Ross, B.S.C. He d. 12 March, 1906, leaving issue,
  Charles Frederick Ross, Barrister-at-Law, of the Inner Temple, b. 9 May, 1879.
  Norah Helen Louisa, b. 13 May, 1876.
(4) Frederick Cartwright (*Nonington, near Dover*), b. 22 Aug. 1850; m. 1st, 13 Jan. 1881, Mary Alice, 3rd dau. of Gilbert F. Traill, J.P., Orkney, and has issue,
  1. Frederick Nepean Traill, b. 1 Nov. 1881; d. 9 May, 1882.
  2. Evelyn Charles Traill, b. 8 Dec. 1882; d. 5 May, 1885.
  3. Martin Nepean Traill, b. 16 April, 1891.
  1. Gladys Mary, b. 25 Dec. 1883.
  2. Honor Elizabeth Traill, b. 4 Jan. 1888.
He m. 2ndly, 1902, Emily Agnes, eldest surviving dau. of C. J. Plumptre, of Fredville Park, near Dover (*see that family*).
(5) John Harington, C.M.G., Lecturer in Japanese at the University of Oxford, late Secretary of Legation and Japanese Secretary of the Embassy at Tokio, b. 1852; m. 1893, Helen Brodie, dau. of C. A. McVean, J.P., of Kilfinichen, Mull, N.B., and has issue,
  1. Hugh Power Nepean, b. 25 March, 1894.
  2. Colin MacVean, b. 2 July, 1896.
  1. Una MacLean, b. 5 June, 1895.
  2. Marjorie Mary, b. 17 Feb. 1898.
  3. Helen Ruth Martin, b. 5 Sept. 1900.
  (1) Norah, m. Lieut.-Col. Charles Oxenden, and has issue.
4. Frederick, C.B., Bengal Civil Service, sometime Commissioner to Gov.-Gen. of India, b. 1818; d. 27 March, 1902.
  1. Lucy, m. 1872, Richard Woodward, Bengal Civil Service.
  2. Honoria, m. 1833, William Hans Sloane Stanley, of Paultons, Hants, and by him (who d. 1879) had issue.
  3. Elizabeth Catherine, m. 1st, 29 May, 1839, William Aubrey de Vere, 9th Duke of St. Albans; and 2ndly, 10 Nov. 1859, Viscount Falkland (*see* BURKE's *Peerage*). She d. 2 Dec. 1893.
1. Honor, m. 1803, Ralph Dutton, who d.s.p. 1804.
2. Mary, m. 1st, Thomas Panton; and 2ndly, Gen. John Gent.
The eldest son,
GEORGE STAMER GUBBINS, of Kilfrush, whose will bears date 2 April, 1797, m. Anne, dau. of Francis Russell, and had issue,
1. JOSEPH, of Kilfrush.
2. George, m. Miss Blood, of co. Clare.
1. Mary, d. unm.
2. Eliza Georgina, m. Rev. W. Evans Hartopp, Rector of Harby, co. Leicester.
The eldest son,
JOSEPH GUBBINS, of Kilfrush, m. Maria, dau. of Thomas Wise, of Cork, and by her (who d. May, 1841) had issue,
1. JOSEPH, of whom presently.
2. Thomas Wise, of Bottomstown, co. Limerick, and Dunkathel, co. Cork, b. 1830; m. 1st, 1855, Mary (who d.s.p. that year), dau. of John Franks, of Ballyscaddanc (*see that family*); and 2ndly, 1857, Frances Gertrude, eldest dau. of Thompson Russell, of Askeaton, co. Limerick. He d. 7 Aug. 1904, having had issue,
  1. Joseph Hartopp, of Dunkathal and Bottomstown, co. Limerick (*Dunkathal, Glanmire, co. Cork*), b. 1858; m. 24 Jan. 1907, Helen Frances Barnard, only dau. of Walter Barnard Byles, of Harefield, Uxbridge, and Princes Gardens, S.W., and has had issue, a son, b. 26 Jan.; d. 5 Feb. 1908.
  2. Russell Dunmore, Lieut.-Col. R.A., b. 1862.
  Frances Gertrude, m. 23 March, 1895, Capt. Edward Honeywood Hughes, son of Gen. Sir William Hughes, K.C.B., of Dunley House, Devon. He d. 1900.
3. John, of Brutee House, co. Limerick, High Sheriff 1888, b. 1839; m. 1889, Edith, dau. of the late Charles B. Legh, of Adlington Hall, co. Cheshire. He d. 20 March, 1906. She d. 25 Aug. 1896.
4. Stamer, of Knockany, Capt. 30th Regt., d. 1878.
1. Anna Georgina Thomasine, m. 29 March, 1855, James Napier Webb. He d.s.p. 1888 (*see that family*). She d. 5 April, 1906.
2. Alice, d. unm. 27 Sept. 1896.
3. Maria, m. March, 1861, Capt. Wray Bury Palliser, of Annestown (*see that family*), and d. 10 Jan. 1896.
4. Henrietta, m. 1855, Simon Dring, of Rocksgrove, co. Cork, who d. 1879, leaving issue (*see* DRING of *Tower Hill*). She d. 7 Oct. 1911.
5. Emily, m. Thomas Browning, orass Cf Caourt, co. Limerick.
The eldest son,
JOSEPH GUBBINS, of Kilfrush, co. Limerick, J.P., High Sheriff 1863, b. 1829; m. 3 Sept. 1863, Frances Thomasine, 2nd dau. of Sir Beresford Burston MacMahon, Bart. She d. 25 Feb. 1909. He d. 20 Feb. 1895, leaving issue,
1. FRANCIS JOSEPH BERESFORD, now of Kilfrush.
2. Frederick William Beresford, late R.E., b. 1868; m. 22 Jan. 1896, Vera, youngest dau. of Robert Law, of New Park, co. Kildare, and has issue,
  1. Thomas Stanier Beresford, b. 2 Nov. 1897.
  2. Roderick Joseph Beresford, b. 1899.
3. Marcus Stamer Beresford, late Lieut. 2nd Dragoon Guards, b. 15 Nov. 1874; m. 26 June, 1901, Nina Alice, dau. of David Gaussen, of Green's Norton Manor, Towchester (*see* GAUSSEN of *Shanemullagh*).
4. Lucius Burston Beresford, Lieut. 3rd Batt. Highland L.I.,

b. 1876; m. 15 April, 1909, Etta Mary, eldest dau. of late Edmund Gibson, of Waitangi, N.Z.
5. Quintus Evelyn Beresford, b. 1879; d. unm. 5 Jan. 1899.
Seat—Kilfrush, Knocklong, co. Limerick.

GUINNESS. *See* BURKE'S PEERAGE, **ARDILAUN, B.** and **IVEAGH, B.**

GUN OF RATTOO.

WILLIAM TOWNSEND JACKSON GUN, of Rattoo, co. Kerry, J.P., High Sheriff 1902, Barrister-at-Law, b. 30 May, 1876, educated at Harrow and at Trin. Coll. Camb., B.A.; s. his grandfather 1893; m. 29 April, 1908, Ethel Winifred, younger dau. of the Rev. Charles Young, M.A., Vicar of Chewton Mendip, Somerset.

Lineage.—REV. WILLIAM GUNN, of Limerick, will proved 1614, m. Eleanor, dau. of Randal Mayawaring, of Peover, Cheshire (Fun. Ent. Ulster's Office 23 May, 1638). She remarried Rt. Rev. Wm. Stears, Bishop of Ardfert, who. d. 21 Jan. 1637. The only son was
WILLIAM GUNN, of Ballykelly, co. Kerry, m. Elizabeth Meredith. Adm. to husband's offspring granted to her 30 April, 1639. Had issue,
WILLIAM GUN, of Liscahane Castle, living 1641, m. the dau. of Samuel Raymond, of Ballyloughrane, co. Kerry, second son of Edward Raymond, of Dunmow, Essex, and Mary, dau. of Anthony Stoughton, and had two sons,
1. WILLIAM, his heir. 2. Richard, d. unm.
The elder son,
WILLIAM GUN, of Rattoo, m. Elizabeth, dau. of Col. Richard Waller, of Cully, co. Tipperary, and d. about 1699 (will dated 30 Sept. 1690, proved 1699) leaving issue,
1. Richard, d.s.p. v.p. 2. WILLIAM, of whom presently.
3. George, of Kilmorna and Gunsborough and of Carrigafoile Castle, co. Kerry, m. 1690, Sarah, dau. of Rev. Thomas Connor, Archdeacon of Ardfert, 1693-1704, and d. 1744 (will dated 17 Oct. 1743, proved 16 April, 1744) leaving issue,
  1. William, of Kilmorna and Gunsborough, b. 1710; m. 1stly, 1737, Elizabeth Anne, dau. of the Hon. Mr. Justice Henry Rose, M.P., of Mount Pleasant, co. Limerick, by whom he had no issue. He m. 2ndly, 30 June, 1739, Elizabeth, eldest dau. and coheir of Isaac Dobson and Ellen Massey his wife, and left issue two daus.,
    (1) Ellen, m. 22 March, 1762, Hon. and Very Rev. Maurice Crosbie, D.D., Dean of Limerick 1771-1809, and d. 1767, leaving issue, Elizabeth, m. Edward Moore, of Mooresfort, co. Tipperary.
    (2) Sarah, m. 1771, Sir Joshua Paul, Bart. (*see* BURKE's *Peerage and Baronetage*).
  2. John, of Cloherbrien, co. Kerry, Capt. in Wolfe's Regt. m. Martha, dau. of Rev. Thomas Collis, Vicar of Dingle, by Avis his wife, dau. of Thomas Blennerhasset, of Castle Conway, and d. about 1756 (will dated 12 June, 1765, proved 16 July, 1766), having by her (who m. 2ndly, Cam Richard Frankland) had a son,
    George, of Kilmorna and Gunsborough, co. Kerry, and afterwards of Mount Kennedy, co. Wicklow (*see* GUN-CUNINGHAME of *Mount Kennedy*).
  3. George, of Ballybunion, m. 1st. 1747, Elizabeth, dau. of James Raymond, of Ballyvegan, and had a son, George, his heir. He m. 2ndly, 1784, Joice, dau. of Robert Leslie, of Tarbert House, and by her had John Leslie, d. unm. The son by the 1st wife, George, of Ballybunion, m. 1774, Arabella, dau. of Rev. Barry Denny, of Ballyvelly, and had, with two daus., Jane Joice, m. 1st, 1812, Capt. Robert Cashell, and 2ndly, William Hikeman; and Arabella, m. John Watts, an only son,
    Barry William, of Plover Hill, m. 5 Sept. 1807, Jane, 2nd dau. of William Wilson, and d. 25 Aug. 1828, leaving an only child, George, of Ballybunion and Plover Hill, J.P., b. 21 Oct. 1808; m. 4 Sept. 1833, Belinda, dau. and co-heir of John Boles Reeves, of Belfort, co. Cork, and d.s.p.
  4. Henry (Rev.) Rector of Annagh and Cloherbrien 1755.
  5. Richard, will dated 1734.
    1. Honora, m. 1746, James Raymond, of Dromin, co. Kerry, and had issue. 2. Margaret.
    3. Sarah, m. 1734, Arthur Blennerhasset.
    4. Elizabeth, m. Richard Morris, of Castle Morris and Ballybeggan, and had issue. 5. Mary, m. Shepherd.
4. Samuel.
5. David, who had a son, George.
1. Anne. 2. Dorothy. 3. Agnes.
The 2nd son,
WILLIAM GUN, of Rattoo, m. 1694, Catherine, dau. of Col. Richard Townsend, by Mary Hyde his wife, and d. (will dated 16 Mar. 1723, proved 25 Nov. 1723) leaving with other issue (Francis; Richard; William; Rebecca; Sarah; and Catherine) a son and heir,
TOWNSEND GUN, of Rattoo, m. Elizabeth, dau. of John Blennerhassett, of Castle Conway, co. Kerry, and dying in 1766 by her left, with two daus. (Catherine, b. 1728, and Elizabeth, b. 1735, m. Thomas, 1st Lord Ventry), an only son,
WILLIAM TOWNSEND GUN, of Rattoo, m. 1st, 7 Dec. 1765, Sarah, eldest dau. of Anthony Stoughton, of Ballyhorgan, co. Kerry, and had issue,
1. TOWNSEND, his heir. 2. Thomas, d. unm.
3. William, m. Margaret, 2nd dau. of Sir William M'Kenny, Bart., and left a dau., Sarah.

IRELAND. Hall.

1. Elizabeth, *m.* 1st, 1783, James Fuller Harnett ; and 2ndly. Maj. William Ponsonby, of Crotta, and had issue by both husbands.
2. Sarah, *m.* Samuel Morris, of Ballybeggan, co. Kerry, and had, with other issue, Georgina, eventually sole heiress, who *m.* Capt. Lloyd Henry de Ruvignes, and had issue.
3. Frances, *m.* Thomas Collis.
4. Penelope, *m.* the Rev. James Mabon ; and had issue.
5. Catherine, *m.* Rev. Stephen Dunlevie ; and had issue.

He *d.* 1812, and was *s.* by his son,
TOWNSEND GUN, of Rattoo, *m.* 1803, Amelia, eldest dau. of William Wilson, and by her (who *d.* 1845) had issue,
1. William Townsend, *b.* 1808 ; *d. unm.* 1837 ; High Sheriff 1834.
2. WILSON, late of Rattoo.
1. Catherine, *m.* 1824, Capt. Whitworth Lloyd, R.N. ; *d.* June, 1875, and left issue.
2. Sarah, *m.* 1806, Augustus Warren ; *d.* 1867. and left issue.
3. Jane, *m.* the Rev. Edward M. Denny, Vicar of Listowel, and left issue.
4. Elizabeth, *m.* 1831, Maj. William Thomas Harrison, and *d.* 1835.

Mr. Gun *d.* 1817, and was *s.* by his 2nd son,
WILSON GUN, of Rattoo, co. Kerry, J.P. and D.L., High Sheriff 1846, *b.* 26 May, 1809 ; *m.* May, 1839, Gertrude Marianne, 2nd dau. of Henry E. Allen, of Hampton Manor, Bath, Somerset, and had issue,
1. Towusend George, *b.* 23 May, 1840, J.P. co. Kerry, High Sheriff, 1870 ; *d.* 25 May, 1875.
2. Henry Allen, J.P., Capt. Royal Engineers, *b.* 22 April, 1842 ; *m.* May, 1875, Elizabeth Esther, 3rd dau. of Henry Beecroft Jackson, of Basford House, Whalley Range, Manchester, and *d.* 22 March, 1878, leaving by her (who *d.* 5 June, 1876) a son,
WILLIAM TOWNSEND JACKSON, now of Rattoo.
1. Emma Frances, *m.* 1 Oct. 1862, George Robert Browne, J.P., of Cahirdown, Listowel. He *d.* 24 Mar. 1904, leaving issue.

Mr. Wilson Gun *d.* 30 April, 1893, and was *s.* by his grandson.

Seat—Rattoo, Lixnaw, co. Kerry.

GUN-CUNINGHAME. *See* CUNINGHAME.

BROWN-GUTHRIE.
See BURKE'S PEERAGE, **ORANMORE, B.**

HACKETT OF RIVERSTOWN.

CHARLES BERNARD HACKETT, of Riverstown, co. Tipperary, Lieut. P.O.W. Yorks. Regt., *b.* 18 April, 1886.

Lineage.—ROBERT HACKETT, of Eglish, King's Co., left by Anne his wife (with several daus., one of whom *m.* Richard Burris, of Ballintemple, King's Co. ; and another, Deborah, *m.* 1813, Robert Robinson, of Tinnikelly), four sons,
1. SIMPSON, of whom presently.
2. William, of Prospect, Parsonstown, *d.* 1830.
3. Michael, of Elm Grove, Parsonstown, *m.* 1799, Jane, dau., of Adam Mitchell, and *d.* 1856, leaving issue,
1. Robert, a Cavalry Officer, *m.* Mary Anne Steele, and *d.s.p.* His widow, *m.* 2ndly, 1838, Joseph Michael Rivers.
2. THOMAS of Whiteford, *m.* 1838, Isabel Jackson, and *d.* 1875, leaving issue,
3. Wellington, an Officer in the Army, *d. unm.*
4. Adam, Lieut. in the Army, *d. unm.*
5. George, an Officer in the Army, *m.* and left issue.
6. Samuel, Col. (retired), late Maj. 38th Regt., *d.* 1891.
7. Richard, of Elm Grove, J.P., *m.* 1st, ——, dau. of Rev. E. FitzGerald, by whom he had a son,
(1) Capt. Frederick, *d.s.p.* 1908.
He *m.* 2ndly, 30 June, 1856, Jemima, eldest dau. of Thomas Sadlier, of Castletown, co. Tipperary, and *d.* 28 Sept. 1871, leaving issue,
(2) Richard, *d. unm.* (3) Henry.
(4) Edward.
(1) Eugenic.
(2) Eleanor, *m.* Frederick Harding.
(3) Adelaide. (4) Annette.

(5) Charlotte, *m.* 1st, 1888, Wm. Fowler, and 2ndly, 1902, Samuel Jones.
1. Ellen, *m.* Capt. Davidson.
2. Jane, *m.* 1845, William Lewis, of Dublin.
4. Isaac, an Officer in the Army, killed at Waterloo.

The eldest son,
SIMPSON HACKETT, of Riverstown, co. Tipperary, *b.* 28 Dec. 1763 ; *m.* 1 May, 1790, Sarah, dau. of Thomas Mitchell, of Fortle Castle, King's Co., and by her (who *d.* 5 Aug. 1839) had issue,
1. Simpson, *b.* 1791 ; *d.* 1795.
2. Robert, 18th Light Dragoons, *b.* 1 Jan. 1796 ; *d.* 22 April, 1816.
3. THOMAS, late of Moor Park.
1. Sarah, *m.* Alexander A. Graydon, of Newcastle House, co. Dublin.
2. Anne Maria, *m.* John Brereton, of Old Court, co. Tipperary.
3. Margaret, *m.* Thomas Hobbs, Capt. 92nd Highlanders, of Barnaboy, King's Co. (*see that family*).
4. Jane, *m.* Robert Seymour Drought, of Ridgemount.
5. Ellen, } *d.* young.
6. Elizabeth, }

Mr. Hackett *d.* 21 Jan. 1848. His 3rd son,
THOMAS HACKETT, of Moor Park, King's Co., and Riverstown, co. Tipperary, J.P. and D.L., High Sheriff of the King's Co. 1841, *b.* 15 Jan. 1798 ; *m.* 1 July, 1830, Jane Bernard, youngest dau. of Bernard Shaw, of Monkstown Castle, co. Cork, and niece of Sir Robert Shaw, 1st bart., of Bushy Park, co. Dublin, and by her (who *d.* 23 Feb. 1857) had issue,
1. SIMPSON, late of Moor Park.
2. Thomas Bernard, of Riverstown, co. Tipperary, Lieut.-Col., formerly Major 23rd R. W. Fusiliers, *b.* 15 June, 1836 ; *m.* 9 July, 1874, Josephine, eldest dau. of the late Rev. Joseph Marshall, of Baronne Court, co. Tipperary (*see that family*). He *d.* 1880. She *d.* 16 Jan. 1910.
3. Robert Henry, Col. (retired) late 90th Foot, *b.* 26 Aug. 1839, *d. unm.* 30 Dec. 1893.
4. CHARLES, late of Riverstown.
1. Jane Louisa, *d.* 3 Feb. 1875.
2. Sara, *m.* Sept. 1880, Rev. John Clifford
3. Emily, *m.* 2 May, 1860, Rev. Milward Crooke, Chaplain to the Forces, and has issue.
4. Louisa, *m.* 18 Feb. 1879, William Denis Browne, 2nd son of Very Rev. Denis Browne, Dean of Emly, and has issue (*see* BURKE'S *Peerage,* SLIGO, M.).
5. Alice. 6. Florence.
7. Helen Agnes, *d. unm.* 29 March, 1884.

He *d.* 13 Jan. 1869. The eldest son,
MAJOR-GEN. SIMPSON HACKETT, of Moor Park, King's Co., J.P. King's Co. and Tipperary, Major-Gen. late Royal Sussex Regt., *b.* 15 June, 1831 ; *m.* 17 July, 1858, Edith Mary, youngest dau. of Major-Gen. Bredin, R.A. She *d.* 1895. He *d.s.p.* 1898. His brother,
LIEUT.-COL. CHARLES HACKETT, of Riverstown, J.P. for King's Co. and Tipperary, Lieut.-Col. (retired) 5th Northumberland Fusiliers, *b.* 4 Jan. 1846 ; *m.* 14 Sept. 1882, Alice Harvey, 2nd dau. of John Prankerd, of Bleadon, Somerset. She *d.* 25 Oct. 1887. He *d.* 2 July, 1909, having had issue,
1. CHARLES BERNARD, now of Riverstown.
1. Ethel Alice.
2. Helen Mary, *d.* an infant 2 April, 1885.

Arms—Sa., three piles pointing to the base arg., the centre one charged with a trefoil slipped vert on a chief gu. a lion passant guardant or. *Crest*—A demi-panther arg. spotted az. collared gu., charged on the shoulder with a trefoil slipped vert and holding in the dexter paw a branch of the last. *Motto*—Virtute et fidelitate.

Seat—Riverstown, Parsonstown.

HALL OF NARROW WATER.

ROGER HALL, of Narrow Water, co. Down, J.P. and D.L., High Sheriff 1901, J.P. co. Armagh, High Sheriff 1900, late Capt. Royal Fusiliers, *b.* 4 Nov. 1864 ; *m.* 4 Feb. 1891, Elvira Adela, youngest dau. of the late John Meade, of Earsham Hall, Bungay, having had issue,

ROGER, *b.* 6 Aug. 1894.
Elizabeth Adela, *b.* 9 Feb. 1892.

Lineage.—This family is of English extraction. WILLIAM HALL settled in Ireland in the 17th century, and *d.* at Red Bay, co. Antrim, 1640, leaving a son,
FRANCIS HALL, of Mount Hall, co. Down, *m.* Mary, dau. of Judge Lyndon, and had issue,
1. ROGER, of whom presently.
2. Edward, ancestor of HALL *of Knockbrack* (*see that family*).
3. Alexander Trevor.
1. Frideswid, *m.* 1681, Chichester Fortescue, of Dromiskin.

The eldest son,
ROGER HALL, of Mount Hall, High Sheriff 1702, *m.* 1686, Christian, dau. of Sir Toby Poyntz, of Acton, co. Armagh, and had issue,
1. TOBY, his heir. 2. Roger.
1. Rose, *m.* 1708, Richard Close (*see* CLOSE *of Drumbanagher*).

The son and heir,
TOBY HALL, of Mount Hall, High Sheriff co. Down 1715, *m.* 1712, Margaret, dau. of the Hon. Robert Fitzgerald, and sister of the 19th Earl of Kildare, and by her (who *d.* 8 Dec. 1758) he left at his decease, 4 May, 1734, two daus., Christian and Elizabeth, and one son,

Hall. THE LANDED GENTRY. 286

ROGER HALL, of Mount Hall, High Sheriff co. Armagh 1739, and co. Down 1740, m. 10 Sept. 1740, Catherine, only dau. of Rowland Savage, of Portaferry, and had issue,
1. SAVAGE, his heir.
1. Dorcas, m. Francis Carleton.
2. Anne, m. Patrick Savage, of Portaferry.
3. Catherine, m. 1765, the Right Hon. William Brownlow, M.P.
4. Elizabeth, m. James Moore (see MOORE of Dromont).
5. Sophia, m. Richard Ainsworth.
The son and heir,
SAVAGE HALL, of Narrow Water, High Sheriff co. Armagh 1795, and co. Down 1800, b. 1763; m. 3 Feb. 1787, Elizabeth, 4th dau. of John Madden, of Hilton, co. Monaghan, and by her (who d. 1801, had issue,
1. ROGER, his heir, of Narrow Water.
2. Savage (Rev.), Rector of Loughall, b. 1798; m. 1831, Anne, eldest dau. of the late William James O'Brien, of co. Clare, and d. 1851, leaving issue,
  1. SAVAGE, 89th Regt. b. 1834; d. 1868.
  2. WILLIAM JAMES, of whom presently.
  3. Roger, Major, late 14th Regt., b. 1840; d. 21 April, 1905.
    1. Margaret Barbara, m. 1858, William Orme, of Owenmore, co. Mayo, who d. Sept. 1876. She d. 16 Dec. 1910.
    2. Elizabeth Grace, m. 1860, Lieut.-Col. H. C. Moore; and d. Feb. 1881.
    3. Annette, d. unm. 1899.   4. Alice.
    5. Emily, d. 1865.
3. SAMUEL MADDEN, late of Narrow Water.
  1. Anne, m. Trevor Corry, of Newry, and d. 1852.
  2. Catharine, m. Capt. Nowlan, dec.
  3. Elizabeth, m. the Rev. W. B. Savage; d. 1867 (see NUGENT of Portaferry).
4. Jane, m. 1842, Rev. Sir Hunt Johnson Walsh, Bart. (see BURKE's Peerage).
The eldest son,
ROGER HALL, of Narrow Water, J.P. and D.L., High Sheriff co. Armagh 1815, and for Down 1816; b. 6 Nov. 1791; m. 10 Nov. 1812, Barbara, 4th dau. of Patrick Savage, of Portaferry, co. Down (see NUGENT of Portaferry). He d.s.p. 20 Sept. 1864, and his wife d. 1869, 1853. His younger brother,
SAMUEL MADDEN FRANCIS HALL, of Narrow Water, J.P. and D.L., High Sheriff 1869, Major 75th Regt., b. 1800; m. 24 Sept. 1845, Anne Margaret (who d. 28 Jan. 1895), youngest dau. of Andrew Savage Nugent, of Portaferry, and d.s.p. 17 Feb. 1873, when he was s. by his nephew,
WILLIAM JAMES HALL, of Narrow Water, co. Down, J.P. and D.L. co. Down, late Major R.A., High Sheriff co. Down 1878, and co. Armagh 1880, b. 16 Sept. 1835; m. 1st, 1 Dec. 1863, Elizabeth Theodosia Catherine, 2nd dau. of the late Rev. William B. Forde, of Seaforde, co. Down, and by her (who d. May, 1866) had issue,
1. ROGER, of Narrow Water.
2. William Charles, Maj. late Royal Welsh Fusiliers, b. 10 May, 1866; m. 6 July, 1901, Olive Edith Kathleen, dau. of Sir Standish O'Grady Roche, 3rd Bart. (see BURKE's Peerage), and has issue,
  1. Barbara Kathleen, b. 11 Jan. 1903.
  2. Olive Mary, b. 14 Oct. 1905.
He m. 2ndly, 28 April, 1875, Florence Selina, youngest dau. of George Brooke, of Ashbrooke, co. Fermanagh, by Lady Arabella his wife, and d. 21 May, 1896, leaving issue,
3. Francis, Capt. late R.A., b. 19 Feb. 1876.

Seat—Narrow Water, Warrenpoint, co. Down. Club—Naval and Military, W.

HALL OF KNOCKBRACK.

MAJOR HENRY THOMAS HALL, of Knockbrack, co. Galway, J.P., High Sheriff 1911, formerly Capt. 4th Batt. Connaught Rangers, some time A.D.C. to the Governor of Jamaica and late Capt. 18th Hussars, served in S. African War 1900-1901, b. 30 Sept. 1859; s. his father 1869; m. 8 Dec. 1886, Elizabeth Anne, eldest dau. of the late Major John Joseph Lopdell, of Raheen Park, Athenry, co. Galway (see LOPDELL of Raheen), and has issue,
Henry Juan, b. 27 July, 1892; d. 11 May, 1893.
Gladys Olive.

Lineage.—EDWARD HALL, of Strangford, 2nd son of Francis Hall, of Mount Hall (see preceding Article), m. Anne Rowley, and d. 1713, leaving issue. The 2nd son,
ROWLEY HALL, of Killeludagh, m. Miss Tipping, and was father of
THE VEN. FRANCIS HALL, LL.D., Rector of Arboe. co. Tyrone, successively Præcentor and Archdeacon of Kilmacduagh, and Vicar-General of that Diocese, m. circa 1780, Christian Traill, and dying circa 1834, left (with other issue, dec.),
1. JAMES TRAIL, Barrister-at-Law, Chairman of the cos of Galway, Monaghan, and Cavan, m. Aug. 1818, Anne Cockerell, only child of John Moubray, grandson of John Moubray, of Cockairny, co. Fife, and d. 21 Nov. 1836, leaving by her (who d. 2 Aug. 1855) issue,
  1. Francis Henry (Rev.), Incumbent of Drumcullin, co. Down, b. 23 Aug. 1820; m. 1st, 27 March, 1849, Mary Letitia, 2nd dau. of the Rev. James McCreight, Rector of Keady, co. Armagh, and d. 10 June, 1881, leaving issue,
    (1) James Traill (Rev.), of Honley, Huddersfield, b. 14 Aug. 1850.
    (2) Francis Henry, C.V.O., C.B., Col. R.F.A., b. 21 March, 1852.
    (3) John Moubray, b. 23 Dec. 1853; d. 9 May, 1900.
    (4) William Thomas, C.S.I. (1904), B.A., LL.B., late I.C.S. (see Knightage), b. 18 Nov. 1855.
    (5) Henry North George, b. 3 Oct. 1857.
    Rev. F. H. Hall m. 2ndly, 2: Dec. 1861, Louisa, dau. of William Henry Armstrong, M.P., of Mount Heaton, King's Co.
  2. James Trail, Lieut.-Col. N. Down Rifles, m. 19 May, 1877, Isabella, widow of Col. Keatinge, Royal Dragoons, and d. 1896.
  3. Thomas Erskine Arthur, Maj.-Gen. in the Army, b. 13 Jan. 1836; m. 28 Dec. 1865, Lady Margaretta Louisa, dau. of Charles, 4th Earl of Castle Stuart, and d. 9 Feb. 1901.
    1. Clara Jane.   2. Henrietta Maria.
2. HENRY, of Mairwarra, now Knockbrack.
3. Francis Tipping, m. Anne Maria Waddington, and at his decease left issue,
  1. Henry Francis (Rev.).
    1. Julia Palmer, m. 10 July, 1838, Thomas Lloyd, of Beechmount. He d. 1873. She d. 29 Sept 1901, leaving issue (see that family).
  2. Anne Maria Christian.
  3. Francis Erskine, m. Rev. Robert Augustus Maunsell, Prebendary of Harristown, co. Kildare, 2nd son of the Ven. William Wray Maunsell, Archdeacon of Limerick (see that family).
    1. Jane Marian Christian.
The 2nd son,
GEN. HENRY HALL, C.B., of Knockbrack, co. Galway, and Merville, co. Dublin, J.P., b. 11 Sept. 1789; m. 3 Oct. 1827, Sara, eldest dau. of Gen. Fagan, Adjutant-Gen. in the Bengal Army, and d. 1875, having by her (who d. 1847) had issue,
1. HENRY EDWARD, Capt., formerly 13th Regt., b. 19 Sept. 1831; served in the Crimea and India; m. 23 Nov. 1858, Annie, only dau. of Major-Gen. Thomas Moore, Bengal Army, and d. Feb. 1869, leaving by her (who m. 2ndly, Giles Eyre Lambert, of Moor Park, 2nd son of Walter Lambert, of Castle Lambert),
  1. HENRY THOMAS, now of Knockbrack.
  2. Charles Henry Edward, b. 16 Nov. 1861.
  3. Arthur Francis, of Caheroyan, Athenry, b. 11 Dec. 1864; m. 28 Nov. 1889, Louisa Jane, 2nd dau. of the late Major John Joseph Lopdell, of Raheen Park, Athenry (see LOPDELL of Raheen), and d. 2 June, 1896, leaving issue,
    Arthur Henry, b. 11 June, 1891.
    Aileen.
  1. Annie Isabella Clara.
2. Christopher James Traill, b. 1839; d. 1854.
1. Eliza Margaret, m. 30 Jan. 1855, the Rev. Macnevin Bradshaw, only son of the late Robert Scott Bradshaw, Barrister-at-Law.
2. Annie Jane.

Seat—Knockbrack, Athenry, co. Galway. Club—Naval and Military.

HALL OF ROWANTREE HOUSE.

JAMES CAMPBELL HALL, of Rowantree House, and Tully House, both co. Monaghan, J.P., D.L., B.A., M.B., B.Ch., Dublin, b. 23 Oct. 1851; m. 9 Feb. 1880, Sarah Frances, only dau. of the late John Harrison Massue Wilson, of Harvest Lodge, Roscrea, and Church Hall, Essex, and Sarah his wife, dau. of James Willington, D.L., of Castle Willington, co. Tipperary.

Lineage.—PERRY HALL, of Tully House, co. Monaghan, left issue, a son,
REV. RICHARD AUGUSTUS HALL, of Tully House, co. Monaghan, Incumbent of Quivry, Kilmore, M.A. Trin. Coll. Dublin, b. 5 Sept. 1823; m. 11 Dec. 1849, Mary, eldest dau. of Thomas Gibson Henry, of Mourne Abbey, co. Down, and d. 9 Nov. 1895, leaving issue,
1. JAMES CAMPBELL, of Rowantree House and Tully House.
2. Thomas G. H., b. 23 Feb. 1853; m. Edith, dau. of —Whitelaw, and has issue, a son and a dau.
3. John A. L., b. 5 Dec. 1855; m. Harriette, eldest dau. of E. M. Tabuteau, and has issue, nine daus.
4. Richard A., b. 1 Oct. 1858; m. Sophie, eldest dau. of John Burnside, and has issue, one son and two daus.
5. Charles W., b. 28 Jan. 1864.

Arms—Arg. on a chevron engrailed between three talbot's heads erased sa. as many trefoils slipped or. Crest—A bear's head couped and muzzled ppr. charged with a trefoil or. Motto—Remember and forget not.

Seats—Rowantree House, and Tully House, Monaghan.

HALL-DARE. See DARE.

HAMILTON OF KILLYLEAGH.

GAWIN WILLIAM ROWAN HAMILTON, of Killyleagh Castle, co. Down, J.P. and D.L., High Sheriff 1875, Col. late 3rd Royal Irish Rifles, and formerly Capt. 7th Dragoon Guards, B.A. Univ. Coll. Oxford, b. 7 March, 1844; m. 19 Oct. 1876, Lina Mary Howley, only dau. of Sir George Howland Beaumont, Bart., of Coleorton, and has,

ARCHIBALD JAMES, served with Imp. Yeom. in S. African War (medal with clasps). b. 30 Sept. 1877; m. 4 July, 1908, Norah, only dau. of late Frederick Abiss Phillips, of Manor House, Stoke d'Abernon, Surrey, and has issue,
Shiela Hermione Katherine, b. 3 Jan. 1911.
Orfla Melita, b. 7 Feb. 1880; m. 10 July, 1901, Arthur Oswald Fisher, of Mickleham, Surrey, and has issue, Eric Arthur; John and Catharine Beatrice.

Lineage.—The HAMILTONS of Killyleagh are the senior male representatives of that branch of the house of Hamilton from which were descended the Earls of Clanbrassil and Viscounts Limerick.

THE REV. HANS HAMILTON, Vicar of Dunlop, Ayrshire, b. 1536; m. Margaret Denham, dau. of the Laird of Weshiels; and dying 30 May, 1608, left,
1. JAMES (Sir), of Killyleagh and Bangor, Serjeant-at-Law, and Privy Councillor to King JAMES I, who was created by patent, dated 4 May, 1622, VISCOUNT CLANEBOYNE; his son and heir, James, 2nd Viscount Claneboyne, was created EARL OF CLANBRASSIL, 4 March, 1647. He was father of HENRY, 2nd Earl of Clanbrassil, who d.s.p. 1675.
2. ARCHIBALD, of whom presently.
3. GAWEN, of Ballygally, a Merchant at Coleraine, who, by Helen Dunlop his wife, was father of JAMES HAMILTON, of Ballygally, who m. Miss Watson, and left a son, REV. ARCHIBALD HAMILTON, of Armagh and Ballough, living 1693, who m. Mary, sister of David Kennedy, of Ballycultra, and had a son, JAMES HAMILTON, of Derryboy, whose will was proved 10 Feb. 1719; he m. Mary, eldest dau. and co-heir of Robert Hamilton, of Killyleagh (3rd son of Hugh Hamilton of Lisbane) and was father of Archibald Hamilton, of Ballynochan, who m. 1736, Alice, dau. of Robert Lambert, of Dumlady, and d. 1741, leaving, with other issue, ROBERT HAMILTON, of Hill of Hills, Curragh, co. Kildare, b. 1737; m. Miss May Harrison, of Liverpool, and d. 1814, leaving with a dau., Emily, wife of John Dennis, nephew of James, Lord Tracton, a son, REV. ARCHIBALD ROBERT HAMILTON, M.A., b. 11 March, 1778, who m. 1815, Jane, 2nd dau. of John Cotter, and d. 1857, leaving issue,
  1. ROBERT HAMILTON, M.D. Cambridge, of Clifton Mount, Jamaica, b. 11 Nov. 1820; m. 1st, Eleanor Anne, dau. of Robert Walkington, which lady d. 6 July, 1871; and 2ndly, 4 Dec. 1872, Katherine Elizabeth, eldest dau. of the late Thomas Land, of Spanish Town, Jamaica.
  2. Archibald Robert (Rev.), Rector of Greenham, Berks, m. Mary Laura, dau. of Rev. Edward Golding, and d. 1869, leaving issue.
    1. Nancy, m. 1st, Rev. Thomas Perrott, and 2ndly, Rev. Canon Alexander Poole, M.A. She d. his widow 8 Jan. 1904.
    2. Jane, m. 1849, Francis Christopher Bland, of Derryquin Castle, co. Kerry.
    3. Catherine Cotter, d. unm.
    4. Emily, m. Rev. Charles Elrington.
  4. JOHN, of Coronary, co. Cavan, and Monella, co. Armagh, ancestor of LORD HOLMPATRICK (see BURKE'S Peerage).
  5. WILLIAM, of Bangor, co. Down, ancestor of the HAMILTONS of Bangor, Tollymore Park, &c.

The 2nd son,
ARCHIBALD HAMILTON, of Halcraig, Denham, co. Lanark, m. 1st, Rachel Carmichael, and had issue,
1. JOHN.
2. JAMES, of Neilsbrook, co. Antrim, who inherited one-fifth of the Earl of Clanbrassil's estates. He m. Agnes Kennedy, and had three daus.,
  1. Rose, m. William Fairlie, but d. without issue.
  2. Rachel, d. unm.
  3. ANNE, m. Hans Stevenson, of Ballyrott, James Stevenson, whose eldest dau. an

STEVENSON, m. Sir John Blackwood, and was created B. DUFFERIN AND CLANEBOYE. Her descendant, FREL TEMPLE HAMILTON BLACKWOOD, Marquess of Dufferin and K.P., is, through her, HEIR-GENERAL of this family, HAMILTON.
3. GAWEN, of whom presently.
4. William, of Killyleagh, d. 1716, without issue.
5. Hugh, of Dublin, Merchant.
Archibald Hamilton m. a second time, and left a dau.,
1. Jane, who m. Archibald Edmonstone, of Braiden Island, Antrim.

His 3rd son,
GAWEN HAMILTON, of Killyleagh, co. Down, m. Jane, da. Archibald Hamilton, and dying 1703, was s. by his son,
ARCHIBALD HAMILTON, of Killyleagh, m. Mary, dau. of Willis Johnston, of Tully, co. Monaghan, and had issue,
1. GAWEN, his heir.
2. William, of Killough, who m. Elizabeth Caddell, and had, two sons, William and David, who both d.s.p., a dau.,
Mary, who m. 1798, William Logan, of Woodlands, co. Dub. and had issue.
1. Susanna, m. Rev. Hamilton Traill, Rector of Killinchy.
2. Jane, m. Peter Fitch of Ballymackney.
3. Mary, m. Acheson Johnston, of Tallyho, son of Sir Wil. an Johnston, of Gifford, co. Down.
Mr. Hamilton was s. at his decease, 25 April, 1747, by his elder son,
GAWEN HAMILTON, of Killyleagh, High Sheriff, co. Down, 177 b. 1729; m. 8 May, 1750, Jane, only child of WILLIAM ROWAN, Barrister-at-Law, and widow of Tichborne Aston, of Beaulieu, co. Lou by whom he had,
ARCHIBALD, his heir.
Sidney, m. Rev. Benjamin Beresford.
Mr. Hamilton d. 9 April, 1805, and was s. by his only son,
ARCHIBALD HAMILTON ROWAN, of Killyleagh Castle, b. 12 May, 1752; m. 6 Oct. 1781, Sarah Anne, dau. of Walter Dawson Carickmacross, co. Monaghan, and had issue,
1. GAWEN WILLIAM ROWAN, of Killyleigh Castle, co. Down, b. 1783; Post-Capt. R.N., C.B.; m. 1817, Catherine, dau. of Gen Sir George Cockburn; and dying 17 Aug. 1834, left issue,
  1. ARCHIBALD ROWAN, of whom presently.
  2. George Rowan, late Capt. 5th Dragoon Guards, b. 1822 d. 4 March, 1902. His widow Caroline Frederica d. 1 Dec. 1907.
    1. Melita Anne, m. 8 Feb. 1844, Capt. Jacob Hierom Sankey R.N., of Coolmore. He d. 1881. She d. 13 July, 1901, leaving issue (see that family).
  2. Sydney, b. 1789; m. a dau. of the late Henry Jackson, o Carrickmacross, and has issue.
  3. Archibald, an Officer in the Army, d. at Gibraltar,
  4. Frederick, R.N., b. 1793; killed on the coast of Spain, 1811
  5. Dawson, b. 1801; m. and has issue.
  1. Jane.
  2. Elizabeth, m. Rev. Sidney Beresford.
  3. Mildred, m. Sir Edward Ryan, Knight of the Order of Maria Theresa.
  4. Harriet, m. Crofton Fitzgerald.
  5. Francesca, m. William Fletcher, son of the late Judge Fletcher and d. 1861, leaving issue,
Mr. Hamilton Rowan d. 1 Nov. 1834, and was s. by his grandson.
ARCHIBALD ROWAN HAMILTON, of Killyleigh Castle, co. Down J.P., High Sheriff, formerly Capt. 5th Dragoon Guard b. 9 Aug 1818; m. 24 Feb. 1842, Catherine Ann, dau. of the ev. George Caldwell, by Harriot his wife, dau. of Sir William Abdy, Bart. and had issue,
1. GAWIN WILLIAM ROWAN, now of Killyleigh Castle.
2. George Rowan, of Wilford, Bray, co. Wicklow, J.P., b. 10 April 1845; Lieut.-Col. (retired), late Lieut. 8th Foot, and Adjutant, 3rd Batn. Royal Irish Rifles, m. 23 Jan. 1873, Helen, eldest dau of J. Maudesley, of Kensington, and has issue,
  1. Sydney Orme, Capt. 3rd Batt. Royal Irish Rifles, late Lieut Royal Garrison Regt., b. 10 Nov. 1877; m. 10 Aug. 1901, Vera youngest dau. of Maj. J. Barnett Barker, and has issue,
    Hans Frederic, b. 21 Jan. 1906.
  1. Catherine Harriot Mona.
  2. Helen Ethelwyn.
3. Sidney Augustus Rowan, Lieut. R.N., b. 1 July, 1846; d. unm. 19 April, 1868.
4. Frederick Temple Rowan, Lieut.-Col. late Major 9th (East Norfolk) Regt., A.D.C. to H.E. Earl Spencer, when Lord Lieut. of Ireland (Culverlands, Farnham, Surrey), b. 17 July, 1850; m. 26 April, 1883, Blanche, only dau. of Admiral Fellowes Gordon, of Knockspock, Aberdeenshire, and has a son, Guy.
1. Harriot Georgina (C.I.), m. 23 Oct. 1862, Frederick Temple. Marquess of Dufferin and Ava, K.P., G.C.B., G.C.M.G., who d. d. 12 Feb. 1902, leaving issue (see BURKE'S Peerage).
2. Helen Gwendoline, m. 4 Oct. 1876, Russell Maule Stephenson, and d. 4 Sept. 1886, leaving issue.
3. Mary Catherine, m. 20 April, 1881, Rt. Hon. Sir Arthur Nicolson, 11th bart., P.C., G.C.B., G.C.M.G., G.C.V.O., K.C.I.E., and has issue (see BURKE'S Peerage).
Capt. Archibald Rowan Hamilton d. 2 May, 1860.

Arms—Gu., three cinquefoils pierced erm. on a chief or, a heart of the first. Crest—A demi-antelope affrontée arg. attired and unguled or, holding between the forelegs a heart gu.
Seats—Killyleigh Castle, co. Down; and Shanganagh Castle, co. Dublin. Clubs—Carlton, and Naval and Military.

HAMILTON OF CORNACASSA.

1. MERVYN JAMES HAMILTON, of Cornacassa, co. Monaghan, J.P., Gordon Highlanders, late Capt. The Lancashire Fusiliers, served with Mounted Infantry, S. African War, 1899-1902 (two medals and clasps), b. eldest Dec. 1879; m. 20 d. in 1909, Hildred Laura, dau. of Gen. Hon. Bernard Ward, .B., of Staple Cross, Christchurch, Hants (see BURKE'S Peerage, BANGOR, V.), and has issue,
1. Phœbe Maxwell.

Lineage.—In the time of the Solemn League and Covenant, James Hamilton, accompanied by one of his brothers, emigrated to Ireland. The brother went to the co. Down, and James established himself at Carravetra, in Monaghan. This ROBERT JAMES HAMILTON, of Carravetra, Clones, co. Monaghan, was father of a 5th son,

1812, ACRE HAMILTON, who m. Dorothy Smith, of Belfast, and had issue,
d. J. 1. Dacre, who m. 1735, Mary, dau. of Edward Owen, of Kilmore, and widow of Joseph Wright, of Gola, and d. 20 April, 1786.
D.L. 2. JAMES (Sir).

The 2nd son,
Sir JAMES HAMILTON, Knt., of Cornacassa, High Sheriff of Monaghan, 1786, m. his cousin, Catherine, dau. of William, 6th son of James Hamilton, by Miss Johnstone his wife, and by her (who D.L.L. 21 Oct. 1822, aged 96) had issue,
1. William Henry, Capt. in the Army, m. Miss Gardner, and 2. DACRE, his successor.
3. JAMES (Rev.), Rector of Cootehill, and afterwards of Ardingly, m.
 1. the widow of Col. Black, and d. 1844.
 2. 4. Skeffington, Capt. in the Army, m. 11 May, 1812, Katharine Salisbury, dau. of the Rev. Robert Montgomery, of Beaulieu, co. Louth, and d.s.p. 1 Oct. 1830.
 1. Sarah, m. Charles Lucas, of Castle Shane, co. Monaghan.
 2. Dorothea, m. Hugh Hawkshaw.
 3. Maria, m. Sir Hedworth Williamson, Bart., of Whitburn, co. Durham.
 4. Olivia, m. Rev. Edward Lucas.
 5. Elizabeth, dec.   6. Jane, dec.
 7. Eleanor, m. Dacre Hamilton, of New Park.
 8. Frances, m. 1st, Col. Lee; and 2ndly, Le Baron de Montague.

The 2nd son,
DACRE HAMILTON, of Cornacassa, High Sheriff 1798, m. Eliza, 4th dau. of Col. Archdall, of Castle Archdall, and by her (who d. 1833) left at his decease, 13 June, 1837, an only son,
JAMES HAMILTON, of Cornacassa, J.P. and High Sheriff 1830; b. 1806; m. 1835, Eglantine Georgina, youngest dau. of Col. Blair, of Blair, co. Ayr, and d. 1877, having had issue,
1. DACRE MERVYN ARCHDALL, late of Cornacassa.
2. Blair Skeffington, b. 1838, Commander R.N.
3. Charles Henry, Royal Artillery, b. 1841, killed accidentally on parade, 6 Oct. 1871.
1. Madeline Charlotte Eliza, m. Sept. 1870, Joseph Pratt, of Cabra Castle (see that family).

The eldest son,
DACRE MERVYN ARCHDALL HAMILTON, of Cornacassa, co. Monaghan, J.P. and D.L., High Sheriff 1864, b. 13 Oct. 1837; m. 1873, Helen, dau. of Walter Nugent, Baron of the Austrian Empire, and d. 1899, leaving issue,
1. MERVYN JAMES, now of Cornacassa.
1. Georgina Eglantine, m. 1st, April, 1893, Charles Slingsby Chaplin, K.R. Rifle Corps, eldest son of Clifford Chaplin, of Borrough Hill, co. Leicester. She m. 2ndly, 31 March, 1906, Harold Arkwright, son of Col. A. C. Arkwright, of Halfeld Place, Witham, and has issue (see ARKWRIGHT of Hampton Court).
2. Ismay Magdelene, m. 17 June, 1908, Capt. Henry Hudson Fraser Stockley, R.M.L.I., youngest son of Col. George Stockley, late R.E.
3. Agnes Elizabeth, m. 5 Jan. 1905, Maxwell, 6th Viscount Bangor, and has issue (see BURKE's Peerage).
4. Edith Louisa.

Arms—Gu., a chevron between three cinquefoils erm. on a canton or, as many holly leaves conjoined vert. Crest—Out of three cinquefoils in fess conjoined or, an oak tree fructed and penetrated transversely in the main stem by a frame-saw ppr., frame and handles gold. Motto—Semper virescens.

Seat—Cornacassa, Monaghan.

HAMILTON OF BALLYMACOLL.

JAMES ARTHUR DURBIN HAMILTON, of Ballymacoll, co. Meath, b. 18 June, 1854; m. 6 Nov. 1883, Julia Sophia, only surviving child of late Commander George Durbin, R.N.

Lineage.—HENRY HAMILTON, of Ballymacoll, co. Meath, 2nd son of JAMES HAMILTON, of Sheephill and Holmpatrick, and younger brother of HANS HAMILTON, M.P., ancestor of Lord Holm Patrick (see BURKE'S Peerage), was b. 16 July, 1760; m. Mary dau. of John Wetherall, of Dublin, and d. Nov. 1844, having had issue,
1. JAMES JOHN, of whom presently.
2. Henry (Rev.), of 17, Devonshire Place, Portland Place, W., M.A. Trin. Coll., Dublin, Ensign 85th L.I., Rector of Thomastown, co. Kildare, for 28 years, b. 1795; m. 1840, Frances Margaret, dau. of Ralph Peters, of Platbridge, Lancashire, and d. 16 Sept. 1874, having had issue,
 1. Henry Blackburne, Col. late Commanding 14th King's Hussars, and formerly in the 6th Dragoon Guards (Carabineers), M.A. Christ Church, Oxford (57, Montagu Square, W., Cumloden, Bournemouth. Clubs—Carlton, Royal Automobile, and Wellington), b. 3 July, 1841; m. 1st, 30 April, 1874, Isabella Lottie, d. and in her issue co-heir of J. K. Wedderburn (see BURKE's Peerage, WEDDERBURN, Bart.), and granddau. of Gen. Sir Thomas McMahon, Bart., G.C.B. She d. 6 Dec., 1881, leaving issue,
  Henry Kellermann HAMILTON-WEDDERBURN which surname he assumed by Royal Licence 14 Jan. 1904 (3, Lygon Place, S.W.), Lieut. Scots Guards, b. 22 Nov. 1881; m. 17 Oct. 1905, Aileen Mary, dau. of Col. A. H. Vincent, of Summerhill, co. Clare (see that family), and has issue,
   Diana Gertrude Aileen, b. 11 Sept. 1910.
  He m. 2ndly, 21 Jan. 1888, Florence Emily, eldest dau. of Lieut.-Gen. C. B. Ewart, C.B., R.E., Lieut.-Gov. of Jersey.
 2. Frederick William Addison, b. 1845; d. 1850.
 3. Arthur John, Lieut. R.N. (Blythewood, Ascot, Jun. United Service, and Constitutional Clubs), b. 1846; m. 1884, Evelyn Louisa, dau. of F. W. Fryer, of West Moors, Dorset, and has issue,
  Hubert Arthur, b. 1894.
  Frances May, b. 1891.
 1. Harriet Mary, d. unm. 1896.
 2. Frances Selina Charlotte, d. unm. 1861.
 3. Helen Isabel (30, Bramham Gardens, S.W.), m. 1881, Frederick W. Cardall (d. 1904) and has issue a son, Hugh Hamilton b. 1885.
3. John, of Grove, co. Meath, m. Katherine Elizabeth, dau. of William Smythe, of Barbavilla, co. Westmeath. She d. 1878. He d. 1847, leaving issue,
 1. Henry Meade, of the Grove, C.B., Lieut.-Gen. late 12th Regt., b. 8 Dec. 1820; m. 5 June, 1845, Henrietta Mary, dau. of the Rev. Sir Erasmus Dixon Borrowes, 8th bart. He d. 14 July, 1895, leaving issue,
  (1) Gilbert Henry Claud, C.B., Col. late 14th Hussars, and Brig.-Gen. South Africa, b. 31 Jan. 1853; m. 1885, Florence Brooks, dau. of Henry Tootal Broadhurst, of Woodhill, Prestwich, and has issue,
   Brian Gilbert, b. 1886.
  (2) Bruce Meade (Sir), K.C.B., K.C.V.O., Lieut.-Gen., Commanding-in-Chief Scottish Command since 1909, late Commanding 3rd Div. 1st Army Corps, late E. Yorks. Regt., has 1st Class Red Eagle, b. 7 Dec. 1857 (Army and Navy, and Travellers' Clubs).
  (3) Hubert Ion Wetherall, C.V.O., C.B., D.S.O., A.D.C. to the King, Major-Gen. Commanding Div. Territorial Army Military Secretary to Viscount Kitchener of Khartoum, late R. W. Surrey Regt. (Army and Navy Club), b. 27 June, 1861.
  (4) Keith Randolph, D.S.O., Major Oxfordshire L.I., b. 28 Feb. 1871; m. 1895, Ella Marcella, dau. of Major John Finlay, late 78th Highlanders, of Castle Toward, co. Argyll (see that family), and has issue,
  (1) Edith Althea (32, Queen Anne's Gate, S.W.), m. 1st, 14 March, 1878, Major-Gen. Sir George Pomeroy Pomeroy-Colley, K.C.S.I., C.B., C.M.G., who d.s.p. 27 Feb. 1881 (see BURKE's Peerage, HARBERTON, V.), and 2ndly, 17 Feb. 1891, Wentworth Blackett, 1st Baron Allendale, who d. 13 Feb. 1907 (see BURKE's Peerage).
  (2) Kathleen Eleanor Laura, m. Rev. Walter Neame, and d.s.p. 1904.
 2. Thomas Rice, Capt. 98th Regt., b. 3 Dec. 1827; m. Anne, dau. of George Baumbach, and was killed in action in Zululand 1879, having had issue,
  (1) Harry Rice, Capt. S. African Constabulary, b. 31 May, 1859; m. Edith, dau. of — Tulett, and d.s.p. 1901. Killed in action at Petrusburg, S. Africa.

Seats—Rowfant, D.S.O., Capt. Thorneycroft's Horse, b. 14 Nov.

1860; *m*. Constance Lodwick. He *d*. 29 June, 1904, leaving issue,
1. Vivian.
2. Meade
3. Geoffrey.
4. Alexander.
(1) Mabel.
(2) Ethel Katherine.
(3) Mary, *m*. Capt. Neill, and has issue.
3. Hans Frederick (Rev.), of Boveen, King's Co., M.A. Oxford, Rector of Woodmansterne, Epsom, Surrey (*Court Haw, Woodmansterne, Surrey*), *b*. 13 Oct. 1829; *m*. 8 April, 1858, Mary Georgina, dau. and co-heir of Charles Barry Baldwin, of Boveen, King's Co., M.P. for Totnes. She *d*. 1 June, 1898, having had issue,
(1) Gawayne Baldwin, of Boveen, Sharavogue, King's Co., J.P., Barrister-at-Law, B.A. Oxford (14, *Old Square, Lincoln's Inn, W.C., and Jun. Carlton Club*), *b*. 20 Aug. 1861; *m*. 3 June, 1897, Agnes, dau. of Lieut.-Gen. Sir Fiennes Middleton Colville, K.C.B. (*see* COLVILLE *of Lullington*), and has issue,
Anthony Baldwin, *b*. 22 April, 1898.
Patricia.
(1) Geraldine Frances.   (2) Evelyn Maud.
(3) Alice Ellinor Mary.
1. Katherine Sara Olivia, *d. unm*.
2. Mary Louisa, *m*. 6 Feb. 1861, William Armit Lees, who *d*. 11 Oct. 1885 (see BURKE'S *Peerage*, LEES, Bart.). She *d*. 4 Jan. 1898.
3. Charlotte Anne, *m*. 1857, Rev. Elias Thackeray Stubbs, and *d*. 2 Jan. 1903, leaving issue.
4. Frances Althea Mary, *d. unm*. 1850.
5. Harriett Isabella, *m*. 1865, Capt. B. Lee Warner, and has issue.
4. Hans Henry, Q.C., of 28, Fitzwilliam Place, Dublin, *m*. 1833, Augusta, dau. of Gen. Sir Frederick Augustus Wetherall, G.C.H, and *d*. 1875, having had issue,
1 Augustus Henry Carr, sometime Capt. R.A., *b*. 1834.
2. Roger Adolphus, Lieut. 10th Bengal Cavalry, killed in Indian Mutiny, 15 April, 1858.
3. Edward Pakenham Robert, Capt. 65th Regt., *d.s.p*. 1870.
4. Lionel Hans.
5. Douglas, *m*. Adeline, dau. of Thomas J. Hamilton, and has issue.
1. Victoria Alexandrina, *m*. 1 June, 1858, Thomas Kemmis, of Shaen, and has issue (*see that family*). He *d*. 1906.
2. Frederica Mary, *m*. 1861, Edward Nicholas Hill, late Capt. 30th Regt., and has issue.
3. Florence, *m*. 15 Nov. 1864, Richard Pierce Butler, late 78th Highlanders, 2nd son of Sir Richard Pierce Butler, 9th bart., and has issue (*see* BURKE'S *Peerage*).
5. Robert, *d. unm*.
1. Mary, *m*. Rear-Adm. Frederick Wetherall, R.N.
2. Isabella, *m*. 6 June, 1818, Rev. Charles Taylor Wade, and had issue (*see* WADE *of Clonebraney*).
3. Harriet, *m*. March, 1825, Rev. Sir Erasmus Dixon Borrowes, 8th bart. and *d*. 1880. He *d*. 27 May, 1866, leaving issue (*see* BURKE'S *Peerage*).
4. Sophia, *d. unm*.   5. Charlotte, *d. unm*.

The eldest son,
JAMES JOHN HAMILTON, of Ballymacoll, co. Meath, *b*. 1788; *m*. 1st, Margaret, dau. of Thomas Carter, of Castle Martin, co. Kildare, and by her had issue,
1. HENRY, late of Ballymacoll.
2. JAMES, late of Ballymacoll.
1. Catherine, *m*. Count Cerrosi, of Florence, and *d*. 1885, leaving a dau.
2. Mary Alicia, *d. unm*. 26 Dec. 1904.
3. Laura Mary, *d. unm*. 1900.

He *m*. 2ndly, 1821, Hon. Anne Geraldine, dau. of John, 26th Baron Kingsale. She *d*. 20 Feb. 1855. He *d*. 1842, having by her had issue,
3. John de Courcy, of Thornham Hall, Norfolk, *b*. 18 April, 1823; *m*. 1850, Anna Chapman, dau. of George Hillhouse, of Combe House, Clifton. She *d*. 4 May, 1905. He *d*. 1895, leaving issue,
1. Henry de Courcy, *b*. 1854, *m*. 1887, Edith, dau. of L J. B. Gregory, and has issue,
(1) John A de Courcy, *b*. 8 Oct. 1896.
(1) Lorna Margaret de Courcy, *m*. 11 Feb. 1910, George Home, of Deli Sumatra.
(2) Rosamund Mary de Courcy, *m*. 16 June, 1909, Henry Hugh Maclean, R.A. (*see* MACLEAN *of Ardgour*).
(3) Brenda de Courcy, *b*. 21 July, 1893.
2. Frederick de Courcy, *b*. 1856, *m*. 1886, Geraldine Elizabeth, dau. of C. Hodgson, of Merlin Park, co. Galway.
3. William Gerald, *b*. 1858; *d*. 1864.
4. James de Courcy, M.V.O., Rear-Admiral R.N. (retired) Chief Officer of the London Fire Brigade since 1903 to 1900, *b*. 1 Feb. 1860; *m*. 23 April, 1901, Mabel Eveline, 2nd dau. of the late William Sang, and has issue,
William Evelyn de Courcy, *b*. 28 Dec. 1902.
Doreen Marie de Courcy, *b*. 21 Nov. 1905.
5. Arthur Hillhouse de Courcy, *b*. 1863, *m*. 1888, Lilian Harriet, dau. of Lancelot Haslupe, and *d*. 14 Aug. 1907, having issue,
Cedric Hans de Courcy, *b*. 23 June, 1891.
Beryl de Courcy.
1. Agatha Geraldine, *b*. 1851; *m*. 1870, Henry James Coldham, of Anmer Hall, Norfolk, who *d*. 1887, leaving issue.
I.L.G.

2. Georgina Mary.   3. Fanny Louisa, *b*. 1861.
4. Alice Maud, *b*. 1865; *m*. 1894, William Schreiber Hu and had issue.
5. Laura Madeline, de Courcy, *m*. 17 June, 1908, Cecil Broon field Kingsley, son of late Henry Kingsley, M.D.
6. Mabel de Courcy, *m*. 1892, Johnston Penny, I.C.S., w *d.s.p*. 1891.
4. Thomas de Courcy, V.C., Maj.-Gen. late 64th Regt., Knt. the Legion of Honour, J.P. co. Gloucester, *b*. 20 July, 1825; *m*. 8 Sept. 1857, Mary Anne Louisa (*Dunboyne, Cheltenham*), dau. of Sir William Baynes, 2nd Bart. He *d*. 3 March, 1908, having had issue,
1. Claud de Courcy, C.B., late A.A.G., India, Col. late R.A., *b*. 23 Sept. 1861; *m*. 17 March, 1887, Jeanie Kathleen, dau. of Patrick Hill Osborne, of Currandooley, N.S.W. He *d.s.p*. 30 Sept. 1910.
2. Roger Baynes, *b*. 1863; *d. unm*. 8 June, 1895.
3. Sidney Whitmore (*Barnato Station Cobar, N.S. Wales*), *b*. 9 June, 1866; *m*. 19 March, 1902, Winifred Agnes Josephine, dau. of Major-Gen. Lewis Percival, late Rifle Brigade, and has issue,
(1) Rowan Charles de Courcy, *b*. 22 Nov. 1903.
(2) James Percival de Courcy, *b*. May, 1905.
(1) Geraldine Agnes de Courcy, *b*. Feb. 1910.
4. Ernest Richard, Acting Sub-Lieut., R.N., *b*. 1869; *d. unm* 1 Dec. 1900.
1. Charlotte Annie, *m*. 27 April, 1882, Rear-Adm. John Salwey Hallifax, of Upton Cottage, Old Alresford, Hants, and has issue. He *d*. 1904.
2. Florence.
3. Gwendoline Louisa, *m*. 9 Dec. 1896, Walter Mackay Staniford, of Whitmuir, Bournemouth.
5. Gerald de Courcy, late Chief Constable of Devon, 1856-91 (19, *Alexandra Mansions, Chelsea, Junior Constitutional Club*), *b*. 10 Oct. 1828; *m*. 1st, 1859, Henrietta Anna, dau. of the late Albany Savile, of Oaklands, Devon, and widow of W. O'B. H. Buchanan She *d*. 1893, leaving a son,
Constantine de Courcy (*Little Hatton, Woking, Surrey, Hatton, Argyllshire, and Oxford and Cambridge Club*), *b*. 1861; *m*. 1887. Eliza Susan Eccles, dau. of the late Capt. R. H. Swinton, R.N., and has issue,
(1) Gerald de Courcy, *b*. 1899.
(1) Evelyn de Courcy, *b*. 1890; *m*. 1911, J. B. McMorland, M.B., Ch.B.
(2) Violet Anna de Courcy, *b*. 1894, *d*. 1900.
He *m*. 2ndly, 11 Jan. 1908, Fanny, only dau. of late George Rusbridger, of Westerton, Sussex.

The eldest son,
CAPT. HENRY HAMILTON, of Ballymacoll, 13th Light Dragoons, *b*. 1811; *m*. 1850, Helen, dau. of Col. Dickson, and *d.s.p*. 19 Aug. 1861. He was *s*. by his brother,
THE REV. JAMES HAMILTON, of Ballymacoll, co. Meath, M.A., Christ's Coll. Camb., Vicar of Melbourn, Cambs., *b*. 1 March, 1817; *s*. his brother 19 Aug. 1861; *m*. 3 March, 1847, Louisa, 4th dau. of Major John James Durbin, of Mainstone Court, Herefordshire, by Anne his wife, dau. of Wyrley Birch, of Wretham, Norfolk, and grand-dau. of Sir John Durbin, of Walton Court, Somerset. She *d*. 1893. He *d*. 9 Feb. 1911, having had issue,
1. Archibald Henry, of Ebor Hall, Cornamona, co. Galway, J.P., co. Mayo, LL.B., M.A. Christ's Coll. Camb., Barrister-at Law, sometime Puisne Judge, Gold Coast, *b*. 22 Dec. 1847; *m*. 14 April, 1885, Mary Ann, dau. of James Parry, and widow of James Archbold Pears-Archbold, of Eland Hall, Northumberland. She *d*. 4 May, 1899. He *d.s.p*. 21 Aug. 1900.
2. JAMES ARTHUR DURBIN, of Ballymacoll.
3. Francis Edmund, M.A., *b*. 22 Feb. 1856; *m*. 28 June, 1883, Florence, youngest dau. of George Benham, and *d*. 9 June, 1887, having had issue,
Geraldine, *b*. 26 May, 1884.
1. Geraldine Louisa, *d. unm*. 30 Aug. 1881.
2. Emmeline Margaret.
3. Josephine Laura, *m*. 12 July, 1883, Charles Frederick Hughes Hallett, and has issue.
4. Florence Anne, *d*. 16 Aug. 1872.

Arms—Gu. a mullet arg. between three cinquefoils pierced erm., on a chief or a heart of the first. Crest—A demi antelope arg. armed and unguled or, charged with a mullet gu. holding between the hoofs a human heart as in the arms. Motto—Quibis ab incepto.

Seat—Ballymacoll, Dunboyne, co. Meath. Residence—Comfort's Place, Blindley Heath Surrey.

HAMILTON OF HAMWOOD.

CHARLES ROBERT HAMILTON, of Hamwood, co. Meath, J.P. Rowlands, co. Meath and Dublin, b. 29 Aug. 1846; m. 10 Sept. 1874, Louisa Caroline Elizabeth, eldest dau. of Francis Thebrooke, of Somerton, co. Dublin, by his wife, the Hon. Henrietta Monck, eldest dau. of the 3rd Viscount Monck, and has had,

1. Charles George, b. 3 June, 1875; d. 2 July, 1877.
2. Gerald Francis Charles, b. 23 June, 1877.
3. Frederick Arthur, b. 15 Dec. 1880.
4. Henry John, b. 25 Sept. 1885; d. 16 Dec. 1885.
1. Eva Henrietta, b. 28 June, 1876.
2. Letitia Marion, b. 20 July, 1878.
3. Amy Kathleen, b. 24 July, 1879.
4. Ethel Grace, b. 1 April, 1882.
5. Constance Louisa, b. 27 June, 1883.
6. Lilian Mary, b. 26 June, 1884, m. 14 June, 1911, John Wroughton Bonham (see BONHAM of Bollintaggart).

Lineage.—CHARLES HAMILTON, youngest son of Alexander Hamilton, of Knock, M.P., by Isabella, dau. of Robert Maxwell, of Innebrogue (see HAMILTON-STUBBER of Moyne), was of Hamwood, co. Meath, and Bishopstown and Clare, co. Westmeath; he m. Elizabeth, dau. of Crewe Chetwood, of Woodbrook, Queen's Co., by Anna his wife, dau. of Allan Holford, of co. Chester, and relict of Ralph Sneyd, of Keele, co. Stafford. Charles Hamilton d. 16 Feb. 1818, having had (with other issue, d.s.p.),

1. CHARLES, of whom presently.
2. Robert, of Liverpool, Merchant, d.s.p. July, 1822.
3. George, of Quebec, and Hawkesbury, Canada, Merchant, and Col. of the local Militia, founded the Hawkesbury Mills, m. Susannah Christianna, dau. of John Craigie, 3rd son of John Craigie, of Kilgraston, Perthshire, and d. 7 Jan. 1839, having had issue,
1. Robert, of Hamwood, Quebec, b. 1 Sept. 1822; m. 31 July, 1845, Isabella, dau. of John Thomson. She d. 12 Sept. 1900. He d. 19 Sept. 1898, having had issue,
(1) George, b. 18 Jan. 1850; m. 1879, Grace Julia Parker, and d.s.p. 6 May, 1880.
(2) John, of Quebec, b. 7 Sept. 1851; m. 25 April, 1877, Ida Mary, dau. of A. C. Buchanan, and grand-dau. of Chief Justice Bowen, of Quebec, and has issue,
1. Constance Naomi, b. 6 May, 1879.
2. Edith Craigie, b. 11 July, 1881.
3. Mary Frances Vera, b. 14 May, 1885.
4. Jessie Irene, b. 2 April, 1887.
(1) Isabella, m. 25 April, 1867, Lieut.-Col. De la Cherois Thomas Irwin, C.M.G., R.A., of Carnagh, co. Armagh, and 170, Cooper Street, Ottawa, Canada, and has issue (see IRWIN of Mount Irwin).
(2) Susan, m. 1873, Walter Gibson Pringle Cassels, K.C., Judge of the Exchequer Court of Canada. 1908.
(3) Robina. (4) Frances, d. unm. 1888.
(5) Jessie, m. Charles Percy Dean, and d. 1886.
(6) Henrietta Margaret, m. 1889, Ven. Archdeacon R. H. Cole, M.A.
2. George, b. 1824; m. 1846, Julia, dau. of His Honour Judge George S. Jarvis, of Cornwall, Ontario (formerly Lieut. 8th Regt.), and d. 1856, having had issue,
(1) George Wellesley, b. 1847; m. Henrietta, dau. of His Honour Judge Sicotte, of Quebec, and d. 1898, having had issue,
George Arthur Sicotte, m. 18 Oct. 1894, Mabel, dau. of Jackson Rae, of Montreal, and has issue,
1. George Cyril Rae, b. 4 March, 1896.
2. George Stratford, b. 1899.
1. Mabel Hope, b. 1898.
Beatrice.
(2) Charles Chetwode (Rev.), Rector of Broome, Stourbridge Worcs., M.A., Oxon., b. 9 Jan. 1851; m. 13 Jan. 1874, Katherine Isabella, eld. dau. of Alexander Davidson Parker, of Edinburgh and Montreal, and has issue,
1. Francis Alexander Chetwode, Capt. Scottish Rifles, b. 29 March, 1875; m. 12 Aug. 1908, Ouida Mary, dau. of Lieut.-Col. Thomas Tryon of Bulwick, Northants (see that family), and has issue,
Joan Alice Chetwode, b. 16 Sept. 1909.
2. Edward Jarvis, b. 29 Jan. 1877; d. 27 Jan. 1894.
3. Hugh Evandale, b. 27 June, 1878; d. 28 Sept. 1881.
4. Charles Chetwode, b. 27 Oct. 1883; d. 24 Jan. 1884.
5. Crewe Chetwode, b. 23 May, 1886.
6. George Rostrevor, b. 11 April, 1888.
7. Eric Knightley Chetwode, b. 6 Feb. 1890.
1. Katherine Grace Chetwode, b. 9 Oct. 1891.
2. Gwendolen Julia Chetwode, b. 2 Oct. 1893.
(3) Robert Craigie, b. 6 July, 1852; m. 28 April, 1875, Charlotte Sherwood, dau. of Right Rev. John Travers Lewis, D.D., LL.D., Archbishop of Ontario, and Anne Henrietta Margaret his wife, dau. of the Hon. Henry Sherwood, Attorney-General of Upper Canada (see LEWIS of Ballinagar), and by her (who d. 26 June, 1903) has issue,
1. Robert Craigie, R.N., b. 4 Feb. 1886.
1. Ethel Maude, m. 8 July, 1897, Wilfred Oswald Faithfull Sergeant, and has issue.
2. Eva Mary, m. 4 June, 1903, Capt. George Henry Bell, Indian Army.
3. Violet Travers. 4. Esmé. 5. Annie May.
(1) Julia, d. unm. 1851.
3. John, of Hawkesbury Mills, Canada, b. 1827; m. 1st, 1852, Rebecca, dau. of the Rev. John Lewis, of Cork, and has issue,
(1) George Chetwode, b. 1857; d. unm. 19 Sept. 1891.
(1) Alice Mary.
(2) Louisa Henrietta, m. 1889, Francis Hilton Green, of Frampton-on-Severn, and has issue.
He m. 2ndly, 1864, Ellen, dau. of William Wood, of Seale Lodge, Surrey, and by her, who d. 3 April, 1873, has issue,
(2) Edmund Charles, late Capt. 3rd Hussars (Somerford Manor, Great Somerford, Wilts, and Naval and Military Club), b. 31 March, 1868; m. 17 Feb. 1892, Adelaide Augusta, dau. of Donald Lorn Macdougall, and has issue,
Honor Beryl, b. 3 Jan. 1893.
(3) Arthur Cyril, b. 17 Jan. 1870; d. 5 Sept. 1888.
(3) Frances Ellen, m. 1891, C. A. Eliot. She d. 1905.
(3) Marion Aston Key, m. 1888, Caledon Forbes Gilder.
4. Charles (Right Rev.), D.D., Bishops College, Lennoxville, D.C.L., Trinity, Toronto, M.A., Oxford, 1857, Bishop of Ottawa, Canada, b. 6 Jan. 1834; m. 25 Feb. 1862, Frances Louisa Hume, dau. of Tannatt Houston Thomson, Deputy Commissary Gen., and Margaret Anne, his wife, dau. of Capt. Ussher, of The Grove, Chippewa, Canada, and has issue,
(1) Charles Robert, b. 15 Aug. 1867; m. Edith Bell, dau. of — Wilson, and has issue,
Charles Hamwood.
Edith Frances Mary.
(2) Hubert Valentine, b. 14 Feb. 1873; m. Mabel Violet, dau. of Henry Caulfeild.
(3) Harold Francis (Rev.), M.A., Ch. Ch. Oxford, D.T., 5 Oct. 1876.
(4) George Theodore, Lieut. R.F.A., b. 5 July, 1881.
(1) Lilian Margaret, b. 16 June, 1869; m. Rev. Lennox Ingall Smith.
(2) Mabel Frances, b. 25 July, 1870; m. E. C. Kirwan Martin.
(3) Ethel Mary, b. 14 Nov. 1871.
(4) Winifred Katherine, b. 22 Aug. 1875; d. 8 July, 1880.
(5) Mary Agnes, b. 17 April, 1878.
5. Francis, b. 1838, d.s.p.
1. Henrietta, m. 1853, Andrew Thomson.
2. Isabella.
4. William Henry, m. 1st, 1821, Bridget, dau. of Beauchamp Colclough, of Kildavin, co. Carlow, and had issue,
1. Henry, b. 1826.
1. Georgina, m. 1849, Walter Scougail, and had issue.
Mr. W. H. Hamilton m. 2ndly, 1831, Margaret, dau. of Archibald McMillan, and had issue, a dau.,
2. Henrietta, m. William King Kains.
5. John, of Liverpool, Merchant, m. 1821, Caroline, dau. of Thomas Frame, of Bostock Hall, co. Chester, and had issue at his decease, 23 June, 1823, one dau.,
Mary Anne, d. unm. 10 July, 1854.
1. Henrietta, m. Maj.-Gen. William Augustus Prevost, C.B., brother of Sir George Prevost, 1st bart. He d.s.p. 8 Aug. 1824.

The eldest son,

CHARLES HAMILTON, of Hamwood, b. 1772; m. 29 April, 1801, Marianne Caroline, dau. of William Tighe, of Rosanna, co. Wicklow, M.P., by Sarah his wife, only child of Sir William Fownes, Bart., of Woodstock, co. Kilkenny, and by her (who d. 29 July, 1861, aged 84) had issue,

1. CHARLES WILLIAM, late of Hamwood.
2. William Tighe, b. 31 March, 1807; m. 27 Sept. 1832, the Hon. Anne Louisa, dau. of the late Major-Gen. Sir William Ponsonby, K.C.B. (by Georgina his wife, dau. of Charles, 1st Lord Southampton). She d. 23 Jan. 1863, leaving issue,
Frederick Fitzroy, b. 1837.
3. Frederick John Henry Fownes, b. 27 July, 1816; m. 22 May, 1860, Frances Catharine, only dau. of Richard Gethin, of Earlsfield, co. Sligo, formerly of the 13th Light Dragoons, and d. 1893, having had issue,
Frederick Evandale Gethin, b. 12 March, 1861; d. young.
Adela Maude Gethin.
1. Sarah, m. 21 June, 1836, the Hon. and Rev. Francis Howard, brother of William, 3rd Earl of Wicklow. He d. 16 Feb. 1847. She d. 15 March, 1892, leaving issue (see BURKE's Peerage).
2. Mary, d.s.p.
3. Caroline Elizabeth, m. 1st, Capt. Trevor Stannus; and 2ndly, 1849, Rev. John William Finlay, of Corkagh, co. Dublin (see that family). He d. 1879. She d. 31 May, 1909.

Mr. Hamilton d. 29 Sept. 1857, and was s. by his son,

CHARLES WILLIAM HAMILTON, of Hamwood, J.P., b. 1 April, 1802; m. 1 June, 1841, Letitia Charlotte, eldest dau. of the late William Henry Armstrong, M.P., of Mount Heaton, King's Co., by Bridget his wife, dau. of Col. Charles MacDonnell, M.P., of New

Hall, co. Clare. She d. 28 June, 1872. He d. 16 Feb. 1880, leaving issue,
  1. CHARLES ROBERT, now of Hamwood.
  2. Edward Chetwood, Major, b. 23 Aug. 1847; m. 4 Jan. 1870, Eleanor Georgina Anna Blanche, dau. of Col. George Gladwin Denniss, 101st Royal Bengal Fusiliers, and has issue,
    1. Edward Charles Bayley, b. 1 May, 1873.
    2. George Chetwood Digby, b. 29 July, 1874.
    1. Blanche Letitia, b. 1 Nov. 1870.
    2. Eleanor Georgina, b. 2 Oct. 1871.
    3. Kathleen Maude Albina, b. 30 Sept. 1877.
  3. Arthur, of Hollybrook, Foxrock, co. Dublin, J.P., formerly Lieut. 12th Regt. (*Kildare Street Club*), b. 16 Aug. 1848; m. 29 Oct. 1874, Alma Louisa Geraldine Isabella, youngest dau. of the late Edward Croker, of Ballynagarde, and Lady Georgiana Croker, and has had issue,
    1. Alick Edward Croker, b. 14 March, 1879.
    2. Robin Arthur Vesey, b. 29 Feb. 1884.
    3. Eric Richard Monck, b. 19 Sept. 1888.
    4. Geoffrey Cecil Monck, b. 8 Dec. 1894.
    1. Aileen, b. 16 Oct., d. 18 Nov. 1875.
    2. Dorothea Alice Letitia.
    3. Rosalie Alma Georgiana.   4. Elsie Marguerite Monck.

Arms—Quarterly: gu. and arg., in the 1st and 4th quarters, three cinquefoils pierced erm., and a canton of the 2nd, charged with a trefoil slipped vert; in the 2nd and 3rd, a lymphad, sails furled and oars out sa. **Crest**—Out of a ducal coronet or, an oak tree fructed and penetrated transversely in the main stem by a framesaw ppr., the frame or and blade inscribed with the word "Through," suspended from one of the branches a shield arg., charged with a trefoil slipped vert. *Mottoes*—(Over): Through; (*under the arms*)—Sola nobilitas virtus.

Seat—Hamwood, Dunboyne, co. Meath. **Residence**—90, Lower Dominick Street, Dublin. *Clubs*—Wellington and Royal Societies, S.W., and Kildare Street, Dublin.

HAMILTON OF BROWN HALL.

JAMES HAMILTON, of Brown Hall, co. Donegal, J.P. and D.L., late Major Donegal Militia, High Sheriff 1849, b. 3 June, 1824; m. Oct. 1863, Dorothea Elizabeth, dau. of William Stewart, M.D., 2nd son of William Stewart, of Hornhead, co. Donegal, by Angel Isabella, dau. of Sir James Galbraith, Bart., of Urney, and has issue,

JOHN STEWART, High Sheriff, co. Donegal, 1898, Capt. late 5th Batt. Royal Innis. Fus., b. Aug. 1864, m. 7 Oct. 1911, Winifred Mary Percy, dau. of late Percy Weston, of Greenfield, East Sheen.

Lineage.—JOHN HAMILTON, of Murvagh, who removed the family residence from Murvagh to Brown Hall in 1697, m. Jane, dau. of Col. Abraham Creighton (ancestor of the Earl of Erne), and d. 1706, leaving, with other issue,
  1. JAMES, of whom presently.
  2. Abraham, b. 1591; d. 1775.
  1. Jane, b. 1683, m. Andrew Cunningham, of Mount Paradise, co. Donegal.
  2. Hester, b. 1701; m. Richard Nesbit, of Woodhill, co. Donegal.
The elder son,
JAMES HAMILTON, b. 1688; m. 1734, Dorothy, dau. of Henry Green, of Ballymacroy, co. Limerick, and d. Jan. 1755, leaving, with other issue,
  1. JOHN, of whom presently.
  2. Henry, Major 56th Regt., served throughout the siege of Gibraltar, and d. 1812.
  1. Jean, m. 1st, John Hamilton, of Castlefin; and 2ndly, William Conyngham, of Springhill, co. Derry.
The elder son,
JOHN HAMILTON, of Brown Hall, b. 1735; m. Isabella, sister of James Stewart, of Killymoon, M.P. for co. Tyrone (*see* STEWART *of Ballymoran*), and d. 1811, having had by her (who d. 1832), with other issue,
  1. JAMES, of whom presently.
  2. Abraham, b. 1773; d. 1861.
  3. William Stewart, b. 1775; m. 1807, Harriet, dau. of Hans Blackwood, afterwards Lord Dufferin, and had issue.
The eldest son,
JAMES HAMILTON, who predeceased his father 1805, was b. 1771; m. 1799, Hon. Helen Pakenham, sister of Thomas, Earl of Longford, and had issue,
  1. JOHN HAMILTON, his heir.
  2. Edward Michael (Rev.), Rector of Drumconrath, b. 1802; m. 2 Dec. 1828, Martha Anne, dau. of Chichester Fortescue, of Dromisken, and sister of Thomas Fortescue, Baron Clermont, and d. 16 May, 1861, leaving issue,
    Chichester, b. 1 Sept. 1835; d. 2 June, 1870.
    Martha Angelina, m. 1861, Rev. Henry Stewart, D.D., Rector of Banbridge, co. Down, who d. 1896, leaving issue.
    1. Catherine, b. 1803; m. Rev. W. H. Foster, Rector of Loughgilly; she d. 1873.
Mr. Hamilton d. 1805. His eldest son,
JOHN HAMILTON, of Brown Hall and St. Ernans, co. Donegal, J.P. and D.L., High Sheriff 1826, b. 25 Aug. 1800; m. 1 May, 1825, Mary, 2nd dau. of Hugh Rose, of Calrossie (who assumed the name of Ross of Cromarty), and by her (who d. 1854) had issue,

  1. JAMES, now of Brown Hall.
  1. Isabella, d. 1840.
  2. Mary, m. F. A. Courbarron, and d. 1877.
  3. Arabella Rose, m. Arthur Hamilton Foster, and d. 6 Oct. 1906.
  4. Helen, m. 1855, Rev. Gustavus de Veer.

Mr. Hamilton m. 2ndly, 1858, Mary, eldest dau. of George Simpson, of Pitcorthie, co. Fife, and by her (who d. 30 Aug. 1906) had issue,
  2. John Pakenham, b. 8 Sept. 1861.
  5. Katherine.
He d. 13 June, 1884.
Seat—Brownhall, Ballintra, Donegal.

HAMILTON OF MOSSVILL.

LIEUT.-COL. WILLIAM JOHN PAUMIER HAMILTON, of Mossvill, co. Donegal, J.P., Lieut.-Col. 3rd Brigade S. Irish Division R.A., late of the 41st Regt., representative of the family of HAMILTON of Ballyfatton, b. 19 Jan. 1852; m. 18 Oct. 1888, Louisa, 3rd dau. of Major Francis D'Arcy Irvine, Indian Army (*see* IRVINE *of Castle Irvine*), and has issue,
  1. JAMES PAUMIER, b. 1898.
  1. Mary Maud Mervyn.
  2. Aline Constance.

Lineage.—WILLIAM HAMILTON, " of Priestfield, in the Realm of Scotland," was granted the privileges of an English subject, 17 Aug. 1617. He was granted the lands of Ballyfatton by Claud, Lord Strabane, 3 June, 9 CHARLES I (1634). He made his will 16 May, 1637, which was deposited in the Castle of Strabane. The Castle was burned by Sir Phelim O'Neill, but materials were afterwards forthcoming to enable the will to be proved at Londonderry, 22 June, 1652. He was taken prisoner by the rebels, and confined at Doe Castle, with Robert Hamilton, the husband of his granddau. Janet. He held lands under the Earl of Abercorn. By his wife Janet Moore he had, with other issue,
WILLIAM HAMILTON, who s. to the Ballyfatton estate; m. Isabella, dau. of Major William Hamilton, of Loughmuck, in Barony of Omagh, and sister of John Hamilton, of Termegan, Strabane. Mr. Hamilton's will, dated 2 Oct. 1680, was proved by his son Patrick 30 June, 1681. He had issue,
  1. WILLIAM, who d.v.p. leaving issue,
    1. WILLIAM, his heir of whom next.
    2. Archibald, Lieut.-Col. in Lord Mountjoy's Regt. of Foot, d.s.p. 1712.
    3. James, a Capt., d.s.p. 1730.
  2. Patrick.
  3. Frederick.   4. John.
  5. James.   6. George.
  7. Charles.   8. Archibald.
  1. Marjory, m. Richard Wilson.
  2. Katherine.   3. Isabel.
  4. Janet, m. Robert Hamilton.
  5. Jean, m. John Lowry, of Aghenis, co. Tyrone.
The above,
WILLIAM HAMILTON, s. his grandfather at Ballyfatton. By Sarah his wife he had issue,
  1. ARCHIBALD, his successor.   2. Charles.
  3. Galbraith.
  1. Anne, m. William Drummond.
  2. Margery.
The eldest son,
ARCHIBALD HAMILTON, of Ballyfatton, Cornet of Dragoons, m. 1st (settlements dated 4 April, 1719), Jane, dau. of Rev. George Nesbitt, of Drumalugh, and had issue,
  1. WILLIAM, of Ballyfatton.
  2. George, in the Army, d.s.p., killed at Almanza.
  1. Sarah, m. John Tredennick, of Camlin.
  2. Letitia, m. William Young, of Coolkeiragh.
Mr. Hamilton m. 2ndly (settlements 16 April, 1746), Letitia Fairlie, and d. 1753 (will dated 24 Feb. 1753), having had further issue,
  3. Archibald, of Dublin, M.D., Pres. of College of Physicians, d. 1777.
  4. Richard.   5. James.
  6. John, Capt. in the Army; killed at Seringapatam, d. unm.
  7. Sampson in the Army, d.s.p.
  8. GALBRAITH, ancestor of HAMILTON *of Castle Hamilton*.
  1. Margery, m. 19 Feb. 1776, Peter Paumier.
His eldest son,
WILLIAM HAMILTON, of Ballyfatton and Eden, co. Donegal, High Sheriff co. Tyrone 1757, m. his cousin, Mary White, of White Hall, co. Antrim, and had issue,
  1. William, d. unm.
  2. JAMES, of whom presently.
The younger son,
JAMES HAMILTON, of Eden, co. Donegal, J.P., b. 1745, m. his cousin, Mary Hamilton, of Fort Stewart, and by her (who d. 1854, aged 94) had issue,
  1. WILLIAM, of whom presently.
  2. James, Alderman of Dublin, Lord Mayor 1779-80, d.s.p.
  3. John, Capt. R.N., m. Miss Richards, of Macmine Castle, co. Wexford, and d.s.p.   4. Charles, d. young.
  5. Timothy, Capt. Irish Brigade, served under Bolivar, and was killed.

T 2

6. George, of Eden, J.P., *d. unm.*
7. Galbraith, of Eden and Ballyfatton, *m.* twice, but *d.s.p.*
1. Margery, *d. unm.* 2. Maria, *d. unm.*
The eldest son,
CAPT. WILLIAM HAMILTON, Rifle Brigade, a gallant and distinguished officer, severely wounded at Ciudad Rodrigo and San Sebastian, leading forlorn hopes, *m.* Mary, dau. of Capt. John Power, 9th Lancers, and had issue,
1. JAMES PAUMIER, of whom presently.
2. William, of Seaview, *m.* 1851, Jane, dau. of Anthony Brownless, and *d.s.p.*
1. Anne Jane, *m.* 1 Jan. 1852, Sir Anthony Colling Brownless, K.C.M.G., LL.D., M.D., F.R.C.S., Chancellor of the University of Melbourne, only son of Anthony Brownless, of Peynitz Hall, Kent. He *d.* 1897. She *d.* 14 Nov. 1889, leaving issue (*see* BURKE's *Colonial Gentry*).
2. Maria Frances, *m.* 1st, James Johnston, 40th Regt., son of George Johnston, and 2ndly, John Smyth Watkins.
The elder son,
JAMES PAUMIER HAMILTON, Recorder of Cork, and County Court Judge and Chairman of Quarter Sessions, E.R. co. Cork, and a Bencher of King's Inns, *m.* 1850, Martha, dau. of Anthony Brownless, of Peynitz Hall, Kent, and grand-dau. of Anthony Brownless, and Anne his wife, dau. of Michael Colling, of Darlington, Durham, and *d.* 1892, leaving an only son,
WILLIAM JOHN PAUMIER, now of Mossvill.

Seat—Mossvill, Glenties, co. Donegal. *Clubs*—Constitutional W.C.; United Service Club, S.W.

HAMILTON OF CASTLE HAMILTON.

WILLIAM JOSEPH HAMILTON, of Castle Hamilton, co. Cavan, J.P. and D.L., High Sheriff 1886, M.A. Trin. Coll. Dublin, Capt. and Hon. Major late 4th Batt. Royal Irish Fus., previously 2nd Vol. Batt. Royal Welsh Fus., *b.* 1850; *m.* 1897, Frances Florence, dau. of the late Charles Stuart Adams, of Glynch House (*see* ADAMS of *Northlands*), and has issue,
WILLIAM GUY LOFTUS, *b.* 1900.

Lineage.—GALBRAITH HAMILTON, of the City of Dublin, 6th and youngest son of Archibald Hamilton of Ballyfatton (*see* HAMILTON of *Mossvill*); *m.* June, 1762, Jane Brooke. He willed dated 29 April, 1783, was proved 13 July, 1791. He left issue two sons and as many daus.,
1. James, *d. unm.*
2. John, of whom hereafter.
1. Martha, *m.* George Maconchy, of Rathmore.
2. Mary, *d. unm.*
The 2nd son,
JOHN HAMILTON, of Larkfield, co. Dublin, *m.* Jane, sister of Thomas Dickson, of Grangeville, and had issue,
1. JAMES of Castle Hamilton. 2. John, *d. unm.*
The elder son,
JAMES HAMILTON, of Castle Hamilton, co. Cavan, J.P., D.L., High Sheriff 1847; *m.* 4 June, 1839, Mary Matilda, dau. of Thomas Dickson, of Grangeville, co. Dublin. She *d.* 1895. He *d.* 1887, having had issue,
1. James, *d.* 14 May, 1904.
2. WILLIAM JOSEPH, now of Castle Hamilton.
3. Robert Claude, *m.* 26 Nov. 1891, Eva Adeline, dau. of the late Charles Stuart Adams, of Glynch House (*see* ADAMS *of Northlands*).
1. Anna Elizabeth, *d. unm.* 2. Elizabeth Matilda, *d. unm.*
3. Mary Katherine. 4. Maude Victoria, *d. unm.*

Seat—Castle Hamilton, Killeshandra, co. Cavan. *Residence*—Drumanny, Killeshandra, co. Cavan.

COLE-HAMILTON OF BELTRIM.

ARTHUR RICHARD COLE-HAMILTON, of Beltrim, co. Tyrone, J.P. and D.L., late Lieut.-Col. Hon Col. commanding. 6th Batt. Royal Irish Rifles, Lieut.-Col. and Hon. Col. (ret.) Special Reserve, late Capt. 7th Hussars and Royal Scots Fusiliers, served in Egypt 1882, and in the Soudan 1885-6, *b.* 29 April, 1859; *m.* 1st, 2 Jan. 1882, Jeannette, eldest dau. of Samuel Moore, of Moorlands, Lancashire, and by her (who *d.* 7 April, 1883) has issue,
WILLIAM MOORE, late Lieut. King's Royal Rifle Corps, served in S. African War, 1902 (medal, with two clasps); *b.* 3 April, 1883; *m.* 1903, Ada Beatrice, dau. of William P. Huddle, and has issue, William Arthur, *b.* 1 Dec. 1906.
Nora, *b.* 1904.

He *m.* 2ndly, 18 Feb. 1884, Florence Alice, dau. of James Duke Hughes, of Brentwood, Surrey, and *s.* his grandfather 1891.

Lineage.—RIGHT HON. SIR CLAUDE HAMILTON, of Baldony, co. Tyrone, 2nd son of Claude, 1st Lord Paisley, and brother of James, 1st Earl of Abercorn, Gentleman of the Chamber, and Privy Councillor, Ireland. He *m.* the dau. and heir of Sir Robert Hamilton, Knt., and *d.* 14 Oct. 1614, leaving with five younger sons, Alexander, Robert, George, Claude, and James, all of whom *d.s.p.*, an elder son and heir,
SIR WILLIAM HAMILTON, Knt., of Manor Elieston, co. Tyrone, who *m.* twice. He was bur. in the church of Baldony. His will, dated 1 May, 1662, was proved 6 May, 1664. The eldest son of his 2nd marriage, with Beatrix Campbell,
CLAUD HAMILTON, of Montaloney, co. Tyrone, had, by Isabella his wife, five daus., 1. Beatrix; 2. Mary; 3. Agnes; 4. Margaret; and 5. Rebecca, and two sons, 1. WILLIAM, his successor; 2. Claud, of Strabane, ancestor of HAMILTON, Bart., of Woodbrook (ext.). Mr. Hamilton, whose will, dated 1 Oct. 1692, was proved 31 Aug. 1695, was s. by his eldest son,
WILLIAM HAMILTON, of Beltrim, co. Tyrone, who left, by Mary his wife, two sons and three daus. His will, dated 2 May, 1739 was proved 2 April, 1747. His son,
CLAUD HAMILTON, of Beltrim, *m.* his cousin, Letitia, dau. of Claud Hamilton, of Strabane, by whom he had,
1. LETITIA, of whom hereafter.
2. Isabella. 3. Beatrix.
Mr. Hamilton, whose will, dated 7 June, 1780, was proved 24 May, 1782, was s. by his dau.,
LETITIA HAMILTON, of Beltrim, *m.* 1780, Hon. Arthur Cole, afterwards COLE-HAMILTON, of Skea, co. Fermanagh, M.P. for the co., High Sheriff 1778, *b.* 8 Aug. 1750, and 2nd son of John, 1st Lord Mount Florence, and brother of William, 1st Earl of Enniskillen. She *d.* 7 Feb. 1823. He *d.* 1810, having had issue. His eldest son,
CLAUD WILLIAM COLE-HAMILTON, High Sheriff co. Tyrone, 1811, *b.* 7 July, 1781; *m.* 10 Oct. 1805, Nichola Sophia, eldest dau. of Richard Chaloner, of Kingsfort, co. Meath, by whom (who *m.* 2ndly, 1826, Joseph Pratt, of Cabra, co. Cavan) he left at his decease, 25 April, 1822, two sons. The elder son,
ARTHUR WILLOUGHBY COLE-HAMILTON, of Beltrim, co. Tyrone, J.P. for cos. Tyrone and Londonderry, D.L. for Tyrone, High Sheriff 1830, formerly Major Royal Tyrone Fusiliers Militia, *b.* 23 Nov. 1806; *s.* his grandmother 1823; *m.* 16 Dec. 1831, Emilia Katherine, dau. of Rev. Charles Cobbe Beresford, and grand-dau. of Hon. John Beresford, and son of Marcus, 1st Earl of Tyrone, and brother of George, 1st Marquess of Waterford, and *d.* 16 Dec. 1891, having by her) who *d.* 19 Nov. 1869) had issue. The eldest son,
WILLIAM CLAUD COLE-HAMILTON, of Ballitore House, co. Kildare, R.M., late Capt. 88th Regt., *b.* 8 Aug. 1833; *m.* 10 June, 1858, Caroline, 7th dau. of Hon. Andrew Godfrey Stuart, and grand-dau. of Andrew Thomas, 1st Earl of Castle Stewart, and *d.v.p.* 26 Nov. 1882, having had, with other issue (*see* BURKE's *Peerage*, ENNISKILLEN, E.), an eldest son,
ARTHUR RICHARD, now of Beltrim.

Arms.—Quarterly: 1st and 4th, arg., at bull passant sa. arms with unguled or, a border of the second charged with eight bezants on a sinister canton, per pale gu. and az. a harp gold, stringed of the field; 2nd and 3rd quarterly, 1st and 4th gu. three cinquefoils pierced erm.; 2nd and 3rd, arg., a ship with sails furled and oars sa.

Seat—Beltrim, Newton Stewart, co. Tyrone.

HAMILTON OF VESSINGTON.

TREVOR BLACKWOOD HAMILTON, of Vessington, co. Meath, late Capt. and Hon. Major 5th Batt. Leinster Regt., *b.* 1860; *m.* 1883, Louisa Hawkes, dau. of George Knox, and widow of Richard Garnett, of Summerseat, co. Meath, and by her (who *d.* 1899) has issue,
Grace Elizabeth.

Lineage.—JAMES HAMILTON, of Vessington and Dunboyne Castle, *b.* 1761; was 3rd son of James Hamilton, of Sheephill and Holm Patrick, co. Dublin (*see* BURKE's *Peerage*, HOLM PATRICK, B.). He *d.* 24 May, 1800, leaving three sons and three daus. The eldest son,
JOHN HAMILTON, of Vessington and Dunboyne Castle, Major Royal Dublin Militia, *b.* 1789; *m.* Sophia, dau. of James Stannus, and *d.* 1844, leaving, with other issue, a third son,
TREVOR RICHARD HAMILTON, of Vessington, co. Meath, J.P., *b.* 1821; *m.* 1854, Elizabeth Catherine, dau. of Hans Hamilton, and Louisa his wife, dau. of 3rd Lord Dufferin and Clandeboye, and *d.* 1901, leaving issue,
1. TREVOR BLACKWOOD, now of Vessington.
2. Henry Stannus, Major late Lancashire Fusiliers (*Walden, Worplesdon, Surrey*), *b.* 9 July, 1862; *m.* 2 Sept. 1891, Mary Constance dau. of late Leonard Gow, J.P., D.L., of Hayston, Lanarkshire.
3. John Douglas, Chief Commissioner of Police and Sheriff at Lagos, W. Africa, and late Major 4th Batt. Royal Irish Fusiliers, formerly Lieut. 14th Hussars, *b.* 28 Aug. 1866.
1. Constance Louisa, *d.* 1908.
2. Kathleen Florence, *m.* 4 Nov. 1891, George Cooper, LL.B., of The Oaks, Preston, Lancashire, who *d.* Dec. 1891.

Arms—Gu. a mullet argent between three cinquefoils pierced erm. on a chief or, a heart of the first, a mullet charged with a crescent for difference. *Crest*—A demi-antelope argent attired or holding between the forepaws a human heart gu. *Motto*—Qualis ab incepto.

Seat—Vessington, Dunboyne, co. Meath.

BARRETT-HAMILTON OF KILMANOCK HOUSE.

GERALD EDWIN HAMILTON BARRETT-HAMILTON, of Kilmanock House, co. Wexford, B.A. Camb., Major 5th Batt. Royal Irish Rifles, J.P. co. Wexford, High Sheriff 1904-5, Barrister-at-Law of the Inner Temple, *b.* 1871 ; *m.* 8 Aug. 1903, Maude Charlotte, only surviving dau. of S. C. Eland, of Ravenshill, Pietersburg, Transvaal, and has issue,

1. FRANK GERALD HILL, *b.* 19 Oct. 1904.
2. Samuel Anthony Frederick, *b.* 1905.
3. Gerald Childers, *b.* 17 April, 1907.
1. Ethel Maude.
2. Geraldine Margaret
3. Anna Vida Mary.

Lineage.—HILL HAMILTON BARRETT, of Dublin (who *d.* 1872) *m.* Sarah dau. of William Hutcheson, of Woodside, co. Armagh, and had issue an only son,

SAMUEL BARRETT-HAMILTON, of Kilmanock House, co. Wexford, J.P. and D.L., High Sheriff, 1887, late Capt. 3rd and 14th Hussars *b.* 1838 ; *m.* 1st, 1865, Alexina, dau. of James Lyall, of Farnock co. Lagark, and 2ndly, 1870, Laura Emilia, dau. of Charles H. Thompson, of the Mount, York. He assumed by Royal Licence 20 Aug. 1887, the additional surname and arms of Hamilton and *d.* 22 Sept. 1906, having had issue by his second wife,

GERALD EDWIN HAMILTON, now of Kilmanock House.

Arms—Quarterly 1st and 4th per saltire gu. and az. a galley, sails furled and oars in action or, between three cinquefoils pierced arg. (HAMILTON) 2nd and 3rd per pale arg. and gu. barry of eight in chief three roses all counterchanged (BARRETT). **Crest**—1. In front of two battle axes in saltire an oaktree fructed all ppr, the trunk transfixed with a frame saw of (HAMILTON). 2. A human heart gu. between two wings conjoined and expanded az. bezantée (BARRETT). **Mottoes**—1. HAMILTON, Through. 2. BARRETT, " Vivit post funera virtus."

Seat—Kilmanock House, Campile (via Waterford), co. Wexford.
Club—Kildare Street.

ORMSBY-HAMILTON OF CABINTEELY HOUSE.

ALFRED HAMILTON ORMSBY - HAMILTON, of Cabinteely House, co. Dublin, J.P. and D.L., High Sheriff, 1905, Barrister-at-Law, of King's Inns, 1879, and Lincoln's Inn, 1899, Junior Crown Prosecutor for cos. Carlow and Kildare, M.A. Trin. Coll. Dublin, late Capt. Louth Rifles, *b.* 14 May, 1852 ; *m.* 7 Sept. 1892, his cousin, Gertrude Uhthoff (Mrs. HAMILTON), only dau. of Thomas Claud George Hamilton, J.P. (*see below*). Mr. ORMSBY-HAMILTON assumed the additional name and arms of HAMILTON by Royal Licence, 19 Nov. 1892.

Lineage (of ORMSBY).—PAUL ORMSBY, of Knockmore, co. Mayo, 4th son of Robert Ormsby, of Cloghans, and Mary Blakeney his wife (*see* ORMSBY *of Gortner Abbey*), *m.* Mary, dau. of Robert Blakeney, of Abbert, co. Galway, and had a son,

CHARLES ORMSBY, of Foxford, co. Mayo, *b.* 1707 ; *m.* Anne, dau. of Rev. James Price, M.A., a Minor Canon of St. Patrick's Cathedral. She *d.* 1783, aged 74. He *d.* 1769, having had issue, a son,

CAPT. JAMES ORMSBY, 45th Regt., *b.* 1737 ; *m.* 1762, Jane, dau. of Capt. Stephen de Gualy, of Languedoc, France. She *d.* 1808, aged 67. He *d.* 1807, having had issue,

1. Charles Montagu (Sir), 1st bart., M.P., Barrister-at-Law, Knighted Jan. 1806. and created a Baronet 29 Dec. 1812, *b.* 23 April, 1767 ; *m.* June, 1794, Elizabeth, dau. of Thomas Kingsbury, and *d.* 3 March, 1818, leaving two sons,
    1. James (Sir), 2nd bart., *d.s.p.* 1 Nov. 1821.
    2. Thomas (Sir), 3rd bart., *b.* 26 May, 1797 ; *m.* 1824, Mary, only dau. of Maj.-Gen. Francis Rebow (formerly Slater), of Wyvenhoe Park, Essex, by Mary Hester his wife, eldest dau. and co-heir of Col. Isaac Martin Rebow, of Wyvenhoe Park, and *d.s.p.* 9 Aug. 1833, when the baronetcy became extinct. His widow *m.* 1835, John Gurdon, of Letton. She *d.s.p.* 17 Sept. 1842 (*see* GORDON-REBOW *of Wyvenhoe Park*).
2. Stephen, Maj. in the Army, *m.* the dau. of Maximilian Favière, of Dublin, and *d.s.p.* 8 May, 1852.
3. James Wilmot (Rev.), *m.* Jan. 1798, Elizabeth, dau. of Sir Hugh Dillon Massy, 1st bart., of Doonass, and *d.* 1831, leaving issue, with four daus. a son,
    James Wilmot, Barrister-at-Law.
4. HENRY, of whom presently.
5. William, Capt. 13th Madras N.I.
6. George, Capt. R.N.
7. John Blosset, Capt. 70th Regt.
1. Charlotte, *m.* — Corneille.
2. Jane, *m.* Rev. Henry Casey.

The 4th son,

THE REV. HENRY ORMSBY, M.A., Rector of Kilskeer, co. Meath, *m.* 1804, Margaret, dau. of Rev. Michael Sandys, Rector of Powerscourt, and *d.* Sept., 1818, leaving issue,

1. John Blosset (Rev.), Domestic Chaplain to the Bishop of Cashel, Rector of Templemore, *b.* 25 May, 1805 ; *m.* 13 Jan. 1839, Martha, 3rd dau. of Rev. Richard Grier, D.D., of Midleton, co. Cork, and *d.* 26 June, 1849, having had issue.
2. William Edwin (Rev.), Vicar of St. Peter's, Drogheda, *b.* 6 July, 1808 ; *m.* 9 Dec. 1839, Ellen, dau. of James Price, and *d.* Nov. 1858, having had issue,
    1. William Edwin, LL.D., J.P., formerly Judge of the High Court, Travancore, *d.* 8 June, 1910.
    2. Francis, Sec. of G.S. and W.R., who *d.* 1909.
3. Charles Montagu, Barrister-at-Law, *b.* 27 Oct. 1810 ; *m.* 13 Dec. 1838, Anne Christina, dau. of Thomas Hutchinson, and widow of George Keough, and had issue.
4. HENRY WILMOT, of whom presently.
5. Edwin Sandys (Rev.), *b.* 12 Nov. 1813 ; *m.* Charlotte, dau. of Simon Armstrong, and had issue
    1. Mary Charlotte, *m.* 19 July, 1838, Rev. Hugh Hamilton, and had issue (*see* HAMILTON-STUBBER *of Moyne*).

The 4th son,

THE RIGHT HON. HENRY WILMOT ORMSBY, P.C., Judge of the Chancery Division of the High Court of Justice in Ireland, 1875-85, *b.* 19 Feb. 1811 ; *m.* 1 Sept. 1840, Julia, dau. of Henry Hamilton, of Tullylish, co. Down (*see* HAMILTON-STUBBER *of Moyne*), and *d.* 17 Sept. 1887, leaving issue,

1. Montague Henry, *b.* 19 March, 1842 ; *d.* June, 1870.
2. George Albert (Right Rev.), D.D., Bishop of Honduras 1893, *b.* Sept. 1843 ; *m.* 1871, Ellen, dau. of the Rev. Canon Scotland, and has issue, a fourth son, Montague Henry, *m.* 5 Dec. 1908, Marian Wallace, dau. of late Col. J. H. Green, C.B.
3. Edwin Robert (Rev.), M.A., *b.* 19 Feb. 1845 ; *m.* 24 Aug. 1869, Esther, dau. of — Procter.
4. John Blosset, *b.* 28 Jan. 1850, *d.* 17 March, 1851.
5. ALFRED HAMILTON, of Cabinteely.
6. Frederick Alexander (Rev.), M.A., Vicar of Christ Church, Clapham, *b.* 9 May, 1854 ; *m.* 20 Feb. 1888, Caroline Ellen Mary, dau. of the late T. H. Fraser. He *d.* 9 Nov. 1901, and left issue.
1. Millicent.
2. Julia Charlotte, *d. unm.* 3 Aug. 1907.
3. Louise, *m.* 8 Feb. 1886, C. Athill Stanuell.

Lineage (of HAMILTON).—GEORGE HAMILTON, of Hampton Hall, co. Dublin, Baron of the Exchequer in Ireland from 1776, sometime Solicitor-General for Ireland, M.P. for Belfast 1769-1776, 3rd son of Alexander Hamilton, M.P., of Knock, co. Dublin, and Newtown Hamilton, co. Armagh (*see* HAMILTON-STUBBER *of Moyne*), *m.* his cousin, Elizabeth, dau. of George Hamilton, of Tyrella, and *d.* 1793, leaving issue,

1. Alexander, of Hampton Hall, co. Dublin, M.P. for Belfast and elsewhere 1789-1799, K.C., *m.* 11 Feb. 1796, Catherine, dau. of Thomas Burgh, Comptroller-Gen. and Commissioner of Revenue, Ireland, and *d.s.p.* 1808.
2. GEORGE, of whom presently.

The younger son,

Rev. GEORGE HAMILTON, of Hampton Hall, co. Dublin, and Tyrella, co. Down, s. his maternal uncle 1796, and his brother 1808 ; *m.* 1796, Anna, dau. of Thomas Pepper, of Ballygarth Castle, co. Meath, by Henrietta his wife, dau. of Stephen Moore, of Barne, and *d.* March, 1833, leaving issue,

1. George Alexander (Right Hon.), of Hampton Hall, co. Dublin, J.P. and D.L., D.C.L., M.P. for the City of Dublin, and subsequently for the University of Dublin, Financial Secretary to the Treasury, 1852, *b.* 29 Aug. 1802 ; *m.* 1 May, 1835, Amelia Fancourt, dau. of Joshua Andrew Uhthoff, of Bath, and *d.s.p.* 1871.
2. THOMAS CLAUD GEORGE, of whom presently.
1. Harriet, *m.* Joseph W. Swan, M.D., of Kingstown, son of William Swan, M.D., of Dublin, and *d.s.p.* July, 1878.

The younger son,

THOMAS CLAUD GEORGE HAMILTON, J.P., co. Dublin, *m.* 1st, 1840, Gertrude Anne, 2nd dau. of Joshua Andrew Uhthoff, e:

Bath, above-mentioned. and 2ndly, Elizabeth, dau. of Richard Spooner, M.P., and d. 1889, having by his 1st wife had issue an only dau.,
GERTRUDE UHTHOFF, m. as above, Alfred Hamilton Ormsby Hamilton.

Arms—Quarterly 1st and 4th gu. three cinquefoils erm. and in the centre chief point a fasces erect ppr. (HAMILTON), 2nd and 3rd gu. a bend between six cross crosslets or, the bend charged for cadency with a mullet az. and thereon a crescent arg. (ORMSBY). *Crests*—1. HAMILTON: Out of a ducal crest coronet of five leaves or, charged on the band with three torteaux fessewise a mount vert thereon an oak tree penetrated transversely in the main stem by a frame-saw ppr., the frame or ; 2. ORMSBY : A dexter arm embowed in armour ppr., purfled or the hand arg., holding a man's leg also in armour couped above the knee also arg. *Mottoes*—1. (Over the Hamilton Crest): Through ; 2. (Over the Ormsby Crest): Fortis qui prudens ; 3. (Under the Arms) : Sola nobilitas virtus.

Seat—Cabinteely House, co. Dublin. *Town Residence*—16, Fitzwilliam Square, Dublin. *Clubs*—Junior Carlton, National, and Constitutional, S.W. ; University, Dublin, and Royal St. George Yacht, Kingstown.

HAMILTON. *See* BURKE'S PEERAGE, **ABERCORN, D.**

HAMILTON-JONES. *See* **JONES.**

HAMILTON. *See* **HAMILTON-STUBBER.**

WALDRON-HAMILTON. *See* **WALDRON.**

HANDCOCK OF CARANTRILA PARK.

GERALD CARLILE STRATFORD HANDCOCK, of Carantrila Park, co. Galway, Major 1st Batt. "The Princess of Wales' Own" Yorkshire Regt., b. 16 Feb. 1858 ; m. Ella Scott, eldest dau. of James Broun, of Orchard Carluke, N.B.

Lineage.—WILLIAM HANDCOCK, of Twyford, in Westmeath, M.P. for that co. in the first Parliament after the Restoration, was appointed one of the Council of Connaught, and obtained a patent in 1680 to erect his estates into a manor, under the designation of the Manor of Twyford. He m. 25 July, 1652, Abigail, dau. of Rev. Thomas Stanley, and sister of Sir Thomas Stanley, by whom he was ancestor of the LORDS CASTLEMAINE. His 5th son,

REV. MATTHEW HANDCOCK, Archdeacon of Kilmore, co. Cavan, b. 1668, was attainted by Parliament, *temp.* JAMES II ; m. June, 1693, Elizabeth, dau. of Sir Elias Best, and d. 1740, leaving issue a son and heir,

REV. ELIAS HANDCOCK, Rector of Kilnafad, co. Cavan, b. 7 April, 1712 ; m. Aug. 1742, Catherine, dau. of Thomas Smith, of Castle Pollard, and d. 1771, having by her (who d. 1781) had issue,
1. WILLIAM, his heir.
2. Mathew, Dep. Surveyor Gen. of Lands and Dep. Muster Master Gen. and Clerk of the Check, Ireland.

His elder son,
WILLIAM HANDCOCK, m. Oct. 1802, Anne Henry, and d. 1828, leaving by her (who d. 1818),
1. WILLIAM HENRY, his heir.
2. JOHN STRATFORD, who s. his brother.

The elder son,
WILLIAM HENRY HANDCOCK, b. 1803 ; m. Sept. 1824, the dau. of T. Kelly, and had issue three daus. He was s. at his death by his brother,

JOHN STRATFORD HANDCOCK, b. 1804 ; m. 1857, Elizabeth Penelope Blair, dau. of Capt. W. G. Kent, R.N., and by her had issue,
1. GERALD CARLILE STRATFORD, now of Carantrila Park.
2. Cecil Henry Kent Stratford, m. 10 Sept. 1892, Alice, only dau. of Professor S. S. Hamill.
3. Herbert William Fenton Stratford, d. 1864.

4. Lionel Bertie Stratford.
5. Claude Henry William George Stratford.
1. Evelyn Anne Henry Stratford, m. 1889, Lieut.-Col. Maurice George Moore, C.B., Connaught Rangers, son of the late George Moore, M.P., of Moore Hall, co. Mayo, and has issue (*see that family*).
2. Mabel Percival Alice Stratford.

Mr. Handcock d. 1872.

Arms—*See* CASTLEMAINE, *Baron.*

Seat—Carantrila Park, Dunmore, co. Galway.

HANDCOCK.

See BURKE'S PEERAGE, **CASTLEMAINE, B.**

HANDCOCK OF GARNAFAILAGH.

THE HON. ROBERT ARTHUR HANDCOCK, of Garnafailagh, co. Westmeath, J.P. and D.L., b. 19 April, 1864 ; m. 16 Jan. 1894, Ethel Violet, only dau. of Col. Sir Edmund Bainbridge, K.C.B., R.A., and has had issue,

RICHARD EDMOND GUY, b. 21 July, 1896 ; d. 11 Nov. 1909.
Violet Louisa, b. 26 May, 1895.

Mr. Handcock is the only surviving brother and heir presumptive of Albert Edward, 5th Baron Castlemaine.

Lineage, Arms, &c.—(*See* BURKE'S *Peerage*, CASTLEMAINE, B.)

Seat—Garnafailagh, Athlone. *Clubs*—Sackville St. (Dublin), Royal St. George's Yacht.

HANFORD-FLOOD OF FLOOD HALL.

MAJOR ROBERT THOMAS HANFORD-FLOOD, of Flood Hall and Farmley, co. Kilkenny, and Woollas Hall, J.P. co. Kilkenny, co. Worcester, Major late 2nd Queen's Royal West Surrey Regt., b. 13 Sept. 1850, s. his brother 11 Aug. 1911.

Lineage.—Hanford, in Cheshire, was the original seat of this family. The elder line became extinct about 1550, and the younger was seated at Woollas Hall, co. Worcester 1567-1860, when it also became extinct in the male line.

LAURENCE HANFORD, 2nd son of Robert Hanford, and 7th in descent from Sir John Hanford, of Cheshire, left by his wife, a dau. of — Pope, a son,

THOMAS HANFORD, of Elmdon, Worcestershire in 1567, m. Margaret, dau. of John Higford, of Dixton, co. Gloucester, by Dorothy, his wife, sister and co-heiress of John Vampage, of Woollas Hall and with her acquired the Woollas Hall estates. He suffered severely for his faith, and his estates were sequestrated by the Crown in lieu of payment of fines as a Popish recusant. He d. 1605, having had issue,
1. Edmund, d.v.p. 1579, bur. at Pershore.
2. JOHN, his heir.
1. Catherine, m. John Whittington, of Notgrove, co. Gloucester.
2. Margaret, m. Thomas Copley, of Bredon's Norton, co. Worcester.

The only surviving son,
JOHN HANFORD, of Woollas Hall, co. Worcester, which he built in 1611, obtained a general pardon from JAMES I, in discharge of the escheat on his estates, m. Anne, dau. and co-heir of Richard Rake, of Allesley, co. Worcester, and widow of John Browne, of Pershore, and d. 17 Aug. 1616, leaving issue,
1. FRANCIS, his heir.
2. Edmund, b. 1603, living at Bristol in 1632, left issue, a son, Tobias, of Virginia, in 1669, and of Shobdon, co. Hereford, s. his cousin John, of Shobdon, 1676, and d. May, 1677, having had a son,
Tobias, of Shobdon, d. an infant 1679, and was s. by his cousin Walter, of Woollas Hall.
3. John, of Shobdon, co. Hereford, living as Shelfield, co. Stafford, 1632, m. Aug. 1639, Eleanor, only dau. and heir of Warnicombe Wigmore, of Shobdon, and d. 1670, leaving an only son,
John, of Shobdon, a minor, 5 July, 1676, and was s. by his cousin, Tobias (*see above*).
1. Margaret, living 1632.
2. Mary, bapt. 1605, m. John Brinckman, of Lane End in the Marsh, Bucks.
3. Anne, living 1632.   4. Jane, living 1632.
5. Dorothy, m. Anthony Hunt, of Longmore, Salop.
6. Elizabeth, living 1632.
7. Catherine, d. unm. 1681.

The eldest son,
FRANCIS HANFORD, of Woollas Hall, b. 1601, m. 1st (then aged 15), Elizabeth (then aged 12), dau. of Thomas Russell, of Rushock, co. Worcester. This marriage was dissolved March, 1617. (She m.

IRELAND.   Harden.

2ndly, John Hornyold, of Blackmore Park, co. Worcester). He *m.* 2ndly, Elizabeth, dau. of Walter Giffard, of Chillington, co. Stafford, and *d.* 1643, having by her (who *m.* 2ndly, 1648, Aylifle White, Barrister-at-Law, and *d.* 1681) had issue,
1. WALTER, his heir.
2. John, of London, living 1697, had a son John, living 1681.
3. Edward, *b.* 1634, living 1664.
4. Thomas, *b.* 1635, living 1664.
1. Anne, *m.* 1654, Edmund Bradshaw, of London, merchant.
2. Margaret, *d.* young.
3. Elizabeth, *b.* 1630, *m.* 1654, Robert Clarke, citizen and merchant of London.
4. Mary, a nun, living 1681.
5. Winifred, *d. unm.* 1679.
The eldest son,
WALTER HANFORD, of Woollas Hall, compounded with the Commonwealth for his estates for the sum of £800 and suffered severely during the Rebellion, *m.* 1651, Frances, dau. and co-heir of Sir John Compton, Knt., of Brambletye, Sussex, and *d.* 16 July, 1679, having had issue,
1. FRANCIS, his heir.
2. Walter, *d.* young.
3. Henry, *d. unm.* 1681.
4. COMPTON s. his brother.
5. John, Collector of Inland Revenue, at Weymouth, *d. unm.* 1705.
6. William, Page of Honour to JAMES II, and Capt. in Lord Galloway's Regt. in Provence, 1698.
7. Charles, *d. unm.* 1731.
8. Philip, living 1711.
9. George, *d.* young, 1681.
10. Edward, of Redmarley d'Abitot. co. Worcester, received a grant of that manor from Lord Plymouth 1702, *b.* 1671 ; *m.* 1717, Frances, dau. of Robert Hornyold, of Blackmore Park, and *d.* 1763, having by her (who *d.* 1728) had issue,
1. Robert, *d.v.p.* 1723.
2. Charles, of Redmarley d'Abitot, *b.* 1721, *m.* 1776, Esther, dau. of John Lockley, of Barton Park, co. Derby, and Boscobel, Salop. She *d.* 1803. He *d.* 28 May, 1794, having had issue,
(1) CHARLES EDWARD, s. to Woollas Hall 1816.
(1) Lucy Elizabeth, *b.* 1778 ; *m.* Charles Parker, of Battle, Sussex, and *d.* 1854.
(2) Elizabeth, *b.* 1779. *d. unm.* 1862.
(3) Esther Maria, *b.* 1780, *m.* — Lemon, and *d.* 1831.
(4) Eleanor, *m.* 7 Feb. 1809, John Raester, of Pershore, surgeon, and *d.* 1810.
1. Frances, *m.* 1763, Daniel Dew, of Pauntley Court, co. Gloucester.
2. Sarah, *d. unm.* 1734.
3. Elizabeth, *m.* 1765, Samuel Niolett, of Gloucester, banker, and *d.* 1812.
11. Vampage, *d.* an infant, 1681.
1. Lucy, *d. unm.* 1727.
2. Mary, living 1679.
3. Dorothy, living 1721.
4. Frances, *d. unm.* 8 April, 1721.
5. Katherine, living 1679.
The eldest son,
FRANCIS HANFORD, of Woollas Hall, *m.* Dorothy, dau. and co-heir of Sir John Cocks, of Crowle, co. Worcester. She *d.* 1722. He *d.* 1682, having had a dau.,
Frances, inherited the Manor of Ruyall's Court in Pershore, and many other lands, *m.* 1708, Charles Somerset, of Powick, and *d.s.p.* 1716.
His brother,
COMPTON HANFORD, of Woollas Hall, sold the Shobdon estates 1685, *m.* 1st, Elizabeth, only dau. and heir of Sir Robert Slingsby, Bart., of Newsells, Herts, and niece of Francis, 1st Earl of Derwentwater, and by her (who *d.* 1694) had issue,
1. EDWARD, his heir.
2. Charles, *b.* 1719, *d. unm.* 1763.
1. Elizabeth, *d. unm.* 1770.
2. Barbara, *d.* an infant, 1694.
3. Mary, *d.* an infant, 1694.
He *m.* 2ndly, Joanna, sister of Joseph de Chaumont, of Brussels and cousin of Mary, widow of Sir George Wintour, Bart., of Huddington, co. Worcester. She inherited from her cousin, Lady Wintour all the furniture and pictures (now at Woollas Hall) belonging to the Wintours, the Gunpowder Plot conspirators. She *d.s.p.* 1717. He *d.* 1722, and was s. by his elder son,
EDWARD HANFORD, of Woollas Hall, who, with his brother, shared the misfortunes of their cousin, the ill-fated Earl of Derwentwater. He *m.* 1718, Elizabeth, dau. and co-heir of John Hurst, of Haverill, Essex, and *d.* 1766, having had issue,
1. EDWARD, his heir
2. James, *b.* 1721, *d. unm.* 9 April, 1795.
3. CHARLES, s. his brother.
1. Eleanor, *b.* 1723 ; *d. unm.* 16 Dec. 1802.
2. Mary, *b.* 1724 ; *d. unm.* 13 Sept. 1775.
3. Elizabeth, *b.* 1728 ; *d.* a nun at Liège 1761.
4. Dorothy, *b.* 1736 ; *d.* a nun at Liège 1761.
The eldest son,
EDWARD HANFORD, of Woollas Hall, *b.* 27 May, 1719 ; *d. unm.* 23 Sept. 1797, and was s. by his brother,
CHARLES HANFORD, of Woollas Hall, *b.* 17 Sept. 1726 ; *m.* Mary, dau. of J. Duffkin, of London, merchant. She *d.* 1823, aged 87. He *d.s.p.* 12 June, 1816, and was s. by his cousin,
CHARLES EDWARD HANFORD, of Woollas Hall, and Redmarley, J.P. and D.L. co. Worcester. *b.* June, 1781 ; *m.* 11 Oct. 1809, Elizabeth, 3rd dau. of James Martin, of Overbury Court, co.

Worcester. She *d.* 5 March, 1844. He *d.* 17 Feb. 1854, having had issue,
1. Charles Edward, *b.* 19 Oct. 1810 ; *d.v.p.* 22 March, 1827.
2. James, *b.* 13 Feb. 1812 ; *d. unm.* 18 Feb. 1840, *v.p.*
3. COMPTON JOHN, his heir.
1. Eleanor, *d.* young, 1824.
2. Elizabeth Henrietta, *d. unm.* 31 Dec. 1833.
3. FRANCES, of whom we treat.
The only surviving son,
COMPTON JOHN HANFORD, of Woollas Hall, *b.* June, 1819 ; *d. unm.* 19 June, 1860, and was s. by his sister,
FRANCES HANFORD, of Woollas Hall, *b.* 27 July, 1823 ; *m.* 18 Nov. 1847, William Lloyd Hanford-Flood, of Farmley, co. Kilkenny, J.P. and D.L. co. Kilkenny, High Sheriff 1849, J.P. co. Worcester, High Sheriff 1871. Mr. Hanford-Flood assumed the originally Lloyd, assumed by Royal Licence 1839, the additional name of Flood and the arms of Flood, name of HANFORD-FLOOD 4 June 1861, and *d.* 3 May, 1892. Mrs. Hanford-Flood *d.* 21 Feb. 1875, having had issue,
1. JOHN COMPTON, late of Flood Hall, and Woollas Hall.
2. ROBERT THOMAS HANFORD-FLOOD, now of Flood Hall.
3. William Compton HANFORD-FLOOD, of Manitoba, Canada, *b.* 22 July, 1861 ; *d. unm.* 27 July, 1903.
1. Anne.
2. Elizabeth.
3. Frances Alice.
4. Sarah Teresa, *d. unm.* 2 Dec. 1885.
5. Mary Frances, *m.* 11 Aug. 1886, Col. Constantine Rodney William Hervey, R.A., and has issue.
COL. JOHN COMPTON HANFORD, C.B., of Flood Hall, co. Kilkenny, and Woollas Hall, co. Worcester, J.P. and D.L. co Kilkenny, late 19th Hussars, B.A. Trin. Coll. Camb., *b.* 22 July, 1840, served in Egyptian War 1882-84 and in Soudan 1884-85, sometime an Assistant Insp. of Remounts, assumed by Royal Licence, 6 May, 1893, the name and arms of HANFORD only, in lieu of HANFORD-FLOOD. He *d.* 11 Aug. 1911, being s. by his brother.

Arms.—Vert, a chevron between three wolves' heads erased arg. Crest—A wolf's head erased arg. Motto—Vis unita fortior est.
Seats—Flood Hall, Thomastown, co. Kilkenny, and Woollas Hall, Pershore, co. Worcester. Club—Junior United Service.

HARDEN OF HARRYBROOK.

RICHARD JAMES HARDEN, of Harrybrook, co. Armagh, J.P. and D.L., High Sheriff 1871, *b.* 23 Dec. 1846 ; *m.* 11 April, 1872, Annie Johnstone, dau. of Joseph Atkinson, J.P. and D.L., of Crowhill, co. Armagh, and has issue,
1. JAMES EDWARDS, Major 3rd Batt. Royal Irish Fusiliers, J.P. co. Armagh, *b.* 24 Aug. 1873 ; *m.* 12 April, 1904, Letitia Grace Campbell, eldest dau. of late Robert Nutter Campbell Connal, of Glasgow, and has issue,
1. Esmé Grace, *b.* 21 Feb. 1906.
2. Amy Margaret.
2. Robert Atkinson. *b.* 27 June, 1875.
3. George Frederick St. Clair (*Sandwell*, *Radlett*), *b.* 26 May, 1878 ; *m.* 23 May, 1907, Violet Emily, 3rd dau. of J. Primrose Lindsay, of Gosforth, Newcastle-on-Tyne, and has issue,
James Lindsay, *b.* 19 March, 1911.
Diana Primrose, *b.* 24 Feb. 1909.
1. Kathleen Annie, *b.* 19 Feb. 1883 ; *m.* 15 Sept. 1909, Dudley G. P. Hornidge, of Calvertown, co. Westmeath, and has issue.
Lineage.—HENRY HARDEN, J.P. and D.L., *b.* 1710 ; *m.* Catherine Hartford, and *d.* 1751, leaving a son,
JAMES HARDEN, *b.* 1741 ; *m.* Mary, dau. and heiress of W. Walker, of Ballybreagh, co. Armagh, and *d.* 1805, leaving issue,
1. Henry, *b.* 1774, Capt. Armagh Militia.
2. ROBERT, of whom presently.
3. John, *b.* 1789, Capt. 17th Foot.
1. Mary Anne, *m.* W. Gray, of Graymount, co. Antrim.
2. Catherine, *m.* Edward Lucas, of Drumnargal.
The 2nd son,
ROBERT HARDEN, of Harrybrook, co. Armagh J.P. and D.L., *b.* 1781 ; *m.* 1804, Ann, dau. of John Hardy, of Longhgall, co. Armagh, and *d.* 1840, leaving issue,
1. JAMES, his heir.
2. Robert Acheson, *b.* 1820 ; *m.* Catherine Hydes.
3. Archibald (Rev.), *b.* 1822; *m.* and had issue an only son, Robert Manners, of Rutland Lodge, Ledbury, who *d.* 2 April, 1910, and whose widow Gertrude *d.* 16 Aug. 1911.
1. Sarah, *m.* Rev. James Hardy, of Moylany, co. Louth.
2. Mary, *m.* John Woodhouse, of Bronté, Liverpool.
The eldest son,
JAMES HARDEN, of Harrybrook, J.P. and D.L., *b.* 1805 ; *m.* 1844, Annabella, dau. of the late Col. Lloyd Edwards, of Nanhorn, co. Carnarvon, and by her (who *d.* 1851) had issue,
1. ROBERT ACHESON, *d. unm.* 1864.
2. RICHARD JAMES, now of Harrybrook.
3. Frederick John, Lieut.-Col. Bedfordshire Regt., *b.* 25 Oct. 1848 ; *d.* 2 June, 1895.
4. George, Lieut.-Col. Royal Sussex Regt., *b.* 2 Feb. 1851 ; *m.* Mabel, dau. of Col. Angelo. She *d.* 7 April, 1907, leaving issue,

1. Frederick.
2. George.
3. Arthur James Victor.
Mr. James Harden d. 1861.
Seat—Harrybrook, Tandragee.

HARE. See BURKE'S PEERAGE, **LISTOWEL, E.**

HARKNESS OF GARRYFINE.

WILLIAM HENRY HARKNESS, of Garryfine and Temple Athea, co. Limerick, late Capt. 5th Dragoon Guards, B.A. Trin. Coll. Dublin, b. 10 Jan. 1854; served in the Zulu Campaign 1879; m. Feb. 1901, Lucy Emily, dau. of Major Lancelot Kiggell, J.P., of Cahara, Glin, co. Limerick.

Lineage.— WILLIAM HARKNESS, of Lismoney, co. Londonderry, whose will, dated 5 April, 1715, was proved 7 Nov. following, m. Mrs. Mary Thaker, widow, and had, with other issue,
  WILLIAM HARKNESS, of Dungannon, co. Londonderry, whose will, dated 19 May, 1746, was proved 10 July following ; m. Margaret Blackley, and had issue,
  1. David.
  2. WILLIAM, of whom presently.
  1. Isabel, Mrs. Hannington, of Dungannon.
  2. Sarah, Mrs. Wright.
The 2nd son,
  WILLIAM HARKNESS, of Garryfine, co. Limerick, previously of Clontarf, and of the City of Dublin, Director of the Bank of Ireland ; m. (marriage licence, 23 March, 1782) Mary, dau. of Capt. Price, and had issue,
  1. William, of Garryfine and Temple Athea, d. unm. 1825.
  2. George, d. unm.
  3. ROBERT (Rev.), of whom hereafter.
  4. Samuel, d. unm.
  1. Margaret, m. James Clarke, of Rutland Square, Dublin, M.D.
The 3rd, but eldest surviving son,
  REV. ROBERT HARKNESS, M.A., of Garryfine and Temple Athea, co. Limerick, Vicar of East Brent, Somerset, m. 1822, Jane Waugh, dau. of Right Rev. George Henry Law, D.D., Bishop of Bath and Wells (by Jane, his wife, dau. of Gen. Adeane, M.P., co. Cambridge), and niece of Edward, 1st Lord Ellenborough, by whom he had issue,
  1. WILLIAM (Rev.), his successor.
  2. George Law (Rev.), M.A., Rector of St. James's, Shaftesbury, m. Frances, dau. of Major Albert D'Alton, and has issue,
    Henry D'Alton, C.B., Col. (retired pay), late Lieut.-Col. and Brev.-Col. commanding 2nd Batt. Welsh Regt., served in South Africa, and wounded at Paardeberg, Feb. 1900 (Forest Lea, Sway, Hants ; Club—Junior United Service), b. 10 March, 1859.
    Janet.
  3. Robert (Rev.), M.A., late Rector of St. Giles, Wimborne, m. Elizabeth, dau. of William Seddon, of Stoneygate House, co. Leicester, and widow of Dr. Toswill, and has,
    1. Robert Law, of Penyard House, Ross, Herefordshire, m. 7 June, 1887, Mary Robina, dau. of the late John Tregonwell, of Anderson and Cranborne, Dorset (see that family).
    2. William Bathurst, Lieut.-Col. R.M.A.
    1. Margaret.
    2. Katherine.
    3. Constance.
  4. Henry Law (Rev.), M.A., Rector of St. Swithin's, Worcester, m. 1st, Agatha, dau. of Edward Clarke, and has issue,
    1. Edward Law, b. 19 March, 1874.
    2. Henty Law, b. 18 May, 1879.
    3. Percy Yarborough, b. 26 Jan. 1884 ; m. 26 Oct. 1905. Gladys Dundas, only dau. of J. Frederick Knowles, of Belair of Bournemouth (see KNOWLES of Colston Bassett).
    1. Agatha Mary, b. 1 Dec. 1875.
    2. Constance Ariel, b. 23 Dec. 1877.
    3. Ariel Law, b. 24 Jan. 1886.
  He m. 2ndly, 1 Dec. 1897, Mabel Stuart, dau. of the late Charles Stuart Smyth.
  5. James Clarke (Rev.), M.A., Vicar of Hawkley, near Liss ; m. 1st, Constance Susan, dau. of G. W. Franklin, M.P. for Poole. She d. Nov. 1879. He m. 2ndly, 11 Aug. 1898, Edith Charlotte, dau. of the late Charles Stuart Smyth. He d. 11 April, 1906.
  1. Jane, m. Rev. Robert Bathurst, son of Gen. Sir James Bathurst, K.C.B.
  2. Mary, m. Henry Jenkinson, son of Admiral Henry Jenkinson, of Alveston, co. Warwick.
  3. Margaret, m. Rev. Frank Synge, son of Rev. Edward Synge.
The eldest son,
  REV. WILLIAM HARKNESS, M.A., of Garryfine and Temple Athae, co. Limerick, Vicar of Winscombe, co. Somerset, m. 1853, Sarah Anne, dau. of John Peebles, Dublin, M.D., and d. 1863, leaving issue,
  1. WILLIAM HENRY, now of Garryfine.
  1. Jane Charlotte, d. 1865.
  2. Grace, m. 15 March, 1882, Thomas Eudo Bellingham, and d. 1 Oct. 1905.
  3. Maud Bellingham.
  4. Florence Law.

Arms—Gyronny of eight or and erm., each piece charged with a crescent alternate gu. and az., over all a lion ramp. sa. Crest—A dove close per pale or and vert holding in the beak an olive branch, also vert fructed gold. Motto—Hope in God.

Seat—Garryfine, co. Limerick. Residences—Cahara, Glin, co. Limerick ; Temple Athea, co. Limerick.

KING-HARMAN OF NEWCASTLE.

COL. WENTWORTH HENRY KING-HARMAN, of Newcastle, co. Longford, J.P. and D.L., High Sheriff 1896, Col. late R.A., and formerly Chief Inspector of Small Arms, b. 27 March, 1840 ; m. 30 May, 1863, Annie Kate, dau. of D. J. Smith, of Kingston, Canada, and has issue,
  1. WENTWORTH ALEXANDER, Major and Hon. Capt. 3rd Batt. Royal Irish Rfles, late Lieut. 1st Batt. Royal Irish Rifles, b. 3 Jan. 1869.
  1. Beatrice Caroline.   2. Lilian Mary.
  3. Annette Maude, m. 15 March, 1900, Capt. Thomas Carson, Royal Irish Rifles, and has issue (see CARSON of Shanroe).

Lineage.—NICHOLAS HARMAN, of Carlow settled in Ireland during the reign of JAMES I. He was one of the first burgesses of Carlow named in the charter granted to that borough by JAMES I in 1614, and was High Sheriff of the co. Carlow in 1619 ; by Mary his wife he was father of
  HENRY HARMAN, of Dublin, who had by Marie his wife (she made her will 5 Jan. 1649, which was proved in the Consistorial Court of Dublin 25 March, 1652, and directs that she should be bur. in St. Bride's Church, Dublin, near her dau. Anne Wall) five sons and as many daus.,
  1. Edward, of Derrymoyle, Queen's Co., M.P. for Carlow, 10 Jan. 1634, whose will, dated 9 June, was proved 16 Sept. 1673. He had two sons,
    1. William, of Derrymoyle, will dated 27 April, 1682, proved 10 Jan. 1684, d.s.p. m. His dau. Katherine, d. 11 Feb. 1757, having m. Capt. Hon. James Fitzmaurice. of Kilmihill, co. Limerick, brother of Thomas, 1st Earl of Kerry, from which marriage was descended FITZMAURICE of co. Carlow.
    2. Hungerford, d.s.p., will proved 1691.
  2. Anthony, d.s.p. before 1684.
  3. THOMAS (Sir), of whom hereafter.
  4. William, of Ince-Conolly, co. Cavan, m. Jane, dau. of Christopher Piers, and had Christopher, of Belenacarriz, co. Cavan, attainted by JAMES II in 1689, ancestor of HARMAN of co. Cavan.
  5. HENRY, ancestor of HARMAN of Palace.
  1. Anne, m. Edward Wall ; b. before 1649, bur. at St. Bride's Church, Dublin
  2. Mary, m. 1st, — Burton, and 2ndly Francis Brereton, of Chapel-Izod.
  3. Jane, d. unm
  4. Margaret, will dated 10 March, 1683, and proved 23 Feb. 1684, m. 1st, — Gormachan, and 2ndly, Capt. Henry Crewkerne, who d. in Carlow, Feb. 1655.
  5. Mabel, m. — Greatrakes.
Mr. Harman d. before 1649. His 3rd son,
  SIR THOMAS HARMAN, Knt. of Athy, knighted by the Lord Deputy, Thomas, Earl of Ossory, 5 June, 1664, was a Major in the Army 1661 ; M.P. for Carlow 1659, and for the borough of Kildare 1661. He obtained a grant of considerable estates in the co. of Longford, under the Act of Settlement by patent dated 4 July, 1667, enrolling 7 Oct. following. He m. Anne Jones, who also obtained a grant of lands under the Act of Settlement in the co. of Carlow, by patent dated 20 July, and enrolled 13 Aug. 1668. He d. 11 Dec. 1667. His will bears date 6 Aug. 1667, and was proved 1 May, 1668. His widow d. 1 June, 1683. They were both bur. in Christ Church, Dublin, having had issue, with a dau., Mary (m. 1st, 1675, Sir Arthur Jones, Knt. of Osberston, co. Kildare ; and 2ndly, William Moreton, D.D., Bishop of Meath), a son,
  WENTWORTH HARMAN, of Castle Roe, co. Carlow, a Capt. of the Battle Axe Guards, 10 Dec. 1683, m. 1st (licence 10 Oct.), 1679,

Margaret, dau. of Garrett Wellesley, of Dangan, and by her (who d. 15 June, 1683) had issue, with two sons one dau., Elizabeth, wife of Conway Blennerhassett. The sons were,
1. Thomas, b. 1681 ; d.s.p.
2. WENTWORTH, of whom hereafter.
Mr. Harman m. 2ndly, June, 1691, Frances, sister and heir of Anthony Sheppard, of Newcastle, co. Longford, by whom (who d. 14 May, 1766, aged 94) he had further issue,
3. ROBERT, successor to his nephew.
4. Francis, d. May, 1714.
5. Anthony, b. 1701, Major in the Army, who had no issue by Charity his wife, who was the sole executrix of his will, dated 14 Aug. 1749.
6. William, d.s.p.
7. CUTTS (Very Rev.), successor to his brother.
1. ANNE, m. as 2nd wife, 1742, Sir Lawrence Parsons, 3rd bart. of Birr Castle (see BURKE'S *Peerage*, ROSSE, E.), and had issue.
Mr. Harman d. 3 May, 1714, and was s. by his eldest son,
WENTWORTH HARMAN, of Moyne, co. Carlow, LL.D., Trinity Coll. Dublin 1718, m. 1714, Lucy, dau. of Audley Mervyn, of Trillick, co. Tyrone, and sister and heir of Henry Mervyn, of same place, by whom (who d. 1737) he had issue,
1. WESLEY, his heir.
2. Thomas, bapt. 16 Jan. 1728, a Cornet of Horse, 1751 ; d.s.p. 9 May, 1765.
1. Wentworth Parsons, b. 25 Oct. 1745, Capt. in the Army ; m. Charlotte, dau. of Paul Winter, of Dublin, and had an only dau., Ann, m. R. B. Deverell.
2. LAWRENCE, of whom hereafter.
Mr. Harman d. 3 Nov. 1757, when he was s. by his eldest son,
WESLEY HARMAN, of Moyle, m. Mary, dau. of Rev. Nicholas Milley, D.D., Prebendary, of Ullard, Diocese of Leighlin, by whom (who m. 2ndly, 7 March, 1763, Rev. Charles Doyne, Rector of Carlow) he had an only son,
Wentworth, who d.s.p. in his father's lifetime.
Mr. Harman d. 6 April, 1758, and was s. by his uncle,
ROBERT HARMAN, of Newcastle, co. Longford, and Millicent, co. Kildare, b. 1699, M.P co. Kildare, 1755, and co. Longford 1761 ; m. Ann, dau. of John Warburton, 3rd son of George Warburton, of Garryhinch, in the King's Co., and d.s.p. 3 Sept. 1765, when he was s. by his only surviving brother,
VERY REV. CUTTS HARMAN, M.A. of Newcastle, Dean of Waterford, bapt. 20 July, 1706, presented to the Deanery 7 March, 1759 ; m. 22 July, 1751, Bridget, dau. of George Gore, of Tenelick, co. Longford, Justice of the Court of Common Pleas in Ireland, and sister of John, Lord Annaly, by whom (who d. 22 Nov. 1762) he had no issue. The Dean presented to his cathedral the very fine organ which it possesses. He d. Jan. 1784, and bequeathed his estates to his nephew, the son of his sister Anne, who m. as above, Sir Lawrence Parsons.
LAWRENCE PARSONS-HARMAN, of Newcastle, M.P. co. Longford, who assumed the additional surname of HARMAN 1792, on s. to his uncle's estates. He was b. 26 July, 1749 ; m. 11 June, 1772, Lady Jane King, dau. of Edward, 1st Earl of Kingston, by whom (who d. 1848) he had an only dau.,
FRANCES, of whom hereafter.
Mr. Parsons-Harman was created 25 Sept. 1792, Lord Oxmantown, and in Feb. 1806, Earl of Rosse, with special remainder, in default of male issue, to his nephew, Sir Lawrence Parsons, 5th bart. of Birr Castle (see BURKE'S *Peerage*, ROSSE, E.). His lordship d. 20 April, 1807, when his peerage passed according to the limitation, and his Harman estates devolved on his only dau. and heir,
LADY FRANCES PARSONS-HARMAN, of Newcastle, who m. 9 Dec. 1799, Robert Edward, 1st Viscount Lorton (see BURKE'S *Peerage*, KINGSTON, E.), by whom (who d. 20 Nov. 1854) she had issue,
1. ROBERT, 2nd Viscount, who s. as 6th Earl of Kingston, 1869 (see BURKE'S *Peerage*).
2. LAWRENCE HARMAN, who s. to the Harman estates, of whom hereafter.
1. Jane, m. 19 July, 1824, Anthony Lefroy, of Carrickglass Manor, co. Longford, LL.D., for many years M.P. for the University of Dublin, eldest son of the Right Hon. Thomas Lefroy, Lord Chief Justice of Ireland, and d. 1 Dec. 1868. He d. 11 Jan. 1890.
2. Caroline, m. 23 March, 1827, Sir Robert Gore-Booth, 4th bart. of Lissadel, and d. 13 Jan. 1828 (see BURKE'S *Peerage*, GORE-BOOTH, Bart.).
3. Frances, m. 8 April, 1834, Right Rev. Charles Leslie, Bishop of Dromore, and d. 28 July, 1835. He m. 2ndly, Louisa Mary, dau. of the Hon. Sir Henry King, K.C.B., and d. 8 July, 1870 (see BURKE'S *Peerage*, KINGSTON, E.).
4. Louisa, d. unm. 1831.
The Viscountess Lorton d. 7 Oct. 1841, when she was s. in her estates by her 2nd son,
HON. LAURENCE KING-HARMAN, of Newcastle, and of Rockingham, co. Roscommon, who assumed the additional surname of HARMAN. He was b. in 1816 ; m. 17 May, 1837, Mary Cecilia, 7th dau. of James Raymond Johnstone, of Alloa, co. Clackmannan. She d. 11 Jan. 1904. He d. 10 Oct. 1875, leaving, with other issue (see BURKE'S *Peerage*, KINGSTON, E.), a 2nd son,
WENTWORTH HENRY, now of Newcastle.

Arms—Quarterly : 1st and 4th sa. a chevron between three rams passant arg. attired or (HARMAN) ; 2nd and 3rd gu. two lions rampant combatant supporting a dexter hand couped at the wrist and erect arg. (KING). Crests—1. Out of a ducal crest coronet or a dexter arm armed and erect in pale ppr. cuff arg. the hand also ppr. grasping two slips of roses, one gu., the other arg. stalked, seeded, and leaved ppr. (HARMAN) ; 2. Out of a ducal crest coronet or a dexter hand erect, the third and fourth fingers turned down ppr. (KING). Motto—Spes tutissima cœlis.

Sea t—Newcastle, Ballymahon, co. Longford.

HARMAN, late OF PALACE.

THOMAS EDWARDS HARMAN, of Carrigbyrne, co. Wexford, J.P., D.L., Major late 2nd Queen's Royal Regt., b. 15 April, 1842 ; m. 15 Jan. 1885, Mary Edith, 4th dau. of Richard Clayton-Browne Clayton, J.P. and D.L., of Carrickbyrne, co. Wexford, and Adlington Hall, co. Lancaster, and has issue,
THOMAS CLAYTON, Lieut. 20th Hussars, b. 17 Oct. 1886.
Catherine Olga Dorothy.

Lineage.—HENRY HARMAN, of Athy, the fifth son of Henry Harman, of Dublin and Carlow (see HARMAN *of Newcastle*), had two sons, George, of Athy (will dated 22 June, 1720), who left two sons, Henry, d. about 1722, leaving surviving issue, an only dau., Harriet, wife of Col. Pope, from whom descended the family of Harman-Pope, of Popefield, Queen's Co. ; Edward (who d.s.p. 1776), and
ANTHONY HARMAN, of Rosetown, co. Kildare, m. the dau. of Joseph Robbins, of Ballyduff, co. Kilkenny, and had, with a younger son, JOSEPH, of whom presently, an elder son, Nicholas, of Rosetown, m. Sarah Masterson, of Moneyseed, co. Wexford, and had, with other issue (who d.s.p.), Anthony, d.s.p. before Dec. 1733, and Masterson, of Ballyroe, m. April, 1742, Martha Minnett, co. Tipperary, and had a son, George, b. 21 May, 1746, and a dau., Mary, bapt. 17 July, 1743. The younger son,
JOSEPH HARMAN, of Ballagh, co. Wexford, removed to that co. and settled there. By Mary his wife he left issue,
1. THOMAS, his successor.
2. John, d. unm., bur. at New Ross, 20 April, 1764.
3. Luke, of Spring Park, Old Ross ; will dated 30 Jan. 1799, proved 18 Feb. 1800.
Mr. Harman, whose will, dated 20 Oct. 1769, was proved 21 June, 1781, was s. by his eldest son,
THOMAS HARMAN, of Ballagh, b. about 1725, who acquired additional property in co. Wexford. He purchased Palace, the family residence, from the Watts family ; m. Deborah, dau. of Joseph Batt, of Grange, co. Wexford, and had issue,
1. Joseph, of Ballagh, m. Mary Shee, who was bur. at New Ross, 17 March, 1770 ; d.s.p.
2. SAMUEL, who carried on the line.
3. Luke, d.s.p. ; will dated 2 May, 1795, proved 4 April, 1801.
1. Mary, b. 26 March, 1752 ; m. (licence 23 July, 1768) Ephraim Hewitt, of Ballylane, co. Wexford ; d. Dec. 1841.
Mr. Harman, whose will, dated 13 April, 1776, was proved 18 Nov. 1778, was s. by his eldest surviving son,
SAMUEL HARMAN, of Palace, b. 1748 ; m. Hannah, dau. of Mathew Hughes, of Wexford, by whom (who d. 10 April, 1825) he had a dau., Deborah, b. 1784 ; d. 25 March, 1806 and an only son,
THOMAS. He d. 21 March, 1816, and was s. by his only son,
THE REV. THOMAS HARMAN, of Palace, ordained 1819, Rector of the Rower, Diocese of Ossory, 1788 ; m. at St. Anne's, Dublin, April, 1813, Sarah Stotesbury, dau. and heiress of John Shearman, by Grace, his wife, dau. and co-heiress of George Stotesbury, of Burris and Ballycarron, co. Kilkenny, by whom (who d. 21 May, 1859) he had issue,
1. SAMUEL THOMAS, his heir.
1. Grace Sophia, m. 3 June, 1833, Robert Tyndall, of Oaklands, co. Wexford (see *that family*).
2. Deborah, b. 25 May, 1815 ; d. 10 Nov. 1817.
Mr. Harman d. 23 Dec. 1871, and was s. by his only son,
SAMUEL THOMAS HARMAN, of Palace, J.P., b. 5 May, 1818 ; m. 17 Oct. 1830, Mary Anne, dau. of John Lloyd Edwards, of Camolin Park, co. Wexford, and Roebuck, co. Dublin, and by her (who d. 6 June, 1885) had issue,
1. THOMAS EDWARDS, his heir.
1. Wilhelmina Sara, d. unm. 20 Sept. 1906.
2. Marion Stotesbury.
Mr. Harman d. 3 Jan. 1882, and was s. by his only son.

Arms—Sa., a chevron between six rams counter passant arg. armed and unguled or. Crest—Out of a ducal coronet or, an arm erect vested az., cuffed arg., the hand ppr. grasping a rose branch stalked and leaved vert, bearing two roses, one gu. the other arg., seeded of the first. Motto—Dieu defend le droit.

Seat—Carrickbyrne, co. Wexford. Club—Kildare St. (Dublin)

STAFFORD-KING-HARMAN OF ROCKINGHAM.

EDWARD CHARLES STAFFORD-KING-HARMAN, of Rockingham, co. Roscommon, second Lieut. Irish Guards, *b.* 13 April, 1891, assumed by Royal Licence, 3 Feb. 1900, the additional surnames and arms of KING-HARMAN.

Lineage.—THE RIGHT HON. EDWARD ROBERT KING-HARMAN, P.C., of Rockingham, co. Roscommon, H.M. Lieutenant of that county, J.P. cos. Longford, Sligo, and Westmeath, M.P. for Sligo 1877-8, for Dublin 1883-5, and for the Isle of Thanet 1885-8, Col. 5th Batt. Connaught Rangers, sometime Lieut. 60th Royal Rifles, *b.* 3 April, 1838, eld. son of the Hon. Laurence Harman King-Harman, of Rockingham (*see* BURKE's *Peerage*, KINGSTON, E.), *m.* 20 Aug. 1861, Emma Frances, dau. of Sir William Worsley, 1st bart. She *d.* 15 May, 1893. He *d.* 10 June, 1888, having had issue,

1. Laurence William, Lieut. 5th Batt. Connaught Rangers, *b.* 23 Nov. 1863 ; *d. unm.* 23 Oct. 1886, *v.p.*
1. Frances Agnes, *m.* 22 May, 1890, Thomas Joseph Stafford, C.B., D.L., F.R.C.S.I., Commissioner of the Local Government Board, Ireland, of 9, Fitzwilliam Square, Dublin, and has issue,
  1. EDWARD CHARLES, of Rockingham.
  2. Cecil William Francis, *b.* 1895.
2. Violet Philadelphia, *d.* young, 28 May, 1867.

Arms—Quarterly 1st and 4th, grand quarters 1st and 4th sa., a chevron between three rams pass. arg. attired or (HARMAN) ; 2nd and 3rd gu., two lions rampant combatant supporting a dexter hand couped at the wrist and erect arg. (KING): 2nd and 3rd per chevron or and arg., a chevron engrailed and a canton gu.(STAFFORD). Crests—1. Out of a ducal crest coronet or a dexter arm armed and erect in pale ppr. cuffed arg., the hand also ppr., grasping two slips of roses one gu. and the other arg., stalked, seeded, and leaved ppr. (HARMAN) ; 2. Out of a ducal crest coronet or a dexter hand erect, the third and fourth fingers turned down ppr. (KING) ; 3. Out of a ducal coronet az., a swan rising ppr. charged with a torteau. (STAFFORD). Motto—Spes tutissima cœlis.

Seat—Rockingham, Boyle, co. Roscommon. Residence—Taney House, Dundrum, co. Dublin. Club—Guards'.

HAROLD-BARRY. See BARRY.

HARRIS OF ASHFORT.

MARY ANNE MADELINE, MRS. MAYNE, EUGENE PORTER HARRIS, and LOUISA EDITH, MRS. MEEKE, tenants in common of Ashfort.

Lineage.—HUGH HARRIS, of Ashfort, co. Armagh, by Margaret his wife, dau. of Right Rev. John Porter, D.D., Bishop of Clogher, had with other issue,
1. John Porter.
2. Hugh.

The elder son,

JOHN PORTER HARRIS, of Ashfort, co. Armagh, J.P., *d.* 1855, being succeeded by his brother,

HUGH HARRIS, of Ashfort, co. Armagh, J.P. and D.L., High Sheriff 1865, Barrister-at-Law, late Capt. Armagh Militia, *b.* 1819 ; *m.* 1844, Lucy, dau. of Richard Williams, of Drumcondra Castle, by whom he left issue at his decease in 1890,
1. Margaret Anne, *m.* Henry Robert King Irwin.
2. MARY ANNE MADELINE, of Ashfort (2, *Arkendale Road, Glasgavry, Kingstown, co. Dublin*) ; *m.* 1870, the late Charles Crawford Mayne, M.D., and has, with other issue,
  Robert Herbert Harris MAYNE, *b.* 1871 ; *m.* 1910.
  Annie Georgina Wilmot.
3. Lucy Henrietta, *d. unm.*
4. EUGENE PORTER.
5. LOUISA EDITH (*Highlands*, 583, *Finchley Road, N.W.*) ; *m.* 1905, Arthur Henry Montgomery Meeke, M.D.

Seat—Ashfort, Tynan, co. Armagh.

HARRIS-TEMPLE. See TEMPLE.

HARRISON OF CASTLE HARRISON.

COL. STANDISH HENRY HARRISON, of Castle Harrison, co. Cork, J.P., served in and commanded 1st and 2nd Batts. The King's Liverpool Regt., commanded 101st Regimental District, Tralee, Record Officer at Lichfield and South Irish Grouped Districts, Cork, with rank of Brig.-Gen., retired June, 1907, educated at Trin. Coll. Dublin, *b.* 27 Feb. 1853 ; *m.* 14 July, 1880, Amy Georgina, 4th dau. of Major-Gen. G. F. de Berry, and has issue,

1. Standish, *b.* 2 Jan. 1882 ; *d.* 29 April, 1882.
2. JOHN DE COURCY, *b.* 2 June, 1886, educated Sandhurst, late Lieut. 2nd Batt. The Royal Irish Regt.
1. Aline Maude, *m.* 1 Nov. 1905, Capt. Thomas Julian Goodlake, 4th R.M. Fus., son of Lieut. William Garrard Goodlake, R.N., and has issue.
2. Amy Kathleen, *m.* 24 June, 1908, Alan Campbell Ferguson, Lieut. A.S.C. (retired), Reserve of Officers, son of Surgeon-Major William Ferguson, A.M.D.
3. Marjorie Isabel.   4. Maureen Standish.
5. Dorothy Patricia.

Lineage.—HENRY HARRISON, of Castle Harrison, co. Cork, brother of William Harrison, one of His Majesty's Commissioners of Revenue, who *d.s.p.*), was collector of Wexford ; his will is dated 3 Sept. 1765. By his wife Elizabeth, he had, with three daus., one son,

WILLIAM HARRISON, of Castle Harrison, *m.* Mary, dau. of John O'Grady, of Kilballyowen, by Mary Elizabeth his wife, eldest dau. and co-heir of Gerald, Lord Kinsale, and had issue,
1. HENRY, of whom presently.   2. Thomas, *d.s.p.*
3. William, Lieut. in the Austrian Service.
1. Mary, *m.* John Harvey, J.P., of Mount Pleasant, Wexford.
2. Elizabeth, *m.* Edward Gladowe.

The eldest son,

HENRY HARRISON, of Castle Harrison, *m.* Sept. 1758, Margaret, dau. of Standish Grady, of Elton, and had issue,
1. William, *d.s.p.*
2. STANDISH HENRY, of whom presently.
3. Henry, of Portsea, *m.* Elizabeth, dau. of Capt. Norton, R.N.
1. Eliza, *m.* John Harold Barry, of Ballyvonear.
2. Catherine Elizabeth Anne.

The 2nd son,

STANDISH HENRY HARRISON, of Castle Harrison, *m.* 1825, Isabella, dau. of Gerald de Courcy O'Grady, of Kilballyowen (*see that family*), and had issue,
1. HENRY, his heir.
2. Gerald de Courcy, *b.* 1828 ; *d.* 10 Nov. 1885.
3. William Thomas, *m.* 26 April, 1866, Christina R. P., dau. of Rev. Pierce Drew, D.D., Rector of Youghal (*see* DREW *of Mocollop*), and *d.* 30 July, 1882, leaving two daus.
  1. Isabella, *d.* 1893.
  2. Alice de Courcy, *m.* Nov. 1904, Capt. Walter Vernon Hume, South Lancashire Regt. (*see* HUME-GORE).
4. Standish, *d.* Dec. 1847.
1. Eliza Thomasina, *m.* 8 March, 1859, Major Henry Call Lodder, 47th Regt.
2. Margaret, *m.* 1867, Arthur Beavor Wynne, F.G.S., and has issue.

Mr. Harrison *d.* 21 Aug. 1865, and was *s.* by his son,

HENRY HARRISON, of Castle Harrison, J.P., *m.* 1 June, 1849, Marianne, dau. of Robert Stein, of Kilbegie, N.B., and by her (who *d.* 1882) had issue,
1. STANDISH HENRY, now of Castle Harrison.
2. Robert Harold (620, *North L. Street, Takoma, Washington, U.S.A.*), *b.* 1860 ; *m.* 1st, 1884, Blanche, dau. of Edwin Clarence Digby, and has a dau.,
  1. Flora, *m.* 1907, George Andrew, U.S.A.
  He *m.* 2ndly, 20 Nov. 1897, at Warrenton, Virginia, U.S.A., Kate, 2nd dau. of late William Muller, of White Hall, Fauquier Co., Virginia, and Weir Gifford, Devonshire, and has further issue,
  1. Standish Harold, *b.* 6 Oct. 1903.
  2. Aline Harold, *b.* 25 Jan. 1900.
3. George Gerald de Courcy, Major 9th Batt. King's Royal Rifle Corps, *b.* 1865 ; *d.* 8 Aug. 1910.
1. Marian Isabella, *m.* 31 July, 1873, Samuel Newburgh Hutchins, of Ardnagashel, J.P. co. Cork, and has issue (*see that family*).
2. Isabella Katherine, *m.* 1st, 1880, John Stewart Gumley, of Battalia. He *d.s.p.* 1881 ; she *m.* 2ndly, Edward French, H.M. Legation, Siam, and *d.* 18 July, 1896.
3. Alexina Frederica Seaton, *d. unm.*
4. Madeline Elizabeth Phillis, *m.* 15 Feb. 1879, Francis Alfred Synes, Lieut. R.N., of Bridport, co. Dorset ; *d.* 26 Sept. 1910.
5. Eliza Thomasina, *d. unm.*   6. Adelaide Mary.

Mr. Harrison *m.* 2ndly, 1884, Emily (*d.* 1 Sept. 1909), dau. of Swithen Fleming, of Middleton, and *d.* 25 Oct. 1884.

Seat—Castle Harrison, Charleville, co. Cork.

HART OF KILDERRY.

WILLIAM EDWARD HART, of Kilderry, co. Donegal, J.P. for Donegal, and High Sheriff 1882, M.A. (Cantab), *b.* 24 Dec. 1844 ; *m.* 1878, Bessie Louisa, eldest dau. of George Johnston Allman, LL.D. She *d.* Nov. 1892, leaving issue,

1. JOHN GEORGE VAUGHAN, Lieut. W. India Regt., *b.* 30 May, 1879.
2. Henry Percyval.   3. Andrew Chichester.
1. Irene Mabel.
2. Frances Edith, *m.* 10 Oct. 1910, Henry Crofton Young.
3. Adelaide Isabel Louisa Bessie.

Lineage.—This family was founded in Ireland by CAPT. HENRY HART, who is stated to have gone from England with the Earl of Essex, in the reign of ELIZABETH. Since its settlement in Ireland it has been connected by intermarriages with the Brookes, Beresfords, and Vaughans.

GEORGE VAUGHAN HART, 5th in descent from Capt. Henry Hart, a Gen. in the Army, and Military Governor of Londonderry and Culmore Forts; *m.* 1792, Charlotte, dau. of John Ellerker, of Ellerker, and by her (who *d.* 1827) had issue,

1. John Richard, *d. unm.* 1838.
2. Henry, *d. unm.* 1850.   3. Edward, *d. unm.* 1836.
4. GEORGE VAUGHAN, of whom presently.
5. William, E.I.C.S., *m.* 29 Jan. 1840, Frances Anne, dau. of Edward Frere, of Clydach, Llanelly, co. Brecon (*see* BURKE'S *Peerage*, FRERE, Bart.), and by her (who *d.* 1898) has issue,
    1. Henry George, *b.* 16 April, 1843; *m.* 9 Aug. 1873, Honoria Letitia, dau. of Sir Henry Montgomery Lawrence, and niece of John, 1st Lord Lawrence (*see* BURKE'S *Peerage*).
    2. Edward Chichester, Col., late R.E., *b.* 5 Aug. 1844; *m.* 25 June, 1872, Maria Eliza, dau. of Lieut.-Col. Julius Brockman Travers, and has issue,
        Henry Travers, Capt. R.A., *m.* 3 Nov. 1908, Phyllis Hope, dau. of Lieut.-Col. H. M. Matthews.
    3. William Ellerker, *m.* 29 Dec. 1874, Katurah Jessie Bruce, dau. of John Bayfield Millington, of Freeston Priory, Lincoln, and *d.* 1891.
    4. George Henry Reeves.
        1. Frances Mary, *m.* 9 Oct. 1861, Major-Gen. Joseph Bonus, Indian Army, and *d.* 1886.
        2. Charlotte Isabella.   3. Edith Vaughan, *d.* 1896.
        4. Mabel Catherine Rivers.
    1. Elizabeth Grant, accidentally burned to death in 1824.
    2. Charlotte, *m.* 6 Feb. 1827, George Gough, of Rathronen, co. Tipperary, *m.* 6 Feb. 1827, son of Very Rev. Thomas Bunbury Gough (*see* BURKE'S *Peerage*, GOUGH, V.). She *d.s.p.* 1827. He *d.* 18 April, 1889.
    3. Frances Alicia Anne, *m.* Rev. Robert Chichester, and *d.* 1867.
    4. Georgina Susanna, *m.* Rev. Edward James Hamilton, and *d.* 1882.

Gen. Hart represented co. Donegal in Parliament for nearly 18 years, and *d.* 1832. His 4th son,

GEORGE VAUGHAN HART, of Kilderry, co. Donegal, J.P. and D.L., a retired Commander R.N., *b.* 7 June, 1805; *m.* 23 Sept. 1835, Jane Maria, dau. of the Rev. George Vaughan Hart, of Glenalla House, Rector of Castlebar; and *d.* 13 May, 1895, leaving issue,

1. WILLIAM EDWARD, now of Kilderry.
2. John Hume, Royal Artillery, *d.* at Hong Kong 1872.
3. George Percival, *d.* 1872.
1. Maria Henrietta *d.* 1860.   2. Charlotte.
3. Elizabeth Jane, *d.* young, 1849.
4. Marianne Vaughan, *d.* 1854.   5. Josephine Frances.
6. Catherine Grace, *d.* 1872.
7. Adelaide Elizabeth Jane, *m.* 1879, Ernest Wilcox, and *d.* 1880.
8. Georgina Susanna. *d.* 1884.

Seat—Kilderry House, Muff, co. Donegal.

HART-SYNNOT. *See* SYNNOT.

HARTLEY OF BEECH PARK.

RICHARD ARTHUR HARTLEY, Beech Park, co. Dublin, Lieut.-Col. 5th Batt. Royal Dublin Fusiliers, *b.* 2 Jan. 1861, Lord of the Manor of Confey, J.P. co. Dublin, served in S. Africa, King's and Queen's medals and five clasps.

Lineage.—SAMUEL HARTLEY, *m.* and had issue,

1. WILLIAM, of whom presently.
2. James, *m.* 26 Jan. 1713-14, Alice, dau. of the Rev. Elias Travers, and by her had issue,
    1. Travers, M.P. for Dublin, *d.* 1796 *m.* 1st, 1747, Anne Spence; 2ndly, 1752, Anne Sibton.
    2. James, Director of the Bank of Ireland, *d.* 1811.

The elder son,

REV. WILLIAM HARTLEY, *b.* 1670, entered T.C.D. 7 July, 1696, settled at Ballyvaghan co. Carlow; *m.* 27 Nov. 1706, Jane, dau. of Rev. Humphry Lloyd (*see* LLOYD *of Lossett*), and had issue, a son,

REV. HUMPHRY HARTLEY, M.A. Trin. Coll. Dublin, *b.* 1711. This Rev. Humphry Hartley *d.* 13 Dec. 1780, and by his wife Honor (who was living 13 Dec. 1780) issue, three sons and one dau.,

1. JAMES, of whom presently.
2. Humphry, *m.* 1785, Anne Agar, and had issue,
    1. William, B.A. T.C.D.
        1. Anne, *d. unm.*
    2. Ellis Agar, *m.* 1809, Henry Ryan, of Kilfera, co. Kilkenny, and left issue.
3. Bartholomew, of Calcutta, *m.* and left issue, a dau.,
    Patience, *m.* — Smith, of Meadop Hall, co. Wexford.

The eldest son,

JAMES HARTLEY, of Tomgar, and Leamore, *m.* 1st, 1780, Christian, eldest dau. of William Hepenstall, of Leamore, co. Wicklow, who *d.* 21 July, 1797, leaving issue,

1. Humphrey, *b.* 31 July, 1785.
2. Travers, *b.* 1 Oct. 1786; *d.* 3 March, 1787.
3. BARTHOLOMEW, of whom presently.
4. Honor, *b.* 19 Nov. 1782.
2. Jane, *b.* 31 Aug. 1788; *d.* 21 March, 1790.
3. Barbara, *b.* 27 Sept. 1789; *m.* 1819, Daniel Desmond, of Ballinasloe, co. Galway, and left issue.

He *m.* 2ndly, 1799, Jane Bourne, of Donnybrook, sister of Frederick Bourne, of Terenure, co. Dublin, and has issue,

4. James, *b.* 15 March, 1800; *d.* 12 Nov. 1800.
5. James, of Fairy Hall, Kent, Director of P. & O. Service; *m.* 1828, Martha Semple, and had issue,
    1. Harry, *m.* — Paton.
    2. James, *m.* — McCready, and had issue, two daus.
        1. Mary Anne, *m.* H. Carson, and has issue.

The 3rd son,

BARTHOLOMEW HEPENSTAL HARTLEY, Capt. 94th and 8th Regts., *b.* Sept. 1791; *m.* 1st, 1823, Eliza, dau. of Richard Wilson, of Ruske, co. Meath, and had issue,

1. RICHARD WILSON late of Beech Park.
2. Bartholomew Hepenstal, *b.* 1826; *m.* Emma Clementina Pitt
    1. Marianne, *m.* Lieut. Neame, late 8th Regt., dec.
    2. Martha, *m.* Arthur Foulger, of Shern Hall, Walthamstow, Essex, and has issue.

He *m.* 2ndly, 1841, Arabella, widow of Col. Jones, and dau. of Richard Blennerhassett and niece of the late Lord Ventry, but by her had no issue. He *d.* 1854. The eldest son,

RICHARD WILSON HARTLEY, of Beech Park, co. Dublin, Lord of the Manor of Confey, J.P. cos. Meath, Kildare (High Sheriff 1880), and Dublin (High Sheriff 1878), Lieut.-Col. late co. Dublin Militia, formerly Capt. in the 8th Regt., *b.* 24 March, 1824; *m.* 19 Jan. 1858, Hester Maria, dau. of Rev. Lambart Watson Hepenstal, of Altadore, co. Wicklow, and *d.* 22 Nov. 1903, leaving issue,

1. Bartholomew, *d.* 5 Feb. 1870.
2. RICHARD ARTHUR, now of Beech Park.
3. Desmond James Lambart, Lieut.-Col. 5th Royal Dublin Fus., late Capt. 19th Regt., served in S. Africa, medal and five clasps, *b.* 29 March, 1862; *m.* 2 Dec. 1908, Araminta Lydia, only dau. of the late Robert Dunscombe, D.L., of Mount Desert, Cork (*see that family*), and has issue,
    Desmond Richard Dunscombe, *b.* 6 Aug. 1911.
    Araminta Beresford.
4. Ralph Legh, Major, King's Regt., served in S. Africa, medal and two clasps, *b.* 15 April, 1864; *m.* at Halifax, N.S., Nov. 1894, Clarina Louise, dau. of W. Slaytor, M.D., of Morris, Halifax, N.S., and has issue,
    Honor Barbara Clarina. *b.* 26 March, 1899.
1. Diana Louisa Hepenstal, *m.* 22 Jan. 1891, Capt. Edward John Marriott Brisco, of Screggan Manor, Tullamore, King's Co., eldest son of Edward John Brisco, of Riverdale, co. Westmeath (*see that family*).

Arms—Arg., on a cross gu., pierced of the field, four cinquefoils or, in the 1st and 4th quarters a martlet sa., and in the 2nd quarter a rose of the second barbed and seeded ppr. **Crest**—Out of a mural crown or, a stag's head ppr. holding in the mouth a rose gu. barbed and seeded ppr. **Motto**—Spectemur agendo.

Seats—Beach Park, Clonsilla, co. Dublin, and Rennafurra, Kenmare, co. Kerry.

HARVEY OF BARGY CASTLE.

JOHN MACLACHLAN HARVEY, of Bargy Castle, co. Wexford, M.A. Trin. Coll. Dublin, *b.* 27 Sept. 1853; *s.* his father 3 May, 1880; *m.* 1881, Mary, dau. of W. F. Littledale, of Whaley Abbey, co. Wicklow, and has issue,

1. BEAUCHAMP BAGENAL, *b.* 19 April, 1890.
2. John James Gascoyne. *b.* 13 Aug. 1892.
1. Cythna Dora de Montmorency Bagenal, *b.* 1888; *m.* Major Irvine, late 44th Regt., and has issue.

Lineage.—AMBROSE HARVEY, styled "the elder of Bridge of Bargy," the name of the townland on which the castle is built, was father of

AMBROSE HARVEY, styled "the younger of Gregherla," who *m.* 1677, Susanna, dau. of Samuel Cambey, and left (with a dau., the wife of John Boxwell, of Lingstown) a son,

REV. WILLIAM HARVEY, Rector of Mulrancan, and Prebendary of Edermine, *b.* 1682; *m.* 1st, Susanna, 5th dau. of John Harvey, of Killiane Castle, M.P. for Wexford 1695, and had issue,

1. Ambrose (Rev.), *b.* 1707; *m.* Elizabeth, dau. of Rev. Pierce Hughes, of Slad. He was disinherited by his father's will. His great-grandson, Jaffray, settled in Canada.
2. John, of Tagunnan, co. Wexford, who was also disinherited by his father's will. He *m.* Jane Russell, and was bur. at Maglas, 18 Aug. 1794, having had issue,
    1. JOHN, of Mount Pleasant, *alias* Tagunnan, who eventually *s.* to the Bargy estates, under the will of his first cousin, James, of Bargy (*see below*).

2. Richard, an Officer of the Army, d. unm.
3. William, of Killiane Lodge, co. Wexford, Treasurer of the co., m. 9 Dec. 1797, Dorothea, 3rd dau. of John Harvey, of Killiane Castle; and d. 5 Sept. 1828, leaving issue seven sons and two daus.,
(1) John, b. 16 Feb. 1803; Treasurer of co. Wexford, m. Harriet, dau. of John Farran, of Sherrington, co. Dublin, and left at his decease four sons and four daus.,
1. William Croker, Treasurer of co. Wexford, m. Mary Anne, dau. of Capt. George Webb, and d. 1872, having had, with two daus., a son and heir, John George Augustus, b. 31 March, 1864.
2. Crosbie.
3. Charles John, of Hilburn, Capt. Wexford Militia, m. Elizabeth, youngest dau. of David Beatty, of Borodale, J.P., d. leaving issue.
4. John James, Lieut.-Col. 24th Regt., d. in India, 1890.
1. Susan. 2. Dora, m. Edward Lloyd, and d. 1889.
3. Isabella, m. John Thomas Beatty, of Woodview, Major Wexford Militia, who d. 18 Aug. 1877. 4. Sarah Maria.
(2) William, b. 31 Oct. 1807; settled at Buenos Ayres, South America, d. 1890.
(3) Joseph, b. 30 Aug. 1809; m. Barbara, dau. of Arthur Meadows, and has one dau.,
Barbara, m. 29 Nov. 1877, John Percy Waddy, Surgeon-Major Royal Irish Regt.
(4) Richard, b. 7 June, 1815. (5) Vigors, b. 15 Oct. 1817.
(6) Robert, b. 17 Nov. 1819. (7) James, b. 7 Dec. 1821.
(1) Sarah, m. 4 July, 1829, Robert Percival, of Great Hayestown, co. Wexford, and has issue, three daus.
(2) Anne, m. Thomas Redmond.
3. FRANCIS, who s. to the estates of his father.
1. Elizabeth, m. John Boxwell, of Lingstown Castle, co. Wexford.
2. Susannah, m. 1st, — Thornton; 2ndly, — Bennett.
3. Catharine, m. 17 Sept. 1737, Thomas Hore, of Pole Hore, co. Wexford and d. 1777.
4. Mary, m. 1st, — Allen; 2ndly, James Moore, of Milne Hill, co. Cavan.

The Rev. William Harvey m. 2ndly, Dorothea, dau. and heiress of Christopher Champney, of Kyle, co. Wexford and had, with other issue,
4. CHRISTOPHER (Rev.), D.D., of Kyle, was incumbent of Rathdowney, Diocese of Ossory, and of Ross, near Ross Carberry, co. Cork; and Prebendary of Edermine, Diocese of Ferns. He m. Dec. 1765, Rachel, dau. of Abraham Nickson, of Munny, co. Wicklow, and niece and heiress of Richard Hutchinson, of Knocklofty, co. Tipperary, and was bur. 20 April, 1796, leaving issue,
1. WILLIAM, of Kyle, Barrister-at-Law, b. about 1767; m. 22 Aug. 1795, Dora, 3rd dau. of Hon. and Very Rev. Maurice Crosbie, Dean of Limerick, 3rd son of Maurice, 1st Lord Brandon, and had issue,
(1) CHRISTOPHER GEORGE, b. 18 Sept. 1797, Mayor of Wexford 1832; d. unm.
(2) James William, of Bromley, co. Wexford, b. 20 Aug. 1798; d. 1873; a Capt. of Guards; m. 10 March, 1824, Frances, only child of Joshua John Pounden, of Fairfield, co. Wexford, Sheriff of Dublin 1798, and by her (who d. 8 May, 1835) had issue,
1. Crosbie William, of Bromley, J.P., co. Wexford, b. 3 Nov. 1831; m. 9 Feb. 1870, Elizabeth Mary Ann dau. of Charles Arthur Walker, of Tykillen, V.L., co. Wexford (see that family), and d. Aug. 1896, leaving a son, Crosbie Charles, b. 1871.
1. Sophia Pyne.
2. Julia Maria, m. James Howlin Graves.
3. Dora Adelaide, m. Edward Hosken Fitzgibbon Royse, Sub-Inspector R.I.C.
4. Mary Anne, m. Edward Thomas Solly Flood, who m. 2ndly, Eliza, dau. of John Harvey, of Bargy Castle and Mount Pleasant.
(3) Maurice Crosbie, R.N., J.P., b. 25 Aug. 1799; d. unm. 25 Nov. 1830.
(4) Percy Lorenzo, of Kyle, b. 8 Oct. 1801; Capt. H.E.I.C.S. Service, J.P. and D.L., and High Sheriff for co. Wexford 1857; m. 1st, Anne, dau. of James Cuppage, and 2ndly, July, 1854. Mary Arabella, dau. of Francis Leigh, of Sion, co. Wexford, and Thornhill, near Bray; by the latter of whom he (who d. 1880) had issue,
1. PERCY LEIGH, of Kyle, b. 2 Oct. 1856.
2. Mary Elizabeth, m. 27 April, 1887, Arthur Kellett, son of Capt. A. Kellett, R.N.
2. Eva Dora, m. 5 Dec. 1888, Col. James McGregor Whitton.
(5) Henry Robert, b. 22 June, 1802, J.P.; m. Eugenie Fannie Félicité, dau. of Mons. Simon Jacques Rochard, of London, and had issue,
1. William Crosbie, Major in the Army, formerly in the 9th Regt., b. 12 March, 1835; m. 2 Nov. 1858, Rosa Cordelia, only dau. of E.S. Horridge, of Cheltenham.
2. James Henry, b. 24 Feb. 1836; d. 9 Dec. 1909; m. Jane Cecil Horton, of Drayton, Toowomba, Queensland, and had issue,
a. HENRY ROBERT, of Kyle, and Glascarrig, and of Gympie, Queensland, b. 9 Dec. 1865; m. 29 Sept. 1888, Emma dau. of John Christopher, of Gympie, Queensland, and has issue,
(a) Percy William.
(b) Herbert Henry.
(c) Robert Crosbie. (d) Cavendish James.

(e) Vivian John.
(a) Rosalie Marie.
b. Cavendish William, b. 24 Feb. 1867; m. Frances Franklin, of Maryborough, Queensland, and has issue.
c. Percy Lorenzo, b. April, 1868; d. unm.
d. Donald Crosbie, b. 6 June, 1869; m. Annie Cochrane, and has issue,
3. Cavendish Gore, b. 21 Aug. 1838; m. 10 Sept. 1862, Emily, dau. of Capt. Thomas Hungerford, R.A.
4. Frances, m. 17 Feb. 1863, Frances Elizabeth, dau. of John Pollock, and had issue. His dau. Kathleen, m. 21 Feb. 1885, Thomas F. Manning, co. Kerry.
1. Dorothea Eugenia, m. 28 Nov. 1861, Edwin Rickard Lloyd.
1. Dorothea, m. 1797, Percy Evans Freke, and was mother of George, 7th Lord Carbery.
2. Rachael m. Capt. Charles Randall, and had a dau., who m. 1858, J. R. T. H. Parker, of Swannington.
The Rev. William Harvey was Mayor of Wexford about 1753. His will was proved in Dublin 1765, and he was s. in his estates by his 3rd son,
FRANCIS HARVEY, of Bargy Castle, was one of the six Clerks in Chancery; he m. Martha, eldest dau. of Rev. James Harvey, of Killiane Castle. His will was proved in Dublin 1792. He was s. by his eldest son,
BEAUCHAMP BAGENAL HARVEY, of Bargy Castle, Barrister-at-Law. This misguided gentleman suffered the extreme penalty of the law for the prominent part he took in the rebellion of 1798, and an act of attainder passed against his property, and received the Royal Assent 6 Oct. 1798 (38 GEORGE III). He d. unm., and was s. by his brother,
JAMES HARVEY, received a re-grant of the old family estates twelve years after the attainder. Dying unm., he bequeathed by his will, which was proved in Dublin, the chief part of the old family estates to his first cousin,
JOHN HARVEY, of Mount Peasant, J.P., Barrister-at-Law, m. Mary (who d. 20 March, 1837), dau. of William Harrison, of Castle Harrison, co. Cork, and had issue,
1. John, in the Royal Navy, d. unm.; killed in action, 1813.
2. William Harrison, Lieut. R.A., who lost an arm at Waterloo, m. Elizabeth Mary, dau. of Col. Paulet Colebrooke, R.A., and d. 18 Aug. 1826, leaving issue,
1. JOHN, heir to his grandfather.
2. William Henry, m. 1845, Maria, dau. of Rev. Mr. Black, of Plymouth, and has four sons and one dau.
3. James Colebrooke, Lieut. 39th Regt., A.D.C. to Sir J. Littler, G.C.B.; killed at the battle of Ferozeshah, 21 Dec. 1845.
1. Agnes Mary, d. 13 May, 1877.
3. George, R.N., drowned at Cork by the upsetting of a boat, unm.
1. Sarah, d. unm. Aug. 1867. 2. Eliza, d. May, 1847.
3. Anne, m. 2 June, 1832, Conolly McCausland Lecky, of Londonderry, d. 14 Feb. 1865.
Mr. Harvey d. 4 June, 1834, and was s. by his grandson,
JOHN HARVEY, of Bargy Castle, and Mount Pleasant, co. Wexford, Capt. R.A., and late Major of the Donegal Artillery, J.P. and D.I., b. 27 Oct. 1816; m. 1st, 11 Nov. 1837, Jane, dau. of Lieut. William Miller, R.A., and had issue,
1. Elizabeth Jane, m. 1871, Gen. Robert Alexander Napper, Bengal Staff Corps, and had issue. She d. his widow 26 Nov. 1911.
2. Henrietta, m. 1862, James Bradish, of Strandfield, co. Wexford, and has issue.
3. Mary Elizabeth, m. 1889, Edward Cartwright, C.E., Kingston, Canada.
He m. 2ndly, 8 June, 1852, Anne, dau. of Pierce William Hughes, of Kilkevan, co. Wexford, and d. 3 May, 1880, leaving issue,
1. JOHN MACLACHLAN, now of Bargy Castle.
2. Edward George Colebrooke, b. 1 Feb. 1855; d. 1893.
3. William James Colebrooke, b. 23 July, 1859.
4. Alexander Maclachlan, b. 22 March, 1861; d. 1887.
5. Harvey de Montmorency, b. Feb. 1864.
6. Robert Roe Fisher, b. 10 April, 1867.
7. Charles Bertie Simons, b. 8 June, 1869.
8. Pierce William George Hughes b. 1871.
4. Anna Beatrice, m. 1885, J. C. Dobbs, of Boston, U.S.A.
5. Florence, m. 1899, Henry Mitchell, of Ontario, Canada, and has issue.
Seat—Bargy Castle, Ballycogley.

HARVEY OF MALIN HALL.

GEORGE MILLER HARVEY, of Malin Hall, co. Donegal, J.P. and D.L., High Sheriff 1870, b. 14 Aug. 1838; m. 11 Aug. 1864, Julia Mary, dau. of William Charles Gage, of Drummond House, co. Derry, and has issue,
1. JOHN, b. 16 July, 1865; m. 23 Oct. 1895, Florita, eldest dau. of J. Digby O'Donoghue, of Montevideo, and has issue,
1. Julia Mary, b. 1 Sept. 1896.
2. Emily Georgina, b. 3 Dec. 1898.
3. Dora, b. 4 June, 1903.

1. Mary Gage, d. unm. 1001.
2. Julia Emily, m. 29 April, 1903, W. Power-Steele.

Lineage.—ROBERT HARVEY, of Londonderry, Storekeeper during the siege of Londonderry, 1688, High Sheriff of the co. 1696, 4th son of JAMES HARVEY, of Dunmore (see HARVEY of Mintiaghs) administered his father's goods and thus became possessed of the confirmation of arms dated 1602, which is now in the possession of his descendant, G. M. Harvey, D.L., of Malin Hall. He had issue
1. JOHN, of whom presently.
2. Samuel, of Londonderry, m. 1st, Ann, dau. of Robert Carey, of Whitecastle, and 2ndly, Jeane —, and d.v.p. 1702, having had issue, Samuel, and Sarah, bur. 21 Oct. 1697.
1. Sarah, m. James Balfour, of Kildrum, and d.s.p. He d. intestate 1718.

The elder son,

JOHN HARVEY, of Londonderry, m. 28 Oct. 1685, Martha Rankin, step-dau. of Capt. Michael Browning, of the "Mountjoy," and had issue,
1. John, m. 20 March, 1722, Elizabeth, dau. of Robert Stewart, of Dungannon, and sister and heir of William Stewart, and d.v.p., having by her (who m. 2ndly, Rev. John Montgomery) had issue, William, Agnes, Rhoda, and Elizabeth.
2. Robert, exor. to his brother John.

He m. 2ndly, Jane, dau. of Richard Godsalve, of Rigmardin, Lancashire, by Ann his wife, dau. of Rev. — Warley, of Irford, co. Gloucester; she d. 28 April, 1706. He m. 3rdly, 10 Oct., 1706, Elizabeth, dau. of Alexander Lecky, Alderman and Mayor of Derry and High Sheriff for the county 1677; she d. 16 Oct. 1708, aged 33.
He m. 4thly, Elizabeth, dau. of Col. Henry Hart, of Kilderry, Inishowen, by Anne his wife, dau. of Sir Tristram Beresford, Bart. (ancestor of the Marquess of Waterford), by whom he had, with other issue,
3. GEORGE, of whom presently.
4. Henry.
5. Thomas (Rev.), who had issue, Thomas and Margaret.

The 3rd son,

GEORGE HARVEY, b. 1713, High Sheriff for Donegal 1754; acquired considerable estate in the manor of Malin, Inishowen, and built Malin Hall. He m. 1740, his cousin, Elizabeth, dau. of Col. George Hart, of Kilderry, and dying 1773, left issue five sons and five daus.,
1. JOHN, his heir.
2. George Hart, d.s.p.
3. George, m. Mary Donne.
4. Thomas.
5. Ludford (Sir), knighted 19 May, 1813; m. Lucy Skinet, and had issue,
  George Ludford (Rev.), who left a son,
    William Hugh Peyton (Rev.), M.A. Oxon, Vicar of Chipping Sodbury, b. 1846; m. 30 April, 1889, Sarah Wilhelmina, widow of the Rev. George Harrison Reade, and dau. of Richard Charles Pratt, of Kinsale, co. Cork (see Family Records).
1. Mary Anne, d. young.
2. Elizabeth, m. W. Stewart.
3. Mary Anne, m. Rev. William Chichester, D.D., Rector of Clonmanny, Inishowen, by whom she had a son, Arthur, of Greencastle, M.P., created a Bart. 13 Sept. 1821, d. unm. 1847.
4. Alice.
5. Anne.

The eldest son,

REV. JOHN HARVEY, of Malin Hall, b. 27 Dec. 1742; m. 16 Oct. 1766 Elizabeth, dau. of Robert Young, of Culdaff, and had eight sons and one dau.,
1. George, d.s.p.
2. George, d.s.p.
3. ROBERT, heir to his father.
4. Edward, m. Rebecca, dau. of George Young, of Culdaffe.
5. John, b. 1772; m. Susan, dau. of George Young.
6. Thomas.
7. Henry.
8. William.
1. Mary Anne, m. Rev. W. Hawkshaw, Rector of Fahan, Inishowen.

He d. 12 May, 1794. His son,

ROBERT HARVEY, of Malin Hall, b. 21 Aug. 1770; m. 14 April, 1801, Barbara Frances, eldest dau. of Robert Gage, of Rathlin Island, co. Antrim, and by her (who d. 23 Aug. 1857) had issue,
1. JOHN, of Malin Hall.
2. Robert, m. 14 May, 1835, Anne Smith, and d. 23 Aug. 1857, having had issue,
  1. Robert.
  2. Charles.
  3. John.
Mrs. Harvey d. 17 March, 1865.
3. George, m. 10 Dec. 1835, Jane Richardson, and has issue,
  1. Robert.
  2. John Auchmuty.
  3. George.
  4. Gardiner.
  1. Mary.
  2. Barbara Emily.
  3. Kate Rosetta.
  4. Susan.
4. Gardiner, m. 28 Aug. 1838, Rosetta Gage, and has issue,
  1. Gardiner.
  2. John.
  3. George.
  1. Kate.
  2. Rosetta.
  3. Barbara Frances.
  4. Annie Susan.
  5. Amy.
  6. Rosa.
1. Mary.
2. Marianne, m. 1 Sept. 1842, Rev. Charles Miller, Rector of Carlingford, son of Rev. George Miller, D.D., Head Master Armagh College.
3. Barbara.
4. Susan, m. 12 July, 1859, James W. Young, M.D.
5. Catherine, m. 6 Nov. 1849, James Alexander, B.C.S.

Mr. Robert Harvey d. 1 Dec. 1820, and was s. by his son,

JOHN HARVEY, of Malin Hall, J.P. and D.L., High Sheriff 1836, b. 24 Jan. 1802; m. 19 April, 1831, Emily, dau. of the Rev. George Miller, D.D., of Armagh, and by her (who d. 22 June, 1839) had issue,

1. Robert, b. 30 June, 1833; d. 5 Feb. 1855.
2. GEORGE MILLER, now of Malin Hall.

He d. 9 July, 1868.

Arms—Gules, on a bend argent, three trefoils slipped vert.
Crest—A lion passant guardant proper, holding in his dexter paw a trefoil slipped vert. **Motto**—Je n'oublierai jamais.
Seat—Malin Hall, co. Donegal.

HARVEY, late OF MINTIAGHS.

EDWARD HENRY HARVEY, late of Mintiaghs, co. Donegal, Barrister-at-Law of the Middle Temple, b. 14 Nov. 1837. In conjunction with his brothers, he sold the Mintiaghs estate in 1879.

Lineage.—JAMES HARVEY, or HERVY, was presumably son of CAPT. GEORGE HARVEY, who had a confirmation of arms and grant of crest 1602, for this confirmation was afterwards in his (James's) possession, and then in the possession of Robert, his 4th son, and is at present in the possession of George Miller Harvey, of Malin Hall (see that family), a descendant (see below). James Harvey was a lessee under Lieut. George Gale, of Dunmore, and his son, George Gale, of Dunmore. His name is written "James Hervy" in a Chancery Bill, Ireland, 20 April, 1673. He d. 17 April, 1667, having had issue, four sons,
1. David, Dunmore, living 1650. His will was made 27 July, 1702; he was bur. 1704, having had by Mary his wife, three sons and a dau.,
  1. David, of who d.v.p., leaving by Rebecca his wife (who m. again) a son and a dau. The said son,
    Robert, of Londonderry, merchant, m. the only child and heir of Capt. Michael Conyngham, and by her, or another wife, had two sons and five daus.,
      1. Michael.
      2. David, of London, b. 1715; d.s.p. 1 July, 1788 (M.I.).
      1. Catharine, m. (contract dated 16 Oct. 1740) John McClintock, of Dublin. She d. 1799. He d. before 22 July, 1760.
      2. Elizabeth, b. 1720; m. 19 Aug. 1742, as 2nd wife, Richard Bateson, Sheriff of Donegal 1761 (see BURKE's Peerage, DERAMORE, B.), and d. 1789, leaving issue. Her son, Sir Robert Bateson-Harvey, assumed the additional name of HARVEY and was created a baronet 12 Aug. 1789 (Irish baronetcy extinct). He d.s.p.l. 1825.
      3. Rebecca, d. unm. Will proved 1792.
      4. Mary, d. unm. Will proved 1795.
      5. Sarah, m. her cousin John Ferguson, of Londonderry, surg., son of Andrew Ferguson, of Burt, by the dau. of John Harvey, of Glendermott. Her son, Sir Andrew Ferguson, was created a baronet, 1801 (Irish baronetcy extinct), and had issue.
    Elizabeth, m. the Rev. Thos. Harvey, of Malin, and had a son, Robert, and a dau.
  2. John, of Glendermott, m. Agnes, dau. of William Maxwell, of Strabane, and had issue,
    (1) William, who left issue, by Helena his wife.
    (2) David (Rev.), d.s.p. 1795, at a great age.
    (1) A dau. m. Andrew Ferguson, of Burt, co. Donegal, and had issue.
  3. George, of Bristol, d.s.p. 1710.
    1. Elizabeth, m. 1685, William McClintock, who d. 1774, leaving issue (see MCCLINTOCK of Dunmore).
  2. John, of Imlick, d.s.p., devising that estate to his nephew William (see below). His will was dated 24 July, 1706.
  3. JAMES, of whom presently.
  4. Robert, storekeeper during the siege of Londonderry. He was administrator of his father's goods and was ancestor of HARVEY of Malin Hall (see that family).

The 3rd son of the above James Harvey or Hervy, of Dunmore, who d. 1667,

JAMES HARVEY, of Dunmore, appears to have m. a second wife, Elizabeth Caldwell, by whom he had 4 daus. He also appears to have removed to the neighbouring townland of Listikell, where he d. 1712, having had issue, three sons,
1. WILLIAM, of whom presently.
2. John, of Dunmore, m. his cousin Jane, younger sister to his brother William's wife, dau. of William McClintock, of Strabane, and had issue,
  1. David.
  2. James, m. 1760, Rose, dau. of Robert McClintock, of Castrues. Her will, proved 1777, his, 1772. They had issue, John, Helen, Jane (will proved 1806), Elizabeth, and Rose Ann.
  1. Elizabeth, d. 1787.
  2. Rebecca.
  3. Mary, m. — Bond.
  4. Margaret, m. John Bond, and had issue.
3. Thomas, of Dunmore.

The eldest son of James, of Dunmore (and of Listikell),

WILLIAM HARVEY, of Imlick, co. Donegal, living in Derry during the siege; m. 30 June, 1708, his kinswoman, Mary, dau. of William McClintock, of Strabane, and d. 16 May, 1734, having by her (who d. 16 April, 1751) had issue, four sons and five daus. The eldest son,

JOHN HARVEY, of Imlick, and of Molenan, in Londonderry, b. 1710; m. (contract 1752) Elizabeth, dau. of William Scott, of Londonderry, and by her (who d. 22 Jan. 1800) had three sons,
1. William, of Molenan, d. unm.
2. John, of Londonderry, d. 1818; m. Isabella Scott, dau. of George Scott, by Elizabeth his wife, dau. of the Rev. Bether King, by his wife, a dau. of Richard Nicolson, who was a brother of Dr. Wm. Nicolson, Bishop of Derry and just before his death was appointed Archbishop of Cashel. He had with other issue,
1. Richard, of Molenan, Sheriff of Londonderry, m. a dau. of Rev. John Vaughan, Master of Malpas School, Cheshire, by whom he had issue,
(1) John Nicholson Harvey, of Molenan, m. his cousin, dau. of Vincent Vaughan, and sister and heir of Vincent Vaughan, of Bell Hatch, by whom he had, with five daus., three sons,
1. Vincent Vaughan, late of Molenan.
2. Richard, b. and d. 1859.
3. William, b. 1862; d. 1891.
3. Thomas, of whom next.
THOMAS HARVEY, of Mintiaghs, Inishowen, co. Donegal, and 16, Portland Place, London, b. 4 March, 1757; m. 4 May, 1789, Maria, 3rd dau. of John Paris, of Wanstead, Essex (by Rebecca his wife, dau. of Rev. Vyner Snell, B.D., of Shenley Hall, Herts, Rector of Doddington), and by her (who d. May, 1841) had four sons and four daus.,
1. JOHN, his heir.
2. Thomas, of Wykeham, Hants, b. 4 Jan. 1794; m. 1st, Harriet, 2nd dau. of Edward Moberly, and sister of Dr. Geo. Moberly, Bishop of Salisbury, and by her (who is dec.) had issue,
1. Edmund, of 46, Chester Square, b. 16 Nov. 1821; m. 19 April, 1864, Agnes Anne, dau. of Rev. Charles Cookson, B.A., Vicar of Maxey, Northants. He d. 24 Aug. 1898.
2. Francis Edward, b. 28 July, 1828; m. 30 Oct. 1861, Maria, dau. of Rev. Charles Cookson, Vicar of Maxey, and d. 7 Dec. 1877, having by her (who d. 8 Jan. 1896) had issue,
(1) Thomas Francis, b. 25 Oct. 1865.
(2) Harry Charles, Major Royal Irish Rifles, B.A. Trin. Hall Camb., b. 20 July, 1868.
(3) Edwin Percy, M.A. Trin. Coll. Camb., b. 25 May, 1874.
(1) Frances Maria.
(2) Harriett Agnes, d. unm. 20 June, 1880.
1. Frances Emily, of Wyckham, deceased.
Mr. Thomas Harvey m. 2ndly, 1 July, 1856, Mary Agnes, dau. of John Barnes, of Catherington, Hants. She d.s.p. July, 1862. He d. 21 Jan. 1876.
3. Archibald Ross, d. young, 3 Nov. 1803, bur. at Wanstead.
4. William Francis, of Purbrook, Hants, b. 8 March, 1805; m. 13 Feb. 1849, Mary Johanna, widow of Andrew Newton, M.D., and dau. of Major-Gen. J. P. Murray, C.B., M.P. (grandson of Alexander, 4th Lord Elibank), and d. 23 April, 1893, having by her (who d. 31 March, 1875) had issue,
Thomas William, b. 30 July, 1852, deceased.
Elizabeth Maria.
1. Rebecca Maria, b. 6 Jan. 1791; m. 27 June, 1833, R. A. Douglas-Gresley, of Salwarpe, co. Worcester, J.P., D.L., who d.s.p. 13 Feb. 1885. She d. 3 March, 1876.
2. Elizabeth, b. 3 July, 1795; d. unm. 19 Oct. 1824, bur. at Wansted.
3. Maria, b. 18 Sept. 1799; d. unm. 14 Aug. 1872, bur at Fareham.
4. Anne, b. 26 Aug. 1811; d. unm. 8 April, 1874, bur. at Farcham.
Mr. Harvey d. 8 Nov. 1819, and was s. by his eldest son,
JOHN HARVEY, of Mintiaghs, and of the Middle Temple, Barrister-at-Law, M.A. Camb., b. 4 Aug. 1792; m. 16 Nov. 1831, Harriet Mary, 2nd dau. of Archibald Paris, of Beech Hill Park, Middlesex (by Margaret Jane Lee, his wife). She d. 13 April, 1884. He d. 12 Feb. 1856, leaving issue,
1. EDWARD HENRY.
2. William Marsh, of Goldington Hall, co. Bedford, Barrister-at-Law (Carlton Club); b. 16 July, 1841.
3. Frederick Mortimer (Rev.), M.A. Trin. Coll. Camb., formerly Rector of Bolnhurst, co. Bedford, b. 24 July, 1845; m. 2 Nov. 1885, Katherine Dorothea (d. 14 April, 1911), dau. of Edward John Parker Jervis, J.P. (see BURKE's Peerage, ST. VINCENT, V.), and has issue,
Ronald Marmaduke Dawnay, b. 16 May, 1887.
1. Mary Frances, m. 25 July, 1860, Rev. Henry Willes Southey, M.A., Vicar of Woburn, co. Bedford, m. d. 9 May, 1900, leaving issue.
2. Eleanor.
3. Florence Elizabeth, d. 22 Feb. 1842, aged 6, bur. at Leamington.
4. Catherine Favell, m. 25 July, 1860, Robert Jubb, formerly of Mintiaghs Lodge, J.P. co. Donegal, and had issue, three daus. She d. and was bur. at Eversley.
5. Louisa.
6. Annie, m. 15 Dec. 1887, Rev. R. S. Tabor, M.A. He d. and was bur. at Cheam.
7. Harriet Caroline, d. unm. Oct. 1879, bur. at Bolnhurst.
8. Emily Julia.

Arms—Gu. on a bend arg. three trefoils slipped vert. and in the sinister chief point a mullet of the second. Crest—A lion passant guardant ppr. holding in his dexter paw a trefoil slipped vert. Motto—Je n'oublieray jamais.

HASTINGS.

See BURKE'S PEERAGE, **HUNTINGDON, E.**

PERRIN-HATCHELL OF FORTFIELD HOUSE.

LOUIS PERRIN-HATCHELL, of Fortfield House, co. Dublin, J.P., High Sheriff co. Carlow 1903, b. 1854, educated at Harrow and at Magdalen Coll. Oxford, Barrister-at-Law, s. his uncle 1901, and adopted the additional name of HATCHELL.

Lineage.—The family of HATCHELL can be traced in the co. of Wexford to the close of the 17th century, and is traditionally stated to have settled in Ireland temp. WILLIAM III.
HENRY HATCHELL, of Wexford, b. circa 1745 (son of Henry Hatchell, also of Wexford, by Mary his wife); m. circa 1769, Mary, dau. of Patrick Lambert, and had issue,
1. Henry, d. unm.
2. JOHN, of whom presently.
3. George, m. Sarah Jane Fitzgerald, dau. of G. Melville, and was father of
George, M.D., Inspector-Gen. of Lunatic Asylums in Ireland, and Surgeon in Ordinary to the Lord Lieutenant of Ireland, m. the dau. of Joseph Stephens, and had issue.
1. Mary, m. William Lewis. 2. Catherine, m. James FitzJames.
3. Margaret, m. James Armstrong.
4. Henrietta, d. unm.
5. Anna, m. Rev. William Hill.
6. Eliza, m. Robert Brenan.
His 2nd son,
THE RIGHT HON. JOHN HATCHELL, of Fortfield House, Terenure, co. Dublin, and Kingsland, co. Wexford, a Commissioner of Charitable Donations and Bequests, P.C., Q.C., Attorney-General for Ireland from 1850 to 1852, and during the same period M.P. for Windsor, b. 1783; m. 1815, Elizabeth, eldest dau. of Richard Waddy, of Kilmacoe, co. Wexford, and Merrion Square, Dublin, and by her (who d. 1848) had issue,
1. JOHN, late of Fortfield House.
1. Penelope, m. 1846, John Perrin, eldest son of the Right Hon. Louis Perrin, Judge of the Queen's Bench in Ireland, of Knockdromin, Lusk, co. Dublin, and d. 11 Feb. 1895, and by him (who d. 1860) has issue,
1. Louis, s. his maternal uncle at Fortfield.
1. Elizabeth Hester. 2. Hester Anne.
3. Mary Margaret.
2. Mary, m. 1860, the Right Hon. Sir Maziere Brady, Bart., Lord Chancellor of Ireland, who d. 13 April, 1871. She d. 26 April, 1891.
3. Elizabeth, d. unm. 1853.
Mr. Hatchell, a distinguished member of the Irish Bar, to which he was called in 1809, was made a K.C. in 1835, appointed Solicitor-General for Ireland in 1847, and promoted to the office of Attorney-General in 1850, which he resigned on the retirement of Lord John Russell's Government in 1852. He d. 14 Aug. 1870. His only son,
JOHN HATCHELL, of Fortfield House, co. Dublin, M.A., Barrister-at-Law, J.P. cos. Dublin and Wexford, D.L. co. Dublin, High Sheriff 1890, b. 1825; M.P. for co. Wexford from 1857 to 1859, and High Sheriff 1859, Private Secretary to the Earl of Carlisle, Lord Lieutenant of Ireland 1859 to 1864, and Principal Secretary to the Lord Chancellor of Ireland 1865 to 1866. He d. unm. 27 Aug. 1901.

Seat—Fortfield House, Terenure. Clubs—United University, S.W., and Kildare Street.

HATTON OF CLONARD.

MAJ.-GEN. VILLIERS HATTON, C.B., of Clonard, co. Wexford, late Grenadier Guards, b. 8 Oct. 1852; m. 30 March, 1897, Emily, only child of Charles Burrall Hoffman, of New York.

Lineage.—The first of the family who settled in the co. Wexford was the
REV. HENRY HATTON, son of Christopher Hatton, of Selby Abbey, in the parish of Welford, co. Northampton. He was b. 1615, and became A.B. of St. John's, Cambridge, 1637, A.M. 1641, and was Prebendary of Clone, in the diocese of Ferns and Leighlin, 1662. His son,
THOMAS HATTON, of Gorey, co. Wexford, m. Sept. 1673, Esther, dau. of Samuel Cambey, and had issue,
HENRY HATTON, of Clonard, co. Wexford, m. circa 1700, Editha, dau. of Thomas Richards, of Rathaspec, co. Wexford, and had issue, four sons and two daus., of whom,
1. LOFTUS, ancestor of HATTON, of Prospect (see that family).

2. John, of whom next.
The second son,
JOHN HATTON, of Clonard, was called to the Bar 1745, High Sheriff co. Wexford 1758. He m. 29 Oct. 1757, Elizabeth, dau. of John Wray, of Castle Wray, co. Donegal, by Elinor, dau. of Sir Arthur Gore, Bart., and had issue, five sons,
1. Henry, of Clonard, m. 1783, Lady Anne Jane Gore, dau. of Arthur, 1st Earl of Arran, but had no issue.
2. William, m. Elizabeth Ross, and had issue,
 1. William, dec.
 1. Louisa, m. Mr. Sandwith, of the Royal Marines.
 2. Isabella Elizabeth Mary, m. Rev. John B. Hildebrand, Rector of Saxby and Stapleford, co. Liecester.
3. GEORGE, of whom presently.
4. John, Major-Gen. in the Army, m. Annetta, dau. of Col. Hodges, and had issue, four sons and two daus.
The 3rd son,
GEORGE HATTON, M.P. for Lisburn, m. Lady Isabella Rachel Conway Seymour, youngest dau. of Francis, 1st Marquess of Hertford (see BURKE's *Peerage*), and had (with a dau., Isabella Elizabeth, m. Baron Grumkau), two sons, Henry John, Commander R.N., dec., and
VILLIERS FRANCIS HATTON, of the co. Wexford, Admiral R.N., M.P. for that co., b. 20 Aug. 1787 ; m. 24 May, 1817, Harriet, dau. of Right Hon. David la Touche, of Marlay, co. Dublin, M.P. for co. Carlow, by the Lady Cecilia Leeson his wife, dau. of the 1st Earl of Milltown, and d. 9 Feb. 1859, having by her (who d. 23 Dec. 1866) had issue,
1. VILLIERS LA TOUCHE, of whom presently.
 1. Cecilia (dec.), m. George Baird, of Stichill House, co. Roxburgh (who d. 1870), and had issue, a son,
 George, dec.
 2. Elizabeth Frances, dec., m. 20 Nov. 1854, Arthur Lowry Cole, C.B., Col. in the Army (who d. 1885), and had issue.
The son,
VILLIERS LA TOUCHE HATTON, of Clonard, co. Wexford, J.P. and D.L., High Sheriff 1862-3, Lieut.-Col. in the Army, late of the Grenadier Guards, b. 15 April, 1824 ; m. 6 Nov. 1850, Rosia Mary, only dau. of the late Sir William Plunkett de Bathe, Bart., and d. 2 Feb. 1897, having by her (who d. 20 May, 1895) had issue,
1. VILLIERS, now of Clonard.
2. William de Bathe, Major late Seaforth Highlanders, b. 25 Dec. 1855 ; m. 10 Jan. 1899, second dau. of the late Major Fraser, of Merlewood, Inverness, N.B.
1. Rosia Mary, m. May, 1900, Rev. David Woodward Whincup, M.A.
2. Madeleine Frances, m. 13 Dec. 1881, Lieut.-Gen. Sir William Henry MacKinnon, K.C.B., C.V.O., late Grenadier Guards.
Arms—Az., on a chevron between three garbs or, an annulet, gu. Crest—A hind statant or, charged with an annulet as in the arms. Motto—Virtus tutissima cassis.
Clubs—Guards', Windham, St. James's, and United Service.

HATTON OF PROSPECT.

JOHN HATTON PORTER-HATTON, of Prospect, co. Wexford, Manager of Provincial Bank of Ireland, Newry, b. 1858 ; m. 1905, Margaret Louisa, widow of David Jackson, of Yokohama, Companion of Imperial Order of Rising Sun (brother of Sir Thomas Jackson, Bart.), and dau. of Robert T. Wright, formerly of Ballinode, co. Monaghan: He assumed the additional surname and arms of HATTON by Royal Licence 5 Oct. 1908.
Lineage.—REV. HENRY HATTON, son of Christopher Hatton, of Selby Abbey, Northamptonshire, b. 1615 ; of St. John's Coll. Cambridge, B.A. 1637, M.A. 1641, Prebendary of Clone, Divine of Ferns 1662, and d. 1669, leaving a son,
THOMAS HATTON, of Gorey, co. Wexford ; m. (licence 18 Sept.) 1675, Esther, dau. of Samuel Cambey, and had issue,
HENRY HATTON, of Wexford, will dated 2 Nov. 1743, proved 10 July, 1747 ; m. circa 1700, Editha (who d. 1747), dau. of Thomas Richards, by Jane, dau. and co-heir of Loftus Codd, of Castletown and Rathaspick (see RICHARDS of *Macmine Castle*), and had four sons and two daus.,
1. LOFTUS, of whom presently.
2. John, of Clonard, ancestor of HATTON of *Clonard* (whom see).
3. Henry.
4. Thomas, b. 1717.
1. Hannah. m. 1730, Christopher Conron, of Welshertown, co. Cork.
2. Esther.
LOFTUS HATTON, of Clonard, b. 1704 ; d. to Feb. 1745, High Sheriff co. Wexford 1730 ; m. 1730, Catherine, dau. of Richard Huson, of Ballyorrell, co. Wexford, and had a son,
HENRY HATTON, of Annagh, co. Wexford, b. 1740 ; m. Sarah, dau. of — Lambe, and had, with a dau., Anne, m. Robert Cooke, of Waterford, a son,
LOFTUS HATTON, of Prospect, co. Wexford ; m. 9 July, 1790, Isabella, dau. of Joshua Nunn, of St. Margaret's, co. Wexford, and had a son,

HENRY HATTON, of Prospect, Capt. Wexford Militia, m. Anne Jane, dau. of Rev. Conolly O'Neill, Rector of Kilforglin, co. Kerry (son of John O'Neill, of Park Hill, co. Donegal), by Dorothea, 3rd dau. of George O'Malley, of Spencer Park, co. Mayo, and had three sons and seven daus.
1. Henry, b. 14 May, 1816 ; d.s.p.
2. Loftus, b. 4 April, 1827 ; d.s.p.
3. John, b. 7 June, 1830 ; d.s.p.
1. Isabella Frances, m. Richard Allen, of Elmville, Wexford.
2. Rebecca Eliza, m. Frederick Robinson, Commander R.N.
3. Anne. 4. Jane Henriette.
5. Susan Arabella, m. William Nalty.
6. Harriette, m. Rev. James Porter, rector of Drumuakilly, co. Tyrone, and had issue,
 John Hatton Porter, who has assumed the name and arms of HATTON.
7. Jemima Jane, m. James R. Crawford, 68th Regt.
Arms—Quarterly 1st and 4th, az., on a chevron between three garbs or an annulet gu. (HATTON), 2nd and 3rd per chevron arg. and sable, three bells counterchanged, a bordure gu. (PORTER). Crests—
1. A hind statant or, charged with an annulet as in the arms (HATTON). 2. A dexter arm in armour embowed in fess ppr. couped at the shoulder, the hand grasping a dagger point downwards ppr. charged on the elbow with a bell sable (PORTER). Mottoes—Virtus tutissima cassis " ; and (over second crest) Vigilantia et virtute.
Seat—Prospect, Clonard, co. Wexford. Residence—Hill Street, Newry. Club—United Counties, Newry.

HAWKINS OF ST. FENTON'S.

HERBERT REGINALD MONTGOMERY HAWKINS, of St. Fenton's, co. Dublin, b. 5 Feb. 1869, only son of James Staples Hawkins, of St. Fenton's, who d. 9 June, 1909, late Lieut. 3rd Hussars, Capt. Dorsetshire Regt., J.P. co Dublin ; m. 22 Sept. 1894, Hilda Nugent, 3rd dau. of Henry Hyde Nugent Bankes, of Wraysbury, Bucks. (*See* BANKES *of Corfe Castle*) and has issue,

1. GEOFFREY ALAN BROOKE, b. 13 July, 1895.
2. Victor Francis Staples, b. Aug. 1904.
3. Audley Reginald, b. 19 Aug. 1904.
1. Lerne Cecilia. 2. Joyce Hilda.
Lineage.—WILLIAM HAWKINS, of Dublin, formerly of London, d. 22 Dec. 1680 ; bur. at St. Werburgh's, Dublin (funeral entry). He m. three times. By his 1st wife he had no issue. He m. 2ndly, Anna, dau. of — Thompson, and by her had two sons and four daus.,
1. John, of Rathfriland, co. Down, High Sheriff 1675, d. to Dec. 1680 ; m. Mary, sister of Sir John Magill, bart., dau. of Lieut. William Johnston by Susanna, dau. of John Magill, of Gill Hall, co. Down, and had, with other issue,
 1. John, assumed the name of MAGILL on succeeding to the Gill Hall estate, High Sheriff co. Down 1700 and 1712, M.P. co. Down 1703-13, b. 1675 ; d. 5 Sept. 1713 ; m. Rose, dau. of Sir Robert Colville, of Newtown, co. Down, and had with other children who d. young, a son,
  ROBERT HAWKINS-MAGILL, of Gill Hall, M.P. for co. Down 1743-45, b. 27 Jan. 1703-4 ; d. 10 April, 1745 ; m. 1st, Aug. 1728, Rachel, widow of Randal, 4th Earl of Antrim, dau. of Clotworthy, Viscount Massereene, and by her (who d. 13 April, 1739) had an only son who d. an infant. He m. 2ndly, 17 Sept. 1742, Lady Anne Bligh, dau. of John, Earl of Darnley, and by her (who m. 2ndly, Dec. 1748, Bernard, 1st Viscount Bangor, and d. Feb. 1789) had an only surviving child and heir,
   Theodosia, m. John, 1st Earl of Clanwilliam.
 2. Acheson.
 3. Robert, High Sheriff for co. Down 1718.
  1. Arabella Susanna, m. George Johnston.
 2. Robert.
1. Anne, d. 17 March, 1702 ; m. 1st, Capt. Oldfield, 2ndly, Sir Andrew Owen ; 3rdly, Arthur, Viscount Loftus of Ely.
2 Judith, m. 1st, 1666, Richard Kenny (d. 1 Oct. 1682) ; 2ndly, Gideon Jacque.
3. Elizabeth, m. Oct. 1677, Sir John Magill, Bart.
4. Mary, d. 1729 ; m. Ephraim Thwaites.

William Hawkins *m*. 3rdly, June, 1665, Grace, dau. of William Thwaites, and by her (who *m*. 2ndly, July, 1681 (as 2nd wife), Sir William Sands, Bart.(*d*. 14 Aug. 1687), and 3rdly, David Clarkson) had four sons,
  3. WILLIAM, of whom presently.   4. Thomas, *b*. 1671.
  5. Samuel, *b*. 1673.   6. Joseph, *b*. 1678
The eldest son,
  WILLIAM HAWKINS, *b*. 1670 ; *d*. 21 Nov. 1736, Ulster King of Arms 13 April, 1698 ; *m*. 1st, 29 Aug. 1692, Lettice, only dau. of Hugh Ridgate, by Lettice his wife, dau. of Sir Richard Carney, Ulster King of Arms 1683-92, and by her (who *d*. 6 June, 1696) had a son,
  William, *b*. May, 1699 ; *d*. 1749, Deputy Ulster King of Arms 1741, Athlone Pursuivant 28 Jan. 1745-6 ; *m*. July, 1720, Margaret, dau. of John Cuthbert, of Ballygall, co. Dublin, *s.p.*
He *m*. 2ndly, 1700, Elizabeth, dau. of James Mutlow, of Woodtown, co. Waterford, and by her (who *d*. 1734) left a son,
  JOHN HAWKINS, *b*. May, 1701 ; *d*. 14 Aug. 1758, Ulster King of Arms, jointly with his father, 19 July, 1722, and *s*. to the office on his father's death, 1736 ; *m*. 1723, Catherine, dau. of William Smith, M.D., of College Street, Dublin, and by her (who *d*. 19 April, 1768) had issue,
  1. JAMES, of whom presently.
  2. John, *b*. 17 Feb. 1727 ; *d. unm.* 1745, Lieut. R. Marines.
  3. William (Sir), *b*. 16 March, 1730 ; *d*. 26 March, 1787, Ulster King of Arms 17 May, 1765, knighted 17 March, 1783 ; *m*. 26 May 1768, Anne, dau. of James Stevenson, of Killyleagh, co. Down, and had issue,
    John Bolton, *d.s.p.* 1831.
    Catherine, *m*. 1881, John Adamson, of Moate, co. Westmeath.
  1. Elizabeth, *m*. Aug. 1753, Rev. Thomas Paul, Dean of Cashel (see PAUL, Bart.).
The eldest son,
  THE RIGHT REV. JAMES HAWKINS, D.D., *b*. 1724 ; *d*. 23 June, 1807, Dean of Emly 1766, Bishop of Dromore 1775, translated to Raphoe 1780 ; *m*. March, 1755, Catherine, dau. of Gilbert Keene, by Alice, dau. of Thomas Whitshed, and had issue,
  1. JOHN, his heir.
  2. William, *b*. 1759 ; *d*. 31 July, 1836 ; *m*. Constantia, dau. of — Brought, and had issue.
  3. James, *b*. 1761 ; *d*. 28 Oct. 1849, of Killincarrig, co. Wicklow, R.N., assumed the name and arms of WHITSHED in addition to Hawkins by Act of Parliament 1791, G.C.B. 1830, created a Baronet 16 May, 1834, Admiral of the Fleet 1844 ; *m*. 11 Dec. 1791, Sophia Henrietta, dau. of Capt. John Albert Bentinck, R.N., Count of the Holy Roman Empire, and by her (who *d*. 20 Jan. 1852) left (with a dau., Renira Antoinette, *m*. 10 March, 1829, Gen. Sir Henry William John Bentinck, K.C.B.) a son,
    SIR ST. VINCENT-KEENE HAWKINS-WHITSHED, 2nd bart., *b*. 28 July, 1801 ; *d*. 13 Sept. 1870 ; *m*. 1 April, 1832, Hon. Elizabeth, 5th dau. of David Montague, 2nd Baron Erskine, and had issue,
    (1) SIR ST. VINCENT BENTINCK HAWKINS-WHITSHED, 3rd bart. *b*. 12 Feb. 1837 ; *d*. 9 March, 1871, when the title became extinct, High Sheriff for co. Wicklow 1867 ; *m*. 8 Dec. 1858, Anne Alicia, 2nd. dau. of the Hon. Rev. John Gustavus Handcock, and by her (who *m*. 2ndly, 11 Dec. 1885, John Percival Hughes) left an only child,
      Elizabeth Alicia Frances, of Killincarrig, *m*. 1st, 27 June, 1879, Col. Frederick Augustus Burnaby (see BURNABY of *Baggrave Hall*), who was killed in action 17 Jan. 1885. She *m*. 2ndly, 1886, John Frederick Main (*d*. 1892) ; and 3rdly, 1900, Francis Bernard Aubney Le Blond, and has issue by 1st marriage.
    (2) Elizabeth Sophia, *m*. 18 Feb. 1857, Col. Arthur Cavendish Bentinck (see BURKE's *Peerage*, PORTLAND, DUKE OF).
    (3) Renira, *m*. 18 Nov. 1862, Rear-Admiral Edwin John Pollard, and left issue (see POLLARD of *Haynford Hall*). He *d*. 1909. She *d*. 30 Aug. 1904.
  4. Thomas (Rev.), *b*. 1766 ; *d*. 17 Jan. 1850, D.D., Dean of Clonfert 1812, Dean of the Chapel Royal, Dublin, 1831 ; *m*. — Fox, and left issue.
  5. Francis, *m*. Helen, dau. of General Barrington, H.E.I.C.S., and left issue.
  1. Elizabeth, *m*. Aug. 1782, Benjamin Ball, of Dublin.
  2. Catherine, *m*. April, 1786, John Puget.
The eldest son,
  THE REV. JOHN HAWKINS. *b*. 1 Aug. 1757 ; *d*. 11 May, 1841, M.A. (Dublin) ; *m*. March, 1792, Anne, 2nd dau. of Alexander Montgomery, of the Hall, co. Donegal (see MONTGOMERY, Bart.), and left issue,
  JAMES, his heir.
  Catherine, *d.s.p.* 20 Jan. 1872 ; *m*. 27 Oct. 1813, Sir Thomas Staples, Bart., Q.C. (see STAPLES, Bart.).
  JAMES HAWKINS, of St. Fenton's, co. Dublin, *b*. 9 Jan. 1797 ; *d*. 25 March, 1880, Barrister, King's Inns, 1819 ; *m*. 23 Aug. 1827, Isabella, dau. of Robert Law, of Dublin, and by her (who *d*. 8 Jan. 1864) had,
  1. John Alexander Whitshed, *b*. 23 June, 1830 ; *d*. 1 May, 1831.
  2. JAMES STAPLES, his heir.
  3. Robert, *d.* young.
  1. Elizabeth, *d*. 28 March, 1883 ; *m*. 25 March, 1861, Robert Francis Ellis, of Magherymore, co. Wicklow (see LESLIE-ELLIS *of Magherymore*).
The 2nd son,
  JAMES STAPLES HAWKINS, of St. Fentons, *b*. 10 Feb. 1837 ; *d*. 9 June, 1909, J.P. co. Dublin ; *m*. 27 July, 1865, Letitia Georgina, dau. of George Frederick Brooke, of Ashbrooke, co. Fermanagh (see BROOKE *of Colebrooke, Bart.*), and had one son and two daus.,
  1. HERBERT REGINALD MONTGOMERY, now of St. Fentons.

1. Kathleen Isabella, *m*. 22 Jan. 1897, Caryl Wentworth Thisleton Wykeham Fiennes (see SAYE AND SELE, *Baron*).
2. Florence Alice, *m*. 19 April, 1906, Capt. Reginald Trevor Roper, Dorsetshire Regt.
  Arms—Per chevron arg. and vert, three hinds trippant ppr. *Crest*—A falcon rising ppr. belled or, perched on a lure of the first stringed arg. and vert. *Motto*—Providence with adventure.
  Seat—St. Fenton's, Sutton, co. Dublin.

HEAD OF DERRYLAHAN PARK.

CHARLES OCTAVIUS HEAD, of Derrylahan Park, late Major R.H.A., *b*. 30 May, 1869 ; *m*. 1908, Alice Margaret, dau. of Charles Threlfall, of Tilstone Lodge, Cheshire.

  Lineage.—MICHAEL HEAD, of the city of Waterford, was sheriff of that city in 1672, and mayor 1684. His brother, the REV. JOHN HEAD, was father of three sons, John, Thomas, and George. His sister Mary was wife of Mr. Higgins. Michael Head *m*. 1st, 1666 (marriage licence dated 3 Oct. 1666), Grace Collins, and had one son,
  1. JOHN, of whom presently.
He *m*. 2ndly, in 1667-8 (marriage licence dated 3 Jan. 1667-8), Elizabeth Hunt, and had issue, one son,
  2. Thomas Head, of Headsgrove, co. Kilkenny, *m*. 1711 (settlement dated 13 April, 1711), Mary, dau. of Rev. John Congrave. He *d.s.p.*, having made his will, dated 23 April, 1723, proved 5 March, 1723-4, and in which he mentions his cousin, Mary Hunt, and limits his estate, first to Thomas Head, and son of his uncle, the Rev. John Head.
The only son by the first marriage,
  JOHN HEAD, of Waterford, *m*. Elizabeth, dau. and heir of Samuel Wade, of Derry, co. Tipperary, and had issue,
  1. MICHAEL, of whom presently.
  2. Samuel, *m*. Elizabeth, dau. of Rt. Rev. Bishop Temson, Bishop of Meath, and widow of Michael Cole, of Castle Lough, co. Tipperary.
  1. Elizabeth.
  2. Grace, wife of Arthur Burdett.
The eldest son,
  MICHAEL HEAD, of Derry Castle, co. Tipperary, *m*. 1733-4 (marriage articles dated 9 Jan. 1733-4), Mary, dau. of O'Neill. His will bears date 16 Oct. 1749, proved 14 Feb. 1749-50, and he had two sons,
  1. Michael, of Derry Castle, *d*. 5 Nov. 1812 ; *m*. Margaret, dau. of Henry Prittie, of Kilboy, and sister of the 1st Lord Dunalley, and had three sons and ten daus.,
    1. Michael, of Derry Castle, *m*. Mary, dau. of John Butler, Capt. in the Army, and had issue,
      (1) Michael, *d.s.p.*
      (1) Maria.   (2) Caroline.
      (3) Emily.   (4) Henrietta.
      (5) Margaret.
    2. Henry Aldborough, Col. 7th Dragoon Guards, *m*. Harriett, dau. of Samuel De la Cherois Crommelin, of Carrowdore Castle, co. Down, and had surviving issue,
      (1) HENRY HASWELL, late senior representative of the family of HEAD *of Derry Castle*, M.D., J.P., ex-President Royal Coll. of Physicians, Ireland ; *m*. 1st, 1858, Mary, dau. of Andrew Mulholland, of Ballywalter Park, co. Down, and sister of 1st Baron Dunleath (see BURKE's *Peerage*). She *d.s.p.* 15 Feb. 1859. He *m*. 2ndly, 1863, Harriett Annette Catherine (*Thornhill, Bray*, co. Wicklow), dau. of Major Andrew Nugent (see NUGENT *of Portaferry*) and Harriet Margaret his wife, dau. of 6th Baron Farnham and widow of 4th Viscount Bangor. He *d*. 13 Jan. 1910, having had issue,
        1. Henry Nugent, Major The Cameronians, senior Representative of the family of HEAD *of Derry Castle (Ferry Quarter, Strangford, co. Down)*, *b*. 4 Feb. 1864 ; *m*. Oct. 1892, Rosa, only dau. of Col. Edward Saunderson, of Castle Saunderson, M.P. (see *that family*), and has issue,
          a. Henry Nugent, *b*. 10 June, 1898.
          b. Edward Saunderson, *b*. 14 Dec. 1907.
          a. Helena Constance.
          b. Angela Nita.
        2. Arthur Edward Maxwell, *b*. 1876.
          1. Gertrude, *m*. 19 Feb. 1908, Edward Sclater, of Kilwarlin House, Hillsborough, co. Down, 5th son of late James Henry Sclater, of Newick Park, Sussex (see *that family*).
          2. Constance, *d*. 1890.
          3. Annette, *m*. 1893, Major R. L. Bower, King's Royal Rifle Corps, formerly of Welham, Yorks, and has issue.
          4. Louise Meriel.
          5. Edith Grace, *m*. 3 Sept. 1895, Robert David Perceval-Maxwell, and has issue (see PERCEVAL-MAXWELL *of Finnebrogue*).
      (1) Harriett.   (2) Charlotte, *m*. Rev. George Courtenay.
      (3) Grace, *m*. her cousin, Henry Darby Head, eldest son of Very Rev. John Head, Dean of Killaloe.
    3. John (The Very Rev.), Dean of Killaloe, *m*. 1815, Susan, dau. of Edward Hawke Darby (see DARBY *of Leap Castle*), and had issue,

(1) Henry Darby Head, *m.* his cousin Grace, dau. of Col. Henry Aldborough Head, and has issue.
(2) John Prittie, Capt. 9th Lancers, *d. unm.*
(3) Michael, *d. unm.* (4) Edward, *d.* an infant.
(5) Edward, Capt. 98th Regt., *m.* Annie, dau. of Capt. Corrigan, and has issue.
(6) Jonathan (Rev.), *m.* Annie, dau. of Col. Shakespear, and has issue.
 (1) Margaret, *d.* an infant.
 (2) Harriet, *m.* Richard Uniacke Bayly, of Ballyre, co. Cork (*see* BAVLY *of Debsborough*).
1. Deborah, *m.* William Causabon Purdon (*see* PURDON *of Tinerana*).
2. Maria, *m.* William Gore. 3. Eliza.
4. Grace, *m.* 1795, Hon. Robert Leeson (*see* BURKE's *Peerage*, MILLTOWN, E.).
5. Catherine, *m.* Rev. Frederick Trench (*see* TRENCH *of Clonfert*).
6. Margaret, *m.* Rev. John Burdett.
7. Matilda. 8. Charlotte, *m.* Sir John Burgoyne, Knt.
9. Theodosia.
10. Louisa, *m.* 1814, Thomas Ford, of Seaford, Barrister-at-Law.
2. JOHN, of whom hereafter.
The 2nd son,
JOHN HEAD, of Ashley Park, co. Tipperary; *m.* Phœbe Toler, sister of the 1st Earl of Norbury, and *d.* 23 June, 1817, leaving a son,
LIEUT.-GEN. MICHAEL HEAD, of Modreeney House, who was *b.* 1770 and *m.* Oct. 1808, Elizabeth, dau. of Edward Ravenscroft, of Portland Place, London, and *d.* 1827, leaving an only child,
WILLIAM J^{HN}Y HEAD, of Derrylahan Park, J.P. and D.L., *b.* 8 Sept. 1809, *m.* 3 Jan. 1860, Isabella, dau. of Nicholas Biddulph, J.P., of Congor House, co. Tipperary (*see* BIDDULPH *of Rathrobin*), by Isabella his wife, dau. of James La Touche, of Dublin, Banker, and *d.* 1888, having had issue,
1. WILLIAM EDWARD, of Derrylahan.
2. John Henry, *b.* 1 Nov. 1866.
3. CHARLES OCTAVIUS, now of Derrylahan.
4. Michael Ravenscroft, *b.* 12 May, 1880.
1. Elizabeth Phœbe, *m.* April, 1882, Rev. George Bennett.
2. Georgina. 3. Isabella Louisa.
4. Anna Septima.
The eldest son,
WILLIAM EDWARD HEAD, of Derrylahan, co. Tipperary, J.P., Capt. Antrim Artillery, *b.* 8 April, 1864; *m.* 1886, Mary Katherine, eldest dau. of Digby Johns, of Rosebrook, co. Antrim.

Seat—Derrylahan Park, Birr, King's Co.

HEARD OF KINSALE.

ROBERT HENRY WARREN HEARD, of Kinsale, and Pallastown, co. Cork. *s.* his father 1897.

Lineage.—This family has long been seated in co. Cork. JOHN HEARD, the first of the name who settled in Ireland, is stated to have come from Wilts with Sir Walter Raleigh, in 1579. He received a grant of lands at Bandon, and *m.* Mary, dau. of John Heans, Provost of Bandon. He is described in his will, which was proved in 1619, as of Bandon Bridges, co. Cork, Gent. Sir Isaac Heard, Garter, states, 1762, in a memorial, still at the Heralds' College, that all John Heard's papers were destroyed in the Irish rebellion 1641. He had issue,
1. HENRY, of whom presently.
2. John, of Bandon Bridge (will proved 1670); *m.* Jane, sister of James Rice, of Bandon, and *d.* 1670, having had issue,
 1. John, *b.* at Bandon 1663; *m.* about 1685, Esther, dau. of John Hawkins, of Cork. She *d.* 1690. He *d.* 1733, having had issue,
  (1) Joseph, *b.* 1686, sailed round the world in the "Duke and Duchess" 1708-11; *m.* Mary, dau. of John Healy, and *d.* 1761, having had issue,
   1. Isaac, *d.* an infant.
   2. Joseph, *m.* Martha, widow of Joseph Russel, of Cork.
   3. Nathaniel, *d. unm.*
   4. Henry, *b.* 1728; *m.* Mary, dau. of Capt. John Teape, and *d.* 1791, having had,
    a. Henry Joseph, *b.* 1761; *d. unm.* 1803.
    b. Isaac, *d.* an infant.
    c. John, *b.* 1766; *d. unm.* 1803.
    a. Susanna, *m.* William Creed, Lieut. 4th King's Own Regt.
    b. Mary, *d.* an infant.

2. Nathaniel, *d.s.p.* in Dublin 1705.
3. Isaac, of Cork, and afterwards of Bridgwater, Somerset, *m.* 1690, Mary, dau. and sole heir of William Massey, of Bridgwater, and *d.* 1704, having had issue,
 (1) John, of Bridgwater and of London, *b.* 1698; *m.* 1726, Elizabeth, only dau. and heir of Benjamin Michell, of Seaside, Branscombe, and Slade, Salcomb Regis, Devon. She *d.* 1778. He *d.* 1759, having had issue,
  1. Isaac (Sir), Garter King of Arms, *b.* 1730; *m.* 1st, 1770, Katherine, dau. of Andrew Tyler, of Boston, U.S. She *d.s.p.* 1783. He *m.* 2ndly, 1787, Alicia, widow of John George Felton, and dau. of Charles Hayes, of Chelsea. He *d.s.p.* 1822.
  2. Benjamin, *b.* 1743; *d. unm.* 1765.
   1. Elizabeth, *m.* James Branscombe, of Exmouth.
   2. Mary, *m.* 1st, Archibald Barnett, who *d.s.p.* 1765, and 2ndly, Charles Lowe, of Cork. She *d.s.p.* 1803.
   3. Jane, m, 1768, Matthew Wade, and *d.s.p.* 1783.
  4. Sarah, *m.* 1768, James Wild, who *d.* 1801, leaving issue.
  (2) Isaac, *d.* an infant.
  (1) Mary, *d.* an infant.
  (2) Elizabeth, *m.* William Knight, of Kingston.
  (3) Jane, *m.* Roger Cave, of Bridgwater.
  (4) Mary, *m.* George Thomas, of Bridgwater, and *d.* 1740, having had issue.
 1. Catherine. 2. Mary.
 3. Alice. 4. Rose.
The elder son,
HENRY HEARD, who was father of
BENJAMIN HEARD, who was father of
ELISHA HEARD, who *m.* about 1686, Margaret St. Leger, and by her had two sons,
1. JOHN, his heir, of whom presently.
2. Elisha, who *m.* 31 Aug. 1717, Anne, dau. of — Cox, of Ballymartle, and had issue,
 1. John, who *m.* 1st, Anne, dau. of Robert Hindston; 2ndly, Abigail, dau. of Richard Pope, and 3rdly, his cousin, Elizabeth Heard; and had issue, John Pope, and Esther, *m.* Joseph Bullen.
 2. Samuel, *m.* Sarah Carthy, of Cork, and had issue,
  1. Margaret, *m.* Henry Austin, of Cork, and had issue.
  2. Mary, *m.* William Bowler, of Milewater, Cork, and *d.s.p.*
The elder son,
JOHN HEARD, was sovereign of Kinsale 1734; *m.* 1707, Anne, dau. of John Bickford, and *d.* 1763, aged 73, having by her (who *d. circa* 1758) had issue,
1. JOHN, of whom presently.
2. BICKFORD, of Ballintubber, co. Cork, *m.* Susan, dau. of John Maunsell, of Limerick. Sheriff of Cork 1767, and by her had issue,
 1. EDWARD, of Ballintubber, Major H.E.I.C.S., *m.* Margaret, dau. of Francis Drew, of Mocollop Castle, co. Waterford, and *d.* 1821, having had issue,
  (1) EDWARD, of Ballintubber, *b.* 1791; *m.* 1824, Jane, dau. and co-heir of Thomas Scott, of Glenbower and Ballydavid, co. Waterford. She *d.* 1864. He *d.* 1861, having had issue,
   1. EDWARD, of Ballintubber, *b.* 1831; *m.* 1857, Mary, dau. of Richard Giffard Campion, of Bushy Park, co. Cork, and *d.* 1901, having had issue,
    a. Edward, *b.* 1850; *d.* 1896.
    b. Richard, of Ballintubber, *b.* 1867; *m.* 1895, Anne, dau. of George Harris, of Spitalfields, co. Cork.
    c. Samuel Bickford, *d.* an infant.
    a. Jane, *m.* James Williamson, of Old Dromore, co. Cork, and has issue.
    b. Lucy, *d. unm.* c. Mary.
    d. Amy, *m.* 1897, her cousin William Scott, of Ardvarna, co. Dublin.
    e. Julia, *d. unm.* f. Arabella.
    g. Elizabeth Frances.
    h. Margaret, *m.* 9 Dec. 1907, Edward John Tilleard, eldest son of late Freeman Tilleard, of East Sheen.
    i. Sophia, *d. unm.*
   2. Samuel Thomas, of Rossdohan, co. Kerry, J.P., D.L., High Sheriff 1908, *b.* 1835; *m.* 1682, Kate, dau. of William Bradley, J.P., M.L.C., of Lindsay and Landsdowne, N.S.W., and has issue,
    a. Edward Severin, Major, late Lieut.-Col. commanding 5th Fusiliers, *b.* 7 March, 1863; *m.* 1893, Georgina Gertrude, dau. of Gen. Beauchamp Henry Whittingham Magrath, and has issue,
     Patrick Beauchamp Valentine, Cadet R.N., *b.* 1894.
     Maureen Kate.
    b. Francis William, Lieut. 4th King's Own, *b.* 1866; *d.* 1889.
    c. Hugh Lindsay Patrick, Capt. R.N., *b.* 1869.
    d. William Beauchamp, *b.* 1877.
    a. Kate Ethel, *m.* 1 June, 1907, Hubert Calisle du Vallon, eldest surviving son of Grosvenor de Jacobi du Vallon, of St. Servan, Brittany.
   1. Julia, *m.* 1870, the late George Harris, of Spitalfields, co. Cork.
   2. Margaret, *d.* 17 Dec. 1909.
   3. Elizabeth, *m.* 1863, Bindon Scott, of Ardvarna, co. Dublin, and has issue.
  (2) Francis Drew, Capt. S. Cork Militia; *b.* 1782, *m.* Ellen, dau. of James Splaine, J.P., of Gurrane, co. Cork, and had issue,
   1. Edward, *d. unm.*
   2. Francis, of Lehena, co. Cork, J.P., Lieut.-Col. 3rd Batt. R. Munster Fus., *m.* Sarah Bradshaw, dau. of George Loane. She *d.* 1891, leaving issue,

  a. Francis George, M.D. *b.* George Loone, J.P.
  a. Sarah Bradshaw. *b.* Ellen Splaine.
  c. Arabella. *d.* Amy Florence.
  e. Mary Webb.
  1. Abigail. 2. Margaret.
 3. Ellen, *m.* Frederick Harrison, of Ballinahina, co. Cork, and had issue.
 (3) Bickford, *d. unm.*
 (1) Arabella, *d. unm.*
 (2) Susan, *m.* Capt. Rickard Lloyd, R.N., and had issue.
 (3) Elizabeth, *m.* William C. Cottrell, of Ballydulea, co. Cork, and had issue.
 (4) Sophia, *d. unm.*
2. John Bickford, *m.* Margaret, dau. of — Doyle, of Dublin, and had issue,
 (1) Henry George, who left one son and two daus.,
  1. Henry James (Rev.), *m.* the dau. of Alexander Bannatyne, of Woodstown, co. Limerick, and has issue,
   a. Alexander St. John.
   b. Robert Bannatyne.
   c. Henry FitzGerald.
   1. Emma, *m.* William W. White.
   2. Susan.
  (2) Christopher. (3) Robert.
  (4) Nevill.
  (1) Grace, *m.* Rev. W. B. Greer, Rector of Waldingham.
3. James Bickford, Major in the Army, *m.* Georgiana Nevill, and had a son,
 (1) James Nevill (Rev.), Rector of Caterham, Surrey; *b.* 1811; *m.* 4 July, 1840, Lady Charlotte Emily Harriet Anne Turnour, elder dau. of 3rd Earl of Winterton. She *d.* 24 April, 1892. He *d.s.p.* same year.
 (2) St. John, Col. H.E.I.C.S., *d. unm.*
  (1) Georgiana, *d. unm.*
  (2) Augusta, *d. unm.*
4. George, Lieut. R.N., *m.* Eliza Williams, and *d.s.p.*
5. Richard, *d.* about 1774.
 1. Anne Elizabeth, *m.* April, 1791, John Arbuthnot, of Rockforest Castle, co. Sligo.
 2. Susanna, *m.* William Bennet, of Arding, near Ross, and had issue.
 3. Martha, *m.* John Swete, of Flotaville, co. Cork, and had issue.
 4. Charlotte, *m.* Alexander Rogers, of Cork, and had issue.
3. Edward, *m.* 1st, Elizabeth, dau. of Capt. Allen, of Cork, who *d.* 1757, leaving an only son, John (Capt.), *m.* Sarah Emerton; 2ndly, Judith, dau. of Rev. William Ellis, sovereign of Clonakilty, and had issue,
 1. Edward, *m.* and had issue.
 2. William, Commander R.N., *m.* his cousin, Anne (*see below*), dau. of William Heard, and *d.s.p.*
  1. Judith, *m.* William Warren, of Hollyhill, and had issue.
  2. Anne, *m.* — Nares.
 4. William, *m.* Sarah, dau. of William Kelly, Attorney-at-Law, and had issue, three daus.,
  1. Sarah, *m.* William Colburne.
  2. Margaret, *m.* George Weir, of Lincoln's Inn.
  3. Anne, *m.* 1st, Major Potter; 2ndly, her cousin, William Heard (*see above*).
1. Margaret, *m.* Thomas Ottiwell, of Kilcullen, co. Kildare, and had an only dau., Anne, who *m.* Richard Moore.
2. Anne, of Kinsale, *d. unm.*, will proved 10 Nov. 1780.
The eldest son,
 JOHN HEARD, of Kinsale; *m. circa* 1736, Bridget, dau. of John Stammers, of Bandon, and had an only child, Elizabeth, 3rd wife of her cousin, John Heard. He *m.* 2ndly, 1755, Rose, dau. of Joseph Wyatt, of Hythe, Hants, and by her (who *m.* 2ndly, — Brabazon) had issue (with four daus., Rose, Esther, Sarah Wyatt, *d.* young, and Sarah, *m.* Robert Warren, an Officer of Dragoons), four sons,
 1. JOHN, of whom presently.
 2. William. 3. James.
 4. Edward, of Compass Hill, Kinsale, Sovereign of Kinsale, 1833-6, *m.* Catherine, dau. of Rev. Richard Griffith, Rector of Kilbrittain, and *d.* 1836, having had issue, two daus., Maria, *d. unm.*, Anne, *d. unm.* 6 March, 1889, and four sons,
  1. Edmund, *d.* young.
  2. John Edward, Capt. 62nd Regt., *m.* Cornelia Pryce, and *d.* in India, leaving a son, Edward.
  3. Richard, of Killybegs, *b.* 1804; *m.* 1st, 1832, Anna Maria, dau. of Robert Lynn, of Belfast, and had issue,
   Robert Lynn, M.D., *b.* 1834; late Assistant-Surgeon, 67th Regt., *m.* 1865, Ellen, eldest dau. of William Haughton, of Moorefield, co. Dublin. He *d.* 31 Aug. 1901, leaving issue.
  Mr. Richard Heard *m.* 2ndly, Caroline, dau. of Richard C. Chambers, of Lifford, who *d.* 1863; 3rdly, 1865, Susanna, dau. of William Allman, of Bandon, and *d.* 1891.
  4. Alexander Wilson Hutcheson, *b.* 1808; *m.* 1st, 1832, Esther Elizabeth Phœbe, 2nd dau. of Eustace Stawell, of Coolmaine Castle, co. Cork, and had issue,
   (1) John Isaac, *b.* 1836; *d.* 1839.
   (2) Alexander Edward Stawell, of Coolmain Castle, Kilbrittain, co. Cork, and of Greenane House, co. Tipperary, *b.* 1842; *m.* 1863, Dorothea, dau. of Samuel Bennett, M.D., of Adelaide House, Bruff, and has had issue,
    1. Samuel Bennett, *b.* 14 Dec. 1865; *d.* 23 March, 1876.
    2. Alexander Eustace Stawell, Major Royal Irish Fusiliers, *b.* 14 Dec. 1867.
    3. Edward St. John, *d.* young.
    4. George Bennett, *b.* 18 March, 1870.
    1. Esther Stawell, *d.* young.
    2. Amy Rebecca, *m.* 19 April, 1905, J hn Norman Sinclair, R.F.A., son of late James Sinclair of Goring, Oxon.

  3. Dorothea Alexandria, *d.* young.
  4. Catherine Stawell, *m.* 25 Oct. 1905, Capt. Philip J. Paterson, R.F.A.
  (3) Stawell Llewellyn, *d.* 22 Aug. 1911.
  (4) Edward S. (5) George. (6) Amyas.
  (7) Charles Leagram (*The Square, Cahir*).
 Mr. Alexander W. H. Heard *m.* 2ndly, Bessie, dau. of Rev. P. Bolton, and has issue,
  (8) Wilson, District Inspector, R.I.C.
The eldest son,
 JOHN HEARD, of Kinsale, whose will was proved 23 July, 1789, *m.* (Setts. dated 10 Jan. 1786) Rachael, dau. of Isaac Servatt, of Kinsale, and by her (who *d.* 12 June, 1819) had issue, Isaac, who *d.* an infant, and
 JOHN ISAAC HEARD, of Kinsale and Ballydaly, co. Cork, M.P. for Kinsale from 1852 to 1858, J.P. and D.L., High Sheriff 1839, *b.* 1787; *m.* 1808, Mary, youngest dau. of Hope Wilkes, of Lofts Hall, Essex, J.P. and D.L., and *d.* 1 Sept. 1862, having by her (who *d.* 16 April, 1850) had issue,
 1. John Wilkes, *b.* 1811; *d.* 1825.
 2. ROBERT, of whom presently.
 1. Martha Ann, *d. unm.* 1834.
 2. Catherine Jane, *d. unm.* 5 Sept. 1883.
 3. Mary, *m.* 3 Jan. 1831, Achilles Daunt, J.P., of Tracton Abbey, and of Compass Hill, Kinsale, and *d.* 20 April, 1884, leaving issue (*see that family*).
 4. Eleanor, *d. unm.* 1840.
The only surviving son,
 ROBERT HEARD, of Kinsale and Pallastown, co. Cork, J.P., High Sheriff 1870, formerly Capt. South Cork Militia, *b.* 27 Nov. 1815; *m.* 8 Feb. 1848, Charlotte, dau. of Sir John Borlase Warren, Bart., and *d.* 12 Sept. 1896, having by her (who *d.* 22 April, 1886) had issue,
 1. John Isaac, *d.* young.
 2. ROBERT WILKES, late of Kinsale.
 3. Augustus Riversdale.
 1. Mary Warren, *m.* 23 Nov. 1876, Sir William Quartus Ewart, Bart., and has issue (*see* BURKE's *Peerage*).
 2. Charlotte, *m.* 6 Dec. 1888, Gilbert, son of Sir Gilbert King, Bart., and had issue (*see* BURKE's *Peerage*).
 3. Catherine Jane, *m.* Sept. 1887, Herbert Eyre Robbins, Ma or Royal Marines, and has issue.
 4. Rachael Eleanor, *d. unm.* 20 June, 1893.
The eldest surviving son,
 ROBERT WILKES HEARD, of Kinsale and Pallastown, co. Cork, *b.* 17 July, 1852; *m.* 20 June, 1888, Charlotte Amyand Powys, elder dau. of Henry Atherton Adams, J.P., of Wynters, Essex, and *d.* 17 April, 1897, having by her (who *m.* 2ndly, 16 Aug. 1898, Richard Charles Pratt, 8th son of Richard Charles Pratt, of Kinsale (*see* BURKE's *Family Records*) had issue,
 1. ROBERT HENRY WARREN, now of Kinsale.
 1. Mary Amyand Powys, *d.* in infancy.
 2. Margaret Marion Atherton.
 3. Mary Evelyn Warren.
 4. Kathleen Vittoria Fiorenza Servatt.
 5. Amyand Dorothy.
 Arms—Arg. on a chevron gu. between three water bougets sa. as many crescents or. *Crest*—A demi-antelope ppr., ducally gorged or, charged on the shoulder with a water bouget as in the arms. *Motto*—Audior.
 Seats—Pallastown and Ballydaly, Kinsale, and The Lodge, Lackamore, co. Tipperary.

HEATON-ARMSTRONG. See ARMSTRONG.

HEIGHINGTON OF DONARD HOUSE.

LIEUT.-COL. WILLIAM HEIGHINGTON, of Donard House, co. Wicklow, J.P., Major and Hon. Lieut.-Col. Wicklow Artillery, *b.* 5 Sept. 1851; *m.* 29 Sept. 1891, Sara Simmonds Henrietta, eldest dau. of the late Robert Cooper, of Collinstown, co. Kildare, and has issue,

Elizabeth Mary Everina.

Lineage.—CUTHBERT HEIGHINGTON, of Donard, co. Wicklow, son or grandson of George Heighington, of Donard (who *m.* by licence 27 Dec. 1670, Anne Wetherelt), administered to his brother, John Heighington, of Donard, 17 Nov. 1757. He had two sons,
1. GEORGE, of whom presently.
2. Thomas, *m.* by licence, 11 May, 1749, Sarah Stubber, but *d.s.p.* Admon. 5 March, 1750.
The elder son,
 GEORGE HEIGHINGTON, of Donard, *m.* Jane Valentine (admon. to her husband 9 Nov. 1742), and had issue,
 1. GEORGE, of whom presently.
 2. Cuthbert.
 3. John, *d.* before 1750.
 1. Mary.
The elder son,
 MAJOR GEORGE HEIGHINGTON, of Donard, whose will, dated 12 March, 1750, was proved 30 June, 1757. He had issue,

IRELAND. Henchy.

1. THOMAS, of whom presently.
2. John.
1. Eleanor. 2. Mary.
3. Margaret.
4. Anne, *m.* 1747, Rev. Anthony Malone (*see* MALONE *of Baronston*).

he elder son,
THOMAS HEIGHINGTON, of Donard, left issue two sons,
1. GEORGE, of whom pres:ntly.
2. Cuthbert, *m.* by licence 12 Feb. 1778, Martha Cooper.

he elder son,
GEORGE HEIGHINGTON, of Donard, *m.* by licence 10 Feb. 1773, Esther, dau. of William Hornidge, of Tulfarris, co. Wicklow, and by her had issue, a son,
WILLIAM HEIGHINGTON, of Donard, *b.* 1800, Mary, dau. of James Critchley, of Grangebeg, co. Wicklow. She *d.* 11 June, 1850. He *m.* 9 May, 1822, having had issue,
1. George. 2. Abraham.
3. WILLIAM, of Donard.
4. Robert Thomas, *d.* 22 Jan. 1847.
1. Sara. 2. Anne.
3. Mary. 4. Martha, *m.* Rev. F. Faris.
5. Elizabeth, *m.* 1840, Rev. Thomas Francis Greene, of Kilranalagh and Baliuroan, co. Wicklow.
6. Emily.

The younger son,
WILLIAM HEIGHINGTON, of Donard, *b.* 1814 ; *m.* 30 Aug. 1848, Elizabeth Eleanor, dau. of Major George Faris, Leitrim Rifles, and *d.* 9 March, 1867, leaving issue,
1. WILLIAM, now of Donard.
2. Robert Cuthbert, *d.* Dec. 1891.
1. Eleanor, *d.* young.
2. Mary, *d.* young.

Seat—Donard House, Dunlavin, co. Wicklow.

HELY-HUTCHINSON. *See* HUTCHINSON.

HEMPHILL OF SPRINGHILL.

The REV. SAMUEL HEMPHILL, D.D., Litt. D. Dublin, M.R.I.A., Rector of Birr and Canon of Killaloe, Professor of Biblical Greek in the University of Dublin 1888–1898, *b.* 5 July, 1859; *m.* 1885, Flora Margaret, eldest dau. of the Rev. Alexander Delap, B.A., of Ray, co. Donegal, and has issue,
1. ROBERT, *b.* 26 Aug. 1888, Trin. Coll. Dublin.
2. Samuel, *d.* in infancy.
3. Richard Patrick, *b.* 1894.
4. Alexander William, *b.* 1896.
1. Annette Noel. 2. Flora.
3. Elizabeth Mary. 4. Margaret Constance.

Lineage—The REV. SAMUEL HEMPHILL, M.A. Edinburgh University, 1726, came to Fethard as Presbyterian Minister in 1728, and the same year purchased Springhill, Killenaule. He *d.* 1761, having *m.* Sarah, dau. of — Semple, and had, with one dau., four sons,
1. William, emigrated to Lancaster, Pennsylvania, in 1760.
2. EDWARD, of whom presently.
3. John, *b.* 1741, Physician of the Infirmary, Cashel ; *d.* 1828 ; *m.* 1766, Elizabeth, dau. and co-heir of Edward Bacon, of Rathkenny, co. Tipperary (*see* BURKE'S *Peerage*, HEMPHILL, B.).
4. Samuel, an Officer in the 14th Dragoons, emigrated to Savannah, Georgia, in 1784.

The 2nd son,
EDWARD HEMPHILL, of Springhill, M.D., Leyden University, *b.* 1735 ; *d.* 1811 ; *m.* 1779, Frances, only dau. of Francis Green Despard, of Killaghy Castle, co. Tipperary, and had issue by her (who *d.* 1807) two sons and a dau.,
1. SAMUEL, his heir.
2. Richard, Solicitor, *b.* 1787 ; *d. unm.* 1869.
1. Elizabeth, *d.* 1869 ; *m.* Col. John Blackmore, 8th Foot.

The eldest son,
SAMUEL HEMPHILL, of Springhill, M.D., Edinburgh University, *b.* 1782 ; *d.* 1866 ; *m.* 1810, Mary, dau. of Robert Backas, of Butlerstown Castle, co. Waterford, and by her (who *d.* 7 July, 1859) had issue,
1. Edward (Rev.), M.A. Trin. Coll. Dublin, *d. unm.*
2. ROBERT, who succeeded.

3. Richard (Rev.), M.A. Trin. Coll. Dublin, Rector of North Strand, Dublin, *b.* 1815 ; *d.* 1885 ; *m.* and left issue, one son, Richard (Rev.), B.A., Rector of Drumshambo, co. Leitrim, *b.* 1848.
4. William Despard, M.D., Edinburgh, *m.* and had issue.
5. Samuel, Solicitor, *m.* and had issue, with three daus., two sons,
1. Samuel R. C., Solicitor (*Sunnyside, Blackrock, co. Dublin*), *b.* 1867.
2. Charles G. C., Maj. Cork Artillery (*Eastmount, Dalkey, co. Dublin*), *b.* 1870.
6. John (Rev.), M.A. Trin. Coll. Dublin, Rector of Knockaney and Canon of Cashel, *b.* 1827 ; *d.* 19 Feb. 1911 ; *m.* 1857, Harriet Hulcatt, and had issue.
1. Ellen, *m.* Rev. Daniel Foley, D.D.
2. Frances, *m.* Rev. B. D. Aldwell, M.A.

The 2nd son,
ROBERT HEMPHILL, of Springhill, Solicitor, *b.* 31 Dec. 1812 ; *d.* 1891 ; *m.* 1858, Annette Sarah, eldest dau. of Samuel Alleyne Rothwell, of Newtown. Kells, co. Meath, by Elizabeth, 2nd dau. of William Irvine, of Gola House, co. Fermanagh (*see* IRVINE *of Killadeas*), and by her (who *d.* 1879) had issue,
1. SAMUEL, present representative.
2. Richard, B.A. Trin. Coll. Dublin, *d.* in Australia.
3. Robert, M.A., LL.B., Trin. Coll. Dublin (*Springhill, Killenaule*), J.P. co. Tipperary, *b.* 1862.
4. William (*Sedgwick Avenue, Kingsbridge, New York, U.S.A.*), *b.* 1864 ; *m.* and had issue.
5. Edward, M.B., B.Ch., Trin. Coll. Dublin, *d.* in Australia. *unm.*
6. Henry, C.E. (*Bangor, co. Down*), *b.* 1872 ; *m.* 1890, Annie Elizabeth, dau. of Rev. S. D. Burnside, of Belfast, and has issue,
1. Robert Edward, *b.* 1906.
2. Henry Douglas, *b.* 1910.
1. Frances Annette, *b.* 1903.
1. Elizabeth Mary.
2. Mary Backas, *m.* Commander C. W. R. Hooper, R.I.M.
3. Annette, *m.* Commander H. E. Kellett, R.N., of Clonacody, co. Tipperary.

Arms—Per fess or and arg., on a fess engrailed between two lion's heads erased contourne az., three estoiles of the second. **Crest**—A cubit arm erect vambraced or, charged with two chevronels az., the hand grasping a short sword ppr. **Motto**—Virtus in arduis.

Residence—The Rectory, Birr, King's Co.

O'CONNOR-HENCHY OF STONEBROOK.

CAPT. HUGH O'CONNOR - HENCHY, of Stonebrook, co. Kildare, and Moyvilla Castle, co. Galway, J.P. and D.L. co. Kildare, High Sheriff 1884, late Capt. 19th Hussars, *b.* 31 May, 1852 ; *m.* 1 Aug. 1887, Virginia Maude, only dau. of Lieut.-Gen. Andrew Browne, C.B., of Moyvilla Castle, co. Galway.

Lineage.—This is a younger branch of the O'CONOR DON'S family. Carbry O'Conor Don was ten years of age at the time of his father Owen Caech O'Conor Don's death in 1485. He *m.* Dervorghil, dau. of Felim Finn O'Conor Roe, and *d.* 1546, leaving issue,
1. Turlogh.
2. Dermot O'Conor Don, made O'Conor Don 1550, *m.* Dorothy, dau. of Teige Buidhe O'Conor Roe, and had issue (*see* O'CONOR DON).
3. Owen Caech O'Conor. 4. Owen Toole O'Conor.
5. FELIM FINN O'CONOR, called Geannach, who follows.

The 5th son,
FELIM FINN O'CONOR, had issue, two sons,
1. Rury, who was the father of Owen O'Conor, who had issue, Connall o'Conor and Dubalthagh o'Conor.
2. FELIM OGE O'CONOR.

The 2nd son,
FELIM OGE O'CONNOR, had issue,
1. Teige, who had issue, Turlogh Callagh.
2. RORY.

The 2nd son,
RORY O'CONOR, of Tobermackey Castle, co. Roscommon, was the father of,
TEIGE O'CONOR, first of Tobermackey Castle, which he assigned, 20 June, 1588, to William Tuite, after which he became of Castlerone or Castleruby, co. Roscommon ; he *m.* 1590, Mary ny Byrne, and *d.* 1607, leaving issue,
HUGH MERGAGH O'CONOR, of Castleruby, *b.* 1592, forfeited Castleruby, transplanted 13 June, 1656, on whose descendants Hugh oge O'Conor Don settled, 30 Aug. 1662, the Clonalis estates after the extinction of the line of Roger Fitz Brian Roe O'Conor ; *d.* 1673, leaving issue,

U 2

Henchy. THE LANDED GENTRY. 308

1. THADY or TERENCE, who follows.
1. Dorothy, *m.* Dermot O'Conor, of Russine.
2. Mary, *m.* Bryan Roe O'Connor, of Corrasduna, 4th son of Sir Hugh O'Conor Don, M.P. (*see that family*).
The only son,
THADY or TERENCE O'CONOR, of Knockleg, then of Tuomona, co. Roscommon, was assigned the townlands of Lisloohrnie, Russine and Knocktegan out of his father's estates under the Act of Settlement, 1677, *m.* Dorothy, and *d.* May, 1720, leaving issue,
TERENCE O'CONNOR, of Tuomona, made will 19 April, 1725; exhibited 18 Jan. 1728, had issue,
   1. Roger, of Tuomona, *m.* previous to 1704, Anne, dau. of William Crofton, 5th son of John Crofton, of Lisdoorne ; he *d.* Aug. 1727. she in 1728, leaving issue,
      Michael, of Tuomona, living 1772. *m.* Bridget, sister of Bryan Farrell, of Ardanra, co. Longford (she *d.* Dec. 1768), and had issue,
         John, of Tuomona, co. Roscommon, *m.* 1772, Winifred, dau. of Simon Dowell, of Gort, co. Roscommon, widow of Ignatius Kelly, of Killaghamore, co. Roscommon, and *d.* June, 1777, leaving issue,
           Peter, of Tuomona, co. Roscommon, J.P. co. Roscommon, *d.* 14 Aug. 1830, *s.p.*
      Margaret, *m.* Jeffrey French, of Rocksavage.
2. DOMINICK O'CONNOR, of Ballintubber, co. Roscommon, who follows.
3. Roger O'Connor, who claimed to be P.P. of Ballintubber, rival P.P. to Magrath.

The 2nd son,
DOMINICK O'CONNOR, of Ballintubber, co. Roscommon, and had issue,
HUGH O'CONNOR, 1st of Ballintubber, then of the City of London, enrolled as a Freeman 17 Jan. 1786, Member of the Wheelwrights Co., *b.* 1730 ; *m.* 21 Dec. 1765, Monica, dau. of Hugh O'Conor, of Galway, and of Douglas, Isle of Man, son of Bryan, 7th son of Dermot O'Connor, of Sylanmore, co. Galway (*see* DONELAN *of Sylanmore*), and *d.* Dec. 1801, buried at St. Pancras 14 Dec. 1801, having by her (who *d.* — Admin. granted 27 Oct. 1812) had issue,
1. Hugh, bapt. 9 Aug. 1771 ; *m.* 15 Feb. 1821, Winefred, dau. of Charles Browne Mostyn, of Kidlington Hall, Oxford. She *d.* 18 March, 1852. He *d.* 23 Oct. 1839, having had issue,
   1. Winefred, *b.* 4 Nov. 1822 ; *m.* 1st, 30 June, 1845, Comte Pierre Raoul Alberic, son of the Marquis de Lubersac. He *d.* 1 Jan. 1847. She *m.* 2ndly, 17 Oct. 1857, Comte d'Agoult, and *d.* 18 March, 1863, having by him had issue,
      (1) Hector Hugues, Count d'Agoult, ex-Lieut. French Navy, Deputy for the Senegal, 1888-1902, *b.* 9 May, 1860 ; *m.* 22 May, 1891, Valentine, dau. of the Marquis d'Estampes, and has issue,
         (1) Beatrice, *b.* 19 Aug. 1858 ; *m.* May, 1886, Count Le Groing de La Romagère.
         (2) Marguérite, *b.* 15 July, 1861 ; *m.* 3 May, 1886, Count André de Charpin-Feugerolles.
      2. Marie Louise, *b.* 3 Oct. 1828 ; *m.* 10 May, 1852, Marquis de Bouillé, and *d.* 12 Dec. 1859, having had issue,
         (1) Claude, Count de Bouillé, *b.* 7 Sept. 1853 ; *m.* 5 June, 1879, Amélie, dau. of the Marquis La Guiche, and *d.* 1908.
         (2) Bertrand Count de Bouillé, *b.* 22 Nov. 1860 ; *m.* 25 April, 1889, Marie Thérèse, dau. of Count d'Hunolstein, and has issue.
         (3) Count François de Bouillé, *b.* 12 Aug. 1866.
         (4) Count Louis de Bouillé, *b.* 19 Oct. 1867.
2. VALENTINE, of whom presently.
3. Dominick, bapt. 11 May, 1775 ; *d.* 17 buried 20 Dec. 1780, M.I. St. Pancras.
3. Malachy Thomas, of La Grande Riviere, Guadaloupe, bapt. 15 April, 1779 ; *m.* 11 Sept. 1822, Marie Françoise, dau. of Jacques Brière de Bretteville, of Martinique. She *d.* 22 May, 1834. He *d.* in Guadaloupe 29 June, 1833, leaving issue,
   1. Malvina, *b.* 6 Nov. 1823 ; *d.* 23 Oct. 1836.
   2. Marie Anna (Aline), *b.* 14 June, 1827 ; *d.* 1836.
1. Honora, *bapt.* 16 July, 1768 ; *m.* 16 Nov. 1797, John Shee, of Ballcredin, co. Kilkenny, and had issue. Will made Nov. 1841. proved 26 Feb. 1846.
2. Eleanor, bapt. 1 Jan. 1770 ; *m.* 2 June, 1797, William Errington, of High Warden, Northumberland, and had issue.
3. Christina, *b.* 1772 ; *m.* Oct. 1800, Capt. James Power, Royal Irish Artillery.
4. Mary, *b.* 1774 ; *m.* 11 Jan. 1801, Anthony O'Brien, son of Dennis Thomas O'Brien ; *d.* 3 Nov. 1835.
5. Juliet, bapt. 26 Oct. 1776.
6. Monica, bapt. 15 May, 1782 ; *d.* 23 May, 1855.

The second son,
VALENTINE O'CONNOR, *b.* 24 Oct., bapt. 7 Nov., 1773 ; *m.* 26 Dec. 1796, Mary, dau. of David Henchy, of Rockfield, Blackrock, co. Dublin (who *d.* 8 May, 1820) (*see that family below*). She *d.* 31 March, 1814. He *d.* 26 Dec. 1829, having had issue,
1. Hugh, *b.* 3 June, 1801 ; *m.* 20 June, 1828, Elizabeth, dau. of Edmund Cashin, of Waterford, and *d.* 1 Feb. 1836, having had issue,
   1. Hugh, *b.* 18 Dec. 1830 ; *m.* 3 Sept. 1863, Julia, dau. of Michael Thunder, of Lagore, co. Meath, and *d.* 3 Aug. 1897, having had issue,
      Mary, *b.* 6 June, 1865 ; *d.* 10 Dec. 1880.
   2. Valentine, late Lieut.-Col. 80th Foot, *b.* 11 Dec. 1831 ; *m.* 1st, 19 July, 1870, Victoria Busfield, dau. of Capt. Crispin, R.N., A.D.C. He *d.* 15 Dec. 1909. She *d.* 17 March, 1883, having had issue,
      (1) William Hugh Francis, of St. Paul's, Minnesota, U.S.A., and of Boynman, Montana, *b.* 28, *bapt.* 31 Aug. 1872 ; *m.* 24 Sept. 1895, Sarah Ann, dau. of the late James Paul, of McKeesport, Pennsylvania, U.S.A., and has issue,
         1. Hugh, *b.* 27 Aug. 1898.
         1. Mary Agnes Victoria, *b.* 7 Aug. 1896.
         2. Monica, *b.* 31 Jan. 1907.
      (2) Cuthbert Edmund Valentine, *b.* 16, *bapt.* 18 July, 1874 ; *m.* 31 July, 1902, Katherine, dau. of Francis Hearn, of Currie, Minnesota, and *d.* 14 Feb. 1905, leaving issue, Eileen, *b.* 24 Sept. 1903.
      (3) Valentine Rickard, *b.* 3 Nov. 1876.
      (4) Charles Joseph Wilfred, *b.* 6, *bapt.* 9 July, 1879 ; *m.* 2 Oct. 1908, Esther Beaumont.
He *m.* 2ndly, 23 April, 1887, Frances, widow of Francis Joseph Lush, and dau. of John Ashton, and by her had issue,
      (5) Cyril Ashton Valentine, *b.* 15, *bapt.* 17 April, 1888.
      (1) Eileen Elizabeth Catherine, *b.* 11 Aug. 1889.
3. Edmund, *b.* 23 Feb. 1835 ; *m.* 21 June, 1861, Mary, dau. of Thomas Lyons. He *d.* 21 Aug. 1905. She *d.* 19 Oct. 1908.
4. Peter, *b.* 9 Oct. 1836 ; *d.* 18 Dec. 1837.
1. Mary Anne, a nun, *b.* 4 Nov. 1829 ; *d.* 19 Aug. 1894.
2. Monica, *b.* 18 May, 1833 ; *m.* 2 April, 1861, the Right Hon. Lord Justice Deasy, and *d.* 24 March, 1880, leaving issue.
2. DAVID, of whom presently.
3. Valentine O'Brien, of Rockfield, co. Dublin, and Ballykisteen, co. Tipperary, High Sheriff of Dublin 1853, *b.* 3, *bapt.* 9 May, 1811 ; *m.* 4 Sept. 1838, Monica, dau. of William Errington, of High Warden, Northumberland, and *d.* 13 Sept. 1873, having had issue,
   1. Valentine, *b.* 12 Dec. 1844 ; *d.* 17 Feb. 1865.
   2. John, twin with Valentine, *d.* 4 May, 1862.
   3. David, *b.* 18 Jan. 1848 ; *d.* 6 July, 1848.
   4. William, *b.* 27 Jan. 1850 ; *m.* 8 May, 1874, Rose, dau. of Edmund Lawless, Q.C., and *d.* 5 April, 1898.
   1. Ellen Mary, *b.* 16 July, 1839 ; *m.* 27 June, 1860, Walter Hussey Walsh, of Cranagh and Mulhussey, co. Roscommon (who *d.* 17 Jan. 1904) (*see that family*). She *d.* 20 Oct. 1911.
   2. Mary Christina, *b.* 9 Mar. 1842 ; *m.* 4 Aug. 1859, Major William Blount, eldest son of William Blount, of Orleton, co. Hereford, and *d.* 24 March, 1874, leaving issue (*see that family*).
   3. Eliza Monica, *b.* 9 March, 1842 ; *m.* 20 Sept. 1868, John Browne, son of Joseph Browne, of Elmgrove, co. Meath. He *d.s.p.* 20 June, 1876. She *d.* 9 Dec. 1905.
   4. Margaret, *b.* 26 July, 1846 ; *m.* 24 June, 1874, Sir Percy Grace, 4th bart , and has issue. He *d.* 16 Aug. 1903.
1. Margaret, *b.* 10 April, 1798 ; *d.* 27 Sept. 1831.
2. Ellen, *b.* 27 May, 1799 ; *m.* 27 Jan. 1824, Percy Magan, and *d.* June, 1860, leaving issue.
3. Mary, *b.* 23 Nov. 1802 ; *m.* 20 Feb. 1837, Baron de Curnieu, and *d.* 4 March, 1863, leaving issue,
   Honorie Emilie Caroline, *m.* Aug. 1861, Etienne, Count de Luppé, eldest son of the Marquis de Luppé, and *d.* 11 April, 1887, leaving issue,
      Pierre, Marquis de Luppé, *b.* 26 May, 1866 ; *m.* 26 May, 1891, Albertine Charlotte Marie, dau. of the Duc de Broglie, and has issue.
4. Monica, *b.* 3 Nov. 1803 ; *m.* 21 July, 1825, Peter Purcell, of Halverstown, co. Kildare, and *d.* 18 March, 1879, leaving issue.
5. Julia, *b.* 4 Aug. 1806 ; *d.* 9 May, 1821.
6. Honoria, *b.* 3 Nov. 1807 ; *m.* 4 Sept. 1832, Capt. Peter Slingsby FitzGerald and *d.* 19 June 1866 (*see* FITZGERALD *of Little Island*).

The second son,
DAVID O'CONNOR-HENCHY, of Stonebrook, co. Kildare, J.P. and D.L., M.P. for co. Kildare 1852-9, High Sheriff 1844, adopted the name of HENCHY, *b.* 23, *bapt.* 29 May, 1810 ; *m.* 10 Jan. 1850, Elizabeth, dau. of Sir John Burke, Bart., of Marble Hill. She *d.* 31 Dec. 1890. He *d.* 1 Dec. 1876, having had issue,
HUGH, now of Stonebrook.
Elizabeth, *b.* 12 Dec. 1850 ; *m.* 6 April, 1875, Sir George Morris, K.C.B., and has issue, a dau., Julia (*see* BURKE'S *Peerage*, KILLANIN, B.).

Arms—Arg. an oak-tree eradicated ppr., in base three lizards passant to the sinister barwise vert.

Seats—Stonebrook, Ballymore Eustace, co. Kildare, and Moyvilla Castle, Oranmore, co. Galway.

FAMILY OF HENCHY.

Lineage.—PETER HENCHY, of Cappagh Castle, co. Clare, *m.* the dau. of O'Brien, and *d.* about 1700, leaving issue,
PETER.
Margaret, *m.* McInerney.

Peter Henchy became possessed of Feenagh, co. Clare, on 14 Aug. 1707, since when he and his descendants were exposed to actions brought by fictitious and genuine Protestant discoverers until the estates were eventually, on 16 Jan. 1786, decreed to John Lindsay, of Lisburn, as the first genuine Protestant discoverer. He made his will 4 Aug. 1732, proved 11 Dec. 1736, and had issue (he *d* 1734),
1. MICHAEL, who follows.
2. Loghlen, *m.* Mary McNamara, will dated 21 April, 1765.
3. Thomas.
1. Elizabeth, *m.* Thomas Amory, of Garriard, co. Kerry.
2. Theresa, *m.* John White.   3. Lucy, *m.* — Gripha.
4. Sarah, *m.* — Quin, of Dromline, co. Clare.
5. Winifred, *m.* — Traitt.

The eldest son,
MICHAEL HENCHY, *d.v.p.*, leaving issue,
1. PETER, who follows.

2. John, of Cratloe, *b.* 1708 ; *m.* a wife (who was *b.* 1727, and *d.* 1807) ; and *d.* 17 April, 1787, M. I. Croghane, Cratloe, leaving issue,
  1. David, of Rockfield, co. Dublin ; *m.* 27 June, 1776, Margaret, dau. of — May, and widow of Thomas Carter, of Leeson Street, Dublin, and *d.* 8 May, 1820 (will dated 17 Nov. 1817 ; codicil dated 16 Aug. 1819), leaving issue,
    Mary, *b.* 4 June, 1778 ; *m.* 26 Dec., 1796, Valentine O'Connor, of Dublin, and *d.* 31 March, 1814, leaving issue (*see preceding pedigree*).
  2. Michael.   3. John.
  4. James, *m.* Margaret —, and had issue,
    (1) David.
    (2) Michael, *m.* 28 Dec. 1788, Judith O'Brien.
  5. Patrick.
  1. Joan, *m.* — Doyle.
  2. A dau., *m.* James Sinnott.

The eldest son,
PETER HENCHY, of Feenagh, co. Clare, *b.* 1706 ; *m.* 1728, Margaret, dau. of Florence Henchy, of Ballycumeen, co. Clare (*b.* 1709 ; *d.* 4 July, 1748), and *d.* leaving issue (assigned Fenagh to his son Donough, 6 Sept. 1763),
1. DONOUGH, who follows.
2. John, living 1777.
1. Margaret, *m.* 28 Oct., 1754, John Fitzmaurice, of Tralee, co. Kerry.
2. Hannah, *m.* 1st. — Vandeleur ; 2ndly, 20 Oct. 1763, St. John Dillon, of Carlow ; 3rdly, 1777, Michael O'Brien, Capt., R.N., son of John O'Brien and Mary, dau. of Luke Magrath, of Dysart, co. Clare, and had issue, Rear-Admiral Donat Henchy O'Brien, R.N.
3. Bridget, *m.* 9 May, 1770, Robert Bradford.

The eldest son,
DONOUGH HENCHY, of Feenagh, co. Clare, *m.* 1st, 18 Jan. 1764, Anne, dau. of John Hickie, of Cappagh Castle, co. Clare, which marriage was subsequently dissolved by the Prerogative Court ; 2ndly, Dorothy, dau. of Patrick Fitzgibbon, of Newcastle, co. Limerick, uncle to 1st Earl of Clare, and *d.* 5 Feb. 1777, leaving issue,
1. PETER FITZGIBBON, LL.D., K.C., 1st of Feenagh, then of Moyarta, co. Clare, forfeited Fenagh, 16 Jan. 1786, *b.* 20 April, 1773 ; *m.* 1st, Eleanor, dau. of — Atkinson, who *d.* 9 Jan. 1831, leaving issue,
  1. Fitzgibbon, M.A., T.C.D., of Moyarta, *d.* 1875.
  1. Eleanor Anne.
  2. Georgina Frederica, *m.* 12 Jan. 1835, 2nd Viscount Frankfort de Montmorency, and *d.* 16 April, 1885, leaving issue (*see* BURKE's *Peerage*).
  3. Caroline, *m.* 30 April, 1832 (settlement 27 April), Edward Basil, 5th son of Sir Henry Brooke, of Colebrook, co. Fermanagh, Bart., Major-General commanding forces in West Indies.
  4. Charlotte, *m.* — Reilly.   5. Henrietta, *unm.*
He *m.* 2ndly, 2 April, 1832, Clara, dau. of Benjamin Jones and widow of 2nd Lord Ventry, and *d.* 11 Jan. 1849 (will made 15 Oct. 1841).
2. Donat, of Ballinvarrassig, co. Cork, Capt., R.N., *m.* 1st. Nov. 1797, Rose, dau. of Peter Carey, of Blackwater, co. Cork, and *d.* 8. Sept. 1854, leaving issue by his 1st wife,
  1. Anne, *b.* 1801 ; *d.* 16 Dec. 1876, *unm.*
  2. Eliza, *b.* 1803 ; *m.* 22 June, 1826, John Robert Scott, and *d.* 24 Feb. 1882.
  3. Emily, *b.* 11 April, 1811 ; *m.* 2 May, 1840, Rev. Edward Kirby, Rector of Randlestown (who *d.* 18 Dec. 1859), and *d.* 22 May, 1905, *s.p.*
  4. Rose, *b.* 1815 ; *m.* John Aitken, and *d.* 23 Feb. 1883.
He *m.* 2ndly, 1830. Agnes, dau. of Robert Cameron, of Glenesk, Midlothian, and had issue,
  1. Donat Cameron, *m.* 31 May, 1851, Maria, dau. of — West and widow of Kershaw, and *d.s.p.* in Australia, 1869.
  2. Robert Cameron, Col. R.A., *b.* 14 March, 1832 ; *m.* 18 Feb. 1866, Emma, dau. of Christopher Penney, of Hazlewood, Clifton, and had issue,
    (1) Donatus, *b.* 1872 ; *d.* 1876.
    (1) Roberta, *m.* 8 Dec., 1897, Henry Hills, of Santiago. California, U.S.A.
    (2) Eileen, *b.* 9 April, 1871 ; *m.* 26 April, 1904, Wilfred James Roberts, of Sherborne, Dorset.
3. John, *d.* 1781.

Arms—Per chevron, or and az. in chief 2 thistles ppr. and in base a lion rampant of the first. *Crest*—An arm in armour erect ppr., the hand also ppr. grasping a baton sa. *Motto*—In te Domine speravi.

HENDRICK-AYLMER. *See* **AYLMER.**

HENN OF PARADISE HILL.

FRANCIS BLACKBURNE HENN, of Paradise Hill, co. Clare, Barrister-at-Law, Resident Magistrate, co. Sligo, J.P. co. Clare, B.A. Trin. Coll. Dublin, *b.* 1848 ; *m.* 28 Oct. 1880, Helen Letitia Elizabeth, dau. of Francis Gore, of Woodlands, co. Clare, and has issue.

1. WILLIAM FRANCIS, *b.* 1892.
2. Thomas Rice, *b.* 10 Nov. 1901.
1. Muriel Helen Isabella Rice, *m.* 26 Nov. 1903, Frederick William O'Hara, J.P., younger son of late Charles William O'Hara, of Annaghmore (*see that family*), and has issue.
2. Lilian Adela Gore.   3. Maud Susan Beatrice.

Lineage.—The family of Henn, one of English origin, has been settled in the co. Clare for upwards of two centuries. RICHARD HENN in 1685 obtained a grant of " Paradise Hill," and various estates in that county, from the then Earl of Thomond.

WILLIAM HENN, 2nd son of Thomas Henn, younger brother and devisee of Richard Henn, the grantee of Paradise Hill, was called to the Irish Bar, and created a Judge of the King's Bench, 1768. He *m.* Miss Elizabeth Parry, and in his will, which bears date 20 July, 1784, and was proved 9 June, 1796, names his three daus., Mary, *m.* Francis Casey, of Seafield, co. Clare ; Susanna, *m.* William Daxon, of Fountain, co. Clare ; Frances, *d. unm.* ; and an only son,

WILLIAM HENN, who became Master of the Irish Court of Chancery 10 July, 1793. He *m.* July, 1782, Susanna, sister of Sir Jonathan Lovett, Bart., of Liscombe Park, Bucks, by whom he left issue,
1. WILLIAM, of whom presently.
2. Jonathan, a Queen's Counsel of high reputation at the Irish Bar, and for many years Chairman of the co. Donegal, *d. unm.*
3. Richard, of Herbert Street, Dublin, Commander R.N., *m.* July, 1841, Maria, dau. of Joseph Atkinson, of Upper Mount Street, Dublin.
1. Eleanor, *d. unm.*
2. Susanna, *m.* April, 1813, Rev. Charles Mayne, of Killaloe, who was the eldest son of the Hon. Judge Mayne.
3. Eliza, *m.* Jan. 1810, Edward Mayne, of Stephen's Green, 2nd son of the Hon. Judge Mayne.
4. Jane, *m.* 10 May, 1826, Walter Hussey Griffith, Barrister-at-Law, of Clare Street, Dublin.
5. Frances, *m.* Jan. 1851, Stephen Collins, Q.C., of Merrion Square, Dublin.

The eldest son,
WILLIAM HENN, who, like his father, became a Master in Chancery in Ireland, 1822, *m.* April, 1809, Mary Rice, eldest dau. of George Fosbery, of Clorane, co. Limerick, by Christiana his wife, dau. of Thomas Rice, of Mount Trenchard, in the same co., by whom he had issue,
1. William, *d. unm.* 1853.
2. THOMAS RICE, late of Paradise Hill.
3. Jonathan Lovett, *d. unm.* 1888.
4. George, '*d. unm.*   5. Richard, *d. unm.*
1. Christiana, *d. unm.* 27 Dec. 1891.
2. Susanna, *d. unm.* 15 Dec. 1891.
3. Mary, *m.* John Stanford, and *d.* 1 Jan. 1891.
4. Ellen, *m.* William Robert La Touche, D.L., of Bellevue, co. Wicklow.
5. Jane, *m.* 24 Sept. 1842, Robert Holmes, of Moycashel (*see that family*). He *d.* 17 Oct. 1870. She *d.* 3 May, 1905, leaving issue.

The 2nd son,
THOMAS RICE HENN, of Paradise Hill, co. Clare, Barrister-at-Law, K.C., J.P. and D.L. co. Clare, County Court Judge, Chairman of Quarter Sessions for co. Carlow 1859, and for co. Galway 1868, Recorder of Galway 1878, *b.* 1814 ; *m.* Oct. 1845, Jane Isabella, 2nd dau. of Right Hon. Francis Blackburne, Lord Chancellor of Ireland (*see* BLACKBURNE *of Tankardstown*). She *d.* 29 April, 1902. He *d.* 7 June, 1901, leaving issue,
1. WILLIAM, Lieut. R.N. (retired), J.P. co. Clare, *b.* 1847 ; *m.* 1877, Susanna Cunninghame-Graham, only surviving child of late Robert Bartholomew, of Broom Hill, co. Dumbarton, and St. Anne's Lodge, Rothesay, Isle of Bute (by his 2nd wife, Susan Cunninghame-Graham, dau. of William Cunninghame-Cunninghame-Graham, of Gartmore (*see that family*), and *d.s.p.* 1 Sept. 1894. She *d.* 16 Oct. 1911.
2. FRANCIS BLACKBURNE, now of Paradise Hill.
3. Thomas Rice, Lieut. R.E., acted as Quartermaster Bombay Sappers and Miners with Afghan Field Force, and fell in action at Maiwand, in Afghanistan, 27 July, 1880, *unm.*
4. Edward Lovett, Ex-Fellow Trinity Hall, Cambridge, *m.* 6 Aug.

Hennessy. THE LANDED GENTRY. 310

1878, Margaret Agnes Vaughan, dau. of Mitchell Henry, of Kylemore Castle, and Stratheden House, London, formerly M.P. co. Galway, and has issue,
    Eric, b. 1891.
5. Richard Arthur Milton, of Castle Troy House, co. Limerick, J.P. co. Clare, Col. (late) Special Reserve and Royal Artillery, b. 8 April, 1855; m. 7 Aug. 1895, Elizabeth Letitia, dau. of Charles Heaton-Armstrong, of George Street, Limerick (see that family),and has issue,
    Marjorie Vera Milton.
6. Henry (Rt. Rev.), D.D., Bishop of Burnley, Hon. Canon of Manchester, formerly Fellow of Trin. Hall, Camb.; m. 1 Nov. 1905, Frances Helen, eldest dau. of the late Rt. Hon. Lord Collins, of Kensington (see COLLINS of Ardualee).
1. Adela Jane, m. Nov. 1884, James Samuel Gibbons, C.B., and d. 28 April, 1893.
2. Mary Rice, d. at Aix-les-Bains, 24 Sept. 1883.

Arms—Gu., a lion rampant arg. on a canton of the last a wolf pass. sa. **Crest**—On a mount vert a hen pheasant ppr. **Motto**—Gloria Deo.

Seat—Paradise Hill, Ennis, co. Clare. *Residence*—Albert House, Sligo. **Clubs**—University, Dublin, and County, Sligo.

HENNESSY OF BALLINDEASIG.

MICHAEL HENNESSY, of Ballindeasig, co. Cork, J.P., b. 16 April, 1851.

Lineage.—JOHN C. HENNESSY, of Knocknaneffe House, co. Cork, J.P., m. Mary Creagh, dau. of Richard Roche Kenifeck, of Ballindeasig, co. Cork, and Alicia his wife, dau. of Mellish Moylan, of Cork, and had issue,
1. MICHAEL, now of Ballindeasig.
2. John Francis, d. unm.
3. Richard Martin, Scholar Trin. Coll. Dublin, B.A., K.C. in Ireland, b. 1854.
1. Alice Mary, a nun.
2. Mary Josephine.
3. Kathleen Mary, m. Herbert Baldwin O'Sullivan Beare, of Clohina, Ballyvourney, co. Cork.

Seat—Ballindeasig, Minane Bridge, co. Cork.

HENNESSY OF BALLYMACMOY.

CHRISTOPHER JAMES HENNESSY, of Bally-macmoy, co. Cork, b. 6 May, 1893.

Lineage.—GEORGE HENNESSY, of Ballymacmoy, co. Cork (son of James Hennessy, of Ballymacmoy, by Helen Nagle, his wife), m. Mary O'Phelan, of co. Tipperary, and by her had (with a dau., m. to Henry Goold) two sons,
1. JAMES, his heir.
2. Charles, of Brussels and Ostende, who m. Margaret O'Murphy, and had two sons: James, who m. Ellen Barrett, but d.s.p.; and Patrick Michael,who m. Miss Danout, of Brussels, and was father of Patrick Hennessy, of Brussels.

The elder son and heir,
JAMES HENNESSY, of Ballymacmoy, m. in 1750, Catherine Barrett, and by her (who d. 1770) had two sons,
1. GEORGE, his heir.
2. Richard, b. at Ballymacmoy in the year 1720, went to Cognac, in France, in 1765. He was an officer in Dillon's Regt., in the French service, and m., 1765, his cousin, Ellen, widow of James Hennessy, of Brussels, and dau. of James Barrett, by Margaret, his wife, sister of Garret Nagle, of Monanymy and Ballyduff, co. Cork, and aunt to the Right Hon. Edmund Burke. He d. 1800, and had, with a dau., Bridget, b. 1767, who d. in France, a son,
James Hennessy, of Cognac, known by some as Jacques, b. 11 Oct. 1765, in Belgium, a few days before his parents sailed for Bordeaux, Member of the Chamber of Deputies for the Department of La Charente until the period of his decease; created a Peer of France, though an Irishman and never naturalised, about the year 1794. He m. Martha, dau. of Monsieur Martell, one of the Deputies for Libourne, and dying 22 April, 1843, left issue,

(1) James, of La Billarderie (Cognac), b. 1795; m. Sophia, dau. of Baron de Marcuil, Ambassador from France to several Courts, and a Peer of France. He d. 1845, having had issue,
1. Maurice, b. 1834; m. Jeanne Foussat (she was b. 1853, d. 1896). He d. 1905, and had issue,
(1) James Richard, of La Billarderie (Cognac), Deputy for Cognac, elected September, 1906, b. 1867; m. 189 Alice Hennessy, his cousin, b. 1874; d. 1901). He h issue,
1. Raymond, b. 1895.
2. Maurice Richard, b. 1896.
1. Irene.   } twins.
2. Madeleine, b. 1894 }
3. Isabelle, b. 1898.
(2) Jean Patrick, of Chateau de St. Brice, electe Deputy for Barbezieux (Charente) 1910, b. 1873; m 1901, Marguerite, dau. of Comte de Mun, Membr Academie Française, and Deputy, and has issue,
1. Patrick, b. 1902.
2. Kilcan, b. 1907.
1. Jacqueline, b. 1904.
(1) Marguerite, b. 1868; m Comte Bruno de Boisgelin. She d. 1892, leaving issue, a dau., Jeanne.
(2) Jacqueline, b. 1870; d.s.p. 1886.
1. Sophia, m. Baron Tard Panvillier, and has issue.
2. Alice, m. Vicomte de Brimont, and has issue.
(2) Auguste Richard, b. 1800; m 1832, Irene, dau. of Baron d'Anthès, of Burgundy, elected Depuré for the Charente Department, 1845 to 1868, then elected Senateur and created Knight of the Legion of Honour, was Col. in the National Guards, Member of the Chamber of Commerce, &c. He d. 1879, having had issue
1. Richard, b. 1835; m. 1872, his cousin, Martha Lucy Hennessy (see below), and d. 1885; served during Siege of Paris, 1870, in Vol. Regt. of Horse Guards, leaving issue,
(1) Richard (Salcote Place, Rye, Sussex; Chateau de Bagnolet, Cognac, France), received a commission in the Militia in Ireland, 1895, entered the Army in 1898, served as Lieut. 2nd Gordon Highlanders during the S. African War, 1899-1901, was wounded severely at the Battle of Elandslaagte, received South African medals, Queen's medal, bearing four clasps, b. 1876; m. 1902, Ethel Frederica, dau. of late Charles Selmes, of Playden, Sussex, and has issue,
1. Richard Francis Blennerhassett, b. 1907.
1. Aileen Frederica, b. 1903.
2. Sheilab Jerne, b. 1905.
(2) George Richard (Compton Manor, Stockbridge, Hants, and Villa Hibernia, Cognac, France), Major 3rd Batt. Cheshire Regt., served in the S. African War, 1901 (Queen's medal, three clasps), entered the 3rd Batt. Cheshire Regt. (Militia), 1895, J.P. for Hants, Member of County Council and High Sheriff of the County (1911), b. 1877, m. 1898, Ethel Wynter, and has issue,
1. James Bryan, b. 1903.
2. Frederick, b. 1906.
1. Dorothy, b. 1899.   2. Violet, b. 1901.
3. Noreen, b. 1909.
(1) Henriette, b. 1873; m. 1892, Comte de la Falaise, He d. leaving issue.
(2) Alice, b. 1874, d. 1901; m. 1893, her cousin, James Hennessy, and has issue (see above).
(3) Lucy, b. 1880; m. 1901, R. Formey de St. Louvent, and had issue. She d. 1908.
2. Jacques Francis, b. 1841.
3. Raymond, b. 1842; d.s.p. 1884.
1. Marguerite, b. 1834; m. Comte de Damremont, Ambassador to the Court of Russia, &c. Had issue.
2. Henrietta, b. 1844; d.s.p. 1864.
(3) Frederick, of Cognac, b. 1807; m. 1842, Julia, dau. of Frederick Perkins, of Chipstead Park, co. Kent. He d. 1878, having had issue,
1. Armand, b. 1845; d.s.p. 1899.
2. Robert, b. 1846; d.s.p. Jan. 1908.
3. Gerard, b. 1859; d.s.p. 1880.
1. Martha Lucy, b. 1854; m. 1st, 1872, her cousin, Richard Hennessy, of Bagnolet, and has issue (see above); and 2ndly, 4 Sept. 1888, Lord James Douglas, 4th son of the 7th Marquess of Queensberry (see BURKE's Peerage), who d.s.p. 5 May, 1891.
(4) George, } twins, d. young.
(5) Ernest, }
(6) Patrick.
(1) Lucy, b. 1808; m. Gabriel Martell, of Cognac. She d.s.p. 1843.
3. James, m. Miss Nagle, and had issue,
1. George, of Cork, m. Miss Stackpole, and had, with a son, James, who d. young, two daus., Mary, a nun, and Georgina, m. to John Coxon, of Flesk Priory, co. Kerry.
2. Athanasius, Col. E.I.C.S., Town-Major of Fort William, and Aide-de-Camp to Lord Minto, d. unm. 1830.
1. Eleanor, d. unm. 1831.
1. Mary, m. John Shea, of the City of Cork, Merchant.
2. Bridget, m. MacWalter Burke, of Curraghnabouly, co. Tipperary.
3. Anne, d. unm.
4. Elizabeth, m. John Comerford.

The eldest son and heir,
GEORGE HENNESSY, of Ballymacmoy, m. his cousin, Anastasia, dau. of John Comerford, of the City of Cork, and had issue,

1. JOHN, his heir.
2. Christopher, who m. Mary, only dau. of — Seton, of Santa Crux, and d. in the West Indies, s.p.
3. James, who d. in 1782 on board Capt. Lawson's ship.
1. Bridget, b. 1760 ; m. 1780, Patrick Lawson, of Banff, captain of the " Lord Holland," East Indiaman, and had issue.
2. Catherine, b. 1764 ; m. Samuel Flanrey, of London, and had issue.

The eldest son and heir,
JOHN HENNESSY, of Ballymacmoy, b. 1761 ; m. Margaret, dau. of Philip Barry, of Burton, and niece to John Barry, of Ballyvoneer, and by her had (with a dau., Catherine, who d. in infancy), two sons,
1. George, d. unm., aged 90.
2. James Hennessy of Ballymacmoy, b. 1795 ; m. 1818, Eliza, dau. of MacWalter Burke, of Curraghnabouly, co. Tipperary, and had issue,
  1. Walter, d. unm.   2. James, d. unm.
  3. George, d. young.
  4. Christopher, of Ballymacmoy, m. 1863, Mary, 5th dau. of Roger Keating Sheehy, of Liskennet, co. Limerick, by his wife, Elizabeth, dau. of Carroll Naish, of Ballycullen House, co. Limerick, and had issue an only son,
    James Walter, of Ballymacmoy, b. 1865 ; m. 1892, Hariette (Ballymacmoy, co. Cork), only dau. of Edward Bryan Sheehy, by his wife, Charlotte, 2nd dau. of Daniel Lombard, of Mount Mary, co. Cork. He d. 1896, leaving issue,
    CHRISTOPHER JAMES, now of Ballymacmoy, b. 6 May, 1893.
    Olive Mary Hope, b. 11 Sept. 1894.
  1. Margaret Eliza, m. Timothy Mahony, of Blarney, co. Cork, and had issue.

Arms—(Recorded in Brussels, 25 July, 1845.) Gu., a boar passant sable. Crest—A hand ppr. vested arg., holding a battle-axe also ppr. Motto—Vi vivo et armis.
Seat—Ballymacmoy, Killavullen, co. Cork.

HENRY OF FORT HENRY.

FREDERICK THOMAS CLIFFORD HENRY, of Fort Henry, co. Tipperary, Principal Clerk in the Charity Commission, b. 20 Oct. 1850 ; m. 20 April, 1881, Catherine Jeanie, dau. of Rev. William Blake Doveton, Vicar of Corston, and has issue,
JOSEPH WINGFIELD, Lieut. Northumberland Fus., b. 20 Feb. 1882, m. 23 April, 1908, Grace, youngest dau. of late Archibald Peel, D.L., and Lady Georgiana Peel, of Westlea, Herts (see BURKE'S Peerage, PEEL, Bart.).

Lineage.—REV. ROBERT HENRY, Presbyterian Minister, at Carrickfergus, and subsequently in Dublin, was ordained 22 April, 1674. He d. 1699. His son,
HUGH HENRY, of Straffan, co. Kildare, and of Dublin, merchant and banker, M.P. for Newtownlimavady 1713, and for Antrim 1715, m. 17 July, 1717, Anne, eldest dau. of Joseph Leeson, and sister of the Earl of Milltown. He d. Dec. 1743, having had issue,
1. JOSEPH, of whom presently.
2. HUGH, of Lodge Park (see HENRY of Lodge Park).
1. Jane, m. 1740, Loftus Jones, of co. Sligo.

The elder son,
JOSEPH HENRY, of Straffan, M.P. for Longford 1761-8, and for Kildare Borough 1770-6, High Sheriff co. Kildare 1771, m. 30 April, 1764, Lady Catherine Rawdon, dau. (and co-heir of her mother) of John, 1st Earl of Moira (see BURKE'S Peerage, LOUDON, E.), and had issue,
1. JOHN JOSEPH, of whom presently.
1. Catherine, d. unm.
2. Helen, d. unm.
3. Anne, m. Henry Widman Wood, of Rosmead, co. Westmeath, and had issue. She d. 15 May, 1798.
4. Louisa, m. Dr. Patrick Plunket, brother of 1st Baron Plunket.
5. Elizabeth, m. — King, and had issue.

The only son,
JOHN JOSEPH HENRY, of Straffan, High Sheriff co. Kildare 1803, m. 1801, Lady Emily Elizabeth FitzGerald, dau. of William Robert, 2nd Duke of Leinster. She d. 8 Feb. 1856. He d. 1835, having had issue,
1. William Wentworth, m. 10 Jan. 1832, Catherine, dau. of Sackville Hatch Lovett, J.P., and d.s.p. 22 June, 1847 (see LOVETT of the Grange).
2. CHARLES JOHN, of whom presently.
3. Hastings Reginald YELVERTON (Sir), G.C.B., Adm. R.N., m. 9 April, 1845, Barbara, suo jure Baroness Grey de Ruthyn, and widow of George Augustus, 2nd Marquess of Hastings. She d. 19 Nov. 1858. He assumed by Royal Licence on his marriage the name of YELVERTON in lieu of HENRY, and d. 24 July, 1878, leaving a dau.,
  Barbara, m. 23 Sept. 1872, 2nd Lord Churston, and had issue (see BURKE'S Peerage).
4. George, m. the dau. of — Ferrers, Treasurer of the Mauritius.
5. Clifford, Capt. 40th Regt., b. 17 Oct. 1817 ; m. 1st, Miss Mason ; and 2ndly, 7 Dec. 1848, Zoë Mary, dau. of Henry Hungerford St. Leger. She d. Nov. 1898. He d. 27 Nov. 1874, having had issue, with two daus.,
  FREDERICK THOMAS CLIFFORD, now of Fort Henry.
  1. Emily Elizabeth, m. John Michael Henry, Baron de Robeck, and d. 21 March, 1859, leaving issue (see BURKE'S Peerage, Foreign Titles).
  2. Geraldine, d. unm.

3. Olivia m. 17 July, 1850, Sir Thomas Seabright, 8th bart. He d. 29 Aug. 1866. She d. 27 June, 1859, leaving issue (see BURKE'S Peerage).

The second son,
CHARLES JOHN HENRY, of Fort Henry, co. Tipperary, m. 25 June, 1838, Lady Selina Constance Hastings, 3rd dau. of Francis, Marquess of Hastings (see BURKE'S Peerage, LOUDON, E.). She d. 8 Nov. 1867. He d. 1879, leaving issue,
1. Mabel.   2. Agnes.   3. Eva.
He was s. at Fort Henry by his nephew, FREDERICK THOMAS CLIFFORD HENRY, now of Fort Henry.

Seat—Fort Henry, Birdhill, co. Tipperary. Town Address—121, Ebury Street, S.W. Club—Junior Carlton.

HENRY OF LODGE PARK.

FREDERICK ROBERT HENRY, of Lodge Park, co. Kildare, b. 10 March, 1862.

Lineage.—HUGH HENRY, of Lodge Park, which he built about 1775, 2nd son of HUGH HENRY, of Straffan, co. Kildare (see HENRY of Fort Henry), m. 21 Aug. 1770, Lady Anne Leeson, dau. of Joseph, 1st Earl of Milltown, and had issue,
1. Joseph, d. unm. 16 June, 1775.
2. Joseph, b. 27 June, 1775 ; d. 1809.
3. ARTHUR, of whom presently.
4. Hugh Robert, of Toghermore, co. Galway, b. 2 Feb. 1790 ; m. 1816, Elizabeth, dau. of Sir Robert Langrishe, 2nd bart. She d. 4 Jan. 1869. He d. 1838, leaving issue,
  1. Hugh, of Firmount, co. Kildare, J.P., b. 1818 ; m. 11 Oct. 1859, Emily Cecilia, his cousin, 3rd dau. of Arthur Henry, of Lodge Park, and d. 29 May, 1888, having had issue,
    (1) Hugh Arthur, of Firmount, Sallins, co. Kildare, J.P., High Sheriff 1909, Capt. 3rd Batt. Royal Dublin Fus., b. 10 Feb. 1869 ; m. 24 Sept. 1904, Eileen, eldest dau. of Sir William Joshua Goulding, Bart. (see BURKE'S Peerage) and has issue,
      Hugh Geoffrey, b. 5 Dec. 1906.
      Eileen Doreen, b. 5 Feb. 1908.
    (2) Arthur, b. 17 March, 1871.
    (1) Elizabeth.
    (2) Selina, m. 3 Jan. 1889, Capt. O'Neill, Royal Dublin Fusiliers.
    (3) Edith Frederica.   (4) Anna Cecilia.
    (5) Emily Georgina.
  2. Robert, of Toghermore, co. Galway, b. 1819 ; m. 31 March, 1859, Isabella Jane, dau. of Rev. Richard Quintus St. George, and d. 30 Dec. 1889, having had issue,
    (1) St. George Charles, C.B., of Toghermore, Major-Gen., late Col. Northumberland Fus. ; served in Dongola Expedition 1896, Nile Expeditions, 1897, 1898, and 1899, and in South Africa, 1899-1902 ; b. 29 Dec. 1860 ; d. unm. 6 Dec. 1909, being s. by his next brother.
    (2) Cecil Robert, of Toghermore and of Crumlin Park, Ballyglunin, co. Galway, High Sheriff 1910, b. 19 Dec. 1862.
    (1) Ethel Maud, m. 1901, Michael Henry Burke, of Ballydugan, co. Galway, and has issue (see that family).
    (2) Frances Amy, d. unm. 19 Feb. 1888.
  3. Joseph (Rev.), D.D., b. 1821, d. unm. 1885.
  4. James, b. 1823, Merchant at Lima ; m. 1855, Anita West, and d. in London 1884, leaving issue,
    James, b. 1857.
    Lilly Anne.
  1. Anne Elizabeth, m. Nov. 1844, Rev. T. Brooke, brother of Sir H. Brooke, 1st bart. He d.s.p. 10 Jan. 1854. She d. June, 1902.
  2. Cecilia, m. 1846, Frederick Ness.
  3. Charlotte, d. unm. 1883.
  4. Frances, m. 1858, Monsieur Bourel, d. in 1863.
1. Elizabeth, m. Sept. 1802, Richard Hornidge, of Tulfaris, and had issue (see that family).
2. Frances, b. 5 June, 1784 ; d. unm. 18 Nov. 1801.
3. Cecilia, b. 10 May, 1786 ; d. unm. 30 March, 1858.

The 3rd son,
ARTHUR HENRY, of Lodge Park, High Sheriff co. Kildare 1820, b. 30 June, 1781 ; m. 1 Feb. 1812, Eliza, 3rd dau. of George Gun-Cuninghame, of Mount Kennedy, co. Wicklow, by Jane his wife ; and d. 4 Sept. 1856, having by her (who d. 28 July, 1853) had issue,
1. FREDERICK HUGH, of Lodge Park.
2. Arthur Robert, Capt. R.N., b. 8 March, 1817 ; d. unm. 31 Oct. 1863.
3. Richard Francis, Lieut. 29th Regt., b. 1 May, 1820 ; d. unm. 6 April, 1879.
4. George Joseph, b. 30 May, 1818 ; d. 30 July, 1818.
5. Charles Stuart, Lieut.-Gen. R.A., C.B., b. 15 Nov. 1822 ; m. 21 Oct. 1871, Hon. Louisa Harriet, eldest dau. of Kenelm, 17th Baron Somerville, and co-heir of her brother, 18th baron. Gen. C. S. Henry d.s.p. 5 Oct. 1892.
6. James William, in Bombay Army, b. 27 April, 1824 ; m. the widow of — Hadan. She d. 1885. He was killed in the Indian Mutiny 4 Oct. 1857.
7. George Cecil, Col. R.A., b. 24 June, 1826 ; m. 3 Aug. 1858, Elizabeth, dau. of Rev. R. Garth, and d. 30 Sept. 1900, having had issue,
  Charles Cecil, b. 1865 ; m. 24 Sept. 1901, Mary, eldest dau. of the late Rev. Frank Kewley.
  Mabel Mary.
8. Robert Edward, Lieut.-Col., late Capt. 86th Regt. ; member

Hepenstal.   THE LANDED GENTRY.   312

of the Hon. Corps of Gentlemen-at-Arms; *b.* 6 March, 1828; *m.* 1867, Frances, only dau. of Rev. J. Macdonald, and *d.s.p.* 19 Feb. 1892.
1. Anne Elizabeth, *b.* 10 Dec. 1813; *d. unm.* 24 April, 1868.
2. Selina Jane, *m.* 14 Sept. 1854, George Whitelocke Lloyd, of Strancally Castle, Cappoquin, co. Waterford, and by her (who *d.* 11 Jan. 1880) had issue (*see* WHITELOCKE-LLOYD *of Strancally Castle*).
3. Emily Cecilia, *m.* 11 Oct. 1859, her cousin, Hugh Henry, of Firmount, and has issue (*see above*).

The eldest son,
FREDERICK HUGH HENRY, J.P., of Lodge Park, co. Kildare, High Sheriff, co. Antrim 1862, and of co. Kildare 1863, late 35th Regt., *b.* 25 April, 1815; *m.* 30 April, 1860, Adolphina Frederica, eldest dau. of Robert Gun-Cuninghame, D.L., of Mount Kennedy, co. Wicklow, and *d.* 25 March, 1888, having had issue,
FREDERICK ROBERT, now of Lodge Park.
Emily Jane, *b.* 13 Sept. 1863; *d.* 27 May, 1865.

Seat—Lodge Park, Straffan, co. Kildare.

DOPPING-HEPENSTAL OF DERRYCASSAN.

LAMBERT JOHN DOPPING-HEPENSTAL, of Derrycassan, co. Longford and of Altadore Castle, co. Wicklow, D.L., J.P., High Sheriff co. Wicklow, 1909, and co. Longford 1910, Major R.E. (ret.), *b.* 3 Aug. 1859.

Lineage.—JOHN DOPPING, of Frampton, co Gloucester, and of Dopping Court, Dublin, *m.* Joan, dau. of John Elliott, of Salop, and had an only son,
ANTHONY DOPPING, of Dopping Court, Dublin, Clerk of the Privy Council in Ireland, Feodary of the Province of Leinster, and Examiner of the Court of Wards, *m.* Margaret, dau. of Gilbert Domvile, M.P. co. Kildare, by Margaret his wife, dau. of Most Rev. Thomas Jones, D.D., Archbishop of Dublin, and Lord Chancellor of Ireland, sister of 1st Viscount Ranelagh, and *d.* 8 July, 1649, having had issue (with a dau., Jane Antonia, *m.* as 2nd wife, Thomas Towers, of Kentstown, co. Meath, *d.* 22 July, 1648). His son,
MOST REV. ANTHONY DOPPING, D.D., Bishop of Meath, of Dopping Court, Dublin, *b.* in Dublin 1614, Fellow Trin. Coll. Dublin and Vice-Chancellor of the University. Consecrated Bishop of Kildare 2 Feb. 1679, translated to the See of Meath by patent dated 14 Jan. 1681, and Chancellor of the University; *m.* by licence, dated 27 Dec. 1670, Jane (*b.* 10 March, 1648), dau. of Samuel Molyneux, and had issue,
1. Samuel, *b.* in Dublin 1671, whose will, dated 7 Dec. 1718, was proved 17 Sept. 1720; *d.s.p.*
2. ANTHONY, of whom hereafter.
1. Margaret, *m.* by licence, dated 8 July, 1701, Henry Osborne, of Dardistown, co. Meath, and had issue. Her will, dated 17 Aug. 1752, was proved 21 Oct. same year.
2. Lucy, *m.* 17 Feb. 1708, John Hamilton, of Caledon, co. Tyrone, and had issue, an only dau. and heiress,
Margaret, *m.* 30 June, 1738, John, 5th Earl of Cork and Orrery.
3. Mary, *m.* by licence, dated 20 Dec. 1721, Arthur Weldon, of Rahenderry, co. Kildare, and had issue.
4. Jane, *m.* 1718, Rev. Peter Leslie, D.D., Rector of Aghogil, co. Antrim, and had issue.

The Bishop of Meath *d.* in Dublin, 25 April, 1697, and was bur. in St. Andrew's Church. His 2nd, and eventually eldest surviving son,
RIGHT REV. ANTHONY DOPPING, Bishop of Ossory, of Dopping Court, Dublin, *b.* in Dublin, 1675, was instituted Dean of Clonmacnois 2 July, 1720, and consecrated Bishop of Ossory 19 July, 1740. He *m.* Dorothea, dau. of Ralph Howard, M.P., of Shelton Abbey, co. Wicklow, ancestor of the Earls of Wicklow, and had issue,
1. ANTHONY, his heir.
1. Jane Lucy, *m.* 29 May, 1742, Riley Towers, of Finglas, co. Dublin, Barrister-at-Law, and *d.* 9 April, 1743, leaving issue.
2. Alice, *d. unm.*   3. Margaret, *d. unm.*
4. Frances, *m.* Sept. 1778, Samuel Molyneux Madden, who *d.* 1783.
5. Katherine, *m.* Robert Lowry, of Melbury, near Caledon. He *d.s.p.* 1764.

The Bishop of Ossery *d.* Jan. 1743, and was bur. in St. Andrew's Church, Dublin. His eldest son,
ANTHONY DOPPING, of Lowtown, co. Westmeath, *m.* 26 Jan. 1756, Alice, dau. of James D'Arcy, of Hyde Park, co. Westmeath, and of Derrycassan, co. Longford, and had (will dated 7 Nov. 1790, and proved 5 Aug. 1794), with two daus., Dorothea and Catherine, who both *d. unm.*, two sons,
1. Samuel Dopping, *b.* 1760; *s.* his father at Lowtown, 1794, and *d.s.p.m.* 6 April, 1822.
2. RALPH, who carried on the line.

Mr. Dopping was *s.* by his eldest son, who *d.* as above, while the family was carried on by the 2nd son,
RALPH DOPPING, of Erne Head and Derryacsson, co. Longford, *b.* 1766, *m.* 1798, Catherine, dau. of Philip Smyth, of Grouse Hall, co. Cavan, and had issue,
1. JOHN, his heir.
2. Henry, of Erne Head, J.P., High Sheriff 1861, *b.* 1807; *m.* Dec. 1836, Frances, dau. of Robert Jessop, of Mount Jessop, co. Longford, and has issue, one son and one dau. (Henrietta Charlotte Martha, *d. unm.* 19 Nov. 1911).
Francis Henry John (Rev.), A.M., Vicar of Colombkill, co. Longford, *b.* 1838; *m.* 28 Oct. 1890, Mary Florence, dau. of Edward Hudson. She *d.* Nov. 1894. He *d.* 13 May, 1907, leaving issue,
Henrietta Charlotte Martha.
1. Mary, *m.* 1826, Rev. Charles Robinson, Rector of Kilglass, co. Longford, *d.* 30 Oct. 1870.
2. Frances, *d. unm.*

Mr. Dopping *d.* 30 June, 1818, and was *s.* by his eldest son,
JOHN DOPPING, of Derrycassan, J.P., High Sheriff 1823, *b.* 1800; *m.* 1822, Frances, dau. of James Henry Cottingham, of Somerville, co. Cavan, and by her (who *d.* Dec. 1867) had issue,
1. RALPH ANTHONY, his heir.
2. John Francis, *b.* 1840; *d. unm.* 1869.
3. James Henry, Lieut.-Col. and Hon.-Col. 6th Batt. Rifle Brigade, J.P. cos. Donegal, Kildare, and Longford, late H.E.I.C.S. (10, *Trafalgar Terrace, Monkstown, Dublin*); *b.* 24 Sept. 1832; *m.* 1st, 23 Nov. 1857, Helen Sarah, 4th dau. of Rev. Charles Moore, of Monasterevan, grandson of Edward, 5th Earl of Drogheda, and by her (who *d.* 1891) has a dau..
1. Charlotte Agnes, *m.* 1879, William Henry Boyd, J.P. and D.L., of Ballymacool, co. Donegal, and has issue (*see that family*).
He *m.* 2ndly, 9 Sept. 1893, Maud Helen, eldest dau. of the late Luke White, of Shrubbs, co. Dublin, and by her has issue,
2. Rosalie White.   3. Jane Emily.
1. Charlotte Henrietta, *m.* 1848, Admiral Edward John Stoll, R.N., and *d.* 1854, leaving issue.
2. Sarah (Haidee) Rose, *m.* 1857, Col. William Creagh, Bombay Staff, and *d.* 1875, leaving issue.

Mr. Dopping, who was drowned 3 April, 1855, was *s.* by his eldest son,
RALPH ANTHONY DOPPING-HEPENSTAL, of Derrycassan, J.P. and D.L., High Sheriff 1859, Hon. Col. Longford Rifles, *b.* 31 Aug. 1823; *m.* 1st, 30 July, 1858, Diana Dalrymple, dau. of the Rev. Lambert Watson Hepenstal, of Altadore, co. Wicklow (*see below*), and had issue,
1. LAMBERT JOHN, now of Derrycassan and Altadore Castle.
1. Susannah Elizabeth Louisa Mary Caroline.
2. Haidee Emily Rose.   3. Diana Charlotte.
He *m.* 2ndly, 10 July, 1867, Anne, 3rd dau. of Richard Maxwell Fox, of Foxhall, co. Longford, D.L. and M.P., and had further issue,
2. Ralph Francis Byron, *b.* 3 Aug. 1868.
3. Maxwell Edward, Major 1st P.W.O. Gurkhas, late Worcester Regt., *b.* 7 March, 1872.
4. Juanita Rose.

Col. Dopping assumed by Royal Licence dated 24 June, 1859 the additional surname and arms of HEPENSTAL, in compliance with the testamentary injunction of his father-in-law, Rev. Lambert Watson Hepenstal, of Altadore, co. Wicklow. He *d.* 1887, and was *s.* by his eldest son, Lambert John Dopping-Hepenstal, now of Derrycassan and Altadore.

FAMILY OF HEPENSTAL.

REV. JOHN HEPENSTAL, of Newcastle, co. Wicklow, *b.* 1699; *m.* 1726, Miss Adair, of Hollybrook, co. Wicklow, and had issue,
1. William, who had issue, two daus.
2. EDWARD, of whom we treat.

The younger son,
EDWARD HEPENSTAL, of Newcastle, *m.* 1759, Jane, dau. of John Lambert, of Kilcrony, and sister of Col. Oliver Richard Lambert, and had issue,
1. John, *d.s.p.*   2. GEORGE, of whom presently.
3. Edward, Lieut. 88th Regt., *d.s.p.*
4. William, Capt. R.N., *d.s.p.*

The 2nd son,
GEORGE HEPENSTAL, of Sandymount, whose will, dated 22 Feb. 1804, was proved 17 Jan. 1806; *m.* April, 1787, Hester Watson, and had (with other issue) a son,
REV. LAMBERT WATSON HEPENSTAL, of Altadore, co. Wicklow, *m.* 1st, 1809, Elizabeth, dau. of William Ball, and had issue,
1. GEORGE RICHARD, *m.* 1863, Mrs. Margaret Murray, widow, and *d.* May, 1869.
2. William, *d. unm.*
1. Jane Anne, *d.* July, 1824.
2. Esther Charlotte, *d.* Aug. 1856.
3. Louisa Diana, *m.* Aug. 1836, Rev. James Peed, Rector of Wexford.
4. Elizabeth Martha, *d.* April, 1853.
5. Susanna Rebecca, *d.* Sept. 1836.
6. Selina Dalrymple, *m.* Jan. 1844, G. Owen Ormsby, Engineer.
7. Emily Mary, *d. unm.* July, 1898.
8. DIANA DALRYMPLE, *m.* 30 July, 1858, Ralph Anthony Dopping, afterwards DOPPING-HEPENSTAL.
9. Hester Maria, *m.* 1858, Major Richard Wilson Hartley.

Mr. Hepenstal *m.* 2ndly, 27 Oct. 1858, Cecilia, dau. of John Berkeley Deane, of Berkeley, co. Wexford (*see* DEANE *of Glendaragh*), and *d.* 1859.

Arms—Quarterly: 1st and 4th, per chevron erm. and arg. on a chevron gu. between in chief a cross-crosslet of the third, and in base an eagle displayed sa. three cinquefoils of the second, for HEPENSTAL; 2nd and 3rd gu., a chevron erm. in base a plate, a chief chequy arg. and az. and a border engrailed or, for DOPPING.
Crest—1st, HEPENSTAL: A pelican in her piety ppr. on the breast

IRELAND.   Herbert.

a cross-crosslet gu.; 2nd, DOPPING: A talbot's head arg. chained or, and gorged with a collar engrailed gu. thereon three bezants, *Motto*—Virescet vulnere virtus.

Seats—Derrycassan, Granard, co. Longford, and Altadore Castle, co. Wicklow. Club—Kildare Street.

HERBERT, late OF MUCKRUSS.

HENRY ARTHUR EDWARD KEANE HERBERT, J.P. co. Kerry, heir male of the family of HERBERT of Muckruss, b. 1867.

Lineage.— Since the merging of the elder branch of the family of CLIVE, by the marriage of the heiress of the last Herbert, Earl of Pow's, with the son of the celebrated General Lord Clive, the chieftainship of the name seems indubitably to rest with HERBERT *of Muckruss*, in co. Kerry, descended from Thomas Herbert, of Kilcuagh, who went to Ireland under the care and patronage of his relative Lord Herbert, of Cherbury and Castle Island, A.D. 1656; which Thomas was the son of Mathew, the son of Sir John, the son of Sir William, the son of Sir Mathew of Colebrook, the lineal descendant from the eldest son of Sir Richard Herbert, of Colebrooke, only brother of the Earl of Pembroke of the first creation. These brothers (as may be read in the pages of Speed and Hollinshed) suffered as Yorkists in the Wars of the Roses. The heir-general of the Earl of Pembroke married into the family of Somerset, Earl and Marquess of Worcester, and Duke of Beaufort. From Sir Richard descended in the younger branches the Lords Herbert of Cherbury, afterwards Earls of Powis, and Herbert, Earl of Torrington, both extinct in the male line, while from a senior, but never ennobled branch, the family of Muckruss and Kilcuagh now remains the existing and legitimate male representative of the famous name of Herbert.

THOMAS HERBERT, of Kilcuagh aforesaid, served as High Sheriff of the co. Kerry, 1659. He *m.* Mary, dau. of Edward Kenny, of Cullen, co. Cork, and had issue,
1. EDWARD, his heir. 2. John, *d.s.p.*
3. ARTHUR, *m.* Mary Bastable, of whom came the widespread branches of HERBERT *of Currens, of Cahirnane, and Brewsterfield* (see HERBERT *of Cahirnane*).

The eldest son,
EDWARD HERBERT, of Muckruss. High Sheriff of Kerry, *m.* 1684, Agnes, dau. of Patrick Crosbie, of Tubrid, and had issue,
1. EDWARD, his heir. 2. John, *d.s.p.*
3. Arthur, *d.s.p.*
1. Elizabeth, *m.* William Hull, of Lemcon, eldest son of Sir William Hull.
2. Margaret, *m.* 1st, 1718, John Leader, of Mount Leader, co. Cork (*see that family*); and 2ndly, the Rev. Stanley Craven.

The eldest son,
EDWARD HERBERT, of Muckross, M.P. for Ludlow, in Salop, A.D. 1756, *m.* the Hon. Frances Browne, dau. of Nicholas, 2nd Viscount Kenmare (see BURKE's *Peerage*), and had issue,
1. THOMAS, his heir.
2. Nicholas (Rev.), *m.* 8 April, 1766, Hon Martha Cuffe, dau. of John, 1st Lord Desart (*see* BURKE's *Peerage*), and by her (who *d.* 1808) left at his decease, 180-, JOHN OTWAY, his heir; Thomas *m.* Lucinda, dau. of the Hon and Rev. Hamilton Cuffe; Nicholas (Rev.), A.M., J.P.; Lucinda, *m.* William Bradshaw; Sophia, *m.* John Mandeville, of Anner Castle; and three other daus., who *d. unm.* The son and heir,

THE REV. JOHN OTWAY HERBERT, *m.* 1796, Honoria Ann, only dau. of Capt. James Russell, H.E.I.C.S., and *d.* 1800, having had an only child,
WALTER OTWAY HERBERT, of Pill House, co. Tipperary, J.P., *b.* Oct. 1798; *m.* 19 Sept. 1822, Mary, only child of John Miles, of Dameren House, Dorset, and by her (who *d.* 26 June, 1848, had issue,
1. JOHN OTWAY (Rev.).
2. Nicholas Sidney, Tipperary Artillery.
1. Margaret Jane, *m.* Nicholas Valentine Maher, of Turtulla, M.P. co. Tipperary.
2. Honoria Anne, *m.* Robert Cope Hardy, Military Train.
3. Edward, M.P. 1760, for Innistioge, co. Kilkenny and Tralee *d.* 2 March, 1770; *m.* 21 July, 1749, Hon. Nichola Sophia Cuffe, eldest dau. of John, Lord Desart, and by her (who *d.* 1818) had issue,
1. Edward (Ven.), Archdeacon of Aghadoe, *m.* 1789, Frances Diana, dau. of R. Standish, and left issue, three sons and four daus.
Edward Thomas (Rev.), Rector of Kilpeacon, *b.* 1793; *m.*

1815, Alice, dau. of Rev. Gustavus Wybrants and half-sister of Rev. Arthur Champagne, and dying 1860, had by her (who *d.* 7 April, 1863),
1. Edward, *d. unm.* 8 Sept. 1847.
2. Gustavus Wybrants, J.P. co. Cork, *b.* 5 March, 1837; *m.* April, 1865, Annie Catherine, 3rd dau. of the Rev. Otway John Herbert, and *d.* Nov. 1886, having by her (who *d.* 1882) had issue,
 a. Edward Sidney, Major The Black Watch (Royal Highlanders, now serving with Egyptian Army, has 3rd Class of the Mejidie, and 4th Class of the Osmanieh, *b.* 6 June, 1866; *m.* 12 Oct. 1905, Alice Gwendolen, youngest dau. of Rt. Hon. Sir John Gorst P.C. (*see* LOWNDES *of Castle Combe*).
 b. Gustavus Otway, *b.* 26 July, 1867; *m.* 1901, Alice, dau. of late Col. John Moorhead McLanahan, and has issue,
  Edward Otway, *b.* 1901.
 c. Henry Arthur Charles (Rev.), Rector of Broughton, co. Lincoln, since 1908, late Chaplain, Indian Establishment, *b.* 26 April, 1871; *m.* 15 Aug. 1907, Penelope Mary Caroline, 2nd dau. of Rev. William Wyatt, Rector of Broughton, Lincs., and has issue,
  Arthur Patrick, *b.* 21 Aug. 1910.
 d. Otway Charles, Capt. Argyll and Sutherland Highlanders, *b.* 1 July, 1877.
 a. Annie Eveline, *m.* 4 July, 1903, Charles William Scott, younger son of the Ven. J. George Scott, D.D., Archdeacon of Dublin, and has issue.
 b. Alice Mabel, *m.* Frank Browne, Clerk of the Peace for co. Wicklow, and has issue.
3. Henry Arthur, *d. unm.* 1861.
1. Emily, *m.* Eyre Powell, and *d.* 1858.
2. Louisa, *m.* Frederick Maunsell. 3. Frances, *d. unm.*
4. Olivia, *m.* 1864, the Rev. A. Pearde Nash.
5. Henrietta, *d. unm.*
6. Nicola Sophia, *m.* 18 June, 1855, George Fosbery, of Clorane, and *d.* 1876, having had issue (*see that family*).
7. Alice, *m.* 1864, N. J. Hobart, M.D., only son of Lieut.-Col. Hobart, E.I.C.S.

(2) Henry (Rev.), Rector of Rathdowney, *b.* 12 Sept. 1795; *m.* 1st, 25 March, 1822, his cousin Harriet, widow of William Pitt Blunden (mother of Sir John Blunden, Bart. (*see* BURKE's *Peerage*), only dau. of Thomas Pope, of Popefield, and by her (who *d.* 1861) had issue, two sons and six daus.,
1. Edward Thomas, *b.* 1824; *d.* 1834.
2. Henry Arthur, *b.* 1826; *m.* 21 Dec. 1850, Grace, dau. of Sir Frederick Pollock, 1st Bart. He *d.* 16 April, 1910, leaving issue,
 a. Henry Arthur, *m.* 1894, Edith S., dau. of Henry H. Mercer, and has issue,
  (a) Henry Arthur, *b.* 1898.
  (b) Charles Edward Mercer, *b.* 26 June, 1904.
  (a) Nicola Sophia Grace.
  (b) Geraldine.
 a. Frances Harriet, *m.* 1888, Godfrey Cornwall Chester Master (*see that family*).
 b. Grace Sophia.
 c. Mary Jane, *m.* 1881, W. H. W. Poole
1. Frances Diana, *m.* 1853, George Pollock, son of Sir F. Pollock, Bart., and *d.* 30 Dec. 1891 leaving issue (*see* BURKE's *Peerage*).
2. Nicola Sophia, *m.* 31 Aug. 1848, Hon. Sir Charles Pollock, Baron of the Court of Exchequer and afterwards a Judge of the High Court, and *d.* 15 Nov. 1855, leaving issue (*see* BURKE's *Peerage*).
3. Jane Dorothea, *m.* Rev. J. Hall Gedge.
4. Alice, *m.* Alfred Gahan. 5. Olivia, *m.* Robert White.
6. Thomasine Elizabeth, *m.* Charles Thompson, J.P. for Queen's Co.

He *m.* 2ndly, 20 April, 1865, Catherine, dau. of the Rev. M. N. Thompson and *d.* 14 Dec. 1874, without further issue.
(3) John (Rev.), *b.* 1800; *m.* 1831, Anne, dau. of W. Stoker, M.D.; and *d.* 1853, leaving, with three other daus.,
1. Edward Otway (Rev.), formerly Vicar of St. John, Middlesboro', Private Chaplain to Earl De la Warr. *m.* 1 Nov. 1902, Rachel Mary, eldest dau. of the late Rev. Richard Hull, Rector of Upper Stondon, co. Bedford.
2. William Henry, Lieut.-Col. late Royal Irish Regt., *b.* 18 June, 1838; *d.* 28 Feb. 1909.
1. Frances Ann, *m.* 26 Dec. 1855, John Robert Day, son of Lieut.-Col. Edward Day, H.E.I.C.S.
(1) Frances Diana, *m.* 1821, Maurice Collis, M.D.; *d.s.p.* 1850.
(2) Nichola Sophia, *m.* 1820, Robert Staveley, and *d.s.p.* 1829.
(3) Olivia, *m.* 1827, Rev. E. Bourke, of Oranmore.
(4) Thomasine, *m.* 1831, William Taylor.
Archdeacon Edward Herbert *d.* 1814.
1. Frances Maria, *m.* 1784, Richard Chaloner, of Kingsfort.
2. Dorothea, *m.* 1776, Francis Warren Bonham, of Ballintaggart.
3. Nicola Sophia, *d. unm.*
4. Catherine, *d. unm.*
1. Agnes, *m.* 1st, Florence McCartie More*; and 2ndly, Edward Herbert, of Currens, *s.p.*

---
* The only son of the marriage, Charles McCartie More, *d. unm.* 1770, and bequeathed the remnant of his estates, including Pallace, once the famed residence of the McCarties, to his kinsman, Thomas Herbert, of Muckruss.

Herbert. THE LANDED GENTRY. 314

2. Helena, *m.* — Hedges, of Macroom Castle, co. Cork.
3. Frances, *m.* John Blennerhassett, of Ballyseedy (*see that family*).
4. Arabella, *d. unm.*
5. Thomasina, *m.* Oct. 1765, Thomas Cuffe, and was mother of Grace Cuffe, wife of Barry Maxwell, 1st Earl of Farnham.
6. Catherine, *m.* Robert Herbert, of the Currens family.

The eldest son,
THOMAS HERBERT, of Muckruss, M.P. for Ludlow, *m.* 1st, Anne, dau. of John Martin, of Overbury, co. Worcester, and by her had issue,
1. HENRY ARTHUR, his heir.
2. Edward (Rev), *m.* Mary Herbert, of Brewsterfield, dau. of Bastable Herbert (*see* HERBERT *of Cahirnane*), and Barbara Fitzgerald, dau. of the Knight of Kerry, and hence descended the Rev. Edward Herbert, Vicar of Killarney.
 1. Frances, *m.* the Rev. Edward Kenny.
 2. Catherine, *m.* the Rev. Mr. Dawson.
 3. Mary, *m.* Rev. Arthur Herbert, brother of R. T. Herbert, of whom descended the Rev. Thomas Herbert, Rector of Killentierna, and his brothers. 4. Anne, *m.* Col. James Kearney.
 5. Emily, *m.* Richard Townsend Herbert, of Cahirnane, as his 1st wife (*see that family*).
Thomas Herbert *m.* 2ndly, Agnes, dau. of Rev. Francis Bland, Vicar of Killarney, and by her had issue,
 3. Thomas, *d.s.p.* 1798, bur. at Worcester Cathedral.
 4. Francis, killed in a duel at Gibraltar, 1797.
 6. Cherry, *d. unm.* 7. Elizabeth.

The eldest son,
HENRY ARTHUR HERBERT, of Muckruss, *m.* Elizabeth, dau. of Lord George Sackville, and sister to the last Duke of Dorset, and had issue a dau., Elizabeth, wife of Major Henry Verelst, and a son and successor,
CHARLES JOHN HERBERT, of Muckruss, *m.* 1814, Louisa Middleton, and had issue,
 1. HENRY ARTHUR, late of Muckruss. 2. Charles, *d.s.p.*
 1. Louisa, *m.* Rev. Edward Stewart, cousin to the Earl of Galloway, and had issue. 2. Emily, *m.* Col. Long, of Bromley Hill.
 3. Jane, *m.* 16 April, 1845, William Henry White Hedges, of Macroom Castle, 3rd Earl of Bantry, and *d.* 7 July, 1898, having had issue (*see* BURKE's *Peerage*). He *d.* 15 Jan. 1884.
 4. Maria, *d.* June, 1872.

He *d.* 1836, and was *s.* by his eldest son,
THE RIGHT HON. HENRY ARTHUR HERBERT, of Muckruss, co. Kerry, Lord-Lieut. and M.P. for that co. and Col. Kerry Militia; Chief Secretary for Ireland from 1857 to 1858 ; *m.* 1837, Mary, dau. of James Balfour, of Whittinghame, East Lothian (*see that family*) by Lady Eleanor his wife, and by her (who *d.* 1893) had issue,
 1. HENRY ARTHUR, late of Muckruss.
 2. Charles, *m.* 1st, Mdlle. de Morny ; and 2ndly, 1874, Helen (who *d.* Nov. 1882), only child of Lieut.-Col. Andrew Spottiswoode.
 1. Eleanor, *m.* 1871, Thomas Thoroton Hildyard, eldest son of T. B. Thoroton Hildyard, of Flintham Hall, Notts.
 2. Blanche.

He *d.* 24 Feb. 1866, and was *s.* by his elder son,
HENRY ARTHUR HERBERT, late of Muckruss, co. Kerry, J.P. and D.L., High Sheriff 1881, M.P. for that co. 1866 to 1880, Major London Irish Rifles, late Capt. Coldstream Guards, *b.* 1840 ; *m.* 20 Oct. 1866, Hon. Emily Julia Charlotte Keane, only child of Edward, 2nd Lord Keane, and by her (who was divorced 28 April, 1882) had issue,
HENRY ARTHUR EDWARD KEANE, present representative.
Kathleen Mary Eleanor, *m.* 21 July, 1894, Capt. A. Morris, late 20th Hussars.

Mr. H. A. Herbert *d.* 14 Aug. 1901.

Arms—Per pale az. and gu., three lions rampant arg., armed and langued or. **Crest**—A bundle of arrows, or, headed and feathered arg., six in saltire, one in pale, girt round the middle with a belt gu., buckle and point extended of the first.

KENNEY-HERBERT late OF CASTLE ISLAND.

UNG·JE·SERVIRAI

The late JOHN KENNEY-HERBERT, of Knocknagore, Castle Island, co. Kerry, J.P., *b.* 15 Feb. 1848 ; *m.* 16 Nov. 1874, Harriett Mary, dau. of Thomas Murdock Green, of Aghadoe, Killagh, co. Cork. She *d.* his widow 3 April, 1904.

Lineage.—EDWARD KENNEY, of Ballymartle and Cullen, co. Cork, a younger son of HENRY KENNEY, of Kenney's Hall and Edermine, co. Wexford, made his will 24 Aug. 1683.
He *m.* Mary Merrill, and had issue,
1. Edward, of Cullen, Sovereign of Kinsale, co. Cork, *m.* Sarah, dau. (or sister) of Capt. Swithen Walton, of Dromore Castle, co. Cork, and had issue,

1. Edward, of Newfort House, co. Wexford, Col. in the Army, High Sheriff of Wexford 1696, J.P., *m.* Frances, only dau. and heiress of her great-uncle, Col. Richard Kenney, of Kenney Hall and Edermine, and had issue,
 (1) Richard, *d.s.p.*
 (2) Henry, of Kenney Hall, *b.* 1699 ; *m.* Elizabeth Dodwell, and *d.s.p.* 12 Dec. 1751.
 (3) Thomas, *d. circa* 1732, leaving an only son, Edward, killed in a duel with Colclough, of Tintern Abbey, *d.s.p.*
 (1) Mary.
 (2) Elizabeth, *m.* John Goodison.
 (3) Katherine, *m.* Charles Morton.
2. John, *b.* 1671, Prebendary of St. Michael's, Cork, *d.* 1712.
3. Thomas, Capt. R.N., killed in action off Brest, 1704.
4. William. 5. Richard.
2. WILLIAM, of whom presently.
1. Jane, *m.* Martin Supple.
2. Mary, *m.* Capt. Meade, of Tassaxon.

The 2nd son,
WILLIAM KENNEY, of Clarab, co. Cork, an Officer in the Army, *m.* Katherine, dau. of Sir Peter Courthope, Knt., of Courtstown and Little Island, co. Cork, and had issue,
1. WILLIAM, of Coolekereen, co. Cork, *d. unm.*
2. JOHN, of whom presently.
1. A dau., *m.* Norris Hoare, of Iveragh, co. Kerry.
2. Mary, *m.* 1st, — Lewis ; 2ndly, Capt. Bedford ; and 3rdly, Lieut. Fourness, co. York, afterwards of Bandon, co. Cork.
3. Jane, *m.* Richard Thornhill, of Castle Kivin, near Mallow.
4. Anne, *m.* Edward Thornhill, of Castle Kivin.
5. Katherine, *m.* Edward Supple, of Supple's Court.

The 2nd son,
THE REV. JOHN KENNEY, M.A., Prebendary of Kilbrittain, co. Cork, *b.* 1701 ; *m.* 3 March, 1727, Judith, dau. of Edward Browne, Mayor of Cork, sister of Most Rev. Jemmett Browne, Archbishop of Tuam, by whom (who *d.* 27 July, 1741) he had issue,
1. Edward, Rector of Movidddy, co. Cork, *b.* 19 Feb. 1729 ; *d. unm.* 23 April, 1818.
2. William, *b.* 4 Aug. 1734 ; *d. unm.*
3. John, *b.* 10 June, 1738 ; *d.* young.
4. JOHN, of whom presently.
1. Judith, *d. unm.* 2. Katherine, *d.* 1812.
3. Mary, *m.* — Foxworthy. 4. Elizabeth, *d.* 1740.
5. Frances, *d. unm.* 6. Jane, *d.* 4 Aug. 1741.

Rev. John Kenney *d.* 1768. His youngest son,
THE REV. JOHN KENNEY, LL.D., Prebendary of Kilbroggan, and Vicar-General of Cork and Ross for 43 years, *b.* at Bantry, 3 Sept. 1739 ; *m.* Mary, dau. of Rev. John Herbert, of Castle Island, co. Kerry (sister of John Herbert, of Castle Island, who *d.s.p.* 1795, and bequeathed his estates to the issue of his sister), and had issue,
1. Edward, Rector of Kilmeen, co. Cork, for 43 years, *b.* 1768 ; *m.* Frances, dau. of Thomas Herbert, of Muckruss, and *d.* April, 1842, having had the following issue,
 1. John (Rev.). 2. Thomas (Rev.).
 3. Robert (Rev.), *m.* Frances Diana, dau. of Henry Standish, and by her (who *d.* 9 March, 1883) had two daus.,
 (1) Isabella. (2) Frances.
 4. Arthur, M.D.
 1. Margaret. 2. Mary, *d.* 24 Feb. 1883.
 3. Frances.
 4. Anne, *m.* 2 April, 1830, Rev. Horace Townsend.
 5. Katherine. 6. Judith.
2. Robert, Capt. and Brigade-Major, *b.* 1770 ; *m.* Annie, dau. of Lieut.-Col. Francis Kearney, and *d.s.p.* 1826.
3. THOMAS, of whom hereafter.
4. Arthur Henry (Very Rev.), Fell. Trin. Coll. Dublin, Dean of Achonry, *b.* 1 Sept. 1776 ; *m.* Feb. 1802, Mary Lusinda, dau. of Robert Herbert (who was brother of above John of Castle Island), and *d.* 27 Jan. 1855, leaving,
 Arthur Robert Kenney-Herbert, Rector of Bourton, near Rugby, *b.* 11 May 1805 ; *d.* 21 June, 1883; *m.* 6 Aug. 1836, Mary Louise, dau. of James Palmer, of Lichfield, by whom (who *d.* 14 Feb. 1851) he had issue,
 (1) Arthur Robert, Col. late Madras Cavalry, *b.* 17 Aug. 1840 ; *m.* Agnes, dau. of Gen. Cleveland, Madras Army, and has with other issue,
 Arthur Cleveland Herbert, Major late Northants Regt., *b.* 1863 ; *m.* 20 June, 1908, Edith Harriet, only dau. of late Richard Stanton Evans, of Lowndes Street, S.W.
 (2) Herbert William, *b.* 23 Sept. 1844 ; *d.* aged 11.
 (3) Edward Maxwell, J.P. Bucks, late Chief Inspector of Schools (6, *Woodfield Road, Ealing, W.*), *b.* 10 Dec. 1845 ; *m.* 6 Jan. 1876, Lady Jane White, dau. of the 3rd Earl of Bantry (*see* BURKE's *Peerage*), and has issue,
 Aubrey Edward, *b.* 1877.
 Doreen Edith Elizabeth.
 (1) Katherine Lucy, *m.* Sept. 1862, Rev. Charles Garth Fullerton.
 (2) Louisa Mary, *m.* Rev. Humberston Skipwith.
 (3) Harriette, *d. unm.* 23 Aug. 1867.
 (4) Mary Lucinda.
1. Judith, *b.* 1772. 2. Mary, *b.* 1774 ; *d. unm.*

Rev. John Kenney *d.* 25 Dec. 1814. His 3rd son,
THE REV. THOMAS KENNEY, Rector of Donoughmore, co. Cork, *b.* 1771 ; *m.* 15 April, 1806, Anne Diana, dau. of Rev. John Kenton Dawson, of Ledbury, co. Hereford, by whom (who *d.* 1825) he had issue,
1. JOHN, of whom hereafter.
2. Edward Herbert, Capt. R.N., *m.* Charlotte Mary, dau. of Capt. George Bignell, R.N., and (*d.* 9 Nov. 1876) left issue,

IRELAND. Herdman.

1. Edward Herbert, b. 26 Feb. 1853; m. 8 March, 1887, Pauline Even, and had issue,
    (1) Edward Herbert, b. 19 Oct. 1891.
    (1) Pauline Charlotte, b. 22 Mar. 1888.
    (2) Mary Georgiana, b. 7 March, 1897; d. 25 Oct. 1897.
    (3) Edith Dora, b. 20 March, 1899; d. 14 Jan. 1910.
2. Arthur Herbert, C.M.G., D.S.O., Col. R.E. (*Stoncleigh, Northam, N. Devon*), served in Afghan War 1879-80 (medal), Nile Expedition 1884-5 (despatches, medal with two clasps, bronze star), and in S. Africa 1899-1900 (despatches, medal with three clasps, D.S.O.), British Commissioner on Anglo-French Frontier Delimitation Commission on River Gambia 1890-91 (thanked by Government), and near Sierra Leone 1891-2 (C.M.G.), b. 4 Jan. 1855.
    1. Charlotte Mary.
3. Thomas Robert, d. Dec, 1831, aged 17.
4. William Shield, Col. E.I.C.S., b. 1821; d. Jan. 1890.
1. Katherine, d. unm. 1833.
2. Mary Anne, d. unm. 1824.
3. Frances Amelia, m. 16 July, 1851, Henry Stewart, Commander R.N., and d.s.p. 21 Oct. 1868.
Rev. Thomas Kenney d. 8 June, 1841. His eldest son,
JOHN KENNEY, b. 14 April, 1809; s. to the Herbert estates on the death of his uncle, Rev. Edward Herbert Kenney, in accordance with the provisions of the will of his maternal grand-uncle John Herbert, of Castle Island, whereupon he assumed, by Royal Licence, 29 June, 1842, the additional name and arms of HERBERT. m. 1843, Jane, dau. of Daniel Humphreys, of Broomfield, co. Cork, and d. 8 Dec. 1873, leaving issue,
1. JOHN, his successor, late of Castle Island.
2. Aune.
2. Jane, m. 30 May, 1876, William King, and d. May, 1890, leaving issue.
3. Frances Amelia, d. unm. 30 June, 1883.
4. Adelaide Rebecca, d. unm. May, 1890.
5. Henrietta Matilda, m. 16 May, 1876, Rev. Neville Kearney.
6. Katherine Louisa. d. unm. 30 Nov. 1881.

Arms—Quarterly: 1st and 4th per pale arg. and sa., three lions rampant, two and one counterchanged, for HERBERT *of Castle Island*; 2nd and 3rd, per pale or and azure a fleur-de-lis between three crescents counterchanged, for KENNEY. Crests—1st, a bundle of twelve arrows in saltier or, headed and feathered arg. belted gu. and buckled of the first; 2nd, KENNEY, a dexter cubit arm erect vested gu. cuffed arg., the hand grasping a paper scroll ppr. Motto—Ung je serviraí.

HERBERT OF CAHIRNANE AND CURRENS.

ARTHUR STEWART HERBERT, of Cahirnane, co. Kerry, J.P., High Sheriff 1900, b. 28 May, 1866; s. his father 1898; m. 14 Dec. 1899, Theresa Selina, dau. of Col. Gerald Boyle (*see* BURKE'S *Peerage and Baronetage*, CORK, E.), and has issue,
1. GEOFFREY RICHARD ARTHUR, b. 28 March, 1902.
2. Christopher Reginald Courtney, b. 23 March, 1906.

Lineage.—ARTHUR HERBERT, of Currens, 3rd son of Thomas Herbert, of Kilcuagh, and Mary Kenny (*see* HERBERT *of Muckruss*), m. Mary, dau. and heir of George Bastable, of Castle Island, and had issue,
1. GEORGE, of whom hereafter.
2. John (Rev.), Rector of St. Paul's, Cork.
3. Thomas (Rev.), Rector of Castle Island, and had issue.
4. Edward.   5. Fiach.
6. Charles, d.s.p.
7. Arthur, of Cahirnane and Brewsterfield, a barrister, m. Lucy, dau. and heir of Francis Brewster, of Brewsterfield, to whose property he s. and purchased CAHIRNANE (originally part of McCarty More's property) from Col. Hussey. He d.s.p. 5 Oct. 1771, and left Brewsterfield to a nephew, from whose descendants it passed eventually by the marriage of the heiress, to Richard Hungerford Orpen (*see* ORPEN *of Ardtully*), and Cahirnane, to his grand-nephew Richard Townsend Herbert, of Currens (*whom see*).
8. Bastable, m. Barbara, dau. of Maurice FitzGerald, the Knight of Kerry.
1. Lucy, m. Francis Markham.
2. Agnes, m. Rev. Thomas Orpen, of Killowen (*see* ORPEN *of Ardtully*), and had issue.
3. Mary, m. 1st, William Supple, and 2ndly, William Lucy.
4. Margaret, m. William Saunders.
5. Charity, m. Richard Chute, of Chute Hall, and had issue (*see that family*).
The eldest son,
GEORGE HERBERT, m. Jane FitzGerald, dau. of Maurice Fitz-Gerald, Knt. of Kerry, and had issue, 1. ARTHUR, of whom presently; 2. Maurice, m. Julia, sister of Viscount Molesworth; 3. George, Major in the Army; 4. Edward, in the Civil Service; 5. Thomas, Capt. 10th Regt.; and 6. John. d. young, and four daus. The eldest son,

THE REV. ARTHUR HERBERT, of Cahirnane and Currens, Rector of Tralee, m. 1st, Helena, 3rd dau. of Col. Richard Townsend, of Castle Townsend, co. Cork, and has issue,
1. ARTHUR TOWNSEND, his heir.
2. Arthur, Rector of Myross, m. Mary, dau. of Thomas Herbert, M.P., of Muckruss, and had issue.
1. Helena, m. 1786, George Daunt, of Newborough, co. Cork.
Arthur Herbert m. 2ndly, Jane, dau. of the Rev. Thomas Collis, and widow of Frederick Mullins, of Burnham, eldest brother of the 1st Baron Ventry, and d. 1760, aged 37, having had issue by her,
2. Frances, m. 1794, Richard Digby, of Cork.
The eldest son,
RICHARD TOWNSEND HERBERT, of Cahirnane and Currens, for many years in the Irish Parliament, s. to Currens on his father's death, and inherited Cahirnane by will from his grand-uncle, Arthur Herbert, of Cahirnane and Brewsterfield. He m. 1st, Emily, dau. of Thomas Herbert, M.P. for Muckruss, and by her had issue,
1. Emily,   2. Anne.
He m. 2ndly, Jane, dau. of Anthony Stoughton, of Ballyhorgan, and had issue,
1. ARTHUR, his heir.
2. Thomas (Sir), K.C.B., Rear-Admiral R.N., b. 1793; served in the China War and afterwards commanded the Naval forces on the S.E. coast of America; was a Lord of the Admiralty from Feb. to Dec. 1852, and M.P. for Dartmouth. Sir Thomas was High Sheriff co. Kerry 1829, and a Deputy-Lieut.
3. Richard (Rev.), d. unm.
4. Charles, General in the Army, served in the Indian Mutiny.
3. Elizabeth, m. Samuel Butcher, Admiral R.N., and had issue,
    1. Samuel Butcher, D.D., Bishop of Meath.
    2. Richard George Butcher, M.D., ex-President of the Royal College of Surgeons, Ireland.
    3. Arthur Butcher, Col. Royal Marines.
    4. John Barlow Butcher, Capt. Royal Marines.
4. Helen, m. Rev. Barry Denny, and has issue.
5. Jane.
6. Penelope Antonia, m. Francis Chute, of Chute Hall. He d. 12 Aug. 1849. She d. 7 May, 1870, leaving issue (*see that family*).
7. Frances.
8. Anne, m. Rev. Browning Drew; and d. 1853.
9. Letitia, m. — Jackson, of co. Tipperary.
10. Mary, m. John Bourchier, of Smithville, co. Tipperary, and had issue (*see that family*).
The eldest son,
REV. ARTHUR HERBERT, of Cahirnane and Currens, Rector of Castle Island, co. Kerry, m. Jane, dau. of Rev. Maynard Denny, of Churchill, by Penelope Stoughton his wife, and d. 1832, having had issue,
1. RICHARD (Rev.), of Cahirnane and Currens, d. unm. 24 Feb. 1875.
2. HENRY, late of Cahirnane and Currens.
3. Arthur, Capt. 62nd Regt.
4. Charles, Major late 58th Regt., C.B., served with distinction in the New Zealand War.
5. Edward, Col. Kerry Regt. of Militia, d. unm. June, 1882.
6. Thomas, m. 1866, Emily, dau. of Lieut.-Col. Colthurst, and has issue,
    1. Arthur Colthurst, Capt. Warwickshire Regt., b. 4 May, 1867.
    2. Percy Thomas Colthurst, Capt. R.A., b. 16 Aug. 1868.
    3. Cecil.
1. Penelope, m. Arthur Maynard Denny, grandson of Admiral Lord Collingwood, and has issue.
The 2nd son,
HENRY HERBERT, of Cahirnane, Currens, and Dunkerron, co. Kerry, J.P., High Sheriff 1879, b. 15 March, 1818; m. 1 Aug. 1865, Katharine Elizabeth, dau. of Rev. Edward Stewart, of Sparsholt, Winchester, by Louisa his wife, eldest dau. of Charles John Herbert, of Muckruss, and d. 18 Jan. 1898, leaving issue,
1. ARTHUR STEWART, now of Cahirnane.
1. Winifred, m. 1895, George Ruttledge, and d. 1896.
2. Kathleen Olive, m. 1901, Herbert Everett.
3. Violet Ina Jane.
4. Gwendolen Egerton.

Arms—(*See* HERBERT *of Muckruss*).

Seat—Cahirnane, Killarney; Dunkerron Castle, Kenmare.

HERDMAN OF SION HOUSE.

EMERSON TENNENT HERDMAN, of Sion House, co. Tyrone, J.P. and D.L., High Sheriff 1890, b. 1842; m. 1864, Frances Alice, dau. of Francis John West, M.D., late Resident Physician, Omagh Lunatic Asylum, and has issue,
1. JOHN CLAUDIUS, Capt. 4th Batt. Royal Inniskilling Fus., b. 1876; m. 1901, Maud Harriet, dau. of Major-Gen. Alexander Clark-Kennedy, of Camus, co. Tyrone.
1. Adelia Maud.
2. Elizabeth Alice, m. 1893, Capt. Ambrose St. Quintin Ricardo, D.S.O., Royal Inniskilling Fusiliers (*see* RICARDO *of Bromesberrow Place*).
3. Frances Evelyn, m. 1889, Frederick W. Sherwin, Capt. Royal Inniskilling Fusiliers.
4. Olive Mary, m. 11 Sept. 1895, Emerson Crawford Herdman, High Sheriff co. Tyrone 1899, only son of the late John Herd-

Herrick.

man (who d. 26 July, 1903), D.L. co. Donegal, High Sheriff 1899-1900 and of co. Tyrone 1894, of Carricklee, Strabane, co. Tyrone.
5. Gertrude Isabel.

Mr. Herdman is the son of James Herdman, of Bath and of Strabane, co. Tyrone, who m. 1840, Elizabeth Suffern, and grand-nephew of the late Sir James Emerson-Tennent, Bart.

Seat—Sion House, Sion, co. Tyrone. *Club*—Ulster, Belfast.

TABUTEAU-HERRICK OF SHIPPOOL.

MARY ELIZA TA-BUTEAU-HERRICK, of Shippool, co. Cork, s. her mother 1903; m. 30 June, 1868, Rev. Augustus Tabuteau, late Capt. 65th Regt., by whom she has issue,
 1. AUGUSTUS WILLIAM, F.R.C.S.I. (228A, *Romford Road, Forest Gate, Essex*), b. 16 July, 1869; m. Jenny Frances, dau. of — Hill, County Inspector, R.I.C., and has issue,
  Thomas Bousfield Herrick, b. July, 1894.
  Olive Frances.
 2. James Hugh, b. 29 March, 1872; m. Alice Catherine, dau. of — Braisted, of Oaklands, California.
 3. Edgar Olivier, b. 22 Jan. 1876.
 4. Frederick Joseph, b. 12 Sept. 1877.
 5. Henry Gordon, late Lieut. Army Veterinary Corps, b. 3 Feb. 1883.
 1. Eilie Augusta, b. 16 Dec. 1874; m. May, 1897, Ernest Edwin Lucas, of Sheffield.
 2. Mary Violet, b. 12 Jan. 1881.

The Rev. Augustus Tabuteau, who was b. 27 Oct. 1840, and served in the Maori War, 1863-65 (medal, mentioned in despatches), adopted the additional surname of Herrick.

Lineage.—(of HERRICK)
JOHN HERRICK, b. 1612, accompanied the Duke of Ormonde to Ireland 1641. He m. twice, and d. 8 Aug. 1689, leaving by his 1st wife, a son, GERSHOM, and by the 2nd, two sons and a dau. John, Francis, and Mary. To his 2nd son, John, he bequeathed an estate in the Barony of Ibane. To his eldest son,
 GERSHOM HERRICK, of Shippool, he devised that estate; this gentleman was b. 1665, and m. 1st, 1693, Susanna, only dau. and heir of Smithin Smart, by Frances his wife, dau. of Edward Riggs, of Riggsdale, co. Cork, by whom he had, with a dau., Mary, five sons,
  1. EDWARD, his heir.
  2. James.
  3. John.
  4. Henry.
  5. George.
Mr. Herrick m. 2ndly, 1715, Margaret, widow of Lieut.-Col. Capel, of Brigadier Sankey's Regt., and had another son,
 6. THOMAS, of Coolkerkey, m. 1749, Catherine, dau. of Jasper Lucas, of Richfordstown, co. Cork, grand-dau. of Thomas Evans, of Milltown Castle, M.P., and had, with four younger sons, Jasper, Thomas, Edward, and Henry, an elder son,
  GERSHOM, of Coolkerkey, m. 1749, Susan, sister of John Rashleigh, of Cloncoose, co. Cork, and with a younger son, Gershom (who m. Miss S. Whitmore), and two daus., Dora and Katherine, who d. unm., an elder son,
   THOMAS, of Coolkerkey, m. 1834, Katherine, dau. of Thomas Wade Foot, of Springfort, co. Cork (see FOOT *of Carrigacunna Castle*), and had issue,
    1. GERSHOM, now of Coolkerkey, Major Royal Lancaster Militia, formerly an Officer in the 5th (Fusiliers), b. 1835; m. 1868, Fanny, dau. of John Nicholls, of Shrewton House, Wilts, and has issue,
     a. Thomas, m. 16 Jan. 1901, Marion Eva, eldest dau. of late Montague C. Barker, of Hampton Court.
     b. Gershom.   a. Kathleene Rashleigh.
    2. Thomas, Capt. 4th West India Regt., d. unm.
     1. Katherine Foot, m. Rev. Thomas Howe, R.N.
Mr. Herrick d. 1730, and was s. by his eldest son,
 EDWARD HERRICK, of Shippool, b. 1694; m. 1728, Elizabeth, dau. of Caleb Falkiner, of the city of Cork, and had six sons and two daus. The 2nd son. Edward, Lieut. R.N., was killed on board the *Dorsetshire*, in Sir Edward Hawke's action, 20 Sept. 1759. The eldest son,
  FALKINER HERRICK, of Shippool, b. 1729; m. 1st, June, 1752, Sarah, eldest dau. of Thomas Bousfield, of Cork, and had issue.
   1. THOMAS BOUSFIELD, his heir.
   2. Francis, Capt. 27th Regt., killed at Guadaloupe, 1795.
   1. Jane, m. Rev. Ambrose Hickey.
   2. Elizabeth, d. unm. aged 36.

Mr. Herrick m. 2ndly, 22 July, 1763, Harriet Graham, and d. 28 June, 1775. He was s. by his son,
 THOMAS BOUSFIELD HERRICK, of Shippool, b. 1754; m. 1788, Annie, only dau. of Henry Moore, of Hoddersfield, co. Cork, and by her (who m. 2ndly, 1798, Daniel Cudmore, and d. 1820) had issue,
  1. William Henry, of Shippool.
  2. Henry Moore, Capt. 45th Regt., killed at Badajos, unm.
  3. Edward, Capt. R.N., b. 18 Oct. 1793; m. 13 Feb. 1836, Charlotte, only dau. of Capt. Thomas Alexander, R.N., C.B., and left issue,
   1. Arthur, 54th Regt., b. 20 Dec. 1836, dec.
   2. Edward, R.N., b. 17 June, 1845.
   1. Charlotte, d. unm.   2. Henrietta, dec.
  1. Ann, m. Jan. 1818, Richard Plummer Davies, Capt. R.N.
Mr. Herrick d. 1796, and was s. by his eldest son,
 WILLIAM HENRY HERRICK, of Shippool, J.P., Capt. R.N., b. 13 Feb. 1784; m. 8 Sept. 1814, Mary, only dau. of Robert De la Cour, of Bear Forest, co. Cork, and by her (who d. 2 July, 1854, aged 60) had issue,
  1. THOMAS BOUSFIELD, late of Shippool.
  2. William Henry, b. 9 Feb. 1824, late Capt. 51st Regt.; m. 22 June, 1848, Anne Sophia, 2nd dau. of Chambre Corker, of Cor Castle, co. Cork, and has a dau., Caroline Victoria Mary.
  3. Benjamin Bousfield (*Hurstbury, Lindfield, Hayward's Heath*), b. 18 Feb. 1826, Major-Gen. Royal Marines; m. 1st, 21 Feb. 1856, Caroline, youngest dau. of Capt. Biggs, of the 60th Rifles, and 2ndly, 25 Feb. 1879, Harriet Stephanie, only dau. of Lieut.-Col. Collingwood Fenwick, 76th Regt. By his 1st wife he has issue,
   Henry Bousfield, m. 22 Jan. 1880, Gwenllian, dau. of Capt. Herbert Lloyd, 21st Madras N.I., youngest son of John W. Lloyd, of Danyralt, co. Carmarthen, and has issue,
    1. Eustace, b. 20 Sept. 1889.
    1. Kathleen Mary Gwenllian.   2. Clare Mary.
    3. Rachael Mary.   4. Betta Mary.
   Alice, m. 1st, 5 Feb. 1879, Sir Peyton E. Skipwith, Bart., and has issue (see BURKE's *Peerage*). Sir Peyton d. 12 May, 1891. She m. 2ndly, 1 June, 1892, John Hugh Ward-Broughton-Leigh, late Maj. 4th Batt. Royal Warwickshire Regt., and by him has issue a son and a dau.
  4. James Hugh, b. 13 Dec. 1830, Capt. West Cork Artillery, d. 1872.
  1. Mary de la Cour, m. 6 Jan. 1836, Richard Corbett, M.D., of Cork, and d. 31 March, 1847.
  2. Annie Harriet, m. 21 Aug. 1841, John Campbell Meade, of Innishannon, co. Cork.
  3. Louisa Josephine Pettitot.
  4. Georgiana Henrietta, m. 1888, William Nicholas Wrixon Becher, D.L., son of the late Sir William Wrixon Becher, Bart.
  5. Catherine de la Cour.
Mr. Herrick d. July, 1863, and was s. by his son,
 THOMAS BOUSFIELD HERRICK, of Shippool, J.P., b. 25 Feb. 1819; d. 6 Feb. 1892. He m. 23 April, 1844, Eliza Anne, second dau. of John Tonson Rye, of Rye Court, co. Cork (see *that family*) to whom he devised his estate and by whom he had issue,
  1. MARY ELIZA, Mrs. TABUTEAU-HERRICK, now of Shippool.
  2. Sophia Eliza, m. 1871, W. F. Burnett, and d. 1876.
  3. Georgina Adelaide, m. D. P. Sarsfield.
  4. Annie Thomasina, m. Lieut.-Col. Charles William Henry Evans, D.S.O., late Royal West Kent Regt. He d. 2 Nov. 1900.
Mrs. Herrick d. 2 Jan. 1903, and was s. by her eldest dau., Mrs. Tabuteau-Herrick, now of Shippool.

TABUTEAU.

PETER TABUTEAU, fled from France to Holland on the Revocation of the Edict of Nantes in 1685, and d. 14 March, 1691. He m. Elizabeth Flanc (who d. 26 June, 1725), and left a son,
 STEPHEN TABUTEAU, b. 10 Dec. 1669; m. 18 May, 1692, Renée (b. Sept. 1667), dau. of Gideon Bion by his wife, Marie La Motte, and had,
  1. Gideon, b. 22 July, 1694; d. at Utrecht 2 Aug. 1698.
  2. AUGUSTUS, his heir.
  1. Anne Renée, b. 2 May, 1701; d. 15 Feb. 1775; m. 10 June, 1725, Daniel Olivier, of London and Rotterdam.
The younger son,
 AUGUSTUS TABUTEAU, b. 24 April 1696; naturalized 27 Feb. 1721, d. in Bengal; m. 6 Aug. 1724, Henrietta Madeleine Brions (b. 6 Aug. 1699; d. 1767), and had two sons and two daus.,
  1. GIDEON, his heir.
  2. Stephen, b. 6 March, 1730; d. 5 June, 1751.
  1. Henrietta, b. 30 Oct. 1725; d. at Tullamore 7 May, 1805.
  2. Anne, b. 8 July, 1731; d. an infant.
The elder son,
 GIDEON TABUTEAU, of Southampton, and afterwards of Tullamore, King's Co., b. 22 March, 1728; d. 27 Dec. 1805; m. 24 Dec. 1753, Mary Butin (b. 10 Oct. 1727; d. 2 March, 1785, at Tullamore), and had a son and a dau.,
  JOSEPH BRIONS, his heir.
  Anne, b. 4 April, 1758; d. 16 May, 1748; m. 22 Oct. 1786, Anthony Mobére, of Amsterdam, who d. 9 Jan. 1801.
The only son,
 JOSEPH BRIONS TABUTEAU, of Tullamore, M.D., b. 18 Feb. 1759; d. 5 April, 1817; m. 20 Jan. 1795, Eleanor, dau. of Benjamin Batt, by Eleanor Elliott his wife, and by her (who was b. 8 Oct. 1765, and d. 17 June, 1825) had issue that survived infancy three sons and a dau.,
  1. Augustus Elliott, of Portarlington, J.P., King's Co., b. 2 Jan. 1797; d. April, 1874; m. 26 March, 1830, Anne Maria Manly, and had,
   1. Augustus Olivier, b. 5 Oct. 1831; d.
   2. Joseph Manly, M.A., M.B. (Dublin), J.P. King's and Queen's Cos. (*Kilmalogue House, Portarlington*), b. 3 Aug. 1844; m.

11 May, 1875, Louise Maria, dau. of Capt. George Grant Webb, 6th R. Dragoons, and has issue,
  (1) Augustus Elliott, *b.* 2 Oct. 1880, Paymaster R.N.
  (2) George Grant, *b.* 19 Nov. 1881, Capt. R.A.M.C.
  (1) Louisa.
  1. Elizabeth, *m.* 11 Oct. 1853, Rev. John Pim, of New Park, co. Kildare.
  2. Ellen, *m.* 1st, 9 July, 1861, Digby William Lawlor, 25th K.O.B. (*d.* 13 May, 1866); 2ndly, Samuel Lane Popham, R.A.M.C.
  3. Henrietta Augusta.   4. Anne Molière.
  5. Sarah Christina.
2. Joseph, *b.* 11 June, 1798; *d.* Sept. 1879, Resident Magistrate, Ireland; *m.* 15 May, 1832, Ellen, 2nd dau. of Thomas Crowe, J.P., of the Abbey, Ennis, co. Clare (*see* CROWE *of Dromore*), and had two sons and a dau.,
  1. Joseph Olivier, *b.* 3 Aug. 1835, C.E.; *m.* 21 June, 1860, Agnes MacIvor Paterson, and has,
    (1) Augustus Joseph Olivier, *b.* 27 March, 1861.
    (2) Henry, *b.* 8 March, 1862.
    (3) Charles, *b.* 3 Feb. 1868.
    (4) Joseph.
    (1) Ellen Mona.
    (2) Beatrice Alice.
    (3) Ida Augusta.
  2. William Augustus (Rev.), *b.* 27 Oct. 1840, formerly Capt. 65th Regt., *m.* 30 June, 1868, Mary Eliza (now of Shippool) eldest dau. of Thomas Bousfield Herrick, of Shippool, *as above.*
    1. Henrietta, *b.* 7 March, 1843; *m.* 16 Dec. 1868, James Daniel Crowe, Col. R.A.M.C. (*Southsea, Hants*).
  3. Bartholomew Molière, of Simmonscourt Castle, co. Dublin, Consul for the Netherlands in Dublin, and Knight of the Lion, *b.* 25 May, 1799; *d.* 6 July, 1869; *m.* 30 Dec. 1824, Mary Jane, dau. of William Mayne, of Freame Mount, co. Monaghan, and by her (who *d.* 8 July, 1876) had fourteen children, of whom eight sons and three daus. survived infancy,
    1. Joseph Molière, *b.* 5 Jan. 1828; *d.* 4 Dec. 1880; *m.* 17 Sept. 1853, Catherine Gamson (*d.* 21 June, 1888), and had,
      (1) Joseph Molière, *b.* 27 Nov. 1854.
      (2) Charles Augustus, *b.* 23 Feb. 1856.
      (3) Walter James, *b.* Dec. 1860.
    2. William Augustus, *b.* 12 Aug. 1832; *d.* in Africa, March, 1854.
    3. Augustus, *b.* 28 Sept. 1833; *d.* 2 June, 1880, Lieut. R.N.; *m.* 28 Oct. 1872, Ida Augusta Barney, and had two daus.,
      (1) Viva Bertha.   (2) Ina Mary.
    4. Anthony Olivier, *b.* 23 Feb. 1835; *d.* 23 Aug. 1897, Lieut.-Col. 93rd Highlanders; *m.* 24 Jan. 1870, Mary Stanley, dau. of John Stanley McGowan, Collector of Customs, Bengal, and by her (who *d.* 11 Nov. 1870) had a dau.,
      Mary Stanley, *d.* 9 Oct. 1876.
    5. Thomas Rooke, *b.* 7 April, 1838, Col. Indian Army.
    6. Richard Mayne, of Oldville, Sandymount, co. Dublin, *b.* 24 Aug. 1840; *m.* 9 Feb. 1866, Constance Gertrude Maria, only dau. of Hon. Patrick Plunket (*see* PLUNKET, Baron), and has,
      (1) Ernest Richard Plunket, *b.* 7 Nov. 1866.
      (2) Lionel Richard Plunket, *b.* 12 March, 1869; *m.* 21 April, 1893, Eva Hamilton, eldest dau. of Keith Hamilton Hallowes, and has three daus.,
        1. Muriel Flora.   2. Norah Constance.
        3. Ruth Eva.
      (3) Harold Richard Plunket, *b.* 16 Sept. 1872.
      (4) Frank Richard Plunket, *b.* 18 Jan. 1883.
      (1) Naomi Constance Plunket.
      (2) Violet Constance Plunket.
      (3) Mabel Constance Plunket.
      (4) Lily Constance Plunket.
    7. Edward Mayne, *b.* 25 Oct. 1841; *m.* 22 Nov. 1865, Anna Rochfort Haynes, and has,
      (1) Thomas Edward, *b.* 20 March, 1871; *d.* 1895.
      (2) Joseph Augustus Molière, *b.* 26 Feb. 1873.
      (3) Richard Arthur, *b.* 17 Nov. 1874.
      (1) Harriette.   (2) Anne.
    8. Molière, of Bembridge, Isle of Wight, *b.* 28 Oct. 1845; *m.* 14 July, 1870, Elizabeth Harriet, only child of Henry McGeough, and has,
      (1) Claude Henry Molière, *b.* 17 Sept. 1873.
      (2) Reginald Molière, *b.* 6 Aug. 1879; Lieut. R.N.; *m.* 30 July, 1910, Rose Margaret Sharpe.
      (3) Rupert Rochfort Molière, *b.* 20 March, 1889.
      (1) Ether Mary Nita.   (2) Kathleen Nita.
      (3) Helen Nita.   (4) Winifred Anne Nita.
      (5) Madeleine Anne Nita.   (6) Renée Nita.
  1. Harriet Thomasine, *d.* 16 Feb. 1861; *m.* 14 Aug. 1856, Col. Arthur Herbert Leahy, R.E. (*see* LEAHY *of Carriglea*).
  2. Ellen, *m.* 3 July, 1855, Rev. John William Robinson, M.A.
  3. Anne Marie, *d.* 29 Dec. 1869; *m.* 26 Jan. 1858, Duncan Macpherson MacNab.
1. John, *m.* 3 Dec. 1833, Thomas Slater Rooke.

Arms—(of TABUTEAU) Arg. a fess gu. between three erm. spots.
Crest—An erm. spot sa.   *Motto*—Toujours sans tache.
Seat—Shippool, near Innishannon, co. Cork.

HERVEY OF KILLIANE.

CHARLES WILLIAM ARTHUR HERVEY, *b.* 26 Jan. 1855; *m.* 11 Feb. 1893, Clare, dau. of the late Sir Edmund Harrison, K.C.B., and widow of I. H. Webster.

Lineage—FRANCIS HARVEY (3rd son of Richard Harvey, of Lyme Regis) Dorset, Merchant, and grandson of John Harvey, of Meldreth, having been taken in arms by Prince Rupert, was committed, with other prisoners, to the jail at Exeter, at the beginning of the rebellion; and on being liberated went to Lyme Regis, and became a merchant in that town, of which he was chosen Mayor, 1644, and admitted a freeman. After the year 1649 he obtained a grant of lands in co. Wexford which were confirmed him under the Act of Settlement. He was M.P. for Clonmines 1661, Mayor of Wexford 1671, and High Sheriff co. Wexford 1666. He *m.* Katharine Plunket, by whom, who *d.* Dec. 1710, he had issue,
  1. JOHN, his heir.
  2. Richard, living at Cork 1663.
  1. Katherine, *m.* Feb. 1676, Joshua Nunn, of St. Margarets.

Mr. Harvey *d.* Nov. 1692, and was *s.* by his son,
JOHN HARVEY, of Killiane Castle, M.P. for Wexford 1695, and High Sheriff of the co. 1694. He *m.* 19 Oct. 1675, Elizabeth, dau. of James Stopford, of Saltersford, co. Chester, and New Hall, co. Meath, ancestor of the Earl of Courtown, and had issue,
  1. JAMES (Rev.), his heir.
  2. Francis, Capt. R.N., *d.s.p.*
  3. William, *d.s.p.*   4. Richard, *d.s.p.*
  5. John, bapt. 18 Feb. 1688, Lieut. 30th Regt., *d.s.p.*
  1. Elizabeth, *m.* Richard Rowe, of Ballyharty.
  2. Katherine, *m.* William Welman, of New Ross.
  3. Mary, *m.* Cornelius Donovan, of Clonmore.
  4. Amelia, *m.* Benjamin Betts, of Wexford.
  5. Susan, *m.* Rev. William Harvey, of Bargy.

Mr. Harvey *d.* Sept. 1707, and was *s.* by his son,
THE REV JAMES HARVEY, of Killiane Castle, Rector of Rathaspect, *b.* 1676; *m.* Martha, dau. of John Beauchamp, of Ballyloughane, co. Carlow, by Katherine his wife, dau. of Bartholomew Vigors, Bishop of Ferns and Leighlin, by whom, who *d.* 23 Dec. 1760, he had issue,
  1. JOHN, his heir.
  2. Vigors, Lieut. 16th Regt., *m.* Sarah, dau. of William Watson, of Pitsmoore, co. York, and *d.s.p.*
  3. James, of Wigan, co. Lancaster, Capt. 7th Regt., *m.* Cecily, dau. and heiress of Robert Leigh, eldest son of Alexander Leigh, of Hindley Hall, and had issue,
    1. Robert John, of Farnham, co. York, Col. in the Army, *m.* Elizabeth, dau. and heiress of Thomas Bickerdyke, of Farnham, co. York, and had issue.
    2. James Leigh, Capt. 33rd Regt.
    1. Martha Cecilia, *d. unm.* 1791.
  4. Francis, *d.s.p.*   5. Bartholomew, *d.s.p.*
  1. Martha, *m.* Francis Harvey, of Bargy Castle.
  2. Katharine, *m.* Philip Palliser, of Castletown.

Mr. Harvey *d.* 16 June, 1760, aged 84, and was *s.* by his son,
JOHN HARVEY, of Killiane Castle, Capt. 16th Regt. of Foot, *m.* Martha Rowe, and dying 1763, left an only child,
JOHN HARVEY, of Killiane Castle, *b.* 1751. High Sheriff co. Wexford 1775; *m.* May, 1772, Dorothy (*b.* 2 Jan. 1756), eldest dau. of Major Loftus Cliffe, and by her (who *d.* 1813) had issue,
  1. VIGORS, his heir.
  1. Anne, *m.* 1st, James Gildea, of Coslough, co. Mayo, and 2ndly, Ralph Nash, of Cahirconlish, co. Limerick.
  2. Martha, *d. unm.*
  3. Dorothy, *m.* 7 Dec. 1798, William Harvey, of Mount Pleasant.
  4. Barbara, *m.* 1st, 1798, Richard Lambart, of Bristol, and 2ndly, Arthur Meadows, of Hermitage.
  5. Mary, *m.* Henry Archer, of Ballyseskin.
  6. Frances, *m.* 1809, Very Rev. Samuel Adams, of Northlands, co. Cavan, Dean of Cashel, and had issue (*see that family*).

Mr. Harvey *d.* 29 May, 1796, and was *s.* by his son,
VIGORS HERVEY, of Killiane Castle, co. Wexford, and of Hamnerton Hall, co. York, B.A. Oxford, *b.* 12 Dec. 1794, who, in 1818, assumed by royal permission, the name of HERVEY in lieu of Harvey. He *m.* 26 Nov. 1816, Frances Margaretta, sister of Sir Charles Shakerley, 1st bart. of Somerford, and by her (who *m.* 2ndly, 1832, Thomas Read Kemp, of Kemp Town, Brighton, M.P., and *d.* 27 Aug. 1861) he left at his decease, 1827, an only child,
CHARLES JOHN VIGORS HERVEY, of Killiane, co. Wexford, *b.* 29 Nov. 1817; *d.* 29 March, 1904; *m.* 24 July, 1839, Martha, dau. of Thomas Read Kemp, of Kemp Town, Brighton, M.P., by Frances his wife, dau. of Sir Francis Baring, 1st bart. of Larkbeer, and by her (who *d.* 9 July, 1900), had issue,
  1. CHARLES WILLIAM ARTHUR, now of Killiane,

1. Lydia, m. 1st, Arthur Hainguerlot, of Chaalis, France. He d. 1892. She m. 2ndly, 1894, Prince Murat, who d. 1901. She d. 1901.
2. Blanche Maud, m. Alfred Goldsmith, of the Mazeraies, France, and has issue. He d. 1908.
3. Marie Augusta, m. John Coupland, of Goscote Hall, Leicester, and has issue.

Arms—Gu., on a bend arg. three trefoils slipped vert. Crest—A cat-a-mountain ppr. bezanté ducally collared or, holding in the dexter paw a trefoil slipped vert. Motto—Je n'oublieray jamais.
Residence—1, Norfolk Crescent, Hyde Park, W.

LUDLOW-HEWITT OF CLANCOOLE.

Rev. Thomas Arthur Ludlow - Hewitt, of Clancoole, co. Cork, J.P., b. 17 May, 1850; assumed by Royal Licence (Heralds' Coll. 1857) the surname and arms of Hewitt upon inheriting the estates of his maternal grandfather; m. 5 Oct. 1882, Edith Anne, only dau. of the late A. R. Hudson, of Wick House, Pershore, co. Worcester, and has issue,

1. Alfred Arthur Thomas, b. 3 Aug. 1884, m. 13 Sept. 1908, Margery, only dau. of late H. Moseley, Linacre Professor, Oxon.
2. Edgar Rainey, Royal Irish Rifles, b. 9 June, 1886.
3. Harry Balfour Cedric, b. 17 May, 1888.
1. Edith Caroline Annette, b. 10 May, 1892.
2. Mary Dorinda Elizabeth b. 7 July, 1894.

Lineage.—Thomas Hewitt, of Clancoole, co. Cork, b. 1668 ; m. Mary Synge, who d. 1706. His 2nd son,
Isaac Hewitt, of Clancoole, inherited the estate at the death, s.p., 1713, of his elder brother, Thomas ; and bad three sons,
1. Thomas. 2. William. 3. George.
His eldest son,
Thomas Hewitt, of Clancoole, b. 1706; m. 1st, Mary, dau. of Col. John Freke, of Garretstown. She d. 7 June, 1737. He m. 2ndly, Dorothy Brome, and was s. by his eldest son,
Isaac Hewitt, of Clancoole, m. 1st, 1756, Mary Bernard, of Castle Bernard, but she d.s.p. He m. 2ndly, Frances Gertrude Wall (who m. 2ndly, William Honnor), and d.s.p., when he was s. by his brother,
Henry Hewitt, of Clancoole, m. Judith Browne, but d.s.p., and was s. by his brother,
Charles Hewitt, of Clancoole, m. Letitia, dau. of James Wall, of Coolnamuck, co. Waterford, and had issue,
1. Thomas Wall, his heir. 2. Charles.
3. Isaac, m. Miss Beamish, of Kilmalroda, co. Cork, and has issue.
He d. 1809, when he was s. by his eldest son,
Thomas Wall Hewitt, of Clancoole, b. 1776 ; m. 1812, Anne Lloyd, of Dongay, and co-heiress of Lloyd of Berghill, Ellesmere ; and d. 1857, leaving an only dau.,
Annette, m. 25 Feb. 1843, Rev. Arthur Rainey Ludlow, of Durrant, co. Devon. He d. 9 Jan. 1890, leaving issue,
1. Thomas Arthur, now of Clancoole.
1. Anne Jane, d. 1908.
2. Katharine Dorinda, m. 12 Feb. 1874, Rev. Francis Rohde Carbonell, Vicar of Fairford, Gloucester, and has issue, two daus.
3. Margaret Lloyd, m. 1882, E. Rouse, M.D., of Bideford, Devon. and has two daus. He d. 1897.
4. Mary Agnes. d. 1855.
5. Agnes Elizabeth, m. 3 March, 1903, Col. J. Millard Eden, late Queen's Own West Kent Regt., of Pebworth, co. Gloucester, and Bournemouth, Hants.

Family of Ludlow.

Christopher Ludlow, 1647, m. Mary Pennell, of Chipping-Sodbury, co. Gloucester, and had, with other issue, a son,
Ebenezer Ludlow, b. 1695 ; m. Mary Adey, and d. 1760, leaving a son,
Daniel Ludlow, b. 1720; m. Rachael, dau. of G. Hardwicke, of Tytherington, Gloucester, and d. 1801, leaving (with other issue) a son,
Ebenezer Ludlow, b. 1744 ; m. Katherine Wallis, of Tortworth, Gloucester, and d. 1769, leaving (with other issue) a son,

Ebenezer Ludlow, of Oaklands, co. Gloucester, Serjeant-at-Law, and Commissioner of the Court of Bankruptcy in England, b. 1777 ; m. 28 Aug. 1804, Jane Rainey, and d. 1851, leaving (with other issue) a son,
Rev. Arthur Rainey Ludlow, b. 7 May, 1810, m. as above, Annette Hewitt.

Arms—Arg., two chevronels indented gu. between three owls ppr. Crest—The trunk of a tree fesswise eradicated ppr. therefrom rising a falcon belled or tretty gu. in the beak an acorn slipped also ppr. Motto—Tam nocte quam die sapere.
Seat—Clancoole, Bandon, co. Cork. Residence—Minety Vicarage, Malmesbury.

HEWITT. See Burke's Peerage, LIFFORD, V.

HEYGATE. See Burke's Peerage, HEYGATE, Bart.

HIBBERT OF WOODPARK.

Robert Fiennes Hibbert, of Woodpark, co. Galway, and Bucknell, co. Oxford, J.P. for Galway, late Lieut. Queen's Bays, b. 1 June, 1860 ; m. 4 Oct. 1887, Florence Jane, only child of the late Philip Villiers-Reade, of Woodpark, co. Galway, and has issue,
1. Leicester Robert, b. 23 Nov. 1888.
2. Aubrey Philip John, b. 19 Dec. 1892.

Mr. Hibbert is the eldest son of the late Col. Frederick Drummond Hibbert, of Chalfont Park, Bucks, who d. 20 Sept. 1897, and Hester Louisa, his wife, who d. 1 July, 1894, dau. and co-heir of Fienness Trotman, of Bucknell Manor, Oxford (see HIBBERT of Crofton Grange).

Lineage.—Philip Reade, of Wood Town, co. Westmeath (eldest son of Rev. Philip Reade), m. 1695, Mary Palmer, of Ballyboggin, co. Kildare, and with a dau., Anne, m. John Hopkins, of Dardistown, co. Meath, had two sons,
1. Philip, his heir.
2. Daniel, m. Jane Purdon, of co. Westmeath.
The elder son and heir,
Rev. Philip Reade, D.D., of Wood Town, b. 1695 ; m. 1st, 1748, Margaret, dau. of Thomas Featherstonhaugh, of Bracklyn Castle, co. Westmeath, and 2ndly, 1770, Elizabeth, dau. of William Smyth, of Drumcree, M.L. co. Westmeath, and by the former only had issue,
1. John, Barrister-at-Law, m. 1787, Martha, only dau. of Francis Hopkins, and sister of Sir Francis Hopkins, Bart., and by her had an only child,
Frances Catherine of Wood Town, co. Meath, who d. unm. 1853.
2. William Francis.
The younger son,
William Francis Reade, of Woodpark, m. 1788, Jane Peacock, only dau. and heir of Edward Borr, of New Park, co. Meath, by Jane his wife, only child and heir of William Peacock, of Tinne Park, King's Co., and had issue,
1. Philip, his heir.
2. Edward Borr, m. Jane, dau. of Robert Carew, of Woodtown, co. Tipperary, and has issue,
1. William. 2. Robert Carew.
3. Philip. 4. Edward.
1. Frances. 2. Jane Peacock.
1. Jane Peacock, d. unm.
2. Maria Peacock, m. Rev. Robert de la Pere Robinson, of Ballynavin Castle, co. Tipperary.
3. Jessie Louisa, d. unm.
Mr. Reade d. 10 Sept. 1801, and was s. by his eldest son,
Philip Reade, of Woodpark, J.P., M.A., Barrister-at-Law, b. 1793; m. 28 April, 1829, Grace, youngest dau. of John Rutherfoord, of St. Doulough's, co. Dublin (the eldest male representative of the Rutherfoords of Ashentilly, co. Perth), and d. 1883, leaving issue,
1. Philip William Villiers, b. Sept. 1839 ; m. 8 March, 1862, Caroline Charlotte, only dau. of Robert Dupré Alexander, and grand-dau. of Sir Robert Alexander, 2nd bart. of the city of Dublin, and d. 21 Aug. 1874, leaving by her (who m. 2ndly, 18 July, 1878, Leicester Hibbert, of Chalfont, co. Bucks) an only child,
Florence Jane, now of Woodpark, m. (as above) 4 Oct. 1887, Robert Fiennes Hibbert.
1. Sarah Rosanna, d. unm. 7 June, 1902.
2. Jane Peacock Maria, m. 6 May, 1853, Joseph C. Rutherfoord, of Lynbury, co. Westmeath, but d. Jan. 1877, leaving issue.

Seat—Woodpark, Scariff, co. Galway. Residence—The Weir House, Alresford, Hants. Club—Army and Navy, S.W.

IRELAND. Hickman.

HICKIE OF KILELTON.

WILLIAM SCOTT HICKIE, of Kilelton, co. Kerry, J.P. co. Kerry, Hon. Col. and Lieut.-Col. commanding 4th Batt. Royal Munster Fusiliers 1892-6, b. 5 July, 1854; m. 27 April, 1887, Constance Mary, dau. of Henry Knight, of Cloakham, Devon, and has issue.

Lineage.—The family of Hickie, or O'Hicky, descend from Eochy Baldearg, of the race of Cormac Cas, King of Munster. They were formerly chiefs of a district in the co. of Clare. The estates of James Hickie, in the Barony of Tulla, co. Clare, were confiscated in 1652, and granted to Cromwellian settlers, the confiscation being confirmed by Act of Settlement, 1666, whereupon his son,
 WILLIAM HICKIE, settled at Kilelton, co. Kerry. His son,
 WILLIAM HICKIE, of Kilelton, m. 1682, Pomel, dau. and coheir of John Edmonds, of Asdee, descendant and representative of Anthony Edmonds, by Margaret O'Conor, dau. of John O'Conor, of Carrigafoyle, "O'Conor Kerry," thus becoming possessed of the lands of East and West Asdee, which escaped confiscation, and the estate of West Asdee came into the possession of the Hickie family. William Hickie was s. by his son,
 WILLIAM HICKIE, of Kilelton, m. 1720, Phillis, dau. of James Trant, of Dingle, by whom he had a son and heir,
 MICHAEL HICKIE, of Kilelton, m. 1767, Margaret, eldest dau. of Pierce Nagle, of Anakissy, co. Cork, and grandson of Pierce Nagle, who was the last Roman Catholic up to the passing of the Emancipation Act, that filled the office of High Sheriff for co. Cork, 1689, and who was brother of Sir Richard Nagle, M.P. for the co. Cork, and Attorney-General to King JAMES II. By Margaret Nagle his wife, Michael Hickie had a son,
 WILLIAM HICKIE, of Kilelton, J.P., b. 1768; m. 26 Nov. 1791, Jane, dau. of William Creagh, of Shanballymore, otherwise Old Court, co. Cork (see CREAGH of Ballyandrew), by whom (who d. 1829) he had issue. He d. 1847, and was s. by his son,
 WILLIAM HICKIE, of Kilelton, co. Kerry, and Janemount, co. Cork, J.P. for the cos. Cork and Kerry, and High Sheriff of the latter co. 1854, b. 4 April, 1796; m. 29 Jan. 1829, Maria, dau. of James Murphy, J.P., of Ringmaron Castle, co. Cork, and d. 11 May, 1856, having by her (who d. 11 Nov. 1869) had issue,
1. WILLIAM CREAGH, of whom presently.
2. James Francis, of Slevoyre, Borrisokane, co. Tipperary, J.P. (Clubs—United Service, Junior United Service), Lieut.-Col. (retired), served in the 7th Royal Fusiliers, b. 15 Aug. 1833; m. 20 Sept. 1862, Lucila Calista, 4th dau. of Don Pablo Lariosy Herreros de Tejada, of Laguna de Cameros, Old Castile; and by her (who d. 6 March, 1880) had issue,
 1. William Bernard, Lieut.-Col. and Bt. Col. commanding 1st Batt. Royal Fusiliers, b. 21 May, 1865.
 2. Arthur Francis (Rev.), late Maj. R.A., b. 28 Oct. 1866.
 3. Carlos Joseph, Capt. King's Own Yorkshire L.I., b. 10 Dec. 1872; m. 3 Sept. 1903, Edith, only dau. of the late Capt. M. H. Thunder, of Coolnagloose, and has issue,
  William Shamus Francis, b. 3 Jan. 1908.
  Dolores Calista, b. 25 July, 1905.
 4. Manuel Domingo, J.P. co. Tipperary, b. 24 Feb. 1875.
 1. Mary Pauline, m. 15 Sept. 1884, Sir Morgan Ross O'Connell, 4th Bart., of Lakeview, Killarney, and has issue (see BURKE'S Peerage).
 2. Amalia Maria Victoria, d. unm. 17 Sept. 1887.
 3. Lucila Concha.
 4. Dolores Mercedes, m. 19 Jan. 1901, Capt. Henry H. P. Deasy, late 16th Lancers, only surviving son of the late Right Hon. Lord Justice Deasy, and has issue.
 1. Mary Josephine, m. 28 Oct. 1853, William J. Murphy, of Richmond, co. Cork, and d. leaving issue.
 2. Jane Anne, d. unm. 28 Feb. 1850.

The elder son,
 WILLIAM CREAGH HICKIE, of Kilelton, co. Kerry, J.P. and D.L., High Sheriff 1873, b. 16 Dec. 1831; m. 29 Sept. 1853, Mary Ann Caroline, only child of the late Charles Davidson Scott (by his wife Jane Farrent Bidwell), and grand-dau. of John Scott, killed on board "The Victory" at the battle of Trafalgar, when Secretary to Lord Nelson, and d. 16 June, 1894, leaving issue.
1. WILLIAM SCOTT, now of Kilelton.
2. Charles Valentine, b. 14 Feb. 1856; Barrister-at-Law, English and Irish Bar; m. 17 Feb. 1887, Alice, dau. of the late James Harding, J.P., of Myrtle Hill, co. Cork. She is deceased.
3. James Francis, b. 2 Dec. 1859; d. 15 Oct. 1881.
4. Robert Eustace, b. 20 Sept. 1861; Physician and Surgeon, deceased.
1. Jane Frances, m. 8 Sept. 1881, Alexander John, 3rd son of Henry Knight, of Cloakham, Axminster, co. Devon, and has issue.
2. Mary Lucilla, d. 5 Feb. 1875.
3. Caroline Teresa.
4. Helen Ursula Creagh, m. 29 Sept. 1896, Joseph Vincent Galway Gaven.
5. Elizabeth Christine.
6. Agnes Lucila Wilhelmine, m. 30 July, 1898, Edward Valentine M'Carthy, of Ardmanagh House, Glenbrook, co. Cork, J.P., grandson of Alexis Richard, kinsman of late Cardinal Patrick, Archbishop of Paris, and has issue,
 Edward Justin Scott Hickie McCarthy, b. 28 Oct. 1899.

Seat—Kilelton, Ballylongford, co. Kerry.

HICKMAN OF FENLOE.

STOPFORD COSBY HICKMAN, of Fenloe, co. Clare, J.P. and D.L., High Sheriff 1909, Major R.A., b. 10 Aug. 1854; m. 1st, 1885, Mary, youngest dau. of Rev. Henry Charles Knightley, Vicar of Combroke, co. Warwick, and by her (who d. Nov. 1889) had issue,

 BERYL STOPFORD MARY, b. 28 Sept. 1889; m. 26 Oct. 1910, William Lewthwaite, elder son of William Lewthwaite, of Broadgate, co. Cumberland (see that family).

He m. 2ndly, 16 Oct. 1899, Mrs. R. Whitting, of 33, Sloane Gardens, S.W.

Lineage.—GREGORY HICKMAN, described in the family pedigree as 3rd son of Walter Hickman, of Kew, Surrey, ancestor of the Earls of Plymouth, was a Merchant of Hamburgh, where he m. Rhoda, dau. of Mr. Felton, Merchant; his 2nd wife was Jane, dau. of Nicholas Hubbert, of Dromore, in Ireland. By the 1st wife Gregory had a son,
1. THOMAS HICKMAN, of Barntic, co. Clare (whose will bears date 16 Sept. 1677); he m. the dau. of John Colpoys, of Ballycar, co. Clare, by whom he had, 1. THOMAS, his heir; 2. Dixie; 3. William, of Cork; 4. Andrew, Lieut. in the Army; 5. George, of Dublin, and four daus., 1. Anne, m. John Harrold, of Dublin, Merchant; 2. Rhoda, m. Hugh Perceval, of Gortnadrome, co. Clare, who d. 14 Sept. 1683 (Funeral Entry); 3. Elizabeth, m. Obadiah Dawson; and 4, Mary, d. unm. The son and heir,
 THOMAS HICKMAN, of Barntic, m. 1st, Gertrude, dau. of Brigadier-Gen. Core, of Clonroad, co. Clare, by whom he had, THOMAS, Capt. in the Army, d. unm., and three daus., Elizabeth, m. Beverly Usher, of Waterford; Jane, m. George Rose, of Cork; and Gertrude; by his 2nd wife, Elizabeth, dau. of Robert Stratford, of Baltinglass, he had three sons, Robert; Edward, who was a Cornet of Horse; and Charles, who d. at the Temple; and two daus., 1. Mary, m. William Wright, of Clontarf; 2. Henrietta, m. Thomas, youngest son of Hugh Hickman, of Fenloe.
 By his 2nd wife Gregory Hickman had, with two daus. (Jane, m. Col. Villiers Harrington, of Bagworth, co. Warwick, by whom she had a dau., Lucy, who was mother of Col. Taylor and Berkely Taylor, and Mary, m. Capt. Bernard, co. of Cork), three sons,
1. HENRY, of Kilmore, co. Clare, m. Elizabeth, dau. of Henry Hart, Commissary-General of Ireland, by whom he had two sons, 1. HENRY, of Kilmore, had a regiment in the reign of Queen ANNE. He m. Margaret, dau. of Sir William Poole, of Poole Hall, co. Devon, and by her had three sons, POOLE, Henry, and William and two daus., Susan, m. Mr. Bowles, an East India Merchant, and Sophia, d. unm. Of the sons, Henry, the 2nd son, was a Capt. in the Welsh Fusiliers, and William, the youngest, a Col. in the same Regt. The eldest son,
 POOLE HICKMAN, m. Mary, dau. of Mountiford Westropp, of Attyflinn, co. Clare, and d. 1753, leaving Henry Hickman, of Kilmore, Col. in the Army (d. 1872), and three daus.,
  1. Elizabeth, m. Robert Westropp, of Fort Anne, co. Clare.
  2. Margaret, m. Patrick Eneland.
  3. Jane.
 2. Walter, m. Bridget, dau. of Godfrey Greene.
3. Hugh. 4. HENRY.

The 4th son,
 HENRY HICKMAN, of Ballyket (who d. 1713), m. Honora, dau. and heir of Morrough M'Mahon, by whom he had three sons, Luke, George, and HUGH, of Fenloe, and three daus., Jane, m. George Colpoys; Katherine, m. Edward Vau Hogart, and afterwards Capt. Randall Jones; and Anne, m. — Gifford, Fort Major of Berwickupon-Tweed. Luke, the eldest son, d. unm.; George, the 2nd, m. Jane, dau. of Charles Fox, of Fox Hall, and by her had three sons, Anthony, of Ballyket, m. Eleanor Finch; Henry; and Fox; and several daus., Honora, m. Edward Turner, of London; Elizabeth, m. Charles Smyth, Collector of the co. Clare; Anne, m. James Fitzgerald, of Stone Hall; and Hester, m. Henry Ward; Mary; and Barbara.

 HUGH HICKMAN, youngest son of Henry Hickman, of Ballyket, and Honora, dau. and heir to Morrough M'Mahon, m. Anne, dau. of George Hastings, of Daylesford, co. Worcester, by whom he left at his decease, 1722, one dau., Mary, m. Sir Edward O'Brien, of Dromoland, co. Clare, and two sons,
1. LUKE, his heir.
2. Thomas, of Brickhill (father of Mary, Countess of Charlemont).

The elder son,
 LUKE HICKMAN, of Fenloe, m. 1728, Gertrude, 2nd dau. and co-heir of Mountiford Westropp, of Attyflin. Their son,

HUGH HICKMAN, of Fenloe, m. 1752, Bridget, dau. of John Bury, of co. Cork, by whom he had nine sons. The 3rd son,
THOMAS HICKMAN, m. 1803, Jane, dau. of Thomas Cosby, and d. 1824, leaving one son,
HUGH PALLISER HICKMAN, of Fenloe, J.P. and D.L., High Sheriff 1860, b. Nov. 1805; m. April, 1843, Sophia Angel St. John, 3rd dau. of Most Rev. Edward Stopford, D.D., Bishop of Meath, and had issue,
1. THOMAS EDWARD STOPFORD, late of Fenloe.
2. STOPFORD COSBY, now of Fenloe.
3. Hugh Palliser, Col. R.A., b. 4 July, 1856; m. 27 March, 1905, Beatrice Helen, widow of Brig.-Gen. E. G. Bingham, R.A. (see that family) and dau. of late Francis Sidney Stephen, of Melbourne, Victoria.
1. Catherine Frances, m. 7 July, 1885, Rev. Robert Humphreys, Dean of Killaloe.
2. Jane Alicia, m. 29 April, 1875, Richard Laurence Whitty, and by him (who d. 2 Nov. 1897) has issue, Hugh Fitzwalter, b. 14 May, 1876.   3. Caroline Amelia, d. unm.
4. Sophia Angel St. John, m. 27 Nov. 1887, Pierce O'Brien, of Durra, co. Clare, and has issue.
Mr. Hickman d. 6 Oct. 1883, and was s. by his eldest son,
THOMAS EDWARD STOPFORD HICKMAN, of Fenloe, co. Clare, J.P., Lieut.-Col. 21st Hussars, formerly in the 14th Hussars, b. Oct. 1844; and d.s.p. 25 Oct. 1892, when he was s. by his brother.

Arms—Per pale indented arg. and az. on the dexter side three roses in pale gu., on the sinister as many in pale of the first.
Seat—Fenloe, Newmarket-on-Fergus.

2. William Newenham, C.E.
1. Kate Christianna.
2. Florence Henrietta, m. 5 Jan. 1875, Edward William Dunlo Croker, Capt. 93rd Highlanders (see CROKER of Ballynagarde). He d. 10 May, 1893, leaving issue. She m. 2ndly, 14 Aug. 1902, Rt. Hon. Hedges Eyre Chatterton, P.C., Vice-Chancellor of Ireland, who d. 30 Aug. 1910.
3. Elizabeth Mary.
The eldest son,
FRANCIS GORE, of Tyredagh Castle, b. Oct. 1800; m. 20 Dec. 1824, Mary, dau. and co-heir of Edmond Browne, of Newgrove, and had issue,
1. FRANCIS, of Tyredagh.
2. Edmond.
3. Thomas Browne.
4. Poole Hickman, m. 31 May, 1911, Frances Louisa, dau. of Capt. George Lloyd Studdert, of Clonderalaw, co. Clare (see STUDDERT of Bunratty Castle).
1. Anne.
2. Letitia Jane.
3. Mary.
4. Christina Emma.
5. Eliza.
The eldest son,
FRANCIS GORE, of Tyredagh Castle, J.P., High Sheriff 1856, m. 30 April, 1855, Ellen, dau. of George Studdert, and had issue,
FRANCIS WILLIAM, now of Tyredagh.

Arms—Per pale indented arg. and az. in the dexter chief a trefoil slipped vert. *Crest*—A talbot sejant arg. collared and chained gu., charged on the shoulder with a trefoil slipped vert.
Motto—Per tot discrimina rerum.
Seats—Tyredagh Castle, Tulla; and Kilmore, Knock.

HICKMAN OF TYREDAGH CASTLE.

FRANCIS WILLIAM HICKMAN, of Tyredagh Castle, and Kilmore, co. Clare, J.P., High Sheriff 1884. b. 1857; m. 1878, Elizabeth, dau. of Pierce O'Brien, J.P., of Durra, co. Clare, and has issue,
1. FRANCIS GORE, b. 1879.
2. Poole Henry.
3. Norman Gore.
4. Victor Gore.
5. Percival Gore, d. 24 April, 1908.
6. Westropp Gore.
1. Elizabeth Trene.

Mr. Hickman assumed the name of HICKMAN in lieu of Gore, by Royal Licence dated 19 Nov. 1878.

Lineage.—JOHN GORE, of Clonroad, co. Clare, m. Jane, dau. of John Taylor, of Ballynorth, co. Limerick, and d. 1700, leaving issue,
1. FRANCIS, his heir.   2. Charles.
1. Ellen, d. unm.
2. Gertrude, m. Thomas Hickman, of Barntic.
3. Susanna, m. 1st, John King, son of Sir William King, Knt.; and 2ndly, Richard Smyth, 4th son of Sir Percy Smyth, Knt. of Ballynatra, co. Waterford.
The elder son and heir,
FRANCIS GORE, of Clonroad, co. Clare, was made a Brigadier-General 1710. He m. Catherine, dau. of Sir Arthur Gore, Bart., of Newton Gore, co. Mayo, and had issue,
1. ARTHUR, his heir.
2. Francis (Rev.), A.M.; ancestor of HUME-GORE, of Derryluscan (see that family).
3. John.
1. Gertrude, d. unm.
2. Ellen.
3. Isabella.
Mr. Gore, whose will is dated 3 Jan. 1733, was s. by his eldest son,
ARTHUR GORE, of Clonroad, m. Mabella, dau. and eventually sole heir of John Cusack, of Kilkessen, and dying 1730, left, with a dau., Jane, m. William Ryves, a son and successor,
FRANCIS GORE, of Derrymore, co. Clare, Col. in the Army, aged 13 at the time of his father's decease, who m. Anne Lewis, and was father of
FRANCIS GORE, of Derrymore, m. 1797, Christianna Emma, dau. of Sir Joseph Peacoke, Bart., of Barntic, co. Clare, and had issue,
1. FRANCIS, his heir.
2. JOSEPH, of Derrymore (see that family).
3. Henry, who was drowned.
4. Charles William, Major 72nd Highlanders, m. Kate, dau. of Hugh Faulkner, of Fort Faulkner, co. Wicklow, and d. 1 Jan. 1881, having had issue,
1. Charles William, Major 76th (2nd West Riding) Regt., m. 7 June, 1883, Edith, dau. of Gen. Knox-Gore, and has issue,
(1) Annesley Charles St. George, b. 31 July, 1886.
(1) Kathleen Madeline.
(2) Oonah Mary Blanche.
(3) Sydney Mary.

HICKSON OF FERMOYLE.

GEORGE ARCHIBALD ERSKINE HICKSON, of Fermoyle, co. Kerry, J.P., b. 21 Nov. 1854; m. 26 Jan. 1884, Lina, youngest dau. of the late Mahony Harte, B.L., of Rockfield, co. Kerry, and has issue,
1. ROBERT CONWAY, b. 26 Oct. 1884.
2. George Lionel O'Hara, b. 9 March, 1887.

Lineage.—REV. CHRISTOPHER HICKSON, descended out of co. Cambridge, was ordained on 20 Dec. 1593, by Maurice O'Brien Ara, first Protestant Bishop of Killaloe, and in 1615 was Treasurer of Ardfert, Rector of Disert, and Vicar of Kilconley, in the same county. Two years later he was appointed Rector of Kilgobbin, and the adjoining parish of Stradbally, in the West of Kerry. Rev. Christopher Hickson m. a dau. of Rev. Thomas Hussey, Vicar of Killiny, and had, with a dau., Katherine, m. Walter, son of Very Rev. Nathaniel Langdon, Dean of Ardfert, a son, Christopher, m. Ellen Stack, of Garrinea, co. Kerry, and adopted the Roman Catholic faith. He is mentioned in the depositions relating to the Insurrection of 1641, preserved in Trin. Coll. Dublin, as "Christopher Hickson, Gentleman, of Knockglass, a rebel and papist," and his certificate of transplantation to Connaught, with seventeen of his family and household, in 1650, is preserved in the Dublin Record Office. He returned to Kerry after 1660, and left issue at his death two sons, ROBERT HICKSON, of Stradbally, whose issue is extinct; and THOMAS HICKSON, of Gowlane, in the parish of Stradbally, m. Katherine, dau. of Walter Hussey, of Castle Gregory, in the same parish, and had (with a dau., m. Maurice FitzGerald, of Liscarney, near Fermoyle) three sons.

JOHN HICKSON, the second, was settled at Tierbrin, in the West of Kerry, in 1712, and soon after acquired the adjacent lands of Fermoyle. He m. Susan, dau. of Daniel FitzGerald, of Ballinruddery, co. Kerry, 3rd son of John FitzGerald, of Ennismore, Knight of Kerry, and his wife Honora O'Brien, dau. of Lord Clare, and by her had five sons,
1. THOMAS, d. young.
2. CHRISTOPHER, of whom presently.
3. James, High Sheriff of Kerry in 1765, m. Rosanna, dau. of John Keane, and had, with other issue, d. unm., two daus.,
1. Mary, m. her first cousin, Robert Conway Hickson, as hereafter mentioned.
2. Rosanna, m. Arthur Blennerhassett, of Fortfield, Kerry, younger brother of Sir Rowland Blennerhassett, 1st bart. (see BURKE's *Peerage and Baronetage*).
4. John, of Tierbrin and Stradbally, co. Kerry, m. Ellen, dau. of Domiinick Trant, of Dingle, by Mary, dau. of Pierse Ferriter, of Ferriter's Cove, near Dingle, and had issue,

1. George, of Hillville, co. Kerry, *d. unm.* 1821.
2. Christopher, *m.* — Moriarty, and had, with other issue, *d. unm.*, a son, John Christopher Hickson, *m.* — Wright, and left a dau., Elizabeth, *m.* David Robertson, E.I.C.S.
3. John, *m.* — Poore, of Cork, and had, with other issue, a dau. *m.* Thomas Coppinger, of Cork.
4. James, *m.* Mary, dau. of John O'Connell, of Kilfinny, co. Limerick, by Avice his wife, dau. of William Hilliard, of Listrim, co. Kerry, and had (with three daus., Christiana, *d.* young ; Maria, *m.* William Busteed, and left surviving issue, John (M.D.), now of Castle Gregory, and Catherine ; Ellen, *m.* Morgan Busteed, M.D., and had no issue) a son, John James, *m.* 1809, Sarah, dau. of Rev. James Day, Rector of Tralee, and Vicar-General of Ardfert and Aghadoe (son of Rev. Edward Day, Rector of Tralee in 1754, by Sarah, sister of James Leslie, Bishop of Limerick and Ardfert), by his wife Margaret, dau. of the MacGillicuddy, of The Reeks, and had surviving issue, two sons and one dau., 1. James, of Hillville, co. Kerry, *m.* his first cousin, Deborah Godfrey, dau. of Rev. Edward Day, Rector of Kilgobbin, and had issue ; he *d.* 1865 ; 2. John, a Barrister-at-Law, *d. unm.* 1874 ; 1. Mary Agnes.
5. Robert, Lieut in the 5th Regt., *m.* Mary Blake, and had issue, two sons,
   (1) George Blake, K.C., *m.* 1st, Anne, relict of William O'Neill, Barrister-at-Law, and had, William, a Barrister-at-Law, now of Leeson Street, Dublin, *m.* 1847, Margaret, dau. of Rev. Edward Day above-mentioned, and had issue, three sons and two daus. ; and *m.* 2ndly, Julia, dau. of C. Delmege, of Castle Park, co. Limerick, by whom he had no issue ; he *d.* 1873.
   (2) Robert, *m.* Margaret Lynch, of Drumcorry, Galway, and has issue several children.
   1. Katherine, *m.* — Mahony, and had no issue.
   2. Mary, *m.* Thomas Day, and had issue a son, John (Rev.), Rector of Milltown, Kerry, *m.* Charlotte, dau. of Sir Barry Denny, 1st bart., and had issue.
   3. Joanna, *m.* Patrick Rice, of Dingle, and had issue.
5. George, *m.* 1747, Mary, only dau. of George Gould, of Cork, by Clara his wife, dau. of Henry Trant, of Dingle, and had an only child, *m.* John Fagan, of Kiltalla, co. Kerry, and had by him six daus., of whom the 2nd, Elizabeth, *m.* Major-Gen. Richardson, and had, with other issue, a dau., Charlotte Louisa, *m* Gen. Sir Charles Van Straubenzee, G.C.B., lately Governor of Malta, and six sons all highly distinguished Officers in the Army.
The 2nd son,
CHRISTOPHER HICKSON, of Fermoyle, *m.* 1745, Elizabeth, dau. of Thomas Conway, and his wife Anne, dau. of Patrick FitzGerald, of Gallerus (younger son of John FitzGerald, Knight of Kerry, and his wife Hon. Katherine Fitzmaurice, dau. of Thomas, 18th Lord Kerry, by Hon. Julia Power his wife. dau. of Richard, 3rd Lord Power, of Curraghmore), and *d.v.p.* at Fermoyle, 24 Feb. 1752, leaving, with other issue, *d. unm.*, an elder son,
ROBERT CHRISTOPHER HICKSON, of Fermoyle, High Sheriff of Kerry 1794 ; *m.* 1770, his first cousin, Mary, dau. of James Hickson, by Rosanna Keane before-mentioned, and had issue,
   1. JAMES, his heir.
   2. Robert Conway, High Sheriff of Kerry 1811, *d. unm.*
   3. George, *d. unm.* 1838.
   1. Mary, *m.* J. Levne, son of Maurice Leyne, by Agnes his wife, dau. of The MacGillicuddy, of The Reeks, and Catherine his wife, dau. of Richard Chute, of Chute Hall, and had issue, an only child,
     Mary, *m.* 7 Feb. 1843, Thomas Stewart. He *d.* 25 Dec. 1866. She *d.* 3 Dec. 1877, having had issue, Alexander, Ensign 74th Highlanders, *d. unm.* in Melbourne, Australia, 25 April, 1879, and Isabella, *b.* 17 March, 1851.
   2. Catherine, *m.* her first cousin, Robert Blennerhassett, and had no issue.
   3. Anne, *m.* John Hilliard, of Scrahan Lodge, co. Kerry, and had an only child,
     Katherine, *m.* Capt. Oliver Day Stokes, of the Indian Army, and had issue.
Mr. Hickson *d.* 1812, and was *s.* by his eldest son,
JAMES ROBERT HICKSON, of Fermoyle, *m.* Teresa, dau. of John Pearl, and had issue.
1. ROBERT CONWAY, his heir.
2. George, *d. unm.*
1. Jane, *d. unm.*
2 Sarah, *m.* Richard Norris, of Belgrave Terrace, Cork, and *d.s.p.*
Mr. Hickson *d.* Feb. 1817, and was *s.* by his eldest son,
ROBERT CONWAY HICKSON, of Fermoyle, High Sheriff of Kerry 1855, *b.* 1812 ; *m.* 1st, 1 Aug. 1831, Agnes, dau. of John Mahony, of Dromore Castle, co. Kerry, by Margaret his wife, dau. of Sir William Godfrey, 1st bart., and had by her no surviving issue. He *m.* 2ndly, 20 April, 1841, Jane, dau. of Capt. Paterson O'Hara, 59th Regt., by Araminta Erskine his wife, sister of Col. James Erskine, C.B., 48th Regt., and dau. of Capt. Archibald Erskine (*see* BURKE'S *Family Records*), and by her (who *d.* 10 March, 1889) had issue,
1. James Robert Conway, Lieut. R.A., *b.* 2 Jan. 1844 ; *d. unm., v.b.* at Madras, 1867.
2. PATERSON O'HARA, his heir.
3. George, *b.* 17 Sept. 1847 ; *d.* 28 Feb. 1850.
4. GEORGE ARCHIBALD ERSKINE, heir to his brother.
1. Araminta Theresa, *m.* 20 Sept. 1866, John Coote Ovens, of Aughnagaddy House, Ramelton, co. Donegal, and Killybegs in that co., late 8th Dragoon Guards. He *d.* 29 May 1894, leaving issue.
2. Jane Sarah Victoria, *m.* 1st, 13 Sept. 1870, Robert Fitzgerald Day, of Beaufort House, co. Kerry, who *d.* 13 March, 1883. She *m.* 2ndly, 22 Oct. 1884, Ernest de Lautour.
3. Theresa Georgina Adelaide, *m.* 16 Sept. 1880, Rev. Joseph Rogerson, E. C. Hodgins, M.A. Cambridge, Vicar of St. James's Birkdale, Lancs., and Hon. Canon of Liverpool, Proctor in York Convocation, and grandson of the Rev. J. Cotter, nephew of Sir James Cotter. Bart., of Rockforest, co. Cork.
4. Sarah Maria Norris, *m.* 66 April, 1881, James Coulton, Capt. Royal Munster Fusiliers, and *d.* 28 March, 1896.
Mr. Hickson *d.* at Fermoyle 4 Nov. 1878, and was *s.* by his eldest surviving son,
PATERSON O'HARA HICKSON, J.P., of Fermoyle, *b.* 5 Oct. 1845 ; *d.* 28 Sept. 1879, when he was *s.* by his brother, GEORGE ARCHIBALD ERSKINE HICKSON, now of Fermoyle.

Arms—Or, two eagles' legs erased a la Quise in saltire, sa., in the centre chief point a trefoil vert. *Crest*—Out of a ducal coronet or, a griffin's head sable beaked of the first charged with a trefoil gold. *Motto*—Fide et fortitudine.
Seat—Fermoyle, near Castle Gregory, co. Kerry. *Residence*—Woodville, Castleisland, Kerry.

HICKSON OF BALLINTAGGART.

COL. ROBERT ALBERT HICKSON, C.B., of Ballintaggart, co. Kerry, Col. Commanding 3rd Regimental District, late of the Buffs, E. Kent Regt., *b.* 15 Sept. 1848 ; *m.* 7 Feb. 1880, Annette Emilie, dau. of the late Thomas William Younghusband, of Bamburgh, N.B., and has issue,
   Eileen Anita.
Lineage.—ROBERT HICKSON, of Dingle, co. Kerry, J.P. and Deputy Governor of the County, High Sheriff 1749, *m.* 1776, Judith, dau. of William Murray, and had issue,
1. JOHN, his heir.
2. Samuel Murray, J.P., *d.s.p.*
3. Robert (Rev.), *m.* the dau. of — Hewson, and had issue.
4. James, of Lansdowne Lodge, who left issue.
5. George (Rev.), who also left issue.
1. Mary, *m.* Peter Bodkin Hussey, Barrister-at-Law.
2. Anne, *m.* Sir William Cox, Knt. of Coolcliffe, co. Wexford.
The eldest son,
JOHN HICKSON, of Grove, Dingle, co. Kerry, J.P. and D.L. High Sheriff 1826, *b.* 20 May, 1782 ; *m.* 4 May, 1813, Barbara, eldest dau. of John Mahony, of Dromore Castle, and had issue,
1. ROBERT, his heir.
2. John Mahony MAHONY, of Tubrid, co. Kerry, J.P., assumed by Royal Licence 11 Dec. 1827, the name and arms of MAHONY.
3. Richard Mahony, of Redcliff, co. Kerry, Capt. in the Army, *m.* 1849, Lucy, dau. of John Curry, and had issue. She *d.* 10 Feb. 1908.
1. Margaret, *m.* William Norcock.
2. Barbara, *m.* Adm. James Bower.
3. Julia, *m.* Sept. 1853, Samuel Murray Hussey, of Edenburn, co. Kerry.
4. Mary Anne, *m.* 1st, Charles Blennerhassett, of Ballyseedy, co. Kerry, and 2ndly, Capt. William Walker.
5. Sarah, *m.* T. Shuldham Henry.
The eldest son,
ROBERT HICKSON, of Ballintaggart, J.P., *m.* Julia Sophia, dau. of William Sadleir Bruère, of Berwick, N.B. He *d.* 1870, leaving a son,
ROBERT ALBERT, now of Ballintaggart.

Seat—Ballintaggart, Dingle, co. Kerry. *Residence*—Commandant's House, Canterbury. *Club*—Naval and Military.

HIGGINSON OF CARNALEA.

HENRY CLIVE HIGGINSON, of Carnalea House, co. Down, *b.* 26 April, 1887 ; *s.* his father 1908.

Lineage.—This family was founded in Ireland by an English gentleman of the name of HIGGINSON, who accompanied the army of WILLIAM III to Ireland, was Col. in the Commissariat Department, and dying at a very advanced age, left issue, of whom
1. PHILIP, Capt. in the Army, *m.* Eleanor Talbot, and had a son,
   PHILIP TALBOT HIGGINSON, *d.* 22 June, 1819, Lieut. 73rd Regt., *m.* 4 Aug. 1764, Margaret, dau. of Richard Taylor, by whom he had issue an only dau.,
     Jane, *m.* her cousin, the Rev. Thomas Edward Higginson (*see below*).
2. THOMAS, of whom hereafter.
The 2nd son,

THOMAS HIGGINSON, settled in co. Wexford, and d. 1756, having m. Mary Colley, by whom he had issue,

REV. THOMAS HIGGINSON, Vicar of Balinderry and Rector of Lisburn, co. Antrim, b. 1722 ; m. Ann Moore, of Boley, co. Wexford, and had issue,
1. THOMAS EDWARD, of whom presently.
1. Sarah Eliza, m. Henry Marmion, of Lambeg, co. Antrim, and had, with other issue, a dau.,
   Sarah Jane Marmion, who m. Robert Potter, of Ardview, co. Down.
2. Maria, m. 22 Dec. 1772, John Johnston, of Belvidere Place, Dublin.
3. Letitia, m. Capt. Greydon, of H.M. Dragoons.

Rev. Thomas Higginson d. 23 May, 1789. His eldest son,
REV. THOMAS EDWARD HIGGINSON, Incumbent of Lambeg, b. 1767; m. 7 Sept. 1788, his cousin Jane, dau. of Philip Talbot Higginson, Lieut. 73rd Regt., Usher in Court of Exchequer (see above), and left issue,
1. THOMAS EDWARD, Solicitor H.E.I.C.S. at Madras, b. 18 July, 1789, m. Fanny Clay, d. at Madras, being father of Lieut.-Col. Thomas Edward Leslie, Madras Staff Corps, who d.s.p. 25 March, 1891, having m. 1st 10 Oct. 1858, Mary Anne, dau. of James Lermitte (see that family), and widow of Major Spier Hughes, and 2ndly, 26 April, 1860, Henrietta Anne, eldest dau. of T. G. Dodson. She d. 1861.
2. Philip Talbot, Capt. 87th Regt. (The Royal Irish Fusiliers), b. 1 Jan. 1791, d.s.p.
3. HENRY THEOPHILUS, of whom presently.
1. Margaret, b. 13 June, 1792, m. 14 Oct. 1820, Rev. Edward Leslie, Rector of Anahilt, co. Down, and Treasurer of Dromore (uncle of Sir John Leslie, Bart., of Glasslough, co. Monaghan), and had issue. She d. 13 Nov. 1872.

Rev. Thomas Edward Higginson d. 22 June, 1819. His 3rd son,
HENRY THEOPHILUS HIGGINSON, of Carnalea House, co. Down, b. 17 March, 1798, M.A. Trin. Coll. Dublin, J.P. for cos. Antrim and Down, Capt. Derriaghy Yeomanry, Sheriff of Carrickfergus, 1849 ; m. 6 Jan. 1825, Charlotte, only surviving dau. and heiress of John McConnell, of Belfast (son of James McConnell, by Elizabeth his wife, only dau. of Andrew Bogle, M.D., of Strabane, co. Tyrone, one of the claimants of the dormant Earldom of Menteith ; see BURKE's Extinct and Dormant Peerage), by Charlotte his wife, dau. of James Potter, of Mount Potter, co. Down. He had issue,
1. JOHN MCCONNELL, of Carnalea.
2. Thomas Edward, b. 12 Jan. 1828, Lieut. 39th Bengal Native Infantry, d. 1850.
3. Charles Henry, b. 4 Jan. 1830 ; m. Maria, dau. of James Potter, of Savannah, Georgia, and Princetown, New Jersey, U.S. (representative of the family of Stewart, of Ballymorran, co. Down), and d. 1860, leaving issue, two sons and four daus.,
   1. James Potter, m. Mary Walker.
   2. Henry Theophilus, d.s.p., 1891.
   1. Charlotte Potter, m. John Hampden Coursen.
   2. Maria Potter, m. Wayland Manning.   3. Katherine Potter.
   4. Frances Potter.
4. Theophilus, C.B., Col. Indian Army, J.P., b. 4 April, 1839 ; m. 1871, Ada, dau. of William Whitla, of Lisburn, co. Antrim (see that family), and d. 30 Aug. 1903, having had issue,
   Harold Whitla, of Church Circle, Farnborough, Capt. Royal Dublin Fusiliers, b. 10 Nov. 1873 ; m. 14 Jan. 1903, Ivy Letitia, 4th dau. of the late James Brown, of Orchard, Carluke, N.B., and has issue,
      James, b. 5 July, 1906.
      Joan Letitia, b. 20 June, 1909.
   Ada Dorothea, m. 27 July, 1910, Edward Hyde Greg, 3rd son of the late Edward Hyde Greg, D.L. (see GREG of Coles Park).
5. Henry Talbot, M.D., b. 16 March, 1841 ; m. 21 April, 1870, Isabella Watson, dau. of Hugh Dobbin. She d. 4 Dec. 1890. He d. 30 Jan. 1891, leaving issue,
   1. Edwin Stuart, b. 9 and d. 20 Sept. 1874.
   2. Hugh, b. 21 Aug. 1877.
   3. Henry Talbot, b. 15 Feb. 1880.
1. Charlotte Potter, b. 13 Dec. 1831, m. 8 Sept. 1862, Thomas Jefferson Thompson, son of Ross Thompson, of Greenwood Park, co. Down. She d. 11 April, 1906, leaving issue.
2. Jane, m. 8 Sept. 1853, Col. John Barton Taylor, son of Lieut.-Gen. Jeremiah Taylor, and by him (who d. 1894) has issue.
3. Dorothea Josepha, m. Charles John, of Dunston House, co. Stafford, Barrister-at-Law, Inner Temple, and B.A. St. John's Coll. Camb. He d. 17 April, 1880, leaving issue.

Mr. Henry Theophilus Higginson d. 20 June, 1869, and was s. by his eldest son,

JOHN MCCONNELL HIGGINSON, of Carnalea House, co. Down, J.P., Registrar of the Diocese of Down, Connor, and Dromore, b. 21 Nov. 1826 ; m. 20 Nov. 1850, Susan Arabella Gertrude, only dau. of Robert Conry, of Clonabee, co. Roscommon, and Lisbrack, co. Longford, Capt. 90th Regt., and d. 14 April, 1891, having by her (who d. 6 April, 1890) had issue,
1. HENRY HARTLAND, late of Carnalea.
2. Charles William Shaw, b. 24 Jan. 1857 ; d. unm. 1903.
3. Thomas Edward, b. 16 Nov. 1860 ; d. 21 June, 1895.
4. Robert Conry, b. 21 Aug. 1863 ; d. 10 Dec. 1886.
1. Gertrude Arabella.
2. Charlotte Augusta, m. 7 April, 1881, Charles John Du Bedat, M.A., son of William George Du Bedat, of Ballybrack House, co. Dublin. He d. April, 1893.

The eldest son,
MAJOR HENRY HARTLAND HIGGINSON, of Carnalea House, co. Down, Major 2nd Batt. N. Staffordshire Regt., b. 3 July, 1855 ; m. 3 June, 1886, Elizabeth Mary (52, Lower Sloane Street, S.W.), youngest dau. of the late Andrew Armstrong, of Kylemore, co. Galway, and St. Andrews, co. Dublin, and d. 31 Aug. 1908, having had issue.
HENRY CLIVE, now of Carnalea.

Arms—Sa., three towers in fess, arg. between six trefoils slipped, three in chief and three in base or. Crest—Out of a tower ppr. a demi-griffin segreant, vert, armed and beaked or Motto—Malo mori quam foedari.

Seat—Carnalea House, Crawfordsburn, co. Down.

HILL. See BURKE'S PEERAGE, DOWNSHIRE, M.

HILLAS OF DOONECOY.

ROBERT WILLIAM GOODWIN HILLAS, of Doonecoy, co. Sligo, J.P. and D.L., High Sheriff 1896, late Capt. and Hon. Maj. Duke of Connaught's Own Sligo Artillery and Prince Albert's Somersetshire L.I., b. 6 Dec. 1856 ; m. 1889, Louisa Clara, dau. of the late John Wyndham Hooper, C.E.

Lineage.—ROBERT WILLIAM HILLAS, of Doonecoy, Templeboy, co. Sligo, and Cregg House, Sligo, J.P. and D.L., left issue, a son,
ROBERT WILLIAM HILLAS, of Doonecoy, co. Sligo, and Farm Hill, Dundrum, co. Dublin, J.P. and D.L. for the former county, High Sheriff 1887, m. 1st, Ella Bazett, dau. of the late R. T. Goodwin, Senior Member of Council, Bombay, and had issue,
1. ROBERT WILLIAM GOODWIN, now of Doonecoy.
2. William Hutchinson, Capt. 3rd Dragoon Guards and 4th Hussars, b. 23 Nov. 1857 ; d. unm. 1897.
3. Thomas Standish HILLAS-DRAKE, m. Muriel Emily, dau. of William Henry Fitzhugh, of 17, Craven Hill Gardens, W.
1. Ella Katherine, m. 1887, Col. Alfred Western Hornsby Drake, late M.S.C., of Thedden Grange, Alton, Hants.
He m. 2ndly, 8 July, 1865, Alice, dau. of Rev. John Grant, and d. 10 Jan. 1888, having issue by her also.

Seat—Doonecoy, Templeboy, co. Sligo.

HINGSTON OF AGLISH.

THE REV. RICHARD EDWARD HULL HINGSTON, of Aglish, co. Cork, Senior Curate of Merton, S.W., b. 24 Oct. 1859 ; m. 25 Sept. 1883, Frances, dau. of D. L. Sandiford, of Ballinlough, co. Cork, and has issue,
1. JAMES HENRY (Rev.), M.A. (Trin. Coll. Dublin), Curate of Queenstown, co. Cork, b. 28 Nov. 1884.
2. Henry Sandiford, M.B., B.S. Lond., b. 27 Nov. 1885.
3. Richard William George, M.B., B.Ch., B.A.O., Lieut. Indian Medical Service, b. 17 Jan. 1887.
4. Francis Perceval Randolph, b. 13 July, 1888.
5. Frederick Becher, b. 11 Nov. 1889.
1. Elizabeth Maria Alleyne, b. 22 Feb. 1891.
2. Marie Selina Priscilla, b. 7 March, 1893.
3. Frances Henrietta, b. 15 Oct. 1895.

Lineage.—JAMES HINGSTON, of the Commissariat Department, son of Maj. James Hingston, an officer in the Parliamentary Army temp. CHARLES I., settled in co. Cork. His son,
JAMES HINGSTON, of Aglish, East Muskerry, co. Cork, which he purchased 1702, m. Helen, dau. of Alderman Morley, of Cork, and had with a younger son Justinian, who d. in Gloucestershire, an elder son,
WILLIAM HINGSTON, of Aglish, m. Elizabeth, dau. of John Webb of Aglish, and had issue,
1. JAMES, his heir.
2. John of the old Castle, d.s.p.
1. A dau., m. Rev. S. Hales, D.D , and had issue.
The elder son,
REV. JAMES HINGSTON, of Aglish, Rector and Preb. of Donoghmore, and Vicar of Clonmeen, co. Cork, J.P., m. 1741, Katherine, dau. of Rev. Benezer Murdock, Rector of Kilshannig, co. Cork, by Elizabeth his wife, dau. of Herbert Love, of Cork, by his wife, the dau. of Col. Randolph Clayton, of Mallow, and Judith, his wife, eldest dau. of Sir Philip Perceval, ancestor of the Earls of Egmont. Mr. Hingston had issue,
1. William, d. unm.
2. Benezer Murdock, Capt. in the Army, m. Priscilla, dau. of — Compton, Sheriff of the State of Pennsylvania, U.S., and had issue,

1. John, *m.* Judith, sister of Col. Limerick, H.E.I.C.S., of Union Hall, co. Cork, and *d.s.p.*
2. Spencer.
3. James, Governor of Cape Coast Castle, Lieut.-Col. Commandant Royal African Corps, served in the 83rd Regt. in the Peninsular War.
4. William, R.N., *d.* in the West Indies.
5. Clayton Low, Comptroller of Westport and Newport, co. Mayo, *m.* Mary Ann, dau. of Rev. John Hingston.
3. JAMES, of whom presently.
4. John (Rev.), Prebendary of Lefinny, *b.* 1762, *m.* 1789, Alicia, second dau. of Arthur Bernard, of Palace Ann, Provost of Bandon, and *d.* 1799, leaving issue,
 1. Arthur Bernard, *d.* young.
 2. Francis Bernard, Lieut. 84th Regt.
 3. James.
 1. Mary Ann, *m.* Clayton L. Hingston.
1. Catherine, *m.* Rev. Thomas Tuckey, and had issue.
2. Helen, *m.* Justician Hingston, and *d.s.p.*
3. Elizabeth, *m.* 19 Jan. 1775, Rev. James Reid.
4. Mary, *d. unm.*
5. Isabella, *m.* 1st, George Brereton, of Carrigslaney, co. Carlow, and by him had issue. She *m.* 2ndly, Sir James Laurence Cotter, 2nd bart., who *d.* 9 Feb. 1829. She *d.* April, 1832, having by him had issue.
The Rev. James Hingston *d.* 1775. His third son,
THE REV. JAMES HINGSTON, LL.D. of Aglish, co. Cork, Vicar General of Cloyne and Rector of Aghabullogue, J.P. co. Cork, *b.* 1755, *m.* Anne, dau. of Rev. William Hoddnet, Rector of Aghadown, and had issue,
 1. JAMES, his heir.
 2. William Hales (Rev.), Prebendary of Coole, *m.* Anne, dau. of Rev. G. S. Cotter, son of Sir James Cotter, 1st bart., and *d.* 1823, having had issue,
  1. James, *d.* young.
  2. George Cotter (Rev.), Rector of Queenstown, co. Cork, *d.* 25 Aug. 1858.
  1. Isabella Charlotte.
  2. Margaret Anna.
  3. Ann Mathilda.
 3. Richard, Lieut. in the Army, killed at Talavera, 1809.
 1. Martha, *m.* Thomas Johnston, of Fort Johnston, and had issue (*see that family*).
 2. Louisa, *m.* William Beamish, of Cork, and *d.s.p.*
 3. Anne, *m.* Linegar Rogers, and had issue.
The eldest son,
REV. JAMES HINGSTON, of Aglish, Rector of Whitchurch, Cloyne, *m.* Lucinda, dau. of Richard Becher, of Hollybrook, co. Cork, and left issue,
 1. JAMES, his heir.
 1. Lucinda, *b.* 24 Sept. 1816; *m.* William Hull, of Lemcon Manor, Skibbereen, co. Cork, and had issue. She *d.* 25 Oct. 1907.
 2. Mary, *m.* Thomas Somerville, of the Prairie, co. Cork, who *d.s.p.* 23 Jan. 1851.
The only son,
JAMES HINGSTON, of Aglish, who built the present residence, *b.* 8 June, 1818; *m.* 3 Nov. 1838, Maria, eldest dau. of Richard Edward Hull, of Lemcon Manor, co. Cork. She *d.* 1 Feb. 1880. He *d.* 7 July, 1873, leaving issue,
 1. James, *b.* 16 March, 1856, settled in America, *d.* 17 March, 1911.
 2. RICHARD EDWARD HULL, now of Aglish.
 1. Henrietta Anna Margaretta, *b.* 30 Nov. 1839; *d. unm.* 14 July, 1879.
 2. Lucinda Mary.
 3. Emily Anne Elizabeth, *b.* 12 Nov. 1854; *d. unm.* 6 Sept. 1883.
 4. Lonisa Caroline, *b.* 30 March, 1861; *d. unm.* 25 Dec. 1907.
 5. Mary Florence Lucinda, *b.* 1 Nov. 1862; *m.* 16 Nov. 1882, Carew O'Grady, J.P. of Carrigmanus House, Goleen, and had issue. She *d.* 16 Feb. 1897.

Arms—Az. a chevron nebuly erm. between in chief two lozenges or, each charged with a leopard's face affrontée of the field and in base a cross patée of the third. Crest—A demi lion rampant per pale nebuly az. and or, holding in its paws a cross patée of the second. Motto—Deum posui adjutorem.

Seat—Aglish, co. Cork. Residence—"Felhampton," Morden Road, Merton, S.W.

HOBBS OF BARNABOY.

HERBERT FRANCIS CLAYTON HOBBS, of Barnaboy, King's Co., Lieut. P. O. W. West Yorks. Regt., *b.* 17 Nov. 1886.

Lineage.—GEORGE HOBBS, of Barnaboy, had, by his wife Eleanor, a dau. and a son,
THOMAS HOBBS, of Barnaboy, *b.* 1712; *m.* a dau. of Richard Pilkington, of Tore, co. Westmeath, and *d.* 1786, leaving issue,
 1. GEORGE, of whom presently.
 2. John, *d. unm.* 1795.
 3. Henry, who *m.* and had issue, two sons.
 4. Thomas, who by his wife Jane had issue, a dau.
 1. Barbara, *m.* to — Mitchell, and had issue, two sons and a dau.
 2. Mary, *d. unm.* 1839.
The eldest son,
GEORGE HOBBS, of Barnaboy, *b.* 1766; *m.* Charlotte Augusta Mathilda, dau. of Bartholomew Creagh, and *d.* 1838, having had issue,
 1. THOMAS, his heir.
 2. Henry, *m.* a dau. of — Bailey, and had issue, 1, Henry; 2, Thomas; 3, George; 1, Matilda.

3. John, *d. unm.* 1824.
1. Rebecca, *m.* 1805, Major-Gen. John Lamont, of Lamont, co. Argyll, and had issue (*see that family*).
The eldest son,
THOMAS HOBBS, of Branaboy, J.P., fought at Quatre Bras (where he was wounded) as Lieut. in 92nd Highlanders; *b.* 1791; *m.* Margaret, dau. of Simpson Hackett, of Riverstown, co. Tipperary (*see that family*), and by her (who *d.* 1896, in her 103rd year) had issue,
1. THOMAS FRANCIS, of whom presently.
2. George Lamont, Major 45th Regt. Sherwood Foresters, *m.* 1864, Frances Margaret, dau. of Robert Brown, F.R.C.S., of Winckley Square, Preston, and *d.* 1871, leaving issue (with a dau. Beatrice).
 George Lamont, Major Connaught Rangers, *b.* 18 June, 1867; *m.* 12 Oct. 1910, Gwladys Ruth, dau. of Dillon Lawson, of the Bank of Ireland, Galway.
3. Simpson Hackett, Capt. late 89th Regt. (*Kylemore, Malvern*); *m.* 1st, 1860, Mary, dau. of Rev. Canon Murphy, by whom he has issue,
 1. Thomas Henry Montague (Rev.), *m.* 1890, Caroline Frances, dau. of Hay Morant, of the Manor House, Ringwood. He *d.s.p.* 4 Dec. 1900.
 2. Simpson Hackett Beresford, Lieut.-Col. Indian Army, Major 14th Bengal Cavalry, *b.* 2 Aug. 1862, *m.* 1899 Kate, dau. of C. Gale, and *d.* 13 Feb. 1907, leaving issue,
  (1) Katherine Audrey, *b.* 1903.
  (2) Joan Beresford, *b.* 1906.
Capt. Hobbs *m.* 2ndly, 1874, Sarah, dau. of James Bailey, of Fulwell, Tyldesley, by whom he had issue,
 3. Charles James Willoughby, Capt. The Sherwood Foresters, served in S. African War 1900-2, *b.* 23 Jan. 1876; *m.* 21 Nov. 1906, Dorothea Jessy, dau. of Major A. Bell, late 48th Regt. and has issue,
  (1) Rosemary Margaret, *b.* 17 Sept. 1909.
  (2) Dorothea Elizabeth, *b.* 24 Nov. 1910.
 4. Reginald Francis Arthur, D.S.O., Capt. R.E., served in South African War 1899-1902 (despatches, medals, D.S.O.), *b.* 30 Jan. 1878; *m.* 29 Aug. 1906, Frances Graham, youngest dau. of late Gen. Sir William Stirling, K.C.B., and has issue,
  (1) Reginald Geoffrey Stirling, *b.* 8 Aug. 1908.
  (2) Peter Graham, *b.* 19 May, 1911.
 5. Edward Neville Bayley, *b.* 25 Sept. 1883, *m.* 1906, Violet Godfrey.
  1. Annie Margaret, *m.* 30 Jan. 1902, William Otway Wilson, 2nd son of Rev. Sumner Wilson, Vicar of Preston Candover, Hants, and has issue.
4. James Cavendish, Capt. late 30th Regt., *m.* 1861, Mary, dau. of Dennis O'Mahoney (he *d.* 24 Dec. 1909), and has had issue,
 1. Edward, *d.* 1890.
 2. Frederick Manoli Baltazzi, Major R.M.L.I., *b.* 11 Dec. 1867, *m.* 1906, ——, widow of Taunton Collins, and *d.* 1911, leaving issue,
  Edward, *b.* 1907.
 1. Kathleen, *m.* 25 July, 1908, W. Hards, of London.
5. Frederick Fitzwilliam Trench, Col. A.P.D., *b.* 27 Dec. 1836, *m.* 1860, Jane Victoria, dau. of John French, of Riversdale, co. Roscommon, and *d.* 20 Jan. 1900, leaving issue,
 1. Frederick. 2. John.
 3. Edward. 4. Arthur.
 5. Charles. 6. Ernest.
 1. Mary. 2. Ina. 3. Edith.
1. Sally, *d. unm.* 1830.
2. Charlotte Augusta Matilda, *m.* Charles, son of Sir John Maginniss, and has issue.
3. Rebecca Lamont, *d. unm.* 1823.
4. Margaret Hobart, *d. unm.* 1847.
5. Anne Amelia, *d. unm.* 1825.
6. Mary Elizabeth, *m.* 1845, Thomas, son of William Bor, of Ballindolan, and has issue.
7. Thomasina, *m.* 1856, George Manifold, son of Daniel Manifold, of Cadamstown, King's Co. She *d.* 24 May, 1907.
8. Sally, *m.* 1855, Thomas, son of Richard Studdert, of Kilkishen.
9. Jane Josephine, *m.* 1859, John, son of James Connell, and has issue.
Capt. Thomas Hobbs *d.* 1842, and was *s.* by his eldest son,
THOMAS FRANCIS HOBBS, of Barnaboy, Col. Commanding 6th Regt., served in the Crimea as Major Royal N. British Fus., *b.* 1829; *m.* 1850, Mary Alicia, dau. of James Connell, and had issue.
1. HERBERT THOMAS DE CARTERET, late of Barnaboy.
2. Percy Eyre Francis, C.M.G., Colonel Army Service Corps, *b.* 18 Feb. 1865; *m.* 17 July, 1889, Eliza Anne, dau. of Henry Hutson, M.D., of Georgetown, B. Guiana, and has issue,
 Carleton Percy, *b.* 18 June, 1898.
 Vera Gwendoline Wolseley, *b.* 15 March, 1891.
 1. Amy Alice Caroline, *m.* Hardress Connell.
Col. Hobbs *d.* 1866 and was *s.* by his elder son,
MAJOR HERBERT THOMAS DE CARTERET HOBBS, of Barnaboy, King's Co., of 62nd and 14th Regiments, Major West Yorkshire Regt., *b.* 28 April, 1857; *m.* 1885, Elizabeth, dau. of W. B. Clayton, M.D., of The Abbey, Athy, and was killed in action at Honing Spruit, S. Africa, 22 June, 1900, leaving issue,
 HERBERT FRANCIS CLAYTON, now of Barnaboy.
 Gladys Mary, *b.* 1892.
Seat—Barnaboy, Frankford, King's Co.

LE HUNTE-HOBSON. See LE HUNT OF ARTRAMONT.

Hodder. THE LANDED GENTRY. 324

HODDER OF RINGABELLA.

WILLIAM MORGAN HODDER, of Ringabella House, co. Cork, Col. late Royal Engineers, *b.* 23 March, 1861; *s.* his father, 1888; *m.* 22 July, 1896, Winifred, only child of John Henry Sylvester, of 16, Melbury Road, Kensington, late of 11th Bengal Lancers, and Deputy Surgeon-General, and has issue,

1. Muriel Winifred Sylvester.   2. Beryl Adeline Sylvester.

Lineage.—COL. JOHN HODDER, of Bridgetown, and his brother, WILLIAM HODDER, of Coolmoor, were settlers in co. Cork before 1641. The former, Col. John Hodder, was sometime agent to Sir Philip Perceval, and the latter, William Hodder, as appears from his will, was *b.* at Millcome (Melcombe Regis), co. Dorset. They had a brother, Edward Hodder, whose dau. was living at Weymouth 1671, and a sister, *m.* William Smart. Both of the settlers passed patent for lands under the Act of Settlement. John obtained two grants of 4,133 acres, and William a grant of 7,364 acres in co. Cork, including the seats of the family, viz., Coolmoor, Ringabrow, or Hoddersfield, Ballea, Ringabella, and Fountainstown. The said John Hodder was Mayor of the city of Cork 1656, and High Sheriff of co. Cork 1657; and his brother, William Hodder, was Mayor 1657, and High Sheriff of the county 1661. John Hodder *d.s.p.* 1673, leaving his estates to FRANCIS, 2nd son of his brother William, having, however, by deed in his lifetime, given Dunkittle and other large estates to his nephew, William Smart.

WILLIAM HODDER (Col. John Hodder's brother), *m.* twice, and *d.* 1665, having had, with junior issue, two sons,
1. WILLIAM, ancestor of the HODDERS *of Ringabella and Fountainstown.*
2. FRANCIS, ancestor of HODDER *of Hoddersfield.*

The elder son,

WILLIAM HODDER, of Ballea Castle, co. Cork, *d.* in England 1689, leaving issue, by his wife Hannah, with six daus., four sons,
1. THOMAS, High Sheriff co. Cork, 1697, who sold Coolmoor to the Newenhams, 1691, and *d.* about 1738.
2. JOHN, of Cork, Merchant.
3. SAMUEL, of Fountainstown, of whom we treat.
4. Benjamin, *d.s.p.* 1729.

The 3rd son,

SAMUEL HODDER, of Fountainstown, *m.* 1694, Elizabeth, dau. of John Boles, of Inch, and *d.* 1737, leaving issue (besides daus., Elizabeth, *b.* 1743; Anne, *m.* Alderman William Busteed; and Mary, *m.* Benjamin Barter, of Anagh) four sons,
1. JOHN, of Ringabella, of whom we treat.
2. Francis, of Fountainstown, *d.s.p.* 1744.
3. William, a Lieut. in Major-Gen. St. Clair's Regt. of Foot, *d. unm.* 1743.
4. GEORGE, of Fountainstown (*see* HODDER *of Fountainstown*).

The eldest son,

JOHN HODDER, of Ringabela, co. Cork, *m.* 1722, Mary, dau. of Edward Bullen, of the Old Head, Kinsale, and *d.* 1742, leaving, with four daus., as many sons, of whom the eldest,

JOHN HODDER, of Ringabella, *m.* 1747, Martha, dau. of Francis Woodley, and had a son and successor,

SAMUEL HODDER, of Ringabella, *m.* 1793, Jane, dau. of George T. Holder, of Fountainstown, and was *s.* by his son,

FRANCIS HODDER, of Ringabella, *m.* Alicia, dau. of William Martin, and left a son,

SAMUEL HODDER, of Ringabella House, J.P., formerly Capt. Royal Cork City Artillery Militia, *b.* 8 Dec. 1820; *m.* 26 April, 1860, Jane, 2nd dau. of W. Morgan, M.D., of Cork, and had issue,
1. WILLIAM MORGAN, now of Ringabella.
2. Samuel, *b.* 17 Sept. 1863.
3. Francis Edward, *b.* 26 March, 1866.
1. Alice, *m.* Rev. Horatio Nelson, B.A., His Majesty's Indian Service. She *d.* April, 1892.
2. Jane Georgina, *d.* young.
3. Anna Hickman, *m.* Surgeon Major J. Crofts, M.D., I.M.S.

Mr. Hodder *d.* 1 Jan. 1888.

Seat—Ringabella House, Carrigaline.

---

and grand-dau. of Sir Thomas Roberts, 1st bart. of Britfieldstown, co. Cork. He *d.* 30 April, 1908, having had issue,
1. GEORGE WALTON, *b.* 8 Feb. 1874.
2. Francis Charles, Lieut. 1st Batt. Leicester Regt., *b.* 24 March, 1876; *d. unm.* 12 Nov. 1899.
3. William Randall, Assist. Paymaster R.N., *b.* 25 Aug. 1877.
4. Gerald Edward, *b.* 5 July, 1886.
1. Ethel Clare, *b.* 12 April, 1889.

Lineage.—GEORGE HODDER, of Fountainstown, co. Cork, youngest son of SAMUEL HODDER, of Fountainstown, and Elizabeth his wife, dau. of John Boles, of Inch, and younger brother of JOHN HODDER, of Ringabella (*see that family*), *m.* the dau. of — Baker, and *d.* July, 1771, having had issue,

GEORGE, his heir.
Elizabeth, *m.* Francis Woodley, of Leeds, co. Cork.

The only son,

GEORGE HODDER, of Fountainstown, J.P., *m.* Jan. 1774, Sarah, dau. and co-heir of William Norris, of Old Court, co. Cork, and had issue,
1. GEORGE, his heir.
2. Francis, of Ballea Castle, *m.* 1815, Anna Matilda, dau. of Thomas Kift, and *d.* 1853, having had issue,
 1. GEORGE FRANCIS, *s.* his uncle.
 2. John Thomas, of Ballea Castle, *b.* 1822; *m.* Feb. 1859, Elizabeth, 3rd dau. of James Morgan, of Prospect Hill, co. Cork. She *d.* 1864. He *d.* 1867, leaving issue,
  (1) Francis John, of Ballea Castle, late Capt. 4th Batt. Royal Irish Regt., *b.* 30 June, 1860; *m.* 4 Jan. 1899, Elizabeth Ada, widow of Major W. Dennehy, and only dau. of the late Samuel Browne, of Clifton, Bristol. She *d.* 14 Jan. 1912, having had issue,
   1. Francis Charles Samuel, *b.* 19 June, 1900.
   2. Cornish Henri, *b.* 20 June, 1905.
  (2) John Thomas, *b.* 22 Dec. 1863.
  (1) Jane Matilda, *m.* 27 July, 1910, James O'Connell, lat of Cornwall Mansions, Chelsea, S.W.
 3. Francis.
 1. Susan, *m.* John Furlong, of Richmond, Fermoy, and had issue.
 2. Sarah, *m.* Philip William Bass.
 3. Jane, *m.* Rev. Mr. Lee.   4. A. dau.
3. John, of Cork, Alderman, *m.* Barbara, dau. of William Martin, and had issue,
 1. George, *m.* Albina, dau. of William Johnson.
 2. Francis.   3. John, *d.s.p.* 1859.
 4. Peter, Capt. R.N.   5. Robert, Lieut. R.N.
6. Michael, Lieut. R.N.
7. Edward, Lieut. 94th Regt., wounded at Waterloo.
1. Jane, *m.* 1793, Samuel Hodder, of Ringabella, and had issue.
2. Anne, *m.* 21 May, 1814, Robert Stevelly.
3. Mary.   4. Sarah.
5. Harriet.

The eldest son,

GEORGE HODDER, of Fountainstown, co. Cork, J.P., *d.s.p.*, and was *s.* by his nephew,

GEORGE FRANCIS HODDER, of Fountainstown, J.P., *b.* 1817; *m.* 12 Jan. 1843, Elizabeth Townsend, dau. of Michael Roberts, of Kilmoney Abbey, co. Cork (*see that family*). She *d.* 3 Feb. 1854. He *d.* 12 March, 1863, having had issue,
1. FRANCIS GEORGE, late of Fountainstown.
2. George Francis, of Lapps Island, Cork, and Briscoe Place, Fermoy, *b.* 25 Feb. 1852; *d.* 24 Oct. 1908; *m.* Deborah, only dau. of the late Robert Briscoe, of Fermoy.
 1. Elizabeth Roberts.
2. Anna Matilda, *m.* 30 Jan. 1868, Thomas Hayes, of Crosshaven House, co. Cork, and has issue.
3. Lydia Mary, *m.* 4 July, 1882, William Ralph Westropp Roberts, Fellow Trin. Coll. Dublin, and has issue (*see* ROBERTS *of Kilmoney*).

Arms—Argent, five pole axes erect in fess ppr.

Seat—Fountainstown, co. Cork. **Residence**—Inveresk, Belfast.

HODDER OF FOUNTAINSTOWN.

The late FRANCIS GEORGE HODDER, of Fountainstown, co. Cork, and Inveresk, Belfast, Resident Magistrate at Belfast, J.P. co. Cork, B.A., exscholar Trin. Coll. Dublin, called to the Irish Bar, Trinity Term, 1871, *b.* 28 July, 1846; *m.* 15 April, 1873, Susan Louisa Florence (now of Fountainstown), dau. of John Drew Atkin, of Castle Park, co. Dublin,

MOORE-HODDER OF HODDERSFIELD.

WILLIAM HENRY JOHN MOORE-HODDER, of Hoddersfield, co. Cork, J.P. and D.L., High Sheriff co. Cork, 1899, *b.* 1 Aug. 1846; educated at Eton; late Lieut. 10th Regt.

Lineage.—FRANCIS *HODDER, 2nd son of the 1st William Hodder, of Ringabella, High Sheriff of co. Cork 1661 (*see preceding Memoirs*), *s.* to the estates by his father's and uncle's wills, and was of Bridgetown and Ringabrow or Hoddersfield. He had issue by his wife Jane, besides three daus., three sons,
1. WILLIAM, of Bridgetown, co. Cork, *b.* 1659; *m.* 1679, Jane, dau. of Major Grove, of Ballyhimock, co. Cork, and *d.* 1686, leaving two daus.,
 1. Frances.   2. Jane.
2. John, of Hoddersfield and Killeagh.
3. FRANCIS, of whom presently.

The youngest son,

FRANCIS HODDER, of Cork, *m.* Aug. 1688, Hannah, dau. of Capt. George Pepper, of Ballygarth, and *d.* 1726, leaving, besides four

daus. (Jane, *m.* Joseph Bullen ; Alicia Hannah, *m.* John Bayly, of Ballymoney, and Elizabeth), with two younger sons, George and Francis, an eldest son,
CAPT. WILLIAM HODDER, of Hoddersfield, *m.* Anne, sister of Capt. Daniel Webb, and had issue,
1. WILLIAM, of whom presently.
1. Hannah.
2. ANNE, *m.* HENRY MOORE, Capt. 48th Foot, and had issue, a son and a dau.,
 WILLIAM HENRY, of whom presently.
 Anne, *m.* Thomas B. Herrick, of Shippool co. Cork (*see that family*).
The only son,
WILLIAM HODDER, of Hoddersfield, *m.* 1st, 23 Dec. 1756, Mrs. Webb ; 2ndly, 19 March, 1763, Anne, dau. of Stephen Grey ; and 3rdly, the Hon. Margaret Lysaght, dau. of Lord Lisle, and *d.s.p.* 1787, leaving his estates to his nephew, William Henry Moore, on condition that he should bear the name and arms of Hodder. His nephew,
WILLIAM HENRY MOORE, who adopted the additional surname of HODDER upon the death of his maternal uncle, and became of Hoddersfield. He *m.* July, 1789, Harriet, dau. of Right Hon. Henry Theophilus Clements (brother to the 1st Earl of Leitrim), by Mary his wife, dau. and heir of Gen. Webb, and had issue,
1. WILLIAM HENRY, his heir.
2. Henry Theophilus (Rev.), D.D., LL.D., Rector of Carrigrohane, *m.* May, 1849, Sarah, dau. of Rev. Thomas Saunders Forster, Chaplain R.N., and *d.s.p.* 1865. She *d.* 25 Oct. 1897.
3. Thomas Eyre, *m.* 29 Feb. 1844, Eliza Hill, dau. of George Blacker. She *d.* 1862. He *d.* 8 April, 1863.
4. John Francis, *m.* Grace, dau. of Andrew Smith, of Burnbank ; and *d.* 1875, having had by her,
 1. William Henry.
 1. Grace, dec. 2. Harriet.
 3. Letitia Grace.
 4. Georgina Caroline Augusta, *d. unm.* 24 Oct. 1906.
1. Catherine, *m.* Rev. John Johnson ; *d.* 1856.
2. Harriet, dec.
3. Anna Maria, dec. 4. Selina, *d.* 1857.
The eldest son,
WILLIAM HENRY MOORE-HODDER, of Hoddersfield, co. Cork, J.P. and D.L., Col. N. Cork Militia, *b.* 1791 ; *m.* 1st, Charlotte Colthurst, of Ardrum, co. Cork, sister of Sir Nicholas Conway Col. thurst, Bart., which lady *d.* 7 March, 1832 ; he *m.* 2ndly, 14 Feb. 1839, Lucy Elizabeth Mary, dau. of Col. Need, of Mansfield Woodhouse, co. Notts (*see* WELFITT *of Langwith*). Col. Moore Hodder *d.* 20 Nov. 1859, having by his 2nd wife (who *d.* 10 Oct. 1898) had issue,
WILLIAM HENRY JOHN, now of Hoddersfield.
Lucy Harriet Fanny, *m.* 19 April, 1866, Col. Charles Fludyer, Grenadier Guards, eldest son of Sir Henry Fludyer, Bart., of Ayston Hall, Rutland. He *d.v.p.* 14 Jan. 1895, *s.p.*

Seat—Hoddersfield, Crosshaven, co. Cork.

HODSON. *See* BURKE'S PEERAGE, HODSON, Bart.

HOLMES LATE OF MOYCASHEL.

ARTHUR HOLMES, *b.* 3 July, 1876, present representative of the family of HOLMES of Moycashel, *s.* his father 1910.

Lineage. — ROBERT HOLMES, of Garryduff (son of Richard Holmes, who was an Officer of Cavalry in the Army of WILLIAM III in Ireland), *d.* in or before 1759, leaving by Elizabeth his wife,
1. Thomas, *d.* in or before 1759.
2. RICHARD, of whom presently.
1. Elizabeth, *m.* — Forbes.
2. Mary, *m.* — Mitchell.
3. Jane, *m.* John Armstrong, of Kilclare.
The 2nd son,
RICHARD HOLMES, *m.* Jane, dau. of — Telford, of Ballylough, and *d. circa* 1783-6, leaving issue,
1. Joseph, *b.* 1745 ; *d.* 1770.
2. Thomas, of Farmhill, co Sligo, High Sheriff 1810, *m.* Anne, sister of Dr. Phibbs, F.T.C.D., and *d.* June, 1818, leaving issue,

1. Richard, of Oakfield, Sligo, *m.* Anne, dau. of Alexander Erskine, and *d.* 1820, leaving issue.
2. Joseph, *d. unm.* 3. Isaac, *d. unm.*
4. Mathew, *d. unm.*
5. William (Right Hon.), P.C., M.P., *b.* 1779 ; *m.* 1807, Helen dau. of John Tew, and widow of Sir James Stronge, and *d* 1853, leaving issue.
6. Robert, *m.* Lucy, dau. of Alexander Watts, of Jamaica, and had issue.
1. Jane, *m.* Richard Meaben, and had issue.
2. Esther Mary, *d. unm.*
3. Elizabeth, *m.* — Petarr, and had issue.
3. William, *d.* 1780. 4. RICHARD, of whom presently.
1. Elizabeth, *d.* 1766, will proved 19 Feb. 1805.
2. Mary, *m.* Peter Longworth, of Bunnahenley, co. Westmeath, and had issue.
The 4th son,
RICHARD HOLMES, of Prospect and Garryduff, High Sheriff 1812, *b.* 1755 ; *m.* 1st, 28 Aug. 1780, Elizabeth, sister of Michael Telford, of Ballylough, co. Westmeath, and had issue, all of whom *d.* young. He *m.* 2ndly, Anne, dau. of John Arbuthnot, of Rockfleet, co. Mayo, and *d.* 31 March, 1822, leaving issue,
1. George Arbuthnot, of Moorock, King's Co., High Sheriff 1810, Lieut. in the Army, was wounded at Corunna, and served in the Walcheren Expedition, *b.* 1788 ; *m.* Feb. 1813, Jane, dau. of John Moore, of Clara, and *d.* Nov. 1847, leaving issue, two daus.,
 1. Jane, *m.* Feb. 1836, Cuthbert John Clibborn, of Moate, who *d.* 1847, leaving issue (*see that family*).
 2. Elizabeth, *m.* 11 Aug. 1842, George Nixon Montgomery, son of Major Alexander Nixon Montgomery (*see* BURKE'S *Family Records,* NIXON).
2. Charles, of Prospect, *b.* 6 July, 1796 ; *m.* Martha, dau. of Edward Molloy, of Dovehill, King's Co., and had issue.
3. ROBERT, of whom presently.
1. Anne, *b.* 1787 ; *m.* Rev. Cuthbert Fetherston, and *d.* 1847, leaving issue.
2. Jane, *b.* 1789 ; *m.* 11 June, 1811, Samuel Lindsey Bucknall, of Turin Castle, co. Mayo, and *d.* March, 1843, having by him (who *d.* 24 April, 1844) had issue.
3. Eliza, *b.* Jan. 1791 ; *m.* 1814, Lieut.-Col. D. J. Hearn, 43rd Regt., and had issue.
4. Sarah, *b.* 1793 ; *m.* 1824, Justin Brennan, 7th Regt.
5. Frances, *b.* 1799 ; *m.* 1823, Rev. W. R. Gresson, and had issue.
6. Susan, *b.* 1801 ; *m.* 1818, Gustavus Jones, of Belville, co. Westmeath, and had issue.
The youngest son,
ROBERT HOLMES, of Moycashel, *b.* 11 Oct. 1803 ; *m.* 24 Dec. 1842, Jane (*d.* 3 May, 1905), 5th dau. of William Henn, of Merrion Square, Dublin, Master in Chancery, and *d.* 17 Oct. 1870, leaving issue,
1. ROBERT WILLIAM ARBUTHNOT.
2. William Henn (225, *Lower Circular Road, Calcutta*), for 25 years in the East Indian Civil Service, *b.* 9 Nov. 1846 ; *m.* Oct. 1872, Rachel, dau. of John Scott Russell, F.R.S., and has issue, Madeline and Beatrix.
3. George Charles Vincent (Sir), K.C.B., K.C.V.O. (*Dornden, Booterstown, co. Dublin*), Chairman of the Board of Works, Ireland since 1901, formerly Secretary of the Institute of Naval Architects, C.E., *b.* 9 Oct. 1848 ; *m.* 22 July, 1880, Louisa Eugenia Greenstreet, dau. of Charles Greenstreet Addison, and has issue, Robert Gerard Addison, *b.* 31 Aug. 1881.
4. Edmond Gore Alexander, *b.* 17 July, 1850 ; *m.* 22 June, 1880. Florence, dau. of Ca pt. P. M. Syme, R.A., and has issue,
 1. Robert Arbuthnot, *b.* 4 June, *d.* Aug. 1883.
 2. Maurice, *b.* 14 June, 1885.
 1. Florence Ruth.
5. Thomas Rice Edward, *b.* 24 May, 1855 ; *m.* 14 Aug. 1888, Eliza Isabel, dau. of Lionel Isaacs, of Mandeville, Jamaica.
6. Charles Leslie Arbuthnot, *b.* 21 Sept. 1858 ; *d. unm.* 1874.
1. Mary Rice, *d. unm.* 13 July, 1902.
2. Eleanor Jane Pamela.
3. Julia Susan Christiana, *m.* 13 Aug. 1885, Walter Kerr, and *d.* leaving a dau., Dorothy.
The eldest son,
SIR ROBERT WILLIAM ARBUTHNOT HOLMES, K.C.B., of Moycashel, co. Westmeath, J.P., Barrister-at-Law, M.A. Trin. Coll. Dublin, Clerk of the Crown and Hanaper 1880-2, and Treasury Remembrancer and Deputy Paymaster-Gen. in Ireland since that year, *b.* 28 Dec. 1843 ; *m.* 28 Dec. 1871, Isabella, only dau. of J. Favière Elrington, LL.D., Q.C., Recorder of Londonderry, and Janet his wife, sister and heir of the late Mordaunt Bisset, of Lessendrum; *see that family*). He *d.* 19 Feb. 1910, having had issue,
1. ARTHUR.
2. Robert, *b.* 18 March, 1890.
1. Edith. 2. Norah.
3. Mabel Evelyn, *m.* 16 Aug. 1906, Rudolph Imelmann, son of Professor Imelmann, of Berlin.
4. Isabella. 5. Evelyn Iris.
6. Harriet.

Arms—Arg. a lion ramp. sa. armed and langued gu., charged on the shoulder with three bendlets or. Crest -A buck's head couped ppr. charged with three bendlets as in the arms. Motto—Dum spiro spero.
Residence—Marlay Grange, Rathfarnham, co. Dublin.

HOLMES OF ST. DAVID'S.

Major Hardress Gilbert Holmes, of St. David's, co. Tipperary, J.P., Major (ret.) P. W. O. Yorks. Regt., served in the Tirah Campaign and in the S. African War, b. 7 July, 1862; m. 17 Sept. 1908, Alys Maude Josephine, dau. of late John Lloyd, of Gloster, King's Co., and has issue,

Gladys Maude Rosaleen.

Lineage.—Peter Holmes, appointed joint Cursitor of the Court of Chancery, Ireland, 1 July, 1646, and Clerk of the Faculties, 6 Feb. 1661, Sovereign of Naas 1673, d. 2 Dec. 1675. He m. Bridget, dau. of Robert Ussher, of Cromlin, co. Dublin, and had three sons and four daus.,

1. Robert, of Clongeny, co. Kildare, Usher of the Court of Exchequer 21 April, 1669, d. Nov. 1683; m. Aug. 1679, Cisley, dau. of John Aylmer, and left a son and a dau.,
   John.
   Bridget, m. — Aylmer.
2. George, of New Hall, co. Kildare, joint Clerk of the Faculties with his father, d.v.p. 13 Nov. 1675; m. Aug. 1674, Lucy, dau. of William Hamilton, of Liscloony, King's Co., and by her (who m. 2ndly, William Talbot (see TALBOT of Mount Talbot)) had two sons,
   1. Peter, of Peterfield, co. Tipperary, b. 1675, High Sheriff of King's Co. 1707, M.P. for Banagher, 1713-14, for Athlone, 1727-31, d. 8 Feb. 1731; m. 1st, Lucy, 2nd dau. of William Sprigg, of Cloonivoe, King's Co., and 2ndly, Anne, widow of Richard Malone and William L'Estrange, dau. of Sir Thomas Crosbie, of Ardfert, co. Kerry. By the 1st wife he had an only son,
      Robert, of Peterfield, co. Tipperary, b. 1706, M.P. for Banagher, 1735, but unseated, d. 22 Jan. 1759; m. Elizabeth, dau. of Richard Malone, of Ballynahown, co. Westmeath, and had issue,
      1. Peter, of Peterfield, High Sheriff of co. Tipperary, 1772, M.P. for Banagher, 1761-90, for Kilmallock 1790-97, and for Doneraile, 1798-1801, d. 1803; m. 4 Feb. 1765, Elizabeth, dau. of Henry Prittie, of Kilboy, co. Tipperary. She d.s.p. 22 May, 1768.
         1. Isabella, m. 21 June, 1742, Thomas Dawson, of Nenagh.
         2. Bridget, m. 1753, John Bayly, of Debsborough, co. Tipperary (see that family).
         3. Jane, m. June, 1757, Owen Moony, of Lackagh, King's Co. (see MOONY of the Doon).
         4. Anne, d. unm. 29 Aug. 1760.
         5. Margaret, d. unm. 3 May, 1765.
   2. George, of Liscloony, of whom presently.
3. Gilbert, of Ovidstown, co. Kildare, d. unm. 1689.
1. Margaret, m. 11 Nov. 1669, Arthur Shepheard.
2. Anne, m. 1678, John Southerne.
3. Mary, d. unm. 1715.
4. Jane, m. 1st, 1685, James Ryan; 2ndly, Cornelius Macenis.

George Holmes, of Liscloony, King's Co., b. posthumous, 1676, High Sheriff of Co. Longford 1712, and of King's Co. 1713, M.P. for Banagher 1727-34, d. 1734; m. 1st, Catherine ———, s.p.; 2ndly, 1 July, 1703, Isabella, dau. of Rev. Andrew Hamilton, of Kilskery, co. Tyrone, by Isabella, dau. of James Galbraith, by whom (who d. in 1758) he had eight sons and four daus.,
1. Audrey, m. 1730, Sarah, dau. of John Saunderson, and d.s.p.
2. Galbraith, of Ballinlough, co. Longford, b. 1706, High Sheriff of co. Longford, 1731, and of co. Cavan, 1737, M.P. for Banagher 1734, but unseated, d. Nov. 1763; m. June, 1742, Dorcas, dau. of Robert Adair, of Hollybrook, co. Wicklow, and had issue,
   1. George, of Ballinlough, High Sheriff of co. Longford, 1768.
   2. Robert, of Willbrook, High Sheriff of co. Longford, 1802.
   3. Galbraith.
   1. Jane, m. Peter Beatty, of Spring Park, co. Longford.
3. Robert, b. 1710; d. unm.
4. George, of Ferbane, living 1756.
5. Gilbert, of Belmount, of whom presently.
6. Henry.
7. James, Capt. 27th Foot, m. Jan. 1769, Frances, widow of Warneford Armstrong, of Ballycumber, King's Co., dau. of — Gray.
8. Richard, m. 31 Aug. 1756, Elizabeth, dau. of Hon. William Molesworth (see Peerage, Viscount Molesworth).
1. Isabella, d. unm. 1790.
2. Elizabeth, m. 1722, Edmund Armstrong, of Gillon, King's Co.
3. Lucy, m. Thomas Armstrong, of Ballylin, King's Co.
4. Jane.

The 5th son,

Gilbert Holmes, of Belmount, King's Co., High Sheriff 1771, d. 1810; m. 4 Nov. 1752, Mary, dau. of Francis Saunderson, of Castle Saunderson, co. Cavan, and by her (who d. 30 Nov. 1771) had three sons,

1. Peter, of Peterfield, co. Tipperary, b. 1765, High Sheriff of co. Tipperary 1795, d. 27 Oct. 1843; m. 17 May, 1796, Henrietta Maria, dau. of Very Rev. James Archibald Hamilton, Dean of Cloyne, and her by (who d. 3 Dec. 1844) had,
   1. Peter, of Peterfield, b. 1798; d. 1 May, 1843; m. Mary Augusta, dau. of Rev.—Postle, and had issue by her (who m. 2ndly, 18 July, 1844, John Hamilton Dundas),
      (1) Peter, of Peterfield, b. 1841; d. unm. 1864.
      (2) Robert Arthur, b. 1842; m. Edith, dau. of Rev. Robert Robinson, and left issue three daus.,
         (1) Mary, m. Rev. Edward Mann Perry, Vicar of Mevagissey, Cornwall.
      2. Alexander.   3. Gilbert.
      4. James Gustavus Hamilton, Col. 9th Lancers, b. 1809; m. Edith, dau. of Rev. Robert Robinson, of Ballynavin, co. Tipperary, and had issue,
         (1) James, d. unm.   (2) Arthur, m.
         (3) Robert.
         (1) ——— m. Dr. Lowe, of Lincoln.
         (2) Lily.   (3) ———, m. Gen. Riach.
   1. Henrietta Mary, b. 1800, deceased.
   2. Elizabeth Catherine, b. 1801; m. 1832, George Goff.
   3. Mary Anne, b. 1803.
   4. Jane Sophia, b. 1806; m. William Mitchell, Queen's Bays.
   5. Maria Julia, m. William Woodley Frederick de Cerjat, of Lausanne.
   6. Julia, b. 1812; m. Vicomte Brenier de Montmorand.
2. Gilbert, of whom presently.
3. Alexander, of Athgavan Lodge, co. Kildare, b. 1780, d. 1840, m. 1880, Jane Hamilton, and had issue,
   Arthur, b. 1801.
   Frances, d. 2 April, 1871; m. 5 June, 1837, Hon. Berkeley Wodehouse, C.M.G. (see Peerage, Kimberley, E. of).
1. Bridget.
2. Mary Anne, b. 1767; m. 1812, Admiral Henry Evans, M.P.
3. Elizabeth, b. 1768; m. 1792, William Harding.

The 2nd son,

The Very Rev. Gilbert Holmes, Dean of Ardfert, m. 1810, Lydia Waller, eldest dau. of Col. Francis Saunderson, of Castle Saunderson; and d. 23 Dec. 1846, having had,
1. Francis S., Major 8th Regt., d. at Kurrachee, in Scinde, India, Aug. 1849.
2. Peter, Lieut. 44th Regt., d. at Mangalor, 1834.
3. Alexander, G. B., R.N., d. 1839.   4. Cecil, d. 1837.
5. Hardress Robert, 66th Regt., d. at St. Anne's, Barbadoes, Sept. 1848.
6. William Bassett, of whom presently.
1. Lydia Catherine, m. 1841, Capt. Lancelot Bayly, of Bayly Farm, co. Tipperary, son of John Bayly, of Debsbro, co. Tipperary.

The youngest son,

William Bassett Holmes, of St. David's, J.P. and D.L., High Sheriff for King's Co. 1874, and for Tipperary 1872, Capt. Tipperary Militia, b. 20 Dec. 1820; m. 29 May, 1856, Elizabeth Deane, eldest dau. of W. L. Barter, of Fort William, co. Cork, and by her (who d. 28 April, 1906) had issue,
1. William Bassett Traherne, late of St. David's.
2. Hardress Gilbert, now of St. David's.
1. Lydia Cecil Frances.
2. Elizabeth Rose, m. 11 Sept. 1902, Arthur Persse Pollok, 2nd son of the late John Pollok, of Lismany (see that family).
3. Henry Henrietta Mary.

Mr. Holmes d. 15 Nov. 1883, being s. by his elder son,

William Bassett Traherne Holmes, of St. David's, J.P., High Sheriff co. Tipperary 1891, b. 11 Aug. 1858; d. unm. 4 Oct. 1906, being s. by his brother.

Arms—Arg., a lion rampant vert.
Seat—St. David's, Nenagh, co. Tipperary. **Clubs**—Naval and Military, Kildare St.

HOMAN-MULOCK. See MULOCK.

HORNIDGE OF TULFARRIS.

Edward Stuart Hornidge, of Tulfarris, co. Wicklow, b. 2 June, 1887; s. his father 1911.

Lineage.—Two brothers, John and James Hornidge, coming from Gloucestershire, settled at Colemanna, co. Carlow about 1656.

James Hornidge, of Colemanna, paid four shillings hearth money in 1664, and d. 1676 (admon. 23 Jan. 1676-7). By Sarah, his wife, he left issue,
1. James, of Killoneen, King's Co., m. Susanna Goodwin, and d. 1733, leaving issue.
2. Richard, of whom presently.   3. William.
1. Sarah.   2. Elizabeth.

The 2nd son,

Richard Hornidge, of Russelstown and Tulfarris, co. Wicklow, m. licence dated 26 Jan. 1699-1700, Hester, dau. of — Hogshaw. He d. 1740 (will dated 17 Sept. 1740, proved 2 Feb. 1740-1). He left issue,
1. William, of Russelstown, m. the dau. of Cuthbert Heighington, and d. March, 1785, leaving a son, Cuthbert, and two daus.
2. Richard, of whom presently.
3. James, d. unm. 9 Feb. 1769.
4. John, d. unm. Feb. 1785.
1. Hester, m. 6 June, 1742, Henry Rainsford.
2. Jane, m. Robert Gilbert, of Humphreystown, co. Wicklow.

The 2nd son,

Richard Hornidge, of Tulfarris, co. Wicklow, D.L., m. Aug. 1759,

Mary, 4th dau. of Hurd Wetherelt, and sister and co-heir of Vans Wetherelt, of Castletown, King's Co. She d. March, 1810. He d. March, 1787, having had issue,
RICHARD, of whom presently.
Frances Emelia, m. March, 1777, Michael Aylmer, of Grangemore and Courtown, co. Kildare (see that family).
The only son,
RICHARD HORNIDGE, of Tulfarris, J.P. and D.L., co. Wicklow, High Sheriff 1789, J.P. co. Kildare, Maj. Wicklow Yeomanry, B.A. Trin. Coll., Dublin, 1786, b. 1764; m. 1st, 1 July, 1788, Isabella Katherine Mary, dau. of Rev. Arthur Grueber, D.D. She d. June, 1795, leaving issue,
1. Isabella, d. unm. Dec. 1800.
2. Martha, m. 21 Aug. 1813, her cousin, John Aylmer, of Courtown.
3. Emily Maria, d. unm. 10 Jan. 1853.
He m. 2ndly, Sept. 1802, Elizabeth, eldest dau. of Hugh Henry, of Lodge Park, co. Kildare (see that family), and by her had issue,
1. RICHARD JOSEPH, his heir.
2. Robert GLEDSTANES, of Twickenham, King's Co., who assumed by Royal Licence, 11 July, 1871, the name and arms of GLEDSTANES, b. 1815; m. 1st, 14 Dec. 1838, Sophia, dau. of John Corry Moutray, of Favor Royal, co. Tyrone, and by her (who d. 1848), had issue,
  1. Moutray GLEDSTANES, of Favor Royal, co. Tyrone, b. 28 April, 1845; m. 15 Jan. 1874, Helen Catherine, dau. of John James Verschoyle, of Tassagart, co. Dublin, and has issue (see GLEDSTANES of Fardross).
  2. Robert, b. 1848.
He m. 2ndly, 1855, Mary, dau. of Mervyn Stewart, of Martray, co. Tyrone (see BURKE's Peerage, STEWART, BART. of Athenry), and d. 1876, having by her had issue,
  3. Cecil Ambrose Frederick (Stanford, Kati Kati, N.Z.), b. 1858; m. 1882, Caroline Jane, dau. of Rev. John Crossley, Vicar of Shankhill, Belfast, and has issue,
    (1) Caroline Edith Phœbe. (2) Mary Florence.
    (3) Isabella.   (4) Helen Louisa.
  4. Edward (Kati Kati, N.Z.), b. 1860; m. 1885, Addeen Emma, dau. of Stephen Goss, and has issue,
    (1) Mary.   (2) Phœbe Kathleen.
    (3) Helen. (4) Dorothy.
  5. Charles Mervyn, b. 1868.
  1. Phœbe, m. 1881, her cousin, Mervyn Archdale Stewart, and has issue (see BURKE's Peerage).
  2. Evelyn, m. 1896, George Charles Wadby Morris.
3. Vance, B.A. Trin. Coll. Dublin, 1840, d. 1887.
4. EDWARD, of whom presently.
1. Cecilia, m. 2 Oct. 1828, Ambrose Upton Gledstanes, of Fardross, co. Tyrone (see that family). She d. 27 June, 1861. He d.s.p. 1871.
5. Louisa Elizabeth, d. unm. 7 Sept. 1881.
The eldest son,
RICHARD JOSEPH HORNIDGE, of Tulfarris, J.P., B.A. Trin. Coll. Dublin, 1824, b. Aug. 1803; d. unm. 9 Oct. 1859, and was s. by his youngest brother,
EDWARD HORNIDGE, of Tulfarris, m. 1857, Phœbe Julia (who d. 1890), dau. of Mervyn Stewart, of Martray (see BURKE's Peerage, STEWART, BART., of Athenry), and d. 29 March, 1874, leaving issue,
1. RICHARD JOSEPH, of Tulfarris.
2. Edward, B.A. Trin. Coll. Dublin, formerly Lieut. 6th Brigade South Irish Div. R.A. (40, Hurlingham Court, S.W., and Dillon House, Downpatrick), b. 18 July, 1865; m. 15 Oct. 1895, Sarah Madelina Frideswide, only child of Spencer Perceval, brother of Robert Perceval-Maxwell, of Finnebrogue (see that family), and has issue,
  1. Frideswida Frances. 2. Kathleen Margaret. 3. Eileen Vivien.
  1. Elizabeth, m. Charles Frederick Moutray, and had issue (see MOUTRAY of Favor Royal).
  2. Frances Cecilia. 3. Louisa Mary, m. 1885, James M. Higginson.
4. Georgina Helen, m. 1888, John Greaves.
5. Edith Phœbe, m. Gerald Lewis.
6. Alice, m. Maj. Lionel K. Carlyon.
The eldest son,
RICHARD JOSEPH HORNIDGE, of Tulfarris, co. Wicklow, J.P., High Sheriff 1899, Capt. 3rd Batt. Royal Dublin Fus., b. 12 Nov. 1863; m. 26 Aug. 1886, Margaret, dau. of J. Cree, of Virginia, U.S.A. He d. 31 Jan. 1911, having had issue,
1. EDWARD STUART, of Tulfarris.
2. Robert.   3. Mervyn Cyril.
1. Phœbe.

Seat—Tulfarris, Blessington, co. Wicklow.

HOUSTON OF ORANGEFIELD.

JOHN BLAKISTON BLAKISTON-HOUSTON, of Orangefield and Roddens, co. Down, Vice-Lieutenant co. Down, J.P. and D.L., High Sheriff co. Down 1860, and M.P. for North Down 1898; b. 11 Sept. 1829; m. 16 Nov. 1859, Marian, 2nd dau. of the late Richard S. Streatfeild, of The Rocks, Sussex, and by her (who d. 1890) has issue,

1. RICHARD, late Capt. 5th Batt. Royal Irish Rifles, b. 7 July, 1864; m. 24 Feb. 1897, Lilian Agnes, dau. of George Jardine Kidston, of Finlaystone, co. Renfrew, and has issue,
  1. JOHN MATTHEW, b. 31 Aug. 1898.
  2. George, b. 12 May, 1900.
  1. Marian.
2. Thomas, b. 12 Sept. 1865.
3. Charles, b. 31 Aug. 1868; m. 1904, Norah Persse.
4. James Edward, Capt. 8th Hussars, b. 18 Nov. 1877.
5. John, Capt. 11th Hussars, b. 18 April, 1881; m. 22 Nov. 1910, Louisa Henriette, dau. of Monsieur Le Conte de St. Ouen, France.
1. Mary Charlotte, m. 6 Aug. 1884, Harry Scarlett, youngest son of W. Scarlett, of Downland, Uckfield, and has issue (see that family).
2. Annie Marian.
3. Dora, m. Feb. 1905, Commander F. Scarlett, R.N., and has issue.
4. Mabel. m. 24 June, 1896, George Hurst Fowler, youngest son of Robert Fowler, of Rahinstown, co. Meath (see that family).
5. Isabel, m. Jan. 1911, Major David Ramsay Sladen, D.S.O., son of General Sladen, of Rhydoldog (see that family).
6. Ethel, m. 20 Aug. 1902, James MacAlpine-Downie, of Appin, Argyllshire, and has issue.
7. Hilda, m. Aug. 1907, George James Bruce, son of Samuel Bruce, D.L., of Norton, Glos., and has issue (see that family).

Mr. Houston s. his father 1857.

Lineage.—WILLIAM HOUSTON, m. 9 Aug. 1732, Elizabeth, dau. of Joshua McGough, of Drumsill, co. Armagh, and had (with two other sons and a dau., all of whom d. unm.) an eldest son,
THOMAS HOUSTON, m. 21 Sept. 1765, Mary, dau. of John Holmes of Belfast, and d. in 1771, leaving one son,
JOHN HOLMES HOUSTON, of Orangefield, co. Down, m. 1792, his cousin, Eliza, dau. of John Holmes, of Belfast. His eldest and last surviving dau.,
MARY ISABELLA HOUSTON, m. 11 July, 1827, Richard Bayly Blakiston, late R.A., afterwards BLAKISTON-HOUSTON, of Orangefield and Roddens, co. Down (b. 13 May, 1793), and had issue,
1. JOHN, now of Orangefield and Roddens.
2. Richard Mathew, d. 1847.
3. Thomas, Capt. 4th Foot, b. 12 Nov. 1833; d. 1860.
4. Charles William, b. 11 May, 1836; d. 1861.
1. Anne, m. 26 Sept. 1849, Matthew Blakiston, eldest son of John Blakiston, of Mobberley Hall, co. Chester (see BURKE's Peerage, BLAKISTON, Bart.).
2. Eliza Houston, d. 1847.
Mr. Blakiston was 5th son of Sir Matthew Blakiston, 2nd bart., by Anne his wife, dau. of John Rochfort, of Clogrenane, co. Carlow, assumed by Royal Licence, on the death of his father-in-law, in March, 1843, the surname of HOUSTON, in addition to his patronymic BLAKISTON. He d. 21 July, 1857. His widow d. 4 Nov. 1873.

Arms—Quarterly: 1st and 4th, or a chevron chequy sa., and arg. between three martlets of the second, for HOUSTON; 2nd and 3rd, arg., two bars and in chief three cocks statant gu., an annulet az. for difference, for BLAKISTON. Crests—1st, a sand-glass ppr. for HOUSTON; 2nd, a cock statant gu. charged with an annulet or, for BLAKISTON. Mottoes—(Over the 1st crest), In time; (under the arms), Do well and doubt not.

Seat—Orangefield, and Roddens, Belfast, co. Down. Clubs—Carlton and Ulster.

HOVENDEN OF GURTEEN.

Lineage.—THOMAS HOVENDEN, of Tankardstown Castle and Ballylehane Castle, Queen's Co., m. Margaret, eldest dau. of Thady FitzPatrick, 4th Baron of Upper Ossory, by Joan his wife, granddau. of James, Earl of Ormonde. He d. 1657. Their son,
JOHN HOVENDEN, of Tankardstown, m. Mary, dau. of Edward Butler, 1st Viscount Galmoye, by Anne his wife, dau. of Edmund Butler, 2nd Viscount Mountgarret. He d. 1680. Their son,
THOMAS HOVENDEN, of Towlerton Park, Queen's Co., d. 1695, having m. Jane, dau. of James Hovenden, of Ballyfoyle, Queen's Co., by Margaret, dau. of Henry Wycombe, co. Wicklow. This James Hovenden, b. 1586, d. 21 Nov. 1637, was the son of John Hovenden, of Killaban to whom and his posterity arms were confirmed and crest granted, in 1585. He was the son of Giles Hovenden who went to Ireland. Thomas and Jane Hovenden had issue, a son,
THOMAS HOVENDEN, of Towlerton Park, and of Gurteen, Tieremane, Ballickmovler, Ballylehane, &c., Queen's Co., m. Letitia Mosley. His will is dated 20 April, 1744. He left issue,
1. JOHN, of whom presently.
2. Piers, of Ballickmovler, m. his cousin, Eleanor, dau. of Henry Hovenden, and sister of Arthur Hovenden, J.P., of Merrymount (whose wife was Mary, dau. of Geo. Hartpole, of Shrule Castle, Queen's Co.), and by her left issue at his death, 10 June, 1800,
  1 William, of Ballickmovler, who s. his father, and d. unm., 24 Sept. 1804, and was s. by his nephew (son of his sister), Francis Hovenden (see below).
  1. Anne, m. 1794, Thomas Phelan, of Naas, co. Kildare, but d.s.p.
  2. Frances, m. her cousin, Henry Hovenden, Attorney-at-Law, and d. 21 July, 1802, leaving issue (see below).
  3. Elizabeth, d. unm. 12 March, 1809.
  4. Eleanor, d. unm.
3. Henry, d. young.   4. Giles, d. young.
  1. Mary, m. Thomas Rutledge, but d.s.p.
  2. Jane, m. 1st, William Greene; and 2ndly, her cousin, Nicholas Hovenden (son of Arthur Hovenden, and his wife Elizabeth Aylmer), by whom (who d. 1810) she had issue.

3. Margaret, m. 1736, George Stanley, of Clonmore, Queen's Co., grandson of Geo. Stanley, and his wife Jane Burdet, aunt to Sir Thomas Burdet, Bart. of Garrahill, co. Carlow, and left issue.
4. Lanceletto, m. Gerald Alley, J.P. Queen's Co.
5. Anne, m. her cousin, Thomas Hovenden, by whom she had a son.

Mr. Hovenden d. 31 Aug. 1744, and was s. by his eldest son,

JOHN HOVENDEN, of Gurteen, m. 1st 8 Dec. 1749, Mary, youngest dau. of Thomas Fitzgerald, of Moret, Queen's Co., by whom he had three daus.,
1. Frances, m. 1st, Stephen Fitzgerald, by whom she had two sons, who both d. unm.; and 2ndly, Bryan Stapleton, Attorney-at-Law, by whom she had issue.
2. Margaret, m. her cousin, Thomas Alley.
3. Lanceletto, b. 1755 ; m. 1776, John Tubbs, of Loftus Hill, co. Dublin, but d.s.p. 19 March, 1834.

Mr. Hovenden m. 2ndly, Agnes, dau. of William Moore, of the Queen's Co., by whom he had issue,
1. John Moore, Capt. Queen's Co. Militia, m. 1802, Delia, dau. of Charles Warner, of Carlow, who d.s.p. 11 June, 1803. He d. 22 March, 1829.
2. Henry, Attorney-at-Law, m. 1st, his cousin, Frances, dau. of Piers Hovenden, of Ballickmoyler, by whom (who d. 21 July, 1802) he had,
   1. Francis, b. 12 July, 1802, s. in 1804 (in right of his mother) to Ballickmoyler, and d. unm. 6 Feb. 1824, when he was s. by his sister, Mrs. Marshall.
   1. Anne, who s. her brother in Ballickmoyler, m. 1st, Thomas Gregory, Attorney-at-Law, by whom she was murdered 3 Sept. 1831 ; and 2ndly, James Jackson Marshall, Attorney-at-Law, who d. 13 Jan. 1857. Mrs. Marshall devised her estate to her half-sister, Miss Florinda M. Hovenden, and d.s.p. 24 March, 1863.

Mr. Henry Hovenden m. 2ndly, Maria, dau. of Charles Warner, and by her (who d. 2 Dec. 1828) left at his death, 5 Dec. 1827, three daus.,
   2. Florinda Maria, b. 6 Dec. 1804, who s. to the estate of her half-sister, Mrs. Marshall, and devised it to her cousin Julia, dau. of Charles Warner Hovenden (see below). She d. unm. 10 May, 1884.
   3. Julia, b. 17 Dec. 1805 ; m. 1847, her cousin, William Hovenden, of Tierernane, but d.s.p. 20 Oct. 1862.
   4. Harriett, m. J. Higgins.
3. Pierce, Capt. 53rd (Shropshire) Foot, d. unm. in Madeira.
4. Moseley, d. 26 June, 1823.
5. Moore, of whom presently.
6. Thomas, of Gurteen, Lieut. Queen's Co. Militia, d. unm. 1869, and was s. by his nephew, Henry Hovenden.
4. Jane, d. unm. March, 1811.

Mr. Hovenden, whose will is dated 20 Dec. 1791, d. 7 Oct. 1797, and was s. eventually in Tierernane, and in the representation of the family, by his 5th son,

MOORE HOVENDEN, of Tierernane, who m. 1812, Julia, dau. of Charles Warner. By her (who d. 1 April, 1865) aged 93, he had,
1. JOHN MOORE, of whom presently.
2. HENRY, of whom presently.
3. Charles Warner, of Ballylehane, b. 1817 ; m. 1839, his cousin, Anne, youngest dau. of Arthur Aylmer Hovenden, of Ashfield Hall, Queen's Co., J.P. and D.L., Queen's Co., and d. in Gurteen, 28 Sept. 1089, leaving by her (who d. 15 March, 1878),
   1. CHARLES, of Gurteen.
   2. William, d. young.
   3. John Moore, b. 2 Jan. 1846 ; m. 22 Sept. 1880, Susan Sarah, eldest dau. of Thomas Robinson, by whom (who d. 30 March, 1885) he had issue,
      (1) HENRY CHARLES, male representative of the family, b. 18 March, 1885.
      (1) Anne Margaret Sophia.
   He m. 2ndly, 15 Sept. 1888, Ida Marion, 2nd dau. of Richard Coote, M.D., and grand-dau. of Sir Charles Coote, Bart., of Donnybrook, by whom he had,
      (2) Ethel Sybil, b. in Gurteen, 27 Jan. 1891 ; d. 30 Dec. 1894.
   He d. 16 Dec. 1895.
   4. Peirce Giles, b. 19 Feb. 1847 ; m. 15 Nov. 1879, Elizabeth, dau. of James George, and has issue,
      (1) Herbert, b. 22 Jan. 1883.
      (1) Edith Annie, d. 17 Feb. 1895.   (2) Florinda.   (3) Violet.
      (4) Raby, d. 18 Dec. 1886.
   5. Henry Butler, b. 23 April, 1853 ; d. unm. 7 Jan. 1878.
   1. Anne Butler, m. 15 Aug. 1875, her cousin, Thomas Stanley Torney, and has issue,
      (1) Hovenden Henry George, b. 10 Oct. 1877 ; d. 7 Jan. 1878.
      (2) Ralph Hovenden, b. 10 Jan. 1881.
      (3) Henry Charles, b. 7 Aug. 1885.
      (4) Percy Stanley, b. 14 Dec. 1887.
      (1) Lettice Caroline Jane.
      (2) Anna Eva.   (3) Julia Maria Alianora.
      (4) Blanche Eveline.
   2. JULIA (see FFOLLIOTT of Tierernane and Ballickmoyler), who s. to the estates of Ballylehane and the Strand, Upper Ballickmoyler, Queen's Co., under the will of her cousin Florinda Maria.
4. William, of Tierernane, b. 1819 ; m. 1847, his cousin Julia, 2nd dau of Henry Hovenden. She d. 20 Oct. 1862. He d.s.p. 26 Nov. 1892, and was s. under his will by his niece Julia, now of Tierernane.

Mr. Moore Hovenden d. 16 Jan. 1845, was s. by his eldest son, JOHN MOORE HOVENDEN, of Tierernane, who d. unm. 1849, having devised his estate to his youngest brother, William, when the representation of the family devolved on his next brother,

HENRY HOVENDEN, of Gurteen, to which property he s. on the death of his uncle, Lieut. Thomas Hovenden ; b. 1814 ; d. unm. 27 Dec. 1889, and was s. by his nephew,

CHARLES HOVENDEN, of Gurteen, m. 1902, Elizabeth Agnes, 4th dau. of Thomas Nolan, of Kilconner, co. Carlow, and d. 1907, leaving issue an only dau.,
Elizabeth Agnes.

HOWARD. See BURKE'S PEERAGE, WICKLOW, E.

HUGHES OF BALLYCROSS.

FREDERIC HUGHES, of Rosslare Fort, and Barntown House, co. Wexford, late Lieut. 3rd Batt. Royal Irish Regt., served in S. African War (medals and clasps), b. 5 Jan. 1874 ; m. 12 Nov. 1902, Anna Margaret, youngest dau. of William Bolton, of The Island, co. Wexford (see that family), and has issue,
1. Eva Frederica.
2. Violet Theodosia.

Lineage.—THOMAS HUGHES, who went from Wales to Ireland during the Commonwealth, is believed, on very strong presumptive evidence, to have been the son of Hugh Piers Hughes, of Penbedw, co. Flint, who d. May, 1677, and who, according to the family pedigree in the possession of Mr. Hughes, of Kinmel Park, had a son, Thomas, who went to Ireland. This Hugh Piers m. Margaret, dau. of Thomas Venables, of Ysceifiog, and was son of Piers Hughes of Penbedw (by Katharine his wife, dau. of Robert Wynn Dolben, of Denbigh), who was 3rd son of Hugh ap Piers, of Plas vn Diserth and Llewerllyd, co. Flint, living 1588, ancestor of Hughes of Kimmel. He had, by Margaret his wife, two sons,
1. PIERCE or PIERS, of whom hereafter.
2. Walter, whose will, dated 16 April, 1671, was proved 4 May following, left by Elizabeth his wife,
   1. Walter, d. intestate, 1700.
   2. Thomas, d. intestate, administration to Mary, his widow, 1700.
   1. Margaret.
   2 Elizabeth, m. Jan. 1695, Isaac Betts.

The eldest son,
PIERCE HUGHES, living 1686, m. Sarah, dau. and heiress of Abraham Deane, of Ballytrent, and St. Margaret's, co. Wexford, acquired with her considerable estates in that co., and had by her (whose will, dated 8 Nov. 1705, was proved 17 Feb. 1709) issue,
1. ABRAHAM THOMAS, his heir.
2. Deane, of Wexford, Merchant, m. April, 1699, Eleanor Lambert, widow of Mr. King, and had a son, Lambert (Rev.), D.D., Chancellor of Christ Church, Dublin, 30 April, 1762. His will, dated 2 Sept. 1770, was proved 21 Jan. 1771 ; d. unm. and was bur. in his Cathedral, 12 Jan. 1771.
3. Pierce (Rev.), Rector of Kilscoran, whose will, dated 15 April, 1746, was proved 2 March, 1754. He m. Elizabeth, dau. of Henry Archer, of Ballyhoge, and had issue,
   1. Benjamin, of Wexford, m. Euphemia, dau. of George Nixon of Belmont, and d. 1798, leaving a son, Pierce (Rev.), Rector of Drogheda, and a dau. Sarah, m. William Daniel, of Fortview, co. Wexford.
   2. Archer, of Slad, m. Elizabeth, dau. of Richard Nunn, St. Margaret's, and had issue,
      (1) Archer, went abroad.
      (1) Elizabeth, m. Thomas Finn.
      (2) Hannah, m. Richard Edward Bolton.
      (3) Mary, m. Arthur Murphy.   (4) Anna
      (5) Frances.   (6) Charlotte.
   1. Elizabeth, m. Rev. Ambrose Harvey, of Bargy.
   2. Mary, m. April, 1736, John Howlin.
4. William, of Wells, m. Mary Graham, and d. intestate, administration granted 8 Aug. 1738.
1. Mary, m. June, 1679, William Ingham, of Lexlip.
2. Margaret, m. Sept. 1686, Richard Nixon, of Belmont.
3. Hannah, m. 1st, Oct. 1680, William Jacob ; and 2ndly, Rev. John Hough, Rector of Kilscoran.
4. Sarah, m. Richard Newton, of Ballynahallo.
5. Bridget, m. Cornelius Donovan, of Comore.
6. Frances, m. Capt. Blake, of Galway.
7. Martha, m. 1st, Dec. 1695, Simon Peare, of Kilmalock ; and 2ndly, Mr. Barry.   8. Jane, d. unm.

Mr. Hughes d. before 1705, and was s. by his eldest son.

ABRAHAM THOMAS HUGHES, of Ballytrent, High Sheriff co. Wexford 1727, *m.* 1st, Nov. 1697, Mary, dau. of William Hore, of Harperstown, co. Wexford, and by her had two daus.,
1. Jane, *m.* April, 1730, Thomas Lee.
2. Sarah, *m.* Dec. 1723, James Howlin, of Ballycronigan.

He *m.* 2ndly, Mary, dau. of Henry Archer, of Ballyhoge, same co., by whom he had issue,
1. HENRY, his heir.
2. Pierce, of Newtown, *m.* (marriage settlement dated 15 Feb. 1735) Margaret, dau. of George Nixon, of Newtown, co. Wexford, *d.* intestate (administration 4 Feb. 1745), and left, with a dau., Sarah, *d. unm.*, two sons,
  1. Abraham, *d. unm.*
  2. George, of Newtown, *m.* 1st, July, 1764, Ellinor, dau. of William Wray, of Castle Wray, and 2ndly, July, 1779, Hannah, dau. of Capt. Fox ; and dying 1799, left by her three sons, of whom the eldest,
    PIERCE WILLIAM, *m.* Sarah, dau. of Samuel Hall, and *d.* May, 1831, leaving issue,
    1. EDWARD (Rev.), D.D., Rector of Castlane, Diocese of Ossory, *m.* Mary, dau. of John Burrowes, of Fir Hill, co. Kildare, and had issue.
    2. George William, *m.* 22 Nov. 1866, Charlotte Frances Proctor, dau. of Edward Townsend, of White Hall, co. Cork, and *d.* 23 May, 1884.
      1. Joanna Matilda.   2. Katherine.   3. Fidelia.
      4. Anne, *m.* 8 June, 1852, Major John Harvey, of Bargy Castle, D.L. co. Wexford.
3. Abraham, went to Barbados, 1752, and *d.s.p.* before 1765.
4. Benjamin, of Hulltown, *m.* Sept. 1742, Sarah, dau. of Henry Bunbury, of Ballyseskin, and *d.* 1765, leaving with two daus., Sarah, *m.* Oct. 1768, William Todd Blake, and Mary (Mrs. Hall), and a younger son, Abraham, *d.s.p.*, an elder son,
  Henry, of Hilltown, *m.* 14 March, 1771, Jane Maria, dau. of Francis Goodall, of Kilcorrall ; and *d.* 1811, having had a son,
    Benjamin, of Kilcorrall, an Officer in the 56th Regt. and the Wicklow Militia, *m.* Jan. 1793, Sarah, dau. of Peter Paul Labertouche ; and *d.* 1805, leaving a dau., Mary Anne, *m.* 29 May, 1832, Tuffnell Carbonnell Barrett, 65th Regt., and two sons,
    1. Henry Francis, of Three Rivers, Canada, Ensign 35th Regt., and Glengarry Canadian Fencibles, *m.* 1812, Mary, dau. of Capt. Edward Cartwright, 60th Regt., and *d.* 1875, having had issue.
    2. Benjamin, settled in Trinidad as a sugar planter, *m.* a Frenchwoman there, and had two sons and five daus., *a.* Henry ; *b.* Abel ; *a.* Sarah ; *b.* Clementina ; *c.* Elizabeth ; *d.* Maria ; *e.* Camilla.
8. Henrietta, *m.* John Goodall, of Willmount.

Mr. Hughes *d.* 1739, and was *s.* by his eldest son,

HENRY HUGHES, of Ballytrent, *b.* 1706 ; *m.* Ellinor, dau. of George Houghton, of Bormount, by Euphemia his wife, dau. and co-heir of Christian Bor, of Bormount, by whom (who *m.* 2ndly, Capt. Connolly Ball) he had issue,
1. HENRY, of Ballytrent, *s.* his father, *m.* Jan. 1766, Mary, dau. of John Goodall, of Willmount, and had issue,
  1. Henry, *b.* 1770, *s.* his father, sold Ballytrent, and went to America.   2. John, *d. unm.*
  3. Abraham, *d. unm.*   4. Edward, went to India.
  1. Mary, *d. unm.*   2. Ellenor, *m.* Nicholas Grey.
  3. Henrietta Maria, *d. unm.*
  4. Euphemia, *m.* William McGuccin, of Belfast, Barrister-at-Law.
2. ABRAHAM, of whom we treat.
1. Euphemia, *m.* Loftus Hough.

Mr. Hughes *d.* intestate before 1746. His 2nd son,

ABRAHAM HUGHES, of Wexford, *m.* 8 Jan. 1767, Jane, youngest dau. of Robert Clifford, of Wexford, by Mary Boyd his wife, dau. of Highgate Boyd, of Rossylare, and Margaret Loftus his wife, sister of Nicholas, 1st Viscount Loftus, and had issue,
1. Henry, Capt. E.I.C.S., *d. unm.*
2. Abraham, Lieut. R.N., *d. unm.*
3. ROBERT, *s.* his father.
4. William, Lieut. 53rd Regt.
5. James, *m.* Miss Lawrence, and had a son,
  Henry, Lieut. 18th Madras Native Infantry, *d. unm.* at Valore, India, 18 April, 1857.
6. Nicholas Loftus, *d. unm.*   7. George, Lieut. 73rd Regt.
1. Mary, *m.* Robert Donovan.
2. Ellinor, *d. unm.*   3. Euphemia.

Mr. Hughes *d.* 1824, and was *s.* by his son,

ROBERT HUGHES, of Ely House, co. Wexford, J.P., *b.* 10 Sept. 1772 ; *m.* 1 Jan. 1797, Anne, 2nd dau. of Capt. Frederick Sparkes, of Crosshue. and *d.* 1854, leaving issue,
1. Robert Wigram, Bengal Civil Service, *d. unm.* 2 March, 1859.
2. FREDERIC (Sir), of whom presently.
1. Georgiana, *m.* 21 March, 1821, John Doran, Major in the 18th Royal Irish Regt.

The 2nd son,

SIR FREDERIC HUGHES, Knt. of Rosslare Fort and Barntown House, co. Wexford, J.P. and D.L., High Sheriff 1889, knighted in 1858, late Capt. 7th Madras Cavalry, and Knight of the Royal Persian Order of the Lion and Sun, F.R.G.S., F.R.A.S., *b.* 1814 ; *m.* 1st, 7 April, 1864, Emily, eldest dau. of William Kraeutler, and by her (who *d.* 13 Dec. 1868) had one child,
1. Frederic William Robert, *b.* 7 Dec. 1868 ; who *d.* an infant, 1869.

Sir Frederic *m.* 2ndly, 22 Nov. 1871, Theodosia, eldest dau. of Edward James, of Swarland Park, co. Northumberland, and *d.* 18 Nov. 1895, leaving further issue,

2. FREDERIC, now of Barntown and of Ballycross, Bridgetown, co. Wexford.
3. Walter Hastings Frederic, *b.* 10 Feb. 1875.
1. Winifred Emily Frederica.
2. Georgina Theodosia, *m.* 21 Aug. 1901, Rev. Henry Crawford Armour, Vicar of Reamington-with-Rock, Northumberland, and has issue, a son, Robert Rowland Crawford, and three daus., Mary Theodosia, *b.* 17 Aug. 1902, Angela Helen, and Cicely Georgina.
3. Myra Kathleen.
4. Gwendolen Loftus.
5. Elinor Clifford, *m.* 11 Oct. 1906, Arden Henry William Llewellyn Morgan, younger son of late Francis Frederick Richard Mansel Morgan, D.L., of Plas Coed Môr, Anglesey (*see that family*).

Arms—Or, on a chevron sa. between three griffins' heads erased gu., a fleur-de-lis, between two mullets pierced of the field,   Crest—A griffin's head erased gu., holding in the beak a fleur-de-lis or. Motto—Verus amor patriæ.
Residences—Ballycross, Bridgetown, co. Wexford ; Upton House, Kilmuckridge, co. Wexford.   Club—Royal St. George Yacht.

HUGHES OF DALCHOOLIN.

EDWIN HUGHES, of Dalchoolin, co. Down, J.P., High Sheriff, co. Roscommon, 1893, and for co. Down 1903, B.A., *b.* 19 Sept. 1851 ; *m.* 8 July, 1886, Emma Sophia, dau. of the late H. P. Rhodes, of Glenoak, co. Antrim, and has issue,
1. THOMAS WILLIAM GILLILAN JOHNSON, Lieut. N. Irish Horse *b.* 30 March, 1889.
1. Isabel May, *b.* 27 April, 1887.
2. Ethel Winifred Gwendoline, *b.* 9 Nov. 1891.

Mr. Hughes is the eldest surviving son of Thomas Hughes, of the Bush, co. Antrim, who was *b.* 3 July, 1808, and *d.* 20 Jan. 1885, and Catharine his wife (who was *m.* 21 Feb. 1837, and *d.* 7 Jan. 1893), dau. of Robert Dalzell.

Seat—Dalchoolin, Craigavad, co. Down.   Club—Ulster, Belfast.

HUMBLE OF CLONCOSKORAINE.

CHARLES NUGENT HUMBLE, of Cloncoskoraine, co. Waterford, J.P. and D.L., High Sheriff 1894, *b.* 1 Feb. 1854, 4th son of Sir John Nugent Humble, 2nd bart., who *d.* 11 June, 1886, and Elizabeth Philippa his wife, who *d.* 27 Sept. 1886, only dau. of George Fosbery, of Clorane, co. Limerick.

Lineage, Arms, &c.—*See* BURKE'S *Peerage*, NUGENT, Bart.

Seat—Cloncoskoraine, Dungarvan, co. Waterford.   Club—Kildare Street.

HUME. *See* DICK.

HUME OF HUMEWOOD.

WILLIAM HUME HUME, of Humewood, co. Wicklow, D.L., J.P., High Sheriff 1896, educated at Christ Church, Oxford, where he graduated with classical honours 1880, was an Attaché in H.M.'s Diplomatic Service, and appointed to the Embassy at Paris 1885, where he served till his resignation in 1892, *b.* 21 April, 1858. He *s.* by devise to the Humewood property of the Right Hon. W. W. Fitzwilliam Hume Dick.

Seats—Humewood, Kiltegan, co. Wicklow, and Thames Ditton House, Surrey.   Residence—24, Avenue des Champs Elysées, Paris. Clubs—Turf, Travellers', and Conservative.

HUME. *See* MACARTNEY OF LISSANOURE.

HUME-GORE. *See* GORE.

HUMFREY OF CAVANACOR.

WILLIAM KNOX HUMFREY, of Cavanacor, co. Donegal, Lieut. Lancashire Fusiliers. *b.* 1891; *s.* his elder brother 23 May, 1912.

Lineage.—JOHN HUMFREY landed in Ireland 15 May, 1655, from Cumberland, and settled at Donard, co. Wicklow. His mother *d.* there 12 Jan. 1664. He *d.* 16 Jan. 1665-6 (*Fun. Entry*), having had, with other issue, a son, HENRY HUMFREY, *m.* 13 Jan. 1657, Catharine, dau. of Francis Rolleston, of Frankfort Castle, and *d.* 4 July, 1709, leaving a son, JOHN HUMFREY, *m.* 19 July, 1712, Elizabeth Henthorn, and *d.* 9 June, 1743, leaving a son, THOMAS HUMFREY, *b.* 28 Jan. 1717, who was father, by Elizabeth Stewart his wife of an only son, HENRY HUMFREY, *b.* 1757, who, dying *unm.* 1 May, 1843, left, by will, his property in Wicklow, Louth and the King's Co., to his kinsman, Benjamin Geale Humfrey (*see below*).

EDWARD HUMFREY, of Clonagh, co. Carlow, 5th son of the first John Humfrey, of Donard, *m.* 1676, Deborah, dau. of Matthew Shepperd, of Killerick, co. Carlow. His will, dated 3 Jan. 1686, was proved 19 Feb. 1686. By her (who *m.* 2ndly, Thomas Bernard, of Clonmulsh) he had a 2nd son,

MATTHEW HUMFREY, of Carlow, *m.* by licence 1704, Martha, dau. of — Isaac. His will, dated 27 Dec. 1736, was proved 15 March, 1738-9. He *d.* 1738, leaving, with three daus., two sons,
1. Matthew, *m.* Jemima, dau. of Bernard, and *d.* 1744 (will dated 8 Feb. 1743, proved 3 July, 1744) leaving an only dau.
   Elizabeth, *m.* 10 June, 1759, Coghill Cramer.
2. JOHN, of whom we treat.

The 2nd son,
JOHN HUMFREY, *m.* 27 April, 1747, Elizabeth, dau. of John Geale, of Mount Geale, co. Kilkenny, and dying 1758, left a son,

WILLIAM HUMFREY, *b.* 1750; *m.* 5 Feb. 1774, Mary, dau. of Alexander Kirkpatrick, of Drumcondra, and by her (who *d.* 1802) left at his decease, 20 Oct. 1829.

1. ALEXANDER, *b.* 1775; *d.* Aug. 1845; *m.* Catherine, dau. of Major Craven, and had issue,
   1. William Charles, *b.* 1802; *m.* Collina, dau. of Major Fortye, and had four sons and one dau.
   2. Alexander John, *b.* 1803; *m.* Caroline, dau. of John Bayley, and had issue.
   3. Thomas Craven, *b.* 1811.
   4. Benjamin, *b.* 1813; *m.* Harriet, dau. of Daniel O'Rorke, and has issue.
   1. Ellen, *m.* Rev. J. F. Morton.
2. BENJAMIN GEALE, of Cavanacor.
1. Anne, *m.* L. Stotesbury; *d.* 1820.
2. Margaret, *d.* 1815.
3. Eliza, *m.* J. M. Reade.
4. Catherine, *d.* 9 Dec. 1815.
5. Mary Anne.

The 2nd son,
BENJAMIN GEALE HUMFREY, of Cavanacor, co. Donegal, Lieut.-Col. in the Army, served in the 45th Regt. during the Peninsular War, for which he had a medal and nine clasps; J.P. and High Sheriff 1848; *b.* 28 Sept. 1793; *d.* Feb. 1865; *m.* 3 July, 1823, Mary (who *d.* June, 1875), only child and heiress of William Keys, of Cavanacor, and had issue,

1. William, *b.* 16 July, 1824; *d.* April, 1826.
2. JOHN KEYS, late of Cavanacor.
3. Alexander, *b.* 9 Aug. 1831; *d.* Feb. 1876, Surgeon-Major 77th Regt., served in the Crimea (three medals); *m.* 10 Aug. 1865, Louisa, 2nd dau. of Rev. J. V. Brabazon, of Rahan Glebe, and had four sons and one dau.
4. Benjamin Geale, *b.* 25 Dec. 1833, late Lieut.-Col. R.A., served in the Crimea (despatches, three medals); *m.* 22 Oct. 1872, Mary Grace, dau. of John Page, of Southend, Essex, and has issue, three sons.
   1. Jane. 2. Mary.
   3. Marion, *m.* 11 Aug. 1853, Joseph Fishbourne, of Ashfield Hall, Queen's Co.; *d.* Nov. 1876.
   4. Elizabeth, *m.* 18 July, 1867, Robert Moore M'Mahon, of Hollymount, Queen's Co.; *d.* Feb. 1878.
5. Kate, *m.* General Brooke Rynd Chambers, of Foxhall, the Indian Army, and *d.* April, 1861.
6. Annie Frances, *m.* 19 Aug. 1873, Rev. Canon John S. M'Clintock, of Croghan House, Lifford, Rector of the Parish of Clonleigh.

The eldest surviving son,
JOHN KEYS HUMFREY, of Cavanacor, J.P., High Sheriff 1868, *b.* 16 June, 1828; late Lieut. 53rd Regt., and Capt. and Adjutant Donegal Militia; *m.* 1st, 6 March, 1857, Bessie Harriet, 2nd dau. of Henry William Wray, of Hollymount, of the Castle Wray branch of that family, and by her (who *d.* 3 Jan. 1859) had a son,
1. BENJAMIN GEALE, now of Cavanacor.

He *m.* 2ndly, 30 Aug. 1865, Maria, 3rd dau. of Falconer Miles, of Merton Sandford, co. Dublin, and *d.* 26 April, 1870, having had further issue,
2. William Keys, Lieut. S.A. Constabulary, served during Riel's Rebellion in Canada (medal) and in S. African War (medals), *b.* 30 Nov. 1866.

1. Alice Mary Lydia, *m.* Charles Frederick Stewart, of Horn Head, co. Donegal. She *d.* 1907, having had issue (*see that family*).
2. Kathleen Mona, *m.* Francis Staunton Blake, eldest son of John Blake, of Craig Castle, co. Galway, and left issue.

BENJAMIN GEALE HUMFREY, of Cavanacor, co. Donegal, Lieut.-Col. and Hon. Col. late commanding 3rd Batt. Leicestershire Regt., and Major retired 17th Foot, commanded his battalion in South African War (Queen's medal with three clasps), *b.* 3 March, 1858; *s.* his father 26 Aug. 1870; *d.* 5 May, 1912; *m.* 15 Jan. 1885, Emily Anne, 2nd dau. of William Knox, H.E.I.C. Service, of Clonleigh, co. Donegal (*see* BURKE's *Peerage*, RANFURLY, E.), and has issue,

1. BENJAMIN, of Cavanacor, *b.* Nov. 1885; *d.* 23 May, 1912.
2. WILLIAM KNOX, now of Cavanacor.
3. Percy Gerald.
1. Mary Isabella, *m.* 31 July, 1911, Guy Allen Colpoys Ormsby-Johnson, Bedfordshire Regt.

Arms—Quarterly: 1st and 4th, gu., a cross botonnée or, for HUMFREY; 2nd and 3rd, arg., on a bend sa. three lozenges of the first on each a saltire gu., for URSWICK. **Crest**—A sphinx sejant ppr. **Motto**—Sic olim.

Seat—Cavanacor, Ballindrait, co. Donegal.

HUMPHRYS OF BALLYHAISE.

NUGENT WINTER HUMPHRYS, of Ballyhaise House, co. Cavan, Lieut. Manchester Regt., *b.* 1885; *m.* 1 Feb. 1911, Blanche Ada de Vivefay, dau. of William Edward Wilson, of Daramona (*see that family*).

Lineage.—WILLIAM HUMPHRYS, of Ballyhaise, co. Cavan, younger brother of Christopher Humphrys of Dromard, was High Sheriff of that co. 1822; by his wife Letitia Kennedy he had issue,
1. Christopher, *b.* 6 Feb. 1786.
2. WILLIAM, who *s.* his father.
3. John, *b.* 1 Dec. 1809; *d.* 1818.
1. Anne, *m.* — Brown. 2. Matilda, *m.* Edward Archdall.
3. Letitia, *m.* — Twigg. 4. Amelia, *m.* — Kempland.
5. Caroline, *m.* — O'Brien.
6. Sophia, *m.* (as his first wife) Thomas Titson Magan, 4th son of Arthur Magan, of Clonearl and Togherson, and *d.* 29 March, 1846, leaving issue (*see that family*).

WILLIAM HUMPHRYS, of Ballyhaise House, J.P. and D.L., High Sheriff 1832; *b.* Dec. 1798; *m.* 1st, Jan. 1826, Anna Maria, dau. of John Pratt Winter, of Agher, co. Meath, and by her (who *d.* 1837) had issue,
1. William, of Ballyhaise.
2. JOHN WINTER, *s.* his brother.
3. Mervyn Archdall, *b.* March, 1830; killed before Delhi in the Indian Mutiny.
1. Anne Elizabeth, *m.* 2 Aug. 1860, Armoric Russell MccGuire. She *d.* 18 June, 1874. He *d.* 15 Feb. 1897.

He *m.* 2ndly, Feb. 1838, Maria Clarissa, dau. of Hugh Moore, of Eglantine House, co. Down (*see* MOORE *of Rowallane*), by whom (who *d.* 5 Oct. 1901) he had,
4. Hugh (Rev.), of Coon, co. Kilkenny, Rector of Eccles-next-the-Sea, Norfolk, and Incumbent of Knocktopher, co. Kilkenny, *b.* 10 Nov. 1838, formerly Capt. 15th Hussars; *m.* 28 April, 1875, Louisa, dau. of Rev. Henry Evans Lombe, of Bylaugh, Park, Norfolk, and has issue,
   1. William Evans Hugh, *b.* 1876, *m.* 29 Aug. 1911, Jessie Alice, dau. of Rev. E. Holliday, Rector of Miles Platting, Manchester.
   2. Julian Shirley Lombe, *b.* 8 June, 1882.
   3. Hugh Everard, *b.* 29 May, 1883.
5. Armitage Eglantine, of Lisagoan, co. Cavan, ¶ J.P.; *b.* Aug. 1843, *m.* 1st, 1867, Maria Victoria, only dau. of James Betty, of Lakefield, Bawnby, co. Cavan; 2ndly, Cecilia, dau. of J. L. Weaver. He *d.* 5 Sept. 1910.
2. Cecilia Letitia, *m.* 25 Nov. 1869, Arthur Shirley Ball, of Geraldstown, co. Meath.
3. Clara, *m.* 5 April, 1865, Clifford Walton, Dep. Assistant Commissary General.
4. Sylvia Priscilla, *m.* Sir Nugent Talbot Everard, Bart., of Randalstown, co. Meath (*see* BURKE's *Peerage*).

Mr. Humphrys *d.* 1872, and was *s.* by his son,
WILLIAM HUMPHRYS, *b.* Nov. 1827; *d. unm.* 5 April, 1877, and was *s.* by his brother,
JOHN WINTER HUMPHRYS, of Ballyhaise House, *b.* 23 Sept. 1829; *m.* 15 Feb. 1854, Priscilla Cecilia (*d.* 4 Jan. 1911), dau. of of the Rev. J. P. Garrett, of Killgaron, co. Carlow, and had issue,
1. WILLIAM, late of Ballyhaise.

2. John Mervyn, b. 10 July, 1858 ; d. 26 Nov. 1874.
3. James Winter, b. 17 April, 1861 ; d. Aug. 1871.
4. Charles Vesey, b. 1 Oct. 1862, Lieut.-Col. West Riding (The Duke of Wellington's) Regiment ; m. 1st, 1891, Florence, eldest dau. of James Chittick Humphrys, of Clare View, Kesh, co. Fermanagh, and by her (who d. 3 Feb. 1904) had issue,
Basil Hardress, b. 1892.
He m. 2ndly, 1905, Marion, dau. of Edwin Owen, of Bantry.
5. Mervyn Archdall, b. 25 Feb. 1864, Major Loyal North Lancashire Regt. ; m. 28 June, 1894, Cecile Clemence, eldest dau. of the late Monsieur Alexandre Gariner.
6. Francis Edward, b. 19 May, 1865 ; m. Maggie, dau. of — Armstrong, of Taurguga, N. Zealand, and has a son,
Mervyn, b. 1888.
7. Arthur Armitage, b. 17 Jan. 1870; m. 14 May, 1903, May, dau. of Samuel Francis White, of Abbeymead, Chertsey.
8. Llewellyn Winter, b. 28 Nov. 1871.
9. Percy Raymond, b. 16 July, 1873 ; m. 29 Dec. 1904, Catherine, dau. of late C. W. Minchener, of Christchurch, N.Z.
1. Caroline Elizabeth, m. 15 April, 1884, John Henry McIllree, I.S.O., Assist. Commissioner Royal N.W. Mounted Police, Canada, son of late Surg.-Gen. J. D. McIllree.
2. Priscilla Cecilia, m. 5 April, 1888, Rev. Thomas Haines Abrahall, M.A., Rector of Ennis, co. Clare.
3. Clara Christina, m. 1893, Whitney Upton Moutray, D.L., of Fort Singleton, co. Monaghan (see MOUTRAY of Favour Royal). He d. 4 Feb. 1904.
4. Anna Maria, m. 15 Sept. 1897, Mervyn Gilbart Smith, Barrister-at-Law.
5. Emily May.
Mr. Humphrys d. 1884. His eldest son,
WILLIAM HUMPHRYS, of Ballyhaise House, co. Cavan, J.P., late Lieut. R.N., b. 17 Nov. 1855 ; m. 1879, Alice, dau. of James Stannard, J.P. of Bricketstown House, co. Wexford, and d. 25 May, 1897, having by her (who m. 2ndly, 1898, Capt. Charles Ulric Sandys, Royal Irish Fusiliers) had issue,
1. WILLIAM, late of Ballyhaise.
2. NUGENT WINTER, now of Ballyhaise.
1. Ethel Elizabeth, m. 19 Nov. 1903, Baptist Barton Crozier, R.A., son of the Primate of Ireland, and had issue,
2. Evelyn Alice.
The eldest son,
WILLIAM HUMPHRYS, of Ballyhaise House, co. Cavan, Lieut. 17th Lancers, b. 1883 ; d. unm. 4 July, 1906, being s. by his brother.

Arms—Gu., a lion rampant, superintending his head a ducal ......et or, on a canton arg. a trefoil vert. Crest—On a ducal coronet an eagle, wings elevated, and endorsed or, armed and membered gu., holding in his dexter claw a broken spear-head of the first. Motto—Optima sperando spiro.

Seat—Bailyhaise House, Cavan.

HUNGERFORD OF INCHODONY.

MARY SANDES HUNGERFORD, of Inchodony (The Island) and Castle Ventry, co. Cork, s. her father 1870.

Lineage.—CAPT. THOMAS HUNGERFORD, of Rathbarry, or The Little Island, about four miles westward of Inchodony, the seat of his descendants, was a cadet of the House of HUNGERFORD of Farley, Somerset, and accompanied his relative, Col. Sir Edward Hungerford, of Farley Castle, in his expedition against Ireland, which started from Chester 27 May, 1647. He was living 1680. By Mary his wife he had,
1. RICHARD, his heir.
2. John (Rev.), of Cahirmore, b. 1658.
3. THOMAS, ancestor of the Cahirmore branch.
1. Elizabeth, m. Achilles Daunt.
2. Margaret, m. Francis Poole, of Mayfield.
3. Jane, m. Thomas Hewitt, jun.

The eldest son,
COL. RICHARD HUNGERFORD, of Inchodony, or The Island, near Clonakilty, is called " cousin " in the will dated 24 May, 1729, of John Hungerford, Lord of the Manor of Hungerford, in England. His own will was dated on or about 5 April. 1725. He m. Mary, dau. of Sir Emanuel Moore, and d. about 1729, leaving issue. The eldest son and heir,
THOMAS HUNGERFORD, m. 1719, Susannah Becher, and d.v.p., leaving issue,
1. RICHARD, his heir.
1. Elizabeth, m. 1733, Capt. Philip Townsend, of Derry, co. Cork.
2. Mary (a legatee in the will of John Hungerford, of Hungerford, in England), m. 1739, the Rev. Horatio Townsend, Rector of Donnoughmore, co. Cork.
The only son,
RICHARD HUNGERFORD, of The Island, and for many years of Foxhall, m. 1st. Mary Becher, and by her had
1. THOMAS, his heir.

2. John of Burren, m. 1771, Anne Daunt, and d. 1803, leaving with other issue a dau. Anne, m. Robert Sealy, of Gortnahorna (see that family) ; Richard, of Cappeen, and,
Emanuel, Capt. S. Cork Militia, formerly Lieut. 32nd Foot, emigrated to Australia, 1828. He was b. 1 Feb. 1785 ; m. 1 Feb. 1813, Catherine, dau. of Dr. Loane, and d. at West Maitland, N.S.W., 1872, having had issue,
(1) John Becher, b. 1814 ; m. 7 June, 1839, Anne, dau. of T. W. M. Winder, and had issue,
1. Emanuel Becher, m. — Blick.
2. John. 3. Percy.
4. Arthur.
1. Frances, m. J. Fitzgerald.
(2) Robert Richard, b. 1816 ; m. 4 Feb. 1839, Ellen Winder, and had issue,
1. William Augustus, m. Caroline Langstaff.
2. Robert. 3. Edward.
4. Hussey Hastings.
1. Kate Agnes.
2. Emma, m. Ven. Archdeacon Tyrrell.
3. Susan, m. Edward Tyrrell.
4. Amelia, m. Charles Simpson.
5. Annie, m. — Greenwood.
6. Helena.
7. Marian, m. J. Davidson.
(3) Emanuel, b. 1818, m. 1st, 4 Feb. 1851, Jane, dau. of Rev. John Boston, and 2ndly, Elizabeth Boston, and had issue,
1. John.
1. Elizabeth. 2. Kate. 3. Maria.
(4) William Moore, b. 1820 ; m. 5 Nov. 1845, Agnes Winder, and had issue,
1. Walter, m. Alice Gill.
2. Melville, m. Josephine Chambers.
3. Lovick.
1. Jessie, m. Rev. A. Newtle.
2. Emily, m. R. Doyle.
3. Jane, m. John Wilkinson.
4. Eva. 5. Louisa Agnes.
(5) Henry, b. 1822 ; d. unm.
(6) Thomas, M.L.A. of Bacrami, Sydney, b. 1823 ; m. 1st, 19 June, 1852, Emma Wood, and had issue,
1. Edmund, m. Beatrice Martin.
2. Cecil Payne, m. Lily Scott.
3. Herbert Blomfield, m. Edith Vaughan.
4. Frederick Richard, deceased.
5. Kenneth Stuart, m. Alice, widow of Francis T. Beamish and dau. of H. J. Hungerford, of Cahirmore (see that family).
6. Thomas, m. Lurline White.
7. Septimus, d. young.
1. Katherine Rachel.
2. Emma Elizabeth, m. Guy Hungerford.
3. Florence Loane, m. Capt. J. Kilpatrick.
4. Rose.
He m. 2ndly, K. Mallow, and had further issue,
8. Becher. 9. Roland.
10. Orpen.
5. Mary Kate, m. G. Macmahon.
6. Ethel Maud, m. E. H. Wilshire.
7. Mabel.
(7) Septimus (Rev.), Incumbent of St. Thomas, Enfield, Sydney, N.S.W., formerly of St. Peter's, Armidale, b. 12 Aug. 1825 ; m. 1 Feb. 1854, Eliza Sophia, dau. of Henry Incledon Pilcher, Solicitor, and has issue,
1. Marcus Orpen, Surveyor, b. 18 June, 1855 ; m. 3 March, 1880, Emily Cherrie, dau. of John Nicholson, and has issue,
a. John. b. Garnett.
c. Geoffrey.
a. Zilla. b. Clare.
c. Dorothea. d. Marjory.
2. Hedley Heber, Solicitor, b. 20 April, 1864 ; m. 4 April, 1894, Edith Mary Martha Flower.
1. Minna Catherine Eliza, b. 23 Aug. 1857 ; m. 1st, 8 Nov. 1881, Charles Walter William MacArthur; 2ndly, 24 Oct. 1894, Francis William Hales, son of Archdeacon Hales, of Tasmania.
2. Annette Jemima, b. 31 Dec. 1859 ; m. 19 Jan. 1882, Lambert Skene Gordon.
3. Miriam Eliza, b. 17 March, 1862.
4. Beatrice Theodora, b. 18 March, 1867 ; m. 5 July, 1892, George Barnewall Hales, son of Archdeacon Hales.
(8) Percy Payne, b. 1830 ; m. 3 Oct. 1869, Emily Smith, and has issue,
1. Percy. 2. Henry.
3. Ernest. 4. Roland Loane.
5. Claud. 6. Septimus Clive.
7. Leslie Gordon.
1. Lily. 2. Laura.
(1) Anne Loane, b. 1827 ; m. 7 May, 1850, Rev. Robert Chapman, and has issue.
(2) Catherine, b. 1834 ; m. 15 Jan. 1857, Edward Swire and has issue.
He m. 2ndly, Mary, dau. of the Rev. Emanuel Hungerford, and by her was father, inter alios, to
3. Richard (Rev.). m. 1775, Mary Hungerford, and by her (who m. 2ndly, Michael French) had an only son,
Richard, b. 1776 ; m. 1794, Isabella Masters, and had a son, Richard, of Carrigeen, m. Mary Cranfield, dau. of Capt. Colin Campbell, 42nd Highlanders, and Eliza his wife, dau. of Col. Hungerford, and had issue,

Hungerford.   THE LANDED GENTRY.   332

1. Richard. 2. Colin Campbell. 3. Alexander George. 4. Thomas Walter, of Greymouth, New Zealand, b. 28 Jan. 1832 ; m. 25 Feb. 1863, Elizabeth Mary, dau. of James Delany, of Clony Castle, and has surviving issue, 1, Richard Colin Campbell, b. 1 Jan. 1865 ; 2, Henry Hungerford John Sealy, b. 29 Feb. 1867 ; 3, Mary Elizabeth Cranfield, b. 12 June, 1869.
 1. Mary Cranfield. 2. Charlotte.

Richard Hungerford d. circa 1784, and was s. by his son,
 THOMAS HUNGERFORD, of The Island, m. 1770, Mary Cranfield Becher, and by her (who d. 1836) had issue,
 1. RICHARD, his heir.
 2. George (Dr.), of Clonakilty, m. 1802, Eliza Hungerford, his first cousin, and by her (who d. 1828) left at his decease, 15 Sept. 1832,
    Richard, m. 1843, Mary, dau. of William Daunt, of Spring Hill, and had issue.
 3. Thomas, of Broomley, near Carragline, m. 1st, Johanna, widow of Henry Hungerford ; and 2ndly, Eliza, dau. of the late Dr. George Daunt, of Cork ; and had issue by his 1st wife,
    1. Thomas William, m. Miss O'Hea.
      1. Eliza Charlotte (dec.), m. O'Donovan Becher.
      2. Mary Cranfield.
    By the 2nd wife he had,
    2. George Daunt.
    3. Georgina Daunt.   4. Catherine Maria.
    5. Susanna Letitia.   6. Charlotte.

The son and heir,
RICHARD HUNGERFORD, of The Island, b. 1771 ; m. July, 1793, Frances Eyre, dau. of Richard Becher, of Hollybrooke, and by her (who d. 12 Sept. 1843) had issue,
 1. THOMAS, late of Inchodony, or The Island.
 2. Richard Becher, m. 18 Sept. 1837, Frances, dau. of John Becher, of Hollybrooke, and d. 21 March, 1904, leaving issue,
    1. Richard Hedges Becher, m. Elizabeth Adams, and has issue,
       (1) Olive Mary Frances.   (2) Ena Muriel.
    1. Susan Becher.   2. Frances Eyre Becher.
 3. John, d.s.p.
 4. William, m. 22 March, 1831, Jane, dau. of Winspeare Toye, and left issue (with four daus., Margaret Toye, m. F. E. Macnamara ; Frances Eyre, d. unm. ; Janie, d. unm. ; and Rachel Jane, d. unm.), three sons,
    1. Richard, Deputy Surg.-Gen. late 53rd Regt., b. 23 March, 1834 ; d. 19 March, 1909 ; m. 12 Sept. 1861, Sarah, dau. of Alexander Grant, and by her (who d. 17 Nov. 1906) had issue,
       (1) William Alexander (5, Gracechurch Street, London, E.C.), b. 18 April, 1870 ; m. 24 May, 1902, Dorothy, dau. of Dr. Elliot, of Chiswick, and has issue,
          Amy, b. 19 Jan. 1907.
       (2) Richard Becher, b. 21 June, 1879 ; m. 12 Aug. 1903, Lilian Irene (d. 2 Sept. 1910), youngest dau. of Rev. Samuel Bell.
       (1) Annie Florence, b. 17 Aug. 1862.
       (2) Frances Eyre, b. 25 Aug. 1864 ; m. 23 March, 1897, her first cousin Winspeare Campbell Augustus Hungerford, and has issue (see below).
       (3) Jane Toye, b. 27 March, 1866.
       (4) Mary Caroline, b. 19 Oct. 1868 ; m. 13 Feb. 1890, Lieut.-Col. Robert Caldwell, R.A.M.C., and has issue, Richard Hungerford, b. 27 Aug. 1892.
    2. William, of Sunmount, and Castle Ventry, co. Cork, J.P., m. 1st, 12 Sept. 1876, his cousin, Frances Eyre, dau. of Thomas Hungerford, of Inchodony (see below), m. 2ndly, 11 Feb. 1904, Ellen Henrietta Lucinda, 2nd dau. of John Richard Hedges Becher, J.P. of Lough Ine. He d. 10 Jan. 1908.
    3. Winspeare Toye, of Shanakill House, Cork, d. 21 May, 1905, having m. 1st, Sophia Spencer, and by her had issue,
       (1) Sophia, m. Sheldon Carter.
       He m. 2ndly, Isabella Fishbourne, and by her had issue, with seven daus.,
       (1) Winspeare Campbell Augustus, m. 23 March, 1897, his first cousin, Frances Eyre, dau. of Deputy Surg.-Gen. Richard Hungerford (see above), and has issue.
          Winspeare Toye, b. 20 Aug. 1898.
          Elizabeth Grant, b. 16 July, 1902.
       (2) Walter Hastings.   (3) Robert Beaconsfield.
       (4) Richard Geoffrey.
 5. George, m. 7 Oct. 1845, Mary Elizabeth Sandes, and left issue,
    1. Mary Georgina.   2. Frances Honoria Sara.
 6. Henry, d.s.p. 10 Oct. 1835.
 7. Becher, who settled in Canada, m. 14 Feb. 1845, Jane Crossley, and had issue,
    1. Richard Becher, m. Mary Large, and had issue,
       (1) Richard Frederick.   (2) Edward Percival.
       (1) Lucy Maria.
    2. William Arthur, m. Emily Deans, and had issue,
       (1) Henry Becher, m. Maria McOongar, and has issue.
       (2) John.   (3) Walter Hastings.
       (1) Edith, m. Rev. Eleazer Sibbald, and has issue.
       (2) Sarah, m. John McDonald.
       (3) Kathleen.
    3. Becher, m. Mabel True Davis.
    4. Arthur Radcliffe Crossley, m. Harriet Folinsbee, and has issue,
       Becher Samuel.
    5. Samuel Gibson Getty.
    6. John Henry, d. unm.   7. Thomas, d. unm.
    8. Walter Francis Hugh Watson, m. Maud Margaret McLaren, and has issue,
       Becher Alexander.

1. Emily, m. Thomas Augustine Gale.
2. Frances Eyre.
3. Mary Caroline, m. George B. Sippi.
4. Jane Crossley.
1. Fanny, d. unm.
2. Susan, m. 4 June, 1836, Winthrop Baldwin Sealy.

Mr. Hungerford d. 16 Feb. 1833, and was s. by his eldest son,
 THOMAS HUNGERFORD, of Inchodony, The Island, co. Cork, J.P., b. 16 Jan. 1795 ; m. 1 Dec. 1842, Caroline, dau. of George Sandes, of Dunowen, co. Cork, and by her (who d. 1 April, 1888), had issue,
 1. Hungerford Richard, d. 1 June, 1855.
 1. MARY SANDES, now of The Island.
 2. Frances Eyre, m. 12 Sept. 1876, her cousin, William Hungerford, of Sunmount and Castle Ventry, Cork (see above), and d. 28 April, 1900.
Mr. Hungerford d. 29 April, 1870.

Arms—Sa., two bars arg. in chief three plates. Crest—Out of a ducal coronet, or, a pepper garb of the last between two sickles. erect ppr. Motto—Et Dieu mon appuy.
Seat—The Island Clonakilty, co. Cork.

———

HUNGERFORD OF CAHIRMORE.

HENRY HUNGERFORD, of Cahirmore, co. Cork, s. his father 1906.

Lineage.—CAPT. THOMAS HUNGERFORD, of Rathbarry (see preceding Memoir), d. 1680, leaving, by Mary his wife, a son,
 THOMAS HUNGERFORD, of Cahirmore, matriculated Trin. Coll. Dublin, 1679, m. 1684, Frances Syng, sister to the Archbishop of Tuam, and had issue,
 1. THOMAS, his heir.
 2. John, m. Catherine, dau. of Henry Jones, of Drombeg House, and was father of
    THOMAS HUNGERFORD, m. Ellen, dau. of Capt. Payne, of Tralee, and had issue,
     JOHN TOWNSEND HUNGERFORD, Solicitor to the Hon. E. I. Co. at Bombay. He m. Mary Anne, dau. of J. Payne, and niece of T. Price, of Ardmoyle, and Clonmore, co. Tipperary, and d. leaving issue,
      1. John Hayes, d. 1823.
      2. TOWNSEND JAMES WILLIAM, Capt. Bengal Artillery, b. 1814.
      1. Ellen, m. Rawson Hart Boddam, Bengal Civil Service, eldest son of R. H. Boddam.
      2. Mary Anne, m. 1st, Ewan Law, Bengal Civil Service, son of Ewan Law, of Horsted Place, Sussex ; d. 1818 ; and 2ndly, 1826, George Williamson, Lieut. H.M.'s 11th Dragoons, and Capt. H. H. the Nizam's cavalry.
      3. Catherine, m. Welby Jackson, Bengal Civil Service, son of Sir John Jackson.

The eldest son,
 COL. THOMAS HUNGERFORD, of Cahirmore, m. 1724, Barbara, dau. of Col. Bryan Townsend, M.P. of Castle Townsend, co. Cork, and by her had a son,
 THOMAS HUNGERFORD, of Cahirmore, J.P., m. 1751, Sarah, dau. of Dr. John Boisseau, a Huguenot, and had by her three sons,
 1. THOMAS, his heir, of Cahirmore.
 2. John, m. Anna, dau. of the late Capt. Richard Blair, of Blair's Cove, and the Abbey, and had issue, one son,
    Thomas John, m. Catherine, dau. of Henry Pyne Masters, and had issue three sons (dec.), and two daus., the eldest, Jane, m. Gustavus Helsham, of St. Mary's Hall, Norfolk, has issue, two sons, Evelyn Hungerford and Somerville, and one dau., Emily Blunt.
 3. Richard, m. twice, and by his 2nd wife, Mary Shaw, had issue, two sons, Richard and Robert, both of whom have issue.

The eldest son,
 THOMAS HUNGERFORD, of Cahirmore, m. 1787, Jane, dau. of Jonas Travers, of Butlerstown, co. Cork, and by her (who m. 2ndly, 1791, the Rev. William Stuart, of Welfield, co. Cork) left at his decease, v.p. 1789, a son and heir,
 THOMAS HUNGERFORD, of Cahirmore, M.A., J.P., b. April, 1789 ; m. 1814, Alicia, dau. of the Rev. Henry Jones, of Drombeg, Rector of Lislee and Kinsale, and by her (who is dec.) had issue,
 1. Thomas, d. aged 18, 1840.
 2. HENRY JONES, of Cahirmore.
 3. Edward, d. unm. 1849.
 1. Catherine Charlotte, d. unm.   2. Jane, d. unm. 1855.
 3. Harriette Alicia, deceased.   4. Martha, d. unm. 1842.
 5. Alice, deceased.

Mr. Hungerford d. 1861. The eldest surviving son,
 HENRY JONES HUNGERFORD, of Cahirmore, co. Cork, B.A. Trin. Coll. Dublin, Barrister-at-Law, J.P., b. 20 Sept. 1825 ; m. 8 Dec. 1856, Mary Boone, eldest dau. of Henry Augustus William Screen Cowper, H.M. Consul-General at Havana, and d. 1905, having had issue,
 1. THOMAS HENRY, of Cahirmore.
 2. Guy, b. 25 Oct. 1861 ; m. 1886, Emma, dau. of Thomas Hungerford, M.L.A. of Baerami, N.S.W.
 3. Edward, b. 10 June, 1863.
 4. Launcelot Machell Travers, R.M., at Dongarra, W. Australia b. Jan. 1865 ; m. Jan. 1893, Alice, dau. of Robert Wardrop, of Dublin.
 5. Gordon, b. 6 Dec. 1865.   6. Arthur Townsend, b. May, 1867.

IRELAND.   Hunt.

7. Geoffrey, *b*. July, 1873; *m*. 27 Sept. 1905, Caroline Agnes Lily, eldest dau. of Lieut.-Col. Hungerford, of Brinkhill, Paignton, S. Devon, and has issue,
   Geoffrey Anthony Walter, *b*. 16 June, 1906.
1. Alice, *m*. 1st, 1877, Francis T. Beamish, son of Sampson Beamish, of Kilmalooda. He *d.s.p*. 6 May, 1897. She *m*. 2ndly, Kenneth Hungerford, son of Thomas Hungerford, M.L.A., of Baerami, Sydney.
2. Ethel, *m*. Henry Thomas Wright, of Fern Hill, co. Cork, and has surviving issue, two sons and three daus.
The eldest son,
   THOMAS HENRY HUNGERFORD, of Cahirmore, co. Cork, *b*. 6 Dec. 1858,; *m*. Margaret Woulfe, dau. of late Rev. Fitzjohn Hamilton, and *d*. 1906, having had issue,
   1. HENRY, present representative.
   2. Thomas.
   1. Vera.
Arms, &c.—Same as HUNGERFORD *of Inchodony*.
Seat—Cahirmore, Rosscarbery, co. Cork.

PHILLIPS-HUNT OF BALLYSINODE.

HENRY FITZMAURICE HUNT PHILLIPS-HUNT, of Ballysinode, co. Tipperary, and of "Standish," Huyton, Liverpool, M.D., *b*. 21 Jan. 1863, s. his kinsman 1907, when as requested in his will he adopted the additional surname of HUNT; *m*. 3 Aug. 1892, Florence Irene, dau. of Dr. Thomas Buxton, and has had issue,
1. ROBERT FITZMAURICE HUNT, *b*. 12 Aug. 1893; *d*. 17 Dec. 1893.
1. Nora Rose Hunt, *b*. 31 July, 1896.
2. Mary Kathleen, *b*. 20 Aug. 1897.

Lineage.—HENRY HUNT, 2nd son of Rev. Vere Hunt, of Glangoole, co. Tipperary, and younger brother of Vere Hunt, of Curragh, ancestor of DE VERE, Bart. (extinct). He *m*. the dau. of Robert Bradshaw, and had issue,
1. VERE DAWSON, of whom presently.
2. Fitz Maurice, ancestor of the HUNTS of Georgia, America.
3. Piercy, *d.s.p*.
4. —, of Ballysinode, co. Tipperary, who left a dau.,
   Jane, *m*. 1816, her cousin, Vere David Urquhart Hunt, of Friarstown (*see that family*).
5. Damer, of Millbrook, co. Tipperary, who left a dau.,
   Mary Ann, *m*. Rev. John Hunt, of High Park, and *d*. 30 March, 1871, leaving issue.
The eldest son,
   VERE DAWSON HUNT, of Cappagh White, co. Tipperary, *m*. Nov. 1773, Elizabeth Davis. His will, dated 12 Dec. 1790, was proved 30 Oct. 1792. He had issue,
   1. Vere Dawson (Moses), of Cappagh White, co. Tipperary, bapt. Moses, but required by his father's will to adopt the names of Vere Dawson; *d*. 1812, having *m*. 1st, Fanny Palmer, dau. of James Short, of Newtown, Queen's Co., and by her had issue,
      1. Vere, *d*. 1842, having *m*. Bessie, dau. of William Vowell, of Clonmel, and had issue,
         (1) Vere Dawson de Vere, *b*. 7 July, 1829; *m*. 14 July, 1852, Elizabeth, dau. of Robert Walker, M.D., of Dublin, and *d*. 9 Dec. 1878, having had issue,
            1. Aubrey de Vere, *b*. 27 Sept. 1858.
            2. William Vere *b*. 4 Dec. 1860.
               1. Jane de Vere.   2. Dixie Vera de Vere.
         (2) William, *b*. May, 1830, who left issue.
      1. Mary, *m*. 1819, Thomas Pennefather, of Marlow, co. Tipperary, and *d*. 2 Jan. 1870.
   Mr. V. D. Hunt *m*. 2ndly, 24 June, 1809, Mary, dau. of Philip Holmes, of New Park, co. Cork, She *d*. 12 July, 1861. He *d*. 12 March, 1829, having by her had issue,
   2. Dawson, *b*. 16 July, 1813; *m*. 4 Oct. 1844, Sarah Pierce, dau. of Thomas Alexander Odell, of Odellville, co. Limerick, and had issue,
      Vere Dawson, *b*. 26 Nov. 1847.
      Meliora Kate, *d. unm*. 2 May, 1870.
   3. Charles, *b*. 23 July, 1814; *d. unm*.
   1. Anne, *m*. 1829, John Bernard.
   2. Bessie, *m*. 1830, John Frewen.
   4. Harriet, *d. unm*.
   5. Jane, *m*. 1837, Lloyd Blackham, and *d.s.p*.
   6. Charlotte, *m*. 1837, John Phillips.
   2. HENRY DAVIS, of whom presently.
   3. Fitz Maurice, of Cappagh, *b*. 1795; *d*. 21 Feb. 1829; *m*. 1827, Dorothea, dau. of Edward Pennefather, of Marlow, co Tipperary, who left a dau.,
      Mary Elizabeth, *m*. 14 July, 1847, Richard Phillips, of Gaile (*see that family*), and *d*. 1885, having had, with other issue, a younger son,
         HENRY FITZMAURICE HUNT PHILLIPS, who adopted the additional surname of Hunt, and is now of Ballysinode.
   1. Mary Elizabeth, *m*. her cousin, Rev. John Hunt, of High Park.
   2 Elizabeth, *m*. — Short.   3. Henrietta.
The 2nd son,
   HENRY DAVIS HUNT, of Ballysinode, Curraheen, co. Tipperary, *b*. 31 Oct. 1789; *m*. March, 1814, Anne, dau. of Robert Ross, M.D. She *d*. 7 Feb. 1856. He *d*. 6 Feb. 1827, leaving issue,
   1. VERE DAWSON, his heir.

2. ROBERT FITZ MAURICE, late of Ballysinode.
   1. Mary, *b*. 13 March, 1815; *d. unm*. 22 Jan. 1879.
   2. Anne Dorothea, *b*. 28 March, 1819; *d. unm*.
   3. Georgina Margaret, *b*. 1821; *m*. William G. Sturgess, Lieut. R.N., and *d*. 14 June, 1853, leaving issue.
The elder son,
   VERE DAWSON HUNT, of Ballysinode, *b*. 28 May, 1816; *d. unm*. 28 Aug. 1840, and was s. by his brother.
   ROBERT FITZ MAURICE HUNT, of Ballysinode, *b*. 28 Aug. 1824; *d. unm*. 11 Oct. 1907, having devised his estates to his kinsman, Henry Fitzmaurice Hunt Phillips, now of Ballysinode.

Seat—Ballysinode, Carraheen, co. Tipperary. *Residence*—"Standish," Huyton, Liverpool.

HUNT OF DANESFORT.

JOSEPH STOPFORD HUNT, of Danesfort, co. Cork, *b*. Sept. 1842.

Lineage. — THOMAS HUNT, Capt. in Col. Chidley Coote's Regt. of Horse in Ireland 1646-49, "of an ancient family in the County Warwick," had a confirmation of arms 28 June, 1647. His "Cromwellian Debenture" is the only one known to be extant (*see* PRENDERGAST's *Cromwellian Settlement in Ireland, 2nd Edn*.). He *d*. before May, 1658, leaving issue by his wife, Esther, who survived him,
1. Henry.
2. Thomas, *m*. and had a dau., Lydia, alive in July, 1685.
3. BENJAMIN, of whom presently.
1. Anne.
2. Esther, *m*. before July, 1685, — Baxter, and had issue living in July, 1685.
3. Sarah, *m*. before July, 1685, James Roberts, of Dublin, and had a dau. living in July, 1685.
The youngest son,
   BENJAMIN HUNT, *m*. 29 April, 1680, Mary, dau. of Robert Percival, of Knightsbrook, co. Meath. He *d*. July, 1685 (will dated 18 and proved 21 July, 1685), leaving issue by his wife, who had predeceased him (buried in St. Michan's, 12 May, 1682).
   PERCIVAL, his heir.
   Elizabeth, *m*. Francis, son of William Cock, of Dublin.
The only son,
   PERCIVAL HUNT, of Larah, co. Kildare, and also the owner of extensive estates in the cos. Dublin and Meath, High Sheriff of Dublin in 1718-19, *m*. 1st, Elizabeth (*b*. 1688; *d*. 6 Feb. 1721), eldest dau. of John Chamney, of Shillelagh, co. Wicklow, and sister of Thomas Chamney, of Platten Hall, co. Louth, and 2ndly, 1725, Christina, dau. of Col. Thomas Hewetson, of Grange Castle, co. Kildare, and widow of Robert Higgins. She *d*. 14 Jan. 1757. By his 1st wife he had,
   1. Benjamin, High Sheriff of Dublin 1740-1, *m*. 1741, Alicia, dau. of William Mercer, of Fair Hill, co. Louth, by Anne Sarah, dau. of John Bailie, of Inishargie, co. Down, M.P. Mr. Benjamin Hunt *d.s.p., v.p*. 31 Aug. 1748. His widow *m*. 2ndly, 9 Dec. 1750 Stephen Cassau, of Sheffield, King's Co. (*see that family*).
   2. Percival, of Milltown, co. Dublin, Lord Mayor of Dublin 1755-6, Lieut.-Col. of the Dublin Militia, stood for the representation of Dublin against Grattan, *m*. 26 March, 1744, Mary Lamprey, and had issue,
      1. Benjamin, Capt. in the Green Horse, *d. unm*.
      2. John Percival, Barrister-at-Law, who left issue all now extinct.
   3. JOHN, of whom presently.
   1. Jane, *m*. Edward Noy, of Newbrook, and had issue one dau., Anne, *m*. 1758, Major-Gen. Arthur Preston, and *d.s.p*. 5 Feb 1831, *actat* 93.
   2. Catherine, *m*. 1731, William Richardson, and had issue.
   3. Elizabeth, *m*. — Murray, and *d.s.p*.
   4. Anne, *m*. 12 Sept. 1768, Alexander Murray, of Bloomsbury, co. Meath, brother to her sister's husband, and *d.s.p*.
   5. Barbara, *m*. 20 April, 1748, John Swan, of Baldwinstown, co. Wexford, and by him (who *d*. 1757) was ancestress of the SWANS of Baldwinstown (*see that family*).
   Mr. Percival Hunt *d*. 2 Feb. 1761, at an advanced age. His 3rd son, JOHN HUNT, of Dublin, *m*. 28 March, 1747, Dorcas, dau. of John Cummin. He owned extensive estates in co. Roscommon and other counties, and *d*. 1800 (will dated 7 June, 1790, proved 5 July, 1800), having had, with other issue who predeceased him,
   1. JOHN, of whom presently.
   2. William, Capt. in the 9th Dragoons, *d.v.p., s.p*.
   1. Elizabeth, *d. unm*. 1843.   2. Anne, *d. unm*. 1838.
   3. Dorcas, *d. unm*. 1839.   4. Charlotte, *d. unm*. 1836.
The eldest son,

Hunt. THE LANDED GENTRY. 334

JOHN HUNT, of 8, Upper Merrion Street, Dublin, and Clermont, co. Wicklow, etc., Barrister-at-Law, *b.* 6 Aug. 1752; *m.* 1784, Anne, eldest dau. of the Rev. Edmund Lombard, M.A., T.C.D., of Lombardstown, co. Cork, Rector of Kilshannig, Diocese of Cloyne, son of James Lombard, of Lombardstown, High Sheriff co. Cork 1750, by Mary, dau. of Capt. James Uniacke, of Mount-Uniacke, co. Cork (*see that family*). Mr. John Hunt *d.* 1844 (will proved 8 Sept. 1844), having had, with other issue who *d.* young,
1. John (Rev.), of Cherrywood, co. Dublin, Rector of Rathmichael and Prebendary of St. Patrick's Cathedral, bapt. 6 Aug. 1786; *m.* 1810, Anna, dau. of William Hore, of Harperstown, co. Wexford, son of Col. Walter Hore, M.P., of Harperstown, by Lady Anne Stopford, dau. of James, 1st Earl of Courtown. Rev. John Hunt *d.* 25 Aug. 1866, leaving by his wife (who *d.* 26 Sept. 1866) issue,
    1. John, *b.* April, 1822, *d. unm.*
    2. William Hore, *b.* May, 1824; *d.s.p.* 30 May, 1900.
    1. Eleanor Catherine, *m.* 1846, Daniel Connelly, Barrister-at-Law. Both *d.s.p.*
    2. Maria, *m.* 1854, the Rev. Robert Cage, Rector of Rathconnell, co. Westmeath, and *d.s.p.* 2 Dec. 1900, her husband having predeceased her.
    3. Anne, *d. unm.* 1906.
    4. Elizabeth, *d. unm.* 1908, *aged* 91.
    5. Cecilia.
2. Edmund, bapt. 22 Aug. 1787; *d.* young.
3. JAMES, of whom presently.
4. Joseph, Barrister-at-Law, of 8, Upper Merrion Street, Dublin, and Summerhill, Enniskerry, co. Wicklow, *m.* 15 Sept. 1835, Mary Sarah, eldest dau. of John Francis Hewson, D.L., of Ennismore, co. Kerry, by his wife Elizabeth, dau. of John Hewson, of Castle Hewson, co. Limerick, and *d.* 2 July, 1852, having had issue,
    1. John Lombard, late Lieut.-Col. commanding 7th Queen's Own Hussars, *b.* 5 Jan. 1841.
    2. William Stopford, of Dromdiah and Aghadoe, Killeagh, co. Cork, J.P. co. Cork, late Assistant Land Commissioner, Ireland, *b.* 3 Nov. 1842.
    1. Mary Elizabeth.
    2. Anne Josephine, *m.* 16 Feb. 1865, Lieut.-Col. Robert Home, C.B., R.E., and *d.* Jan. 1879, leaving issue.
5. William Stopford, *m.* 1831, Anne, dau. of Graves Chamney Swan, of Newtown Park, co. Dublin, Barrister-at-Law (*see* SWAN *of Baldwinstown*), by Mary, dau. of the Rev. Edmund Lombard, M.A., T.C.D., of Lombardstown, and *d.* 22 Dec. 1837, having had by her (who *d.* 1864) one son,
    John William (Rev.), of Portarlington, *d.* 16 July, 1876, having had issue two daus.,
    (1) Wilhelmina Stopford, *m.* 28 July, 1879, Herbert W. F. de Schmid, Capt. South Devon Militia, son of the Baron de Schmid.
    (2) Dora Anne, *d. unm.*
6. Edmund Lombard, of Ballymanton, Gort, and Headford, co. Galway, J.P. co. Galway, *m.* 25 March, 1841, Catherine Elizabeth, dau. of Capt. Robert Powell, of Cloonraher, co. Sligo, and *d.* 1 Oct. 1860, having had by her (who *d.* 20 Sept. 1897) aged 85) issue,
    1. John Percival, Lieut.-Col., retired pay, R.A.M.C., F.R.C.S., Ireland, M.D. University of Glasgow, and Barrister-at-Law, Lincoln's Inn, *b.* 29 Oct. 1844; *m.* 1st, 16 June, 1868, Emily Anne, dau. of Thomas Harpur, of Cecil Hills, N.S.W., and formerly of Lime Park, co. Tyrone, and 2ndly, Lilian, dau. of Henry Eames, M.D., Trin. Coll. Dublin, and has issue by his 1st wife only.
    2. Robert Edmund, M.D., *d. unm.* June, 1904.
    1. Elizabeth Frances, *m.* 11 Aug. 1881, Abraham Sandys Connellan, of St. Peter's Port, Guernsey, L.R.C.S. Ireland, and by him (who *d.* 1890) has issue.
    2. Annette Louisa, *m.* 1 June, 1871, Cuthbert Henry Cooke Huddart, M.B., B.A., T.C.D., of Shoyswell Manor, Sussex, 3rd son of George Augustus Huddart, J.P., D.L., of Brynkir Hall, co. Caernarvon, and by him (who *d.* 24 Aug. 1900) has issue.
    3. Mary Catherine, *m.* 2 April, 1868, William Mascall Kenrick, of Broome, Fleet, Hants, late 67th Regt. and 7th Fusiliers, and by him (who *d.* May, 1905), has issue.
7. Percival, M.A., M.B., T.C.D., Physician to Sir Patrick Dun's Hospital, Dublin, *b.* 29 May, 1802; *d. unm.* 4 March, 1848.
    1. Elizabeth Dorcas, *d. unm.* 5 May, 1865.
    2. Dorcas, *d. unm.* 25 Sept. 1871.
    3. Anne, *m.* 1830, Maurice Hewson, Capt. R.N., and had issue (*see* HEWSON *of Ovington Park*).
    4. Mary, *d. unm.* 22 July, 1879.

The 3rd son,
JAMES HUNT, of Aldworth and Danesfort, co. Cork, *m.* 12 June, 1834, Anna Catherine Elizabeth, dau. of Rev. William Stopford, of Abbeville, co. Cork, Rector of Garrycloyne, Diocese of Cloyne, by Abigail, dau. of Eyre Evans, of Miltown Castle, co. Cork, and Ash Hill Towers, co. Limerick, grandson of the Right Rev. James Stopford, D.D., Bishop of Cloyne, and by her (who *d.* 8 March, 1896) had issue,
1. John James, *d. unm.* 19 March, 1864, aged 29.
2. William Eyre, *d. unm.* 9 March, 1860, aged 23.
3. EDMUND LOMBARD, of Danesfort.
4. JOSEPH STOPFORD, now of Danesfort, *b.* Sept. 1842.
5. James Stopford, of Ballymagooly, co. Cork, *b.* 22 March, 1845; *m.* 29 Aug. 1877, Rosa Jane, only dau. of the Rev. John Evans Lewis, M.A., Rector of Mointaghs, Diocese of Dromore, by Margaret Jane, dau. of Henry Swanzy, of Rockfield, co. Monaghan (*see* BURKE'S *Family Records*).
6. Percival, of Eglantine, co. Cork, *b.* 1849; *m.* 17 Aug. 1876, his cousin, Angelina Josephine, dau. of the Rev. Joseph Stopford, of Ferney, co. Cork, by Elizabeth, dau. of Simon Dring, of Rockgrove, co. Cork, and by her (who *d.* 13 Oct. 1884) has issue,
    1. James Stopford, late Lieut. 9th Batt. King's Royal Rifles, *b.* 1 May, 1878.
    2. Joseph William Lombard, Lieut. R.N., *b.* 30 Aug. 1879; *m.* 19 Oct. 1904, Florence Evelyn, only dau. of Capt. Digby Tighe, and has issue,
        (1) Leslie Percival Lombard, *b.* 14 July, 1905.
        (2) William, *b.* 1911.
    3. Edmund Lombard, *b.* 20 March, 1883.
1. Abigail Mary Angelina, of Mountprospect, co. Cork, *m.* 22 Nov. 1877, her cousin, Lieut.-Col. George Eyre Massy, 5th Fusiliers, son of Eyre Massy, of Glenville, co. Limerick. He *d.* 25 Dec. 1896, leaving issue.
2. Anne Elizabeth, of Danesfort, co. Cork, *d.* 30 Jan. 1912.
3. Elizabeth Ellen Lombard, *m.* 28 Sept. 1882, her cousin, Edward Horatio Phibbs Maunsell, of Newborough, co. Limerick, and by him (who *d.* 23 July, 1899) had issue (*see* MAUNSELL *of Ballywilliam*).

Mr. James Hunt, of Danesfort, *d.* 26 Oct. 1869, and was *s.* by his eldest surviving son,

EDMUND LOMBARD, of Danesfort, *b.* 15 April, 1838; *d.* 17 May, 1911, being *s.* by his brother.

Arms—Sa. a chevron between six leopards' faces or, on a chief of the last a lion passant holding in the dexter paw a serpent ppr. **Crest**—Out of a ducal coronet or, an arm gu., the hand grasping the pommel and hilt of an armed sword. **Motto**—Credentibus nil difficile.

Residence—Danesfort, near Mallow, co. Cork.

HUNT OF CUMMER MORE.

VERE DAVID URQUHART HUNT, of Cummer More, Kilcommon, co. Tipperary, J.P., Assistant Land Commissioner, *b.* 2 Nov. 1856; *m.* 1st, 31 Oct. 1878, Elizabeth, only dau. of Arthur Russell, of Lemonfield, same co. which lady *d.* 29 May, 1885. He *m.* 2ndly, 7 Nov. 1888, Zillah Edith, only dau. of the late William Bredin, J.P., of Castlegarde, Pallasgreen, co. Limerick, and has issue,

1. WILLIAM, *b.* 24 Oct. 1890.
1. Lillah Edith.
2. Annie Vera.

Lineage—WILLIAM HUNTE, of Gosfield, co. Essex (*vide* Visitation of Essex, 1614), *m.* Ellen Cracherode, of Cust Hall, Toppesfield, in the same county. He *d.* 12 Aug. 1552, and his wife 12 Sept. 1578, both being bur. in Gosfield Church. They had eleven children of whom the eldest son,

HENRY HUNTE was High Sheriff of Essex. He *m.* 2 April, 1573, at Gosfield, "Jane Vere," who is stated in the Visitation of Essex, 1558 (Harl. MS. 1137) to have been youngest dau. of Aubrey de Vere, 2nd son of John, Earl of Oxford, K.G. They had issue,
1. William, *b.* 1577; *d.* 1578.
2. JOHN, of whom next.
3. Edward.
4. Henry.
1. Dorothy.
2. Agnes, *m.* Thomas Whitbread, of Whight Notley, co. Essex.

The eldest surviving son,
JOHN HUNT, Capt. in the Army, *b.* 1582, took service in Ireland, and was one of "the 49 officers." His commission, dated 24 April, 1650, speaks of him as Colonel. He had issue a son,

VERE HUNT, of Ballycholan, and subsequently of Glangoole, co. Tipperary, and of Curragh Chase, co. Limerick. He took part in the siege of Youghal. In 1657 and 1660 he was appointed one of the Commissioners of co. Limerick for raising the supplies then demanded for the public service. He *d.* at Curragh, at an advanced age, leaving by Mary his wife (who administered to her husband 24 June, 1681), two sons, Henry, of whom later, and John. The younger son,

JOHN HUNT, of Glangoole, co. Tipperary, and of Curragh Chase, *b.* 1633; *m.* 1st, the dau. of the Rev. John Hicks, Rector of Kilcooley, co. Tipperary, and by her had issue,
1. VERE, his heir.
2. William, *m.* Mary, dau. of John Bury, of Shannon Grove, co. Limerick, and had issue.
3. John.
4. Daniel.
1. Alice, *m.* Peter Agar.
2. Susan, *m.* Rev. Henry Royse.
3. Gertrude, *m.* — Tennison.

. WILLIAM, his heir.
 John (Rev.), of High Park, co. Tipperary, d. March, 1837; m. 1st, Mary Elizabeth, dau. of Vere Hunt, of Cappagh-White (who d.s.p.); and 2ndly, 1812, Mary Anne, dau. of Damer Hunt, of Milbrook, co. Tipperary, by whom (who d. 30 March, 1871) he had issue,
1. Vere, of High Park, J.P., b. 8 June, 1814; m. 1st, March, 1859, Maria, dau. of Hugh Brady Bradshaw, of Philipstown, co. Tipperary, by whom (who d. 1863) he had a dau.,
  (1) Jenny, b. 5 Nov. 1861.
He m. 2ndly, 2 Aug. 1869, Frances Augusta, dau. of Hugh Massy Yielding, of Woodlands, Tarbert, co. Kerry, and had issue,
  (1) Vero Robert, b. 26 Nov. 1875.
  (2) Mary, b. 15 April, 1871.
  (3) Fanny, b. 3 Sept. 1872.
2. FitzMaurice (Rev.), m. Frances, dau. of Rev. Arthur Hyde, Rector of Mohill, co. Leitrim.
1. Mary Anne, m. Robert Holmes Philips, of Oakhampton, co. Tipperary.
2. Wilhelmina, m. Rev. James Marten.
3. Fanny Margaret.
3. Thomas, m. March, 1798, Dorothea, dau. of John Bloomfield, of Redwood, co. Tipperary, by whom he had issue,
  1. Vere, d. unm.   2. Thomas Bloomfield.
  3. Robert, of Cloghadromin, and Green Hill, co. Limerick, and 83, George's Street, Limerick, J.P., High Sheriff of the city 1840 and 1841, b. 31 Aug. 1814; m. 1833, Maria, dau. of George Bonynge Rochfort, of Pierstown, co. Westmeath. She d. 1885. He d. 1895, having had issue,
   (1) Thomas Rochfort, of Cloghadromin, b. 9 Aug. 1834, Lieut.-Col. late 17th Regt.; m. 1865, Elizabeth Frances, dau. of Robert Ringrose Gelston, M.D., of co. Limerick, and has issue,
    a. Thomas Aubrey, b. 1876.
    b. Cecil Vere, b. 9 March, 1879.
    c. Rochfort Vere, b. 11 May, 1880.
    d. Godfrey Bloomfield, b. 19 Jan. 1883.
     a. Edith Gelston.   b. Kathleen Frances.
    c. Walter Caroline, m. Walter Richardson Fox, son of George E. Fox, of Hillsides, Plymouth, and has issue.
    d. Gwendoline Maria.
   (2) George Gerald, b. 10 Sept. 1840, Commander R.N., d.s.p.
   (3) William Lewis, b. 31 March, 1843; m. 1867, Mary, dau. of Luke Brady, of Brookville, co. Clare, and has issue, with three daus.,
    a. Robert Windham, m. 20 Nov. 1909, Aileen Melita, eldest dau. of Gen. Charles Elmhirst, C.B.
    b. Henry Brady, m. 13 Jan. 1898, Lady Ernestine Mary Alma Georgiana Brudenell-Bruce, elder dau. of 5th Marquess of Ailesbury, and has issue,
     Hamo.
    c. George.
   (1) Ellen Anne, m. 1868, Lieut.-Gen. Vere Hunt Bowles.
   (2) Frances Dorothea, m. 1861, Lieut.-Gen. Charles Elmhirst, C.B.
   (3) Meriel Kate, m. 1869, Alexander Caulfeild, Gren. Guards.
   (4) Maria Sarah, m. 1877, Peter Gerald Griffin, of Altavilla, co. Limerick.
  4. Rochfort.
  1. Frances, d. unm.   2. Anne, m. and left four sons.
1. Mary, m. Robert Ross, and had a dau.
2. Anne, m. her cousin, Henry Davis Hunt.
Mr. Hunt was s. by his eldest son,
WILLIAM HUNT, of Friarstown, m. Elizabeth, dau. and heiress of David Urquhart, of Newhall, co. Cromarty, and had issue,
1. VERE DAVID URQUHART, his heir.
2. William Henn, b. 31 Dec. 1795; m. 31 Aug. 1836, Ellen, dau. of George Bonaye Rochfort, of Pierstown, co. Westmeath, and d. Oct. 1867, leaving two sons and three daus.,
  1. William Robert, b. 4 Aug. 1837; d. unm.
  2. Rochfort Vere (Major), of Ligadoon, b. 26 July, 1842; m. 17 Sept. 1868, Lydia, only dau. and heir of John Houston, of Prospect Villa, Rathgar, co. Dublin, and has a dau.,
   Emily Anne Urquhart, b. 8 Feb. 1873.
  1. Anna Maria, b. March, 1839.   2. Jane, b. 1841.
  3. Elizabeth Harrison, b. 29 Aug. 1847.
Mr. Hunt was s. by his eldest son,
VERE DAVID URQUHART HUNT, of Friarstown, b. 13 Jan. 1794; m. 1816, Jane, dau. of Henry Hunt, of Ballysinode, and d. 5 Oct. 1854, having had by her (who d. Aug. 1860) eight sons and one dau.,
1. William, b. 1818; d. unm. 1834.
2. Henry, b. Sept. 1820; d. unm. April, 1866.
3. Vere, b. 1822; d. unm. 2 Dec. 1844.
4. George Hodges, of co. Limerick, b. June, 1824; m. 3 Jan. 1856, Susan, dau. of Rev. Godfrey Massy, Rector of Bruff, co. Limerick, and d. 4 Nov. 1862, leaving issue,
  1. VERE DAVID URQUHART, now of Cummer More.
  2. Godfrey Massy, Col. (ret.) (Cappagh House, Cappowhite, co. Tipperary), b. 29 May, 1859; m. 14 Dec. 1904, Alice, dau. of William L. Hunt, of 83, George Street, Limerick, and has issue,
   (1) Meriel Dorothy.
   (2) Susan Mary.
  3. George Hodges, b. 18 March, 1861.
5. John Thomas Urquhart, of Friarstown, b. July, 1829; m. 14 Nov. 1867, Annie Dunscombe Russell (Friarstown House, Limerick), only dau. of Henry Purdon Wilkinson, of Limerick. He d. 29 March, 1898.
6. EDMOND LANGLEY, of Curragh Bridge, co. Limerick, b. 12 May, 1831; d. 1 July, 1911; m. 1st, 26 April, 1859, Anne Matilda, younger dau. of Samuel Dickson Power, of Monroe, J.P. co. Tipperary, by whom he had a son,
  1. Vere Valentine, LL.B., b. 14 Feb. 1860.
He m. 2ndly, 17 March, 1864, Annie B. C., dau. of Lieut.-Col. Francis William Dillon, 18th Regt. (Royal Irish), by whom he has further issue,
  2. Francis Dillon, Major A.V.D., b. 27 March, 1867; m. Dec. 1895, Geraldine, dau. of Richard Uniacke Bayly, of Ballyre, co. Cork, and Ballinaclough, Nenagh, and has issue,
   Geraldine Annie.
  3. Edmond Langley, C.M.G., L.R.C.P.I. and L.R.C.S.I. (Accra, Gold Coast, W. Africa), served as Civil Surgeon in S. African War, 1899-1902, b. 22 April, 1868; m. 8 Aug. 1907, Florence, dau. of late James Hird, of Montrose, and has issue,
   Edmund Robert Langley, b. 1 Aug. 1910.
  4. Henry, Surgeon, R.N., b. 5 Aug. 1869.
  5. Edward Dillon, b. 29 Aug. 1870.
  6. William Power, F.S.I., b. 9 Oct. 1871.
  7. Rochfort Noel, Capt. R.A.M.C., b. 7 Dec. 1872.
   1. Annie Henrietta, b. 9 Oct. 1877; m. 23 Nov. 1898, Wilfred Bennett Davidson-Houston, Maj. 5th Batt. Royal Dublin Fus., Commissioner for S. Ashanti, Gold Coast, 2nd son of the late Rev. Bennett Clear Davidson-Houston, Vicar of St. John's Church, Dublin, and has issue, Wilfred Edmond Clear, b. 1 Sept. 1901.
  7. FitzMaurice, b. 1836.
  8. Samuel Bradshaw, Surg.-Col., late Indian Medical Service (75, George Street, Limerick), b. 5 Nov. 1840; m. 8 April, 1869, Emma Matilda, dau. of Frederick Clarke, of Beau Coin, Jersey, and has issue,
   1. Frederick John Robert, Barrister-at-Law, of the King's Inns, Dublin, Judge of the High Court of Judicature, Travancore, and Fellow of the University of Madras, Madras, India, b. 5 Jan. 1871; m. Dec. 1900, Signe, dau. of Lauritz Bronn, of Christiania, Norway, and has issue,
    Vere John Urquhart, b. 7 Dec. 1906.
   2 Vere Henry Wilson, b. 2 Feb. 1872; d. 27 May, 1878.
1. Elizabeth Mary, m. Mathew Shine.
Arms—Az., on a bend between two water bougets or, three leopards' faces gu. Crest—A leopard's face ppr. Motto—Labor omnia vincit.
Seat—Cummer More, Kilcommon, co. Tipperary. Residence—Carnaballa Lodge, Doon, co. Limerick.

HURLY OF GLENDUFFE.

JOHN CONWAY HURLY, of Glenduffe, Tralee, co. Kerry, J.P., b. 1862; m. 2 June, 1891, Maud Isabel, dau. of Rev. George William Grogan, M.A., and by her (who d. 1892) had issue,
ROBERT WILLIAM CONWAY, b. 18 March, 1892.

Lineage.—DENNIS HURLY, of Knocklong, co. Limerick, "a descendant of the brother of Sir Thomas Hurly, of Knocklong, in the county of Limerick, baronet, or of Maurice Hurly, his father," according to Black Jack's Book, by John Blennerhassett, of Ballyseedy. He held a commission in the Kerry Militia. He m. 1701, Anne, 5th dau. of Robert Blennerhassett, 2nd son of John Blennerhassett, of Ballyseedy, co. Kerry, by his wife Avice Conway, 2nd dau. and co-heiress of Edmund Conway, of Castle Conway, Killorglin, and had issue,
1. THOMAS, his heir.
2. CHARLES, heir to his brother.
3. John, d. young.
4. Dennis, d. young.
5. William, d. young.
1. Alice.   2. Avis.   3. Sara.
The eldest son,
THOMAS HURLY, m. Alice, dau. of his uncle, Thomas Blennerhassett, by Jane Darby, and by her had issue, three daus.,
1. Anne, d. unm.
2. Alice, m. Arthur Browne, of Ventry, co. Kerry, and had issue.
3. Jane, m. John Mason, of Ballydowney.
Thomas Hurly was s. by his brother,
CHARLES HURLY, m. Alice Fitzgerald, sole dau. and heiress of Edmond Fitzgerald, of Murriregane, and by her had two sons, THOMAS and JOHN, and one dau., m. Thomas Langley. He was s. by his eldest son,
THOMAS HURLY, m. his cousin, Letitia Browne, 2nd dau. of Arthur Browne and Alice Hurly, and had one son, Charles, who d. young. His brother,
JOHN HURLY, Clerk of the Crown and Peace for Kerry, s. his brother Thomas, and m. 18 May, 1784, Mary Conway, only surviving child of Edmond Conway and Christian Rice. She d. 15 July, 1825. He d. 26 Nov. 1829, leaving issue,

He *m.* 2ndly, the dau. of — Bowles. His will dated Oct. 1736, was proved 17 May, 1737. By his 2nd wife he had issue,
5. Thomas.
6. Henry, *d.* 1796, having *m.* 1747, Grace Forsyth, by whom he had issue (with a dau. Susanne, *m.* James Kearney, of Blancheville, co. Kilkenny), two sons,
  1. Charles, Lieut. R.N., *d. unm.* 1803.
  2. James, *d.* 1819, having *m.* 1797, Mary Seaton, by whom (who *d.* 1818) he had issue (with a son Charles, *m.* a dau. of Baron Pfeilitzer, a son Thomas and four daus., Elizabeth, Maria, Harriette and Jemima) an eldest son,
    Henry (Rev.), M.A. (Trin. Coll. Dublin), Rector of Virginia, co. Cavan, and Vicar General of Elphin, *b.* 26 May, 1792; *d.* 22 May, 1861; *m.* 12 March, 1823, Rose Anne Adair and by her (who *d.* 18 Nov. 1879) he had issue (with four daus., Rose Anne, Mary Harriet, Ellen Maria and Isabella), three sons,
      1. James (Rev.), M.A. (Trin. Coll. Dublin), Rector of Castle Blakeney, co. Galway, *b.* 1825; *m.* 1879, Eleanor Margaret Adair and *d.s.p.* 4 May, 1894.
      2. Henry Leslie, Major and Adjutant 7th West York R.V., late Lieut. 67th Regt., *b.* 21 Jan. 1829; *d.* 17 Dec. 1880; *m.* 1st, 1855, Anne Caroline, dau. of John S. Hulbert, of Stakes Hill Lodge, Hants, and by her (who *d.* 1857), had issue,
        a. Henry de Vere (Rev.), B.A. Camb., Rector of Ahascragh (*The Rectory, Ahascragh, co. Galway*), *b.* 12 March, 1856; *m.* 20 July, 1882, Mary Caroline, dau. of Rev. Peter William-Browne, Rector of Blackrock, Lancs., and has issue,
          (a) Henry Leslie, *b.* 21 April, 1890.
          (a) Alice Kathleen, *b.* 15 Sept. 1883.
          (b) Eleanor Caroline, *b.* 21 July, 1885.
          (c) Vera Mary, *b.* 11 Dec. 1886.
      He *m.* 2ndly, 1860, Mary Stewart, dau. of Rear-Adml. Hay, of Belton, Haddingtonshire, and by her (who *d.* 1903) had further issue,
        b. James Hay, *b.* 6 June, 1861; *d.* 2 Nov. 1908.
        c. Thomas Aubrey, *d. inf.*
        d. Edward Leslie, late Capt. R.E., *b.* 11 Jan. 1867.
        e. Charles Adair.
        a. Mary Stewart, deceased.
        b. Isabella Baird, *d.* 1900.
        c. Jane Evelyn, deceased.
        d. Rosa Louise.
      3. Thomas Adair, *b.* 1830; *d.* 1906; *m.* 1857, Caroline, dau. of Sir Ross Mahon, Bart. (*see* BURKE's *Peerage*).
7. James.
8. George.
4. Elizabeth, *m.* — Foster.
5. Anne, *m.* — Odell.
6. Mary, *m.* — Sprigg.
7. Penelope, *m.* — Halpin.
8. Rebecca.
9. Lucy.
10. Dorothea.
11. Amelia.

The eldest son,
THE REV. VERE HUNT, of Glangoole, *m.* in 1712, Constantia, eldest dau. of Sir William Piers, 2nd bart. of Tristernagh, Westmeath (*see* BURKE's *Peerage*, PIERS, *Bart.*) and granddau. (maternally) of William Fitzmaurice, Lord Kerry, by whom he had four sons,
1. VERE, his heir.
2. Henry, from whom descend the branch of the family settled at Cappagh, co. Tipperary, and the HUNTS *of Georgia, &c.* (*see* HUNT *of Ballisinode*).
3. John, *m.* the dau. and co-heir of William Turvin, of Tennor, co. Tipperary.
4. William, *m.* the dau. of — Lane.

The Rev. Vere Hunt *d.* in 1759, and was bur. at Kilcooley Abbey, co. Tipperary. He was *s.* by his eldest son,
VERE HUNT, of Currah, co. Limerick, and of Glangoole, co. Tipperary; *m.* 1st, Katherine, dau. of William Chadwick, of Ballinard She *d.s.p.* He *m.* 2ndly, 29 May, 1760, Anne, 2nd dau. of Edmund Browne, of New Grove, co. Clare, by whom he had two sons and a dau.,
1. VERE, 1st bart.
2. John Fitzmaurice, who *m.* 1st, Jane, 3rd dau. of William Henn, of Paradise, co. Clare (*see that family*); and 2ndly, 1799, Frances, dau. of Col. Lane, by both of whom he had issue.
1. Jane, *m.* John Hamilton Lane, of Lanespark, co. Tipperary, and had issue. She *d.* 1807.

He was *s.* at his decease by his elder son,
SIR VERE HUNT, 1st bart of Currah, who was created a BARONET OF IRELAND, 4 Dec. 1784. He *m.* 4 March, 1784, Elinor, only dau. of the Right Hon. and Right Rev. William Cecil, Lord Glentworth, Bishop of Limerick, and sister of Edward, 1st Earl of Limerick (*see* BURKE's *Peerage*), by whom (who *d.* 25 Dec. 1820) he had an only son, AUBREY, the 2nd Bart. Sir Vere raised and commanded three regiments of infantry, the 135th of the line, a levy, and the co. Limerick fencibles. He was returned to the Irish Parliament in 1797. He purchased Lundy Island in 1803. He *d.* 11 Aug. 1818, and was *s.* by his son,
SIR AUBREY DE VERE, 2nd bart., *b.* 28 Aug. 1788, who assumed by royal licence, dated 15 March, 1832, the surname and arms of DE VERE only. He sold Lundy Island in 1830. He *m.* 12 May, 1807, Mary, elder dau. of Stephen Edward Rice, of Mount Trenchard, co. Limerick (*see* BURKE's *Peerage*, MONTEAGLE, B.), and Catherine his wife, sole heir of Thomas Spring, of Ballycrispin, co. Kerry, by whom (who *d.* 11 Feb. 1856) he had issue,
1. VERE EDMOND, 3rd bart.
2. STEPHEN EDWARD, 4th and last bart.
3. Aubrey Thomas, LL.D., author of *The Waldenses*, and other poems, *b.* 10 Jan. 1814; *d. unm.* 20 Jan. 1902.

4. William Cecil, Capt. R.N., *b.* 20 April, 1823; *m.* 8 July, 1852. Sophia, dau. of John Allen, of Burnham, and *d.* 2 Feb. 1869.
5. Frances Horatio, Maj. in the army and Capt. R.E., *b.* 12 Oct 1828. *d.* 22 Aug. 1865; *m.* 4 Nov. 1856, Anne Celestine (*St. Clerans, co. Galway*), youngest dau. and eventual heiress of James Hardiman Burke, of St. Clerans, co. Galway, and sister of the eminent Australian explorer, Robert O'Hara Burke, and by her (who *m.* 2ndly, 20 Feb. 1873, the Rev. Charleton Maxwell, J.P., formerly Rector of Leckpatrick, co. Tyrone, who *d.* July, 1895), had issue three daus.,
  1. Mary, *m.* 1st, 1879, Major William Utting Cole, 3rd Dragoon Guards, who *d.* 1892, leaving issue; and 2ndly, 19 April, 1894, Capt. Herbert William Studd, D.S.O., 2nd Batt. Coldstream Guards (*Guards', Travellers', Bachelors' Clubs*), and has issue.
  2. Eleanor Hester, *m.* 9 July, 1885, Sir Frederick William Shaw 5th bart., of Busby Park (*see* BURKE's *Peerage*, SHAW, Bart.).
  3. Margaret Elizabeth, *m.* 1886, Francis Joyce, who *d.* May, 1890, leaving issue.
1. Elinor Jane Alicia Lucy, *m.* 14 Feb. 1835, Hon. Robert O'Brien (who *d.* 5 March, 1870), 4th son of Sir Edward O'Brien, Bart., and brother of Lucius, 13th Lord Inchiquin, and *d.* 5 March, 1889, aged 76, leaving issue,
  1. Aubrey Stephen O'BRIEN, R.M., Maj. late 60th Rifles, *b.* 4 May, 1837; *m.* 10 Aug. 1871, Lucy Harriette (*Currah Chase, Adare, co. Limerick*), only dau. of Maj.-Gen. Wynne, R.E. She assumed by royal licence, 1899, the name of DE VERE in lieu of O'BRIEN. He *d.* 18 Dec. 1898, leaving issue,
    (1) Robert Stephen Vere DE VERE, of Currah Chase, Adare, co. Limerick, LL.B., Camb., Barrister-at-Law who has assumed (together with his mother) by royal licence, 1899, the name of DE VERE in lieu of O'BRIEN (*Wellington Club*), *b.* 23 July, 1872; *m.* 26 Sept. 1906, Isabel Catherine, only surviving child of the Right Rev. Handley Carr Glynne Moule, D.D., Bishop of Durham.
    (2) Eva Mary, *d. unm.* 15 Aug. 1892.
  2. Robert Vere O'BRIEN, of Ballyalla, Ennis and Monare, Foynes, Barrister-at-Law, Clerk of the Peace for Clare (*Athenaeum and Kildare Street Clubs*), *b.* 20 Oct. 1840; *m.* 10 July, 1883, Florence Mary Arnold Forster, dau. of William Delafield Arnold, Director of Public Instruction in the Punjaub, and adopted dau. of the late Right Hon. William Edward Forster, M.P., and has issue (*see* BURKE's *Peerage*, INCHIQUIN, B.).
    1. Mary Ellen Vere, *m.* 2 Jan. 1868, Charles Spencer Perceval, Barrister, who *d.* 29 Jan. 1889 (*see* BURKE's *Peerage*, EGMONT, E.).
    2. Charlotte Alice Vere, *d. unm.* 9 March, 1903.
    3. Eleanor Grace Katharine, *m.* 25 Oct. 1870, William T Monsell, R.M., who *d.* 1887, leaving issue.
  2. Mary Theodosia Cecil, *d. unm.* 1830.
  3. Catherine Louisa, *d. unm.* 1834.

Sir Aubrey was author of *Julian the Apostate*, and *The Duke of Mercia*, dramatic poems published in 1822 and 1823, and of *A Song of Faith*, and other poems, published in 1842, and of *Mary Tudor*, a dramatic poem. He *d.* 5 July, 1846, and was *s.* by his eldest son,
SIR VERE EDMOND DE VERE, 3rd Bart., *b.* 12 Oct. 1808; *m.* 9 Jan. 1838, Mary Lucy, eldest dau. of Rowland Standish, of Scaleby Castle, Cumberland, and of Farley Hill, Berks, by Lucy his wife, dau. of Edmund, 1st Earl of Limerick. She *d.* 16 Jan. 1892. Sir Vere *d.s.p.* 23 Sept. 1880, and was *s.* by his brother,
SIR STEPHEN EDWARD DE VERE, 4th Bart., of Currah Chase, co. Limerick, B.A. Trin. Coll. Dublin, Barrister-at-Law, M.P. for Limerick 1854 to 1859, and High Sheriff of the co. 1870; *b.* 26 July, 1812; *s.* his brother as 4th bart. 1880. In May, 1898, Sir Stephen and his younger and only surviving brother, Aubrey de Vere, both being unmarried and aged respectively 86 and 88, conveyed their respective life estates to their nephew, Maj. Aubrey Stephen O'Brien (*see above*). Sir Stephen *d. unm.* 1904, when the baronetcy became extinct, having been previously *s.* by his nephew (*see* DE VERE *of Currah Chase*).

We now return to
HENRY HUNT, of Ligadoon, near co. Limerick, living in 1730, elder son of Vere Hunt, of Williamstown, co. Limerick, and brother of John Hunt, of Glangoole, ancestor of DE VERE, Bart. (*see above*). He had issue, three sons and two daus.,
1. John, of Ligadoon, whose will is dated 18 Aug. 1759, *d.s.p.*
2. HENRY, of whom hereafter.
3. Robert, *d.* intestate, leaving one son,
  Robert, of Inchirourke, *m.* Gertrude, dau. of Edmund Browne, of New Grove, co. Clare.
1. Anne, *m.* (settlement dated 13 and 14 Jan. 1726) Vere Royse, of Nantenan, co. Limerick.
2. Another dau., *m.* Rev. Thomas Widenham, of Milford, co. Limerick.
The 2nd son,
HENRY HUNT, of Friarstown, obtained that estate from Henry Ingoldsby, of Cartown, 24 April, 1730. He *m.* Margaret, dau. of Daniel Widenham, and had issue,
1. VERE, his heir.
2. Daniel, of Ballygaddy, co. Galway.
3. Henry, of Clorane, co. Limerick, *m.* (settlement dated 21 and 22 Oct. 1773) Arabella Matthews, of co. Kilkenny.
1. Dorothea, *m.* 13 Nov. 1764, George Bowles, son of Sir William Bowles.
Mr. Hunt, whose will is dated 26 Feb. 1762, was *s.* by his eldest son,
VERE HUNT, of Friarstown, a minor at his father's death, *m.* (settlement dated 5 March, 1761) Anne, dau. of William Maunsell, co. Limerick, and had issue,

HUSSEY OF WESTOWN.

ANTHONY ALOYSIUS STRONG HUSSEY, of Westown, co. Dublin, J.P., b. 21 June, 1850 ; m. 28 Oct. 1884, Mary, only dau. of Richard Henry Sheil, of Liverpool, and has a dau.,
Mary Mabel.

Lineage.—PETER HUSSEY, 2nd son of James Hussey, Baron of Galtrim, by Mary his wife, dau. of Richard Aylmer, of Lyons (see HUSSEY of *Rathkenny*), m. Mary, only dau. and heir of Bartholomew Bellew, of Westown, co. Dublin, and had a son,
LUKE HUSSEY, of Westown, father of
COL. EDWARD HUSSEY, of Westown, m. Mabel Barnewall, and had issue,
1. JAMES, his heir.
1. Mabel, m. Matthias Barnewall, of Castletown.
2. Catherine, m. Sir Andrew Aylmer, Bart. of Balrath, co. Meath, and by him (who d. 5 Nov. 1740) left at her decease, 1746, with other issue, a dau.,
Mabel Aylmer, m. John Strong, of Mullafin, co. Meath, and had, with seven dans., five sons,
(1) Andrew. (2) Simon, a priest.
(3) John, a priest.
(4) GERALD, of whom presently, as the inheritor of the Westown estates. (5) Robert.
The eldest son,
JAMES HUSSEY, of Westown, co. Dublin, and of Courtown, co. Kildare, m. Catherine, dau. of Richard Parsons, Viscount Rosse, and by her (who d. March, 1766) had issue. He d. 1759, and was s. by his son,
EDWARD HUSSEY, of Westown, m. 1743, Isabella, eldest dau. and co-heir of John, Duke of Montagu, and relict of William Montagu, Duke of Manchester, and assumed, at the decease of his father-in-law, the name and arms of MONTAGU. In 1753 he was installed a Knight of the Bath ; in 1762 created a Peer of Great Britain, as BARON BEAULIEU, of Beaulieu ; and in 1784, advanced to be EARL BEAULIEU. By the co-heiress of Montagu, his lordship had an only son. John, who d. unm., and one dau., Isabella, who also d. unm. 1772. He d. 1802 (when the peerage expired), and was s. in the Irish estates by his brother,
RICHARD HUSSEY, of Westown, who d. unm. having devised his property to his cousin (the grandson of Catherine Hussey, by her husband, Sir Andrew Aylmer, Bart.),
GERALD STRONG, who assumed in consequence the name and arms of Hussey. Mr. Strong Hussey m. 1781, Mary, dau. of Anthony Lynch, of La Vally, co. Galway, and had issue,
1. ANTHONY, his heir.
1. Margaret, m. 1812, Francis Magan, of Emoe, co. Westmeath.
2. Isabella, m. 1814, Col. William Meall, E.I.C.S., and d. leaving two daus.
Mr. Strong Hussey d. 30 Nov. 1811, and was s. by his son,
ANTHONY STRONG HUSSEY, of Westown, J.P. and D.L., b. 24 Aug. 1782 ; m. 19 Aug. 1811, Mabel, eldest dau. of Malachi Donelan, of Ballydonelan, co. Galway, and by her had issue,
1. Gerald Richard, d. 8 Dec. 1859.
2. MALACHI STRONG, of whom presently.
3. Anthony, Maj. in the Austrian Service.
4. Edward Patrick, m. 21 Oct. 1857, Margaret Mary, 2nd dau. of the late Richard Butler Mackenna, of Gloucester Place, Portman Square, London. 5. Richard.
1. Mary, a nun. 2. Mabel, a nun.
3. Margaret, a nun.
4. Isabel, a nun, d. 31 Oct. 1909.
Mr. Hussey d. 12 July, 1859. The second son,
MALACHI STRONG HUSSEY, of Westown, J.P. and D.L., High Sheriff 1867, b. 20 May, 1815 ; m. 21 Aug. 1849, Charlotte Isabella, 2nd dau. of Richard FitzGerald, of Muckridge House, Youghal, and had issue,
1. ANTHONY ALOYSIUS, now of Westown.
2. Henry James, b. 8 Oct. 1854, B.A. Trinity College, Dublin.
1. Emily Geraldine, m. 5 Aug. 1882, Thomas FitzGerald Murphy, 2nd son of James George Murphy, of The Grange, co. Meath (see *that family*). He d. 25 Feb. 1907.
2. Mabel Mary Lousia, m. James FitzGerald (who d. 1885), 2nd son of Thomas FitzGerald, of Fitzwilliam Place, Dublin, and nephew of the late Lord FitzGerald.
Mr. M. S. Hussey d. 14 March, 1880.

Arms—Barry of six erm. and gu., on a canton of the last a cross or. Crest—On a mount vert, a hind passant arg. under a tree ppr. Motto—Cor immobile.
Seat—Westown, near Ballybriggan.

HUSSEY OF EDENBURN.

SAMUEL MURRAY HUSSEY, of Edenburn, co. Kerry, J.P. cos. Kerry, Cork, and Limerick, High Sheriff of Kerry 1868, and D.L. for Kerry, b. 17 Dec. 1824 ; m. 30 Aug. 1853, Julia Agnes, 3rd dau. of John Hickson, of The Grove, Dingle, J.P., D.L. co. Kerry, by Barbara Mahony, his wife, and has issue,
1. John Edward, J.P., High Sheriff of Kerry 1880, b. 13 Dec. 1856 ; m. 1896, Gladys Marianne, 2nd dau. of the late James Buckley, D.L., of Brynycaern, Carmarthen. He d.v.p. 24 July, 1905, having had issue,
HUBERT MURRAY, b. 1898.
Eileen.
2. Maurice FitzGerald, J.P. for cos. Mayo, Roscommon, and Kerry, b. 4 Nov. 1858 ; m. Mabel, dau. of Capt. Henry Meux Smith, and has issue,
1. Maurice Henry Murray, b. 9 Aug. 1896.
2. John Edward, b. 6 July, 1902.
1. Mary, m. 1st, 1883, Maj. James Ormsby Sherrard (S. Staffordshire Regt.), and by him (who d. 1884) has a son,
James Ormsby, Lieut. R.H.A., b. 1884 ; m. 1910, Priscilla Harding, of Boston, U.S.A.
She m. 2ndly, 2 June, 1894, Major-Gen. Hamilton Bower, C.B., late 17th Bengal Cavalry.
2. Charlotte.
3. Eileen Margaret.
4. Florence Barbara, m. Donald Nicolls, J.P., of Burntwood, near Winchester, and has issue.
5. Julia Agnes.

Lineage.—HUBERT HUSSEY, of Castle Gregory, co. Kerry, d., according to a *post-mortem* inquisition, 3 Feb. 1610, seised of several lands near Dingle in that co. His eldest son, NICHOLAS HUSSEY, of Castle Gregory, m. Katherine Gerald, and was father of
MEILER HUSSEY, of Castle Gregory, b. 1583, who was found by the inquisition to be aged 27 at his grandfather's death ; he m. Frances, dau. of Capt. Thomas Spring, the first of that name who settled at Kerry, by Annabella his wife, dau. of John Brown, the "Master of Awney," and had issue,
1. NICHOLAS, s. his father ; d. 30 July, 1625, leaving one dau., Ellena, b. posthumous, 26 Sept. 1626 ; d. 25 Jan. 1627.
2. WALTER, his heir.
1. Annabella. 2. Ellen.
The second son,
WALTER HUSSEY, of Castle Gregory, was found by inquisition *post-mortem*, taken 27 March, 1627, to be heir to his niece ; he m. Katherine FitzGerald, of Kilmurray, and had issue,
1. NICHOLAS, his heir. 2. John.
3. Hubert.
1. Katherine, m. Oliver Hussey, of Rabeg, co. Kerry, and had issue. 2. Frances, m. Thomas Hickson, of Gowlane.
Walter Hussey garrisoned Minard Castle against Oliver Cromwell's forces, and was blown up with all his men. His eldest son,
NICHOLAS HUSSEY, of Castle Gregory, was deprived of his estate ; he m. Mabel, dau. of Nicholas Browne, of Cooleleave, 3rd son of Sir Nicholas Browne, Knt. of Molahiff, and had several children including a son Richard, who m. Joanna Rice. His cousin and brother-in-law,
OLIVER HUSSEY, of Rha, m. his cousin Katherine, eldest dau. of Walter Hussey, of Ballybeggan Castle and Minard Castle, and had two sons,
1. WALTER.
2. Edward, who had two sons, Edward and Patrick, both d.s.p. male.
The elder son,
WALTER HUSSEY, of Ballingown, made his will 31 Oct. 1728 ; he m. Ellen Fitzgerald, and had,
1. Edward, whose male issue failed. 2. MAURICE.
The second son,
MAURICE HUSSEY, of Dingle, m. his cousin, Mary, dau. of Richard Hussey and Johanna Rice (see *above*), and had two sons, JOHN and Edward, and a dau., Alice. His elder son,
JOHN HUSSEY, of Dingle, m. Helen Bodkin, of Annagh, co. Galway, and had four sons, of whom three d. unm. The survivor,
PETER BODKIN HUSSEY, of Farrinakilla, co. Kerry, J.P., D.L., d. 1836 ; m. 10 Dec. 1804, Mary, dau. of Robert Hickson, of The Grove, near Dingle, J.P. and D.L. co. Kerry, and by her (who d. 1857) had issue,
1. John. 2. James.
3. Edward, m. Julia, dau. of Rev. Robert Hickson, and had issue,
1. Peter, Lieut. R.A., d.s.p.
2. Edward Robert, Lieut.-Col. R.E., d. unm.
4. Robert, Lieut.-Col. R.E.
5. SAMUEL MURRAY, now of Edenburn.
1. Mary.
2. Ellen, m. 1st, Robert FitzGerald, son of the Knight of Kerry, and had a dau., Maria, who m. Capt. W. Percy. Ellen m. 2ndly, Col. T. A. Tennant.
3. Anne.
4. Julia, m. 11 Aug. 1838, Sir Peter George FitzGerald, Bart., Knight of Kerry, and had issue (see BURKE's *Peerage*).

Seat—Edenburn, Gortatlea, co. Kerry. Residence—18, Elvaston Place, S.W. Club—Carlton.

HUTCHINS OF ARDNAGASHEL.

SAMUEL NEWBURGH HUTCHINS, of Ballylicky and Ardnagashel, co. Cork, J.P., Barrister-at-Law, b. 16 April, 1834 ; m. 31 July, 1873, Marianne Isabella, eldest dau. of Henry Harrison, of Castle Harrison, J.P. (see *that family*), by his wife Marianne, dau. of Robert Stein, of Kilbegie, N.B., and has issue,
1. RICHARD, J.P. co. Cork, Capt. 4th Batt. Royal Munster F., b. 27 July, 1870 ; m. 9 July, 1910, Isobel Alice Edith, dau. of John Peacock, and has issue, Mary Patricia Rachel.
2. Samuel, Capt. Army Service Corps, late Lieut. 18th R. Irish Regt., b. 30 Aug. 1877.
3. Emanuel, M.R.C.V.S., b. 12 Jan. 1882.
4. Francis Harold, b. 17 Feb. 1887.
5. Thomas Arthur, b. 20 July, 1888.

IRELAND. Hussey.

1. ROBERT CONWAY, his heir.
2. JOHN, s. his brother.
1. Letitia, m. Rowland Blennerhassett, 4th son of Sir Rowland Blennerhassett, Bart.
2. Alice, m. Alexander Elliott.
3. Christian, m. James Magill.
4. Lucy, d. unm.
5. Arabella, d. young.
6. Mary, m. Barry Collins.

The elder son,
The Rev. ROBERT CONWAY HURLY, Rector of Killiney, Vicar-General and Surrogate of the Diocese of Ardfert and Aghadoe, d. unm., and was s. by his only brother,
JOHN HURLY, of Bridge House, and Glenduffe House, Tralee, co. Kerry, Clerk of the Peace and J.P. for Kerry; m. 19 May, 1814, Anna Maria Theresa, only dau. of Col. Hugh Hill, of Mount Mill, co. Armagh, by Elizabeth Kirwan his wife, eldest dau. of the learned Richard Kirwan, of Cregg Castle, co. Galway, President of the Royal Irish Academy, and d. 19 June, 1854, having had issue,
1. ROBERT CONWAY, of whom presently.
2. Hugh Richard Kirwan, dec.
3. John, of Fenit House, co. Kerry, J.P., m. 18 Dec. 1853, Elizabeth Augusta, widow of William Dundas Boyd, Lieut. 14th Light Dragoons, and 3rd dau. of Colquhoun Grant, of Kinchirdy, Morayshire. She d. Aug. 1881. He d. Oct. 1878, leaving issue,
1. John Charles Dennis, of Fenit House, Fenit, co. Kerry, J.P., High Sheriff 1888, b. 25 July, 1864.
1. Elinor Mary Augusta, m. 30 Aug. 1881, Samuel Gordon Fraser, of Askive, Kenmare, co. Kerry.
2. Augusta Hobart, m. 10 April, 1894, Harnett John Fuller, 2nd son of James Franklin Fuller, of Glashnacree, Kenmare, co. Kerry, and has issue (see that family).
1. Elizabeth.
2. Maria Theresa, m. Hugh Bradshaw.
3. Alice, m. Rev. John Scott.
4. Letitia, m. Richard Fitzgerald.

The eldest son,
ROBERT CONWAY HURLY, of Bridge House, Tralee, and Glenduffe, co. Kerry, J.P., b. 2 June, 1815; m. 1st, 27 May, 1845, Dorcas, eldest dau. of the late Arthur Blennerhassett, of Ballyscedy, M.P. co. Kerry; and 2ndly, 1860, Annie, 2nd dau. of William Comyns, of Witheridge, co. Devon, by whom he had issue,
1. JOHN CONWAY, now of Glenduffe.
2. Maurice Randall, Major Indian Army, b. 12 June, 1864; m. 20 Aug. 1890, Norah, dau. of Robert Fitzmaurice, M.D., of Clogbers, Tralee.
3. Francis Thomas Barnwall (Rev.), b. 2 Aug. 1866; d. 17 Feb. 1897.
1. Roberta Mary Conway, b. 30 Aug. 1870.
He d. 11 Sept. 1870. His widow m. 2ndly, 1873, the Rev. John Ross, M.A., Vicar of Caynham, Salop.

Arms—Az., on a fess between three cross-crosslets or, a dexter hand couped between two mullets gu., quartering FITZGERALD and CONWAY. Crests—1st, a naked arm embowed holding a sword wavy, all ppr.; 2nd, Out of an antique Irish crown or, a naked arm embowed ppr. holding a cross-crosslet gold. Motto—Dextra cruce vincit.
Seat—Glenduffe, Tralee.

HUSSEY OF RATHKENNY.

ALGERNON FREDERICK EDWARD THOMAS HUSSEY, of Rathkenny, co. Meath, b. 14 Aug. 1849.

Lineage.—WALTER HUSSEY, of Albright Hussey, Shropshire, obtained in 1155 a grant of Crown Land in Pencrig, in Staffordshire. He m. Matilda, dau. of Henry de Lee, and d. before Easter, 1172, leaving issue,
1. Ralph Lud of Albright Hussey, Shropshire, who had issue.
2. William, m. Laetitia, dau. and heir of Gilbert de Hadnall and widow of Nigel de Barastre.
3. HUGH, who follows.

Sir HUGH received a grant, from King John, of land between Grange Gorman and the Liffey, in Dublin, in 1200 confirming previous grant by Prince John in 1185; also of Galtrim in Barony of Deene, co. Meath, from Hugh de Lacie; gave, in 1207, 200 marks and 2 palfreys to have the Manor of Pencrig, which he granted in 1215 to Henri de Londres, Archbishop of Dublin, and d. before Dec. 1226, leaving issue,
1. Walter Hussey of Galtrim, co. Meath.
2. MAURICE, who follows.

MAURICE HUSSEY was given as hostage in 1206; had issue, Hugh Hussey, Lord of Galtrim, co. Meath, "nephew and heir of Walter Huose," one of the pledges for Walter de Lacy in 1226, was s. by
ADAM de HUSSEY, Lord of Galtrim, who had issue,
Sir HUGH HUSSEY, Kt., "son and heir of Adam de Hosey, Lord of Galtrim," released 24 Dec. 1316, to Holy Trinity Church, the Grange of Gylgorman (Cal. Ch. Ch. Deeds No. 195). He was summoned to Parliament in 1294 as Baron of Galtrim (Mem. Rolls), and had issue,
WILLIAM HUSSEY, Baron of Galtrim, m. Beatrix, and had issue,
Sir JOHN HUSSEY, Kt., Baron of Galtrim, summoned to Parliament 25 March and 22 Nov. 1374, and 22 Jan. 1377, and was slain at Kinsleagh, leaving issue,
1. Sir John Hussey, Baron of Galtrim, had issue Paula.
2. EDMUND HUSSEY, who follows.
1. Margaret.
2. Joan, m. Thomas Bathe.

I.L.G.

EDMUND HUSSEY, Baron of Galtrim, summoned to Parliament 11 Sept. 1380, and 29 April, 1382. He d. 24 Jan. 1384, leaving issue by his wife Matilda,
1. Paul.
2. PETER, who follows.
1. Margaret, m. Robert O'Rell, who s. to Galtrim in 1390.
PETER HUSSEY, Baron of Galtrim, who m. 1st, Anne, dau. of John Cusack, of Lismullen; and 2ndly, a dau. of the House of Leinster. He d.s.p. 14 RICHARD II, and was s. by
MATTHEW HUSSEY, Baron of Galtrim, into which manor with that of Moyle-Hussey, or Mul-Hussey, and divers other lands he had a pardon of intrusion 5 July, 1403; Sheriff of Meath 8 HENRY IV. in July, 1406, he had licence to settle the manor of Mul-Hussey on NICHOLAS HUSSEY and his heirs male (see HUSSEY WALSH of Cranagh and Mul Hussey), and d. 1418, leaving issue, by his wife Margaret, dau. and heir to Pettyt of Rathkenny, two sons, Thomas, who d. without issue, and
WALTER or NICHOLAS HUSSEY, who in May, 1403, had a pardon of intrusion into the manor of Galtrim. By Mary his wife, dau. of Sir Edward Eustace, Knt., of Castle Martin, co. Kildare, he had,
1. Thomas Hussey, Baron of Galtrim, m. Matilda Plunkett; d. 9 HENRY IV.
2. Nicholas, Baron of Galtrim 1433.
JOHN HUSSEY, Baron of Galtrim, m. Catherine Plunket, dau. of the House of Dunsany, and had
PATRICK HUSSEY, Baron of Galtrim, m. Anne Delahyde, and had issue, a son,
NICHOLAS HUSSEY, Baron of Galtrim, m. Catherine, eldest dau. of Sir Christopher Barnewall, Bart. of Crickston, and had issue,
SIR PATRICK HUSSEY, Baron of Galtrim, who was living in the reigns of Queen MARY and Queen ELIZABETH. He was knighted 1548, m. Catherine, dau. of John, 3rd Lord Trimleston, and had
1. Nicholas, Baron of Galtrim, Sheriff of Meath 11 and 12 HENRY VIII., who d. without issue.
2. JAMES, Baron of Galtrim, who d. 1603, leaving by Mary his wife, dau. of Richard Aylmer, of Lyons, two sons,
1. PATRICK, his heir, of whom hereafter.
2. Peter, m. Mary, only dau. of Bartholomew Bellew, of Westown, co. Dublin, who d. 29 Sept. 1623, and was ancestor of the HUSSEYS of Westown (see that family).
1. Mary, m. George Aylmer, of Cloncurry.
2. Ruth, m. Taaffe of Ballybregan.

His grandson,
PATRICK HUSSEY, Baron of Galtrim, eldest son of James, by Mary Aylmer his wife, m. Margaret, dau. of Robert Rochefort, of Kilbride; he made a settlement of his estate 26 May, 1617, M.P. Meath, 1619, signed his will 31 Dec. 1634, d. soon after, and was bur. in the church of Galtrim, having had issue, five sons and seven daus., 1. HUGH, his heir; 2. James; 3. Robert; 4. John; 5. Edward; 6. Ignatius; 1. Eleanor; 2. Bridget; 3. Genet; 4. Elizabeth; 5. Ismay; 6. Anne; and 7. Catherine. The eldest son,
HUGH HUSSEY, Baron of Galtrim, who was living after the restoration of King CHARLES II., m. 1st, a dau. of Dowdall of Brownstown; and 2ndly, Elizabeth, dau. of James, the 1st Earl of Roscommon, and had two sons,
1. MATTHIAS.
2. Peter.

The elder son,
MATTHIAS HUSSEY, d. before his father, 1633, leaving by his wife Catherine, dau. of Hussey of Westown (who re-married with Christopher Barnewall, of Newstown, co. Meath), a son,
JAMES HUSSEY, styled Baron of Galtrim, d. Jan. 1776, a minor at his father's death, living 1699, m. Penelope, dau. of Francis Stafford, of Portglenone (by Sarah his wife, dau. of Sir James MacDonnel, of the House of Antrim), and had issue,.
1. STAFFORD.
2. Patrick.

The elder son,
STAFFORD HUSSEY, Baron of Galtrim, m. Anne, dau. of Simon Kirwan, of Castle Hacket, co. Galway, by Mary his wife, dau. of Thomas Nugent, styled Lord Riverston, and had issue,
1. JOHN, his heir.
2. Nicholas.
3. THOMAS, s. his brother.

The eldest son,
JOHN HUSSEY, of Rathkenny, co. Meath, styled Baron of Galtrim, m. Anne, dau. of Ralph Hansbey, of Tick Hill Castle, Yorkshire, and relict of Patrick D'Arcy, of Stydalt, co. Meath. He d.s.p. 1803.

His brother,
THOMAS HUSSEY, of Rathkenny, b. 1749; s. his brother 1803; m. 4 Aug. 1777, Lady Mary Walpole, younger dau. of Horatio, Earl of Orford, by Lady Rachel Cavendish his wife, dau. of William, 3rd Duke of Devonshire. She d. 1 April, 1840. He d. 25 March, 1825, and was s. by his only son,
EDWARD THOMAS HUSSEY, of Rathkenny, b. 1778; m. Aug. 1803, Anne Frances (d. 2 Sept. 1866), elder dau. of Sir Edmund Bacon, of Raveningham, Norfolk, Premier Baronet of England, and had issue,
EDWARD HORATIO, late of Rathkenny.
Annabella Maria, d. young.

Mr. Hussey d. 27 Sept. 1846. His only son,
EDWARD HORATIO HUSSEY, of Rathkenny, J.P., b. 5 May, 1807; m. 17 Dec. 1840, Hon. Frederica Maria Louisa Irby, 4th dau. of George, 4th Lord Boston, and by her (who d. 13 July, 1885) had issue,
1. HORATIO GEORGE, late of Rathkenny.
2. ALGERNON FREDERICK EDWARD THOMAS, now of Rathkenny.

He d. 1 May, 1876, and was s. by his elder son,
HORATIO GEORGE HUSSEY, of Rathkenny, co. Meath, J.P., b. 26 June, 1846; d. unm. 30 June, 1902.

Arms—Barry of six erm. and gu. on a canton of the last a cross or. Crest—A stag under an oak tree.
Seat—Rathkenny, Slane, co. Meath.

Y

Tipperary, *m.* 6 Sept. 1784, Sarah, dau. of James Hutchinson, of Timoney (*see below*), and *d.* 1820. She *d.* 1794, having had issue,
1. William Henry, of Knockballymagher, *b.* 1792 ; *m.* 1st, 1821, Sarah, dau. of John Birch, of Shee Hills, co. Tipperary, and by her had an only dau.,
   a. Sarah Anne, *s.* her father at Knockballymagher, *m.* Edward C. Minchin, of Greenhills, co. Tipperary.
He *m.* 2ndly, 1832, Eliza Hannah, dau. of George Waller, of Prior Park, co. Tipperary, and *d.* 21 Nov. 1842, having by her [who *m.* 2ndly, 22 Oct. 1844, John Dawson Hutchinson, of Timoney (*see below*)] had issue,
   a. Thomas William Henry, Capt. 9th Lancers, *b.* 8 March, 1833 ; *d.s.p.*, killed at Lucknow, 19 March, 1858.
   b. Eliza Selina Maria, *m.* 1st, 6 Aug. 1857, Hugh Hamon Massey O'Grady, of Castle Garden, co. Limerick, who *d.* 8 Dec. 1859, leaving issue. She *m.* 2ndly, 1862, William Bredin, J.P., and *d.* 2 Aug. 1878, having by him had issue.
   c. Georgina Wilhelmina Henrietta, *m.* 18 July, 1867, Richard Warburton, D.L., of Garryhinch, King's Co., and *d.* 1891, leaving issue (*see that family*).
      1. Christiana.   2. Lydia.
   3. Anne, *m.* 1811, John Waldron Watson, of Spafield, co. Tipperary, M.D.
   4. Maria Isabella.
   (3) John, *d.* young.
   (1) Elizabeth, *d.* young.
   (2) Anne, *m.* John Duckett, of Philipstown.
   (3) Mary.   (4) Martha.
2. JOHN, who *s.* to Timoney.
1. Mary, *d. unm.* 17 April, 1706.
2. Elizabeth, *d. unm.* 1705.
Mr. Hutchinson *m.* 2ndly, 8 Aug. 1694, Sarah, widow of Richard Pearce, of Limerick, and *d.* 18 Sept. 1718. He was *s.* at Timoney by his younger son,
JOHN HUTCHINSON, of Timoney, co. Tipperary, *m.* 18 June, 1715, Mary, dau. of Paul Chanders, and *d.* 18 May, 1753, leaving issue,
1. JAMES, his heir.
2. Benjamin, *b.* 1720 ; *d.* 1791.   3. John, *b.* 1731.
1. Mary.   2. Elizabeth, *d.* 1792.

The eldest son,
JAMES HUTCHINSON, of Timoney, *b.* 20 July, 1716 ; *m.* 15 Oct. 1748, Christina, dau. of John Pim, of Lacca, Queen's Co., and *d.* 11 Aug. 1791. She *d.* 1795, leaving issue,
1. WILLIAM, of whom presently.
2. John, *b.* 19 Jan. 1763.
1. Mary, *m.* 1779, Robert Powell, of Ratoath, co. Meath.
2. Sarah, *m.* 6 Sept. 1784, her cousin, Thomas Hutchinson, of Knockballymagher, and *d.* 1794, leaving issue (*see above*).

The elder son,
WILLIAM HUTCHINSON, of Timoney, J.P., and High Sheriff co. Tipperary, *b.* 9 Sept. 1757 ; *m.* 10 June, 1791, Anna, dau. and co-heir of John Dawson Coates, of Dublin, and *d.* 6 June, 1832, leaving issue,
1. JOHN DAWSON, his heir.
2. James, of Dungar, *d.s.p.* 9 March, 1839.
3. William, *d.s.p.* 1814.
4. Samuel Dawson, of Mount Heaton, King's Co., *m.* 14 Aug. 1843, Mary, only dau. of John Lloyd, and niece maternally and heiress of William Peisley Vaughan, of Golden Grove. He assumed by Letters Patent the surname of LLOYD-VAUGHAN. She *d.* 31 Jan. 1845. He *d.* 1855, leaving issue (*see* VAUGHAN *of Golden Grove*).
5. Frederick, *d.s.p.* 7 April, 1858.
6. Joseph Fade, of Dungar, King's Co., J.P., formerly High Sheriff of King's Co. and Carlow.
7. Samuel Summers, of Beechy Park, co. Carlow, *m.* 6 July, 1858, Matilda Jane, dau. of Rev. Charles Collins, Rector of Milstead, and Anne Matilda his wife, dau. of Lawrence Creagh, of Castle Park, co. Tipperary, and *d.* 1881, having by her (who *d.* 15 April, 1902) had issue,
   1. Frederick William, of Brooklands House, The Avenue, Cambridge, and Beechy Park, co. Carlow, M.A. and B.Ch. Camb., late Lieut. 8th Batt. King's Royal Rifles (Carlow Militia), *b.* 11 Jan. 1868; *m.* 20 June, 1891, Georgina Aurora Fanny, eld. dau. of Col. Sir John Louis, 3rd bart., and has issue,
      Aurora Margaret.
   1. Magdalene Blanche, *d.* an infant.
   2. Margarita Theodora Eirene, *m.* 28 Oct. 1903, Rev. William Henry Frazer, D.D.
8. Samuel, *d.s.p.* 19 Feb. 1857.   9. William, *d.s.p.* 1836.
1. Eliza Dawson, *d. unm.* 9 April, 1864.
2. Christiana, *m.* 1826, Frederic Lidwell, of Dromard, and *d.* 1833, leaving issue.
3. Sarah Summers, *m.* 1819, John Dawson Duckett, of Ducketts Grove (*see that family*).   4. Maria.
5. Anna, *m.* 7 June, 1840, Michael Head Drought, of Harristown, Queen's Co.   6. Sophia, *m.* 1831, John Pim, of Lacca.
7. Henrietta.
8. Louisa, *m.* 20 Feb. 1840, Frederick Adolphus Jackson, of Inane, co. Tipperary.   9. Amelia.
10. Charlotte, *m.* 1844, Capt. Samuel John Gosselin, 49th Regt., of New Lodge, co. Meath.

The eldest son,
JOHN DAWSON HUTCHINSON, of Timoney Park, co. Tipperary, J.P., *b.* 1796; *m.* 1st, 15 Dec. 1840, Elizabeth Anne, dau. of John Lloyd, of Lloydsborough. She *d.s.p.* 3 March, 1840. He *m.* 2ndly, 22 Oct. 1844, Eliza Hannah, dau. of George Waller of Prior Park (*see that family*), and widow of William Henry Hutchinson, of Knockballymagher (*see above*), and *d.* 21 Dec. 1881, having by her had issue,
Anna Christiana, *m.* 13 July, 1867, Anthony Parker, of Castle Lough, co. Tipperary (*see* PARKER *of Bally Valley*), and *d.* 18 Oct. 1871, leaving issue.
1. STANDISH GRADY JOHN, now of Timoney.
1. Anna Christiana, *b.* 20 May, 1868 ; *d.* 12 Aug. 1871.
2. Elizabeth Margaret, *b.* 29 May, 1871.

Arms—Quarterly 1st and 4th quarterly Gu. and az. crusily or a lion rampant arg. (HUTCHINSON); 2nd and 3rd Sa. a stag's head caboshed between two flaunches arg. in the centre chief point a mullet or (PARKER). Crests—1. Out of a ducal crest coronet or a cockatrice wings addorsed ppr. (HUTCHINSON); 2. A stag salient ppr., charged with a mullet as in the arms (PARKER). *Motto*—Fideli certa merces.

Seats—Timoney Park, Roscrea, Tipperary; Castle Lough, Nenagh, co. Tipperary, and Cardtown, Mountrath, Queen's Co. *Club*—Kildare Street.

HYDE OF LYNNBURY.

GUSTAVUS ROCHFORT HYDE, of Lynnbury, co. Westmeath, J.P., High Sheriff 1910, educated at Radley and Cambridge, M.A., C.C.C., *b.* 20 Feb. 1858 ; *m.* 1st, 10 April, 1888, Annie Martha, eldest dau. of Marlborough Parsons Berry, of Clooneen, King's Co. She *d.* 19 Aug. 1889, leaving a dau.,
  1. Annie Frances Jane.

He *m.* 2ndly, 25 April, 1901, Nellie, 2nd dau. of Edwin C. Wharton, of Attleborough, and by her has issue,
  1. EDWARD ROCHFORT, *b.* 27 Aug. 1904.
  2. Gustavus Patrick Rochfort, *b.* 2 Feb. 1906.
  3. Charles Humphrey Rochfort, *b.* 23 Dec. 1907.
  2. Mary Constance.

Mr. Hyde is the eldest son of the late Gustavus William Rochfort Wade, of Dublin (who *d.* 28 March, 1897), and Mary his wife (who *d.* 15 Oct. 1899), dau. of Rev Edward Mayne, and grandson of the late Thomas Wade of Carrowmore, co. Galway (who *d.* 26 Oct. 1865). Mr. Hyde assumed by Royal Licence, 15 Sept. 1898, the name and arms of HYDE in lieu of WADE.

Lineage.—*See* WADE *of Carrowmore*.

Arms—Az. on a chevron between three lozenges or, a hurt for distinction, on a canton of the field, three escallops of the second between two flaunches erm., a canton gu. for distinction. Crest—A falcon rising sable belled and jessed or, charged on the breast with a bezant for distinction. *Motto*—Soyez Ferme.

Seats—Lynnbury, Mullingar, co. Westmeath, and Hatherley Brake, Cheltenham. *Club*—Hibernian United Service, Dublin.

HYDE, late OF CASTLEHYDE.

MRS. SARAH HYDE, *m.* 20 Sept. 1859, Richard Edward Beck, formerly Capt. 89th Regt., of Derwyn, co. Monmouth, who *d.* 26 Oct. 1887. His widow assumed by Royal Licence, dated 7 Dec. 1888, for herself and her issue, the surname and arms of HYDE in lieu of BECK, in compliance with the will of her uncle, JOHN HYDE of Creg.

Lineage.—This is a branch of the family of HYDE,

IRELAND.   Hutchinson.

1. Mary.
2. Frances Newburgh, m. 25 Nov. 1899, Capt. Edmund Hyde Smith, R.N., eldest son of Major-Gen. E. D. Smith, and has issue, Richard Edmund Hyde, b. 29 June, 1900, and Samuel Newburgh Hyde, b. 24 Sept. 1903.
3. Alicia Isabella, m. 27 April, 1911, Capt. John McDouall Harkard, Royal Dublin Fus., 2nd son of William Haskard, of Florence.
4. Margaret Ellen.
5. Aline Katherine, d. 16 April, 1909.
6. Madeline, d. young, 9 Dec. 1885.
7. Ellen Madeline.   8. Marian Geraldine.

Lineage.—RICHARD HUTCHINS, of Blackrock, near Bantry, who went to Ireland during the Civil War, served under the Earl of Orrery 1666, and was appointed by Act of Parliament, 9 WILLIAM III, one of the Commissioners of Poll Tax. He m. Barbara Burridge, and d. 1701, leaving issue by her (who d. 1716), with three daus., two sons,

1. THEOPHILUS, of Kametringane, of whom presently.
2. Benjamin, of Berehaven, m. Elizabeth, dau. of Col. Thomas Raddy, of Quanning, and had issue.

The elder son,

THEOPHILUS HUTCHINS, of Kametringane, Berehaven, m. Margaret, sister of Hugh Hutchinson, and had issue. His son and heir,

THOMAS HUTCHINS, of Ballylicky, m. 1726-8, Katherine, eldest dau. of Beversham Harman, of Laharen, by his wife Margaret Palmer, and d. 1754, leaving issue by her (who d. 1804) an only child,

THOMAS HUTCHINS, of Ballylicky, J.P., b. 1735; m. 14 March, 1759, Elinor, only child and heiress of Arthur Hutchins, of Thomastown and Cregane Castle, co. Limerick, and d. 4 Feb. 1787, having had issue by her (who d. 22 March, 1814) twenty-one children, of whom survived,

1. EMANUEL, of Cregane, J.P., b. Feb. 1769; d.s.p. at Damascus, 22 Nov. 1839.
2. Arthur, of Ardnagashel, J.P., b. Aug. 1770; m. 15 March, 1802, Matilda, dau. of John O'Donel, of Erris, and Ann, sister to Sir Nial O'Donel. He d. 17 Aug. 1838, leaving issue by her (who d. 24 Oct. 1827, aged 51),
    1. Thomas, of Roughty, b. 29 Dec. 1802; m. 23 July, 1832, Charlotte, dau. of Edward Orpen, of Killowen, and d. 19 Oct. 1875, leaving issue,
        Arthur, b. 28 May, 1848; d. unm.
        Elizabeth Charlotte Matilda, d. 10 Jan. 1908.
    2. Arthur, of Ballylicky, J.P., b. Sept. 1805; d. 12 Jan. 1889.
    3. Richard, b. 1 April, 1815; d. 7 Dec. 1887.
    1. Margarette Anne, of Barnstaple, d. 29 Aug. 1869.
    2. Matilda, d. 21 Feb. 1856.
    3. Ellen, of Barnstaple, d. 6 April, 1890.
    4. Katherine, d. 19 July, 1840.
    5. Mary, d. 6 April, 1854.
3. Thomas Massy, of Ballylicky, b. 1778; d. 18 July, 1815.
4. SAMUEL, of Ardnagashel, by the will of his brother, Emanuel, s. to the family estates.
    1. Katherine, b. 1765; d. June, 1789.
    2. Ellen, b. 17 March, 1785; well known as a botanist, d. 10 Feb. 1815.

The 4th son,

SAMUEL HUTCHINS, of Ardnagashel and Fortlands, J.P., b. 29 Sept. 1786; m. 1st, 22 Sept. 1822, Frances Camac (b. 17 June, 1795), 2nd dau. of Arthur Robert Camac Newburgh, of Ballybaise, co. Cavan, by his wife Eliza Mariamne, only child and heiress of Jacob Camac, of Greenmount, co. Louth, Lieut.-Col. H.E.I.C.S., and by her (who d. 16 Sept. 1839) had issue,

1. EMANUEL, late of Ardnagashel.
2. Samuel, b. 3 Oct. 1825; d. 27 Jan. 1828.
3. SAMUEL NEWBURGH, now of Ballylicky.
4. Robert Arthur, b. 5 Feb.; d. 24 April, 1837.
5. Francis Arthur, J.P. cos. Kent and Hants, late Lieut.-Col. 4th Hussars (*The Orchard, Crofton, Fareham, Hants*), b. 11 Feb. 1839; m. 30 April, 1890, Alice Evelyn, only child of David Dowie, of Hurst Lea, Kent, and has issue,
    1. Arthur Newburgh, b. 10 April, 1891; d. 20 Aug. 1908.
    2. Robin Leslie, b. 18 May, 1897.
    1. Daphne Kathleen.
1. Frances Mary Elizabeth, d. unm. 15 Oct. 1902.
2. Louisa Ellen, m. 1859, William Shore Smith (now Nightingale), of Embley, Hants, and Lea Hurst, co. Derby, and has issue,
    1. Samuel, b. 27 Nov. 1860.
    2. Louis Hilary, b. 11 July, 1866; m. 21 April, 1903, Helen Johanna, 2nd dau. of James Spencer-Bell, of Fawe Park, Keswick.
    1. Rosalind Frances Mary, m. 1892, Vaughan Nash, C.B., and has issue.
    2. Margaret Thyra Barbara, m. Dec. 1904, Harry Lushington Stephen, Judge of the High Court of Calcutta, 3rd son of late Sir James Fitzjames Stephen, Bart. (*see* BURKE's *Peerage*).
3. Alicia Maria.

Mr. Hutchins m. 2ndly, 28 May, 1842, Mary (b. Nov. 1814), only surviving dau. of the late Peter Burrowes, Chief Commissioner of the Court for the Relief of Insolvent Debtors, M.P. for Enniscorthy in the last Irish Parliament, by Anne Drake, of Newport, Isle of Wight (his 2nd wife), and by her (who d. 24 Jan. 1849) had issue,

6. Peter Burrowes, Barrister-at-Law, b. 5 March, 1843; d. 4 Aug. 1901.
7. Elliot Burrowes, b. 2 April, 1845; m. 18 Sept. 1897, Gertrude Elizabeth, 2nd dau. of Joshua Wall, of Handsworth, Staffordshire, and Caroline Beadman hi- wife. He d. 1 July, 1905, leaving issue, Kathleen Mary Burrowes.
4. Mary Burrowes, b. 11 Jan. 1849; d. 25 Feb. 1855.

Mr. Samuel Hutchins d. 18 June, 1862. His eldest son, EMANUEL HUTCHINS, of Ardnagashel and Fortlands, J.P., b. 19 July, 1823; d. unm. 9 Sept. 1880, and was s. by his brother.

Seats—Ballylicky and Ardnagashel, Bantry.

HELY-HUTCHINSON OF SEAFIELD.

JOHN HELY-HUTCHINSON, of Seafield and Lissen Hall, co. Dublin, J.P. and D.L., High Sheriff 1872, b. 20 Nov. 1836; m. 25 Feb. 1865, Mary Louisa, eldest dau. of Robert Tottenham, of Annamult, 2nd son of Charles Tottenham, of Ballycurry, co. Wicklow (*see that family*), and has issue,

1. COOTE ROBERT, late Lieut.-Col. 6th Batt. Royal Fus. b. 6 Feb. 1870.
2. Richard George, Major Royal Fus., b. 3 March, 1871; m. 20 April, 1899, Alice, only dau. of the late William Cunningham, of Somerset, Belfast.
1. Ethel Mary, b. 3 March, 1868; d. unm. 6 May, 1886.
2. Cecil Frances Katharine, b. 3 March, 1869.
3. Eleanor Blanche, b. 27 July, 1872.

Mr. Hely-Hutchinson is the elder son of the late Capt. the Hon. Coote Hely-Hutchinson, R.N., who d. 6 May, 1842. and Sophia his wife (who d. 30 April, 1896), dau. of Rev. Sir Samuel Synge Hutchinson, bart., and nephew of John, 3rd Earl of Donoughmore.

Lineage, Arms, &c.—*See* BURKE's *Peerage*, DONOUGHMORE, E.

Seats—Seafield, Donabate. and Lissen Hall, Swords, both co. Dublin. *Club*—Sackville Street, Dublin.

PARKER-HUTCHINSON OF TIMONEY.

STANDISH GRADY JOHN PARKER-HUTCHINSON, of Timoney Park and Castle Lough, co. Tipperary, and of Cardtown, Queen's Co., J.P., D.I., co. Tipperary, High Sheriff Queen's Co. 1894, High Sheriff co. Tipperary 1908, M.A. Magdalen Coll. Oxford, b. 9 Jan. 1870; assumed by Royal Licence the additional name and arms of HUTCHINSON, 17 April, 1891; m. 30 Sept. 1903, Mary Eleanor, eldest dau. of Capt. J. Hill Poe, of Riverston, co. Tipperary (*see that family*), and has issue,

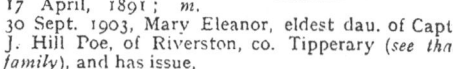

1. Honor, b. 9 March, 1907.
2. Mary Christiana.

Lineage.—(Of PARKER): Mr. PARKER-HUTCHINSON is head of the family of PARKER, of Castle Lough. Refer to the family of PARKER, of Bally Valley (of HUTCHINSON): JAMES HUTCHINSON, a Capt. in CROMWELL's Army, founded this family in Ireland, and settled at Knockballymagher, co. Tipperary, in 1653. He was b. at Kirkby Stephen, Westmorland, and was the son of John and Isabel Hutchinson. He m. 1st. Mary, dau. of John Godfrey, of King Walton, co. Hereford, and by her had a son,

1. JAMES, his heir.

He m. 2ndly, 19 Nov. 1653, Mary, dau. of John Sandford, of Castle Dee, co. Donegal, and d. 20 Sept. 1689, having by her (who d. 1691) had issue,

2. David, b. 17 Nov. 1655, left issue,
    1. Mary.   2. Abigail.
    1. Susannah.   2. Martha.
3. Rebecca.

His elder son,

JAMES HUTCHINSON, of Knockballymagher, and Timoney, co. Tipperary, m. 1st, 10 Jan. 1681, Mary, dau. of John Bennet, and by her (who d. 12 Oct. 1690) had issue,

1. James, of Knockballymagher, m. 23 Feb. 1712, Anne, dau. of Thomas Duckett, of Philipstown, co. Carlow, and d. 13 March, 1738. She d. 15 Oct. 1739, leaving, with other issue, two sons,
    1. JAMES, his heir, b. 28 Sept. 1715; d. unm. 25 May, 1780.
    2. Thomas, s. his brother; b. 7 Feb. 1721; m. 4 May, 1750, Elizabeth, dau. of Jonathan Hutchinson, and d. 17 Oct. 1788. She d. June, 1799, leaving issue,
        (1) James, his heir, b. 7 July, 1751; d.s.p. 1791.
        (2) Thomas, heir to his brother, J.P. and D.L. co.

Y 2

South Denchworth, and afterwards of Kingston Lisle, both in Berks (see CLARKE's *Hundred of Wanting*), of whom was SIR GEORGE HYDE, of Kingston Lisle, K.B., *temp.* JAMES I. JOHN HYDE, of South Denchworth, *d.* 21 July, 1447. His son, JOHN HYDE, is the first who appears in the Visitations. His great-grandson, OLIVER HYDE, who *d.* 4 Oct. 1516, was father of

WILLIAM HYDE, who *m.* Margery, only dau. and heir of John Cater. She received a grant of the Cater arms and crest 20 April, 1559. They had issue, a son,

WILLIAM HYDE, of Denchworth and Kingston Lisle, Berks., *m.* Alice, dau. of Sir Thomas Essex, of Lambourne, a descendant of Henry de Essex, Baron of Raleigh *temp.* HENRY II, and granddau. of William, Baron Sandys, K.G. He *d.* 1567. His second son,

ARTHUR HYDE, settled in Ireland *temp.* ELIZABETH, and obtained a grant (Letters Patent 26 Jan. 1588) of 12,000 acres of confiscated lands in co. Cork as a seignory to be held by the name of HYDE for ever. He *m.* Elizabeth, dau. and sole heir of John Pates, of Buckingham, and *d.* 1600, having had issue, 1. ARTHUR (Sir), of whom presently ; 2. Thomas ; 1. Susan, *m.* Sir Richard Southwell, Knt., of Limerick ; 2. Helen, *m.* Thomas Hyde ; 3. Catherine, *m.* 1st, Robert Gore, and 2ndly, Cornelius O'Garvan ; and 4. Frances, *m.* Richard Pilkington. The elder son,

SIR ARTHUR HYDE, Knt., of Carrigoneda, co. Cork, *m.* Helen, dau. of Anthony Power, of co. Waterford, and *d.* 1644, having had two sons,

1. WILLIAM, his heir.
2. ROBERT, of Caherdrinna Castle, co. Cork, *m.* a dau. of —— Arriball, and was father of

ANTHONY HYDE, Capt. R.N., *m.* 1st, a dau. of the noble family of Southwell, which lady *d.s.p.* ; and 2ndly, Dora, dau. of Col. Harrison, of Castle Harrison, and *d.* 1720, leaving a son,

ROBERT BOYLE HYDE, Lieut. R.N., of Ardmayle House, co. Tipperary, *b.* 1718, *m.* Catherine, dau. of Anthony Walsh, of Tully or Ivy Park, and *d.* 1802, leaving a son,

ARTHUR HYDE, of Mitchelstown, co. Cork, *b.* 1752, who *m.* 1776, Mary, dau. of Robert Jones, of Whitefort House, Holycross, co. Tipperary, and by her (who *d.* 1842) left at his decease, 1808, a son,

CAPT. HENRY BARRY HYDE, 96th Regt., Judge of the High Court of Admiralty, and Acting Governor of Sierra Leone, *b.* 1785 ; *m.* 16 July, 1816, Amelia, dau. of Major Cole, of Newport, Isle of Wight, and *d.* 10 Jan. 1831, leaving a dau. Amelia, *m.* 17 June, 1867, Sir R. Arthur Arnold, M.P., Vice-Chairman London County Council, who *d.* 20 May, 1902, and a son,

HENRY BARRY HYDE, F.S.S., of Ealing, *b.* 2 June, 1820 ; *m.* 24 Feb. 1852, Mary Anne (who *d.* 16 Feb. 1889), dau. of Golding Bird, of Derry, and *d.* 28 Aug. 1906, and had issue,

(1) Henry Barry (Rev.), M.A., Vicar of Bovey Tracey, Devon, Archdeacon of Madras, 1905-10, *b.* 31 May, 1854 ; *m.* 18 Jan. 1887, Hilda Dixon, dau. of W. Sheppard, M.R.C.S., and has issue,

1. Henry Barry, *b.* 16 Sept. 1890.
2. Anthony, *b.* 2 Oct. 1900.
1. Wymarke Frances Mary.

(2) Clarendon Golding (Sir), *b.* 5 Feb. 1858, of the Middle Temple, Barrister-at-Law, M.P. for Wednesbury 1906-10, Knt. Bach. (*Longworth House, Berks*), Lord of the Manor of East and West Longworth, J.P., Berks ; *m.* 27 July, 1886, Laura Adrie, eldest dau. of Rev. Canon George Thomas Palmer, Rector and R.D. of Newington, S.E., Canon of Rochester, and has issue one dau.,

Margery Laura, *m.* 7 June, 1910, John K. L. Fitzwilliams, R.H.A., and has issue,

(1) Violet (a deaconess). (2) Amelia.
(3) Eva, *m.* Robert D. Thomson, of the Pool House, Groby, co. Leicester.
(4) Geraldine, *m.* Rev. Canon A. H. B. Brittain, M.A., Vicar of Whittlebury cum Silverstone. He *d.* 9 Oct. 1911.
(5) Mabel.

Sir Arthur Hyde was *s.* at his decease by his eldest son,

WILLIAM HYDE, of Carrigoneda, *m.* Catherine, dau. of Robert Tynte, of co. Cork, eldest son of Sir Robert Tynte, Knt., and with other issue, had

1. ARTHUR, of whom presently.
2. John, *m.* Susanna Rowlston, and had two sons and two daus.,
1. Arthur. 2. William.
1. Katherine. 2. Helen.
1. Katherine, *m.* Sir Henry Spottiswood, eldest son of James Spottiswood, Lord Bishop of Clogher.
2. Elizabeth, *m.* James Spottiswood, 2nd son of the Bishop of Clogher.
3. Susan, *m.* Anthony, son of Sir John Dowdall, of Kilfinny, Knt.

The elder son,

ARTHUR HYDE, of Castle Hyde, co. Cork, J.P., High Sheriff 1670, living 1669, *m.* Elizabeth, dau. of Sir Richard Gethin, Bart., and *d.* 1688, leaving with five daus. (1. Sarah, *m.* William Causaban, of Youghal ; 2. Deborah, *m.* John Brown, of Kilbolan ; 3. Elizabeth, *m.* Foulke, of Kilvokery, co. Cork ; 4. Catherine ; and 5. Gertrude, *m.* 1699, Robert Gore, of Sligo) and two younger sons, William and Richard, an elder son,

ARTHUR HYDE, of Castle Hyde, J.P., who *m.* 1st, 3 Oct. 1695, Joan, dau. of Richard Yeats, of Youghal, and by her had, with a dau. Elizabeth, *m.* Alderman John Lucas, of Youghal, a son and heir,

1. ARTHUR, of whom presently.

He *m.* 2ndly, Mary, dau. of Col. George Evans, of Carrass, co. Cork, and by her had, with two daus., Mary and Jane, two sons,

2. George, *m.* Sophia, sister of Col. Frederick Hamilton, and had issue, Rev. Arthur Hyde, Incumbent of St. Anne's, Shandon, *m.* 14 Oct. 1756, Anne, dau. of Benjamin Green, of Youghal, and *d.* 1805, having had, with six daus. (1. Alice ; 2. Anne, *d.* 1760 ; 3. Sophia, *m.* 1800, Rev. Edward Spread, Vicar of Ahern, co. Cork ; 4. Mary Elizabeth, *m.* 5 Feb. 1789, Daniel Conner, of Manch (*see that family*) ; 5. Anne, *b.* 1706 ; and 6. Jane, *m.* 1790, William Jackson, of Youghal), a son,

Arthur (Rev.), Vicar of Killarney, *m.* 1st, 1787, Sarah, dau. of Geo. French, of French Park ; and 2ndly, 1809, Louisa Piersey. By the latter he had one dau., Lucy, of Belleview, Youghal, and by the former,

(1) Arthur, Vicar of Mohill, *m.* Frances, dau. of Sir Hugh Crofton, Bart., and had issue,

1. Arthur (Rev.), Canon of Elphin and Rector of Tibohine, *m.* 23 Oct. 1852, Elizabeth, dau. of Ven. John Orson Oldfield, Archdeacon of Elphin. He *d.* 29 Aug. 1905, having had issue,

a. Arthur, *d.* 1879.
b. John Oldfield, *d.* 1896.
c. Douglas, *m.* and has issue.
a. Annette, *m.* 4 Dec. 1902, John Cambreth Kane, son of John Kane, of the Castle, Mohill.
1. Frances, *m.* Nov. 1860, Ven. FitzMaurice Hunt, Archdeacon of Ardagh. He *d.* 1889.
2. Sarah.
3. Barbara, *m.* 5 Oct. 1864, L. F. S. Maberly, and has issue,
4. Anne, *m.* 1859, John Kane, of the Castle, Mohill, and had issue (*see* KANE *of Drumreaske*).
5. Emily.

(2) Frederick, J.P., *m.* Elizabeth, dau. of Francis Christopher Bland, of Derryquin, and had a son,

Arthur, *m.* Louisa, dau. of Thomas Harnett Fuller, and has Arthur ; Thomas ; and Frances.

(3) John, M.D., *m.* and had issue.
(4) George, *m.* and had issue.

3. John, of Creg Castle, co. Cork, who *m.* Joanna Condon, and had a son and three daus.,

1. William, of Templenoe, co. Cork, *m.* Catherine Lane, and *d.* 1790.
1. Elizabeth, *m.* — Pooley.
2. Sarah, *m.* Ambrose Lane, of Kilkenny.
3. Mary, *m.* John Alleyne, of Coolprebane, co. Tipperary.

Mr. Hyde *d.* 6 Oct. 1720, and was *s.* by his eldest son,

ARTHUR HYDE, of Castle Hyde, who *m.* Anne, only dau. and heir of Richard Price, of Ardmayle, and of Clonmore, co. Tipperary, and had issue (with three daus., Jane, *m.* May, 1749, the Hon. Richard Barry, son of James, Earl of Barrymore, and *d.* 19 Oct. 1751 ; Anne ; and Deborah, both *d. unm.*) three sons,

1. Arthur, of Castle Hyde, who *d. unm.* 22 Dec. 1772.
2. William.
3. JOHN, eventual successor to the family estates.

The last,

JOHN HYDE, of Castle Hyde and of Creg, *m.* Sarah, dau. of Benjamin Burton, of Burton Hall, co. Carlow, by Lady Anne Ponsonby his wife, dau. of William, Earl of Bessborough, and had issue,

1. JOHN, late of Castle Hyde.
2. William, *d.* in the East Indies, 1790.
1. Anne, *m.* Col. William Stewart, son of Sir Annesley Stewart, Bart. of Fort Stewart, co. Donegal, *d.s.p.*
2. Catherine, *m.* John Leslie, dec.
3. Mary, *m.* Benjamin Woodward, dec.
4. Sarah, *m.* 9 June, 1798, Henry, Earl of Shannon, and *d.* Sept. 1820.

The elder son,

JOHN HYDE, of Castle Hyde, co. Cork, High Sheriff 1808 ; one of the Esquires of the Order of St. Patrick to the Earl of Shannon, at the Installation, 29 June, 1809 ; *m.* 1801, Hon. Elizabeth O'Callaghan, 2nd dau. of Cornelius, 1st Lord Lismore, and by her (who *d.* 10 Aug. 1824) had issue surviving,

1. JOHN, late representative of the family.
2. Cornelius, *d. unm.*
1. Frances, dec.
2. SARAH, *m.* 1st, 11 April, 1836, William Cooke-Collis, J.P., of Castle Cooke (*see that family*), and by him, who *d.* 18 Oct. 1842, she had issue,

1. SARAH, *s.* her uncle.
2. Mary Matilda, *m.* Major-Gen. E. D. Smith, formerly A.Q.M.G. Dublin District, and *d.* 29 Jan. 1881.
3. Elizabeth Geraldine, *m.* 1st, Major John McDonald Cuppage, 89th Foot, and 2ndly, 4 Aug. 1868, Arthur W. Spens, Capt. 71st Regt., 3rd son of Archibald Spens, of Lathallan Park, co. Stirling, and *d.* 27 Jan. 1896.

Mrs. Cooke-Collis *m.* 2ndly, Capt. Spencer Cosby Price, son of Thomas Price, of Clementhorpe, co. York, and *d.* 18 Dec. 1843, leaving issue three daus. and co-heirs (*see* BURKE's *Peerage*, RUGGE-PRICE, Bart.).

3. Elizabeth (*d.* 1868), *m.* Robert McCarty, of Carrignavar, co. Cork, who *d.* 1867.
4. Louisa, *m.* William Penrose, of Lehane-Trehan ; *d.* 1857.

Mr. John Hyde *d.* 1832, and was *s.* by his eldest son,

JOHN HYDE, of Creg and Castle Hyde, co. Cork, J.P. and D.L., High Sheriff, *b.* 1803 ; *d. unm.* 1885, when he was *s.* by his niece, SARAH (widow of Capt. Richard Edward Beck), who has assumed, in accordance with his will, the name and arms of HYDE by Royal Licence.

Arms—Quarterly, 1st and 4th, gu., two chevronels arg. (HYDE) ; 2nd and 3rd, arg., a chevron engrailed az. between in chief two lion's heads erased ppr. langued gu., and in base a lymphad oars in action ppr. (COLLIS). Crest—A lion's head erased sa. bezantée. Motto—De vivis nil nisi verum ; de mortuis nil nisi bonum.

IEVERS OF MOUNT IEVERS.

JAMES BUTLER IEVERS, of Mount Ievers, and now of Quinville Abbey, co. Clare, J.P. co. Limerick, b. 31 Oct. 1844; m. 1st, 3 July, 1866, Elizabeth Buchanan, 2nd dau. of Robert Blackwell, of The Prairie, co. Down, and by her (who d. 25 Jan. 1898) has issue,

EYRE HERBERT, now of Mount Ievers, co. Clare, and Glanduff Castle, co. Limerick, J.P., late Capt. and Hon. Major 5th Batt. R. M. Fus., b. 30 April, 1867; m. 11 Sept. 1902, Frances Hetty Webb, only dau. of the late Herbert Webb Gillman (see GILLMAN of Clonteadmore), and has issue,
  1. Eyre Herbert, b. 1 July, 1904.
  2. James Henry Gillman, b. 13 Feb. 1910.
  1. Mildred Vivian.
  2. Annie Muriel Elizabeth.
Mildred, m. 20 July, 1901, A. H. Villiers, Natal Carabineers.

He m. 2ndly, 1 Feb. 1899, Ernesta Carlotta Nina, younger dau. of Surg.-Gen. George Whitla (see WHITLA of Ben Eaden).

Lineage.—This family is descended from HENRY IEVERS, who settled in Clare in 1643. He was clerk to the King's Commissioners for settling the quit rents, and afterwards became the Deputy Receiver (Dineley's Journal, 1680). He was a magistrate and High Sheriff of that co., in which he held considerable landed property. He m. Elizabeth, dau. of Capt. Stephens, of Ballysheen, and d. 28 Oct. 1691, leaving issue,
1. Henry.
2. John, J.P. and High Sheriff for Clare 1709, and M.P. for the co. 1715-31; m. Ellen, only dau. of Augustine Fitzgerald, of Moy Castle, and had issue,
  1. Henry, Col. of the Clare Militia Dragoons, J.P. for Clare 1718, High Sheriff 1720, High Sheriff of Limerick 1743, and Mayor of that city 1746. m. his cousin Elizabeth, dau. of Col. Fitzgerald, of Silver Grove, co. Clare, and d. 1752, leaving issue,
    (1) John Augustin, High Sheriff of Limerick 1790, Col. 30th Regt., in which he served for 38 years, was wounded at Bunker's Hill 1775, and d. in 1791.
    (2) Henry Norton, Major 30th Regt., led the forlorn hope at the taking of Belle Isle 1761.
    (1) Anna Maria, m. Rev. J. Wilson, of Moygallow, co. Clare.
    (2) Jane, m. Capt. Henry Keane.
    (3) Dorothea, m. Henry Bridgeman, of Woodfield, co. Clare.
  2. Augustin, m. Susan, dau. of — O'Brien; d. 1769.
  3. William, m. Alice, dau. of — Brereton; d. 1770.
  4. Thomas, m. Sophia, dau. of — Stewart.
  1. Mary, d. unm. 1730.   2. Elizabeth, d. unm. 1777.
  3. Jane, m. — Wilson.
  4. Lucy, m. Sir Thomas Prendergast.
3. William.   4. Thomas.
5. Robert.   6. GEORGE, of whom presently.
7. Ambrose.
1. Ellen.

The 6th son,
GEORGE IEVERS, m. dau. of — Seward, of co. Cork, and had issue,
1. ROBERT, of whom presently.
2. George, m. Anne, dau. of Lancelot Gubbins, of Maidstown Castle, and niece of Gen. Lord Blakeney.
3. Henry, d. unm. 1803.

The eldest son,
ROBERT IEVERS, m. Mary, dau. of — Parsons, of Cragbeg, co. Limerick, and d. 1783, having by her (who d. 1775) had issue,
1. Henry. 2. Richard, m. the dau. of — Holmes.
3. John Henry, m. 1791, Ellen, dau. of — Wilson.
4. GEORGE, of whom presently.
1. Mary, m. 1782, James, eldest son of William Butler, of Castle-crine, co. Clare.   2. Anne, d. unm.
3. Frances, m. Major Fitzgerald, of Carrigoran, co. Clare.

The youngest son,
GEORGE IEVERS, m. 1785, Eleanor, dau. of James Butler, of Castlecrine, co. Clare, and d. 22 March, 1868, having by her (who d. 1 Nov. 1805) had issue,
1. Robert, m. 1813, Isabella Henrietta, dau. of — Fitzgerald, of the Leinster family, and by her had two daus.
2. William, m. 24 Feb. 1831, Anne, dau. of Lucius Wilson, of Springfield, co Clare, and d.s.p. 17 Oct. 1849.
3. George, d. 7 Dec. 1828.
4. Thomas, of the 8th Regt., d. unm. 12 Dec. 1832.
5. James, m. his cousin Elizabeth, dau. of Richard Ievers, of Green Park.
6. EYRE, of whom presently.
1. Mary, m. 1824, Capt. Richard Shinkwin, 10th Regt., and d. 1843.
2. Elizabeth, d. unm. 1 Oct. 1863.
3. Jane, m. 1826, James Cree, of Limerick, and d. 1872, leaving issue.

The youngest son,
EYRE IEVERS, of Mount Ievers, co. Clare, J.P. cos. Clare and Limerick, b. 1 March, 1797; m. 28 April, 1842, Mildred (d. 1903), dau. of Maurice Newnan, of Moyge, co. Cork, and d. 27 Sept. 1860, having by her (who d. 12 Dec. 1903) had issue,
1. JAMES BUTLER, of whom presently.
2. Eyre, b. 25 July, 1848; m. 7 March, 1871, Jane Perrier, eldest dau. of John Osborne, of Lindville, co. Cork, and has issue,
  1. Francis, b. 10 April, 1873; m. 10 March, 1897, Catherine Macbeth.

  2. James Butler, b. 26 Aug. 1877; m. 18 April, 1906, Dorothy, 2nd dau. of F. B. Henson, of Hilden Grange, Toubridge.
  3. Osburne, b. 27 Feb. 1879.
  4. George Julian, b. 21 March, 1883.
  1. Catherine Osburne, m. 23 May, 1896, George Butler, of Buenos Aires.   2. Mildred.
  3. Jane Besnard, m. 8 Dec. 1898, Herbert N. Lowther, of Calcutta.   4. Madeline.
3. George Maurice, of Inchera, co. Cork, b. 29 Jan. 1850; m. 22 May, 1878, Phoebe Elizabeth, dau. of Very Rev. James Hastings Allen, Dean of Killaloe, and d. 27 June, 1908, leaving issue,
  1. George Frederick, b. 19 Aug. 1882; m. 11 Dec. 1907, Ada Augusta, 3rd dau. of Rev. T. R. Matthews, of Crookstown, co. Cork, and has issue.
  2. Sydney Gladstone, b. 25 May, 1886.
  1. Agnes Georgina, m. 12 Jan. 1898, Augustus Warren, only son of Col. Sir Augustus Riversdale Warren, Bart., of Warrens Court, co. Cork (see BURKE's Peerage).
  2. Maud St. Leger, m. 28 July, 1900, Henry Williamson Leader, of Mount Leader, and has issue (see that family).
  3. Sybil, m. 28 Sept. 1910, the Hon. Hector J. Atkinson, Capt. Royal Irish Fus., 3rd son of the Right Hon. Lord Atkinson, of Glenwilliam.
4. William, b. 3 Sept. 1851; m. 4 Aug. 1880, Georgina, dau. of Charles Langley Tuthill, of Ballyteigue, co. Limerick, and d. 5 April, 1897, leaving issue,
  1. Hugh William, b. 17 July, 1883.
  2. Charles Langley, b. 2 Dec. 1884.
  1. Helena.   2. Clare Charlotte.
  3. Margaret Hope Tuthill.
5. Philip Glover, Major R.A.M.C., b. 25 May, 1853; m. 1st, 15 Feb. 1883, Alice Margaret, dau. of James Chadwick, of Hoar Abbey, co. Tipperary. She d. 1883. He m. 2ndly, 15 June, 1897, Gertrude Marie Fitzgerald, dau. of J. Fitzgerald Studdert, R.M., late 85th K.L.I. (see STUDDERT of Bunratty), and d. 3 June, 1909, leaving issue,
  Philip de Clare, b. 1 April, 1898.
1. Mary Shinkwin.
2. Mildred, m. 7 Jan. 1871, Rev. F. Hewson Wall, LL.D., of Arlington, Portarlington, Queen's Co., Rector of Aldingham, Ulverston, Lancs.
3. Elizabeth Anne, m. 26 May, 1880, Rev. Sinclair Carolin, M.A., Rector of Wyvenhoe, Colchester, and has issue.

Seat—Quinville Abbey, Quin, co. Clare. **Club**—Clare Club, Ennis.

INNES-CROSS. See CROSS.

IRVINE OF CASTLE IRVINE.

WILLIAM D'ARCY IRVINE, of Castle Irvine, co. Fermanagh, formerly Capt. 67th Regt., J.P. and D.L., High Sheriff 1885; b. 1823; m. 1858, Louisa, dau. of Capt. Cockburn, R.A., and has had issue,
1. William D'Arcy, Lieut. 99th Regt., and 3rd Batt. R. Innis. Fus., served in the Zulu War, d. unm. 25 Sept. 1879.
2. CHARLES COCKBURN D'ARCY, Major North Irish Horse, Capt. North of Ireland Imperial Yeomanry, late Capt. 3rd Batt. Inniskilling Fus., High Sheriff 1886, b. 1863; m. 1stly, 13 March, 1884, Fanny Kathleen (d. 10 Dec. 1910), dau. of Lieut.-Col. Jesse Lloyd, of Ballyleck, co. Monaghan, by whom he had issue
  1. CHARLES WILLIAM, Lieut. Leinster Regt., late 3rd Batt. Royal Irish Rifles, b. 1885.
  2. Henry Cockburn, b. 1886.
  1. Violet Kathleen, b. 1888.
He m. 2ndly, 31 Jan. 1912, Mildred, youngest dau. of late Henry Haward, of Bramford, Suffolk.

Lineage.—CHRISTOPHER IRVINE, a Lawyer, bred at the Temple, London, was the first of the family who settled in Ireland, upon a grant, from King JAMES VI. of Scotland and I. of England, of lands in Fermanagh. He built Castle Irvine, which was burnt by the rebels in 1641. He lived till after the Restoration, and d. in 1666, at an advanced age. He m. his cousin, Blanche, dau. of Edward Irvine, Laird of Stapleton (see IRVING of Bonshaw), and had issue,
1. Christopher, M.D., b. 1618, Physician-General to the States of Scotland, Historiographer to King CHARLES II., m. Margaret, dau. of James Wishart, Laird of Pittarow, 2nd son of Sir James Wishart, and Lady Jean Douglas, 3rd dau. of William, 9th Earl of Angus, and d. 1693, leaving issue,
  1. Christopher, M.D., of Castle Irvine, b. circa 1642; s. to the Castle Irvine estates on the death of his uncle, Sir Gerard. He was High Sheriff co. Fermanagh 1690, and M.P. for the co. from 1703 to 1713; m. Phoebe, dau. of Sir George Hume, Bart., of Castle Hume, and widow of Henry Blennerhassett, of Cavendish Castle, and d.s.p. 9 May, 1714. She d. 1710.
  2. James, Surgeon-General, of Dumfries, m. Miss Maxwell, and had one son,
    Christopher, who d. young.
  3. Thomas, m. Sydney, dau. of Lancelot Carleton, of Rossfad (see that family), and d.s.p. 1694.
  4. John, d. unm. circa 1698.

2. Gerard (Sir), of Ardscragh, co. Tyrone, Lieut.-Col. in King Charles II.'s service before his Restoration, created a bart. 31 July, 1677, d. at Dundalk Camp 1689, a Lieut.-Col. in the Earl of Granard's Regt. in King William's service; m. 1st, Catherine, dau. of Adam Cathcart, of Bandoragh, Scotland, and of Drumslager, co. Tyrone (she d.s.p.); and 2ndly, Mary, dau. of Major William Hamilton, and by her (who d. 1685) had issue,
1. Christopher, b. 1654; m. Deborah, dau. and co-heiress of Henry Blennerhassett, of Castle Hassett, co. Fermanagh, and d. 1680 v.p.s.p. 2. Charles, Lieut. of Horse, d. unm. 1684.
3. Gerard, drowned at Enniskillen School.
1. Margaret, m. John Crichton.
3. Lancelot, d. unm. 4. William, of whom presently.
1. Margaret, m. 1st, Col. Richard Bell, co. Dumfries, and had issue; 2ndly, Capt. Thomas Maxwell; and 3rdly, David Rynd, of Derryvullen, co. Fermanagh (see Rynd of Ryndville).
2. Marion, m. 1st, Andrew Johnston, 2nd son of James Johnston, Laird of Beirholme, co. Dumfries; 2ndly, her cousin, Launcelot Carleton, of Rossfad, and had issue (see that family); and 3rdly, Capt. John Somerville.

The 4th son,
William Irvine, of Ballindulla, was a Lieut. of Horse under King Charles II at the battle of Worcester, where he was wounded; and High Sheriff for co. Fermanagh 1681. He m. 1st, Elizabeth, dau. of Herbert Gledstanes, a Col. under Gustavus Adolphus, King of Sweden, and Governor of Walgast, and had issue,
1. Christopher, of whom afterwards.
2. John, ancestor of the Irvines of Killadeas (see Irvine of Killadeas).
3. Charles, Lieut.-Col., m. 8 March, 1698, Margaret King, sister of William King, D.D., Archbishop of Dublin, and d.s.p. 1745.
4. Lancelot, Lieut. in Brigadier Wolseley's Regt. of Inniskilling Horse; d. unm. 1701.
1. Elizabeth, m. 1st, Samuel Eccles; and 2ndly, — Mayne, co. Fermanagh.
2. Margaret, m. William Humphreys, of Dromard, who was attainted by James II. in 1689.
3. Mary, m. James Johnston, High Sheriff co. Fermanagh 1707.
4. Katherine, m. Merrick Medge, of Greenhill, co. Fermanagh.
5. Magdalene, m. Robert Johnston.
Mr. Irvine m. 2ndly, Anne Armstrong, and by her had further issue,
5. Gerard, Capt., of Greenhill, m. Alice Forster, and d.s.p. 21 March, 1755.
6. Rebecca, d. young.

The eldest son,
Christopher Irvine, commonly called Colonel Irvine, s. (on the failure of the issue male of his uncles, Dr. Irvine and Sir Gerard Irvine) to the Castle Irvine estates in 1714, and was High Sheriff co. Fermanagh 1716. He d. 1723, having m. 1st, 1683, Mary, dau. of Rev. Dr. Bernard, and by her had two daus., Mary (Mrs. Hamilton) and Elizabeth; and 2ndly, 1693, Dorothy Anne, dau. of Jeffry Brett, by whom he left at his decease,
1. Christopher.
2. Charles, m. 1st, Susan Ferguson, by whom he had, John, d. unm., and Elizabeth (Mrs. Humphreys); 2ndly, Anne Irvine, by whom he had, John; and 3rdly, Elizabeth Grant, who d.s.p.

The elder son,
Christopher Irvine, of Castle Irvine, High Sheriff for Fermanagh 1725, b. 15 April, 1697; m. 1718, 1st, Dorcas, dau. of Col. Alexander Montgomery (see Montgomery of Beaulieu), but by her had no issue. He m. 2ndly, 1727, Elinor, dau. and ultimately co-heir of Audley Mervyn, of Trillick, co. Tyrone (by Hon. Olivia Coote, dau. of Richard, 1st Lord Colloony), and by her (who d. July, 1767) had issue,
1. William, his heir.
2. Henry, m. 1759, Harriett, dau. of Benjamin Bunbury, of Kilfeacle, and had a dau., Mary, m. Col. John Caulfeild, of Donamon (see Burke's Peerage, Charlemont, V.).
1. Olivia, d. unm. 2. Mary, d. unm.
3. Elizabeth, d. unm.
4. Elinor, m. June, 1766, Oliver Nugent, of Farrenconnell.

Mr. Irvine d. 1755. The elder son,
Col. William Irvine, of Castle Irvine, b. 15 July, 1734; Member for Ratoash in the Irish House of Commons, was High Sheriff co. Fermanagh 1758 and of Tyrone 1768. He m. 1st, 10 Dec. 1755, Hon. Flora Caroline Cole, dau. of John, 1st Lord Mount Florence (see Burke's Peerage, Enniskillen, E.); she d. 20 Oct. 1757, leaving a son, Christopher, d. young. He m. 2ndly, 23 Feb. 1760, Sophia, dau. of Gorges Lowther, of Kilrue, co. Meath (by Judith his wife, dau. of John Usher and Mary his wife, only dau. of George, 1st Lord St. George), and had eight sons and eight daus.,
1. Gorges Marcus, of whom presently.
2. William Henry (Rev.), Rector of Tara and Dunshaughlin, co. Meath, J.P. for that co., b. 1763; m. Elizabeth, dau. of James Hamilton, of Sheephill, co. Dublin, and d. 1839, leaving by her (who d. 26 April, 1859) issue,
(1) Gorges Lowther (Rev.), Rector of Rathregan, co. Meath, m. Dec. 1827, Henrietta Florence, dau. of Christopher Edmund John Nugent, of Bobsgrove, and d. Nov. 1838, having by her (who d. 13 March, 1834) had two daus.,
(1) Sophia, m. John Galwey Holmes, of Rockwood, co. Galway, and d.s.p.
(2) Henrietta, m. Clement Hammerton, M.D., and d.s.p.
2. St. George Caulfeild (Rev.), Rector of Kilmessan, co. Meath, m. Elizabeth Anne, eld. dau. of Nathaniel Preston, of Swainstown, co. Meath, and had an only child, Georgina Elizabeth, m. 1st, Hull Browning Reid, who left issue; and 2ndly, 1863, Lieut.-Col. George William McNalty, C.B., M.D., late R.A.M.S. (19, Lansdowne Road, Lee, S.E.), and has issue.

3. James, Comm. R.N., of Hardwick Place, Dublin, d. unm. Nov. 1867.
4. Henry, of Rosslare, co. Wexford, and Kilmore, co. Tyrone, b. 1802; m. 1829, Elizabeth, dau. of Ebenezer Racford Rowe, of Ballyharty, co. Wexford, and d. 1891, leaving issue,
(1) John William Henry, of Mervyn, co. Wexford, b. 1831; m. Mary Field Gray and had issue,
1. Hans William Henry (Vine Lodge, Great Western, Victoria), M.P. Federal House of Representatives, J.P., b. 2 Aug. 1856; m. Mary Jane Robinson.
2. Arthur Hamilton, of Victoria, m. Maria Watson.
1. Evelyn Edith, b. 10 Sept. 1854; m. Tristan Opie, of Ballarat, Victoria.
2. Charlotte Jane, m. 1906, Hon. Robert Mathew Fitzmaurice-Deane-Morgan, eldest surviving son of Lord Muskerry (see Burke's Peerage).
(2) William Henry, late Capt. 3rd Regt. (Buffs), m. Maria Jane, dau. of Arthur Edward Knox, of Castlerea (see Knox of Mount Falcon), by Lady Jane Parsons, his wife, dau. of Lawrence, 2nd Earl of Rosse, and has a dau., Edith.
5. Hans, M.B., d. unm.
1. Charlotte, d. unm. 1874. 2. Harriet, d. unm.
3. Caroline, m. Rev. John Lowe, Rector of Dunshaughlin, co. Meath.
3. Christopher Henry Hamilton, R.N., b. 1766; d. unm.
4. George St. George, Major in the Army, of Balinahown, co. Wexford, High Sheriff 1804, b. 1771; m. 1st, Bridget, dau. of Maurice Howlin D'Arcy, of Cooline, co. Wexford; she d.s.p. He m. 2ndly, Frances, dau. of Robert Doyne, of Wells, co. Wexford (see that family), and had issue,
1. Edward Tottenham, of St. Aidan's, co. Wexford, J.P. and D.L., High Sheriff co. Wexford 1861, late Capt. 16th Lancers, b. 1832; m. 1861, Elizabeth Beatrice, dau. of Edward Gonne Bell, of Streamstown, co. Mayo, and d. 22 Sept. 1903, having had issue,
a. Edward St. George Tottenham, Lieut. 4th Batt. Connaught Rangers, formerly 16th Lancers, b. 12 Feb. 1883; m. 31 Oct. 1906, Hon. Flora Fitzmaurice-Deane-Morgan, only dau. of 4th Lord Muskerry (see Burke's Peerage), and has issue,
Patricia Elizabeth Flora, b. 1907.
a. Mary Sophia Georgina, b. 13 Feb. 1863; d. 8 Jan. 1864.
b. Florence Constance, b. 17 Nov. 1875; m. 16 Oct. 1906, Charles FitzGerald Harvey.
c. Beatrice Brenda, b. 22 Sept. 1877.
1. Frances Eleanor D'Arcy, m. 1856, Rev. Charles Elrington.
2. Sophia Maria, m. 1st, 1852, James Butler, of Castle Crine; 2ndly, 1860, Col. I. H. Graham, and d. 8 May, 1887.
5. Henry William, b. 1772; m. Rebecca Cooke, and had an only dau.,
Rebecca, m. David Onge.
6. Audley Mervyn, b. 1774; killed at Pondicherry.
7. John Caulfeild, Capt. in the Army, J.P. co. Cork, b. 1781; m. Mary Broderick, dau. and co-heir of Henry Mitchell, of Mitchellsfort, co. Cork, and relict of Grice Smyth, of Ballinatray (see that family); and d.s.p. 1850.
8. Hugh Lowther, b. 1783; killed at Monte Video.
1. Sophia Maria, m. Capt. Carew Smith.
2. Elinor Jane, m. Henry Gonne Bell.
3. Florence Elizabeth Anne, m. 8 Nov. 1784, William Rathborne, of Scripplestown, co. Dublin (see that family). He d. 1810.
4. Olivia Emily, m. 5 April, 1794, George Lenox Conyngham, of Springhill, and had issue (see that family).
5. Frances Mary, m. Jones Irwin, of co. Sligo.
6. Harriett, m. John Carleton, of Mohill, co. Leitrim.
7. Letitia St. Patricia Mervyn, m. Col. Alexander Stuart, only son of Gen. James Stuart.
8. Elizabeth Henry, m. 1st, Ebenezer Radford Rowe, of Ballybarty, of Wexford; and 2ndly, Samuel Green.
Col. Irvine d. May, 1814. His eldest son,
Major Gorges Marcus Irvine, of Castle Irvine, b. 26 Nov. 1760; m. 31 March, 1788, Elizabeth, dau. and heir of Judge D'Arcy, of Dunmow Castle, co. Meath (by Elizabeth his wife, dau. and heir of Richard Nugent, of Robbinstown). (The D'Arcy's of Dunmow, of whom Mr. D'Arcy-Irvine is the heir-general, were descended from the baronial house of D'Arcy, afterwards Earls of Holderness. (see D'Arcy of Hyde Park).) By the heiress of D'Arcy (who d. 1829), Major Irvine had five sons and five daus.,
1. William D'Arcy, of whom hereafter.
2. Richard, E.I.C., b. 1791, d.s.p.
3. Gorges Marcus (Rev.), b. 8 July, 1800; m. 20 Sept. 1823, Selina Agnes, dau. of Judge Vaughan. She d. 7 Dec. 1873. He d. 29 Nov. 1854, having had issue,
1. Thomas George Henry Mervyn (Rev.), Canon of Goulburn, N.S.W., b. 20 July, 1825; m. 10 Nov. 1854, Harriet, dau. of Gen. Strover, and d. 1895, leaving issue six sons and four daus.,
(1) St. George Henry.
(2) Somerset William, m. Emily Carew and had issue, Arthur, dec.
(3) Arthur Trevor, m. Fanny Stoyles, and has issue,
1. Trevor. 2. Carol.
(4) John Lowther, m. and has issue three sons.
(5) Gerard Addington (Ven.), Archdeacon of Cumberland, N.S.W., m. Bessie Atkinson Langley, and has issue,
1. Dudley Charles. 2. Thomas Gerard.
1. Mona D'Arcy. 2. Dorothy Harriet.
(6) Malcolm Mervyn, Barrister-at-Law.
(1) Emily, m. E. R. Vickerman.
(2) Harriett, m. E. M. Zouch.
(3) Minnie, m. C. B. Middleton.

(4) Georgina Lilly, *m.* Cecil Bertram, 2nd son of Rt. Hon. Sir Frederick Matthew Darley, P.C., late Chief Justice and Lieut.-Gov. of New South Wales (*see* BURKE'S *Colonial Gentry*).
2. William Frederick, M.D., *b.* 1830; *m.* 1st, 1867, Bertha Bond, dau. of C. Uther; and 2ndly, 1869, Alice Maria Uther, and *d.* 1892, leaving three sons and two daus.,
(1) Reginald Uther, *m.* 1889, Alice E. Johnson.
(2) St. George Trevor Nixor.
(1) Florence Edith.
(2) Ethel Bertha, *m.* 1906, J. G. Schreiber.
(3) Blanche Evelyn.
3. St. George Caulfield (Sir), K.C.B., Adm. (retired), *b.* 23 May, 1833; *m.* 30 April, 1868, Katherine, dau. of Adm. Sir Horatio Austin, K.C.B.
4. John, Commander R.N., of Carra Leena, Rathmullan, co. Donegal, *b.* 2 June, 1835; *d.* 11 April, 1907; *m.* 16 Jan. 1873, Hau, dau. of Hamilton Porter, by Ellen Esther, his wife, dau. of Capt. Nesbitt, and had a dau. Blanche Alexandra, *m.* 29 Nov. 1900, Reginald St. George Smalbridge Bond, Staff Surgeon, R.N., M.B., C.M., F.R.C.S.
1. Adelaide Maria, *b.* 19 Dec. 1836; *d. unm.* 24 Jan. 1901.
2. Louisa, twin with her sister.
4. St. George, *b.* 1801; *m.* Catherine Fennell, and had issue.
5. Somerset, R.N., *b.* 1809; *m.* a dau. of Abraham Hargrave, of Cove, co. Cork, and *d.s.p.* 1850.
1. Louisa, *b.* 1791.
2. Elizabeth, *b.* 1795; *m.* Marquise Fernando Incontri, of Florence.
3. Susanna Amelia, *b.* 1797; *d. unm.* 1870.
4. Sophia, *b.* 1799; *m.* Arthur, Viscount Dungannon (*see* BURKE'S *Peerage*), and *d.* 21 March, 1880.
5. Letitia, *b.* 1805; *d. unm.* 5 April, 1884, aged 78.
Major Irvine *d.* 28 Nov. 1847, and was *s.* by his eldest son,
WILLIAM D'ARCY IRVINE, of Castle Irvine, Lieut. 1st Dragoon Guards, served at Waterloo, *b.* 22 Jan. 1793, adopted the surname of D'ARCY. He *m.* 1817, Maria, dau. of Sir Henry Brooke, 1st bart. of Cole Brooke, co. Fermanagh (*see* BURKE'S *Peerage*), and by her (who *d.* 18 July, 1838) had issue,
1. HENRY MERVYN D'ARCY IRVINE, his heir.
2. Richard D'Arcy, Treasurer of co. Fermanagh, *d. unm.* 1857.
3. WILLIAM D'ARCY, heir to his nephew.
4. Francis D'ARCY, Major H.M. Indian Army, *m.* 1854, Margaret Rebecca, dau. of Col. Sewell. He *d.* 12 Jan. 1889, leaving issue,
1. William, J.P., of Brisbane, Queensland, *b.* 13 Oct. 1860; *m.* 30 Dec. 1884, Elizabeth Maxwell, and has issue,
(1) Arthur Somerset Francis, *b.* 29 April, 1886.
(2) William Mervyn Maxwell, *b.* 14 Sept. 1889.
(3) Gerald Huntley, *b.* 23 May, 1893.
(4) Lionel St. George Somerset, *b.* 1 Sept. 1900.
(1) Henrietta Margaret, *b.* 10 June, 1888.
2. Frank, of New South Wales, *b.* 14 July, 1862; *m.* Edith Griffith, and has issue,
Mervyn.
3. Robert, of New South Wales, J.P., *b.* 28 Feb. 1866; *m.* Clara Nicholson, and has had issue,
(1) Robert Hastings dec.
(2) John Irvine.
(1) Norah
4. Judge, Commander R.N., *b.* 31 July, 1867; *m.* Hettie, dau. of Col. H. C. Creak, and has issue,
(1) Kenneth Judge.
(2) Another son.
1. Maria Elizabeth, *b.* 9 April, 1855; *m.* 21 June, 1904, Professor William Snow Burnside, Fellow Trin. Coll. Dublin.
2. Henrietta, *b.* 24 Dec. 1856; *m.* 6 May, 1897, Rev. Walter Auchinleck Stack, 3rd son of Rt. Rev. Charles Maurice Stack, Bishop of Clogher (*see that family*).
3. Mary, *b.* 1859; *d.* infant.
4. Louise, *b.* 21 July, 1863; *m.* 18 Oct. 1888, Lieut.-Col. W. J. P. Hamilton, of Mossvill, co. Donegal, and has issue (*see that family*).
5. Sophia, *b.* 6 April, 1865; *m.* Charles Caldecott, M.D.
6. Maude, *b.* 18 Feb. 1871; *m.* J. F. McKettrick, M.D.
5. Arthur D'Arcy, Capt. in the Fermanagh Militia.
6. John D'Arcy, Capt. R.N., *m.* 3 Oct. 1865, Ellen Lucy, dau. and heir of Adm. Sir William James Hope-Johnstone (*see* BURKE'S *Peerage*, LINLITHGOW, M.), and *d.* 1885, having had issue,
1. Arthur Osborne, *b.* 14 Aug. 1867; *m.* 1901, Laura, dau. of — Hindshaw.
2. FitzRoy William Hope, *b.* 5 Aug. 1873; *m.* 1903, Marian B., dau. of — Wilkinson.
1. Eleanor Maria.
2. Kathleen Cecilia.
3. Alice Evelyn, *d. unm.* 1891.
4. Edith Mary, *m.* 1897, Hugh Fortescue Hooper.
5. Grace Douglas.
6. Mary Catherine.
7. Violet Leigh.
1. Elizabeth, *m.* 1846, John Caldwell Bloomfield, of Castle Caldwell, co. Fermanagh, and had issue (*see that family*). He *d.* 27 Feb. 1897. She *d.* 10 March, 1874.
2. Maria, *d.* 29 July, 1893.
Mr. Irvine *d.* 23 June, 1857, and was *s.* by his eldest son,
HENRY MERVYN D'ARCY IRVINE, of Castle Irvine, High Sheriff co. Tyrone 1851, who by Royal Licence, 27 April, 1861, assumed the additional surnames and arms of MERVYN and D'ARCY. He *m.* 16 Oct. 1862, Huntly Mary, eldest dau. of Hon. Francis Prittie, and by her (who *d.* 2 March, 1864) left at his death, 1 July, 1870, a son,
HENRY HUNTLY D'ARCY IRVINE, of Castle Irvine, *b.* 14 Aug. 1863; *d. unm.* 9 Jan. 1882, and was *s.* by his uncle, WILLIAM D'ARCY IRVINE, now of Castle Irvine.

Seat — Castle Irvine, Irvinestown.

IRVINE OF KILLADEAS.

JOHN GERARD CHRISTOPHER IRVINE, of Killadeas, co. Fermanagh, D.L., J.P., High Sheriff 1891, Major late 3rd Batt. Royal Inniskilling Fusiliers, served in S. African War 1900–1, *b.* 25 Aug. 1865; *m.* 20 Dec. 1886, Georgina Emma Matilda, dau. of Capt. Mervyn Archdale, M.P., of Castle Archdale, co. Fermanagh, and has issue,
1. GERARD MERVYN FREDERICK, *b.* 21 Jan. 1888.
2. John, *b.* 7 July, 1896.
1. Marjorie Matilda.

Lineage. — WILLIAM IRVINE, of Ballindullagh, 3rd son of Christopher Irvine, of Castle Irvine (*see that family*), *m.* Elizabeth, dau. of Herbert Gledstanes, Col. under GUSTAVUS ADOLPHUS, and *d.* 1691, leaving with other issue,
1. CHRISTOPHER, who *s.* his cousin, and was ancestor of IRVINE of Castle Irvine.
2. JOHN, who *s.* his father, of whom presently.
The 2nd son,
JOHN IRVINE, of Cooles and Killadeas, co. Fermanagh, *m.* 1st, Elizabeth, dau. of J. Hamilton, and by her had issue,
1. CHRISTOPHER, his heir.
1. Margaret, *m.* Rev. Alexander Smyth, and *d.* 1766.
He *m.* 2ndly, Catherine, dau. of Launcelot Carleton, of Rossfad, and by her (who *d.* 1733) had issue,
2. John, *d. unm.* 1728.
2. Magdalen, *m.* Gerard Macgregor, and *d.* 1720.
3. Katherine, *m.* John Coulson, of Belmount.
4. Dorothy Maria, *d. unm.* 1718.
5. Sydney, *m.* Christopher Crowe.
6. Sophia, *d. unm.* 1725.
His will bears date 10 July, 1716, and was proved 7 Nov. same year.
The eldest son,
MAJOR CHRISTOPHER IRVINE, of Cooles and Rockfield, High Sheriff co. Fermanagh 1734, *m.* Jane, dau. of Rev. William Greene, of Dresternan, co. Fermanagh, and Shanballyholly, co. Limerick, and *d.* 1760, having had issue,
1. JOHN, his successor, of whom presently.
2. Gerard, of Greenhill, *m.* 1st, 1751, Anne, dau. of Andrew Hamilton, of Ballinadonell, co. Donegal; and 2ndly, Sarah, dau. of John Moutray, of Favor Royal, co. Tyrone, and *d.* 1795, leaving issue, six sons and five daus., of whom,
1. Arthur Henry, Col. York Hussars, *m.* Maria Williams; *d.s.p.*
2. Andrew, *d. unm.*
3. William, Capt. 52nd Regt., *m.* Anne, dau. of Henry Major, of Greenford, co Donegal, and had issue, three sons and four daus.,
(1) Arthur, Lieut. 77th Regt., *d. unm.*
(2) William, of Blackrock.
(3) Henry, *d. unm.* 1840.
(1) Anne, *d. unm.* 1864.
(2) Elizabeth, *m.* Samuel Alleyne Rothwell.
(3) Letitia, *d. unm.*
(4) Rebecca, *m.* R. Denny.
4. Hamilton, of Greenhill, co. Fermanagh, J.P. and D.L., High Sheriff 1799, *b.* 21 Oct. 1768; *m.* Feb. 1798, Elizabeth, dau. of John Sandys, of Drimnacor, co. Longford, and *d.* 25 May, 1846, having by her (who *d.* 1858) had issue,
(1) Arthur Henry, of Greenhill, *b.* 16 Oct. 1808; *d. unm.* 1862.
(2) Gerard, *d. unm.*
(3) Hamilton John, *d. unm.*
(1) Letitia.
(2) Elizabeth
(3) Anne Hannah.
(4) Catherine Angelina.
5. John, *d.* young.
6. Thomas Gledstane, *d. unm.*
1. Catherine.
2. Elizabeth.
3. Anne.
4. Sophia Jane.
5. Letitia, *m.* 2 Sept. 1793, James King, brother of Sir A. B. King, Bart., of Corrard.
1. Elizabeth, *m.* 1744, William Rhynd.
The eldest son,
JOHN IRVINE, of Rockfield, co. Fermanagh, High Sheriff of Fermanagh 1763, *m.* 1745, Catherine, eldest dau. of Right Rev. Joseph Story, Bishop of Kilmore, and had issue four sons and three daus.,
1. Christopher, *d. unm.*
2. Joseph, *d. unm.* 5 April, 1797.
3. GERARD, his heir.
4. William, of Cookstown, co. Tyrone, Capt. 5th Royal Irish Dragoons, and Major Royal Tyrone Fusiliers. He *d.* 1830, leaving two sons and a dau.,
1. William John (Rev.), Rector of Kilmoon, co. Meath, *m.* 1834, Catherine Charlotte (*d.* 1870), dau. of Capt. Thomas Boyes, of 76th Regt., and *d.* 1870, leaving with seven daus., two sons, the eldest of whom,
William Stewart, *m.* 1873, Mary Louisa, dau. of Rev. Henry Theophilus Hobson, of Muckeridge House, Youghal, first cousin of Lord Clermont, and has issue.
2. Charles, Lieut.-Col. 38th Regt., *m.* Mary, dau. of Lewis Gollock, and *d.* 1864. She *d.* 24 April, 1897, leaving issue,
(1) Henry, C.B., J.P., Lieut.-Col. and Hon. Col. 3rd Batt. Royal Inniskilling Fusiliers (*Strathlomond, Omagh, co. Tyrone*), *b.* 1 July, 1849; *m.* 1 Sept. 1875, Edith, dau. of Capt. David White, Royal Tyrone Fus., J.P., of Lisonally, co. Tyrone, and has issue,
1. Frederick Henry, *b.* 1876.
2. Arthur Gerard, *b.* 1878.
(2) Arthur.
(3) George.
(1) Anne.
1. Katherine Elizabeth Sophia, *m.* Col. Charles Bailey, R.E., and *d.* 1865, leaving issue.
1. Deborah, *d. unm.* 1804.

2. Elizabeth, m. 1787, Rev. Charles Fleetwood, and d. 1820.
3. Sophia, d. unm. 1836.
Mr. Irvine d. 1787, and was s. by his eldest surviving son,
GERARD IRVINE, of Rockfield, co. Fermanagh, b. 1749, Deputy-Governor of co. Fermanagh, and High Sheriff 1803, Capt. 47th Regt., with which regiment he served in the American War, and was at the battle of Bunker's Hill. He m. Catherine, dau. of Robert Hassard, of Skea, co Fermanagh, by Jane his wife, dau. of George Nixon, of Nixon Hall (see BURKE's *Family Records*), and d. 3 March, 1835, having had by her (who d. 17 Dec. 1839) issue,

1. JOHN, his successor, of whom presently.
2. Robert, d. 1823. 3. William, d. 1 Feb. 1850.
4. Arthur Henry (Rev.), of Spring Hill, co. Tyrone, d. 1867.
5. George, Capt. 33rd Regt. of Bengal N.I., d. 1866.
1. Jane, m. Thomas Hemsworth, of Abbeville, co. Tipperary.
2. Catherine, m. 25 Sept. 1817, Michael Hugh Tuthill, M.D., Surgeon R.A., who d. 8 Oct. 1845.

The eldest son,
JOHN IRVINE, of Rockfield or Killadeas, co. Fermanagh. J.P. and D.L., Major Royal Tyrone Fusiliers Regt. of Militia, High Sheriff co. Fermanagh 1819; b. 9 Jan. 1788; m. 4 Jan. 1817, Sarah, eldest dau. of Thomas Towers, of Bushy Park, co. Tipperary; and d. 5 June, 1860, having by her (who d. 11 May, 1874) had issue,

1. Gerard, d. unm. 30 July, 1840.
2. JOHN GERARD, late of Killadeas.
3. Christopher (Rev.), Incumbent of Listimnaghan, co. Tyrone, b. 7 Sept. 1825, and d. unm. 29 Dec. 1905.
4. Thomas, d. 9 July, 1840.
5. Charles Dopping, of Rockfield, Hokianga, New Zealand, b. 23 Nov. 1833; d. 1911; m. 1876, Lucy, dau. of John McLachlan, and had issue,
  1. Charles Henry Howard, b. 23 Nov. 1876.
  2. Christopher William, b. 27 Jan. 1884.
  3. Gerard John Malcolm, b. 27 Oct. 1891.
  4. John Duncan Lancelot, b. 8 Sept. 1896.
  1. Florence Ethelreda, m. 27 April, 1905, Donald McIntyre, of Tunatahi, eldest son of John McIntyre, of Nairne, co. Hokianza, N.Z.
  2. Minna Sophia.
  3. Blanch Charlotte, d. unm. Feb. 1909.
  4. Mary Modlin. 5. Dorothy Beatrix.
  6. Sarah Lucy. 7. Catherine Deborah.
6. Malcolm Edward, d. 11 July, 1839.
7. Arthur Benjamin (Rev.), late Vicar of Longcot, Faringdon, Berks. b. 8 May, 1838; d. 1908; m. 23 July, 1862, Louisa Caroline, dau. of Cheyne Brady, and had issue,
  1. Arthur Gerard Cheyne, b. 26 April, 1864; m. 1 May, 1895, Charlotte Ellen, dau. of Thomas Stamps, of Berwood, Erdington, co. Warwick.
  2. John George Christopher, b. 11 May, 1865.
  3. Maziere Cheyne William, b. 13 April, 1868.
  4. William Carleton, b. 3 June, 1871.
  1. Amelia Mary. 2. Constance Anna.
  3. Louisa Winnifred.
8. Duncan Malcolm, of Fernshaw, Dungannon, co. Tyrone, J.P., late Capt. 17th Regt., b. 3 Oct. 1839; m. 6 Oct. 1868, Jane Caroline, eldest dau. of Capt. Marcus Knox, R.N., youngest son of Colonel Knox, of Prehen, co. Derry (see *that family*), and has issue, a dau.,
  Catherine Sarah Helen, b. 24 April, 1879; m. 13 Nov. 1901, John George Burnett, of Powis, Aberdeenshire, only son of George Burnett, Lyon King of Arms (see BURNETT *of Kemnay*), and has issue, George Irvine Leslie, b. 10 April, 1903.
1. Mary, d. unm. 13 July, 1890. 2. Kathleen, d. unm. 1845.
3. Caroline Sophia, m. 18 May, 1865, Most Rev. Joseph Ferguson Peacocke, D.D., Archbishop of Dublin, and has issue (see BURKE's *Peerage*).
4. Sarah Elizabeth, d. young, June, 1841.

The eldest surviving son,
JOHN GERARD IRVINE, of Killadeas, co. Fermanagh, J.P. and D.L. for that co., High Sheriff 1852, J.P. co. Tyrone, High Sheriff 1878, Col.-Comm. 3rd Batt. Roy. Innis. Fus.; b. 25 Dec. 1823; m. 15 Dec. 1860, Elizabeth, dau. of William Daniell, of Ballymackney, co. Monaghan, and Manor Hassett Lodge, co. Fermanagh, J.P. co. Louth. He d. 13 March, 1902, having by her (who d. 1 Dec. following) had issue,
1. JOHN GERARD CHRISTOPHER, now of Killadeas.
2. William Peregrine Daniell, late Lieut. Royal Inniskilling Fus., b. 1869.
3. Arthur Launcelot Carleton, late Lieut. Royal Inniskilling Fus., b. 1870.
4. Charles Edward Stannus, b. 1873.
5. Geoffrey George Vaughan, b. 1874.
1. Mary Elizabeth Geraldine, m. 9 Feb. 1892, Frederick Viveash Maude, J.P., and son of Gen. Cornwallis O. Maude (see BURKE's *Peerage*, DE MONTALT, E.). 2. Caroline Sarah Sophia.
3. Kathleen Margaret Matilda, d. 25 Nov. 1909.
4. Elsie Beatrice Blanche.

Seat—Killadeas, Ballinamallard, co. Fermanagh.

IRWIN OF MOUNT IRWIN.

HENRY CROSSLEY IRWIN, of Mount Irwin, co. Armagh, J.P., B.A. Queen's Coll. Oxford, late Bengal Civil Service, b. 25 July, 1848; m. 16 Aug. 1881, Constance Harriet Catherine, dau. of the late Lieut.-Col. G. A. J. McClintock, of Fellows Hall, co. Armagh (see McCLINTOCK *of Rathvinden*), and Catherine Caroline Brownlow his wife, dau. of Sir James Matthew Stronge, Bart., and has issue,

1. GEORGE VALENTINE CROSSLEY, Lieut. Royal Inniskilling Fus., b. 25 Feb. 1883.
2. Henry Mark, b. 10 March, 1885.
3. Felix Miles Patrick, b. 10 Sept. 1893.
1. Harriet Josephine Elizabeth, b. 11 April, 1888.
2. Georgie Catherine Joyce, b. 13 Oct. 1889.
3. Alison Constance Frances, b. 9 Oct. 1891.

Lineage.—WILLIAM IRWIN, of Mount Irwin, co. Armagh son of James Irwin and grandson of William John Irwin who obtained a grant of the lands of Carnagh, co. Armagh 1680, and d. 1718), m. Sarah, dau. of James Manson, of Fairview (now called Tynan Abbey), co. Armagh, and d. 1737, having had issue,
1. William, d. unm.
2. Arthur, High Sheriff co. Armagh 1759, m. Alice, dau. of Thomas Kelly, of Dawson's Grove, co. Armagh, and d. 1795, having had issue, with three daus., who d. unm., seven sons,
  1. William, of Carnagh, co. Armagh, m. 1785, Eliza, dau. of — Owens, of Stone House, co. Louth, and d. 1835, having had issue,
    (1) Acthur, d. unm. 1836.
    (2) John Robert, of Carnagh, J.P., High Sheriff 1844, b. 1788; m. 12 July, 1840, Elizabeth Emily, dau. of Nicholas De La Cherois Crommelin of Carrowdore Castle, co. Down (see *that family*), and Elizabeth his wife, 2nd dau. of 2nd Lord Ventry, and d. 1872, having had issue,
      1. William Arthur, of Carnagh, High Sheriff co. Armagh 1886, Capt. 11th Regt., b. 9 July, 1841; m. 1870, Eliza, dau. of Col. Brown, and d s p 9 May, 1896.
      2. De La Cherois Thomas, C.M.G., of Carnagh, Lieut.-Col. late R.A., and late commanding Royal Canadian Artillery (170, Cooper Street, Ottawa, Ontario, Canada), b. 31 March, 1843; m. 25 April, 1867, Isabella, dau. of Robert Hamilton, of Hamwood, Quebec (see HAMILTON *of Hamwood*), and has issue,
        a. Arthur De La Cherois, b. 30 Nov. 1885.
        b. Robert Hamilton, b. 28 Nov. 1887.
        c. William Eric Crommelin, b. 24 Jan. 1890.
        a. Isabel Gladys.
      3. John Frederick, Maj. E. Lancashire (59th) Regt., b. 15 Sept. 1847; m. the dau. of Dr. Stannistreet, and d.s.p. 1901.
      4. FitzJohn Robert, M.D., of Kilkeel, co. Down, Surg. Monaghan Militia, b. 1849; m. 1880, Sarah (Saidee), dau. and co-heir of André Allen Murray Ker, of Newbliss, co. Monaghan (see *that family*), and d. 1882, leaving issue,
        FitzJohn Murray, of Beech Hill Mouaghan, Capt. Monaghan Militia, formerly 3rd Royal Inniskilling Fus., High Sheriff 1910, b. 1881.
        Ethel Elizabeth, b. 1882.
      5. Edmund Herbert De Moleyns, Manager of Merchants Bank, Canada, at Sherbrooke, P.Q., b. 1856; m. Mary, dau. of Thomas Boyer, of Barrie, Ontario, and has issue,
        a. Basil, b. 1892. b. Cyril, b. 1898.
      6. Arthur Constantine, b. 1854, d. 1862.
      1. Elizabeth Emily. 2. Alice Anna Clara.
    (1) Alicia, d. unm. 1873.
    (2) Eliza, d. unm. 1889.
  2. Daniel, d. unm. 3. Robert, d. unm.
  4. Arthur, d. and infant.
  5. Arthur, m. Sarah Owens, and d.s.p. 1844.
  6. Thomas, d. unm. 7. Stronge, d. unm.
  8. ROBERT, of whom presently.
The youngest son,
ROBERT IRWIN, of Mount Irwin, co. Armagh, m. the dau. of — Nevin, and had issue, four sons,
1. Blayney (Rev.), Rector of Laracor, co. Meath, m. the dau. of — Cairnes, and had issue,
  Robert (Rev.), m. Elizabeth Caroline, dau. of Edward Purdon, of Lisnabin, co. Westmeath (see *that family*), and had issue, six sons and six daus.
2. WILLIAM, of whom presently. 3. Robert, d. unm.
4. Thomas, Lieut. 89th Foot, d. unm.

The 2nd son,
WILLIAM IRWIN, of Mount Irwin, co. Armagh, High Sheriff 1817,

Irwin. THE LANDED GENTRY. 346

b. 1769; m. 1807, Sarah, dau. of Samuel De La Cherois-Crommelin, of Carrowdore Castle, co. Down (*see that family*). He d. 1848, having had issue, with four other daus., who d. *unm.*,
1. William George, b. 1813; d. 1850.
2. Samuel De La Cherois Crommelin, b. 1814; d. 1884; m. 1845, Elizabeth, dau. of Rev. William Raine, of Swimbrook, Oxon., and has issue,
   Surtees, J.P. Cheshire (*Park House, Knutsford, Cheshire*), b. 1849; m. 1878, Genevieve, dau. of A. Palmer, U.S.A.
3. Thomas Hastings, b. 1815; d. 1867; m. 1852, Frances, dau. of William Brook, J.P. of Huddersfield, and has issue,
   1. De La Cherois Hastings, M.I.M.E. (*The Wyelands, Buxton, Derbyshire*), b. 1855; m. 1881, Nona Louisa, 7th dau. of Rev. F. B. Wright, M.A., and grand-dau. of Sir Thomas Pasley, Bart., R.N. (*see* BURKE's *Peerage*), and has issue,
      (1) Clinton De La Cherois, Capt. 2nd Batt. Manchester Regt., b. 1882; m. 1 June, 1910, Everilda, dau. of Hatt Cook, of Hartford Hall, Cheshire.
      (2) Philip Hastings, Lieut. R.N., b. 1884.
      (3) Patrick Hugh, b. 1888.
      (4) Thomas Whitmore Crommelin, b. 1896.
      (1) Una Kathleen. (2) Eileen.
   2. Basil Hastings (*The Lindens, Colchester*), b. 1859.
4. HENRY, of whom presently.
1. Elizabeth Helen, b. 1809; m. Maj. Francis Crossley, and had issue, three sons and one dau.

The fourth son,
HENRY IRWIN, of Mount Irwin, b. 29 Aug. 1816; m. 1846, Harriet Josephine, dau. of George Ogle Laurence Jacob, H.E.I.C.S., and Mary Ann his wife, dau. of Rev. Joseph Miller. She d. 6 Feb. 1877. He d. 31 Jan. 1883, having had issue,
1. HENRY CROSSLEY, now of Mount Irwin.
2. George Robert, C.S.I., Indian Civil Service, Gen. Superintendent of Thuggy and Docoity Department 1900-3, educated at Uppingham and Christ Church, Oxford, b. 2 April, 1855 (*East India U.S. Club*).

Arms—Arg., on a fess engrailed gu. between three holly leaves vert, a trefoil slipped or. *Crest*—A fore-arm vambraced, charged with a trefoil as in the arms, the hand grasping a thistle all ppr. *Motto*—Nemo me impune lacessit.
Seat—Mount Irwin, Tynan, co. Armagh. *Club*—Savile.

IRWIN OF DERRYGORE.

JOHN ARTHUR IRWIN, of Derrygore, co. Fermanagh, J.P., High Sheriff 1888, b. 1 Jan. 1854; s. his brother 1880.

Lineage.—GEORGE IRWIN, lived in Derrygore, and d. there 1791. He m. Ellen Logan, and by her (who d. 1792) had, with other issue, a youngest son,
ACHESON IRWIN, b. 11 Nov. 1760; who resided at Derrygore. He m. 1790, Catherine Wilson, and by her (who d. Nov. 1837) had issue,
1. George Acheson, d. *unm.* 1817.
2. EDWARD, late of Derrygore.
3. Acheson, of Clonaveil, co. Fermanagh, d. 1855; leaving issue, a son,
   George (Sir), of Cumberland Lodge, Headingly, Yorks, Knt., J.P. for W.R. Yorks, b. 1832; m. 1861, Flora Adelaide, dau. of Capt. Thomas Jacob Smith, of Manor House, co. Salop, and d. 11 June, 1899.
4. James Stuart, d.s.p. 1844.
1. Letitia, m. John Bartley, and has issue.
2. Ellen, m. Charles Ashenhurst, and has issue.
3. Catherine, m. Ralph Stone, and has issue.
4. Mary Anne, m. William Emery, and has no issue.

His eldest surviving son,
EDWARD IRWIN, of Derrygore, co. Fermanagh, J.P. for that co. and High Sheriff 1862, also J.P. for the borough of Leeds, co. York, b. March, 1795; m. June, 1847, Hannah, dau. of Thomas Baynes, of Leeds, and d. 1874, having had issue,
1. EDWARD, of whom presently.
2. JOHN ARTHUR, now of Derrygore.
3. Acheson Harcourt, b. 3 March, 1858; d. 1 May, 1909.
1. Rose, m. 1877, Thomas Miller, and has issue a son, Hugh Montgomery.
2. Hannah.

The eldest son,
EDWARD IRWIN, of Derrygore, J.P., b. 1848; m. 26 Dec. 1878, Annie Brunskill, 4th dau. of Samuel N. Elliott, of Mount Galpine, Dartmouth, and widow of William Fawcett Brunskill, of Polsloe and Buckland-tout-Sainte-Devon. He d.s.p. 15 June, 1880, and was s. by his brother,
JOHN ARTHUR, now of Derrygore.

Arms—Arg., a mural crown gu. between three holly leaves ppr. *Crest*—A mailed arm fessways holding in the hand a thistle and a holly leaf all ppr. and charged on the arm with a crescent gu. *Motto*—Nemo me impune lacessit.
Seat—Derrygore, Enniskillen.

IRWIN OF RATHMOYLE.

ARTHUR JOHN IRWIN, of Rathmoyle, co. Roscommon, Deputy Director, Royal Survey, Siam, B.A. Trin. Coll. Dublin, b. 13 May, 1868; s. his father 20 Nov. 1909; m. 16 Dec. 1896, Josephine, dau. of Hugh Gerald Byrne, and has issue,
1. RICHARD ARTHUR, b. 29 Dec. 1897.
2. Edward Vincent, b. 27 Sept. 1902.

Lineage. — JOHN IRWIN, of Ballinderry, b. 1618; d. at an advanced age 20 June, 1720; m. 1690, Susanna, dau. of Jones, of Stone Park, co. Roscommon, and left, with other issue, a son,
ARTHUR IRWIN, of Fernhall, b. 1692; d. 1785; m. 1748, Eleanor, dau. of Gerald Dillon, of Rathmoyle, co. Roscommon, and d. 1785, leaving issue,
1. Alexander.
2. Patrick, of Fernhall, b. 1757; d. 1807, leaving issue.
3. RICHARD, of Rathmoyle.
4. Thomas, d. in Jamaica 1803.
1. Eleanor, b. 1759; m. E. Howley, of Seaview, co. Sligo.
2. Mary, d. 19 Jan. 1779.

The second son,
RICHARD IRWIN, of Rathmoyle, b. 1758; d. 1818; m. 1st, 1801, Sarah, dau. of Edmund Burke, of Ballynakill, by whom (who d. in childbed) he had a son,
1. Arthur, who d. 1802.

He m. 2ndly, 1804, Margaret, dau. of Valentine Dillon, of Tenelick, co. Longford, and had further issue by her (who d. 1837),
2. RICHARD, his heir.   3. Valentine, b. 1808; d. 1846.
4. John, b. 1809, J.P. co. Roscommon; m. 1840, Margaret, dau. of Luke Harkan, of Raheen, co. Roscommon, and d. 1884, leaving issue.
5. James, d. in Australia.
1. Eleanor, m. 1835, John White, of Nantenan, co. Limerick, and d. 1863, leaving issue (*see that family*).
2. Margaret, a nun, d. *unm.* 1864, aged 50.

Mr. Irwin d. 1818, and was s. by his eldest son,
RICHARD IRWIN, of Rathmoyle, b. 1806; High Sheriff co. Roscommon 1832; m. 27 Feb. 1832, Mary, dau. of John Kelly, D.L., of Rockstown, co. Limerick, and Ballintlea and Firgrove, co. Clare (*see* KELLY *of Rockstown Castle*), by whom (who d. Dec. 1861) he had issue,
1. RICHARD, his heir, of Rathmoyle.
2. John, b. 1836; d. 24 April, 1908.
3. Valentine, late Magistrate at Kuttack, Bengal, b. 1838; m. 1871, Mary, dau. of John Scully, and d. 1873, leaving issue, a dau., Kathleen Mary.
1. Mary, a nun, d. 1862, aged 23.
2. Katherine, a Nun, d. 1903.   3. Margaret, a nun.
4. Frances.   5. Eleanor, d. 1875.

Mr. Irwin d. 7 Jan. 1867, and was s. by his eldest son,
RICHARD IRWIN, of Rathmoyle, J.P., High Sheriff 1864, Col. late 5th Batt. Connaught Rangers, b. 23 Nov. 1832; s. his father 1867; m. 16 June, 1866, Cecilia Olivia, dau. of Philip O'Reilly, D.L., of Coolamber, co. Westmeath (*see that family*), and d. 20 Nov. 1909, having had issue,
1. ARTHUR JOHN, now of Rathmoyle.
2. Francis Joseph (Rev.), of the Society of Jesus, b. 9 June, 1869.
3. Henry John (Rev.), of the Society of Jesus, M.A., D.Litt. London, b. 24 June, 1870.
4. Valentine Philip, b. 18 Oct. 1874.
5. Cyril James, B.A. Oxford, Indian Civil Service, b. 4 Jan. 1881.
1. Mary, a nun.   2. Rosalie.

Arms—Arg., a trefoil between three holly leaves slipped vert. *Crest*—A dexter cubit arm in armour, the hand grasping a thistle all ppr. *Motto*—Haud ullis labentia ventis.
Seat—Rathmoyle, Castlerea, co. Roscommon.

IZOD OF CHAPEL IZOD.

Col. WILLIAM HENRY IZOD, of Chapel Izod House, co. Kilkenny, J.P. and D.L., High Sheriff 1885, late Lieut.-Col. Com. and Hon. Col. 5th Batt. Royal Irish Regt., formerly Col. R.A., *b.* 24 Dec. 1837.

Lineage.—RICHARD IZOD, who was possessed of the manor of Kilfera, co. Kilkenny, in 1667, left by Anne Brabant, his 2nd wife, a son,

LIONELL IZOD, of Chapel Izod (or Grovebeg), co. Kilkenny, *m.* Elizabeth Cochrane, grand-dau. and heiress of John Kevane, of Grovebeg, co. Kilkenny, who was the son of the Rev. J. Kevane, Kyvane or O'Kyvane, Prebendary of Aghour 1619 and of Mayne 1637, in the Diocese of Ossory, descended from the old tribal family of O'Keveny, of Cranagh, co. Kilkenny, mentioned in the Annals of the Four Masters. This John Kevane, *b.* 1627, *d.* 1712, had held the lands of Grovebeg, &c., from the Duke of Ormonde before 1672, and purchased the fee farm grant of these and other lands from James, Duke of Ormonde, by deed dated 1711. Lionell Izod *s.* him in 1712, and left issue, an elder son,

WILLIAM IZOD, of Chapel Izod (or Grovebeg), *b.* 1707, *m.* Elizabeth Waring. She *d.* 1770. He *d.s.p.* 1789, and was *s.* by his brother,

KEVAN IZOD, of Wilton, co. Cork, and afterwards of Chapel Izod, *d.* 1797, leaving issue two daus.,
1. Lucia, *m.* Charles Henry Leslie.
2. ELIZABETH, heiress to her uncle William, *m.* 1773, Lorenzo Nickson, son of Abraham Nickson, of Munny, and had with several daus., one son, WILLIAM, of whom presently.

The grandson,

WILLIAM (Nickson) IZOD, of Chapel Izod, High Sheriff 1810, adopted the name of Izod under deed of settlement, *b.* 1782; *m.* 21 June, 1811, Darkey, dau. of Thomas Hemsworth, of Abbeyville, co. Tipperary, and by her (who *d.* 10 June, 1834) left at his decease, 22 Aug. 1848, an only son and heir,

LORENZO NICKSON IZOD, of Chapel Izod, J.P. and D.L., at one time High Sheriff, *b.* 4 June, 1812; *m.* 20 March, 1837, Elizabeth Catherine, dau. of the late Sir Henry Robert Carden, Bart., of Templemore House (*see* BURKE's *Peerage*). She *d.* 23 April, 1908, having had issue,
1. WILLIAM HENRY, now of Chapel Izod.
2. John Craven, *b.* 19 Dec. 1839; *d.* 1 Sept. 1882.
3. Henry, Lieut. R.N., *b.* 12 May, 1841; *d.* 1 Aug. 1864.
4. Francis Lorenzo (Rev.), *b.* 11 Jan. 1844; *d.* 23 April, 1882.
5. Frederick Kevan, late Lieut.-Col. 4th Batt. Leinster Regt., *b.* 8 Nov. 1845; *d.* 1904; *m.* 13 March, 1880, Mary Frances, eldest dau. of the late John Hamill Stewart, of Ballyatwood, co. Down, and Fulwood Park, Cheltenham. He *d.* 8 May, 1909, having had issue,
  1. Kevan William, Lieut. Loyal North Lanc. Regt., *b.* 1885.
  1. Lucia Elizabeth. 2. May Constance.
6. Lionel, *b.* 16 Feb. 1858; *m.* Ethel, dau. of — Roberts, and has issue, three sons.
1. Edith Harriet Sophia, *m.* 7 Dec. 1876, Evans Charles Johnson, of Madras Civil Service, son of the Ven. Archdeacon J. E. Johnson, D.D., and *d.* 6 Nov. 1900, leaving issue.
2. Lucy Kate, *d. unm.*
3. Caroline Frances (*Chapel Izod House, Stoneyford*)
4. Julia, *m.* 1885, Fleetwood Rynd, of Mount Armstrong, co. Kildare. She *d.* 17 July, 1901, leaving issue (*see that family*).
5. Sarah Elizabeth, *d.* 14 June, 1888.

Mr. Izod *d.* 4 Feb. 1884, and was *s.* by his eldest son, WILLIAM HENRY, now of Chapel Izod.

Seat—Chapel Izod House, Stoneyford, co. Kilkenny.

JACKSON OF CARRAMORE.

PERCY VAUGHAN JACKSON, of Carramore House, co. Mayo, *b.* 22 Sept. 1862; *m.* 1906, Geneviève Louise, dau. of Sir James Spearman Winter, K.C.M.G., Barrister-at-Law, K.C., of St. John's, Newfoundland, and has issue,

OLIVER JAMES VAUGHAN, *b.* 6 July, 1907.

Lineage.—FRANCIS JACKSON, described as a younger son of Joseph Jackson, of Sneyd Park, Kent, is stated to have passed over into Ireland as Capt. of Dragoons in CROMWELL'S Army, and to have purchased extensive landed property in the barony of Tyrawley, co. Mayo, which shortly after the Restoration was confirmed to him and his heirs, by patent of CHARLES II. He *d.* 1678, leaving by Elizabeth his wife, a son,

OLIVER JACKSON, of Enniscoe, *m.* Jane, dau. of Dr. King, Archbishop of Tuam, and had two sons,
1. John, *b.* 1681, killed in a duel 1704, leaving no issue.
2. OLIVER, who *s.* his father.

He *d.* 1691, and the estates eventually devolved on his son,

OLIVER JACKSON, of Enniscoe, *m.* Catherine, dau. of Simon Owens, of co. Louth, and had three sons,
1. GEORGE, his heir. 2. Oliver, *d. unm.* 1785.
3. William, *d. unm.* 1802.

The eldest son,

GEORGE JACKSON, of Enniscoe, Dep. Gov. of co. Mayo, *b.* 1717, *s.* his father Feb. 1722. He *m.* 22 Nov. 1758, Jane, dau. of the Right Hon. James Cuff, of Ballinrobe, M.P. co. Mayo, sister and heir of James, Lord Tyrawley, and niece of Arthur, Earl of Arran, and had issue,
1. GEORGE, his heir.
2. James, *b.* 1765, a military officer, *m.* Mary, dau. of — Perry, of Cork, and *d.* 1825, leaving two daus.
  1. Jane, *m.* William de Mesurier, of Guernsey.
  2. Mary Perry.
3. Francis, *b.* 1769; *m.* Eliza, dau. of John Martin, of Cleveragh, co. Sligo, and *d.* 1834, leaving a son, George Francis, and other issue.
4. Oliver Cuffe, Major in the Army, *m.* 10 Sept. 1812, Sarah, dau. of Humphrey Jones, of Mullinabro', co. Kilkenny, and had George Humphrey and other issue.
  1. Elizabeth *m.* John Ormsby, of Gortner Abbey, and *d.* 1830.
  2. Anne, *m.* William Orme, of Abbeytown, co. Mayo.

Mr. Jackson *d.* 1789, and was *s.* by his son,

GEORGE JACKSON, of Enniscoe, *b.* 1761, Col. of the North Mayo Militia, and Member for co. Mayo in the Irish and Imperial Parliaments. He *m.* 1783, Maria, only dau. and heir of William Rutledge, of Foxford, co. Mayo, and had issue,
1. WILLIAM, his heir, of Enniscoe, Col. of the North Mayo Militia, *b.* 1787; *m.* Jane Louisa, dau. of Col. Blair, of Blair, co. Ayr, M.P., and by her (who *d.* 1817) left at his decease, 1822, an only dau. and heir,
  MADELINE EGLANTINE, *m.* 1834, Mervyn Pratt, of Cabra Castle, co. Cavan, J.P. and D.L., and has issue.
2. GEORGE, of whom presently.
3. James (Sir), Gen., G.C.B., Col. King's Dragoon Guards, served in the Peninsula, at Waterloo, in India, and in Arabia, and at the Cape of Good Hope as Commander of Forces, and Lieut.-Governor. Sir James received the war medal with nine clasps for Busaco, Fuentes d'Onor, Ciudad Rodrigo, Badajos, Salamanca, Vittoria, Pyrenees, Nivelle, and Nive; he *d.* 31 Dec. 1871.
4. Francis, Major 85th Regt., served in the campaigns of Holland, dec.
5. Andrew (Rev.), *m.* Mary Louisa, dau. of the Rev. Edwin Stock, son of Dr. Stock, Bishop of Waterford, and *d.* leaving a son, George William, B.A.
6. Oliver, *m.* 1849, Eleanor, widow of Walter James Burke, and dau. of the Hon. Frederick Cavendish.
1. Barbara, *m.* Thomas Carey, of Rozel, Guernsey.
2. Jane, *m.* Christopher Carlton, of Market Hill.
3. Mary, dec.
4. Elizabeth, *m.* Thomas Orme, of Abbeytown.
5. Anne, *m.* William Orme, of Glenmore.
6. Sarah, *d. unm.* 7. Belinda Cuff, *d. unm.*

Col. Jackson *d.* 1805. His 2nd son,

GEORGE JACKSON, Col. of the North Mayo Militia, *m.* 1804, Sidney, only child and heir of Arthur Vaughan, of Carramore, co. Mayo, a descendant of the Vaughans of Wales, and had issue,
1. GEORGE VAUGHAN, his heir, of Carramore.
2. William (Very Rev.), Dean of Killala, *m.* 1st, 1847, Julia de Villiers; and 2ndly, 1866, Susan Anne, dau. of Courtnay Kenny, J.P., of Ballinrobe, and *d.* 1885, leaving issue,
  1. William Vaughan, *b.* 22 Aug. 1867; *d.* 29 Oct. 1893.
  2. James Vaughan, *b.* Oct. 1869; *d.* 31 Dec. 1870.
  1. Sidney.
3. Francis, in the Indian Army, *d. unm.* 1843.
4. OLIVER VAUGHAN, of Carramore.
5. James Vaughan, Capt. North Mayo Militia, *m.* Frances, second dau. of Thomas Jones, of Castletown (*see* JONES *of Arduaree*), and *d.* 1872, having by her, who *d.* 4 March, 1902, had issue,
  1. George Vaughan, *b.* 1847; *m.* 1879, his cousin Sidney Vaughan, dau. of the late Oliver Vaughan Jackson, of Carramore House. He *d.* 8 Dec. 1901.
  2. Herbert Francis, of Potter's Bar, Middlesex, *b.* 23 March, 1859; *m.* 4 May, 1885, Amy Mackintosh Priestley, dau. of Robert Priestley, and has issue,
    Frances Iris Madeline Vaughan, *b.* 17 Feb. 1886.
  1. Anna Rebecca. 2. Sidney Vaughan.
  3. Frances Alice. 4. Elizabeth.
7. Henry King, killed hunting, *d. unm.* 1833.
1. Maria Louisa, *m.* Major Walter Butler.

Col. Jackson *d.* 1836. His eldest son,

GEORGE VAUGHAN JACKSON, of Carramore, M.A., J.P. and D.L., Col. of North Mayo Militia, Assistant Poor Law Commissioner, *b.* 19 Sept. 1806; *d. unm.* 30 Jan. 1849; and was *s.* by his brother,

OLIVER VAUGHAN JACKSON, of Carramore House, J.P. and D.L., High Sheriff 1869, Capt. 6th Dragoon Guards (Carabineers), *b.* 2 April, 1811; *m.* 24 March, 1851, Elizabeth, eldest dau. of Thomas Jones, of Castletown, co. Sligo, J.P. and D.L. (*see* JONES *of Arduaree*), and *d.* 24 May, 1887, having had issue,
1. Arthur George, *d.* 1855. 2. Oliver Vaughan, *d.* 1859.
3. GEORGE JAMES VAUGHAN, late of Carramore.
4. PERCY VAUGHAN, now of Carramore.
1. Anne Elizabeth, *d. unm.* 1862.

2. Sidney Vaughan, *m.* 1879, her cousin George Jackson, eldest son of the late Sidney Vaughan Jackson. He *d.* 8 Dec. 1901. She *d.* 1 July, 1906.
3. Frances, *d. unm.* 1859.
4. Olivia Frances Vaughan, *d. unm.* 1861.
5. Alexandra Eva Vaughan.
6. Ida Gertrude Vaughan.

The elder surviving son,
GEORGE JAMES VAUGHAN JACKSON, of Carramore House, J.P., *b.* 19 March, 1860; *d. unm.* 10 April, 1898, and was *s.* by his brother.

Arms—Arg., on a chevron sa. between three hawks' heads erased az. as many trefoils slipped or quartering CUFF, AUNGIER, RUTLEDGE, VAUGHAN, and VAUGHAN *of Wales. Crest*—A horse passant arg. charged on the shoulder with a trefoil slipped vert. *Motto*—Celer et audax.

Seat—Carramore, Ballina, co. Mayo.

JACKSON. See MORTON-JACKSON.

JAMESON OF WINDFIELD.

MAURICE EYRE FRANCIS BELLINGHAM JAMESON, of Windfield, co. Galway, *b.* 9 May, 1888.

Lineage.—WILLIAM JAMESON, of Alloa, co. Clackmannan, *m.* 25 Nov. 1737, Helen Horne, of Thomanean, co. Kinross, and had, with other issue, a son,
JOHN JAMESON, Sheriff Clerk of Clackmannanshire, *b.* 1740; *m.* 1763, Margaret, elder sister of James Haig, of Blairhill, co. Perth, and Lochrin, Midlothian, and *d.* 1824, leaving issue,
1. Robert, *b.* 17 June, 1771, Sheriff Clerk of Clackmannanshire, *d. unm.* 1847.
2. John, of Prussia Street, Dublin, *b.* Aug. 1773; *m.* Isabella, dau. of John Stein, and *d.* 1851, having had issue,
   1. John, of St. Marnock's, co. Dublin, J.P., High Sheriff City of Dublin 1869, *m.* Anne, dau. of William Haig, and *d.* 1881, leaving issue,
      John, of St. Marnock's, M.A. Trin. Coll. Dublin, J.P. and D.L. co. Dublin, High Sheriff 1880, *m.* 1870, Elizabeth, eldest dau. of Thomas Collins Banfield.
   2. James, of Delvin Lodge, *m.* Lucy, dau. of William Cairnes, of Stameen, co. Meath, and had issue. She *d.* 22 July, 1907.
   3. William (Rev.), of Holly Bank, *m.* April, 1849, Elizabeth, dau. of Arthur Guinness, of Beaumont, co. Dublin, and has issue.
   4. Andrew, Sheriff Clerk of Clackmannanshire, *m.* Miss Cochrane, and had issue.
   5. Henry, *m.* Margaret, dau. of Andrew Philip, and has issue.
   1. Isabella, *m.* Major William Cairns, 48th Regt.
3. William, of Merrion Square, Dublin, *b.* 29 July, 1777; *d.s.p.*
4. JAMES, of whom presently.
5. Andrew, *b.* 18 Aug. 1783; *m.*, and had issue,
   Annie, *m.* Signor Marconi, Banker, of Bologna, Italy, and has issue,
   (1) Alfonso.
   (2) Guglielmo, LL.D., D.Sc., created Chevalier by the KING OF ITALY for his invention of Wireless Telegraphy. Has the order St. Ann of Russia, Commander of St. Maurice and St. Lazarus and Grand Cross of the Order of Crown of Italy (*Marconi House, Strand, W.C.;* 203, *Knightsbridge, W. Clubs*—*Bath; Royal Automobile*), *b.* 1875; *m.* 16 March, 1905, Hon. Beatrice, 6th dau. of 14th Baron Inchiquin (*see* BURKE'S *Peerage*), and has issue.
1. Margaret, *m.* 1801, William Robert Robertson (*see* family *of* ROBERTSON *of Prendergast*). 2. Helen, *d. unm.*
3. Anne, *m.* Major Francis Stupart, of the 2nd North British Dragoons.
4. Jennett, *m.* 1812, John Woolsey, of Milestown, co. Louth, who *d.* 1853.

JAMES JAMESON, *s.* to the fortune of his immediate elder brother, William, of Merrion Square, and purchased the estate of Windfield, co. Galway, and the demesne of Montrose, co. Dublin. He *m.* 28 Sept. 1815 Elizabeth Sophia, youngest dau. of the Rev. William Woolsey, of Prioriland, co. Louth, by his wife Mary Anne, youngest sister of Sir William Bellingham, of Castle Bellingham, co. Louth, Bart., and had issue,
1. JOHN, his heir.
2. William, of Montrose, co. Dublin, *b.* 19 Dec 1818; *m.* 20 March, 1855, Emily St. Leger, 2nd dau. of Major-Gen. Arthur Henry O'Niell, of St. Anne's, co. Dublin, and *d.* 26 Oct. 1896, leaving issue,
   1. James Arthur Henry, of Montrose, co. Dublin, *b.* 24 Dec. 1855; *m.* 9 Jan. 1886, Edith Caroline, 2nd dau. of George Augustus Haig, of Pen Ithon, co. Radnor, and has issue (*see that family*).
   2. William Bellingham, High Sheriff co. Louth 1904, *b.* 21 Aug. 1859; *m.* 21 Nov. 1891, Evelyn Constance, 3rd dau. of John Scarlett Campbell, of 1, Queen's Gate Place, S.W., and has issue,
      (1) William Scarlett, *b.* 3 Sept. 1899.
      (1) Joan Mary, *b.* 6 Dec. 1892.
      (2) Nora Evelyn, *b.* 20 June, 1895.
   3. Charles Villiers, *b.* 29 May, 1870; *d.* 28 Jan. 1910; *m.* 27 Jan. 1898, Frances Dora, dau. of Alexander Shirley Montgomery, of Bally Keil, co. Down, and had issue,
      (1) Nancy Thomasina Evelyn, *b.* 4 July, 1899.
      (2) Joyce Emily Pearl, *b.* 4 April, 1901.
   1. Helen Maud, *m.* 1879, James F. Jameson, of Windfield (*see below*).
   2. Emily Constance, *m.* 25 July, 1876, the late Col. Eyre Macdonald Stuart Crabbe, C.B., Grenadier Guards, of Glen Eyre, Hants. She *d.* 1 June, 1904, leaving issue. He *d.* 8 March, 1905.
   3. Nora Frances, *m.* April, 1890, Capt. Edward Sylvester Gilman, of Mallow, co. Cork.
   4. May Astel Rosina, *m.* 15 Nov. 1890, Sir Henry Edward Dering, 10th Bart., and has issue (*see* BURKE'S *Peerage*, DERING, Bart.).
   5. Aileen Elizabeth Eyre St. Leger, *m.*—Fraser, of Felixstowe.
3. James, of Airfield, co. Dublin, *b.* 4 Aug. 1821; *m.* 10 Jan. 1849, Alicia Trimleston, dau. of Robert Robertson, Advocate and Sheriff Substitute of co. Stirling, by Alicia Catherine his wife, eldest dau. of Rev. Charles Eustace, heir to the Viscounty of Baltinglass, and *d.* 16 Oct. 1889, leaving issue,
   1. James Robert, Lieut.-Col. 3rd Batt. R. I. Fusiliers, *b.* 4 Dec. 1849, late Lieut. 14th Uhlans, in the service of the German Emperor; *m.* 1880, Martha, only dau. of Herr Florke, of Hanover, and has issue,
      (1) James Frederick, *b.* 5 Sept. 1881; *m.* 4 Oct. 1911, Emma Elizabeth, youngest dau. of John Galbraith.
      (2) Robert Trimleston, *b.* 2 Jan. 1889.
      (1) Helen Alice Adolphina Martha.
   2. William Frederick, *b.* 27 Jan. 1851; *m.* 1st, 3 Aug. 1876, Ida, dau. of Henry Haig, and by her (who *d.* 26 July, 1882) has issue,
      (1) George Stanley Byng, *b.* 5 Sept. 1880.
      (1) Nina Seton. (2) Olive Frederica Wolseley.
   He *m.* 2ndly, 27 Oct. 1887, Blanche Violet Nasmyth only dau. of Alexander Macbean, formerly H.B.M. Consul for West Tuscany and the district of Rome. She *d.* 1893. He *m.* 3rdly, 7 July, 1911, Theresa, widow of the late Lieut.-Col. Fincham.
   3. John Eustace, of Taney House, Dundrum, co. Dublin, J.P., Maj. late Worcestershire Y.C., 18th Regt. and 20th Hussars, M.P. for West Clare 1895-1905 (*Chigwell Hall, Essex;* 25, *Cranley Gardens, S.W.; Nav. and Mil. Club*), *b.* 22 March, 1852; *m.* 22 July, 1875, Mary Elizabeth, 2nd dau. of John Bond Cabbell, D.L., of Cromer Hall, Norfolk, and has issue,
      (1) William Kenneth Eustace, Capt. R.F.A., *b.* 15 May, 1876; *m.* 14 June, 1909, Elsie Lilian, dau. of late Rev. John Banks Weeks Butler, M.A., Rector of Maresfield, Sussex (*see* BUTLER *of Standen Manor*).
      (2) John Bond Cabbell Eustace.
      (3) Arthur Henry Ronald Eustace.
      (4) Benjamin Bond Cabbell.
      (1) Margaret Bond Cabbell Eustace.
      (2) Mildred Mary Eustace, *m.* 21 July, 1900, Sir Valentine Raymond Grace, 5th Bart., and has issue (*see* BURKE'S *Peerage*).
      (3) Alice Evelyn Eustace, *m.*
      (4) Irene Eustace, *m.* 26 Sept. 1907, Lawrence Lydall Savill, eldest son of Philip Savill, J.P., of The Woodlands, Chigwell Row, Essex.
      (5) Victoria Georgina Eustace.
      (6) Eva Aileen, *d.* young.
      (7) Kathleen Clare Eustace.
   4. Sydney Bellingham, late Col. Seaforth Highlanders (82, *Christchurch Road, Tulse Hill, S.W.*), *b.* 1 March, 1857; *m.* 9 Aug. 1887, Ethel Theodora, only dau. of Kelynge Greenway, of Halloughton Hall, co. Warwick, and has issue,
      (1) Ian Herbert Sydney, *b.* 23 April, 1888.
      (2) Alastair Durnford Murray, *b.* 22 Nov. 1892.
      (3) Harry Roderick Victor, *b.* 29 Aug. 1897.
      (4) Edward Nigel, *b.* 23 Jan. 1901.
      (1) Ethel Mabel, *b.* 20 July, 1889.
      (2) Isobel Theodora, twin with her sister, *d.* young.
      (3) Helen Rosalind, *b.* 2 March, 1904.
   5. Charles O'Brien, Capt. 6th Batt. R.I. Rifles (*Monasterevan, co. Kildare*), *b.* 22 Nov. 1866; *m.* 1st, 1890, Georgina Phillips, dau. of Rawdon Macnamara, M.D., and by her (who *d.* Dec. 1891) has issue,
      (1) Charles Eustace, *b.* 4 Dec. 1891.
      (1) Phyllis Mary.
   He *m.* 2ndly, 1 July, 1901, Norah Mary Marvel, dau. of Rev. Joseph Seymour Eagar, and by her has issue,
      (2) Norah O'Brien Sydney, *b.* 21 Nov. 1902.
   1. Alicia Katherine Nina, *d.* young, 31 May, 1855.
   2. Helen Lucy, *d. unm.* 3 Nov. 1883.
   3. Alice Arabella, *m.* 19 Jan. 1882, George Stanley Byng, 8th Viscount Torrington, and *d.* 19 Dec. 1883, leaving one dau.
   4. Mabel Elizabeth, *d.* young, Nov. 1865.
   5. Ida Isabel, *m.* July, 1883, Robert Boeufvé, Vice-Consul of the Republic of France, and has issue.
4. Robert O'Brien, late Capt. of the 11th Hussars, *b.* 17 June, 1828; *m.* July, 1870, Emily Margaret, 3rd dau. of Major Mitchell, and *d.* 24 Aug. 1890, leaving issue.

1. Mary Anne, m. 11 Aug. 1860, Arthur Dake Coleridge, Fellow King's Coll. Camb., Clerk of Arraigns, Midland Circuit, and has issue.   2. Elizabeth Sophia.

Mr. Jameson, who was a Director of the Bank of Ireland and Deputy-Governor at the time of his death, 24 Aug. 1847, was s. in his estates of Windfield by his eldest son,

REV. JOHN JAMESON, of Windfield, co. Galway, M.A. of Queen's Coll. Oxford, b. 17 July, 1816 ; m. Jan. 1845, Isabella Anne, eldest dau. of Lieut.-Gen. Sir Harry David Jones, Royal Engineers, G.C.B., Commander of the Legion of Honour of France, and d. 1872, leaving issue,
1. JAMES FRANCIS, late of Windfield.
2. Harry William, Lieut.-Col. Commanding 6th Batt. Royal Irish Rifles, b. 5 Sept. 1851 ; m. 1887, Anne Maria, dau. of Isaac Atkinson, of Whitchaven, and has issue.
3. Arthur Bellingham, b. 15 June, 1864 ; m. 2 Aug. 1904, Charlotte Annette, younger dau. of late George Potts, of Boscombe, Hants.
    1. Charlotte Elizabeth, m. Kelynge Greenway, late of Halloughton, co. Warwick, and had issue.
    2. Edith Sophia Inkerman, m. Thomas Mack, late Lieut. 17th Lancers, of Tunstead Hall, Norfolk, and has issue.

The eldest son,

JAMES FRANCIS JAMESON, of Windfield, co. Galway, J.P., late Major 4th Batt. Connaught Rangers, and Lieut. 7th Dragoon Guards, b. 5 June, 1848 ; m. 1879, Helen Maud, eldest dau. of William Jameson, of Montrose, co. Dublin, and d. 1896, leaving issue,
MAURICE EYRE FRANCIS BELLINGHAM, now of Windfield.

Arms—Az. a saltier or, cantoned in chief and flanks by Roman galleys ppr., and a bugle horn in base of the second. Crest—A Roman galley ppr., the sail gu. charged with a lion passant guardant or. Motto—Sine metu.

Seat—Windfield, Menlough near Ballinasloe.

JENINGS OF IRONPOOL.

LIEUT.-COL. ULICK ALBERT JENINGS, late Army Med. Service, of Ironpool, co. Galway, J.P. for co. and City of Dublin, b. 27 Jan. 1842 ; s. his father 1873 ; m. 1877, Isabel, dau. of Simon Mac-Namara Creagh (see CREAGH of Dangan) by his wife Charlotte, dau. of Capt. Thomas Leader, J.P., of Ash Grove, co. Cork, by whom he has issue,
1. ULICK CREAGH, b. 1879.
2. Herbert Creagh, Capt. 5th Lancers, b. 1882.
3. George Pierce Creagh, Lieut. 1st Batt. K. Shropshire L. I., b. 1885.

Lineage.—The pedigree is given in O'Ferrall's Linea Antiqua down to 1709, and was registered by Betham, Ulster, in 1814.

WILLIAM OGE BURKE, "Athankip," 2nd son of Richard de Burgo, Lord of Connaught, m. Una, dau. of Felim, son of Cathal Crobh Dearg, King of Connaught, and had three sons,
1. Sir William, ancestor of the Earl of Mayo.
2. JOHN, of whom below.
3. Philip, father of four sons,
    1. Gilbert or Gibbon, ancestor of the family of MacGibbon or Gibbons.
    2. Philip, ancestor of MacPhilbin or Philips.
    3. Theobald, ancestor of Sliocht Tibbot, of Magh-odhar.
    4. Meyler, ancestor of MacMeyler.

JOHN BOURKE, the 2nd son of William oge, whose descendants were called from him, MacSeonin or McJonine, was father of,
JOHN (MIAGH) McJONINE, father of
JOHN (BOY) McJONINE, father of
WILLIAM McJONINE, father of
MEYLER OGE BURKE, father of
RICKARD McJONINE, father of
THEOBALD (BOY) McJONINE, of Tobberkeigh (Blindwell), co. Galway, received a pardon from the Crown 6 July, 1584. He was outlawed for rebellion 17 June, 1595, and his estate forfeited, but was again pardoned 6 May, 1598. He had three sons,
1. RICKARD (OGE), his heir.
2. John, pardoned 6 July, 1584.
3. Edmund (Owny), of Owlter, slain in rebellion 24 June, 1600, and his estate confiscated.

The eldest son,

RICKARD (OGE) McJONINE, of Tobberkeigh and Fartagar, took a prominent part in the affairs of Connaught in the latter half of the 16th century, and was in rebellion from 1586 to 1597, for which he was outlawed. He was included in the pardons to his father, but again rebelling, he was taken prisoner and executed in Aug. 1599. He m. Shily, dau. of Sir Hubert Burke, of Glinsk, and had a son,

THEOBALD, McJONINE, who was slain 26 Dec. 1600, and was father of
RICKARD McJONINE, father of
REDMOND McJONINE, whose estate, comprising the lands of Sylaun, Tysan and Carraghan (Castlegrove), Lissanauny and Lissaleen, was forfeited in 1650, he left two sons,
1. ULICK, his heir.
2. Theoba'd, who d. unm. ; his will dated 20 May, 1707, proved at Tuam 29 May, 1717.

The elder son,
ULICK McJONINE or JONINE, of Polleniren (Ironpool), whose will dated 5 May, 1716, was proved at Tuam 25 April, 1722, left four sons and four daus.,
1. RICKARD, his heir.   2. Patrick.
3. Redmond
4. Edmond, m. a dau. of Walter Blake, of Beagh.
1. Cicely.   2. Mary.
3. Kate, m. John Buckley.   4. Honora.

The eldest son,
RICKARD JONINE, of Polleniren and Cloonteen, whose will dated 15 April, 1725, was proved at Tuam 5 May following, m. (art. 28 Feb.) 1703, Catherine, dau. of Andrew Browne, of Laracoragh, co. Galway, and had issue, four sons and a dau.,
1. ULICK. his heir.   2. Andrew.
3. Dominick, of Liskeevy, d. 1789.   4. Theobald.

The eldest son,
ULICK JONINE, of Polleniren, whose will, dated 15 Dec. 1749, was proved at Tuam 14 Jan. 1750, m. Mary, dau. of Walter Bourke, of Creaghduff, and left with four daus., an only son,
RICKARD JONINE or JENINGS, of Ironpool, a minor at his father's death. He m. Julia, dau. of Martin Kirwan, of Blindwell, and left an only son,
ULICK JENINGS, of Ironpool, d. 1847 ; m. (sett. 6 April), 1796, Elizabeth, 7th dau. of John Bodkin, of Castletown, co. Galway, and had five sons and a dau.,
1. Richard, J.P. cos. Galway and Mayo, b. 1799 ; d. 26 Dec. 1870 ; m. 11 Jan. 1843, Mary Clare (d. 13 April, 1877), eldest dau. of Thomas Mark Lyster (see LYSTER of Rocksavage), and had issue,
    1. Richard St. John Lyster, b. 24 June, 1849 ; d. 14 Nov. 1872.
    1. Harriette Mary Lyster, d. 9 Nov. 1872.
    2. Lysbeth Graciana Lyster ("Bess") (Royal Terrace House, Kingstown, co. Dublin).
    3. Marie Fiona Lyster.
2. GEORGE, who succeeded.
3. Thomas, b. 1809 ; d. 1873, M.A. Dublin 1831, Barrister-at-Law; m. 1841, Elizabeth, widow of William Buchanan, and dau. of Samuel Simcocks, of West House and Dove Park, co. Galway, and left an only son,
    ULICK ALBERT, now of Ironpool.
4. John R., L.R.C.S.I., d. 1840 ; m. 1838, his cousin Anne, eldest dau. of John J. Bodkin, of Kilclooney, M.P. for Galway, and left a son, Ulick Richard, d.s.p. 1862.
5. Dominick, m. Catherine, eldest dau. of Francis Jenings, of Lissaleen. He d.s.p. 1852. She d. 15 March, 1883.
1. Catherine, m. Francis Burke, and had issue (see BURKE of Ower).

The 2nd son,
GEORGE JENINGS, of Ironpool, b. 1809 ; m. 1841, Elizabeth (d. 8 Aug. 1885), dau. of Francis Jenings, of Lisaleen, co. Galway, and d.s.p. 23 Jan. 1883, when he was s. by his nephew.

Arms—Or, a cross gu., in the 1st and 4th quarters a dexter hand couped, in the 2nd and 3rd a lion rampant sa. Crest—A cat's head affrontée erased sa., charged on the neck with a cross crosslet or. Motto—Ung Roy, ung Foy, ung Loy.

Seat—Ironpool, Tuam, co. Galway. Residence—Mervue, Monkstown, co. Dublin. Club—Royal St. George Yacht, Kingstown.

JERVIS-WHITE. See WHITE.

JESSOP OF DOORY HALL.

GEORGE HENRY JESSOP, of Doory Hall, co. Longfield, and Marlfield, b. 5 Feb. 1852 ; s. his cousin, Catherine Jessop, at Marlfield, 1891 ; and his sister at Doory Hall, 6 Nov. 1911.

Lineage.—ANTHONY JESSOP, d. 24 Dec. 1767 ; m. 1749, Bridget, dau. and heir of Christopher Donelly, of Portwiny, co. Roscommon, by Anne his wife, dau. of Edward Harward, and by her had, with three daus. and a son, William, who d. unm., another son,
JOHN JESSOP, of Doory Hall, m. 1779, Mary Anne, dau. and co-heir of Robert Fetherston, of White Rock, and had two sons,
1. JOHN HARWARD, of whom hereafter.
2. ROBERT FETHERSTON (Rev.), Rector of Kilglass, co. Longford, m. 1811, Catherine, dau. of Sir Thomas Fetherston, Bart., of Ardagh, and d. 1842, leaving issue by her (who d. 1858),

Jocelyn. THE LANDED GENTRY. 350

1. JOHN HARWARD, of Marlfield, co. Dublin, J.P. co. Westmeath and Dublin, High Sheriff co. Longford 1853, M.A., Barrister-at-Law, b. 1826; d. 18 Oct. 1888.
    1. CATHERINE, of Marlfield, d. unm. 1891, and was s. by her cousin GEORGE HENRY JESSOP (see below).
    2. Elizabeth, d. Oct. 1880.
The eldest son,
JOHN HARWARD JESSOP, of Doory Hill, m. 1806, Frances, only child and heiress of Sir Frederick Flood, Bart., M.P. (by Frances his wife, youngest dau. of Sir Harry Cavendish, Bart.), and widow of Richard Solly, of Essex, and had issue,
  1. FREDERICK THOMAS, his heir.
  2. Robert (Rev.), of Blackrock, co. Dublin, m. 1st, 1836, Susan, dau. of the Hon. Pennefather, Baron of the Court of Exchequer in Ireland, and by her (who d. 1837) had one son, William, b. 1837, d. 7 April, 1899. He m. 2ndly, Isabella, dau. of Capt. Hort, and by her had a son, Robert. He d. 1847.
  1. Frances Flood, m. 1827, the Hon. and Rev. John Gustavus Handcock, Rector of Annaduff, co. Leitrim, 3rd son of the 2nd Lord Castlemaine.
  2. Maria, m. 1833, the Rev. Nicholas Devereux, D.D., of Ballyrankin House, co. Wexford. He d. 1867.
  3. JANE, m. 1834, Matthew Thomas Derinzy, of Clobemon Hall, co. Wexford. He d. 1851.
Mr. Jessop d. Aug. 1825, and was s. by his eldest son,
FREDERICK THOMAS JESSOP, of Doory Hall, J.P. and D.L., High Sheriff 1835, b. 26 Aug. 1811; m. 12 July, 1836, Elizabeth, dau. of Peter Low, by Louisa his wife, dau. of Sir Richard Butler, 7th bart., of Cloughrennan, co. Carlow, and by her (who d. 1869) had issue,
  1. FRANCIS JOHN, his heir.
  2. Frederick Flood, b. 17 Sept. 1844; d. unm. 1869.
  3. GEORGE HENRY, now of Doory Hall.
  1. Louisa, late of Doory Hall.
  2. Elizabeth, m. 1867, Thomas William De Butts Armstrong, Chief Engineer of the Central Provinces of India, son of Rev. W. C. Armstrong, of Moydow, co. Longford. He d. 1878, leaving one son,
    William Meredith Howard Armstrong, Major A.S.C., b. 1868; m. 27 April, 1898, Mabel Mary, only surv. dau. of the late Major Geo. R. A. Moore, Madras Staff Corps.
  3. Frances Flood.   4. Mary Kathleen.
Mr. Jessop d. 1868, and was s. by his eldest son,
FRANCIS JOHN JESSOP, of Doory Hall, Lieut. 2nd Regt., b. 30 May, 1837; d.s.p. 1875. His estates devolved on his eldest sister, LOUISA JESSOP, late of Doory Hall.
LOUISA JESSOP, of Doory, co. Longford, s. her brother, Francis, 1875; d. 6 Nov. 1911, being s. by her brother, George Henry.

Arms—Quarterly, 1st, vert three mullets arg. (JESSOP); 2nd, arg. two lions' rampant combatant supporting a dexter hand couped gu. in base a salmon in the sea ppr. on a chief az. three mullets of (DONELLY); 3rd, Az. a lion rampant arg. debruised by a fess or charged with three roses gu. barbed vert (HARWARD); 4th, Gu. a chevron between three ostrich feathers arg. (FETHERSTON); 5th, Arg. two bars gu. on a canton of the last a lion rampant or (LANCASTER); 6th, Arg. three bucks' heads cabosbed gu. (COLENWOOD); 7th, Sa. a wolf ramp. arg. in chief three estoiles or (WILSON); 8th, Vert a chevron between three wolf's heads erased arg. on a canton (for CAVENDISH) sa. within a bordure arg. three buck's heads caboshed of the last attired or (BC); 9th, Arg. a cross az. in the first quarter five ermine spots (WARDEN); 10th, Or on a chief vert three pheons of the field (CROMPTON). Motto—In Deo confido.

Seat—Doory Hall, co. Longford.

JOCELYN. See BURKE's PEERAGE, RODEN, E.

JOHNSON OF ROCKENHAM AND SKAHANAGH.

WILLIAM JOHNSON, of Rockenham, co. Cork, J.P. and D.L., High Sheriff 1902, Lieut.-Col. late Rifle Brigade, b. 19 Jan. 1829; m. 1859, Maria, dau. of Henry St. George Osborne, of Dardinstown Castle, co. Meath, and has issue,

GEORGINA SUSAN MARY, m. 1885, Brev. Col. Montagu Grant Wilkinson, C.V.O., late King's Own Scottish Borderers, and d. 16 June, 1908, leaving issue,
  Violet Helen Grant.

Lineage.—This family derives descent from William Johnston or Johnson, a native of Scotland, who settled in Ireland circa 1670. He left issue, two sons, WILLIAM and George; the younger son, George, d. leaving one son, NOBLE JOHNSON, who d. at Cork, 21 Dec. 1755, leaving by Frances his wife, three daus., his co-heiresses, Catherine, m. William Blennerhasset, of Ballyseedy; Frances, m. 1760, John Lindsay, of Lindville; and Anne, m. Heyward St. Leger, of Heyward's Hill.

WILLIAM JOHNSON, elder son of the first settler, m. Elizabeth, dau. of Henry Mannix, and had issue,
  1. Jonas, d.s.p.
  2. WILLIAM, of whom presently.
The 2nd son,
WILLIAM JOHNSON, m. 1734, Anne, dau. of the Rev. Valentine French, Prebendary of Kilaspugmullane, and Dean of Ross, and d. 1764, leaving issue,
  1. Valentine, d. unm.
  2. Savage, d. unm.
  3. NOBLE, of whom presently.
  1. Anne, m. Daunt, of Tracten Abbey.
The 3rd son,
NOBLE JOHNSON, Mayor of Cork 1809, and one of the Governors of the City, m. Anne, dau. of Arthur Easton, and had issue,
  1. WILLIAM, his heir.
  2. Noble, Col. 87th Fusiliers, killed in the battle of Monte Video when in command of his regiment, m. Elizabeth, dau. of Col. O'Kelly, co. Galway, and had one child,
    Noble Eliza.
  3. Henry, m. Mary Daunt, of Tracton.
  1. Anne, m. Rev. Thomas Spread Campion, D.D., Rector of Knockmourne.
  2. Elizabeth.
  3. Mary.
  4. Emily.
  5. Frances.
The eldest son,
WILLIAM JOHNSON, a Deputy-Governor of the city of Cork, and its High Sheriff 1815, m. Sarah, dau. of John Martin, of Killacloyne, co. Cork, and d. 1827, leaving issue,
  1. NOBLE, his heir.
  2. John (Rev.), Prebendary of Killanully, b. 1800; m. Catherine, dau. of Col. Moore Hodder, of Hoddersfield; and d.s.p. 1837.
  3. William, of Vostersburg, J.P., D.L., and High Sheriff of Cork 1861, b. 26 March, 1815; m. 14 Oct. 1845, Ann, dau. of John Smithwick, of Ratheloghcen, co. Tipperary, by his wife Cherry, dau. of Col. Pennefather, of Cashel, and d. 1888, leaving issue,
    1. Noble William, of Ballinglanna, Glanmire, co. Cork, J.P., Secretary to the Grand Jury co. Cork, b. 5 Nov. 1846; m. 1st, 28 April, 1873, Mary Louisa, dau. of late Eyre Powell, of Clareville, co. Limerick, and by her had a son d. 1876, and a dau. d. 1878, an only surviving dau.,
      (1) Evelyn Herbert, b. April, 1878.
    He m. 2ndly, 29 March, 1885, Mary, dau. of Capt. Richard Townshend Gray, late 50th Regt., and by her has issue,
      (1) William Richard, b. 3 Oct. 1888.
      (2) Mildred, b. 23 Dec. 1885.
    2. George, Lieut. 99th Regt., b. 8 April, 1850, killed at the battle of Gingilhovo, Africa, in 1879.
    3. William, b. 7 Feb. 1858.
    4. Valentine Francis, b. 17 March, 1860.
    5. Walter Berwick, b. Nov. 1861.
    1. Cherry Pennefather.
    2. Sarah, m. James Shee, of Ballyreddan, and left issue.
  4. George Charles Jefferyes (twin with William), J.P., Commander R.N., served in the campaign in Syria 1840, for which he received two medals, and d. unm. 1882.
  1. Eliza, m. John Topp, and d. 1865.
  2. Anne, m. John Roberts, of Ardmore.
  3. Barbara, m. William Ricketts D'Altera, and had issue.
  4. Albinia, m. her cousin George Hodder.
  5. Jane, m. Richard Roberts, Lieut. R.N.
The eldest son,
NOBLE JOHNSON, of Rockenham, co. Cork, b. 9 Jan. 1798; m. 1828, Susan, dau. of Joseph Bullen, of Kinsale, and had issue,
  1. WILLIAM, now of Rockenham.
  2. Joseph Bullen, b. Jan. 1833; m. 1858, Eloise, dau. of Capt. Robert Atkins Rogers, of Coolfadda House, and has issue,
    Noble Bullen, m. 20 Nov. 1905, Madeline Mary, 5th dau. of Lieut.-Col. de Pentheny O'Kelly, and has issue,
      Madeleine, b. 8 Aug. 1906.
    Alice, m. 31 Oct. 1891, Capt. Arthur Hemming Robeson (Governor's House, H.M. Prison, Galway), late Wilts Regt., son of Archdeacon Robeson, of Bristol, and has issue,
      (1) Arthur Vyvyan, b. 11 Feb. 1894.
      (1) Muriel Charlotte Pearl, b. 14 Sept. 1901.
      (2) Roma Alice Hemming, b. 15 Oct. 1908.
  1. Susan, m. 1881, Capt. Richard Townsend Gray, J.P., of Lota Ville, co. Cork.   2. Sarah Kate.
Mr. Noble Johnson d. 1880, and was s. by his eldest son.

Arms—Arg., a saltier sa. between a lymphad in chief of the second, and a tower in base gu., on a chief engrailed of the last three cushions or. Crest—On a mural crown ppr. a spur erect or, between two wings expanded arg., each charged with an annulet gu. Motto—Nunquam non paratus.

Seat—Rockenham, Passage West, co. Cork. Residence—6, Ashbrook Terrace, Leeson Park, Dublin.

JOHNSTON OF BALLYKILBEG.

WILLIAM JOHNSTON, of Ballykilbeg, co. Down, b. 14 Sept. 1876; m. 1904, Wilhelmina Galway, and has with other issue,

WILLIAM, b. 1904.

Lineage.—WILLIAM JOHNSTON, of Killough, m. 26 Aug. 1760, Ann, dau. of Matthew Brett, of Killough, son of the Rev. Jasper Brett, Prebendary of Rasharkin, and Chancellor of Connor, by Mary his wife, dau. of John McNeal, Dean of Down, and Lucretia his wife, dau. of Francis Marsh, Archbishop of Dublin, cousin of Edward Hyde, Earl of Clarendon, the grandfather of Queens MARY and ANNE. The son and heir of the marriage of William Johnston and Ann Brett his wife was

WILLIAM JOHNSTON, J.P., of Ballykilbeg, m. 15 May, 1787, Mary Anne Humphreys, and d. 8 Aug. 1796, having had by her (who d. 1848), besides other children, a son,

JOHN BRETT JOHNSTON, of Ballykilbeg, co. Down, m. 17 March, 1828, Thomasina Anne Brunette, dau. of the late Thomas Scott, and by her (who d. 13 Feb. 1852) had issue,
1. WILLIAM, late of Ballykilbeg.
2. Robert Barclay Macpherson, b. 1830; d. 1854.
3. Charles Crochley, b. 14 May, 1835.
4. John Brett, b. 1839; d. 1868.
1. Elizabeth, d. 1852.
2. Mary Anne Brunette, m. 9 Aug. 1860, Hunt Walsh Chambre, J.P., and d. 8 Feb. 1912, leaving issue (see CHAMBRE of Dungannon).
3. Thomasina Isabella, m. 29 June, 1864, Sir Arthur Graham Hay, Bart., of Park, and by him (who d. 18 Nov. 1889) has issue, three sons and five daus.

Mr. Johnston d. 8 March, 1853, and was s. by his eldest son,

WILLIAM JOHNSTON, of Ballykilbeg, co. Down, M.A., M.P. for Belfast 1868 to 1878, and for South Belfast 1885-1902, late Inspector of Irish Fisheries, b. 22 Feb. 1829; m. 1st, 22 Feb. 1853, Harriet, dau. of Robert Allen, of Kilkenny, by whom he had issue,
1. John Brett McNeal, b. 2 Feb. 1854; d. 29 June, 1857.
2. William Henry Colclough, b. 7 Nov. 1855; d. 11 July, 1864.
1. Mary Louisa.   2. Thomasina Elizabeth Macpherson.

He m. 2ndly, 10 Oct. 1861, Arminella Frances, dau. of Rev. Thomas Drew, D.D. He m. 3rdly, 4 May, 1863, Georgiana Barbara, youngest dau. of Sir John Hay, of Park, 7th bart., and had by her (who d. 6 Aug. 1900) issue,
2. Lewis AUDLEY MARSH, of Ballykilbeg.
3. Charles, b. 17 Feb. 1867; m. 10 Oct. 1888, Vera, dau. of General V. Jellhovsky.
4. WILLIAM, now of Ballykilbeg.
3. Georgiana Audley Hay, m. 2 Sept. 1891, John Brereton.
4. Harriet Ann Brunette, d. 1874.
5. Ada Catherine, m. 1904, Samuel A. P. Brew.
6. Ina, d. 26 Sept. 1888.

He d. 17 July, 1902, and was s. by his eldest surviving son,

LEWIS AUDLEY MARSH JOHNSTON, of Ballykilbeg, co. Down, J.P., Acting Treas. M.E.C. and M.L.C. of Hong-Kong 1903-5, and Postmaster-General there 1903-8, b. 12 Sept. 1865; m. 26 Jan. 1903, Emily Sophia, youngest dau. of the late Rev. Thomas Jones, Rector of Tullaniskien, co. Tyrone. He d s p 1908.

Seat—Ballykilbeg, co. Down.

JOHNSTON OF FORT JOHNSTON.

HENRY GEORGE JOHNSTON, of Fort Johnston, co. Monaghan, B.A. Oxon., b. 8 July, 1860; m. 27 July, 1892, Beatrice, dau. of the late Rev. John Eccles, Rector of Drogheda. She d. 14 April, 1910, leaving issue,
1. WILLIAM CUTHBERT, b. 18 Feb. 1894.
2. John Eccles, b. 22 Sept. 1895.

Lineage.—Mr. Shirley, in his History of co. Monaghan, states that WILLIAM JOHNSTON, whose name occurs among the gentlemen of co. Monaghan in the census of 1659 as residing in the parish of Donagh in that co., appears to have been the progenitor of this family. One of their oldest possessions in the parish of Donagh was Stramore, now called Fort Johnston. The direct representative in 1688 was Baptist Johnston, of Trough, who was second in command to Matthew Anckettll, at the battle of Drumbanagher. He d. leaving two daus. and co-heirs. His uncle,

HECTOR JOHNSTON, of Stramore, was buried at Donagh, leaving a son,

JAMES JOHNSTON of Stramore and Tullycallick, who was s. by his son by Marjory his wife,

GEORGE JOHNSTON, of Fort Johnston, b. 1728; m. Margaret, dau. of Sir Richard Baxter, Knt., by whom (who d. 12 Feb. 1813, aged 76) he had two sons,
1. John, of Cork, M.D., m. a sister of Sir Anthony Perier, Knt., of Cork, and d.s.p.   2. THOMAS, who s. to the estate.

Mr. Johnston d. 21 Dec. 1818. His 2nd son,

THOMAS JOHNSTON, of Fort Johnston, m. 1st, 1796, Martha, eldest dau. of Rev. James Hingston, Rector of Whitchurch (see HINGSTON of Aglish), by whom he had issue,
1. HENRY GEORGE, his heir.   2. Thomas Hodnet, d. unm.
1. Anna Matilda, m. 23 July, 1830, Nicholas Dunscombe, of King Williamstown, co. Cork, and d. 24 Oct. 1865, leaving issue (see DUNSCOMBE, of Mount Desert).
2. Maria, m. Rev. Richard Graves Meredith, Rector of Timoleague, co. Cork, and d. 1848.

Mr. Johnston m. 2ndly, Rosalinda, only dau. of John O'Connell, of Dublin, and by her he had one dau.,
3. Rosalinda, m. 28 June, 1860, Thomas Franklin, and d.s.p. Oct. 1862.

Mr. Johnston d. 1841, and was s. by his eldest son,

HENRY GEORGE JOHNSTON, of Fort Johnston, J.P., High Sheriff 1859, b. March, 1798; m. 5 Oct. 1820, Maria, dau. of Walter Young, of Monaghan, and by her (who d. 1 Dec. 1866) had issue,
1. WALTER YOUNG, his heir.
2. Henry, b. 1 Sept. 1827; d. unm. 1855.
3. William Young, b. 7 April, 1833, Ensign 30th Regt., was present at the battle of Alma, and d. next day of cholera.
1. Matilda, m. Julius Brockman Travers, Depôt Paymaster at Chatham, and has issue.
2. Elizabeth Anna, m. 10 July, 1850, Robert McKinstrey, M.D., Governor of Lunatic Asylum, Armagh, and d. 1872, leaving issue.
3. Louisa Martha, m. 5 Dec. 1855, Edward William Lucas, of Raconnell, co. Monaghan, who d. 20 Sept. 1862, leaving issue (see LUCAS of Castle Shane).
4. Maria Alice, m. 1 July, 1862, Joseph John Henry Carson, 2nd son of Thomas Carson, Bishop of Kilmore, Elphin, and Ardagh, Dean of Kilmore, and has issue (see CARSON of Shanroe). He d. 3 Dec. 1907.

Mr. Johnston d. July, 1869, and was s. by his eldest son,

REV. WALTER YOUNG JOHNSTON, of Fort Johnston, B.A., Rector and Prebendary of Connor 1868-88, b. 5 Oct. 1823; m. 1st, 24 Dec. 1851, Martha, eldest dau. of Nicholas Dunscombe, J.P., of King Williamstown, co. Cork, and by her (who d. 5 Feb. 1855) had a dau.,
1. Martha Dunscombe, m. 17 June, 1884, Thomas Herbert Knowles Duff, elder son of Thomas Duff, of Aberlour and Cannes, and d. 2 May, 1900, leaving a son, Kenneth Dunscombe Johnston Duff, b. 31 March, 1885.

He m. 2ndly, July, 1857, Frances Palmer, 4th dau. of the late Rev. Henry Murphy, Minor Canon of Down Cathedral, and d. 20 May, 1901, having had issue,
1. HENRY GEORGE, now of Fort Johnston.
2. William Walter Harding, b. 16 June, 1862; d. 11 Jan. 1887.
3. Frederick Thomas Crommelin, b. 31 March, 1864; m. 25 April, 1900, Evangeline De la Banka, eldest dau. of the late Capt. Donald Macmillan, R.N., and has issue.
4. Walter Herbert, b. 27 Oct. 1865; m. 25 March, 1903, Marjorie Hilda Douglas, 3rd dau. of the late John Connell, Surveyor of Auckland.
5. Francis Hector, b. 31 Dec. 1871.
6. John Alexander, b. 28 Feb. 1876; m. 1 June, 1904, Catherine Hazel Douglas, 2nd dau. of the late John Connell, Surveyor of Auckland, N.Z., and has issue.
7. Percy Lucas, b. 31 May, 1877; d. July, 1878.
2. Frances Maria, m. June, 1882, Edward Mulgan, M.A., 2nd son of Rev. H. Mulgan, Auckland, New Zealand, and has issue.
3. Louisa Mary, m. 21 Sept. 1900, Dr. Edward Anstie Bewes, younger son of the late Col. Wyndham Bewes, 73rd Regt., and has issue.
4. Mary Kathleen, m. 24 April, 1901, Nutcombe Jeanes Evered, 4th son of Capt. J. G. C. Evered, of Barford Park, co. Somerset.
5. Flora Gertrude, d. 14 July, 1887.
6. Grace Violet, m. 22 March, 1893, Carl Paul Rudolf Recknagel, Min. Ex. Freiberg, Germany, and has issue.
7. Isabel Henrietta.   8. Adela May, d. 1898.

Seat—Fort Johnston, Glasslough, co. Monaghan. Residence—Devonshire Square, Bandon, co. Cork.

JOHNSTON OF KILMORE.

GEORGE HAMILTON JOHNSTON, of Kilmore, co. Armagh, and Blackhall, co. Dublin, B.A. Trin. Coll. Dublin, Lieut.-Col. late East Yorks. Regt. and Reserve of Officers, b. 26 Oct. 1847.

Lineage.—WILLIAM JOHNSTON, an architect sent from Scotland to superintend the restoration of public buildings injured during the Rebellion of 1641, m. Miss Campbell (who d. in Derry during the siege), and left issue, two sons and one dau.,
1. WILLIAM, of whom presently.
2. Alexander, served, like his elder brother, in the defence of Londonderry; m. Elinor Fleming, and d. 1736, bur. at Armagh Cathedral, leaving a son,

William, b. 1699; m. 1729, Susanna, dau. of Rev. Nathaniel Weld, and settled at Bordeaux, where his descendants still reside.

1. A dau., *m.* Rev. William English, of Armagh and Carrickfergus, son of John English, of Dublin, by Rose his wife, dau. of Lieut.-Col. George Blacker, of Carrick Blacker.
The elder son,
WILLIAM JOHNSTON, *b.* about 1660, a staunch supporter of WILLIAM III., served at the siege of Derry. He *d.* 1753 and was bur. at Armagh Cathedral, leaving an only son,
EDWARD JOHNSTON, *b.* 31 Oct. 1700 ; *m.* 1 June, 1720, Mary, dau. of Capt. John Johnston, of Drumconnell, co. Armagh (who served at the siege of Derry and was attainted by the Parliament of JAMES II), and *d.* 1771, leaving a son,
WILLIAM JOHNSTON, of Armagh, *b.* 3 Feb. 1728; *d.* 1792; *m.* 1757, Margaret, dau. of James Houston, and by her had issue,
 1. Richard, of Eccles Street, Dublin, and Ballinteer, co. Dublin, *b.* 1759 ; *m.* 30 Sept. 1780, his cousin Susanna, dau. and co-heir of Robert Barnes, son of Rev. John Barnes, of Armagh (by Mary, dau. of Rev. William English, of Armagh and Carrickfergus), and uncle of Gen. Sir Edward Barnes, G.C.B. and M.P., formerly Governor of Ceylon, and subsequently Commander-in-Chief of India. She was *b.* 1766, and *d.* 1799. He *d.s.p.* 20 March, 1806.
 2. Francis, of Eccles Street, Dublin, *b.* 1760, M.R.I.A., founded the Royal Hibernian Academy of Arts, 1824. He *m.* Anne, dau. of Robert Barnes (sister of his elder brother's wife). He *d s.p.* March, 1829.
 3. William, of Armagh, *b.* 1764 ; *m.* Margaret, dau. of John Arthur Donnelly, of Blackwatertown, co. Armagh, and *d.* 1797, leaving an only child,
  Margaret, *m.* 1st, 1818, Col. Charles Douglas Waller, R.A., of West Wickham, Kent, who *d.* 23 June, 1826, leaving issue ; and andly, 23 Jan. 1833, William Lodge Kidd, who *d.* 2 April, 1851 (she *d.* 1881).
 4. ANDREW, of whom below.
The youngest son,
ANDREW JOHNSTON, of Barnhill, Dalkey, President of the Royal College of Surgeons, Ireland, *b.* 1770 ; *m.* 1 July, 1806, Sophia, only child of George Cheney, of Holywood, co. Kildare, and St. Stephen's Green, Dublin (*d.* 9 Oct. 1868), and *d.* Aug. 1833, having had issue,
 1. Francis Samuel, *b.* 11 July, 1811 ; *m.* May, 1840, Mary, dau. of Thornton Gregg, of Oldtown, co. Longford, and *d.* 1861. His widow *d.* 1888.
 2. William, of Williamstown, co. Meath, M.A., *b.* 24 March, 1813 ; *m.* 1837, Jane, dau. of Thornton Gregg (sister of his eldest brother's wife), and *d.* 30 May, 1889. His widow *d.* 1892.
 3. George, M.D., of St. Stephen's Green, Dublin, President of the Royal College of Physicians, Ireland, *b.* 12 Aug. 1814 ; *m.* 2 Feb. 1843, Henrietta, dau. of John Williamson, of Milbeach House, Monkstown, co. Dublin, and *d.* 7 March, 1889, having had issue. 4. RICHARD, late of Kilmore.
 5. Andrew, *b.* 10 Jan. 1819 ; *d.* 9 June, 1838.
 6. Robert, *b.* May, 1822, served in the 7th Dragoon Guards during the second Kaffir War, for which he had a medal ; *m.* 1854, Jane, dau. of Henry Phillips. He *d.* 25 Aug. 1901. She *d.* 11 Aug. 1909.
 7. Henry Benjamin, Col. Commanding Antrim Artillery Militia, *b.* 4 Sept. 1831 ; *d.* 25 June, 1890.
 1. Henrietta, *m.* Sept. 1832, Rev. Francis Gregg, D.D., of Oldtown, co. Longford (she *d.* 1884). 2. Anne, *d.* 4 April, 1820.
The 4th son,
REV. RICHARD JOHNSTON, M.A., of Kilmore, co. Armagh, *b.* 5 April, 1816 ; *m.* 1st, 1844, Augusta Sophia, last surviving child of Rev. George Hamilton, M.A., Rector of Killermogh, Queen's Co., and grand-dau. of Right Rev. Hugh Hamilton, D.D., F.R.S., of Newtown-Hamilton, co. Armagh, Bishop of Ossory (*see* HAMILTON-STUBBER *of Moyne*), by whom (who *d.* 30 April, 1860) he has issue,
 1. GEORGE HAMILTON, now of Kilmore.
 2. Andrew Edmund, *b.* 23 Nov. 1848 ; *m.* 6 Sept. 1877, Constance Mary, youngest dau. of John Samuel Graves, of Woodbine Hill, Honiton, Devon (*see* GRAVES-SAWLE, BURKE'S *Peerage and Baronetage*), and has issue,
  1. George Paul Graves, *b.* 4 March, 1881.
  1. Katherine Hester. 2. Isabel Mary.
  3. Constance Ella.
 3. Francis Burdett (Rev.), M.A., Vicar of Waltham Abbey, co. Essex (*Athenæum Club*), *b.* 25 March, 1850.
 4. Henry Augustus, Barrister-at-Law, B.A. Trin. Coll. Dublin, J.P. co. Armagh (*Garrick and Kildare Street Clubs*), *b.* 11 Nov. 1851.
 1. Sophia. 2. Isabella Selina. 3. Augusta.
Mr. Johnston *m.* 2ndly, 27 May, 1862, Hester, eldest dau. of Robert William Lowry, J.P. and D.L., of Pomeroy, co. Tyrone, and Belmore, co. Westmeath (she *d.* 1 June, 1876) ; and 3rdly, July, 1883, Olivia Frances Grafton, eldest dau. of Robert Westley Hall-Dare, D.L., of Theydon Bois, Essex, and Newtownbarry, co. Wexford (*see that family*). He *d.* 27 Nov. 1906.

Arms—Quarterly : 1st and 4th, JOHNSTON, arg. a saltier sa. between in chief a trefoil slipped vert and in base a heart ensigned with an imperial crown ppr. on a chief gu. three cushions or ; 2nd CHENEY, az., six lions rampant, three, two, and one, arg., armed and langued gu., on a canton erm. a bull's scalp ppr. 3. HAMILTON viz., quarterly, gu. and arg., in the 1st and 4th quarters three cinquefoils pierced erm. and a canton of the second charged with a trefoil slipped vert. in the 2nd and 3rd quarters a lymphad, sails furled oars in action sa. *Crest*—An arm in armour embowed, the hand grasping a sword all ppr. charged on the elbow with a spur rowel gu. *Motto*—Nunquam non paratus.
Seat—Kilmore, Richhill, co. Armagh.

JOHNSTON OF MAGHERAMENA.

JAMES CECIL JOHNSTON, of Magheramena Castle, and of Glencore House, co. Fermanagh, High Sheriff 1910, late 14th Hussars, served in S. Africa 1900-2, Deputy Ranger of the Curragh of Kildare since 1910, Master of the Horse to H.E. the Lord Lieut. since 1910, *b.* 1880 ; *m.* 28 Oct. 1903, Violet Myrtle, dau. of S. A. Walker Waters, Assist. Inspector-Gen. Royal Irish Constabulary, and has issue,
1. MYRTLE, *b.* 7 March, 1909.
2. Marjorie Helen, *b.* 18 Jan. 1911.

Lineage.—WALTER ROE JOHNSTONE, of Mawlick, co. Fermanagh, High Sheriff of that county 1679, attainted 1689, made his will 11 Aug. 1693. He had five sons,
 1. Francis, of Limerick, Capt. in the Army, whose will, dated 24 July, 1695, was proved in 1699, by Sarab his wife. He had two sons and three daus.,
  1. Walter, of Kilmore, J.P. co. Fermanagh 1718, *m.* Letitia, dau. of Rev. John Leslie, D.D., of Tarbert, co. Kerry (*see that family*), and had issue,
   (1) Francis, of Kilmore, whose will was proved 12 April, 1743.
   (2) James.
   (1) Marianna, *m.* John Sinclair, of Holy Hill, co. Tyrone.
   (2) Jane. (3) Mary.
  2. Francis, of Derrycholought, co. Fermanagh, High Sheriff 1731 and 1732, *m.* 1710, Anne, dau. of Robert Clarke and widow of John Archdale, of Drumin, co. Fermanagh, and by her (whose will, dated 22 June, 1761, was proved 29 Feb. 1768) had issue,
   (1) Francis. (2) Robert. (3) Walter.
   (4) Clarke. (5) William.
   (1) Elizabeth.
   (2) Ann, *m.* 1752, Stephen Betty.
   (3) Alice.
  1. Mary. 2. Sarah.
  3. Ellis.
 2. James, of Magheramena, *m.* Frances Cathcart, and *d.s.p.* 1731.
 3. George. 4. HUGH, of whom hereafter.
 5. Edward, of Leittim, Capt. in the Army, *m.* the dau. of Thomas Armstrong, and had,
  1. Francis. 2. Hugh.
  1. A dau., *m.* — Martin.
The 4th son,
REV. HUGH JOHNSTON, of Templecarne, co. Fermanagh, made his will 9 May, 1691, and left a son,
FRANCIS JOHNSTON, of Magheramena, *d.* 1737, leaving, by Frances his wife, several children,
1. James. 2. Walter.
3. Hugh. 4. Francis.
5. JOHN.
1. Mary. 2. Grace.
3. Lettice.
His 5th son,
CAPT. JOHN JOHNSTON, left by Anne his wife (*m.* 1756), two sons, of whom,
ROBERT JOHNSTON, Q.C., *m.* 14 Oct. 1806, Letitia, dau. of Sir William Richardson, Bart., of Castle Hill, co. Tyrone, and dying 15 Aug. 1813, left issue,
1. JAMES, his heir.
1. Anna Maria, *m.* 1827, Lieut.-Col. George Knox, D.L., of Prehen, co. Londonderry, and had issue (*see that family*).
2. Harriette, *m.* Henry Daniel, of Auburn, co. Westmeath.
3. Letitia Mary, *m.* 23 Sept. 1835, John Lennox Macartney, son of Capt. James Macartney, 18th Hussars, and nephew of Maj.-Gen. Sir Eccles Nixon (*see* BURKE'S *Family Records*).
The son,
JAMES JOHNSTON, of Magheramena Castle, J.P. and D.L., High Sheriff, *b.* 16 Sept. 1817 ; *m.* 24 May, 1838, Cecilia, dau. of Thomas Newcomen Edgeworth, of Kilshrewly, co. Longford, and had by her (who *d.* 1876) issue,
1. ROBERT EDGEWORTH, his heir.
1. Letitia Marian, *m.* 1868, Charles P. Webber, 2nd son of C. Tankerville Webber, and Lady Adelaide Webber.
2. Rosetta, *m.* Joshua J. Pim, of Brennanstown House, Cabinteely, co- Dublin. She *d.* 13 May, 1909.
Mr. Johnston *d.* 1873, and was s. by his only son,
ROBERT EDGEWORTH JOHNSTON, of Glencore House, High Sheriff 1877, *b.* 17 Dec. 1842 ; *m.* 26 April, 1873, Edythe Grace, dau. of John Reynolds Dickson, of Woodville, and Tullaghan House, co. Leitrim, and had by her (who *d.* 14 Jan. 1887), with other issue,
JAMES CECIL, now of Magheramena Castle.
Mr. Johnston *d.* Aug. 1882.
Seat—Magheramena Castle, co. Fermanagh.

JOHNSTON OF GLYNN.

RANDAL WILLIAM JOHNSTON, of Glynn, co. Antrim, Major, Reserve of Officers, late 5th Batt. Royal Irish Rifles, late Capt. King's Own Scottish Borderers, *b.* 8 Sept. 1858 ; *s.* his father 19 Feb. 1885.

Lineage.—GEORGE JOHNSTON, of Glynn, attainted in 1689 in the Parliament of King JAMES in Dublin, was *s.* by

353   IRELAND.   Johnstone.

WILLIAM JOHNSTON, of Glynn, High Sheriff co. Antrim, 1723. He is supposed to have been the elder brother of JAMES JOHNSTON, who m. Elizabeth, dau. of James Leslie, of Leslie House, co. Antrim (see LESLIE *of Ballibay*), and d. 1707, leaving issue,
1. William, b. 1691; d. before 1707.
2. HENRY, of Glynn.
3. George, b. 1698; d. 1747; m. 1731, Ann, dau. of Robert Lindsey, of Sligo (she d. 1735), and had issue,
   Robert, d. 1759.
   1. Elizabeth, b. 1693; d. before 1707.
   2. Rose, b. 1695.   3. Jane, b. 1696.
   4. Mary, b. 1697.   5. Elizabeth, b. 1700.
   6. Katherine, b. 1701; d. before 1707.
The 2nd son,
HENRY JOHNSTON, of Glynn, b. 1694; m. 1724, Anne Stewart, and had issue,
1. James, who was drowned at sea coming home from St. Croix.
2. ADAM BLAIR, his successor.
   1. Isabella, m. Daniel Fleming.
   2. Jane, m. Capt. William McCleverty, R.N.
   3. Mary, m. Henry M'Kedy.
   4. Ellen, m. Rev. James Dunbar; d. 1766.
His 2nd son,
ADAM BLAIR, of Glynn, m. 1760, Margaret, dau. of Robert Johnston of Aghadunvane. co. Leitrim, and had issue,
1. Robert, b. 1761; d. unm. 1802.
2. Henry Leslie, Capt. Royal Marines, d. unm. at Ajaccio, Corsica, 1794.
3. James, E.I. Co.'s Navy, killed in a mutiny at sea near Penang; 1805.
4. Peter Leslie, Lieut. 45th Regt., d. unm. 1796.
5. William, Midshipman, drowned.
6. Arthur Trevor, d. young.
7. RANDAL WILLIAM McDONEL, of Glynn.
8. Adam Blair, b. 1781; d. in West Indies, unm.
   1. Jane, m. James Stephenson.
   2. Anne, m. 1797, Rev. George Birch, Incumbent of Comber, co. Down.
   3. Penelope Lucy Leslie, m. Capt. Walker, 42nd Highlanders and Major Renfrew Mil.
The 7th son,
RANDAL WILLIAM McDONEL JOHNSTON, of Glynn, b. 1777; m. 9 June, 1806, Isabella Anna Jane (d. 1850), dau. of George Birch, of Ballybeen, co. Down. He d. 1838, having had issue,
1. Adam Blair, b. 3 April, 1808, Lieut. 46th Madras N.I.; d. unm. Nov. 1828.
2. George Birch, late of Glynn.
3. Robert, b. 23 Oct. 1812; m. Anna Causer, and d. in West Indies, 1840.   4. James Birch, b. 8 Jan. 1814; d. young.
5. Randal William McDonel, b. 16 March, 1817; d. unm. 1850.
   1. Charlotte Catherine Birch, b. 1 Jan. 1810; d. unm. 1895.
   2. Margaret. b. 29 Dec 1814; d. young.
   3. Isabella Jane, b. 28 Nov. 1818; m. 14 April, 1846, her cousin James Walker.
   4. Margaret, b. 31 Oct. 1820; m. June, 1852, Michael Andrews. She d. Oct. 1905.
   5. Sarah Hill, b. 30 Sept. 1822; m. Feb. 1850, William Purden. She d. 17 Feb. 1908.
His 2nd son,
GEORGE BIRCH JOHNSTON, of Glynn, co. Antrim, J.P., b. 20 March, 1811; m. 9 April, 1856, Jane Waring, dau. of Thomas Kelly Evans, son of Edward Evans, of Gortmerron, co. Tyrone, and d. 19 Feb. 1885, having had issue,
1. RANDAL WILLIAM, now of Glynn.
2. Thomas Kelly Evans, b. 1 May, 1860, Col. R.A. (retired); m. 19 March, 1891, Margaret Ross, eldest dau. of Archibald Gray, and has issue,
   Randal William McDonnell.
   Margaret Gray.
3. George Birch, b. 28 Sept. 1866.
4. Charles McGarel, b. 3 May, 1876; m. Nov. 1908, Margaret Thompson, and has issue,
   A dau.
   1. Elizabeth Thomasina Evans, m. 26 June, 1884, Rev. Robert Lauriston Lee, and has issue,
   2. Isabella Eva.   3. Charlotte Maria.
Seat—Glynn House, Glynn, co. Antrim.

———

JOHNSTON OF KINLOUGH HOUSE.

JAMES JOHNSTON, of Kinlough House, co. Leitrim, J.P. and D.L., High Sheriff 1884; b. 20 Nov. 1858; m. 9 July, 1890, Rebecca Ceely, dau. of Maurice Ceely Maude, of Lenaghan Park, co. Fermanagh (see BURKE'S *Peerage*, DE MONTALT, E.), and has issue,
1. William James, b. 27 Dec. 1891; d. 14 Dec. 1893.
2. ROBERT CHRISTOPHER, b. 17 Jan. 1896.

Lineage.—ROBERT JOHNSTON, of Kinlough House, co. Leitrim, and 23, Mountjoy Sq., Dublin, b. 1768; m. Florence, dau. of Henry Rathborne, of Dunsinea, co. Dublin, and d. 22 March, 1843, having had, with other issue,
1. WILLIAM, of whom presently.
2. Henry (Ven.), M.A., Archdeacon of Elphin, and Vicar of Boyle, co. Roscommon, b. 1821; m. 1852, Letitia Jemima, dau., I.L.G.

of Joseph Meredith, of Cloonamahon, co. Sligo, and Jane Walker his wife. She d. Feb. 1900. He d. 1882, having had issue,
1. Robert St. George, of Laurel Lodge, Randalstown, co. Antrim, b. 6 March, 1852; m. March, 1899, the Countess Ada von Rhoden.
2. Henry Joseph, C.I.E., Supdt. Eng. P.W.D., India, m. Sept. 1893, Maude E. Bloomfield, of Thornville, Carlow, and d. 13 March, 1905, leaving issue,
   Iris Maude, b. 31 Dec. 1897.
3. Meredith, of Kildevin, Streete, co. Westmeath, J.P., B.A. Trin. Coll. Dublin, b. Oct. 1859; m. Feb. 1890, Edith Mary Jane, dau. of Robert Blakeney Wise, and Mary Letitia Grace Yeats his wife, and has issue,
   Meredith St. George Corbet, b. Nov. 1893.
   1. Jane Sophia, m. 1st, 1889, William Frazer, F.R.C.S.I., M.R.I.A.; and 2ndly, Rev. John E. Webb, of Christ Church, Harrow Road, W.
4. St. George Robert, of Mount Prospect, Kinlough, and Towney Corry, Drumshambo, co. Leitrim, and Ballaghnagrisheen, Menlough, co. Galway, J.P. cos. Longford and Leitrim, High Sheriff for the latter 1897, B.A. Trin. Coll. Dublin, b. 1826; m. 1856, Annette Catherine, 2nd dau. of William Tredennick, of Fortwilliam, co. Donegal (see TREDENNICK, of Camlin). He d. 18 Nov. 1911.
The eldest son,
WILLIAM JOHNSTON, of Kinlough House, co. Leitrim, and Mountjoy Sq., Dublin, J.P. co. Leitrim, High Sheriff 1850, b. 21 Sept. 1814; m. 1856, Sarah Jane, dau. of Rev. William Percy, Rector of Carrick-on-Shannon, and d. 15 Feb. 1888, having had issue,
1. JAMES, of Kinlough.
   1. Florence Elizabeth, b. 13 Sept. 1857; m. 25 July, 1875, Lieut.-Col. Robert Howard-Brooke, of Castle-Howard, Ovoca, co. Wicklow. She d.s.p. May, 1893 (see BURKE'S *Peerage*, BROOKE, Bart.).
   2. Sophia Mary.
   3. Emma Caroline.
   4. Lucy Katherine.
Seat—Kinlough House, Kinlough, co. Leitrim.

———

JOHNSTONE OF SNOW HILL.

JOHN DOUGLAS JOHNSTONE, of Snow Hill, co. Fermanagh, b. 21 March, 1874; m. 1903, May, youngest dau. of late Patrick Murphy, of St. Andrew's, Milltown. He served during the Mashonaland 1897 with the British S. African Co., also during the S. African War with the R.S.A. Field Force.

Lineage.—WILLIAM JOHNSTONE settled in Ireland about the year 1660, and m. Prudence, dau. of William Goodfellow, of co. Derry, by whom he had one son,
JAMES JOHNSTONE, of co. Fermanagh, m. Joanna Gunnis, co. Donegal, and (with a younger son, Christopher, Surgeon of the 17th Lancers, who was father of Christopher Johnstone, Col. of the 8th Hussars) had an elder son and heir,
JAMES JOHNSTONE, of Snow Hill, m. Anne, dau. John Johnstone, of Adragoole House, co. Leitrim, and had issue,
1. JOHN DOUGLAS, his successor.
2. Andrew, Lieut. 8th Hussars, d. unm. at Calcutta, 1810.
   1. Margaret, m. 1st, Capt. W. Johnstone, of the 63rd Regt.; and 2ndly, Gilbert Burrington.
   2. Mary, m. July, 1793, Francis Lloyd, eldest son of George Lloyd, of Mount Catharine, co. Limerick.
Mr. Johnstone d. 1808, and was s. by his son,
JOHN DOUGLAS JOHNSTONE, of Snow Hill, b. May, 1769; m. 1798, Samina, youngest dau. of Samuel Yates, of Moone Abbey, co. Kildare, by his 2nd wife, Catharine, sister of Sir Richard Johnston, Bart. of Gilford, co. Down, and d. Nov. 1842, leaving issue,
1. JAMES DOUGLAS, b. 1803; m. 1828, Charlotte, eldest dau. of John Devereux, of Ballyrankin House, co. Wexford, Major Wexford Militia, and d. 3 Aug. 1840, leaving a dau., Samina Maria, m. 1st, William Wainwright Braddell, of Bullingate, co. Wicklow; and 2ndly, 29 July, 1882, John Daly Devereux, of Ballyrankin, J.P. co. Wexford, and an only son,
   JOHN DOUGLAS JOHNSTONE, who s. his grandfather, 1842, and d. unm. 22 July, 1862.
2. Richard Gosford, b. 1807; d. in Upper Canada, April, 1810.
3. John Douglas, C.B., Major-Gen. in the Army, Col. of the 33rd Regt., served through the campaign in the Crimea, and lost an arm at the first attack on the Redan, 18 June, 1855; m. 1830, Caroline, eldest dau. of the Rev. A. O'Beirne, D.D. She d. 1878. He d. Sept. 1863, leaving issue,
   1. JOHN DOUGLAS, late of Snow Hill.
   1. Samina, m. Capt. Charles C. Barrett, late of the 33rd Regt.
   2. Caroline, m. the Rev. Dr. Stanley, D.D.
4. Fairholme, d. 1832.   5. SAMUEL YATES, of whom presently.
6. William, d. young.
   1. Catherine, d. unm.
   2. Anna Douglas, m. 1837, to her cousin, Francis Bateman Lloyd, of Barranaigue and Moneymohill, co. Limerick, and had issue.
   3. Samina, m. 1829, William Worthington, eldest son of Sir William Worthington, of the city of Dublin, Lord Mayor 1795-6.
The 5th son,

z

Johnstone. THE LANDED GENTRY. 354

SAMUEL YATES JOHNSTONE, of Snow Hill, co. Fermanagh, J.P. and D.L., M.A., Barrister-at-Law, *b.* 12 July, 1815 ; *s.* his nephew John Douglas Johnstone, 1862 ; *d. unm.* 25 March, 1895, and was *s.* by his nephew,

COL. JOHN DOUGLAS JOHNSTONE, of Snow Hill, co. Fermanagh, J.P. and D.L., and High Sheriff 1891, Col. late Duke of Wellington's West Riding Regt. and Royal Sussex Regt., and 101st Regtl. District, served in the Crimean and Abyssinian Campaigns, *b.* 13 Dec. 836 ; *m.* 20 Jan. 1869, Hon. Augusta Anna Margaretta, dau. of Thomas Oliver, 12th Lord Louth (*see* BURKE's *Peerage*). He *d.* 10 Jan. 1906. She *d.* 27 Aug. 1907. They had issue,
1. JOHN DOUGLAS, now of Snow Hill.
1. Anna Maria, *d.* 1874.
2. Randalena Augusta Caroline, *d. unm.*

Seat—Snow Hill, Lisbellaw. co. Fermanagh. *Club*—Primrose, S.W.

JOHNSTONE OF BAWNBOY HOUSE.

ROBERT HENRY JOHNSTONE, of Bawnboy House, co. Cavan, J.P. and D.L. for that co. and J.P. co. Leitrim. *b.* 1849 ; *m.* 1872, Mary Elizabeth, only child of Thomas Blackstock, and has issue,

ARTHUR HENRY, M.I.C.E., B.A., a District Engineer of the E. Indian Railway, *b.* 1873 ; *m.* 1st, Amy (*d.* 1905), dau. of Major E. Jones, late Indian Army ; 2ndly, 1 Oct. 1907, Lilian Margaret, elder dau. of late John Frederick Roberts, of Buenos Aires, and has issue, a dau.

Mr. Johnstone is the eldest son of the late Capt. John Johnstone, 70th Regt., of Swanlinbar, co. Cavan, J.P. (son of Robert Johnstone, who *d.* 1864), by Isabella Eccles his wife, dau. of Capt. John Jameson, 70th Regt., Clonkeen, co. Monaghan.

Seat—Bawnboy House, Cavan.

JONES, late OF HEADFORT.

COL. THOMAS JOHN JONES, R.A., of Moolum, co. Kilkenny, served in Egypt 1882 (mentioned in despatches, medal, star, and 3rd Class Medjidieh), *b.* 16 Dec. 1839 ; *m.* 7 Oct. 1869, Margaret Gertrude, dau. of Sir Theophilus Shepstone, K.C.M.G., and by her (who *d.* 19 June, 1910) had issue,
1. BRYAN JOHN, Capt. Leinster Regt., served in S. Africa 1900-2 (despatches), *b.* 13 May, 1874 ; *m.* 3 Aug. 1911, Grace, only dau. of the late Samuel Henry Stephens, C.I., R.I.C.
2. Eustace Henry, Capt. R.H.A., served in China Expedition 1900, *b.* 2 Oct. 1875.

Lineage.—BRYAN JONES, of the city of Dublin, Auditor at Wars, M.P. for Baltimore 1639-49, descended from an ancient family in Wales, had a grant of lands from King JAMES I. in 1622. He *m.* Elizabeth, dau. of Walter White, of Pitcherstown, co. Kildare, and by her (who *d.* 14 Aug. 1681) had issue,
1. WALTER, his heir.
2. Nicholas, of the city of Dublin, M.P. for Naas 1692 ; *m.* 24 June, 1673, Elizabeth, dau. of John Sargeant, and *d.* Oct. 1695, leaving issue,
  1. Bryan, bapt. 7 Oct. 1675, bur. 28 Sept. 1676.
  2. John, *d.* 29 April, 1678.
  3. Thomas, bapt. 14 Oct. 1680 ; *m.* 1701, Jane, dau. of Elnathan Lum, M.P., of Lumville, King's Co., and *d.s.p.*, bur. 28 Dec. 1720.
  4. Walter, bapt. 6 Nov. 1681, *d.s.p.*
  5. James, bapt. 27 July, 1683. *d.* young.
  6. Arthur, bapt. 13 Nov. 1684, bur. 29 Oct. 1685.
  7. William, bur. 26 July, 1685.
  1. Katherine, bapt. 19 Aug. 1674 ; *m.* Benjamin Chetwode, M.P., and *d.* 1695, leaving a dau.
  2 Elizabeth, *m.* Capt. R. Carthy, and had issue.
  3. Jane, bapt. 16 Nov. 1677 ; *m.* 1st, Rev. Ralph Vigors, and 2ndly, W. Wilson, and had issue.
  1. Mary, *m.* Robert Aickin.

Bryan Jones *d.* 7 Nov. 1671, and was *s.* by his elder son,

WALTER JONES, of Dublin, Auditor of War, High Sheriff co. Leitrim 1682 ; *m.* 13 Jan. 1661, Elizabeth, only surviving child and heir of Rev. William Heward *alias* Hayward, *alias* Hayworth, of Dublin. He *d.* 17 Feb. 1687, having had issue,
1. Thomas, *d.* 1663.
2. THEOPHILUS, of whom presently.
3. Bryan, B.A., M.B., T.C.D., *b.* 7 Oct. 1667 ; *m.* 30 Jan. 1694, Elizabeth, dau. of Edward Crofton, of Mohill, co. Leitrim, and had issue,
  1. Walter, *m.* 1718, Jane Scott, of Cork.
  2. Theophilus, *d.* 1756 ; *m.* 1st, 20 Jan. 1726, Anne, dau. of John Bingham, of Dublin, and had issue,
    (1) Walter, of Lavagh, Drumsna, co. Leitrim ; *m.* 1767, Charlotte Cunningham, of Dublin.
    (2) Bolton, of Headfort, B.A. Trin. Coll. Dublin.
  He *m.* 2ndly, Dec. 1750, Elizabeth, dau. of John Lawder, of Bonnybeg, and by her had issue,
    (3) William Vaughan, of Summerhill. *b.* 1751 ; left issue.
    (4) John, of Headfort, and Lisduff Castle, co. Leitrim, *b.* 1752 ; *m.* Oct. 1794, Abigail, dau. of William Johnstone, of Headfort, and *d.* 1847, having had issue,
      1. Charles, of Taish House, co. Leitrim, *b.* Jan. 1798 ; *m.* 16 Oct. 1828, Jane, dau. of Morgan Meakom, of Mohill. She *d.* 1878. He *d.* 1870, having had issue,
        a. John, of Kilmore House, co. Roscommon, and Gort Lodge, co. Leitrim, *b.* 1831 ; *m.* 1860, Charlotte, dau. of Robert Browne, of Burren Mills, Oak Park, co. Carlow, and *d.* 27 May, 1906, having had issue,
          (a) Bolton Charles, LL.D., T.C.D., of Lincoln's Inn, Barrister-at-Law (8, *Victoria Road, Upper Norwood, Surrey*), *b.* 2 Nov. 1861.
          (b) Theophilus John, *d.s.p.*, bur. 15 Feb. 1880.
          (c) Arthur Henry (*Doneraile, co. Cork*), *b.* 1 June, 1870.
          (d) Walter Alfred, J.P., Ph.D. (*Mount Browne, Strokestown*), *b.* 10 Aug. 1878 ; *m.* 26 Aug. 1907, Birdie Jane G., widow of late Arthur Browne, J.P., LL.B., of Mount Browne, co. Roscommon, and dau. of Robert Ffrench, J.P. of Larchgrove, co. Roscommon.
          (a) Harriette Eva, *m.* April, 1900, Frederick Marsh.
        b. Charles Augustus, of Taish House, *m.* Margaret Blair, and had issue, with a dau., a son, Charles.
        c. William, *m.* 1st, the dau. of William Algeo, of Manor Hamilton, and had issue, William. He *m.* 2ndly, Isabella Mary, dau. of John Booth, of Fenagh, and *d.* 1896, and had issue a son, John, and a dau., Mary, *m.* 1909, Garnett Murphy.
        a. Eliza, *m.* 7 Nov. 1853, David Noble, of Mohill. She *d.* 18 Sept. 1890. He *d.* 9 Oct. 1898, leaving issue.
        b. Maria, *d.s.p.*   *c.* Jane, *m.* — Boyce.
        d. Anne, *m.* James Allen.   *e.* Matilda, *d.s.p.*
      2. William, of Lower Lisduff House, *m.* 1828, Katherine, dau. of Morgan Meakorn, of Lurga. She *d.* 1859, having had issue,
        a. William.   *b.* Arthur, of Lisduff.
        c. Thomas.   *d.* John.
        a. Eliza.   *b.* Emily.
      3. Arthur, *b.* 2 Feb. 1808 ; *m.* Sarah, dau. of Frank Noble, and *d.s.p.*
      4. Bolton Theophilus, *d.* young.
      1. Phœbe, *b.* 26 Nov. 1801 ; *m.* 13 March, 1827, Edward Thorpe, of Drumsna, and had issue.
      2. Anne, *m.* John McClaughery, of Ballykenny, and had issue.
    (5) Edward, of Lavagh, *d.* 1836, leaving a son, the Rev. R. Jones, Rector of Kilmore ; *m.* Mary Dunbar, and *d.* 1840.
    (6) Bryan, *d.s.p.*
    (1) Anne, *m.* 1806, Robert Crofton.
4. William, of Headfort, High Sheriff co. Leitrim 1688, *b.* 25 Oct. 1668.
5. John, *b.* 15 April, 1670.
6. Nicholas (Rev.), bapt. 29 May, 1678, Parish Priest at Donabate.
1. Sarah, bapt. 25 April, 1671.
2. Elizabeth, bapt. 12 Aug. 1673.
3. Mary, bapt. 19 March, 1674-5.
4. Anne, *b.* 23 April, 1680.
5. Jane, *b.* 15 Jan. 1681.

The eldest surviving son,

THEOPHILUS JONES, B.A. Trin. Coll. Dublin, *b.* 2 Sept. 1666, sometime of Bealanamore, co. Leitrim, and afterwards of Headfort, co. Leitrim, M.P. for Sligo 1692 and co. Leitrim 1695-1736. He *m.* 1692, Margaret, dau. of Nicholas Bolton, of Brazeel, co. Dublin, and widow of John Edkins, of Roper's Resi. He *d.* 15 April, 1736, having had issue,
1. WALTER, his heir.
2. Bolton of Drumard, co. Leitrim ; *m.* 1739, Elizabeth, dau. of Hugh Crofton, M.P., of Mohill, and *d.* 1782, having had issue, with two daus.,
  1. Bolton, *d. unm.*
  2. Thomas (Rev.), of Drumard, Rector of Drumliffen, Carrick-on-Shannon, M.A., T.C.D., *m.* 1780, Elizabeth, dau. of John Arabin, of Dublin, and had issue,
    (1) Bolton, *d.* an infant, Oct. 1782.
    (2) Theophilus Bolton, of Drumard, J.P., Major H.E.I.C.S., *m.* 1819, Anne Frances, dau. of Capt. Swain, H.E.I.C.S., and *d.* 1850, having had issue with two daus., Frances, *d. unm.*, and Mary Percy, *m.* George Devenish,

Thomas Josiah (Rev.), M.A., T.C.D., Rector of Tullyniskin, co. Tyrone, b. 1820; m. 1864, Letitia Eleanor, dau. of John Percy, of Garadice, and d. 1889, having had issue,
  a. Theophilus Percy, M.B., Major R.A.M.C., b. 6 Jan. 1866; m. 1896, Ella Isabella, dau. of Major Watts, R.A., and has issue, two sons.
  b. Gervais Bolton, M.D., T.C.D., District Surgeon in Natal, m. 1898, Edith Sophia Greer, and has issue a son, and a dau.
  c. Thomas Bushe (*Banbury, West Australia*), m. 1901, Grace Allum, and has issue, two sons.
  d. Henry Arabin (Rev.), M.A., T.C.D., Rector of Tyrella, co. Down, m. 18 Jan. 1911, Mabel, dau. of John Joseph Hickmott, of The Court, Longfield, and has issue, a dau.:
    a. Letitia Frances. m. 17 March, 1894, Robert Jones Devenish, B.A. Trin. Coll. Dublin, and has issue.
    b. Isabel Mary.
    c. Lavinia Adelaide, m. Steven Brereton Martin, M.A., LL.B., and has issue.
    d. Emily Sophia, m. 26 Jan. 1903, Lewis Audley Marsh Johnston, J.P. (*see* JOHNSTON *of Ballykilbeg*).
(3) Thomas, of Dromard, m. 1830, the dau. of George Percy, of Corduff, and had issue,
  1. William Percy, of Dromard, d. 17 July, 1908; m. 1853, the dau. of — Duke, of Mohill, and had issue,
    a. Bolton, of Dromard, Lieut. 4th Batt. Connaught Rangers, m. Mrs. C. W. Pope and left issue,
      (a) Theodore Bolton, d. unm.
      (b) John Bolton.
    o. William Percy, L.R.C.S.I.
  2. John George, of Kilbracken House, Carrigallon, co. Leitrim, and had issue,
    Thomas George, of Kilbracken.
  3. Thomas George, m. a dau. of — Percy, of Corduff, and left issue.
(1) Harriette.
(2) Elizabeth, m. John Devenish.

The elder son,
WALTER JONES, of Headfort and of Dublin, High Sheriff co. Leitrim 1718, B.A., T.C.D., m. 1722, Olivia, elder dau. and co-heir of Hon. Chidley Coote, of Coote Hall, co. Roscommon, and grand-dau. of Richard, 1st Lord Coloony, and d. May, 1756, having had issue,
1. THEOPHILUS, his heir.
1. Margaret, b. 21 March, 1724; m. 22 March, 1754, Chidley Morgan, 2nd son of Mark Anthony Morgan, M.P., and had issue.
2. Catherine, m. 3 Jan. 1758, Sir Nathaniel Barry, 2nd bart., M.D., and had issue.
3. Elizabeth, m. Edward Crofton.
4. Frances, m. Oct. 1760, Lieut.-Gen. Thomas Bligh, M.P., brother to John, 1st Earl of Darnley. He d.s.p. Aug. 1775.

The only son and successor,
THE RIGHT HON. THEOPHILUS JONES, of Headfort, a Privy Councillor in Ireland, M.P. for co. Leitrim 1767-8, for Coleraine 1769-76, for co. Leitrim 1776-83, for Monaghan 1783-90, and for co. Leitrim 1790-1802, m. 1st, 29 March, 1754, Lady Catherine Beresford, dau. of Marcus, 1st Earl of Tyrone, and widow of Thomas Christmas, by whom (who d. 28 March, 1763) he had issue,
1. WALTER, his heir.
2. Theophilus, of Bolton Row, London, Vice-Admiral of the Red, b. Sept. 1760; d. unm. Nov. 1835.
3. James (Rev.), of Merrion Square, Dublin, Rector of Urney, Diocese of Derry, M.A., T.C.D., m. 1st, Lydia, dau. of Theobald Wolf, K.C., and had by her (who d. in 1793) four sons and two daus.,
  1. Theophilus, of Dublin, Barrister-at-Law, M.A., T.C.D., d. unm. 1867.
  2. Theobald, of Aghadowney, Admiral R.N., M.P. co. Londonderry 1830-57, b. 1790; d. unm. 1868.
  3. James (Rev.), M.A., T.C.D., Chancellor of Armagh 1840, and Rector of Kilmore, co. Armagh, m. Isabella, dau. of Rev. Thomas Quin, of Wingfield, co. Wicklow. She d. 24 May, 1886. He d. 24 Jan. 1871, having had issue,
    (1) James, b. 10 June, 1863, Ellen Danniell, and d. 26 Aug. 1902, leaving issue, James, Jane, and Anne, d. 1887.
    (2) THOMAS JOHN, now of Moolum (*see above*).
    (3) John George, Admiral R.N., b. 9 June, 1844; has issue,
      1. James, Lieut. R.N., b. 1880. 2. John Fleming, b. 1891.
    (1) Ellen Catherine.
    (2) Isabella Elizabeth, d. unm. 28 April, 1878.
  4. Walter, of Belmont, Lifford, and of Harcourt Street, Dublin, m. 1825, Rebecca Anne Galbraith, and had issue,
    (1) James (Rev.), d.s.p.
    (2) Walter, d.s.p.
    (3) Theophilus, Capt. the Buffs, d.s.p. 5 Aug. 1907; m. Jane, dau. of Rev. John Colthurst, Rector of Boveva, Derry. She d. 6 Oct. 1905.
    (4) Theobald, m. and had issue, three sons and two daus.
    (5) John, Lieut. R.N., d.s.p.
    (1) Rebecca, d. unm. 1888.
    (2) Catherine, d. unm. (3) Harriet.
1. Elizabeth, m. Rev. E. Atkinson, d.s.p.
2. Catherine, d. unm.
Rev. James Jones m. 2ndly, 1 Oct. 1796, Anne, dau. of Sir Robert Blackwood, Bart. (by Dorcas his wife, Baroness Dufferin and Claneboye), and relict of the Very Rev. John Ryder, Dean of Lismore, son of John Ryder, D.D., Archbishop of Tuam. Mr. Jones d. in 1835, and was buried at Urney.
The Right Hon. Theophilus Jones m. 2ndly, 1768, Anne, dau. of Col. John Murray, M.P. for Monaghan (by Mary his wife, dau.

of Sir Alexander Cairnes, Bart., and widow of Cadwallader, Lord Blayney), and had by her one son, Henry, who d. young, and two daus., Maria, d. unm., and Anne, d. in infancy. Mr. Jones d. 8 Dec. 1811, and was s. by his eldest son,
WALTER JONES, of Bealanamore, co. Dublin, Headfort, co. Leitrim, Cork Abbey, co. Wicklow, and Hayte Place, Kent, Col. Leitrim Militia, High Sheriff co. Leitrim 1795, and M.P. for Coleraine, b. 29 Dec. 1754; m. 8 Oct. 1805, Katherine Penelope, dau. and co-heir of Rev. Lascelles Iremonger, Vicar of Chadford, co. Southampton, and d. 1839, having had five daus., his co-heirs,
1. MARIA SOPHIA, b. 7 Sept. 1806; m. 27 Feb. 1838, Henry Shovel Marsham, Admiral R.N., son of Hon. and Rev. Jacob Marsham (*see* BURKE's *Peerage*, ROMNEY, E.), and s. to Headfort and Bealanamore. They assumed the surname of JONES. She d.s.p. 21 Dec. 1861. He d. 26 Oct. 1875.
2. KATHERINE PENELOPE, of Headfort and Bealanamore, b. 29 Oct. 1807; d. unm., and was s. by her nephew, George Marsham.
3. ELIZABETH MARCIA, b. 21 Oct. 1810; m. 4 June, 1833, Rev. George Frederick John Marsham, M.A., Rector of Allington, Maidstone, Kent (who was b. 2 June, 1806, and d. 29 Jan. 1842), 5th son of Hon. and Rev. Jacob Marsham, D.D., Canon of Windsor, Prebendary of Rochester and Wells, and grandson of Robert, 2nd Earl of Romney (*see* BURKE's *Peerage*, ROMNEY, E.), and d. 29 April, 1849, leaving with other issue, an only son,
GEORGE MARSHAM, now of Hayle Place, and of Headfort House (*see that family*).
4. Sophia, d. unm. Feb. 1890.
5. Anne, m. William Moore, of Wierton, and d.s.p. 1882.

Arms—Gu., three lioncels rampant guardant or, armed and langued az., on a quarter of the second, a fret of the first. Crest—A talbot's head couped arg., langued and chained gu. Motto—Deus fortitudo mea.

Seat—Lisnawilly, Dundalk.

HAMILTON-JONES OF MONEYGLASS.

EMMELINE ANNIE MABELLA, MRS. TOBIA, of Moneyglass House, co. Antrim, and Jonesborough, co. Armagh, b. 12 April, 1885; m. 29 April, 1910, Arturo Tobia, M.D., Capt. 13th Regt. Artillery, and Cavalieri of the Crown of Iltay, 3rd son of Diament Tobia, of Pinnico, Italy.

Lineage.—MORRES JONES (grandson of Morres Jones, of Ystrad, *temp.* CHARLES II.), m. Anne, dau. of Capt. William Dobbyn, of Duneane House, Toome, by Sarah his wife, sister of "French John" O'Neill, of Shane's Castle, and cousin-german of Jane, wife of Arthur Baron Dawson, of Castle Dawson. Mr. Jones, to whom French John O'Neill granted, as a portion with his niece, a lease in perpetuity of the lands of Moneyglass, d. 15 Sept. 1735, leaving issue, two daus., Mary, d. 1 March, 1755, and Anne, d. 9 April, 1765, and an only son,
THOMAS MORRES JONES, "The Bumper Squire Jones" of Carolan's Muse, m. 1740, Elizabeth, dau. of Robert Cope, of Loughgall, co. Armagh, M.P. for Armagh (*see that family*), and d. Dec. 1760, leaving an elder son,
ROBERT MORRES JONES, who d. unm. 1775, and was s. by his next brother,
THOMAS MORRES JONES, of Ivybrook, b. 1746; m. 1770, Letitia Hamilton, of Glenawly, co. Fermanagh, and by her (who d. *circa* 1814) had issue, four sons and eight daus.,
1. William Morres, d.s.p.
2. Thomas Morres Hamilton, Capt. of the Moneyglass Volunteers, d. from the effects of a fall from his horse. He m. June, 1804, Marianne, dau. of Humphrey Nixon, of Nixon Lodge, and grand-dau. of the Rev. Andrew Nixon, of Belturbet, Vicar of Ahamplisty, but d.s.p. 1807. She m. 2ndly, 1811, Edward Hudson, and had issue.
3. KENRICK MORRES, his heir.
4. Robert Morres, a Lieut. in the Army, d. unm. June, 1794.
1. Elizabeth, m. 1809, Mark Kerr O'Neill, Barrister-at-Law, of Flowerfield, Coleraine, grandson of Felix O'Neill, of Neil's Brook, Randalstown.
2. Mary, m. Rev. William Babington.
3. Ann, m. Capt. Mitchell.
4. Britannia, m. 11 June, 1807, Capt. Humphrey Stewart Nixon, of Nixon Lodge, co. Cavan, nephew of the Right Hon. Sir John Stewart, Bart., M.P.
5. Emma, m. Alexander O'Hara.
6. Letitia, m. Henry O'Hara.
7. Harriet, m. Rev. Charles Henry Crookshank, and d. April, 1868.
8. Helen, m. Capt. Alexander McManus, of Mount Davy's, co. Antrim; she d. 29 March, 1870.
Mr. Jones d. 27 May, 1818, and was s. by his son,
KENRICK MORRES JONES, b. 1785, who assumed his maternal name of HAMILTON; he m. 1818, Mabella, dau. of Major Charles Hill, of Bellaghy Castle, co. Londonderry, and by her (who m. 2ndly, 1837, Lieut.-Col. Arthur Kennedy, 18th Hussars, of Cultra, co. Down, and d. 9 May, 1868) had issue,
1. THOMAS MORRES, his heir.
2. John Charles Hill, Lieut.-Col. 54th Regt., and afterwards Commanding 14th Brigade Depôt at Liverpool, b. 30 March, 1824; m. 15 Jan. 1861, Evelina Gray, only dau. of Col. Alexander William MacKenzie, of the 48th and 18th Regts., and d.s.p. 3 Sept. 1876.

Jones. THE LANDED GENTRY. 356

1. **Mabella**, *m.* 4 April, 1843, Meredith Chambré, of Hawthorn Hill, co. Armagh, J.P., and had issue (see CHAMBRÉ of *Dungannon*).

Mr. Hamilton Morres Hamilton Jones *d.* 31 March, 1830, and was *s.* by his elder son,

THOMAS MORRES HAMILTON-JONES, of Moneyglass House, co. Antrim, Jonesborough, co. Armagh, and The Cottage, co. Fermanagh, 7th Dragoon Guards, J.P. for cos. Antrim, Derry, Armagh, Fermanagh, and Down, and D.L. co. Armagh, served the office of High Sheriff for each of the cos. of Armagh, Antrim, Down, and Fermanagh, *b.* 2 April, 1821; *m.* 4 Aug. 1859, Sara Ellen, only dau. of Lieut.-Col. Edward Day, H.E.I.C.S., of the family of Day, of Kerry, widow of Capt. Francis Spring, of the 24th Regt. of Foot, who was killed in action during the Indian Mutiny, 1857 (leaving a son, William Edward Day, Capt. 24th Regt., who *d.* 13 June, 1886, and a dau., Anne E.), and had issue,

1. KENRICK JOHN CHARLES, of Moneyglass.
2. ARTHUR HENRY MORRES (*Glenderg, Seymour Park, Plymouth*), *b.* 3 June, 1866, Capt. 1st Batt. South Wales Borderers; *m.* 19 July, 1892, Kathleen Travers, 4th dau. of Benjamin Ormsby, of Beaumont, Blackrock, co. Dublin, and has had issue,
   1. Edward Morris, *b.* at Cairo, 27 Feb. and *d.* 5 March, 1893.
   2. Kenrick Morris, *b.* 1894.
   3. Leslie Morris, *b.* 12 July, 1900.
   1. Eileen Sarah, *b.* 28 April, 1897.
1. Mary Lizzie Mabella, *m.* 1st, 6 June, 1890, James B. Byrne, Barrister-at-Law, only son of John A. Byrne, Q.C., of Dublin; he *d.s.p.* 25 Sept. 1891. She *m.* 2ndly, 4 Oct. 1892, her cousin Richard R. G. Crookshank, of Purneah, Bengal, and has issue, a son, Thomas Hamilton, *b.* 19 June, 1893.
2. Emmeline Hawtrey Sara, *m.* 5 June, 1895, Capt. Charles Godby, R.E., eldest son of Major-Gen. J. Godby, late R.A., and has issue.
3. Adeline Ida Sara, twin with Emmeline, *m.* 7 Jan. 1892, Joseph George Auriol Kane, M.D., only son of William F. de Visnes Kane, of Drumreaske, co. Monaghan (see *that family*). He *d.s.p.* 5 April, 1896.

Mr. Hamilton Jones *d.* 3 Sept. 1881, and was *s.* by his elder son,

KENRICK JOHN CHARLES HAMILTON-JONES, of Moneyglass House, co. Antrim, and Jonesborough, co. Armagh, J.P., Capt. 4th Batt. Royal Irish Rifles, *b.* 31 July, 1860; *m.* 22 Aug. 1882, Hannah, dau. of P. McErlain, of Toome, and *d.* 15 Jan. 1887, leaving two daus.,

1. MARY SARA LOUISA, *b.* 31 Aug. 1883; *d.* 20 May, 1899.
2. EMMELINE ANNIE MABELLA, now of Moneyglass.

Seats—Moneyglass House, Toomebridge, co. Antrim; Jonesborough House, Flurrybridge, co. Armagh. Postal Address—91, Via Vinti Settembre, Rome.

JONES OF MULLINABRO'.

JOHN HAWTREY JONES, of Mullinabro', co. Waterford, *b.* 20 Oct. 1843.

Lineage.—FRANCIS JONES, of Mullinabro', co. Kilkenny, who had a grant of that estate and other lands in cos. Kilkenny and Waterford, 4 Oct. 1666, under the Act of Settlement, *m.* Margaret dau. of Bayley, of Castlemoor, co. Cork, and had issue,

1. JOHN, *b.* 6 April, 1651.
2. William, of Parkswood, co. Waterford, *b.* 11 March, 1662.
1. Mary, *b.* 12 Dec. 1652. 2. Frances, *b.* 22 March, 1655.
3. Dorothy, *b.* 12 July, 1667.

He *d.* 25 Nov. 1670, and was *s.* by his son,

JOHN JONES, of Mullinabro', *m.* 7 Aug. 1684, Sarah, dau. of Humphrey Minchin, of Shanagarry, co. Tipperary, and had issue,

1. Francis, *b.* 30 March, 1687; *d.* young.
2. HUMPHREY, *b.* 6 Aug. 1688.
3. John, *b.* 7 Jan. 1690; *d.* 25 Dec. 1691.

He was *s.* by his eldest surviving son,

HUMPHREY JONES, of Mullinabro', J.P. and High Sheriff for co. Kilkenny 1752; *m.* 1st, 13 April, 1721, Eleanor, dau. of Nicholas Toler, of Graig, co. Tipperary, and by her (who *d.* Nov. 1726) had issue,

1. JOHN, his heir.

He *m.* 2ndly, 20 May, 1729, Mary, dau. of John Morris, of Harbour View, co. Waterford, and by her had issue,

2. Humphrey, *b.* 1 Feb. 1730; *d.* young.
3. Humphrey, *b.* 4 Feb. 1736, killed at battle of Quebec.
4. Morris, *b.* 21 July, 1737.
1. Sarah, *b.* 28 Feb. 1731; *m.* 1st, 1749, Edward Whitby; 2ndly, 1753, Rev. William Dennis.
2. Mary, *b.* 8 Sept. 1732; *m.* John Andrews, of King's Co.
3. Anne, *b.* 20 May, 1735.

He *d.* 20 Sept. 1761, and was *s.* by his son,

JOHN JONES, of Mullinabro', *b.* 10 May, 1723, High Sheriff co. Kilkenny 1762; *m.* 1750, Rebecca, dau. of William Morris, J.P. co. Waterford, by Martha his wife, dau. of Richard Reade, of Rosenara, co. Kilkenny, and by her had issue,

1. HUMPHREY, *b.* 30 Sept. 1759; *d.* 12 Feb. 1820.
1. Sarah, *b.* 1754; *m.* John Carew, of Ballinamona, co. Waterford.
2. Mary, *m.* William King; *d.* 1815.
3. Rebecca, *b.* 18 June, 1756.
4. Eleanor, *b.* 1761; *d.* 25 May, 1822.
5. Anne, *b.* 13 Sept. 1760; *m.* Rev. John Hughes.
6. Henrietta, *b.* 1762. 7. Margaret, *b.* 1767.

John Jones *d.* 9 Dec. 1788, and was *s.* by his son,

HUMPHREY JONES, of Mullinabro', *b.* 30 Sept. 1759; *m.* 1st, 30 Sept. 1790, Anne, eldest dau. and co-heir of Rev. Ralph Hawtrey, Rector of Gaulskill, co. Kilkenny, the representative of the eldest branch of the ancient family of Hawtrey, of Escott and Ruislip, Middlesex, and by her (who *d.* 7 Nov. 1806) had issue,

1. John Hawtrey, *b.* 20 Oct. 1791; *d.v.p.* 12 March, 1803.
2. Ralph Hawtrey, *b.* 15 Feb. 1795, killed by a fall from his horse 29 Jan. 1817; *d.v.p.* 3. HUMPHREY, his heir.
4. JOHN HAWTREY, *s.* his brother.
1. Sarah, *b.* 7 April, 1793; *m.* 10 Sept. 1812, Major Oliver Cuffe Jackson.
2. Rebecca, *b.* 15 Feb. 1799; *m.* Jan. 1822 (as 1st wife), William Henry Gabbett, of Caherline, co. Limerick. She *d.* 1828, leaving issue (*see that family*).
3. Mary Anne, *b.* 15 Aug. 1801; *m.* Nov. 1825, George Ormsby, of Gortner Abbey, co. Mayo, and had issue (*see that family*).
4. Eleanor, *b.* 10 July, 1805; *d.* Jan. 1826.
5. Anne Charlotte, *b.* 5 Nov. 1806.

Humphrey Jones *m.* 2ndly, 19 Nov. 1811, Lucy, only dau. of Samuel Newport, and by her (who *d.* 23 Sept. 1877) had issue,

5. Samuel Humphrey, *b.* 28 Jan. 1813.
6. Marmaduke, *b.* 9 March, 1817; dec.
6. Lucy Jane, *b.* 8 Sept. 1814; *d.* March, 1860.

He *d.* 12 Dec. 1820, and was *s.* by his eldest surviving son,

HUMPHREY JONES, of Mullinabro', *b.* 23 Sept. 1802; *d. unm.* 24 Nov. 1825, and was *s.* by his brother,

JOHN HAWTREY JONES, of Mullinabro', J.P. and D.L., High Sheriff 1833, *b.* 23 Dec. 1803; *m.* 24 Aug. 1840, Annie, dau. of William Milward, of Waterford, and *d.* 19 April, 1899, having by her (who *d.* 30 Oct. 1888) had issue,

1. JOHN HAWTREY, now of Mullinabro'.
2. William Milward, R.M., *b.* 12 March, 1846; *d.* 21 July, 1909.
3. Henry Hawtrey, Inspector Royal Irish Constabulary, *b.* 19 April, 1851; *m.* Mary Wesley, and *d.* 9 Oct. 1903, having had issue, two daus., of whom Constance Evelyn, *m.* 20 April, 1911, Harold Ernest Skeffington.
4. Francis, *b.* 18 April, 1854.
1. Marion Jane, *b.* 19 May, 1841; *d.* 27 Aug. 1858.
2. Annie Eliza, *b.* 22 Aug. 1842. 3. Emily, *b.* 26 Oct. 1848.

Seat—Mullinabro', Waterford.

BENCE-JONES OF LISSELAN.

REGINALD BENCE-JONES, of Lisselan, co. Cork, J.P. and D.L., High Sheriff 1894, *b.* 4 Nov. 1865; *m.* 9 Oct. 1890, Ethel Annie, youngest dau. of D.C. Da Costa, of Barbados, West Indies, and has issue,

1. CAMPBELL WILLIAM WINTHROP, *b.* 21 April, 1894.
2. Philip Reginald, *b.* 12 Jan. 1897.

Lineage.—WILLIAM JONES, of Blackrock, Cork, *m.* Eleanor, dau. of William Winthrop, of Cork, Mayor of Cork 1744, and had issue.

WILLIAM, his heir.
Alicia, *m.* Nov. 1795, Rev. Morgan Donovan, of Montpellier, The O'Donovan.

The only son,

LIEUT.-COL. WILLIAM JONES, 5th Dragoon Guards, of Lisselan, co. Cork, and Theberton Hall, Saxmundham, *m.* 1811, Mathilda, dau. of the Rev. Bence Bence, of Thorington Hall, Suffolk, Rector of Beccles, and *d.* 6 Aug. 1843, leaving issue,

1. WILLIAM BENCE, his heir.
2. Henry Bence, F.R.S., M.D., D.C.L. of 84, Brook Street, London, *b.* 1813; *m.* 28 May, 1842, Lady Millicent Acheson, dau. of Archibald, 2nd Earl of Gosford. He *d.* 20 April, 1873. She *d.* 29 Aug. 1887, leaving issue,
   1. Henry Robert (12, *Victoria Square, S.W., and New University Club*), *b.* 18 April, 1844.
   2. Ralph Noel, *b.* 1845; *d. unm.* 17 Feb. 1866.
   3. Archibald Bence, M.A., Barrister-at-Law (56, *Upper Berkeley Street, W.*; 11, *King's Bench Walk, Temple, E.C.*; *Athenæum, Garrick, and Arts Clubs*), *b.* 24 July, 1856; *m.* 1 June, 1901, Hon. Susan Ludlow Cordelia Lopes, eldest dau. of 1st Lord Ludlow, and has issue,
      Millicent Cordelia Susan, *b.* 1903.
   1. Millicent Mary (12, *Victoria Square, S.W.*).
   2. Olivia Mary (46, *Montagu Square, W.*).
   3. Edith Mary, *m.* 1889, Edward James Stapleton, of Warbrook, Eversley, Hants, who *d.* 1896.
3. Frederick Pembroke, *m.* Emma, dau. of W. Delmar, of The Elms, Canterbury.

The eldest son,

WILLIAM BENCE-JONES, of Lisselan, co. Cork, J.P., M.A., Barrister-at-Law, *b.* 5 Oct. 1812; *m.* 6 July, 1843, Caroline, dau. of William Dickinson, of Kingweston, M.P. for Somerset. She *d.* July, 1886. He *d.* 22 June, 1882, having had issue,

1. WILLIAM FRANCIS BENCE, his heir.
2. REGINALD BENCE, now of Lisselan.
1. Caroline Sophia, *m.* 16 Aug. 1877, Francis Henry Blackburne Daniell, only son of Capt. George Daniell, R.N., and Alice Catherine his wife, dau. of the Right Hon. Francis Blackburne, Lord Chancellor of Ireland.
2. Mary Lilias, *m.* 1 Feb. 1886, Rev. R. H. Charles, M.A., son of D. H. Charles, M.D., of Cookstown.
3. Philippa Frances, *m.* Aug. 1885, Sir Frederick Albert Bosanquet, K.C., Common Serjeant of the City of London and has issue (*see* BOSANQUET *of Dingestow*).

The elder son,

WILLIAM FRANCIS BENCE-JONES, of Lisselan, co. Cork, b. 9 March, 1856; d. unm. 20 Nov. 1883, and was s. by his only brother.

Seat—Lisselan, Clonadilty, co. Cork. *Club*—United University.

JONES OF ARDNAREE.

HENRY HASTINGS JONES, of Ardnaree, co. Mayo, J.P. cos. Mayo and Sligo, High Sheriff co. Sligo 1890, late Capt. 4th Batt. King's Own Royal Lancaster Regt., formerly Lieut. 3rd Batt. Connaught Rangers, b. 12 April, 1865 ; m. 27 March, 1899, Alice Carrie, dau. of the late Richard Harvey, of Aliwal North, Cape Colony, and Commissie Drift, Orange River Colony, and has had issue,
1. THOMAS GEORGE CLAYTON VAUGHAN, b. 4 Nov. 1907.
2. Lawrence Charles Kennedy Vaughan, b. 4 Dec. 1909.
1. Marjorie Christian Helena Vaughan, b. 11 Sept. 1900; d. 7, Jan. 1901.
2. Marjorie Helena Elizabeth Vaughan, b. 16 Feb. 1906.

Lineage.—THOMAS JONES, of Ardnaree, co. Mayo, High Sheriff co. Sligo 1707, m. Mary, sister of Thomas Smith, of Mullpit, co. Galway. His will, dated 16 March 1710, was proved 9 Jan. 1716. He had issue,
1. GEORGE, his heir.
2. Thomas, m. Rebecca, dau. of James Barrett, and d.s.p. His will was dated 4 March, 1719.
3. Arthur. 4. Charles.
1. Mary, m. Francis Waldron, of Cartron and Scurmore, co. Roscommon, and had issue (*see that family*).

The eldest son,
GEORGE JONES, of Ardnaree, whose will is dated 1720. He left issue by Christian his wife (who m. 2ndly, Edward Ormsby) with four daus., two sons.
1. Thomas, of Ardnaree, m. Mary, sister of Arthur Vaughan, of Carramore, co. Mayo. His will, dated 14 Sept. 1749, was proved 30 June, 1750. He d.s.p.
2. VAUGHAN, of whom we treat.

The younger son,
VAUGHAN JONES, of Scurmore and Ardnaree, s. his brother, and left issue, by Ann his first wife: 1. THOMAS, of whom presently. 2. George. 3. Charles; and 1. Anne. He m. 2ndly, 1758, Catherine, dau. of Robert Bowne, of Fortland, co. Sligo, and by her he was ancestor of the family of JONES of Fortland. He d. 1798. The eldest son,
THOMAS JONES, of Ardnaree, m. 1779, Frances, 4th dau. of Col. Fergus Kennedy, and d. 1838, leaving a son,
THOMAS JONES, of Ardnaree and Castletown, co. Sligo, J.P. and D.L. cos. Mayo and Sligo, High Sheriff 1835, m. Anne, dau. of T. J. Atkinson, of Cavangarden, co. Donegal, and left issue,
1. THOMAS, of Ardnaree.
1. Elizabeth, m. Capt. Oliver Vaughan Jackson, of Carramore (*see that family*).
2. Frances, m. Sidney Vaughan Jackson (*see JACKSON of Carramore*).
3. Anne, m. Capt. Hamilton, R.N.

The only son,
MAJ. THOMAS JONES, of Ardnaree, J.P. and D.L. co. Sligo, J.P. co. Mayo, Maj. 4th Royal Irish Dragoons, m. 10 Feb. 1863, Anne Eliza, dau. of Ralph Walters, M.P., of Newcastle-on-Tyne. She d. 7 April, 1886. He d. June, 1868, leaving issue,
1. HENRY HASTINGS, now of Ardnaree.
2. Thomas Frederick Newcome, Capt. 4th Royal Irish Dragoon Guards, b. 3 Aug. 1866 ; killed in action near Jamrud on the Afghan front, 10 Oct. 1897, d. unm.
3. Walter Vaughan, late Major 4th Batt. Royal Inniskilling Fus., b. 2 Jan. 1868 (*Junior United Service Club*).

Arms—Per pale az. and gu., three lions rampant between as many mullets arg., a bordure engrailed or. *Crest*—A buck statant arg. charged with a trefoil slipped az., between the attires a bugle horn stringed of the last. *Motto*—Cervus lacessitus leo fit.

Seats—Ardnaree, Ballina, co. Mayo; Rathlee, Easky, co. Sligo. *Club*—Constitutional.

JONES, late OF JONESBORO', CO. MEA

FREDERICK WILLIAM NOBLE JONES, b. 1 Jan. 1862; m. 1 Jan. 1889, Edith Maude, dau. of Edward Turner, of Sydney, N.S.W., son of William Turner, of Bedfont, Middlesex, and has had issue,
1. ERIC EDWARD NOBLE, b. 20 Sept. 1889 ; d. 1 Jan. 1910.
2. Frederick James Noble, b. 17 Dec. 1898.
1. Kathleen Helen Noble, b. 26 Feb. 1892 ; d. 15 Jan. 1908.

Lineage. — WILLIAM JONES, of Crossdrum, co. Meath, will dated 8 June, 1703, left issue,
1. AMBROSE, of whom next.
2. Thomas.
1. Mary, m. Joseph Raphson. 2. Frances.

AMBROSE JONES, of Drewstown, co. Meath, will dated 4 1732, proved 3 July, 1734 ; m. Elizabeth, dau. of and left issue,
1. WILLIAM, of whom next.
2. Thomas, of Oldcastle, co. Meath, will dated 22 April, 1; proved 12 April, 1738 ; m. Pinninah, dau. of
3. Ambrose, of Liss, co. Meath, Lieut. R.N., will dated 10 N 1764, proved 10 Jan. 1765, and 6 Feb 1767 ; m. Hannah, d of—St. Clair, of Oldcastle (who m. 2ndly, mar. lic. 1768, Re Towers), and had issue,
 1. Mary, m. Richard Davis.
 2. Margaret, m. — Henery.
 3. Martha, m. — Leet.
 4. Sarah, m. — Folliott.
 5. Anne, m. — Notley.

WILLIAM JONES, of Newtown, co. Meath, will dated 6 Jan. 174 codicils 17 May, 1748, and 15 Aug. 1749, proved 16 Sept. 174 m. mar. lic. 21 Jan. 1723, Sarah, dau. of Edward Rotherham. H will dated 18 Aug. 1757, proved 26 Sept. 1757, left issue,
1. Edward, of The Grove, co. Meath, will dated 29 June, 178 proved 18 June, 1787 ; m. mar. lic. 19 Aug. 1761, Mary, dau. of — Irvine.
2. Ambrose, of Jonesboro or Kilcunny, near Kells, co. Meath d. March, 1786, will dated 22 April, 1783, proved 13 Dec. 1786 m. mar. lic. 1767, Elizabeth, dau. of — Jones, who d. 7 April, 1790 aged 58, leaving issue,
 FREDERICK EDWARD, of whom next.
 Elizabeth Amelia, m. mar. lic. 13 Jan. 1787, James Cusack, of of Jamestown, co. Meath.
3. John, of Newtown, will dated 21 Nov. 1798, proved 29 Nov. 1803 ; m. April, 1759, Elizabeth, dau. of George Hardman, Alderman of Drogheda.
 1. Elizabeth, d. unm. before 1757.
 2. Jane, d. unm. admon. 15 Jan. 1768.
 3. Sarah, m. mar. lic. 1767, Edward Jones.

FREDERICK EDWARD JONES, of Jonesboro, co. Meath, d. 15 May, 1813, will dated 1801, proved 1813 ; m. mar. lic. 11 Feb. 1793 Margaret, dau. of — Holdcroft, and left issue,
1. FREDERICK AMBROSE, of whom next.
2. Henry Robert, d. 1815.
1. A dau. 2. A dau.
3. A dau. 4. A dau.

FREDERICK AMBROSE JONES, of Jonesboro, co. Meath, b. 19 Dec. 1793; d. 5 Oct. 1836 ; m. 1831, Mary, dau. of Frank Noble, of Doonera, Mohill, co. Leitrim, left issue,
FREDERICK AMBROSE NOBLE, of whom next.
Maria Teresa, d.s.p.
FREDERICK AMBROSE NOBLE JONES, of Evelyn Mansions, Victoria, b. 29 Nov. 1833 ; d. 6 Feb. 1904 ; m. 1856, Helen, dau. of James Ellaway, of Bristol, left issue,
FREDERICK WILLIAM NOBLE (*see above*).

Arms—Or, three lions rampant guardant gu., armed and langued az., on a canton vert, a fret of the first. *Crest*—A talbot's head couped arg. langued gu., collared vert fretty or. *Motto*—Deus Fortitudo Mea.

Residence—" Jonesboro," Gerrards Cross, Bucks.

JOYCE OF CORGARY.

WALTER JOYCE, of Corgary, co. Galway, J.P., b. 25 June, 1865.

Lineage.—The descent of the family from a remote period is very fully given in Mac Firbis' " Genealogies," and also in the pedigree of Gregory Joyce, certified 17 Sept. 1790, by Ulster King of Arms (Pedigrees, Ulster's Office, Dublin Castle).

1. s Joyce, of Galway, m. Elizabeth Lynch, and was father of
Rik Joyce, of Galway, m. Jane Aylward, and d. 1754, leaving
Ddaus., one m. MacDonnel; another Ulick Burke; and Bridget,
Mr. ird, Martin Blake; also five sons,
s. b Pierce, his successor.   2. Mathew, M.D.
TRobert.   4. Thomas.
AntGregory.
nagEldest son,
Pierce Joyce, m. 1761 (settlement dated 29 Jan.), Frances, dau.
Hi hn Kelly, of Limerick (see Kelly of Rockstown Castle and
an more), and by her, who predeceased him, had issue,
da Walter, his heir.   2. John, d. 1818.
of Jane, m. 1787, James Blake, of Cregg Castle, co. Galway.
whse Joyce d. 1786, and was s. by his eldest son,
so Alter Joyce, of Merview and Corgary, J.P. co. Galway, a
amber of the Irish Volunteers of 1782, b. 1763; m. 1st. 1 Sept.
3, Margaret, dau. of Peter Daly, of Clooncha, co. Galway, by
wife, Helen, dau. of Philip Roche, and by her, who d. 1803, had
son and two daus.,
1. Walter, his heir.
. Frances, a nun in the Presentation Convent, Galway, d. 1840.
2. Helen, m. Charles Lynch, D.L., of Barrycurran Castle, co. Mayo;
'. 1845.
. Joyce m. 2ndly, 1806, Helen, dau. of Thomas Appleyard, by
wife Helena, dau. of Michael Kelly, of Limerick, by whom he
t issue,
2. Pierce, of Mervue (see that family).
3. Thomas Appleyard, of Rahasane Park, co. Galway, J.P.,
High Sheriff 1852, b. 18 June, 1819; m. 1844, Julia Frances, only
child of Major Bisshopp, 10th Regt., K.H., by Julia his wife, dau.
of William Talbot, of Castle Talbot, co. Wexford, and d. 1878,
leaving issue,
    1. William Walter Patrick, of Rahasane Park, b. 26 Feb. 1845,
    Major (retired) late Prince of Wales' Own (W. Yorkshire) Regt.
    2. Thomas Appleyard, b. 23 July, 1848.
    3. Frederick Talbot, b. 1 Jan. 1850.
    4. Arthur Edward, b. 10 May, 1851.
    5. Edward Aloysius Gonzaga, b. 24 June, 1857.
N   1. Elizabeth Helena Mary.   2. Julia Thomasina, dec.
    3. Agnes Mary Pia.
H1. Helen, m. 1835, Charles Lynch.   2. Christina.
4 3. Eliza, m. 1832, Cornelius J. O'Kelly, and is dec.
1 4. Theresa, m. 1838, Ambrose O'Kelly, and is dec.
  5. Mary Aloysia, dec.
Ir. Joyce d. 4 July, 1853, and was s. by his eldest son,
Walter Joyce, of Corgary, co. Galway, b. 1801; m. 12 Jan. 1829,
hristina, dau. of John Kelly, D.L., of Ballintlea, co. Clare, and by
er (who d. Jan. 1859) had issue,
    1. Walter, his heir.   2. John, of Nagilka, co. Galway.
    3. Peter, d. unm.   4. James, of Rockstown, co. Limerick.
    1. Mary.
    2. Christina, a nun, Laurel Hill Convent, Limerick.
Ir. Joyce d. at Toulouse, France, 18 Feb. 1871, and was s. by his
ldest son,
Walter Joyce, of Corgary, co. Galway, J.P., b. 1 June, 1831;
1. 18 July, 1859, Louisa, dau. of James Daly, of Castle Daly, J.P.
o. Galway; by his wife Margaret, dau. of Hubert Dolphin, of Turoe
ee Dolphin of Turoe), and had with other issue,
Walter, now of Corgary.
Ir. Joyce d. 1883, and was s. by his eldest son, Walter Joyce,
ow of Corgary.

Seat—Corgary, Castle Blakeney, co. Galway.

JOYCE OF MERVUE.

Pierce John Joyce, of Mervue, co. Galway,
.P., High Sheriff of Galway Town 1867, b. 5 Nov.
844; m. 16 June, 1875. Selina Henrietta, dau. of
harles George Mahon. J.P. and D.L., of Mount
leasant, co. Mayo, and by her (who d. 1898) has
ad issue,

1. Pierce Charles, Capt. Connaught Rangers, b. 23 June, 1878.
2. Henry Ross, b. 21 Nov. 1881; d. 1882.
1. Henrietta Kathleen, b. 18 June, 1876

Ir. Joyce is eldest son of Pierce Joyce, of Mervue,
.P. and D.L., who d. 14 Oct. 1883, by Jane Mary
is wife, dau. of Francis Blake, of Cregg Castle, co.
alway.

Seat—Mervue, Galway.

KANE OF DRUMREASKE.

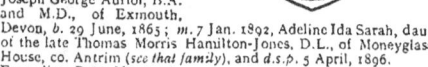

William Francis
de Vismes Kane, of
Drumreaske, co. Monaghan, M.A., J.P. and
D.L., High Sheriff
1865 and 1909, b.
9 April, 1840; m.
1st, 2 Sept. 1862,
Amelia Maria Jane,
only dau. of the Rev.
Charles James Hamilton, Incumbent of
Kimberworth, co.
York, and by her
(who d. March, 1901)
has issue,

Joseph George Auriol, B.A.
and M.D., of Exmouth,
Devon, b. 29 June, 1865; m. 7 Jan. 1892, Adeline Ida Sarah, dau.
of the late Thomas Morris Hamilton-Jones, D.L., of Moneyglass
House, co. Antrim (see that family), and d.s.p. 5 April, 1896.
Emmeline Rosa Margaret.

He m. 2ndly, 26 Nov. 1902, Hon. Louisa
Catherine, dau. of 1st Lord Bateman and widow
of Col. Henry Green Wilkinson, Scots Fus. Guards.

Lineage.—In the year 1715, Joseph, son of Matthew Kane,
of Dublin, drew up for the information of posterity, a pedigree which
gives the names and marriages of his ancestors, and sets forth that
Hugh O'Kane (who m. Mary, dau. of O'Connor Faly), with his
youngest brothers, Manus and Roderick (mentioned in Sir H.
Docwra's Narration), went out of Ulster into Leinster about the
year 1570. His father, Roderick M'Manus O'Kane (m. Mary,
dau. of O'Donnell), whose ancestry is given in McFirbis and
elsewhere, was chieftain of O'Kane's country, which included the
county of Derry, and possessed several strongholds, the most noted
of which were the castles of Limavady, Enagh, and Dungiven, co.
Derry, and Dunseverich, in the co. Antrim. His son, Sir Donell
O'Kane, who m. Una, dau. of O'Neil, Earl of Tyrone, was
treacherously seized by the English, 1607, and d. in the Tower of
London in 1626, under charge of high treason of which he was
never convicted, but his property was divided among the civic
companies of London.

The above-mentioned Hugh was great-grandfather of
Matthew Kane, of Dublin, who d. 1690, and left, by Sarah his
wife, two sons.
1. Joseph Kane, Lord Mayor of Dublin 1725, who d. without
male issue.
2. Nathaniel Kane, Lord Mayor of Dublin 1734, who established, in connection with David Digues La Touche, the Bank of
Kane and La Touche, in Dublin. He m. Martha, only dau. of
Ephraim Thwaites, of Dublin, and by her (who d. 27 July, 1741)
had issue,
    1. Nathaniel, b. 12 Aug. 1750; d.v.p. unm.
    2. Joseph, of whom presently.
    1. Elizabeth, m. 1737, Matthew Weld, of Dublin, whose dau.
    Esther, m. the Right Rev. John Brinkley, Astronomer Royal
    of Ireland, Lord Bishop of Cloyne.
    2. Martha, d. unm., will proved 1765.
    3. Mary, m. June, 1727, Alderman John Walker, Lord Mayor
    of Dublin 1744-5.
    4. Esther, d. 24 Aug. 1752.

His grandson,
Joseph Kane, of Baggot Street, Dublin, and Harold's Cross,
near Dublin (2nd son of Nathaniel Kane, Lord Mayor of Dublin),
was called to the English Bar; he m. Mrs. Mary Maxwell (née
Church), and had issue,
1. Nathaniel, his heir.
2. Joseph Thomas, m. 1st, Mrs. Elizabeth Stock, which lady
d.s.p.; and 2ndly, Frances, eldest dau. of the Rev. John Crossley
Seymour, Vicar of Cahirelly, and had issue, one son and three
daus.; he d. 1837.
3. John Daniel, Lieut.-Col. 4th The King's Own Regt., Inspecting
Field Officer of Yeomanry and Volunteers from 1803, served in
Nova Scotia 1793, and in the Exped. to the Helder, b. 20 May,
1770; m. 1st, 11 April, 1795, Louisa Phillips, and by her (who d.
Apr.l, 1807) had a son.
    1. John Joseph, of the Grange, Monmouth, Lieut. 4th The
    King's Own Regt., Capt. and Adjt. of the Royal Monmouthshire Militia, served in America, 1814-1, and Army of Occupation, France, where he was A.D.C. to Brig.-Gen. Brooke,
    b. 31 May, 1796; m. 3 Dec. 1827, Sarah Ann, sole surviving
    child and heiress of Richard Willis, Major of the Monmouth
    Local Militia, and Ann his wife, dau. and eventual co-heir of
    Thomas Apperley, of Scudamore, Herefordshire. She d.
    14 May, 1886. He d. 1 Oct. 1876, leaving issue,
        (1) John Fielding Willis, Capt. 48th Regt., b. 3 Nov. 1833;
        d. unm. in India, 1 Feb. 1880.
        (2) Richard Nathaniel (Rev.), M.A. Oriel Coll. Oxford,
        Rector of Suckley, co. Worcester, J.P., b. 24 Aug. 1835;
        m. 19 May, 1874, Mary Evans, elder dau. of the late
        Thomas Rowley Hill, of St. Catherine's Hill, Worcester,
        and Suckley, Worcestershire, M.P., and has issue,

1. John Feilding Hill, 2nd Lieut. Rifle Brigade, *b.* 22 Oct. 1876 ; *d. unm.* on service on N.W. Frontier, India, 23 Oct. 1897 (Indian Frontier medal).
2. Richard Willis Hill, of Suckley, Worcs., *b.* 25 Sept. 1879 ; *m.* 2 Feb. 1911, Phyllis Mary, youngest dau. of Richard Barrett, of Merton Park, Surrey, and has issue, a son, *b.* 11 Dec. 1911.
3. Christopher Rowley Hill, *b.* 3 Jan. 1890.
1. Kathleen Mary, *m.* 10 April, 1901, William Gerald Woolrych, of Woolthorpe, Queensland, 4th son of the Rev. William H. Woolrych, Vicar of Crowle, co. Worcester, and has issue.
2. Mabel Grace, *m.* 1905, Clement Michael Spurling, and has issue.
3. Sarah Joyce, *m.* 1908, Frederick Roberts, of Cricklewood, Proserpine, N. Queensland, and has issue.
4. Margaret Feilding, *m.* 27 Jan. 1909, George Seton Briscoe, 4th Worcestershire Regt., son of late J. G. Briscoe, of Ballincollig, co. Cork.
5. Bridget Stanhope.
(3) Edward, *b.* 1 May, 1837 ; *d.* 25 March, 1906 ; *m.* 1865, Mora Inez Bellini, and had issue,
Robert Edward Bellini, *b.* 1865.
Lily Sarah Beatrice.
(4) Charles George, Lieut.-Col. late 9th Regt., assumed the name of BAGNALL-O'CAHAN in lieu of KANE, *b.* 5 March. 1839 ; *m.* 0 June, 1877, Emma Anne, only child and heiress of Rev. Henry Bagnall, Rector of Great Barr, Stafford.
(5) Francis William Feilding, Lieut.-Col. late 3rd Regt. (the Buffs), assumed the name of FEILDING-KANE, 1885, *b.* 6 June, 1841 ; *m.* 17 Feb. 1876, Maud Legh, only dau. of John Plunkett, of Rathmore Abbey, co. Meath. He *d.s.p.* 15 March, 1909.
(6) Robert, *b.* 26 Aug. 1843, late 16th Regt. ; *m.* 23 Jan. 1869, Henrietta, eldest dau. of C. J. Coursol, Judge of Sessions of Peace, Montreal, Canada, and grand-dau. of Sir Etienne Tasché, and *d.* 29 April, 1900, leaving issue,
1. Robert Joseph Willis, *b.* 11 Aug. 1871 ; *d.* 4 Jan. 1877.
2. Roderick Auguste Coursol, Capt. 3rd Regt. Victoria Rifles of Canada, *b.* 1 Sept. 1875.
1. Mary Sarah Henriette. 2. Alice Mary Clare.
(1) Sarah Anne (*The Grange, Monmouth*).
(2) Louise Mary, *d.* an infant.
(3) Ellen (*The Grange, Monmouth*).
2. Eleanor Jessé, *b.* and *d.* April, 1807.
1. Louisa, *d. unm.*   2. Caroline, *d. unm.*
3. Augusta, *m.* George Michael McGuire, and had issue.
4. Matilda, *d. unm.*
5. Emma, *m.* Frederick Dunbar, Capt. 39th Foot, and had issue. 6. Susan Hester, *d. unm.*
7. Ellen, *d.* young.
Col. J. D. Kane *m.* 2ndly, Eliza, dau. of John Morgan, of Birch Grove, co. Glamorgan, only widow of Capt. George Morgan, of the Foot Guards, only son of Gen. George Morgan, of Weald Side, Essex, by whom he had no issue ; he *m.* 3rdly, Anna, dau. of Henry Belson, of Dublin, and sister of General Belson, by whom he had one son,
3. Henry John Belson, C.E., *d.* 14 March, 1884.
Col. John Kane *d.* 11 Aug. 1847.
1. Matilda, *m.* Capt. William Moore, of H.M. Regt. of Royal Irish Artillery, cousin of the Marquess of Drogheda ; *d.* without issue.
2. Esther, *m.* Robert Creed, of Osbertstown.

The eldest son,
NATHANIEL KANE, of Baggot Street, Dublin, and Harold's Cross, near Dublin, Lieut.-Col. H.M. 4th Regt., *m.* 1802, Elizabeth, eldest dau. of Francis Nisbett, of Derrycarne, co. Leitrim, and by her (who *d.* 1858) had issue,
1. JOSEPH, his heir.
2. Nathaniel, Capt. 62nd Regt., *d.* 6 Sept. 1844.
3. Francis, M.A. T.C.D., Rector of Fenagh, co. Leitrim, *m.* 1864, Anne, dau. of Rev. J. Shea, of Dublin, and *d.* 1885.
4. John, of The Castle, Mohill, B.A. T.C.D., J.P. and D.L. of co. Leitrim, *b.* 1810 ; *m.* 1st, 1839, his cousin, Matilda, dau. of Matthew Nisbett, D.L., J.P., of Derrycarne, co. Leitrim, and by her (who *d.* 1861) had issue,
1. Matthew Nisbett Gordon, *b.* 1845, Major late Seaforth Highlanders.
2. John Cambreth, *b.* 1849 ; *m.* 4 Dec. 1902, Annette, dau. of Rev. Arthur Hyde, Canon of Elphin (*see* HYDE *of Castle Hyde*).
1. Elizabeth Mary, *d.* 1858. 2. Madeline Mary.
Mr. John Kane *m.* 2ndly, 1859, Anne, dau. of Rev. Arthur Hyde, Rector of Mohill, and *d.* 1880, leaving by her a son,
3. Arthur Hyde, Major R.A., *b.* 6 Sept. 1870 ; *m.* 1908, Marian Fletcher, and has issue.
5. William, M.D., *m.* Caroline Ann, 3rd dau. of Gen. Charles Dallas, Governor of St. Helena, which lady *d.s.p.* 1862.
6. Matthew, A.M., M.D., Surgeon-Major H.M. Indian Army, of H.M. Mint, Bombay, *b.* 26 April, 1817 ; *m.* 1842, Catherine Eliza Clementina, eldest dau. and co-heiress of William G. Kirkpatrick, of Isleworth, and *d.* 1892, leaving issue,
1. Nathaniel Henry Kirkpatrick, B.A., M.D., *b.* 1847 ; *m.* 1884, Kathleen Marion, dau. of William Elphick, M.R.C.S., of Plaistow, Essex, and *d.* 1896, leaving issue.
2. Francis Richard Pennefather, *b.* 10 July, 1854, Lieut.-Col. E. Surrey Regt., *m.* 1887, Joanna, dau. of Rev. W. Grey Smith, of Over Dinsdale, Yorkshire.
1. Elizabeth Catherine, *m.* 1878, Charles A. White, and *d.* 1895, having had issue.
2. Emily Matilda Christine, *d.* 1874.

3. Helen Strachey, *d.* 1851.
4. Annie Caroline, *d.* 1851. 5. Nissa Georgina.
6. Edith Maria, *m.* 1892, Kenneth McLaren, M.B.
7. Ella Marcia, *d.* 1879.
Col. Kane *d.* in 1826, and was *s.* by his eldest son,
JOSEPH KANE, of Baggot Street, Dublin, and Withycombe Grange, Devon, *b.* 1803, *m.* 1837, Eliza Jane, Mademoiselle de Vismes, only dau. of Col. the Count de Vismes of the Coldstream Guards (*see* BURKE's *Peerage, Foreign Titles*), by Mrs. Hall, *née* Salt, his wife, sister to Dr. Salt, the celebrated traveller, and *d.* 1841, having by her (who *m.* 2ndly, 1844, the Rev. Thomas Shelford, Fellow of Corpus Christi College, Cambridge, and Rector of Lambourne, Essex, and *d.* 1853, leaving a dau., Emmeline Susan) had issue,
1. Nathaniel de Vismes, *d.* in infancy, 1839.
2. WILLIAM FRANCIS DE VISMES, now of Drumreaske.
1. Eliza Jane Margaret, *d. unm.* March, 1861.

Arms—Gu., three fishes haurient arg., in the centre chief point an estoile or. Crest—A naked arm embowed ppr. charged with an estoile gu. and holding a sword also ppr.

Seat—Drumreaske House, Monaghan.

KAVANAGH OF BORRIS.

WALTER MACMORROUGH KAVANAGH, of Borris, co. Carlow, J.P. and D.L. co. Carlow, High Sheriff 1884, J.P. co. Kilkenny, and High Sheriff co. Wexford 1893, M.P. for co. Carlow 1908-10, late Capt. 5th Batt. Royal Irish Rifles, *b.* 14 Jan. 1856 ; *m.* 1 Feb. 1887, Helen Louisa, dau. of Col. John S. Howard, and has issue,

1. ARTHUR THOMAS, Lieut. 7th Hussars, *b.* 12 Jan. 1888.
2. Dermot, *b.* 9 Jan. 1888.

Lineage.—DERMOT MACMORROUGH, King of Leinster, whose lineage is traced to far distant times, *d.* May, 1170, and was father, with a dau., Princess Eva, of DONELL CAOMHANAGH, or Donel the Handsome. King of Leinster, who was the immediate ancestor of this powerful Irish sept. His descendants were elected Kings of Leinster down to the reign of HENRY VIII., and the Chief was acknowledged as "The MacMorrough" by the English. Donell was slain 1175, and was *s.* by his son,
DONNELL OGE CAVANAGH, who was given as a hostage to Roderick O'Conor, King of Ireland, and was slain by him. His son,
MORTAGH KAVANAGH MACMORROUGH, was slain at Arklow in 1281, and was *s.* by his son,
MORTAGH KAVANAGH, elected King of Leinster, who was summoned to attend EDWARD II. against the Scots 1314. His descendant, according to the pedigree registered in Ulster Office,
ART BOY KAVANAGH, of Borris and St. Molins, co. Carlow, and Poulmonty, co. Wexford, *temp.* EDWARD IV., had two sons,
1. CAHIR, his successor.
2. Moriertagh mac Art boy, ancestor of KAVANAGH, of Templeudigan and Ballyleigh, the representative of whom, JOHN BAPTIST KAVANAGH, Baron of Ginditz in Bohemia, *d.* 1774, leaving issue.
The elder son,
CAHIR MAC ART BOY KAVANAGH, of Borris, Lord of Ballyanne, co. Wexford, Captain of his nation, was created by patent, dated 8 Feb., 1 and 2 MARY I., Baron of Ballyanne for life. He left issue,
1. Morough or Morgan, called Bacragh, or the lame, Baron of Cowellelleyn, *d.s.p.*
2. Gerald, a hostage for his father, 1537.
3. Dermot, created by patent, dated 18 March, 2 and 3 PHILIP and MARY, Tannist, or successor to his brother, *d.s.p.*
4. BRIAN, who carried on the line.
5. Crean, a hostage for his brother 1556.
1. Honora, *m.* Rowland Masterson, of Ballyshannon, co. Wexford.
Lord Ballyanne *d.* before 1554. His 4th son,
BRIAN MAC CAHIR KAVANAGH, of Borris and Poulmonty, was in rebellion 1572. He *m.* Elinor, dau. of Hugh Byrne, of Rathangan, co. Wicklow, and had issue,
1. MORGAN, his heir.
2. Edmond, of Ballyknockstaggard, co. Carlow, whose line is extinct.
3. Gerald, of Ballybrannagh, ancestor of KAVANAGH, of Rocksavage and Inch, and HENRY KAVANAGH, a Baron of the Kingdom of Austria.
4. Morish, of Ballybrack, whose line is extinct.

Keane. THE LANDED GENTRY. 360

1. Elinor, *m.* Donel Kavanagh, "Spainagh," of Clonmullen. Brian Kavanagh *d.* 1575, and was *s.* by his eldest son,
MORGAN KAVANAGH, of Borris and Poulmonty, who *m.* 1st, Hon. Elinor Butler, dau. of Edmund, 2nd Viscount Mount Garratt, and had issue,
1. BRIAN, his successor. 2. Charles.
3. Edmund. 4. Arthur.
He *m.* 2ndly, Joan, dau. of Nicholas Morres, of Templemore, co. Tipperary, by whom he had an only dau.,
1. Joan.
He *d.* 19 June, 1636, and was *s.* by his eldest son,
BRIAN KAVANAGH, of Borris, who *m.* 1st, Elinor, dau. of Sir Thomas Colclough, Knt. of Tintern Abbey, by whom he had two daus.,
1. Elinor. 2. Anne.
He *m.* 2ndly, Elinor, dau. of Sir Edward Blancheville, Knt., of Blanchevillestown, co. Kilkenny, and had issue,
1. MORGAN, his heir.
3. Elizabeth, *m.* Hon. John Fitzpatrick, son of Brian, 6th Lord Upper Ossory. 4. Alice.
5. Mary, *m.* Charles Kavanagh, of Carrickduff, 2nd son of Sir Morgan Kavanagh, of Clonmullen.
Mr. Kavanagh *d.* 1 Dec. 1662, and was *s.* by his son,
MORGAN KAVANAGH, of Borris, who *m.* Mary, dau. of John Walsh, of Piltown, co. Waterford, and was *s.* by his only son,
MORGAN KAVANAGH, of Borris, who *m.* 1st, Frances, dau. of Sir Lawrence Esmonde, 2nd bart. of Ballytrammon, and had issue,
1. BRYAN, his successor. 2. Henry, *d.* 28 April, 1741.
3. Charles, General in the Austrian Army, Governor of Prague 1766.
He *m.* 2ndly, Margaret, dau. of Hervey Morres, of Castle Morres, co. Kilkenny, and had another son,
4. Hervey, of Ballyhale, co. Kilkenny, *m.* April, 1732, Mary, dau. and heir of John Meade, of Ballyhale; *d.* 1740, leaving, with a dau., Mary, *m.* Luke Masterson, of Moneyseed, co. Wexford, a son,
Morgan, of Ballyhale, *m.* Lady Frances Butler, dau. of Walter Butler, of Garryricken, and sister of John, 17th Earl of Ormonde and Ossory, and *d.* 1817, having had (with two daus., Elinor, *m.* 17 March, 1792, George Lidwill, of Dromard, and *d.* 2 Sept. 1802, leaving issue; and Margaret, *d. unm.*) a son,
Walter Hervey, of Ballyhale, *m.* Mary, dau. of Edward Newland, of St. James' Square, London, and *d.* 1853, leaving, with five daus., a son,
Morgan, of Ballyhale, *m.* Elizabeth, dau. of James Gordon Grant, and *d.v.p.* 1848, leaving Morgan Butler, of Seville Lodge, co. Kilkenny, J.P., and Merrion Square, Dublin, Barrister-at-Law, *b.* 25 June, 1815; *m.* 10 Aug. 1875, Katie, only surviving child of Eugene Shine, of Seville Lodge, and *d.* 8 Oct. 1882, having by her (who *m.* 2ndly, 23 July, 1883, John Francis Moriarty, K.C., First Serjeant at-Law) had issue, 1. MORGAN BUTLER, *b.* 23 May, 1876; 2. Eugene Rupert, *b.* 10 Jan. 1878; 3. Henry, *b.* 14 March, 1879; 4. Walter, *b.* 3 April, 1880; 1. Mary, *m.* Michael Quinlan, Surgeon in the Army; 2. Nano, *m.* John P. Byrne, of Ballybohill.
Mr. Kavanagh *d.* 1720, and was *s.* by his eldest son,
BRYAN KAVANAGH, of Borris. *m.* Mary, dau. of Thomas Butler, of Kilcash, and sister of the 15th (*de jure*) Earl of Ormonde, and dying 1741, left, with six daus., of whom the eldest, Margaret, *m.* Richard Galwey, a son,
THOMAS KAVANAGH, of Borris, *m.* 1755, Lady Susanna Butler, sister of John, 17th Earl of Ormonde, and *d.* 1790, having had issue,
1. Walter, who *d.s.p.* 1813. 2. Brian, *d.s.p.*
3. Morgan, *m.* 1792, Alicia, only child of Michael Grace, of Gracefield, Queen's Co., and *d.s.p.* 1804.
4. THOMAS, of whom presently.
1. Helena, *m.* Sept. 1782, James Archbold, of Davidstown.
2. Mary, *m.* George Butler, of Ballyraggett. 3. Honora.
The 4th son and eventual inheritor,
THOMAS KAVANAGH, of Borris House, *b.* 10 March, 1767, M.P. for the city of Kilkenny in the last Irish Parliament, and subsequently representative for co. Carlow in the last two Parliaments of GEORGE IV. and 1st WILLIAM IV.; *m.* 1st, 24 March, 1799, Lady Elizabeth Butler, dau. of John, 17th Earl of Ormonde, and by her (who *d.* 1822) had issue, a son, Walter, who *d.* 1836, and nine daus., of whom six *d. unm.*; the other three were, Anne, *m.* Henry Bruen, of Oak Park, co. Carlow, and *d.* 1850; Susanna, *m.* Major Richard Doyne; and Grace, *m.* John St. George Deane, of Berkeley Forest, co. Wexford, and *d.s.p.* Mr. Kavanagh *m.* 2ndly, 28 Feb. 1825, Lady Harriet Margaret Le Poer Trench, dau. of Richard, 2nd Earl of Clancarty, and left at his decease, 20 Jan. 1837,
1. THOMAS, of Borris. 2. CHARLES, of Borris.
3. ARTHUR, of Borris.
1. Harriet Margaret, *m.* Col. W. A. Middleton, C.B., R.A.; *d.* 7 May, 1876.
The eldest son,
THOMAS KAVANAGH, of Borris, *d. unm.* in Australia, March, 1852, and was *s.* by his brother,
CHARLES KAVANAGH, of Borris, *b.* 28 Jan. 1829; *d. unm.* Feb. 1853, and was *s.* by his brother,
THE RIGHT HON. ARTHUR MACMORROUGH KAVANAGH, of Borris, Lord-Lieut. of that co., sworn one of H.M. Most Hon. Privy Council in Ireland 1886, M.P. co. Wexford 1866-8, and co. Carlow 1869-80, J.P. and D.L., High Sheriff co. Kilkenny 1856, and co. Carlow 1857, *b.* 25 March, 1831; *m.* 15 March, 1855, Frances Mary, only surviving child of Rev. Joseph Forde Leathley. She *d.* 2 June, 1908. He *d.* 1889, having had issue,
1. WALTER MACMORROUGH, now of Borris.
2. Arthur Thomas MacMorrough, *b.* 27 Aug. 1857; *d.* 1882.

3. Charles Toler MacMurrough, C.V.O., C.B., D.S.O., Col. late 10th Hussars, *b.* 25 March, 1864; *m.* 1895, Mary, dau. of S. Perry, of Woodroffe, co. Tipperary (*see that family*), and has issue.
4. Osborne MacMorrough, third Sec. to the British Embassy, *b.* Aug. 1869; *d. unm.* 15 Dec. 1897.
1. Eva Frances MacMorrough, *m.* 27 July, 1882, Cecil Alexander, son of the Archbishop of Armagh, and *d.* 27 Sept. 1896. He *d.* 31 March, 1910, having had issue (*see* ALEXANDER *of Forkhill*).
2. May Sabina MacMorrough, *m.* Henry Stock, of Knolle Park, Liverpool.
3. Agnes Mary MacMorrough, *m.* 17 Nov. 1886, Henry Bruen, eldest son of the Right Hon. Henry Bruen, P.C., of Oak Park, co. Carlow (*see that family*).
Arms—Arg., a lion passant gu. in base two crescents of the last. Crest—Between the horns of a crescent, a garb gu. Motto—Siothchain agus fairsinge, *i.e.*, Peace and plenty.
Seats—Borris House, Borris, co. Carlow, and The Lodge, Ballyragget, co. Kilkenny. Clubs—Carlton and Sackville Street, Dublin.

KEANE OF BEECH PARK.

MARCUS THOMAS FRANCIS KEANE, of Beech Park, co. Clare, J.P. and D.L., High Sheriff 1905, *b.* 31 July, 1854; *m.* 28 July, 1903, Henrietta Mary, dau. of the late Major William Mills Molony, D.L., of Kiltanon, co. Clare (*see that family*), and has issue.
MARCUS WILLIAM, *b.* 2 Jan. 1906.
Helen Louise.

Lineage.—This branch of the Keane family came from co. Londonderry at the time of the plantation of Ulster.
OWEN KEANE settled at Ballyvoe, near Ennis, about the middle of the 17th century. He *m.* Judith, a dau. of Robert Shaw, of Galway, and had one son,
ROBERT KEANE, *b.* 1690; *m. circa* 1730, Mary, dau. of Robin Keane, of Ross, co. Clare, and had three sons,
1. Robert, whose sons *d.s.p.* 2. CHARLES, of whom we treat.
3. Patrick, who *m.* Anne, dau. of Robert Crowe, of Ennis.
The 2nd son,
CHARLES KEANE, of Corbally, co. Clare, *m.* 1766, Anne, dau. of Robert Harding, of Limerick, and dying 1802, left (with two daus., Mary, *m.* Robert Creagh, of Dangan, and Anne, *m.* William Power, two sons, CHARLES KEANE, Major R.A., who *d.* in the West Indies, 1812, without issue, and
ROBERT KEANE, of Beech Park, J.P., *b.* 1774; *m.* Dec. 1799, Jane, eldest dau. and co-heiress of Thomas Delahunty, by his wife Susan, only dau. and heiress of James Colpoys, of Crusheen, and by her (who *d.* 9 Feb. 1842) had issue,
1. Charles, M.D., *m.* 1832, Sarah, dau. of Andrew James Watson, and *d.v.p.s.p.* 16 Aug. 1832. His widow *m.* 2ndly, George Ellis, M.D., of Dublin, and *d.* in 1870.
2. FRANCIS NATHANIEL, of Hermitage, near Ennis, J.P., *b.* 27 Oct. 1803; *m.* July, 1827, Hannah Maria (who *d.* 3 July, 1883), dau. of Sir Christopher Marrett, Knt. of Limerick, and *d.* 18 May 1880, having had issue,
1. Robin, *d. unm.* Dec. 1856.
2. Christopher Marrett, *d. unm.* March, 1857.
3. Charles, Capt. 86th Regt., *d. unm.* April, 1876.
4. FRANCIS BURTON of Hermitage, J.P., *b.* 17 Oct. 1844; *m.* 14 Nov. 1871, Mary, dau. of W. G. Gubbins, of Castle Troy, co. Limerick, and widow of Isaac North Bomford, of Gallow and Ferrans. She *d.* 15 Jan. 1895. He *d.* 20 Aug. 1908, having had issue,
(1) Francis Thomas, *b.* 24 Aug. 1872, dec.
(2) Charles Owen, *b.* 11 Sept. 1875; *m.* 1907, Alice, youngest dau. of Thomas O'Gorman, of Buncrangy.
(3) Robert Giles, *b.* 17 June, 1882; *m.* 28 March, 1904, Eliza Sophia, eldest dau. of late Francis Weldon Walshe, J.P., of Piltown, co. Kilkenny, and *d.* leaving a dau., Lorraine.
(1) Mary Sarita, *m.* 9 June, 1897, W. J. Macnamara (*see* MACNAMARA *of Doolen*).
(2) Olive Maria.
(3) Ethel Frances.
5. William Henry, *d.* young.
1. Hannah Maria.
2. Jane, *m.* 6 Oct. 1863, Walter James Pollard, Capt. R.N., son of William D. Pollard, of Castle Pollard, co. Westmeath. He *d.* 27 June, 1879, leaving issue (*see* POLLARD-URQUHART).
3. Sarah.
4. Susannah, *d.* 17 March, 1897.
3. Thomas, of Kilballyowen, co. Clare, J.P., *m.* Anne, dau. of

Thomas Crowe, of the Abbey, Ennis, and *d.s.p.* 1870. She *m.* 2ndly, Rev. G. W. Tyrrell, and *d.* 1876.
4. Giles, late Col. 86th Regt., *m.* Sept. 1861, Mary, dau. of George Ellis, and *d.s.p.* in Sept. 1867. She *m.* 2ndly, 1870, Maj.-Gen. H. W. Holland, C.B., and *d.* 1881.
5. Robert, of Dublin, *m.* Mary Anne, dau. of John Code. She *d.* June, 1882. He *d.* 1873, having had three daus.,
 1. Mary Letitia, *m.* Joseph Parkinson.
 2. Jane, *m.* 13 Oct. 1875, A. G. Parkinson.
 3. Anne, *m.* Edward Moore.
6. MARCUS, *s.* to Beech Park.
7. William (Rev.), Rector of Whitby, Yorkshire, *b.* Feb. 1818; *m.* Nov. 1853, Elizabeth, dau. of the Hon. John Fryer Thomas, Member of Council at Madras. She *d.* 26 March, 1908. He *d.* 24 May, 1873, having had issue,
 1. John Thomas, *b.* 4 Oct. 1854.
 2. Robert Keane Charles, *b.* 22 Feb. 1856, dec.
 3. Marena William Alison, dec.
 1. Hilda Elizabeth, *m.* 4 Aug. 1878, Rev. George Carter, of Farnborough, and has issue.
 2. Jane Maria Colpoys, *m.* 1 May, 1879, Espine Ward, and has issue.
8. Henry. *m.* 1864, Aphra, dau. of John Locke, of Newcastle, co. Limerick, and relict of Alexander Casey, of Shandrum, co. Clare. She *d.* 1877. He *d.* 1884, leaving a dau..
 Aphra Jane, *m.* James Gloster, of Rock Vale, co. Limerick.
 1. Anne, *m.* Thomas Pilkington, of Waterpark, Ennis, and *d.* 1875.
 2. Susannah, *m.* 1826, John Armand Dubourdreu, and *d.* 20 Nov. 1842. He *d.* 1843.
 3. Maria, *m.* 25 Nov. 1844, Rev. Charles Ward, Vicar of Kilmaley, and had issue.
 4. Jane, *m.* 1851, John Rutherford, of Kinsborough, Parsonstown.
 5. Charlotte, *d. unm.* 10 Nov. 1893.
Mr. Keane *d.* 1839, and was *s.* at Beech Park by his 6th son,
 MARCUS KEANE, of Beech Park, co. Clare, J.P., *b.* 7 Feb. 1815; *m.* 9 Nov. 1847, Louisa Isabella, 3rd dau. of Nicholas Westby, of Clare (*see* WESTBY *of Roebuck Castle*), and by her (who *d.* 3 Oct. 1894) had issue,
 1. Percival William, *b.* 12 Sept. 1848; *m.* 25 Sept. 1873, Mary Frances, only dau. of Rev. Robert Ellis, of Rash House, co. Tyrone. He *d.* 28 April, 1910, having had issue by her (who *d.* 29 July, 1911), a dau., Isabella Louisa.
 2. Robert Charles George, *b.* 5 Nov. 1851; *d.* 6 Nov. 1858.
 3. MARCUS THOMAS FRANCIS, now of Beech Park.
 4. Granville Giles, *b.* 17 July, 1861; *d.* in Batavia, 21 July, 1882.
 5. Frederic Colpoys, Capt. Carmarthen and Clare Artillery (73, *Goldington Avenue, Bedford*), *b.* 11 March, 1868; *m.* June, 1898, Rose Dorothea, dau. of the late Maj.-Gen. William Roberts Farmar, of Bedford House, Southampton (*see* FARMAR *of Bloomfield*), and has issue,
 1. Anthony Colpoys, *b.* 6 July, 1899.
 2. Marcus Hugh, *b.* 23 Nov. 1901.
 3. Granville, } twins, *b.* 24 July, 1905.
 4. John Colpoys, }
 5. Nicholas Colpoys, *b.* 17 Feb. 1908.
 1. Jane Mary, *d.* young, 6 Oct. 1857.
 2. Louisa Caroline.
Mr. Marcus Keane *d.* 29 Oct. 1883.
Arms—Quarterly: Gu. and or, in the 1st and 4th quarters a salmon naiant arg.; in the 2nd and 3rd quarters a tree vert. **Crest**—A wild cat rampant guardant ppr. gorged with an antique Irish crown or, and charged on the shoulder with a trefoil vert. **Motto**—Felis demuleta mitis.
Seats—Beech Park, Ennis; and Doon Dahlin, Carrigabolt, co. Clare. **Club**—Kildare Street, Dublin.

BUTLER-KEARNEY OF DROM.

CHARLES JAMES BUTLER-KEARNEY, of Drom, co. Tipperary, and of Three Castles, co. Kilkenny, High Sheriff co. Kilkenny 1903, Lieut.-Col. late R. Munster Fusiliers, assumed the additional surname and arms of KEARNEY, by Royal Licence dated 30 April, 1876, upon *s.* to a moiety of the estates of his cousin, James Charles Kearney, *b.* 25 Oct. 1851; *m.* 5 June, 1873, Georgina Hannah, youngest dau. of the late Robert Clarke, of Bansha Castle, co. Tipperary (*see* CLARKE *of Craiguenoe*), by Anne his wife, dau. of Capt. R. Butler, 27th Regt., and has issue,

1. Charles James, *d.* an infant, 1874.
2. THEOBALD WILLIAM, late Lieut. 2nd Batt. Leinster Regt., *b.* 15 May, 1876.
3. Trench Frank, *b.* 20 Dec. 1877.
4. George Fitzwalter, *b.* 15 Dec. 1881.
1. Mary Violet.

Lineage (*of* KEARNEY).—REV. JOHN KEARNEY, D.D., Vicar-General of the Diocese of Ossory, and Vicar of Dunkitt by patent dated 11 March, 1637. He held the lands of Garranbehy under the Duke of Ormonde. He *m.* Judith, dau. of Capt. David Serment, of Lismacteigue, co. Kilkenny, J.P., and made his will 3 Feb. 1665, which was proved 27 Feb. 1665. He left two sons and two daus.,
 1. RICHARD, his heir.
 2. John, *d.* 1693, leaving a son, Hugh, and three daus., Mary, Elizabeth, and Anne.
 1. Elizabeth, *m.* Hugh Drysdale, D.D., Archdeacon of Ossory.
 2. Mary.
REV. RICHARD KEARNEY, of Parkstown, co. Kilkenny, Rector of Dysertinoon and Rosbercon, *d.* Sept. 1690, having had issue by his wife Elizabeth Stewart (with a dau., Elizabeth), three sons,
 1. JAMES, his heir. 2. John, *b.* 1667. 3. Richard.
The eldest son,
 JAMES KEARNEY, of Kearney Bay, co. Kilkenny, *m.* Katherine, dau. of Benjamin Alcock, and had issue,
 1. BENJAMIN, his successor.
 2. Richard, of Waterford, who, by his wife, Miss Fleming, had issue,
 James, of Watertord, who *m.* Anne, dau. of William Alcock, of Wilton, co. Wexford, and had issue,
 William, of Waterford, who *m.* Martha, dau. of Charles Backas, M.D., of Waterford, and had issue, two sons,
 1. William Richard, *b.* 1805 } both of whom *d. unm.*
 2. Richard James,
 1. Martha, *m.* Capt. William Moore, R.N.
 2. Anne, *m.* Capt. Henry Bolton, R.N.
 3. Nicholas, left a son, Benjamin.
The eldest son,
 BENJAMIN KEARNEY, of Blanchville, High Sheriff co. Kilkenny 1761, *d.* 1784, having had issue by his wife, Anne, dau. and heir of Fitzgerald, of Brambleston, co. Kilkenny.
 1. JAMES, of whom presently. 2. John, *d.s.p.*
 3. Michael, *m.* Gertrude, dau. of Thomas Hickman, and had issue, eight children. 4. Richard.
 1. Mary, *m.* 14 July, 1756, Nicholas Aylward, of Shankhill Castle, co. Kilkenny.
The eldest son,
 JAMES KEARNEY, of Blanchville, High Sheriff co. Kilkenny 1782, *m.* Susanna, dau. of Henry Flunt, State Apothecary, and had issue,
 1. Benjamin James, *b.* 1774; *a.s.p.*
 2. JAMES, of whom presently.
 3. John, *m.* Anne Waller, dau. of Rev. Cadogan Keatinge, and with three daus., Waller, Anne, Susan, left one son,
 John Cadogan, Major in the Army, killed in China.
 4. Charles, Lieut.-Col. of the Queen's Bays, *b.* 1798; *m.* 8 Oct. 1829, Mary Anne, dau. of the Hon. George Eyre Massy, and *d.* 1871.
 1. Elizabeth, *m.* 1805, Nicholas Aylward, of Shankhill Castle, and was mother of JAMES KEARNEY AYLWARD, of Shankhill Castle, who assumed the additional surname of KEARNEY, 1876.
 2. Anne, *m.* 1815, Rev. Theobald Butler (*see below*), whose grandson, CHARLES JAMES BUTLER, of Drum, co. Tipperary, assumed the additional surname of KEARNEY, 1876.
The 2nd, but eldest surviving son,
 SIR JAMES KEARNEY, K.C.H., of Blanchville, Lieut.-Col. 2nd Regt. of Dragoon Guards, and eventually a Lieut.-Gen. in the Army and Col. of the 7th Hussars, *b.* 1777; *m.* Margaret, dau. of Clayton Bayley, of Gowran, co. Kilkenny, and by her, who pre-deceased him, had issue,
 1. JAMES CHARLES, his heir.
 1. Mary, *d. unm.* 2. Susan, *d. unm.*
 3. Catherine, *d. unm.*
 4. Margaret, *m.* Charles Tottenham, of MacMorrogh, and *d.* 27 Feb. 1852.
 5. Anne Waller, *m.* 9 June, 1842, Rev. Hans Atkinson, and *d.* 14 Aug. 1844, leaving an only dau., Alice, *m.* Rev. Joseph Stewart (*see* STEWART *of Ballymenragh*).
Sir James *d.* 23 Feb. 1814, and was *s.* by his only son,
 JAMES CHARLES KEARNEY, of Blanchville, Lieut. 2nd Regt. of Dragoon Guards (Queen's Bays), High Sheriff co. Kilkenny 1855-56, *b.* 4 Jan. 1814. Mr. Kearney *d.s.p.* 1876, when his estates devolved on his cousins, JAMES KEARNEY AYLWARD, of Shankhill, and CHARLES JAMES BUTLER, of Drom, who both assumed, by Royal Licence 1876, the additional surname and arms of KEARNEY.

Lineage (*of* BUTLER).—THEOBALD BUTLER, of Killoskehan, co. Tipperary, 3rd son of James 2nd Lord Dunboyne, and Margaret, his second wife, dau. of the 4th Earl of Thomond, *m.* Eleanor, dau. of — O'Meagher, of Rouleabane, co Tipperary, and *d.* before 1660, leaving issue,
 1. JAMES, of whom presently.
 2. Thomas, *m.* Catherine, dau. of Edmund Butler, of Belacaring, and was great-grandfather of James Butler, Capt. in the French Service and Knight of St. Louis in 1735.
 3. Piers, ancestor of the BUTLERS *of Priestown, of Maiden Hall, co. Kilkenny, and of Waterville, co. Kerry* (*see those families*).
The eldest son,
 JAMES BUTLER, of Killoskehan, and Drom, co. Tipperary, restored to his estate in 1661, *m.* Margaret, dau. of — Bourke, and had a son,
 JAMES BUTLER, of Killoskehan and Drom, *m.* the dau. of — Dalton, and had a son,

Kelly. THE LANDED GENTRY. 362

RICHARD BUTLER, of Wilford and Drom, *m*. Margaret, dau. of Morgan O'Brien, and had issue,
1. THEOBALD, of whom presently.
2. Piers, of Glasshouse, who left issue.
3. James, of Park, co. Tipperary, ancestor of BUTLER *of Park*.

The eldest son,
THEOBALD BUTLER, of Wilford, whose will dated 1794, was proved 8 May, 1795, *m*. 1st, Bridget, dau. of Edmund Butler, of Wilton, co. Kilkenny, and by her had two daus.,
1. Bridget, *m*. John Willington, of Killoskehan.
2. Anne, *m*. her cousin, William Butler, of Park.

He *m*. 2ndly, Elizabeth, dau. of Edward Lee, of Waterford, and by her had issue,
1. Theobald, *d. unm. v.p.*
2. WILLIAM, of whom presently.
3. James, of Lisduffe, co. Tipperary, *m*. Catherine, dau. of — Howley, of Killenaule, co. Tipperary, and left two daus.
4. Francis, of Moncouill, co. Tipperary, and Castletown, Queen's Co., *m*. Hannah, dau. of Robert White, of Aghavoe, Queen's Co. (*see* WHITE *of Charleville*), and *d*. 1815, leaving issue.
5. Edward, of Drangan, co. Tipperary.
6. Richard.   7. Piers.
8. Mary, *m*. 1st, 1787, John, 12th Baron Dunboyne, sometime Bishop of Cork, and 2ndly, John Hubert Moore, and *d*. Aug. 1860, aged 96.
4. Elizabeth, *m*. Thomas McLoughlin.

He *m*. 3rdly, Mary, dau. of James Hackett, and by her had issue,
5. Elinor, *m*. Rev. John Aldwell, of Moyne, co. Tipperary.
6. Catherine.   7. Frances.

The eldest surviving son,
WILLIAM BUTLER, of Wilford, and Drom, *m*. Caroline, dau. of Hugh, 1st Lord Massy. She *d*. 1837. He *d*. 3 Jan. 1802, having had issue,
1. THEOBALD, his heir.
1. Caroline, *m*. Hugh Barret.
2. Emma.
3. Frances, *m*. Valentine Browne, of Galway.
4. Mary Anne.
5. Jane.
6. Bridget.

The only son,
REV. THEOBALD BUTLER, of Drom, *m*. 1815, ANNE, dau. of JAMES KEARNEY, of Blanchville, co. Kilkenny (*see above*), and had issue,
1. WILLIAM, his heir.
2. James, *m*. 21 June, 1851, Emily Dorothea, dau. of Charles Putland, of Bray Head, co. Wicklow (*see that family*), and had issue, an only child,
 Emily Mary Eliza, *m*. April, 1894, Hector J. C. Toler-Aylward, of Shankill Castle, co. Kilkenny (*see that family*).
3. Theobald.
1. Anne.   2. Catherine.
3. Elizabeth.

The eldest son,
WILLIAM BUTLER, of Drom, *b*. 1819, *m*. 1842, Catherine, only dau. of John Lloyd, of Lisheen Castle, co. Tipperary, and *d*. 1870, having had issue,
1. CHARLES JAMES, now of Drom.
2. Francis, *b*. 1853.
1. Amelia, *m*. Charles E. Clarke.
2. Emma Anne.

Arms—Quarterly: 1st and 4th, arg., three lions rampant gu. on a chief az. between two pheons or, a gauntleted hand in fess of the last, holding a dagger of the first, pommel and hilt gold, for KEARNEY; 2nd and 3rd, or, a chief indented az. three escallops in bend counterchanged, for BUTLER. *Crest*—1st, KEARNEY, A gauntleted hand in fess, holding a dagger arg., pommel and hilt gold ; 2nd, BUTLER, Out of a ducal coronet or, a plume of five ostrich feathers arg., issuant therefrom a demi-falcon also arg., motto over, Timor Domini fons vitæ. *Motto*—Sustine et abstine.

Seats—Drom, co. Tipperary, and Three Castles, co. Kilkenny. *Club*—Junior Army and Navy, W.

KELLY OF MUCKLON.

MAJOR ARTHUR DILLON DENIS KELLY, of Mucklon, Ballyforan, co. Galway, and Weston, Duleek, co. Meath. THE O'KELLY, Major late 1st Batt. Border Regt., J.P. co. Meath. *b*. 5 Dec. 1853 ; *m*. 17 April, 1895, Henrietta, youngest dau. of the late Hon. Chichester Thomas Skeffington, brother of John, Viscount Massereene and Ferrard, K.P.

Lineage.—The representative of this family claims to be chief of his name as being the eldest descendant of William Boy, 21st or 27th O'Kelly, founder of the Abbey of Kilconnel (*see* the recorded pedigree in Ulster's Office, vol. 1, p. 166).

BRYAN KELLY, of Ballyforan, *m*. Jane Oshaldistone, and left issue,
1. Hugh, of Ballyforan, *b*. 1655 ; *m*. Elizabeth, dau. of — Harborne, and *d*. July, 1689, having by her (who *m*. 2ndly, Rev. William Hodson, Rector of Belturbet) had issue,
 1. Bryan, of Ballyforan, *m*. 8 Oct. 1703, Elizabeth, dau. of Daniel Molyneux, of Ballymulvey, co. Longford, and *d*. 1706, having by her (who *m*. 2ndly, Rev. Lemuel Shuldham, and 3rdly, Buckley Butler) had issue,
  (1) Katherine, *m*. 1st, John Hawkins, and 2ndly, James Smith.   (2) Elizabeth, *m*. William Hewetson.
 2. Hugh, of Ballyforan, *d.s.p.*
 3. Edmund, of Ballyforan, *m*. Bridget McHugo, and *d*. Jan. 1745-6, leaving issue,
  Hugh, *m*. 3 July, 1750, Mary, dau. of Dominick Daly, of Benmore, co. Galway, and had issue,
   1. Edmund, of Ballyforan, *m*. 22 July, 1779, Clara, dau. of Sir Charles ffrench, 1st Bart., of Castle ffrench, co. Galway (*see* BURKE'S *Peerage*, FFRENCH B.), and *d*. 1794, leaving a dau., Clara Rosetta, *m*. Anthony D'Arcy, of Gurteen, co. Galway, who *d*. 1815.
   2. Daniel, *d*. 1794.   1. Mary.
  Elizabeth, *m*. 1752, Stephen Donellan, who *d*. 1794.
 4. Daniel, of Ballyforan, *d.s.p.* o Aug. 1759.
 5. Denis, *d.s.p.*   6. Robert, *d.s.p.*
 1. A dau., *m*. Redmond O'Fallon.
2. WILLIAM, of whom presently.
3. Daniel, Capt., living 1709, left issue.

The 2nd son,
CAPT. WILLIAM KELLY, of Mucklon, co. Galway, living 1714, left issue, a son,
DANIEL KELLY, of Mucklon, also living 1714, who left a son,
WILLIAM KELLY, of Mucklon, *m*. Elizabeth, dau. of Bryan Mahon, of Castlegar, co. Galway, and *d*. 2 March, 1748, leaving issue,
1. Denis, of Mucklon, *m*. 22 July, 1752, Prudence, dau. of Carncross Nesbitt, and *d.s.p.* 1 Dec. 1785.
2. Ledwith, of Imlagh, co. Roscommon, *d.s.p.* 11 Nov. 1756.
3. DENIS, of whom presently.   4. Bryan.
1. Elinor, *m*. Edmund McDermot   2. Elizabeth.
3. Catherine.

The third son,
DENIS KELLY, of Mucklon, *b*. 1734 ; *m*. 1772, Catherine, dau. of Richard French, Lord Mayor of Dublin, and *d*. 1813, leaving issue,
1. Denis, of Mucklon, *m*. Lucy, dau. of H. P. L'Estrange, of Moystown, and *d.s.p.* 1820.
2. George, *d.s.p.* Sept. 1851.
3. Edward, scholar at Trinity Coll. Dublin, and afterwards a surgeon in the Army, lost at sea, *d.s.p.*
4. RICHARD, of whom presently.
5. James, *m*. Anne, dau. of E. Roper, and *d*. March, 1847, leaving issue,
 1. Denis (Rev.), *d.s.p.*
 2. Robert, Capt. 83rd Regt., whose issue is settled in New Zealand.
 1. Catherine, *m*. 22 June, 1833, Richard Pennefather Lloyd, and had issue (*see* LLOYD *of Rockville*).
6. William, Lieut. 66th Regt., carried the regimental colour at Talavera, *d*. of wounds.
7. John, Lieut. R.N., *d*. at the Cove of Cork, 1810.
1. Lucy, *m*. E. Roper.

The 4th son,
COL. RICHARD KELLY, of Weston, co. Meath, of the 24th Regt., commanded the 66th Regt. at the Battle of Talavera. m. in Ceylon, 1814, Anne, dau. of Francis Thomé, and *d*. 18 June, 1846, having by her (who *d*. 30 Sept. 1861) had issue,
1. RICHARD (Sir), of whom presently.
2. Francis James, of Weston, co. Meath, J.P., *b*. 19 Sept. 1819; *m*. 9 Jan. 1862, Catherine, dau. of Benjamin Geale Brady, of Mount Geale, co. Kilkenny. He *d*. 22 July, 1908.
 1. Annie Maria, *m*. Feb. 1857, H. Battersby, of Larkfield, co. Westmeath, who *d.s.p.* 1868 (*see* BATTERSBY *of Laughbawn*). She *d*. 18 Dec. 1910.
 2. Catherine Elizabeth, *d. unm.* 1 July, 1892.

The elder son,
GEN. SIR RICHARD DENIS KELLY, K.C.B., of Mucklon, Ahascragh, co. Galway, and Shrublands Earley, Berks, Gen. in the Army, and Col. of the Border Regt., *b*. 9 March, 1815 ; *m*. 2 March, 1848, Ellen Susanna, dau. of Sir William Dillon, Bart. of Lismullen, co. Meath, and *d*. 2 July, 1897, leaving by her, who *d*. 8 Feb. 1903, issue,
1. ARTHUR DILLON DENIS, now of Mucklon.
2. Richard Makdougall Brisbane Francis, C.B., D.S.O., Col. R.A., Comdg. Artillery Southern Defences Territorial Force since 1909, *b*. 24 Sept. 1857 ; *m*. 10 Dec. 1887, Mary Piercy, dau. of Major-Gen. P. Bedingfeld, R.A., and has issue,
 1. Ethel Beatrice Bedingfeld.   2. Stella Agnes Piercy.
1. Ellen Catherine, *m*. 6 Jan. 1870, Rev. Walter James Tait.
2. Annie Louisa, *m*. 7 Jan. 1875, Capt. Charles Lacon Harvey, 71st H.L.I., and *d.s.p.* 8 Dec. 1875.
3. Sophia Henrietta, *m*. 25 July, 1872, Major Hamilton William Wetherell Spooner, J.P., of Sunnyside, Leamington, late 94th Regt., and has issue.
4. Beatrice Frances, *m*. 4 Feb. 1892, Francis Arthur Beauchamp, and has issue (*see* BURKE's *Peerage and Baronetage*, PROCTOR-BEAUCHAMP, Bart.).

Arms—Az. a tower triple towered, supported by two lions rampant arg. as many chains descending from the battlements between the lion's legs or. *Crest*—An enfield statant vert. *Motto*—Turris fortis mihi Deus.

Seats—Mucklon, Ballyforan, co. Galway, and Weston, Duleek, co. Meath. *Club*—United Service.

KELLY OF ROCKSTOWN CASTLE.

BASIL JAMES ROCHE KELLY, of Rockstown Castle, and Islandmore, co. Limerick, J.P., High Sheriff 1900, Major and Hon. Lieut.-Col. Reserve of Officers, Capt. Limerick City Artillery, b. 22 March, 1877.

Lineage.—According to a pedigree of this family in Ulster's Office, Dublin Castle, certified 7 Nov. 1772,
BRAZILL O'KELLY, of Clone, co. Kilkenny, m. Mary, dau. of Sir Richard Shee, Knt. of Upper Court (see O'SHEE of Garden Morris), and bad, with other issue, a son,
LAURENCE KELLY, m. Mary, 6th dau. of Michael Langton, of Grenan, Queen's Co., and Kilkenny, and grand-dau. of Nicholas Langton, M.P. of Kilkenny, 1613 (see LANGTON of Dangannmore), and by her (who was b. 3 Aug. 1646, and d. 7 Oct. 1682) he had nine children,
1. BRAZILL, of whom presently; 2. Michael; 3. Ignatius; 4. William; 5. John; 6. James; 1. Anstace; 2. Ann; 3. Mary. About the time of the Revolution some members of the family settled in Limerick. Laurence Kelly's eldest son,
BRAZILL or BRASSELL KELLY, d.s.p. at Limerick, 7 March, 1702, and was bur. at St. Mary's Cathedral. Administration of his property was granted, 19 Dec. 1702, to his brother and next-of-kin,
JOHN KELLY, b. at Birr, 1672, m. Helena, dau. of John Morony, and grand-dau. of Patrick Morony, of Fanningstown, co. Limerick, and by her (who d. Nov. 1760) had issue,
1. LAURENCE, his heir, m. 1 Oct. 1759, Mary, sister of Richard Harrold, of Pennywell, Limerick; and d.s.p. 1776. He bequeathed all his property to his wife.
2. Martin, who settled at Cadiz, in Spain, where he was m.
3. MICHAEL, of whom presently.
1. Mary, m. Nicholas McInerheny, of Copavilly, co. Clare, and left issue.
2. Catherine, m. Martin Killikelly, son of Bryan Killikelly, of Castle Lydican, co. Galway, and left issue.
3. Anstace, m. (settlement dated 3 Nov. 1744) Lewis Collin, of Dublin, and had issue an only child,
Margaret Helen, m. Oliver Dolphin (see DOLPHIN of Turoe).
4. Helena, m. (licence dated 12 July, 1726) Dominick Killikelly, of Bilbao in Spain, younger brother of the above Martin Killikelly, and had issue, an only son, Bryan Paul de Killikelly of Bilbao; and a dau., Kate, m. George Moore, of Moore Hall (see that family).
5. Jane, m. James Creagh, of Limerick; d. 20 March, 1759, and left issue.
6. Margaret, b. 1724; m. 16 April, 1751, Philip Roche.
7. Frances, m. 29 Jan. 1761, Pierce Joyce, of Galway, and had issue (see JOYCE of Corgary).

John Kelly d. July, 1765. His 3rd son,
MICHAEL KELLY, b. 1727; m. 6 June, 1753, Christian, dau. of John Roche, of Limerick and Ballintlea, co. Clare, by Ann his wife, dau. of Philip Stackpoole, of Mountcashel, co. Clare, a near kinsman of the Duc de Stacpoole (see ROCHE of Granagh Castle), and by her (who d. 5 May, 1785, aged 51 years) had issue,
1. JOHN PETER, of whom presently.
2. Thomas, of Shannonview, co. Limerick, bapt. 17 Dec. 1781; m. 8 May, 1816, Letitia, dau. of John Phillip Roche (see ROCHE of Granagh Castle), and d. 12 Jan., 1869, in his 88th year, leaving by her (who d. 20 Nov. 1823) issue,
 1. Margaret, m. 1846 (settlement 21 Feb.), Francis Greene, of Athassell Abbey, co. Tipperary, and has issue.
 2. Christiana.
1. Helena, bapt. 27 Sept. 1758; m. 6 Oct. 1779, Thomas Appleyard, son of John Appleyard, of Athlunkard, co. Clare, and had issue.
2. Jane, bapt. 25 Feb. 1765; m. (settlement dated 31 Dec. 1791) John Greatrakes, of Rathkeale, co. Limerick, and left issue.
3. Catherine, bapt. 23 July, 1766; m. John O'Halloran, and left issue.   4. Christian, bapt. 11 Feb. 1771; d. young.
5. Mary Annie, d. unm.
6. Frances, bapt. 7 Aug. 1778; m. 14 May, 1808, Charles McNamara; and d. 24 Nov. 1871, in her 93rd year, leaving issue.
Michael Kelly d. 22 April, 1785, aged 58 years. His eldest surviving son,
JOHN PETER KELLY, of Ballintlea and Firgrove, co. Clare, D.L., b. 29 June, 1775; purchased, in 1811, the estates of the Ingoldsby Massy family, co. Limerick. He m. 28 Aug. 1799, Mary, dau. of James Lyons (see LYONS of Croome House), and by her (who d. 15 March, 1830) had issue,
1. Michael, d. young.
2. JAMES MICHAEL, of whom presently.
2. Mary, d. young, 15 April, 1806.
2. Christiana, m. 13 Jan. 1829, her cousin, Walter Joyce, of Corgary, co. Galway, and d. Jan. 1859, having had issue (see that family).

3. Mary, b. 26 Dec. 1812; m. 27 Feb. 1832, Richard Irwin, of Rathmoyle. She d. Dec. 1861, having had issue (see that family). John Kelly d. 18 Feb. 1871, in his 96th year, and was s. by his only surviving son,
JAMES MICHAEL KELLY, of Rockstown Castle, Donore, Castle Bagot and Cahircon, co. Clare, b. 2 Feb. 1808; High Sheriff co. Limerick 1841; M.P. for Limerick 1844 to 1847; m. 6 May, 1834, Frances Maria, dau. of Edward Roche, of Trabolgan, co. Clare, and only sister of Edmond Burke, Lord Fermoy, Lord-Lieut. and Custos Rotulorum of co. Cork, and had issue.
1. JOHN JOSEPH ROCHE, of whom presently.
2. Edward Roche, of Donore, co. Kildare, and of Johnstown, co. Cork, J.P., m. 1st, 1881, Anna Louisa, only dau. of Thomas John Quill, of Caherin, co. Kerry (she d. 1882), and 2ndly, 1884, Lillie Marie, dau. of William Roche, and has issue, a son, b. 1885, and a dau., Nellie, m. 24 April, 1911, James Dillon Roche, R.A.M.C.
3. James FitzJames, of Ballintlea, co. Clare, J.P., m. Jane, sister of J. P. White, D.L., of Nantenan, and had issue. He d. 19 Dec. 1911.
4. Michael Roche, of Firgrove, co. Clare, J.P., m. 4 Aug. 1875, Mary, 2nd dau. of Edmond Smithwick, J.P. and D.L., of Kilcreene, Kilkenny, and has issue,
 1. James Roche, High Sheriff co. Clare 1911.
 2. Edmund Roche, Lieut. 1st Batt. Royal Irish Regt., b. 11 April, 1881.
 1. Helen Mary.
5. Edmond Burke Roche, of Castle Bagot, co. Dublin, J.P.
6. Thomas, a barrister, d s.p.
1. Margaret Honoria, d. young.   2. Mary.
3. Frances Rose, m. Feb. 1878, Richard O'Reilly, of Colamber, co. Westmeath, and d., leaving issue.
James Kelly d. 18 Aug. 1875. His eldest son,
JOHN JOSEPH ROCHE KELLY, of Rockstown Castle, and Islandmore, co. Limerick, J.P. and D.L., High Sheriff 1879, b. 5 April, 1835; m. 1st, 5 June, 1865, Helen Maria Agnes, only child of John Joseph Preston, of Bellinter, nephew and heir-at-law of Lord Tara (see PRESTON of Pellinter), and by her (who d. 28 July, 1873) had issue,
1. James Preston, } both d. in infancy.
1. Sarah,
He m. 2ndly, 2 June, 1875, Kate O'Donnell, dau. of Francis Murphy of Kilcairne, J.P. co. Meath, and d. 5 Sept. 1898, leaving by her who d. 1902, issue,
2. BASIL JAMES, now of Rockstown.
3. Algernon James, Lieut. Limerick City Artillery.
2. Augusta Eleanor Mary.
3. Hilda Frances, m. 24 Feb. 1903, Lewis Morley, son of C. Morley, D.L., of Milfort, Portlaw.
4. Violet.

Arms—Az., two lions supporting a tower triple towered arg.,
Crest—An enfield passant vert.   Motto—Turris fortis mihi Deus.

Seat—Islandmore, Croome, co. Limerick

KELLY OF GLENCARA.

FRANCIS HUME KELLY, of Glencara, co. Westmeath, B.A. Univ. Coll. Oxford, b. 1840, J.P., Major late 9th Batt. Rifle Brigade (Westmeath Militia); m. 1876, Gertrude Annie, only child of G. Murdoch, of Belvedere, Menai Bridge, Anglesey, North Wales, and has issue,
1. FRANCIS VANDELEUR HUME, B.A. Trin Hall, Camb., Capt. 3rd Batt. N. Staffs. Regt., b. 1877.
2. George Harvey, Capt. 2nd Batt. N. Staffs. Regt., b. 1879.

Lineage.—The Kelleys of Glencara claim descent from the Kellys of Cargins, co. Roscommon, through MICHAEL O'KELLY, who settled in the barony of Kilkenny West, co. Westmeath, 1685, and subsequently became proprietor of Kellybrook, barony of Rathconrath, in same co.
HUBERT KELLY, of Kellybrook, b. 1725; m. Arabella, dau. of William Meares, of Annsgrove, and d. 1810, leaving issue,
1. JOHN, of Kellybrook.
2. CHARLES, who purchased Glencara and other properties.
3. Hubert, M.D., of Birr, King's Co., b. 1763, m. Julia, dau. of Jeremiah Hanks, of Birr, and d. 1847, leaving issue,
 1. Charles, b. 1803, d. 1881.
 2. Edmund Meares, M.A., K.C., b. 1807, m. 1811, Georgiana Eliza (who d. 1896), dau. of Richard Thomas Goodwin, senior Member of Council, Bombay. He d. 23 Oct. 1903, having had issue,
 (1) Hubert Goodwin, b. 1845, m. Madeline, dau. of Oliver Flood, of Mountrath, Queen's Co., and d. 1902, leaving issue, Alfred Spencer, b. 1892, and Georgiana.

(2) Edward Drake, late Capt. 3rd Batt. Leinster Regt., b. 1854 ; m. Kathleen A., dau. of Francis Molton, and has issue, Yvonne, m. 1909, Le Baron René Sebire de Vaucourt, and has issue,
Odette.
(3) Harford Alfred Cater, b. 1856.
(4) Spencer Litton Hall, LL.D. (16, *Idrone Terrace, Blackrock, Dublin*), b. 1859, m. 1899, Frances Sarah Alexander, dau. of John Alexander Bell, of Frescati, Blackrock, and Jimbour Darling Downs, Queensland, and grand-dau. of the late Sir Andrew Armstrong, Bart. of Gallen Priory, and has issue,
   a. Edmund Alexander Charles Harford, b. 1900.
   b. John Hubert Thomas Robert, b. 1903.
(1) Anney Eliza.
3. Alfred, b. 1813, m. Louisa, dau. of Thomas Manly, of Tullamore, King's Co., and d. 1891, leaving issue,
(1) Alfred Hubert, M.D., R.N., b. 1853, d. 1891.
(1) Henrietta Julia. (2) Mary Louisa.
4. Jeremiah Hubert, M.D., b. 1815, m. Susan, dau. of Josiah Jones. He d. 5 April, 1910.
1. Jane, d. 1883.
2. Arabella, m. Robert Chadwick, of Birr, and *d.s.p.*
3. Frances, m. John Cossart, of Villa Franca, Dalkey, co. Dublin, and left issue.
4. Matilda, d. 1892.
5. Elizabeth, m. Col. Gilbert Hogg, K.T.S., K.S.F., of Gillstown, co. Roscommon, who served in the Spanish Legion, and d. 1867, leaving issue.
The 2nd son,
CHARLES KELLY, of Glencara, m. 1790, Katherine, dau. of William Johnson, of Headford House, co. Leitrim, by Katherine his wife, dau. of Robert Hume, of Lisanoure Castle, and d. 1839, having had issue,
1. William Meares, d. unm. 2. Charles, d. unm.
3. ROBERT HUME, late of Glencara.
4. John Hubert, of Lunestown, co. Westmeath, J.P., m. 1831, Hannah, dau. of Theobald Fetherstonhaugh, of Mosstown, co. Westmeath, and d. 1881, leaving issue,
Charles, of Lunestown, J.P., High Sheriff 1883 ; b. 1834 ; m. 1860, Emily Florence, 2nd dau. of John W. H. Lambert, of Aggard.
1. Arabella.
2. Katherine, m. Currell Smyth, eld. son of Robert Smyth (*see* SMYTH *of Gaybrook*), and had issue.
3. Clementina. 4. Julia.
5. Maria, m. 6 July, 1831, John Devenish-Meares, of Mearescourt, J.P. and D.L., and d. leaving issue (*see* MEARES *of Meares Court*).
6. Harriet.
The 3rd son,
ROBERT HUME KELLY, of Glencara, M.A., Barrister-at-Law, J.P., and High Sheriff 1867, b. 1800 ; m. 1830, Isabella Olivia, dau. of Capt. Oliver Isdell, of Coilinstown, J.P., Capt. Longford Mil., by Anne his wife, dau. of James Creagh, of Cahirbane, co. Clare, and had issue,
1. FRANCIS HUME, now of Glencara.
2. Robert Vandeleur, C.B., J.P., co. Westmeath, Lieut.-Col. N. S. Wales Army Med. Corps, F.R.C.S.E., Knt. of Grace of the Order of St. John of Jerusalem (*Kellyswood, Balmoral, N.S.W., and Union Club, Sydney*), b. 26 July, 1843 ; m. 13 June, 1877, Annie Holmes, dau. of William Fetherstonhaugh, of Grouse Lodge, co. Westmeath (*see* FETHERSTONHAUGH *of Brachlyn Castle*), and has issue,
Robert Hume Vandeleur, Lieut. R.F.A., b. 13 April, 1878.
Frances Mary Vandeleur.
3. Harvey Hamilton HARVEY-KELLY, who assumed the additional name of HARVEY, Col. Indian Army, F.R.G.S., b. 29 Dec. 1845 ; m. Dec. 1876, Constance, dau. of General Dunsterville, Indian Army, and d. 13 March, 1903, leaving issue,
1 Harvey St. George Hume, Capt. Indian Army, b. 10 Oct. 1880.
2. Charles. 3. Gilbert Isdell.
1. Hubert, Lieut. Indian Army.
1. Aileen, m. 1st, Alan Daly, who d. in India Feb. 1903, leaving a dau. She m. 2ndly, 25 March, 1905, Alexander Brodrick Leslie-Melville, elder son of Alexander Samuel Leslie-Melville, and has issue (*see* BURKE's *Peerage*, LEVEN, E.).
1. Katherine, m. Rev. Frederick Armitage, and has issue, 1. Allan Leathley ; 2. Lionel ; 1. Diana ; 2. Winifred.
2. Diana Louisa, m. Edward Armitage, son of Leathley Armitage, late of Farnley Hall, co. York, and has issue, 1. John Leathley, Major Royal Inniskilling Fusiliers, b. 7 Dec. 1887 ; 2. Edward Hume, Lieut.-Col. R.A., b. 28 Jan. 1859 ; 1. Katherine, m. 1892, Major Lawrence Brook Hollinshead, Royal West Kent Regiment.
Mr. Kelly d. Sept. 1868.
Arms—Az. two lions arg. chained or, supporting a tower of three turrets of the second, in the centre chief point a mullet of the third. Crest—An enfield passant vert, charged on the shoulder with a mullet of the arms. Motto—Turris fortis mihi Deus.
Seat—Glencara, Mullingar, co. Westmeath. Club—Kildare Street, Dublin.

KELLY OF ST. HELEN'S.

The late WILLIAM EDWARD KELLY, of St. Helen's, co. Mayo, J.P. and D.L., High Sheriff 1898, b. 3 April, 1843 ; m. 18 June, 1885, Edith Mary (now of St. Helen's), dau. of the late Ven. John Cather, Archdeacon of Tuam, and d. 16 Nov. 1909, having had issue,
PHILIP EDWARD, Lieut. Royal Irish Fus., b. 5 April, 1889.
Dorothy Isabel Edith Mary, b. 18 Oct. 1887.
Lineage.—JOHN WILLIAM KELLY, of St. Helen's, Westport, co. Mayo, and 32. Gardiner's Place, Dublin, J.P. co. Mayo, son of William Kelly, of Grange, near Galway (who d. 26 Feb. 1839), b. 17 April, 1817 ; m. 1840, Mary Adelaide, dau. of John Scott, of Limerick. She d. 15 Nov. 1890. He d. 3 April, 1884, having had issue,
1. WILLIAM EDWARD, now of St. Helen's.
2. John William, b. 22 Sept. 1845 ; d. unm. 28 Nov. 1880.
3. Richard, b. 28 April, 1848 ; m. 3 June, 1878, Marie, only dau. of Rev. George Barton, and has issue,
John Upton, Lieut. Wilts Regt., b. 18 Sept. 1882.
Mona, b. 9 May, 1879.
4. Edward David, Lieut. R.H.A., b. 11 Feb. 1850 ; d. unm. 20 April, 1880.
1. Helen Mary, b. 9 Aug. 1841.
2. Mary Charlotte, b. 6 Jan. 1856 ; m. 14 Oct. 1886, Hugh Stuart Moore, of 7, Fitzwilliam Square, Dublin, and has issue three daus., 1. Ethel ; 2. Marjory ; and 3. Helen Noel.
Seat—St. Helen's, Westport, co. Mayo. Residence—32, Gardiner's Place, Dublin. Club—New, Cheltenham.

KELLY-KENNY. See KENNY.

KEMMIS OF SHAEN.

THOMAS HENRY KEMMIS, of Shaen, Queen's Co., J.P., D.L., late Capt. Royal Fusiliers, b. 11 July, 1860 ; m. 17 Nov. 1904, Mary Caroline, eldest dau. of late Charles Stewart Trench, of Clay Hill, Virginia, U.S.A., and has issue,
1. WILLIAM FREDERICK, b. 6 Dec. 1905.
1. Victoria Mary, b. 24 Oct. 1908.
2. Elizabeth Gertrude, b. 21 Jan. 1911.
Lineage.—THOMAS KEMMIS, of Shaen Castle, Killeen, Straboe, Rossnaclough, and Clonin, Queen's Co., b. 1710 ; m. Susan (who d. 12 Aug. 1804), dau. of John Long, of Derrynaseera, and d. 16 July, 1774, leaving issue,
1. JOHN, of Shaen, and Rossnaclonagh, and other lands in Queen's Co., Treasurer of the county, b. 6 July, 1747 ; m. 7 Aug. 1775, Margaret, dau. of Charles White, of Aghavoe, Queen's Co. She d. 1827. He d. Jan. 1800, leaving issue,
1. Charles, of Rossnaclonagh, Queen's Co., *d.s.p.* 2 Dec. 1837.
2. Thomas (Rev.), of Straboe, *d.s.p.* 30 May, 1839.
2. Mary, b. 1791 ; d. 1826.
3. Susannah, m. Martin McDonald.
2. James, Major-Gen. in the Army, served in the Peninsular War (medal with clasp), *d.s.p.* 2 April, 1820.
3. THOMAS, of whose descendants we treat.
4. Joshua, of Knightstown, b. 9 Feb. 1755, J.P., High Sheriff 1795 ; m. Catherine, dau. of the Ven. Archdeacon Smyth, LL.D., and d. Aug. 1818, leaving by her (who d. 31 Dec. 1857) issue,
1. Joshua, of Knightstown, J.P., *d.s.p.* 1843
1. Alicia, m. 17 May, 1831, Rev. Gustavus Warner, M.A.
2. Catherine Henrietta, m. March, 1828, Rev. William Betty (who d. 19 July, 1857), M.A., of Knightstown.
5. William Edward, of Killeen, Clonin, &c., Treasurer of the Queen's Co., 4 March, 1758 ; *d.s.p.* 7 Nov. 1848.
1. Elizabeth, d. young.
The 3rd son,
THOMAS KEMMIS, J.P., of Shaen Castle, Killeen, &c., Crown and Treasury Solicitor for Ireland, Patron of Rosenallis, b. 4 May, 1753 ; m. 11 Sept. 1773, Anne, dau. of Henry White, of Dublin, and d. 16 Jan. 1823, having by her (who d. 29 Sept. 1810) had issue,
1. THOMAS, his heir.
2. Henry, M.A., Q.C., Assistant-Barrister and Chairman of the Quarter Sessions of Kilmainham, M.P. for Tralee 1800, b. 19 Sept. 1776 ; m. 1804, Maria, dau. of Arthur Dawson, of Castle Dawson, co. Londonderry, M.P., and d. 18 March, 1857, having had by her (who d. 27 Aug. 1849) issue,
1. Thomas Arthur, of Croham Hurst, Croydon, Surrey, J.P., late Capt. Grenadier Guards, M.P. for East Looe 1832 ; b. 16 March, 1806 ; m. 14 Sept. 1833, Henrietta Anne, dau. of Col. Charles Kemeys Kemeys-Tynte, M.P., of Halswell House, Somerset. He d. 25 Dec. 1858. She d. 24 March, 1880, leaving an only son,
Arthur Henry Nicholas, of Croham Hurst, Croydon, Surrey, late Capt. 1st Somerset Militia, J.P. and D.L. for Surrey, and J.P. for King's Co., High Sheriff of King's Co., 1862, b. 13 July, 1834 ; m. 11 July, 1862, Emma Jane, dau. of E. Collins.

IRELAND. Kemmis.

2. Henry Richard, B.A., Barrister-at-Law, b. 10 Oct. 1811; m. 1848, Laura Charlotte, dau. of Arthur Male, of Bellevue, co. Stafford, and by her (who d. 2 Nov. 1862) had issue,
(1) Jasper Henry. (2) Edward Robert.
(1) Mary Frances.
(2) Alice Louisa, m. Rev. William H. Walker, Rector of Nacton, Norfolk. (3) Helen Laura, m. William Kennedy.
(4) Isobel. (5) Maude Susan.
3. WILLIAM, of Ballinacor (see that family).
4. James, of Derry and Meelick, Queen's Co., and of Choisy, near Paris, M.A. Trin. Hall, Camb., b. 9 March, 1791; m. 1818, Mary Alice, dau. of Geo. Losh, of Chatlet, Rouen, and d.s.p. July, 1848.
5. Richard, d. an infant.
1. Anne, m. 15 May, 1800, Richard Warburton, of Garryfinch, Queen's Co., J.P. and D.L. Mrs. Warburton d. 29 Aug. 1852, and her husband 15 July, 1853.
2. Susannah, m. 21 Dec. 1802, William Talbot, of Mount Talbot, J.P. and D.L. co. Roscommon, who d.s.p. 1851. Mrs. Talbot d. 30 Aug. 1831.
3. Mary, m. 1st (lic. 10 Feb. 1801) Sir Arthur Cardeu, Bart. (see BURKE's *Peerage*); and 2ndly, Joseph Smith, of Mount Butler, co. Tipperary, Capt. 26th Regt.; and d.s.p. 20 June, 1857.
4. Elizabeth, d. an infant.
The eldest son,
REV. THOMAS KEMMIS, B.A., of Shaen Castle and Brockley Park, Queen's Co., Patron of Rosenallis, b. 10 Aug. 1774; m. Mary, dau. and heir of Arthur Riky, of Airfield, co. Dublin, and d. 4 Oct. 1827, leaving issue,
1. THOMAS, his heir.
2. Arthur, of Sydney, Australia, m. Aphra, dau. of James Raymond, J.P., of Hollywood, co. Limerick, and had issue.
3. Henry, B.A., of Tasmania, Australia, m. twice, and had issue.
1. Mary, m. Charles Hogan, M.A., of Dublin, one of the six Clerks of the Court of Chancery in Ireland, and has issue.
The eldest son,
THOMAS KEMMIS, of Shaen Castle and Straboe, Patron of Rosenallis, J.P., High Sheriff 1832, b. Aug. 1798; m. 18 Aug. 1834, Mary Henrietta, eldest dau. of Rev. Robert Blackwood Jelly, of Portarlington, and by her (who m. 2ndly, 1856, Sir Henry Marsh, Bart.. M.D., and d. 24 March, 1880) had issue,
1. THOMAS, of Shaen Castle.
2. Robert, R.N., b. 1839, d. unm. 1860.
3. William, late 84th Regt., of Los Rosas, Argentine Republic, b. 24 Jan. 1841; m. 1876, Annie Jane Loretta, 2nd dau. of Wilfrid Latham, of Los Alamos, Buenos Aires, and d. 17 June, 1900, leaving issue.
Arthur William Marsh, Capt. 10th D.C.O. Lancers (Hodsons' Horse), Indian Army, late Lieut. Royal Irish Regt., b. 7 July, 1881.
4. Arthur, Capt. late 15th Regt., b. 1842; d. unm. 18 March, 1881.
1. Jane, d. unm. 1857.
Mr. Thomas Kemmis d. 1844. His eldest son,
THOMAS KEMMIS, of Shaen, Queen's Co., J.P. and D.L., High Sheriff 1860, b. 14 May, 1837; m. 1 June, 1858, Victoria Alexandrina, eldest dau. of Hans H. Hamilton, Q.C., of 26, Fitzwilliam Place, Dublin (see HAMILTON *of Ballymacoll*), and d. 17 Sept. 1906, having had issue,
1. THOMAS HENRY, now of Shaen.
1. Augusta Mary.
2. Helen, d. an infant.
Seat—Shaen, near Maryborough, Queen's Co.

KEMMIS OF BALLINACOR.

WILLIAM HENRY OLPHERT KEMMIS, of Ballinacor, co. Wicklow, J.P., High Sheriff 1904, Major late R.A., late Lieut.-Col. commanding Wicklow R.G.A. (Mil.), b. 15 March, 1864; m. 12 April, 1888, Francis Maude, 2nd dau. of Rev. Charles Beauclerk, M.A., Chaplain of Holy Trinity Church. Boulogne, and has issue,
1. WILLIAM DARYL OLPHERT, b. 19 Jan. 1892.
2. Thomas Steinman, b. 19 July, 1902.
1. Karolie Kathleen, b. 27 June, 1900.
Lineage.—WILLIAM KEMMIS, of Ballinacor, co. Wicklow, and Killeen, Queen's Co., Crown and Treasury Solicitor for Ireland (see KEMMIS *of Shaen*), b. 23 Oct. 1777; m. 11 May, 1805, Ellen, 2nd dau. of Nicholas Southcote Mansergh, J.P., of Greenane, co. Tipperary (see that family), and by her (who d. 10 June, 1815), had issue,
1. WILLIAM GILBERT, late of Ballinacor.
2. Thomas, Barrister-at-Law, of Killeen, Coolbanagher, Queen's Co., Crown and Treasury Solicitor for Ireland, b. 19 April, 1807; m. 17 June, 1839, Elizabeth Anne, only dau. of Rev. Charles Lambe Palmer, of Rahan, co. Kildare; he d. 18 Dec. 1868, having by her (who d. 24 March, 1893) had issue,
1. William Palmer, b. 1 April, 1840; d. 15 Nov. 1847.
2. Thomas, of Killeen, J.P., b. 29 Jan. 1842; d.s.p. 8 May, 1869. 3. Charles, b. 18 Nov. 1844; d.s.p. 31 Oct. 1861.
4. Gustavus Richard, b. 3 May, 1846; d. 19 Oct. 1862.

5. William, C.M.G., M.V.O., of Killeen, Portarlington, Queen's Co., J.P. and D.L., High Sheriff 1886, Lieut.-Col. and Hon. Col. 4th Batt. Lancaster Regt., served in S. African War 1900-1, mentioned in despatches (*Everton Grange, Lymington, Hants, Junior United Service and Kildare St. Clubs*), b. Feb. 1861; m. 1894, Ellen Mary Gwendoline, only dau. of the late Algernon Warner, of 23, Stanhope Gardens, S.W., and has issue,
Harry William Algernon, b. 1894.
1. Elizabeth. 2. Frances Gertrude, d. 14 Sept. 1878.
3. Louisa Rosalie, d. unm. 7 July, 1893. 4. Florence Jane.
3. George (Rev.), B.A., of Corrigeen and Clopoke, Vicar of Oregan, formerly Midshipman R.N., b. 4 June, 1808; m. 23 April, 1835, Caroline, dau. of Rev. John Olphert, of Ballyconnell, co. Donegal, and d. 8 June, 1880, having by her (who d. 28 Nov. 1856) had issue,
1. WILLIAM, late of Ballinacor.
2. John Olphert, late Capt. 15th Regt., b. 5 Nov. 1837; m. 14 Oct. 1863, Mary Louisa, dau. of William Needham, Barrister-at-Law, of Fredericton, New Brunswick, and has issue,
(1) George Richard, b. 20 July, 1865; d. May, 1868.
(2) John William Henry Shore, b. 19 July, 1867; m. 25 Feb. 1896, Maud Mary, dau. of Col. R. W. Elton, and has issue a dau.
(3) Charles Edward, b. 19 Jan. 1876.
(1) Helen Valetta, b. 29 Jan. 1870.
(2) Maud Mary, b. Jan. 1872; m. 1st, 21 March, 1901, Maj. A. R. L. Hayward, A.S.C.; and 2ndly, 5 Oct. 1910, Arthur Frederick White, son of James White, of Forest Hill.
3. Thomas (Rev.), M.A., b. 21 Oct. 1839; m. 1st, 5 Aug. 1873, Penelope, dau. of Robert Roberts, of Monkstown, and by her (who d. Oct. 1875) had a dau.
(1) Ethel Constance, b. 23 Sept. 1875.
He m. 2ndly, 13 June, 1877, Letitia M. F., dau. of Capt. H. L. Pendleton, Louth Militia. She d. 2 June, 1897. He d. 19 July, 1892, having by her had issue, with a son, who d. young, a dau.
(2) Violet Harrie de Burgh, m. 4 Aug. 1897, her cousin Lewis G. N. Kemmis, formerly of Ballycarroll (see below).
4. George, late Capt. 13th Regt., b. 16 Oct. 1840; m. 23 Sept. 1869, Maria Frances Catherine, dau. of Admiral Michael de Courcy, C.B., and d.s.p. 24 May, 1885.
5. Henry Marcus, M.D., of Bridgwater, b. 19 July, 1846; m. 27 Oct. 1870, Mary Frances, only dau. of John Armstrong, of Kingstown, and d. 12 June, 1902, leaving issue,
(1) Herbert George, m. 7 Sept. 1901, Aimée Fetherston, dau. of the late Thomas Bourchier Bolton. (2) Charles Tynte.
(3) John Garnet, d. an infant. (4) Henry Olphert.
(1) Georgina Florence, m. Philip Scott Surtees. She d. 12 Jan. 1909.
6. Arthur, of Corrigeen, b. 28 June, 1850.
7. Edward Richard, b. 7 Nov. 1856; d.s.p. at Natal, 8 Jan. 1877.
1. Anna Benjamina, m. Owen Andrew Armstrong, and d. 28 Sept. 1887.
2. Caroline, m. 28 March, 1878, Hon. Arthur Hill Trevor de Montmorency, 4th son of the 4th Viscount Mountmorres, and has issue (see BURKE's *Peerage*). He d. 1 Jan. 1910.
4. Richard, b. 26 Feb. 1813; d. unm. 24 April, 1887.
5. James, d. an infant.
1. Elizabeth, m. 16 Jan. 1827, William Charles Quin, Barrister-at-Law, an Ecclesiastical Commissioner, son of Rev. Thomas Quin, of Burleigh, co. Wexford, and d. 26 Sept. 1889, leaving issue. He d. 26 April, 1871.
Mr. Kemmis d. 20 July, 1864, and was s. by his son,
WILLIAM GILBERT KEMMIS, of Ballinacor, co. Wicklow, J.P. and D.L., High Sheriff co. Wicklow 1835, and Queen's Co. 1852, B.A., b. 11 June, 1806, and d. unm. 10 Aug. 1881, when he was s. by his nephew,
COL. WILLIAM KEMMIS, of Ballinacor, for co. Wicklow, and Ballycarroll, Queen's Co., J.P. and D.L. for the former co., Col. late R.A., b. 8 Aug. 1836; m. 20 Aug. 1862, Ellen Gertrude de Horne Christy, eldest dau. of George Steinman Steinman, F.S.A., of Sundridge, Kent, and d. 3 Feb. 1900, leaving issue,
1. WILLIAM HENRY OLPHERT, now of Ballinacor.
2. Marcus Steinman (Rev.), Rector of Conington with Knapwell, Ely, M.A. Magd. Coll. Oxford, b. 29 May, 1867; m. 22 Sept. 1892, Eliza Jane, eldest dau. of the Rev. Canon Chorlton, M.A., Vicar of Pitsmoor, Sheffield, Canon of York Minster.
3. Lewis George Nicholas, formerly of Ballycarroll (10. *Bardwell Road, Oxford*), J.P., co. Wicklow, B.A., Wadham Coll. Oxford, b. 21 Nov. 1870; m. 4 Aug. 1897, his cousin, Violet Harrie de Burgh, dau. of the late Rev. Thomas Kemmis, M.A. (see above), and has issue,
1. LEWIS WILLIAM, b. 12 July, 1898.
2. Alan Nicholas Albert, b. 30 Nov. 1900.
4. Edward Bernhard, B.A., Wadham Coll. Oxon., Barrister-at-Law, b. 11 June, 1873; d. unm. 9 Oct. 1907.
5. Gilbert (Rev.), Incumbent of Killeavy, co. Down, M.A. St. John's Coll. Oxford, b. 4 June, 1875; m. 20 May, 1903, Geraldine Josephine, elder dau. of Joseph Carson, J.P., of Cloncorn House, Clones, co. Monaghan.

Seat—Ballinacor, Rathdrum, co. Wicklow.   Club—Kildare St.

KENNEDY OF BARONRATH.

ROBERT KENNEDY, of Baronrath, co. Kildare, H.M. Lieut. for that co., J.P. co. Dublin, b. 5 Aug. 1828; m. 1855, Alice, dau. of Rev. Henry Gray (son of the Bishop of Bristol), by Lady Emilie Caroline his wife, sister of the 2nd Earl of Limerick, and has issue,

1. JOHN HENRY, formerly Capt. 3rd Batt. Royal West Kent Regt., late Capt. 97th Regt. (Attleborough Lodge, Norfolk), b. 5 March, 1859; m. Rose, dau. of Maj.-Gen. H. Parke, R.M.A., and widow of Col. Henry Thornhill, R.H.A.
2. Edward Robert, b. 1860; m. Doris, dau. of E. Lumsdaine, of Sydney, N.S. Wales, Australia.
3. Francis William, Capt. R.N., b. 1863; m. 30 Aug. 1898, Amy, dau. of Col. H. H. Goodeve, late R.A.
4. Robert Gray, Capt. Lancashire Fus., b. 27 March, 1867; m. 11 Feb. 1891, Jane (Killuntin, Fermoy), dau. of the late John Nicholson. He d. 15 Oct. 1910.

Mr. Kennedy is the youngest son of Sir John Kennedy, 1st bart. (who d. 15 Oct. 1848), by Maria his first wife (who d. 7 Nov. 1828), dau. of William Beauman, of Dublin.

Lineage.—See BURKE'S Peerage, KENNEDY, Bart.

Arms—Sa. on a fesse between three helmets close arg., a fox courant ppr. Crest—An armed arm embowed holding a branch of oak, all ppr. Motto—Adhaero virtuti.

Seat—Baronrath, Straffan, and Newcastle Lodge, co. Kildare.

KENNEDY OF CULTRA.

ROBERT JOHN KENNEDY, C.M.G., of Cultra, co. Down, M.A. Univ. Coll. Oxford, J.P. and D.L., F.R.G.S., entered H.M.'s Diplomatic service 1874, Attaché at Madrid 1874-6, Sec. at Constantinople, 1877-9, Sec. at St. Petersburg 1879-1881, Chargé d'Affaires in Bulgaria 1882-4, in Roumania 1886-8, Sec. of Legation in Persia 1888-93, and now Minister Plenipotentiary and Ambassador Extraordinary to the Republic of Uruguay, South America, formerly H.M.'s Minister Resident at Cettinge, Montenegro, was in attendance on the Shah of Persia during his visit to England, has the Jubilee medal 1897, and the Coronation medal 1902, late Lieut. Royal N. Down Militia, b. 24 Dec. 1851; m. 9 Aug. 1883, Hon. Bertha Ward, 3rd dau. of Henry William Crosbie, 5th Viscount Bangor, and has issue,

1. Mary Grace Enid, b. 3 May, 1884.
2. Bertha Catherine Maud, b. 1885.
3. Kathleen Matilda, b. 1888.
4. Lucy Emily Harriette, b. 1893.

Lineage.—HUGH KENNEDY, of Ballycultra, co. Down, M.D. (will dated 1683, proved 1685), m. Mary, dau. of Arthur Upton and had issue

JOHN KENNEDY, who purchased the estate of Cultra from the Earl of Clanbrassil, 1671. He m. Martha, dau. of William Stewart, of Ballylawn, co. Down, and aunt of Robert, 1st Earl of Londonderry, and was s. by his son

HUGH KENNEDY, of Cultra, m. 1741, Mabel, dau. of John Curtis, of Dublin, and sister of John Curtis, of Mount Hanover, co. Meath, and had issue,

JOHN, his heir.
Mary, m. Jan. 1774, John Crawford, of Crawfordsburn, and left issue (see that family).

He was s. by his son,

JOHN KENNEDY, of Cultra, J.P., High Sheriff 1769, M.A., Glasgow m. Elizabeth, dau. of Rev. Henry Cole, of Brookville, co. Fermanagh (by Mary, dau. of Henry Brooke, of Colebrooke), and niece of the 1st Lord Mount Florence, by whom he had,

1. HUGH, his heir.
2. Henry, d. in India.
3. John, of Dunbrody, co. Wexford, J.P., m. 1st, Maria, dau. of Col. Call ; and 2ndly, Elizabeth, dau. of Michael Harris. By his 1st wife, he had, with other children who d. unm.,

1. Francis Augustus, of Ruane, co. Wexford, b. 1819, Capt. in the Wexford Militia ; d. unm. 1876.
1. Henrietta Maria, m. 1841, Philip Jocelyn Newton, of Dunleckney, J.P. and D.L.
2. Georgina, m. Charles Henry Doyne, of St. Austin's Abbey.

4. Arthur, Lieut.-Col. 18th Hussars, m. 1837, Mabella, dau. of Maj. Charles Hill, of Bellaghy Castle, co. Derry, and widow of Kenrick Morres Hamilton-Jones, of Moneyglass, and by her (who d. 9 May, 1868) had three daus.

1. Elizabeth Caroline Thomasina, m. 12 June, 1862, Sir Anthony C. Weldon, 5th bart. of Rahenderry, and had issue (see BURKE'S Peerage).
2. Adeline, d. unm.
3. Louisa Emily Georgina, m. 11 Nov. 1902, Robert Edward Percy Winton, of Scremby Hall (see that family).

5. Langford, sometime H.E.I.C.S., m. 20 July, 1846, his cousin, Alicia, eldest dau. of David Verner, of Churchill, co. Armagh (see BURKE'S Peerage, VERNER, Bart.), and widow of Handcock Montgomery, 5th son of Major Alexander Nixon-Montgomery, of Bessmount Park, co. Monaghan, and d. 1 t. 1850, having had issue by her (who d. 8 Aug. 1859).

1. Langford de Grey, b. 1 July, 1847 ; d. 7 Nov. 1864.
2. Charles William, Barrister-at-Law (Scot's Hill House, Crossley Green, Herts), b. 6 July, 1850 ; m. 8 July, 1884, Florence Eliza, 2nd dau. of Rowland Hunt, of Borcatton Park, Salop (see that family).

1. Henrietta Frances Alicia, m. 1 Aug. 1871, Col. Francis Weldon, Indian Staff Corps, 6th son of Sir Anthony Weldon, 4th bart. (see BURKE'S Peerage), and has issue.

6. William, Dep. Mil. Auditor-Gen. of Bengal, d. 1846 ; m. Miss Blair.
7. Alexander, Capt. R.N.
8. Charles Pratt, Political Agent at Simla, d. 1875 ; m. 1838, Charlotte Anett.
9. Thomas.
10. Robert, Colonial Sec. of Bermuda, d. 1864.
1. Selina, m. 1822, William Unett, D.L.
2. Another dau., m. Marcus Langford McCausland, and had issue (see McCAUSLAND of Drenagh).

Mr. Kennedy, who, after the death of the 8th Earl of Cassillis, was a claimant for the title, d. 1802 and was s. by his eldest son,

HUGH KENNEDY, of Cultra, J.P., High Sheriff 1802, m. 1st, 1799, Grace Dorothea, dau. of Thomas Hughes, of co. Tipperary (by Dorothea, dau. of Sir Edward Newenbam), by whom he had issue,

1. John Hughes, d. 1839.   2. ROBERT STEWART, his heir.
3. Thomas Henry, d. 1864.
4. Arthur Edward (Sir), G.C.M.G., C.B., Governor of Queensland, m. Georgina, dau. of J. Macartney, and d. 1883, having by her (who d. 1874), had issue,

1. Arthur, d. 1884 ; m. 2 Aug. 1860, Laura Elizabeth Amabel Walrond, eldest dau. of Mr. Justice Downing Bruce, one of H.M. Judges for the Island of Jamaica, and had issue, two sons and a dau.,
   (1) Arthur.   (2) Bruce.
   (1) Georgina.

1. Elizabeth, m. 17 June, 1867. Richard James, 4th Earl of Clanwilliam, and had issue (see BURKE'S Peerage).
2. Georgina.

5. William Hugh, Capt. R.N., b. 1812 ; m. 1 April, 1841, Georgina, dau. of Sir Charles Paget, brother of the 1st Marquess of Anglesey; and d. 13 Oct. 1864, leaving by her (who d. 8 Nov. 1901) a dau., Elizabeth Georgina Frederica, m. 7 Nov. 1863, Michael Francis Knighton Seymour, son of Admiral Sir Michael Seymour, G.C.B., and d. 1 July, 1876. He d. 1909, and had issue (see BURKE'S Peerage, CULME-SEYMOUR, Bart.).

6. George Augustus, d. 1816.
1. Elizabeth, m. the late Rev. Herbert Kynaston, D.D., High Master of St. Paul's School, and d. 1872.
2. Frances, m. Rev. Frederick Downes Panter. She d. his widow 1 Feb. 1905.
3. Grace, m. Arthur Woodgate, and d. 9 May, 1900.
4. Emily Jane, m. Donald Mackenzie Douglas.
5. Dorothea, m. 1831, Capt. Samuel Price.

He m. 2ndly, Sophia, dau. of William John Lowe, by Sophia, dau. of Richard, 4th Viscount Boyne, and had issue,

7. Frederick.   8. Hugh.
6. Sophia Jane, m. 1853, Rev. Joseph Marshall, and had issue (see MARSHALL of Baronne Court). She d. 21 Sept. 1905. He d. 25 Dec. 1865.
7. Georgina, d. unm.   8. Edith, d. unm.
9. Florence, m. Capt. Samuel James Morton, 6th Dragoon Guards, elder son of the Rev. James Morton, of Little Island (see that family).
10. Augusta, m. 1st, R. Manderson, E.I.C.S. ; 2ndly, Gen. Ouseley.

Mr. Kennedy d. 1850, and was s. by his eldest son,

ROBERT STEWART KENNEDY, of Cultra, b. 1807 ; m. 5 Sept. 1849, Anne Catherine, dau. of Michael Edward Ward, of Bangor Castle (see BURKE'S Peerage, BANGOR, V.), by Lady Matilda Stewart his wife, dau. of 1st Marquis of Londonderry, and d. 6 July, 1854, having by her (who d. 20 June, 1904) had issue, two sons and one dau.,

1. ROBERT JOHN, now of Cultra.
2. Edward Henry, b. 1854 ; d. 1857.
1. Grace Emily.

Seat—Cultra Manor, Holywood, co. Down. Residence—British Legation, Montevideo, South America. Clubs—Travellers' and St. James's ; Ulster, Belfast ; Royal Ulster Yacht, and Royal North of Ireland Yacht.

KENNEDY.   See BURKE'S PEERAGE, **KENNEDY**, Bart.

FITZGERALD-KENNEY OF KILCLOGHER.

WILLIAM LIONEL CREAN NICHOLAS DE KENNE FITZGERALD-KENNEY, of Kilclogher, co. Galway, late 4th Batt. Connaught Rangers, b. 23 Nov. 1872; s. 31 Oct. 1877; m. 1896, Josephine, 3rd dau. of D. M. Delmas, of San Francisco, and has issue,

1. DELPHIN HENRY.
2. Lionel James.

Lineage.—The first patent of lands to this family in Galway is dated 29 Jan. 22 JAMES I., being a grant of the Abbey of Athenry, &c.

NICHOLAS KENNE, KENNY, or KENNEY, went with the cadets of many Somersetshire families to Dublin; he m. Anne Nevill, of Wexford. Their 3rd son (the descendants of the others being extinct),

NICHOLAS KENNEY, of Kenney's Hall, co. Wexford, m. Anne Synott, of an ancient Wexford family, and had issue,

NICHOLAS KENNEY, of Kenney's Hall and Dublin, who d. 1590. He m. the heiress of Hassan (heirs of the Hay family), and had,

NICHOLAS KENNEY, of Kenney's Hall and Edermine, co. Wexford, several times a Royal Commissioner, and Escheator and Feodary-General of, and last who held that office for, all Ireland, to Queen ELIZABETH (1596) and JAMES I. He received Edermine Manor, co. Wexford, and large grants of lands by patents dated 18 Feb. 1610, and 16 Jan. 1616. He d. 1621, having had issue by his wife Anne (dau. or sister of Michael Kettlewell, Deputy-Treasurer of Ireland, of the old family originally of Kettlewell, co. Cork), HENRY, his successor, and EDWARD KENNEY, of Newcastle, near Lyons, co. Dublin, Dep.-Escheator 1610, who d. 1617. The elder son,

HENRY KENNEY, of Kenney's Hall and Edermine, M.P. for Newcastle, d. 16 July, 1650; m. Frances Barry, sister of James, Lord Santry, and had (with EDWARD, of Ballymartle and Cullen, Capt. WILLIAM, of whom later, and three daus., of whom Elizabeth m. Hon. Raymond Fitzmaurice) an eldest son,

COL. RICHARD KENNEY, of Kenney's Hall and Edermine, M.P., High Sheriff co. Wexford; d. 1 Oct. 1682: his will making dispositions " so that his estates may be preserved in the name and blood of the Kenneys as it is in this place and county by many descents." His line (which married into that of his brother Edward of Cullen, made many distinguished alliances, and produced the gallant Thomas Kenney, R.N., Captain of the *Falmouth*, killed in 1704) expired about the close of the last century with Col. Edward Kenney, of Newford and Edermine. We revert to the 3rd son of Henry Kenney and Frances Barry,

CAPT. WILLIAM KENNEY, of Kenneyswood, co. Cork, m. his cousin-german, Jane, dau. of Edward Kenney, of Newcastle, and had issue,

CAPT. JAMES KENNEY, of Grange, co. Wexford, b. 1653; d. 9 Jan. 1679; m. Alice, only child of Robert Taylor, of Dublin, great-grandson of Robert (son of James Taylor, of Swords, co. Dublin), by Elizabeth Golding his wife, grand-dau. of Lord Howth, and through him inheriting, by two lines, the Plantagenet blood (see BURKE's *Royal Descents*), and had a son,

JAMES KENNEY, of Wexford, who m. Ellen, dau. of Edward Whitmore, of Ballyteigne, and had with others, who d.s.p., a son,

JAMES KENNEY, of Wexford, b. 1710; d. 1771; m. Catherine (d. 1782), dau. of Capt. Thomas O'Kelly, of King JAMES's Army (by his wife Catherine Masterson, of the Fernes family), grand-nephew of Col. Richard O'Kelly, of Kilclogher, co. Galway, who forfeited that estate, purchased back by the only son of said James, of whom descendants still exist, viz.,

WILLIAM KENNEY, of Kilclogher and Keelogues, &c., co. Galway, Ballivtarsney, co. Wexford, Longwood, co. Meath, and 15, Gardiner's Place, Dublin, b. 1755; m. 1789, Bridget Fitzgerald (d. 28 Aug. 1842), dau. and heiress of John Daly, of Dalybrook, co. Kildare, by Julia his wife, dau. of Gerald Fitzgerald, of Rathbone, co. Meath, and Clare, dau. of Sir John Bellew, Bart. Mr. Kenney d. 22 Jan. 1830, leaving issue (among others, d.s.p.),

1. JAMES FITZGERALD, of whom presently.
2. THOMAS HENRY, of Ballyforan House, co. Roscommon, Derrymore, King's Co., and the Chateau de la Vrilliere, in Touraine, d. 21 Dec. 1864; m. 2 May, 1827, Sophie, dau. of the Comte de Montlivault, and had by her (who d. 7 April, 1871), with two daus., an only son,
James Louis Lionel, Chevalier de Kenney, of the French Navy, Knight of the Legion of Honour and of St. Stanislaus, b. 6 Sept. 1829, who gallantly led the French at Ning-po, 1862, and there d. unm., of his wounds, 28 May. That city has given his name to a street, and in his honour the Emperor NAPOLEON III. called a vessel of war *The Kenny*.
1. Clare, m. 16 July, 1823, Hon. Gonville ffrench, of Claremont, co. Roscommon, and d. 12 Oct. 1864, s.p. He d. 29 April, 1866.

The eldest son,

JAMES FITZGERALD KENNEY, of Kilclogher, and Keelogues, &c., co. Galway, Longwood, co. Meath, and Merrion Square, Dublin, J.P., Lieut. 8th or King's Regt. (war medal for services in West Indies), Lieut.-Col. in foreign service, Chevalier du Temple, b. 21 April, 1790; m. 24 Jan. 1814, Jane Olivia, only dau. of William Thomas Nugent of Pallas, called Lord Riverston, and sister of Anthony Francis, Earl of Westmeath (see BURKE's *Peerage*), which lady d. 27 Dec. 1842, their issue being (with three daus. and one son, d. infants),

1. William Nugent, Capt. 11th (North Devon) Regt., d. unm. 18 Dec. 1850, bur. at Skebanagh, co. Galway, where a chapel was erected to his memory by his brother James.
2. JAMES CHRISTOPHER FITZGERALD, late of Kilclogher and Keelogues.
3. Nugent Thomas, of Hermitage Park, co. Dublin, who assumed by royal sign manual the surname and arms of KINGSMILL, of Hermitage Park, co. Dublin, m. 22 June, 1865, Isabel, dau. and heiress of Col. Sir John Kingsmill; and d. 22 Dec. 1872, leaving issue (see KINGSMILL *of Hermitage Park*).
1. Julia Mary Fitzgerald Kenney, d. 17 Aug. 1879.

Lieut.-Col. Kenney d. 29 Feb. 1852, and was s. by his son,

JAMES CHRISTOPHER FITZGERALD KENNEY, of Kilclogher, J.P., B.A. Trin. Coll. Dublin, Barrister-at-Law, M.R.I.A., m. 17 Aug. 1870, Helena Mary, dau. and co-heir of the late Major Patrick Crean Lynch, D.L. of Clogher House, co. Mayo, and Hollybrook, by Marcella his wife, dau. of the late Sir Michael Dillon Bellew, Bart. of Mount Bellew. She d. 26 May, 1903. He d. 31 Oct. 1877, leaving issue,

1. WILLIAM LIONEL CREAN NICHOLAS DE KENNE, now of Kilclogher.
2. Henry James Christopher Emmanuel de Kenne, d. unm.
3. Gilbert Richard Julian Gerald de Kenne, d. 22 Nov. 1880
4. James Christopher, of Clogher House, Ballyglass, co. Mayo, J.P., B.A., Barrister-at-Law, b. 30 April, 1878.
1. Marcella Jane Antonia Mary de Kenne.
2. Helena Julia Olivia Anna de Kenne.

Arms—Per pale or and az., a fleur-de-lis between three crescents all counterchanged. Crests—Out of an earl's coronet or, a demi-arm erect sleeved gu., with a white cuff, holding in the hand a roll of parchment ppr. Mottoes—In 1667, over the crest, Teneat, luceat, floreat; and beneath the shield, Vi, virtue, et valore; now in general the former alone. Some of the family bore, Dei dextra dabit.

KENNEY-HERBERT. See HERBERT.

KENNY OF BALLINROBE.

STANHOPE LLOYD KENNY, of Ballinrobe, co. Mayo, Deputy Conservator of Forests, Indian Forest Service, b. 16 March, 1874; s. his father 30 Jan. 1910.

Lineage.—The first of this family who settled in Ireland, circa 1660, m. a dau. of John Gray, an Englishman, and was father of

THOMAS KENNY, of Ballinrobe, who m. 20 Oct. 1698, Frances, dau. of David Courtney, and grand-dau. of the Rev. John Courtney, M.A., Rector of Ballinrobe, and by her (who d. 25 Feb. 1766) he left at his decease, 11 Dec. 1725, a son,

COURTNEY KENNY, of Roxborough, Ballinrobe, Capt. Lieut. in Col. Cuff's Regt. of Militia Dragoons, b. 14 April, 1702; m. 1st, Eliza Thompson, who d.s.p.; and 2ndly, Anne, dau. of the Rev. John Rogers, co. Down, and by her (who d. 5 Dec. 1772) had issue,

1. Thomas, b. 11 Oct. 1734; m. 9 Jan. 1757, Eliza, dau. of the Very Rev. William Crowe, D.D., Dean of Clonfert, by Emilia his wife, sister of George, Lord Carbery. He d. 28 Oct. 1812, aged 78; and his wife 29 July, 1814, aged 78, having had issue,
   1. William, Lieut.-Col. 11th Madras Native Infantry, m. Martha, relict of George Cunning, Chief at Cuddalore; and d. 1803, of wounds received leading the storming party at Gawilghur, having had issue,
   (1) William, late Major 73rd Regt., m. Miss Inge, of co. Leicester.
   (2) Eyre, Lieut.-Col. 80th Regt., unattached.
   2. Thomas, m. a dau. of Rev. Vesian Pick, Rector of Johnstown, and had issue,
   Edward, of Ballyornan, co. Wicklow, Lieut.-Col. 89th Regt., retired full pay; m. Mary Anne, dau. of Capt. Courtney Kenny (see below), and had issue,
   1. Edward, } Lieuts. 84th Regt. (both d. in India).
   2. Henry, }
   1. Mary Jessie.
3. David Crowe, Lieut.-Gen. E.I.C.S., d. 20 Aug. 1847, aged 65, leaving William and Maria.
4. Courtney Crowe, Capt. 9th Regt., m. a dau. of Gen. Geils. He was shot acting as Engineer at the siege of Burgos, leaving issue,
   (1) Henry, who m. and had two daus., Euphemia and Edith.
   (2) Thomas, Lieut.-Col. and Assistant Adjutant-Gen. 2nd Madras European Infantry, m. and had issue, Courtney, late 88th Regt., and others.

(3) James William Gammell, Col. 13th N.I., m. 1st, 4 May, 1837, Eliza, 2nd dau. of Lieut. Beatty, 62nd Rgt., and 2ndly, 3 Aug. 1847, Margaret Rosborough, 3rd dau. of Maj. Alexander Rennick of Derryargan, co. Fermanagh. She d. 17 Aug. 1858.
  (1) Mary Anne, m. Major Edward Kenny (see above).
  (2) Jessie, m. Capt. Geils, d.s.p.
2. COURTNEY, of whom presently.
3. John, m. Frances, dau. of Lemuel Shuldham.
1. Frances, m. Arthur Stanhope.
2. Anne, m. Gregory Cuff, J.P. of Creagh, co. Mayo.
3. Hannah, m. John Garnet.
Mr. Courtney Kenny d. 17 Sept. 1779. His 2nd son,
  COURTNEY KENNY, J.P. of Roxborough, Ballinrobe, b. 21 April, 1736; m. 23 April, 1775, Susanna, dau. of Stanhope Mason, of Moira, co. Down, and by her (who d. 6 July, 1806, aged 55) had issue,
  1. COURTNEY, of Ballinrobe.
  2. Mason Stanhope, M.D., J.P. of Halifax, co. York, b. 29 Nov. 1786; m. Aug. 1812, Sophia, dau. of William Fenton of Spring Grove, co. York, and d. 25 April, 1865, leaving issue,
    1. William Fenton, J.P., b. 18 Sept. 1815; m. Agnes Ramsden, dau. of John Rhodes Ralph, J.P. of Halifax, and had issue, Courtney Stanhope and Charles. The elder son, Courtney Stanhope Kenny, F.B.A., LL.D., M.P. for West Riding of Yorkshire, Barrister Division, 1885-9, Barrister, Fellow of Downing Coll., Cambridge, and Professor of Law, Cambridge University, b. 18 March, 1847; m. 1876, Emily Gertrude, dau. of William Wood Wiseman, of Ossett, Yorks.
    2. Lewis Stanhope (Rev.), M.A., Rector of Kirkby Knowle, b. 3 Jan. 1827; m. Arabella, dau. of Lieut.-Col. Walker, and d. 1881, having had issue.
      1. Emily Anne, m. Rev. Godfrey R. Ferris, M.A., late Rector of Hulcott.
    3. John, m. Miss Lovelock, and d. 27 Oct. 1819.
    1. Anne, m. Major Maxwell, Northampton Fencibles.
    2. Susan, m. Thomas Gildea, Clerk of the Peace, Mayo.
    3. Maria, m. John Clarke, of Dublin.
    4. Brilliana, m. William Griffith, J.P. co. Sligo.
Mr. Courtney Kenny d. 10 March, 1809. His eldest son,
  COURTNEY KENNY, of Ballinrobe, co. Mayo, J.P., b. 27 Sept. 1781; m. 16 Dec. 1816, Louisa, dau. of William Fenton, of Underbank and Spring Grove, co. York, and by her (who d. 15 Aug. 1841) had issue,
  1. Courtney, b. March, 1818; d. 1824.
  2. George Frederick, b. 18 June, 1821; d. 1826.
  3. STANHOPE WILLIAM FENTON, late of Ballinrobe.
  4. Lewis Fenton, C.E., b. 18 June, 1831.
  1. Sarah Louisa.
  2. Susan Anne, m. 1866, Very Rev. William Jackson, M.A., Dean of Killala.
  3. Emma Sophia, d. 14 April, 1911.
  4. Maria, m. 1866, Rev. Henry Vereker.
  5. Caroline, m. 1864, George Johnstone Darley, C.E., of Dublin.
He d. 15 March, 1863. The eldest surviving son,
  STANHOPE WILLIAM FENTON KENNY, of Ballinrobe, co. Mayo, J.P., B.A. Trin. Coll. Dublin, b. 1 July, 1827; m. 4 Dec. 1867, Mary Anne, 3rd dau. of Guy Lloyd, of Croghan, co. Roscommon, J.P. and D.L. (see that family). He d. 30 Jan. 1910, having by her (who d. 5 Nov. 1893) had issue,
  1. Courtney, Lieut. R.A., b. 22 Feb. 1869; d. unm. 7 June, 1894.
  2. STANHOPE LLOYD, now of Ballinrobe.
  3. Lewis Fenton (4, Anglesea Road, Dublin), b. 21 July, 1875; m. 6 Sept. 1910, Henrietta Norah Margaret, youngest dau. of the late Robert Joy, of Millmount, Banbridge, co. Down and has issue,
    Mary Elizabeth, b. 12 Aug. 1911.
  1. Susannah Louisa Fenton.
Residence—Ballinrobe, co. Mayo.

KELLY-KENNY OF TREANMANAGH.

GEN. SIR THOMAS KELLY-KENNY, G.C.B., G.C.V.O., of Doolough Lodge, co. Clare, J.P. and D.L., Gen. in the Army and Adjt.-Gen. to the Forces, Col. Queen's Royal West Surrey Regt., assumed in 1874 the additional name of KENNY, served in China 1860, in Abyssinia 1867-68, and in S. Africa 1899-1901, b. 27 Feb. 1840. Sir Thomas is the son of the late Matthew Kelly, D.L., of Kilrush, co. Clare.

Residence—Doolough Lodge, co. Clare. Town Residence—136, Ashley Gardens, S.W. Clubs—Army and Navy, and Arthur's.

KER OF MONTALTO.

RICHARD WILLIAM BLACKWOOD KER, of Montalto, and Portavo, co. Down, J.P. and D.L., High Sheriff 1880, M.P. for Down 1884, and for Eastern Division 1885-90, formerly Capt. 1st Royal Dragoons, b. in 1850; m. 1876, Edith Louisa, dau. of William George Rose, of Wolston Heath, co. Warwick, and has issue,
  DAVID ALFRED WILLIAM, late Lieut. Carbiniers, 6th Dragoon Guards, b. 28 Nov. 1878.

Lineage.—DAVID KER, of Portavo, purchased Montalto from the Earl of Moira. By Maddelena, his wife, he left a son and heir, DAVID KER, of Portavo and Montalto, co. Down, J.P. and D.L., who represented Athlone, and afterwards Downpatrick in Parliament, and purchased the De Clifford property in 1844; m. 22 Feb. 1814, Lady Selina Sarah Stewart, dau. of the 1st Marquess of Londonderry (see BURKE's Peerage), and d. 30 Dec. 1844, leaving issue,
  1. DAVID STEWART, of Montalto and Portavo, co. Down.
  2. Richard John Charles Rivers, J.P. and D.L., M.P. for Downpatrick, sometime in the Diplomatic Service, m. 1856, Rose Jane, eldest dau. of Nicholson Calvert, of Hunsdon, co. Herts, and Quintin Castle, co. Down, and left with other issue a youngest dau., Olga, m. 1892, Rear-Adml. George Fowler King-Hall, C.V.O., eldest son of late Adml. Sir William King-Hall, K.C.B.
    1. Catherine Anne Frances, m. 6 Feb. 1840, Mathew Anketell, of Anketell Grove, co. Monaghan, D.L. She d. 28 Feb. 1887. He d. 8 May, 1870, leaving issue (see that family).
    2. Madeline Selina, m. 8 Oct. 1844, William Robert Anketell, of Quintin Castle, co. Down. She d. 8 April, 1878. He d. 9 March, 1880, leaving issue (see ANCKETILL of Ancketill's Grove).
The eldest son,
  DAVID STEWART KER, of Montalto, co. Down, M.P. for that co., J.P. and D.L., High Sheriff co. Down 1852, and co. Antrim 1857, b. 1817; m. 1st, 1 March, 1842, Hon. Anna Dorothea Blackwood, youngest dau. of Hans, 3rd Lord Dufferin, and by her (who d. 27 Oct. 1862) had, with other issue,
  1. ALFRED DAVID, his heir.
  2. Charles, d. unm.
  3. RICHARD WILLIAM BLACKWOOD, now of Montalto.
  4. Henry, d. unm. 1890.
  5. Edward.   6. Robert.   7. David, deceased.
  8. Hamilton Chichester (Rev.), m. Emily, dau. of Rev. Mr. Bateman.
    1. Selina Frances Imogene, m. 29 Sept. 1868, John William Perceval Maxwell, who d. 21 Nov. 1875, leaving issue (see that family).
    2. Helen.
    3. Violet, m. 1872, William Molyneux Rose, of Wolston Grange (see that family).
He m. 2ndly, 12 July, 1869, Caroline Hellena, eldest dau. of Parsons Persse, of Castle Turven, co. Galway. Mr. Ker d. 8 Oct. 1878; his eldest son,
  ALFRED DAVID KER, of Montalto and Portavo, Capt. 12th Lancers, J.P., High Sheriff 1877, b. 1843; m. 4 March, 1871, Hon. Eva Frances Caroline (Cremelle Court, Milborne Port, Somerset; 12, Grosvenor Place, S.W.), elder dau. of Thomas, Lord Deramore, by his wife, Hon. Caroline Elizabeth Anne, dau. of 4th Lord Dynevor, and d. 8 Dec. 1877, leaving issue,
  1. Sybil Anna.
  2. Eva Winifred Selina, m. 27 Nov. 1897, Wilmot Inglis-Jones, of Derry Ormond (see that family).
  3. Kathleen Elianore Mary.
  4. Eva Cecil Violet.

Seat—Montalto and Portavo, Ballynahinch, co. Down. Club—Carlton.

MURRAY-KER OF NEWBLISS HOUSE.

MARY ISABELLA MURRAY-KER, of Newbliss House, co. Monaghan, younger dau. of the late André Allen Murray, D.L., s. her mother 1900.

Lineage.—JAMES MURRAY, of Beech Hill, co. Monaghan, m. Margaret, sister of the Ven. Dr. André Allen, Archdeacon of Clogher, and d. 1828, having had issue,
  ANDRÉ ALLEN MURRAY, of Loughhoona, ex-Scholar T.C.D., and Barrister-at-Law, m. Jan. 1818, Rebecca, 2nd dau. of Rev. William Moffatt, Rector of Currin and Drumcrin, and d. 9 Sep., 1827, leaving issue,
  1. ANDRÉ ALLEN, late of Newbliss House.
  2. William, of Beech Hill, co. Monaghan, J.P., d. unm. 1899.
  3. Robert, M.R.C.S.I., m. Annie (who d. 18 April, 1911), dau. of Charles Cambie, J.P. of Castletown, co. Tipperary, Barrister-at-Law, and d. 7 Feb. 1854, leaving issue,
    André Allen.
    Roberta Jane, m. Rev. Henry Heard, Rector of St. Michael's, Bath.
The eldest son,
  ANDRÉ ALLEN MURRAY-KER, of Newbliss House, co. Monaghan, J.P. and D.L., High Sheriff 1844, b. 28 Oct. 1818; m. 2 Nov. 1854, Marianne, only dau. of the Rev. Richard Foster, by Mary Ker his wife, niece and heiress of Andrew Ker, M.D., of Newbliss House. Dr. Ker s. his brother ALEXANDER KER, Barrister-at-Law, who built the present family mansion in the year 1814. They were sons of Rev. ANDREW KER, Rector of Aghabog, and grandsons of ROBERT KER (1751), who is mentioned in Dr. Reid's History of the Presbyterian Church of Ireland (vol. III., p. 343) as having assisted the introduction of Seceders to Newbliss. Mr. A. A. Murray-Ker assumed the additional name of KER on his marriage, and d. 21 Oct. 1892. His widow d. 9 Feb. 1900, having had issue,

1. Andrew, b. 8 April, 1858; d. 18 Oct. 1861.
1. Sarah, of Beech Hill, co. Monaghan, m. 1880, Fitzjohn Robert Irwin, M.B. of Kilkeel, co. Down, son of the late John Robert Irwin, of Carnagh House, co. Armagh, and by him (who d. 1882) had issue (see IRWIN *of Mount Irwin*).
2. MARY ISABELLA, now of Newbliss.

Seat—Newbliss House, Newbliss, co. Monaghan.

KING OF BALLYLIN.

HENRY LOUIS KING, of Ballylin, King's Co., J.P. King's Co., High Sheriff 1903. b. 1860; eldest son of Ross Mahon, of Ladywell and Harriett his wife, dau. of Rev. Henry King, of Ballylin, s. his uncle, John Gilbert King, of Ballylin, and assumed by Royal Licence 17 May, 1901, the name and arms of KING in lieu of his patronymic, MAHON; m. 10 May, 1904, Winifred Harriette, only surviving dau. of William Somerset Ward, of Dublin (see BURKE'S *Peerage*, BANGOR, V.), and has issue,
1. GILBERT MAHON, b. 1905.
1. Harriet Mary, b. 1906.
2. Winifred Alice, b. 1909.

Lineage.—This family, and that of Sir Gilbert King, Bart., of Charlestown, is one and the same, descended from EDWARD KING, b. at Stukeley, co. Huntingdon, 1577, elected Fellow of Trin. Coll. Dublin, 1593, two years after its foundation, and consecrated Bishop of Elphin 1611. He d. 1638, and was bur. in Elphin, where he built a castle, and acquired landed property in the neighbourhood. The Bishop m. twice, and left sons and daus., among them JOHN KING, of Boyle, co. Roscommon, whose dau., Anne, m. Dominick French, of Dungar, or French Park, co. Roscommon, and
JAMES KING, of Charlestown, co. Roscommon, High Sheriff and M.P. 1657, m. Judith, dau. of Gilbert Rawson. His son,
GILBERT KING, of Charlestown, M.P., b. 1658; m. Mary, dau. of Dominick French, of French Park; she was grand-dau. of John King, of Boyle. His son,
JOHN KING, High Sheriff and M.P. 1703 to 1728, d. 4 Nov. 1778, having m. twice, 1st, Miss Shaw, of Newford, co. Galway, and 2ndly, 18 Jan. 1770, Rebecca, dau. of John Digby, of Landentown, co. Kildare (son of Bishop Simon Digby, and grandson of Essex Digby, Bishop of Dromore, who was son of Sir Robert Digby and Baroness Letice Fitzgerald, of Offally). His son,
JOHN KING, of Fermoyle, co. Longford, was the first of the family who came to Ballylin, m. twice, 1st, 6 Nov. 1748, Alice, dau. of Ross Mahon, of Castlegar, co. Galway; 2ndly, Frances Digby. He had issue, John, of Ballylin, M.P. for Jamestown, b. 1760; Gilbert, m. Elizabeth, dau. of Joseph Henry, of Straffan, co. Kildare; Jane, m. Abraham Creighton, 1st Lord Erne; and Rebecca, who m. April, 1771, her cousin GILBERT KING, Major 5th Dragoon Guards, son of Gilbert King, by Sarah, dau. of John French, of French Park, co. Roscommon, who fought at the battle of Quebec 1759, and by him left, with a dau., Harriet, m. the Rev. John Eagles, a son and heir,
REV. HENRY KING, of Ballylin, King's Co., b. 1799, who s. to Ballylin at the decease of his maternal uncle, m. 5 June, 1821, Harriett, youngest dau. of John Lloyd, of Gloster, King's Co., for many years M.P. for that co., and sister of the Countess of Rosse (see LLOYD-VAUGHAN *of Golden Grove*), and by her (who d. 1846) had issue,
1. JOHN GILBERT, late of Ballylin.
1. Harriett, m. Ross Mahon, of Ladywell, eldest son of Rev. Henry Mahon, Rector of Tissauran, King's Co., and Anne, his wife, dau. and co-heir of Rev. Abraham Symes, Rector of Carnew, co. Wicklow, and grandson of Ross Mahon, of Castlegar (see BURKE'S *Peerage*, MAHON, Bart.), and Anne, his wife, dau. of John, 1st Earl of Altamount (see BURKE'S *Peerage*, SLIGO, M.). He d. 1892. She d. 1868, leaving issue,
  1. HENRY LOUIS, now of Ballylin.
  2. Ross, b. 1865, d. 1903. 3. George Gilbert, b. 1866.
  1. Harriet Anne. 2. Louisa Mary Anne.
2. Jane, m. 12 Oct. 1853, the Rev. Sir William R. Mahon, 4th Bart., of Castlegar, co. Galway. He d. 14 Aug. 1893. She d. 7 June, 1895, and had issue (see BURKE'S *Peerage*).
3. Mary, m. 6 Dec. 1854, Henry William, 5th Viscount Bangor, and was accidentally killed 31 Aug. 1869, leaving issue (see BURKE'S *Peerage*).
The Rev. Henry King d. 1857. His only son,
I. L. G.

JOHN GILBERT KING, of Ballylin, King's Co., J.P. and D.L., High Sheriff 1852, M.P. 1865-8, b. 19 Dec. 1822; d. unm. 9 Jan. 1901, and was s. by his nephew, Henry Louis Mahon (now King), of Ballylin.

Arms—Sa., a lion rampant double queued or. Crest—An escallop gu. Motto—Spes tutissima cœlis.
Seat—Ballylin, Ferbane, King's Co. Clubs—Kildare Street, Dublin, and Royal St. George Yacht.

KING. See BURKE'S PEERAGE, KINGSTON, E.

KING-EDWARDS. See EDWARDS.

KING-HARMAN. See HARMAN.

KING-SEALY. See SEALY.

KINGAN OF GLENGANAGH.

WILLIAM SINCLAIR KINGAN, of Glenganagh, co. Down, b. 6 Dec. 1876; s. his father 1911.

Lineage.—WILLIAM KINGAN, of Silverstream, White Abbey, co. Antrim, had issue, a son,
SAMUEL KINGAN, of Glenganagh, co. Down, J.P. and D.L., b. 24 Feb. 1824; m. Nov. 1875, Jane, dau. of the late John Sinclair, of The Grove, Belfast, and d. 13 May, 1911, having by her (who d. 24 Dec. 1901) had issue,
1. WILLIAM SINCLAIR, now of Glenganagh.
2. Thomas Davison, b. 7 Nov. 1879.
1. Elizabeth Janie Sinclair.
2. Mary Ethel.

Arms—Az. a fess indented arg. between an antique crown in chief or and in base two dexter hands clasped and conjoined, that on the dexter ringed on the third finger with a royal signet all ppr. Crest—Two dexter hands clasped and conjoined as in the arms thereon a lion rampant guardant or. Motto—A favore regis nomen.
Seat—Glenganagh, Bangor, co. Down.

KINGSMILL OF HERMITAGE PARK.

JULIAN CLAUD DE KENNE BRUCE KINGSMILL, of Hermitage Park, co. Dublin, Capt. late R.H.A., served in Black Mountain campaign (medal with clasp), personally thanked for his services on the Indian Frontier 1888, b. 11 May, 1866; s. his father, 1872; m. 24 June, 1893, Emily Lydia, eldest dau. of the late James Marsland, son of the late John Marsland, of White Hall, co. Gloucester, and has issue,

1. Robert Percy Willmott George, b. 1904; d. 18 Nov. 1905.
2. EDWARD GEORGE WILLIAM, b. 7 April, 1906.
3. Nigel John de Kenne, b. 22 July, 1908.

Kingsmill.

1. Margaret, b. 9 June, 1896.
2. Isabel Augusta Helena Olivia, b. 30 Jan. 1898.
3. Emily Mary Anne Teresa Lydia, b. 17 July, 1900.
4. Lilian Julia, b. 23 July, 1910.

Lineage.—This family, whose original name was Castlemayne, resided at Basingstoke, Hants, from the 12th to the 16th century, having received a grant of the Royal Mill there, from which they derive their name.

RICHARD KINGSMILL, Bailiff of Basingstoke 1456, and lessee of Basingstoke hospital property, from Merton Coll. 1455-79, was s. by his son,

RICHARD KINGSMILL, of Doberton Manor, collector of the subsidy for South Hants 1463, and Bailiff of Basingstoke 1464 and 1487. He entertained for a night, 4 Nov. 1501, Catherine of Arragon with her suite at his house at Basingstoke, on her way to be married to Prince Arthur. He d. May, 1511, bur. in St. Michael's church, Basingstoke, having, by Alice his wife, had issue, a son,

SIR JOHN KINGSMILL, of Freifolk, Hants, Judge of the Common Pleas, 2 July, 1503, m. Jane, dau. of Sir John Giffard, of Itchell, Hants, and d.v.p. 1509 (will proved 20 May, that year), leaving issue

SIR JOHN KINGSMILL, of Sydmonton Court, Hants, which he acquired by purchase from the Crown 31 and 35 HENRY VIII. He m. Constance, dau. of John Goring, of Barton, Sussex, and d. 20 July, 1556, having by her (who d. 16 May, 1581) had issue,

1. WILLIAM, of whom presently.
2. Richard (Sir), of Highclere, m. 1st, Alice, dau. of Richard Fauconer, of Hurstbourne, Hants, and widow of Thomas Wroughton, of Overton, Wilts, and by her had issue, one child,
   Constance, of Highclere and Burghclere, m. Sir Thomas Lucy, of Charlecote, and had issue (see that family).
   He m. 2ndly, 13 Oct. 1574, Elizabeth, dau. of Daniel Woodroof, Alderman of London, and widow of Rev. George Stonehouse. Sir Richard d. 1600, and was bur. with great pomp in Highclere church (funeral entry, Coll. of Arms, I., 16, f. 103).
3. Roger, d.s.p. 1591.   4. Edward, d.s.p.
5. Henry, the traveller and writer, d.s.p. 1577.
6. John, Fellow of Magdalen Coll. Oxon, 1564, Vicar-Gen. of the Diocese of Winchester 1566, and Master Greatham Hospital, Durham, 1585, b. 1537; d. 1590.
7. George (Sir), of Malshanger, Hants, Judge of the Common Pleas, 8 Feb. 1599, knighted 23 July, 1603; m. Sarah, dau. of Sir James Harrington, of Exton, and widow of Francis, Earl of Huntingdon, and d.s.p. 1606. She m. 3rdly, Edward, Lord Louch.
8. Andrew, Fellow of All Souls, Oxford, 1558, d. at Lausanne, Sept. 1569.
9. Thomas, Fellow of Magdalen Coll. Oxford, and Professor of Hebrew 1569, m. a dau. of — Cuthbert, of English, co. Oxford, and had issue,
   1. John (Sir), of Enham, co. Donegal, Capt. of Horse in Ireland 1610-29, knighted at Dublin 29 June, 1617, acquired large estates in co. Donegal, and d.s.p. at Kentbury, Berks, 9 March, 1646.   2. Andrew, d.s.p.
   3. Samuel, Chancellor-at-Law, bapt. 5 Jan. 1578; d s.p. 1638.
   4. William (Rev.), D.D., of Enham and Alresford, b. 1579; m. Margaret, dau. of — Pistor, Rector of Havant, Hants, and had issue,
      (1) John, of Andover, Major in the Andover Regt., b. 1626; was twice m., and d. 1694, leaving issue,
         1. William, d.s.p.   2. John, d.s.p.
         1. Mary, m. Edward Evans, D.C.L.
         2. Ann, m. her cousin, J. Taswell.
         3. Constance, m. Sept. 1684 (as his first wife), William Grove, of Castle Shanaghan, and d. 1687 (see GROVE of Castle Grove).
         4. Frances, m. 1st, — Phillip, and 2ndly, John Brind.
         5. Eleanor, b. 1671; m. — Hodder.
      (1) Elizabeth, m. 1st, Thomas Toking, of London, and 2ndly, James Taswell, of Lymington.
      (2) Bridget, of Enham, m. her cousin, Daniel Kingsmill (see below).
         1. Constance, m. Richard Guppy, of Sandridge Hill Park, Wilts, and d.s.p.
10. Arthur, d.s.p.
1. Constantia.
1. Jane, m. Richard Cooper, of Paulett, co. Somerset, and d. 1599, leaving issue.
2. Alice, m. 24 June, 1563, Dr. James Pilkington, Bishop of Durham, who d. 23 Jan. 1575.   4. Anna.
5. Katherine, m. Sir Richard Norton, of East Tisted, Hants, and d. 1611, leaving issue. He d. 1591.
6. Margaret, m. John Thornburgh, of Cottesden, Hants, and had issue.
7. Mary, m. Edward Goddard, of Woodhay, Hants, and was bur. 8 Oct. 1600.

The eldest son,

SIR WILLIAM KINGSMILL, Sheriff of Hants 1564, b. 1526; m. Bridget, dau. of George Raleigh, of Thornburgh, Warwick, and was bur. 11 Dec. 1592, having by her (who d. 12 Aug. 1607) had issue,

1. WILLIAM, of whom presently.
2. Thomas, of Enborne, Berks, m. Judith, dau. of Ciprian de Valeria, of Andalusia, and d. 1613, having by her (who m. 2ndly, Edward Prescott, of London) had a dau.,
   Ann, m. Gyles Coys, of North Oxendon, Essex.
3. Richard, of Jesus Coll. Oxford 1575, left a dau., Frances.
4. Robert, M.A., and Fellow of All Souls, Oxford 1578.
5. Ferdinand, Capt. in the Army, served in Ireland, temp. ELIZABETH, bapt. 8 Feb. 1566; bur. 14 May, 1617.
6. Francis (Sir), bapt. at Kingsclere, b. Jan. 1570, served in Ireland under Sir G. Carew in 1601-2, acquired lands at Ballybeg Abbey, co. Cork, and was knighted at Dublin March, 1603. He d. 25 July, 1620, leaving issue,

1. Henry, b. 1607; d. 22 April, 1621.
2. Francis, b. 1612; d.s.p. 20 Aug. 1640.
3. William, of Ballybeg Abbey, co. Cork, M.P. for Mallow 1634-41, one of the 1649 officers, m. Dorothy, dau. of Sir Warham St. Leger, and d. 1650, leaving issue,
   (1) William, of Mallow, m. 1683, Susanna, dau. of Richard Myers, from whom the Kilkenny and Canadian branches of the family descend.
   (2) John, d.s.p.
   (3) Thomas, Sheriff of Cork 1697; d. 1702, leaving issue.
   (1) Sydney, m. Sir Thomas Fortescue, from whom the Earls Claremont.
   (2) Mary, m. Ulysses Burgh, Bishop of Ardagh,
   (3) Lavinia, m. Matthew Pennefather, of Gort, and had issue.
   1. Ann, m. Francis Smith, of Kilcoursie, co. Cork, and had issue.
   2. Dorothea, m. 1st, Thomas Fleetwood, who d. 7 Oct. 1631, leaving issue, and 2ndly, Alexandre Marchant, Sieur de St. Michel, by whom she was mother of Elizabeth, m. 1 Dec. 1655, Samuel Pepys, the famous author of the Diary, and d.s.p. 10 Dec. 1669.
7. George, of Wattington, Berks, Capt. in the Army in Ireland, d.s.p. 1639.   8. John, bapt. 16 April, 1578; d. young.
1. Constance, m. Richard Fiennes, Lord Saye and Sele, and had issue.
2. Eleanor, bapt. 12 June, 1571; m. her cousin, Sir Henry Goring, of Burton.
3. Bridget, bapt. 28 Sept. 1572; m. Sir Thomas Norris, 5th son of Henry, Lord Norris, and had issue.
4. Katherine, bapt. 25 July, 1574; m. 11 March, 1593, Sir Anthony Palmer.   5. Frances, m. 1581, John Croker, of Barton.

The eldest son,

SIR WILLIAM KINGSMILL, of Sydmonton, Sheriff of Hants 1602 and 1613, knighted at the Charterhouse 11 May, 1603, entertained JAMES I. and his Queen at Sydmonton Court 18 and 19 Aug. 1603; m. Ann, dau. and co-heir of William Wilks, of Hodnell, co. Warwick, and widow of Anthony Dryden, and d. 30 June, 1618, leaving issue,

1. William, bapt. 22 Feb. 1578; d. 24 May, 1603.
2. HENRY, of whom presently.
3. Richard (Sir), of Malshanger House, who was bur. at Kingsclere, 1 May, 1663, leaving issue,
   1. Henry, bapt. 19 Aug. 1624.
   1. Dorothy, m. 30 March, 1639, John Fanshawe, of Parsloes, and had issue.
   2. Ann, m. Sir Robert Howard, son of the Earl of Berkshire.
4. George, of Easthorpe, Essex, m. Ann, dau. of Thomas Blagrove, and had issue,
   George, b. 1647; m. 31 May, 1676, Elizabeth, dau. of Humphrey Jones.
   Ann, d. 1652.
5. Walter, d. Dec. 1592.
6. Joshua, bapt. 7 Nov. 1593, left issue by Margaret his wife, three children.
1. Anna, m. 28 Oct. 1615, Humphrey Foster, and d. 1673. He d. 1663.
2. Constance, m. Sir Thomas Baker, of Wettingham Hall, Suffolk.
3. Margaret, bapt. 30 Aug. 1598; m. Sir John Woodward, of Weston-under-Edge, and d. 1664.
4. Francis, m. 1634, Sir Guy Foster, of Hanslope, Bucks, and had issue.
5. Bridget, m. 3 Nov. 1614, Sir Henry Colt, of Colt Hall, Suffolk, and had issue.
6. Elizabeth, bapt. 29 June, 1581; m. Sir Edward Tyrrell, of Thornton, Bucks, and had issue.
7. Eleanor, bapt. 30 May, 1583; m. Sir Timothy Tyrrell, of Oakely, Bucks, and d. 24 May, 1641, leaving issue.
8. Martha.   9. Judith.

The second son,

SIR HENRY KINGSMILL, of Sydmonton, b. 1587, knighted 8 Feb. 1610; m. 20 Dec. 1610, Bridgett, dau. of John White, of Southwick, Hants, and d. 22 Oct. 1624, having by her (who d. 4 Sept. 1672) had issue,

1. WILLIAM, of whom presently.
2. Henry, of Enham, Hants, Capt. in the King's Army, killed at Edgehill, 1642.
3. John, of Sandleford, Berks, B.A. Trin. Coll. Oxon, m. Rachel, dau. of Henry Pitt, and d. 15 July, 1687, leaving issue,
   1. Robert, of Sandleford, d.s.p. 13 July, 1697.
   2. Henry, of Sandleford, d.s.p. 1710.
4. Thomas.
5. Daniel, b. 1622; m. 1st, Bridgett, dau. of the Rev. William Kingsmill, D.D. (see above), and 2ndly, 4 Nov. 1672, Abigail Robinson, of Inkpen, Berks. H= d. 1679, leaving issue by his first wife,
   1. William, of Bristol, d. 1717.   2. Daniel, of London, d. 1715.
   1. Mary.   3. Elizabeth.
   3. Bridgett.   4. Catherine.

The last male heir of their several lines, William Kingsmill, d. young about 1784, but the senior female line, on the death of the last baronet, Sir Robert Kingsmill, of Sydmonton Court, without male heirs 1825, s. to the manors and estates of Sydmonton, Woodcote, and Lichfield, Hants, under a double testamentary devise and entail pursuant to the will of Sir William Kingsmill, 1698 (see below).

1. Bridget, bapt. 21 Dec. 1622; m. Richard Lord Gorges, Baron Dundalk, and d. about 1700.   2. Anne, d. in France.

The eldest son,

SIR WILLIAM KINGSMILL, of Sydmonton, Sheriff of Hants 1643, b. 1613; m. Anna, dau. of Sir Anthony Haslewood, of Maidwell, and d. 3 Sept. 1661, having by her (who m. 2ndly, Sir Thomas Ogle) had issue,

1. WILLIAM, of whom presently.
1. Bridget, d. 3 Jan. 1719.
2. Ann, b. April, 1661, Maid of Honour to Queen MARY; m. 14 May, 1684, Heneage, 4th Earl of Winchelsea, and d.s.p. 5 Aug. 1720.

The only son,

SIR WILLIAM KINGSMILL, of Sydmonton, b. 1660, knighted 28 Oct. 1680; m. 1st, 8 June, 1681, Frances, dau. of Alderman Thomas Coldwall, of London. She d. 4 July, 1689, leaving issue,
 1. William, of Sydmonton, bapt. 12 Nov. 1683; d. unm. 8 Jan. 1766.   2. Thomas, b. 10 Feb. 1686; d. 30 April, 1687.
 3. Henry, bapt. Jan. 1687; d.s.p. 20 May, 1710.
 1. Frances, m. 1682; Hugh Corry, of Newtown, co. Down, and d. 8 Sept. 1721, leaving issue,
  1. William d.s.p. 1763.   2. Henry, d.s.p. 1738.
  1. Catherine, d. young.   2. ELIZABETH, of whom presently.
He m. 2ndly, Rebecca —, and was bur. at Kingsclere 26 Nov. 1698, having by her (who d. 20 May, 1727) had issue,
 2. Rebecca, d. 26 Nov. 1696.
 3. Penelope, m. Rev. John Waterman, of Barkham, Berks, Rector of Arbenfield, and had issue, one dau.,
  Rebecca, m. 1st, Laurence Head Osgood, of Winterton, Berks, who d.s.p. 1766. She m. 2ndly, Richard Brickenden, of Malshanger, Sheriff of Hants, 1788. She d.s.p. 1780.

His grand-dau.,

ELIZABETH CORRY, of Sydmonton, m. before 1766, CAPT. ROBERT BRICE (or Bruce), R.N. (afterwards Admiral Sir Robert Bruce-Kingsmill, Bart.), second son of Charles Brice, of Castle Chichester, co. Donegal. He was a very distinguished naval commander, and friend of Nelson's, and was presented with the freedom of the cities of Dublin and Cork, when on the Irish station, for capturing Irish frigates. He was created a baronet 24 Nov. 1800, with remainder to his nephew. His wife d.s.p. 1783. He d.s.p. 23 Nov. 1805, and was s. by the only son of his brother Edward Bruce, principal Surveyor of the Revenue in the Port of Belfast (who also by Royal Licence dated 19 Dec. 1787, had taken the name and arms of KINGSMILL, and d. 4 July, 1796). He was

MAJOR SIR ROBERT BRUCE-KINGSMILL, Bart., of Sydmonton Court, of the Bristol Light Cavalry, b. 1772; d. 1825; m. June, 1795, Elizabeth, dau. and heiress of Charles Newman, of Calcutta, by whom he left a dau. and heiress,

ELIZABETH CATHERINE BRUCE-KINGSMILL, b. Sept. 1797; m. 10 June, 1824, John Woodham, of Cavendish Square, London, Barrister-at-Law, sometime Treasurer for co. Southampton, who by Royal Licence dated 8 April, 1824, took the additional name and arms of KINGSMILL, on his union with their representative, and having by a subsequent Royal Licence, dated 8 Dec 1825, renounced the name of Woodham and was COL. SIR JOHN KINGSMILL, Knt., J.P., of Hermitage Park, Commander of the Battle-Axe Guards of the Castle of Dublin; Knighted 5 Oct. 1830, and d. 23 Oct. 1859, having by her (who d. 23 May, 1865), a dau. and heiress,

ISABEL AUGUSTA BRUCE, m. 22 June, 1865, Thomas Nugent Kingsmill (formerly KENNEY), son of Lieut.-Col. James FitzGerald Kenney, of Kilclogher (see that family), and nephew of the 9th Earl of Westmeath (see BURKE'S Peerage), and d. 22 Dec. 1872, leaving issue,

JULIAN CLAUD DE KENNE BRUCE KINGSMILL, now of Hermitage Park.

Mr. Kenney had assumed the surname of KINGSMILL and the arms of Kingsmill and Kenney quarterly by Royal Licence dated 18 Jan. 1866.

Arms—Quarterly: 1st and 4th, arg. semée of cross-crosslets fitchée, sa. a chev. ermines between three fers de moline pierced of the second, a chief in the third (for KINGSMILL); 2nd and 3rd, per pale or and az. a fleur-de-lis between three crescents all counter-changed, a crescent for difference (for KENNEY). Crests—1st, a cubit arm, erect, vested arg. cuffed ermines, in the hand ppr. a fer de moline as in the arms (for KINGSMILL), 2nd, out of an earl's coronet or a cubit arm erect vested gu. cuffed arg. the hand grasping a roll of parchment ppr. the arm charged with a crescent arg. for difference, (for KENNEY).   Motto—Do well, doubt nought.

Seat—Hermitage Park, Lucan, co. Dublin. Residence—Newton House, Newton, Lanarkshire.

KIRKWOOD OF WOODBROOKE.

COL. JAMES NICHOLSON SODON KIRKWOOD, of Woodbrook, co. Roscommon, and of Curramabla, co. Sligo, J.P., Col. (ret.) Indian Army, b. 4 Jan. 1846; m. 1880, Minnie Charlotte, 4th dau. of late Major Home Fergusson, of The Park, Elie, Fifeshire, and has with other issue,

CHARLES HOME KINGSTON, Capt. 23rd Cav. (Frontier Force), Indian Army, b. 1882.

Lineage.—JAMES KIRKWOOD, of Woodbrooke, J.P., b. 1731 (son of Thomas Kirkwood, of Woodbrooke, by Eleanor his wife, dau. of the first Archdeacon Carey, and grandson of Michael Kirkwood, of Killukin, by his wife, Elizabeth Jackson, of Enniscoe, co. Mayo), m. 25 Sept. 1762, Catherine, only dau. of Samuel Kirkwood, of Moyne Abbey, co. Mayo, and d. 1791, leaving a son and successor,

THOMAS KIRKWOOD, of Woodbrooke, J.P., High Sheriff 1808; m. 15 Feb. 1798, Anne, dau. of James Knott, of Battlefield, co. Sligo, and by her (who d. 1836, aged 68) had issue,
 1. JAMES, his successor.
 2. Thomas, of Cloongoonagh (see KIRKWOOD of Cloongoonagh).
 3. Harloe, d. unm. July 1850.
 1. Joanna, m. Charles Gallagher Moore, 2nd son of George Moore, Barrister-at-Law, of Mountjoy Square, Dublin.
 2. Mary, m. Edward Fraser, of Annagh, co. Sligo.

The eldest son,

JAMES KIRKWOOD, of Woodbrooke, co. Roscommon, b. 1800, J.P. and D.L., High Sheriff 1848; m. 7 Oct. 1839, Sarah Mary Dodd, eldest dau. of Capt. James Nicholson Sodon, 24th Regt., J.P. and D.L., only son of Thomas Sodon, J.P. of Moneygold, co. Sligo, for fifty years Provost of Sligo, and had issue,
 1. THOMAS YADEN LLOYD, of Woodbrooke.
 2. JAMES NICHOLSON SODON, now of Woodbrooke.
 3. Kingston Dodd Lloyd, b. 20 July, 1851; d. 1886.
 1. Isabella Matilda Emily, m. 6 April, 1869, John Law Hackett, J.P., of Ardcarne House, co. Roscommon.
 2. Annina Mary.   3. Sarah Carey Lydia Adelaide.
 4. Joanna.

Mr. Kirkwood d. 25 June, 1857. His eldest son,

COL. THOMAS YADEN LLOYD KIRKWOOD, of Woodbrook, co. Roscommon, J.P. and D.L., and High Sheriff co. Roscommon 1873, and J.P. co. Sligo, Col. late Comm. 5th Batt. Connaught Rangers, b. 19 Sept. 1843. He d. 14 Jan. 1911, and was s. by his brother.

Arms—Gu. on a chevron or, between three fetterlocks arg. a pheon between two mullets pierced sa. Crest—A pheon sa, charged with a mullet or.   Motto—Spes mea in Deo.

Seats—Woodbrooke, Boyle, co. Roscommon; and Curramabla, co. Sligo.

KIRKWOOD OF CLOONGOONAGH.

MAJOR THOMAS MOORE KIRKWOOD, of Cloongoonagh, co. Roscommon, Major Indian Army, b. 4 Feb. 1865; m. 9 Sept. 1905, Olive Muriel, youngest dau. of Gilbert Joseph Talbot, County Inspector Royal Irish Constabulary, and has issue,

GEOFFREY MOORE TALBOT, b. 17 Oct. 1906.
Olive Adelaide Ethel.

Lineage.—THOMAS KIRKWOOD, of Cloongoonagh, co. Roscommon, 2nd son of THOMAS KIRKWOOD, of Woodbrooke (see that family), b. 1803; m. 18 April, 1831, Judith Mary, dau. of John Kirkwood, of Rathfarnham, Dublin. She d. 19 Feb. 1858. He d. 2 May, 1854, having had issue,
 1. ANDREW SAMUEL, now of Cloongoonagh.
 2. Thomas Moore, Surg.-Maj. A.M.S., b. 21 Nov. 1839; m. Annabelle Edith, only dau. of Gen. Pottinger, of Mount Pottinger, co. Leitrim, and d. 1886, leaving issue,
  1. Emily Moore.
  2. Edith Frances, m. 13 April, 1907, Barry Neame, 7th son of George Neame.
 1. Anna Mary, m. 19 May, 1852, Gen. J. Long, A.S.C.
 2. Sidney Elizabeth, m. Capt. J. S. Cullen, Leitrim Rifles.
 3. Emily Frances.
 4. Frances Harriett Caroline, m. Lieut.-Col. E. Morrell, 44th Regt. She d. 22 June, 1890.

The eldest son,

ANDREW SAMUEL KIRKWOOD, of Cloongoonagh, co. Roscommon, J.P., b. 15 Feb. 1834; m. 12 May, 1864, Mary Harriette, youngest dau. of the late John MacMunn, M.D., of 2, Rutland Square, Dublin, and d. 8 Nov. 1902, having had issue,
 1. THOMAS MOORE, now of Cloongoonagh.
 2. Torton Andrew, Major Indian Army, b. 29 Aug. 1871.
 3. Sinclair Francis, Major Waterford Art., b. Aug. 1873; m. 3 June, 1902, Violet Caroline Josephine, only dau. of the late Lieut.-Col. Joseph Thackwell, of Aghada Hall, co. Cork (see that family), and has issue,
  Esther.
 4. Andrew Samuel, Lieut. 1st Batt. Royal Irish Rifles, b. 6 June, 1875; m. 6 June, 1906, Violet Mabel, dau. of Edward Sinclair Snow, of Homestead, co. Dublin, and has issue,
  Violet Mabel.
 5. William Clarke, Capt. Indian Army, late Lincoln Regt., b. 12 March, 1880.
 6. Howard Monypenny, Indian Police, late Lieut. 6th Batt. Rifle Brigade, b. 30 Oct. 1884.
 1. Judith Mary, m. 26 April, 1897, W. Morony, of Ellesmere, Boyle, co. Roscommon.
 2. Rosabel Sinclair, m. 2 Oct. 1884, Lieut.-Col. H. L. Donovan, A.M.S.
 3. Mary Howard, m. 20 July, 1893, John Wills, of Willsbrook, Lucan, co. Dublin.
 4. Muriel Morrell, d. unm. 20 March, 1901.

Arms—See KIRKWOOD of Woodbrooke.

Seat—Cloongoonagh, Carrick on Shannon, co. Roscommon.

KIRWAN OF CREGG.

DENIS AGAR RICHARD KIRWAN, of CREGG, Lieut. R.N., b. 1878, s. his uncle 1904; m. 1904, Dorothy Marjory, dau. of John Dallender, of New York.

Lineage.—WILLIAM KIRWAN, who settled in the town of Galway, 1488, d. there 1499, leaving two sons,
1. THOMAS REAGH, of whom presently.
2. Patrick, Warden of Galway.

The elder,
THOMAS REAGH KIRWAN, d. 1545, and was father of
THOMAS KIRWAN, Alderman of Galway in 1542, who had two sons,
1. ANDREW, his successor.
2. Stephen, ancestor of KIRWAN of Castle Hackett.

The elder son,
ANDREW KIRWAN, of Galway, m. Anastacia French, and d. 1578, leaving with a younger son, William Oge, an elder son and heir,
PATRICK KIRWAN, Alderman of Galway, m. Jane Brown, and had, with two other sons, Robert and Thomas, three sons,
1. ANDREW, his heir.
2. Edward, called "Airgid," or of the Silver, who m. Anastacia Blake, and was ancestor of KIRWAN of Dalgin, and MAITLAND KIRWAN of Gelston.
3. Robert, of Galway, m. Mary, dau. of Nicholas Martin, of Galway, and d. 23 Dec. 1626, leaving issue,
   1. Nicholas, of Galway.
   2. Richard.
   3. Joan.
   3. Margery.
   3. Robert.
   2. Agnes.

He d. 1608, and was s. by his eldest son,
ANDREW KIRWAN, m. Margaret French, and d. 1644, having had issue, three sons and as many daus.,
1. PATRICK, his heir.
2. Martin, of Knock, m. Mary, dau. of Sir Thomas Blake, 2nd bart. of Menlo, and had a son,
   JOHN KIRWAN, m. Bridget Netterville, and dying 1691, left two daus., one of whom m. her cousin, Thomas Kirwan; and the other, her cousin, Ambrose Kirwan.
3. William, of Cloondroon, m. and had issue, 1. Patrick; 2. John; 3. Andrew, whose only son, William, was father of an only son, Andrew Kirwan, who dying s.p., this branch became extinct.
1. Giles, m. Sir Richard Blake, Knt. of Galway.
2. Mary, m. Dominick Lynch, gent. of Galway.
3. Katherine.

The eldest son,
PATRICK KIRWAN, of Cregg, m. Eliza, dau. of Andrew D'Arcy, of Galway, and d. 1679, leaving a son and successor,
MARTIN KIRWAN, of Cregg, m. 1668, Eliza, dau. of Ambrose Bodkin, of Corobeg, and had issue,
1. PATRICK, his heir.
2. Andrew.
3. Ambrose, m. his cousin, the dau. of John Kirwan, of Hillsbrook, and had a dau.,
   Margaret, m. Thomas Browne.
4. Thomas, m. his cousin, the dau. of John Kirwan, of Knock, and had,
   1. Martin Fitz-Thomas, d. 1771. 2. Ambrose.
   3. JOHN, of Hillsbrook, m. Mary Mahon, and had issue,
      (1) JOSEPH, of Hillsbrook, m. 1800, Mary, eldest dau. and co-heiress of Edward Lynch, of Hampstead, and d. without male issue, 1827. Of his daus. and co-heiresses,
         1. Mary, m. Capt. Euseby Kirwan.
         2. Julia, m. Edward Browne.
         3. Eliza, m. James, 7th Viscount Netterville.
      (2) MARTIN, of Knockdromadough and Stowe Lodge, co. Galway, m. 18 July, 1806, Maria, dau. of Myles Burke, of the Island of St. Eustacia, and had issue,
         1. JOHN JOSEPH ANDREW, of Castlecomer, co. Kilkenny, and Stowe Lodge, co. Galway, Barrister-at-Law, Resident Magistrate, co. Kilkenny, J.P. and D.L. co. Galway, b. 31 Oct. 1811; m. 11 June, 1832, Mary Isabella, only dau. of Major William Burke, of Quansborough, by Lady Matilda St. Lawrence, his wife, dau. of William, 2nd Earl of Howth, and co-heiress of her mother, Lady Mary Bermingham, 2nd dau. and co-heiress of Thomas, Earl of Louth, 22nd Baron Athenry. By this lady (who d. March, 1869) he had, 1, Martin Fitz-John, Capt. City of Dublin Militia, b. 25 Sept. 1835; d.s.p. 11 Nov. 1865; 2, William Joseph, Lieut. in the Galway Militia, b. 13 Nov. 1837; m. 1861, Kate, dau. of Edmund Kirwan, of Woodfield (see below), and d. June, 1862, leaving issue, one dau., Mary Lydia; 3, ANDREW FITZ-JOHN, an Officer in Australia, b. 13 July, 1839; 4, Henry, b. 18 March, 1841; 1, Matilda Harriet Josephine, m. her cousin, Joseph Burke, of Roscommon, and had issue.
         2. Myles, Barrister-at-Law, of Glenrock, m. 1838, Maria, his cousin, only dau. of John Kirwan, and d.s.p. 1846.
         3. Martin, an Officer in Portugal.
         4. Henry John, J.P. of Gardenfield, co. Galway, m. Mary Martyn, and has a son, Henry.
         1. Mary, m. 1838, James Blakeney, and has issue.

2. Barbara, m. Henry M'Donell, of Streamsfort, and has issue.
(1) Matilda, m. Walter Blake, of Menlo.
(2) Theresa, m. 1775, William Burke, of Ower.
(3) Juliana, m. George William Lyster (see LYSTER of Rocksavage).

Mr. Kirwan d. 1705, and was s. by his eldest son,
PATRICK KIRWAN, of Cregg, m. 23 March, 1703, Mary, dau. of Richard Martyn, of Birch Hall, and had issue,
1. MARTIN, his heir. 2. George, killed in a duel in France.
3. Richard Moy, of Woodfield, m. Christian Maria, dau. of Nicholas Bermingham, of Barbesford. He fought at the battle of Fontenoy with the Irish Brigade. He d. 1779, leaving four sons and three daus. His eldest son, MARTIN, of Woodfield, J.P., m. Bedelia, dau. of Michael McCann, of Dunmore, and d. 1820, leaving issue,
   1. Edmund b 1803; m. Lydia, dau. of John Waters, Lieut. 21st Royal Fus., of Parkmore Lodge, Ballinglass, co. Wicklow, and d. in Paris 1887, leaving,
      (1) Martin Waters, Lieut. Glamorganshire Militia, and afterwards Capt. in Foreign Legion of France, served through the Franco-Prussian war. He d. in New York 10 Nov. 1899, leaving issue, a dau.
      (2) Nicholas John, Lieut. Glamorgan Militia, d. 1865.
      (1) Kate, m. 1861, William Joseph Kirwan, son of John Joseph Andrew Kirwan, of Castlecomer (see above).
      (2) Christian, m. Capt. Stephens. (3) Lydia.
   2. Nicholas John, of Sandymount House, co. Galway, b. 1809; m. 9 Feb. 1858, Mary Ellen, dau. of John Waters, Lieut. 21st Royal Fus., of Parkmore Lodge, Ballinglass, co. Wicklow, and d. 1888, leaving issue,
      (1) Edmund Martin, b. 1860.
      (2) John Waters (Hon.), M.H.R. for Kalgoorlie in the first Australian Commonwealth Parliament, and as member of that Parliament granted in 1904 the right to retain the title of "Hon" for life (Kalgoorlie), and J.P. East Coolgardie, b. 1866.
      (1) Dorinda, m. Louis Henry Brindley, J.P., and has issue.
      (2) Lydia, m. Robert J. Kirwan, B.A., B.E., eldest son of Henry Kirwan, J.P., of Gardenfield, co. Galway, and has issue.
   3. Richard, of Ashfield, co. Dublin, b. 1809; m. Dorinda, dau. of John Waters, of co. Carlow, and d. 1872, leaving,
      Patrick Bermingham, d. 1891.
   4. Patrick, b. 1813; d. 1839.
   5. Austin b. 1815; emigrated to U.S.A., and d. 1887, leaving issue.
4. Anthony, killed in Galway.
5. Edmund, killed in a duel in India. 6. Andrew, of Curragh.

Mr. Kirwan, who was living in 1746, was s. by his eldest son,
MARTIN KIRWAN, of Cregg, m. Mary French, and had four sons,
1. Patrick, d. 1756.
2. Richard, LL.D., of Cregg, Pres. Roy. Irish Society, a distinguished writer on chemistry, geology, and the kindred sciences, and one of the first natural philosophers of his time, m. 1757, Anne, dau. of Sir Thomas Blake, Bart. of Menlo, and d. in 1812, leaving two daus.,
   1. Maria Theresa, m. 21 Jan. 1793, John Thomas, 15th Lord Trimlestown, and d. 12 Oct. 1824, leaving issue (see BURKE's Peerage). 2. Elizabeth, m. Mr. Hill.
3. Andrew, Major in the Army, d. 1813. 4. Hyacinth.

The youngest son,
HYACINTH KIRWAN, m. Elizabeth Frances, dau. of Patrick Blake, a younger son of the family of Blake, of Tower Hill, co. Mayo. and dying in 1800, left issue,
1. PATRICK, inherited the family property at the decease of his uncle, Richard Kirwan, LL.D.
2. Richard, Capt. h.p. 94th Regt., m. Ellen, dau. and heir of George Bond, Barrister-at-Law, and had issue,
   1. Richard, b. 1830, m. 1860, Rose Helen, dau. of Rev. Barrett Lampet, of Great Bardfield, and d. 1872, having had issue,
      (1) Robert Mansel (Rev.), M.A. Oxon., Chaplain Bengal Ecclesiastical Establishment, b. 1861; m. 29 Oct. 1902, Marguerite Theodora, dau. of Henry Trenton Wadley.
      (2) Ernest Cecil (Rev.), Rector of Guildford, Surrey, b. 1867.
      (3) Lionel Edward, of Madras, b. 1869; m. 8 Feb. 1903, Evelyn Waller, dau. of E. W. Stoney, of Madras, and has issue,
         1. Patrick Lionel, b. 1905. 2. Ralph Bertram, b. 1908.
         1. Hyacinth Ethel, b. 22 Oct. 1903.
      (4) Bertram Richard, Major R.A., b.17 May, 1871; m. Helen, dau. of Gen. Hogg, Indian Army, and has issue,
         Rudolph Charles Hogg, b. 1903.
         Kathleen Helen, b. 1899.
      (5) Gerald William Claude, b. 1872.
      (1) Eleanor Augusta Mary, m. 1897, Reginald Barlow Plumer, Mysore Civil Service.
   2. George, Capt. King's Own Scottish Borderers, d. 1901.
   3. Robert, Capt. Royal Marine Art., d.s.p. 1860.
      1. Ellen, m. James Cooch, Royal Fusiliers, and d. 1909.
3. Andrew Hyacinth, Capt. h.p. 66th Regt., m. Charlotte, 2nd dau. of Francis Eld, of Seighford Hall, co. Stafford.
4. John, R.N., d. 1825.
1. Elizabeth Frances, m. 1818, T. Macquoid.

The eldest surviving son,
PATRICK KIRWAN, of Cregg, co. Galway, b. 19 Dec. 1787; m. 9 Aug. 1811, Louisa Margaret, 4th dau. of Dominick Geoffrey Browne, of Castle Macgarrett, co. Mayo, and sister of Dominick, 1st Lord Oranmore, and by her (who d. 1826) had issue,
1. RICHARD ANDREW HYACINTH, his heir.

2. Edward (Rev.), Vicar of Wootton Wawen, co. Warwick, b. Aug. 1814; m. Louisa, only dau. of Thomas Macquoid.
3. John Henry (Rev.), M.A., Rector of St. John's, Cornwall, b. 25 Dec. 1816; m. Fanny, 3rd dau. of Rear-Admiral James Dacres, and d. 13 June, 1899, leaving issue.
  Henry, Commander R.N. (ret.), m. Kathleen Whistler, and has issue, two daus.
4. Hyacinth (Rev.), Chaplain with Field Force under General Sir Colin Campbell before Lucknow, b. 28 July, 1820; d. unm. April, 1858.
1. Henrietta Theresa, m. Feb. 1838, Rev. George Dacres Alexander Tyler, and had issue.
2. Louisa Margaret, m. (as his second wife) 17 April, 1838, Henry B. Brownlow, Bengal Civil Service, youngest brother of Charles, 1st Lord Lurgan, and d. 29 Feb. 1840 (see BURKE's *Peerage*).
3. Elizabeth Frances Charlotte, m. Rev. T. A. Voules, and has issue.
4. Mary Ann Georgiana, m. the late George A. Lawrence, and has issue, George Patrick Charles, Barrister-at-Law, d. 18 April, 1908, m. 8 Aug. 1883, Hon. Hildegarde Davey, dau. of Lord Davey, and has issue.
5. Isabella Catherine Louisa, d. unm. 5 Nov. 1910.
Mr. Kirwan d. 31 Dec. 1847, and was s. by his eldest son,
  RICHARD ANDREW HYACINTH KIRWAN of Bawnmore, co. Galway, J.P., High Sheriff 1855, late Capt. Galway Militia, late Lieut. 5th and 7th Fus., b. 30 May, 1813; m. 29 April, 1839, Agnes Jane, 3rd dau. of John Thompson, of Laurence Town, co. Down, and by her (who d. 14 March, 1884) had issue,
1. MARTIN ORANMORE, his heir.
2. John Denis, Major R.H.A., b. 22 Oct. 1852; m. Jan. 1877, Georgiana Constance, dau. of E. Talbot Agar, of Milford House, Hants. She d. 24 March, 1909. He d. 6 June, 1891, leaving issue,
  1. DENIS AGAR RICHARD, now of Cregg.
  1. Eileen Constance, b. 1877; m. 1905, Capt. A. T. Dickenson, Indian Army, and has issue.
  2. Hyacinth Maud, b. 1882; m. 24 Feb. 1906, Lieut. Cecil John Charles Street, R.A., only son of late Gen. Street, C.B., and has issue
  3. Audrey Theodora Agnes, b. 1888; m 25 May, 1909, Capt. A. C. Halahan, Essex Regt, 2nd son of late Col. S. H. Halahan, and has issue.
1. Helen Louisa Elizabeth, m. 1st, 12 Sept. 1860, Thomas Donaldson, 3rd K.O. Hussars, who d. 13 July, 1867, leaving issue,
  1. Walter Kirwan, b. 1863.
  2. Gerald Kirwan, b. 1865; m. 1897, Ada, dau. of William Miller, of Melbourne.
  3. Thomas Kirwan, b. 1867; d.s.p. 16 March, 1893.
  1. Helen Louisa, m. 1st, Capt. Frederick Ind, R.A., who d. 1887, and 2ndly, 7 July, 1891, Capt. Wellesley George Pigott, late Rifle Brigade, and has issue (see BURKE's *Peerage*, PIGOTT, Bart.).
Mrs. Donaldson m. 2ndly, 1870, A. C. Wolseley-Cox, J.P., of Clara, King's Co., late 12th Lancers, and d. 28 Aug. 1903, having by him had an only child,
  4. Reginald Garnet Wolseley, b. 1872.
3. Henrietta Frances, m. 5 Jan. 1865, Major-Gen. Richard Blundell Hollinshead Blundell, late 3rd K.O. Hussars, and has issue,
  1. Henry Leigh, Lieut. Rifle Brigade, b. 1869; d. 2 Feb. 1896.
  2. Dermot, M.V.O., Capt. King's Royal Rifle Corps, b. 27 Feb. 1874; m. 15 June, 1901, Eugénie Sybil, dau. of W. H. Dudley Ward (see BURKE's *Peerage*, DUDLEY, E.). He d. 26 Oct. 1910.
  1. Henrietta, m. 6 June, 1889, Rear-Admi. Sir Colin Keppel, K.C.V.O., C.B., D.S.O., R.N., Equerry to H.R.H. the Duke of Saxe-Coburg and Edinburgh, and has issue (see BURKE's *Peerage*, ALBEMARLE, E.).
Mr. Kirwan b. 3 Jan. 1886. His eldest son,
  MARTIN ORANMORE KIRWAN, of Bawnmore, co. Galway, b. 26 April, 1847; d. unm. 17 May, 1904, and was s. by his nephew.

Arms—Arg., a chevron sa. between three Cornish choughs ppr.
Crest—A Cornish chough as in the arms. Motto—J'aim mon Dieu, mon roy, et mon pais.

Seat—Baunmore, Clare Oalway, co. Galway.

KNOX OF PREHEN.

The late GEORGE KNOX, of Prehen, co. Londonderry, J.P. and D.L., for cos. Donegal and Londonderry, High Sheriff co. Donegal 1862; Lieut.-Col. late Comm. Londonderry Artillery, b. 1832; m. Rose Virginie Grimm, of Neuchâtel, Switzerland, and d. 29 Nov. 1910, having had issue,

1. EUGENIE, m. Ludwig von Scheffler, Doctor of Philosophy, and has issue,
  1. George Carl Otto Louis.
  1. Manon.   2. Virginie.
2. AUGUSTA GEORGINA, m. 2 Sept. 1896, Molyneux William Shuldham, of Moigh House, Ballymulvey co. Longford (see that family).

Lineage.—This would now appear to be the direct representative line of the ancient and extended family of KNOX, the founder of that name.
  ADAMUS, son of Uchtred, obtained from the High Steward *temp.* ALEXANDER II. King of Scots, 1214 to 1249, grants of the lands of Knock, Ranfurlie, Griefie Castle, Craig End, &c., in the barony and county of Renfrew. The descendants of Adamus assumed the surname of Knox, derived, according to *Patronymica Britannica*, page 182, from the lands of Knocks, or Knox, Knock being Gaelic for round-topped hill. For many generations they were seated at the castle of Ranfurlie, the ruins of which lie between Glasgow and Greenock. Adamus had a son,
  JOHANNE DE KNOX, he had an eldest son,
  UTRED DE KNOCX, whose son was,
  ALANUS DE KNOCKIS, *temp.* Robert Bruce, who had a son,
  SIR JOHN DE KNOX, Lord of Ranfurly. He m. 1371, the 2nd dau. and co-heiress of Sir David Fleming of Biggar. Their son was
  ROBERT DE KNOCK, who had a son,
  UCHTRED DE KNOCKS, who had a son,
  JOHN DE KNOCKS, who by his wife, the only child of Sir Robert Maxwell, of Calderwood, by Elizabeth, co-heiress of Sir Robert Dennistoun, had a son,
1. UCHTRED.
The eldest son,
  UCHTRED KNOX, of Craig Ends, m. Agnes, dau. of Lord Lyle, and had two sons.
  1. UCHTRED, his heir.
  2. George, m. Janet, dau. of — Fleming, of Barrochan, and had two sons,
    1. John the Reformer.
    2. William, Minister of Cockpen, m. and had issue.
  UCHTRED KNOX, m. Janet, dau. of Lord Sempill, and had,
  1. UCHTER, who s. him.
  2. William, styled of Silvyland, ancestors of the family of KNOX, of Brittas, of Rappa Castle, of Mount Falcon, of Grace Dieu, and of Greenwood Park, &c., and of the EARLS OF RANFURLY.
The eldest son,
  UCHTER KNOX, of Ranfurlie, m. Isabella, dau. of — Cunningham of Craigends, and had two sons,
  1. JOHN, of Ranfurlie, whose son,
    UCHTER, of Ranfurlie, s. his father, and was s. by his son,
    JOHN, of Ranfurlie, who was father of
    UCHTER, of Ranfurlie, sold his estate to Lord Cochrane, and d.s.p. male.
  2. ANDREW, who eventually carried on the family.
The 2nd son,
  RIGHT REV. ANDREW KNOX, was consecrated Bishop of the Isles 1605, and Bishop of Raphoe, Ireland, 1610. The Bishop had a grant of the monastery and lands of Rathmullen, co. Donegal, 1614. He m. Elizabeth, dau. of Sir Ralph Bingley, Knt. of Rosquil, co. Donegal, and had issue,
  1. Thomas (Right Rev.), D.D., Bishop of the Isles 1622, m. Dec. 1625, Prudence, dau. of Peter Benson, of Shragmore, co. Derry, and had issue. The heiress of his line, Katherine, dau. of Andrew Knox, of Rathmacnee, co. Wexford, m. 1735, John Grogan, of Johnstown, same co.
  2. ANDREW, of whom hereafter.
  3. John (Rev.), of Ballygonnah, co. Donegal, m. Jane, dau. of George Downham, D.D., Bishop of Derry, and d. 31 March, 1643, leaving a son,
    George, b. 1621, Provost Marshal of the besieged army of Derry, 1689; d. Dec. 1690, leaving by Mary, his wife, two sons,
      (1) Thomas.
      (2) George.
  4. Claud (Rev.), Administrator to his father, 1638.
  5. James, Administrator to his father, 1633.
The Bishop of Raphoe d. 17 March, 1632. His 2nd son,
  ANDREW KNOX, of Rathmullen, m. Rebecca, dau. of Lieut.-Col. Robert Galbraith, of Dowish, co. Londonderry, and had issue,
  1. ANDREW, his heir.
  2. Robert, whose will is dated 2 Sept. 1711. m. the sister of John French, and had a son, William; a dau., Rebecca; and another, m. Conyngham.
Mr. Knox was s. by his eldest son,
  ANDREW KNOX, of Rathmullen, Major in the besieged army of Derry, attainted by the Parliament of JAMES II., 1689. By Mary his wife he left a son and successor,
  GEORGE KNOX, of Rathmullen, and of Munnymore, co. Donegal, whose will, dated 11 May, 1739, was proved 29 July, 1741. He m. Mary Wray, and had two sons, ANDREW, his heir, and a younger son (from whom descended Letitia, dau. of Rev. George Knox, Rector of Strabane, mother of Gen. Sir Henry Montgomery Lawrence and John Laird Mair, Baron Lawrence, Viceroy of India, 1864). The eldest son,
  ANDREW KNOX, of Rathmullen and Munnymore, 27 years M.P. for Donegal, and Col. in the Army, whose will, dated 10 May, 1772, was proved 13 Dec. 1774. He m. Honoria, dau. and heiress of Andrew Tomkins, of Prehen, co. Londonderry, and had (with a dau., Mary Anne, shot by John Macnaughton, 10 Nov. 1760) a son, his heir,
  GEORGE KNOX, of Prehen, m. 1762, Jane, dau. of Thomas Mahon, of Strokestown, co. Roscommon, and sister of Maurice, 1st Lord Hartland, by whom he had issue,
  1. ANDREW, his heir.
  2. Thomas (Rev.), m. Ellen, dau. of Redmond Dillon, of Ashbrook, co. Dublin, and had two sons,
    1. George, b. 1806, appointed, 1847, Resident Magistrate co. Sligo; m. 1827, Caroline Catherine, dau. of Charles Hawkes, of Brierfield, co. Roscommon, and d. 13 Jan. 1874, leaving by her (who d. 8 July, 1874) a son, Thomas Conroy, b. 1852.
    2. Thomas.

Knox. THE LANDED GENTRY. 374

3. Maurice, of Farn, co. Roscommon, *m.* Anne Maple, dau. of James Wilson, of Derks, co. Meath, and had issue,
  1. George (Rev.), Rector of Donamon, co. Roscommon, *m.* Frances Holmes, and had issue,
    Maurice, *b.* Jan. 1847, Surgeon-Major in the Army; *m.* 27 Sept. 1880, Edith, dau. of Major-Gen. George Noble Cave, Bengal Army (*see* CAVE *of Cleve Hill*).
    Janet.
2. Maurice Wilson, late of Kilmarnock, co. Wexford, J.P., *b.* 5 Nov. 1805; *m.* 1831, Elizabeth, dau. and heiress of Francis White, of Oldstone, co. Antrim, and by her (who *d.* 25 Nov. 1880) had issue,
  (1) Francis William White, *b.* 11 Oct. 1847; *m.* July, 1871, Annie, dau. of George Hudson, of Templecarrig, co. Wicklow, and has issue,
    1. George Henry Hudson, *b.* 23 Feb. 1874.
    2. Francis William White, *b.* 10 April, 1876.
    3. Richard Beresford, *b.* 1 July, 1879.
    4. Maurice Wilson, *b.* 22 June, 1883.
    5. Beresford Hubert, *b.* Sept. 1885.
    1. Isabella Frances, *b.* 2 May, 1872.
  (2) Maurice, *d.* Nov. 1858.
  (1) Jane, *m.* Nov. 1869, William Topham, and *d.* 26 June, 1870. He *d.* 23 Sept. 1871, aged 39.
  (2) Frances, *m.* 2 Dec. 1854, Charles James Nicholson.
  (3) Bessie, *m.* 3 July, 1862, Robert Boyd.
  (4) Hannah Magdalen, *m.* Nov. 1856, James Brown Hornor Boyd, Lieut.-Col. 17th Regt.
  (5) Jemima Mabel, *m.* 13 Nov. 1869, George Pemberton Pigott.
  (6) Mary, *m.* 20 May, 1869, Lieut.-Col. Albert Greenland, 2nd Batt. Essex Reg., Pompadours, who *d.* 26 Nov. 1883, aged 43.
  (7) Anne Charlotte, *m.* 1880, George Graves Bowring.
1. Hannah, *m.* her cousin, William Knox.
2. Jane.
3. Anne, *m.* George Devenish.
4. Alexander, Capt. Donegal Militia, *m.* Miss Lyneham, and had a son,
  William, *m.* his cousin, Hannah, dau. of Maurice Knox, of Farn.
1. Mary Anne, *m.* Thomas Conroy.
Mr. Knox *d.* 23 Aug. 1840, and was *s.* by his eldest son,
ANDREW KNOX, of Prehen, Col. of the Donegal Militia, M.P. in the Irish Parliament at the Union, *m.* June, 1790, Mary, dau. of Dominick McCausland, of Daisy Hill, co. Derry (*see* MCCAUSLAND, *of Drenagh*), and had issue,
1. GEORGE, his heir.
2. Dominick, *m.* Miss Dysart.
3. Andrew (Rev.), of Birkenhead, *m.* Miss Cox, and had issue.
4. Marcus, Capt. R.N., *m.* Jane, dau. of William Edie, of Thornhill, J.P. co. Tyrone, and *d.* 11 Jan. 1885, leaving two daus.,
  1. Jane Caroline, *m.* 6 Oct. 1868, Duncan Malcolm Irvine, Capt. 17th Regt. (*see* IRVINE *of Killadeas*).
  2. Mary Dorothea Dawing, *m.* 18 May, 1867, Rev. Henry Johnson.
5. Thomas, *m.* Mary Anne, dau. of George Franks, and has issue.
1. Jane, *m.* Capt. Hay, R.N.
2. Honoria, *m.* Ven. Chas. Galway, Archdeacon of Derry, who *d.* 13 March, 1882, aged 90.
3. Mary, *d. unm.*
4. Caroline, *m.* R. Rickards, of Clengallow, co. Glamorgan.
5. Benjamina, *m.* Capt. Loeffel, Belgian Service.
Mr. Knox *d.* 1840, and was *s.* by his eldest son,
GEORGE KNOX, of Prehen, Capt. 2nd Dragoon Guards, J.P. and D.L. cos. Londonderry and Donegal, *m.* 1827, Anna Maria, dau. of Robert Johnstone, of Magheramena Castle, co. Fermanagh, and *d.* 1828 (*see that family*), leaving issue,
  1. GEORGE, late of Prehen.
1. Letitia Mary, *m.* 22 Sept. 1863, Alexander Shuklham, Capt. and Major Londonderry Militia. He *d.* March, 1876, leaving issue (*see that family*). She *d.* 29 July, 1883.
2. Harriett.

Seat—Prehen, Londonderry.

KNOX OF BRITTAS.

JOHN FREDERICK KNOX, late Lieut. R.N., *b.* 1876.

Lineage.—This is a branch of the family of KNOX, of Prehen.

WILLIAM KNOX, styled of Silvyland, the second son of Uchtred Knox and Janet Semple (*see preceding Memoir*), *m.* the heiress of Silvyland, which is situate near the Clyde, below Glasgow. He had a son,

WILLIAM KNOX, of Silvyland, who had two sons,
1. JOHN, who *s.* him.
2. MARCUS, ancestor of the family of Knox, of which the earl of Ranfurly is head (*see* BURKE'S *Peerage*, RANFURLY).

The eldest son,

JOHN KNOX, of Silvyland, *s.* his father, and had two sons,
1. THOMAS, of Silvyland, his heir, who was *s.* by his son, William, of Silvyland, *d.* 1622, leaving a son, Alexander, of Silvyland, *d.s.p.* the last mentioned of Silvyland.
2. WILLIAM, of Lifford, of whom hereafter.

The 2nd son,
WILLIAM KNOX, of Lifford, co. Donegal, settled in Ireland, and his descendants acquired large estates in Mayo. He *m.* a lady named Campbell, and by her left at his decease. 1650 (with three daus.), two sons,
1. JOHN (Sir), Sheriff of Dublin 1675, and Lord Mayor 1685-6, knighted 6 Feb. 1685; *m.* Hannah, dau. of Pierce Moore, of Raheenduff, Queen's Co. (*see* MOORE *of Cremorgan*), and *d.s.p.* 1687. Lady Knox *m.* 2ndly, Henry Mervyn, of Trellick, co. Tyrone.
2. WILLIAM, of whose descendants we treat.

The 2nd son,
WILLIAM KNOX, of Castlerea, co. Mayo, *b.* 1630, whose name appears in the loyal addresses from that county to CHARLES II., 1682 and 1683; *m.* 1st, Mary, only dau. of Roger Palmer, of Castle Lacken, co. Mayo, and had by her,
1. Francis, of Moyne Abbey, co. Mayo, his heir.
2. ARTHUR (*see* KNOX *of Mount Falcon*).
3. Richard, of Lissadrone, co. Mayo, *d.s.p.* 1754.
1. Mary, *m.* 1705, Thomas Bell, Alderman of Dublin, and Lord Mayor 1702.
He *m.* 2ndly, Elizabeth, eldest dau. and co-heir of John Crofton, of Rappa Castle, and had issue,
4. WILLIAM, of Dublin, Clerk of the Crown, of the Peace, and of Assizes for the province of Connaught, *m.* 1733, Mary, dau. of Henry Osborne, of Dardistown, co. Meath, and left issue.
5. John.

His eldest son,
FRANCIS KNOX, of Moyne Abbey, co. Mayo, High Sheriff 1718, *m.* Dorothy, 4th dau. and co-heir of Maurice Annesley, of Little Rath, co. Kildare, nephew of Arthur, 1st Earl of Anglesey, and had by her,
1. Thomas, *d. unm. v.p.*
2. JAMES, of whom presently.
3. FRANCIS, of Rappa Castle (*see* KNOX *of Rappa*).
1. Sarah, *m.* Francis Blake.
2. Dorothy, *b.* 15 Nov. 1729; *m.* Thomas Rutledge, of Killala.
3. Ellinor, *b.* 22 Nov. 1730; *d. unm.*
4. Mary Anne, *b.* 3 May, 1728; *d. unm.* 1800.

Francis Knox *d.* 1730. His eldest surviving son,
JAMES KNOX, of Moyne Abbey, co. Mayo, High Sheriff 1758, *b.* 22 July, 1724; *m.* Dorothea, dau. of Peter Ruttledge, of Cornfield, and *d.* Dec. 1806, having had issue,
1. Francis, of Moyne Abbey, K.C., Assistant Barrister, co. Sligo, M.P. for Philipstown 1797, *b.* 1754; *d. unm.* 12 April, 1821.
2. JOHN, of whom presently.
3. William, H.E.I.C.S., *d.* aged 19.
4. James, Capt. 51st Foot, *d.* at Armagh.
1. Elizabeth, *m.* Dowell O'Reilly of The Heath.
2. Dorothy, *d. unm.* Aug. 1807.
3. Mary Anne. 4. Charity.

The second son,
JOHN KNOX, of Summerhill, Dublin, and of Moyne Abbey, co. Mayo, *b.* 1755; *m.* 1806, Sarah, dau. of Daniel Grehan, and *d.* 25 Dec. 1837 (will dated 3 Aug. 1836, proved 17 Jan. 1837), having had issue,
1. Francis Blake, of Moyne, *m.* 1st, 17 July, 1834, Jane, eldest dau. of George Mayhall Knipe, of Erne Hill, co. Cavan. He *m.* 2ndly, 18 May, 1839, Elizabeth Mary, 2nd dau. of William Hutchinson, of Bullock Castle, co. Dublin. His will, dated 17 Aug. 1850, was proved 26 April, 1851. He had issue,
  1. Harry Blake, of Moyne, and 80, Ulverton Road, Dalkey, J.P. co. Mayo.
  2. William Raymond, *d.* 5 July, 1907.
  3. Ernest Edward, of Rahara, co. Roscommon, *m.* 10 Dec. 1873, Evelyn Florence, eldest dau. of William W. Bentley, of Sydenham.
  4. Francis Albert Blake, *d.* 15 April, 1908; *m.* 1873.
2. WILLIAM, of whom presently.
3. George, Barrister-at-Law.
1. Sarah, *m.* 1825, Rev. Edward Leet.
2. Anne, *m.* 1827, John Ryan Hunter.
3. Frances, *m.* 1831, John Andrew Nolan.
4. Dorothea, *m.* Jan. 1839, Samuel McClintock, of Perrymount, co. Tyrone (*see* MCCLINTOCK *of Seskinore*).

The second son,
COL. WILLIAM KNOX, of Brittas Castle, Thurles, co. Tipperary, J.P., late 13th Light Dragoons, *b.* 1808, *m.* Georgina, youngest dau. of Rev. William Grogan, D.D., of Slaney Park, co. Wicklow, Rector of Baltinglas (*see* BURKE'S *Peerage* CROGAN, Bart.). She *d.* 1878. He *d.* 1892, having had, with other issue,
1. John Hunter, Lieut.-Col. 14th Hussars, *m.* 1878, Ada Kathleen, dau. of Edward Tipping, of Bellurgan, co. Louth, and *d.* 1885.
2. FITZROY, late of Brittas Castle.

His son,
FITZROY KNOX, of Brittas Castle, co. Tipperary, J.P. and D.L., *m.* 1875, Maude (*now of Brittas*), dau. of John Anthony Woods, of Benton Hall, Northumberland, and *d.* 3 April, 1911, having had, with other issue,

JOHN FREDERICK (*see above*).

Arms—Gu. a falcon wings expanded within a bordure engrailed or, on a canton of the last, a fess chequy arg. and az. *Crest*—A falcon close on a perch all ppr.

Seat—Brittas Castle, Thurles, co. Tipperary. *Club*—Kildare Street.

KNOX OF RAPPA CASTLE.

RONALD ANNESLEY KNOX, of Rappa Castle, co. Mayo, b. 1891; s. his uncle 1897.

Lineage.—FRANCIS KNOX, b. 16 July, 1726, 3rd son of Francis Knox, of Moyne Abbey (*see preceding memoir*), settled at Rappa Castle, co. Mayo, of which co. as well as of Sligo he served as High Sheriff. He m. 25 March, 1761, Mary, dau. and co-heir of Paul Annesley Gore, of Belleek, M.P. co. Mayo (brother of Arthur, 1st Earl of Arran), and by her (who d. 31 Oct. 1818) had issue,
1. ANNESLEY GORE, of Rappa Castle, his heir.
2. Francis, J.P., d. unm. 1803.
3. JAMES, of Broadlands Park, co. Mayo, ancestor of the Knox-Gore family (*see* SAUNDERS-KNOX-GORE *of Belleek*).
4. Henry William, of Netley Park, co. Mayo, Capt. 6th Dragoon Guards, High Sheriff co. Mayo 1810, m. 2 July, 1806, Jane, eldest dau. of Rev. William Rogers, D.D., of Kells, co. Meath, and d. 6 Oct. 1816, having by her (who d. 13 Feb. 1835) had issue,
  1. Henry William, of Netley Park, J.P. and D.L., High Sheriff 1845, b. 9 Dec. 1809; m. 1st, 7 Dec. 1835, Isabella Antoinette, youngest dau. of John Peel, of Burton-on-Trent, co. Stafford, which lady d. 19 Dec. 1838; and 2ndly, 1842, Eliza, eldest dau. of the O'Grady, of Kilballyowen, and d.s.p. 24 Sept. 1859.
  2. William Henry, d. 1847.
  3. Annesley Gore, d. unm. 26 Oct. 1863.
  1. Mary Mina, of Netley, m. 28 March, 1833, her cousin, James Annesley Knox, and has issue (*vide infra*).
  2. Harriette, m. Charles Kirkwood, of Bartra House, co. Mayo, Capt. R.N.
  3. Eleanor, m. 2 July, 1845, Henry Augustus Knox, and d. 1892, leaving issue (*see below*).
5. Arthur, of Bushfield, co. Mayo, b. 1785; m. Barbara, eldest dau. of Joseph Lambert, of Brookhill (*see that family*), and had issue,
  Elizabeth, m 18 Oct, 1833, Annesley Knox, of Rappa, and d. 1876, leaving issue (*see below*).
6. John, of Greenwood Park, J.P. co. Mayo, High Sheriff 1852, and Major North Mayo Regt., b. 3 Nov. 1786; m. 26 Aug. 1830, Jane, 3rd dau. of Samuel Handy, of Bracca Castle, co. Westmeath, by Jane his wife, eldest dau. of William Orme, of Abbeytown, co. Mayo, and d. 10 March, 1861, having by her (who d. 19 Aug. 1894) had issue,
  1. John Henry, his heir, of Greenwood Park, b. 25 Aug. 1842; d. unm. 28 July, 1875.
  2. Samuel Handy, b. 20 Aug. 1846; d. unm. 1 Aug. 1869.
  1. Jane Caroline, m. 19 July, 1867, Major James Paget, of Knockglass, co. Mayo, and has issue.
  2. Adelaide, m. Col. Orme, of Glenmore, co. Mayo, late 16th Lancers, and has issue.
  3. Rosa Matilda.   4. FLORENCE, late of Greenwood Park.
1. Eleanor Anne, m. John Knox, of Mount Falcon.
2. Dorothea Henrietta, m. Henry Bruen, of Oak Park, M.P. co. Carlow (*see that family*).
3. Elizabeth, m. 28 Aug. 1787, Robert Rutledge, of Broomfield.
4. Mary, m. William Handy, of Bracca Castle.
5. Anne, m. 14 Nov. 1803, Anthony Gildea, of Port Royal.
6. Charity, m. 23 May, 1815, William Orme, of Glenmore.

Mr. Knox d. 1813, and was s. by his eldest son,

ANNESLEY GORE KNOX, of Rappa Castle, b. 11 Jan. 1768; m. 28 Jan. 1793, Harriette, sister of Sir Ross Mahon, Bart., and by her (who d. Nov. 1840) had issue,
1. ANNESLEY, of Rappa Castle.
2. St. George Caulfeild (Rev.), Rector of Dromard, b. 1800; m. Dec. 1836, Ann Cordelia, dau. of Rev. Richard Quintus St. George, and d. 7 Dec. 1864, having had issue,
  1. Richard Annesley, late Col. 4th King's Own Regt., b. 1837; d. June, 1901.
  2. Hercules Frances, of Rosslare, co. Sligo, and Carogh House, Naas, co. Kildare, b. 1844; m. 1870, Harriet Elizabeth (who d. 24 May, 1884), 3rd dau. of Rev. John James Fox (who d. 1870), Rector of Kinawley (*see* Fox *of Fox Hall*), by Harriet Louisa his wife (who d. 24 Sept. 1871), eldest dau. of Rev. Charles Cobb Beresford (*see* BURKE's *Peerage*, WATERFORD, M.), and has issue surviving,
    (1) Richard Frederick Beresford, b. 16 Feb. 1878, Capt. 2nd Royal Dublin Fus., served in S. African War 1900-1902, Queen's medal with 3 clasps, King's medal with 2 clasps, seconded with 4th King's African Rifles, Uganda.
    (2) Hercules John, b. 2 Aug. 1880, B.A. Trin. Coll. Dublin, M.D., B.Ch., B.A. and L.M. Univ. Dublin, West Derby, Liverpool.
    (1) Ella Harriet St. George.
    (2) Elise Frances Beresford.
    (3) Anita Henrietta.
    (4) Selina Maud Beresford, m. 19 April, 1904, Capt. Henry Eliardo de Courcy-Wheeler, of Robertstown, co. Kildare (*see that family*).
3. James Annesley, J.P., of Netley Park, co. Mayo, m. 28 March, 1833, his cousin, Mary Mina, dau. and eventual heiress of Henry William Knox, of Netley Park, and had issue, three sons and two daus.,
  1. James Fitzroy, Capt. Sligo Rifles Militia, b. 13 Oct. 1838; d. unm. 14 Aug. 1872.
  2. Granville Henry, of Errew Grange, co. Mayo, b. 18 June, 1840; m. 5 July, 1862, Ellen, dau. of Richard Frederick Farrer, and has issue,
    (1) Annesley Frederick Granville, b. 18 June, 1863.
    (2) Herbert Dudley Wilton, b. 15 Aug. 1866.
    (3) Arthur Somerset Girtin, b. 10 Feb. 1872.
    (4) Frederick FitzRoy Farrer, b. 26 June, 1873.
    (5) James Lionel Richard, b. 5 Aug. 1876.
    (1) Constance Mina.
    (2) Gertrude Ethel.
    (3) Hilda Maud Emma.
    (4) Dora Ellen.
  3. Lionel William.
  1. Jane Harriet, m. 24 May, 1855, Albert Henry Knox, Paymaster Sligo Militia, and has issue (*see* KNOX *of Mount Falcon*).
  2. Constance Mina, m. Edward Knox Leet, late Capt. North Mayo Regt., and had issue.
4. John, of Broadlands Park, co. Mayo, b. 17 Dec. 1802; m. 3 Feb. 1847, Henrietta Adelaide, dau. of Anthony Gildea, of Clooncormac House, co. Mayo. She d. 28 April, 1878. He d. 18 July, 1874, having had issue,
  1. James Annesley, d. unm. 1872.
  2. John Anthony, b. 1850, m. 1875, Margaret, dau. of Francis Carroll, of Ballintain, co. Mayo, and has issue,
    (1) James Annesley, b. 20 March, 1876.
    (2) Godfrey FitzRoy, b. 22 Sept. 1877.
    (1) Harriette Adelaide.
5. Henry Augustus, of Palmerston, co. Mayo, b. 13 Feb. 1807; m. 2 July, 1845, Eleanor, dau. of Henry William Knox, of Netley Park, and d. 1887, having by her (who d. 1892) had, with other issue,
  1. Reginald Henry, J.P., of Netley Park, and Palmerston, co. Mayo, b. 24 Aug. 1846; m. 26 Oct. 1876, Sarah Elizabeth dau. of Rev. Edwin Smith, M.A., Chaplain to the Forces, and has issue,
    Reginald Edwin Henry, Lieut. 3rd Batt. Connaught Rangers, and Royal Garrison Regt., b. 5 Aug. 1877; m. Gwlladys Laleah Keith, only dau. of L. J. K. McGhee, of Kent Park, Halifax, Nova Scotia, and d. 10 March, 1908.
    Edith Lilian, b. 22 April, 1880.
  2. St. George James, b. 24 Sept. 1855; m. 15 Sept. 1904, Florence Isabel, 4th dau. of Albert Henry Knox, of Hollywood, (*see* KNOX *of Mount Falcon*), and has issue,
    (1) Cyril Albert St. George, b. 23 June, 1905.
    (2) Maurice Edward Desmond, b. 11 Feb. 1910.
    (1) Anna Isabel Violet.
  3. Edmond Francis Annesley, b. 2 Nov. 1850.
  1. Emilie Jane.
6. Francis William, b. 23 Dec. 1811.
1. Anne Elizabeth.   2. Maria.
3. Harriette, m. April, 1833, James Knox Gore.
4. Jane.   5. Emily.

Mr. Knox d. 4 July, 1839, and was s. by his eldest son,

ANNESLEY KNOX, of Rappa Castle, J.P. and D.L., High Sheriff 1829, b. 1798; m. 18 Oct. 1833, Elizabeth, dau. of Arthur Knox, of Bushfield, co. Mayo, and by her (who d. 1876) had issue,
1. ANNESLEY ARTHUR, his heir.
2. Ross Mahon, b. 16 June, 1850, m. Violet, 2nd dau. of the late Capt. Alfred C. Knox, and had issue,
  RONALD ANNESLEY, now of Rappa Castle.
3. Robert Henry, b. 20 Oct. 1851.
4. Richard Francis, b. 20 May, 1853.
5. Arthur Lionel, dec.
1. Bessie Barbara, d. 20 Dec. 1908.
2. Harriette Lucy, d. unm.
3. Emma Louisa, m. 8 Sept. 1863, Capt. Charles Knox Kirkwood, R.A., of Bartra House, co. Mayo, and d. 14 Jan. 1876.
4. Francis Maria, dec.
5. Isabella Jane, m. 14 May, 1880, John Singleton Darling.
6. Lucy Anne.

Mr. Knox d. 21 Feb. 1878, and was s. by his eldest son,

ANNESLEY ARTHUR KNOX, of Rappa Castle, co. Mayo, D.L., High Sheriff 1884, b. 24 Feb. 1838; d. unm. 1897.

Arms—Gu., a falcon wings expanded within a bordure engrailed or, on a canton of the last a fess chequy arg. and az. *Crest*—A falcon close on a perch all ppr.

Seat—Rappa Castle, near Ballina.

KNOX OF MOUNT FALCON.

UTRED AUGUSTUS KNOX, of Mount Falcon, co. Mayo, J.P. cos. Mayo and Sligo, and D.L. of the latter co., High Sheriff of co. Mayo 1875, b. 19 April, 1825; m. 16 Aug. 1875, Agnes Frances Nina, dau. of Sir Francis Arthur Knox-Gore, 1st bart. of Belleek Manor, co. Mayo, by his wife, Sarah, dau. of Col. Chas. N. Knox, of Castle Lacken, co. Mayo. She d. 17 April, 1906, having had issue.

1. UTRED ARTHUR FREDERIC, Lieut. Royal Irish Rifles, b. 1 May, 1885.
1. Sarah Augusta.
2. Maud Anna Theodora, m. 9 June, 1909, Harry Jones Bristow, son of Very Rev. John Bristow, Dean of Connor.

Knox.   THE LANDED GENTRY.   376

3. Ruth Lilian.
4. Agnes Nina.
5. Olive Gore, *m.* 1 June, 1911, J. B. A. Drought, Royal Irish Rifles, son of J. A. H. Drought, of Delaford Manor, Ives, Bucks.
6. Gladys Mary.

Lineage.—ARTHUR KNOX, 2nd son of William Knox, of Castlerea, by Mary Palmer his wife (*see* KNOX *of Bruttas*), served as High Sheriff co. Mayo 1732-3. He *m.* 8 May, 1724, Hannah, 3rd dau. and co-heir of Roger Palmer, of Palmerston, co. Mayo, by Charity his 2nd wife, 2nd dau. and co-heir of Maurice Annesley, of Little Rath, co. Kildare, and *d.* 16 May, 1743. leaving a dau., Sydney, *m.* Matthew Vaughan, of Carramore, and a son,

JOHN KNOX, of Castlerea, J.P., M.P. for Donegal from 1761 to 1769, and Castlebar from 1769 to 1774, served as High Sheriff for Sligo 1752, and for Mayo 1763, *b.* 1728; *m.* 25 May, 1750, Anne, 4th dau. of the Right Hon. Sir Henry King, Bart., by Isabella his wife, sister of Richard, Viscount Powerscourt, and had by her (who *d.* 29 March, 1803) two sons and three daus.,
1. Arthur, of Castlerea, *b.* 13 Sept. 1759. who settled at Woodstock, co. Wicklow (an estate purchased from Lord St. George), High Sheriff for that co. 1791, for Mayo; and a Magistrate for both cos.; *m.* 23 June, 1781, Lady Mary Brabazon, eldest dau. of Anthony, 8th Earl of Meath, and *d.* 23 Oct. 1798, leaving issue,
   1. John, of Castlerea and Woodstock, J.P. and D.L., *b.* 13 May, 1783, High Sheriff of co. Wicklow 1809, and co. Mayo 1821; *m.* 12 March, 1808, Maria Anne, only dau. of Major John Knox, of Mount Falcon, by his 1st marriage, and *d.* 31 Dec. 1861, having by her (who *d.* 1 June, 1861) had issue,
      (1) Arthur Edward, of Castlerea and Trotton, Sussex, *b.* 28 Dec. 1808, an Officer in the 2nd Life Guards, *m.* 12 Dec. 1835, Lady Jane Parsons, elder dau. of Laurence, 2nd Earl of Rosse and *d.* 23 Sept. 1886, leaving issue,
         1. Lawrence Edward, M.P. for Sligo, D.L., Capt. 11th Foot, and Major of Militia, *b.* 7 Nov. 1836; *m.* 13 Aug. 1858, Clara Charlotte, 2nd dau. of Major Ernest Knox, of Killala, co. Mayo, and *d.s.p.* 24 Jan. 1873. She *d.* 3 April, 1908.
         2. Arthur Henry, R.N., *b.* March, 1852.
         1. Maria Jane, *m.* 30 Nov. 1875, Capt. William Irvine, 3rd Regt., and has issue (*see* IRVINE *of Castle Irvine*).
         2. Alice, *m.* 31 March, 1864, Col. Horace Parker Newton, R.A., and has issue.
         3. Helen, *m.* 26 April, 1869, C. J. Fletcher, late 18th Hussars, and has issue.
      (2) Ernest, Maj. N. Mayo Mil., *m.* 12 July, 1836, Charlotte Catherine, dau. of James Knox Gore, of Broadlands Park, co. Mayo, and *d.* 8 Sept. 1883, leaving issue.
      (3) Robert Augustus (Rev.), *m.* 1842, Octavia Gertrude, youngest dau. of Rev. R. J. Hallifax, only son of Dr. Hallifax, Bishop of St. Asaph; and *d.s.p.* 1876.
      (4) Edward William John, Capt. 75th Regt., killed at siege of Delhi, 1857; *m.* 1854, Charlotte Emily, dau. of Major Gardiner, of Farm Hill, co. Mayo, and had issue.
      (5) Alfred Charles, Capt. 73rd Regt., *m.* 1855, Victoria Anne, dau. of Col. Arthur Hunt, R.A., and *d.* 25 June, 1893, leaving issue.
   2. Edward, *b.* 2 Nov. 1786, a Field Officer in the Army; *d. unm.* 1849.
   3. Arthur (Rev.), *b.* 22 Nov. 1793; *m.* Nov. 1820, Mary, dau. of the Right Hon. Dennis Daly, of Dunsandle, co. Galway.
   1. Mary, *d. unm.* July, 1798.
   2. Anne, *m.* Edward William Scott, Barrister-at-Law.
2. JOHN, of whom presently.
1. Isabella, *m.* Xaverius Blake, of Oranmore, co. Galway.
2. Hannah, *m.* 29 July, 1775, James Wilson, of Parsonstown, co. Meath.
3. Anne, *d. unm.* 14 Sept. 1788.

Mr. Knox *d.* 24 Feb. 1774. His 2nd son,
JOHN KNOX, of Mount Falcon, co. Mayo, and of Grace Dieu, co. Dublin, and of Dublin, Major in the Sligo Regt. of Militia, *b.* 10 March, 1764; *m.* 1st, 24 Dec. 1786, Eleanor Anne, eldest dau. of Francis Knox, of Rappa Castle, co. Mayo, by Mary his wife, 4th dau. and co-heir of Annesley Gore, M.P. for co. Mayo (brother to Arthur, 1st Earl of Arran), and by this lady (who *d.* 20 March, 1790) had (with a dau., Maria Anne, *m.* 12 March, 1808, John Knox, of Woodstock, co. Wicklow, and Castlerea, co. Mayo) two sons,
1. JOHN FREDERIC, his heir.
2. Francis, *b.* 1790; *d.* young (1793).

Major Knox *m.* 2ndly, 14 April, 1811, Catharine, 2nd dau. of Richard Chaloner, of Kingsfort, co. Meath, and by her had further issue (*see* KNOX *of Grace Dieu*). Major John Knox *d.* 11 July, 1821, and was *s.* by his eldest son,

JOHN FREDERICK KNOX, of Mount Falcon, co. Mayo, Lieut.-Col. of the Sligo Militia, J.P. and D.L. cos. Mayo and Sligo, High Sheriff of Mayo 1823, and of Sligo 1824, *b.* 28 Feb. 1789; *m.* 28 Jan. 1819, Anna Maria, eldest dau. of James Knox Gore, of Broadlands Park, co. Mayo, by his wife, Lady Maria Louisa, dau. of Arthur Saunders, 2nd Earl of Arran, and by her (who *d.* 7 Jan. 1887) had issue,
1. Frederic Edgar, *b.* 29 April, 1822; *d. unm.* 28 Oct. 1867.
2. UTRED AUGUSTUS, now of Mount Falcon.
3. Albert Henry, of Hollywood, co. Mayo, Capt. Sligo Rifles, *b.* 10 Feb. 1827; *m.* 24 May, 1855, Jane Harriett, eldest dau. of James Annesley Knox, of Crosspatrick, co. Mayo (*see* KNOX *of Rappa*), and by her (who *d.* 23 June, 1897) has issue,
   1. Albert Frederick James, *b.* 20 May, 1856.
   2. Ernest Henry (*see* KNOX *of Greenwood*).
   3. Alfred Douglas, *b.* 18 May, 1861.

1. Mina Eleanor Anna, *b.* 11 Jan. 1858; *d. unm.* 29 March, 1893.
2. Constance Louisa.
3. Edith Kathleen Zinna, *m.* 3 June, 1897, William Henry Roberts, L.R.C.S. and P. Ed., of 63, Lower Mount Street, Dublin, and has issue, Maiben Albert William, *b.* 21 April, 1904, and Shirley Douglas Knox, *b.* 26 July, 1905.
4. Florence Isabel, *m.* 15 Sept. 1904, St. George James Knox, of Palmerston, Killala, co. Mayo, and has issue (*see* KNOX *of Rappa*).
5. Emily Mabel.
6. Nina Gwendoline.
4. Alfred William, *b.* 5 May, 1829; *d. unm.* 8 June, 1910.
5. Alberic Edward, *b.* 17 Sept. 1831; *m.* 4 June, 1868, Emily Adela, dau. of Sheffield Grace Philip Fiennes Betham, of Monkstown, co. Dublin, Dublin Herald, 2nd son of Sir William Betham, Ulster King of Arms, and *d.* 11 Jan. 1870, having by her (who *m.* 2ndly, 16 Nov. 1880, Arthur Richard Frederic Exham, M.D.) had issue, one dau.,
   Grace, *m.* 21 Aug. 1890, John St. Clair Upton, of Market Drayton, youngest son of Rev. Robert Upton, Rector of Moreton Say, Shropshire, and grandson of Thomas Everard Upton of Leeds and Bramhope Manor, Yorks, and has issue,
   1. John Alberic Everard, *b.* 30 June, 1891; 2. Robert Babington Everard, *b.* 5 April, 1896; 3. Joseph Annesley Everard, *b.* 13 April, 1899; and 1. Ruby Grace Apelina.
6. Ernest Adolphus, *b.* 25 April, 1834; *d. unm.* 17 April, 1904.
7. John Ethelred, *b.* 7 March, 1836; *d. unm.* 25 Oct. 1886.
1. Eleanor Louisa, *m.* 1872, George W. Frazer.

Lieut.-Col. Knox *d.* 20 Sept. 1871, and was *s.* by his eldest surviving son, the present UTRED AUGUSTUS KNOX.

Arms—Gu., a falcon wings expanded within a bordure engrailed or, on a canton of the last a fess chequy arg. and az. **Crest**—A falcon close on a perch all ppr. **Motto**—Moveo et proficio.

Seat—Mount Falcon, near Ballina, co. Mayo.

KNOX OF GREENWOOD.

ERNEST HENRY KNOX, of Greenwood Park, co. Mayo, J.P., *b.* 25 May, 1859; *m.* 28 April, 1892, Ada Josephine, 2nd dau. of Henry Alexander Cowper, of Trudder, Newtownmount Kennedy, and has issue,
1. Ada Evelyn Elizabeth.
2. Zinna Ethel.

Mr. E. H. Knox, who purchased the Greenwood Estate from his cousin, Miss Florence Knox, is the second son of Albert Henry Knox, of Hollywood, co. Mayo (*see* KNOX *of Mount Falcon*), and his wife, Jane Harriett, eld. dau. of James Annesley Knox (*see* KNOX *of Rappa*).

Lineage and Arms—*See* KNOX *of Mount Falcon.*

Seat—Greenwood Park, Crossmolina, co. Mayo.

KNOX OF GRACE DIEU.

LIEUT.-COL. RICHARD KNOX, of Grace Dieu, co. Dublin, and Holt Hatch, Alton, Hants, Lieut.-Col. late 13th Hussars; *b.* 23 Dec 1848; *s.* his father 3 Jan. 1892; *m.* 1882, Mary Eliza, only child of Clement Milward, Q.C., of Alice Holt, Hampshire, and has issue,
CLEMENT UCHTER, *b.* 27 Feb. 1890.

Lineage.—MAJOR JOHN KNOX, of Mount Falcon, co. Mayo, and of Grace Dieu, co. Dublin, and of Dublin (*see* KNOX *of Mount Falcon*), *b.* 1764; *m.* 14 April, 1811, as his second wife, Catherine, 2nd dau. of Richard Chaloner, of Kingsfort, co. Meath, *d.* 11 July, 1821, having by her (who *d.* 1876) had issue,
1. RICHARD, of Grace Dieu.
2. Edward Chaloner, of Silverton, Monkstown, co. Dublin, J.P. and D.L. co. Tyrone, J.P. co. Dublin, Capt. Tyrone Militia, *b.* 29 Jan. 1815; *m.* 15 Oct. 1856, Alice Hewitt Caroline, dau. of Acheson St. George, of Wood Park, co. Armagh, by his 2nd marriage with Jane, dau. of Hon. and Very Rev. John Hewitt, Dean of Cloyne. He *d.s.p.* 4 April, 1896.
3. Robert John. of Cahirleske and Ballaghtobin, J.P. for co. Kilkenny, *b.* 1 Sept. 1817, Capt. 6th Dragoon Guards; *m.* 6 April, 1854, Philippa Allen, dau. of Frederick Lindsay, of Loughry, co. Tyrone. She *d.* 27 July, 1907. He *d.* 1901, leaving issue,
   1. Robert Chaloner, of Ballaghtobin, J.P. co. Kilkenny, Col. Kilkenny Militia, *b.* 5 Feb. 1855.
   2. Frederick William (Rev.), *b.* 5 May, 1856; *m.* 1892, Eva Basile, dau. of Rev. Henry G. C. Browne (*see* Peerage, KILMAINE, B.).
   3. Lindesay, of Bonnettstown, co. Kilkenny, J.P., High Sheriff 1905, *m.* dau. of Major-Gen. Dennis.
   1. Catherine Frances.   2. Agnes Charlotte.
   3. Philippa.   4. Alice.
   5. Sophia Janette.   6. Flora Blanche Marianne.

7. Mary Herbert, *m*. 29 April, 1908, William Archibald Richardson.
1. Catherine Anne, *d*. young.
2. Frances Maria. *m*. William Pitt Blunden, of Bonnettstown House, co. Kilkenny, brother of Sir John Blunden, Bart., and had issue (*see* BURKE'S *Peerage*).
3. Eliza, *m*. 22 April, 1839, Sir John Blunden, Bart., of Castle Blunden, co. Kilkenny, and had issue (*see* BURKE'S *Peerage*).

The elder son,
LIEUT.-GEN. RICHARD KNOX, of Grace Dieu, co. Dublin, and Strathdurn, Cheltenham, Col. 18th Hussars; raised, and for many years commanded, the 18th Hussars, *b*. 28 May, 1812; *m*. 1844, Mary Letitia, dau. of Col. and Brigadier-Gen. Bryce McMaster, H.E.I.C.S., and had issue,
1. RICHARD, now of Grace Dieu.
2. Francis Robert Bonham, late Major Hyderabad Cavalry Contingent, *b*. 13 Jan. 1851; *m*. 1875, Edith, dau. of F. P. Chappell, and *d*. 19 Aug. 1903, leaving issue,
   Kate Millicent Gladys.
3. Horace Chaloner, *b*. 17 May, 1854, Public Works Department, India.
4. Charles William, *b*. 26 March, 1858; late Major Hampshire Regt.
5. Eustace Chaloner, *b*. 19 March, 1860, Lieut.-Col. and Brev. Col. 18th Hussars, *d*. 18 Feb. 1902.
6. Walter Frederick, *b*. 29 Oct. 1866; *m*. 30 Sept. 1897, Elfleda Ethel, dau. of late Rev. H. Rich, of Carlrooke Hall, Norfolk.
1. Mary Letitia, *m*. 1868, T. Walsh, A.M.D., and *d*. 1876, leaving issue.   2. Catherine, *d*. unm.
Lieut.-Gen. Richard Knox *d*. 3 Jan. 1892, and was *s*. by his eldest son,

Arms—Same as KNOX *of Mount Falcon*.
Residence—Holt Hatch, Alton, Hants. *Clubs*—United Service, Army and Navy, S.W., and Cavalry, W.

KNOX OF CLONLEIGH.

CAPT. WILLIAM KNOX, of Clonleigh, co. Donegal, J.P. and D.L. for that co., High Sheriff 1896, and J.P. co. Tyrone, late Capt. 21st Hussars and 4th Batt. East Surrey Regt., *b*. 17 Sept. 1858. Capt. Knox is the only son of the late William Knox, Madras C.S., of Clonleigh, co. Donegal, J.P. (who *d*. 27 Oct. 1867), by Gertrude his first wife (who *d*. 16 May, 1860), dau. of Thomas Dabine, R.N., and great grandson of the Rt. Rev. William Knox, D.D., Bishop of Derry, 4th son of Thomas, 1st Viscount Northland.

Lineage.—*See* BURKE'S *Peerage*, RANFURLY, E.
Arms—Gu. a falcon volant or, within an orle wavy on the outer and engrailed on the inner edge arg. *Crest*—A falcon close standing on a perch ppr. *Motto*—Moveo et proficior.
Seat—Clonleigh, Ballindrait, co. Donegal. *Clubs*—Naval and Military and Cavalry, W.; Kildare Street, and Royal St. George Yacht, Dublin.

KNOX OF CREAGH.

COL. CHARLES HOWE CUFF KNOX, of Creagh, co. Mayo, J.P. and D.L., High Sheriff 1873, M.A. Ch. Ch. Oxford, Hon. Col. 3rd Batt. Connaught Rangers, formerly Capt. 8th Hussars, *b*. 1841; *m*. 30 Sept. 1869, Henrietta Elizabeth, dau. of the Right Hon. Sir William Gibson Craig, 2nd bart., P.C., having had issue,
1. Charles William Cuffe, Capt. Rifle Brigade, *b*. 25 Dec. 1870; *m*. 17 Oct. 1905, Violet Ileene Cassandra, only dau. of Lieut.-Col. Richard Frederick Meysey-Thompson, late Rifle Brigade, of Nunthorpe (*see* BURKE'S *Peerage*, KNARESBOROUGH, B.). He *d.v.p.* 25 Jan. 1910.

2. HENRY HOWE, *b*. 1871; *m*. 17 Oct. 1906, Ada, only child of Sidney Bryan, of Kenilworth, Port Elizabeth, and has issue, A dau.
3. Gerald Vivian Cuff, Commander R.N., *b*. 29 April, 1875; *m*. 6 Feb. 1907, Muriel Campbell, youngest dau. of Major John Finlay, of Castle Toward, Argyllshire (*see that family*), and has issue,
   Ian Charles, *b*. 5 Dec. 1907.
1. Louisa Gertrude, *m*. 20 Nov. 1902, Capt. Walter Charles Lascelles, D.S.O. (*see* BURKE'S *Peerage*, HAREWOOD, E.).

Lineage.—ALEXANDER KNOX (son of William Knox, who *d*. intestate, son of Alexander Knox), said to have sold Silvyland, co. Renfrew, settled in co. Donegal, and is said to have had issue two sons,
1. William, of Ashmoyne, co. Donegal, will dated 3 Aug., proved 13 Oct. 1710. He had issue,
  1. Alexander, of Ballynamore, who had issue,
   (1) John, of Ashmoyne and Ballynamore.
   (2) William.
   (3) Adam.
  2. William, of Drommachill and Woodhill.
  3. Ralph, of Bannach.
  4. John, who had two daus., Rebecca and Barbara.
2. ALEXANDER, of Ballybofey.
The second son,
ALEXANDER KNOX, of Ballybofey, co. Donegal, will dated 11 Jan. 1741, proved 15 Sept. 1742, left issue, by Mary his wife, who *d*. before him,
1. William, of Cloghan.
2. Alexander, of Ballybofey, will dated 12 Nov. 1753, proved 1756, left issue,
  1. William, of Ballybofey, *s*. his father.
  1. Nicola Sophia, *m*. John Gregory.
  2. Mary, in New England, 1753.
3. Oliver.
1. A dau., *m*. — McCurry.
2. Margaret, *m*. — Gallagher.
3. Mary, *m*. Arthur Ingram.
The eldest son,
WILLIAM KNOX, of Cloghan, co. Donegal, *d*. intestate, admon. granted 3 Nov. 1760. He left issue, by Margaret his wife, a son,
JAMES KNOX, of Kilcaddan, co. Donegal. Will dated 16 Nov. 1769, proved 24 Oct. 1775. He left, by Martha his wife,
1. WILLIAM, of Kilcaddan.
2. Carncross, of Ballybofey, *d*. before 1775.
3. Robert, living 1775.
1. Margaret, *m*. before Nov. 1769, Nicholas Spence.
2. Elizabeth, living 1775.
3. Martha, living 1775.
The eldest son,
WILLIAM KNOX, of Kilcaddan, co. Donegal, High Sheriff 1776, *m*. Sept. 1778, Elizabeth, only child of Charles Nesbitt, of Scurmore, co. Sligo. Her will, dated 16 May, 1783, was proved 11 Jan. 1791. They had issue, a son,
COL. CHARLES NESBITT KNOX, of Scurmore, co. Sligo, and Castle Lacken, co. Mayo, High Sheriff for the former 1810, and for the latter 1831, *m*. 1810, Jane Cuff, testamentary heiress of James, Lord Tyrawley. His will, dated 4 Dec. 1857, was proved 27 Sept. 1860. He *d*. 14 Feb. 1860, leaving issue,
CHARLES, his heir.
Sarah, *m*. 4 Aug. 1829, Sir Francis Arthur Knox-Gore, 1st bart., of Belleek, co. Mayo, and *d*. 8 May, 1888. He *d*. 21 May, 1873, leaving issue (*see* SAUNDERS-KNOX-GORE *of Belleek*).
The only son,
COL. CHARLES KNOX, of Cranmore, Ballinrobe, co. Mayo, High Sheriff 1860, Col. North Mayo Militia, *b*. 1817, *m*. (setts. dated 18 May, 1839) Lady Louisa Catherine Browne, dau. of Howe Peter, 2nd Marquess of Sligo. She *d*. 14 Dec. 1891. He *d*. 14 March, 1867, leaving issue,
1. CHARLES HOWE CUFF, now of Creagh.
2. Howe James, Lieut.-Col. late Royal Munster Fus., *b*. 23 Jan. 1843; *d*. 6 March, 1910.
3. Hubert, I.C.S., *b*. 1845.
1. Philippa.

Seat—Creagh, Ballinrobe, co. Mayo. *Clubs*—Carlton, and Army and Navy.

KNOX OF DUNGANNON.

THOMAS GRANVILLE KNOX, of Dungannon, co. Tyrone, J.P. and D.L., Capt. 3rd Batt. Queen's Regt., *b*. 22 Dec. 1868; *m*. 24 Feb. 1897, Hon. Harriet Georgiana Lucia Agar-Ellis, dau. of the 5th Viscount Clifden, and has issue,
Constance Georgiana.

Mr. Knox is the only son of Col. the Hon. William Stuart Knox, D.L., M.P., of Dungannon, co. Tyrone (who *d*. 15 Feb. 1900), and Georgiana his wife, dau. of John Bonfoy Rooper, of Abbot's Ripton, Hants, and grandson of 2nd Earl of Ranfurly.

Lineage, Arms, &c.—*See* BURKE'S *Peerage*, RANFURLY, E.
Residence—11, St. James's Court, S.W. *Club*—Arthur's.

KNOX. *See* BURKE'S PEERAGE, **RANFURLY, E.**

Knox.   THE LANDED GENTRY.   378

KNOX-BROWNE. *See* **BROWNE.**

───◆───

SAUNDERS-KNOX-GORE. *See* **GORE.**

───◆───

PERY-KNOX-GORE. *See* **GORE.**

───◆───

KYLE OF LAUREL HILL.

HENRY GREVILLE KYLE, of Laurel Hill, co. Derry, educated at Merton Coll. Oxon., B.A. 1894, M.B. and B.Ch. 1899, M.A. and M.D. 1910, Surgeon, General Hospital, Bristol, *b.* 18 April, 1869.

Lineage.—The Kyle family, formerly settled in Ayrshire, N.B., became possessed, at the time of the settlement of Ulster (early in the 17th century) of the lands of Camnish, co. Londonderry.
  SAMUEL KYLE, of Camnish, *b.* 1686; *m.* 1720, Mary Buchanan, and *d.* 1769, having had issue,
    1. John, *b.* 1724; *m.* 1755, Mary Haslett, and *d.* 1805, having had issue,
      1. Samuel, *b.* 1756; *d. unm.*   2. Joseph, *b.* 1757; *d.* 1794.
      3. John, *b.* 1765; *m.* 1797, Isabella Rogers, by whom he had two sons and three daus., one of the latter *m.* Samuel Lowry.
      4. James, Surgeon R.N., *b.* 1766; *d. unm.* 1794.
      5. Arthur, *b.* 1767; *m.* Martha Colquhoun, and *d.* 1835, having had issue, John; Alexander; and two daus., one of whom *m.* Dr. Clarke, of Kilrea.
      6. William, *b.* 1768; *d. unm.* in America, 1835.
      1. Johanna, *m.* 1785, William Haslett, of Derry.
    2. William, *b.* 1727; *m.* 1757, and had one son and two daus.
    3. James, *b.* 1729; *m.* Lœtitia Clinton, and *d.* 1815, having had issue,
      1. John, *b.* 1754; *m.* Mary Bibby, and *d.* 1802.
      2. Samuel, *b.* 1755; *d. unm.*
    4. ARTHUR, of whom presently.
    5. Samuel, of Dungiven, co. Derry, *b.* 1735; *m.* 1st, 1765, Jane Boyle, by whom he had,
      1. Thomas, *b.* 1766; *m.* Jane MacDougall, and *d.* 1813, having had issue, one son and four daus.
      2. Samuel, *b.* 1770; successively Scholar, Fellow, and Provost of Trin. Coll. Dublin, D.D., Lord Bishop of Cork, Cloyne, and Ross (1831); *m.* 1801, Anne, dau. of William Duke Moore; *d.* 1848, and was bur. in Trin. Coll. Chapel. He had issue,
        (1) Samuel Moore, *b.* 1801; Sch. Trin. Coll. Dublin, D.D., Vicar-Gen. of Cork, Cloyne, and Ross, Treasurer of Leighlin, and Archdeacon of Cork; *m.* 1833, Jane Cotter, of Ashton, co. Cork, and *d.* 1890, having by her had issue,
          1. Samuel, Col. R.A., *b.* 17 Aug. 1834; *d.* 1898.
            1. Rebecca Catherine, *m.* Wyrley Birch, of Wrotham Hall, Norfolk.   2. Annette.
          3. Catherine, *m.* Col. Frederick Hardy.
        (2) William Cotter, *b.* 1802, M.A., LL.D. Trin. Coll. Dublin, Barrister-at-Law, Secretary to the Commissioners of Education and Endowed Schools in Ireland, J.P. co. Roscommon; *m.* Louisa, dau. of Capt. Rea (1st Royal Regt.), of St. Colombs, co. Derry, and *d.* 1879, having by her (who *d.* 1850) had issue,
          1. Westwood Henry, *b.* 1840; *d. unm.* 1878.
          2. Edmund Lombard, Lieut. 45th Regt., *b.* 1842; *d.* in active service in Burmah 1872.
          3. John Charles, Lieut. 9th Foot, *b.* 1844; *d.* at Simon's Town, Cape of Good Hope, in 1866, while quartered there.
          4. William Blacker Hamilton, *b.* 1846; *m.* 1882, Miss Lane, and has issue,
            a. William Victor Blacker.
            a. Eleanor Louisa.   *b.* Joan.   *c.* Irene Gladys.
          1. Elizabeth Sophia, *d. unm.* 9 Aug. 1911.
          2. Louisa Anne Jane.
        (3) Henry Stopford, *m.* Julia Esther, dau. of John Green, of Cockermouth, and *d.* 1865, leaving a son,
          Henry Egerton, who *m.* and has issue, Julia Hallam, *b.* 1887.
        (4) Hallam D'Arcy, *b.* 1815; *d. unm.* 1857, at Peshawur, India, in command of the 27th Regt.
        (5) John Torrens (Rev.), Rector of Clondrohid, co. Cork, and Canon of Cloyne, *d. unm.* 1883.
        (1) Alice Dorothea, *m.* Rev. T. Moore.
        (2) Annette, *m.* William Westwood Chafy, of Feltwel Place, Norfolk.
        (3) Jane Elizabeth, *m.* Gen. George Wynell-Mayow, C.B., of Bray, co. Cornwall, and of Hanworth, co. Norfolk.
        (4) France Mary, *d.* 16 Nov. 1895.
        (5) Emily Elizabeth, *m.* 7 Nov. 1847, as his 1st wife, Sir Francis William Brady, Bart., and *d.* 4 Aug. 1891. He *d.* 26 Aug. 1909, leaving issue (*see* BURKE's *Peerage*, BRADY, Bart.)
The 4th son,
  REV. ARTHUR KYLE, *b.* 1733; *m.* 1770, Martha, dau. of James Wood, by his wife Maria Lœtitia, 2nd dau. of Rev. Robert Higinbothom, of Laurel Hill, co. Derry (James Wood was brother to Robert Wood, the celebrated traveller, who discovered the ruins of Balbec and Tadmor, and was Under-Secretary of State in 1759, in Lord Chatham's Government), and *d.* 1808, having by her (who *d.* 1774) had issue,
    1. ROBERT, *b.* 1771; *m.* 1st, 1800, Margaret Fulton, and by her (who *d.* 1807) had issue, Arthur, Martha, Margaret, who all *d.* in infancy, and Maria Lœtitia, *b.* 1805; *d.* 1817. Mr. Kyle *m.* 2ndly, 1810, Ellen, youngest dau. of Rev. George Murray, and *d.* 1831, being *s.* by his nephew, HENRY KYLE, of whom hereafter.
    2. SAMUEL, of whom we treat.
The younger son,
  SAMUEL KYLE, *b.* 1772; *m.* his cousin Martha, youngest dau. of Rev. Henry Wright, M.A., by his wife Martha, eldest dau. of Rev. Thomas Higinbothom, Rector of Pettigo, co. Fermanagh, and by her (who *d.* 1812) had issue,
    1. Arthur, *d. unm.*
    2. Henry Wright, *d. unm.*
    3. Samuel, *d. unm.*
    4. Robert Wood, *b.* 1799, in Holy Orders, M.A. Dub., Vicar of Holy Trinity, Guernsey; *m.* 1826, Georgina Jane, 2nd dau. of Rev. George Horan (by his wife Jane Nixon), and *d.* 1851, having by her (who *d.* 1868) one son,
      Arthur Wood, *b.* 1827; *d. unm.* at Melbourne, 1858.
    5. HENRY, of whom hereafter.
    1. Maria Lœtitia Wood, *b.* 1897; *m.* 1825, Rev. William John Knox, M.A., and *d.* 1886, having had issue. He *d.* 1839.
    2. Rachael Anna, *d. unm.*
    3. Martha Eleanor, *d. unm.*
    4. Anna Lily, *d. unm.*
    5. Emily Higinbothom, *m.* 1831, John Little, of Stewartstown, co. Tyrone, who *d.* 1889. She *d.* 1875, leaving issue.
Mr. Kyle *d.* 1814, at Capel Curig, N. Wales, and was bur. there. His 5th son,
  HENRY KYLE, of Laurel Hill, J.P. and D.L. co. Londonderry, High Sheriff 1868, was *b.* 13 June, 1811; *s.* his uncle, Robert Kyle, 1831; *m.* 1836, his cousin Elizabeth Mary, 3rd dau. of William Thompson, of Oatlands, co. Meath (*see* THOMPSON *of Clonfin*), and by her (who *d.* 24 June, 1865) had issue,
    1. ROBERT (Rev.), of whom presently.
    2. Henry, *b.* 1841; *d. unm.* 1866.
    3. William Thompson, of Kylesbrae, Buxted, Sussex, *b.* 7 April, 1849; B.A. Trin. Coll. Dublin, Jun. Moderator and Medalist 1871, Barrister-at-Law 1874; *m.* 30 July, 1889, Caroline Elizabeth Auchinleck, only child of Rev. Thomas Lewis, B.A., Vicar of Udimore, Sussex.
    1. Anne Elizabeth.
    2. Ellen, *m.* 9 Sept. 1873, Rev. Frederick William Hogan, M.A., Vicar of All Saints', Hillsborough, co. Down, and has issue, four sons and four daus.
    3. Frances Martha.
    4. Georgina Higinbothom.
Mr. Kyle *d.* 13 April, 1878, and was *s.* by his eldest son,
  REV. ROBERT KYLE, of Laurel Hill, co. Derry, J.P., *b.* 26 Dec. 1837; *m.* 30 April, 1868, Kathleen, 2nd dau. of William Wilson Carus-Wilson, of Casterton Hall, Westmorland, and *d.* 10 Feb. 1898, having by her (who *d.* 16 Dec. 1892) had issue,
    1. HENRY GREVILLE, now of Laurel Hill.
    2. Francis Carus, *b.* 2 Sept. 1872; *m.*   , *d.* 1909, leaving issue, John Arthur, *b.* 1898.
    3. Robert Wood, *b.* 5 March, 1875.
    1. Mary Alice Kathleen.

Seat—Laurel Hill, Coleraine. *Residence*—31, Westbury Road, Bristol.

───◆───

POWER-LALOR OF LONG ORCHARD.

GEORGE RICHARD POWER-LALOR, of Long Orchard, co. Tipperary, late Lieut. Tipperary Artillery, *b.* 29 Aug. 1864; *m.* 22 Nov. 1910, Stella, widow of Edward Wells Keegan, and dau. of George Browne, of Brownestown (*see that family*).

Lineage.—The O'Lalors, or Lalors, are of Milesian origin. At an early period they migrated, with the O'Mores, from Ulster to the extensive district of Leix, in the Queen's Co., of which county the O'Mores became powerful princes, and, under them, the O'Lalors were influential chieftains, possessing considerable landed property, between Stradbally and Maryborough. Their principal seat was at Disert, near the rock of Dunamase. Thence a branch sprung which settled in the co. of Tipperary.
  DIONYSIUS LALOR, of Ballymoney, was a member of this family. His name was signed to the new form of oath and declaration of the Confederate Catholics of Ireland, dated 10 Jan. 1646, o.s., amongst the signatures of several other personages, who are styled by historians " veluti comitiales in Domo Communium."
  The first member of the O'Lalor family who became a resident in co. Tipperary was
  JEREMIAH LALOR, *b.* 1626, who removed from Disert, Queen's Co., about the year 1666, after having taken a prominent part in

defending the fortress of Dunamase against the Parliamentarians during the war of 1641. He held the rank of Major in the Irish forces, and his father was nephew to Winifred, dau. of O'Lalor, of the Queen's co., and wife of John Crosbie, Bishop of Ardfort, who d. 1621. The lands of Farran-g-cahill, near Templemore, and also several other denominations in that neighbourhood, were Major Jeremiah Lalor's estates. Farrenaghahill at the present day pays a chief-rent to his descendant, Mr. Power-Lalor, of Long Orchard after mentioned. Major Jeremiah Lalor, although then far advanced in years, fought as a volunteer under King JAMES II. at the Boyne. After he had become resident in co. Tipperary, he m. Judith, dau. of Kedragh O'Meagher, of Boulebane Castle, same co., and had issue five sons. He d. 9 July, 1709, aged 83. His eldest son,

JEREMIAH LALOR, of Barnagrotty, King's Co., m. the dau. of Samuel Smith, of Lisduffe, co. Tipperary, and had two sons,
1. JOHN, of Long Orchard, of whom presently.
2. Jeremiah, of Barnagrotty.

The eldest son,
JOHN LALOR, of Long Orchard, and Cregg, co. Tipperary, m. Elizabeth, sister of John Doherty, of Outrath, co. Tipperary, and d. 9 May, 1782, aged 75, leaving issue,
1. THOMAS, of Cregg, co. Tipperary, J.P., and a Deputy-Governor of cos. Tipperary and Kilkenny, m. Bridget, dau. of Edmund Power, of Garnavilla, and d. 27 May, 1812, leaving issue,
  1. Thomas Edmund, of Cregg, J.P. and D.L. High Sheriff 1840-1, m. Anne, dau. of Richard Power, of Carrick-on-Suir. She d. 31 Jan. 1848. He d. 22 Feb. 1847, leaving issue,
    (1) THOMAS, of Cregg, J.P. and D.L., Vice-Lieutenant co. Tipperary. High Sheriff 1860, J.P. cos. Kilkenny and Waterford, Gentleman-at-Arms to H.E. the Earl of Bessborough when Lord-Lieut. of Ireland. He d. 8 Jan. 1890, and was s. by his sister.
    (2) John, 12th Infantry, d. 11 Nov. 1850, aged 26.
    (3) Nicholas, d. 18 Oct. 1848, aged 22.
    (1) Mary Anne, of Cregg, d. unm. 1890, and was s. by her niece.
    (2) Eliza, m. 1856, William O'Meagher, of Kilmoyler.
    (3) Louisa, m. Clement Sadleir, of Castleblake, co. Tipperary, and had issue. Their eldest dau., Annie Mary, s. to Cregg 1890.
  1. Maria, m. D'Arcy Mahon.
  2. Alice, m. John Power of Churchtown.
2. Nicholas, of Dunmore and Ballyragget, co. Kilkenny, m. Cecilia, dau. of Ulick Burke, of Meelick, co. Galway, and d.s.p. 29 June, 1768.
3. JOHN, of Crannagh and Long Orchard, of whom presently.
4. Jeremiah, of Glasshouse, m. 1st, Lydia, dau. of William Smith, of Burriscastle, Queen's Co., by whom he was father of John, of Gurteen, co. Tipperary, who m. Sarah, dau. of Edward Kennedy.
He m. 2ndly, Anne, dau. of John Doherty, of Outrath, co. Tipperary.
5. James, of Riverstown, m. Miss Bray, a niece of Dr. Thomas Bray, Roman Catholic Archbishop, and had by her a dau., Alicia.
6. Joseph, a law student, d. young and unm.
1. Bridget, m. Noble Luke Usher, of Gurteen, co. Tipperary, and d.s.p.
2. Alice, m. William Keating, of Brookley, co. Tipperary, and d.s.p.
3. Susan, d. unm.

The 3rd son,
JOHN LALOR, of Crannagh and Long Orchard, co. Tipperary, J.P. and Deputy-Governor, m. Mary, dau. of Thomas Phelan, of Nodstown, co. Tipperary, and had issue,
1. John Thomas, b. 1793; d. unm. 1823.
2. Thomas Phelan, Barrister-at-Law, d. unm. 4 June, 1825.
1. ANASTATIA PHELAN, of whom hereafter.
2. Mary, m. 1827, Richard Montesquieu Bellew, M.P., brother of the 1st Lord Bellew, and d.s.p. 1828.

Mr. Lalor d. 7 Sept. 1828. His eldest dau.,
ANASTATIA PHELAN LALOR, m. 1st, 1815, Edmond Power, of Gurteen, co. Waterford, and had issue,
1. JOHN WILLIAM, who s. his father at Gurteen (see DE LA POER of Gurteen le Poer).
2. EDMOND JAMES, who assumed the additional surname of LALOR, of whom hereafter.
3. Richard Francis, m. Sara Gordon, of Virginia, North America, and had two daus.,
  1. Anastatia.   2. Mary.
1. Mary, m. 13 Aug. 1846, Henry Petre, of Dunkenhalgh, D.L. co. Lancaster, and d. 1 Jan. 1880.
2. Eleanor, m. 1843, Patrick William Power, of Pembroke's Town, co. Waterford.

Mrs. Power m. 2ndly, Right Hon. Richard Lalor Shiel, M.P., and d. 4 Aug. 1852. Her 2nd son,
EDMOND JAMES POWER-LALOR, of Long Orchard, J.P. and D.L. co. Tipperary, High Sheriff 1857, Capt. 1st Dragoon Guards, s. to his maternal grandfather's estates, and assumed by Royal Licence 8 July, 1853, the surname and arms of his mother's family. He was b. 18 Oct. 1817, and m. 1858, Mary Frances, dau. of George Ryan, of Inch House, D.L., co. Tipperary, and had issue,
1. GEORGE RICHARD, now of Long Orchard.
2. Edmond George, b. and d. 1860.
1. Mary Anastatia, m. 2 Sept. 1879, Capt. William Gervase de la Poer, of Glen Poer, late 65th Regt. She d. 27 Aug. 1908.
2. Coralie Evelyn Mary, m. 2 Jan. 1889, William Anthony Burke (Ballybrack House, co. Dublin), 4th son of the late Sir Thomas Burke, Bart. of Marble Hill, and d. 9 Feb. 1910, leaving issue (see BURKE's Peerage).

3. Evelyn Letitia, b. 1868; d. 1871.
4. Helen Georgiana, d. 1874.   5. Grace Mary, d. 1879.

Mr. Power-Lalor d. 4 Aug. 1871, and was s. by his son.

Arms—Quarterly: 1st and 4th, or, a lion rampant guardant gu.; 2nd, arg., a chief indented sa.; 3rd, arg., on a chief gu. three escallops of the first. Crests—1st, An arm embowed vested gu. cuffed vert, the hand ppr. grasping a short sword also ppr.; 2nd, a stag's head affrontée or, between the horns a crucifix ppr. Mottoes—Fortis et fidelis : and Per crucem ad coronam.
Seat—Long Orchard, Templemore, co. Tipperary.

LAMBART OF BEAU PARC.

See BURKE'S PEERAGE AND BARONETAGE.

LAMBERT OF AGGARD.

CHRISTOPHER RICHARD THOMAS LAMBERT, late of Aggard, co. Galway, J.P., b. 29 Oct. 1868. He emigrated to Australia, and is m.

Lineage.—This family traces its descent from that of Maj.-Gen. Lambert, of Carlton in Craven, Yorks. His eldest son left an only dau. and heiress, Frances, m. 1701, Sir Thomas Middleton, 2nd bart. of Belsay (see BURKE's Peerage and Baronetage).

JOHN LAMBERT, of Carlton in Craven, Yorks, an Officer in Lord Clanricarde's Regt. in the Duke of Ormonde's Army in Ireland in 1660, m. (setts. dated 23 June, 1659) Mary, dau. of — French. He had a lease of Creg Clare from the Earl of Clanricarde in 1669, and d. 1683, leaving a son and a dau.,
CHARLES, of whom presently.
Mary, m. Robert French, of Rahassane.

The only son,
CHARLES LAMBERT, of Creg Clare, m. Janet, dau. of Walter Taylor, of Ballymacragh, and was killed at the siege of Derry, leaving two sons.
1. WALTER, of whom presently.
2. Joseph, ancestor of the Mayo branch (see LAMBERT of Brookhill).

The elder son,
WALTER LAMBERT, of Creg Clare, co. Galway, d. 17 May, 1770; m. 1st, Miss Hamilton, and had an only son,
1. Charles, of Creg Clare, m. 1742, Margaret, dau. of Dominick Browne, of Castle Macgarrett, co. Mayo, and had, with others, who d. unm.,
  1. Walter, of Creg Clare, m. 1st, 2 March, 1778, Honoria, dau. of Luke Dillon, of Clonbrock (by the Lady Honoria Burke, his wife, dau. of John, Earl of Clanricarde), and sister of 1st Lord Clonbrock. She d.s.p. He m. 2ndly, 1784, Catherine, dau. and co-heir of James Staunton, of Waterdale, and d. 21 Sept. 1822, leaving issue,
    (1) James Staunton, of Creg Clare and Waterdale, M.P. for Galway 1826-33, J.P. and D.L., High Sheriff 1814, b. 5 March, 1789; m. 25 Sept. 1832, Hon. Camden Elizabeth MacClellan, only child of Camden Gray, last Lord Kircudbright and d. 1 July, 1867, having by her (who d. 1 July, 1874) had issue,
      1. Walter MacClellan, late Capt. 41st Regt., b. 31 Aug. 1833; d. unm.
      2. Charles James, b. 11 Oct. 1837; d. unm. 6 Feb. 1855.
      3. Thomas Camden, Lieut.-Col. Donegal Artillery Militia, b. 5 Oct. 1841; m. Rose, dau. of William Armstrong, of Toronto, and d.s.p. 21 Jan. 1894. She m. 2ndly, 18 June, 1895, Sir George Albert de Hochpied Larpent, 3rd and last bart., who d.s.p. 18 May, 1899.
      4. Robert, b. 4 Feb. 1844; m. 22 April, 1862, Mary Ann Alice, youngest dau. of the late Thomas Newman, of Bath, and has issue,
        a. Sydney Robert Emelius, b. 11 April, 1864.
        b. Charles Edward, b. 2 July, 1865, dec.
        c. James Staunton, b. 4 May, 1867, dec.
        d. Thomas William, b. 22 April, 1879.
        e. Robert Staunton MacClellan, b. 9 April, 1884.
        a. Isabella, b. 22 July, 1871; m. Frederic Clinton, only son of the late Col. H. Clinton, of Earlsby Park, and grandson of the late Gen. Sir W. H. Clinton, G.C.B. (see BURKE's Peerage, NEWCASTLE, D.).
        b. Violet Mary, b. 28 Aug. 1881.
      5. James Henry, b. 5 Sept. 1851; m.
      1. Sarah Elizabeth, m. 2 Oct. 1858, Charles Edward Lewis, of St. Pierre, co. Monmouth, D.L. (see that family).
      2. Harriette, m. 2 Oct. 1856, Lieut.-Gen. Somerset Molyneux Wiseman Clarke, C.B., late 93rd Highlanders, and has issue.
      3. Katherine Isabella, b. 21 Sept. 1839; d. unm. 4 Dec. 1854.
    (2) Thomas Dominick, b. July, 1791.
    (1) Harriet, d. unm. 1829.
    (2) Maria Margaret, d. unm. 1853.
    (3) Emily, d. unm. 1830.
  1. Elizabeth, m. John Burke, of Tyaquin.
  2. Catherine, m. — Wilson, of Belvoir, co. Clare.
  3. Ellice, m. April, 1780, Joseph Donelan, of Killagh, co. Galway, and d. Aug. 1823, leaving issue (see that family).

Lambert. THE LANDED GENTRY. 380

Walter Lambert *m*. 2ndly, Miss Martin, of Tullyra, and had issue,
2. JOHN, of whom presently.
3. PETER, ancestor of LAMBERT, of Castle Ellen (*see that family*).
4. Thomas, *m*. the dau. of — Wood, of Chappell Field, co. Sligo, and had issue,
 1. Walter, of Castle Lambert, *m*. 1791, Elizabeth, 3rd dau. of Burton Persse, of Persse Lodge, now Moyode Castle, co. Galway, and *d*. Dec. 1824, leaving issue,
  Walter, of Castle Lambert, J.P., D.L., and High Sheriff 1828, *b*. 10 Sept. 1795; *m*. 21 Oct. 1817, Ann, eldest dau. of Col. Giles Eyre, of Eyre Court Castle, and *d*. 9 Aug. 1867, leaving issue,
   (1) THOMAS EYRE, of Castle Lambert, co. Galway, J.P., late Capt. 38th Regt., *b*. 25 April, 1820; *m*. 19 Aug. 1850, Sarah, 3rd dau. of John Wilson Trousdell, of Fort House, Kilrush, co. Clare, by Sarah, his wife, dau. of Thomas B. Persse.
   (2) Giles Eyre, of Moor Park, *m*. 1st, 1 May, 1850, Mary Jane, only child of Francis Rea, of Richview, Sandymount, co. Dublin, and by her had a dau.,
    Ada, *m*. 14 March, 1876, her cousin, William Fetherstonhaugh Lambert, of Donalstone House, Ballyglunin (*see below*).
   Mr. G. E. Lambert *m*. 2ndly, Annie, dau. of Maj.-Gen. Thomas Moore and widow of Capt. Henry Edward Hall.
   (3) Walter, *m*. and settled in America.
   (4) Richard, *m*. 6 Dec. 1870, Jean Mary, dau. of James Fraser, of Achnagairn, co. Inverness, and *d*. 6 June, 1898.
   (1) Annie Sophia, *d*. 27 March, 1908, having *m*. July, 1837, John Edmund O'Moore, 2nd son of O'Moore, of Cloghan Castle, King's Co.
   (2) Anchoretta Maria, *m*. 1848, P. Savage, youngest son of James Savage, of Finglass Wood, co. Dublin.
   (3) Ada, *m*. 1855, William Henry Price, eldest son of Dr. Price, of Dublin.
 2. John, *m*. Jane, only dau. of Col. Peyton, of Raheen, co. Leitrim, and had issue, six sons and two daus.
 3. Richard, of Lyston Hall, Essex, formerly Surgeon in the R.A., *b*. April, 1807; *m*. 27 June, 1828, Elizabeth Charlotte Louisa, eldest dau. and heir of John Campbell, of Lyston Hall, Accountant-General of the Court of Chancery, and *d*. 25 Jan. 1878, leaving issue,
  (1) JOHN CAMPBELL, of Lyston Hall, in the War Office, *m*. 18 Dec. 1867, Catherine Elizabeth, eldest dau. of Robert Chambré Vaughan, of Burlton Hall, co. Salop, and has issue,
   Archibald Vaughan Campbell, *b*. 27 Oct. 1868.
   Annie Elizabeth, *b*. 17 March, 1870.
  (2) Richard Blake, Comm. R.N.
  (3) Walter Miller, Capt. R.M.A.
  (1) Elizabeth Blackwell Campbell, *m*. 27 May, 1851, Wynn R. Williams, late Lieut. 4th Dragoon Guards, eldest son of Robert Vaughan Wynne Williams, of Bedford Place.
  (2) Anne Henrietta Campbell, *m*. Major-Gen. Hawkins, Bombay N.I.
  (3) Julia Campbell, *m*. 22 July, 1869, Capt. Robert Gordon Sanders Mason, late of the 8th Regt.
 4. Parsons, dec.
 5. Charles, dec. } *m*. and settled in America.
 6. Robert,
 1. Sarah, *m*. 1st, 1816, Charles Barry, 2nd Baron Clanmorris; and 2ndly, 29 May, 1830, Edward S. Hickman.
 2. Bessy, *m*. Matthew St. George, of Kilcolgan Castle, co. Galway.
 3. Anna Maria, *m*. 1825 (as his second wife), Richard Rathborne, of Ballymore, co. Galway, and had issue (*see* RATHBORNE, *late of Scripplestown*).
 4. Margaret, *m*. 1805, George Boate, of Duck's Pool, co. Waterford.
 5. Anne, *m*. Henry Lambert.
 1. A dau., *m*. Francis Butler, of Creg.
 2. A dau., *m*. Morgan, of Monksfield.

The 2nd son,
JOHN LAMBERT, of Milford, co. Galway, *m*. Mary, dau. of Sir Henry Burke, Bart. of Gliusk (*see* BURKE'S *Peerage*), and *d*. 1787, leaving issue,
1. Walter, of Kilquain, *d.s.p.*
2. HENRY of Aggard of whom presently.
3. Thomas, of Milford, *m*. 5 Sept. 1805, Lydia, dau. of Cuthbert Fetherstonhaugh, of Mosstown, Ballymore, and *d*. 1822, leaving issue,
 1. JOHN WALTER HENRY, of Aggard, *s*. his uncle.
 2. Cuthbert Fetherstonhaugh, *d. unm*.
 1. Mary Ann, *m*. 1824, Major Cuthbert Barlow, Paymaster 27th Foot.   2. Lydia, *m*. George Marshall, E.I.C.S.
 3. Cecilia, *m*. Col. W. Nixon, E.I.C.S.
 4. Charlotte, *m*. Capt. Henry Marshall, E.I.C.S.
1. Jane, *d. unm*.   2. Eliza, *d. unm*.
3. Letitia, *m*. John Fallon, of Runnemead, co. Roscommon.
4. A dau., *m*. Edmund Kelly, of Scregg.

The eldest surviving son,
HENRY LAMBERT, of Aggard, co. Galway, *d.s.p.* 1820, and was *s*. by his nephew,
JOHN WALTER HENRY LAMBERT, of Aggard, co. Galway, J.P., High Sheriff 1855, *b*. 5 Oct. 1811; *m*. 11 Feb. 1833, Anne, only dau. of William Fetherstonhaugh, of Derrahiney, co. Galway. He *d*. 8 April, 1899, having by her (who *d*. 20 Feb. 1859) had issue,
1. THOMAS WALTER, late of Aggard.
2. John Henry, of Remount Hill, Ballinasloe. co. Galway, J.P., *b*. 16 Dec. 1844; *m*. 8 Sept. 1881, Adelaide, 4th dau. of William Tombs Dewé, of Coates, co. Gloucester, and has issue,

 1. Charles Henry, *b*. 20 July, 1882.
 2. Ralph Gore, *b*. 23 Dec. 1887.
 3. John Hastings Wolfe, *b*. 28 May, 1891.
 1. Miriam Constance Dewé.
 2. Mary Adelaide.   3. Gwendoline Muriel.
3. William Fetherstonhaugh, of Donalstone House, Ballyglunin, co. Galway, B.A., M.D., M.Ch., L.M., T.C.D., *b*. 20 Nov. 1852; *m*. 14 March, 1876, Ada. 2nd dau. of Giles Eyre Lambert, of Moor Park (*see above*). He *d*. 30 May, 1907, having had issue,
 1. John Giles Henry, *b*. 24 July, 1878.
 2. William Clare Fetherstonhaugh, *b*. 28 April, 1887.
 1. Mabel Lizzie, *b*. 11 Nov. 1876; *d*. 21 April, 1900.
 2. May, *b*. 8 Sept. 1881.
 3. Violet Ada, *b*. 27 Feb. 1883; *m*. 29 Oct. 1907, Thomas Paterson Naismith.
 4. Ada Mary Jane, *b*. 8 Jan. 1885.
 5. Eva Annie Maud, *b*. 20 Sept. 1891.
1. Anne Caroline, *d. unm*. 1911.
2. Charlotte, *m*. Lieut.-Col. Cuthbert Barlow, 10th Foot.
3. Emily Florence, *m*. 1860, Charles Kelly, of Luneston, Westmeath, J.P.
4. Elizabeth Jane, *m*. Thomas Barlow, I.C.S.
5. Marian Marcella, *m*. Major Charles Brereton, R.A., and *d*. March, 1869, leaving issue.
6. Adelaide, *d*. 11 May, 1910; *m*. Rev. Robert O'Callaghan, now Vicar of Mapleton, Hull.
7. Fanny, *d. unm*. 3 Sept. 1899.
8. Alice, *m*. Jones Lamprey, of Southsea, M.B., Surgeon-General late 67th Regt.

The eldest son,
THOMAS WALTER LAMBERT, of Aggard and Kilquaine, co. Galway, *b*. 24 March, 1841; *m*. 31 May, 1865, Elizabeth, 3rd dau. of Christopher St. George, of Tyrone Hosue. She *d*. 3 Dec. 1910. He *d*. 11 March, 1902, leaving issue,
1. CHRISTOPHER RICHARD THOMAS, late of Aggard.
2. John Walter Henry Charles, *b*. 20 Nov. 1871, now of Kilquaine, Craughwell, co. Galway, *m*. Mary, dau. of Rev. John Foot, and has issue,
3. Cuthbert Harold, *b*. 24 Aug. 1876.
4. Harry William Reginald, *b*. 17 May, 1878; *m*. 1 Aug. 1911, Lily, dau. of T. Scanlan, of Shannon Lodge, Bandon.
1. Olivia Bessie Josephine, *m*. 1898, Walter Mortimer Dyas, of Piercetown House, Kells, co. Meath.
2. Charlotte Norah Barlow, *m*. 20 Sept. 1898, Major William Thomas Conway Poole, Indian Army, 2nd son of the late Lieut.-Col. M. Conway Poole, Deputy-Commissioner of Rangoon, and of Mrs. Conway Poole, of Kingsleigh, Harrow-on-the-Hill. She *d*. 12 Sept. 1911.
3. Anne Marion, *m*. 30 March, 1897, William Astle Ryan, of Cahore, co. Wexford. She *d*. 9 Sept. 1908, having had issue,
 1. Beaumont Astle, *b*. 6 March, 1898.
 2. William Astle, *b*. 13 Sept. 1905.
 1. Eleanor Blanche Lambert, *b*. 24 Oct. 1900.
 2. Anne Marion Fetherstonhaugh, *b*. 8 Oct. 1902.
4. Adelaide St. George, *m*. 6 Feb. 1901, Robert Sparrow, Resident Magistrate, Enniskillen (*Fort Lodge, Enniskillen*), and has issue.
5. Guendoleyne Lizzie.
6. Ethel Beatrice, *d*. young.
7. Beatrice Helena.

LAMBERT OF CASTLE ELLEN.

WALTER PETER LAMBERT, of Castle Ellen, co. Galway, Lieut. Connaught Rangers, *s*. his father 1894; *b*. 8 Jan. 1891.

Lineage.—PETER LAMBERT, son of Walter Lambert, of Creg Clare (*see* LAMBERT *of Aggard*), *m*. Miss Carroll, of Ardagh, and had issue,
WALTER PETER LAMBERT, *m*. Miss Tubbs, and had several sons. The eldest,
PETER LAMBERT, *m*. 1st, 1810, Eleanor, eldest dau. of Thomas Seymour, of Ballymore Castle (*see that family*), and by her (who *d*. 20 Nov. 1828) had issue.
1. WALTER PETER, of Castle Ellen.
2. Thomas Seymour, *d. unm*.   3. Peter, *d. unm*.
1. Isabella, *m*. May, 1851, Edward Henry Carson, of Dublin, and had, with other issue, the Right Hon. Sir Edward Henry Carson, P.C., K.C., M.P., Solicitor-Gen.
Mr. Lambert *d*. 17 Jan. 1844, having had by his second wife, two daus.,
2. Ada Constance, *m*. 26 May, 1857, Sir George Moyers, Lord Mayor of Dublin 1881.
3. Louisa Maria, *m*. April, 1853, Henry J. S. Bowdler.

His eldest son,
WALTER PETER LAMBERT, of Castle Ellen, co. Galway, J.P. and D.L., High Sheriff 1859, *b*. 4 Nov. 1816; *m*. 5 March, 1846, Elizabeth, only child of William McO'Boy, of Stump Hill, co. Cork, and *d*. 19 Oct. 1892, having by her (who *d*. 7 Jan. 1903) had issue,
1. PETER FITZWALTER, late of Castle Ellen.
2. William, *b*. 29 Dec. 1856; *d*. July, 1865.
1. Kate, *m*. 1879, Capt. William W. Weston, 7th Dragoon Guards, and is dec.

The only surviving son,
PETER FITZWALTER LAMBERT, of Castle Ellen, co. Galway, J.P., High Sheriff 1891, *b*. 8 Dec. 1848; *m*. 7 July, 1887, Julia Mary,

eldest dau. of Col. Henry Alexander Hewetson, of Auchnacloy, co. Dublin, and *d.* 24 Feb. 1894, leaving issue,
1. WALTER PETER, now of Castle Ellen.
2. Henry Alexander, Midshipman R.N., *b.* 23 March, 1892.
3. William Robert, *b.* 29 July, 1894.
1. Amelia Lizzie.   2. Mary Georgiana.
Seat—Castle Ellen, Athenry, co. Galway.

LAMBERT OF BROOKHILL.

ALEXANDER FANE-LAMBERT, of Brookhill, co. Mayo, Lieut. Royal Field Artillery, *b.* 15 Nov. 1887.

Lineage.—JOSEPH LAMBERT, of Toher and Thomastown in 1694, son of John Lambert and Janet his wife, dau. of Walter Taylor (*see* LAMBERT *of Aggard*). He *m.* 1699, Anne, dau. of Peter Rutledge, of Cornfield, co. Mayo, and had a son,
  FRANCIS LAMBERT, of Toher and Thomastown, *b.* 1703; *m.* 1st, 15 April, 1747, Rebecca, dau. of Thomas Lindsey, of Turin Castle, co. Mayo, and sister of Thomas Lindsey, of Hollymount, and had by her a son, JOSEPH, his heir; and two daus.; the elder, Letitia, *m.* Thomas Elwood, of Ashford Park, co. Galway; and the younger, *m.* Francis Goodwin. Mr. Lambert *m.* 2ndly, Miss Ormsby, of co. Mayo, and *d.* 1790, having had by her a son, Francis, R.N., *m.* Miss Banks, and had issue. The only son of the first marriage,
  JOSEPH LAMBERT, of Brookhill, High Sheriff of Mayo 1796, *b.* 1749; *m.* 1st, 1780, Barbara, dau. of Thomas Ruttledge, of Bloomfield, and sister and heir of Robert Ruttledge, M.P., of the same place, and by her had issue,
  1. Thomas, who *d. unm.*
  2. FRANCIS (Rev.), of Bloomfield, co. Mayo, J.P., *b.* 1788; assumed the name and arms of RUTTLEDGE; *m.* 9 June, 1819, Margaret, dau. of Col. Henry Bruen, M.P., of Oak Park, and had issue (*see* RUTTLEDGE *of Bloomfield*).
    1. Barbara, *m.* Arthur Knox, of Bushfield, co. Mayo, and had issue (*see* KNOX *of Rappa Castle*).
  Mr. Lambert *m.* 2ndly, 1790, Mary, eldest dau. of Rev. Alexander Clendinning, D.D., Prebendary of Tuam, and Rector of Westport, and by her had issue,
  3. Joseph, late of Brookhill, J.P., *b.* 1793; *d. unm.* 1855.
  4. ALEXANDER CLENDINNING, of whom presently.
  3. Eleanor, *m.* David Ruttledge Courtenay, Barrister-at-Law, and had issue.
  4. Rebecca, *d. unm.*
  5. Letitia, *m.* John Vevers, R.N.   6. Elizabeth, *d. unm.*
  7. Georgiana, *m.* Charles Bowen, of Milford (*see* BOWEN MILLER *of Milford*).
  Mr. Lambert *d.* 1813. His 4th son,
  ALEXANDER CLENDINNING LAMBERT, of Brookhill, co. Mayo, J.P. and D.L., Treasurer of the co. for fifty years, *b.* 7 Nov. 1805; *m.* 12 Sept. 1848, Emma Maria, dau. of Guy Lenox Prendergast, formerly Member of Council, Bombay, and M.P. for Lymington, and had issue.
  1. JOSEPH ALEXANDER, late of Brookhill.
  2. GUY LENOX BENCE-LAMBERT, C.M.G., of Thorington Hall, Suffolk, and Dernasliggan, Leenane, co. Galway, J.P. co. Galway, and J.P., D.L. co. Suffolk, late Lieut.-Col. Commanding 3rd Connaught Rangers, assumed by Royal Licence 1884, additional name of BENCE (*Carlton Club*), *b.* 30 Dec. 1856; *m.* 23 Jan.1884, Ida Millicent, dau. and co-heir of the late Henry Bence, J.P. and D.L.,of Thorington Hall, Suffolk (*see* BENCE *of Kentwell*).
    1. Emma Mary Louisa, *d. unm.* 1898.
    2. Flora Marion.   3. Louisa Matilda.
    4. Florence Amy, *m.* 14 Dec. 1882, Harvey Trewythen Brabazon Combe, son of Boyce Harvey Combe, of Oaklands, Sussex, and has issue (*see* COMBE *of Oaklands*).
  Mr. Lambert *d.* 27 Sept. 1892.
  Col. JOSEPH ALEXANDER LAMBERT, of Brookhill, co. Mayo, J.P. and D.L. High Sheriff co. Mayo 1906, Commanded the 2nd Dragoon Guards (Queen's Bays), *b.* 7 April, 1855; *d.* 1907; *m.* 10 Feb. 1887, Grace Susan, elder dau. of the late William Dashwood Fane, of Fulbeck Hall, Lincolnshire (*see* BURKE'S *Peerage*, WESTMORLAND, &.) and has issue,
  1. ALEXANDER FANE, now of Brookhill.
  2. Guy William, *b.* 1 Dec. 1889.
  3. Francis John, Lieut. R. N., *b.* 12 March, 1891.
  4. Jeffrey Maurice, *b.* 23 Jan. 1900.
  1. Grace Mary Blanche.   2. Joan Millicent.
  3. Ida Patricia Emma.

Arms—Gu., a cross-crosslet or, between three cinquefoils pierced arg. Crest—A centaur ppr. charged on the shoulder with a cross-crosslet, or. Motto—Ut quocunque paratus.

Seat—Brookhill, Claremorris, co. Mayo.

LAMBERT OF CARNAGH.

GEORGE HENRY LAMBERT, of Carnagh, co. Wexford, J.P., co. Anglesey, late Capt. Royal Anglesey Eng. Mil., *b.* 8 Aug. 1866; *m.* 28 Sept. 1897, June, dau. of Francis Augustine Leigh, of Rosegarland (*see that family*), and has issue,
HENRY FRANCIS, *b.* 17 Sept. 1898.

Lineage.—NICHOLAS LAMBERT, of Carnagh, co. Wexford, *m.* Marian, dau. of Richard Stafford, of Rahayle, and left issue,
  1. Patrick, of Dunmaine House, co. Wexford, Clerk of the Crown, Commanded a Regt. at the battle of the Boyne 1660, Escheator of the Province of Connaught, High Sheriff co. Wexford 1683, M.P. for Taghmon in the Irish Parliament 1692. He obtained grants of land in 1683 and in the same year a grant of arms from Ulster. He *m.* 1st, Mary, dau. of William Talbot, Mayor of Wexford 1630, by whom he had an only son. He *m.* 2ndly, Nov. 1682, Mary Story (who *m.* 2ndly, Lieut.-Col. Robert Dixon, of Calverstown, co. Kildare). His only son,
    Arran, an officer in General Langston's Regt. 1711, J.P. 1707, *m.* 1713, Catherine, dau. of William Jones, of Waterford, and *d.* 1747 (his widow *m.* Mathias Reilly, of Dublin), having had issue with a dau., Catherine, a son,
      Lewis Jones, of Dublin, Barrister-at-Law, *d.* 1781, having *m.* Jane Woods, by whom he had issue,
        1. William, *d.* 1807; *m.* 1788, Mary, dau. of William Bernard, of Carlow, by whom he had issue,
          a. Lewis Jones, B.A., Trin. Coll. Dub. of Parkswood, *d.* 1876; *m.* Georgina, youngest dau. of Richard Anderson, of Kilternan Abbey, Carrickmines, by whom he had issue,
            (*a*) Louis Jones, Col. U.S. Army. Killed in action.
            (*b*) Richard Anderson, B.A. Trin. Coll. Dub., M.D. Edin. (11, *Pleasants Street, Dublin*).
            (*c*) William Henry, of Parkswood, Waterford.
          b. Bernard, M.D.
          c. Thomas, *d.* young.
          a. Jane, *m.* Major Thomas Odell.
          b. Jemima, *m.* her cousin, Richard Bernard.
          c. Anne, *m.* Thomas Devonport.
        2. Lewis Jones.   3. Frederick.
  2. JAMES, of Carnagh, of whom below.

The younger son,
JAMES LAMBERT, of Carnagh, *m.* Anstace, dau. and heir of Nicholas Sutton, of Ballykerogemaure, and acquired through her the Carnagh estates, in the barony of Bantry. His will, dated 2 Feb. 1697, was proved 23 May, 1700. He left issue,
  1. Nicholas, Capt. in the Army of JAMES II, was killed at Limerick 1691, *s.p.*
  2. PATRICK, of whom presently.
  1. Mary, *m.* James Molony, of Kiltanon.
  2. Margaret, *m.* 6 Oct. 1676, Richard Bolger.
  3. Catherine, *m.* Thomas Houghton, of Kilmanock.
  4. Madeline, *m.* Morgan Kavanagh, of New Ross.
The only surviving son,
PATRICK LAMBERT, of Carnagh, *m.* by licence 23 Jan. 1698, Catherine White. He *d.* 1 Jan. 1729, leaving two sons and a dau. His elder son,
JAMES LAMBERT, of Carnagh, *d.s.p.* at Bath, Oct. 1757, and was s. by his brother,
HENRY LAMBERT, of Carnagh, *m.* Margaret, dau. of Thomas FitzSimon, of the house of Glencullen, co. Dublin. She *d.* 1791. He *d.* 17 Feb. 1774, leaving issue, with another son,
  1. PATRICK, his heir.
  2. James, of Bantry Lodge, *m.* 1st, 30 June, 1774, Maria, dau. of John Kennedy, and had issue,
    1. James, Lieut. R.N., *d.* 1836.
    2. Henry Patrick, *m.* 1810, Christina, dau. of Peter Strange. She *d.* 1846. He *d.* 1858, leaving a dau.,
      Margaret, *d. unm.* 1866.
  He *m.* 2ndly, Aug. 1780, Begnet, dau. of George Lattin, of Morristown Lattin, and by her had three sons, who *d.s.p.*, and three daus.
    1. Christina, *m.* 16 Aug. 1766, Edward Bolger, of Ballinabarna, co. Kilkenny, and had issue.
    2. A dau., *m.* Joseph Anthony, of Waterford, and had issue.
The eldest son,
PATRICK LAMBERT, of Carnagh, *m.* 1781, Mary Anne, eldest dau. of George Lattin, of Morristown Lattin, co. Kildare. She *d.* 10 Sept. 1838. He *d.* 7 July, 1808, leaving issue,
  1. HENRY, his heir.
  2. Ambrose, of New Grove, co. Kilkenny, *b.* 1789, *m.* 1823, Eliza, dau. of John Snow, of Larkfield, co. Kilkenny. She *d.* 3 Nov. 1868. He *d.* 5 July, 1856, leaving issue,
    1. Ambrose, of New Grove, co. Kilkenny, J.P., *b.* 1827, *m.* 1864, Mary, dau. of Francis Coppinger, and *d.* 11 Aug. 1878, leaving issue,
      (1) Ambrose, *b.* 1865.
      (2) Nicholas Henry, of Dysertmore, co. Kilkenny, J.P., *b.* 1867.
      (3) Henry, *b.* 1868, *d.* 1893.
      (4) Francis, *b.* 1874, *d.* 1896.
      (5) Bertrand, *b.* 1878, *m.* 19 Jan. 1899, Hon. Margaret Barnewall, youngest dau. of the late Charles Barnewall, of Meadstown, and sister of Lord Trimlestown (*see* BURKE'S *Peerage*).
      (1) Mabel.
      (2) Ethel, *m.* 1896, Fritz Weber, of Cologne.

Langford. THE LANDED GENTRY. 382

2. Henry, b. 1831, m. 1853, Catherine, dau. of Myles McSwiny. She d.s.p. 1894.
3. Sydenham John, Col. R.E. (3, *Maitland Park Villas, Haverstock Hill, N.W.*), b. 15 April, 1842; m. 1871, Emily, dau. of Gen. David Pott, C.B., Bengal Staff Corps (see POTT *of Todrig*), and has issue,
   (1) Edward, b. 1874.
   (2) Henry, b. 1875, d. 1888.
   (3) Robert, b. 1878.
   (4) Ambrose, b. 1881.
   (5) Arthur, b. 1889, d. 1890.
   (1) Kathleen.
1. Eliza, d. unm. 1806.
2. Mary, d. 18 March, 1906.
3. Augusta, a nun.   4. Margaret, a nun.
1. Catherine, m. March, 1811, Gerald Aylmer, of Lyons, and had issue. Her dau. Letitia, m. (as his second wife) 9 Oct. 1844, Charles Barnwell, J.P., Meath. She d. 3 March, 1886, leaving with other issue Christopher Patrick and Charles, 17 and 18 Lords Trimlestown (see BURKE's *Peerage*).
2. Margaret, d. unm. 21 July, 1862.
3. Lettitia, a nun, d. 8 May, 1854.
4. Jane, m. 2 June, 1840, Awley Banon, M.D. of Irishtown, co. Meath, and d.s.p. 11 Feb. 1874.   He d. 1867 (see BANON *of Broughall Castle*).
The eldest son,
HENRY LAMBERT, of Carnagh, J.P. and D.L., M.P. for co. Wexford, b. 1 Sept. 1786, m. 11 June, 1835, Catherine, youngest dau. of William Talbot, of Castle Talbot, and sister of Maria Theresa, Countess of John, 16th Earl of Shrewsbury. She d. 16 March, 1883. He d. 20 Oct. 1861, leaving issue,
1. HENRY PATRICK, late of Carnagh.
2. George Thomas (Sir), Knt., C.B., Governor of Christ's Hospital and formerly Director of the estates and finances of Greenwich Hospital, 1885-1901, created C.B. 1887, and knighted 1903 (7, *Park Place, St. James', S.W.; White's and Arthurs' Clubs*), b. 9 Nov. 1837.
1. Mary Jane, m. P.J. Lynch, of Churchtown House, co. Dublin, and d. 1882, leaving issue.
2. Anne, m. 1st, 27 Jan. 1870, Edwin Richard, 3rd Earl of Dunraven, K.P., who d. 6 Oct. 1871. She m. 2ndly, 26 April, 1879, Hedworth, 2nd Lord Hylton, who d. 31 Oct. 1899.
3. Catherine, d. unm. 8 March, 1857.
4. Juliana Margaret, m. 1871, Edward Gerald More O'Ferrall, D.L., of Lissard, co. Longford, and has issue (see *that family*).
5. Letitia, d. unm. 1 Jan. 1906.
6. Frances.
The elder son,
HENRY PATRICK LAMBERT, of Carnagh, co. Wexford, J.P. and D.L., High Sheriff co. Wexford 1864, and co. Anglesea 1868, b. 2 Dec. 1836; m. 23 Sept. 1863, Elizabeth, eldest dau. of the late Thomas Williams, of Tan-y-Craig, Anglesea. She d. 12 Sept. 1893. He d. 22 June, 1896, leaving issue,
GEORGE HENRY, now of Carnagh.
Gwendoline Elizabeth Moneda.

Arms—Quarterly 1st and 4th vert a lamb arg.; 2nd and 3rd erm. an eagle displayed gu. Crest—A sagittary per pale gu. and arg. charged with a trefoil vert, the bow and arrow or. Motto—Deus providebit.
Seats—Carnagh, New Ross, Wexford, and Tan-y-Graig, Pentraeth, Anglesey.

COPLEN-LANGFORD OF KILCOSGRIFF.

RICHARD COPLEN-LANGFORD, of Kilcosgriff Castle, co. Limerick, and Shean, co. Clare, J.P. for the former co., b. 1853; s. his mother 1884, and his father in 1887. He m. 24 Aug. 1898, Sophia, eldest dau. of the late Charles Alphonse Massy J.P. of Goondaroo, N.S. Wales and Farran, co. Limerick (by Charlotte Renton his wife, dau. of Dr. Bute Stuart, of Parramatta, N.S.W.), and grand neice of the late Eyre Massy of Glenville, co. Limerick.

Lineage.—WILLIAM LANGFORD of Gurteengary, co. Limerick, living there 1678, was appointed one of the Commissioners for raising supplies in 1695 and 1698. He left issue.
1. William, m. 1703, Gertrude, who d. 1734 (the only lady who was ever made a Freemason), dau. of John St. Leger, of Doneraile, co. Cork, by his wife, Lady Mary Chichester, dau. of the Earl of Donegal, sister of Arthur, 1st Viscount Doneraile, and widow of Richard Aldworth, of Newmarket (see *that family*), and had issue.
2. JAMES, of whom we treat.
3. Francis, m. 1728, Mary, dau. of Capt. Robert Lloyd, of Newcastle, co. Limerick, by Elizabeth his wife, dau. of William De Burgh, Prebendary of Croagh and Rector of Newcastle West, and had a dau., Sarah, m. Major France Drew, of Drewscourt (see *that family*).
4. John, of Tullagha, left a son, Jonas, of Antigua, who left an only dau., Elizabeth, m. Peter Brooke, of Mere Hall, co. Cheshire.
5. Robert, living at Kilcosgriff, 1719.
1. Susannah, m. (settlement dated 20 Oct. 1677) Capt. John Coplen, of Kilcosgriff, co. Limerick, who d.s.p., having bequeathed his estates to his wife's brother, James Langford, on condition that he assumed the additional name of Coplen.
2. Jane, m. 1735, O'Dell Conyers, of Castletown Conyers.
The second son,
JAMES COPLEN-LANGFORD, of Kilcosgriff, co. Limerick, m. Mary, dau. of Major Nicholas Monckton of Kilmore, by his wife Jane O'Dell, and had issue,
1. JOHN, of whom presently.   2. Richard.
The elder son,
JOHN COPLEN-LANGFORD, of Kilcosgriff and Shanagolden, co. Limerick, m. Elizabeth, widow of Henry Freeman, of Freemount, co. Cork, dau. of Rev. George Studdart, Rector of Rathkeale and Chancellor of Limerick Cathedral, by his wife Mellicent Rose, sister to Henry Rose, Lord Chief Justice of the King's Bench, and by her had issue,
1. JOHN, of whom presently.
2. George, of West Park and Reen, co. Kerry, an officer in the Army, will dated 1814.
The elder son,
JOHN COPLEN-LANGFORD, of Kilcosgriff and Rowell, co. Limerick, m. 21 Oct. 1756, Jane, dau. of William Fosberry, of Castletown and Curraghbridge, co. Limerick, and had issue,
1. RICHARD COPLEN, of whom presently.
2. Francis (Rev.), B.A. T.C.D., Rector of Kilcornan, m. Margaret Stewart, and by her had issue,
   1. John Thomas, M.A. T.C.D., b. 13 March, 1810.
   2. Francis (Rev.), Rector of Newbridge, co. Kildare, m. Miss Parkinson, of Cheltenham, and had issue,
      Francis, Major late 85th Regt., b. 15 March, 1842.
   3. George, M.D., of Adare, co. Limerick, d.s.p.
3. George, of Maun, co. Kerry, m. his cousin, — Fosberry, and d.s.p.
4. Robert, of Rowell, co. Limerick, m. Dora, dau. of John Brereton, of Rathurles, co. Tipperary, and had issue a son,
   John Brereton Langford, b. 11 Aug. 1805; m. Emma, dau. of Col. Hughes, of Mardanash, Essex, and had issue, with a dau., a son, Arthur, B.A. J.P. Dublin, m. and has issue.
5. John.
6. Edward, of Stonehall, co. Limerick, and Besborough, co. Clare, Capt. Royal Limerick Yeomanry, B.A., T.C.D., m. Elizabeth, dau. of Rev. — Spellicy, Rector of Ennis, co. Clare, and by her had issue,
   1. John, J.P., m. 1826, Mary, dau. of William Cox, of Ballynoe, co. Limerick, and had issue, three sons and three daus.
      1. Henrietta, m. 25 July, 1835, Col. Frank Dillon, 18th Regt.
      2. Maria, m. 1 March, 1840, Robert Hunt, J.P., of Inchirourke, co. Limerick.
      3. Millicent, d. unm.
   1. Elizabeth, m. Robert Nesbitt, of Fort Nesbitt, co. Tipperary.
   2. Melicent, m. Rev. Richard Standish, of Frankfort, co. Limerick, son of Sir Thomas Standish.
   3. Jane, d. unm.
The eldest son,
RICHARD COPLEN-LANGFORD, of Kilcosgriff Castle, co. Limerick, and Beechwood Park, co. Tipperary, J.P., Capt. 66th Foot, b. 1761, m. 1784, Catherine, dau. of Cooper Crawford, J.P., of Fermoyle, and d. 30 March, 1845, leaving issue,
1. RICHARD COPLEN, of whom presently.
2. John, of Ballycormick and Shanagolden, d.s.p.
3. William, Col. 51st Regt., served in Peninsular War and Indian Army, m. and had issue.
4. Cooper, killed in the American War, s.p.
5. George, of Pallintoher, co. Tipperary, m. 1828, Maria, youngest dau. of Rev. Henry Bayley, of Bayley's Farm, co. Tipperary, and had a son,
   John Crawford, Capt. 17th Foot, b. 1829; m. 20 Sept. 1854, Margaret, dau. of James Gibbon, of Aberdeen, and had issue,
   (1) George, Capt. R.N., d.s.p.
   (2) John Crawford, m. Margaret Euphemia Lowther, and has issue.
   (3) James Gibbon, d.s.p.
   (4) William, m. 1906, Alice Evans, and has issue,
      1. Arthur, b. 1907.   2. Cyril Coplen, b. 1909.
      1. Gwendoline.
   (5) Charles, D.S.O., Capt. late 8th Hussars, b. 1873; m. 1906, Agnes, dau. of Joseph Matterson, J.P., of Castle Troy, co. Limerick, and has issue, Richard Crawford, b. 1907.
   (6) Henry.
   (1) Mary, m. Col. Garstin, I.S.C.
   (2) Maria m. Col. Ray, Army Pay Dept., late Warwickshire Regt.
   (3) Margaret Douglas, m. Sydney Smith, Inspect.-Gen. of Police, India.
   (4) Leonarda m. Richard Mansergh Martin.
   (5) Elizabeth.   (6) Isabel, d. unm.
1. Elizabeth, m. George Finch, of Crecora, co. Limerick, son of William Finch, of Kilcolman, co. Tipperary (see *that family*).
2. Jane, m. John Langford Locke, of Newcastle, son of the Rev. Mr. Locke.   3. Henrietta, d. unm.
4. Catherine, d. unm.   5. Mary, d. unm.
6. Millicent, d. unm.
The eldest son,
THE REV. RICHARD COPLEN-LANGFORD, of Kilcosgriff Castle and Ballycormick, co. Limerick, Rector of Miltown Malbay, co. Clare, M.A. T.C.D., m. Elizabeth, dau. of Cooper Crawford, of Fermoyle, co. Tipperary. and d. Sept. 1856, leaving issue,
1. RICHARD COPLEN, of whom presently.
1. Bessie, m. John O'Donoghue, Barrister-at-Law, and author of *The Historical Memoirs of the O'Brien Family*, etc.
2. Henrietta, m. — Fitzgerald, Inspector of National Schools in Ireland, son of the Rector of Ennis, co. Clare.
3. Sarah, d. unm.
The only son,
RICHARD COPLEN-LANGFORD, of Kilcosgriff Castle, Ballycormick, and Shanagolden, co. Limerick, b. 23 July, 1821; m. 7 July, 1853, Geraldine Eliza, dau. and heiress of Major Charles Creagh, 12th

Lancers, J.P. of Carrigery, co. Clare (*see that family*), by Louisa, his wife, dau. of Charles Costello, D.L. of Edmonstown, co. Mayo, and by her (who *d*. 31 March, 1884) had issue,
1. RICHARD, now of Kilcosgriff Castle.
2. Charles Creagh, *b*. 1855; *m*. 17 June, 1877, Alice Charlotte, dau. of the late John Willington, J.P. of Castle Willington, co. Tipperary, and has issue three daus.
   1. Lily.
   2. Louisa, *m*. Rev. John Yates, M.A., Rector of Miltown, co. Clare.
   3. Maud.
3. Thomas Crawford (*Glenville, Ardagh, co. Limerick*), *b*. 1857; *m*. 12 Dec. 1903, Frances Mary, eldest dau. and heir of Jonathan Bruce Massy, J.P., of Glenville, co. Limerick, and has issue,
   1. Richard Massy Coplen, *b*. 1905.
   2. Jonathan Bruce Massy, *b*. 1908.
   1. Frances Massy.   2. Mary Creagh.
1. Margaret Louisa, *m*. Robert Hunt, of Inchirourke, co. Limerick, J.P., and has issue two sons.
Mr. Richard Coplen-Langford sold the Ballycormick and Shanagolden estates in 1852, and *d*. 13 Sept, 1887, when he was *s*. by his son RICHARD, now of Kilcosgriff Castle.

Seats—Kilcosgriff, co. Limerick; Lough Naminna Lodge, Ennis, co. Clare. *Club*—County, Limerick.

LANGLEY OF COAL BROOK.

The late GEORGE LANGLEY, of Coal Brook, co. Tipperary, J.P. and D.L., and J.P. co. Kilkenny, *b*. 9 June, 1838; *s*. his brother 1868; *m*. Oct. 1862, Katherine Elizabeth, dau. of Rev. George Peacocke, Rector of Holycross, and *d*. 12 April, 1907, having had issue, three daus.,

1. Katherine Georgina, *m*. Dec. 1888, E. Lt. Maunsell, who *d*. 1896.
2. Elizabeth Dorothea Villiers, *m*. 27 March, 1894, Edward Theodore Alms, of Holway, Taunton, and has issue, three sons and one dau.
3. Henrietta, *m*. 25 March, 1896, Capt. C. W. Grey, and has issue, one dau.

Lineage.—HENRY LANGLEY, a Lieut. in Capt. Thomas Ask's troop in Col. Hierom Sankey's Regt. of Horse in CROMWELL'S Army, went to Ireland 1649 from Prestwich, Lancashire, and was put into possession of lands in the barony of Slievardagh, co. Tipperary, 1655. He was the son of Deodatus Langley, who was the son of Rev. William Langley, Rector of Prestwich 1569-1611, who was descended from the Langleys of Agecroft Hall, co. Lancaster. His wife's name was Ann, and his sister, Dorothy Langley, was of Bury, co. Lancaster. Henry Langley, bapt. 23 Aug. 1618, whose will bears date 2 Feb. 1666, was dead 1667. His son,
CHARLES LANGLEY, of Lisnamrock, co. Tipperary, to whom his father left lands in the barony of Slievardagh, *d*. before 29 March, 1723, when his will was proved. He left a son.
HENRY LANGLEY, of Lisnamrock, made a deed of settlement, dated 30 Oct. 1742, and by Anne his wife had issue,
1. CHARLES, his heir.
2. HENRY, of Priestown, co. Tipperary, ancestor of the family of LANGLEY *of Brittas Castle*.
3. Lawrence, Capt. R.N.; *d. unm*.
4. Thomas, of Archerstown, co. Tipperary, *m*. 1780, Catherine, dau. of John Nicholson, of Tutulla, co. Tipperary, and *d*. 1807, having had,
   1. Henry, of Archerstown, Capt. (late Tipperary Yeomanry), *m*. 1815, Lydia, eldest dau. of Richard Levinge, of Belmont, co. Kilkenny, and *d*. 28 Dec. 1858, having had surviving issue,
   Henry, of Archerstown, Thurles, co. Tipperary, J.P., *b*. 20 Oct. 1815; *m*. 7 Aug. 1860, Catherine Maria Victoria, dau. of John Toler, M.D., and *d*. 3 March, 1899, having by her (who *d*. 21 May, 1899) left issue.
     1. Henry Oliver, B.A. (Dublin), J.P. of Archerstown House, Thurles, *b*. 7 July, 1863; *m*. 27 Sept. 1899, Ethel Maud, dau. of John Max, of Maxfort, co. Tipperary, and has issue,
       Henry Richard, *b*. 16 Nov. 1901.
       Mary Katharine Toler, *b*. 16 Nov. 1900.
     2. Thomas Finlow, *b*. 16 Sept. 1870.
       1. Catherine Elizabeth Boswell, *b*. 17 July 1862; *m*. 18 Sept. 1893, Frederick Foster.
     2. Lawrence.   3. Thomas.
     1. Blanch.   2. Anna Maria.
     3. Catherine.
1. Rachel, *m*. — Blackmore, of co. Kildare.
2. Mary, *m*. Richard Clutterbuck, of Bannoxtown.
Henry Langley's son and successor,
CHARLES LANGLEY, of Lisnamrock, whose will, dated 13 Oct. 1791, was proved 21 March, 1793, *m*. June, 1744, Alice, dau. of John Croker, of the family of CROKER *of Ballinagarde*, co. Limerick (her will was proved 1793), and had, with other issue,
1. HENRY, his heir.
2. Charles, *d. unm*.
3. Thomas.
4. Lawrence, *m*. a dau. of Going, of Ballyphilip.
The eldest son,
HENRY LANGLEY, of Lisnamrock, co. Tipperary, *m*. Frances, dau. of Jeremiah Jackson, of Fanningstown, co. Limerick, and *d*. 1808, leaving by her (who *d*. 1802) issue,

1. CHARLES, his heir.
2. Jeremiah, *m*. Lydia, eldest dau. of Godfrey Taylor, of Noan, co. Tipperary, and had issue,
   1. Henry, Lieut. E.I.C. Navy, murdered in a mutiny at sea.
   2. Charles.
   1. Frances.
   2. Lydia, *m*. Lieut. George Jackson, R.N.
1. Catherine, *m*. George Tuthill, of Ballyteigue, co. Limerick, and had issue.
The eldest son,
CHARLES HENRY LANGLEY, of Lisnamrock and Coal Brook, a Deputy-Governor of co. Tipperary, *b*. 1772; *m*. 24 July, 1794, Frances, dau. of Col. John Bagwell, of Kilmore, co. Tipperary, and had by her (who *d*. 1846) issue,
1. HENRY, his heir.
2. Charles, *b*. 1799; *d. unm*.
3. John, J.P., *b*. 1810; *d. unm*.
4. Hamilton William, *b*. 1817, *m*. Isabella, dau. of Ion Studdert, of Elm Hill, co. Clare, and *d*. in Buenos Ayres, 1867, leaving issue,
   1. Charles, *d.s.p.*
   2. Ion.
   3. Hamilton.
   4. Henry.
   5. George.
   1. Emily, *m*. John Fraser.   2. Frances.
1. Frances, *m*. 16 Feb. 1816, William Atkinson, D.L., of Rehins, co. Mayo.   2. Isabella, *d*. young.
3. Catherine, *m*. Piercy Bagwell, Comm. R.N., and *d.s.p.*
4. Elizabeth, *d*. young.
5. Jane, *m*. Rev. David Whitty, of Rathvilly, and has issue.
6. Gertrude, *m*. Rev. William Whitty, M.A., of Cromwell's Ford, co. Carlow, and has issue.
7. Dorcas Henrietta, *m*. 1840, James Nixon, of Clone, co. Kilkenny, J.P., and has issue.
Mr. Langley *d*. 10 April, 1831, and was *s*. by his eldest son,
HENRY LANGLEY, of Coal Brook and Lisnamrock, *b*. 1797; *m*. 9 April, 1832, his cousin Elizabeth Dorothea, dau. of George Tuthill, of Ballyteigue, co. Limerick, and *d*. 16 Aug. 1860, having had by her (who *d*. Aug. 1870) three sons,
1. CHARLES HENRY, of Coal Brook, *d. unm*. 7 Aug. 1868.
2. GEORGE, late of Coal Brook.
3. Henry Percy, *d*. young, 11 June, 1844.

Seat—Coal Brook, New Birmingham, co. Tipperary.

LANGLEY, formerly OF BRITTAS CASTLE.

ADMIRAL GERALD CHARLES LANGLEY, present representative of the family, *b*. 13 Oct. 1848; *m*. 11 April, 1893, Juanita Maxwell, dau. of the late A. G. Scott, of Ashbrooke, Edinburgh, and has issue,
1. HENRY FITZROY GRACE, *b*. 14 Jan. 1895.
2. Gerald Maxwell Bradshaw, *b*. 14 Dec. 1895.
3. Algernon Albert Miles, *b*. 6 June, 1900.
1. Geraldine Marion, *b*. 31 March, 1897.
2. Lina Merlin Juana, *b*. 14 Jan. 1902.

Lineage.—HENRY LANGLEY, of Priestown (now called Langley Lodge), co. Tipperary (2nd son of Henry Langley, of Lisnamrock, who was son of Charles Langley, and grandson of Lieut. Henry Langley, of Col. Hierom Sankey's Regt. of Horse in CROMWELL'S Army), *m*. Margaret, dau. and heiress of Oliver Grace, of Brittas Castle, who was grandson of John Grace, of Brittas Castle, by Joan his wife, dau. of Thomas Butler, of Brittas, great-grandson of Tibbott Butler, brother of Edmund, Lord Dunboyne, whose father, John Grace, Baron of Courtstown, was representative of the great Anglo-Norman family of Grace. By Margaret his wife, Henry Langley had issue,
1. HENRY GRACE, of Brittas Castle, *m*. 1st, Sophia, dau. of Tenison; 2ndly, Mary, dau. of John Bagwell, of Marlfield, co. Tipperary, M.P., and *d.s.p.*
2. OLIVER, of whom presently.
3. Lawrence Grace, *m*. 1st, Anne, dau. of Richard Moore, of Barne, co. Tipperary, and had issue,
   HENRY AUGUSTUS, of Brittas Castle, and Langley Lodge, Capt. 6th Dragoons, *d.s.p.*
Mr. Langley *m*. 2ndly, Susanna, dau. of Godfrey Taylor, of Noan, co. Tipperary, but had no issue by her.
The 2nd son,
OLIVER LANGLEY, *m*. 1783, Elizabeth Butler, and left issue at his decease, 1825,
1. HENRY, his heir.
2. Richard, Lieut. in the Army.

3. Oliver (Rev.).
4. Lawrence, m.
5. John, m. Mary, dau. of Natt. Taylor, of Somerville, co. Tipperary, and had issue,
   1. Susanna.
   2. Helena.
   3. Adelaide.
1. Margaret, m. Richard Phillips.
2. Mary, m. John Hurst.

The eldest son,

HENRY LANGLEY, of Brittas Castle, Major in the Army, m. 7 May, 1807, Maria, dau. of Henry Penton, of Pentonville, Middlesex, M.P. for Winchester, and d. 12 Oct. 1834. She d. Feb. 1862, leaving issue,
1. HENRY, late representative of the family.
2. Oliver Grace, formerly Col. 16th Regt., m. Marie, dau. of J. E. Wilkinson, of Potterton Hall, co. York, and d. 3 Dec. 1895, leaving issue, one son and one dau.
   1. Elizabeth Maria, m. Col. Henry Penton, of Pentonville, and has issue (see that family).
   2. Catherine Fanny, m. 20 Sept. 1837, Percy Jocelyn Gough, 5th son of Very Rev. Thomas Bunbury Gough (see BURKE'S Peerage, GOUGH, V.). She d. 1882. He d. 27 Jan. 1905, having had issue, five sons and three daus.
   3. Mary, m. William Perry, of Woodrooff, Clonmel, J.P. and D.L., and d. 1886, having had issue, one son and two daus.
   4. Sophia, d. unm.
   5. Isabella Petronella, m. Col. Edward Bagwell Purefoy, of Greenfields, J.P. and D.L. for Tipperary, and d. 1859.

The eldest son,

HENRY LANGLEY, J.P. and D.L., late 2nd Life Guards, b. 19 Sept. 1820; m. 15 Dec. 1845, Harriet Maria, only child of James Bradshaw, M.P. for Canterbury, and d. 14 April, 1902, having had issue,
1. Henry Fitzroy James, b. 8 Dec. 1846, and Sec. of Legation at Buenos Ayres; d. unm. 30 Nov. 1884.
2. GERALD CHARLES, present representative.
3. Hubert Boyle, b. 5 March, 1852; d. unm. 1873.
4. Walter Louis Frederick Goltz, C.B. of the Foreign Office, b. 22 Feb. 1855; m. 30 Aug. 1894, Gertrude Mary, youngest dau. of the late W. Ramsay, and by her (who d. 6 Aug. 1895) has issue,
   Hubert Francis Grace, b. 30 July, 1895.
5. Algernon Arthur, b. 25 March, 1863; m. April, 1894, Minnie, dau. of — Robertson, of U.S.A.
6. Claude Spencer, b. 25 Sept. 1867; m. 15 Feb. 1897, Blanche, widow of Major Thomas Armstrong Gough, and dau. of John William Fletcher, Bengal Army.
1. Grace.
2. Isabel Augusta Kitty, m. 6 Dec. 1898, Adm. Albert Baldwin Jenkings, eldest son of the late Henry Jenkings, of Courlands, Lostwithiel, co. Cornwall.
3. Florence.
4. Constance Laura Mary, m. Jan. 1880, C. J. Smith, and had issue, two sons and a dau.
5. Marion Frances Charlotte, m. 15 Dec. 1904, John Charles Miles, Fellow of Merton College, Oxford, Barrister-at-Law.

Arms—Arg., on a fess sa, a crescent or, in chief three hurts, quartering GRACE of *Brittas Castle*; gu., a lion rampant per fess arg. and or. *Crest*—A cockatrice, wings addorsed sa., combed, wattled, and spurred gu., charged with a crescent or. *Motto*—Fide sed cui vide.

Residence— Lhassa, Camberley, Surrey.   *Club* — United Service.

LANGRISHE.

See BURKE'S PEERAGE, **LANGRISHE, Bart.**

LA TOUCHE OF BELLEVUE.

The late MAJ. PETER LA TOUCHE, of Bellevue, co. Wicklow, and Drumhearney, co. Leitrim, J.P. and D.L. co. Leitrim, High Sheriff 1900, J.P. co. Wicklow, late Maj. 5th Batt. Royal Dublin Fus., b. 23 Aug. 1864; d. 13 March, 1904; m. 30 April, 1902, Sophia Dora Elizabeth, elder dau. of Maj. C. R. W. Tottenham, of Woodstock, Newtown, Mount Kennedy (see that family). She m. 2ndly, 17 Jan. 1907, Joseph Frederick Cowper, son of late H. A. Cowper, of Dublin.

Lineage.—The family of La Touche was established in Ireland by DAVID DIGUES DE LA TOUCHE, a Huguenot, who settled in that kingdom after the Revocation of the Edict of Nantes, having served first as volunteer and afterwards as Lieut. and Capt. in the Princess Anne's Regiment of Infantry. He was the 4th son of a noble Protestant family of the Blesois, which possessed considerable estates between Blois and Orleans, and in other parts of France. He first fled to Holland, where a branch of his family had for some time been established, and shortly afterwards embarking with the Prince of Orange, served the Irish campaign under him. At the conclusion of the war, Mr. La Touche, with many of his countrymen, settled in Dublin. He m. twice; by his 2nd wife he had no issue, but by the 1st (whom he m. 5 July, 1690), Judith Biard, dau. of Noé Biard and Judith Chevalier his wife, he had, with two daus., issue,
1. DAVID, of whom presently.
2. James Digges, of Dublin, m. 1st, 1735, Elizabeth, dau. of David Chaigneau, and had issue by her an only child,
   1. Elizabeth Wilhelmina, wife of Robert Barry, 3rd son of Sir Edward Barry, Bart.
He m. 2ndly, 1743, Matilda, dau. of William Thwaites (will dated 17 Nov. 1752, and proved 29 Sept. 1761), and had issue by her,
   1. William Digges, of Dublin, m. Grace, dau. of John Puget, of London, and had issue,
      (1) James Digges, of Sans Souci, co. Dublin, m. Isabella, dau. of Sir James Lawrence Cotter, Bart., and left issue at his decease, 1827,
         a. William Digges, of Dublin, m. 13 Sept. 1842, Louisa, dau. of Christopher L'Estrange-Carleton, of Market Hill, co. Fermanagh (see that family), and left issue,
            1. James John Digges (Sir), K.C.S.I., B.A., T.C.D., Bengal C.S., Lt.-Gov. United Provinces of Agra 1901-6 (14, Gledhow Gardens, S.W.), b. 16 Dec. 1844; m. 1873, Julia, dau. of Thomas Wade Rothwell.
            2. Christopher Digges, of 40, Merrion Square, Dublin, b. 1856.
         b. John George Digges.
         c. Edmond Robert Digges, Barrister-at-Law.
         a. Isabella Digges, m. 1839, Nicholas Biddulph, of Congor (see that family). She d. 29 Dec. 1886.
         b. Grace Digges.   c. Elizabeth Digges.
      (2) William Digges, d. unm.
      (3) Thomas Digges, m. Anne, dau. of — Needham.
      (1) Esther, m. Rev. Benjamin Waller.
      (2) Elizabeth, m. Rev. Caesar Otway.
      (3) Grace, m. Rev. George Edmond Cotter.
   2. Peter Digges, of Belfield, co. Dublin, m. 1789, Charlotte, dau. of George Thwaites, and had issue,
      (1) Peter Digges, m. Mary Anne, dau. of Dodwell Browne.
      (2) John James Digges (Rev.).
      (3) George Digges, m. Frances, dau. of Rev. Caesar Otway, and had issue.
      (4) Theophilus Digges, d. unm.   (5) William Digges, d.s.p.
      (1) Elizabeth.
      (2) Emily, m. John Brennan, a Six-Clerk in Chancery.
      (3) Frances.   (4) Harriett.
      (5) Sophia.
   3. Theophilus Digges, of Dublin, d. unm. 1777.
   4. David Digges, of Dublin, d. unm. 1778.
Mr. La Touche d. 17 Oct. 1745, and was s. in the bank which he had established in Dublin, by his son,

DAVID LA TOUCHE, b. 31 Dec. 1703, who had been educated in Dublin with his relation Digues de la Motte, of Rotterdam, He m. 8 Feb. 1724-25, Mary Anne, dau. of Gabriel Canaseele, and had issue,
1. Gabriel David, b. 1728; d.v.p.
2. DAVID (Right Hon.), of Marlay.   3. James, b. 1730; d.v.p.
4. JOHN, of Harristown (see LA TOUCHE of Harristown).
5. PETER, of Bellevue, M.P., sat for many years in Parliament as Knight of the Shire for Leitrim. He m. 1st, 24 Dec. 1766, Rebecca, only dau. of Robert Vicars, of Grantstown, Queen's Co., which lady d.s.p. 1786; and 2ndly, Elizabeth, dau. of Richard Vicars, of Lavally, which lady d.s.p., having survived her husband a considerable time. Having no issue, Mr. La Touche adopted Peter (the 4th son of his brother, the Right Hon. David La Touche, of Marlay).
6. Gabriel, b. 26 Dec. 1734.   7. Matthew, b. 1738.
1. Mary Anne, b. 1726; m. 10 May, 1772, Lieut.-Col. Philip Roberts.
2. Martha, b. 1736.
3. Elizabeth, twin with Martha.   4. Judith, b. 1742.
Mr. La Touche d. Feb. 1875. The eldest son,

THE RIGHT HON. DAVID LA TOUCHE, of Marlay, co. Dublin, many years M.P. for his own borough of Newcastle and other places, b. 1729; m. 18 Feb. 1762, Elizabeth, dau. of the Right Rev. George Marlay, D.D., Bishop of Dromore, son of Chief Justice Marlay, and by her (who was first cousin to the Right Hon. Henry Grattan) had issue,
1. DAVID, of Marlay, Col. of the Carlow Militia, M.P. for that co., m. 24 Dec. 1789, Lady Cecilia, dau. of the Earl of Milltown, and left issue,
   1. DAVID, d. unm. 1830.
   2. John (Rev.), Vicar of Mountrath, m. and had issue.
   3. George, b. 1798; m. and had issue.
   4. Peter, Major 7th Bengal N.I., m. 1st, 1829, Fanny, dau. of Brigadier-General William George Maxwell, C.B., of Dalswinton. Dumfries, by whom (who d. at Kiatah, India, 22 Jan. 1830) he had issue, one son, b. 19 Jan. 1830; d. an infant. He m. 2ndly, at Capetown, 11 Sept. 1832, Ellen Maria, dau. of Charles Bestandig, of German extraction, from Göttingen. He d. 16 May, 1849, having by her (who d. at Bath, 1 July, 1845) had issue,

(1) Cecil D'Urban, Colonel and Commandant of the Poonah Horse, *b.* 11 July, 1834; *m.* 23 April, 1855, Agnes Emma, only dau. of Benjamin Proctor Rooke, M.D., and *d.* 19 Sept. 1900, leaving issue, two daus.
(2) Charles Blunt, Capt. Bombay Staff Corps, *m.* 1866, Wilhelmina, dau. of William Müller, of Shenley, Herts, had issue, one dau. only. He was killed in action at Macherba Kattywar, India, 29 Dec. 1867.
(3) William Paget, *b.* 6 June, 1838, at Nusserabad, India, Lieut.-Gen. Indian Army; *m.* 2 Nov. 1866, Frances Gertrude, 2nd dau. of Gen. Sir Anthony B. Stransham, G.C.B., by whom he has had issue, Charles Burdett Malcolm, and seven other children, of whom Henrietta Mary *m.* 1888, Col. Sir William Sinclair Smith Bisset, K.C.I.E., R.E.
5. William, *d. unm.*
6. Robert, Capt. in the Army, *m.* and had issue.
7. Cecil, *d. unm.*
1. Elizabeth, *m.* William, 3rd Lord Brandon.
2. Harriett, *m.* 24 May, 1817, Villiers Francis Hatton, Rear-Admiral R.N., and had issue (*see* HATTON *of Clonard*).
3. Frances, *d. unm.*   4. Emily.
5. Mary.
2. George, *d. unm.* 1823.
3. John David, *b.* 2 Jan. 1772; *m.* March, 1799, Anne Caroline, dau. of Charles Tottenham, of New Ross, co. Wexford, and *d.* Aug. 1838, leaving issue,
1. DAVID CHARLES, late of Marlay, *b.* 18 April, 1800, Col. co. Dublin Militia, J.P. and D.L., High Sheriff of Wicklow 1838, and of the co. and city of Dublin 1843; *d. unm.*
2. Charles John, *b.* 21 March, 1811; *m.* June, 1850, Mademoiselle Marie de Fouchier, and has a son, John David, *b.* May, 1861.
1. Frances Caroline Sarah, *d.* 1877.
2. Elizabeth Louisa, *d.* 1891.
3. Anne Caroline, *d. unm.* 1844.
4. PETER, of whom hereafter, as successor to his uncle of Bellevue.
5. Robert, Lieut.-Col. of the Carlow Militia, and for some years M.P. for Carlow, *b.* 1783; *d.s.p.*   6. William, *d.* young.
1. Elizabeth, *m.* 1781, Robert, 3rd Earl of Lanesborough.
2. Harriet, *m.* Sir Nicholas Colthurst, 3rd bart. of Ardrum, co. Cork.
3. Emily, *m.* Nov. 1790, Col. George Vesey, of Lucan House, co. Dublin.
4. Anne, *m.* George Jeffreys, of Blarney Castle, co. Cork.
5. Maria, *m.* 1801, the Right Hon. Maurice Fitzgerald, Knight of Kerry.
Mr La Touche *d.* June, 1817. His 4th son,
PETER LA TOUCHE, of Bellevue, *b.* 1777; *m.* 1806, the Hon. Charlotte Maud, dau. of Cornwallis, 1st Viscount Hawarden, and by her (who *d.* 3 Dec. 1874, aged 92) had issue,
1. PETER, his heir.
2. Cornwallis, *d.* 1837, in India.
3. WILLIAM ROBERT, of Bellevue.
4. Ashley, *m.* 2 May, 1861, Sarah Julia, dau. of Col. Sir William Cox, of Coolcliffe, and *d.* 1876, leaving issue, one dau., Annette.
5. Charles Henry, *d.* 1876.
6. FRANCIS, *s.* his brother William Robert.
7. James, *d.* 1852.
8. OCTAVIUS, *s.* his brother Francis.
9. John Alexander, *d.s.p.* 18 March, 1892.
1. Isabella, *d. unm.* 10 June, 1891.   2. Charlotte, *d.* 1911.
3. Mary.
4. Eliza, *m.* 1851, Rev. James Godley. He *d.* 30 April, 1910. She *d.* 4 Nov. 1908, leaving issue (*see* BURKE'S *Peerage*, KILBRACKEN, B.).   5. Elizabeth, *d.* young.
Mr. La Touche *d.* 11 Feb. 1830, and was *s.* by his son,
PETER LA TOUCHE, of Bellevue, *d.s.p.* 1856, and was *s.* by his brother,
WILLIAM ROBERT LA TOUCHE, of Bellevue, co. Wicklow, D.L. for co. Leitrim, J.P. for Wicklow, High Sheriff for Wicklow 1860, and for Leitrim 1858, *b.* 30 June, 1810; *m.* 13 July, 1867, Ellen, 4th dau. of William Henn, Master in Chancery, by Mary Rice his wife, eldest dau. of George Fosbery, of Clorane, co. Limerick, and *d.s.p.* 17 Jan. 1892, and was *s.* by his eldest surviving brother,
FRANCIS LA TOUCHE, of Bellevue, co. Wicklow, and Drumhearney, co. Leitrim, J.P. and D.L., High Sheriff co. Leitrim, *b.* 1815; *d. unm.* July, 1897, and was *s.* by his only surviving brother,
MAJOR OCTAVIUS LA TOUCHE, of Bellevue, co. Wicklow, and Drumhearney, co. Leitrim, *b.* 27 March, 1824; *m.* 1860, Elizabeth Cecilia, dau. of George La Touche. She *d.* 25 April, 1891. He *d.* 28 Dec. 1897, leaving issue,
1. PETER, late of Bellevue.
2. Mary (*Delgany, co. Wicklow*).
2. Frances Cecilia, *m.* 12 Aug. 1801, Arthur Montford Archer, M.D., now of Bellevue, High Sheriff co. Leitrim 1910.
3. Charlotte Isabella, *m.* 1 Aug. 1902, Loftus Adam Studdert, 2nd son of Robert O'Brien Studdert, of Cullane.

Arms—Arg., a pomegranate slipped in pale ppr. on a chief gu. two mullets of the field. *Crest*—A mullet or. *Motto*—Quid verum atque decens curo et rogo.

Seats—Bellevue, Delgany, co. Wicklow; and Drumhearney, Leitrim.

LA TOUCHE OF HARRISTOWN.

ROBERT PERCY O'CONNOR LA TOUCHE, of Harristown, co. Kildare, J.P., *b.* 12 July, 1846; *m.* 9 Feb. 1870, Lady Annette Louise, 2nd dau. of John, 3rd Earl of Clonmell (*see* BURKE'S *Peerage*).
I.L.G.

Lineage.—JOHN LA TOUCHE, of Harristown, co. Kildare, M.P., 2nd surviving son of David Digges La Touche, of Marlay (*see* LA TOUCHE *of Bellevue*), *m.* 9 Dec. 1763, Gertrude Fitzgerald, dau. of Robert Uniacke, of co. Cork (who took the name and arms of FITZGERALD), and had issue,
1. ROBERT, his heir.
2. John, many years M.P. for co. Leitrim, *d. unm.*
1. Gertrude, *m.* Francis Matthew, 2nd Earl of Llandaff.
2. Marianne, *m.* Ralph Peter Dundas.
The elder son,
ROBERT LA TOUCHE, of Harristown, M.P. for co. Kildare, *m.* 17 April, 1810, Lady Emily Le Poer Trench, youngest dau. of William Power Keating, 1st Earl of Clancarty, and by her (who *d.* 1816) had issue,
1. JOHN, late of Harristown.
2. Robert, twin with John, *d. unm.* 8 Sept. 1846.
3. William, *b.* 1815; *d. unm.* 10 Jan. 1867.
1. Anne, *d.* young.
2. Gertrude, *m.* 1811, her cousin, Stanley McClintock, son of John McClintock, of Drumcar, by his wife, the Lady Elizabeth Le Poer Trench.   3. Emily, *d.* young.
Mr. La Touche *d.* May, 1844.
JOHN LA TOUCHE, of Harristown, co. Kildare, J.P. and D.L., High Sheriff cos. Kildare 1846, and Leitrim 1850, *b.* 15 Sept. 1814; *d.* 17 Sept. 1904; *m.* 16 May, 1843, Maria (who *d.* 1904), only child of Rose Lambart Price, of Trengwainton, co. Cornwall, eldest son of Sir Rose Price, Bart.; and Catherine his wife, widow of the 2nd Earl of Desert, and had issue,
1. ROBERT PERCY O'CONNOR, now of Harristown.
1. Emily Maria, *m.* 27 June, 1865, Hon. Bernard Matthew Ward, Major 32nd Light Infantry, 4th son of Viscount Bangor, and *d.* 1 June, 1868, leaving issue (*see* BURKE'S *Peerage*).
2. Rose Lucy, *d. unm.* 25 May, 1875.
3. Emily, *d.* 1907.

Arms, &c.—Same as LA TOUCHE *of Bellevue*.

Seats—Harristown, Brannoxtown, Newbridge; Newbury, Kilcurren, co. Kildare. *Clubs*—Marlborough, Kildare Street.

LAW OF KILLALOE.

The late PATRICK FRANCIS LAW, of Killaloe, co. Clare, *b.* 28 Aug. 1836; *m.* 9 July, 1868, Julia (now of Killaloe), youngest dau. of Henry Taylor Jones, of Chatham and Hoo, Kent (*see* BURKE'S *Peerage*, JONES, Bart.), and Caroline Munster his wife, dau. of Maj.-Gen. Wulff, and widow of Sir Richard Hardinge, 1st bart. He *d.* 3 Dec. 1909, having had issue,
1. CECIL ARBUTHNOT, Capt. Duke of Edinburgh's Wilts Regt., B.A. Oriel Coll. Oxford, *b.* 25 Jan. 1872; *m.* 29 April, 1902, Mary Theresa Forestier, 2nd dau. of Arthur George Walker, late Bengal C.S., son of George James Walker, 13th Dragoons (*see* BURKE'S *Peerage*, FORESTIER-WALKER, Bart.).
2. Walter Henry Patrick, Capt. Army Service Corps, B.A. Oriel Coll. Oxford, *b.* 14 Feb. 1876; *m.* 12 Dec. 1905, Dorothy, 2nd dau. of John Arthur Brooke, of Feray Hall, Huddersfield, and Fearn Lodge, Ardgay, and has issue,
Patrick John, *b.* 28 March, 1910.
Sheila Dorothea, *b.* 23 Sept. 1907.

Lineage.—MICHAEL LAW, eldest son of Samuel Law, of Carriglee, near Strabane, co. Tyrone, raised a troop of horse for WILLIAM at the Battle of the Boyne, 1690. He *m.* 2 Feb. 1692, as his 2nd wife, Sarah, dau. of Daniel Eccles, of Shannock, co. Fermanagh (*see* McCLINTOCK *of Seskinore*). He had issue, a son,
THE REV. SAMUEL LAW, Rector of Omagh, co. Tyrone, *d.* Sept. 1760; *m.* 1719, Anne, dau. of Rev. Robert Gurney, D.D., Rector of Comber, co. Derry, and had issue,
1. Michael, M.D., of Raphoe, co. Donegal, Surg. Enniskillen Light Dragoons, 1760. His will is dated 10 April, 1790. He had issue,
1. Samuel (Rev.), *m.* Mary, dau. of Rev. James Montgomery, Archdeacon of Rapho, and had a dau.,
Dorothea, *m.* 1805, James Sinclair, of Hollyhill, and had issue (*see that family*).
2. Robert William, *m.* 1791, Elizabeth, dau. of Capt. Wm. Johnstone, 48th Regt., of Malheny, co. Dublin, and *d.* 1828 (will proved 19 March, 1829), leaving four sons and four daus., of whom Michael *m.* 1833, Sarah Anne, dau. of Crofton Vandaleur FitzGerald, and a dau., Elizabeth, *m.* 1830, Right Rev. John Gregg, Bishop of Cork.
1. Nicola Anne, *m.* Jan. 1797, Lieut.-Col. Peter Maxwell, of Birdstown, co. Donegal, and had issue.
2. ROBERT, of whom we treat.
The younger son,
THE REV. ROBERT LAW, D.D., Rector of Midleton, co. Cork, and St. Mary, Dublin, Senior Fellow, T.C.D., *m.* 1st. 26 Sept. 1767, Amelia Span, and by her had, with another son (*d.* an infant),
1. FRANCIS, of whom presently.
Dr. Law *m.* 2ndly, Eliza, dau. of Alexander Hamilton, of Knock, co. Dublin, and by her had issue,
2. Robert, of Brookville, *m.* Sarah, dau. of S. Watson, and widow of Robert Roberts, and had a son, Hamilton Robert, *d. unm.*
1. Elizabeth, *m.* 21 Sept. 1802, Major the Hon. Charles Murphy, who *d.* 17 Sept. 1859, leaving issue (*see* BURKE'S *Peerage*, MANSFIELD, E.).
Dr. Law's will is dated 21 Dec. 1787. His eldest son,

2 R

Lawder. THE LANDED GENTRY. 386

Rev. Francis Law, Vicar of Attanagh, Queen's Co., and Rector of Cork, b. 1768; m. 5 Nov. 1795, Bellinda Isabella, 2nd dau. of Patrick Comerford, of Sumnerville, co. Cork, and d. 1807 (will dated 11 Oct. 1796, proved 21 Jan. 1803) having had issue,
1. Patrick Comerford, of whom presently.
2. Robert, M.D., Professor of Medicine, Trin. Coll. Dublin, b. 3 Nov. 1798; m. Eleanor, dau. of Rev. George Vesey, D.D., of Derrabard House, co. Tyrone (*see that family*). She d. 21 Oct. 1889. He d. 23 April, 1875, having had issue, with two sons who d. young,
    Isabella Barbara, m. 6 Sept. 1875, Maj.-Gen. George Baret Stokes, of Mounthawk, co. Kerry. She d. 9 July, 1891, leaving issue (*see that family*).
3. Francis (Rev.), Incumbent of Samlesbury, Lancashire, B.A. Queens' Coll. Cambs., b. 4 June, 1800; m. 1st, 6 May, 1828, Marianne, dau. of Gen. Alexander Cuppage, of Clare Grove, co. Dublin (*see Cuppage of Mount Edwards*), and by her had issue,
    Francis, b. 27 Feb. 1829; m. 30 Jan. 1866, Ruth, dau. of Thomas Lee, of Blackheath, Kent, and d. 21 Nov. 1898, leaving issue,
      (1) Francis Arthur, b. 1 June, 1867; m. 20 Feb. 1897, Rose Anne Livingston.
      (2) William Henry, b. 20 Sept. 1869; d. 4 Nov. 1876.
      (3) Robert Archie, b. 18 Nov. 1877.
      (1) Ruth Ellen, m. 28 Nov. 1889, George Egerton Metcalf.
      (2) Minnie Louisa, d. unm. 22 Oct. 1897.
      (3) Florence Marianne.
He m. 2ndly, 15 Nov. 1865, Sophia Elizabeth Wahl, widow of — Perkins. She d. 17 Dec. 1877. He d. 20 Sept. 1881.
4. Samuel, b. 2 Jan. 1803; d. an infant.
1. Amelia Teresa, m. 31 July, 1837, Rev. Arthur Wynne, son of the Rev. Richard Wynne (*see Wynne of Hazlewood*), and d.s.p. 25 Oct. 1868.
2. Isabella, d. an infant, 22 Sept. 1802.
3. Elizabeth, m. Thomas Roberts, and had issue.

The eldest son,
The Rev. Patrick Comerford Law, Rector of North Repps, Norfolk, and Chaplain to the Marquess of Cholmondeley, B.A. Trin. Coll. Dublin, b. 21 Aug. 1797; m. 17 Oct. 1828, Frances, 2nd dau. of Right Rev. Alexander Arbuthnot, D.D., Bishop of Killaloe. She d. 19 Nov. 1857. He d. 15 April, 1869, having had issue,
1. Francis Patrick, b. 1 Oct. 1830; d. 29 March, 1832.
2. Alexander Patrick, M.A. Corpus Christi Coll., b. 14 Jan. 1832; d. 30 Oct. 1895.
3. Patrick Francis, late of Killaloe.
4. Arthur Arbuthnot, b. 30 May, 1840; d. 1 March, 1841.
5. Robert Arbuthnot (Rev.), Rector of Gunthorpe with Bale, Norfolk, b. 28 Feb. 1842; m. 20 Jan. 1870, Agnes, only dau. of Rev. Chancellor John Henry Sparke, of Gunthorpe Hall. She d. 18 June, 1892. He d. 11 Dec. 1889, having had issue,
    1. Arbuthnot Patrick Astley, b. 5 July, 1872.
    2. Hubert Henry Bingham, b. 25 Oct. 1873.
    3. Alexander Delaval Hamilton, b. 18 Oct. 1874.
6. William Arthur, Dramatic Author, late Lieut. Royal Scots Fus. (*The Homestead, Parkstone, Dorset*), b. 22 March, 1844; m. 7 July, 1877, Fanny, dau. of John Holland, and has issue,
    Hamilton Patrick John Holland, b. 12 July, 1879; m. 9 Oct. 1907, Frances Dora, only dau. of Rev. Cecil Brereton, Rector of Hardham, and Burton-cum-Coates, Sussex, and has issue,
      (1) Frances Marcia.
      (2) Eileen Merial.
1. Georgiana Anne, m. 22 Jan. 1870, Rev. Theophilus John Fenton, M.A. She d.s.p. 7 March, 1895.
2. Frances Amelia, m. 14 Aug. 1862, Henry Charles Hull, B.A., Barrister-at-Law, and d. 5 Oct. 1883, leaving issue.
3. Isabella Susan, d. unm. 14 Jan. 1885.
Residence—

LAWDER OF LAWDERDALE.

James Ormsby Lawder, of Lawderdale, co. Leitrim, J.P. and D.L., High Sheriff 1909, M.Inst.C.E., late Public Works Dept. India, b. 22 Nov. 1847; m. 2 Nov. 1872, Jane Eliza, dau. of Rev. Edwin Thomas, Vicar of Carlingford, co. Louth, and has issue,
1. Cecil Edward, late Lieut. R.F.A., b. 6 May, 1877; m. 26 Jan. 1909, Violet Wood, 2nd dau. of J. Basden Orr, of Kelvinside, Glasgow.
    1. Violet, d. young, 15 Dec. 1889.
    2. Pearl Edith.

Lineage.— William Lawder, of West Barns, Dunbar, co. Haddington, younger son of Sir Robert Lawder, of the Bass, and Isabel, his wife, dau. of John, 1st Lord Hay of Yester, m. Jonet Liddell, administration of her estate 10 Dec. 1576. He d. 1556, leaving issue,
1. Maurice, of whom later.
2. Robert, Bailie of Dunbar 1576, m. Janet, dau. of James Douglas, of Knightsryhne, and d. Nov. 1600.
3. Hugh, Capt., Bailie of Dunbar 1580, m. Janet Kirkcaldy.
4. William, Bailie of Dunbar 1565.
5. John.

The eldest son,
Maurice Lawder, of Belhavin and West Barns, Bailie of Dunbar 1561, M.P. for Dunbar 1585, m. 1st, Nicholas Home (d. 10 July, 1569), and had issue,
1. William, of whom we treat.
2. John, d.v.p.
3. Robert, Capt., of Tyninghame, m. Margaret Home (d. 15 July, 1580), and d. 12 Nov. 1597, leaving issue.
    1. Jonet.
    2. Helen, m. John Aytoun, of Haddington.
    3. Margaret.
4. Nicholas, m. Andrew Waldie, of Leith.
He m. 2ndly, Margaret Hamilton, who d.s.p. 2 Nov. 1580; and m. 3rdly, Alison Cass, by whom he had,
5. Jonet, m. 1st, Sir Claude Hamilton, Bart., of Castle Hamilton, co. Cavan; 2ndly, Sir Arthur Forbes, Bart., of Castle Forbes, co. Longford.
6. Isobel, m. Lawrence Simpson, of Craighouse, Edinburgh.
He d. 8 Aug. 1602. His eldest son,
William Lawder, of Belhavin and West Barns, Bailie of Dunbar 1602, m. 1st, Elizabeth Hepburn, by whom he had,
1. Alexander, of whom later.
2. William, Bailie of Dunbar 1620, m. Christian Knowes, and d. circa 1623, leaving issue.
He m. 2ndly, Margaret, dau. of James Hume, of Friarlands, Dunbar, and had by her,
3. James.
He d. 30 March, 1618, at Clonyen, Killeshandra, co. Cavan. His eldest son,
Alexander Lawder, of Belhavin, West Barns, and Clonven, m. Katherine Pringle (d. 20 Nov. 1603), and d. 24 June, 1631, leaving issue,
George, of whom next.
Violet, m. James Kirkwood, of Dunbar.
The only son,
George Lawder, of Belhavin and West Barns, Haddington and Derindrehed or Mount Lawder, co. Cavan, m. 1st, Elspeth Lawder (d. March, 1606), by whom he had,
1. Robert, of Belhavin, m. Mary, dau. of Patrick Douglas, of Standingstone, and d. 1657, leaving issue.
    1. Jane.
He m. 2ndly, Agnes Bothwell (d. April, 1612), and had by her,
2. James, of West Barns, M.P. for Dunbar 1645-96, m. Agnes Home.
    2. Catherine.
He m. 3rdly, Isobel ———, by whom he had,
3. William, Capt., of whom we treat.
4. Launcelot, of Ardunction, co. Fermanagh, J.P., m. Elizabeth Wray, of Ards, co. Donegal, and d. 15 Nov. 1674, leaving issue.
5. Andrew, of Cor, co. Cavan.
6. John, of Kiltubbrid, co. Leitrim.
7. George, of Bawnboy, co. Cavan.
He d. 1640. His 3rd son,
William Lawder, of Bawnbow and Drumdiege, High Sheriff co. Cavan 1681, was, with his nephew Launcelot, attainted by the Parliament assembled by James II at Dublin in 1689. His will was proved 1 June, 1698. By his wife, Dorothy Trench, who predeceased him, he left issue,
1. William, of Bonnybeg, co. Leitrim, High Sheriff 1699, 1704, 1706 and 1712, m. Catherine, dau. of Arthur Auchmouty, of Brianstown, co. Longford, and left issue. His will dated 5 Nov. was proved 5 Dec. 1715. From him is descended William Sidney Lawder, of Bonnybeg.
2. Frederick, of whom we treat.
3. James, of Kilmore, co. Roscommon, High Sheriff co. Leitrim 1713 and co. Roscommon 1721, m. 1st, Deborah, dau. of John Dogherty, and 2ndly, Dorcas, widow of Thomas Auchmouty, of Brianstown, and dau. of Samuel Townley, and d. 1 May, 1740, leaving issue, four daus. His will, dated 1 July, 1746, was proved 22 Sept. 1750.
    1. Jane, m. Thomas Hame, of Bawn, co. Cavan.
    2. Anne.
    3. Sidney.
    4. Catherine, m. James Kirkwood, of Owengallis, co. Cavan.
The 2nd son,
Frederick Lawder, of Cor, co. Cavan, High Sheriff co. Leitrim 1705, m. Rebecca, dau. of David Rynd, of Derryvolan, co. Fermanagh (*see Rynd of Ryndville*), and had issue,
1. William, of Dublin, m. Elizabeth Rayson, and d.s.p.
2. Thomas, of Rose Hill, co. Cavan, m. Anne, dau. of Robert Hume, of Lissanover, co. Cavan, and d. 10 Oct. 1775, leaving issue,
    1. James, d.s.p.   2. Hume (Rev.), d.s.p.
    1. Eliza, m. George Neal.
    2. Phœbe, m. George Pendred.
    3. Anne, m. David Gumley.
3. Frederick, of whom we treat.
4. Christopher, of Lowfield, co. Roscommon, m. Priscilla, dau. of John Crozier, of Dunbar, co. Fermanagh, and left issue.
5. James, d.s.p. in India.
The 3rd son,
Frederick Lawder, of Mough House (now Lawderdale), co. Leitrim, m. 1744, Rebecca, dau. of Christopher Rynd, of Fenagh, co. Leitrim. His will was proved 16 Jan. 1801. He had issue,
1. Rynd, of whom next.
2. Henry, of Waterford, m. Margaret Dwyer, and d.s.p.
3. Frederick, d.s.p.   4. James, d.s.p.
1. Deborah.   2. Phœbe, m. G. Quail.
3. Rebecca.
The eldest son,
Rynd Lawder, of Mough House, b. 6 Jan. 1746; m. Mary, dau. of John Beatty, of Coolagherty, co. Longford. She d. 12 Feb. 1814. He d. 9 Oct. 1811, having had issue,
1. John, his heir.

2. **Frederick**, settled in the United States, and *m.* Margaret Reid, of Virginia, and *d.* 6 May, 1866, leaving issue.
3. **Rynd**, Surg. 7th Hussars, *m.* Dora Mitchell, of Drumlish, co. Monaghan, and *d.s.p.* 11 July, 1836.
4. **James**, Surg. H.E.I.C.S., *b.* 9 March, 1788; *m.* 1 Dec. 1820, Anna Maria, dau. of Rev. James Wilmot Ormsby, Rector of Bray, and *d.* 21 Feb. 1860, and by her had issue,
  1. **Edward James**, General Madras Staff Corps, *b.* 5 Nov. 1821; *m.* 30 Jan. 1845, Dora Jane, eldest dau. of Thomas Moore-Lane, M.D., Madras Medical Department. She *d.* 27 May, 1877. He *d.* 2 March, 1900, having had issue,
    (1) JAMES ORMSBY, now of Lawderdale.
    (2) Edward J. G., *b.* 10 May, 1849; *m.* 28 Nov. 1885, Margaret, 5th dau. of G. Ellis, Madras Civil Service, and has issue,
      1. Noel, Lieut. Bedfordshire Regt., *b.* 12 Oct. 1886.
      1. Mildred. 2. Iris. 3. Beryl.
    (3) Thomas, Lieut. and Adjt. 96th Regt., Deputy Commissioner Perak, Straits Settlements, *b.* 8 Nov. 1851; *d. unm.* 23 Jan. 1888.
    (4) Charles, Indian Postal Dept., *b.* 14 July, 1853; *m.* 1 July, 1901, Mary, eldest dau. of Robert Arkwright, of Knuston Hall, Northants, and has issue,
      1. Robert, *b.* 12 May, 1906.
      1. Dorothy. 2. Clare.
    (5) Francis, *b.* 14 May, 1862; *m.* 31 Dec. 1888, Elizabeth, dau. of H. D. Maclead, and has issue,
      1. Patrick, R.N., *b.* 2 March, 1891.
      2. Keith, R.N., *b.* 17 April, 1893.
      3. Edward, *b.* 10 March, 1895.
    (6) Arthur, *b.* 21 April, 1866; *m.* 1 Dec. 1892, Blanche, dau. of J. Luff, of Old House, Blandford, and has issue,
      Rynd, *b.* 3 March, 1895.
      Dora.
    (1) Anna Maria, *m.* 6 June, 1866, Sir George Clement Bertram, late Bailiff of Jersey.
    (2) Dora, *m.* 27 July, 1874, F. G. Bertram, late 86th Regt.
    (3) Eliza Kate.
    (4) Edith, *m.* 7 Dec. 1889, C. E. Wilkinson, of the Batch, Flax Bourton.
    (5) Elizabeth.
  2. William, *d.* young.
5. **William Henry**, of Drumdart, co. Leitrim, 32nd Foot, *m.* Ursula, dau. of Matthew Nesbitt, of Derrycarne, co. Leitrim, and *d.* 22 June, 1869, leaving issue.
  1. Rebecca, *m.* James Irwin. 2. Maria, *d. unm.*
  3. Marcella, *d. unm.* 4. Margaret, *d. unm.*
The eldest son,
JOHN LAWDER, of Mough, *b.* 10 Feb. 1776; *m.* 21 Aug. 1816, Ellen, dau. of Matthew Nesbitt, of Derrycarne, co. Leitrim. She *d.* 23 June, 1867. He *d.* 28 Nov. 1853, having had issue,
  1. Rynd, *b.* 13 Oct. 1818; *d.s.p.* 14 May, 1872.
  2. MATTHEW NESBITT (Rev.), *s.* his brother William.
  3. John, *b.* 28 Nov. 1821; *d.s.p.* 12 Sept. 1908.
  4. James, Capt. Madras Army, *b.* 14 Jan. 1823; *d.s.p.* 9 May, 1860.
  5. WILLIAM, of whom next.
  6. Francis, *b.* 22 June, 1828; *d.s.p.* 13 July, 1884.
  7. Henry, *b.* 1 Oct. 1830; *d.s.p.* 21 March, 1894.
  8. Edward, *b.* 19 Sept. 1840; *d.s.p.* 16 May, 1849.
  1. Ellen, *m.* Gen. William Gabbett, Madras Horse Artillery, and *d.* 17 March, 1862.
  2. Margaret, *d. unm.* 11 Oct. 1858.
The 5th son,
WILLIAM LAWDER, of Mough, *s.* his father and changed the name of his residence to Lawderdale, J.P., D.L. co. Leitrim; *b.* 18 Aug. 1824; *d.s.p.* 16 May, 1876, and was *s.* by his brother,
THE REV. MATTHEW NESBITT LAWDER, of Lawderdale (Mough), *b.* 9 March, 1827; *m.* Oct. 1848, Anne, dau. of John Gumley, and *d.s.p.* 9 Sept. 1881, when he was *s.* by his cousin JAMES ORMSBY LAWDER, now of Lawderdale.

Seat—Lawderdale, Ballinamore, co. Leitrim.

LAWLESS.
See BURKE'S PEERAGE, **CLONCURRY, B.**

LAWRENCE OF LISREAGHAN.

DENIS JOHN LAWRENCE, of Lisreaghan, co. Galway, J.P. co. Galway, *s.* his brother 1905; *b.* 18 —; *m.* 1882, Eliza Jane (who *d.* 1897), dau. of Edward Parsons, of Oxton, Cheshire, and has had issue,

Ethel Margaret.

Lineage.—JOHN LAWRENCE, with his younger brother Walter, afterwards governor of the gaol and city of Naas (*see Fiants*), ELIZABETH, 23 April, 1586, Rolls Office, Dublin), came to Ireland in the retinue of Sir John Perrott, Lord President, in 1571 (*see Patent Rolls*). He *m.* the dau. of O'Madden, Lord of Longford, co. Galway

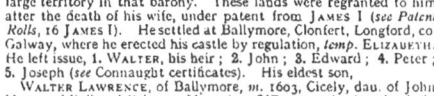

captain of his nation and last chief of his name, and by her acquired large territory in that barony. These lands were regranted to him after the death of his wife, under patent from JAMES I (*see Patent Rolls*, 16 JAMES I). He settled at Ballymore, Clonfert, Longford, co. Galway, where he erected his castle by regulation, *temp.* ELIZABETH. He left issue, 1. WALTER, his heir; 2. John; 3. Edward; 4. Peter; 5. Joseph (*see* Connaught certificates). His eldest son,
WALTER LAWRENCE, of Ballymore, *m.* 1603, Cicely, dau. of John Moore, of Ball and Brie, co. Mayo (*see* O'DONOVAN'S *Annals of the Four Masters*), and Lady Mary de Burgh, dau. of the Earl of Clanricarde (*see Patent Rolls*, JAMES I, *and also* CHEVALIER O'GORMAN'S *MS. ped. of the Earls of Clanricarde, at Laurencetown*). He left issue an only son,
JOHN LAWRENCE, of Ballymore and Lisreaghan, *m.* 1st, 1640, a dau. of John O'Donelan, of Ballydonelan, co. Galway, by whom he had Walter and James, who both *d.v.p.*; 2ndly, Mabella, dau. of Killagh O'Kelly, of Aughrim, co. Galway, eldest son and heir of Feartanah O'Kelly, chief of his name (*see Fun. Cert.* 1038), and had a dau., Mabella, *m.* J. Kelly, of Ballagh, co. Galway; 3rdly, Mary, dau. of Gerald McCoghlan, eldest son and heir of Sir John McCoghlan, of Cloghan, chief of his name, and Lord of the Country of Delvin Arra, now the Barony of Garry Castle, King's Co. (*see Fun. Cert.* 1 May, 1635), by the Lady Honora Burke his wife, dau. of Richard, 4th Earl of Clanricarde and St. Albans, and by her had a son and heir, WALTER, and three daus., who *d. unm.*, Honora, Christian, and Dorothy. His estates were seized and sequestrated by the usurped powers in 1641, but a part of them was restored by patent dated 6 Aug. 29 CHARLES II, enrolled 26 Aug. 1677. He *d.* at Ballymore Castle, 1675, and was bur. at Clonfert (will dated 23 Sept. 1675). His widow *m.* 2ndly, James Deane, and *d.* 1714. He was *s.* by his only son,
WALTER LAWRENCE, of Lisreaghan, *m.* 1673, his cousin Cicely, dau. of Col. Garrett Moore, of Cloghan Castle, King's Co., by his wife, the Lady Margaret, 2nd dau. of Richard, 6th Earl of Clanricarde, and the Lady Elizabeth Butler his wife, dau. of Walter, 11th Earl of Ormonde, and by her (who *m.* 2ndly, John Kelly) left at his decease, 1677 (with a dau. Honoria, *m.* H. Pelly, of Kill, co. Galway), two sons, minors, John, *d.s.p.*, under age, and
WALTER LAWRENCE, of Lisreaghan, *m.* Mary, dau. of Nicholas Arcedekne, of Gortnamona, co. Galway, and dying 1706, left issue,
  1. JOHN, of whom presently.
  2. Peter, Rear-Admiral R.N., a distinguished officer (*see* CHARNOCK, *Biographia Navalis*), *b.* 1702; *d.s.p.*, of Woodfield, Eyrecourt, 1768, bur. at Clonfert.
The elder son,
JOHN LAWRENCE, of Lisreaghan, *b.* 1698; *m.* 20 April, 1727, Mary, only dau. and heir of John Scott, of Greenish and Cappavarnagh, co. Galway, and of Montserrat, West Indies, by his wife, Anastasia, dau. of Robert ffrench, of Rahasane, co. Galway, and dying 1730, was *s.* by his only son,
WALTER LAWRENCE, of Lisreaghan, *b.* 1729; *m.* 1 May, 1760, Margary, only dau. of Edmond Netterville, of Longford, co. Galway and had issue,
  1. Peter, *b.* Aug. 1762; *d.s.p.* July, 1790.
  1. Maria, *d. unm.* 1803.
Mr. Lawrence *m.* 2ndly, Aug. 1791, Catharine, dau. of John D'Arcy, of Ballykine, co. Mayo, by Margaret his wife, widow of Charles Blake, of Merlin Park, and youngest dau. of Dennis Daly, of Raford, co. Galway, and granddau. of Michael, 10th Earl of Clanricarde, and by her had issue,
  1. WALTER, late of Lisreaghan.
  2. Matilda Margaret, *m.* 1822, Thomas Seymour of Ballymore Castle, co. Galway, and has issue.
Mr. Lawrence *d.* Oct. 1796, and was *s.* by his son,
WALTER LAWRENCE, of Lisreaghan, J.P., High Sheriff 1801-2, *b.* 15 Dec. 1793; *m.* 1 March, 1813, his 1st cousin Georgiana, 3rd dau. of Charles Blake, of Moyne, and Coolcon, co. Mayo, and of Merlin Park, co. Galway, by his wife Georgina, eldest dau. and coheir of Sir George Browne, 6th bart. of The Neale, co. Mayo (eldest brother of John, 1st Baron Kilmaine), by Anastatia his wife, dau. of Denis Daly, of Raford, and the Lady Anne de Burgh his wife, dau. of Michael, 10th Earl of Clanricarde, and *d.* 21 Sept. 1873, having by her (who *d.* 1863) had issue,
  1. Walter, late Capt. 41st Regt., subsequently Capt. Galway Militia, *m.* 1848, Olivia, eldest dau. of Sir Michael Dillon Bellew, Bart., and *d.* 1863, leaving by her (who *d.* 10 Jan. 1874) a dau., Honora Mabel Angela, *m.* 29 July, 1868, Charles Ormsby Blake de Burgh, of Coolcon, co. Mayo (*see that family*), and *d.* 1873, leaving issue.
  2. John, *d.* 22 Feb. 1872.
  3. CHARLES, late of Lisreaghan.
  4. Peter, *d.* 3 Sept. 1907.
  5. DENIS JOHN, now of Lisreaghan.
  6. George Edward. 7. Henry William
  1. Georgiana.
  2. Catherine Elizabeth, *m.* John Clarke.
  3. Mary Dorothy. 4. Margaret Mabella.
  5. Frances Cicely. 6. Anne Helena Christian.
  7. Adelaide Bridget Octavia.
The 3rd son,
REV. CHARLES LAWRENCE, of Lisreaghan, co. Galway, formerly Vicar of Thurton, Diocese of Norwich, and Chaplain to the Bishop of Carlisle, F.S.A. (Ireland), and F.R.G.S., formerly commissioned in the Austrian Hussars; *b.* 28 Oct. 1828 *m.* 26 Feb. 1806, Cecil, youngest dau. of Gen. Sir Charles Wale, K.C.B., of Shelford, co. Cambridge. She *d.s.p.* Jan. 1881. He *d.* 6 July, 1905.

Arms—Quarterly: 1st and 4th arg., a cross raguly gu., for LAWRENCE; 2nd and 3rd sa., a catherine-wheel between two crescents in chief and a trefoil in base or, for SCOTT. **Crest**—A demi-turbot tail erect ppr. **Motto**—Pro rege Saepe, pro patria Semper.
Seat—Lisreaghan (or Bellevue), Lawrencetown, co. Galway.

Leader.   THE LANDED GENTRY.   388

LEADER OF DROMAGH CASTLE.

WILLIAM NICHOLAS LEADER, of Dromagh Castle, co. Cork, J.P. and D.L., High Sheriff 1908, B.A. Trin. Coll. Camb., b. 1853, late Lieut. Scots Greys; m. 21 June, 1881, Hon. Eleanor Burke Roche, eldest dau. of Edmund, 1st Lord Fermoy (see BURKE'S *Peerage*).

Lineage.—About the middle of the 17th century, two brothers HENRY and JOHN LEADER, settled in the co. Cork. The younger brother, JOHN, was ancestor of the LEADERS *of Keale*, co. Cork. (*whom see*). The elder,

HENRY LEADER, purchased very considerable estates in the co. Cork, amongst others, the family residence of Mount Leader. He m. 1689, Margaret, dau. of Thomas Radley, by Mabella Chinnery his wife, and d. circa 1738, having had issue,

1. JOHN, of Mount Leader, b. 1698; m. 1718, Margaret, 3rd dau. of Edward Herbert, of Kilcow, co. Kerry, and d. circa 1732, leaving by his wife (who m. 2ndly, Rev. Craven Stanley), with six daus., of whom the eldest, Mary, m. Richard Edward Hull, of Leamcon, three sons, 1. EDWARD, whose only son, John Leader, sold Mount Leader to his cousin William Leader (see below); 2. Thomas; and 3. Richard, Capt. in the Army, of Oldcastle, co. Cork.
2. Thomas, b. 1700; d. 1727.
3. HENRY, of Tullig, co. Cork, of whom presently.
1. Mary, m. 1711, John Purcell, of Gurtenard.
2. Margaret, m. Charles O'Keefe, of Cullen.
3. Marvella, m. John Leader, of Keale.

The 3rd son,

HENRY LEADER, of Tullig, co. Cork, b. 1705; d. 2 Feb. 1771; m. 1741, Christabella, dau. of William Philpott, of Dromagh, co. Cork, and by her (who d. 1794) left issue,

1. JOHN, b. 1742; d. 1801. He m. 20 Oct. 1767, Deborah, eldest dau. of Emanuel Hutchinson, of Mount Massy, and had an only son, HENRY LEADER, formerly of Illy, co. Donegal, and of Adelaide Road, Dublin, b. 1768; m. Mary, dau. of the Rev. Thomas Stewart, and d. 1844, leaving one son and five daus., 1. HENRY, of Dromaneen, near Kanturk, co. Cork (m. 1835, Sarah, dau. of Thomas Woodcock, Banker of Wigan, and d. 1873, leaving William, of Dromaneen, b. 1837, and other issue); 1. Elizabeth. d. unm.; 2. Deborah, m. 1845, John Allen; 3. Mary, m. 1844, William Ribton Ward; 4. Charlotte, m. Francis Foster, of Rushine Lodge, co. Donegal; and 5. Margaret, m. Aug. 1834, John Herbert Orpen, M.D.
2. WILLIAM, of Mount Leader (which he purchased from his cousin John Leader), J.P., b. 1743; d. April, 1828; m. April, 1768, Margaret, dau. of Warham St. Leger, of Heyward's Hill, and by her (who d. Feb. 1828) had issue,
   1. NICHOLAS PHILPOT, M.P. for Kilkenny, m. Margaret, dau. and co-heir of Andrew Nash, of Nashville, co. Cork, and d. 1836, leaving by her (who d. 8 Oct. 1858),
      (1) NICHOLAS PHILPOT, late of Dromagh Castle, J.P., M.P., d. 31 March, 1880, aged 69.
      (2) William, J.P., of Rosnalee, Kanturk, co. Cork, m. 29 June, 1847, Dorothea, dau. of Richard MacGillycuddy of the Reeks (see that family), and d. 1860, having had issue,
         1. WILLIAM NICHOLAS, now of Dromagh Castle.
         2. Francis Henry Mowbray, b. 1855; m. 1879, Agnes, dau. of — Brodrick, and has issue.
            1. Dora Margaret, m. 1877, George Ware.
            2. Margaret, m. 1883, Henry Bruce Armstrong.
      (3) Henry, . 1815; m. 1st, 1841, Margaret, dau. of John Birmingham Miller, Q.C., and has issue, two sons, and a dau., Maria Winifred; m. 1864, Rev. Edward Lavallin Puxley, who d. 30 June, 1909, leaving issue (see PUXLEY of *Danboy*). He m. 2ndly, 1864, Annette, dau. of Rev. Thomas Ellison and sister of J. W. Ellison Macartney, M.P. (see that family).
      (1) Margaret, m. John Newman, eldest son of Adam Newman, of Dromore, co. Cork.
      (2) Elizabeth, m. 14 April, 1849, Sir George Richard Waldie-Griffith, Bart. of Hendersyde Park, co. Roxburgh. He d. 8 May, 1889. She d. 19 Aug. 1903, leaving issue.
   2. Worham (Rev.), Rector of St. Anne's, Shandon, Cork, m. Henrietta, dau. of Robert Atkins, of Firville, co. Cork, and d.s.p.
   3. William (Rev.), Curate of St. Peter's, Cork, d. unm.
   4. HENRY, of Mount Leader, m. Aug. 1830, Elizabeth Anna, 2nd dau. of Rev. Charles Eustace, of Robertstown, co. Kildare, claimant of the Baltinglass Peerage (see that family), and d. 5 April, 1868, leaving by her (who d. 1858) an only child,
      HENRY EUSTACE LEADER, of Mount Leader, J.P., Capt. 16th Lancers, b. 1833; m. 1st, Oct. 1868, Helen Augusta, youngest dau. of the late Lieut.-Col. Williamson, of Carrowkeal, co. Cork; and d. 1 June, 1876, having by her (who m. 2ndly, 1878, Charles Arthur Duncan, Barrister-at-Law) had issue,
         1. HENRY WILLIAMSON, of Mount Leader, co. Cork, J.P., b. 18 July, 1869; m. 28 July, 1900, Maud St. Leger, 2nd dau. of George M. Ievers, of Inchera, co. Cork, 3rd son of Eyre Ievers, of Mount Ievers (see that family), and has issue,
            a. Maud Ievers.   b. Violet Eustace.
         2. Lionel Frederic, Capt. 8th King's (Liverpool Regt.), b. 10 Sept. 1870; m. 2 Oct. 1897, Mabel Campbell, only dau. of E. Butler Rowley, of Manchester, and has issue,
            Eustace Lionel, b. 1 Oct. 1898.
            Marvella Hilda, b. 12 Dec. 1902.
         3. George Eustace, d. young.   4. Roland William.
         1. Elizabeth, m. 1799, Rev. Matthew Purcell, of Burton, Cork.

2. Harriet, m. Matthias Henley, of Mount Rivers, co. Cork, and d.s.p. 1833.
3. Emilia, m. 1810, John Rye Coppinger, of Carhue, co. Cork, and d.s.p. 1832.
4. Louisa, m. Richard Harris Purcell, of Annabella.
2. Henry, of Tullig, m. Mary Kearney, and d. in 1809, leaving issue, an only child,
   Henry, who d.s.p.
4. Nicholas, who went to America.
1. Elizabeth, m. Joseph Barry, M.D., of Mallow.
2. Christabella, m. Christopher Hendley, of Mount Rivers.
3. Catherine, d.s.p. 1772.   4. Marvella, d.s.p, 1773.

Seat—Dromagh Castle, Kanturk, co. Cork. **Clubs**—Carlton, Kildare Street.

LEADER OF KEALE.

JOHN LEADER, of Keale, Millstreet, co. Cork. Capt. 2nd Batt. Bedfordshire Regt., b. 31 July, 1876; m. 25 March, 1909, Evelyn Maude, only child of Lieut.-Col. Hon. John Pleydell-Bouverie (see BURKE'S *Peerage*, RADNOR, E.).

Lineage.—The ancestor of this family, JOHN LEADER, left issue by his wife (who m. 2ndly, George Chinnery, of Gortnageenia, now Flintfield, co. Cork. see CHINNERY-HALDANE *of Glenzagles and Flintfield*), two sons, Henry and John, who in the 17th century settled with their mother in co. Cork. HENRY LEADER was ancestor of the LEADERS *of Dromagh* (see that family). The other son,

JOHN LEADER, settled at Keale, co. Cork, m. circa 1690, Jane, dau. of Thomas Radley, and had issue, an only son,

JOHN LEADER, of Keale, co. Cork, m. 1st, 1733, Marvella, dau. of his uncle, Henry Leader, and by her had issue, an only son,
1. Henry, who d. unm.
He m. 2ndly, 1750, Jane, dau. of Thomas Radley, of Knockrur, by Margaret Purdon his wife, of the ancient family of Lurgan Race, co. Louth, and d. 1766, leaving surviving issue,
2. John, of Keale, J.P., b. 1758; m. 1795, Johanna, dau. of Dennis McCartie, of Rathduane, co. Cork, the lineal descendant of McDonogh McCartie Lord of Duhallow, and by her had issue,
   John, of Keale, J.P., b. 1797; m. Elizabeth, dau. of Edward Herrick, of Bellmount, co. Cork, and d.s.p. 1839.
   Albina, m. — Murphy.
3. LEONARD, of whom presently.
1. Jane, m. Edward Sullivan.
2. Margaret, m. William Philpot.

The younger son,
LEONARD LEADER, of Stakehill, co. Cork, J.P., b. 1762; m. 1796, Sarah, dau. of Benjamin White, of Knockanemore, co. Cork, and d. 1845, having had issue,
1. JOHN, of whom presently.
2. Benjamin, of Stakehill, co. Cork, J.P., b. 28 April, 1815; m. Maria, dau. of — Stuart, and d.s.p. 1902.
   1. Mary, d. 1890.
   2. Anne, m. Rev. Francis Cooper, M.A., Curate of Drumitariff, co. Cork, son of Thomas Cooper, of Cooperville, and Anne, his wife, dau. of Rev. John Sullivan, and had issue.
   3. Margaret.   4. Sarah.
   5. Charlotte, m. William Sullivan, of Sunville, co. Cork, and had issue (see LEADER *of Stake Hill*).

The elder son,
JOHN LEADER, of Keale, M.D., J.P., b. 3 Sept. 1807; m. 7 May, 1836, Margaret, eldest dau. of Capt. Thomas Radley, of Rockville, co. Cork, and d. 28 Jan. 1880, having by her had issue,
1. Leonard, of Keale, b. 17 April, 1837; d. unm. 11 Jan. 1889.
2. JOHN, of whom presently.
3. Thomas Radley, b. 4 June, 1846, lost at sea, 1865.
4. Benjamin Tartarine, b. 23 Sept. 1847.
5. Richard Radley, M.D., b. 19 March, 1851; m. 18 Nov. 1879, Elizabeth Mary, youngest dau. of Dr. Nicholas Warburton White, and has issue,
   1. John Radley, b. Sept. 1880; d. 10 April, 1906.
   1. Elizabeth Maud.   2. Margaret Warburton.
   3. Frances.   4. Constance.
6. Nicholas, of Keale House, co. Cork, Lieut.-Col. Reserve of Officers and Lieut.-Col. (retired) R.A.M.C., F.R.C.S., b. 15 April, 1852.
7. Henry Warburton, b. 8 Oct. 1859; d. 4 April, 1869.
1. Alice, m. 2 Jan. 1869, Francis Bernard MacCarthy.
2. Sarah, d. Nov. 1852.   3. Katharine.
4. Mary, d. 1849.
5. Mary Warburton, m. 7 Nov. 1879, Capt. Herbert F. Hill, 44th Regt.
6. Sarah, m. 28 Oct. 1890, George Emmanuel Irving.
7. Jane.
8. Elizabeth, m. 18 July, 1908, Henry Herrick Warren, 4th son of Major-Gen. Richard Warren, late R.E., son of Rev. Robert Warren (see BURKE'S *Peerage*).

The 2nd son,
SURG.-MAJOR JOHN LEADER, of Keale, co. Cork, served in the 2nd Batt. 19th Regt., J.P. co. Cork, b. 23 June, 1843; m. 26 Aug. 1875, Annie Margaret, eldest dau. of Robert McMurray, J.P., of Roxborough, co. Limerick, and d. 12 Sept. 1892, having by her had issue,
1. JOHN LEADER, now of Keale.
2. Robert Ripley, Lieut. West India Regt., b. 15 March, 1878.
1. Kathleen.   2. Winifred, d. 1881.

Surg.-Major Leader s. to the Keale estate on the death of his brother Leonard in 1889.

Seat—Keale, Millstreet, co. Cork.

LEADER OF STAKE HILL.

THE REV. LEONARD LEADER LEADER, of Stake Hill, co. Cork, M.A., b. 13 Dec. 1866, assumed by Royal Licence 1903, the name of LEADER only, and the arms of LEADER quarterly, with his paternal arms of SULLIVAN; m. 11 April, 1893, Ellen Jane, dau. of William Stockings, of Stony Stratford, Bucks, and has surviving issue,

1. LEONARD WILLIAM LEADER, b. 6 June, 1895.
2. Donald Benjamin Leader, b. 3 Sept. 1899.
1. Elsie Muriel Gertrude.

Lineage.—THE REV. JOHN SULLIVAN, son of Thomas Sullivan, m. Anne Carey, and had issue,
1. Carey, in holy orders.
2. Francis, left issue.
3. WILLIAM, of whom presently.
4. John, in holy orders.
5. George, Professor of Botany, T.C.D.

The 3rd son,
REV. WILLIAM SULLIVAN, Rector of Kilnagross and Desert, Prebendary of Templebryan, m. Margaret, dau. of William Scott, and had with eight daus., an only son,
WILLIAM SULLIVAN, of Sunville, and Castletown-Kinneigh, co. Cork, m. Charlotte, 5th dau. of Leonard Leader, of Stake Hill (see LEADER of *Keale*), and sister of Benjamin Leader, of Stake Hill (who d. 1901), and had issue,
1. William, m. Mary Josephine, dau. of James Franklin Bland, of Derryquin, co. Kerry (*see that family*), and had issue, four sons and four daus.
2. LEONARD, of whom presently.
3. John Howe, dec.
4. Benjamin Leader, dec.

The 2nd son,
REV. LEONARD LEADER SULLIVAN, B.A. Dublin, m. 1 Jan. 1866, Mary Louisa Leader, of Stake Hill, and had issue,
1. LEONARD LEADER, now of Stake Hill.
2. Benjamin Leader, dec.
1. Charlotte Leader.

Arms—Quarterly 1st and 4th arg. on a fesse sa. between three ogresses each charged with an escallop of the field, a lion's head between two boars', all erased or, a bordure engrailed gu. (LEADER); 2nd and 3rd. per fesse the base per pale, in chief or a dexter hand couped at the wrist gu. grasping a sword erect entwined with a serpent ppr. between two lions rampant respecting each other of the second, in the dexter base vert a buck trippant of the first, in the sinister per bend arg. and sa. a boar passant counterchanged (SULLIVAN). **Crest**—An arm embowed vested paly of six vert and gu. holding in the hand a branch of three roses ppr. **Motto**—Probum non poenitet.

Seat—Stake Hill, Clonbanin Cross, co. Cork.

LEAHY OF SOUTHILL.

Lineage.—JOHN LEAHY, of Southhill, co. Kerry (son of John Leahy, b. 1737; d. 27 April, 1791), J.P. co. Kerry, b. 1772; d. 23 June, 1846; m. 2 Feb. 1809, Elizabeth, dau. of Richard Ashe, of Ashgrove, co. Cork, and by her (who d. 22 March, 1864) had eight sons and three daus.,

1. John, of Southhill, co. Kerry, B.A. (Dublin), Q.C., b. 16 Nov. 1809; d. 13 Oct. 1874; m. 1851, Matilda Emma (d. 15 Sept. 1907), dau. of William White, of Shrubs, co. Dublin (*see* WHITE *of Cloone Grange*), and left an only son,
John White, of Southhill, B.A. Oxon., J.P., D.L., High Sheriff 1877, b. 29 May, 1852; d. 6 Sept. 1907; m. 27 Sept. 1906, Agnes Caroline (*now of Southhill*), dau. of Thomas Elmer Cole, of Wingland, Norfolk, s.p.
2. Richard, b. 1 Sept. 1811; d. 18 March, 1865; m. 28 Oct. 1841, Eleanora, dau. of Rev. Edward Nash, of Ballycarty, co. Kerry, and left issue,

1. John Richard, b. 28 April, 1850; m. 2 Dec. 1879, Sara Florence Wilhelmina, eldest dau. of Major-Gen. William Andrew Armstrong, and has issue,
(1) Richard Armstrong, b. 2 May, 1883.
(2) Austin George, b. 10 Aug. 1884; m. 26 July, 1909, Louisa, dau. of —Giron, of Hermosville, Mexico.
(3) John Cecil Robert, b. 10 Aug. 1886.
(1) Evelyn Ethel, m. 16 Jan. 1907, Major Austin Samuel Cooper, of Killenure Castle, co. Tipperary (*see that family*).
(2) Clementina Violet.
(3) Eleanora Eileen.
2. Edward NASH, of Ballycarty, co. Kerry, J.P., Lieut.-Col. late Essex Regt., b. 16 Oct. 1851, assumed the name of NASH instead of Leahy on succeeding to the Ballycarty estate in 1878; m. 19 Nov. 1884, Constance Louisa, dau. of John Radcliffe, of Moorfields, Willington, Manchester,' and has issue,
3. Richard, b. 13 Dec. 1854; d. 19 Jan. 1881.
4. Charles Edward, b. 6 March, 1856; m. 24 Jan. 1881, Isabella dau. of Jerome Quill, of Tralee, and has issue.
5. Henry, b. 6 July, 1857.
6. Robert Nash, b. 6 Aug. 1860; m. 11 April, 1895, Annie May, dau of Dr. Kenneth Millican.
1. Clementina, m. 17 April, 1873, De Courcy Daniel Denny (d. 16 Dec. 1878).
2. Elizabeth, d. 1843.
3. Frances, m. 15 Sept. 1868, Major-Gen. Charles Patrick Stokes.
4. Sarah Anne, m. Nov. 1875, Alexander McHinch, C.I.E. (d. Nov. 1890).
5. Mary.   6. Eleanora.
7. Elizabeth.   8. Emily Pett.
3. Edward, of Flesk, Killarney, J.P., b. 30 Aug. 1815; d. 3 Aug. 1870, B.A. (Dublin), *unm.*
4. David, b. 3 June, 1817; d. 11 Jan. 1866; m. 1st, Jane, widow of Capt. Mundell, dau. of John Bourchier; and 2ndly, Frances M. White.
5. Henry, of Flesk, co. Kerry, b. 8 Oct. 1819; d. 20 May, 1870, *unm.*
6. Thomas, of Carriglea, co. Kerry, J.P., b. 25 Jan. 1823; d. 3 Dec. 1903, *unm.*
7. Arthur, of Flesk, co. Kerry, Col. R.E., b. 5 Aug. 1830; d. 13 July, 1878; m. 1st, 14 Aug. 1856, Harriet Thomasina, dau. of Bartholomew Molière Tabuteau, of Simmonscourt, co. Dublin (*see* TABUTEAU-HERRICK *of Shippool*), and by her (who d. 1862) had,
1. Arthur Herbert (92, *Ashdell Road, Sheffield*), b. 25 March, 1857, M.A., late Fellow and Bursar, Pembroke Coll. Cambridge, Professor of Mathematics and late Dean of the Faculty of Pure Science, University of Sheffield.
2. Edward Arthur, b. 1860; d. young.
1. Mary Jane, d. young 5 Nov 1907.
He m. 2ndly, 11 Sept. 1866, Eliza Thomasina, only dau. of Thomas Poynter, of Doctor's Commons, and had issue,
3. HENRY GORDON, of Carriglea, co. Kerry, J.P., Major Royal Artillery, b. 21 Jan. 1868; m. 1st, 12 July, 1899, Aline Mina, only dau. and heir of the late Capt. Henry Raymond Pelly, R.E. (*see* BURKE's *Peerage*, PELLY, Bart.), and had issue by her (who d. 29 April, 1901),
(1) Kathleen Elizabeth.
He m. 2ndly, 3 Aug. 1905, Ellen Elizabeth, dau. of William Johnson, of Fortfield, Lansdowne Road, Cheltenham, and has
(1) ARTHUR GORDON POYNTER, b. 1906.
(2) Edith Constance.
4. Kenyon Arthur (*Victoria, Rhodesia*), b. 6 March, 1871; m. 1902, Elizabeth Alice, dau. of Charles John Leahy (*see below*).
5. Charles John, b. 22 May, 1872; d. 20 June, 1894, Lieut. R.A.
6. Philip Fraser Arthur, b. 9 Oct. 1875; d. 3 April, 1897, Lieut. Leinster Regt.
7. Thomas Bernard Arthur, b. 13 June, 1878, Capt. R.M.A., m. 24 Nov. 1904, Agnes Wentworth, dau. of Mordaunt A. de B. Stevens, M.D., of Nice, and has issue,
(1) Thomas, b. 25 Dec. 1908.
(1) Geraldine Clara Marguerite.   (2) Rose Maria.
2. Beatrice Marion.
8. Charles John, b. 2 April, 1833; d. 15 Jan. 1866; m. 1862 Susan, dau. of William Thornton, of Cork, and left issue,
Charles Albert, b. 22 Feb. 1863; d. 14 Nov. 1896, Capt. R.E., served in Soudan.
Elizabeth Alice, m. 1902, Kenyon Arthur Leahy (*see above*).
1. Elizabeth, b. 20 Aug. 1813; d. *unm.* 31 Aug. 1893.
2. Mary, b. 6 Feb. 1821; d. 9 June, 1886; m. 1847, Most Rev. Samuel Butcher, D.D., P.C., Bishop of Meath, who d. 1876, leaving issue.
3. Frances, b. 25 May, 1825; d. 1832.

Arms—Gu., a lion rampant or, armed and langued az. in chief a fleur-de-lys arg. between two roses of the last, barbed and seeded ppr. **Crest**—A demi lion rampant gu., armed and langued az., holding in the paws a sceptre or. **Motto**—Fortiter et Fideliter.

LECKY OF BEARDIVILLE.

HUGH LECKY, of Beardiville, co. Antrim, J.P., b. 21 Oct. 1839; m. 13 Jan. 1876, Rebecca Mary, dau. of Robert Crookshank, of Glenmanus House, Portrush, and has issue,

1. HUGH, b. 18 April, 1880; m. July, 1905, Annie Margaret, youngest dau. of Anthony Traill, LL.D., Provost of Trin. Coll. Dublin, of Ballylough, co. Antrim, and of Marlfield, co. Down (see that family).
2. Robert, b. 12 July, 1882.
3. Randall, } twins, b. 15 Jan. 1885.
4. James,
1. Olivia, m. 1907, Edward Clement Price, and has issue.

Lineage.—This family is of Scotch extraction, and settled in the co. of Derry in the 17th century.

CAPT. ALEXANDER LECKY, who served at the siege of Londonderry, was father of

HARRY LECKY, of Agivy, co. Derry, m. 1715, Mary (d. 1777), dau. of Randal McCollum, of Limnalary, Glenarm, co. Antrim, and had a son,

HUGH LECKY, of Agivy, m. 1765, Elizabeth, dau. of the Rev. John Gage, of Rathlin, co. Antrim, and d. 1796, having had issue,
1. JOHN GAGE, his heir.
2. Hugh, b. 1773; m. Sept. 1803, Elizabeth, dau. of James Orr, of Keeley, co. Londonderry; and d. 17 June, 1817, having had by her (who d. 14 April, 1865) issue,
 1. HUGH, heir to his uncle.
 2. James Orr, m. 1855, Harriett, dau. of John Knox, of Rushbrooke, and is dec.
 3. John Gage, Lieut.-Col., late of the 38th Regt.; m. 1846, Tamazina, dau. of William Edie, of Thornhill, co. Tyrone, is dec.
 4. Andrew, } twins, dec.
 5. William,
 6. Conolly, m. 1866, Mace Wynne, dau. of William H. Hawker, and widow of Lieut.-Col. Cuddy, 55th Regt., and is dec.
1. Mary, m. John Caldwell, M.D., Londonderry.
2. Anne, m. John Ball, of Dublin, Barrister-at-Law.

The elder son,

JOHN GAGE LECKY, of Agivy and Bushmills, b. 1772; m. Elizabeth, dau. of Rev. Oliver McCausland, and d.s.p. 1819, when he was s. by his nephew,

HUGH LECKY, of Beardiville, co. Antrim, High Sheriff 1835, b. 29 Aug. 1804; m. Aug. 1837, Matilda, dau. of G orge Hutchinson, of Ballymoney, co. Antrim, and by her (who d. 9 Jan. 1883) had issue,
1. HUGH, now of Beardiville.
2. George, Col. Indian Army, b. 20 July, 1841; m. 17 Aug. 1865, Harriett Frances, dau. of A. Macaulay Dobbs, and has issue,
 1. Charles Hugh, b. 22 Sept. 1867.
 2. Harry Francis, b. 1870. 3. John Gage, b. 1872.
 4. Arthur Macaulay, Lieut. R.N., b. 1881; m. 2 Nov. 1907, Evelyn, dau. of Col. Arthur Jackson, late 18th Royal Irish.
 5. Marcus Daly, b. 1883. 6. Harold Alexander.
 1. Mary Matilda Eva, m. 1891, Major William Keane Richardson, Cheshire Regt., and has issue, Hugh Keane, b. 1892, and Dorothy.
3. John Gage, Lieut.-Col. late 75th Regt., b. 1814; m. Jan. 1880, Amelia Mary, dau. of Rev. H. Ozanne, of Guernsey, and has issue,
 1. John Gage, b. 1883. 2. Averell.
 3. Hugh McCollum. 4. William.
 1. A dau., b. 1891.
4. Harry, b. 1846.
1. Elizabeth, d. 13 Jan. 1910.
Mr. Lecky d. 11 Feb. 1881, and was s. by his eldest son.

Seat—Beardiville, Coleraine.

LECKY OF BALLYKEALEY.

JOHN RUPERT FREDERICK LECKY, of Ballykealey, co. Carlow, Member of the Middle Temple, and Lieut. 7th Batt. Royal Fusiliers Special Reserve, b. 1885; s. 6 Aug. 1908.

Lineage.—This is an ancient family deriving originally from co. Stirling, and settled in Ireland since the reign of ELIZABETH. The estates of Ballykealey, co. Carlow, have been in their possession for more than 200 years.

ROBERT LECKY, of Kilnock, co. Carlow, son of James Lecky, of the same place, d. 1786, leaving a son,

JOHN LECKY, of Ballykealey, m. 1780, Elizabeth, dau. of Jacob Goff, of Horetown, co. Wexford, and by her (who d. Jan. 1842) had issue,
1. Robert, d. young. 2. JOHN JAMES, of Ballykealey.
1. Eliza, m. June, 1809, John Watson, of Kilconner House, co. Carlow, and d. leaving issue.
2. Mary, m. James Forbes Russell, and d. leaving issue.
3. Anne, m. J. Phelps, and d. leaving issue.
4. Jane Sophia, d. unm.
5. Sarah Maria, m. J. Christy, of Stramore House, co. Down, and d. leaving issue. 6. Hannah Matilda, d. unm.
7. Lydia Matilda, m. Richard Goff, of Tottenham Green, co. Wexford.

Mr. Lecky, of Ballykealey, d. Dec. 1799, and was s. by his son,

JOHN JAMES LECKY, of Ballykealey, J.P. and D.L., High Sheriff 1828, b. 2 Oct. 1790; m. 13 July, 1825, Sarah Lucia, only dau. of John Smyth, of Balby, co. York, and of Marlborough Place, Surrey, and had issue,

JOHN FREDERICK, late of Ballykealey.

Mary Elizabeth Adelaide, v. 21 June, 1853, Very Rev. Francis Metcalf Watson, Dean of Leighlin, and d. 10 March, 1878, leaving one dau., Sarah Lucia Watson, b. 1856.

Mr. Lecky, d. 1 Feb. 1878. His only son,

JOHN FREDERIC LECKY, of Ballykealey, co. Carlow, J.P. and D.L., High Sheriff 1864, b. 25 May, 1826; m. 28 July, 1853, Frances Margaret Fetherstonhaugh, only dau. of John Beauchamp Brady, of Myshall, co. Carlow (see CORNWALL-BRADY—HARTSTONGE-WELD of Rahinbawn), and had issue,
1. JOHN RUPERT ROBERT, late of Ballykealey, late Lieut. 8th Hussars, b. 18 Feb. 1855; d. 10 Oct. 1908; m. July, 1884, Florence Mary, eldest dau. of Rev. Frederick Henry Snow Pendleton, Rector of St. Sampson's, Guernsey, and had issue,
 JOHN RUPERT FREDERICK, now of Ballykealey.
2. Frederic Beauchamp, D.S.O., Col. (ret.) R.H.A., b. 11 Oct. 1858.
3. Frederic James Smith, b. 26 Feb. 1861; d. 24 Sept. 1906, Col. Comm. Tipperary Artillery; m. July, 1889, Haidee Susan, dau. of the late Col. Roberts, of Newtown, co. Waterford.
4. Robert St. Clair, b. 11 Feb. 1863, Lieut.-Col. R.H.A.; m. 3 April, 1900, Muriel Edith, dau. of John Goldney, I.C.S., and has issue a son, b. 19 Oct. 1908.

Mr. Lecky d. 6 Aug. 1908.

Seat—Ballykealey, Tullow, co. Carlow.

LEE, late OF BARNA.

ALBERT HENRY LEE, late of Barna (Newport), co. Tipperary, b. 27 April, 1853; s. his father 10 Jan. 1861; m. 28 Aug. 1883, Raby Beatrice, only dau. of Henry Godfrey James, of Ballyvourneen, co. Limerick, and granddau. of Capt. James, of the 35th Regt., and has issue,

HENRY WILLIAM JAMES, b. 16 Dec. 1893.
Susan Kate.

Lineage.—HENRY LEE, of Cragg Castle, purchased in 1668 the lands of Barna, Barony of Owny and Arra, co. Tipperary, from Richard Dingle and Robert Child, and d. circa 1698, leaving, with two daus. (who s. to Cragg Castle), a son,

EDWARD LEE, of Barna, m. Mary, dau. of Benjamin Lane, of co. Tipperary, and d. 1702, leaving a son,

BENJAMIN LEE, of Barna, co. Tipperary, who (by Martha his wife) left two daus., Elizabeth, m. John Spunner, of King's Co., and Mary, m. James McCarol, of Cnol, co. Tipperary, and an only son,

EDWARD LEE, of Barna, m. Elizabeth, dau. of Daniel Ryan, of Ballymackeogh (see that family), and widow of William Keating, of Cranna. His will, dated 29 March, 1724, was proved 1726. By his wife, who survived him, he left, with another son, Edward, an elder son,

HENRY LEE, of Barna, under age at his father's death, m. 10 Feb. 1747, Mary, dau. of Evan Phillips, of Killeen (Mount Rivers), co. Tipperary, and d. 1803, leaving issue,
1. GEORGE, his heir.
2. Evan, of Lodge, co. Tipperary, m. Alice, dau. of Saunders Young, of Ballysiely, co. Clare, and had issue.
3. Henry, Lieut.-Col. Royal Marines, m. the dau. of Power of Clonshire, co. Limerick, and had issue.
4. William. 5. Richard.
1. Susan, m. Stumbles Philips, of Mount Philips, co. Tipperary, and had issue.
2. Elizabeth, m. George Cornwall, of Old Park, co. Cork, and had issue.
3. Mary, m. — Ware, of Bandon.
4. Catherine, m. — Frewen, of Castle Connell.
5. Nessy, m. Pierce Ryan, M.D., and had issue.

The eldest son,

GEORGE LEE, of Barna, m. 19 Feb. 1778, Alice, dau. and co-heir of John Norris, of Limerick, and left at his decease, June, 1815,
1. HENRY, his successor.
2. John, an Officer 3rd Dragoons, m. 1st, Emma, dau. of Henry Bevan, of Camas, co. Limerick, by whom he had issue,
 1. William Norris, of Bettyville, co. Limerick, m. his cousin, Alicia, dau. of James Thomas Dickson, and had surviving issue,
 (1) John Theodore Norris (Rev.), M.A., Trin. Coll. Camb., Rector of Alwalton, Peterborough, formerly of Hardwicke, Cambridge, m. 3 Jan. 1882, Mary, dau. of William Cuppaidge, M.D., and has issue,
  a. William Cuppaidge Norris, Lieut. Indian Army, b. 6 July, 1884.
  b. Frederick Harry Norris, Cape of Good Hope Civil Service, b. 4 Nov. 1885.
  c. Robert Stephen Norris, b. 3 March, 1887.
  d. Arthur Oldfield Norris (Rev.), b. 6 Aug. 1888.
  e. Dionys John Norris, b. 9 Oct. 1892.
  a. Alicia Mary Beatrice, b. 15 Oct. 1890.
 (2) William, d. unm.
 (1) Anne, d. 1910; m. Joseph Bevan, of Glen Bevan, co. Limerick
 (2) Mary, m. Charles FitzGerald Tuthill.
 (3) Alice, m. Robert Reeves Tuthill. (4) Stephanie.
 1. Elizabeth, m. 1st, George Henry Heard, one of the six Clerks in the Court of Chancery, and had issue. She m. 2ndly, Hamilton Geale, Barrister-at-Law, of Darragh, co. Cork, brother of the Countess Fortescue. 2. Alice, dec.
 3. Anna, m. Lieut.-Col. Francis Russell, H.E.I.C.S., and d. leaving issue.

He m. 2ndly, Ellen, dau. of Edmund Morony, of Ballyclough, co. Clare, by whom he had a dau., Ellen, d. unm. He d. 1835.

3. WILLIAM (Rev.), D.D., Scholar of Trin. Coll. Dublin (1799), appointed 1825 to the Rectory of Hore Abbey, Diocese of Cashel ; became successively Rector of Moyaliffe, Vicar of Emly, and, 1829, a Vice-Choral of Cashel. He *m.* 1813, Jane, dau. of Richard White, of Greenhall, co. Tipperary, and *d.* 1835, having had issue,
  1. William (Ven.), D.D., Professor of Ecclesiastical History in the University of Dublin, Fellow of Trin. Coll. and Archdeacon of Dublin. He *m.* Anne, dau. of William English, of Farmley, co. Tipperary, and had issue,
    (1) William (Rev.), M.A., Vicar of Holy Trinity, Gosport, *m.* 29 July, 1880, Margaret Alexandrina, 3rd dau. of Sir Andrew Clark, 1st bart., M.D. (*see* BURKE'S *Peerage*), and has issue.
    (2) Thomas Richard, Barrister-at-Law, B.A. Pembroke Coll. Camb., *b.* 1855.
    (3) Henry, dec.
    (4) Alice.   (2) Anne.
    (3) Jane, *d. unm.*
  2. George, *m.* Agnes, dau. of John Brown, of London, by whom he had issue,
    (1) George John, dec.
    (2) Albert Benjamin Henry, dec.
    (1) Agnes Maria.   (2) Rosalie Alice.
    (3) Mary.   (4) Florence.
    (5) Helen.
  3. Richard (Rev.), *m.* Jane, dau. of Robert H. Ievers, of Castle Ievers, cc. Limerick (*see that family*) ; and *d.* 1850, leaving issue,
    (1) Richard (Rev.), D.D., M.A., Head Master of Christ's Hospital, London, 1876-1902.   (2) William *dec.*
    (1) Jane.   (2) Maria.
  4. Henry, *m.* Maria, dau. of Robert H. Ievers, and *d.* March, 1903, leaving issue,
    (1) William Henry *dec.*   (2) Robert.
    (3) Henry.
    (1) Maria.   (2) Jane Henrietta.
    1. Anne Lætitia, *dec.*   2. Alice, *d.* young, *unm.*
  4. Richard, *d. unm.* 1842.
  5. Edward, of Dublin, *m.* Elizabeth, dau. of M. Ryan, of Tyrone House, co. Tipperary, and *d.* 1860, leaving by her, who predeceased him, an only child, Elizabeth, *m.* Capt. Falkiner.
  1. Anne, *m.* James Thomas Dickson, Barrister-at-Law, and by him, who is dec., had issue
His eldest son,
HENRY LEE, of Barna, J.P., Cornet 5th Dragoons, *b.* 2 March, 1779 ; *m.* 2 Jan. 1808, Maria, 2nd dau. of Christopher Crofts, of Stream Hill, Doneraile, co. Cork (*see* CROFTS *of Velvetstown*), and *d.* 18 Jan. 1848, leaving issue by her (who *d.* 1868),
  1. HENRY ALBERT, his heir.   2. George Augustus.
  3. Charles Edward.
  1. Anne.   2. Alicia Maria.
  3. Catherine Louisa.   4. Charlotte, dec.
  5. Emily.
  6. Maria Louisa, *m.* Samuel de Vere Hunt, M.D. of Limerick.
His eldest son,
HENRY ALBERT LEE, M.D., of Barna, *b.* 2 Aug. 1818 ; *m.* 31 July, 1852, Susan Kate, eldest dau. of John Benn, of Dromore House, near Newport, co. Tipperary, and *d.* 10 Jan. 1861, having by her (who *m.* 2ndly, Surg.-Major Abbott, A.M.S.) had issue,
  1. ALBERT HENRY, now of Barna.
  2. William Alexander, Lieut.-Col. R.A.M.C., *b.* 13 Aug. 1854 ; *m.* Annie, dau. of Col. Addison Potter, of Heaton Hall, Newcastle-on-Tyne, and has issue,
    Charles Stewart.
  3. George John Francis, *b.* 12 April, 1856 ; *d.* 3 March, 1865.
  4. Henry Ewer, *b.* 11 Feb. 1858 ; *d.* 14 Aug. 1897.
Residence—11, Longford Terrace, Monkstown, co. Dublin.

LEE-NORMAN. *See* NORMAN.

LEECH, late OF CLOONCONRA.

HENRY BROUGHAM LEECH, M.A., LL.D., late Fellow of Gonville and Caius Coll. Camb., of the King's Inns, Barrister-at-Law, ex-Regius Professor of Laws, Trin. Coll. Dublin, late Registrar of Deeds and Registrar of Titles in Ireland, *b.* 15 Nov. 1843 ; *m.* 1 June, 1875, Annie Louisa, dau. of William Garbois, and has issue,
  1. ARTHUR GRAVES, Capt. R.A., LL.D. Trin. Coll. Dublin, *b.* 17 Sept. 1877 ; *m.* 19 July, 1911, Amy Mary, dau. of Charles Booth, of Woolwich.

  2. Henry Brougham, M.D., *b.* 14 July, 1879.
  3. William John, R.H.A., *b.* 10 April, 1881.
  4. Cecil John Farran, Lieut. R.A., *b.* 25 April, 1882.
  5. Frederick George, *b.* 1 July, 1884 ; *d.* 8 Dec. 1906.
  1. Kathleen Mary Angel.

Lineage.—GEORGE LEECH, settled in Ireland *circa* 1667, at Rosserk, co. Mayo. He *m.* Elizabeth, eldest dau. of Samuel Nicholson, of Castle Connor, co. Sligo, and left an only son,
JOHN LEECH, of Frankfort, co. Sligo, *b.* 1694 ; *m.* Mary, eldest dau. of Robert Orme, of Carne, co. Mayo, and by her (who *d.* 10 Dec. 1796, aged 80), had issue, besides several daus., of whom Mary, the eldest, *m.* 1759, James Wood,
  1. JOHN, his heir.   2. ROBERT.
  3. James, *b.* 1746 ; *d.* at Stoke Newington, 21 Feb. 1826, aged 80.
Mr. Leech *d.* 2 June, 1770, aged 76, and was *s.* by his eldest son,
JOHN LEECH, of Rathroan, co. Mayo, J.P. and Deputy-Governor of the co. of Sligo, and of Dublin, *b.* 1742 ; *m.* 1760, Elizabeth, eldest dau. and co-heir of Samuel Ansdell, and by her (who was *b.* 9 June, 1742, and *d.* 4 Feb. 1834, in her 92nd year) had issue to survive, two daus., Marianne, *b.* 1775 ; *m.* 1808, Richard Perceval Moulson ; Lydia, *d. unm.* ; and one son, WILLIAM ANSDELL, his heir. Mr. Leech *d.* 8 Aug. 1822, aged 80, and was *s.* by his son,
WILLIAM ANSDELL LEECH, of Rathroan, co. Mayo, a Collector of H.M. Customs in Ireland, *b.* 11 July, 1777 ; *m.* 15 May, 1806, Mary, 2nd dau. of Charles Atkinson, of Rehins, co. Mayo, and *d.* 19 Oct. 1837, leaving issue,
  1. JOHN (Rev.), his heir.
  2. Charles, of Hermitage, co. Sligo, and Upper Merrion Street, Dublin, Barrister-at-Law, M.A. T.C.D., Q.C., *b.* 16 Dec. 1810 ; *m.* 19 Aug. 1840, Anna Maria, 2nd dau. of Hunt Walsh Chambré, of Hawthorn Hill, co. Armagh, and *d.* 29 Nov. 1890, leaving issue,
    1. William Ansdell, of New Zealand, *b.* 11 June, 1841 ; *m.* Elizabeth, dau. of Thomas Gill, and has issue,
      Grace.
    2. Hunt Walsh, M.A., T.C.D., *b.* 4 Dec. 1842 ; *m.* 28 Aug. 1879, Theodosia, widow of John Quentin Davies, Bombay S.C., and dau. of the late Rev. John Colthurst (*see* BURKE'S *Peerage and Baronetage*, COLTHURST, Bart.), and has issue,
      Charles Reginald Colthurst.
      Ethelberta Theodosia.
    3. Charles, *b.* 28 June, 1844 ; *m.* 15 Sept. 1874, Eben, dau. of William Harpur Lepper, and has issue,
      (1) Charles Ansdell.
      (2) Ernest Chambré.
      (3) Douglas.
      (1) Eilene Hilda Macaulay, *m.* 11 April, 1907, Col. William T. Johnston, R.A.M.C.
      (2) Mary Nina.
    4. Thomas Archibald, *b.* 19 April, 1853 ; *m.* Mary, dau. of W. Deane-Freeman, and *d.* 8 July, 1897, leaving issue.
    5. John, *b.* 22 May, 1857, LL.B. T.C.D., K.C., *m.* Sarah Frances, dau. of George Hudson Greaves.
      1. Rebecca Olivia, *m.* 11 Sept. 1872, Henry A. Macaulay, and has issue.
      2. Anna Maria, *m.* 27 Aug. 1879, Edmund Shackleton, and *d.* 12 Jan. 1882, leaving issue.
      3. Emily Edith, *m.* Edmund Figgis, and has issue.
    3. William Ansdell, *b.* 23 Dec. 1812 ; *m.* 7 Nov. 1855, Eleanor, 2nd dau. of George Gibson, of Lower Pembroke Street, Dublin, by Elizabeth, eldest dau. of John Gibson. She *d.* Aug. 1896. He *d.* Sept. 1897, leaving issue,
      1. William Ansdell, *b.* 21 Aug. 1857.
      2. George Gibson, *b.* 7 Nov. 1859.
      3. Arthur Henry William, *b.* 12 July, 1862.
      1. Elizabeth Marian Susanna.
      2. Florence Catherine Sinclair.
      3. Madaline Eleanor.   4. Mabel Wilhelmina.
      5. Ada Frederika Orme.
    4. Edward, *b.* 9 Oct. 1814, B.A. T.C.D. ; *m.* 3 Oct. 1855, Wilhelmina Fredericka, dau. of Richard Hammersley, of Corrolantry, King's Co., J.P.
    5. Arthur Henry (Very Rev.) of Ballycloughduff, co. Westmeath, M.A. T.C.D., Dean of Cashel, *b.* 23 March, 1817 ; *m.* 18 Dec. 1845, Ellen, 2nd dau. of Thomas Maunsell Wilson, of Cahirconlish House, co. Limerick, by Isabella his wife, younger dau. of Charles Stanley, 1st Viscount Monck, and sister to the Earl of Rathdowne, and by her (who *d.* 1 Sept. 1881) had issue,
      1. William Thomas Atkinson, *b.* 2 April, 1860 ; *d.* 27 April, 1860.
      1. Isabella Monck, *d. unm.* 11 Aug. 1878.
      2. Mary Wilhelmina Monck, *d. unm.* 7 April, 1897.
      3. Eleanor Elizabeth, *d.* Oct. 1893.
      4. Henrietta Maria, *m.* 1880, Rev. Walter Brocas Lindesay, LL.D., and has issue.
      5. Edith, *m.* her cousin Graves Atkinson Leech (*see below*), and has issue.
    6. James Ansdell, *b.* 27 Nov. 1818 ; *d.* in Spain, 6 May, 1855.
    1. Mary, *d. unm.* 20 April, 1880.
    2. Elizabeth, *m.* Aug. 1846, William Crawford Poole, M.D. of Ardmore, co. Waterford.
    3. Catherine Anne, *d. unm.* 1886.
    4. Marianne Charlotte, *m.* 11 Dec. 1844, the late Henry Connor White, of Golden Hills, co. Tipperary, Registrar of the Royal Dublin Society, and *d.* 31 May, 1877.
    5. Maria Isabella *m.* 1st, 27 Feb. 1845, William Thomas Lloyd, of Upper Mount Street Crescent, Dublin, A.M. T.C.D., Barrister-at-Law (who *d.* 13 Dec. 1857) ; and 2ndly, 9 Oct. 1860, Richard Augustine FitzGerald Studdert, and *d.* 31 Dec. 1892.
The eldest son,
REV. JOHN LEECH, of Clöonconra, co. Mayo, M.A., D.D., T.C.D., *b.* 30 Aug. 1808 ; *m.* 9 May, 1839, Mary, 2nd dau. of William Darley,

of St. John's, co. Dublin, and by her (who d. 23 March, 1889) had issue,
1. WILLIAM ANSDELL, late of Cloonconra.
2. HENRY BROUGHAM, present representative.
3. Joseph Farran (*Beechwood, Pendleton, Lancashire*), b. 25 July, 1845; m. 1st, 19 Aug. 1879, Beatrice Jane, dau. of James Seccombe, of Trenodden, co. Cornwall. She d. 23 Feb. 1887, leaving a dau.,
1. Beatrice Mary Seccombe.
He m. 2ndly, 16 July, 1888, Alice Elizabeth, youngest dau. of the Rev. Joseph Walker, M.A., Rector of Great Billing, and Catherine Augusta, his wife, dau. of Adm. Sir William Carroll, K.C.B., and has issue,
1. Hugh Ansdell Farran, b. 28 April, 1889.
2. Cecil Darley Farran, b. 21 Nov. 1892.
3. Noel Leslie Farran, b. 22 Nov. 1902.
2. Sylvia Louise Ruthven.
4. Frederick John (*Enniscorthy, co. Wexford*), b. 30 Jan. 1847; m. 22 Aug. 1877, Lily, dau. of the Rev. Canon Wolseley, Rector of Kilrush, and has issue, John Wolseley; Grace Elizabeth Mary; and Muriel.
5. Graves Atkinson (*Danesfield, Dollymount, co. Dublin*), b. 13 Nov. 1850, B.A. Trin. Coll. Dublin; m. 1st, 23 July, 1878, Annie, dau. of David Smyth, of Gallony House and Artegervan, co. Tyrone, and by her (who d. 3 April, 1892) had issue,
1. Elizabeth Mary Rachel. 2. Margaret Grace.
He m. 2ndly, his cousin Edith, dau. of Very Rev. A. H. Leech, Dean of Cashel (*see above*), and by her has a dau.,
3. Eleanor Mary.
1. Anna Darley, m. 5 March, 1867, Henry James Bourchier, of Baggotstown, co. Limerick, and has issue (*see that family*).
2. Mary Walter Barbara Farran, m. 3 Oct. 1873, William Fleming Mease Smyth, of Gallony House, co. Tyrone.
3. Elizabeth Catherine, m. 28 Jan. 1884, Hunt Walsh Chambré Leech, LL.D., Barrister-at-Law, and has issue, John and Catherine Mary Richarda. 4. Richarda King.
The Rev. John Leech d. 1 Aug. 1889, and was s. by his son,
REV. WILLIAM ANSDELL LEECH, of Cloonconra, co. Mayo, B.A. Emmanuel Coll. Camb., Barrister-at-Law, b. 30 Sept. 1842; m. Mary, widow of J. Walker, and d. 21 Nov. 1895, leaving a dau., Laura.

Arms—Erm., a trefoil vert, on a chief indented gu. three ducal coronets or. *Crest*—Out of a ducal coronet or, charged with a trefoil vert, an arm erect ppr., grasping a snake environed about the arm also vert. *Motto*—Virtute et valore.
Residence—55, Castletown Road, West Kensington.

LEECH, late OF KIPPURE.

JOHN CYRIL LEECH, of Hurdcote House, Wilts, Lieut. 8th Hussars, b. 29 April, 1890.

Lineage.—ROBERT LEECH, of Lumme, in the parish of Ashton, Lancashire, d. in 1608, leaving by Katherine his wife, a son,
JOHN LEECH, of Lumme, who d. 1640, leaving a son,
JOHN LEECH, of Hurst, Ashton, Lancashire, b. 30 Oct. 1597; m. 27 Oct. 1621, Anne Marland. His monument in Ashton Church, bears the family arms and an inscription, recording his descendants at the time of his death. He was bur. 16 Oct. 1689, leaving an eldest son,
JOHN LEECH, of Hurst, b. 20 March, 1624; was s. by his son,
JAMES LEECH, of Hurst, who by Anne his wife left issue, a son,
JOHN LEECH, of Audenshaw, Ashton, who left issue by Jane his wife, a son,
JOHN LEECH, of Newton, Mottram, Cheshire, b. 15 July, 1717; m. 1753, Lydia Heape, and d. 1808, having had issue,
1. JOHN, his heir.
1. Sarah, d. unm. 2. Anne, m. James Schofield, of Newton.
3. Mary, m. John Hague, of Ashton.
The only son,
JOHN LEECH, of The Croft, Dukinfield, Cheshire, b. 1755; m. 1801, Elizabeth, dau. of John Turner, of Ashton, and widow of Samuel Bates of Newton, and d. 21 Nov. 1822, having had two sons and a dau.,
1. JOHN, his heir. 2. William, b. 1803; d. 20 Dec. 1812.
1. Elizabeth, b. 1806; m. John Ashton, son of James Ashton, of Newton, Cheshire (*see* BURKE'S *Peerage*, ASHTON of Hyde, B.).
The only surviving son,
JOHN LEECH, of Gorse Hall, Dukinfield, Cheshire, b. 20 Oct. 1802; m. 6 June, 1832, Jane, dau. of Thomas Ashton, of Hyde, Cheshire (*see* BURKE'S *Peerage*, ASHTON, B.), and d. 23 April, 1861, having had issue,
1. JOHN, his heir. 2. Ashton b. 19 Oct.; d. Nov. 1841.

3. William, b. 24 Aug. 1836; m. 4 March, 1873, Rosalie, dau. of Richard Ansdell, R.A., of Moy, Inverness, and d. 8 March, 1887, leaving issue,
1. William Harold, b. 22 Jan. 1874.
2. Guy Ansdell, b. 22 Oct. 1877.
1. Mabel Rosalie, twin with William Harold.
2. Gwendoline, b. 18 May, 1879.
3. Sybil Helena, b. 1 June, 1880.
1. Mary, b. 10 Sept.; d Dec. 1840.
2. Jane, b. 14 June, 1833; d. unm. 29 Nov. 1876.
3. Harriet, b. 20 Aug. 1834; m. 14 Feb. 1870, Frederick Burton, younger son of James Burton, of Ingleton, Yorks.
4. Elizabeth, b. 9 Nov. 1837; m. 17 May, 1862, Walter Potter, son of Edmund Potter, F.R.S., D.L., of Denting, Glossop, and Campfield Place, Hatfield. She d. 14 Jan. 1865.
5. Helen, b. 15 April, 1839; m. 8 Aug. 1863, Rupert Potter, younger son of the above-mentioned Edmund Potter.
The eldest son,
JOHN LEECH, of Gorse Hall, b. 5 Aug. 1835; m. 17 Jan. 1860, Eliza, dau. of Henry Ashworth, of the Oaks, Bolton-le-Moors (*see* ASHWORTH *of Birtenshaw*), and d. 20 Oct. 1870. leaving issue,
1. JOHN HENRY, his heir, late of Kippure.
2. Stephen, Minister Resident in Cuba since 1909 (*Club, Travellers'*), b. 8 July, 1864; m. 15 July, 1902, Hon. Alice Florence Murray, 3rd dau. of 10th Lord Elibank. This marriage was annulled 1909.
1. Ethel, b. 4 Jan. 1861; m. 18 Nov. 1890, Rev. Sir William Hyde Parker, 10th bart. of Melford Hall, Suffolk (*see* BURKE'S *Peerage and Baronetage*).
The elder son,
JOHN HENRY LEECH, of Kippure Park, co. Wicklow, and of Hurdcote House, Wilts, F.R.G.S., F.L.S., F.Z.S., b. 5 Dec. 1862; m. 13 April, 1889, Beatrice Ellen, only child of Benjamin Leatt Nias, of Philadelphia, U.S.A., and d. 29 Dec. 1900, leaving issue,
JOHN CYRIL, present representative.
Kathleen Ethel, b. 21 June, 1891.

Arms—Erm., a rose gu. barbed and seeded ppr. on a chief indented of the second three ducal coronets or. *Crest*—An arm erect ppr. grasping a snake entwined about the arm all ppr. *Motto*—Virtus est venerabilis.

Seat—Hurdcote House, Wilts.

LEESON-MARSHALL. *See* MARSHALL.

LEFROY OF CARRIGGLAS.

LIEUT.-COL. AUGUSTINE HUGH LEFROY, of Carrigglas Manor, co. Longford, J.P., D.L. for that county, High Sheriff 1909, and of the Lodge, Boxted, Colchester, J.P. Essex, late 45th Regt., b. 22 July, 1839; s. his brother 1902; m. 23 March, 1878, Isabel Mary, eld. dau. of John Hebblethwaite, of St. Clair, Cheltenham, and has issue,

1. HUGH PERCIVAL THOMSON, Capt. R.E., b. 6 Oct. 1880.
2. Longlois Massy, b. 26 Oct. 1885.
3 Augustine George Victor, Midshipman R.N., b. 3 March, 1887; d. 8 March, 1904.
1. Mary Elizabeth, b. 30 Jan. 1879.
2. Kathleen Grace, b. 22 April, 1883; m. 19 Jan. 1910, Benjamin St. George Lefroy, of Derryeashel, Longford (*see below*).

Lineage.—The Lefroys are of Flemish extraction, and emigrated from Cambray to England in the time of the Duke of Alva's persecutions and settled at Canterbury. The first settler, in this country, about 1569, was ANTOINE LEFROY. His descendant in the fourth generation,
THOMAS LEFROY, of Canterbury, b. 1680; m. Phœbe (b. 1679), dau. of Thomas Thomson, of Kenfield, by Phœbe his wife, dau. of William Hammond, of St. Alban's Court, Kent, and granddau. of the Right Hon. Sir Dudley Digges, of Chilham Castle, Kent, Master of the Rolls, and d. 3 Nov. 1723, having by her (who d. 1761) had a son,
ANTHONY LEFROY, of Leghorn and Canterbury, b. 10 Dec. 1703; m. 1738, Elizabeth, sister of Benjamin Langlois, M.P., many years Under Secretary of State, and had (with one dau., Phœbe, m. to an Italian nobleman, Del Medico Staffetti, Count de Carrara) two sons,
1. ANTHONY, Lieut.-Col. 9th Dragoons, b. 1742; m. 15 Nov. 1765, Anne, dau. of Col. Gardiner, and d. 8 Sept. 1819, having had issue,

IRELAND. Lefroy.

1. THOMAS LANGLOIS, of whom presently.
2. Anthony, late Capt. 65th Regt., b. 1777, and d. 1857, having m. 1798, Elizabeth Wilkin and by her had with other issue,
Thomas Edward Preston, M.A., Q.C., b. 13 Aug. 1815; m. 9 Sept. 1846, Anna Jemima, eldest dau. of Rev. Benjamin Lefroy, Rector of Ashe, and by her (who d. 17 Oct. 1855) had William Chambers, M.A. Oxon, Barrister-at-Law, late Chief Administrative Inspector of Secondary Schools, J.P. Hants (*Goldings, near Basingstoke*), b. 2 Feb. 1849; m. 1896, Clara Frances, dau. of late Lieut.-Col. C. H. Pierse. She d.s.p. 31 Aug. 1907.
3. Benjamin, of Cardenton House, co. Kildare, J.P., Capt. R.A., b. 1782; d. 1869; m. 1stly, 31 Oct. 1807, Margaret, dau. of Philip Savage, of Kilgibbon, co. Wexford, and niece of Lord Callan. He m. 2ndly, 1817, Katherine Tessier de la Nauze, and had with other issue,
George, b. 1826; m. Phœbe Baldwin, and d. 30 Sept. 1896, leaving with other issue,
Benjamin St. George (*Derrycashel, Clondra, Longford*), b. 1 Jan. 1865; m. 10 Jan. 1910, Kathleen Grace, younger dau. of Col. A. H. Lefroy, of Carrigglas (*see above*).
(1) Lucy, m. 11 Sept. 1858, Robert Exham Turbett, o Owenstown House, co. Dublin, and Kilmackshane, co. Galway. He d. March, 1889, leaving issue.
(2) Mary Jane, now of Cardenton House.
He m. 3rdly, 1831, Isabella Telford and had with other issue,
Robert, J.P., late Capt. 97th Regt., b. 1834; d. 6 Jan. 1907; m. 1872, Maud, only child of John Willoughby Sneyd Cole, of Broonfield, co. Dublin, and had issue,
1. Robert Willoughby (Rev.), B.A. (Dub.), 1903, b. 8 Nov. 1877.
2. Francis Buchanan, b. 12 June, 188·, Lieut. Leinster Regt. m. 7 June, 1011, Œnone Florence Mary, dau. of Hon. Hickman, Molesworth, Judge of Supreme Court, Victoria (*see* BURKE'S *Peerage*, MOLESWORTH, V.).
1. Sydney Maud, m. 21 Sept. 1910, Capt. Malcolm B. Riall, West Yorks. Regt.
4. Christopher, b. 1784, Midshipman R.N., killed in action on board H.M.S. "Sans Fiorenzo" 14 Feb. 1805
5. Henry (Rev.), M.A., Vicar of Santry, near Dublin, b. 5 May, 1789; m. 1814, Dorothea, 2nd dau. of John, The O'Grady, of Kilballyowen (*see that family*). She d. 1865. He d. 29 Jan. 1876, having had issue,
(1) Anthony O'Grady (Hon.), C.M.G., late Treasurer W. Australia, b. 24 March, 1816; m. 1852, Mary, dau. of Col. Bruce, and d. 21 Jan. 1897, having had issue,
1. Henry Bruce (Hon.), C.M.G., Agent-General for West Australia, b. 24 March, 1854; m. 1880, Rose Agnes, dau. of the late Charles Wittenoon, J.P. West Australia, and had three sons and one dau. She d. 17 April, 1902. He m. 2ndly, 23 Nov. 1904, Madeleine Emily Stewart and dau. of Rev. William Stewart Walford, Vicar of St. Mary's-at-the-Quay, Ipswich, and has issue a son b. 29 Nov. 1907.
2. Anthony Langlois O'Grady, b. 1863; d. unm. 20 Jan. 1877.
1. Minnie. 2. Dorothea.
3. Emily, m. 1888, Arthur Williams.
(2) Gerald de Courcy, b. 4 Oct. 1819; m. 1852, Elizabeth, dau. of William Brockman, and settled in Australia, and d. 15 Dec. 1877, having had issue two sons and six daus.
(1) Henry Maunsell, of Fern Hollow, Killaloe, co. Tipperary, J.P. cos. Tipperary and Clare, b. 13 Jan. 1826; m. Feb. 1860, Ellen, dau. of James Shine, of Ballymacreese, co. Limerick, and had issue,
1. Henry, b. 8 Dec. 1860; m. Sept. 905, Minnie, dau. of F. John Minchin, J.P. of Annagh, co. Tipperary and Soberton Manor, Hants (*see that family*).
2. James, b. 3 Oct. 1865.
3. Gerald, b. 1867; d. unm. 15 Jan. 1891.
4. Claud, b. 11 March, 1871; d. unm. 6 March, 1905.
1. Dorothea O'Grady.
2. Hester Margaret, m. 1897, Courtney Oulton, C.I., R.I.C., and has issue.
(1) Eliza Waller, d. unm. 23 Dec. 1875.
(2) Ann Langlois, m. 1847, James Stein, of Chalmington, Dorset, and Kennetpans, N.B., and d. 1868, having had issue.
(3) Mary Elizabeth O'Grady, d. unm. 1 Oct. 1875.
(4) Dorothea Thomasina, d. unm. 28 Feb. 1901.
1. Lucy, b. 1768; m. 1803, Hugh Ryves Baker, of Massy Lodge, co. Tipperary, and d. 1853, and had issue.
2. Phœbe, b. 1770; m. 1825, Capt. Butler, of Castle Comer, co. Kilkenny, and d.s.p. 1839.
3. Sarah, b. 1773; m. 1799, Capt. Courtenay, of Grange, co. Antrim, and had issue. She d. 1836.
4. Eliza, b. 1780; m. 1811, Richard Sadlier, of Scalaheen, co. Tipperary, and d. 1867 leaving issue.
5. Anne, b. 1786; m. 1817, Major Power, and d.s.p.
2. Isaac Peter George, Fellow of All Souls', Oxford, Rector of Ashe and Compton, Surrey, b. 12 Nov. 1745; m. 1778, Anne, eldest dau. of Edward Brydges, of Wootton Court, Kent, by Jemima, his wife, dau. and co-heir of William Egerton, LL.D., grandson of John, 2nd Earl of Bridgewater, and by her (who d. in 1804) left at his decease, Jan. 1806,
1. John Henry George, of Ewshott House, Hants, Rector of Ashe, Hants and Compton, Surrey, b. 12 Jan. 1782; m. 1806, Sophia, youngest dau. of Rev. Charles Jeffreys Cottrell, and d. 5 Sept. 1823, leaving issue,
(1) George, d. unm. 1824.
(2) CHARLES EDWARD, of Ewshott House, otherwise Itchel Manor, Crondall, Hants, J.P., M.A. Ch. Ch. Oxon, Barrister-at-Law, Secretary to the Speaker of the House of Commons, Taxing Officer of that House 1856, b. 9 March, 1810; s. his brother George 1824; m. 1845 Janet, dau. and heir of James Walker, LL.D., F.R.S., C.E., and d. 17 April, 1861, leaving with other issue, a son,
CHARLES JAMES MAXWELL LEFROY, of Itchel Manor, Hants, late Capt. 14th Hussars, b. 12 Sept. 1848; m. 14 Aug. 1872, Elizabeth Catherine, eldest dau. of Alfred Henry McClintock, M.D., of Merrion Square, Dublin (*see* M'CLINTOCK, *of Rathvinden*), and d. 2 Nov. 1908, having had issue,
1. Charles Alfred Henry, b. 4 June, 1873.
2. George Langlois, b. 22 Aug. 1874; m. 16 Dec. 1903, Almina, younger dau. of G. Campbell, of Manitoba.
3. CECIL MAXWELL, Commander R.N., b. 2 Feb. 1876.
4. Harold Maxwell, M.A., F.Z.S., F.E.S., Etymologist for India, b. 20 Jan. 1877; m. 22 Jan. 1904, Kathleen Hamilton 2nd dau. of late William O'Meara, Provost Marshal of British Guiana and has had issue,
Anthony Cecil, b. 7 July, 1907.
Gladys Kathleen, d. inf. 3 June, 1905.
5. Evelyn, b. 16 March, 1879; m. 9 May, 1906, Ethel Muriel Richards.
6. Patrick Egerton, Lieut. R.N., b. 1889.
1. Kathleen Margaret, b. 8 Dec. 1882; m. 4 Aug. 1904, Capt. Philip E. Lewis, R.A., eldest son of Col. J. Lewis, late R.E.
(3) Anthony Cottrell (Rev.), M.A., Vicar of Longdon, co. Worcester, b. 1811; m. 1841, Anne, dau. of John Rickman, and has four daus.
(4) John Henry (Sir), Gen., R.A., K.C.M.G., C.B., F.R.S., LL.D., F.S.A., Governor of Bermuda 1871 to 1877, and of Tasmania 1880-81, b. 1817; m. 1st, 16 April, 1846, Emily Merry, dau. of Sir John Beverley Robinson, Bart. of Toronto, Canada, and by her (who d. 29 June, 1859) had two sons and two daus. He m. 2ndly, 12 May, 1860, Charlotte Anna, dau. of Col. Dundas, of Fingask, and widow of Col. Armine Mountain, C.B., and d. 11 April, 1890 (*see Colonial Gentry*).
(5) Henry Maxwell, of West Australia, b. 1818; d. 18 July, 1879, having m. 1853, Annette Bate, and left issue.
(6) Frederick, d. Oct. 1828.
(1) Ann, m. 1829, John, 1st Lord Rathdonnell. She d. 22 Dec. 1889. He d.s.p. 17 May, 1879.
(2) Frances Phœbe, m. 1842, Sir George Kettilby Richards, K.C.B., Barrister-at-Law, and d. 22 Sept. 1859, having had issue, a son and five daus.
(3) Ann Sophia, m. 1852, Rev. Ernest Hawkins, B.D., Canon of Westminster, and d.s.p. 1897.
(4) Lucy, b. 1819; d. Aug. 1837.
(5) Isabella Elizabeth, m. 1854, Rev. C. Frederick Seymour, Rector of Winchfield, Hants. She d. 20 April, 1887, and had issue.
2. Christopher Edward, Barrister-at-Law, British Commander at Surinam for Suppression of Slave Trade, b. 25 Nov. 1785; d. unm. 3 July, 1856.
3. Benjamin (Rev.), Rector of Ashe, b. 13 May, 1791; m. 1814, Jane Anne Elizabeth, eldest dau. of Rev. James Austen, Rector of Steventon, Hants (and niece of Jane Austen, the authoress), and dying 1829, left issue, George Benjamin Austen, and six daus., of whom the 2nd Julia Cassandra, m. 1861, Sir George Kettilby Rickards, K.C.B., late Counsel to the Speaker of the House of Commons.
1. Lucy, m. 18.1, the Rev. Henry Rice, of Norton Court, near Faversham. She d. 11 March, 1862, leaving issue.

The grandson,

THE RIGHT HON. THOMAS LANGLOIS LEFROY, LL.D., of Carrigglas Manor, Lord Chief Justice of Ireland, b. 8 Jan. 1776; m. 16 March, 1799, Mary, only dau. and heir of Jeffry Paul, of Silver Spring, co. Wexford, member of the younger branch of the family of Sir Robert Paul, Bart., and had issue,
1. ANTHONY, of Carrig-glas Manor.
2. THOMAS PAUL, s. his brother.
3. Jeffry (Very Rev.), M.A. Trin. Coll. Dublin, Dean of Dromore, b. 25 March 180·; m. 2 May, 1844, Helena eldest dau. of the Rev. Frederick Trench (*see* BURKE'S *Peerage*, ASHTOWN, B.), by Lady Helena his wife, sister of George James, 6th Earl of Egmont. She d. 7 May, 1898. He d. 10 Dec. 1885, having had issue.
1. Thomas Charles Perceval, b. 7 May 1845; m. 25 June, 1873, Isabella Napier, elder dau. of Alexander Hastie, of Carnock, co. Fife, M.P. for Glasgow, and d. 18 June, 1893, leaving issue,
(1) Charles Jeffry Alexander, b. 1 Aug. 1876.
(2) Bertram Perceval, D.S.O. (1901), Capt. Royal Warwickshire Regt., b. 18 May, 1878.
(3) Robert Napier, Lieut. Middlesex Regt., b. 7 Dec. 1881; d. 14 Nov. 1904.
(1) Annette Helena, b. 24 Nov. 1874.
(2) Eileen Mary, b. 18 March, 1880; d. unm. 7 Feb. 1904.
2. Frederick Anthony (Rev.), M.A. Trin. Coll. Camb., Hon. Canon Gloucester Cathedral, 1909, Vicar of Haresfield, Stonehouse, Gloucestershire, b. 10 Dec. 1846; m. 5 May, 1881, Henrietta, eldest dau. of George Gurney, of Eastbourne, Sussex, and has issue,
(1) George Frederick, b. 15 Feb. 1882; m. 12 Aug. 1908, Elaine, dau. of Surg.-Gen. H. Beaman, I.M.S., and has issue.
Jeffry Ardern, b. 14 June, 1909.

Legge. THE LANDED GENTRY. 394

(2) Charles Edwin, b. 1 July, 1883.
(3) Robert Philip Perceval, b. 4 Jan. 1888.
(1) Annie Kathleen, b. 12 March, 1865.
(2) Helena Mary, b. 15 Sept. 1891.

3. Jeffry Arthur, b. 18 Aug. 1852; m. 4 April, 1877, Sallie Watson, eldest dau. of John Montague, of Richmond, Virgina, and d. 16 Jan. 1884, leaving issue,
Helena Trench, b. 18 Aug. 1878; m. 17 Nov. 1897, Clifford Randolph Caperton, and has issue.
4. George Alfred (Right Rev.), D.D. Trin. Coll. Camb., Bishop of Lahore, b. 11 Aug. 1854.
5. Francis Paul, LL.B., Trin. Coll. Camb., Barrister-at-Law, b. 11 Jan. 1857; m. 2 Sept. 1884, Beatrice Mary, 4th dau. of Francis Shand, of Woolton, co. Lancaster, and d. 16 Nov. 1896, having had issue,
(1) Edward Jeffry, b. 15 Jan. 1893.
(2) Francis Perceval, b. 29 Oct. 1895.
(1) Norah Beatrice, b. 1 Oct. 1885; d. 22 May, 1889.

3. Edward Heathcote (65, Belgrave Road, S.W.), b. 15 Jan. 1859; m. 31 July, 1894, Lilian Wyndham, 4th dau. of Sir Herbert Barnard.
1. Helena Mary, b. 7 June, 1848.
2. Mary Frances, b. 3 Feb. 1850; m. 5 Sept. 1889, Henry Paul Loftie.
4. George Thomson, late Treasurer to the Ecclesiastical Commissioners, High Sheriff of Longford, 1846, b. 26 May, 1811; m. 10 Dec. 1869, Mary, widow of William Martley Blackburne, of Tankardstown, co. Meath, and dau. of Rev. William Thorp, D.D., and d.s.p. 19 March, 1890.
1. Jane Christmas, b. 24 June, 1802; d. unm. 3 Aug. 1896.
2. Anne, b. 25 April, 1804; d. unm. 24 Feb. 1885.
3. Mary Elizabeth, b. 19 Dec. 1817; d. unm. 23 Jan. 1890.

Lord Chief Justice Lefroy, one of the most distinguished Lawyers of his time, was called to the Bar 1797, and appointed a Bencher of the King's Inn, 1819. He sat in Parliament as Member for the University of Dublin from 1830 till his elevation to the Bench, which took place 1841, when he was appointed a Baron of the Exchequer. He became Lord Chief Justice 1852, and d. 4 May, 1869. His eldest son,

ANTHONY LEFROY, of Carrig-glas Manor, J.P. and D.L., LL.D., M.P. for the University of Dublin 1858 to 1870, and for co. Longford 1830 to 1837, and 1841 to 1847. High Sheriff co. Longford 1850, b. 21 March, 1800; m. 10 July, 1824, Hon. Jane King, eldest dau. of Robert Edward, 1st Viscount Lorton, and grand-dau. of Robert, 2nd Earl of Kingston, and d. 11 Jan. 1890, having by her (who d. 14 Dec. 1868) had issue,
1. Thomas, b. 1 July, 1826; d. 1 March, 1828.
1. Frances Jane, m. 22 March, 1849, Col. Sir David Carrick Robert Carrick-Buchanan, K.C.B., D.L., of Drumpellier, co. Lanark. He d.s.p. 8 Feb. 1904. She d. 2 June, 1911.
2. Mary Louisa, m. 26 June, 1852, Lieut.-Col. the Hon. William L. P. Talbot, who d.s.p. 12 Aug. 1881, 7th son of James, 3rd Lord Talbot de Malahide.

Mr. Lefroy was s. by his brother,

THOMAS PAUL LEFROY, of Carrig-glas Manor, Q.C., M.A., County Court Judge of Down, Chancellor of the Diocesan Court of Down, Connor and Dromore, Bencher of the King's Inns; b. 31 Dec. 1806; m. 1 July, 1835, Hon. Elizabeth Massy, dau. of Hugh, 3rd Lord Massy, and by her (who d. 30 July, 1874) had issue,
1. THOMAS LANGLOIS HUGH, late of Carrig-glas.
2. AUGUSTINE HUGH, now of Carrig-glas.
3. Anthony William Hamon (Rev.), B.A., Rector of Appleshawe; b. 14 Jan. 1847; m. 23 May, 1876, Sarah Jane, dau. of John Wickham Flower, of Park Hill, Croydon. She d. 9 Feb. 1909, leaving issue,
Anthony Langlois Massy, b. 15 Feb. 1880.
Frances Jane, b. 18 May, 1877.
4. Charles Edward, Col. formerly commanding 6th Batt. Rifle Brigade, b. 27 Nov. 1852; m. 23 Oct. 1895, Alice Constance, only child of the late Colin John Campbell, Scots Greys, of Colgrain, co. Dumbarton (see hat family), and has issue,
1. Theodore Charles Geoffrey, b. 25 Jan. 1900.
1. Aileen Muriel.
2. Constance Elizabeth.   3. Gladys Mary.
5. George Henry, b. 4. Aug.; d. Sept. 1854.
6. Alfred Henry, LL.B., Trin. Coll. Cambridge, Barrister-at-Law (The Briars, Kingston-on-Thames), b. 23 Feb. 1856; m. 3 June, 1891, Geraldine Mary, only dau. of the late Patrick Panton, of Rothnersham Court, Kent, and Edenbank, co. Roxburgh, and has issue,
1. Pauline Mary Elizabeth.
2. Rosemary Geraldine Massy.
1. Margaret Everina, b. 8 Nov. 1837; m. 25 Jan. 1872, Rev. Henry N. Collier, M.A., Vicar of East Finchley, and has issue,
1. Arthur Henry Lefroy, b. 13 Dec. 1874; 2. Cecil Massy, b. 24 Aug. 1876; m. 1908, Elsie Emelyn Fisher, and has issue; and 1. Mary Everina, b. 20 Jan. 1873; m. 1900, Pierre Francois.
2. Mary Georgina, b. 21 Aug. 1841; d. unm. 13 Feb. 1871.
3. Millicent Elizabeth, b. 6 May, 1843; d. unm. 18 March, 1864.
4. Grace Elizabeth, b. 7 March, 1845; m. 27 Dec. 1883, Maj.-Gen. William Hatt Noble, late R.E., who d. 14 Oct. 1903. She d.s.p. 27 April, 1904.
5. Frances Anna, b. 6 Sept. 1849; d. unm. 2 Jan. 1874.

His Honour Judge Lefroy d. 29 Jan. 1891. The eldest son,

THOMAS LANGLOIS HUGH LEFROY, of Carrig-glas Manor, co. Longford, J.P. and D.L., High Sheriff 1892, M.A., Barrister-at-Law, b. 26 April, 1836; m. 16 Jan. 1894, Dorothy Winifred dau. of Robert Carrex, of Carrey, co. Carnarvon, D.L. He d.s.p. 29 Nov. 1902. She m. 2ndly, 3 April, 1907, William McGowan.

Arms—Quarterly: 1st and 4th, vert, fretty of eight pieces arg. on a chief of the second, a hood or cap (allusive to the badge assumed by the party opposed to the Duke of Alva) between two wyverns gu., for LEFROY; 2nd and 3rd, az., a chevron or, between three crescents arg. on a chief gu. three mullets of the third, for LANGLOIS. Crest—A demi-wyvern gu. langued and armed az. Motto—Mutare sperno.

Seats—Carrigglas Manor, near Longford; The Lodge, Boxted, Colchester. Club—Junior United Service, S.W., Hibernian United Service, Dublin.

LEGGE-BOURKE. See BOURKE.

LE HUNTE OF ARTRAMONT.

SIR GEORGE RUTHVEN LE HUNTE, K.C.M.G., of Artramont House, co. Wexford, Barrister-at-Law, M.A. Trin. Coll. Camb., H.M. Colonial Service, Fiji, President of the Island of Dominica; Member of the Executive Council of the Leeward Islands, Colonial Secretary of Barbados, Colonial Secretary of Mauritius, 1897, Lt.-Gov. of British New Guinea, 1898-1903, Gov. of S. Australia, 1903-1909, Gov. Trinidad, 1909, b. 20 Aug. 1852; m. 14 Feb. 1884, Caroline Rachel, dau. of John Clowes, of Burton Court, co. Hereford, and has a son.

JOHN, Lieut Hampshire Regt., b. 11 Aug. 1886.
Editha Rachel, b. 7 Oct. 1891.

Lineage.—RICHARD LE HUNTE, bapt. at Little Bradley 10 Aug. 1620 (son of Sir George Le Hunte, of Little Bradley Suffolk, by Elizabeth his wife, dau. of Sir John Peyton), went to Ireland as a Col. in the Army of CROMWELL, and Capt. of his Body Guard. This last commission, dated 1649, is still extant. He settled at Cashel, co. Tipperary (High Sheriff 1657), and was M.P. for that city 1661. He m. Mary, dau. and heiress of Thomas Lloyd, of Cileyfedd, co. Pembroke (who d. 1688), and had issue,
1. GEORGE, his heir
2. Charles, m. Jane, dau. of Lieut.-Col. Oliver Jones, and left issue.
1. Elizabeth, m. John Buckworth, of Cashel!
2. Jane, m. Samuel Hughes
3. Margaret, m. Francis Bolton.

GEORGE LE HUNTE, b. 1663, Alice, dau. and heir of Francis Legge, of Cappagh, co. Tipperary, and d. 27 May, 1697, leaving issue,
1. Richard, of Llanrian, co. Pembroke, M.P. for Enniscorthy, High Sheriff co. Wexford 1712.
2. Francis, of Brenanstown, co Dublin, M.D., one of the founders of the Royal Dublin Society, s. his brother Richard. He m. Susanna, dau of Major Daniel French, of Belturber, co. Cavan, and widow of John Britton, and d 1 Dec. 1750, leaving an only son,
Richard, of Artramont, M.P. for Wexford Borough 1771-1783 B.A. Trin. Coll. Dub., Barrister-at-Law; d.s.p. 1783 devising Artramont to his cousin Major George Le Hunte (see below).
3. William (Rev.), B.D. Rector of Kidderminster, and d. 1746.
4. GEORGE, of whom presently.
5. Thomas, Barrister-at-Law, M.P. for Wexford.
1. Anne, m. Humphrey French, Lord Mayor of Dublin, M.P. for Dublin 1733-6.
2. Elizabeth, m. Rev. Mr. Browne.
3. Jane, m. George Warburton, of Garryhinch.

The 4th son
GEORGE LE HUNTE, of Ballymartin, co. Wexford, m. Martha, dau. of Lieut.-Col. Oliver Jones, an heiress, and dying 1741, left issue. The 2nd son,
GEORGE LE HUNTE, of Artramont, co. Wexford, had issue by Alicia Mary Corry his wife.
1. RICHARD, his heir.
2. WILLIAM AUGUSTUS, of whom presently.
3. Charles, b. 2 June, 1788.
4. Francis (Sir), Knt., J.P., twin with Charles, d. unm. 1860.
1. Anne, m. Simon Purdon, of a collateral branch of the Purdons of Tinerana.
2. Editha, m. Sir Henry Meredyth, 3rd bart. of Carlandstown.

Mr. Le Hunte d. 1799, and was s. by his son,

RICHARD LE HUNTE, of Artramont, b. 25 Feb. 1769; m. Miss Morgan, co. Pembroke, and had,
1. Maria Alicia. m: 1820, Samuel Meade Hobson, K.C., son of Samuel Meade Hobson, of Muckridge, co. Cork, and d. 10 May, 1883, aged 81. He d. 1835, having had issue,

1. SAMUEL LE HUNTE HOBSON, of Artramount, co. Wexford, and Dunbane, co. Tipperary, and of Aston Lodge, Bournemouth, J.P. co. Cork, formerly 17th Lancers, b. 9 Dec. 1823, d. unm. 19 Aug. 1906.
   1. Sophy, b. 2 Jan. 1821; m. Capt. Lindesay Shedden, 17th Lancers.
   2. Louisa Hobson, b. 2 June, 1829; m. Maj. Graves C. S. Lombard, late 16th Regt., and d. 29 Aug. 1900.
   2. Sophia, m. Capt. William Doyle, son of Gen. Doyle.
   3. Louisa Editha, m. 8 Feb. 1831, William H. B. J. Wilson, of Knowle Hall, co. Warwick.

Mr. Le Hunte was s. in his estates by his three daus. and coheirs. His brother and heir male,

WILLIAM AUGUSTUS LE HUNTE, b. 25 Oct. 1774, High Sheriff co. Wexford 1817; m. 1st, Martha (or Patty), only dau. of George Warburton, of Garryhisch, King's Co., M.P., but by her had no issue. He m. 2ndly, Isabella Maria, eldest dau. of Lieut.-Col. Huson, Wexford Militia, by whom (who d. 1809) he had a dau.,
   1. Alicia (commonly called Isabella), m. Rev. Robert Cooper, Rector of Agbade, and d. 16 Sept. 1883, aged 74.

He m. 3rdly, Henrietta Eliza, dau. of Rev. Joseph Miller, and d. 1820, leaving issue,
1. GEORGE, of whom presently.
2. WILLIAM AUGUSTUS, of Knocknalier, J.P., b. 28 Jan. 1819; d. unm. 14 March, 1878.
3. Francis (Rev.), b. 8 Jan. 1820; Rector of St. Mary's, New Ross, co. Wexford; m. 12 Jan. 1860, Eleanor Barbara, dau. of George Robert Magrath, of Rutland Square, Dublin, and d. 2 Jan. 1900.
2. Harriet Josephine, d. young.
3. Patty Warburton, d. young.
4. Maria, d. unm. 21 Oct. 1884.
5. Marianne, d. unm. 4 Jan. 1900.
6. Editha Christian, m. Rev. Yarburgh Gamaliel Lloyd, of Sewerby, Yorks, who has taken the name of GREAME.

The eldest son,
GEORGE LE HUNTE, of Artramont House, co. Wexford (which he purchased from his cousins), J.P. and D.L., and High Sheriff 1838, M.A. Trin. Coll. Cambridge, b. 15 June, 1815; m. 5 Aug. 1845, Mary, 5th dau. of the Right Hon. Edward Pennefather, Lord Chief Justice of Ireland (see PENNEFATHER of Rathsallagh). She d. 8 May, 1900. He d. 1891, having had issue,
1. GEORGE RUTHVEN (Sir), now of Artramont House.
2. Richard, Lieut. R.N., b. 8 Sept. 1854; d. unm. 1876.
1. Mary Harriet.
2. Ellen Lily.
3. Margaret Dora.

Arms—Vert, a saltire or. Crest—A lion sejant or. Motto—Parcere prostratis.

Seat—Artramont House, Castlebridge, co. Wexford. Club—Travellers'.

LEIGH OF ROSEGARLAND.

FRANCIS ROBERT LEIGH, of Rosegarland, co. Wexford, J.P., late 3rd Batt. Royal Irish Regt., b. 27 April, 1853; m. 19 March, 1903, Elizabeth Scott, dau. of the late Barton Bell, of Blackhall, Lanark. N.B., and has issue,
1. FRANCIS EDWARD, b. 1907.
2. Robert, b.
1. Augustine Anne Leigh, b. 25 Dec. 1903.
2. A dau.
3. A Dau.

Lineage.—FRANCIS MACLAOIGHSIGH, MACLYSACH, MACLYE, or LYE, petitioned for a lease of the dissolved monastery town and lands of the Holy Cross of Killeigh, near Geashill, King's Co., 1551, and obtained a lease of them next year; two months after, 30 Nov. 1552, he obtained a grant of English liberty to enable him to hold the lands. He m. the dau. of John O'Carrol, and had issue,
1. JOHN, his successor.
2. Arthur, living in 1612, and mentioned in his brother's will in remainder to his estates.
3. Francis, in the Army, appointed 6 Sept. 1579.
4. Henry, living in 1612.

Francis MacLaoighsigh or Lye was dead in 1573, and his lands were in possession of his eldest son,

JOHN MACLAOIGHSIGH, LYE, or LY, who having a perfect knowledge of the English language as well as the Irish, was appointed Interpreter to the State, and was granted for his services as interpreter, by patent dated 9 May, 1584, 20 Queen ELIZABETH, the fee of the monastery of Killeigh, which he then held under the lease made to his father, and obtained a grant of Rathbride, co. Kildare, dated 1 June, 1591. He m. Amy, dau. of George FitzGerald, of Ticroghan, co. Meath, and sister of Sir Edward FitzGerald, Knt. of the same place, and had issue,
1. JOHN, his heir.   2. Andrew, a minor in 1612.
1. Katherine, m. James FitzGerald, of Osberston, co. Kildare.

2. Mabel.   3. Mary.
4. Margaret.   5. Bridget.
6. Amy.   7. Ellen.

John MacLaoighsigh, or Ly, d. 7 May, 1612, and was bur. at the Cathedral of Kildare, where his tombstone still remains. He was s. by his eldest son,

JOHN LEIGH, of Rathbride, who with his mother having alienated some of his father's lands, got a pardon for alienation dated 14 Dec. 1613. He had by his wife, whose name was Dowdall, the following issue,
1. FRANCIS, his heir.
2. Robert, who was abroad with CHARLES II during CROMWELL's time, and after the Restoration, as a reward for his faithful and loyal services, got a grant of the manor of Rosegarland, co. Wexford, by the several letters patent dated 18 May, 1668, and 9 Sept. 1669, and by other letters patent the manors of Colpe, alias Newbawn, Longrague, Garry Richard, 3,344 acres, and other lands in the cost Wexford and Kildare. He m. Oct. 1673, Margaret, dau. of Sir Cæsar Colclough, 2nd bart. of Tintern Abbey, co. Wexford, aud sister and heir of Sir Cæsar Colclough, 3rd and last bart., by whom (who d. 1722) he had no issue. On his marriage he assumed the additional name and arms of COLCLOUGH. By his will, dated 4 May, 1694, and proved 11 June, 1695, he bequeathed his estates to his nephew, as below.
1. Mabel, m. 1675, James Barnewall.

John Leigh d. abroad and intestate. Administration was granted 5 May, 1660, to his eldest son,

FRANCIS LEIGH, of Rosegarland. who was appointed Escheator-General of Leinster by letters patent dated 22 July, 1663, and M.P. for the borough of Kildare, 1689. Having supported JAMES II, he was attainted of high treason in 1691, when all his lands were forfeited. He m. Feb. 1662, Judith, dau. of Henry Spencer, by whom he had,
1. ROBERT, who was executor and heir of his uncle, Robert Leigh-Colclough, d. unm.; administration granted to his brother Francis, 7 Nov. 1724.
2. John, of Dublin, d. unm.; administration granted to his brother Robert, 20 July, 1700.
3. Andrew, of Friarstown, co. Kildare, d. unm.; administration granted to his brother Francis, 30 Nov. 1706.
4. FRANCIS, of whom presently.
1. Judith, d. unm. 1700.

The 4th son,
FRANCIS LEIGH, of Rathangan, co. Kildare, s. his brother in the Wexford estate, and became of Rosegarland. He m. 1st, Sept. 1699, Alice, widow of John Rawlins of Rathangan, by whom (who d. 1702) he had no issue; he m. 2ndly, Miss Carew, by whom he had issue,
1. JOHN, his heir.
2. Robert, a Free Burgess of New Ross 1730, d. unm. 1734.
3. Andrew, a Free Burgess of New Ross 1735, d. unm. 1745.
1. Cecilia, m. 1729, Joseph, 1st Earl of Milltown, and d. 1737.
2. Judith, d. unm. 1738.   3. Mary.

Mr. Leigh d. 1727, and was s. by his eldest son,

JOHN LEIGH, of Rosegarland, M.P. for New Ross from 1727 to 1758; m. July, 1727, Mary, dau. of John Cliffe, of Mulrancan, co. Wexford, by whom he had
ROBERT, his heir.
Grace, m. 20 May, 1758, Anthony, 8th Earl of Meath, and d. 20 Oct. 1812.

Mr. Leigh, whose will, dated 2 April, 1751, was proved 27 Sept. 1758, was s. by his only son,

ROBERT LEIGH, of Rosegarland, b. 1729, M.P. for New Ross from 1759 to 1800, D.L. co. Wexford, and appointed Lieut.-Col. of the Wexford Militia 1763; m. 9 Feb. 1750-1, Arabella, dau. of Robert Leslie, of Glasslough, co. Monaghan, by whom he had,
1. FRANCIS, his heir.
2. Charles, Major in the Army, d. unm.
3. Joseph, of Tinnakilly, co. Wicklow, Collector of the town of Wicklow, 1799, m. Aug. 1797, Mary, dau. of Stephen Radcliffe, Judge of the Prerogative Court, and had issue,
   1. Stephen, d. unm.
   1. Ellen, m. 10 Feb. 1836, Charles Arthur Walker, of Tykillen, V.-L. co. Wexford, M.P.   2. Arabella.
   3. Mary Anne.
1. Arabella, m. June, 1782, Ponsonby Tottenham, M.P. for Fethard, and d. 2 Aug. 1806.

Mr. Leigh, whose will, dated 10 April, 1802, was proved 10 May, 1803, was s. by his eldest son,

FRANCIS LEIGH, of Rosegarland, b. 1755, Collector of Wexford 1794, Sovereign of New Ross 1799. He m. Dec. 1788, Grace, dau. of Richard Baldwin, by whom he had,
1. John Robert, m. Feb. 1822, Dorothea Anne, dau. of Edward FitzGerald, of Carrigoran, co. Clare; and d. in his father's lifetime, 7 July, 1827, leaving by her (who m. 2ndly, 7 Sept. 1832, Hervey Francis de Montmorency; see BURKE's Peerage, FRANKFORT, V.),
   1. FRANCIS AUGUSTINE, late of Rosegarland.
   2. Charles Edward, b. 1823, formerly in the 90th Foot; m. 1853, Elizabeth Anne, dau. of — Parker, of Hanslope Park, co. Bucks, and d.s.p. at Paris, Nov. 1867.
2. Charles, b. 1797; d. unm. 1821.
3. Francis, of Siou, co. Wexford, b. 1808; High Sheriff of Wexford 1837; m. June, 1830, Mary Martin, dau. of John Southcote Mansergh, of Grenane, co. Tipperary (see that family), and d. 20 Feb. 1882, having had issue,
   1. Francis Charles, formerly Lieut. Wexford Militia, b. 1851, d. 1902.
   2. John Robert, d. unm.   3. Charles, d. unm.
   4. Leslie Cecil Hore.

1. Grace Mary, m. George King, Major 53rd Regt.
2. Mary Arabella, m. July, 1854, Percy Lorenzo Harvey, of Kyle and Lonsdale, co. Wexford, who d. 1880 leaving issue (see HARVEY of Bargy Castle).
3. Elizabeth Kate Ellen, d. unm.
4. Dorothea Olivia, d. unm.
1. Cecilia, m. Major-Gen. Thomas Hore, and d. 28 July, 1868.
2. Grace, b. 1791; d. 1798.   3. Mary, d. unm.

Mr. Leigh, who was M.P. for Wexford from 1793 to 1802, d. 1839, when he was s. by his grandson,

FRANCIS AUGUSTINE LEIGH, of Rosegarland, co. Wexford, J.P. and D.L., High Sheriff 1867, formerly Lieut. 10th Hussars, b. 24 Nov. 1822; m. Augustine, dau. of Mons. Charles Perrier, of Metz, in the Province of Lorraine, and by her (who d. 22 Nov. 1880) had issue,
1. FRANCIS ROBERT, now of Rosegarland.
2. Edward, Major Hampshire Regt., b. 25 Aug. 1867.
1. Rose Jane, m. 3 June, 1903, F. King.
2. Frances.
3. Jane, m. 28 Sept. 1897, G. H. Lambert, of Carnagh, co. Wexford (see that family).

Mr. Leigh s. his grandfather 1839, and d. 1900.

Arms—Arg., two bars az. a bend compony counter-compony gu. and or. Crest—A dexter hand lying fesswavs couped at the wrist holding a sword erect impaling three gory heads all ppr. Motto—Conlan-a-bu.

Seat—Rosegarland, New Ross, co. Wexford.

LEIGH-WHITE. See WHITE.

LENDRUM OF MAGHERACROSS.

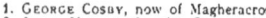

GEORGE COSBY LENDRUM, of Magheracross, co. Fermanagh, J.P., D.L. co. Fermanagh, High Sheriff 1875, J.P. co. Tyrone, High Sheriff 1882, b. 22 April, 1846; m. 10 Dec. 1878, Antoinette Frances, eldest dau. of Antoine Sloet Butler, C.B., late Capt. 7th Dragoon Guards, and has issue,
1. JAMES BUTLER, b. 14 Sept. 1880.
2. George Waller, b. 5 Aug. 1882.
3. Marcus Beresford, b. 11 Oct. 1883.
4. Alan Cane, b. 11 July, 1885.
1. Anne, m. 7 Feb. 1905, Alexander George Dalgety (see DALGETY of Lockerley Hall).

Lineage.—JAMES LENDRUM, of Corlea, co. Tyrone, was father of

GEORGE LENDRUM, of Moorfield, co. Tyrone, m. Mary, dau. of John Story, of Corick, near Clogher, co. Tyrone, elder brother of Right Rev. Joseph Story, D.D., Bishop of Kilmore, and had issue,
1. JAMES, his heir.   2. Thomas (Rev.).
3. Joseph (Rev.), Prebendary of Coolstuffe, Diocese of Ferns, co. Wexford.   4. John, Major H.E.I.C.S.
1. John, m. 22 Dec. 1767, John Richards, of Dublin, Barrister-at-Law, and d. 1822, leaving issue,
  1. John (father of John William Richards, of Barnagh, co. Mayo (see RICHARDS of Macmine).
  2. George (Rev.), Rector of Coolstuffe (father of John Richards, of Macmine, co. Wexford).
  1. Hannah, m. Mr. Hamilton, of Sea View, co. Donegal.
  2. Frances Anne, m. Rev. Thomas Skelton.
2. Anne, d. unm.
3. Rebecca, m. Rev. Hugh Nevin, LL.D., Rector of Derryvolan, co. Fermanagh, Prebendary of Kilskerry, Diocese of Clogher.

The eldest son,
JAMES LENDRUM, fixed his residence at Magheracross, co. Fermanagh, and changed its name to "Jamestown." He m. 1st, Nov. 1770, Ann, dau. of William Young, of Coolkeiragh House, co. Derry, by Letitia Hamilton his wife; and 2ndly, July, 1812, Margaret Young, of Loughesk, co. Donegal. By the former lady Mr. Leadrum had (with a dau., Letitia, who d. unm.) an only son,

GEORGE LENDRUM, of Jamestown, J.P. and D.L., High Sheriff co. Fermanagh 1806, and Tyrone 1819, b. 24 Aug. 1776; m. 28 April, 1805, Mary Jane, 3rd dau. of Henry Coddington, of Oldbridge, co. Meath, by Elizabeth his wife, dau. of Lathom Blacker, of Rathescar, co. Louth, and had issue,
JAMES, his successor.
Elizabeth, m. Aug. 1831, the Rev. Cosby Stopford Mangan, Incumbent of Derrynoose, co. Armagh.

Mr. Lendrum d. 22 Oct. 1855, and was s. by his son,
JAMES LENDRUM, of Magheracross, J.P. and D.L. for cos. Fermanagh and Tyrone, High Sheriff co. Fermanagh 1835, and co. Tyrone 1837, B.A. Cantab. 1830 (Trin. Coll.), b. 12 Jan. 1806; m. 2 Nov. 1843, Anne, eldest dau. of Samuel Vesey, of Derrabard, and by her (who d. 1876) had issue,

1. GEORGE COSBY, now of Magheracross.
2. James Vesey (twin with George), Maj. Seaforth Highlanders, m. Constance Eccles, and d. 2 Nov. 1890, leaving issue, one son, Charles.   3. William Trevor, b. 4 July, 1854.
4. Samuel Edward Lathom, b. 10 Sept. 1855; d. 30 April, 1879.
1. Rosabelle Frances, m. C. R. Walker, 21st Fusiliers, and has issue, two sons and one dau.
2. Mary Jane Waller, m. D. Carleton, late Capt. 21st Fusiliers, and had issue, three sons and one dau.
3. Elizabeth Alice, d. 15 Oct. 1906.

Arms—Gu., three garbs or, on a chief arg., as many woolpacks, sa.   Crest—On a mount vert, a dove holding an olive branch in its beak all ppr.   Motto—La paix.

Seat—Magheracross (the ancient name restored), Ballinamallard, co. Fermanagh.   Residence—Corkil, Kilskeery, co. Tyrone.

RYAN-LENIGAN OF CASTLE FFOGERTY.

JOHN VIVIAN RYAN-LENIGAN, of Castle ffogerty, co. Tipperary, J.P. and D.L., High Sheriff 1887, late Lieut.-Col. Commanding Tipperary Artillery Militia, assumed by Royal Licence, Dec. 1878, the additional surname of LENIGAN, in compliance with the testamentary injunction of his cousin, Penelope Elizabeth Marie Lenigan, of Castle ffogerty, b. 1831.

Lineage.—The chief of the sept in 1583,
CONOHER NA SURY O'FFOGERTY, of Munroe, co. Tipperary, was father of
DONOUGH O'FFOGERTY, who was slain in battle at Lateragh (his father then living) 26 Nov. 1583, and was the Donough who m. Ellen Purcell, of the ancient baronial family of Logsmoe, and lies bur. in the Abbey of Holy Cross, to which he was a considerable benefactor. He was s. by his son,
DONALD O'FFOGERTY, of Munroe, surnamed Grany (or the Illfavoured), whose son and heir,
DONOUGH O'FFOGERTY, of Inchy O'ffogerty, Fishmoyne, and Bally ffogerty (now Castle ffogerty), left two sons,
1. ROGER, his successor.
2. William, of Fishmoyne, Physician to His Majesty King CHARLES II, who, under the charge of being concerned in the Meal-Tub Plot, was imprisoned in the Tower, and d. there s.p. in 1665. This is the gentleman described in the Act of Settlement as Ensign William ffogerty, and who under that Act is included amongst those exempted from confiscation. His will bears date in 1666.

The eldest son and heir,
ROGER O'FFOGERTY, of Inchy O'ffogerty, m. a dau. of Cashuy, and was s. by his son,
TEIGE, or TIMOTHY, O'FFOGERTY, of Bally ffogerty, &c., m. Margaret, dau. of Burke, of Barrycurry (of the family of Lord Brittas), and had issue,
1. CORNELIUS, his heir.
2. Thomas, m. Anne, dau. of James Magrath, of Derrymore, and had a son, Magrath ffogerty, who was father of Thomas ffogerty and grandfather of Magrath ffogerty, of Ballinlonty, and of Philip ffogerty, Barrister-at-Law.
3. John.   4. Dionysius, a priest.
5. Malachy, Doctor of the Sorbonne and Prefect of the College of Lombard, Paris, anno 1705.

The eldest son and heir,
CORNELIUS FFOGERTY, of Castle ffogerty, b. 14 May, 1661, Capt. in the Army of King JAMES II; m. in 1696, Mary, dau. of Michael Kearney, of Milestown, co. Tipperary, and dying in 1730, was s. by his son,
TEIGE, or TIMOTHY, FFOGERTY, of Castle ffogerty, who d.s.p. at the age of 50, in 1747, and was s. by his brother,
THOMAS FFOGERTY, of Castle ffogerty, m. Christian, dau. and eventual heir of James Meyler, of Sallymount, co. Kildare, and had issue,
1. JAMES, his heir.
2. Thomas, Capt. in the Regt. of Ultonia, in the Spanish service, d. unm. in 1781.
1. ELIZABETH, m. WILLIAM LENIGAN, of Zoar, co. Kilkenny, and by him (who d. 23 Nov. 1768) left an only son,
THOMAS LENIGAN.

Mr. ffogerty d. 1758, and was s. by his eldest son.
JAMES FFOGERTY, of Castle ffogerty, who, having conformed to the Established Church, served the office of High Sheriff for co. Tipperary, 1783. He d. unm. 1788, when his sister, ELIZABETH LENIGAN, became his heir, and the estates passed through her to her only son,
THOMAS (JEAN BAPTISTE) LENIGAN, who thus became " of Castle ffogerty." This gentleman m. 1st, in April, 1794, Peniel, dau. of Edmund Armstrong, of Buncraggy, co. Clare (by his wife Hannah, sister of Robert Henry Westropp), and by her (who d. April, 1804, had issue,
1. JAMES, of Castle ffogerty.
2. Edmund, b. 8 Aug. 1798; d. unm. 6 June, 1836.
1. Anna Elizabeth, m. 1824, John Denis Ryan, Lieut. 13th Dragoons, 2nd surviving son of George Ryan, of Inch, co. Tipperary (see that family). He d. 1863. She d. 28 June, 1865, leaving issue,
  1. George, Lieut.-Col. late commanding 70th Regt.
  2. JOHN VIVIAN, now of Castle ffogerty.

3. Valentine, Hon. Major-Gen. (retired), late Lieut.-Col. North Staffordshire Regt., b. 19 Oct. 1833, has had issue by Bertha, his wife, who d. 10 Sept. 1903,
(1) Valentine John Eustace, of Thomastown Park, King's Co., High Sheriff 1910, Lieut. R.A., b. 12 Dec. 1882.
(2) Lionel, d. in India, April, 1903.
1. Penelope, d. unm. 25 Dec. 1887.
2. Nina. 3. Emma.
4. Marian. 5. Elizabeth.
2. Elizabeth, d. unm. 1883. 3. Henrietta.
Mr. Lenigan m. 2ndly, Clarinda, dau. of John O'Reilly, of Mount Street, Dublin, and had by her two other daus.,
4. Mary, a nun. 5. Rosetta.
He d. 2 Aug. 1825, and was s. by his son,
JAMES LENIGAN, of Castle ffogerty, J.P. and D.L., M.R.I.A., M.A. of Trin. Coll. Dublin, b. 23 June, 1797; m. 30 April, 1825, Eleanor Frances, dau. of John Evans, and sister of William Evans, M.P. for Leominster, by whom he had two daus.,
1. Sarah Ellen Henrietta, d. at Munich, in Bavaria, 30 March, 1842.
2. PENELOPE ELIZABETH MARIE, of Castle ffogerty, who d. at Badgstein, Austria, 3 Aug. 1878, having devised her estates to her cousin, the present Lieut.-Col. J. VIVIAN RYAN-LENIGAN, of Castle ffogerty.

Seat—Castle ffogerty, Thurles.

BARRETT-LENNARD.

See BURKE'S PEERAGE, **BARRETT-LENNARD**, Bart.

LENOX-CONYNGHAM. See CONYNGHAM.

LENTAIGNE OF TALLAGHT.

JOSEPH HUSSEY NUGENT LENTAIGNE, J.P. co. Dublin, B.A. Trin. Coll. Dublin, Barrister-at-Law, Clerk of the Crown, and Hanaper and Permanent Sec. to the Lord Chancellor of Ireland, b. 30 May, 1847.

Lineage.—This family is of ancient descent in Normandy. MICHEL LENTAIGNE m. Magdalene Brenet, and d. 1695, leaving (with a younger son, Michel, Sieur des Moulins) an elder son,
RICHARD LENTAIGNE, Sieur de la Croix, m. Jeanne, dau. of Pierre Haye, Sieur de la Lorière. She d. 1741. He d. 1720, leaving,
1. Gabriel, a Capucin.
2. Pierre, b. 1687; m. 1710, Marie Le Roy, who d. 1768. He d. 1732, and was ancestor of Lentaigne, Counts de Logivière.
3. Robert, b. 1689; d. 1724; his only dau., Jeanne, d. unm.
4. Jean Richard, b. 1697; d. 1773; m. Anne Magdeleine, dau. of Jacques Lehot Duférage, and had issue (with two daus., one m. 1771, M. Augustin de Marescot de Villeuil, and the other, M. de Quéens), Antoine Charles, m. 1774, Marie Therese Foucques, de Marencour; and the Rev. Jacques Lentaigne, D.D., Curé de St. Sauveur, and Rector of the University of Caen, who d. in Dublin, 25 Jan. 1802. 5. JEAN FRANÇOIS, of whom hereafter.
1. Ambroise, m. 1723, Raulin le Montier, Sieur de la Bectière.
The 5th son,
JEAN FRANÇOIS LENTAIGNE, Capitaine de la Compagnie de St. Etienne de Caen, b. June, 1699; d. 1780; m. 27 March, 1724, Marie Anne Lehot Duférage. Their eldest son,
PIERRE FRANCOIS LENTAIGNE, "Lieut. de Dragoons," et Juge Consul, b. 24 Feb. 1725; m. 1766, Anne Marguerite, b. 1740, dau. of Guillaume François Paisant Duclos, son of Jean Paisant Duclos, by Rachel his wife (m. 1701; d. 1710), dau. of Elie de Cussy, and d 14 May, 1802, leaving issue,
1. JEAN FRANÇOIS, b. 11 Sept. 1768, guillotined 1793.
2. Joseph, b. 8 Jan. 1770; guillotined 1793.
3. BENJAMIN, of whom we treat.
4. Simeon, b. 1775; m. 1807, Rose, dau. of Jean Edouard Blacher, by Marie Anne Mitchelle Delaunay his wife, and d. 1845, leaving two sons,
1. Abel Edouard Marie, b. 11 Oct. 1808, Chevalier de la Legion d'Honneur, Juge al Tribunal Civil de Caen, et Conseiller à la Cour Impériale, d. 1877, leaving one son,
Edward. Juge à la Cour Civile de Falaise.

2. Ismael Jean Zachurie Simeon, b. 2 April, 1820; d. 1874, leaving two daus.,
(1) Marie, m. 30 April, 1877, M. Edouard Valbrey.
(2) Louise, m. 27 Oct. 1878. M. Lucien Noel.
1. Jeanne, m. 1791, Nicholas Hervieu Duclos, and left issue.
The 3rd son,
BENJAMIN LENTAIGNE, M.D., F.R.C.P., b. 14 Feb. 1773, emigrated in 1792 to England, and settled as a physician in the city of Dublin; m. 24 July, 1799, Maria Therese, dau. and eventually heir of John O'Neill, Catholic Delegate, 1792 (of the O'Neills of Lower Clanaboy), son of Patrick Francis O'Neill, by Catherine his wife, dau. of Hugh Macquire, of Churchtown, of the line of Tempo. By her (who d. 24 May, 1820) Dr. Lentaigne had three sons and one dau.,
1. JOHN (Right Hon. Sir), P.C., C.B., of Talaght.
2. Joseph (Very Rev.), M.A. Trin. Coll. Dublin, and University of Melbourne, N.S.W., formerly a Barrister, afterwards in Holy Orders of the Church of Rome, b. 27 July, 1805; d. Dec. 1885.
3. Benjamin Plunkett, b. 1809; d. in infancy.
1. Mary Anne, d. unm. 11 Dec. 1867.
Dr. Lentaigne d. 19 Oct. 1873. His son,
RIGHT HON. SIR JOHN FRANCIS O'NEILL LENTAIGNE, P.C., C.B., of Tallaght, co. Dublin, J.P. and D.L. for co. Monaghan, High Sheriff of the latter co. 1844, Knt. of the Order of Pius IX, B.A., Inspector-General of Prisons in Ireland 1854-77, and Commissioner of National Education, b. 21 June, 1803; m. 13 Sept. 1841, Mary, dau. and co-heir of Francis Magan, J.P. of Emoe, Westmeath, and by her (who d. 8 May, 1887) had issue,
1. JOSEPH HUSSEY NUGENT, present representative.
2. Victor Walter (Rev.), b. 27 Oct. 1848.
3. John Vincent O'Neill (Sir), B.A., Trin. Coll. Dublin, L.K.Q.P.I., F.R.C.S.I. (42 Merrion Square, Dublin), b. 19 July, 1855; m. 20 Feb. 1882, Phillis Mary (d. 1893), only dau. of the late John W. Coffey, and has issue,
1. Edward Charles. 2. Benjamin.
3. A son, b. 11 Dec. 1887.
1. Mary Sydney.
4. Henry Ængus Westenra, Trin. Coll. Dublin, b. 19 Aug. 1857; m. 6 Oct. 1885, Emily, eldest dau. of the late — Hepburn, of Bothwell House, Sydney, Australia, and d. 18 Aug. 1887, leaving issue. 5. Benjamin Plunkett, b. 28 March, 1865.
1. Mary Theresa, a Sister of Charity.
2. Margaret Mary, a nun.
Sir John d. 12 Nov. 1886.

Arms—Or, on a chevron az. between three martlets sa. a fleur-de-lis of the 1st, a chief of the 2nd, charged with three mullets arg. quartering O'NEILL and PLUNKETT. Crest—A dove with wings endorsed ppr. charged on the breast with a mullet arg. and holding in the bill a fleur-de-lis or and charged on the breast with a mullet az. Mottoes—Dieu ayde. Over the crest—Pro fide, rege, et patria pugno.

Seat—Tallaght, co. Dublin. Club—Stephen's Green, Dublin.

LESLIE OF TARBERT HOUSE.

ROBERT LESLIE, of Tarbert House, co. Kerry, J.P. and D.L., High Sheriff 1864, late Capt. Kerry Militia, b. 1825; m. 1867, Melicent Agnes, eldest dau. of the late Richard Chute, D.L., of Chute Hall, co. Kerry, and has issue.
1. CECIL ROWLAND, J.P. co. Kerry, High Sheriff 1911, Capt. and Hon. Major 3rd Batt. Royal Munster Fus., b. 1874.
2. Walter Edward, b. 1876.
1. Theodora Rose. 2. May.

Lineage.—JOHN LESLIE accompanied to Ireland, with his brother James, their cousin-german, John Leslie, D.D. Oxon, who was translated from the see of Orkney, and made Bishop of Raphoe in 1633. All three took an active part against the rebels in 1641. The above-mentioned John Leslie m. Catherine, dau. of Rev. Alexander Conyngham, Dean of Raphoe, and had (with a dau., Catherine, m. Rev. James Hamilton, Archdeacon of Raphoe) a son,
JOHN LESLIE, who raised in 1688, a company of Foot and a troop of Dragoons, and at their head performed services so important that the King rewarded him by grants of estates. He m. Marion, dau. of Rev. Humphrey Galbraith, by Mabel his wife, 4th dau. of Sir Paul Gore, Bart., of Manor Gore, and d. in 1700, leaving issue,
1. John, who fell at Aughrim, d. unm.
2. JAMES, of whom presently.
3. George (Rev.), D.D., Rector of Clones and afterwards of Kilmore, m. 1711, Margaret, sister of Col. Alexander Montgomery, M.P., of Convoy House (see MONTGOMERY of Beaulieu), and had issue,
1. James (Rev.), D.D., Prebendary of Durham.
2. George LESLIE-MONTGOMERY, of Ballyconnell, co. Cavan, M.P. for Strabane 1761-8, and for co. Cavan 1769-87, s. his maternal uncle at Ballyconnell and assumed the name and arms of MONTGOMERY, m. 1752, Hannah, 2nd dau. of the Right Hon. Nathaniel Clements, M.P., and sister of 1st Earl of Leitrim, and d. 1787, leaving issue,
(1) George, d. unm.
(2) Hannah, m. Rev. Joseph Story.
(2) Alicia, m. Nathaniel Sneyd, M.P., and d.s.p.
(3) Mary, d. unm. (4) Nathalina, d. unm.
1. Margaret, d. unm.
2. Catherine, m. William Hamilton, of Dunnymana, co. Tyrone.

and had two children. Her dau. Margaret, m. 1 Oct. 1763, John Enery, of Bawnboy, co. Cavan, High Sheriff for that co. 1759, and for co. Fermanagh 1764, and had a son, Lieut.-Col. John Enery, of Bawnboy, who s. to Ballyconnell, and a dau., Maty Enery, m. 10 Sept. 1793, Adam Nixon, 3rd son of Alexander Nixon, of Nixon Hall, co. Fermanagh.
1. Elizabeth, d. young.
2. Isabella, m. Thomas Knox.
3. Lettice, m. Walter Johnston, of Kilmore, co. Fermanagh, and had issue (see JOHNSTON *of Magheramena*).
4. Catherine, m. Thomas Enraght.

The son and heir,
JAMES LESLIE, settled in Kerry, and m. Sarah, dau. of Col. Kellie, and had, with a dau., three sons,
1. John, his heir, left an only dau.,
   Lucy, who m. Robert FitzGerald, Knt. of Kerry.
   John was s. by his brother.
2. JAMES, of whom presently.
3. Robert, m. Aphra, dau. of Richard Babington, and had a son,
   ROBERT, of whom presently, and three daus.

The 2nd son,
THE RIGHT REV. JAMES LESLIE, D.D., Bishop of Limerick and Prebendary of Durham, inherited the estates at the death of his brother John. He m. Joyce, dau. of Anthony Lyster, and sister and co-heir of Thomas Lyster, of Lysterfield, co. Roscommon, and d. 24 Nov. 1770, aged 64. She d. 8 Feb. 1773, aged 62 (will dated 5 Oct. 1772, proved 6 July, 1780), leaving issue,
1. EDWARD (Sir), of whom presently.
2. Richard (Rev.), s. in right of his mother to her half of the Lysterfield estates.
   1. Mary Anne, m. Francis Warren Bonham.
   2. Catherine, m. 1779, James Scott of Willsboro, co. Derry, and had issue (*see that family*).
   3. Martha, m. July, 1785, Rev. James Lowry, of Rockdale, co. Tyrone.

The elder son,
SIR EDWARD LESLIE, Bart., of Tarbert House, co. Kerry, M.P. for Old Leighlin, was created a bart. 3 Sept. 1787. He m. Anne, dau. of Col. Cane, of the Royal Dragoons, M.P. for Tallagh, and left at his decease a dau. and heir,
Catherine, m. 16 June, 1807, Lord Douglas Gordon Hallyburton of Pitcur, who d. 25 Dec. 1841. She d. 2 Oct. 1851 (see BURKE's *Peerage and Baronetage*, HUNTLY, M.).
Sir Edward was s. by his cousin-german,
ROBERT LESLIE, of Tarbert House, co. Kerry, son of Robert Leslie, and Aphra Babington his wife. He m. 1790, Frances Anne, dau. of Pierse Crosbie, of Ballyheigue Castle (*see that family*), and had issue, three sons and two daus. The eldest son,
ROBERT LESLIE, of Tarbert House, b. 1792; m. 1823, Margaret, dau. of William Sandes, of Pyrmont, co. Kerry, and d. 1827, having by her (who m. 2ndly, 20 May, 1841, Lieut.-Col. James Duff Paterson, afterwards MacIver Campbell, of Asknish (*see that family*) had issue,
ROBERT, now of Tarbert House.
Aphra, m. Com. Spencer H. Pickard. R.N., and had one son and two daus.

Seat—Tarbert House, Tarbert, co. Kerry.

LESLIE OF BALLYWARD.

JOHN LESLIE, of Ballyward Lodge, Banbridge, co. Down, formerly Lieut. 5th Fusiliers and Capt. Donegal Militia, b. 31 May, 1839; m. 11 Feb. 1862, Harriet Anne, 3rd dau. of Sir David William Barclay, 3rd Bart. (see BURKE's *Peerage*), and has issue,

May Florence de Rune, m. 9 Aug. 1888, Col. Frank Robert Lowth, C.B., late Lincolnshire Regt., and has issue,
1. Francis Robert Leslie, Lieut. Lancashire Fus., b. 1889.
2. John Leslie, b. 1890.
3. Norman Charles Leslie, b. 1891.
4. William Barclay Leslie, b. 1893.
1. Doris May Leslie.

Lineage.—SIR WILLIAM LESLIE. Knt, 4th Baron of Balquhain, descended from a common ancestor with the Earls of Rothes, was knighted at the coronation of JAMES I. He m. 1st, Elizabeth, dau. of Sir Alexander Fraser of Lovat, and had issue,
1. Alexander, from whom the family of Leslie of Balquhain, co. Aberdeen,
2. WILLIAM, of whom presently.
1. Galdaea, m. John Barclay, of Garthlie, co. Aberdeen.
Sir William m. 2ndly, Agnes, dau. of Alexander Irvine, of Drum,

and by her was ancestor of Leslie, of Wardis, Bart.; Leslie, of New Leslie; Leslie, of Kininvie; and Leslie, Viscount Baigownie. He m. 3rdly, Euphemia, dau. of Sir William Lindsay, of Cairnie, Fifeshire, and by her was ancestor of Leslie, of Pitcaple. The younger son by his first marriage,
WILLIAM LESLIE, of Kincraigie, co. Fife, m. Mary, dau. of Francis Ross, of Auchlossin, co. Aberdeen, and had an only son,
WILLIAM LESLIE, of Kincraigie, co. Fife, m. Elizabeth, dau. of Robert Strachan,.of Balhousie, co. Forfar, and had issue,
1. ALEXANDER, of whom presently.
2. Patrick, of Lochtolloch, co. Aberdeen.   3. James, d.s.p.
1. Elizabeth, m. John Lichton, of Ulisheavin, co. Forfar.

The eldest son,
ALEXANDER LESLIE, of Kincraigie, m. Margaret, dau. of George Gordon, of Halhead, co. Aberdeen, and had issue,
1. GEORGE, of whom presently.
2. John, of Durno, co. Aberdeen, m. 1st, Johanna, dau. of John Gordon, of Braco, and had issue. He m. 2ndly, the dau. of John Patterson, of Edinburgh, but by her had no issue.
1. Margaret, m. George Leslie, of Crichie.

The elder son,
GEORGE LESLIE, of Kincraigie, m. Mary, dau. of Patrick Leith, of Edingarrock, and had issue,
1. PATRICK (Sir), of whom presently.   2. Alexander.
1. Isabella, m. Alexander Leslie, of Warthelle.
2. Margaret, m. Alexanderson, of Edinburgh.
3. Elizabeth, m. Walter Mearnes, of Aberdeen.

The eldest son,
SIR PATRICK LESLIE, Knt., of Kincraigie, Provost of Aberdeen, m. Jane, dau. of John Leslie, 10th Baron of Balquhain, and had issue,
1. George, of Kincraigie, m. Magdalen, dau. of William Wood, of Bonnietoun, Midlothian, and had issue.
2. JOHN, of whom we treat.

The second son,
JOHN LESLIE, of the City of Aberdeen, m. Margery, dau. of William Strachan, of Tippartie, co. Banff, and had issue,
1. PATRICK, of whom presently.
2. William, settled and d. in America.
1. Isabella, m. 1st, — Forbes, of Touch, and 2ndly, William Guthrie, of Guthrie.
2. Margery, m. William Leslie, of Wardis.

The elder son,
PATRICK LESLIE, settled in Ireland, m. Mary, dau. of John Forbes, of the City of Aberdeen, and had issue, a son,
JOHN LESLIE, of Durosamount, now called Kincraigie, co. Donegal, who settled in Ireland about 1705, and had issue, with a dau., Margaret, wife of — Ritchie, a son,
CHARLES LESLIE, of Kincraigie, co. Donegal, m. Elizabeth, dau. of John Griffith, of Dublin, and who left issue, a son,
THE VEN. CHARLES LESLIE, D.D., Archdeacon and Vicar-General of Diocese of Raphoe, m. Elizabeth, dau. of James Grove, of Grove Hall, co. Donegal, and d. 1781, leaving issue,
1. Charles, d.s.p.
2. John (Rev.), of Kincraigie, co. Donegal, d. unm.
3. Robert Grove, d. unm. before his brother John.
1. JANE, of whom presently.

The only dau.,
JANE LESLIE, heiress in her issue to her brothers, m. 1795, William Beers, of Ballygorian and Ballyward, co. Down, son of William Beers, and grandson of Philip Beers, and d. 23 Dec. 1833, having by him (who d. 8 Aug. 1829) had issue,
1. FRANCIS CHARLES, of whom presently.
2. William Philip, b. 31 Jan. 1797; d. 30 May, 1797.
3. William, of Brook Cottage, Newcastle, co. Down, J.P., b. 3 June, 1798; m. 1st, Mary Keown, and 2ndly, Elizabeth Davidson and d. 3 Oct. 1880, leaving issue.
4. Leslie, b. 18 May, 1799; d. unm. 1 May, 1826.
5. John, of Leslie Hill, co. Donegal, J.P., b. 5 Sept. 1800; m. 25 June, 1830, Catherine Anna, dau. of William Colquhoun, of Green Cottage, co. Donegal, and d. 14 July, 1888, leaving issue.
6. Philip Grove, b. 11 Sept. 1801; d. in New Zealand.
7. James Annesley (Rev.), Rector of Drumballyroney, co. Down, b. 5 April, 1805; m. Alice Elizabeth, dau. of Capt. Banks, R.N., and d. 9 June, 1880, having issue.
1. Elizabeth, d. unm. 24 April, 1876.

The eldest son,
FRANCIS CHARLES LESLIE (formerly Beers), of Ballyward, co. Down, and Kincraigie, co. Donegal, b. 4 Jan. 1796; assumed by Royal Licence 8 March, 1850, the surname and Arms of LESLIE, in lieu of his patronymic; m. 5 May, 1837, Hannah Theodosia, dau. of Lieut.-Col. Charles Thompson, of the 27th Regt., and d. 23 Jan. 1866, having by her (who d. 27 Jan. 1867) had issue,
JOHN, now of Ballyward.
Harriet Jane, m. 3 Sept. 1863. William Malo de Rune Barclay, late 24th Foot. 3rd son of Sir D. W. Barclay, Bart., and has issue (*see* BURKE's *Peerage*).

Arms—Arg. on a fess between two cross-crosslets fitchée, az. three buckles or, a crescent gu. for difference. Crest—A griffin's head couped ppr. charged with a cross-crosslet fitchée arg. Motto—Firma spe.

Residence—Ballyward Lodge, Banbridge, co. Down.

LESLIE OF BALLIBAY.

EDWARD HENRY JOHN LESLIE, of Ballibay, co. Monaghan, J.P. D.L., co. Monaghan, High Sheriff 1908, b. 11 Aug. 1880, entered the Foreign Office 1902.

Lineage.—GEORGE, 4TH EARL OF ROTHES (see BURKE'S *Peerage*), m. 3rdly, Agnes, dau. of Sir John Somerville, and widow of John, 2nd Lord Fleming, and had issue,
1. ANDREW, 5th Earl (ancestor of the Earls of Rothes).
2. JAMES LESLIE, b. 1530; m. Jane, dau. of Sir James Hamilton of Evandale. His eldest son,

THE MOST REV. HENRY LESLIE (or LESLEY), D.D., b. 1580, educated at Aberdeen settled in Ireland, 1614, where he was ordained 8 April, 1617. He was Chaplain to King CHARLES I, with whom he shared his great adversities (see Harris' *Ware*, ed. 1737). He had a younger brother, George, a Prebendary of Lismore, and Rector of Ahoghill, co. Down. In 1619 the Crown presented him to the Prebend of Connor, which, 1627, he resigned for the Deanery of Down. He was also made Treasurer of St. Patrick's, Dublin, and, 1635, was advanced to the Bishopric of Down and Connor, whence at the restoration he was translated to Meath. He d. 7 April. 1661, having m. Jane Swinton, and left issue,
1. Robert (Right Rev.), D.D., Bishop of Raphoe and of Clogher, m. Nichola, dau. of Sir Francis Hamilton, Bart., of Castle Hamilton, co. Cavan, and d. 10 Aug. 1672, leaving an only child, Jane, m. 20 May, 1678, Cromwell Ward.
2. JAMES, of whose line we treat.
3. William, of Prospect, co. Antrim, m. Mary, dau. of John Echlin, of Ardquin (see *that family*) and d. 1698, leaving with three other daus.,
Sarah, who m. John Corry, M.P., of Castle Coole, ancestor of the Earl of Belmore.
1. Mary, m. 1st, Robert Echlin, of Ardquin, co. Down, and 2ndly, Sir Robert Ward, Bart., of Bangor.
2. Margaret, m. Sir Albert Conyngham, ancestor of Marquess Conyngham.

The 2nd son,
JAMES LESLIE, of Leslie House, co. Antrim, b. 24 Nov. 1624; m. 8 Nov. 1650, Jane, dau. of John Echlin, of Ardquin, co. Down, and Mary Strafford, his wife, and d. 1704, and was s. by his eldest son,

THE VEN. HENRY LESLIE, D.D., Archdeacon of Down, b. 4. Nov. 1651, Chaplain to the Duke of Ormonde, Lord-Lieut. of Ireland. In 1680 he obtained a Prebend in the Cathedral of Down, which he resigned, 1695, for the Archdeaconry. He m. 16 July, 1676, Margaret, dau. and heiress of Peter Beaghan, of Ballibay, and d. 1733. leaving issue,
1. PETER, his successor.
2. Edmund, M.P. for Antrim, m. his cousin Martha Corry, and d.s.p. 1764.
1. Penelope, m. 1714, Edmund Francis Stafford, of Brownstown, co. Meath, and had an only dau., Anne, b. 25 Dec. 1715; m. Arthur, 1st Viscount Dungannon, and was grandmother of Arthur, 1st Duke of Wellington.

Archdeacon Leslie d. 1733, and was s. by his son,
REV. PETER LESLIE, b. 1686, Rector of Ahoghill, co. Antrim; m. Jane, dau. of Anthony Dopping, D.D., Bishop of Meath, and had issue,
1. HENRY, his heir.
2. James, of Leslie Hill, co. Antrim, b. 1728; m. 1st, Mrs. Hamilton, and 2ndly, Nov. 1789, Sarah Fleming; but d.s.p. 1796.
3. Samuel, Major 14th Regt., d. unm.
4. EDMOND, Ven. Archdeacon of Down (see LESLIE *of Leslie Hill*).
1. Margaret, m. Very Rev. Hill Benson, Dean of Connor, 1753, who d. 1775.
2. Jane, m. Rev. Mr. Stewart.

The eldest son,
REV. HENRY LESLIE, of Ballibay, co. Monaghan, LL.D., b. Oct. 1719, Prebendary of Tullycorbet, Clogher, and afterwards Prebendary of Tandragee, in the Cathedral of Armagh: m. 1753, Catherine, dau. of Very Rev. Charles Meredyth, Dean of Ardfert, and d. 1803, leaving issue,
1. Peter Henry, b. 1755; killed in action in America.
2. CHARLES ALBERT, his heir.
1. Catherine Letitia, m. William Foster, Bishop of Clogher, brother of Right Hon. John Foster, Speaker of the Irish House of Commons, who was created Lord Oriel.

The only surviving son,
CHARLES ALBERT LESLIE, of Ballibay, co. Monaghan, b. 23 May, 1765; m. July, 1799, Ellen, youngest dau. of Richard Magenis, of Waringstown, co. Down, and left at his decease, 1838, an only surviving child,

EMILY ELEANOR WILHELMINA, of Ballibay, b. 1838; m. 1st, 1 Feb. 1828, her cousin, Arthur French, of Clonsilla, co. Dublin (b. 1 Nov. 1802), son of Robert Henry French, by Charlotte (m. 1798), dau. of William Reynell, of Castle Reynell, Westmeath, and grandson of Arthur French, of French Park, co. Roscommon (see BURKE'S *Peerage*, DE FREYNE), and by him (who d. 6 March, 1843) had issue,
1. ROBERT CHARLES (now LESLIE), late of Ballibay.
2. Charles Albert Leslie Attila FRENCH, late Col. 2nd Dragoon Guards, b. 5 Oct. 1842; m. 19 June, 1873, Agnes, dau. of Samuel Laing, M.P., and has issue,
1. Charles Albert, late Capt. 2nd Dragoon Guards, b. 24 Feb. 1876.
2. Cecil, b. 1879.
1. Helena Charlotte, m. 1851, James Blake, of Cregg Castle, co. Galway.
2. Albertine Caroline, m. James Ryan, dec.
3. Henrietta Victoria Alexandria, m. 1863, Col. Charles Kendal Bushe, late 59th Regt. (d. Sept. 1911), and has issue (see BUSHE *of Glencairn*).

She m. 2ndly, 1844, her cousin, the Rev. John Chas. William Leslie, son of James Leslie, of Leslie Hill, co. Antrim (see LESLIE *of Leslie Hill*), and by him (who d. 29 Nov. 1877) had issue,
3. Ferdinand Seymour, b. Oct. 1845. B.A. Oriel Coll. Oxford, Lieut. 1st King's Dragoon Guards; d. 29 Nov. 1880.
4. Marion Adelaide, m. Walter Raleigh Trevelyan, of Emsworth House, Hants, who d. July 1898, leaving issue.

Mrs. Leslie d. 26 Aug. 1884.
ROBERT CHARLES LESLIE, of Ballibay, co. Monaghan, and Kilclief, co. Down, J.P. and D.L. co. Monaghan, High Sheriff 1854, b. 30 Nov. 1828; m. at Paris, 5 Jan. 1867, Charlotte Philippa Mary (who d. 20 April, 1908), dau. of Capt. Edward Kelso, of Kelsoland and Horkesley Park, Essex, by his wife, Frances Letitia Philippa, heiress of Barrington Purvis, of Porters Hall, Essex (see KELSO *of Kelsoland*), and had issue,
1. Theodore Barrington Norman, 2nd Lieut. Grenadier Guards, b. 2 Feb. 1878; d. unm. 4 Dec. 1899, of wounds received at the battle of Belmont, S. Africa.
2. EDWARD HENRY JOHN, now of Ballibay.
1. Mabel Edith, m. 15 May, 1891, John Henry Foster Vesey-Fitzgerald, of Moyvane, co. Kerry, K.C., and has issue (see *that family*).

He assumed by Royal Licence, 25 June, 1885, the surname and arms of LESLIE, in compliance with his maternal grandfather's will. He d. 23 March, 1904, and was s. by his eldest son.

Arms—Quarterly: 1st and 4th, arg., on a bend az. three round buckles or, for LESLIE; 2nd and 3rd, arg., a lion rampant sa., for ABERNETHY. Crest—An angel ppr. Motto—Grip fast.

Seat—Ballibay House, co. Monaghan. *Town Residence*— 10, Douro Place, Kensington, W. *Club*—Marlborough.

LESLIE OF LESLIE HILL.

JAMES GRAHAM LESLIE, of Leslie Hill, Ballymoney, co. Antrim, and Seaport Lodge, Portballintine, Bushmills, J.P. and D.L., High Sheriff 1907, Barrister-at-Law (Gray's Inn), some time Head of a Dept. in the Office of the Crown Agents for the Colonies, b. 14 Nov. 1868; s. his uncle 1904; m. 31 Aug. 1901, Grace, only dau. of the late J. Lamont Brodie, of Wimbledon, and has issue,
1. SEYMOUR ARGENT SANDFORD, b. 9 June, 1902.
1. Grace Margaret Hester, b. 10 July, 1905.
2. Mary Etheldritha (Audrey), b. 23 Nov. 1906.

Lineage.—THE VEN. EDMUND LESLIE, D.C.L., appointed Archdeacon of Down, 1782, and also a prebendary of Connor, b. Nov. 1735, 4th son of Rev. Peter Leslie (see LESLIE *of Ballibay*); m. 1st, Jane, dau. of John Macnaghten, of Benvarden, co. Antrim, and had by her four sons and a dau.,
1. Peter, d. in England.
2. Bartholomew, d. in India 1790.
3. JAMES, of whom presently.
4. Edmund, d. in India 1793.
1. Mary, m. 7 July, 1794, Rev. Gregory Boraston.

Archdeacon Leslie m. 2ndly, Eleanor, dau. of George Portis, of London, and had by her,
5. George, m. Elizabeth, dau. and heir of Rev. Francis Hutcheson, D.D., of Donaghadee, co. Down, by whom he left at his decease, 1831,
1. Edmund Francis, of Donaghadee, co. Down, J.P., B.A. of Trin. Coll. Dublin, and formerly Capt. North Down Rifles,

Leslie. THE LANDED GENTRY. 400

b. 1817; s. 1853; m. 1855, Florinda, dau. of R. B. Bagley, and widow of Nathaniel Alexander, of Portglenone, formerly M.P. for co. Antrim, by whom (who d. 24 May, 1861) he had a dau., Elizabeth Florinda, who d. 19 April, 1862. Mr. E. F. Leslie d. 7 Feb. 1862.
2. George, of Donaghadee, Lieut.-Gen. Royal Artillery, b. 22 April, 1825; m. 1855, Albina Jane, dau. of James Shaw, a Judge of the Supreme Court of Calcutta. She d. 20 Jan. 1873. He d. 22 Feb. 1897, leaving with other issue,
George Francis, Lieut.-Col. 4th Batt. Rifle Brigade, b. 16 July, 1856; m. 24 Sept. 1884, Aimée, dau. of John Graham Berry, of Broomfield, co. York.
1. Mary Ellinor, m. 1842, William Thomas Poe, of Solsborough, Tipperary, and had issue (see POE of Riverston).
2. Elizabeth, d. young.
3. Ellen, m. 1854, Daniel de la Cherois, D.L., of the Manor House, Donaghadee, co. Down, and d. 4 Dec. 1891, leaving issue (see that family).
6. Henry (Very Rev.), Dean of Connor from 1823 to 1848, when he resigned for preferment in England. He m. Mrs. Harriette Inglis, and d.s.p. 1848.
7. Samuel, Rear-Admiral R.N., m. Martha, dau. of George Vaughan, and d.s.p. Sept. 1851.
2. Ellen, m. Rev. Stephen Dickson, youngest son of William Dickson, D.D., Lord Bishop of Down and Connor; and d. in giving birth to her dau. Ellen, who m. Dr. Christian, and d. 23 Aug. 1868, leaving a dau., Selina.

Archdeacon Leslie's eldest surviving son,
JAMES LESLIE, J.P. and D.L., s. to the estates of Leslie Hill upon the demise of his uncle, James Leslie, 1796. In 1790 he was High Sheriff for co. Antrim. He was b. 17 July, 1768; m. 28 Feb. 1795, Mary, dau. of Adam Cuppage, of Donicloney, co. Down, and d. 17 April, 1847, having by her (who d. 1 Feb. 1847) had issue,
1. JAMES EDMUND, of Leslie Hill.
2. Henry, M.A., Trin. Coll. Dublin, J.P. for co. Antrim; b. 2 April, 1803; m. 30 Aug. 1840, Harriet Ann, eldest dau. of Capt. Thomas Job Seyer Hanmer, R.N., of Holbrook Hall, Suffolk, and d. 5 July, 1864, having by her (who d. 7 Feb. 1887) had issue,
1. Henry Hanmer, b. 1 Dec. 1853; d.s.p.
1. Mary Emily, d. unm.
2. Helen Maria, m. 28 July, 1878, Frederick Weldon, of 53, Queen's Gate Gardens.
3. Constance Harriet Augustus, m. Dudley Jeffery, and d.s.p. 21 May, 1885. 4. Edith, d. unm.
3. Francis Seymour, of the Home Office, b. 24 Nov. 1805, d. 17 July, 1881.
4. John Charles William (Rev.), b. 25 June, 1808; m. Emily Eleanor Wilhelmina, widow of A. French, and dau. and heiress of Charles Albert Leslie, of Ballibay, and d. 29 Nov 1877, and had issue (see LESLIE of Ballibay).
5. Bartholdus George Albert, b. 1 April, 1812, d. 21 Dec. 1815.

The eldest son,
JAMES EDMUND LESLIE, of Leslie Hill and Seaport Lodge, co. Antrim, J.P. and D.L., High Sheriff 1854, b. 3 April, 1800; m. 14 April, 1823, Sarah, youngest dau. of the Right Rev. Daniel Sandford, D.D., Bishop of Edinburgh, and by her (who d. 20 Dec. 1864) had issue,
1. James Sandford, b. 10 Aug. 1824; d. Jan. 1829.
2. Henry Erskine, b. 15 Nov. 1825; d. 10 Feb. 1829.
3. EDMUND DOUGLAS, late of Leslie Hill.
4. Daniel Sandford, b. 5 March, 1830; d. 28 Dec. 1830.
5. Seymour Montague, late of the Probate Office, London, b. 14 Nov. 1835; m. 1st, 30 Oct. 1866, Louisa, youngest dau. of William Graham, of Fitzharris, Berks, by whom (who d. 7 June, 1869) he had issue,
1. JAMES GRAHAM, now of Leslie Hill.
1. Sarah Harriett Penelope, an Hon. Sister of the Order of St. John of Jerusalem.
He m. 2ndly, 22 Oct. 1878, Sarah Alice, youngest dau. of George Vincent, of Westminster, by whom he had issue,
2. Edmund Vincent, b. 6 Dec. 1879.
2. Alice Emma.
Mr. S. M. Leslie d. 17 Nov. 1891.
6. Francis Macnaghten, b. 7 Feb. 1838, late Capt. and Hon. Major, 4th Batt. R.I. Rifles, late Lieut. in the H.E.I.C.S., and in H.M.'s 105th, 103rd, and 63rd Regts., d.s.p. 16 Sept. 1908.
7. Erskine Douglas, b. and d. June, 1839.
1. Frances Mary, m. 10 Feb. 1864, Rev. Andrew George Gilmore, Rector of Selworthy, Somerset, who d. 24 Nov. 1883.
2. Mary Wilhelmina.
3. Sarah Agnes (Satara, Eastbourne), m. 23 Sept. 1862, Col. Sir Herbert Bruce Sandford, R.A., K C.M.G., who d. 1 Feb. 1892 (see SANDFORD of Sandford). 4. Jane Elizabeth.
Mr. Leslie d. 17 Jan. 1881. His 3rd son,
EDMUND DOUGLAS LESLIE, of Leslie Hill, Ballymoney, co. Antrim, and Seaport Lodge, Bushmills, J.P. and D.L. co. Antrim, Lieut.-Col. and Hon. Col. 4th Batt. Royal Irish Rifles, b. 22 Sept. 1828; m. his father 1881, and d. unm. 27 Jan. 1904, and was s. by his nephew (see above).

Arms.—Quarterly 1st and 4th, arg., on a bend az., three buckles or, 2nd and 3rd arg. a lion rampant sa. Crest—An angel ppr., vested and winged or.
Seats—Leslie Hill, Ballymoney, co. Antrim; and Seaport Lodge, Portballintrae, Bushmills.

L SLIE. See BURKE'S PEERAGE, **LESLIE**, Bart.

LESLIE-ELLIS. See **ELLIS.**

L'ESTRANGE, formerly of CLONSHEEVER.

LIEUT.-COLONEL FRANCIS ADOLPHUS L'ESTRANGE (retired) R.A.M.C., b. 1842; m. 17 Sept. 1879, Annie, eldest surviving dau. of Hon. William Macdonald, of Water Valley, and Moore Hall, Jamaica.

Lineage.—The earlier generations of the family are recorded in the Herald's *Visitations of Norfolk* (see BURKE'S *Landed Gentry*, LE STRANGE *of Hunstanton*).

SIR THOMAS LE STRANGE, of Hunstanton, Norfolk, High Sheriff 1532, m. Anne, dau. of Nicholas, Lord Vaux, of Harrowden, and had with four daus., seven sons,
1. Nicholas (Sir), of Hunstanton, Knighted 1547, d. 20 Feb. 1580; m. 1st, Ellen, dau. of Sir William Fitz William, of Milton, Northants, and had issue. He m. 2ndly, Catherine, dau. of John Hyde, of Hyde, Dorset, s.p. His eldest son,
Hamon, d. 7 Oct. 158-; m. Elizabeth, dau. of Sir Hugh Hastings, of Elsing, Norfolk, and was father of
Nicholas (Sir), of Hunstanton, Norfolk, and Athleague, co. Roscommon, Knighted in Ireland 5 Jan. 1588-9; m. 1st, Mary, dau. of Sir Robert Bell, of Ipwell, Baron of the Exchequer; 2ndly, Anne, widow of Sir George Chaworth, dau. of Sir John Pastow. He d. 15 Dec. 1591, leaving issue (see L'ESTRANGE *of Hunstanton*).
2. Richard, m. Anne dau. of John Astley, and had a son,
THOMAS, of whom hereafter.
3. William. 4. John. 5. Roger. 6. Henry.
7. Thomas (Sir), of Loughseudy, co. Westmeath, High Sheriff 1558, Knighted by the Lord Deputy Aug. 1584; d. 14 March 1582, will dated 66 Feb. 158), m. Margaret, widow of Nicholas Shaen, dau. of — Bath, s.p.

THOMAS LE STRANGE, of Castle Strange, co. Roscommon, nephew of Sir Thomas Le Strange, living 1616; m. Elizabeth ——, and left a son,
HAMON LE STRANGE, of Castle Strange, d. before 7 March, 1639; m. Dorothy, dau. of Sir John Moore, of Croghan, King's Co., and by her (who m. 2ndly, Richard St. George, of Athlone) had a son and a dau.,
THOMAS, his heir.
Elizabeth, m. John Crofton, of Kilbryan, co. Roscommon.

The only son,
THOMAS LE STRANGE, of Castle Strange, will dated 18 Sept. 1651, proved 1653; m. and left two sons,
1. Henry, of Moystown, King's Co., d. 1666; m. Elizabeth, dau. of William Sandes, of Dublin (see SANDES *of Sallow Glen*), and was ancestor of the family of L'Estrange, of Moystown.
2. WILLIAM, of whom next.

The younger son,
WILLIAM L'ESTRANGE, of Castle Cuffe, Queen's Co., will dated 4 March, 1676, proved 1 Nov. 1677; m. Grany, dau. of — Malone, and had four sons and a dau.,
1. Charles, of Linisky, d. before 1731; m. Alice, dau. of — Rochfort, and left an only child, Thomasine.
2. Thomas, of Hallain Hall, d. before 18 June, 1673, unm.
3. ROBERT, of Kcoltown. 4. Henry.
1. Mary, m. Thomas Moony, of Turin.

The 3rd son,
ROBERT L'ESTRANGE, of Keoltown, co. Westmeath, was father of
JOHN L'ESTRANGE, of Keoltown, whose will dated 14 Jan. 1694, was proved 1741. He m. Susanna, dau. of Rev. John Harrison, and had with five daus., three sons,
1. Joseph, d.s.p. 1705.
2. Robert, of Keoltown, m. Susanna, dau. of Rev. William Hodson, of Anna, co. Cavan, and had issue by her (who m. 2ndly, Michael Swift) ancestor of L'Estrange, of Keoltown.

The 3rd son,
JOHN L'ESTRANGE, of Boardstown, co. Westmeath, will dated 26 June, 1736; m. Esther, dau. of John Smith, of Violetstown, co. Westmeath, and had a son,
EDWARD L'ESTRANGE, of Boardstown, m. Mary, dau. of John Cooke, and had issue,
1. Samuel, of Boardstown, b. 1757; m. 1740, Anne, dau. of Stephen Bomford, of Rahinstown, co. Meath, and left issue.
2. Richard, of Frankbrook, d.s.p. 1743.
3. John, of Churchtown and Downdaniel, m. and left issue, two daus.
4. EDMUND, of Clonsheever, of whom presently.
1. Anne, m. — Falkiner.
2. Mary, m. 1st, Edward Osbrey; 2ndly, John Smith.
3. Esther.

The 4th son,
EDMUND L'ESTRANGE, of Clonsheever, co. Westmeath, m. Alicia, dau. of — Ussher, and was father of

EDMUND L'ESTRANGE, of Clonsheever, *m.* his 1st cousin Anne, dau. of John L'Estrange, of Churchtown, and Downdaniel, and had four sons,
1. Edmund, of Churchtown and Downdaniel, *m.* Sept. 1785, Anne, dau. of William Osbrey, and left three daus. and co-heirs,
   1. Anna Maria, *m.* 1812, Patrick Isdell.
   2. Frances Ellen, *m.* 1814, Thomas Walsh.
   3. Eliza, *m.* Capt. George Walsh, 45th Regt.
2. John (Rev.), Rector of St. Werburgh's, Dublin, *d. unm.*
3. Ussher, *d.* young.
4. ANTHONY.

The 4th son,
ANTHONY L'ESTRANGE, of Dublin, *b.* 1768; *d.* 3 Jan. 1848; *m.* Margaret, dau. of —Harrison, by Sarah, dau. of Thomas Denham, and had three sons and two daus.,
1. Edward, Major-Gen. 14th and 70th Regts., served in the Peninsula and India.
2. FREDERICK, of whom next.
3. Francis, M.A. Dublin 1832, F.R.C.S.I., Surgeon Antrim Artillery, *b.* 1803; *d.* 6 Jan. 1875; *m.* 1830, Catherine Eliza, dau. of John Mathews (she *d.* 24 Aug. 1865). and had issue,
   1. Edward Napoleon, Col. late Cheshire Regt. and Royal Scots Fus., *d.* 26 June, 1890; *m.* 1st, Margaret Innes, of Manchester, and had,
      (1) Francis.
      (2) Henry Innes, Lieut. late Leinster Regt.
      (3) George, *d.* in America.
      (4) Ernest, Natal Police.
      (1) Adelaide, *m.* 11 April, 1890, Capt. John Thomas Cramer, of Ballindinisk, co. Cork (*see that family*).
      (2) Margaret.
   Col. E. N. L'Estrange *m.* 2ndly, Belinda Emily, 4th dau. of Isaac North-Bomford, of Gallow Ferrans, co. Meath (*see that family*), and had a son,
      (5) Edward Bomford, Capt. Leinster Regt.; *m.* 12 Feb. 1910, Hiliare Frances Elizabeth, youngest dau. of William Ireland de Courcy-Wheeler, M.D., of Robertstown House, co. Kildare (*see that family*).
   2. George Wellington, Col. (ret.) late Com. 8th Batt. Rifle Brigade.
      1. Catherine, *m.* Capt. W. Sheffield Hardinge, Cheshire Regt.
      2. Olivia Massereene, *m.* W. W. Babington, of Cork.

The 2nd son,
FREDERICK L'ESTRANGE (2nd son of Anthony L'Estrange), Lieut. R.N., *b.* 1798; *d.* 10 Aug. 1871; *m.* 1829, Frances Amelia (who *d.* 11 May, 1877), dau. of John Matthews, and had two sons and two daus.,
1. FRANCIS ADOLPHUS, present representative of this family.
2. Albert Halahan, Lieut.-Col. (ret.) R.A.M.C., *b.* 1844; *m.* 1886, Martha, dau. of Henry Alexander Taylor, and has four sons,
   1. Frederick Henry Paget, *b.* 1888.
   2. Francis Albert, *b.* 1889, } twins.
   3. Henry Rowland, *b.* 1889, }
   4. Albert Cecil Taylor, *b.* 1891.
1. Margaret.   2. Elizabeth.
Arms—Gu., two lions passant guardant arg.   Crest—A lion passant guardant or.   Motto—Memento mei.
Residence—Istalia, Ailesbury Road, Dublin.

CARLETON L'ESTRANGE OF MARKET HILL.

ARTHUR HENRY L'ESTRANGE, of Kevinsfort, co. Sligo, *b.* 8 July, 1865; *m.* 11 July, 1900, Mabel, youngest dau. of late M. G. Newton, of Earl's Court Square, S.W., and widow of Ronald John Neville, of New South Wales.

Lineage.—LANCELOT CARLETON, of Rosstad, Enniskillen, co. Fermanagh; *m.* Mary, dau. of William Irvine, of Castle Irvine, (*see that family*), and had issue,
1. Lancelot, of Rosstad, High Sheriff co. Fermanagh 1683, and for Donegal 1686; *m.* Mary, dau. of John Cathcart, co. Fermanagh; and *d.* 1695, having had six sons, none of whom left male issue except the 5th, viz.,
   Christopher, of Newry, co. Down, *m.* Katherine, dau. of Henry Ball, of Donegal, and had two daus., Ann, *m.* John Rotton, of Dublin, and Conally, *m.* Alexander Crawford, of Milwood, co. Fermanagh (their dau. Katherine, *m.* 1785, Beauchamp Colclough, of Kildavin, co. Carlow), and four sons, the 3rd of whom,
      SIR GUY CARLETON, K.B., Gen. in the Army, was created 21 Aug. 1786, LORD DORCHESTER (*see* BURKE'S *Peerage*).
2. CHRISTOPHER, of whom presently.
Mr. Carleton was killed in the Civil War in the service of CHARLES I. His 2nd son,
CHRISTOPHER CARLETON, of Market Hill, co. Fermanagh, *m.* Anne, dau. and heir of Rev. George Hamilton, Rector of Devenish, and dying 1716, left three sons,
1. Alexander, J.P., cos. Fermanagh and Meath, *d.s.p.* 13 Nov. 1745.
2. GEORGE, of whose line we have to treat.
3. Lancelot (Rev.), A.M., Chaplain to a Dragoon Regt. serving in

Spain, and Rector of Padwoth, Berks, 1715, *m.* Barbara, dau. of Thomas Twitty, of Clunes, co. Worcester, and *d.* 14 Oct. 1730, leaving a son, Alexander Carleton, banker, of London, *d. unm.* 10 May, 1775, and a dau. Cecilia.
The 2nd son,
GEORGE CARLETON, of Market Hill, J.P., High Sheriff co. Monaghan, *m.* Catherine, dau. of John Creighton, of Aughlane, co. Fermanagh, and had issue,
1. John, *d.s.p.*
2. Alexander, Barrister-at-Law, *m.* 1771, Evelyn, dau. of Gilbert Pepper, co. Meath, and had three sons,
   1. George James, Lieut. Marines.
   2. William, *d.s.p.*   3. John.
3. CHRISTOPHER, of whom hereafter.
4. William, of Enniskillen, J.P., *d.* 1778.
5. George (Rev.), M.A., Chaplain 67th Foot, left a son, George.
Mr. Carleton *d.* 1747. His 3rd son,
CHRISTOPHER CARLETON, of Market Hill, J.P., *m.* Henrietta Maria, dau. of Col. Creighton, and *d.* 1779, having had a son, George, who *d.* young, and three daus., Henrietta, *d. unm.* 1762; Vincentia, *d. unm.* 1787; and
MARY CARLETON, of Market Hill, *m.* 1765, HENRY PEISLEY L'ESTRANGE, of Moystown, King's Co., and had issue; the 2nd son, CHRISTOPHER L'ESTRANGE, assumed the surname of CARLETON at the decease of his mother, 1830, and became of Market Hill. He was *b.* Feb. 1776; *m.* 8 May, 1808, Jane, dau. of Col. Jackson, M.P. of Enniscoe, co. Mayo, and had issue,
1. HENRY, *d. unm.* 31 Oct. 1830.
2. GEORGE L'ESTRANGE CARLETON, his heir.
3. CHRISTOPHER CARLETON L'ESTRANGE, of Market Hill.
4. William Jackson L'Estrange.
5. Guy James L'Estrange (Rev.).
1. Mary, *m.* 10 Aug. 1848, Right Hon. John George, one of the Judges of the Court of Queen's Bench in Ireland.
2. Janette, *m.* 20 Sept. 1837, William Orme, of Owenmore, co. Mayo; and *d.* 30 Aug. 1850.
3. Elizabeth Henrietta, *d.* 7 Oct. 1835.   4. Alice.
5. Louisa, *m.* 13 Sept. 1842, William Digges La Touche, of Stepnen's Green, and had issue (*see* LA TOUCHE *of Bellevue*).
6. Sidney Fanny, *m.* 16 May, 1843, Robert Orme, of Mountanvil, co. Dublin.   7. Sarah, *d. unm.* 8 April, 1838.
Major Carleton, High Sheriff of Fermanagh 1811, *d.* Sept. 1843, and was s. by his eldest son,
GEORGE L'ESTRANGE CARLETON, of Market Hill, *b.* 1811; *d. unm.* 19 Sept. 1881, and was s. by his brother,
CHRISTOPHER CARLETON-L'ESTRANGE, of Market Hill, J.P., *m.* 19 Feb. 1852, Charlotte Annie, dau. of Arthur Brooke Cooper, of Cooper's Hill, co. Sligo, and by her (who *d.* 22 Oct. 1887) had issue,
1. CHRISTOPHER ARTHUR, his heir.
2. ARTHUR HENRY, now of Market Hill.
3. Edmund, *b.* 14 Aug. 1867; *d.* 25 Dec. 1909.
4. Henry George, *b.* 8 April, 1869; *m.* 24 July, 1901, Evelyn Mary, dau. of Owen Wynne, of Hazelwood, co. Sligo (*see that family*).
1. Janeta Frances.   2. Elizabeth Mary.
3. Charlotte Louisa, *m.* Major James Campbell, and *d.* 3 Feb. 1885.
4. Alice Margaret, *m.* 30 Aug. 1900, G. M. Eccles, of Moneygould, co. Sligo.
Mr. Carleton-L'Estrange *d.* 11 Feb. 1889. The eldest son,
CHRISTOPHER ARTHUR CARLETON-L'ESTRANGE, of Woodville, co. Sligo, J.P., *b.* 1 July, 1856; *m.* 21 Sept. 1887, Annie, dau. of the late Roger Dodwell Robinson, and *d.s.p.* May, 1900.
Seat—Kevinsfort, co. Sligo.   Residence—35, Coleherne Court, London, S.W.   Club—Royal Societies.

LEWIN OF CASTLEGROVE.

THOMAS FREDERICK LEWIN, of Castlegrove, co. Galway, J.P. cos. Mayo and Galway, High Sheriff co. Mayo 1908, and late Lieut. 4th Batt. Connaught Rangers.

Lineage.—THOMAS LEWIN, of Cloghans, son of Thomas Lewin, of Croom, co. Limerick, *m.* 1656, Elizabeth, dau. of Edward Yea, of Lanefadon, Wales, and in 1663 purchased Cloghans. His will dated 17 Jan. 1678, proved 9 April, 1686. He left issue,
1. JOSEPH, his heir.
2. Arthur, *d.* 1686, leaving a dau. Mary.
3. Thomas, *d.* before 1686.
1. Elizabeth, *m.* John Clarke.
Mr. Lewin *d.* 1690. The eldest son,
JOSEPH LEWIN, of Cloghans, *m.* 1685, Ann, dau. of Robert Bell, of Streamstown, and had issue,
1. THOMAS, his heir.   2. JOHN, *d.s.p.*
1. Elizabeth.
The eldest son,
THOMAS LEWIN, of Cloghans, *m.* 1714, Christina, dau. of B. King, and had issue,
1. THOMAS, his heir.
2. Henry, a cavalry officer, *d.s.p.*, killed in the battle of Fontenoy.   3. CARRIQUE, of whom presently.
4. Francis, *d.s.p.*
The eldest son,

THOMAS LEWIN, of Cloghans, High Sheriff of Mayo 1745, m. 1740, Barbara, dau. of John Ross Lewin, of Fortfergus, co. Clare, and had issue,
1. THOMAS, his heir.
  1. Anne, m. 1776, George Ross Lewin, of Ross Hill, co. Clare, who d. 1822, leaving issue (see that family).
  2. Susan, m. John Westropp, of Mellon, co. Limerick.

The only son,
THOMAS LEWIN, of Cloghans, High Sheriff of Mayo, m. 1770, Elizabeth, dau. of Harrison Ross Lewin, of Fortfergus, co. Clare, and had issue,
1. Jane, m. 1st, Capt. Horsfall, 39th Regt.; and 2ndly, Col. John Scrope Colquitt, of the Grenadier Guards.
2. Barbara, m. Ralph Benson, of Lutwyche Hall, co. Salop, some time M.P. for Stafford (see that family).
3. Anna, d. unm.

Mr. Lewin left no male issue. His uncle,
CARRIQUE LEWIN, son of the 2nd Thomas Lewin, of Cloghans, m. 1745, Margaret, dau. of James Gallagher, and had issue, a son,
JAMES LEWIN, of Oaklands, m. 1780, Ann, dau. of Edward Elwood, of Ballymore, co. Sligo, and had issue,
1. James, Capt. 30th Foot, who m. and had one son,
  James St. George, Lieut. 61st Regt., d.s.p. 1849, in India.
2. THOMAS, of whom presently.
3. Carrique, Lieut. 71st Regt., d.s.p. 1844.

The 2nd son,
THOMAS LEWIN, of Cloghans, served a few years as an Officer 30th Regt., but quitted the army on the reduction after Waterloo. He m. 1823, Anna, dau. of Westropp Ross Lewin, of Cornfield, co. Clare, and d. 1873, having had issue,
FREDERIC THOMAS, of Cloghans and Castlegrove.
Georgina, m. 1851, George Ellis, late Lieut. 52nd Light Infantry.
FREDERIC THOMAS LEWIN, of Cloghans, co. Mayo, and of Castlegrove, co. Galway, J.P. and D.L. for former co., High Sheriff 1886, and J.P co. Galway, High Sheriff, 1892, b. 1828 ; m. 1867, Lucy Emma, dau. of William Byrom Corrie, of Cheltenham, and d. Nov. 1904, having by her (who d. 1880) had issue,
1. THOMAS FREDERIC, now of Castlegrove.
2. ARTHUR CORRIE, now of Cloghans, co. Mayo (see that family).
3. Frederic Henry, B.A. Oxon.
1. Constance Mary, m. 26 Oct. 1898, Edgar Harris, son of Samuel Harris, of Clifton.
2. Lucy Emily, m. 21 April, 1898, Wilfred Tighe, 2nd son of Col. Tighe, D.L., of Rossanagh, co. Wicklow (see TIGHE of Woodstock).
3. Gwynneth Maud, m. 24 Aug. 1893, Capt. Herbert C. Fergusson, Highland L.I., son of Chaworth Fergusson, of Blackwood, co. Westmeath.
4. Alice Christina, m. 30 April, 1902, Cyril Edward Browne, M.A., 3rd son of Lord Richard Howe Browne, and has issue (see BURKE's Peerage, SLIGO, M.).
5. Emma Marian Edith, m. 18 Oct. 1900, William Raymond Heaven (see HEAVEN of Forest of Birse).

Seat—Castlegrove, Tuam, co. Galway.

LEWIN OF CLOGHANS.

MAJOR ARTHUR CORRIE LEWIN, D.S.O., of Cloghans, co. Mayo, Major 3rd Batt. Connaught Rangers, late 19th Hussars and formerly Capt. King's Liverpool Regt., served in S. Africa 1899-1902 with first Batt. Mounted Infantry (despatches twice, Queen's Medal with five clasps, King's Medal with two clasps, D.S.O.), b. 26 July, 1874 ; m. 14 Nov. 1900, Norah Constance, youngest dau. of late William Higgin, of Rosganna, co. Antrim, and has issue,
1. PATRICK WILLIAM, b. 31 Dec. 1903.
2. Thomas Chippendall Colquitt, b. 13 Aug. 1908.

Major A. C. Lewin is the second son of the late Frederick Thomas Lewin of Cloghans, co. Mayo, and of Castlegrove, co. Galway (see that family), who d. 1904, by his wife Lucy Emma, dau. of William Byrom Corrie of Cheltenham, who d. 1880, and s. to the Cloghans Estate at the death of his father.

Lineage—See LEWIN of Castlegrove.
Seat—Cloghans, co. Mayo.

ROSS-LEWIN OF ROSS HILL.

REV. GEORGE HARRISON ROSS-LEWIN, of Ross Hill, co. Clare, of Gortakillen, co. Limerick, and Garrane, co. Tipperary, M.A. (Durham), Vicar of Benfieldside, co. Durham, Rural Dean, and Hon. Canon of Durham Cathedral, b. 18 Dec. 1846.

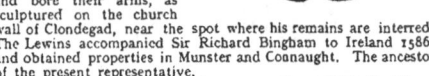

Lineage.—GEORGE Ross, of Fortfergus, High Sheriff co. Clare 1664, b. 1625, was the first possessor of the family seat in Clare. He claimed descent from the noble and once powerful Rosses of England, and bore their arms, as sculptured on the church wall of Clondegad, near the spot where his remains are interred. The Lewins accompanied Sir Richard Bingham to Ireland 1586, and obtained properties in Munster and Connaught. The ancestor of the present representative,
JOHN ROSS-LEWIN, of Fortfergus, co. Clare, High Sheriff co. Clare 1724, m. Elizabeth Hastings. Of this marriage there were issue,
1. HARRISON, of whom presently. 2. George Hastings.
3. Herman.
1. Mary.
2. Barbara, m. 19 Feb. 1740, Thomas Lewin, of Cloghans, co. Mayo, and left issue.
3. Susannah, m. 14 Sept. 1745, Palmes Westropp, and had issue.

Mr. J. Ross-Lewin is honourably mentioned in Mr. J. A. FROUDE'S English in Ireland, vol. 1. p. 424. Mrs. Ross Lewin d. 1734, and Mr. Ross Lewin d. 1757, and was s. by his only surviving son,
HARRISON ROSS-LEWIN, of Fortfergus, High Sheriff 1755, m. Hannah, dau. of John Westropp, of Lismehane (afterwards Maryfort), co. Clare, and sister of Ralph Westropp, of Attyflin, and d. 20 Nov. 1775, having had issue,
1. John, of Fortfergus, m. Eleanor, dau. of George Stacpoole, of Edenvale, co. Clare, and d. 1792, leaving three sons and several daus.,
  1. John, d. in the West Indies.
  2. William, who also d. a minor in the West Indies.
  3. George, Cornet 17th Light Dragoons, m. Caroline, dau. of Col. O'Toole, by the Lady Catherine Annesley his wife, and had an only son.
    1. Anna, m. Capt. Charles John Whyte, son of John Whyte, of Loughbrickland ; and 2ndly, John Louis Auriol, of Clifton.
    2. Jane, m. Dr. Barnard, Bishop of Limerick ; and 2ndly, Col. Hay.
    3. Mary Anne, m. Rev. Charles Dunbar Whitehead Massy, of Summerhill, co. Clare, son of Sir Hugh Massy, Bart. of Doonas.
    4. Leonora, m. Major Marley. 5. Louisa, m. J. Walker.
    6. Wilhelmina, m. J. Saunders Benwell, 21st Light Dragoons.
    7. Eliza, m. M. Stacpoole. 8. Frances Eleanor.
2. GEORGE, of whose family we treat.
3. Westropp, of Cornfield, co. Clare, J.P., m. Margaret, dau. of Edward Morony, of Cork, and had issue,
  1. Henry, Lieut. 70th Foot, m. Jane, dau. of M. Pereira, and had issue.
  2. Edward, Lieut. and Adjutant 9th Foot, killed at the storming of St. Sebastian, 1813.
  3. Francis Nathaniel Burton, m. Susannah, dau. of William Kenny, and had issue. 4. Westropp, d.s.p. at Ascension, 1838.
  1. Margaret, m. Edward Greene, of Snugville, co. Clare.
  2. Maria, m. Gen. Aylmer. 3. Frances.
4. Anna, m. 1823, Thomas Lewin, of Cloghans, who d. 1873, leaving issue (see that family).
5. Jane, m. Major Ellis, 93rd Highlanders.
6. Georgina, m. 1st, Joseph Cripps, of Limerick, and Wellington Lodge, co. Clare ; and 2ndly, Edward Morony.
4. Ralph, Lieut. 5th Foot and on the Staff, m. Archange, dau. of M. Baubie, of Quebec, and d.s.p.
5. William, d.s.p.
6. Harrison, M.A., m. Eliza, dau. of Gen. Hardwick, and had issue.
1. Jane, m. 1779, Capt. James Ness, of Osgodvie, co. York, and had issue.
2. Hannah, m. 1781, Robert Burdett, of Slates, co. York, and had issue.
3. Elizabeth, m. Thomas Lewin, of Cloghans, co. Mayo.
4. Susanna, d. unm.
5. Anna Maria, d. unm.

The 2nd son,
GEORGE ROSS-LEWIN, of Ross Hill, co. Clare, Cornet 14th Dragoons, m. 1776, Anne, dau. of Thomas Lewin, of Cloghans, co. Mayo (see that family), and had issue,
1. Harrison, d.v.p.
2. HENRY, his heir.

3. Thomas, Lieut. 32nd Regt., had Peninsula medal with eight clasps, and was wounded at Sarrozin, in Spain, and at Waterloo ; *m*. Frances, dau. of Daniel O'Grady, of Shannon Park, *d.s.p.*
4. George, *d.s.p.*
1. Eliza, *d. unm.*
2. Barbara, *m*. Rev. Charles Thomas Gladwin, and had issue.

Mr. Ross-Lewin *d*. 1822, and was *s*. by his eldest surviving son,

HENRY ROSS-LEWIN, of Ross Hill, Major in the Army, J.P., *b*. 1778. He was present at eleven general actions and sieges, including the battles of Quatre Bras and Waterloo, and was wounded in the last charge at Salamanca. He *m*. Anne, dau. of William Burnett, of Eyrescourt, by Christina Mary his wife, dau. of Edward Donelan, of Hillswood, co. Galway, and by her (who *d*. 31 Dec. 1876) had issue,
1. GEORGE (Rev.), his heir.
2. Henry, of Donogrogue Castle, co. Clare, *m*. Jane Stamer, dau. of George C. Hodges, of Donogrogue Castle, co. Clare, and *d.s.p.*
3. Charles Massey, *d.s.p.* 8 Sept. 1870.
4. John Dillon, Lieut. 30th Regt., mortally wounded at the close of the battle of Inkerman, 5 Nov. 1854.
1. Georgina, *m*. William Stephen Morgan, of Old Abbey, co. Limerick, J.P., who *d*. 1871, leaving issue.
2. Maria Christina, *m*. 1st, 1847, Comm. Frederick Lowe, R.N., who *d s.p.* 1861 ; and 2ndly, Rev. Thomas Westropp, Rector of Ardcanny, M.A., who *d*. 1876.
3. Charlotte Augusta.
4. Mary Julia, *m*. Francis Lowe, son of W. Lowe, of the Middle Temple, by his wife Eliza, dau. of John Manley, and has issue, three sons.

Major Ross-Lewin *d*. at Ross Hill 27 April, 1843, and was *s*. by his eldest son,

REV. GEORGE ROSS-LEWIN, of Ross Hill, co. Clare, M.A., J.P., formerly in the R.N., *b*. 1810 ; *m*. 20 March, 1844, Grace, dau. of Henry Sargint, of Castleview, co. Tipperary, by Anne his wife, dau. of Richard Sadleir, of Tipperary, and *d*. 1885, having by her (who *d*. 1871) had issue,
1. HENRY HASTINGS (Rev.), late of Ross Hill, *b*. 25 Feb. 1845 ; *d. unm.* 24 Aug. 1887.
2. GEORGE HARRISON, now of Ross Hill.
3. Richard Sargint Sadleir (Rev.), B.A., Rector of Kilmurry, co. Limerick, Canon of Limerick Cathedral and Rural Dean, *b*. 17 Aug. 1848 ; *m*. 16 Aug. 1877, Louisa, dau. of Frederick Maunsell.
4. Robert O'Donelan (Rev.), M.A., Chaplain R.N., Hon. Canon of Newcastle Cathedral and Rural Dean, Rector of Wark-on-Tyne, Northumberland, *b*. 26 March, 1850 ; *m*. 18 May, 1897, Katherine Mary Beatrice, eldest dau. of John Wilson Walton Wilson, J.P., of Shotley Hall, Northumberland, and has issue,
Francis Henry Westropp, *b*. 3 March, 1898.
Lucy Marian, *b*. 4 Oct. 1899.
1. Anne Thomasina.   2. Mneme Geraldine Mabel.

Arms—Arg. a bend engrailed sa. between two trefoils slipped vert. Crest—A demi lion sa. holding between the paws a trefoil slipped vert. Motto—Consilio ac virtute.

Seat—Ross Hill, Kildysart, co. Clare. Residence—St. Cuthbert's Vicarage, Shotley Bridge, co. Durham.

LEWIS OF BALLINAGAR.

JOHN MICHAEL AYLWARD LEWIS, of Ballinagar, co. Galway, J.P., High Sheriff 1903, *b*. 1 Feb. 1854 ; *s*. his father 1873 ; *m*. 4 Dec. 1889, Catherine Frances, only dau. of Edward Jonas Greene, of Newstead, co. Dublin, and has issue,

JOHN AYLWARD, *b*. 23 July, 1893.
Kathleen Adelaide, *b*. 29 Aug. 1890.

Lineage—DAVID LEWIS settled in Ireland about the middle of the the 17th century, at Waterford, of which city he became Alderman. He was Sheriff in 1695, and filled the office of Mayor five times. He *d*. 1718, leaving issue by his wife Sarah (who *d*. 1730),
1. William (Ven.), Archdeacon of Kilferona, *b*. 1692 ; *m*. Elizabeth, dau. of Richard Buckner, of Waterford, and *d*. 4 July, 1767, leaving by her (who *d*. Jan. 1788) issue,
1. William (Rev.), *b*. 1725 ; *m*. 29 May, 1765, Mary, dau. of Col. Clarke of Surrey, and he had issue,
William (Rev.), *b*. 1767 ; *m*. 25 May, 1795, Anne, dau. of Frances Ryves, of Ryves Castle, co. Limerick, and *d*. 5 Feb. 1859, leaving issue,
1. William Buckner (Rev.), British Chaplain at Smyrna, *b*. 1798 ; *d*. 3 Jan. 1870 ; he *m*. 17 July, 1826, Margaret, dau. of W. C. Purdon, of Tinnerana, co. Clare, and had issue, 1, William ; 1, Mary ; 2, Arabella, *m*. 2 May, 1854, Walter M. Pengelley, Lieut. Indian Navy ; 3, Adelaide, *m*. July, 1858, Rev. Rowland Cousins.
2. Richard, Capt. 94th Regt., *m*. 1844, Margaret, dau. of A. Campbell ; *d*. 30 Sept. 1844.
1. Dora, *d. unm.* 7 Dec. 1887.   2. Mary.
2. David (Rev.), *b*. 1730 ; *d*. 1759.
1. Anne, *m*. 8 March, 1760, Col. Gore, of Derrymore, co. Clare.
2. Dorothea, *m*. 1st, Feb. 1758, Gen. Crumpe ; and 2ndly, 14 Oct. 1792, Lord Glentworth, Bishop of Limerick, and *d*. Aug. 1802.
3. Elizabeth, *m*. 30 Dec. 1762, Rev. William Maunsell, D.D., of Limerick.

2. David, of Waterford, High Sheriff 1740, *m*. 20 Sept. 1740 Mary Shiel, of Dublin, and *d*. 1754, leaving issue,
1. David.   2. Samuel.
3. THOMAS, of whom presently.   4. James (Rev.), *d. unm.*

The third son,

THOMAS LEWIS, of Oldcastle, co. Cork, *m*. 21 Nov. 1728, Joan, dau. of Francis Radley, of Knockraur, co. Cork, and had issue,
1. HENRY, of whom presently.
2. Thomas, *m*. 1762, Elizabeth, dau. of Richard Edward Hull, J.P., of Lemcon Manor, co. Cork, and *d*. 1808, having by her (who *d*. 1773) had issue,
1. Richard Hull, of Seaforth House, co. Cork, Lieut. 68th Regt., *b*. 1764 ; *m*. 16 March, 1791, Christiana, dau. of John Sweetenham, of Mardyke House, co. Cork, and *d*. 23 Oct. 1835, leaving by her (who *d*. 26 Dec. 1849) issue,
(1) William, Lieut. 19th Regt., *b*. 10 Oct. 1793 ; *m*. 1st, 1 July, 1824, Christiana (*d*. 30 Jan. 1826); dau. of Robert Bird, of Bantry, by whom he had issue, a dau.,
1. Mary, *m*. 5 Feb. 1853, Dr. Abraham Tuckey, of Bantry, *d*. 20 May, 1876.
He *m*. 2ndly, 24 April, 1827, Sarah (*d*. 10 Dec. 1874), dau. of Robert Boyle Warren, of Kinsale, and *d*. 17 Oct. 1883, leaving issue,
1. Richard Hull, *b*. 7 March, 1828, Col. in the Army, late 20th Regt. ; *m*. 10 Aug. 1858, Georgina, dau. of John Tonson Rye, of Rye Court, co. Cork, and *d*. 3 April, 1888, leaving issue,
a. Percy John Tonson, C.M.G., Lieut.-Col and Brev.-Col. late A.S.C., formerly Lieut. Royal Artillery, *b*. 5 April, 1861 ; *m*. 14 July, 1892, Maud, dau. of Richard Griffith, of Glenmore, Cheltenham. He *d*. 28 Oct. 1910, having had issue, a dau., Muriel, *b*. 6 July, 1893.
b. Richard Hull, *b*. 14 March, 1870, Capt. Royal Engineers ; *m*. 24 Sept. 1895, Frances, dau. of Rev H. B. Swabey and *d*. 30 Oct. 1910.
a. May, *m*. 3 Sept. 1889, Major Charles R. Browne.
b. Claire, *m*. 18 Oct. 1890, Henry C. Jenkins, Fleet Paymaster R.N.
c. Georgiana, *m*. 7 Jan. 1896, James C. Ward.
1. Sarah, *m*. 25 June, 1850, Richard C. Pratt, of Kinsale, and *d*. 8 July, 1855.
2. Christiana, *m*. 6 May, 1852, Capt. Johnstone Napier, 74th Regt., and *d*. 5 Feb. 1856.
(2) John Henry, Lieut. 1st Ceylon Regt., *b*. 1794 ; *m*. 21 June, 1825, Patience, dau. of T. Long, of Seaview, co. Cork, and *d.s.p.* 11 Feb. 1827. She *d*. 6 Oct. 1872.
(3) Thomas, Lieut. 48th Regt., *b*. 1796 ; *m*. Alicia, dau. of Capt. Dalton, of Ross Castle, co. Clare ; *d.s.p.* 4 June, 1837.
(4) Stephen, Lieut. 73rd Regt., *b*. 1797 ; *m*. 8 Dec. 1819, Eliza (*d*. March, 1831), dau. of Dr. Millar, of Six Mile Bridge, co. Clare, and *d*. 26 July, 1880, leaving issue,
1. John Riggs Millar, Deputy-Surgeon-General A.M.S., *b*. 1821 ; *m*. Mary, dau. of Judge Jervis, of Canada, and *d*. 13 Aug. 1898, having had issue, John George Stephen, Surgeon-Major A.M.S., *b*. 3 Oct. 1857 ; *d*. 16 July, 1897.
2. Stephen, *b*. 1825 ; *m*. 1st, Isabella, dau. of Thomas Crumpe, of Chorley, Salop (who *d*. 29 May, 1880), and had issue,
a. Henry Stephen, *b*. 1857 ; *m*. 15 Oct. 1889, Frances, dau. of Charles H. Minchin, and has issue,
Stephen Henry, *b*. 29 July, 1890.
b. Richard Crumpe, *b*. 15 April, 1865, Surgeon-Capt. A.M.S.
a. Marian, *m*. 8 April, 1880, John Dorman.
He *m*. 2ndly, 21 Aug. 1883, his first cousin, Catherine, dau. of Henry Lewis, and *d*. 1 Dec. 1896.
3. James Henry, Surgeon A.M.S., *d. unm.* 1 July, 1867.
(5) Henry, *b*. 1801 ; *m*. Mary (*d*. 16 Jan. 1882), dau. of Ralph Bracken, and *d*. 25 May, 1849, leaving issue,
1. Richard Hull, *m*. 9 Aug. 1877, Ellen, dau. of Thomas Babbington, and *d s.p.*
2. Henry Ralph, late Lieut. 11th Regt., *m*. 9 Nov. 1859, Eliza, dau. of Robert Dunne, of Kinsale, and has issue, Minnie, *m*. 26 Feb. 1889, Harry H. Primrose.
1. Alice, *d. unm.* 12 June, 1897.
2. Matilda, *d. unm.* 1 April, 1896.
3. Mary, *d. unm.* 1908.
4. Catherine, *m*. 21 Aug. 1883, her cousin, Stephen Lewis (*see above*).
(1) Marv, *m*. 27 July, 1820, Major Crooke, 25th Regt., and *d*. 25 June, 1891.
(2) Catherine, *m*. 1st, 9 Sept. 1824, Capt. Sandys, 24th Light Dragoons ; and 2ndly, 12 Aug. 1841, Col. Lowth, C.B., 38th Regt., A.D.C. to the Queen.
2. Tonson (Rev.), *b*. 1766 ; *m*. 28 July, 1791, Mary, dau. of Richard Blair, of Blair's Cove, Bantry, and *d*. 1841, leaving issue,
(1) Richard Blair, *m*. 6 June, 1815, Constance Bennet, who *d*. 3 March, 1857.
(2) Thomas.
1. Elizabeth, *m*. 19 Jan. 1790, Richard Blair, of Blair's Cove, co. Cork.
3. Francis, *m*. 10 Jan. 1784, Anne, dau. of William Gardner, of Youghal, co. Cork, and *d*. 1813, having by her (who *d*. 21 Jan. 1836) had issue,
Francis Richard, *b*. 1800 ; *m*. 3 Sept. 1831, Maria, dau. of Dr. Potter, and *d*. Feb. 1843, having by her (who *d*. 1 Feb. 1852) had issue,
James Potter, M.D., of Gloucester Crescent, London, *b*. 19 Jan. 1834 ; *m*. 16 June, 1864, Halgena, dau. of Matthias Hare LL.D., and *d*. 30 May, 1890, leaving issue,
1. Halgena.   2. Mary.   3. Theodora.

Lewis. THE LANDED GENTRY. 404

1. Catherine, *m.* 10 Feb. 1766, John Hopkins, of Macroom, co. Cork.

The eldest son,
HENRY LEWIS, *b.* 1732; *m.* 9 April, 1771, Margaret (*d.* 26 April, 1787), dau. of Richard Edward Hull, J.P., of Leincon Manor, co. Cork, and *d.* 27 June, 1810, leaving issue (with a dau. Mary, who *d. unm.* 18 May, 1866), an only son,
RICHARD LEWIS, *b.* 15 Feb. 1772; *m.* 26 Oct. 1797, Catherine, dau. and ultimately sole heiress of John Travers, J.P., of Garrycloyne Castle, co. Cork, and *d.* 27 July, 1812, leaving by her (who *d.* 15 Sept. 1847),
  1. John (Rev.), *b.* 10 Sept. 1798; *m.* 15 Nov. 1823, Rebecca, dau. of John Lawless, of Cork, and *d.* 29 Oct. 1833, leaving by her (who *d.* 14 Feb. 1891),
    1. John Travers Lewis (Right Rev.), D.D., LL.D., Archbishop of Ontario, late Metropolitan of Canada, *b.* 20 June, 1825; *m.* 1st, 22 July, 1851, Anne, dau. of Henry Sherwood, Attorney-General of Upper Canada, and *d.* by her (who *d.* 1886) had issue,
      (1) John Travers, *b.* 29 Oct. 1857; *m.* 22 Oct. 1884, Ethel, dau. of Collingwood Schreiber, C.M.G.
      (1) Charlotte Sherwood, *m.* 28 April, 1875, Robert Craigie Hamilton, and *d.* 1903, leaving issue (*see* HAMILTON *of Hamwood*).
      (2) Rebecca, *m.* 4 Feb. 1889, Llewellyn F. Lloyd.
    He *m.* 2ndly, 20 Feb. 1889, Ada, dau. of Evan Leigh, of Manchester, and *d.* 6 May, 1901.
    2. Richard Pyne, M.D., *b.* 24 Jan. 1827; *m.* 17 March, 1857, Millicent, dau. of Alexander O'Dell.
    3. Rowland, *b.* 18 Sept. 1828. 4. Zachery, *b.* 18 July, 1832.
    1. Mary, *m.* 16 Sept. 1850, U. C. Lee.
    2. Rebecca Louisa, *m.* 11 Sept. 1852, Hon. John Hamilton, M.L.C. 3. Annie.
  2. RICHARD TONSON, of whom presently. 3. Henry, dec.
  4. Robert Travers, M.D., *b.* 21 Oct. 1805; *m.* 15 Sept. 1831, Mary, dau. of Henry Longworth, of Castletown, Queen's Co., and *d.* 3 Jan. 1852 (she *d.* 10 Oct. 1844), leaving issue,
    1. Robert.
    2. Richard Moore, *m.* Ellen, dau. of J. E. Gameau.
    3. John David.
    1. Jane, *m.* 16 Jan. 1857, Henry D. Murray, son of Sir Patrick Murray, Bart. (*see* BURKE's *Peerage and Baronetage*).
  5. William Hull, M.D., J.P., *b.* 28 Oct. 1806; *m.* 25 May, 1837, Anne, dau. of William Roe, and *d.* 2 June, 1875, having by her (who *d.* 27 April, 1896) had issue,
    1. William Roe, *b.* 1841; *m.* 1869, Anna (*d.* 29 May, 1875), dau. of W. H. Jones, County Inspector R.I.C., and has issue,
      (1) William Henry Jones, *b.* Sept. 1872.
      (1) Mary Elizabeth, *b.* 26 April, 1870; *m.* 8 Sept. 1898, Berkeley W. R. Dunn.
      (2) Anna Jones, *b.* 23 May, 1875; *d. unm.* 27 Nov. 1900.
    2. Robert, *d.* 1910. 3. Richard.
    4. Frederick, *m.* Frances Smythe. 5. Rowland, *d.s.p.* 1856.
    1. Catherine. 2. Rebecca. 3. Hannah.
    1. Jane, *m.* 10 May, 1827, Thomas Alleyn Browne, of Rockborough, Muskerry, and *d.* 13 June, 1827.
    2. Margaret, *m.* 15 Feb. 1844, Rev. W. Meade, Vicar of Kinsale, and *d.* 11 Dec. 1892. 3. Catherine, *d. unm.* 9 Aug. 1861.

The 2nd son,
RICHARD TONSON LEWIS, *m.* 17 June, 1824, CICELY CONNOLLY (*d.* 4 Feb. 1844), only child and eventual sole heiress of Capt. J. M. Aylward, of Ballinagar, co. Galway (*see below*), and *d.* 23 Oct. 1851, leaving issue (with a dau. Olivia Barbara, who *d. unm.* 8 Nov. 1895) an only son,
JOHN MICHAEL AYLWARD LEWIS, of Ballinagar, J.P. co. Galway, *b.* 12 March, 1827; *m.* 7 April, 1853, Hannah, dau. of Thomas Roberts White, and *d.* 26 May, 1873, leaving issue,
  1. JOHN MICHAEL AYLWARD, now of Ballinagar.
  2. Thomas White, M.D. Trin. Coll. Dublin, *b.* 8 Jan. 1855; *d.* 8 April, 1907.
  3. Richard George, Lieut. Galway Militia, *b.* 19 Feb. 1857; accidentally drowned in Lough Derg, 31 Jan. 1881.
  4. Robert Travers, M.B. Trin. Coll. Dublin, *b.* 19 March, 1859; *m.* 3 Sept. 1890, Emily, dau. of Thomas Twamley, and *d.* 2 Dec. 1906, having by her had issue,
    1. Richard George, *b.* 15 April, 1895.
    1. Iva Gwendoline, *b.* 7 June, 1891.
    2. Cicely Travers, *b.* 19 June, 1892; *d.* 19 May, 1893.
    3. Margerie, *b.* 23 July, 1893; *d.* 22 Jan. 1894.
    4. Norah Frances, *b.* 13 Oct. 1897.
    5. Violet Mary, *b.* 8 June, 1900.
  5. Henry Hull, B.A. Trin. Coll. Dublin, J.P. co. Galway, *b.* 15 Dec. 1860.
  6. George White, Maj. and Brevet Lieut.-Col. Worcestershire Regt., *b.* 29 May, 1863.
  1. Annie. 2. Hannah Blanche.

FAMILY OF AYLWARD.

The lands of Faithlegg, co. Waterford, with other lands in the same county, granted to the AYLWARDS at the Anglo-Norman invasion of Ireland in 1177, remained with the Aylward family for nearly five centuries. John Aylward, Mayor of Waterford 1650, the last possessor, was transplanted to Connaught by CROMWELL, and settled at Ballinagar. He *m.* 1639, Margaret, dau. of Alderman William Dobbyn, of Waterford, and *d.* 1662, leaving issue,
PETER AYLWARD, of Ballinagar, *b.* 1653, who obtained (29 CHARLES II.) a grant from the Crown of the Ballinagar estate, co. Galway. He *m.* Elizabeth, dau. of Christopher French (afterwards St. George) of Tyrone, co. Galway, and had issue,
  1. JOHN, his heir. 2. James.

3. Mathew, *d. unm.* 1739.
1. Jane, *m.* Walter Joyce, of Galway.
2. Honora, *m.* Gerald Dillon, of Dillon Grove, co. Roscommon, and *d.* 1743.
3. Margaret, *m.* 1st, John Leonard, of Carha, co. Galway; 2ndly, Patrick Fitzgerald, of Kilnecorren, co. Mayo.

The eldest son,
JOHN AYLWARD, of Ballinagar, *m.* Barbara, dau. of Garrett Nugent, of Dysert, Westmeath, and *d.* July, 1731, leaving by her (who *d.* Feb. 1765) issue,
  1. JOHN FRENCH, his heir.
  2. NUGENT SYLVESTER, who *s.* his brother.
  3. MICHAEL WIDMAN, who *s.* his brother.
  1. Elizabeth, *m.* Patrick Byrne, Ballyteskin, Queen's Co.
  2. Mary, *m.* 9 Feb. 1755, Francis French, of Dublin.
  3. Barbara, *m.* Edward O'Brien, of Ballysoblona, co. Westmeath.
  4. Bridget, *m.* 2 Nov. 1752, John Blake, of Ross, co. Clare.

The eldest son,
JOHN FRENCH AYLWARD, of Ballinagar, *d. unm.* 30 Sept. 1755, and was *s.* by his brother,
NUGENT SYLVESTER AYLWARD, of Ballinagar, *b.* 1728; *m.* 5 Feb. 1757, Catherine, dau. of Patrick French (now St. George), of Tyrone, co. Galway, and by her (who *d.* 27 Dec. 1786) had issue,
  Mary, *m.* 1st, 23 Feb. 1780, Edmund Blake, of Ballyglunin Park, co. Galway; and 2ndly, 19 July, 1788, Col. John Blake, of Furbo, co. Galway; she *d.* 1789.
Mr. Aylward *d.* 10 Aug. 1783, and was *s.* by his brother,
MICHAEL WIDMAN AYLWARD, of Ballinagar, who had served for some time in the Spanish Army, for which he was outlawed, but received (38 GEORGE II.) the royal pardon. He *m.* 1st, Sarah, dau. of Patrick French (now St. George), of Tyrone, co. Galway; and 2ndly, 16 Dec. 1784, Jane, dau. of Hyacinth Daly, of Killimore Castle, co. Galway, and by her (who *d.* 13 Jan. 1835) had issue,
  Michael, *b.* 1785; *d. unm.* 27 April, 1824.
Mr. Aylward (whose widow re-married, Capt. Averell Lecky, 14th Light Dragoon Guards, of Castle Lecky, co. Londonderry) *d.* 10 June, 1785, leaving issue by his first wife,
  1. JOHN MICHAEL NUGENT, his heir.
  1. Barbara (*d.* 24 Dec. 1822), *m.* 9 Jan. 1802, William Mahony of Rockvale, co. Cork.
  2. Mary, *m.* 1st, 9 Jan. 1802, William Burke, of Moyglass, co. Galway; and 2ndly, 17 Jan. 1808, Thomas L. Whistler, Surgeon A.M.S.

The son and heir,
JOHN MICHAEL NUGENT AYLWARD, of Ballinagar, Capt. 5th Dragoon Guards, *b.* 15 Nov. 1780; *m.* 29 Nov. 1803, Jane (*d.* 7 May, 1864), dau. of Anthony Lambert, of Alnwick, Northumberland, and *d.* 28 Sept. 1861, leaving issue (with a dau., CICELY CONNOLLY, who *m.* 17 June, 1824, Richard Tonson Lewis, *see family of Lewis*), an only son and heir,
JOHN MICHAEL AYLWARD, of Ballinagar, *b.* 13 March, 1809; *m.* 12 Dec. 1831, Mary (*d.* 25 Dec. 1864), dau. of Thomas Higgins, of Caropadin, co. Galway, and *d.* 14 April, 1867, *s.p.* when the Aylward property passed under settlement to his nephew, the late JOHN MICHAEL AYLWARD LEWIS, of Ballinagar.

Seat—Ballinagar, Loughrea, co. Galway.

LEWIS OF INNISKEEN AND SEATOWN.

HENRY OWEN LEWIS, of Inniskeen, co. Monaghan, and Seatown, co. Dublin, J.P. and D.L., M.P. for Carlow 1874-80, High Sheriff co. Monaghan 1885, B.A. Trin. Coll. Dublin, *b.* 26 Sept. 1842; *m.* 1st, 8 Aug. 1866, Frances Sophia, only child and heiress of Francis Charles Elsegood, of Upper Brook Street, Grosvenor Square, and by her (who *d.* 13 April, 1900) has issue,
  1. Henry Owen, *b.* 12 Sept. 1867; *d.* an infant.
  2. ARTHUR FRANCIS OWEN, D.S.O., Governor of H.M. Prison, Mountjoy, Major late 4th Batt. Lancashire Fus., and Capt. (retired) late P.W.O. Yorkshire Regt., served through S. African War, *b.* 6 Aug. 1868; *m.* 6 Jan. 1896, Kathleen, dau. of William Henry, R.I.C.
  3. Francis Owen, Lieut. 14th Bombay Infantry, *b.* 17 Aug. 1869; *m.* Joanna Somerset, dau. of Sir Charles Farquhar Shand, LL.D., Chief Justice of the Mauritius. He was killed in action near Gras Pan, South Africa, 24 Nov. 1899, leaving issue,
    FRANCIS ARTHUR HARVEY OWEN, *b.* 1888.
    Margaret Frances, *b.* 1889.

4. Cyril Alexander Owen, D.S.O., M.L.C. Cape Colony, and Capt. (retired) late Maj. Comm. Cape Colony Cyclist Corps; served through S. African War; *b.* 28 Jan. 1871; *d. unm.* 10 Nov. 1905.
1. Frances Isabella Sophia Mary Owen, *m.* 2 March, 1897, Sir AlfredMoloney,K.C.M.G., late Governor of Trinidad and Tobago.
2. Frederica Sophia Elizabeth Mary Owen, for whom His Majesty the King of Hanover stood sponsor, *m.* 23 Jan. 1894, John Joseph Chevers, D.L. of Killyan, and has issue (*see that family*).

Mr. Lewis *m.* 2ndly, 21 Feb. 1903, Baroness Louise von Robendorff.

Lineage—FRANCIS LEWIS settled in Ireland about the middle of the 17th century, and acquired property in the counties of Kildare, Meath, and Queen's Co. He *m.* Elizabeth Bedurda, and was father of

WILLIAM LEWIS, of Tullygory, co. Kildare, *m.* Margaret, dau. of Francis Roberts, by Jean O'Kelly his wife, and was *s.* by his son,

MICHAEL LEWIS, of Tullygory, *m.* Susanna, dau. of Edmund Jones, M.P. for Duleek 1696, by Rebecca his wife, dau. of William Crutchley, of Crutchley Hall, co. Stafford, and had a son and successor,

ROBERT LEWIS, of Dublin and of Queen's Co., *m.* Anne, dau. of Arthur Gambell, of Washbrook, co. Westmeath, M.P. for Ballyshannon, by Elizabeth his wife, dau. of Major John D'Alton, of Dunuel Castle, co. Westmeath. By Anne Gambell his wife Robert Lewis had a son and heir,

MICHAEL LEWIS, of Spring Hill, co. Dublin, *b.* 1750; *m.* 1786, Anne, only dau. of Richard Frizell, of Beaufort House, co. Dublin, and had issue by her (who *d.* 1825),
1. WILLIAM, of Harlech, co. Dublin, and of Kilcullen, co. Kildare, *m.* Dora, dau. of John Cassidy, of Monasterevan, and *d.* 1850, leaving issue,
 1. JOHN HARVEY, of Kilcullen. co. Kildare, J.P. and D.L. for Middlesex, High Sheriff co. Kildare 1857, M.P. for Marylebone 1861-74, M.A. Trin. Coll. Dublin, 1838, *b.* 1814; *m.* 1st, 27 Aug. 1840, Emily Owen, only child of George Ball, of Richmond, Surrey, which lady *d.s.p.* 11 Nov. 1850. He *m.* 2ndly, 1851, Jane Isabella, dau. of William Brown, and *d.s.p.* 1889.
 2. William, Clerk of the Crown, co. Kildare, *b.* 1818; *m.* 1845, Jane, dau. of Michael Hackett, of Elm Grove, King's Co., and *d.* 1878, leaving issue,
 (1) William, of Haddington House, Kingstown, co. Dublin, *b.* 1849. (2) Harvey.
 3. Edward Valentine.
 1. Mary Anne, *m.* 1839, Robert Morellet Alloway, J.P. of the Derries, Queen's Co.
2. ARTHUR GAMBELL, of whom presently.
3. Richard, *m.* 1st, Emily, dau. of J. Osborne; 2ndly, Anna Maria, dau. of Thomas Taylor, of Polygon House, Southampton, and 3rdly, Frances Tyler, niece of Admiral Sir Charles Tyler, and left issue.
4. Robert, R.N., *m.* Elizabeth, 3rd dau. of Sir Richard Onslow, 1st bart., K.B., Vice Admiral of England and Gen. of Marines, and *d.* 1840, leaving issue. She *d.* at Brighton, 25 Nov. 1861.
5. Edward, *m.* his cousin, Henrietta, dau. and co-heir of H. Loftus Frizell, and *d.* 1874, leaving issue.
6. Edmond Jones (Rev.), *m.* Elizabeth, dau. of the Rev. William Lyster, and niece of James, Bishop of Dromore, and *d.* 1877, leaving issue.
1. Anne, *m.* Major J. Fielding Sweeny, and *d.* 1877, leaving issue.
2. Eleanora, *m.* Major F. Bernard Sweeny, and *d.* 1882.
3. Charlotte, *m.* Capt. Stuart, and *d.* 1837.
Michael Lewis *d.* 1824. His 2nd son,

LIEUT.-COL. ARTHUR GAMBELL LEWIS, D.L. and J.P., High Sheriff of Monaghan 1847, and Longford 1854, *b.* 7 Dec. 1790; *m.* 1st. 1820, Hester, 2nd dau. of Richard Westenra, of Rutland Square, Dublin, uncle of the 2nd Lord Rossmore, by whom (who *d.* 1837) he had issue,
1. Maurice Peppard Warren, LL.D., *b.* 1821; *d. unm.* 1865.
He *m.* 2ndly, 1841, Henrietta, relict of the Hon. Richard Westenra, 2nd son of the 1st Lord Rossmore, and only child and heiress of Henry Owen Scott (*d.* 1797), of Scotstown, co. Monaghan, by Olivia his wife, 2nd dau. and co-heir of John Owen, of Racconnell, near Monaghan, by whom (who *d.* 1860) he had
2. HENRY OWEN, now of Inniskeen and Seatown.
Col. Lewis, who had served in the 68th Regt., and was subsequently Lieut.-Col. of the Monaghan Militia, *d.* 22 Sept. 1869.

Arms—Sa., on a chevron erm. between three spear-heads arg. a crescent gu. **Crest**—Out of a ducal coronet ppr. a plume of five ostrich feathers alternately gu. and az. charged with a chevron or, thereon a crescent gu. **Motto**—Bidd Llu Hebb Llydd.

Seat—Inniskeen, Monaghan. **Residence**—52, Cranley Gardens, S.W. **Club**—Junior Carlton.

LIDWILL OF DROMARD.

ROBERT ARTHUR LIDWILL, of Dromard, co. Tipperary, J.P., B.A. Trin. Coll. Dub., called to the Irish Bar 1899, Major 3rd Royal Fusiliers, *b.* 15 April, 1871; *m.* 11 Aug. 1909, Edith Gustava, youngest dau. of Robert Gabbett Parker, of Ballyvalley, co. Clare (*see that family*).

Lineage.—JOHN LIDWILL, of Shannaghmore, co. Tipperary (son of Robert Lidwill, of Shannaghmore, by Mary his wife, sister of Launcelot Caulfield), who purchased property to a large extent at Castle Dermot, co. Kildare. He *m.* Eleanor, dau. of Thomas Cooke, of Painstown, by Ellen his wife, eldest dau. and co-heir of Nicholas Purcell, baron of Loughmore, co. Tipperary, and had issue,
1. GEORGE, his heir.
2. Thomas, who *m.* (settlement dated 1736) Jemima, dau. and heiress of Mark Cowley, of Clonmore, and Cormackstown, co. Tipperary, and *d.* 1782, leaving, with four daus., as many sons,
 1. John, of Rushall, Queen's Co., *m.* Anne Fitzpatrick, of Ballybooden, and had issue.
 2. Mark, of Clonmore, Cormackstown and Annfield, High Sheriff of Tipperary 1779; *m.* 8 Dec. 1774, Lucy, dau. of Michael Scanlan, of Ballyneha, co. Limerick, J.P., and had issue.
 3. George, a Capt. in the Roden Fencibles, *m.* Mary, dau. of O'Brien Butler, of Bansha Castle, co. Tipperary, and *d.s.p.*
 4. Thomas, of Clonmore, *m.* 14 Jan. 1774, Elizabeth Julia, dau. of John O'Grady, of Kilballyowen, by Mary his wife, dau. and co-heir of Gerald de Courcy, Lord Kingsale, and left an only dau. and heiress,
 Mary Margaret, *m.* Henry Grove Grady, of Bellwood, co. Tipperary.

John Lidwill, of Shannagbmore, *d.* 2 Jan. 1769, aged 66. Their eldest son and heir,

GEORGE LIDWILL, of Lissannure, co. Tipperary, *m.* Miss Sall, of Cashel, a co-heiress, and had two sons,
1. JOHN, his heir.
2. Robert, of Lissannure, *m.* Hester, dau. of Joseph Gubbins, of Kilfrush, co. Limerick, and *d.* 1790.
The elder son and heir,

JOHN LIDWILL, of Dromard, co. Tipperary, commonly known as "Black Jack," *m.* Catherine, dau. of Patrick Fitzpatrick, of Ballybooden, of the noble family of Upper Ossory, and co-heiress of her brother Timothy Fitzpatrick, of Ballybooden, and *d.* 1807, aged 74, leaving with other issue,
1. GEORGE, his heir. 2. John Lidwill.
The elder son,

GEORGE LIDWILL, of Dromard, a well-known littérateur and politician, High Sheriff Tipperary 1807, *m.* (licence dated 17 March, 1792) Elinor, dau. of Morgan Kavanagh, of Ballyhale, co. Kilkenny (*see* KAVANAGH *of Borris*), by Lady Frances Butler his wife, sister of John, Earl of Ormonde, and left (with two daus., Frances and Catherine) two sons, FREDERICK and Henry. The latter *d. unm.* She *d.* 2 Sept. 1802. He *d.* 1839. His elder son,

FREDERICK LIDWILL, of Dromard, *m.* 1826, Christiana, dau. of William Hutchinson, of Timoney, co. Tipperary, and *d.* 1858, having by her (who *d.* 1833) had issue (with a dau., Anna, who *m.* 1853, Capt. W. J. Hoare, 7th Royal Fusiliers, and *d.* 1856, leaving a dau., Anna Maria) a son, GEORGE, now of Dromard.

MAJOR GEORGE LIDWILL, of Dromard, co. Tipperary, J.P., late Capt. 19th Regt., served in the Eastern Campaign of 1845-5, in Turkey and the Crimea, in the Light Division; was present at the battles of Alma and Inkerman. He was *b.* 1828; *s.* his father 1868; *m.* 14 Oct. 1863, Edith Wheatley, dau. of Henry Adams, of Kersington, by whom (who *d.* 22 March, 1877) he had issue,
1. George John Frederick, *b.* 20 Oct. 1869; late Lieut. 19th Princess of Wales' Own Hussars.
2. ROBERT, ARTHUR, now of Dromard.
1. Eleanor, *m.* 1883, Major-Gen. Watt, late 64th Regt.
2. Edith Margaret. *m.* 25 Jan. 1899, Henry Hewson Fetherstonhaugh, son of the late Capt. Harry Fetherstonhaugh, of Tullamore (*see* FETHERSTONHAUGH *of Carrick*), and has issue.
He *m.* 2ndly, 1882, Mary, dau. of late John Newell, of Fartield Addiscombe, who *d.* 29 June, 1906. He *m.* 3rdly, Margaret J. Williams, and *d.* 14 Oct. 1908, and was *s.* by his second son.

Arms—Arg., fretty gu., on a chief engrailed az. a leopard passant guardant between two fleurs-de-lys or. **Crest**—A demi lion sa. crowned with an Irish crown or, and charged on the shoulder with a fleur-de-lys as in the arms. **Motto**—Vis unita fortior.

Seat—Dromard, Templemore, co. Tipperary. **Club**—University (Dublin).

LINDESAY, late OF LOUGHRY.

Lineage.—The first who settled in Ireland, upon the confiscation of the O'Neils in Ulster, were two brothers, BERNARD LINDESAY, of Lough Hill, co. Haddington, Gentleman of the Bedchamber to King JAMES VI, and ROBERT LINDESAY, Chief Harbinger to that monarch, sons of THOMAS LINDESAY, of Kingswark, in Leith, which Thomas held several offices of high honour and trust, as well as emolument, under MARY, Queen of Scotland, and her son, King JAMES VI, such as Searcher-General of Leith, in 1562, which he resigned in favour of his son, Bernard, on 15 Oct. 1594. In Oct. 1580, he held the office of Snowdon Herald, and is also described as Snowdon Herald on 15 Oct. 1594. King JAMES provided, not only for him, but his family, by pensions, &c.: to his daus., Agnes and Elizabeth, out of the rents and tithes of the Abbey of North Becwick; also to his sons, Bernard, Thomas, and Robert, from other lands belonging to the Friars of Linlithgow. Thomas Lindesay, the Snowdon Herald and Searcher General of Leith, was living 15 Oct. 1594. (*See* WILSON's *Memorials of Edinburgh*, LORD LINDSAY's *Lives of the Lindsays*, and CASSELL's *Edinburgh*). His son,

ROBERT LINDESAY, of Leith, Chief Harbinger and Comptroller of the Artillery to King JAMES I in Scotland, obtained from that monarch a grant of the manor and lands of Tullahoge, Loughry, &c., co. Tyrone, by Patent dated 21 June, 1611. He *m.* Janet Acheson, and by her (who survived him, and was living 1619) he had a son and successor,

ROBERT LINDESAY, of Loughry and Tullahoge, who obtained a second patent of the said manor and lands of Loughry and Tullahoge, described therein as Manor Lindesay, in the 14th year of the reign of CHARLES I., and who built the mansion house of Loughry in 1632, which was burnt by the rebels in 1641, and rebuilt by him in 1671. He was an Officer in the Royal Army at the battle of Worcester. He *m.* Margaret, dau. of James Richardson, of Castle Hill, co. Tyrone, and *d.* 18 May, 1674, aged 70, having had issue (with three daus.) three sons;

1. ROBERT, of whom presently.
2. Alexander, of Cahoo, present with his brother Robert at the siege of Derry, in defence of which city he is stated to have lost his life, 1689. From him descended

WALTER LINDESAY, of Glen View, co. Wicklow, J.P. for cos. Wicklow and Dublin, Barrister-at-Law, *b.* 10 April, 1808; *m.* 1st, 1830, Thomasine Jane, only dau. of Robert Jephson, and niece of Sir Richard M. Jephson, 1st bart., which lady *d.* 1830; 2ndly, 28 March, 1838, Harriet Cole, 2nd dau. of William Cornish, of Marazion, Cornwall, D.L. and J.P., and *d.* 1877, leaving issue,

(1) Walter Brocas (Rev.), M.A., LL.D., *b.* 25 Dec. 1848; *m.* 1st, 1871, Agnes, dau. of Rev. Robert Gibbings, D.D. She *d.* 1879. He *m.* 2ndly, 1881, Henrietta Maria, dau. of Very Rev. A. H. Leech, M.A., Dean of Cashel, and has issue, Walter, Brocas, and Ellen.
(1) Nora Cole.   (2) Harriet Mary Ann Foster.
(1) Frances Honora.

3. William, described in a deed of 1667 as having "gone to parts beyond sea."

The elder son,

ROBERT LINDESAY, of Loughry and Tullahoge a refugee and defender in Derry during the siege, *m.* Anne, dau. of John Morris, of Bellville, co. Tyrone, and *d.* 1691, leaving issue,

1. Robert, of Loughry and Tullahoge, M.P. co. Tyrone, 1726, Judge of the Common Pleas 1733, *b.* 1679. This gentleman was the intimate friend of Dean Swift.* He *m.* 1707, Elizabeth, dau. of Edward Singleton, of Drogheda, and sister of Henry Singleton, Lord Chief Justice of the Common Pleas, Ireland, and afterwards Master of the Rolls in that kingdom, and had issue, one son and one dau.,

Robert, *d.* an infant.   Anne, *d. unm.*

2. JOHN, of whose line we treat.

The eldest son, Judge Lindesay, having *d.s.p.* 1742, was *s.* by his brother,

JOHN LINDESAY, of Loughry and Tullahoge, *b.* 1686; *m.* 1744, Elizabeth, dau. of Rev. Bellingham Mauleverer, Rector of Maghera, co. Derry, and grand-dau. of William Nicolson, Archbishop of Cashel, and *d.* 1761, leaving a son and successor,

ROBERT LINDESAY, of Loughry and Tullahoge, M.P. for Dundalk, 1781, a Deputy-Governor of Tyrone, Assistant-Barrister co. Tyrone, *b.* 11 April, 1747; *m.* 6 July, 1775, his second cousin, Jane, eldest dau. and co-heir of Thomas Mauleverer, of Arncliffe Hall, co. York, and by her (who was *b.* 24 July, 1753, and *d.* 18 April, 1824) had issue,

1. John, Lieut. 16th Regt., and afterwards Lieut.-Col. Royal Tyrone Militia Mayor of Cashel 1825, *b.* 20 Feb. 1780; *m.* Maryanne (who *d.* 25 Dec. 1873), dau. of Richard Pennefather, of New Park, co. Tipperary, M.P. for Cashel; and *d.* in the lifetime of his father, 6 Nov. 1826, leaving an only son,

JOHN LINDESAY, D.L., Lieut. 23rd, and afterwards Lieut. in the 7th Royal Fusiliers, High Sheriff 1840, *b.* 16 March, 1808; *s.* to the family estate on the death of his grandfather 1832. He *m.* 31 May, 1836, Harriott Hester (who *d.* 18 March, 1878), dau. of the Right Hon. Charles Watkin Williams-Wynn, M.P., of Langedwin, brother to Sir Watkin Williams-Wynn, Bart., M.P., of Wynnstay, co. Denbigh, but *d.s.p.* 7 Aug. 1848, and was *s.* by his uncle, FREDERICK LINDESAY, late of Loughry.

2. ¶Robert, *d.* an infant.
3. FREDERICK, of Loughry, J.P. and D.L., M.A., Barrister-

---

* See Sir Walter Scott's *Life of Swift*. Robert Lindesay was the "eminent lawyer" of Swift's works. A summer house known as "Swift's House," in which he wrote some of his works, still stands at Loughry.

---

at-Law, High Sheriff 1859, *b.* 2 Jan. 1792; *m.* 1st, 23 Sept. 1823, Agnes Cornish Bayntun, eldest dau. and co-heiress of Sir Edwin Bayntun Sandys, Bart. of Miserden Park, co. Gloucester, and Hadlington Hall, co. Oxford, and by her (who *d.* 10 May, 1842) had issue,

1. Robert Sandys, late 30th Regt., Capt. Royal Tyrone Fusiliers Militia, *d.* Feb. 1870.
2. FREDERICK JOHN SANDYS, of Loughry, Major formerly 3rd Dragoon Guards, 4th Hussars and 17th Regt., *b.* 1830; *d.* 16 Oct. 1877, and was *s.* by his brother.
3. Thomas Edward, Lieut. 22nd Bengal Native Infantry, killed in India, 10 June, 1857.
4. JOSHUA EDWARD CHARLES COOPER, late of Loughry, J.P. and D.L., Lieut.-Col. 3rd Batt. East Lancashire Regt., late 30th Regt., *b.* 14 Feb. 1838; *d.* 1 Feb. 1893, and was *s.* by his cousin.

1. Jane Mauleverer Agnes, *d. unm.* 20 July, 1840.
2. Philippa Allen, *m.* Capt. Robert John Knox, J.P., late of the Carabineers (6th Dragoon Guards), and of Cahirleske, co. Kilkenny, and has had issue, three sons and eight daus. He *d.* 30 Oct. 1901. She *d.* 27 July, 1907.
3. Agnes Sarah, *m.* John Bagwell, of Lisronagh, co. Tipperary. He *d.* 29 Jan. 1898. She *d.* 21 Feb. 1901, leaving issue (1) Frederick Taylor, *w.* 11 Jan. 1894, Hilda, dau. of John Turnly, of Drumnasole, co. Antrim, and has issue; (2) Edward; (3) John Percy, *d. unm.* 9 April, 1891; (1) Blanche, *m.* 7 Aug. 1884, R. F. Harrison, K.C., (2) Pauline, *m.* 30 Jan. 1892, Philip Wade; (3) Edith, *m.* April, 1889, Capt. Hinde, 12th Royal Lancers; (4) Alice, *d. unm.* 23 Dec. 1895. He *m.* 2ndly, Nov. 1856, Charlotte, 4th surviving dau. of Henry Charles Boyle Mac-Murrough Murphy, late of Hume Street, Dublin, by Susan his wife, dau. of John Jacob, M.D., of Maryborough, Queen's Co., and *d.* 10 July, 1871, having had issue,
5. William Frederick (Rev.), B.A. Oxon, Rector of St. Cuthbert's Church and Chaplain of H.M. Prison, Bedford, *b.* 1857; *d.* 14 Feb. 1907.
6. Charles de la Poire Crawford, C.E., *b.* 1 July, 1863; *m.* 26 Dec. 1889, Amy Carleton, dau. of George Howard Bigg Wither (*see* BIGG-WITHER *of Manydown*), and has had issue,
    (1) Hugh Howard, *b.* 24 Nov. 1892
    (2) Robert Noel Carleton, *b.* 25 Dec. 1897.
    (1) Frances Mabel Amy, *b.* 10 Oct. 1895; *d.* 5 Oct. 1896.
7. Alexander Robert Knox, *d.* an infant.
8. Victor Edward Hugh, Major Indian Medical Service, *b.* 24 May, 1869; *m.* 6 June, 1898, Frances Helen Levine, dau. of Major W. Merrick Fowler, 61st Foot, of Strode Manor, Dorset, and has issue,
    (1) Frederick Hugh Byres, *b.* (twin) 9 May, 1908; *d.* 2 June, 1909.
    (2) Robert John Byres, *b.* 8 Nov. 1910.
    (1) Enid Katharine Jessie, *b.* 18 May, 1900.
    (2) Dorothy Mauleverer, *b.* 14 Feb. 1905.
    (3) Helen Loughry, *b.* (twin) 9 May, 1908; *d.* 31 May, 1908.
9. Robert Thomas Mauleverer, *b.* 1870; *m.* 26 Oct. 1894, Louisa, youngest dau. of the late John Barnard, of Cotham, Bristol, and by her has issue,
    Elizabeth Katharine, *b.* 16 Dec. 1895.
4. Flora Charlotte Helena, *m.* 24 May, 1893, Rev. Octavius Frederick Pigot, Chaplain of H.M. Prison, Wandsworth.
5. Emmeline Stuart, *m.* 3 July, 1894, Ernest Henry Godfrey, only surviving son of the late Valentine Godfrey, of Glaston, Rutland, and has issue.
6. Charlotte Philippa Bendreda, *d.* an infant, June, 1866.
7. Alexandra Philippa Anna, *m.* Major Vivina Boase Bennett, Indian Medical Service, and has issue.

4. Thomas (Rev.), Rector of Upper Cumber, *b.* 25 Dec. 1794; *m.* 1st, 1 Dec. 1835, Harriet Catherine, dau. of the Hon. and Right Rev. Richard Ponsonby, Lord Bishop of Derry, and sister of William, 4th and last Lord Ponsonby of that creation. She *d.* Dec. 1836. He *m.* 2ndly, 28 March, 1840, Elizabeth, dau. and co-heiress of Henry Coddington, of Donore (*see* CODDINGTON *of Oldbridge*), by his wife Eleanor Hamilton, of Brown Hall. She *d.* 5 Nov. 1885. He *d.* 2 March, 1860, leaving issue,
1. Robert Thomas, *b.* 15 Jan. 1841; *d. unm.* 20 Jan. 1862.
2. HENRY RICHARD PONSONBY, of Loughry, co. Tyrone, and of Donore, Ivy Bridge, South Devon, Lieut.-Col. Reserve of Officers, late 60th Rifles and 20th Regt., educated at Rossall School and Trin. Coll. Dublin, *b.* 27 July, 1843; *s.* to the Loughry property by will of his cousin, the late FREDERICK JOHN SANDYS LINDESAY, of Loughry; *m.* 20 July, 1898, Frances Mary, dau. of the Rev. J. Irwin, Rector of Hurworth-on-Tees. He *d.s.p.* 1 Sept. 1903.
3. Thomas (*Auckland, New Zealand*), *b.* 4 Feb. 1845; *m.* 1 Aug. 1874, Inez Eva Isabel, dau. of Lieut.-Col. the Hon. Ponsonby Peacocke, of Hawthornden, Howick, New Zealand, and has had issue, four sons and three daus.
4. Frederick, *b.* 18 Jan. 1848; *m.* Dec. 1874, Mary S., dau. of P. H. Delamotte, and has had issue, three sons and three daus.
5. John, *b.* 20 Jan. 1851.
6. Abraham Hamilton, Lieut. R.N., *b.* 6 April, 1852; *d. unm.* 17 April, 1888.
7. Edward, Major, late Royal Scots and Loyal North Lancashire Regt., *b.* 6 Sept. 1853; *m.* 20 Sept. 1892, Eva, dau. of Surg. Gen. James Davis, I.M.S., and has issue, Henry James Coddington, Thomas, Hamilton, and Edward Mauleverer.
8. William O'Neill (Rev.), M.A., late Rector of Upper Cumber, co. Derry, formerly Rector of Barons Court, co. Tyrone, *b.* 5 Jan. 1857; *m.* 20 April, 1898, Priscilla Sarah, dau. of G. J. Buck.

1. Ellen Jane.
2. Elizabeth Frances, *m.* 12 Aug. 1869, Charles Stewart, of Hornhead, co. Donegal, and *d.* 5 March, 1881, leaving issue (*see that family*).
3. Isabella, *m.* 20 April, 1875, Henry Wilton, D.I., R.I.C., and has issue.
1. Jane, of 28, Imperial Square, Cheltenham.
2. Sarah, *m.* James Cranbourne Strode, cousin, both by father and mother, to the 2nd Marquess of Salisbury, *d.* 31 Oct. 1851.
3. Eliza, *m.* Col. Joshua Cooper, of Markree (*see that family*).
4. Mary, *m.* Bellingham Mauleverer, *d.* Nov. 1858.
5. Fanny, *m.* Col. O'Neill. 6. Anne, *d. unm.*
Mr. Lindesay *d.* 6 Jan. 1832.

LINDSAY OF GLASNEVIN.

LIEUT.-COL. HENRY GORE LINDSAY, of Glasnevin House, co. Dublin, J.P. and D.L. cos. Dublin and Brecon, C.C. co. Dublin, Lieut.-Col. Brecon R.V. 1861-83, formerly Capt. Rifle Brigade and Chief Constable of Glamorganshire, *b.* 26 Aug. 1830; *m.* 14 May, 1856, Hon. Ellen Sarah Morgan, dau. of Charles, 1st Lord Tredegar (*see* BURKE'S *Peerage*), and has issue,

1. HENRY EDZELL MORGAN, C.B., late Capt. R.E., now Lieut.-Col. Commanding Royal Monmouthshire Royal Reserve Engineers, J.P. Glamorgan and co. Dublin (*Ystrad Mynach, Cardiff, and Naval and Military Club*), *b.* 13 Feb. 1857; *m.* 24 July, 1889, Ellen Katherine, eldest dau. of George William Griffiths Thomas, of Ystrad Mynach, Giamorgan, and has issue,
   1. George Walter Thomas, *b.* 29 Jan. 1891.
   2. Claud Frederic Thomas, *b.* 20 Jan. 1892.
   3. Archibald Thurston Thomas, *b.* 17 June, 1897.
   4. David Edzell Thomas, *b.* 28 March, 1910.
   1. Ellen Blanche, *b.* 22 Dec. 1893.
   2. Nest Jessie, *b.* 23 May, 1898.
2. Claud Gore, Lieut. R.N., *b.* 15 April, 1859; *d. unm.* 15 Dec. 1886.
3. Lionel Arthur, Chief Constable of Glamorganshire, late Egyptian Gendarmerie 1884-9 (*Canton, Cardiff*), *b.* 27 March, 1861.
4. David Balcarres, Capt. Gloucestershire Hussars (*Willesley House, Tetbury, Gloucester, and White's Club*), *b.* 15 Feb. 1863; *m.* 11 Jan. 1898, Grace Maud, dau. of George Miller, and has issue.
   1. Mandeline, *b.* 2 Jan. 1899.
   2. Juliet Mary, *b.* 27 Jan. 1904.
   3. Winifred Laura, *b.* 24 May, 1907.
5. Walter Charles, M.V.O., Capt. 3rd Batt. Royal Dublin Fus., Gentleman in Waiting to the Lord Lieutenant of Ireland, High Sheriff co. Kilkenny, 1911 (*Ballyhinch House, Thomastown co. Kilkenny. Clubs—White's, Kildare Street*), *b.* 11 March, 1866; *m.* 24 March, 1897, Lady Kathleen Butler, only dau. of Charles Henry Somerset, 6th Earl of Carrick, and has issue,
   1. Doreen, *b.* 29 June, 1899.
   2. Kathleen, *b.* 7 Aug. 1902.
6. George Mackintosh, Capt. Rifle Brigade, served in South Africa, 1901-2 (despatches, medal), *b.* 3 July, 1880.
   1. Ellen Rosamond Mary, *m.* 16 Nov. 1898, Charles Ernest Alfred French Somerset, 7th Earl of Carrick, and has issue (*see* BURKE'S *Peerage*).

Col. Lindsay is the elder surviving son of the late George Hayward Lindsay, of Glasnevin House, co. Dublin, J.P. and D.L., High Sheriff 1862 (who *d.* 5 Jan. 1886), and the Lady Mary Catherine Gore (who *d.* 28 April, 1885), sister of 4th Earl of Arran, K.P., and grandson of the Hon. and Rt. Rev. Charles Dalrymple Lindsay, D.D., Bishop of Kildare, 6th son of John, 5th Earl of Balcarres.

Lineage.—*See* BURKE'S *Peerage*, CRAWFORD AND BALCARRES, E.

Seat—Glasnevin House, Dublin. *Clubs*—Army and Navy, and Kildare Street.

LINDSEY-FITZPATRICK. *See* FITZPATRICK.

LITTLE OF STEWARTSTOWN.

EMILY KYLE LITTLE, of Stewartstown, co. Tyrone, 2nd dau. of the late Samuel Little, J.P., eldest son of John Little, of Stewartstown, *s.* her aunt 1901.

Lineage—The family of LITTLE has been settled in co. Tyrone for the last two hundred years.

ALEXANDER LITTLE, of Legacurry, *b.* 1729; *m.* 1755, Ann, eldest dau. of Samuel Eliot, of Tullybogue, and *d.* 11 April, 1773, having by her (who *d.* 24 Sept. 1790) had issue,

1. SAMUEL, of whom hereafter.
2. James, *b.* 1758; *m.* Belinda, dau. of William Park, of Rocklodge, co. Tyrone, and had issue,
   Elizabeth, *m.* Samuel Jones, of Tullybogue, and had one son, James Little.
3. John, *b.* 1760; *d.s.p.* 1780.

The eldest son,

SAMUEL LITTLE, of Stewartstown, *b.* 1756, an Officer of the 1st Tyrone Regt. of Volunteers, *m.* 1783, Sarah Eliot, 2nd dau. of Samuel Park, of Stewartstown, and Anna Carson his wife (the "beautiful Anna Carson"), and *d.* 2 June, 1828, having by her (who *d.* 8 Aug. 1845) had issue,

1. John, *b.* 10 Oct. 1790; *d.* 1796.
2. JOHN, of whom hereafter.
1. Anna, *d.* in infancy. 2. Jane, *d.* in infancy.
3. Sarah Anne, *d.* in infancy.
4. Mary, *m.* 27 Dec. 1814, Charles William, 2nd son of William Hardy, of Loughgall, co. Armagh, J.P.; an Officer of the Armagh Regt. of Light Infantry, and *d.* 1 868, leaving issue by him,
   1. Samuel Little, *b.* 30 Oct.1815, M.D., F.R.C.S.; *m.* 1850, Mary, dau. of Robert Montgomery, M.D., and *d.* 29 Oct. 1863, leaving, with other issue, Henry and Emma.
   2. William, *b.* 19 July, 1817; *d.* young.
   3. John, *b.* 7 Nov. 1823, Capt. 3rd West Indian Regt.; *d.* 9 Sept. 1851.
   4. Charles Henry, *b.* 1823, M.D., settled in Australia.
   1. Sarah Jane, *d.* young.
   2. Elizabeth Anne, *m.* 10 Dec. 1846, Thomas Falkner Fleetwood, and has had issue,
      (1) Thomas, *b.* 29 Oct. 1847.
      (2) Charles Henry H., *b.* 25 Nov. 1848.
      (3) William John, *b.* 12 Sept. 1850.
      (4) George Samuel, *b.* 8 Aug. 1852, *d.* young.
      (5) Arthur Little, *b.* 24 Feb. 1856; *d.* 1863.
      (6) Edwin James, *b.* 8 Sept. 1858; *d.* 1860.
      (1) Mary Sybella, *d.* 1883. (2) Henrietta Elizabeth.
      (3) Emma.
   3. Mary, *d.* young from an accident.
5. Elizabeth Anna, *d.* 1874.
6. Sarah Jane, *m.* 12 Dec. 1823, Rev. Robert Allen, D.D., and *d.* 23 Feb. 1858, leaving issue,
   1. John Little, *b.* 28 Dec. 1824; *d.* 3 June, 1846.
   2. Samuel, *b.* 23 June,1826, M.D.; *m.* 23 July, 1863, Elizabeth, eldest dau. of Samuel Gibson, and *d.* 20 Nov. 1874, having by her (who *d.* 23 May, 1884) had issue,
      Samuel Gibson, *b.* 9 June, 1864; *d.* young.
      Sarah.
   3. Robert Austen, *b.* 23 Dec. 1829, M.D., Surg.-Major Army Medical Staff and 71st H.L.I.; *m.* 18 Jan. 1859, Mary Franklin, dau. of Andrew Risk, of Manweny, co. Donegal, and *d.* 4 Dec. 1876, leaving issue,
      (1) Robert Franklin, *b.* 21 Feb. 1860, Capt. R.E.; *m.* 11 Dec. 1886, Alice Gordon, dau. of Surg.-Gen. Jackson, and has issue,
         Robert Austen, *b.* 18 Sept. 1887.
      (2) Sydney Glen, *b.* 30 March, 1863, Surg. Army Medical Staff. (3) Charles William, *b.* 8 Aug. 1868.
7. Margaret, *d.* 3 June, 1867. 8. Eleanor, *d.* young.

The eldest surviving son,

JOHN LITTLE, of Stewartstown, *b.* 8 March, 1803; *m.* 1831, Emily Higinbotham, youngest dau. of Samuel Kyle, and by her (who *d.* 9 Feb. 1875) had issue,

1. SAMUEL, J.P., *b.* 3 July, 1833; *m.* 1861, Hannah, eldest dau. of Bryan Padgett Gregson, of Caton, Lancashire, J.P. and D.L., and *d.v.p.* 1880, leaving issue,
   1. Bryan Padgett Gregson, *b.* 9 March, 1862; *d.* 1887.
   2. JOHN, *b.* 26 April, 1867; *m.* 4 Nov. 1895, Agnes Stuart, dau. of Sir John Usher, Bart., J.P. and D.L., of Norton and Wells, Roxburghshire, and has issue,
      (1) John, *b.* 30 Dec. 1897.
      (1) Ellen Mary. (2) Joan Kathleen Bulmer.
   3. Samuel, *d.* in infancy.
   1. Hannah Gibson.
   2. EMILY KYLE, now of Stewartstown.
   3. Margaret Maudsley, *d.* 3 Jan. 1884.
   4. Ellen Murray, *d.* 3 Aug. 1870.
   5. Mary Eveline.
   6. Kathleen Alice, *m.* 4 June, 1902, Arthur James Meidrum, D.L. of Dechmont, co. Linlithgow, and has issue.
2. Robert Kyle, *b.* 4 Dec. 1834, Capt. 97th and 22nd Regts. (served in the Crimea and in the Indian Mutiny); *m.* 1868, Dora, eldest dau. of James Irvine, of Springfield, co. Tyrone, and *d.* 15 Jan. 1880, leaving issue,
   1. John, *b.* 1 July, 1875.
   2. Sydney Hamilton, *b.* 9 May, 1880.
   1. Mary Ormsby. 2. Emily Kyle.
   3. Ellinor Murray. 4. Hannah.
3. John, *b.* 23 Nov. 1835, Capt. 20th Regt. (served in the Crimea and in the Indian Mutiny); *d. unm.* 10 April, 1858, at the Field Hospital, Cawnpore.
4. Henry Alexander, C.B., Lieut.-Gen. in the Army, served in the Crimea and the N.W. Frontier campaign (1864-5), and in the Burmese war (1888-9); *b.* 14 Aug. 1837; *m.* 1866, Ellen Wade, eldest dau. of the late David Peter Thompson, J.P., of Stonestown and Park, King's Co. (*see* THOMPSON *of Clonfin*), and *d.* 7 Sept. 1908, leaving issue,
   John David George, *b.* 24 Feb. 1868; *d.* 10 Jan. 1907.
   Gerard Eleanor.
5. Charles William, *b.* 26 Oct. 1838; *d.* young.
6. William John Knox KNOX-LITTLE (Rev.), *b.* 1 Dec. 1839, M.A. Camb., Vicar of Hoar Cross, Staffordshire 1885-1907, Canon

of Worcester; m. 1866, Annie, eldest dau. of Henry Gregson, J.P., of Moorlands, Lancaster, and has issue,
  1. Arthur Henry Alban Knox, b. 17 June, 1867; m. 1894, Ethel, dau. of James Sykes Wright, and has issue,
    (1) William John Knox, b. 18 March, 1909.
    (1) Marjory Knox.   (2) Mary Knox.
  2. Francis Gore Knox, b. 25 July, 1875; d. 28 Feb. 1908.
  3. Harold Edward Knox, b. 14 Feb. 1877.
  4. Walter Lawrence Wood Knox, b. 4 Sept. 1878.
  5. William John Knox, b. 7 Feb. 1881.
  6. Charles Hugo Knox, b. 21 Nov. 1887.
  1. Rose Emily Knox, m. 26 Nov. 1901, Frederick Usher, D.L. of Broomhouse, Duns, Berwickshire, 4th son of Sir John Usher, Bart., and has issue (see BURKE's *Peerage*).
  2. Rhoda Edith Knox, m. 31 July, 1900, Col. Hon. Richard Thompson Lawley, C.B., 2nd son of 3rd Baron Wenlock (see BURKE's *Peerage*).
  3. Ethel Annie Knox.
  4. Mary Catherine Knox, d. 13 Aug. 1909.
7. Francis Lawrence Gore, b. 27 Aug. 1841, Major late R.A., formerly Chief Constable of Preston, Lancashire, m. Jan 1871, Clara Hester, 3rd dau of John Reynolds Dickson, J.P. of Woodville, co. Leitrim, and Kilbarron, co. Donegal, and has issue,
  1. John Francis Gore, b. 9 Jan. 1873.
  2. William Hyacinth Patrick Gore, b. 16 March, 1876; m. 14 Sept. 1905, Clara Frances, dau. of David McAlpin, of Bothesby, Carlisle, and have issue,
    Hester Elizabeth.
  1. Clara Edythe Gore.
  2. Violet Audley Gore, m. 14 June, 1906, Edward Bridges, only son of Rev. E. W. Harford, Canon Residentiary of Wells, and has issue.
  3. Mary Gore, d. 5 Jan. 1910.
  4. Joan Emily Gore.
8. Arthur Wood, b. 9 Aug. 1843; d. 28 May, 1863.
9. Charles Hardy (Rev.), Vicar of Peasedown St. John, Somerset, b. 29 April, 1845, M.A. Oxon. and Dublin, British Chaplain at St. Petersburg 1880-5; Vicar of St. Martin, Brighton, 1887-1903; m. 1873, Mary Ellen (d. 7 May, 1908), 3rd dau. of Bryan Padgett Gregson, J.P. and D.L., of Caton, Lancashire, and has issue,
  Charles Hardy, b. 18 June, 1874; m. 29 July, 1900, Marie Margaret, eldest dau. of Patrick Park Macindoe, of Park Hill, Dalmuir, N.B., and d. Dec. 1910, leaving by her one dau.
  Mary Hardy.
He m. 2ndly, 27 Sept. 1910, Gertrude, youngest dau. of late Henry Pedley, of Crogthorne, Tenterden, Kent.
10. Sydney Hamilton, b. 23 June, 1840, M.A. Oxford, Consul General at Madrid, formerly in Holy Orders; m. 1875, Edith Mary, eldest dau. of John Locke Stratton, of Turweston House, Bucks. She d. 21 Dec. 1907. He d. 8 June, 1905, leaving issue,
  1. Sydney Knox Hamilton, b. 23 Feb. 1878; d. unm. 19 Sept. 1903.
  2. John Hamilton, b. 28 Jan. 1880; d. young.
  3. Henry Charles Hamilton, b. 21 Dec. 1880.
  4. Francis Hamilton, b. 18 Jan. 1883.
  5. Wilfrid Joseph Hamilton, b. 18 Jan. 1887.
  1. Mary Bridgett Hamilton.
  2. Edith Agnes Hamilton, d. young.
11. Emilius George Higinbotham (Rev.), b. 6 April, 1853, M.A. Dublin, sometime assistant British Chaplain at St. Petersburg, Rector of All Saints, Inveraray, N.B.; m. 1880, Dorothy, youngest dau. of Jonathan Hardcastle, J.P., of Blidworth Dale, Notts.
1. Ellen Murray, late of Stewartstown.
Mr. John Little d. 8 Jan. 1889, and was s. at Stewartstown by his only dau.,
ELLEN MURRAY LITTLE, of Stewartstown, co. Tyrone, who d. unm. 11 Sept. 1901, and was s. by her niece, EMILY KYLE LITTLE, now of Stewartstown.

Seat—Stewartstown, co. Tyrone.

LITTON OF ARDAVILLING.

EDWARD FALCONER LITTON, of Ardavilling, co. Cork, b. 4 May, 1896; s. his father 1902.

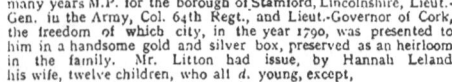

Lineage.—THOMAS LITTON, of Dublin, was b. 1657; he m. 1710, Gertrude, dau. of P. Verdoen, a descendant of an ancient family of Dutch extraction, and d. 24 Dec. 1741. His will was dated 16 Dec. 1741. He was s. by his son and heir,
THOMAS LITTON, of Oldtown, co. Kildare and of Ballyfermot, co. Dublin, b. 27 Feb. 1718, and called to the Irish Bar 1742. He m. 14 Aug. 1742, Hannah, dau. of Ralph Leland (by Hannah Cooke his wife), niece of the Rev. John Leland, D.D., well known as one of the most eminent theologians of his day, and sister of John Leland, for many years M.P. for the borough of Stamford, Lincolnshire, Lieut.-Gen. in the Army, Col. 64th Regt., and Lieut.-Governor of Cork, the freedom of which city, in the year 1790, was presented to him in a handsome gold and silver box, preserved as an heirloom in the family. Mr. Litton had issue, by Hannah Leland his wife, twelve children, who all d. young, except,
  1. Thomas, Barrister-at-Law, d. unm.
  2. EDWARD, of whom hereafter.
  1. Hannah, m. 12 March, 1785, to Richard Weld, of Lodge (now called Eastwood), co. Carlow.

The son,
EDWARD LITTON, of Ballyfermot, co. Dublin, b. 5 Feb. 1754, was Capt. in the 37th Regt. of Foot, in which he served with distinction in the American War, having been present at the battle of Bunker's Hill 1775. He m. 1783, Esther Charlotte, dau. of Very Rev. Daniel Leatablere, D.D., Dean of Tuam, and d. July, 1808, leaving issue,
  1. THOMAS, m. Anne, dau. of Lorenzo Izod Nickson, of Chapel Izod, co. Kilkenny, and niece of Christiana (in her own right) Baroness Donoughmore, of Knocklofty; d. in Dec. 1859, leaving issue two sons, Edward Thomas, and Lorenzo Nickson; and three daus., Elizabeth Charlotte Letablere, Mary Hannah, and Anne Nickson. The eldest son,
    EDWARD THOMAS, J.P., m. 1st, Anne, dau. of Lieut.-Col. Hugh Gore Edwards, 27th Regt., of Raveagh, co. Tyrone, J.P., by whom he had no issue; and 2ndly, Georgina, dau. of William Minchin, of Annagh, co. Tipperary, by whom (who d. 27 March, 1910) he has issue, with three daus., two sons, Thomas Edward and WILLIAM HENRY FREDERICK (5, *Rosetti Mansions, Cheyne Walk, S.W.*), b. 13 Aug. 1864; m. 1886, Catherine, dau. of Major Blayney Thomas Winslow, J.P., of Mount Prospect, Derrylin, co. Fermanagh, and has issue,
      Edward Leslie, b. 1887.
  2. DANIEL, of whom presently.
  3. Edward (Right Hon.), of Altmore, co. Tyrone. Master in Chancery, and many years representative in Parliament for the borough of Coleraine, m. Sept. 1812, Sophia, dau. of the Rev. Henry Stewart, D.D., Rector of Loughgilly, co. Armagh, and niece of the Right Hon. Sir John Stewart, 1st bart. of Ballygawley, M.P., by whom he had, with other issue,
    1. Edward Arthur (Rev.), M.A., Rector of Naunton, co. Gloucester, m. Anne, dau. of Rev. Carus Wilson, of Casterton Hall, Westmorland, and d. Sept. 1897, leaving issue one son, Edward John Letablere, and two daus. Rev. Edward Arthur Litton obtained a double first-class at Oxford, an Oriel fellowship, was Bampton Lecturer, and author of several theological works of great merit.
    2. Richard Weld, Capt. in the 30th and 31st Regts., served in the Crimea in 1855-6. He d. 28 Jan. 1905, having m. 1859, Mary, 3rd dau. of Sir Hugh Stewart, 2nd bart. of Ballygawley, M.P. for Tyrone, and by her (who d. Jan. 1871) has one surviving dau.,
      Agnes Mary Henrietta, who m. 1885, William Lyster Smythe (see SMYTHE of *Barbavilla*).
    1. Sophia Augusta, m. 23 Feb. 1865, to Major the Hon. Edward Sydney Plunkett, 95th Regt., son of Thomas, 11th Lord Louth, and d. 15 April, 1877.
    2. Charlotte Emily, m. 1st, to Rev. Armitage Forbes, by whom she had issue two sons; and 2ndly, 1850, to John Turnly, of Drumnasole, co. Antrim, J.P. and D.L., and has issue.
    3. Harriett Louisa, m. to Lieut.-Col. John Kenneth Mackenzie, 60th Rifles, of Belmaduthy, co. Ross, and has issue.
    4. Mary Letablere, m. 10 April, 1844, to William Carus Wilson, of Casterton Hill, co. Westmorland, and has issue.
    5. Emily Frances, m. 4 June, 1856, to Gen. St. George Mervyn Nugent, of Farrancennell, who d. 29 May, 1884, leaving issue.
  4. John, of Ardavilling, co. Cork, M.A. and J.P., m. Vescina, dau. of Rev. William Hamilton, D.D., Rector of Clondevadock, co. Donegal, J.P., and d.s.p.
  1. Mary, m. Joseph Gabbett, J.P., Barrister-at-Law, author of GABBETT's *Digest of The Statute Law* and *Treatise on the Criminal Law*.

The 2nd son,
DANIEL LITTON, m. Jane, dau. of Falconer Minchin, of Annagh, co. Tipperary, and d. Dec. 1875, leaving by her (who d. 1859) one son and three daus.,
  1. EDWARD FALCONER LITTON, of Ardavilling.
  1. Helena Maria, m. Charles Langley Tuthill, of Ballyteigne, co. Limerick, and has issue.
  2. Charlotte Esther.
  3. Jane Hannah, m. Rev. John Luther, A.M., of Ballyorgan, co. Limerick, and has issue.

His 2nd son,
EDWARD FALCONER LITTON, of Ardavilling, co. Cork, M.A., Q.C., J.P. cos. Cork and Wicklow, and M.P. co. Tyrone 1880 to 1881, b. 1827; m. 1st, 3 July, 1851, Bridget Elizabeth, dau. of Capt. Christopher Tuthill, R.N., and had by her (who d. Dec. 1859) three daus. and three sons,
  1. Daniel Leland, b. 19 March, 1852; d. without issue.
  2. Edward Christopher, b. 19 May, 1858; d. unm.
  3. Robert Tuthill, of Melbourne, Australia, b. 20 Dec. 1859; m. 1891, Dorinda, only dau. of the late Major Arthur Wilkinson, C.B., and d.s.p. Feb. 1896.
  1. Grace Mary, d. unm.   2. Jane Anna, d. unm.
  3. Elizabeth Dorcas, m. 6 Dec. 1881, Capt. Monier Williams Skinner, R.E., and has issue.
He m. 2ndly, 5 March, 1861, Lizzie, dau. of Rev. Mark Clarke, by whom (who d. Jan. 1873) he had,
  4. EDWARD DE L'ESTABLÈRE, late of Ardavilling.
  5. Marshal William, b. 28 July, 1869; m. 1896, Elizabeth Catherine

Dorothea, dau. of George S. Nason, of Sandyhill Tallow, co. Waterford, and has issue,
George Edward, *b.* July, 1897.
4. Maria Charlotte, *m.* 1889, Charles Deane Oliver, C.E., of Rockmills Lodge, Mallow, co. Cork, and has issue.
5. Esther Maud Vareilles, *d. unm.* 17 Aug. 1900.
6. Helen Frances, *d. unm.*
7. Charlotte, *m.* 26 Aug. 1893, Francis Stewart Dobbs, of Greystones, co. Wicklow, and has issue.
He *m.* 3rdly, 2 Feb. 1875, Mary, dau. of Henry Lee, of Savile Row, London. by whom (who *d.* 1 Jan, 1876) he had a son,
6. Francis Henry, *b.* 28 Dec. 1875; *m.* 25 Aug. 1903, Olive, youngest dau. of Anthony Joseph MacDermott, of the Park, Killarney (*see* MACDERMOTT *of Ramore*).
He *m.* 4thly, 10 April, 1877, Adelaide, dau. of Clifford Trotter, of Bermingham, co. Galway, by whom he had one dau.,
8. Adelaide Kathleen.
Mr. Litton was appointed a Land Commissioner under the Land Act (1881); and a Judge of the Supreme Court in Ireland 1890. He *d.* 27 Nov. 1890, and was *s.* by his son,
EDWARD DE L'ESTABLÈRE LITTON, of Ardavilling, co. Cork, J.P., Barrister-at-Law, *b.* 19 Nov. 1864; *m.* 2 Aug. 1894, Ida Kathleen, youngest dau. of Samuel Gordon, M.D., ex-Pres. R.C.P.I., and *d.* 27 June, 1902, leaving issue,
1. EDWARD FALCONER, now of Ardavilling.
2. Roy Vareilles, *b.* 3 Oct. 1897.

Arms—Erm., a crescent gu., on a chief indented az. three ducal coronets, or. Crest—Out of a ducal coronet, or, an ermine's ..., erm. Motto—Prudentia gloriam acquirit.
Seat.—Ardavilling, co. Cork. *Residence*—4, Herbert Street, Dublin.

LLOYD OF CROGHAN.

JOHN MERRICK LLOYD, of Croghan House, co. Roscommon, J.P., D.L., High Sheriff for co. Leitrim 1902 and for co. Roscommon 1911, M.A. Trin. Coll. Dublin, *b.* 1846; *m.* 5 July, 1900, Frances Emily, dau. of John Henry Darley, of Ferney, co. Dublin. He *s.* his brother 1906.

Lineage.—CAPT. OWEN LLOYD, of Croghan, co. Roscommon, M.P. for Boyle, 1661, the first possessor of that estate, *b.* 1633, at Cavetown, co. Roscommon, was eldest son of Thomas Lloyd, of co. Leitrim, who migrated from Wales to Ireland under the auspices of his kinsman, Sir Ralph Bingley. He *m.* Elizabeth, dau. of Richard Fitzgerald, of Castle Dod, co. Cork, and left at his decease, 1664 (will proved 1685), three sons and three daus.,
1. Thomas, of Croghan, Col. in the Army, served in the War against JAMES II, and was present at the battle of the Boyne, *m.* Margaret, dau. of Sir John Cole, Bart., but *d.s.p.* 1699 (will proved that year).
2. Owen (Rev.), D.D., Dean of Connor, Senior Fellow of Trin. Coll. Dublin, Professor of Divinity, *b.* 1664, *d.* 1743.
3. RICHARD, of whom we treat.
1. Elizabeth, *m.* Daniel Hodson.
2. Honora, *d. unm.*
3. Elizabeth, *m.* 1694, Rev. George Digby.
The 3rd son,
RICHARD LLOYD, *b.* 1662, entered Trin. Coll. Dublin, 10 May, 1677, Speaker of the Upper House of Assembly, Jamaica, and Lord Chief Justice of that Island, where he *m.* Mary Guy, an heiress, and had two sons and two daus. Chief Justice Lloyd was *s.* by his 2nd, but eldest surviving son,
GUY LLOYD, of Bylaugh Hall, Norfolk, *m.* Mary Copping, of Essex, and *d.* about 1768 (will proved that year), having had issue,
1. RICHARD, *s.* to his father.
2. Henry (Rev.), *m.* Diana, dau. of Thomas Bullock, of Hingham in Norfolk.
1. Mary, *m.* Thomas St. John.
Mr. Lloyd was *s.* by his son,
RICHARD LLOYD, of Bylaugh Hall, Norfolk, Col. Norfolk Militia, *m.* Elizabeth, dau. and sole heir of Thomas Jecks, of Bawdeswell Hall, and had issue,
1. GUY, his successor.
2. Richard, *b.* 1772; *m.* Sarah Harriet, dau. of Peter Elwin, of Thurning Hall, Norfolk, and had, with other issue, Richard Hastings Elwin.
3. Henry, *m.* Sarah, eldest dau. of J. Stephenson Cann.
4. Merrick, R.N., killed on board H.M.S. *Sirius*, under Nelson, in 1805, before Malta, *s.p.*
1. Bridget, *m.* the Rev. Dr. Bulwer, Rector of Cawston, Norfolk.
2. Letitia, }
3. Katharine, } of Pawdeswell Hall, and demesne lands thereto
4. Eliza, } annexed.

5. Margaret, *m.* Robert Bircham.
6. Diana, *m.* the Rev. James Stoughton, M.A., Rector of Sparham.
7. Jane, *m.* the Rev. Thomas Dade, Rector of Broadway and Bincombe, Dorset.
Col. Lloyd *d.* 1811 (will proved that year), and was *s.* by his eldest son,
GUY LLOYD, J.P., of Croghan House, co. Roscommon, *b.* 19 Aug. 1766; *m.* 17 Nov. 1799, Martha, dau. of William Bircham, of The Ollands, Norfolk, and *d.* 1842, leaving issue,
1. GUY, his successor.
1. Sarah Bircham, *m.* 14 Dec. 1835, the Rev. William Atthill, of Brandiston Hall, Norfolk, and *d.* 1837.
2. Elizabeth, *m.* 10 Dec. 1825, the Rev. Philip Francis, M.A., of Stibbard Lodge, Norfolk.
3. Murtha, *d.* 7 March, 1871.
The son and heir,
GUY LLOYD, J.P. and D.L., of Croghan House, High Sheriff for co. Roscommon 1833 and for Leitrim 1847, *b.* 30 Dec. 1803; *m.* 26 May, 1827, Susanna Martha, youngest dau. of John Stephenson Cann, of Wramplingham, Norfolk. She *d.* 1868. He *d.* 12 Nov. 1890, leaving issue,
1. GUY, late of Croghan.
2. JOHN MERRICK, now of Croghan.
3. William Richard (Rev.), M.A. Trin. Coll. Dublin, Rector of Mickleham, Surrey, *b.* 1848; *m.* 17 Jan. 1884, Evelyn Minnie, dau. of G. A. Fuller, of the Rookery, Dorking, Surrey.
1. Sarah Martha, *d. unm.* 1881.
2. Susan Ellen.
3. Mary Anne, *m.* 4 Dec. 1867, Stanhope William Fenton Kenny, J.P., of Ballinrobe, co. Mayo, and *d.* 5 Nov. 1895, having had issue (*see that family*).
4. Elizabeth Bertha, *m.* 1858, Joseph Fulton Meade, J.P., of Eastwood, co. Wicklow, who *d.* 19 Jan. 1897. She *d.* 17 Jan. 1907.
5. Emma Jane, *d. unm.* 1892.
6. Katharine Edith, *d. unm.* 1896.
7. Frances Dorothea, *d.* 1909.   8. Alice Octavia.
9. Emily Muriel Knyvett, *m.* 3 Jan. 1884, the Rev. Annesley W. Streane, D.D., Fell. of Corpus Christi Coll. Camb.
The eldest son,
GUY LLOYD, of Croghan House, co. Roscommon, J.P. and D.L., High Sheriff co. Roscommon 1867, and for co. Leitrim 1869, *b.* 13 April, 1833; *m.* 31 Oct. 1865, Elizabeth, dau. of Sir Gilbert King, Bart. of Charlestown, co. Roscommon, and *d.* 25 Aug. 1906, having had issue,
Elizabeth, *d.* an infant 1885.

Arms—Az., a chevron or, and a chief erminois. *Crest*—An eagle displayed with two heads sa., armed and langued gu.
Seat—Croghan House, Boyle, co. Roscommon.

LLOYD OF BEECHMOUNT.

MAJ.-GEN. THOMAS FRANCIS LLOYD, of Beechmount, Rathkeale, co. Limerick, J.P. and D.L., High Sheriff 1894, Major-Gen. in the Army (retired); formerly Col. commanding 2nd Regtl. District, and Lieut.-Col. commanding 98th Regt.; sometime A.A.Q.M.G. Cork District; *b.* 21 April, 1839; *m.* 26 May, 1870, Mary Henrietta, dau. of Christian Allhusen, D.L., of Stoke Court, Bucks (*see that family*), and has had issue,

Thomas Henry Eyre, Capt. Coldstream Guards, *b.* 2 May, 1871; *d. unm.*, distinguished himself for his bravery in S. Africa, where he was Assistant Staff Officer to Col. Benson's column, and was killed in action at Brakenlaagte, Eastern Transvaal, South Africa, 25 Oct. 1901.

Lineage.—THOMAS LLOYD, of Towerhill, co. Limerick, was Lieut. in the Army in 1652, *m.* Eleanor, dau. of Rev. Richard Burgh, D.D., and had a son,
WILLIAM LLOYD, *m.* Jane, dau. of Thomas FitzGerald, and had a son,
REV. THOMAS LLOYD, *m.* 1st, his cousin Mary, dau. of Rev. Rickard Burgh, of Dromkeen, Prebendary of Kilbragh (*see* DE BURGH *of Oldtown*), and by her had issue,
1. Rickard (Rev.), of Castle Lloyd, *m.* Mary, dau. of William Armstrong, of Mealiffe (*see that family*), and had issue,
1. Thomas (Rev.), *m.* Elizabeth, dau. of Thomas FitzGerald, Knight of Glyn (*see that family*), and had issue.
2. Edward (Rev.), Rector of Fethard.

Lloyd. THE LANDED GENTRY. 410

3. William, Barrister-at-Law, *d.* 1783.
4. John, Serjeant-at-Law, *d.* 1835.
1. Alice. 2. Eliza.
3. Mary, *m.* Joseph Gabbett, of High Park, who *d.* 16 July, 1818. She *d.* 15 Jan. 1830, leaving issue (*see* GABBETT *of Cahirline*).
2. William, of Tower Hill, *m.* Anne, dau. of Thomas Lloyd, of Killodrumin, co. Limerick, and left issue.
3. Edward, *m.* the dau. of C. Minchin, and left issue.
He *m.* 2ndly, Frances, dau. of John Bateman, of Altavilla, co. Limerick, and by her had a son,
4. THOMAS, of whom we treat.

The youngest son,
COL. THOMAS LLOYD, of Beechmount, which he purchased in 1805; *m.* Ellen, dau. and heir of Thomas Lloyd, of Dromsalla, co. Clare, and by her had issue,
  1. William, R.N., drowned at sea, *d.s.p.*
  2. THOMAS, of whom presently.
  3. Richard, Lieut.-Col. 84th Regt., *m.* Jane, dau. of George Gough, of Woodstown, co. Limerick, and sister of Field-Marshal Hugh, 1st Viscount Gough, P.C., K.P., G.C.B., &c. (*see* BURKE's *Peerage*), and was killed at the passage of the Nive in 1813, leaving an only dau. This gallant officer was frequently mentioned in despatches. "I ought particularly to report on the good conduct of the 84th Regt. under Lieut.-Col. Lloyd" (*Wellington's Despatches, vol.* viii. *p.* 423). "Major Hoystead claims precedence since the death of that excellent and gallant officer, Lieut.-Col. Lloyd of the 84th Regt." (*Wellington's Supplementary Despatches, vol.* viii. *p.* 432). "Lieut.-Gen. Sir John Hope reports most favourably of the conduct of all the officers, and particularly mentions Maj.-Gens. Robinson and Bradford and Lieut.-Col. Lloyd, 84th Regt., who was unfortunately killed" (*Wellington's Despatches, vol.* xi. *p.* 369).
  4. John (Rev.), Rector of Cashel, *m.* Elizabeth, dau. of Thomas Barclay, of Ballyslattery, co. Clare, and had issue,
    1. Thomas, Barrister-at-Law, *m.* Anne Barclay, and had issue,
      (1) John, *d. unm.*
      (2) Richard, Col. late 36th Regt., *b.* 7 March, 1833; *m.* Marion Bennett, and has issue.
      (3) Thomas, Lieut.-Col. late 35th Regt., *b.* 25 July, 1841; *m.* Emma Studdert, and has issue.
      (1) Millicent, *d. unm.* (2) Georgiana, *d. unm.*
    1. Anne, *m.* Robert Maunsell, of Merrion Square, Dublin, who *d.* 1876, leaving issue (*see* MAUNSELL *of Ballywilliam*).
    2. Ellen, *m.* 1828, George Studdert, of Clonderalaw, who *d.* 1857, leaving issue (*see* STUDDERT *of Bunratty*).
  5. Edward, Capt. 91st Argyllshire Regt., *d.* on the West Coast of Africa.
  6. Hugh, Capt. 65th Regt., *d.* in the West Indies.
  7. Arthur, Gen. in the Army, was in the 98th Regt. under Gen. Abercrombie, and *d.* in Egypt 1860; *m.* the dau. of Monck Mason.
  1. Jane, *m.* Sept. 1811, Rev. John Talbot Crosbie, of Ardfert, and had issue (*see that family*).
  2. Ellen, *m.* Charles Smith, of Ballinanty, co. Limerick, D.L., and had issue,
    William, *m.* Charlotte, sister of 4th Baron Gwydyr (*see* BURKE's *Peerage*).

The 2nd son,
THOMAS LLOYD, of Beechmount, co. Limerick, D.L., M.P. for that county 1826-30, *m.* 1797, Catherine, dau. of Eyre Evans, of Miltown Castle (*see that family*), nephew of George, 1st Lord Carbery (*see* BURKE's *Peerage*), and *d.* 1830, having by her (who *d.* 14 Feb. 1848) had issue,
  1. THOMAS, of whom presently.
  2. Eyre, of Prospect, Castle Connell, and New Garden, co. Limerick, J.P. and D.L., *b.* 1803; *d.* 4 May, 1876; *m.* 10 May, 1827, Anne Hutchinson (*d.* 1877), dau. of Capt. Hugh Massy, grandson of John Massy, of Glenville, 2nd son of William Massy, of Stoneville (*see* BURKE's *Peerage*, CLARINA, B.), and had issue,
    1. Thomas, Capt. 87th Regt., *d.* 1 April, 1900; *m.* 1854, Anne Cooper (*d.* 1862), only child of James Cheese, of Huntington Court, Herefordshire, and had issue, Eyre Edmond, *b.* 1856, *d.* 1862; Anne Geraldine, *m.* 1st, Wilbraham E. E. Morley; 2ndly, 1884, Gen. A. B. Crosbie, Royal Marines (retired list) (*Harestock House, Winchester*), eldest surviving son of Capt. W. A. Crosbie, Rifle Brigade.
    2. Eyre, M.A. Trin. Coll. Dublin and Cambridge, Barrister-at-Law of the Inner Temple, *m.* 1864, Sarah, 2nd dau. of Rev. Samuel Paynter, Rector of Stoke Guildford, Surrey, and 13 Bolton Street, Piccadilly (*see* PAYNTER *of Gale House*), and *d.* 9 June, 1895, having had issue,
      (1) Samuel Eyre Massy, Lieut.-Col. Commanding 3rd Batt. Suffolk Regt., served in S. Africa 1899-1902 (despatches, medals, brevet of Major) (*Yendlands, Felsham, Suffolk*; *Carlton and Army and Navy Clubs*), *b.* 31 July, 1867; *m.* 7 Aug. 1890, Annie Eliza, 4th dau. of Edward Madoc-Jones, of Glentworth, Oswestry, Salop, and has had issue,
        1. Vera Lillian Mary Massy, *b.* 7 May, 1891.
        2. Violet Nancye, *b.* April, 1893.
        3. Isola Lucinda Eyre, *b.* 21 Aug., *d.* 25 Dec. 1898.
      (2) Eyre Evans, *b.* 28 May, 1870; *m.* 1893, Minnie Annora, 5th dau. of Edward Madoc-Jones, of Glentworth, Oswestry.
    3. Hugh Massy, Major 14th Regt., *d. unm.* 1873.
    4. Arthur, drowned in the Shannon 1862, *unm.*
    5. Rickard, *d.* young.
    1. Anne, *d.* young.
    2. Catherine Lucinda, *m.* 1st, Capt. John D'Olier George, 60th King's Royal Rifles, of Cahore, co. Wexford; 2ndly, Cecil Roche, Barrister-at-Law. She *d.* 1886.

1. Catherine, *m.* George Meares Maunsell, of Ballywilliam (*see that family*).
2. Eliza, *m.* Rev. Edward Hemming.

The elder son,
THOMAS LLOYD, of Beechmount, J.P. and D.L. co. Limerick, and J.P. cos. Clare and Tipperary, *b.* 1798; *m.* 1st, 1825, Anne, dau. of Edmund Burke, of Ballyvoreen, and by her had issue.
  1. Thomas, *d.s.p.*
  1. Jane, *d. unm.*, accidentally shot by her *fiancé.*
  2. Catherine, *m.* John Maunsell, of Edenmore, Raheny, and has issue (*see* MAUNSELL *of Ballywilliam*).
He *m.* 2ndly, 10 July, 1838, Julia Palmer, dau. of Capt. Francis Hall (*see* HALL *of Knockbrack, co. Galway*), and *d.* 1873, leaving by her (who *d.* 29 Sept. 1902) issue,
  2. THOMAS FRANCIS, now of Beechmount.
  3. Arthur Rickard, *m.* 21 Oct. 1869, Theodosia, dau. of Capt. John Talbot, of Mount Talbot, D.L. (*see that family*), and by her (who *d.* 3 Jan. 1894) has issue,
    1. John Arthur Thomas, *m.* 1 June, 1904, Isabel Keith, eldest dau. of David Campbell, of Glasgow.
    2. Henry Talbot, Capt. Royal Marine Light Infantry, served under Adm. Seymour in the attempt to relieve the Legations at Pekin (despatches), and was killed in action at Tientsin, China, July, 1900.
    3. Arthur Eustace.
    1. Diana.
  4. Henry Hall, *b.* 1844; *d.* 1898; *m.* 1st, 1872, Ellen, dau. of Rev. Charles Childers, and 2ndly, 12 March, 1890, Frances Catherine, dau. of Col. E. S. Bayly, of Ballyarthur (*see that family*). She *d.* 17 Jan. 1896.
  1. Julia Clara Henrietta, *m.* Henry Herbert Edwards. She *d.* his widow 3 March, 1905, having had issue,
    1. Herbert. 2. Reginald Llewellyn.
    1. Eleanor.
  2. Anna Maria, *m.* 1887, Charles Buchanan Ker.

Arms—Gu., a lion ramp. reguardant between two flaunches or, each charged with three cinquefoils sa. **Crest**—On three cinquefoils in fess or a lion rampant reguardant gu. **Motto**—Vi et virtute.

Seat—Beechmount, Rathkeale, co. Limerick. **Club**—United Service.

LLOYD OF GLOSTER.

JOHN HARDRESS LLOYD, of Gloster, King's Co., J.P., High Sheriff 1906, late Capt. 21st Lancers, *b.* 14 Aug. 1874; *m.* 5 Aug. 1903, Adeline, dau. of the late Sir Samuel Wilson, formerly M.P. for Portsmouth.

Lineage.—JOHN LLOYD, of Gloster, King's Co., J.P. and D.L., High Sheriff 1866, *s.* by will 1860 to the estates of Col. Hardress Lloyd, of Gloster, M.P. for King's Co.; *m.* 14 Nov. 1872, Susannah Frances Julia, 2nd dau. of John Thomas Rosborough Colclough, of Tintern Abbey, J.P. and D.L. co. Wexford (*see that family*), and had issue,
  1. JOHN HARDRESS, now of Gloster.
  2. Evan Colclough, Capt. 1st Batt. Royal Irish Regt., *b.* 4 Jan. 1877.
  3. Llewellyn Wilfrid Medhop, Lieut. 2nd Batt. Royal Irish Regt., *b.* 27 July, 1879.
  1. Mary Louisa Arthurina Gwendoline Colclough, *b.* 28 Aug. 1873.
  2. Susan Frederica Lillian Mary, *b.* 4 Sept. 1875; *m.* 5 Jan. 1899, Lieut.-Col. Edwin Charles Barnes Cotgrave, Central India Horse.
  3. Alice Maude Josephine, *b.* 14 April, 1878; *m.* 17 Sept. 1908, Major Hardress Gilbert Holmes, of St. David's, co. Tipperary (*see that family*).
  4. Myrtle Susan, *b.* 9 Aug. 1883.
Mr. Lloyd *d.* 26 Jan. 1883, aged 50.

Seat—Gloster, Roscrea, King's Co.

LLOYD late OF LLOYDSBORO'.

JOHN FORTESCUE LLOYD, of Fortescue and Cranagh Castle, co. Tipperary, *b.* 1887; *s.* his father 1902.

Lineage.—JOHN LLOYD, of Lloydsboro', co. Tipperary, son of Joseph Lloyd, by Mary Otway his wife. He *m.* Elizabeth, dau. of John Blunden, and was father of
JOHN LLOYD, of Cranagh, *d.* 4 Nov. 1744; *m.* 2 Sept. 1746, Deborah, dau. of Thomas Clutterbuck, of Bannixtown, co. Tipperary, and had issue,
  1. JOHN, of Cranagh and Lloydsboro', *m.* Amy Brazier, and left an only dau.,
    Debby Anne, *m.* her cousin JOHN LLOYD, of Lloydsboro'.
  2. Thomas, *m.* Judith Maher, and had issue,
    1. George Richard, *m.*
    2. Horatio, *m.* and *d.* leaving issue.
  3. Richard, A.M., Rector of Clononty, co. Tipperary, afterwards of Northam Cottage, North Devon, *b.* Dec. 1754; *m.* 16 Sept. 1788, Priscilla, dau. of Rev. John Lord, Rector of Clonkelly, and *d.* 8 Jan. 1830, leaving issue by her (who was *b.* 17 Oct. 1760, and *d.* 4 Feb. 1837),

1. George William Aylmer, C.B., Lieut.-Gen. H.E.I.C.S., Col. 28th Bengal N.I., commanded the Bengal Volunteers in the China war 1841-2 ; *b.* 4 July, 1789 ; *m.* March, 1824, Caroline, 2nd dau. of Capt. William Bruce, H.E.I.C.S., Resident at Bushire ; and *d.* 4 July, 1865.
2. John, Comm. R.N., and J.P. of Cowaka and Paubula, near Eden, Twofold Bay, New South Wales, *m.* 19 Jan. 1824, Sarah Robinson, and had issue,
  (1) ARTHUR, of Northam House, Bideford, North Devon, and Adelaide, South Australia, *b.* 30 Dec. 1824 ; *m.* 1st, 30 Oct. 1858, his cousin Elizabeth Lucy, eldest dau. of Rev. Charles Lloyd, which lady *d.* 1874 ; and 2ndly, 1878, Catherine, 2nd dau. of Capt. James Clyde, 96th Regt., and has issue by the former,
    1. Priscilla Emelia, *m.* 1884, William Scott Owen, of Cefn-wifed, Newtown, co. Montgomery.
    2. Isabella Anne Caroline.
  (2) William, Civil Engineer, East Indies, *b.* 24 May, 1826.
    (1) Priscilla Amelia, *m.* 28 Sept. 1847, Major William Ellison Wardon, 2nd Bengal N.I., eldest son of Lieut.-Col. George Warden, Bengal Army, and by him (who *d.* 12 June, 1857) has one dau.,
      Priscilla Emilia Jane.
3. Arthur Forbes, M.A., Rector of Instow, Devon, *m.* 1825, Harriet, dau. of Thomas Furley Forster, of Walthamstow ; and *d.* 3 July, 1860, having had issue,
  (1) Arthur Forster, of South Australia, *b.* 1826 ; *m.* 30 Dec. 1851, Jean, youngest dau. of James Gordon Morgan, M.D., of Barnstaple, and has issue,
    1. Arthur, *b.* 1 April, 1856.
    2. A son, *b.* 1858.
    1. Jane, *b.* 1852.
    2. Mary Elizabeth, *b.* 1854, dec.
  (2) Richard, of Morphett Vale, South Australia, *b.* 1827 ; *m.* 19 June, 1856, Marcella Adelaide Cornelia, dau. of James Elton, of North Stoke, co. Oxford, and has a son,
    Richard Elton, *b.* 26 March, 1857.
  (3) Benjamin Furney, of Morphett Vale, South Australia, *b.* 1836.
  (4) George Aylmer, of Morphett Vale, South Australia, *b.* 1840.
  (5) Thomas Furney, *b.* Feb. 1845.
  (6) Edward.
  (1) Harriet Mary, *m.* 6 March, 1855, Charles Constantine Bruce, of Adelaide, South Australia, only surviving son of Capt. William Bruce, H.E.I.C.S. She *d.* 3 April, 1855.
  (2) Isabella. (3) Emily.
  (4) Adelaide. (5) Susanna.
  (6) Priscilla Lord.
1. Priscilla Emilia, *b.* 25 July, 1790, of Northam Cottage ; *d.* at Seorole, Benares, 13 Sept. 1846.
2. Isabella Anne, of Northam House, North Devon.
4. HENRY JESSE, of whom presently.
5. Frederick, of Ballymacrease, *m.* Julia, dau. of Thomas Vereker, of Roxborough (see BURKE's *Peerage*, GORT, V.), and by her (who *d.* 1747) had issue,
  1. Johns, of Lisheen Castle, co. Tipperary, and of Madoc Hastings, Canada West, J.P., *m.* 1st, Catherine, dau. of John Rotton, of Bath, and had issue,
    (1) CHARLES HENRY, of Lisheen Castle, Templemore, J.P., *b.* 1821 ; *s.* 1856 ; *m.* 1st, 1846, Anne, dau. of Major George Jackson ; 2ndly, 1849, Anna, dau. of Fergus Langley, and *d.* 1887, leaving by her, with other issue, a son,
      CHARLES EDWARD, of Lisheen Castle, J.P., *b.* 1854 ; *m.* 1885, Louisa Dorset, dau. of the late Charles W. S. Shultze.
    (2) Frederick, in Canada.
    (1) Catherine, *m.* William Butler, of Drom, co. Tipperary.
  2. Frederick, Lieut. R.N.
  3. Henry Vereker, formerly Bengal Cavalry, *m.* Miss Jopp, *d.s.p.*
  4. Charles (Rev.), formerly Chaplain at Prince Edward's Island, afterwards Curate of St. John the Evangelist, Durdham Down ; *m.* 17 Sept. 1826, Elizabeth, dau. of William Tyeth, of Phillibead, near Bideford, Devon, and had issue,
    (1) Charles Frederick, Lieut. 3rd West India Regt., *m.* 29 Sept. 1858, Jessica Mary, eldest dau. of Alexander Dunscombe, M.D., of The Grange, Antigua, West Indies, and Clifton.
    (2) William of New York, *m.* 1 Nov. 1828, Caroline Tupper.
    (3) John Vereker, in Australia.
    (1) Elizabeth Lucy, *m.* 30 Oct. 1858, her kinsman, Arthur Lloyd, of Northam House, Bideford, Devonshire, and Australia (mentioned above).
    (2) Julia Henrietta Camilla.
    1. Julia, *m.* George Duncan. 2. Camilla.
  3. Harriet, *d. unm.*
1. Elizabeth, *m.* Rev. Charles Tuckey, and has four sons and four daus.
2. Deborah, *m.* July, 1781, Gorges Hely, and has six sons and seven daus.
The 4th son,
HENRY JESSE LLOYD, of Castle Incy, co. Tipperary, *m.* Ellen, dau. of Thomas Garde, of Ballina Curra, co. Cork, and dying 1816, left issue,
  1. JOHN, of Lloydsboro'. 2. Thomas, *d. unm.*
3. Henry, of Farrinrory, co. Tipperary, *m.* 1822, Harriet Amelia, youngest dau. of Sir John Craven Carden, 1st bart., and by her (who *d.* 10 April, 1879) has issue,
  1. Jesse, of Ballyleck House, co. Monaghan. J.P., High Sheriff 1863, Lieut.-Col. Monaghan Militia, late Capt. 47th Regt., *b.* 23 Feb. 1824 ; *m.* 14 Dec. 1853, Ellen, eldest dau. of George Vincent, of Ermagh, co. Clare, and *d.* 25 Jan. 1896, having by her (who *d.* 1886) had issue,
    (1) Henry Craven Jesse, *b.* 8 Feb. 1855 ; *d. unm.*
    (1) Josephine, *m.* 1884, John Porter Porter, of Jamestown, co. Fermanagh.
    (2) Coralie.
    (3) Fanny Kathleen, *m.* 1884, Charles Cockburne, eldest son of William D'Arcy-Irvine, of Castle Irvine.
  1. Frances Maria, *m.* 26 March, 1840, Andrew Wauchope, of Niddrie Marischall, Midlothian, and *d.* 25 June, 1858, leaving issue.
  2. Josephine Julia Helen, *m.* 1st, 19 May, 1846, Henry Robert, 3rd Lord Rossmore ; and 2ndly, 18 June, 1863, Major G. W. Stacpoole, of Eden Vale, co. Clare.
  3. Coralie Augusta Frederica, *m.* 17 June, 1848, William Fitzwilliam Burton, of Burton Hall, co. Carlow.
4. William, *m.* Kate, only dau. of John Harris, of Waterford, and had issue.
1. Mary Anne, *m.* Rev. Thomas Hoare, youngest son of Sir Edward Hoare, 2nd bart., Annabelle.
2. Eliza Lucy, *m.* Mr. Morris, and *d.s.p.*
The eldest son,
JOHN LLOYD, of Lloydsboro' and Cranagh, B.A. of Trin. Coll. Dublin, *b.* 16 March, 1790 ; *m.* 21 July, 1810, Debby Ann, dau. of John Lloyd, of Cranagh ; *d.* 9 Feb. 1868, having had issue,
  1. JOHN JESSE, his heir.
  2. Richard Jesse, Lieut. 59th Regt., *d. unm.* 14 Oct. 1847.
  1. Elizabeth Anne, *m.* 15 Dec. 1840, John Dawson Hutchinson, of Timoney Park, co. Tipperary, and *d.s.p.* 3 March, 1842.
  2. Eliza Ellen, *m.* John Stratford Collins, Barrister-at-Law, and *d.* 17 Nov. 1862, leaving issue.
He *d.* 11 Jan. 1864, and was *s.* by his eldest son,
JOHN JESSE LLOYD, of Lloydsboro' and Cranagh, *m.* Mary, dau. of Edward Nathaniel William Fortescue, of Fallapit, and *d.* 1871, leaving by her (who *d.* 1888), with a dau., three sons,
  1. HENRY JESSE, late of Lloydsboro', J.P., and High Sheriff 1881, *b.* 1845 ; *m.* 12 June, 1883, Mary Alice, dau. of William Butler, of Park, co. Tipperary, and *d.s.p.* 1893.
  2. RICHARD, late of Fortescue, *b.* 1850, *d.s.p.* 1898.
  3. EMLYN FORTESCUE, *s.* his brother.
The youngest son,
CAPT. EMLYN FORTESCUE LLOYD, of Cranagh Castle, High Sheriff 1898, late Capt. 22nd Regt., *b.* 1850 ; *m.* 1882, Henrietta Eliza, only dau. of Capt. Robilliard, R.N., of Val des Portes, Alderney, and *d.* 28 Nov. 1902, leaving issue,
  JOHN FORTESCUE, now of Fortescue.

Seats—Fortescue, and Cranagh Castle, near Templemore, co. Tipperary.

LLOYD OF LOSSETT.

CLIFFORD BARTHOLOMEW LLOYD, of Lossett, co. Cavan, B.A., *b.* 18 Aug. 1845 ; *m.* 1st, 5 May, 1870, Isabella Maria, dau. of Major Des Vœux, of Portarlington, Queen's Co., and by her (who *d.* 1892) has issue,
  1. WILMOT HUMPHREY CLIFFORD, B.A., *b.* 15 July, 1879.
  1. Beatrice Anna Caroline Isabelle Clifford, *m.* 1st, 7 May, 1891, Leslie Tufnell Peacocke (Capt. 5th Batt. Connaught Rangers), and has issue, a son,
    Hugo Leslie.
She *m.* 2ndly, 24 Nov. 1902, Capt. Eardley Wilmot Brooke, A.S.C., formerly 60th Rifles (see BROOKE *of Dromavana*).
  2. Alice Elizabeth Clifford, *m.* 18 Dec. 1900, George Pakenham Stewart, only son of Capt. E. P. Stewart, of Laragh, Killiney, late Seaforth Highlanders, and has issue,
    Douglas Arthur Pakenham.
    Evelyn Ella.

He *m.* 2ndly, 7 Oct. 1896, Edith Emily Marguerite, youngest dau. of Thomas Fitz Herbert, of Blackcastle, co. Meath (see that family).

Lineage.—ROBERT LLOYD, *b.* 6 June, 1533 ; *m.* Mary, dau. of J. Jones, of Denbigh, and had a son,
ROBERT LLOYD, Treasurer of the Cathedral of St. Asaph 1624, *b.* 4 Oct. 1560, at Llanrhaidar-yn-Mochnant, co. Denbigh ; *m.* Jane, dau. of Christopher Ewer, of St. Asaph, had, with other issue,
ROBERT LLOYD, his 3rd son, *b.* 10 June, 1602 ; *m.* Anna, dau. of Rev. John Williams, and had,
  1. Robert, *b.* 6 Nov. 1653.
  2. HUMPHREY (Rev.), of whom hereafter.
  3. Richard, *b.* 30 Sept. 1660 ; *d.* 3 May, 1728.
  4. John, *b.* 28 June, 1663. 5. Lewis, *b.* 26 Oct. 1666.
  6. Griffin, *b.* 11 Jan. 1668.
The 2nd son,
REV. HUMPHREY LLOYD, *b.* 30 May, 1656, went to Ireland from Wales, between 1680 and 1683, and settled at New Ross, co. Wex-

Lloyd.
THE LANDED GENTRY.
412

fo:..] where he resided at "The Abbey House," also at Folly House, of which he had a lease dated 4 July, 1705 ; will dated 11 April, 1727, proved Nov. 1727. He signed the Address of the New Ross Corporation to WILLIAM III. 18 Aug. 1696, and was made a Free Burgess of the town 3 Nov. 1716. He m. Elizabeth Ball (who was b. 10 June, 1665), and had issue,

1. Robert, b. Feb. 1693 ; d.s.p. vita patris.
2. Richard (Rev.), M.A. Trin. Coll. Dublin, Rector of Rathcormack, co. Cork, 1742, b. 4 Jan. 1699. He m. 31 March, 1727, Elizabeth, dau. of Christopher Forward, of Fermoy, same co. ; and d. April, 1775, leaving by her (who d. 26 Nov. 1778),
    1. RICHARD, of Tullygreen House, b. 14 Jan. 1732 ; m. Jane, dau. of Thomas Austen, of Waterfall, co. Cork, and by her (who was b. 5 Oct. 1744) had,
        (1) Richard, b. 1764, d. 1766.
        (2) RICHARD (Rev.), J.P., Prebendary of Killanully, co. Cork, b. 27 May, 1767 ; m. 20 March, 1802, Mary, dau. of James Franklin Morrison, of Cork, by Elizabeth his wife, dau. of Ven. Michael Davies, Archdeacon of Cloyne, and d. 6 Feb. 1840, leaving a dau., Elizabeth Mary Annie, b. 1806 ; m. 11 Sept. 1829, Capt. John George Elphinstone, H.E.I.C. ; and a son,
            RICHARD, Barrister-at-Law, b. 23 Sept. 1807 ; m. 15 Oct. 1836, Margaret, dau. of Edmond Knapp Piersy, of Charleville, co. Cork, and d. 5 April, 1879, leaving, with a dau., Annie Piersy, m. 1st, 1863, William Austin Morrison, and 2ndly, 1867, Robert Villiers George, M.D.
            a. Richard Morrison, b. 21 Jan. 1839 ; d.s.p. Dec. 1896.
            b. Edmond George Knapp Piersy, V.D., of Passage West, co. Cork, Col., Staff Officer of the North London Vol. Brigade and of the 1st London Vol. Infantry Brigade, now a member of the Territorial Force Association of the County of London, served in S. Africa 1900–2, b. 15 Dec. 1842 ; m. 20 Feb. 1873, Emma Susanna, dau. of Benjamin Johnson, M.D., and has,
                Langford Newman, D.S.O., M.R.C.S. and L.R.C.P., Capt. R.A.M.C., served in S. Africa 1899-1901 (mentioned in despatches, D.S.O.), b. 28 Dec. 1873.
        (1) Elizabeth, b. 9 July, 1768 ; m. 21 Dec. 1799, Owen Lloyd, of Smith Hill, co. Roscommon, and d. Dec. 1804.
        (2) Mary, b. 28 Nov. 1769 ; m. Andrew Elphinstone, R.N., M.D., and d. 10 Oct. 1831.   (3) Barbara, d. unm.
    2. Christopher, b. 21 May, 1738 ; m. 10 July, 1768, Elizabeth Bateman, and d. 11 March, 1792, leaving
        (1) Richard Bateman, b. 1770 ; m. 19 April, 1795, Elizabeth, widow of Capt. Trant, and d. 1822, leaving
            1. Mountiford Staughton, Major-Gen. in the Army, was present at Waterloo (medal).   2. Richard Augustus.
        (2) Christopher, had two sons, and as many daus.
        (3) Staughton.
        (1) Elizabeth, b. 23 March, 1771 ; m. Capt. Bateman, R.N.
    3. William, b. 1734 ; d. 1736.
    4. Samuel, b. 3 May, 1742 ; m. Hannah, dau. of Thomas Austen.
    1. Elizabeth, b. 1733 ; d. 1734.
    2. Barbara, b. Jan. 1746 ; m. Lieut. Stephen Sandys, R.N.
3. BARTHOLOMEW (Rev.), of whom hereafter.
1. Jane, b. 8 Jan. 1683, d. May, 1737 ; m. 27 Nov. 1706, Rev. William Hartey (see HARTLEY of Beech Park).
2. Elizabeth, b. 19 Feb. 1688, m. 2) Nov. 1706, Rev. John Acheson, M.A., Rector and Vicar of Rosbercon, co. Kilkenny, who d. Dec. 1726.
3. Mary, b. 21 June, 1695 ; m. 4 April, 1716, John Batt, Attorney-at-Law, and d. 1773.
4. Anne, b. 6 July, 1697 ; m. 24 June, 1724, Henry Moore.
5. Frances, b. 28 June, 1703 ; d. 1 Oct. 1778.

Rev. Humphrey LLoyd d. 15 April, 1727. His 3rd, but 2nd surviving son,

REV. BARTHOLOMEW LLoyd, of Abbey House, New Ross, was b. 13 Jan. 1707 ; admitted a Freeman of New Ross, 1 Oct. 1722, and entered Trin. Coll. Dublin, 8 June, 1726. He m. 22 June, 1732, Ann, dau. of Robert Clifford, of Wexford, by Elizabeth, his wife, only dau. of Thomas Kyrle, of Clonneene, co. Cork (see MONEY-KYRLE of Homme House). He had issue,

1. Bartholomew, b. 30 Aug. 1733 ; d. 12 Sept. 1748.
2. HUMPHREY, of whom hereafter.
3. Robert, b. 1 June, 1738.
4. Clifford, b. 15 March, 1741 ; d. 2 Nov. 1742.
5. John (Rev.), Vicar of Ferns, Rector of Kilbride, and Prebendary of Clone, Diocese of Ferns, b. 25 July, 1743 ; d. 16 June, 1781.
    1. Anne b. 15 Aug. 1736.
    2. Rachel, b. 1739.

Rev. Bartholomew LLoyd d. 26 April, 1783. His eldest surviving son,

HUMPHREY LLoyd, of New Ross b. 4 Aug. 1735 ; m. (mar. lic. 22 Nov. 1766) Margaret, dau. of Borbidge, of Deralossory, co. Wicklow, and had issue,

1. BARTHOLOMEW (Rev.), of whom hereafter.
2. John, b. 24 Dec. 1774 ; m. Margaret, dau. of Rev. William Hall, Rector of Wexford, and had issue,
    1. Robert (Rev.), m. Mrs. Majeveston, widow, and had a son, Robert (Rev.), m. the dau. of Rev. John Bridge, Rector of Ballyconnor.
    2. Horatio Nelson.   3. Bartholomew, m. Miss Daly.
    1. Letitia, m. Dr. William Reeves.
    2. Matilda, m. Rev. John Bridge, Rector of Ballyconnor.
    3. Margaret, m. William R. Digby.
3. Robert, b. 6 Jan. 1785 ; m. Charlotte Elizabeth, dau. of Rev. J. Ball, Rector of Attanagh, co. Kilkenny, and had,
    1. Bartholomew.
    1. Margaret, m. 15 Dec. 1846, John Tuthill, of Kilmore, co. Limerick (see VILLIERS-TUTHILL).
    2. Susan Penelope, m. Rev. Robert McKee, Rector of Fethard, co. Wexford.
    3. Maria, d. unm.
4. Rachel, bapt. at New Ross, 7 Nov. 1779.
2. Anne, m. — Kane.
3. Harriet, m. Allan Nesbit, of Stephen's Green, Dublin.
4. Frances, m. — Shaw.
5. Mary, m. Peter Barnewall Sullivan, and had issue.

Mr. Humphrey LLoyd d. 5 Oct. 1786. His eldest son,

REV. BARTHOLOMEW LLOYD, D.D., Provost of Trin. Coll. Dublin, and President of the Royal Irish Academy, was b. 5 Feb. 1772 ; became a Scholar of Trin. Coll. 1790, a Fellow 1796, and was appointed Provost 1831 ; will dated 25 July, 1821, proved 1838. He m. July, 1799, Eleanor, dau. of Patrick McLaughlin, of Dublin, and of Dunshaughlin, co. Meath, and Kilmartin, co. Dublin, elected but did not serve as Sheriff of Dublin 1779. They had issue,

1. HUMPHREY (Rev.), of whom presently.
2. Bartholomew Clifford, of Lossett, co. Cavan. LL.D., Q.C., Chairman of Quarter Sessions, co. Waterford, b. 1808 ; m. 1st, 21 Sept. 1844, at the British Embassy, Paris, Caroline Hamilton, only dau. of Right Hon. William Brooke, P.C. of Dromavana, co. Cavan, Master in Chancery, and one of the Commissioners of the Great Seal in Ireland, and his wife Emily Margaret, sister of Edward Wilmot Chetwode, of Woodbrooke, Queen's Co. (see that family), and by her (who d. 1864) had issue,
    1. CLIFFORD BARTHOLOMEW, now of Lossett.
    2. William Chetwode, Lieut.-Col. formerly 20th Hussars, served in Soudan 1884–5, b. 24 Nov. 1846 ; d. 12 June, 1909 ; m. Catherine, eldest dau. of Thomas Garnett, of Furze Hill Lodge, Brighton, and has issue,
        (1) Chetwode, Lieut. Hampshire Regt.   (2) Hugh.
        (3) Humphrey.
    3. Humphrey Wilmot, Barrister-at-Law of The King's Inns, b. 28 Feb. 1848 ; m. Kate, only dau. of Col. Graham, H.E.I.C.S. He d. 2 Oct. 1908.
    4. Alfred Robert, b. 31 July, 1854, Major late Bedfordshire Regt., served Chitral Relief Force 1895 (medal and clasp), S. African War 1900 (medal and two clasps); m. 27 Aug. 1903, Helen Elizabeth, dau. of the late George Goodchild, of the British Embassy, St. Petersburg, by his wife, dau. of late Baron Mond, of Mendlova, Finland.
    5. Arthur Brooke, Barrister-at-Law, of the Inner Temple, London (32, Grainger Street West, Newcastle-on-Tyne), b. 22 Jan. 1856.
    6. Frederick Charles, Lieut.-Col. commanding 2nd Batt Lincolnshire Regt., served in S. Africa 1900–2 in command 7th Batt. Mounted Infantry (mentioned in despatches, Brevet Major, Queen's medal and five clasps, King's medal and two clasps), b. 10 Oct. 1860 ; m. Millicent, youngest dau. of Thomas Garnett, and has issue,
        Clifford Humphrey, Lieut. R.A.
        Vera Millicent.
    1. Emily Janet, m. Skeffington John Wynne, Col. A.P.D. (see WYNNE of Hazlewood).
    2. Constance Eleanor.   3. Florence Caroline.
    4. Caroline Alice Elizabeth, m. Anson Schomberg, Rear-Adml. R.N.

He m. 2ndly, Oct. 1869, Anna Maria, dau. of Major Sackville Brownlow Taylor, 6th Regt. ; and d. 28 April, 1872.

3. Robert Clifford, Col. in the Army, b. 1809 ; m. Annie (d. 18 March, 1908), dau. of Capt. George Savage, 13th Light Dragoons, and had issue,
    1. Charles Dalton Clifford Lloyd, b. 13 Jan. 1844 ; Barrister-at-Law, late a Resident Magistrate in Ireland, and afterwards Minister of the Interior, Egypt, m. 30 April, 1867, Isabel Henrietta, only dau. of Capt. Henry Sabine Browne, of the Rifle Brigade, and 85th Light Infantry.
    2. Humphrey George Clifford, b. 19 June, 1845.
    3. Arthur Clifford, Lieut.-Col. late 45th Regt., b. 11 Feb. 1849.
    4. Wilford Neville, M.V.O., of His Majesty's Body Guard, Lieut.-Col. late R.A., J.P. Cheshire, b. 15 Sept. 1855 ; m. 21 July, 1891, Ella Margaret, only dau. of the Very Rev. Arthur Purey-Cust, Dean of York, and Lady Emma Purey-Cust (see BURKE'S Peerage, BROWNLOW, E.), and has issue,
        1. Grace Eleanor Coltman, m. 1860, Maurice Cross, Judge at Negapatam, India, who d. Dec. 1884.
        2. Emily Johanna Frances, m. Ferdinand Beauclerk, Capt. R.E.
4. John Frederick (Rev.), Archdeacon of Waitemata, and Minister of St. Paul's Church, Auckland, New Zealand, afterwards Rector of Newton Wold, Diocese of Lincoln, b. 1810 ; m. 23 Aug. 1851, Sarah Greer, and d. 8 Sept. 1875, leaving issue,
    1. John Frederick, b. 20 Jan. 1854 ; m. Nellie, dau. of Dr. Quinter, M.D., of Grosmont House, Yorks., and has issue.
    2. Charles Patterson, b. 9 Feb. 1861.
    3. Humphrey Selwyn, b. 13 Sept. 1870 ; m. Caroline, eldest dau. of William Hutton Perkins, and has issue.
    1. Alice Mary, m. — Dew-Smith, of Cambridge.
    2. Margaret Anna, m. W. Marshall.
    3. Frances Edith.
    4. Ethel Mary, m. Walter Dobell.
1. Eleanor, b. 1801 ; a. unm. 13 Jan. 1881.
2. Harriett, b. 1803 ; m. Rev. Maurice Hime, and had, with other issue, Right Hon. Sir Albert Henry Hime, P.C. (1902), K.C.M.G. (1900), Hon. LL.D. Camb., Edin., and Dub., formerly Prime Minister, Natal, Vice-Pres. Royal Colonial Institute, Hon. Lieut.-Col. R.E. (ret.) (58, Burton Court, S.W.), b. 29 Aug.

1842; *m.* 1866, Josephine Mary, dau. of the late J. Searle of Plymouth, and has issue.
3. Anne. 4. Elizabeth, *b.* 1808 (twin).
5. Maria.
6. Margaret, *m.* 13 July, 1841, Rev. Richard Verschoyle, Rector of Derry Vollen, co. Fermanagh, and brother to the late Bishop of Kilmore (*see* VERSCHOYLE *of Castle Shanaghan*).
Dr. LLoyd *d.* 24 Nov. 1837, and was *s.* by his eldest son,
REV. HUMPHREY LLOYD, D.D., F.R.S., of Victoria Castle, Killiney, co. Dublin, *b.* 16 April, 1800; Scholar of Trin. Coll. Dublin 1819, Fellow 1824, and Provost 1867. He was the author of the *Wave Theory of Light*, and several other scientific works. In 1874 he received the order " Pour le Merite " from the German Emperor, was also President Royal Irish Academy. He *m.* 14 July, 1840, Dorothea Maria Redfoord (who *d.* 21 April, 1905), only dau. of Rev. James Bulwer, Rector of Hungworth, co. Norfolk; and sister of James Bulwer, late M.P. Cambridge; and *d.s.p.* 17 Jan. 1881, and was *s.* by his nephew.

Arms—Or, a lion rampant regardant sa., on a canton az. a cross pattée fitchée of the first. *Crest*—A demi-lion rampant regardant sa. charged on the shoulder with a trefoil slipped or. *Motto*—Tendit in ardua virtus.
Residence—Victoria Castle, Killiney, co. Dublin. *Clubs*—Constitutional, S.W., University, Dublin, and Royal St. George Yacht, Kingstown.

LLOYD OF ROCKVILLE.

WILLIAM LLOYD, of Rockville, Drumsna, co. Roscommon, J.P. and D.L., High Sheriff 1889, late Capt. and Hon. Major. 5th Batt. Connaught Rangers, *b.* 8 July, 1858; *m.* 28 Jan. 1884, May Brodribb (who *d.* 25 July, 1907), dau. of Major William Lancelot Hutchinson, by Louisa his wife, dau. of Capt. Samuel Bush Brodribb, 2nd son of William Brodribb, J.P., of Camely House and Stantonwick, co. Somerset, and has issue,
1. WILLIAM HUTCHINSON, late Lieut. 9th Batt. King's Royal Rifle Corps, High Sheriff co. Roscommon 1909, *b.* 2 April, 1885.
2. Coote Richard Fitzgerald, *b.* 2 July, 1887.
3. Gwendoline Elizabeth May.

Lineage.—OWEN LLOYD, High Sheriff of co. Roscommon 1719, *b.* 1660; *m.* 12 Jan. 1703, Susanna, dau. of Thomas Yeadon, of Castlerea, co. Roscommon, and had issue,
1. OWEN, his heir.
1. Isabella, *m.* Lewis Hicks.
2. Mary, *m.* Thomas Digby, of Drundaff, co. Roscommon.
3. Sarah.
The only son,
OWEN LLOYD, of Carrickena, now Rockville, co. Roscommon, High Sheriff 1751, *b.* 22 May, 1714; *d.* 1778; *m.* 1st, 19 April, 1740, Susannah, dau. and co-heir of Richard Blackburne, of Carrickena, and had issue, *b.* 8 Dec. 1770, Anne, widow of William Devenish, of Rush Hill, dau. of Francis Fetherston, of Whiterock, co. Longford (*see* FETHERSTONHAUGH *of Bracklyn Castle*). The children of the 1st wife were,
1. Owen, of Grange, High Sheriff 1775, *b.* 7 March, 1743; *d.v.p.* 21 Feb. 1777; *m.* 4 Aug. 1770, Emily, dau. and co-heir of Edward Nicholson, of Primrose Grange, co. Sligo, and left two sons,
  1. Owen, of Rockville, will dated 5 Feb., ⎫
     proved 1 May, 1793, *unm.*   ⎪ Both *d.* at Lisbon.
  2. John Thomas, of Rockville, will dated   ⎬
     18 Sept. 1795, proved 4 March, 1796, *unm.* ⎭
2. WILLIAM, who *s.* his nephew.
3. John Yeadon, of Anneville, co. Roscommon, High Sheriff 1786, will dated 9 Dec. 1797, proved 13 Jan. 1798; *m.* Catherine, dau. of John Crofton, of Lissadorn, co. Roscommon, and had issue,
  1. Owen, of Lissadorn, D.L., *m.* Harriet, dau. of Arthur French, of French Park (*see* DE FREYNE, Baron), and left with other issue,
    Morgan George (Sir), K.C.B. 1911, C.B. 1897, Col. 3rd Batt. Royal Irish Rifles, J.P., co. Wexford (*Residence*—*Belvedere, Tenby, S. Wales*), *b.* 1843, *m.* 1870, Emily Olivia, dau. of Thomas Bell, of Brook Hill, co. Wexford, and has issue.

2. Thomas. 3. John Yeadon.
1. Anne.
2. Susanna, *m.* William Lloyd (*see below*).
3. Anne Catherine.
4. Thomas (Rev.), *m.* Dorothy, dau. of Thomas Digby, of Drumdaff, co. Roscommon, and had issue,
  1. Owen, of Fairview, *m.* Eliza, dau. of Benjamin Bunbury, of Kilkenny, and had issue,
    (1) Thomas William.
    (1) Jane. (2) Dorothea.
  1. Mary, *m.* Thomas George Digby, of Drumdaff.
  2. Susanna, *m.* Garret Parkinson, Surgeon Clare Militia.
1. Jane, *m.* 21 May, 1768, William Phibbs, of Hollybrook, co. Sligo (*see* PHIBBS *of Lisheen*).
2. Susanna, *m.* 9 Oct. 1767, William Handcock, M.P. for Athlone 1761–76 (CASTLEMAINE, Baron).
3. Mary, *m.* 13 Nov. 1781, Gilbert Ormsby, of Grange, co. Roscommon (*see* ORMSBY *of Gortner Abbey*).
4. Sarah, *m.* Rev. William Thompson.
5. Abigail, *m.* Jan. 1779, Rev. William Phibbs, of Abbeyville, co. Sligo.
6. Anne, *m.* 10 June, 1777, John Armstrong, of Bellevue, King's Co.
The 2nd son,
WILLIAM LLOYD, of Rockville, High Sheriff 1800, *b.* 21 Jan. 1748; *d.* 1818; *m.* 7 Dec. 1771, Mary Hampton, dau. of Sacheverel Jones, by his wife Jane Hampton, of Henlys, Beaumaris, and had issue,
1. OWEN, his heir.
2. William, *m.* Susanna, dau. of Owen Lloyd, of Lissadorn (*see above*).
3. Thomas Jonas.
1. Mary Hampton, *m.* 1799, Coote Mulloy, of Hughestown, co. Roscommon (*see* O'MULLOY).
2. Susanna. 3. Jane.
4. Sarah, *m.* 3 May, 1810, Molloy McDermott Roe (*see* MACDERMOTT *of Alderford*).
5. Emma. 6. Emily.
The elder son,
OWEN LLOYD, of Rockville, High Sheriff 1818, Lieut.-Col. Roscommon Militia, *b.* 7 March, 1774; *d.* 12 April, 1840; *m.* 31 Dec. 1801, Catherine, dau. of Col. Richard Pennefather, of New Park, co. Tipperary (*see* PENNEFATHER *of Rathsallagh*), and had issue,
1. WILLIAM, his heir.
2. Richard Pennefather, M.A. (Dublin), Barrister, *m.* 22 June, 1833, Catherine, dau. of James Kelly (*see* KELLY *of Mucklon*), and had issue, two daus.
3. Thomas, *m.* and had issue.
4. Matthew Pennefather, Major 59th Regt., *m.* Amy, dau. of Edward Morgan, and had one son and three daus.,
  1. Owen Edward Pennefather, V.C. (1894), C.B. (1910), Surgeon-Gen. A.M.S., *b.* 1 Jan. 1854; *m.* Florence Maria, dau. of Richard Spread Morgan, of Brdlestown, co. Cork.
    1. Maria Amelia, *m.* 6 Feb. 1877, Rev. Daniel Gabbett Westropp, M.A. (*see* WESTROPP *of Attyflin*).
    2. Mary Hampton Wall, *m.* Robert Harloe Fleming, M.D.
    3. Susan, *m.* Mark Bloxham Cooper, Barrister.
5. Robert, *m.* Frances, dau. of Daniel Kelly, of Cargins, co. Roscommon, and had with other issue, *d.* young,
  1. Owen, *m.* Josephine, widow of — Mallon, dau. of — Eakins, and has issue living three sons,
    (1) Owen Francis. (2) William.
    (3) Frederick.
  2. Daniel Kelly, *d. unm.*
  1. Mary Hampton, *m.* Frederick Walter Franklin.
1. Mary, *m.* Rev. William Wall.
2. Anna, *m.* Benjamin Grant.
3. Catherine, *m.* Oct. 1833, Rev. James Wentworth Mansergh (*see* MANSERGH *of Grenane*).
The elder son,
WILLIAM LLOYD, of Rockville, *b.* 28 Feb. 1803; *m.* 22 Sept. 1829, Anna, only dau. of Major Acheson Montgomery Moore, co. Tyrone, descendant of Sir Archibald Acheson, 1st Baron Gosford, and *d.* 7 Jan. 1870, leaving two sons,
1. OWEN RICHARD NATHANIEL, of whom presently.
2. Acheson Montgomery, *b.* 26 Oct. 1831; *m.* 18 Jan. 1865, Catherine, dau. of Rev. James Wentworth Mansergh, co. Tipperary (*see* MANSERGH *of Grenane*), by his wife Catherine, dau. of Col. Owen Lloyd, of Rockville (*see above*), and has issue, one son,
  William Owen, *b.* 29 July, 1866.
The elder son,
MAJOR OWEN RICHARD NATHANIEL LLOYD, *b.* 7 July, 1830; *m.* 20 Sept. 1855, Frances Maria, dau. of William Hutchinson, M.D., of Carrick-on-Shannon, by Mary Susanna his wife, dau. of Capt. Coote Mulloy, D.L., of Hughestown, co. Roscommon. He *d.* 17 Nov. 1863, having by her (who *d.* 2 Oct. 1885) had issue,
1. WILLIAM, now of Rockville.
2. John Charles, *m.* Margaret, dau. of — Waldron, and has issue, Owen John Montgomery.
  Frances Maria.
1. Anna Montgomery, *m.* Rev. William Kennedy Brodribb, B.A., Rector of Putley, Herefordshire, and by him has issue, Owen Adams Kennedy, and Eanswith Alice Kennedy, dec.

Arms—Az. a chevron or, and a chief erminois. *Crest*—An eagle displayed with two heads, sa. armed and langued gu.

Seat—Rockville, Drumsna, Roscommon. *Club*—Kildare Street.

LLOYD OF STRANCALLY CASTLE.

The late GEORGE WHITELOCKE WHITE-LOCKE-LLOYD, of Strancally Castle, co. Waterford, and Calton, co. York, D.L. W.R. of York, J.P. for the former co. and High Sheriff thereof 1859, b. 30 May, 1830, educated at Trin. Coll. Camb.; m. 1st, 14 Sept. 1854, Selina Jane, dau. of Arthur Henry, of Lodge Park, co. Kildare (and Eliza his wife, dau. of George Gunn, of Mount Kennedy, co. Wicklow), and by her (who d. 11 Jan. 1860) has issue,

1. WILLIAM WHITELOCKE, of Glandore, co. Cork, late Lieut. 24th Regt., b. 5 May, 1856; m. 25 June, 1885, Catherine Anna Mona, dau. of Very Rev. Henry William Brougham, D.D., Dean of Lismore, and d. 24 Nov. 1897, leaving issue,
   PERCY GAMALIEL, Lieut. (on probation) 5th Batt. Leinster Regt., b. 7 Aug. 1890.
   Winifred Lucy Selina, b. 23 May, 1886.
1. Eveline Selina, m. 1st, John William Williams; 2ndly, 29 June, 1910, Samuel Bright Willioms, of Wilcot, Broadstairs.
2. Augusta Frances Jane, m. 1st, 14 July, 1898, Robert Barlow, M.R.C.S., of Orlebar, St. Peter's, Kent; 2ndly, 4 Jan. 1910, John Gordon Davis, of Parkville, Ramsgate.
3. Selina Mary, m. 1st, Matthew Manton; 2ndly, 8 April, 1905, Kenlm Digby, of The Limes, St. Peter's, Ramsgate.

Mr. Lloyd m. 2ndly, 7 Feb. 1861, Lady Anne Margaret Butler, 2nd dau. of Richard Somerset, 3rd Earl of Carrick. She d.s.p. 15 May, 1901. He took by Royal Licence, 1880, the additional surname and arms of WHITELOCKE. He m. 3rdly, 3 Nov. 1904, Anna Maria (now of Strancally Castle), of Buttevant Castle, co. Cork, only surviving dau. of the late George Wheeler Bennett, of Ashbrook, co. Limerick, and d. 14 May, 1910.

Lineage.—GAMALIEL LLOYD, of Mattersey, co. Nottingham, d. 1 Nov. 1661, leaving issue by his wife, Anne Briggs, of Wigan, co. Lancaster,
1. GEORGE, his heir. 2. Gamaliel.
3. William, whose representatives are now the BOOTHS of Glendon, co. Northbants. 4. John.
1. Anne, m. Joseph Smethurst, and had a numerous posterity.
The eldest son,
GEORGE LLOYD, b. 1650, settled at Manchester, and d. 1728, leaving by his wife, Martha Whittaker, of Newton Heath, co. Lancaster, an only surviving child,
GAMALIEL LLOYD, of Manchester, merchant and manufacturer, d. 1749, leaving by Elizabeth his wife, dau. and co-heir of John Carte, M.B., of Manchester, who d. 30 Sept. 1763, an only child,
GEORGE LLOYD, M.A. Cantab, F.R.S., D.L. for West Riding of York, who purchased Hulme Hall, near Manchester, and resided at Barrowby, near Leeds, where he d. 4 Dec. 1783. He m. 1st, Eleanor, dau. of Henry Wright, of Offerton, co. Chester (by Purefoy his wife, dau. of Sir Willoughby Aston, Bart.), and by her had an only child,
1. JOHN, F.R.S., of Snitterfield, m. Anne, dau. and heir of James Hibbins, M.D., and had issue,
   1. GEORGE, of Welcombe House, co. Warwick, High Sheriff 1806, b. 7 March, 1768; d. unm. 11 July, 1831.
   2. JOHN GAMALIEL, Bencher of the Middle Temple, s. his brother in Welcombe House, High Sheriff co. Warwick 1832; d. unm. 1837.
      1. Charlotte, m. 4 May, 1802, Rev. Thomas Warde.
      2. Purefoy, d. unm.
Mr. Lloyd m. 2ndly, Susannah, dau. of Thomas Horton, of Chadderton, co. Lancaster, sometime Governor of the Isle of Man under the Earl of Derby, and father of Sir William Horton, Bart., and had issue,
2. GAMALIEL, his heir.
3. GEORGE (see LLOYDS of Stockton Hall).
4. Thomas, of Horsforth Hall (see LLOYD of Cowesby).
1. Susannah, m. Rev. Henry Wray, and has two sons and a dau.
2. Elizabeth, m. 1780, Thomas Bateson, and had an only son, Robert, created a Baronet.
The eldest son of the 2nd marriage,
GAMALIEL LLOYD, Alderman of Leeds, and Mayor 1799, b. 26 May, 1744, resided at Bury St. Edmunds, and afterwards in Great Ormond Street, London, where d. 31 Aug. 1817. By his wife Elizabeth (m. about 1780 or 1781), dau. of James Attwood, he had issue, with two daus., Mary Horton, m. Stephen John Winthrop, M.D.; Anne Susannah, m. Leonard Horner, F.R.S., an only son,

WILLIAM HORTON LLOYD, F.L.S., possessor of estates in cos. York, Lancaster, and Derby, b. 10 Feb. 1784; m. 13 April, 1826, Mary (who d. 18 Feb. 1882), 6th and youngest dau. of George Whitelocke, of Seymour Place, Bryanston Square, London, and Fortoiseau, near Paris (a great-grandson of Sir Bulstrode Whitelocke), by Mary his wife, dau. of David Roche, Alderman of Limerick, and d. 18 Feb. 1849, having had issue, Gamaliel, b. 12 June, 1827; d. 6 Nov. 1830; and the late GEORGE WHITELOCKE WHITELOCKE-LLOYD, of Strancally Castle.

FAMILY OF WHITELOCKE.

Lineage.—JOHN WHITELOCKE, of an old Berkshire family possessed for several generations of a considerable property in Berks as well as in cos. Oxford and Buckingham, was living in the reign of HENRY VI, and m. 1459, Agnes, only dau. and heir of ROBERT DE LA BECHE (the last male descendant of the De la Beche family of co. Buckingham, whose progenitor WILLIAM DE LA BECHE is mentioned in deeds of 15 and 31 HENRY III), and was s. by his son,
WILLIAM WHITELOCKE, living 1509, who left by his wife, whose name was Cowdry, a son,
RICHARD WHITELOCKE, living 1543. By his wife, who was of the family of Grove, near Plunges, he had issue,
1. William (Rev.), Fellow and Vice-Provost of King's Coll. Camb., Vicar of Frescott, diocese of Chester, and Canon of Lichfield, d. unm. at Lichfield, aged 80 years.
2. John, m. at 45 years of age the dau. of Planer, of Okingham, co. Berks, who was then aged 17, and had,
   1. William, Lord of the Manor of Beches, co. Berks and Beches Lands, co. Oxford, m. Ursula, dau. of George Beresford, by Mary his wife, dau. of John Colte, and had a son,
   William, Lord of the Manor of Beches, at Visitation, Bucks, 1634.
   2. John, one of the King's household in the Wafery, m. the widow of his kinsman, Rev. William Whitelocke, Vicar of Sunning. 3. De la Beche, living 1634.
3. Heirom, who d. aged over 60 years, leaving a son,
   William (Rev.), M.A. Oxford, Vicar of Sunning, and Prebendary of Wells and Lichfield, left by his wife (who m. 2ndly, John Whitelocke, of the King's household) a son,
   William, living 1634.
4. RICHARD, ancestor of the line treated of here.
Mr. Whitelocke was party to deeds made 10 HENRY VII and 1 HENRY VIII. His youngest son,
RICHARD WHITELOCKE, of London, was b. at Beches about 1533, became a Merchant, and was made free of the "Merchant Adventurers." He m. 7 Feb. 1563, Joan, dau. of John Colte, of Hertford, and widow of Mr. Brockhurst, of London, Merchant (who d. of the plague, 5 Queen ELIZABETH), by whom (who m. 3rdly, Thomas Price, of London, Merchant, and d. 21 Feb. 1606) he had issue,
1. Edmund, b. 10 Feb. 1564, Capt. of Infantry, served in Provence. Was indicted for high treason with Robert, 1st Earl of Essex, but was discharged; accused of being concerned in the Gunpowder Plot, 1605; d.s.p. 1608.
2. Richard of Elbing, in Spruceland, Sweden, b. 28 Dec. 1565, sent to Dantzic at the age of 16; m. Katherine Dambits, of Elbing, and d. 1624, leaving with two daus., Katherine, m. — Smith, of Clundby, and another m. Capt. Potley, as many sons,
   1. James, b. in Elbing 1608.
   2. John, b. in Elbing about 1614, father of
      John Jacob Whitelocke, b. 1657, whose son,
      Clement, m. Marie Behmer de Metzdorph, and had three sons, 1. John, b. 13 Sept. 1744, Major in the service of the King of Sweden, and Knt. of the Order of the Sword; m. Marie Lindmark, and was killed by a canon ball while commanding a ship of the line against Russia, 3 June, 1790, leaving one son, Charles Otto, Aide-de-Camp to the King of Sweden, b. 27 Sept. 1789, and d. at Florence, Italy, about 1840; 2. Paul, Major in the Artillery of Sweden, Knight of the Sword; b. 1748, d. unm. 1810; 3. Charles, b. 1754, m. Sophie Lindmark, and d. 1780, leaving a son, Gustave, b. 1776, who left Sweden, and has never since been heard of.
3. William, b. posthumous 28 Nov. 1570, entered the military service; served under Sir Francis Drake, and was slain in a fight with the Spaniards 1597.
4. James (Sir), twin with William, of whom hereafter.
Mr. Whitelocke d. at Bordeaux, 7 Nov. 1570. His youngest son,
SIR JAMES WHITELOCKE, Knt., of Fawley Court, co. Buckingham, J.P. of that co. and Oxford, was b. posthumous, a twin with his brother William, in St. Thomas's Street, St. Dunstan-in-the-East, London. He was educated as St. John's Coll. Oxford, of which he was elected a Fellow Nov. 1589. Admitted to the Middle Temple 2 March, 1592; called to the Bar Aug. 1600; appointed Chief Justice of Chester 14 June, 1620; Serjeant-at-Law 18th same month; knighted at Theobalds 29 Oct. 1620; and sworn in a Justice of the King's Bench 18 Oct. 1624. Sir James m. 9 Sept. 1602, ELIZABETH BULSTRODE (b. 31 July, 1575; d. 28 May, 1631), dau. of Edward Bulstrode, of Hedgeley Bulstrode, co. Buckingham, by Cecily his wife, sister of Sir John Croke, Knt. of Chilton, co. Buckingham, M.P., Speaker of Queen ELIZABETH's last Parliament, and Justice of the King's Bench, and grand-dau. of Thomas Bulstrode, of Hedgeley Bulstrode. By her he had issue,
1. BULSTRODE (Sir), his heir.
2. James, b. 17 May, 1612; d. before 1619.
1. Elizabeth, b. 6 Oct. 1603; m. 24 May, 1623, Sir Thomas Mostyn, Knt. of Mostyn, and was mother of
   Sir Roger Mostyn, 1st bart. of Mostyn.
2. Mary, b. 17 May, 1606; d. 5 June, 1611.
3. Cicely, b. 10 March, 1607; m. 3 July, 1632, Edward Dixon, of Hilden in Tunbridge, co. Cambridge.

IRELAND. Loftus.

4. Joan, b. 6 Aug. 1609 ; d. at Beaconsfield, 8 May, 1610.

Sir James d. 22 June, 1632, and was s. by his son,

SIR BULSTRODE WHITELOCKE, Knt. of Fawley Court, and of Chilton Lodge, co. Wilts, created by CHRISTINA, Queen of Sweden, a Knight of the Order of Amaranth, b. 6 Aug. 1605. Entered Oxford University at sixteen, the Middle Temple at eighteen, and was admitted a barrister 1626. He was M.P. for Stafford 1629, for Great Marlow 1640, for Oxford 1654, and for co. Buckingham 1656. In 1632 he was appointed Recorder of Abingdon, and was deputed 1642 on the breaking out of the Civil War, to prevent the execution of a Royal array in co. Oxford. In 1644 he was member of the commission to treat with the King, and a Commissioner of the Admiralty 1645. He garrisoned Phyllyscourt against the King 1646. Was appointed one of the Commissioners of the Great Seal 2 March, 1648 ; Serjeant-at-Law, 2 Oct. following ; and was sent by OLIVER CROMWELL as Ambassador to Sweden 2 Sept. 1653, which post he resigned in 1654. He was summoned to OLIVER CROMWELL'S " Other House " by writs, 11 Dec. 1655, and was created a Viscount by a patent, dated 21 Aug. 1657. After the death of CROMWELL, he was appointed, 27 Oct. 1659, one of the Committee of safety " for the Preservation of the Peace " ; and the same year was made First Commissioner of the Great Seal. At the Restoration he retired from public life, and was granted a free pardon by CHARLES II, and presented by His Majesty with his Coronation Bible and Prayer Book. Sir Bulstrode m. 1st, June, 1630, Rebecca, dau. of Alderman Thomas Bennett, of London, by whom (who d. 16 May, 1634) he had a son,

1. James (Sir), of Trompington, b. 13 July, 1631, Col. of Horse, knighted by OLIVER CROMWELL, 6 Jan. 1650, M.P. co. Oxford, 12 July, 1654 ; m. Mercy, dau. and co-heir of George Pyke, of Trompington, co. Cambridge, and d. Oct. 1701, leaving,
  1. Bulstrode, aged about 40 in 1696, d. unm.
  2. George, unm. 1703.
  3. James Bulstrode, unm. 1703.

Sir Bulstrode m. 2ndly, 10 Nov. 1634, Hon. Frances Willoughby, dau. of William, 3rd Lord Willoughby, of Parham, by whom (who d. 16 May, 1649) he had issue,

2. William (Sir), Knt. of Phyllyscourt, Henley-on-Thames, co. Oxford, bapt. 28 Dec. 1636, Barrister of the Middle Temple, M.P. for Wenlock, knighted at Whitehall, 10 April, 1689 ; m. Mary, dau. of Sir Thomas Overbury, Knt. of Burton-upon-the-Hill, co. Gloucester ; and d. Nov. 1717, having had issue,
  1. Overbury, d. unm. Dec. 1693.
  2. William, of the Middle Temple, m. Anne, dau. of Edward Nowell, Secretary to the Excise Commissioners ; and d. 27 July, 1709, having had an only dau.,
    Anne, d. April, 1699.
  3. Bulstrode, d. unm.   4. James, d. unm. Feb. 1677.
  1. Anne, m. 1681, Sir Thomas Noel, 3rd bart. of Kirby Mallory ; and d. 8 Jan. 1737.
  2. Mary, m. William Harmar, of the Middle Temple, gentleman.   3. Frances, d. unm. June, 1680.
  4. Hester, m. Edward Sherwood, of Henreth, co. Berks.
  5. Dorothy, d. unm. March, 1721.
  6. Elizabeth, m. William Wiseman, of Sparsholt Court, co. Berks.   7. Henrietta, d. Oct. 1710.
  8. Diana.
3. Willoughby, b. 1626 ; d. unm.
4. Bulstrode, b. 1648 ; d. unm.
1. Frances, bapt. 30 Dec. 1635.
2. Elizabeth, bapt. 11 Jan. 1637.
3. Mary, bapt. 4 April, 1639 ; m. George Nevill, of Sheffield Park, co. Sussex, and was mother of George, 11th Lord Abergavenny (see BURKE'S Peerage).
4. Cicely, bapt. 9 Jan. 1641.
5. Hester, bapt. Aug. 1642 ; m. Mr. Seawen, a Welshman.
6. Anne, m. Abraham Hill, of Shilton, co. Devon.

Sir Bulstrode m. 3rdly, 11 Sept. 1650, Mary Carleton, of Surrey, widow of Rowland Wilson, by whom he had further issue,

5. Samuel, of Chilton Foliatt, co. Wilts, b. 1651 ; m. Elizabeth, dau. of Robert Gough, of Vernham Dean, co. Southampton ; and d. May, 1690, leaving by her (who d. Oct. 1702) two sons and as many daus.,
  1. Samuel, of Chilton Foliatt, bapt. 23 Dec. 1675 ; m. 1st, Elizabeth Trotman, who d.s.p. April, 1700 ; and 2ndly, at Westminster Abbey, 6 Feb. 1703, Katharine, dau. of John Dolben, and grand-dau. of Most Rev. John Dolben, D.D., Archbishop of York ; and d. April, 1743, leaving by her (who d. Oct. 1722), twelve children, viz.,
    (1) John, of Chilton Foliatt, sold the estate, and d. unm.
    (2) Samuel, d. unm. 1741.   (3) Gilbert, d. 1747.
    (1) Katherine, b. 9 Nov. 1703 ; d. unm.
    (2) Anne, m. Rev. Mr. Gifford, Rector of Nufford, co. Oxford.
    (3) Elizabeth, b. 1706 ; d. 30 Oct. 1777.
    (4) Necettie, b. 1709 ; d. 26 April, 1781.
    (5) Mary, b. 1711 ; d. unm. 25 April, 1802.
    (6) Henrietta, b. 1714 ; d. 21 Dec. 1797.
    (7) Mulso, b. 1715 ; d. 15 Dec. 1812.
    (8) Charlotte, m. Charles Garrard.
    (9) Judith, b. 1722 ; d. 26 Aug. 1807.
  2. Bulstrode, of Everleigh, co. Wilts, b. 1678, whose will is dated 26 Aug. 1732 ; d.s.p.
    1. Frances, m. Walter Parker, of Highworth.   2. Mary.
6. CARLETON, of whom hereafter.
7. Stephen, a Six-Clerk in Chancery, d.s.p.
8. Bigley, b. 6 Nov. 1653 ; d. May, 1686.
9. John, b. 26 Sept. 1656.
7. Frances, b. 17 May, 1655 ; m. 11 Sept. 1672, Sir Francis Pile, 4th bart. of Compton Beauchamp.
8. Rebecca, b. 7 May, 1658.

Sir Bulstrode d. 1675, and was bur. at Chilton Foliatt, near Hungerford, co. Wilts, which place he had purchased, 1660. His sixth son,

CARLETON WHITELOCKE, of Hersham, co. Surrey, and Salisbury Square, London, bapt. 21 June, 1652 ; m. 1st, Katherine, dau. of Sir Andrew Henley, 1st bart. of Henley, who d. 1637, leaving four daus.,
1. Ruth.   2. Katharine, b. 1683.
3. Elizabeth, b. Sept. 1687.
4. Mary, m. William Russell, of Fleet Street, London.

Mr. Carleton Whitelocke, m. 2ndly, Maty, dau. of Herbert Alwyn, of London, Merchant, and widow of Thomas Mitchell, of Greyford, co. Kent, by whom he had another dau., Agnes de la Beche, b. Aug. 1700, and d. Dec. next year, and a son, his successor,

JOHN CARLETON WHITELOCKE, of Priorswood, co. Dublin, bapt. 29 Sept. 1699, joined the Army as Ensign, 29 Sept. 1719, and was afterwards Major in Col. Burrell's Regt. He m. 15 April, 1725, Anne, dau. of George Roche, of St. Mary's, Limerick, M.P. for that city, and had issue,
1. GEORGE, his successor.
2. Bulstrode, b. Feb. 1726 ; d. 1736.
1. Anne, d. unm.   2. Frances, d. 1748.
3. Katherine, m. Walter Bermingham ; and d. 15 Dec. 1769.

Major Whitelocke d. 4 July, 1776. His only surviving son,

GEORGE WHITELOCKE, of Wokingham, co. Berks, Gloucester Place, London, and Fortoiseau, near Paris, was bapt. at St. Thomas's Church, Dublin, 4 May, 1750, and eventually became heir male of SIR BULSTRODE WHITELOCKE. He m. Mary, dau. of David Roche, Limerick, and aunt of Sir David Roche, 1st bart. of Carass, and d. 12 Jan. 1831, having had issue,
1. BULSTRODE, his heir, d.s.p. 1867.
2. JAMES, of Amboise, Touraine, France, heir to his brother, d. unm. 30 Nov. 1879.
3. George, of Harewood Square, London, d. unm. 24 June, 1879.
4. De la Beche, bapt. 16 Sept. 1791 ; d. unm. 1858.
1. Henrietta, b. 1785 ; d. Sept. 1790.
2. Anne, d. unm. 1856.   3. Georgina, d. unm. 1835.
4. Frances, d. unm. Dec. 1861.
5. MARY WHITELOCKE, b. 12 Aug. 1797 ; m. 13 April, 1826, WILLIAM HORTON LLOYD, of Calton, co. York, by whom (b. 10 Feb. 1784 ; d. 18 Feb. 1849) she left at her decease (18 Feb. 1882) one surviving son,

GEORGE WHITELOCKE WHITELOCKE-LLOYD, late of Strancally Castle, who, on the death of his maternal uncle, James Whitelocke, having become representative of the WHITELOCKE family, assumed by Royal Licence, dated 13 Jan. 1880, the additional surname and arms of WHITELOCKE.

Arms—Quarterly : 1st and 4th counter-quartered—1st and 4th, LLOYD, ar. three lions dormant in pale sa. ; 2nd and 3rd, WHITELOCKE, az. a chev. engr. between three eaglets close or, for WHITELOCKE-LLOYD ; 2nd, az. a chev. engr. between three eaglets close or, for WHITELOCKE ; 3rd, arg. on a bend gu. three stags' heads cabossed or. for DE LA BECHE. Crests—1st, LLOYD, a demi-arm in scale armour, the hand naked ppr., cuffed arg., grasping a lizard vert ; 2nd, WHITELOCKE, on a tower vairé ar. and gu., an eaglet, wings endorsed or.—Motto over—Quodcunq. evenerit optimum. Motto—Ar ol gwaith gorphvys.

Seat—Strancally Castle, Tallow, co. Waterford, and Buttevant Castle, co. Cork.

LLOYD-VAUGHAN. See VAUGHAN.

LOFTUS OF MOUNT LOFTUS.

JOHN EDWARD BLAKE LOFTUS, of Mount Loftus, co. Kilkenny, J.P., High Sheriff 1908, Capt. 4th Batt. R. Irish Regt., by Royal Licence, 11 June, 1910, he and his younger brother were authorised to continue the name of LOFTUS and to bear the arms of Loftus quartered with those of Murphy, b. 1876 ; m. 1903, Pauline May, only dau. of August Lichtenstadt, and has issue,

1. FRANCIS COATES CREAGH, b. 23 May, 1908.
1. Bettina Idrone Dorothy, b. 1906.
2. Ludovica Patricia Alice, b. 28 Feb. 1910.

Lineage.—SIR EDWARD LOFTUS, of Mount Loftus, co. Kilkenny (son of Nicholas, Viscount Loftus, of Ely), Capt. in Conway's

Lombard. THE LANDED GENTRY. 416

Regt., M.P. for Jamestown 1761-68, LL D. (Dublin) Honoris causa 1766, was created a Baronet of Ireland 16 July, 1768, High Sheriff of co. Tyrone 1777, co. Wexford 1784, and d. May, 1818. He m. 18 March, 1758, Anne, elder dau. and heir of Rev. Paul Read, of Drumnabrigh, co. Tyrone, Rector of Leckpatrick, who d. Aug. 1818, leaving four sons and two daus.,
1. NICHOLAS, 2nd bart.
2. Edward, Lieut. 4th R. Irish Dragoons, left a dau., Mary, m. Matthew Murphy.
3. Henry, Cornet in the Army.
4. FRANCIS HAMILTON, 3rd bart.
1. Mary, d. Oct., 1839; m. May, 1783, Rev. Edward Cary, of Munfin, co. Wexford.
2. Elizabeth, d. unm. April, 1844.
The eldest son,
SIR NICHOLAS LOFTUS, 2nd bart., of Mount Loftus, High Sheriff of co. Kilkenny 1801 and co. Wexford 1805, Lieut.-Col. Kilkenny Militia, d. 16 Aug., 1832, and was s. by his only surviving brother,
SIR FRANCIS HAMILTON LOFTUS, 3rd bart., of Mount Loftus, Capt. Kilkenny Militia, d. unm. 12 March, 1864, having devised his estates to the dau. of his brother Edward.
MARY MURPHY, dau. of Edward Loftus and wife of MATTHEW MURPHY, who s. to Mount Loftus, d. 25 June, 1869, and left three sons and two daus.,
1. JOHN, who s. 2. Peter.
3. Paul Edward.
1. Anne, m. 18 Dec. 1858, Hyacinth Chevers Plunkett, K.C., d. 22 May, 1911, Father of the Irish Bar.
2. Maria Joesphine.
The eldest son,
JOHN MURPHY, of Mount Loftus, J.P. cos. Wexford and Kilkenny, High Sheriff 1873, d. 12 Oct. 1881. He m. Belinda Olivia, 2nd dau. of Pierse Creagh, of Mount Elva and Bryan's Castle, co. Clare (see CREAGH of Dangan), and by her (who m. 2ndly, 1887, Maurice Lindsay Coates, of Springfield, Belfast) left three sons and a dau., who assumed the name of Loftus.
1. FRANCIS COCHRANE, his heir.
2. JOHN EDWARD BLAKE, now of Mount Loftus.
3. Pierse Creagh.
4. Linda, d. 1887.
5. Nora, m. 1908, Robert Alexander Gardiner, of Sagtikos Manor, Long Island, New York.
The eldest son,
FRANCIS COCHRANE LOFTUS, of Mount Loftus, who assumed the name of Loftus, Capt. R. Inniskilling Fusiliers, killed at Colenso, South Africa, 1899, and was s. by his brother.

Arms—Quarterly 1st and 4th sable a chevron engrailed erm. between three trefoils slipped arg., a bordure wavy of the last (for LOFTUS); 2nd and 3rd quarterly arg. and gu. in the 1st and 4th, a lion rampant of the 2nd, in the 2nd and 3rd a garb or, over all a fess embattled counter embattled sable (for MURPHY). **Crest**—A boar's head erased and erect per pale wavy arg. and sable. **Motto**—Loyal au mort.

Seat—Mount Loftus, Goresbridge, co. Kilkenny. **Clubs**—Kildare Street Club and Windham Club, St. James's, S.W.

LOMBARD OF SOUTH HILL.

ROGER EDWARD FITZGERALD-LOMBARD, late Capt. 5th Batt. Rifle Brigade, formerly Lieut. Royal Artillery, B.A. Trin. Coll. Dub., b. 22 May, 1878; m. 5 Sept. 1903, Maud Elizabeth, dau. of A. F. Pitel, of The Wintons, East Croydon, Surrey, and has issue,
1. James Cotter Roger, b. Jan. 1905.
2. Dermot Michael Barry, b. 5 Aug. 1906.
1. Helen Mary.
2. Jeannette Giuglia Laura Charlotte Mason.

Capt. Lombard served in the S. African War (Queen's Medal and four clasps). He adopted the additional surname of Fitzgerald by Deed Poll.

Lineage—REGINALD LE LUMBARD circa 1210 was father of DONATUS LE LUMBARD, whose son, THADDEUS had a son,
JOHN LUMBARD, who received the freedom of the city of Cork 1340. He was Sheriff of co. Cork 1355 and 1358, and Mayor of the City of Cork 1380 and 1389. His son GREGORY was father of DAVID, who had issue two sons,
1. EDWARD, of whom next.
2. NICHOLAS, of whom later.
EDWARD LUMBARD had a son,
WILLIAM LUMBARD, who had issue,
1. James, of Lumbardslande (or Lombard's Castle), Buttevant, who had issue,
   Gregory, of Lumbardslande, who m. Ellen, dau. of — Barry, and had issue,
   (1) John, of Lumbardslande, Buttevant.
   (2) Nicholas.
   (3) Peter, of Buttevant.
2. Edmund, Clerk of the Court of Chancery.
1. Ellinor, m. James FitzNicholas Barry.
The younger son of David Lumbard, the aforesaid,
NICHOLAS LOMBARD, had issue,
1. John.
2. Edmund, who had issue by his wife Catherine a son, Piers.
3. PIERS, of whom next.
1. Ellice, m. Philip FitzJohn Barry.
The third son,
PIERS LOMBARD, who was Bailiff of Cork, 1529, had issue,
1. JAMES, of whom next.
2. David, whose will was proved 1582 by his wife Alsone Tyrry, he left issue.
The elder son,
JAMES LOMBARD, Bailiff of Cork 1584 and 1595, had issue,
1. James, Mayor of Cork 1645. Will proved 1652, d.s.p. having m. 1638, Ellen Archdeacon. He built Monkstown Castle, co. Cork, and was the last Catholic Mayor before the penal laws.
2. William.
3. David, Sheriff of Cork 1626, living 1642.
4. Nicholas, Sheriff of Cork 1614. Will dated 1626, proved 24 Feb. 1627. By Ellen his wife he was ancestor of LOMBARD of Lombardstown.
5. EDWARD, of whom next.
1. Anne, 2. Jenett.
3. Joan.
4. Ellen, m. Michael Morrogh.
The youngest son,
EDWARD LOMBARD, Councillor of Cork 1626, whose will is dated 1642, proved 12 Feb. 1643, had issue with three daus., Catherine Anstace, and Eleanor, and an elder son John, a younger son,
NICHOLAS LOMBARD, who had issue with a son Nicholas, a younger son,
WILLIAM LOMBARD, a Capt. in Sir Wm. Browne's Kerry Regt., 1689. He had issue with an elder son Nicholas, a younger son,
ÆNEAS LOMBARD, who married a dau. of Griffin and by her had issue, with a dau. (m. — Council), three sons,
1. Roger.
2. Æneas, who left issue.
3. NICHOLAS, of whom next.
NICHOLAS LOMBARD, of Knockagand (born circa 1730 or 1720), whose will was proved at Ardfert (diocesan court) in 1811. By Catherine his wife he had issue with four daus. who m. respectively John Behane, John Cronin, David Curtain and Timothy Connor),
1. JAMES of Woodville, of whom next.
2. Richard.
3. Nicholas, who left issue.
4. Æneas, through whose marriage in 1791 with Margaret Harnett Woodville came into the Lombard family.
The eldest son,
JAMES LOMBARD, of Woodville, by his wife Johanna Dillon had issue,
1. James, b. 1775, will dated 1833; d. 1834; m. Julia de Courcy (b. 1798) and whose issue is now extinct in the male line.
2. ROGER, of Woodville, of whom presently.
3. John, b. 1782; m. Mary de Courcy and left issue.
1. Mary, m. Daniel Mahony.
2. Honora, m. Richard Norris.
3. Anne, m. Edward King.
4. Johanna, m. Daniel McCarthy.
5. Julia, m. Patrick Hussey.
The second son,
ROGER LOMBARD, of Woodville, b. 1780, d. after 1824 or before 1835, by his wife Jane Fitzgerald whom he m. in May, 1809, had issue,
1. Æneas, b. 1811; d.s.p.
2. JAMES FITZGERALD, of South Hill, b. 1817, of whom next
3. Edward Fitzgerald, m. Hanna Teresa Sheehan and had issue.
4. William,
1. Mary Anne, b. 1813. 2. Anne, b. 1815.
3. Margaret, b. 1817. 4. Honora.
5. Julia.
The second son,
JAMES FITZGERALD LOMBARD of South Hill, co. Dublin, J.P., M.R.I.A., Chevalier Legion d'Honneur, b. 1817; d. 1901, having m. 1st, Margaret Tuite, by whom he had issue,
1. James William Lombard, b. 1845; m. Mary Darcy, who d.s.p.
1. Mary (twin with above), m. 1870, William M. Murphy, of Dartry, co. Dublin, J.P., late M.P. for a Division of Dublin City. She d. 1900.
He m. 2ndly, 1873, Sarah, dau. of late Michael Barry, M.R.I.A., Barrister-at-Law, Professor of Law, Queen's University of Ireland (see BARRY of Firville), and by her had issue,
2. ROGER EDWARD (see above).

Arms—Per pale az. and fusilly arg. and sa. on the dexter a dimidiated eagle displayed grasping by the string a bugle horn all or, and charged on the breast with an antique crown gu. in chief two rescents of the fourth. **Crest**—A lion rampant gu. on the shoulder an escutcheon arg., charged with a bugle-horn sa., stringed vert. **Motto**—Aut vincere aut mori.

Seat—South Hill, co. Dublin. **Residence**—9, Corrig Avenue, Kingstown, co. Dublin. **Clubs**—Junior Army and Navy, Hibernian United Service, Edward Yacht, Kingstown.

LONGFIELD OF LONGUEVILLE.

RICHARD EDMUND LONGFIELD, of Longueville, co. Cork, J.P. and D.L., High Sheriff 1887; M.A. Trin. Coll. Cambridge; b. 6 June, 1842; m. 19 Sept. 1872, Alberta Charlotte, dau. of Sir W. H. Russell, LL.D., and has issue,

1. RICHARD WILLIAM, Capt. late 3rd Dragoon Guards, b. 18 Dec. 1873.
2. Lewis, b. 7 Dec. 1874; m. 27 Sept. 1897, Olive Katie Oahe, only child of J. Murray Dobson, and has issue,
   1. Theodore, b. 9 July, 1899.
   2. Richard James, b. 2 Jan. 1901.
3. Charles Edmund, b. 31 Aug. 1885.
1. Sibyl Mary, b. 13 June, 1877; m. 10 Jan. 1899, Major William Percival Monkhouse, M.V.O., R.H.A., youngest son of the late Rev. John Monkhouse, Rector of Church Oakley, near Basingstoke.
2. Muriel Alberta, b. 8 Sept. 1878; m. 3 July, 1899, Wyrley Edwin George Wyrley-Birch (see that family).

Lineage.—JOHN LONGFIELD, of Denbigh, Wales, 1652, afterwards of the city of Dublin, d. intestate; administration granted 8 March, 1669-70. He had two sons,
1. Robert, b. in Denbigh, 1652, obtained an extensive grant of lands in cos. Westmeath, Meath, Clare, under the commission of grace, by patent dated 15 April, 1685. He resided at Kilbride, co. Meath, and d. 1710, leaving issue, which became extinct in the male line on the death of his great-grandson, Robert Longfield, in 1790.
2. John, ancestor of the Longueville and Castle Mary families.

The 2nd son,
JOHN LONGFIELD, jr., b. 1653, settled at Castle Mary, near Cloyne, co. Cork, and d. 22 April, 1730, leaving by Mary his wife, dau. and co-heir of William Hawnby, of Mallow.
1. ROBERT, of Castle Mary, J.P., b. 1688; m. 1731, Margaret, dau. and co-heir of Richard Geering, of Dublin, M.P., and d. 11 March, 1765, aged 67, having had issue,
   1. JOHN, of Castle Mary, b. 3 July, 1733; m. (licence dated 10 March, 1755), Alice, dau. of Thomas Tilson, and left at his decease an only son,
      ROBERT, of Castle Mary, M.P. for borough of Donegal, m. April, 1778, Elizabeth, sister of the 1st Lord Lismore, and dau. of Thomas O'Callaghan, of Shanbally, co. Tipperary, by his 2nd wife, Hannah, dau. of John Rogerson, Lord Chief Justice of the King's Bench, and d.s.p.
   2. RICHARD, of Longueville, co. Cork, J.P., High Sheriff for co. Cork, 1758, M.P. for Charleville 1761, and afterwards for co. Cork, 1734. He was created, 1795, BARON LONGUEVILLE *of Longueville*, and in 1800 advanced to the VISCOUNTY OF LONGUEVILLE. His lordship, who was Governor of co. Cork and a Representative Peer for Ireland, m. 8 Nov. 1756, Margaret, dau. of Richard White, and aunt to Richard, 1st Earl of Bantry, but d.s.p. 23 May, 1811, when the honours expired. She d. April, 1809.
      1. Anne, m. 26 Feb. 1753, Roger Conner, of Connerville (see CONNER of Manch).
   2. John, of whom presently, as of Longueville.
   3. Hawnby, of Cork, m. 29 June, 1733, Mary, dau. of Christopher Vowell, of Ballyorane, co. Cork, and d. 31 July, 1741, leaving by her (who had predeceased him, Sept. 1738) an only child, Susanna, b. 19 Feb. 1734-5; m. Richard Parker.
   4. William, of Cork, b. 1710, who, by Mary Goodman his wife (b. 23 Nov. 1719; d. 5 Aug. 1739) had at his death, 1777, an only child, John Longfield, M.D., of Cork, m. 1775, Elizabeth, dau. of John Conroy, and aunt to the 1st Baronet of that name, and had (with other children, who d.s.p.) a 3rd son,
      Robert, m. April, 1815, Mary, 2nd dau. of John Martin, of Cork, and had an only child and heir,
      Mary Elizabeth, who m. 1838, her 1st cousin, David Beatty, of Borodale, co. Wexford.
   1. Helena, m. 1708, Theodore Vansevenhoven, of Cork.
   2. Elizabeth, m. John Tooker, of Ballindinish, co. Cork.
   3. Anne, m. (sett. dated 4 Nov. 1735), Richard Uniacke, of Mount Uniacke, co. Cork, and d. July, 1787, leaving issue (see *that family*).
   4. Mary, m. 1720, Walter Lavitt, of co. Cork.
   5. Henrietta, m. Rev. Thomas Squire.
   6. Deborah, m. Nov. 1731, James Peirce, of co. Cork.
   7. Bryana, m. Rev. William Bucknor, of Croom, co. Limerick.

The 2nd son,
JOHN LONGFIELD, of Longueville, J.P., b. 24 June, 1695; m. 12 Sept. 1738, Susanna, dau. of Montifort Westropp, and left at his decease, 5 April, 1765, two sons,
1. JOHN, his successor, of whose line we treat.
2. MOUNTIFORT, ancestor of the family now of Castle Mary (*refer to that Memoir*).

The elder son,

I.L.G.

JOHN LONGFIELD, of Longueville, J.P., High Sheriff co. Cork 1775, M.P. for Mallow, b. 5 July, 1741; m. 24 June, 1764, Elizabeth, dau. of William Foster, and 1st cousin of the Right Hon. John Foster, created Lord Oriel, by whom he had issue,
1. JOHN, his successor.
2. William, b. 1768, Barrister-at-Law 1794, d.s.p.
3. Mountifort (Rev.), Vicar of Desertserges, co. Cork, and many years J.P. for that co., m. 1st, Nov. 1796, Grace, dau. of William Lysaght, by whom he had issue,
   1. John, m. Miss Cotter, and had issue.
   2. Mountifort (Right Hon.), P.C., Q.C., J.P., LL.D. of Trin. Coll. Dublin 1831 (B.A. 1823, M.A. 1829, LL.D. 1831), became a Fellow of that College 1825, and Professor of Political Economy, 31 Oct. 1832. He resigned his Fellowship for the Professorship of Feudal and English Law, 29 Nov. 1834. This eminent jurist was appointed, 1847, a Commissioner of the Incumbered Estates Court, and, 1858, Judge of the Landed Estates Court. He was b. 1802; m. 1845, Elizabeth, dau. of Andrew Armstrong, and d. 1884. She d. 1882.
   3. Robert, of Merrion Square, Dublin, M.A. of Trin. Coll. Dublin, called to the Irish Bar, 1884, appointed Q.C. 1852, elected M.P. for Mallow 1859, b. 1810; m. 1840, Charlotte, dau. of George Stawell, of Crobeg, co. Cork, and d. 1868.
      1. Elizabeth, m. 4 June, 1822, Daniel Conner, of Manch (see *that family*), and has issue.
      2. Margaret, m. — M'Carthy. 3. Grace, m. Thomas Beasley. The Rev. Mountifort Longfield m. 2ndly, Mary Ann, dau. of Col. William Conner, and had further issue,
   4. Richard (Rev.), Rector of Mogeely, m. Wilhelmina, dau. and co-heir of the Rev. James Gollock, and d. March, 1898, having had issue,
      (1) Mountifort, b. 1859; d. 1865.
      (2) Richard William Fred, b. 1861; m. 1898, Maria Louisa, dau. of Rev. Thomas Henry Gollock, of Forest, co. Cork, and has issue,
         Grace Wilhelmina.
      (3) James Mountifort, Capt. Reserve of Officers, late King's Regt., b. 1866.
      (4) George Francis (Rev.), b. 1868.
      (5) Claude Robert (Rev.), b. 1871; m. 12 July, 1899, Anna Arabella, dau. of John Bomford, of Oakley Park, co. Meath (see *that family*), and d. 1903, leaving issue,
         Richard Charles, b. 17 April, 1901.
      (6) William Elrington, late Capt. R.E., Assistant Director of Railways, Soudan, b. 1874; m. 1908, Maude Kirkby, dau. of Ralph B. Bagnall-Wild, of Costock (see *that family*).
   5. George (Rev.), D.D., M.A., Fellow Trin. Coll. Dublin, 1842; m. 28 July, 1859, Mary Webb, eldest dau. of Nathaniel Webb Ware, and d. 3 Nov. 1878, leaving issue,
      (1) Mountifort Gooree, Barrister-at-Law, b. 5 June, 1864.
      (2) Eleanor Charlotte Elizabeth.
      (2) Mary Louisa Beatrice.
   6. Henry, m. Eleanor, dau. of N. Webb Ware, and d. 17 Dec. 1898, leaving issue,
      (1) Henry Foster, m. 1894, Cherry Frances Pennefather, dau. of Capt. R. L. Warren.
      (1) Elizabeth, m. 1910, Thomas Delapere Homan, M.D.
      (2) Elinor Mary Augusta, m. 19 Feb. 1898 (her cousin), John Edmund Longfield (see below).
   7. William, J.P. co. Cork, b. 1821; m. 1865, Frances Catherine, eldest dau. of Rev. Richard Longfield Conner, of Downdaniel, Rector of the St. Anne's, Snandon. He d.s p. July, 1905.
   8. Charles, M.A., B.E., Trin. Coll. Dublin, d. 1898.
   9. Thomas, B.A. Trin. Coll. Dublin, d. 1909.
   10. Foster, Lieut.-Col. 8th Regt.
   4. Mary, d. 1886.
   5. Francis Patience, m. 29 April, 1861, Gen. John Longfield, C.B., and d. 28 July, 1903, leaving issue (see below).
4. Robert (Rev.), Rector of Mourne Abbey, co. Cork, d.s.p. 1807.
5. HENRY, of Waterloo, co. Cork, J.P., m. Mary, only dau. and heiress of John Powell, of Sea Court, co. Cork, and d. 1851, leaving issue,
   1. JOHN POWELL, late of Waterloo, J.P., B.A. of Trin. Coll. Dublin, late Lieut.-Col. Royal Cork Artillery Militia, b. 1815; m. 1848, Louisa (d. 24 July, 1906), 6th dau. of Rev. Matthew Purcell, of Burton, co. Cork.
   2. Henry, of Sea Court, Timoleague, co. Cork, b. 1828; m. 30 April, 1857, Eliza Augusta, only child and heir of William Purcell, of Altamira, co. Cork, and d. 16 Feb. 1871, leaving issue,
      (1) William Henry, Lieut. Lincolnshire Regt., b. 1859; d. unm. 9 Oct. 1888.
      (2) Alfred Purcell, Maj. R.F.A., b. 6 Dec. 1862; m. 12 April, 1898, Constance Ada, dau. of the late Professor James Saunders, of Edinburgh, and has issue,
         1. Ada Kathleen, b. 27 Oct. 1899.
         2. Violet, b. 1905.
      (3) Mountifort, of Sea Court, Timoleague, co. Cork, J.P., D.L., High Sheriff 1906, b. 12 Feb. 1866; m. 6 Jan. 1891, Geraldine Spencer, only dau. of Henley J. Edwards, late Ind. Navy.
      (1) Mary, m. 1885, Stuart Banks Roupell, Capt. R.N.
      (2) Kathleen Augusta, m. 1889, Alfred Robinson MacMullen.
   3. Robert, d. unm. 1864.
   1. Elizabeth, m. John Power, of Roskeen, co. Cork, J.P.
   2. Rachel, m. Rev. William Neligan, LL.D., Rector of St. Mary's, Shandon, co. Cork.
   3. Mary, m. 1st, Robert Longfield, of the Castle Mary branch (which see), and 2ndly, 1854, George, 2nd son of Thomas Lucas, of Richfordstown, co. Cork.

2 D

Longfield. THE LANDED GENTRY. 418

4. Patience, *m.* 6 Jan. 1848, Daniel Conner, of Manch, co. Cork (*see that family*).
5. Dora, *m.* Edward Francis Roche, J.P., of Johnstown House, co. Cork.
1. Patience, the 1st wife of John Wallis, of Drishane Castle, co. Cork. 2. Elizabeth, *m.* George Stawell, of Crobeg, co. Cork.
Mr. Longfield *d.* 1815, and was *s.* by his eldest son,
JOHN LONGFIELD, of Longueville, Lieut.-Col. in the Army, J.P. and High Sheriff 1829, *b.* May, 1767; *m.* 15 Oct. 1797, Eleanor, dau. of John Lucas, of Mount Lucas, King's Co. (*see that family*), and by her (who *d.* Nov. 1858) had issue,
1. RICHARD, of Longueville.
2. John, of Kilcoleman, Bandon, co. Cork, C.B., General (retired), Col. 8th Regt., *b.* 1804; *m.* 29 April, 1861, Frances Patience, dau. of Rev. Mountifort Longfield, of Churchill, Rector of Desertserges, co. Cork. She *d.* 28 July, 1903. He *d.* 27 Feb. 1889, leaving a son,
John Edmund, of Kilcoleman, co. Cork, J.P. co. Cork., B.A. Trin. Coll. Dublin, formerly Capt. 9th Batt. King's Royal Rifle Corps, *b.* 14 April, 1865; *m.* 19 Feb. 1898 (his cousin), Elinor Mary Augusta, dau. of Henry Longfield, of Mallow, co. Cork (*see above*), and has issue,
(1) John Foster, *b.* 15 July, 1906.
(1) Eleanor Frances Beatrice, *b.* 10 June, 1899.
(2) Margaret Lilian, *b.* 20 March, 1908.
Gen. Longfield *d.* 27 Feb. 1889.
1. Margaret Eleanor, *m.* 21 Aug. 1820, Thomas Wood Craster, D.L., of Craster Tower, co. Northumberland, who *d.* 1867, leaving issue (*see that family*).
2. Elizabeth, *m.* 1836, Rev. Edmund Lombard, and *d.* Dec. 1892.
Col. Longfield *d.* 18 Oct. 1842, and was *s.* by his son,
RICHARD LONGFIELD, of Longueville, co. Cork, J.P. and D.L., High Sheriff 1833, Member for co. Cork in the last Parliament of WILLIAM IV, 1835-7, *b.* 7 May, 1802; *m.* 1st, 7 Jan. 1832, Harriet Elizabeth, dau. of John M'Clintock, M.P., of Drumcar, co. Louth, by the Lady Elizabeth his wife, and by her (who *d.* 27 April, 1834) had an only child,
1. John, 89th Regt., *b.* 29 Nov. 1832; *d. unm.* returning from the Crimea, 20 Oct. 1855.
He *m.* 2ndly, 31 Aug. 1847, Jemima Lucy, dau. of Wyrley Birch, of Wretham Hall, Norfolk, by Catherine Sarah his wife, dau. of Jacob Reynardson, of Holywell, co. Lincoln, and by her (who *d.* 15 Jan. 1892) had issue,
2. RICHARD EDMUND, now of Longueville.
3. Augustus Henry, of Waterloo, Mallow, co. Cork, Lieut.-Col. (retired), late 1st Batt. Norfolk Regt., *b.* 5 May, 1845; *m.* 28 June, 1883, Florence Amy, younger dau. of Richard Nicholas Percival, of Springfield, Sandbach, Cheshire, and has issue,
John Percival, M.V.O., Lieut. Norfolk Regt., *b.* 27 Oct. 1885.
Kathleen Mary Noel, *b.* 29 Dec. 1886; *d.* 20 Nov. 1910.
4. Lewis Pryor, *b.* 4 March, 1848; *d.* 27 Sept. 1856.
1. Catharine Elinor, *d. unm.* 30 June, 1870.
2. Johanna Jemima.
Mr. Longfield *d.* 18 June, 1889.

Arms—Gu. a chevron erm. between seven crosses-crosslet fitchée, three in chief and four in base arg. *Crest*—Out of a ducal coronet or, a demi-lion rampant gu. *Motto*—Parcere subjectis.
Seat—Longueville, near Mallow, co. Cork. *Clubs*—New University, S.W. and Kildare Street, Dublin.

LONGFIELD OF CASTLE MARY.

LIEUT.-COLONEL MOUNTIFORT JOHN COURTENAY LONGFIELD, of Castle Mary, co. Cork, J.P. and D.L. High Sheriff 1909, educated at Eton and Oxford, Major and Brevet Lieut.-Col. (retired) late 2nd Life Guards, *b.* 16 Oct. 1858; *m.* 10 Jan. 1891, Alice Elizabeth, 2nd dau. of James Mason, of Eynsham Hall, co. Oxford, and has issue,
1. Rita Narcissa, *b.* 29 Nov. 1891; *m.* 20 July, 1911, Capt. Hon. Cyril Myles Ponsonby, M.V.O., Gren. Gds., 2nd son of the Earl of Bessborough (*see* BURKE's *Peerage*).
2. Norah Mary, *b.* 1893. 3. Cynthia Evelyn.

Lineage.—For the earlier portion of this pedigree, refer to LONGFIELD *of Longueville*. The younger son of John Longfield, of Longueville,
MOUNTIFORT LONGFIELD, who inherited the estates of Castle Mary from his cousin Lord Longueville, *b.* 22 Aug. 1746; *m.* (licence 22 June, 1778) Frances, dau. of John George Bateman. He was Col. of the City of Cork Militia, M.P. for Enniscorthy, and many years for Cork. He *d.* 8 June, 1819, having had issue, two daus., Margaret and Letitia, and three sons,
1. Richard, *m.* Maria, dau. of Henry Bruen, of Oak Park, co. Carlow, and *d.* 1819, leaving two sons, who both *d. unm.* 1833.
2. John, *d.s.p.* 3. ROBERT, of whom we treat.
The 3rd son,
REV. ROBERT LONGFIELD, of Castle Mary, *m.* Cherry, dau. of Thomas Hugo, of Drumeen, co. Wicklow, and had issue,
1. MOUNTIFORT, of Castle Mary.
2. Robert, a Lieut. in the Army, *m.* Mary, dau. of Henry Longfield, of Waterloo, co. Cork, and by her (who *m.* 2ndly, George Lucas) left at his decease, 1849, one dau.,
Mary Jane.
3. William Henry, Col., *m.* Elizabeth Mary (*d.* 2 Nov. 1909), dau. of Mathew Brinkley, of Parsonstown, co. Meath, and had issue, one son and two daus.,

1. William Mountifort, Capt. Hants Imp. Yeom., *m.* 23 Sept. 1884, Constance Madeline Frances, dau. of John Arthur Macartney, of Waverley, Queensland (*see* BURKE's *Peerage*, MACARTNEY, Bart.), and was killed in action in S. Africa 4 June, 1901, leaving issue,
William Brinkley Macartney, *b.* 26 Nov. 1886.
Constance Madeline Frances.
1. Florence Letitia, *m.* 25 Nov. 1871, Robert Dillon Hare, of Ballymore, Queenstown, co. Cork, J.P., and has issue (*see* BURKE's *Peerage*, LISTOWEL, E.).
2. Edith Caroline, *m.* W. Alexander.
4. Thomas Hugo (Rev.), Rector of St. Paul's, Cork, *d. unm.* 17 March, 1869.
1. Frances Anne, *m.* Richard Beare Tooker, J.P., Capt. Royal Cork City Artillery Militia, and *d.* 28 April, 1866, having had issue.
2. Cherry, *m.* 1851, William Oliver Jackson, of Ahanesk and Castleview, co. Cork, and *d.* 1862, leaving issue.
3. Margaret, *d. unm.* 4. Emily, *d. unm.* 1854.
5. Elizabeth, *m.* 13 Aug. 1853, Maziere John Brady, Barrister-at-Law, 2nd son of the Right Hon. Sir Maziere Brady, Bart., Lord Chancellor of Ireland, and *d.* 10 April, 1894, leaving issue (*see* BURKE's *Peerage*, BRADY, Bart.). He *d.* 3 Sept. 1903.
The Rev. R. Longfield *d.* 1843, and was *s.* by his eldest son,
MOUNTIFORT LONGFIELD, of Castle Mary, J.P., D.L., High Sheriff 1855, *m.* 1840, Caroline Augusta, sole surviving child of George Courtenay, of Ballyedmond, co. Cork, and by her (who *d.*) had issue,
1. MOUNTIFORT JOHN COURTENAY, now of Castle Mary.
1. Narcissa Caroline.
2. Cherry Elizabeth, *d. unm.* 31 March, 1906.
3. Louisa Margaret, *m.* 19 April, 1869, the late Major George Sackville Berkeley, R.E., eldest son of Robert Berkeley, Q.C., 40, Upper Mount Street, Dublin, and *d.* 25 Nov. 1901, leaving issue, one son.
4. Anne Catherine, dec.
5. Margaret Eleanor, dec.
6. Emily Blanche Mary, *m.* 1 Oct. 1872, Henry Philip Constantine Dillon, Lieut. R.E., eldest son of the Hon. Constantine Dillon. She *d.* 13 Sept. 1903, leaving issue, two sons and one dau. (*see* BURKE's *Peerage*, DILLON, V.).
7. Letitia Geraldine, *d. unm.* 21 June, 1903.
8. Caroline Augusta Rose, dec.
9. Adeline Maude Felicia, *m.* 4 June, 1874, Col. Charles Augustus Rochfort-Boyd, C.M.G., R.E., 2nd son of George Augustus Rochfort-Boyd, of Middleton Park, co. Westmeath, (*see* BOYD-ROCHFORT). She *d.* 6 May, 1902, leaving issue.
10. Frances Amy Georgina, *d. unm.* 24 Feb. 1905.
11. Alice, } twins, dec.
12. Clara, }
He *d.* 8 Nov. 1864.

Arms, &c.—Same as LONGFIELD *of Longueville.*
Seat—Castle Mary, near Cloyne, co. Cork.

DAMES-LONGWORTH OF GLYNWOOD.

TRAVERS ROBERT DAMES-LONGWORTH, of Glynwood, co. Westmeath, *b.* 20 Dec. 1896; *s.* his father 17 March, 1907;

Lineage.—FRANCIS LONGWORTH, of Creggan Castle, was *s.* by his son,
FRANCIS LONGWORTH, of Creggan Castle, who *d.* 1742, leaving issue,
1. John. 2. George.
3. FRANCIS.
The 3rd son,
FRANCIS LONGWORTH, of Creggan Castle, *m.* Elizabeth, dau. and co-heir of Thomas Dames, of Rathmoyle, King's Co., and *d.* 1804, having had issue,
1. JOHN, of Creggan Castle, *m.* 1787, Alicia Margaret, dau. of Lord Kilmaine. 2. FRANCIS, of whom presently.
3. THOMAS, J.P. King's Co., who assumed the name of DAMES, *b.* 1768, *m.* 1788, Jane, dau. of Mansel Burke, and *d.* 5 Sept. 1825, leaving issue (*see* DAMES *of Greenhill*). The eldest son,
FRANCIS, of Greenhill, King's Co., J.P. and D.L., High Sheriff 1832, *b.* 25 Dec. 1789; *m.* 1st, 5 June, 1830, Anna, youngest dau. of Rev. Travers Hume, D.D., and by her (who *d.* 21 Sept. 1835) had issue,
(1) THOMAS, now of Greenhill (*see* DAMES *of Greenhill*).
(2) FRANCIS TRAVERS, *s.* his cousin JOHN LONGWORTH, of Glynwood (*see below*).
(1) Elizabeth, *d.* an infant, 1835.
Mr. Francis Longworth Dames *m.* 2ndly, 13 Aug. 1839, Elizabeth Selina, youngest dau. of Ralph Smyth, of Gaybrook, co. Westmeath, and *d.* 6 Oct. 1863, leaving issue by her (who *d.* 13 June, 1885) (*see* DAMES *of Greenhill*).
4. George, *m.* Anne Phillips. 5. William, *d.* 1855.
1. Eliza, *m.* Rev. Samuel Lucas. 2. Catherine, *m.* J. Bailey.
3. Mary, *m.* John Wakeley, of Ballyburly, King's Co.
The 2nd son,
FRANCIS LONGWORTH, of Glynwood, *m.* 1st, 3 Jan. 1795, Sarah, dau. of John, 1st Lord Kilmaine, and 2ndly, Anne, dau. of James Whitaker of Sparkbrook, co. Warwick, and had issue,
1. Francis, *d.* 1856. 2. JOHN, of whom hereafter.
3. Thomas (Rev.), Vicar of Broomfield, Shrewsbury, *m.* Emma, dau. of Thomas Charles Bridges, of The Lodge, Salop, and *d.* 1865.

4. George, d. 1847.
1. Alicia Harriet, m. Henry Norwood Trye, of Leckhampton Court, co. Gloucester, and d. 1866.
2. Anne, m. Col. Young, of Barton End, co. Gloucester.
His and son,
JOHN LONGWORTH, of Glynwood, d.s.p. 1881, and was s. by his cousin,
FRANCIS TRAVERS DAMES-LONGWORTH, of Glynwood, co. Westmeath, High Sheriff co. Westmeath 1882, and for co. Galway 1890, Her Majesty's Lieutenant and Custos Rotulorum of the co. Westmeath J.P. for King's Co., Roscommon, Westmeath, Kildare, Dublin, and Donegal; M.A. of Trin. Coll. Dublin, Q.C. 1872, and formerly Bencher of the Society of the King's Inns, b. 26 April, 1834; s. to the estates of the late John Longworth, of Glynwood; m. 1 Aug. 1860, Frances Tennison, eldest dau. of William Noble, of Annagirt, co. Monaghan, and d. 3 Dec. 1898, having by her (who d. 8 Nov. 1895) had issue,
1. EDWARD TRAVERS, of Glynwood.
2. Francis, M.A. Trin. Coll. Camb., Asst. Master at Charterhouse School, b. 6 Oct. 1862.
1. Mary Louisa, m. 5 Sept. 1888, Langer Meade Loftus Owen, K.C., of Ellesmere, Hunter's Hill, Sydney, N.S.W., only child of the late Hon. Sir William Owen, Primary Judge in Equity in N.S.W., and has issue (see KYNASTON of Hardwicke).
The elder son,
EDWARD TRAVERS DAMES-LONGWORTH, of Glynwood, co. Westmeath, J.P. and D.L., High Sheriff 1900, J.P. co. Roscommon, B.A. Oxon., Barrister-at-Law, b. 23 May, 1861; m. 15 Dec. 1891, Hester Anne, eldest dau. of the late Frederick Pepys Cockerell, and d. 17 March, 1907, having had issue,
1. TRAVERS ROBERT, now of Glynwood.
1. Hester Frances.   2. Pamela Frederica.
3. Paulina Pepys.
Seats—Glynwood and Creggan, Athlone.

LONGWORTH-DAMES. See DAMES.

LOPDELL OF RAHEEN.

ROBERT HUGH OSWALD LOPDELL, of Raheen Park, co. Galway, b. 21 May, 1901; s. his father 1911.

Lineage.—JAMES LOPDELL, of Ballyline and Emlagh, co. Galway, removed from England, temp. CHARLES II., and purchased land in co. Galway, where he settled. He m. Jane, sister of John Fennell, of Windy House, co. Kilkenny, and d. in 1682, leaving issue,
1. JOHN, from whom descend Lopdells of Mulpit and Derryowen.
2. Christopher, of whom we treat.
The younger son,
CHRISTOPHER LOPDELL, d. before 1741, and was bur. at Kiltartan, co. Galway, leaving a dau. (m. Dr. Richard Reeves, of Ennis), and three sons,
1. James, of Cranagh, d.s.p. 1741.
2. CHRISTOPHER, of Raheen and Derryowen.
3. John, of Athenry, co. Galway, m Elizabeth, sister of Thomas Faircloth, of Hallenecraggy, co. Galway, and d. 21 May, 1795, leaving with two daus. (Deborah and Patty), four sons,
  1. CHRISTOPHER, of Raheen, of whom presently.
  2. James, d. unm. June, 1811.
  3. William, d.s.p. 5 July, 1845.
  4. Joseph, of Athenry, m. May, 1791, Matilda, only dau. of Robert Ormsby, of Eden Hall, co. Galway, and d. March, 1821, leaving by her (who d. 1845), with two daus. (Catherine, d. unm. 15 Oct. 1875; and Martha, m. Sept. 1823, Capt. William Rogers, of Caraminna, co. Galway), three sons,
    (1) JOHN, of Raheen, of whom hereafter.
    (2) Robert Ormsby, d. unm. 1830.
    (3) James, m. Nov. 1825, Harriett Amelia, dau. of Col. Fleming, and d.s.p. in 1828.
The eldest surviving son,
CHRISTOPHER LOPDELL, of Raheen and Derryowen, b. 1697; d. unm. 8 April, 1801, aged 104 years. By his will, dated 3 Nov. 1800, he entailed Derryowen, co. Clare, on his kinsman, Christopher Lopdell, and Raheen, co. Galway, and other estates, on his nephews, the sons of his brother John, the eldest of whom,
CHRISTOPHER LOPDELL, of Raheen, d.s.p. Sept. 1801, and was s. by his nephew,
JOHN LOPDELL, of Raheen Park, B.A., J.P., b. 25 Feb. 1792, called to the Irish Bar 1818; m. 9 Jan. 1823, Jane, eldest dau. of Peter Blake, of Corbally Castle, co. Galway, by Mary his wife, 2nd dau. of the Hon. John Browne, sixth son of the 1st Earl of Altamont, and by her (who d. 25 April, 1879) had issue,
1. JOHN JOSEPH, of Raheen.
2. Henry Robert (Rev.), incumbent of Kilmastulla, co. Tipperary, b. 13 April, 1832; d. 31 July, 1906.
3. James, b. 27 May, 1836.
4. Francis Blake, County Inspector R.I.C., b. 22 Dec. 1846; d.s.p. 10 Nov. 1911; m. 24 April, 1877, Charlotte Raby, dau. of Thomas R. Grey, of Greyford, Borrisokane, co. Tipperary.
1. Maria, d. unm. 2 May, 1891.
2. Elizabeth, d. unm. 25 Feb. 1898.
3. Louisa, d. unm. 3 Feb. 1895.

4. Emily Alice, m. 12 March, 1867, Willioughby Newton, of Newton Park, co. Wicklow (see NEWTON of Killymeal).
5. Matilda, m. 22 Feb. 1877, Rev. Francis Costello, incumbent of Ballymackey, Tipperary.   6. Jane, d. 11 Oct. 1887.
Mr. Lopdell d. 3 Oct. 1871, and was s. by his eldest son,
JOHN JOSEPH LOPDELL, of Raheen Park, J.P., Major in the Galway Militia, b. 13 Jan. 1826; m. 16 April, 1861, Catherine Mary, only surviving dau. of John Adams, of Ballydevitt, co. Londonderry, J.P., D.L., and High Sheriff for that co. in 1862, and by her had issue,
1. JOHN ROBERT, of Raheen.
2. Christopher Thomas (3, Wellington Park, Belfast), b. 6 March, 1870.
3. James Adams, b. Aug. 1872; d. 17 Nov. following.
4. James, b. 7 April, 1874; m. 22 Aug. 1905, Tillie, dau. of James F. Marsh, of Rockdale, Manchester.
1. Lizzie Anne, m. 8 Dec. 1886, Major Henry Thomas Hall, late 18th Hussars, of Knockbrack, Athenry, co. Galway, J.P., eldest son of the late Capt. Henry Edward Hall, of the 13th Regt., and has issue (see HALL of Knockbrack).
2. Louisa Jane, m. 1st, 28 Nov. 1889, Arthur Francis Hall, of Caherovan, Athenry, youngest son of the above-named Capt. Henry Edward Hall, and has issue, (see HALL of Knockbrack). He d. 2 June, 1896. She m. 2ndly, 20 July, 1898, Humphrey Bradshaw (who d. 24 Sept. 1907), son of Rev. McNevin Bradshaw.
3. Katie Frances, m. 11 Sept. 1895, Charles Cecil Yeldham, D.I., R.I.C., and d. 11 April, 1897.
4. Mabel Violet, m. 27 April, 1905, Harold E. Henderson, D.I.R.I.C., son of Very Rev. William George Henderson, L.D., Dean of Carlisle.
5. Hilda Gladys, m. 5 June, 1907, Fred. A. Britten, D.I.R.I.C.
Major John Joseph Lopdell, d. 8 Oct. 1891. His eldest son,
JOHN ROBERT LOPDELL, of Raheen Park, co. Galway, J.P., Lieut.-Col. 4th Batt. The Connaught Rangers, b. 27 Jan. 1866; m. 19 Aug. 1893, Lavinia Susan, eldest dau. of Peter J. Blake, of Galway, and great-grand-dau. of Peter Blake, of Corbally, and d. 28 May, 1911, having had issue,
1. John Aubrey, b. 27 May, 1894; d. 28 Aug. 1895.
2. ROBERT HUGH OSWALD, now of Raheen.
2. Zelie Marguerite, b. 20 July, 1895.
3. Dorothy Noel, b. 14 Jan. 1898.
Seats—Raheen Park, Athenry, co. Galway, and Ballydevitt, co. Londonderry.

LOW OF KILSHANE.

FRANCIS SIMON Low, of Kilshane, co. Tipperary, D.L. co. Tipperary, late Lieut. 2nd Life Guards, b. 4 Aug. 1870; m. 11 March, 1896, Anna Eleanor Isabel, eldest dau. of the late Stephen Moore, D.L., M.P. of Barne, co. Tipperary (see that family), and has issue,

SIMON FRANCIS, b. 2 May, 1904.
Sylvia Louise Maud.

Lineage.—SIMON Low, of Cork, and Galbally, co. Limerick, son of John Low, who settled in co. Tipperary; m. 1st, Grace, dau. of — Kennelly, and by her had an only child,
1. Mary, m. Thomas Maunsell Rose, of Aghabeg, co. Limerick, who d. 12 Oct. 1831, leaving issue (see that family).
He m. 2ndly, Aug. 1783, Elizabeth, dau. of Peter Blackmore, and d. about 1808 (will proved that year), having by her (who d. 1800) had issue,
1. JOHN, of whom presently.
2. Peter, of Lowtown, co. Limerick, ancestor of Low of Sunvale (see that family).
The elder son
JOHN Low, of Kilshane, co. Tipperary, who had a confirmation of arms to him and the descendants of his father, m. Anne, dau. of Thomas Wise, of Cork, and by her had issue,
1. Simon, d. unm.
2. FRANCIS WISE, of Kilshane.   3. Henry, d. unm.
1. Elisabeth, d. unm.   2. Anna, d. unm.
The eldest surviving son,
FRANCIS WISE Low, of Kilshane, co. Tipperary, and Sillahertane, co. Kerry, J.P. and D.L., co. Tipperary, High Sheriff 1871, J.P. co. Kerry, b. 1810; m. 1st, 23 Oct. 1860, Valentine Henrietta, 2nd dau. of the late Henry Stuart Burton, of Carigaholt Castle, co. Clare (see that family). She d. 1 July, 1861, having had issue,
1. Cecilia Elizabeth, d. an infant 1 July, 1861.
He m. 2ndly, 9 Aug. 1864, Sara Louise, 2nd dau. of John Trant, D.L., of Dovea (see that family), and d. 14 Aug. 1904, having by her had issue,
1. FRANCIS SIMON, now of Kilshane.

2. Henry F., Capt. 3rd Batt. Durham L.I., served in S. Africa 1899-1901, *m.* 5 March, 1904, Eva Mary, dau. of late Sir Harry Bullard, M.P.

Arms—Arg. on a bend vert three wolves' heads erased or, each charged with an annulet gu. *Crest*—A wolf's head as in the arms. *Motto*—Facta non verba.

Seats—Kilshane, co. Tipperary ; Rookery Park, Yoxford, Suffolk. *Club*—Naval and Military.

LOW OF SUNVALE.

The late LIEUT.-COL. JOHN MAXWELL LOW, of Sunvale, co. Limerick, late Duke of Wellington's Regt., and formerly of the Duke of Cornwall's L.I., *b.* 20 Nov. 1844; *m.* 27 Feb. 1890, Anna Workman, dau. of Henry Hogan, of Montreal. He *d.* 24 Jan. 1912, having had issue,

1. JOHN, *b.* 30 Nov. 1896.
1. Kathleen, *b.* 14 Jan. 1895.
3. Georgiana Violet, *b.* 26 Nov. 1899.
2. Anna, *b.* 27 June, 1898.
4. Mona Marion, *b.* 31 May, 1902.

Lineage.—PETER LOW, of Lowtown, co. Limerick, J.P. and D.L., 2nd son of Simon Low, of Galbally, co. Limerick *(see Low of Kilshane)*, by Elizabeth Blackmore his 2nd wife (who *d.* 1800), *m.* 1811, Louisa, eldest dau. of Sir Richard Butler, Bart. of Garryhundon and Ballintemple, co. Carlow, and had issue,

1. JOHN, his heir.
2. Richard Butler, late Capt. 53rd Regt., *m.* 1849, Anna, dau. of Montifort Westropp, of Mellon, co. Limerick, and by her (who *d.* 1858) had issue, two sons and three daus. He *d.* Nov. 1868.   3. Henry, *b.* 1826; *d.* 1860.
1. Sarah, *m.* 18 Aug. 1831, William Mussenden, of Larchfield, co. Down, D.L., *d.* 22 April, 1868.
2. Elizabeth, *m.* 12 July, 1836, Frederick Thomas Jessop, of Doory Hall, co. Longford, D.L., both dec.
3. Louisa, *m.* Thomas Waring, of Waringfield, co. Down, who *d.* 1877, leaving issue.
4. Katherine, *m.* Feb. 1850, Robert Ruttledge, of Bloomfield, co. Mayo, D.L., and *d.* June, 1856, leaving issue.
5. Henrietta, *m.* Charles George Mahon, of Mount Pleasant, co. Mayo, D.L.

Mr. Low *d.* 1842. His eldest son,

JOHN LOW, of Sunvale, J.P. and D.L., High Sheriff 1852, M.A. Trin. Coll. Dublin 1833, Barrister-at-Law, *b.* 8 Jan. 1813 ; *m.* 2 Dec. 1841, Sophia Georgiana, only dau. of George Mahon, of Mount Pleasant, co. Mayo, by Sophia his wife, eldest dau. of David Ker, of Portavo and Montalto, co. Down, and *d.* 1880, leaving by her (who *d.* 4 April, 1902) issue,

1. GEORGE PETER, of Sunvale, co. Limerick, B.A. Oriel Coll. Oxford, late Capt. 8th Hussars, *b.* 20 July, 1843 ; *s.* his father 1880 ; *d.* 20 May, 1894 ; *s.* by his brother.
2. JOHN MAXWELL of Sunvale.
1. Sophia Georgiana, *d. unm.* 1 March, 1848.
2. Henrietta Catherine, *m.* 27 Jan. 1868, W. J. Scarlett, of Island of Gigha, Argyllshire, late Capt. 5th Dragoon Guards, and *d.* 1885, leaving issue, sons and daus.

Arms—Arg., on a bend vert three wolves' heads erased or, each charged with an annulet gu. *Crest*—A wolf's head as in the arms. *Motto*—Facta non Verba.

Seat—Sunvale, Kilmallock, co. Limerick, *Town Address*—7, Queensberry Place, S.W.

LOWRY OF POMEROY.

ROBERT THOMAS GRAVES LOWRY, of Pomeroy House, co. Tyrone, J.P. and D.L., High Sheriff 1896, late Major 1st Dragoon Guards, *b.* 16 Jan. 1857.

Lineage.—This is a junior branch of the Earl of Belmore's family.

REV. JAMES LOWRY, of Tullyhog, *b.* 1707, 4th son of Robert Lowry, of Ahenis (ancestor of the Earls BELMORE), by Anne his wife, dau. of the Rev. James Sinclair, of Hollyhill, co. Tyrone, was Rector of Clogherny, co. Tyrone, where he *d.* 1757. He *m.* Hester, eldest dau. of John Richardson, M.P., of Rich Hill, co. Armagh, and sister of Mary, Viscountess Gosford. By her (who *d.* 1771) he had issue,

1. ROBERT, of Pomeroy.
2. John, Rector of Clogherny, *m.* 1772, Susannah, only child and heiress of the Rev. George Underwood, Rector of Kencott, co. Oxford, and has issue,
   1. The Rev. James Lowry, Rector of Clogherny, *b.* 3 April, 1773 ; *d.* 4 Nov. 1852. He *m.* Harriett, dau. of James Duberley, of Hensham Hall, co. Oxford, by whom (who *d.* 5 Jan. 1843) he had issue, an only child.
      1. Harriet Martha, *m.* William Owen Jackson, Barrister-at-Law, dec.   She *d.* 1 June, 1870, without issue.
      2. Jane Lowry, *m.* 1805, Charles Frederick Barnwell, now dec. She *d.* 1 Sept. 1862, leaving issue.
3. JAMES, from whom the ROCKDALE branch.
4. Hester, *m.* Thomas Dickson, M.P. of Woodville, co. Leitrim.

The eldest son,

ROBERT LOWRY, of Pomeroy, *b.* 2 Oct. 1748 ; *m.* 1777, Elizabeth, dau. of Major William Tighe, of Ballyshannon. She *d.* 1822. He *d.* 17 May, 1802, leaving issue,

1. James, 14th Light Dragoons, *b.* May, 1778 ; *d. unm.* 1807.
2. ROBERT WILLIAM of Pomeroy.
3. John, formerly 8th Regt., *o.* 4 July, 1789 ; *d.* 29 April, 1888.
4. Armar, 45th Regt., wounded at Orthes, *b.* 20 Feb. 1791 ; *d.* 18 June, 1876.
5. William, of Drumreagh, near Dungannon, co. Tyrone, formerly Commander R.N., *b.* 24 Feb. 1793 ; *m.* 1819, Isabella (who *d.* 21 Nov. 1873), dau. of the Rev. James Graham, Rector of Pomeroy and Mullinagore, co. Tyrone, and *d.* 10 April, 1875, leaving issue,
   1. Robert William, C.B., of Aghnablaney, co. Fermanagh, Lieut.-Gen. in the Army, late Lieut.-Col. 47th Regt., served in the Crimea, and has medal with three clasps, Turkish medal, and 5th class of the Medjidie, and Canadian medal for expedition against the Fenians 1866, Knight of Grace of St. John of Jerusalem, was Resident of Zante 1853-4, *b.* 20 March, 1824, *m.* 9 June, 1853, Emily Rohesia, dau. of Sir Henry G. Ward, G.C.M.G., Lord High Commissioner Ionian Islands, Governor of Madras, &c., and *d.* 8 June, 1905, leaving issue,
      (1) Robert Swinburne, Rear-Adm. R.N., commanding Royal Naval War College, Portsmouth, *b.* 4 March, 1854 ; *m.* 12 Dec. 1893, Helena Macgregor, dau. of Thomas Greer, of Sea Park *(see that family)*, and has issue,
         Robert Graham, *b.* 18 Aug. 1899.
      (2) William Henry, Col. Indian Army, *b.* 2 Dec. 1855.
      (3) Henry Wrad, *b.* 20 Jan. 1859, Lieut.-Col. Indian Army ; *m.* 1 March, 1907, Sophia Mackenzie Stephenson Jellie, B.A., 2nd dau. of Dr. Stephenson Jellie, B.Sc., Ph.D.
      (4) Charles Ernest Corry, *b.* 6 Sept. 1863 ; *m.* 16 April, 1887, Kathleen Rose, dau. of John Perrier, and has issue,
         1. Phylis Evelyn.
         2. Kathleen May.
      (5) Arthur Cole, *b.* 18 Sept. 1864, Commander R.N., *m.* 7 Jan. 1903, Ethel Mary Louisa, dau. of Col. C. W. A. Harcourt Wood, of Carleton Lodge, Pontefract *(see WOOD of Gwernyfed)*, and *d.s.p.* 3 Dec. 1903.
      (6) James Herbert, late Capt. Indian Army, *b.* 14 May, 1866 ; *m.* Charlotte Louise, dau. of P. Bury Ramsbotham.
      (7) Ernest Ward, *b.* 15 Feb. 1871 ; *m.* Margaret Duggan.
         (1) Emily Hope.   (2) Mary Georgina.
   2. William John, Lieut. R.N., *b.* 5 May, 1828 ; *d. unm.* 1864.
   3. James Armar, late Capt. 47th Regt., *b.* 9 Aug. 1832 ; *d.* 24 April, 1861. He went through the Crimean campaign.
   4. John Henry, *b.* 14 Sept. 1834.
   5. Armar Graham, of Farlough Lodge, co. Tyrone, Lieut.-Col., late Major 8th King's Regt., formerly Capt. 41st Regt., with which he served in the Crimea (medal with three clasps, Turkish medal, and 5th class of the Medjidie). He was *b.* 11 Sept. 1836 ; *m.* 10 Dec. 1869, Margaret, dau. of Robert Newton *(see NEWTON of Kellymeal)*, and *d.s.p.* 24 Oct. 1900. She *d.* 23 Jan. 1912.
      1. Elizabeth.
      2. Isabella Hester, *m.* 17 Nov. 1864, John Toler, M.D., and has issue.
      3. Mary Grace, *d. unm.* 20 Feb. 1857.
1. Everina, *d.* an infant.
2. Hester, *b.* Nov. 1780 ; *d.* 4 March, 1863.
3. Elizabeth, *d. unm.* 19 Jan. 1867.
4. Maria, *d. unm.*

The eldest surviving son,

ROBERT WILLIAM LOWRY, of Pomeroy House, J.P. and D.L., High Sheriff co. Tyrone 1812, *b.* 1787 ; *m.* 6 Feb. 1815, Anna, eldest dau. of Admiral Samuel Graves, the elder brother of Sir Thomas Graves, K.B., and by her (who *d.* 23 Dec. 1875) had issue,

1. ROBERT WILLIAM, late of Pomeroy House.
2. John Fetherstonhaugh, of Belmore, co. Westmeath, Doraville, co. Tyrone, and Fitzwilliam Place, Dublin, B.A. Brasenose Coll. Oxford, Barrister-at-Law, J.P., *b.* 18 July, 1818 ; *m.* 12 Sept. 1854, Dorothea Eliza, dau. of William John Moore, and relict of George Folliott, of Vicars Cross, Cheshire, and *d.* 5 Feb. 1883, having by her (who *d.* 10 Sept. 1892) had issue, a dau.,
   Anna Graves Fetherstonhaugh, *m.* 22 Sept. 1885, Marmaduke W. C. Cramer Roberts, of Sallymount, co. Kildare, and has issue *(see that family)*.
3. Thomas Graves, R.E., killed at Sebastopol, 7 June, 1855.
1. Hester, *m.* 27 May, 1862, the Rev. Richard Johnston, of Kilmore, co. Armagh, and *d.* 1 June, 1876.
2. Eliza Catherine, *m.* 9 Jan. 1856, Capt. John Herbert Armstrong, of Kilclare, King's Co., who *d.* 17 Aug. 1873, leaving issue. *d.* 9 Jan. 1890.

IRELAND.   Lucas.

3. Anna Jane, *m.* 2 April, 1868, John Malone, of Baronston, co. Westmeath. He *d.* 30 July, 1894, leaving issue (*see that family*).

Mr. R. W. Lowry *d.* 16 Nov. 1869, and was *s.* by his son,

ROBERT WILLIAM LOWRY, of Pomeroy House, co. Tryone, B.A. Brasenose Coll. Oxford, J.P. and D.L., M.R.I.A., Barrister-at-Law, High Sheriff 1849, *b.* 30 Dec. 1816; *m.* 1st, 7 July, 1852, Frances Elizabeth, youngest dau. and co-heir of Benjamin Humphrey Geale Brady, of Mount Geale, co. Kilkenny, and by her (who *d.* 23 Nov. 1877) had issue,
1. Robert Geale, *b.* 22 Oct. 1853; *d.* 1 April, 1854.
2. ROBERT THOMAS GRAVES, now of Pomeroy House.
 1. Mary Anna Catherine, *m.* 25 April, 1888, Lieut.-Col. C. M. Alexander, of Termon, co. Tyrone, and has issue.
 2. Letitia Maria Isabella.

He *m.* 2ndly, 21 Dec. 1880, Dorothea Elizabeth, 2nd dau. of George Folliott, of Vicars Cross, co. Chester, and *d.* 10 Feb. 1899.

Arms—Sa., a cup arg. with a garland of laurel between two branches of the same, all issuing thereout ppr. *Mottoes*—Floreant Lauri (above); Virtus semper viridis (below).

Seat—Pomeroy House, Pomeroy, co. Tyrone.

LOWRY OF ROCKDALE.

EDWARD LESLIE BARN-
WELL LOWRY, of Rockdale,
co. Tyrone, D.L., High
Sheriff 1905, Vice-Lieut.
1906, late Capt. 41st,
31st, and 81st Regt.,
served in Crimea (two
medals and Medjidie), *b.* 27
May, 1837; *s.* his brother
1897; *m.* 1st, 27 April,
1865, Eliza, only child of
Thomas John Taylor, of
Earsdon, Northumberland.
She *d.* 23 Dec. 1869, leaving
issue,

1. Evelyn Eliza.
2. Mary Emily.

He *m.* 2ndly, 18 June, 1872, Edith Clara Halyma, only child of Samuel Saunders, of Alexandria, and by her (who *d.* 16 Feb, 1904) had issue,
1. James Taylor, late Lieut. Inniskilling Fus., *b.* 21 Aug. 1875; *d.* from illness contracted on service in S. Africa, 19 Sept. 1900.
3. Hilda Clare Leslie.
4. Joice Leslie, *m.* 3 Aug. 1904, Edward Turnour Master

Lineage.—JAMES LOWRY, of Rockdale, co Tyrone (3rd son of the Rev. James Lowry, of Desortcreight (*see* LOWRY *of Pomeroy*), *m.* 1785, Martha, dau. of the Right Rev. James Leslie, D.D., Bishop of Limerick, by his wife Joice, sister and eventual heir of Thomas Lyster, of Lysterfield, co. Roscommon, and by her (who *d.* Dec. 1831) had issue,

JAMES, of whom presently.

Hester, *m.* to William Chaigneau Colvill, an eminent merchant in Dublin and a Director of the Bank of Ireland.

Mr. Lowry *d.* 7 Jan. 1790, and was *s.* by his son,

JAMES LOWRY, of Rockdale, *b.* 1787; *m.* 1st, Harriet, youngest dau. of Thomas Pepper, of Ballygarth Castle, co. Meath, and by her (who *d.* 18 April, 1834) had issue,
1. JAMES CORRY, his heir.
2. Edward Leslie, *b.* 1811; *d. unm.* 9 Nov. 1833.
3. Thomas William, *b.* 1814; *d. unm.* 31 July, 1852.
4. Hercules, *b.* 1817; *d. unm.* 27 July, 1851.
5. Armar, *b.* 8 May, 1821, formerly Capt. 30th Regt.; *m.* Jane, 2nd dau. of Joseph Greer, of The Grange, co. Tyrone, and *d.* 20 March, 1898, leaving issue,
 1. Mary Jane, *d.* 30 Jan. 1861.
 2. Harriet Pepper, *m.* 11 April, 1872, Frederick Stutfield, and has issue.
6. Octavius, *b.* 25 Dec. 1824, late Capt. 96th Regt., Maj. in the Army; *m.* 24 Nov. 1851, Arabella (*d.* 26 Feb. 1906), 5th dau. of James Jones, of Mount Edward, co. Sligo, and *d.* 19 Nov. 1852, leaving issue,
 1. Thomas Pepper Ernest, *b.* 7 Oct. 1852, late Maj. 1st West India Regt.
 2. William Hay Talbot, Canadian Mounted Police, late Lieut. Galway Militia, *b.* 2 Dec. 1854, killed in action at Battleford, 3 May, 1885.
  1. Edith Julia Vivian, *m.* 20 April, 1910, Lieut.-Col. W. K. J. Dobbin, I.A. (retired).
  2. Florence Emily Joice, *m.* Jan. 1891, Major F. Wintle, Indian Army, and had issue.
7. Robert, *b.* 5 Nov. 1826; *m.* 17 June, 1852, Louisa, dau. of Thomas Braddell, and *d.s.p.* 15 Aug. 1864. She *d.* Feb. 1892.
 1. Henrietta Martha, *m.* 28 Aug. 1852, her cousin Henry Lowry Barnwell, who *d.* 20 March, 1858. She *d.* 20 Oct. 1872.
 2. Charlotte, *d. unm.* July, 1834.
 3. Joice, *m.* 1st, her cousin Edward Leslie Colvill, and 2ndly,

Henry Loftus Tottenham, and *d.* 27 Sept. 1892. He *d.* 26 April, 1896.
4. Georgina, *m.* 16 Jan. 1852, William Acton. He *d.* 9 Jan. 1896. She *d.* 31 Oct. 1905, having had issue.
5. Mary Louisa Pepper, *d. unm.* 11 Aug. 1860.

Mr. Lowry *m.* 2ndly, 15 June, 1835, Emily, eldest dau. of Joseph Greer, of The Grange, co. Tyrone, and by her (who *d.* 22 April, 1851) had issue,
8. Henry MacGregor, *b.* 17 Dec. 1838, Col. (ret.) late 12th Regt.; *m.* 1st, 24 April, 1867, Margaret Eliza, eldest dau. of Ranulph Dacre, and had by her (who *d.* 29 Jan. 1893) issue,
 1. Henry Dacre, Major Dorsetshire Regt., *b.* 24 Aug. 1868; *m.* 17 June, 1908, Kathleen, dau. of Lieut.-Col. Rochfort Hunt.
 2. Hubert Leslie, *b.* 1870.

He *m.* 2ndly, 3 Jan. 1894, Annie Elizabeth Woodville. He *d.* 19 Feb. 1907.
6. Emily, *m.* 25 Oct. 1873, John Richardson, of Trewmount, co. Tyrone.   7. Martha Leslie, *d.* 3 July, 1862.

Mr. Lowry *d.* 14 June, 1847, and was *s.* by his eldest son,

JAMES CORRY LOWRY, of Rockdale, Q.C., Master of the Court of Exchequer in Ireland, *b.* 1 Nov. 1809; *m.* 1st, 1832, Dorinda, 2nd dau. of James Jones, of Mount Edward, co. Sligo, Capt. Sligo Militia, and by her (who *d.* 8 Feb. 1845) had issue,
1. JAMES CORRY JONES, late of Rockdale.
2. EDWARD LESLIE BARNWELL, now of Rockdale.
3. Thomas Pepper, *b.* 18 July, 1839; *d.* Jan. 1847.
4. George Pepper, *b.* 22 July, 1843; *d.* 1 Feb. 1882.
5. John Robert Colvill, *b.* 19 Dec. 1844, B.A. T.C.D., Indian Medical Staff; *m.* 26 April, 1871, Constance, dau. of William T. B. Lyons. He *d.* 12 July, 1873.
 1. Harriett, *m.* 30 Jan. 1858, Michael Obins Seeley Jones, who *d.* 5 April, 1860. She *d.* 27 April, 1882.
 2. Eliza, *m.* 29 Sept. 1868, John J. Twigg, K.C.

Mr. Lowry *m.* 2ndly, 1848, Ellen, widow of Frederick Gamble, and 3rdly, 20 Aug. 1850, Jane, eldest dau. of Booth Jones, of Streedagh, co. Sligo, and *d.* 20 June, 1869, having by her had issue a son,
6. Somerset Thomas Corry (Rev.), Rector of Wonston, Micheldever, Hants, *b.* 21 March, 1855; *m.* 1 Feb. 1816, Hon. Alice Venables Vernon, dau. of the 6th Lord Vernon, and has issue, Hugh Vernon, *b.* 3 Feb. 1897.

The eldest son,

JAMES CORRY JONES LOWRY, of Rockdale, co. Tyrone, J.P. and D.L. co. Tyrone, High Sheriff 1874, Vice-Lieut. 1889-92, sometime Capt. R.A. and Col. Commanding Donegal Artillery Militia, *b.* 26 June, 1835; *m.* 20 Oct. 1863, Elizabeth Jackson, 2nd dau. of Thomas Greer, of Tullylagan, co. Tyrone, and widow of the Rev. Thomas F. Bushe, and *d.* 9 Dec. 1897, having by her (who *d.* 25 Nov. 1888) had issue,
1. Dorinda Florence, *m.* 1 March, 1892, Thomas MacGregor Greer, only son of Thomas Greer, of Sea Park, co. Antrim, and has issue two daus. (*see that family*).
2. Mina Ethel, *m.* 9 Aug. 1899, Maj. W. Lenox-Conyngham, Worcester Regt., eldest son of Sir William Lenox-Conyngham, K.C.B., of Spring Hill, and has issue (*see that family*).

Arms and *Mottoes*—Same as LOWRY *of Pomeroy*.

Seat—Rockdale, Tullyhogue, co. Tyrone.

LUCAS OF RATHEALY.

HENRY LUCAS, of Rathealy, co. Cork, J.P., late Maj. 3rd Batt. Royal Munster Fusiliers, formerly Capt. 45th Regt., *b.* 28 July, 1827; *m.* 6 Sept. 1864, Emma, dau. of William Whitla, of Lisburn, co. Antrim, and has issue,
1. Arthur Hyde, *b.* May, 1865; *d.* 3 Jan. 1891.
2. HENRY JOHN, *b.* 1866.
3. Frederick Whitla, *b.* 1870; *m.* 2 Aug. 1911, Violet, only child of Dr. William B. Mackay.
4. Reginald, *b.* 1877.
 1. Ada Elizabeth, *m.* Lieut.-Col. John J. Russell, R.A.M.C., and has issue.
 2. Nellie.   3. Mary.

Lineage.—The Rathealy branch of the Lucas family settled at Youghal about the year 1640.

JASPER LUCAS, a merchant of Youghal, *d. circa* 1630, *m.* Jane, dau. of John Atkins, of Minehead, Somerset, and was father of

JASPER LUCAS, *m.* 11 May, 1685, Jane, eldest dau. of Samuel Hayman, of Youghal, and widow of John Vaughan, of the same town, and by her (who *d.* 13 Dec. 1718) has issue,
1. JOHN, his heir.
2. Jasper, ancestor of LUCAS, of Richfordstown, represented by JOHN RASHLEIGH LUCAS, J.P.
3. Samuel, bur. at Youghal, 27 Dec. 1694.
4. Atkin, bapt. 1 Jan. 1697; *d.* Feb. 1700.
1. Elizabeth, *m.* Dec. 1701, Henry Rugge, of Ballydaniel, Recorder of and M.P. for Youghal.

He *d.* 9 Sept. 1710, and was *s.* by his eldest son,

JOHN LUCAS, an Alderman of Youghal, *m.* 19 Oct. 1714, Elizabeth, eldest dau. of Arthur Hyde, of Castle Hyde, and had issue, ARTHUR HYDE, his heir; three other sons, who *d. unm.*; and two daus., Jane, *m.* Alderman James Uniacke, of Youghal; and Elizabeth, *m.* Hull Attfield. He *d.* 12 June, 1732, and was *s.* by his eldest son, ARTHUR HYDE LUCAS, of Grange, near Fermoy, *b.* 6 March, 1715 -6.

He *m.* 4 June, 1750, Jane, dau. of John Smyth, of Rathcoursey, and by her (who *d.* 1805) had issue,
1. ARTHUR.
1. Henrietta, *m.* 1st, 1774, Thomas Bernard, of Palace Anne, and 2ndly, Richard Perry, of Cork, and *d.* 1838.
2. Elizabeth, *b.* 1753; *d. unm.* 1838.
He *d.* 13 May, 1788, and was *s.* by his surviving son,
ARTHUR HYDE LUCAS, of Rathealy, *b.* 3 Oct. 1757; *m.* 3 Sept. 1806, Frances, dau. of Henry Adams, of Cregg, Fermoy, and had ssue,
1. ARTHUR HYDE, his heir.
2. John, *b.* 30 Aug. 1816; *m.* Mary, dau. of Laurence Corban, of Kilworth, co. Cork, and *d.* 1 Dec. 1857, leaving Arthur John and Mary Corban.
3. HENRY, now of Ratbealy.
1. Anna, *d. unm.*   2. Harriette, *d.*
3. Frances, *d.* 1877.
4. Emma Jane, *m.* 10 Feb. 1855, Samuel Smith, M.D., and *d.* 11 Oct. 1855.
5. Sarah Maria, *d.* April, 1890.
6. Catherine, *d. unm.* 26 Sept. 1859.
Mr. Lucas *d.* 4 Sept. 1830, and was *s.* by his eldest son,
ARTHUR HYDE LUCAS, of Rathealy, J.P., late Capt. 45th Regt. and Col. Cork Militia, *b.* 28 Oct. 1812; *m.* July, 1864, Elizabeth Frances, dau. of Rev. Samuel Adams, of Cregg, Fermoy, and *d.s.p.* 12 Nov. 1880, when he was *s.* by his brother.

Residence—Rathealy, Fermoy.

LUCAS-CLEMENTS. *See* CLEMENTS.

LUCAS-SCUDAMORE. *See* SCUDAMORE.

LUDLOW-HEWITT. *See* HEWITT.

LYLE OF KNOCKTARNA.

THE REV. JOHN LYLE, of Knocktarna, co. Londonderry, Rector of Kildolla, co. Londonderry 1885-89, *b.* 14 March, 1817; *m.* 1st, 1851, Elizabeth, dau. of Rev. Andrew M'Creight, Rector of Belturbet, co. Cavan; She *d.* 1852. He *m.* 2ndly, 1857, Elizabeth, eldest dau. of Maj. Thomas Scott, of Willesboro, co. Londonderry, and has issue,
1. HUGH THOMAS, D.S.O., Lieut.-Col. and Bt. Col. Royal Welsh Fus., D.L. co. Londonderry, *b.* 24 April, 1858; *m.* 24 June, 1886, Alice Fanny, dau. of Sir Warren Hastings D'Oyly, Bart. (*see* BURKE's *Peerage*), and has issue,
  1. HUGH D'OYLY, *b.* 4 July, 1895.
  1. Kathleen Annie, *b.* 4 Nov. 1888.
  2. Phyllis Mary, *b.* 23 Dec. 1897.
2. John Cromie, *b.* 1862; *m.* 1896, Amy, only dau. of the late Col. Meyrick, and has issue,
  1. John Charlton, *b.* 1901.
  1. Marjorie, *b.* 1897.   2. Eleanor Joan, *b.* 1902.
3. Thomas William, *b.* 1865.
4. Charles Acheson, *b.* 1867; *d.* 1888.
5. George Herbert, *b.* 1870.
1. Kathleen Annette.   2. Florence Emily.
3. Harriette.
Lineage.—HUGH LYLE, of Coleraine, sometime an officer in a Dragoon Regt., said to have come originally from Renfrewshire, *m.* before 1717, Eleanor, dau. of Hugh Bankhead, of Kilotin, co. Londonderry, and by her had issue,
1. HUGH, his heir.
1. Elizabeth, *m.* Hugh Carmichael, of Dublin.
2. Martha, *m.* — Bryan.
The only son,
HUGH LYLE, of Coleraine, *b.* 20 Feb. 1717; *m.* 6 July, 1749, Eleanor, dau. of Samuel Hyde, of Belfast, son of John Hyde, of Haughton, Cheshire, and by her had issue,
1. HUGH, of whom presently.
2. SAMUEL, ancestor of LYLE *of Cairnagariff*, and LYLE *of the Oaks*.
3. James, of Philadelphia.
1. Mary.   2. Eleanor.
The eldest son,
HUGH LYLE, of Jackson Hall, co. Londonderry, *b.* 30 Dec. 1756, *m.* Sarah, dau. of Thomas Greg, of Belfast, and *d.* 1812, leaving issue,
1. HUGH, of whom presently.
2. Thomas.   3. Samuel.
1. Elizabeth.   2. Eleanor.
3. May.   4. Sarah, *m.* 1828, Ross Thompson Smyth.
The eldest son,
HUGH LYLE, of Knocktarna, co. Londonderry, *m.* Harriet, dau. of John Cromie, of Cromore, co. Londonderry, and left eight sons and five daus.; of these
1. Hugh Thomas, *b.* 1 Nov. 1815; *d. unm.* 1834.
2. JOHN (Rev.), now of Knocktarna.
3. James Acheson, of Portstewart, co. Londonderry, J.P. cos. Antrim and Londonderry, *b.* March, 1818; *m.* 1st, 12 Aug. 1851, Sarah Jane, dau. of Andrew Mulholland, D.L., of Ballywalter, co. Down (*see* BURKE's *Peerage*, DUNLEATH, B.). She *d.s.p.* 30 March, 1853. He *m.* 2ndly, 12 Nov. 1861, Emily Octavia (*Glandore Lodge, Kilrea, co. Antrim*), dau. of the Hon. and Rev. Henry Ward, Rector of Killinchy, co. Down (*see* BURKE's *Peerage*, BANGOR, V.), and *d.* 29 Nov. 1900, leaving by her (who *m.* 2ndly, Henry Thomas Finlay, of Corkagh, *see that family*),
  1. Henry, I.C.S., *b.* 5 June, 1865; *m.* 2 April, 1903, Lucy, dau. of the late Henry Higgins, M.R.C.S., L.R.C.P., of Heathfield, Peel, Isle of Man.
  2. Sydney James, of Derganagh, Ballycastle, co. Antrim, J.P., *b.* 13 Jan. 1871; *m.* 30 April, 1904, Fanny Edith Florence, dau. of late Thomas Spotswood Ash, of The Manor House, Kilrea.
  1. Alice Harriett Cromie, *m.* 11 Aug. 1891, Denis Robert Park-Beresford, of Fenagh House, co. Carlow, D.L. (*see that family*).
4. Thomas Cromie, *b.* March, 1819; *d.* 1854.
5. George Robert, *b.* 1821; *m.* 1883.
6. Henry, *b.* 1826; *d.* 1844.
7. Edward Augustus (Rev.), M.A., Perpetual Curate of Kircubbin, co. Down, *b.* 1830; *m.* 16 Oct. 1865, Andrina, dau. of Andrew Mulholland, D.L. of Ballywalter, co. Down (*see* BURKE's *Peerage*, DUNLEATH, B.). She *d.* 1881. He *d.* 1897.
8. Octavius Godfrey, *b.* 1831, *d.* 1879.
1. Anne Frances, *m.* Rev. Fielding Ould. She *d.* 1899.
2. Sarah Olivia, *m.* Rev. Townley Blackwood Price, who *d.* 1902, leaving issue.
3. Harriet Ellen, *m.* Rev. George V. Chichester, and *d.* :888.
4. Ellen Jane, *m.* Rev. James Bedd Scott, who *d.* 1896.
5. Frances Louisa, *m.* 2 April, 1851, John Mulholland, 1st Baron Dunleath. He *d.* 11 Dec. 1895. She *d.* 23 Feb. 1909, leaving issue (*see* BURKE's *Peerage*).

Seat—Knocktarna, co. Londonderry.

LYLE OF CAIRNAGARIFF.

MAJOR GEORGE SAMUEL BATESON LYLE, of Cairnagariff, co. Donegal, Major R.A., *b.* 23 July, 1865; *m.* 1886, Grace Adelaide, 2nd dau. of William Lysaght, of Beechmount, Mallow, and has issue a son,
CECIL, *b.* 25 April, 1887.
Lineage.—SAMUEL LYLE, of The Oaks, High Sheriff co. Fermanagh 1806, 2nd son of Hugh Lyle, of Coleraine (*see* LYLE *of Knocktarna*) and Eleanor his wife, dau. of Samuel Hyde. He was *b.* 13 April, 1761; *m.* 17 Aug. 1787, Esther, dau. of John Acheson, of Londonderry (who *d.* 4 Feb. 1844), and *d.* 25 Dec. 1815, leaving issue,
1. HUGH, of Cairnagariff.
2. Acheson, of The Oaks, Londonderry, Lieut. and Custos Rotulorum for that co. (*see* LYLE *of The Oaks*).
3. Samuel, *b.* 18 Feb. 1801; *m.* 2 May, 1843, Margaret, dau. of John Stephenson, of Knockan, co. Londonderry, and *d.* 18 Aug. 1868, leaving issue.
4. James, *d. unm.*
1. Eleanor, *d. unm.*
2. Sarah, *m.* Thomas Batt, of Rathmullen, co. Donegal.
3. Mary, *m.* Henry Sole Sandys.
The eldest son,
HUGH LYLE, of Cairnagariff, co. Donegal, Treasurer of co. Londonderry, *m.* Catherine, dau. of Thomas Bateson, of Cartruse, co. Donegal, and sister of Sir Robert Bateson, Bart., and had issue a son,
HUGH CHETHAM LYLE, of Cairnagariff, co. Donegal, J.P., High Sheriff 1881, Lieut.-Col. R.A., *b.* 1835; *m.* 5 June, 1860, Juanita Henriquita, eldest dau. of Admiral Duntze, and *d.* 30 Aug. 1897, having had issue,
1. Hugh, *d.* in infancy.
2. GEORGE SAMUEL BATESON, now of Cairnagariff.
3. Henry Duntze, Capt. late R.A., *b.* 6 Dec. 1866.
4. Hugh, late Kitchener's Scouts, *b.* 28 July, 1875.
1. Juanita Henriquita, *d.* in infancy.
2. Catherine, *m.* 21 Aug. 1895, Albert John Palmer, of Fairford Park, co. Gloucester.
3. Gertrude Caroline, *m.* 11 June, 1896, A. F. Cooke, of Government House, co. Londonderry.
4. Rosario Theresa, *m.* 18 Aug. 1890, E. G. Newell, of the Wilderness, Moville, Londonderry.
5. Eva Gwendoline, *m.* 7 June, 1893, Robert A. Wilson, of Glendarroch, co. Donegal.

Seat—Cairnagariff, Moville, co. Donegal.

LYLE OF THE OAKS.

The late JAMES ACHESON LYLE, of The Oaks, co. Londonderry, J.P. and D.L., B.A. Trin. Coll. Dublin, Barrister-at-Law, *b.* 4 Feb. 1827; *m.* 16 Aug. 1851, Ida Elizabeth, 2nd dau. of the Rev. Francis Ruttledge, of Bloomfield, co. Mayo (*see that family*), and *d.* 11 April, 1907, having had issue,
1. Acheson Francis Acheson, Maj. Shropshire L.I., *b.* 24 April, 1855; *m.* 9 April, 1896, Stella Marguerite, dau. of J. B. Worgan, of Darjeeling, E. Indies, and *d.* 30 July, 1902, leaving issue,
  ACHESON MERVYN ACHESON, *b.* 14 March, 1898.
2. Felton Harvey James Acheson. *b.* 25 May, 1861.
3. Francis Acheson, *b.* 4 March, 1865.
1. Margaret Eleanor Acheson, *b.* 27 April, 1853; *m.* 5 Jan. 1876, her cousin, Hugh Lyle, of Larchmount, Londonderry, eldest son of Samuel Lyle, junior. He *d.* 25 Oct. 1897, leaving issue,

1. Hugh Norman, Lieut. 20 Madras N.I., b. 11 Nov. 1877; d. unm. 21 May, 1903.
2. Geoffrey Samuel.
   1. Augusta Margaret Eleanor.
   2. Esther Florence. 3. Ida Emily.
2. Eleanor Ida Acheson, b. 18 Feb. 1863.

Lineage.—SAMUEL LYLE, of The Oaks Lodge, co. Londonderry, High Sheriff co. Fermanagh 1806, 2nd son of Hugh Lyle, of Coleraine (see LYLE of Knocktarna), b. 13 April, 1761; m. 17 Aug. 1787, Esther, dau. of John Acheson, of Londonderry. She d. 4 Feb. 1844. He d. 25 Dec. 1815, leaving issue (see LYLE of Cairnagurriff). His 2nd son,

ACHESON LYLE, of The Oaks, co. Londonderry, H.M. Lieut. and Custos Rotulorum of that county, b. 14 March, 1795; m. 5 April, 1825, Eleanor, 2nd dau. of James Warre, of Randalls Park, Surrey, by Eleanor his wife, dau. of Thomas Greg, of Belfast. She d. 29 April, 1876. He d. 22 April, 1870, leaving issue,
1. JAMES ACHESON, of The Oaks.
1. Georgina Acheson, m. 11 Nov. 1856, the late Lieut.-Col. J. Ponsonby Cox, R.E. She d. 23 Aug. 1903.
2. Eleanor Augusta Acheson, m. 1st, 4 Sept. 1855, Capt. Felton Frederick William Hervey, 13th Light Dragoons, who d.s.p. 31 March, 1861 (see BURKE'S Peerage, HERVEY-BATHURST, Bart.). She m. 2ndly, 9 Jan. 1869, Samuel Greg Rathbone, of Allerton, Lancashire (see RATHBONE of Greenbank).
3. Esther Emily Acheson, m. 6 Feb. 1862, William Rathbone, late M.P., of Greenbank, Lancashire, and has issue (see that family).
4. Florence Acheson, m. 4 Aug 1874, Very Rev. George Galbraith, of Clanaboyan, co. Tyrone, Dean of Derry.

Seat—The Oaks, Londonderry.

LYNCH OF BARNA.

MARCUS NICHOLAS LYNCH, of Barna, co. Galway, J.P., D.L., High Sheriff 1869, formerly Lieut. 33rd Regt., b. 12 Sept. 1836; m. 8 May, 1867, Blanche (d. 18 May, 1908), only dau. of Count Juliuz Marylski, of Leuczyca, Duchy of Posen, Poland, and had issue,
1. NICHOLAS MARCUS, b. 16 April, 1868, Capt. S. Lanc. Regt., served in W. Africa (medal and clasps), S. Africa (including relief of Ladysmith) (medal and clasps), d. on active service 1900, unm.
2. John Arthur, b. 5 July, 1874; d. unm. 25 June, 1892.
1. Ida, a nun. 2. Ethel, a nun.
3. Violet, a nun.

Lineage.—The greater portion of the Barna property came into the Lynch family by the marriage of the direct ancestor of the present proprietor with the heir of the O'HALLORANS, the foundations of whose castle are still to be seen.

MARCUS LYNCH, of Barna, descended from the marriage of William Lynch and the heir of O'Halloran, m. 1684, Elizabeth, dau. of Oliver Browne, of Coolaron, and was father of

NICHOLAS LYNCH, of Barna, m. 1719. Mary, dau. and heir of Neptune Lynch, of Lettermullin, co. Galway. Their only son,

MARCUS LYNCH, of Barna, m. 1st, 1742, Anstace (who d. March, 1766), dau. of Maurice Blake, of Ballinafad, co. Mayo (see that family), and had issue, with three daus. (of whom Julia, m. 1784, Hyacinth D'Arcy, of Kiltulla), two sons, the younger of whom, James, d. leaving one dau. and heir, who m. Maurice Blake, of Ballinafad, co. Mayo. Mr. Lynch m. 2ndly, 2 Jan. 1767, Surna, only dau. of Patrick French, of Cloghballymore. His will, dated 28 Nov. 1787, was proved 6 July, 1795. He was s. by his elder son,

NICHOLAS LYNCH, of Barna, m. 1765, Catherine, only dau. and heir of Henry Blake, of Ballinahill, co. Galway, 2nd son of Blake, of Lehinch, co. Mayo, and by her had one son with five daus., of whom the eldest m. 1800, Lawrence Comyn, of Woodstock and Kilcorney (see that family).

MARCUS BLAKE LYNCH, of Barna, m. 1st, Jan. 1792, Jane Mary, dau. of Mark Byrne, of Mullinahack, Dublin; and 2ndly, 1796, Catherine, 2nd dau. of John Segrave, of Cabra, co. Dublin (see that family), by whom at his death, Jan. 1829, he left issue, five daus. (Catherine, Jane, Frances, Clarinda, and Henrietta) and an only son,

NICHOLAS LYNCH, of Barna, D.L., High Sheriff of Galway 1843, b. 22 Feb. 1804; m. 24 Nov. 1835, Eliza, 2nd dau. of Stephen Grehan, of Rutland Square, Dublin, by Margaret his wife, dau. of George Ryan, of Inch (see that family), and by her (who d. 10 March, 1857) had issue,
MARCUS NICHOLAS, now of Barna.
Margaret.
Mr. Lynch d. 22 Nov. 1862.

Seat—Barna, Galway.

LYNCH OF DURAS.

JOHN WILSON LYNCH, of Duras and Renmore, co. Galway, Hon. Maj. Galway Militia, D.L. for Galway, and J.P. for Galway co. and town, and for co. Clare, was High Sheriff for Galway 1858, Clare 1866, and for Galway co. 1870, b. 1831; m. 1865, Fanny, 2nd dau. of Sir Thomas N. Redington, K.C.B., of Kilcornan (see that family), and has issue,

1. Mark, B.A. Ch. Ch. Oxford, b. 1866, and d. 1892.
2. THOMAS DAVID, b. 1870; m. 1901, Henrietta Kathleen, dau. of Pierce John Joyce, of Mervue, co. Galway (see that family) and has had issue,
   Mark Florimond, b. 1905; d. an infant.
   Maureen, b. 1906.
3. William Patrick.
1. Ellen, d. 1905. 2. Fanny.

Lineage.—MARK LYNCH, of Renmore, co. Galway, b. 1684; m. Jane, only dau. of Nicholas Biggs, of Jamaica, and had two sons,
1. PATRICK, his heir. 2. Nicholas, d.s.p.
The elder son and heir,

PATRICK LYNCH, of Renmore, b. 1714; m. 1747, Anne, sister of Sir Charles ffrench, Bart., of Castle ffrench, and aunt of Thomas, 1st Baron ffrench, and by her had, with two daus., who both d.s.p., two sons,
1. MARK, of whom presently.
2. Matthew, Barrister-at-Law.
The elder son,

MARK LYNCH, of Duras, co. Galway, b. 1755; m. 1785, Barbara, only child of Stephen Burke, of Ower, co. Galway (see that family), and by her had one son,
1. PATRICK MARCUS LYNCH, late of Duras.
He m. 2ndly, 1792, Victoire, dau. of Richard Wolsey Cormick, of Wolsey Park, in the island of Grenada, by Lucy Barbara his wife, sister of Sir George Leonard Staunton, Bart., and by her had issue at his death, 1822,
2. GEORGE STAUNTON, of Clydagh House, co. Galway (refer to LYNCH-STAUNTON).
3. HENRY CORMICK, Capt. H.E.I.C.S., Madras, b. 1801; m. 1838, Charlotte, dau. of J. Brock Wood, of Huntingdon Hall, co. Chester, and had a son,
   George Staunton, of Purbrook House, Cosham, Hants, J.P., late Capt. 14th Hussars (Clubs: Naval and Military, S.W.; Royal Yacht Squadron), b. 1839; m. 1870, Margaret, youngest dau. of Rev. James Kirkpatrick, of Hollydale, Keston, Bath, and had issue,
   Henry George, Capt. 5th Fus., m. 27 April, 1907, Helen Grace, widow of Major George Alban Williams, S. Staffs. Regt.
   Capt. Lynch s. to the estate of Leigh Park, near Havant, Hants, 1859, on the death s.p. of his cousin Sir G. T. Staunton, Bart. (see STAUNTON), and d. in the same year, having assumed the additional name and arms of STAUNTON.
4. Richard Marcus, of Glenard, co. Galway, J.P., m. Georgina, dau. of the Rev. G. Varenne, D.D., Rector of Staplehurst, Kent, and d. 12 June, 1894, leaving a dau., Anna Varenne, m. Maj. Foster, late 19th Regt.
5. Charles ffrench, dec.
1. Lucy, m. Richard Martyn, of Galway, dec.
2. Jeannette Victoire, m. the late Abraham F. Royse, 2nd son of Thomas Royse, of Nantenant House, co. Limerick.
3. Margaret, d. unm.
The eldest son,

PATRICK MARCUS LYNCH, of Duras and Renmore, J.P., High Sheriff 1845, b. 1785; m. 1820, Ellen, only dau. of John Wilson, of Belvoir, co. Clare, and had issue,
1. JOHN WILSON, now of Duras.
2. William Joseph, an Officer 19th Regt., b. 1835; d. 1874.
1. Barbara, m. 1851, Lieut.-Col. Geoghegan, H.E.I.C.S. She d. 1903.
2. Ellen, m. 1855, Edward Thomas Stapleton, and d. 1892.
3. Eliza, d. 1906. 4. Mary Jane.
5. Fanny.
He d. 1864.

Seats—Duras, Kinvarna, co. Galway; Renmore, Galway; Belvoir, Six-Mile Bridge, co. Clare. **Clubs**—United Service, Dublin, Galway County, and Clare County.

LYNCH OF PARTRY.

COL. HENRY BLOSSE LYNCH, of Partry House, co. Mayo, J.P., High Sheriff 1911, Col. late Dorsetshire Regt., b. 16 Dec. 1856; s. his father, 1884; m. 16 June, 1898, Emily Gwendolyn, youngest dau. of Ogilvie Blair Graham, D.L., of Larchfield, co. Down (see that family), and has issue,

HENRY PATRICK BLOSSE, b. 30 April, 1899.
Louise Gwendolyn Blosse, b. 25 Oct. 1905.

Lineage.—ARTHUR LYNCH, of Partry, 3rd son of Sir Robert Lynch, of Currendalla Castle, co. Galway, 2nd Bart., Mayor of Galway, 1638, M.P. for that place 1639 and 1641 (see BURKE'S Peerage, LYNCH-BLOSSE, Bart.), by his wife Ellis, 3rd dau. of Sir Peter French, Kt., settled with his mother, Lady Lynch, at Partry

Lynch. THE LANDED GENTRY. 424

in 1667, that estate being assigned to her in lieu of dower. He *m.* Joan, eldest dau. of Sir John Browne, of The Neale, and *d.* 1691, being *s.* by his son,
  JOSEPH LYNCH, of Partry, who *m.* Anstace, dau. of Maurice Blake, of Ballinafad, co. Mayo (*see that family*), and *d.* 1721, being *s.* by his son,
  MICHAEL LYNCH, of Partry, who *m.* Anstace, 3rd dau. of Patrick Blake, of Corbally, co. Galway, and *d.* 1771, being *s.* by his son,
  JOSEPH LYNCH, of Partry, who *m.* Margaret Maria, dau. of John Blake, of Ballinafad. He *d.* 1785, being *s.* by his son,
  HENRY BLOSSE LYNCH, of Partry, Maj. 73rd Foot, who *m.* Elizabeth, dau. of Robert Finnis, of Hythe, Kent, and *d.* 1845, having had issue,
    1. JOHN FINNIS, of Partry.
    2. Robert Blosse.
    3. HENRY BLOSSE, of Partry.
    4. EDWARD PATRICK, of Partry.
    5. Thomas Ker.
    6. Stephen, *d.* 11 Oct. 1896, aged 76.
The eldest son,
  JOHN FINNIS LYNCH, of Partry, J.P., Barrister-at-Law, who *d. unm.* 1855, and was *s.* by his brother,
  HENRY BLOSSE LYNCH, C.B., of Partry, Capt. Indian Navy, was second in command Euphrates Expedition, 1834, and in command of Indian Naval Squadron, 1842, and in command of squadron of steam frigates on the River Irrawaddy, taking part in the capture of Rangoon and the relief of Martaban; *b.* 24 Nov. 1807; *m.* Aug. 1838, Caroline, dau. of Col. Robert Taylor, of the Bombay Army, H.M.'s Minister of Bagdad, and had issue,
    1. Quieted Finnis, *b.* 1850; *d. unm.*
      1. Rose.   2. Alice.
      3. Caroline.
He *d.* 1872, and was *s.* by his brother,
  EDWARD PATRICK LYNCH, of Partry, Lieut.-Gen. of the Bombay Army, distinguished himself in Persia, and for his services received the Firman (Royal Letter) of thanks from the King, and the Order of the Lion and the Sun. Politically employed in Afghanistan, in Belgaum during the Mutiny, commanded his regt. at the taking of the fort of Shaik Othman (mentioned in despatches), commanded at Aden, Assurghur, Brig.-Gen. at Ahmednuggur and Deesa; J.P. co. Mayo; *m.* Emily Elizabeth, dau. of Capt. Stirton, of Earlswood House, Reigate, Surrey, and by her (who *d.* 1 May, 1902) had issue,
    1. HENRY BLOSSE, now of Partry.
    2. Sarah Jane, *m.* Col. Scott, Bengal Staff Corps, Deputy Commissioner, and has issue, three sons and five daus.
    2. Elizabeth, *m.* Col. E. S. Marryott, R.E. Bombay, and has issue, two sons and three daus.   3. Louisa Caroline.
    4. Constance Emily, *m.* Dr. C. O'Rorke, and has issue, two sons and three daus.
    5. Alice Victoria, *m.* George G. Soote, W.S.
Gen. Lynch *d.* 23 May, 1884.

Arms—Az., a chevron between three trefoils slipped or.
Crest—A lynx passant cowarded ppr. **Motto**—Semper constant et fidelis.

Seat—Partry House, Ballinrobe, co. Mayo.

LYNCH OF CLONMAINE HOUSE.

MAURICE FRANCIS LYNCH, of Clonmaine House, co. Cork, J.P., *b.* 15 Feb. 1844; *m.* 18 Nov. 1883, Mary, dau. of Peter Mac Donough, of Kilmacdonough, Youghal, co. Cork, and Mary Conway his wife, and has issue,
  1. PATRICK MICHAEL, *b.* 15 March, 1887.
  2. Maurice, *b.* 13 May, 1888.
  3. Charles, *b.* 30 Oct. 1889.
  4. Peter, *b.* 17 March, 1891.
  5. Michael James, *b.* 17 Dec. 1892.
  6. Edmund, *b.* 6 Oct. 1896.
  1. Eileen Daisy, *b.* 25 Nov. 1884.
  2. Mary, *b.* 24 Jan. 1886.
  3. Winifred, *b.* 21 March, 1894.
  4. Frances, *b.* 11 March, 1897.
  5. Agnes, *b.* 31 July, 1898.
  6. Teresa, *b.* 11 April, 1900.
  7. Marcella, *b.* 17 Feb. 1903.

Lineage.—EDMUND LYNCH, of Kilcredan, Ballyrussel, and Lisquinlan, Midleton, co. Cork, left issue a son,
  MICHAEL LYNCH, of Kilcredan and Lisquinlan, *b.* 1803; *m.* 22 Feb. 1841, Ellen Beausang, dau. of James Stanton, of Ladysbridge, and Norah Beausang, his wife, of Ightermurrough Court, Castlemartyr, co. Cork. She *d.* 26 July, 1882. He *d.* 4 June, 1864, having had issue,
    1. Edmond, *b.* 1842, *d.* young.
    2. MAURICE FRANSIS, of Clonmaine House.
    3. James, *b.* 1848; *d. unm.* 8 Dec. 1877.
    4. Patrick Michael (Rev.), author of works on Social Problems and Historical and Religious Subjects, *b.* 17 March, 1850.
    5. Michael, *b.* 1851, *d.* young.
    1. Margaret, *b.* 24 June, 1845; *m.* March, 1882, J. J. Hartnett, of Dungourney, co. Cork, and has issue: 1. John Joseph, *b.* 21 Aug. 1885; 1. May Blossom, *b.* 28 March, 1884; and 2. Agatha, *b.* 10 Feb. 1889.
    2. Joanna, *b.* 10 June, 1852; *m.* 1883, P. J. Motherway, of Ballymacoda, co. Cork, and has issue: 1. Joe, *b.* 1890; 1. Mary Frances, *b.* 28 March, 1885; 2. Anna, *b.* Feb. 1888; and 3. Bride, *b.* 1 Feb. 1892.
    3. Ellen Agnes, a nun in Presentation Convent, Youghal, known in religion as Sister Mary Frances Regis, designed the lace fan carried by Queen Victoria at the Golden Jubilee. She *d.* 26 Sept. 1895.
    4. Mary, *b.* 1858.

Seat—Clonmaine House, Castlemartyr, co. Cork.

LYNCH-ATHY. *See* ATHY.

LYNCH-STAUNTON. *See* STAUNTON.

LYONS OF OLD PARK.

WILLIAM HENRY HOLMES LYONS, of Old Park, J.P. co. Antrim, High Sheriff 1904, D.L. Belfast, *b.* 31 July, 1843; *m.* 5 Jan. 1888, Mary Eliza (Lily). eldest dau. of George Evans, of Gortmerron House, co. Tyrone, and has issue,
  1. WILLIAM HOLMES ST. JOHN, *b.* 28 Dec. 1888; *m.* 27 Dec. 1907, Doris Margaret, youngest dau. of George A. Walpole, F.R.C.S., of Gormanston, Tasmania.
  1. Vera Patricia Mabel, *b.* 16 March, 1890.
  2. Evyleen Sarah Evans.
  3. Lily Eileen.

Lineage.— DAVID LYONS, of Belfast (the son of THOMAS LYONS, who was *b.* 1624, and *d.* 30 Jan. 1693, and was bur. at Shankhill, near Belfast), had, by Kate his wife (who *d.* 1735), DAVID, of whom presently, and Anne, *m.* Thomas Foster. He *d.* 26 June, 1717, and was *s.* by his son,
  DAVID LYONS, of Old Park, Belfast, *b.* 1701; *m.* 1st, Mary, dau. of Elias Boyd, and by her (who *d.* 13 Aug. 1739, aged 33) had issue. By his 2nd wife, Jane (who *d.* 22 Aug. 1777), he had issue,
    1. THOMAS, of whom presently.
    2. Henry, of 2, Mountjoy Square, Dublin, *b.* 1764; *m.* 27 July, 1786, Eliza, dau. of Rev. Robert Smith, of Drogheda, co. Louth, and *d.* May, 1814. She *d.* 5 May, 1789. They had, with other issue, Thomas and William, who both *d.* young.
    8. William.
    1. Mary, *m.* Samuel Ashmore, of Belfast, and had issue.
    2. Anne, *m.* July, 1775, John Brown, of Peter's Hill and Solitude, co. Antrim, High Sheriff for that co. 1783, and had issue.
    8. Eleanor, *m.* Frederick Holmes, Barrister-at-Law, of the Middle Temple, London, and had issue.
    4. Elizabeth, *m.* 1775, James Bell, of Willmount.
    5. Jane, *d.* young, 12 Aug. 1772.
    6. Sarah, *d. unm.* April, 1828.
David Lyons *d.* 6 July, 1772. His eldest son,
  THOMAS LYONS, of Old Park, *b.* 1747; *m.* 4 July, 1778, Sarah, dau. of Andrew Armstrong, of Clara, King's Co. and Dublin, by Elizabeth his wife, dau. of Francis Longworth, of Greggan, co. Westmeath, and by her (who *d.* 4 March, 1818) had issue,
    1. HENRY, his heir.
    2. WILLIAM HOLMES, *s.* to his brother.
    3. Edward Forbes, *d.* young 1. Jan. 1800.
    1. Eliza, *d. unm.* 1840.
    2. Juliana, *d. unm.* 1837.
Thomas Lyons *d.* 8 June, 1806, and was *s.* by his eldest son,
  HENRY LYONS, of Old Park, *b.* 1779; *d. unm.* 2 May, 1839, and was *s.* by his brother,
  WILLIAM HOLMES LYONS, of Old Park, *b.* 1781; *m.* 4 Feb. 1810, Anne, dau. of Rev. William Bristow, Vicar of Belfast, and Sovereign of the town, by Rose his wife, dau. of George Cary, of Red Castle, co. Donegal, and by her (who *d.* 31 Jan. 1853) had issue,
  WILLIAM THOMAS BRISTOW, of Old Park.
    Sarah, *b.* 30 Aug. 1818; *d.* 7 March, 1905.
Mr. Lyons *d.* 12 Feb. 1849, and was *s.* by his only son,
  WILLIAM THOMAS BRISTOW LYONS, of Old Park, and Brookhill, J.P. and D.L., High Sheriff co. Antrim 1866, *b.* 12 Aug. 1812; *m.* 24 Feb. 1840, Julia Maria, dau. of James Jones, of Mount Edward, co. Sligo, and by her (who *d.* 16 Dec. 1900) had issue,
    1. WILLIAM HENRY HOLMES, now of Old Park.
    2. Robert Colvill Jones (*Lime Hill House, Tunbridge Wells*), *b.* 26 Oct. 1844, formerly an officer 43rd Light Infantry, served in New Zealand War (medal); *m.* 8 Dec. 1869, Helen Caroline, dau. of John Le Mottée, one of the Judges of the Royal Court of Guernsey, and has issue,
      1. Cecil Colvill, *b.* 17 Sept.; *d.* 18 Dec. 1871.
      2. Edward Colvill, *b.* 9 Jan. 1873; *m.* 10 Sept. 1901, Sybil Hill, eldest dau. of Henry N. Miers, of Ynyspenllwch, Swansea Valley, Glamorganshire, and 34, Philbeach Gardens, W. (*see that family*), and has issue,
        Robert Henry Cary, *b.* 20 April, 1905.
        Pamela Adelina, *b.* 12 Oct. 1910.
      3. Guy Cary (*Rosecrans, Tasmania*), *b.* 16 Oct. 1875; *m.* 15 Aug. 1901, Heather Mary, eldest dau. of the late H. T. T. Salvin, of Croxdale Hall, co. Durham (*see that family*), and has issue,
        (1) Roger Salvin, *b.* 19 April, 1902.

(1) Marjorie, b. 29 Oct. 1903.
(2) Helen, b. 12 June, 1905.
(3) Marie, b. 19 Nov. 1906.
(4) Madeleine, b. 15 Jan. 1910.
(5) Phœbe, b. 9 April, 1911.
   1. Muriel, m. 9 June, 1904, Frank Fleming, J.P., 2nd son of Sir John Fleming, of Dalmunzie, Aberdeenshire, and has issue.
3. Henry Kenneth Thomas (*Denver, U.S.A.*), b. 6 June, 1850; m. 7 Feb. 1903, Geraldine, dau. of John Edward Fitzgerald, and has issue,
   Henry Fitzgerald, b. 21 April, 1904.
   Maureen Elise, b. 13 Aug. 1908.
4. James Eristow, b. 1 Oct. 1853 ; m. 8 Oct. 1885 ; Margaret Julie, dau. of Jules Festu-Villiaumez, of Calvados, Normandy, and d. 9 Aug. 1905, leaving by her (who d. 6 May, 1902) issue,
   1. William Barry, Lieut. 18th Royal Irish Regt., b. 11 July, 1887.
   2. James Henry, b. 28 Feb. 1889.
5. Clarence Edward, b. 10 Feb. 1856 ; d. same year.
   1. Eliza, m. 28 March, 1865, Robert Cunningham Thomson, of Castleton, Belfast, J.P. for co. Antrim, formerly Capt. 2nd Queen's Own Regt., who d. 9 Oct. 1884.
   2. Julia Maria, d. 1 Jan. 1850.   3. Dorinda Anna Henrietta.
4. Edith Arabella Louisa Florence, m. 9 June, 1877, Lieut.-Col. Henry Martin Moorsom, M.V.O., late Rifle Brigade, son of Capt. W. S. Moorsom, formerly 52nd Light Infantry, and grandson of Admiral Sir Robert Moorsom, K.C.B., M.P.
5. Constance Adela Hastings, m. 1st, 26 April, 1871, John Robert Colvill Lowry (who d s.p. in India, 18 July, 1873), 4th son of James Corry Lowry, Q.C., of Rockdale, co. Tyrone ; and 2ndly, 13 May, 1875. John Bath Allanson, of Bryn Seiant, co. Carnarvon, eldest son of Thomas Allanson, of Tals Kyddy, St. Columb, Cornwall, and has issue.
6. Julie Marie Louise.
Mr. William Thomas Bristow Lyons d. 4 June, 1887.

Arms—Arg. a lion ramp. az. *Crest*—A demi-lion rampant holding in the dexter paw a fleur-de-lis arg. *Motto*—In te, Domine, speravi.

Seats—Brookhill, Lisburn ; and Old Park, Belfast. *Residence*—Richmond Lodge, Strandtown, co. Down.

LYONS OF CROOM.

JAMES DENIS LYONS, of Croom House, co. Limerick, J.P., High Sheriff 1911, late Capt. 13th Hussars, b. 28 Sept. 1877 ; m. 8 July, 1908, Mary Josephine, elder dau. of late James Campsie Dalglish and Mrs. Dalglish Bellasis, and has issue,
   HENRY ANTHONY MONTAGU, b. 13 Jan. 1910.

Lineage.—JAMES O'LYNE settled at Croome, co. Limerick, and d. at Croome House 1740, leaving, with one dau., a son, his successor.

DENIS LYNE, or LYONS, of Croome House, b. 1689 ; m. 1723, Mary Lenham, by whom (who d. 29 Dec. 1774) he had issue,
1. James, b. 1729, settled in Limerick, and m. 20 Oct. 1757, Mary, dau. of David Hourigan, and d. 8 June, 1783, having had issue,
   1. Denis, b. 4 Nov. 1761 ; d. unm. 6 Nov. 1826.
   2. David, b. Sept. 1765 ; d. unm. 1799.
   3. James, b. 20 Oct. 1767 ; d. unm. Sept. 1841.
   4. Christian, d. unm. 16 Dec. 1836.
   1. Johanna, m. 29 June, 1801, Richard England, and d.s.p. June, 1836.
   2. Mary, m. 28 Aug. 1799, John Kelly, and d. 15 March, 1830, leaving issue (*see* KELLY of *Rockstown*).
2. DENIS, of whom hereafter.
1. Catherine, m. 14 June, 1760, James Scully, of Kilfeacle, co. Tipperary, and d. 30 June, 1818, leaving issue (*see* SCULLY of *Mantle Hill*).
2. Mary, m. 5 Aug. 1768, John Canny, of Ballycasey, co. Clare, and d. 25 Nov. 1823, leaving issue.
Mr. Lyons d. 22 Nov. 1777. His 2nd son,
DENIS LYONS, of Croome House, J.P., b. 1749 ; m. 9 Aug. 1779, Christian, eldest dau. of Thomas Casey, M.P., by whom (who d. Aug. 1823) he had issue,
   1. Denis, b. 6 Oct. 1782 ; d. unm. 30 March, 1803.
   2. Thomas, b. 9 May, 1784 ; d. young.
   3. JAMES DENIS, his successor.
   4. Henry, b. 27 June, 1786 ; d. unm. 10 March, 1837.
   5. John, b. 2 July, 1789 ; m. 21 Sept. 1819, Helen, dau. of D. Daly, who d. 26 Jan. 1875. He d. 18 June, 1828, and had issue,
      1. John Edward, b. 27 June, 1823 ; m. 24 Oct. 1868, Gertrude, dau. of Rev. F. Hewson, and d. 10 Oct. 1877.
         1. Christian, m. 1852, Thomas Gallwey.
         2. Helena, m. 1854, Daniel Cronin Coltsmann, of Glenflesk Castle, Killarney.

6. Thomas, b. 26 Jan. 1795 ; d. unm. 1822.
1. Helen, m. 20 Oct. 1802, Roger Scully, and d. April, 1860.
2. Johanna, m. 15 Oct. 1811, Daniel Clanchy, of Charleville, and d. 30 Dec. 1840.
3. Christian, d. 3 Jan. 1855.   4. Mary, d. Jan. 1820.
Mr. Lyons d. 5 July, 1809, and was s. by his eldest surviving son,
JAMES DENIS LYONS, of Croome House, J.P., D.L., High Sheriff 1853, b. 5 July, 1785 ; m. 31 March, 1818, Bridgette, eldest dau. of John Kennedy, of Limerick, by whom he had issue,
1. Denis, b. 21 May, 1822 ; d. unm. 16 Nov. 1841.
2. John, b. 10 Aug. 1823 ; d. unm. 10 April, 1848.
3. HENRY, of Croome House,
4. Thomas Casey, Lieut.-Gen. in the Army, C.B., Gov. and Commander-in-Chief, Bermuda, b. 9 July, 1829 ; m. 6 Jan. 1863, Helen, dau. of George Young, of Apley Towers, Ryde, and d. 10 Sept. 1897, leaving issue,
   Henry George, b. 11 Oct. 1861 ; m. 8 July, 1896, Helen Julia Hardwick.
   Helen Amy, m. 12 July, 1894, Lieut.-Col. Arthur John William Dowell, of the Royal Berkshire Regt., son of Admiral Sir William M. Dowell, K.C.B.
5. James, Capt. R.A., b. 3 Feb. 1832 ; d. 12 June, 1862.
6. Edward, b. 28 Nov. 1836, Col. R.A. ; m. 15 May, 1862, Alice Smith.
1. Anna Maria, m. 10 Feb. 1840, George Sampson, of St. Catherine's, co. Clare, and has issue.
2. Christina, m. 3 July, 1844, James Morrogh, of Old Court, co. Cork.
3. Mary Jane, d. 12 April, 1825.   4. Helena.
5. Bessie, d. 4 Nov. 1841.
6. Frances Hortense, d. 26 April, 1857.
7. Wilhelmina, m. 29 April, 1876, Michael Russell, of Glenmore, co. Cork, and d. 14 March, 1877.
Mr. Lyons d. 2 April, 1853, and was s. by his eldest surviving son,
HENRY LYONS, of Croome House, J.P., D.L., High Sheriff 1860, b. 18 May, 1828 ; m. 14 May, 1873, Olivia Millicent, eldest dau. of Lord Robert Montagu, P.C. (*see* BURKE's *Peerage*, MANCHESTER, D.), by his 1st wife, Ellen Mary, only child of John Cromie, of Cromore, co. Londonderry, and had issue,
1. JAMES DENIS, now of Croom House.
2. Henry Montagu, b. 6 July, 1882.
3. John Cromie, b. 18 Sept. 1883.
1. Mary Eleanor.
2. Olivia Millicent, m. 23 April, 1904, Capt. J. Seawell Cape, younger son of late W. F. Cape, of Ireby, Cumberland, and has issue.   3. Ethel Christine Bertha.
Mr. Lyons d. 1885.

Arms—Arg., on a mount vert, between four fleurs-de-lys az., a lion rampant gu. *Crest*—A plate charged with a lion rampant gu. collared and chained or. *Motto*—Virtute et fidelitate.

Seat—Croom House, Croom, co. Limerick. *Clubs*—Cavalry and County (Limerick).

LYONS OF LEDESTOWN.

JOHN CHARLES GEOFFREY PILKINGTON LYONS, of Ledestown, co. Westmeath, B.A. Trin. Coll. Dub. 1908, b. 17 Nov. 1883.

Lineage.—In the reign of JAMES I CAPT. WILLIAM LYONS purchased the estate of Clonarrow, afterwards called River Lyons, and other lands in King's Co., and received a grant, 3 CHARLES I, of the townland of Tullynally, with part of the great wood of Fercall, King's Co.

HENRY LYONS, of River Lyons, m. Anne, 6th dau. of George Rochfort, of Gaulstown, by Lady Elizabeth Moore his wife, youngest dau. of Henry, 3rd Earl of Drogheda, and had three daus.,
1. Anne, m. John Nixon.
2. Elizabeth, m. July, 1762, Robert Barry, M.P. for Charleville.
3. Henrietta, m. 1780, Robert Garden.
Henry Lyon's brother,
JOHN LYONS, Maj. in the Army, purchased Ledestown, co. Westmeath, 1715. He m. Elizabeth, relict of Lieut.-Col. Richard Ashe, and dau. of Henry Williams, Deputy-Governor of Antigua, and had issue,
1. CHARLES, his heir.
2. JOHN, afterwards Capt. in the Army, m. Dorothea, dau. of Hugh Montgomery, and had three sons, of whom the 2nd, Hugh, took the additional name of MONTGOMERY, and was ancestor of LYONS-MONTGOMERY of *Belhavel* (*see that family*).
3. Henry, of Belmont, Deputy-Clerk of the Council and Deputy Muster-Master-General, m. and had an only child, Louisa, m. 1752, Chambré Brabazon Ponsonby, only son of Maj.-Gen. the Hon. Henry Ponsonby, brother of the 1st Earl of Bessborough.
4. Samuel, settled in Antigua, and is presumed to have been ancestor of the Lords LYONS.
1. Margaret, m. Hans Widman, of Hanstown, co. Westmeath.
2. Mary, m. Hugh Bowen, of Mullingar.
3. Anne, m. Isaac Smith, of Anneville.
4. Elizabeth, m. Glasgow Thompson.
The eldest son,
CHARLES LYONS, of Ledestown, High Sheriff co. Westmeath 1731, Col. of Militia, m. 1723, Christiana, dau. of Robert Mason, of Mason Brook, co. Galway, and had issue,
1. JOHN, his heir.
2. Charles, Maj. 60th Regt., d. unm. 1799.
1. Margaret, m. 1764, Theophilus Bolton.
2. Alicia, d. unm.
The elder son,

JOHN LYONS, of Ledestown, High Sheriff 1778, m. 1765, Caroline, 3rd dau. of Lieut.-Col. John Degennes, of Portarlington, and had issue,
1. CHARLES JOHN, Capt. 12th Light Dragoons, b. 1766; m. 1791, Mary Anne, youngest dau. of Sir Richard Levinge, 4th bart., and by her (who m. 2ndly, 1798, Anthony Adams Reilly, of Roebuck, co. Cavan, and d. 1855), he left at his decease, v.p., May, 1796, an only child,
JOHN CHARLES LYONS, of Ledestown.
2. John Robert, Capt. 69th Regt., d. unm. 1801.
3. Tenison, Capt. 12th Dragoons, b. 1769; m. 1812, Eleanor, dau. of David Frazer, Barrister-at-Law, and d. 1832, leaving issue.
4. Henry, d. young.
1. Margaret Christiana, m. 1806, Rev. Samuel Auchmuty.
2. Caroline, m. 1812, Mark Anthony Levinge, and d. 11 March, 1856. He d. 1847.
3. Frances, d. unm. 1793.
Mr. Lyons d. 1803, and was s. by his grandson,
JOHN CHARLES LYONS, of Ledestown, J.P. and D.L., High Sheriff 1816, Capt. Westmeath Militia, b. 22 Aug. 1792; m. 1st, 14 March, 1820, Penelope Melesina, only dau. of Hugh Tuite, of Sonna, and by her (who d. 10 Feb. 1855) had issue,
1. Charles, b. 7 Feb. 1821; d. unm. 24 Feb. 1859.
1. Mary Ann Melesina, m. 1848, James Malley.
He m. 2ndly, 12 Nov. 1856, Frances Ellen, 3rd dau. of Thomas Walsh, of Belleview, co. Westmeath, and had further issue,
2. JOHN CHARLES, of Ledestown.
3. Charles John, b. 17 Feb. 1863; m. 24 June, 1896, Cora Alicia, dau. of Charles Graham Persse (see PERSSE of Moyode).
2. Caroline Constance, m. 1885, the late William Owen Daly, late Leinster Regt., and has issue.
3. Mary Ann Camilla, m. — McMaster, Consul at Durban, who was killed during the S. African War.
Mr. Lyons d. Sept. 1874, and was s. by his son,
JOHN CHARLES LYONS, of Ledestown, co. Westmeath, J.P., b. 1 Feb. 1861; m. 29 Nov. 1882, Evelyn Maude, dau. of Frederick Pilkington, of Newberry Hall, co. Kildare, and had issue,
1. JOHN CHARLES GEOFFREY PILKINGTON, now of Ledestown.
1. Gladys Maude Pilkington, b. 14 June, 1887.
2. Coral Cecil Constance, b. 27 Sept. 1889.
Mr. J. C. Lyons d. 27 Aug. 1908, and was s. by his only son.

Seat—Ledestown, Mullingar, co. Westmeath.

LYONS-MONTGOMERY. See MONTGOMERY.

LYSTER OF ROCKSAVAGE.

Lineage.—JOHN LISTER, or LYSTER, de Derby, living 6 EDWARD II. (1312), m. Isabel, dau. and co-heir of John Bolton de Bolton, in Craven. He had a son,
RICHARD LYSTER, of Derby, and of Barnoldswick, &c., Yorks. Had a grant of de Bolton lands in Midhope, from his mother, July 1384; d. before 1404-5, when his widow Katherine released lands in Derbyshire to their son,
JOHN LYSTER, of Barnoldswick and Midhope, living 1383, will 21 Oct. 1434, pr. 4 July, 1435; m. Katherine, dau. of Laurence Shuttelworth, and had with other issue (see Visitation of Yorks, 1563) a second son,
LAURENCE LYSTER, of Myddop, m. before 1334, Ellen, dau. of Chris. Banister, and had issue, a son,
CHRISTOPHER LISTER, or LYSTER, of Midhope, d. before April, 1509, having m. 1467, Joan dau. of Sir Walter Calverley, of Calverley, Yorks, by Agnes his wife, dau. of Sir John Tempest, Knt., of Bracewell (see TEMPEST of Broughton). He left issue, three sons,
1. William Lister, or Lyster, of Midhope and Thornton, ancestors of the LISTERS of Burwell (see that family).
2. THOMAS, of whom presently. 3. Nicholas, a priest.
The 2nd son,
THOMAS LYSTER, or LISTER, of Arnoldsbiggin, living 1492, m. Isabel, dau. and heir of Roger de Cliderow, of Cliderow, and by her had (with a dau.) Jane, mother of the celebrated Cardinal-Archbishop William Alan), an only son,
THOMAS LISTER, or LYSTER, of Arnoldsbiggin and of Westby Hall, Gisburne, Yorks, m. Lucie, dau. and co-heir of Thomas Westby of Westby; and d. 1540-1 (will dated 14 March, 1540, proved at York, 10 Jan. 1541), leaving issue, two elder sons,
1. Thomas, of Westby, ancestor of Lord Ribblesdale (see BURKE's Peerage). 2. ANTHONY, of whom presently.
The 2nd son,
ANTHONY LYSTER, or LISTER, of Newsholme, Gisburne, Yorks (will 21 July, pr. 22 Sept. 1576), left issue by Margaret, his wife, who survived him,

1. Thomas, of Newsholme, m. Alice, widow of — Lancaster, and had issue (will dated 18 Aug.it587, proved at York, 10 Sept. 1587).
2. Anthony, of Newsholme (will dated 13 Aug. 1588, proved at York, 4 Oct. 1588), d.s.p.
3. John, living 13 Aug. 1588, left issue.
4. WALTER, of whom presently.
1. Alice, m. Edmund Danser, of Gisburne.
The youngest son,
WATLER LISTER, of Milton, co. Roscommon, where he was granted lands by James I., b. at Westby, bapt. at Gisburne, 5 Dec. 1566; went to Ireland as Secretary to Hon. Geoffrey Osbaldeston, of Osbaldeston, co. Lanc., Chief Justice of the Province of Connaught, whose dau. Debora he m.; he d. 28 Jan. 1622, bur. in Camm Ch., co. Roscommon, M.I. (will, 28 Jan, 1622-3, proved 28 June, 1623), leaving, with a dau., Ellin, a son,
ANTHONY LISTER, a minor in Jan. 1622-3, living 1680, who m. 1st, Miss Blood, who was murdered with her children by the rebels in 1641. He m. 2ndly, Christiana, dau. of — Kilkenny, and by her had issue,
1. THOMAS, of whom presently.
2. John, of Corkip, co. Roscommon, from whom the family of LYSTER of Lysterfield.
The elder son,
THOMAS LISTER, of Grange, Athleague, &c., co. Roscommon, m. 1st, the dau. of The O'Kelly, and by her had issue,
1. William, of Athleague, and Castle Coote, co. Roscommon, High Sheriff 1714, d. 1722; m. Margaret, dau. of Bryan Gunning, of Castle Coote, and widow of John Edwards, of Dublin, and by her (who m. 3rdly, Francis Houston, of Ashgrove, and 4thly, Theobald, Viscount Bourke, of Mayo, who d. 25 June, 1741, and d. 9 June, 1771) had issue,
1. John, of Athleague, b. posthumous Nov. 1722; d. unm. 28 Nov. 1753.
1. Elizabeth, d. unm. 1790.
2. Jane, d. 1788, having m. Christopher Kirwan, of Ash Park. who assumed the name of LYSTER, and had issue.
3. Margaret, m. 1st, 17 Feb. 1752, William O'Dwyer, who took the name of LYSTER, and d. 18 May, 1789. She m. 2ndly, Richard Rumbold, who also took the name of LYSTER. She m. 3rdly, James West, of Fort William, co. Roscommon, who likewise took the name of LYSTER. She d.s.p., will dated 6 Feb. 1809, proved 21 Dec. 1812.
2. Anthony, of Lysterfield, d. 1746, having m. 1st, Elizabeth, dau. and heir of Richard Warren, and by her had issue,
1. Thomas, of Lysterfield, m. July, 1742, Mary, only dau. of Boleyn Whitney, K.C., M.P. of Naas. co. Kildare, and d.s.p.
1. Joyce, m. James Leslie, D.D., Bishop of Limerick; and d. 8 Feb. 1773, having by him (who d. 24 Nov. 1770) had issue (see LESLIE, of Tarbert, and LOWRY of Rockdale).
He m. 2ndly, Mary, dau. of Patrick French, of Monivea, by Jane his wife, dau. of Simon Digby, Bishop of Elphin; and d. 4 Feb. 1745, having by her had,
2. Elizabeth, m. Robert Robinson, M.D., who took the name of Lyster, and had issue (see BURKE's Peerage, ASHTOWN).
3. JOHN, of whom presently.
He m. 2ndly, 7 March, 1718, Alice, dau. of Dodwell Browne. This lady m. 1st, Dominic Wade; 2ndly, Sir John Aylmer, Bart., who d. April, 1714; 3rdly, Thomas Lyster (as above); and 4thly, Rev. Oliver Carter. Her will is dated 20 Oct. 1743, and proved 24 June, 1748. Thomas Lister d. 28 Aug. 1726, having by her had issue,
4. Thomas, of Grange, ancestor of the LYSTERS of Grange, of whom hereafter (see below).
5. George, b. 29 July, 1722.
The 3rd son,
JOHN LYSTER, of Rocksavage, co. Roscommon, eventually heir male of his father, living 4 July, 1727, d. 1755; m. May, 1718, Elizabeth, dau. of Dixie Coddington, of Holm Patrick, co. Dublin (see that family) and had issue,
1. Dixie, d. unm. 2. JOHN, of whom presently.
3. Henry, M.D., of Bath, and of Kilbride, co. Wicklow, m. Mary, dau. and eventually sole heir of John Alen, of St. Woolstans, co. Kildare, and had issue,
1. John (Rev.), D.D., of Dublin and Bath, Rector of Clonpriest, co. Cork; M.A., Oxon, 1778, Chaplain to the Marquis of Buckingham, Lord Lieutenant, and to the Earl of Mountmorris, b. 1754; m. 1778, Mary Aleyne, dau. of Thomas, Cameron, B.A., M.D. Oxon., of Worcester, and d. 30 June, 1820, having by her (who d. 4 Oct. 1826) had issue,
(1) Henry Alen, Royal Irish Artillery, b. 1782, m. Elizabeth, dau. of Adm. Saunders, and d. 7 Oct. 1827, having had issue,
1. Henry Alen, d.s.p.
2. Thomas Lyttelton, Midshipman, R.N., d.s.p. 1842.
(2) Lyttelton, of Union Hall, and of Lysterfield, Skibbereen, co. Cork, Bucks Militia 1806, 3rd Bengal Native Infantry 1807-12, 1st Royal Surrey Regt. 1812, subsequently Capt.; J.P. co. Cork; b. 1789; m. 15 Aug. 1811, Charlotte Cameron, dau. of Rev. Paul Limrick, D.D., and d. 20 Feb. 1850, having by her (who d. 14 May, 1849) had issue,
1. Lyttelton Henry, of Union Hall and Dublin, 1st Royal Surrey Regt., b. 21 July, 1814; m. 19 March, 1846, his first cousin, Jane, dau. of Charles Lyster (see below), and d. 24 Nov. 1890, leaving issue,
a. Lyttelton Annesley Alen, b. 16 Oct. 1858.
a. Marion Georgina, m. 18 Oct. 1877, Rev. Edward Denny, Rector of Laracor (who d. 1906 and has issue) (see BURKE's Peerage).
b. Louisa, m. 15 Feb. 1884, William Williams, of Arodstown House, co. Meath.
c. Matilda.
d. Adeline.

IRELAND. Lyster.

2 George Annesley, of Posilipo, Monkstown, co. Dublin, *b* 10 July, 1828 ; *d.* 2 Oct. 1910 ; *m.* 25 May, 1860, Marian, dau. of Patrick Morgan, County Inspector R.I.C. (who died 8 Oct. 1910), and by her had issue,
  Henry Cameron (Rev.), B.D., Rector of Enniscorthy, Canon of Ferns, Rural Dean, *b.* 12 Feb. 1862 ; *m.* 1 Sept. 1892, Anna Frances Elizabeth, dau. of Rev. Francis Digby Marsh, M.A., and has issue,
    a. George Francis Marsh, *b.* 16 May, 1902.
    a. Constance Deborah Marsh, *b.* 30 May, 1894.
    b. Charlotte Cameron, *b.* 18 June, 1898.
1. Louisa, *m.* 1st, 24 March, 1830, Rev. William O'Neill ; 2ndly, George Ogilvie, and *d.* 31 Dec. 1894. and had issue.
2. Anne Judith, *m.* Rev. Joseph Rawdon Henderson, and *d.* 1864, leaving issue.
3. Pauline, *d.* 1904, having *m.* 1st, 21 Jan. 1855, Yelverton Baker, and had issue ; 2ndly, 17 April, 1865, Michael J. O'Brien.
(3) Charles Frederick, of Riverstown, co. Cork, Lieut. Royal Marines, 1810-14, afterwards 1st Royal Surrey Regt., *m.* 1814, Elizabeth, dau. and eventually co-heir of Deane Hoare, of Cork (*see Peerage*), and *d.* 14 Feb. 1855, having by her (who *d.* 10 July, 1867) had issue,
1. Henry Alen, *b.* 13 April, 1816 ; *m.* 30 Dec. 1856, Isabella Franklyn, dau. of Rickard Lloyd, Comm. R.N., and *d.* 27 Nov. 1872, having by her (who *d.* 1 June, 1867) had issue, Charles Rickard, *b.* 4 May, 1860 ; and Arabella.
2. Charles, *b.* 4 Feb. 1820 ; *m.* 17 Sept. 1861, Susan, dau. of Henry Howard, and *d.* 16 July, 1866, having by her (who *m.* 2ndly, James Graig, of Lindalfiv, Kent) had issue, Charles Dean, *b.* 30 Aug. 1862 ; and Norman Howard, *b.* 27 June, 1864, killed in South Africau War, where he served as a volunteer, 1900, *unm.*
3. Dean, *b.* 23 Feb. 1824 ; *d.* young.
4. Robert, *b.* 7 Nov. 1826 ; *d.* young.
5. Fred Lyttelton, *b.* 2 May, 1829 ; *m.* 9 July, 1853, Elizabeth, dau. of Capt. Boyle Travers Hill, who *d.s.p.* 1902.
6. William, *b.* 11 March, 1832 ; *m.* Alice Howard, and *d.s.p.*
1. Jane, *m.* 19 March, 1846, her first cousin, Lyttelton Henry Lyster (*see above*).
2. Mary Anne, *m.* 1 Dec. 1855, Thomas Merrick, and has issue.
3. Charlotte, *m.* 4 Nov. 1864, Richard O'Callaghan, and by him (who *d.* 18 July, 1874) had issue.
(1) Mary Anne (or Marion), *b.* 1779 ; *d.* 28 April, 1840, having *m.* 13 Oct. 1794, Sir James Crofton, Bart., who *d.* 1840, leaving issue (*see* BURKE's *Peerage and Baronetage*).
(2) Louisa Susanna, *m.* 1 Dec. 1819, Capt. George Thompson, 16th Lancers, and *d.* Sept. 1852, leaving issue.
(3) Georgina, *m.* 1807 Peter North, and *d.s.p.* Sept. 1864.
(4) Augusta, *m.* Rev. Henry Rogers, and had issue.
(5) Caroline, *m.* Terence Fitton, of Gawsworth, Cheshire, and had issue.
(6) Lucy, bapt. 8 Feb 1781, *d.s.p.*, having *m.* 1804, Robert Richardson.
2. William, living 1765, *m.* the widow of Alan Reilly, of Miltown, co. Meath, who *d.* 1800.
3. Henry, *m.* Margaret, dau. of Thomas Burroughs, and had a son, Alfred, living 1798, who *m.* and had four children.
1. Mary, *m.* 1780, Henry Tisdall, and had issue.
2. Charlotte *m.* — Eames.
4. William (will dated 17 Dec. 1875, proved 22 Nov. 1788), *m.* 1780, Mary, dau. Rev. T. William Tisdall, and had issue,
1. John Brabazon, Commissioner of Wide Streets, Dublin, *d.* 1803, having *m.* 1792, Emily Letitia, dau. Benjamin Neale Bayly (*see* BAYLY *of Debsboro*), and had issue,
(1) Elizabeth, *d.* 1831, having *m.* 1814, Capt. Richard Adams, of Dunheston, co. Cavan (*see that family*), and had issue.
(2) Letitia, *b.* 1800 ; *m.* 1823, Edmund F. Dayrell, 4th Dragoon Gds., of Lillingstone Dayrell, Bucks, High Sheriff 1845 (*see that family*). and had issue.
(3) Kate, *d.* 1866, having *m.* 1833, Cosby, brother of Capt. Richard Adams (*above*), and had issue.
2. Mark Anthony, *m.* Elizabeth Myles, dau. Myles Dowdall (by Elizabeth Lyster), and had two daus.
3. Rev. William, B.A., Rector of Cloghran, *b.* 1768 ; *d.* 1833, having *m.* Priscilla, sister of Right Hon. Sir Gore Ouseley, Bt., G.C.H., F.R.S., &c., and had issue.
4. Chaworth, Capt. Dublin Artillery, South Fingal Cavalry, 1801, *d.* 1860, having *m.* 1821, Anne, dau. Thomas Keightley, who *d.* 1860, having had, with other issue,
(1) Alfred Chaworth (*West Heath, Abbey Wood, Kent*), *m.* 1857, Elizabeth, dau. Capt. C. L. Kennett, and has issue,
1. Cecil Rupert Chaworth (70, *Wimpole Street, W.*), M.R.C.S., *b.* 1859.
2. Gerald Keightley, *b.* 1861.
1. Beatrice Isabella Keightley, *m.* 1883, George Todd, and has issue.
(2) Chaworth Edward, M.D., F.R.S.I., *b.* 1835 ; *d.* 1881, leaving issue, two daus.
(1) Emma, *m.* 1st, 1849, Arthur Nolan, M.D., and had issue ; *m.* 2ndly, 1878, Alfred Hudson, M.D., Physician H.M. in Ireland.
1. Elizabeth, *m.* 1795, James Saunin, D.D., Bishop of Dromore, (*see that family*), and had issue.
5. Thomas (Rev.), D.D., Secretary to the Dublin Society, *m.* 1770,

Elizabeth, dau. of Sir Fielding Ould, M.D. His will was proved 1808. He had an only child Fielding, Bar.-at-Law, *b.* 1774 ; *d.* 1803.
1. Anne, *m.* 1756, Rev. James Kyan, and had issue.
2. Elizabeth, *d.s.p.* having *m.* Rev. Samuel Whalley.
3. Fridsweed, *m.* Mark Hearne, and had issue.
4. Catherine, *m.* Robert Travers.
5. Mary, *m.* 1766, M. Prendergast.
6. Dorothy.
The second son,
  JOHN LYSTER, of Rocksavage and of Wexford, *b.* 30 March, 1725 ; *m.* by licence, 5 Dec. 1754, Jane Ducasse, and *d.* 4 May, 1816, having by her (who *d.* 10 Sept. 1812) had issue.
1. JOHN HENRY, of whom presently.
2. Henry Dixie, Capt. of Militia, *b.* 24 April, 1760 ; *d. unm.* 1793.
3. Stephen (Rev.), Rector of Kilnamanagh, *b.* 18 June, 1763 ; *m.* 8 April, 1795, Margaret Corristinea, dau. of — Fry, of Frybrook, co. Roscommon, and had issue,
  1. Catherine Jane, *d. unm.* 7 Aug. 1886.
  2. Jane, *d. unm.* 18 June, 1866.
  3. Mary, *d. unm.* 13 June, 1884.
  4. Margaret, *d. unm.* 15 Nov. 1900.
4. Thomas, of Rocksavage, Lieut.-Col. in the Army, *b.* 21 Sept. 1764 ; *d. unm.* 20 Nov. 1844.
5. William John, Capt. in the Army, *b.* 27 Aug. 1765 ; *m.* 1st, Martha, dau. of John Hatton, of Ballymartin, co. Wexford, who *d.* 1818). He *m.* 2ndly, Emily Letitia, dau. of Benjamin Neale Bayly, and widow of John Brabazon Lyster, of Dublin ; she was bur. 21 March, 1849. Capt. W. J. Lyster *d.* Aug. 1849, having had by his 1st wife two sons,
  1. Armstrong, *b.* 1803, settled in United States of America ; *d.* 1876, having *m.* 1834, Anne Isabella, dau. Capt. Isdell, of Sanders Court, co. Wexford, and had issue,
    (1) Isdell Dayrell, *b.* 1836 ; *d.* 1888, having *m.* 1866, Eliza Patterson, and had issue, seven sons,
      1. Thomas William, *b.* 1867, present head of the family.
      2. Richard Dayrell.   3. John Armstrong.
      4. George.   5. Edmund.
      6. Gregory Croston.   7. Antoine Clerk.
    (2) William John, *d.s.p.*
    (3) Edmund Francis, *m.* and has issue, in United States of America.
    (4) Armstrong Browne, *m.* and has issue in United States of America.
  2. Rev. William Narcissus, B.A., *b.* 1805 ; *m.* 1832, Ellen, dau. John Cooper, of Birchgrove, co. Wexford, and had three sons,
    (1) William John, late Lieut.-Col. Conundz. 21st Infantry United States of America Army, *d.* 1805, leaving issue.
    (2) Henry Francis Le Hunte, Major United States of America Army, *d.* 1894, leaving issue.
    (3) Theodore Gordon.
6. Mark Anthony (Rev.), *b.* 17 May, 1767 ; *d.* 15 May, 1849.
7. David James, of Dublin, *b.* 19 Nov. 1769 ; *d. unm.* 22 Oct. 1853.
1. Elizabeth Magdalen, *m.* 1 Oct. 1781, Robert Swift, and *d.* Dec. 1822, leaving issue.
2 Jane Fridsweed, *d.* young 7 June, 1760.
3. Louisa Deborah, *d.* young 5 June, 1760.
4. Anne Hester, *m.* Very Rev. Thomas Paul, Dean of Cashel, and *d.s.p.* 6 Dec. 1839.   5. Mary, *d.* in infancy Nov. 1768.
The eldest son,
  JOHN HENRY LYSTER, of Summerhill, co. Dublin, Barrister-at-Law of the Irish Bar from 1783, *b.* 8 Jan. 1759 ; *m.* 3 June, 1790, Catherine Dorothea, dau. Benjamin Neale Bayly, and *d.* 11 Dec. 1808, having by her (who was bur. 31 Aug. 1650) had issue,
1. John Dixie, Lieut. 100th Regt., *b.* 17 April, 1792 ; *d. unm.* bur. 14 Nov. 1825.
2. Benjamin O'Neal, Capt. R.A., *b.* 8 March, 1795 ; *m.* Mary Hill, of Halifax, Nova Scotia, and *d.* 1842, having had issue.
3. Thomas George, *b.* 15 Dec. 1797 ; *d. unm.* 18 June, 1823.
4. HENRY, of whom presently.
5. Walter Stephen, *b.* 2 Jan. 1803 ; *d.* 1825.
1. Letitia Jane, *m.* 1818, Rev. Richard Bermingham, and *d.s.p.* 16 July, 1882.
2. Catherine, *d.* in infancy, 8 May, 1794.
3. Catherine Dorothea, of Rocksavage, *d. unm.* 23 Jun. 1883.
4. Jane Elizabeth *d.* young, 12 March, 1815.
5. Anne Frances, *d. unm.* 11 Aug. 1868.
6. Isabella, *m.* 14 Nov. 1833, Col. William Toole, of Curracloe, co. Wexford, and *d.* 9 May, 1868, leaving issue.
The fourth son,
  REAR-ADMIRAL HENRY LYSTER, *b.* 3 Sept. 1799, entered R.N. 1811, Capt. 1845, Rear Admiral 1863 ; *m.* 3 April, 1831, Eliza, second dau. of Gen. John Hatton, and *d.* 27 Oct. 1864, having by her (who was bur. 6 Aug. 1855) had issue,
1. HENRY JOHN, of Rocksavage, co. Roscommon, Col. R.A., *b.* 21 Sept. 1851 ; *d.s.p.* 6 March 1903.
2. Frederick Charles, *b.* 24 Jan. 1855 ; *d.* 10 April, 1856.
1. Annette Thomasina, *d. unm.* 18 March 1908.
2. Isabella Catherine, *d. unm.* 24 July, 1860.
3. Victoria Jane.
4. Eliza Jeanette.
We now return to
  THOMAS LYSTER, of Grange, co. Roscommon, High Sheriff 1739 and 1745, fourth son of Thomas Lyster, of Grange, co. Roscommon, by Alice his second wife, dau. of Dodwell Browne (*see above*). He was *b.* 29 Dec. 1719 ; *m.* 1743, Bridget, dau. of Thomas Fitzgerald, of Turlough, co. Mayo (*see that family*), and *d.* 1790 (will dated 15 Nov., proved 15 Dec. that year) leaving issue,
1. ANTHONY, of whom presently.

MacAdam. THE LANDED GENTRY. 428

2. John, living 17 March, 1798.
3. Thomas, Ensign 39th Regt., *d. unm.* 1798 (will, dated 17 March, 1798, proved 20 April, 1799).
4. George William, *m.* Juliana, dau. of John Kirwan, of Hillsbrook (*see* KIRWAN *of Stowe Lodge*), and had an only child,
Thomas Mark, *d.* 1817, having *m.* Harriette, dau. and co-heir of Peter Bourke, of Ballinew, co. Mayo, by whom he had issue,
(1) George, *d.* aged 18.
(2) Thomas Mark, *d.* 19 April, 1862; *m.* 1843, Kathleen Boyne Brynan, of Derreen, King's Co., by whom (who *d.* 20 June, 1859) he had an only child, *d. inf.*
(1) Mary Clare, *d.* 13 April, 1877; *m.* 11 Jan. 1843, Richard Jenings, eldest son of Ulick Jenings, of Ironpool, and had issue (*see that family*).
(2) Julia, *d.* 30 Nov. 1898.

The eldest son,
CAPT. ANTHONY GEORGE, of Grange, Ensign 28th Regt., 1772, Capt. Fifeshire Fencibles, *b.* 21 Jan. 1759; *m.* Anna, McLellan, and *d.* 1797 (will dated 26 Sept. 1797, proved 10 July, 1800), having by her (who *d.* Jan. 1842, aged 87) had issue,
1. THOMAS ST. GEORGE, of whom presently.
2. Anthony, of Stillorgan Park, Dublin, *b.* 1797; *m.* Marcia Deborah, 5th dau. of James Tate, of Ballintaggart, co. Wicklow, and *d.* 5 Jan. 1880, having by her (who *d.* 17 Jan. 1893) had issue,
 1. Harry Hammon, of Stillorgan Park, co. Dublin, V.C., C.B., Lieut.-Gen. Indian Army, *b.* 24 Dec. 1810; *d.* 1904.
 2. William George, of Reading, Berks, *b.* 27 May, 1834.
 3. John Lionel, C.E., *b.* 1838; *m.* 20 Dec. 1892, Gertrude Agnes, dau. of Admiral Sir Francis William Sullivan, 6th Bart. K.C.B., C.M.G. He *d.* 12 Dec. 1908, leaving issue a dau., Ruth.
 1. Emily Sophia, *b.* 22 Dec. 1825; *m.* 31 July, 1845, Sir George Samuel Jenkinson, 11th Bart., and *d.* 23 Feb. 1892, having by him (who *d.* 19 Jan. 1892) had issue (*see* BURKE's *Peerage*, JENKINSON, Bart.).
 2. Georgina Alicia, *b.* 29 April, 1827; *m.* 10 Oct. 1854, Capt. Julius Alexander Sartoris, 16th Lancers (who *d.* 3 Aug. 1863), leaving issue.
 3. Louisa Charlotte, *b.* 27 May, 1837; *d.* 1839.
1. Bridget Harriet, *m.* Michael English Graham, and *d.s.p.* 1862.
2. Anna Maria, *b.* 1785; *m.* 1816, James Collins, son of the Rev. Emanuel Collins, and *d.* 23 Aug. 1885, leaving issue.
3. Belinda, *d. unm.* 13 May, 1858.
4. Alicia Anna, *m.* John North, M.D., and *d.* 1 March, 1847, leaving issue.
5. Helen, *m.* Capt. Robert Denny, 3rd Buffs, and had issue.
6. Sophia, *b.* 1790; *m.* 30 Oct. 1812, the Rev. Sir Harcourt Lees, 2nd Bart., and *d.* 11 Aug. 1874, leaving issue (*see* BURKE's *Peerage*, LEES, Bart.). He *d.* 7 March, 1852.
7. Louisa, *m.* 1825, Capt. William Hammond, and had issue,

The eldest son,
THOMAS ST. GEORGE LYSTER, of Grange, Maj. 6th Dragoon Guards, previously Capt. 74th Highlanders, *b.* 1777; *m.* Sophia Sarah, dau. of Lieut.-Gen. Henry Lyster, A.D.C. to KING GEORGE III, Coldstream Guards, and *d.* 17 Nov. 1850, having by her (who *d.* 12 May, 1857, aged 80) had issue,
1. St. George Lumley, Lieut. R.E., *b.* 5 April, 1806; *d. unm. v.p.* at Demerara, 7 Sept. 1841.
2. Arthur O'Neil, Lieut. 46th Regt., *b.* 15 Aug. 1807; *d.* 26 March, 1897.
3. William Durham, Lieut. R.N., served in Pedroite Army in Portugal 1837-42, *b.* 28 Oct. 1800; *d. unm.* 13 Dec. 1852.
4. Henry, Knt. of the Royal and Military Order of St. Ferdinand, Maj. British Auxiliary Legion in Spanish War of Succession, *b.* 16 Nov. 1810; *m.* 7 May, 1841, Harriet, dau. of Admiral Henry Hume Spence, R.N., and *d.* 15 May, 1881, having had issue,
 1. Harriet Alicia, *b.* 11 Jan. 1849; *d. unm.* 21 Aug. 1860.
 2. Sophia Sarah, *b.* 7 June, 1853; *d.* 29 June, 1862.
 3. Graciana, *b.* 28 Aug. 1856; *m.* (as *below*) 24 June, 1877, her cousin Frederick Edward Lyster, and has issue. She *m.* 2ndly, Ernest de Blois Brenton.
5. FREDERICK TORRENS, late representative of the Grange branch.
6. Anthony Greenwood, Capt. H.E.I.C.S., *b.* 19 July, 1814; *d. unm.* 6 June, 1857.
7. Septimus, served in War of Succession in Spain, Ensign 94th Regt. 1836, Lieut.-Col. Commander 1868, *b.* 27 April, 1817; *m.* 2 Jan. 1844, Elizabeth, dau. of Maj. George Horton, 94th Regt., and *d.* 20 July, 1880, leaving by her (who *d.* 27 May, 1902) issue,
 1. William Henry (*Roscommon, Camberley*), Lieut.-Col. Indian Army, Brig.-Gen. Commanding Nagpur District 1898-9, *b.* 5 Aug. 1846; *m.* 17 May, 1875, his cousin Alice, dau. of James Collins, and grand-dau. of James Collins and Anna Maria Lyster his wife, and has issue,
  Cecil Julius Hamilton, *b.* 1 Dec. 1878, Capt. Indian Army; *m.* 1909, Cecily Agnes, dau. of Foster Kinloch Cunliffe (*see* BURKE's *Peerage*, CUNLIFFE, Bart.), and has issue,
   David Anthony, *b.* 2 Aug. 1911.
  Maud Alice, *b.* 10 Jan. 1880; *m.* 11 Feb. 1909, Commander Kenneth Gofton-Salmond, R.N., son of late Robert Gofton-Salmond, and has issue.
 2. Frederick Leslie, Surgeon, *b.* 20 April, 1850; *d. unm.* 22 April, 1890.
 3. John Charles, *b.* 20 Sept. 1855; *m.* 27 Dec. 1894, Edith, dau. of Norris Adams Bradley.
 4. Arthur Edward (*The Yews, Great Baddow, Chelmsford*),

M.R.C.S., J.P. Essex, *b.* 28 Nov. 1861; *m.* 14 Feb. 1887, Lucy, dau. of William Eddowes, and widow of -- Gillitlic, and has issue,
 (1) Arthur Lumley St. George, Lieut. R.N., *b.* 27 April, 1888.
 (2) Ronald Guy, *b.* 8 Sept. 1889.
 (3) Lionel Charles, *b.* 2 May, 1893.
 (1) Dorothy. (2) Phyllis.
5. Alfred James, of Constantinople, *b.* 18 Aug. 1866; *m.* 1887, Marie Antionette, dau. of G. de Anino, and has had issue,
 (1) Henry Newbolt, *b.* 6 March, 1888.
 (2) James Leslie, *b.* 14 May, 1890; *d.* young.
 (3) Frederick John, *b.* 9 March, 1897.
 (1) Edythe Marie Valerie.
1. Sophia Harriet, *b.* 22 Oct. 1848; *m.* 23 April, 1868, Arthur Edwin Temple Longhurst, late 60th Rifles.
2. Frances Henrietta Elizabeth, *b.* 13 June, 1857; *m.* 11 March, 1880, William Goldby, and has issue.
3. Alice, *b.* 4 July, 1864; *d.* 3 Sept. 1867.
1. Sophia Amelia, *b.* 24 Oct. 1815; *m.* 1847, Capt. Timothy Thornhill, and had issue.
2. Emma, *b.* 9 July, 1819; *m.* 25 Oct. 1848, Charles Porteous, H.E.I.C.S., and had issue. He *d.* 1 May, 1885.

The fifth son,
COL. FREDERICK TORRENS LYSTER, of Warren House, Starcross, co. Devon, served in the Wars of Succession in Spain and Portugal, 1833-40, Knight of St. Ferdinand, and a Don in Spain, 50th Regt. 1841, Maj. 21st Scots Fus. 1864, Col. Commanding 1870-74, *b.* 30 March, 1813; *m.* 1st, 23 Jan. 1846, Ellen, 2nd dau. of Edward W. Lake, and bv her (who *d.* 26 March, 1859) had issue,
1. FREDERICK EDWARD, of Garden City, Long Island, U.S.A., formerly Ensign 30th Regt., *b.* 2 Nov. 1846; *m.* 24 June, 1877, his first cousin Graciana, dau. and co-heir of Henry Lyster (*see above*), and *d.* leaving issue,
 Frederic St. George, *b.* 15 Feb. 1879.
2. Charles Bybie (6, *Barnfield, Crescent, Exeter*), Maj. late the Buffs (East Kent Regt.), *b.* 20 May, 1852; *m.* 13 Oct. 1885, Alice, only dau. of James Bindloss, M.R.C.S., of Prestwich, Manchester, and has issue,
 1. Anthony St. George, P.W.D. Punjab, India, *b.* 13 March, 1888.
 2. Lumley FitzGerald, *b.* 21 Oct. 1890.
 3. Harry Stratford Gore, *b.* 29 July, 1894; *d.* 18 Feb. 1895.
 1. Sybil, *b.* 13 Sept. 1886. 2. Rosamund, *b.* 3 Dec. 1889.
3. Arthur Walter, Maj. late 3rd Goorkhas, *b.* 26 July, 1853; *d.* 15 July, 1911.
4. William O'Brien, late R.N. (*Glatton Hall, near Peterborough*), *b.* 9 June, 1857; *m.* 21 Sept. 1887, Mary, dau. of James Ross, of Perth, and has issue,
 1. Mary Elizabeth, *b.* 17 June, 1890.
 2. Dorothea Lake, *b.* 22 Dec. 1891.
 3. Winifred Annette, *b.* 18 Sept. 1893.
1. Ellen Elizabeth, *b.* 22 April, 1851.
2. Emily Mariamne, *b.* 3 Nov. 1858; *m.* 7 Oct. 1890, Herbert Weston Sparkes, and has issue.
He *m.* 2ndly, 3 Oct. 1860, Frances Jemima, 2nd dau. of Capt. Charles Reed, 8th Hussars, of Westerfield, Sussex, and *d.* 17 Sept. 1902.

Arms—Quarterly: 1st and 4th, erm., on a fesse sa. three mullets or (for LYSTER); 2nd and 3rd, gu., a chevron between three mullets arg. in the dexter and sinister chief points, a bird bolt in pale or (for BOLTON). *Crest*—Issuing from a ducal coronet or, charged with a cross humettée gu. a stag's head ppr. *Motto*—Retinens vestigia famae.

MACADAM OF BLACKWATER.

CAPT. PHILIP BOWER MACADAM, of Blackwater House, co. Clare, late 3rd West York L.I. and of the 59th Regt., with which he served in Afghan War 1879-80, *b.* 6 Oct. 1856; *s.* his father 1906.

Lineage.—PHILIP MACADAM, purchased the estate of Blackwater, in co. Clare, from James Craven, in 1684. He *d.* 1694, and was *s.* by his son,
PHILIP MACADAM, who *d. unm.* 24 June, 1729, and his next brother, John Craven MacAdam, a naval officer, having been killed (*unm.*) in the South Seas, he was *s.* by his only surviving brother,
THOMAS MACADAM, of Churchland House, *m.* Honor, dau. of Terence Grace O'Ryan, of co. Tipperary, and *d.* 1752, leaving with other issue, an eldest son,
PHILIP MACADAM, of Churchland, *m.* 2 Aug. 1755, Catherine, 2nd dau. of Rev. Bassett Dickson, of Knockdrumassell, co. Limerick, and left issue, with other daus. (who *d. unm.*), two sons,
1. THOMAS, his heir.
2. John, *m.* the dau. of G. Vincent, of Parteen House, co. Clare.
1. Matilda, *m.* Major E. Collis, 58th Regt.

The eldest son,

THOMAS MACADAM, of Churchland House, and Blackwater, b. 21 Jan. 1762; m. 1st, 1783, Jane, only dau. and heir of Petre Tyndale, of Dublin, and by her (who d. 1793) left issue, with one dau., two sons,
1. PHILIP, his heir.
2. Thomas Hutchinson, b. 1792; m. 1827, Charlotte, 4th dau. of John Lannigan Stannard, of The Grange, co. Kilkenny, and d. 1836, leaving issue,
  1. Thomas Stannard, m. 1860, Mary, dau. of John Brown, J.P., of Clonboy House, co. Clare (see that family).
  2. Robert Stannard, dec.
    1. Charlotte.   2. Jane, d. unm.
Mr. MacAdam m. 2ndly, 1796, Catherine, dau. of J. Dickson, of Limerick, by whom he left issue, an only child,
8. David Hastings, b. 1798, deceased.
Mr. MacAdam d. 1825, and was s. by his oldest son,
PHILIP MACADAM, of Blackwater House, b. 1789, Capt. 3rd West York Militia; m. 1825, Elizabeth, 3rd dau. of John Lannigan Stannard, of The Grange, co. Kilkenny, and d. 2 Sept. 1855, leaving issue,
1. THOMAS JOHN STANNARD, of Blackwater House.
2. Philip Henry, m. 1864, Helen, dau. of the late Miles O'Reilly, Q.C., of The Willows, Hamilton, Upper Canada, Judge of London County, Upper Canada, and d. 6 July, 1895, leaving issue, with a son, d. young,
  1. Kathleen.   2. Helen, dec.
3. John Stannard, Brigade Surg. Lieut.-Col. Army Medical Staff (retired), b. 1838; d. 23 April, 1904; m. 23 June, 1875, Mary D., dau. of B. T. Bovell, of Barbadoes, W. Indies,
  1. Elizabeth Matilda, m. 1 Dec. 1875, William Thomas Waller, J.P., of Prior Park, co. Tipperary (see that family). She d. 26 Nov. 1906. He d. 19 March, 1878.
  2. Catherine.
  3. Matilda, m. 5 July, 1865, Henry Vereker, 3rd son of Major John Vereker, of Limerick, and d. 10 July, 1871, leaving issue (see BURKE'S Peerage, GORT, V.).
The eldest son,
LIEUT.-COL. THOMAS JOHN STANNARD MACADAM, of Blackwater House, co. Clare, Lieut.-Col. (retired) late 3rd Batt. York and Lancaster Regt., J.P. cos. Clare, Limerick, and Sussex, High Sheriff co. Clare 1890, b. Sept. 1827; m. 1st, 11 Jan. 1855, Elizabeth Chivers, 2nd dau. of the late John Seddon Bower, of Broxholme House, co. York, and by her (who d. 9 Oct. 1856) has issue,
1. PHILIP BOWEN, now of Blackwater.
He m. 2ndly, Sept. 1858 Ellen Jane only dau. of the late Capt. William D'Arcy Preston R.N. J.P. of Borde Hill House Sussex (see PRESTON of Askham Bryan) and d. 14 March, 1906, having by her (who d. 11 June, 1909) had issue
2. Francis Robert Preston, Capt. Prince of Wales' Own West Yorkshire (14th) Regt., b. 26 Aug. 1859; d. from the effects of a fall from his horse, in York Barracks, 22 July, 1893.
3. Walter, Lieut.-Col. R.E., b. 20 Feb. 1865; m. 22 Dec. 1909, Mary Moore, dau. of W. M. Hutchison, late of Heronsgate, Herts, and has issue a dau., Honor.
4. Raymond D'Arcy, b. 1867; d. young.
  1. Charlotte Honor, m. 2 Oct. 1903, Peter David FitzGerald, 3rd son of Sir Peter FitzGerald, Bart., Knt. of Kerry (see BURKE'S Peerage).
  2. Grace Elizabeth, m. 23 March, 1892, Col. Edward Hart Dyke, late R.A., and has issue (see BURKE's Peerage, DYKE, Bart.).

Arms—Vert, a cross calvary, in the dexter chief a mullet, and in the sinister a crescent, all or. Crest—On a mount vert, a cock ppr., in the bill a cross, as in the arms. Motto—In hoc signo vinces.
Seat—Blackwater House, co. Clare. Club—Naval and Military.

MACAN OF DRUMCASHEL.

ARTHUR MACAN, of Drumcashel, co. Louth, J.P., D.L., High Sheriff 1882, late Capt. 6th Batt. Royal Irish R.fles, b. 25 July, 1852; m. 7 Aug. 1877, Mary Louisa, eldest dau. of Lieut.-Col. William Johnston Bellingham, of Bowling Green, Castle Bellingham, co. Louth, and has issue,
1. ARTHUR HENRY, b. 1 July, 1883.
2. Hugh Turner, b. 8 April, 1886.
  1. Sybil Norah, b. 18 June, 1878.
  2. Joan Florence, b. 5 May, 1887.
  3. Elsie Winifred, b. 13 June, 1889.

Lineage.—ROBERT MACAN (eldest son of Thomas MacCann, of Armagh) got the remnant of the family estates, viz., Carriff, co. Armagh. He m. 1783, Hannah Bagwed, by whom (who d. 1824) he left at his decease, in 1808, three sons,
1. Thomas, d. unm. in India.
2. Turner, of Carriff, m. Harriet, dau. of the Rev. Wetenhall Sneyd, of Newchurch, Isle of Wight, and d. 1835, leaving issue, Turner Arthur, of Carriff, co. Armagh, and Elston Lodge, Bedford, J.P., b. 1826, m. 1855, Florence, dau. of Henry Lawes Long, of Hampton Lodge, Hants, and d. 1889, leaving, with other issue,
  (1) William Arthur of Carriff b. 1850; m. 1886 Lucy Eugenie dau. of Sir Claude William de Crespigny Bart. He d. 17 Oct. 1818, having had with other issue, William Reginald Harry, b. 1887; d. 20 Feb. 1905.
  (2) Ralph E., m. 4 Feb. 1907 Dorothy Elizabeth, eldest dau. of late Hon. Greville Theophilus Howard (see BURKE's Peerage SUFFOLK E.).
  (1) Florence Catherine, m. 1879 Humphrey Pocklington Senhouse, eldest son of Joseph Pocklington Senhouse of Netherhall. He d. 20 Dec. 1903, leaving issue (see that family).
3. RICHARD, of whom we treat.
The 3rd son,
RICHARD MACAN I.C.S. of Drumcashel m. 28 Nov. 1848 Caroline Helene, dau. of Prof. Macaire, of Geneva, and by her (who d. 25 Jan. 1901) had issue,
1. ARTHUR, now of Drumcashel.
2. George.   3. Richard.
  1. Caroline.
  2. Eliza, m. 1881, John Gascoigne Lillie, and has issue.
  3. Edith m. 7 March 1894, Henry Dyke Marsh, Major late 82nd Foot, Military Knt. of Windsor, son of late Capt. Edward Marsh, Indian Army, of Ivychurch, Kent, and Nethersole, Somersetshire. He d. 17 Aug. 1907, leaving issue.
  4. Annie.
Mr. Macan d. 13 Oct. 1879, and was s. by his eldest son.

Seat—Drumcashel, Castle Bellingham, co. Louth. Clubs—Junior Carlton, S.W., and Sackville Street, Dublin.

MACARTNEY OF LISSANOURE.

CARTHANACH GEORGE MACARTNEY, of Lissanoure, co. Antrim, J.P., educated at the Charterhouse and Sandhurst R.M.C., b. 11 Aug. 1869; s. his father 29 Aug. 1874; m. Aug. 1890, his cousin Margaret Tryphena Mabel, eldest dau. of Townley Patten Hume Macartney Filgate, of Lowtherstone, co. Dublin (whom see), and has issue,
1. DERVOCK GEORGE AUCHINLECK, b. 1 Dec. 1891; d. 26 Sept. 1900.
2. George Travers Lucy, b. 29 Oct. 1896.

Lineage.—Of the Auchinleck branch of the ancient Scottish family of Macartney, MacCartney, or MacCarthy, was GEORGE MACCARTNEY, m. 1522, Margaret, dau. of Godfrey MacCullogh, of Fleet Bank, Kirkcudbright. His son,
PATRICK MACCARTNEY, m. the dau. of John McLellan, and had an eldest son,
BARTHOLOMEW MACCARTNEY, of Auchinleck, Kirkcudbright, in 1597; m. 1587, Mary, only dau. of John Stewart, of Auchinleck, and had a son,
BARTHOLOMEW MACCARTNEY, m. Catherine, dau. of George Maxwell, and d.v.p. leaving a son,
GEORGE MACARTNEY, a Capt. of Horse, b. at Auchinleck, removed to Ireland 1649, and settled in co. Antrim, where he acquired a large estate, represented Belfast in Parliament. In 1678 he served as High Sheriff, and in 1688, proclaimed King WILLIAM and Queen MARY at Belfast, for which he was soon after obliged to fly to England, and was attainted of King JAMES' Parliament held at Dublin 1689. He was restored on the settlement of the Kingdom. He m. 1st, Jane, dau. of St. Quintin Calderwood, and had issue (with three daus., of whom two d. unm., the youngest m. William Lockhart),
  1. James, M.P. for Bridport 1692-5, one of the Judges of the Court of Common Pleas in Ireland, b. 1651; d. 1727; m. 1st, Frances Ireby (d. 1683-4), by whom he had no surviving issue. He m. 2ndly, Alice Cuit, and by her (who d. 1725) had issue,
James, M.P. for Longford and Granard 1713-1760, b. 1692; d. in Hanover 1770, having m. 1715, Catherine Coote, by whom he had issue,
  (1) Francis, M.P. for Blessington 1749; m. 1748, Henrietta Gardiner and d.s.p.v.p.
  (2) Coote, d. unm.
  (1) Alice   (2) Catherine
  (3) Frances, m. 1748, Fulke Greville, of Wilbury, Wilts.
  (4) Mary, m. 2 June, 1761, Sir William Henry Lyttelton, 7th Bart., created Baron Westcote of Ballymore, co. Longford, and Baron Lyttelton. She d. 28 May, 1765, leaving issue (see BURKE's Peerage, COBHAM, V.).
  2. Arthur, m. Jane Chalmers, and had issue,
    1. George, M.P. for Belfast 1721, d. unm.
    2. James, Merchant in Bristol, d. unm.
    3. Charles, Merchant in Dublin, m. Margaret McCullock, of Piedmont, in Antrim, and had issue,
      Arthur, b. 1744.
      Margaret.
      1. Eleanor, m. Rev. Francis Tredell.
      2. A dau., m. Capt. Coleman.
    3. A dau., d. unm.
    3. John, d. young.   4. Bartholomew, d. young.
    5. George, d. young.   6. St. Quintin, d. young.
He m. 2ndly, Elizabeth, dau. of Sir Stephen Butler, and had issue (with a son, Chichester, d.s.p.),

Macartney. THE LANDED GENTRY. 430

GEORGE MACARTNEY, M.P. for Belfast for 54 years, called to the Bar 1700, High Sheriff co. Antrim, Deputy Governor and Col. of a Regiment of Militia Dragoons, b. 7 Feb. 1671; *m.* 1st, 1700, Letitia (*d.* 1721), dau. and co-heir of Sir Charles Porter, Lord Chancellor of Ireland. He *m.* 2ndly, Elizabeth Dobbin (*d.s.p.*), and *d.* 1754, and 1757, leaving by his 1st wife (with a son, Charles, *d.s.p.* 17 Oct. a son, Hugh, of Ch. Ch. Coll.) a son,
GEORGE MACARTNEY, who *m.* 1732, Elizabeth, dau. of the Rev. John Winder, and had issue,
1. GEORGE MACARTNEY, Earl Macartney, Viscount Macartney, of Dervock, Lord Macartney, Baron of Lissanoure, in Ireland, and of Parkhurst and Auchinleck in Great Britain, Knight of the most honourable military order of the Bath, and of the most ancient and royal order of the White Eagle of Poland, one of H.M.'s most honourable Privy Council, Principal Secretary to the Lieutenancy of Ireland in the administration of Lord Townsend 1769, Capt.-Gen. of Grenada 1775, Governor of Fort St. George, East Indies, 1779, of Bengal 1785, and later of Madras, and Ambassador Plenipotentiary to the Empress of Russia, Col. of a Regiment of Militia Dragoons, and Custos Rotulorum of the co. of Antrim, b. May, 1737, was created BARON MACARTNEY 1770, and promoted Earl 1794; *m.* 1 Feb. 1768, Lady Jane Stewart, 2nd dau. of John, Earl of Bute, and *d.s.p.* 1806, when his titles became extinct.
1. Letitia, *m.* Godfrey Echlin, and *d.s.p.*
2. Elizabeth, *m.* John Blaquier, Major of Dragoons, and *d.* 1782, leaving an only dau.,
ELIZABETH, of whom we treat.

His grand-dau.,
ELIZABETH BLAQUIER (niece of Earl Macartney), *m.* 1785, the REV. TRAVERS HUME (son of Gustavus Hume, of Dublin, State Surgeon, who *m.* 22 Oct. 1756, dau. of Rev. Boyle Travers, D.D.), who was bur. 1757, and *d.* 1805, leaving issue,
1. GEORGE, who assumed the surname and arms of MACARTNEY.
2. Gustavus Thomas, *b.* 1794, served in the R.A. at the battle of Waterloo, and was afterwards in the 15th Hussars and 6th Dragoon Guards; *d. unm.* 1846.
3. John, *b.* Oct. 1795; *m.* 1st, Anna Waller, dau. of John Parker, by whom he had one son, Arthur, late 79th Highlanders, *b.* 21 June, 1840, and two daus., Mary, *m.* Capt. Hickey, 1st Bengal Lancers, and Elizabeth. He *m.* 2ndly, Elizabeth, dau. of Major Stewart, of the Rifles, by whom he had one son, John Stewart, *b.* Aug. 1856, Capt. South Staffordshire Regt. He *d.* 1859.
4. Robert (Rev.), *m.* 2 June, 1823, Mary, 3rd dau. of Michael Harris, and by her (who *d.* 1862) had issue,
1. Arthur, of Dawson Street, Dublin, *b.* 17 Aug. 1824; *m.* 14 June, 1854, Elizabeth, 2nd dau. of Robert F. Rynd, of Ryndville, co. Meath, and has,
(1) Arthur Robert, Capt. Duke of Wellington's West Riding Regt., *b.* 21 Nov. 1856; *m.* 16 Jan. 1888, Violet Margaret Isabel, only dau. of Major-Gen. Hugh Rowlands, C.B., V.C., of Plastirion, co. Carnarvon.
(1) Mary. (2) Florence Elizabeth.
2. Gustavus (Sir), Lieut.-Col., Knt. Legion of Honour, Lieut. Hon. Corps Gentlemen-at-Arms, *b.* 1826; *m.* 18 July, 1857, Ellen Catherine (now Lady Hume-Gore), dau. and co-heir of Charles Vernon, and had issue (*see* HUME-GORE *of Derryluskan*).
3. Robert (Sir), K.C.B., Lieut.-Gen., Knt. Legion of Honour, *b.* 23 Nov. 1828; *m.* 1872, Jane, dau. of R. Brown, and widow of Capt. Harris, of Indian Army.
4. John Richard, Major Gen. (retired), Knt. Legion of Honour.
5. Walter, Capt. late 38th Regt.
1. Elizabeth, *m.* G. D. Pakenham, late Capt. 4th Bengal Light Cavalry.
1. Elizabeth, *m.* 1806, Henry Brooke, and *d.* 1823.
2. Georgiana, *m.* 1808, George Richard Golding, Capt. 4tb Dragoon Guards, dec.
3. Alicia, *m.* 1823, Major-Gen. Oldfield, K.H., dec.
4. Anna, *m.* 1830, Francis Longworth Dames, of Greenhill, King's Co., and *d.* 1835 (*see that family*).

The eldest son,
GEORGE MACARTNEY, of Lissanoure, J.P. and D.L., M.P. co. Antrim, *b.* Oct. 1793; *m.* May, 1828, Ellen, only surviving child and heir of Townley Patten Filgate, of Lowtherstone, co. Dublin, and Droingoolton, co. Louth, and by her (who *d.* 1847) had issue,
1. GEORGE TRAVERS, his heir.
2. Townley Patten Hume Macartney Filgate, of Lowther Lodge, co. Dublin (*see* FILGATE *of Lowther Lodge*).
1. Martha Ellen, *m.* 1852, Townley Filgate, M.A., of Arthurstoun, co. Louth, and *d.* March, 1885, leaving issue.
2. Elizabeth Jane, *d. unm.* 9 Oct. 1910. 3. Anne Sophia.
This gentleman, whose patronymic was HUME, assumed by Royal Licence 8 Oct. 1814, the surname and arms of MACARTNEY, under the will of his grand-uncle, Earl Macartney. He *d.* 20 Oct. 1869, and was *s.* by his eldest son,
GEORGE TRAVERS MACARTNEY, of Lissanoure, J.P. and D.L., formerly Capt. 15th King's Hussars, *b.* Feb. 1830; *m.* 3 Oct. 1865, Henrietta Frances, 3rd dau. of Robert Smyth, of Gaybrook, co. Westmeath (*see that family*), and had issue,
1. CARTHANACH GEORGE, his heir.
1. Helen Henrietta, *b.* July, 1866; *m.* Sept. 1890, Alexander G. Robins, and had issue, John Macartney, *b.* June, 1894.
2. Mabel Constance, *b.* Sept. 1871.
3. Frances Rose, *b.* July, 1873.
Mr. Macartney *d.* 29 Aug. 1874, and was *s.* by his son, CARTHANACH GEORGE MACARTNEY, now of Lissanoure.

Arms—Or, a buck trippant gu. attired arg. within a bordure of the second. **Crest**—A cubit arm erect, the hand grasping a rose-branch in flower, all ppr. **Motto**—Mens conscia recti.

Seat—Lissanoure Castle, Killagan, co. Antrim.

ELLISON-MACARTNEY OF MOUNTJOY GRANGE.

RIGHT HON. WILLIAM GREY ELLISON - MACARTNEY, P.C., of Ballydownfine, co. Antrim, and of Mountjoy Grange, co. Tyrone, B.A. Oxon, Barrister-at-Law, Parliamentary Sec. to the Admiralty 1895-1900, Dep.Master and Controller of the Mint since 1903, a Public Works Commissioner and a member of the Pensions Commutation Board, M.P. for S. Antrim, 1885 - 1903. High Sheriff 1908, *b.* 7 June, 1852; *m.* 5 Aug. 1897, Ettie Myers, eldest dau. of the late John Edward Scott, of Outlands, and Devonport, and has issue,
1. John Arthur Mowbray, *b.* 12 March, 1903.
1. Phœbe Katherine, *b.* 18 June, 1898.
2. Mildred Esther, *b.* 25 April, 1900.

Lineage (of the family of ELLISON).—Towards the end of the reign of JAMES I, THOMAS ELLISON, a younger son of an eminent merchant of Newcastle-on-Tyne, went over to Ireland, and settled in the north-west part of that country. He had issue, a son,
THOMAS ELLISON, of Castletown, co. Mayo, who had issue, a son,
REV. THOMAS ELLISON, *m.* 1731, Mildred dau. of Nathaniel Cooper, of Cappagh, and Old Grange, co. Kilkenny, by whom he had issue,
1. William, of Rockland, co. Mayo, *m.* Miss Fyvie, and *d.s.p.*
2. JOHN, of whom presently.
3. Thomas (Rev.), LL.D., Rector of Castlebar, *m.* Florinda Norman, and left issue, three sons, Thomas, William, R.N. and Frederick, all *d. unm.*, and five daus., Catherine, Florinda (*m.* Dr. William Latham, of Antrim), Lavinia, Susan, and Phoebe.
4. Bingham, *m.* Miss Crampton, and had issue, one son, Thomas, R.A., *d. unm.*, and a dau., Charlotte, *m.* Rev. Pierce Goold, and had issue,
1. Anne, *m.* George Bingham, co. Mayo, and had issue, three daus., the eldest of whom *m.* Dr. Arbuthnott, Bishop of Killaloe. The 2nd *m.* 1st, Col. Vesey, and by him had an only dau., *m.* Sir Robert Arbuthnott; and 2ndly, James, Kirkland, by whom she had a dau., Anne. The 3rd dau. of Mrs. Bingham *m.* John, Lindsey Bucknall, of Turin, co. Mayo, and had issue.

The 2nd son,
REV. JOHN ELLISON, D.D., Fellow of Trin. Coll. Dublin, Rector of Cleenish, Diocese of Clogher, and afterwards Rector of Conwall, Diocese of Raphoe, *m.* 1776, Anne, dau. of John Olphert, of Ballyconnell, co. Donegal, and had issue,
1. Thomas (Rev.), Prebendary Killamery, Diocese of Ossory, *m.* 1st, 1803, Mrs. Elizabeth Cox, widow, by whom he had one dau., Martha, *d. unm.*; and 2ndly, 1815, Catherine, 2nd dau. of ARTHUR CHICHESTER MACARTNEY, by whom he had,
1, JOHN WILLIAM, who assumed the additional surname and arms of MACARTNEY.
2. Arthur, *d. unm.*
1. Annete Anna Maria, *m.* 1864, Henry Leader, of Clonmoyle, co. Cork (*see* LEADER *of Dromagh*), and *d.s.p.* 1896.
2. Eleanor, *d. unm.*
2. John (Rev.), Rector of Killymard, *m.* his cousin, Amelia, dau. of Wybrants Olphert, of Ballyconnell, co. Donegal, and had issue,
1. John Wybrants.
1. Anna Maria, *d. unm.*
2. Anne, *d. unm.*
3. Henry, R.A., *d. unm.*
1. Anne, *m.* Charles Colhoun, of Carrickballydory, who left issue, one son and four daus. (*see that family*).

The elder son,
JOHN WILLIAM ELLISON-MACARTNEY, of Mountjoy Grange, co. Tyrone, M.P. co. Tyrone 1874 to 1885, Barrister-at-Law, J.P. and D.L. cos. Tyrone and Fermanagh, High Sheriff co. Armagh 1870, *b.* 2 May, 1818; *m.* 27 May, 1851, Elizabeth Phœbe, eldest surviving dau. of the Rev. John Grey Porter, of Kilskeery, co.Tyrone, Belleisle, co. Fermanagh, and Clogher Park, co. Tyrone (eldest son of the Right Rev. John Porter, formerly Bishop of Clogher), by his wife, Margaret Lavinia, dau. of Thomas Lindsey, of Hollymount House, co. Mayo, and of Lady Margaret Eleanor Lindsey, dau. of Charles, 1st Earl of Lucan, and by her (who *d.* 22 Dec. 1902) has issue,
1. WILLIAM GREY (The Right Hon.), P.C., now of Mountjoy Grange.
2. Thomas Stewart PORTER, of Clogher Park (*see* PORTER *of Clogher Park*).
3. Arthur Hubert, of Kenwood, Sonoma Co., California, U.S.A., *b.* 28 March, 1857.
4. Henry John, *b.* 26 March, 1859; *d. unm.* 1890.
Mr. Ellison assumed by Royal Licence, 4 April, 1859, the additional

urname and arms of MACARTNEY, on the death of his maternal uncle, the Rev. W. G. Macartney.

Lineage (of the family of MACARTNEY).—GEORGE MACARTNEY, *i.* 1640 (son of George Macartney, of Blacket, Scotland, who settled it Belfast 1630). He *m.* Martha Davies, and had two sons,

1. George, who served under the Duke of Marlborough and Prince Eugene, had the misfortune to act as second to Lord Mohun when the latter fought the celebrated duel with the Duke of Hamilton, in which both the Duke and Lord Mohun lost their lives. At the time of his death he was Lieut.-Gen. in the Army, Commander-in-Chief of the Forces in Ireland, Governor of Portsmouth, and Col. of the Carabineers.
2. ISAAC, of whom we treat.

The 2nd son,

ISAAC MACARTNEY, possessed a large estate in the north of Ireland, and served as High Sheriff of co. Antrim 1690. He was b. 671 ; *m.* 1699, Anne, sister and co-heir (with her sister, the wife of John Macdowal, of Freuga, and grandmother of Patrick Macdowal, Earl of Dumfries) of John Haltridge, of Dromore, Downside, M.P. for Killyleagh, and had issue,

1. George, High Sheriff of Antrim 1740, Sovereign of Belfast 1749, *d.* 1776, having *m.* a dau. of Rev. Wm. Reid, Rector of Muff, co. Derry, and had issue,
    1. William, *d. unm.*
    2. George (Rev.), LL.D., J.P., Vicar of Antrim, *b.* 1740 ; *m.* Mildred Brown, and *d.* 1821, leaving issue,
        (1) Arthur Chichester (Rev.), Vicar of Templepatrick and Belfast, was formerly Capt. R.A., *m.* 1816, Catherine, dau. of Merton Woollett and *d.* 1843, leaving by her (who *d.* 1854) two sons and one dau. (Louisa, *m.* Rev. R. Oulton),
            1: Arthur Chichester, *b.* 1817 ; *d. unm.* 1875.
            2. William Merton, *b.* 1819, Barrister-at-Law ; *m.* 1847, Henrietta, elder dau. of John Hitchcock, J.P., of Antrim House, Antrim, and *d.* 1860, having by her (who *d.* 1862) had issue,
                a. John Merton, Major late Dorset Regt., *m.* 1884, Ethel, dau. of Col. Frank Crossman, Bengal Cavalry, and by her (who *d.* 1887) has issue,
                    (a) Frank Alan George, *b.* 1884.
                    (b) Kenneth Chichester, *b.* 1885.
                    (a) Beryl Violet Kathleen.
                b. William Merton Closworthy, *m.* Emily Rewkin, and *d.s.p.* 1887.
                c. Henry Frederick Tucker, Capt. Bengal Cavalry, *b.* 1857 ; *m.* Eveline, dau. of Chadwick Ward, by whom he has issue, three daus.
                a. Henrietta Rosina Catherine, *m.* Rev. James Pöe.
                b. Althea Florence Violet, *m.* 1893, Col. Lionel Edmund Lushington.
        (2) William, *d.s.p.*
        (3) Joseph, *m.* his cousin Maria, dau. of Sir John Macartney, Bart., and had issue,
            1. George, *m.* Mollie Graham.
            2. John, Col. 17th Lancers, *d. unm.* 1891.
            3. William Isaac. *m.* Henrietta, dau. of Richard Davie, of Killyhevlin, co. Fermanagh, and left, with other issue, Edward Henry, M.P., Brisbane, Australia.
            4. Arthur, killed in retreat from Cabul, *d.s.p.*
            1. Georgiana, *m.* Sir Arthur Edward Kennedy, G.C.M.G., and *d.* 1874, leaving issue.
            2. Maria, *m.* R. Coulson, R.M. Sligo, and *d.* 1891.
        (4) Clotworthy, *d.* leaving issue, three daus.
        1. Anne, *m.* John Nicholson, and *d.* 1800.
        2. Elizabeth.
        3. Barbara, *m.* Thomas Reade.
    2. WILLIAM, of whom hereafter.
    1. Anne, *d. unm.* 1742.
    2. Grace, *m.* Sir Robert Blackwood, Bart., and had issue (see BURKE's *Peerage*, DUFFERIN, M.).

WILLIAM MACARTNEY, of Lish, co. Armagh, M.P. for Belfast 1747-1761, *b.* 1715 ; *m.* 1743, Catherine, dau. (by Elizabeth Montgomery his wife) of Thomas Bankes, of the family of Bankes, or Corfe Castle, Dorset, and *d.* 1797, having had issue,

1. ARTHUR CHICHESTER, his heir.
2. John, of Lish, co. Armagh, created a Bart. 22 July, 1799 (see BURKE's *Peerage*).
    1. Anne, *d. unm.* 2. Julia, *d.s.p.*
3. Jane, *m.* Simon Langley, and left issue.
4. Margaret, *m.* Abel Harris.

The elder son,

ARTHUR CHICHESTER MACARTNEY, of Lish, co. Armagh, and of Murlough, co. Down, K.C., Chief Remembrancer of the Court of Exchequer, *b.* 1744 ; *m.* 1779, Anna, dau. of Rev. Samuel Lindsey, of Turin Castle, co. Mayo, and by her (who *d.* 1841) had issue,

1. WILLIAM GEORGE, M.A., Vicar of Killead, co. Antrim, *d.s.p.* 12 Nov. 1858, having devised his property to his nephew, JOHN WILLIAM ELLISON-MACARTNEY (*see above*).
1. Frances, *m.* W. Huband, and had issue.
2. Catherine, *m.* 1815, the REV. THOMAS ELLISON (*ut supra*), and *d.* Oct. 1836.
3. Anne, *d. unm.* 1855.
4. Letitia, *d. unm.* 1855.
5. Matilda, *d. unm.* 1857.
Mr. Macartney *d.* 29 Sept. 1827.

Arms—Quarterly : 1st and 4th, or, a buck trippant gu. within a bordure of the last, for MACARTNEY ; 2nd and 3rd gu., on a chevron between three eagles' heads erased, arg. a trefoil slipped vert, for ELLISON. **Crests**—1st. A cubit arm erect, the hand grasping a rose branch in flower, all ppr., for MACARTNEY ; 2nd, a buck's head erased ppr. charged on the neck with a trefoil slipped vert, for ELLISON ; over the 1st crest, on an escroll, the motto, Stimulat sed ornat. *Motto*—Spe gaudeo.
Seat—Mountjoy Grange, co. Tyrone. *Residence*—Royal Mint E.C. *Clubs*—Carlton, S.W., and St. Stephen's.

MACARTNEY-FILGATE. *See* FILGATE.

MACAULAY OF RED HALL.

JOHN MACAULAY, of Red Hall, co. Antrim, J.P. and D.L., High Sheriff 1891, *b.* 23 June, 1823 ; *m.* 1 Feb. 1853, Jane Callwell, dau. of Patrick Agnew, of Kilwaughter and Larne, co. Antrim. She *d.* 26 June, 1899, and has issue.

1. ROBERT HELENUS, *b.* 21 Nov. 1854 ; *m.* 1883, Sarah W., youngest dau. of the late William Richardson, of Brooklands, Belfast, and has issue.
    1. ROBERT KEITH AGNEW, Lieut. R.E., *b.* 26 March, 1884.
    2. John Mortimer William, *b.* 8 April, 1885.
    1. Irene Vera Muriel.
2. Agnew McNeil, *b.* 31 July, 1858.
1. Elizabeth Agnew, *m.* 1880, Robert Ewing, J.P., of Burton Grange, co. Hertford, and 12, Durham Villas, Kensington, W.
2. Helen Elizabeth White.
3. Edith May Agnew, *m.* 27 Sept. 1888, Edmund Cecil Henry Arundel St. John-Mildmay. He *d.s.p.* 15 Sept. 1889 (see BURKE's *Peerage*, ST. JOHN-MILDMAY, Bart.).

Lineage.—JAMES MACAULAY, J.P., of Benneagh, Crumlin. *m.* 1785, Jane (who *d.* 1842), dau. of Thomas Hyndman, of Ballyronan, co. Derry, and *d.* 1839, leaving a son,

ROBERT MACAULAY, of Glenoak, Crumlin, and of Larne, co. Antrim, who *m.* 1807, Helena, dau. of Jasper White, of Limerick, and had issue,

1. JASPER, of Leigh Hill House, Cobham, Surrey, *m.* 1865, Sarah, dau. of H. Boyd, of Newry, and *d.* 19 March, 1893, aged 72.
2. JOHN, now of Red Hall.
1. Helena, *m.* 1832, James Hunter Robertson.
2. Robina, *m.* 1847, Houston Russell, who *d.* 1883.
3. Emily, *m.* 1854, William Sharman Crawford, who *d.* 1879.
Mr. Macaulay *d.* 1864.

Seat—Red Hill, Ballycarry, co. Antrim. *Residence*—28, Park Place, Cheltenham. *Clubs*—Junior Carlton and Ulster.

McCALMONT OF ABBEYLANDS.

MAJOR - GEN. SIR HUGH McCALMONT, K.C.B., C.V.O., of Abbeylands, co. Antrim, J.P. co. Antrim and for co. Kilkenny, M.P. for N. Antrim 1895-9, *b.* 9 Feb. 1845 ; *m.* 29 Sept. 1886, Hon. Rose Elizabeth, youngest dau. of John Charles, 4th Lord Clanmorris, and has issue,

DERMOT HUGH BINGHAM, Lieut.7th Hussars, *b.*10 April, 1887.

Gen. McCalmont, formerly of the 9th Lancers, and 7th Hussars, served in the Red River Expedition; in the Ashanti War (1870); in the Russo-Turkish War of 1877-8, and was present at the siege of Kars (Turkish medal and brevet of Major) ; in the South African War (1879), for which he received the medal and clasp, and brevet of Lieut.-Col. ; in the Afghan War 1879 (mentioned in despatches) ; in the Egyptian War of 1882, and present at Kassassin and Tel-el-Kebir (mentioned in despatches, medal with clasp, bronze star, and 3rd class Medjidie), and

McCarthy.

commanded the Light Camel Regt. in the Soudan Expedition of 1884-5 (mentioned in despatches, clasp, promoted Colonel, and created C.B.), Gen. McCalmont commanded the 4th D.G. from 1888 to 1892 ; and was in command of Cork District 1898-1903.
Lineage.—THOMAS MCCALMONT of the Farm, Closeburn Castle-Caron, co. Antrim, had issue,
1. THOMAS, of whom presently.
2. James, of Susquehanna, Pennsylvania, U.S.A., b. circa 1707 ; m. Hannah Blair, and was ancestor of the McCALMONTS of Larne, co. Antrim.
3. John, of Clarkestown, co. Antrim, and afterwards of Delaware, U.S.A., b. 1 May, 1709 ; m. a dau. of — Latimer, of co. Tyrone, and was ancestor of the McCALMONTS of Pennsylvania ; he d. 1779.
4. Robert. 5. Hugh.
The eldest son,
THOMAS MCCALMONT, of the Farm, co. Antrim, b. circa 1700, and was drowned near Delaware, U.S.A., leaving, with a dau. Margaret, an only son,
ROBERT MCCALMONT, of Newtown, co. Antrim, m. 1764, Margaret, dau. of Hugh Mumford, of Dremalis, co. Antrim, and by her, who d. 1768, had issue,
1. HUGH, of Abbeylands, of whom presently.
2. James, a Surgeon, b. 1772, killed by an explosion on board ship off the coast of Africa.
The eldest son,
HUGH MCCALMONT, of Abbeylands, co. Antrim, b. 31 Dec. 1765 ; m. 13 Jan. 1807, Elizabeth Allen, dau. of Thomas Barklie, of Inver, co. Antrim, and by her (who d. 16 Dec. 1871, aged 94) had issue,
1. Robert, of Gatton Park, b. 3 Jan. 1808 ; m. 23 Oct. 1835, Margaret, dau. of William Cairns, of Cultra, co. Down, and d.s.p. 2 Dec. 1883. His widow d. 30 Dec. 1889.
2. THOMAS (Rev.), of Highfield, Hants, B.A. Trin. Coll. Dublin, and Worcester, Oxon, b. 28 Jan. 1809 ; m. 1st, 6 June, 1833, Sarah, 2nd dau. of Rev. William Blundell, Rector of St. Anne's, Liverpool, and by her (who d. 24 Aug. 1836) had issue,
 1. HUGH BARKLIE BLUNDELL, of Hampton Court, co. Middlesex, Barrister-at-Law, b. 24 Aug. 1836 ; m. 8 Aug. 1860, Edith Florence, dau. of Martin Blackmore, of Rosenheim, Bonchurch, Isle of Wight, and had issue,
  (1) HARRY LESLIE BLUNDELL, of Cheveley Park, co. Cambridge, J.P. and D.L., J.P. for Suffolk, Lieut.-Col. and Hon. Col. 6th Batt. Royal Warwickshire Regt., formerly Lieut. Scots Guards and M.P. for E. Cambridgeshire, b. 30 May, 1861 ; m. 1st, 9 Dec. 1885, Amy Hyacinth, dau. of Major-Gen. John Miller, late of the 13th Hussars. She d.s.p. 29 Nov. 1889. He m. 2ndly, 5 July, 1897, Winifred, widow of William Atmar Fanning, and dau. of Gen. Sir Henry De Bathe, Bart. He d.s.p. 8 Dec. 1902, and was s. by his widow, at whose death, the estates will pass to Dermot Hugh Bingham McCalmont, only son of Sir Hugh McCalmont, K.C.B. (see above).
  (1) Ethel Elizabeth, b. 9 Aug. 1862 ; m. 21 April, 1888, James Shaw Robinson, son of Sir William Robinson, K.C.S.I., and has issue.
  (2) Margaret Anna, b. 25 Dec. 1863 ; m. 21 Oct. 1884, James Ernest Rawlins, of Hanford, California, and has issue.
  Mr. Hugh Barklie Blundell McCalmont d. 24 June, 1888. His widow m. 22 May, 1890, Frederick John Partridge. She d. 26 Nov. 1910.
 Mr. Thomas McCalmont m. 2ndly, 30 Oct. 1844, Emily Georgina, youngest dau. of Frederick Hill, of the 1st Life Guards, and by her (who d. 1871) had issue,
 2. Frederick Haynes, D.C.L., Barrister-at-Law, of the Inner Temple, b. 13 Oct. 1846 ; d. unm. 4 Nov. 1880.
 3. Alfred Leighton, of Highfield, Hants, J.P. and Mayor of Southampton 1877, b. 28 May, 1851 ; d. unm. 26 Nov. 1878.
 4. BARKLIE CAIRNS, C.B., of Highfield, Southampton, J.P., heir male of the family of McCALMONT, Col. Comm. 5th Batt. Royal Warwickshire Regiment, formerly Capt. 6th Foot 1878-95, served in South Africa 1901-2 (despatches, medal with two clasps, C.B.) ; (Warborne, Lymington, Hants ; Army and Navy, Naval and Military and Royal Yacht Squadron Clubs) ; b. 22 Nov. 1860 ; m. 28 Oct. 1884, Catherine Madeline de Courcy, dau. of Lieut.-Col. Severus William Lynam Stretton, late 40th Regt., by Catherine Adela his wife, dau. of John, 28th Baron Kingsale, and has issue,
  (1) Madeline Josephine de Courcy, b. 25 March, 1886.
  (2) Kathleen Elaine, b. 12 Sept. 1888.
  (3) Dorothy Barklie, b. 12 Nov. 1890.
  (4) Madeline Stretton, b. 1893.
 1. Georgina Elizabeth, b. 28 Sept. 1845 ; d. 12 Jan. 1850.
 2. Florence Emily, b. 27 March, 1852 ; m. 30 Dec. 1875, Capt. Alexander James Corse-Scott, of Highbold, late 79th Highlanders and Indian S. C., and has issue, Evangeline Katherine Florence, b. 30 May, 1880.
 3. Evangeline Elizabeth, b. 23 April, 1854.
 Rev. Thomas McCalmont d. 16 March, 1872.
3. Hugh, of Abbeylands, b. 26 March, 1810 ; d. unm. 9 Oct. 1887.
4. John, b. 26 Oct. 1814 ; d. unm. 30 July, 1834.
5. Barklie, b. 23 Aug., d. 6 Sept. 1816.
6. JAMES, of Abbeylands.
1. Jane, b. 24 Jan. 1812 ; d. 5 April, 1818.
2. Margaret Jane, b. 27 Nov. 1817 ; d. unm. 30 Aug. 1845.
3. Elizabeth, b. 5 May, 1821 ; d. unm. 29 May, 1840.
4. Rosanna, b. 7 Aug. 1823 ; m. Sept. 1851, John MacGildowney, J.P. and D.L., of Clare Park, co. Antrim, and d. 4 Nov. 1879. He d. 30 Oct. 1887.
Mr. Hugh McCalmont d. 20 Oct. 1838. His youngest son,

JAMES MCCALMONT, of Abbeylands and Breen, co. Antrim, J.P., b. 9 June, 1819 ; m. 27 April, 1843, Emily Anne, dau. of James Martin, J.P., D.L., of Ross, co. Galway, and by her had issue,
1. HUGH (Sir), of Abbeylands.
2. James Martin, Hon. Col. Antrim Garrison Art., Capt. late 8th Hussars, formerly A.D.C. to Lord-Lieut. of Ireland, M.P. for East Antrim since 1885 (Residence—Magheramorne, co. Antrim. Clubs—Carlton, Ulster and Kildare Street), b. 23 May, 1847 ; m. 14 Oct. 1880, Mary Caroline, dau. of Col. Robert William Romer, of Denbigh, and has issue,
 Robert Chaine Alexander, Major Irish Guards, b. 29 Aug. 1881 ; m. 16 Nov. 1907, Mary Caroline, dau. of Andrew Skeen, M.D.
 Margaret, b. 25 Sept. 1888.
Mr. James McCalmont d. 18 July, 1849. His widow m. 12 Oct. 1853, Augustine Hugh Barton, of Rochestown, co. Tipperary, who d. 23 Oct. 1874, leaving issue (see BARTON of Grove). She d. 30 Nov. 1907.
Arms—Gu. a cross vair arg. and az. betw. four fleurs-de-lis or. Crest—A griffin's head erased ppr. charged with a fleur-de-lis or. Motto—Nil desperandum.
Seat—Abbeylands, White Abbey, Belfast. Clubs—Carlton, Army and Navy, Kildare Street, and Royal St. George Yacht.

McCARTHY OF SRUGRENA ABBEY.

SAMUEL TRANT MCCARTHY, of Srugrena Abbey, co. Kerry, J.P., High Sheriff 1912, was in Madras C.S. 1863-90, b. 1842 ; m. 1st, 1875, Dorcas Louisa, dau. of the late Richard Newman. She d. 1894, leaving issue,
1. Eileen, b. 1 Jan. 1876.
2. Kathleen, b. 13 June, 1877 ; m. 1905, Joseph Carroll, and has issue.

He m. 2ndly, 1899, Ebba, widow of Count Axel Otto De la Gardie, of Maltesholm, Sweden.
Lineage.—TEIG-NA-MAINISTREACH MCCARTHY MOR, who d. 1413, left two sons,
1. Donal an Dainn McCarthy Mor, who left issue.
2. CORMAC, of Dunguil.
The younger son,
CORMACK MCCARTHY, of Dunguil, was father of
DONAL RUADH MCCARTHY, father of
DONAL OGE MCCARTHY, father of
CORMACK MCCARTHY, of Dunguil, who had two sons,
1. Donal, of Dunguil, who left three sons,
 1. Donogh. 2. Teig.
 3. Donal oge.
2. CALLAGHAN, of whom next.
The younger son,
CALLAGHAN MACCORMAC MCCARTHY, d. 1613, having had issue,
1. Donal. 2. CORMAC, of whom next.
The younger son,
CORMAC MCCARTHY, was father of
DONAL or DANIEL MCCARTHY, of Srugnena in 1656. He had two sons,
1. Charles, m. 1672, Ellen, dau. of Cornelius McGillycuddy.
2. DONAL, who carried on the line.
The younger son,
DONAL BUIDHE, or DANIEL, MCCARTHY, of Srugnena, d. 1752, leaving,
CHARLES MCCARTHY, of Srugrena, father of,
ANDREW MCCARTHY, of Srugrena, who m. a dau. of Myles Mahony, of Castlequin, and had,
ANDREW MCCARTHY, son of CHARLES MCCARTHY and grandson of DANIEL MCCARTHY, Domhnal Buidhe (who d. 1752). He m. the dau. of Myles Mahony, of Castlequin, and had issue,
1. DANIEL, his heir.
2. Jeremiah, m. 1788, Eleanor, dau. of Edward Segerson, of Cove, and had three sons, Andrew, William, and Daniel.
3. William, Lieut.-Col. in the Army, m. Ellen, dau. of Charles Geoffrey O'Connell, of Ballinablown, and had issue.
 1. Honora, m. — De Courcey. 2. Eliza, m. — O'Connell.
 3. Catherine, m. — Egan.
The eldest son,
DANIEL MCCARTHY, m. 1777, Frances, dau. of Samuel Blennerhasset, of Tralee, and had issue,
1. SAMUEL, his heir.
1. Ellen, m. Samuel Hilliard, and had issue.
2. Frances, m. — Mahony, and had issue.
The only son,
SAMUEL MCCARTHY, m. 1806, Lucy, dau. of Theobald Spotswood, and d. 1840, having had issue,
1. DANIEL, his heir.
2. William, m. Isabella Grasse, and had issue.
 1. Fanny, m. — Tharr. 2. Ellen, m. J. Jewell.
 3. Mary, m. — Ashe. 4. Lucy, m. W. Campbell.
 5. Alice, a nun. 6. Kitty.
7. Teresa, m. — Quadling.
The elder son,
DANIEL MCCARTHY, m. 1841, Ellen, dau. of Patrick Trant, of Waterview, Portmagee, and had issue,
1. SAMUEL TRANT, his heir 2. Daniel, d. unm. 1887.
3. William Patrick Trant, b. 1853 ; m. 1892, Harriett, dau. of — Bentley. She d. 1897. He d. 1901, leaving issue,

McCausland.

1. Daniel, b. 1 June, 1893. 2. William, b. 26 July, 1894.
3. Samuel, b. 9 March, 1897.
1. Clara, d. young. 2. Lucy.
3. Ellen, d. unm. 1871.
Seat—Srugena Abbey, Cahirciveen, co. Kerry.

MacCARTHY-O'LEARY. See O'LEARY.

MacCARTIE OF CARRIGNAVAR.

LIEUT.-COL. FREDERICK FITZGERALD MacCARTIE, C.I.E., of Carrignavar, co. Cork, B.A., M.B., Trin. Coll. Dublin, Lieut. - Col. Indian Medical Service, Assay Master to H.M. Mint, Calcutta, served in Afghan War 1879-80 (medal); b. 6 Aug. 1851; m. 1882, Julie Charlotte, dau. of John Adrian Vanrenen, and has issue,

1. Sheila (Eileen) de Courcy.
2. Geraldine Fitzgerald.

Lineage.—M'CARTY, of Carrignavar, is the chief of his name, and representative of the oldest existing branch of the once sovereign House of M'Carty. The first who bore the appellative of M'Carty, or son of CATAGH, was the grandfather of DIARMOD M'CARTY MORE, whom the English found in possession of Cork, and who swore fealty, gave hostages, and subjected his kingdom to HENRY II. Diarmod was slain by Theobald Butler, founder of the House of Ormonde, in 1186. His successors were DONALD, CORMAC FIGUN, DONALD RUB, DONALD OGE, and CORMAC, all of whom were distinguished as M'CARTY MORE (or GREAT), an adjunct continued in this senior branch until 1556, when DONALD M'CARTY MORE, the 7th in descent from the eldest son of the last mentioned Cormac, was created Earl of CLANCARE, in Kerry, on resigning his estates to Queen ELIZABETH, from whom he again received the investiture of them," "to hold of the Crown of England in the English manner." This stock of the M'Carty More is extinct for more than a century; but the above Cormac More had a 2nd son, DERMOD, 1st Chief of Muskerry, and founder of that potent house, who was killed by the O Mahonys, 1367. From him sprung in succession, as Chiefs of Muskerry, TEIGE-CORMAC, d. 1374; TEIGE, 1448; CORMAC LAIDHIR (the Stout), 1494; CORMAC OGE LAIDHIR, who defeated the Earl of Desmond at the battle of Morne Abbey 1521, and d. 1536; TEIGE, d. 1565; DERMOD, d. 1570. His son,
CORMAC, of Muskerry, had his residence at the Castle of Blarney, and d. 1616, leaving two sons,
1. CORMAC OGE, of Muskerry, created VISCOUNT MUSKERRY 15 Nov. 1628. He d. in London 1640, leaving (with a dau. Elena, wife of John Power, ancestor of Frances Power, wife of Richard French, of Garbally) a son,
DONOGH, 1st Earl of CLANCARTY, whose male line is extinct.
2. DONALD, or DANIEL.
The 2nd son of Cormac,
DONALD, or DANIEL M'CARTY, built the Castle of Carrignavar, His son, by Katherine his wife, a dau. of Stephen Meade,
CHARLES (CORMAC) M'CARTY, of Carrignavar, m. Catherine, dau. of David Roche, 7th Viscount Fermoy, and was s. at his decease by (the son of his son Daniel and Elizabeth Matthews his wife) his grandson,
CHARLES M'CARTY, of Carrignavar, m. Lucy, dau. of Morgan Kavanagh, of Borris, but dying without issue 1761, he was s. by his nephew,
DANIEL M'CARTY of Carrignavar (son of Daniel M'Carty and Grace Fitzgerald his wife), m. 1751, Elizabeth Geraldina, dau. of Gerald, 24th Lord Kingsale, and had issue,
1. JUSTIN, d.s.p. 1775.
2. ROBERT, s. to his brother.
1. Elizabeth, m. Maurice Uniacke Atkin, of co. Cork.
Mr. M'Carty d. 1763. His 2nd son,
ROBERT M'CARTY, of Carrignavar, m. 1784, Jane, dau. of Joseph Capel, of Cloghroe, and had issue,
1. JUSTIN, his heir. 2. Joseph, d. unm. 1821.
1. Elizabeth, m. 24 Aug. 1811, Joseph Deane Freeman, of Castlecor, co. Cork (see DEANE, late of Glendaragh).
Mr. M'Carty d. 1823. His son,
JUSTIN M'CARTY, of Carrignavar, J.P., b. 19 March, 1786; m. 29 May, 1810, Isabella, dau. of Caleb Falkiner, eldest son of Sir Riggs Falkiner, 1st bart., by whom he had surviving issue,

I.L.G.

1. Robert, b. 14 April, 1811; m. Elizabeth, dau. of John Hyde, of Castle Hyde, co. Cork, and d. 1867, having had issue,
1. Justin, d. unm. 22 May, 1898.
2. Charles, d. unm. 1877.
1. Bessy, m. Capt. Horace Townsend. 2. Florence.
3. Geraldine. 4. Marie. 5. Ellioner.
2. JUSTIN, late of Carrignavar.
3. Frederick Caleb, M.D., m. 1st, 1845, Frances Anne, dau. of John Samuel Beamish, of Mount Beamish; and 2ndly, Jane, dau. of George O'Driscoll, and left by the latter one dau.,
Isabella de Courcy.
4. Joseph (Rev.), Vicar of Wilton, co. York, late in the H.E.I Co.'s Military Service, m. Mary Frances, dau. of the Ven. William Thompson, Archdeacon of Cork. She d. his widow 8 Sept. 1910. He left issue,
1. Charles Falkiner, I.C.S., Private Sec. to Lord Wenlock, Governor of Madras, b. 1848, d.s.p. 1900.
2. Joseph Fitzgerald, Lieut. 1st Batt. Durham L.I., d. unm. 1886.
3. Gerald de Courcy, of Shrub Hill, co. Surrey, late Capt. 4th Batt. Princess of Wales' Own Yorkshire Regt., b. April, 1867; m. 20 Oct. 1890, Irma, Countess Zichy, only dau. of Count Ernest Zichy, of Ferind a, Hungary, and left issue,
Douglas Marie Geraldine, b. 12 Aug. 1891.
1. Mary.
2. Ella Farquhar, m. Rev. Henry Wilson, and has issue.
3. Bessie Ross, m. Major S. C. Peile, Inspector-Gen. of Police, Burmah, and has issue.
4. Flora Theodosia.
5. Anna Justina.
1. Lydia, m. Lowther Forrest, H.E.I.C.S., and is dec.
2. Jane, m. 1st, Rev. Horace Townsend; and 2ndly, 1845, William Burton Leslie, of Court Macsherry, co. Cork, and is dec.
3. Isabella, m. Alexander Ross, H.E.I.C.S., and has issue.
4. Elizabeth, dec.
5. Mary Geraldine, m. 1st, Thomas Charles Morton, Barrister-at-Law; and 2ndly, 2 Jan. 1848, William Brownrigg Elliot, grandson of Gilbert, 1st Baron Minto, and d. 22 June, 1904. He d. 14 July, 1900, leaving issue (see BURKE's Peerage, MINTO, E.).
6. Rose, m. George Pakenham, and is dec.
7. Ellinor.
He d. 1861. His second son,
JUSTIN MacCARTIE, of Carrignavar, co. Cork, J.P., Barrister-at-Law, b. 24 March, 1815; m. 18 Jan. 1848, Louisa, dau. of Edward Fitzgerald, Major H.E.I.C.S., and d. 20 Feb. 1900, having had issue,
1. Gerald Falkiner, B.A. Trin. Coll. Dublin, Barrister-at-Law, b. 1848; d.s.p. 17 Nov. 1890.
2. FREDERICK FITZGERALD, now of Carrignavar.
3. Robert Capel, b. 20 Sept. 1856.
4. Justin Charles, b. 4 Feb. 1860; m. 1883, Lilian, dau. of J. Boyd, and has issue,
Lilian.
1. Isabella, m. 9 March, 1885, A. P. Gould.
Arms—Arg., a stag trippant gu., attired and unguled or. Crest—A dexter arm couped above the elbow erect, in chain mail cuffed arg., and hand holding up a lizard, all ppr. Motto—Forti et fideli nibil difficile.

Seat—Carrignavar, co. Cork.

McCAUSLAND OF DRENAGH.

MAURICE MARCUS McCAUSLAND, of Drenagh, co. Londonderry, J.P. and D.L., High Sheriff 1908, b. 9 April, 1872; m. 9 April, 1902, Eileen Leslie, 2nd dau. of the late Robert Alexander Ogilby, D.L. of Pellipar House (see that family), and has issue,

1. CONOLLY ROBERT, b. 11 July, 1906.
1. Helen Laura, b. 6 April, 1903.
2. Eileen Mary, b. 29 Jan. 1910.

Lineage. — ANDREW MACAUSLANE was grand father of
COL. ROBERT McCAUSLAND, of Fruit Hill, near Newtownlimavady, styled his "cousin" in the will of Capt. Oliver McCausland, of Strabane, of which he was left executor and also a legatee. He had estates in the parish of Cappagh, co. Tyrone, and s. under the will of the Right Hon. William Conolly to considerable property in co. Derry. He m. July, 1709, Hannah, dau.

2 E

of William Moore, of Garvey, and relict of James Hamilton, jun., of Strabane, and by her left surviving issue, at his death, circa 1734,
1. CONOLLY, his heir.
2. Marcus, of Daisy Hill (Newtownlimavady), b. 7 Oct. 1717; m. a dau. of Dominick Heyland, and had issue, with others,
  1. Robert, of Coleraine, m. May, 1767, Miss Smith.
  2. Conolly, of Daisy Hill, and subsequently of Learmount.
  3. Dominick, of Daisy Hill, m. Jan. 1769, Mary, co-heir of Archdeacon Benjamin Bacon, of Glebe Hall, and had issue,
    (1) Robert, who assumed the name of BACON, and d.s.p.
    (2) Marcus Langford, m. a dau. of John Kennedy, of Cultra, (see that family), and had issue,
      1. Marcus (Rev.), Rector of Birr, King's Co., b. 27 Jan. 1802; m. 24 Aug. 1832, Fanny Georgina, dau. of the Hon. and Right Rev. Edmund Knox, Bishop of Killaloe, and d. 1881, having by her (who d. 31 Dec. 1894) had issue,
        a. Marcus Langford, Col. late 11th Foot, b. 14 Aug. 1834.
        b. Edmund Bacon, b. 21 Aug. 1836; m. 1865, Mary Emma Gunn, and has issue,
          (a) Marcus, b. 1866.
          (b) Langford, b. 1867.
          (c) John.
          (d) Percy.
          (e) William.
        c. William Henry, Col. late Queen's Own Cameron Highlanders, b. 11 Aug. 1838; m. 4 Jan. 1893, Edith Mary Adelaide, dau. of the late Rev. James Gram Biine, Rector of Lower Harcres, Kent (see BURKE'S Family Records). He d. 30 Dec. 1905, leaving issue,
          (a) Eileen Maud, b. 27 Dec. 1893.
          (b) Mary Cares', b. 21 July, 1895.
        d. John Kennedy, Major, late A.P.D., late Capt. King's Own Borderers, b. 26 May, 1846.
        e. Francis Harry Ernest, d. young.
        f. Charles Knox, twin, d. young.
        a. Charlotte Ann, m. Thomas Woods, M.D., of Birr, King's Co., and has issue. She d. 1 March, 1894. He d. 5 Jan. 1905.
        b. Maria Caroline; m. 1868, Walter Melville Derwent Wright, Capt. Madras Artillery, and has issue.
        c. Jessy Elizabeth, dec.
      2. John Kennedy, C.B., Lieut.-Gen. H.E.I.C.; b. 1 June, 1803.
      3. Dominick, Q.C., LL.D., b. 20 Aug. 1806; m. Emily Panter, and d. 1873, leaving issue,
        a. Marcus Francis Henry, Col. R.A., b. 26 Feb. 1839; m. 1st, Laura, dau. of Col. Hugh Mitchell, and by her (who d. 1875) had issue,
          (a) Cecil Frank, Capt. 3rd Batt. Essex Regt., b. 1872. He m. 2ndly, Julia Ann, dau. of — Eckley, of Credenhall Park, Herefordshire, and by her (who d. 9 Jan. 1904) had issue,
          (b) Dominick Eckley, M.A. Oxford, b. 1879.
          (c) Marcus Eckley, Lieut. R.E., b. 3 Jan. 1881.
          (a) Elizabeth Eckley, m. Capt. Richard Waring, and has issue (see WARING of Waringstown).
        b. Dominick Downes, b. 1845; m. Agnes Falkner, and d. 1887, leaving a dau.,
          Muriel, m. Maj. Swan.
        c. Ernest John (Rev.), Rector of Drayton, Beauchamp, Bucks, b. 1847, d. 1887.
        a. Emily Sarah, b. 1842.
      4. William Henry (Rev.), b. 5 Nov. 1808.
        1. Elizabeth, d. young.
    (1) Mary, m. 1799, Lieut.-Col. Knox, of Prehen, M.P. for Donegal, and had issue (see that family).
    (2) Letitia, m. 1802, Rev. John Hill, and was mother of the late Sir George Hill, Bart. of St. Columb.
    (3) Anne, m. 1807, Rev. John Olphert, of Ballyconnell.
3. Frederick, of Streeve Hill, m. 1st, Rachael Hillhouse, and had, with others, ABRAHAM, of Culmore, and CONOLLY, of Streeve. Mr. McCausland m. 2ndly, Jane Cochrane, relict of John Anderson, of Londonderry, by whom he had two daus., Sarah, m. Pitt Skipton, and Jane, m. James Anderson. His will, dated 18 Nov. 1763, was proved 23 Jan. 1784. His 3rd son,
CONOLLY McCAUSLAND, of Streeve Hill, co. Derry, m. Sarah, dau. of Marcus McCausland, of Daisy Hill, and d. 26 March, 1796, having by her (who d. 28 Dec. 1821) had issue,
  (1) FREDERICK, of Bessbrook, co. Derry, m. 21 Jan. 1814, Theodosia, dau. of John Stirling, of Walworth, co. Derry, and had issue,
    1. CONOLLY, Major-Gen. late R.E., b. 22 Jan. 1815; m. 14 Aug. 1855.
    2. John Stirling, b. 23 May, 1818; d. 24 Dec. 1844.
    3. Abraham, b. 28 Jan. 1829; d. 12 July, 1847.
  (2) Robert, m. Matilda, widow of Thomas Dallas.
  (3) Marcus, d. Sept. 1822.
  (1) Elizabeth, m. Hugh Boyle.
  (2) Rachel, m. Marcus Gage.
  (3) Sarah, m. Rev. Thomas Twigge.
  (4) Mary.
1. Sarah, b. 2 June, 1710; m. William Smith.
2. Rebecca, b. 4 Aug. 1711; m. 4 Dec. 1726, John McClintock, of Dunmore.
3. Hannah, b. 25 Dec. 1712; m. 1739, James Stirling, of Walworth, co. Derry.

The eldest son,
CONOLLY McCAUSLAND, of Fruit Hill, b. 21 Nov. 1713; m. 10 Feb. 1742, Elizabeth, dau. of Thomas Gage, of Magilligan, and eventually sole heir to her brother Hodson Gage, of Bellarena, and d. 27 June, 1794, aged 80, leaving issue,
1. CONOLLY, his heir.
2. Marcus, b. 28 Aug. 1755; s. under the will of his mother to the Bellarena estates, and assumed the name of GAGE. He m. Julia Stirling, and d. leaving issue,
  1. Conolly Gage, of Bellarena, D.L., m. 1827, Henrietta, dau. of Thomas Tyndall, and d. 1843, leaving an only dau. and heir,
    MARIANNE, m. 1851, Sir F. W. Heygate, Bart., M.P. for co. Derry, and has issue.
  2. James, d. unm.
  3. Hudson, d. unm.
  4. Marcus, of Streeve Hill, m. Rachel, dau. of Conolly McCausland, of Streeke Hill. He d. 1856, leaving an eldest son and heir,
    MARCUS GAGE, of Ballynacree House, co. Antrim, J.P., m. 1854, Harriet, dau. of William Lenox Conyngham, of Spring Hill, co. Londonderry.
  5. Robert (Rev.), Rector of Desertoghill, m. Ann, dau. of the Rev. John Olphert, and had, with other issue, a son,
    MARK GAGE, of Ballynahinch, co. Down, J.P.
  6. William Charles, of Drummond, co. Londonderry, J.P., m. 1838, Mary, dau. of Rev. John Olphert, and has issue.
  1. Julia, m. 1826, Sir Hugh Stewart, Bart.
1. Hannah, b. 3 Oct. 1751; m. 11 Nov. 1778, William Lecky, M.P. for Derry, and d. 1826, leaving issue.
2. Elizabeth, b. 16 April, 1753; m. 1776, Thomas Skipton, of Beech Hill, otherwise Skipton Hall, and d.s.p. 1800.
3. Sarah, b. 27 Jan. 1759; m. 1777, George C. Kennedy, who, on succeeding to the Skipton Hall estate at his cousin's death, assumed the name of SKIPTON. She d. 1823, leaving issue.
4. Sydney, b. 25 March, 1760; d. young.

The elder son,
CONOLLY McCAUSLAND, of Fruit Hill, b. 3 Aug. 1754; m. 15 Jan. 1778, Theodosia, sister to Maurice, Lord Hartland, and dau. of Thomas Mahon, of Strokestown House, by Jane, dau. of Maurice, Lord Brandon, and by her (who d. 3 May, 1822) had issue,
1. MARCUS, his heir.
2. Conolly Robert, Lieut. R.H.A., b. 5 Nov. 1789; d. at Poonah, 17 Aug. 1817.
3. Frederick Hervey, b. 18 Dec. 1793; d. 17 Nov. 1817.
1. Jane, m. Rev. Gustavus Hamilton, Rector of Drumachose, co. Derry, and nephew of the Right Hon. Sackville Hamilton, and had issue.
2. Elizabeth, m. J. Ross, of the Lodge, Newtownlimavady; d.s.p.
3. Eleanor, d. unm. 12 Dec. 1818.
4. Theodosia, m. Charles, son of Thomas Tyndall, of The Fort, and d. 1825, leaving issue.

Mr. McCausland, who had assumed the name of GAGE, in 1816, d. 1827, aged 72, and was s. by his eldest surviving son,
MARCUS McCAUSLAND, of Fruit Hill, D.L. co. Derry, b. 24 April, 1787; m. 5 Sept. 1815, Marianne, dau. of Thomas Tyndall, of The Fort, near Bristol, and by her (who d. 22 Aug. 1864) had issue,
  1. CONOLLY THOMAS, late of Drenagh (Fruit Hill).
  1. Marianne, m. 2 Jan. 1845, John Talbot, D.L., of Mount Talbot, and had an only child, Mary Annie Jane Theodosia, m. 21 Oct. 1869, Arthur Rickard Lloyd, of Beechmount (see that family).
  2. Theodosia Sydney, m. 16 April, 1846, Edward Senior.
  3. Henrietta Caroline, m. 16 Aug. 1849, Edwin Henry Vaughan, and d. 24 July, 1897.
  4. Katherine Geraldine, m. 17 April, 1850, Thomas Tertius Paget, and d. 5 April, 1869.
  5. Eleanor Georgiana, m. 15 Sept. 1851, George Bright, and d. in India, 4 Sept. 1852.
  6. Julia, d. Oct. 1825.
  7. Georgiana, d. 14 Aug. 1836.
  8. Adelaide, m. 5 Aug. 1866, Oliver Claude Pell.

Mr. McCausland d. 18 Jan. 1862, and was s. by his only son,
CONOLLY THOMAS McCAUSLAND, of Drenagh, co. Londonderry, J.P. and D.L., High Sheriff 1866, late Capt. Derry Militia, b. 13 May, 1828; m. 8 June, 1867, Hon. Laura St. John, 2nd dau. of St. Andrew, 14th Baron St. John of Bletsoe. He d. 25 June, 1902, leaving issue,
  1. MAURICE MARCUS, now of Drenagh.
  2. Patrick, late Capt. 1st Batt. Leinster Regt. b. 18 June, 1874.
  3. Edmund Thomas William, Lieut. 3rd Queen Alexandra's Own Gurkha Rifles, b. 11 Dec. 1883.
  1. Eleanor Marianna Katharine, m. 19 July, 1907, Ralph Hackett, son of Col. Hackett, of Brooklawn, Chapelizod, Dublin.
  2. Lucia, m. 4 Jan. 1899, Rev. Reginald Gibbs, Vicar of Clifton Hampden, Berks, son of Rev. John Lomax Gibbs, of Speen House, Newbury (see BURKE'S Peerage, ALDENHAM, B.).
  3. Geraldine, m. 10 Oct. 1910, Henry Burroughes Ford, 31st Punjabis, Indian Army, son of the late Capt. Charles Wilbraham Ford, Bengal Army.
  4. Julia Sydney, m. 8 Oct. 1902, Richard Ashmur Blair Young, Capt. Royal Inniskilling Fus., of Coolkeiragh, Londonderry, and has issue (see that family).
  5. Lettice Theodosia.
  6. Emily Octavia.

Arms—Or, a boar's head erased between three boars passant az. **Crest**—A boar's head erased az. armed or, langued gu. and charged with a crescent of the second. **Motto**—Virtus sola nobilitat.
Seat—Drenagh (formerly Fruit Hill), Limavady, co. Londonderry. **Club**—New Oxford and Cambridge, W.

IRELAND. McClintock.

McCAUSLAND OF DRIMBAWN.

CAPT. EDWARD OLIVER McCAUSLAND, of Drimbawn, co. Mayo, J.P. cos. Galway and Mayo, late Capt. 16th Lancers, *b.* 19 June, 1851.

Lineage.—ALEXANDER M'AUSLANE (grandson of M'Auslane, of Glendouglas, on the shores of Lock Lomond, Dumbartonshire, in Scotland, who migrated to Ireland *temp.* JAMES I), served in the Army in Ireland before 1649 and settled in Tyrone, when he possessed the Manors of Ardsrath, Mountfield, etc. He *m.* Genet, dau. of Edward Hall, of New Grange, co. Meath, and *d.* 1675. His elder son,

OLIVER M'AUSLANE, M.P. for Strabane, and High Sheriff co. Tyrone, 1687, *m.* Jane, dau. of James Hamilton, and had a son,

OLIVER McCAUSLAND, who possessed large estates in co. Donegal, and *d.* 1722, leaving an eldest son,

JOHN McCAUSLAND, of Strabane, and the Manors of Stranorlar and Castlefin, M.P. for Strabane 1725-7, *m.* Amy Jane, dau. of Thomas Norris, and *d.* 1728, having had issue,
1. OLIVER, his heir.
2. Rebecca, *m.* Rev. John Hamilton.
3. Mary, *m.* Dr. Moore, of Londonderry.

The only son,

OLIVER McCAUSLAND, of Strabane. M.P. for Strabane 1729-31, *m.* Anne Jane, dau. of William Hamilton, of Waterhouse, and *d.* 1756, having had issue,
1. JOHN, his heir.
2. Oliver, *m.* Jane, dau. of William Murray, of Mount Murray, co. Meath, and had a son, who *d.s.p.*, and five daus.
   1. Margaret.
   2. Alice, *m.* Gen. Charles Eustace.
   3 Anne Jane, *m.* Edward Shaw, of Coolcor, co. Kildare.

The elder son,

JOHN McCAUSLAND, of Strabane, M.P. for co. Donegal, *m.* 12 Feb. 1757, Elizabeth, dau. of Rev. William Span, of Ballinacove, and *d.* Nov. 1804, having had issue,
1. Oliver (Rev.), Rector of Finlagan, co. Londonderry, *b.* 6 Nov. 1747; *m.* 1785, Hannah, dau. of Redmond Conyngham, of Letterkenny, co. Donegal. She *d.* 1846. He *d.* 1 Sept. 1846, leaving issue.
2. WILLIAM JAMES, of whom presently.
1. Catherine, *m.* 1791, William Conyngham, 1st Lord Plunkett, Lord Chancellor of Ireland. She *d.* 14 March, 1821. He *d.* 5 Jan. 1854, leaving issue.

The second son,

WILLIAM JAMES McCAUSLAND, of Morville, co. Dublin, and 27, Fitzwilliam Square, Dublin, *m.* Susan, dau. of Rev. J. Waters, and had issue a son,

SIR RICHARD BOLTON McCAUSLAND, of Drimbawn, Ballinrobe, co. Mayo, and 61, Fitzwilliam Square, Dublin, Recorder of Singapore, 1856-66, and afterwards Clerk of Custodes in Lunacy in Ireland, Barrister-at-Law, M.A. Trin. Coll. Dublin, *b.* 1810; *m.* 1841, Fanny Mary (*d.* 19 Jan. 1906), eldest dau. of Edward Netterville Blake, D.L., of Castlegrove, co. Galway, and *d.* 8 June, 1900, having had issue,
1. EDWARD OLIVER, now of Drimbawn.
2. Richard Bolton, F.R.C.S.I. (79, *Merrion Square, Dublin*), *b.* 1865; *m.* 1897, Charlotte, only child of the late Professor Charles E. Browne Séquard, of Paris, and has issue,
   Charles Edward, *b.* 4 Oct. 1898.
1. Annie, *m.* Col. C. E. Souper.
2. Susan, *m.* Robert McDonnell, F.R.S.
3. Fanny, *m.* Richard Waller, Ind. C.S., and has issue.
4. Louisa.   5. Kathleen, *d. unm.* 29 May, 1902.

Seat—Drimbawn, Ballinrobe, co. Mayo. *Town Residence*—61, Fitzwilliam Square, Dublin. *Clubs*—Army and Navy, and Kildare Street.

McCLINTOCK OF RATHVINDEN.

ARTHUR GEORGE FLORENCE McCLINTOCK, of Rathvinden, co. Carlow, J.P. cos. Wicklow, Kildare, Down, and King's Co., D.L. Carlow, late Lieut. 26th Cameronians, *b.* 16 April, 1856; *m.* 3 July, 1877, Susan, 3rd dau. of Joshua Heywood-Collins, J.P. of Kelvindale, co. Lanark, and Lagarie, co. Dumbarton, and has issue,

1. ARTHUR GEORGE, Capt. 5th Royal Irish Lancers, *b.* 30 April, 1878; *m.* 1908, Millicent, only dau. of James Alexander Toomey, and has issue,
   Elizabeth Dawn.
2. John Heywood Jocelyn, late Lieut. 18th Hussars (*Mahons-town House, Kells, co. Meath*), *b.* 21 Oct. 1880; *m.* 6 Dec. 1904, Mary Catherine, only dau. of Col. H. Torkington of Willey Park, Farnham, and has issue,

1. John William Jocelyn, *b.* 5 Dec. 1905.
1. A dau., *b.* 12 Nov. 1911.
3. Robert Le Poer, Lieut. Gordon Highlanders, *b.* 19 Aug. 1882.
4. Edward Stanley, *b.* 7 Oct. 1889.
5. Ronald St. Clair, *b.* 13 July, 1892.
1. Jane Catherine Gladys.

Lineage.—ALEXANDER McCLINTOCK, of Trinta, co. Donegal, (only son of Alexander McClintock, who came from Argyllshire and purchased in 1597 the estates in Donegal) *m.* 1648, Agnes Stenson, dau. of Donald Maclean. She *d.* 6 Dec. 1696. He *d.* 6 Sept. 1670, leaving issue,
1. JOHN, his heir.
2. WILLIAM, ancestor of McCLINTOCK *of Dunmore* (see that family).

The elder son,

JOHN McCLINTOCK, of Trinta, *b.* 1649; *m.* 11 Aug. 1687, Jenet, 4th dau. of John Lowry, of Ahenis, co. Tyrone, and *d.* 3 Sept. 1707, leaving issue,
1. John, *b.* 1 Feb. 1689; *d.* young.
2. Alexander, of Drumcar, co. Louth, *b.* 30 Sept. 1692; *m.* Rebecca, dau. of William Sampson, of Dublin, and *d.s.p.* 25 May, 1775.
3. JOHN, of whom presently.
4. Robert, *b.* 27 Oct. 1702; *m.* Helen, dau. of William Harvey, and had issue.

The third son,

JOHN McCLINTOCK, of Trinta, *b.* 27 March, 1698; *m.* Susannah Maria, 2nd dau. of William Chambers, of Rock Hall, co. Donegal, and had issue,
1. William, *m.* Francelina, 3rd dau. of James Nesbitt, of Green Hills, and had issue.
2. James, of Trinta, *b.* 17 Aug. 1739; *m.* 1762, Dorothea Beresford, only dau. and heiress of Henry McCullagh, of Ballyarten, co. Derry, and had issue.
3. JOHN, *s.* his uncle at Drumcar.
4. ALEXANDER, of Newtown, co. Louth, ancestor of the family of McClintock of Seskinore (*see that family*).
1. Francelina, *m.* William Keyes, of Cavancor, co. Donegal.
2. Rebecca, *m.* L. O'Hara, of Brookfield, co. Donegal.
3. Catherine, *m.* 1st, James Nesbitt, and 2ndly, Benjamin Fenton.
4. Anne, *m.* April, 1766, Rev. John Young, and had issue (*see* BURKE's *Peerage*, YOUNG, Bart.).

The third son,

JOHN McCLINTOCK, of Drumcar, co. Louth, M.P. for Enniskillen, 1783-90, and for Belturbet, 1790-7, *b.* 1 Jan. 1742; *m.* 11 May, 1766, Patience, dau. of William Foster, of Rosy Park, M.P. (*see* BURKE's *Peerage*, FOSTER, Bart.), and *d.* Feb. 1799, having had issue,
1. JOHN, his heir.
2. Alexander (Rev.), Rector of Newtown Barry, co. Wexford, *b.* 6 Jan. 1775; *m.* 1790, Anne, dau. of Mervyn Pratt. He *d.* 6 Aug. 1836, having had issue,
   1. Henry Fitzalan (Rev.), M.A., rector of Macloneigh and Kilmichael, diocese of Cork; *d. unm.* Oct. 1879.
   2. Lowry Cole (Rev.), M.A., rector of The Neale, and prebendary of Kilmeen, diocese of Tuam; *d. unm.* 2 April, 1876.
   3. Alexander Edward, *m.* 17 June, 1862, Mary Selina, dau. of Major Edward Cottingham, late 28th Regt., J.P., inspector-gen. of Prisons in Ireland, and has one son,
      William Maxwell, late Capt. 6th batt. Royal Irish Rifles, *b.* 16 July, 1868; *d.s.p.* 1898.
   1. Annette, *d. unm.* 24 Oct. 1899, in her 100th year.
   2. Frances Hester, *d. unm.* Oct. 1881.
   3. Louisa, *d. unm.* June, 1882.
   4. Elizabeth Cholmondeley, *m.* in 1846, Edward Beaufort, son of the Rev. William Lewis Beaufort, LL.D., and has issue.
   5. Lucy Hester, *d. unm.* May, 1891.
   6. Hester, *m.* 11 Feb. 1840, Walter Hussey de Burgh, D.L. of Donore House, co. Kildare, and Dromkeen House, co. Limerick, and *d.* 27 June, 1858. He *d.* 19 Oct. 1862, leaving issue (*see that family*).
3. William Foster, *b.* 18 Oct. 1777; *m.* in 1803, Mary, dau. of Major-General Helden, and *d.* in 1838, having had issue,
   1. William Charles Helden Foster, *d. unm.* Jan. 1890.
   2. Richard, *m.* Maria, dau. of Capt. James Watson Boys, 64th Regt., and has issue,
      (1) Charles Claude Cope, *b.* 18 Jan. 1866.
      (1) Charlotte Maud Mary Louisa.
      (2) Bessie Anne.
      (3) Ethel Mary Dagmar.
   3. John Augustus, *m.* Ellen, dau. of Stewart Crawford, M.D., of Bath. She *d.* 25 Aug. 1879.
   4. Walter, *m.* 5 Dec. 1864, Frances Delia Sophia, eldest dau. of Arthur Wilcox Manning, and niece of Sir William Montagu Manning, K.C.M.G., Judge of the Supreme Court of New South Wales, and has issue,
      (1) Arthur Walter William Foster, *b.* 25 Oct. 1865.
      (2) John Leopold Bunbury, *b.* 9 April, 1871.
      (3) George Augustus Helden, *b.* 21 April, 1878.
      (1) Frances Mary Ellen.
      (2) Maud Harriett.
   1. Henrietta, *m.* Cope Garnett, J.P., of Green Park, co. Meath, and *d.s.p.*
   2. Sarah, *d. unm.*   3. Mary.
   4. Catherine.   5. Frances, *d. unm.*
4. Henry, 3rd Dragoon Guards, *b.* 28 Sept. 1783; *m.* Dec. 1809, Elizabeth Melesina, dau. of Ven. George Fleury, D.D., Archdeacon of Waterford. She *d.* 29 Jan. 1853. He *d.* 27 Feb. 1843, having had issue,
   1. Francis Leopold (Sir), Admiral, K.C.B., F.R.S., LL.D.

McClintock. THE LANDED GENTRY. 436

D.C.L., Hon. Freeman of the City of London, A.D.C. to Queen Victoria 1868-71, Admiral Superintendent Portsmouth Dockyard 1872-7, Comm.-in-Chief on North American and West Indian Stations 1879-82, an elder brother of Trinity House, a distinguished Arctic navigator; knighted, 1860, for his services in discovering the fate of the Franklin Expedition, *b.* 8 July, 1819; *m.* 12 Oct. 1870, Annette Elizabeth, 2nd dau. of R. Foster Dunlop, of Monasterboice House, co. Louth, by Anna, his wife, sister of 10th Viscount Massereene and Ferrard, and *d.* 17 Nov. 1907, having had issue,
 (1) Henry Foster, B.A. Oxon., Capt. 24th Middlesex R.V., *b.* 11 Aug. 1871.
 (2) John William Leopold, Commander R.N., *b.* 26 July, 1874.
 (3) Robert Singleton, Brevet-Major R.E., *b.* 26 July, 1876; *m.* 15 July, 1909, Mary Howard, youngest dau. of late Gen. Sir Howard Cranford Elphinstone, V.C., K.C.B.
 (1) Anna Elizabeth, *b.* 3 June, 1873; *m.* 19 Nov. 1902, Bernard Eyre Greenwell, eldest son of Sir Walpole Greenwell, Bart. (see BURKE's *Peerage*), of Marden Park, Surrey (*see that family*).
 (2) Elizabeth Florence Mary, *b.* 18 Aug. 1882.
2. Alfred Henry, M.D., LL.D., *b.* 21 Oct. 1821; *m.* 2 May, 1848, Fanny, dau. of John Loftus Cuppaidge, and *d.* 21 Oct. 1881, leaving issue,
 (1) Leopold Alfred, Maj. late R.A., *b.* 7 Sept. 1853; *m.* 1 March, 1881, Jane Bunbury, dau. of Rev. J. Lewis Moore, D.D., Vice-Provost Trin. Coll. Dublin, and has issue,
  1. Patience.   2. Jane.
 (2) Frederic Foster, M.A., *b.* 27 March, 1859.
 (1) Florence, *d. unm.*
 (2) Elizabeth Catherine, *m.* 14 Aug. 1872, Capt. Charles James Maxwell Lefroy, of Itchell Manor, Hants, late 14th Hussars, and has issue. He *d.* 7 Nov. 1908 (*see* LEFROY *of Carrig-glas*)
 (3) Frances Edith, *m.* — Wilson, M.D., of Harrismith, S. Africa.
 (4) Caroline Frances, *m.* 30 Oct. 1891, Capt. Sir William Longfield Brady, 4th Bart. (*see* BURKE's *Peerage*, BRADY, Bart.).
3. Theodore Ernest, lieut.-col. in the army, *b.* 9 March, 1829; *m.* 5 Nov. 1863, Anna Maria, dau. of George Carmino Holden, of H.M. Ordnance Department, and had issue,
 (1) Frederic William, *b.* 10 Aug. 1864; *m.*, and has issue.
 (2) Edgar Stanley Victor, *b.* 18 Sept. 1865; *m.* 19 April, 1898, Augusta Julia dau. of H. L. Inskip.
 (1) Agnes Laura.
4. Charles Fortescue, R.I. Constabulary, *b.* 13 June, 1836; *d.* 1907.
1. Isabella Marion, *b.* 1812; *m.* 1st, 14 Sept. 1838, T. Shallcross Battersby (who *d.* 17 March, 1847), and 2ndly, 11 Oct. 1848, E. Spencer Dix, M.A., J.P., Barrister-at-Law who *d.* 14 Jan. 1876.
2. Anne Louisa, *m.* 1832, F. Hall Tipping (who *d.* 1874), 2nd son of Edward Tipping, of Bellurgan Park, co. Louth.
3. Emily Caroline, *m.* 1st, 24 Jan. 1840, Capt. Charles Henry Paget, R.N. (who *d.* 26 May, 1845, leaving issue), eldest son of Vice-Admiral the Hon. Sir Charles Paget, G.C.B. (*see* BURKE's *Peerage*, ANGLESEY, M.). She *m.* 2ndly, 19 July, 1848, Lieut.-Col. J. B. Gardiner, late 17th Regt.
4. Rosa Melisina, *d.* 25 June, 1911, having *m.* B. Willis Richardson, and has issue.
5. Florence Gertrude, *m.* 1849, George Alloway, M.D., and had issue.
6. Emma Patience, *m.* 19 Nov. 1854, H. Torrens Dix, and has issue.
7. Emily Anna Foster, *m.* 1857, G. Crozier, M.A., who *d.* 1874.
1. Mary Anne, *m.* 1 Jan. 1787, Mathew Fortescue, of Stephenstown House, co. Louth, and had issue.
2. Elizabeth, *m.* 31 Dec. 1801, Lieut.-Col. Henry Le Blanc.
3. Rebecca, *m.* 1799, Edward Hardman, eldest son of Edward Hardman, M.P.
4. Fanny, *m.* 1798, Theophilus Clive, and had issue.

The eldest son,
 JOHN MCCLINTOCK, of Drumcar, M.P., *b.* 14 Aug. 1770; *m.* 1st, 11 July, 1797, Jane, only dau. of William Bunbury, M.P., of Moyle, co. Carlow, and by her (who *d.* 28 April, 1801) had issue,
 1. JOHN, created BARON RATHDONNELL (*see* BURKE's *Peerage*).
 2. William Bunbury MCCLINTOCK-BUNBURY, of Lisnavagh, father of 2nd BARON RATHDONNELL (*see* BURKE's *Peerage*).
 1. Catherine, *m.* Rev. George Gardner, Rector of St. Leonards, and *d.* 5 June, 1834.
Mr. John McClintock *m.* 2ndly, 15 April, 1805, Lady Elizabeth Trench, dau. of William, 1st Earl of Clancarty, and by her (who *d.* 30 May, 1877) had issue,
 3. Frederick William Pitt, M.A., Barrister-at-Law, *d. unm.* 1834.
 4. Charles Alexander, Capt. 74th Regt., *d. unm.* 9 Dec. 1833.
 5. Robert Le Poer (Rev.), M.A., Rector of Castle Bellingham, co. Louth, *b.* 10 Aug. 1810; *m.* 29 July, 1856, Maria Susan, only dau. of Charles Alexander Heyland, and *d.s.p.* 30 June, 1879. His widow *m.* 2ndly, 1 Feb. 1883, Francis Burton Owen Cole, D.L., of Llys Merichion, co. Denbigh (*see* COLE *of Stoke Lyne*).
 6. Henry Stanley, of Kilwarlin House, co. Down, J.P. cos. Antrim, Down, and Kildare, late of the Royal Horse Artillery, formerly Major Antrim Artillery, *b.* 1812, *m.* 1839, Gertrude, only dau. of Robert La Touche, M.P., of Harristown, co. Kildare, by Lady Emily his wife, dau. of William, 1st Earl of Clancarty. She *d.* 22 March, 1864. He *d.* 9 Sept. 1898, having had issue,
  1. FREDERICK ROBERT (7, *Ormonde Gate, Chelsea, S.W.*), *b.* 31,

Aug. 1842; *m.* 1 Feb. 1877, Lucy Antonia, younger dau. of Sir Anthony Cleashy, Baron of the Exchequer 1868-79.
 2. Charles Edward, of Glendaragh, co. Antrim, J.P., Lieut.-Col. late 6th Batt. Royal Irish Rifles, *b.* 11 May, 1844; *m.* 2 Aug. 1881, Blanche Louisa, dau. of Robert Foster Dunlop, of Monasterboice, co. Louth, and has issue,
  (1) Stanley Robert, Capt. Gordon Highlanders, *b.* 17 May, 1882.
  (2) William Frederick Charles, *b.* 21 Nov. 1883; *d.* 1908.
  (3) Edward Louis Longford (Rev.), *b.* 21 Feb. 1886.
 3. Francis George Le Poer (Rev.), Rector of Drumcar, and Dean of Armagh, M.A. Camb., *b.* 8 Oct. 1853.
 1. Emily, } twins.
 2. Gertrude,
7. GEORGE AUGUSTUS JOCELYN, of whom presently.
2. Anne Florence, *m.* 21 April, 1828, Very Rev. Hugh Usher Tighe, D.D., Dean of Derry, and had issue (*see* TIGHE *of Mitchelstown*).
3. Harriette Elizabeth, *m.* 1832, Richard Longfield, of Longueville, co. Cork, and *d.* 27 April, 1834, leaving issue (*see that family*).
4. Emily Selina Frances, *m.* 16 Nov. 1841, John Wandesforde, D.L., of Castlecomer, co. Kilkenny (who *d.s.p.* 26 June, 1856). She *d.* 20 Jan. 1909.

Mr. John McClintock *d.* 5 July, 1855. His 7th son,
 LIEUT.-COL. GEORGE AUGUSTUS JOCELYN MCCLINTOCK, of Fellows Hall, co. Armagh, J.P., who served in the 52nd Light Infantry, and was Lieut.-Col. of the Sligo Rifles, *b.* 22 May, 1822; *m.* April, 1850, Catherine Caroline Brownlow, dau. of Sir James Mathew Stronge, Bart., and *d.* 24 Dec. 1873, leaving issue,
 1. ARTHUR GEORGE FLORENCE, now of Rathvinden.
 1. Constance Harriet Catherine, *m.* 16 July, 1881, H. C. Irwin, of Mount Irwin, co. Armagh, and has issue (*see that family*).
 2. Amy Isabella.   3. Isabella.
 4. Mary Alice, *m.* Thomas Lonsdale, and has issue.

Arms—Per pale gu. and az. a chevron erm. between three escallops that in the dexter chief or, that in the sinister chief arg. and that in base per pale of the fourth and last. **Crest**—A lion passant arg. **Motto**—Virtute et labore.
Seat—Rathvinden, Leighlinbridge co. Carlow. **Clubs**—Carlton, Kildare Street.

McCLINTOCK OF HAMPSTEAD HALL.

WILLIAM KERR MCCLINTOCK, of Hampstead Hall, co. Londonderry, Col. commanding 1st Batt. Royal Berkshire Regt., with which he served in Egypt 1882, Soudan 1885 and 1886, S. Africa 1899-1900 (Egyptian medal, two clasps, Khedive's Bronze Star, S. African medal with two clasps), *b.* 10 Oct. 1858; *m.* 15 April, 1895, Edith Mary, dau. of William Rowland Swanston, of Newcastle-on-Tyne, and has issue,
1. William Kerr, *b.* 7 March, 1896.
1. Violet Kerr, *b.* 22 Nov. 1902; *d.* 27 Jan. 1903.
2. Anne Kerr, *b.* 3 Aug. 1904.
3. Margaret Kerr, *b.* 6 Oct. 1908.

Lineage.—JOHN MCCLINTOCK, son of John McClintock, of Hampstead Hall, by Sarah his wife, dau. of James Acheson, *m.* Margaret, dau. of Robert Alexander, merchant of Londonderry. She *d.* 1819. He *d.* 1802, having had issue,
1. WILLIAM KERR, of Hampstead Hall.
2. John.   3. Robert.
4. Hugh, *m.* Mary, dau. of — Hawthorn, of Dublin, but *d.s.p.*
5. James, Capt. 88th Connaught Rangers and Adjutant of the Londonderry Militia.
6. Samuel, of Gransha Lodge, co. Londonderry, *m.* Mary, dau. of Rev. Andrew Cochran, Rector of Lower Fahan, co. Donegal, and had issue,
 1. John Samuel (Rev.), Rector of Clonleigh, co. Donegal, *m.* 1st, Anne, dau. of Col. Benjamin Humphry, of Cavanacor, co. Donegal and 2ndly Elizabeth, dau. of Commander Edward Harvey, R.N., but *d.s.p.*
 2. Acheson.
 1. Mary, *m.* John Atkinson, of Ballynewry House, co. Armagh, and has issue, Ben., Major R.H.A., *m.* Loctitia Janet Emily only dau. of E. K. Norman, J.P., D.L. of Mistley Lodge, Essex (*see* ATKINSON *of Cangort*).
 1. Eliza, *m.* Andrew Beatty, of Londonderry.
 2. Anne, *d. unm.*
 3. Jane.

The eldest son,
WILLIAM KERR MCCLINTOCK, of Hampstead Hall, co. Londonderry, J.P., *b.* 22 Feb. 1788; *m.* June, 1818, Sarah, eldest dau. of William Macky, of Londonderry, and had issue,
1. John Kerr, J.P., *b.* 8 June, 1820, left issue.
2. William Kerr Macky, *b.* 21 July, 1821; *d.* 1857.
3. THOMPSON MACKY, of Hampstead Hall.
4. Kerr, *b.* 21 Sept. 1827, dec.
1. Sarah, *d. unm.*   2. Anne, *d. unm.*
3. Ellen Macky, *d. unm.* 4 Nov. 1908.
4. Louisa, *d. unm.*

The 3rd son,
THOMPSON MACKY MCCLINTOCK, of Hampstead Hall, co. Londonderry, J.P. cos. Donegal and Londonderry, late Capt. 87th Royal

Irish Fus., b. 2, June, 1826; m. 19 June, 1856, Sarah Maria, elder dau. of Rev. John Conyngham McCausland, Rector of Clonmore, Louth, and Sarah Anne his wife, dau. of Edward Elsmere and Sarah de Renzi his wife, of Clobemon Hall and Baltinglass, co. Wexford. He d. 9 April, 1904, having had issue,
1. WILLIAM KERR, now of Hampstead Hall.
2. John Conyngham, of Tiernaleague House, Carndonagh, and St. Helens, Buncrana, co. Donegal, J.P. and D.L., High Sheriff 1902, late Londonderry Royal Field Artillery, Capt. Reserve of Officers (*Northern Counties Club, Londonderry*), b. 15 Sept. 1862; m. 7 March, 1885, Alice, dau. of Eugene Aubry, M.D., of Havre, and has issue,
　1. Dorothy Marie, b. 11 Sept. 1890.
　2. Alice Marie, b. 2 Nov. 1892.
3. Kerr, of the Imperial Light Horse, b. 5 Aug. 1867, killed in action at Elandslaagte S. Africa, 21 Oct. 1899, *unm.*
4. Edward Elsmere, b. 8 Sept. 1871; m. 26 March, 1909, Frances Charlotte, younger dau. of Maurice Charles Hime, LL.D., of Buncrana, and has issue,
　1. Maurice Kerr, b. 12 Feb. 1907.
　1. Stella Mary, b. 18 Feb. 1905.
1. Sarzh Louisa, m. 8 April, 1886, William Parker Halliley, of Carlabeck, Ceylon, and has issue,
　1. Elsmere Hans, b. 4 Jan. 1887.
　2. William Sydney, Lieut. Royal Warwickshire Regt., b. 7 Feb. 1888.
　3. Alan Kerr McClintock, Sub-Lieut. R.N., b. 19 Aug. 1889.
　4. Hubert Claude, b. 10 Sept. 1898.
2. Ada Elsmere, m. 10 April, 1890, James Faulkner, Lieut. 6th Batt. Worcestershire Regt., of Charlton House, Pershore, Worcs., and has issue,
　1. James Elsmere, b. 26 Jan. 1891; d. 14 Feb. 1901.
　2. William Carey, b. 2 Oct. 1895; d. 1907.
　3. Walter Douglas, b. 16 Aug. 1898.
　1. Eleanor Mary.
3. Sydney Maria, m. 3 Oct. 1905, Thomas Hall, Winsley Chambers of Innishowen Lodge, Marton, Yorks, son of Thomas Chambers of Abertoyle, Londonderry.
4. Elizabeth Maude, b. 30 May, 1870; d. Jan. 1874.
Seat—Hampstead Hall, co. Londonderry. *Residence*—Redvers House, Newcastle-on-Tyne. *Clubs*—Army and Navy, Kildare Street.

M'CLINTOCK OF DUNMORE.

COL. WILLIAM M'CLINTOCK, of Dunmore, co. Donegal, J.P., High Sheriff 1903, late Lieut.-Col. R.A., Superintendent R.G.P. Factory, Waltham Abbey 1892-4, b. 16 May, 1841; m. 1st, 15 May, 1873, Elizabeth Esther, dau. of Samuel Lyle, of Oaks Lodge, Londonderry, and by her (who d. 26 March, 1875) has a son,

ROBERT LYLE, D.S.O., Capt. and Brevet-Major R.E., b. 26 March, 1874; m. 11 Nov. 1908, Jennie Margaret, dau. of Sir George Casson-Walker, K.C.S.I., I.C.S.

He m. 2ndly, 27 Aug. 1877, Isabella, 4th dau. of the late George FitzMaurice, R.M.

Lineage.—WILLIAM MCCLINTOCK, of Dunmore, co. Donegal, 2nd son of Alexander McClintock, of Trintagh, by Agnes Stenson Maclean his wife, dau. of Donald Maclean (*see* BURKE's *Peerage*, RATHDONNELL, B.), b. 1657, m. 1685, Elizabeth, only dau. of David Harvey, of Dunmore, co. Donegal (*see* HARVEY *of Mintiaghs*), and d. 1724, leaving issue,
1. JOHN, who s. him in the estate of Dunmore.
1. Mary, m. 30 June, 1708, William Harvey, of Imlick, co. Donegal, and had issue (*see* HARVEY *of Mintiaghs*).
2. Elizabeth, m. Nathaniel Alexander, of Caledon, co. Tyrone, whose youngest son was created Earl of CALEDON (*see* BURKE's *Peerage*).
3. Margaret, m. 1730, William Stinson, of Knockan, co. Derry.
4. Jane, m. John Harvey, of Dunmore, and had issue (*see* HARVEY *of Mintiaghs*).
The son and heir,
JOHN MCCLINTOCK, of Dunmore, held the commissions of Capt. in the Militia of Donegal and Tyrone, bearing date respectively 27 and 30 Dec. 1745, m. 4 Dec. 1728, Rebecca, dau. of Robert McCausland, of Fruit Hill, co. Londonderry, and has issue,
1. ROBERT, his heir.　　2. William, 103rd Regt., d. *unm.*
1. Hannah, m. 1st, Brent Spence, and 2ndly, 17 June, 1762, Sir Hugh Hill, Bart., M.P. of Old Walworth.

2. Lydia, m. Andrew Ferguson, M.P., of Burt House.
3. Elizabeth, m. Rowley Heyland, of Castle Roe.
4. Jane, d. *unm.* 27 Feb. 1802.
The son and heir,
ROBERT MCCLINTOCK, of Dunmore, J.P. of the co. Donegal, and a Capt. in the Militia, of Donegal and Tyrone, High Sheriff of Tyrone 1759, and of Donegal 1764, m. 16 May, 1760, Alice, dau. and heiress of Andrew Patton, of Springfield, co. Donegal, and by her (who d. 14 April, 1820) had issue,
1. John, Capt. 69th Regt. and Donegal Militia, d. *unm.*
2. Andrew, Rector of Kanturk and Newmarket, Diocese of Cork, Cloyne, and Ross, d. *unm.* 1807.
3. WILLIAM, of whom presently.
4. Thomas, b. 1774, d. *unm.* 1845.
1. Alicia Anne, m. W. L. J. Spencer, and d.s.p. He d. 1844.
The 3rd son,
WILLIAM MCCLINTOCK, b. 1773; m. 8 March, 1802, Catherine, dau. and heiress of Benjamin Ramage, of Cloughole, co. Derry. She d. 30 May, 1810. He d. 17 Feb. 1825, having had issue,
1. ROBERT, his heir.　　2. Benjamin, d. *unm.* 1827.
1. Margaret, m. 1840, the Rev. John Gage Ball, Rector of Killea.
The eldest son,
ROBERT MCCLINTOCK, of Dunmore, J.P. cos. Donegal and Londonderry, and D.L. of the co. of Donegal, High Sheriff 1835, b. 13 Dec. 1804; m. 30 Dec. 1833, Margaret, 3rd dau. of Robert Macan, of Ballynahone House, co. Armagh, and by her (who d. 1893) had issue,
1. ROBERT, late of Dunmore.
2. WILLIAM, now of Dunmore.
3. Benjamin, Major late Shropshire Light Infantry, b. 27 Aug. 1843; d. 8 July, 1911.
4. Charles, b. 15 June, 1849, M.D., F.R.C.S.E.; d. *unm.* 27 Oct. 1885.
1. Letitia.
2. Alice, m. 17 April, 1860, John Acheson Smyth, of Ardmore, co. Londonderry. He d. 24 July, 1874, leaving issue.
3. Margaret Elizabeth, m. 20 May, 1862, Holt Waring, of Waringstown, J.P. (*see that family*).
4. Emma, m. 23 Sept. 1878, Rev. John Goold Adams, Incumbent of Clooney, co. Derry (*see that family*).
5. Anna Mary, m. 27 June, 1876, Rev. Henry Stevenson.
6. Isabel, m. 29 July, 1875, Col. Baptist Johnston Barton, D.L., of Greenfort, co. Donegal, and has issue (*see that family*).
Mr. McClintock d. 6 Dec. 1859. The eldest son,
ROBERT MCCLINTOCK, of Dunmore, co. Donegal, J.P. and D.L., High Sheriff 1878, B.A., b. 27 June, 1838; m. 19 Oct. 1881, Jessie Macleod, dau. of C. W. W. Alexander, and d. 24 April, 1899, leaving issue,
1. Hilda Margaret, b 25 Nov. 1883; m. 24 Jan. 1906, Frederick Ernest Grubb, and has issue (*see* GRUBB *of Ardmoyle*).
2. Vera, b. 17 Feb. 1884; m. 12 Dec. 1910, Richard Grubb.
3. Madeline, twin with Vera, d. *unm.* 2 Feb. 1910.

Arms—Per pale gu. and az., a chevron erm. between three escallops, that in the dexter chief or, in the sinister arg., and in base per pale of the fourth and last. *Crest*—A lion passant arg. *Motto*—Virtute et labore.

Seat—Dunmore, near Londonderry. *Club*—Army and Navy.

McCLINTOCK OF SESKINORE.

JOHN KNOX MCCLINTOCK, of Seskinore and Ecclesville, co. Tyrone, J.P., D.L., High Sheriff 1891, Lieut.-Col. commanding 3rd Batt., late Major 4th Batt. Royal Inniskilling Fusiliers, b. 8 Feb. 1864; m. April, 1893, Amy Henrietta, eldest dau. and co-heiress of John Stuart Eccles, D.L. of Ecclesville, co. Tyrone (*see below*), and has issue,

Leila Isobel Eccles.

Lineage.—JAMES PERRY, of Welsh descent, had a free farm grant of the lands of Moyloughmore, from Sir Audrey Mervyn, 26 June, 1662. He had three sons,
1. Francis, of Tityreagh, near Omagh, m. Elizabeth, 5th dau. of John Lowry, of Ahenis, or Pomeroy, co. Tyrone (*see* BURKE's *Peerage*, BELMORE, E.), and d.s.p.
2. Samuel, m. 1st, Catherine, eldest dau. of John Lowry, of Pomeroy, above mentioned, and by her had issue. He m. 2ndly, Isabella, only dau. of Hector Graham, of Lee Castle, Queen's Co., and Coolmain House, co. Monaghan, and by her had a son and a dau. viz.,
　Edward, Capt. in the Army, m. his 1st cousin Margaret, dau. of George Perry, and d. at Lisbon, leaving two daus.,
　　(1) Catherine, d. *unm.*
　　(2) Angel, m. William Brooke, M.D., and had issue.
　Catherine, m. Col. Henry Richardson, of Rich Hill, co. Armagh, and Russfad, co. Fermanagh.
3. GEORGE, of whom presently.
The 3rd son,
GEORGE PERRY, of Moyloughmore, m. Angel, dau. of Rev. James Sinclair, of Holyhill, near Strabane, and had issue,
1. SAMUEL, of whom presently.
2. George, m. the dau. of Crawford, of Cooley, co. Tyrone, and had issue,

1. Sinclair, *m.* Miss Dick, and had issue.
2. George, *m.* Miss Porter.
 1. Mary, *m.* Oliver Speer.
1. Margaret, *m.* as above, her cousin, Capt. Edward Perry.
2. Letitia, *m.* — Johnston. 3. A dau., *m.* -- Dick.
The eldest son,
SAMUEL PERRY, of Perrymount and Mullaghmore *m.* the dau. of Olphert, of Ballyconnell House, co. Donegal, and had issue,
GEORGE, of whom presently.
Mary, *m.* Dec. 1781, Alexander McClintock, of Newtown, co. Louth, who was *b.* 30 March, 1746, younger brother of John McClintock of Drumcar (*see* BURKE'S *Peerage*, RATHDONNELL, B.), and by him had issue, with three daus., two sons,
 1. John, of Newtown, co. Louth, *d. unm.* 1845.
 2. SAMUEL, heir to his uncle.
The only son,
GEORGE PERRY, of Perrymount and Moyloughmore, Cornet of Horse, *b.* 1762; *m.* Mary, dau. of John Burgess, and niece of Sir John Smith Burgess, Bart. (*see Extinct Baronetage*), and *d.s.p.* when he was *s.* by his nephew, the 2nd son of his only sister Mary,
SAMUEL MCCLINTOCK, of Newtown, co. Louth, and Seskinore, co. Tyrone, J.P. for both cos., High Sheriff co. Louth 1843, sometime Lieut. 18th R.I. Regt., *b.* 1790; *m.* 1st, Jane, dau. of Lieut.-Col. Lane. She *d.* 1837. He *m.* 2ndly, Jan. 1839, Dorothea, 4th dau. of John Knox (*see* KNOX *of Moyne Abbey*), by whom he left at his decease, 13 Dec. 1852, two sons,
1. GEORGE PERRY, of whom presently.
2. Samuel John, *d.* 1856.
The elder son,
GEORGE PERRY MCCLINTOCK, of Seskinore, co. Tyrone, D.L., J.P., Lieut.-Col. and Hon. Col. 4th Batt. Royal Inniskilling Fusiliers, High Sheriff co. Tyrone 1865, 1st Class Resident Northern Nigeria, late Capt. and Brevet-Major 1st Batt. Seaforth Highlanders, *b.* 6 Nov. 1839; *m.* 2 May, 1860, Amelia Harrietta, dau. of Rev. Samuel Alexander, of Termon, co. Tyrone, by his wife Charlotte, dau. of Rev. Charles Cobbe Beresford, Rector of Termon (*see* BURKE'S *Peerage*, WATERFORD, M.). She *d.* 23 June, 1906. He *d.* 26 Dec. 1887, having had issue,
1. BERESFORD GEORGE PERRY, *b.* 15 Feb. 1861; *d.s.p.* 31 Jan. 1870. 2. JOHN KNOX, now of Seskinore.
3. Harry Edward, *b.* 11 Oct. 1865; *d.* 2 April, 1866.
4. Augustus, D.S.O., *b.* 18 Dec. 1866, 1st Class Resident Northern Nigeria, late Capt. and Brevet-Major 1st Batt. Seaforth Highlanders.
5. Leopold Arthur, late Capt. 3rd Batt. Innis Fusiliers, *b.* 23 Nov. 1868; *d.* 11 June, 1906.
6. Hubert Victor, *b.* 24 July, 1870; *m.* 19 Feb. 1902, Charlotte Fraser, youngest dau. of George Pim Malcolmson, of Woodlock, co. Waterford, and *d.* 15 Aug. 1910, having had issue,
 1. Herbert Victor, *b.* 1904.
 2. James Leopold Perry, *b.* 3 Sept. 1908.
7. Guy Reginald, late Lieut. Innis. Fus., *b.* 6 Nov. 1876.
1. Dorothea Selina Navarra, *m.* Edward C. Thompson, M.P., F.R.C.S.I.
2. Amelia Charlotte Olivia, *m.* John Willis, 2nd son of the late Gen. Sir George Willis, G.C.B.
3. Eleanor Harriette Woodrop, *m.* Capt. George Peacock, West India Regt.
4. Madeline Frances Edith.
5. Florence Beatrice Hanna, *m.* Capt. Audley Willis, 3rd Batt. Hampshire Regt., 3rd son of the late Gen. Sir George Willis, G.C.B.

FAMILY OF ECCLES.

Lineage.—JOHN ECCLES, of Kildonan, co. Ayr, living 1618, *m.* Janet Cathcart, of the Carleton family, and had two sons, John and Gilbert. The elder, JOHN ECCLES, of Kildonan, a devoted Royalist, continued the senior line of the family at Kildonan, while the younger,
GILBERT ECCLES, of Shannock, co. Fermanagh, High Sheriff 1665, and for co. Tyrone 1673, *b.* 1602, settled in Ireland *temp.* CHARLES II, and acquired large estates in cos. Tyrone and Fermanagh. He *d.* 26 July, 1694, leaving issue,
1. Daniel, of Shannock, High Sheriff 1675. *m.* (articles dated March, 1670) Sarah, dau. of William Moore, of Tullavin, co. Cavan, and *d.v.p.* March, 1688, having had issue,
 1. Gilbert, of Shannock, High Sheriff 1696 and 1698.
 2. William. 3. Chichester.
 1. Mary, *m.* Rev. Adam Nixon, M.A., Rector of Aghalurcher, co. Fermanagh. and was grandmother of Major-Gen. Sir Eccles Nixon, H.E.I.C.S.
 2. Sarah, *m.* 2 Feb. 1692, Michael Law, of Coleshill, co. Fermanagh.
 3. Hester. 4. Jane. 5. Anne.
2. CHARLES, of whom presently.
3. Joseph, of Rathmoran, High Sheriff 1712.
The 2nd son,
CHARLES ECCLES, of Fintona, co. Tyrone, to whom his brother, Joseph Eccles, of Rathmoran, co. Fermanagh, by his will, dated 3 Aug. 1709, and proved 17 Sept. 1723, devised the Fermanagh estates. He was High Sheriff co. Tyrone 1694, and J.P. for the same in the reigns of Queen ANNE and GEORGE I. He *d.* intestate, and administration was granted 7 Nov. 1726, to his son,
DANIEL ECCLES, of Fintona, *b.* 1692, High Sheriff co. Tyrone 1720; *m.* 1718, Mary, dau. of Thomas Lowry, of Ahenis, and *d.* 1750, leaving issue,
1. CHARLES, his heir.
2. ROBERT, who had the Fermanagh estate, *d.* 7 June, 1762; *m.* 23 April, 1753, Miss Boggs, and had,
 1. Daniel. 2. Joseph, *d.s.p.*

3. James Lowry, *m.* Miss Parry, and had,
 1. John, *d.s.p.* 2. Charles, of Shannock
 1. Jane, *m.* Rev. Alexander Auchinleck.
 2. Mary, *m.* — Lucas.
4. Mervyn, *d.s p.*
1. Anne, *m.* — Coyne, and *d.s.p.*
2. Frances, *m.* 1740, John Dickson, of Ballyshannon, co. Donegal (*see* DICKSON *of Woodville*).
3. Mary, *m.* — Delamere, and *d.s.p.*
4. Elizabeth *m.* 1st, Dr. Draydon; 2ndly, 11 May, 1759, Capt. Ley, and *d.s.p.*
5. Margaret, *m.* — Smyth.
6. Isabella, *m.* Rev. Francis Lucas, Rector of Drumgoon.
Mr. Eccles, whose will, dated 10 Nov. 1747, was proved 2 July, 1750, was *s.* by his eldest son,
CHARLES ECCLES, of Ecclesville, Fintona High Sheriff co. Tyrone 1709, *m.* Rebecca Anne Stewart, of Bailieborough Castle, and by her (who *d.* 26 April, 1790) had issue, three sons,
 1. DANIEL, his heir. 2. John, *d.s.p.*
 3. Charles (Rev.), drowned at Bath.
Mr. Eccles *d.* 30 Dec. 1763, and was *s.* by his eldest son,
DANIEL ECCLES, of Ecclesville, co. Tyrone, *b.* 1746, High Sheriff 1772; *m.* 28 Feb. 1773, his cousin Anne, dau. of John Dickson, of Ballyshannon (*see* DICKSON *of Woodville*), and by her (who *d.* 11 March, 1819, aged 73) had issue,
1. CHARLES, *b.* 1777, High Sheriff for co. Tyrone 1802; *d.v.p.s.p.* 15 Dec. 1807. 2. JOHN DICKSON, of whom presently.
3. Gilbert William, *b.* 4 Sept. 1784; *d.s.p.*
4. Daniel, *b.* 15 March, 1787; *d.* 1869, aged 81.
5. Thomas, *b.* 29 June, 1791; *d.s.p.* 6. James Eccles.
1. Frances, *b.* 7 Dec. 1775; *m.* her cousin Charles Lucas.
2. Anna Rebecca, *b.* 13 June, 1779; *d. unm.*
3. Mary, *b.* 11 May, 1781; *m.* 3 March, 1810, her cousin Rev. James Lowry Dickson (*see* DICKSON *of Woodville*).
4. Elizabeth Letitia Sarah, *b.* 14 July, 1786; *d.* 27 Sept. 1833; *m.* 1813, William Newcombe.
5. Hester, *b.* 28 April, 1789; *m.* 1817, William Dickson, and by him (who *d.* 10 July, 1854) had issue.
Mr. Eccles *d.* 31 July, 1808, and was *s.* by his eldest surviving son,
JOHN DICKSON ECCLES, of Ecclesville, J.P., *b.* 22 Sept. 1783; *m.* 30 Oct. 1810, his cousin Jemima, 3rd dau. of Thomas Dickson, of Woodville, co. Leitrim (*see that family*), by his wife Hester Lowry, and by her (who *d.* 19 April, 1879) had issue,
1. DANIEL, *d.s.p.* 2. CHARLES, his heir.
2. Thomas Dickson, *b.* 3 Aug. 1818; *d.s.p.* Dec. 1848.
4. John, *b.* 20 Aug. 1821; *d.s.p.* 1845.
5. James William, *b.* 14 April, 1824; *d.s.p.* Feb. 1853.
6. Robert Gilbert (Rev.), *b.* 10 June, 1826, Rector of Kilbrogan, *m.* Nannie, dau. of Col. Dickson, and has issue.
1. Hester Catharine, *b.* 26 March, 1814; *d. unm.* 7 Dec. 1868.
2. Anna Jemima, *b.* 21 March, 1817; *d. unm.* 17 Sept. 1835.
3. Eliza Frances Wilhelmina, *b.* 12 July, 1829; *m.* Rev. Benjamin Newcombe, and *d.* Jan. 1865.
Mr. Eccles *d.* 12 Oct. 1830, and was *s.* by his eldest son,
CHARLES ECCLES, of Ecclesville, J.P., D.L., High Sheriff 1835, *b.* 9 April, 1813; *m.* 9 April, 1840, Isabella, dau. of Edward Blake, J.P., D.L., of Castle Grove, co. Galway, and by her (who *d.* 30 Dec. 1859) had issue,
1. JOHN STEWART, his heir.
2. Charles Edward, Capt. Donegal Militia Artillery, *b.* 20 Oct. 1850; *m.* 11 Dec. 1883, Mathilda Theodosia, dau. of Thomas Richardson Browne, of Aughentaine (*see that family*). He *d.* 1897.
3. Robert Gilbert, *b.* 25 Oct. 1854; *d.* young.
1. Annie Henrietta, *b.* 25 Jan. 1849; *m.* Connolly William Browne Lecky, 3rd son of Thomas R. Browne, of Aughentaine, D.L. 2. Gertrude Marian, *b.* 9 June, 1852; *d.* 19 June, 1852.
3. Constance Isabella, *b.* 8 Oct. 1856; *m.* Capt. James Vesey Lendrum, Seaforth Highlanders (*see* LENDRUM *of Maghercross*), and by him (who *d.* 2 Nov. 1890) had a son, Charles.
Mr. Eccles *d.* 4 Nov. 1869, and was *s.* by his eldest son,
JOHN STEWART ECCLES, of Ecclesville, D.L., *b.* 6 Oct. 1847; *m.* 23 May, 1871, Frances Caroline, dau. of Thomas Richardson Browne, of Aughentaine Castle, co. Tyrone, J.P., D.L. (*see that family*), and *d.* 1886, having by her (who *d.* 1887) had issue,
1. Charles Raymond, *b.* 22 Aug. and *d.* 4 Sept. 1872.
1. AMY HENRIETTA FRANCES, *b.* 22 April, 1874; *m.* as above, 1893, JOHN KNOX MCCLINTOCK.
2. ROSE ISABEL DE MONTMORENCY, *b.* 5 Jan. 1876; *m.* 19 Dec. 1906, Carfrac Hamilton Dolmage, Capt. 21st Lancers (*see* DELMEGE *or* DOLMAGE *of Rathkeale*).
3. ANNIE THEODOSIA HESTER, *b.* 8 Feb. 1878; *m.* Jan. 1900 Capt. Leigh Sadleir Stoney, J.P. 4th Royal Irish Fus., of Forrest, Mountmellick, Queen's Co. (*see* STONEY *of The Downs*).

Arms—Per pale gu. and az., a chevron erm. between three escallops, that in the dexter chief or, in sinister arg., and in base per pale of the fourth and last. Crest—A lion passant arg. Motto—Virtute et labore.

Seat—Seskinore, Omagh; Ecclesville, Fintona. Club—Junior Conservative, S.W.

McCORKELL OF GLENGALLAUGH.

MAJ. HENRY JOHN McCORKELL, of Glengallaugh, co. Londonderry, D.L., High Sheriff 1902, late 5th Batt. Royal Inniskilling Fus., b. 10 Nov. 1842. Maj. McCorkell is son of the late Archibald McCorkell, of Glengallaugh (who d. 12 March, 1854), by Mary his wife (who d. 3 Dec. 1884), eldest dau. of Henry John Walker, of Clocannon House, co. Roscommon; who d. 29 Jan. 1906. He had one sister, Marie.

Seat—Glengallaugh, Londonderry. Club—Jun. United Service.

MAC DERMOT OF COOLAVIN.

CHARLES EDWARD MAC DERMOT, of Coolavin, J.P. and D.L., styled THE MAC DERMOT, PRINCE OF COOLAVIN,* B.A. Trin. Coll. Dublin, Barrister-at-Law, late Lieut. 8th Brig. N. Irish Division, R.A., b. 29 Dec. 1862; m. 10 Oct. 1894, Caroline Mary, dau. of John Whyte, of Loughbrickland, J.P. and D.L. (see that family), and by her has issue,

1. HUGH MAURICE, b. 28 Sept. 1896.
2. Charles, b. 20 Feb. 1899.
3. Cyril, b. 4 July, 1902; d. 26 June, 1904.
4. Dermot b. 14 June, 1906.
5. Basil, b. 19 Feb. 1908; d. 27 March, 1908.
1. Moira Madelaine, b. 11 March, 1910.

Lineage.—The MAC DERMOTS, the O'CONORS, and other powerful families derived a common origin from Murryach, surnamed Mullathan, who reigned over Connaught in the 7th century. The Mac Dermots were possessed of a large territory known as "Mac Dermot's Country," including a considerable portion of the cos. of Roscommon and Sligo, and some districts in Mayo, until deprived of the greater part of their patrimony by the confiscations which followed the Cromwellian and Williamite wars.

MAOLRUANA MOR, brother of Connor, King of Connaught, described in the ancient annals as "Prince of Moylurgh," was the prepositus of the race as distinguished from the O'Conor or elder branch descended from the above-mentioned Conor. His (Maolruna's) son led the sept at the battle of Clontarf in 1014.

DERMOT, or DIARMAID (dia, god; armaid, of arms), was the lineal descendant of Maolruna in the sixth generation. He d. in 1165, distinguished alike for valour and wisdom, and was s. by his son,

CONOR MAC DERMOT, or MACDIARMAID, son of Dermot, with whom the surname of Mac Dermot thus originated. He was s. by his son,

TOMALTACH NA CARRIGE, or TIMOTHY OF THE ROCK, so called from the fortress he built in 1204 on the island in Lough Key, near his chief mansion house, called from that fortress, Port-na-Carrige. The direct filiations between him and Bryan Mac Dermot next mentioned are Cormac, Conor, Gilla-Christ (Jamulus Christi), Malrony, Tomoltach, Conor, Hugh, Roderick, Teig, Roderick, who d. in 1540, and was s. by his son,

BRYAN MAC DERMOT, Chief and Prince of Moylurg, m. Sarah, dau. of O'Conor Sligo, and niece of O'Donel, Prince of Tyrconnel, and was father of

BRYAN MAC DERMOT, the younger, of Carrige Mac Dermot, the family seat, now Rockingham, in the possession of the King-Harmans. Bryan being under age at the time of his father's death, the family patrimony was put in wardship, and in the Patent Rolls of the 3rd year of the reign of JAMES I. he is described in connection with this wardship as chief of his name. In the 13th year of the same reign a grant by patent was made him of the lordships, manors, and advowsons, comprising Rockingham, in the Barony of Boyle, and large territories in the cos. of Roscommon and Sligo. This patent, richly illuminated, covers sixteen skins of parchment, and is in the possession of the present Mac Dermot of Coolavin, together with the articles entered into upon the marriage of the same Bryan with Margaret Burke, of Clanrickarde. He had issue by her, two sons, Terence and Charles. Terence, who d. unm., by indented deed, dated 1640, assigned the family patrimony, including 389 quarters, to his brother,

* The family title was originally Prince of Moylurg, Tiroile, Airteach, and Clancuain, as may be learned from the books of LECAN, BALLYMOTE, and KILIONAN, and the annals of Lough Key, the writings of Doctor O'CONOR, BURKE'S Hibernia Dominicana, &c. Driven from his ancient patrimony during the Cromwellian wars, the then chief of the race removed to Coolavin, on the shores of Lough Gara. This title has since been territorially connected with the portion of the family possessions which escaped confiscation. It is one of the few Irish titles still surviving, and has been distinctively borne by the chief of the name for a period extending over eight centuries.

CHARLES MAC DERMOT, of Port-na-Carrige, styled Cathal Roe, who became Chief and Prince of Moylurg, and m. Eleanor, youngest dau. of O'Mulloy, of Ughterera, co. Roscommon. During the Cromwellian wars this Charles was an active adherent of the Stuart cause, which led to the forfeiture of the chief part of his patrimony. Driven from his fortress of The Rock, he removed to Coolavin, on the shores of Lough Gara. In 1689, his eldest son, Hugh, garrisoned Sligo at his own expense in the interests of JAMES II, and in Sept. 1690, he was again restored to the family inheritance. The order under which he was restored to possession is dated Sept. 1690; it bears the signature of Theobald, Viscount Dillon, as Lord-Lieut. of the co. of Roscommon, and it directs possession to be given him, Charles, of the Castle of Carrige Mac Dermot, the Castle and Stronghold of Conbo, and other lands which are therein described as his "Ancient Inheritance." This document is in the possession of The Mac Dermot of Coolavin. After the battle of Aughrim, where his son, Hugh, fought, and was taken prisoner, he was again driven from Roscommon. He was s. by his eldest son,

HUGH MAC DERMOT, of Coolavin, m. Elizabeth Kelly, of the family of Aughrim, and had a son and successor,

CHARLES MAC DERMOT, of Coolavin, m. Catherine Dillon, of the family of Clonbrock, and was s. by his son,

MYLES MAC DERMOT, of Coolavin, m. Bridget, dau. of Charles O'Conor, the historian, and was s. by his son,

HUGH MAC DERMOT, of Coolavin, m. 16 July, 1793, Elizabeth, dau. of Denis O'Conor, of Belanagare (see O'CONOR DON), and was s. by his son,

CHARLES JOSEPH MAC DERMOT, m. Arabella Mary, only child of Hyacinth O'Rorke, the representative of the ancient and once-powerful House of O'RORKE, of Breffny, and had issue,
1 HUGH HYACINTH O RORKE (Right Hon.), the late Mac Dermot.
2. John Baptist Natheus, Professor of All Hallows' Coll. Drumcondra, b. 1835.
3. Charles Borromeo Molua, b. 1849.
4. Joseph Augustine, b. 1842.
1. Atharacta Mary Agnes.
2. Josephine Elizabeth.
3. Victoria Julia.
4. Fanny Emily.
5. Arabella Maria.

He d. 5 Sept. 1873, and was s. by his son,

THE RIGHT HON. HUGH HYACINTH O'RORKE MAC DERMOT, of Coolavin, co. Sligo, P.C., J.P. and D.L., Q.C. styled THE MAC DERMOT, Prince of Coolavin, Solicitor-General for Ireland 1886, Attorney-General and member of the Privy Council 1892, b. 1 July, 1834; m. 1st, 1 Dec. 1861, Mary, dau. of Edward Howley, of Belleek Castle, J.P. and D.L. by his wife, Mary Anne, sister of Sir John Ennis, Bart. and by her (who d. 1871) had three sons,
1. CHARLES EDWARD, the present Mac Dermot.
2. Hugh.
3. Roderick.

He m. 2ndly, 25 March, 1872, Henrietta Maria, dau. of Henry Blake, by his wife, Anna, dau. of Patrick Burke, of Dancsfield, co. Galway, and niece of P. J. Blake, Q.C., and d. 6 Feb. 1904, having by her had five sons,
4. Henry Blake, m. 30 Dec. 1911, Gladys, dau. of Frederick Lowenadler, of Badgemore, Henley-on-Thames.
5. Percy.
6. Bernard, d. in S. Africa, 1902.
7. Dermot.
8. Francis.

Arms—Arg. three boars passant, azure, armed, bristled, and ungued or. Crest—A boar's head erased azure. Motto—Honore et virtute.

Seat—Coolavin, Monaster-aden, co. Sligo. Clubs—Stephen's Green; Royal St. George (Yacht), Kingstown.

MACDERMOTT OF ALDERFORD.

THOMAS CHARLES MACDERMOTT, of Alderford, co. Roscommon, "MACDERMOTT ROE," J.P. cos. Sligo and Roscommon, High Sheriff co. Roscommon, 1875, b. 16 Feb. 1847.

Lineage.—Mulroony Mor, a younger son of Tiege, King of Connaught, who d. 956, and brother of Conor, King of Connaught, ancestor of O'Conor Don, founded the clan Mulroony, consisting, besides the Mac Dermotts, of the Mac Donachs, Lords of Tir Oilel, &c. Mulroony's son, Murtagh, Prince of Moylurgh, was direct ancestor of the family of Mac-Dermott-Roe, the representative of which, at the commencement of the 17th century, was Conor, alias Cornelius McDermott-Roe, who had a grant from the Crown, 20 Nov. 1605, upon his surrender of the four quarters of Camagh, and the two quarters of Kilmactrany. He was father of Charles Duff McDermott-Roe, who m. a Burke, of co. Galway, and was father of

HENRY BACCACH McDERMOTT ROE, of Kilronan, co. Roscommon, who had a grant from King CHARLES II. He m. Mary, dau. of John Fitzgerald, of Turlogh, co. Mayo (see that family), and had issue,

MacDermott. THE LANDED GENTRY. 440

1. Henry, of Kilronan, *m.* Miss O'Donnell, of Mayo, and had a dau., Elizabeth, *m.* Aug. 1741, Col. Robert Maguire, of Tempo, co. Fermanagh.
2. JOHN, of whom we treat. 3. Thomas, Bishop of Ardagh.
4. Matthew, M.D., *m.* Miss MacDermott, of Ballinvilla, and had one son,
   Charles, M.D., who *d.* at Jamaica.
5. Charles, *m.* Eleanor, sister of Charles O'Conor, of Bealanagar, the historian, and had issue,
   1. Charles. 2. Henry.
   1. Mary.

The 2nd son and heir,
JOHN MCDERMOTT-ROE, of Kilronan and Camagh, living 1717; *m.* Julia French, of Cusquinny, and had issue,
1. Charles, *d. unm.* 2. THOMAS, of whom hereafter.
1. Celia, *d. unm.*

The 2nd son and heir,
THOMAS MCDERMOTT-ROE, of Camagh (Alderford), *b.* 21 Dec. 1744; *m.* Jan. 1777, Margaret, dau. of Coote Molloy, of Hughstown, co. Roscommon, and *d.* 21 Dec. 1823, having had issue,
Roscommon, and *d.* 21 Dec. 1823, having had issue,
1. FFRENCH, his heir.
2. Molloy, *m.* 3 May, 1810, Sarah, dau. of William Lloyd, of Rockville, co. Roscommon, and had issue,
   1. Thomas Charles, *b.* 1815; *m.* Dora, dau. of Thomas Digby, of Drumdaff, co. Roscommon, and *d.s.p.* 28 Sept. 1841.
   2. William, *b.* April, 1817; *d.* 1831.
   1. Sarah, *m.* Capt. Hœner de Marniel, of the Belgian Grenadier Guards. 2. Mary, *m.* Alonzo Lawder, of Clonfonla.
   3. Hester. 4. Julia.
   1. Margaret, *d. unm.* 2. Cecilia, *d. unm.*

The elder son,
FFRENCH MCDERMOTT-ROE, of Camagh, otherwise Alderford, *m.* Katherine, dau. of Archibald Fraser, and *d.* Oct. 1824, having by her (who *d.* 16 Aug. 1850) had issue,
1. Thomas, *d. unm.* 16 March, 1847.
2. WILLIAM FFRENCH, of whom presently.
1. Margaret, *m.* Aug. 1829, Rev. Richard Meade Swift, Incumbent of Mountfield, co. Tyrone.
2. Cecilia, *m.* 3 June, 1841, Charles Thompson, of Mount Dodwell, co. Sligo.
3. Katherine Peyton, *m.* 3 Dec. 1840, Meredith Thompson, of Knockodoo House, co. Sligo.

The 2nd son,
WILLIAM FFRENCH MACDERMOTT-ROE, of Alderford, *m.* 15 Feb. 1846, Esther Maria, dau. of Richard White, of Whitehall, co. Dublin, and had issue,
1. THOMAS CHARLES, now of Alderford.
2. Ffrench Fitzgerald, late Capt. 4th Brigade S. Irish Div. R.A., *b.* 26 May, 1848; *m.* 1st, 26 July, 1862, Marian, dau. of Robert Reid, R.I.C., who *d.* 1885; he *m.* 2ndly, June, 1891, Agnes Kathleen, dau. of Bernard Daly, of Hazelbrook, co. Dublin.
3 Fitzgerald, *b.* 4 May, 1850.
4. William Andrew, *b.* 27 Jan. 1852.
5. Edward Charles, *b.* 29 March, 1853.

Arms—Arg., on a chevron gu. between three boars' heads, erased az., as many crosses-crosslet or. **Crest**—A demi-lion rampant couped sa. holding a sceptre or. **Motto**—Honor et virtus.

Seat—Alderford, Ballyfarnan, near Boyle.

MACDERMOTT OF RAMORE.

JAMES FRANCIS MACDERMOTT, of Ramore, co. Galway, J.P. and D.L., High Sheriff 1880, *b.* 11 Oct. 1836; *m.* 27 Jan. 1876, Elizabeth Lucy, dau. of the late John Hutchinson, of Appleton Lodge, Warrington, Lancashire, and has issue,
1. James Robert, *b.* 24 March, 1881.
2. Charles John, *b.* 25 Feb. 1883; *d.* 16 June, 1884.
3. George Anthony, *b.* 27 April, 1884.
4. Michael Austin, *b.* 12 May, 1887.
1. Mary Elizabeth, *b.* 16 Sept. 1885.
2. Lucy Isobel, *b.* 13 June, 1888.
3. Anna, *b.* 19 April, 1891.

Lineage.—MAJ. ANTHONY JAMES MACDERMOTT, of Ramore, co. Galway, an officer of the Austrian Service, *m.* Anne Barbara, younger dau. of Robert Garvey, of Rouen, France, and *d.* 18 March, 1830, having had issue,
JAMES ANTHONY MACDERMOTT, of Ramore, an officer in the 20th Light Dragoons, *b.* 1792; *m.* Mary Agnes, only dau. of James Blake, of Creg Castle, co. Galway, by Jane his wife, dau of Walter Joyce, of Mervue, same county. She *d.* 17 April, 1866. He *d.* 4 March, 1868, having had issue,
1. JAMES FRANCIS, now of Ramore.
2. Anthony Joseph, *b.* 25 Dec. 1838; *m.* 4 July, 1873, Liza, dau. and co-heir of Maj. Patrick Crean Lynch, of Clogher, co. Mayo, and Marcella his wife, dau. of Sir Michael Dillon Bellew, Bart., of Mount Bellew. She *d.* 27 Feb. 1882, having had issue,
   1. Anthony, Lieut. R.N., *b.* 7 Jan. 1878.
   2. Eric, *b.* 25 April, 1880.
   3. James Robert, *b.* 26 July, 1876; *d.* an infant.
   1. Marie Marcella, *b.* 6 May, 1874; *m.* 29 Feb. 1904, Gregory Stapleton, Lieut. R.N., 2nd son of late Hon. Bryan J. Stapleton (*see* BURKE's *Peerage*, BEAUMONT, B.).

2. Anna Carmella, *b.* 17 July, 1875.
3. Olive, *b.* 23 Feb. 1882; *m.* 25 Aug. 1903, Francis Henry Litton, son of the late Edward Falconer Litton, Q.C., of Ardavilling, co. Cork (*see that family*).
Mr. A. J. MacDermott *m.* 2ndly, Charlotte, dau. of S. Browne, of Loftus Hill, Yorks.
1. Jane, a nun, *b.* 21 April, 1840.
2. Anne Georgina, *b.* 13 Aug. 1842; *m.* 14 Sept. 1870, Charles Dessain, of Malines, Belgium, and has issue.
3. Georgina, a nun, *b.* 6 Aug. 1845.

Seat—Ramore, Killimore, Ballinasloe, co. Galway.

MACDONNELL OF NEW HALL AND KILKEE.

CHARLES RANDAL ARMSTRONG MACDONNELL, of New Hall, and Kilkee, co. Clare, J.P., D.L., late Clare Artillery, Barrister-at-Law, *b.* 24 March, 1862; *s.* his father Nov. 1883; *m.* 28 March, 1896, May Eva Louisa, dau. of the late Richard Stacpoole, D.L., of Edenvale, co. Clare (*see that family*), and has issue,

A dau., *b.* 31 Oct. 1898.

Lineage.—DANIEL MACDONNELL, of Kilkee, was possessed of the estate of Kilbreckan and considerable property in co. Galway, and in the liberties of the city of Limerick, and was living at Kilkee 1671. He *m.* Penelope (whose sister, Honora, *m.* Connor, 2nd Viscount Clare, of Carrigaholt), 3rd dau. of Daniel O'Brien (More), of Dromore, and Dough, co. Clare (by Eleanor his wife, dau. of Edmond Fitzgerald, Knight of Glynn), by whom he had issue, two sons and two daus. He *d.* about 1675, *v.p.* The elder son,
JAMES MACDONNELL, of Kilkee, served as a Capt. in Lord Clare's Regt. of Dragoons, but on the accession of WILLIAM III he relinquished the Catholic cause, and, having given to his adhesion to that monarch, he secured to himself his estates. In 1695, he was appointed one of the Commissioners for collecting the poll tax in co. Clare. He *m.* about 1683, Elizabeth, dau. of Capt. Nicholas Bromby, of Newcastle, co. Limerick (by Harriet his wife, dau. of Henry Edgeworth, of Lizzard, co. Longford), and by her (who *d.* Jan. 1720) he had four sons and one dau. James MacDonnell *d.* at an advanced age Dec. 1714. The 3rd son,
CHARLES JAMES MACDONNELL, of Kilkee, *s.* his brother Randall 1726, and was High Sheriff of Clare 1728; he *m.* 8 Oct. 1718, Elizabeth, only child of Capt. Christopher O'Brien, of Ennistymon, co. Clare (by his first marriage, with Elizabeth, dau. of Theobald Mathew, of Thomastown, co. Tipperary, ancestor of Lord Landaff), by whom he had issue, one son and two daus.; he *d.* Oct. 1743. Mrs. MacDonnell *d.* 28 April, 1788, aged 89 years. Their eldest son,
CHARLES MACDONNELL, of Kilkee, *b.* 1736, High Sheriff of Clare 1760, was Lieut.-Col. of co. Clare Militia Dragoons, and (1765) *s.* Sir Edward O'Brien in the representation of the co.; he was subsequently (1768) M.P. for Ennis, which seat he held up to the time of his death. Killone Abbey, otherwise called New Hall, was purchased by him, 1764, from his maternal uncle, Edward O'Brien, and from that time became the principal residence of the family. He *m.* 1 Jan. 1760, Catherine, 3rd dau. of Sir Edward O'Brien, Bart., of Dromoland, co. Clare (by Mary his wife, dau. of Hugh Hickman, of Fenloe, co. Clare), and by her (who *d.* 25 July, 1818, aged 74) had issue, three sons and three daus.,
1. CHARLES, of whom presently.
2. Edward, of Kilmurry, co. Clare, Col. in the Army, Quartermaster-Gen. of Canada, *b.* 1776; *m.* 1797, Anne, eldest dau. of Sir John Johnson, Bart., Superintendent-Gen. of Indian Affairs in British North America, and *d.* at Montreal, 30 Oct. 1812, leaving issue by his wife (who survived him, and *d.* 31 Jan. 1848), four sons and five daus.
3. Randal, Capt. R.N., *d. unm.* at Lucca, 1806.
1. Mary, *m.* 1787, George Synge, of Rathmore.
2. Eliza, *m.* 1789, Cornelius Bolton, M.P., of Faithieg.
3. Henrietta Ann, *m.* 1799, Charles Hamilton, of The Leasowes.
Mr. MacDonnell *d.* 25 April, 1773, and was *s.* by his son,
CHARLES MACDONNELL, of New Hall and Kilkee, *b.* 1761, Lieut.-Col. Comm. of the Earl of Belvidere's Regt., who, during the American War raised a Regt. of Volunteers, which he commanded in Canada. He was M.P. for co. Clare, and at the time of his death sat for the borough of Yarmouth. In 1802, he was appointed a Commissioner of Accounts. He *m.* 17 Feb. 1785, Bridget, 3rd dau. of John Bayly, of Debsborough, co. Tipperary, and *d.* 6 Sept. 1803, having had issue by his wife (who *d.* 15 March, 1800, aged 38) with other children, who all *d.* young,
1. JOHN, his heir.
2. Edward Richard, *b.* 17 March, 1792, served during the Peninsular war in the 2nd Queen's Royal Regt. and afterwards in 93rd Highlanders. He *d. unm.* 28 March, 1821.

1. Bridget, *m.* 7 April, 1809, William Henry Armstrong, M.P., of Mount Heaton, King's Co. (*see that family*). She *d.* 20 Oct. 1860, aged 70, having by him (who *d.* 21 Sept. 1835) had, with other issue, a 2nd surviving son, WILLIAM EDWARD, who *s.* his uncle.

The elder son and heir,

JOHN MACDONNELL, of New Hall and Kilkee, J.P. and D.L., *b.* 14 Oct. 1789, served as a Volunteer in Spain during the Peninsular War on the staff of Gen. Carroll, High Sheriff co. Clare 1821. Mr. MacDonnell *d. unm.* at New Hall, 29 June, 1850, aged 61, leaving by will the whole of his estates in Clare and Galway to his nephew,

WILLIAM EDWARD ARMSTRONG MACDONNELL, of New Hall and Kilkee, co. Clare, J.P. and D.L., Lieut.-Col. Comm. co. Clare Militia, High Sheriff 1853, *b.* 10 May, 1826; assumed by Royal Licence, dated 18 May, 1858, the additional surname and arms of MACDONNELL; *m.* 20 July, 1858, Hon. Juliana Cecilia O'Brien, eldest dau. of Lucius, 13th Baron Inchiquin, and had issue,

1. CHARLES RANDAL, now of New Hall and Kilkee.
2. Lucius Gerald, *b.* 14 Sept. 1864.
3. Edward Ronald, *b.* 8 July, 1867.
4. William Henry, *b.* 10 April, 1870.
5. Aubrey George, *b.* 21 Feb. 1873; *d.* 4 Dec. 1898.
1. Mary Gertrude.   2. Nora Grace, *d. unm.* 5 July, 1889.
3. Violet Maude.

He *d.* 11 Nov. 1883, and was *s.* by his eldest son.

Arms—Quarterly: 1st and 4th grand quarters, for MACDONNELL: 1st or, a lion rampant gu.; 2nd or, a dexter arm issuant from the sinister fess point out of a cloud ppr., in the hand a crosscrosslet fitchée erect az.; 3rd arg. a lymphad with the sails furled sa.; 4th per fess az. and vert, a fish naiant in fess ppr. In the centre chief point a crescent gu.; 2nd and 3rd grand quarters, for ARMSTRONG, gu., three dexter arms vambraced and embowed ppr., hands clenched also ppr., in the centre chief point a mullet or. *Crests*—1st, for MACDONNELL, a dexter arm embowed fessways vested or, cuffed arg., the hand holding a cross-crosslet fitchée erect az., the arm charged with a crescent gu. 2nd, for ARMSTRONG, a dexter arm vambraced fessways and embowed ppr. charged with a mullet gu. the hand grasping an armed leg couped at the thigh and bleeding also ppr. *Motto*—Toujours pret.

Seats—New Hall, near Ennis, and Liscrona House, near Kilkee, co. Clare. *Club*—Kildare Street.

McDONNELL OF KILSHARVAN.

JOHN MCDONNELL, of Kilsharvan, co. Meath, J.P., B.A. Cantab., Major Royal Meath Regt., *b.* 2 Nov. 1878, *s.* his uncle 1904.

Lineage of MCDONNELL.—JOHN MACDONNELL, 2nd son of John, Lord of the Isles by his wife the Princess Margaret, dau. of ROBERT II, King of Scotland, was founder, about the year 1380, of the clan "Ian Vore," or "Clandonald South," whose chiefs were also stlyed Lords of Dunyveg, Isla, Kintyre, and the Glens of Antrim.

ALEXANDER MACDONNELL, 6th chief who invaded Ulster with 8,000 men in 1532, had by his wife, a dau. of the Lord of Ardnamurchan, five sons, of whom JAMES, 7th chief, *m.* Lady Agnes Campbell, dau. of Colin, 3rd Earl of Argyll, and was slain in 1565, leaving issue, a son Angus, Lord of Kintyre. James MacDonnell transferred, however, his Irish possessions to his brother, Sorley Buy, father to the 1st Earl of Antrim.

COLL-DHU MCDONNELL, eldest brother of James, the 7th chief, *m.* a dau. of McQuillan, Lord of Dunluce, and was father to GILLESPIE, Chief of Iona and Collinsay, whose son, by his wife, a dau. of O'Cahan (O'Kane), of Loughlinch,

COLL (KITTAGH) MCDONNELL, was at the head of the clan "Ian Vore," and was besieged in the Castle of Dunyveg and put to death by Archibald, Marquis of Argyll, in 1647. He *m.* a dau. of McDonnell, of Sanda, and was father of

SIR ALEXANDER MCDONNELL, Montrose's celebrated Lieut.-Gen., who having survived the Royal cause in Scotland, was killed in Ireland while second in command of the Royal forces at Knock-naness, co. Cork, 13 Nov. 1647. He *m.* a dau. of McAllister, of the family of Loup, and had issue,

1. COLL, of Kilmore, in the Glens of Antrim.
2. Archibald, of Glassmullin, a Capt. in Lord Antrim's Regt., who distinguished himself and was wounded at Aughrim. He *m.* Anne, dau. of Stewart, of Redbay Castle, and from him descended the McDONNELLS *of Glassmullin.*

The eider son,

COLL MCDONNELL, *m.* Anne, dau. of McGee, of Murlough, co. Antrim, and was *s.* by his son,

ALEXANDER MCDONNELL, of Kilmore, living 1738, *m.* 1st, a dau. of McDonnell, of Knappin, and had issue (with another son, Alexander, *d. unm.*),

1. Randal, *d. unm.*
2. Michael, *m.* Elizabeth, dau. of A. Steward, of Ballintoy, and was father of
JAMES MCDONNELL, of Belfast, and Murlough, co. Antrim, M.D., who left by his 1st wife, Elizabeth, dau. of J. Clarke, of Belfast,
(1) ALEXANDER (Sir), Bart., P.C. M.A. Ch. Ch. Oxford, of Lincoln's Inn, Barrister-at-Law, Resident Commissioner at the Board of National Education in Ireland, created a bart. 1872, in consideration of his long and distinguished career in the public service in Ireland, *m.* Barbara, dau. of Hugh Montgomery, of Benvarden, co. Antrim, and widow of Richard Staples, which lady *d.* 1865. He *d.s.p.* 1875, when the baronetcy became extinct.

(2) JOHN, M.A. T.C.D., a retired Commissioner of the Irish Local Government Board; *s.* his brother, the Right Hon. Sir Alexander McDonnell, P.C. 1875; *m.* 1826, Charity, dau. of the Rev. Robert Dobbs, and *d.* 20 Jan. 1892, leaving issue

1. JAMES, of Murlough, co. Antrim, and Kilsharvan, co. Meath, Barrister-at-Law, M.A. T.C.D., *b.* 1826; *m.* 1859, Rose Anna, dau. of William Cairns, of Cultra, co. Down, and *d.* 25 Nov. 1904, having by her (who *d.* April, 1872) had issue,
   a. Matilda Helen.
   b. Rose Charity, *d.* 1865.
   c. Frances Emily Catherine, *d.* 1866.
   d. Margaret Wilhelmina Cairns, *m.* 23 Jan. 1912, Alexander John McDonnell Pilkington (*see* PILKINGTON *of Tore*).

2. Robert, M.D., F.R.S., President of the College of Physicians in Ireland 1877, *m.* 1st, Mary M., dau. of Daniel Molloy, of Clonbeala, King's Co., which lady *d.s.p.* 1869; and 2ndly, 21 June, 1877, Susan, 2nd dau. of Sir R. B McCausland, and *d.* 6 May, 1889, having had a son, JOHN, now of Kilsharvan, Drogheda, *b.* 2 Nov. 1878; *s.* his uncle James in that estate 1904.

3. Alexander, C.E., *b.* 1829; *m.* 1867, Isabelle Blanche, dau. of George St. Leger Grenfell, and *d.* 3 Dec. 1903, having had issue,
   a. Ian Alaster, *b.* 1868.
   b. James Riversdale, *b.* 1872; *m.* 1903, Florence Marie, dau. of Henry de Blaquiere, of Fiddane House, co. Galway.
   a. Marie Louise.

4. Randall William, Q.C., *b.* 1833, *m.* Sara Martha, dau. of John Carlisle, of Belfast, and *d.* 1874, having had issue
   a. Alaster Colla, *b.* 1867.
   b. John Carlisle, *b.* 1868.
   c. Randall William.
   d. Robert, *d.* 1908.
   a. Minna, *m.* William Derington Turner.

5. Richard Carmichael, *b.* 1836; *d.* same year.
6. William Dobbs, *b.* 1845; *m.* his cousin, Rose Charity, 3rd dau. of Richard Reeves (*see* REEVES *of Bessborough*).
1. Wilhelmina Charity, *m.* 12 May, 1855, Henry Pilkington, Q.C., of Tore, co. Westmeath. He *d.* 23 May, 1899. She *d.* 16 July, 1902, leaving issue (*see that family*).
2. Elizabeth Penelope, of Monavert, co. Antrim.
3. Rose Emily.
4. Catherine Anne Stewart, *d.* Jan. 1904.
5. Barbara Montgomery.

(1) Katherine Anne, *m.* Andrew Armstrong, of Kilsharvan, co. Meath, and had issue, 1. George Andrew, *b.* 1825, killed in India, 1845; 1. Elizabeth Penelope, *m.* Right Hon. Mountifort Longfield, P.C., Judge of the Landed Estates Court, Ireland; 2. Katherine; 3. Emily, and 4. Charity.

Alexander, of Kilmore, *m.* 2ndly, Anne, dau. of Elease McVeagh, of Dinnadoon, and had further issue,

3. JOHN, of Kilmore (*see that family*, now SILVERTOP).

Seat—Kilsharvan, Drogheda. *Clubs*—Kildare Street; Oxford and Cambridge.

McDONNELL (NOW SILVERTOP) OF BRACKNEY AND KILMORE, IN GLENS OF ANTRIM.

WILLIAM ALEXANDER SILVERTOP, of Kilmore, co. Antrim, B.A. Camb., Lieut. 20th Hussars, *b.* 1884; *s.* his uncle 1905. He is the 2nd son of late Henry Thomas Silvertop, of Minster Acres, Northumberland (*see that family*), who *d.* 17 Dec. 1893, by Rachel Mary Josephine (who *d.* 1908), only child of Alexander McDonnell, of Kilmore (*see below*).

Lineage and **Arms** of SILVERTOP.—*See* SILVERTOP *of Minster Acres.*

Lineage (*of* MCDONNELL)—JOHN MCDONNELL, 3rd son of Alexander McDonnell, of Kilmore (*see* MCDONNELL *of Kilsharvan*), who *s.* by family arrangement to the possession of Kilmore. He *m.* Rose, dau. of George Savage, of Down, and dying 25 Dec. 1803, was *s.* by his son,

RANDAL MCDONNELL, of Kilmore and Brackney, *m.* Mary, dau. of Archibald MacElheran, of Glassmullin, co. Antrim, grand-dau. of Alexander McDonnell, of Glassmullin, and had issue, four daus. and two sons,

1. ALEXANDER, his heir.   2. JOHN, late of Kilmore.

Mr. McDonnell was *s.* by his son,

ALEXANDER MCDONNELL, of Kilmore and Dublin, *m.* Nov. 1851, Margaret, dau. of Alexander McMullin, of Cabra House, co. Down, and *d.* 24 Nov. 1862, leaving a dau.,

RACHAEL MARY JOSEPHINE, heir of her mother's estate in co. Down, and *d.* 12 Feb. 1908, having *m.* 19 Jan. 1882, Henry Thomas Silvertop, of Minster Acres, Northumberland, and by him (who *d.* 17 Dec. 1893) had with other issue (*see that family*) a 2nd son,

WILLIAM ALEXANDER SILVERTOP, now of Kilmore.

Mr. Alexander McDonnell was *s.* in his own estate by his brother,

MacDonnell. THE LANDED GENTRY. 442

JOHN McDONNELL, of Kilmore, Glenariff, co. Antrim, Col. and Hon. Col. (retired), J.P. and D.L., Knight of St. Gregory, b. 1823; m. 2 July, 1870, Hon. Madeleine O'Hagan, dau. of Thomas, Lord O'Hagan, K.P. She d.s.p. 14 Oct. 1875. He d. 13 Sept. 1905, being s. by his nephew.

Seat:—Kilmore, Glenariff, co. Antrim. Club—New.

MACDONNELL OF DUNFIERTH.

FRANCIS WILLIAM JOSEPH MACDONNELL, of Dunfierth, co. Kildare, J.P., late Capt. 3rd Batt. Royal Dublin Fus., b. 1870; m. 9 Aug. 1898, Teresa, dau. of Sir John Lawson, 2nd Bart., of Brough Hall, and has issue,

1. FRANCIS EDWARD ANTHONY, b. Oct. 1899.
2. Edward Henry Patrick, b. 22 Feb. 1902.
1. Joan Agnes Mary.

Lineage.—JAMES MACDONELL, of Cahir, co. Mayo, m. Cecilia, dau. of Francis Egan, and left issue a son,
SIR FRANCIS MACDONNELL, of Dunfierth, Enfield, co. Kildare, m. 1817, Bridget Mary, eldest dau. of James O'Connor, of Madrid. He d. 23 April, 1840, having had issue,

1. James, b. 1819, d. 1853.
2. FRANCIS EDMOND JOSEPH, late of Dunfierth.
3. Thomas, Lieut. R.N.
4. Edward.
5. Percy.
6. Henry Joseph, 12th Regt.
7. Robert John, 81st Regt.
1. Mary Anne, a nun.
2. Julia Mary.
3. Eliza Mary, a nun.

The 2nd son,
FRANCIS EDMOND JOSEPH MACDONNELL, of Dunfierth, co. Kildare, J.P. for that county, High Sheriff 1866-67, and J.P. co. Meath, b. 7 March, 1823; m. 1st, 2 June, 1859, Eleanor Mary, only child of Henry MacNamara, of Barbados and Belfast. She d.s.p. 21 April, 1861. He m. 2ndly, 28 Nov. 1865, Georgina Mary, only surviving dau. of James Gernon, of Athcarne Castle, co. Meath (see that family), and d. 1878, having by her had issue,
FRANCIS WILLIAM JOSEPH, now of Dunfierth.
Mary Josephine Julia Henrietta.

Seats:—Dunfierth, Enfield, and Rathangan Lodge, Kildare. Club—Kildare Street.

McDONNELL. See BURKE'S PEERAGE, ANTRIM, E.

McDONOGH OF WILMONT HOUSE.

FRANCIS JOSEPH McDONOGH, of Wilmont House, co. Galway, J.P., b. 18 June, 1844; m. 19 March, 1865, Kate Mary, dau. of the late Thomas Bodkin, M.D., of Eastland House, Tuam, co. Galway, and has had issue,

1. MATTHEW JOSEPH, b. 26 Jan. 1867.
2. Thomas Aloysius, b. 19 June, 1870.
3. Joseph Patric, b. 19 Feb. 1875.
4. Francis James, b. 5 Jan. 1877.
5. Allen, b. 1879.
6. Charles, b. 1882.
7. Jack Edward.
1. Mary Esmina, b. 1868; d. 17 March, 1873.
2. Esmina Mary.

Lineage.—FRANCIS McDONOGH, of Wilmont House, co. Galway, held lands at Gort, and was s. by his eldest son,
MATHEW McDONOGH, of Wilmont House, d. 1779, leaving with another son, James, a son and heir,
ALLEN McDONOGH, of Wilmont House, J.P. co. Galway, m. Mary, dau. of Thomas Doolan, of Derry, King's Co., and by her had issue,
1. MATHEW, of whom presently.
2. William, d.s.p.
3. Thomas; b. 1 Sept. 1805; d.s.p.
4. Allen, of Athgarvan Lodge, co. Kildare, m. Charlotte Elizabeth, only dau. and eventually sole heiress of the late George Houghton, of Leicester, and has an only dau.,
Charlotte Murray Houghton, who m. 1871, John Pym Yeatman, of Cedar Villa, High Barnet, Herts, and of the Temple, Barrister-at-Law, and has issue (see YEATMAN of Stock House).
1. Eleanor.
2. Hannah.
3. Frances Elizabeth.
4. Margaret.

Mr. McDonogh d. July, 1825, and was s. by his eldest son,
MATHEW McDONOGH, of Wilmont House, J.P. co. Galway, Capt. 10th Hussars, d. 1875, m. Jemima, dau. of James Lynch, M.D. of Loughrea, co. Galway, and had an only son,
FRANCIS JOSEPH McDONOGH, now of Wilmont House.

Seat—Newpark House, Kilmeague, co. Kildare.

MACEVOY OF TOBERTYNAN AND MOUNT HAZEL. See DE STACPOOLE.

MACFARLANE late OF HUNSTOWN HOUSE.

MAJOR JAMES FRANCIS LENOX MACFARLANE, Major Cork Artillery, late Capt. 3rd Dragoon Guards; b. 7 April, 1845; m. 1871, Elizabeth Odette, dau. of Manners McKay, 3rd Dragoon Guards, of Moreen, co. Dublin, by his wife, dau. of Benjamin Bunbury, of Lisbryan, co. Tipperary, and has issue,

1. WALTER HENRY MANNERS, of Melbourne, Australia, b. 1872; m. 1898, Doris, 3rd dau. of the late Roderick Travers, of Aramore, Queensland.
2. Charles Selby Lenox, b. 1873.
1. Maud Alice Bunbury, m. D. O'Conel Fitzsimon, of Glancullen, co. Dublin.

Lineage.—MALCOLM MACFARLANE, was nephew, it is stated, of Col. John MacFarlane, of that ilk, whose three brothers, Major Andrew, Archibald and Walter, were killed at Malplaquet, serving under the Duke of Marlborough. He m. about 1725, Janet Drummond, grand-dau. of James Drummond, 4th Earl of Perth, created Duke by JAMES VII, and d. about 1729, leaving a son,
FRANCIS MACFARLANE, b. 1727, who was at Prestonpans 1746, where he was beside Col. Gardiner when that gallant officer was killed. Purchasing some property in Ireland, he settled at Stirling, co. Meath. To this Francis, his "cousin" Walter MacFarlane of that ilk, the learned genealogist, transmitted a copy of the family pedigree. He m. 1st, 1766, Jane Hastie, of Edinboro, by whom he had (with a dau. Jane, who m. Mr. Bevan, of Wales, and d.s.p.) three sons,
1. HENRY LAWES, his heir.
2. James Hepburn, of Stutton House, Suffolk, Post Capt. R.N., Signal Lieut. to Lord Howe, on the Glorious 1 June, 1794, b. 30 May, 1769; m. 1803, his cousin Mary, dau. of James Hastie, of London, and had issue,
  1. Francis James, an Officer in the R.N., d. in the West Indies.
  1. Mary Anne, d. unm.
  2. Elizabeth Frances, m. Francis John MacFarlane, Lieut.-Col. late 3rd Dragoon Guards (see below).
3. Francis, of Longford and Pacefield, co. Dublin, b. 1771; m. 1832, Maria, dau. of — James, of Bristol, and had issue,
  Francis Thomas, b. 2 July, 1835; d. 1883, at Kingston, Jamaica.
  Jane Hastie, m. George Tinckler, of London.

Mr. MacFarlane m. 2ndly, 1793, Mary Richardson, and by her had a son and a dau.,
4. Edward North, of Mount Pleasant, co. Dublin, b. 13 March, 1704; m. Lucy, dau. of James Barker, and has issue,
  Francis Edward, Lieut.-Col. A.M.D., b. 1836.
  Caroline.
1. Mary, m. 1817, Richard Barker, son of Oliver Barker, of Clonard, the grandson and heir of Richard Barker, of Croboye-East, and had issue.

The eldest son,
HENRY LAWES MACFARLANE, of Stirling, co. Meath, and Hunstown House, co. Dublin, b. 28 May, 1767; m. 14 April, 1815, Mary, dau. of Ross Maguire, of Oak Park, Castleknock, and by her (who d. March, 1837) had issue,
1. Malcolm Francis, b. 16 Jan. 1816; d.s.p. 11 Jan. 1827.
2. HENRY JAMES, of Hunstown House.
3. Francis John, Lieut.-Col. late 3rd Dragoon Guards, b. June, 1819; m. May, 1852, his cousin Elizabeth Frances, dau. of Capt. James Hepburn MacFarlane, of Stutton House, Suffolk, Post Capt. R.N. He d. 19 Dec. 1894. She d. 27 May, 1896, leaving a dau., Mary Elizabeth.
1. Catherine, d. 31 Oct. 1868, unm.

Mr. MacFarlane d. Jan. 1851, and was s. by his 2nd son,
HENRY JAMES MACFARLANE, of Hunstown House, co. Dublin, and Fallagh Erin, co. Tyrone, educated at Trin. Coll. Dublin, B.A. 1837, LL.D. 1852, J.P. cos. Dublin and Tyrone, High Sheriff co. Dublin 1877, b. 3 July, 1817; m. 1st, 27 Aug. 1840, Jane, dau. of Hamilton Stuart Wallace, of Shergrim, co. Tyrone, by Margaret his wife, sister to Colin Campbell, then of Tanderagee Castle, and had issue,
1. JAMES FRANCIS LENOX.
1. Charles James Napier, M.A. (Trin. Coll. Dublin), late Capt. Cork Artillery, J.P. co. Dublin, of Newbury House, co. Dublin, and Carrickmourne, co. Kilkenny (Newbury House, Raheny, co., Dublin), b. 15 Nov. 1851; m. 20 July, 1889, Annie Mary (Ninah), dau. of Joseph Francis Stirling, Capt. R.N., son of Admiral Charles Stirling, of Faskine, co. Lanark, and grandson of Admiral Sir Walter Stirling (see BURKE'S Peerage, STIRLING, Bart.), and had issue,
  Joseph Francis Stirling, b. 27 April, 1890.
  Dorothy Mary.
3. Henry William Hamilton, M.A., T.C.D., formerly Lieut. 3rd Dragoon Guards, b. 8 April, 1854, served in Egypt (medal and Khedive's star); m. 5 July, 1888, Margaret Ellen Susannah, dau. of the late Rev. James Bird, D.D., Rector of Foulsham, Norwich, and grand-dau. of Sir William Procter-Beauchamp, Bart., and has issue.
  1. Wallace Bird, b. 2 April, 1894.
  1. Laura Beauchamp Violet.
  2. Marian Geraldine.
1. Mary, d. unm. 7 July, 1902.
2. Jane Moore.
3. Elizabeth Frances, d. unm. 14 Oct. 1894.
4. Marion Agnes Hinds.
5. Eva, d. unm. 7 June, 1877.

Mr. H. J. MacFarlane *m.* 2ndly, 24 Nov. 1891, Elizabeth Mary. dau. of Lieut.-Gen. Augustus St. John Clerke, K.H., by Louisa his wife, dau. of Very Rev. Holt Waring, of Waringstown, co. Down, and *d.* 29 June, 1901.
Residence—Cobblehill, Victoria B.C.

MacGEOUGH-BOND. *See* BOND.

MacGEOUGH-BOND-SHELTON. *See* SHELTON.

M'GILDOWNY OF CLARE PARK.

HUGH MCCALMONT MCGILDOWNY, of Clare Park, co. Antrim, J.P. co. Antrim, *b.* 18 May, 1854; *m.* 30 Oct. 1905, Mary Rose, dau. of Rev. Thomas Alexander Cameron, M.A., V.D., Hon. Chaplain 2nd Vol. Batt. The Black Watch, of Farnell, Forfarshire, and has issue,

1. HUGH CAMERON, *b.* 10 April, 1907.
2. John Ralph Lyon, *b* 18 Feb. 1910.

Lineage.—JOHN M'GILDOWNY, of Ballycastle, son of Edmund M'Gildowny, of Ballynaglough, *m.* Mary Gray, and had issue,
1. John, of Clare Park. 2. CHARLES, of whom presently.
3 Edmund, of Clare.
1. Mary, *m.* John Montgomery Casement, and *d.* 1843, leaving issue (*see* CASEMENT *of Magherintemple*).
The 2nd son,
CHARLES M'GILDOWNY, of Clare Park, *m.* 9 March, 1819, Rosetta, dau. of E. D. Boyd, of Ballycastle, and *d.* 24 Jan. 1842, leaving an only son and heir,
JOHN M'GILDOWNY, of Clare Park, J.P. and D.L., High Sheriff 1843, late Capt. Antrim Militia, *b.* Feb. 1820 ; *m.* 1851, Rose Anna, dau. of Hugh McCalmont, of Abbeylands, co. Antrim (*see that family*), and by her (who *d.* Nov. 1879) had issue,
1. CHARLES, late of Clare Park.
2. HUGH MCCALMONT, now of Clare Park.
3. John Edmund (23, *West Cliff Terrace, Ramsgate*), *b.* 1861.
4. Robert, Lieut. R.H.A., *b.* 1864 ; *d. unm.* 1889.
5. William, Capt. R.A., *b.* 1870 ; *m.* 15 June, 1901, Nora, eldest dau. of Lieut.-Col. Duncan Spiller, of Reading, and has issue, Edmund, *b.* 4 July, 1902.
1. Elizabeth Margaret (23, *West Cliff Terrace, Ramsgate*), *b.* 1857. Mr. M'Gildowny *d.* 1887. His eldest son,
CHARLES M'GILDOWNY, of Clare Park, co. Antrim, *b.* 1852, *d.* , and was *s.* by his brother.

Seat—Clare Park, near Ballycastle, co. Antrim. *Clubs*—Royal Thames Yacht ; Sackville Street, Dublin.

MACGILLICUDDY OF THE REEKS.

DENIS DONOUGH CHARLES MACGILLICUDDY OF THE REEKS, late Lieut. R.N., *b.* 14 May, 1852 ; *s.* his brother 1871 ; *m.* 1881. Gertrude Laura, 2nd dau. of Edmond Miller, of Ringwood, Mass., U.S.A., and has issue,

1. Ross KINLOCH, Lieut. 4th Royal Irish Dragoon Guards, *b* 1882 ; *m.* Helen Victoria, dau. of Edward Courage, of Shenfield Place, Essex, and has issue, John Patrick, *b.* 1909.
2. Richard Hugh, *b.* 1884.

Lineage—CORNELIUS or CONNOR MCGILLYCUDDY, *b. circa* 1580 ; *d.* by shipwreck 1630, having *m.* 1st, Joan, dau. of John Crosbie, Bishop of Ardfert (*see* CROSBIE *of Bullyheigne*), and 2ndly, Sheelah, dau. of David Oge McCarty, of Dunguile, by whom he had a son, Niell, and a dau. By his 1st wife he had, with other issue,
DONOGH or DONATUS MCGILLICUDDY, of Carnbeg Castle, co. Kerry, *b.* 1623. He was Sheriff of Kerry 1686, and obtained a grant of arms from Carney, Ulster, 1688. He *m.* 1641, Marie, youngest dau. of Daniel O'Sullivan, of Dunkerron, co. Kerry, and *d. circa* 1695, having had issue,
1. CORNELIUS, his heir.
2. Daniel, Capt. in Col. Monck's Regt., *d.* 1705, having *m.* Lucretia, dau. of Derryck Von Dachelaer, by whom he had issue,
 1. DENNIS, who eventually *s.*
 2. Cornelius.
He *d.* 1695, and was *s.* by his elder son,
CORNELIUS MCGILLICUDDY, *m.* Elizabeth McCarty, and *d.s.p.* 1712, being *s.* by his cousin,
DENNIS MCGILLICUDDY, *m.* 1717, Anne, dau. of John Blennerhassett, of Killorglin Castle, by whom he had issue, with four daus.,

1. DENNIS, of whom next.
2. CORNELIUS, who *s.* his brother.
3. John, *d.s.p.* 4. Philip, *d.s.p.*
He *d.* 1730, being *s.* by his eldest son,
DENNIS MCGILLICUDDY, *b.* 1718 ; *d. unm.* 1735, being *s.* by his brother,
CORNELIUS MCGILLICUDDY, *b.* 1720 ; *m.* 16 July, 1745, Catherine, dau. of Richard Chute, of Tulligaron, by whom he had issue,
1. Denis, *b.* 31 Oct. 1747 ; *d. unm.*
2. RICHARD, who *s.* his father.
3. FRANCIS, who *s.* his brother.
4. Daniel, *b.* Feb. 1753, who *m.* 1st, Elizabeth, dau. of Conway Blennerhassett and Elizabeth Lacy, but had no issue by her; he *m.* 2ndly, 1811, Sophia, dau. of Sir Barry Denny, Bart., and by her (who *d.* 1832) had issue,
 1. Daniel De Courcy, of Tralee, co. Kerry, J.P., *b.* 18 Aug. 1815 ; *m.* Sept. 1839, Lucinda Margaret, dau. of Richard Morphy, Esq. of Tralee, and had issue,
  (1) Daniel De Courcy, *b.* July, 1840.
  (2) Richard Edward, *b.* May, 1850.
  (3) Henry Arthur, *b.* Nov. 1852.
  (4) Edward Abram, *b.* Nov. 1854.
  (5) Arthur Orpen, *b.* Nov. 1856.
  (6) Francis John, *b.* June, 1860.
  (1) Sarah Lucinda, *m.* 1 Oct. 1867, the Rt. Rev. Raymond De Audemer Orpen, D.D., Bishop of Limerick, Ardfert, and Aghadoe, son of Sir Richard John Theodore Orpen, of Dublin, and of Ardtully, Kenmare, co. Kerry, and *d.* 4 July, 1891, having had Issue (*see that family*).
  (2) Sophia Elizabeth.
 Arabella, *m.* Aug. 1843, Edward Morphy, son of Richard Morphy, of Tralee, co. Kerry, and has issue, four sons and one dau.
 2. Sophia, *m.* 22 May, 1834, Rev. Henry Denny, Rector of the Parish of Ballinahaglish, co. Kerry, son of Sir Edward Denny, 3rd Bart., and *d.* 17 Jan. 1890, and by him (who *d.* 25 Sept. 1877) had issue (*see* BURKE's *Peerage*).
5. Eusebius, *b.* May, 1754, who had issue five sons, Richard, Daniel, Francis, Eusebius, and James, and also four daus., Ellen, Catherine, Charity, and Margaret.
6. Cornelius, *b.* July, 1762.
1. Charity, wife of Edward Collis.
2. Mary Anne, *d. unm.*
3. Margaret, wife of the Rev. James Day.
4. Ruth, *d.s.p.* 5. Avis, *d.s.p.*
6. Agnes, wife of Maurice Leyne, M.D., J.P. of Tralee.
The eldest son,
RICHARD MCGILLICUDDY, of The Reeks, High Sheriff co. Kerry 1793, *b.* 1750 ; *m.* 1780, Hon. Arabella Mullins, dau. of Thomas, 1st Lord Ventry (*see* BURKE's *Peerage*). She *d.* 1821. He *d.s.p.* 1826, being *s.* by his brother,
FRANCIS MCGILLICUDDY, of The Reeks, *b.* 17 Aug. 1751 ; *m.* Catherine, relict of Darby McGill, and dau. of Denis Mahony, of Dromore, co. Kerry. He *d.* 6 April, 1827, having had issue,
1. RICHARD, his heir. 2. Denis.
3. Daniel.
1. Frances. 2. Mary Catherine.
3. Elizabeth.
RICHARD MCGILLICUDDY, of The Reeks, *b.* 1 Jan. 1790 ; *m,* 1st, 1814, Margaret, only dau. of John Bennett, M.D. She *d.* 1849, having had issue,
1. Dorothea, *m.* 29 June, 1847, William Leader, of Rosnalea, Kanturk, co. Cork, and had issue (*see* LEADER *of Dromore*).
He *m.* 2ndly, 6 Nov. 1849, Anna, dau. of Capt. John Johnstone, 3rd Light Dragoons, of Mamstone Court, Herefordshire, by whom he had issue,
1. RICHARD PATRICK, late of The Reeks.
2. DENIS DONOUGH CHARLES, now of The Reeks.
3. John, Major 4th Batt. Royal Munster Fus. (*Ballinagroun, co. Kerry*), J.P., D.L. co. Kerry, *b.* 1855 ; *m.* 1890, Emily Jane. dau. of R. Hudson, of Bache Hall, Chester, and has issue,
 Anthony John, *b.* 1874.
 Anna Emily.
4. Charles, *b.* 8 Nov. 1857, and *d.* 1906, having *m.* Louisa, dau. of Rev. J. FitzGerald, and widow of J. Aldworth.
5. Niell (*Pendennis, Bournemouth*), *b.* 22 July, 1860 ; *m.* Jadwiga, dau. of Adolphus Janasy of Plohoem, Warsaw, and has issue,
 1. Adolphus Richard Niell, *b.* 1887.
 1. Naomi Anna, *m.* 1910, Cedric Scott, and has issue.
 2. Esther Amy. 3. Sylvia Ruth.
1. Agnes, *m.* 1884, George Stoker, M.D., J.P. (14, *Hereford Street, Mayfair*), son of Abraham Stoker, and has issue.
2. Anna Catherine, *m.* 1878, Capt. George Joseph Metcalfe, 4th Royal Irish Dragoon Guards, son of J. Metcalfe, of Metcalfe Park, Kildare, and has issue.
3. Mary Ruth, *m.* 1889, Major Clement Heigham, 1st Batt. West Yorkshire Regt., son of Major Heigham, of Hunston Hall, and has issue (*see that family*).
4. Sylvia Emily (23, *Chelsea Gardens, Sloane Square, S.W.*).
He *d.* 6 June, 1866, and was *s.* by his eldest son,
RICHARD PATRICK MACGILLICUDDY, of The Reeks, *b.* 15 July, 1850 ; *d. unm.* 1871, and was *s.* by his brother (*as above*).

Arms—Gu. a wyvern or. *Crest*—A representation of MacGillicuddy's Reeks, co. Kerry, ppr. *Motto*—Sursum corda. *Seat*—The Reeks, Killarney. *Residence*—Bawnchrone, Beaufort, co Kerry.

McKENNA OF ARDOGENA.

JOSEPH EMANUEL MCKENNA, of Ardogena, co. Waterford, b. 1858; s. his father 15 Aug. 1906.

Lineage.—MICHAEL MCKENNA, of Dublin, had an eldest son, SIR JOSEPH NEALE MCKENNA, of Ardogena, co. Waterford, J.P. and D.L. co. Cork, J.P. co. Waterford, M.P. for Youghal 1865-68, and 1874-85, and for S. Monaghan 1885-92, Barrister-at-Law, Knighted 1867, b. 1819; m. 1st, 1842 Esther Louisa, dau. of Edmund Howe, of Dublin. She d. 1871, having had with other issue,

JOSEPH EMANUEL, now of Ardogena.
Helen Josephine, m. 31 Jan. 1877, Daniel O'Connell, of Ballynabloun, co. Kerry, son of Charles O'Connell, and has issue (see that family).

Sir Joseph m. 2ndly, 28 July, 1880, Amelia Anne (d. 1 July, 1907), only child of the late George Keats Brooks, and widow of Richard Warner Hole, of Shelthorpe Hall, Loughborough, and Quorndon, co. Leicester. He d. 15 Aug. 1906.

Seat—Ardogena, Youghal.

MACKY OF BELMONT.

FRANCIS COFFIN MACKY, of Belmont, co. Londonderry, J.P. co. Donegal, and J.P. and D.L. co. Londonderry, High Sheriff co. Donegal 1888, Capt. late 3rd Dragoon Guards, b. 22 Aug. 1847; m. 1st, 7 Oct. 1873, Frances Caroline, dau. of Rev. George Robinson, M.A., and by her (who d. 4 Sept. 1874) had issue,

1. FRANCIS CHARLES THOMPSON, b. 26 Aug. 1874.

He m. 2ndly, 20 Dec. 1881, Emma Clara, dau. of John Barré Beresford, J.P. and D.L., of Learmount and Ashbrook, co. Londonderry, and by her has further issue,

2. John Barré Beresford, Lieut. Royal Warwickshire Regt., b. 15 Aug. 1889.
1. Eleonora Caroline Lucia, b. 26 Oct. 1882; m. 28 Feb. 1907, His Honour Judge Cooke, K.C.
2. Frances Mary, b. 8 June, 1884; d. 19 April, 1886.
3. Gladys Kathleen, b. 19 Aug. 1887.
4. Emma Clara, b. 30 April, 1892.

Lineage.—WILLIAM MACKAY, of Belmont, m. 8 Sept. 1796, Ann, dau. of James Porter, and d. 25 Nov. 1849, having by her (who d. 3 Feb. 1853) had issue, a son and heir,
JAMES THOMPSON MACKY, of Belmont, co. Londonderry, and Castlefin, co. Donegal, J.P. and D.L. co. Londonderry, High Sheriff 1860, and J.P. co. Donegal, b. 1 Jan. 1800; m. 4 July, 1843, Caroline, dau. of Admiral Francis Holmes Coffin, of Alwington House, Stonehouse, Devonshire, and by her (who d. 19 Oct. 1889) had issue,
1. William, b. 1844; m. 1867, Florence Mary, dau. of John Hamilton Colt, of Gartsherrie, Lanarkshire (see that family), and has had issue,
  1. Francis Hamilton Osborne, b. 1869; d. 1879.
  1. Florence, dec.   2. Violet Julia.
2. FRANCIS COFFIN, now of Belmont.
1. Caroline, m. 1886, Maj.-Gen. Sarsfield Green, R.H.A., who d. 1892.

Mr. James Thompson Macky d. 4 Nov. 1885.

Seat—Belmont, Derry, co. Londonderry. Club—Naval and Military.

McMAHON OF HOLLYMOUNT.

ROBERT MOORE MCMAHON, of Hollymount, Queen's Co., J.P., b. 23 Sept. 1831; m. 1st, Aug. 1867, Elizabeth, dau. of Col. Benjamin Gale Humfrey, of Cavanacor, Strabane, and by her (who d. Feb. 1878) has had with other issue,

1. Alexander St. Leger, b. 10 June, 1869; d. unm. March, 1903.

He m. 2ndly, 4 Oct. 1881, Alice Emma, dau. of Rev. Canon G. R. Winter, Vicar of Swaffham, Norfolk, and has further issue,

2. Robert, b. and d. 11 Jan. 1887.
1. Helen m. 1 June, 1909, Donald Ramsey Macdonald, R.F.A. only son of Dudley Ward Macdonald, of Hallatrow Court, Somerset, and has issue,
  John Robert Somerled, b. 21 Oct. 1910.
2. Kathleen   3. Alice, d. an infant.
4. Augusta Mary.   5. Phyllis.
6. Joan Ethel.

Lineage—ALEXANDER MCMAHON, m. 1746, Diana Corry, and had issue,
CHARLES MOORE MCMAHON, m. 1784, Isabella Clarges, and d. 1830. His son,

MAJOR ALEXANDER ST. LEGER MCMAHON, of Hollymount, m. Catherine Fishbourne, and had issue,
1. ALEXANDER RUXTON, of Hollymount.
2. ROBERT MOORE, s. his brother.
3. Charles Joseph, Gen. R. (late Madras) Artillery, b. 13 Aug. 1833; m. Mary Louisa, dau. of Richard Lewis, of Hobart, Tasmania.
1. Isabella Clarges.

His eldest son,
MAJOR-GEN. ALEXANDER RUXTON MCMAHON, of Hollymount, co. Carlow, b. 1829; m. 1st, 1856, Horatia Anna, dau. of Capt. Davies, R.N., and had issue, a dau., Horatia; 2ndly, 1862, Jemima Fanny, dau. of Gen. Morden Carthew, C.B., of Denton Lodge, Norfolk, and had issue, Ethel, Mary, and Violet. He was formerly a Col. in the Madras Staff Corps, a Deputy Commissioner in British Burmah, and Political Agent at the Court of H.M. the King of Burmah. He d. 28 Dec. 1899.

Seat—Hollymount, Carlow.

McMAHON. See BURKE'S PEERAGE, McMAHON, Bart.

MACMAHON-CREAGH. See CREAGH.

MACMURROUGH-MURPHY. See MURPHY.

MACNAGHTEN.
See BURKE'S PEERAGE, MACNAGHTEN, Bart.

MACNAMARA OF DOOLEN.

HENRY VALENTINE MACNAMARA, of Doolen and Ennistymon House, co. Clare, J.P. and D.L., High Sheriff 1885, B.A. Trin. Coll. Camb., b. 14 Feb. 1861; m. 26 April, 1883, Edith Elizabeth, youngest dau. of Sir Daniel Cooper, Bart., G.C.M.G., and by her has issue,

1. FRANCIS, b. 20 Feb. 1884; m. Mary, eldest dau. of the late Edouard Majolier, of Congénies Zard, France, and has issue, John, b. 1908.
2. Valentine, b. 14 June, 1887.
3. George, b. 23 May, 1890.
1. Violet Elizabeth.
2. Edith Eileen, m. Oct. 1910, R. F. Cruise, District Inspector R.I.C. son of late H. J. Cruise, of Rahoad, co. Meath.
3. Doreen Finola.   4. Mavis Nesta.

Lineage.—This is a branch of the ancient Milesian family of Macnamara, of co. Clare, which was resident at Ballynacraige Castle.

BARTHOLOMEW MACNAMARA, of Muraghlin, Barony of Burren, co. Clare, 6th son of Teigue Macnamara, of Ballynacraige, was b. at Ballymacraige 1685; m. Dorothy, dau. of William Brock, Mayor of Galway, and had issue,
1. WILLIAM, of whom presently.   2. Michael, d.s.p.
3. Teigue, d.s.p.
4. John, m. Margaret, dau. of Anthony, Macdonogh, Capt. in the Duke of Berwick's Regt., and had issue.

The eldest son,
WILLIAM MACNAMARA, of Doolen, co. Clare, b. at Glannynpagh 1714; m. Catherine, dau. and heir of Francis Sarsfield, of Doolen, co. Clare, and by her had issue,
1. FRANCIS, of whom presently.   2. William, d.s.p.

The elder son,
FRANCIS MACNAMARA, of Doolen, b. 1750; m. Jane, dau. of George Stamer, of Carnelly, co. Clare, by Honor his wife, dau. of Christopher O'Brien, of Ennistymon, and Mary, his 2nd wife, dau. of Sir Randall MacDonnell, Bart. He had issue,
1. WILLIAM NUGENT, his heir.
2. Richard, late 20th Dragoons, m. Mrs. Peyton, widow of Col. Peyton, and sister and co-heir of George Nugent Reynolds.
3. George.   4. Francis.
5. John.
6. Burton (Sir), Admiral R.N., of Tromeroe, co. Clare, J.P., b. 1794; m. 1832, Jane, dau. of Daniel Gabbett, of Strand, co. Limerick, and d.s.p. 1876.
1. Honoria, d. unm.   2. Dora, m. William Calcutt.

The son and heir,
WILLIAM NUGENT MACNAMARA, of Doolen, M.P. for Clare, b. 1775; m. 1798, Susannah, dau. and eventually co-heir of the Hon.

MAGAN OF CLONEARL.

The late AUGUSTA ELIZABETH MAGAN, of Clonearl, King's Co., and Killyan, co. Meath, only sister of the late William Henry Magan, of Clonearl, M.P. co. Westmeath, Capt. 4th Light Dragoons; s. to Clonearl and Killyan upon the death of her mother, 11 Sept. 1880, and d. 25 Oct. 1905.

Lineage.—MORGAN MAGAN, of Cloney, co. Westmeath, brother of Richard Magan, of Emoe, had issue,
1. THOMAS, his heir.
2. MORGAN, successor to his brother.
  1. Susannah, m. 1st, Sir Arthur Shaen, Bart., of Kilmore, co. Roscommon, and 2ndly, Robert Dillon, of Clonbrock.

The elder son,
THOMAS MAGAN, of Togherston, a Commissioner in the years 1695, 1697, and 1698, for raising a supply in Westmeath for King WILLIAM III, m. Sarah Morgan, and d.s.p. 1710; when he was s. by his brother,
MORGAN MAGAN, of Togherston (whose will, dated 8 Jan. 1737, was proved 3 Aug. 1738). By Elizabeth his wife he had issue,
1. Thomas, d.s.p.
2. Hubert, d.s.p.
3. William, d.s.p.
4. Edward, d.s.p.
5. Morgan, d.s.p.
6. ARTHUR, his heir.
1. Eliza, m. James Daly, of Castle Daly.
2. Sarah, m. Nov. 1729, John Meares, of Meares Court, and had issue (see that family).
3. Ann, m. John Fetherstonhaugh, of Dardistown.
4. Frances, m. George Montgomery, of Killee.

The 6th son,
ARTHUR MAGAN, of Clonearl, High Sheriff of Westmeath 1759, b. 1721; d. 14 Sept. 1777; m. 20 July, 1754, Ann, dau. of Hugh Henry, of Straffan, co. Kildare, and had issue,
1. Edward, d.s.p. 1779.
2. Hugh Henry, b. 1760.
3. ARTHUR, who carried on the line.
1. Aune, d. unm.
2. Harriet, d. unm.

The youngest son,
ARTHUR MAGAN, of Clonearl, and Togherston, b. 26 July, 1756; m. Hannah Georgina, dau. and co-heir (with her sister, Eliza Anne, wife of Charles, Lord Castlecoote) of Rev. Henry Tilson, D.D., of Eagle Hill, co. Kildare, and had issue,
1. Edward, d. young.
2. WILLIAM HENRY, his heir.
3. Arthur, Capt. R.N., of Portland Lodge, Brixton, b. 1794; m. Catherine Smith, of London, and d. 8 Feb. 1870, having had issue, an only child,
Georgina Elizabeth, m. 3 Feb. 1840, John Henry Brummell, son of William C. Brummell.
4. Thomas Tilson, Capt. in the Army, b. 1798; d. 27 Aug. 1870. He m. 1st, Sophia Willoughby, dau. of William Humphrys, and sister of William Huruphrys, of Ballyhaise (see that family), by whom (who d. 29 March, 1846) he had issue,
1. Arthur, Capt., b. 4 Sept. 1833; d.s.p.
2. Tilson Shaw, Lieut.-Col. Madras Staff Corps, b. Aug. 1841; m. 18 Feb. 1871, Mrs. Davey, and d. 26 Oct. 1887, leaving issue.
1. Letitia, d. unm. 2 Dec. 1833.
2. Georgina Tilson, d. unm. 5 Dec. 1833.
3. Adelaide Charlotte, d. unm. 19 Dec. 1869.
He m. 2ndly, 10 Jan. 1850, Louisa O'Grady, and had further issue,
3. Thomas O'Grady Tilson. b. 1 Jan. 1853.
4. Francis William, b. 31 Jan. 1861; m. 30 Dec. 1903, Caroline Olensted, dau. of Edward Maynard Marshall of Charleston, S. Carolina, U.S.A.
4. Emily Louisa.
5. Clara Cecilia.
6. Georgina Matilda.
5. George Percy, of Doning, co. Carlow, m. Ellen, dau. of Valentine O'Connor, of Dublin, and d. 1857, leaving issue,
1. Arthur, Capt., b. 1825; d. unm. 3 April, 1874.
2. Percy, of Kilcleagh Park, co. Westmeath, J.P., b. 20 Aug. 1828; m. 20 Sept. 1865, Annie Katherine, dau. of Rev. Edward Richards (see RICHARDS of Ardmine). He d. 26 Dec. 1903, leaving issue,
(1) Percy Tilson, b. 13 Nov. 1867.
(2) Arthur Tilson Shaen, of Correal, Roscommon (Kildare St. Club), b. 21 May, 1880; m. 22 Jan. 1906, Kathleen Jane, eldest dau. of Assheton Biddulph, of Moneyguyneen (see BIDDULPH of Rathrobin), and has issue,
  1. William Morgau Tilson, b. 13 June, 1908.
  1. Annie Sheelah, b. 4 Dec. 1906.
  2. Violet Mary, b. 11 Dec. 1909.
(1) Emily Georgina. (2) Muriel Rozel.
(3) Rachel Evelyn. (4) Violet Augusta.

I.L.G.

3. Thomas Tilson, b. 1830; d. unm.
4. Henry, b. 1831; d. young. 5. Henry Augustus, b. 1832.
6. Edward William, b. 1835; d.s.p.
7. Hugh Tilson, b. 1840; d. unm. 7 Jan. 1874.
8. Albert Edward, b. 1843; d. unm.
9. Valentine John, b. 1845; d. unm. July, 1872.
1. Georgina, d. 2. Mary Monica.
3. Ellen. 4. Charlotte Elizabeth, d. unm.
5. Henrietta, d. unm. 6. Flora Emily.
7. Harriet Honoria.
6. Henry (Rev.), d.s.p.
1. Charlotte, d. unm. 2. Eliza, d. unm.
3. Harriett, d. unm.
4. Louisa, m. Augustus, Baron von Retzenstein, Col. Hanoverian Life Guards.
5. Emily, m. George Medlicott, and had an only dau., Louisa, who m. 21 Dec. 1858, Hon. J. P. Vereker, and has two sons and two daus. (see BURKE'S Peerage, GORT, V.).
6. Henrietta, m. R. Hawksworth, Queen's Co.

Mr. Magan d. 1808, and was s. by his eldest son,
WILLIAM HENRY MAGAN, of Clonearl, High Sheriff of Westmeath 1820, b. 1790; m. 1817, Elizabeth Georgina, relict of Col. Thomas Lowther Allen, of Killyan, head of the ancient and distinguished House of Loftus, and had issue,
1. WILLIAM HENRY, of Clonearl, b. 31 Jan. 1819; m. 4 Aug. 1849, Lady Georgiana Charlotte Keppel, dau. of William Charles, 4th Earl of Albemarle, and d.s.p. 1860. She d. March, 1854.
2. Dudley, d. unm.
1. AUGUSTA ELIZABETH, late of Clonearl and Killyan.

Arms—Arg., a chevron between three boars passant az. tusked, hoofed and bristled or. Crest—A boar's head couped az. tusked and bristled or. Motto—Virtute et probitate.

Seats—Clonearl, King's Co.; Eagle Hill, co. Kildare; Woodlawn, Foray, co. Wicklow; and Killyan Manor, co. Meath.

MAGENIS OF FINVOY LODGE.

RICHARD HENRY COLE MAGENIS, of Finvoy Lodge, co. Antrim, and of Drumdoe, co. Roscommon, Lieut. 3rd Batt. Royal Irish Rifles, b. 20 April, 1888; s. his father 1908.

Lineage.—RICHARD MAGENIS, of Dublin, m. Alicia, dau. of William Caddell, of Downpatrick, and had issue,
1. RICHARD, his heir.
2. Henry, d. 10 Sept. 1759.
1. Mary, m. 21 Aug. 1754, Isaac Espinasse.
2. Jane.
3. Alicia, m. Arthur French, of French Park.

Mr. Magenis, whose will, dated 16 Jan. 1754, was proved 9 March, 1757, was s. by his eldest son,
RICHARD MAGENIS, of Waringstown, m. 1st, 5 Feb. 1760, Miss Wray, who d. same year, and 2ndly, 31 Dec. 1761, Elizabeth, dau. and heir of Col. William Berkeley, brother of the celebrated George Berkeley, D.D., Bishop of Cloyne, and by her (who d. 5 April, 1831) had issue,
1. RICHARD, his heir.
2. William (Very Rev.), Dean of Kilmore.
1. Ellen, m. 1799, Charles Albert Leslie, of Ballibay.
2. Louisa, m. William Richardson, of Rich Hill, M.P. for Armagh.
3. Emily, m. Very Rev. John French, Dean of Elphin.
4. Alice. 5. Harriette.

Mr. Magenis d. 1807, and was s. by his eldest son,
RICHARD MAGENIS, of Chanter Hill, co. Fermanagh, M.P. for Enniskillen, b. 1763; m. 1st, 1788, Lady Elizabeth Anne Cole, dau. of William Willoughby, 1st Earl of Enniskillen, by whom (who d. 26 May, 1807), he had issue,
1. RICHARD WILLIAM, his heir.
2. William John Cole, dec.
3. Henry Arthur, Lieut.-Col. 87th Royal Irish Fusiliers, b. July, 1795; m. 11 June, 1828, Joseph Crusle Elise, dau. of M. J. Damain de Kerostan, Brittany, France, and d. 14 Nov. 1852, leaving by her (who d. 25 Dec. 1887) issue,
1. RICHARD HENRY, heir to his uncle.
2. Frederick Arthur, Lieut. 28th Regt., b. 1836; d. 25 Nov. 1857.
3. HENRY COLE, of Finvoy.
4. Edward Cole, late of Finvoy, b. 18 Oct. 1841; m. 22 Dec. 1885, Cicelev, dau. of Joseph Hornby Birley, J.P., of Brookside Newton-le-Willows (who d. 15 Nov. 1894). He d. 8 June, 1908, leaving issue,
(1) RICHARD HENRY COLE, now of Finvoy Lodge.
(1) Marjorie Elise, b. 1 Jan. 1887.
(2) Sheila Frances, b. 13 May, 1891.
(3) Cicely, b. 13 Oct. 1894.

Magill. THE LANDED GENTRY. 450

1. Elizabeth Anne Florence, *m.* 1863, Col. Edward Meurant, late 83rd Regt., who *d.* 19 Oct. 1898. She *d.* 9 Dec. 1898.
4. John Balfour, *m.* Frances Margaretta, widow of George Ede, of Merry Oak, Southampton, and dau. of the late Judge Moore, of Lamberton Park, Queen's Co., and *d.* 1862, leaving two daus.,
  1. Florence, *d.* 1871.
  2. Geraldine, *m.* 31 Aug. 1864, Col. Leonard Howard Lloyd Irby. and *d.* 18 April, 1882, leaving issue (*see* BURKE's *Peerage*, BOSTON, B.).
5. Arthur Charles (Sir), G.C.B., H.M. Minister at Lisbon, *d.* 4 Feb. 1867.
1. Anne Louise, *m.* 19 May, 1821, David Albemarle Bertie Dewar, of Doles, Hants, and Great Cumberland Place, London, and *d.* 1855. He *d.* Nov. 1859, leaving issue (*see* BURKE's *Family Records*).
2. Elizabeth Anne, *m.* James Wilmot Williams, of Heringston, Dorset, and *d.* 1882.
3. Florence Sarah, *d. unm.*
4. Florence Catherine, *m.* 9 June, 1823, John Ashley Warre, of Cheddon, co. Somerset, and West Cliffe House, Ramsgate, and *d.* 1837.

Mr. Magenis *m.* 2ndly, Elizabeth Callander, widow of Col. Dashwood, and dau. of James Callander, of Craigforth, co. Stirling, and Ard Kinlos, co. Argyll, and had further issue,
6. Frederick Richard, *b.* 1816 ; *d. unm.* 1866.

He *d.* 6 March, 1831, and was *s.* by his eldest son,
RICHARD WILLIAM MAGENIS, of Harold Hall, Beds, late Major 7th Fusiliers, J.P. and D.L., High Sheriff 1830, *b.* 19 Nov. 1789 ; *m.* 28 Aug. 1821, Ann Maria, eldest dau. and co-heir of William Shepherd, of Bradbourne, Kent. He *d.s.p.* Dec. 1863, and was *s.* by his nephew,
RICHARD HENRY MAGENIS, of Finvoy Lodge, co. Antrim, J.P. cos. Cambridge and Antrim, High Sheriff 1868, Major 90th Light Infantry and Lieut.-Col. Commandant Antrim Militia Artillery, *b.* 15 Aug. 1831 ; *m.* 14 June, 1860, Lady Louisa Anne Lowry-Corry, dau. of Armar, 3rd Earl Belmore. He *d.s.p.* 4 Aug. 1880, and was *s.* by his brother,
MAJ.-GEN. HENRY COLE MAGENIS, of Finvoy Lodge, co. Antrim, J.P. and D.L., High Sheriff 1887, Major-Gen. (retired) late R.H.A. *b.* 10 Sept. 1838 ; *s.* his brother 4 Aug. 1880, and *d. unm.* 30 Oct. 1906, and was *s.* by his brother.

Arms—Vert, a lion rampant or, on a chief arg. a dexter hand, couped gu. *Crest*—A boar passant ppr. *Motto*—Sola salus servire Deo.

Seats—Drumdoe, Boyle, co. Roscommon ; Finvoy Lodge, Ballymoney, co. Antrim. *Clubs*—Hibernian United Service, Dublin, and Ulster, Belfast.

MAGILL OF LYTTLETON.

WILLIAM JAMES NAPIER MAGILL, of Lyttleton and Griffinstown House, co. Westmeath, J.P., Col. Commanding Dublin Artillery Militia, *b.* 22 March, 1834 ; *m.* 10 July, 1867, Isabel, dau. of James Stirling, of Ballawley Park, co. Dublin, and by her (who *d.* 19 Dec. 1891) has issue.

1. LENNOX NAPIER, *b.* 28 Aug. 1868.
2. William Henry Napier, *b.* 28 Jan. 1871.
3. George Napier, *b.* May, 1885.
1. Eva Isabel Napier, *m.* 11 Oct. 1905, Claud O'Hagan, son of Thomas O'Hagan, of 11, Lancaster Gate, W.
2. Alice Ismea Napier.

Lineage.—GEORGE MAGILL. Capt. 5th Dragoons and Westmeath Militia, *m.* Dec. 1790, Hester (who *d.* 1846), 5th dau. of Col. John James Nugent, of Clonlost, co. Westmeath, and Elizabeth his wife, sister to William Le Poer Trench, 1st Earl of Clancarty, and *d.* 1808, leaving a son,
WILLIAM MAGILL, of Littleton, co. Westmeath, J.P., *b.* 28 Nov. 1797 ; *m.* 23 April, 1833, Harriette Caroline, youngest dau. of Thomas Stannus, of Carlingford, co. Louth, and Portarlington by Caroline his wife, 2nd dau. of Hans Hamilton, M.P., of Sheephill (now Abbotstown), co. Dublin, and by her (who *d.* 24 Nov. 1879) had issue,
1. WILLIAM JAMES NAPIER, now of Lyttleton.
1. Emily Caroline, *m.* 5 Feb. 1861, Theophilus Lucas-Clements, D.L., of Rathkenny, co. Cavan, and *d.* March, 1870, leaving issue, one son and two daus. (*see that family*).
2. Caroline Harriette, *m.* 2 Dec. 1858, Col. Robert Caulfeild, 7th Madras Cavalry, of Camolin House, co. Wexford, and has issue, five sons and three daus.
Mr. Magill *d.* 22 May, 1876.

Seat—Lyttleton, near Ballymahon, and Griffinstown House, co. Westmeath.

MAGILL OF CHURCHTOWN.

STEPHEN JAMES MAGILL, of Churchtown, co. Kerry, *b.* 1867 ; *s.* 1905.

Lineage.—DARBY MAGILL, otherwise Macgillicuddy, of Dunkerron, co. Kerry, *m.* 1767, Catherine, dau. of Denis Mahony, of Dromore Castle, co. Kerry, and by her (who *m.* 2ndly, Richard MacGillycuddy, of the Reeks) had issue,
1. JAMES, his heir.
2. Darby, *m.* Sarah, dau. of — Trant, of Dingle.
The elder son,

JAMES MAGILL, of Dunkerron Castle, co. Kerry, *m.* 1st, Shine Lawlor, *s.p.* He *m.* 2ndly, Mary, dau. of Capt. Nathaniel Weeks, and had one son and two daus.,
1. JAMES, his heir.
2. Catherine, *m.* 13 Sept. 1830, Rev. Anthony Denny, Archdeacon of Ardfert, and *d.* 16 Feb. 1866, leaving issue (*see* BURKE's *Peerage*, DENNY, Bart.).
2. Jane, *m.* Rev. Henry Sandes, Rector of Ballycuslane.

He *m.* 3rdly, 16 March, 1810, Christine, 3rd dau. of John Hurly, Clerk of the Crown and Peace for co. Kerry (*see* HURLY *of Glenduffe*), and had two sons and four daus.,
2. John. 3. Darby.
3. Sara, *unm.* 4. Lucy, *m.* William Sandes.
5. Carolina, *m.* Capt. Stapleton, R.N.
6. Letitia, *m.* Capt. Collingwood, R.N.

The eldest son,
JAMES MAGILL, of Ballinskea House, co. Meath, *d.* 7 Oct. 1837 ; *m.* 18 Feb. 1833, Frances, dau. of Henry Purdon, and had,
1. JAMES MACGILLICUDDY, his heir.
1. Catherine, *m.* Thomas Tighe Mecredy.
2. Mary Jane, *unm.*

The only son,
JAMES MACGILLICUDDY MAGILL, of Churchtown, co. Kerry, *b.* 18 July, 1837 ; *d.* 22 June, 1905, Capt. 2nd Queen's Royal Regt. J.P. co. Kerry ; *m.* 22 Feb. 1866, Honoria Elizabeth, dau. of Stephen Creagh Sandes, of Tralee, and had seven sons and six daus.,
1. STEPHEN JAMES, now of Churchtown.
2. James Ponsonby, *b.* 1868, C.E.
3. Henry Patrick, *b.* 1871, Capt. Loyal N. Lancs. Regt.
4. Falkener Sandes, *b.* 1874 ; *d.* 1881.
5. William Dermott, *b.* 1883, Natal Police.
6. George Sandes, *b.* 1885.
7. Maurice FitzGerald Sandes, *b.* 1888.
1. Frances Mary. 2. Honoria Elizabeth, *d.* 1873.
3. Nora Kathleen.
4. Emily Alice, *m.* Thomas Lister Coltman, of Burbush, Hants.
5. Elizabeth Anna. 6. Margaret.

Seat—Churchtown House, Beaufort, Killarney.

MAHER OF BALLINKEELE.

GEORGE MAURICE MAHER, of Ballinkeele, co. Wexford, D.L., Capt. late 7th Dragoon Guards, *b.* Oct. 1847.

Lineage.—JOHN MAHER, of Tulla MacJames, near Templemore, co. Tipperary, *m.* Catherine, dau. of William Lanigan, of co. Kilkenny, by Mary, his 2nd wife, dau. of Charles Gore, of Garryhiggen, 6th son of Sir Paul Gore, Bart., and had three sons and one dau.,
1. NICHOLAS, of Turtulla, *m.* Miss Smyth, of Callan, and had issue,
  1. JOHN, late of Tullamaine Castle, co. Tipperary, *m.* Catherine, dau. of W. Prendergast, of Greenmount, but *d.s.p.* 1850.
  2. Valentine, of Turtulla, co. Tipperary, J.P. and M.P. for that co., *b.* 17 May, 1780 ; *d. unm.* 1844, having bequeathed a considerable portion of his property to his cousin, Nicholas Maher.
  1. Marianne, *m.* Edmund Smyth, and had two sons, (1) Edmund, and (2) Lorenzo.
  2. Eliza, *m.* Col. Fallon.
2. MATTHIAS, of whose line we treat.
3. Gilbert, of Loughmore, *m.* Miss Burke, of Summer Hill, and had issue,
  John, who *m.* Mary, eldest dau. of John Byrne, of Boolibeg, and *d.* in 1822, leaving two daus.,
    (1) Mary Anne, *m.* William Strang Loughnan.
    (2) Margaret, *m.* Robert M'Garry, of Cappagh House, near Dublin.

Margaret, *m.* Thomas Maher, of the city of Cashel, and had a son, Nicholas Valentine Maher, of Turtulla, J.P., M.P. for co. Tipperary 1844-52, *m.* 1845, Margaret Jane, dau. of Walter Otway Herbert, of Pill House, co. Tipperary, and *d.s.p.* 1871. His widow *d.* 1882.

The 2nd son,
MATTHIAS MAHER, of Ballymullen, Queen's Co., *m.* 2 Feb. 1799, Anne, dau. of Maurice O'Donnell, of Carrick-on-Suir, and by her (who *d.* Dec. 1813) left at his decease, 12 Jan. 1824,
1. JOHN, his heir. 2. Matthias, J.P.
1. Mary Anne, *m.* Peter Pentheny O'Kelly.
2. Margaret, *d. unm.* 1838.

The eldest son,
JOHN MAHER, of Ballinkeele, J.P. and D.L., High Sheriff 1853, and M.P. co. Wexford, *b.* 24 July, 1801 ; *m.* 24 Oct. 1843, Louisa

IRELAND. Mahon.

Catherine, dau. of George Bourke O'Kelly, of Acton House, Middlesex, by Mary his wife, dau. of Peter Pentheny, co. Kildare, and had issue,
1. MATTHIAS AIDAN, late of Ballinkeele.
2. GEORGE MAURICE, now of Ballinkeele.
3. John Pentheny, b. April, 1849; d. unm. 3 June, 1879.
4. William Stanislaus, b. April, 1851; m. 1897, Maren, dau. of Kristen Laursen, of Gathaab, Denmark, and has with other issue, John Charles, b. 1898.
5. Augustine, b. May, 1652; d. 4 Dec. 1863.
1. Mary Anne, b. 22 March, 1845; d. unm. 11 April, 1863.
2. Louisa Ellen, m. 19 Nov. 1885, Francis Thunder.
Mr. Maher d. 28 May, 1860, and was s. by his eldest son,
MATTHIAS AIDAN MAHER, of Balinkeele, co. Wexford, J.P. and D.L., High Sheriff 1878, b. 5 May, 1846; d. unm. 1901.

Arms—Az., two lions rampant combatant or, supporting a sword in pale ppr., in base two crescents of the second. Crest—On a mount vert, a hawk rising, belled and hooded ppr., on each wing a crescent or. Motto—In periculis audax.

Seat—Ballinkeele, near Enniscorthy, co. Wexford. Clubs—Cavalry; Hibernian United Service, Dublin.

MAHON OF CORBALLY.

BRYAN ELIDORE STACPOOLE MAHON, of Corbally, co. Clare, and Crag Brien, co. Clare, Lieut. Northumberland Fusiliers, b. 22 Nov. 1890.

Lineage.—JAMES MAHON, had no issue by his 1st wife, Katherine, who d. 1747. He m. 2ndly, Maria, only dau. of Charles Minchin, of Honeymount, co. Tipperary, and by her had issue, CHARLES, his heir, and Clarinda, m. 1779, Richard Janns, and had issue. Mr. Mahon d. 1783. His son,
CHARLES MAHON, was called to the Irish Bar, 1781, and was appointed Assistant Barrister of co. Clare 1796. He m. 1785, Rebecca, eldest dau. of Thomas Crowe, by whom (who d. 1836) he had issue,
1. THOMAS, his heir.
2. Charles, of Cahircalla, Treasurer co. Clare, b. 1789; m. Eliza Timmins; d.s.p. 1874. His widow d. 1886.
3. Robert, of Ashline, b. 1793; m. Elizabeth F. Morgan, who d. 1874; he d.s.o. 1858.
4. James, b. 1802; m. twice, and had issue.
1. Maria, b. 1794; m. 1817, Garrett Parkinson, and had issue.
Mr. Mahon d. 1822, and was s. by his eldest son,
THOMAS MAHON, J.P., High Sheriff co. Clare 1812, b. 1788; m. 1812, Alicia, dau. of William Minchin, of Greenhills, co. Tipperary, and by her (who d. 1851) he had issue,
1. CHARLES, his heir.
2. William, d. young.
3. John, C.E., b. 1823; m. Louisa, dau. of John Gabbett, of Shepperton, co. Clare, and d. 1877, leaving issue, 1. Thomas, m. but d.s.p. 1898; 2. John; 3. Charles, m. 1894, Marie Amelie, dau. of G. F. Blumberg, and has issue; and 1. Louisa.
4. Thomas, b. 1832, Col. R.A.; m. 30 Aug. 1855, Katharine Elizabeth, dau. of James Edward Ferguson Murray, R.N. (see BURKE's Peerage), and d. 22 Aug. 1879, having by her (who d. 20 March, 1893) had issue,
1. Charles Edward, Capt. B.S.C., b. 29 June, 1856; m. 5 Feb. 1883, Sophia, dau. of Admiral Sir Leopold Kuper, G.C.B., and d. 21 April, 1886, leaving issue.
2. Reginald Henry, C.B., Col. R.A., b. 5 May, 1859; m. 8 Aug. 1888, Alice Geraldine, dau. of Lieut.-Gen. Stephen Henry Edward Chamier, C.B., R.A., and has issue.
3. Ernest Leonard, b. 26 Jan. 1864; m. 1893, Frances Emmeline, dau. of William Scott Watson, of Burnhead, and has issue (see that family).
1. Alicia Georgina. 2. Kathleen Elsie.
3. Dorothy Rebecca, m. Major G. Cox.
4. Mabel Agnes, m. 1892, Capt. William Scott Watson, of Burnhead, Roxburghshire, N.B., and has issue (see that family).
5. Maud Sybil, m. Rev. G. Warne.
1. Rebecca, d. unm. 1850.
Mr. Mahon d. 1847, and was s. by his eldest son,
CHARLES MAHON, of Corbally, J.P., Lieut. Clare Militia, b. 1818; m. 1844, Jane, 2nd dau. of Very Rev. William Henry Stacpoole, D.D., Dean of Kilfenora, and d. 1850, leaving issue by her (who d. 3 Jan. 1879),
THOMAS GEORGE STACPOOLE, late of Corbally.
Francis Georgina, d. unm. 1871.
The only son,
THOMAS GEORGE STACPOOLE MAHON, of Corbally, co. Clare, Vice-Lieut. co. Clare, J.P. and D.L., High Sheriff 1880, B.A. Trin. Coll. Oxford, Barrister-at-Law, b. 11 July, 1848; m. 8 June, 1886, Hon. Geraldine Mary O'Brien, eldest dau. of Edward Donough, 14th Lord Inchiquin, and has issue,
1. BRYAN ELIDORE STACPOOLE, now of Corbally.
1. Hester Charlotte. 2. Geraldine Frances Jane.
Mr. T. G. S. Mahon d. 10 Oct. 1906, and was s. by his only son. His widow m. 2ndly, 21 Oct. 1908, as his 2nd wife John Blood, of Ballykilty, co. Clare (see that family).

Seat—Corbally, Quin, co. Clare.

PAKENHAM-MAHON OF STROKESTOWN.

HENRY PAKENHAM-MAHON, of Strokestown, co. Roscommon, J.P. and D.L., High Sheriff 1895, late Capt. Scots Guards, b. 13 July, 1851; m. 13 Jan. 1890, May, only dau. of Lieut.-Col. Sidney Burrard, late Gren. Guards (see BURKE's Peerage, BURRARD, Bart.), and has issue,
Olive, b. 7 Sept. 1894.

He s. on the death of his father 28 March, 1893, to the Ballyfeeny, Strokestown estates, and to his grandmother's Mount Sandford estates in cos. Roscommon, Westmeath, and Dublin. The Strokestown property with special clause concerning the present deer park, and also the Mount Sandford property, are held under grants from CHARLES II.

Lineage.—CAPT. NICHOLAS MAHON, an Officer, in CHARLES I's Army, who was distinguished for his loyalty in the civil wars, m. Magdalene, dau. of Arthur French, of Movilla Castle, co. Galway, and had issue,
1. JOHN, his heir.
2. Peter (Rev.), Dean of Elphin, m. Catherine, grand-dau. of Sir Arthur Gore, Bart.
3. Nicholas, m. 14 Feb. 1709, Eleanor, dau. of Henry, 5th Lord Blayney (by Margaret Moore his wife, eldest sister of John, 1st Lord Tullamore), and had issue, Nicholas, m. 3 Dec. 1736, Mary, only dau. of Cadwallader, 7th Lord Blayney, and Elizabeth, m. Nov. 1734, Charles, 8th Lord Blayney.
Mr. Mahon d. 10 Oct. 1680, and was s. by his eldest son,
JOHN MAHON, m. 11 Feb. 1697, Eleanor, dau. of Sir Thomas Butler, Bart., and was s. by his eldest surviving son,
THOMAS MAHON, M.P., for the borough of Roscommon 1739-63, and for the co. 1763-82. He was 42 years in the Irish Parliament, and was Father of the House, b. 1701; m. 16 Jan. 1735, Jane, eldest dau. of Maurice, Lord Brandon, and had issue,
1. MAURICE, his heir.
2. Thomas (Rev.), b. 3 June, 1740; m. Honoria, dau. of Denis Kelly, of Castle Kelly, and d. 19 March, 1811, leaving issue,
1. Thomas, b. 1785; m. 1820, Catherine, dau. of the Hon. Robert Annesley, and d.s.p. March, 1825. She d. 1822.
2. DENIS, of whom presently.
3. John, b. 1793; m. April, 1831, Leonora, dau. of Rev. Armstrong Kelly, of Castle Kelly, and had issue,
(1) Thomas Kelly, b. April, 1832.
(2) John, b. April, 1833.
(3) Denis, b. Dec. 1835.
(1) Leonora.
1. Anne, m. William Richardson, of Prospect House, co. Louth.
1. Anne, m. David Ross, of Beaufort.
2. Jane, m. George Knox.
3. Theodosia, m. 1778, Connolly M'Causland, of Frinthill, co. Londonderry (see M'CAUSLAND of Drenagh).
Mr. Mahon d. 13 Jan. 1782, and was s. by his elder son,
MAURICE MAHON, M.P., b. 21 June, 1738, created a Peer of Ireland as BARON HARTLAND, of Strokestown, co. Roscommon, 10 July, 1800; m. 17 June, 1765, Catherine, dau. of Stephen, 1st Viscount Mount Cashell (see BURKE's Peerage, MOUNT CASHELL, E.). She d. March, 1834, leaving,
1. THOMAS, his heir.
2. Stephen, Lieut.-Gen., b. 6 Feb. 1768; d.s.p. 27 May, 1828.
3. MAURICE, heir to his brother.
Lord Hartland d. 4 Jan. 1819, and was s. by his eldest son,
THOMAS, 2ND BARON HARTLAND, Lieut.-Gen. in the Army, b. 2 Aug. 1766; m. 16 Aug. 1811, Catharine, dau. of James Topping, of Whatcroft Hall, Cheshire, but d.s.p. 8 Dec. 1835, and was s. by his only surviving brother,
MAURICE, 3RD BARON HARTLAND, in Holy Orders, b. 6 Oct. 1772; m. 24 Nov. 1813, Jane Isabella, dau. of William Hume, M.P., of Humewood, but d.s.p. 11 Nov. 1845. She d. 12 Dec. 1838. His cousin and heir,
MAJOR DENIS MAHON, of Strokestown, co. Roscommon, b. 12 March, 1787; m. 17 Sept. 1822, Henrietta, dau. of Right Rev. Henry Bathurst, Bishop of Norwich, and was barbarously murdered 1847, leaving issue, Thomas, b. 30 Oct. 1831; d. unm., and GRACE CATHERINE, now of Strokestown House. His only dau. and heir,
GRACE CATHERINE MAHON, m. 11 March, 1847, HENRY SANDFORD PAKENHAM, J.P. and D.L. co. Roscommon, High Sheriff 1830, late 8th Hussars, eldest son of the Hon. and Very Rev. Henry Pakenham, Dean of St. Patrick's (see BURKE's Peerage, LONGFORD, E.), by Elizabeth his wife, niece and co-heir of Henry, 2nd Baron Mount Sandford (see BURKE's Extinct Peerage). He assumed by Royal Licence, 26 March, 1847, the additional surname and arms of MAHON, and d. 28 March, 1893, leaving issue,

1. HENRY, now of Strokestown.
1. Henrietta Grace, *m.* 9 March, 1874, W. H. Foster, late M.P. for Bridgnorth, and has issue (*see* FOSTER *of Apley*).
2. Florence, *d. unm.* 7 Dec. 1900.
3. Maud.

Arms—Quarterly of eight 1 and 8 grand quarters quarterly i and iv, or a lion ramp. az. armed and langued gu., for MAHON; ii and iii, quarterly or and gu. in 1st quarter, an eagle displayed vert, for PAKENHAM, 2. the same arms of Pakenham; 3. per chevron or and erm., in chief two boars' heads erased sa., for SANDFORD; 4. arg. on a bend indented sa., cotised az., three fleurs-de-lis of the field, each cotise charged with three bezants, for CUFF; 5. erm., a griffin segreant az., for AUNGIER; 6. per bend crénellé arg. and gu., for BOYLE; 7. MAHON as in grand quarters. *Crests*—An heraldic tiger, passant, holding in the dexter paw a broken tilting lance ppr. for MAHON. *Motto*—*Periculum fortitudine evasi.*

Seat—Strokestown, co. Roscommon. *Residence*—35, St. George's Road, Eccleston Square, S.W. *Clubs*—Carlton, Guards, and Kildare Street.

MAHON OF BALLYDONELAN AND KILEREENY.

GEORGE CHARLES KER MAHON, of Ballydonelan Castle and Kilereeny, co. Galway, J.P., *b.* 31 Oct. 1852; *m.* 1st, 27 April, 1889, Wilhelmina (who *d.* 1898), only child of William Persse, Queen's Bays, son of Capt. William Persse (*see* PERSSE *of Roxborough*), He *m.* 2ndly, 20 March, 1906, Caroline Marcia Ciceley, dau. of the late Lord Henry Vere Cholmondeley and granddau. of 3rd Marquis of Cholmondeley (*see* BURKE'S *Peerage*).

Lineage (*see* BURKE'S *Peerage*).—THE VERY REV. JAMES MAHON, of Weston-Ahascragh, co. Galway, Dean of Dromore, and previously of Tuam, younger brother of Sir Ross Mahon, 1st bart. (*see* BURKE'S *Peerage*), and 4th son of Ross Mahon, of Castlegar, co. Galway, and Lady Anne Browne his wife, only dau. of John, 1st Earl of Altamont (*see* BURKE'S *Peerage*, SLIGO, M.), *b.* 1773; *m.* Frances Catherine, dau. of David Ker, D.L., M.P. of Montalto and Portavo (*see that family*), and *d.* March, 1837, having had issue,
1. JOHN DENIS FITZ JAMES KER, of Ballydonelan.
1. Fanny, *m.* Alexander Napoleon de Pothonier.
2. Sophia Madeline, *m.* 1841, Robert St. George, 3rd son of Sir Richard Bligh St. George, 2nd bart. She *d.* 31 March, 1901. He *d.* 28 June, 1893, having had issue (*see* BURKE'S *Peerage*).
The only son,
JOHN DENIS FITZ JAMES KER MAHON, of Ballydonelan Castle, Loughrea, co. Galway, J.P., *b.* 1819; *m.* 7 July, 1850, Harriet Salisbury, dau. of Capt. John Dillon, J.P., of Johnstown, co. Roscommon, 5th Dragoon Guards, and Sarah Salisbury his wife, dau. of Sir Richard Bligh St. George, 2nd bart. She *d.* 28 Oct. 1893. He *d.* 28 Jan. 1900, having had issue,
1. James Fitz John Ker, *b.* 24 April, 1852; *d. unm.* 8 April, 1879, *v.p.*
2. GEORGE CHARLES KER, now of Ballydonelan.

Arms—Per fesse sa. and arg. an ostrich counterchanged, holding in the beak a horse-shoe or. *Crest*—A dexter arm in armour embowed ppr. garnished or, the gauntlet grasping a sword wavy arg., pomel and hilt gold. *Motto*—Moniti meliora sequamur.

Seats—Ballydonelan, Loughrea, and Kilereeny, Ballinasloe, co. Galway. *Clubs*—British Empire, S.W., Royal St. George Yacht, Kingstown.

MAHON. *See* BURKE'S PEERAGE, **MAHON**, Bart.

MAHONY OF KILMORNA.

GEORGE PHILIP GUN MAHONY, of Kilmorna and Gunsborough, co. Kerry, M.A. Oxon, J.P., High Sheriff 1876, *b.* 14 May, 1842.

Lineage.—It appears from old Irish records and from MSS. that KEAN, 12th Lord of Kinealmeaky in direct descent, and also of Iniskean, so called from him, 24th in direct descent from Olioll Olum, King of Munster in the 3rd century *m.* Sabha, dau. of Brian Boroimhe, King of Munster, who was killed at the battle of Clontarf A.D. 1014, and had issue a son,
MAHONY, Lord of Kinealmeaky, from whom this family derive their name of O'MAHONY. His son,
BRODCHON O'MAHONY, was the first who bore the surname after the general assumption under the law of Brian Boroimhe. Eighth in descent from him,
DERMOD O'MAHONY, Lord of Kinealmeaky, also Lord of Rathlean, was called More, or Great. His son,
DERMOD O'MAHONY (to whom and his brother Donnell his father left Ross Broin and eighteen townlands, but of which they were dispossessed by their elder brother, Finghin), settled in Desmond about 1335. His descendants were styled Slioght Mergagh. His son,
JOHN (or SHANE) O'MAHONY MERGAGH, of Desmond, *m.* Shela, dau. of Aodh (or Hugh) O'Connell, chief of his name, and their son,
DERMOD O'MAHONY MERGAGH, of Desmond, living in 1442, *m.* Sabina, dau. of O'Sullivan Mor, of Dunderron, by Margaret, dau. of Finin McCarthy. Their son,
CONOR O'MAHONY MERGAGH, of Desmond, party to treaty of peace 1477, *m.* Mary, dau. of Geoffrey O'Donoghue, of Clonflesk, by Elinor, dau. of Donald McCarthy, and had issue,
TIEGUE O'MAHONY MERGAGH, who signed a treaty with the Lord Deputy, Lord Leonard Grey, in 1536, and was Seneschal of Desmond under the Earl of Desmond. He *m.* Honora, dau. of Dermod O'Sullivan Beare, by Lady Eleanor FitzGerald, dau. of Gerald, Earl of Kildare, and their seventh son,
DONOGH O'MAHONY, was father of Conor, who went to the Netherlands; Maolmuadh, most of whose sons settled in Spain; and KEAN, who left a son, David, father of Cornelius, whose son,
DAVID MAHONY, of Knockavony, co. Kerry, had six sons, of whom
CORNELIUS MAHONY, of Knockavony, co. Kerry, will dated 24 Sept. 1722; died soon after, bur. at Brosna; *m.* 2ndly, Mary dau. of Gerald FitzGerald, Knt. of Glyn, and had issue,
DAVID, of whom presently.
Ellen, wife of Daniel Duggan, of Knocknaseed, co. Kerry.
The son,
DAVID MAHONY, of Carrigeen, co. Kerry, and of The Castle, New Castle, co. Limerick, *b.* 1712;[*] *m.* 1743, Catherine, dau. of Pierce de Lacy, of Dromada, co. Limerick, a General in the service of King JAMES II, and Col. of a Regiment (whose family gave so many distinguished generals and diplomatists, the Generals and Counts de Lacy, to Austria, Russia, and Spain), by Annabella, dau. of Robert Goold, of Knocksaun, co. Cork. He *d.* 1779, and had issue,
1. Cornelius, *d.s.p.*   2. PEIRCE.
The 2nd son,
PEIRCE MAHONY, of The Castle, New Castle, co. Limerick, and of Wood Lawn, co. Kerry, J.P. cos. Kerry and Limerick, *b.* 1750; *m.* 1st, Catherine, dau. of Bryan Sheehy, of Gardenfield, co. Limerick, by whom he had issue,
1. Bryan, an Officer in the Irish Brigade, afterwards incorporated in the British service, in which he was killed in action at the storming of Guadaloupe.
2. Cornelius, Capt. in the 45th Regt., *m.* Mary, dau. of Francis Arthur, and *d.s.p.*
3. Philip, *d. unm.* in Paris.
1. Mary, *m.* Philip Hunt, of Loughborough, co. Leicester, a Capt. in the Army, and had issue a son, an Officer in the Army, killed in the Kaffir War.
Mr. Peirce Mahony *m.* 2ndly, 21 Feb. 1792, Anna Maria, dau. of John Maunsell, of Ballybrood House, co. Limerick (*see* MAUNSELL *of Thorpe Malsor*), by his 2nd wife, Catherine, dau. of the Rev. Thomas Widenham, of the Castle Widenham family, and by this marriage, had issue,
4. PEIRCE, of Wood Lawn and Kilmorna.
5. David, of Grange Con, co. Wicklow, *b.* 22 Feb. 1795; *m.* Oct. 1824, Margaret, dau. and co-heir of William Perry, of Gambonstown, co. Tipperary, and *d.s.p.* 1845.
He *d.* 1819, and was *s.* by his son,
PEIRCE MAHONY, of Wood Lawn and Kilmorna, co. Kerry, J.P., D.L., at one time M.P. for Kinsale, and a member of the Royal Irish Academy, *b.* 19 Dec. 1792; *m.* 10 Jan. 1815, Jane, only dau. of Edmund Kenifeck, of Seafort, co. Cork, by Mary Creagh. Their issue was

---

[*] Collateral with this branch were the Mahonys of Batterfield, co. Kerry, of whom Marion, dau. and heir of James Mabony, of Batterfield, by Margaret his wife, *m.* 1796, William J. Harte, of Coolruss, co. Limerick, who *d.* 1814, leaving, with other issue, J. Mahony Harte, of Batterfield, whose daus. (by Lina, his wife, dau. of Ministerial Rath Achenbach, of Carlsruhe) and co-heirs were Marion, *m.* Robert FitzGerald, 2nd son of Sir Peter FitzGerald, Bart., Knt. of Kerry, and Lina, *m.* George A. Hickson, of Fermoyle, co. Kerry.

1. PEIRCE K. MAHONY, of whom presently.
2. David, of Grange Con, co. Wicklow, M.A., J.P. and D.L., High Sheriff co. Wicklow 1868, b. 14 Jan. 1820; d. unm. 3 Aug. 1900.
1. Anna Maria, b. and d. Oct. 1815.
2. Maria, m. 10 Jan. 1844, Lieut.-Col. Francis W. Johnstone, son of James Raymond Johnstone, of Alva (see BURKE's *Peerage*, JOHNSTONE, Bart.). He d. 9 Aug. 1888. She d. 24 May, 1901, leaving issue,
  1. Montague Cholmeley, b. 28 Sept. 1844.
  2. Peirce de Lacy Henry, late of Indian Civil Service, M.A. Oxford, Barrister-at-Law, b. 25 May, 1848; m. 24 Oct. 1888, Jessie, dau. of James Sime.
    1. Barbara, twin with Montague, d. young.
    2. Alice Jane, m. 17 Dec. 1901, her cousin Peirce Charles de Lacy Mahony (see below). She d. 29 June, 1906.
    3. Edith Lucy Maria, m. 12 Dec. 1888, Leonard Barnard, and has issue.
He d. Feb. 1853, and his widow d. 16 July, 1860. Their eldest son, PEIRCE K. MAHONY, of Kilmorna and Gunsborough, J.P., High Sheriff co. Kerry 1844, b. 4 Oct. 1817; m. 15 Nov. 1839, Jane, 3rd dau. of Robert Gun Cuningham, D.L., of Mount Kennedy, co. Wicklow (see *that family*) by his 1st wife, Elizabeth, only child and heir of Archibald Hamilton Foulkes, of Coolawinna, in the same co., and had issue,
1. Peirce Robert George Gun, b. 13 Sept. 1840; d. May, 1844.
2. GEORGE PHILIP GUN, now of Kilmorna and Gunsborough, s. his grandfather 1853.
3. Peirce Charles de Lacy, of Grange Con, co. Wicklow, s. his uncle 1900, and adopted the name of O'MAHONY, J.P., D.L., M.P. North Meath 1886-92, b. 9 June 1850; m. 1st, 24 April, 1877 Helen Louise, only child of Maurice Collis, M.R.I.A., by Martha Jane, dau. of Richard Montgomery, and by her (who d. 26 July, 1899) has issue,
  1. Peirce Gun, M.R.I.A., of Kilmurry, Castle Island, co. Kerry, Barrister-at-Law, Cork Herald of Arms 1905-10, b. 30 March, 1878; m. 1903, Ethel Tindall, younger dau. of late J. J. Wright, M.D., of Malton, Yorkshire.
  2. Dermot Gun, b. 2 April, 1881.
Mr. Peirce C. de L. O'Mahony m. 2ndly, 17 Dec. 1910, his cousin Alice Jane, dau. of Lieut.-Col. Francis W. Johnstone (see *above*). She d. 29 June, 1906.
Mr. Peirce K. Mahony d. 21 July, 1850, and his widow, who m. 2ndly, 8 April, 1856, Col. William Henry Vicars, late of 61st Regt., d. 12 Nov. 1873, leaving issue by her 2nd marriage, three sons and one dau. (see GUN-CUNINGHAME *of Mount-Kennedy*).

Arms:—Quarterly: 1st and 4th, quarterly, 1st and 4th or, a lion rampant, az.; 2nd per pale arg. and gu. a lion rampant counter-changed; 3rd arg., a chevron gu. between three snakes erect wavy sa.; 2nd and 3rd, arg. a fess gu., surmounted by a bendlet az., for DE LACY. Crest:—Out of a coronet of nine balls an arm vambraced embowed, the hand bare grasping a sword, ppr., piercing a fleur-de-lys or. Ancient crest, a dexter arm embowed, grasping a flaming sword ppr. *Motto*—Lasair romhuin a buad. *Badge*—The De Lacy knot.

Seat—Kilmorna, co. Kerry. Clubs—Windham, S.W.; and Kildare Street, Dublin.

MAHONY OF LOTA BEG.

MARTIN FRANCIS RONAYNE MAHONY, of Lota Beg, and Ardfoile, co. Cork, J.P., b. 1 Sept. 1867; m. 26 April, 1894, Teresa Mary, dau. of Thomas Breen, and has issue,
1. MARTIN FRANCIS RONANYE, b. 28 Feb. 1895.
2. Francis Sylvester, b. 12 May, 1902.
1. Helen Marie, b. 11 July, 1896.
2. Gertrude Mary, b. 30 Aug. 1897
3. Dorothy Mary, b. 4 Nov. 1898.
4. Teresa Mary, b. 2 May, 1900.

Lineage.—MARTIN MAHONY, of Levanagh, Blackrock, co. Cork, left issue a son,
MARTIN FRANCIS MAHONY, of Lotamore, co. Cork, b. Dec. 1831; m. Nov. 1864, Mary, dau. of Christopher Copinger, Q.C., County Court Judge. She d. Sept. 1882. He d. April, 1882, having had issue,
1. MARTIN FRANCIS RONAYNE, now of Lota Beg.
2. Christopher Copinger, b. Dec. 1870.
3. Edward Ronayne, of Marysboro', Glanmire, co. Cork, J.P., b. 25 Nov. 1872; m. 20 Sept. 1898, Elizabeth Mary, eldest dau. of Andrew Nugent Comyn, of Ballinderry (see *that family*), and has issue,
  1. Edmond Ronayne, b. 3 July, 1899.
  2. Geoffrey John, b. 21 Nov. 1901.
  1. Mary Elizabeth. 2. Winifred Mary.
1. Catherine Mary, b. 13 June, 1866; m. 1893, Staff-Surg. Michael Ronan, R.N), who d. 1897.
2. Elizabeth Anastasia, b. 28 June, 1869; m. 1897, Lieut.-Col. W. MacNamara, R.A.M.C., P.M.O., Pretoria, South Africa.

Seat—Lota Beg, Glanmire, co. Cork.

MALONE OF BARONSTON.

COL. JOHN RICHARD MALONE, of Baronston, co. Westmeath, J.P. and D.L., High Sheriff 1896, late 12th Lancers, late Col. Commanding 6th Batt. Rifle Brigade, b. 1846; m. 1st, 11 July, 1872, Hon. Charlotte Mildred (she was divorced in 1892, and m. 2ndly, 1892, Count C. de Beaumont d'Autichamp), dau. of Hon. John Yarde Buller, and sister of John, 2nd Lord Churston, and has issue,

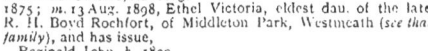

1. JOHN RICHARD MORDRED HENRY L'ESTRANGE, Capt. Reserve of Officers, b. 12 Aug. 1875; m. 13 Aug. 1898, Ethel Victoria, eldest dau. of the late R. H. Boyd Rochfort, of Middleton Park, Westmeath (see *that family*), and has issue,
  Reginald John, b. 1899.
2. Roderick O'Connor Vivian Henry Vere, late Lieut. Royal Irish Fus., and Indian Army, served in the South African War, 1900-2, b. 28 June, 1879; m. 29 Aug. 1905, Nicholina Frances, only dau. of John Dill.
3. Victor Mildred Charles, b. 15 June, 1881.

Col. Malone m. 2ndly, 1893, Catherine Cecil, dau. of Major J. W. Percy, late Norfolk Regt., and has issue,
4. Henry Anthony Percy, b. 18 June, 1894.
5. Richard Maurice Fitzgerald, b. 10 May, 1897.
6. Barbara Grace Maria Patricia.

Lineage.—EDMOND MALONE, of Ballynahown, m. 1569, Margaret, dau. of Richard D'Alton, of Milltown, and was father of
EDMOND MALONE, of Ballynahown, m. 1st, 1599, Rose, dau. of John Coghlan the Maw, and 2ndly, Catherine Pettyt. By the latter he had a son, John, of Cartrons (who m. Mary, dau. of John Browne, of the Neale), and a dau. Mary, m. John Dillon; and by the former he was father of a son and heir,
EDMOND MALONE, of Ballynahown, m. 1617, a dau. of Garrett Byrne, and left a son and successor,
EDMOND MALONE, of Ballynahown, m. 1644, Mary, dau. of Brazel Fox, of Kilcoursy, and had two sons,
1. EDMOND, his heir.
2. Anthony, of Baronstown, m. 1673, Mary, dau. of John Reilly, of Lismore, co. Cavan, and grand-dau. of the Earl of Roscommon. He was father of
  Richard, of Baronstown, b. 1674, the celebrated lawyer and orator; m. 2. April, 1698, Marcella, dau. of Redmond Molady, by Mary his wife, dau. of John Malone, of Cartrons, and had issue,
    (1) Anthony (the Right Hon.), M.P., Prime Serjeant and Chancellor of the Exchequer 1757-60, m. 1733, Rose, dau. of Sir Ralph Gore, Bart., Speaker of the House of Commons, but d.s.p. 8 May, 1776.
    (2) Edmond, M.P., Judge of the Court of Common Pleas in Ireland, m. 1736, Catherine, dau. and heir of Benjamin Collier, of Ruckholts, Essex, and d. 1775, leaving two sons,
      1. RICHARD, Baron Sunderlin, in the Peerage of Ireland, so created 1785; d.s.p. 1817 (see BURKE's *Extinct Peerage*).
      2. Edmond, the commentator on Shakespeare, d. 1812.
    (3) Richard, M.P., 2nd Serjeant at-Law, m. Anne, dau. and co-heir of Henry Malone, of Litter, and had issue,
      Henry, m. 1765, Catherine, dau. of Richard Plunket, and had a son, Richard, of Pallas Park, and a dau. Alice, b. 1767, m. Henry O'Connor. At the death of her brother this lady resumed her maiden name of MALONE, and retained possession of Baronstown until her death, 1866.
      Mary, m. 1753, John O'Connor, of Mount Pleasant (see O'CONNOR-MORRIS, *of Mount Pleasant*).
    (1) Anne Jane Frances. (2) Mary, m. Theobald Dillon.
    (3) Margaret, m. John Hussey.
    (4) Marcella, m. John Reilly.

The elder son of Edmund Malone and Mary Fox his wife,
EDMOND MALONE, of Ballynahown, m. 1674, Anne, dau. of Henry L'Estrange, of Moystown, King's Co., and had (with a dau., Mary, m. Anthony Daly) three sons,
1. RICHARD, of Ballynahown.
2. Henry, of Litter, King's Co., d. 1739, leaving by Margaret L'Estrange his wife, two daus., his co-heirs,
  1. Anne, m. Richard Malone.
  2. Elizabeth, m. Henry L'Estrange, of Moystown, M.P. for Banagher, and their great-grandson, Edmund L'Estrange, of Tynte Lodge, m. Lady Henrietta Susan Lumley, sister of Richard, 9th Earl of Scarborough, and d. 1866, leaving with other issue, REV. SAVILE RICHARD WILLIAM L'ESTRANGE-MALONE, Mus. Bac. T.C.D., Minor Canon of Worcester 1881-5,

Manley. THE LANDED GENTRY. 454

and Rector of Dalton Holme, b. 1838; m. 10 Oct. 1876, Frances Mary, 2nd dau. of George Savile Foljambe, of Osberton, Notts (see BURKE'S *Peerage*, LIVERPOOL, E.). He d. 16 Sept. 1908, leaving with other issue, a 2nd dau., Selina Constance L'Estrange, m. 18 Aug. 1909, Major Harold Charles Thoroton Hildyard, R.F.A., eldest son of Lieut.-Gen. Sir H. J. T. Hildyard, K.C.B. (*see* HILDYARD *of Flintham Hall*).
3. Anthony, m. Bridget, dau. of Henry Talbot, and had issue,
  1. Richard, m. Mary, dau. and co-heir of Acheson Moore, of Ravella, co. Tyrone, and relict of Roger Palmer, but d.s.p.
  2. Edmond, Major 47th Regt. m. Mary, eldest dau. of Richard Malone, and widow of John O'Connor, and had issue,
    (1) Anthony, d. 1787.
    (1) Elizabeth, m. Henry Sneyd, 6th son of Ralph Sneyd, of Keele, co. Stafford.
    (2) Maria.
The eldest son of Edmond Malone, and Anne L'Estrange, his wife,
RICHARD MALONE, of Ballynahown, m. 1717, Anne, dau. of Sir Thomas Crosbie, of Ballyheigue, co. Kerry (*see that family*), and had issue,
1. Edmond, M.P. for Ardfert, m. Ruth Judge, of Gageborough, and d.s.p. 1759.
2. HENRY, his heir.
3. Anthony (Rev.), of Cartrons, m. Anne, eldest dau. of Major George Heighnington, of Donard, co. Wicklow (*see that family*), and had a son,
Edmond, of Cartrons, m. 1st, the dau.of Henry White, and 2ndly, Anne, youngest dau. of John O'Connor, of Mount Pleasant, aunt of the Countess of Desart, and had issue,
  (1) Anthony.
  (2) Henry, Capt. 40th Regt., killed in the battle of the Pyrenees.
  (3) Edmond, b. 1785, Lieut. R.N.; m. Mary Anne, dau. of W. B. Taylor, of Yarmouth, and d. 1863, leaving issue,
    1. Robert Edmond, Paymaster R N., m. 1st, 1846, Frances Anne Stepney Maume; and 2ndly, 1854, Anne, dau. of William Turner, M.D., of Grantham (which lady d. 16 April, 1868), and d. Nov. 1874.
    2. Richard (Rev.), M.A., late Vicar of Potton, Beds, 1876-87, b. 1820, m. 1849, Jane Wilmot, dau. of Gen. Robyns, K.H., of Penzance. She d. 1896. He d. 7 June, 1908, leaving issue,
      a. John Henry Edmond, b. 1854; d. 1861.
      b. Cecil Richard Robyns, Maj. late Worcester Regt., of Trevavler, Penzance, b. 29 Oct. 1859; m. 6 Oct. 1892, Nora, eldest dau. of the late S. T. G. Downing, Barrister-at-Law, and has issue,
        (a) Edmond Cecil Downing, b. 21 Dec. 1894.
        (b) Brian Wilmot L'Estrange, b. 29 Aug. 1896.
      a. Elizabeth Wilmot Marion, b. 1851, d. 1878.
      b. Maria Jane Maude.
      c. Ethel Ada Julia.
      d. Wilmot Edith Catherine.
    3. William, drowned.
    4. Anthony, Lieut.-Col. late R.M.L.I., m. 1st, Mary, dau. of Charles Edwards, of Totnes, and by her (who d. 25 Jan. 1868) has a dau. Minnie; and 2ndly, 23 Nov. 1869, Eliza Carter (who d. 1909), elder dau. of Sir William C. Hoffmeister, of Clifton House, Cowes, Isle of Wight, and has issue,
      a. Robert Joseph Gee, b. 1871.
      b. Henry L'Estrange (Cartrons, Heber Road, Cricklewood, N.W.), b. 20 Sept. 1873; m. 8 June, 1901, Ethel Gertrude, dau. of H. R. Vincent, of Jacobstowe, Devon, and has issue,
        (b) Anthony Vincent L'Estrange, b. 17 Aug. 1907.
        (a) Richard Vincent L'Estrange, b. 1910.
        (a) Iris L'Estrange, b. 5 May, 1903.
      a. Florence Hoffmeister.
      b. Anne Wade.
    1. Marianne, d. 1898.
    2. Elizabeth, d. 1904.
    3. Harriette, m. G. Kingston, M.A., of Toronto, and has issue, George Malcolm and Alice. She d. 1909.
    4. Julia, m. B. Cherrman, M.A., of Toronto.
      1) Elizabeth, m. Major Peter Warburton, 96th Regt., 2nd son of Col. Warburton, of Garryhinch, and has issue, 1. Anne, m. Col. Wade; 2. Martha; and 3. Elizabeth.
      (2) Anne, m. Robert French, grandson of the Very Rev. W. French, Dean of Ardagh, of Abbey Boyle and Oak Port, in Roscommon, and has issue, Anne, m. A. Hector, and had issue.
      (3) Mary, m. J. Hamilton.
1. Elizabeth, m. Robert Holmes, of Peterfield.
The 2nd son,
HENRY MALONE, of Ballynahown, m. Anne, dau. of Morres Jones of Moneyglass, and had a son,
EDMOND MALONE, of Ballynahown, m. 1774, his cousin Mary, eldest dau. of John O'Connor, of Mount Pleasant, King's Co., and had issue,
1. EDMOND, of whom presently.
2. John, d. unm. 1836.
3. Henry, m. Mary Anne, widow of — Hamilton, and dau. of Francis Enraght Moony, of the Doon, and d.s.p. 1843.
  1. Maria, d. unm.   2. Anne, d. unm.
His eldest son,
EDMUND MALONE, of Ballynahown, co. Westmeath, Capt. in the Black Horse, m. 1813, Henrietta, dau. of John Chomley, of Belcamp, co. Dublin, and dying 1818, left issue,
1. Edmond, d. unm. 1836.

2. JOHN RICHARD, late of Baronston.
1. Harriette, d. unm.
The only surviving son,
JOHN RICHARD MALONE, of Baronston, co. Westmeath, J.P. and D.L., High Sheriff 1852, b. 1817; m. 1st, 1844, Elizabeth, dau of Col. Henry Peisley L'Estrange, of Moystown, King's Co., and by her (who d. 1847) had issue,
1. JOHN RICHARD, now of Baronston.
2. Henry I. L'Estrange, Lieut.-Col. late 16th Lancers, formerly A.D.C. to the Lord-Lieut. of Ireland, b. 1847; m. 29 July, 1884, Grace Agnes, youngest dau. of Francis Brooke. of Summerton, co. Dublin (*see that family*), and d. 1894. His widow m. 25 July 1908, Hermon John Francis Headfort Lindsey-FitzPatrick, of Hollymount, co. Mayo (*see that family*).
He m. 2ndly, 2 April, 1868, Anna Jane, youngest dau. of Robert William Lowry, D.L., of Pomeroy, co. Tyrone, and Belmore, co. Westmeath. Mr. Malone d. 30 July, 1894.

Arms—Vert a lion rampant between three mullets arg. *Crest*— A man in armour, spear in hand, resting on the ground, all ppr. on the sinister arm a round shield or. *Motto*—Fidelis ad urnam.
Seat—Baronston, Ballinacargy, Mullingar; and Shinglass, Ballymore, Moate, co. Westmeath. *Clubs*—Cavalry, Naval and Military, and Kildare Street.

MANLEY OF WHITEHOUSE.

HENRY CUNNINGHAM MANLEY, M.D., of Whitehouse, co. Antrim, b. 6 June, 1844; m. 12 Jan. 1866, Annabella, dau. of George Tate, of Wellington Park House, Belfast, and has issue,

HENRY TATE, Capt. Lancs. Fus., b. 22 Nov. 1869.
Margaret Elizabeth Madeline Tate.

Lineage.—WILLIAM MANLEY, of Hemyock, d. 1663, leaving issue,
1. Joseph, of Upottery, admon. to Jane, his widow.
2. William, of Wrot Backland, bur. there 28 Dec. 1708, left, by Joan, his wife,
William, m. Joan and left a dau.
3. ROBERT, of whom presently.
The 3rd son,
ROBERT MANLEY, of Hemyock, m. 1st, Dorothy, and 2ndly Bridget, living 1684, and bur. 4 May, 1685 (will dated 14 Aug. 1684, proved 1685), leaving by his 1st wife,
1. ROBERT, of whom presently.
1. Joane.   2. Alice, bapt. 13 Aug. 1668.
The only son,
ROBERT MANLEY, of Windsor, bapt. 18 March 1670; m. 16 Aug. 1700, Joan Churley, of Uffenlin. He was bur. 14 April, 1747 (will dated 1746, proved 1750) leaving issue,
1. Robert, bapt. 22 Dec. 1701, d.s.p.
2. William, bapt. 21 June, 1712, d.s.p.
3. Henry, bapt. 5 Jan. 1704; m. 14 Feb. 1724-5, Joan Jervis, and had issue,
  1. Robert, m. Sarah Hall, and had issue,
    Sarah, m. — Strong, of Tiverton.
  2. Henry, bapt. 22 May, 1729, who had issue, Gen. Manley, of Plymouth; Adm. Manley, of Plymouth, and Capt. Manley, 33rd Regt., who m. Miss Wynan, and d. at Cheltenham.
  3. William (Rev.), bapt. 20 May, 1721; bur. 4 June, 1775.
  4. James, Lieut.-Col. Somerset Militia, m. Leonora Langley, and had issue,
    (1) James, drowned at sea.
    (2) George, b. 9 Sept. 1764; m. Anna Maria Barberini, and d. 1793 (will proved 1794), leaving issue, one son,
      1. George, m. 1st, dau. and co-heir of Benj. Waddington, of Llanover; and 2ndly, Sarah Emerson, dau. and heir of William Stackey, of Swaffham, Norfolk; and 3rdly, the dau. of — Trenchard, and by his 2nd wife had,
        (1) George, m. 1st, Isobel Watts, dau. of — Russel; and 2ndly, Charlotte Middleton, and by her had issue,
          1. George, d.s.p.
          2. William, m. M. F. Radcliff, and has a dau., Marie.
          3. Marmaduke, m. E. Middleton, and has three children.
          4. Hubert.
          1. Isabel, m. J. D'Arcy Hartley, and has issue.
          2. Mary, m. H. Walmesley, and has issue.
          3. Florence, d.s.p.
          4. Emily, m. C. Walmesley, and has issue.
          5. Laura.   6. Amy Angela.
        (1) Emily m. —. Redmond, and had issue.
        (3) Robert.   (4) Henry.
        (1) Betty.   (2) Anne.
        1. Anne d. unm. 1718.   2. Elizabeth, d. unm. 1766.
        3. Mary, m. John Darley.
        4. Joan, m Lieut.-Col. Thomas Darch.
    4. Nicholas, bapt. 12 June, 1706; bur. 21 May, 1784 unm.
    5. EDWARD, of whom presently.
    1. Dorothy, m. 7 Jan. 1774, Thos. Osmund, of Willand.
    2. Patience, bapt. Oct. 1717; m. Jonathan Waldron, of Hemyock.
    3. Elizabeth, m. — Tratt, of Buckland, St. Mary.
    4 Joan, d. unm.
    5. Eleanor, m. Will'am Churchill, and d.s.p.
    6. Mary, m. Rev. — Richards, of Tiverton.
The youngest son,
EDWARD MANLEY, of Windsor, bapt. 9 Sept. 1721; m. 18 Feb. 1742, his 1st cousin, Joan Chorley, and had,

Mansergh.

1. Henry Chorley (Rev.), Inc. of Bradford, Somerset, *m.* 5 March, 1818, the dau. of — Maddox, and *d.* 1828, aged 76, leaving,
    1. Edward (Rev.), *m.* Charlotte Jenkins, of Sudbury, and *d.* Nov. 1841, leaving one son,
       Henry, *d. unm.* 9 Jan. 1836.
    2. Henry, *d. unm.* in America.
    3. Robert, of Sudbury, *m.* the dau. of — Pearce, of Sudbury. She *d.* 1830, leaving,
       (1) Robert, who left issue,
          1. Robert. —
          2. Edward. — In Australia.
             1. Anne. —
       (2) Charles Orlando, *m.* Elizabeth Williams, and had,
          1. Charles Williams.
          1. Eliza Dulciedella.   2. Anaie Marie.
       (3) Edward, *d. unm.*
       (1) Mary Anne, *d. unm.* 9 Nov. 1864.
       (2) Maria, *m.* Sept. 1854, H. Hallett, and *d.s.p.*
       (3) Dulcibella, *d. unm.*
    4. William Henry, *d.* young.
    5. Richard, *d.* young.
    6. Charles, *m.* the dau. of Mortimer, of the Isle of Wight, and *d.* 1816, leaving,
       (1) Charles Maddox, left issue, a son,
       (2) Nicholas, *m.* Jane Petergale, and had seven children.
       (3) Mortimer, *m.* Lydia Horpon.
       (4) Henry John, *m.* 1st, Kate Francis, and had two children. He *m.* 2ndly, Celia Coleridge.
       (5) Hardwick Stowe, *b.* 2 March, 1826.
       (1) Mary Arabela, *d.* 30 Aug. 1869.
       (2) Emma,   (3) Emilie.
       (4) Anne   (5) Dulcibella, *m.* — Hiscock.
    7. Nicholas, Maj., 20th Regt. (Calcutta), *d. unm.* 23 May, 1823, aged 37.
       1. Anne, *m.* 11 Nov. 1828, Lieut. Williams, 1st Royal Veteran Batt.
       2. Elizabeth, *d. unm.*
    2. Edward, of whom presently.
    1. Mary, *d.* young.
    2. Joan, *m.* — Gore, of Uffculin.
    3. Elizabeth.

The youngest son,
EDWARD MANLEY, *b.* 1747 ; *m.* Anne Perry, dau. of Thomas Pearce and Eliza, his wife. She *d.* 20 June, 1823. He *d.* 1780, leaving,
1. John Pearse, LL.D., *m.* Mary Richards, of Sudbury. He *d.* 25 Nov. 1823, aged 51, leaving,
   1. George Pearse, *m.* 27 Sept. 1824, Mary, dau of Rev. H. Jones, of Cumotson, North Wales. He *d.* 1842, leaving,
      (1) John Henry Jones.
      (2) George Frederick Jonas, *d. unm.*
   2. John Henry, *d.* young.
2. Edward, *d.* young.
3. HENRY, of whom presently.
1. Anne, *d.* young.

The youngest son,
HENRY MANLEY, Capt. 63rd L.I., of Sidmouth, Devon, and of Lakefield, Belmont, co. Down, and Silverstream House, co. Antrim, *m.* the dau. of — Crawford, of Belfast, and had issue,
1. Hugh Pearse, *b.* 1809 ; *m.* Mary, dau. of Rev. H. Jones, and widow of George Pearse Manley.
2. HENRY JOHN, of whom presently.
1. Elizabeth Pearse, *b.* 19 Dec. 1805.
2. Anne, *b.* 31 Oct. 1807.

The younger son,
HENRY JOHN MANLEY, of Lisburn, *b.* 4 March, 1811 ; *m.* 26 July, 1843, Anna, dau. of Richard Waring, of Belfast. She *d.* Jan. 1889. He *d.* Jan. 1875, having had issue,
1. HENRY CUNNINGHAM, of whom presently.
2. Hugh Crawford, *b.* 2 Feb. 1847 ; *m.* Margaret (*Prospect House, Donoghdu, co. Down*), dau. of — Tate ; *d.* March, 1900, having had issue,
   1. George Tate.
   1. Rowena Mabel.   2. Margaret Robinson.

Seat—Whitehouse, near Belfast.

MANSERGH OF GRENANE.

PHILIP ST. GEORGE MANSERGH, of Grenane, co. Tipperary, *b.* 12 May, 1863 ; *s.* his brother 22 Jan. 1906 ; *m.* 23 April, 1907, Ethel Marguerite Otway Louisa, only dau. of the late Major Charles Stepney Perceval Egmont Mansergh, 40th Regt., of Clifford, Castletownrocke (*see below*), and has with other issue,

1. CHARLES OGILVY MARTIN SOUTHCOTE, *b.* 22 March, 1908.
2. Philip Nicholas Seton, *b.* 27 June, 1910.

Lineage.—MRS. REBECCA MANSERGH, dau. of Rev. James Redman, of Halton, Yorks (by Agnes Otway his wife), and sister of Col. Daniel Redman, M.P., for co. Kilkenny, had three sons,
1. BRYAN, of whom presently.
2. Robert, of Kilkenny, who left by Edith his wife, administratrix of his property (bond dated 11 June, 1691, *Richmond Wills, Lonsdale Deanery*), an only son,
   George, of Cashel, co. Tipperary, admitted a freeman of that city 27 Jan. 1675, Alderman 15 June, 1683, on roll for Mayor 27 July, 1708, resigned his Aldermanship 11 April, 1710, under his hand and seal, and was bur. in Rock of Cashel Cathedral, *d.s.p.*, left in remainder the estate of his uncle James.
3. James, of Macrony Castle, Fermoy, co. Cork, Capt. of Horse, who obtained grants of land under the Act of Settlement, and amongst them the lands of Macrony. He signed a proclamation issued at Cork 18 Feb. 1659 (SMITH'S *History of Cork*). He *d.* 19 Sept. 1703 (will dated 13 Jan. 1701, proved 12 Dec. 1704) leaving issue,
   1. George, executor to his father's will, left no issue by Elizabeth Wheeler his wife.
   1. Eleanor, *m.* 1684, Nicholas Southcote,* of Grenane, co. Tipperary, and had issue.
   2. Dorothy, *m.* 1681, Alexander Grove, of Ballyhinock, co. Cork, son of Major Ion Grove, of that place, and had a son, Ion, *b.* 1685-8 ; *m.* 1710, Arabella, dau. of Robert Blennerhasset, and *d.* between 1728 and 1734, leaving an eldest son, Robert, *m.* 1741, Mary Ryland, and *d.* 1764 (leaving a dau., Mary, *m.* 1766, 1st Earl Annesley), and a dau., Elinor, *m.* 1735, John FitzGibbon, from whom the Lords Clare, the Lords Decies, and Lord Holmpatrick.
   3. Mary, *d. unm.*

The above-mentioned
BRYAN MANSERGH, of Ballybur, co. Kilkenny (who migrated to Ireland, with the above-mentioned James Mansergh), obtained a grant of lands under the Act of Settlement in the cos. of Meath and Kilkenny. He was High Sheriff co. Kilkenny 1681-2, and J.P. He *m.* Catherine, dau. of Daniel Wentworth, and had issue,
1. DANIEL, of whom presently.
2. George, of Coolgrange, co. Kilkenny, *m.* 1744, Sarah, 4th dau. of Patrick Wemyss, M.P., of Danesfort, co. Kilkenny. His will dated 1748, was proved 1754.
3. Wentworth.
4. Bryan (Rev.), Curate of Tipperary from 25 Oct. 1789, *d. unm.* 27 Dec. 1805 ; bur. in Tipperary.
1. Lemon.   2. Rebecca.
3. Margaret, *m.* 6 April, 1798, John Manx, of Dublin.

The eldest son,
DANIEL MANSERGH, of Macrony Castle, co. Cork, J.P. for that co. *temp.* GEORGE I, *m.* (*as above*) his cousin Mary, dau. and eventual co-heiress of Nicholas Southcote, of Grenane. His will bears date 30 Nov. 1724, and was proved 1 April, 1725. He left issue,
1. James, of Macrony, co. Cork, Major 8th Dragoons, under age 1728 ; *m.* 1st (setts. dated 20 June, 1728) Elizabeth, dau. of John Gifford, of Ahern, co. Cork, and by her had a dau.,
   Catherine, *m.* 2 Feb. 1757, Samuel Bayley.
He *m.* 2ndly, 11 July, 1749, Mary, dau. of Lieut.-Gen. Richard St George, Commander of the Forces in Ireland. His will, dated 2 Feb. 1770, was proved 21 March, 1774. He left issue by her,
   Richard St. George Mansergh, of Headford, co. Galway, who assumed the name of ST. GEORGE ; *m.* Anne Stepney, of Durrow, and was murdered by the Rebels, 1797.
2. NICHOLAS, of whom presently.
3. Bryan, Capt. Lieut. 2nd Regt. of Horse, who left issue, three sons,
   1. James.   2. Nicholas.   3. Henry.
1. Eleanor, *m.* Jonathan Lovett, of Liscombe, Northampton, and Kingswell, Tipperary, and *d.* 2 Dec. 1786, leaving issue (*see that family*).

The 2nd son,
NICHOLAS MANSERGH, of Grenane, co. Tipperary, *m.* 9 Dec. 1750, Elizabeth, dau. of Richard Lockwood, of Indaville and Castle Leake, Cashel. His will is dated 6 Jan. 1767, and proved 6 Aug. 1768, and hers is dated 27 Sept. 1775, and proved 25 Jan. 1776. She *d.* 6 March, 1795, bur. in Tipperary. They had issue,

---
* His father, THOMAS SOUTHCOTE, of Bovey Tracey, co. Devon (son of Thomas Southcote, of Bovey, by Susan, his 2nd wife, dau. of Sir Thomas Kirkham, and grandson of John Southcote, of Bovey), left by Grace his wife, four sons (*see Visitation of Devon*, 1620), 1, Francis ; 2, Anthony ; 3, Henry, and 4, NICHOLAS. The 4th son,
NICHOLAS SOUTHCOTE, of Mountsadivy, co. Devon, and Grenane, co. Tipperary, *b.* about 1613 ; *m.* at St. Peters le Poor, London, 16 Oct. 1647, Mary, 3rd dau. of James Perceval, ancestor of the Earls of Egmont (by Alice his wife, dau. of William Chester, of Amesbury, co. Gloucester), and grand-dau. of James Perceval, of Weston, co. Somerset (who *d.* 26 May, 1594). His will was proved 1679 (Pub. Record Off., Dublin). He left, with other issue, an eldest son,
NICHOLAS SOUTHCOTE, of Grenane, co. Tipperary, *m.* 1684, Eleanor, dau. of James Mansergh, of Macrony (*see text*), and *d.* before 1724 (will proved that year in Cashel Diocesan Court), leaving issue,
1. James, *b.* 20 March. 1685 ; *d.* 2 Jan. 1703 ; bur. in Tipperary (M.I.).
2. Mansergh, *b.* 2 Oct. 1700 ; *d.* 28 March, 1710 ; bur. in Tipperary (M.I.).
1. Mary, *m.* her cousin Daniel Mansergh, of Macrony Castle, co. Cork, and had issue (*see text*).
2. Anne, *d. unm.*
3. Eleanor, *m.* John Massy Dawson, of New Forest (Ballinacourte), co. Tipperary (will dated 7 June, 1751 ,proved 13 Jan. 1752), *d.s.p.*

Mansergh. THE LANDED GENTRY. 456

1. NICHOLAS SOUTHCOTE, of whom presently.
2. Daniel, of Cashel, High Sheriff for co. Tipperary, 1789, *m.* June, 1788, Catherine, dau. of Kingsmill Pennefather, of Cloneyharp, co. Tipperary, M.P. for Cashel in the Irish Parliament, by the Hon. Mary Lysaght his wife, and *d.* 10 June, 1823, aged 50, having by her (who *d.* 17 Nov. 1834) had issue,
  1. NICHOLAS, late of Macrony Castle, co. Cork, J.P. cos. Cork and Tipperary, M.A. Trin. Coll. Dublin, B.A. 1811, M.A. 1815, Barrister-at-Law 1813, last Recorder of Cashel 1836, *b.* 20 May, 1789; *d.* Oct. 1865.
  2. Daniel, Capt. in the Army, of Ballyshean, Cashel. *m.* 1st, 22 Aug. 1836, Miss Budd, of Kilkenny, and by her had issue, two sons and two daus. One of the sons, Henry, *d.* 1889. He *m.* 2ndly, Eleanor Jane, dau. of George Riall, of Parsonstown, and by her (who *d.* 21 Aug. 1893) had issue,
     Helen Elizabeth Frances.
  3. James Wentworth (Rev.), Rector of Kilmore, Diocese of Cashel. *m.* 31 Oct. 1835, Catherine, 3rd dau. of Col. Owen Lloyd, of Rockville, co. Roscommon (*see that family*). She *d.* 27 Sept. 1891. He *d.* 1847, leaving issue,
     (1) Daniel James, of Grallagh Castle, Thurles, co. Tipperary, J.P., Col. Comm. South Tipperary Artillery Militia, formerly served as Ensign in 19th Regt., *b.* 3 Nov. 1836; *d.* 27 April, 1907; *m.* 3 July, 1866, Margaret, 3rd dau of Austin Cooper, of Camas, Cashel, co. Tipperary.
     (2) Owen Lloyd, of Liskeveen, Thurles, J.P. co. Tipperary, *b.* 12 April, 1838; *m.* 1st, 1875, Margaret, 2nd dau. of William Going, of Ballyphilip (*see that family*); 2ndly, Nov 1883, Miss M Going, of Liskeveen, and took the name of GOING, and *d.s.p.* 3 Oct. 1892.
     (3) Nicholas, *b.* 25 Oct. 1852, Ensign 59th Regt.; *d. unm.* 27 Oct. 1870.
     (1) Catherine, *b.* 21 March, 1841; *m.* 18 Jan. 1865, Acheson Montgomery Lloyd, and has issue (*see LLOYD of Rockville*).
  1. Mary, *m.* Edward Pennefather, of Marlow, and had issue.
  2. Margaret, *m.* Major Jacks, 7th Dragoons, and *d.s.p.* 2 May, 1844.
  3. Elizabeth, *m.* Lieut.-Col. Richard Pennefather, M.P. for Cashel, of New Park (*see PENNEFATHER of Rathsallagh*). She *d.* 10 Dec. 1827. He *d.* May, 1831.
  4. Catherine, *d.* young, 7 Aug. 1794.
  5. Catherine, *m.* Richard Martin, of Castle Jane, Glanmire, Cork, and has issue.
3. James, Major 32nd Regt., *d. unm.* 3 April, 1808.
4. Bryan, *m.* Elizabeth, dau. of William Gabbett, of Caherline, co. Limerick (*see that family*), and had issue,
   1. James, of Limerick (will dated 26 May, 1798, proved 29 Jan. 1813). He *d.s.p.*
   1. Ellen, *d. unm.*
   2. Dorothy, *m.* Jan. 1796, Archibald Redfoord, B.L., of Shroland, co. Kildare, and had issue.
5. George, Capt. 22nd Regt., *m.* 1st, a dau. of George Dacre, of York, and had issue,
   1. Lewis, of Riversdale, co. Kildare, *m.* the dau. of — Henn, of Paradise, co. Clare.
   2. George, of Riversdale, co. Kildare, *m.* Mary, 2nd dau. of George Studdert, of Kilkeshen, co. Clare (*see STUDDERT of Bunratty Castle*).
     1. Maria, *m.* Robert Rawson, of Glassealy, co. Kildare, County Treasurer of Kildare.
     2. Jane Elizabeth, *m.* 1786, James Blacker, of Dublin, J.P. (*see that family*).
Capt. George Mansergh *m.* 2ndly, Miss Wolfe, who *d.s.p.* June, 1835.
6. Mathew Wentworth, Attorney-at-Law, *d. unm.* 22 Oct. 1803.
1. Jane Elizabeth, *d.s.p.* 6 March, 1795.

The eldest son,
NICHOLAS SOUTHCOTE MANSERGH, of Grenane, J.P.., *m.* 22 March, 1770, Elizabeth, dau. of John Carden, of Templemore, and sister of Sir John Craven-Carden, Bart., and *d.* March, 1818 (will dated 4 July, 1815), leaving issue,
1. JOHN SOUTHCOTE, of whom presently.
2. Nicholas, *d.s.p.* bur. in Tipperary.
3. Robert, of Friarsfield, Capt. in the Army, *m.* 15 Aug. 1814, Jane, dau. of John Hare, of Deerpark, Cashel, and *d.s.p.*
4. John, of Tipperary, *d.* 14 Feb. 1825, aged 54, bur. in Tipperary.
5. James, Lieut. in the Army, bur. in Tipperary 22 Jan. 1804.
6. Daniel, Capt. 48th and formerly 38th Regts., *m.* Elvira Waterhouse, and had, with other issue
   1. John Craven Carden, Major late 6th Regt., *m.* 1st, 1850, Frances Penelope, dau. of Wallis Adams, of Kilbree, Cloyne, co. Cork. She *d.* in South Africa 1852. He *m.* 2ndly, 7 Feb. 1856, Lucinda Maria Georgina, 3rd dau. of William Smith, of Capetown, Private Secretary to H.E. Sir Benjamin Durban, Governor of Cape Colony. Major Mansergh *d.* 11 Dec. 1886, leaving issue,
     (1) Cornwall Lewis Warwickshire (*Wynberg, Cape Town, S.A.*), *b.* 25 Nov. 1863; *m.* 22 Jan. 1891, Zoldelinda, dau. of Goert Van Rheede, R.M., and Civil Commissioner of Stellenbosch, and has issue.
     (1) Florence Nightingale, *m.* John Hector Straith, and has issue.
     (2) Ellen Alice Maria Wentworth Waterhouse.
   2. Francis, *b.* 1807; *d.* 1871; *m.* Elıza, only dau. of Capt. Daniel Hainersley, 48th Regt., and by her (who *d.* 1866) had issue, three sons and four daus.,
     (1) John Craven, *m.* Annie, dau. of Dr. O'Shannesy.
     (2) Nicholas Southcote, *d.* young.
     (3) Francis.
     (1) Emily Mary, *m.* John Stanistreet, of Rock Lodge, Limerick, and has issue.

(2) Ellen, *m.* John Turton Pierpoint Meadows, and has issue.
(3) Mary, *m.* William Harbrow, of Warren Park, Melbourne, and has issue.
(4) Elizabeth, *m.* 9 May, 1878, Charles Henry Folliott Fowke, son of Dr. Thomas Fowke, of Graiseley, co. Wolverhampton, and has issue.
3. Peter, of Melbourne, *m.* Mary Anne, dau. of Surgeon Blair. She *m.* 2ndly, John Neale.
   1. Penelope. 2. Elizabeth. 3. Priscilla.
7. Robert, *m.* Susan, 2nd dau. of William N. M'Namara, M.P. for Clare, of Doolen, co. Clare (*see that family*).
1. Ellen, *m.* 11 May, 1805, William Kemmis, of Ballinacor, and *d.* 10 June, 1812, leaving issue (*see that family*).
2. Clarinda, *d. unm.* 3. Letitia, *d. unm.*

The eldest son,
JOHN SOUTHCOTE MANSERGH, who resided at Grenane, Tipperary, J.P. cos. Cork and Tipperary, High Sheriff 1800, *m.* 7 Jan. 1795, Mary, only dau. and heiress of Richard Martin, of Clifford, co. Cork (*see MARTIN of Wiche*), and by her (who *d.* 3 Sept. 1811) had issue,
1. Nicholas Southcote, *b.* 9 Jan. 1799; *d.* young.
2. RICHARD MARTIN SOUTHCOTE, his heir, of whom presently.
3. Charles Carden, of Clifford, co. Cork, J.P., Lieut. 3rd Dragoon Guards, M.A. Trin. Coll. Dublin, *b.* 2 Oct. 1802; *m.* Jan. 1830, Elizabeth, dau. of Capt. Loftus Otway Bland, R.N., of Bath, and *d.* 14 Dec. 1873, having by her (who *d.* 1876) had issue,
   1. John Loftus Otway, Major 44th Regt., *b.* 1835; *d.s.p.* 1863.
   2. Charles Stepney Perceval Egmont, Major 40th Regt., of Clifford, Castletown Roche, *b.* 31 Oct. 1841; *m.* 26 March, 1870, Helen, dau. of George Ogilvy, of The Cove, co. Dumfries, and *d.* 1879, having by her (who *m.* 2ndly, 1886, Col. Walter Luttrell Mansel, 40th Regt. (*see MANSEL-PLEYDELL of Whatcombe*) had issue,
     Loftus Charles Ogilvy, of Clifford, Castletownroche, co. Cork, Lieut. R.N., *b.* 2 March, 1873, drowned in Submarine A1, 1904.
     Ethel Marguerite Otway Louisa, *m.* 23 April, 1907, Philip St. George Mansergh (*see above*).
   3. Arthur Henry Wentworth, of Marlacoo, Portadown, co. Armagh, J.P. cos. Leicester and Armagh, Col. and Lieut.-Col. Commandant 1st Vol. Batt. Leicester Regt., late Major 17th Regt., *b.* 29 April, 1844; *m.* 27 Feb. 1878, Bessie Hornor, only child of the late Col. J. B. H. Boyd, commanding 2nd Batt. Leicester Regt., and has issue,
     Bryan Hornor, *b.* 22 Jan. 1892.
   4. Neville Frederick, Major 6th Regt., *b.* 1845; *m.* 22 June, 1870, Anne Elizabeth, only dau. of James Gibbs, of Clifton, and *d.* 1883, leaving issue,
     (1) Charles James Carden, *b.* 17 Feb. 1874.
     (2) Neville Stepney St. George, *b.* 5 July, 1876.
     (3) John Loftus Otway, Lieut. 18th Royal Irish Regt., *b.* 24 May, 1878.
     (1) Lillian Jane Elizabeth, *m.* 14 July, 1897, Henry Esme Bedford, son of the Rev. W. K. R. Bedford (*see BEDFORD of Sutton Coldfield*).
   5. St. George Dyson, of Rock Lodge, Ballyhooley, co. Cork, *b.* 7 March, 1848; *m.* 11 March, 1882, Alice Emma, widow of William Yates Peel, Scots Guards, grandson of Sir Robert Peel, 1st bart., and has issue,
     (1) Perceval St. George, *b.* 15 Dec. 1882; *d.* 12 June, 1910.
     (2) Robert Otway, Lieut. 18th Royal Irish Regt., *b.* 12 Jan. 1885.
     (3) Arthur Neville, *b.* 10 Nov. 1887.
     (4) John Loftus, *b.* 23 Jan. 1891.
     (1) Olivia Alice. (2) Mary Thomasina Maud.
     (3) Adelaide.
   1. Sarah Mary, *m.* 1860, Capt. George Bunbury, 50th Regt., of Woodville, Nenagh, co. Tipperary, and had issue.
   2. Mary Adelaide Catherine, *m.* 1858, Major John Lawrie, late 82nd and 18th Regts., and has issue. He *d.* 5 Jan. 1881.
   3. Elizabeth Frances Olivia.
   4. Georgina Constance Antoinette, *m.* Nov. 1884, Robert Cole Bowen, of Bowen's Court (*see that family*). She *d.s.p.* 8 July, 1886.
4. John Craven, of Rocksavage, Cork, J.P. cos. Cork and Tipperary, late Hon. Lieut.-Col. and Paymaster R.A., *b.* 10 Oct. 1805; *m.* 1st, 1832, Anna, dau. of John Louis van Wilmsdorff Richards of Rathnaspeck, co. Wexford (*see RICHARDS of Macmine*), and by her (who *d.* 10 Nov. 1844) had issue,
   1. John Lewis, of Melbourne, *b.* 21 Aug. 1833; *m.* 20 July, 1863, Hannah Wilks, and has issue,
     (1) John Lewis. (2) Richard Martin.
     (1) Emily Peel. (2) Anne.
     (3) Elizabeth Sarah. (4) Henrietta.
     (5) Clara.
   2. Henry Charles, of Rocksavage, co. Cork, J.P., Major 39th Regt., *b.* 1 Feb. 1835; *d.* 29 July, 1911; *m.* 1st, 2 Nov. 1865, Emily (who *d.* 25 Nov. 1907), dau. of Right Hon. William Yates Peel, and grand-dau. of Sir Robert Peel, 1st Bart. Major Mansergh *m.* 2ndly, 14 Aug. 1909, Rebecca Elizabeth, elder dau. of the late Edward Hoare, of Glanauore, co. Cork (*see BURKE's Peerage, HOARE, Bart.*).
   3. Thomas, *d.* young, 8 Aug. 1836.
   4. Wilmsdorff George, Paymaster, 53rd Regtl. District, and formerly of 18th Hussars, *b.* 27 Sept. 1837; *m.* 18 June, 1878, Sarah Richarda, 4th dau. of Richard Philips, of Mountrivers, co. Tipperary, and *d.* 2 March, 1893, leaving issue,
     (1) Wilmsdorff George, *b.* 8 Dec. 1880.
     (2) Henry Craven, *b.* 20 Dec. 1885.
     (3) Neville Southcote, *b.* 3 Sept. 1889.
     (1) Anna Victoria Wilmsdorff, *m.* 28 June, 1904, Capt.

IRELAND. Mansfield.

Richard Ludwig Bagge, D.S.O., only son of Herbert Bagge (*see* BURKE's *Family Records*).
Mr. J. C. Mansergh *m.* 2ndly, 1855, Jane Anne, dau. of Major John Campbell, 74th Regt., and *d.* 30 Dec. 1896, leaving issue,
  5. Southcote Campbell, *b.* 27 Dec. 1857; *m.* July, 1890, Frances, dau. of James Moody, of Redruth, Cornwall.
  6. Randal Martin St. George, Capt. North Tipperary L.I., *b.* 27 May, 1859.
  5. Southcote, of Grallagh Castle, Thurles, J.P., 50th Regt., *b.* 8 May, 1807; *m.* 1 June, 1841, Anna Matilda, dau. of Col. Rawston Stepney, of Abington, co. Limerick, and relict of William Nicholson, of Turtulla, co. Tipperary, and *d.s.p.* May, 1881. She *d.* July, 1861.
  1. Elizabeth, *b.* 1 Jan. 1796; *m.* Edward Beatty, of Heathfield, co. Wexford, and *d.* 1871, having had issue.
  2. Catherine, *b.* 21 July, 1797; *m.* 21 April, 1817, George Walker, Comm. R.N., of Fermoy, co. Cork, and *d.* 5 May, 1860, having had issue.
  3. Mary Martin, *b.* 23 Nov. 1803; *m.* June, 1830, Francis Leigh, of Sion, co. Wexford, and *d.* 13 Sept. 1868, leaving issue (*see* LEIGH *of Rosegarland*).
Mr. Mansergh *m.* 2ndly, Charlotte, youngest dau. of John Carey, of Straw Hall, Fermoy, and *d.v.p.* 14 Sept. 1817, having by her had an only son,
  6. Robert John Southcote, who *d.s.p.* 31 May, 1871.
The eldest surviving son,
RICHARD MARTIN SOUTHCOTE MANSERGH, of Grenane, Tipperary, J.P., *b.* 14 Nov. 1800; *m.* 1st, 25 Feb. 1822, Jane Rosetta, 2nd dau. and co-heir of Robert Bomford, of Rahinstown, co. Meath (*see that family*), and by her (who *d.* 20 Feb. 1836) had issue,
  1. JOHN SOUTHCOTE, late of Grenane.
  2. Robert George, *b.* 17 April, 1825; *d. unm.* at Cheadle, Cheshire, 29 May, 1869.
  3. Richard St. George, of Friarsfield, Tipperary, *b.* 25 Feb. 1833; *m.* 5 Aug. 1858, Sophia Elizabeth (who *d.* 1905), eldest dau. of the late Richard Oliver Ellard, of Newton-Ellard, co. Limerick. She *d.* 1905. He *d.* 9 Aug. 1897, leaving issue,
    1. RICHARD SOUTHCOTE, late of Grenane.
    2. PHILIP ST. GEORGE, now of Grenane.
    1. Charlotte Rosetta.
  1. Maria Annette, *b.* 24 April, 1828; *m.* 1865, Joseph E. K. Nadin, M.R.C.S.E., of Tipperary, and had issue. She *d.* 13 Feb. 1900. He *d.* 27 May, 1900.
  2. Jane Rosetta, *b.* 12 March, 1830; *m.* 23 April, 1852, William Lane, of Lanes Park, Thurles, co. Tipperary, and has issue.
Mr. Mansergh *m.* 2ndly, 26 April, 1843, Christine, eldest dau. of Rev. Richard Mauleverer, Rector of Tipperary, and *d.* 24 March, 1876, having by her (who *d.* 21 Nov. 1854) had issue,
  4. Richard Charles William, Lieut. 11th Regt., *b.* 24 July, 1846; *m.* at Grahamstown, Cape of Good Hope, 6 July, 1869, Emma, dau. of J. Standen, of Grahamstown, Cape Colony, and *d.* 16 Oct. 1883, leaving issue,
    1. Dora Christine, *b.* 10 Sept. 1870.
    2. Constance Mary, *b.* 26 July, 1872; *m.* 21 Aug. 1895, T. A. R. Purchas. She *m.* 2ndly, William Bruce.
    3. Olive de Burg, *b.* 1 March, 1874; *m.* 24 March, 1903, Arthur Bertram Baines, 3rd son of Lieut.-Col. J. E. Baines, of Dinan, Brittany.
    4. Annette Louisa, *b.* 24 April, 1876; *d.* 16 June, 1877.
  5. James Wentworth, *b.* 12 Sept.; *d.* 30 Sept. 1847.
  6. Richard Mauleverer, Lieut. R.N., *b.* 20 Dec. 1851.
  3. Christine Maria, *b.* 16 April, 1844; *m.* 30 April, 1868, William F. H. Majendie, Lieut. 31st Regt., eldest son of Rev. Stuart Majendie, Rector of Barnwell, Northamptonshire, and *d.* 8 Nov. 1906, leaving issue. He *d.* 5 July, 1893.
  4. Elizabeth Mary, *b.* 11 April, 1845; *m.* 17 March, 1874, Philip Oliver Ellard, J.P., eldest son of the late Richard Oliver Ellard, of Newton-Ellard, co. Limerick, and had issue. He *d.* 2 May, 1877. She *d.* 21 Sept. 1898.
  5. Martha Letitia, *b.* 3 Sept. 1849; *m.* 16 March, 1869, George Edward Moore Taylor, late 44th Regt., and has issue.
The eldest son,
JOHN SOUTHCOTE MANSERGH, of Grenane, Tipperary, J.P. and D.L., Hon. Col. 4th Batt. South Lancashire Regt. and formerly Lieut. 2nd Dragoon Guards (Queen's Bays) and 62nd Regt., *b.* 28 June, 1823; *m.* 24 July, 1851, Mary Elizabeth, only dau. of Charles Walter Wyatt, of Bôd-Erw, St. Asaph, co. Flint. She *d.* 8 March, 1899. He *d.s.p.* 8 Feb. 1899, and was *s.* by his nephew,
RICHARD SOUTHCOTE MANSERGH, of Grenane, co. Tipperary, J.P., *b.* 25 Oct. 1859; *s.* his uncle 8 Feb. 1899, and *d.* 22 Jan. 1906, and was *s.* by his brother.

Arms—Quarterly of eight: 1st, arg. a bend raguly gu. between three arrows points downwards of the last flighted and barbed or (MANSERGH); 2nd, arg., a chevron engrailed gu., between three cootes sa. (SOUTHCOTE); 3rd, per pale gu. and arg., on a chevron between three mullets as many talbots all counterchanged (MARTIN); 4th, arg., on a bend between two lions rampant sa., a wyvern wings displayed of the first (RUDINGE); 5th, per pale or and arg., an escutcheon within an orle of eight martlets sa. (BROWNLOW); 6th arg., a stag courant ppr., on a chief vert three mullets of the first (O'DOHERTY); 7th, az., on a chevron arg. three mullets sa. (ROBERTS); and 8th, az. on a fess erm. three cross-crosslets fitchée gu. (BOMFORD). **Crest**—Out of a ducal crest coronet ppr. charged with a label of three points gu. a demi-lion rampant arg. gorged with a collar raguly of the second, holding in the dexter paw an arrow point downwards of the last, flighted and barbed or. **Motto**—Tout jour pret.

Seat—Grenane, Tipperary.

MANSFIELD OF MORRISTOWN LATTIN.

GEORGE MANSFIELD, of Morristown Lattin, co. Kildare, J.P., D.L., High Sheriff 1874, *b.* 12 Feb. 1845; *m.* 2 Aug. 1877, Alice Adéle d'Audebard de Ferussac, eldest dau. of Count d'Audebard de Férussac, of Paris, by his wife Alice Thorn, and has had issue,
  1. EUSTACE LATTIN MANSFIELD, Capt. 3rd Batt. Royal Dublin Fus., previously Capt. 3rd Batt. Royal Dublin Fus., J.P., *b.* 1879; *m.* 1911, Mabel Edith Clare, 3rd dau. of late Thomas Guy Paget, of Ibstock and Humberstone (*see that family*).
  2. Henry Marie Lattin, *b.* 1881.
  3. Alexander Lattin, *b.* 1882; *m.* 1907, Alice, 3rd dau. of Ambrose More O'Ferrall, of Balyna, co. Kildare (*see that family*), and has issue,
    Alexander George, *b.* July, 1908.
  4. Bertrand Lattin, *b.* 1885; *d.* 1887.
  5. Tirso Louis Marc Lattin, *b.* 1888.
  1. Mary Alice Philomena.
  2. Marguerite Cécile, *m.* 2 Feb. 1905, Richard Morton Wood, Inniskilling Dragoons, eldest son of Col. Wood, Docklands, Ingelstone, *d.* Jan. 1908. She *m.* 2ndly 28 Oct. 1911, Edward John Nettleford, 5th Dragoon Guards, son of the late Edward Nettleford, Brightwell Park, Wallington.

Lineage.—From an inquisition p.m. taken at Dungarvan 1579, it appears that
WILLIAM MANSFIELD, *d.* 1567, seised of Killongford and several other lands on co. Waterford, held of the Crown *in capite*, and that he left by his wife Ellisin Ny Donnell McGrath, who survived him, a son,
EDMUND MANSFIELD, *b.* 1550, who *m.* Catherine, dau. of John FitzGerald, Lord of the Decies, by his wife Hellen, dau. of Maurice Fitz-Gibbon, the White Knight, and by her had issue,
  1. MARGARET, of whom presently.
  2. Catherine, *m.*— Dalton. The lands of Ballyharrohane, co. Waterford were conveyed to her by her father in 1603.
The elder dau.,
MARGARET MANSFIELD, *m.* 1599, WALTER MANSFIELD, Fitz-Edmund Fitz-Walter, of Ballinamultina, co. Waterford (Inq. at Tallow, co. Waterford, 1622, reciting grant of Ballinamultina to Walter Mansfield). They had issue,
EDMUND MANSFIELD, on whom his father, by deed dated 23 July, 1591, settled Ballinamultina. He *m.* Oct. 1621, Ellenor, dau. of Richard Nugent, of Cloncoskraine, co. Waterford, and dying in 1623, left an only son,
WALTER MANSFIELD, of Ballinamultina, named in the deed of 1591, who *m.* 1640, Helena, dau. of Nicholas Power, of Kilballykiltie, co. Waterford. This Walter, who was one of the "Fortynine" officers, suffered much during the Commonwealth, his property having been confiscated, and he was himself transplanted to Connaught. His son,
RICHARD MANSFIELD, *s.* him, and recovered a portion of the family estate at the Restoration; *m.* 1681, Dorothea, dau. of Matthew Hore, of Shandon, co. Waterford, and left, with other issue, an eldest son,
JOHN MANSFIELD, *m.* Jane, dau. of James Eustace, of Yeomanstown. co. Kildare, and by her had issue, with two daus., a son,
ALEXANDER MANSFIELD, *m.* Anne, dau. of David Power, of Knockaderry, co. Waterford, and had issue,
  1. JOHN, of whom hereafter.   2. David, *d.s.p.*
  1. Jane, *m.* Thomas Sherlock, of Butlerstown Castle, co. Waterford.
The elder son,
JOHN MANSFIELD, having inherited a portion of the property of the Eustaces of Yeomanstown, in right of his paternal grandmother, removed to co. Kildare, and *m.* Elizabeth, dau. of Walter Woulfe, of Rathgormack, co. Waterford, by Frances Ryan, of Inch, co. Tipperary, his wife, and left two sons and a dau.,
  1. ALEXANDER, of whom presently.
  2. Walter Henry, of Yeomanstown, co. Kildare, and Rathgormack, co. Waterford, *m.* 1813, Frances, 2nd dau. of Owen Mac Dermott, of Great Denmark Street, Dublin, by Frances Laffan his wife, and *d.* 1849, having by her (who *d.* 1883) had issue,
    1. John Alexander, *b.* 1814; *d.s.p.* 1860.
    2. Walter George, of Tinhalla, Capt. R.N., *m.* 1853, Anne, only dau. and heir of Maurice Ronayne, of Knockaderry and Tinhalla, co. Waterford, by Anne his wife, dau. of Nicholas Power, of Snowhill, co. Kilkenny, and *d.s.p.* 1873.
    3. Owen, *b.* 1818; *m.* 1847, Jane, dau. of William E. Wright, and by her (who *d.* 1883) had issue, and *d.* 1888.
    4. Octavian, J.P., Landscape, co. Waterford, *b.* 1826; *d.* 1890.

5. Edward Oswald, Landscape, co. Waterford, b. 1828.
6. Eustace Henry, formerly Col. Comm. Kildare Militia, b. 1829, d. 1903.
1. Eliza Mary, d. 1852. 2. Fanny Mary.
3. Emily Jane Mary.
1. Frances, d.s.p. 1840.
The eldest son,
ALEXANDER MANSFIELD, of Morristown Lattin, b. 1786 ; m. Pauline, only dau. and heir of Patrick Lattin, of Morristown Lattin, co. Kildare, by Elizabeth Snow (of Drumdowny, co. Kilkenny) his wife, and had issue,
1. GEORGE PATRICK LATTIN, of Morristown Lattin.
2. Alexander John, of the English Bar, b. 1826; m. 14 July, 1863, Maria, eldest dau. of Sir John Howley, Q.C., H.M. First Serjeant in Ireland. He d. 14 Oct. 1901.
3. William Henry, Capt. 44th Regt., d. of wounds received before Sebastopol 1855.
4. Richard Walter, Major late Kildare Militia, d. 1893.
5. Edmund Alexander, Major late co. Dublin Militia.
1. Eliza Pauline, m. 1837, George Thunder, youngest son of Patrick Thunder, of Lagore, co. Meath. Mr. Thunder d. 1877. Mrs. Thunder d. 1878, leaving issue (see that family).
Mr. Mansfield d. in 1842. His eldest son,
GEORGE PATRICK LATTIN MANSFIELD, of Morristown Lattin, J.P. and D.L., High Sheriff 1851, b. 19 Dec. 1820 ; m. 31 Nov. 1843, Mary Frances Constantia, dau. of George Bourke O'Kelly, of Acton House, Middlesex, and by her (who d. 9 June, 1853) had issue,
1. GEORGE, now of Morristown Lattin.
1. Pauline Mary, d. 15 Jan. 1854. 2. Maude Mary.
Mr. Mansfield d. 1889.

Arms—Arg., three bars sa., the first bar charged with a wyvern of the field. Crest—An arm embowed in armour, holding a short sword, all ppr. Motto—Turris fortitudinis.

Seat—Morristown Lattin, Naas, co. Kildare. Clubs—MotorClub, and Kildare Street, Dublin.

MANSFIELD OF CASTLE WRAY.

FRANCIS HARCOURT MANSFIELD, of Castle Wray, co. Donegal, formerly in the N.W. Mounted Police, Canada, b. Sept. 1861.

Lineage.—RALPH MANSFIELD, a Capt. in the Army, was the first of the family who settled in Ireland, and was granted by JAMES I in 1614, by patent, 1000 acres, called Killaneguirdon (now called Killygardon), part of which has ever since been in the possession of the family. Ralph was s. by his son,
JOHN MANSFIELD, who m. Miss Leigh, of Norbury Booth, and had issue, one son, GEORGE, and two daus., Anne, m. — Goodwin, co. Londonderry, and Sarah, m. — Parke, co. Sligo. The son,
GEORGE MANSFIELD, m. Miss Rhoda Johnston, of Kilmore, co. Fermanagh, and had issue, five sons,
1. Ralph (Rev.), d. unm.
2. FRANCIS, of whom presently.
3. George, of Laught.
4. Charles, m. the dau. of Edmund Evans, and had one son, Kingsmill Evans Mansfield, who d. unm.
5. Johnston, m. Miss Young, of Lough Esk, co. Donegal, and had several sons and daus., all of whom d. unm. except Robert, who m. Miss Darran, of co. Sligo, by whom he had a very numerous family. The present representative of this branch of the family is Robert Mansfield, of Kilmore Lodge, co. Tyrone, J.P., b. 1814, and s. his brother 1884.
The 2nd son,
CAPT. FRANCIS MANSFIELD, of Mount Hall, m. Elizabeth Montgomery, grand-dau. of Hugh, 2nd Viscount Montgomery, of Great Ards, co. Down, and by her had issue,
1. RALPH, of whom presently.
1. Anna Helena. 2. Martha, m. Lieut. Thelwell Howell.
The son,
REV. RALPH MANSFIELD, m. the dau. of — Johnston, of Drumkeen, co. Fermanagh, and had issue,
1. FRANCIS, of whom presently.
1. Elizabeth, m. William Wray, of Oak Park, co. Donegal.
2. Grace, m. John McClintock.
The son,
FRANCIS MANSFIELD, of Castle Wray, m. May, 1789, Margaret West, grand-dau. of John Leonard, of co. Fermanagh, and had with others, who d. unm.,
1. Ralph, Capt. 15th Hussars, d. 12 Nov. 1854.
2. David d. unm. in India. 3. FRANCIS, his heir.
1. Margaret. 2. Rhoda.
3. Elizabeth.
4. Jane, m. Oct. 1830, Sir James Stewart, 8th bart. of Fort Stewart.
5. Anna Helena, m. Robert M. Tagart, of Wood Brook, co. Tyrone. 6. Frances Letitia.
7. Grace Octavia, m. David Fussell.
The 3rd son,
FRANCIS MANSFIELD, of Castle Wray and Ardrummon House, co. Donegal, J.P., D.L., b. 19 Nov. 1796 ; m. 6 April, 1832, Mary, 3rd dau. of Sir Samuel Hayes, 2nd bart. of Drumboe Castle, co. Donegal. She d. 15 Dec. 1874. He d. 19 Feb. 1884, leaving issue,
1. FRANCIS STEWART, of Castle Wray.
2. Ralph Mansfield, b. 1838 ; d. 1894.
3. James Charles Henry, Capt. Welsh Regt., b. 1 May, 1841 ; m. 1881, Jane, dau. of Dr. Coates, M.D., and d. 28 Feb. 1889.

4. Edmund Christopher, of Ardrummon House, co. Donegal, J.P., High Sheriff 1906, B.A., Trin. Coll. Dublin, b. 26 May, 1851 ; m. 29 April, 1890, Minnie Frances, dau. of the late John Coote Ovens, of Aghnagaddy House, co. Donegal, J.P., of the 5th Dragoon Guards, and grand-dau. of Robert Conway Hickson, D.L., of Fermoyle, co. Kerry, and d. 21 Feb. 1907, leaving issue,
1. Edmund Francis Hayes, b. 11 Nov. 1891.
2. James Alexander, b. 21 Feb. 1893.
3. Richard George Henry, b. 24 Oct. 1894.
1. Muriel Mary.
2. Winifred, b. 19 March, d. 3 April, 1902.
1. Eliza. 2. Mary Jane.
The eldest son,
FRANCIS STEWART MANSFIELD, of Castle Wray, co. Donegal, B.A. Trin. Coll. Dublin, J.P. and D.L., High Sheriff 1859, Lieut.-Col. late 5th Batt. Royal Inniskilling Fus., b. 26 Feb. 1833 ; m Oct. 1860, Anna Philippa, eldest surviving dau. of George Simon Harcourt, M.P., of Ankerwyke, Bucks (see that family), and had issue,
1. FRANCIS HARCOURT, now of Castle Wray.
2. Ralph Chandos Henniker, b. Sept. 1862 ; m. Nov. 1908, Letitia Helen Mousley, dau. of the late Walter Mousley, of Strathfieldsaye, Hants.
3. Henry Bevan, b. May, 1865.
4. Edward James, b. Sept. 1868 ; d. Nov. 1891.
5. Robert, b. Nov. 1869.
1. Jessy Gertrude Anne, m. 1 June, 1887, George Rawdon Maurice Hewson, of Dromahair, co. Leitrim, J.P.
2. Isabel Mary, m. 12 Aug. 1896, Sir Harry Jocelyn Urquhart Stewart, Bart. of Fort Stewart, co. Donegal (see BURKE'S Peerage).
3. Emily Anna Phillippa, m. April, 1898, Henry Edward Wynne, J.P., of Ernecliffe, Enniskillen, and has issue (see WYNNE (now PERCIVAL) of Haslewood).
Mr. F. S. Mansfield d. 21 Oct. 1909, and was s. by his eldest son.

Seat—Castle Wray, Letterkenny, co. Donegal.

MAPOTHER OF KILTEEVAN.

THOMAS AUSTIN PATRICK MAPOTHER, of Kilteevan, co. Roscommon, J.P. and D.L., High Sheriff 1868.

Lineage.—RICHARD MAYPOWDER, b. at Mickleham, co. Dorset, settled in co. Roscommon, temp. ELIZABETH, and was High Sheriff 1585, was granted the lands of Killenboy, Kilteevan, and others by Patent dated 11 Jan. 1613, to hold for ever by service of one knight's fee. He m. Margaret, dau. of Capt. Thomas Woodhouse, of Abreton or Kingswood, Stafford, and d. June, 1630 (Fun. Entry) having had issue,
1. THOMAS, of whom presently.
2. Woodhouse, m. Alson, dau. of James Lodge, of Dublin.
3. Sarah, m. John Crofton, of Lisadurn, co. Roscommon, who d. 16 Sept. 1639, leaving issue. (See BURKE'S Peerage, CROFTON, B.)
2. Anne, m. Sir Matthew de Renzy, and d. 20 Aug. 1659.
3. Eleanor, m. William Marson, of Clonetragh, co. Roscommon.
4. Mary, m. 1st, William Ormsby, of Clonesilly, co. Roscommon, and 2ndly, William Crofton.
The eldest son,
THOMAS MAYPOWDER, of Killenboy, m. Catherine, dau. of — Fesier, of Paris, and d. before 1653, leaving issue : 1. RICHARD, his heir ; 2. James ; and 3. John. The eldest son,
RICHARD MAYPOWDER, of Killenboy, m. Elizabeth, dau. of John Chevers, of Killyan, co. Galway. She d. Sept. 1690. He d. at a very advanced age 1711, having had a son,
PATRICK MAPOTHER, of Kilteevan, m. 1st, Mary, dau. of Gerald Dillon, of Strokestown, co. Roscommon, by whom he had two daus. He m. 2ndly, Eleanor, dau. of Edmund Nugent, of Carlandstown, co. Westmeath. She d.s.p. He m. 3rdly, Susanna, dau. of Christopher Irwin, of Oran, co. Roscommon, and by her had a son, who d. young and two daus. He m. 4thly, Anne, dau. of Edward Crofton, of Longford House, co. Sligo (see BURKE'S Peerage, CROFTON, Bart.), and by her had three sons,
1. EDWARD, his heir.
2. HENRY, s. his brother.
3. Patrick.
The eldest son,
EDWARD MAPOTHER, of Kilteevan, m. 1st, Frances, dau. of John Kelly, of Conlyon, co. Galway. She d.s p. 4 March, 1765. He m. 2ndly, June, 1768, Frances, dau. of Robert Ormsby, of Rocksavage, co. Roscommon. She d.s.p. May, 1781. He m. 3rdly, Anne, dau. of James Crofton, of Longford House (see BURKE's Peerage), and d.s.p. 1802, when he was s. by his brother,
HENRY MAPOTHER, of Kilteevan, m. Margaret, dau. of Charles Croghan, of Tonragee, co. Roscommon, and had, with other issue, a son,
EDWARD MAPOTHER, of Kilteevan, d. 28 April, 1835 ; m. April, 1784, Penelope, dau. of John Taylor, of Swords, co. Dublin, and had, with other issue, a son,

JOHN EDWARD MAPOTHER of Kilteevan, m. 9 Aug. 1824, Catherine, dau. of Owen O'Conor Don, The O'Conor Don, of Belanagare, co. Roscommon, and had, with other issue, a son,
THOMAS AUSTIN PATRICK, now of Kilteevan.
Arms—Sa. a griffin passant, wings elevated arg. between three escallops or.
Seat—Kilteevan House, co. Roscommon.

MARLAY OF BELVEDERE.

CHARLES BRINSLEY MARLAY, of Belvedere, co. Westmeath, M.A. Trin. Coll. Camb., J.P. and D.L., High Sheriff cos. Westmeath 1853 and 1906, Louth 1863, and Cavan 1885, b. 1831; s. to the settled estates of Robert, 1st Earl of Belvedere, and assumed the name and arms of ROCHFORT, by Royal Licence, 30 Nov. 1867, but does not use that surname.

Lineage.—The first of the family whom we find on record is JOHN MARLAY, of Newcastle-on-Tyne, merchant. By his wife Elizabeth (who m. 2ndly Mark Shaftoe, of the same place), he left issue,
1. Simon, who appears to have d. unm.
2. WILLIAM, of whom presently.
1. Eleanor, m. Ralph Carr, of Cocken, co. Durham.

The 2nd son,
WILLIAM MARLAY, a merchant, of Newcastle-on-Tyne, b. 1590; d. 1609, and was bur. at Newcastle-on-Tyne. He left issue, by Catherine his wife (who d. 1620), an only son,
SIR JOHN MARLAY, of Newcastle-on-Tyne, merchant, and Alderman. He served as Mayor of that town five times between the years 1637 and 1662, and received the honour of knighthood at Berwick 26 July, 1639. He defended that town for King CHARLES I 1644, being Governor of it, but was obliged to surrender. He d. 1673, having m. Jane, sister to Edith, wife of Richard Hedworth, merchant, of Newcastle-on-Tyne, by whom he had a son,
ANTHONY MARLAY, of Creevan, co. Longford, m. Elizabeth, 2nd dau. of Robert Morgan, of Cottlestown, co. Sligo, and had issue,
1. THOMAS (Right Hon.), Lord Chief Justice of the Court of King's Bench in Ireland, whose will, dated 1753, was proved 1756; m. 1707, Mary, dau. of Charles De Laune, of Dublin, and had issue,
   1. Thomas, of Celbridge, co. Kildare, d. before 1784.
   2. Anthony, Barrister-at-Law, Commissioner of Appeals, m. 26 Oct. 1740, Martha, dau. of William Usher, of Usher's Quay, and by her (who d. 1763) left an only dau. and heir,
   Letitia, m. 8 Feb. 1765, Sir Richard Wolseley, 2nd bart. (see BURKE's Peerage).
   3. Robert.   4. Richard, Bishop of Waterford, d. unm. 1802.
   1. Elizabeth.
   2. Mary, m. James Grattan, Recorder of Dublin, and M.P. for that city, and was mother of the Right Hon. Henry Grattan, M.P.   3. Alice, m. 1748, Michael Leving, of Colverstown.
2. Robert.   3. John.
4. GEORGE, of whose line we treat.

The 4th son,
THE RIGHT REV. GEORGE MARLAY, D.D., Bishop of Dromore, consecrated 1745. m. Elizabeth Dunlevy, and d. 8 April, 1763, leaving a dau., Elizabeth, m. 1762, Right Hon. David Latouche, and a son,
GEORGE MARLAY, of Twickenham, Middlesex, Major in the Army, m. Lady Catherine Butler, dau. of Brinsley, Earl of Lanesborough, by Lady Jane Rochfort his wife, only dau. of Robert, 1st Earl of Belvedere, and d. 14 April, 1826, leaving with two daus. (Elizabeth, d. unm. 1848, and Catherine, m. Rev. Calvert Fitzgerald Moore, of Twickenham), a son and successor,
GEORGE MARLAY, of Cavendish Square, b. 1791, Lieut.-Col., C.B., A.D.C. to Sir Edward Paget, m. 1828, Catherine Louisa Augusta, dau. of James Tisdall, of Bawn, co. Louth (descended from James Tisdall, of Bawn, to whom and his brothers arms were assigned by St. George, Ulster, 1679), by his wife Catherine Maria Dawson, afterwards Countess of Charleville, and d. 1830, having had issue,
1. James, d. 1843.
2. CHARLES BRINSLEY MARLAY, now of Belvedere.
1. Catherine Louisa Georgina, m. 10 June, 1851, John James Robert, 7th Duke of Rutland, K.G., P.C., G.C.B., and d. 7 April, 1854, leaving issue (see BURKE's Peerage).

Arms—Quarterly: 1st and 4th, az. a lion rampant arg., armed and langued gu. (ROCHFORT); 2nd and 3rd, barry of eight or and gu., a bordure az. charged with eight martlets of the first (MARLAY). **Crests**—1. A robin redbreast ppr. (ROCHFORT); 2. An eagle displayed ppr. (MARLAY). **Mottoes**—Nulli præda sumus; and Cando; dat viribut alas.
Seat—Belvedere, Mullingar, co. Westmeath. **Residence**—St. Katherine's Lodge, Regent's Park. **Clubs**—Carlton and Travellers'.

MARSH OF JERPOINT.

COL. JEREMY TAYLOR MARSH, of West Jerpoint, co. Kilkenny, Col. R.E. (ret.), b. 14 May, 1841; m. 15 Sept. 1864, Rachel Gertrude, only child of Charles Ferdinand Smyth, of Endsleigh, co. Surrey. She d. 17 March, 1905, leaving issue,
1. Francis Charles, Capt. and Brevet Major Queen's Own W. Kent Regt., b. 20 Sept. 1866, killed at the capture of Burmi, N. Nigeria, 27 July, 1903.
2. James Reynolds Maxwell, Major Lincoln Regt., b. 5 March, 1868; d. 29 Oct. 1907.
3. JEREMY TAYLOR, Capt. A.S.C., late Middlesex Regt., b. 16 Dec. 1871; m. 9 June, 1906, Constance Mary, only dau. of Arthur Holland Robinson, of 31, Onslow Gardens, S. Kensington, and has issue,
   Jeremy Taylor, b. 28 May, 1909.
4. Digby Cecil, late Manchester Regt., b. 16 Aug. 1877.
5. Roland Henry, Capt. 18th Tiwana Lancers, b. 25 March, 1879.
6. Gilbert Howe Maxwell, Capt. 41st Dogras, b. 30 July, 1882.
1. Evelyn Caroline Gertrude.
2. Emily Frances, m. 29 April, 1896, William Moseley Fenton Mellor, son of William Moseley Mellor, of Lingdale, Claughton, Cheshire, and has issue.
3. Gertrude Clifford, m. 2 July, 1903, Graves W. Eves, A.M.I.C.E., eldest son of the Rev. Canon Eves, of Maryborough, Queen's Co., and has issue.
4. Hilda Gordon Maxwell.

Lineage.—FRANCIS MARSH, of Edgeworth, co. Gloucester, m. Anne, dau. of William Aylesbury, and aunt of Frances, Countess of Clarendon, mother of ANNE, Duchess of York, 1st wife of JAMES II. The grandson of this marriage,
FRANCIS MARSH, D.D., Archbishop of Dublin, b. 23 Oct. 1626; m. Mary, dau. and co-heir of Jeremy Taylor, Bishop of Down and Connor, and had issue,
1. Francis, who left two daus.
2. JEREMY, of whose line we treat.
1. Barbara, wife of Francis Cauntrell.

The 2nd son,
THE VERY REV. JEREMY MARSH, Dean of Kilmore, m. 1st, Henrietta Catherine, dau. of Henry Dodwell, by whom he had an only dau., Mary, wife of John Digby, of Landenstown, co. Kildare; he m. 2ndly, Elizabeth, dau. of Simon Digby, Bishop of Elphin, and had by her a dau., Frances, wife of the Rev. William French, and a son, JEREMY, his heir. The Dean m. 3rdly, Judith, dau. of Francis Butler, and had by her a son, Francis (who d. unm. 1772). Dean Marsh d. 1734. His son and heir,
REV. JEREMY MARSH, Rector of Athenry, in the Diocese of Tuam, m. Jane, dau. of Patrick French, of Monivea, co. Galway, and had issue,
1. FRANCIS, his heir.
2. ROBERT, Rector of Killynan, co. Galway, father of Sir HENRY MARSH, M.D., created a bart. in 1839, whose only son, Sir Henry Marsh, 2nd bart., d.s.p. 27 May, 1868.
3. Digby, Senior Fellow of Trin. Coll. Dublin, d. unm. 1791.
4. Jeremy, m. Rachael, dau. of Col. Hugh Montgomery, of Rose Mount, Grey Abbey, and had issue,
   1. Jeremy Digby, Capt. 90th Regt., m. Mary Anne Dickson, dau. of Rev. George Dowse, D.D., and had issue.
   2. Hans Stevenson.
   3. Digby, Rear-Adm. R.N., m. Adelaide, dau. of John Robley, of Tobago, West Indies, and had issue,
      (1) Willoughby Digby, Col. R.E., of Brown's Barn, co. Kilkenny, b. 16 Sept. 1831; m. 1st, Margaret Isabella, dau. of Stephen Falside Carmichael, M.D., and by her had issue,
         1. Digby, b. 1 Sept. 1860; m. Fannie, dau. of — Beresford, M.D., of Hartford, Conn., U.S.A., and d.s.p.
         2. Henry Carmichael, b. 4 Feb. 1865; m. 9 Jan. 1894, Caroline Julia Chambers (who d. 1 Jan. 1910), dau. of William Henry Deane, and has issue,
            a. Willoughby Digby Henry, b. 24 July, 1900.
            a. Margaret Caroline Snowvia.
            b. Grace Rachel Montgomery.
            c. Rosamond Adelaide Ussher.
            d. Eileen Beatrice Cecil.
            e. Mary Carmichael Patricia Ouseley.
         3. Francis Stevenson, M.A., LL.B. T.C.D., b. 26 Jan. 1872.
            1. Laura, d. young.
      He m. 2ndly, 10 Aug. 1880, Elizabeth, 3rd dau. of the late Francis Marsh, of Springmount (see below), and by her has issue,
         2. Anna Adelaide Caroline.
      (2) Hans Stevenson St. Vincent, Capt. 33rd Foot, killed before Sebastopol, 24 June, 1855.

(1) Maria Adelaide, *m.* 1861, Capt. William Kemp, of Lyminster House, Arundel.
(2) Rosamond.
4. Robert, Lieut. R.N., *d. unm.*
5. Francis, Capt. late 11th Foot, *m.* Isabella, dau. of — Wilson, and had issue, six sons and one dau., settled in Australia.
1. Elizabeth, *m.* Rev. Simon Digby, of Osberstown.
2. Frances, *m.* Joshua Hearn, of Hearnsbrook.
3. Nichola, *m.* Rev. Cecil Crampton.
The eldest son,
FRANCIS MARSH, Barrister-at-Law, *m.* 9 Sept. 1775, Anne, only dau. and heiress of Neptune Vero, and *d.* Jan. 1829, having had issue (with a dau.), two sons,
 1. JEREMY, his heir.   **2.** Digby, who *m.* and left two daus.
The elder son,
REV. JEREMY MARSH, Rector of Ballintober, Queen's Co., *m.* 1815, Sarah, dau. of Richard Connell, and by her (who *d.* 25 July, 1823) left at his decease, 2 Nov. 1830, two daus., Anne and Sarah, and one son,
FRANCIS MARSH, of Springmount, Queen's Co., J.P., *b.* 11 June, 1817 ; *m.* 17 July, 1838, Anna Maria, youngest dau. of Arthur Maxwell, of Dublin, and by her (who *d.* 19 Feb. 1890) had issue,
 1. JEREMY TAYLOR, present representative.
 2. Arthur, *b.* 25 April, 1844 ; *m.* 28 July, 1870, Rachel, eldest dau. of Andrew M'Cullagh, and has issue,
  1. Francis, *b.* 16 Sept. 1872 ; *d. unm.* 17 Jan. 1906.
  2. Arthur Torrens, *b.* 29 Oct. 1876.
  1. Rachel Kathleen.   2. Anna Ethel.
  3. Emily Cecil Clare.
 3. Francis, *b.* 15 Aug. 1846 ; *d.* 7 Aug. 1863.
 4. Henry, C.I.E., M.I.C.E. (Chief Engineer P.W.D. India, retired) (33, *Barkston Gardens, South Kensington*), *b.* 8 Sept. 1850 ; *m.* 1st, 2 Sept. 1879, Alice Matilda, dau. of Very Rev. W. Smyth-King, Dean of Leighlin, and had by her (who *d.* 14 Oct. 1881),
  1. Cecil Henry, I.C.S., *b.* 3 Aug. 1880.
  2. Percy William, I.C.S., *b.* 14 Oct. 1881.
He *m.* 2ndly, 3 Jan. 1884, Helen Elizabeth, only dau. of Rev. Henry Freke, Rector of Stackallan, co. Meath, and by her has issue,
  3. Harry Francis Freke, Lieut. 2nd K.E.O. Gurkhas, *b.* 25 Aug. 1886.
  1. Vera Evelyn Selina, *m.* 3 June, 1906, Selwyn Howe Freemantle, I.C.S., 2nd son of Adm. Sir Edmund Robert Fremantle, G.C.B., C.M.G. (see BURKE'S *Peerage*, COTTESLOE, B.).
  2. Gladys Helen Mildred.
 5. Robert Maxwell, C.E., P.W.D. India, of Springmount, Queen's Co., J.P., late Major 4th Batt. Leinster Regt., *b.* 7 Sept. 1852 ; *m.* 7 Feb. 1893, Ellen, only surviving child of the late Edmund Bowyer, of Freshford, Somerset, and has issue,
  1. Stephen Gilbert Bowyer, *b.* 26 Dec. 1893.
  2. Robert Maxwell Owen, *b.* 31 July, 1896 ; *d.* 16 Nov. 1911.
  1. Gertrude Mary, *b.* 19 Jan. 1912.
 6. Cecil Crampton, *b.* 30 Jan. 1856 ; *d.* 30 Jan. 1875.
 7. George William, *b.* 11 Nov. 1858 ; *m.* 6 Feb. 1884, Anna Beverley, eldest dau. of Col. Beverley Robinson, of New Brunswick. He *d.* 11 Nov. 1886, leaving issue,
  1. Constance, *d. unm.*
  2. Violet, *m.* George William Clements, who *d.* 1909, leaving issue.
 1. Caroline Anne, *d.* 25 April, 1862.
 2. Anne Maria, *d.* 12 Oct. 1871.
 3. Elizabeth, *m.* 10 Aug. 1880, Willoughby Digby Marsh, Col. R.E. (*see above*).
Mr. Marsh *d.* 25 Feb. 1879, and was *s.* by his son,

Arms—Gu., a horse's head couped or, between two trefoils in chief and a fleur-de-lis in base arg. *Crest*—A griffin's head couped az. gorged with a ducal coronet, or, in the beak a rose arg. seeded gold, slipped, leaved, and beaked vert. *Motto*—Nolo servile capistrum.
Residence—Black Hill, Abbeyleix, Ireland. *Club*—Naval and Military.

LEESON-MARSHALL OF CALLINAFERCY HOUSE.

MARKHAM RICHARD LEESON-MARSHALL, of Callinafercy House, co. Kerry, J.P. and D.L., High Sheriff 1890, B.A. New Coll. Oxon, Barrister-at-Law, Capt. 3rd Batt. Royal Munster Fus., *b.* 24 Dec. 1859 ; *m.* 1st, 9 Aug. 1890, Mabel Edith, eldest dau. of Sir John Fermor Godfrey, Bart., and by her (who *d.* 2 May, 1892) has issue,

 Mary (May), *b.* 19 May, 1891.

He *m.* 2ndly, 1907, Meriel Anne, only dau. of Sir George Frederick John Hodson, 3rd Bart. (*see* BURKE'S *Peerage*).

Lineage.—ROBERT LEESON, *b.* April, 1746, son of Hon. Robert Leeson, 2nd son, by his 3rd wife, of Joseph, 1st Earl of Milltown (see BURKE'S *Peerage*, MILLTOWN, E.), *m.* Jan. 1820, Elizabeth, only surviving dau. and heiress of Ralph Marshall, of BallymacAdam, co. Kerry, and had, with other issue,
RICHARD JOHN LEESON, *b.* 11 April, 1828, who took the surname of MARSHALL, under the will of his uncle, John Markham Marshall, by Royal Licence, 10 Feb. 1852 ; *m.* 23 Sept. 1858, Rebecca (Zeena), dau. of Ven. Ambrose Power, Archdeacon of Lismore, and *d.* 27 Aug. 1877, leaving (with three daus., Mary Henrietta, Grace Elizabeth, and Edith Susan) a son, the present MARKHAM RICHARD LEESON-MARSHALL, of Callinafercy House.

FAMILY OF MARSHALL.

TRISTRAM MARSHALL, came to Kerry in the expedition of Sir Charles Wilmot, 1602, and marrying Mary, dau. of Maurice Fitz-Gerald, of BallymacAdam Castle, co. Kerry, settled there. His son,
JOHN MARSHALL, *m.* Jane, dau. of Florence McCarty, of Clodane ; was driven out by the Irish in the great rebellion of 1641, returned as a Capt. in Cromwell's Army, and re-settled at BallymacAdam Castle, co. Kerry. His son,
RALPH MARSHALL, *m.* Elizabeth, dau. of Arthur Brown, of Ballyneatig, co. Kerry, a Cromwellian officer. His son,
RALPH MARSHALL, *m.* Jane, dau. and heiress of John Purcell, of Gortenard, co. Cork. His son,
JOHN MARSHALL, *m.* Lucy, sister of the Hon. Robert Day, a Judge of the King's Bench. His son,
RALPH MARSHALL, High Sheriff co. Kerry 1799, *m.* Jane, only dau. and heiress of John Markham, of Brewsterfield, co. Kerry ; and was killed in the Peninsular War, leaving a son, John Markham, who *d. unm.* 1832, and a dau.,
ELIZABETH MARSHALL, *m.* Jan. 1820, Robert, son of Hon. Robert Leeson, youngest son of Joseph, 1st Earl of Milltown, and had, with other issue,
RICHARD JOHN LEESON (who took the name of MARSHALL, as above), *m.* 23 Sept. 1858, Rebecca (Zeena), dau. of Ven. Ambrose Power, Archdeacon of Lismore, and *d.* 27 Aug. 1877, leaving (with three daus.) a son, MARKHAM RICHARD LEESON-MARSHALL.

FAMILY OF MARKHAM.

JOHN MARKHAM, an Officer in Cromwell's army, settled in Ireland. His son,
CAPT. JOSHUA MARKHAM, of Killaha Castle, co. Kerry, *m.* Mildred, grand-dau. and co-heir of Sir Francis Brewster, of Brewsterfield, co. Kerry, and *d.* 1717. His son,
JOSHUA MARKHAM, of Nunstown, *m.* Hester, dau. and heiress of William Godfrey, of Callinafercy, co. Kerry. His son,
JOHN MARKHAM, of Brewsterfield and Callinafercy, High Sheriff co. Kerry 1784, *m.* Elizabeth, dau. of Geoffry " The O'Donoghue of the Glynn " by his wife Elizabeth, dau. of " The McCarty More." His only dau.,
JANE MARKHAM, *m.* Ralph Marshall, of BallymacAdam, co. Kerry (*see above*).

Arms—Quarterly 1st and 4th : Barry of six arg. and sa., on a canton erm. an escutcheon of the second charged with a trefoil slipped or, a crescent gu. for difference (MARSHALL) ; 2nd Gu. a chief nebulée arg., the rays of the sun issuing therefrom ôr (LEESON) ; 3rd Or, on a chief az. a demi-lion arg., holding between his paws a harp of the first (MARKHAM). *Crests*—1st A demi-man in armour affrontée ppr. holding in his dexter hand a baton sa. tipped or, charged on the breast with a rose gu. girded with a sash of the last, a crescent as in the Arms for difference (MARSHALL) ; 2nd A demi-lion ramp. gu. holding in his paws a sun or, partially eclipsed by a cloud ppr. (LEESON), 3rd A winged lion sejeant guardant arg., wings addorsed, holding between his forepaws a harp or, his head encircled with a plain glory of the last (MARKHAM). *Motto*—Sapere aude.
Seat—Callinafercy House, Milltown, co. Kerry. *Clubs*—New University, S.W. ; Kildare Street, Dublin.

MARSHALL OF BARONNE COURT.

WILLIAM KENNEDY MARSHALL, of Baronne Court, King's Co., J.P. and D.L., High Sheriff 1886, *b.* 12 March, 1858 ; *m.* 27 May, 1881, Ada Elizabeth, only dau. of Michael Den Keatinge, D.L. of Woodsgift, co. Kilkenny, by Adelaide, dau. of Col. Grogan, of Seafield, co. Dublin, and has issue,
 1. GILBERT KENNEDY, Lieut. 3rd Batt. Leinster Regt., *b.* 28 May, 1888.
 2. William George, *b.* 13 May, 1899.
 1. Eva Josephine.
 2. Esmé Georgina Ermyntrude.
 3. Ada Iris.

Lineage.—JOSEPH MARSHALL, of Glenkeen, co. Tyrone, *b.* 1700 ; *m.* Miss Simpson, of co. Armagh, and had a son, Joseph, who *d. unm.*, and a dau., Sarah, of Glenkeen, *s.* her father, *m.* Matthieu Louis, Baron de Periguy de Quenieux (Admiral *temp.* Louis Philippe), and *d.* 1850, and was *s.* by will by her cousin, REV. JOSEPH MARSHALL (*see below*).
REV. CORNELIUS MARSHALL, who was a cousin of Joseph Marshall, of Glenkeen, *m.* Margaret, dau. of Rev. John Brydge, and by her had issue,

1. JOSEPH, of whom presently.
2. John (Rev.), of Wark, Northumberland.
3. James.
4. Robert, *m.* Miss Swayne, and had a son, Robert George Swayne, Col. late R.A., *b.* 13 April, 1841.
1. Anna, *d. unm.*   2. Jane, *m.* J. Bell.
3. Sophia Ward, *m.* Richard Bolton, of Castle Ring, co. Louth.

The eldest son,

THE REV. JOSEPH MARSHALL, of Baronne Court, J.P. for King's Co. and for co. Tipperary, sometime R.N., *b.* 1801; *m.* 1853, Sophia Jane (who *d.* 21 Sept. 1905), dau. of Hugh Kennedy, of Cultra, D.L. co. Down (*see that family*), and by her had issue,

1. WILLIAM KENNEDY, now of Baronne Court.
1. Josephine. *m.* 9 July, 1874, Lieut.-Col. Thomas Bernard Hackett, V.C., of Riverstown, co. Tipperary, J.P., late Royal Welsh Fusiliers (*see that family*). He *d.* 1880. She *d.* 16 Jan. 1910.
2. Georgina, *m.* 1st, 1877, Col. William Grogan Graves, of Cloghan Castle, King's Co., by whom she had issue (*see* GRAVES *of Cloghan Castle*); 2ndly, 17 Oct. 1891, James Kingston Barton, late of Greenhill, co. Kilkenny, and has issue by him.
3. Sophia Margaret, *m.* 1883, A. R. Hutchinson, R.M., of Kiltorkan, co. Kilkenny, late Major Royal Welsh Fusiliers; and *d.* 1885, leaving issue, Muriel Eleanor Sophia.

Rev. Joseph Marshall *d.* 25 Dec. 1865.

Seats—Baronne Court, Birr, and Woodsgift, co. Kilkenny.

MARSHAM OF HEADFORT.

GEORGE MARSHAM, of Hayle Place, Kent, and Headfort House, co. Leitrim, B.A. Merton Coll. Oxford, J.P. and D.L. cos. Kent and Leitrim, and High Sheriff of the latter co. 1878, *b.* 10 April, 1849.

Lineage. — WALTER JONES, of Bealanamore, co, Dublin, Headfort, co. Leitrim, Cork Abbey, co. Wicklow, and Hayle Place, Kent, Col. Leitrim Militia, High Sheriff co. Leitrim 1795, and M.P. for Coleraine, eldest son of Right Hon. Theophilus Jones (*see* JONES *late of Headfort*), *b.* 29 Dec. 1754; *m.* 8 Oct. 1805, Katherine Penelope, dau. and co-heir of Rev. Lascelles Iremonger, Vicar of Chadford, co. Southampton, and *d.* 1839, having had five daus., his co-heirs,

1. MARIA SOPHIA, *b.* 7 Sept. 1806; *m.* 27 Feb. 1838, Henry Shovel Marsham, Admiral R.N., son of Hon. and Rev. Jacob Marsham (*see* BURKE'S *Peerage*, ROMNEY, E.), and s. to Headfort and Bealanamore. They assumed the surname of JONES. She *d.s.p.* 21 Dec. 1861. He *d.* 26 Oct. 1875.
2. KATHERINE PENELOPE, of Headfort and Bealanamore, *b.* 29 Oct. 1807: *d. unm.*, and was *s.* by her nephew, George Marsham.
3. ELIZABETH MARCIA, *b.* 21 Oct. 1810; *m.* 4 June 1833, Rev. George Frederick John Marsham, M.A., Rector of Allington, Maidstone, Kent (who was *b.* 9 June, 1806, and *d.* 29 Jan. 1852), 5th son of Hon. and Rev. Jacob Marsham, D.D., Canon of Windsor, Prebendary of Rochester and Wells, and grandson of Robert, 2nd Earl of Romney (*see* BURKE'S *Peerage*, ROMNEY, E.), and *d.* 29 April, 1849, leaving issue,

1. GEORGE MARSHAM, now of Hayle Place.
1. Catharine Elizabeth, *m.* 1st, 23 Jan. 1866, Rev. William Gale Townley, of Beaupré Hall, Norfolk, who *d.s.p.* 4 Sept. 1869; and 2ndly, 11 May, 1880, Hon. Edward Kenyon, son of 2nd Baron of Kenyon. He *d.* 21 Oct. 1894.
2. Marcia Elizabeth Maria, *d. unm.* 25 Dec. 1898.
3. Frances Penelope, *m.* 20 June, 1876, Rev. Cloudesley Dewar Bullock Marsham, Vicar of Stoke Lyne and Caversfield, co. Oxford, 3rd son of Robert Bullock Marsham, D.C.L., Warden of Merton Coll. Oxford, eldest son of the above-mentioned Hon. and Rev. Jacob Marsham. She *d.* 9 Feb. 1890, leaving issue,
    (1) Cloudesley Henry, *b.* 10 Feb. 1879.
    (2) Francis William, *b.* 13 July, 1883.
    (1) Jessie Catharine.   (2) Constance Elizabeth.
4. Elizabeth Isabella Sophia, *d. unm.* 1 Sept. 1883.
4. Sophia, *d. unm.* Feb. 1890.
5. Anne, *m.* William Moore, of Wierton, and *d.s.p.* 1882.

Arms—Quarterly: 1st and 4th arg., a lion passant in bend gu. between two bendlets az., for MARSHAM; 2nd and 3rd gu., three lioncels rampant guardant or, armed and langued az., on a quarter of the second a fret of the first, for JONES. *Crest*—A lion's head erased gu. *Motto*—Non sibi sed patriæ.

Seats—Hayle Place, Maidstone, Kent; and Headfort House, Leitrim. *Clubs*—Carlton, Junior Carlton.

MARTIN OF ROSS.

MISS BARBARA ZAVARA MARTIN, of Ross, co. Galway, *s.* her father 1905.

Lineage.—About the year 1590 ROBERT MARTIN the lineal ancestor of the present holder, was in possession of the estates now held by that gentleman. Robert Martin thus referred to served the office of High Sheriff 1607, and being elected Mayor of Galway, *d.* during his year of office, 20 April, 1621. He was *s.* by his eldest son,

JASPER MARTIN, who *d.* 1629. By inquisition made in 1635, it was found that Jasper Martin *d.* 12 April, 1629, seised of the lands of Ross, and several other denominations in the West of Galway, all which descended to his son and heir,

ROBERT MARTIN, of Ross, High Sheriff 1644. Having adhered to the cause of CHARLES I, upon the conquest of Galway, 1654, he was dispossessed of his house in the town of Galway, and his property in the suburbs by Sir Charles Coote, commanding the Parliamentary troops, who occupied it, and this house, and the other property of Mr. Martin, were granted to Edward Eyre, who was Judge-Advocate of the Force under Sir Charles Coote, and was also intruded into the Recordership of the town by the expulsion of the gentleman who held that office. Mr. Martin made an effort to be restored to his house and property upon the restoration of CHARLES II, but without success, although he held the King's warrant under his own signature to that effect. (For an account of this proceeding of Mr. Martin, see the *Journals of the Irish House of Commons*, vol. I. 439.) Mr. Martin had issue,

1. JASPER, his successor.
2. James, of Maghery, co. Galway, *m.* (articles dated 22 June, 1667) Mary, eldest dau. of Marcus D'Arcy, of Cloghrane, co. Galway, and *d.s.p.*
3. Richard, ancestor of MARTIN *of Ballinahinch*.

He *d.* 1700, and was *s.* by his eldest son,

JASPER MARTIN, of Ross, who *d.* 1710, and was *s.* by his son, NICHOLAS MARTIN, who *m.* 1st, Jane, dau. of Anthony French, of Clough, co. Galway; and 2ndly, Margery, dau. of Robert Browne, of Breaghfy, co. Mayo; he *d.* 1731, and was *s.* by his eldest son of his 1st marriage,

JASPER MARTIN, of Ross *d. unm.* 1749, and was *s.* by his half-brother, eldest son of the 2nd marriage of his father,

JAMES MARTIN, of Ross, who *m.* 1726, Barbara, dau. of Farragh M'Donnell, of Ballycallagh, co. Mayo, and by her (who *d.* 1772) had a son and successor, JASPER, and a 2nd son, NICHOLAS. Mr. Martin, *d.* June, 1775, and was *s.* by his eldest son,

JASPER MARTIN, of Ross, who *d. unm.* 1783, and was *s.* by his brother,

NICHOLAS MARTIN, of Ross, who *m.* Elizabeth, dau. of Robert O'Hara, of Leneboy, co. Galway, and by her had issue,

1. James, *d. unm.*   2. ROBERT, his heir.
3. Richard.

Nicholas Martin *d.* 1811, and was *s.* by his son,

ROBERT MARTIN, of Ross, who *m.* Marian, dau. of John Blackney, of Ballyellen, co. Carlow, and of the city of Waterford, and by her (who *d.* 1855) he left at his decease, 10 June, 1868, one son and two daus.,

1. JAMES, his heir.
1. Elizabeth, *m.* Arthur Ussher, of Ballysaggartmore, co. Waterford.
2. Marian, *m.* Arthur Bushe, 4th son of the Right Hon. Charles Kendal Bushe, Lord Chief Justice of Ireland.

The son and heir,

JAMES MARTIN, of Ross, D.L. and J.P., High Sheriff 1826, M.A. Trin. Coll. Dublin, *b.* 1804, *m.* 1st, 1824, Anne, dau. of Thomas Higinbotham, of Dublin, and by her had five daus.,

1. Mary, *m.* Thomas Barklie, of Inverhouse, Larne.
2. Emily, *m.* 1st, 27 April, 1843, James McCalmont, of Abbeylands, co. Antrim, who *d.* 18 July, 1849, leaving issue (*see that family*), and 2ndly, 12 Oct. 1853, Augustine Barton of Rochestown, who *d.* 23 Oct. 1874, leaving issue (*see* BARTON *of Grove*). She *d.* 30 Nov. 1907.
3. Elizabeth, *d.* 10 March, 1906; *m.* William Kennedy, of Annefield.
4. Maud, *m.* Henry Callwell, who *d.* 25 April, 1908.
5. Josephine, *d. unm.*

He *m.* 2ndly, 28 March, 1844, Anna Selina, dau. of Charles Fox, of New Park, co. Longford, and grand-dau. of Lord Chief Justice Bushe and of Mr. Justice Fox, of the Court of Common Pleas in Ireland, and by her (who *d.* 8 Feb. 1906) has issue,

1. ROBERT JASPER, of Ross.
2. James Richard Charles, J.P., *b.* 24 Dec. 1854; *m.* 10 June, 1885, Amy Geraldine, eldest dau. of Major-Gen. Charles Herbert, late Bengal Staff Corps.
3. Charles Fox, *b.* 14 Aug. 1859; *m.* Lucy, dau. of R. Sherwood, who *d.* 1894.
6. Katharine Annesley, *m.* 10 Oct. 1882, Commander Edward Hamilton Currey.
7. Geraldine Charlotte Louisa, *m.* Rev. E. Hewson, Rector of Gowran.
8. Selina Rosanna, *d. unm.* 17 Jan. 1909.
9. Edith Sydney, *m.* 22 Nov. 1882, Cuthbert Pilkington Dawson, of Groton House, co. Suffolk, Lieut.-Col. late 2nd Dragoon Guards. She *d.* 18 Feb. 1908.
10. Gertrude Isabel, *d. unm.*   11. Violet Florence.

The eldest son,

ROBERT JASPER MARTIN, of Ross, co. Galway, J.P., B.A. Trin. Coll. Dublin, *b.* 17 June, 1846; *m.* 1886, Amelia Constance, widow of Victor Baddeley Roche, of Killuntin, co. Cork, and dau. of J. J. Schmidt, of Thornfield, co. Lancaster, and *d.* 13 Sept. 1905, and was *s.* by his only child,

Martin. THE LANDED GENTRY. 462

Barbara Zavara, now of Ross.

Arms—Az., a cross Calvary arg., the dexter arm terminating the sun in splendour or, and the sinister in a decrescent of the last.
Crest—An estoile of six points or. **Motto**—Sic itur ad astra.
Seat—Ross, near Moycullen, co. Galway.

MARTIN OF WICHE.

John Charles Martin, b. 1857, m. Margaretta, dau. of J. Brian, and has issue.

Lineage.—John Martin, of Wiche, co. Worcester, living towards the end of the 15th and beginning of the 16th centuries, m. Margaret, dau. and co-heir of Humphrey Rudinge, of Wiche, and had two sons, Gilbert and John. The elder has

Gilbert Martin, of Creckers, co. Bedford, m. Catherine Boteler, dau. of George Boteler, of Sharnbrooke, co. Bedford, by Mary Throckmorton his wife, and had

George Martin, of Wiche, seated there 1627; m. Alice, 5th dau. of Dr. James Caulfeild, and sister of William, 2nd Lord Charlemont, and had

John Martin, of Lurgan, co. Armagh, M.P. for Charlemont in the Irish Parliament in 1639 and for several years subsequently. By Katherine his wife (who d. in 1667) he had two sons and one dau.,
1. Ffulke, of whom presently.
2. John, who left a dau., Jane.
1. A dau., m. 1656, Roger Lyndon, of Carrickfergus, and had issue.

Mr. Martin d. 1656. His son and heir,

Ffulke Martin, of Brownlow Derry, co. Armagh, Major in the Army, a distinguished officer in the Civil Wars of the period, m. 1650, Eleanor, dau. and co-heir of Sir William Brownlow, Knt., and had issue,
1. Robert, of Lurgan, b. 1653; m. Alice Warren, and had issue at his decease in 1717,
   1. Francis, d. unm.
   2. Standish, of Dublin, d. unm. 1755.
      1. Alice, m. Joseph Clinch, of Dublin, and had issue,
      2. Johanna, m. 1st, George Barnwall, co. Westmeath, and had issue. She m. 2ndly, Joseph Bony, and had issue.
2. Miles, of whom presently.
1. Katherine, m. William Smith, 3rd son of James Smith, of Lisnagwny.
2. Eleanor, m. William Lowther.
3. Anne.
4. Dowglas Martin.

Major Martin d. 1679. His 2nd son,

Miles Martin, b. 1660, was Officer in the army of William III. and fought at the Boyne and Limerick. He settled first in co. Kerry, where he m. in 1706, Elizabeth, dau. and co-heir of Richard M'Laughlin, by Catherine Blennerhassett his wife. Mr. Martin by this marriage acquired considerable estates in the cos. of Cork and Kerry. He sold the Cork estates and purchased land in the city of Cork, where he went to reside. He left issue, one son and three daus.,
1. Henry, of whom presently.
1. Eleanor, m. William Hilliard, of Tralee.
2. Catherine.
3. Agnes.

Mr. Martin d. 1735. His only son,

Henry Martin, an eminent merchant in the city of Cork, b. 1710, sold his Kerry estates and purchased property in the city of Cork. He m. 1743, Elizabeth, dau. of John de la Cour, of Cork, and had issue,
1. Richard, of Clifford, co. Cork, b. 29 Feb. 1744; m. 1773, Catherine, only dau. and heir of Randal Roberts, of Bridgetown, and d. 1823, having had an only dau. and heir,
   Mary, m. 7 Jan. 1795, John Southcote Mansergh, of Grenane, Tipperary (see that family).
2. Henry, of Bordeaux, b. 1745; m. Miss Dickson, of Ballyshannon, co. Donegal, and d. 15 Nov. 1837, having had issue,
   1. Robert, d. unm.
   2. Henry, of Bordeaux, m. in France, but had no issue.
   1. Elizabeth, m. Isaac, Count D'Egmont, and had issue.
3. John, of whom presently.
4. Charles, twin brother of John, b. 1755; m. Esther, dau. and co-heir (with her sister, Susannah Millerd, wife of Rev. Francis Orpen) of Hugh Millerd, of Monard, co. Cork. He d.s.p. 1821, having devised his estates in the co. and city of Cork to his nephew, Archdeacon Martin.
1. Mary, m. Rev. Maurice O'Connor, and d.s.p. 1844.
2. Elizabeth, m. Daniel Dickson, Captain Wexford Militia, and d.s.p. 1844.

Mr. Martin d. 1773. His 3rd son,

John Martin, of Blackrock, co. Cork, b. in 1755; m. 31 Dec. 1791, Mary, dau. of Aylmer Allen, of Woodview, High Sheriff of Cork, 1780, and had issue,
1. Henry (Rev.), Rector of Larne, co. Antrim, b. 1794; m. 1830, Jane, dau. and heir (with her sister, Anne, wife of James Martin, of Ross, co. Galway) of Thomas Higinbotham, of Mountjoy Square, Dublin. He d.s.p. 1859.
2. John Charles, of whom presently.
3. Aylmer Richard, of Vernon Mount, Cork, b. 1798, High Sheriff of Cork 1831. He was also Chamberlain of the City to the time of his death. He m. 23 Oct. 1824, Henrietta, dau. of Robert O'Donoghue, of Cork, and d. 2 April, 1841, leaving issue,
   1. John, of Upper Mount Street, Dublin, m. 17 April, 1854, Eliza, dau. of John Robinson, Treasurer of co. Longford, and has issue,
      (1) Aylmer Richard, d. 1865.
      (2) John, d. 1891.
      (3) Thomas, d. 1866.
      (4) Aylmer, d. 1867.
      (1) Elizabeth, m. Rev. Simon Carter Armstrong, and has issue.
      (2) Henrietta, m. her cousin Surg.-Capt. Richard Crofts, and d. 1893, leaving issue.
      (3) Ruth, m. Surg.-Capt. James Rose, and has issue.
   2. Robert James, of Dublin, b. 20 July, 1829; m. 12 Aug. 1862, Sarah William, dau. of William Crooke Ronayne, of Cork, and d. 10 Jan. 1865, leaving a son,
      Aylmer Caulfeild (Rev.) (The Rectory, Kanturk, co. Cork), b. 7 Aug. 1864; m. 5 Aug. 1897, Elizabeth Louisa, elder dau. of Thomas Wilson Strangman, of Kilnoith, Shanagarry, co. Cork, and has issue,
         a. Aylmer Robert, d. young.
         b. Rudinge Caulfeild, b. 8 Sept. 1901.
         c. Charles Wilson, b. 28 March, 1906.
         a. Catherine Lydia Caulfeild, b. 1 Oct. 1898.
         b. Sarah Louisa, b. 2 April, 1909.
   3. Thomas, M.A., m. 1st, Jane, dau. of Capt. Bredin; and 2ndly, Anna Maria, dau. of Richard Dunbury, and had issue, Aylmer, d. 1869; Charles; Thomas; and three daus.
   4. Charles, B.A., J.P., m. 1881, Mynce, dau. of Rev. J. B. Webb.
   1. Elizabeth, m. 10 May, 1849, her cousin Geo. Crofts, and has issue.
4. Charles Rudinge (Rev.), b. 1803; m. 1826, Susan, dau. of Robert Bomford, of Rahinstown, co. Meath, and with her sisters, co-heirs of their brother, George Robert Bomford. He d. 1847, and left issue four sons,
   1. John Charles, d. unm.
   2. Robert, formerly Capt. in the 74th Highlanders, d. unm.
   3. Charles Nassau, Major-Gen. in the Royal Engineers, severely wounded at Sebastopol, received the Legion of Honour, b. 12 July, 1832; m. 10 Feb. 1863, Anna Maria, dau. of Peter Horrocks, of Penwortham Lodge, J.P. and D.L. (see Horrocks of Mascalls), and by her (who d. 4 June, 1891) has issue,
      (1) Charles Francis, Capt. Highland L.I., d.s.p. 24 Dec. 1893.
      (2) Charles Rudinge.
      (1) Ethel.   (2) Eileen.
   4. George Henry (Rev.), M.A., Rector of Agher, m. 20 Dec. 1859, his cousin Edith Agatha, dau. of Ven. John Charles Martin (see below), and d. 12 Dec. 1896, having by her (who d. 1893) had issue, with four sons, who d.s.p., four daus.,
      (1) Susan Maria, m. Rev. C. Mease, and d. 1891.
      (2) Agatha Edith, m. Capt. H. Stanuell, 21st Regt., and has issue.
      (3) Mary Louisa.
      (4) Frances Georgina, m. Sept. 1898, Rev. R. T. M. Clifford.
5. Richard, Barrister-at-Law, b. 1809; m. 10 Jan. 1838, Catherine, youngest dau. of Robert O'Donoghue, of Cork, and d. 29 Oct. 1859, having had issue, one son and three daus.,
   1. John Charles (Rev.), Rector of Dowra, co. Cavan.
   1. Mary Elizabeth.   2. Henrietta, d. unm. 1872.
   3. Catherine, m. A. Luxmore.
1. Elizabeth, m. David Beatty, of Borodale, co. Wexford, Capt. in the Army, who was present at Talavera. He d. in 1855, having had issue.
2. Mary, m. Robert Longfield, only surviving son of John Longfield, of Cork, M.D., and had an only dau. and heir, Mary Elizabeth Longfield, m. her first cousin David Beatty, of Borodale, and had issue.

Mr. Martin d. Dec. 1811. His 2nd son,

The Venerable John Charles Martin, D.D., F.T.C.D., Archdeacon of Kilmore, and Rector of Killeshandra, co. Cavan, b. 1797; m. 23 Jane, 1829, Agatha, only dau. of Right Rev. Richard Mant, D.D., Bishop of Down and Connor, and by her (who d. 4 Sept. 1875) had issue,
1. John Charles (Rev.), late of Killeshandra.
2. Richard Luther, m. 23 Sept. 1856, Mary Olivia Henrietta, dau. of Rev. John Taylor, LL.D., and d. Nov. 1872, leaving issue,
   1. John Charles, present representative.
   2. Richard D'Olier (Rev.), b. 1859; m. 10 July, 1888, Catherine Mary Clifford, and has issue,
      (1) Denys Richard, b. 11 Oct. 1892.
      (2) Laurence Henry, b. 7 Aug. 1897.
      (3) Marcus Francis Clifford, b. 25 April, 1900.
      (1) Mary, b. 18 June, 1895; d. same year.
   3. Aylmer Ffulke, b. 1864; m. Violet, dau. of Humphrey Minchin, and has issue.
   4. Walter de la Cour, b. 1869; m. Mabel, dau. of — Campbell, and has issue.
   5. Francis Jeffrey Cockburn, b. 1871.
   1. Theodosia Agatha, m. Rev. F. R. Burrows, and has issue.

2. Maud Mant, *m.* Rev. James Ferguson, and has issue.
3. Anna Helen.
4. Henrietta, *m.* Rev. H. Stewart, and has issue.
3. Henry Francis John (Rev.). Scholar T.C.D., Rector of Killeshandra, *d.* 6 Oct. 1906 ; *m.* 2 Nov. 1865, Barbara, dau. of Robert Collins, of Ardsallagh, co. Meath, and has,
  1. John Charles Collins, *b.* 1867.
  2. Robert Collins, *b.* 1869.
  3. Arthur Henry Mant. (Rev.), *b.* 1870 ; *d. unm.* 18 Jan. 1897.
  4. Joseph Clarke Collins, *b.* 1872 ; *m.* 21 June, 1905, Nora Kathleen, 4th dau. of Charles Stuart Adams.
    1. Mary Roberta, *d.* 1868.
4. Frederick Walter, *d.s.p.* 1863.
5. Charles William Wall, LL.D., Indian Civil Service (retired), *m.* 19 Dec. 1866, Gertrude Honoria, dau. of W. M. Hickson, R.M., and *d.* 18 April, 1907, having had issue,
  1. Charles Henry, *b.* 1870.
  2. John Fitzgerald Uniacke, *b.* 1872.
  3. William Frederick, *b.* 1874.
  4. Neville Brownlow, *b.* 1880, *d.* 1883.
  5. Clive Victor, *b.* 1883.
  1. Gertrude Louisa, *m.* H. Gass, Inspector of Forests, India.
  2. Adela Rose O'Neill, *m.* J. Wallis, of Herbert Hill, Dundrum.
  3. Ethel Mary.   4. Olivia Maria.
  5. Beryl Edith.   6. Maud Eileen.
  7. Nesta Violet, *d. unm.* 1890.
6. Caulfeild Aylmer, LL.D., Director of Public Instruction in Bengal, *m.* Oct. 1870, Isabella Emily, dau. of Frederick Beatty, of Lakeview, co. Wicklow, and has issue,
  1. Frederick Walter (Rev.), *b.* 1874.
  1. Mabel Beatty.   2. Kathleen Olivia.
  3. Emily.
  4. Florence, *m.* 6 Dec. 1898, Ernest Bignold, of Darjeeling.
7. Brownlow Rudinge, M.D., *m.* Jan. 1875, Mary Jane Johnstone, and has issue,
  1. Brownlow Rupert, *d.* 1884.
  2. Reginald Victor, *b.* 1889.
  1. Agatha Mary.
  2. Edith Evelyn, *d.* 1880.
  3. Elsie Georgina Mary.
  4. Muriel Barbara Regina.
  5. Adela Freda.
1. Elizabeth Mary Adelaide, *m.* 1st, 1850, Rev. Christopher Adamson, who *d.s.p.* 1856, and 2ndly, G. M. Hearne, M.D., and *d.* 1891, leaving issue.
2. Edith Agatha, *m.* 20 Dec. 1859, her cousin Rev. George Henry Martin, M.A., Rector of Agher co. Meath, and *d.* 1893. He *d.* 12 Dec. 1896, leaving issue *(see above)*.
3. Mary Emily, *b.* 1847.
4. Olivia Frances, *m.* 20 July, 1865, R. H. Clifford, Bengal Civil Service, who *d.* Oct. 1876, leaving issue.
5. Adela Neville, *m.* 1 Nov. 1881, Edward Dobbs, LL.D., Deputy Conservator of Forests in India, and has issue.

Archdeacon Martin *d.* 17 Jan. 1878, and was s. by his eldest son,

Rev. JOHN CHARLES MARTIN, M.A. Trin. Coll. Dublin, *b.* 28 Dec. 1831 ; *d. unm.* 10 April, 1899.

Arms—Quarterly : 1st and 4th, MARTIN, per pale gu. and arg., on a chevron between three mullets, as many talbots, counterchanged ; 2nd and 3rd, RUDINGE, arg., on a bend between two lions rampant sa., a wyvern, wings overt, of the first.

WOOD-MARTIN OF CLEVERAGH.

WILLIAM GREGORY WOOD-MARTIN, of Cleveragh, co. Sligo, J.P. and D.L., High Sheriff 1877, Col. late Commanding the Duke of Connaught's Own Sligo Artillery, R.G.A., 1883-1902, A.D.C. to the King, and formerly to Queen Victoria and King Edward VII, late Lieut.44th Regt., author of numerous archæological and historical works, *b.* 16 July, 1847 ; *m.* Nov. 1873, Frances Dora (who *d.* 7 Nov. 1905), eldest dau. of Roger Dodwell Robinson, J.P., of Wellmount, co. Sligo, and has issue,
  1. JAMES ISIDORE, Capt. Northamptonshire Regt., attached to the Egyptian Army, Lieut.-Col. commanding 9th Sudanese, served in the war in S. Africa 1899-1902 (Queen's medal with three clasps, King's medal with two clasps), operations in the province of Bahr-el-Gazal, Sudan, 1905 (medal and clasp, Order of the Medjidieh, mentioned in despatch to the Khedive 1908), *b.* 3 Sept. 1874.
  2. Henry Roger Bromhead.
  3. Gregory Gonville Cuffe, Lieut. R.N.
  4. Francis Winchester, Capt. Suffolk Regt., served in the war in S. Africa 1899-1902 (Queen's medal with three clasps, King's medal with two clasps), *b.* 27 Feb. 1880.
  1. Frances Nora.   2. Annette Kathleen.

Lineage.—In the year 1551, Thomas Wood received from EDWARD VI a grant of the Abbey of Tyntern and the lands adjoining for " his long and painful service in the wars." In 1583, ELIZABETH granted a pension to Richard Wood " for long and faithful service."

The first of this family who appears to have settled in Sligo was THOMAS WOOD, Constable of the Crown Castle of Ballymote, and High Sheriff co. Sligo 1592. He was sent to England with despatches by Sir R. Bingham, Lord President of Connaught, to Lord Burleigh, Queen ELIZABETH'S Minister. In a Chancery Inquisition taken at Sligo 9 June, 1610, Thomas Wood claimed the lands of Clonyganvin. George Wood was High Sheriff co. Sligo 1619. THOMAS WOOD, *b. circa* 1602, a Cornet in Capt. Morgan's troop in Col. Richard Coote's Regt. of Horse 1642-60. Thomas Wood obtained considerable grants of land at Castle Laccan and Castle Connor, in the barony of Tireragh, also in the parish of Kilmacteige, barony of Liney, co. Sligo. He *m.* a dau. of Ven. Robert Brown, Archdeacon of Killala, and Rector of Skyrne, co. Sligo, and *d.* 1692. Major Edward Wood, of Court, co. Sligo, son of Cornet Wood, was a distinguished Officer during the Revolution of 1688. He commanded a regiment which he raised in co. Sligo, was present at Newtownbutler, commanded the main body at the battle of Boyle, and defended the Castle of Sligo against Sarsfield. His name is of frequent occurrence in the pamphlets of the period. He *m.* Anne, dau. of Henry St. George, of Athlone, and *d.s.p.* He bequeathed Lochans, co. Kilkenny, his wife's property, to the St. George family, hence the name " Woodsgift."

The elder branch of this family became extinct in the male line at the death of Richard Wood, whose dau. and heir, ELIZABETH, *m.* 1st, 1776, William H. Cooper, of Cooper's Hill, co. Sligo, and 2ndly, Very Rev. William Digby, of Geashill, Dean of Clonfert, whose descendant, Kenelm Digby, of Shaftesbury House, now possesses a portion of the original grant.

Another branch became extinct in the male line on the death of CHARLES WOOD, of Leekfield, whose dau. and heir, Sarah, *m.* Daniel Webb Webber, Q.C., of Merrion Square, Dublin.

Members of the family served successively as High Sheriffs of co. Sligo in the years 1592, 1619, 1683, 1684, 1717, 1784, 1791, 1798, 1826, and 1877.

JAMES WOOD, a younger son of Cornet Thomas Wood, *m.* a dau. of Ven. Archdeacon Laynge, and *d.* 1732, having had, with other issue,

JAMES WOOD, *b.* 1702 ; *d.* 1781 ; *m.* Catharine, dau. of Comm. Walker, R.N., and had, with other issue, a son,

JAMES WOOD, *b.* 1732 ; *m.* Mary, dau. of John Leech, of Frankfort, and had, with five daus., two sons,
  1. JAMES, his heir.
  2. John, *m.* 1802, Dorothea, dau. of Rev. Charles Grove, Rector of Templeboy, Diocese of Tuam, and left at his decease,
    James GROVE, of Castle Grove, co. Donegal, J.P. and D.L., High Sheriff 1855, who adopted the name of GROVE on s. to the Castle Grove estate, *b.* 1803 ; *m.* 1843, Frances Judith, dau. of Robert Montgomery, of Convoy House, co. Donegal, by Maria Frances Stewart his wife, niece of Robert, 1st Marquess of Londonderry, and had issue,
      (1) John Montgomery Charles, J.P., *b.* 1847.
      (2) Robert Thomas, *b.* 1850.   (3) Charles William, *b.* 1853.
      (1) Dorothea Alice.   (2) Frances Mary Ellen.
  Mary, *m.* 10 July, 1827, Henry Alexander Godfrey, son of Sir John Godfrey, 2nd bart. of Kilcoleman Abbey, co. Kerry, and *d.* 1882, leaving issue, two daus., Dora Frances and Mary Susan Ellen.

The elder son,

JAMES WOOD, of Woodville, *b.* 1762 ; *m.* 1796, Judith, dau. and heir of William Coristine, of Cleveragh, co. Sligo, and had,
  1. JAMES, his heir.   2. William, *d. unm.* 1852.
  3. Abraham, *d. unm.* 1832
  1. Margaret, *d. unm.*   2. Mary, *d. unm.* 1873.
  3. Judith Coristine, *m.* 1823, Sir Edmond De Gonville Bromhead, 3rd bart. of Thurlby Hall, co. Lincoln, and *d.* 12 June, 1873.

Mr. Wood *d.* 1814, and was *s.* by his eldest son,

JAMES WOOD, of Woodville, J.P., High Sheriff 1826, *b.* 20 June, 1797 ; *m.* 1st, 28 Nov. 1833, Rhoda, youngest dau. of Sir Edmond Nugent, of Airfield, co. Dublin, and had by her a son,
  1. James Edmond, *b.* 1834 ; *d.s.p.* 1859.

He *m.* 2ndly, 1842, Anne, dau. of Abraham Martin, of Cleveragh, co. Sligo, and *d.* 16 July, 1873, having had by her (who *d.* 20 July, 1897) a son,
  2. WILLIAM GREGORY, now Wood Martin, of Cleveragh.

Lineage *(of* MARTIN *of Cleveragh)*.—This family settled in co. Sligo in the 17th century, where they possessed considerable property.

JOHN MARTIN, only son of ARTHUR MARTIN, left two sons,
  1. CHARLES, his heir.
  2. Arthur, an officer in the Army of WILLIAM III.

The elder son,

CHARLES MARTIN, *b.* 1662 ; *d.* 17 Oct. 1734, having had issue,
  1. ABRAHAM, his heir.
  2. Charles, *b.* 1713 ; *d.* 11 Feb. 1768.

The elder son,

ABRAHAM MARTIN, of Cleveragh, *b.* 1705 ; *m.* 1st, 8 March,

Martley. THE LANDED GENTRY. 464

1724, Elinor, dau. of John Jameson, and by her had two daus., of whom the elder *m.* Rev. William Boyd. He *m.* 2ndly, 2 Aug. 1741, Judith, dau. of William Clarke, of Westport, co. Mayo, and *d.* 30 Oct. 1776, leaving issue,
1. JOHN, his heir.
2. Frederick, *b.* 24 July, 1757; *d.* 7 Aug. 1780.

The elder son,
JOHN MARTIN, of Cleveragh, High Sheriff 1782, *b.* 3 Aug. 1742; *m.* 22 Feb. 1770, Elizabeth, dau. of Thomas Shuttleworth, and *d.* 25 Nov. 1799, leaving issue, with other daus., who *d. unm.*,
1. ABRAHAM, his heir.
2. Charles, *b.* 29 July, 1773; *d.* 20 Dec. 1850.
3. Henry (Rev.), Rector of Aughrim, *b.* 20 May, 1790; *m.* the dau. of D. Jones, of Banada Abbey, co. Sligo, and *d.* 1 Feb. 1845.
1. Elizabeth, *m.* Francis Jackson.

The eldest son,
ABRAHAM MARTIN, of Cleveragh, J.P. and D.L., High Sheriff 1805, *b.* 17 June, 1772; *m.* 29 Nov. 1804, Alicia, dau. of Gregory Cuffe, of Creagh, co. Mayo, and *d.* 18 Nov. 1853, leaving issue,
1. JAMES, of whom presently.
2. John, J.P. and D.L., M.P. for Sligo 1832-7; *d. unm.* 28 Feb. 1846.
3. Gregory Cuffe, *m.* 23 Oct. 1835, Anna Louisa, dau. of Thomas Jones, of Ardnaglass, co. Sligo, and *d.* 31 Aug. 1844, leaving issue, with others, who *d.* young.
ABRAHAM, heir to his uncle.
Anne, *m.* May, 1859, Henry Byne, and had issue.
1. ANNE, of whom presently.
2. Elizabeth, *m.* Rev. Edward Day, of Beaufort, co. Kerry, and *d.s.p.* 23 Oct. 1894.

The eldest son,
JAMES MARTIN, of Cleveragh, co. Sligo, J.P. and D.L., sometime Capt. 3rd Light Dragoons, *b.* 21 Feb. 1816; *m.* 29 Nov. 1854, Isabella Charlotte Louisa, eldest dau. of Col. Thomas Kingscote, of Kingscote Park, co. Gloucester (*see that family*), by his 1st marriage with the Lady Isabella Somerset, dau. of the 6th Duke of Beaufort, and *d.s.p.* 21 March, 1860. She *d.* 22 June, 1907. His nephew,
ABRAHAM MARTIN, of Cleveragh, co. Sligo, J.P. and D.L., High Sheriff 1862, Capt. 11th Regt., *b.* 30 Jan. 1838; *m.* 1871, Florence, dau. of Col. Pitt Kennedy, and *d.s.p.* 19 April, 1874. He was *s.* (under the will of James Martin) by his aunt,
ANNE MARTIN, who *m.* 1842, JAMES WOOD, of Woodville (*see that family above*). She assumed by Royal Licence, 1874, in compliance with the will, the additional name and arms of MARTIN, for herself and her issue, and *d.* 20 July, 1897, leaving a son,
WILLIAM GREGORY, now of Cleveragh.

Arms—Quarterly: 1st and 4th, sa., a chevron between three crescents arg., for MARTIN; 2nd and 3rd, arg., an oak tree fructed growing out of a mound in base, all ppr., in the dexter chief point a crescent gu., for WOOD. **Crests**—1st, MARTIN, A lion rampant ppr. holding in the dexter paw a crescent or; 2nd, WOOD, a demi-savage ppr. wreathed about the temples and loins vert, and charged on the breast with a crescent gu., in his dexter hand an oak tree fructed, and in his sinister a club resting on his shoulder, all also ppr. **Mottoes**—Hinc fortior et clarior; above, Fructu cognoscitur arbor.
Seats—Cleveragh, Bloomfield, and Woodville, co. Sligo.
Clubs—Army and Navy; Sligo (County).

MARTLEY late OF BALLYFALLON.

WILLIAM GIBSON MARTLEY, M.A. Balliol College, Oxford, and Trinity College, Dublin, *b.* 21 Nov. 1859; *m.* 25 April, 1891, Ethel, dau. of Joshua Clarke, Q.C., County Court Judge, of Dublin.

Lineage.—The ancestor of this family, long settled in Meath, was father of
JOHN, of whom presently.
Alice, *m.* 1681, Roger Lloyd, of Dollardstown, and had a dau.
Catherine, *m.* 3 July, 1707, Athanasius Cusack, of Moyaugher, co. Meath.

The son,
JOHN MARTLEY, of Ballyfallon, co. Meath, *m.* Margery, dau. of James Cusack, of Clonard, co. Meath (*see* CUSACK *of Gerardstown*). He *d.* 9 Dec. 1729, aged 87 (will dated 10 May, proved 27 Nov. 1729), and his tombstone is in Athboy Church. He had issue,
1. William, of Ballyfallon, *m.* Anne Tandy, and *d.s.p.*
2. JOHN, of whom presently.
1. Margery, *m.* Henry Cusack, of Clonard.
2. A dau., *m.* James Tuite, of Tennor, co. Meath.

The younger son,
JOHN MARTLEY, of Ballyfallon, *m.* 1744, Clementina, eldest dau. of the Rev. Robert Meares, Rector of Almoritia, 3rd son of Lewis Meares, of Meares Court, co. Westmeath (*see that family*), and by her (who *d.* Jan. 1789) had three sons and four daus., viz.,
1. John, *d. unm.*, will dated 6 Dec. 1791, proved 20 Jan. 1792.
2. WILLIAM, of whom presently.
3. James Frederick, M.D., of Kells, co. Meath, *m.* 1788, Henrietta Maria Hopkins (who *d.* 1833), and *d.* May, 1813, having had four sons and two daus.,
1. John, Q.C., Recorder of Cork, Sch. Trin. Coll. Dublin 1809, B.A. 1811; *m.* 1821, Isabella Jane, dau. of William Hopkins, and *d.* Oct. 1839, having by her (who *d.* 26 Dec. 1862) had issue,
(1) James Frederick, Attorney-General at Melbourne, *m.* 26 Oct. 1854, dau. of the Rev. James Lever, Rector of Ardnurcher, co. Meath.

(2) John, Capt. 56th Regt., afterwards of The Grange, Lillooet, British Columbia, *m.* Maria, dau. of Adm. Ballingall, and by her (who *m.* 2ndly, William Armit Eyre, son of John Eyre, of Eyre Court, co. Galway (*see that family*)) left a son, Arthur.
(3) William Henry, M.D., *d.* 1860.
(1) Isabella, *m.* her 1st cousin, George Hopkins, and *d.* 1901, leaving issue.
(2) Anne, *d.* 31 Jan. 1874. (3) Henrietta.
2. Henry, Q.C., Judge of the Landed Estates Court, Dublin, M.A. Trin. Coll. Dublin, *m.* Marianne, dau. of Robert Cary Hamilton M'Naghton, of Magherabuoy, co. Derry, and *d.* 4 March, 1859, having had by her (who *d.* 9 June, 1873) three sons and six daus.,
(1) Robert Henry, B.A., *m.* 18 July, 1867, Selina Grace, youngest dau. of Maj. Henry Waring, of Waringstown, co. Down (*see that family*). She *d.* 4 Dec. 1904. He *d.* 5 May, 1878, leaving a son,
Henry Lancelot (Rev.), M.A. Oxon, Vicar of West Crawley, Sussex, *m.* 9 July, 1895, Frances Enid, dau. of the Rev. James George Bullock, M.A., and has a son and two daus.,
a. Averell.
a. Varina. *b.* Audrey.
(2) John, B.A., Barrister-at-Law, *m.* 6 Oct. 1881, Frances Elizabeth, dau. of Henry Howarth, of Lisbon, and *d.s.p.* 26 Aug. 1882.
(3) Henry Frederick, Solicitor, *m.* 5 Jan. 1886, Constance Eva, youngest dau. of George Vandeleur, of Ballynamona, co. Limerick (*see* VANDELEUR *of Kilrush*).
(1) Mary Charlotte, *m.* 6 July, 1868, the Rev. Gerald Ormsby Vandeleur, of Ballynamona, Rector of Ravenstone, Ashby-de-la-Zouche, and has issue (*see* VANDELEUR *of Kilrush*). He *d.* 24 May, 1903.
(2) Henrietta Maria, *m.* 14 Nov. 1865, the Rev. Richard Lockwood Giveen, M.A., Vicar of St. Mark's, Clerkenwell, London, and has four sons. He *d.* 17 Dec. 1910.
(3) Isabella Jane, *m.* 26 June, 1872, the Rev. Henry Watters Carson, B.D., Rector of Santry, Dublin, son of the Right Rev. Thomas Carson, D.D., Bishop of Kilmore (*see* CARSON *of Shanroe*). He *d.s.p.* 1 Sept. 1895.
(4) Marion.
(5) Alice Anne, *m.* 3 Jan. 1871, Yelverton Dawson, M.D., of Bellevue, Mallow, and has issue.
(6) Clemena Elizabeth, *m.* 25 Feb. 1880, Alfred Charles de Burgh, son of the Rev. William de Burgh, D.D. (*see* DE BURGH *of Oldtown*), and has one dau.
3. James. 4. Francis, *d.v.p.*
1. Jane, *d.* 24 May, 1870.
2. Clemena, *m.* John Kelly, of Dublin.
1. Ann, *m.* (setts. dated 17 Dec. 1780) the Rev. Francis Johnston, of Tremont, Newry, co. Down.
2. Mabella, *m.* 1791, William Hopkins.
3. Jane, *m.* 1786, William Wynne.
4. Elizabeth, *m.* — Sheridan.

Mr. Martley *d.* 1797 (will proved 1 Aug.), and was *s.* by his eldest surviving son,
WILLIAM MARTLEY, of Ballyfallon, *m.* 1st, in July, 1789, Alicia, dau. of Francis Hopkins, of Darvistown, co. Meath, and had an only dau.,
Jane, *m.* 1809, the Right Hon. Francis Blackburne, Lord Chancellor of Ireland, and *d.* Sept. 1872, having had issue (*see* BLACKBURNE *of Tankardstown*).
He *m.* 2ndly, 1798, Elizabeth, dau. of Richard Rothwell, of Rockfield, and Berford, co. Meath (*see* ROTHWELL *of Rockfield*), and *d.* (will proved 14 April, 1807), leaving by his 2nd wife an only son,
JOHN MARTLEY, of Ballyfallon, matriculated at St. Mary's Hall, Oxford, 22 May, 1817, aged 17; *m.* 1818, Jane, dau. of John Rothwell, of Cannonstown, co. Meath, by Catherine, dau. of Thomas Prendergast (*see* ROTHWELL *of Rockfield*), and had by her (who *d.* Aug. 1837) issue,
1. WILLIAM, of whom presently.
2. John Rothwell, Senior Ensign 66th Regt, N.I., *d.* in India, 5 Aug. 1845.
3. FRANCIS BLACKBURNE, *s.* his brother.
4. Charles, *d. unm.* 5. Richard, *d.s.p.* 1892.
1. Kate Isabella, *d. unm.* 4 Dec. 1871.
2. Elizabeth Jane, *m.* 5 April, 1848, James Francis Erskine, J.P., of The Yews, Newry, youngest son of the Rev. Josiah Erskine, B.A., Rector of Knockbride, co. Cavan (*see* BURKE'S *Family Records*), and *d.* 6 July, 1883, having had two sons and one dau., viz.,
1. John Francis, Lieut. R.A., *d. unm.* 13 Aug. 1878.
2. Robert, *m.* 30 Nov. 1882, Anne Emily, dau. of the Rev. Thomas Francis Greene, M.A., of Kilranalagh, co. Wicklow (*see* HEIGHINGTON *of Donard*), and has four children.
1. Marianne, *m.* 2 Jan. 1880, the Rev. James Jackson Sherrard, B.D., Vicar of Nynagh, Banagher.

Mr. Martley *d.* 31 Aug. 1841, and was *s.* by his eldest son,
WILIAM MARTLEY, of Ballyfallon, *m.* 13 May, 1852, Mary Jane, eldest dau. of John Friday, of Brenchley, Kent, and *d.* 6 Feb. 1874, when he was *s.* by his brother,
FRANCIS BLACKBURNE MARTLEY, of Ballyfallon, J.P. co. Meath, Registrar of the High Court of Judicature in Ireland, *b.* 1829; *m.* 22 Oct. 1853, Elizabeth (*d.* 23 Sept. 1908), dau. of William Gibson, of Rockforest, co. Tipperary, and Gaulstown, co. Meath, J.P., by Louisa, dau. of Joseph Grant, Barrister-at-Law (*see* GIBSON *of Rockforest*), and had issue,
1. John, *d.* at school at Marlborough, 9 March, 1870.
2. WILLIAM GIBSON.
3. Francis Charles, late of Ballyfallon, M.A., M.D., Cantab. (6, Prince Edward Mansions, Bayswater, W.), *b.* 20 Jan. 1865;

m. 27 Sept. 1892, Adelaide Amelia, dau. of Edward Strangman, of Kilcop, co. Waterford, and has,
   1. John Francis, *b*. 29 July, 1893.
      1. Mary.   2. Nannette.
1. Louisa Katherine, *d*. young 20 Jan. 1857.
Mr. Martley *d*. 24 Aug. 1894, and was *s*. by his son, the present representative.
Residence—134, High Street, Poplar, E.

MARTYN OF TULIRA.

EDWARD JOSEPH MARTYN, of Tulira, co. Galway, sometime J.P. and D.L., High Sheriff 1886, *b*. 31 Jan. 1859; *s*. his father 5 April, 1860.

Lineage.—OLIVER MARTYN, M.P. for Galway 1689, left issue three sons,
1. RICHARD, his heir.
2. Peter, *m*. Miss Browne, and had issue,
   1. OLIVER, who *s*.
   2. Geoffrey, *d. unm.*
   3. Richard, *d. unm.*
   4. John, *d*. Jan. 1764; *m*. Mary Anne Lynch, of Tubber, co. Galway, and had a son,
      EDWARD, who *s*.
3. John, of Doebeg, *d*. 1767; *m*. Anne, dau. of Anthony Blake, and had issue,
   Thomas, of Doebeg, *d*. 1753; *m*. Cecilia (*d*. 1776), dau. of William O'Fallon, of Cleonaugh, co. Roscommon, and had,
   Peter, of Doebeg, *d*. 1796; *m*. Judith (*d*. 1801), dau. of James McDonnell, of Taughnaugh, co. Mayo, and had issue,
     1. Thomas, of Doebeg, a Col. in the Austrian service.
     2. Robert, Major in the Austrian service, *m*. 22 May, 1802, Antoinetta, dau. of Christopher Gaál, of Gayla, Hungary, and had two sons,
       a. Edward, *b*. 1818; *m*. Franzisca Herzog, and left two daus.
       b. Victor Francis Thomas, *b*. 21 Dec. 1825; *d*. 1883; *m*. 1862, Augelica, dau. of Joseph Pickler, of Hungary, and had,
         (*a*) Francis Albert, *b*. 9 March, 1864, of Szabadka, Hungary, *m*. 18 Aug. 1889, Chatarine, dau. of Jacob Vukorits, of Szabadka.
         (*b*) Arthur, *m*. Grizella Piatsek, and has issue.
         (*a*) Angelica, *m*. Jenö Bogyay.
     3. Peter, Capt. in the Austrian service.
     1. Sarah, *m*. Cunningham McAlpine, of Douglass, co. Tyrone.

The eldest son,
RICHARD MARTYN, of Tulira, *d.s.p.* 1740, and was *s*. by his nephew,
OLIVER MARTYN, of Tulira, *m*. 8 July, 1748, Frances, dau. of John Donnellan, of Ballydonnellan, co. Galway, *d.s.p.* 1768, and was *s*. by his nephew,
EDWARD MARTYN, of Tulira, *m*. 1798, Mary, eldest dau. of Andrew Browne, of Mount Hazel, co. Galway, and had issue,
1. JOHN, late of Tulira.
2. Andrew, of Spiddal, co. Galway, *m*. 1863, Mary, eldest dau. of Oliver Dolphin, of Turoe, co. Galway, and *d*. 1878, leaving issue, Mary, *m*. 27 Feb. 1897, Capt. Fitzroy Hemphill (*see* HEMPHILL *of Rathkenny*), and has issue.
3. Peter, Capt. in the 88th Regt., *d. unm.* 24 March, 1866.
  1. Jane, *m*. John R. Corballis, Q.C.
  2. Mary Anne, *m*. James Balfe, J.P., of Runnamoat, co. Roscommon, and *d*. leaving issue (*see* BALFE *of South Park*).
Mr. Martyn *d*. 1836, and was *s*. by his son,
JOHN MARTYN, of Tulira, co. Galway, J.P., *b*. Aug. 1801; *m*. 17 Feb. 1857, Annie Mary Josephine, dau. of James Smith, J.P., of Masonbrook, co. Galway. He *d*. 5 April, 1860. She *d*. 12 May, 1898, leaving issue, two sons,
1. EDWARD JOSEPH, now of Tulira.
2. John, Lieut. 3rd Dragoon Guards, *b*. 19 March, 1860; *d*. 5 March, 1884.

Arms—Az., a cross Calvary arg. between in dexter chief the sun in splendour or, and in the sinister chief the moon in crescent of the second. **Crest**—An estoile of six points or. **Motto**—Sic iiur ad astra.
Seat—Tulira, Ardrahan, co. Galway. **Club**—Kildare Street, Dublin.

MASSEY. *See* BURKE'S PEERAGE, **CLARINA, B.**

MASSEY-DAWSON. *See* **DAWSON.**

MASSEY-WESTROPP. *See* **WESTROPP.**

I.L.G.

MASSY OF GRANTSTOWN HALL.

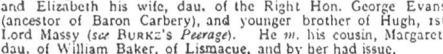

COL. HARRY STANLEY MASSY, C.B., F.R.G.S., of Grantstown Hall, co. Tipperary, Assistant-Adjt.-Gen. 7th Div. E. Command in India 1904-6, Col. (ret.) late commanding 19th Bengal Lancers, Indian Army, *b*. 12 July, 1855; *m*. 1 Oct. 1894, Geraldine Elinor, dau. of George Massy, of Glenville, co. Limerick, and has issue,
EYRE FITZGERALD FRANCIS, *b*. 11 Nov. 1907.
Geraldine.

Lineage.—THE REV. GODFREY MASSY, of Mount Sion, Vicar of Dysart, and Prebendary of Limerick, 3rd son of Col. Hugh Massy, of Duntrileague, co. Limerick, and Elizabeth his wife, dau. of the Right Hon. George Evans (ancestor of Baron Carbery), and younger brother of Hugh, 1st Lord Massy (*see* BURKE'S *Peerage*). He *m*. his cousin, Margaret dau. of William Baker, of Lismacue, and by her had issue,
1. Hugh, of Mount Sion.
2. WILLIAM, of whom presently.
3. Elizabeth.

The 2nd son,
REV. WILLIAM MASSY, of Glenwilliam, co. Limerick, Prebendary of Dysart, Rector of Clonbeg, *m*. 1st, the dau. of Michael Scanlan, of Ballinaher, co. Limerick, and by her had issue,
1. Godfrey, Capt in the Army, *d. unm.*
2. George, of Glenwilliam Castle, co. Limerick, *m*. 1st, Lucinda Clenchy, who *d*. April, 1818. He *m*. 2ndly, 1 June, 1819, dau. of Col. the Right Hon. William O'Dell, M.P. She *d*. 16 Dec. 1846, leaving issue.
3. Hugh, of Stagdale, co. Limerick, *m*. Mary, only child of John Lane. She *d*. 20 Feb. 1826. He *d*. 14 March, 1814, leaving issue.
He *m*. 2ndly, Nov. 1772, Elizabeth, dau. of Henry Bevan, of Camass, co. Limerick, and by her had issue,
4. WILLIAM, of whom presently.
5. Henry, of Woodfort, co. Cork, *m*. 1st, Mary, dau. of Thomas Buchanan, and 2ndly, Hester, dau. of James O'Connor, of Brook Lodge, co. Cork, and had issue.
6. Eyre, an Officer in the Army, *d. unm.*
7. Charles, ancestor of MASSY *of Kingswell* (*see that family*).
He *m*. 3rdly, the widow of — Creed, and 4thly, Jane, dau. of Robert Hoare, of Factory Hill, co. Cork. She *d.s.p.* 24 Dec. 1827. He *d*. 1822. His 4th son,
REV. WILLIAM MASSY, Prebendary of Dysart, *m*. 1st, Catherine, dau. and heir of J. Dwyer, and by her had issue,
1. William Godfrey, *m. unm.*
  1. Alicia, *m*. Henry Adams.
He *m*. 2ndly, Elizabeth, dau. of Capt. Joseph Evans, and *d*. 14 Nov. 1833, having by her had issue,
2. HENRY WILLIAM, of whom presently.
3. Charles William, Maj. in the Militia, *d.s.p.* 8 Oct. 1881.
4. Godfrey William Hugh, of Castlerea, co. Tipperary, Maj. 19th Foot, Knight of the Legion of Honour, *m*. 31 Jan. 1856, Louisa Emma, dau. of Robert George Maunsell, of Limerick, and widow of Francis William, 6th Earl of Seafield, and *d*. 4 June, 1862, having by her (who *m*. 3rdly, 5 July, 1864, Lord Henry Loftus, and *d*. 2 Aug. 1884) had a son,
  Godfrey Lennox Eyre, late Capt. Connaught Rangers, *b*. 24 Dec. 1856.
5. Hugh Francis, Capt. 19th Regt., *m*. 3 Dec. 1864, Beatrice Louisa, dau. of Thomas Johnstone Barton, of Glendalough House, co. Wicklow (*see that family*). She *d*. 23 Jan. 1893, having had issue,
  1. Hugh Eyre Barton, *b*. 25 June, 1866.
  2. Godfrey William Edward, *b*. 16 March, 1873; *m*. 15 Feb. 1911, Eva Susan, dau. of William Bolton, of The Island (*see that family*), and widow of Hon. Hamilton Robert Tilson Grogan Fitzmaurice Deane-Morgan (*see* BURKE'S *Peerage*, MUSKERRY, B.).
    1. Dora Isabel.   2. Violet Georgina.
    3. Beatrice Erskine.
2. Elizabeth Frances, *m*. 1846, George Latham Bennett, of Glenefy, co. Limerick, and had issue.
3. Frances, *m*. Thomas Hobbs Williams, of Snowden, Devon, late 74th Highlanders.

The eldest son by the 2nd marriage,
HENRY WILLIAM MASSY, of Grantstown Hall, and of Rosanna, co. Tipperary, J.P. cos. Tipperary and Limerick, Maj. Tipperary Artillery Militia, *b*. Jan. 1816; *m*. Feb. 1838, Maria, dau. of Patrick Cahill. She *d*. March, 1886. He *d*. 20 Nov. 1895, having had issue,
1. WILLIAM GODFREY DUNHAM, of Grantstown.

2 G

Massy. THE LANDED GENTRY. 466

2. Charles Francis, Lieut.-Col. Indian Army, *b.* 10 June, 1847; *m.* 1873, Alice, younger dau. of Maj.-Gen. Sir Thomas Seaton, K.C.B., and has issue,
  1. Seaton Dunham, 2nd Lieut. Princess Alexandra of Wales' Own Yorkshire Regt., *b.* 25 April, 1882.
    1. Ella, *m.* P. D. Agnew, Indian Civil Service, Deputy Commissioner, Punjab.
    2. Alice Seaton, *m.* 17 Nov. 1903, Capt. Charles Walter Tribe, 38th Dogras, Indian Army, son of Ven. Archdeacon W. Tribe.
3. HARRY STANLEY, now of Grantstown Hall.
4. Percy Hugh Hamon, Col. late 6th Dragoon Guards (57, *Drayton Gardens, S.W.*), *b.* 6 Nov. 1857; *m.* 28 July, 1888, Rosamond Amabel Nora, dau. of the late Sir Carey Knyvett, K.C.B., and has issue,
  Cynthia Rosamond Emeline.
1. Anna.
2. Elizabeth Frances, *m.* 1867, Col. William James Massy, Norfolk Regt.
3. Maud, *m.* 1874, Rev. Charles Swynnerton, Chaplain to the Forces, Bombay, and *d.* 1882, leaving issue.
4. Amy Evans, *m.* 18 Oct. 1884, Thomas Watt Smyth, M.A., I.C.S., Judge of the Chief Court of the Punjab, and has issue (*see* SMYTH *of Duncira*).

The eldest son,
LIEUT.-GEN. WILLIAM GODFREY DUNHAM MASSY, C.B., of Grantstown Hall, co. Tipperary, J.P. and D.L., High Sheriff 1899, C.C. South Riding, Tipperary, and District Councillor Tipperary Rural Div., LL.D. Dublin University, Lieut.-Gen. in the Army and Col. of the 5th Royal Irish Lancers, Knight of the Legion of Honour, late commanding the Forces in Ceylon, *b.* 24 Nov. 1838; *m.* 20 Nov. 1869, Elizabeth Jane, elder dau. of Maj.-Gen. Sir Thomas Seaton, K.C.B., of Ackworth House, East Bergholt, Suffolk, and by her issue,
  Gertrude Annette Seaton, *m.* 1st, 21 Sept. 1893, Col. James George Cockburn, A.A.G. Chatham, who *d.* 30 Jan. 1900. She *m.* 2ndly, 27 Dec. 1903, Capt. Godfrey W. Massey, of Cahervillahow Golden, co. Tipperary.
Gen. Massy served in the Crimea, 1855 (dangerously wounded at the Redan, despatches, medal with clasps, Legion of Honour, Turkish medal), and in the Afghan War, 1879-80 (despatches, medal with two clasps). He *d.* 20 Sept. 1906, and was *s.* by his brother.

Arms—Arg. on a chevron between three lozenges sa. a lion passant or. Crest—A bull's head gu. issuing out of a ducal coronet or. Motto—Pro libertate patriæ.

Seat—Grantstown Hall, Tipperary. Club—United Service, S.W.

MASSY late OF KINGSWELL.

RICHARD ALBERT HAMON MASSY, late of Kingswell House, Tipperary, *b.* 1899.

Lineage. — CHARLES MASSY, youngest son of Rev. William Massy, of Glenwilliam (*see* MASSY *of Grantstown*), *m.* 1808, Margaret Spread, dau. of John Cummins, of Ballygran, co. Limerick, and *d.* 1811, having by her (who *d.* 1854) had issue,
1. William Charles, of Castleview, co. Tipperary, *m.* 1st, his cousin Maria, dau. of Henry Massy, of Woodfort; and 2ndly, Maria, dau. of Benjamin Bradshaw, of Gambenstown, and by her had issue,
  William Charles, *d. unm.* Aug. 1878.
  Frances Isabella, *m.* Rev. F. D. Burnside, of Belfast, and had issue.
2. JOHN, of whom presently.

The younger son,
JOHN MASSY, of Kingswell House, co. Tipperary, J.P. cos. Tipperary and Limerick, *b.* 18 July, 1810; *m.* 11 Aug. 1832, Alicia, dau. of Capt. Richard Chadwick, of Chadville, co. Tipperary. She *d.* 22 June, 1874. He *d.* 1894, having had issue,
1. Charles Henry, *d.* serving with his (the 77th) regiment during the Russian War, in his 20th year.
2. RICHARD ALBERT, of whom presently.
3. John, *b.* 1848; drowned at Kilkee, 6 Aug. 1864.
  1. Margaret Alicia, *m.* 11 Aug. 1857, Gen. George Wheeler (*d.* 1910), son of Gen. Sir Hugh Massy Wheeler, K.C.B., and is dec.
  2. Alicia Victoria, *m.* 30 June, 1863, James George Deck, son of George Deck, of Wellington, New Zealand, and is dec.
  3. Melian Rebecca, *m.* 20 Sept. 1871, Maj.-Gen. Henry Wyllie, C.S.I., Ind. Army. She *d.* 9 Nov. 1905.
  4. Frances Elizabeth, *m.* 1st, March, 1879, Hugh Baker, of Lismacue, co. Tipperary, who *d.* 9 July, 1887. She *m.* 2ndly, Sept. 1888, Major Ralph Hall Bunbury.
The 2nd son,

RICHARD ALBERT MASSY, J.P. co. Leitrim, late Lieut. 60th Rifles, Resident Magistrate co. Kerry, *b.* 22 Feb. 1840; *m.* 21 April, 1869, Matilda, only dau. of Capt. George Minchin, R.N., of Rock Abbey, Cashel, and *d.* 25 Sept. 1889, having issue,
1. JOHN GEORGE ALBERT, of Kingswell.
2. GEORGE GODFREY HAMON, late of Kingswell.
  1. Maude Alice Beatrice.
  2. Alberta, *d.* 1904.

The elder son,
JOHN GEORGE ALBERT MASSY, of Kingswell House, Tipperary, Capt. 18th Royal Irish Regt., *b.* 27 Jan. 1870, and *d.* 24 July, 1908, in India, and was *s.* by his brother,
GEORGE GODFREY HAMON MASSY, of Kingswell House, *b.* 28 March, 1874; *m.* Florence Caroline, 2nd dau. of Charles A. Clarke, of Kingstown, co. Dublin, and *d.* 21 May, 1910, and was *s.* by his son,
RICHARD ALBERT HAMON MASSY, now of Kingswell House.

Arms—Arg., on a chevron between three lozenges sa. a lion passant or. Crest—A bull's head gu. issuing out of a ducal coronet or. Motto—Pro libertate patriæ.

MASSY. *See* BURKE'S PEERAGE, **MASSY, B.**

MAUDE. *See* BURKE'S PEERAGE, **DE MONTALT, E.**

MAUNSELL OF LIMERICK.

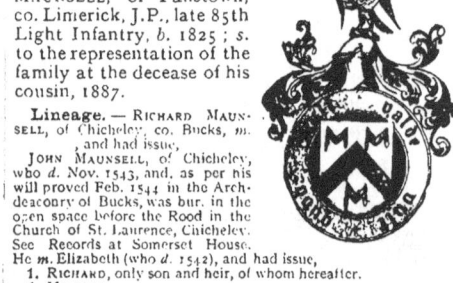

LIEUT.-COL. ROBERT MAUNSELL, of Fanstown, co. Limerick, J.P., late 85th Light Infantry, *b.* 1825; *s.* to the representation of the family at the decease of his cousin, 1887.

Lineage. — RICHARD MAUNSELL, of Chicheley, co. Bucks, *m.* , and had issue,
JOHN MAUNSELL, of Chicheley, who *d.* Nov. 1543, and, as per his will proved Feb. 1544 in the Archdeaconry of Bucks, was bur. in the open space before the Rood in the Church of St. Laurence, Chicheley. See Records at Somerset House.
He *m.* Elizabeth (who *d.* 1542), and had issue,
1. RICHARD, only son and heir, of whom hereafter.
  1. Margery.
  2. Cecily, *m.* 1539, Charles Goodred.
  3. Joan.
RICHARD MAUNSELL, of Chichely, Bucks, *m.* 1st, 5 Aug. 1535, Margaret, 2nd dau. of Sir Thomas Fairlax, of Walton and Gilling Castles, and widow of William Sayre, of Worsall. He *m.* 2ndly, Joan, dau. of Thomas Potter, of Newport Pagnell. He *d.* 6 Nov. 1559 (will proved 7 Dec. 1559), leaving issue,
1. THOMAS, of whom presently.
2. John, of Haversham, ancestor of the Mansels of Cosgrove Hall.
3. Rudolph, *d.* young.
  1. Olivia, *b.* 1542. 2. Elizabeth, *b.* 1546.
The eldest son,
THOMAS MAUNSELL, of Chichely, Bucks, matriculated at Magdalen Coll. Oxon. 1550, M.A. 1554, *b.* 1536; *m.* 11 Sept. 1567, Agnes, dau. of John Moreton, of Oundle, and widow of William Everell, and *d.* 5 April, 1582, leaving issue,
1. John, of Thorp Malsor, who *d.* 19 Oct. 1625. He had two sons, John and Thomas. His grandson, Robert, *m.* Judith, dau. of Thomas Brooks, of Oakley, but *d.s.p.* By his will (dated 1704) he left his estate to his nephew Robert, with remainder to his cousin Thomas, 3rd son of John Maunsell, of Ballyvoreen, co. Limerick (*see below*).
2. THOMAS, of whom presently.
3. Richard, of Emberton, co. Bucks, and Losemore, co. Gloucester, *w.* 1623, Dorothy, dau. of Henry Mordaunt, of Thunderley, and widow of Humphry Phipps, and *d.s.p.* 1631.
  1. Maria, *m.* Daniel Comry.
  2. Martha, *m.* Henry Edwards. 3. Elizabeth, *m.* — Petit.
The 2nd son,
THOMAS MAUNSELL, of Vandy, Bucks, Mocollop, co. Waterford, and Derryvillane, co. Cork, *b.* 17 April, 1577, matriculated at Magdalen Hall, Oxford 1594. He was of Barnard's Inn and admitted to Gray's Inn 1599. Served in the fleet against the Spanish Armada and retiring in 1609, settled in Ireland. He *m.* Alphra, dau. of Sir William Crayford, of Mongam Magna, Crayford, Kent. Admon. of his estate was granted in Ireland, 20 April, 1661. He had issue,

1. THOMAS, of whom presently. 2. Walter.
3. John, of Ballyvoreen, Capt. in Cromwell's Life Guards, wounded at Naseby, *m.* 1st, 1656, Mary, dau. of George Booth, and 2ndly, a dau. of — Campbell. By his 2nd wife he was ancestor of the family of MAUNSELL *of Thorp Malsor (see that family).*
4. Boyle, of Gaulstown, or Kilbroney, co. Kilkenny, *m.* Elizabeth, who left issue, now extinct in the male line.
5. Richard, of the Inner Temple, London, living 23 Aug. 1642; *d. unm.*
1. Alphra, *m.* George Peacocke, of Graigue, co. Limerick.
2. Anne, *m.* 1630, Very Rev. Robert Naylor, Dean of Lismore, and afterwards of Limerick.
3. Sarah, *m.* — Ridgate.
4. Catherine, *m.* Theophilus Eaton.
5. Alice, *m.* — Andrews.
6. Mary, *m.* Richard Bettesworth.

The eldest son,
COL. THOMAS MAUNSELL, of Mocollop, in the Royal Army, greatly distinguished himself for the defence of Mocollop Castle in 1650. He *m.* 1651, Margaret, widow of Thomas Hutchins, of Mitchelstown, and dau. of Leonard Knoyle, of Ballygally, co. Waterford. His will is dated 6 May, 1686. He had issue,
1 THOMAS, of whom presently.
2. John, Capt. R.N., *d.v.p., unm.*
1. Sara, *m.* Thomas Seward.
2. Aphra. *m.* Henry Carter, M.D. 3. Aphra, *m.* John Downing.

The elder son,
COL. THOMAS MAUNSELL, of Mocollop, also in the Royal Army, got grants of land 1663, in Galway and Limerick, *m.* Anne, eldest dau. of Theophilus Eaton, of Dublin. His will is dated 8 July, 1690. By her (who *m.* 2ndly, John Ryves) he had issue,
1. Thomas, of Annaghrosty, J.P. co. Limerick, High Sheriff 1697, *d. unm.* 1711.
2. Joseph, of Curagh, co. Galway, *m.* 1st, the dau. of — Tierney, and 2ndly, the dau. of — FitzGerald, of Stone Hall, co. Limerick, and had issue extinct in the male line. His dau. Anne *m.* Anthony Burke, of Springfield, and had issue a son, Maunsell Burke, whose dau. Jane *m.* 1798, Thomas Longworth-Dawes, of Greenhill (*see that family*).
3. John Causidice, of Cork, High Sheriff 1719, *m.* 1709, Elizabeth Campion and had issue, which also became extinct in the male line. His will is dated 20 Jan. 1747. His son, Richard (Rev.), had an only dau. and heir, Elizabeth, *m.* John Thomas Waller, of Castletown (*see that family*).
4. RICHARD, of whom presently.
5. William, ancestor of MAUNSELL *of Spa Hill (see that family).*
6. Edwin, *d. unm.* 7. Theophilus, *d. unm.*
1. Margaret, *m.* 1st, 6 Feb. 1692, John Widenham, of Castletownroche, and 2ndly, 1709, Rev. Richard Verling, and had issue.
2. Anne, *m.* Rev. Daniel Widenham, of Ballinamona, and had issue.
3. Mary, *m.* Henry Ormsby, of Ballymartin.
4. Katherine, *m.* her cousin James Knight, of Dublin, and had issue.

The 4th son,
RICHARD MAUNSELL, settled at Limerick, and represented that city from 1740 to 1761, Mayor of Limerick 1734. High Sheriff 1743. He *m.* 1st, Margaret, dau. of Thomas Twigg of Donnybrook Castle (*see* TWIGG, *formerly of Thorndale*), and had issue,
1. THOMAS, his successor.
1. Anne, *m.* 1st, Col. Edward Taylor, of Ballynort, co. Limerick, M.P. for Askeaton, and had issue, two daus.; 2ndly, John Tunnadine, Master in Chancery, M.P. for Askeaton.
Mr. Maunsell *m.* 2ndly, Jane, eldest dau. of William Waller, of Castle Waller, co. Tipperary, and had issue,
2. Richard, of Ballywilliam, co. Limerick (*see* MAUNSELL *of Ballywilliam*).
3. John, Gen. in the Army, who commanded the 56th Regt. at the siege of Havannah 1762, and led the party who stormed the Morro; he was twice married, but *d.* in New York, July, 1795, *s.p*
4. William (Rev.), D.D., of Limerick, *m.* Elizabeth, 3rd dau. of Ven. William Lewis, Archdeacon of Kilfenora (*see* LEWIS *of Ballinagar*), and had issue,
1. Richard (Rev.), *m.* Anne Crump, and had a son, Richard John William.
1. Elizabeth, *m.* 1798, as his 2nd wife, Richard Chute, of Chute Hill, co. Kerry, and had issue (*see that family*).
2. Dorothea Grace, *m.* Thomas Maunsell, M.P., of Plassy, and had issue.
3. Jane, *m.* Anthony Samuel Raymond, and had issue.
5. Eaton, Sheriff of Limerick 1760, Mayor 1779, *d. unm.*
6. Edward, *d. unm.*
Mr. Maunsell *d.* 1773, and was *s.* by his only son by his first marriage,
THOMAS MAUNSELL, LL.D., Barrister-at-Law, King's Counsel, Counsel to the Commissioners of Customs, and M.P. for Kilmallock, *m.* Dorothea, youngest dau. of Richard Waller, of Castle Waller, and had issue,
1. Richard, who *d.* in America, *unm.*
2. THOMAS, of Plassy, co. Limerick, M.P. for Johnstown, *m.* 1 Oct. 1767, Mary, eldest dau. of John Rochfort, of Clogrenan, co. Carlow, but had no issue. He *m.* 2ndly, Dorothea Grace, dau. of Rev. William Maunsell, D.D., and *d.* leaving two daus., his co-heirs,
1. ELIZABETH DOROTHEA, who *m.* her cousin Maj. Robert Hedges Eyre Maunsell.
2. DOROTHEA JANE, *m.* John Dunlevie.
3. ROBERT, of Bank Place, of whom presently.
4. George (Very Rev.), D.D., Dean of Leighlin, *m.* Helena, dau.

of Richard Hedges Eyre, of Macroom Castle and Mount Hedges, co. Cork, and had issue,
1. Thomas (Rev.), M.A., *m.* Miss Blackmore, and had issue two daus.,
(1) Elizabeth, *m.* 1831, Thomas Godfrey Phillips, of Beechmount, co. Tipperary (*see* PHILLIPS *of Gaile*).
(2) Helena, *m.* John Burnett.
2. Robert Hedges Eyre, a Maj. in the Army, *m.* his cousin Elizabeth Dorothea, dau. and co-heir of THOMAS MAUNSELL, of Plassy, and had (with four daus., Grace, *m.* George Smith; Helena; Emily; and Georgina, *m.* John L. Phelps) one son, Richard.
3. George, a Capt. in the Army, *m.* Maria Wilhelmina Frederica, dau. of the Baron Von Hardenburgh, and had a son, Robert, and two daus., Louisa, *m.* Isidore Blake, Barrister-at-Law, and Maria.
4. Richard, LL.B., Barrister-at-Law *m.* 1808, Lady Catherine Hare, youngest dau. of William, Earl of Listowel, and *d.* 17 March, 1819, leaving issue (with two daus., Mary Grace, *m.* Rev. Richard Davies, and Louisa Hare), five sons,
(1) Robert Hedges (Rev.), who assumed the surname of EYRE on succeeding to a portion of the estates of his great-uncle Robert Hedges Eyre, and *m.* 5 Feb. 1836, Anna Maria, dau. of Eyre Evans, D.L., of Ash Hill, co. Limerick, and had issue, Robert Hedges MAUNSELL-EYRE (Rev.), Vicar of Congresbury, near Bristol, and has issue,
a. Listowel Frehe.
b. Richard Hedges.
a. Anna Julia Moncrieffe.
(2) William Hare, *m.* 1st, Fanny, dau. of Patrick ffrench, of Dublin, and had issue; and 2ndly, 6 Sept. 1859, Harriette, eldest dau. and co-heir of the Rev. W. H. Fleming, of Nullamore.
(3) George, late Capt. 94th Regt., *m.* Elizabeth, dau. of Brigadier-Gen. Conway.
(4) Richard, late Lieut. 7th Fusiliers, *m.* Maria, dau. of Maj. Odell, of The Grove, co. Limerick.
(5) Edward Eyre, Capt. R.N., *m.* 1 March, 1859, Louisa, only dau. of Samuel Waller, of Cuckfield and Brighton, and had issue. His eldest dau., Florence Catherine, *m.* 27 April, 1887, Rev. Theodosius Boughton-Leigh, M.A., Rector of Bradfield, co. Suffolk; and his youngest dau., Alice Hare, *m.* 11 April, 1882, Thomas Montagu Morrison Wylde, Lord Truro (*see* BURKE'S *Peerage*).
5. Edward Eyre (Rev.), M.A., Vicar of Galway, of Fort Eyre, co. Galway, *m.* 1818, Elizabeth, dau. of Thomas Studdert, J.P. and D.L., of Bunratty Castle, co. Clare, and has issue, a dau. Helena, *m.* the Venerable Charles Goold Butson, Archdeacon of Clonfert, and four sons,
(1) Edward Eyre, J.P., Barrister-at-Law, High Sheriff 1854, of Fort Eyre, *b.* 16 May, 1823; *m.* 1867, Alicia, only dau. of George Minchin, of Busherstown Castle, King's Co., and *d.* 1876.
(2) George William, J.P., Maj. 4th Batt. Connaught Rangers, *m.* Alys, only dau. of Gen. Sir Michael Creagh, K.H., and has issue,
1. Charles Edward Osborne, *d. unm.*, aged 40.
2. Herbert Henry Creagh, *d. unm.* aged 18.
3. William Granville Eyre, accidentally killed, aged 23, *unm.*
4. George Frederick Massy, *d.* young.
5. Edward Whitford Eyre, *m.* 1902, Marion, dau. of Capt. Tyrrell-Smith, and has issue,
a. Herbert Edward Creagh.
b. William Charles Eyre.
a. Haidee Cathleen. *b.* Winifred Eleanor Eyre.
6. Harry Butson, J.P., of Nigel, Transvaal, Capt. Southern, Mounted Rifles, late Civil Surgeon in S. African War, *b.* 1865; *m.* 1893, Miriam, dau. of A. D. Gilson, late 76th Regt., R.M., Natal, and has issue,
a. Herbert Edward Eyre.
a. Zoe Alys. *b.* Errol Creagh.
c. Audrey Evelyn.
7. George Christmas (*Cape Town*).
8. Octavius Studdert, late Civil Surgeon in S. Africa, 1899-1902 (*Clarinda Park, Kingstown, co. Dublin*).
9. Frederick Osborne Eyre, *d.* an infant.
10. James Henry Creagh, *d.* young.
(3) Richard Hedges Eyre, dec.
(4) Charles Studdert, late Capt. 82nd Regt., *d.* 1904.
1. Henrietta Margaret Eyre, *m.* 1805, the Rev. William Atthill, M.A., of Brandiston Hall, co. Norfolk, and had issue.
2. Emily, *m.* Henry Watson, 2nd son of George Watson, of Ballydartin House, co. Carlow.
1. Blanche, *m.* Maunsell Sargeant; *d.s.p.*
2. Margaret, *m.* Robert Going, of Traverston Hall.
3. Elizabeth, *m.* Henry White.
4. Dorothea, *m.* William Long Kingsman.
Upon the decease of Thomas Maunsell, of Plassy, leaving daus. only, the representation of the family of Maunsell devolved upon that gentleman's next brother,
ROBERT MAUNSELL, of Bank Place, H.E.I.C.S., Chief of the Council of Gangam, and subsequently Member of the Supreme Council of Madras. He *m.* 1782, Anne, only dau. and heiress of John Maxwell Stone, also Chief of Gangam, grandson and heir of the Hon. John Maxwell, 2nd son of John, 3rd Earl of Nithsdale, and by her (who *d.* Oct. 1848) had issue,
1. ROBERT GEORGE, his heir.
2. George, Lieut.-Col. 3rd Dragoon Guards, *d. unm.* 4 Sept. 1849.
3. HENRY, of Fanstown, J.P., Barrister-at-Law, High Sheriff for the City of Limerick 1848, and for the co. 1851; *m.* March, 1821,

Eliza, dau. of Pryce Peacocke, by Jane Ellard, of Fairyfield, Kilmallock, his wife, and d. 1876, having by her (who d. 24 Nov. 1867) had issue,
1. ROBERT, present representative.
2. William Pryce, of Fairyfield, Kilmallock, B.A. Trin. Coll. Dublin, Barrister-at-Law (5, Martello Terrace, Kingstown), b. 1828; m. Nov. 1861, Richarda, dau. of late Richard Gabbett (see GABBETT of Cahirline), and has issue,
   (1) Richard, C.E., B.A. Trin. Coll. Dublin, b. 1 April, 1864; d. 14 July, 1901.
   (2) Henry Rhys, Solicitor, B.A. Trin. Coll. Dublin, b. 2 Feb. 1877; m. 1905, Frances Geraldine, dau. of late Arthur Cooper Jenkinson, and has issue,
      William Arthur Rhys, b. 1906.
   (1) Gwendoline Frederica, m. 29 Nov. 1893, C. M. Courtney, who adopted the name of GABBETT, and has issue.
   1. Emma Frederica, m. 23 Jan. 1884, Charles Warren, Lieut. R.N., who d. 16 July, 1885.
   2. Henrietta.
4. Charles, d. unm. 1814.
5. Frederick, Gen. in the Army, Col. 85th King's Light Infantry, b. 1793; m. 13 Nov. 1834, Alicia, 2nd dau. of Thomas Studdert, J.P. and D.L., of Bunratty Castle, co. Clare. She d. 1885. He d. 18 Oct. 1875, leaving a son,
   ROBERT GEORGE STONE, of Gortbwee and Cloran, co. Limerick, and Amberd, Dean Park, Bournemouth, J.P. co. Clare and Bournemouth, late Maj. Limerick Artillery, Militia and formerly Lieut. 85th and 50th Regts. (Jun. Constitutional Club), b. 20 Oct. 1842; m. 1st, 1 Dec. 1870, Henrietta Peyton, dau. of Benjamin Peyton Sadler, Capt. R.N., which lady d. 12 Sept. 1871; and 2ndly, 7 Oct. 1873, Anna Margaret, dau. of Henry Spaight, J.P. of Affock, co. Clare, by whom he has issue,
      (1) Frederick Henry Robert, Lieut. King's Shropshire L.I., b. 16 Jan. 1888.
      (2) Robert George Frederick, b. 25 March, 1891.
      (1) Henrietta Frederica Maria.
      (2) Alicia, m. 12 April, 1899, Lieut. John Henry Stainton Burder, R.N., who d. 2 Sept. 1902, leaving a dau.
      (3) Grace, m. 7 June, 1907, Edward How White, M.D., and has issue.
      (4) Anna Constance.
      (5) Mary Helen Maxwell.
6. Septimus.
1. Anna, m. 20 March, 1805, Eyre Evans, of Ash Hill Towers, co. Limerick.
2. Maria, m. 16 June, 1817, the Hon. John Massy, youngest son of Hugh, 2nd Lord Massy, and d. 28 May, 1880.
3. Eliza, d. unm. 30 Dec. 1832.
4. Grace, m. 8 Oct. 1833, the Rev. James Charles Fitzgerald, of Shepperton, co. Clare.
Mr. Maunsell d. 1 Feb. 1832, aged 87, and was s. in his landed estates by his eldest son,
ROBERT GEORGE MAUNSELL, of Limerick, m. 1st, 28 Aug. 1813, Mabella, 2nd dau. of Standish Grady, of Elton, co. Limerick, brother of the Countess of Ilchester, and by her had issue,
1. ROBERT THOMAS, his heir, d.s.p. 22 Sept. 1850.
2. STANDISH GRADY, d.s.p. 1874.
3. GEORGE, late representative, Maj. H.E.I.C.S., d. Dec. 1887.
1. Anne Stone.
2. Louisa Emma, m. 1st, 17 Aug. 1843, Francis William, 6th Earl of Seafield, who d. 30 July, 1853; 2ndly, 31 Jan. 1856, Maj. Godfrey William Hugh Massy, 19th Regt., who d. 4 June, 1862; and 3rdly, 5 July, 1864, Lord Henry Loftus, who d.s.p. 28 Feb. 1880. She d. 2 Aug. 1884, aged 60.
3. Maria, d. 10 Jan. 1851.
4. Georgiana, m. 15 Aug. 1849, Hon. Lewis Alexander Ogilvie Grant, and d. 1885, leaving issue (see BURKE's Peerage, SEAFIELD, E.).
5. Mabella.   6. Emma.
7. Eliza Grace, m. 14 June, 1860, the Rev. T. H. Gollock, M.A., of Forest, co. Cork.
Mr. Maunsell m. 2ndly, 28 Oct. 1834, Maria, eldest dau. of John Minton, and by her had issue,
4. John, Lieut. R.A., b. 20 April, 1836; m. 2 June, 1864, Elizabeth, dau. of Rev. S. T. Hartman, and d. 27 Aug. 1867, leaving issue,
   1. Lily Mary, d. 27 May, 1894.
   2. Mary Edith.
8. Martha Sophia Edith, m. William Stopford Maunsell, late R.A., and has issue (see MAUNSELL of Ballywilliam).
Mr. Maunsell d. 3 Oct. 1838.

Arms—Arg., a chevron between three maunches sa. Crest—a hawk rising ppr. Mottoes—Quod vult valde vult; Honorantes me honorabo.
Residence—78, George Street, Limerick.

MAUNSELL OF BALLYWILLIAM.

GEORGE EDWARD SCARLETT MAUNSELL, of Ballywilliam, co. Limerick, b. 1871.

Lineage.—RICHARD MAUNSELL, of Ballywilliam, co. Limerick, eldest son (by his 2nd wife, Jane, eldest dau. of William Waller, of Castle Waller, co. Tipperary) of Richard Maunsell, M.P. for Limerick from 1742 to 1761 (see MAUNSELL of Limerick), m. 18 June, 1745, Helena Maria, eldest dau. of Daniel Toler, of Beechwood, and half-sister of John, 1st Earl of Norbury, and had issue,

1. DANIEL, his heir.
2. Richard, m. Rebecca, dau. of Nicholas Smith, of Castle Park, near Limerick, and had issue,
   1. Richard (Rev.), m. Sarah, dau. of Benjamin Hawkshaw, of Falleen, Tipperary.
   2. Nicholas, m. 1st, Sophia Secretain, a Jersey lady, and 2ndly, Ursula, dau. of James Kinsley.
   3. John, d. unm.
   4. Charles, m. thrice, and had issue.
   1. Elizabeth, m. William Ryves.
   2. Helena Maria, m. 13 Jan. 1806, Charles Rolleston, of Silverhill, King's Co.
   3. Rebecca, d. unm.
3. JOHN (see MAUNSELL of Oakeley Park).
4. George, m. 1st, Miss Smith, aunt of Viscount Guillamore, and had a dau., m. Thomas O'Grady. He m. 2ndly, Miss Mogarth, first cousin to the Earl of Dunraven, and had by that lady,
   1. Richard (Rev.).
   2. John (Rev.), m. Elizabeth, dau. of James Butler, of co. Clare, and has issue.
   3. George.   4. Thomas.
   5. Edward.   6. Robert.
   7. Frederick.   8. William.
   9. Windham.
   1. Frances.   2. Elizabeth.
1. Jane, m. William Gabbett, of Caherline.
Mr. Maunsell, of Ballywilliam, d. 1790, and was s. by his son,
DANIEL MAUNSELL, of Ballywilliam, m. 18 Feb. 1779, Sarah, 2nd dau. and co-heir of George Meares, of Lion Hill, co. Dublin, and had issue,
1. Richard William, b. 22 Oct. 1783; d. 3 June, 1787.
2. GEORGE MEARES, of Ballywilliam.
3. Daniel, d. young, 31 March, 1787.
4. John, b. 1788; d. 1812.
5. William, b. 1789; d. unm.
6. Daniel Henry (Rev.), of Balbriggan, co. Dublin, b. 17 July, 1791; m. Louisa, dau. of John Richardson, of Mount Panther, co. Down. She d. 2 Jan. 1858. He d. 15 July, 1834, having had issue,
   1. Henry Daniel, Col. in the Army, b. 21 March, 1824; m. Emily, dau. of Rev. J. M. Butt. She d. 1866. He d.s.p.s. 11 June, 1894.
   2. John, b. 31 July, 1827; d. 18 July, 1837.
   3. Frederic Richard (Sir), K.C.B., Gen. R.E., Col. 1st King George's Own Sappers and Miners, b. 4 Sept. 1828; m. 1863 Mary Alexandrina, dau. of Don Manuel Velez, of New Granada. She d. 7 April, 1883, leaving issue,
      (1) Frederick Guy, Maj. R.A., b. 14 Feb. 1864; m. 1896, Hilda, dau. of H. Irwin, and has issue,
         Frederick Richard Guy, b. 22 Oct. 1898.
         Alexandrina Velez, b. 17 Dec. 1900.
      (2) Manuel Charles, Capt. R.A., b. 8 March, 1866; m. 29 Jan. 1892, Alice Blanche Mary, dau. of Lieut.-Col. de Pentheny de Pentheny-O'Kelly, and has issue,
         1. Charles Frederick, b. 8 Feb. 1893.
         2. Edgar Joseph Arundell, b. 24 Aug. 1896.
         1. Ida Margaret.
         2. Ysabel Frances.
      (3) Francis, b. 6 June, 1867; m. 1894, Mary Warner, and has issue,
         Frederick.
      (1) Louisa Jane Mary Alice Florence, b. 1863.
      (2) Mary Agnes, b. Feb. 1865; d. Oct. 1866.
      (3) Margaret Mary, b. 21 July, 1868; m. 1888, Daniel O'Leary, and has issue.
      (4) Ysabel Mary.
   4. John Richardson, Col. R.E., b. 17 June, 1834; m. 1864, Augusta, dau. of Col. H. Sandwith, and d. Dec. 1887, leaving issue,
      (1) John Boyd, Lieut. R.A., b. 1867, d. 1891.
      (2) Debonnaire Frederick, b. 1870.
      (1) Louisa Frances, b. 1365, d. 1366.
      (2) Edith Eleanor, b. 1869, d. 1870.
      (3) Eleanor Frances, b. 6 Aug. 1876.
      (4) Florence Mabel, b. March, 1881.
   1. Jane, b. 2 Sept. 1826; m. 1867, Gen. James Brind, R.A., and d.s.p. 6 Nov. 1908.
   2. Louisa, b. 11 Dec. 1830; m. 1857, H. B. Medlicott, B.A., and has issue.
7. Francis Richard (Rev.), Rector of Castle Island, co. Kerry, b. 27 Feb. 1793; m. Sarah, dau. of Edward Kelly, of Moate, and d. 1874, having had issue,
   1. Daniel Edmund Knox, dec.
   2. Richard Savage, dec.
   3. George Henry Clonbrook, dec.
   1. Mary Isabella, m. 31 March, 1846, James George Godfrey, son of Sir John Godfrey, Bart. (see BURKE's Peerage and Baronetage).
   2. Sarah Louisa, m. 18 April, 1849, Rev. Edward Fitzgerald Day, of co. Kerry, son of the Hon. Robert Day, Judge of the King's Bench.
   3. Letitia Maria, d. unm.
   4. Julia Allen, m. 10 April, 1861, Maj. Henry Marcus Beresford, son of the Most Rev. M. G. Beresford, and has issue (see BURKE's Peerage, WATERFORD, M.).
   5. Victoria Elizabeth, m. 1st, 12 April, 1861, John Henry Herbert St. John, 20th Regt., and by him has issue. She m. 2ndly, 1880, Henry Richard Sewart Bolton, of Tullydonnell, co. Louth (see that family). He d.s.p. 9 April, 1910.
8. Edward Charles, b. 8 March, 1794; m. Charlotte Heming, and d. 1857, had issue,
   1. Daniel.   2. Edward.

3. George, dec.
1. Sarah, d. unm.
2. Isabella.
3. Marian.

9. Robert, of Merrion Square, Dublin, b. 9 Aug. 1795; m. 1st, Anne, eldest dau. of the late Rev. John Lloyd, and niece of Thomas Lloyd, of Beechmount, late M.P. for co. Limerick, and d. 1876, having had issue,

1. Daniel, in the Army, m. 26 May, 1853, Anna Lucinda, dau. of Robert Billing.
2. John, J.P., of Edenmore, Raheny, co. Dublin, b. 1824; m. 1st, 1851, Catherine Lucinda, dau. and heir of Thomas Lloyd, of Beechmount, J.P. She d. 1862, leaving issue,
 (1) Edmund Robert Lloyd, M.A. and LL.B. Trin. Coll. Dublin, Barrister-at-Law, of 70, Lower Leeson Street, Dublin, b. 18 Oct. 1852; m. 13 Aug. 1879, Annie Rachael, dau. of Joseph Emerson Dowson, and d. 2 Nov. 1886, leaving issue,
  1. Arthur Edmund Lloyd, B.A. LL.B., Trin. Coll. Dublin Barrister-at-Law, of Lemonfield House, co. Limerick, and Ballyvourheen (12, Gerald Road, Eaton Square, S.W.), b. 26 May, 1880.
  1. Eileen Lucinda Elizabeth.
  2. Gwenodlen Josephine.
 (2) John Drought, Maj. Army Pay Dept., m. 17 Feb. 1885, Euphemia Sullivan, dau. of Maj. Robert Bush, 96th Regt. (see BURKE'S *Family Records*).
 (3) Frederick William.
 (4) Eyre Lloyd.
 (1) Annie Mary.

He m. 2ndly, 16 Dec. 1863, Emily Roche, only child of Archibald John Stephens, Q.C., LL.D., Recorder of Winchester, and had, with other issue, a son,
 (5) Archibald John Stephens, Major Royal Warwickshire Regt., b. 8 Sept. 1864.
 (2) Kathleen Isabella, m. 26 Sept. 1895, Herbert Stanley Ballance, M.D., of Weston-super-Mare, 3rd son of Charles Ballance, of Clapton, Middlesex.

He m. 3rdly, 1883, Annie, dau. of Rev. George Peacock, Rector of Gaile. He d. 15 Sept. 1899.
1. Elizabeth, m. 10 June, 1851, Capt. Robert Mayne, grandson of Judge Mayne.
2. Isabella, m. William Boyne Butt, M.D., son of Rev. John M. Butt.

Mr. Robert Maunsell m. 2ndly, Fanny, eldest dau. of Francis Dwyer, late Six Clerk, Court of Chancery, and had issue,
3. Francis Richard, m. 15 Sept. 1869, Louisa Jane, dau. of Humphrys Jones, of Carrickaderry, co. Monaghan (see BURKE's *Family Records*, SWANZY). He d.s.p. 25 Feb. 1900. She d. 13 Sept. 1899.
4. Albert Edward.
3. Fanny Barbara Maria.

He m. 3rdly, Louisa, dau. of the late James Douglas, of co. Antrim, and had issue, a son,
5. George Meares.

10. Thomas (Rev.), b. 14 Aug. 1797; m. Alice, dau. of T. F. Maunsell, of Ballybrood, co. Limerick, and had issue,
1. Thomas, dec.
2. Charles.
3. George, dec.
4. Samuel, dec.
5. Horatio, dec.

11. Horatio (Rev.), b. 23 Nov. 1798; m. Louisa, dau. of Rev. Mr. Marriot, of Canterbury, and d. 1852, having had issue,
1. Horatio.
2. Edward Henry.
3. Arthur.
4. John.
1. Louise.
2. Dora.
3. Jane.
4. Selina.
5. Eugenie.

1. Isabella Meares, m. 26 Feb. 1812, Edward Smyth, 2nd son of Rev. Thomas Smyth, D.D., and was s. by his son,
GEORGE MEARES MAUNSELL, of Ballywilliam, High Sheriff 1835, B.A. Oriel Coll. Oxford 1807, b. 1785; m. 1st, 19 Dec. 1817 Catherine, dau. of Thomas Lloyd, of Beechmount, late M.P. co. Limerick, and had issue,

1. DANIEL MEARES, of Ballywilliam, co. Limerick, B.A., J.P., b. 26 Oct. 1819; m. 21 June, 1858, Eliza, dau. of Christopher Delmege, J.P., of Castle Park, co. Clare, and d.s.p. 16 Dec. 1898.
2. THOMAS, of Ballywilliam.
3. George Meares, d. young, 9 March, 1830.
4. Richard, b. 7 Jan. 1829; m. 9 March, 1858, Jane Maria, dau. of William Ledmon, M.D., of Maghlgass, co. Kerry. He d. 10 Jan. 1864. She d. 20 March, 1903, leaving issue,
1. George William, Col. late Queen's Own Royal West Kent Regt. (3, *Clarendon Place, Hyde Park Gardens, W.*) b. 18 Feb. 1859; m. 6 Oct. 1894, Anne Pauline Clementina, 2nd dau. of John Phillips Thomas, of Warneford Place, Wilts.), and has issue,
 (1) Aileen Edith Pauline, b. 4 Sept. 1895.
 (2) Beryl Lola, b. 15 Nov. 1897.
2. Frances Richard, C.M.G., Lieut.-Col. R.A., late Mil. Attaché at Constantinople, b. 14 Feb. 1861.
1. Catherine, m. 26 May, 1840, William Phibbs, of Seafield, co. Sligo. He d. 1881. She d. 30 Nov. 1903, leaving issue (see PHIBBS *of Lishcen*).

He m. 2ndly, 15 Oct. 1833, Mary Josepha Anne, dau. of Rev. William Stopford, Rector of Blarney, co. Cork, and d. 1871, having had issue,
5. William Stopford, Col. late R.A., b. 2 Oct. 1834; m. Martha Sophia Edith (d. 11 April, 1907), youngest dau. of Robert George Maunsell (see MAUNSELL *of Limerick*), by his second wife, Maria, dau. of John Minton, and has issue,
1. Maria Elizabeth Sophia Edith.
2. Edith Mary Victoria.
3. Kathleen Frances Harriette.

6. George Joseph, late Capt. 15th Foot, b. 25 Aug. 1836; m. 9 Aug. 1862, Anna Jane, elder dau. of Francis M. Enraght Moony, of The Doon, King's Co. (see that family).
7. Edward Horatio Phibbs, of Newborough, co. Limerick, b. 26 July, 1841; m. 28 Sept. 1882, his cousin Elizabeth Dilen Lombard, dau. of James Hunt, of Danesfort, co. Cork (see that family), and d. 23 July, 1899, having had issue.
1. Philip, d. young.
2. James.
3. Edward.

2. Abigail Mary Angelina, m. 31 Jan. 1861, Robert James Enraght Moony, of The Doon, King's Co., J.P. and D.L. for that co., and J.P. co. Westmeath, and has issue (see that family).

The 2nd son,
MAJ.-GEN. SIR THOMAS MAUNSELL, K.C.B., of Ballywilliam, co. Lmerick, Maj.-Gen. in the Army (ret.), late 28th Regt. b. 10 Sept. 1822; m. 1865, Amy Louisa Elizabeth (*Burghclere, Newbury, Berkshire*), dau. of Col. Robert Edward Burrowes, K.H., of Bourton Court, Somerset, and d. 4 July, 1908, leaving issue,
1. GEORGE EDWARD SCARLETT, now of Ballywilliam.
2. Philip Mountstuart Aitchison, b. 1874.
1. Louisa Amy Catherine Augusta.
2. Cicely Marion Grace.

Arms—Arg., a chevron between three maunches sa. *Crest*—A hawk rising ppr. *Mottoes*—Honorantes me honorabo; and Quod vult valde vult.

Seat—Ballywilliam, near Rathkeale, co. Limerick. *Residence*—Burghclere, Newbury, Berkshire.

MAUNSELL OF OAKLY PARK.

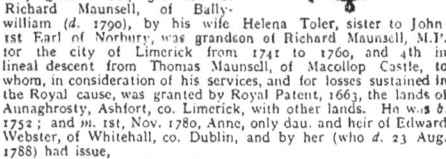

RICHARD JOHN CASWELL MAUNSELL, of Oakly Park, co. Kildare, and Blackwater, co. Clare, B.A. Trin. Coll. Dublin, Barrister-at-Law, J.P. co. Kildare, b. 2 May, 1878; s. his father 1907.

Lineage.—JOHN MAUNSELL, Barrister-at-Law, of Carrickoreely, co. Limerick, and of Portarlington, Queen's Co., 3rd son of Richard Maunsell, of Ballywilliam (d. 1790), by his wife Helena Toler, sister to John 1st Earl of Norbury, was grandson of Richard Maunsell, M.P. for the city of Limerick from 1741 to 1760, and 4th in lineal descent from Thomas Maunsell, of Macollop Castle, to whom, in consideration of his services, and for losses sustained in the Royal cause, was granted by Royal Patent, 1663, the lands of Annaghrosty, Ashfort, co. Limerick, with other lands. He was b. 1752; and m. 1st, Nov. 1780, Anne, only dau. and heir of Edward Webster, of Whitehall, co. Dublin, and by her (who d. 23 Aug. 1788) had issue,
1. RICHARD, b. 23 Aug. 1785.
2. Edward, b. 1786; d. young.
1. Anne, m. 13 Oct. 1832, Very Rev. Sir John Wolseley, Bart., Dean of Kildare, of Mount Wolseley, co. Carlow, and d.s.p. 14 Dec. 1860 (see BURKE's *Peerage*).

Mr. Maunsell m. 2ndly, 20 June, 1793, Anne, youngest dau. of the Very Rev. Richard Handcock, Dean of Achonry, and sister to William, 1st Viscount Castlemaine; she d.s.p. 1839. Mr. Maunsell d. 27 July, 1829, at Oakly Park, and was s. by his only son,
RICHARD MAUNSELL, of Oakly Park, J.P., High Sheriff of Kildare 1841, b. 23 Aug. 1785; m. 1 June, 1807, Maria, only dau. of John Woods, of Winter Lodge, and sister of George Woods, of Milverton Hall, co. Dublin, and by her (who d. 2 March, 1850) had issue,
1. JOHN, his heir.
2. GEORGE WOODS, of Oakly Park and Ashford, co. Limerick, s. his brother.
3. Richard Dixie (Rev.), of Whitehall, and 25, Ailesbury Road, co. Dublin, Rector of Innislonnagh, Tipperary, m. 10 Feb. 1859, Alicia Fanny, dau. of Malcolm Laing, of Spanish Town, Jamaica, formerly of Passdale, Orkneys, nephew of Malcolm Laing, the historian of Scotland; and d. 7 Dec. 1885, having had issue,
1. Richard Edward, m. 1895, Lucie Eleanor, dau. of S. A. W. Waters, Assist. Insp.-Gen. R.I.C., and has issue,
 Richard Lucius Dixie, } (twins), b. April, 1900.
 Helena Cecil,
2. Malcolm Laing.
3. John George, d. 1874.
4. Alexander Copland Dixie, d. 1880.
1. Maria Helena, d. 1874.
2. Alice Emily, m. 8 Sept. 1887, Rev. William Somerville Somerville-Large, and d. Sept. 1888, leaving a dau., Alice Emily.
3. Laura Gwendoline, d. 1874.
4. Frances Cecil.
5. Violet Augusta Caroline.
4. Edward Beauchamp, Capt. 39th Regt., killed 12 July, 1855, in the trenches before Sebastopol, and bur. on Cathcart's Hill.
5. Warren Cecil (Rev.), of Hodgestown co. Kildare, Rector of Thomastown, co. Kildare, d. 20 May, 1872.
6. Frederick Webster (Rev.), of Shrule, Queen's Co., Rector of Symondsbury, Bridport, Dorset, m. 15 Oct. 1857, Emily Caroline (d. Jan. 1873), dau. of Malcolm Laing, as above, and has issue,

Maunsell.   THE LANDED GENTRY.   470

1. Edward Beauchamp, m. 26 Jan. 1900, Maud, dau. of late Mrs. W. B. Jackson of Park Grange, Cheltenham.
2. Richard Cecil.
3. Frederick Baker Laing, m. 1906, Ethel Anna Mary (who d. Dec. 1911), dau. of C. G. Nantes, of Delapré, Bridport.
1. Laura Beatrice.   2. Frances Emily, d. 19 Dec. 1869.
3. Louisa Isabella.   4. Maria Gertrude, d. 31 Dec. 1869.
5. Emily Caroline.   6. Alicia Barbara.
1. Hannah, d. unm. 7 March, 1842.
2. Anne Jane, d. unm. 1882.
3. Fanny, d. unm. 1880.   4. Helena Maria.
5. Louisa Augusta, m. 28 June, 1860, Rev. Malcolm Strickland Laing, late Chaplain to H.M. European Forces in India, Vicar of Hinton St. Mary's, Dorset.
Mr. Maunsell d. 25 Nov. 1866, and was s. by his eldest son,
  JOHN MAUNSELL, of Oakly Park, co. Kildare, and Carrickoreely, co. Limerick, J.P., High Sheriff 1868 (the 1st year H.R.H. the Prince of Wales was at Punchestown), b. Nov. 1810 : d. unm. 29 March, 1882, when he was s. by his brother,
  GEORGE WOODS MAUNSELL, of Oakly Park, co. Kildare, and of Ashford, co. Limerick, J.P. and D.L., High Sheriff co. Kildare (the 2nd year H.R.H. was at Punchestown) 1885, M.A., Barrister-at-Law, b. 1815 ; m. 4 Aug. 1842, Maria, eldest surviving dau. and co-heir of Mark Synnot, of Monasteroris House, King's Co., and Grove House, Clapham, Surrey, and d. 25 April, 1887, having by her (who d. 8 Dec. 1893) had issue,
1. RICHARD MARK SYNNOT, of Oakly Park.
2. George John Synnot, b. 1846 ; d. 1863.
1. Anna Mary Synnot, m. 25 Sept. 1873, Alan Cameron Bruce Pryce, of Duffryn, St. Nicholas, 10, Glamorgan, and has issue (see PRYCE of Duffryn). He d. May, 1907.
2. Maria Augusta Synnot, d. 24 Dec. 1894.
Mr. Maunsell d. 25 April, 1887, and was s. by his son,
  RICHARD MARK SYNNOT MAUNSELL, of Oakly Park, co. Kildare, and Blackwater, co. Clare, J.P. cos. Kildare (High Sheriff 1891) and Clare, late Capt. 1st (Royal) Dragoons, b. 22 Oct. 1843 ; m. 1st, Marie Lucy, eldest dau. of Alexander Copland, of Wingfield, Berks (which lady d.s.p. 11 Jan. 1875): and 2ndly, 26 Feb. 1877, Mary Eliza, dau. and heiress of the late Samuel Caswell, J.P. of Blackwater, co. Clare, and by her (who d. 30 Aug. 1892) has issue,
  RICHARD JOHN CASWELL, now of Oakly Park.
  Marie Norah.
He m. 3rdly, 6 Feb. 1894, Georgina MacKenzie, 2nd dau. of the late Joseph Richard Middleton, Capt. H.E.I.C.S. He d. 31 Dec. 1907. She d. 31 May, 1908.

Arms—Arg., a chevron between three maunches sa. **Crest**—A hawk rising ppr. **Motto**—Honorantes me honorabo.
Seats—Oakly Park, Celbridge, co. Kildare ; and Blackwater, co. Clare. **Town Address**—55, Lower Baggot Street, Dublin.

MAUNSELL OF SPA HILL.

ROBERT GEORGE MAUNSELL, of Spa Hill, Limerick, b. 15 Dec. 1842 ; m. 17 Feb. 1869, Dorothea Jane (d. 24 Oct. 1911), dau. of Thomas Warren White, of Kingstown and Caherblonick, co. Clare, Barrister-at-Law, Crown Prosecutor for co. Leitrim, by Elizabeth his wife, dau. of Robert Persse of Roxboro', co. Galway, and has issue,

1. ROBERT CHARLES BUTLER, M.B., B.Ch., F.R.C.S.I., Surgeon of Mercer's Hospital, Examiner in Surgery, T.C.D. (32, Lower Baggot Street, Dublin), m. 26 July, 1911, Eleanor, dau. of James Hanna, of Kilmore, co. Monaghan.
2. Arthur Persse Gabbett (Rev.), B.D., Chaplain Indian Ecclesiastical Establishment, m. 15 Jan. 1906, Amabel Staveley, eldest dau. of Chas. Randel Narindin, late Commr. of Rajshahi.
3. Dudley Philip Winthrop, B.A., Barrister-at-Law
1. Dora Frances Elizabeth, m. 1895, as his 2nd wife, Rev. Canon Robert Irvine Ford, B.D., Rector of Castlerea, co. Roscommon, and has issue, two sons and two daus.
2. Elizabeth Georgina.

Lineage.—WILLIAM MAUNSELL, of Ballinamona, co. Cork, 5th son of Col. Thomas Maunsell, of Mocollop, and Ann Eaton his wife (see MAUNSELL of Limerick), m. by licence 7 July, 1713, Alice, dau. of Rev. John Norcott (or Northcote), of Ballygarret, Mallow, co. Cork. Admon. was granted to his widow 2 May, 1718. By her (who m. 2ndly, 1720, William Breretou, of Carrickslany, co. Carlow) he left issue,
1. John, whose dau. m. May, 1753, Lifford White, ancestor of Col. Maunsell White, of New Orleans.
2. WILLIAM, of whom we treat.
1. Anne, m. John Norris, and left issue.
The younger son,
  WILLIAM MAUNSELL, of Caherdavin, Maryville, and Flag House, Limerick, an Officer in the Royal Limerick Regt. 1744-1762, m. 1st, Mary Sealy, of Cork, and had issue,
1. Anne, m. 5 March, 1761, Vere Hunt, of Fryarstown, and had issue (see that family).
2. Eliza, d. unm.

He m. 2ndly, 4 Nov. 1761, Bridget, dau. of William Winthrop, Mayor of Cork. He d. 23 Nov. 1798 (will dated 25 April, 1796), having by her had issue,
1. WILLIAM, of whom presently.
3. Mary, m. Sept. 1782, Robert Reeves, of Dublin (see REEVES of Besborough).
4. Sarah, m. Dr. John Vize, of Limerick.
5. Alice, m. William Ricketts Hughes, of Cork.
6. Frances, m. her cousin David Roche of Carass, and d. April, 1818, leaving issue (see BURKE's Peerage, ROCHE, Bart.).
The only son,
  WILLIAM MAUNSELL, of Caherdavin, Maryville, and Castle Park, an Officer, Royal Limerick Regt. 1804, m. 1st (setts dated 31 Dec. 1790), Dorothea, dau. of William Gabbett, of Caherline, and Jane his wife, dau. of Richard Maunsell, of Ballywilliam, and by her had issue,
1. William (Rev.), Rector of Kilmurry, m. Frances, dau. of Rev. William Lewis, and had issue,
  1. William Francis (Rev.), Rector of Kildimo, b. 12 Aug. 1820 ; m. 14 Sept. 1847, Rebecca Caroline, eldest dau. of Rev. Richard Dickson, of Vermount, Clarina, co. Limerick, Rector of Kilkeedy, Limerick. She d. 27 April, 1853. He d. 10 June, 1895, having had an only son,
    William Dickson DICKSON, of Kildimo House, and Mulcair, co. Limerick, J.P., Col. late City of Limerick Art, assumed the name of DICKSON by Royal Licence 1901, b. 27 April, 1853 ; m. 17 Feb. 1897, his cousin Frances Louisa, dau. of Rev. Lewis Montagu Maunsell, Rector of Kilskyre, and had issue (see DICKSON of Kildimo).
  2. Richard, Lieut.-Col., J.P., late of Dubbo, N.S.W., b. 1822 ; d. 5 March, 1907 ; m. Annie Mary, 2nd dau. of Capt. Alexander Livingstone and had issue (settled in New South Wales),
    (1) Lewis Livingstone.
    (2) Richard Dillon, m. 1894, Anne Churchward, and has issue,
      1. Allan Richard.   2. Massy.
    (3) Edward Montagu, b. 1869.
    (1) Frances Rebecca, m. 1st, 1870, John Corsane Robinson, Lieut. R.A., and had issue. She m. 2ndly, Maj. George Rowland Gambier, R.H.A.
    (2) Elizabeth Mary Dora, m. Louis Becke, and has i sue.
    (3) Eveline Annie Ryves, m. 1895, Sydney Robert Morris, and has issue.
    (4) Ethel Mary Ursula, m. 1898, Harley C. Antill, and has issue.
  3. Lewis Montagu (Rev.), Rector of Kilskyre, co. Meath, b. 1823 ; m. Mary Letitia, dau. of Rev. Richard Bell Booth, and had issue,
    (1) Frances, m. 17 Feb. 1897, her cousin Col. William Dickson Dickson, of Kildimo, and has issue (see above).
    (2) Mary, m. G. Gilchrist, LL.D., and has issue.
  4. Francis Edwin, Maj. in the Army, b. 1825 ; m. 1849, Ellen Catherine Stephenson, and had issue,
    (1) Francis Edwin, Lieut. 2nd West India Regt., m. Miss Coffey, and d.s.p.
    (2) Arthur Munro, Maj. late Royal Munster Fus., b. 5 Feb. 1852 ; m. Mary Thompson, and has issue.
    (3) Edward Lewis, Lieut.-Col. R.A.M.C., b. 3 Nov. 1853, m. E. O'Callaghan.
2. Richard, Midshipman R.N., killed in action.
3. John, of Clonmoyle, m., and left issue (settled in New Orleans).
4. Winthrop, d. unm.
5. JOSEPH GABBETT, of whom presently.
1. Briget, m. — Wilson, of Rhynanna, co. Clare, and had issue.
2. Dorothy, m. Samuel Bell Kingsley.
3. Jane, d. unm.
4. Helena Maria, d. young 1807.
He m. 2ndly, Elizabeth, dau. of William Marcus Jackson, and by her had issue,
5. George, d. unm.
5. Elizabeth, d. unm.   6. Mary, d. unm.
The youngest son by 1st wife,
  JOSEPH GABBETT MAUNSELL, b. 25 Dec. 1803 ; m. 1st, Anne, dau. of Samuel Bevan, of Camass, co. Limerick, and by her (who d. 20 Oct. 1832) had issue,
1. Daniel Gabbett, b. 1832, d. young.
He m. 2ndly, Jan. 1835, Sarah Maria, widow of George Dodd, Solicitor, and dau. of Bannister Chambers, of Corbally House. Limerick, and d. Jan. 1868, having by her had issue,
2. Theophilus Alfred, d. an infant Dec. 1836.
3. Samuel, d. young.
4. Joseph Gabbett, d. unm. 1857.
5. Richard Johnston, m. Frances, widow of Henry Prettie Bayly, and dau. of Richd. Massy Yeilding, of Bellevue House and Glenstar co. Limerick, but d.s.p.
6. ROBERT GEORGE, of Spa Hill.
1. Charlotte, d. an infant Sept. 1836.

Arms—Arg. a chevron between three maunches sa. **Crest**—A falcon rising ppr., jessed and belled or. **Mottoes**—1. (Under the Arms) Quod vult valde vult. 2. (Over the Crest) Honorantes me honorabo.
Residence—Chicheley, Ulverton Road, Dalkey.

PERCEVAL-MAXWELL OF FINNEBROGUE AND GROOMSPORT.

ROBERT DAVID PERCEVAL-MAXWELL, of Finnebrogue, co. Down, J.P. and D.L., High Sheriff 1911, formerly Major North of Ireland Imperial Yeomanry, b. 29 March, 1870; s. his grandfather 1905; m. 3 Sept. 1895, Edith Grace, dau. of Henry Haswell Head, M.D. (see HEAD of Derrylahan), and has issue,
1. JOHN ROBERT, b. 24 Jan. 1896.
2. Richard Henry, b. 30 Oct. 1897.
3. Patrick Edward, b. 2 May, 1900.
4. Brian Stephen David, b. 2 Jan. 1908.

Lineage.—THE VERY REV. WILLIAM PERCEVAL, Archdeacon of Cashel and Dean of Emly, 2nd son of George Perceval, Registrar of Prerogative Court, Dublin, ancestor of PERCEVAL of Temple House, Sligo (see that family), b. 14 Dec. 1671; m. 5 April, 1708, Catherine, dau. of Henry Prittie, of Silvermines, co. Tipperary. She d. 3 Dec. 1730. He d. 29 Aug. 1734, leaving issue,
1. Kene (Rev.), D.D., Vicar of Powerscourt and Castle Kaock.
2. WILLIAM, of whom presently.
3. Charles (Rev.), Rector of Mitchelstown, b. 7 Dec. 1713; d. 9 Aug. 1785.
1. Catherine, m. 22 Oct. 1737, Brewster Langlin.

The 2nd son,
WILLIAM PERCEVAL, Barrister-at-Law, b. 24 June, 1711; m. 1st, 1838, Elizabeth, dau. of John Croker, of Dublin. She d.s.p. June, 1739. He m. 2ndly, 30 June, 1748, Elizabeth, dau. of Robert Ward. She d. 30 Nov. 1770, leaving issue,
1. Charles (Rev.), of Burton, co. Cork, Rector of Churchtown, co. Cork, who left issue,
   1. Helena, m. 1806, John Crosbie Graves, who d. 13 Jan. 1835, leaving issue (see GRAVES of Cloghan).
   2. Caroline, m. 20 Nov. 1820, Charles Perceval, 63rd Regt. (see below).
2. William, Capt. 104th Regt., b. 9 Sept. 1754; m. 15 Oct. 1784, Jane, 2nd dau. of John Brereton, of Rathgilbert, and d. 10 Sept. 1793, leaving issue,
   1. William John, Capt. 9th Regt., b. 2 July, 1789; m. 2 April, 1818, Mary, dau. of Arthur Brereton, of Limerick. She d. 15 Feb. 1867. He d. 2 Nov. 1848, leaving issue,
      (1) William, M.D., b. 10 April, 1819; d. unm.
      (2) Arthur (Rev.), Rector of Wakerley, Stamford, B.A., T.C.D., b. 7 Nov. 1821; m. 4 Aug. 1848, Emilie Caroline, dau. of George Bevill Granville Grenfell, and has issue.
      (3) Henry, b. 21 Sept. 1826; m. 1 May, 1850, Harriette, dau. of John Echlin, of Echlinville, co. Down, and has issue.
      (1) Elizabeth. (2) Jane.
      (3) Emma.
   2. Charles, Lieut. 63rd Regt., b. 26 March, 1793; m. 20 Nov. 1820, his cousin, Caroline, dau. and co-heir of Rev. Charles Perceval, of Burton, co. Cork (see above). She d. 3 Dec. 1861. He d. 16 Jan. 1849, having had issue,
      (1) Charles William, M.D., b. 1 Nov. 1827; m. 28 July, 1868, Charlotte Alice, only child of Major Henry Shaw, and has issue.
      (2) Caroline, m. 19 July, 1849, Rev. Francis P. Studdert, Rector of St. Patrick's, Limerick, and has issue.
3. ROBERT, of whom we treat.

The youngest son,
ROBERT PERCEVAL, b. 30 Sept. 1756, Physician-General to His Majesty's Forces in Ireland during Lord Talbot's Viceroyalty, and Professor of Chemistry in Trin. Coll. Dublin. He m. 9 May, 1785, Anne, eldest dau. of John Brereton, of Rathgilbert, and dying 3 March, 1839, left issue, an only child,
REV. WILLIAM PERCEVAL, of Kilmore Hill, co. Waterford, and Annefield, co. Dublin, b. 9 April, 1787; m. 9 Sept. 1809, Anne, eldest dau. of John Waring Maxwell, of Finnebrogue, co. Down, descended from a younger son of the Very Rev. Robert Maxwell, Dean of Armagh (see MAXWELL of Ballyrolly), from whose eldest son, Robert, Bishop of Kilmore, descends the Baron Farnham (see BURKE'S Peerage). He d. 20 April, 1880, having by her (who d. 5 May, 1861) had issue,
1. ROBERT, of Finnebrogue and Groomsport.
2. John Maxwell, C.B., of Dillon House, Downpatrick, Gen. in the Army, Col. 12th Regt., b. 25 Sept. 1814; m. 12 April, 1853, Catharine Isabel, eldest dau. of the Hon. and Very Rev. Robert Maude, Dean of Clogher, and Archdeacon of Dublin (see BURKE'S Peerage, HAWARDEN, V.), and d. 24 Jan. 1900, having by her (who d. 27 May, 1887) had issue,
   1. William Frederick, Lieut. 12th Regt., b. 20 Oct. 1856; d. unm. 27 May, 1880.

2. Richard Douglas (Kary Hill, Downpatrick), C.E., J.P., b. 25 June, 1858; m. 27 Aug. 1901, Ethelwyn Mary, only dau. of Maj. J. N. Blackwood Price, J.P., D.L., of Saintfield, co. Down (see that family), and has issue,
   (1) Richard John, b. 26 July, 1902.
   (2) Michael Charles, b. 16 Feb. 1907.
3. Edward Maxwell, D.S.O., Col. R.A., b. 13 Aug. 1861; m. 1st, 1894, Marion, dau. of R. L. Bowles, M.D., J.P., and by her (who d. 1895) has issue,
   (1) Robert Rawnsley Maxwell, b. 1895.
He m. 2ndly, 1906, Norah, dau. of the late Adm. R. C. Mayne, C.B., R.N., and by her has issue,
   (2) John Richard, b. 13 April, 1909.
   (1) Diana, b. 29 Dec. 1907.
4. Claude John, D.S.O., Maj. R.A., b. 28 Sept. 1864; m. 14 April, 1898, Isabel Gordon, only dau. of Col. F. de L. Morison, of Bognie, Aberdeenshire, and has issue,
   (1) Margaret Aileen, b. 26 Feb. 1902.
   (2) Rachel Mary, b. 12 Jan. 1906.
   (3) Grace Jean Maxwell, b. 17 Jan. 1910.
5. Charles Cecil, Maj. R.E., b. 9 Sept. 1866; m. 11 Dec. 1902, Eleanor, dau. of the late Rev. E. A. Askew, of Greystoke, Cumberland.
6. Philip, Capt. R.A., b. 16 Jan. 1873; m. 4 July, 1900, Barbara Rose, dau. of the late Thomas Leach, Q.C., and has issue,
   Rosaline.
1. Agnes Maude, m. 31 Aug. 1881, Lieut.-Col. Percy Herbert Johnston, C.M.G., M.D., R.A.M.C., and has issue.
2. Florence Martha, m. 11 July, 1900, Hon. Edward Herber Scott Napier, 4th son of Robert, 1st Lord Napier of Magdala (see BURKE'S Peerage).
3. Isabel Henrietta, m. 1902, Rev. F. W. Wood, M.A., of Inch, co. Wexford.
3. Richard, of Kilmore Hill, Waterford, b. 24 Sept. 1819; d. 1898.
4. Spencer, b. 7 March, 1821; m. 21 June, 1865, Elizabeth, dau. of William Mussenden, of Larchfield, co. Down, and d. 7 May, 1872, leaving a dau.,
Sara Madalene Frediswid, m. 15 Oct. 1895, Edward Hornidge, and has issue (see HORNIDGE of Tulfarris).
5. William, C.E., b. 4 April, 1825; d. 5 Oct. 1905; m. 17 July, 1852, Sarah, dau. of Henry Going, of Tipperary, 3rd son of Rev. John Going.
6. Charles Frederick, M.D., b. 4 Jan. 1827; d. unm. 21 March, 1877.
1. Anne Sarah, d. unm. 20 Oct. 1873.
2. Maria Dorothea, m. 1 Jan. 1836, Rev. John Corry Moutray, Rector of Erigleckeerough, 2nd son of J. C. Moutray, of Favour Royal, co. Tyrone, and d. 23 Sept. 1864, leaving issue.
3. Caroline, d. unm. 15 Sept. 1871.
4. Madelina, d. unm.

ROBERT PERCEVAL-MAXWELL, of Finnebrogue and Groomsport House, co. Down, and Moore Hill, co. Waterford, B.A., Oxford, J.P. and D.L. co. Down, J.P. co. Waterford, High Sheriff co. Down 1841, and co. Waterford 1864, late Major Royal N. Down R.M., b. 24 June, 1813; m. 19 Sept. 1839, Helena Anne, only dau. and heiress of William Moore, of Moore Hill, co. Waterford, son of the Hon. William Moore, 2nd brother of the 1st Earl Mountcashel, and by her (who d. 22 Jan. 1888) has issue,
1. John William, of Tyrella, co. Down, High Sheriff 1873, b. 24 Oct. 1840; m. 29 Sept. 1868, Selina Frances Imogene, eldest dau. of David Stewart Ker, of Monalto, co. Down, and d.v.p. 21 Nov. 1875, leaving issue,
   ROBERT DAVID, now of Finnebrogue,
   Anna Violet Madelina, b. 21 June, 1875; d. unm. 22 Aug. 1902.
2. William John, of Moore Hill, Tallow, co. Waterford, J.P. and D.L., High Sheriff 1878, late Capt. 3rd Hussars, b. 2 Nov. 1841; m. 1st, 8 Aug. 1871, Lady Louisa Arabella Hastings, 3rd dau. of Francis Theophilus Henry, 13th Earl of Huntingdon, which lady d.s.p. 3 Feb. 1873; and 2ndly, 20 Oct. 1874, Isabella Mary, eldest dau. of Richard Chearnley, of Salterbridge, co. Waterford (see that family). He d.v.p. 11 Aug. 1902, having had issue,
   1. William Moore, of Moore Hill, Tallow, co. Waterford, J.P. and D.L., High Sheriff 1908, formerly Capt. 9th Batt. King's Royal Rifle Corps, b. 10 Oct. 1877.
   2. Richard John, b. 2 Oct. 1887; d. 8 Jan. 1888.
   1. Beatrice Mary, b. 1875. 2. Violet Isabel, b. 1876.
   3. Helen Frances, b. 29 Aug. 1880; d. 16 Oct. 1885.
   4. Maude Helena. 5. Norah Selina.
3. Robert, b. 19 March, 1849; d. unm. 1873.
4. Stephen Richard Nassau, b. 4 Nov. 1850; m. 28 July, 1884, Mabel Henrietta, 3rd dau. of Joseph Richardson, of Glenmore, co. Antrim, and has issue, Nigel.
5. Henry Spencer, of Lansdowne Lodge, Kenmare, co. Kerry, b. 18 Sept. 1861; m. 7 Dec. 1899, Hyacinthe Mary, dau. of Vice-Adm. Gerard Napier (see that family), and has issue,
   1. Edward Napier, b. 7 Jan. 1901.
   2. Gerard Henry Aubrey, b. 24 May, 1903.
   1. Oonah Hyacinthe, b. 14 April, 1902.
1. Mary Elizabeth, m. 27 June, 1865, Percy Scott Smyth, of Headborough, co. Waterford, and has issue.
2. Madelina Dorothea, m. 27 Dec. 1873, Lieut.-Col. Frank Galloway, R.A., and has issue.
3. Helena Anne, m. Sept. 1892, Major-Gen. W. E. Warrand, R.E., D.L., of Westhorpe, Southwell, Notts (see that family). He d. 22 Oct. 1910.
4. Harriette Louisa, m. 22 June, 1871, C. Purdon Coote, of Ballyclough Castle, and Bearforest, co. Cork, who d. 20 Sept. 1893, leaving issue (see that family).
5. ISABELLA MARIA, now of Groomsport House, Groomsport, co. Down.

Maxwell. THE LANDED GENTRY. 472

6. ANNA CAROLINE, now of Groomsport House, Groomsport, co. Down
7. Alicia Catherine, *m.* 3 July, 1901, Rev. Benjamin Finch White, B.A., Rector of Inch, son of the late Finch White, Q.C., of Dublin. This gentleman, whose patronymic is PERCEVAL, assumed by Royal Licence 25 July, 1839, the additional surname and arms of MAXWELL, and *d.* 9 July, 1905, and was *s.* by his grandson.

Arms—Quarterly: 1st and 4th, arg., a saltire sa., on a chief of the last three pallets of the first, for MAXWELL; 2nd and 3rd, arg., on a chief indented gu. three crosses pattée of the first. *Crest*—A stag's head and neck erased ppr. *Motto*—Je suis prêt.

Seat—Finnebrogue., Downpatrick *Clubs*—Carlton; Kildare Street, Dublin; Ulster, Belfast.

MAXWELL OF BALLYROLLY.

THEODORE MAXWELL, of Ballyrolly, co. Down, B.Sc. Lond., B.A. and M.D. Camb., *b.* 29 March, 1847; *m.* 9 Sept. 1873, Elizabeth Eyre, dau. of Dr. John Eyre Ashby, of Enfield, and has a son,
ARNOLD ASHBY, *b.* 1874.

Lineage.—THE VERY REV. ROBERT MAXWELL, Dean of Armagh, 2nd son of Sir John Maxwell, Knt., of Calderwood, in Scotland (*see* BURKE's *Peerage*, FARNHAM, B.), *m.* 1st, Susan Armstrong, and 2ndly, Isabel, dau. of Seton, of Lathrisk, and had issue,
1. ROBERT, ancestor of the Lords FARNHAM.
2. HENRY, of whom presently.
3. James, of Mullatinny (Elm Park), co. Armagh, *m.* Jane Norris, and had two sons, of whom the eldest,
Henry, of Mullatinny, *m.* his cousin, Margaret, dau. of Dr. Robert Maxwell, Bishop of Kilmore and Ardagh, and had two daus., of whom the younger,
Margaret, *m.* 1st, Sir Robert Maxwell, of Ballycastle, who *d.s.p.*, and 2ndly, Capt. James Butler, of Bramblestown, co. Kilkenny, and had a dau., Catherine, *m.* Rev. Samuel Close (*see* CLOSE *of Drumbanagher*).
1. Elizabeth, *m.* Robert Berkeley, D.D., Dean of Clogher.
2. Phœbe.

The 2nd son,
HENRY MAXWELL, of Finnebrogue, *m.* Jane, 3rd dau. of Right Rev. Robert Echlin, Bishop of Down and Connor (*see* ECHLIN *of Ardquin*), and by her (who *m.* 2ndly the Ven. William Fullerton, Archdeacon of Armagh), had issue. He was grandfather of
RIGHT HON. HENRY MAXWELL, of Finnebrogue, co. Down, *m.* 1st, Jane, dau. of Rev. Henry Maxwell, Rector of Dertynoose, co. Armagh, and sister of John, 1st Lord Farnham, but by her had no issue. He *m.* 2ndly, Dorothea, dau. of Edward Bryce, of Kilroot, co. Antrim, by whom he had issue,
1. Patrick, his successor, who *d. unm.* 1749.
2. Robert, successor to his brother, ancestor in the female line of PERCEVAL-MAXWELL *of Finnebrogue* (*see preceding article*).
3. EDWARD, of whom hereafter.
1. Margaret, *m.* James Adair.
He *d.* 12 Feb. 1729-30. His 3rd son,
GEN. EDWARD MAXWELL, of Ballyrolly, co. Down, Gen. in the Army, Col. 67th Regt., was father of
EDWARD PHINEAS MAXWELL, of Ballyrolly, Capt. in the 49th Regt., *b.* 1745; *m.* 30 Oct. 1781, Frances Tapson, who *d.* 21 July, 1828, aged 69. He *d.* 21 Feb. 1818, aged 73. His son,
EDWARD MAXWELL, of Ballyrolly, was a Judge in the Bengal Presidency and a Member of the Supreme Court of Judicature. He *m.* 1st, 20 Aug. 1817, in India, Emilia (who *d.* 26 July, 1822), dau. of Alexander Walker, M.D., of Edinburgh, and 2ndly, 21 Jan. 1826, Rosina Hogg, and *d.* at Berhampore, East Indies, 19 Aug. 1826, leaving by his 1st wife a son and successor,
REV. EDWARD MAXWELL, of Ballyrolly, co. Down, M.A. Trin. Coll. Camb., formerly Rector of High Roding, Essex, *b.* 1 June, 1818; *m.* 1st, 13 Feb. 1845, Mary Hogg, dau. of Alexander Jaffray Nicholson, M.D., of Lisburn (by his wife, Clara Hogg), and sister of Brigadier-Gen. J. Nicholson, by whom (who *d.* 29 Dec. 1889) he had issue,
THEODORE, now of Ballyrolly.
He *m.* 2ndly, Elizabeth, widow of Joseph Clissold, of Clifton, and *d.* without further issue, 8 March, 1900.

Arms—Arg., a saltire sa., a chief paly of six of the first and second, a crescent for difference. *Crest*—A buck's head erased ppr., a crescent for difference. *Motto*—Je suis prêt.

Residence—Woolwich Common, Kent.

MAXWELL OF CORDUFF.

GEORGE MAXWELL, of Corduff, co. Dublin, Royal Irish Constabulary, *b.* 1874; *m.* 5 May, 1909, Edith Frances, eldest dau. of John Radcliffe Battersby, of Loughbawn, co. Westmeath (*see that family*).

Lineage.—ARTHUR MAXWELL, of Brookend, co. Tyrone, and Killyfaddy, left a son,
REV. GEORGE MAXWELL, Vicar of Askeaton, co. Limerick, 1838-1870, *b.* 27 Aug. 1809, ordained 30 Nov. 1832, Curate of Askeaton 1833-8; *m.* Margaret Anne, dau. of John Francis Hewson, D.L., of Ennismore, Listowel, co. Kerry. She *d.* 5 March, 1881. He *d.* 8 Jan. 1870, having had issue,
1. ARTHUR, now of Corduff.
2. John Francis, of Rostrevor, co. Down, J.P., M.A. Trin. Coll. Dublin, *b.* Aug. 1843.
1. Elizabeth Caroline, *m.* 30 Aug. 1870, Rev. Edmund L. Eves.
2. Margaret Anne.
ARTHUR MAXWELL, of Corduff, co. Dublin, J.P., B.A. Trin. Coll. Dublin, *b.* 1842; *m.* 1873, Ellen Jervois (*now of Corduff*), youngest dau. of Henry Owen Becher, of Aughadown, Skibbereen, co. Cork, and *d.* 29 Nov. 1909, having had issue,
1. GEORGE, now of Corduff.
2. Arthur Henry, *b.* 1876; *m.* 7 Sept. 1908, Vere Anna Estelle Beresford, dau. of Leuric Cobbe.
1. Ellen Harriette.   2. Margaret Anna.

Seat—Corduff, Donabate, co. Dublin.

MAXWELL OF FORTLAND.

COL. THE HON. HENRY EDWARD MAXWELL, D.S.O., of Fortland, co. Cavan, J.P. and D.L., High Sheriff co. Cavan 1910, Lieut.-Col. commanding 2nd Batt. The Black Watch 1903-7, served in S. Africa 1899-1902, *b.* 27 Nov. 1857; *m.* 10 Aug. 1887, Edith, dau. of Col. Robert Godolphin Cosby, of Stradbally (*see that family*), and has issue,
RICHARD SYDNEY SOMERSET, *b.* 29 May, 1893.
Ismay Alice, *b.* 19 May, 1888.

Col. Maxwell is the 2nd son of the late Hon. Richard Thomas Maxwell, of Fortland, co. Cavan (who *d.* 22 Jan. 1874), and Charlotte Anne his wife (*d.* 1 March, 1910), 2nd dau. of Rev. Henry Preston Elrington, D.D., Rector of Templeshambo, Col. Maxwell, who is the only brother of 11th Baron Farnham, was granted a patent of precedence as a baron's son 14 May, 1897.

Lineage and Arms—*See* BURKE's *Peerage*, FARNHAM, B.

Seat—Fortland, Mount Nugent, co. Cavan. *Clubs*—Naval and Military; Kildare Street, and Royal St. George Yacht.

MEADE OF BALLYMARTLE.

RICHARD JOHN MEADE, of Ballymartle, co. Cork, B.A., J.P., *b.* 18 April, 1865.

Lineage.—This family is said to be of ancient Irish extraction (*see* BURKE's *Peerage*, CLANWILLIAM, E.).
ROBERT MEADE (2nd son of Lieut.-Col. William Meade, by Elizabeth his wife, dau. of Sir Robert Travers, and brother of Sir John Meade, ancestor of the Earl of CLANWILLIAM), assisted in raising a regiment of foot for the service of King WILLIAM III, his commission bearing date 1694. He *m.* Frances, dau. and co-heir of Sir Peter Courthorpe, of Courtstown and of Little Island, co. Cork, appointed Governor of Munster, by CHARLES II 1669 (by Margaret his wife, dau. of Thomas Daunt, of Owlpen and Gortigrenane), and had issue (with a dau. Joanna, who *m.* J. Nesbitt, M.D., and *d.* leaving issue) one son,
THE VERY REV. WILLIAM MEADE, of Ballymartle, Dean of Cork, Rector of Ballymartle, Dunderrow, and Ringroane, *b.* 1686, *m.* Feb. 1719, Helena, dau. of Bryan Townsend, of Castle Townsend,

IRELAND. Meade.

o. Cork (by Mary his wife, dau. of Edward Synge, Bishop of Cork, Cloyne, and Ross, and sister of Edward Synge, Archbishop of Tuam), and *d.* (will dated 29 Nov. 1762, was proved 31 May, 1764) eaving issue,
1. JOHN, Rector of Ballymartle, 1752. He purchased from his cousin John, 1st Earl of Clanwilliam, 1787, the family estates of Ballymartle and Ballintober, &c. *m.* 1st, 1748, Katherine, dau. of Rev. John Moore, of Innishannon, and 2ndly, 1766, Susanna, dau. of Rev. Horace Townsend, Rector of Donoughmore. He *d.s.p.* 1800.
2. Robert, Rector of Dunderrow, *b.* 1722, *m.* 1753, Charlotte, dau. of James Nesbitt, Surgeon, and *d.* Feb. 1799, leaving issue,
  1. Joanna, *d. unm.*
  2. Helena, *m.* Rev. Horace Townsend, of Derry, and left issue, one dau., Joanna, *m.* Thomas Poole, of Mayfield.
3. Richard, Barrister-at-Law, *d. unm.* 1769.
4. William (Rev.), Rector of Ringcurran, *b.* 1728, *m.* 1759, Martha, dau. of Col. Richard Bourne, of Burren, and *d.* 1769, leaving issue,
  1. RICHARD, of whom hereafter.
  2. William, M.D., *m.* Catherine, dau. of Hewitt Poole, of Mayfield, and *d.s.p.*
  3. JOHN (see MEADE *of Ballintober*).
  4. Robert (Rev.), Rector of Ballymoney, co. Cork, *b.* 1768, *m.* Eliza, dau. of Robert Travers, and *d.* 1852, leaving issue,
    (1) William Robert (Rev.), Vicar of Kinsale, *m.* Margaret, dau. of Richard Lewis, and *d.s.p.* 1852.
    (2) Robert, *d. unm.*
    (1) Barbara Helena, *m.* Rev. William De Courcy Meade, Rector of Dunmanway, and *d.* 1814, leaving issue.
    (2) Martha Bourne, *d. unm.* 1859.
    (3) Elizabeth, *d. unm.*
  1. Martha, *d. unm.* 1832. 2. Helena, *d. unm.* 1843.
His grandson,
REV. RICHARD MEADE, Rector of Ballymartle, *s.* his uncle, John, in the Ballymartle estates, &c.; *m.* Dorothea, dau. of Adam Newman, of Dromore, and by her (who *d.* 1815) had issue,
1. WILLIAM RICHARD, late of Ballymartle.
2. John, Fellow of Trin. Coll. Dublin, *d. unm.* 29 June, 1835.
3. Richard Newman, Capt. H.E.I.C.S., fell at the battle of Meanee, in Scinde, 1843.
4. Robert Henry (Rev.), B.A., Incumbent of Rincurran, co. Cork, *b.* 25 Sept. 1809 ; *d. unm.* 1890.
5. Horace Townsend Newman, M.D., of Churchill House, Queenstown, *d. unm.* 1861.
6. Adam Newman, *m.* June, 1859, Louisa Sophia, dau. of Daniel Conner, of Manch (*see that family*), and *d.* 1878, leaving issue,
  1. ROBERT.
  2. RICHARD JOHN, now of Ballymartle.
  3. Adam Daniel Conner, *m.* July, 1909. Ella Nora, dau. of Richard Ashe, of Ashton, co. Cork.
  1. Elizabeth Mary.
  2. Dorothea Martha, *m.* 8 Jan. 1884, Col. Frederick Trenchard Thomas Fowle, C.B., R.A.
  3. Louisa Susanna Helena.
  1. Mary Townsend, *d.* 1880. 2. Susanna Helen, *d. unm.* 1858.
Rev. Richard Meade *d.* 1814, and was *s.* by his eldest son,
WILLIAM RICHARD MEADE, of Ballymartle, co. Cork, J.P. and D.L., M.A., Barrister-at-Law, *b.* 1804; *d. unm.* 20 Jan. 1894, and was *s.* by his nephew, RICHARD JOHN, now of Ballymartle.

Arms—Gu., a chevron erm. between three trefoils slipped arg. **Crest**—An eagle displayed with two heads sa., armed or. **Motto**—Toujours prest.
Seat—Ballymartle, Kinsale, co. Cork.

MEADE OF BALLINTOBER.

JOHN JOSIAS MEADE, of Ballintober, co. Cork, *b.* 26 Sept. 1858; *s.* his father 1898.

Lineage.—(See MEADE *of Ballymartle*.)

JOHN MEADE, of Ballintober, 3rd son of Rev. WILLIAM MEADE, Rector of Ringcurran, *s.* his uncle, John, in that estate, which had been purchased by the latter from his cousin, the Earl of Clanwilliam. He was *b.* 1767; *m.* Alice, dau. of the Ven. Chambré Corker, of Ballymaloe and Glanmire, co. Cork, Archdeacon of Ardagh, and grand-dau. of Dr. Browne, Archbishop of Tuam, and *d.* 1816, having had issue,
1. JOHN (Rev.), his heir.
2. William, Rector of Inchinabacky, *m.* Anne, dau. of Robert Warren, and has issue.
3. Richard, of Kildare Street, Dublin, *m.* Catherine, dau. of William Stephens, and *d.* April, 1860, leaving, with other issue, an eldest son,
  Josiah Dunne, *d. unm.* 1868.

4. Edward Southwell, *d. unm.*
1. Eliza, *d. unm.* 2. Martha Helena, *d. unm.*
The eldest son,
REV. JOHN MEADE, of Ballintober, co. Cork, J.P., Rector of Leighmoney, *b.* 26 July, 1792; *m.* 26 July, 1816, Sarah, only child of George Wood, of Riverview, and by her (who *d.* Feb. 1873) had issue.
1. JOHN, late of Ballintober.
2. Richard William, Surgeon-Major in the Army, served in the 88th Regt. in the Crimea and Indian Mutiny; *d. unm.* 10 July, 1896.
3. Edward Southwell, *d. unm.* 1862.
1. Eliza Anne, *m.* 1st, Waller Bates, late 65th Regt.; and 2ndly, Hardwicke Evans, and *d.* Jan. 1892.
2. Alice Corker, *d. unm.* 5 June, 1895.
He *d.* Jan. 1864, and was *s.* by his eldest son,
JOHN MEADE, of Ballintober, co. Cork, J.P., *b.* 18 March, 1819; *m.* 10 Sept. 1851, Eliza, dau. of Richard Meade, of Dublin. She *d.* 25 Jan. 1907. He *d.* 16 Jan. 1898, leaving issue,
1. Richard Percy, *b.* 22 April, 1857; *d. unm.* 1883.
2. JOHN JOSIAS, now of Ballintober.
3. William George, *b.* 11 April, 1862; *m.* Eliza, dau. of Frederick Bullock, and has issue,
  1. Kathleen Alice. 2. Dorothea Lucia.
  3. Margaret Emily.
4. Pierce, *b.* 1863; *d.* 1864.
5. Robert Jocelyn, *b.* 21 Jan. 1871.
6. George Waller, *b.* 17 Jan. 1872.
1. Catherine Eliza, *b.* 1855; *d. unm.* 1875.
2. Eliza Lucia. 3. Sarah Helena.
4. Alice Hardy.

Arms—(See MEADE *of Ballymartle*).
Seat—Ballintober, Ballinhassig, co. Cork.

MEADE OF BURRENWOOD.

CAPT. JOHN PERCY MEADE, of Burrenwood, co. Down, and Earsham Hall, Norfolk, D.L. co. Down, High Sheriff 1897, and J.P. cos. Norfolk and Suffolk, late Capt. Oxfordshire L.I., *b.* 17 May, 1847; *m.* 2 Jan. 1894, Helena Frances, eldest dau. of Sir Allen Johnson Walsh, 4th bart., and has issue,
1. JOHN WINDHAM, *b.* 28 Nov. 1894.
2. Robert Percy, *b.* May, 1896.
1. Helena Theodosia Kathleen.

Capt. Meade is the elder son of the late John Meade, of Burrenwood, co. Down (who *d.* 5 May, 1886), and Elvira his wife, dau. of Robert Ibbetson, and grandson of Gen. the Hon. Robert Meade, of Burrenwood (and Anne Louisa his wife, dau. of Gen. Sir John Dalling, Bart.), 2nd son of John, 1st Earl of Clanwilliam.

Lineage.—See BURKE'S *Peerage*, CLANWILLIAM. E.

Arms—1st and 4th grand quarters, gu. a chevron erm. between three trefoils slipped arg. (MEADE), 2nd and 3rd grand quarters, quarterly 1 and 4, az. three pewits arg. (MAGILL), 2nd and 3rd, per chevron arg. and vert three hinds trippant ppr. (HAWKINS), a crescent for difference. **Crest**—An eagle displayed with two heads sa. armed or. **Motto**—Toujours prest.
Seats—Earsham Hall, Norfolk; Burrenwood, co. Down. **Clubs**—Carlton, Army and Navy.

MEADOWS OF WEXFORD AND THORNVILLE, co. WEXFORD.

ABRAHAM JAMES HOWLIN MEADOWS, of Thornville, co. Wexford, J.P., *b.* 8 July, 1853, formerly Lieut. in the Wexford Regt. of Militia, served in the S. African Campaign in 1901-2 as Capt. in the 5th Victorian Mounted Rifles (S. African medal with three clasps), now Hon. Major; *m.* 1st, 13 Sept. 1876, Helen, 2nd dau. of the late Thomas McDowell, of Armagh. She *d.s.p.* 3 Jan. 1879. He *m.* 2ndly, 20 Aug. 1881, Catherine Evangeline (who *d.* 5 Aug. 1886), only surviving dau. of the late John Lloyd, of Patrick's Hill, Cork, by whom he had issue,

1. Fraser, *b.* 14 Dec. 1882.
2. Daunt, *b.* 3 April, 1885.
3. Violet, *b.* 2 Aug. 1886; *d.* 7 Sept. 1886.

He *m.* 3rdly, Nov. 1906, at Montreal, Canada, Sarah Louisa, 4th dau. of Thomas McDowell aforesaid.

Lineage.—WILLIAM MEDDOWS, or Meadows, of Wexford, co. Wexford, by his will, dated 10 Jan. 1721, and proved 10 March, 1726, desired to be bur. in St. Iberius Church, Wexford, and mentions his sister Mary Chambers, his three sons and a dau. By his wife Catherine, whom he *m.* Aug. 1697, he left issue,

1. ARTHUR, of whom presently.   2. John.
3. James, bapt. 4 Aug. 1706.
1. Catherine.

The eldest son,
ARTHUR MEADOWS, of Wexford, *b.* 1698-9; *d.* 8 Feb. 1780; *m.* 18 April, 1722, Mary, eldest dau. of Joseph Chambers, of Taylorstown Castle, co. Wexford (see CHAMBERS *of co. Meath*), by whom he had issue,

1. Joseph, *b.* 23 July, 1723; *d.* before 18 March, 1729.
2. William, *b.* 22 June, 1728; *d.* ante 1766; *m.* 1762, Elizabeth, sister of Saml. Hiett, of Dublin, and had issue, a son, William, of Liverpool, *d.* 1813, and a dau., *m.* Wm. Wilson, and *d.s.p.* 1853.
3. ARTHUR, his successor, of whom presently.
4. Joseph, of Newbay, co. Wexford, *b.* 6 Sept. 1730; *d.* Oct. 1799, *m.* 1771, Eleanor (*d.* Aug. 1790), dau. of Charles Frizell, of Whitestown, co. Wexford, and of Annaville, co. Wicklow. He had issue,
   1. Arthur Frazer, of Newbay, *b.* about 1776; *d.* 26 March, 1852;
   m. 11 Feb. 1802, Alice, dau. of Abraham James Howlin, of Castlepalliser, and Ballycronigan, co. Wexford (*see that family*), and had issue, a son, JOSEPH, of whom later.
      1. Anne, *m.* 16 Feb. 1802, John Emerson, and had issue.
      2. Mary, *b.* 1779; *d.* young.
      3. Eleanor, *b.* 1781; *d.* Jan. 1796.
      4. Penelope, *b.* 1786; *d.* 9 July, 1866; *m.* 1810, as his 2nd wife, Joseph Lichtburne, of Harcourt Lodge, Trim, co. Meath.
5. Anthony, *b.* 1 Oct. 1734.
1. Catherine, *b.* 10 Sept. 1725; *d. unm.* 1796.
2. Sarah, *b.* 15 May, 1727; *d.* young.
3. Mary, *b.* 6 Feb. 1738-9; *m.* 1766, Thomas Finn.

The 3rd son,
ARTHUR MEADOWS, of Whitestown, and of Wexford, Mayor of Wexford 1794-5; *b.* Sept. 1729; will dated 22 Aug. 1797, proved 7 Sept. 1797; *m.* 1st, 1760, Margaret, dau. of Samuel Batt, of Ozier Hill, co. Wexford (*see BATT of Purdysburn*), by whom (who *d.* 27 Aug. 1771) he had, with two children who *d.* young, a son and successor,

1. ARTHUR, of whom presently.

He *m.* 2ndly, 24 Nov. 1774, Anne, dau. of Edward Percival, of Gurrygibbon, co. Wexford (*see* PERCIVAL *of Barntown*), by Jane, sister of William Charleton, of Ballykelly, co. Wexford, and had further issue,

2. William, Lieut. Staffordshire Militia, *b.* 10 June, 1778; *d.* 21 Aug. 1866; *m.* Johanna, dau. of Joseph McCarthy, of Killarney, and had issue,
   1. Joseph McCarthy, of Wolfe Hill, Queen's Co., and subsequently of Dublin, Mining Engineer, *b.* 1824; *d.* 1905· *m.* April, 1870, Sarah Hanlon, formerly Byrne, widow, and had issue a son, Joseph Percival, *b.* Nov. 1881 and a dau., Anne Josephine.
   2. Arthur, *b.* Oct. 1831; *d.s.p.* 1884.
   3. William, *b.* 1827.
   1. Mary, *m.* Thos. O'Brien.
   2. Anne Percival, *m.* John Reynolds.
   3. Kate, *d. unm.* 1869.   4. Hannah, *d. unm.* 1852.
   5. Norah, *d. unm.* 1874.
3. Edward, of Ballyteigue Castle, *b.* 29 Nov. 1779; *d.* intestate April, 1854; *m.* 22 Sept. 1804, Elizabeth, dau. of — Berry, of Sarshill, and widow of John Henry Colclough, of Ballyteigue Castle, co. Wexford (*see* COLCLOUGH *of Tintern Abbey*), and by her (who *d.* 16 Nov. 1826) had two sons,
   1. Arthur, *b.* 1 Aug. 1805; *d.* in India about 1848.
   2. Edward of Ballyteigue Castle, *b.* 27 July, 1811; *d.* Aug 1863, *s.p.*; *m.* 1844, Mary, dau. of Henry Archer, of Ballyseskin, co. Wexford.
4. Joseph, *b.* Jan. 1785; *d.* Feb. of same year.
1. Jane, *b.* 26 Dec. 1775; *d.* Aug. 1783.
2. Mary, *b.* 10 March, 1777, *d.* young.
3. Anne, *b.* 9 Jan. 1781; *m.* 1805, William Bolton, of Dublin. She *d.* 30 July, 1810, having had a dau., Anne, who *d.* young. He *m.* 3rdly, 1786, Frances, dau. of — Hyde, and widow of John Colley, of Ballywalter, co. Wexford (*see* POUNDEN *of Ballywalter*), but by her had no issue. He *d.* 22 Aug. 1797, and was *s.* by his eldest son,

ARTHUR MEADOWS, of Whitestown or Hermitage, co. Wexford, *b.* 24 Oct. 1770, Mayor of Wexford 1803-4, 1817-18, 1818-1819. High Sheriff co. Wexford 1808, Capt. Wexford Regt. of Militia. He was prominent among those whom the rebels seized in the Rebellion of 1798, and narrowly escaped the cruel death which they inflicted upon their victims, on the bridge of Wexford, on Wednesday, 20 June, 1798 (see his personal account in *Ireland, its Scenery, Character, &c.*, by S. C. Hall, Vol. II, pp. 171-2). Mr. Meadows *m.* 1st, 19 Aug. 1796, Barbara, dau. of Maurice Howlin D'Arcy, of Coolcul, co. Wexford, and sister of Edward Howlin D'Arcy, of Coolcul, shot by the rebels near the gates of Ballynahown, by her (who *d.* 20 March, 1805) he had, with several children who *d.* young, two daus., Margaret, *b.* 27 Dec. 1800; *d. unm.* 1 Oct. 1840, and Eleanor D'Arcy, *b.* 27 April, 1802; living *unm.* Nov. 1854. He *m.* 2ndly, 17 March, 1807, Barbara, widow of Richard Lambart, of Bristol, and 4th dau. of John Harvey, of Killiane Castle, co. Wexford (see that family who assumed the name of HERVEY in 1818) and by her (who *d.* Feb. 1878) had with other issue who *d.* young,

1. Barbara, *b.* 7 June, 1811; *d.* 17 July, 1868; *m.* 29 July, 1845, Joseph Harvey, of Wellington College, Wexford, and had issue.
2. Jane, *b.* 10 April, 1820; *m.* Surgeon Thomas Mawe, H.E.I.C.S., and had issue.
3. Dorothy, *b.* 15 Nov. 1822; *m.* Thomas Dartnell.
4. Charlotte, *b.* 16 Oct. 1825; *m.* Charles Cole, and had issue.

He *m.* 3rdly, 1840, Margaret Phelan, by whom he had no issue, and *d.* 21 July, 1844, having no male issue, the representation of the male line of the family in co. Wexford, devolved upon,

JOSEPH MEADOWS, of Carcur, and later, through his wife, of Thornville, co. Wexford, Clerk of the Peace of co. Wexford, only son, as above-mentioned, of Arthur Frazer Meadows, of Newbay. He was *b.* 5 July, 1800; *m.* 7 Oct. 1842, his mother's distant cousin Anne, eldest dau. of John Lloyd, of Thornville, co. Wexford, and eventually sole heiress of her brother Henry Howlin Lloyd. He *d.* 13 July, 1877, having had issue by his wife, who *d.* 12 May, 1896,

1. John Lloyd, *b.* 1843; *d.* 9 March, 1845.
2. Arthur, of the Rectory, Carne, co. Wexford, B.A. Trin Coll. Dublin, *b.* 7 Sept. 1844.
3. Joseph, of Moortown, co. Wexford, B.A., C.E., Trin. Coll. Dublin, F.R.G.S.I., *b.* 19 Jan. 1847; *m.* 9 April, 1877, Emily Mary, dau. of the Rev. James Peed, Rector of Wexford, and has issue,
   1. Henry Lloyd, of Coolonghter, *b.* 27 Jan. 1878.
   2. Louisa Mary.
   3. Blanche Anna Mabella, *m.* Rev. Arthur Ivan Greaves, Vicar of Leicester, and has issue.
4. Henry Lloyd, of Ballyrane, co. Wexford, M.A. Trin. Coll. Dublin, F.R.A.S., Clerk of the Crown and Peace for co. Wexford, *b.* 3 June, 1851; *m.* 29 April, 1890, Olive Maud, eldest dau. of Edward J. Nunn, of Silverspring, co. Wexford, and has issue, Annie Frances.
5. ABRAHAM JAMES HOWLIN (*see above*), to whom his brothers and sister disposed of their interest in Thornville.
6. Edward, *b.* 23 Dec. 1857.
1. Mary Lloyd, of Bushville, co. Wexford, *m.* 23 Sept. 1875, John Lloyd, M.D., who *d.* in India, Surgeon-Major B.M.S.

Arms—Az., a chevron or, between three pelicans' wings endorsed, vulning themselves ppr., on a canton of the second three cinquefoils of the field. **Crest**—Out of a coronet or a demi-eagle displayed pean. **Motto**—Mea dos virtus.

Seat—Thornville, Ballycogley, co. Wexford.

MEARES OF MEARES COURT.

JOSEPH LEYCESTER DEVENISH-MEARES, of Meares Court, co. Westmeath, B.A. 1859, B.E. 1859, M.A. 1863, Trin. Coll. Dublin, formerly a Civil Engineer, J.P. cos. Armagh, Down and Westmeath, High Sheriff Westmeath, 1912, *b.* 14 March, 1838; *s.* his brother 1907; *m.* 19 Oct. 1864, Frances Georgina (who *d.* 9 Aug. 1907), dau. of Basil George Brooke, J.P. of Dungannon, and has issue,

1. JOHN FREDERICK, B.L., Middle Temple and King's Inn, *b.* 18 Feb. 1866; *m.* 6 July, 1900, Harriette Frances, dau. of R. A. Handcock.
2. Basil, C.E., *b.* 29 June, 1868; *m.* Feb. 1896, Bessie, dau. of R. O'Flaherty, C.E., and *d.* 5 Oct. 1907, leaving issue, Basil John, *b.* 11 Jan. 1898.

3. Leycester, b. 18 May, 1870 ; d. same year.
4. Leycester Francis, Capt. Imp. Yeom., b. 15 March, 1873.
5. Arthur William, b. 18 Dec. 1874.
6. William Lewis, b. 17 March, 1886.
1. Grace Maria. 2. Ethel Isabella.
3. Florence. 4. Frances Stuart Irene.
5. Sophie Constance.

Lineage.—JOHN MEARES, of Whitbourne, near Corsley, co. Wilts, b. about 1560; had by Eleanor his wife (with an elder son, whose representative, Robert Meares, of Hackney, Middlesex, was living at the Visit. Wilts. 1614) a younger son,
LEWIS MEARES, of Rowlandstown, co. Westmeath, b. at Corsley, 1625, an Officer in the Army, sent to quell the Rebellion in Ireland 1641, who obtained a grant of the lands of Rowlandstown, now called Meares Court, co. Westmeath, and of Cornamuckla, co. Longford, by patent dated 3 Dec. 1667. He rebuilt and endowed the church of Almoritia, or Ballymorin, adjoining Meares Court. He m. 1st, 1648, Mary, dau. of Samuel Palmer and widow of Capt. Smyth, and by her had issue,
1. Lewis, his heir.
2. Richard, b. 12 March, 1654 ; m. Katherine, dau. of William Jones, of Rathconrath, and left issue.
3. John, b. 24 Dec. 1657 ; m. Katherine, dau. of Giles Vandeleur, of Rahaline, co. Clare.
  1. Ann, m. Francis Conduit.
  2. Elizabeth, m. Robert Conduit.
Mr. Meares m. 2ndly, Elizabeth Large, but by her had no issue. His will was dated 1699, and he was s. by his eldest son,
LEWIS MEARES, of Meares Court, b. in Dublin, 26 May, 1651 ; m. 27 Jan. 1678, Thomasine, dau. of Capt. John Jones (2nd son of Henry, Bishop of Meath), and grand-niece of Sir Theophilus Jones, Privy Councillor temp. CHARLES II, and had issue,
1. JOHN, his heir.
2. Lewis, b. Oct. 1684, will dated 28 Feb. 1713.
3. Robert (Rev.), b. 18 Sept. 1688, Rector of Almoritia, co. Westmeath, m. Anne Wakely, of Ballyburly, and made his will 10 May, 1738. He had issue,
  1. William, of Togherstown, b. 8 Feb. 1732 ; m. 1768, Katherine Martha, dau. of Rev. Fletcher Piers, and d. Oct. 1801, leaving a son,
    George Galbraith, of Millgrove, co. Roscommon, b. 27 Nov. 1783 ; m. April, 1805, Lady Mary Elizabeth King, dau. of Robert, 2nd Earl of Kingston, and had, with other issue, three sons,
    1. Robert King, d.s.p.
    2. William Piers, b. 3 Nov. 1818, Col. H.E.I.C.S., m. Mary Ada Montrilli, and d. 20 Dec. 1869, leaving, with three daus. (Mary Ada Douglas, Eleanor, and Mary William Anna), a son, GEORGE GERALD MEARES, heir male of the family.
    3. George Richard James, of Sinduri, India, b. 26 May, 1814 ; m. Caroline Alicia Nicholson, and d. 8 Aug. 1867, leaving issue,
      a. George Robert King, b. 26 Oct. 1841.
      b. Charles William, b. 10 April, 1846 ; m. Eliza Martha Mary Hampton, and has, 1, Charles Robert, b. 16 Oct. 1867 ; 1, Ellen Caroline Mary ; and 2, Caroline Charlotte.
      c. William Edward, b. 14 Dec. 1848 ; m. 15 Dec. 1874, Rose Reed.
      d. Gerald FitzGerald John, b. 7 Oct. 1850.
      e. Henry James Palmer, b. 23 July, 1853.
      f. Percy Nicholson, b. 28 Jan. 1856.
      g. Cecil Furlong Eddis, b. 1 Feb. 1858.
      a. Caroline Furlong, d. unm.
      b. Eleanor Mary, m. H. F. Payne.
      c. Charlotte Ellen Louisa, m. 13 June, 1866, George Annesley Glascott (see GLASCOTT of Aldertown, Killowen, &c.).
      d. Isabella. e. Mary Ann.
  2. Charles (Rev.), b. 26 Feb. 1734 ; m. 1st, Katherine Hamilton, widow of Rev. Francis Goldsbury, of Larkin, co. Meath, by whom he had no issue, and 2ndly, Oct. 1774, Elizabeth, dau. of Andrew Nixon, of Cavan, by whom he had,
    Robert, d.s.p. at Bristol, 1795.
    Lucinda, m. Rev. Thomas Conolly Coane, of Clifton, co. Gloucester.
    1. Clementina, m. 1744, John Martley, of Ballyfallan, co. Meath, ancestor of the Martleys of Ballyfallan, and d. Jan. 1789, leaving issue (see that family).
    2. Arabella, m. H. Kelly.
    3. Anne, m. 1739, Rev. Currell Smyth (see SMYTH of Gaybrook).
    4. Elizabeth, m. 1st, — Ormsby, and 2ndly, her cousin John Meares, of Meares Court.
4. Peyton, b. 14 Jan. 1694 ; d.s.p. 1722.
5. Edward, b. 4 Jan. 1702, had one dau., Margaret, m. William Granger.

Mr. Meares (whose will is dated 28 Feb. 1713) was s. by his eldest son,
JOHN MEARES, of Meares Court, b. 7 Aug. 1682 ; m. 1st, 17 Dec. 1705, Katherine, dau. of John Wakely, of Ballyburly, King's Co., and had issue,
1. JOHN, his heir.
2. Charles, of Dalystown, d.s.p.
3. Peyton, who had a son, Blacket, Capt. in the Army, d.s.p. 1796, and a dau. Katherine, m. Henry Brooke, of Rantavan House, co. Cavan.
4. George, m. Miss Jones, and had a dau., Jane.
5. Edward. 6. Lewis.
1. Elizabeth, b. 2 Oct. 1706, Mrs. Crofton.
Mr. Meares m. 2ndly, 14 May, 1726, Margaret, sister of Edward Eyre, of Eyre Court, co. Galway, and widow of Hon. Charles Annesley, but by her had no issue. He d. 1742, and was s. by his eldest son,
JOHN MEARES, of Meares Court, High Sheriff 1748, b. 28 May, 1709 ; m. 1st, Nov. 1729, Sarah, dau. of Morgan Magan, of Clonearl and Togherstown (see that family), and by her (who d. 1762) had
1. Thomas, b. July, 1732 ; d. 1734.
2. JOHN, his heir.
1. Henrietta, b. 6 Aug. 1719 ; d. unm.
2. Katharine, b. 17 Oct. 1720 ; m. John Devenish, of Portlick, co. Westmeath, and had eight sons and five daus. Of these, the 3rd son,
  WILLIAM DEVENISH, got the Meares Court estate under his uncle's will.
3. Susanna, m. Rev. William Fleming.
4. Mary Rose, m. Anthony Lennon.
5. Elizabeth, d. unm. 1806. 6. Jane, d. unm.
7. Thomasine, m. Rev. F. H. Goldsbury, of Boyle, and d. 1809.
Mr. Meares m. 2ndly, his cousin Elizabeth, dau. of Rev. Robert Meares, Rector of Almoritia, but had no further issue. He was s. by his only surviving son,
JOHN MEARES, of Meares Court, High Sheriff 1783, Capt. Westmeath Yeomanry, b. 4 June, 1742 ; m. 30 May, 1771, Mary, dau. of John Vandeleur, of Kilrush, co. Clare, and d.s.p. 1790, having by his will devised his estate of Meares Court to his nephew,
WILLIAM DEVENISH, J.P., of Meares Court, who adopted the surname of MEARES. He was b. 22 July, 1759 ; m. 21 Sept. 1791. Deborah, dau. of Joseph Coghlan, of Kilumney, co. Cork, and d. 6 Jan. 1844, having by her (who d. 1834) had issue,
1. JOHN, his heir.
2. Matthew (Rev.), m. 1821, Augusta, dau. of Charles Devenish, and had issue.
  1. Catherine, m. 1813, Rev. Frederick A. Potter, Rector of Rathconrath, and d.s.p.
  2. Mary Anne, m. Robert Sandys, of Crevagh, co. Longford, and d.s.p.

The eldest son,
JOHN DEVENISH-MEARES, of Meares Court, J.P. and D.L. co. Westmeath, High Sheriff 1862, b. 12 Oct. 1795 ; m. 6 July, 1831, Maria, dau. of Charles Kelly, of Charleville, co. Westmeath (see KELLY of Glencara), and d. July, 1876, having by her (who d. 30 Aug. 1869) had issue,
1. WILLIAM LEWIS, late of Meares Court.
2. John Henry Gouldsbury, Surgeon-Major in the Army, b. 29 Jan. 1836 ; m. 21 June, 1860, Thomasine, dau. of Capt. W. Smith, 68th Regt., and d.s.p. Jan. 1877.
3. JOSEPH LEYCESTER, now of Meares Court.
1. Charlotte Maria, m. 24 July, 1866, John North-Bomford, of Ferrans and Gallow, co. Meath. She d.s.p. Oct. 1881 (see that family).
2. Florence Anne Lever, m. Dec. 1876, Henry Goff Carey, and d. July, 1877, leaving issue.
The eldest son,
WILLIAM LEWIS DEVENISH-MEARES, of Meares Court, co. Westmeath, J.P. and D.L., High Sheriff 1885, Major-Gen. in the Army formerly Lieut.-Col. 20th Regt., served during the siege and fall of Sebastopol, b. 6 April, 1832 ; m. Nov. 1870, Katherine Charlotte, dau. of George Folliott, of Vicars Cross, co. Chester. She d. 25 Sept. 1905, and he m. 2ndly, 27 Oct. 1906, Florence, dau. of Rev. Francis Wellington Moore, Vicar of Duffield, Derbyshire. He d.s.p. 18 June, 1907, and was s. by his brother.

Seat—Meares Court, Mullingar, co. Westmeath. Clubs—United Counties, Newry.

MEDLEN OF LOWLANDS.

GEORGE AUSTIN MEDLEN, of Lowlands, Roscrea, Tipperary, J.P. King's Co. and co. Tipperary, High Sheriff for former co. 1900, b. 5 Oct. 1835 ; m. 1st, 7 May, 1867, Anna Doolan, dau. of the late Capt. James Sheppard, of Clifton House, Tipperary, by Mary his wife, dau. of Thomas Doolan, of Wingfield, co. Tipperary. She d. March, 1896. He m. 2ndly, Oct. 1897, Mary, eldest dau. of James Tertius Donovan, of Parsonstown House, Slane, co. Meath. Mr. Medlen is the 2nd son of the late DERRY LEWIS MEDLEN, and Mary his wife, dau. of George Austin and grandson of RICHARD MEDLEN.

Seat—Lowlands, Roscrea, co. Tipperary.

MEDLICOTT OF DUNMURRY.

JAMES EDWARD MEDLICOTT, of Dunmurry, co. Kildare, J.P., b. 19 Dec. 1827 ; m. 12 Oct. 1859, Margaret (who d. 1904), dau. of Joshua Henry, Davidson, M.D. Edinburgh, H.M. Physician in Ordinary, and has issue,
1. HENRY EDWARD, b. 12 Jan. 1863.
2. Edward James, b. 16 March, 1876 ; d. 21 Sept. 1887.
3. Richard Frederick Cavendish, b. 9 July, 1877.

Medlycott. THE LANDED GENTRY. 476

4. Charles Francis Lewis, b. 25 July, 1880.
5. George Herbert, b. 6 June, 1885.
1. Annie Stuart, d. young, 1867.
2. Elizabeth, m. 21 June, 1883, Thomas Browning Reeves, of Athgarvan, J.P., co. Kildare.
3. Mary Graydon, m. 29 Jan. 1896, William Calvert Andrew, of Sydney.
4. Helen Mackenzie. 5. Annie Catherine Stuart.
6. Harriet, m. 22 March, 1902, Richard Ebenezer Nunn Bailey, late Lieut. 3rd Batt. Royal Inniskilling Fusiliers, younger son of Thomas Bailey, R.N., J.P., of Mulladuff, co. Fermanagh.
7. Margaret Cecil, m. 22 April, 1908, James Watson Fleming, of Derreen, co. Longford.

Lineage.—Thomas Medlicott, of Abingdon, J.P. and D.L., bapt. 9 March, 1627, M.P. for Abingdon 1668, was presented with a parliamentary medal at the Coronation of William III and Mary II, 11 April, 1689. He had issue,
1. James, from whom descends in the female line Medlycott, Bart. of Ven House (see Burke's *Peerage and Baronetage*).
2. Charles, of Cottingham, co. Northampton, who had, by Barbara his wife,
Thomas, of Cottingham, m. Anne, dau. of Richard Buckley, and had an only son, who d.s.p. and two daus., his co-heirs, Anne Barbara, m. George Hill, of Rothwell, co. Northampton, Serjeant-at-Law, and Elizabeth, m. Rev. John Hill, LL.D., Rector of Thorpe and Kilmarsh, co. Northampton, and Prebendary of Windsor, and d. 19 Sept. 1798.
3. Edmund, living 1722.
4. George, of whom we treat.
5. Thomas, of Binfield, co. Berks, ancestor of Medlycott *of Rocketts Castle and Waterford* (see that family).

Mr. Medlycott d. 13 Dec. 1713, in his 89th year. His 4th son,
George Medlicott, of Tully, co. Kildare, b. 1649, purchased from John Berkeley, Lord Fitzharding, 1712, the estate of Youngstown and Dunmurry, co. Kildare. He m. Elizabeth, dau. of Edward Bagot, of Harristown, and had by her (who d. 29 Dec. 1725), with seven daus., as many sons,
1. James, of Youngstown, d. 1718.
2. Edward, of Moortown, co. Kildare ; d. 10 May, 1762, leaving by Dorcas his wife, five sons, whose line is extinct.
3. Ossory (Rev.), b. at Bandon, 1683 ; m. 1st, Hannah, dau. of Major-Gen. John Pepper, and had an only son, John Pepper, d.s.p., and 2ndly, 23 Sept. 1729, Margaret, dau. and heir of John Bradeston, and widow of Edward Pakenham, of Pakenham Hall.
4. John, of Ballysax, m. Feb. 1727, Mrs. Hester Withers, widow, of Tully, co. Kildare, and d.s.p.
5. Samuel, of Dunmurry, of whom hereafter.
6. George, who had a son, George, b. 1705.
7. Thomas, will proved 1738.

Mr. Medlicott d. 26 June, 1717, aged 68. His 5th son,
Samuel Medlicott, of Dunmurry, had, by Mary his wife (who d. 1730), with five daus., four sons,
1. James, of Ardsrath and Youngstown, LL.D. ; d. unm. 25 Dec. 1771, having (by an indenture dated to Dec. 1770) assigned all his estates to Charles Dowling, of Redhills, co. Kildare, who thereupon adopted the name of Medlicott. He was b. 1705 ; m. Sarah, dau. of Joshua Paul Meredith, and d. intestate 12 Feb. 1811, aged 106 years. leaving three daus. (one of whom, Sarah, m. 16 Nov. 1801, John Grogan, Barrister-at-Law, and d. 20 Oct. 1819, leaving a son, Sir Edward Grogan, Bart.), and one son, James Medlicott, of Youngstown, who d. unm. 1812, and bequeathed the Medlicott estates back to the family.
2. Edward, who continued the line as hereafter.
3. George.
4. Samuel, m. Oct. 1765, Angelice Irwin.

Mr. Medlicott d. 1737. His 2nd son,
Edward Medlicott, of Dunmurry, had two sons and two daus.,
1. James, his successor.
2. Joseph, of Nealstown, co. Dublin, m. 5 March, 1785, Katherine, dau. of Lieut.-Col. Robert Wood, M.P. He d. March, 1816, leaving issue,
1. George, of Rutland Square, Clerk of the Peace, co. Kildare, m. Emily, dau. of Arthur Magan, of Clonearl, and had an only dau.,
Louisa, m. 21 Dec. 1858, Hon. John Prendergast Vereker, son of John Prendergast, 3rd Viscount Gort, and has issue.
2. Edward, settled at Lisbon, m. there, and d. leaving,
(1) Joseph.
(2) William. (3) Edward.
(1) Frances.
3. James, d. unm.
4. Samuel (Rev.), Rector of Loughrea, co. Galway, m. Charlotte, dau. of Henry Benedict Dolphin, co. Galway, and d. 1858, leaving issue by her (who d. 1 May, 1884, aged 79),
(1) Joseph George. (2) Henry Benedict.
(3) Samuel (Rev.), M.A., Rector of Bowness, co. Cumberland.
(1) Anne, m. Rev. George Augustus Froderick Armstrong.
5. Joseph (Rev.), Vicar of Potterne, co. Wilts, b. 1798 ; m. 6 Dec. 1838, Dionysia Meliora, dau. of Richard Godolphin Long, of Rood Ashton, co. Wilts, and d. 1871, having had issue,
(1) Henry Edmonstone, of Sandfield, co. Wilts, J.P., M.A. Oxford, b. Jan. 1840 ; m. April, 1874, Kate D'Oyley, dau. of Alexander Robinson Gale, of Stanton Lodge, near Bury St. Edmunds, co. Suffolk, and has issue,
1. George Godfrey, b. 26 Dec. 1877 ; d. 1883.
2. Walter Sandfield, b. 28 Aug. 1879 ; m. 5 Oct. 1910. Lavender, only dau. of Sir Alfred E. Pease, of Pinchinthorpe, Yorks, Bart. (see Burke's *Peerage*).
3. Henry Edward, b. 24 July, 1882, Capt. 3rd Skinner's Horse, I.A. ; m. 7 June, 1910, Clare, dau. of Sir Martin le Marchant Gosselin, G.C.V.O., K.C.M.G., C.B., of Blakesware, Herts (see *that family*).
4 Stephen, R.N., b. 22 May, 1892.
1. Kate Josephine, m. 11 Dec. 1899, Henry Paton Rogers, Capt Wiltshire Regt,. who d. at Bloemfontein 13 May, 1900.
(2) Walter Edward (Rev.), M.A. (*Whingarth, Shedfield, Hants*), late Vicar of Swanmore 1871-1907, co. Hants, b. 23 June, 1841 ; m. 30 June. 1868, Edith Louisa, dau. of Rev. Robert Sumner, and grand-dau. of Charles Sumner, D.D., Bishop of Winchester, and has issue,
1. Robert Sumner (Rev.), Vicar of Portsmouth, b. 2 May, 1869 ; m. 24 May, 1905, Ellen Douglas, dau. of late John James Irvine, of Waterford, Cape Colony, and King Williamstown, and has issue,
a. Robert Irvine, b. 24 and d. 25 Jan. 1908.
a. Ellen Douglas, b. 24 and d. 25 Jan. 1908.
b. Joan Douglas, b. 26 Aug. 1910.
2. Walter Barrington, b. 12 Oct. 1872 ; m. 24 April, 1900, Hilda Fothergill, 2nd dau. of the late W. Fothergill Robinson, Q.C., Vice-Chancellor of the Duchy of Lancaster, and has a dau.,
Eleanor Betty, b. 1 April, 1901.
1. Margaret Edith. 2. Grace Katharine.
1. Elizabeth, m. Feb. 1768, John Bell.
2. Grace, m. Feb. 1772, Robert Bell.

Mr. Medlicott was s. at Dunmurry by his elder son,
James Medlicott, of Dunmurry, b. 1737 ; m. 1st, Dec. 1774, Jane, dau. of Alexander Wood, and had an only issue,
1. Alexander, an officer in the Kildare Militia, who went to India, m. and d. there u.p., without surviving issue.

Mr. Medlicott m. 2ndly, Feb. 1784, Mary, dau. of Thomas Graydon, and had further issue,
2. Edward, his successor. 3. James, R.N., d. unm.
4. George, H.E.I.C., d. unm.
5. Thomas, m. Martha Williams, d.s.p.
6. Graydon, settled in North America, m. Hester, dau. of Rev. John Grant, and has, with five daus., one son, John James.
1. Mary Anne, d. unm. 2. Elizabeth, m. Rev. William Cox.
3. Katherine, d. unm. 4. Letitia, d. unm.
5. Jane, d. unm. 6. Frances, d. unm.

Mr. Medlicott, who s. to the remainder of the family estates in 1812, d. 1827, aged 90, and was s. by his eldest surviving son,
Edward James Medlicott, of Dunmurry, J.P., m. Feb. 1827, Anne, dau. of Solomon Speer, of Graniteheld, co. Dublin (by Anne his wife, dau. of Richard Donovan, of Ballymore, co. Wexford), by whom (who d. 22 Aug. 1866) he had issue,
1. James Edward, now of Dunmurry.
2. Edward Richard, Sub-Inspector Royal Irish Constabulary, d. unm. 25 Nov. 1872.
3. Richard Solomon, m. 9 March, 1882, Louisa Mary, dau. of A. T. H. Banks, M.D.
1. Annie, b. 31 Oct. 1829 ; m. 1857, Walter Bagot, and d.s.p. 6 Aug. 1878.

Mr. Medlicott d. 11 Jan. 1868, and was s. by his eldest son.

Seat—Dunmurry, Kildare.

MEDLYCOTT OF ROCKETTS CASTLE.

John Thomas Medlycott, of Rocketts Castle, co. Waterford, Capt. 3rd R.I. Regt., late Lieut. 1st South Staffordshire Regt. (38th), b. 20 Jan. 1868 ; m. 18 Nov. 1896, Mary Fraser, eldest dau. of George P. Malcomson, of Woodlock, co. Waterford, and has issue,
1. John Thomas, b. 16 Nov. 1902.
2. George Bradford, b. 27 Sept. 1905.
1. Florence Mary, b. 27 March, d. 2 April, 1898.
2. Constance Mary, b. 23 June, 1899.
3. Florence Maud, b. 1901.
4. Lilian Keith, b. 28 April, 1909.

Lineage.—Thomas Medlycott, of Binfield, Berks, and afterwards of Dublin, 3rd son of Thomas Medlicott, of Abingdon, Berks (see Medlicott *of Dunmurry*), was bapt. 22 May, 1662. He was M.P. for Milbourne Port 1706, and for Westminster 1708-10 and 1713, also Chief Commissioner of Revenue in Ireland. In 1698 he got from James, Duke of Ormonde, lands in the cos. of Kilkenny and Tipperary, and in 1699, lands in co. Waterford, and March, 1701, purchased from the Earl of Arran lands in co. Mayo. He had a dau., Anne, m. Dec. 1715, Right Hon. Edward Riggs, M.P. for Killybegs, and a son,
Thomas John Medlycott, of Newport Pratt, co. Mayo, m. Frances Philippa Seigneaux, of Lausanne, in Switzerland, and by her (who d. 8 Nov. 1750) had a son,
John Thomas Medlycott, of Newport Pratt, co. Mayo, and afterwards of Rocketts Castle, co. Waterford, m. 21 June, 1787, Elizabeth, only dau. of William Lockwood, of Clerihan Castle, co. Tipperary, and d. 25 April, 1827, leaving (with four daus., 1. Frances, m. Cornelius Sullivan, of Upper Merrion Street, Dublin ; 2. Maria ; 3. Jane, m. Dawson French, of Tullamore, Queen's Co. ; and 4. Susan, m. Rev. George Stanley Monck, Rector of Clonegam, co. Waterford, and d. his widow, 18 April, 1887, aged 86) a son and heir,

REV. JOHN THOMAS MEDLYCOTT, of Rocketts Castle, J.P., b. 9 Oct. 1789; m. 19 June, 1820, Mary, eldest dau. of Ambrose Isher Congreve, of Mount Congreve, co. Waterford. and d. 1877, leaving issue,
1. JOHN THOMAS, of whom presently.
1. Anne, m. 4 Feb. 1845, George Augustus Quentin, Major late 10th Hussars, son of Sr George Quentin, Lieut.-Col. 10th Hussars. She d. 8 Sept. 1903.
2. Elizabeth, m. Rev. James Rumsey, M.A., of Pembroke College, Oxford. 3. Ellen.
4. Susan, m. Rev. Richard Neville, Rector of Stradbally.
5. Louisa, d. 14 Nov. 1868. 6. Maria.
His only son,
JOHN THOMAS MEDLYCOTT, of Rocketts Castle, co. Waterford, B.A., J.P. and D.L., b. 13 Aug. 1823; m. 1st, 2 May, 1867, Florence Caroline, dau. of Sir William Coles Medlycott, 2nd bart. of Ven, by whom (who d. 30 Jan. 1868) he had a son,
1. JOHN THOMAS, now of Rocketts Castle.
He m. 2ndly, 28 April, 1874, Marianna, 4th dau. of Samuel King, of Mount Pleasant, Waterford, and d. 5 Feb. 1896, having by her (who d. 19 June, 1894) had issue,
2. William, b. 21 Nov. 1876; m. 25 Oct. 1901, Selena Mary, only dau. of the late George Stewart Phillips, of Otterston, Fifeshire, N.B.
3. Mervyn, b. 16 Sept. 1879; m. 1 Aug. 1907, Vera, dau. of Maurice Gubbay, of 16, Grosvenor Gardens, W.
Seat—Rocketts Castle, Portlaw, co. Waterford.

MEREDITH OF DICKSGROVE.

RICHARD MEREDITH, of Dicksgrove, co. Kerry, J.P. High Sheriff 1886, b. 19 Feb. 1841; m. 16 June, 1874, Mary Elizabeth (who d. 18 March, 1909), eldest dau. of Stephen Huggard, of Lismore House, Tralee, co. Kerry, Clerk of the Crown and Peace, co. Kerry, and has issue,
1. WILLIAM JOHN, Lieut. 3rd Batt. Royal Munster Fus., b. 23 June, 1876.
2. Stephen John (Parkmore, co. Kerry), b. 23 June, 1876 (twin); m. 11 June, 1902, Elizabeth, dau of P. Shannon, B.A., and has issue,
Richard, b. 29 June, 1905.
3. Richard Charles, b. 17 July, 1877.
4. Thomas, b. 20 April, 1881.
5. Manus Buckle, b. 6 Sept. 1890.
6. Wilfred, b. 11 Nov. 1895.
1. Rose Helen.
2. Mary Clare.
3. Marion Elizabeth.
4. Maud Catherine, d. young.
5. Nora Gertrude.
6. Alice Anne.
7. Kathleen Eileen.
8. Eileen, d. young
Lineage.—RICHARD MEREDITH, 2nd son of David Meredith, of Gowress, co. Montgomery, settled in Ireland, m. Anne, only dau. and heir of William Browne, of Totteridge, Herts, by Frances his wife, eldest dau. of Richard, 2nd Lord Herbert, of Chirbury, and d. 1752, leaving issue,
1. Richard, of Tierneygore, High Sheriff 1731, m. Honora, 2nd dau. of Maurice FitzGerald, Knight of Kerry, and had issue. This line is now extinct.
2. WILLIAM, of Dicksgrove.
1. Frances, d. unm.
2. Anne, m. Robert Langford, son of Francis Langford, of Gardenfield, co. Limerick.
The second son,
WILLIAM MEREDITH, of Dicksgrove, co. Kerry, High Sheriff 1736, m. 1737, Marian, youngest dau. of Maurice FitzGerald, Knight of Kerry, and had issue,
1. RICHARD, of whom presently.
2. John, m. Gertrude, dau. of Courtland Skinner, of New Jersey, and had issue.
3. Robert, d.s.p.
4. Maurice, d.s.p.
1. Anne.
2. Elizabeth, m. 11 March, 1764, John Bateman, of Holly Park, co. Kerry.
3. Margaret, m. 1st, James Mabony, of Butterfield, and 2ndly, Sir Richard Hart, of Coolruss, co. Limerick.
4. Frances, m. Robert Coote, of Cork.
5. Honora, m. 11 Jan. 1773, George Twiss, of Cordell, co. Kerry. He d. 2 April, 1802, leaving issue.
The eldest son,
RICHARD MEREDITH, of Dicksgrove, High Sheriff 1766, m. 3 Nov. 1770, Lucy, dau. of Arthur Saunders, of Killarney, and had issue,
WILLIAM, his heir.
A dau., m. Manus Blake, of Garacloon, co. Galway.
The only son,
WILLIAM MEREDITH, of Dicksgrove, J.P., High Sheriff 1803, b. 28 July, 1771; m. 1801, Alicia, dau. of Richard Orpen, of Ardtully, co. Kerry. She d. 1821. He d. 1 June, 1819, having had issue,

1. RICHARD, his heir.
2. Robert FitzGerald (Rev.), M.A., Rector of East Chelborough and Hadstock, co. Dorset, b. 1815; m. 1852, Mary Russell (who d. 1868), dau. of Samuel Cox, of Beaminster, and had issue.
3. Manus Blake, b. 16 June, 1817; m. 1844, Anne, dau. of Thomas Casebourne, of Armagh, and d. 15 Nov. 1856, leaving issue.
1. Anne, m. William Harnett, of Sandville, co. Kerry, and had issue.
2. Marian Maria.
3. Catherine.
The eldest son,
RICHARD MEREDITH, of Dicksgrove, J.P., b. 1803; m. 1st, Louisa dau. of Maj. Juxon. She d. 1826, having had issue a son,
1. William, m. and had issue.
He m. 2ndly, 23 Aug. 1837, Rose Helen, dau. of William Hill Buckle, of the Mythe, co. Gloucester. She d. 21 June, 1861. He d. 4 Sept. 1857, having by her had issue.
2 RICHARD, now of Dicksgrove.
3. John Robert, b. 6 June, 1813; d. unm. 3 Jan. 1895.
Seat—Dicksgrove, Farranfore, co. Kerry.

METGE OF ATHLUMNEY.

CAPT. ROBERT HENRY METGE, of Athlumney, co. Meath, Capt. late Welsh Regt., b. 15 Dec. 1875.
Lineage.—PETER METGE (or de la Metgeé), of Navan, a Huguenot, who left France and settled at Athlumney after the revocation of the Edict of Nantes, was of an old Protestant family possessed of considerable estates in Brittany (the name was originally spelled " de la Metgeé," but the final e has been dropped by later generations). His will, dated 17 Nov. 1733, was proved 21 Feb. 1735, He m. Joyce Hatch (d. 23 Jan. 1735, aged 60), and d. 1 Feb. 1735, aged 70, having had issue,
1. PETER, his heir.
1. A dau., m. William Thompson, of Clonfin, co. Longford (see that family).
2. Martha, m. Thomas Barry.
3. Anne, m. (setts. dated 22 and 23 June, 1737), Robert Beatty, of Coolnorty, co. Longford, who d. 15 Dec. 1754, leaving issue.
4. Joyce. m. — Dalton.
His only son,
PETER METGE, of Athlumney, d. 29 Oct. 1774, will dated 27 June, 1772, proved 22 Feb. 1777; m. Anne Lyon, of the Strathmore family, and by her had, with eight daus., four sons,
1. PETER. 2. JOHN.
3. Daniel Augustus, d. July, 1779.
4. Ludlow
1. Mary, m. 21 Sept. 1764, Rev. Richard Barry.
2. Jane, m. 19 Oct. 1771, Thomas Bowater.
3. ——, m. Thomas Barry.
4. Hester, m. Nov. 1789, William Henry Clayton Cowell.
5. Joyce, m. Dec. 1774, Rev. Mark Foster.
6. Isabella, m. Maurice Neligan.
7. Martha, m. 1791, George O'Reilly.
8. Christiana, m. 1st, 7 June, 1775, John Rogers; 2ndly, 1787, George Bartley.
The elder son,
PETER METGE, Baron of the Exchequer, M.P. for Boyle, m. Sophia Jane, 2nd dau. of Sir Marcus Lowther Crofton, Bart., and by her (who d. Dec. 1777) had an only son, Peter, b. 9 Sept. 1777, who d.v.p., unm. March, 1794, and a dau., who d. unm., and was s. by his brother,
JOHN METGE, of Athlumney, Navan, and Warrenstown, Dunboyne, Capt. 4th Dragoons, M.P. for Dundalk in the Irish Parliament, and for Boyle in the Imperial Parliament, and Deputy Auditor-General of the Irish Treasury. He m. 1st, Aug. 1777, Hon. Mary, widow of Edmund Costello, dau. of Francis, 21st Baron of Athenry, s.p. By his 2nd wife, Henrietta, dau. of Henry Cole Bowen, of Bowen's Court (see that family), he had issue,
1. PETER PONSONBY, of Athlumney.
2. John Charles, of Sion, m. Eliza Ibbetson, dau. of Henry Cole, of Twickenham, and d. 1870, having by her (who d. 1896) had (see COLE of Stoke Lyne) issue,
1. John Owen, dec.
2. Francis Burton, of Ladywell, Athlone, co. Westmeath, and Dardistown, Killucan, co. Westmeath, m. Anne, eldest dau. of Henry Cole Bowen, and by her (who d. 1897) has issue,
(1) Charles, b. 1871. (2) John.
(3) Hearty (twin).
(1) Anne. (2) Henrietta Cole.
(3) Frances Burton (twin).
3. PETER PONSONBY, now of Rathkea, co. Tipperary (Killinure, co. Westmeath), m. Julia, dau. of W. Westropp Brereton, Q.C., and has issue,
(1) Peter Ponsouby, d. 1906.
(1) Geraldine. (2) Janet Lyon.
(3) Henrietta Ibbetson.
4. Robert Henry, late of Athlumney.
1. Elizabeth Ibbetson Cole.
2. Henrietta Cole, m. 31 March, 1874, George Charles Mulock, of Kilnagarna, King's Co., and had issue, one son and three daus. (see that family).
3. Louisa Charlotte, m. J. Preston Walsh, late 38th Regt.

Miller. THE LANDED GENTRY. 478

3. Robert Henry, dec.
1. Louisa Cole, *m.* Rev. Robert Thompson, of Greenmount, Rector of Navan, dec. (see THOMPSON *of Rathnally*).
2. Isabella, dec.
The eldest son,
PETER PONSONBY METGE, of Athlumney, Navan, co. Meath, *d.s.p.* 10 Nov. 1873, and was *s.* by his nephew,
ROBERT HENRY METGE, of Athlumney, co. Meath, J.P., LL.B., Barrister-at-Law, M.P. co. Meath 1880-4, *b.* 1850; *m.* 1stly, 1874, Frances Thomasina Virginia, dau. of the Rev. Charles Lambart, Rector of Navan, son of Gustavus Lambart, of Beauparc (*see* BURKE'S *Peerage*, CAVAN, E.) and by her (who *d.* 1891) had issue,
  1. ROBERT HENRY, now of Athlumney.
  2. Pierre Ponsonby, *b.* 1878; *m.* Nancy Graves, and has issue.
  3. Radulphe Cole, late Lieut. 5th Batt. Leinster Regt., *b.* 1881.
  4. Selwyn Ibbetson Cole, *b.* 1886.
  5. Noel Cole, *d.* 1887.
  6. Francis Charles Cole, *b.* 1889.
  1. Virginia Maria Frances Cole.
  2. Louisa Charlotte Cole, *m.* 23 March, 1904, Major Richard William Everard, only son of Col. Sir Nugent Talbot Everard, 1st Bart. of Randalestown, co. Meath, and has issue (*see* BURKE'S *Peerage*).
  3. Eileen Mary Cole, *m.* Edward Emanuel Lennon, M.D., F.R.C.P.I., of Merrion Square, Dublin, and has issue.
  4. Ethel Cole.
  5. May Cole, *m.* Capt. Murray Trant Elderton, and has issue.
  6. Edith Cole, *m.* Walter Montgomery Nielson, of Queenshill, Kirkcudbrightshire.
  7. Gladys Ibbetson Cole, *m.* 3 Aug. 1910, Major W. F. Sweny, of 7th Fus., son of Col. Sweny, of Toronto, Canada.
He *m.* 2ndly, 1892, Lilian Margaret, only dau. of Richard Combridge Grubb, of Cabir Abbey, co. Tipperary (*see* GRUBB *of Ardmayle*), and *d.* 19 Sept. 1900, having by her had issue,
  8. Lilian Gwendaline Cole.   9. Dorothy Elise Cole.

Seat—Athlumney, Kilcairne, co. Meath.

MILLER OF MILFORD AND BLINDWELL.

The late ORMSBY BOWEN-MILLER, of Milford, co. Mayo, and Blindwell, co. Galway, B.A. Trin. Coll. Dublin, J.P. and D.L. for co. Mayo, High Sheriff 1892 and 1893, and J.P. co. Galway, *b.* 18 May, 1832; *m.* 1st, 26 Nov. 1884, Elizabeth Mira, dau. of Gen. William Irwin, of St. Catherine's Park, co. Kildare, which lady *d.s.p.* 14 Jan. 1886. He *m.* 2ndly, 25 April, 1890, Monica Mary (*now of Blindwell*), dau. of Oliver Dolphin, of Turoe, co. Galway, and widow of Thomas Staunton Kirwan, D.L., of Blindwell, co. Galway, and *d.s.p.* 8 April, 1910.

Lineage.—ROBERT MILLER, of Ballycushion, co. Mayo, *b.* 1618, having joined the Parliamentary Forces, went to Ireland, under CROMWELL'S command, where he settled at Ballycushion. There is a tradition that CROMWELL, on his return to England, sent Mr. Miller an original picture of himself in oil, which is now at Milford. Mr. Miller and his son Robert contributed to the success of WILLIAM III's army at Aughrim, carrying on negotiations with Sir John Bingham, who, at the crisis of the battle, deserted JAMES II, and passed over with his regiment of horse to the enemy. Robert Miller, senior, served as High Sheriff of Mayo 1681, 1693, and 1695. He *m.* Rebecca Gonne, of Farmhill, co. Mayo, and *d.* 1698, leaving by her (who *d.* 1703),
  ROBERT, of Milford.
  Lettice, *m.* James Stirling.
The son,
ROBERT MILLER, of Milford, High Sheriff 1703, *m.* 1697, Sarah, dau. of John Bingham, of Newbrook, co. Mayo, and had issue,
  1. ROBERT, of Milford.
  2. James, of Ballynew, *m.* Anne, dau. and co-heir of Thomas Croasdaile, of Cloghstoken, co. Galway.
  3. Gilbert, of Dowias, Queen's Co.
  4. John.
  1. Dorothy, *m.* 1st, — Palmer, of Palmerstown, co. Mayo; and 2ndly, 1723, Thomas Cox.
  2. A dau., *m.* Major-Gen. Owen Wynne, of Hazlewood, co. Sligo, who *d.s.p.* 28 Feb. 1737.

3. Sarah, *m.* Thomas Lindsey.
He *d.* 1718, and was *s.* by his eldest son,
ROBERT MILLER, of Milford, who *m.* 1710, Jane, 3rd dau. and co-heir of Thomas Croasdaile, of Cloghstoken, co. Galway, and had issue,
  1. ROBERT, of Milford.
  2. CROASDAILE, heir to his brother.
  1. Mercy, *d. unm.*
The elder son,
ROBERT MILLER, of Milford, High Sheriff co. Mayo 1735, dying *unm.* 1747, was *s.* by his brother,
CROASDAILE MILLER, High Sheriff 1750 and 1756, who *m.* 28 Feb. 1756, Anne, 5th dau. of Sir John Bingham, Bart., and sister of Charles, 1st Earl of Lucan, and *d.* 1783, having by her (who *d.* 1782) had issue,
  1. ROBERT, *d. unm.*   2. GEORGE, of Milford.
  3. CROASDAILE CHARLES, subsequently of Milford.
  1. Elizabeth, *m.* 1800, Christopher Bowen, and *d.* 1815, having by him (who *d.* 1828) had issue,
    1. Christopher (Rev.) (*see* BOWEN *of Hollymount*).
    2. CROASDAILE, of whom presently.
    3. Charles, *m.* Georgina, dau. of Joseph Lambert, of Brookhill, co. Mayo, and *d.* 1871, leaving issue.
    4. Robert, *m.* Jane, dau. of — Courtenay, of Dromselk, co. Down, and *d.* 1881, leaving issue.
    5. William, *d. unm.*   6. Edward, *d. unm.* 1873.
    1. Anne, *d. unm.* 1876.
    2. Elizabeth Louisa, *d. unm.* 1834.
  2. Marcia, *m.* Rev. A. Wilson, of Milbrook.
The 2nd son,
GEORGE MILLER, of Milford, Lieut.-Col. 7th Dragoon Guards, dying *unm.* 1808, was *s.* by his next brother,
CROASDAILE CHARLES MILLER, of Milford, Brig.-Gen., *b.* 1772; *m.* Anne Jones, but *d.s.p.* in Portugal 1811, and was *s.* by his nephew,
CROASDAILE BOWEN, who assumed, by Royal Licence, dated 1 Feb. 1812, the additional surname and arms of MILLER. He was *b.* 1802, and *m.* 22 Oct. 1828, Catherine Anne, 2nd dau. of Thomas Ormsby, of Knockmore, co. Mayo, and by her (who *d.* 1896) had issue,
  1. CROASDAILE CHARLES, of whom presently.
  2. ORMSBY, now of Milford.
  1. Anne, *m.* 1851, John Yeadon Ormsby, of Ballinamore, co. Mayo, and has issue, 1. Anthony; 2. Charles Croasdaile; 3. John Yeadon; 4. George; 5. Thomas; 1. Anne; 2. Kate; 3. Isabel; 4. Elizabeth; 5. Edith.
  2. Elizabeth, *m.* Mark Perrin, of Knockdromin, co. Dublin, son of the Right Hon. Mr. Justice Perrin.
  3. Catherine.
  4. Croasdailla, *m.* Rev. John William Burke, of Brampton, Huntingdon (*see* BURKE *of Ballydugan*).
Mr. Bowen Miller *d.* 19 April, 1837, and was *s.* by his elder son,
CROASDAILE CHARLES BOWEN-MILLER, of Milford, J.P. and D.L., High Sheriff 1870, *b.* 1829; *d. unm.* 14 March, 1880, and was *s.* by his brother,
ORMSBY BOWEN-MILLER, late of Milford.

Arms—Quarterly: 1st and 4th, erm., three wolves' heads erased az., for MILLER; 2nd and 3rd, gu., a stag trippant arg., pierced in the back with an arrow and attired or, for BOWEN. Crests—1st, A wolf's head erased, as in the arms, for MILLER; 2nd, A falcon close ppr., belled or, for BOWEN. Motto—Nil conscire sibi.

Seats—Milford, Hollymount. co. Mayo; and Blindwell, Tuam, co. Galway.

MILWARD OF TULLOGHER.

CLEMENT ARCHER JOHN MILWARD, of Tullogher. co. Kilkenny, *b.* 1905; *s.* his father 1908.

Lineage.—CLEMENT MILWARD, of Alvechurch, co. Worcester, a Capt. in the Parliamentary Army, and one of the Committee of Parliament who came to Worcester, upon the surrender thereof 25 July, 1646. He was possessed of lands in the Manor of Alvechurch, as a copyholder under the Bishop of Worcester, *temp.* CHARLES II. He settled in co. Wexford; *m.* Elizabeth, dau. of William Plunkett, and had issue,
  1. CLEMENT, of Dublin, who *s.* to his father's estates in cos. Worcester and Wexford, and *m.* Anne, dau. of George Stowall but *d.s.p.* By his will, dated 5 Dec. 1707, and proved 21 Oct. 1709, he devised his property to his wife for life, with remainder to his next brother.
  2. THOMAS, who carried on the line.
  1. Elizabeth, *m.* Aug. 1697, Henry Archer of Ballyhoge.
  2. Winifred, *m.* March, 1698, Gervaise Clifford.
  3. Margaret, *m.* Dec. 1799, William Gifford, of Polemaloe, and *d.* 4 May, 1718.
Mr. Milward acquired considerable estates in the cos. of Wicklow and at Enniscorthy and Ballyharran, co. Wexford, and left them by his will, dated 12 Nov. 1694, and proved 6 Feb. 1697, to his eldest son. His 2nd son,
THOMAS MILWARD, of Ballyharran, co. Wexford, *s.* to the estates at the death *s.p.* of his elder brother. He *m.* 1st, Oct. 1696, Hannah Smith, by whom he had no issue; and 2ndly, July, 1697, Sarah Wellman, heiress of Tullogher, co. Kilkenny, by whom he had issue.

1. Clement, b. 4 July, 1702 ; d.s.p. in Africa, June, 1722.
2. William, b. 15 Aug. 1703 ; d.s.p. in Africa, June, 1722.
3. Henry, his heir.
4. John, b. 14 Oct. 1713.
1. Elizabeth, b. 20 April, 1698.
2. Sarah, b. 6 June, 1699.
3. Anne, b. 16 Sept. 1700.
4. Lucy, b. 4 July, 1705.
5. Winifred, b. 20 Oct. 1707 ; m. Rickard Donovan, of Clonmore, who d. 1781.
6. Anne, b. 20 May, 1715.
7. Mary, b. 16 June, 1716.

Mr. Milward, whose will was dated 1 May, proved 25 Aug. 1731. was s. by his eldest surviving son,

HENRY MILWARD, of Ballyharran, b. 25 Oct. 1711 ; m. 20 Dec. 1734, Beata, dau. of James Webb, Dublin, and had issue,
1. HENRY, his heir.
2. Thomas, b. 23 Nov. 1744.
1. Sarah, b. 2 March, 1737.
2. Beata, b. 4 June, 1740.
3. Elizabeth, b. 9 Oct. 1741 ; m. Henry Archer, of Ballyseskin, and d. 1829.

Mr. Milward d. Aug. 1758, and was s. by his son,
HENRY MILWARD, of Ballyharran, b. 5 March, 1742 ; m. June, 1767, Elizabeth, dau. of Henry Archer, of Ballyseskin, and had issue,
1. HENRY, his successor.
2. Thomas, b. 20 July, 1774 ; d. unm.
3. CLEMENT, who s. his brother.
1. Beata, b. 22 Sept. 1769, m. Christopher Hore Hatchell.
2. Elizabeth, b. 1 Feb. 1773.
3. Lettice, b. 7 Oct. 1775.
4. Sarah, b. 1777.

Mr. Milward d. 18 Dec. 1777, and was s. by his eldest son,
HENRY MILWARD, of Ballyharran, J.P., Major Wexford Militia, b. 4 March, 1772 ; m. 1812, Miss Elizabeth Cooth Whitmarsh, of Bath, and d.s.p. at Southampton, 1842, when he was s. by his only surviving brother,
CLEMENT MILWARD, of Tullogher, co. Kilkenny, Rear Admiral R.N., b. 7 Sept. 1776 ; m. 1816, Elizabeth, dau. of Charles Dawson, of Charlesfort. co. Wexford, and grand-dau. of Walter Dawson, of Clare Castle, co. Armagh (see BURKE'S Peerage, DARTREY, E.), by whom (who d. 1854) he had issue,
1. Henry (Rev.), Rector of Rodney Stoke, Somerset, Rural Dean and Prebendary of Wells Cathedral, m. 1st, Jan. 1846, Eliza Anne (dec.), dau. of Rev. John Pedder, of Churchtown, co. Lancaster, and d. 5 May, 1876, leaving three daus.,
1. Eliza Margaret.
2. Anne Maria.
3. Jane Deborah.
2. Charles Richard, B.A. Trin. Coll. Dublin, and Proctor of the Ecclesiastical and Admiralty Courts in Ireland ; d. unm. Jan. 1848.
3. CLEMENT, of Alice Holt.
4. Thomas Walter ,C.B., Lieut.-Col. R.A., and Col. in the Army, Aide-de-Camp to Queen Victoria, b. 18 June, 1825 ; m. 24 June, 1852, Olivia Maria, dau. of David Beatty, of Penzance, co. Wexford, and d. 31 Dec. 1874, leaving by her (who d. 5 Nov. 1887) issue,
1. CLEMENT HENRY, of Tullogher.
2. Frederick David, Major Lancashire Fusiliers, b. 10 Sept. 1862 ; m. 5 Dec. 1899, Evelyn Maude, dau. of H. Hilton, of London.
3. Arthur Dawson, b. 13 July, 1865.
4. Thomas Walter, Capt. Essex Regt., b. 10 April, 1867, served in S. Africa, and wounded at Paardeberg, d. unm. 10 May, 1900.
5. Harry Dacres, Major Worcester Regt., b. 1 July, 1871.
1. Elizabeth Mary.
2. Anne Olivia.
3. Clementina Blanche.
5. William, b. 12 March, 1827 ; d. unm.
6. DAWSON ARCHER, of whom presently.
1. Deborah Elizabeth, d. unm.
2. Anna Louisa, d. unm 7 Jan. 1907.

Admiral Milward d. 1857.
CLEMENT MILWARD, of Alice Holt, co. Southampton, of the Middle Temple, Barrister-at-Law, Q.C., b. 20 Aug. 1821 ; m. 8 May, 1856, Elizabeth Jane, only dau. and heir of John Pearson, of Ulverston, and has a dau.,
MARY ELIZA, m. 22 Nov. 1882, Lieut.-Col. Richard Knox, 13th Hussars, eldest son of Lieut.-Col. Richard Knox (see KNOX of Grace Dieu), and has issue,
Clement Uchter, b. 27 Feb. 1890.

Mr. Milward d. Nov. 1890. His brother,
DAWSON ARCHER MILWARD, of Tullogher, and Lavistown, co. Kilkenny, J.P., b. 8 May, 1829 ; s. 1890 ; d.s.p. 11 Sept. 1897.
MAJOR CLEMENT HENRY MILWARD, of Tullogher, co. Kilkenny, Major R.A., b. 8 Oct. 1860 ; m. 12 Oct. 1893, Louise Mary, dau. of the late John Yardley, of Chesterfield, Lichfield, and d. 4 July, 1908, leaving issue, an only son,
CLEMENT ARCHER JOHN MILWARD, now of Tullogher.

Seat—Tullogher, co. Kilkenny. Residence—The Old House, Kibworth, Leicestershire ; 4, Priory Grove, The Boltons, London, S.W.

MINCHIN OF ANNAGH.

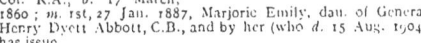

FALKINER JOHN MINCHIN, of Annagh, co. Tipperary, and Holywell, Hants, Lord of the Manor of Soberton, J.P. co. Tipperary, M.A. Trin. Coll. Dublin, b. 15 Nov. 1831 ; m. 1st, 15 July, 1858, Margaret Mary Anne, eldest dau. of William Adams Reilly, of Belmont, Mullingar, co. Westmeath. She d. 1888, having had issue,
1. William Reilly, Capt. late Queen's Own Royal West Kent Regt., b. 2 May, 1859 ; d.s.p. 11 Sept. 1909.
2. FREDERICK FALKINER, Col. R.A., b. 17 March, 1860 ; m. 1st, 27 Jan. 1887, Marjorie Emily, dau. of General Henry Dyett Abbott, C.B., and by her (who d. 15 Aug. 1904) has issue,
1. Henry Falkiner, Lieut. R.N., b. 5 Feb. 1889.
2. Frederick Frank, 2nd Lieut. Connaught Rangers, b. 16 June, 1890.
1. Violet Marjorie, b. 7 Dec. 1887.
He m. 2ndly, 20 Sept. 1905, Caroline Jane Royds, dau. of John Lloyd, of Astwick Manor, Hatfield, Herts, and has issue,
3. Richard Humphry Lloyd, b. 15 Feb. 1907.
2. Margaret Doreen, b. 8 May, 1910.
1. Helen Frances Georgina, m. June, 1883, William Trumperant Potts, J.P., of Correen Castle, co. Roscommon, and has issue.
2. Minnie, m. Sept. 1895, Harry Lefroy, of Killaloe.
3. Georgina Louisa, m. Sept. 1890, John Cecil Bruce, C.E., of Lesseragh, co. Tipperary, and has issue.

He m. 2ndly, 26 Sept. 1893, Louisa Margaret, dau. of Rev. Samuel Forbes Auchmuty, late Rector of Blunsdon, Wilts.

Lineage.—CHARLES MINCHIN,* of Moneygall, Capt. in the Parliamentary army, purchased the Annagh estate from Maj. Solomon Cambie 1669, and the Ballinakill estate from Sir R. Stephens 1680. He m. the sister of Col. Walcott, of Croagh, co. Limerick (who was executed for his share in the Rye House Plot). He d. 1681 (will proved 18 Nov. 1681), leaving issue,
1. Thomas, of Busherstown, King's Co., b. 1658 ; d. 1686 ; m. 1680, Elizabeth, dau. of Hon. Richard Butler, by Anne, dau. of Edward Wolley, Bishop of Clonfert, and left three daus.,
1. Ann, m. Archdeacon Thomas Parnell, D.D., the poet.
2. Jane, m. William Broughton.
3. Elizabeth, m. Butler Townshend.
2. Humphrey, of Ballinakill, and afterwards of Busherstown, King's Co., M.P. for co. Tipperary, temp. WILLIAM III., High Sheriff co. Tipperary 1696, b. 1660 ; m. Rebecca, dau. of Joshua Paul, of Bogh, co. Carlow. His will was proved 30 Sept. 1733. He had issue,
(1) Humphrey, of Ballinakill, which he sold, and purchased Holywell, Soberton, Hants, obtained private Acts of Parliament, 11 and 12 GEORGE III., to sell portions of his private property, M.P. for Tipperary in the Irish Parliament and afterwards M.P. for Okehampton in the English Parliament 1751 and 1772 and for Boisseny and Tintagel 1790-96, Col. of the North Hants Militia ; m. 4 Aug. 1750, Clarinda, dau. of George Cuppaidge, of Dublin, and d. 1796, leaving issue,
1. Paul, Admiral, R.N., of Holywell, m. Mary, dau. of H. Dalrymple, of North Berwick, and d.s.p.
2. Spencer, Lieut. R.N., killed in battle of Copenhagen, d.s.p.
3. George, d.s.p.
4. Henry, of Holywell, m. 1st, 1796, Elizabeth, elder dau. of John Guitton, of Little Park, Hants. She d. 1813, leaving issue,
a. Henry James Bunbury, of Holywell, d.s.p. 1869, leaving his English estates to his nephew, the present FALKINER JOHN MINCHIN, of Annagh.
b. Champneys (Rev.), m. Ellen, dau. of Thomas Oshorne, of Southampton, and d. 188c, leaving issue,
(a) Ellen, m. 1865, Capt. C. E. Sheriff, Indian Army, and has issue,
(b) Eliza Caroline.
(c) Maria Frederica.
(d) Julia.

* Charles Minchin had a brother Ambrose Minchin, whose four daus. m. respectively David Cambie, Boyle Minchin, William Hingsdoll, and William Lane. He had also three sisters, who m. respectively Edward Parry, of Limerick ; Joseph Pike, of Cork ; and Oliver Newhouse, of Kilkerran, co. Tipperary.

Minchin. THE LANDED GENTRY. 480

 c. Frederic Calder, Col. 67th Bengal N.I., *d.s.p.* 1871.
 a. Harriet, *m.* S. S. Taylor, of Upham, Hants.
 b. Fanny, *m.* Rev. J. Kelly.
 c. Georgina, *m.* 1829, William Minchin, of Annagh, who *d.* 1843, leaving issue (*see below*).
 d. Louisa, *d. unm.*
 e. Caroline, *m.* Rev. R. Clarke, of Geashill, King's Co. Mr. Henry Minchin *m.* 2ndly, Edith Maitland, who *d.s.p.*; and 3rdly, Caroline Mackett, by whom he had issue,
  d. Charles, Lieut. 88th Regt., *d.s.p.*
  f. Emily, *m.* Jonathan Clarke.
  g. Maria, *m.* Capt. John King, of Warnford, Hants.
 1. Henrietta, *m.* Sir T. Champneys, Bart. of Exton.
 2. Georgina, *m.* T. Smith, of Southampton.
 3. Louisa, *m.* John J. Pigou, of Ham Common, Surrey.
 (2) Paul, *d.s.p.*
 (1) Rebecca, *m.* Nov. 1760, Daniel Toler, of Beechwood, co. Tipperary, M.P. She *d.* Sept. 1800. He *d.* June, 1790, leaving issue (*see* BURKE's *Peerage*, NORBURY, E.).
 (2) Elizabeth, *m.* Rev. C. Woodward.
2. HUMPHREY, of Busherstown, ancestor of Minchin of Busherstown (*see that family*).
3. George, Capt. H.E.I.C.S., *m.* Jane, dau. of Rev. J. Hemsworth, and left
 Harriet, *m.* Dec. 1774, William Woodward, of Cloghprior, co. Tipperary.
 1. Rebecca, *m.* 1717, John Carden, of Templemore (*see* BURKE's *Peerage*, CARDEN, Bart.).
 2. Anne, *m.* 1733, Thomas Bernard, of Ratho, co. Carlow.
 3. Sarah, *m.* 1738, J. Anderson, of Dublin.
 4. Sophia, *m.* 1737, Benjamin Hobart, of Carlow.
3. Charles, *d.s.p.*
4. JOHN, of whom presently.
5. William, of Greenhills, whose descendants are settled in New Zealand (*see* BURKE's *Colonial Gentry*).
6. Edward, of Glenahilly, had issue, a son,
 Walcot, *m.* Jane, dau. of John Stoyte, of Street, co. Westmeath, and had issue,
  Charles, *m.* Elizabeth, dau. of Hugh Massy, of Stoneville, co. Limerick, Town Major-Comm. of Police, and had issue, Humphrey, *b.* 9 Nov. 1750; *d.* 15 June, 1830; *m.* 14 Jan. 1775, Frances Catherine, dau. of Major Joseph Sirr, Town Major of Dublin 1762-7, and sister of Major Henry Charles Sirr, Town Major of Dublin 1796-1827. He left issue,
   Francis Joseph, of Woodville, co. Tipperary, Castle Kelly, co. Kilkenny, and Fitzwilliam Square, Dublin, *b.* 29 Oct. 1780; *d.* 13 May, 1836; *m.* 22 May, 1804, his cousin Louisa Elizabeth Frances, dau. of Major William Hall, Town Major of Dublin 1771, and had issue,
    Henry Charles (Rev.), M.A., of Woodville and Castle Kelly, Vicar of St. Mary de Lode, Gloucester, *b.* 26 Nov. 1811; *d.* 16 Aug. 1881; *m.* 23 April, 1851, Anne Jane, elder dau. of John Jones, M.R.C.S., R.N., and by her (who *d.* 22 Nov. 1901) had issue,
    1. Charles Humphrey (Rev.), Rector of Bladon and Woodstock, Domestic Chaplain to the Duke of Marlborough, *b.* 26 April, 1855; *m.* 2 Nov. 1893, Susan Dowding.
    2. Hugh Dillon Massy, Lieut.-Col. Indian Army, *b.* 26 Nov. 1857; *d.* 16 July, 1904; *m.* 5 Sept. 1889, Caroline Frances Stephens Loder, and had issue,
     (1) Hubert Charles Loder, Lieut. Indian Army, *b.* 16 July, 1890.
     (2) Hugh Charles Stephens, *b.* 4 Feb. 1893.
     (3) Reginald Humphrey.
    3. Harry Christopher Montague, M.A. Oxon (*Gorsedene, Farnham*), *b.* 26 Dec. 1861; *m.* 4 Oct. 1904, Olivia Juliana, dau. of Rear-Adm. Reginald Yorke (*see* BURKE's *Peerage*, HARDWICKE, E.).
    1. Louise Henrietta Eden, *m.* 20 Feb. 1879, James George Frederick Hughes-Bonsall, of Glanrheidol, Cardiganshire, J.P., D.L., and has issue.
1. Anne, *m.* Edward Ross, of Clondelaw, co. Clare.
2. Jane, *m.* Richard Bourke, LL.D., of Palmerston, co. Kildare (*see* BURKE's *Peerage*, MAYO, E.).

The 4th son,
JOHN MINCHIN, of Annagh, co. Tipperary, High Sheriff 1733, *m.* 1699, Penelope, dau. of Joseph Cuffe, of Castle Inch, co. Kilkenny (*see* BURKE's *Peerage*, DESART, E.), and left issue,
 1. CHARLES, his heir.
 2. Humphrey, of Inch, *m.* 1737, Anne, dau. of Alderman Thomas Barnes, of Kilkenny.
 3. John, *m.* Elizabeth, dau. of James Lane, of Killeen, co. Tipperary, and had issue two sons.
 4. Boyle, *m.* the dau. of Ambrose Minchin.
 1. Penelope, *m.* Thomas Minchin.
 2. Jane, *m.* Henry Stotesbury, of Ballydoole, co. Kilkenny.
 3. Mary, *m.* Michael Lewis.
The eldest son,
CHARLES MINCHIN, of Annagh, *m.* 1725, Catherine Jane, dau. of John Greene, of Old Abbey, co. Limerick, and was killed in a duel 1736, leaving issue,
 1. JOHN, his heir.
 1. Abigail, *m.* Edward Lloyd, of Eyon, co. Limerick.
 2. Anne, *m.* Francis Sergeant.
 3. Penelope, *m.* Christopher Carr, of Limerick.
The only son,

JOHN MINCHIN, of Annagh, *m.* 20 March, 1755, Caroline, dau. of Caleb Falkiner, and sister of Sir Riggs Falkiner, 1st Bart. (*see* BURKE's *Peerage*), and left issue,
 1. Charles, Capt. 27th Regt., *d.s.p.*
 2. FALKINER, of whom presently.
 3. Frederick Boyle.
 4. Edward, Lieut. R.N., *m.* Elizabeth, niece of Sir John Wentworth, Governor of Nova Scotia.
 5. George, Capt. 85th Regt., *d.s.p.*
 1. Mary, *m.* T. Moore. 2. Caroline, *m.* J. Weekes.
 3. Catherine, *m.* Guy Luther.
The 2nd son,
FALKINER MINCHIN, of Annagh, Capt. 27th Regt., *b.* 1757; *m.* 1786, Maria, dau. of William Gabbett, of Caherline, co. Limerick, and *d.* 1825, having had issue,
 1. JOHN, of Annagh, *d.s.p.*
 2. WILLIAM, of whom presently.
 3. Charles (Rev.), *d.s.p.*
 1. Jane, *m.* Daniel Litton, of Dublin.
 2. Caroline, *m.* Rev. Maurice FitzGerald Hewson
 3. Maria, *m.* Richard Chadwick.
 4. Catherine, *m.* Daniel Creagh Harnett.
 5. Dora, *m.* Robert Harding.
The 2nd son,
WILLIAM MINCHIN, of Eversham, co. Dublin, *b.* 1793; *m.* 1829, Georgina, dau. of Henry Minchin, of Holywell House, Hants (*see above*). She *d.* 1884. He *d.* 1843, leaving issue,
 1. FALKINER JOHN, now of Annagh and Holywell.
 2. Henry, *d.s.p.*
 3. William Burnet, late R.I.C., *b.* 29 July, 1838.
 4. Frederick Richard, *b.* 30 June, 1840; *m.* 1899, Adelaide Isabella, dau. of Walter Raleigh Trevelyan (*see* BURKE's *Peerage* TREVELYAN, Bart.).
 1. Georgina, *m.* 1858, Edward Thomas Litton, of Dublin.
 2. Clarinda Georgina. 3. Mary Caroline.

Arms—Erm., a chevron with two couple closes gu., between three fleurs-de-lys az. *Crest*—A naked arm embossed, couped at the shoulder, the hand grasping a baton or. *Motto*—Regarde la mort. (The descendants of the late Mrs. Minchin quarter the following arms for Reilly of Belmont, viz., Vert, a dexter hand appaumée, couped at the wrist, dropping blood, supported by two lions rampant or. *Crest*—An oak tree eradicated, entwined by a snake ascendant, all ppr. *Motto*—Fortitudine et prudentia.)

Seats—Annagh, Coolbawn, Borrisokane, co. Tipperary, and Holywell House, Hants.

MINCHIN OF BUSHERSTOWN.

RICHARD MINCHIN MINCHIN, of Busherstown, King's Co., J.P., late Capt. 4th Batt. Royal Irish Regt., *b.* 15 Sept. 1870, assumed the name of MINCHIN under the will of his uncle George John Minchin in 1897; *m.* 20 Dec. 1899, Rebecca Sarah Minchin, only child by his first marriage of Johnston T. Stoney, J.P. of Emell Castle, Cloughjordan, King's Co. (*see* BUTLER-STONEY *of Portland Park*), and has issue,
 1. RICHARD GEORGE EDWARD, *b.* 20 Jan. 1901.
 2. Humphrey Johnstone de Vere, *b.* 30 June, 1908.
 1. Alice Rebecca Winifred, *b.* 1 Feb. 1903.
 2. Aubrey Beatrice de Vere, *b.* 3 Jan. 1905.

Lineage.—HUMPHREY MINCHIN, of Ballynakill, co. Tipperary, and afterwards of Busherstown, King's Co., M.P. co. Tipperary *temp.* WILLIAM III, *b.* 1660, 2nd son of Charles Minchin, of Moneygall, (*see* MINCHIN *of Annagh*), had his armorial bearings entered in Ulster's Office in 1720. He *m.* Rebecca, dau. of Joshua Paul, of Bogh, co. Carlow, and made his will, 30 Sept. 1733. He left with other issue (*see* MINCHIN *of Annagh*), a son,
HUMPHREY MINCHIN, of Busherstown, *m.* 11 June, 1736, Catherine, dau. of Godfrey Greene, of Greeneville, co. Kilkenny (*see that family*), and *d.* Feb. 1777, having had issue, with eight daus.,
 1. JOHN, of Busherstown.
 2. Humphrey. 3. Paul.
 4. Joshua. 5. George.
His eldest son,
JOHN MINCHIN, of Busherstown, High Sheriff of King's Co. 1768, *m.* Miss Ellard, and had issue,
 1. Richard, Capt. of Dragoons, *d. unm.*
 2. GEORGE, of Busherstown.
 1. Rebecca, *m.* William Minchin, of Greenhills, co. Tipperary, and had issue (*see* BURKE's *Colonial Gentry*).
His 2nd son,
GEORGE MINCHIN, of Busherstown, High Sheriff of King's Co. 1828, *b.* 1784; *m.* Elizabeth Agnes, dau. of John Studdert, D.L., of Elm Hill, co. Limerick, by whom (who *d.* 1863) he had issue,
JOHN, his heir.
Alicia, *m.* 1867, Edward Eyre Maunsell, of Fort Eyre, co. Galway (*see* MAUNSELL *of Limerick*).
The only son,
JOHN MINCHIN, of Busherstown, J.P., an Officer 48th Regt., *b.* 1814; *m.* 1842, Anne, dau. of Robert Hall, of Innismore Hall, co. Fermanagh, and Merton Hall, co. Tipperary, and *d.* 1851 having had issue,

1. GEORGE JOHN, of whom presently.
1. Elizabeth Agnes, *m.* 1863, Richard J. Gabbett, J.P., of Caherline House, co. Limerick (*see that family*).
2. Alice Anne, *m.* 1868, Major R. T. Welch, J.P. of Monkstown Park, co. Dublin, son of R. Welch, of Monkstown Castle, and by him (who *d.* 1902) has issue, with four daus., two sons,
  1. RICHARD MINCHIN, now of Busherstown.
  2. George Cecil de Vere.
is only son,
GEORGE JOHN MINCHIN, of Busherstown, King's Co., J.P. and .L., High Sheriff for that co. 1870, and J.P. for cos. Tipperary and Limerick, educated at Trin. Coll. Dublin, B.A. 1867, M.A. 1875, *b.* 1 April, 1845; *m.* 15 June, 1876, Edith Margaret (who *m.* 2ndly 1 Aug. 1906, Major Henry Sheil, late R.A.), elder dau. and co-heiress of Benjamin Bunbury Frend, of Boskell, co. Limerick, and grand-niece of Field-Marshal Hugh, 1st Viscount Gough, and *s.p.* 16 Aug. 1897, and was *s.* by his nephew Richard Welch, who has assumed the name of MINCHIN.

Seat—Busherstown, Dunkerrin, Roscrea.

MINNITT OF ANNAGHBEG.

CHARLES FREDERICK ROBERT MINNITT, of Annaghbeg, *b.* 9 Aug. 1869; *m.* 1 Aug. 1908, Winifred May, dau. of Thomas Buddle, of Auckland, New Zealand.

Lineage.—The founder of the Irish branch of the Minnitt family was
CAPT. JOHN MINNITT, of Mount Minnitt, co. Limerick. He *m.* and had issue, The elder son,
ROBERT MINNITT, of Knygh Castle, Blackfort, and Annaghbeg, all co. Tipperary, *m.* Jane, dau. of John Kent, of Poleran, co. Kilkenny, Collector of Waterford, and had issue,
1. Caleb, murdered at Cranagh Duffe, Dowhara, 2 April, 1707, *d.s.p.*
2. JOHN, of Ballyallow, Annaghbeg, and Carny, co. Tipperary, Capt. in the Army, *b.* 1695; *m.* 1713, Mary, dau. of James Gubbins, of Kilfrush, co. Limerick, and had a son and three daus.,
   1. JAMES, of Ballyallow and Annaghbeg, *d. unm.*
   1. Mary, *m.* 1743, George Hastings, of Ballyvalley, co. Clare.
   2. Eliza, *m.* her cousin John Cardeu, of Coolrue and Killard.
   3. Jane, *m.* 1st, Mr. Carr, of Limerick; 2ndly, Zachariah Ledger, of Terryglass, co. Tipperary; and 3rdly, Isaac Jacques.
3. ROBERT, of whom hereafter.
1. Martha, *m.* 1694, Richard Powell, of Newgarden, co. Limerick.
2. Hannah, *b.* 1681; *m.* 1700, Charles Atkins, eldest son and heir of Richard Atkins, of Currakerry West, co. Cork.
3. Abigail, *b.* 1685, *m.* 1707, Edward Despard, of Cranagh, Queen's Co., eldest son of William Despard, of Coolbally.
4. Grace, *b.* 1688, *m.* 1707, Henry Fletcher, of Shannon Hall, co. Tipperary.
Robert Minnitt *d.* 31 May, 1709. His 3rd son,
ROBERT MINNITT, of Knygh and Blackfort, purchased Ballyallow and Annaghbeg from his nephew, James; *b.* 1697, *m.* 1717, Anne, dau. and co-heir of Rev. Paul Ducloss, Rector of Rathdowny, Queen's Co., of an eminent French family, and left at his decease, 1773, five sons and two daus.,
1. PAUL, of Blackfort, *b.* 1720, *d. unm.* 1792.
2. Robert (Rev.), Rector of Tulla, co. Clare, *b.* 1723; *m.* his cousin Eleanor, 2nd dau. of William Devereux, of Deerpark, co. Clare, by Margaret, eldest dau. of Robert Atkins, of Fountainville, co. Cork, and *d.* 27 Jan. 1783, having by her (who *d.* 1777 or 1778) had issue, a son, Robert, who *d.* young, and a dau. and heir,
  Anne, of Blackfort, who *m.* 1806, William Fitzgerald, of Adrival, co. Kerry, Barrister-at-Law.
3. Caleb, *b.* 1728, *m.* 1761, his cousin Elizabeth, dau. of John Carden, of Killard, and had issue.
4. John, *b.* 1730, *m.* 1772, Miss Harding, of Clonlea, and *d.* 1782, having had issue,
   1. Paul, settled in Van Diemen's Land, *b.* 1774, *m.* Debora Fletcher, and *d.* about 1840, leaving with four daus.,
     David Fletcher, *b.* 1824, *m.* Georgina McKee.
   2. William, *b.* 1777, *m.* the dau. of John Palmer, of Glanacurragh Castle, King's Co. and *d.* 1841, leaving with other issue, John Robert Minnitt, Barrister-at-Law, *b.* 1817, *d.* 1886.
5. JOSHUA, of Annaghbeg.
1. Margaret Martha, *m.* William Molloy, of Dove Hill, King's Co.
2. Abigail, *m.* Robert Molloy, of Streamstown.
The 5th son,
JOSHUA MINNITT, of Annaghbeg, *b.* 29 March, 1734; *m.* 1776, Anna, dau. of George Tuthill, of Faha, co. Limerick, and had issue. Mr. Minnitt *d.* 5 June, 1778, and was *s.* by his son,
JOSHUA MINNITT, of Annaghbeg, *b.* 1 Jan. 1778; *m.* 1805, Mary Toler, dau. and co-heir of Capt. Nicholas Toler Kingsley, 8th Regt., and by her (who *d.* 1852) had issue,
1. JOSHUA ROBERT, his heir.
2. George Powell, *d. unm.* 1830.
3. William Hastings, *m.* Araminta, dau. of Rev. James Metge, and *d.* 25 Dec. 1878, leaving one surviving dau.
4. Edmund, *b.* 1820, *m.* 1854, Eliza, dau. of Capt. Robert Rowan, and left one son and four daus.
5. John Christopher, Capt. 31st Regt., *b.* 1823, *m.* 1st, 1847, Dora Jones, and by her (who *d.* 1851) had two sons; and 2ndly,

I.L.G.

1853, Mary, dau. of John Baldwin, of Clay House, Halifax, co. York, and by her had two sons and three daus. He *d.* 1887.
1. Eliza, *m.* 31 July, 1834, Maurice Studdert, of Lodge, co. Tipperary.
2. Anna, *m.* 30 Sept. 1834, Rev. Robert Willson Rowan, of Mount Davys, co. Antrim, and had issue (*see that family*).
3. Mary, *d. unm.* 1848.
4. Eleanor, *m.* Oct. 1855, William Galwey, son of the Archdeacon of Derry.
Mr. Minnitt *d.* April, 1830, and was *s.* by his eldest son,
JOSHUA ROBERT MINNITT, of Annaghbeg, J.P., *b.* 9 Aug. 1806; *m.* 19 May, 1834, Elizabeth, 3rd dau. of Sir Charles Forster Goring, Bart., of Highden, co. Sussex, and by her (who *d.* 1901) had issue,
1. Joshua Charles, *b.* 1835, *d.* 1836.
2. CHARLES GORING, late of Annaghbeg.
3. Robert, *b.* 1838, *d.* 1839.
4. Joshua Robert, M.B., *b.* 24 May, 1844; *m.* 1880, Katherine Marion, dau. of Capt. Saunders, and by her (who *d.* 1884) had one surviving dau.
5. George Godolphin Caleb, *b.* 6 Feb. 1849; *m.* 1871, Isabella, dau. of W. T. Webb, and has issue, one son and four daus.
1. Mary, *m.* 1879, Robert Standish Wolfe, of South Hill, Nenagh.
2. Elizabeth, *m.* 1872, J. R. Headech, and has issue.
3. Bridget, *d. unm.* 1909.   4. Anna.
Mr. Minnitt *d.* 1882, and was *s.* by his son,
MAJOR CHARLES GORING MINNITT, of Annaghbeg, co. Tipperary, Major 18th Royal Irish Regt., *b.* 2 Aug. 1836; *m.* 15 Aug. 1865, Elizabeth Frederick, dau. of Sir Frederick Whitaker, of Auckland, New Zealand. He *d.* 29 June, 1903, leaving issue,
1. CHARLES FREDERICK ROBERT, now of Annaghbeg.
2. Walter Alfred, *b.* 5 July, 1875; *m.* 1909, Martha Myer, and has issue a daughter.
1. Elizabeth Augusta, *m.* Robert Dyer, and has issue.
2. Mary.   3. Anna.

Seat—Annaghbeg, Nenagh. Residence—Auckland, New Zealand.

MOLLOY OF CLONBELA.

LAURENCE BOMFORD MOLLOY, of Clonbela, King's Co., J.P., *b.* 2 Jan. 1845; *m.* 3 Feb. 1869, Amy Frances, 3rd dau. of Rev. John Gemley, of London, Canada, and by her (who *d.* 14 Dec. 1895) has issue,
1. Robert Laurence, *b.* 4 March, 1870; *d.* 1 June, 1892.
1. Mary Macaulay, *b.* 18 Feb. 1872; *m.* 29 Oct. 1904, Lewen Francis Barrington Weldon, Egyptian Civil Service (*see* BURKE'S *Peerage*, WELDON, Bart.), and has issue,
  Olivia Mary.
2. Amy Frances, *b.* 19 May, 1873; *m.* 23 Oct. 1905, Rev. G. Cruddas, of Nether Warden, Northumberland, and has issue William Lawrence Molloy, *b.* 23 Jan. 1907, Amy Patricia, and Noreen Maud.
3. Evelyn Maud, *b.* 25 Oct. 1874.
4. Harriet Elizabeth, *b.* 6 July, 1879; *m.* 16 April, 1909, George Lloyd Cruddas, eldest son of Rev. G. Cruddas, of Nether Warden, Northumberland, and has issue, Elizabeth Molloy.

Lineage.—This family represents the sept of the O'Mulloys of Fircall, or "Mulloy's Country." The sept descended from Fiachada, 3rd son of Niall of the Nine Hostages, Monarch of Ireland 371, and derived the name from Maolmhuaidh, Chief of the territory of Feara Ceall (now Fircall), who was slain in 1019.
ART O'MOLLOY was father of
DANIEL MOLLOY, of Streamstown and Clonbela, who was granted Coulemore by patent 22 Dec. 1629. He *m.* Mary, dau. of Nicholas Herbert, of Killyan, King's Co., and was *s.* by his son,
EDWARD MOLLOY, of Streamstown and Clonbela, who was in Spain 1651-62. He was living in 1701, when he successfully claimed his estate before the Trustees at Chichester House. His grandson,
EDWARD MOLLOY, of Clonbela, *d.* after 1752, having had issue two sons. The elder,
DANIEL MOLLOY, of Clonbela, *m.* 31 July, 1752, Susanna, dau. of Peter Daly, of Kilcleagh, co. Westmeath, and *d.s.p.* 18 Jan. 1760, when he was *s.* by his brother,
JOHN MOLLOY, of Clonbela, *m.* 4 June, 1755, Anne, dau. and co-heir of Edward Bomford, of Hightown, co. Westmeath, with whom he acquired property in Westmeath, and had a son,
LAURENCE BOMFORD MOLLOY, of Clonbela, *m.* 1788, Elizabeth, dau. of Rev. John Mulock, D.D., of Bellair, King's Co. (*see* MULOCK *of Kilnagarna*), and left issue,
1. JOHN (Rev.), his heir.
2. DANIEL, successor to his brother.
3. Thomas HOMAN-MULOCK, of Bellair, King's Co., who assumed by Royal Licence the name and arms of HOMAN-MULOCK (*see that family*).
1. Anne, *m.* 1818, Alured L'Estrange, son of Lieut.-Gen. L'Estrange, and *d.s.p.* 1819.
Mr. Molloy *d.* 1805, and was *s.* by his eldest son,
REV. JOHN MOLLOY, of Clonbela, who *d. unm.* 1818, and was *s.* by his brother,
DANIEL MOLLOY, of Clonbela, J.P. King's Co., *m.* 16 May, 1834, Julia Henrietta, only dau. of James Higginson, of Cushendun Lodge, co. Antrim, Maj. 10th Regt., and *d.* 25 April, 1856, leaving issue,
1. Laurence, *d.* in infancy.
2. LAURENCE BOMFORD, the present representative of the family.

2 H

Molony. THE LANDED GENTRY. 482

3. James, d. 16 May, 1849.
1. Mary Macaulay, m. Robert Macdonnell, M.D., and d.s.p. 8 March, 1869.
2. Elizabeth Mulock, d. 8 July, 1856.
3. Anne Homan, m. 3 June, 1876, Maj.-Gen. Walter Weldon, and has issue.
4. Harriet, d. 24 Aug. 1856.
Seat—Clonbela, Birr, King's Co.

MOLONY OF CRAGG.

ALICE LYDIA MOLONY, of Cragg, co. Clare, s. her father 1901.

Lineage. — JOHN O'MOLONY, d. 1 May, 1610, leaving a son,
JOHN O'MOLONY, m. the dau. of McMahon, of Clonderalaw, co. Clare, and had issue,
1. JAMES, his heir.
2. John (Rev.), b. 1617, D.D., Canon of Rouen, in France, made Bishop of Killaloe in 1671, and translated to Limerick in 1688. For his adherence to the cause of JAMES II, he was attainted in 1696, and retired to France, where he died at Issy, 3 Sept. 1702 (will dated 22 Nov. 1701). He was a founder of the Irish College at Paris, and a benefactor of the College of Louis Le Grand, endowing in the latter by a foundation deed, dated 8 Aug. 1701, free bursaries for certain Clare and Limerick families to whom he was related, with a preference for relations and othrs of the name of O'Molony.

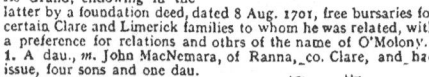

1. A dau., m. John MacNemara, of Ranna, co. Clare, and had issue, four sons and one dau.
2. A dau., m. — Dwyer, and had a dau.
3. Vui, m. — Blake, and had two sons.

The eldest son,
JAMES O'MOLONY, left issue at his decease four sons and two daus.,
1. Daniel, of Ballysheen, co. Clare, Capt. in O'Brien's Regt., killed at the siege of Limerick, and his property sequestered.
2. Denis, Barrister-at-Law, of Gray's Inn, b. 1650; d. unm. 11 Dec. 1726 (will dated 30 Nov. 1726, and proved 10 Jan. 1726-7).
3. JAMES, of whom presently.
4. John Baptiste (Rev.).
1. Eleanor, m. Edmond Nihell, and had issue.
2. Honora, m. Florence MacNemara, of Ardcloony, co. Clare, and had issue.

The 3rd son,
JAMES MOLONY, of Kiltanon and Ballinahinch, J.P., an Officer in Col. O'Brien's Regt. of Foot, of JAMES II's Irish Army. His property was saved him by the clause in the Treaty of Limerick, exempting from attainder those within its walls. He built the family vault at Tulla, dated 2 June, 1702, which is still the burying place of the Molonys of Cragg. He m. 1st, Joan Molony, and by her had issue,
1. JOHN, of whom presently.
He m. 2ndly, Mary, dau. of James Lambert, of Carnagh, co. Wexford, and by her had issue,
2. JAMES, ancestor of the family of MOLONY of Kiltanon (whom see).
He m. 3rdly, Mary, dau. of Kennedy Brien, of Killernan, co. Limerick (widow of Daniel Ryan, of Moanageenagh, co. Clare, and of Richard Butler, of Knocktopher, co. Kilkenny). She d.s.p.
He m. 4thly, Christian, sister of Peter Martin, and by her had issue,
3. Richard, of Loughboro', co. Clare.
4. Thomas, m. Mrs. Sibella Blake, and d. 1729, leaving a dau. Christian.
5. Andrew, of Clonbrick.
6. STEPHEN, ancestor of the MOLONYS of Ballinahinch.
1. Margaret, d.s.p. 2. Catherine, d.s.p.
3. Mary, m. Henry Brady, of Kilcorney and Bemskea, co. Galway, and had issue, ancestor of Brady of Myshall, co. Carlow,
Mr. Molony d. at Ballinahinch, and his will was proved in Dublin, 4 July, 1733. His eldest son by his 1st marriage,
JOHN MOLONY, m. (setts. dated 5 May, 1713) Anstace, dau. of William McNemara, of Rathanny, co. Limerick, and d.v.p. in 1724, leaving by her (who d. 1726) with three daus., issue,
1. James, of Cragg, m. Anne O'Dwyer, and d.s.p. Oct. 1759. Will dated 20 Oct. 1759.
2. William, d. unm. 1760.
3. John, of Tulla. His only son, John, d. without issue.
4. Patrick, who succeeded to Cragg under a deed of settlement dated 20 Jan. 1732, and of whom presently.
5. Andrew, m. Arabella Massy, and had issue,
  1. James Massy, of Rathluba, co. Clare, m. Susanalva Molony, and had issue one dau.
  2. Hugh.

3. MacNamara; he was presented in 1773, to one of the Bursaries founded by Bishop O'Molony, in the College of Louis Le Grand, Paris.
1. Elinor. 2. Anstace.
The 4th son,
PATRICK MOLONY, s. to Cragg on the death of his eldest brother, and m. (settlement dated 28 Feb. 1746) Elizabeth, dau. of Thomas Cusack, of Fortanemore, co. Clare, and niece of John Cusack, of Kilkishen, and d. 19 April, 1799, leaving issue,
1. JOHN, his heir.
2. James, of Fortanemore, m. 16 Feb. 1789, Marcella, dau. of Bartholomew O'Connell, of Kilgory, co. Clare, and d. Feb. 1841, having had issue, now extinct in the male line.
1. Margery, m. Thomas O'Grady, and d. 6 July, 1793, having had issue.
The elder son,
JOHN MOLONY, of Cragg, m. (settlements dated 4 July, 1771) his cousin Dilliana, dau. of Henry Brady, of Killcorney, and d. 11 May, 1805. She d. 21 June, 1806, leaving issue,
1. PATRICK, of whom presently.
2. Henry, d.s.p. 1823.
3. James, was presented in 1789, to one of the Bursaries founded by Bishop O'Molony at the College of Louis Le Grand. He was an Officer in the French Army during the Revolutionary Wars, and d. unm. 1 Feb. 1843.
4. William, d.s.p. 1822. 5. Hugh, d.s.p. 1836.
1. Mary, m. James Barry, of Rockstown, co. Limerick (settlement dated 10 Feb. 1812), and by him (who d. 25 July, 1828) had issue three daus., Dilliana, Mary, and Alice (see BARRY of Sackville).
The eldest son,
PATRICK MOLONY, J.P., of Cragg, m. 2 Oct. 1808, Alice (d. 17 March, 1847), eldest dau. of Chartres Brew, of Applevale, co. Clare, and had issue,
1. JOHN PATRICK, of whom presently.
2. Chartres Brew, m. 10 Nov. 1841, his cousin Alice, dau. of James Barry, of Rockstown, and d. 24 July, 1875, having by her (who d. 30 Sept. 1871) had issue,
  1. Harry, m. 19 Dec. 1868, Charlotte Eliza, dau. of John Carver Coates, and d. 17 Jan. 1880, leaving issue,
    (1) Chartres Aylmer.
    (2) Harry Brereton, B.A. (Dub.).
    (3) Percival John (Rev.), B.A. (Dub.).
  2. James Barry, m. 21 Nov. 1872, Ellen, dau. of John Butler Greene, and d. 31 Dec. 1904, leaving issue,
    (1) John Chartres, M.A. (Madras Civil Service), m. 6 July, 1904, Frances, dau. of William Adams, J.P. of Drumelton, co. Cavan, and has issue, 1. Chartres James Chatterton, and 1. Mary Frances Adams.
    (2) James Georges Massy, m. 6 Sept. 1910, Anne, dau. of John Kay, of East View, Preston.
    (1) Alice.
    (2) Eileen Mabel, m. Francis C. Pilkington.
  3. Chartres Brew, d. unm. 1879.
  4. John, F.R.C.P.I., J.P. co. Armagh, m. 1st, Ethel Constance, dau. of Hugh Lyons-Montgomery, D.L., of Belhawel, co. Leitrim (see that family). She d. 28 Oct. 1891. He d. 7 April, 1906, leaving issue,
    (1) Otho Hugh Chartres, Capt. Indian Army, m. 17 March, 1908, Eileen Owen, only child of Col. E. Ffrench Owens, Leinster Regt.
    (2) John Barré de Winton, M.D. (Edin.).
  He m. 2ndly, 27 Feb. 1900, Mary Macaulay, dau. of Charles Henry Higginson, of Springmount and Rockforest, co. Antrim, and d. 7 April, 1906.
  5. Godfrey Massey, m. 11 Oct. 1882, Clara Penrose, dau. of Sir John Coode, K.C.M.G. 6. Alfred.
  1. Mary.
3. Henry, d. unm.
4. James, F.R.C.S.I., m. 11 May, 1848, Rebecca, dau. of Michael Greene, of Ennis. She d. 10 June, 1896. He d. 14 Sept. 1893, having had issue,
  1. Charles, d. unm. 9 Dec. 1859.
  2. Henry, B.A., M.D., m. 24 April, 1889, Geraldine, dau. of Edmund Morony, of Odell Ville, co. Limerick (see that family), by Helena his wife, only dau. of John Odell.
  3. John (Rev.), B.A., Rector of Moffatt, N.B., m. 27 March, 1884, Charlotte Jane, dau. of Andrew Patterson, of Abbotsford Crescent, Edinburgh, and has issue,
    (1) James Alexander. (2) Andrew Chartres Brew.
    (3) Adrian Charles.
  4. FitzJames, m. 15 May, 1886, Louisa Basil, dau. of Charles Townley, of Townley House, Ramsgate, and has issue, James Townley.
  5. Charles William, d. unm. 15 Jan. 1880.
  1. Jane Dilliana, d. unm. 17 May, 1892.
  2. Alice Maude, m. 4 Nov. 1875, Robert Spaight, of Affock, co. Clare, and had issue (see SPAIGHT of Derry Castle). She d. 22 Nov. 1906.
  3. Anne Ellen.
1. Rebecca, m. 2 Nov. 1833, John Trousdell, and d. 15 Aug. 1880, having had issue.
2. Dilliana, d. unm. 16 July, 1883.
3. Alice, d. young, Feb. 1840.
Mr. Molony d. 9 Oct. 1832, and was s. by his eldest son,
JOHN PATRICK MOLONY, of Cragg, J.P., m. (settlement dated 12 Feb. 1838) Anna, dau. of Denis Canny, J.P. of Clonmony, co. Clare, and d. 22 Feb. 1851, leaving issue,
1. PATRICK JOHN, late of Cragg.
2. Denis William, d. unm. 1874.
3. John, J.P. of Bendemeer Yuelba, Queensland, m. 2 April

1881, Mary, dau. of the late Richard Harney, of Melbourne (and step-dau. of Thomas Nugent Fitzgerald), and *d.* 20 Oct. 1902, leaving issue,
1. Harry.
2. Fergus, *d. unm.* 31 Dec. 1904.
   1. Eileen.
   2. Alice.
   3. Clare.
   4. Anna.
   5. Winifred.
4. Henry Mostyn, of Murgoo, Murchison, Western Australia, *m.* Aug. 1889, Lizzie Itystein, and *d.* 17 July, 1903, leaving issue, Mostyn, and other sons.
1. Ellen Mary.   2. Mary.
3. Alice, *d. unm.* 5 Jan. 1906.
PATRICK JOHN MOLONY, of Cragg, co. Clare, J.P., B.A. Dublin nd Cantab., *b.* 19 Feb. 1839; *m.* 17 Oct. 1870, LYDIA ANNE, ow of Cragg, dau. of Richard Galwey, of Herbert Place, Dublin, nd *d.* 26 Aug. 1901, leaving issue,
ALICE LYDIA, now of Cragg.

Arms—Quarterly: 1st and 4th, az., a quiver erect holding three rrows between two bows palewise, all or; 2nd and 3rd, gu., two lions ampant, supporting a staff all ppr. *Crest*—An arm vambraced mbowed, the hand gauntleted grasping a short sword all ppr., he forearm charged with a trefoil slipped az. *Motto*—In domino et non in arcu meo sperabo.

Seat—Cragg, Tulla, co. Clare.

MOLONY OF KILTANON.

WILLIAM BERESFORD MOLONY, of Kiltanon, co. Clare, High Sheriff 1908, formerly Capt. King's Own Royal Lancaster Regt., *b.* 25 Aug. 1875, *s.* his father 1891; *m.* 22 Feb. 1905, Lena Mara Annie, only dau. of George Wright, of Hevsham Lodge, Lancashire, and of Coverham Abbey, Yorkshire.

Lineage.—JAMES MOLONY, of Kiltanon, only son of JAMES MOLONY, of Kiltanon and Ballinahinch (*see* MOLONY *of Cragg*), by his 2nd wife, Mary, dau. of James Lambert. He *m.* (settlements dated 4 and 5 Nov. 1720) Elizabeth, widow of Major Morgan Ryan, and 2nd dau. and co-heir of Thomas Croasdaile, of Cloghstoken, co. Galway, by Mercy his wife, dau. of Col. Richard Ringrose, of Moynoe House, co. Clare, and had issue,
1. JAMES, his heir.
2. CROASDAILE, *b.* 1719; *m.* (settlement dated 1756) Catherine, dau. of Henry Gonne, Clerk of the Peace, and dying 1799, was *s.* by his son,
HENRY GONNE MOLONY, Barrister-at-Law, *b.* 1759; *m.* 1786, Caroline, dau. of Thomas Walker, Master in Chancery, by Caroline his wife, dau. of the Hon. Bysse Molesworth, and *d.* 1821, leaving issue,
(1) CROASDAILE, of Granahan, *b.* 18 July, 1788; *m.* 1816, Charlotte, dau. of Col. Thomas Halcott, H.E.I.C.S., and *d.* 1867, leaving issue,
 1. CROASDAILE, of Granaban, *b.* 1818; *m.* 1864, Johanna Isabella, youngest dau. of Henry Martin Blake, of Windfield, co. Mayo (*see* BLAKE *of Renvyle*), and *d.s.p.* 1870.
 2. Henry, *d.* 31 Oct. 1904, aged 85.
 3. Charles Walker (Rev.), Rector of West Worlington, Devon, *b.* 4 June, 1822; *m.* 27 Aug. 1853, Adelaide, dau. of Sir William Russell, Bart., M.D. She *d.* 27 March, 1885. He *d.* 2 July, 1888, leaving issue,
  a. Croasdaile Charles Russell, *b.* 5 Oct. 1854; *d.* 29 March, 1876.
  b. Henry William Eliott (Rev.), Vicar of Great Ilford, Essex, *b.* 14 Sept. 1858; *m.* 29 Dec. 1891, Edith Gertrude Marion, dau. of Rev. George Edmund Tatham, and has issue,
   (*a*) Brian Charles, *b.* 25 Oct. 1892.
   (*a*) Edith Irene, *b.* 10 March, 1895.
   (*b*) Iva Clare Marion, *b.* 15 Sept. 1896.
   (*c*) Margaret Adelaide, *b.* 23 Sept. 1898; *d.* 9 Sept. 1900.
   (*d*) Agatha Mary, *b.* 30 July, 1900.
  c. Cecil Heathorn Lindsay, *b.* 16 Oct. 1859; *d.* Nov. 1895.
  d. Eustace Cyril, *b.* 3 July, 1862; *m.* March, 1888, Frances French.
  e. Charles Winfrid Brian, *b.* 4 Aug. 1865.
  f. Clement Arthur, Capt. R.A., *b.* 14 Sept. 1867; killed in action, 24 Feb. 1898.
  g. Basil Edmund, *b.* 19 Jan. 1871; lost at sea, June, 1888.
  a. Jane Eliza Lewin, *m.* 1892, John French, son of Gen. French.
  b. Claudine Charlotte, *m.* 15 Aug. 1883, Rev. C. H. Stone, and has issue.
  c. Blanche Frances Agatha, *m.* 10 July, 1889, John Backhouse Alcock, I.C.S., and has issue.
 4. Thomas, *d.s.p.*
 1. Henrietta, *m.* 1st, Robert Fannin, of Dublin, who *d.* leaving issue; and 2ndly, 1844, Joliffe Tufnell, who *d.* 1886, leaving issue.
(2) Henry Gonne, *b.* 1801; *m.* 13 Dec. 1823, Hannah, dau. of Rev. Arthur Knox, Rector of St. Catherine's, Dublin, and of Bray, in Wicklow, and *d.* 31 July, 1888, having by her (who *d.* 18 Nov. 1841) had issue,
 1. Henry Gonne, bur. 8 Nov. 1827, aged five days.
 2. Arthur Knox, *b.* 1 Nov. 1832.
 3. Henry Campbell, *b.* 1836; *d.* at St. Louis, America, 1866.
 4. William John, *b.* about 1838; *m.* living in New Zealand.
  1. Caroline, *d.* at Milan, 5 July, 1889.
  2. Henrietta Elizabeth, *d.* at Swords, Aug. 1855.
  3. Hannah, *d.* 30 May, 1836.
  4. Julia, *m.* about 1874, Samuel Murray Going, of Liskeveen House, co. Tipperary. 5. Maria, *d.* 29 March, 1851.
  6. Jane, a nun in the Cistercian Convent, Wimborne.
(1) Caroline, *m.* Capt. William Richards, 5th Dragoon Guards.
(2) Catherine, *m.* the Right Hon. John Richards, a baron of the Exchequer in Ireland, and *d.* leaving issue.
3. Lambert, Barrister-at-Law, *d.* 14 Jan. 1771; *m.* 18 Nov. 1768, Jane, dau. of Rev. Mr. Browne, of Waterford, by whom he had an only dau. and heir,
Elizabeth Croasdaile, *m.* James Ledwith, of Ledwithstown, co. Longford.
1. Jane, *m.* 6 Oct. 1756, her cousin Ringrose Drew, of Drewsborough, co. Clare.
Mr. Molony was *s.* by his eldest son,
JAMES MOLONY, of Kiltanon, *b.* 1717; *m.* 8 Aug. 1751, Mary, dau. of Arthur Weldon, of Rabeenderry, Queen's Co., and had issue,
1. JAMES, his heir.
2. Arthur, in the H.E.I.Co.'s C.S., *d. unm.*
3. Walter Weldon, *m.* Mary, dau. of — Spelisy, M.D., and had issue,
 1. Walter, a Stipendiary Magistrate, *m.* Miss Kelly, and had issue, with three other sons and five daus.,
  (1) Walter Weldon, an Officer I.C., *m.* 1845, Frances Doyne, only dau. of Capt. Francis Thompson, of Killibandrick, co. Cavan, and had issue,
  William Walter Francis, *b.* 1848, served in the R.I.C. and after became Capt. in the R.I. Fusiliers; *m.* Mary Eliza (Mai) Molony, his cousin, and has issue,
   a. Walter William, *b.* 1878, served as Lieut. in the 1st Connaught Rangers during S. African War 1899-1902, afterwards Capt. in the A.S.C.; *m.* July, 1905, Edith Lowcay, only dau. of Col. H. Norcock, late R.M.L.I., and has issue,
    (*a*) Desmond Walter, *b.* 6 May, 1907.
    (*b*) Arthur Corser, *b.* 20 Nov. 1909.
   a. Edith Frances, *m.* Aug. 1903, Ewen Reginald Logan, Barrister-at-Law and Stipendiary Magistrate in S. Africa and after in B. E. Africa, younger son of the late Francis Logan, Barrister-at-Law, of Cliffe Side, Bournemouth.
    b. Annie Beryl.
 2. Arthur (Rev.), Rector of Derrylorne, *m.* Heaner, dau. of Edward Croker, and had issue by her, who *d.* 1837.
 3. James, *d.* in India, *unm.*
 1. Anne.   2. Eliza, *m.* John Croker.
4. Lambert, a Judge in the service of the H.E.I.C., *m.* Miss King, of Corrard, co. Fermanagh, and had issue,
 1. Chidley.
 2. Henry Anthony, served in the Army as Ensign and Lieut., and Adjutant H.M. 50th Foot, was through the Sikh campaign of 1844-5, and present at Moodkee, Ferozeshah, Aliwal, and Sabraon; *d.* at Meerut shortly after the conquest of the Punjaub, having *m.* Emily, dau. of Henry Vinall, of Chatham, Kent, and by her had (with two daus.), Emily Maria Mouatt, *b.* 1846; and Honoria Harriet Wilmot, *b.* 1847) two sons,
  (1) Henry Andrew, *b.* 1843.
  (2) Chidley Kearnan (*Kiltanon House, Kimberley*), *b.* at Cawnpore, 1845, served in Royal Navy, passing for rank of Paymaster in 1867, afterwards at the Admiralty Office, having retired from R.N. after having served on the Australian, Home, and West Coast of Africa stations, is a J.P. for Kimberley, South Africa, and Town Clerk of that important Borough. Served in his civil capacity through the siege of Kimberley and mentioned in despatches by General Kekewich; *m.* 1871, Emma, 3rd dau. of the late Selwyn Schofield Sugden, formerly Deputy Governor of H.M. Convict Prison at Gibraltar, and by her has issue,
   1. Chidley Selwyn Anthony, *b.* 1873, served through the siege of Kimberley as Lieut. of a Special Corps (raised by himself) of Cape Colonials and mentioned in despatches by General Kekewich; *d.* 1910.
   2. Henry Lambert, *b.* 1876; *d.* an infant.
   3. Ernest Andrew, *b.* 1881.   4. George, *d.* in infancy.
   5. Frederick Sugden, *b.* 1886.
   1. Emily Catherine, *b.* 1875
 1. Anna Maria, *m.* — Yonge.
5. Weldon John (Rev.), Rector of Dunleckney, co. Carlow, *m.* 20 March, 1804, Mary, dau. of Rev. Samuel Preston, Rector of Ballbracken, Vicar of Monasterevan, and Prebendary of Harrow town, and had issue,
 1. Stewart Weldon, Capt. Madras Light Cavalry, *d. unm.* 1837.
 2. Weldon Samuel, *m.* 15 Aug. 1849, Harriet, dau. of Sir Anthony Weldon, Bart., and has issue,
  (1) Anthony Weldon.   (2) Stewart Arthur.
  (3) Weldon Charles, *b.* 16 Nov. 1853; *m.* 9 Aug. 1883, Eleanor Anne, eldest dau. of Commissary-Gen. Edwards, by his 2nd wife, Anne, dau. of Dr. Harrison, of Hume Street, Dublin, and has issue,
   1. Alexander Weldon, *b.* 5 June, 1884.
   2. Claude.   3. Bertram.
   1. Eileen.

2 H 2

Monck.   THE LANDED GENTRY.   484

(1) Harriette Mary, m. John Percy Gordon Maynard, of Ratoath Manor, co. Meath.
(2) Emily Frances.
(3) Florence Helen, m. 1893, Major Alexander.
(4) Constance Anna, m. 5 Jan. 1887, Rev. Robert Mease, M.A., of St. Mark's, London, and d. 1890.
3. Charles Preston, Col. E.I. Staff Corps, m. 23 Nov. 1855, Rosa Elizabeth, eldest dau. of Sir Thomas Fetherston, Bart., and d. 1888, leaving, with three daus., a son,
  Charles Stewart, b. 1856.
1. Mary, m. Rev. John Alexander, LL.D., Rector of Carne, Diocese of Ferns.
2. Elizabeth, m. Capt. James Beveridge Harris.
3. Letitia.   4. Lucy.
5. Ellen.
6. Charles.   7. Edmund.
1. Elizabeth.

Mr. Molony was s. by his son,

JAMES MOLONY, of Kiltanon, High Sheriff of Clare 1802, b. 1752; m. 1780, Selina, dau. of Rev. John Mills, of Barford, co. Warwick, and by her (who d. in 1825) had issue,
1. JAMES, his heir.
2. Charles Arthur, b. 1790, H.E.I.Co.'s C.S., Chief Commissioner of the Districts of the Nerbudda, d. unm. in India, 1824.
3. Edmund, b. 1794, H.E.I.Co.'s Secretary to the Government of Bengal: m. 1815, Frances Rosina, dau. of Henry Creighton, of Goarmalty, East Indies, and d. in India, 1830, leaving issue,
  1. Charles Arthur (Rev.), M.A., Vicar of St. Lawrence, Rams-gate, b. 1816; m. 1872, Mary Emily Jane, dau. of R. D. Parker, late H.E.I.Co's C.S., and d. 1895, leaving issue,
    (1) Edmund Parker, m. 19 Aug. 1902, Charlena Jean, dau. of the late Charles Murray Gibson, of Ontario, and has issue a son, b. 17 Nov. 1903.
    (2) Henry James Creighton.
    (3) John Charles Arthur Deane.
    (4) Percy William.
    (1) Rosina Mary, m. 10 June, 1908, Frank Mainwaring Furley, eldest son of Walter Furley, of Canterbury.
    (2) Katharine.
  1. Frances, m. 1845, A. E. Gayer, LL.D., Q.C. (who d. 1877), and has issue (1) Edmund Richard, in Holy Orders; (2) Arthur, in Holy Orders; (1) Lucy Harriette; (2) Edith Mary.
  2. Selina, d. unm. 1898.
1. Selina, d. unm. 1864.   2. Mary, d. unm. 1826.
3. Harriet, d. an infant.
4. Anne, m. Rev. W. Butler, of Doon, co. Clare, and d.s.p. 1846.
5. Lucy, d. unm. 1855.

Mr. Molony d. 12 Oct. 1823, and was s. by his son,

JAMES MOLONY, of Kiltanon, J.P. and D.L., High Sheriff 1828, b. 18 Aug. 1785; m. 1st, 17 Feb. 1820, Harriet, 3rd dau. of William Harding, of Baraset, co. Warwick, and had by her (who d. 8 Oct. 1826),
1. James, b. 1822; d. 1834.
2. WILLIAM MILLS, his heir.
1. Harriet, d. an infant.

He m. 2ndly, 15 April, 1828, Lucy, 2nd dau. of Sir Trevor Wheler, Bart., of Leamington, Hastings, co. Warwick, and had by her (who d. 14 May, 1855),
3. Frances Wheler (Rev.), b. 5 April, 1829; m. 19 Oct. 1853, Harriet, dau. of Capt. George Baker, R.N. She d. 11 April, 1910. He d. 1860, leaving issue,
  James Arthur, b. 29 Aug. 1854; m. 1876, Annie, dau. of J. W. Hague, of Enon Valley, Pennsylvania, and has issue, Francis Wheler, b. 1887, and four daus.
4. Edmund Weldon, H.E.I.C.S., b. 27 March, 1830; m. 1863, Frances Selina, dau. of A. Edward Gayer, LL.D., Q.C.; and d. 30 Jan. 1888, leaving issue,
  1. Edmund Alexander, Indian Civil Service, b. 1866; m. 1898, Blanche, dau. of Herbert Smith, of Barla, East Indies.
  2. Frederick Arthur, b. 1875.
  1. Eleanor Mary, m. 2 July, 1904, George Whitly Gayer, Indian Police, 3rd son of late Surg.-Major Edward Gayer, I.M.S.
  2. Mary, d. an infant.   3. Lucy Selina.
  4. Alice Helen.   5. Lilian Edith.
5. Trevor Charles, Capt. R.A., b. 21 April, 1832; m. 26 Dec. 1862, Helen, 2nd dau. of W. F. Chicheley Plowden, of Ewhurst, Hants, and d.s.p. 24 Jan. 1871.
6. Frederick Beresford, H.E.I.C.S., b. 15 June, 1833; m. 13 Oct. 1858, Eleanor Jane, dau. of A. Edward Gayer, LL.D., Q.C.; and d. at Madras 13 Nov. 1868, leaving issue,
  1. Francis Arthur, Major R.E., b. 1863; m. 1888, Katharine Mary, dau. of J. W. Grigg, of Tamerton Foliot, co. Devon, and has two sons and two daus.
  2. Herbert James (Rt. Rev.), Bishop of Mid-China, b. 1865; m. 1st, 1869, Eva, dau. of the late Rev. M. Collisson. She d. 12 Sept. 1897. He m. 2ndly, 6 Aug. 1908, Gertrude Elizabeth, widow of Rev. J. W. Goodwin and dau. of Rev. S. D. Stubbs, M.A., Vicar of St. James', Pentonville.
  1. Mary Selina.
  2. Eleanor Harriett, d. an infant.
  3. Eleanor Florence, m. 1st, 1892, Surg. Lieut.-Col. Horatio Scott, who d. 1895. She m. 2ndly, 25 Aug. 1906, Francis Mackenzie Ogilvy, of Bayswater.
  4. Agnes Freda Helen, m. 1 Feb. 1908, Edward Millington Synge, son of late Rev. F. Synge.
7. Charles Mills, C.B., Col. in the Army, of St. Catharine's Priory, Guildford, late Commissary-General, and formerly Capt. R.A., b. 26 Jan. 1836; m. 1866, Eliza, dau. of Andrew Hamilton, of Streatham. He d. 14 Aug. 1901, leaving issue,

1. James Rowland Hamilton, b. 1867; m. 12 Jan. 1895, Emma Charlotte, 2nd dau. of the late Arthur Wienbolt, of Fassifern, Queensland, and has issue,
  (1) Trevor James, b. 7 July, 1897.
  (2) Marcus Vandeleur, b. 18 Dec. 1898.
  (1) Clara Elizabeth, b. 7 Aug. 1902.
2. Trevor Charles Wheler, D.S.O., Major R.F.A., b. 28 July, 1868; m. 31 Oct. 1899, Beatrice Annie, youngest dau. of Major-Gen. W. H. Beynon, and has issue,
  (1) Trevor St. Patrick, b. 6 Sept. 1900.
  (2) Charles Beynon, b. 15 Jan. 1906.
  (3) Norman, b. 14 April, 1907.
  (1) Pearl, b. 21 July, 1903.
3. Charles Vandeleur, Capt. R. West Kent Regt., b. 19 July, 1870.
1. Margaret Hamilton, d. 1879.
8. Marcus, J.P., b. 1838; m. 1862, Christina Emma, dau. of Francis Gore, of Tyredagh Castle, co. Clare, and d.s.p. 1886.
2. Mary, m. 3 Jan. 1856, Arthur Vandeleur, Major R.A., of Rathaline, co. Clare, who d. 1860, and has issue,
  1. Lucy, m. 1881, A. B. Stoney, Barrister, and has issue, (1) James Arthur; (2) Arthur Vandeleur; (1) Mary Evelyn.
  2. Emily Harriet, m. 1884, Lord George H. Loftus, and d. 1896, leaving issue, Adam John St. George, and Anna Mary Kathleen.
3. Lucy Anne, d. an infant, 4 July, 1836.
4. Harriet Selina, m. 1859, Ven. Thomas Fitzgerald French, Rector of Castle Connell, and Archdeacon of Killaloe, who d. 1884, leaving issue, 1, Fitzgerald Charles, b. 1861; 2, Riversdale Sampson, b. 1862; 3, Deane, b. 1864; 4, Arthur James Pascoe (Rev.), b. 1865; 5, Raymond William, b. 1867; 6, Frederick Beresford, d. an infant; 7, Harry O'Donovan, b. 1872; 1, Lucy Selina; 2, Agnes Melian.

Mr. Molony d. at Leamington 7 July, 1874, and was s. by his eldest surviving son,

WILLIAM MILLS MOLONY, of Kiltanon, co. Clare, J.P. and D.L., late Major 22nd Regt., High Sheriff 1865; b. 24 April, 1825; m. 8 Nov. 1865, Marianne Marsh, elder dau. and co-heir of Robert Fannin, of Leeson Street, Dublin, by his wife Henrietta, dau. of Croasdale Molony, of Granahan, and by her (who d. 27 Jan. 1880) had issue,
1. James Edmund Harding, b. 23 July, 1873; d. 29 Dec. 1879.
2. WILLIAM BERESFORD, now of Kiltanon.
1. Henrietta Mary, m. 28 July, 1903, Marcus Keane, D.L., of Beech Park, co. Clare, and has issue (see that family).
2. Iva Kathleen, m. 10 June, 1896, Capt. John R. Longley, 1st Batt. East Surrey Regt., son of the late Charles T. Longley, of the Madras Civil Service, and has issue, Charles Raynsford.
3. Selina Charlotte, d. 18 Jan. 1880, aged 9.
4. Maud Alice, d. 5 Jan. 1880, aged 7.

Major W. M. Molony d. 7 Sept. 1891, and was s. by his only surviving son.

Seat—Kiltanon, near Tulla, co. Clare.

MONCK. *See* BURKE'S PEERAGE, **MONCK, V.**

MONTAGU OF CROMORE.

ROBERT ACHESON CROMIE MONTAGU, of Cromore, co. Londonderry, J.P. cos. Londonderry and Antrim, late Lieut. R.N., b. 29 Aug. 1854; m. 24 Nov. 1880, Annie Margaret, dau. of Gilbert McMicking, of Miltonise, co. Wigton, and has issue,
1. JOHN MICHAEL CROMIE, b. 22 Aug. 1881; m. 1907, Libia Maria, dau. of Señor Martin Montes, of Quilmes, Argentine Republic.
2. George Frederick, Lieut. R.N., b. 12 March, 1883.
3. Cuthbert Francis, b. 29 May, 1884.
4. Austin Robert, b. 26 May, 1885.
5. Walter Philip, b. 7 May, 1886.
6. Gilbert Paul, b. 30 June, 1887.
7. Alexander Cyril, Sub-Lieut. R.N., b. 17 Sept. 1890.
1. Mary Helen, b. 5 Feb. 1889; d. 13 Feb. 1892.
2. Mary Emily Winifred, b. 26 June, 1892.

Mr. Montagu is the eldest son of Lord Robert Montagu, P.C., D.L. (who d. 6 May, 1902), by Ellen Mary his 1st wife (who d. 11 July, 1857), dau. and heir of John Cromie, of Cromore, co. Londonderry, and grandson of George, 6th Duke of Manchester.

Lineage Arms &c.—*See* BURKE'S *Peerage*, MANCHESTER, D.

Seat—Cromore, Portstewart.

MONTGOMERY OF GREY ABBEY.

MAJOR-GEN. WILLIAM EDWARD MONTGOMERY, of Grey Abbey, co. Down, J.P. and D.L., High Sheriff 1900, late Scots Guards, served in Zulu War, 1879, at Ulundi, b. 18 July, 1847; m. 22 June, 1891, Iberta Victoria, dau. of Gen. the Right Hon. Sir Henry Ponsonby, G.C.B., P.C. (see BURKE'S *Peerage*, ESSBOROUGH, E.).

Lineage.—This is the Braid stane line of the noble House of CLINTON.
ROBERT MONTGOMERY, 2nd son of Alexander, Master of Montgomery, and brother of Alexander, 2nd Lord Montgomery, ancestor of the Earls of Eglinton, obtained for his patrimony, from his grandfather, Alexander, 1st Lord, the lands of Braidstane, and thus became its laird. He was s. by his eldest son,
ROBERT MONTGOMERY, 2nd Laird of Braidstane, *d.s.p.* and was s. by his brother
ALEXANDER MONTGOMERY, 3rd Laird of Braidstane, who *d.s.p.*, and was s. by his only surviving brother,
ADAM MONTGOMERY, 4th Laird of Braidstane, who was s. by his son,
ADAM JOHN MONTGOMERY, 5th Laird of Braidstane. *m.* the eldest dau. of Sir John Colquhoun, of Luss, and d. about 1550, having had four sons, of whom,
1. ADAM, whose eldest son, SIR HUGH MONTGOMERY, 6th Laird of Braidstane, was raised to the Peerage of Ireland, 1622, as Viscount MONTGOMERY, and Earl of Mount Alexander of the Great Ardes, co. Down, a title now extinct.
2. ROBERT.

The younger son,
ROBERT MONTGOMERY, was father of
JOHN MONTGOMERY, who settled in Ireland in the early part of the reign of King JAMES I. He m. an heiress of the family of Stewart, in Scotland, and was father of
✠ HUGH MONTGOMERY, of Maghera, co. Derry, M.P. for Newtownards. He left two sons,
1. HUGH, his heir.   2. John.
The elder son,
HUGH MONTGOMERY, of Maghera, m. a dau. of Sir Robert McClelland, by whom he had several daus., and an only son, his successor,
WILLIAM MONTGOMERY, of Maghera, m. Mary, eldest dau. and co-heir of Capt. James Macgill, of Kirkistown, co. Down, and had, with one dau., Lucy, d. unm. 1701, an only son, his successor,
WILLIAM MONTGOMERY, m. 1st, 1719, Catherine, dau. of Edward Hall, of Strangford, and by her (who d. 1723) had,
1. Edward, who d. 1726.   2. WILLIAM, his heir.
He m. 2ndly, 1725, Elizabeth, dau. of Samuel Hill, of Bucks. By this lady (who d. 1789) he had (with three daus., 1. Mary, m. 1749, Robert Maxwell, of Finnebrogue, co. Down, *d.s.p.* 1755 ; 2. Anne, m. James Dobbin, of Donaghadee, d. 1812 ; and 3. Catherine, m. 1754, George Matthews, of Springvale, co. Down) four sons,
3. Hugh, d. unm. 1765.   4. James, d. unm. 1796.
5. Robert, d. unm. 1758.
6. Samuel, Lieut.-Col. 12th Regt., m. Elizabeth dau. of Rev. George Drury, and *d.s.p.*
Mr. Montgomery d. 1755, and was s. by his 2nd son,
WILLIAM MONTGOMERY, of Grey Abbey, M.P. for Hillsborough, m. 1749, Susanna, dau. and sole heir of John Jelly, of Rathmullen, co. Down, and had issue,
1. William, Major 40th Regt., killed in America, 8 Sept. 1781.
2. HUGH, heir to his father.   3. Edward, R.N., d. unm.
4. Francis, Capt. 67th Regt., d. unm. 1808.
1. Dorcas, d. unm. 1824.
Mr. Montgomery d. Nov. 1799, and was s. by his eldest surviving son,
REV. HUGH MONTGOMERY, of Grey Abbey, b. 1754 ; m. 1782, the Hon. Emilia Ward, youngest dau. of Bernard, 1st Viscount Bangor (by his wife, Lady Anne Bligh, dau. of John, Earl of Darnley), and has issue,
1. WILLIAM, his successor.
2. Hugh Bernard, Capt. in the Guards, was severely wounded at Waterloo, of which he never recovered ; d. 2 May, 1817.
3. Edward (Rev.), Rector of Portaferry, and Chancellor of the Diocese of Down, d. unm. 1825.
4. Arthur Hill, of Tyrella, co. Down, D.L. and J.P. of that co., m. May, 1825, Lady Matilda Anne Parker, 3rd dau. of Thomas, 5th Earl of Macclesfield. She d. 25 May, 1883. He d. 1867, having had issue,
 1. Hugh Parker, of Tyrella, co. Down, Major-Gen. in the Army, late Lieut.-Col. 60th Rifles, b. Sept. 1829 ; d. 29 Dec. 1901.
 2. Arthur Hill Sandys, Lieut.-Col. late Rifle Brigade, lately commanding the Provisional Batt., b. 27 Oct. 1841 ; m. 1873, Constance Anne Katharine, eldest dau. of Robert Bryce Hay, and has issue,
  Patrick, b. 1876,
  Mabel Violet Blanche, m. 3 July, 1894, Percy Downes, 3rd son of Rev. William Downes, of Combe Raleigh, Devon.
 1. Amelia Maria Eliza, d. 1898.   2. Frances Arabella Louisa.
5. John Charles, Barrister-at-Law, d. 19 Dec. 1845.
6. Francis Octavius, Major 45th Regt., and Col. Comm. Royal Down Rifles, m. 6 Oct. 1842, Arabella Catherine, dau. and co-heir of Kean Osborne, Capt. 5th Dragoon Guards, by his wife, the Hon. Theodosia Ward, grand-dau. of Bernard, 1st Viscount Bangor, and d. 19 April, 1885.
7. George Augustus Frederick Sandys, Lieut. R.N., d. 18 March, 1827.

1. Anne Catherine, d. unm. 1802, aged 17.
2. Emilia Georgiana Susanna, m. 4 Feb. 1817, James Myles Reilly, Barrister-at-Law, youngest son of John Reilly, of Scarvagh, co. Down (see that family), and had issue.
Mr. Montgomery d. at Grey Abbey, 30 March, 1815, and was s. by his eldest son,
WILLIAM MONTGOMERY of Grey Abbey, J.P. and D.L., High Sheriff co. Down, 1824, m. March, 1817, Lady Amelia Elizabeth Parker (who d. 5 Feb. 1881), 2nd dau. of Thomas, 5th Earl of Macclesfield ; he d. 3 May, 1831, and was s. by his only child,
HUGH MONTGOMERY, of Grey Abbey, J.P. and D.L., High Sheriff 1845, b. 26 June, 1821 ; m. 20 Oct. 1846, the Lady Charlotte Elizabeth Herbert, 2nd dau. of Edward, 2nd Earl of Powis, K.G. She d. 15 May, 1906. He d. 29 May, 1894, leaving issue,
1. WILLIAM EDWARD, now of Grey Abbey.
2. Robert Arthur, C.V.O., C.B., Major-Gen. R.A., *p.s.c.*, Vice-Pres. Ordnance Board 1908–10, G.O.C. Transvaal 1906–8, formerly Commanding R.A. Southern District, late Deputy-Director-General of Ordnance (*Pentrepant Hall, Oswestry*), b. 7 Sept. 1848 ; m. 11 Jan. 1881, Maria Maud, 2nd dau. of Richard Gosling, of Ecclesfield, Ashford, co. Middlesex.
3. Percy Hugh Seymour, of the Chinese Imperial Customs Service, b. 8 March, 1856 ; d. unm. 26 Sept. 1902.
4. Francis Henry, b. 2 Sept. 1857.
5. George Fitzmaurice, of the Chinese Imperial Customs Service, b. 27 Jan. 1861 ; m. 1905, Mildred Mary, dau. of the Rev. Prependary and Hon. Mrs. Clayton, and has issue,
 1. Hugh, b. 1906.
 2. Sheila.
1. Lucy Florentia.
2 Edith Cecilia, m. 5 Sept. 1878, Colonel Henry Charles Geast Dugdale, late Rifle Brigade (d. Sept. 1911), and has issue (see DUGDALE: *of Merivale Hall*).
3. Charlotte Henrietta Emily, m. 2 June, 1874, Robert J. Harrison, of Caerhowel, co. Montgomery, D.L., Lieut.-Col. 4th Batt. South Wales Borderers, who d. 6 June, 1896, leaving issue (see that family).
4. Evelyn Mary.

Seat—Grey Abbey, Newtownards, co. Down.   Club—Carlton.

MONTGOMERY OF KILLEE.

WILLIAM MONTGOMERY, of Killee, co. Cork, b. 14 Sept. 1868 ; m. 27 Jan. 1897, Frances, only child of William Collis, late of Lismore, co. Kerry, and has issue,

WILLIAM COLLIS, b. 1899.

Lineage.—REV. JAMES MONTGOMERY, Chaplain of Grey Abbey, co. Down, was among the followers of Hugh Montgomery, Laird of Braidstane (created 3 May, 1622, Viscount Montgomery, of Ardes), when he removed to Ireland at the Plantation of Ulster. His son,
HUGH MONTGOMERY, of Ballynagown, co. Down, m. Elizabeth, dau. of Lindsay, of Dromrod, and had issue. His 2nd son,
HUGH MONTGOMERY, was at first put to sea by his father, and made two voyages to America. He afterwards entered the Army, and served under WILLIAM III in Ireland, and in 1702, was in the Duke of Ormonde's Troop of Horse, and served in Flanders, and in England. He m. Elizabeth Howard, widow of Col. Francis De la Rue (a Frenchman, who served under WILLIAM III, and had a grant by patent, dated 28 Sept. 1699, of Killee and other lands in co. Cork and elsewhere, and who d. 1701, leaving an only son, Wriothesley De la Rue, *d.s.p.* 1734), and by her had an only son,
GEORGE MONTGOMERY, of Killee, co. Cork, to whom his half-brother, Wriothesley De la Rue, devised all his estates, m. Frances, dau. of Morgan Magan, of Togherstown, co. Westmeath, and had issue by her, who d. Nov. 1778.
1. Thomas, *d.s.p.*   2. John, *d.s.p.*
3. GEORGE, of whom hereafter.
4. Hugh, m. and had issue, who settled at the Cape of Good Hope.
1. Elizabeth, m. Arthur Duhig, Barrister.
2. Katherine, *d.s.p.*
The 3rd son,
GEORGE MONTGOMERY, of Killee, co. Cork, m. 1787, Mary Quin, of Loloher, Cahir, co. Tipperary, and had issue,
1. Thomas, m. Katherine Franks, and *d.s.p.*
2. John, killed at the battle of Talavera.
3. George, *d.s.p.*
4. WILLIAM QUIN, of whom hereafter.
5. Arthur, *d.s.p.* 1847.
1. Maria, *d.s.p.* 1830.
The 4th son,
REV. WILLIAM QUIN MONTGOMERY, of Killee, m. 1840, Alice, dau. of Rev. P. Sleeman, of Whitechurch, co. Devon, and d. 1869, having had issue,
1. GEORGE, his heir.
2. Thomas Bedford, Agent to Hor. Irish Soc. (*Government House, Londonderry*), m. 20 Oct. 1874, Dorothea Maria, dau. of Samuel Riall, of Annerville, co. Tipperary (see that family), and has issue,
 1. Arthur Samuel, b. 5 April, 1877.
 1. Amy Maria, b. 9 Feb. 1879, m. 14 April, 1901, Thomas A. D. Best, Capt. Royal Inniskilling Fus., son of late W. J. Best, of Malabar Hill, Bombay.
 2. Violet Aileen Riall, b. 15 Oct. 1897.

3. William Hugh (Rev.), Rector of Sutcombe, Holsworthy, co. Devon, *m.* Adela Auber, of Bovey Tracey, same co., and had issue, two sons and two daus.
1. Katherine, *d.s.p.*
2. Grace, *d.s.p.*
3. Amy, *d.s.p.*
4. Mary, *d.s.p.*

The eldest son,
GEORGE MONTGOMERY, of Killee and Careysville, co. Cork, J.P., B.A. Trin. Coll. Dublin, *b.* 12 July, 1843; *m.* 1866, Elizabeth Jane, dau. and heir of Edward Keily Carey, of Careysville, co. Cork, and *d.* 4 Sept. 1910, having had i ue,
1. WILLIAM, of Killee.
2. Edward Hugh, of Careysville, co. ork, M.D. (Trin. Coll. Dublin), *b.* 10 Nov. 1871; *m.* 12 July, 1894, Lilla, dau. of W. Perrott, and has issue,
Edward Henry, *b.* March, 1896.
3. George Howard (*Rose Hill, Broomfield, Bridgwater*), *b.* 21 Aug. 1874; *m.* 26 April, 1906, Mabella, eldest dau. of Hugh Arthur Birley, of Woodside, Knutsford, and has issue,
Arthur George Carey, *b.* 4 July, 1910.
4. Thomas Alexander, late Gloucester Regt., *b.* 8 Oct. 1876; *m.* 25 Gladys eldest dau. of Col. Francis, and has issue,
1. Thomas, *b.* Jan. 1908.
2. George Edward, *b.* Jan. 1909.
1. Margaret Elizabeth, *b.* 1867; *m.* 21 July, 1892, Major Herbert Sturges Barlow, late 1st Batt. Seaforth Highlanders (Ross-shire Buffs), and has issue,
Robert George, *b.* Aug. 1893, and Hilaré Margaret, *b.* 10 Oct. 1898.
2. Grace Alice, *b.* 26 April, 1885.

Seat—Killee, Mitchelstown, co. Cork.

MONTGOMERY OF BEAULIEU.

RICHARD JOHNSTON MONTGOMERY, of Beaulieu, co. Louth, J.P., High Sheriff 1910, *b.* 7 July, 1855; *m.* 25 March, 1890, Maud Helena Collingwood (now of Rokeby Hall, co. Louth), only dau. of the late Sir John Stephen Robinson, Bart., C.B., of Rokeby Hall, and has issue.

1. John Gerald Richard Collingwood, *b.* 6 Feb., *d.* 9 Feb. 1892.
2. Bertram Richard Thomas, *b.* 15 June, *d.* 19 June, 1896.
3. Maud Rosa Mabella, *b.* 27 May, 1900; *d.* 6 Feb. 1901.

Mrs. R. J. Montgomery *s.* by family settlement to the Rokeby Hall property in Louth on the death *s.p.* of her brother Sir Gerald William Collingwood Robinson, 4th bart. of Rokeby, 31 May, 1903.

Lineage.—ALEXANDER MONTGOMERY, who first settled in Ireland, came at the invitation of Viscount Montgomery, and was Prebendary of Doe, co. Donegal, but turned soldier, and got a command. By his wife Margaret, dau. of Very Rev. Alexander Conyngham, Dean of Raphoe (who *d.* 18 June, 1675), he had two sons,
1. JOHN.
2. William.

The elder son,
JOHN MONTGOMERY, Major in the Army, *d.* 1679, leaving by Dorcas his wife (who *m.* 2ndly, Rev. Andrew Leslie), a dau., Margaret, who *m.* Rev. George Leslie, D.D., and had a son, George Leslie Montgomery, M.P. co. Cavan, who *s.* to the Cavan estates, and a son and heir,
JOHN MONTGOMERY, Major in the Army, *m.* 1st, Catherine, dau. of Rev. James Auchinleck, and by her had,
1. JOHN.
2. Alexander, Col. of Convoy, co. Donegal, and Ballyconnell, co. Cavan, *m.* a dau. of Henry Percy, of Seskin, co. Wicklow, but *d.s.p.* 1729, having devised the Donegal estates to his cousin, Alexander Montgomery, of Convoy.

Major John Montgomery *m.* 2ndly, Katherine, Lady Moore, relict of Sir William Moore, 2nd bart., of Ross Carbery, and dau. of Sir John Perceval, 3rd bart., of Burton. The eldest son,
JOHN MONTGOMERY, of Cragan, Major in the Army, had three sons,
1. John, Major in Col. Echlin's Regt. of Dragoons, whose male descendants became extinct.
2. ALEXANDER, of whom we treat.
3. Robert (ancestor of MONTGOMERY *of Bessmount*, co. Monaghan), of Anarea, co. Monaghan, *m.* Isabella, dau. of James Leslie, and had a son, Alexander, of Bessmount Park, co. Monaghan, who left two daus. and co-heiresses,
1. Mary, *m.* 1758, Alexander Nixon, of Nixon Hall, co. Fermanagh, and had, with other issue, a second son,
Alexander MONTGOMERY, of Bessmount, co. Monaghan, assumed the name of MONTGOMERY; *m.* 1807, Eliza, dau. of Arthur Stanley, and had issue,
1. Alexander, of Bessmount, *b.* 17 May, 1808; *m.* 8 Oct. 1846, Henrietta, dau. of Major Randal Stafford, of Tully, co. Cavan. He *d.* 25 June, 1881, leaving a son,
Alexander, *m.* Mary, dau. of Dr. Banks, and *d.* 28 Dec. 1878, leaving a son,
Alexander Randal William, *b.* 27 Oct. 1878.
2. Arthur Henry, of Crieve House, co. Monaghan, *m.* 29 April, 1851, Henrietta Frances, dau. of Rev. Francis Chomley, and *d.* 2 Dec. 1859, leaving issue.
3. Robert, *d.* 5 July, 1843.
4. George, M.D., of Dublin, *m.* 11 Aug. 1842, Elizabeth, dau. of George Arbuthnot Holmes, of Moorock, King's Co., and *d.* 4 Nov. 1869, leaving issue.
5. Handcock, *m.* 23 May, 1838, Alicia, dau. of David Verner, and niece of Sir William Verner, and *d.* 8 May, 1839, leaving an only son,
Alexander Verner, Capt. late 7th Royal Fus.
6. Mark Anthony, Ensign 67th Regt., *d. unm.* 26 April, 1844.
1. Anna Maria, *m.* 15 June, 1832, George Alcock Nixon, M.D., grandson of Alexander Nixon, of Nixon Hall.
2. Mary, *m.* 8 June, 1841, Robert Adams, M.D.
3. Elizabeth, *m.* 23 May, 1845, James Power, of Colehill House, co. Longford.
4. Jane Caroline.
, Anne, *m.* Col. George Vaughan, of Villa, co. Down (see VAUGHAN *of Quilly*).

The 2nd son,
ALEXANDER MONTGOMERY, of Ballyleck, M.P. co. Monaghan, 1713-15 and 1715-23, High Sheriff co. Monaghan, *m.* before 1696, Elizabeth, dau. and heir of Thomas Cole, of Ballyleck, and *s.* to the Ballyleck estate through her. He *d.* 1723, leaving issue,
1. Thomas, M.P. for Lifford (whom he disinherited for marrying without consent), *m.* Mary Franklin, and had issue,
1. Alexander John, Capt. in the Army, M.P. co. Donegal for thirty-two years, *d.* Sept. 1800; inherited the Convoy estate from his cousin, Alexander Montgomery, of Convoy.
2. John, of Lisbon.
3. Richard, a Capt. in the Army, emigrated to America, and there *m.* a dau. of Judge Livingston, joined the Americans in the war of Independence, and became a Gen. of great distinction; killed at Quebec 31 Dec. 1775. His remains were removed to New York, and a monument erected in St. Paul's Church there at the expense of Congress. He left no issue.
1. Sarah, *m.* Charles, 4th Viscount Ranelagh.
2. JOHN, of whom presently.
3. Matthew, killed by a fall from his horse.
4. Robert, of Brandrum, co. Monaghan, *m.* Sarah Maxwell, of Falkland, co. Monaghan, and had issue,
Robert, *m.* about 1779, Frances, dau. of George Fraser, of Cuba House, and Judith Desgennes, his wife, and had issue,
(1) Robert, of Convoy House, J.P. and D.L., High Sheriff 1819, *b.* March, 1780; *m.* 10 June, 1811, Maria Frances, only surviving dau. of Alexander Stewart, of Ardes House, by Lady Mary Moore his wife, 3rd dau. of Charles, 1st Marquess of Drogheda, and *d.* 1846, leaving issue,
1. Robert George, of Convoy House, J.P. and D.L., High Sheriff 1840, Hon. Col. Donegal Militia Artillery, *b.* 1814; *d. unm.* 1900.
1. Mary Elizabeth, *m.* Rev. Charles Boyton, D.D., F.T.C.D. Rector of Tullyaguish, and vicar-general of Raphoe. He left an only son, Rev. William Charles Boyton, M.A. Camb., Canon of St. Patrick's Cathedral, Canon of Derry Cathedral and Rector of Templemore, *b.* 1838, who *s.* to Convoy, 1900.
2. Frances Judith, *m.* 1843, James Grove Wood, of Castle Grove, co. Donegal, J.P. and D.L., who afterwards adopted the name of Grove on succeeding to the Castle Grove estate, and has issue.
(2) George, *m.* Maria, dau. of John Rutherford, and had issue, four sons and two daus.,
(3) Alexander Richard, Capt. in the Army.
(1) Judith Susanna, *m.* Thomas Montgomery, Capt. R.N.
1. Dorcas, *m.* Christopher Irvine, of Castle Irvine.
2. Sarah, *m.* Godfrey Wills, of Willsgrove.
3. Elizabeth, *m.* 1720, John Moutray, of Favour Royal, and had issue (*see that family*).

The 2nd son,
JOHN MONTGOMERY, of Ballyleck, co. Monaghan, M.P. for that co. 1723-27, High Sheriff 1726, *m.* Mary Cox, Maid of Honour to GEORGE II's Queen, and *d.* 1733. By Mary his wife (who *m.* 2ndly, Dr. Clements, Vice-Provost of Trin. Coll. Dublin, and M.P. for the University), he left issue,
1. JOHN, of Ballyleck, M.P. co. Monaghan Oct. to Dec. 1741; *d.* 1741.
2. Alexander, of whom next.

The younger son,
ALEXANDER MONTGOMERY, of Ballyleck, M.P. for Monaghan 1743-61, 1768-75, and 1776-83, High Sheriff 1747, Gen. of Volunteers; *m.* 1st, 1746, Catherine, dau. and co-heir of Col. Hugh Montgomery Willoughby, of Carron, co. Fermanagh (last heir in remainder to the Viscounty of Montgomery of the Great Ards, extinct on the death *s.p.* of the Earl of Mount Alexander in 1757). By her he had issue,
1. John, of Ballyleck, Col. Monaghan Mil., M.P. co. Monaghan 1783-90 and 1790-7, High Sheriff 1777; *m.* Salisbury, dau. and co-heir of Thomas Tipping, of Beaulieu. He *d.s.p.* 1797.
2. Hugh, Col. Madras Army, *d.* 1795, leaving a dau., who *m.* William James.
3. ROBERT, of whom presently.

He *m.* 2ndly, Eleanora, dau. and co-heir of Acheson Moore, of Garvey, co. Tyrone, and by her had issue,
4. Nathaniel, of Garvey, ancestor of MONTGOMERY-MOORE, of Garvey (*see that family*).
1. Sidney, *d. unm.*
2. Maria, *d. unm.*

The 3rd son,
REV. ROBERT MONTGOMERY, of Beaulieu, co. Louth, Rector of Monaghan for thirty years; *m.* Sophia Mabella, dau. and co-heir of Thomas Tipping, of Beaulieu and Bellurgan, co. Louth, by Sophia his wife, dau. of William Aston, by Salisbury his wife, dau. and heir of Henry Tichborne, Lord Ferrard, of Beaulieu (*see* BURKE's *Extinct Peerage*). He *d.* 1825, leaving issue,

1. ALEXANDER, his heir.
2. Thomas, Capt. R.N., m. 1815, Judith Susanna, dau. of Robert Montgomery, of Convoy, and has issue,
　1. Robert John, Barrister, m. Anne, dau. of Samuel Lindsay Bucknall, of Turin Castle, co. Mayo, and has issue.
　2. Thomas Alexander, m. Elizabeth Beaumont, dau. of William James.
　3. Alexander George, Surgeon 46th Regt., m. Mary, dau. of Col. Dennis, C.B., Bengal H.A., and left issue.
　4. George Samuel, C.S.I., Lieut.-Gen. Bombay Army, m. Letitia, dau. of Rev. Charles Gayer, and had issue. She d. 1894. He d. Jan. 1898. His dau. Evelyn, m. 7 Sept. 1881, Col. Arthur Bouverie Stopford, R.A. (see BURKE's Peerage, COURTOWN, E.).
　5. John Willoughby.
　1. Frances Mary.
　2. Sophia Louisa, m. Samuel Gordon, M.D.
1. Katharine Salisbury, m. 11 May, 1812, Capt. Skeffington Hamilton, who d.s.p. 1 Oct. 1830 (see HAMILTON of Coonacassa).
The elder son,
REV. ALEXANDER JOHNSTON, of Beaulieu, assumed the name of JOHNSTON in lieu of Montgomery and the Arms of JOHNSTON only by Royal Licence, 14 July, 1813, having m. 1st, 21 March, 1809, Margaret, dau. and heir of Andrew Johnston, of Littlemount, co. Fermanagh, by Rose his wife, dau. of Jason Hassard, of Skea. She d. 15 Oct. 1824, having had issue,
1. Robert Willoughby, b. 31 Oct. 1811; d. 28 Feb. 1826.
2. RICHARD JOHNSTON, of whom presently.
3. Thomas Tichborne, b. 14 March, 1815; m. Laura, dau. of — Armstrong, and had issue,
　1. Alexander.　　2. Richard.
　3. Robert.
　1. Margaret.
4. Alexander John, b. 21 Feb. 1820; d. 15 Dec. 1880; m. 12 Sept. 1855, Alice, dau. of Gustavus Jones, of Belleville, Westmeath. He d. 15 Dec. 1880, leaving issue,
　1. Richard Tichborne, b. 21 April, 1857; m. 10 June, 1903, Belinda Mary, youngest dau. of John Gilbert Cockburn, and has issue,
　　Alexander Richard Tichborne, b. 16 Aug 1907.
　　Frances Salisbury Tichborne.
　2. John Alexander Moore, b. 5 June, 1867; m. 10 April, 1895, Florence Mary, dau. of Rev. Richard Legge Tyner, Rector of Annadown, co. Galway.
　3. Robert Willoughby.
　1. Margaret Jane, m. Robert Roscoe Nuttall, and d. 13 Aug. 1894.
　2. Alice Elizabeth Frances, m. 3 March, 1881, Walter Blake Kirwan Tyner, son of the Rev. R. L. Tyner.
　3. Rose Sidney Sophia, m. H. Sweetman, M.D.
5. Arthur Andrew, d. young.
1. Rosa, m. 8 Feb. 1832, William Pentland, son of George Pentland, of Blackhall, Louth.
2. Sophia Mabella, m. 29 Sept. 1846, George Henry Pentland, of Blackhall, co. Louth, and d. 17 Aug. 1897, aged 81, leaving issue. He d. 1882.
3. Maria Jane, m. 27 July, 1867, William Gustavus Burroughes, and d. 1 Feb. 1895.
4. Sidney Katherine Salisbury, m. 12 Feb. 1840, Henry St. George Smith, of Piperstown, co. Louth, and had issue. He d. 16 Dec. 1899. She d. 14 March, 1902.
Rev. Alexander Johnston m. 2ndly, 12 Jan. 1827, Charlotte Isabella, dau. of John Forster, brother of Sir Thomas Forster, Bart. She d.s.p. 1 July, 1840. He d. 2 Jan. 1856. His 2nd, son,
RICHARD THOMAS MONTGOMERY, of Beaulieu, J.P., High Sheriff 1855, sometime Lieut. 3rd Light Dragoons, b. 6 Jan. 1813; m. 11 Sept. 1845, Frances Barbara (d. 23 Feb. 1909), dau. of St, George Smith, of Greenhills, co. Louth, and d. 27 Feb. 1890, leaving issue,
1. RICHARD JOHNSTON, now of Beaulieu.
2. Willoughby Aston, b. 31 Aug. 1858; m. Miss Hunter, and has issue,
　1. Willoughby Tichborne, b. 1896.
　2. Richard Aston, b. 20 Oct. 1900.
3. Tichborne St. George Roger, b. 28 May, 1860.
1. Emily Hannah, m. 30 May, 1872, Very Rev. Lucius H. O'Brien M.A., Dean of Limerick, nephew of Lucius, 13th Lord Inchiquin.
2. Rose Sophia Mabella, d. unm. 25 Nov. 1885.
3. Sydney Wilhelmina Salisbury, m. 12 April, 1888, James Watt, of Claragh, co. Donegal, and has issue.
4. Violet Marguerite, m. 8 June, 1898, her cousin Alexander Johnston Smith, son of H. St. G. Smith, of Piperstown.

Seats—Beaulieu, near Drogheda; and Rokeby Hall, Dunleer, co. Louth. Residence—Killineer House, near Drogheda.

MONTGOMERY OF BLESSINGBOURNE.

HUGH DE FELLENBERG MONTGOMERY, of Blessingbourne, co. Tyrone, M.A. Ch. Ch. Oxon. J.P. and D.L. for co. Tyrone, J.P. co. Fermanagh, High Sheriff for co. Fermanagh 1871, and for co. Tyrone 88, late Capt. Fermanagh Militia, b. 14 Aug. 1844; '4 March, 1870, Mary Sophia Juliana, youngest dau. of Hon. and Rev. John Charles Maude, Rector of Enniskillen, and has had issue,
1. HUGH MAUDE DE FELLENBERG, Major R.A., b. 5 Dec. 1870; m. 20 Dec. 1894, Mary, 2nd dau. of the late Edmund Langton, and Mrs. Massingberd, of Gunby, co. Lincoln (see that family), and has issue,
　1. Hugh Edmond Langton, b. 30 Oct. 1895.
　2. Peter Stephen, b. 1909.
　1. Mary Langton, b. 1897.
　2. Elizabeth, b 1900.
　3. Anne, b. 1903.
2. Archibald Armar, Major R.A., b. 6 Dec. 1871; m. 21 April, 1896, Diana, youngest dau. of the late Edmund Langton and Mrs. Massingberd, of Gunby (see that family).
3. Geoffrey Cornwallis, b. 1874; m. 4 April, 1899, Elsie Katherine, eldest dau. of E. Tindal Atkinson, K.C., and had issue,
　1. Robert Edward, b. 1904; d. 1907.
　1. Joan, b. 1899.
　2. Ruth Mary, b. 1902; d. 11 Sept. 1907.
　3. Joyce, b. 1905.
4. Francis Trevilian, b. 1875; d. 4 March, 1887.
5. Charles Hubert, b. 1876.
6. Maurice William de Fellenberg, b. and d. 1878.
7. Walter Ashley, b. 1882.
8. Ralph Noel Vernon, Lieut. R.H.A., b. 1884.
1. Mary Millicent, b. 1873; d. 1874.

Lineage.—HUGH MONTGOMERY was settled at Derrybrosk, or Derrybrusk, co. Fermanagh, by his kinsman, George Montgomery, D.D., Bishop of Clogher and Meath about 1618. He had a son,
NICHOLAS MONTGOMERY, b. about 1615, Laureatus of Glasgow University 1634, Lieut. in Sir James Montgomery's Regiment, and afterwards Rector of Carrickmacross, of Derrybrosk, or Derrybrusk, co. Fermanagh, and d. about 1706, leaving with two younger sons, Robert, of Derrybrusk, Capt. in the Army, and Andrew, who s. his father as Rector of Carrickmacross, and a dau. Catharine, who m. Capt. Alexander Acheson, an elder son,
HUGH MONTGOMERY, of Derrygonnelly, Capt. of Horse under WILLIAM III, b. 1651; m. Katherine, dau. and heir of Richard Dunbar, of Derrygonnelly (by his wife Anna Catharina, dau. of Lars Grubbe Stjernfelt, a cousin of King Gustavus Adolphus, of Sweden, and widow of Ludovic Hamilton, Baron of Deserf, in Sweden), and great-grand-dau. of Sir John Dunbar,* Knt., of the same place, and had issue,
1. NICHOLAS, m. 1st Angel, dau. and heir of William Archdall, of Castle Archdall, co. Fermanagh, and assumed the surname of ARCHDALL. By her (who d. 1747) he had an only son Mervyn, of Castle Archdall (see that family). He m. 2ndly, Sarah, dau. of — Spurling, of London, and had four sons, and four daus,
　1. Robert.
　2. Richard, B.A. Dub., M.P. for Ardfert 1790–97, Killybegs 1798–1801, Kilkenny 1801–2, Dundalk 1802–6, d. 8 Feb. 1824; m. Nov. 1780, Anna Maria Montague, and left issue by her, who d. 16 Sept. 1805.
　3. Nicholas, d. 25 Jan. 1825; m. Aug. 1782, Sarah Arabella Abigail, dau. of Rev. Samuel Meade, by Abigail, dau. of Walter Cope, of Drumilly, and assumed the name of COPE (see COPE of Drumilly).
　4. Edward.
　1. Catherine, d. 21 June, 1810, m. 26 Sept. 1777, James Byrn, of Park, co. Carlow; who d. March, 1824, and had issue, Nicholas, d. 3 May, 1849; m. 9 Aug. 1812, Elizabeth, dau. of Peter Burtchaell, of Coolroe, co. Kilkenny, and had issue.
　　Augusta, m. 12 May, 1816, Patrick Burtchaell.
　2. Sarah.
　3. Augusta, m. 1778, Rev. Jonathan Bruce.
　4. Elizabeth.
2. HUGH, of whom hereafter.
3. Richard, of Monea, co. Fermanagh.
1. Sarah, m. Brockhill Green.
2. Anne, m. Thomas Beaghan, of Dublin.
3. Jane, m. Thomas Clarke Dover, of Dublin.
4. Margaret, m. Hugh O'Donnell, of Larkfield, the representative of the Earls of Tyrconnell, of the 1st creation (see O'DONOVAN'S Annals of the Four Masters).
5. Sidney.
Mr. Montgomery's will, dated 10 Feb. 1720, was proved 14 June, 1723. His 2nd son,
HUGH MONTGOMERY, of Derrygonnelly, m. Elizabeth, dau. of Ven. William Armar, Archdeacon of Connor (by Martha his wife, dau. of Capt. William Leslie, of Prospect), and sister of Margetson Armar, of Castle Coole, co. Fermanagh, and d. before 1739, leaving a son,
HUGH MONTGOMERY, of Castle Hume, b. 1739; m. 1778, Mary, dau. of Sir Archibald Acheson, 1st Viscount Gosford, and d. 1797 (will, dated 29 July, 1791, proved 1797), leaving issue, two sons and a dau.,
1. HUGH, his successor.　2. Archibald Armar, b. 1783; d.s.p.
1. Mary Milicent, b. 1787; d. unm. 1868.
The eldest son,
HUGH MONTGOMERY, of Blessingbourne, Capt. 18th Dragoons, Lieut.-Col. Fermanagh Militia, b. 1779; m. 1821, Maria Dolores Plink, of Malaga, Spain, and d. 1838, leaving an only son,

---

* This Sir John Dunbar, original plantation grantee of the manor of Dunbar, or Drumcrow, in the barony of Magherabov, co. Fermanagh, Sheriff in 1626, and again in 1632, seems to have been a person of importance. He appears to have come from Avoch, in Ross-shire, and to have descended from Patrick Dunbar, Chancellor of Aberdeen, 7th son of Sir Alexander Dunbar, of Westfield.

HUGH RALPH SEVERIN MONTGOMERY, of Blessingbourne, b. 1821; m. 1843, Maria Philipina, dau. of Philip Emmanuel de Fellenberg, of Hofwyl, sometime Landamman of the Republic of Berne, and by her (who d. 1846) left at his decease, 1844, a son and heir, the present
HUGH DE FELLENBERG MONTGOMERY, of Blessingbourne.
Seat—Blessingbourne, Fivemiletown, co. Tyrone.

MONTGOMERY OF BENVARDEN.

JOHN ALEXANDER MONTGOMERY, of Benvarden and Potters Walls, co. Antrim, J.P. and D.L., High Sheriff 1910, late Major 4th Batt. Royal Irish Rifles, b. 3 Dec. 1866; s. his father in 1893; m. 16 Oct. 1900, Elizabeth Ferguson, dau. of the late Canon Newland, Rector of Buncrana, and has issue,
1. JOHN ALEXANDER JAMES, b. 26 April, 1904.
1. Elizabeth Barbara Ethne, b. 17 July, 1901.
2. Isabel Frances Ellen, b. 9 April, 1903.

Lineage.—ROBERT MONTGOMERY, of Glenarm, b. 13 Oct. 1711; m. 8 July, 1742, Isabella Stewart, and by her had issue,
HUGH MONTGOMERY, of Glenarm, b. 12 April, 1743; m. 2 April, 1785, Margaret, dau. of Robert Allen, of Killymaudle, and had issue by her (who d. 17 Nov. 1835),
1. JOHN, his heir.
2. Hugh, of Ballydrain, co. Antrim, m. Emily, dau. of John Ferguson, of Ballysillan, and d. 1867, having had issue, six sons and one dau (see MONTGOMERY of Ballydrain).
3. Alexander, of Potters Walls, co. Antrim; d.s.p.
1. Thomas, of Birch Hill, co. Antrim, J.P., formerly in the 16th and 9th Lancers; d.s.p.
1. Barbara, m. 1st, Richard Staples, son of the Right Hon. John Staples, of Lissan, and 2ndly, 1826, the Right Hon. Sir Alexander Macdonnell. 2. Isabella, d. 1854.
3. Marian. 4. Victoria.
Mr. Montgomery d. 13 Oct. 1832, and was s. by his eldest son,
JOHN MONTGOMERY, of Benvarden, J.P. and D.L., b. 24 Dec. 1790; m. 5 March, 1819, Jane, dau. of Sir Andrew Ferguson, Bart., and had surviving issue,
1. ROBERT JAMES, his heir.
1. Barbara Anne, m. 27 Dec. 1876, as his second wife, Very Rev. Andrew Ferguson Smyly, Dean of Derry (see SMYLY of Camus), who d. 1897. She d. 25 April, 1911.
2. Isabella Dorothea, d. unm. 23 Aug. 1908.
Mr. Montgomery d. 7 Dec. 1876, and was s. by his only son,
ROBERT JAMES MONTGOMERY, of Benvarden and Potters Walls, co. Antrim, High Sheriff 1867, and J.P. and D.L. co. Antrim, High Sheriff 1870, formerly Capt. 5th Dragoon Guards, served in the Crimea, b. 1829; m. 28 Jan. 1864, Elizabeth, dau. of James Robert White, of White Hall, co. Antrim, and by her (who d. 30 Aug. 1893) had issue,
1. JOHN ALEXANDER, now of Benvarden.
2. Francis James, Capt. 4th Royal Irish Rifles, b. 14 Oct. 1869; m. 12 Dec. 1908, Eva, elder dau. of J. S. Talbot, late Col. Shropshire Light Infantry, and has issue,
Hugh Ainslie, b. 22 April, 1910.
1. Janet Maude.
2. Elizabeth Barbara Isabel, m. 28 Jan. 1901, Henry I. Stuart, of Rockwood, Queensland, 4th son of the late C. G. Stuart, of Ballyhivistock, co. Antrim. He d. 15 Aug. 1902, leaving a son.
Mr. R. J. Montgomery d. 13 May. 1893, and was s. by his eldest son.
Seats—Benvarden, Dervock, and Potters Walls, Antrim.

LYONS MONTGOMERY OF BELHAVEL.

HENRY WILLOUGHBY STEWART LYONS-MONTGOMERY, of Belhavel, co. Leitrim, late Lieut. Leitrim Militia, b. 16 Sept. 1850; m. 6 April, 1876, Jane Singer, only child of Capt. Travers Crofton, of Lakefield (see that family).

Lineage. — CAPT. JOHN LYONS, of Drogheda, 2nd son of John Lyons, of Ledestown, co. Westmeath, by Elizabeth his wife, dau. of Henry Williams, Deputy-Governor of Antigua, m. Dorothea, dau. of Hugh Montgomery, son of Sir Thomas Montgomery, Knt., and had issue,
1. John, killed in a duel, 17 March, 1754.
2. HUGH, of whom presently.
3. Charles, Town Major of Halifax, whose dau. Clementina m. Rev. John Achmuty, Rector of Trim.
The 2nd son,

HUGH LYONS, assumed the name of MONTGOMERY. He m. Feb. 1773, Catherine, dau. of Richard, 4th Viscount Boyne, and had issue,
1. HUGH, his heir.
2. Charles (Rev.), Rector of Innismagrath, Diocese of Kilmore, m. 26 June, 1815, Emily, dau. of Humphrey Nixon, of Nixon Lodge, co. Cavan, and niece of the Right Hon. Sir John Stewart, Bart., M.P., of Athenry, co. Galway. He d. 3 Sept. 1859, having had issue,
1. Hugh, m. 11 June, 1856, Henrietta Constance, youngest dau. of the Rev. Henry Lucas St. George, Rector of Dromore, co. Tyrone, and had issue,
Henry Lucas St. George, b. 2 Nov. 1859; d. 2 Jan. 1887.
Emily Laura, m. 17 Sept. 1898, William Stewart Archdale (see ARCHDALE of Castle Archdale).
2. Humphrey, Lieut. Cavan Militia; d. 26 Nov. 1905.
3. Charles Nixon, b. 1825; d. 10 May, 1843.
1. Anna, d. 27 Sept. 1896.
2. Sophia, d. 28 Aug. 1896.
3. Catherine.
4. Emily, m. 19 Feb. 1844, John O'Donnell, of Larkfield, co. Leitrim.
5. Elizabeth, m. 27 Dec. 1858, Rev. Julius S. Hearn, son of the Rev. William Edward Hearn, Vicar of Kildrumferton, Diocese of Kilmore.
1. Georgina, m. 19 Oct. 1797, Jones W. Irwin.
2. Elizabeth, m. 1795, Capt. Nathaniel Cooper, 68th Regt., of Cooper Hill, co. Meath.
3. Catherine, m. March, 1799, Thomas Norman (see that family).
Mr. Lyons-Montgomery d. 1792, and was s. by his son,
HUGH LYONS-MONTGOMERY, of Belhavel, co. Leitrim, m. 27 Jan. 1812, Elizabeth, dau. of the Very Rev. Stewart Blacker, of Carrick Blacker, co. Armagh, Dean of Leighlin, and by her (who m. 2ndly, Monsieur de Champre) had issue,
1 HUGH, his heir.
2. Stewart Lambert, Lieut.-Col. Scots Fusiliers, late 10th Royal Hussars, m. a dau. of Gen. Young, H.E.I.C.S., and left issue,
Hugh Frederick, C.B., of Camusdarrach Arisaig, co. Inverness, Col. Indian Army, b. 5 Jan. 1856; m. 15 Oct. 1891, Catherine Mary, dau. of Æneas R. Macdonell, of Morar, co. Inverness, who d. 22 May, 1911.
Constance Mary, m. 30 Dec. 1882, Lieut.-Col. H. W. Apperly, late 9th Lancers.
3. Charles, Lieut.-Gen. Bengal Staff Corps, b. 6 Feb. 1824; m. Miss Masters, of Calcutta.
1. Elizabeth, m. 1st, Joseph May, of Hale, co. Southampton, and 2ndly, Robert Maxwell, of Islanmore, co. Limerick.
2. Caroline, m. Adolphus Cavagnari, Major in the French service.
3. Sophia, m. 1840, John Barré Beresford, of Learmount and Ashbrook, co. Derry.
4. Louisa, m. Ralph Smith, of Greenhills, co. Louth.
Mr. Lyons-Montomery d. 26 April, 1826, and was s. by his eldest son,
HUGH LYONS-MONTGOMERY, of Belhavel, co. Leitrim, J.P. and D.L., High Sheriff 1840, M.P. for the co., b. 1816; m. 26 June, 1840, Elizabeth, dau. of Henry Smith, of Annesbrook, co. Meath, and by her (who d. 30 Sept. 1899) had issue,
1. Hugh, Lieut. 45th Regt., d. in Thungor, 10 March, 1874.
2. HENRY WILLOUGHBY, now of Belhavel.
3. Lambert de Winton, b. 1854; m. 19 Feb. 1909, Mabel Frances, dau. of George Bordes.
4. Alfred Otho, drowned in South Africa, Feb. 1878.
5. Kynaston Forster Walter, Capt. British South Africa Company's Forces, late 2nd Dragoon Guards, served in Bechuanaland Exped. 1884-5, Mashonaland Exped. 1890 (despatches), Pondoland Exped. 1894, Rhodesia Rebellion 1896 (despatches), Boer War 1900-2 (Cambridge, South Africa Medal), b. 22 April, 1859; m. 1 Sept. 1903, Marion Elizabeth, 3rd dau. of late John Robinson Reid, of Charlie's Hope, Rosebank, Cape Colony, and has issue,
Hugh Neil, b. 10 Oct. 1905.
Beatrice, b. 27 March, 1904.
1. Elizabeth, m. 30 Oct. 1865, Richard Ruxton Fitzherbert, of Blackcastle (see that family).
2. Caroline Matilda, dcc.   3. Ada Louisa Mary.
4. Eveleen Clemina, m. 19 March, 1873, Arthur Vesey Fitzherbert (see FITZHERBERT of Blackcastle).
5. Henrietta Emily Anna, m. 17 April, 1890, Lieut.-Col. J. K. Kirsteman, late 100th Regt.
6. Florence Maud, m. 19 March, 1873, Folliott Barton, son of Lieut.-Col. William Barton, 2nd Life Guards, of the Waterfoot, co. Fermanagh (see that family).
7. Norma Wilhelmina, m. 1873, W. A. Peyton, and d. 1876.
8. Ethel Constance m. John Molony, and d. 28 Oct. 1891, leaving issue (see MOLONY of Cragg).
9. Beatrice Cecilia Blanche.
Mr. Lyons-Montgomery d. 16 July, 1882.

Arms—Quarterly: 1st and 4th grand quarters, quarterly 1st and 4th az., three fleurs-de-lis or; 2nd and 3rd, gu., three gem rings or, gemmed az., over all an escutcheon arg., charged with a trefoil slipped vert, for MONTGOMERY; 2nd grand quarter, az., three battle-axes erect, two and one, arg., for BATTEN; 3rd grand quarter per fesse or and az., three lions rampant, within a tressure flory, all counterchanged, for LYONS. Crest—A cubit arm erect, vested gu., cuffed arg., grasping a broken tilting-spear, the point falling downwards, ppr. Motto—Patriæ infelici fidelis.

Seat—Belhavel, Killargue, co. Leitrim (viâ Dromahaire).

MONTGOMERY OF BALLYDRAIN.

HUGH WYNDHAM MONTGOMERY, of Ravensdale, co. Kildare, High Sheriff 1911, late Lieut. 17th Lancers, b. 1875; m. 1898, Lena, dau. of the late Thomas Benyon Ferguson, by his wife Hon. Emma Amelia, sister of 12th Viscount Falkland (see BURKE's *Peerage*), and has issue,

1. GEORGE WYNDHAM CLAUD, b. 1899.
2. Noel Hugh, b. 1910.
1. Shelagh Blanche, b. 1904.
2. Daphne Lena, b. 1906.

Lineage.—HUGH MONTGOMERY, of Ballydrain (2nd son of Hugh Montgomery of Glenarm—see MONTGOMERY of *Benvarden*) m. Emily, dau. of John Ferguson, of Ballysillan, and d. 1867, having had by her, with four other sons, a 5th and a 6th son, THOMAS and GEORGE. The 5th son,

THOMAS MONTGOMERY, of Ballydrain, co. Antrim, J.P. and D.L., High Sheriff 1885, b. 1837; m. 1866, Isabella Folingsby (now of *Ballydrain*), dau. of the late Rev. Thomas Walker, and d. 29 Nov. 1909, having had issue,

1. HUGH FERGUSON, Capt. 4th Batt. Royal Irish Rifles, b. 1806; d.v.p. 21 Jan. 1908.
1. Emily Sarah.
2. Mary Isabella, d. 21 Dec. 1891.
3. Florence Jane, m. 28 Jan. 1896, William Gordon Crawford, eldest son of William CRAWFORD, of Crawford (see *Crawfordsburn*).
4. Eva Victoria, m. 27 May, 1901, Arthur Dupuis, son of Rev. George Dupnis, of Sessay, Yorks.
5. Blanche Marjorie, m. 19 Sept. 1900, Capt. Nicholas Delacherois Cromnelin, 5th Batt. Royal Irish Rifles (see *that family*). She d.s.p. 1 Feb. 1909.
6. Ellen Georgina.

The 6th son of Hugh Montgomery and Emily Ferguson,

GEORGE MONTGOMERY, b. 1843; m. Blanche, 3rd dau. of John Evelegh Wyndham, of Sock Dennis, Somerset, and had an only son,

HUGH WYNDHAM, of Ravensdale, co. Kildare.

Lineage—See MONTGOMERY of *Benvarden*.

Seat—Ravensdale, co. Kildare.

MONTGOMERY-MOORE. See MOORE.

MOONY OF THE DOON.

GEORGE MEARES STOPFORD ENRAGHT-MOONY, of The Doon, King's Co., J.P. King's Co., b. 31 March, 1868; s. his father 5 Sept. 1892; m. 16 Sept. 1902, Henrietta Georgina Ethel, eldest dau. of George Charles Mulock, late D.I., R.I.C., 5th son of the late Thomas Mulock, of Kilnagarna, King's Co. (see *that family*), and has issue,

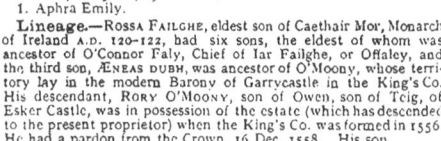

1. OWEN ROBERT MULOCK, b. 9 July, 1903.
2. Edward Ross, b. 14 Sept. 1909.
3. Desmond Stopford Mulock, b. 8 June, 1911.
1. Aphra Emily.

Lineage.—ROSSA FAILGHE, eldest son of Caethair Mor, Monarch of Ireland A.D. 120-122, had six sons, the eldest of whom was ancestor of O'Connor Faly, Chief of Iar Failghe, or Offaley, and the third son, ÆNEAS DUBH, was ancestor of O'Moony, whose territory lay in the modern Barony of Garrycastle in the King's Co. His descendant, RORY O'MOONY, son of Owen, son of Teig, of Esker Castle, was in possession of the estate (which has descended to the present proprietor) when the King's Co. was formed in 1556. He had a pardon from the Crown, 16 Dec. 1558. His son,

OWEN O'MOONY, of Esker Castle, was father of

JOHN O'MOONY, of Esker Castle, father of

OWEN O'MOONY, of Esker Castle, included in a pardon 6 May, 1602. He surrendered his estate and had a re-grant from the Crown of Esker, Corracullin, Doon, &c., by Patent dated 26 Aug. 1637. He d. 1640, leaving three sons and a dau.,

1. EDMUND, his heir, d. unm. 1643.
2. JOHN, of Carrocollin, s. his brother and d. 1649. His will, dated 20 May, 1648, was proved 13 Oct. 1663. He m. Mary, dau. of — Carroll, and left an only son,

OWEN, of whom presently.

3. Matthew, a Capt. in the King's service, named as an Ensignman in the Acts of Settlement and Explanation.
1. Margery, m. Charles O'Melaghlin, representative of the ancient Kings of Meath.

The grandson,

OWEN MOONY, of Esker Castle, The Doon, &c., b. 1647, was restored to his estate as an innocent by decree of the Court of Claims in 1663. He m. (settlements dated 1 and 2 May), 1666, Elisa, dau. of Hugh Flattery, of Streamstown, King's Co., and d. 24 April, 1716, leaving two sons and three daus.,

1. OWEN, of whom presently.
2. William, of Lackagh, d. unm., will dated 11 Dec. 1756, proved 1764.
1. Mary, b. 1682; d. April, 1752; m. 1710, John Moony, of Lackagh, who d. April, 1752 (son of Edmund Moony, a Capt. in King James II's army, who d. 20 Dec. 1689); and had an only son, OWEN, of Doon, High Sheriff of King's Co. 1772, d. 7 May, 1789, admon. 30 May, 1791; m. 1757, Jane, dau. of Robert Holmes, of Johnstown (see HOLMES of *St. David's*), and left an only child,

Isabella, m. 18 Sept. 1783, William Carroll, of New Lawn, co. Tipperary, who assumed the additional name of Moony, and was High Sheriff of the King's Co. 1792.
2. Alice, m. Anthony Molloy, of Galduss, King's Co.
3. Honora, m. Charles Molloy.

The elder son,

OWEN MOONY, of The Doon, b. 1673; m. 1700, Mary, dau. of John Coghlan and niece of Francis Coghlan, of Kilcolgan, King's Co., and d. 20 April, 1755. His will, dated 4 Sept. 1753, was proved 6 May, 1755. He left two sons and one dau.,

1. JOHN, his heir, d.s.p. March, 1759.
2. EDMUND, s. his brother; m. Anne Riley, but d.s.p.
1. Matilda, m. JAMES ENRAGHT, of Ballyclare, King's Co. (who was b. 1684, and d. 1736), and had two sons,
1. FRANCIS, of whom presently.
2. Owen, of Banagher, d. 1808, having m. and left issue.

The grandson,

FRANCIS ENRAGHT-MOONY, of The Doon, assumed the additional name of MOONY on succeeding in 1789. He was b. 1744, m. Helen, dau. of Robert Mulock, of Bellair, King's Co., and d. 1802, leaving by her, who d. 21 Oct. 1815, aged 74, a son and a dau.,

ROBERT JAMES, of whom presently.

Mary Anne, m. 1st, — Hamilton; m. 2ndly, Henry Malone (who d. 1843).

The only son,

ROBERT JAMES ENRAGHT-MOONY, of The Doon, b. 1770, J.P. and D.L. King's Co., High Sheriff 1794, m. June, 1794, Isabella, eldest dau. of John Drought, of Whigsborough, King's Co., and d. 22 Nov. 1842, leaving by her (who d. 16 Oct., 1836), one son and five daus.,

1. FRANCIS MOONY, of whom presently.
1. Isabella Georgina, d. young.
2. Sarah Isabella, d. 18 Nov. 1838.
3. Susanna Elizabeth, d. 28 June, 1843; m. 19 March, 1833, Lundy Dickinson, Commander R.N., of Spring Lawn, King's Co.
4. Eleanor Mary Anne, m. 1st, John Whitly Frazer, R.A.; and 2ndly, 24 Jan. 1844, Charles Dillon Fry, who d. 26 Oct. 1885.
5. Matilda Frances, d. 23 Sept. 1838; m. 12 Jan. 1836, Rev. Simon Charles Foot, M.A., Rector and Vicar of Knocktopher, co. Kilkenny (see FOOT *late of The Rower*).

The only son,

FRANCIS MOONY ENRAGHT-MOONY, of The Doon, b. 1795, J.P. King's Co., High Sheriff 1820; m. 22 Dec. 1820, Catherine, dau. of Lundy Foot, of The Rower, co. Kilkenny, and Orlagh, co. Dublin (see *that family*), and d. 23 Feb. 1857, having by her (who d. 19 Oct. 1870) had issue,

1. ROBERT JAMES, of whom presently.
2. Jeffery Francis, d. young.
3. John Drought (Rosewarne, Dawlish Road, Teignmouth, S. Devon), late Lieut. 13th Somersetshire, L.I., served as Captain in the Colonial Force during the Kaffir War of 1879-80 (Medal and clasp), m. 16 Aug. 1862, Elizabeth Anna, dau. of David Davies, late 90th Regt., and has issue,
1. Francis Herbert Greenock, b. 9 April, 1865, late Resident British Commissioner of Swaziland; m. Mary L. Stevens.
2. David Robert, b. 11 Oct. 1866; killed in Matabele War 15 June, 1896.
3. John Owen William, b. 23 March, 1870; m. Sophia Barnard.
4. Hugh O'Neill, b. 17 Aug. 1881.
1. Katherine Louisa Isabella, m. 14 Dec. 1898, Edward Gardiner Powell.
2. Rose Gwendaedd, b. 3 June, 1816; m. Capt .C .R. Nettleton.
3. Edith Violet, b. March, 1876; m. 9 June, 1903, Major Alfred Edmond Weld, R.A.M.C., elder son of Matthew Richard Weld, late I.C.S.
4. Gladys Wharton, b. 23 June, 1883.
1. Anna Jane, m. 9 Aug. 1862, George Joseph Maunsell, Capt. 15th Regt.
2. Isabella Sarah, m. 3 June, 1874, John William Tarleton, of Killeigh, King's Co. (see *that family*).

The eldest son,

ROBERT JAMES ENRAGHT-MOONY, of The Doon, b. 19 Oct. 1830; d. 5 Sept. 1892; B.A. Trin. Coll. Dublin 1854, J.P., D.L. King's Co., High Sheriff 1855, J.P. co. Westmeath; m. 31 Jan. 1861 (Abigail Mary) Angelina, younger dau. of George Meares Maunsell, of Ballywilliam, co. Limerick (see *that family*), and had issue,

1. Francis Owen, d. 1 April, 1870.
2. GEORGE MEARES STOPFORD, now of The Doon.
3. Robert James, b. 13 Sept. 1869.

1. Mary Maud, m. 9 April, 1890, William Morley Philip Aldborough Reamsbottom, of Aldborough House, King's Co., and Larkspur Park, Kati Kati, New Zealand.
2. Katherine Isabella, m. 21 Oct. 1903, Wilfrid Perry, of Lisderg, Belmont, King's Co.
3. Hilda Angelina.

Arms—Chequy gu. and arg. in chief, a trefoil slipped vert.
Crest—Out of a coronet an arm in armour erect, the hand grasping a tilting-spear all ppr. Motto—Sola virtus nobilitat.
Seat—The Doon, Athlone.

MOORE OF BALLYDIVITY.

JAMES STEWART-MOORE, of Ballydivity, co. Antrim, M.A. Trin. Coll. Dublin, J.P. and D.L., High Sheriff 1880, b. Nov. 1847 ; s. his father 1870 ; m. 11 Jan. 1871, Elizabeth, dau. of Charles Stuart, of Ballyhivistock, co. Antrim, and has issue,
1. JAMES, b. 18 June, 1876.
2. Charles Francis, b. 1 Dec. 1878.
1. Ethel, b. 3 Dec. 1877. 2. Mary, b. 14 Feb. 1880.
3. Katherine Frances, b. 21 April, 1883.

Lineage.—ANDREW STEWART settled in Ireland after the battle of Culloden, 1746. His son, JAMES STEWART, m. Jane, only dau. of James Moore, of Ballydivity, and was father of
JAMES STEWART-MOORE, of Ballydivity, High Sheriff co. Antrim 1798. He m. 1792, Margaret, dau. of the Ven. William Sturrock, Archdeacon of Armagh, and d. 1845, having had issue,
1. JAMES STEWART-MOORE, his heir.
2. John, of Moyarget, co. Antrim, J.P., Lieut.-Col. H.E.I.C.S., m. Elizabeth, dau. of Alexander Dunlop, of Drumnagresson, co. Antrim, and had issue,
   1. Mary, m. 16 Sept. 1879, Valentine Ball, C.B., who d. 15 June, 1895, leaving issue (see BURKE's Family Records).
   2. Frances, m. William Dunlop.   3. Elizabeth.
   4. Jane, m. James Stuart, and d. 1893.
   5. Margaret, d. unm.
   6. Catherine, m. Francis Turnly Gage.
3. Henry, d. unm.
1. Harriett, m. 31 March, 1831, Major William Stewart, 30th Regt., and had issue.
2. Jane, m. John Owens, and had issue.
3. Elizabeth, m. Thomas Robinson, and had issue.

The eldest son,
JAMES STEWART-MOORE, of Ballydivity, co. Antrim, J.P. and D.L., High Sheriff 1849, Capt. 11th Hussars, served in the Peninsula, at Waterloo, and in India, b. 1793 ; m. 1845, Frances, dau. of Henry Richardson, of Somerset, co. Londonderry, and d. 1870, leaving by her (who d. 1876),
1. JAMES, now of Ballydivity.
2. Henry, b. 1850; d. 14 Sept 1908 ; m. June, 1882, Emily, dau. of Butler Giveen, J.P. and D.L. of Cooldaragh, co. Antrim,
1. Margaret, m. Lieut.-Col. H. Tracey, R.A.
2. Catherine Elizabeth, m. 1867, Anthony Traill, M.D., Provost of Trin. Coll. Dublin (see TRAILL, of Ballylough).

Seat—Ballydivity, Ballymoney, co. Antrim.

MOORE OF BARNE.

RANDAL KINGSMILL MOORE, of Barne, co. Tipperary, J.P. and D.L., High Sheriff 1904, late Lieut. 3rd Batt. Leinster Regt., b. 12 Feb. 1873 ; s. his father 1897 ; m. 3 April, 1909, Lilian Julietta Mabson, youngest dau. of the late Henry John Simonds, of The Rectory, Caversham.

Lineage—In the reign of JAMES I (about 1620) RICHARD MOORE came over to Ireland, and settled at Clonmel, co. Tipperary, about 1635. He was High Sheriff co. Waterford 1666, and Tipperary 1675. His will (dated 17 April, 1690) was proved 10 Sept. 1690, by his wife Margaret, by whom he had issue, two sons,
1. STEPHEN, ancestor of the Earls of MOUNTCASHELL.
2. THOMAS, of whom we treat.

The 2nd son,
THOMAS MOORE, of Chancellorstown, co. Tipperary, High Sheriff 1698, m. Eleanor, dau. of Richard Covert, of the city of Cork, Alderman, by Christian his wife, dau. of Nicholas King. His will is dated 21 April, 1702, and proved 2 March, 1703. By his wife (who re-married with James Harrison, of Cloughjordan, co. Tipperary) he had issue,
1. STEPHEN, of whom hereafter.
2. Guy, of Abbey, co. Tipperary, High Sheriff co. Tipperary 1722, b. 1691 ; m. 1717, Mary, elder dau. and co-heir of Childley Coote, and had issue,
   1. Guy Moore Coote, father of Guy Moore Coote.
   2. Thomas Childley Moore, m. 7 May, 1765, Honora, dau. of — Bryan.
      1. Mary.   2. Elizabeth, m. Lieut.-Col. Daniel Webb.
   3. Robert, of Ardmovie and Mooremount, m. Elinor, 2nd dau. and co-heir of Childley Coote, and had a son, Thomas Bob Moore.
   4. Thomas, of Moore Hall, co. Cork, and of Marlfield, co. Tipperary, d. 27 Sept. 1752 ; m. 1721, Mary, dau. of Richard Moore, of Cashel, and had issue,
      1. Stephen, High Sheriff co. Tipperary 1757, m. 12 Feb. 1751, Alicia, younger dau. of Sir Robert Maude, Bart.
      2. Richard, b. 1725.
      1. Elizabeth, m. Sir Arthur Newcomen, Bart.
      2. Sophia, m. — Preston.
      3. Anne, m. Sir James May, Bart.   4. Mary, d. young.
   5. Covert.
   1. Elleanor.   2. Christian.
   3. Lydia, m. John Lapp, of Waterford.
   4. Margaret.

The eldest son,
COL. STEPHEN MOORE, of Barne, co. Tipperary, b. 1689 ; m. Nov. 1712, Judith, dau. of Richard Dowdeswell, of Poole Court, co. Worcester. His will bears date 12 Feb. 1747, and was proved 23 Nov. 1750. He left issue,
1. Richard, of Barne, High Sheriff co. Tipperary 1744. He m. 24 Feb. 1741, Henrietta, youngest dau. of the Right Hon. Sir Thomas Taylor, Bart., and by her (who d. May, 1783) left issue at his decease, 8 Aug. 1771,
   1. Thomas, of Barne (whose will is dated 17 Nov. 1780, and was proved 25 May, 1781), m. 15 March, 1777, Charlotte, dau. of Conway Spencer, of Tremary, co. Down, who, after Mr. Moore's decease, m. 24 Oct. 1788, George Augustus, and Marquess o Donegal, and d.s.p.
   2. Stephen, High Sheriff co. Tipperary 1786, d. unm. He was for many years M.P. for Clonmel, and after the Union, held the office of Comptroller-General of Ireland.
   3. Richard (Very Rev.), M.A., Dean of Emly, b. 6 June, 1776 ; will dated 9 Oct. 1816, proved 8 June, 1818 : d. unm.
      1. Henrietta, m. Thomas Pepper, of Ballygarth Castle, co. Meath.
      2. Salisbury, m. her cousin Stephen Moore, of Chesterfield, and Marfield, co. Tipperary.
      3. Elizabeth, m. Joseph Boultbee, of Springfield, co. Warwick.
      4. Anne, m. Lawrence Langley, of Brittus, co. Tipperary.
      5. Charity, m. 8 March, 1790, Richard Long, of Longfield, co. Tipperary.   6. Mary, d. unm.
2. STEPHEN, of whom we treat.

The younger son,
STEPHEN MOORE, of Chancellorstown, Capt. in the Army, m. Margaret Kellet, of co. Tipperary, and had issue,
1. STEPHEN, of whom presently.
2. Richard, who m. three times, and left at his decease, 1826, a son, Richard, and a dau., Mary Anne.
1. Margaret.   2. Mary.

The elder son,
STEPHEN MOORE, of Grenane, co. Waterford, and Chesterfield and Marlfield, co. Tipperary, High Sheriff co. Tipperary 1784, m. his cousin Salisbury, dau. of Richard Moore, of Barne, and had issue,
1. STEPHEN, of whom presently.
2. RICHARD (see MOORE of Killashee).
3. Thomas, Capt. 18th Foot, d. unm. 13 June, 1851.
4. Edward, d. unm.   5. William, d. 1872.
1. Harriet, d. unm. Dec. 1851.   2. Elizabeth, d. unm. 1876.

The eldest son,
STEPHEN MOORE, of Barne, Lieut.-Col. 5th Dragoons, High Sheriff 1832, b. 1782 ; m. June, 1805, Eleanor, dau. of Henry Westry of Dublin, and by her (who d. 1859) had issue,
1. STEPHEN CHARLES, his heir.
2. Richard, b. 1811 ; d. unm. 1850.
3. Henry, b. 1816 ; m. 26 Nov. 1857, Emily, only dau. of the Right Hon. Justice George, of Cahore, co. Wexford, and d. 17 March, 1877, leaving,
   1. Stephen George, b. 12 Feb. 1862.   2. Henry, b. 1866.
   1. Eleanor Constance.

Mr. Moore d. 20 Nov. 1860, and was s. by his eldest son,
STEPHEN CHARLES MOORE, of Barne, J.P. and D.L., High Sheriff 1867, b. 12 March, 1808 ; m. 25 May, 1833, Anna, dau. and co-heir of Col. Kingsmill Pennefather, of New Park, co. Tipperary, and by her (who d. 31 Dec. 1887) had issue,
1. STEPHEN, his heir.
2. Richard Albert, b. 19 May, 1848 ; m. and living in Queensland.
3. Charles Henry Algernon, b. 8 Aug. 1851 ; m. Mary, dau. of Gen. Foster.
1. Anna Maria, m. Dec. 1866, Col. Charles Thornhill, R.A., and has a son, Charles.
2. Katherine Grace, m. 25 Aug. 1870, Sir Francis John Milman, 4th bart., of Levaton, and has issue.
3. Elmina Constance, m. 5 Jan. 1875, Henry Burroughs, of Boston, Mass., and has issue.

Mr. Moore d. 10 April, 1873. The eldest son,
STEPHEN MOORE, of Barne, co. Tipperary, J.P. and D.L., High Sheriff 1885, J.P. co. Waterford, M.P. co. Tipperary 1875-80,

formerly Capt. 63rd Regt., b. 23 Aug. 1836; m. 1st, 1 Oct. 1867, Anna Maria, only surviving child and heiress of Wilmer Wilmer, of 24, Wilton Crescent, London, and by her (who d. 22 Dec. 1886) had issue,
1. Stephen Wilmer, b. 19 Nov. 1868; d. 17 June, 1877.
2. Randal Kingsmill, now of Barne.
3. Stephen Thomas Wilmer, late Lieut. 16th Lancers, assumed by Royal Licence, 6 Feb. 1903, the surname and arms of Wilmer, in lieu of those of Moore, b. 7 Feb. 1881; d. 17 May, 1909.
1. Anna Eleanor Isabel, m. 11 March, 1895, Francis S. Low, of Kilshane, co. Tipperary.
2. Geraldine Elma, m. 23 March, 1909, J. S. Leadam, Recorder of Grimsby.
3. Mary Augusta, m. 11 March, 1903, Capt. Noel Arbuthnot Thomson, Seaforth Highrs.
4. Stephanie Hilda Grace, m. 21 Nov. 1901, Rev. John Carleton Steward, Rector of North Runcton, Norfolk, 2nd son of the late John Steward, of East Carleton Manor, Norfolk.
Mr. Stephen Moore m. 2ndly, 11 July, 1888, Martha Mary, dau. of the late John Morgan, of Brampton Park, Hunts. He d. 9 July, 1897.

Arms—Quarterly: 1st and 4th, sa., a swan close arg. membered or, within a bordure engrailed of the second, Moore; 2nd and 3rd gu., a chief or, over all a bend ermine, Pennefather. **Crest**—A goshawk seizing a coney, both ppr. *Motto*—Vis unita fortior.

Seat—Barne, near Clonmel.

MOORE OF DROMONT.

The late Hugh Stuart Moore, of Dromont, co. Tyrone. J.P., M.A., b. 26 Feb. 1848; m. 4 Oct. 1886, Mary Charlotte, dau. of John William Kelly, of St. Helen's, Westport, co. Mayo (see *that family*), and d. 10 Jan. 1906, leaving issue,
1. Ethel Mary Christian.
2. Marjory Cecil. } Now of Dromont.
3. Helen Noel Stuart.

Lineage.—Early in 1600 three brothers supposed to be of the family of Mure of Rowallane, migrated from Scotland to Ireland. One settled at Dromont, co. Tyrone, one at Drum, co. Down, and the other at Drumlough in the same county.

John Moore, of Dromont, co. Tyrone, son of the first settler there, left issue, two sons and two daus.,
1. William, his heir.
2. Robert, of Bawn, co. Tyrone, m. and left a son, John.
1. Margaret, m. — Hanna. 2. Mary, m. — Lanu.

The eldest son,
William Moore of Dromont, served in Derry during the siege 1689, m. Rebecca, dau. of John Lowry, of Ahenis, co. Tyrone (see Burke's *Peerage*, Belmore, E.), and d. 1748, having had issue,
1. John, his heir.
2. Robert.
3. James, m. Elizabeth, dau. of Roger Hall, of Mount Hall (see Hall of Narrow Water).

The eldest son,
John Moore, of Dromont, m. 1740, Jane, dau. of Gilbert Jackson, of Newtown, co. Down, and d. 1777, having had issue, a son,
William Moore, of Dromont, m. 1775, Anne, dau. of Rev. Hugh Mulligan, and d. 1787, having had issue,
1. John, his heir.
2. Hugh, of whom presently.
3. William John Jackson, d. unm.
1. Rebecca. 2. Jane Elizabeth.
3. Mary.   4. Anne.

The eldest son,
Capt. John Moore, of Dromont, Royal Tyrone Regt. of Militia, d.s.p., and was s. by his brother,
Hugh Moore, of Dromont, Major Royal Tyrone Regt. of Militia, m. his cousin Letitia Maria, dau. of Maj. Edward Moore, and niece of Lieut.-Gen. James Moore, K.H., of Drumlough, co. Down, for twenty-six years Equerry to H.R.H. Edward Duke of Kent, and descended from that branch of the family which settled at Dromlough. Mr. Moore d. 1849, having had issue,
1. James Hamilton, his heir.
2. Cecil m. Emily, dau. of George Battye, of Camden Hill, and has issue,
   1. Hugh Hamilton.
   2. Cecil John Montague.
   1. Frederica.   2. Emily, d. unm.
3. Edward, d. unm.
4. William, d. unm.
5. Stuart, killed in the Indian Mutiny while serving in the Carabineers.
1. Mary Anne, d. unm.
2. Elizabeth Maria Fanny, d. unm.

The eldest son,
James Hamilton Moore, of Dromont, m. 21 July, 1841, Anne Christian, dau. of Joseph Abbott, and great grand-dau. of John Moore, of Drumlough, and had issue,
1. Hugh Stuart, late of Dromont.
2. Joseph Henry Hamilton, County Court Judge of co. Tipperary, Barrister-at-Law, formerly Fellow of Hertford Coll. Oxford (*Dromin, Delgany, co. Wicklow*), b. 24 May, 1852; m. 1st, 7 Aug. 1888, Ethel Florence, dau. of Henry Cope Colles, Barrister-at-Law, and by her (who d. 26 June, 1900) has issue,

1. James Stuart Hamilton, b. 31 Aug. 1891.
2. Henry Geoffrey Hamilton, b. 6 Sept. 1894.
1. Dorothy Hamilton.
He m. 2ndly, 22 Sept. 1903, Gertrude, dau. of the late F. W. Tweed, of Horncastle, Lincolnshire, and by her has issue,
3. Hugh Frederick Hamilton, b. 13 Nov. 1904.
3. James Cecil Hamilton (Rev.), b. 9 Jan. 1856; d. unm.
4. William Stuart, d. young.
1. Letitia Maria.
2. Anne, d. unm.
3. Florine Elizabeth, m. 1887, Rev. William Arthur Hayes, Canon and Chancellor of Dromore Cathedral, and has issue, Doris Cecil Anne.

Residence—Kilternan Grange, Kilternan, co. Dublin.

MOORE OF MOORE LODGE.

William Moore, of Moore Lodge, co. Antrim, b. 22 Nov. 1864, M.A. T.C.D., K.C., J.P. and D.L. co. Antrim, called to the Irish Bar Nov. 1887, and to the English Bar 1899, a Bencher King's Inns, M.P. Antrim Northern Div. from 1899 to Jan. 1906, and for Armagh Co., Northern Div., from Nov. 1906, Parliamentary Priv. Sec. to the Chief Secretary for Ireland 1902-3; m. 15 Sept. 1888, Helen Gertrude, 4th dau. of Joseph Wilson, of Clonmore, co. Dublin (D.L., co. Armagh), and has issue,
1. William Samson, b. 17 April, 1891.
2. Joseph Roger, b. 25 March, 1895.
1. Nina Mary Adelaide, m. 17 Aug. 1911, Norman Colum Patrick (see Patrick *of Dinmimming*).

Lineage.—James Moore, migrated from Cumberland in the reign of James I, and settled at Ballinacreemore, parish of Ballymoney, co. Antrim. His grandson,
James Moore, of Ballinacree, was a member of the Society of Friends, and was distrained for tithes each year, 1675-82, by the priest of Ballymoney (see Stockdale's *A Great Cry of Oppression*, published 1683). His will, dated 29 Dec. 1727, was proved by his three sons,
1. William, settled in 1702, at Killead in same co., of which he was High Sheriff in 1718. He m. Miss Clotworthy, and had a son, John, of Moore's Grove, who was High Sheriff in 1733, and was grandfather of Capt. Roger Moore, of Killead, who was High Sheriff in 1750, and who in conjunction with Capt. Thomas Thompson in 1760, marched a contingent of 173 volunteers from Killead and the district round Antrim to oppose the landing of the French at Carrickfergus.
2. James, of Ballinacree.
3. Joseph, of whom presently.

The third son,
Joseph Moore, of Rosnashane, co. Antrim, m. 1706, Susan Breddy (Brady), of Grange, in same co., and had issue,
1. William, his successor.
2. James, of Desertderrin, ancestor of Moore *of Moore Fort*.
3. John, b. 1712, ancestor of Moore *of Lischeihan*.
4. Joseph, b. 1716, of Ahoghill, line extinct.
5. Samson, of Moore Lodge, High Sheriff 1767; d. 1775.
6. George.

The eldest son,
William Moore, of Rosnashane, b. 4 Aug. 1708; m. Elizabeth Courtenay, of Glenburn, and, with three daus., had two sons,
1. Joseph, his heir.
2. William, of Killagan, co. Antrim, High Sheriff 1778; m. the dau. of Rev. J. Warren, Rector of Kilrea, co. Londonderry, and had two sons,
   1. Samson, of Moore Lodge, subsequently of Ballinacree, Capt. in the Antrim Regt., High Sheriff 1809, m. Sarah, dau. of William Warren, and d.s.p.
   2. William, of Moore Lodge, Officer in the 3rd Dragoons, afterwards Capt. in the Antrim Regt., High Sheriff 1808. He succeeded his brother Samson in the Moore Lodge estates on the accession of the latter to the Ballinacree estates. He m. 3 Sept. 1789, Elizabeth, dau. of Richard Rothe, of Mount Rothe, co. Kilkenny, and was s. by his son, George, on whose death, unm., Moore Lodge was inherited by his cousin, William Moore, M.D., of Moore Lodge.

The elder son,
Joseph Moore, of Rosnashane, Barrister-at-Law, m. Susan, dau. of Joseph Courtenay, of Glenburn, and had issue, two daus., Elizabeth, d. unm.; and Alice (Mrs. Clarke, of Tumarobert), and three sons,
1. William, d. young.
2. Thomas, Midshipman R.N., drowned.
3. Samson, his successor.

The 3rd, but only surviving son,
Samson Moore, of Rosnashane, Capt. in the Finvoy Yeomanry; m. 1787, Jane Ramadge, of Mullens, and d. 1832, leaving issue,
1. Thomas, an Officer in the Antrim Regt., d. unm.
2. Alexander, his successor.
3. William, Lieut. 71st Regt. and 54th Regt., d. in Burmese War, 1827.
4. Joseph, d. young.
1. Elizabeth, m. 1842, R. Young, of Hillmont, co. Antrim, and d. 1875.

Moore. THE LANDED GENTRY. 492

2. Jane, *d. unm.*
3. Martha, *d. unm.*
4. Alice, *m.* 1831, James W. Armstrong, of Culmore House, co. Antrim, J.P., and *d.* 1892, leaving issue.

The 2nd son,
ALEXANDER MOORE, M.D., of Rosnashane (which property was sold at his death), *m.* 1821, Mary, dau. of Rev. B. Mitchell, and great-grand-dau. of James Moore, of Desertderrin, and *d.* 1830, having by her (who *d.* 1897) had issue,
1. WILLIAM, late of Moore Lodge.
2. Samson, *d. unm.*
3. Alexander, Col. in the Army, U.S.A., *m.* Mary, only dau. of Gen. D. Taylor, U.S.A., and has issue, a son, Daniel Tyler.
4. George, *d.* leaving a son, George, dec.
5. Thomas, *m.* Mary, eldest dau. of William Moore, of Moore Fort, co. Antrim (*see that family*), and by her (who is dec.) had issue,
  1. Samson.
  1. Mary Violet.   2. Alice Warren.
  3. Sara Emily.
6. Courtenay (Rev.), M.A., Rural Dean, Rector of Mitchelstown, co. Cork, and Canon of Cloyne, *m.* Jessie Mona, dau. of Capt. Benjamin Duff, 92nd Highlanders (and Emma his wife, dau. of Comm. Gen. Haines, of Kirdford, Sussex), eldest son of Garden Duff, of Hatton Castle, by his wife Louisa, eldest dau. of the 6th Baron Duffus, and has issue,
  1. Courtenay Edward.   2. Alexander Duff.
  1. Harriet Emma.   2. Jessie Louisa.
  1. Mary, *d. unm.* 1893.   2. Jane.
  3. Elizabeth, dec.

The eldest son,
WILLIAM MOORE, of Moore Lodge, co. Antrim, J.P., M.D., High Sheriff co. Antrim 1890, was President of the King and Queen's Coll. of Physicians, Ireland, 1883-1884, late "King's" Professor of Medicine, Trin. Coll. Dublin, appointed Physician-in-Ordinary to the Queen in Ireland 1885, *b.* 13 Nov. 1826; *m.* 3 Sept. 1863, Sydney Blanche, dau. of Capt. Abraham Fuller, of Woodfield, King's Co., by Frances Anna his wife, dau. of Edmund Bigoe Armstrong, of Castle Armstrong, King's Co., and *d.* 17 April, 1901, leaving issue,
1. WILLIAM, now of Moore Lodge.
2. John, *b.* 31 Jan. 1866; *m.* 1894, Catherine Peck McClargherty of Seguin, Texas, and has two daus. and two sons, Roger and John, and *d.* 1909.
3. Alexander, Major Indian Army, *b.* 5 Jan. 1868; *m.* 1st, 11 Aug. 1893, Katharine Mary Maud, only dau. of Surg.-Major Marratt. She *d.* 1895, leaving issue, one son,
  Alexander William Uvedale.

He *m.* 2ndly, A. Cherry, dau. of the late Judge Cherry, I.C.S.
4. George Abraham, B.A., M.D., T.C.D., *b.* 24 March, 1869, Major R.A.M. Corps; *m.* 12 Sept. 1899, Helena Catherine Georgina, dau. of Surg.-Gen. George Whitla (*see* WHITLA *of Ben Eaden*), and has issue,
  1. George Frederick William, *b.* 24 July, 1901.
  2. John Ernest Clotworthy, *b.* 23 July, 1903.
  3. Roger Whitla, *b.* 17 May, 1909.
  1. Sybil Barbara.
5. Sydney William, *b.* 17 June, 1872, B.A., T.C.D.; *m.* Ida Sherwood, dau. of Mark Wilson, J.P. Carnlough, co. Antrim, and has issue,
  Roger Francis Bryanton, *b.* 13 Dec. 1906.
  Sydney Eileen.
6. Roger Clotworthy, *b.* 12 Feb. 1875; *d.* Jan. 1894.

Seat—Moore Lodge, Ballymoney, co. Antrim. **Residence**—3, Lower Merrion Street, Dublin. **Clubs**—Carlton, Sackville Street (Dublin), Ulster (Belfast).

MOORE OF MOORE HALL.

GEORGE AUGUSTUS MOORE, of Moore Hall, co. Mayo, High Sheriff 1905, *b.* 24 Feb. 1852; *s.* his father 1870.

Lineage.—GEORGE MOORE, Vice-Admiral of Connaught, *temp.* WILLIAM III, son of Thomas Moore, and Mary his wife, dau. of John Apadam, of Flint. He *m.* Catherine, dau. of Robert Maxwell, of Castle Teyling, Scotland, by Editha his wife, dau. of Sir John Dunbar, and was father of
GEORGE MOORE, of Ashbrook, co. Mayo, living 1717, *m.* Sarah dau. of Rev. John Price, of Foxford, by his wife, Editha Machen, of the city of Gloucester, and by her had two sons,
1. George, of Clongee.
2. JOHN, of whom we treat.

The younger son,
JOHN MOORE, of Ashbrook, *b.* about 1700; *m.* Jane, dau. of Edmund Athy, by Margaret his wife, heir of Philip Lynch, of Renville co. Galway, and had issue,
1. Robert, *d.s.p.* 1783.
2. GEORGE, of whom presently.

3. Edmund, of Moor Brook, co. Mayo, living 1790, had two sons, Thomas and George.
1. Sarah, *m.* — Shee, and had issue, George.
2. Jane, *m.* Roger Palmer.

His 2nd son,
GEORGE MOORE, of Moore Hall and Ashbrook, and Alicante, Spain, *b.* 1729; *m.* about 1765, Catherine, dau. of Dominick de Killikelly, of Castle Lydican, co. Galway, by Helen his wife, dau. of John O'Kelly, of Clone, co. Kilkenny, and *d.* 1799, leaving issue,
1. John, *b.* 1769, joined the rebellion of 1798, and was elected President of the Republic of Connaught, *d.s.p.* 1799.
2. GEORGE, of whom presently.
3. Thomas, *b.* 1775, *d.s.p.* 1830.
4. Peter, *d.s.p.* 1850.

The 2nd son,
GEORGE MOORE, of Moore Hall, *b.* 1773; *m.* 26 Aug. 1807, Louisa, dau. of the Hon. John Browne, 6th son of John, 1st Earl of Altamont, and *d.* 1840, having had issue,
1. GEORGE HENRY, his heir.
2. John, *b.* 1812; *d.s.p.* 1829.
3. Arthur Augustus, *b.* 1817; *d.s.p.* 1845.

The eldest son,
GEORGE HENRY MOORE, of Moore Hall, J.P. and D.L., M.P. co. Mayo, High Sheriff 1867, *b.* 19 April, 1810; *m.* 1851, Mary, eldest dau. of Maurice Blake, of Ballinafad, co. Mayo, and by her (who *d.* 23 May, 1895) had issue,
1. GEORGE AUGUSTUS, now of Moore Hall.
2. Maurice George, C.B., Col. Connaught Rangers, *b.* 10 Aug. 1854; *m.* 1889, Evelyn, eldest dau. of the late J. Stratford Handcock, of Carantrila Park, co. Galway (*see that family*), and has issue,
  1. Maurice George Henry Patrick, *b.* 1894.
  2. Ulick Augustus George, *b.* 1896.
3. Augustus George Martin, *b.* 1856; *d.* 27 Dec. 1910; *m.* 1891, Justina, dau. of the late Sir John Monckton, Town Clerk of the City of London, and had issue,
  1. Peter Augustus John Falkland, *b.* 1891.
  2. Reginald Maurice, *b.* 1892; *d.* same year.
4. Henry Julian, *b.* 1864.
1. Nina Mary Louisa, *m.* 1885, John Kilkelly, of Mossfort, co. Galway, and has issue.

Mr. Moore *d.* 19 April, 1870.

Arms—Arg., a chevron gu., between three moorcocks ppr. **Crest**—On a coronet or, a moorcock ppr. **Motto**—Fortis cadere cedere non potest.

Seat—Moore Hall, Ballyglass, co. Mayo.

MOORE OF MOORE FORT.

JOHN MOORE, of Moore Fort, co. Antrim, J.P. New Zealand, *b.* 9 May, 1854; *s.* his brother 1910; *m.* 30 Dec. 1884, Amy Elizabeth, 2nd dau. of the late John Ncholls, of Chester, and has issue,
WILLIAM GEOFFREY, *b.* 12 Nov. 1885.
A dau.

Lineage.—This is a branch of MOORE *of Moore Lodge*, descending from
JAMES MOORE, of Desertderrin, co. Antrim, 2nd son of Joseph Moore, of Rosnashane, *b.* 1710; *m.* Miss Lindsay, and had a son,
JAMES MOORE, of Moore Fort, who was father of
JAMES MOORE, of Moore Fort, *m.* 15 Nov. 1813, Mary, dau. of the Rev. Lindsay Hall, Rector of Donegore, and by her (who *d.* 31 Aug. 1838) had issue,
1. WILLIAM, of Moore Fort.
2. Lindsay, *d.* young.   3. James, *d.* young.
1. Mary, *m.* the Rev. Michael Fox Dudgeon, Vicar of Cratfield, Suffolk.
2. Alicia, *d. unm.* 25 April, 1886.
3. Sarah, *d. unm.* 12 Sept. 1848.

Mr. Moore *d.* 18 Sept. 1847, and was *s.* by his son,
WILLIAM MOORE, of Moore Fort, LL.D., Barrister-at-Law, J.P., High Sheriff 1847, *b.* 28 Oct. 1818; *m.* 2 April, 1846, Mary Shuldham, eldest dau. of John Hill, J.P., of Bellaghy Castle, Castledawson, co. Derry, and by her (who *d.* 24 Nov. 1872) had issue,
1. James, *b.* 22 Dec. 1848; *d.* 3 April, 1853.
2. WILLIAM, late of Moore Fort.
3. JOHN, now of Moore Fort.
4. George Kenrick, Major Army Pay Department, *b.* 11 Sept. 1857; *m.* twice, and *d.* 20 Oct. 1896, and has one son and two daus.
1. Mary, *m.* 2 April, 1872, Thomas Moore, son of Alexander Moore, M.D., of Rosnashane, and *d.* 9 Nov. 1882, leaving issue, one son and three daus. (*see* MOORE *of Moore Lodge*).

2. Sarah, *m.* 27 June, 1888, James Kilroe, and has three daus.
3. Elizabeth, *b.* 29 Feb. 1856.

Mr. Moore *d.* 30 March, 1889. His 2nd son,
   WILLIAM MOORE, of Moore Fort, co. Antrim, late R.N., *b.* 3 June, 1752; *m.* 20 Dec. 1888, Adeline C. H. P., 2nd dau. of Col. H. S. B. Bruce, of Ballyscullion House, Castledawson; *d.* 21 Jan. 1910, being *s.* by his brother.

Arms—Az., on a chief engrailed or an annulet between two mullets gu. *Crest*—Out of a mural coronet, ppr. charged with an annulet gu., a Moor's head in profile, also ppr. the temples encircled with a wreath arg. and az. *Motto*—Fortis cadere cedere non potest.

Seat—Moore Fort, Ballymoney, co. Antrim. *Residence*—Riverbank, Napier, New Zealand. *Clubs*—Hawkes Bay; Napier, both in New Zealand.

MOORE OF KILLASHEE.

LIEUT.-COL. RICHARD ST. LEGER MOORE, C.B., of Killashee, co. Kildare, J.P., High Sheriff 1899, late 9th, 12th, and 5th Lancers, commanded 17th Batt. Imp. Yeom. in S. African War, and Master of the Kildare Hounds 1883-97, *b.* 12 July, 1848; *m.* 3 April, 1873, Alice Geraldine, 3rd dau. of Joseph Pratt Tynte, D.L., of Tynte Park, co. Wicklow (*see that family*), and has issue,
1. RICHARD STEPHEN TYNTE ST. LEGER, Lieut. 12th Lancers, *b.* 16 Jan. 1890.
1. Geraldine Fanny Louisa, *b.* 3 April, 1874; *m.* 10 Nov. 1897, Capt. Lionel Charles Warren, Royal Munster Fusiliers, and has issue.
2. Evelyn Emma Cecilia, *b.* 25 Oct. 1875.
3. Violet Florence Grace, *b.* 9 March, 1881.

Lineage.—THE RIGHT HON. RICHARD MOORE, P.C., one of the Judges of the Court of Queen's Bench, in Ireland, the second son of STEPHEN MOORE, of Grenane (*see* MOORE *of Barne*), *b.* 1783; *m.* 1st, Fanny, dau. of the Rev. Thomas Bligh, aud by her had a son,
1. RICHARD, of whom presently.
Judge Moore *m.* 2ndly, Wilhelmina, youngest dau. of William Westby, of Thornhill, co. Dublin, and by her (who *d.* 13 March, 1860) left at his decease, 31 Dec. 1857, one son and one dau.,
2. William Westby, of Higham, Bournemouth, co. Hants, J.P. and D.L., A.D.C. to the Earl of Eglinton the Earl of Carlisle, when Lords-Lieutenant of Ireland, *b.* 1826; *m.* 1st, 25 June, 1863, Louisa Susan Anne, dau. of the Hon. G. M. Fortescue, of Dropmore, by whom (who *d.* 31 March, 1864) he had a dau.,
   Anne Constance Louisa, *m.* 13 Oct. 1893, Capt. W. G. Wyld, Hampshire Regt., who *d.* 16 July, 1900, leaving issue,
      John William Fortescue, *b.* 22 Aug. 1894.
   Honoria Cecil Annie, *b.* 10 Jan. 1896.
He *m.* 2ndly, 21 July, 1868, Isabella Sophia Ann, dau. of Hon. Granville Dudley Ryder. She *d.* 31 Jan. 1884.
1. Fanny, *d. unm.* 3 Sept. 1861.

The eldest son,
   RICHARD MOORE, of Killasbee, co. Kildare, J.P., *b.* 1818; *m.* 9 Sept. 1847, Emma Frances, dau. of Richard Sharpe, of Appscourt, Surrey, and by her (who *d.* 16 Jan. 1889) had issue,
1. ST. LEGER, now of Killashee.
2. Stephen Blyth, Capt. Royal Scots and Major Imp. Yeom., *b.* 15 July, 1850; *m.* 25 May, 1881, Hester Marion, dau. of A. Wedderburn. He *d.* on active service, South Africa, 5 June, 1901, leaving issue,
   1. Stephen, *b.* 7 March, 1884.
   1. Marion Hester, *b.* 24 June, 1882.
   2. Eileen, twin with her brother.
3. Edward Francis William, *b.* 9 July, 1857.
1. Florence Henrietta Fanny, *b.* 2 April, 1859; *d. unm.* 29 Sept. 1887.

Mr. Moore *d.* 2 June, 1881.

Arms—(See MOORE *of Barne*).

Seat—Killashee, Naas, co. Kildare. *Clubs*—Army and Navy; Cavalry; Kildare Street, Dublin.

MOORE OF MOLENAN.

CAPT. ROBERT LYON MOORE, of Molenan, co. Londonderry, and Cliff, co, Fermanagh, Capt. 3rd Hussars, has the Order of the Medjidie 4th Class, *b.* 1868; *m.* 15 July, 1907, Sally, eldest dau. of Gen. John A. Halderman, U.S. Army, and widow of Edwin Wilson.

Lineage.—This family of Moore is descended from James Mure who settled in Ireland in the 17th century, and was the son of William Mure, of Caldwell, co. Ayr. James Mure had a numerous family, of whom the eldest son, William, *s.* his uncle, William Mure, 4th Laird of Glenderstown, and Samuel, who changed his name to Moore on taking his diploma in Glasgow University in 1724. This Samuel Moore practised as a medical man in cos. Donegal and Derry, and was the direct ancestor of the MOORES *of Molenan*.

ROBERT MOORE, *m.* 1775, Anne Scott, and *d.* in America, in the early part of the present century. His son,

WILLIAM MOORE, of Molenan, *m.* 1835, Elizabeth, dau. of Robert Maxwell, of Armagh, and *d.* 1853, leaving issue,
1. ROBERT LYON, late of Molenan.
2. Samuel Maxwell, *d.* 3 June, 1899.
1. Wilhelmina Elizabeth, *m.* W. Green, of Government House, Londonderry, and *d.s.p.*

The elder son,
ROBERT LYON MOORE, of Molenan, co. Londonderry, and Cliff, co. Fermanagh, J.P. and D.L. co. Londonderry, J.P. co. Donegal, High Sheriff co. Derry 1877, High Sheriff co. Donegal 1886, educated Trin. Coll. Dublin, B.A. 1860, M.A. 1865, called to the Irish Bar 1860, *b.* 1836; *m.* 1867, Mary Elizabeth Moore (*of Molenan, Londonderry*, and *Cliff, Belleek, co. Fermanagh*), dau. of the late John Munn, J.P. He *d.* 28 May, 1902, leaving issue,
1. ROBERT LYON, now of Molenan.
2. William Maxwell Scott, *b.* 1870; *m.* 1895, Ida May, dau. of Alfred D. Smith, of New York, U.S.A.
3. Walter, *b.* 1871; *d.* 6 Nov. 1901.
1. Mary Elizabeth Henrietta.
2. Patience Violet Holford.

Seats—Molenan, co. Londonderry, and Cliff, Belleek, co. Fermanagh.

MOORE OF MOORESFORT.

CHARLES JOSEPH HENRY O'HARA MOORE, of Mooresfort and Aherlow Castle, co. Tipperary, J.P., *b.* Nov. 1880.

Lineage. — CHARLES MOORE, son of Arthur Moore, of Crookedstone, co. Antrim, by Mary O'Hara his wife, purchased Mooresfort, co. Tipperary, and was M.P. and J.P. for that co. He was *b.* 17 June, 1804; *m.* 12 Jan. 1835, Marian Elizabeth, dau. of John Story, and had issue,
1. CHARLES HENRY O'HARA, dec.
2. ARTHUR JOHN, of Mooresfort.
1. Marian Edith, *d. unm.* Aug. 1899.
2. Helena Blanche, a nun.
3. Laura Mary, *m.* 12 Aug. 1862, Capt. George Augustus Vaughan, son of the Hon. George Laurence Vaughan, and nephew of John, 3rd Earl of Lisburne, and *d.* 9 Jan. 1898, leaving issue.
Mr. Moore *d.* 15 Aug. 1869. His 2nd son,
ARTHUR JOHN MOORE, of Mooresfort, co. Tipperary, J.P. and D.L., M.P. for Clonmel 1874-85, and for Derry 1899-1900, High Sheriff 1877, created a Count by H.H. the Pope 1879, a Commander of the Order of St. Gregory, and Chamberlain to His Holiness, *b.* 15 Sept. 1849; *m.* 7 Feb. 1877, Mary Lucy Clifford, dau. of Sir Charles Clifford, 1st Bart., of Hatherton Hall, co. Stafford (*see* BURKE'S *Peerage*), and *d.* 5 Jan. 1904, having had issue,
1. ARTHUR JOSEPH CLIFFORD, *b.* July, 1878; *d.* 8 July, 1900.
2. CHARLES JOSEPH HENRY O'HARA, now of Mooresfort.
1. Edith Mary.

Arms—Az., on a chief engrailed or, a rose gu., barbed and seeded ppr., between two mullets pierced of the third. *Crest*—Out of a mural crown ppr., a Moor's head also ppr., wreathed about the temples arg. and az. and charged in the neck with a rose gu., barbed vert. *Motto*—Fortis cadere cedere non potest.

Seats—Mooresfort, and Aherlow Castle, Bansbee, Tipperary. *Residence*—64, Prince's Gate, S.W. *Club*—Wellington.

MOORE OF MANORKILBRIDE.

JOSEPH FLETCHER MOORE, of Manorkilbride, co. Wicklow, J.P. and D.L., High Sheriff 1894, M.A. Trin. Coll. Dublin, Barrister-at-Law, *b.* 2 Dec. 1835; *m.* 5 Dec. 1861, Jane, dau. of James Atkinson, of Longford Terrace, Monkstown, and Belfast, New South Wales, and has issue,
1. Thomas Brown, Lieut. R.E., *b.* 26 April, 1865; *d. unm.* 24 March, 1895.
2. JOSEPH SCOTT, Col. Army Service Corps, *b.* 14 Oct. 1866; *m.* 9 Jan. 1902, Violet Grace Hastings Wheler, only dau. of the late Charles Wheler Wheler, of Ledston Hall, co. York.
3. George Fletcher, *b.* 10 Oct. 1869; *m.* 1899, Lillie, dau. of D. J. Abercrombie, of Jeneriffe, Brisbane.
4. Nithsdale Carleton Atkinson, Lieut. R.N., twin with his brother, *b.* 10 Oct. 1874.
5. James Maxwell, *b.* 1879; *d.* 11 Feb. 1890.
1. Emily Elizabeth, *m.* 30 April, 1906, Rev. Hubert Poer, M.A., son of the late S. Beresford Poer, of Belleville Park, Waterford.

2. Bertha Mary, *m.* 7 March, 1894, Lt.-Col. Edward Humphrey Bland, R.E., and has issue (*see* BLAND *of Blandsfort*).
3. Ada Catherine, *m.* 23 Jan. 1900, Ernest Lucas, of 21, Grimston Gardens, Folkestone, son of Sir Thomas Lucas, Bart. (*see* BURKE'S *Peerage and Baronetage*).
4. Louisa Anne Fletcher.

Lineage.—This family, which is of Scottish origin, settled in the North of Ireland about 1650.
JOSEPH MOORE, of Bond's Glen, co. Londonderry, *m.* 1794, Anne, dau. of George Fletcher, of Tottenham, co. Middlesex, and *d.* 1852, leaving by her (who *d.* 1803) a son,
JOSEPH SCOTT MOORE, of Manorkilbride, co. Wicklow, J.P., High Sheriff 1866, *b.* 1796; *m.* 1832, Elizabeth, dau. of Thomas Browne, of Ardwick, near Manchester, and by her (who *d.* 12 Sept. 1886) had issue,
JOSEPH FLETCHER, now of Manorkilbride.
Mr. Moore *d.* 9 March, 1884, and was *s.* by his only son, JOSEPH FLETCHER MOORE, of Manorkilbride.

Seat—Manorkilbride, co. Wicklow. *Club*—University, Dublin.

MONTGOMERY-MOORE late OF GARVEY.

GEN. SIR ALEXANDER GEORGE MONTGOMERY-MOORE, K.C.B., High Sheriff 1904, D.L. for co. Tyrone and J.P. Belfast, Gen. in the Army, Col. of the 18th Hussars and later of 4th Hussars, *b.* 6 April, 1833; *m.* 30 Sept. 1857, the Hon. Jane Colborne, youngest dau. of Field-Marshal John, 1st Lord Seaton, G.C.B. Gen. Montgomery-Moore was A.D.C. to Comdr. of the Forces in Ireland, commanded the 4th Hussars, was Assistant-Adjutant-General of the Dublin District, commanded the Belfast and S.E. Districts, and the troops in Canada from 1893 to 1898; was in command of Aldershot District 1899 to 1900.

Lineage.—JOHN MURE, of Caldwell, co. Ayr, *s.* to his inheritance in 1539, and *m.* 1st, Lady Isabel Montgomery, dau. of Hugh, 1st Earl of Eglinton; and 2ndly, Christian, dau. of Ninian, Lord Ross, of Hawkhead. From him sprang the subsequent line of MURE *of Caldwell*, and also that of MURE *of Glanderstown*.
WILLIAM MOORE, of Glanderstown, co. Renfrew, *m.* about 1620, Jean, dau. of Rev. Hans Hamilton, and sister of James, Earl of Clanbrassil, and had, with other issue,
WILLIAM MOORE, of Garvey, to whom, in 1667, a patent of Clonkeen, and subsequently Fassaroe Castle, Wicklow, and Garvey, co. Tyrone, was granted as a reward for his loyalty to CHARLES I. He served as High Sheriff co. Tyrone 1664. His son,
JAMES MURE (or MOORE), of Garvey or Fassaroe, High Sheriff 1697, was attainted and his estates confiscated by JAMES II in 1688; and fought at the siege of Derry, and was wounded when defending the North Gate. His son,
JAMES MOORE, of Garvey and Fassaroe, High Sheriff 1701, who *m.* Mary, dau. of Sir Arthur Acheson, Bart., and dying intestate 1710, was *s.* by his son,
ACHESON MOORE, of Garvey, Revella, co. Tyrone, and Fassaroe, co. Wicklow, High Sheriff 1712, M.P. for Bangor, co. Down, who *m.* 17 April, 1723, Sidney, dau. of Edward Wingfield, of Powerscourt, and sister of Richard, 1st Viscount Powerscourt, and by her (who *d.* 10 Dec. 1727) left issue,
1. JAMES, of Garvey, bapt. 6 Aug. 1726; *d. unm.* 1759.
1. ELEANOR, of whom hereafter.
2. MARY, *m.* 1st, 26 June, 1753, Roger Palmer, of Palmerstown, co. Mayo; and 2ndly, Richard Malone, 2nd son of Lord Sunderlin, *d.s.p.*
3. SIDNEY, *b.* 10 Dec. 1827; *m.* 25 April, 1751, Hodson Gage, of Ballyreena, co. Derry, and had one dau., who *d.* young.

The eldest dau.,
ELEANOR MOORE, *m.* 27 July, 1756, ALEXANDER MONTGOMERY, of Ballyleck, Gen. of Volunteers, M.P. for Donegal (*see* MONTGOMERY *of Beaulieu*), and had two daus., Sidney and Maria, who both *d. unm.*, and a son,
NATHANIEL MONTGOMERY, of Garvey, Revella, and Fassaroe, High Sheriff 1786, M.P. for Strabane and afterwards co. Tyrone, and Col. Tyrone Militia, which he commanded in the Rebellion of 98. He assumed in right of his mother, the surname and arms of MOORE. He *m.* 1785, Mary Anne, dau. of Alexander Boyd, of Ballycastle, co. Antrim, by Anna Maria his wife, dau. of Sir Archibald Acheson, Bart., Viscount Gosford, and by her (who *d.* 24 Dec. 1813) had issue,
1. ALEXANDER JAMES, his heir.
2. Acheson, Major Tyrone Militia, *b.* 17 Oct. 1788; *m.* 1813, Eliza, dau. of Richard Pennefather, of New Park, co. Tipperary, and by her (who *m.* 2ndly, Sir John Judkin Fitzgerald, Bart.) he left one dau. Anne, *m.* William Lloyd, of Rockville, co. Roscommon.
3. Nathaniel, *b.* 3 Nov. 1789; *m.* Agnes Cox, of Exeter, and *d.s.p.* 1823.
4. Robert, J.P. and D.L. co. Tyrone, and High Sheriff 1834, *m.* 1840, Annie Maria Wilhelmina, dau. of Baron de Wolmaar, and *d.* 1873, having had issue,
1. Frederick Acheson, *m.* 1st, Mary, dau. of Thomas Frosser, by whom he had issue,

Alexander Acheson, *m.* 24 April, 1900, Brillianna Stanhope, dau. of the late John Cotter Atkins, of Carrig, Queenstown. Mabel.
He *m.* 2ndly, Lilly, dau. of Edward Byam Martin, U.S. America.
2. Alexander Willoughby.   3. Robert Tichborne.
1. Annie Emmeline Acheson.
2. Amy Rose Blanche Willoughby.
5. James, *d.* young.
1. Anna Maria, *d. unm.* 1813.
2. Sydney, *m.* Thomas Smallcombe, of Bath, and *d.* 1838.
3. Ellen, *m.* Col. De Naucaze, of the French Service, only son of the Marquis de Naucaze, of Auvergne.

NATHANIEL MONTGOMERY-MOORE, who sat in the last Irish Parliament for co. Tyrone, and voted for the Union, *d.* 4 Dec. 1834, and was *s.* by his son,
ALEXANDER JAMES MONTGOMERY-MOORE, of Garvey and Fassaroe, *b.* 15 Feb. 1786; *m.* 24 April, 1832, Susanna, youngest dau. of George Matcham, of Ashfold Lodge, Sussex, by Catherine his wife, sister of Horatio, 1st Viscount Nelson, and by her (who *d.* 1885) had issue,
1. ALEXANDER GEORGE, now of Garvey.
2. Acheson, *d.* young.
Mr. Montgomery-Moore *d.* 1836.

Residence—Gipsy Lodge, Norwood, S.E. *Clubs*—Carlton and United Service, S.W.

MOORE OF CREMORGAN.

HENRY MOORE, of Cremorgan, Queen's Co., J.P. and D.L., High Sheriff 1883, B.A. Trin. Coll. Dublin, *b.* 1843.

Lineage.—This family derives from the O'MORES, Chieftains of Leix, now the Queen's Co. Cearnach O'More, lord of Leix, was slain 1017, from him descended Rory O'More, who warred with the English *temp.* ELIZABETH.
MURTAGH OGE O'MORE, who was son, or grandson, of Lisagh MacConnell O'More, who was slain in 1530, eldest son of Connell MacMelaghlin O'More, Chieftain of Leix 1523-37, had a grant from the Crown of Raheenduff in 1562 and Cremorgan in 1570. He *d.* 2 May, 1589, having *m.* Honora O'Lalor, and had three sons and a dau.,
1. Patrick, of Cremorgan, attainted for High Treason 1598.
2. JOHN, of whom presently.
3. Murtagh, living 1585.
1. *m.* Dermot O'Lalor, of Rathnagecragh, Queen's Co.

The 2nd son,
JOHN MOORE, of Killenevar, Queen's Co., *d.* 11 Nov. 1636, and was bur. in St. Patrick's Church, Stradbally (Fun. Entry). He *m.* Margaret, dau. of Connor O'Hickey, of Bolton, co. Kildare, and left two sons and six daus.,
1. JOHN OGE, his heir.
2. Pierce, of Raheenduff, *m.* Mary, dau. of Francis Edgeworth, Clerk of the Hanaper (*see* EDGEWORTH *of Edgeworthstown*), and by her, who *m.* 2ndly, John Pigott (*see* PIGOTT *of Cappard*) had two sons and two daus.,
1. John (Rev.), Archdeacon of Cloyne 1665-82, *d.* 1702, by his 1st wife had four sons. He *m.* 2ndly, 1675, Joan, dau. of William Weldon, of Raheenderry (*see* WELDON, Bart.), and had an only dau., Elizabeth, who *d.* young. There were
(1) Francis (Rev.), M.A. (Dublin), *b.* 1664; *d.* 1729, Rector of Athy, and of Innishannon; *m.* Catherine, dau. of William Weldon, of Raheenderry, and left by her (who *d.* 1754) two daus. and co-heirs,
1. Catherine, *m.* Feb. 1723, Col. William Caulfeild.
2. Elizabeth, *m.* Robert Percy, of Snugborough, co. Wicklow.
(2) Pierce, matric. Trin. Coll. Dublin 19 June, 1680, aged 17.
(3) Charles.
(4) John (Rev.), M.A. (Dublin), Treasurer of Cork, *b.* 1675, *d.* 1749; *m.* Anna Maria, dau. of John Folliott, and had three sons and four daus.,
1. John, matric. Trin. Coll. Dublin 9 July, 1722, aged 17.
2. Pierce, B.A. (Dublin) 1733.
3. Charles (Rev.), M.A. (Dublin), *b.* 1717; *d.* Nov. 1753, Rector and Vicar of Innishannon; *m.* Mary, dau. of Col. Christopher Rogers, and left two daus.,
a. Martha, *m.* Edward Wilmot (*see* WILMOT-CHETWODE *of Woodbrook*).

b. Catherine, *m.* 1st, 3 April, 1766, Sir Robert Waller, 1st Bart. (*d.* 1780) ; *m.* 2ndly, 2 June, 1783, Rev. Jerome Alley, Rector of Beaulieu.
1. Anna Maria, *m.* Boyle Travers.
2. Hannah, *m.* 1738, Thomas Corker.
3. Frances, *m.* 1741, Joseph Ledbetter.
4. Catherine, *m.* 1748, Rev. John Meade (*see* MEADE *of Ballymartle*).

2. Roger, of Johnstown, co. Dublin, M.P. for Mullingar 1692-93 and 1695-99, *d.* Jan. 1704-5 ; *m.* Nov. 1667, Elizabeth, dau. of Anthony Stoughton, Clerk of the Castle Chamber (*see* STOUGHTON *of Owlpen*), and had three sons and four daus.,
 (1) John, *d.v.p., s.p.*
 (2) Boyle, *d.* 1742 ; *m.* Catherine, dau. of Sir Richard Cox, Bart., Lord Chancellor of Ireland, and had, with a son, Boyle, who *d.* an infant 1710, two daus. and co-heirs,
  1. Mary, *m.* July, 1745, Rev. Frederick Trench, of Baltinakill.
  2. Elizabeth, *m.* April, 1749, Rev. Hugh Dawson.
 (1) Honora, *m.* 1st, Samuel Foley, Bishop of Down ; *m.* 2ndly, Oct. 1696, Thomas Whitley.
 (2) Elizabeth, *m.* Feb. 1693-4, Col. Henry Edgeworth, of Lissard, co. Longford.
 (3) Frances, *m.* Rev. Ezekiel Burridge ; *d.s.p.* 1708.
 (4) Hannah, *m.* Arthur Ormsby, of Cumine, co. Sligo.
 (5) Anne, *m.* 1st, Rev. Benedict Scroggs, F.T.C.D. (who *d.* 1696) ; *m.* 2ndly, John Carey.
1. Frances, *m.* 7 May, 1657, Christopher Lovet, Lord Mayor of Dublin 1676-77 (*see* LOVETT *of The Grange*).
2. Hannah, *m.* 1st, Sir John Knox, Lord Mayor of Dublin 1685-86 (*see* KNOX *of Brittas*) ; *m.* 2ndly, Henry Mervyn, of Trillick, co. Tyrone.
3. Elizabeth, *d. unm.*
4. Dorothy, *d. unm.*
1. Margaret, *m.* Richard Jacob, of co. Kildare.
2. Honora, *m.* Keadagh Moore, of co. Tipperary.
3. Catherine, *m.* John Dempsy, of King's Co.
4. Grania, *m.* Murtagh Dempsy, of Queen's Co.
5. Dorothy, *unm.*
6. Una, *m.* Oliver Grace, of Kilmainham, Queen's Co.

John Moore *m.* a second time, but had no further issue. The elder son,

JOHN OGE MOORE, of Ballydavis, Queen's Co., *d.* 18 Jan. 1668-9 ; *m.* Susan, dau. of James Hovenden, of Queen's Co. His will, made 14 Jan. 1668-9, was proved at Leighlin 9 June, 1669. He left three sons and four daus.,
1. BARTHOLOMEW, his heir.
2. John. 3. Lewis.
1. Margaret, *m.* Con Magenis.
2. Elizabeth, *m.* Pierce Purcell.

The eldest son,

BARTHOLOMEW MOORE, of Raheenduff and Cremorgan, *d.* before 1700 ; *m.* Mary, dau. of Henry Walsh, of Ballybrin, co. Kildare, and had three sons,
1. LEWIS, his heir.
2. Henry, who left two sons, LEWIS, who *s.* his uncle, and James,
3. John, living 1746.

The eldest son,

LEWIS MOORE, of Cremorgan, High Sheriff of Queen's Co. 1736; *m.* before 1717, Frances, dau. of — Stafford, but had no issue. His will, dated 8 July, 1746, was proved 11 Aug. following. He was *s.* by his nephew,

LEWIS MOORE, of Cremorgan, High Sheriff 1760, *d.* 23 Oct. 1775 ; *m.* 20 Jan. 1746, Christian, dau. of Pierce Moore, of Lorau, Queen's Co., and by her (whose will, dated 12 June, 1783, was proved 13 Sept. 1787) had four sons and three daus.,
1. HENRY, his heir. 2. John.
3. Pierce, *d.* Dec. 1775 ; *m.* —, dau. of — Marsh, and left au only dau., Elizabeth, *m.* Rev. Mr. Sillery.
4. Lewis.
1. Elizabeth, *m.* — Christian.
2. Elinor. 3. Susan.

The son and heir,

HENRY MOORE, of Cremorgan, High Sheriff 1784, *m.* 12 Aug. 1800, Anne, dau. of Mark Scott, elder brother of John, 1st Earl of Clonmell. She *d.* 7 July, 1829. He *d.* 31 Oct. 1815, having had issue,
1. Lewis, of whom presently.
2. Henry, C.B., Lieut.-Col. Bengal N.I., *b.* 1803.
3. Thomas, of Highthorn, co. Dublin. Maj.-Gen. Bengal Light Cavalry, *b.* 12 Dec. 1809 ; *m.* 28 Nov. 1836, Isabella Maria, dau. of Josiah John Hogg, Surg. H.E.I.C.S., and had surviving issue, Anne, *m.* 1st, 23 Nov. 1858, Capt. Henry E. Hall, 13th Regt., who *d.* 16 Feb. 1869, leaving issue (*see* HALL *of Knockbrack*). She *m.* 2ndly, Giles Evre Lambert, of Moor Park (*see* LAMBERT *of (Aggard)*).
4. Pierce, Barrister-at-Law, *d. unm.* 1857.
5. Mark, Madras C.S., *d. unm.* 1834.
1. Margaret, *m.* 28 Sept. 1825, Sir Samuel Osborne-Gibbes, 2nd Bart., and *d.* 20 Jan. 1847, leaving issue.
2. Mary, *d. unm.* Dec. 1861.
3. Charlotte, *d. unm.* 1857.

The eldest son,

LEWIS MOORE, of Cremorgan, J.P. and D.L., High Sheriff 1828, *b.* Feb. 1801 ; *m.* Mary Sarah, 2nd dau. of Capt. Charles Lancelot Sandes, of Indiaville, Queen's Co. She *d.* Dec. 1859. He *d.* 1880, having had issue,
1. HENRY, his heir.
2. Charles, *b.* Dec. 1844.
3. Lewis.

1. Minna, *m.* 24 Oct. 1868, the Right Hon. Dodgson Madden, P.C., Judge of the High Court of Justice[1]. She *d.* 1 May, 1895 (*see* MADDEN *of Hilton Park*). He 15 Sept. 1896, Jessie Isabelle, dau. of Richard Warbu of Garrybinch, King's Co. (*see that family*).
2. Anne, *m.* 1877, William Henry Atkinson, of H[2] Queen's Co. (*see* ATKINSON *of Cangort*).
3. Margaret.

Arms—Vert, a lion rampant and in chief three (**Crest**—An arm fessways erased vested or, the hand g sword erect impaling three gory heads all ppr. **Motto**— fidelis et audax.

Seat—Cremorgan, Timahoe, Queen's Co.

MOORE OF ROWALLANE.

HUGH ARMYTAGE MOORE, of Rowallane, cc J.P., *b.* 10 March, 1873 ; *m.* 10 Nov. 1910 Christian, eldest dau. of Kerneth Mathics 50, Prince's Gate, London, S.W.

Lineage.—CAPT. HUGH MOORE, of the 9th Dragoon: Col. Muir, who served in WILLIAM III's army and obt grant of lands in Ireland, *d.* 23 Aug. 1777, leaving an eldes

JOHN MOORE, *m.* Deborah, dau. of Robert Isaac, of Holyw co. Down, and Anne his wife, dau. of James Bailie, of Inisha She *d.* 16 Feb. 1806, aged 76. He *d.* 5 Feb. 1800, aged 74, lea a son,

HUGH MOORE, of Eglantine House, and Mount Panther, Down, Capt. 5th Dragoon Guards, and Col. of the Eglantine Y manry (which he raised) in the Irish Rebellion, *m.* 7 Nov. 17 Priscilla Cecilia, dau. of Robert Armytage, of Kensington, widow of Robert Shaw, of Terenure, co. Dublin (*see* BURKE's P. *age*, SHAW, Bart.). She *d.* April, 1849. He *d.* 29 July, aged 86, leaving issue,
1. JOHN ROBERT, his heir.
2. William Armytage, of Armore, co. Cavan, *b.* 17 Oct. 1 *m.* 1st, Jane Ada, dau. of Thomas Ball, Master in Chancer Ireland. She *d.s.p.* He *m.* 2ndly, Mary E., dau. of W. H. Met and widow of H. D. Lockwood, and *d.* Feb. 1883, having by (who *m.* 3rdly, 1902, Frank Hardcastle, D.L., of 87, Lanc Gate, London, late M.P. for West Houghton Divi of L shire) had issue,
 1. HUGH ARMYTAGE, now of Rowallane.
 2. John Reginald Rowallane, *b.* 25 March, 1876
 3. Charles Armytage, *b.* 27 April, 1880.
 1. Priscilla Cecilia Armytage, *m.* 2 July, 189 Hugh, 5th Earl Annesley. He *d.* 15 Dec. 1908 (*see* BURKE's *Peerage*).
 2. Ethel Armytage, *m.* 28 June, 1890, William She *d.s.p.* 29 June, 1891 (*see* FRENCH *of Cloonigu*
1. Jane Deborah, *d. unm.* 6 Dec. 1863.
2. Priscilla Cecilia, *m.* 15 July, 1828, William Rich: Annesley. He *d.* 25 Aug. 1838. She *d.* 29 March, 1 issue (*see* BURKE's *Peerage*).
3. Caroline Anne Elizabeth, *m.* 5 Nov. 1834, Rev. Garrett, of Kilgarrron, co. Carlow.
4. Maria Clarissa, *m.* (as his second wife) Feb. 1838, Humphrys, of Ballyhaise, co. Cavan, who *d.* 1872, leaving (*see that family*).

The eldest son,

JOHN ROBERT MOORE, of Rowallane, co. Down, M.A., *b.* 4 O 1801 ; *m.* 1850, Jane, dau. of R. Morris, of Carmarthen and wido of Henry Davidson. She *d.* 1856. He *d.s.p.*, and was *s.* by hi nephew.

Seat—Rowallane, Saintfield, co. Down.

MOORE. *See* BURKE's PEERAGE, **DROGHEDA, E.**

MOORE-BRABAZON. *See* **BRABAZON.**

MOORE-HODDER. *See* **HODDER.**

MORE-O'FERRALL. *See* **O'FERRALL.**

DEANE-MORGAN.
See BURKE's PEERAGE, **MUSKERRY, B.**

MOROGH-BERNARD. *See* **BERNARD.**

MORONY OF ODELL VILLE.

the ND MORONY, da ll Ville, co. lea , J.P., b. 21 H 1832; m. 14 Br 1860, Helena 18 only child of M dell, of Odell F co. Limerick. s issue,

Helena, m. 26 1884, her cousin. Vereker Lloyd y, B.E., and has *below*).
ldine, m. 24 April, enry Molony, M.D.

Me age.—PIERS y, of Cloonenagh, T , held lands in the t Killard, West Clare, He m. Margaret who d. his widow Fe 1706. His will was ed 1078. He had issue, EDMUND, of whom reser tly.

. Piers, of Limerick, m. Catherine Brown. She d. 31 Dec. 723. He d. 17 May, 1728, having had issue,
1. Edmond.
. Andrew, d.s.p. 24 July, 1723.
. A dau., m. — MacNamara, of co. Clare.
. Catherine, m. Thady Quin, of Adare, co. Limerick.

er son,
OND MORONY, of Kilmacduane, co. Clare, J.P. (1687), m. , dau. of James Macnamara, and had issue,
Pierce, of Kilmacduane, d.s.p.
John, ancestor of the MORONYS of Dunaha, co. Clare.
THOMAS, of whom we treat.

youngest n,
OMAS MORONY, of Miltown Malbay and of Kilmacduane, WILLIAM of — Meade, of Bruree. co. Limerick, keen, and
Tyrone, wa sently.
served as J rtugal, d. unm.
JAMES M. m. the dau. of — Kilkelly, and d. 1697, was a her cousi and fought leaving iss f Ennis.
the North omyn, of Milford, co. Clare, and had JAMES N Percy Frenc
m. Mary, d. n). ry Miller, of Toonagh, co. Clare, and was s. b ne m. 2ndly, Christopher Carr, of Limerick.
ACH id
co. W e issu Y, of Kilmacduane and Miltown Malbay, co. m. 1 ED d st, 14 April, 1752, Ann, 2nd dau. of John Westropp, cour re (now Maryfort), co. Clare. She d. 31 July, 1764, (wh vin Lis
, as, ancestor of the MORONYS of Miltown Malbay, co. Clare.
, ropp (Rev.), d. unm.
. in, Lieut. Clare Militia, m. 1810, Catherine Leonard, dau. James Bourke, of Castle Bourke, co. Mayo, and had issue.
4. Ralph, of Faro, co. Clare, m. 1795, Ellen, dau. of John Woolfe, of Cahirush, co. Clare, and had issue.
1. Jane, m. 1st, 23 March, 1771, Exham Vincent, of Limerick, and had issue. She m. 2ndly, Joseph Cripps, of Limerick, and d 1795.
2. Mary Anne, m. Amos Vereker, of Limerick, and had issue.
3. Hannah, m. Thomas Devonport Hunt, of Kilrush, and had ue.
Eliza, m. 17 Dec. 1790, James Kerin, of Ennis, and d.s.p.
m. 2ndly, 1768, Blanche, dau. of Thomas Vincent, of Limerick, d. 9 July, 1783, having had issue,
EDMOND, of whom presently.
Exham, Capt. Limerick Militia, m. Catherine, dau. of Robert hnston, of Crocknacrieve, Fermanagh, and had issue.
Ralph, d. unm.
Blanche, m. 5 April, 1792, Capt. Barclay Westropp, and d issue.
Susan, m. Bryan MacMahon, of Limerick, and had issue.
Morony d. at Parteen, Limerick, 6 Aug. 1778, aged 55. His er son by the second marriage,
EDMOND MORONY of Ballyclough, Limerick, J.P. cos. Clare and imerick, Lieut. 9th Foot, m. 28 April, 1790, Christian, dau. of ichard Phillips, of Mount Rivers, co. Tipperary, and by her had sue,
1. EDMUND, of whom presently.
2. William, of Fortlawn, co. Mayo, m. Dec. 1852, Matilda, dau. of Capt. James Nicholson Soden, of Moneygold, co. Sligo. She d. 16 Aug. 1892. He d. 13 April, 1886, leaving issue,
1. Henry Vereker Lloyd, B.E. (Q.U.I.), M.Inst.C.E., m. 26 Aug. 1884, his cousin, Eliza Helena, dau. of Edmund Morony, of Odell Ville (*see above*), and has issue,
Helen Mary Matilda, LL.B. (Dublin).
2. William, m. 26 April, 1897, Judith Mary, dau. of Andrew Kirkwood, of Cloongoonagh, c

3. Exham, m. 14 June, 1888, Emily Helena, dau. of James Peacocke, of Dooneen, co. Limerick, and has issue,
(1) Emily Helena.
(2) Geraldine.
(3) Matilda.
4. James Nicholson Soden, m. 12 June, 1895, Emma, dau. of Rev. Henry Vereker, of Omeath, co. Louth, and has issue, William Vereker.
1. Isabel Dodd, m. 12 June, 1895, A. C. Larminie, J.P., of Castlebar, co. Mayo, and has issue.
1. Anne, m. Henry Vereker, of Dublin, and had issue.
2. Elizabeth, m. Vere Hunt, of Clorane, co. Limerick, and d.s.p.
3. Ellen, m. John Lee, of Betty Ville, co. Limerick.
4. Blanche, m. 1st, 14 April, 1840, John Morony, who d.s.p. 1844. She m. 2ndly, 1846, Francis Morony, and d.s.p. 1861.
The elder son,
EDMUND MORONY, of Ballyclough, co. Limerick, Lieut. Limerick Militia, m. 1st, 1 April, 1831, Geraldine, dau. of Andrew Castle, of Ennis, and by her had issue,
1. EDMUND, of Odell Ville.
2. Francis William, Lieut. Limerick Militia, d. unm. 15 Sept. 1858.
1. Geraldine, m. 1855, James Peacocke, of Dooneen, co. Limerick, and had issue.
He m. 2ndly, 7 April, 1856, Julia, 3rd dau. of William Johnston Westropp, of Roxborough, Limerick. She d.s.p. 21 April, 1885. He d. at Odell Ville, 31 Oct. 1867, aged 74.

Arms—Az. three cross crosslets or between as many boars' heads couped above the shoulders arg. langued gu. Crest—A lion rampant arg. holding a sceptre or. Motto—Amicis semper fidelis.

Seat—Odell Ville, Ballingarry, co. Limerick.

O'CONNOR-MORRIS OF GORTNAMONA OR MOUNT PLEASANT.

MAURICE LINDSAY O'CONNOR MORRIS, of Gortnamona, King's Co., J.P., B.A. Dublin 1887, and Barrister-at-Law King's Inn, sometime Priv. Sec. to Lord Ashbourne, Lord Chancellor of Ireland, b. 23 March, 1865.

Lineage (of MORRIS). BENJAMIN MORRIS, of Waterford, J.P., m. Isabella Smyth, of the same place, and had three sons 1. WILLIAM; 2. BENJAMIN, 3rd Horse, m. 30 April, 1774, dau. of John Sheppard; and 3. John. The eldest son, WILLIAM MORRIS, of Waterford, J.P., m. Martha, dau. of Richard Reade, of Rosseoara, co. Kilkenny, and by her had four sons,
1. Benjamin, d.s.p.
2. Richard, d. unm.
3. WILLIAM, of whom presently.
4. GEORGE WALL, Deputy-Governor co. Waterford (who assumed the additional surname of WALL on succeeding to the estates of his father-in-law), m. Jane, eldest dau. and heir of James Wall, of Clonea Castle, co. Waterford, and had a son,
RICHARD WALL, of Rockenham, co. Waterford, J.P., High Sheriff 1843-4, m. 1st, 1827, Jane, dau. of Jesse Lloyd, of Lloydsborough, co. Tipperary, and 2ndly, 1840, Eliza, only dau. of Edward Roberts, J.P. of Killoteran, co. Waterford, and d. 1870, having had by the latter, with other issue, a son, GEORGE WILLIAM, of Rockenham, J.P., b. 1844; d.
; m. 1871, Sibella, youngest dau. of Samuel King, of Mount Pleasant, co. Waterford, and left issue a son, Richard Wall, b. 1876.
The 2nd son,
WILLIAM MORRIS, of Harbourview, co. Waterford, J.P., m. 1st, Jane Hackett, by whom he had a dau. Martha Jane, m. A. M. Alcock. He m. 2ndly, 1785, Mary, dau. of Shapland Carew, of Castleboro', co. Wexford, M.P., ancestor of Lord Carew, and by her had issue,
1. William, of Rossenarra, co. Kilkenny, D.L., who assumed the name and arms of READE.
2. Shapland Carew, of Harbourview, co. Waterford, D.L., m. Letitia, dau. of Rev John Kennedy.
3. BENJAMIN, of whom presently.
4. Richard Lieut. R.N., m. Eliza, 2nd dau. of Very Rev. the Dean of Waterford, and by her had issue,
1. Mary Anne, m. C. S. Tandy.
2. Elizabeth, m. William J. Tulloh.
3. Dorothea Anne, m. 26 April, 1823, William G. Sheppard.
The 3rd son,
REV. BENJAMIN MORRIS, b. 1790; m. 24 Oct. 1822, Elizabeth, 4th dau. and co-heir of Maurice Nugent O'Connor, of Mount Pleasant, her (who d. 24 Nov. 1861) had issue, amona.

", Maurice O'Connor, late Deputy-Postmaster-General of the island of Jamaica, b. 17 Feb. 1 27 ; m. 4 Feb. 1873, Mary Childs lau. of Col. Greenhuffe, and d. 19 May, 1901, leaving issue,
  1. Francis Joseph Maurice Nugent, b. 2 Dec. 1875.
  2. Geoffrey Bertram Henry William, b. 7 Dec. 1886.
1. Maria Catherine O'Connor, m. 16 Jan. 1875, W. H. Bishop, and d. Nov. 1898.
v. Benjamin Morris d. 30 Oct. 1846.
Lineage (of O'Connor).—In the year 1689,
Col. John O'Connor, of Cappaghgarane, or Gortnamona, was P. for the Borough of Philipstown in the Parliament assembled in Dublin by James II, and, it is supposed, was slain at the battle o Aughrim. He had three sons,
  1. Maurice, of whom presently
  2. Gerald, an officer in the French service.
  3. Thomas, who d.s.p.
T he eldest son,
Maurice O'Connor, gave the modern name of Mount Pleasant to a portion of the family estate. He m. circa 1725, Mary, 3rd dau. o Peter, 4th Earl of Fingall, and by her (who d. 1750) had issue,
John O'Connor, of Mount Pleasant, High Sheriff of King's Co., 1 59 ; m. 21 Sept. 1732, Mary, eldest dau. of Richard Malone, Serjeant-at-Law, and niece of the Right Hon. Anthony Malone, (see Malone of Baronston), and by her had issue,
  1. Maurice Nugent, of whom presently.
  2. Richard.
  3. John, of Ballycumber, m. Cathrine D'Alton, widow of — Netterville, by whom he had with other issue,
    1. John, who d. unm.
    2. Henry, m. 1544, Elizabeth, dau. of John Robinson, R.N., and niece of Admiral Hercules Robinson, of Rosmead, co. Westmeath, D.L., and d. 1852, having by her (who m. 2ndly, 1863, George Armstrong, and 3rdly, 1890, John Smith) had issue,
      (1) Maurice Nugent (Egremont, Ballybrack, co. Dublin, Junior United Service Club, London), Major late Royal Scots and Royal Irish Fusiliers, b. 8 July, 1840 ; m. 8 Dec. 1886, Lily, 2nd dau. of Sir John Henry Morris, K.C.S.I. He d. 24 Feb. 1905, leaving issue,
        Richard Nugent, b. 21 Aug. 1889.
      (2) Stanhope Edward, m. the dau. of Hon. H. Smith, of Melbourne.
      (3) Henry King (Rev.), M.A. Oxon., d.s.p. 1893.
      (1) Gertrude, m. Edward Ord Tandy, Deputy Surgeon-Gen., son of Master Tandy, Court of Chancery, Dublin, and has issue.
  4. Henry, m. 1816, Alicia, dau. of Henry Malone, of Pallas, and d. 1834.
  1. Mary, m. 1774, Edmond Malone, of Ballynahown, and had issue.
  2. Frances, m. Philip Stepney.
  3. Anne.   4. Jane.
Mr. O'Connor d. circa 1765, and was s. by his eldest son,
Maurice Nugent O'Connor, of Mount Pleasant, High Sheriff King's Co. 1783, and High Sheriff co. Westmeath 1797, m. 3 May, 1794, Maria, eldest dau. of Sir Thomas Burke, Bart., of Marblehill, co. Galway, and by her had issue,
  1. John, d.s.p. 1814.
  1. Catherine, m. 1st, 17 Oct. 1817, John Otway, 2nd Earl of Desart, who d. 22 Nov. 1820 ; 2ndly, Jan. 1824, Rose Lambart Price, eldest son of Sir Rose Price, Bart., and d. 11 Feb. 1874.
  2. Mary, m. 1826, Hugh Morgan Tuite, of Sonna, and had issue.
  3. Julia, d. unm. Nov. 1850.
  4. Elizabeth, m. Rev. B. Morris, and had issue (as above).
Mr. O'Connor d. 1818, when his estates devolved upon his four daus. as his co-heirs. The King's Co. estate of Mount Pleasant, recently restored to its old name of Gortnamona, has become vested through his youngest dau. Elizabeth, in Mr. O'Connor-Morris.
His Honour William O'Connor-Morris, of Gortnamona or Mount Pleasant, King's Co., B.A., J.P., Barrister-at-Law, County Court Judge and Chairman of Quarter Sessions, cos. Roscommon and Sligo, b. 26 Nov. 1824 ; s. his father, the Rev. William Ould, of Mount Pleasant, Rector of Rincurran, in the Diocese of Cork and Cloyne, 20 Oct. 1846 ; m. 16 March, 1858, Georgiana Kathleen (who d. 24 June, 1910), eldest dau. of George Hayward Lindsay, of Glasnevin, co. Dublin, D.L., and the Lady Mary Lindsay (see Burke's Peerage, Crawford and Balcarres, E.), and d. 3 Aug. 1904, leaving issue,
  1. Maurice Lindsay O'Connor, now of Gortnamona.
  1. Louisa Sudley Elizabeth, d. 3 Nov. 1859.
  2. Mary Augusta Caroline, twin with her sister.
  3. Elizabeth Georgiana Catherine.
  4. Emily Alice Henrietta, d. 20 April, 1864.
  5. Gertrude Ellen Charlotte.
  6. Kathleen Margaret Helen, d. 18 Feb. 1880.
Arms—Quarterly : 1st and 4th, gu. two swords points upwards in the arg. pomels and hilts or between as many garbs in pale of th 1st, banded sa. (Morris) ; 2nd, arg., an oak tree eradicated ppr. (O Connor) ; 3rd, sa., a bend arg. in the sinister chief a tower triple towered of the second (Plunkett). **Crest**—On a Roman fasces a man's head affrontée couped below the shoulders, all ppr. **Motto**—Festina lente.
Seat—Gortnamona, or Mount Pleasant, Tullamore, King's Co.

I.L.G.

MORRIS OF BALLINABOY.

James Timothy Aloysius Morris, of Ballinaboy, co. Galway, J.P., b. 16 June, 1844 ; m. 17 May, 1881, Anna Maria (who d. 2 July, 1907), dau. of George Stacey, of Tottenham, and has issue.
  1. George Philip, Capt. 30th Lancers (Gordon Horse), b. 12 March, 1882.
  2. Anthony James Hellier, B.A. Oxon., b. 17 Nov. 1883.
  3. Charles Sebastian, Lieut. R.N., b. 24 March, 1886.
  4. James Francis, Lieut. R.N., b. 29 Jan. 1889.
Lineage.—James Anthony Morris, of Ballinaboy, co. Galway, eldest son of Capt. Anthony James Morris, R.N., b. 1710 ; m. Eleanor, dau. of Anthony Staunton, of Galway and d. 1840, leaving issue,
  1. Anthony James, of whom presently.
  2. Ellen, m. Mathew Concys ; d.s.p.
  2. Mary, d. unm.
  3. Cecilia Jane, m. Marquis de Recende, and left issue.
The only son,
Anthony James Morris, of Ballinaboy, b. 1822 ; m. Elizabeth Catherine, dau. of James Hardy, and Catherine Lynch his wife. She d. 23 Sept. 1854. He d. 11 May, 1898, leaving issue,
  1. James Timothy Aloysius, now of Ballinaboy.
  2. Anthony, d. unm.   3. John, d. unm.
  4. William Michael, m. Catherine, dau. of Daniel De Vere Hunt, and has issue, a son and three daus.
    1. Catherine Bedelia, m. July, 1882, John J. O'Connor, and d. 20 Nov. 1905, leaving a dau.
Residence—Ballinaboy, Clifden, co. Galway.

MORRIS. *See* Burke's Peerage, **KILLANIN, B.**

MORRISON OF COOLEGEGAN.

Lieut.-Col. Richard Hobart Morrison, of Coolegegan, King's Co., Lieut.-Col. late 18th Hussars, formerly D.A.A.G. Malta, served in S. Africa 1900-2 (two medals and four clasps), b. 26 Nov. 1856 ; m. 11 July, 1889, Louise C. C. Buchanan, dau. of Herman R. de Ricci, of Moulsey House, Surrey, and has issue,
  1. Richard Fielding, 2nd Lieut. R.F.A., b. 30 April, 1890.
  2. Robert Herman Grant, Midshipman R.N., b. 11 May, 1891.
  3. Charles Colquhoun, b. 25 March, 1893.
Lineage.—Sir Richard Morrison, Knt., Member of the Royal Irish Academy, Founder and Vice-President of the Royal Institute of the Architects of Ireland, son of John Morrison, of Middleton, co. Cork, b. 1767 ; m. 1790, Eliza, dau. of the Rev. William Ould, D.D., Rector of Philipstown, King's Co., and grand-dau. of Sir Fielding Ould, Knt., M.D., an eminent Dublin physician in the 18th century, and by this lady (who d. 1854) had issue,
  1. John, M.D., an Officer, 1st Royal Dragoons, dec.
  2. William, an eminent architect, dec.
  3. Richard, m. 1823, Elizabeth, dau. of Robert Jones, of Springfield, co. Dublin, and d. 1857, leaving by her (who d. 1859),
    1. Richard Fielding, late of Coolegegan.
    1. Eliza Alicia, d. unm.
    2. Clara Frances, m. Sir Thomas Crawford, K.C.B., M.D., late Director-General Army Medical Staff, and d. 1860.
    3. Mary Evelina, m. Thomas Smith, of Drumlane, co. Meath, and has issue.
    4. Ada Charlotte, m. Gen. Clement Alexander Edwards, C.B., Col. 18th Royal Irish Regt., and has issue.
  4. Fielding (Rev.), Vicar of Corcomohide, Diocese of Limerick, dec.
Sir Richard Morrison d. 31 Oct. 1849, and was s. by his grandson,
Richard Fielding Morrison, of Coolegegan, King's Co., J.P. co. Dublin, Lieut.-Col. late 4th Royal Irish Lancers, b. 20 June, 1829; m. 20 Dec. 1853, Jane, dau. of Colquhoun Grant, M.D. of Kinchurdy, Morayshire, N.B. (a descendant of the Grants of Grant, chiefs of the ancient clan), and d. 19 July, 1902, having by her (who d. 12 June, 1903) had issue,

Morton. THE LANDED GENTRY. 498

1. RICHARD HOBART, now of Coolegegan.
2. Colquhoun Grant, Colonel, late a Major, in The Royal Dragoons, served in S.A. War (medal and clasp), b. 28 Jan. 1860, Col. R. F. Morrison, who was formerly a Capt. in the 51st Light Infantry (having sold out of the army 1857, and re-entered it as Cornet in the 16th Lancers, 1858), served with the 19th Regt. (light Division) in the Eastern Campaign of 1854, including the battle of Alma and siege of Sebastopol.
Richard Fielding Morrison s. on the death of his father in 1857, to the estate of Coolegegan, which had been in the possession of the family of his grandmother, Lady Morrison, for two centuries.

Arms—Or, on a cross per cross, sa. and gu., four fleurs-de-lis, arg., in the 1st quarter a crescent of the third. Crest—On a mural crown, gu., an eagle's head and neck between two wings, displayed arg., the neck and each wing charged with a fleur-de-lis, sa. Motto— Utile et dulce.

Club—Army and Navy.

MORTON OF LITTLE ISLAND.

VILLIERS ST. CLARE MORTON-JACKSON, of Little Island, co. Tipperary, b. 18 March, 1867; m. 9 June, 1910, Cherry Roma Anne, of Ahanesk Midleton, co. Cork, widow of Major N. H. Sadleir-Jackson. They adopted the additional surname of JACKSON 9 June, 1910.

Lineage.—SAMUEL MORTON, of Little Island, co. Tipperary, b. 4 Dec. 1764; d. 11 May, 1830, leaving issue, a son,
THE REV. JAMES MORTON, of Little Island, b. 17 Dec. 1794; m. 1st, 12 May, 1820, Catherine, dau. of Mathew Villiers Sankey, of Coolmore, Fethard, co. Tipperary (see that family). She d. 24 Sept. 1831, having had issue,
1. Samuel James, Capt. 6th Dragoon Guards (the Carabineers), b. 28 Sept. 1822; m. Florence, dau. of Hugh Kennedy, of Cultra (see that family). He d. 1860.
2. MATHEW VILLIERS SANKEY, late of Little Island.
1. Mary Amelia, m. 23 Dec. 1848, George Whitehead, of Babbicombe, Devon.
2. Catherine Anne, m. Lieut.-Col. R. Oriando Kellett, of Clonacody, Clonmel.
3. Elizabeth Adelaide, b. 17 Jan. 1831.
He m. 2ndly, 1842, Caroline, dau. of — Duddle, and d. 14 Aug. 1870, having by her had issue,
4. Anna Maria, m. Lieut.-Col. G. Wood, of Dorklands, Essex.
The 2nd son,
MATHEW VILLIERS SANKEY MORTON, of Little Island, co. Tipperary, J.P. and D.L. for that county, J.P. co. Waterford, and J.P. Queen's Co., High Sheriff for the latter 1871, late Capt. 35th Royal Sussex Regt., served in Burmah 1856 and in the Indian Mutiny 1857 (medals), b. 16 Oct. 1825; m. 24 Jan. 1863, Lucy Eleanor, dau. of the late Richard Moore, of Clonmel, and d. 31 Oct. 1907, leaving issue,
1. VILLIERS ST. CLARE, of Little Island.
2. Richard Charles, b. 27 Feb. 1868; m. Eleanor, dau. of — Higson.
3. Henry Elrington, b. 17 June, 1869; m. Emma, dau. of — Blennerhassett.
4. Algernon, b. 12 Nov. 1871.
1. Evelyn Villiers, m. Rev. A. Delap.
2. Lucy Eleanor, m. 9 Oct. 1901, Capt. J. C. Livingston-Learmonth, R.F.A.
3. Mary Sankey.

Seat—Little Island, Clonmel. Club—Hibernian United Service (Dublin).

MOUTRAY OF FAVOUR ROYAL.

ANKETELL MOUTRAY, of Favour Royal, co. Tyrone, D.L., J.P. for cos. Tyrone and Monaghan, High Sheriff co. Tyrone 1877, and for co. Monaghan 1903, b. 20 Aug. 1844; m. 1 July, 1873, Gertrude Madelina, 3rd surviving dau. of the late Mathew John Anketell, of Anketell Grove, co. Monaghan (by his wife, Catherine Anne Frances, dau. of D. Ker, of Montalto, co. Down), and has had issue,
1. John Corry, b. 31 Aug. 1878; d. 4 April, 1879.
2. ANKETELL GERALD, Lieut. 1st Batt. The Connaught Rangers, b. 5 Aug. 1882; m. 11 Feb. 1908, Mary Lilitia, 4th dau. of late Major John Grant, of Rathconrath House, co. Westmeath.
1. Anne Gwendoline Stella Eliza, b. 7 July, 1875; d. unm. 31 Aug. 1902.

Mr. Moutray s. his father in 1886, under the will of the late Anketell Moutray, eldest son of John Corry Moutray.

Lineage.—ROBERT MOUTRAY, of Roscobie, Fifeshire, 9th laird of Seafield, in Fifeshire, descended from Robert Multrave or Multrie who had a Royal Charter 1443, confirming to him the lands of Seafield and Markinch. Robert Moutray m. Anne, only dau. of Sir James Erskine of Favour Royal, co. Tyrone, to whom that estate was granted by JAMES I., grandson of John Erskine, Earl of Mar (see BURKE's Peerage), and had a son,
JOHN MOUTRAY, of Aghamoyles, alias Favour Royal, co. Tyrone. m. his cousin, Anne, dau. of the Rev. Archibald Erskine (son of Sir James Erskine), through whom the Moutray family acquired Favour Royal (see LORD BELMORE's Parl. Memoirs of Fermanagh and Tyrone, p. 162), and had a son,
JAMES MOUTRAY, of Favour Royal, High Sheriff co. Tyrone 1682, and M.P. for Augher 1692-1703, m. Deborah, dau. of Henry Mervyn, M.P., of Trillick, son of Sir Audley Mervyn, M.P., Speaker of the Irish House of Commons. His will bears date 12 March, 1718, proved 1719. He had issue,
1. JAMES, his heir. 2. Anketell.
1. Anne, m. George Gledstanes, of Daisy Hill.
2. Sarah, m. 13 June, 1717, Charles Stewart, of Baillieborough.
The son and heir,
JAMES MOUTRAY, of Favour Royal, High Sheriff co. Tyrone 1695; m. 1698, Rebecca, eldest dau. of Col. James Gorry, of Castlecoole, co. Fermanagh, and was father of
JOHN MOUTRAY, of Favour Royal, High Sheriff co. Tyrone 1721, b. April, 1701; d. June, 1779; m. 1720, Elizabeth, dau. of Alexander Montgomery, of Ballyleck, co. Monaghan (see MONTGOMERY of Beaulieu), and had issue,
1. James, of Favour Royal and Killibrick, M.P. for Augher 1761, and 1769, High Sheriff co. Tyrone 1762; m. Hester, sister of Thomas Knox, 1st Viscount Northland, and d.s.p. 17 May, 1777.
2. ANKETELL, of whom presently.
3. Leslie, of Killibrick, m. Jane. dau. of William Wray, of Castle Wray, co. Donegal, and left issue,
 1. Leslie, of Killibrick, who left, with other issue, Leslie.
 2. James, d. unm.
 3. Alexander, who left five sons.
4. John.
 1. Mary, d. unm.
 2. Rebecca, m. William Reid.
 3. Catherine, m. Henry Wray.
 4. Sarah, m. Gerald Irvine (see IRVINE of Killadeas).
 5. Elizabeth, m. Humphrey Jones, of Belturbet.

The 2nd son,
REV. ANKETELL MOUTRAY, of Favour Royal, m. 1768, Catherine, eldest dau. of Thomas Singleton, of Fort Singleton, co. Monaghan, by his 1st wife, the dau. of Oliver Anketell, of Anketell Grove, and d. circa 1801, having had one son, JOHN CORRY, and six daus., all of whom d. unm. except the 3rd, Isabella, who m. Whitney Upton Gledstanes, of Fardross. The only son and heir,
JOHN CORRY MOUTRAY, of Favour Royal, J.P. and D.L., High Sheriff co. Tyrone 1794, b. 29 Sept. 1771; m. 27 April, 1793, Mary Anne Catherine, 2nd dau. of Major Ambrose Upton, of Hermitage, co. Dublin, and had issue,
1. ANKETELL, of Favour Royal.
2. JOHN JAMES, late of Favour Royal.
3. Whitney, of Fort Singleton, co. Monaghan (see MOUTRAY of Fort Singleton).
4. Thomas (Rev.), b. 5 Dec. 1806; m. 20 Oct. 1842, Eliza, dau. of Andrew Crawford, of Auburn; d.s.p. 1843.
5. William (Rev.), b. 2 Oct. 1811; d. unm. 27 April, 1882.
6. Henry, of Killymoon Castle, Cookstown, co. Tyrone, J.P., b. 13 March, 1814; m. 1855, Barbara, eldest dau. of Mervyn Stewart, of Martray House, and d. Feb. 1875, leaving issue,
 1. Mervyn Stewart Thomas, now of Killymoon, J.P., b. 23 Aug. 1865; m. 1891, Helena Claudine, younger dau. of the Rev. Mervyn Wilson, Rector of Camus, and has issue,
  Barbara Claudine.
  1. Frances Vesey.
  2. Beatrice, m. 1887, Daniel James Wilson, B.A., Barrister-at-Law, son of Rev. Mervyn Wilson, Rector of Camus.
1. Catherine, d. unm.
2. Margaret, m. 23 June, 1810, Sir James Richardson Bunbury, Bart., of Aughercastle, who d. 4 Nov. 1851, leaving issue.
3. Isabella, m. 1820, Robert Waring Maxwell, of Killyfaddy, co. Tyrone, and d.s.p.
4. Sophia, m. 14 Dec. 1838, Robert Hornidge, of Twickenham, King's Co., who assumed by Royal Licence 1871, the name and arms of GLEDSTANES. She d. 1848. He d. 1876, leaving issue (see GLEDSTANES of Fardross).
Mr. Moutray d. 26 April, 1859, and was s. by his son,
ANKETELL MOUTRAY, of Favour Royal, High Sheriff co. Tyrone 1855, b. 11 May, 1797; d. s.p. Oct. 1869, and was s. by his brother,
REV. JOHN JAMES MOUTRAY, of Favour Royal, M.A., b. 15 April, 1802; m. 1 Jan. 1836, Maria Dorothea, 2nd dau. of the Rev. William Perceval, of Kilmore Hill, co. Waterford, and by her (who d. Sept. 1864) had issue,
1. JOHN MAXWELL (Rev.), M.A., LL.D., b. 1 Feb. 1837; d. 19 July, 1908; m. 1864, Jane, dau. of David Harrel, of Mount Plasant, co. Down, and has,
 1. John Corry Anketell, b. 1866, d. 1869.
 2. WILLIAM PERCEVAL, M.A., T.C.D., Sub-Inspector Basutoland Mounted Police, served in S. African War in Cape Mounted Rifles (medal with four clasps). While assisting Sub-Inspector Sutherland to arrest a violent native in Maseru on 20 Jan. 1910, he received a gun-shot wound which proved fatal some hours later. Sutherland was shot and killed on the spot. He was b. 4 July, 1872; m. 29 Jan. 1903, Maud, dau. of Charles Cowen, and left issue,
  William Whitney Maxwell, b. 18 July, 1906.
  Eileen Mary Perceval, b. 9 March, 1904.
 1. Anna Helena, b. 22 Sept. 1868.

2. Robert Percevа!, Capt. R.N., *b*. 22 Nov. 1840 ; *d. unm.* 10 Feb. 1896.
3. **William Henry**, *b*. 1842 ; *m*. 1871, Margaret Wilson, in Canada, and has issue,
   1. William Robert Maxwell, *b*. 1884.
   1. Mary Upton, *b*. 1872.   2. Anna Caroline, *b*. 1873.
   3. Elizabeth.   4. Margaret.
   5. Emily.
4. ANKETELL, now of Favour Royal.
5. Charles Frederick, B.A., T.C.D., of Summerhill, Clogher, co. Tyrone, J.P. co. Monaghan, *b*. 31 Oct. 1846 ; *m*. 12 Sept. 1888, Elizabeth, eldest dau. of the late Edward Hornidge, of Tullarris, co. Wicklow, and has issue,
   Frederick Charles, *b*. 23 June, 1889.
   Elizabeth Phœbe Gladys, *b*. 1 July, 1891.
1. Anna Maria Sophia, *b*. 5 Sept. 1849.
2. Mary Elizabeth, *b*. 12 Sept. 1851 ; *m*. 10 Aug. 1889, Algernon Thomas Fetherstonhaugh Briscoe, of Lake House, co. Westmeath, and has issue.
3. Caroline Helena, *b*. 21 April, 1858.
Mr. Moutray *d*. 20 June, 1886, and was s. by his 4th son.

Seat—Favour Royal, Aughnacloy, co. Tyrone.

MOUTRAY OF FORT SINGLETON AND AUBURN.

The late WHITNEY JOHN UPTON MOUTRAY, of Fort Singleton, co. Monaghan, and Auburn, co. Dublin, J.P. and D.L. co. Monaghan, M.A. Trin. Coll., Dublin, Barrister-at-Law, *b*. 5 Jan. 1849 ; *d.s.p.* 4 Feb. 1904 ; *m*. 28 June, 1893, Clara Christina (*now of Fort Singleton, co. Monaghan*), dau. of the late John Winter Humphrys, of Ballyhaise, co. Cavan.

Lineage.—The lineal ancestor of this family settled in Ireland about 1644. By his wife, a sister of John Corry, of Castlecoole, co. Fermanagh, ancestor of the Earls of Belmore, he left a son,

LAWRENCE CRAWFORD, of Carrowmacmea, one of the gentlemen of co. Fermanagh attainted in 1689 by King JAMES's Irish Parliament as adherents of the Prince of Orange. His will was dated 10 Jan. 1727-28. He *d*. 1731, leaving issue,
1. WILLIAM, of Snowhill, co. Fermanagh, who *d*. in 1749, leaving issue,
   1. Ralph, of Snowhill, High Sheriff 1741, *b*. 1711 ; *m*. 22 Jan. 1738-39, his cousin Margaret, dau. of Robert Crawford and Alice Hassard his wife (*see below*), and *d*. July, 1768, leaving an only child, Alicia, *m*. 20 March, 1759, John French, of Frenchpark, co. Roscommon, M.P. for that co., who *d.s.p.* 1775 (*see* BURKE's *Peerage*, DE FREYNE, B.).
   2. Henry, *b*. 1713, settled in America.
   3. Laurence.
   1. Jane, *m*. — Leonard, and had issue, a son, William.
   2. Anne.
   3. Margaret, *m*. Jason Hassard, of Carne, co. Fermanagh, and by him had a son, William, of Carne, High Sheriff co. Fermanagh 1772.
2. Robert, of Aughnacloy, near Brookborough, co. Fermanagh, High Sheriff, *m*. Alice, dau. of Capt. Jason Hassard, J.P. of Skea and Mullymeskar, co. Fermanagh (*see* BURKE's *Family Records*), and *d*. 1734, leaving issue, a son and a dau.,
   Jason, of Lawrencetown, co. Meath, High Sheriff co. Fermanagh 1735, B.A. Trin. Coll. Dublin 1732, *b*. 1710 ; *m*. 1737, Jane, dau. of Robert Maxwell, of Dunmurry, co. Cavan, by Isabella, dau. of James Maxwell, of Fellows Hall, co. Armagh, and son of Robert Maxwell, Bishop of Kilmore, and *d*. 1769, leaving
   (1) Robert of Lawrencetown, *m*. 1759, Miss Tucker, of Petersville.
   (2) John, of Lawrencetown, *m*. 1765, Elizabeth Vincent. Codicil to his will was dated 1805. He left
      1. Jason (Rev.), of Lawrencetown, B.A. Trin. Coll. Dublin 1790, *m*. 1797, Henrietta, dau. of Henry Rowley, of Maperath, co. Meath. His will is there dated 1829. He left issue, (1) John ; (2) Henry ; (3) James ; (4) Edward ; (5) Jason ; and (1) Henrietta.
      2. Robert.
      3. Richard, *m*. a dau. of John Crawford, an officer in the R.A., and *d.v.p.*
      4. John.
      1. Anne.
      2. Jane.
   (3) Ralph Henry, of Ballyhally, co. Cavan, *m*. 1773, Catherine Thompson, and left issue,
      1. Jason, of Ballyhally, and Marino Terrace, Clontarf, *m*. 1808, Catherine, dau. of Gustavus Brooke, of Dublin, and sister of Henry Brooke, of Brookehill, co. Donegal. She *d*. 1 Jan. 1860. He *d*. 20 March, 1846, leaving,
         a. Jason, of Ballyhally, *m*. 4 July, 1842, Susanna, sister of Thomas Young (afterwards Brooke), of Lough Esk, co. Donegal, and *d.s.p.* 4 June, 1877. She *d*. 13 Jan. 1877.
         a. Angel Elizabeth, *d*. Feb. 1892.

b. Elizabeth, *m*. Nov. 1836, Archibald James Somerville, 2nd son of Capt. William Somerville, by Elizabeth, dau. of Col. Henry Bellingham, of Castle Bellingham, co. Louth. She *d*. 23 Sept. 1883. He *d*. 7 Feb. 1871.
c. Catherine Henrietta, *d*. 5 June, 1887.
d. Sophia, *d*. 4 Jan. 1903.
2. Ralph Henry, *m*. Miss Fontaine, and had two daus.,
   a. Catherine, *m*. 1826, George Fontaigne.
   b. Maria, *m*. 1832, Robert Knox, of London and Capetown, and had with other issue : Rt. Hon. Sir Ralph Henry Knox, P.C., K.C.B., late Permanent Under-Sec. for War (*see* BURKE's *Peerage*), and Harriette, *m*. 10 Dec. 1874, Hon. Harry de Vere Pery, 6th son of 2nd Earl of Limerick (*see* BURKE's *Peerage*).
3. John.
1. Maria, *m*. — Aiken.
(1) Annabella, *m*. 1782, Gilbert Bethell.
(2) Margaret, *m*. — Fleming.
Margaret, *m*. 22 Jan. 1738-39, her cousin Ralph Crawford, of Snowhill (*see above*).
3. Henry, of Millwood, co. Fermanagh, High Sheriff 1738, *m*. a dau. of Capt. Alexander Acheson, and *d*. 1755, leaving issue,
   Alexander, of Millwood, High Sheriff 1762, *d*. 1767. He *m*. Conolly, dau. of Christopher Carleton, and sister of Guy, 1st Lord Dorchester, and by her (who *m*. 2ndly, Sir Patrick King) left issue,
   (1) Guy Henry, Lieut. 23rd Light Dragoons, *d. unm.* 1785.
   (2) Alexander, of Millwood, *m*. 1st, Dorothea Jones, and 2ndly, Elizabeth Evans (or Scriven), and *d*. 1812, leaving two sons,
      1. Alexander Fitzgerald, of Millwood, J.P. and D.L., High Sheriff 1830.
      2. Guy Henry, *d*. 1872.
   (3) Christopher.
   (1) Anne, *m*. 1782, Henry Colclough, of Mount Sion, co. Carlow, and had issue (*see* COLCLOUGH *of Tintern Abbey*).
   (2) Catherine, *m*. 1785, Beauchamp Colclough, and had issue.
4. JAMES, of whom presently.
5. John (Rev.).
1. Rebecca, *m*. John Irvine, of Enniskillen.
2. Mary, *m*. — Johnston.
3. Anne, *m*. — Spear.
4. Margaret, *m*. 8 April, 1711, James Corry, of Carrowmacmea, co. Fermanagh.

The 4th son,

JAMES CRAWFORD, of Enniskillen, High Sheriff co. Fermanagh 1739, *b*. 1682 ; *d*. 21 Oct. 1753, leaving issue by his wife Isabella,
1. ANDREW, his heir.
1. Martha, *d*. 1804 ; *m*. 1737, Col. Richard Graham, of Culmaine, co. Monaghan, and Derrynoose, co. Armagh, and had a son, Richard, *d. unm. v.p.*
2. Isabella, *m*. Thomas Singleton, of Fort Singleton, co. Monaghan, and had issue, Thomas, *b*. 1760, and a dau., Isabella, *m*. John Moutray Jones, and *d.s.p.*
3. Elizabeth, *m*. William Black, and left issue.

The only son,

ANDREW CRAWFORD, *m*. his cousin Catherine, dau. of Henry Crawford, and *d*. 1793, leaving issue,
1. JAMES, his heir.
1. Annabella, *b*. 1760 ; *m*. her cousin Thomas Singleton, of Fort Singleton, and *d*. 1 Dec. 1842, leaving by him (who *d*. 8 April, 1836) an only child, Isabella, *b*. 3 Sept. 1783 ; *m*. 28 Aug. 1802, her cousin Andrew Crawford, of Auburn, and *d*. 9 Dec. 1868. He *d*. 4 Jan. 1845, leaving issue (*see below*).

The only son,

JAMES CRAWFORD, of Auburn, co. Dublin, *b*. 29 July, 1755 ; *m*. 22 Oct. 1776, Francis Dorothy, elder dau. of George Vernon, of Clontarf Castle, co. Dublin, and *d*. 25 Nov. 1816, leaving with three daus., who *d*. young,
1. ANDREW, his heir.
2. George, Maj. 33rd Regt., *b*. 20 Nov. 1778 ; *d*. 25 Dec. 1808, *unm*.
3. James Archdall, Capt. 59th Regt., *b*. 5 April, 1784 ; *m*. 10 Sept. 1818, Uliana Fowell, eldest dau. of George Watts, of Bath, and *d*. 10 Aug. 1845, leaving issue,
   George Arthur, Maj. 4th Royal Lancashire Militia, *b*. 5 Dec. 1827 ; *m*. 19 Aug. 1862, Anna, youngest dau. of David Walker, of co. Dublin, Deputy Judge-Advocate-General of the Army, by his wife Anna, eldest dau. and co-heir of William Meeke, of Beddington, Surrey, formerly M.P. for Penrhyn, and *d*. 9 June, 1893, leaving issue, George Reginald, Elizabeth Anna, *d*. 23 Oct. 1886, and Caroline Isabel.
   Elizabeth Uliana, *b*. 29 Aug. 1830 ; *m*. 1854, Auchmuty James Richardson, of Richfort, co. Longford, J.P., and *d.s.p.* 16 April, 1855.
4. John Henry, an officer 34th Regt., *b*. 27 June, 1793 ; *d. unm.* 31 March, 1846.

The eldest son,

ANDREW CRAWFORD, of Auburn, *b*. 28 July, 1777 ; *m*. 28 Aug. 1802, his cousin Isabella, only child of Thomas Singleton, of Fort Singleton (*see above*). She *d*. 9 Dec. 1868. He *d*. 4 Jan. 1845, leaving issue,
1. THOMAS, his heir.
2. ANDREW JONES, s. his brother.
1. ANNABELLA, *m*. 20 April, 1843, WHITNEY MOUTRAY, J.P., 3rd son of John Corry Moutray, J.P. and D.L., of Favour Royal, co. Tyrone (*see that family*). He *d*. 14 Dec. 1882. She *d*. 31 Dec. 1891, having had issue,

Mulcahy.

1. WHITNEY UPTON, now of Fort Singleton and Auburn.
2. John Thomas, b. 18 April, 1851.
2. Louisa Frances, m. 1834, William Donnelly, C.B., late Registrar-General for Ireland, and has issue.
3. Eliza Catherine, m. 20 Oct. 1842, Rev. Thomas Moutray, 4th son of John Corry Moutray. He d. 1843, leaving no issue.

The elder son,
THOMAS SINGLETON, of Fort Singleton, co. Monaghan, and Auburn, co. Dublin, formerly Lieut. 16th Regt., D.L. and J.P. for co. Monaghan, of which he was Sheriff in 1839, b. 1 March, 1807. Mr. Singleton, whose patronymic was CRAWFORD, assumed the name of SINGLETON by royal licence, 26 Jan. 1843, on succeeding to the estates of his maternal grandfather, and d.s.p. 14 May, 1881. His brother,
ANDREW JONES CRAWFORD, of Fort Singleton, co. Monaghan, J.P., b. 15 Nov. 1809; m. 1859, Mary, dau. of William Macreary, and d.s.p. 4 Oct. 1896. He was s. by his nephew.

Seats—Fort Singleton, Emyvale, co. Monaghan, and Auburn, Malahide, co. Dublin.

MULCAHY OF ABBEY VIEW.

JAMES PRENDERGAST MULCAHY, of Abbey View, co. Tipperary, J.P. co. Waterford, b. July, 1840; m. 18 Nov. 1879, his cousin Mary Julia, dau. of William Roberts Mulcahy, of Corabella House, Newcastle, co. Tipperary (and Mary Julia his wife, dau. of Thomas O'Donoghue, of Clocristie, co. Carlow), and great grand-dau. of Thomas Mulcahy, D.L., of Burgesland, and has issue,

1. FRANCIS ALPHONSO, b. 1 Jan. 1883.
2. William Roberts, b. 21 April, 1895.
1. Frances Mary. 2. Mary Julia.
3. Isabella Jane. 4. Evelyn Maud.
5. Charlotte. 6. Margaret Anne.
7. Agnes Josephine Augustine.

Lineage.—ROGER MULCAHY, of Ballymakee, co. Waterford, b. 1591; m. Ellen, dau. of Daniel Magrath, of Ballinamult, and had issue,
1. Nicholas, of Ardfinnan, co. Tipperary, beheaded in Cromwell's Camp during the seige of Clonmel.
2. THOMAS MOORE, of whom we treat.

The younger son,
THOMAS MOORE MULCAHY, m. Ellen, dau. of Pierce Power, and had with other issue, a son,
EDMUND MULCAHY, m. Mary, dau. of James O'Grady, of Ashish, and had a son,
THOMAS MULCAHY, m. Ellen Cassans, of Queen's Co., and had issue, three sons,
1. THOMAS, of whom presently.
2. John, of Ballymakee, m. the dau. of Thomas Quin, of Loloher Castle, co. Tipperary.
3. Edmund, from whom descends Mulcahy of Ballybrien.

The eldest son,
THOMAS MULCAHY, of Burgesland, Newcastle, co. Tipperary, Deputy-Governor of that co. in 1793, the first year Catholics were eligible for the commission, m. Anne, dau. of Gen. Sir Thomas Roberts, of Darrow House, Stradbally, co. Waterford. His son,
FRANCIS MULCAHY, of Noan House, Nedding, and Kossmore, co. Tipperary, b. 1784; m. 1812, Frances Mary, dau. of Charles Prendergast, of Carrick-on-Suir, co. Tipperary. She d. 1863. He d. 1862, having had issue,
1. Charles.
2. Francis, m. 1850, the dau. of Samuel Jellicoe, of Cahir, and d. 17 March, 1892, leaving a dau.
3. John, J.P. cos. Tipperary and Waterford, m. 1859, the dau. of James Barry, of Frogmore House, co. Cork.
4. JAMES PRENDERGAST, of Abbey View.
5. Frederick, d. young.
6. William, d. young.
1. Margaret Anne, d. unm.
2. Harriet Jane, m. 1855, Edmund O'Dwyer, of Liscahill Lodge, Thurles.
3. Isabella, m. 1852, Capt. Wainwright. Both, with their family, were massacred at Cawnpore, 1857.
4. Jane, m. 1857, John Prendergast, of Clonmel, and has issue.
5. Charlotte, m. 1846 Thomas O'Dwyer, B.L. of Mount Bruce, co. Tipperary, and has issue.

Seat—Abbey View, Clonmel.

MULHOLLAND.

See BURKE'S PEERAGE, DUNLEATH, B.

MULLOY OF HUGHESTOWN.

WILLIAM DUKE GORGES O'MULLOY, of Hughestown, co. Roscommon, b. 21 Oct. 1877; m. 2 May, 1898, Marguerite, dau. of Alexander Paul, of Aberdeen, and has issue,
1. CHARLES DUKE PAUL, b. 22 Nov. 1900.
1. Marguerite Norah Aileen, b. 18 Aug. 1906.
2. Emily Louisa Frances, b. 6 May, 1909.

Lineage.—CAPT. ANTHONY MULLOY (10th in descent from Hugh Mor, or Great O'Mulloy, Lord of the Territory of Fercall, chief of his name, emigrated to the co. of Roscommon in the early part of ELIZABETH'S reign, and procured a large grant of land, including the Manor of Ughterthiera (now Coote Hall), etc. He m. Honora Dowell (of the family of Dowell, of Mantua House), and d. 20 July, 1603, leaving a son,
WILLIAM O'MULLOY, who is styled by Lodge, in his Peerage of Ireland, The Great O'MULLOY, of Ughterthiera, co. Roscommon) High Sheriff 1621 and 1641. He m. Margaret Clifford, and had two sons and three daus. The 2nd son,
CONOR MULLOY, m. Jane, dau. of Richard Ruttledge, of Belleek, near Ballyshannon, and had a son,
THEOBALD MULLOY, who held the commission of Capt. of Horse in King WILLIAM'S Army at the Battle of the Boyne (1690). He m. 1st, the dau. of — King. She d.s.p. He m. 2ndly, Frances Harloe, and by her had two sons,
1. CHARLES, of whom presently.
2. William, who d. at Exeter, a Capt. in the Army.

Capt. Theobald Mulloy, High Sheriff to the co. of Roscommon 1691-93, d. 1734, and was s. by his son,
CHARLES MULLOY, who served in some of WILLIAM'S wars, and the siege of Vigo, where he was wounded. He m. Hester Adams, and d. 1760, aged 92, leaving three sons. The only surviving son,
COOTE MULLOY, of Hughestown, b. 1720, Cornet in Hamilton's Dragoons. He m. May, 1745, Margaret, dau. of James Dodd, of Ardagh (of the family of Dodd, of Cloverley Hall, Salop), by Martha his wife, grand-dau. of Arthur Achmuty, of Brianstown, co. Longford, and d. 7 Jan. 1796, leaving issue,
1. TOBIAS, of whom presently.
2. James (Rev.), d. unm.
3. Coote, A.D.C. to Gen. Eustace at the Battle of Gemappe, dec.
4. William, of Oak Port, co. Roscommon, J.P., b. 27 Oct. 1765; m. 12 Dec. 1796, Frances, dau. of Arthur French, of French Park, M.P., and had issue,
  1. Coote, of Oak Port, High Sheriff 1843, d. unm. 1850.
  2. William, m. 1855, Anne, dau. of Daniel Kelly, of Cargins, co. Roscommon, and had a dau.,
    Mary Emily Margarette.
  3. Arthur Edward, 64th Regt., d. 1853, leaving a son.
  1. Alice, d. unm. 2. Margarette, d. unm.
  3. Frances Louisa, d. unm. 4. Jane, d. unm.
1. Hester, m. Andrew Kirkwood, of Castletown.
2. Margaret, m. Thomas M'Dermott Roe, of Alderford, co. Roscommon.
3. Rebecca, m. John Phibbs, of Lisconny.
4. Helen, m. Rev. Peter Birmingham.

The eldest son,
TOBIAS MULLOY, of Hughestown, barrister, b. 6 May, 1748; m. Susannah, dau. of Col. Arthur Roche, son of George Roche, M.P. for Limerick, and d. 20 Feb. 1825, leaving issue,
1. COOTE, of whom presently.
2. Charles (Rev.), Rector of Colooney Glebe, co. Sligo; m. 15 May, 1820, Margaret, sister of Sir Robert King, Bart., of Charlestown, co. Roscommon, and d. April, 1832, leaving issue.
  1. Charles, dec. 2. Coote.
  3. Robert.
  1. Caroline.

The elder son,
COOTE MULLOY, of Hughestown, D.L. for Roscommon, m. 1799, Mary, eldest dau. of William Lloyd, of Rockville co. Roscommon, and d. Oct. 1841, having by her (who d. 1856) had issue,
1. COOTE CHARLES, of whom presently.
2. William James, m. 6 March, 1837, Anne, eldest dau. of the late Hamilton Gorges, of Kilbrew, and had issue,
  William Gorges, b. Oct. 1839.
  Emily Louisa, m. 10 April, 1871, Col. William Hutchinson Mulloy, of Hughestown (see below).
1. Mary, m. William Hutchinson, F.R.C.S.I.
2. Hessy, m. Hugh Chambers.
3. Margaret, m. John Moore.

The elder son,
REV. COOTE CHARLES MULLOY, of Hughestown, co. Roscommon, m. 1st, 1831, Alice, dau. of Robert King Duke, of Newpark, co. Sligo, and by her (who d. 1844) had issue,
1. Coote, d. unm. 10 March, 1857.

2. Robert, d. unm. 1849.
3. WILLIAM HUTCHINSON, late of Hughestown.
1. Mary, d. unm. 1883.
2. Elizabeth Anne, m. 27 May, 1868, Walter Henry Keating, of Newcastle, co. Westmeath, J.P., and has issue.
He m. 2ndly, 15 Sept. 1857, Catherine Reddish, eldest dau. of Edward Stopford, D.D., Bishop of Meath, and d. 23 May, 1882.
WILLIAM HUTCHINSON MULLOY, of Hughestown, co. Roscommon, and of Kelvedon, Reading, Col. (retired) late R.E., b. 6 Jan. 1839; m. 1st. 10 April, 1871, Emily Louisa, dau. of W. J. Mulloy, Rector of Ballysonnan, Kildare, and by her (who d. 6 Aug. 1880) had issue,
1. Coote Charles, d. 1874.   2. Robert Coote, d. 1873.
3. Charles Coote, Lieut. R.W.K. Regt., b. 28 Nov. 1875; d. in South Africa 14 March, 1901.
4. WILLIAM DUKE GORGES, now of Hughestown.
1. Alice Mary.
He m. 2ndly, 24 April, 1883, Edith Louisa Cortlandt, dau. of the Hon. H. Trotter, H.M. Colonial Service. He d. 23 Jan. 1909, having by her had issue,
5. Noel Frank Coote, b. 28 Feb. 1886.
2. Edith Katharine Cortlandt.

Arms—Arg. a lion rampant sa. between three trefoils gu. **Crest**—A greyhound sa. gorged with a collar or, running by an oak tree ppr.   **Motto**—Carrurlagus doagh aboo.
Seat—Hughestown, co. Roscommon.   **Residence**—29, Hampstead Hill Gardens, London, N.W.

MULOCK OF KILNAGARNA.

JOHN CHARLES METGE MULOCK, of Kilnagarna, King's Co., b. 4 Sept. 1875; s. his uncle Thomas Mulock, 26 Jan. 1900; m. 3 Sept. 1907, Alice Blanche Maude, dau. of James Hunter, of Edinburgh.

Lineage.—The Mulocks appear to be descendants of an old Irish family, who, in the reign of HENRY V., assumed the name of Myllok from the lands held by them at Myllok, now Meelick, on the Shannon, and obtained the customary letters patent to enable them to enjoy the benefits of English law, and hold their lands by English tenure.
The surname of the family in course of time came to be written Mullock, and eventually Mulock; and in the middle of the 17th century the representative of the family was
THOMAS MULLOCK (or MULOCK), of Ballynakill, near Meelick, co. Galway, who left issue,
1. THOMAS, of whom we treat.   2. Nicholas.
The elder son,
THOMAS MULOCK, of Moate, co. Westmeath, m. 1st, Frances Meares, and 2ndly, Margaret Conran, and by the latter left issue,
1. JOHN, m. Aug. 1720, Ann, dau. of Robert Drought, of Park, King's Co., and d.s.p. 1757, devising Kilnagarna and other estates in the King's Co. to his next brother Thomas, and Bally-ard (or Bellair) to his nephew, Rev. John Mulock, son of his younger brother Robert.
2. THOMAS, of whom hereafter.
3. Robert (see HOMAN-MULOCK of Bellair).
The 2nd son,
THOMAS MULOCK, of Dublin, and afterwards of Kilnagarna, b. 1700; m. May, 1744, Mary, dau. of James Lawless, of Shankill, co. Dublin.   He s. to the Kilnagarna estates on the death of his brother John in 1757, and d. 1777, leaving issue,
1. THOMAS, of whom hereafter.
2. Robert, of Dublin, and afterwards of Bath, m. Maria Sarah Horner, and d. 1837 leaving (with nine daus.),
  1. Thomas Samuel, b. 1789; m. 7 June, 1825, Dinah, dau. of Thomas Mellard, and d. 11 Aug. 1869, having had issue,
    (1) Thomas Mellard, b. 18 Nov. 1827; d. unm. 22 Feb. 1847.
    (2) Benjamin Robert, b. 18 June, 1829; d. unm. 1863.
    (1) Dinah Maria, the authoress of John Halifax, Gentleman, and many other well-known works of fiction; m. 1865, George Lillie Craik, and d.s.p. 12 Oct. 1887. He d. 25 Oct. 1905.
    2. William, m. twice, and d. 1855, leaving five children.
3. William, of Ballinagore, co. Westmeath, m. Alicia Holmes, and d. 1827, leaving issue,
  1. William Henry, who assumed the surname of HOLMES in addition to Mulock, one of the Hon. Corps of Gentlemen-at-Arms, and Capt. in the Royal London Militia, m. 10 Nov. 1869, Jessie, dau. of George Cobham, M.D., and d.s.p. 17 Sept. 1871.
  2. Thomas Edmonds, C.B., Col. late 70th Foot, m. 24 Jan. 1861, Julia Florentia, dau. of Capt. John Sturt, R.E., of Crichel, by his wife Alexandrina, dau. of Gen. Sir Robert Sale, G.C.B., and d. 9 Sept. 1893, having had issue,
    (1) Henry Edmonds, b. 1861; d. unm. 1885.
    (2) Alfred Sale, b. 1862; d. unm. 1884.
    (3) Frederick Charles, b. 18 May, 1866; m. 1893, Maud, dau. of Col. G. Cadogan Thomson, 1st Bengal Cavalry, and has issue,
      1. Evelyn Edmonds, b. 22 Oct. 1893.
      2. John Sale, b. 23 Nov. 1900.
    (1) Eileen Florentia, m. 18 June, 1903, Henry George Bagnall Vane, son of the late Hon. George Vane, C.M.G.
    (2) Julia Nina, m. 1898, Robert Menzies.
    1. Mary, m. 1831, Hilary Frederick d'Estrange.
The eldest son,

THOMAS MULOCK, of Kilnagarna, b. 1746; Sch. of Trin. Coll. Dublin 1764, B.A. 1766, Barrister-at-Law; s. his father at Kilnagarna 1777; m. 4 Dec. 1790, Frances Henrietta Dorothea, dau. of Samuel Judge, of Ballyshiel, King's Co., by his wife Frances, dau. of Henry Otway, of Castle Otway, co. Tipperary (see BURKE'S Peerage, OTWAY, Bart.), and d. 20 March, 1827, having had issue,
1. THOMAS, of whom hereafter.
2. Mary, m. 1 April, 1834, Edward Bewley, M.D., of Moate, co. Westmeath, and d. 17 Oct. 1857, leaving issue, Sir Edmund Thomas Bewley, LL.D., late a Judge of the Supreme Court of Judicature in Ireland, and Louisa Frances.
3. Jane Martha, m. 26 Dec. 1820, Torriano Francis l'Estrange, and d. 30 Jan. 1822, leaving issue a son, Thomas.
4. Harriet, d. unm. 1 July, 1822.
5. Catherine Louisa, m. 11 June, 1829, Rev. James Paul Holmes, and d. 9 July, 1886, leaving issue: 1. Rev. John Gordon Holmes; 2. Col. Thomas James Paul Holmes; 1. Frances Harriet; 2. Louisa Lucy, m. 1872, Col. Caleb Shera Wills, C.B., and d. 1885; 3. Mary Anne Sophia, m. Philip H. Miller, A.R.H.A.
The only son,
THOMAS MULOCK, of Kilnagarna, b. 25 June, 1829, Rev. Henry 1827; m. 11 June, 1833, Sophia Mary Anne, dau. of Rev. Henry Mahon, Rector of Tissauran, Lemanaghan, and Ferbane (see BURKE'S Peerage, MAHON, Bart.), d. 4 May, 1860, having had issue by her (who d. 3 Feb. 1889).
1. THOMAS, of whom hereafter.
2. Henry Louis, b. 10 Jan. 1836.
3. Robert, b. 23 May, 1843; d. unm. 2 July, 1864.
4. William (twin with Robert), d. unm. 4 Nov. 1858.
5. George Charles, b. 6 May, 1845; m. 31 March, 1874, Henrietta Cole, dau. of John Metge, J.P., of Sion House, co. Meath (see METGE, of Athlumney), and d. 14 March, 1903, leaving issue,
  1. JOHN CHARLES METGE, now of Kilnagarna.
  1. Henrietta Georgina Ethel, m. 18 Sept. 1902, George Meares Stopford Enraght-Moony, of The Doon, King's Co. (see that family).
  2 Sophia Eliza Edith.   3. Emily Cole.
6. Edward Ross, R.N., b. 22 March, 1847; m. 4 Feb. 1890, Georgina, dau. of Rev. George Chute, of Roxborough, co. Kerry, and Market Drayton, Salop, and d. 1 July, 1890. He had issue, a posthumous son,
  Edward Ross, b. 30 Nov. 1890.
7. Charles James, B.A., b. 30 Sept. 1848.
8. Frederick Arthur, b. 22 May, 1851; d. unm. 2 Jan. 1876.
9. Francis John, b. 28 June, 1853; d. unm. 6 Sept. 1886.
1. Anne Harriet, m. 22 Oct. 1857, Joseph Daniel Dickenson, of Hillview, Canterbury, New Zealand, late of 4th K.O. Regt.
2. Frances Jane.
3. Sophia Mary Anne, d. unm. 8 May, 1898.
The eldest son,
THOMAS MULOCK, of Kilnagarna, B.A.; b. 27 May, 1834; s. his father 1860, and d. unm. 26 Jan. 1900, when he was s. by his nephew.
Residence—Kilnagarna, Athlone, co. Westmeath.

HOMAN-MULOCK OF BELLAIR.

WILLIAM BURY HOMAN-MULOCK, of Bellair, King's Co., J.P. and D.L. for that co. and J.P. for Westmeath, High Sheriff King's Co. 1895, late H.M.I.C.S. (Bombay), b. 19 April, 1841; s. his father 1889.

Lineage.—ROBERT MULOCK, 3rd son of THOMAS MULOCK of Moate, Westmeath, and younger brother of Thomas Mulock, of Kilnagarna, (see that family). He had issue,
1. JOHN, of whom hereafter.
1. Helena, m. Francis Enraght-Mooney, of The Doon, King's Co. (see that family).
2. Elizabeth.
3. Frances, m. Thomas Grattan, M.D.
The only son,
REV. JOHN MULOCK, of Bellair (or Ballyard), King's Co., s. to that property by devise of his uncle, John Mulock, of Kilnagarna (see that family), b. 1722; m. 1st, March, 1753, Emily Frances, eldest dau. of Hurd Wetherall, of Castletown, King's Co., and by her had issue,
1. Hurd, Barrister-at-Law, d. unm. 1806.
2. John, d. 1805, leaving issue, from whom is descended Sir William Mulock, of Toronto, Postmaster-General of Canada.
1. Frances Emilia, m. 10 May, 1778, Henry Pilkington, of Tore (see PILKINGTON, of Tore).
The Rev. John Mulock m. 2ndly, 18 Feb. 1764, Anne, dau. and heir of Richard Homan of Moate and Surock, co. Westmeath, and through her acquired the Homan property, and by her had issue,
3. THOMAS HOMAN, of whom presently.

Mulock. THE LANDED GENTRY. 502

2. ELIZABETH, *m.* 22 Feb. 1788, Lawrence Bomford Molloy, of Clonbelamore, King's Co. (*see that family*), and *d.* 1804, leaving issue,
  1. John (Rev.), *b.* 1790 *d. unm.* 1818.
  2. Daniel, *b.* 1793 ; *m.* 16 May, 1834, Julia Harriet, only dau. of Major James Higginson, 10th Regt., and *d.* 25 April, 1856, leaving issue.
  3. THOMAS, of whom presently.
  1. Anne Homan, *m.* 1818, Alured L'Estrange, son of Major-Gen. L'Estrange, and *d.s.p.* 1819.
3. Mary, *d. unm.* 1828.
The Rev. John Mulock *d.* 1803. His 3rd son,
THOMAS HOMAN MULOCK, of Bellair, High Sheriff of King's Co. 1816, *b.* 1770 ; *m.* Catherine Frances, (who *d.* 1845), youngest dau. of Thomas Berry, of Eglish Castle, King's Co. ; *d.s.p.* 1843, and was *s.* by his nephew,
THOMAS HOMAN-MULOCK (formerly MOLLOY), of Bellair, *b.* 5 May, 1798, who assumed by Royal Licence, 14 Feb. 1843, the name and arms of HOMAN-MULOCK. He was High Sheriff of King's Co. 1849 ; *m.* 5 Feb. 1828, Frances Sophia, dau. of John Berry, of Cloneen, King's Co. (eldest son of Thomas Berry, of Eglish Castle, by Elizabeth, his wife, dau. of William Bury, uncle of the 1st Earl of Charleville, and by her (who *d.* 12 Aug. 1863) had issue,
  1. Thomas Homan Mulock, *b.* 8 June, 1830 ; *d.* 1844.
  2. John Berry, *b.* 28 April, 1832 ; *m.* 21 Nov. 1883, Anne Selina, dau. of Lieut.-Col. Owen Lloyd Ormsby (Connaught Rangers), of Ballinamore, co. Mayo, and *d.s.p.* 1885.
  3. Thomas Lawrence, *b.* 6 March, 1834 ; *d.* 1854.
  4. Richard Homan, *b.* 6 Feb. 1836.
  5. Lawrence Bomford, *b.* 23 Jan. 1840 ; *d.* 1863.
  6. WILLIAM BURY, now of Bellair.
  7. Henry Pilkington, H.M.I.C.S., *b.* 8 Jan. 1846.
  8. Homan Mulock, *b.* 3 March. 1847 ; *d.* 1861.
  9. Francis Berry, of Ballycumber (*see* HOMAN-MULOCK *of Ballycumber*).
  10. George Phillips, C.E., *b.* 16 July, 1851 ; *m.* 1st, 17 July, 1877, Clara Frances Lugsdin. She *d.* 28 March, 1882, leaving issue,
    1. George Francis Arthur, R.N., *b.* 7 Feb. 1882.
    1. Clara Frances. 2. Nellie Bell.
    3. Nina Annie Litchfield, *d. unm.* 8 Feb. 1899.
He *m.* 2ndly, 26 Oct. 1883, Jane Elizabeth, dau. of Capt. James Collister, and *d.* 16 March, 1898, having by her had issue,
  2. Henry Collister, *b.* 9 Oct. 1891.
  1. Frances Elizabeth, *b.* 8 Dec. 1828 ; *d. unm.* 1848.
  2. Elizabeth Georgina, *m.* 1 June, 1858, Peter Macfarlane Syme, Capt. R.A., and *d.* 1869, leaving issue,
    Charles Mulock, *d.* 1884.
    Florence Mary, *m.* 1880, E. A. Holmes, H.M.I.S., and has issue.
  3. Mary Mulock, *m.* 1st, 12 Sept. 1863, George Winter Price (who *d.s.p.* 1865), and 2ndly, 20 July, 1867, Frederick Pepys Cockerell, son of Charles Robert Cockerell, R.A. (*see* BURKE'S *Peerage*, COCKERELL-RUSHOUT, Bart.), and has issue,
    1. Robert Rennie Pepys, Barrister-at-Law, *b.* 29 Nov. 1869 ; *m.* Oct. 1897, Violet Helen, dau. of Col. James Lawrence Montgomery, and grand-dau. of Sir Robert Montgomery. He *d.* 6 Aug. 1902.
    2. Frederick William Pepys, B.L., *b.* 10 July, 1786.
    3. Laurence Homan Mulock Pepys, Capt. 60th Royal Berks Regt., *b.* 15 Oct. 1878 ; *m.* 1909, Florence Octavia, dau. of George H. Greenwood, and widow of John Wright, of Dunedin, New Zealand.
    1. Anne Hester, *m.* 15 Dec. 1891, Edward Dames-Longworth, and has issue (*see* DAMES-LONGWORTH *of Glynwood*).
    2. Frances Mary, *m.* 2 April, 1902, Capt. Henry Cecil Noel, 17th Lancers (*see* BURKE'S *Peerage*, GAINSBOROUGH, E.).
  4. Hester Jane, *m.* 14 Nov. 1865, Alfred Austin, Poet Laureate, D.L. for Herefordshire, Barrister-at-Law, of Swinford Old Manor, Ashford, Kent.
  5. Anne Homan, *m.* 27 Feb. 1866, Arthur Challis Kennard, son of Robert William Kennard, M.P. (*see* KENNARD, *late of Crawley Court*).
    1. Arthur Molloy, D.S.O., R.H.A. (*Club*—*Naval and Military*).
    2. Howard William, Diplomatic Service, British Embassy, Washington.
    1. Nina Frances, *m.* 1896, James Augustus Grant, M.P. Egremont, Cumberland, eldest son of Col. Grant, of Househill, Nairn.
    2. Hester Charlotte.
Mr. Thomas Homan-Mulock *d.* 25 June, 1889, and was *s.* by his son, WILLIAM BURY, now of Bellair.

Arms—Quarterly, 1st and 4th az., a cross moline quarter-pierced, and in the dexter chief a letterlock arg., for MULOCK ; and 3rd vert, on a chevron arg., between three pheons points downwards or, as many trefoils slipped ppr., for HOMAN. **Crest**—A lion passant az., in the dexter paw a cross crosslet fitchée gu. **Motto**—In hoc signo vinces.
Residence—Bellair, Ballycumber, King's Co. **Clubs**—E. I. United Service, S.W., and Kildare Street, Dublin.

HOMAN-MULOCK OF BALLYCUMBER.

FRANCIS BERRY HOMAN-MULOCK, of Ballycumber House, King's Co., J.P., High Sheriff 1902, late Bengal Civil Service (North-West Provinces and Oudh), *b.* 26 July, 1848 ; *m.* 14 Aug. 1878, Ethel Annie, dau. of the Right Hon. Sir Edward Nicholas Coventry Braddon, P.C., K.C.M.G., late Premier of Tasmania, and has issue,
  1. EDWARD HOMAN, Vice-Consul Alexandria, Levant Consular Service, *b.* 20 Oct. 1881 ; *m.* 6 June, 1910, Elsie Mabel, eldest dau. of J. Hume Henderson, of Cheniston Gardens, W.
  1. Frances Ethel, *m.* 16 Oct. 1900, Claude Beddington, of 26, Seymour Street, W., Brevet Lieut.-Col. Westmorland and Cumberland Imp. Yeom., and has issue,
    Guy Claude, *b.* 2 Feb. 1902.
    Sheila Claude, *b.* 23 May, 1906.
  2. Enid Hester Nina.

Mr. F. B. Homan-Mulock is the 9th son of the late Thomas Homan-Mulock, of Bellair, and Frances Sophia, his wife, dau. of John Berry, of Cloneen (*see* HOMAN-MULOCK *of Bellair*).

Arms—*See* MULOCK *of Bellair*.
Seat—Ballycumber House, King's Co. **Club**—Kildare Street Dublin.

MURPHY OF THE GRANGE.

GEORGE FITZGERALD MURPHY, of The Grange, co. Meath, J.P., B.A. London, *b.* 12 Sept. 1849 ; *m.* 3 June, 1884, Lady Mary Louisa Plunkett, dau. of Arthur James, 10th Earl of Fingall.

Lineage.—JAMES GEORGE MURPHY, of The Grange, Dunsany, co. Meath, *m.* Mary Eliza, dau. of Col. FitzGerald, of Geraldine, Athy, co. Kildare. She *d.* 1888. He *d.* 1858, having had issue,
  1. GEORGE FITZGERALD, now of The Grange.
  2. Thomas FitzGerald, of Fradswell Hall, Stafford, *b.* Oct. 1851 ; *m.* 5 Aug. 1882, Emily Geraldine, eldest dau. of Malachi Strong Hussey, of Westown (*see that family*). He *d.* 25 Feb. 1907.
  3. James FitzGerald, Capt. late Royal Dragoons (43, *Park Lane*, *W.*).
  4. Francis Joseph, Major late R.A. (4, *Down Street*, *Piccadilly*, *W.*), *b.* 14 Feb. 1855.

Seat—The Grange, Dunsany, co. Meath. **Clubs**—Orleans and Sackville Street Club.

MURPHY OF KILBREW.

REGINALD FRANCIS BRUDENELL MURPHY, of Kilbrew, co. Meath, Capt. 4th Batt. Scottish Rifles (Mil.), *b.* 1880.

Lineage.—WILLIAM MURPHY, of Mount Merrion, co. Dublin, and of Kilbrew and Ballymaglasson, co. Meath, *b.* 1771 ; *m.* 1797, Margaret, dau. of Bryan Reilly, by Mary, his wife, dau. of Thadeus Ford, and sister of Elizabeth Ford, who *m.* Edward Madden, and left two children. Dr. Richard R. Madden, the distinguished writer, and Eliza Cogan, mother of Right Hon. William Henry Ford Cogan, M.P. for co. Kildare from 1852 until 1880. By Margaret his wife (who *d.* 1833), Mr. Murphy left (with five daus., of whom Catherine the eldest, *m.* John Johnson, of Warrenstown, co. Meath, and *d.s.p.*) four sons,
  1. JOHN WILLIAM, of whom presently.
  2. William, *m.* 1840, Margaret, dau. of Matthew O'Conor, of Mount Druid, co. Roscommon, and *d.* at Florence, 1843, leaving two daus.,
    1. Louisa Margaret, *m.* the late Richard D'Arcy, of New Forest, co. Galway.
    2. Emily.
  3. Charles James, *d. unm.* 1849.
  4. James, of Mount Merrion, co. Dublin, *d. unm.* 1860.
Mr. Murphy *d.* 2 Sept. 1849. His eldest son,
JOHN WILLIAM MURPHY, of Ballymaglasson, *m.* 15 April, 1828, Frances Catherine, only child of Christopher Johnson (son of Johnson of Warrenstown, co. Meath), a Gen. in the Austrian service and Governor of Gratz, by his wife, Frances, widow of Sir James Nugent, Bart. of Donore, dau. of John Nugent, of Ballincarrow, co. Westmeath, by Mary, dau. of Nicholas Coyne, of Coyneville, and sister of Lawrence Coyne Nugent, and by her (who *d.* 9 March, 1885) had issue,

1. WILLIAM, his heir.
2. John Christopher, of Mullen, co. Roscommon, and Osberstown, co. Kildare, J.P., High Sheriff co. Roscommon 1880, and co. Kildare 1890, b. 5 May, 1835; m. 11 Sept. 1867, Margaret Mary Frances, only child (by Margaret his wife, dau. of Stephen Grehan) of Francis John Connell, of Calla, co. Galway, and Bettyville, co. Wexford (son of John Agnew Connell, and Margaret his wife, sister of Sir Francis Goold, Bart., of Old Court, co. Cork, and widow of O'Neill Segrave, of Cabra), and d. 14 April, 1909, leaving issue,
  1. John Francis Joseph, b. 18 July, 1868.
  2. William Agnew, b. 23 July, 1869.
  1. Margaret Mary Clare.   2. Evaleen Mary Teresa.
1. Mary, d. young.
2. Frances Ellen, d. unm. 9 Dec. 1888.
3. Margaret, d. unm. 1847.
Mr. Murphy d. 22 March, 1852. His eldest son,
WILLIAM MURPHY, of Kilbrew, co. Meath, b. 4 Jan. 1834; m. 2 Aug. 1856, Anna Helen, dau. of Maurice Blake, of Ballinafad, co. Mayo, and had issue,
  1. WILLIAM, late of Kilbrew and Mount Merrion.
  1. Helen.
  2. Edith Victoria, m. 5 Dec. 1885, Major de Witt Jebb, late 60th Rifles, son of Charles Jebb, late 60th Rifles.
Mr. Murphy d. 1 May, 1885, and was s. by his only son.
WILLIAM BRUDENELL MURPHY, of Kilbrew, co. Meath, and Lullimore, co. Kildare, J.P. for that co., High Sheriff co. Roscommon 1818, b. 1857; m. 1878, his cousin, Mary Antoinette, dau. of Capt. Maurice Lynch Blake, of Ballinafad, co. Mayo, and d. 8 Feb. 1909, having issue,
  1. REGINALD FRANCIS BRUDENELL, now of Kilbrew.
  2. Vere Anthony Evelyn Brudenell, now of Lullimore, Rathangan, co. Kildare (*Mount Merrion, Blackrock, co. Dublin*).
  1. Fenella Mary Brudenell.

Arms—Per pale arg. and gu., on a fess engrailed, between four lions rampant, two garbs, all counterchanged. *Crest*—On a mount vert, a lion rampant gu. bezantée, holding in the forepaws a garb or. *Motto*—Fortis et hospitalis.
Seat—Kilbrew, co. Meath. *Residence*—Mount Merrion, Blackrock, co. Dublin.

MacMURROGH-MURPHY. *See* O'MORCHOE.

MUSGRAVE.
See BURKE'S PEERAGE, **MUSGRAVE**, Bart.

MURRAY-KER. *See* KER.

NAGLE OF CLOGHER.

GARRETT THOMAS NAGLE, of Clogher, co. Cork, J.P., Resident Magistrate for co. Antrim, Barrister-at-Law, B.A. Trin. Coll. Dublin (1876), b. 5 Feb. 1853; m. 14 Dec. 1882, Marcella, dau. of John Harold Barry, D.L., of Ballyvonare, co. Cork (*see that family*), and has issue,
1. Garrett John Harold, b. 24 Nov. 1891; d. 19 Aug. 1892.
2. GILBERT D'ANGULO, b. 5 June, 1893.
1. Mary Margaret, b. 24 March, 1889.
2. Adela Marie Carmel, b. 9 July, 1895.
3. Felicee Pauline, b. 19 April, 1898.

Lineage.—GARRETT NAGLE, of Clogher, m. Mary, dau. of Richard Purcell, and had three sons,
  1. EDMUND, his heir.   2. Edward.
  3. Robert.
The eldest son,
EDMUND NAGLE, of Ballinamona Castle, m. Catherine, dau. of — Fitzgerald, of Ballykennelly, and had issue,
  1. GARRETT, his heir.   2. Richard.
  3. Michael, m. Miss Butler.
  1. Catherine, m. John Howard, of Castle Park.
  2. Eliza, m. David Nagle, of Flemingstown, co. Tipperary.
The eldest son,
GARRETT NAGLE, of Ballinamona Castle, m. 1754, Elizabeth, dau. of Patrick Nagle* of Shanballyduff, and d. 1790, leaving issue,
  1. GARRETT, his heir.
  2. Edmund, m. 1793, Teresa, dau. of William Creagh, of Oldtown.
  3. Patrick, d. unm.
  1. Ellen, m. Garrett Nagle, of Dunmahon.

---

* His sister, Mary, m. Richard Burke, and was mother of the Right Hon. Edmund Burke.

2. Catherine, m. Garrett Cotter of Carker.
3. Jane, m. Richard Burke, of Springvale.
4. Eliza.   5. Mary.
The eldest son,
GARRETT NAGLE, of Ballinamona Castle, J.P., b. 24 June, 1756; m. 30 Jan. 1808, Maria, dau. of Richard Harold, of Pennywell, co. Limerick, and d. 10 Aug. 1853, having by her (who d. 20 Nov. 1834) had issue,
  1. GARRETT, his heir.
  2. Edmund, m. 11 Feb. 1843, Ellen, dau. of John Nagle, of Cregg, and had a dau.
  3. Patrick, m. Sarah, dau. of William Harmer Low, of Granagh, and had issue.
  1. Maria, m. 20 July, 1841, Garrett Graham, M.D., of High Mount.
  2. Eliza, m. 16 April, 1837, David Cagney, J.P., of Park Garriff.
  3. Jane.   4. Fanny.
  5. Anna Maria.   6. Lucy.
  7. Tamsen.
The eldest son,
GARRETT NAGLE, of Clogher House, co. Cork, J.P., b. 16 Nov. 1809; m. 9 July, 1840, Margaret, dau. of John Neligan. He d. June, 1866. She d. 19 April, 1899, leaving issue,
  1. GARRETT THOMAS, now of Clogher.
  1. Cherry, d. unm. May. 1867.   2. Maria Frances.
  3. Margaret Theresa.

Seat—Clogher House, near Doneraile, co. Cork. *Residence*—Avondale, Fitzwilliam Park, Belfast.

NAPER OF LOUGHCREW.

WILLIAM LENOX NAPER, of Loughcrew, co. Meath, High Sheriff 1911, late Capt. Royal Horse Guards, Capt. Reserve of Officers, D.L., b. 4 Jan. 1879; m. 9 July, 1902, Adela Mary Charlotte, eldest dau. of the late Col. the Hon. W. R. Trefusis, C.B., Scots Guards (*see* BURKE'S *Peerage*, CLINTON, B.), and the Lady Mary Trefusis (*see* BURKE'S *Peerage*, BUCCLEUCH, D.).

Lineage.—JAMES NAPER (4th son of Sir Nathaniel Naper, M.P., of More Critchell, Dorset, and grandson of Sir Robert Naper, Chief Baron of the Exchequer of Ireland 1593). High Sheriff of co. Meath 1671; m. Dorothy, dau. of Anthony Petty, of Romsey, Hants, and sister of the celebrated Sir William Petty, ancestor of the Marquess of Lansdowne. By this lady he left at his decease 4 Oct. 1676 (*Funeral Entry*), three sons and two daus.,
  1. William, of Loughcrew, b. 1661; d. unm. 20 May, 1708.
  2. JAMES, who s. his brother.
  3. Robert, Lieut.-Gen., will dated 18 March, 1737, proved 16 June, 1747; m. Anne, dau. of Richard Bickerstaff, of Dublin, and had two sons and two daus.,
      1. William, d.s.p.   2. Robert, d.s.p.
      1. Dorothy, d. unm.
      2. Elizabeth, m. 14 Dec. 1750, George Evans, of Portrane, co. Dublin.
  1. Elizabeth, m. Oct. 1682, Right Hon. Thomas Bligh, M.P., of Rathmore, co. Meath (*see* BURKE'S *Peerage*, DARNLEY, E.).
  2. Frances, m. July, 1688, Lieut.-Gen. Right Hon. Richard Ingoldsby.
The 2nd son,
JAMES NAPER, of Loughcrew, High Sheriff co. Meath 1703, d. 1718; m. 1st, March, 1684, Elizabeth, dau. of James Tandy, of Drewstown, co. Meath, and by her had two daus.,
  1. Dorothy, m. —. Ormsby.
  2. Sarah, m. Feb. 1708, Thomas Whyte, of Redhills, co. Cavan.
He m. 2ndly, July, 1695, Elizabeth Barry, s.p. He m. 3rdly, Anne, dau. of Sir Ralph Dutton, 1st Bart. of Sherborne, co. Gloucester, and had by her (who d. 1720) two sons and a dau.,
  1. JAMES LENOX, his heir.
  2. William, of Billsborough, co. Meath, d. unm. 1741.
  3. Anna Maria, m. Sept. 1734, Dillon Pollard, of Castle Pollard, co. Westmeath.
The elder son,
JAMES LENOX NAPER, of Loughcrew, b. 1712, High Sheriff co. Meath 1740 who assumed the surname and arms of DUTTON. He m. 1st, Sept. 1734, Catherine, dau. of Henry Ingoldsby, by whom he had an only child,
  1. John, who d. unm. 1771.
He m. 2ndly, Jane, dau. of Christopher Bond, of Newland, co. Gloucester, by whom he had issue,
  2. JAMES, of Sherborne, M.P. co. Gloucester 1780, who was elevated to the Peerage as Baron SHERBORNE 1784 (*see* BURKE'S *Peerage and Baronetage*).
  3. WILLIAM, who inherited the Naper estates.

4. Ralph, b. 1755; m. Honor, dau. of Joseph Gubbins, of Kilfrush, and d.s.p. 1804.
1. Anne, m. 1760, Samuel Blackwell, of Ampney Park, co. Gloucester.
2. Mary, m. 1759, Thomas Master, of Cirencester.
3. Frances, m. 1771, Charles Lambart, of Beau Park, co. Meath.
4. Jane, m. 1776, Thomas W. Coke, of Holkham, created Earl of LEICESTER.

Mr. Dutton d. 8 Sept. 1766, aged 63, and was s. in his Irish estates by his 2nd son, William, who resuming the name and arms of NAPER, became

WILLIAM NAPER of Loughcrew. He was b. 1749; m. 5 June, 1787, Jane, dau. of Rev. Ferdinando Tracy Travell, of Upper Slaughter, co. Gloucester, and dying 28 Nov. 1791, left one dau., Jane, m. 26 Sept. 1815, Sir George Cornewall, 3rd bart. of Moccas Court, co. Hereford, and one son,

JAMES LENOX WILLIAM NAPER, of Loughcrew, co. Meath, J.P. and D.L., High Sheriff 1822, b. 18 Feb. 1791; m. 3 May, 1824, Selina, 2nd dau. of Sir Grey Skipwith, 8th bart. of Newbold Hall, co. Warwick, and by her (who d. 12 Sept. 1880) had issue,
  1. JAMES LENOX, late of Loughcrew.
  2. William Dutton, Lieut.-Col. 1st Vol. Batt. Devonshire Regt., formerly Major 11th Foot., J.P. Devon, b. 13 Oct. 1830; m. 6 Dec. 1876, Jane, only dau. of Richard Wyatt Edgell, of Milton Place, Surrey, and Lympstone, Devon.
  1. Lelia Jane, m. 1870, Lieut.-Col. John Nicholas Coddington, of Oldbridge, and d. 1 Feb. 1879.
  2. Anna Selina.

Mr. Naper d. 2 Sept. 1868. His elder son,

JAMES LENOX NAPER, of Loughcrew, co. Meath, J.P. and D.L., High Sheriff 1853, Major Meath Militia, b. 5 Dec. 1825; m. 5 April, 1877, Hon. Katherine Frances Rowley, only dau. of Clotworthy, 3rd Baron Langford. She d. 13 Jan. 1879. He d. 4 Dec. 1901, leaving issue, a son,

WILLIAM LENOX, now of Loughcrew.

Arms—Arg., a saltire engrailed gu. between four roses of the second seeded or barbed vert. *Crest*—A dexter arm erect, couped at the elbow, vested gu., turned up arg. grasping a crescent ppr.

Seat—Loughcrew, near Oldcastle, R.S.O., co. Meath. *Club*—Guards.

NASH OF FINNSTOWN.

RICHARD GRAINGER NASH, of Finnstown and Howth, co. Dublin, J.P., b. 25 Jan. 1860; m. 17 Feb. 1909, his cousin, Caroline Margaret Noël, dau. of Evan Browell Jeune, J.P., of Whaddon Manor, Gloucester, and Manor House, Lynmouth, co. Devon (see SYMONS-JEUNE of Watlington Park), and has issue,

RICHARD GRAINGER JEUNE, b. 17 Jan. 1910.

Lineage—PATRICK NASH (or Naish), of Kanturk, co. Cork, m. about 1690, the dau. of Richard Purcell, of Cork. His son,

JOHN NASH, of Rockfield (or Ballyheen), co. Cork, m. 1725, Mary, dau. of Jonas Barry, of Cork, and co-heir (with her sister Eliza, who m. 16 Aug. 1733, Francis Yelverton, father of Barry, 1st Viscount Avonmore), and had issue,
  1. John, of Ballymagooly, co. Cork, witnessed a deed 26 June, 1772; m. 1st, 30 Jan. 1768, Elizabeth, dau. and co-heir of William Nugent, of Clonlost, co. Westmeath by Ursula his wife, dau. of Richard Aglionby, Registrar of Carlisle, and had issue,
    1. Mary Anne, m. by licence, 24 Sept. 1798, her cousin, James Nugent, of Dublin, and had issue.
    2. Catherine, m. by licence, 20 Sept. 1790, Robert Courtenay, of Ballyedmond, co. Cork, and d. 1799, having had issue (see SMITH-BARRY of Ballyedmond). 3. Ellen, d. unm.
  He m. 2ndly, by licence, 2 Sept. 1780, Mary, dau. of Samuel Carbery Egan, of Cork, and by her had a dau.,
    4. Amelia, m. Capt. Richard Griffin. From this marriage descends the Nash-Griffin family.
  He m. 3rdly, by licence, 2 Aug. 1794, Mary, dau. of Sir James Esmonde, 7th Bart., and widow of Matthew White, of Scarnagh, co. Wexford. By her he had no issue. His will, dated 21 Sept. 1799, was proved 3 July, 1802.
  2. THOMAS, of whom presently.
  3. Michael, of Corrigoon House, co. Cork, m. by licence, 11 Aug. 1789, Marcella, dau. of William Devereux, of Deer Park, co. Clare, and Margaret his wife, dau. of Robert Atkins, of Fountainville, co. Cork. His will, dated 10 July, 1801, was proved 1804. By her (who m. 2ndly by licence, 5 Sept. 1806, Col. John Watling, 39th Regt.), Mr. Nash left issue,

1. John Michael, d. unm. bur. 9 Oct. 1846. Will dated 21 Sept. 1845, proved 6 Feb. 1849.
2. Robert Atkins (Rev.), Rector of Hamerton, co. Huntingdon, bapt. 29 Oct. 1795; d. unm. 1843. Will dated 13 July, 1839, proved 8 Feb. 1844.
3. William, of Danville, co. Cork, b. 1797; m. 28 Feb. 1824, Ellen (who d. 1868), only dau. of Florence Mahony, of Sunday's Well, Killarney, co. Kerry, and was bur. 16 March, 1871, having had issue,
  (1) Michael, b. 6 Oct. 1826; d. 1835.
  (2) Florence, Lieut. 6th Regt., b. 1827; d. unm. 3 May, 1870.
  (3) John, b. 1828; d. Feb. 1840.
  (4) William (Rev.), B.A. Camb., Rural Dean and Rector of Old Somerby, Grantham, b. 14 Jan. 1831; m. 21 Aug. 1862, Louisa Arthur, dau. of John Gregory, Governor of the Bahamas, and by her (who d. 9 July, 1892) had issue. He d. 3 June, 1905, leaving,
    1. William Devereux Gregory, B.A. New Coll. Oxford, b. 23 July, 1863; m. 19 Dec. 1907, Ida Agnes Marsden, dau. of the late Rev. W. B. R. Jacobson, and d. 1 May, 1910, leaving issue,
      William Kenneth, b. 11 Jan. 1909.
    2. Robert John Villeneuve, b. 9 Dec. 1870; d. 6 Sept. 1871.
    3. Philip Arthur Manley, b. 20 Aug. 1875; m. 14 Sept. 1911, Louisa Constance, dau. of the late Gerard Philip Torrens.
    1. Kathleen Louisa, m. Rev. Harry Wilson Bonstead, D.D. (Magdalen Coll. Oxon), of the Rectory, Basingstoke, son of the late John Bonstead, J.P., Cumberland.
    2. Edith Henrietta, d. unm. 20 Oct. 1899.
    3. Mabel Harriet, m. 9 June, 1892, George Harry le Maistre, P. W Dept. India, eld. son of Rev. G. le Maistre, of Jersey, and has issue.
    4. Winifred Ellen, m. 19 June, 1902, John Douglas Wynne Griffith, eldest son of William Douglas Wynne Griffith, D.L., of Garn, co. Denbigh, and has issue (see that family).
  (5) Robert Atkins, b. 9 June, 1838; d. unm. lost at sea, 1860.
  (1) Ellen, m. 1858, Paul Lawless, of Boonbyjan, Queensland (who d. 1865), and has issue.
1. Caroline Margaret, d. unm. 1879.
1. Catherine, b. 1746; m. by licence, 29 April, 1774, William Shearman, of Cork. He was bur. Jan. 1814. She was bur. 25 Jan. 1824.

The 2nd son,

THOMAS NASH, of Rockfield, co. Cork, m. by licence, 21 Jan. 1777, Barbara, dau. of Denis O'Callaghan, of Glynn, co. Cork, by Mary his wife, dau. of Robert O'Callaghan, of Clonmeen, co. Cork, and widow of Henry Daunt, of Cork, and was bur. 14 Feb. 1827, having had issue,
  1. John, of Rockfield, m. by licence, 14 Sept. 1809, Elizabeth, dau. of Christopher Crofts, of Velvetstown, co. Cork. His will, dated 10 May, 1832, was proved 15 Dec. 1832. She was bur. 10 Jan. 1872. He was bur. 20 Aug. 1832, having had issue.
    1. Thomas John, bapt. 12 Jan. 1812; d. young.
    2. John, bapt. 27 May, 1815; d. young.
    3. Christopher Crofts, b. 1824; d. unm., bur. 12 July, 1873.
    1. Maria, bapt. 6 Dec. 1812; d. young.
    2. Barbara, bapt. 25 May, 1816; d. young.
    3. Mary, bapt. 21 July, 1821; bur. Sept. 1831.
    4. Eliza, m. Richard Sherlock, of Ballyrobbinmore, co. Cork, and had issue. She d. 20 July, 1873.
  2. Thomas, d. unm., bur. 15 Feb. 1832.
  3. Patrick, m. 7 Oct. 1819, Catherine, dau. of — Cummins. She was bur. 6 April 1823. He d.s.p., bur. 7 Nov. 1839.
  4. Denis O'Callaghan, b. 1797; d. unm., bur. 26 Dec. 1873.
  5. Michael, m. 15 Oct. 1826, his cousin Charity, dau. of — Shearman. He was bur. 7 May, 1858, having had issue.
    1. Thomas, R.N., bapt. 11 Dec. 1827; d. unm.
    2. William R.N., bapt. 23 Sept. 1830; d. unm.
    3. John, bapt. 19 Aug. 1832; d. young.
    1. Catherine, bapt. 1 Jan. 1829, d. young.
  6. JAMES, of whom presently.
  1. Mary, m. 5 Feb. 1807, her cousin Robert Crofts, of Velvetstown, co. Cork (see that family), who d. 21 May, 1818, leaving issue. She was bur. 17 May, 1864.
  2. Barbara, m. 8 Jan. 1814, William Sharpe, of Glenmount, co. Cork. He was bur. 29 July, 1841. She d.s.p., bur. 14 April, 1833.
  3. Eleanor, m. by licence, 9 Nov. 1808, her cousin Denis O'Callaghan, of Cork, and had issue.
  4. Catherine, d. unm., bur. 3 Nov. 1865.
  5. Amelia, m. 6 June, 1829, George Kirkland Tivy, of Rossacon, co. Cork. He was bur. 16 April, 1861. She was bur. 11 April, 1879, having had issue.
  6. Eliza, m. 1833, her brother-in-law, William Sharpe, of Glenmount (see above). She was bur. 4 Nov. 1850, having had issue.

The youngest son,

JAMES NASH, of Rockfield and Tullig, co. Cork, m. 29 July, 1826, Anne, dau. of Christopher Cudmore, of Cork, and was bur. 23 Aug. 1849, having by her (who d. 21 May, 1878) had issue, a son,

THOMAS JAMES NASH, of Rockfield, and Tullig, co. Cork, and Howth and Finnstown, co. Dublin, b. 8 June, 1827; m. 8 July, 1856, Juliet Isabella, dau. of Richard Grainger, of Elswick Hall, Newcastle-on-Tyne, by Rachel, his wife, dau. of Joseph Arundel. He d. 8 Aug. 1887 (will dated 21 Oct. 1882, proved 26 Nov. 1887), having had issue,
  1. Thomas, b. 24 Oct. 1858; d. unm., bur. 15 April, 1880.

2. RICHARD GRAINGER, now of Finnstown.
3. James, b. 26 June, 1863.
4. Charles Arundel, b. 26 Nov. 1864.
5. George Denis (Rev.), M.A., B.D. Trin. Coll. Dublin, Vicar of St. Jude's, Dublin, b. 11 May, 1866; m. 21 Sept. 1904, Lily, widow of J. D. Bradshaw, M.A., M.B. (Oxon), of London.
6. William Henry, b. 25 May, 1868.
7. Edward, b. 24 Sept. 1869.
1. Rachel Grainger, d. unm. 17 June, 1878.
2. Anne Theodosia, m. George Napier Ferguson, J.P., M.A., Barrister-at-Law, and has issue. He d. 4 May, 1902.

Arms—Arg., a chevron vert between three doves, each holding in the bill an olive branch all ppr. Crest—A boar passant paly of six arg. and gu. Motto—Vi et virtute.

Seats—Finnstown, Lucan, and Howth, both co. Dublin.

NEALE OF NEWINGTON.

SAMUEL NEALE, of Christianstown, co. Kildare, b. 5 Dec. 1867.

Lineage—SAMUEL NEALE, of Newington House, Christianstown, co. Kildare, d. 1845, having had, with other issue, a son,
JOSEPH MANLEY NEALE, of Newington House, Christianstown, b. 10 Sept. 1837; m. Nov. 1865, Annjin Georgina, dau. of George Nelson Wheeler, of Annesborough House, Robertstown, co. Kildare (see DE COURCY-WHEELER of Robertstown), by whom he had issue,
1. SAMUEL (see above).
1. Willianiza Florence Christiana De Courcy.
2. Laura Elizabeth, m. 25 July, 1910, Rev. Mervyn Benjamin Archdall Byrn, Rector of Kilmeague, co. Kildare, 4th son of the late Rev. Richard Archdall Byrn, of Braganza, Carlow, by Marie Wetzlar, his wife, dau. of Rev. Richard Meade Swifte, B.A., Incumbent of Mountfield, Omagh (see SWIFT of Swifts-heath).
3. Evelina Annjin, b. 1885; d. 1900.
He d. 1911, and was s. by his only son.

Seat—Newington House, Christianstown, Newbridge, co. Kildare.

NELIGAN (late PUTLAND) OF BRAY HEAD.

JOHN GEORGE NELIGAN, of Bray Head, co. Wicklow, Lieut. (retired) R.N., b. 1881; m. 1906, Vera Legge, dau. of late Alfred Legge Newcombe, and has issue,

VERA PATRICIA.

Lineage.—THOMAS PUTLAND, of Dublin, m. 1684, Meriel, dau. of Thomas Sisson, and d. 1722, leaving issue. The eldest son,
THOMAS PUTLAND, of Dublin, b. 3 May, 1686; m. 1708, Jane, dau. of John Rotton, of Dublin, and d. in the lifetime of his father, 31 March, 1721, having had issue. The eldest son,
JOHN PUTLAND, of Dublin, b. 1709; m. 22 July, 1738, Catherine, dau. and eventually co-heir of Sir Emanuel Moore, Bart., of Ross Carberry, co. Cork, M.P., and by her (who d. July, 1764) had issue,
1. GEORGE, of whom presently.
2. John. 3. Thomas.
4. William.
1. Jane Emily, m. William Graydon, of Killeshe.
2. Katherine. 3. Emilia.
4. Elizabeth.
5. Meriel, m. 12 Sept. 1778, Benjamin Newbury.
6. Martha, m. John Roberts, of Shankill, co. Dublin.
7. Anne.
Mr. Putland d. Dec. 1773, and was s. by his eldest son,
GEORGE PUTLAND, b. Oct. 1745, who m. Jan. 1779, Catherine, dau. of the Hon. John Evans, of Bulgaden Hall, co. Limerick, brother of George, and Lord Carberry, and had issue,
1. GEORGE, his heir.
1. Kitty, m. John Hall. 2. Emily, m. William Graydon.
Mr. Putland d. June, 1811, and was s. by his elder son,
GEORGE PUTLAND, of Bray Head, who m. 1816, Anna Dorothea, dau. of Hampden Evans, of Portrane, co. Dublin, and dying s.p. Nov. 1841 (this widow survived until 1857), was s. by his brother,
CHARLES PUTLAND, of Bray Head, co. Wicklow, J.P., b. Jan. 1785; m. March, 1812, Constance, eldest dau. of the Hon. George Massy, and d. 25 Dec. 1859, having had issue,
1. CHARLES, late of Bray Head.
2. George, b. May, 1826; d. unm.
1. Emily Dorothea, m. 21 June, 1851, James Butler, and had issue (see BUTLER-KEARNEY of Drom).
2. Georgina, m. Dec. 1851, Walter Gahan; d. 4 April, 1910.
3. Caroline, m. 30 Oct. 1866, William Bernard Shaw.
4. Eliza, m. 1862, Major Charles Fitzgerald Studdert, of Newmarket, co. Clare.
The elder son,
CHARLES PUTLAND, of Bray Head, co. Wicklow, J.P., b. Oct. 1813; m. 1 June, 1835, Charlotte, dau. of Admiral Christian, R.N., and by her (who d. 1845) had issue,
1. GEORGE, of Bray Head, b. 8 March, 1841; d.s.p. 1876.
1. Charlotte Mab, m. 1879, Rev. John West Neligan, M.A.,

eldest son of Rev. Maurice Neligan. D.D., of Dublin. He d. 1902. She d. 10 Oct. 1880, leaving issue,
1. CHARLES WALTER, late of Bray Head.
2. JOHN GEORGE, now of Bray Head.
3. Maurice Wilder. 4. George Ernest.
5. Eric Claude 6. Lancelot Victor.
He m. 2ndly, 19 April, 1849, Georgina, dau. of the late Sir James C. Anderson, Bart., of Buttevant Castle, co. Cork, and d. 1874, having by her (who d. 15 March, 1883) had two daus.,
2. Constance, m. 10 July, 1879, Rev. George Beresford Power, Incumbent of Kilfane, Thomastown, co. Kilkenny, 3rd son of the Ven. Ambrose Power, Archdeacon of Lismore, grandson of Sir John Power, Bart., of Kilfane, co. Kilkenny, and has issue,
1. Georgina Mary, m. 7 Nov. 1911, Capt. Randolph George Gethin (see GETHIN, Bart., BURKE'S Peerage and Baronetage).
2. Kathleen Madi, d. 15 July, 1903.
3. Georgina Dorothea, m. 30 Jan. 1879, Devaynes Smyth (d. 13 Feb. 1912), of Bray Head, Bray, only surviving son of William Monsell Smyth, of Oakwood House, King's Co., and Elizabeth Lucy his wife, dau. of Charles Humphrey Minchin, of Rutland, King's Co., and grandson of Devaynes Smyth, of Oakwood, King's Co., and has issue,
1. Charles Devaynes, Capt. 2nd Batt. Royal Irish Rifles, b. 5 Dec. 1882; m. 8 Nov. 1911, Dorothy Margaret, dau. of George Hotblack, of Shiels Court, Brundall, Norfolk.
2. Algernon Beresford, Lieut. 2nd Batt. K.O. Yorks L.I., b. 11 Jan. 1884.
Mr. Putland d. 1874, and was s. by his g and s in,
CHARLES WALTER NELIGAN, F.R.G.S., of Bray Head, District Commissioner East African Protectorate, b. 10 Nov. 1879; d. 13 Aug. 1910, being s. by his brother.

Seat—Bray Head, co. Wicklow. Residence—242, Lauderdale Mansions, Maida Vale, N.W. Club—Junior Naval and Military.

NEEDHAM. See BURKE'S PEERAGE, KILMOREY, E.

BEAUMONT-NESBITT OF TUBBERDALY.

EDWARD JOHN DOWNING BEAUMONT-NESBITT, of Tubberdaly, King's Co., J.P. and D.L., High Sheriff 1892, b. 20 Nov. 1860; m. 30 April, 1890, Helen, dau. of Frederick Freeman Thomas, of Ratton, Sussex, by his wife, Mabel, 3rd dau. of Viscount Hampden, and has issue,
1. FREDERICK GEORGE, b. 26 March, 1893.
2. Wilfrid Henry, b. 2 Sept. 1894.
1. Violet Catherine, b. 4 Feb. 1891.
2. Eileen Mabel, b. 12 June, 1898.

Lineage.—JOHN DOWNING, of Bellaghy and Rowesgift, co. Derry, b. 1700; m. Aune, dau. of Rev. J. Rowe, D.D., and had issue,
1. ALEXANDER CLOTWORTHY, his heir.
2. Dawson, ancestor of the family of FULLERTON of Ballintoy (which see).
1. Sarah, m. to Charles Dawson, H.M. Inspector of Customs for Ireland, 3rd son of Joshua Dawson, of Castle Dawson, M.P. for Wicklow, and Sec. for Ireland, temp. Queen ANNE. They had issue,
John Dawson, Rear-Admiral R.N., who m. his first cousin, Medicis, eldest dau. of Alexander Clotworthy Downing, of Bellaghy, and had, among other issue,
Thomazine, m. in 1826, to Rev. John Bradshaw, Incumbent of Lambeg, co. Antrim; she d. in 1883, leaving an only surviving child,
Thomazine, m. to Rev. Thomas George Beaumont, M.A., whose eldest son, EDWARD BEAUMONT-NESBITT, is the present possessor of the estates.
The eldest son,
REV. ALEXANDER CLOTWORTHY DOWNING, of Bellaghy and Rowesgift, Rector of Lockpatrick, co. Derry, m. Tamison, dau. of James Nesbitt, of Tubberdaly, King's Co., and had with other issue, a dau., Medicis, who m. her first cousin, Rear-Admiral John Dawson, ancestress of EDWARD BEAUMONT-NESBITT, now of Tubberdaly, and a son,
JOHN DOWNING NESBITT, of Tubberdaly, assumed the additional surname of NESBITT on inheriting the Nesbitt estates in the King's Co. and cos. Roscommon and Galway, m. in 1802, Jane, dau. of Gen. Brady, R.A., of Leixlip House, co. Kildare, and had with other issue,
1. Alexander, who d. unm.
2. WILLIAM GEORGE, his heir.
1. CATHERINE TAMISON, who s. her brother.
2. Jane, m. to Francis, Count de Lusi, and d.s.p. 1875.
3. Mary Anne, d. unm. 1873.
Mr. Downing Nesbitt d. in 1847, and was s. by his son,
WILLIAM GEORGE DOWNING NESBITT, of Tubberdaly, who d. unm. 1857, and was s. by his eldest sister,
CATHERINE TAMISON, who d. unm. in 1886, and was s. by her cousin,
EDWARD BEAUMONT, who adopted the additional surnames of DOWNING and NESBITT.

FAMILY OF BEAUMONT.

GEORGE BEAUMONT, m. 1815, Alice, dau. of James Akroyd, of Brook House, near Halifax, and d. 1858, leaving by her (who d. in 1882) a son,

REV. THOMAS GEORGE BEAUMONT, M.A., J.P., late Rector of Chelmondiston, Suffolk, who m. Tamazine, dau. of Rev. John Bradshaw, Incumbent of Lambeg, co. Antrim. He d. 15 April, 1908, having had issue,
1. EDWARD JOHN, now of Tubberdaly.
2. George (*Uplands, Farnham, Surrey*), m. 1893, Cecilia, dau. of the late R. Chalmers.
3. Henry Hamond Dawson, 1st Secretary in Diplomatic Service, b. 4 Feb. 1867; m. 12 Aug. 1908, Henrietta Louisa Baldwin, dau. of late Col. Edward Baldwin Wake, 21st Light Dragoons (*see* BURKE's *Peerage*, WAKE, Bart.).
1. Alice Mary, m. Rev. B. W. Allen, of Kempsey Vicarage, Worcester.
2. Mabel, m. Rev. Bernard Parker, of Rattery Vicarage, South Brent.

Seat—Tubberdaly, Edenderry. *Clubs*—Travellers', S.W., and Kildare Street, Dublin.

NETTLES OF NETTLEVILLE.

ROBERT NETTLES, of Nettleville, co. Cork, b. Feb. 1876; s. his father 1885.

Lineage.—JOHN NETTLES, of Toureen, co. Waterford, of an ancient English family, went to Ireland 1630, from co. Hereford, and had a grant of lands, by patent from CHARLES II., in cos. Cork and Waterford to the amount of 1,253 acres, which was enrolled 8 Nov. 1666. He was High Sheriff, co. Waterford, 1670. He m. Mary, dau. of Valentine Greatrakes, of Affane, co. Waterford, and had issue,
1. JOHN, his heir.
2. Robert, of Ballyduff, co. Waterford, and of Mahallagh, and Nettleville, co. Cork.
  1. Ruth, m. Barry Drew, of Ballyduff, co. Waterford.
  2. Mary, m. Rev. Patricius Christian, of Old Grange, co. Waterford.
3. Penelope, m. Henry Wallis, of Drishane, co. Cork.
4. Elizabeth, m. Col. Richard Croker, of Curryglass, co. Waterford.

Mr. Nettles (whose will dated 20 April, 1680, was proved 1684) was s. by his eldest son,

JOHN NETTLES, of Toureen, co. Waterford, Major in the Army, High Sheriff 1690-1; he m. Ellen, dau. of Capt. Thomas Evans, and sister of Sir William Evans, Bart., and left at his decease 1715, one son and one dau.,

JOHN, his heir.
Mary, m. Lieut. Edward Jones, of Youghal, co. Cork.

Mr. Nettles d. 1715, and was s. by his only son,
JOHN NETTLES, of Toureen, co. Waterford, Mahallagh and Beare Forest, cc. Cork; he m. Martha, dau. of Robert Ryves, of Rathlogan, co. Kilkenny, and of Ryves Castle, co. Limerick, and d. 12 May, 1726, leaving issue,
1. JOHN RYVES, his heir.
2. Robert (Rev.), Rector of Ballinamona, near Mallow, co. Cork, m. 1st, Jane, eldest dau. of John Bowerman, of Coolyne, co. Cork, and by her (who d. 1762) he had issue, two daus., co-heirs,
  1. Jane, m. her cousin, William Nettles.
  2. Elizabeth, m. 1783, Kilner Baker.

Rev. Robert Nettles, m. 2ndly, Jane, 2nd dau. of Francis Drew, of Drew's Court, co. Limerick, and had no issue by her.

Mr. Nettles was s. by his eldest son,
JOHN RYVES NETTLES, of Toureen and Beare Forest, m. 1738, Catherine, 2nd dau. of John Bowerman, of Coolyne, and d. Nov. 1785, having had issue. The 3rd son was a distinguished officer, Lieut.-Col. Harry Nettles, of the 23rd Dragoons, who d.s.p. 1811. Mr. Nettles s. to Nettleville at the decease of his cousin. His eldest son,

ROBERT NETTLES, of Nettleville, Capt. 10th Foot, J.P. co. Cork, m. 1769, Esther, dau. of John Conran, of Dublin, and had (with three daus.), RICHARD NEVILL, his heir, and four other sons, all of whom were killed accidentally, or in battle, one of them, William, Ensign 52nd L.I., at Waterloo, whilst carrying the KING'S Colour.

Mr. Nettles d. 1831, and was s. by his eldest son,
RICHARD NEVILL NETTLES, of Nettleville, J.P., m. 17 April, 1804, Anne, dau. of Daniel Gibbs, of Derry, co. Cork, and grand-dau. of Sir Robert Warren, 1st bart. of Warren's Court and had issue,
1. ROBERT, of Nettleville.
1. Mary, d. Dec. 1876. 2. Anne.
3. Esther, m. 1836, Rev. Hume Babington, Rector of Moviddy, co. Cork, and d. April, 1878.
4. Frances, m. Nov. 1829, John Hawkes, of Kilcrae, co. Cork, and d. 1874.

Mr. Nettles d. 21 April, 1851. His only son,
ROBERT NETTLES, of Nettleville, J.P., b. 31 March, 1805; m. 20 Aug. 1835, Elizabeth Walton, dau. of Thomas Knolles, of Oatlands, and had issue,

RICHARD, late of Nettleville.
Mr. Nettles d. 1885. His only son,
RICHARD NETTLES, of Nettleville, co. Cork, J.P., b. 1836; m. May, 1872, Esther Elizabeth, dau. of Rev. Hume Babington, Rector of Moviddy, co. Cork, and d. 1885, leaving issue,
1. ROBERT, now of Nettleville.
1. Esther, b. Oct. 1882; m. 1909, Percy H. Taylor, of Knockanemore Ovens.

Seat—Nettleville, Killinardrish, co. Cork.

NEVILLE OF AHANURE AND ROCKFIELD

The late MAJOR ROBERT NEVILLE, of Ahanure, co. Kilkenny, and Rockfield, co. Dublin, Major in the Army, joined the 51st Regt. in 1843, served in the Crimea and at Scutari on the Staff of Sir Henry Storks, b. 1824; m. 1857, Emma Helsham, now of Ahanure and Rockfield, only surviving child of William Helsham-Candler-Brown, of St. Mary's Hall, Tinley, co. Norfolk, and Ahanure, co. Kilkenny. He d. 28 Nov. 1907, having had issue,

1. WILLIAM CANDLER, D.S.O., Col. 1st Batt. Cheshire Regt., b. 22 Jan. 1859; m. 5 Jan. 1892, Amy, youngest dau. of Colin Ross, of Gruinards, Rothshire, and has issue,
  Robert Arthur Ross, b. 17 Dec. 1896.
  Maud Christian.
2. Brent Richard Robert (Rev.), M.A., T.C.D., Rector of St. Lawrence, Ventnor, I. of Wight 1902-7, b. 24 Sept. 1861; m. 3 Jan. 1891, Margaret, youngest dau. of Joseph Shaw, of Woodleigh, Cheltenham, and Temple House, Celbridge, co. Dublin, and has issue,
  1. Kathleen Charlotte. 2. Margaret Evelyn.
  3. Violet Muriel.
1. Emma Catherine Alice.
2. Maud Charlotte Elizabeth Anne, m. 22 Sept. 1896, Atbelstan Robert Pryce, late Capt. 13th Hussars, of Cyfronydd, Montgomery and Abertlefenny, co. Merioneth.

Lineage.—RICHARD NEVILL, settled in co. Kildare in 1649, where he purchased estates and became of Phornauts (or Furnace). He m. Margaret, dau. of Sir William Usher, and d. 13 Sept. 1682, Fun. Entry, will dated 13 Sept. 1682, leaving issue, all named in the will,
1. RICHARD, his heir, of Furnace, d. 10 April, 1750; m. (licence 25 Sept. 1683), Katherine, dau. of Richard Barry, and sister of James Barry, uncle of the 1st Lord Santry, and by her had with four sons, Richard, Francis, James, and Paul, who d. unm., an only dau. and heir,
  Mary, m. Col. Edward Jones, who assumed the surname of NEVILLE, and by him was grandmother of Richard Neville of Furnace, M.P., whose eldest dau. and co-heir, Henrietta, m. 1st, Edward Dering, eldest son of Sir Edward Dering, 7th Bart. of Surrenden Dering, and had issue (*see* BURKE's *Peerage*); and 2ndly, 15 Jan. 1840, Sir William Geary, 2nd bart. of Oxon Hoath, and by him had issue (*see* BURKE's *Peerage*).
2. Robert, m. Mary, and d.s.p. will dated 7 Aug. 1686.
3. GARRETT, of whom we treat.
4. John, of Newrath, co. Wicklow, whose will, dated 15 May, 1730, was proved 18 April, 1735. He m. Elizabeth Riggs, of Riggsdale, and left issue,
  1. Richard.
  1. Alice.
  2. Anne, m. 1st, John Perry, of Woodrooffe; and 2ndly, 23 Dec. 1723, Rev. Thomas Somerville, and had issue (*see that family*).
  3. Catherine, m. 20 Nov. 1728, Harding Parker, of Passage West, who d. 1750, leaving issue (*see that family*).
  4. Judith, m. — Parker, of the Abbey.
1. Alice, m. (licence) 27 July, 1678, Capt. Thomas Twigg.
2. Bridget, m. — Ryves.
3. Mary.

The 3rd son,
GARRETT NEVILL, m. a sister of Richard Skellern, of an ancient Welsh Family, and had two sons and a dau.,
1. THOMAS. 2. Parnell.
1. Anna, m. 1721, Gorges Hely, of Foulkscourt, co. Kilkenny. His will, dated 11 Aug. 1736, was proved 20 Jan. 1737. He d. 1737. His eldest son,

THOMAS NEVILL, of Nevill's Grove, co. Dublin, m. Sarah, dau. of Brent Smyth, of Dublin, and by her, who m. 2ndly, Rev. Smith Loftus, left at his decease, 1745, two sons,
1. GARRETT, his heir.
2. Brent, of Ashbrook, co. Dublin, m. Frances, dau. of James Dance, and has issue,
  1. Brent, m. Catherine, dau. of John Mapas, of Killiney Castle, co. Dublin, and d. 1836, leaving by her, who d. 1880,
    (1) WILLIAM ALEXANDER (Rev.), M.A., of Moyfin, co. Meath, Canon of St. Canice, Kilkenny, and Incumbent of Inistiogue and the Rower, b. July, 1814; d. 21 Dec. 1907; m. Dec. 1844, Katherine Sarah, dau. of Rev. Josiah Crampton, M.A., Rector of Castleconnel, and Dora his wife, dau. of J. Waller, of Castletown, co. Limerick, and had issue,

Newenham

1. William Brent, Col. (ret.) 4th Batt. Royal Irish Fusiliers, d. 30 Sept. 1911; m. and left issue.
2. Richard.
3. Josiah Philip Crampton, Major 14th Bengal Lancers.
    1. Katherine Dorothea Elizabeth.
    2. Pamela Charlotte Jane Meriel.
    (2) ROBERT, late of Ahanure.
    (3) Thomas Josias (1546, *Williams Street, Denver, Colorado, U.S.A.*), b. 9 Dec. 1834; m. 1855, Amelia Elizabeth, dau. of Col. Leander Ransome, of San Francisco, California, U.S.A., and d. 1885, leaving issue an only dau.
        1. Constance Maude, m. 1884, Stephen Rickard, of Denver, Colorado, U.S.A., and has issue.
            1. Brent Neville, b. 1885.
            2. Stephen Darcy, b. 1886.
            3. Hubert Greville, b. 1889.
            (1) Jane Frances.   (2) Kate.
    (3) Georgina.
    2. Richard (Rev.), Rector of Clonpriest, Cork, m. Anne. dau. of Col. William Gore, of The Heath, co. Kildare, and had issue. His 3rd dau. Meriel Anne, m. 1852, Sir George Frederick John Hodson, 2nd bart. of Hollybrook, co. Wicklow.
    3. Garrett (Sir), Sheriff of Dublin: 1819-20, knighted 22 March, 1820; m. Eltrida, dau. of Joshua Nunn, of St. Margaret's, co. Wexford.
        1. Jane, m. 1799, Sir Robert Hodson, 1st bart. of Hollybrook, co. Wicklow.   2. Meriel, m. James Kearney, of Dublin.
        3. Frances, m. Rev. Edward Semple, Rector of Kesh, co. Fermanagh.
    1. Elizabeth, d. unm. (will proved 14 June, 1759).

The elder son,
GARRETT NEVILL, of Marymount, co. Kilkenny, m. 1 Jan. 1765, Mary, eldest dau. of William Hodson, and sister of Sir Robert Hodson, 1st bart. of Hollybrook, and d. 1823, aged 83, leaving issue,
1. THOMAS, of Annamult, co. Kilkenny, m. Rebecca, dau. and heir of Ambrose Power, and d.s.p. 1835.
2. ROBERT, heir to his brother.   3. Parnell, d. unm.
    1. Sarah, m. — Sheares.
    2. Mary, m. Rev. George Miles, of Summerhill, co. Tipperary.
    3. Elizabeth, m. Edmond Theobald Mandeville Butler.
    4. Catherine, m. Rev. M. N. Thompson.
    5. Mary, d. unm.

The 2nd son,
ROBERT NEVILLE, of Marymount, J.P., High Sheriff co. Kilkenny 1842, m. 30 Sept. 1811, Catherine, dau. of John Langley, of Lickfin, co. Tipperary, and had issue,
1. THOMAS, his heir.
2. Garrett, m. 1847, Triphena Clark Smyth, d.s.p.
3. Robert, m. 1854, Mary, dau. of Rev. Piers Edward Butler, and d. 1873, leaving issue.
    1. Robert, of Sydney, N.S.W.
    2. Thomas Percy, d. in S. Africa.
    3. Francis Richard, m. 19 Sept. 1901, Adelaide, dau. of Patton and has issue,
        Claude, b. 13 June, 1905.
        Dorothy Mary.
    1. Catherine Mary.   2. Frances Sarah.
    3. Alice Louisa, m. William Anderson Patchell, and has issue, William Neville, and Alice Mary Frances Violet.
    1. Eliza, m. 1840, Theobald Butler of E. T. M. Ville.
    2. Sarah, m. 1844, John Langley, of Lickfin.
    3. Anna Maria. m. 1854. Arthur St. George.

Mr. Neville d. 14 Sept. 1842, and was s. by his eldest son,
THOMAS NEVILLE, of Borrismore House, J.P. and D.L., b. 20 March, 1818; m. 15 Oct. 1846, Isabella Ann, dau. of Thomas Edward Villiers Tuthill, of Rathgar Mansion, co. Dublin (see TUTHILL, *formerly of Kilmore*), and d. 1884, leaving an only dau., ANNE, m. 1876, Joseph William Thacker, J.P., son of Ven. the Archdeacon of Ossory.

Arms—Barry of four arg. and az. on a saltire of the first. **Crest**—Out of a ducal coronet or, a bull's head pied, attired of the first, charged with a rose. **Motto**—Ne vile velis.
Seats—Ahanure, co. Kilkenny; Rockfield, Ballybrack, co. Dublin.

NEVILLE-BAGOT. See BAGOT.

NEWENHAM OF COOLMORE.

WILLIAM THOMAS WORTH NEWENHAM, of Coolmore. co. Cork, J.P., Capt. and Hon. Major late 3rd Batt. Royal Munster Fusiliers, b. 10 Jan. 1853; m. 17 Jan. 1888, Lilian Maud, only dau. of Hatton Ronayne O'Kearny, of Lochiar, Cork, and has issue,
1. PERCY WORTH, b. 9 June, 1890.
2. Henry Edward Worth, b. 3 March, d. 25 Dec. 1893.
3. William Eyre Worth, b. 31 March, 1894.

1. Violet Maud, b. 28 Feb. 1889; m. 22 Nov. 1911, Walton Jennings, Major R.G.A., youngest son of the late Robert Jennings, of Cork.
2. May Lillian, b. 19 July, 1891.

Lineage.—EDMUND NEWENHAM, the first who settled in Ireland m. Jane, dau. of John Desmyniers, the 2nd Lord Mayor of Dublin. His eldest son, Robert, d. without male issue. The 2nd son,
JOHN NEWENHAM, settled in co. Cork; he served as Sheriff of the city of Cork 1665, and Mayor 1671. He obtained a grant of lands in co. Limerick and liberties of the City of Cork, under the Commission of Grace, 1685, and made large purchases of estates during his lifetime. He m. 1672, Jane, dau. of John Hoder. His will bears date 29 Jan. 1695, and was proved 21 Aug. 1706. He had, with four daus., a son,
THOMAS NEWENHAM, of Coolmore, m. May, 1695, Elizabeth, dau. of Thomas Blackall, of Dublin, and had issue, three sons:
1. WILLIAM, his heir; 2. Francis, m. Isabella, dau. of John Hodder, of Cork; 3. Robert, m. Sept. 1759, Elizabeth, dau. of Rev. George Synge; and six daus. The eldest son,
WILLIAM NEWENHAM, of Coolmore, m. 1726, Dorothy, dau. and heiress of Edward Worth, of Rathfarnham Castle, co. Dublin, Baron of the Exchequer in Ireland, and had issue,
1. THOMAS, of whom presently.
2. William Worth, b. 20 Aug. 1731, d. young.
3. Edward (Sir), b. 5 Nov. 1734; m. 4 Feb. 1754. Grace Anne, dau. of Sir Charles Burton, Bart. He was M.P. for Dublin in the Irish Parliament, and was knighted 10 Nov. 1764. He d. 1814, having had eighteen children, of whom,
    1. Robert O'Callaghan, was editor of *Sketches in Ireland*.
    2. Burton, m. 1800, Maria, sister of Sir William Burdett.

Mr. Newenham d. 1738, and was s. by his eldest son,
THOMAS NEWENHAM, of Coolmore, b. 13 May, 1729; m. 1st 11 Aug. 1750, the Hon. Susanna Wandesford, dau. of Christopher Viscount Castlecomer and by her (who d. 1754) had no issue. He m. 2ndly, 11 March, 1760 (Sept. 1759), Elizabeth, eldest dau. of William Dawson, son of Joshua Dawson, of Castle Dawson, and by her (who d. 24 Dec. 1763) had issue,
1. WILLIAM WORTH, of whom hereafter.
2. Thomas, Major of Militia, b. 2 March, 1762; m. 1783, Mary Anne, dau. of Edward Hoare, of Factory Hill, co. Cork, and dying 10 Oct. 1831, left issue,
    1. THOMAS (Rev.), Rector of Kilworth, of whom hereafter, as successor to his cousin-german, WILLIAM HENRY WORTH NEWENHAM.
    2. Robert, of Sandford, co. Dublin, b. 20 Aug. 1786; m. 18 June, 1810, Jane, dau. of Edward Hoare, of Factory Hill, co. Cork, and dying 19 July, 1836, left issue by her (who d. April, 1830) four sons and three daus.,
        (1) Thomas, b. 13 Feb. 1813; d. unm. 19 April, 1852.
        (2) EDWARD HENRY, late of Coolmore.
        (3) Robert, b. 6 March, 1826; d. unm. 29 March, 1847.
        (4) William Henry, of Maryborough Park, co. Cork, late Capt. 63rd Regt., with which he served in the Crimean War (medal and four clasps), b. 21 March, 1830; m. 1st, 17 Aug. 1865, Emily Maria, only dau. of Robert J. Berkeley, Q.C., and by her (who d. 24 Oct. 1873) had a son,
            Harry Edward Berkeley, b. 22 Dec. 1866.
        He m. 2ndly, 3 Sept. 1880, Hon. Louisa Jane Edwardes (40. *Belgrave Road, S.W.*), dau. of William, 3rd Baron Kensington, and d. 21 July, 1893.
            (1) Mary Anne, b. 23 July, 1814; d. 7 Dec. 1888.
            (2) Frances, b. 29 April, 1816; d. unm. 1856.
            (3) Jane, b. 9 March, 1820, m. 1847, Gen. Clement Edwards, C.B., of Ballyhire, and d. 20 Nov. 1855, leaving two daus.
                1. Louisa, m. 21 Jan. 1818, Capt. Charles Dilkes, R.N., C.B. and d. 22 April, 1845, leaving a son,
                    Charles O'Bryan.
    1. Sarah Maria, m. 23 Aug. 1782, Sir Richard Butler, 7th bart. of Ballintemple.

Mr. Newenham d. 1766, and was s. by his son,
WILLIAM WORTH NEWENHAM, of Coolmore, b. 5 Feb. 1761; m. Louisa, 4th dau. of Henry Sandford, and sister of George, 1st Lord Mount Sandford, and had issue,
1. WILLIAM HENRY WORTH, of whom presently.
2. Thomas, b. 4 Oct. 1788; d. 1799.
3. George, b. 1792; d.s.p. 7 Dec. 1815.
1. Mary, b. 12 Aug. 1786; d. Oct. following.

Mr. Newenham d. 1 Dec. 1814, and was s. by his eldest son,
WILLIAM HENRY WORTH NEWENHAM, of Coolmore, b. 10 June, 1785; m. 25 July, 1807, Catherine, only dau. of Robert Stearne Tighe, of Mitchelstown, and by her (who d. Feb. 1858) had no issue. He d. 4 Sept. 1842, and was s. at Coolmore by his cousin-german,
REV. THOMAS NEWENHAM, Rector of Kilworth, b. 14 Oct. 1784, who d. unm. 5 April, 1849, and was s. by his nephew,
REV. EDWARD HENRY NEWENHAM, M.A., of Coolmore, co. Cork, J.P., b. 16 Aug. 1817; m. 15 Nov. 1849, the Lady Helena Adelaide Moore, 2nd dau. of Stephen, 3rd Earl Mountcashel, and has issue,
1. WILLIAM THOMAS WORTH, now of Coolmore.
2. Edward Arthur Worth, b. 19 Jan. 1857; d. unm. 4 May, 1900.
1. Anne Maria Jane, d. 28 April, 1861.
2. Helena Adelaide Isabella, d. 6 July, 1873.
3. Edith Sophia, b. 7 April, 1863.

The Rev. Edward Henry Newenham d. 25 Oct. 1892.

Seat—Coolmore, Carrigaline, co. Cork. **Club**—Union.

NEWMAN OF NEWBERRY MANOR.

JOHN ROBERT BRAMSTON PRETYMAN-NEWMAN, of Newberry Manor and Kilshannig House, co. Cork, J.P. and D.L., High Sheriff 1898, B.A. Trin. Coll. Camb., M.P. Enfield Division, Middlesex, 1910, late Capt. 5th Royal Munster Fusiliers, he has adopted the additional surname of PRETYMAN, b. 22 Aug. 1871; m. 1st, 24 Aug. 1895, Olivia Anne, 2nd dau. of the Most Rev. Lord Plunket, D.D. (see BURKE'S Peerage and Baronetage). She d.s.p. 24 Jan. 1896. He m. 2ndly, 8 Sept. 1898, Geraldine, only child of the late Col. William Pretyman, 60th Rifles (see PRETYMAN of Orwell Park).

Lineage.—ROBERT NEWMAN, who lived and died at Fifehead, Magdalen, and was bur. in the chancel of the church, had, by Alice his wife (whose will is dated 1556), four sons,
1. ROBERT, ancestor of the NEWMANS of Fifehead.
2. RICHARD, of whom presently.
3. Henry.   4. Thomas.

The 2nd son,
RICHARD NEWMAN, lived at Charlton Musgrave, Somerset, and was father of
RICHARD NEWMAN, of Queen's Camel, Somerset. He m. Agatha, dau. of Humphrey Pole, and had issue,
HUMPHREY NEWMAN, of Wincanton, who m. Dorothy, dau. of Sir Thomas Phelips, Knt., of Barrington, and had issue,
1. Thomas.   2. RICHARD, of whom presently.
3. Humphrey.   4. James.
1. Elizabeth.   2. Dorothy.
3. Joan.   4. Agatha.

The 3rd son,
RICHARD NEWMAN, was resident in the city of Cork 1651, and in 1663, was J.P. for the co. He purchased from Sir Richard Kyrle the estate of Drumineene, and settled there. "In 1686, he passed patent for the castle property of Drumineene and several other lands in co. Cork, and four messuages in the city of Cork; said lands to be erected into a manor called the manor of Newbury." He m. previous to 1651, Sarah, dau. of Richard French, of Cork (ancestor to FRENCH of Cuskinny), and had issue. Richard Newman's will bears date 12 Nov. 1691, and was proved 27 Jan. 1693-4. His eldest son,
RICHARD NEWMAN of Newbury, m. Elizabeth, dau. of J. Dillon, and had issue,
1. DILLON, of whom presently.
2. Adam, of London, who settled in Ireland, and purchased the Dromore estate. He m. Miss Knapp, and dying s.p., bequeathed it to his nephew, Adam, 2nd son of Dillon Newman.
3. Charles, d. unm.
1. Margaret, m. 1711, John Dillon, of Quartertown, co. Cork, and d.s.p.
2. Judith, m. Rev. John Smith, and had issue.

The eldest son,
DILLON NEWMAN, of Newbury, J.P. co. Cork, m. Martha, dau. of Col. Thomas Becher, of Sherkin, co. Cork, by Elizabeth Turner his wife, and had issue,
1. Richard, High Sheriff of the co. 1737, m. Catherine, dau. of Col. William Cassaubon, and had issue, three daus.,
 1. Isabella Sarah, m. Right Hon. Silver Oliver, of Castle Oliver, M.P. for Killmallock, and left issue.
 2. Elizabeth, d. unm.
 3. Martha, d. unm.
2. ADAM, of whom hereafter.
1. Elizabeth, m. 1st, Meade Dunscombe, of Mount Desart, and 2ndly, Alderman R. Travers, and left issue by both marriages.
2. Susannah, m. 5 Oct. 1727, Peter Graham, of Dromore and Conveymore, co. Cork.
3. Dorothea, m. 1st Swithin White, of Rochefortstown, and 2ndly, Benjamin Bousfield, of Ashadown.

Mr. Dillon Newman made his will 11 May, 1733, which was proved 19 Dec. 1733. His 2nd son,
ADAM NEWMAN, J.P., s. his uncle, Adam, in the Dromore estates, and, on his brother Richard's death without issue male, he also s. to the Newbury estates. He m. Mary, dau. of John Carleton, of Darling Hill, co. Tipperary, and had issue. The 3rd son,
ADAM NEWMAN, m. 21 April, 1768, Mary, dau. of Rev. Horace Townsend, Rector of Donoughmore, by Mary, his wife, dau. of Richard Hungerford, of the Island, and had issue,
1. ADAM, of Dromore.
2. Richard, m. Jane Harriet, dau. of James Langton, of Bruree House, co. Limerick. On his brother Adam succeeding to the Dromore estates, he came into possession of the Clahane property which was purchased by Dillon Newman 1708. He d. 1830, leaving issue,
 1. Adam, of Monkstown Castle, co. Cork, J.P., b. 1808; m. 1834, Mary, dau. of Adam Perry Perry, and has issue, Richard, b. 1836.
 2. Richard Meade, dec.
 3. Horace Townsend (Rev.), d. unm.
 4. Henry Richard, dec.
 5. Amos Langton, an Officer in H.E.I.C.S., dec.
 1. Anna Langton.   2. Jane Maria.
3. Horace Townsend (Very Rev.), Dean of Cork, m. Charlotte, dau. of Denis Daly, of Dunsandle, and Lady Harriet Maxwell his wife. He d.s.p. 1864, and his wife d. March, 1866.
1. Mary, d. unm.   2. Susan, d. unm.
3. Elizabeth, m. William Webb, and d.s.p.
4. Jane, d. unm.
5. Dorothea, m. Rev. Richard Meade, of Ballymartle, and d. leaving issue.
6. Harriet, m. William Beamish, of Mount Prospect, 2nd son of Samuel Beamish, of Mount Beamish, and d. leaving issue,

The eldest son,
ADAM NEWMAN, of Dromore, s. at the death of his uncle, John Newman, to the Dromore and Newbury estates. He m. 1803, Frances Dorothea, dau. of Rev. Robert Dring, of Rockgrove, and had issue,
1. JOHN, b. 1812; m. Margaret, dau. of Nicholas Philpot Leader, of Dromagh Castle, and d.s.p. 13 Aug. 1844, having by her (who d. 12 Dec. 1884) had issue,
 1. JOHN ADAM RICHARD, late of Dromore.
 1. Margaret, d. unm.
 2. Frances Dorothea (Fanny), m. 22 Feb. 1870, Capt. Henry E. Bridges, late 4th Royal Irish Dragoon Guards.
 3. Geraldine Elizabeth, m. April, 1865, Col. William Pretyman, late 60th Rifles She d. 14 Jan. 1909. He d. 5 Oct. 1894, leaving issue (see PRETYMAN of Orwell Park).
2. Robert.
1. Eleanor, d. unm.
2. Mary, m. 1st, Richard Townsend, M.D., and 2ndly, Rev. Adam Beamish, and d. leaving issue by both marriages.
3. Eliza, m. 1827, William Hume Franks, of Carrig Park, and d. leaving issue.
4. Frances, m. Samuel Philip Townshend, of Garrycloyne, co. Cork, and d. leaving issue.

Mr. Newman d. 6 Aug. 1859, and was s. by his grandson,
JOHN ADAM RICHARD NEWMAN, of Dromore House, co. Cork, J.P. and D.L., High Sheriff 1874. B.A. Magd. Coll. Camb. 1866, b. 5 Aug. 1844; m. 17 Aug. 1870, Elizabeth Matilda (Maud), younger dau. of the late Lieut.-Col. Robert Bramston Smith, D.L., of Pencraig, Anglesey, and 31, Upper FitzWilliam Street, Dublin, by Elizabet Charlotte, his wife, dau. of Sir Richard John Griffith, 1st bart. of Munster Grillagh, and had issue,
1. JOHN ROBERT BRAMSTON, now of Newberry Manor (Dromore).
2. Richard Griffith Oliver, M.V.O. 4th class (1909), Capt. North Irish Horse (special reserve), late Capt. 7th Dragoon Guards, b. 19 Jan. 1876; m. 3 June, 1903, Beatrice Margery, dau. of late Harry Clegg, D.L., of Plas Llanfair House, Anglesey.
1. Grace Frances, m. 20 Aug. 1895, Henry Charles Villiers Stuart, D.L., of Dromana, co. Waterford (see that family). He d. 8 Sept. 1908. She m. 2ndly, 25 July, 1910, Sir Alexander Kay Muir, 2nd bart., of Deartson, Perthshire (see BURKE'S Peerage).

Mr. J. A. R. Newman d. 14 Oct. 1893.

Arms—Arg., a chevron between three demi-lions passant, gu. a chief az. **Crest**—An eagle's head erased az. charged with an escallop or. **Motto**—Magna vis fidelitatis.

Seat—Newberry Manor, near Mallow, co. Cork. **Town Residence**—79, Eaton Square, S.W. **Clubs**—Carlton and Wellington.

NEWTON (now VESEY) OF DUNLECKNEY MANOR.

ANNE HENRIETTA, MRS. W. M. VESEY, of Dunleckney Manor, co. Carlow, eldest surviving dau. and co-heir of the late Philip Jocelyn Newton, D.L., of Dunleckney; s. her father 1895; m. 16 Oct. 1871, William Muschamp Vesey, of Upton House, co. Carlow, J.P. (who d. 25 Sept. 1880), youngest son of the Hon. and Rev. Arthur Vesey, 2nd son of 1st Viscount de Vesci (see BURKE'S Peerage), and has issue,

1. PHILIP SYDNEY, Hon. Lieut. in the Army, late Capt. 8th Batt. King's Royal Rifle Corps, b. 9 March, 1873; m. 1902, Blanche, dau. of Edmund Nicholas Power, of Tramore House, co. Waterford.
2. Charles, b. 7 Feb. 1874; d. 1 Nov. 1911.

Lineage.—This family, of Lancashire origin, settled in Ireland 1688.
BRYAN NEWTON, of Busherstown, co. Carlow, Registrar of the Diocese of Leighlin, son of Capt. Edmund Newton, of Lancashire. His will, dated 31 Oct. 1709, was proved 13 Dec. that year. He left, by Anne his wife, two sons and a dau.,
 1. Edmund (Rev.).
 2. BARTHOLOMEW, of whom we treat.
 1. Mary.
The younger son,
BARTHOLOMEW NEWTON, of Busherstown, co. Carlow, m. Frances, dau. of Peter Budds, of Ganagh, Queen's Co. She d. 1754. He d. 1749, having had one son and two daus.,
 1. JOHN, his heir.
 1. Elizabeth, m. by licence, 10 Nov. 1735, Chamberlain Walker.
 2. Anne, m. by licence 15 June, 1741, Samuel Budds.
The only son,
JOHN NEWTON, of Busherstown, m. 1730, Elizabeth. dau. of Francis Lodge, co. Kilkenny, and city of Dublin, and founded the family residence at Bennekerry, a short distance from the town of Carlow, which, though still in the family's possession, is not now the family seat. John d. 1748, leaving an eldest son,
BARTHOLOMEW NEWTON, of Bennekerry, m. 1767, Anne, dau. of Philip Bernard, by whom he acquired considerable property in the county of Carlow. He d. 1780, leaving (with a dau. Catherine) two sons,
 1. John, of Bennekerry, Col. of the Carlow Militia, High Sheriff 1797, d. unm.
 2. PHILIP, of whom we treat.
The 2nd son,
PHILIP NEWTON, of Dunleckney, High Sheriff co. Carlow, 1796, m. Oct. 1785, Sarah Bagenal, heiress of Dunleckney. She d. 17 Jan. 1832. He d. Oct. 1833, leaving issue,
 1. WALTER, of whom presently.
 2. Philip, of Bennekerry, who assumed the name and arms of BAGENAL (see BAGENAL of Benekerry).
 3. Beauchamp Bartholomew, of Rathwade, co. Carlow, High Sheriff 1850, m. Isabella, dau. of Lieut.-Col. Arthur Forbes, 32nd Regt. He d.s.p. She m. 2ndly, James Kearney Aylward, D.L., of Shankill Castle, co. Kilkenny, who d.s.p. 1 Feb. 1884 (see that family).
 4. John, of Bagenalstown, co. Carlow, High Sheriff 1856, m. Janet Forbes, and d.s.p.
 5. Henry, of Mount Leinster (see NEWTON of Mount Leinster).
 1. Elizabeth, d. unm.   2. Sarah Anne, d. unm.
The eldest son,
WALTER NEWTON, of Dunleckney, m. 22 March, 1817, Anne, 5th dau. of the Hon. George Jocelyn, 2nd son of Robert, 1st Earl of Roden. She d. 1857, leaving issue, a son and a dau.,
 PHILIP JOCELYN, his heir.
 Thomasine Jocelyn, m. 22 Nov. 1853, Marchése Don Odnardo Frederic Raffael Gadalera di Martano, and d. 1880.
Mr. Newton d. 28 Aug. 1853. The only son,
PHILIP JOCELYN NEWTON, of Dunleckney Manor, co. Carlow, J.P. and D.L., High Sheriff 1846, b. 23 March, 1818; m. 1st, 18 Nov. 1841, Henrietta Maria, dau. of John Kennedy, of Dunbrody, co. Wexford, and Cultra, co. Down, and by her had issue,
 1. Maria Charlotte Augusta, d. 2 May, 1888.
 2. ANNE HENRIETTA (Mrs. Vesey), now of Dunleckney Manor.
 3. Adeline Sarah, m. 17 April, 1876, Arthur N. Forbes Gordon, 79th Highlanders, of Rayne, co. Aberdeen; and d. 21 Feb. 1879, leaving issue (see that family).
He m. 2ndly, 1 July, 1851, Emily, youngest dau. of Sir Daniel Toler Osborne, Bart., by Lady Harriet his wife, sister of William, 1st Earl of Clancarty, and d. 20 April, 1895, having by her (who d. 31 Dec. 1886) had issue,
 4. Harriette Philippa, m. 9 Jan. 1873, Richard Bagwell, D.L., eldest son of John Bagwell, M.P. of Marlfield, co. Tipperary, and has issue (see that family).
 5. Emily Georgina, m. 6 Dec. 1882, Fitzgibbon Trant, eldest son of John Trant, D.L., of Dovea, co. Tipperary, and has issue (see that family).

Arms—Az., two ostrich feathers in saltire between three boars' heads erased arg., tusked or, in the centre chief point a cross-crosslet of the last. Crest—Out of a ducal coronet or, a boar's head between two ostrich feathers arg., the neck charged with a cross-crosslet az. Motto—Pro patria.

Seat—Dunleckney Manor, Bagenalstown.

NEWTON OF KILLYMEAL.

ROBERT NEWTON, of Killymeal House, co. Tyrone, J.P., b. 19 Nov. 1876; m. 11 Feb. 1902, Edith Florence, dau. of Charles Roark, and has issue,
 1. ROBERT CHARLES, b. 9 Oct. 1905.
 2. John Lowry Courtenay, b. 7 Oct. 1909.
 1. Edith Margaret, b. 6 April, 1903.
 2. Norah Alicia, b. 8 Aug. 1904.
 3. Elizabeth Mary, b. 3 April 1907.

Lineage.— RYCHARDE NEWTON, Town Clerk of Carrickfergus, 1595, who had allotments of parts of corporate property 1595, a portion of which is still in possession of the family. His son,
RICHARD NEWTON, Sheriff of Carrickfergus 1598, 1600, and 1601, m. a dau. of John, and sister of Andrew Willoughby, and was father of
MARMADUKE NEWTON, Sheriff of Carrickfergus 1624 and 1632, whose son,
RICHARD NEWTON, of Galgorm co. Antrim, m. Margaret, sister of John and Willoughby Chaplin, and d. 1700, having had four sons, the eldest, Marmaduke, High Sheriff of Carrickfergus 1687, and Mayor 1692-3, d.v.p.s.p. The 2nd son,
ANDREW NEWTON of Galgorm, Sheriff of Carrickfergus 1718, m. his cousin, Margaret, dau. of John Chaplin, by Mary, his wife, dau. of Alderman Andrew Willoughby, and had issue, a son,
HENRY NEWTON, of Galgorm, m. Sarah, sister of Rev. Joseph Fraser, of Carrickfergus, and (besides a son, Willoughby Chaplin, who d.s.p.) was father of
ANDREW NEWTON, first of Galgorm, co. Antrim, and afterwards of Coagh, co. Tyrone, J.P. for cos. Tyrone and Londonderry, b. 1749; m. Margaret, dau. of Robert Hamilton, of Mintlone, co. Armagh, and by her (who d. 12 Feb. 1820) had issue,
 1. Henry, b. 10 June, 1779; m. Eliza Crookshank, otherwise Ledlie, and had, besides three daus., Margaret, Beatrice Walkinshaw and Jane, a son, Andrew, M.D., who m. Mary Johanna, dau. of Maj.-Gen. James Murray, C.B. and left a son, Capt. James Patrick Murray, Bombay Native Infantry, d. unm.
 2. ROBERT, of whom we treat.
 3. Andrew, of Coagh, b. there 26 Jan. 1785, went to reside at Dungannon. He m. 22 Jan. 1811, Jane, dau. of Joseph Courtenay, of The Grange, co. Antrim, and d. 11 June, 1872, aged 87, leaving by her (who d. 20 March, 1863) issue,
  1. Courtenay, of Killymeal House, co. Tyrone, J.P., b. 19 Feb. 1814; m. 1st, 10 Jan. 1837, Frances, dau. of Rev. Thomas Stanley Monck, Rector of Clonegam, co. Waterford (who d. 15 March, 1839), and 2ndly, 12 Feb. 1856, Anne, dau. of Richard Howard, of Mitcham, Surrey. She d. Nov. 1875. He d. 4 May, 1877, having by her had issue,
   (1) Andrew Willoughby, of Killymeal House, J.P., M.A., Barrister-at-Law, b. 14 Jan. 1849; m. 15 Aug. 1872, Blanche, eldest dau. of John Howard of Sampford Peverell, co. Devon. and d. 11 Aug. 1895, leaving issue,
    1. Courtenay Howard, b. 15 May, 1874; m. 29 June, 1901, Berthe Eugenie Lintilhac.
    2. Willoughby John, d. an infant.
    3. Andrew Winstanley, b. 12 Sept. 1879.
    1. Annie Adelaide, b. 6 Sept. 1877; m. 7 Aug. 1901, Rev Francis Algernon Drake.
   (2) Courtenay, d. an infant.
   (1) Mary Howard, m. 16 April, 1869, Henry Russell Kelly of Dungannon. (2) Anna, d. 30 April, 1862.
  2. Andrew James, b. 2 March, 1816, emigrated to New Zealand, and d. in Sydney, July, 1855, having m. Mary Jane Searight, by whom he had issue, Andrew, Searight, and Sarah Darley.
  3. Robert William, of Bellevue House, co. Londonderry, J.P. for the cos. of Tyrone and Derry, b. 8 May, 1818; m. 11 Feb. 1847, Catherine Johanna Voss, dau. of Capt. John Moore Tittle, J.P., late of Farm Hill, Coleraine. She d. 12 May, 1878. He d. 1895, having had issue,
   (1) Andrew Courtenay, b. 7 Jan. 1850.
   (2) Robert William, b. 17 Aug. 1855.
   (3) John Moore, b. 7 May, 1860.
   (4) Thomas, b. 4 June, 1865; d. 24 May, 1866.
   (5) Willoughby Marmaduke, b. 15 Jan. 1868.
   (1) Johanna Catherine Voss, m. 4 July, 1867, William Gregory Lawrence, J.P., Bannfield, Coleraine, and d. 7 July, 1869, leaving issue, one son, Samuel Lawrence.
   (2) Jane Adelaide.   (3) Susan.
   (4) Mary Elizabeth Frances, d. young, 10 Jan. 1859.
   (5) Margaret,
   (6) Annie, d. 12 July, 1874, } twins.
  1. Mary Anne.   2. Margaret.
  3. Jane.
 4. Willoughby Chaplin, b. 13 May, 1789; m. 23 July, 1844, Mary Anne, eldest dau. of Capt. Henry Oulton, of the 57th Regt., and d. 1868, leaving a son,

Willoughby Chaplin, of Newton Park, Wicklow, b. 8 Dec. 1845; m. 12 March, 1876, Emily Alice, dau. of John Lopdell, of Raheen Park, co. Galway (see that family), and d. 17 Aug. 1880, leaving issue,
(1) Willoughby Chaplin, Capt. Middlesex Regt., b. 6 July, 1870; m. 15 Jan. 1903, Elizabeth, dau. of Surg. Lieut.-Col. A. Maxwell Adams, R.A.M.C., and has issue,
Willoughby Chaplin, b. 31 July, 1904.
(2) John Frederick, b. 4 June, 1876; m. 20 Jan. 1909, Phyllis, youngest dau. of Albert Staten, of Utah, U.S.A., and has issue,
John Rowland, b. 6 Dec. 1910.
(1) Maud Mary, d. 10 March, 1909.
(2) Frances Jane Louisa, m. 8 Nov. 1900, Francis William Digby McClean, Lieut. Army Service Corps.
(3) Emily Caroline, m. 27 July, 1909, Arthur Edwin Orpin.
(4) Blanche Howard.
1. Beatrice, m. Richard Oulton, and d. 1838.
2. Frances, m. Robert Smith, and d. 17 Dec. 1876.
3. Catherine, m. Charles Sheils, of London, afterwards of Liverpool, and d. 29 Nov. 1800.
4. Eliza, m. James Scott, of Bloomhill, co. Tyrone.
Mr. Newton d. 11 April, 1826. The second son,
ROBERT NEWTON, b. 24 Dec. 1782; m. Alicia, dau. of Rev. J. Paul, Rector of Ballinderry, co. Tyrone, and d. 14 Feb. 1831, leaving issue,
1. ROBERT, his heir.
1. Jane, d. unm. 21 June, 1702.
2. Margaret, m. 10 Dec. 1869, Lieut.-Col. Armar Graham Lowry, of Fairlough Lodge, Dungannon (see LOWRY of Pomeroy). He d.s.p. 21 Oct. 1900.
The only son,
ROBERT NEWTON, of Cough, co. Tyrone, J.P., went to reside at Dungannon, and purchased Killymeal House from his cousin, Andrew Willoughby Newton (see above), b. 25 Oct. 1831; m. 27 April, 1864, Elizabeth, dau. of W. P. Geoghegan, M.D. She d. 13 Nov. 1909. He d. 8 May, 1900, leaving issue,
1. ROBERT, now of Killymeal.
2. John Orr (Fairlough Lodge, Dungannon), b. 5 Oct. 1880.
1. Alicia, b. 1 June, 1865; d. 15 May, 1908.
2. Annie Louisa, b. 22 May, 1866; m. 19 April, 1899, John Porter Colquhoun Crossle.
3. Francis Elizabeth, b. 22 March, 1869.
4. Norah Mary, b. 6 Nov. 1871; m. 18 Dec. 1896, John Galwey Dysart.

Arms—Arg., in chief two lions gambs erased sa., each grasping a key ppr., and in base a lion rampant gu., charged on the breast with a cross pattée of the field. *Crest*—A martlet sa., charged on the breast with a cross pattée arg. *Motto*—Faveat Fortuna.

Seat—Killymeal House, co. Tyrone.

NEWTON OF BALLYBEG.

JAMES HIBBERT NEWTON, of Ballybeg, co. Wicklow, b. 1 Sept. 1879.

Lineage.—THOMAS NEWTON, b. in England, 10 Jan. 1661, settled at Boston, Massachusetts, in 1688, and became Attorney-General for Massachusetts Bay 1720-1. His son,
HIBBERT NEWTON, was ruined in the war of American Independence, and his family settled in Nova Scotia. One of his sons,
PHILLIPS NEWTON, 48th Regt., went to Ireland with his regiment. His son,
HIBBERT NEWTON, 62nd Regt., settled at New Ross, co. Wexford, m. Margaret, dau. of Francis Glascott, of Pilltown, co. Wexford. He d. 26 Oct. 1795, having had issue four sons. The youngest son,
HIBBERT NEWTON, of Ballinglen, co. Wicklow, J.P., Lieut. 32nd Regt., bapt. 5 Dec. 1790; m. 1817, Dorothea, dau. of James Gildea, of Coslough, co. Mayo. She d. 1 June, 1867. He d. 1861, having had issue,
1. Hibbert, Barrister-at-Law, b. 7 Aug. 1821; m. Susan Liddiard, and had issue,
 1. Hibbert Henry.
 2. George Perceval.
 1. Catherine.
2. James Gildea, b. 17 May, 1823; d.s.p. 29 Feb. 1856.
3. Phillips, of Loughnavoy, co. Galway, and Ballinglen, co. Wicklow, J.P. co. Carlow, b. 9 Nov. 1824; m. 14 Oct. 1865, Martha Westby, eldest dau. of Maj. James Perceval, of Barntown (see that family), and d. 6 June, 1892, having had issue,
 1. Hibbert Perceval, b. 5 March, 1877.
 1. Dorothy Mary Perceval, d. unm. 13 Oct. 1903.
 2. Jane Phoebe Westby.
4. GEORGE GLASCOTT, of Ballybeg.
5. John Vigors Harvey, b. 20 April, 1830; m. Susan Liddiard, and d. 1887, leaving issue,
 1. Henry Gildea. 2. Frederick James.
 3. Thomas George. 4. Francis Harvey.
6. Francis William, b. 10 June, 1832; d.s.p. in Australia, 1903.
1. Anne Frances, d. unm. 31 Dec. 1886.
2. Dorothea Mary Sophia, m. 13 Nov. 1883, Louis Montford, of Killinure, co. Wicklow.
3. Eliza Margaret, d. unm. 13 Dec. 1910.
4. Barbara Araminta Martha, m. 1860, George Aickin, C.E., of New Zealand.
5. Margaret Wright, m. 1861, William Jubb, and d. 1865.
The 4th son,

MAJOR GEORGE GLASCOTT NEWTON, of Ballybeg, co. Wicklow, J.P., late Major 12th Regt., b. 8 May, 1828; m. 14 Oct. 1871, Anne Westby, dau. of Major James Perceval, of Barntown, co. Wexford (see that family), and d. 19 June, 1910, leaving issue,
1. JAMES HIBBERT, now of Ballybeg.
2. George Perceval, b. 29 April, 1884.
3. Francis Phillips, b. 6 Sept. 1888.
1. Anne Catharina. 2. Dorothea Eliza.
3. Barbara Mary. 4. Martha Westby.
5. Araminta.
6. Jane Frances, m. 20 July, 1894, Rev. W. J. M'Combe, Vicar of North Willingham, Lincs.

Seats—Ballybeg, Rathdrum, co. Wicklow; Ballinagilky, co. Carlow; and Bolacoir, co. Wexford.

NEWTON (now BUTLER) OF MOUNT LEINSTER.

ETHEL ELIZABETH JANE, MRS. BUTLER, now of Mount Leinster, co. Carlow, m. 1895, Charles Richard Butler, and has issue,
1. James Humphrey, b. 30 June, 1897.
2. EDWARD CHARLES WALTER, b. 30 May, 1900.
3. Beauchamp Henry, b. 7 Jan. 1902.
1. Blanche Adelaide.

Lineage.—HENRY NEWTON, of Mount Leinster, co. Carlow, youngest son of Henry Newton and Sarah Bagenal, his wife, of Dunleckney, co. Carlow (see NEWTON of Dunleckney), m. 30 April, 1835, Elizabeth Jane, dau. of Rev. Charles William Doyne, Rector of Fethard (see DOYNE of Wells), and d. 1863, having had issue,
1. PHILIP CHARLES, of whom presently.
1. Charlotte Elizabeth Sarah, m. 1st, Capt. T. J. Mitchell, King's Dragoon Guards, and 2ndly, 22 Nov. 1877, H. T. Rees-Mogg, and has issue (see that family).
2. Caroline Susan Henrietta, m. 27 Oct. 1863, Robert Westley Hall-Dare, of Newtownbarry, who d. 18 March, 1876, leaving issue (see that family).
3. Adelaide Georgina, d. unm. 1896.
The only son,
PHILIP CHARLES NEWTON, of Mount Newton, co. Carlow, J.P., High Sheriff 1869, b. 10 Sept. 1837; m. 1st, 1 Aug. 1864, Mary Garrett, dau. of John William Bathe. She d. 1875, leaving issue,
1. HENRY PHILIP, of Mount Leinster.
1. ETHEL ELIZABETH JANE, now of Mount Leinster, co. Carlow.
2. Ada Mary.
3. Isabella Caroline.
He m. 2ndly, 24 Oct. 1891, Ellen, dau. of George Hougham Skelton, of Langton House, Cheltenham. He d. 23 Feb. 1902. The only son,
HENRY PHILIP NEWTON, of Mount Leinster, co. Carlow, J.P., High Sheriff 1904, b. 27 March, 1868, and d. 7 April, 1905, and was s. by his sister.

Seat—Mount Leinster, Borris, co. Carlow.

NICHOLSON OF BALRATH BURRY.

JOHN HAMPDEN NICHOLSON, of Balrath Burry, co. Meath, J.P., High Sheriff 1895, b. 29 June, 1871; m. 1 Aug. 1894, Florence Isabel, 3rd dau. of Thomas Rothwell, of Rockfield, Kells, and has issue,
1. CHRISTOPHER HAMPDEN, b. 15 Sept. 1903.
2. John Armytage, b. 18 June, 1905.
1. Joyce Frances, b. 19 Aug. 1902.

Lineage.—This family came originally out of co. York. GILBERT NICHOLSON, of Bare and Poulton, of Lyndall, in Lonsdale, and of Barton and Easterton, in Westmorland, m. Grace, dau. and co-heir of Gyles Curwen, of Poulton Hall (descended from CURWEN of Workington), and had issue,
1. FRANCIS, d.v.p., leaving a son,
HUMPHRY, who s. his grandfather.
2. Giles.
1. Grace, m. Thomas Brathwaite, of Boamont, near Lancaster.
Gilbert Nicholson d. 1605, and was s. by his grandson,
HUMPHRY NICHOLSON, who was father of

GILBERT NICHOLSON, sometime of Poulton, co. Lancaster, and of the city of Dublin, b. 1620, a Lieut. in the Royal army before 1649, and one of the forty-nine officers, whose arrears of pay were paid up after the Restoration, " for service done by them to His Majesty, or to his Royal father, as commissioned officers in the wars of Ireland, before the 5th day of June, 1649." By the Act of Settlement he received grants of land in co. Monaghan, which he sold, and bought Balrath Burry, in 1669. He afterwards resided in Dublin, and d. 20 April, 1709, in the 89th year of his age. He and his wife Mary, dau. of Sir Thomas Worsop, Knt., are bur. in Christ Church Cathedral, and on their tombstone appear the arms and crest still used by the family. The issue of the marriage were,
1. Christopher, of the Middle Temple, entered 16 June, 1630. He d. in London 1688, without issue by Jane his wife.
2. THOMAS, of whom presently.
3. John, m. and had issue, two sons and two daus.

The 2nd, but eldest surviving son,
THOMAS NICHOLSON, of Balrath Burry, M.A. Ch. Ch. Oxford 1685, b. 1662, inherited Balrath Burry in 1709, and was executor of his father's will. In 1692, he was a Commissioner for co. Meath, under 4 WILLIAM and MARY, cap. 33, and High Sheriff of the co. 1704. He m. 1st, 3 Feb. 1691, Mary, dau. of John Beauchamp, and had, with other issue, who d. young, a dau. whose issue. Margaret, was 2nd wife of Sir Richard Steele, Bart. of Hampstead. He m. 2ndly, 11 July, 1700, Elizabeth, dau. and co-heir of John Wood, of Garelony, and had issue,
1. CHRISTOPHER, of whom presently.
2. John, d.s.p.   3. Thomas, d.s.p.
4. Gilbert, d.s.p.

He m. 3rdly, Rose, widow of Simeon Pepper, of Ballygarth, but by her had no issue. The eldest son,
CHRISTOPHER NICHOLSON, of Balrath Burry, High Sheriff co. Meath, 1735, d. 24 Aug. 1775 ; m. 1st, 25 Oct. 1723, Elinor, only dau. of Simeon Pepper, of Ballygarth, by Rose his wife, dau. of Hon. Oliver Lambart, of Painstown, and granddau. of Charles, 1st Earl of Cavan, and had issue,
1. JOHN, of whom presently.
2. Thomas, m. and had one son,
   John, m. Eliza, dau. of — Harris, of The Moor, near Exeter, and had three daus.
3. George, Major in the Buffs.
4. Christopher.
5. Hampden, m. 19 Jan. 1764, Sarah, dau. of Rev. Arthur Ormsby, and d.s.p.
   1. Rose.   2. Christian.
3. Emilia, m. March, 1753, John Andrews, of Rath, King's Co.

He m. 2ndly, 27 Dec. 1751, Mary, dau. of Oliver Lambart, of Painstown, but by her (who d. 23 March, 1771) had no issue. His eldest son,
JOHN NICHOLSON, of Balrath Burry, Capt. in the Coldstream Guards, b. 27 July, 1724 ; m. 18 Sept. 1766, Anna Maria, dau. of Sir Samuel Armytage, 1st bart., of Kirkleys, co. York (see BURKE's Peerage), relict of Thomas Carter (see CARTER of Shaen Manor) and had issue,
1. CHRISTOPHER ARMYTAGE, his heir.
2. Gilbert, b. 21 March, 1771 ; d. unm.

He d. 29 March, 1782, and was s. by his elder son,
CHRISTOPHER ARMYTAGE NICHOLSON, of Balrath Burry, M.A., D.L., J.P., High Sheriff co. Meath, 1791, b. 10 July, 1768 ; m. 1st, 16 May, 1796, Catharine, dau. of William Newcome, D.D., Archbishop of Armagh and Primate of all Ireland, by Anna Maria his wife, dau. and co-heir of Edward Smyth, of Callow Hill, co. Fermanagh, 2nd son of Ven. James Smyth, Archdeacon of Meath, and had issue,
1. JOHN ARMYTAGE, his heir.
2. Christopher Hampden, Lieut.-Col. Grenadier Guards, b. 10 March, 1803 ; d. unm. 21 Feb. 1866.
3. William (Rev.), Rector of Welford, Berks, b. 1 July, 1805 ; d. 15 Dec. 1878.
4. Gilbert Thomas, J.P., b. 3 March 1819 ; m. 7 July, 1853, Grace Frances, dau. of Ven. Robert Alexander, Archdeacon of Down.
   1. Anna Maria, d. unm.

He m. 2ndly, 16 Feb. 1826, Anna, dau. of George Lenox Conyngham, of Springhill, co. Londonderry, by Olivia his wife, dau. of Wm. Irvine, of Castle Irvine, co. Fermanagh, and had issue,
5. Armytage Lenox, J.P., of Lisdhu, near Dungannon, b. 17 Oct. 1834.
2. Olivia, d. an infant.
3. Sophia Elizabeth.

He d. 18 Dec. 1849, and was s. by his eldest son,
JOHN ARMYTAGE NICHOLSON, of Balrath Burry, M.A., L.M., M.R.I.A., D.L., J.P., High Sheriff co. Meath 1827, b. 2 June, 1798 ; m. 21 July, 1824, Elizabeth Rebecca, dau. of Nathaniel Alexander, D.D., Bishop of Meath (nephew of James, 1st Earl of Caledon), by Anne, his wife, dau. and heir of the Right Hon. Sir Richard Jackson, of Forkhill, co. Antrim, by Anne, his wife, sister of John O'Neill, 1st Viscount O'Neill, and had issue,
1. CHRISTOPHER ARMYTAGE, his heir.
2. Nathaniel Alexander, M.A. Trin. Coll. Oxford, b. 5 Dec. 1826 ; d. unm. 15 Feb. 1874.
3. John Hampden (Rev.), M.A., Curate of Welford, b. 27 June, 1831 ; d. unm. Dec. 1870.
4. William Newcome, M.A., b. 22 May, 1833 ; m. 15 Dec. 1874, Amabel Margaretta, dau. of Reginald Thistlethwayte Cocks, of the Castleditch family, and of Henrietta Pole his wife, dau. of William Stuart, late of Aldenham Abbey, and Tempsford Hall.
5. Gilbert de Poulton, M.A., M.D., b. 8 April, 1835 ; m. 12 Aug. 1876, Minna Anna Bertha (née Bruxwitz), and d. 6 July, 1899, leaving issue,

1. Gilbert William de Poulton, b. 3 April, 1878.
1. Angelica Bella Elizabeth.
2. Katharine Anne O'Neill.
1. Katharine, m. 13 Sept. 1859, William Stuart, of Aldenham Abbey, and of Tempsford Hall, and d. Oct. 1881, leaving issue,
2. Anne, m. 1 March, 1860, Samuel Sanderson, of Clover Hill, co. Cavan (see that family).

Mr. Nicholson d. Dec. 1872, and was s. by his eldest son,
CHRISTOPHER ARMYTAGE NICHOLSON, of Balrath Burry, M.A. J.P. and D.L., High Sheriff 1856, b. 17 June, 1825 ; m. 25 March, 1858, Frances Augusta, eldest dau. of Hon. Augustus Henry Macdonald Moreton (see BURKE's Peerage, DUCIE, E.), by Mary Jane his wife, dau. and co-heir of Sir Charles Macdonald Lockhart, 2nd bart. of Lee, Carnwath, and Largie, and Emilia Olivia his wife, dau. of Sir Charles Ross, 6th bart., of Balnagowan, by Lady Mary FitzGerald his wife, dau. of William Robert, 2nd Duke of Leinster. She d. 5 Nov. 1902. He d. 19 Oct. 1887, leaving issue,
1. GILBERT MORETON, of Balrath Burry, co. Meath, b. 9 March 1860, formerly Lieut. Grenadier Guards, d. unm. 5 Nov. 1898.
2. JOHN HAMPDEN, now of Balrath Burry.
1. Mary Jane, m. 16 June, 1898, John Edward Fowler Sclater, of Hillsborough, co. Down, 5th son of James H. Sclater, of Newick Park (see that family). She d. 14 Nov. 1906.
2. Elizabeth Katharine.
3. Emilia Olivia, m. 1893, R. Arthur Alexander.

Arms—Erm., on a pale sa. three martlets arg. Crest—A leopard sejant arg., spotted sa., thrust through the neck with a demilance ppr. Motto—Pro republica.

Seat—Balrath Burry, near Kells, co. Meath.

NICHOLSON OF BALLOW.

GEORGE PERCY STEELE-NICHOLSON, of Ballow, co. Down, and Falmore, co. Donegal, b. 15 Feb. 1872.

Lineage.—The first of this family, located in Ireland, settled at Ballymagee, near Bangor, co. Down, in the reign of King JAMES I. He had (with two daus., the elder, wife of Thomas McMullan) two sons. The elder,
WILLIAM NICHOLSON, of Ballow, co. Down, b. 1591 ; m. Miss Janet Brown (who d. at the age of 80, 1680), and had issue,
1. John, d.v.p. 1655.
2. HUGH, his successor.

Mr. William Nicholson d. 5 April, 1665. His younger son,
HUGH NICHOLSON, of Ballymagee, m. Miss Isabel Orr, and by her (who d. 1696) had issue, four sons and two daus.,
1. WILLIAM.   2. JOHN.
3. James, of Ballymagee, b. 1663 ; m. Jane, dau. of Francis Allen, Collector of Customs at the port of Donaghadee, and d. 9 Dec. 1727, leaving issue, three sons and two daus.,
   1. Francis.   2. James.
   3. Archibald.
   1. Margaret.   2. Isabel.
4. Henry.
1. Margaret, m. William Glenholme, of Ballymascaw, co. Down, and had issue.
2. Mary.

Mr. Nicholson was s. by his eldest son,
WILLIAM NICHOLSON, of Ballow, b. 1659 ; m. Eleanor, dau. of James Dunlop, of Bangor, and by her (who d. 1720) had issue, two sons. Dying 3 Jan. 1794, he was s. by the elder,
HUGH NICHOLSON, of Ballow, b. 1 Nov. 1697 ; d. unm. 25 Aug. 1722, and was s. by his brother,
WILLIAM NICHOLSON, of Ballow, b. 23 Oct. 1699 ; m. Mary, dau. of Hugh Whyte, of Ballyree, co. Down (by his 2nd wife Anne, eldest dau. of Alexander Hamilton, of Ballyvernon, by his wife Isabel, eldest dau. of John Blackwood of Ballyleidy co. Down, ancestor of the Earl of Dufferin). By that lady (who m. 2ndly, Patrick Clealand, of Ballymagee, and d. 29 Oct. 1787, aged 84) he had issue,
1. HUGH, heir to his father.
2. WILLIAM, heir to his brother.
3. ROBERT DONALDSON, who s. his brother William.
1. Susanna, b. 1729 ; m. Hugh Jackson, of Ballywooley, co. Down and had issue.
2. Margaret Maxwell, b. 1734 ; m. Robert Gawen Steele, and d. 18 March, 1805, leaving by him (who m. 2ndly, Mary Carmichael, and d. 23 March, 1814) with other issue.
   WILLIAM NICHOLSON STEELE, who inherited the Nicholson property on his uncle William's will.

Mr. Nicholson d. 17 June, 1740, and was s. by his son,
HUGH NICHOLSON, of Ballow, who d. during his minority, 1743, and was s. by his brother,
WILLIAM NICHOLSON, of Ballow, b. 1728 ; m. 1st, 1744, Agnes, dau. of John Cleland, of Whithorn, co. Wigtown, and widow of

Richard Rose, a Lieut. in the H.E.I.C.S.; she d. 11 July, 1775. He m. 2ndly, 1777, Sarah, dau. of George Wells, of Belfast but had issue by neither. He d. 5 April, 1793, having devised his estates, failing issue of his brother Robert, to his nephew, WILLIAM NICHOLSON STEELE, who eventually succeeded. He was s. by his brother,

ROBERT RONALDSON NICHOLSON, of Ballow, who dying unm. 5 Sept. 1803, was s. by his nephew,

WILLIAM NICHOLSON STEELE-NICHOLSON, J.P., of Ballow, b. 5 April, 1772, who assumed the additional surname of NICHOLSON in compliance with the testamentary injunction of his uncle, 5 April, 1793; he m. 27 Feb. 1807, Isabella, 6th dau. of Jacob Hancock, of Lisburn (by his wife Elizabeth, dau. of Thomas Phelps, of Dublin, and his wife Sarah, only child of Issachar Willcocks, of that city, banker) and by her (who d. 5 Aug. 1872) had issue,

1. ROBERT, his heir.
2. John, b. 26 Oct. 1812, of Melbourne, Australia, dec.
3. William, b. 21 Sept. 1817; m. 22 July, 1856, Jane Frances, 4th dau. of Thomas Benjamin Middleton, of Dublin, and d. 30 Dec. 1889.
4. JAMES, of Ballow (see below).
5. Charles, b. 21 May, 1828; d. 27 Dec. 1846.
1. Elizabeth, m. 10 Dec. 1852, James Dowsett Rose-Cleland, of Rath Gael, co. Down, J.P. and D.L., and has issue (see that family).
2. Margaret, d. unm. 1892.
3. Mary, m. 1st, 11 April, 1861, Hugh Moore, of Nootka Lodge, Carlingford, co. Louth, who d. 6 July, 1866; she m. 2ndly, 7 Oct. 1868, Andrew Frederic Dunsterville, Capt. Argyll and Bute Artillery Militia.
4. Isabella.
5. Emily.

Mr. Nicholson d. 8 Nov. 1840, and was s. by his eldest son,

ROBERT STEELE-NICHOLSON, of Ballow, co. Down, M.A., J.P., Barrister-at-Law, b. 22 July, 1809; m. 16 Feb. 1841, Elizabeth Jane, youngest dau. of Walter Nangle, of Clonbaron, co. Meath, and d. 30 July, 1870, having had issue,

1. Hugh, b. 25 Jan. 1842; d.v.p. 2 Dec. 1851.
2. WALTER, b. 17 July, 1843; d.s.p. 1873.
3. EDWARD, b. 23 March, 1845, eventually s. to Ballow, which he sold, and emigrated to Port Elizabeth, South Africa.
4. Robert, b. 20 Aug. 1847; m. 20 Oct. 1874, Isabella Hamilton, dau. of James D. Rose Cleland, of Rath Gael House, co. Down (see that family), and has issue,
  1. Robert Jocelyn.
  2. Richard Barcroft Reinhard.
  1. Wini Helen, d. unm. 1893.
  2. Isabel Lola Josephine Ismag.
  3. Elizabeth Gertrude Agnes.
5. William Otway, b. 31 Dec. 1849; m. 27 Oct. 1874, Laura Levingstone, dau. of Edward Wheelock, of New Orleans, North America, and has issue,
  1. Wheelock, b. 6 June, 1876.
  2. Maurice William, b. 31 Dec. 1877.
  1. Virginia Plesanto.
  2. Marion Elizabeth.
6. Hugh, b. 20 Oct. 1854, lost at sea in the Innisfallen.
7. Gilbert Hamilton, b. 26 Sept. 1860.
1. Catherine Elizabeth, m. 12 April, 1881, Frederick Barcroft, of Stangmore House, Dungannon, co. Tyrone, and has issue,
  Gilbert Evelyn, b 14 June, 1883.
  Jane Malcomson.
2. Isabel Frances, d. 20 Nov. 1875.

JAMES STEELE-NICHOLSON, of Ballow, co. Down, and Falmore, co. Donegal, purchased the family mansion of Ballow after the death of his eldest brother Robert in 1873, b. 5 Feb. 1819; m. 30 Dec. 1870, Maria Katherine, dau. of George Augustus Chichester Macartney, of Glendarragh, co. Donegal, by Caroline his wife, dau. of Frank Whittle, D.L., of Muckamore, co. Antrim, and d. 1899, having had issue,

1. GEORGE PERCY, of Ballow.
2. William Herbert Hamilton, b. 27 Nov. 1875.
3. Robert Charles Henry, b. 1 Oct. 1878.
4. Arthur John Macartney, b. 18 Dec. 1880.
5. Alfred Francis James, b. 5 Nov. 1885.
1. Caroline Edith, m. 4 Nov. 1896, Sydney H. Guilford, son of the late Thomas Guilford, J.P., of The Grove, West Molesey, Surrey, and has issue.
2. Maria Kathleen Isabel.
3. Conwaianna Georgina.
4. Margaret Ethel Louise.
5. Mary Elizabeth Maud Grace.
6. Florence Emily.
7. Evelyn Dorothy.

Family of Steele.

JOHN STEELE, of Portavo and Carnelea, co. Down, b. about the year 1655; m. Mary, dau. of James Blackwood, of Bangor, and had issue,

1. James, of whom nothing is known.
2. JOHN.
1. Mary, m. John Crawford, of Holestone, co. Antrim, and had issue.
2. Margaret.

Mr. Steele d. 1721. His 2nd son,

JOHN STEELE, of Belfast, m. 23 Nov. 1721, Isabel, dau. of Alexander Hamilton, of Ballyvernon, co. Down, and his wife Isabel, eldest dau. of John Blackwood, of Ballyleidy, co. Down, ancestor of the Earl of Dufferin, and by her (who d. 15 May, 1739) had issue, eight sons. Mr. Steele d. 1740. His last surviving son,

ROBERT GAWEN STEELE, of Ballymacarret, co. Down, b. 11 March, 1733; m. 1st, Margaret Maxwell, dau. of William Nicholson, of Ballow, and by her (who d. 1805) had issue,

1. Hamilton, b. 21 June, 1768; d. unm. 1807.
2. WILLIAM NICHOLSON, his successor.
3. Robert, b. 22 March, 1775; d. unm. 1806.
1. Mary, b. 24 Feb. 1770; m. Hugh Kearns, and d. 9 Feb. 1833, leaving issue.

Mr. Steele m. 2ndly, May, 1806, Mary, dau. of Richard Walker, gent. of Todstown, co. Down, but had no other issue. He d. 73 March, 1814, and was s. by his only surviving son, William Nicholson Steele-Nicholson, of Ballow who had previously inherited the Nicholson property, and assumed that surname.

Arms—Gu., two bars erm. in chief three suns in glory or. Crest—Out of a ducal coronet or, a lion's head erminois. Motto—Deus mihi Sol.

Seat—Ballow House, near Bangor, co. Down.

NICHOLSON OF CRANNAGAEL.

HENRY PERCY NICHOLSON, of Crannagael, co. Armagh, b. 9 July, 1866; s. his father 1907.

Lineage.—REV. WILLIAM NICHOLSON, M.A., of Tallbridge, Cranagill, co. Armagh, Rector of Derrybrughas, settled in Ireland, and was murdered in the Irish Rebellion, 1641. He m. Elizabeth Percy. Their son,

JOHN NICHOLSON, of Cranagill, who purchased the lands of Breaheaville and Derry, co. Tyrone, 12 Dec. 1632, and was murdered with his father at Cranagill, leaving a son,

WILLIAM NICHOLSON, of Cranagill, who joined the Society of Friends, b. 1632; m. Isabella Gilbert. She d. 1718. He d. 24 Jan. 1715, having had issue,

1. JOHN, of whom presently.
2. Thomas } both killed at the siege of Derry, 1688-9.
3. James }
4. Abraham, d. young.
5. Jacob, m. Elizabeth Gilbert, and had issue, from whom descends the Tallbridge branch.
1. Prudentia, d. young.
2. Sarah, b. 1682; m. 20 Sept. 1701, Robert Hodgson, of Lurgan.
3. Elizabeth, m. William Brownlow.
4. Jane, m. George Fox.

The eldest son,

JOHN NICHOLSON, of Derrycaw, where he built the house, 1698, m. Margery Brownlow, and d.v.p. 2 Dec. 1704 (will dated 10 Dec. 1703), having had issue,

1. William, of Derrycaw, b. 1683, d. 1719, leaving issue by Mary his wife. He was ancestor of the Derrycaw branch.
2. James, b. 1686.
3. JOHN, of whom presently.
4. Isaac, b. 24 June, 1693.
5. Benjamin.
6. Thomas, of Kincary, m. 26 April, 1729, Isabella Richardson, of Eagerlougher. From him descends the Kincary branch.
1. Isabel, b. 1 Sept. 1684; m. 18 Jan. 1701, Joseph Robson, of Lurgan.
2. Elizabeth, b. 1688, m. Jonathan Richardson, of Eagerlougher, and d. 1784.

The 3rd son,

JOHN NICHOLSON, of Hall's Mill, near Lawrencetown, co. Down, b. 13 Jan. 1691; m. 20 July, 1710, Mary Walker, of Lurgan, and by her had issue,

1. John, b. 31 March, 1704; d. unm.
2. Jonathan, b. 1718-9, d. young.
3. Benjamin, b. 1724.
4. Thomas, b. 5 June, 1730; m. 1 March, 1761, Christian, dau. of Robert Jaffray. She d. 1778. He d. 8 June, 1794, leaving issue, from whom descend the Stramore and Banford branches.
5. William, b. 1732, d. young.
6. JAMES, of whom presently.
1. Sarah, b. 12 May, 1712; d. an infant.
2. Mary, b. 15 Feb. 1716; m. 4 Jan. 1741, William Richardson, of Stramore.

The youngest son,

JAMES NICHOLSON, of Dublin, who purchased, 1760, The Hill portion of Cranagail from John Nicholson, of Tallbridge, b. 3 Dec. 1734; m. 1st, 1755, Ruth Morton, of Grange, and 2ndly, 1777, Sarah — and d. 1779, having by his first wife had issue,

1. JOSEPH, of whom presently.
2. Samuel, d. young.
3. James, m. 1st, 1791, Lydia Clibborn, of Moate, co. Westmeath, and 2ndly, 1797, Anna Greer, of Rhouchill, co. Tyrone. She d. 1844. He d. 1838, leaving issue,
  1. Edward, m. 1844, Eleanor Boardman, of Grange, and had a dau., Anna Greer, m. Samuel Cross, of Killyman.
  1. Sarah, m. Jonathan Pike, of Beechgrove (see PIKE of Glendanary).
  2. Anna, d. unm.
  3. Jane, d. unm.
  4. Huldah, m. 28 May, 1829, Thomas Abbott, of Limerick.
  5. Charlotte, m. 1828, Thomas Greer, of Dungannon.
1. Sarah, m. 1750, Jonathan Richardson, of Lisburn.
2. Ruth, m. Edward Harpur, of Gorestown.

The eldest son,

JOSEPH NICHOLSON, of Dublin, afterwards of Bernagh, Grange, co. Tyrone, and finally of Bessbrook and Cranagill, co. Armagh, b. 1758; m. 27 June, 1782, Abigail, dau. of James Hogg, of Lisburn. She d. 1806, aged 40. He d. 1817, having had issue, with others, who d. young.

1. James, b. 1783, d. an infant.
2. James, of Keady, co. Armagh, b. 1784; d. unm. 23 April, 1831.
3. JOSEPH, of whom presently.
4. Thomas, b. 1784, m. Elizabeth Barrington, and d. at Springfield, Pennsylvania.
5. John, d. in New York.
1. Mary, b. 1788, m. Joshua Hoare Beule, of Cork.
2. Ruth, b. 1790, d. unm.

The 3rd son,

IRELAND. Noble.

JOSEPH NICHOLSON, of Cranagill, co. Armagh, J.P., b. 31 March, 1786; m. 10 Nov. 1810, Elizabeth, dau. of George Roe, of Mountoe, co. Armagh. She d. 25 March, 1869. He d. 16 April, 1805, aving had issue,
1. Joseph, b. 1811, d. 1830.
2. George Roe, b. 1817, d. young.
3. Charles James, b. 15 Nov. 1823; m. 2 Dec. 1854, Frances, dau. of Maurice Knox, J.P., of Arthurstown, co. Wexford. She d. 11 July, 1881. He d. 12 Jan. 1891, without surviving issue.
4. HENRY JOSEPH, of Cranagill.
1. Elizabeth, b. 1816, d. 1824.
2. Charlotte Matilda, b. 1819, d. 1821.
3. Frances Elizabeth, b. 1824, d. 1854.
The 4th son,
HENRY JOSEPH NICHOLSON, of Crannagael, co. Armagh, J.P., b. 2 March, 1832; m. 5 Aug. 1865, Emma, dau. of Andrew Macallum, of Nottingham. She d. 29 March, 1897. He d. 19 Sept. 1907, leaving issue,
1. HENRY PERCY, now of Crannagael.
2. George Edward Roe, b. 26 Feb. 1873.
3. Thomas Maccallum, Capt. Indian Army, 59th Scinde Rifles, Frontier Field Force, late 6th Punjab Infantry, b. 11 March, 1877; m. 15 Oct. 1899, Jessie Elizabeth Beatrice Blair, dau. of James Francis Hitchman. She d. 2 June, 1907, leaving issue, a son.
1. Mary Frances Josephine, m. 31 July, 1902, Robert Richard Atkinson, J.P. of Summer Island, Loughall (see ATKINSON of Crowhill).
Seat—Crannagael, Loughgall, co. Armagh.

NIXON OF CRAGBEG.

JAMES HAMILTON FITZ GERALD NIXON, of Cragbeg, co. Limerick, and of Mount Prospect, co. Cavan, J.P. co. Carlow, late Lieut. R.N.R., F.R.G.S., and younger brother of Trinity House, b. 26 May, 1850; m. 13 Oct. 1887, Kathleen Margaret Alsager, youngest dau. of Henry Alsager Pollock, of Alsager, Cheshire, and Goremount, Glenary, co. Antrim, and has issue a son and a dau.,
GEORGE ALSAGER FITZGERALD, b. 26 March, 1892.
Obré Alsager FitzGerald, b. 15 Aug. 1888.
Lineage.—ADAM NIXON, settled in co. Fermanagh temp. JAMES I, and was bur. at Enniskillen 18 Nov. 1669, leaving a son,
GEORGE NIXON, of Granshagh, co. Fermanagh, whose will dated 5 Jan., was proved 2 Feb. 1702. His 2nd son,
THOMAS NIXON, of Kingetown, co. Fermanagh, m. 1st, Lucy Percy, and 2ndly, Mary, widow of — Borrough. His will, dated 6 Sept., 1738, was proven 9 June, 1739. By his first wife only he had issue, three sons and three daus. (see BURKE's Family Records). His youngest son,
REV. ANDREW NIXON, of Nixon Lodge, Drumlane, co. Cavan, Vicar of Ahemlish, B.A. Trin. Coll. Dublin, b. 1710, He m., by licence, dated 10 March, 1737, Marianne, dau. of — French, of Dunshauglin, co. Meath. He d. 6 Jan. 1774, having by her (who d. 13 March, 1775) had issue,
1. Humphrey, of Nixon Lodge, co. Cavan, J.P. High Sheriff 1777, Lieut. 51st Foot, b. 1740, m. 8 Aug. 1781, Anne, sister of the Right Hon. John Stewart, 1st Bart., of Ballygawley, and d. 12 June, 1810, leaving issue.
2. Mathew, of Ballyhaise, co. Cavan, m. 1769, Elizabeth Mee, and d.s.p. He was bur. 3 Jan. 1800.
3. Adam, of Ahemlish, co. Cavan, Ensign 53rd Foot 1767, Cornet 13th Light Dragoons 1770, m. Rose, dau. of Richard Phepoe, and had issue,
Richard Phepoe, Lieut. 19th Foot, d. 11 June, 1910.
3. GEORGE, of whom presently.
1. Anne, m. about 1765, Henry Swanzy, of Avelreagh, co. Monaghan (see BURKE's Family Records). He d. 25 March, 1792. She d. 4 Feb. 1822.
2. Frances, d. unm.
3. Barbara, m. 8 Dec. 1778, Isaiah Corry, of Ballytrain, co. Monaghan.
The youngest son,
GEORGE NIXON, of Lurgan Lodge, Virginia, co. Cavan, and Graan, co. Fermanagh, J.P. co. Cavan, High Sheriff co. Fermanagh, 1785, m. 1st, 14 April, 1774, Elinor, dau of Robert Beatty, of Coolnarby, co. Longford, by Anne, dau. of Peter Metge, of Navan, co. Meath. The d. May, 1779. He m. 2ndly, 23 Aug. 1779, Elizabeth, dau. of James Johnston, of Enniskillen, and d. April, 1805, leaving issue,
1. Andrew, of Lurgan Lodge, J.P. cos. Cavan and Meath, Barrist r-at-Law, m. Frances Matilda, dau. of Rev. Charles Hare, D.D., Rector of Ballymoney, co. Antrim, and had issue.
2. William, whose will was proved 13 June, 1840.
3. Humphrey, Lieut. 96th Regt., who left issue.
4. JAMES, of whom presently.
5. Adam, d. 6 Jan. 1843.
1. Jane, d. 10 Aug. 1859.
2. Elizabeth, m. 22 Oct. 1814, Aldebert J. D'Oisy, of Paris, and d. 23 June, 1826.
3. Mary Anne.
The 4th son,

JAMES NIXON, of Ballyjamesduff, co. Cavan, Lieut. R.N., left one son and two daus.,
1. GEORGE, of whom presently.
1. Annabella, m. 6 Dec. 1860, Robert Hanna, of Dublin; d. 2 Feb. 1911.
2. Eliza, m. 23 June, 1864, Richard Dempsey, of Mount Prospect co. Cavan. She d. 15 May, 1908.
The only son,
GEORGE NIXON, M.D., of Antrim, b. 17 March, 1820, m. 5 June, 1845, Elizabeth, dau. of Espine Ward, of Dublin, and Harriet his wife, dau. of Charles FitzGerald, of Navinstown, co. Kildare, and Merrion Square, Dublin, and d. 18 April, 1862, having had issue, a son and a dau.,
JAMES HAMILTON FITZGERALD, now of Cragbeg.
Harriett Anna Elizabeth, m. 13 April, 1871, Robert Augustus Milliner.
Seats—Cragberg, Clarina, co. Limerick, and Mount Prospect, Mount-Nugent, co. Cavan.

NOBLE OF GLASSDRUMMOND.

SHIRLEY NEWCOME NOBLE, of Glassdrummond, co. Fermanagh, formerly Lieut 5th Batt. Leinster Regt., b. 7 June, 1865; s. his father 1892.
Lineage.—JAMES NOBLE, of Glassdrummond, whose arms were "or, two lions passant in pale sable between two flaunches azure, over all on a fesse gules, three bezants," d. in 1720, leaving issue, amongst others,
1. MUNGO, of whom presently.
2. James, of Clontivern, near Clones, co. Monaghan, m. 1743, Mary, dau. of Richard Legh, of Duhatt, co. Fermanagh, and d. without issue, in 1770, leaving his property of Clontivern to his nephew, the Rev. Mungo Henry Noble.
The eldest son,
MUNGO NOBLE, m. May, 1725, Prudence, dau. of Patrick Bredin, of Drumcagh, co. Fermanagh, and had issue, two sons and two daus., namely,
1. JAMES, of whom presently.
2. Jerome, b. about 1728, entered the Army as ensign in 28th Irish Regt. of Foot, and was present at the capture of Quebec. He lost a leg at Martinique in 1762, and d. with the rank of Major 1784. He m. Miss Elizabeth Crawford, of Springfield, co. Fermanagh, and had issue,
1. Mungo, entered the Army, and was Col. of the 67th Regt. in 1795. He m. Miss Phillipse, dau. of Frederick Phillipse, of Phillipseburg, New York (sister of Maria Eliza, 5th Viscountess Strangford, and Charlotte Elizabeth, wife of Sir Henry Allen Johnstone, Bart.), by whom he had a son, Frederick, who entered the H.E.I.C. Service, and d.s.p., and a dau., Eliza, who d. unm. at Bath, 1867.
1. Margaret. m. 1st, Col. Black, H.E.I.C.S., and had issue, She m. 2ndly, Rev. James Hamilton, D.D., Rector of Cootehill, co. Cavan, and had further issue.
2. Prudentia, m. 1st, Col. Powell, by whom she had no issue; and 2ndly, her cousin, Major Samuel Noble, son of William Noble, of Donagh, and grandson of Arthur Noble, of Drumrane, and had issue.
1. Susanna, m. 1748, John Paumier, a French Huguenot who had settled in Ireland after the revocation of the Edict of Nantes, and had issue.
2. Jane, m. Rev. Mark Noble, of Enniskillen, and had eighteen children, all of whom d. young.
Mungo Noble m. 2ndly, 1741, Mary, dau. of Rev. William Leslie, of Agnavea, co. Fermanagh, and by her had two sons and one dau.,
3. William, Vicar of Holy Trinity, Cork, d.s.p. 1806.
4. Mungo, entered H.E.I.C. Service, and d. unm.
3. Letitia, d. unm.
Mungo Noble d. in 1754, and was s. by his eldest son,
JAMES NOBLE, of Glassdrummond, High Sheriff 1755, b. 1727; m. 1755, Catherine, eldest dau. of WILLIAM WALLER, of Allenstown, co. Meath, and eventually heiress in her issue to Waller of Allenstown. She d. March, 1791, having had issue, four sons and five daus., namely,
1. MUNGO HENRY, of whom presently.
2. William, d.s.p. 1778.   3. James, b. 1768; d.s.p. 1793.
4. Robert Thomas, b. 1772; d.s.p. 1793.
1. Anna Maria, b. 1758; d. Jan. 1809; m. Rev. Dean Browne, of Elpin, and had issue.
2. Susan, b. 1762; d. unm. 17 Nov. 1828.
3. Leonora, b. 1764; d. unm. 1788.
4. Prudence, d. young, 5 Aug. 1792.

5. Mary Martha, b. 2 June, 1778; d. 31 Dec. 1864; m. 1799, Rev. Thomas Sutton, Rector of Clongill, co. Meath, and had issue, one dau.
James Noble d. in Aug. 1780, and was s. by his eldest and only surviving son,
REV. MUNGO HENRY NOBLE, of Glassdrummond, b. 1759, Rector of Clongill, co. Meath; m. 21 Jan. 1794, Maria, only child of "the Right Hon. and Most Rev. William Newcome, D.D., Lord Archbishop of Armagh and Primate of all Ireland, by his 1st wife, Susanna, only surviving child and heiress of Sir Thomas D'Oyly, 3rd bart. of Chislehampton, co. Oxon. On the death, in 1773, of her grand-uncle, the Rev. Sir John D'Oyly, 4th bart., the late heir male, Miss Newcome became *ex parte materni*, sole heir-general to D'Oyly, of Chislehampton. On the death of Robert Waller in 1809, the property of Allenstown, co. Meath, devolved upon the Rev. Mungo Henry Noble, in right of his mother, Catherine Waller, whereupon he assumed the surname and arms of WALLER, in addition to those of Noble. By his wife, Maria Newcome (who d. at Allenstown, 12 April, 1858), Mungo Henry Noble Waller had issue, six sons and two daus., namely,
1. William Henry, b. 1 July, 1795, s. his father at Allenstown in 1831; and d.s.p. 17 June, 1837.
2. ROBERT, of whom presently.
3. James, to whom the reversion of Allenstown was left by his brother William Henry, and who thereupon assumed the surname and arms of WALLER (*see* WALLER *of Allenstown*).
4. Mungo, b. 13 Dec. 1801; d. 17 April, 1802.
5. Mungo (2nd son so named), b. 9 Oct. 1805; d.s.p. 4 July, 1824.
6. John, b. 11 July, 1809, entered Holy Orders, and was for some years Curate of Athboy, co. Meath, d.s.p. 1835.
1. Susanna, d. an infant, 17 Nov. 1797.
2. Maria, b. 6 Sept. 1803; d. *unm.* 17 May, 1857.
Mungo Henry Noble Waller d. 16 June, 1831, aged 72, and was s. in his Fermanagh property by his 2nd son,
REV. ROBERT NOBLE, of Glassdrummond, Rector and Vicar of the united parishes of Athboy, Kildalky, Girley, Rathmore, and Moyagher, co. Meath, b. 29 Aug. 1796; m. 25 Oct. 1833, Catherine (d. 3 Dec. 1904), eldest dau. of the Rev. James Annesley Burrowes, Rector of Castleconnor, co. Sligo, by his wife, Catherine Stock, dau. of Joseph Stock, D.D., Bishop of Killala, by his wife, Catherine Smyth, dau. of Edward Smyth, of Callow Hill, and grand-dau. of James Smyth, Archdeacon of Meath, and Catherine Vesey, dau. of John Vesey, Archbishop of Tuam (*see* SMYTH *of Gaybrook*). Robert Noble and his wife Catherine had eleven children,
1. WILLIAM HENRY, of whom presently.
2. John D'Oyly, b. 17 Nov. 1835; m. 26 Aug. 1869, Helen, dau. of Stafford Frederick Kirkpatrick, of Kingston, Canada, and grand-dau. of Alexander Kirkpatrick, of Coolmine House, co. Dublin, by whom he had issue,
1. Robert Kirkpatrick, b. 9 June, 1870.
2. Stafford D'Oyly, b. 25 Oct. 1871.
3. James Burrowes, b. 17 Feb. 1873.
4. Ernest Annesley, b. 20 Nov. 1876.
3. James Burrowes, b. 2 March, 1839; d. June, 1849.
4. Edwin St. George, b. 19 Oct. 1842.
5. Robert D'Oyly, b. 6 July, 1846.
6. Arthur Annesley Burrowes, b. 16 Jan. 1850; d.s.p. 29 June, 1875.
7. Ernest Newcome, b. 22 March, 1852; d.s.p. 29 March, 1880.
8. Shirley Waller, b. 25 Dec. 1854; d. 15 June, 1859.
1. Helen Catherine, m. 18 Aug. 1863, Rev. Graham Craig, Rector of Tullamore and Dean of Clonmacnoise, son of Stuart Craig, of Banbridge, co. Down, and has issue.
2. Emily Mary, m. 25 Aug. 1864, Robert Stewart Craig, son of Stewart Craig, of Banbridge, co. Down, and has had issue.
3. Maria Louisa, m. 7 April, 1877, her cousin, Edmond Noble Waller of Allenstown, co. Meath (*see that family*).
The Rev. Robert Noble d. Oct. 1870, and was s. by his eldest son,
WILLIAM HENRY NOBLE, of Glassdrummond, co. Fermanagh, Major-Gen. Royal Artillery, b. 14 Oct. 1834; m. 11 July, 1861, Emily, eldest dau. of Frederick Marriott, of Taunton, Somersetshire, by his wife, Mary Anne, only dau. and heiress of Francis Gibbons, of Wellingborough, and had issue, two sons and five daus., namely,
1. SHIRLEY NEWCOME, now of Glassdrummond.
2. Vere D'Oyly, late 27th Inniskillings, b. 7 Feb. 1867; m. 24 Jan. 1895, Dora Mary Robinson, only dau. of H. J. R. Pease, of Hesslewood (*see that family*) and has issue,
1. Henry Francis D'Oyly, b. 23 June, 1896.
2. Geoffrey Waller, b. 4 Nov. 1900.
1. Mawde Lettice.
2. Ethel Emily D'Oyly, d. 29 Nov. 1865.
3. Violet Alice Agnes, m. 24 Nov. 1894, James Montagu Oldham, of Ormidale, Ascot, son of the late Rev. Oldham Oldham, and has issue.
4. Phyllis D'Oyly, m. 29 Aug. 1895, Edward Byas Sheppard, son of Samuel Gurney Sheppard, of Leggatts, Herts, and has issue.
5. Sybil Cholmley Waller.
Major-Gen. Noble d. 17 May, 1892, and was s. by his eldest son.
Arms—Vert, on a fesse or, between three leopards' faces argent, a fleur-de-lis between two annulets sable. Crest—A dove arg. holding in her beak a ring or gemmed az. Motto—Mortem quam dedecus.
Seat—Glassdrunmond, co. Fermanagh.

NOLAN OF BALLINDERRY.

The late JOHN PHILIP NOLAN, of Ballinderry, co. Galway, J.P., M.P. for Galway Co. and North Galway 1874–1895, and 1900–06, late Lieut.-Col. R.A., b. 3 Aug. 1838. d. 29 Jan. 1912.

Lineage.—THOMAS NOLAN, of Ballinrobe Castle, co. Mayo, which was attacked by the Bourkes in 1589 (Cal. State Papers). The attack was repulsed and the town fired. He also owned Iskeroue and another castle and two manors in co. Sligo (Inq. 1629 and 1633; and Patents, JAMES I, p. 343). He d. 18 June, 1628, seised of Ballinrobe Castle, leaving by Agnes Martin, who survived him,
1. Gregory, son and heir 1628, High Sheriff co. Mayo 1623, elected Agent for co. Mayo to the Catholic Convention of Kilkenny, and confiscated by Cromwell (Clanricarde Memoirs, II. Vol. Ormonde; and Book of Explanations for the Transplantations).
2. JOHN, of whom we treat.

The younger son,
JOHN NOLAN, was in possession of Iskerone and the manors in co. Sligo in 1632 (Strafford Survey) which he seems to have purchased from his brother (Inq. 1633). He was transplanted to the neighbourhood of Ballinderry, co. Galway, and to 5,600 acres in Mayo. He m. Mary Skerrett (Vol. III., *Transplanters' Certificates*, and Vol. V. *Connaught Certificates*), and had PATRICK and Andrew. The eldest son,
PATRICK NOLAN, of Ballinderry, had several confirmatory grants of land in the cos. of Mayo and Galway *temp.* CHARLES II. (*Records of the Rolls, vol.* XII., Ulster's Office). He m. 1667, Anne, dau. (by Mary his wife, dau. of Sir Dominick Browne of Carra Browne, co. Galway) of Sir John Browne, Bart., of The Neale, ancestor of the noble Houses of Kilmaine and Sligo, and had, with other issue,
JOHN NOLAN, of Ballinderry, m. Feb. 1709, Ellis, 2nd dau. of William Brabazon, of New Park, co. Mayo, capt. of a troop of horse in King JAMES II.'s Army, and one of the Commissioners for the capitulation of Limerick, by Mary his 1st wife, dau. of George Browne, of The Neale, and left a son and heir,
PATRICK NOLAN, of Ballinderry, m. (settlement dated 11 Nov. 1734) Ellis, dau. of Peter Martyn, of Tullyra Castle, co. Galway, by Magdalen, his wife, dau. of Geoffrey Browne, of Castle McGarrett. He was s. by his son,
JOHN NOLAN, of Ballinderry, m. Margaret, dau. and heir of James French, of Port-a-Carron, Lough Corrib, co. Galway, and was father of a son and successor,
JOHN NOLAN, of Ballinderry, m. Sept. 1809, Mary, dau. of John Browne, of Castle Moyle, and by her (who d. 1852) had a son,
JOHN NOLAN, of Ballinderry, J.P., m. Sept. 1836, Mary Anne, dau. of Walter Nolan, of Loughboy (descended also from Thomas Nolan of Ballinrobe Castle and Iskerone), and d.v.p. April, 1847, leaving issue,
1. JOHN PHILIP, now of Ballinderry.
2. Walter Raymond, of Claremadden, co. Galway (as heir to his maternal grandfather), late Col. 17th Lancers, b. 31 Aug. 1839; d. 30 Aug. 1905.
3. Francis, Q.C., b. 14 Dec. 1841; d. 17 May, 1895.
4. Philip, Indian C.S., b. 22 Sept. 1844; m. Frances Georgina (83, *Sloane Street, S.W.*), dau. of Francis Berkeley Drummond, H.E.I.C.S., 4th son of John Drummond, of London, Banker (*see* BURKE's *Peerage*, PERTH, E.). He d. 28 April, 1902, having had issue,
1. Raymond Philip Drummond, b. 1 July, 1883.
2. Noel John Philip, b. 27 Oct. 1897.
1. Stella Agnes Drummond.
5. Sebastian Michael, of Castle Moyle, Tuam, co. Galway, b. 17 March, 1846; d. 1 April, 1907.
6. Edward, late Lieut. 18th Hussars, b. 5 Dec. 1847; d. 1890.
1. Elizabeth.

Arms—Or on a cross, between four swords, in pale gu., a lion rampant of the first. Crest—A demi-lion rampant or. Motto—Cor unum via una.

Seat—Ballinderry, Tuam. Club—Army and Navy.

NORMAN OF GLENGOLLAN.

CHARLES NORMAN, of Glengollan, co. Donegal, D.L. and J.P., High Sheriff 1910, Lieut. N. Irish Horse, b. 16 May, 1879.

Lineage.—SAMUEL NORMAN, of Londonderry, Mayor of that city 1672, 1673, and 1674, m. 1st, Margaret, dau. of William Latham, Recorder of Londonderry, and had, with daus., a son, CHARLES NORMAN, b. 1666, M.P. for Londonderry 1703, 1713, and 1715, and [ayor 1707 and 1723; *d.s.p.*; his will was proved 1731. Samuel Norman *m.* 2ndly, Elizabeth, dau. of John Gage, of Magilligan, co. Derry, and left issue at his decease, 17 May, 1692, a son,

ROBERT NORMAN, of Dublin, M.P. for Derry 1733, and Mayor 1715. He *m.* Sarah, dau. of the Very Rev. John Bolton, of Lagore, co. Meath, Dean of Derry, and left issue at his decease, about 1743.

1. Thomas, of Lagore (Rev.), *b.* 1715; *m.* 1746, Anne, dau. of Rev. Peter Ward, Chaplain to the Lord-Lieutenant, and (with three other sons *d.* young) had issue,
    1. Robert (Rev.), of Lagore, *d.s.p.* April, 1771.
    1. Sarah, *m.* Thomas Lee (son of William Lee, by Elizabeth Lucas his wife, and grandson of Robert Lee, by Margaret Patten) and left at his decease in 1800 (with three daus.) a son, THOMAS LEE NORMAN, of Corbollis, co. Louth, J.P. and D.L., High Sheriff 1820, *d.* 1875, aged 85 (*see that family*).
    2. Annie, *d. unm.*
    3. Florinda, *m.* 1st, Francis Lucas, and 2ndly, her cousin, Charles Norman.
    4. Elizabeth, *d. unm.*
    5. Frances, *m.* Rev. Robert Norman (*see below*).
2. Frederick.
3. Marcus, *m.* July, 1760, Sarah, dau. of William Gamble.
4. CONOLLY, of whom presently.
1. Florinda, *m.* Charles Gardiner, and was mother of Luke Gardiner, created Viscount Mountjoy.

The 4th son,

CONOLLY NORMAN, of Dublin, *m.* Sept. 1762, Anne, dau. of Luke Gardiner, and had issue,
1. Charles, *m.* his cousin, Florinda, dau. of Rev. Thomas Norman, and *d.s.p.* 1800, having devised his estates to his brother, Thomas.
2. THOMAS, of whom hereafter.
3. Robert (Rev.), *m.* Frances, dau. of Rev. Thomas Norman (*see above*).
4. Luke, of Dublin, *m.* Anne, dau. of Alexander Worthington, and has issue,
    1. Conolly, of Fahan House, co. Donegal, *m.* Georgiana, dau. of George Wilson, of Essex, and *d.* 1890, having by her (who *d.* 1889) had,
        (1) Luke, of Fahan House, Col. Donegal Militia, late 69th Regt., J.P. co Donegal, *m.* 14 April, 1874, Elizabeth, dau. of Alexander Edwards, of Dublin.
        (2) Conolly, *d.* 1890.
        (3) Robert William, *m.* 27 April, 1889, Mary Florence, dau. of James Robert Stewart, of Gortleitragh, co. Dublin, and has, with other issue,
            1. Luke Gardiner, *b.* 1890.
            2. Conolly George.
            3. Robert Warren.
            4. Dudley.   5. Patrick.
            1. Georgiana Eleanor.
        (1) Frances, *m.* Edward Bennett, Professor of Surgery at the University of Dublin.
        (2) Annie, *m.* 3 Oct. 1878, Thomas Norman, of Glengollan (*see below*).
        (3) Georgiana, *m.* Charles T. Tunnard, of Frampton House, co. Lincoln.
        (4) Mary Krause, *m.* W. Garfit, of Boston, co. Lincoln.
        (5) Elizabeth, *m.* Christopher Tunnard.
    2. Charles, *d.* under age.
    3. Alexander, Q.C., Barrister-at-Law, *m.* Charlotte Sarah, dau. of Robert Law, of Great Denmark Street, Dublin, and left, with several daus., a son, LUKE ALEXANDER LEE-NORMAN, of Corbollis (*see* LEE-NORMAN *of Corbollis*).
    4. Luke.   5. Augustus Patrick.
    1. Eleanor, *m.* Thomas Lloyd.
    2. Florinda, *d. unm.*   3. Margaret, *d. unm.*
    4. Elizabeth.

The 2nd son,

THOMAS NORMAN, devisee of his brother Charles's estate, *m.* March, 1790, Catherine, dau. of Hugh Lyons (who assumed the name of MONTGOMERY), by Catherine his wife, dau. of Richard, 4th Viscount Boyne, and by her (who *d.* 1825) left at his decease, 1833,
1. CHARLES, his heir.
2. Hugh (Rev.), Rector of Augbanunshin, *b.* 1808; *m.* Anne, dau. of William Ball, of Buncrana, and *d.* 1875, leaving issue,
    1. Thomas, late I.C.S. (*Oakfield, Weston Park, Bath*), *m.* 1871, Annie, dau. of John Carpenter, and has issue,
        (1) Harold Hugh, Capt. R.A.M.C., *b.* 8 Aug. 1875, served in South African War 1899-1902.
        (1) Maud, *m.* 1906, Rev. S. P. Duval, Vicar of Colne, Lancashire.   (2) Ida.
    2. William, *d.* 1877.
    3. Hugh, *d.* 1875.
    4. John Gage (Rev.) (9, *Cambridge Gardens, Kilburn, N.W.*), *b.* 14 June, 1851; *m.* 3 Oct. 1895, Tryphosa, dau. of the late Francis John Lace, J.P., of Stoneappe, Yorks.
    5. Conolly, M.D., *b.* 1853; *d.s.p.* 23 Feb. 1908; *m.* 1881, Mary Emma, dau. of — Kenny.
    6. Charles, *b.* 1856; *d.* in N. S. W., 1894.
3. Thomas, *d.* under age.
1. Anne, *m.* Robert Maxwell, of Middle Gardiner Street, Dublin, and *d.s.p.* 1880.
2. Catherine, *m.* 21 Feb. 1837, Thomas Kough, of Enniscorthy, co. Wexford, and *d.* 1885, leaving issue.
3. Florinda, *m.* 14 Feb. 1843, Livingstone Thompson, of co. Armagh, and *d.* Feb. 1896, leaving issue.

The eldest son,

CHARLES NORMAN, J.P. for co. Donegal, Lieut. Royal Scots Greys, *m.* 27 April, 1829, Anna Eliza, eldest dau. of Edward Kough, of New Ross, co. Wexford, and *d.* Aug. 1843, leaving an only child,

THOMAS NORMAN, of Glengollan, J.P. and D.L., High Sheriff 1864, Capt. (retired) Donegal Militia, *b.* 5 March, 1835; *m.* 3 Oct. 1878, Annie, 2nd dau. of Conolly Norman, of Fahan House, co. Donegal (*see above*), and *d.* 13 May, 1895, having by her (who *d.* 8 April, 1881) had issue,

CHARLES, now of Glengollan.
Annie, *b.* 23 March, 1881.

Seat—Glengollan, Fahan, Londonderry.

LEE-NORMAN OF CORBOLLIS.

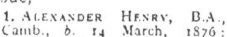

LUKE ALEXANDER LEE-NORMAN, of Corbollis, co. Louth, J.P. and D.L., High Sheriff 1881, Vice-Lieut. co. Louth 1897, M.A. Trin. Coll. Dublin, *b.* 7 April, 1839; *m.* 30 Dec. 1873, Frances Charlotte, dau. of the late Rev. Francis Hewson, Rector of Dungans-town, co. Wicklow, and has issue,

1. ALEXANDER HENRY, B.A., Camb., *b.* 14 March, 1876; *m.* 1904, Alys, eldest dau. of Robert Henry Sturrock Reade, of Wilmont, co. Antrim, and has issue,
    Frances Emily
2. Francis Thomas, *b.* 10 Sept. 1887.
1. Geraldine Mary, *m.* 1906, Cosmos Charles Richard Nevill, Capt. Royal Warwickshire Regt.

Mr. Lee-Norman is the only son of the late Alexander Norman, Q.C. (*see* NORMAN *of Glengollan*), by Charlotte Sarah his wife, dau. of Robert Law, of Dublin. He *s.* his cousin, THOMAS LEE-NORMAN, of Corbollis, who was son of Thomas Lee (son of William Lee, by Elizabeth Lucas his wife, and grandson of Thomas Lee, by Margaret Patten his wife, and great-grandson of Robert Lee), who *m.* Sarah, eldest dau. of Rev. Thomas Norman, of Lagore, and grand-dau. of Robert Norman, M.P. for Derry (*see* NORMAN *of Glengollan*). He assumed the name and arms of LEE-NORMAN by Royal Licence, 9 March, 1876.

Arms—Quarterly: 1st and 4th, or, a chevron between three lions' faces gu. for NORMAN; 2nd and 3rd, arg., a chevron gu. between three leopards' faces ppr. for LEE. Crests—1st, a lion passant guard. ppr. for NORMAN; 2nd, A demi-lion rampant grasping a sceptre all ppr. Motto—Honor virtutis præmium.

Seat—Corbollis, Ardee, co. Louth.

NORTH-BOMFORD. *See* BOMFORD.

NUGENT OF FARREN CONNELL.

COL. OLIVER STEWART WOOD NUGENT, D.S.O., of Farren Connell, co. Cavan, J.P. and D.L., Col. late King's Royal Rifle Corps, A.D.C. to the King, *b.* 9 Nov. 1860; *m.* 7 Feb. 1899, Catherine Percy, dau. of the late Thomas Evans Lees, of Beaucroft, Wimborne, Dorset (*see* BURKE'S *Peerage*, LEES, Bart.), and has issue,

1. OLIVER ST GEORGE PERCY *b* 30 Nov 1899.
1. Marian Catherine Trefiania, *b.* 31 May, 1903.
2. Alison Joan Elliott, *b.* 22 May, 1909.

Lineage.—OLIVER NUGENT, of Ballina, 3rd son

Nugent. THE LANDED GENTRY. 516

(by Marian, his wife, dau. of Nicholas, Lord Howth) of Sir Christopher Nugent eldest son and heir-apparent of Richard, 12th Lord Delvin, *m.* 1st, Anne, 2nd dau. of Christopher, 6th Lord Dunsany, by whom he had one son, CHRISTOPHER, ancestor of the NUGENTS *of Balinna*. He *m.* 2ndly, Miss Browne, of co. Westmeath, and by her was father of

WILLIAM NUGENT, of Rathanwear, *m.* Alison, dau. of Sir James Fitzsimon, of Tullynally, and had two sons,
1. OLIVER.
2. JAMES.

The former,

OLIVER NUGENT, of Enagh, co. Cavan, *m.* Joan, dau. of Christopher Nugent, of Kilmore, and by her had two sons,
1. Nicholas, of Enagh.
2. ROBERT, of whom we treat.

The latter,

ROBERT NUGENT, of Farren Connell, *b.* 1640; *m.* Margaret, dau. of Richard Dease, of Turbotstown, co. Westmeath, and had, with two daus., one son,

OLIVER NUGENT, of Bobsgrove, *b.* 1676; *m.* Catherine, dau. of Col. John Reilly, of Garryrocock, co. Cavan, and by her had, with three daus., a son and heir,

ROBERT NUGENT, of Bobsgrove, High Sheriff 1762, *b.* 5 Oct. 1703; *d.* 20 Jan. 1770; *m.* 2 Sept. 1740, Anastatia, dau. of Michael Lincoln, and had three sons,
1. OLIVER, his heir.
2. Richard, Capt. 31st Regt., and afterwards an Officer in the Russian Service, *b.* 1745; *d. unm.* 11 July, 1794.
3. Christopher, Capt. 49th Regt., *b.* 1746.

The eldest son,

OLIVER NUGENT, of Bobsgrove, High Sheriff 1788, *b.* 20 Oct. 1741; *m.* 24 June, 1766, Eleanor Mervyn, dau. of Christopher Irvine, of Castle Irvine, co. Fermanagh, and by her had issue,
1. Oliver, an officer in the Army, *b.* 1771; *d. unm.* 1794, *v.p.*
2. Richard, an Officer R.A., *b.* 1774; *d. unm.* 1794, *v.p.*
3. Robert William, Capt. Royal Irish Artillery, *d.s.p.* 1794.
4. CHRISTOPHER EDMOND JOHN, of whom presently.
1. Mervyn, *m.* the Very Rev. John William Keatinge, Dean of St. Patrick's, nephew to the 1st Lord Oriel, and *d.* March, 1811.
2. Henrietta Catherine Blanche, *m.* June, 1799, James O'Reilly, of Baltrasna, co. Meath, and *d.* April, 1823.

Mr. Nugent *d.* 10 July, 1813, and was *s.* by his youngest and then only surviving child,

CHRISTOPHER EDMOND JOHN NUGENT, of Bobsgrove, co. Cavan, an Officer of Dragoons, *b.* 22 June, 1777; *m.* 13 June, 1803, Sophia Maria Anne, eldest dau. of William Rathborne, of Scripplestown, co. Dublin, by Florence Elizabeth Anne his wife, dau. of William Irvine, M.P., of Castle Irvine, co. Fermanagh, and had issue,
1. OLIVER, *b.* 17 June, 1804; *m.* 30 Oct. 1837, Sophia Anna Maria, 2nd dau. of Robert Johnston, of Kinlough House, co. Leitrim, and dying 5 June, 1840, left a son,
   EDMOND ROBERT, of Kilrue, *b.* 8 Feb. 1839; *m.* 15 Dec. 1864, Ida Margaret, 3rd dau. of John Rowe, of Ballycross, D.L. co. Wexford, and *d.s.p.* 1876.
2. William Gavin, an Officer in the Madras Engineers, *b.* 17 June, 1805; *d. unm.* 24 Dec. 1828.
3. Edmond (Rev.), Vicar of Denn, co. Cavan, *b.* 17 Oct. 1808; *m.* 2 Dec. 1840, Frances (who *d.* 30 July, 1885), dau. of Matthew Nisbett, of Derricarne House, co. Leitrim, and *d.* 1 Nov. 1854, leaving a dau., Sophia Mary, *d. unm.* 27 March, 1911.
4. Robert George, *b.* 14 Oct. 1812; *d.* 29 Jan. 1835.
5. RICHARD, of Kilrue, J.P., co. Meath, *b.* 17 Aug. 1822; *m.* 5 Dec. 1848, Amelia St. George, dau. of Edward Stopford, D.D., Bishop of Meath, and *d.* 1891, having by her (who *d.* 25 April, 1879) had issue,
   1. Edward Stopford Edmond Richard, *b.* 23 Feb. 1851; *d.* 29 April, 1862.
   2. Richard Oliver William Beresford, *b.* 21 July, 1852; *d.* 9 Sept. following.
   1. Sophia Maria Anne Catherine.
   2. Amelia St. George Eugenie Hortense Catherine.
   3. Evelyn Florence Mervyn Irvine, *d.* 5 Jan. 1860.
6. ST. GEORGE MERVYN, of Farren Connell.
1. Henrietta Florence, *m.* Dec. 1827, Rev. Gorges Lowther Irvine, eldest son of Rev. William Henry Irvine, and grandson of Col. Irvine, M.P., and *d.* 13 March, 1834.
2. Sophia Letitia, *d.* young, 9 Nov. 1817.

Mr. Nugent, who was J.P. for co. Cavan, and served as High Sheriff 1821, *d.* 20 Feb. 1853. His youngest son,

ST. GEORGE MERVYN NUGENT, of Farren Connell, co. Cavan, Major-Gen. in the Army, severely wounded at Sobraon, *b.* 19 Jan. 1825; *m.* June, 1856, Emily Frances, dau. of Right Hon. Edward Litton, Master in Chancery in Ireland, M.P. Coleraine, and had issue,
1. Christopher Oliver St. George, *b.* 1857; *d.* 1858.
2. St. George Richard Litton, *b.* 1859; *d.* 1865.
3. OLIVER STEWART WOOD, now of Farren Connell.
4. Cyril Mervyn, *b.* 1 May, 1862; *d.* 1889.

Gen. Nugent *d.* 29 May, 1884.

Arms—Erm., two bars gu. Crest—A cockatrice rising vert, tail nowed, combed and wattled gu. Motto—Decrevi.

Seat—Farren Connell, Mount Nugent, co. Cavan. Clubs—Carlton, Army and Navy, and Kildare Street.

NUGENT OF PORTAFERRY.

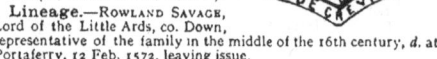

LIEUT.-COL. JOHN VESEY NUGENT, of Portaferry House, co. Down, J.P. and D.L., Lieut.-Col. (retired), formerly Capt and. Brevet-Major 51st K.O. Yorkshire L.I., *b.* 16 July, 1837; *s.* his brother 1905; *m.* 19 Jan. 1886, Emily Georgiana (who *d.* 2 April, 1909), dau. of the late Herbert Langham, of Cottesbrooke Park, Northamptonshire (*see* BURKE'S *Peerage*, LANGHAM, Bart.).

Lineage.—ROWLAND SAVAGE, Lord of the Little Ards, co. Down, representative of the family in the middle of the 16th century, *d.* at Portaferry, 12 Feb. 1572, leaving issue,
1. PATRICK, his heir.
2. Rowland, whose son, PATRICK SAVAGE, was father, with other issue, of two sons, John and Robert, of whom the elder,
   JOHN SAVAGE, of Ballyvarley, *m.* and had, with other issue,
   (1) PATRICK, of whom presently, as heir to Portaferry.
   (2) JAMES, *s.* his nephew at Portaferry.
   (3) Hugh, ancestor of SAVAGE *of Ballymadun*, co. Dublin.
   (1) Margaret, *m.* Hugh Trevor, and had issue.
3. Edmund, of Carney. 4. Richard, *d.s.p.*
5. James.

The eldest son,

PATRICK SAVAGE, Lord of the Little Ards, *b.* 1535; *m.* Anne Plunkett, and dying 31 Dec. 1603-4, left two sons,
1. ROWLAND, his heir. 2. PATRICK, *s.* his brother.

The elder son,

ROWLAND SAVAGE, Lord of the Little Ards, *m.* 20 April, 1604, Rose, dau. of George Russell, of Rathmullen, co. Down, and *d.* 25 June, 1619, leaving an only dau., *m.* Charles O'Hara, of co. Antrim, who *d.* 1639. He *d.* 25 June, 1619, and was *s.* by his brother, PATRICK SAVAGE, of Portaferry, *m.* 1623, Jean, only dau. of Hugh, 1st Viscount Montgomery, and by her (who *d.* 1647) had
1. HUGH, his heir.
1. Elizabeth, co-heir to her brother, *m.* George Wilton, of Gaulstown, co. Westmeath.
2. Sarah, co-heir to her brother, *m.* 1st, Sir Bryan O'Neill, Bart. of Bakerstown, so created for his gallantry at Edgehill, and had issue. She *m.* 2ndly, Richard Rich.

Patrick Savage *d.* 1644, and was *s.* by his son,

HUGH SAVAGE, of Portaferry, *d. unm.* 10 Feb. 1683, and was *s.* in the representation of the family by his cousin,

PATRICK SAVAGE, of Derry, and afterwards of Portaferry, who, by his wife Anne, dau. of F. Hall, of Narrow Water, co. Down, left issue,
1. Patrick, *d.* 13 June, 1712.
2. Rowland, *d.* 13 May, 1723; *m.* 1718, Margaret, dau. of Nicholas Price, of Saintfield, co. Down, by her (who *d.* April, 1721) he left an only dau.,
   Catherine, *m.* 10 Sept. 1740, Roger Hall, of Narrow Water, co. Down. 3. EDWARD, his heir.
4. Francis, *d.* 8 Jan. 1722.
5. Catharine, *m.* John Moore, of Drumbanagher.

Patrick Savage *d.* 13 Sept. 1724, aged 82, and was *s.* by his son,

EDWARD SAVAGE, of Portaferry, *d. unm.* 18 March, 1725, and was bur. at Portaferry. His uncle and successor,

JAMES SAVAGE, of Portaferry, *m.* Mabel, dau. of Edmund Magee, of Lisburn, co. Antrim, and was *s.* by his elder son,

JOHN SAVAGE, of Portaferry, *m.* Catharine, dau. of James Price, of Saintfield, co. Down, and had a son, James, who *d.* young. At his deccase he was *s.* by his brother,

ANDREW SAVAGE, of Portaferry, *m.* Margaret, sister and co-heir of Governor John Nugent, and dau. of Andrew Nugent, of Dysart, co. Westmeath, by his wife, the Lady Catherine Nugent, dau. and co-heir of Thomas, 4th Earl of Westmeath, and had a son and heir,

PATRICK SAVAGE, of Portaferry, High Sheriff 1763, *m.* 1765, Anne, dau. of Roger Hall, of Narrow Water, and by her had issue,
1. ANDREW, his heir.
2. Patrick Nugent, *m.* Harriet, dau. of Rev. Henry Sandiford, and had issue,
   1. Henry, who settled in Australia.
   2. Andrew, Capt. Marine Artillery, *b.* 1811.
   2. Anne, *m.* 1841, James Charles Price, of Saintfield.
   2. Harriet.
3. Roger Hall, Capt. R.N., *d. unm.*
4. John Lavallin, *d. unm.*
5. William (Rev.), Rector of Shinrone, King's Co., *m.* Elizabeth, dau. of Savage Hall, of Narrow Water (*see that family*), and had issue, four sons and three daus.
   1 Barbara, *m.* 10 Nov. 1812, Roger Hall, of Narrow Water (*see that family*).
   2. Dorcas Sophia.

Mr. Savage *d.* 7 March, 1797, and was *s.* by his eldest son, who, on inheriting the property of his great uncle, John Nugent, of Dysart, in 1812, assumed the surname of NUGENT, and became,

ANDREW NUGENT, of Portaferry, co. Down, J.P. and D.L., High Sheriff 1808, Lieut.-Col. of the North Down Militia, *b.* 3 June, 1770;

IRELAND. Nuttall.

m. 13 June, 1800, Hon. Selina Vesey, youngest dau. of Thomas, 1st Viscount de Vesci, and by her (who *d.* 7 Oct. 1857) had issue,
 1. PATRICK JOHN, his heir.
 2. Thomas Vesey, *b.* 1807 ; *m.* 1835, Frances Helen, eldest dau. of Sir James M. Stronge, 2nd bart. of Tynan Abbey, co. Armagh. She *d.* 8 July, 1908. He *d.* 1890, leaving issue,
  1. Andrew Robert, R.N., *b.* 22 June, 1836 ; *d.* Oct. 1856.
  2. Edmond Henry Stuart, *b.* 26 Jan. 1849 ; *m.* 25 March, 1885, Grace, youngest dau. of E. N. Conant, of Lyndon Hall, Oakham, and has issue, Roland Thomas. *b.* 19 June, 1886.
   1. Isabella Frances.
  2. Selina Florence, *m.* 15 Dec. 1864, Sir Edward Wingfield Verner, Bart., of Corke Abbey, near Bray, co. Dublin, and *d.* May, 1911, leaving issue.
 3. Andrew Savage, of Strangford, co. Down, a Major in the Army, late 36th Regt., J.P. and D.L. for that co., High Sheriff 1867, *b.* 28 May, 1809 ; *m.* 4 Oct. 1841, Hon. Harriet Margaret Maxwell, 2nd dau. of Henry, 6th Lord Farnham, and widow of Edward Southwell, 3rd Viscount Bangor, and *d.* 1889, having by her (who *d.* July, 1870) had issue,
  1. Walter Andrew, Lieut. R.E., *b.* 28 Dec. 1846 ; *d.* 1870.
  1. Harriet Annette Catherine, *m.* Feb. 1863, Henry Haswell Head, M.D., of Fitzwilliam Square, Dublin, and by him (who *d.* 13 June, 1910) had issue.
  2. Miriam Dora, *d. unm.* 9 Feb. 1902.
 4. Arthur, *b.* Dec. 1810 ; *m.* 1st, Charlotte, only dau. of Maj.-Gen. Brooke, of Colebrooke, co. Fermanagh, brother of Sir Henry Brooke, Bart., and by her (who *d.* 1870) had issue,
  Selina Catherine, *m.* 28 April, 1869, Hugh Sidney Baillie, eldest son of Right Hon. Henry James Baillie, of Redcastle, Rossshire, and *d.* 5 Nov. 1871.
 He *m.* 2ndly, 7 Dec. 1876, Isabella, 2nd dau. of John Tisdall, of Charlesfort, co. Meath. He *d.* 1896.
 5. Charles Lavallin William, Major-Gen. in the Army, *b.* 1815 ; *m.* Charlotte Alicia, dau. of Major-Gen. Pitt, and *d.* 1884, leaving issue,
  1. Charles, R.E., *b.* 1850, killed in action at Cabul 1879.
  2. George, Capt. R.A., *b.* 1852 ; *d.* 1898.
  3. Arthur, of Bally Edmond, co. Down, late Major Royal Fus., *b.* 1856 ; *m.* April, 1893, Elizabeth, dau. of Capt. Douglas, of Bellevue, Rostrevor, and has, with other issue, Arthur Charles, *b.* 1894.
  4. William Lavallin, *b.* 1858 ; *m.* 1897, Ethel, dau. of Rev. J. Pillars.
  5. Rowland, Capt. R.N., *b.* 1861 ; *m.* Frances, dau. of F. Rutherford.
  6. Walter Thomas Henry, Lieut. Hampshire Regt., *b.* 1868 ; killed in action in Burmah 1889.
  7. Raymond Andrew, Capt. R.N., *m.* 1906, Adelaide Georgina, dau. of Major F. D. Forde.
  1. Amy Selina, *m.* 1882, Lieut. F. Laye, R.N. He *d.* 1884.
  2. Edith Charlotte.
  3. Mabel, *m.* 1890, G. McRobert, and *d.* 1908, leaving issue.
 1. Selina Elizabeth, *m.* 17 June, 1836, Sir James Stronge, 3rd bart. of Tynan Abbey. He *d.s.p.* 11 March, 1885. She *d.* 23 July, 1903.
 2. Anne Margaret, *m.* Sept. 1845, Samuel Madden Francis Hall, of Narrow Water, late Major 75th Regt. He *d.s.p.* 17 Feb. 1875. She *d.* 28 Jan. 1895.
Lieut.-Col. Nugent *d.* 2 Feb. 1846, and was *s.* by his eldest son,
 PATRICK JOHN NUGENT, of Portaferry, Lieut.-Col. of the North Down Militia, and High Sheriff co. Down 1843, *b.* 1804 ; *m.* 29 April, 1833, his cousin, Hon. Catherine Vesey, dau. of John, 2nd Viscount de Vesci, and by her (who *d.* 27 Feb. 1882) had issue,
 1. ANDREW, late of Portaferry.
 2. JOHN VESEY, now of Portaferry.
 3. Arthur Vesey, late 17th Regt., *b.* 2 March, 1841 ; *d.s.p.* 21 Dec. 1894.
 1. Frances Isabella, *m.* April, 1862, Capt. George Barrington Price, late of the Scots Greys. He *d.* 22 Jan. 1910.
Mr. Nugent *d.* Nov. 1857. His eldest son,
 LIEUT.-GEN. ANDREW NUGENT, of Portaferry House, co. Down, J.P. and D.L., High Sheriff 1882, Lieut.-Gen. in the Army, Col. of the Royal Scots Greys, *b.* 30 March, 1834, and *d.* 10 July, 1905, and was *s.* by his brother.

Arms—Erm., two bars gu. **Crest**—A cockatrice, wings expanded, tail nowed vert. combed and wattled gu. **Motto**—Decrevi.

Seat—Portaferry, co. Down.

NUGENT. *See* BURKE'S PEERAGE, **WESTMEATH, E.**

NUTTALL OF TITTOUR.

JOHN WILLIAM McINTOSH NUTTALL, of Tittour, co. Wicklow, J.P., B.A. (T.C.D. 1864), *b.* 3 Dec. 1841 ; *m.* 23 Sept. 1884, Katherine Rebecca Fetherstonhaugh, eldest dau. of the late John Fetherstonhaugh Briscoe, J.P., of Grangemore, co. Westmeath.

Lineage.—RAPHE NUTTALL, of Tottington, *m.* Alice, widow of Laurence Crompton, of Brightmet, co. Lancaster, and *d.* 1634, having had issue,
 1. Thomas, of Tottington, aged 52 years, when he entered his pedigree (1664), and had the arms of Nuttall (anciently Notogh of Notogh, co. Lancaster) confirmed to him, 11 March, 1664 ; *m.* Margaret, dau. of William Orrell, of Turton, co. Lancaster.
 2. LAURENCE, of whom presently.
 3. Ralph, clerk in holy orders.

The 2nd son,
 LAURENCE NUTTALL, of Tottington (will dated 17 July, JAC. II. 1685, proved by his widow, 10 July, 1686), *m.* Margaret, dau. of Henry Woode, of Milhouse, and by her (whose will, dated 20 Aug. 3 JAC. II. 1687, was proved 23 May, 1688, at Chester) had issue,
 1. Thomas, of Tottington, *m.* Eleanor, dau. and co-heir of John Taylor, Horridge Hall, Oldham, co. Lancaster. His will was dated 14 March, 1726, and proved at Chester.
 2. CHRISTOPHER, of whom presently.
 1. Alice, *m.* John Crompton.

The 2nd son,
 CHRISTOPHER NUTTALL, Major in Stanwax's Regt., formerly Capt. 12th Foot, *m.* Elizabeth, dau. of — Henley, and had issue,
 1. John, mentioned in the will of his brother Thomas, 1707.
 2. Thomas, a Lieut. in Col. Lindsay's Regt. ; his will, dated 19 Aug. 1707, was proved 23 Oct. same year, in London.
 3. JAMES, of whom hereafter.
 1. Mary Fetherstone, } mentioned in the will of their brother
 2. Hannah, } Thomas, 1707.

The 3rd son,
 JAMES NUTTALL, of Dublin, gent., living 1753, Capt. 12th Regt. of Foot, *m.* about 1707, Anne, dau. of John Hunter, of Ballysorrell, co. Tipperary (*s.* to the estate of Dromardbegg from her father), and had issue,
 1. CHRISTOPHER, of whom presently.
 2. John, of Mount Nebs, co. Wexford, Capt. 60th Regt., *m.* 25 July, 1771, Elizabeth, 2nd dau. of John Gowan, of co. Wexford, and *d.* 23 Oct. 1773 (will dated 16 Sept. and proved 19 Nov. 1773). He had an only child,
  Mary Anne, *m.* James Burkitt, of Sea View House, Clonevin, co. Wexford, and has issue.
 3. Thomas, of Dublin, *m.* Mary, dau. of James Williams, and had issue.
 1. Mabella, *m.* William Alley, and had issue.

The eldest son,
 CHRISTOPHER NUTTALL, of Drumard, co. Tipperary, *m.* Dec. 1736, Sarah (*b.* 3 Dec. 1701 ; *d.* 24, and was bur. 25 Jan. 1775), dau. and co-heir of Capt. George Barker, and had issue,
 1. GEORGE BARKER, of whom afterwards.
 2. James, *b.* 5 Oct. 1741 ; *m.* Sarah Wilson, and had issue.
 3. Christopher, of Donnybrook Road, Dublin, an Officer in the Army, *b.* 7 Sept. 1743 ; *d. unm.* at Donnybrook, 20 July, 1782 ; will dated 16 and proved 26 July, 1782.
 1. Martha Ann, *b.* 4 Dec. 1739 ; *m.* 23 June, 1768, Lieut. Thomas Bell, and had issue.
Mr. Nuttall (whose will was dated 10 March, 1772, and proved in Dublin, 4 July, 1775) *d.* 28, and was bur. 30 June, 1775. His eldest son,
 GEORGE BARKER NUTTALL, of Tittour, co. Wicklow, and Merrion Street, Dublin, J.P., Cornet in his Majesty's 2nd Regt. of Horse, *b.* at Drumard House, co. Tipperary, 19 Jan. 1738 ; *m.* 10 Sept. 1769, Anne (*b.* 1751 ; *d.* 12 April, 1804), dau. of Dr. John Freeman, of co. Oxford, and had issue,
 1. Robert Henry, *b.* 28 Dec. 1770, at St. Stephen's Green, Dublin ; bapt. 11 Feb. 1771 ; an Officer of the 38th Regt. of Foot ; was killed whilst leading the Grenadiers when fighting against the French at St. Lucia, West Indies, 1796.
 2. JOHN CHRISTOPHER, of whom hereafter.
 3. Henry Quin, *b.* 4 June, 1776 ; bapt. 30 June following ; *d.* young.
 4. George, *b.* 8 Oct. ; bapt. 15 Oct. 1787 ; an Officer in the Army, killed on active service, 28 May, 1813, at Sacketts Harbour, Lake Ontario.
 5. Thomas, *b.* 23 Feb., bapt. 13 March, 1791 ; *d.* 15 Jan. 1792.
 1. Isabella Mary Anne, *b.* 2 April, 1772 ; bapt. 21 April, 1772 ; *d. unm.* 15 Jan. 1847.
 2. Jane, *b.* 23 July, 1773 ; bapt. 17 Aug. same year ; *d. unm.* 12, and was bur. 15 Nov. 1830. Her will, dated 2 April, 1828, was proved 24 Sept. 1851, at Dublin.
 3. Elizabeth, *b.* 5 July, 1778 ; *d. unm.* 30, and was bur. 31 July, 1778.
 4. Anne Margaret, *b.* 8 June, and bapt. 8 July, 1781 ; *m.* — Bradley, and had issue.
 5. Elizabeth Mary, *b.* 8 Aug., bapt. 2 Sept. 1782 ; *d.* 27 Feb. 1817.
 6. A dau., *b.* 3 Sept. 1793 ; *d.* 1 Sept. 1794.
Mr. Nuttall (whose will was dated 18 Oct. 1804) *d.* at Merrion Street, 6 Feb. 1806. His 2nd son,
 JOHN CHRISTOPHER NUTTALL, of Tittour, Newtown-Mount-Kennedy, co. Wicklow, *b.* at Drumbane, 25 Oct., and bapt. 22 Nov. 1774 ; J.P. co. Wicklow ; *s.* to the paternal estates on the death of his elder brother, retired from active service with rank of Major. 1819 ; *m.* 21 July, 1808, Dorothea Annabella, 3rd and youngest dau. of Daniel Falkiner, of Abbotstown, co. Dublin, and co-heir of her brother, Col. Sir Frederick Falkiner, Bart., M.P. By her (who *d.* 24 March, 1860) he had issue,
 1. JOHN FREEMAN, of whom afterwards.
 2. George Frederick William, *b.* 15 April, 1813 ; *m.* 6 May, 1841, Maria Margaret, dau. of Capt. Thomas Harris, 45th Regt., and niece of Sir Henry Brooke, Bart. of Colebrook, co. Fermanagh. He *d.s.p.* 25 Aug. 1885.

O'Beirne. THE LANDED GENTRY. 518

3. Robert Kennedy, M.D. (Aberdeen), and L.R.C.S.I., b. 9 April, 1815, bapt. 11 May following; m. Magdalena (who d. 14 Sept. 1911, age 77), eldest dau. of John Parrott, late of San Francisco, banker, and d. 21 May, 1881 (bur. at Laurel Hill Cemetery, San Francisco), having had issue,
  1. John Robert Kennedy, b. 12 and bapt. 25 Dec. 1854, in St. Mary's Cathedral, San Francisco; m. 18 June, 1884, Hilda, only dau. of Samuel Wolf Roscustock, of San Francisco. He d.s.p. 4 June, 1908.
  2. George Henry Falkiner (3, *Cranmer Road, Cambridge*), b. 5 and bapt. 22 July, 1862; M.D. (California); Ph.D. (Göttingen), M.A. (*Hon. causa*) and Sc.D. (Cantab.), F.R.S., late Fellow of Christ's Coll., Fellow Magdalene Coll., Quick Professor of Biology, Univ. of Cambridge; m. 26 April, 1895, Paula Carola Minda, dau. of Hans Friedrich von Oertzen (Chamberlain to the Grand Duke of Mecklenburg-Strelitz), of Kittendorf, by his wife Alma Marie, Baroness von Kothen, and has issue,
    (1) George Robert Hans Falkiner, b. 24 July, 1896.
    (2) Winfred Lawrence Freeman Falkiner, b. 17 July, 1897.
    (3) Carmelite Alma Magdelina Falkiner, b. 2 Feb. 1902.
3. Robert Tiburcio, b. 5, and bapt. 12 Dec. 1868; d. 10, and bur. 14 June, 1869, in Dresden, Saxony.
  1. Zelia Maria Magdalena, b. 6 Sept. 1857; m. 10 May, 1880, Alphonse Louis Pinart (d. 13 Feb. 1911), from whom she afterwards obtained a divorce, had issue,
    Nadinie Carmelita Nuttall, m. 14 Dec. 1904, Arthur E. S. Laughton, son of Sir John Knox Laughton.
  2. Carmelita Dorothea, b. 12 Nov. 1859; m. 11 Nov. 1880, James Valentine Coleman, of San Francisco, and d.s.p. 9 July, 1885.
  3. Roberta Louise, b. 14 Nov. 1870, m. 12 Dec. 1902, Franz Maximilian Ludwig, Baron Von Rigal-Grunland, Chamberlain to H.M. the German Emperor, and has issue.
1. Maria Elizabeth Josepha, b. 15 May, 1809; m. 4 May, 1830, John Frederick Clarke, M.D., F.R.C.S.I., Inspector-General of Bengal Hospitals, and d. 15 Oct. 1834, leaving issue. He d. and was bur. 1 Nov. 1848.
2. Henrietta Jemima, m. 13 July, 1837, William Philips, Barrister-at-Law, and d. 21 Aug. 1891, leaving issue. He d. 26 Feb. 1857.
Mr. Nuttall d. 7 Nov. 1849. His eldest son,
JOHN FREEMAN NUTTALL, of Tittour, b. 3 June, 1819; J.P. co. Wicklow; m. 1 Aug. 1838, Lucinda Helena, dau. of William M'Intosh, of St. Stephen's Green, Dublin, and by her (who d. 16 Jan. 1887) had issue,
1. JOHN WILLIAM MCINTOSH, now of Tittour.
2. Æneas Falkiner, of Culleenamore, Sligo, b. 18 June, 1847; bapt. 3 Jan. 1848; m. 16 July, 1889, Ellinor Kate, relict of William Knox Barrett, of Culleenamore, and 5th dau. of the late Rev. William Travers Homan, and has issue,
  1. Freeman Æneas Falkiner, b. 20 Jan. 1891.
  2. Ino Lawrence Kennedy, b. 15 March, 1892.
  3. Travers Homan Ercildoune, b. 28 Oct. 1895.
  4. Orrell Hyde Herbert, b. 22 Nov. 1898.
  1. Iris Nello Carmelita, b. 9 June, 1894.
3. Frederick Freeman, b. in Dublin 11 June, 1851; m. 7 April, 1886, Louisa Gertrude Ada, eldest dau. of Conte Thomas Schiassi, of Bologna, Italy, and d.s.p. 25 April, 1897.
4. Edward James Macpherson, b. 14 Feb. 1856.
5. Henry Evelyn Barker, b. 14 May, 1861; m. 31 March, 1892, Alice Beatrice, dau. of Thomas Hammond, and has issue,
  1. John Henry Falkiner, b. 2 June, 1896.
  2. Frederick James Freeman, b. 29 Nov. 1899.
  3. Arthur Bryan Barker, b. 16 April, 1904.
  1. Dorothea Madeline Beatrice, b. 24 April, 1893.
  2. Lucinda Sarah Evelyn, b. 2 Feb. 1895.
1. Anna Dorothea, m. 19 April, 1877, John Harrison, of Dromore, co. Down, J.P., and has issue.
2. Georgina Mary, b. 12 Oct. 1843.
3. Kennetta Lucinda, b. 12 June, 1849.
4. Robina Elizabeth, m. 27 Jan. 1883, Daniel O'Connell, of Surmount, co. Cork, and has issue.
5. Madeline Annabella, m. 20 June, 1883, William Thomas Brabazon, of Johnstown House, Johnstown, co. Meath, and has issue.
6. Helena Isabella, b. 22 Jan. 1858.
Mr. Nuttall (whose will, dated 23 May, 1866, was proved 26 May, 1879) was accidentally drowned at Howth, co. Dublin, 19 Dec. 1878.

Seat—Tittour, Newtown Mountkennedy, co. Wicklow.

O'BEIRNE OF JAMESTOWN.

HUGH JAMES O'BEIRNE, C.V.O., C.B. of Jamestown, co. Leitrim, J.P. and D.L., Councillor of Embassy at St. Petersburg, sometime Chargé d'Affaires, b. 7 Sept. 1866.

Lineage.—FRANCIS O'BEIRNE, of Jamestown (son of Hugh O'Beirne, who d. 1813, by his wife, the dau. of — Keon, of Keonbrook co. Leitrim), m. 2 March, 1826, Winefred Nolan, and by her (who d. 1852) had issue,
1. HUGH, late of Jamestown.
2. Francis, of Jamestown, co. Leitrim, Col. late 2nd Dragoon Guards, late M.P. co. Leitrim, d. 11 April, 1899.

1. Mary, m. 1852, Capt. George Talbot, C.B., of Knockmullen, Chief Commissioner of the Metropolitan Police. Dublin, 1877-82 (see TALBOT *of Castle Talbot*). She d. 25 Feb. 1908, leaving issue,
2. Fanny, m. J. M. Monahan, Q.C., eldest son of the Right Hon. Lord Chief Justice Monahan, and has issue.
3. Julia, m. John Ball, M.P., eldest son of Right Hon. Judge Ball. She d. his widow 17 Dec. 1905.
Mr. O'Beirne d. 1854. His eldest son,
HUGH O'BEIRNE, of Jamestown, co. Leitrim, J.P. and D.L., High Sheriff 1855, m. 26 Jan. 1858, Elizabeth, dau. of Right Hon. J. H. Monahan, Lord Chief Justice of the Court of Common Pleas in Ireland, and had issue,
1. FRANCIS, late of Jamestown Lodge.
2. HUGH JAMES, now of Jamestown.
3. Joseph, b. 12 July, 1874; d. unm. 21 Aug. 1895.
4. George John, b. 24 Dec. 1877; d. 10 Sept. 1883.
1. Mary Frances Josephine, d. 1875.
2. Frances Geraldine Julia, d. 1875.
Mr. O'Beirne d. 16 Sept. 1880, and was s. by his eldest son,
FRANCIS O'BEIRNE, of Jamestown, b. 28 Dec. 1864; d. unm. 1889, when he was s. by his brother.

Seat:—Jamestown, Drumsna. *Residence* British Embassy, St. Petersburg.

O'BRIEN OF CAHIRMOYLE.

WILLIAM DERMOD O'BRIEN, of Cahirmoyle, co. Limerick, D.L., President Royal Hibernian Academy, b. 10 June, 1865; m. 8 March, 1902, Mabel, dau. of late Sir Philip Smyly (see SMYLY *of Camus*), and has issue,
1. BRENDAN EDWARD, b. 11 Jan. 1903.
2. David Lucius, b. 6 Aug. 1904.
3. Horace Donough, b. 24 June, 1911.
1. Mary Elinor, b. 1 Feb. 1907.
2. Rosaleen Brigid, b. 29 Jan. 1909.

Lineage.—SIR EDWARD O'BRIEN, 4th bart. of Dromoland, M.P. for Ennis 1795-1800 and for co. Clare 1802-26, b. 17 April, 1773; d. 13 March, 1837; m. 12 Nov. 1799, Charlotte, eldest dau. and co-heir of William Smith, of Cahirmoyle, and by her (who d. 28 Sept. 1856) had, with other issue (see BURKE's *Peerage*, INCHIQUIN, B.), a 2nd son,
WILLIAM (SMITH) O'BRIEN, M.P., of Cahirmoyle, who d. 18 June, 1864; m. 19 Sept. 1832, Lucy Caroline, his wife, who d. 13 June, 1861, dau. of Joseph Gabbett, of High Park. They had, with other issue (see BURKE's *Peerage*), an eldest son,
EDWARD WILLIAM O'BRIEN, of Cahirmoyle, co. Limerick, J.P. and D.L., High Sheriff 1869, B.A., T.C.D., b. 24 Jan. 1837; d. 22 Jan. 1909; m. 1st, 8 Sept. 1863, Mary Spring, and dau. of the Hon. Stephen Edmund Spring-Rice, of Mount Trenchard, co. Limerick, and sister of Thomas, Lord Monteagle, and by her (who d. 25 April, 1868) had issue,
1. WILLIAM DERMOD, of Cahirmoyle.
1. Ellen Lucy.
2. Lucy Mary, m. 24 Jan. 1894, Arthur Beresford Cane, Barrister-at-Law, of the Inner Temple, and has issue.
Mr. O'Brien m. 2ndly, 31 Jan. 1880, Julia Mary, dau. of the late James Garth Marshall, of Leeds and Coniston, Lancashire, by Mary Alicia Pery his wife, dau. of 1st Lord Monteagle, and by her (who d. 2 March, 1907) had issue,
2. Edward Conor Marshall, b. 3 Nov. 1880.
3. Aubrey Ulick Marshall, Lieut. R.F.A., b. 7 June, 1882.
3. Katharine Jenny. 4. Margaret Ernestine.

Arms—Quarterly: 1st and 4th gu., three lions passant guardant in pale, per pale or and arg.; 2nd arg., three piles meeting in point issuing from the chief gu.; 3rd or, a pheon az. Crest—Issuing from a cloud an arm embowed, brandishing a sword arg, pomel and hilt or. Mottoes—Over the crest, "Lamh laidir an uachtar," and "Vigueur de dessus."

Seat—Cahirmoyle, Ardagh, co. Limerick. Club—Kildare Street, Dublin.

O'BRIEN OF BALLYNALACKEN.

TORLOGH O'BRIEN, of Ballynalacken Castle, co. Clare, J.P., High Sheriff 1906, b. 1868.

Lineage.—TORLOGH, or TERENCE O'BRIEN, of Leitrim, m Elizabeth, dau. of Henry O'Brien of Bealagh Corick, by Catherine his wife, sister of Col. Maurice O'Connell, and had issue,

1. TURLOUGH, of whom presently.
2. John, who m. Miss Foster, and had a son, Terence, who d.s.p.
1. Catherine, a nun.

The elder son,
TURLOGH, or TERENCE O'BRIEN, of Cross (subsequently called Elm Vale), m. Eleanor, dau. of Murtagh O'Hogan, of Cross, by Eleanor Butler his wife, niece of Sir Toby Butler, Knt., M.P., Chief Commissioner of the Irish at the capitulation of Limerick, and had issue,

1. John, of Elm Vale, co. Clare, m. Margaret Macnamara, and d.s.p. 1792. His will, dated Feb. in that year, was proved 20 Dec. following.
2. JAMES, of whom presently.

The 2nd son,
JAMES O'BRIEN, of Elm Vale, co. Clare, s. his brother; m. Feb. 1791, Margaret, dau. of Peter Long, by Anne his wife, elder dau. of Stephen Roche, of Limerick, and by her (who m. 2ndly, Cornelious O'Brien, M.P. for Clare, and d. 6 April, 1839) left issue,

1. JOHN, of whom presently.
2. Peter, of Limerick, b. Sept. 1799; m. Emily, dau. of Edward Shiel, and sister of the Right Hon. Richard Lalor Shiel, and d.s.p. Sept. 1855.
3. Terence, b. Dec. 1802; d. unm. March, 1820.
4. James, one of the Judges of the Queen's Bench in Ireland, and M.P. for Limerick 1854 to 1858. b. 27 Feb. 1806; m. 9 July, 1836, Margaret, dau. of Thomas Segrave, and d. 1882, leaving,
   1. John Henry, b. 25 Feb. 1855; d. 19 May, 1905.
   1. Anne, a nun.   2. Margaret, a nun.
   3. Mary, m. Henry J. Monahan, 2nd son of Lord Chief Justice Monahan.   4. Clara, a nun.
5. Emily.

Mr. O'Brien d. 21 Feb. 1806, and was s. by his eldest son,
JOHN O'BRIEN, of Elm Vale, and afterwards of Ballynalacken, M.P. for Limerick 1841 to 1852, High Sheriff co. Clare 1836, b. 6 Dec. 1794; m. 12 June, 1827, Ellen, dau. of Jeremiah Murphy, of Hyde Park, co. Cork, and by her (who d. 19 Dec. 1860) had issue,

1. JAMES, of Ballynalacken Castle.
2. Jerome, late 28th Regt., b. 1835; m. 1867, Elizabeth, dau. of Robert Clarke, of Bansha, J.P. co. Tipperary (see CLARKE of Graignenoe), and d. 1892, having had issue,
   1. TORLOGH, now of Ballynalacken.
   2. James, b. 1876.
   1. Nathalie, m. 15 July, 1909, Godwin Butler Meade Swifte, of Swiftsheath, co. Kilkenny. D.L. (see that family).
3. John, a Cistercian monk, d.s.p. 1889.
4. William, Indian R.H.A., d. unm.
5. Peter, LORD O'BRIEN, Lord Chief Justice of Ireland, created a bart. 28 Sept. 1891, and raised to the Peerage 16 June, 1900 (see BURKE's Peerage).
6. Terence, d. unm.
1. Margaret, m. James Martin, of 90, Fitzwilliam Square, Dublin.
2. Ellen, m. Robert Daniell, J.P. of New Forest, co. Westmeath.
3. Catto, a nun, dec.   4. Anna, a nun.

Mr. O'Brien d. 6 Feb. 1855. His eldest son,
JAMES O'BRIEN, of Ballynalacken Castle, co. Clare, J.P. and D.L., High Sheriff 1858, b. 9 Jan. 1832; m. 1865, Georgina, dau. of G. Martyn, and widow of Francis Macnamara Calcutt, J.P., M.P., of St. Catherine's, co. Clare, and d. 1904, being s. by his nephew.

Arms—Gu., three lions passant guardant in pale, per pale or and arg. a chief of the 2nd. **Crest**—An arm embowed vested az., brandishing a sword arg., pommelled and hilted or, charged with a fasces in pale ppr. **Motto**—Vigueur de dessus.

Seat—Ballynalacken Castle, Lisdoonvarna, co. Clare. **Club**—Kildare Street.

O'BRIEN. See BURKE's PEERAGE, **INCHIQUIN, B.**

O'BRIEN. See BURKE's PEERAGE, **O'BRIEN, Bart.**

STAFFORD-O'BRIEN. See **STAFFORD-O'BRIEN OF BLATHERWYKE, NORTHANTS.**

O'BYRNE late OF ALLARDSTOWN AND CORVILLE.

EDWARD ALEXANDER O'BYRNE, of Annfield and Buolick, co. Tipperary, a Count of Rome, b. 1865; m. 1 Sept. 1892, Rose Emily, 4th dau. and co-heiress of Joshua James Netterville, J.P. (see MacEvoy of Tobertynan and Mount Hazel), and has issue,

1. JOHN EDWARD, b. 23 Aug. 1894.
2. Terence, b. 11 March, 1911.
1. Eleanor.   2. Elizabeth.   3. Geraldine.
4. Rose Mary.

Lineage.—JOHN BYRNE of Mullinahack, Dublin, one of the brothers, seven in number, who were partners in the great and extensive firm of "John Byrne & Co. of Mullinahack," m. Elizabeth, only dau. of Henry Byrne, of Allardstown and Mount Byrne (who d. 22 March, 1796), and Mary Anne Colman, his wife, and grand-dau. of Henry Byrne, who d. 18 Dec. 1761. The issue of the marriage consisted of one son and two daus.,

1. EDWARD HENRY, s. to Allardstown and Corville.
1. Elizabeth Mary.   2. Pauline, m. Capt. Edward Hunter.

The only son,
EDWARD HENRY O'BYRNE, of Allardstown and Corville, also of St. Gery, near Toulouse, France, b. 18 Dec. 1800; m. 24 Nov. 1828, Gertrude de Rey, dau. of John de Rey, Marquis de St. Gery, by his wife, Mary Christine MacCarthy, and d. leaving issue,

1. JOHN, Count O'Byrne.   2. Edward, d. unm. 1890.
3. Henry, m. 1873, Elizabeth du Bourg, and d. 25 March, 1898, leaving issue, with four daus.,
   1. Henry.   2. Edward.
   3. Gabriel.
1. Mary, m. 9 Feb. 1860, the Comte de Maistre, and had an only son.

JOHN O'BYRNE, of Allardstown, co. Louth, and Corville, co. Tipperary, J.P., a Count of Rome, b. 1835; m. 17 April, 1864, Eleanor, dau. of the late Count von Hübner, late Austrian Ambassador to France and Rome, and d. 27 Sept. 1905. leaving issue,

1. EDWARD ALEXANDER, now of Annfield and Buolick.
2. Patrick Joseph, of Corville, Roscrea, co. Tipperary, b. 30 Aug. 1870; m. 18 Aug. 1897, Bernadette 4th dau. of the late John Boland, and has issue,
   Muriel.
1. Mary, m. 12 Oct. 1886, John Appleyard O'Kelly, of Gurtray, co. Galway, and has issue.
2. Gertrude, m. Henri Soleille, of Toulouse, France.
3. Eleanor, m. 1 June, 1897, Patrick Joseph Boland, eldest son of the late John Boland, and has issue.
4. Bridget.
5. Ita.   6. Dymphna.

Seat—Villa Erin, St.-Jean-de-Luz, France.

O'CALLAGHAN OF MARYFORT.

JOHN O'CALLAGHAN, of Maryfort, and Fort Anne, co. Clare, J.P. and D.L., late Col. Commandant Clare Artillery, and formerly Capt. 62nd Foot, b. 3 May, 1829; m. 24 March, 1859, Mary Johnson, eldest dau. of John Westropp, of Attyflin, co. Limerick, and has issue,

GEORGE O'CALLAGHAN-WESTROPP, of Coolreagh, Bodyke, co. Clare, last Col. Commanding Clare Artillery, late Capt. 1st Batt. Royal Irish Rifles, Aide-de-Camp to the King, b. 18 Feb. 1864, assumed by Royal Licence, dated 8 June, 1885, the surname of WESTROPP, in addition to and after that of O'Callaghan, and the arms of WESTROPP, quarterly with those of O'CALLAGHAN, in compliance with the will of his maternal uncle, Capt. Ralph Westropp. He m. 27 March, 1895, Henrietta Cecile Rose, only dau. of the late Capt. George Augustus Barrington Godbold, 27th Inniskilling Fusiliers, by Henrietta his wife, dau. of James Foster Vesey-Fitzgerald, D.L., of Moyriesk, co. Clare (see that family), and has issue,
1. Rose Mary Hope.
2. Hilda Daphne.
3. Geraldine Henrietta Iris.

O'Callaghan. THE LANDED GENTRY. 520

Lineage.—The O'Callaghans derive their descent and name from CEALLACHAN CAISIL, the famous King of Munster in the 10th century. The O'CALLAGHANS *of Cadogan* are a branch of O'CALLAGHAN *of Clonmeen* and *Drumaneen*, co. Cork.

DONOUGH O'CALLAGHAN, of Duhallow, co. Cork, claimed descent from CEALLACHAN CAISIL, King of Cashel, who defeated the Danes of Limerick in 952, and was chief of the Eoghanists. Donough *d.* 1572. His 2nd son,

CONOR O'CALLAGHAN, of Drummaneen, co. Cork, confirmed in his estates by Queen ELIZABETH, 7 Dec. 1594. His son,

KELLADAN O'CALLAGHAN, was father of

CAHIR O'CALLAGHAN, named " Modarta," of Drummaneen, 1644. His son,

DONOUGH O'CALLAGHAN, *m.* Ellen, dau. and co-heiress of Callaghan, The O'Callaghan, of Clonmeen, and his wife Joan, dau. of James, Duke of Ormond. Donough was a member of the Kilkenny confederacy, and was transplanted to Mountallon, co. Clare, and confirmed in same by Act of Settlement, 1665. His son,

DONOUGH O'CALLAGHAN, of Mountallon and Kilgorey, under leases, 16 Nov. 1675. His will dates 31 March, 1698. He *d. ante* 1700, leaving, with other issue, by his wife, Mary, a son,

DANIEL O'CALLAGHAN, of Mountallon and Kilgorey, *m.* Catherine, dau. of Nicholas Purcell, of Loughmoe, and by her (who *d.* 1731) he had,
 1. Donough, of Kilgorey, *m.* 1742, Hannah, dau. of Christopher O'Brien, of Newhall, and had two sons,
  1. Daniel, who *d. unm.* 1772, in Dublin.
  2. Edmond, of Kilgorey, who *m.* 11 June, 1785, Helen, dau. of Denis O'Brien, of Dublin, by whom he had issue, four daus.,
   (1) Bridget, *m.* Thomas Reilly.
   (2) Catherine, *m.* Thomas, Earl of Kenmare.
   (3) Helen, *m.* James Bagot, of Castle Bagot.
   (4) Elizabeth, *m.* Gerald Dease.
 2. CORNELIUS, of whom we treat.

He *d.* at Kilgorey, 1724. His son,

CORNELIUS O'CALLAGHAN, of Kilgorey, 1745, *m.* Olivia, dau. of Henry Brady, of Kilconry, and was living 1790 ; bur. at Tulla. He left issue,
 1. Donatus, *m.* 14 Aug. 1790, Charlotte, dau. of John Bayly, of Debsborough.
 2. JOHN, of whom hereafter.
 3. Charles, of Ross, co. Clare, *m.* 22 July, 1791, Anne Purdon, of Belkelly.
 4. CORNELIUS, of Ballinahinch, Tulla, co. Clare, *m.* 1st, Harriet dau. of Edward O'Brien, 3rd son of Sir Edward O'Brien, 2nd bart. (*see* BURKE's *Peerage*, INCHIQUIN, B.). She *d.s.p.* He *m.* 2ndly, Frances Westby, dau. of Henry Brady, and *d.* Oct. 1829, having by her (who *m.* 2ndly, 1844, Rev. Lord William Somerset, 6th son of the 3rd Duke of Beaufort, K.G., and *d.* 31 Aug. 1854) had issue,
  Charles George Martin, of Ballinahinch, co. Clare, J.P. and D.L., High Sheriff 1855, Capt. 1st Dragoon Guards, *b.* 1821 ; *m.* 1856, Marian, dau. of J. Kelly, of Dublin, and *d.* 29 Oct. 1895, having by her (who *d.* 1871) had issue,
   (1) Frances, *m.* Lieut. E. Loder, and *d.* Aug. 1879, leaving issue.
   (2) Nora Kathleen, *m.* 28 April, 1886, Capt. Edgar Waldegrave Brodie, late 60th Rifles (*see* BURKE's *Peerage and Baronetage*), and has issue.
  Mary, *m.* 1848, Henry Bourchier Osborne Savile, C.B., Capt. late R.A. She *d.* 1870, leaving issue (*see that family*).
 5. Henry.
 1. Christian, *m.* Richard Creagh, of Dangan, co. Clare.

The 2nd son,

JOHN O'CALLAGHAN, of Kilgorey, High Sheriff of Clare 1807, *b.* 1754 ; *m.* 1st, 1 Dec. 1784, Catherine, dau. of George Colpoys, of Ballycarr, and eventually heiress to those estates, by whom he had issue,
 1. Cornelius, *b.* 27 Sept. 1786 ; *d. unm.* 29 April, 1824.
 2. GEORGE, his heir.
 3. Donat, *b.* 15 July, 1789, *d.* in infancy.
 4. John, of Knockagrady, *b.* 25 Sept. 1791 ; *m.* the widow of — Boucher, and dau. of Vesey Daly, of Galway. She *d.s.p.* 27 June, 1872.

He *m.* 2ndly, 14 March, 1795, Catherine, niece of Sir Lucius O'Brien, Bart., and dau. of Capt. Edward O'Brien, of Ennis, and had issue,
 5. Edward, of Coolready, *m.* Miss Sampson, and *d.s.p.* in 1841.

John O'Callaghan, who was also of Coolready, and lastly of Lismehan, now of Maryfort, *d.* 22 Oct. 1818. His eldest surviving son,

GEORGE O'CALLAGHAN, of Maryfort, *b.* 15 June, 1788 ; *m.* 31 Oct. 1824, Mary, 2nd dau. of Robert Westropp, of Fortane, co. Clare, and by her (who *d.* 7 Jan. 1887) had issue,
 1. JOHN, now of Maryfort and Fortane.
 2. Robert, *b.* 26 Oct. 1833.
 3. Cornelius, *b.* 15 Jan. 1835, *d.* 12 April, 1836.
 4. Cornelius, *b.* 12 Oct. 1836, Private Secretary to Governor of Queensland, late Capt. 1st West India Regt. ; *d. unm.* 10 Dec. 1895.
 5. Donatus, now in Sydney, *b.* 5 Aug. 1841.
 1. Catherine, *m.* 1852, Ralph Westropp, of St. Catherine's late Ensign 68th Light Infantry, and *d.* 24 May, 1898, leaving issue.
 2. Georgina, *d. unm.* 6 Jan. 1856.
 3. Anna.
 4. Frances, *m.* 1st, Andrew Lysaght, LL.D., and 2ndly, Major William Cassius Clifford, and has issue.
 5. Mary, *d. unm.* 1907.

Mr. O'Callaghan *d.* 31 Jan. 1849.

Arms—Arg., in base a mount vert, on the dexter side a burst of oak trees, there from issuant a wolf passant towards the sinister, all ppr. *Crest*—A naked arm embowed, holding a sword entwined with a snake all ppr. *Motto*—Fidus et audax.

Seats—Maryfort and Fortane, Tulla, co. Clare. *Clubs*—Army and Navy, S.W., and Hibernian United Service, Dublin.

O'CALLAGHAN OF CAHIRDUGGAN.

CORNELIUS RICHARD O'CALLAGHAN, J.P., of Cahirduggan, co. Cork, *b.* 1869 ; *m.* 1895, Charlotte Hudson, dau. of the late Sir Edward Hudson-Kinahan, Bart., of The Manor, Glenville, co. Cork, and has issue.
 1. CORNELIUS EDWARD ALEXANDER, *b.* 1897.
 1. Emily Frances Grace.   3. Charlotte Ivy Cecile.

Lineage.—DENIS O'CALLAGHAN, the direct ancestor of this family, had, with two daus., Mary, wife of Ralph Dore, and Ellen, wife of John Fowlue, two sons, namely CORNELIUS, of whom hereafter, and Roger. The 2nd son, ROGER O'CALLAGHAN, of Derrygallon, co. Cork, *m.* 1713 (marriage licence dated 14 Oct. 1713), Ellen, youngest dau. of John Gillman, by Mary his wife, dau. of Col. Heyward St. Leger (*see* GILLMAN *of Clonteadmore*). He *d.* in 1747, leaving issue by her (who survived him).
 1. Denis, of Glynn, co. Cork, *m.* 1748, Mary, dau. of Robert O'Callaghan, of Clonmeen, J.P., and relict of Henry Daunt. He *d.* 1760, having had issue by her (who survived him),
  1. Roger, of Glynn, *b.* 1750 ; *m.* June, 1775, his 1st cousin, Catherine, dau. of Thomas Knolles, of Killeighy, and had issue, with daus., an only son, Denis, who *d. unm.*
  2. Cornelius, *m.* July, 1782, Frances, dau. of Quaile Welsted, of Ballywalter, and had issue.
   1. Elizabeth.   2. Anne.
   3. Ellen.

The elder son of the first-named Denis,

CORNELIUS O'CALLAGHAN, of Dromskehy, *m.* 1706 (marriage licence dated 14 Oct. 1706), Barbara, dau. of John Gillman and sister of Ellen, wife of his brother Roger. He *d.* 1749, and by his said wife (who survived him) had issue,
 1. DENIS, of whom presently.
 1. Judith, *m.* April, 1738, George Foott, of Millford, co. Cork, and had issue.
 2. Mary, *m.* Robert Holmes, of Shinanagh, co. Cork, and had issue.

The only son,

DENIS O'CALLAGHAN, of Dromskehy, *b.* 1708 ; *m.* 1753, Elizabeth, dau. of Thomas Bennett, and relict of William Withers, and by her (who *d.* 1783) left issue at his decease in 1792, an only child,

CORNELIUS O'CALLAGHAN, Dromskehy, and afterwards of Cahirduggan, *b.* 1756 ; *m.* 1781, Mary, only child of Henry Davies (son of Ven. Michael Davies, Archdeacon of Cloyne, and grandson of the Very Rev. Rowland Davies, Dean of Cork). He *d.* 1831, and by her (who predeceased him) had issue,
 1. DENIS, of Cahirduggan, *b.* 1787, of whom presently.
 2. Cornelius, of Rockville, co. Cork, J.P., *b.* Oct. 1788 ; *m.* Sept. 1844, Mary, dau of Peter Campbell, of Cork, and had issue.
 3. Leslie, of Ashgrove, co. Cork.
 4. Richard.
 1. Barbara, *d. unm.*
 2. Mary, *m.* William Bell, M.D., and had issue.
 3. Frances, *d. unm.*
 4. Ellen, *m.* Edward Foott, J.P., and had issue.

The eldest son,

DENIS O'CALLAGHAN, *b.* 1787 ; *m.* 1831, Sarah, dau. of Arthur Pyne, of Ballyvolane, co. Cork, and had issue,
 1. CORNELIUS, of Cahirduggan.
 2. Arthur Pyne, in Holy Orders, *m.* 1869, Dorothea Louisa, dau. of Rev. William Masters Pyne, Rector of Oxted, Surrey.
 3. Denis.   4. Jasper Pyne.
 5. Thomas.
 1. Mary, *m.* Thomas Waggett, of Queenstown.
 2. Elizabeth (twin), *unm.*   3. Barbara (twin), *unm.*
 4. Sarah, *unm.*   5. Dora.
 6. Emily, *m.* William H. Revell, Res. Magistrate, New Zealand.

The eldest son,

CORNELIUS O'CALLAGHAN, J.P. of Cahirduggan, *b.* 1836 ; *m.* 1867, Frances Anne (who *d.* 3 June, 1910), dau. of Richard Shee, J.P., of Ballyreddin, co. Kilkenny. He *d.* 1881, having had issue,
 1. CORNELIUS RICHARD, now of Cahirduggan.
 2. Thomas Marcus, *b.* 1873 ; *m.* 1896, Gertrude Mary Willoughby, only child of late Col. Howden Briggs, 6th Bombay Native Infantry, and has issue.
 1. Ellen Maria, *m.* 1st, William Campbell Bourke, of Fermoy, who *d.* She *m.* 2ndly, Norman Bourke, of Kilworth, and has issue.
 2. Sarah Henrietta, *m.* Philip Creagh, and has issue.

Seats—Cahirduggan, Midleton, co. Cork.

O'CARROLL OF ATHGOE PARK.

FREDERIC JOHN CHRYSOSTOM JOSEPH LOCKE O'CARROLL, of Athgoe Park, co. Dublin, J.P., B.A. Trin. Coll. Dublin, Barrister-at-Law, b. 27 Jan. 1843; m. 29 April, 1874, Margaret Mary Theresa, dau. of William Thompson, of Clare Hall, co. Dublin, by Anna Maria his wife, dau. of J. MacLornan, and has had issue,

1. FREDERIC WILLIAM JOSEPH, Capt. 5th Batt. Royal Dublin Fus., b. 13 April, 1876.
2. John Augustine MacCarthy, b. 28 Aug. 1877.
3. William Thomas, b. 4 Dec. 1881.
4. Oscar Francis, b. 27 May, 1888.
5. Walter Cormac Locke, b. 14 Sept. 1893.
1. Margaret Mary Frances.
2. Anne Kathleen Marie, d. 11 July, 1880.
3. Kathleen Eily.   4. Violet Mary.

Lineage.—The O'Carrolls descend from Kian, son of Oilioll Olium, King of Munster, who d. A.D. 234, and are the leading family of the Clan Kian race. They were chiefs of Ely O'Carroll. Teige O'Carroll was created Baron of Ely in A.D. 1552. Kerball, from whom the name—which signifies "a warlike champion" (vide Gilbert's National MSS., Part 3, xxxb.)—is derived, was 23rd in descent from Kian. The first of the name led the Elians at the battle of Clontarf. Teige O'Carroll, a celebrated chief of the clan. 14th in descent from Kerball, was slain at the battle of Callan, A.D. 1407. He made a pilgrimage to Rome, and on his return visited the Courts of Richard II, and the King of France. In A.D. 1395 he defeated the forces of King Richard II, which had invaded Ely under the command of Roger Mortimer, Earl of March, afterwards Lord Deputy. He was married to Joan, dau. of James, 2nd Earl of Ormonde, great-grandson of King EDWARD I., of England. His grandson, John O'Carroll, was chief A.D. 1489; Donough, son of John, A.D. 1536 (A.F.M.). Teige, son of Donough, was married to Sarah, dau. of Teige More O'Brien, son of Conor O'Brien, of Thomond, by Alice, dau. of Maurice Fitzgerald, 10th Earl of Desmond, through which alliance the descendants of Teige O'Carroll trace also to King EDWARD I. Kian, son of Teige, was slain besieging Leap Castle, which had been occupied by a rival branch of the family. His son,

DUNOUGH O'CARROLL,* of Buolebrack Castle, in Ely O'Carroll, 4th in descent from John O'Carroll, chief of his name, who d. 1489 (see Annals of the Four Masters, and Fun. Entries, vol. VIII., p. 241, Ulster's Office), was transplanted by CROMWELL (see Connaught Certificates, IV. 60), and had a grant of the lands of Beagh, in the co. Galway. His grandson and heir,

JOHN O'CARROLL, the son of Daniel, m. Margaret, dau. of Andrew O'Crean, by Margaret, dau. of 17th Lord Atheury, and had issue, among others,

1. DANIEL (Sir), of Beagh, Knt. of St. Jago, in Spain, created a baro.t. was Lieut.-Gen. of H.M. Forces. His descendant, Sir John Whitley Christopher O'Carroll, 6th Bart., d.s.p. at Hildersheim in Germany, 2 June, 1835, when the title became extinct.
2. REDMUND, of whom we treat.

The youngest son,

REDMUND O'CARROLL, of Ardagh, co. Galway, whose will was proved 17 July, 1755, m. Susanna, dau. of Robert O'Carroll, of Emmell Castle, by Frances, dau. of James Talbot, of Mount Talbot, Esq. (this Robert was son and successor of Anthony "Fada" O'Carroll, the celebrated Jacobite leader), and had issue, with a

dau. Elizabeth (who m. 1st, Sir Joseph Burke, Bart. of Glinsk, and 2ndly, Sir John Burke, Knt. of St. Jago), a son and heir,

REMY or REDMUND O'CARROLL (will proved 21 April, 1815), m. dau. of — O'Carroll, of Emly, co. Tipperary, and had, with other issue, a son and heir,

JOHN O'CARROLL, m. July, 1803, Anne* (who d. 19 June, 1853), dau. and co-heir of John Locke, of Athgoe Park, and d. 1819, leaving issue,

1. Redmond, Peter, m. 26 July, 1834, Mary, dau. of Henry Michael Goold, only brother of Sir George Goold, Bart., and d. 1847, leaving issue,
   1. John (Rev.), a priest, d. 1889.
   2. Francis (Rev.), d. 1886.
2. FREDERICK FRANCIS, of whom presently.
1. Anna, m. Carroll Naish, of Ballycullen, co. Limerick, and had a son, the Right Hon. John Naish, Lord Chancellor of Ireland 1885-6.

The younger son,

FREDERICK FRANCIS O'CARROLL, m. at Castlecoote, co. Roscommon, June, 1841, Catherine (d. 5 Feb. 1865), dau. of Joseph MacCarthy, of Killeshandra, co. Cavan, by Susan, dau. of Edmund Dowell, by Catherine, dau. of John Plunkett, of Mount Plunkett. Mr. O'Carroll d. 17 April, 1889, leaving an only son,

FREDERIC JOHN CHRYSOSTOM JOSEPH, now of Athgoe Park.

Arms—Arg., two lions rampant combatant gu. supporting a sword erect ppr. pomel and hilt or, for O'CARROLL (quartering for LOCKE, per fesse az., and or, a pale counterchanged, three falcons rising two and one of the second, each holding in the beak a fetter-lock sa. ; and for WARREN, chequy or and az. on a canton arg. a lion rampant gu.). Crest—On a stump of an oak tree, sprouting, a falcon rising ppr. belled or. Motto—In fide et in bello fortis.

Seat—Athgoe Park, Hazelhatch, co. Dublin. Residence—Powerstown House, Goresbridge, co. Kilkenny.

O'CONNELL OF DARRYNANE ABBEY.

DANIEL O'CONNELL, of Darrynane Abbey, co. Kerry, J.P. and D.L., High Sheriff 1860, b. 20 Nov. 1836; m. 25 April, 1861, Isabella Ellen, dau. of Denis Shine Lawlor, of Grenagh House, co. Kerry, and sister of D. A. Lawlor Huddleston, of Gawston (see that family), and by her (who d. 26 Aug. 1903) has issue, surviving,

1. ISABELLA MARY.
2. Kathleen
3. Margaret Gertrude.
4. Eileen Mary.
5. Frances Mary.

Mr. O'Connell served in the Royal Navy from 1850 to 1853.

Lineage.—From the district of Upper and Lower Connello, co. Limerick, the O'Connells removed to Iveragh, in the Western extremity of Kerry, and remained there for a considerable period, until the rebellion of 1641 transplanted them to the co. of Clare.

---

* This lady descended from

WILLIAM LOCKE (descended from Theophilus Locke, of Colmanstown); he m. Catherine, dau. of William Allen, of Palmerston, co. Kildare. His son,

PATRICK LOCKE, m. Alison, dau. of Michael Sarsfield, of Sarsfieldstown, co. Meath, and d. 12 Nov. 1635, leaving a son,

WILLIAM LOCKE, m. Catharine, dau. of Nicholas Cheevers, of Donakarney, co. Meath, 2nd son of Sir Christopher Cheevers, and d. 1649. His son,

JOHN LOCKE, restored as an Innocent, m. Anne Nugent, and d. 15 April, 1685, leaving a son,

PATRICK LOCKE, of Colmanstown and Athgoe, co. Dublin. His will, dated 16 Oct. 1703, was proved 27 Jan. 1704. He left, by Margaret his wife, a son,

JOHN LOCKE, of Colmanstown and Athgoe, m. 7 Nov. 1726, Lucy, dau. and heiress of John Warren, of Curduff, co. Dublin. She d. 22 May, 1770. He d. 8 Nov. 1747, leaving a son,

JOHN LOCKE, m. 12 Sept. 1762, Magdalen, dau. of Matthew Lynch, of Drumcong, co. Galway, and left issue,

1. Peter, m. 1st, 8 May, 1789, Eliza, dau. of — Kennedy, of Johnstown-Kennedy, and sister of Charles Kennedy, and 2ndly, Margaret, dau. of John Esmonde, and sister of Sir Thomas Esmonde, Bart., and d.s.p. 1833.
2. Richard, d.s.p., Admon. 10 Aug. 1801.
1. Lucy, m. John Deane Skerrett, of Ballinduff, co. Galway, by whom she had issue, who d.s.p.
2. Margaret, d.s.p.
3. Anne, m. as above, JOHN O'CARROLL.

---

* From Donogh O'Carroll, son of William the Fair, Chief of Ely, who d. A.D. 1377 (A.F.M.), descended CHARLES CARROLL, of Carrollton, Maryland, the most influential and the last survivor of the signers of the American Declaration of Independence. He d. 1833, leaving issue,

Charles, who was father of another

Charles, m. the dau. of Robert Henry Lee Governor of Maryland, and had two sons and a dau.,
(1) Charles, of Carrollton.
(2) John Lee (Hon.), Governor of Maryland.
(1) Louisa, m. George Cavendish Taylor.

Mary, m. Richard Caton, of Philadelphia, and by him had four daus.,

1. Mary Anne, m. 1st, Robert Paterson (whose sister Elizabeth was first wife of Jerome Bonaparte, King of Westphalia). She m. 2ndly, 29 Oct. 1825, Richard Colley, Marquis Wellesley, K.G., Lord Lieutenant of Ireland, to whom an exemplification of the O'Carroll arms was given by Sir W. Bectham, Ulster, 14 July, 1826. She d.s.p. 17 Dec. 1853.
2. Elizabeth, m. 25 May, 1836, George William, Lord Stafford, and d.s.p. 29 Oct. 1862.
3. Louisa, m. 1st, 1817, Sir Felton Elwall Hervey Bathurst, 1st bart., and 2ndly, 24 April, 1828, Francis Godolphin D'Arcy, 7th Duke of Leeds. She d. 8 April, 1874.
4. Emily, m. John McTavish, British Consul at Baltimore, U.S.A.

JEFFREY O'CONNELL, Lord of Bally Carbery, who by letters mandatory of JAMES I. was constituted High Sheriff of the co. Kerry, and d. 25 April, 1635, having had two sons,
1. Maurice, who was transplanted by Cromwell to Brentree, co. Clare, and had two sons, Maurice, of Brentree, Col. of the King's (JAMES II.'s) Guards, killed at Aughrim in 1691, and John, Lieut. King's Regt., killed at Derry 1689. This branch became extinct on the death of Rickard, of Brentree, in 1749.
2. DANIEL, of whom presently.

The 2nd son,
DANIEL O'CONNELL, of Ahavore, having taken no part in the insurrection of 1641, preserved his estate. He *m.* Alice, dau. of Christopher Segerson, of Ballinskelligs Abbey, co. Kerry, and by her had two sons,
1. JOHN, his heir.
2. Maurice, who *d.* 1715 (his grandson, Rickard, was Capt. in the Legion of Maillebois, in the service of Holland).

The elder son and heir,
JOHN O'CONNELL, of Ahavore and Darrynane, raised a company of foot for the service of JAMES II., and embodied it in the regiment of his cousin, Col. Maurice O'Connell. He signalized himself at the siege of Derry, as well as at the battles of the Boyne and Aughrim, and returning to Limerick, was included in the capitulation of that city. He *m.* Elizabeth, dau. of Christopher Conway, of Clahane, co. Kerry, and *d.* 1741, having had three sons,
1. DANIEL, of whom presently.
2. MAURICE, of Tarmons, co. Kerry, *m.* Mary, dau. of O'Sullivan Beare, of Berehaven, and had with other issue, a son, Maurice, Baron O'Connell, Col. in the Austrian Service, and Chamberlain to the Empress Maria Theresa, *b.* 1740, *d.* at Vienna 1831, and a dau., *m.* her cousin, Charles O'Connell, and had a son, Gen. Sir Maurice O'Connell, K.C.H., *m.* Mary, dau. of Admiral William Bligh, and *d.* 1848, leaving, with other issue, a son, Sir Maurice Charles O'Connell, Capt. 28th Regt., President of the Legislative Council of Queensland, Knt. of San Ferdinando Isabella and Charles III., and *d.s.p.* 1878, aged 66.
3. Jeffrey.

The eldest son,
DANIEL O'CONNELL, of Darrynane, *m.* Mary, dau. of O'Donoghue Dhuv, of Anwys, co. Kerry, and had twenty-two children, of whom the following arrived at maturity,
1. John, *m.* the dau. of O'Falvey, of Faha, co. Kerry, and *d.* 9 May, 1851, aged 26, leaving a dau.
2. MAURICE, successor to his father.
3. Morgan, of Carhen, in the Barony of Iveragh, *b.* 1739, *m.* April, 1771, Catherine, dau. of John O'Mullane, of Whitechurch, co. Cork, and dying 1809, had (with six daus., Mary, *m.* Jeremiah M'Carthy, of Woodview, co. Kerry; Honora, *m.* Daniel O'Sullivan, of Reendonegan, co. Cork ; Catherine, *m.* Humphrey Moynihan, of Rathbeg, co. Kerry ; Ellen, *m.* Daniel O'Connell, of Tralee ; Bridget, *m.* Miles M'Swiney, of Keumare ; and Alicia, *m.* 1820, William Francis Finn, M.P. for co. Kilkenny) four sons,
  1. DANIEL, successor to his uncle.
  2. Maurice, *b.* 1776, entered the British Army, and *d.* on the expedition to St. Domingo, in 1797.
  3. John, of Grenagh, co. Kerry, *b.* 1779 ; *m.* Feb. 1806, Elizabeth, dau. and heiress of William Coppinger, of Ballyvolane and Barry's Court, and *d.* 1859, having by her (who *d.* 21 Dec. 1863) had issue, two sons and two daus.,
    (1) MORGAN JOHN, of Ballylean Lodge, co. Clare, and Barry's Court, co. Cork, M.P. for co. Kerry 1835-53, Barrister-at-Law, *b.* 27 Aug. 1811 ; *m.* 21 Feb. 1865, Mary Anne, only dau. of Charles Bianconi, D.L., of Longfield, co. Tipperary. She *d.* 28 Jan. 1908. He *d.* 2 July, 1875, leaving a son,
      JOHN (CHARLES COPPINGER) BIANCONI (*Lacknashannagh Mills, Killysart*), J.P. co. Cork and Clare, now of Ballylean and Barryscourt, who on succeeding to the estate of Longfield at the death of his mother under the will of her father adopted the surname of BIANCONI by Deed Poll 27 April, 1908 ; *b.* 19 Oct. 1871 ; *m.* 10 Jan. 1894, Arabella, dau. of T. P. Hayes, of 42, Lansdowne Road, Dublin, and has issue,
        a. Helen, *b.* 14 Nov. 1895.
        b. Mary, *b.* 22 Dec. 1896.
        c. Una, *b.* 3 Sept. 1898.
    (2) John Dominick Patrick (Rev.), *b.* 25 March, 1828 ; *d.* 1872.
    (1) Jane, *m.* 1st, Charles, The O'Donoghue of the Glens, co. Kerry, Chief of the name, and 2ndly, M'Carthy O'Leary, D.L., and had issue.
    (2) Catherine, *m.* Samuel Vines, and has issue.
  4. James (Sir), of Lake View, Bart. (see BURKE's *Peerage and Baronetage*).
4. Connell, *b.* 1741, drowned at sea, 1765.
5. Daniel, Count O'Connell, Peer of France, Grand Cross of St. Louis, *b.* May, 1745, entered the French service in the Royal Swedois Regt. in 1761, and in 1769 was transferred to Clare's (afterwards Berwick's) Regiment of the Irish Brigade, with which he served in Europe and in the Mauritius until 1778, when he was re-appointed to the Royal Swedois as Lieut.-Col. and was present in that capacity at the sieges of Port Mahan and Gibraltar ; at the latter he was on board one of the famous floating batteries and was severely wounded. He was subsequently appointed Colonel Commandant of the Regiment of Salm-Salm, a member of a committee to revise the system of infantry tactics in the French Army, and was created a Chevalier of the Order of St. Louis. On the downfall of LOUIS XVI., Count O'Connell returned to England and was appointed Col. of the 4th Regt. of the Irish Brigade which command he retained until the corps was disbanded. He

d. July, 1833, at his stepson-in-law's chateau, near Blois, on the Loire, aged 88, holding the rank of General in the French and Colonel in the English service.
1. Elizabeth, *m.* Timothy M'Carthy, of Liss, co. Kerry.
2. Honora, *m.* Charles Sugrue, of Ferinoyle Castle, co. Kerry.
3. Abigail, *m.* Major O'Sullivan, of the Austrian service.
4. Mary, *m.* James Baldwin, of Clonhinna, co. Cork.
5. Ellen, *m.* Arthur O'Leary, of Raleigh, co. Cork.
6. Catherine, *m.* Mortogh O'Sullivan, of Coulagh.
7. Anne, *m.* Maurice O'Connell, of Lative, and *d.s.p.*
8. Alice, *m.* Thomas Segerson, of Ballinskelligs, Abbey, co. Kerry.

Mr. O'Connell *d.* 4 Oct. 1770, and was *s.* by his eldest son,
MAURICE O'CONNELL, of Darryane, Deputy Governor of Kerry, *m.* Mary, dau. and co-heir of Robert Cantillon, of co. Limerick, but dying without issue 1825, at the age of 97, was *s.* by his nephew, the celebrated
DANIEL O'CONNELL, M.P., of Darrynane Abbey, Barrister-at-Law, and Q.C., holding the rank, by patent, of precedency immediately after the first Serjeant at the Bar in Ireland, *b.* at Carhen, near Cahirciveen, 6 Aug. 1775 ; *m.* 3 June, 1802, his cousin, Mary, dau. of Edward O'Connell, M.D., of Tralee, and by her, (who *d.* 31 Oct. 1836) had issue,
1. Maurice, M.P. for Tralee, *m.* 1832, Frances Mary, only dau. of John Bindon Scott, of Cahircon, co. Clare, and *d.* 18 June, 1853, leaving issue,
  1. DANIEL, present representative.
  2. John Maurice, *b.* 12 April, 1839 ; *m.* 9 Aug. 1873, Mary, only dau. of Daniel M'Cartie, of Ardnageeha, co. Cork, and has (with four daus.), had issue,
    (1) Daniel Maurice, *b.* 18 Sept. 1878 ; *d.s.p.* 1893.
    (2) Maurice, *b.* 1888.
  1. Fanny, *d. unm.* 1878.
  2. Mary, *m.* 25 Nov. 1858, Daniel MacCartie, of Headfort, co. Kerry, and has issue.
2. Morgan, M.P. for co. Meath, and Registrar of Deeds, &c., in Ireland, *b.* 31 Oct. 1804 ; *m.* 23 July, 1840, Kate Mary, dau. of Michael Balfe, of South Park, co. Roscommon, and *d.s.p.* 20 Jan. 1885.
3. John, M.P. for Clonmel, and afterwards Clerk of the Hanaper in Ireland, *m* 28 March, 1838, Elizabeth, dau. of Dr. Ryan, of Jubilee Hall, co. Dublin, and by her (who *d.* 9 April, 1876) had
  1. Daniel, *d.s.p.* 1 June, 1872.
  2. John, *m.* Mary, dau. of Judge Baldwin, Q.C., and has issue.
  3. Morgan John Joseph, Capt. 1st Hampshire Regt., *b.* 27 Oct. 1845 ; *d. unm.* 22 Sept. 1881.
  1. Elizabeth, *m.* 9 Aug. 1869, James Sullivan, and has issue.
  2. Mary, *m.* 26 Nov. 1867, Andrew Nugent Comyn, of Ballinderry, co. Galway, J.P., and *d.* 6 Feb. 1910, leaving issue (*see that family*).
  3. Eily, a nun, dec.
  4. Kathleen, *m.* 29 July, 1885, Major Michael Joseph Balfe, of South Park, co. Roscommon, and has issue (*see that family*).
  5. Alice.
He *d.* 24 May, 1858.
4. Daniel, formerly M.P. for Tralee, &c., *m.* Oct. 1866, Ellen Mary, dau. of E. Foster, of The Elms, Cambridge, and *d.* 14 June, 1897, leaving issue,
  1. Daniel John Foster, *b.* Jan. 1873.
  2. Maurice Francis, *b.* March, 1874.
  3. Geoffry Owen Morgan, *b.* Feb. 1876.
  1. Eily Mary Foster. 2. Mary Bessie Katbleen.
1. Ellen. *m.* Christopher Fitzsimon, of Glancullen, M.P. for co. Dublin, J.P. and D.L., and *d.* 27 June, 1883, leaving issue.
2. Catherine, *m.* 7 Oct. 1832, Charles O'Connell, M.P. for co. Kerry (who *d.* 20 Jan. 1877), son of Daniel O'Connell, of Ballynabloun, co. Kerry. She *d.* 19 Aug. 1891, leaving issue (*see that family*).
3. Elizabeth, *m.* Nicholas Joseph Ffrench, who *d.* 3 Feb. 1893.
Mr. O'Connell *d.* at Genoa 15 May, 1847.

Arms—Per fesse arg. and vert, a stag trippant ppr. between three trefoils slipped counterchanged. Crest—A stag's head erased arg., charged with a tr. foil slipped vert. Motto—Ciall agus Neart.
Seat—Darrynane Abbey, Waterville, co. Kerry.

O'CONNELL OF BALLYNABLOUN.

DANIEL O'CONNELL, of Ballynabloun, co. Kerry, *b.* 6 Jan. 1842 ; *m.* 1st, 28 Feb. 1867, Milly, only dau. of Joseph Lindsay Curtis, of Cork. She *d.* 1 June, 1870, having had two daus., both deceased. He *m.* 2ndly, 31 Jan. 1877, Helen Josephine, 2nd dau. of Sir Joseph Neal McKenna, of Ardogena, co. Cork, and 67, Lancaster Gate, and by her has issue,
1. CHARLES, Staff Surgeon R.N., *b.* 19 June, 1878.
2. Donald, Solicitor, *b.* 8 July, 1879.
3. Maurice Geoffry, *b.* 14 Dec. 1885.
1. Esther.
2. Ellen Eveline, *m.* 21 June, 1910, Gilbert Moorhead.
3. Teresa Constance.

Lineage.—CHARLES O'CONNELL, of Ballynabloun, co. Kerry, M.P. for that county, son of Daniel O'Connell, of Ballynabloun, Cahirciveen, co. Kerry, *b.* 12 Aug. 1805 ; *m.* 7 Oct. 1832, Kate, 2nd dau. of Daniel O'Connell, M.P., of Darrynane Abbey, the Liberator (*see that family*). She *d.* 19 April, 1891. He *d.* 20 Jan. 1877, having had issue,

IRELAND. O'Conor.

1. DANIEL, now of Ballynabloun.
2. Charles Francis Xaviar, b. 2 Dec. 1846; d. unm 17 Feb. 1875.
1. Mary, a nun, deceased.
2. Theresa, d. young.
3. Kate, a nun, deceased.
4. Betsey, d. young.
5. Eileen, m. 29 Dec. 1870, Keogh Cullen.
6. Teresa, m. 18 April, 1876, Thomas Downes.

Residences—Ballynabloun and the Bungalow, Derriana Lake, Masterguihy, co. Kerry. *Clubs*—Junior Conservative and Mallow Club.

O'CONNELL. *See* BURKE'S PEERAGE, **O'CONNELL, Bt.**

O'CONNOR. *See* **O'CONNOR-MORRIS.**

O'CONNOR-HENCHY. *See* **HENCHY.**

O'CONOR DON.

O'CONOR DON, DENIS CHARLES JOSEPH O'CONOR, of Belanagare and Clonalis, co. Roscommon, H.M. Lieut. of that co., J.P., High Sheriff 1898, B.A. and LL.B. London Univ., Barrister-at-Law England and Ireland, b. 26 Oct. 1869.

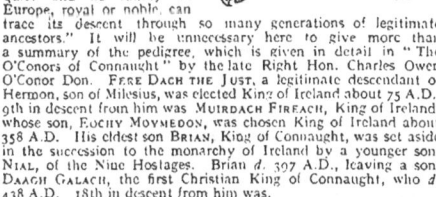

Lineage.— Of the O'Connor family O'Donovan says "No family in Ireland claims greater antiquity and no family in Europe, royal or noble, can trace its descent through so many generations of legitimate ancestors." It will be unnecessary here to give more than a summary of the pedigree, which is given in detail in "The O'Conors of Connaught" by the late Right Hon. Charles Owen O'Conor Don. FERE DACH THE JUST, a legitimate descendant of Hermon, son of Milesius, was elected King of Ireland about 75 A.D., 9th in descent from him was MUIRDACH FIREACH, King of Ireland, whose son, EOCHY MOYMEDON, was chosen King of Ireland about 358 A.D. His eldest son BRIAN, King of Connaught, was set aside in the succession to the monarchy of Ireland by a younger son, NIAL, of the Nine Hostages. Brian d. 397 A.D., leaving a son, DAAGH GALACH, the first Christian King of Connaught, who d. 438 A.D. 18th in descent from him was,
CONCOVAR or CONOR, King of Connaught (son of Teign of the Three Towers), from whom the family name of O'CONOR is derived. He d. 971, leaving a son,
CATHAL O'CONOR, who is said to have reigned for thirty years but was forced to submit to Brian Boru, King of Munster, who assumed the chief sovereignty. Cathal d. a monk, 1010. His son,
TEIGN O'CONOR, of the White Steed, became King of Connaught in 1015, and d. 1030. His son,
HUGH O'CONOR, of the Broken Spear, King of Connaught, who acknowledged the supremacy of the Monarch of Ireland. He was killed in battle near Oranmon, co. Galway, 1067. His son,
RODERIC O'CONOR, called "Rory of the Yellow Hound," King of Connaught, was after an eventful reign blinded by O'Flaherty in 1092, when he was forced to abdicate. He d. in the Monastery of Clonmacroix, 1118. His son,
TURLOUGH MOR O'CONOR, King of Connaught, and afterwards Monarch of Ireland, was inaugurated as King of Connaught at the ford of Termon, 1106, and having subdued the other provincial Kings, reigned supreme over all Ireland after the battle of Moin-mor, near Emly, in 1151. He m. 1st, Tailltin, dau. of Morrough O'Melaghlin, King of Meath, and by her (who d. 1128) had, with other issue, a son RODERIC. He m. 2ndly, 1131, Dervorgilla, dau. of Donnell McLoughlin, Monarch of Ireland, and by her (who d. 1151) had a son, CATHAL CROVEDFARG of whom presently. He m. 3rdly, Durcoulagh, dau. of Melachlin O'Mulroony. She d. 1169. Turlough O'Conor d. 1156. His son,
RODERIC O'CONOR, King of Connaught and Monarch of Ireland, after the death of Murlough McLoughlin. In his reign occurred the English invasion of Ireland in 1170, which culminated in the treaty of Windsor in 1175, whereby the Kings of England became lords paramount to Ireland, and Roderic held the Kingdom of Connaught as vassal of the English Crown. Roderic eventually abdicated in favour of his son, Conor Moinmoy, 1186, and d. in the Monastery of Cong, 1198. Conor Moin moy was killed 1189, and his son, Cathal Carrach, sometime King of Connaught, who was slain 1201, leaving issue. The latter was s. by his great uncle,
CATHAL CROVEDFARG, King of Connaught, son of Turlough Mor O'Conor, who submitted to King John. He m. Mor, dau. of O'Brien, King of Munster, and d. 1224. His eldest son,
HUGH O'CONOR, King of Connaught, m. Rainault, dau. of Auley O'Ferrall, and was murdered 1228. His son,
RORY or RODERIC O'CONOR, who was never King of Connaught, for during his lifetime the sovereignty was held by his uncle Felim. He was accidentally drowned, 1244. His eldest son,
OWEN O'CONOR, who for a few months was King of Connaught, and was slain, 1274, by his cousin Rory, son of his uncle Turlough. His younger son,
HUGH O'CONOR, King of Connaught, acknowledged by the Irish in 1293, though the superiority was claimed by the English King and a great part of Connaught was in the hands of the De Burghs. He m. Finola, dau. of Turlough O'Brien. She d. 1335. He was killed 1309. His sons FELIM, ancester of O'Conor Roe, and TURLOUGH, were successively Kings of Connaught. The latter, TURLOUGH O'CONOR, King of Connaught, m. 1st, Devorgal, dau. of Hugh O'Donnell, Prince of Tyrconnell. He divorced her 1339 and m. 2ndly, Slaine, dau. of O'Brien. He d. 1342, having had issue, two sons, HUGH and RORY, who were subsequently rulers of the Irish in Connaught, and two daus., Finola, wife of O'Kelly, and Una, wife of O'Reilly. The elder son,
HUGH O'Conor, King of Connaught 1315-53; m. Margaret, dau. of Walter de Burgh. She d. 1365. He d. 1356. His son, of Felim,
TURLOUGH OGE O'CONOR, called O'CONOR DON, to distinguish him from his cousin, another Turlough (grandson of Felim), who was called O'Conor Roe. At the death, in 1834, of Roderic, King of Connaught, the kingdom was divided between the two cousins, each of whom claimed the sovereignty of the whole province, and from that date the heads of each branch were called respectively O'Conor Don and O'Conor Roe. O'Conor Don presented himself before RICHARD II at Waterford, and there as Captain of Nation, made his submission to the King 29 April, 1305. He m. Evaine, dau. of O'Kelly, and was killed 1406, by Cathal Duv, son of O'Conor Roe. He was s. in the chieftainship by his son HUGH, who appears to have been s. by his brother,
FELIM GEANCACH O'CONOR DON, who m. Edwina, dau. of O'Conor Sligo, and d. 1474. His son,
OWEN CAECH O'CONOR DON from 1476, m. Devorgilla, dau. of Felim Finn, O'Conor Roe, and d. 1485. His son,
CARBRY O'CONOR DON, b. 1475; d. in Ballintober, 1546, leaving issue, DERMOT, afterwards O'Conor Don, and Turlough, who d. 1582. The elder son,
DERMOT O'CONOR DON, chief of his sept after 1550, m. Dorothy, dau. of Teige Buidhe O'Conor Roe, and had issue, 1. Con, who was killed 1563; 2. Turlough, who d. 1583; and 3. HUGH (Sir), his heir. Dermot O'Conor Don, who d. 1385, was the last of the O'Conors who exercised independent jurisdiction over Connaught. His son and heir,
SIR HUGH O'CONOR DON was b. in 1541, and on his father's death in 1585, compounded with the Lord-Deputy, Sir John Perrott, for all his estates, and was knighted by the Earl of Essex. Sir Hugh was the first Knight of the shire returned to Parliament for the co. of Roscommon. He m. Mary, dau. of Brian O'Rourke, Lord of Breffny, and d. in 1627, leaving four sons,
1. CALVACH O'CONOR DON, of Ballintobber, his heir, whose male line became extinct.
2. HUGH OGE O'CONOR, of Castlereagh, m. Jane, dau. of Theobald, Lord Dillon, and dying, 1662, left an elder son,
  DANIEL O'CONOR, of Clonalis, who left, by Anne Birmingham his wife, dau. of Edward, 17th Lord Athenry, one son,
    ANDREW O'CONOR, of Clonalis, co. Roscommon, who became O'Conor Don. He m. 3 March, 1692, Honora, dau. of Col. Luke Dowell, of Mantua, and by her (who d. 11 Nov. 1708) had two sons,
    1. DANIEL, of Clonalis, d. 17 March, 1769, leaving (with two daus., Jane, wife of William Eccles, and Elizabeth, d.s.p. 1816, and two younger sons, Thomas and Hugh, both d.s.p.) two elder sons, DOMINICK O'CONOR DON, his heir, who d.s.p. in 1795, and was s. by his brother, ALEXANDER O'CONOR DON, of Clonalis, who dying without issue 1820, was s. in the title of O'Conor Don by his kinsman, OWEN O'CONOR, of Belanagare, as hereafter.
    2. Thomas, an Officer in the French service, made Knight of St. Louis for his bravery at the battle of Fontenoy, d.s.p.
3. CATHAL, of whose line we treat.
4. Bryan Roe O'Conor, of Corrasduna (see O'CONNOR of Rathnore). Sir Hugh O'Conor d. 1632, at a very advanced age. His 3rd son,
CATHAL O'CONOR, of Belanagare, co. Roscommon, b. 1597; m. Anne, dau. of William O'Molloy, of Aughterfire, and dying 1634 was s. by his eldest son,
MAJOR OWEN O'CONOR, of Belanagare, Governor of Athlone under JAMES II., d. in the Castle of Chester, 1692. He m. Ellinor dau. of Roger O'Ferrall, of Mornine, co. Longford, widow of Sir Oliver Tuite, 2nd Bart., and d. without male issue 1692, when the estate passed to his brother,
CHARLES OGE O'CONOR, of Belanagare, m. Cecilia, dau. of Fiachra O'Flynn, of Ballinlough, and dying in 1696, was s. by his son,
DENIS O'CONOR, of Belanagare, b. 1674; m. Mary, dau. of Tiernan O'Rourke, Chief of Breffny, and left at his decease, 30 Jan. 1750,
1. CHARLES, his heir.
2. Daniel, an Officer in the French service. 3. Roger (Rev.).

4. Hugh. 5. Matthew (Rev.).
1. Catherine, m. Thomas Durkan.
2. Mary, m. O'Higgin, of Caropaden.
3. Eleanor, m. Charles M'Dermott.
4. Anne, m. M'Dermott Roe.

The son and heir,
CHARLES O'CONOR, of Belanagare, b. 1710, a learned and distinguished antiquary, m. 8 Dec. 1731, Catharine, dau. of John O'Fagan, and had (with a dau., Bridget, m. Miles M'Dermott, of Coolavin, and d. 1777) two sons,
1. DENIS, his heir.
2. Charles, of Mount Allen, co. Roscommon, b. 1736, d. 1808, leaving by his wife, a dau. of John Dillon, of Dublin, two sons, Thomas, settled at New York (father of Charles, Barrister-at-Law, in America), and Denis, and a dau., Catherine; the two latter d. in North America.

Mr. O'Conor d. 1 July, 1790, and was s. by his elder son,
DENIS O'CONOR, of Belanagare, who was appointed Deputy-Governor of Roscommon, b. 1732; m. 1760, Catherine, dau. of Martin Browne, of Cloonfad, co. Roscommon, and by her (who d. 1817) had issue,
1. OWEN, his heir.
2. Charles (Very Rev.), D.D., a learned antiquary, who long resided at Stowe as Chaplain to Mary Elizabeth, Marchioness of Buckingham, wife of George, 1st Marquess of Buckingham, b. 15 March, 1764; d. 1828. 3. Martin, d. young.
4. Denis, Lieut. 13th Dragoons, b. 4 Oct. 1870; d. in Jamaica, unm. 5. Roderick, b. 27 July, 1772; d. unm.
6. Matthew, b. 18 Sept. 1773; m. Priscilla Forbes, and left Denis and other issue (see O'CONOR of Mount Druid).
1. Catherine, m. 9 Dec. 1790, Charles Lyons, of Lyonstown, and d. 1795, leaving a son, Robert, and a dau., Alicia, both dec.
2. Mary, m. 1 Feb. 1795, Con O'Donel, of Larkfield, and had a son, John O'Donel.
3. Bridget, d. unm.
4. Elizabeth Frances, m. 16 July, 1793, Hugh M'Dermot, of Coolavin, The Mac Dermot.
5. Eleanor Anne, d. unm.
6. Alicia, m. John Sheil, of Ballyshannon, M.D.

Mr. O'Conor d. 1804, and was s. by his eldest son,
OWEN O'CONOR, of Belanagare, M.P. for co. Roscommon, who, on the death of his kinsman, Alexander O'Conor Don, s.p. Dec. 1820, s. to the title of O'CONOR DON, as head of the family, b. 6 March, 1763; m. 20 June, 1792, Jane, dau. of James Moore, of Mount Browne, co. Dublin, and by her (who d. 8 April, 1804) has issue,
1. DENIS, his heir.
2. Edward, m. 1835, Honoria, dau. of Major Blake, of Tower Hill, co. Mayo (see that family), and had one son, who d. in infancy.
1. Jane.
2. Catherine, m. 9 Aug. 1824, John Edward Mapother, of Kiltevan, co. Roscommon (see that family).

O'Conor Don d. 1831. His eldest son,
DENIS O'CONOR DON, of Belanagare and Clonalis, M.P. for co. Roscommon, b. May, 1794; m. 27 Aug. 1824, Mary, dau. of Major Maurice Blake, of Tower Hill, co. Mayo, and by her (who d. 1841) had issue,
1. CHARLES OWEN, the late O'CONOR DON.
2. Denis Maurice, M.A., LL.D., Barrister-at-Law, M.P. co. Sligo, 1868-83, J.P. co. Roscommon, and High Sheriff 1865, b. 24 July, 1840; m. 5 Aug. 1873, Ellen Isabella (Ashley Moor, Orleton, R.S.O., Herefordshire), eldest dau. of Rev. W. T. Kevill Davies, of Croft Castle, co. Hereford, and d. 26 July, 1883, leaving issue, Charles William, b. 17 Dec. 1878.
1. Jane, a nun, d. 1851.
2. Kate, a nun, d. 1901. 3. Josephine, a nun, d. 1899.
4. Eugenia, a nun. 5. Dionysia, a nun, d. 1897.

O'Conor Don d. 22 July, 1847. His elder son,
O'CONOR DON, THE RIGHT HON. CHARLES OWEN O'CONOR, P.C., of Belanagare, and Clonalis co. Roscommon, H.M. Lieutenant of that co., J.P., High Sheriff 1884, J.P. co. Sligo (High Sheriff 1863), M.P. for the co. 1860-80, LL.D., a member of the Senate of the Royal University and a Commissioner of Intermediate Education in Ireland, b. 7 May, 1838; m. 1st, 21 April, 1868, Georgina Mary, dau. of Thomas Aloysius Perry, of Bitham House, co. Warwick, and by her (who d. 18 Aug. 1872) has had issue,
1. DENIS CHARLES JOSEPH, O'CONOR DON.
2. Owen Phelim, b. 10 Dec. 1870.
3. Charles Hugh, b. 24 Jan. 1872; m. 9 Jan. 1904, Ellen Letitia, eldest dau. of Edward More-O'Ferrall, of Lisard, Edgworthstown, co. Longford (see MORE-O'FERRALL of Balyna).
4. Roderick Joseph, b. 24 Jan. 1872; d. 1878.

O'Conor Don m. 2ndly, 1879, Ellen, dau. of John Lewis More O'Ferrall, of Lissard, co. Longford (see MORE-O'FERRALL of Balyna), and d. 30 June, 1906.

Arms—Arg., an oak tree eradicated and acorned ppr. Crest— An arm embowed in armour, holding a sword all ppr. Supporters—Two lions rampant gu. each gorged with an antique crown and charged on the shoulder with a harp of Ireland or.

Seats—Belanagare, French Park, and Clonalis, Castlerea, co. Roscommon. Chambers—1, Garden Court, Temple, E.C. Clubs— Reform and Athenæum.

O'CONNOR (OR O'CONOR) OF RATHMEW AND CLUNYGRASSIN.

THOMAS RODERICK O'CONNOR, of Rathmew and Clunygrassin, co. Roscommon, and of Dalton, Northumberland, b. 4 May, 1849; s. 1879 to family estates of Rathmew and Clunygrassin on death of his father (see below).

Lineage—This branch of O'CONNORS (or O'CONORS) is a branch of the great House of O'Conor, in which vested the sovereignty of Connaught. They are lineally descended from Sir Hugh O'Connor, of Ballintobber Castle, co. Roscommon (the acknowledged representative of the last Kings of Ireland), through his 4th son, Capt. Bryan O'Connor, of Corrasduna, co. Roscommon (see O'CONOR DON).

CAPT. BRYAN O'CONNOR, of Corrasduna, who became seised and possessed of the lands of Beagh and Cloonycarney under his father's will, forfeited them with others, 1641, and it appears from the Book of Survey and Distribution of Estates then forfeited, that, by a decree made in Athlone, 5 Sept. 1655, founded on the claim of Col. Roger O'Connor, Bryan's son, that those estates were restored to his mother, Mary (dau. of Hugh O'Connor, of Castlerubay (see O'CONNOR-HEUCHY), for life, with reversion to himself and his heirs. Again, from the Book of Postings on the sale of lands forfeited in 1688 it appears that Roger O'Connor forfeited the said lands of Beagh and Cloonycarney.

COL. ROGER O'CONNOR, who held the commission of Col. in JAMES II's Army (which commission still remains in the possession of his heir-in-law), m. Elizabeth, dau. of O'Shaughnessy, of Gort, and d. at Douay, 1730, leaving issue,
1. OWEN, his heir.
1. A dau., m. Louis, Marquis de Vienne.
2. Margaret, m. Bernard Fallon, of Ballina.

The only son,
OWEN O'CONNOR settled at Corrasduna, co. Roscommon, and was the common ancestor of the various lines of the family immediately before us. He m. Catherine, dau. of Edmund McDermot, of Emla, co. Roscommon, and dying 1766, left four sons and three daus.,
1. RODERICK, of Ballycahir, of whom later.
2. Thomas, of Milton, J.P., High Sheriff 1767 (who attained the rank of Major in the French service), returned to Ireland, and m. 1st, 18 Sept. 1749, Mary, dau. of Gerald Dillon, of Dillon's Grove, co. Roscommon, by whom he had issue,
  1. RODERIC, his heir, of whom next. 2. Owen, Capt.
  1. Honora. 2. Catherine. 3. Margaret.
He m. 2ndly, Miss O'Flynn, by whom he had no issue. He d. 1800.
3. Dennis, of Willsbrook; m. Sarah, dau. of William Irwin of Leabeg, and left issue.
4. Bernard (Rev.).
1. Catherine, m. Hugh O'Connor brother of Charles O'Connor, of Belanagare.
2. Mary, m. Joseph Plunkett, of Castle Pluukett, co. Roscommon.
3. Sabina.

The eldest son and heir of Thomas, of Milton, above mentioned,
RODERIC O'CONNOR, of Milton, m. 1st, Anne Sparks, an English lady, by whom he left no issue, and 2ndly, Bridget, widow of Col. Thomas Wills, of Willgrove, co. Roscommon, and dau. of James Browne, of Brownevile, co. Galway. By her he left issue,
1. RODERIC, of whom next.
2. Dillon. 3. Richard.
4. Aylward, m. 14 May, 1832, Mary, dau. of Bindon Blood, of Cranagher, co. Clare (see that family), and left issue,
  1. Roderic, d.s.p. 2. Bindon Blood.
  3. Aylward Owen Blood, LL.D., d. 12 Oct. 1911; m. Margaret, dau. of William Bindon-Blood, of Cranagher (see that family), and has issue,
    (1) Aylward Robert. (2) William Owen.
  4. William Frederic, s.p.
  5. Dillon s.p.
  1. Elizabeth Anne, d. 2 Nov. 1908.
1. Jane, d. unm. 2. Maria, m. Dr. Kelly.

The eldest son,
RODERIC O'CONNOR, of Milton, Barrister-at-Law, b. 1794; High Sheriff co. Roscommon 1839; m. 1824, Cecilia, dau. of John MacDonnell, of Carnacon, co. Mayo, by Celia his wife, 4th dau. of John Dolphin, of Turoe, co. Galway, and d. 1868, leaving issue,
1. RODERICK JOSEPH, late of Milton, J.P.
2. Alfred John. 3. Eugene.
1. Cecilia. 2. Ellen.

The eldest son,

RODERIC JOSEPH O'CONNOR, of Milton, J.P., High Sheriff co. Roscommon 1863, b. 1825; m. 1854, Eleanor Mary, eldest dau. of Joseph Browne, J.P., of Elm Grove, co. Meath, by Ellen his wife, 2nd dau. of Edward Murphy, of Ballinacloon, co. Westmeath, and d. 1893, leaving issue,
1. RODERIC ANTHONY, b. 1860.
2. Joseph Owen Edward.
1. Ellen Mary. 2. Cecilia.
3. Mary Josephine.
4. Eliza, m. 1st, Capt. Fred W. Mallins, and 2ndly, 27 Jan. 1908, Henry O'Connell Fitzsimon.

We now return to the eldest son of Owen O'Connor, of Corasduna, (*see above*),
RODERIC O'CONNOR, of Ballycahir, m. Mary, dau. of John Fallon, of Cloonagh, co. Roscommon, and d. at Ballycahir, 7 Feb. 1781, leaving issue three son and two daus.,
1. Bernard, d. unm.
2. THOMAS, his eventual heir.
3. Patrick, d. unm.
1. Jane, m. Andrew Browne, of Mount Hazel, co. Galway, and had issue,
   1. Nicholas, m. Ellen, dau. of Sir Thomas Burke, 1st bart., of Marble Hill,
   2. Andrew, m. Mary, dau. of M. Blake,
   3. Roderic, who m. his cousin Maria, dau. of Thomas O'Connor, of New Garden, co. Galway.
   4. Bernard, of Mount Bernard, who d. unm.
   1. Mary, who m. 1798 Edward Martyn, of Tullyra Castle.
   2. Jane, unmarried.
2. Elizabeth.

The 2nd son,
THOMAS O'CONNOR, of New Garden, 2nd son of Roderic, of Ballycahir, m. Margaret, dau. of Peter O'Flanagan and Maria Daly, of Braughel Castle, his wife, and d. 2 Aug. 1832, leaving issue,
1. Roderic, of Rathmew and Clunygrassin, co. Roscommon, bapt. 5 April, 1791 ; m. 1833, Mary Anne, dau. of Rev. William Bell Moises, M.A., Vicar of Felton, co. Northumberland, and Awthorne, co. York, by Mary his wife, dau. of John O. de, of Weetwood, Northumberland, and niece of Julian Anne, Countess of Rodeu, and d. November, 1879, leaving by her (who d. Oct. 1884),
   1. THOMAS RODERICK, now of Rathmew and Clunygrassin.
   1. Julian Anne. 2. Emily, deceased.
3. Thomas Nicholas, bapt. 5 Nov. 1793.
1. Maria. 2. Jane, bapt. 22 April, 1795.
3. Fanny, bapt. 21 June, 1796.
4. Bridget, bapt. 15 Nov. 1800.

The 2nd son,
PATRICK O'CONNOR, of Dundermott, J.P., High Sheriff 1854, m. 2 July, 1832, Jane, 2nd dau. of Christopher French, of Frenchlawn, co. Roscommon, J.P., by Harriet, his wife, dau. of Joseph McDonnel, of Caranacon, co. Mayo, and had issue,
PATRICK HUGH, of Dundermott.
Roderic Thomas, b. 16 May, 1839 ; d. 1858.
NICHOLAS RODERICK (late of Dundermott), J.P., C.B., C.M.G, K.C.B., Chargé d'Affaires, Pekin, 1883, Washington 1885, at one time H.B. Minister at Pekin, afterwards at Constantinople, b. 3 July, 1843 ; m. Minna Margaret, eldest dau. of J. H. Hope-Scott (*see* BURKE's *Peerage*, LINLITHGOW, M.), and niece of Duke of Norfolk, K.G. ; d. 19 March, 1908, bur. at Scutari, leaving issue,
   1. Fearga Victoria Mary. 2. Muriel Margaret.
   3. Eileen Winifred Madeline.
Mr. O'Connor d. 23 Oct. 1860, and was s. by his eldest son,
PATRICK HUGH O'CONNOR, of Dundermott, co. Roscommon, J.P. and D.L., High Sheriff 1860, b. unm. 31 May, 1877, and was s. by his brother Nicholas Roderick (*above*).

Arms—Arg., an oak tree eradicated ppr., supported by two lions rampant combatant sa., in chief an ancient Irish crown or, and in base three lizards passant to the sinister barwise vert. *Crest*—Out of an Irish crown, as in the arms, an arm embowed in armour, the hand grasping a sword all ppr. *Motto*—Lamh chrodha Eirenn. *Residence*—Dalton, Northumberland. *Club*—New, Cheltenham.

O'CONOR OF MOUNT DRUID.

CHARLES MATHEW O'CONOR, of Mount Druid, co. Roscommon, J.P. and D.L., High Sheriff 1877, b. 2 Feb. 1847 ; s. his father 1862 ; m. 12 April, 1894, Alice, dau. of the late James Hale, of Temple View, co. Sligo. She d. 7 June, 1907, leaving issue,

Finola Mary.
Gertrude Gwendoline.

Lineage—This branch of the illustrious House of O'Conor comes next immediately after that of the chief, O'CONOR DON.

MATTHEW O'CONOR, of Mount Druid, Barrister-at-Law (6th son

of Denis O'Conor, of Belanagare, and brother of Owen O'Connor, on whom the title of O'CONOR DON devolved in 1820), m. Dec. 1804, Priscilla Forbes, and by her (who d. 16 June, 1853) had issue,
1. DENIS, of Mount Druid.
2. Arthur, of The Palace, Elphin, co. Roscommon, J.P., High Sheriff 1857, m. March, 1853, Katherine, dau. of Maurice Blake, of Ballinafad, co. Mayo (*see that family*), and d. 1870, having had issue,
   1. ARTHUR MATHEW, J.P., of The Palace, Elphin, b. 8 June, 1855.
   2. Charles Matthew, b. 1859 ; d. 2 Jan. 1912.
   3. Maurice Matthew.
   1. May. 2. Ann.
3. Martin, b. Aug. 1817 ; d. unm.
4. Owen, d. unm. 5. Matthew, b. 1821.
1. Priscilla, m. 1st, 1845, John Chester, of Kilsarine, co. Louth, and 2ndly, 1854, Edward Howley, of Belleek Castle, co. Mayo.
2. Catherine, d. 1889, unm.
3. Alicia, d. unm. 4. Mary Jane, d. unm.
5. Anna, d. unm. 1893.
6. Margaret, m. 1840, William Murphy, of Kilbrew, co. Meath, and Mount Merrion, co. Dublin. He d. s.p. 1901.
Mr. O'Conor d. 8 May, 1844, and was s. by his son,
DENIS O'CONOR, of Mount Druid, co. Roscommon, J.P. and D.L., High Sheriff 1836, b. 12 May, 1808 ; m. 31 May, 1841, Margaret Emily, eldest dau. of the late Nicholas Mahon Power, M.P., of Faithlegg House, co. Waterford (*see that family*). She d. Aug. 1900. He d. Dec. 1862, leaving issue,
1. CHARLES MATHEW, now of Mount Druid.
2. Owen Denis, b. 28 Oct. 1851 ; d. 24 March, 1907.
3. Denis A., b. 23 Sept. 1853.
1. Gertrude Mary, m. 15 June, 1876, Hon. Charles Nugent, 3rd son of Anthony, 9th Earl of Westmeath. He d.s.p. 8 Nov. 1906 (*see* BURKE's *Peerage*).
2. Eva.

Arms—Arg., an oak-tree eradicated and acorned ppr. *Crest*—An arm embowed in armour, holding a short sword all ppr.
Seat—Mount Druid, Castlerea, co. Roscommon. *Club*—Hibernian United Service, Dublin.

O'CONOR OF CHARLEVILLE.

EDMOND O'CONOR, of Charleville, co. Louth, J.P. and D.L., High Sheriff Louth 1894, Cavan 1908, late Lieut. 6th Batt. Royal Irish Rifles, b. 11 April, 1868 ; m. 23 April, 1891, Maud, eld. dau. of Daniel James O'Connell, of Grenagh, co. Kerry, and Frances his wife, dau. of Denis Shine Lawler, of Castle Lough, and has
1. RICHARD DANIEL, b. 6 March, 1892.
2. Edmond Henry, R.N., b. 12 July, 1893.
3. Evelyn John, b. 25 June, 1896.

Lineage—JOHN O'CONOR, m. Emily, dau. of Brian O'Reilly, 3rd son of Colonel John O'Reilly, M.P. for Conlyn, co. Cavan, by whom he had issue,
1, PATRICK (SIR), of whom presently.
1. Margaret, m. 1775, her first cousin, Dowell O'Reilly, of Heath House, Queen's Co., and d. the year of her marriage. Her husband m. Elizabeth Knox, and was ancestor of the O'REILLYs *of Heath House*.
2. Anna Maria, m. 1777, her first cousin, Mathew O'Reilly, of Knock Abbey (who m. 2ndly, 1789, Margaret Dowdall, and had issue, William, b. 1792, s. 1841, to Knock Abbey on the death of his half-brother Mathew, and d. 1844, and was s. by his son, Myles, now of Knock Abbey), and had issue,
   1. Matthew, of Knock Abbey, b. 1779, m. 1830, Susan, dau. of the Hon. George de la Poer Beresford, and d.s.p. 1841.
   1. Anna Maria, m. Richard Dease, and had issue, Mathew O'Reilly, of Dee Farm (now Charleville), co. Louth, M.P., b. 1819, and s. to a portion of the O'Reilly estates on the death of his uncle, Mathew O'Reilly, of Knock Abbey, in 1841, and d.s.p. 1887, having bequeathed them, together with a large personalty, to go towards paying the National Debt. The personalty was devoted to this object, but the estates passed by an entail made in 1777, on the marriage of Anna Maria O'Conor and Mathew O'Reilly (*see above*), to EDMOND O'CONOR, now of Charleville.

The only son,
SIR PATRICK O'CONOR, m. a dau. of John Terry, of Cork, and left issue,
1. Richard (Sir), Rear-Admiral, K.C.B., b. 1785, m. 1816, Hannah dau. and co-heiress of John Ross (a director of the East India Company), of Carshalton, Surrey, and had issue,
   1. Edmund Nagle Therry Ross, Capt. H.E.I.C.S., b. 1823, d.s.p. 1855.
   2. John Ross, Lieut. 16th Lancers, b. 1829, d.s.p. 1845.
   3. John, Capt. 6th Dragoons (Inniskillings), d. unm. at Berne, 1857.
   1. Elise Ross, m. 1834, Conrad Rudolf Count de Wattevillle de Loins, and had issue.
   2. Ellen Ross, d. unm. in Venice, 1882.
   3. Emily Clunes Ross, m. 6 Jan. 1855, Sir Maurice James O'Connell, 2nd bart. He d. 15 Jan. 1896, leaving issue (*see* BURKE's *Peerage*). She d. 23 Jan. 1907.
2. PATRICK, of whom presently.
1. Louisa, m. Henry O'Brien, of Kilcor, and had issue.
2. Emily, m. July, 1801, W. K. Crawford, M.D.

The younger son,

Odell.   THE LANDED GENTRY.   526

PATRICK O'CONOR, b. 1784, m. 1819, Margaret, dau. and co-heiress (twin with her sister, Hannah, Lady O'Conor), of John Ross, of Carshalton, and had issue,
1. RICHARD, of whom presently.
1. Louisa Ross, m. 1852, Baron Charmot de Breissant.
2. Hannah Ross, m. 1847, Baron von Wullersdorff d'Urbair, Admiral in the Austrian Service, Minister of Commerce, and at one time Plenipotentiary at the Court of St. James.
The only son,
RICHARD ROSS O'CONOR, Major in the 17th Regt., b. 1820 ; m. 1867, Angèle, dau. of Jules Beaurain de Seyssel, and d. 1877, leaving an only child,
EDMOND, now of Charleville.
His widow m. 2ndly, Count de la Noue, formerly State Councillor to the Emperor NAPOLEON III.

Seat—Charleville, Dunleer, co. Louth.

ODELL OF KILCLEAGH PARK.

LIEUT.-COL. THOMAS SMIJTH ODELL, of Kilcleagh Park, co. Westmeath, 3rd Batt. Highland Light Infantry, b. 16 Dec. 1866 ; m. 12 Sept. 1895, Henrietta Cecilia, younger dau. of Maj. David Dunlop Urquhart, of Strawberry-hill, King's Co., and has issue,

THOMAS URQUHART, b. 22 July, 1898

Lineage.—JOHN ODELL, of Ballingarry, co. Limerick, a Major in the Army whose mother, Jane Odell, was dau. of Sir Edward Mervin, Knt., obtained a grant of estates in the co. of Limerick containing 1,679 A. 3 R. 12 P. by patent dated in 1667. He was J.P. 1665, High Sheriff 1678-9, and M.P. for the borough of Askeaton in 1692. He m. Elizabeth Cane, and had issue,
1. John, of Bouldoragh, co. Limerick, and afterwards of Bannah, co. Kerry, who d. in the lifetime of his father intestate, and administration was granted to his widow, 6 July, 1691. He m. (articles dated 2 Feb. 1692-3, and settlement in pursuance thereof dated 8 Nov. 1693) the Hon. Constance Fitzmaurice, 4th dau. of William, Lord Kerry, and sister of Thomas, 1st Earl of Kerry, and by her (who m. 2ndly, Sampson Cox, of Ballynoe) had an only son,
John, of Pallace, who in his will dated 9 Jan. 1723-4, and proved 26 Feb. 1725-6, desires that he should be interred with his father at Ardfert. He d. 9 Jan. 1725-6, having m. (settlement dated 2 Dec. 1720) Anne, dau. of the Hon. James Fitzmaurice, of Bannah, by whom he had issue,
(1) Thomas, of Shannon Grove, who by his will dated 29 Oct. 1761, and proved 6 July, 1763, devised his estate to Thomas Odell, 2nd son of John Odell, of Fortwilliam, alias Bealdurogy. He m. Constance, dau. of Robert Fennell, of Curraghbane, co. Cork, but by her (whose will dated 30 Oct. 1789, was proved 3 March, 1823) he had no issue.
(2) John, d. an infant previously to 1729.
(3) Fitzmaurice, m. Eleanor, dau. of John Spread, of Ballycamnon, co. Cork, but by her (who made her will as widow of said Fitzmaurice, 15 Oct. 1762) he had no issue.
(4) William, living in 1729.
(1) Catherine, m. to the Rev. William John Bowen.
2. WILLIAM, of whom presently.
1. Judith, m. Capt. Charles Conyers.
2. Mary, m. 1st, Capt. John Browne, and 2ndly, John Langton.
3. Grissell, m. Henry Graydon, of Elvastown, near Blessington.
John Odell, of Ballingarry, made his will 19 Feb. 1699, which was proved 20 April, 1700. His 2nd son,
WILLIAM ODELL, of Bealdurogy, co. Limerick, J.P., d. intestate, and administration was granted to his widow, Anne, 19 Oct. 1722. He m. Anne, dau. of John Hunt, of Glangoole, co. Tipperary, sister of the Rev. Vere Hunt, and grandaunt of Vere Hunt, who was created a Baronet 1784, and by her had issue,
1. JOHN, his heir.   2. Edward.
3. William.   4. George.
1. Elizabeth.   2. Anne.
The eldest son and heir,
JOHN ODELL, of Fortwilliam, alias Bealdurogy, co. Limerick, High Sheriff for that co. 1751 ; m. 1st, (articles dated 19 July 1748), Elizabeth, youngest dau. of Robert Fennell, of Curraghbane, co. York, and by her had an only child, Frances, m. Francis Drew, of Drewsborough, co. Clare. He m. 2ndly, 28 Aug. 1751, Jane, dau. of John Baylee of Loughgur by her (who d. Sept. 1756) had issue
1. William of the Grove co. Limerick High Sheriff 1779, and M.P. for that co. in 1797 Governor and Custos Rotulorum a Col. and a Lord of the Admiralty m. Aphra dau. of John Crone (by Frances his wife dau. of Robert Fennell of Curraghbane), and by her (whose will, dated 8 March, 1811, was proved 23 March, 1815) had issue,
1. John of the Grove co. Limerick, d. unm.
2. Robert Spread, m.
3. Thomas, Barrister-at-Law, m. Mildred, dau. of John Hewson and had issue,
(1) William, Barrister-at-Law, m. Miss Scanlan.
(2) Francis, in Holy Orders.
(1) Mildred, m. William Browne.
(2) Aphra, d. unm.
4. Henry, a Major of Dragoons, d. unm. His will, dated 19 Oct. 1819, was proved 19 April, 1826.
5. William, an Officer in Dragoons, d. unm. intestate. Administration granted to his father 24 April, 1826.
6. Crone, m. Anne, dau. of Thomas Odell, of Ballingarry.
7. Edward, m. Maria, dau. of Capt. William Bernard, of co. Carlow.
1. Constance, m. John Browne, of Bridgetown, co. Clare. and Danesfort, co. Limerick.
2. Frances, m. Michael Scanlan, of co. Limerick.
3. Aphra, m. Samuel Stephen Raymond, of Riverstown, co. Kerry.
4. Eliza, m. 1st, George Massey, of Glan-William, and 2ndly Daniel Power.
5. Charlotte, d. unm.   6. Anne, d. unm.
2. THOMAS, of whom presently.
1. Catherine, m. Rev. Richard Gibbings, of Gibbings Grove, co. York.
2. Anne, m. Cornel Vereker, of Dunesfort.
John Odell, of Bealdurogy, made his will 16 Oct. 1759, which was proved 11 Dec. 1761. His 2nd son,
THOMAS ODELL, of Ballingarry, to whom Thomas Odell, of Shannon Grove, limited his estate by will dated 1761, m. Sarah, dau. of Thomas Westropp, of Ballysteen (by Jane his wife, dau. of Edmond Browne, of New Grove, co. Clare, by Jane Westropp, of Attyflin, his wife), and had issue,
1. Thomas, a Major, m. Miss Lambert, of co. Wexford.
2. JOHN, of whom presently.
3. Edmond, m. Jane, dau. of the Rev. Richard Gibbings. This Edmond assumed the name of WESTROPP.
4. Henry.   5. Another son.
6. William, m. Phœbe, dau. of John Brown.
1. Jane, m. 1st, Henry Baylee, of Loughgar, and 2ndly, Major Henry Bayley, and 3rdly, — Abbot.
2. Sarah, m. — Fitzgibbon.
3. Catherine, m. 1st, Henry B. Thornhill, of Castle Kevin, co. Cork ; 2ndly, Francis Roche ; and 3rdly, James Carmichael.
4. Anne, m. Crone Odell.
The 2nd son,
JOHN WESTROPP-ODELL, Lieut. R.N., m. at St. Margaret's, Westminster, 26 March, 1802, Philadelphia, dau. of Charles Smijth, and had a son,
THOMAS ALEXANDER ODELL, of Peckham Rye, Surrey, bapt. at Ballingarry, co. Limerick, 16 March, 1803 ; m. at Camberwell, 3 Oct. 1827, Deborah Bartlett Crowte Scruton, and had issue,
1. THOMAS SCRUTON, of Kilcleagh Park.
2. John, a Merchant in China, m. 1863, Elizabeth Robinson, dau. of Richard Bird, of Liverpool.
The elder son,
THOMAS SCRUTON ODELL, of Kilcleagh Park, co. Westmeath, b. 4 May, 1829 ; m. 1st, 6 Jan. 1858, Ellen, eldest dau. of John Bird, of Chester (who d.s.p. 4 Aug. following), and 2ndly, 27 Sept. 1864, Madeleine, 2nd dau. of Thomas Roe, of Coolfin, Queen's Co., and had by her an only surviving child,
THOMAS SMIJTH, now of Kilcleagh.

Arms—Per chevron or and arg., three crescents gu. Crest—A dexter arm embowed in armour, the hand holding a sword all ppr., the arm charged with two crescents in pale gu. Motto—Pro patria invictus.

Seat—Kilcleagh Park, Moate, co. Westmeath.

O'DONOGHUE OF THE GLENS.

GEOFFREY O'DONOGHUE, "O'Donoghue of the Glens," co. Kerry, b. 16 Jan. 1859 ; s. his father 1889 ; m. 1895, Maud, youngest dau. of William Charlton of Clonmacnoise House, King's Co., and has issue,
1. GEOFFREY, b. 8 Oct. 1896.
1. Maud Mary.
2. Nora Kathleen, b. 13 Sept. 1898.

Lineage.—The O'Donoghues are descended from the Royal House of Munster, and several distinguished chieftains of the name from the 10th to the 13th century are mentioned in the annals of Innisfallen, wherein they are styled Kings and Princes of the Eoganacht of Lough Lein. The O'Donoghues were divided into two

branches, the O'Donoghues of Lough Lein, now presumed to be extinct, and the O'Donoghues of the Glens. In the 14th century, GEFFREY O'DONOGHUE, of The Glynn, was chief of his name. He left two sons, Rory O'Donoghue, of The Glynn, Chief of his name 1450 (left a son, Daniel O'Donoghue, of The Glynn, who *d.s.p.*), and TEIGE O'DONOGHUE, father of GEFFERY O'DONOGHUE, Chief of his name, who was *s.* by TEIGE O'DONOGHUE, the father of JEFFERY O'DONOGHUE, of Killaher, in Kerry, attainted 1603, restored 1609, who by his wife Honora, dau. of M'Mahon, had (with a dau., Sheela, wife of Auliff O'Leary, of Dromeer, co. Cork), a son and successor, TEIGE O'DONOGHUE, of Glenflesk, co. Kerry, living 1628, the father of GEFFREY O'DONOGHUE, of Killaher, *alias* O'DONOGHUE, of The Glynn, who at his decease 1655, left, with a younger son, Teige, of Laherne, co. Kerry, an elder son and successor,

GEFFREY O'DONOGHUE, O'DONOGHUE of The Glens 1655, *m.* Alice Coppinger, and by her (who survived him) left three sons,
1. DANIEL, of whom presently.
2. Florence.   3. Geffrey.
In his will, which bears date 19 Jan. 1677, and was proved 22 March, 1678, he describes himself as "Geffrey O'Donoghue, *alias* O'Donoghue." His eldest son,

DANIEL O'DONOGHUE, O'DONOGHUE of The Glens, claimant to a portion of the Kerry estate 1700, and then described as eldest son and heir of Geffrey, was a distinguished Officer in the Army of King JAMES II. He *m.* Mary, dau. of Dermot M'Carthy, of Drishane, co. Cork, and had (with a dau., Elizabeth, wife of Francis Eager), a son and successor.

GEOFFREY O'DONOGHUE, O'DONOGHUE of The Glens, who *m.* Elizabeth, dau. of Randal M'Carthy More, by Mary his wife, dau. of Charles M'Carthy, of Cloghroe, co. Cork, and had,
1. DANIEL, of whom presently.
2. Timothy, *d.s.p.* 1 Aug. 1758.
  1. Alice, *m.* Edward O'Duffy.
  2. Elizabeth, *m.* John Markham.
3. Ellen, *m.* Charles McCarthie, of Headfort, co. Kerry.
4. Mary, *m.* Charles McCarthy, of Lyradane, co. Cork, son of Timothy McCarthy, of Lyradane, by Joan, dau. of Denis McCarthy, of Dooneen.

O'DONOGHUE *d.* 12 Sept. 1758, and was *s.* by his elder son,
DANIEL O'DONOGHUE, O'DONOGHUE of The Glens, who became, at the death, *unm.* in 1770, of his cousin, Charles M'Carthy More, representative of the great house of M'Carthy More. He *m.* Margaret, only surviving child of Murtogh M'Mahon, of Clonina, co. Clare, by Mary M'Donnell his wife, and by her (who *d.* Dec. 1788) had issue, at his decease 1800 (with a dau. Mary, who *d. unm.*), an only son and successor,

CHARLES O'DONOGHUE, O'DONOGHUE of The Glens, *b.* 1777 ; *m.* Mary, dau. of James Morrogh, of Cork, and by her (who *d.* April, 1845) had issue,
1. CHARLES JAMES, of whom presently.
2. Daniel, *d. unm.*
  1. Margaret, *d. unm.*   2. Mary, *d. unm.*
3. Jane, *m.* Sir James O'Connell, 1st bart. of Lakeview, co. Kerry, and *d.* 15 April, 1867.
4. Ellen, *m.* Jeremiah Stack Murphy, co. Cork.

O'DONOGHUE *d.* 21 Feb. 1808, and was *s.* by his elder son,
CHARLES JAMES O'DONOGHUE, O'DONOGHUE of The Glens, *m.* Jane, only dau. of John O'Connell, of Grenagh, co. Kerry, and niece of DANIEL O'CONNELL, Q.C., M.P., and by her (who *m.* 2ndly, John McCarthy O'Leary, of Coomlegane, co. Cork), left issue at his decease, 1 May, 1833, an only child,

DANIEL O'DONOGHUE, "O'DONOGHUE of The Glens," co. Kerry, M.P. for Tralee 1865 to 1885, and for Tipperary 1857 to 1865. *b.* 1833 ; *m.* 1858, Mary Sophie, dau. and co-heir of Sir John Ennis, 1st bart. (*extinct*) of Ballinahown, co. Westmeath, and by her (who *d.* 1891) had issue,
1. GEOFFREY, now The O'Donoghue.
2. Charles, *b.* 1860 ; *d.* 25 Jan. 1903.
3. Daniel, *d.* 1888.   4. John.
5. Angus, *d.* 1908.
1. Florence.

The O'Donoghue *d.* 1889, and was *s.* by his eldest son.

Arms—Vert, two foxes combatant arg., on a chief of the second an eagle volant sa. **Crest**—An arm in armour, embowed, holding a sword entwined with a snake, all ppr.

Seat—The Glens, Flesk, co. Kerry. **Residence**—Ballinahown Court, Athlone.

O'DONOVAN OF CLAN CATHAL.

MORGAN WILLIAM O'DONOVAN, C.B. (Civ.), THE O'DONOVAN, Chieftain of the ancient Irish sept of O'DONOVAN of Clan Cathal, J.P. and D.L. co. Cork, High Sheriff 1892, B.A. Magdalen Coll. Oxford, Lieut.-Col. and Hon. Col. Comdg. 4th Royal Munster Fusiliers (late South Cork Militia) *b.* 11 Feb. 1861 ; *m.* 9 July, 1892, Mary Eleanor, only dau. of the Rev. J. Yarker Barton, M.A., Chaplain to the Forces, and has issue.

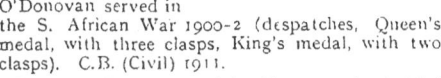

1. MORGAN JOHN WINTHROP, *b.* 2 May, 1893.
2. Miles Henry, *b.* 26 June, 1895.
3. Victor Teige, *b.* 20 June, 1897.
1. Eleanor Melian Frances.

O'Donovan served in the S. African War 1900-2 (despatches, Queen's medal, with three clasps, King's medal, with two clasps). C.B. (Civil) 1911.

Lineage.—This sept, one of the oldest among the aboriginal Irish, was originally located in co. Limerick, and after their removal from that county possessed an extensive territory, called the Cantred of Hy Donovan, situated between the towns of Bantry, Dunmanway, Rosscarbery, and Skibbereen, in the present barony of Carbery, and south-west of the co. of Cork. Keatinge traces its descent from the oldest branches of his Hibernian genealogy, and places their escutcheon as thirteenth in his armorial tables. Mr. Gough, in his edition of Camden's *Britannia*, following the account given by Dr. Smith, the Historian of the county of Cork, published 1750, says :— " The Irish antiquarians allow but eight families of royal extraction in Munster, of which they place four in Carbery, which comprehended all the south-west part of this county (Cork)." Of these were MacCarthy, O'Mahon or Mahown, O'Donovan, and O'Driscol. The sept in ancient times ruled over Hy Fidhgeinte, a territory extending along the banks of the river Maigue, co. Limerick, on which stood the Castle of Crom. Driven from their territory by the Fitzgeralds and De Burghos after the invasions of 1172, they settled in the barony of Carbery, co. Cork, where the estates of the present Chieftain are situate.

CATHAL, Chief of Hy Fidhgeinte, was slain by Callaghan Cashel, King of Munster, A.D. 964, and was *s.* by his son,

DONOVAN, who ruled as Chief 977 ; from him the sept took their tribe name. Seventh in descent from DONOVAN was

CROM O'DONOVAN, *The O'Donovan*, who was in possession of the castle of Crom, standing on the banks of the river Maigue, co. Limerick. According to the genealogies of MacFirbis, he had three sons, from whom descend all the families of O'Donovan and Donavan. These sons were,
1. CATHAL, ancestor of the Chieftain.
2. ANESLIS, who had four sons,
  1. Donough Mor.   2. Rickard.
  3. Walter.
  4. Raghnal, ancestor of the Sloicht Aneslis Mc Icroim O'Donovan, who possessed Gleann a Chroim, or Crom's Glen. The representative of this branch *temp.* Queen ELIZABETH, DONEL MCCNOGHER BOY MCANESLIS O'DONOVAN, of Glen l'Chroim, according to an inq. port mort. taken at Cork 21 Sept. 1625, *d.* 3 Jan. 1602.
3. LOCHLIN, ancestor of the sept of O'DONOVAN of *Clan Loghlin*, who possessed a territory containing thirty-six ploughlands lying between the river Roury and Glandore Harbour. He had a son and successor,
  DONNCHADH, or DONOUGH O'DONOVAN, of Loch Crott, whose lineal descendant and representative,
    DONEL NA CARTAN O'DONOVAN, of Cloghatradbally Castle, adjoining Glandore Harbour, was *Chief of Clan Loghlin temp.* Queen ELIZABETH, according to an inq. post mort. taken at Bandon Bridge 14 Aug. 6 CHARLES I. He *d.* 10 May, 1580 leaving a son, Donel Oge na Cartan O'Donovan (*see* DONOVAN of *Ballymore*).

O'Donovan was killed by the O'Mahonys A.D. 1254, according to the *Annals of Innisfallen*. His eldest son,
  CATHAL O'DONOVAN, *The O'Donovan*, *s.* as Chieftain. From him the senior line of the sept were known as "Clan Cathal." The sixth Chieftain in descent from him was

CATHAL O'DONOVAN, *The O'Donovan*, temp. HENRY VII. (From his near kinsman, Teige O'Donovan, of Gorteenither, descended O'DONOVAN, of O'Donovan's Cove, co. Cork, the representative of whom, Timothy O'Donovan, of O'Donovan's Cove, d. without surviving male issue 16 March, 1874, aged 84, and was s. by his nephew, RICHARD O'DONOVAN, son of Richard O'Donovan, of Fort Lodge, J.P. co. Cork, by Maria O'Sullivan his wife.) O'Donovan was s. by his son,

DONEL O'DONOVAN, *The O'Donovan*, who was known as " Done, nag-Croiceann," or Donel of the Hides, so called from having been, when a child, wrapped up in cow hides to conceal him from the enemies of his father. He was inaugurated Chieftain by McCarthy Reagh, Chieftain of Carbery 1560, and d. 1584, when he was s. by his son,

DONEL O'DONOVAN, *The O'Donovan*, inaugurated by McCarthy Reagh, who delivered him the white wand, and was recognised by Lord Chancellor Adam Loftus, 12 Feb. 1592, as Chieftain lawfully inaugurated according to the Irish custom. He surrendered his territory of Clan Cathal to JAMES I. 1608, and received a re-grant of the entire of it 1615.* He m. Joanna, dau. of Sir Owen MacCarthy Reagh, Knt. of Carbery, and had seven sons,

1. DANIEL, his successor.
2. TEIGE, of Rahine and Drishane, m. Joane Goggin, and d. 1639, leaving a son,
   MURROGH DONOVAN, of Littuclicky, m. Jane Galway, by whom he had seven sons. The eldest son,
   CORNELIUS DONOVAN, m. 1684, his cousin, Helena, only child of Daniel O'Donovan, *The O'Donovan*, by his 1st wife, Victoria Coppinger, and had a son,
   MORGAN DONOVAN, of Ballincallah, B.A. Oxon, J.P., b. 1687; m. 1733, Mary, dau. of Thomas Ronayne, of Hodnettswood, and had issue,
   1. MORGAN, his heir.
      1. Mary, m. John Townsend Becher, of Creagh, co. Cork, and had issue.
      2. Anne, m. Warden Flood, of Paulstown Castle, co. Kilkenny, M.P., Judge of the Court of Admiralty, Ireland.
   The only son,
   MORGAN DONOVAN, of the city of Cork, s. his father 1759. He m. 1766, Melian Towgood, dau. of Savage French, of Marino, co. Cork (see FRENCH of Cuskinny), by whom (who d. 1813) he had issue,
   1. MORGAN (REV.), of whom hereafter, was Chieftain on the death of Gen. Richard O'Donovan 1829.
   2. Savage, M.D., m. Miss Jagoe, and d.s.p. 1807.
   3. Philip, d. unm. Dec. 1837.
   4. Sampson Towgood, d. unm. 1809.
3. Murrogh, of Carrigarruffe, ancestor of O'DONOVAN, of Malaga, in Spain, who registered his pedigree in Ulster's Office 1771.
4. Donogh, ancestor of O'DONOVAN of Cooldurragh, co. Cork.
5. Dermod.
6. Richard, ancestor of O'DONOVAN, of Donovan Street, Cork.
7. Readagh, ancestor of Clan Keady Donovan, from whom descend O'DONOVAN, of Lisheens and of Ardahill.

O'Donovan d. about 1638, and was s. by his eldest son and heir, DANIEL O'DONOVAN, *The O'Donovan*, m. Gyles, dau. of Sir Roger O'Shaughnessy, Knt. of co. Galway. O'Donovan was stripped of all his estates by OLIVER CROMWELL, a part only of which were restored to his son under CHARLES II. He d. 1660, and was s. by his son,

DANIEL O'DONOVAN, *The O'Donovan*, Col. in the service of JAMES II., M.P. for Baltimore 1689, of which he was also Portreeve. He distinguished himself in 1689, by his zealous and steady exertions in the cause of JAMES II.; among other actions, defending Charlesfort at Kinsale with vigour. He surrendered the keys of it into the Earl of Marlborough's own hand, and finally made honourable terms. He m. 1st, Victoria, dau. of Capt. Coppinger, by whom he had an only child, Helena, who m. her cousin, Cornelius Donovan, ancestor of the present chieftain, and 2ndly, Elizabeth, dau. of Major Touson, by whom he had,
1. Daniel, } both d. young.
2. Barry, }
3. RICHARD, his successor.
4. Cornelius, d. 1737.

O'Donovan d. 1705, and was s. by his son,
RICHARD O'DONOVAN, *The O'Donovan*, m. 1703, Ellinor Fitzgerald, dau. of the Knight of Kerry, by whom he had issue,
DANIEL, his heir.
Elizabeth, m. Sylvester O'Sullivan, MacFineen Duff, of co. Kerry.

O'Donovan was s. by his son,
DANIEL O'DONOVAN, *The O'Donovan*, m. 1st, Anne, dau. of James Kearney, of Garrettstown, co. Cork, by whom he had no issue, and 2ndly, 1763, Jane, dau. of John Becher, of Hollybrook, by whom he left issue,
1. RICHARD, his successor.
2. John, an Officer in the Army, killed 1796, in the Maroon war, in Jamaica, unm.
   1. Helen, m. John Warren, son of Sir Robert Warren, 1st bart. of Warren's Court, and d.s.p. 1840.
2. Jane, d. unm. 1833.

O'Donovan, by his will, dated 1770, devised a remainder in his estates on failure of the male issue of his sons, " to his kinsman, Morgan Donovan, of the city of Cork." He did so to fulfil a mutual

---

* O'DONOVAN built Castle Donovan in the Hills, three miles north of Dromoleague, co. Cork, in the north wall of which is a block of limestone, containing the memorial IHS MARIA . DOD . IC . 1626 . DOC, in raised letters two and a half inches long. The castle is still standing, though much dilapidated, and has ninety-two steps leading to the battlements.

---

agreement between Morgan's father and him, that on failure of the male issue of either branch, the survivor should inherit, in order to preserve the family estates to whoever should be chieftain of the sept. He was s. by his son,

RICHARD O'DONOVAN, *The O'Donovan*, b. 1768, Gen. in the Army, served with honour in the 6th Dragoons in the campaigns in Flanders and Spain. He m. Emma Ann, dau. of Robert Powell, by whom he had no issue. O'Donovan suffered a recovery of his estates, and left the ancient estates of Clan Cathal to his wife absolutely. He d. Nov. 1829, when his chieftaincy reverted to the descendant of the 2nd son of Donel, the Chieftain, who d. 1638.

MORGAN O'DONOVAN (REV.), *The O'Donovan*, Chief of Clan Cathal, Rector of Dundurrow, co. Cork, b. 1769; m. Nov. 1795, Alicia, eldest dau. of William Jones, of the City of Cork, by Elinor his wife, youngest dau. of William Winthrop, of Cork, by Alicia Wrixon his wife, and by her (b. 1777 ; d. 29 Aug. 1847) had issue,
1. MORGAN WILLIAM, his successor.
2. William Jones, b. Jan. 1799 ; d. unm. Aug. 1852.
3. HENRY WINTHROP, successor to his brother.
1. Melian, m. Jan. 1839, Richard Henry Hedges Becher, of Hollybrook, J.P. co. Cork, afterwards of Lakelands, and d.s.p. 28 May, 1859.
2. Eleanor, m. June, 1839, William Lemuel Shuldham, J.P. of Coolkelure, Dunmanway, co. Cork, who d. 25 March, 1847.

O'Donovan d. 17 Oct. 1839, and was s. by his eldest son,
MORGAN WILLIAM O'DONOVAN, *The O'Donovan*, Barrister-at-Law, b. 21 Aug. 1796 ; m. 2 July, 1844, Susanna, 2nd dau. of William Armstrong Creed, of Ballybrack, co. Cork, and by her (who d. Nov. 1864) had a dau.,
Melian, who d. Jan. 1846.

O'Donovan d. 16 Dec. 1870, and was s. by his only surviving brother,
HENRY WINTHROP O'DONOVAN, *The O'Donovan*, Chieftain of the ancient Irish sept of O'Donovan of Clan Cathal, M.A., J.P. and D.L., High Sheriff 1889, b. 1 Jan. 1812 ; m. 15 July, 1848, Amelia, dau. of Gerald De Courcy O'Grady, of Kilballyowen, co. Limerick, The O'GRADY (*see that family*), and had by her (who d. 26 May, 1896) issue,
MORGAN WILLIAM, his successor.
Anne Melian, m. 21 June, 1883, Allan Neason Adams, Capt. King's Own Scottish Borderers (25th Regt.), and by him (who d. 31. Dec. 1893) had a son, Henry William Allan Adams, Lieut. R.N., b. 13 June, 1884 ; m. 20 Aug. 1907, Gladys Amabella, only dau. of late Col. H. C. Macdonald, 108th Regt.

O'Donovan d. 24 May, 1890.

Arms—Arg., a dexter arm couped above the wrist, vested gu., cuffed of the first, the hand grasping a sword in pale, the blade entwined with a serpent descending all ppr. *Crest*—An eagle rising or. *Mottoes*—Adjuvante Deo in hostes ; Vir super hostem (a translation of the ancient slogan, or call to war, of the sept, viz., Giolla ar a-namhuid a-bu.)

Seat—Liss Ard, Skibbereen, co. Cork.

O'FARRELL OF DALYSTON.

CHARLES RICHARD JOHN O'FARRELL, of Dalyston, co. Galway, J.P., High Sheriff 1906, b. 22 Sept. 1875. s. his father 1892.

Lineage.—The Farrells, now of Dalyston, claim descent from the O'Ferrals of Mornin and Bawn, co. Longford, who were of the Clan Boy. The old Castle of Mornin still stands, and here the family were resident in 1688. Shortly after, on the defeat of King JAMES II., they were dispossessed and their property confiscated. On a tombstone in the churchyard of Moydow, co. Longford, the burial place of the O'Ferralls of Mornin and Bawn, are inscribed the names of Robert O'Farrell, of Bawn, and of his wife, Alice, and also that of James O'Farrell, of Minard (son of Robert and Alice O'Farrell, of Bawn), who d. 26 Nov. 1771, aged 86. This James is the first of the name of O'Farrell who resided at Minard. He never married, and on fixing his residence at Minard, took his sister to live with him. This lady m. a namesake of her own, and had several children, viz., 1, RICHARD O'FARRELL, who d. at an advanced age in France ; 2, Robert, who d. at Minard ; 1, Alice, who m. Charles Evers, and was mother *inter alios*, of Mary, the wife of JAMES FARRELL, of Minard ; 2, Elizabeth, who m. Peter Farrell, of Coldragh ; and another dau., who m. a Mr. Dalton. At the decease of James O'Farrell, of Minard, 26 Nov. 1771, the whole of his property devolved on his sister, from whom it passed to her son, ROBERT, at whose death it was divided between the husbands (Charles Evers and Peter Farrell) of his sisters, Alice and Elizabeth.

JAMES FARRELL who m. some time about 1772, Mary, dau. of Charles and Alice Evers, was son of Patrick O'Farrell, who accompanied James O'Farrell, the first of Minard, to that place, and resided with his wife and family at Minard to the time of his death, 1780. Mr. James Farrell occupied a portion of the farms of Minard and Lorath, and *d.* 17 Jan. 1789, aged 38, being bur. at Moydow. His son,

CHARLES FARRELL, *b.* at Minard, co. Longford, 24 Aug. 1774, took the degree of M.D. at the University of Edinburgh 1798, and was much distinguished in the medical profession. He passed many years in high official position in the East. Dr. Farrell *d.* 1855, having bequeathed his extensive property to his nephew,

CHARLES GEORGE O'FARRELL, of Dalyston, co. Galway, J.P., *b.* 1825; *s.* to the estates of his late maternal uncle, Charles Farrell, of Dalyston, and assumed in consequence by Royal Licence, 21 Feb. 1855, the surname and arms of FARRELL instead of his patronymic CARROLL, and subsequently, 28 Jan. 1857, by Royal Licence, resumed the name of O'FARRELL in lieu of that of FARRELL; *m.* 20 Jan. 1870, Kate Mary Constance, only dau. of James William MacLoghlin, of Ballyglass, co. Westmeath, and had issue,
1. CHARLES RICHARD JOHN, now of Dalyston.
2. Richard.   3. Henry.
4. Frederick.
1. Kathleen Maud Mary.
2. Ethel, *m.* Claude W. R. Hutchinson, of Eggleston Hall, Durham.

Mr. C. G. O'Farrell (who was son of John Carroll, of Edgeworthstown, co. Longford, by Margaret his wife, dau. of James Farrell, of Minard) *d.* 1892, and was *s.* by his son.

Arms—Per fesse or and vert a lion rampant counterchanged on a canton gu. an Irish harp of the first. **Crest**—On an Eastern crown or, a greyhound courant per pale arg. and sa., gorged with a collar, therefrom a broken chain, both gu. **Motto**—Cu Reabtha.

Seat—Dalyston, near Loughrea, co. Galway.

MORE-O'FERRALL OF BALYNA.

EDWARD GERALD MORE-O'FERRALL, of Balyna, co. Kildare, and Lisard, co. Longford, J.P. and D.L., High Sheriff 1882, *b.* 1846; *m.* 1871, Juliana Margaret, dau. of Henry Lambert, M.P., of Camagh, co. Wexford, and has, with other issue,
1. JOHN, *b.* 1872.
2. Gerald More (*Balyna, Moyvalley, R.S.O.*), *m.* 23 Oct. 1907, Geraldine Mary, eldest dau. of late Lord Maurice FitzGerald (*see* BURKE's *Peerage*, LEINSTER, D.), and has issue,
    Edward George, *b.* 5 Aug. 1908.
1 Ellen Letitia, *m.* 9 Jan. 1904, Charles Hugh O'Conor, 3rd son of Right Hon. O'Conor Don, P.C. (*see that family*).

Lineage.—CHARLES O'MORE, of Balyna, *d.* 1601, leaving (by Margaret Scurlock his wife) two sons and a dau.,
1. Roger, Col. Confederated Catholics 1646, *m.* Jane, dau. of Sir Patrick Barnewall, Knt. of Turvey, and had issue,
    1. Charles, Col. in the Army, killed at Aughrim 12 July, 1691, *d.s.p.*
    1. Anne, wife of Patrick Sarsfield, of Lucan, and mother of PATRICK, EARL OF LUCAN.
    2. Eleanor, wife of Daniel MacMoragh Kavanagh.
    3. Mary, wife of Tirogh O'Neill.
    4. Elizabeth, wife of Christopher Bealing.
2. LEWIS, of whose line we treat.
1. Margaret, *m.* Thomas Plunkett, of Clonebrancy.

The 2nd son,
LEWIS MORE (Col.), one of the Confederated Catholics in 1646, *m.* Mary, dau. of Philip MacHugh O'Reilly, and was father of ANTHONY MORE of Balyna, who *m.* Anne, dau. of Alexander Hope, of Mullingar, and had (with a dau., Mary, wife of Capt. Conor O'Reilly) two sons,
1. LEWIS, his heir.
2. Roger, whose will (dated 1 March, 1746) was proved 9 Jan. 1748. He *m.* Elinor, dau. of William Wright and had issue,
    1. Anthony O'More, Gen. in the Spanish service.
    1. May, wife of Robert Daly, of Caulfield.
    2. Mary, wife of Packington Edgeworth, of Longwood.

The elder son,
LEWIS MORE, of Balyna, *m.* Alicia, dau. of Con O'Neill, and had (with a dau., Mary, Maid of Honour to the Queen of Spain, *m.* — Ward, of Madrid) a son and heir,
JAMES MORE, of Balyna, whose will bears date 13 Dec. 1778, by Mary, his wife (*d.* 30 July, 1771), dau. of Ambrose Madden, of Derryhoran, he left an only dau. and heir,
LETITIA MORE, who *m.* 19 April, 1751, RICHARD O'FERRALL (whose sister, Catherine, *m.* George Lattin, of Morristown), only son of Ambrose O'Ferrall, by Jane Dillon, his wife, and dying 1778 (her husband survived till 1790), left (with several daus., Mrs. Boulger, Mrs. Morris, Mrs. Taylor, Mrs. Pallas, of Grouse Hall, co. Cavan, and Mrs. Nugent, of Killasona, co. Longford) three sons,
1. AMBROSE, his heir.
2. James, Major-Gen. in the Austrian service, *d.* 1828, aged 75.
3. Charles, Col. in the Sardinian service, *d.* 1831, *m.* Margaret, dau. of John Whyte of Leixlip (*see* WHYTE *of Loughbrickland*).

The eldest son,
AMBROSE O'FERRALL, of Balyna, *m.* 1796, Anne, only child of John Bagot, of Castle Bagot, co. Dublin, by Anne, his 1st wife, only dau. and heir of W. Walsh, of Kilmurry, co. Meath, by Elizabeth Nangle his wife, and by her (who *d.* 1810) had issue,

1. RICHARD MORE (RIGHT HON.), of Balyna House.
2. John Lewis More, of Lissard, co. Longford, and Granite Hall, co. Dublin, J.P., D.L., M.A., Barrister-at-Law, Commissioner of Metropolitan Police, Dublin, *m.* 1836, Clare, dau. of Thomas Seagrave, of Cabra, co. Dublin, and *d.* 21 Jan. 1881, leaving
    1. EDWARD GERALD MORE, of Lissard and Balyna, to which latter estate he *s.* on the death of his cousin.
    1. Mary.   2. Maria.
    3. Ellen, *m.* 1879, The Right Hon. O'Conor Don, P.C. (*see* O'CONOR DON).
3. James More, *d. unm.*   4. Robert More (Rev.), *d.* 1834.
5. Edward More, of Kildangan, co. Kildare, High Sheriff co. Kildare, 1856-7, *m.* 1849, Susan, only child of Dominick O'Reilly, of Kildangan Castle, co. Kildare, and by her (who *d.* 1854) left at his decease, 1875, an only son,
    Dominick More O'Ferrall, of Kildangan, High Sheriff co. Kildare, J.P. and D.L., 1879, *b.* 1854; *m.* 1898, Annie, dau. of Col. Francis MacDonnell, C.B., of Plas Newydd, co. Monmouth, and has issue,
    (1) Roderic Charles, *b.* 25 July, 1903.
    (2) Francis Ambrose, *b.* 15 Aug. 1904.
    (3) Edward Roger, *b.* 30 May, 1906.
1. Mary Ann, *d. unm.*   2. Letitia, a nun.
3. Louisa, *d. unm.*   4. Catherine, *d.* 1886.
5. Rose Anna (dec.), *m.* Thomas Errington, of Clintz, co. York.

Mr. O'Ferrall *m.* 2ndly, 1811, Margaret, youngest dau. of Francis Dunne, of Brittas, Queen's Co., which lady *d.* 1826. He *d.* 1835, aged 83, and was *s.* by his eldest son,

RIGHT HON. RICHARD MORE O'FERRALL, of Balyna, co. Kildare, P.C., J.P. and D.L., *b.* 1797; *m.* 28 Sept. 1839, Hon. Matilda Southwell, 2nd dau. and co-heir of Thomas Anthony, 3rd Viscount Southwell, K.P., and by her (who *d.* 25 May, 1882) had issue,
AMBROSE, late of Balyna, co. Westmeath.
Maria Anne, *m.* 19 July, 1860, Sir Walter Nugent, Bart., of Donore.

Mr. More-O'Ferrall, who was M.P. for co. Kildare 1830-47, and for co. Longford 1859-65, was appointed a Lord of the Treasury 1835, Secretary to the Admiralty 1839, and Secretary to the Treasury 1841. From 1847 to 1851 he held the office of Governor of Malta. He *d.* 27 Oct. 1880. He was *s.* by his son,

AMBROSE MORE-O'FERRALL, of Balyna, co. Kildare, J.P. and V.L., Baron 1876, of Carlow, High Sheriff 1887, *b.* 26 Sept. 1846; *m.* 24 Oct. 1872, Jessie Frances, dau. of Patrick Robert Gordon-Canning, of Hartpury Court, co. Gloucester. He *d.* 16 April, 1911, having had issue,
1. Mabel, *b.* 1873; *m.* 1896, Major E. J. C. Dease eld. son of Edmund Gerald Dease, D.L., of Rath (*see that family*).
2. Violet, *b.* 1874.
3. Alice, *b.* 1880, *m.* 1907, Alexander Lattin Mansfield, son of George Mansfield of Morristown, Lattin, and has issue (*see that family*).

He was *s.* by his cousin, as above.

Arms—Quarterly: 1st and 4th vert, a lion rampant or (O'FERRALL); 2nd and 3rd vert, a lion rampant in chief three mullets or (O'MORE). **Crests**—1. On a ducal coronet or, a greyhound springing sable (O'FERRALL).   2. A dexter hand couped gules (O'MORE). **Motto**—Cu reu bhaid.

Seats—Balyna House, Enfield, co. Kildare, and Lisard, Edgeworthstown. **Club**—Kildare Street.

OGILBY OF ARDNARGLE AND PELLIPAR HOUSE.

ROBERT JAMES LESLIE OGILBY, of Ardnargle, Limavady, and Pellipar House, Dungiven, co. Londonderry, J.P. and D.L., High Sheriff 1911, formerly Lieut. 2nd Life Guards, *b.* 27 Nov. 1880.

Lineage.—This branch settled in Ireland at the Plantation. All the records of the family (originally Ogilvie) were destroyed by fire in Scotland in the year 1784. The original residence was at Calhame, in Aberdeenshire.

JOHN OGILVIE, M.D., Aberdeen, settled in Limavady, was a great friend of the celebrated Bishop Burnett, *m.* Elizabeth Agnew, of the Scottish family of that name, who settled in co. Antrim. He was *s.* by his son,

ALEXANDER OGILBY, who changed the spelling of the name from Oglivie, *m.* 1st, Ann Smith, and by her had issue,
1. ALEXANDER, his heir.
1. Mary Ann, *m.* 1st, John Boyle, of Bridge Hill, Newtown-Limavady, and had issue (*see that family*). She *m.* 2ndly, Charles

Harris, of London, and by him had issue. She d. 28 Nov. 1773. Mr. Alexander Ogilby m. 2ndly, Mary Campbell, and by her had issue,
2. George, m. 1st, Mary, dau. of Michael Ross, by his wife Hester Steer, and by her had issue,
  1. Alexander, d.s.p.
  2. Robert, d.s.p.
Mr. George Ogilby m. 2ndly, Miss Smyth, and had issue, one dau.
3. Robert, of Spring Hill, Newtown-Limavady, M.D., m. Jane, 2nd dau. of James Alexander, by his wife Elizabeth Ross, and had issue,
  1. William Law, m. his cousin, Elizabeth, eldest dau. of John Power and Ann Ross, and had issue, one son and six daus.
  2. Alexander, d.s.p. 3. Robert, d.s.p.
  1. Elizabeth, m. her cousin, John Moore, eldest son of Nicholas Moore and Mary Boyle, and had issue.
  2. Mary, d.s.p.
Mr. Alexander Ogilby was s. by his eldest son,
ALEXANDER OGILBY, m. Mary, eldest dau. of James Alexander, of Newtown-Limavady (whose family came originally from the shire of Clackmannan in Scotland), by his wife Elizabeth Ross and had issue,
  1. JOHN, his heir.
  2. Alexander of Kilcatten, d. 1846, s.p.
  3. James, d.s.p.
  4. William, d.s.p.
  5. Robert, of Pellipar House, Dungiven, purchased the entire Manor of Limavady from the Conolly family, also large properties in the co. Tyrone, and estates at Woolwich in Kent. He was also lessee of the estates of the Skinners' Company in the co. of Londonderry. His will, dated 11 Oct. 1838, was proved 28 Nov. 1839. He m. 1st, 1782, Mary, dau. of John Marland, of Dublin. She d.s.p. 1784. He m. 2ndly, 5 Oct. 1809, Joice, eldest dau. of James Scott, of Willsboro', co. Londonderry, by his wife Catherine Leslie, and by her had issue,
    1. Alexander, m. (setts. dated 10 July, 1833) Isabella, only dau. of the Rev. William Curwen, of Bryanston Square, London, and had issue,
      Isabella, m. 26 Aug. 1863, Charles, 3rd Baron Ellenborough. She d. 22 April, 1874. He d. 9 Oct. 1890, leaving issue.
    2. James, of Pellipar House, Dungiven, b. 1812; d. 17 Aug. 1885, s.p., intestate.
  6. David (Sir), b. 3 Aug. 1755, served in Volunteers, entered East India Service in 1781, trained at Lockies Royal Military Academy, Chelsea, served in India for 22 years, and retired as Major. Knighted, 29 Jan. 1804, by Earl Hardwicke, Lord Lieutenant, for his conspicuous services; m. twice, and had issue,
    1. David Fitzroy.
    2. Robert Edwin, m. Louise Elizabeth Paullin, and had issue,
      (1) Clarence Maud.
      (2) Edith Alice, m. twice.
      (3) Grace Stanton Titcombe.
    3. Leslie James Deskford.
  7. Leslie of Strangemore, Dungiven, d.s.p.
  1. Ann, d.s.p. 2. Elizabeth, d.s.p.
  3. Mary, m. James Ross, 2nd son of Michael Ross, and d. 1843, leaving issue.
  4. Jane, m. Andrew Ferguson, of Burt, co. Donegal. She d.s.p 1 Oct. 1856.
Mr. Ogilby was s. by his eldest son,
JOHN OGILBY, of Ardnargle. Newtown-Limavady, b. 1846, m. Jane, dau. of James Simpson, of Armagh, and had issue,
  1. Alexander, d.s.p. 2. John, d.s.p.
  3. JAMES, his heir. 4. David, d.s.p.
  5. Leonard, m. Elizabeth Darley, and had issue, two sons.
  6. ROBERT LESLIE, of whom presently.
  7. William, m. Miss Kenny, and d.s.p.
  1. Ann, m. Mr. Jameson, and had issue.
  2. Jane, m. 1809, her cousin, John Ross and had issue.
  3. Mary, m. her cousin, William Stuart Ross, and had issue.
Mr. Ogilby was s. by his 3rd son,
JAMES OGILBY, of Ardnargle, Newtown-Limavady, m. Bridget Rush, and d.s.p. 1849 (will dated 23 March, 1848). Mr. Ogilby was s. by his brother,
ROBERT LESLIE OGILBY, of Ardnargle, J.P. and D.L. co. Londonderry, High Sheriff 1854, b. 1798, m. 1844, Elizabeth Matilda, dau. of Major William Henry Rainey, H.E.I.C.S., and by her (who d. 24 June, 1903), had issue,
  1. ROBERT ALEXANDER, his heir.
  2. John W. H., d.s.p. 3. David Leslie.
  1. Margaret Harriet, d. unm. 19 April, 1908.
  2. Jane Ann, d. unm. 25 July, 1908.
  3. Elizabeth, d.s.p.
  4. Mary Isabella, m. 13 May, 1895, Capt. Marmaduke Langdale Kelham, R.N., of Bleasby Hall (see that family).
Mr. Ogilby d. 21 May, 1872, and was s. by his eldest son,
ROBERT ALEXANDER OGILBY, of Ardnargle, Limavady, and Pellipar House, Dungiven, J.P. and D.L. co. Londonderry, High Sheriff 1887, Capt. 4th King's Own Regiment, served in Zulu War. Under the will of his great uncle, Robert Ogilby (see above), he s. on the death of his cousin, James Ogilby, to the Limavady, Pellipar, Tyrone and Woolwich estates, b. 15 Jan. 1850; m. 23 Oct. 1875, Helen Sarah, 2nd dau. of the Rev. George Bomford Wheeler, M.A., Rector of Ballysax, co. Kildare, and had issue,
  1. ROBERT JAMES LESLIE, now of Ardnargle and Pellipar.
  1. Ethel Maude, m. 29 June, 1898, Edward Maurice FitzGerald Boyle, eldest son of Major Alexander Boyle, J.P., of Bridge Hill, Limavady, and has issue (see that family).
  2. Eileen Leslie, m. 9 April, 1902, Maurice Marcus McCausland, J.P. and D.L. co. Londonderry, of Drenagh, Limavady, eldest son of Conolly Thomas McCausland, D.L., by his wife, the Hon.

Laura St. John, dau. of 11th Baron St. John, of Bletsoe, and has issue (see that family).
3. Mabel Norah, m. 3 Jan. 1906, Major George De la Maine Crocker, Royal Munster Fusiliers.
4. Esther Gladys, d.v.p. 21 May, 1900.
5. Mildred Constance, m. 17 June, 1908, Capt. Lionel St. Helier Morley, Sherwood Foresters, son of late Col. Morley, 79th Highlanders, and has issue.
Mr. Ogilby d. 14 April, 1902.

Arms—Arg. a lion passant guardant gu. between two crescents, one in chief and the other in base az. Crest—A lion rampant gu. armed and langued az. supporting a tilting spear entwined with a string of trefoils ppr.
Seats—Ardnargle, Limavady, and Pellipar House, Dungiven. Clubs—Cavalry, and Bachelors.

O'GORMAN OF BELLEVUE.

COLONEL NICHOLAS PURCELL O'GORMAN, of Bellevue, co. Clare, late 10th (Lincoln) Regt., b. 16 Dec. 1845; m. 1884, Florence Ellen, dau. of Cairns Daniel, C.S.I., Commissioner, Indian C.S.

Lineage.—JAMES O'GORMAN, of Ennis, b. 1717; m. 1760, Susanna Mahon, of Limerick, who was third in descent from Col. Nicholas Purcell, who commanded the cavalry at Aughrim, and was one of the signatories to the Treaty of Limerick. (Madame de Crequy in the tenth volume of her Souvenirs mentions the O'Gormans as amongst forty-one of the families of " ancienne Chevalerie " long anterior to 1399.) By Susanna his wife (who d. 1812) he left at his decease, 1787. a son,
NICHOLAS PURCELL O'GORMAN, Q.C., Chairman and Assistant-Barrister, co. Kilkenny, m. 1st, 1810, Frances Anne, dau. of Charles Smith, of Castle Park, co. Limerick, by whom (who d. 1824) he had issue,
  1. NICHOLAS SMITH, of whom presently.
  2. Purcell, of Springfield, near Waterford, B.A., M.P. for that city, 1874-80, Major in the Army, late of the 90th Foot, b. 1820; m. 1853, Sarah (d. 18 Feb. 1910), 2nd dau. of Thomas Mellor, of Ashton, co. Lancaster, and d. 1888, leaving issue, one son and two daus.
    1. Susan Frances, m. 1850, Major Edmund Moore Mulcahy, who d. 1880.
Mr. O'Gorman m. 2ndly, 1827, Mary Power, of Ballygallane, Lismore, by whom he had three children.
  3. Alexander.
  2. Fanny. 1. Kate.
He d. 1857. His eldest son,
NICHOLAS SMITH O'GORMAN, late of Bellevue, co. Clare, B.A., J.P., High Sheriff 1878, Barrister-at-Law, b. 1814; m. 1843, Margaret, dau. of Michael Kenny, of Dysert and Holywell, co. Clare. She d. 29 April, 1899. He d. 24 Oct. 1894, leaving issue,
  1. NICHOLAS PURCELL, now of Bellevue.
  1. Mary Susan Frances, d. unm.
  2. Frances Mary Barbara.

Residence—Solars, Chiddingfold, Surrey. Club—United Service, S.W.

O'GRADY OF KILBALLYOWEN.

WILLIAM DE RIENZI O'GRADY, Chief of his name, b. 17 June, 1852.

Lineage.—The Milesian family of O'Grady is one of the most ancient of co. Limerick. Dr. O'BRIEN, Roman Catholic Bishop of Cloyne, in his Irish and English Dictionary, p. 514 (see also KEATING, vol. ii. p. 401, ed. 1809), assigns CONAL EACHLUATH, King of Munster, A.D. 366, 6th in descent from Oilliol Olum (of the race of HEBER, the eldest son of MILESIUS, King of Spain, who colonized Ireland), as the common ancestor of the O'Gradys and the O'Briens; but the latter having subsequently, in the person of BRIEN BOROIMHE, the renowned monarch of Ireland, established an ascendant power in North Munster, or Thomond, of which they became hereditary rulers, the O'Gradys acknowledged their paramount sway, and were arrayed as dynasts, or chiefs of a sept, under the banners of these provincial princes. The O'Gradys diverging in process of time, from the parent stock of Kilballyowen, spread into the various collateral branches of Cappercullen, Elton Grange, Lodge, Rahan, Cahir, Mount Prospect, &c.
In the interval between 1276 and 1310, the chieftainship of the sept vested in
DONALD O'GRADY, who fell in battle 1309. leaving a son,

IRELAND   O'Grady.

Hugh O'Grady, who acquired the same year, in marriage with the dau. and heir of O'Kerwick, Chief of Anlan Cliah, the lands of Kilballyowen, which have since remained the principal residence of his descendants. His son and heir,
William O'Grady, of Kilballyowen, m. Elizabeth, Fitzgerald, dau. of the Knight of Glyn, and was father of
Daniel O'Grady, of Kilballyowen, whose son (by his wife, dau. of O'Hine, Lord of Cahinelly Castle),
Gillyduff O'Grady, of Kilballyowen, m. Eleanor, dau. of William Vernon, of Kilmallock, co. Limerick, and had a son and successor,
Matthew O'Grady, of Kilballyowen, m. Alicia, dau. of Thomas Fitzgibbon, the White Knight, and left a son,
Donogh O'Grady, of Kilballyowen, whose wife was Margaret, dau. of Sir Thomas Browne, Knt. of Camas, co. Limerick. By an extant deed, bearing date 1612, Donogh O'Grady, made a settlement of his estates on his three sons, Darby, Morrogh, and Brien. He was s. by the eldest,
Darby O'Grady, of Kilballyowen, m. 1633, Faith, dau. and co-heir of Sir Thomas Standish, of co. Lancaster, and of Bruff, co. Limerick, by whom he left three sons,
1. Thomas, his heir.
2. Standish, ancestor of O'Grady of Elton and Cappercullen, from a younger branch of which descended Deane Grady and Grove Grady.
3. Darby.

The eldest son,
Thomas O'Grady, of Kilballyowen, m. 1st, Frances, dau. of John Anketell, by the Lady Lucy Touchet his wife, dau. of Mervin, 2nd Earl of Castlehaven, and 2ndly, 1680, Mrs. Ellice Everard, widow, dau. of John Walsh, of co. Tipperary, By his 1st wife he had John, his heir, and Thomas, from whom spring O'Grady of Rakan and Grange. The elder son,
John O'Grady, of Kilballyowen, m. 1st, 1698, Catherine, dau. of Thady Quin, of Adare, co. Limerick, and had one son,
1. Thomas, his heir.

He m. 2ndly, Honora, dau. of Major-Gen. Patrick Alen, of St. Wolstan's, and left by her three sons and two daus.,
2. Standish, m. Honora, dau. and co-heir of Jeremiah Hayes, of Cahir, co. Limerick, and had issue,
1. John, of Cahir, High Sheriff co. Limerick, 1781, d.s.p.
2. Darby, of Mount Prospect, Sheriff co. Limerick, 1785. He m. 30 May, 1763, Mary, dau. of James Smyth, Collector, of Limerick, and had a very numerous offspring, the eldest of whom, Standish O'Grady, was raised to the Peerage as Viscount Guillamore, 1831 (see Burke's Peerage).
3. James, m. Honora Scanlan, and was ancestor of O'Grady of Ballingarry.   4. Patrick, d. unm.
1. Lucy, m. Mathew O'Hea, of Kilkeran, co. Cork.
2. Mary, m. William Haly, of Ballyhaly, co. Cork.

O'Grady was s. by his eldest son,
Thomas O'Grady, of Kilballyowen, m. 1718, Anne, dau. of John Horrish, of The Grange, of Ballybohill, co. Dublin, and left issue,
1. John, his heir.
2. Darby, who served in India, He m. Rose Segrave, of the ancient House of Cabra. co. Dublin, and had issue.
3. Gilbert, an Officer in the French Service, d.s.p.
4. Denis, an Officer in the Austrian Service, d.s.p.
5. Standish, m. 1750, Eliza, dau. of Edward Deane, of Dangan, co. Kilkenny, and of Terenure, co. Dublin, Member in the Irish Parliament, by whom he had one son John O'Grady, of Harstonge Street, Limerick ; and a dau. Eliza, who m. James Bennett, of Ballintona, co. Limerick, whose dau. Mary, m. George Gough Gubbins, eldest son of Joseph Gubbins, of Maidstown Castle, co. Limerick.
1. Mary, m. Henry Harrison, of Castle Harrison.

The eldest son,
John O'Grady, of Kilballyowen, m. 28 March, 1751, the Hon. Mary Elizabeth de Courcy, eldest dau. and co-heir of Gerald, 24th Lord Kingsale, and had (with three daus., Julia, m. Thomas Lidwell, of co. Tipperary ; Margaret, m. David Hearn, of Shanakill, co. Waterford ; and Ellen, d. unm.) a son and successor,
Gerald De Courcy O'Grady, of Kilballyowen, m. Elizabeth Thomasina, dau. of John Thomas Waller, of Castletown, co. Limerick, M.P., and had issue,
1. John Thomas, Lieut. 11th Light Dragoons, d.v.p. 8 Oct. 1811, while serving in the Peninsular War.
2. Gerald De Courcy, his heir.
3. John Waller, of Fort Etna, co. Limerick, R.N., J.P., b. 22 Nov. 1796 ; m. 1 Dec. 1824, Caroline, dau. of George John Veitch, of Kelso, N.B., and had issue (of whom the eldest son settled in Canada, and the younger children all emigrated to the United States of America),
1. Gerald De Courcy (Rev.), of Fort Etna, co. Limerick, and afterwards Chaplain of H.M. Forces at Chambly, Canada, and Archdeacon of the Diocese of Montreal, Canada, b. 22 Oct. 1826 ; m. 17 Nov. 1853, Charlotte Knox, youngest dau. of the late Rev. William Agar Adamson, LL.D., Chaplain and Librarian to the Legislative Council of Canada, and d. 18 Aug. 1862, leaving issue,
(1) John Waller de Courcy (Winnipeg, Canada), b. 26 Sept. 1854 ; m. 3 June, 1885, Katherine Frances, dau. of Lieut.-Col. Joseph Stopford Maunsell, D.A.G., New Brunswick, Canada, and has issue,
1. Gerald Francis de Courcy, b. 10 Aug. 1887.
2. George Waller de Courcy, b. 21 Sept. 1888.
3. John Medley de Courcy, b. 23 Oct. 1889.
4. William Agar de Courcy, b. 27 Oct. 1891.
5. Herbert Standish de Courcy, b. 5 Aug. 1899.

6. Donald Guy de Courcy, b. 5 Nov. 1901.
1. Kathleen Francis de Courcy.
2. Anna Faith de Courcy.
3. Nora Mooney de Courcy.
(2) Gerald de Courcy (Toronto, Canada), b. 31 May, 1856, m. 6 June, 1883, Geraldine, youngest dau. of Edward Carter, Q.C., Barrister-at-Law, of Montreal, Canada, and has issue,
1. Gerald de Courcy, b. 28 July, 1884.
2. Edward Waller de Courcy, b. 6 March, 1886.
3. Standish de Courcy, b. 9 Sept. 1889.
4. Brien de Courcy, b. 5 Nov. 1891.
1. Kathleen de Courcy.
2. Edith Geraldine de Courcy.
(1) Charlotte Kathleen de Courcy.
(2) Edith Faith de Courcy, d. unm. May, 1877.
2. Bolton Waller.   3. George John.
4. John de Courcy.   5. Standish Fitzwaller.
1. Elizabeth Caroline.   2. Edith Faith.
4. John de Courcy (Rev.), of Knockany, co. Limerick, b. 21 June, 1800 ; m. 7 Nov. 1836, Eliza, 2nd dau. of R. J. Peel, of Burton-on-Trent, and d. 1 April, 1856, having by her (who d. 7 Nov. 1898) had issue,
1. Gerald De Courcy, b. 21 March, 1835 ; m. 1 June, 1867, Jessie Georgiana, dau. of P. D. Souper, of Trinidad, and has issue.
2. Henry Knox, Capt. Madras Army, d. unm. 1873.
3. Peel, b. 22 July, 1842.
1. Agnes Antoinette Peel, m. 26 Oct. 1864, Maj.-Gen. Robert Fowler Butler, of Barton Hall, Staffordshire, and d. 1900, leaving issue.
1. Mary Elizabeth, m. Alexander Rose, Capt. R.N. (see Rose of Ahabee).
2. Dorothea, m. Rev. Henry Lefroy, brother of the Right Hon. Thomas Lefroy, Lord Chief Justice of Ireland.
3. Isabella, m. her cousin, 1825, Standish Harrison, of Castle Harrison, co. Cork, and had issue (see that family).

O'Grady d. 1812, and was s. by his eldest surviving son,
Gerald De Courcy O'Grady, of Kilballyowen, co. Limerick, J.P. and D.L., High Sheriff 1821, m. March, 1813, Anne, only child of William Wise, of Cork (by his 1st wife, the dau. of Samuel Austen), and by her (who d. 1849) had issue,
1. William de Courcy, his heir.
2. Henry Blakeney De Courcy, b. 16 Feb. 1825 ; m. Mary Grace, dau. of Major Mackintosh.
3. Standish De Courcy, Capt. late 64th Regt., b. 16 Feb. 1826 ; m. 1st, 31 March, 1864, Charlotte, youngest dau. and co-heir of George Powell Houghton, of Kilmarnock, and by her had a son,
1. Gerald de Courcy, b. 7 March, 1865 ; d. s.p. 4th May, 1886, He m. 2ndly, 24 Oct. 1871, Isabella, dau. of Rev. William Shepherd, and by her had issue. He d. 25th Aug. 1901.
2. Standish de Courcy, b. 27 July, 1872, Major R.A.M.C., m. 7 June, 1911, Esther Alice only dau. of Col. Philip Dayne Vigors, of Holloden, co. Carlow (see that family).
3. Henry de Courcy, b. 26 Aug. 1873 ; m. 3 Feb. 1908, Sybil, eldest dau. of Col. T. Macpherson, late Indian Army.
4. Donald de Courcy, b. 31 May, 1881.
1. Eveleen de Courcy, b. 13 Dec. 1875.
2. Angela de Courcy.
1. Eliza, m. 1842, Henry Knox, of Netley Park, co. Mayo.
2. Anne, m. Richard Bourke, son of Gen. Sir Richard Bourke, K.C.B.
3. Thomasina, m. Standish Thomas O'Grady, of Landscape, co. Clare, and d. 1862, leaving issue.
4. Isabella, m. Rev. Carew Smyth O'Grady, son of Darby O'Grady, of Aghamarta, co. Cork (see that family), who d. 1887, leaving a dau., Ann.
5. Amelia, m. 15 July, 1848, Henry Winthrop, The O'Donovan, and had issue (see that family).
6. Geraldine, d. unm.

O'Grady d. 6 Sept. 1863, and was s. by his eldest son,
William De Courcy O'Grady, of Kilballyowen, Chief of his name, M.A. Trin. Coll. Dublin, b. 23 Feb. 1816 ; m. 13 Sept. 1841, Anna Grogan, only dau. of Thomas De Rinzy, of Clobennon Hall, D.L. co. Wexford, and d. Nov. 1873, having by her (who d. 14 March, 1895) had issue,
1. Thomas De Courcy, of whom presently.
2. William De Rinzy, Chief of his name.
3. John De Courcy, C.B., of Kilballyowen (Kilballyowen, near Bruff, co. Limerick), b. 1 Nov. 1856, Lieut.-Col. late Connaught Rangers, served in the South African Campaign, in the Zulu and Boer affairs, where he was severely wounded ; m. 4 Jan. 1892, Evelyn Wanda, youngest dau. of the late Major-Gen. A. Mattei, C.M.G.
1. Anne Geraldine, m. 4 Feb. 1870, John Edward Le Mottee, Capt. late 56th Regt. ; and d. Aug. 1871.
2. Catherine Frances, m. 4 March, 1878, Arthur Winthropp Gubbins, of Kiewitahi, co. Piako, Auckland, New Zealand, younger son of George Gubbins, of Miltown, co. Limerick. Her 1902, leaving issue a dau., Beatrice.

The eldest son,
Thomas De Courcy O'Grady, of Kilballyowen, co. Limerick, Chief of his name, b. 17 Dec. 1844 ; m. 1 Sept. 1877 Elizabeth Jane, only dau. of Major Richard Doyne, of Hermitage, co. Dublin. She d. Feb. 1896. He d.s.p. 21 March, 1898, and was s. by his brother.

Arms—Per pale gu. and sa., three lions passant in pale, per pale arg. and or. Crest—a horse's head erased s., maned or. Motto—Vulneratus non victus.

Seat—Kilballyowen, near Bruff, co. Limerick.

O'GRADY OF CARNELLY.

GUILLAMORE O'GRADY, of Carnelly, co. Clare, b. 18 Nov. 1877, B.A. (Dublin) 1901, M.A. 1908, called to the Bar, King's Inns 1903, Lieut. South Irish Horse, Dublin Herald of Arms 1908.

Lineage.—EDWARD SMYTH O'GRADY, 3rd son of Darby O'Grady, of Mount Prospect, co. Limerick, by Mary his wife, dau. of James Smyth, and younger brother of the Right Hon. Standish O'Grady, Lord Chief Baron, Ireland, created VISCOUNT GUILLAMORE 1831 (see O'GRADY of *Kilballyowen* and BURKE's *Peerage*, &c.), B.A. (Dublin) 1800, Barrister, King's Inn 1802, Assistant Barrister for co. Waterford, d. 5 Oct. 1835; *m.* 1800, Mary, dau. of William Stamer, of Carnelly, co. Clare, and by her (who d. 4 Dec. 1871) had three sons and a dau.,
1. Standish Stamer, B.A. (Dublin) 1826, Barrister King's Inns 1826, Commissioner of Bankrupts, killed in a duel 1830 ; *unm.*
2. EDWARD STAMER, of whom presently.
3. William, 16th Lancers, d. 1841.
1. Julia, m. 1st, 1840, Wellington Anderson Rose, of Foxhall, co. Tipperary (*see* ROSE *of Ahabeg and Foxhall*), and 2ndly, 1856, Sir Edward FitzGerald, 3rd bart (extinct), of Carrigovan, co. Clare.

The 2nd son,
EDWARD STAMER O'GRADY, of Clenagh, co. Clare, b. 12 April, 1811 ; d. 17 July, 1865 ; Inniskilling Dragoons and 4th Dragoon Guards ; *m.* 22 Aug. 1837, Wilhelmina, only dau. of Richard Anderson Rose, of Ahabeg and Foxhall (*see that family*), and had three sons and three daus.,
1. EDWARD STAMER, his heir.
2. Richard Rose, Capt. 44th Regt., b. 13 Oct. 1842 ; d. 4 July, 1880.
3 Henry George, b. 1844 ; d. 2 Feb. 1862.
1. Maria. 2. Mary Elizabeth.
3. Wilhelmina, *m.* 26 Sept. 1871, William Frederick Swindell, of Melyniog, Wales.

The eldest son and heir,
EDWARD STAMER O'GRADY, of Clenagh, co. Clare, Surgeon, M.Ch. (Dublin) 1859, b. 23 Nov. 1838 ; d. 18 Oct. 1897; *m.* 11 Sept. 1873 Minnie, eldest dau. of John Bishop, of Kinsale, and had issue,
1. Edward Stamer, b. 7 Sept. 1874, now of Clenagh.
2. GUILLAMORE, now of Carnelly.
3. Cantwell, b. 25 March, 1879 ; d. an infant Sept. 1879.
4. Tuite, b. 4 June, 1880 ; d. March, 1893.
5. De Courcy, b. 7 April, 1888.
1. Ada Rose, b. 11 April, 1876 ; d. April, 1886.
2. Ina. 3. Eva.

Arms—*See* O'GRADY *of Kilballyowen.*

Seat—Carnelly, co. Clare. *Residence*—49, Fitzwilliam Square, Dublin; Office of Arms, Dublin Castle. *Clubs*—Cavalry, W., Kildare Street, Dublin ; R. St. George Yacht, Kingstown.

O'GRADY OF AGHAMARTA CASTLE.

SELINA HELENA O'GRADY, of Aghamanta Castle, co. Cork, s. her father in 1886.

Lineage.—DARBY O'GRADY, J.P. and D.L., 6th son of Darby O'Grady, of Mount Prospect, co. Limerick (*see* O'GRADY *of Kilballyowen*), and brother of Standish, 1st Viscount Guillamore (*see* BURKE's *Peerage*), *m.* Jan. 1813, Ellen, dau. of Denis George, Baron of the Irish Court of Exchequer, by his wife Dorothea, dau. of the Rev. Edward Moore, Archdeacon of Emly, and by her (who d. 1857) had issue,
1. STANDISH DARBY, of whom presently.
2. Denis George, of Pattenstown, co. Wexford, b. 1815 ; *m.* 1 May, 1858, Hon. Jane Stewart, 3rd dau. of Walter Hore, by his wife, the Baroness Ruthven, and d.s.p. 11 Nov. 1872.
3. Edward George (Rev.), b. 1817; *m.* Emily, dau. of Rev. Edward Croker, and d. 1880, leaving issue,
   Mary Jane, *m.* — Collins, M.D.
4. Carew Smyth (Rev.), b. 9 Nov. 1818 ; *m.* 26 April, 1849, Isabella, 4th dau. of The O'Grady, of Kilballyowen (*see that family*). She d. He d. 1897, leaving issue,
   Anne Isabella.
5. Rupert, b. 1820 ; d. *unm.*
6. William, b. 1822 ; d. 1831.
7. Thomas, of Nothwood, Rochestown, co. Cork, J.P., b. 1825 ; *m.* 1853, Elizabeth, dau. of Henry Peard, of Carrigan Hall, co. Waterford, and d. leaving issue,
   1. Thomas Dermot, Lieut. 73rd Regt., b. 16 Dec. 1854 ; d. *unm.* 16 Aug. 1877.
   2. Richard Peard, b. 31 July, 1856 ; *m.* 1903, Jeanie, dau. of — Atkins.
   3. William, b. 2 April, 1858 ; d. 1861.
   4. Rupert George, b. 18 Feb. 1861.
   5. Standish Thomas, b. 19 May, 1865 ; *m.* Jeanie Caroline —.
   1. Louise Alexandra Elizabeth, *m.* 1891, George Carleton Foott, of Carrigacunna Castle, co. Cork, and d.s.p.
8. Dudley, of Ballynort, co. Limerick, b. 22 Dec. 1827 ; *m.* 1st, Prudence, dau. of Thomas Evans Davenport, of Ballynacourty House, co. Limerick. She d.s.p. 1864. He *m.* 2ndly, 25 Feb. 1868, Helen Hare, dau. of the late Berkeley Vincent, of Summerhill, co. Limerick (*see that family*). She d. 3 May, 1907. He d. 1883, having had issue,

1. Standish Darby, b. 2 Feb. 1870.
2. Dudley Vincent, b. 7 May, 1876.
1. Helen Louisa, *m.* 7 June, 1899, Edgar Leek Phelps, 3rd son of John Lecky Phelps, of Waterpark (*see that family*).
1. Dorothea Louisa, *m.* William Lloyd, of Tower Hill, co. Limerick, and d.s.p. 1882.
2. Ellen, *m.* 1848, Henry Braddell Croker, of Dromkeen, co. Limerick, and d. 1849, having had issue,
   1. Edward, *m.* his cousin, Matilda Croker, and d.s.p. 1910.
   2. John Crokes Major ret. Royal Munster Fusiliers ; *m.* 1870, Bethia M. Shepherd, and had issue.
   1. Ellen, *m.* T. Gelston, M.D., who d.
   2. Gertrude Jane, d.
   3. Louisa, d.

Mr. O'Grady d. 26 May, 1857. His eldest son,
STANDISH DARBY O'GRADY, of Aghamarta, J.P. co. Cork, Barrister-at-Law, b. 1813 ; *m.* Jan. 1856, Selina Mildred, dau. of Rev. Edward Groome, and Frances his wife, dau. of Col. Uniacke, of Woodhouse, co. Waterford, and grand-dau. of Right Hon. John Beresford, brother of the 1st Marquess of Waterford. She d. 10 Sept. 1861. He d. 1886, leaving issue,
1. SELINA HELENA, now of Aghamarta.
2. Ellen Louisa, *m.* 29 June, 1880, George Thomas Ingelheim Gould, of Upwey, co. Dorset, Capt. late R.E. (*see that family*), and has issue,
   1. George Ingelheim, Lieut. E. Surrey Regt., b. 20 June, 1882.
   2. Standish Charles, 89th Punjahbs Indian Army, b. 3 Jan. 1885.
   3. Hubert Louis, b. 15 Nov. 1885.
   1. Helena Frances Irma.
3. Fanny Eveline.

Arms—*See* O'GRADY *of Kilballyowen.*

Seat—Aghamarta Castle, co. Cork.

O'GRADY OF LANDSCAPE.

Capt. GILBERT O'GRADY, of Landscape, co. Clare, J.P., late 78th Highlanders, b. 11 Feb. 1847 ; s. his father 1876.

Lineage.—THOMAS O'GRADY, 4th son of DARBY O'GRADY, of Mount Prospect, co. Limerick, and brother of Standish, 1st Viscount GUILLAMORE (*see* BURKE's *Peerage*), *m.* Helen, dau. of Simon Dring of Rockgrove, co. Cork, and had issue,
1. STANDISH THOMAS, of whom presently.
2. Robert Dring, Capt. 30th Regt., *m.* 1852, Eliza, dau. of Rev. J. Hobson, and d. 1862, having by her (who d. July, 1866) had issue,
   1. Thomas Robert, b. 17 Nov. 1852.
   2. Standish Thomas, R.N., b. 5 July, 1855.
   3. Robert Dring, b. 19 Aug. 1860.
   4. Hubert Charles, b. 28 May, 1862.
   1. Emma Josephine, *m.* 14 June, 1876, B. Phepoe, and has issue.
3. Thomas (Rev.), Vicar of Hognaston, co. Derby, b. 1 Dec. 1816 ; *m* 11 Oct. 1841, Mary Julia, dau. of W. Purser Freme, of Wepre Hall, Flint, and d. 1886, having had issue,
   1. Thomas, b. 11 Aug. 1842 ; d. 5 July, 1861.
   1. Anna Helena, *m.* 28 April, 1870, Samuel A. Hall, and has issue.
   2. Eleanor Elizabeth (*Wimborne Lodge, Bournemouth*), *m.* 7 Nov. 1865, Henry Graham Lloyd, of West Felton Grange, Salop, and had issue.
4. James Smith, b. 2 Feb. 1824 ; *m.* 12 June, 1862, Mary Frances, dau. of Berkeley Vincent, of Summer Hill, co. Clare.
1. Eleanor, *m.* 7 Dec. 1833, Christopher Musgrave Ussher, of Camphive, co. Waterford, and has issue.

The eldest son,
STANDISH THOMAS O'GRADY, of Landscape, co. Clare. B.A. Trin. Coll. Camb., Barrister-at-Law, b. 6 Sept. 1811 ; *m.* May, 1843, Thomasina, dau. of Gerald de Courcy, The O'Grady, of Kilballyowen, and by her (who d. 30 April, 1862) had issue,
1. GILBERT, now of Landscape.
2. Robert Henry Rodolph, b. 10 Aug. 1848 ; d. *unm.* 1885.
3. John Newman, b. 25 Jan. 1850 ; d. *unm.* May, 1888.
4. Carew Standish, b. 23 April, 1860 ; d. *unm.* 1 July, 1889.
1. Geraldine Anne.
2. Helena Eliza, *m.* 14 Oct. 1880, P. R. Sband, of Swathellic, Ceylon.
3. Diana Eleanor, *m.* 1884, Capt. Percy Wildman-Lushington, 1st Batt. King's Own Scottish Borderers, and has issue.
4. Amelia Maria.

Mr. S. T. O'Grady d. 13 Sept. 1876.

Arms—*See* O'GRADY *of Kilballyowen.*

Seat—Landscape, co. Clare. *Club*—Naval and Military.

O'GRADY. *See* BURKE's PEERAGE, **GUILLAMORE, V.**

O'HARA OF ANNAGHMORE.

CHARLES KEAN O'HARA, of Annaghmore, co. Sligo, H.M. Lieutenant for that county, and Custos Rotulorum, High Sheriff 1886, late Major 3rd York and Lancaster Regt., educated at Eton, *b.* 10 Dec. 1860.

Lineage.—CORMAC O'HARA, of Coolany, co. Sligo, who *m.* Una, dau. of — Gallagher, of co. Galway, and *d.* 24 Oct. 1612, leaving issue, two sons, viz.,
1. TEIGE, of whom hereafter.
2. Cormac O'Hara, of Mollane, co. Sligo, *m.* Catherine, dau. of O'Reilly, of co. Cavan, and *d.* 1642, having had issue by her,
  1. Oliver, *m.* and had issue. He went into rebellion, and forfeited his lands.
  2. Bryan.
3. Cormac O'Hara, Oge, of co. Sligo, *m.* Mary, dau. of Hugh O'Flaherty, of Moycullen, in Iar, Connaught, an ancient family in co. Galway, and had issue, a son,
  Hiberius O'Hara, of Ballyhara, or Cursallagh, co. Sligo, living 1688, *m.* Elizabeth, eldest dau. of William Taaffe, Capt. of Infantry in the Confederate Army of the Catholics of Ireland during the Civil Wars of 1641, ancestor of Viscount Taaffe, and by her had a son,
   Roderick O'Hara, of Ballyhara or Cursallagh, co. Sligo, who *m.* Anne, dau. and heir of — Forde, of Grevagh, co. Leitrim, and was father of
    Charles Herbert O'Hara, who was a Capt. in the Cæsarean Royal Harrecian Legion of Infantry, and afterwards Col. of the Regt. of Ladogo, *m.* at Prague, 1 July, 1750 Maria, Theresa Challons, of the ancient family of De Challons, of Burgundy, in the kingdom of France. He *d.* at Vibourg, in Finland, in the year 1774, having had issue,
     Anthony, Maria Marcellus O'Hara, Lieut.-Col. of the Regt. of Bellosersky, in the service of her Imperial Majesty the Empress of Russia, Knt., of the Order of Malta, and of the Imperial Order of Saint Wladimir, *t.* at Cenoa, 6 April, 1751.
1. Catherine.   3. Annabella.

The eldest son,
TEIGE O'HARA BOY, of Leiny, co. Sligo, High Sheriff 1608, *m.* Sheela, dau. of O'Rourke, and *d.* 5 Oct. 1616, having had issue, two sons, the elder, Teige, of Coolany, co. Sligo, *b.* April, 1612, and *d. unm.* 25 July, 1634. The younger,
KEAN O'HARA, of Coolany, and Annaghmore, co. Sligo, High Sheriff 1665, *s.* his brother Teige in the family possessions, *m.* 1st, Anne, dau. of Sir Adam Loftus, Knt., and relict of Richard, son and heir of Sir Laurence Parsons, Knt., of Birr, and by her had issue,
1. Adam, of Annaghmore, High Sheriff 1616, *m.* Isabella, dau. of Sir Francis Gore, Knt., of Artamon, co. Sligo, by Anne, dau. and heir of Capt. Robert Parke, of Sligo. He *d.* 17 Sept. 1687, leaving an only dau. and heir,
  Anne, who *m.* Ven. Toby Caulfeild, Archdeacon of Killala, and son of Capt. Thomas Caulfeild, of Donamon, co. Roscommon, 7th son of William, 2nd Lord Charlemont.
2. Charles, *s.* to the estates on the death of his brother Adam. He *d.* without issue, 1703, and by his will devised his estates to his half-brother, Kean.

Kean O'Hara *m.* 2ndly, Rose, widow of William Crofton, dau. and heir of John Newman, of Dublin, and by her (who *m.* 3rdly, Sir John Peyton, Bart., Governor of Ross Castle, co. Kerry) had (at his decease in 1675) a son.
KEAN O'HARA, High Sheriff co. Sligo 1703, *s.* to the family estates on the death of his two elder brothers without male issue, *m.* Eleanor, dau. of Theobald Mathew, and sister of George Mathew, of Thomastown, co. Tipperary. Mr. Kean O'Hara made a settlement to himself, for life, with remainder to his son and sons in tail male of said estates. By his said wife (whose will bears date 13 Jan. 1733) he had issue,
1. CHARLES, of whom presently.
2. Kean, of Kinsaly, co. Dublin, *m.* Anna Maria (*d.* 31 Feb. 1779), dau. of George Mathew, and relict of Theobald Mathew, jun., of Thomastown, and had issue, an only child,
  Charlotte, *m.* Eyre Trench, of Ashford, co. Roscommon.
3. Adam.

The eldest son,
CHARLES O'HARA, of Annaghmore, High Sheriff 1740, *m. circa* 1742, Lady Mary Carmichael, eldest dau. of James, 2nd Earl of Hyndford, and sister of William Carmichael, D.D., Archbishop of Dublin, and by her (who *d.* 1759) had issue (at his decease, 3 Feb. 1776), two sons, the younger of whom William, was a Capt. R.N., and *d. unm.* 1790. The elder,

CHARLES O'HARA, of Annaghmore, M.P. for co. Sligo, and one of the Governors of the co., *b.* 26 April, 1746; *m.* Margaret, dau. and heir of John Cookson, M.D., of co. York, and had issue,
1. CHARLES KING O'HARA, of Annaghmore, co. Sligo, *b.* Oct. 1785, who, by his will, devised his estates to his nephew, Charles Cooper, on condition that he should take the surname and quarter the arms of O'Hara.
1. Mary.
2. JANE FRANCES, of whom presently.
3. Charlotte, *m.* 1812, Robert Digby.

The 2nd dau.,
JANE FRANCES O'HARA, *m.* 1810, Arthur Brooke Cooper, of Cooper's Hill, co. Sligo, son of Arthur Cooper, of Cooper's Hill, by Sarah his wife, dau. of Guy Carleton, of Rossfad, co. Fermanagh, and grandson, by Jane Cunningham his wife, of William Cooper, of Cooper's Hill, who was a descendant of the same family as "Cooper of Markree." She *d.* 21 July, 1874, aged 94, leaving issue, two sons and four daus.,
1. Arthur Brooke, *m.* Elizabeth Trulock. She *d.* 21 July, 1859. He *d.v.p.* 12 June, 1845, leaving a dau.,
  Katherine Jane, *m.* J. Cole.
2. CHARLES WILLIAM, of whom presently.
1. Margaret Sarah, *d.* 19 Feb. 1888.
2. Mary Jane Caroline, *d.* 31 Dec. 1877.
3. Jane Henrietta, *m.* Feb. 1850, Lieut.-Col. Alexander M'Kinstry, and *d.* in America, 8 Feb. 1867, leaving a son, Arthur, and other issue,
4. Charlotte Anne, *m.* 19 Feb. 1852, Christopher Carleton L'Estrange, and left issue.

Mr. Cooper *d.* 4 Dec. 1854. His 2nd son,
CHARLES WILLIAM O'HARA, of Annaghmore and Cooper's Hill, co. Sligo, J.P. and D.L., M.P. for that co. 1859 to 1865, High Sheriff 1849, *b.* 30 Oct. 1817; *m.* 28 Oct. 1858, Annie Charlotte, eldest dau. of Richard Shuttleworth Streatfeild, of The Rocks, Uckfield, Sussex and *d.* 5 April, 1898, having by her (who *d.* 12 March, 1882) had issue,
1. CHARLES KEAN, now of Annaghmore.
2. Arthur Cooper, of Cooper's Hill, Riverstown, co. Sligo, J.P. High Sheriff 1903, *b.* 8 Feb. 1862.
3. Richard Edward (*Glenelg, Queensland, Australia*), *b.* 7 June, 1863.
4. Wiliam Henry, *b.* 14 March, and *d.* 5 May, 1866.
5. Henry Streatfeild, *b.* 26 Feb. 1870; *d.* 14 Oct. 1878.
6. Alexander Perceval (*Chicago*), *b.* 16 May, 1871.
7. Frederick William, High Sheriff co. Sligo 1911, J.P. cos. Sligo and Down (*Cultibar, Coolancy, co. Sligo*), *b.* 27 April, 1875; *m.* 26 Nov. 1903, Muriel Helen Isabella Rice, dau. of Francis Blackburne Henn, of Paradise Hill (*see that family*), and has issue,
  1. Donal Frederick, *b.* 5 Nov. 1904.
  2. Francis Cooper, *b.* 21 Sept. 1906.
8. Errill Robert, Capt. Army Service Corps, *b.* 6 Sept. 1879; *m.* 25 Feb. 1911, Moneen, youngest dau. of Capt. William Bond of Newton Bond, co. Longford.
1. Charlotte Jane, *b.* 19 Oct. 1859; *m.* 3 Feb. 1881, Alexander Perceval, of Temple House, co. Sligo (*see that family*).
2. Mary, *b.* 6 Nov. 1864; *d.* 16 Sept. 1879.
3. Annie Frances, *b.* 30 May, 1867; *d.* 10 Sept. 1882.
4. Emily Margaret, *b.* 8 Aug. 1868; *d. unm.* 8 July, 1897.
5. Jane Marian, *b.* 24 Oct. 1872; *m.* 8 May, 1901, Cecily Maude, of Lenaghan, Enniskillen (*see* BURKE'S *Peerage*, HAWARDEN, V.).
6. Kathleen, *b.* 27 June, 1876; *m.* 5 Jan. 1901, Bertram Phibbs, Lieut. R.N. (*see* PHIBBS *of Seafield*).

Mr. O'Hara, whose patronymic was Cooper, assumed by Royal Licence, 27 Nov. 1860, the surname of O'Hara, in compliance with the testamentary injunction of his uncle Charles King O'Hara of Annaghmore.

Arms—Quarterly: 1st and 4th vert, on a pale radiant or a lion rampant sa., for O'HARA; and 2nd and 3rd, gu., on a bend between six lions rampant or, a crescent sa., for COOPER. Crests—1st, a demi lion rampant erm., holding between the paws a chaplet of oak-leaves ppr., for O'HARA; 2nd, a man's bust in profile, couped at the shoulder ppr., on the head an Irish Crown or, and charged on the neck with a crescent sa.; Motto over, Vincit amor patriæ, for COOPER. Motto—Virtute et claritate.

Seat—Annaghmore, Coollooney, co. Sligo. Clubs—Kildare Street, Dublin; Junior Constitutional, W.; Royal St. George Yacht, Kingstown; Sligo County, Sligo; and Roscommon County, Boyle.

O'HARA OF COOPERSHILL.

ARTHUR COOPER O'HARA, of Coopershill, co. Sligo, J.P., High Sheriff 1903, *b.* 8 Feb. 1862. He is the 2nd son of the late Charles William O'Hara, of Annaghmore and Cooper's Hill (*see that family*), by his wife Annie Charlotte, eldest dau. of Richard Shuttleworth Streatfeild, of The Rocks, Uckfield, Sussex.

Lineage and Arms.—See O'Hara of Annaghmore.
Seat—Coopershill, Riverstown, co. Sligo. Club—County, Sligo.

O'HARA late OF O'HARA BROOK.

THE RIGHT REV. HENRY STEWART O'HARA, D.D., late of O'Hara Brook, co. Antrim, BISHOP OF CASHEL, EMLY, WATERFORD AND LISMORE, b. 6 Sept. 1843; m. 13 Feb. 1872, Hatton Thomasina, dau. of Thomas Scott, D.L., of Willsboro, co. Londonderry. His lordship, who was Rector of Coleraine 1869-94, Chancellor of Connor Cathedral 1884-98, Canon of St. Patrick's Cathedral 1897, and Dean of Belfast 1899, was consecrated Bishop of the united diocese of Cashel, Emly, Waterford and Lismore, 1900.

Lineage—GEORGE TAIT, who m. Catherine, only dau. and heiress of Cormac O'Hara, of Drummulley, co. Cavan, was father of
CHARLES O'HARA, Capt. in Gen. Bragg's Regt., J.P. and High Sheriff co. Antrim 1758, m. 1752, Helen, dau. of Alexander Duncan of Lundie, N.B., and had a son,
HENRY O'HARA, of O'Hara Brook, b. 1759, J.P., Lieut.-Col. of the Antrim Militia, and High Sheriff 1785, who m. 1st, 1782, Amy Lloyd, by whom he had a son, Richard, Lieut. R.A., d. in Jamaica, 1812, and two daus., Katherine and Mary. He m. 2ndly, 1792, Eleanor Dunn, and by her had issue,
1. CHARLES, of whom presently.
2. William, Lieut. 35th Regt., d. unm. in the West Indies, 1827.
3. Henry Robert, d. unm. 1854.
4. JAMES DUNN, s. his brother.
1. Eleanor, m. M. Sankey, and is dec.
2. Helen Elizabeth, m. Capt. M. Crofton, R.N., and d. 1876.
3. Grace, m. Rev. William Kearney, and d. 1885.
4. Anne Martha, d. unm. 1855.
5. Louisa, m. Thomas Crofton, R.N., and d. 1883.
6. Maria, m. Robert Maddock.

Mr. O'Hara m. 3rdly, 1808, Sophia Thwaites, but had no issue by her. He d. 20 Jan. 1823. His eldest son,
CHARLES O'HARA, of O'Hara Brook, co. Antrim, J.P., High Sheriff 1833, b. 13 April, 1797; m. Sept. 1823, Margaret, eldest dau. of Arthur Innes, of Dromantine, co. Down, and had issue,
1. Arthur, b. 11 Dec. 1828; d. 23 June, 1866.
2. William, Capt. 40th Regt., b. 31 March, 1830; d. 7 May, 1859.
3. James, late 62nd Regt., b. 4 Nov. 1835; d. unm. 6 Oct. 1870.
2. Anne, m. W. T. Latham, M.D., and d. 13 Aug. 1869.
2. Ellen Sophia, m. 1862, Rev. William Armstrong, Incumbent of Scarva, and d. 3 May, 1889, leaving issue.

Mr. C. O'Hara d. 19 March, 1873, leaving no male issue surviving, and was s. by his brother,
REV. JAMES DUNN O'HARA, of the Castle, Portstewart, and O'Hara Brook, co. Antrim, b. 4 Dec. 1801; m. Nov. 1842, Caroline Deffel, dau. of William Alves, of Enham Place, Hants, and d. 13 Aug. 1893, having by her had issue,
1. HENRY STEWART, present representative.
2. William James, b. 23 June, 1857; m. Oct. 1887, Cecilia, dau. of Peter Connellan, D.L., of Coolmore co. Kilkenny (see that family), and has issue,
  Henry Desmond, b. 1892.
  Ethne Lilian.
1. Sarah Caroline.
2. Helen Sophia.
3. Caroline Elizabeth, d. unm. 1872.

Residence—The Palace, Waterford.

O'HARA OF LENABOY.

LIEUT.-COL. JAMES O'HARA, of Lenaboy, co. Galway, Lieut.-Col. Army Pay Department, late Capt. 2nd Dragoon Guards, served in S. African War 1899-1902 (despatches twice); b. 16 Nov. 1865; m. 2 April, 1902, Margaret McBeath, eldest dau. of the late W. Chalmers Carmichael, and has issue,
  Margaret Rose, b. 23 July, 1903.

Lineage.—JOHN O'HARA, a Capt. in the Army, and Town Major of Galway, served in Spain at siege of Vigo, &c., as Aide-de-Camp to Sir Charles O'Hara, afterwards Lord Tyrawley. He d. in 1729, leaving three sons,
1. JAMES, his heir, b. 1717.
2. Geoffrie, a Capt. in the E.I.Co.'s navy.
3. John.

The eldest son,
JAMES O'HARA, of Lenaboy, was Mayor of Galway in 1747; m. 1744, Elizabeth, dau. of Robert Shaw, and had fourteen children four of whom survived him. Of these were,
1. JAMES, his heir.
2. Robert, of Raheen, m. a dau. of Walter Taylor, of Castle Taylor, and had seven sons and five daus.

The eldest son,
JAMES O'HARA, of Lenaboy, b. 1748, Recorder of Galway for sixty years; m. Jan. 1789, Margaret, dau. of Richard Moore, who d. 1814. He d. Nov. 1838, aged 90 years, and was s. by his son,
JAMES O'HARA, of Lenaboy, M.P. for Galway, b. 1796; m. 15 April, 1823, Anne, dau. of Hon. and Most Rev. Power Le Poer Trench, last Archbishop of Tuam, and grand-dau. of William Power Keating, 1st Earl of Clancarty, by whom (who d. 11 March, 1870) he had issue,

1. JAMES, his heir.
2. Richard, Lieut.-Col. late R.A.
1. Anne, m. Rev. James Lancaster (dec.), Rector of Attanagh, and d. having had issue.
2. Margaret, dec.
3. Elizabeth, m. 30 Oct. 1865, John Temple Reilly, of Scarvagh, co. Down. He d. 30 Jan. 1903, leaving issue (see that family).
4. Emily, m. 27 Dec. 1871, Right Rev. James O'Sullivan, D.D., Lord Bishop of Tuam, and is dec.

Mr. O'Hara d. Dec. 1838, and was s. by his eldest son,
JAMES O'HARA, of Lenaboy, co. Galway, J.P. and D.L. for Galway town, High Sheriff 1863, and J.P. co. Galway, and High Sheriff 1879, Lieut.-Col. late commanding 5th Brigade North Irish Division R.A., formerly Capt. 2nd Dragoon Guards, b. 27 Sept. 1832; educated at Eton; m. 16 Dec. 1864, Blanche Fanny, dau. of the late Rev. Sebastian Gambier, Vicar of Sandgate, and grand-dau. of the late Sir James Gambier, Consul-Gen. at the Hague, and d. 14 Aug. 1902, leaving by her (who d. 31 March, 1903) issue,
1. JAMES, now of Lenaboy.
2. James Geoffrie Musgrave, P.W.D., India, b. 3 April, 1869; m.
3. James Power, b. 1 March, 1872; d. unm. 18 May, 1898.
4. James Fitzgerald William, b. 11 March, 1875.
1. Rose.
2. Blanche Ismay, d. 19 July, 1883, aged 4 years.

Seat—Lenaboy, co. Galway. Clubs—Army and Navy and Kildare Street, Dublin.

O'HARA OF MORNINGTON.

CAPT. PATRICK HENRY AUGUSTUS O'HARA, of Mornington, co. Westmeath, J.P., Capt. (retired) East Surrey Regt., b. 26 April, 1859; m. 30 Nov. 1893, Elizabeth Mary, 2nd dau. of Patrick Boland, of Dublin, and has issue,
1. PATRICK GILBERT WARWICK, b. 29 March, 1897.
2. Owen John Aloysius, b. 21 June, 1901.
1. Eileen Mary Augusta, b. 1 Dec. 1894; d. 13 March, 1895.

Lineage.—PATRICK O'HARA, of Mornington, Crookedwood, co. Westmeath, son of Henry O'Hara, of Ballylesson, co. Antrim, b. 1826; m. 13 April, 1858, Augusta Frances, dau. of Warwick Lake. She d. 29 June, 1895. He d. 21 July, 1860, having had issue,
PATRICK HENRY AUGUSTUS, now of Mornington.
Augusta Elizabeth Mary, m. 14 April, 1891, Lieut.-Col. Gilbert Lavallan Nugent, of Jamestown Court, Castletown, Geoghegan, co. Westmeath, commanding 6th Batt. Rifle Brigade.

Seat—Mornington, Crookedwood, co. Westmeath.

O'KELLY OF GURTRAY.

JOHN APPLEYARD O'KELLY, of Gurtray, co. Galway, J.P., b. 21 Dec. 1848; s. his brother 1877; m. 12 Oct. 1886, Mary, dau. of Count O'Byrne, of Allardstown, co. Louth, and Corville, Roscrea (see that family), and has issue,
1. JOHN DOMINICK, b. 5 Aug. 1887.
2. Ambrose Alexander, b. 23 Aug. 1888.
3. Gerald Edward, b. 11 March, 1890.
4. Joseph Henry, b. 4 Jan. 1892.
5. Raphael Patrick, b. 16 Sept. 1893.
6. Alban Brendan, b. 17 Oct. 1896.
7. Donal Patrick, b. 11 Nov. 1901.

Lineage.—DONNCHADH, or DONOGH O'KELLY, son of Maelseachlain O'Kelly, Prince or Chief of Hy-Many, by Finola his wife, dau. of O'Conor Don, s. his brother, Tadhg, or Teige, as Chief of Hy-Many, in the year 1410; but after enjoying the dignity for fourteen years, he was slain by his own nephews, who rebelled against his government. He was the 24th O'Kelly, and lived at Tyaquin. He left two sons, TADHG and BREASAL. The elder,
TADHG, or TEIGE O'KELLY, Chief of Hy-Many, and 26th O'Kelly, was s. in the chieftainship by his brother, BREASAL, who was the 27th O'Kelly, and d. 1464. Teige m. a dau. of Thomas Burke, of Moyne, and had a son,
MAELSEACHLAINN, or MALACHY O'KELLY, 28th O'Kelly, and Chief of Hy-Many, one of the most celebrated men of his race, who erected the Castles of Gallagh Monivea and Garbally, and took

leading part in the warfare which was waged in 1504 by the Lord Deputy the Earl of Kildare against Mac-William Burke, of Clanicarde, and which was terminated by the victory of Knockdoe. Maelseachlainn *d.* 1511. He *m.* Mabel, dau. of Teige Roe O'Kelly, of Callow, and was father of

TADHG DUBH, or TEIGE DUFF, of Gallagh, Chief of Hy-Many, *m.* 1st, the dau. of Donogh O'Kelly, and had by her a son, AEDH, or HUGH, Lord Abbott of Knockmoy, and a dau. Catherine, *m.* the Lord Bermingham. He *m.* 2ndly, Una, dau. of MacDermot, of Moylurg, and by her had two sons,
1. William, of Mullaghmore, *m.* the dau. of Meyler Boy Bermingham, and had a son, Teige, ancestor of the O'KELLYS *of Mullaghmore*, now extinct.
2. DONNCHADH, of Gallagh.

Tadgh Dubh *d.* 1513. His 2nd son,
DONNCHADH REAGH O'KELLY, of Gallagh, *m.* Una, dau. of John Roe Burke, of Beamore, and was father of
CONCHOBHAR NAG CEARDHACH O'KELLY, of Galagh, who appears to have been one of the sub-chiefs of Hy-Many, and was living 1585. He *m.* Honora, dau. of Richard Boy O'Kelly, of Moate, and dying about the year 1612, left (with five daus.), a son and successor,
TEIGE O'KELLY, of Gallagh, whose wardship, as appears from patent roll, 10 JAC. I., was granted to Lady Ursula Bourke, widow of Sir Thomas Bourke, Knt. He *m.* 1st, Mary, dau. of Henry, son of Sir Hubert Burke, and had a son, DONOGH REAGH, of whom presently. He *m.* 2ndly, Julia, dau. of Sir Dermot O'Shaughnessy, and by her had (with a dau. Margaret, *m.* Col. Charles Kelly, 9th Lord of the Manor of Screen) a son, John MacTeige, *m.* Anne, dau. of Dermot Daly, of Killimore, and had a son, Donogh. The elder son,
DONNCHADH REACH O'KELLY, of Gallagh, *m.* Eleanor, dau. of Sir Ulick Burke, Bart., of Glinsk, and was father of
CAPT. WILLIAM O'KELLY, of Gallagh, living 1688, who, driven from the Castle of Gallagh, after the battle of Aughrim, first settled at Tycooly. He *m.* Elizabeth, dau. of Robert Dillon, of Clonbrock, and had (with a dau. Eleanor) three sons, Conor, FESTUS, and Patrick. The 2nd,
FESTUS O'KELLY, of Tycooly, Count of the Holy Roman Empire 1767, *m.* Joanna, dau. of John Dillon, of Kingdare, and had two sons,
1. CONNOR, his heir.
2. Dillon John, an Officer in the Austrian and Hungarian service, eminently distinguished on many occasions, particularly by his gallant and successful defence of Konnopisht Castle, in Bohemia. In consideration of his services, the Emperor Francis conferred on himself and on his father, Festus O'Kelly, of Tycooly, the dignity of COUNT OF THE HOLY ROMAN EMPIRE. The title was given with a reversion to Festus, as his son Dillon had no issue. Count Dillon O'Kelly *m.* about the year 1755, Marian, Countess of Klenowa and Baroness de Jenovey, a favourite of the Empress Maria Theresa, and widow of His Excellency Count de Witby, Hereditary Treasurer of Bohemia, but had no issue. Count O'Kelly was afterwards Ambassador from the Emperor of Germany to the Elector of Saxony. He became also Grand Chamberlain, and was invested with various other orders and honours of the empire. He *d.* in Germany 1811, leaving the bulk of his property to his nephew, Festus O'Kelly, of Tycooly. The elder son,
CONNOR O'KELLY, of Tycooly, Count of the Holy Roman Empire, *m.* 1766, Margaret, dau. of John Moore, of Annabeg, and sister of Garrett Moore, of Cloghan Castle, King's co., and had two sons, FESTUS and JOHN, and five daus., Mary, Jane, Eliza, Anne, and Susanna. The elder son,
FESTUS O'KELLY, of Tycooly, Count of the Holy Roman Empire, *b.* 1771 ; *m.* 1795, Marian, dau. aud, in her issue, heir of Ambrose O'Madden, of Anna Cala, directly descended from the family of Longford Castle, and dying 4 April, 1834, left two sons,
1. CORNELIUS JOSEPH, of Galiagh Castle, co. Galway, J.P., High Sheriff 1851, *b.* 15 Sept. 1806 ; *m.* 10 Oct. 1831, Eliza, dau. of Walter Joyce, of Mervue, and *d.* 18 Aug. 1892, having had issue,
  1. FESTUS IGNATIUS, *b.* 23 July, 1832 ; *m.* 1863, Theresa Mary, dau. of James Daly, of Castle Daly, co. Galway, and *d.v.p.* 1888, leaving issue,
    (1) CORNELIUS DENIS, of Gallagh, late Capt. 4th Batt. Connaught Rangers, *b.* 9 Aug. 1 65 ; *d.* 1895.
    (2) Edward Joseph, *b.* Dec. 1868 ; *d.* 1902.
  2. Cornelius Joseph, settled in Australia, *b.* 8 Feb. 1835.
  3. Edward Anthony, *b.* 6 Aug. 1842.
  4. Walter Francis Maurice, *b.* 20 Sept. 1844 ; *m.* Catherine, dau. of Richard D'Arcy, of Wellfort, co. Galway, and *d.* Feb. 1880. She *d.* March, 1900, leaving issue,
    (1) Walter Joseph, J.P., co. Galway (*Knockavanine, Tuam, co. Galway*), *b.* 25 June, 1876.
    (2) Richard Mary, *b.* 15 May, 1880.
    (1) Kathleen Isidore.
  1. Helen Theresa, *m.* 1855, Thomas J. Bodkin, J.P., of Kilclooney, who *d.* 1868, leaving issue.
  2. Marian, *m.* Dominick G. Bodkin, of Kilclooney.
  3. Christina Mary, *m.* 20 Nov. 1865, James Dermot Daly, of Castle Daly, co. Galway, and has issue.
  2. AMBROSE, of whom presently.

The 2nd son,
AMBROSE PATRICK O'KELLY, of Gurtray, J.P. cos. Galway and Roscommon, *b.* Feb. 1806 ; *m.* 23 April, 1836, Theresa, dau. of Walter Joyce, of Mervue, and *d.* 21 Nov. 1863, having by her (who *d.* July, 1851) had issue,
1. Ambrose Michael Madden, J.P. co. Galway, *b.* 29 Sept. 1842 ; *d.* 12 Dec. 1867.
2. William Patrick, of Gurtray, J.P. co. Galway, *b.* 9 March, 1844 ; *d.* 29 April, 1876.

3. JOHN APPLEYARD, now of Gurtray.
4. Gerald Alban, *b.* 26 Oct. 1849 ; *m.* Eleanor, dau. of Moore Higgins, of Ottawa, Canada, and *d.* 24 Aug. 1881.
  1. Theresa Mary, *d.* 3 Aug. 1908.
2. Helen Christina.
3. Mary Aloysia, *m.* Sept. 1867, Thomas Aliaga Kelly, of St. Grellans, Monkstown, co. Dublin (descended from Colla O'Kelly, of Castle Kelly), and *d.* 4 Nov. 1907, leaving issue.

Arms—Az., two lions rampant combatant arg., chained or, supporting a tower of three turrets of the second. **Crest**—An enfield vert. **Motto**—Turris fortis mihi Deus.

Seat—Gurtray, Portumna, co. Galway.

MACCARTHY-O'LEARY OF COOMLAGANE.

JOHN MACCARTHY-O'LEARY, of Coomlagane, co. Cork, Capt. S. Lancashire Regt., *b.* 30 June, 1881.

Lineage.—DERMOT MCCARTHY, of Carhue and Dooneen, son (according to the family pedigree) of Donogh MacCarthy, of Drishane, *m.* previous to 1635, Eleanor, dau. of Darby O'Callaghan, of Kilpeader, co. Cork, and by her was father of
DONOGH MCDERMOT MCCARTHY, of Dooneen (mentioned in the will of his uncle, Cahir O'Callaghan, dated 1679), *m.* Jane Radley, of Knockrour, co. Cork, and had (with a son, Daniel, the father of Dermot and Justin) a son and successor,
DENIS MCCARTHY, of Dooneen, *b.* 1677 ; *m.* Jane, dau. of J. Barrett, of Barrett's Country, and *d.* 24 June, 1761, aged 84, leaving issue (with four daus., one of whom, Joan, *m.* Timothy McCarthy, of Lyradane), three sons,
1. JUSTIN, of whom hereafter.
2. Denis, *m.* Ellen, dau. of Daniel McCarthy, and had issue,
  1. Denis.   2. Charles.
  1. Mary.   2. Catherine.
  3. Jane.
3. ALEXANDER, of Knocknagrae, co. Cork, *b.* 1718, an Officer in Lord Clare's Irish Brigade, in France, who fought in 1745 under the banner of the young Chevalier. He *m.* Mary, dau. of Daniel Duggan, of Mount Infant, co. Cork, and *d.* 1802, aged 84, leaving issue,
  1. Denis, who had, with other issue, Florence, of Crookhaven, father of Thomas, of New York, Barrister-at-Law.
  2. Florence, Capt. in the H.E.I.C.S., *d.* 1778.
  3. Daniel, Major in the Austrian service, *d.* of wounds received at the taking of Dusseldorff by the French.
  4. Justin, Capt. in the H.E.I.C.S., *d.* in India, 1788.
  5. ALEXANDER, of Cork, *b.* 25 March, 1771 ; *m.* Eliza, dau. of Stephen Fagan, and by her (who *d.* 30 May, 1829) had (with junior issue) a son,
    ALEXANDER, *b.* 1800, Barrister-at-Law, M.P. for the city and afterwards for the co. of Cork, High Sheriff 1856 ; *d. unm.*
  1. Ellen, *m.* Denis Mahony, of Islandtougher.
  2. Mary, *m.* Martin Lawlor, of Killarney.
  3. Jane, *m.* 1st, — O'Driscoll, and 2ndly, Capt. Coghlan, of Crookhaven.

The eldest son,
JUSTIN MCCARTHY, *m.* 1730, Anne, dau. of Charles McCarthy, of Lyradane, co. Cork, and had issue (with a dau. Jane), a son,
DENIS MCCARTHY, of Glynn, co. Cork, *b.* 1731 ; *m.* 1st, 1770, Anne, dau. of Felix McCarthy, of Springhouse, co. Tipperary, and by her (who *d.* 1780) had issue,
1. DENIS, of whom presently.
1. Ellen, *m.* Albert Stubbeman, of Cork.
2. Mary, *m.* Timothy Mahony, of Cork.

Mr. McCarthy *m.* 2ndly, Helen, only child of the O'LEARY, of Millstreet, who *d.s.p.*, having devised the estates to her stepson, DENIS MCCARTHY, on condition of his assuming the name of O'LEARY. Mr. McCarthy *d.* 1824, and was *s.* by his son,
DENIS MCCARTHY O'LEARY, of Coomlagane, *b.* 1774 ; *m.* 1812, Leonora, dau. of John Howley, of Richill, co. Limerick. She *d.* 1832. He *d.* Oct. 1829, leaving issue,
1. JOHN, of whom presently.
2. Charles, *b.* 1817, *m.* 1840, Kate, dau. of Daniel O'Connell, of Kilgorey, co. Clare, and *d.* 1893, leaving issue.
3. William, 71st Highland L.I., *b.* 1818 ; *d. unm.* 1844.
4. Alexander, *d. unm.* 1827.
5. Thomas, *d. unm.*
6. Felix Joseph, of Montenotte House, co. Cork, J.P. cos. Cork and Clare, formerly Resident Magistrate, *b.* March, 1829 ; *m.* 15 Feb. 1855, Maria, dau. of William Hodnett, and has issue,
  1. William Serle, Capt. Argentine Navy, *b.* 5 Dec. 1855.
  2. Felix Denis Francis, Lieut.-Col. R.E., *b.* 11 Nov. 1857.
  3. Charles, Electrical Engineer, *b.* Nov. 1860.
  4. Augustus, Executive Engineer, P.W.D., India, *b.* June, 1863.
  5. Morgan John, Major R.F.A., *b.* 25 Nov. 1867.
  1. Emily, *m.* 1857, Maurice O'Connell, of Kilgorey, co. Clare, and *d.* 1855.
  2. Anna, *d. unm.* 1902.

The eldest son,
JOHN MCCARTHY-O'LEARY, of Coomlagane, co. Cork, J.P. cos. Cork and Kerry, D.L. co. Cork, High Sheriff 1884, *b.* 19 Sept. 1814 ; *m.* 29 Oct. 1839, Jane, eldest dau. of John O'Connell, of Grenagh, co. Kerry, and relict of O'Donoghue of the Glens. She *d.* 15 March, 1897. He *d.* 1896, having had issue,

1. John Arthur, late of the 34th Regt., b. 3 Aug. 1840; m. 4 March, 1869, at Brussels, La Comtesse Anna de Villegas de St. Pierre Jette, and d. 1870, leaving issue,
    John, India Forest Service, b. 1869.
    Madeleine Felicia.
2. Denis Charles, J.P., Barrister-at-Law, b. Oct. 1841; m. 1874, Frances, dau. of John P. Rowe, of Victoria; and d. at Melbourne, July, 1886.
3. WILLIAM, late of Coomlagane.
4. Maurice Charles, b. March, 1854, Barrister, King's Inns, 1881.
1. Elizabeth Mary.   2. Leonora Mary, d. 1859.
3. Amy Jane, d. 19 March, 1873.   4. Lucinda, dec.

The 3rd son,
LIEUT.-COL. WILLIAM MACCARTHY-O'LEARY, of Coomlagane, co. Cork, J.P., Lieut.-Col. 1st Batt. S. Lancashire Regt., b. 6 Jan. 1849; m. 2 July, 1878, Mary, dau. of Heffernan Considine, D.L., of Derk, co. Limerick (see that family). He was killed in action at Pieter's Hill, S. Africa, 27 Feb. 1900, leaving issue
1. John, now of Coomlagane.
2. Heffernan William Denis, Lieut. Royal Irish Fusiliers, b. 2 Aug. 1885.
3. William, b. 9 April, 1894.
1. Mary Helen.   2. Amy.

Seat—Coomlagane, near Millstreet, co. Cork.

OLIVER formerly OF CASTLE OLIVER.

CECIL RYDER OLIVER, b. 11 Feb. 1887; s. his father 1909.

Lineage.—CAPT. ROBERT OLIVER, Cloghanodfoy, co. Limerick, M.P. for Limerick, 1661, whose arms, with his wife's, are recorded 4 Aug. 1653, in Ulster's Office. He was granted land under the Act of Settlement 1666. He m. 1st, Bridget, a descendant of Philip Ormsby, of Partney, Lincolnshire, and by her had a son and a dau.,
1. CHARLES, of whom presently.
1. Mary, m. Thomas Sadleir, of Sopwell Hall, co. Tipperary.

He m. 2ndly, Valentina, dau. of Sir Claud Hamilton, of Cocknow, and widow 1st of Col. Charles Blount, and 2ndly of Col. Knight, and had further issue,
2. Henry.
3. Christopher.
4. Valentine Blount.
2. Anne.

His will, dated 5 Feb. 1678-9, was proved 13 May, 1679. His eldest son,
CHARLES OLIVER, of Cloghanodfoy, co. Limerick, High Sheriff 1692, and M.P. 1693, b. 1646; m. 1670, Elizabeth, dau. of Sir Percy Smyth, Knt., of Ballynatray, co. Waterford, and dying 13 April, 1706, left a son and successor,
ROBERT OLIVER, of Cloghanodfoy, M.P. co. Limerick 1715, and Col. of Limerick Militia, b. 1671; m. 1st, 1702, Katherine, dau. of the Hon. Sir Robert Southwell, Clerk to the Privy Council and Secretary of State for Ireland; she d.s.p. He m. 2ndly, 1705, Susanna, 2nd dau. and co-heir of James Knight, and dying 1738, aged 67, left, besides two daus. (Jane, m. Boyle Aldworth, of Newmarket, and Elizabeth, m. James Ellard, of Newtown), three sons,
1. ROBERT, of Cloghanodfoy (Castle Oliver), M.P. 1727, m. 1734, Jane, dau. and co-heir of John Silver, and d. 1745, leaving a dau., m. 3 Dec. 1767, Standish O'Grady, of Elton, and a son,
THE RIGHT HON. SILVER OLIVER, of Castle Oliver, M.P. for co. Limerick, 1768 and 1776, High Sheriff 1764, m. 4 Feb. 1759, Isabella Sarah, dau. and co-heir of Richard Newman, of Newbury, co. Cork. She d. 1777. He d. 1799, leaving issue,
(1) RICHARD PHILIP, of Castle Oliver, who assumed by Royal Licence the surname of GASCOIGNE (see that family).
(2) Charles Silver, of Inchera, High Sheriff 1791, M.P. for co. Limerick 1797, m. 1805, Maria Elizabeth, dau. of Abraham Morris, of Dunkettle, and d. 1817, leaving issue,
  1. Silver Charles, 10th Hussars, of Inchera, m. 1830, Ellen, dau. of John Cochrane, of Rochsoles, Renfrew, and d. 1878, having had issue one dau., Ellen, m. 1st, 1857, Capt. Jonas Morris (who d. Oct. 1862); and 2ndly, 1865, William Lewis Grant, of Dalvey on the Spey. He d. 1888.
  2. Abraham Morris, d. unm. 1851.
  3. Richard Phillip Gascoigne.
  1. Thomasine, m. Rev. Benjamin Jacob. She d. 1888.
  2. Isabella, m. M. du Chable, and d. 1897.
  3. Maria Elizabeth, m. 1841, Godfrey Baker, of Fortwilliam, and d. 1901, having had issue.
(3) Silver, M.P. for Kilmallock 1797, d.s.p. at Vienna 1834.
(4) Robert, of Darrington, co. York, m. Mary Sarah Shepley, dau. of Edmund Barker, and widow of William Sotheran, M.P., and d. 1834, leaving,
  1. Richard, Capt. Royal Horse Guards, m. the dau. of H. Ramsden, of Orton Hall, Tadcaster, and d. 1889.
  2. Robert Edmund, Capt. Royal Horse Guards, d. unm.
  (1) Catherine, m. 1780, Henry, Lord Mount Sandford, and d. 1818.
  (2) Jane, m. 1789, Hon. and Rev. William Sandford, brother of Lord Mount Sandford, and had issue, one son and two daus.
  (3) Isabella Sarah, m. John Waller, of Castletown, M.P., who d. 1836.
  (4) Elizabeth, d. unm.
  (5) Susanna, m. Rev. Hans Hamilton, D.D.
2. Philip, of Kilfinan, M.P. for Kilmallock, 1747, m. 1748, Lucy, dau. of R. Gray, and d. 1769, leaving two daus.,
  1. Lucy, m. 1780, Venerable William Maunsell, Archdeacon of Kildare.
  2. Elizabeth, m. 1775, Charles Coote, of Mount Coote, and d. 1820.
3. JOHN, of whom we treat.

The 3rd son,
THE VEN. JOHN OLIVER, Archdeacon of Ardagh, b. 1720; m. 1761, Elizabeth, dau. of John Ryder, D.D., Archbishop of Tuam, and by her (who d. 1 May, 1822, aged 82) had issue,
1. JOHN, of whom presently.
2. Robert Dudley, Admiral R.N., b. 1766; m. 1805, Mary, only dau. of Sir Charles Saxton, Bart., and d. 1 Sept. 1850, having by her (who d. 16 June, 1848) had issue,
  1. Charles Saxton, R.N., b. 1807; d. 4 Jan. 1827.
  2. John, of Circourt, Berks, J.P. and D.L., b. 1809; m. 1st, 1837, Emma Matilda, only dau. of Col. Morgan, of Llandough Castle, co. Glamorgan, which lady d. 31 Dec. 1837; and 2ndly, 1849, Lucy Diana, dau. of Col. Thomas Maunsell, M.P., of Thorpe Malsor, Northampton, and d. 1887, having by her (who d. 1892) had issue, one son,
    Robert Dudley Maunsell, b. 1852.
  3. Richard Aldworth, Admiral R.N., b. 6 Dec. 1811; m. 16 March, 1852, Flora Hutchins, only dau. of Col. Daniel Hutchins Bellasis, and d. 1889, having by her (who d. 17 May, 1871) had issue,
    (1) Richard John Erskine, of Shilton House, Shilton, Coventry (Clubs—Naval and Military; Cavalry), late Capt. 20th Hussars, who, under the will of his maternal uncle, takes the name of BELLASIS. He has s. jointly with his four brothers and one sister to the Circourt property, Berks, b. 30 Jan. 1854; m. 15 Nov. 1899, Gwendoline Mary, eldest dau. of Lieut.-Col. Edward Woollcombe-Adams (see WOOLLCOMBE-ADAMS of Anstey Hall), and has issue,
      1. Richard, b. 15 Sept. 1900.
      2. John, b. 4 Dec. 1904.
    (2) Algernon Hardy, Commander R.N., b. 24 Sept. 1855; m. 14 Nov. 1895, Mary Beatrice, dau. of John Dudley Oliver, of Cherrymount (see below).
    (3) Robert Dudley, b. 30 Oct. 1856.
    (4) Godfrey Ryder, b. 9 June, 1859; m. 27 Nov. 1900, Blanche Cicely, eldest dau. of the late Edward Falkener, of Glanymor, co. Carmarthen, and has issue,
      1. Godfrey Charles Saxton, b. 16 Aug. 1901.
      2. Robert Ormsby, b. 3 Dec. 1902.
      3. Cicely Falkener, b. 24 Dec. 1904.
    (5) Charles Augustus, b. 16 Oct. 1861; m. 11 Jan. 1911, Hilda Margaret, youngest dau. of Lieut.-Col. Edward Woollcombe-Adams (see WOOLLCOMBE-ADAMS of Anstey Hall).
    (1) Flora, m. 1893, Commander W. H. W. Grove, R.N., and has issue.
  4. William Disney, Barrister-at-Law, b. 1817; d. 1883.
  5. Charles Dudley, Capt. 30th Regt., b. 1821; d. at Tangier, 1854.
  6. James Hewitt, Lieut.-Col. Dublin Militia, b. 1823; d. 8 Sept. 1902.
  1. Mary, b. 1815; d. unm. 1834.
  2. Elizabeth, b. 1819; d. unm. 1846.
3. Charles Deane, of Spa Hill and Rockmill Lodge, b. 1771; m. 1805, Sarah, dau. of Capt. Jonathan Bruce Roberts, and d. 15 Feb. 1829, having had issue.
  1. Richard Charles Deane, of Rockmill Lodge, co. Cork, J.P., b. 7 May, 1821; m. 1859, Katherine, dau. of the Ven. Archdeacon Hawtayne, and d. 1880, having had issue by her (who d. 6 Oct. 1911) two sons,
    (1) Charles Deane, b. 1861; m. 1888, Maria Charlotte, dau. of Justice Edward Falconer Litton, and has issue,
      1. Richard Edward Deane, b. 1890.
      1. Elizabeth Catherine Deane, b. 1895.
      2. Kathleen Maude Deane, b. 1897.
      3. Margaret Silver Deane.
    (2) Richard John Deane (Rev.), Chaplain to the Forces, b. 1863.
  1. Anne (who d. 1845) m. Rev. John Aldworth, of Glanworth.
  2. Elizabeth, m. James Hill, and d. 4 Jan. 1887, aged 78, leaving issue.
  3. Mary, d. unm. 1870.
  4. Alicia, m. Capt. St. Leger Aldworth. She d. 1870.
  5. Sarah Agnes, d. unm. 1886.
4. Richard, b. 1776; d. 1791.
5. Silver (Rev.), Rector of Loughgall, co. Armagh, b. 1778; m. 1823, Alicia Maria, dau. of Samuel Madden, of Hilton, and d. 1844. She d. 1851.
6. Nathaniel Wilmot, Major-Gen. R.A., b. (posthumous) April, 1779; m. 1st, 1811, Eliza, dau. of Rev. Michael Baxter, and by her (who d. 1815) had a dau., Eliza, b. 19 March, 1814; m. Rev. Chambre Townshend. Major-Gen. Oliver m. 2ndly, 1817, Marianne, dau. of Dudley Baxter. He d. 10 Jan. 1854. She d. 16 Jan. 1863.
1. Alicia, b. 15 March, 1762; m. James, 2nd Viscount Lifford, Dean of Armagh, and d. 15 March, 1845, leaving issue (see BURKE's Peerage).
2. Susanna, b. 1764; d. unm. 31 Aug. 1819.

2. Anne, b. 1765; m. William Disney, Q.C., and d. 1848. He d. 1847.
4. Elizabeth, b. 1770; m. 1793, Robert Rogers Aldworth, of Newmarket Court, co. Cork, and d. 1842.
Mr. Oliver d. 23 Nov. 1778; his eldest son,
REV. JOHN OLIVER, of Cherrymount, Rector of Swepstone, co. Leicester, b. 1763; m. 1st, 11 May, 1807, Sarah Catherine, dau. of Dudley Baxter, of Atherstone, co. Warwick, and by her (who d. 19 April, 1821) had issue,
1. JOHN DUDLEY, of whom presently.
2. Richard, b. 21 Jan. 1812; d. 7 Jan. 1822.
3. Charles, b. 18 Sept. 1816; d. 14 Aug. 1821.
4. Henry Ryder, b. 14 April, 1818; d. 16 April, 1821.
5. Dudley, b. 10 Feb. 1821; m. 30 April, 1857, Anna Marie, dau. of Herr Johan Walter Steill, of Goutenschwyl, Canton of Aargau, Switzerland, and d. 19 Jan. 1894. She d. 1883.
 1. Elizabeth, b. 1808; d 1867
 2. Alicia Marianne, b. 1810; d. 7 June, 1860.
 3. Susan Catherine, b. 1813; m. 2 May, 1843, William Hall, of Atherstone, and d. 1867. He d. 1880.
 4. Anna Maria, b. 1815; m. 15 July, 1841, Rev. James William King Disney, and d.s.p. 1884. He d. 1877.
 5. Isabella, b. 1819; m. 22 Dec. 1840, Lieut.-Col. Henry Murray, R.A., and d. 1870, leaving issue. He d. 1864.
Mr. Oliver m. 2ndly, 2 Jan. 1826 Elizabeth Martha Caroline dau. of Robert Creswell of Ravenstone, but by her (who d. 9 May, 1859) had no further issue. He d. 16 June, 1832, and was s. by his eldest surviving son,
JOHN DUDLEY OLIVER, of Cherrymount, co. Wicklow, J.P., b. 23 July, 1809; m. 1st, 25 Feb. 1834, Mary Susanna, 4th dau. of Valentine Green, of Normanton-le-Heath, co. Leicester, and by her (who d. 25 Sept. 1853) had issue,
1. JOHN RYDER, late of Tigroney.
2. Charles Valeutine, Major 66th Foot, b. 9 March, 1836; d. at Candahar, 10 Oct. 1880.
3. Edward Dudley, Capt. 51st Foot, b. 25 June, 1837; d. 1 Aug. 1865, in India.
4. Henry James, Capt. 56th Regt., b. 5 July, 1838; m. 23 May, 1864, Frances Martha, dau. of Capt. Thomas Graves, R.N., and by her (who d. 8 Nov. 1885) left at his decease, 12 April, 1879,
  1. Edward Graves Indian Forest Dept. b. 26 Aug. 1866; m. 1891 Flora Ingle, and has issue,
    Henry Herbert Montague b. 1897.
    Frances Alice Margaret b. 17 Jan. 1895.
  2. Herbert Mortimer, b. 28 Aug. 1868.
5. Hans Mortimer, late Lieut. 3rd Buffs, b. 7 Dec. 1843; m. 1885 Harriet widow of H. C. Wilcox of Detroit, and dau. of G. W. Cobb, of Mineral Point, Wisconsin.
6. Robert Wilmot, b. 6 Dec. 1844; d. 16 Oct. 1911; m. 1879, Kate, dau. of P. Butler Aldrich, of Michigan, and has a dau., Beatrice, b. 12 Oct. 1882.
7. Theodore b. 8 May; d. 20 May, 1846.
8. Oswald, b. 17 Oct. 1849; m. 1st, 1881, Mary, dau. of J. F. Wikoff, of Illinois, and by her (who d. 1896) had a dau., Mary Dorothy. He m. 2ndly, July, 1898, Irene, dau. of — Briggs.
9. James William, Indian Forest Dept., b. 7 Dec. 1850.
 1. Susanna Eleanor, b. 11 July, 1840; m. 3 April, 1866, Rev. John Woollam, eldest son of John Woollam, of St. Albans, and had issue. He d. 1909.
 2. Mary Theodosia, b. 4 July, 1841; m. 1 July, 1865, Henry Hodgson, of Currarevagh, and had issue. He d. 31 May, 1903.
 3. Frances Georgiana, b. 22 July, 1842; m. 15 April, 1868, Frederick Lewis Roy, late of Nenthorn, Kelso. He d.s.p. 17 Feb. 1906.
 4. Catherine, b. 30 Dec. 1847.
He m. 2ndly, 22 Oct. 1857, Elizabeth, 2nd dau. of Rev. Wyndham Carlyon Madden, Rector of Bergh Apton, Norfolk, and by her (who d. 30 June, 1860) had issue,
5. Mary Beatrice, b. 21 Dec. 1858; m. 14 Nov. 1895, Lieut. A. H. Oliver, R.N. (see above).
He m. 3rdly, 5 April, 1866, Sydney, 4th dau. of Wliam Tongue, of Comberford Hall, co. Stafford, and by her (who d. 29 Jan. 1909) had issue,
9. Dudley b. 14 Aug. 1867.
Mr. Oliver d. 18 Dec. 1870. His eldest son,
MAJOR-GEN. JOHN RYDER OLIVER, C.M.G., late R.A., of Tigroney (Cherrymount), co. Wicklow, b. 16 Dec. 1834; m. 1st, 19 April, 1864, Georgina Frances, dau. of G. M. Harrison, of Stanground Manor, Hunts, and by her (who d. 9 Nov. 1874) had issue
1. John Charles Arthur, b. 22 April, 1871; d. 4 Feb. 1875.
He m. 2ndly, 30 June, 1880, Mary, dau. of W. G. Hinds, of Kingston, Canada, and d. 10 Feb. 1909, having had issue by his 2nd wife,
2. CECIL RYDER, b. 11 Feb. 1887.
3. Charles Aldworth, b. 10 Sept. 1889.
1. Mary Beatrice Lucy, b. 3 April, 1883.

Arms—Or, on a chevron between two pellets in chief sa. and a mullet naiant in base ppr., a crescent arg. Crest—A hand holding a branch of olive, ppr. vested gu. doubled arg. Motto—Ito tu et fac similiter.

Residence—24, Glazbury Road, West Kensington.

OLPHERT OF BALLYCONNELL.

SIR JOHN OLPHERT, Knt., C.V.O., of Ballyconnell, co. Donegal, LL.B. Trin. Coll. Dublin, J.P. and D.L, co. Donegal, late Capt. 5th Batt. Royal Inniskilling Fusiliers, Gentleman-in-waiting to Lords Carnarvon, Londonderry and Zetland, Lords-Lieut. of Ireland, Gentleman Usher to Earl Cadogan, and to the Earl of Dudley, b. 2 Sept. 1844; m. Dec. 1869, Frances Susan, only dau. of the late Robert Burrowes, M.P., of Stradone, co. Cavan, and has issue,
Geraldine Constance, m. 29 June, 1898, Capt. Bertrand Gosselin, R.H.A., and has issue.
Lineage.—WIBRANTZ OLPHERTZEN, Gen., went over to Ireland from Holland in the reign of CHARLES I., in whose household he is stated to have been. He received from that king a large grant of property and the manor of Ballyness in co. Donegal 1633, which is still part of that now held by the present descendant.
WYBRANTS OLPHERT, High Sheriff of co. Donegal 1720, m. Mary Hodson, and had, with three daus., four sons,
1. JOHN, his heir.
2. RICHARD, m. 1st, his cousin, Miss Hodson, and 2ndly, 1783, Barbara, 2nd dau. of William Blacker, of Carrick Blacker, co. Armagh, and had issue by her,
  1. Richard (Rev.), m. 1st, 1809, his cousin, Anne, eldest dau. of Sir Francis Macnaghten, Bart., and by her had, with other issue, d. young,
    (1) RICHARD, of Milburn House, and Dungiven, co. Londonderry, B.A., J.P., co. Sligo, late Capt. 40th Foot, b. 1818; m. 1849, Elizabeth Henrietta, 2nd dau. of John FitzHerbert Ruxton, of Ardee House, co. Louth, dec.
    (2) Henry, Lieut.-Col. R.A., m. Louisa, dau. of Col. Stedman, and d. 1860.
    (3) Francis Montgomery, of Mount Shannon, co. Sligo. M.A., J.P., b. 1822; m. 1858, Mariana, eldest dau. of Owen Wynne, of Ardaghowen, co. Sligo. He d. 1897.
    (1) Letitia, d. 1831.
    (2) Eliza Jane, m. 1840, Rev. Theodore Dunkin; d. 1842.
  Rev. Richard Olphert m. 2ndly, 1834, Mary, dau. of John Nicholson, of Stramore House, co. Down, and d. 1849, leaving by her an only dau.,
    (3) Isabella, m. Capt. George F. Coryton, late 10th Regt., son of Gen. Coryton, and had issue, of whom, Richard Wybrants, m. 17 Sept. 1901, Claire Azema, dau. of Peter Hennis Green.
  2. WILLIAM, of Dartrey, co. Armagh, Barrister-at-Law, m. Rosanna, 3rd dau. of Edward Atkinson, M.D., of Armagh, by Mary, his wife, only sister of Dr. James Macartney, and had issue,
    (1) Richard Marmaduke.   (2) Edward, d. 1820.
    (3) William (Sir), K.C.B., V.C., Gen. R.A., b. 8 March, 1822; m. Alice Maria, dau. of Gen. Cautley, Bengal Army, and d. 30 April, 1902, leaving, with other issue, a son,
      William Cautley, Major Royal Scots (Lothian Regt.), b. 1862.
    (1) Mary, d. unm. 1862.   (2) Barbara.
  3. Edward, Bengal Army, d. unm.
  1. Letitia, m. 1st, Col. Hall, 28th Regt., and 2ndly, Arthur Irwin Kelly, of Armagh, and d. 1826.
  2. Mary, m. 1817, Samuel Thompson, of Muckamore Abbey, co. Antrim, who d. 1838, and their 3rd son, Samuel Thompson, of Muckamore Abbey, m. Maria Hannah, dau. of Robert Smyth, of Gaybrook, co. Westmeath (see that family), and has John, b. 1867, and other issue.
3. Wybrants.   4. Thomas, d. unm.
The eldest son,
JOHN OLPHERT, of Ballyconnell, co. Donegal, High Sheriff 1747, m. Letitia, dau. of Rev. Andrew Hamilton, D.D., Archdeacon of Raphoe, and Sarah his wife, only dau. and heiress of Henry Conyngham, of Castle Conyngham, co. Londonderry. He had, with other issue,
1. WYBRANTS, his heir.
1. Anne, m. 1776, Rev. John Ellison, D.D., Rector of Chevenish, and had issue (see ELLISON MACARTNEY of Mountjoy Grange).
2. Mary, m. 1 June, 1771, Rev. William Lodge, of Armagh.
The son and heir,
WYBRANTS OLPHERT, of Ballyconnell, High Sheriff 1789, m. 1779, Anne, dau. of Thomas Smith, of The Lodge, co. Londonderry, and had issue,
1. JOHN, of Ballyconnell House.
2. Thomas Wybrants, m. Mary, dau. of Rev. Dr. Lodge, of Armagh, and d.s.p.
1. Amelia, m. 1812, the Rev. John Ellison.
The elder son,
REV. JOHN OLPHERT, of Ballyconnell House, Rector of Drumachose, co. Londonderry, b. 22 Jan. 1789; m. 28 July, 1807, Anna Benjamina, dau. of Dominick McCausland, of Daisy Hill, co. Londonderry, and had issue,
1. WYBRANTS, of Ballyconnell.
2. John, Lieut. R.A., b. 7 Nov. 1815; d. unm. 6 March, 1844.
3. Thomas (Very Rev.), M.A., Dean of Derry, and Incumbent of Urney, near Strabane, b. 10 Dec. 1819; m. 28 April, 1857, Julia, eldest dau. of Sir Hugh Stewart, M.P., 2nd bart., of Ballygawley House, co. Tyrone, and d. 1901, leaving issue,
  1. John (Rev.), Rector of Urney, Canon of Derry, b. 11 Feb. 1858; m. 1896, Maud, dau. of the late Capt. Montgomery Archdall (52nd Light Infantry), of Drumadravy, co. Fermanagh, and has issue.

2. Hugh Stewart, India Telegraph Department, *b.* 1 Feb. 1859; *m.* 1890, Juliet Mary, dau. of Conolly Marcus Gage, J.P., of Drummond House, co. Londonderry (*see that family*).
3. Wybrants, *b.* 4 Feb. 1861.
4. Thomas Richard, *b.* 17 Jan. 1863; *d.* 1899.
5. Alfred Frederick, *b.* June, 1866; *m.* 27 April, 1904, Charlotte O'Brien, dau. of late Michael Houghton Kiernan, of Richmond, Surrey.
6. Herbert Ernest, *b.* June, 1874.
1. Anna Julia, dec.   2. Alice Letitia.
3. Mary Henrietta Caroline.
1. Mary, *m.* 27 Dec. 1838, William C. Gage, J.P., of Drummond House, Bally Kelly. He *d.* 1882. She *d.* 1887, leaving issue.
2. Anna, *m.* 7 June, 1832, Rev. Robert Gage, and *d.* Dec. 1896.
3. Caroline, *m.* 23 April, 1835, Rev. George Kemmis, Vicar of Rosenallis, and *d.* 1856.
4. Letitia, *m.* 24 Oct. 1848, Samuel Frederick Adair.
Rev. John Olphert *d.* 5 June, 1851, and was *s.* by his son,
WYBRANTS OLPHERT, of Ballyconnell, co. Donegal, J.P. and D.L., High Sheriff 1842, B.A. Trin. Coll. Dublin, *b.* 27 March, 1811; *m.* 13 July, 1843, Marianne Constance, 3rd dau. and co-heir of Robert Fannin, and by her (who *d.* 22 March, 1880) had issue,
1. JOHN (Sir), now of Ballyconnell.
2. Wybrants, 14th Foot, *b.* 19 Sept. 1847.
3. Robert Fannin, *b.* 2 April, 1851; *m.* 1882, Frances Sophia, younger dau. of Richard Warburton, D.L., of Garryhinch, King's Co., and has, with other issue,
   Wybrants, *b.* 1883.
4. Albert Thomas, *b.* 2 Oct. 1854; *m.* 9 Nov. 1893, Alice, elder dau. of Samuel Frederick Adair. He *d.s.p.* 18 June 1904,
1. Marianne Constance, *d.* 22 March, 1864.
2. Anna, *m.* 11 June, 1873, Thomas Butler Stoney, J.P., of Oakfield Raphoe, co. Donegal, and has issue (*see that family*).
3. Florence Balfour, *m.* 7 Oct. 1875, William Wildman Kettlewell, J.P., of The Court, East Harptree, co. Somerset, and has issue.
Mr. Wybrants Olphert *d.* 21 Sept. 1892, aged 81.

Seat—Ballyconnell House, Falcarragh, co. Donegal. *Clubs*—Kildare Street, and Junior Conservative.

O'MORCHOE OF OULARTLEIGH.

ARTHUR MACMURROGH-MURPHY, " of Oulartleigh,' co. Wexford, "THE O'MORCHOE," Chief of his sept, *b.* 4 Jan. 1835; *m.* 19 Nov. 1863, Susan Elizabeth, dau. of Thomas Bradley, M.D., of Kells Grange, co. Kilkenny, by his wife Sophia, dau. of Robert Wolfe, of Tentore, Queen's Co., and has had issue,

1. THOMAS ARTHUR MACMURROGH O'MORCHOE (Rev.), M.A. T.C.D., Incumbent of Kilternan, co. Dublin, who has resumed the name of O'MORCHOE by Deed Poll 3 Sept. 1895, *b.* 22 March, 1865; *m.* 8 April, 1891, Anne, dau. of John George Gibbon, LL.D., of Kiltennell, co. Wexford (*see* GIBBON *of Neston*), and has issue,
   1. Arthur Donel MacMurrogh, *b.* 3 June, 1892.
   2. Kenneth Gibbon, *b.* 16 Feb. 1894.
   3. Nial Francis Creagh, *b.* 26 Sept. 1895.
   4. Maurice Gethin, *b.* 11 Jan. 1901.
   1. Dorothy.   2. Honor Gertrude.
   3. Kathleen.
2. Arthur MacMurrogh, L.R.C.P.I., *b.* 22 Sept. 1866; *d. unm.* 18 April, 1899.
3. William MacMurrogh, *b.* 12 July, 1868.
1. Sophia Rebecca MacMurrogh, *m.* 1st, 28 Aug. 1888, Francis Richard Wolfe, eldest son of Rev. Prebendary R. R. Wolfe, M.A., of Leighon, co. Devon, and Lord of the Manor of Ilsington, and by him (who *d.* 11 April, 1899) has issue, a dau. Louise Susan. She *m.* 2ndly, 11 Feb. 1903, Raymond William French, 5th son of the late Ven. Thomas Fitzgerald French, Archdeacon of Killaloe (*see* FRENCH *of Cuskinny*), and has issue,
   1. Raymond Arthur, *b.* 7 Aug. 1911.
   1. Mary Dring.   2. Sheela O'Morchoe.
2. Gertrude Susan MacMurrogh, *d.* young, 29 June, 1882.
3. Edith MacMurrogh, *m.* 2 Aug. 1899, James Robinson, son of the late Archibald Robinson, Taxing Master, High Court of Justice in Ireland, and has issue,
   1. Archibald, *b.* 14 Jan. 1902.
   2. Herbert James, *b.* 12 Dec. 1903.
   1. Audry Gertrude.   2. Gwenda Katie.
4. Mary Augusta MacMurrogh.

Lineage.—The "Rental" of the 9th Earl of Kildare of date 1518 A.D. (Harlean Coll. B. Museum No. 3756), which is an account of the duties leviable by the Earl of Kildare as Lord Deputy upon the Irish Chiefs under his protection, sets forth his duty upon " O'Morowe's countrie, called Ofhelome" (*i.e.*, Hy-Feliuny) " upon the O'Morow for his defense yearly at Mich. XX Kyne or XMKC. The Wilde Orcharde *alias* the Owfforde Lyan " (*i.e.*, Oulartleigh). This estate which this chief held has since passed from father to son to the present time. By Indenture 10 May, 1536, the Chief, Donel O'Morchoe, entered into agreement with Sir Leonard Gray, Knt., Lord Deputy on behalf of the King, to hold his countrie from the King as his feudal lord and to be maintained in his Chiefship by the Lord Deputy. (Memo. Rolls, 28 H. VIII. M. 6.) The retinue of the Chief at this time appears from the tract in the British Museum written previous to 1576, " O'Moroghowe lord of Yphelim 16 horse and 40 kerne." In the return of the " Chief Irish Captains of Ireland " (Carew, S. P., vol. 6, 1515 A.D.), the Chief of this family is described as " O'Mwrgho of Ifeline " (*i.e.*, Hy-Feliuny). The pedigree which is on record in Ulster's Office, Dublin Castle, establishes the descent of this family from Donel Mor, or the " Great," who was the O'Morchoe *temp.* HENRY VIII. and the last independent Chief of his name.

The pedigree starts with this DONEL MOR, or the " Great," who as recorded in the Funeral Entry of 1637 " was O'Morchoe." He was made a feudal lord by the Indenture of 1536 A.D. and was assessed to pay " Kildare's duties" for the defence of his country (S.P. 1537). He was possessed of Oulartleigh, as mentioned in the assessment, and had, with other elder sons,

CORMAC O'MORCHOE, who *s.* to Oulartleigh, named in the State Paper (Carew) 1608 as " Cormac Mac Daniel of Oulartleigh " (*i.e.*, Cormac, son of Donel), and one of the " chief gentlemen of the Barony of Ballaghkeen, co. Wexford." He was granted a pardon in 1550 as " son of Donald O'Merchowe, Capt. of this nation " (Fiants Ed. VI). His son,

HUGH " BALLAGH " O'MORCHOE, of Oulartleigh, referred to in the grant of his estate subsequently made to his son and heir, in which grant his son is referred to as " Brian MacHugh Ballagh O'Murcho, gentleman of Oulartleigh."

BRIAN O'MORCHOE, son of Hugh " Ballagh " or freckled Hugh, had a grant by patent Anno 15 James I. under the commission to remedy defective titles, of the lands of Oulartleigh Mor, Tenneberny, Ballymabodagh, Coolknockmore, Coolneboy, in the Barony of Ballaghkeen and territory of the Murrows, co. Wexford. He made a deed of entail 1634 and forfeited all his lands after the Rebellion of 1641, which were granted in trust for his son to Richard Kenny. His son,

ART O'MORCHOE *s.* to Oulartleigh and his other lands under the entail of 1634, and under a grant made under the Act of Settlement to Richard Kenny, his brother-in-law. He *m.* Bridget Kenny, dau. of Richard Kenny. His son,

DANIEL MORCHOE, of Oulartleigh, *s.* under the entail made by his grandfather in 1634. He *m.* Dorcas, dau. of John Burroughs. By his will, dated 26 May, 1679, is shown the transition of the ancient name O'Morchoe to Murphy, and also in Chancery Bill filed by his son Arthur Murphy, in which he refers to his father as " Daniel Murphy, *alias* Morchoe." His son,

ARTHUR MURPHY, of Oulartleigh, O'MORCHOE, Chief of his sept, *m.* 1st, Elizabeth, dau. of Thomas Knox, of Tagunnon, co. Wexford, and great-grand-dau. of the Right Rev. Thomas Knox Bishop of the Isles, by whom he had a dau.,

Dorcas, *m.* John Giffard, of Great Torrington, co. Devon, and had issue. Her great grandson is the 1st Earl of Halsbury, Lord Chancellor of England (*see* BURKE's *Peerage*).

He *m.* 2ndly, 17 April, 1704, Elizabeth, dau. of William Turner, by whom he had eight sons and four daus. His will is dated 1761. His 2nd son,

WILLIAM MURPHY, of Oulartleigh, O'MORCHOE, Chief of his sept, who *s.* on the death of his eldest brother, Daniel (who *d.* in his father's lifetime), and his nephew James (who *d.s.p.* May, 1759, aged 19): *m.* June, 1727, Elizabeth, dau. of John Hawkins, Ulster King of Arms, and had issue,
1. ARTHUR.
2. Cary, *m.* Aug. 1769, Louisa, dau. of George Nixon, of Newtown, co. Wexford.

The elder son,
ARTHUR MURPHY, of Oulartleigh, O'MORCHOE, Chief of his sept, *m.* (lic. dated 29 Jan. 1766) Esther, dau. of John Pounden, of Enniscorthy, and by her had two sons and three daus. The elder son,

ARTHUR MURPHY, of Oulartleigh, O'MORCHOE, Chief of his sept, *m.* (lic. dated 18 March, 1791) Margaret, dau. of Rev. Shapland Swiny, Rector of Templeshambo, co. Wexford, and *d.* (will dated 5 Sept. 1805 leaving issue, one son and two daus. The son,

ARTHUR MACMURROGH MURPHY, of Oulartleigh, O'MORCHOE, Chief of his sept. *m.* 1st, Elizabeth, dau. of John Millet, of Lismarta, co. Tipperary, which lady *d.s.p.* in 1828. He *m.* 2ndly, 20 Feb. 1834, Rebecca, dau. of Rev. John Bagwell Creagh (*see* CREAGH *of Ballyandrew*), and *d.* 21 Aug. 1867, leaving, by Rebecca his wife (who *d.* 11 Jan. 1889), a son,

ARTHUR MACMURROGH MURPHY, the O'Morchoe, now " of Oulartleigh."

Arms—Arg., a hawthorn tree eradicated vert, fructed gu., on a chief of the last a lion passant, or.

Residence—Kerrymount House, Foxrock, Dublin.

O'NEILL-POWER. *See* POWER.

O'NEILL. *See* BURKE's PEERAGE, O'NEILL, B.

O'REILLY OF EAST BREFNY.

MYLES JOHN O'REILLY, b. 23 Jan. 1860; s. his father 1911.

Lineage.—RAGALLAGH (the son of CATHALAN, Prince of Brefny, and grandson of DUBH CRON, a leading chief against the Danes, who was eldest son of MAOLMORDHA, Dynast of East Brefny, lineally descended from BRIAN, the 4th Milesian King of Connaught) s. his father in the Government of Muintir Maolmordha A.D. 981, and commanded the Royal Army during the reign of Maolseachluin until the dethronement of that prince, in 1002, in favour of Brian Boroimhe, from which period Ragallagh accompanied that celebrated chief in all his expeditions, and at length fell with him at the battle of Clontarf. Ragallagh's son and successor,

ARTEN, Prince of East Brefny, was father of

TARGAILEE, Prince of East Brefny, who was the first that assumed the name of UA RAGALLAGH or O'REILLY. From this time, too, the principality of East Brefny went by the appellation of Brefny O'Reilly, and that of West Brefny by that of Brefny O'Ruark, until both were converted into shire ground, called counties, by Queen ELIZABETH, under the government of Thomas, Earl of Sussex. A.D. 1562, at which time the eastern division was called the co. of Cavan, and the Western the co. of Leitrim. Our limited space precludes us from entering minutely into the history of the subsequent O'Reillys, Princes of Brefny, until we come to

MAOLMORDHA O'REILLY, elected Chief of East Brefny in 1536, d. 1565; m. Marcella, dau. of Hugh duff O'Donell, Chief of Tyrconnell, and by her (who d. 1582) had seven sons,
1. Hugh Connellagh (Sir), elected Chief 1565, knighted June, 1570, and d. 1583; m. three times, and left issue.
2. Donal, slain 1565, left issue.
3. EDMUND, of whom next.
4. John.
5. Owen, of Tullyvin.
6. Cathoir.
7. Philip, the Prior.

EDMUND O'REILLY, of Kilnacrott. He m. twice; 1st, a dau. of the noble house of Plunkett, and 2ndly, a dau. of that of Nugent, and had several children. From his youngest son, Turlough, sprang the SCARVA family (which see). He d. April, 1601. His 3rd son,

JOHN O'REILLY, m. Catherine, dau. of James Butler, and dying 1621, left a son,

BRIAN O'REILLY, m. Mary Plunkett, and d. 1631, having had (with three other sons, Cathal; Eogan, d.s.p.; and Hugh, an eldest son,

MAOLMORDHA, or MYLES O'REILLY, an able Military Officer during the civil wars of 1641, killed at the head of his troops in 1644, leaving, by Catherine his wife, dau. of Capt. Charles O'Reily, of co. Leitrim (with two younger sons, Philip and Edmund), an elder son,

JOHN O'REILLY, of Conlyn and Garryrocock, co. Cavan, and subsequently of Ballymacadd, co. Meath, M.P. for co. Cavan 1689, who raised a regiment of Dragoons at his own expense for the service of King JAMES II. He m. Margaret, dau. of Owen O'Reilly, and d. 17 Feb. 1716, having had (with two daus.) five sons,
1. CONOR, of Garryrocock, co. Cavan, Capt. in his father's Regt. of Dragoons, m. 2 May, 1692, Mary, dau. of Luke O'Reilly, of Tomogh, co. Cavan, and d.s.p. May, 1723.
2. MYLES, m. Aug. 1698, Mary Barnewell, by whom he had (with two daus., Mary, m. Philip Tuite, of Newcastle, co Meath, and Margaret, m. Walter Dowdall, of Cloune, co. Meath) three sons,
  1. JOHN, his heir, d.s.p. 1767.
  2. Dominick.
  3. Francis, d.s.p.
He d. June, 1731.
3. BRYAN, of whom we treat.
4. Owen, or Eugene, who m. and had a son, James.
5. THOMAS, ancestor of the Baltrasna branch (which see).

The 3rd son,

BRYAN O'REILLY, of Ballenrink, Capt. in his father's Regt. of Dragoons, m. Margaret, dau. of Col. Luke M'Dowell, of Montach, co. Roscommon, and by her (who d. 30 Nov. 1755) had six sons. Capt. O'Reilly d. 6 Sept. 1748, in his 72nd year. His eldest son,

MYLES O'REILLY, of Tullystown, co. Westmeath, m. 1740, Sarah, dau. of Willam Fitzsimons, of Garadice, co. Meath, and had (with a dau Margaret, m. the Baron de Bellegarde, Seigneur de Laran, &c., of Toulouse, in France) three sons,
1. John Alexander, Lieut.-Col. of the Regt. of Hibernia, in CHARLES IV., King of Spain's service, m. Mary Lalor, of Crana, co. Tipperary, and d.s.p. 1801.
2. DOWELL, of whom presently.
3. MATTHEW (ancestor of O'REILLY of Knock Abbey).
Mr. O'Reilly d. in Dublin 4 Feb. 1775, aged 67 years. The 2nd son,

DOWELL O'REILLY, of Heath House, Queen's Co., m. 1st, 6 May, 1775, Margaret, dau. of John O'Connor, of the city of Dublin, but by her (who d. in the same year) had no surviving issue. He m. 2ndly, March, 1780, Elizabeth, dau. of James Knox, of Moyne, co. Mayo, by Dorothy Rutledge his wife, and had issue,
1. MYLES JOHN, his heir.
2. James Fitzsimons, Capt. 13th British Regt., and Col. of a Spanish regt., killed in a sortie from the town of Tolosa, in Spain, unm.
3. Alexander, d. young.
4. Dowell, Capt. R.N., a distinguished Naval Officer, m. Jane, dau. of Dr. Digory King Marshall, of Truro, Cornwall, and left at his decease, 1817, one son,
  Dowell Knox, Capt. 69th and 85th Regts., m. Katherine, only dau. of James G. Cavenagh, of Wexford, Surgeon Royal Staff Corps, and d. in the West Indies, having by her (who d. 1858) two children, who d. in infancy.
1. Dorinda, d. unm.
2. Elizabeth, m. Stephen Hastings Atkins.
3. Margaret, m. Aug. 1820, her cousin William O'Reilly, of Knock Abbey Castle, and d. 1842.
4. Sarah, d. unm.

Mr. O'Reilly d. 13 Nov. 1838, and was s. by his eldest son,

MYLES JOHN O'REILLY, D.L., of the Heath House, b. 15 Dec. 1780; m. 16 Jan. 1829, Elizabeth Anne, elder dau. of the Hon. and Rev. George de la Poer Beresford, son of William, 1st Lord Decies, Archbishop of Tuam, by Elizabeth FitzGibbon, his wife, sister of Lord Chancellor Clare, and had issue,
1. MYLES GEORGE, his heir.
2. George Beresford, b. 30 March, 1832; m. 1867, Harrietta, dau. of H. Adams, of Santa Fé de Bogota U.S. Colombia.
3. Henry Tristram, an Officer H.E.I.C.S., b. 30 Nov. 1836; m. 1862, Miss Hickson, dau. of Rev. E. Hickson, of co. Cork, and d. 1890.
1. Susan Rachel, of the Heath House, m. William Porter.
2. Elizabeth Ellen, m. James Deakin, M.D., Surgeon 70th Foot.

Mr. O'Reilly d. 1857. The eldest son,

MYLES GEORGE O'REILLY, of East Brefny, late Capt. North Cork Rifles, J.P. co. Leitrim, b. 30 Oct. 1829; m. 1st, 1858, Elizabeth, dau. of George Brunskill, of The Lodge, Turnham Green, and by her (who d. 1881) had issue,
1. MYLES JOHN, b. 23 Jan. 1860.
2. Edmund Adalbert, b. 5 Dec. 1879.
1. Melanie Georgina.
2. Gwendoline Berestord, m. 25 Oct. 1887, Stanley Mundey.
3. Brunéhault Mildred Elizabeth, m. 1890, Dr. Sidney Harvey.
4. Guinevere Hilda, m. 15 Oct. 1898, Henry Faraday Welton, 2nd son of William Shakespeare Welton, of 46, Canfield Gardens, N.W.
5. Elizabeth Beresford.

He m. 2ndly, 1899, Sarah Anne, dau. of Joseph Wormald, of Leeds, and d. 1911.

Arms—Quarterly: 1st and 4th vert. two lions or, supporting a dexter hand couped and dropping blood ppr.; 2nd and 3rd, arg., on a mount an oak with a snake descending its trunk ppr. **Crest**—An oak tree eradicated entwined by a snake ascendant ppr. **Motto**—Fortitudine et prudentia.
Seat—The Heath House, co. Leitrim. **Residence**—7, Denmark Terrace, Brighton, Sussex.

O'REILLY OF KNOCK ABBEY.

WILLIAM JOSEPH O'REILLY, of Knock Abbey, co. Louth, J.P. and D.L., Commissioner of Education in Ireland, Resident Magistrate for co. Cavan, b. 16 Feb. 1864; s. his father, Feb. 1880.

Lineage.—This is a branch of the ancient Milesian House of O'REILLY, PRINCES OF EAST BREFNY.

MATTHEW O'REILLY, of Knock Abbey, co. Louth, 3rd son of Myles O'Reilly, of Tullystown (see preceding Memoir), m. 1st, 1877, Anne Maria, dau. of John O'Conor Failghe, of Dublin, and had issue,
1. MATTHEW, his heir.
2. John, b. Nov. 1780; d. unm. March, 1830.
1. Anna Maria, m. Richard Dease, M.D., and was mother of MATTHEW O'REILLY DEASE, of Dee Farm, co. Louth, J.P. and D.L., High Sheriff cr. Louth 1857, and for co. Cavan, 1861, and M.P. for Louth 1868-74, b. 1819.
Mr. O'Reilly m. 2ndly, Nov. 1789, Margaret, dau. of Myles Dowdall, of Carne Isle, co. Meath, by his wife, Elizabeth Lyster, of New Park, co. Roscommon, and by her had,
3. Myles, b. 1791; d. unm. Oct. 1822.
4. WILLIAM, of whom presently.
5. Walter, Col. in the Army, C.B., b. Sept. 1793; m. 14 Nov. 1827, Harriett, Duchess of Roxburgh, widow of James, 5th Duke, d.s.p. 4 March, 1844.
6. Dowell, Attorney-General of Jamaica, b. May, 1795; d. unm. 1855.
7. Richard Anthony, a Judge in Jamaica, b. March, 1814; d. unm. 1860.
2. Elizabeth, d. unm. 1854.

Mr. O'Reilly d. 1 Jan. 1817, and was s. by his eldest son,

MATTHEW O'REILLY, of Knock Abbey, b. May, 1779; m. Feb. 1830, Susan Anne, dau. of Hon. and Rev. George de la Poer Beresford, but dying without issue, June, 1841 (his widow m. 2ndly, 2 June, 1842, Gerald S. Fitzgerald, of Mount Offaley), was s. by his brother,

WILLIAM O'REILLY, of Knock Abbey, J.P. and M.P. for Dundalk 1832-35, b. Sept. 1792; m. Aug. 1820, Margaret, 4th dau. of Dowell O'Reilly, of the Heath House, Queen's Co., and had issue,

MYLES WILLIAM PATRICK, his heir.
Elizabeth Margaret, d. unm. 1873.

Mr. O'Reilly d. 1844, and was s. by his only son,

O'Reilly. THE LANDED GENTRY. 540

MYLES WILLIAM PATRICK O'REILLY, of Knock Abbey, co. Louth, J.P. and D.L., High Sheriff 1848, J.P. co. Dublin, B.A. London, LL.D. Rome 1847, Capt. Louth Militia, M.P. for co. Longford, 1862-79, Assistant Commissioner Intermediate Education, b. 13 March, 1825; m. 3 Aug. 1859, Ida, 2nd dau. of Edmund Jerningham, of 43, Rutland Gate, Hyde Park, London, and by her (who d. 20 April, 1878) had issue,
1. WILLIAM JOSEPH, now of Knock Abbey.
2. Edmund Joseph, b. 24 April, 1866, killed in S. Africa, 24 March, 1902.
3. Charles Myles, Major Indian Army, b. 4 Jan. 1869; m. 27 Feb. 1899, Sibyl, dau. of the Hon. Bryan John Stapleton (see BURKE's *Peerage*, BEAUMONT, B.), and has issue,
 1. Bryan Myles William Patrick, b. 22 May, 1900.
 2. Charles Hugh, b. 5 July, 1908.
 1. Ida Wilhelmina, b. 15 June, 1902.
 2. Frideswide, b. 4 July, 1903.
4. Francis Joseph, b. 1 Oct. 1872; m. 2 Nov. 1896, Alice Langrishe, and has issue,
 1. Myles Francis, b. 7 Dec. 1897.
 2. Lawrence, b. 10 Aug. 1907
1. Mary Pia Walburga, b. 8 Dec. 1860.
2. Edith Mary, b. 20 Jan. 1862.
Mr. O'Reilly d. 6 Feb. 1880.

Arms, &c.—(See O'REILLY *of East Brefny*.)
Seat—Knock Abbey, Dundalk, co. Louth. *Club*—Hibernian United Service, Dublin.

O'REILLY OF BALTRASNA.

JAMES O'REILLY, of Baltrasna, co. Meath, J.P., eldest son of Edward Watts-Russell, by Alicia his wife, dau. and co-heir of Anthony O'Reilly, of Baltrasna, b. 1869; s. to this property under the will of his maternal grandfather, and adopted the surname of O'REILLY; m. 18 , and has with other issue,

A son, b. 18

Lineage.—This is another branch of the princely House of O'Reilly.

THOMAS O'REILLY, of Ballgarny, youngest son of John O'Reilly (see O'REILLY *of East Brefny*), was in his father's regiment; he m. 1691, Rosa, dau. of Luke M'Dowell, of Montagh, co. Roscommon; and d. 1756, having had issue,
1. Patrick, d.s.p.
2. Philip, a Friar of the Order of St. Dominick.
3. JAMES, of whom presently.
4. Thomas, of Roebuck, co. Cavan, d. Feb. 1786, leaving an only dau. and heir, who m. Capt. Adams, who took the name of O'REILLY, and became O'REILLY *of Belmont*.
5. Connor, d.s.p.
6. Dominick, b. May, 1719; Lieut.-Gen. in the Spanish service and Chamberlain to H.R.H. Don Antonio, Infanta of Spain.
7. Nicholas, Capt. in the Spanish service, died in Spain.
8. Alexander (Count), b. at Baltrasna 1722, Generalissimo in the Spanish service, Capt.-Gen. of Andulasia, Governor of Cadiz, Inspector-Gen. of Infantry, Commander of the Order of Calatrava, and Grandee of Spain of the First Class. He m. Donna Rosa los Casas, and d. 1794. His eldest son, PETER PAUL, COUNT O'REILLY, m. the Countess of Buena Vista, and d. at the Havannah, leaving issue,
 1. DON MANUEL COUNT O'REILLY,* Marquess of Buena Vista, Grandee of Spain, &c.
 2. Don Pedro, Capt. of Cavalry and Aide-de-Camp to his uncle, the Duke of Baylon, at Madrid.
 3. Don Ferdinand.
 1. Rosa, m. M. de Henela.
 2. Maria de la Concepcion.
The 3rd son,
JAMES O'REILLY, of Baltrasna, m. Catherine, dau. of Philip Tuite, of Newcastle, co. Meath, and d. 5 Jan. 1786, leaving (with a dau.), Mary, m. James O'Reilly, of Millcastle, co. Westmeath) two sons, THOMAS, his heir, and Anthony, b. 30 April, 1746; d.s.p. Sept. 1803. The former,
THOMAS O'REILLY, of Baltrasna, J.P., an Officer in the Army, b. 22 April, 1741; m. March, 1773, Margaret, dau. of the Hon. Mr. Justice Robert Sibthorp, of Duncany, co. Louth, by Marianne his wife, dau. of Gen. Cochrane, and niece to Thomas, 8th Earl of Dundonald, and by her (who d. 1823) had issue,

* Count O'Reilly succeeded to the dukedom of Baylen, held by the well known Glen. Castanos.

1. JAMES, his heir.
2. Robert, b. 10 March, 1779; d. 1788.
3. Thomas, b. 21 Feb. 1780; d. unm.
4. Anthony Alexander, b. 23 Sept. 1781, Col. in the Army; m. 5 Aug. 1799, Anne, dau. of Edward Graves, of Maryborough, and had (with two daus., Anne, m. Capt. Leeson, H.E.I.C.S., and Catharine, m. Col. M'Clean, 27th Regt.) five sons,
 1. Thomas.
 2. James, m. Miss Henricks, of Somerset, Cape of Good Hope, and had issue.
 3. John Robert, Cape Mounted Rifles.
 4. George. 5. Anthony.
5. Stephen, b. 1786; d.s.p.
6. John Roberts, Lieut. R.N., b. 9 April, 1794; who by Anne his wife, had issue, a dau., Georgiana Geraldine, m. Albert Haseltine, R.N.
1. Marianne Margaret. 2. Catherine, d. unm.
Mr. O'Reilly d. Dec. 1805, and was s. by his eldest son,
JAMES O'REILLY, of Baltrasna, J.P., b. 22 June, 1775; m. 1 Oct. 1799, Henrietta Catherine Blanche, youngest dau. of Oliver Nugent, of Farren Connell, co. Cavan and had issue,
1. James, b. 5 July, 1800; d.s.p. 9 Sept. 1825.
2. Thomas, b. 11 Feb. 1804; d. 24 June, 1822.
3. ANTHONY, of Baltrasna.
4. Robert John, of Millcastle, co. Westmeath, Barrister-at-Law, b. 9 July, 1813; m. 1st, 30 Dec. 1842, Florence Tankerville, dau. of Godfrey Kneller, of Donhead Hall, Wilts, and 2ndly, 29 Aug. 1857, Eleanor Grace, 2nd dau. of Sir Norton Joseph Knatchbull, Bart., and d. 18 Dec. 1879, leaving a dau., Kathleen Mary.
 1. Henrietta Catharine, m. Richard Bolger, of Ballard, co. Westmeath, and has issue.
 2. Caroline Blanche, m. William B. Stoker, Barrister-at-Law, d.s.p.
 3. Selina, d. unm. 21 Nov. 1829.
 4. Louisa Marianne Mervyn, d. unm. 24 May, 1827.
Mr. O'Reilly served as High Sheriff for Meath in 1803, and for Cavan in 1804. He d. 19 March, 1853, and was s. by his son,
ANTHONY O'REILLY, of Baltrasna, co. Meath, J.P. and D.L., b. 23 June, 1812; m. 14 May, 1836, Alicia Maria, dau. of Capt. John Fortescue, by Margaret his wife, dau. of Sir John Meredyth, Bart., of Newtown, co. Meath, and by her (who d. 20 Feb. 1858) had issue,
1. JAMES WILLIAM FORTESCUE, b. 3 Oct. 1841; d. June, 1855.
1. Caroline Maria, m. 12 Sept. 1861, William Mark Miller Fortescue, late of the 6th Rifles (of the Clermont family), and d.s.p. 20 Sept. 1862.
2. Alicia Margaret, m. 28 Dec. 1867, Edward Watts-Russell, youngest son of Jesse Watts-Russell, of Ilam Hall, co. Stafford, and d. 20 Feb. 1908, leaving, with other issue,
 JAMES (now JAMES O'REILLY, of Baltrasna).
3. Harriet Georgina, m. 20 June, 1865, Matthew R. Weld O'Conor, of Viewmount, Longford, and has issue.
4. Florence Henrietta, m. 6 Dec. 1871, John Archibald Murray, Capt. 97th Regt., of Hornby Hall, Lancaster, and has issue.
5. Edith Sophia, m. 3 Oct. 1878, Capt. Philip Barne, late 60th Rifles, 2nd son of Frederick Barne, of Sotterley and Dunwich, Suffolk.
6. Olivia Blanche, m. 12 Jan. 1869, William George Clayton Wade (d. 1882), eldest son of Robert Craven Wade, of Clonebrany, co. Meath, and had issue. She m. 2ndly, Frederick P. Dixon, and d. 20 Oct. 1910.
7. Eva Cornelia, m. 16 April, 1879, Albert Beauchamp Astley Cooper, youngest son of Sir Astley Cooper, Bart., and has issue (see BURKE's *Peerage*).
Mr. O'Reilly was High Sheriff co. Cavan 1845. He d. 1874.

Arms (of WATTS-RUSSELL, Heralds' Coll.)—Quarterly 1st and 4th erm., a lion rampant gu., collared arg., on a chief az. three roses of the field (RUSSELL); 2nd and 3rd az., a bend engrailed erminois between two crescents or, a canton gu. for distinction (WATTS). **Crests**—1. Upon a mount vert, a goat passant erm., collared gu. (RUSSELL); 2. A demi-lion rampant or, charged on the shoulder with a cross patée az., the paws supporting an escutcheon of the last thereon a fesse erminois between three fleurs-de-lis in chief and a cross patée in base of the first, on an escroll issuant from the escutcheon the word "Amici" and in the mouth of the lion a slip of oak ppr.
Seat—Baltrasna, Oldcastle, co. Meath. *Residence*—Williamstown, Oldcastle.

O'REILLY OF CASTLE WILDER.

JOSEPH RICHARD O'REILLY, of Castle Wilder, co. Longford, and Sans Souci, co. Dublin, J.P. and D.L. co. Longford, High Sheriff 1867, Barrister-at-Law, B.A. Trin. Coll. Dublin, b. 1843; m. 9 July, 1873, Frances Mary Ursula, youngest dau. of Sir James Power, 2nd bart., of Edermine, and has issue,
1. JOSEPH JAMES, b. 12 Feb. 1875.
2. Reginald John, b. 2 June, 1877; d. young.
3. Henry James Joseph, b. 1880.
4. Bertram Thomas Joseph, b. 1883.
5. Herbert Joseph, b. 1886.
6. Charles Reginald, b. 9 April, 1891.
1. Jane Mary Joseph.
2. Hilda Mary.

Mr. O'Reilly is the eldest son of the late Richard Pearce O'Reilly, M.D., F.R.C.S.I., of Castle Wilder and Sans Souci, D.L. co. Longford (who d. 1870), by Olivia his wife, dau. of Nicholas Kenney, of Rocksavage, co. Monaghan.

Seats—Castle Wilder, co. Longford, and Sans Souci, Booterstown, co. Dublin. Club—Hibernian United Service.

O'REILLY OF COLAMBER.

PHILIP O'REILLY, of Colamber, co. Westmeath, J.P. and D.L. for that co. and J.P. co. Longford, High Sheriff, 1869, b. 10 April, 1836; m. 9 Sept. 1865, Anna Maria, younger dau. of the late Sir Percy Nugent, 1st bart., of Donore, and has issue,

1. PERCY PHILIP, late Capt. 6th Batt. Rifle Brigade, b. 1870; m. 18 Jan. 1900, Alice Eleanor, 2nd dau. of the late Major Rochfort Hamilton Boyd-Rochfort, of Middleton Park, co. Westmeath (see that family), and has issue,
   1. Philip Rochfort, b. April, 1902; d. 1 March, 1911.
   2. Charles Valentine, b. 4 Nov. 1909.
      1. Beryl.   2. Mona.   3. Viola.
1. Mary.
2. Olivia, m. April, 1891, her cousin, Capt. Richard P. O'Reilly, 5th Batt. Connaught Rangers, of Clondrisse, co. Westmeath.
3. Emily, m. 1893, Maj. E. F. Blakeney, Army Service Corps, and has issue.
4. Mildred, m. 21 May, 1902, Lieut.-Col. Gordon Napier Caulfeild, D.S.O., Gurkha Rifles (see BURKE's Peerage, CHARLEMONT, V.).

Lineage.—PHILIP O'REILLY, of Colamber, Rathowen, co. Westmeath, left, with other issue, a son,
PHILIP O'REILLY, of Colamber, co. Westmeath, J.P. and D.L.; m. Cecilia, dau. of the late John Ball. She d. 1893, having had issue,
1. Richard, d. 1901.
2. PHILIP, of Colamber.
3. John, 18th Royal Irish Regt., d. 1858.
4. James, Lieut.-Col. late Royal Army Medical Corps, M.B. 1. Mary, m. 1855, George Grehan, of Clonmeen, co. Cork. She d. 1859. He d. 1886, leaving issue (see that family).
2. Cecilia Olivia, m. 16 June, 1866, Col. Richard Irwin, of Rathmoyle, and has issue (see that family).
3. Fanny, m. George Stapleton, of Wyvern, Killiney, co. Dublin, and d. circa 1885.

Seat—Colamber, Rathowen, co. Westmeath. Clubs—Hibernian United Service, Dublin, and Raleigh, W.

ORME OF OWENMORE.

CHRISTOPHER GUY ORME, of Owenmore, co. Mayo, and Enniscrone, co. Sligo, J.P. and D.L. for the former co., High Sheriff 1910; b. 23 Aug. 1858; s. his brother 1903; m. 17 Jan. 1907, Hon. Mary Kathleen Morris, dau. of Lord Morris and Killanin (see BURKE's Peerage, KILLANIN, B.), and has issue,

1. ROBERT WILLIAM MARTIN, b. 20 Dec. 1908.
1. Lettice Frances, b. 29 Dec. 1907.
2. Cicely Dorothea.

Lineage.—WILLIAM ORME, of Hanse Hall, by Longden Green, in the co. of Stafford, descended from a family long settled in co. Chester, m. 1612, Grace, dau. of Nicholas Hurt, of Casterne, co. Stafford, and d. 1623, leaving a son,
WILLIAM ORME, of Hanse Hall, who being a Royalist, suffered heavy fines and imprisonment at the hands of OLIVER CROMWELL He lived to witness the Restoration, and had a confirmation of his arms from Dugdale, Norroy, 1665. He m. Anne, dau. of Thomas Brudenell, of Staunton Weevill, co. Leicester, and had issue,
1. THOMAS, his heir, s. to Hanse Hall; d. 22 May, 1716, without surviving issue.
2. William, Col. in the French Army, d. 1676.
3. JAMES, of whom presently.
4. Robert, d. unm.
1. Dorothea, m. John Huckley, of Leicester.
He d. 14 Aug. 1665. His 3rd son,
JAMES ORME, settled circa 1671, in the co. of Mayo, where he purchased considerable estates. He m. Elizabeth, dau. of Thomas Barrow, of co. Cork, and had issue, two sons,
1. ROBERT, his heir.

2. William, of Ballintobber, whose will is dated 21 Nov. 1727, m. Dorothea, dau. af Robert Fleming, of Achonry, co. Sligo, and had issue,
   1. William, of Ballintobber, Major in the Army, High Sheriff, co. Mayo, 1775, d. unm.
      1. Elizabeth, m. 1759, her cousin, William Orme, of Falgarriff.
      2. Dorothea, m. Matthew Fleming, of Old Rock.
Mr. Orme d. 1707, and was s. by his eldest son,
ROBERT ORME, of Carne, co. Mayo, m. 1703, Elizabeth, dau. of James Johnston, and by her left issue, four sons and three daus.,
1. Thomas, of Carne, b. 1705; m. June, 1754, Elizabeth, dau. of William Atkinson, of Forgeny, co. Longford, and sister of Col. Atkinson, and d. Jan. 1780, leaving an only son and successor, William, of Abbeytown, co. Mayo, b. 1757, m. 19 June, 1785, Anne, 2nd dau. of George Jackson, of Enniscoe, co. Mayo, and d. 20 May, 1813, leaving issue,
   (1) Thomas, of Abbeytown, Major North Mayo Militia, b. 7 June, 1787; m. 23 May, 1814, Elizabeth, 4th dau. of Col. George Jackson, M.P. of Enniscoe, co. Mayo, and d. 12 June, 1826, leaving (with three younger sons, George; Thomas, Ensign 96th Regt., d.s.p. 1839; James, R.A.; and a dau., Marian) an eldest son, his heir, WILLIAM HENRY, of Abbeytown, M.A., Brevet-Major, s. as representative of this family in Ireland, and d.s.p.
   (2) William, of Glenmore, co. Mayo, b. 16 Nov. 1789; m. 1st, 23 May, 1815, Cherry, youngest dau. of Francis Knox, of Rappa Castle, co. Mayo, by Mary, his wife, dau. and co-heir of Annesley Gore, of Belleek, co. Mayo, brother of Arthur, 1st Earl of Arran, and by her (who d. 10 May, 1817) had issue, two sons,
      1. William Knox, of Glenmore, Ballina, co. Mayo, b. 23 May, 1816, formerly Col. in the Army; d. 1869. He left issue, an only son William John Henry Knox, who d. 31 July, 1901, aged 26.
      2. Francis Knox, B.A., Barrister-at-Law, b. 23 April, 1817 had two sons, who went to Australia.
   He m. 2ndly, 13 March, 1826, Anne Emily, 5th dau. of Col. George Jackson, of Enniscoe, by Maria his wife, only dau. and heir of William Rutledge, of Foxford, co. Mayo, and d. 20 Aug. 1836, leaving by her two sons and a dau.,
   3. Thomas, b. 26 May, 1827; d.s.p. 30 Nov. 1846.
   4. George, b. 13 Oct. 1829.
   1. Maria Sidney.
   (1) Jane, m. 5 Dec. 1803, Samuel Handy, of Bracca Castle, co. Westmeath.
   (2) Elizabeth, m. 1804, William Fetherston, of Carrick, co. Westmeath.
2. James, of Fairfield, co. Mayo, m. Catherine, dau. of Robert Hillias, of Seaview, co. Sligo, and d. without male issue.
3. WILLIAM, of whom hereafter.
4. Robert, who settled in America, in Jones County, and became a Member of Congress.
1. Mary, m. John Leech, of Frankfort, co. Sligo.
2. Margaret, m. Thomas Paget, of Knockglass, co. Mayo.
3. Lettice, m. Robert Atkinson.
The 3rd son,
WILLIAM ORME, of Falgarriff, co. Mayo, m. 1759, Elizabeth, dau. of William Orme, of Ballintobber, by his wife, Dorothea, dau. of Robert Fleming, of Achonry, co. Sligo, and by her (who d. 1 Jan. 1818, aged 87) left issue,
1. Robert, of Milbrook, High Sheriff 1806, m. Dorothea, dau. of Matthew Fleming, of Old Rock, who d. 18 Aug. 1831. He d.s.p. 29 Nov. 1833.
2. WILLIAM, of whom hereafter.
The 2nd son,
WILLIAM ORME, of Belleville, co. Mayo, J.P., m. 3 Sept. 1806, Isabella, dau. of John Ormsby, of Gortner Abbey, same co., and by her (who d. 1847) had issue,
1. WILLIAM, his heir.
2. ROBERT, successor to his brother.
3. John Ormsby, m. Mary Jane, dau. of Rev. Richard St. George, Vicar of Crossmolina, co. Mayo, and has issue,
   1. William Richard, Capt. in the Army.
   1. Isabella.   2. Dorothea Jane.
   3. Annette.
1. Elizabeth.   2. Dorothea.
3. Jane.   4. Isabella Maria.
Mr. William Orme d. 24 Aug. 1840, and was s. by his eldest son,
WILLIAM ORME, of Owenmore, co. Mayo, J.P., b. 16 Feb. 1810; m. 1st, 10 Oct. 1837, Janette, dau. of Christopher Carleton L'Estrange, of Market Hill, co. Fermanagh. She d.s.p. 30 Aug. 1850. He m. 2ndly, 16 Feb. 1858, Margaret Barbara (d. 17 Dec. 1910), eldest dau. of Rev. Savage Hall, Rector of Loughgall, co. Armagh and d.s.p. 20 Sept. 1876, when he was s. by his brother,
ROBERT ORME, of Owenmore, co. Mayo, and Enniscrone, co. Sligo, J.P. and D.L., co. Sligo, b. 1815; m. 16 Feb. 1843, Sidney Frances, dau. of Major Christopher Carleton L'Estrange, of Market Hill, co. Fermanagh. She d. 1899. He d. 1877, leaving issue,
1. ROBERT WILLIAM, late of Owenmore and Enniscrone.
2. CHRISTOPHER GUY, now of Owenmore and Enniscrone.
3. Albert L'Estrange, of The Red House, Matlock, Derbyshire, b. 1864; m. 1900, Marie, dau. of John Goodwin, of Rockside, Derbyshire, and d. 11 July, 1909, leaving issue,
   Christopher Robert L'Estrange, b. 1903.
1. Janet Georgina, m. 1882, Claude Brownlow, of Killynether, co. Down.
The eldest son,
ROBERT WILLIAM ORME, of Owenmore, co. Mayo, and Enniscrone, co. Sligo, J.P. and D.L. for the former co., High Sheriff 1901, and J.P. co. Sligo, High Sheriff 1879, b. 1 April, 1856; d. unm. 20 June, 1903.

Ormsby.   THE LANDED GENTRY.   542

Arms—Az., an eagle displayed between three pole-axes or. **Crest**—A dolphin embowed az., fins and tails or, surmounted of a pole-axe as in the arms. *Motto*—Fortis et fidelis.

Seats—Owenmore, Crossmolina, co. Mayo, and Enniscrone, Ballina, co. Sligo. *Clubs*—Royal Automobile, W.; Kildare Street, Dublin.

ORMSBY OF GORTNER ABBEY.

Lineage.—JOHN ORMSBY, of Louth, co. Lincoln, *m.* Rose, dau. and co-heir of William Wood of Farlesthorpe, co. Lincoln, and had issue,
1. William, *bur.* at Louth, 27 July, 1584; *m.* Alice, dau. of Thomas Daldorne. She was bur. at Louth 30 July, 1580.
2. EDWARD, of whom next.
3. Thomas, killed at Leith.
4. John, killed at siege of Newhaven.
   1. Joane, *m.* Richard Norman.

The 2nd son,
EDWARD ORMSBY, of Woodgrange, Essex, "Dorophorus" to Queen ELIZABETH, *d.* at Newhaven (Havre de Grace) 1563, will dated 21 March, 1562; *m.* Elizabeth, dau. of Robert Moffitt, and by her (who *m.* 2ndly, Andrew Smith) was father of
HENRY ORMSBY, settled in Ireland in the reign of Queen ELIZABETH. He *m.* 1st, Susan Kelke, by whom he had three sons,
1. EDWARD, of Tobervaddy, co. Roscommon, J.P., High Sheriff of cos. Galway and Mayo 1655, whose will is dated 13 July, 1664. By Sarah, his wife, he had,
ROBERT ORMSBY, Major in the Army, *m.* 1st, the dau. of Gilbert, of Kilminchy, in Queen's Co., and 2ndly, Miss Ware, and *d.v.p.* 12 April, 1664, leaving, with other issue,
(1) Edward (Sir), of Tobervaddy and Shrule, co. Mayo; *m.* Feb. 1663, Jane, dau. of David Murray, and *d.s.p.* 1683.
(2) GILBERT ORMSBY, of Tobervaddy, J.P., *s.* his brother Sir Edward Ormesby, M.P., *m.* Sarah, dau. of Arthur Hill of Hillsborough, co. Down, and had, with other issue,
SIDNEY ORMSBY, of Grange, co. Roscommon, *m.* Susan, dau. of Owen Lloyd, of Rockville, same co., and had issue,
a. GILBERT ORMSBY, of Grange, High Sheriff co. Roscommon 1770, *m.* 1st, Catherine, dau. of Very Rev. Peter Mahon, Dean of Elphin, by whom he had (with a dau. Catherine, *m.* Henry Kelly) a son, Sidney (Rev.), of Grange, *m.* twice, and had issue, Gilbert Ormsby; *m.* 2ndly (mar. lic. 13 Nov. 1781), Mary, dau. of Owen Lloyd, of Rockville, co. Roscommon, by whom he had another son.
b. OWEN ORMSBY (Rev.), of Ballymascanlon, co. Louth, *m.* 19 Oct. 1803, Anne, dau. of Rev. William Phibbs, of Abbeyville, co. Sligo, and *d.* Dec. 1834, leaving issue,
(*a*) WILLIAM (Rev.), M.A., of Kilmore, co. Roscommon, *b.* 9 Aug. 1810; *d.* 31 March, 1905; *m.* 1st, Dorah, dau. of Owen Thomas Lloyd, of Hermitage, co. Roscommon, by whom he had no surviving issue, and 2ndly, Henrietta Armstrong, by whom he had, 1, Alexander, *d.* 1864; 2, Watson; 3, George; 1, Emily, *d.* 1866. He *m.* 3rdly, Annie Hodgson, and by her has, 1, Henry, *d.* June, 1900; 2, Robert; 3, Oswald; 4, Sidney, *d.* Jan. 1909; 1, Emma; 2, Mary; 3, Edith.
(*b*) GEORGE, of Onehunga Lodge, Auckland, New Zealand, *m.* Jan. 1844, Selina (*d.* 18 Dec. 1901), dau. of Rev. Lambert Watson Hepenstal, of Altadore, co. Wicklow, and *d.* 4 April, 1861, aged 47, leaving
1. Lambert Hepenstal (Sir), Knt. 1903, M.D., F.R.C.S.I., President of the Royal College of Surgeons in Ireland, 1902, 1903, and 1904 (92, Merrion Square, Dublin, and Constitutional Club, London), *b.* 19 July, 1849; *m.* 16 July, 1874, Anastasia (*d.* 20 Jan. 1911), dau. of the late John Dickinson, of Greenfields, co. Dublin, and has issue,
(1) Owen, *b.* 11 July, 1875; *d.* 8 Oct. 1895.
(2) Gilbert John Anthony, Major R.A.M.C., *b.* 16 Sept. 1876.
    (1) Alice Maud Mary, *b.* 17 Feb. 1878; *d.* 1 May, 1897.
    (2) Stella Beatrice, *b.* 14 Nov. 1880.
1. Isabel, *b.* 29 May, 1845; *d.* 6 Sept. 1875.
2. Emily, *b.* 4 April, 1847; *d.* 24 June, 1870.
3. Louisa.   4. Selina Maria.
(*c*) Robert, went to New Zealand, 1844, *m.*, and has issue.
(*d*) Arthur, *m.* but *d.s.p.* 1888.
(*a*) Harriett, *m.* James Irwin, of Dungannon.
(*b*) Anne, *d.* 1863.   (*c*) Isabel, *d. unm.* 1890.

2. Anthony, ancestor of ORMSBY of *Rathlee*.
3. MALBY, of whom hereafter.

Henry Ormsby *m.* 2ndly, Elizabeth Newman, widow of Thomas Crompton, and had further issue,
4. John, of Cloghkilberg.
5. William, ancestor of ORMSBY of *Willowbrook*, co. Sligo, represented by Lord Harlech.
6. THOMAS, ancestor of ORMSBY of *Ballinamore* (see that family).

The 3rd son,
MALBY ORMSBY, of Cloghans, co. Mayo, *m.* Ross O'Naughten, and was *s.* by his son,
JOHN ORMSBY, of Cloghans, *m.* Winifred Jordan, and had, with a younger son, Stephen, of Castle Dargan, whose will is dated 15 May, 1702, an eldest son, his heir,
ROBERT ORMSBY, of Cloghans, *m.* Mary Blakeney, and had (with three daus., Elinor, Mary, and Lettice) four sons,
1. JOHN, his heir.
2. Joseph, of Ballymacreen, co. Sligo.   3. Oliver.
4. Paul, of Knockmore, co. Mayo (see ORMSBY-HAMILTON of *Cabinteely*).

Robert Ormsby *d.* 1700, and was *s.* by his eldest son,
JOHN ORMSBY, of Cloghans and Gortner Abbey, High Sheriff co. Mayo 1719, *m.* 1st, Henrietta Bingham, of Newbrook, and 2ndly, Frances Vesey, and had, with other issue,
WILLIAM ORMSBY, of Gortner Abbey, co. Mayo, *m.* Isabella, youngest dau. of Thomas Palmer, of Carrowmore, co. Mayo, by Eleanor Jackson, his wife, and had issue (with others, who *d. unm.*),
1. JOHN, his heir.
1. Hannah, *m.* William Palmer, of Richmond, co. Mayo.
2. Elizabeth, *d. unm.*

William Ormsby *d.* Oct. 1790, at a very advanced age, and was *s.* by his only son,
JOHN ORMSBY, of Gortner Abbey, High Sheriff 1783. He *m.* circa 1785, Elizabeth, eldest dau. of George Jackson, of Enniscoe, co. Mayo, by Jane, his wife, dau. of the Right Hon. James Cuff, M.P., and sister of James, Lord Tyrawley, and by her (who *d.* 1830) had issue, with nine other daus., who all *d.* young or *unm.*,
1. JOHN, his heir.
2. GEORGE, of whom hereafter, as heir to his brother.
3. James, 25th Light Dragoons, *m.* Jane, dau. of George Rowan, of Ratharney, co. Kerry, by Elizabeth, his wife, dau. of A. S. Raymond, of Ballyloughrane, co. Kerry, and had issue,
    1. John.   2. George.
    3. William, Capt. 3rd West India Regt.
4. Horatio Nelson (Rev.), M.A., Vicar of Carriganleary, Mallow, *b.* 1 Feb. 1809; *m.* 16 Dec. 1835, Judith Elizabeth, dau. of Becher Fleming, of Newcourt, co. Cork, by Judith Barbara his wife, dau. of Richard Somerville, of Drishane, and had issue,
    1. John Becher, Col. late R.A., *b.* 20 Jan. 1839. His wife, Fanny Louisa, *d.* 23 April, 1909.
    1. Judith Elizabeth, *m.* 1862, Rev. James Galwey.
    2. Elizabeth.   3. Maria Frances.
1. Elizabeth, *m.* 1802, her cousin, Thomas Palmer, of Sommerhill, co. Mayo, High Sheriff 1809, and had issue.
2. Isabella, *m.* 1805, William Orme, of Belleville, co. Mayo, and had issue.

The eldest son,
JOHN ORMSBY, of Gortner Abbey, co. Mayo, J.P. and D.L., *s.* his father and was High Sheriff 1811. Dying Aug. 1817 (aged 23 years) *unm.* he was *s.* by his brother,
GEORGE ORMSBY, of Gortner Abbey, co. Mayo, 3rd Dragoon Guards, J.P. and D.L., and for some years Vice-Lieutenant, High Sheriff 1827. He *m.* 1825, Marianne, 3rd dau. of Humphrey Jones, of Mullinabro, co. Kilkenny (*see that family*), by Anne his wife, eldest dau. of the Rev. Ralph Hawtrey, and had issue,
1. JOHN, his heir.
1. Annabella, *d.* 1852.   2. Elizabeth Rebecca, *d.* 1888.
3. MARIANNE, late of Gortner Abbey, *d.* at Bournemouth 1909.

Mr. Ormsby *d.* 1836. The only son, JOHN ORMSBY, of Gortner Abbey, co. Mayo, J.P., *b.* 1828, *d.s.p.*

Arms—Gu., a bend between six crosses-crosslet or. **Crest**—A dexter arm embowed in armour ppr., holding in the hand a man's leg couped at the thigh, also in armour and ppr. *Motto*—Fortis qui prudens.

ORMSBY OF BALLINAMORE.

ANTHONY ORMSBY, of Ballinamore, co. Mayo, J.P., D.L., *b.* 7 April, 1855; *s.* his father Jan. 1888.

Lineage.—THOMAS ORMSBY, of Cummin, co. Sligo, 6th son of Henry Ormsby, by his 2nd wife (*see* ORMSBY *of Gortner Abbey*). *m.* Una, dau. of Teige O'Hara, of Lisavilly, co. Sligo, and had, with other issue,
1. ANTHONY, of whom hereafter.
2. Christopher, who had a grant of the estate of Ballinamore by patent from the Crown, as appears by the certificate of 6 April, 29 CHARLES II., 1677, granting to him, his heirs, and assigns for ever, the land specified in said certificate, which lands said Christopher was and had been in previous possession of. He *m.* his cousin Margaret, dau. of Edward Ormsby, of Tobbervaddy, and *d.s.p.*, leaving his property by will, dated 1687, to his nephew, Adam Ormsby.

3. Henry, of Red Hill, co. Mayo, *m.* Catherine, dau. of Capt. Lewis Jones, and was ancestor of ORMSBY *of Red Hill.*
Thomas Ormsby *d.* 13 March, 1662 (*Funeral Entry*). His eldest son,
ANTHONY ORMSBY, of Cummin, co. Sligo, High Sheriff 1672, *m.* Jane, dau. of Henry Crofton, of Mohill, co. Leitrim, and had issue,
1. Adam, of Cummin, co. Sligo, High Sheriff 1695, and Ballinamore, co. Mayo, heir to his uncle Christopher. He held a commission in Lord Kingston's Regt., *m.* Hannah, dau. of Col. Roger Moore, of Woodville, and *d.s.p.*, and devised by his will (dated 16 April, 1733) his estates to his nephews, Thomas and ANTHONY, sons of his brother John. The Sligo and Roscommon estates went to Thomas, and Ballinamore to ANTHONY (*see below*).
2. Thomas, *d.s.p.*
1. Ursula.
3. JOHN, of whom hereafter.
2. Mary.
3. Jane.
Anthony Ormsby's will is dated 20 Nov. 1672. His 3rd son,
JOHN ORMSBY, *m.* Anne, dau. of Sir Robert Gore, of Newton, and *d.* intest. 1733, leaving issue,
1. Thomas, of Cummin, High Sheriff co. Mayo 1738, Sligo 1739, ancestor of the ORMSBYS *of Cummin.*
2. ANTHONY, of whom presently.
1. Anne, *m.* — Trumble, of Sligo. Her will dated 1753.
2. Hannah, *m.* Edward Drury, of Loughscur.
3. Frances, *m.* — Matthew.
The 2nd son,
ANTHONY ORMSBY, of Ballinamore, Capt. in Bingham's Regt. of Horse and High Sheriff co. Mayo 1739, *m.* June, 1737, Sarah, dau. of Thomas Lindsay, of Turin, co. Mayo, and *d.* 1797, having had issue,
1. THOMAS, his heir.
2. Christopher, *m.* Jane, dau. of William Rutledge.
3. Adam.
1. Anne.
The eldest son and heir,
THOMAS ORMSBY, of Ballinamore, High Sheriff 1780; *m.* June, 1762, Elizabeth, dau. of Thomas Rutledge, of Cornfield, co. Mayo, and *d.* 1822, having had issue,
1. ANTHONY, his heir.
2. Thomas of Knockmore, *b.* 1768, *m.* 1796, Anne, dau. of Owen O'Malley, of Spencer Park, co. Mayo, and had issue,
 1. Anthony, *d. unm.*
 2. George, *m.* Susanna Semple, and *d.s.p.*
 3. Thomas, *d. unm.*
 1. Elizabeth, *d. unm.* 1873.
 2. Catherine Anne, *m.* 1828, Croasdaile Bowen Miller, of Milford, co. Mayo (*see that family*).
3. Peter Rutledge, M.D., *b.* 1776; *m.* Mary, dau. of Owen Lloyd, of Ardagh, co. Sligo, and had issue,
 1. Thomas, Capt. 92nd Regt., *d. unm.*
 2. Owen Lloyd, Lieut. Col. in the Army, Capt. 88th Regt., *m.* Selina Margaret, dau. of Alexander E. Graydon, of Newcastle House, co. Dublin, and *d.* 1 Feb. 1876, leaving,
  (1) Ormsby Gore, *d. unm.* 1879.
  (2) Sarah, *m.* 1st, John Harvey Adams, of Northlands, co. Cavan, and 2ndly, Edward Gibbs Poingdestre, of Granville Manor, Jersey.
  (3) Mary Alice.
  (4) Anne Selina, *m.* John Barry Mulock, M.D., eldest son of Thomas Homan Mulock, of Bellair.
 3. Anthony, Lieut.-Col. late 80th Regt., Military Knight of Windsor, *d.* 26 Feb. 1872. His widow, Selina, *d.* 25 Feb. 1905.
4. Adam, Lieut.-Col. 40th Regt., *b.* 1775; *d. unm.*
5. George, *m.* Elizabeth, dau. of Christopher Ormsby, and relict of Francis Elwood, of Strandhill, co. Mayo, and had Elizabeth.
6. John, *d. unm.*
7. Christopher, *b.* 1784; *d. unm.*
1. Sarah, *m.* July, 1787, Charles Phibbs, of Lisconney (*see* PHIBBS *of Lisheen*).
2. Anne, *m.* 1798, Owen Phibbs, of Merrion Square, Dublin, and had issue (*see* PHIBBS *of Lisheen*).
3. Mary, *m.* John Irwin, of Camlin, co. Roscommon.
The eldest son and heir,
ANTHONY ORMSBY, of Ballinamore, Lieut.-Col. North Mayo Militia, *m.* 1st, May, 1806, Rebecca, dau. of Thomas Elwood, of Ashford, co. Mayo, and by her had issue,
1. THOMAS, his heir.
1. Letitia, *d. unm.*
2. Elizabeth, *d. unm.*
He *m.* 2ndly, July, 1817, Anne, dau. of John Yeadon Lloyd, of Lisadurn, co. Roscommon, and *d.* 1823, having by her had two sons,
2. ANTHONY, of whom presently.
3. JOHN YEADON, heir to his brother.
The eldest son,
THOMAS ORMSBY, of Ballinamore, co. Mayo, *d. unm.* 1836, and was *s.* by his half-brother,
ANTHONY ORMSBY, of Ballinamore, co. Mayo, High Sheriff 1849, *b.* 1820; *d. unm.* 1882, and was *s.* by his brother,
JOHN YEADON ORMSBY, of Ballinamore, co. Mayo, J.P., B.A. Trin. Coll. Dublin, *b.* 1822; *m.* 5 Nov. 1851, Anne, dau. of Croasdaile Bowen-Miller, of Milford, co. Mayo, and had issue,
1. ANTHONY, now of Ballinamore.
2. Charles Croasdaile, *b.* 13 May, 1856.
3. John Yeadon, *b.* 24 Sept. 1864; *m.* 1889, Susie, dau. of R. Graham, of Toronto, and has issue,
 1. John Anthony Ninion, *b.* 1893.
 2. Gerald Yeadon, *b.* 1895.
 1. Ottilie.
4. George, *b.* 3 April, 1868; *m.* 17 Feb. 1909, Margaret Fanny, dau. of late Major-Gen. G. T. Hilliard.

5. Thomas, *b.* 30 May, 1871; *m.* 1896, Lucy Mary, dau. of Capt. Thomson, of Salruck, co. Galway, and has issue,
 John Yeadon, *b.* 1900.
 Elizabeth Mary.
1. Anne.
2. Katherine.
3. Isabel.
4. Elizabeth Anna.
5. Edith.
Mr. Ormsby *d.* 7 Jan. 1888.
Arms—Gu., a bend between six crosses-crosslet or. **Crest**— A dexter arm embowed in armour ppr., holding in the hand a man's leg couped at the thigh, also in armour and ppr. **Motto**— Fortis qui prudens.
Seat—Ballinamore House, Kiltimagh, Swinford, co. Mayo. **Clubs**—Royal Societies, S.W.; Sackville Street.

ORMSBY-HAMILTON. *See* HAMILTON.

ORPEN OF ARDTULLY.

RAYMOND WILLIAM ORPEN, of Ardtully, co. Kerry, M.D. West African Medical Staff, *b.* 29 Nov. 1875; *s.* 7 Nov. 1911.
Lineage—The family of Orpen claims great antiquity.
ROBERT ORPEN, said to be the son of Sir Richard de Erpingham Orpen, of Norfolk, a Royalist, killed at Naseby, who after the defeat of the King on that field, fled to Ireland. He appears, by an inquisition dated 1661, to have resided at Neflaherolin (now named Killorglin), co. Kerry. He *m.* Lucy Chichester, and had issue,
1. RICHARD, his heir.
2. Robert, who returned to England, and *d.* there.
1. Rachael, *m.* John Mayberry.
2. Dorcas, *m.* Francis Crumpe.
3. Margaret, *m.* Robert Bowen.
The eldest son,
RICHARD ORPEN, of The White House, co. Kerry, was the first of the family who settled on the River Kenmare. In 1688, after the abdication of the English throne by JAMES II., Mr. Orpen garrisoned his house at Killowen, and received into it all the neighbouring Protestant families; but Capt. Phelim M'Carthy, with three thousand Irish soldiers, appearing before the gates of the garrison, the besieged after some time, and when no hope remained of succour, surrendered. Mr. Orpen effected his escape to England, and returned the following year as a commissary, with the rank of Capt. in the Army of WILLIAM III. He fought at the Boyne, and soon after retired with his family to Killowen, having been appointed a Magistrate for Kerry. He *m.* Isabella, dau. of Rev. Thomas Palmer, and had issue,
1. THOMAS (Rev.), his heir.
2. Richard, of Ardtully, co. Kerry, *m.* Grace, dau. of John Riggs, co. Cork, and had issue,
 1. Richard, of Ardtully, *m.* 1st, 1766, Anna, dau. of Horace Townsend, of Bridgemount; 2ndly, Miss Laplant; and 3rdly, 1794, Alice, dau. of John Ryves Nettles, of Nettleville, co. Cork. By the 1st wife only he had issue, five sons and two daus.,
  (1) Richard, of Ardtully, who assumed the additional surname of TOWNSEND. He *m.* 1811, the Hon. Anna Mullins, dau. of William, 2nd Lord Ventry, and had a dau.,
   Anna Sarah, *m.* Adrian Taylor.
  (2) Horace Townsend, *m.* Miss Elizabeth Kite, and had a dau.,
   Anna, who *d.* young.
  (3) Edward, *m.* Maria, dau. of Daniel Crumpe, and had issue,
   1. Richard, *m.* Miss Browne.
   2. Samuel, *m.* a dau. of William Forster, of Stoughton, co. Kerry.
   3. Daniel.
   1. Grace, *m.* John Wood.
   2. Mary.
   3. Anne.
   4. Lucinda.
  (4) Samuel, of Woodville, *m.* 5 Aug. 1805, Sophia, dau. of Thomas Hungerford, of The Island, and by her (who *d.* Oct. 1830) had issue,
   1. Richard Hungerford, of Brewsterfield, Killarney, and Woodville, Kilgarvan, co. Kerry, J.P., B.A. Trin. Coll. Dublin, *b.* 11 April, 1807; *m.* 16 Aug. 1832, Frances Diana, dau. of Rev. Bastable Herbert, of Brewsterfield, and had issue,
    a. Arthur Herbert, *b.* 8 Sept. 1833; *m.* 5 June, 1862, Jane Sophia, dau. of Col. Henry Spencer, and has issue,
     (*a*) Arthur Cecil Herbert, *b.* 3 Dec. 1871.

Orpen. THE LANDED GENTRY. 544

(a) Mary Frances Beatrice, *m.* 19 July, 1895, Humphrey, son of T. Craddock.
(b) Jane Sophia Spencer.
(c) Guldys Herbert, *m.* 15 Sept. 1905, Lieut. B. H. Jones, Royal Indian Marines.
b. Richard Hungerford, *b.* 15 Aug. 1844 ; *m.* 10 Sept. 1867, Maria Martha Taylor, and has issue,
  (a) Bastable Herbert, *b.* 5 June, 1869.
  (a) Adriana Mary.   (b) Rose Olivia Victoria.
  (c) Frances Diana.   (d) Mary Geraldine.
  (e) Ierne Cornelia Georgiana.
a. May, *m.* 11 Aug. 1859, H. Wheatley, and *d.* 12 Nov. 1863, leaving issue.
2. Thomas Hungerford, M.D., *b.* 13 June, 1810 ; *m.* 18 Aug. 1836, Margaret Augusta Owen, and had,
  a. Mary Elizabeth.
  b. Frances Geraldine, *m.* L. Bolton, M.D.
  c. Sophie, *m.* A. Court.
  d. Thomasine, *m.* Dr. Allen, R.N.
1. Sophia Anne, Maria Cranfield Hungerford, *m.* 1830, George Beamish.
(5) Henry, of Gortagas, co. Kerry, Capt. in the Army, *m.* Letitia Beecher, and had issue,
  1. Richard Beecher, *m.* and had issue, one dau.
  2. Thomas Allen Beecher, *d.s.p.*
  3. Edward, *m.* — Heatley, and had issue,
    a. William.
    b. Richard.
    c. Edward.
    d. Samuel (Rev.), who had issue, Mark and Francis.
    a. Elizabeth.
4. Henry, of Bridgeville Park, co. Kerry, *m.* Rachael Harman.
  1. Mary Anne.   2. Letitia Amelia.
(1) Anne, *m.* Richard Rye, of Ryecourt.
(2) Alice, *m.* William Meredith, and had issue.
1. Grace, *m.* Daniel Crumpe.
2. Agnes, *m.* Thomas Wright, of Glengariff, co. Cork.
3. Margaret.
3. Robert, *m.* Eliza Smith, and had two sons and two daus.,
  1. Richard.   2. Lovel, who went abroad.
  1. Mary, *d. unm.*   2. Sarah, *m.* Major King, of Killarney.
4. George.   5. Abraham, Port Surveyor, of Kenmare.
6. Raymond, *d. unm.* 1774. This gentleman, an indefatigable genealogist, compiled about 1745, a most extensive pedigree of his family.

Mr. Richard Orpen, of the White House, co. Kerry, who *m.* Isabella Palmer, was *s.* at his decease by his eldest son,

REV. THOMAS ORPEN, of Killowen, Rector of Kenmare, and adjoining parishes, *m.* Agnes, dau. of Arthur Herbert of Currens, and had issue,
1. RICHARD (Rev.), M.A., of Killowen, co. Kerry, and Frankfort, co. Cork, Rector of Valentia, *m.* Mary, dau. of Matthew Hutchinson, and relict of James French, by whom (who *d.* 1804) he left at his decease, at Bordeaux, 1770, one son and three daus.,
  1. Richard Thomas, High Sheriff co. Cork, *d. unm.*
  1. Mary, *m.* 1st, Capt. John Travers, of Fir Grove, co. Cork, and 2ndly, Gen. the Hon. William Mordaunt Maitland,
  2. Charlotte, *m.* Oct. 1790, Thomas Quin, K.C.
  3. Sophia, *m.* 1797, Philip Oliver Ellard, Capt. Fencible Regt.
2. Arthur, lost at sea, with his wife and only child.
3. Thomas, *d.* in Trin. Coll. Dublin.
4. George, a Military Officer, severely wounded at the battle of Minden. He *m.* Lucy, dau. of Nathaniel Bland, of Derryquin Castle, and had issue,
  1. Thomas, Capt. Kerry Militia, *d. unm.* 1829.
  2. Henry Francis, Major 60th Regt., killed at Talavera, *unm.*
  1. Lucy, *m.* Alexander Strange, Capt. of Dragoons, and had issue.
5. Edward, *b.* 1741, who resided at the family mansion of Killowen, and was Major in a volunteer Regt. ; *m.* Eleanor Connor (who *d.* 22 March, 1839), and had issue (*see* ORPEN *of Exeleigh*).
6. JOHN HERBERT, M.D., an eminent Physician of the city of Cork, *m.* Hannah, dau. of Emmanuel Hutchinson, Barrister-at-Law, and *d.* April, 1799, having by her (who *d.* 1808) had issue,
  1. THOMAS HERBERT, M.D. of Dublin, *m.* Penelope, dau. of David Thompson, of Oatlands, co. Meath, and had issue,
    (1) JOHN HERBERT ORPEN, of St. Stephen's Green, Dublin, Barrister-at-Law, M.A., LL.D., *b.* 1805 ; *m.* 2 Sept. 1840, Ellen Susanna Gertrude, dau. of Rev. John Richards, of Grange, co. Wexford (*see* RICHARDS *of Monksgrange*), and *d.* 3 Sept. 1888, leaving by her (who *d.* 1855) issue.
1. JOHN RICHARDS, B.A., Barrister-at-Law (*St. Leonard's, Killiney, co. Dublin*), *b.* 23 April, 1844 ; *m.* 1st, 4 July, 1867, Sarah Constance, dau. of Henry Leader, of Wyelands, Buxton, and by her (who *d.* 2 Oct. 1884) had issue,
  a. JOHN HERBERT (Rev.), M.A. (*Thurston Vicarage, Bury St. Edmunds*), *b.* 30 Sept. 1868 ; *m.* 14 June, 1900, Ada Mary, dau. of Capt. Edward Pakenham Stewart, of Laragh, Killiney, co. Dublin, and has issue,
    (a) Christopher Charles Stewart, *b.* 9 March, 1904.
    (b) John Edward Leader, *b.* 2 March, 1908.
    (a) Mary Stewart, *b.* 29 May, 1902 ; *d.* in infancy.
  b. Henry Stewart, *b.* 31 Aug. 1870 ; *m.* 25 Nov. 1902, Eleanor C. Lance.
  c. Charles Hutchinson (*Longsoal, Bara Hapjam, Upper Assam*), *b.* 17 July, 1872 ; *m.* 22 Aug. 1906, Gwendolyn Constance Kirwan, only dau. of Rev. Henry Ashe, Rector of Duleek, co. Meath, and has issue,
    Girsha Lilith Constance, *b.* 10 Oct. 1907.
  d. Hugh Massey, *b.* 5 April, 1877 ; *d.* 13 June, 1880.

a. Ethel Constance, *b.* 8 Feb. 1881 ; *m.* 31 Oct. 1906, Capt. John Baillie Barstow, R.E., son of H. C. Barstow, I.C.S., of Hazelbush, York, and has issue.
Mr. J. R. Orpen *m.* 2ndly, 25 March, 1904, Rosa Charlotte, dau. of Francis Rowden, B.A., of Hastings, Barrister-at-Law, and by her has issue,
  Dorothy Esther Penelope, *b.* 22 Jan. 1905.
2. Thomas Herbert (Rev.), M.A. Camb., Vicar of Great Shelford, Cambs., formerly Tutor of Selwyn Coll. and Fellow of Pembroke Coll. Camb., *b.* 8 Sept. 1847 ; *m.* 25 June, 1879, Amy Octavia, dau. and co-heir of Rev. J. H. A. Gwyther Philipps, of Picton Castle, Haverfordwest, co. Pembroke (*see* BURKE's *Peerage*, PHILIPPS, Bart., *of Picton Castle*), and has issue,
  a. Theodore Cecil, Cape C.S., *b.* 21 June, 1880.
  b. John Hugh, late Lieut. Royal Fusiliers, *b.* 19 July, 1882.
  c. James Denys (Rev.), *b.* 1 Aug. 1883.
  d. Henry Fabian, *b.* 14 May, 1889.
  e. Walter Selwyn, *b.* 20 July, 1893.
  a. Angela Mary Kathleen, *b.* 27 Aug. 1886.
3. Richard Theodore, Col. R.E., *b.* 4 March, 1849 ; *d. unm.* 28 Nov. 1906.
4. Goddard Henry, of Monksgrange, Enniscorthy, co. Wexford, B.A., Barrister-at-Law, *b.* 8 May, 1852 ; *m.* 18 Aug. 1880, Adela Elizabeth, only child of Edward Moore Richards, of Grange, co. Wexford, and has issue,
  Edward Richards, *b.* 20 Oct. 1884.
  Lilian Iris, *b.* 13 Feb. 1883.
1. Penelope Jane, *d. unm.* 25 Oct. 1904.
2. Ellen Elizabeth, *m.* 16 Sept. 1873, Davys Tuckey, Barrister-at-Law, of Ardglas, Dundrum, co. Dublin, and *d.* 27 Oct. 1902. She *d.* leaving issue, Charles Orpen, Arthur and Ellen Marguerite.
(2) Henry, *d.s.p.*
(1) Anna Sophia, *m.* 1834, John Thompson Young, of Philpotstown, co. Meath (who *d.* 1850), and *d.* 1897 *s.p.*
2. John Emanuel, of Kantuck (Rev.), M.A., *b.* 1779 ; *m.* Frances, dau. of Richard Ashe, and by her (who *d.* 1839) had issue,
  (1) John Herbert, of Lisheens, co. Cork, M.D., J.P., *m.* 1834, his cousin, Margaret Leader, and *d.s.p.* 1862.
  (2) Richard Ashe, *d. unm.* 1892.
  (3) Emanuel, *d. unm.* 1853.
  (4) Robert, *d. unm.* 1853.
  (1) Fanny Sophia, *m.* 1834, William Smith, of Cork, and *d.* 6 April, 1883 having had issue.
  (2) Eliza, *d. unm.*
  (3) Hannah, *d. unm.* 1878.
  (4) Margaret Lucy, *m.* Thomas Palmer, and *d.s.p.* 10 April, 1906.
  (5) Alice, *m.* Richard Ashe, of Coolebane, co. Cork, and *d.* 1851.
3 Emanuel Hutchinson, of Mount Tallant, *m.* 1831, Letitia dau. of Rowland Bateman, of Oak Park, co. Kerry, *d.s.p.* 1063.
1. Hannah Agnes, *d. unm.*   2. Frances, *d. unm.*
3. Sophia, *d. unm.*
4. Margaret Lucy, *m.* Capt. Henry Odlum (who *d.* 1840) and *d.s.p.* 1862.
7. FRANCIS (Rev.), B.A., Vicar of Kilgarvan, co. Kerry, Rector of Dungourney, co. Cork, and Incumbent of Douglas, near Cork. He *m.* 21 March, 1780, Susanna, dau. and co-heir of Hugh Millerd, of Monard, Alderman of Cork. She *d.* 13 March, 1830, and he *d.* 1805, leaving issue,
1. Arthur George, Barrister-at-Law, *d.s.p.* at Edinburgh, 25 April, 1813.
2. RICHARD JOHN THEODORE (Sir), Knt. of Ardtully, co. Kerry, *b.* 6 Nov. 1788, *m.* 17 May, 1819, Eliza, eldest dau. of Rev. Richard Stack, D.D., Fellow of Trin. Coll. Dublin, and *d.* 4 May, 1876, having had issue,
  (1) Francis Fitz-Richard, B.A., Barrister-at-Law, *b.* 16 July, 1827 ; *d. unm.* 25 Jan. 1858.
  (2) RICHARD HUGH MILLERD, late of Ardtully.
  (3) Arthur Herbert, of Oriel, Stillorgan, co. Dublin, M.A. of Trin. Coll. Dublin, *b.* 29 Dec. 1830 ; *m.* 3 Oct. 1861, Anne, eldest dau. of Right Rev. Charles Caulfeild, Bishop of Nassau, and has issue,
1. Richard Francis Caulfeild, B.A. Trin. Coll., *b.* 24 Dec. 1853 ; *m.* 7 March, 1890, Violet, 2nd dau. of Col. Robert Caulfeild, of Camolin House (*see* BURKE's *Peerage*, CHARLEMONTE, V.).
2. Charles St. George, B.A., Trin. Coll. Dublin, *b.* 12 Dec. 1864 ; *m.* 27 Aug. 1901, Cerise Maria, 4th dau. of the late John Henry Darley, of Stillorgan, and has issue,
  (1) Arthur Frederick St. George, *b.* 19 March, 1903.
  (1) Cerise Mary, *b.* 27 March, 1904.
  (2) Grace Anne, *b.* 19 Nov. 1905.
  (3) Kathleen Hilda, *b.* 27 Jan. 1910.
3. Arthur Herbert Stack, LL.D., Trin. Coll. Dublin, *b.* 27 July, 1872.
4. William Newenham Montague, A.R.A. and R.H.A., *b.* 27 Nov. 1878 ; *m.* 8 Aug. 1901, Grace, youngest dau. of Walter John Knewstub, of Highgate, and has issue,
  a. Mary, *b.* 23 Sept. 1902.
  b. Christine Violet, *b.* 6 Sept. 1906.
1. Grace Mary, *b.* 5 Feb. 1870 ; *m.* 1897, Thomas Jackson, and has issue.
2. Elizabeth Ida, *b.* 26 March, 1875 ; *d.* 16 Oct. 1879.
(4) Charles William de Erpingham, B.A., Barrister-at-Law, *b.* 21 Sept. 1833 ; *d. unm.* 10 Oct. 1867.

(5) William Newenham Morris, *b*. 31 Jan. 1835, Major 77th Foot; *d. unm*. 26 Nov. 1870.
(6) Raymond d'Audemer (Rt. Rev.), D.D., Bishop of Limerick, Ardfert, and Aghadoe, *b*. 27 Aug. 1837; *m*. 1 Oct. 1867, Sarah Lucinda, dau. of Daniel de Courcy MacGillycuddy, J.P., of Day Place, Tralee (*see* MACGILLICUDDY *of the Reeks*), and by her (who *d*. 4 July, 1891) had issue,
1. Richard Theodore, B.A., T.C.D., District Judge, Jamaica, *b*. 13 Oct. 1869; *m*. Oct. 1909, Victoria Maud, dau. of Alfred Henshaw, of St. Philips, Clonskeagh, Dublin.
2. Charles William MacGillycuddy, B.A., T.C.D., M.D., Indian Medical Service, *b*. 11 June, 1871; *d. unm*. 1 May, 1900.
3. Henry Arthur Herbert (Rev.), M.A., T.C.D., Rector of Adare, co. Limerick, *b*. 12 May, 1874.
1. Lucinda Elizabeth, *b*. 14 June, 1877.
(1) Mary, *m*. 12 Feb. 1846, George Hall Stack, of Mullaghmor, Omagh, and *d*. March, 1880, leaving issue.
(2) Theodora Elizabeth, *m*. 14 Jan. 1851, Rev. James Going, Vicar of Kilgarvan, co. Kerry, *d.s.p*. 17 Sept. 1880.
(3) Emily Georgiana, *m*. 26 Nov. 1859, William Plunket Stack, C.E., and *d*. 25 May, 1861, leaving issue.
(4) Cornelia Susanna Sarah.
(5) Elizabeth Ida Rebecca, *m*. 12 June, 1866, John R. Blacker, Capt. 18th Royal Irish, and *d*. 14 Sept. 1901, having had issue, one son.
3. Charles Edward Herbert (Rev.), M.D., F.R.C.S. (London), F.R.C.S (Dublin), member of various literary societies, the philanthropic founder of the National Institution for the Deaf and Dumb at Claremont, Glasnevin, near Dublin, *b*. in Cork, 31 Oct. 1791, took orders and emigrated to the Colony of the Cape of Good Hope, landed at Cape Town 11 March, 1848, reached Port Elizabeth 26 April, 1848, and was 1st Rector of Christ Church, Colesberg; *d*. at Port Elizabeth 20 April, 1856. He *m*. 10 Dec. 1823, Alicia Frances, widow of Rev. Conolly Coane, of Bath, eldest dau. of Major Henry Charles Sirr, Town Major of the city of Dublin, and by her (who was *b*. 18 March, 1796, and *d*. at Grahamstown, 4 Dec. 1869) had issue,
(1) Francis Henry Samuel, of St. Clair, J.P., M.L.A., Barkly West, and previously Surveyor-Gen. of Griqualand West, *b*. 22 Oct. 1824; *m*. 23 Oct. 1855, Sarah Anne (who was *b*. 10 Dec. 1834, and *d*. 17 April, 1906), eldest dau. of Alexander Hugh Murray, of Colesberg, and *d*. 22 Feb. 1893, having had issue,
1. Charles Edward Herbert, Cape Civil Service, J.P., *b*. 25 Aug. 1856; *d. unm*. 21 Dec. 1910.
2. Francis Hugh Raymond *b*. 7 Nov. 1861.
3. Arthur Edward, *b*. 22 May, 1863; *d*. 11 June, 1863.
4. Redmond Newenham Morris, C.M.G., M.L.A. Cape Town, Maj. Late Orpen's Horse, J.P. (*Hilldown, P.C. Campbell, Cape Province, South Africa*), *b*. 22 May, 1864; *m*. 7 May, 1906, Dora Agnes, dau. of the late Abraham Difford, of Cape Colonial C. S., and has issue,
Francis Newenham Garrett, *b*. 23 July, 1911.
Elizabeth Theodora Sarah, *b*. 27 April, 1907.
1. Alicia Frances Charlotte, *b*. 5 March, 1858; *m*. 8 Aug. 1882, Rev. Robert Herbert Godwin, M.A. Oxon, Provost of St. John's, Umtata, Tembuland, youngest son of B. C. Godwin, of Winchester, and has issue,
a. Anthony Herbert Orpen, *b*. 17 Jan. 1884, *d*. 10 Feb. 1884.
b. John Charles Raymond, *b*. 18 July, 1888.
c. Edgar Theodore Harold, *b*. 3 March, 1895.
a. Constance Mary Geraldine, *b*. 3 Aug. 1890.
2. Emily Grace Gordon, *b*. 30 March, 1860; *d*. 16 Aug. 1861.
3. Lilian Grace Ida, *b*. 22 March, 1866.
4. Florence Rose Mary, *b*. 12 April, 1868; *d*. 1 Sept. 1870.
5. Katharine Irene Theodora, *b*. 13 July, 1870.
6. Mary Grace Geraldine, *b*. 4 Nov. 1874; *d*. 10 Jan. 1875.
7. Geraldine Grace Mary, *b*. 4 Nov. 1874; *d. unm*. 29 April, 1892.
(2) Charles Sirr, of Smithfield, Orange River Colony, J.P., *b*. 29 April, 1826; *m*. 17 March, 1854, Rosetta (who was *b*. 24 Dec. 1832; *d*. 17 Dec. 1873), eldest dau. of William Lucas, of Grahamstown, and *d*. 4 Aug. 1887, having by her had issue,
1. Conolly D'Arcy D'Erpingham, *b*. 15 Sept. 1858; *d*. 14 Feb. 1898.
2. Emanuel Isidore, *b*. 22 July, 1864; *d*. 15 Aug. 1864.
3. Charles Evelyn Claremont, *b*. 14 Oct. 1865; *m*. 17 Aug. 1892, Jessie, dau. of Cumberland John Hill, and has issue,
a. Frank, *b*. 4 July, 1893.
a. Amy Eulalie, *b*. 14 Feb. 1896.
b. Evelyn, *b*. 15 April, 1900; *d*. 4 June, 1911.
c. Irene Eöa, *b*. 27 Nov. 1903.
d. Florence Estelle, *b*. 16 March, 1908.
4. Arthur Beverly Morris, *b*. 30 Sept. 1868; *d*. 6 June, 1869.
5. Lionel Edward, *b*. 23 Feb. 1871; *d*. 12 Oct. 1871.
1. Alicia Louisa Herbert, *b*. 30 Dec. 1855; *m*. 13 Nov. 1878, George Gough Wallace, of Stutterheim, Orange Free State, and has issue,
a. Vivienne Rose Maud, *b*. 10 Oct. 1879; *m*. 13 March, 1901, Walter Reuben Harvey, and has issue.
b. Alicia Eulalie, *b*. 9 Nov. 1882.
c. Madeline, *b*. 14 Jan. 1885; *d*. 22 July, 1889.
d. Helen Agnes, *b*. 16 June, 1890.
2. Eulalie Theodora Ida, *b*. 7 Sept. 1860; *m*. 25 July, 1883, Herman Wilhelm Wohlers, M.D., of Smithfield, Orange Free State, and *d*. 16 May, 1889, leaving issue, two daus.,
a. Rose, *b*. 27 April, 1884.
b. Wilhelmina Ida, *b*. 23 Sept. 1887, and *d*. 5 March, 1888.
3. Rosa Isidore Evangeline, *b*. 24 June, 1863; *d*. 3 July, 1863.
(3) Arthur Richard, J.P., Cape Civil Service, *b*. 1 July, 1827; *m*. 1st, 26 Nov. 1856, Emma Haddon, dau. of John Grice, of Durban, Natal, and by her (who *d*. 18 July, 1868) had issue,
1. Robert Moriarty, *b*. 19 May, 1858; *m*. 19 Sept. 1898, Helena Alida, dau. of Peter François de Villiers, of Paarl, Cape Colony, and has issue,
a. Arthur Moriarty, *b*. 1 July, 1899.
b. Terence Francis Moriarty, *b*. 11 Oct. 1907.
2. Edward Grice, Cape Civil Service, *b*. 6 June, 1865; *m*. 4 Dec. 1907, Mabel Isabel, dau. of Dr. Herbert Mearns, of Observatory, Capetown, and has issue,
a. Mavis Isabel, *b*. 30 Oct. 1908.
b. Esmé Claire, *b*. 8 June, 1910.
3. Alfred Richard, *b*. 30 Jan. 1867.
4. Arthur Francis, *b*. 23 March, 1868; *m*. 1st, 4 Jan. 1894, Edith Anne, dau. of Isaac Short; 2ndly, at Melsetter in Rhodesia, 12 Jan. 1910, Mary Eliza, dau. of David Malcolmson, of Belfast, Ireland, and has issue,
Francis Lisle, *b*. 6 June, 1911.
1. Marian May, *b*. 4 Aug. 1862.
He *m*. 2ndly, 23 Aug. 1878, Alice Louisa, dau. of James Attwell, of Battlesden, Victoria, Cape Colony, and *d*. 4 Sept. 1899, leaving further issue,
5. James Havelock, *b*. 8 Aug. 1879; *m*. 19 April, 1909, Eileen Akerman, dau. of Tom Barry, of Lismore, Swellendam, Cape Colony, and has issue,
James Barry, *b*. 27 July, 1911.
Colleen Barry, *b*. 4 March, 1910.
6. William Hugh, *b*. 11 June, 1882.
7. Harold Gill, *b*. 16 Dec. 1886; *d*. 27 June, 1889.
8. Thomas Herbert, *b*. 7 Sept. 1890.
9. Leo Graham, *b*. 18 Oct. 1892.
10. Clarence Patrick, *b*. 30 March, 1896.
11. Maxham St. Clair, *b*. 8 June, 1898.
2. Muriel Louisa, *b*. 9 Jan. 1881.
3. Gladys Fickling, *b*. 30 April, 1884; *m*. 20 April, 1911, John George Douglas Hoets, eldest son of J. C. Hoets, of Plumstead, Capetown.
4. Florence Angela, *b*. 29 Sept. 1888.
(4) Joseph Millerd, J.P., M.L.A. of Avoca and Snowdon, Barkly East, Cape Colony, *b*. 5 Nov. 1828; *m*. 31 March, 1859, Elise Pauline, dau. of Rev. Samuel Rolland, President of the Paris Evangelical Missionary Society, Basutoland, and has issue,
1. Raymond Hugh Millerd, *b*. 5 March, 1871; *d*. 28 Sept. 1862.
2. Reginald Joseph Eugene, *b*. 24 Dec. 1864; *m*. 3 May, 1887, Grace Sophia, dau. of Edward Richard Carlisle, and has issue,
a. Bernard George Overton, *b*. 23 June, 1888; *m*. 6 Aug. 1910, Ethel, dau. of John Devine, of Caledon, and his wife, Mary Taylor, of Swellendam.
b. Oswald Claude, *b*. 30 Aug. 1895; *d*. 9 April, 1900.
c. Eric Millerd, *b*. 13 Oct. 1901.
a. Violet Madeline, } twins, *b*. 23 Oct. 1890.
b. Iris Vivienne,
3. Hope Rolland, *b*. 13 Dec. 1867; *m*. 22 July, 1890, Jane Elizabeth, dau. of Michael Little, I.C.S., and has issue,
Cecil Joseph Rolland, *b*. 29 March, 1902.
Kathleen Ethel, *b*. 27 Aug. 1905.
4. Claude Emile, *b*. 7 Jan. 1871; *m*. 26 Dec. 1893, Caroline Ianthe, dau. of Edmund Richard Carlisle, and has issue,
Harold Claude Millerd Orpen, *b*. 7 Sept. 1898.
5. Leander Joseph John, M.D., Assistant Director of Health, Salisbury, Rhodesia, *b*. 27 Feb. 1877.
1. Emily Minna Cecile, *b*. 14 Jan. 1860; *d*. 23 Oct. 1861.
2. Helen Agnes Josephine, *b*. 1 May, 1863; *m*. 11 July, 1887, The Hon. Col. Charles Preston Crewe, C.B., J.P., M.L.A., only son of Capt. Frederic Crewe, 7th Madras Infantry, and has issue,
a. John Frederic Preston Crewe, *b*. 23 Feb. 1894; *d* 23 May, 1897.
b. Ranulphe Orpen Crewe, *b*. 23 May, 1898.
a. Leila Pauline Crewe, *b*. 3 June, 1888; *d*. 23 June, 1892.
3. Madeleine Elise Emily, *b*. 22 Nov. 1874; *m*. 22 Jan. 1901, Arthur Herbert Holland, son of Benjamin H. Holland, Registrar of Deeds, Capetown, and has issue,
Douglas Orpen Huntly Holland, *b*. 7 Sept. 1901.
(5) Richard John Newenham, of Holdernesse, Cape Colony, M.L.A., J.P., the first traveller to explore the Kallahar Desert (*i.e.*, Wilderness) together with the late Sir Edward Shelley, in 1852–1853), *b*. 28 Jan. 1830.
(6) Henry Martyn Herbert, C.M.G., J.P., Paymaster-Gen. of the Cape of Good Hope, 1876–98, *b*. 24 Jan. 1831; *m*. 8 Sept. 1857, Harriott Eloise (*d*. 29 March, 1877), dau. of George Edward Joseph, of Pavo Park, Somerset, Cape Colony, J.P., at Cape Town. He *d*. 10 Jan. 1908, leaving issue,
1. Herbert Edward Richard, *b*. 10 June, 1858; *d*. 19 May, 1869.
2. Ernest Charles Henry, *b*. 5 Nov. 1859; *m*. 21 Jan. 1889, Mary Luttig, dau. of J. M. Crosby, and *d*. 30 Jan. 1903, leaving issue,
Cyril Herbert, Cape C.S., *b*. 18 Dec. 1890.
3. Arthur George Francis, *b*. 5 April, 1862; *d*. 20 Nov. 1862.

4. Harry Millerd Erpingham, *b.* 25 June, 1863 ; *m.* 29 Sept. 1891, Elizabeth Susan, dau. of Peter Lange, and widow of Robert Scholtz, and has issue,
    a. Gerald Erpingham, *b.* 4 Aug. 1895.
    a. Irene Erpingham, *b.* 26 Sept. 1892.
    b. Doris Erpingham, *b.* 14 May, 1897.
5. Theodore George Herbert, *b.* 15 Nov. 1870,
6. Lionel Emmanuel, *b.* 27 April, 1872 ; *d. unm.* 19 April, 1901.
7. Gerald Edward D'Arcy, *b.* 2 Jan. 1875 ; *m.* 22 Jan. 1901, Constance Maud, dau. of T. H. Lawton, and has issue,
    a. D'Arcy Devenish, *b.* 7 Nov. 1901.
    b. Norman D'Arcy, *b.* 17 Nov. 1905.
    c. Gerald Henry D'Arcy, *b.* 19 Feb. 1909.
    d. Leslie D'Arcy, *b.* 19 June, 1910.
    a. Eileen D'Arcy, *b.* 6 April, 1903.
    b. Constance D'Arcy, *b.* 15 June, 1907.
1. Zaidée Eliza, *b.* 29 Jan. 1861 ; *m.* 1st, 4 Jan. 1883, Norris Edmund Wallace, B.A., T.C.D., Barrister-at-Law (who *d.* 19 May, 1883), 3rd son of Rev. Thomas Wallace, of Belfield, co. Dublin. She *m.* 2ndly, 5 May, 1903, William Frederick Stamper, who *d.* 12 Aug. same year.
2. Agnes Maud, *b.* 20 April, 1865 ; *m.* 22 Dec. 1891, Joshua Andreas Joubert, B A., Barrister-at-Law (who *d.* 26 Nov. 1910), and has issue : *a.* Herbert John Joubert, *b.* 30 Oct. 1892 ; *b.* Noel Francis Joubert, *b.* 15 April, 1894 ; *c.* Raymond James Joubert, *b.* 21 Oct. 1895. *a.* Joyce Marie Eloise Joubert, *b.* 9 Jan. 1903 ; *b.* Lorraine Joubert, *b.* 30 Aug. 1905.
3. Eloise Harriott, *b.* 27 Feb. 1867 ; *m.* 10 May, 1894, Capt. William Alexander Barnett, N. Staffs. Regt. (who *d.* 21 Sept. 1910), and has issue, Zaidée Alexandra, *b.* 26 July, 1902.
4. Edith Alice, *b.* 20 Oct. 1869.
(7) Theodore Robert Morrison, *b.* 12 Sept. 1835 ; drowned 29 Jan. 1863, in Orange River, by the upsetting of his boat.
(1) Susannah Alicia Mary, *b.* 24 July, 1833 ; *d.* 1 April, 1837.
(2) Alicia Emily Catharine, *b.* 6 July, 1838 ; *d.* 24 Dec. 1906 ; *m.* 22 Jan. 1862, Lieut.-Col. Owen Henry Strong, 10th Regt. of Foot, only son of Major Henry Strong, of Iffley, co. Oxfordshire, and has issue,
    1. Henry, R.N.R., *b.* 16 Nov. 1862.
    2. Owen Charles Herbert, Cape Civil Service, *b.* 24 Dec. 1864 ; *m.* 3 Aug. 1908. Winifred Sarah, eldest dau. of Rev. J. Whiteside, of Uitenbage, Cape Colony, and has issue, Ethel Alice Owen, *b.* 7 Aug. 1909.
    3. Edgar Hugh, of Bulawayo, Rhodesia, J.P., M.R.C.S. (Eng.), L.R.C.P. (Lon.) ; *b.* 8 Feb., 1867, *m.* 29 April, 1905, Agnes Beryl. dau. of W. A. H. Holland, J.P., of Grahamstown, Cape Colony, and has issue.
    4. Samuel, *b.* 20 Dec. 1874, *d.* 6 Feb. 1875.
    1. Ethel Alice Emily, *b.* 22 Sept. 1869, *d.* 27 March, 1876.
1. Susannah Maria Frances, *d. unm.* 6 Feb. 1853.
2. Emilia Grace Caroline, *m.* 1816, John Gordon, M.D., of Dublin, *d.s.p.*
3. Rebecca Newenham Millerd, *m.* 31 Jan. 1805, Henry Gage Morris, Rear-Admiral R.N., and had issue (*see* MORRIS *of* York).
4. Cornelia, *d. unm.*
1. Isabelle.   2. Mary.
3. Cherry, *m.* James, son of Nathaniel Bland, of Derryquin Castle.
4. Margaret Lucy, *d. unm.*
5. Lucy, *m.* Conway Blennerhasset.
6. Agnes, *m.* Rev Walter Stewart.
RICHARD HUGH MILLERD ORPEN, of Ardtully, co. Kerry, M.A., *b.* 7 Nov. 1829 ; *m.* 5 Jan. 1871, Amy Noble, eldest dau. of Thomas Horwood, of St. Anne's Road, Stamford Hill, London, and *d.* 2 Jan. 1907, having had issue,
1. RICHARD HUGH HORWOOD, late of Ardtully.
2. RAYMOND WILLIAM, now of Ardtully.
1. Amy Eliza, *b.* 17 Nov. 1874.
2. Constance Marion, *b.* 10 July, 1877.
3. Nora Edith, *b.* 20 Sept. 1878 ; *m.* 1909, — Dudgeon, M.D.
4. Olive Mabel, *b.* 10 June, 1880.
5. Mary Winifred, *b.* 20 Aug. 1884.
6. Ida Grace Victoria, *b.* 31 March, 1887.
RICHARD HUGH HORWOOD ORPEN, of Ardtully, co. Kerry, *b.* 22 Sept. 1873 ; *d. unm.* 7 Nov. 1911, when he was *s.* by his brother.

Arms—Quarterly, 1st and 4th : Per pale az. and or, a lion rampant counterchanged, in the dexter chief point a cross-crosslet of the second (for ORPEN) 2nd and 3rd : Erm. afess az. between three wolves' heads erased sa. (for MILLERD). *Crest*—A demi-lion rampant or, charged on the shoulder with a cross-crosslet sa. *Motto*—Veritas vincet.

Seat—Ardtully, Kenmare, co. Kerry.

ORPEN-PALMER. *See* **PALMER.**

O'SHEE OF GARDENMORRIS.

MAJOR RICHARD ALFRED POER O'SHEE, C.M.G. (1911) of Gardenmorris, co. Waterford and Sheestown, co. Kilkenny, British Commissioner Anglo-Portuguese Boundary, Anglo-French Boundary (Lake Chad) Major, R.E., served with Benin Exped. 1897 (despatches, medal with clasp, Brev.-Major), and in West Africa 1897-8 (clasp), *b.* 6 Aug. 1867.

Lineage. — ODANUS O'SHEE, chief of his name in the 10th century, is styled in a pedigree, attested in 1582 by Robert Cooke, Clarenceux King of Arms, " Lord of The Cantred of Texnane O'Shee, in Kerry, and of the manors of Cloran O'Shee, Clone O'Shee, and Drangan O'Shee, in Tipperary," to which co. they seem to have emigrated in the 13th century.

ODONEUS O'SHEE, chief of his name (and the 10th in a direct line from the above Odanus), styled also, in the same pedigree Lord of Cramp's Castle and Sheesland, in Tipperary, obtained with his three brothers, William, Edmund, and John, letters of denization from Roger Mortimer, Earl of March and Ulster, dated at Clonmel, 6 Nov. 1381, which were confirmed by King HENRY VI. by letters patent, dated at Naas, 18 Nov. 35 HENRY VI., to his great-great-grandson,

RICHARD SHEE, father (by his wife, Rose Archer) of

ROBERT SHEE, who settled at Kilkenny, where he was a merchant and Burgess, and filled the office of Sovereign in 1499. He fell at the battle of Moyallow, 6 Aug. 1500, and left by his wife, Catherine Sherlock, a son,

RICHARD SHEE, Burgess of Kilkenny, *m.* Joan, dau. and heir of Elias Archer, of New Ross, and had five sons and three daus. The eldest son,

ROBERT SHEE, of Bonnestown, co. Kilkenny, J.P., *m.* Margaret Rothe, and had, with six daus., five sons,
1. RICHARD, his heir.
2. Elias, of Kilkenny, described by Holinshed, as " Elias Sheth, borne in Kilkennye, sometime scholer of Oxford, a gentleman of a passing wit, a pleasant conceited companion, full of mirth without gall. He wrote in English divers sonnets." He was ancestor of George Shee, *m.* Mary, dau Martin Kirwan of Blindwell co. Galway, and *d.* 1752, having issue,
(1) Anthony, of Castlebar, grandfather of Sir George Shee, Bart. of Dunmore, who *d.s.p.* 1870.
(2) Martin, of Dublin, *m.* Mary, eldest dau. and co-heir of John Archer, and was father of
Sir Martin Archer Shee, Knt., D.C.L., President of the Royal Academy, an official trustee of the British Museum F.R.S., Honorary Member of the Royal Hibernian Academy and of the Academies of New York, Charleston, and Philadelphia. *b.* 23 Dec. 1769 ; *m.* 6 Dec. 1797, Mary, eldest dau. of James Power, of Youghal, co. Cork, and *d.* 19 Aug. 1850, having by her had issue,
a. George Archer, *b.* 21 June, 1800 ; *m.* 17 Oct. 1842, Jane Seymour, 3rd dau. of Sir Thomas Joseph De Trafford, 1st bart., and *d.* 1879.
b. Martin Archer, Q.C., *b.* 14 Nov. 1804 ; *m.* Louisa Catherine, 2nd dau. of John Richard Barrett, of Milton House, Berks.
c. William Archer, *b.* 28 Aug. 1810 ; *m.* Harriet, widow of Col. William Cubitt, and dau. of George Harcourt, and had issue,
(a) Martin Archer (*The Lawn, Nailsworth, Glos.*), *b.* 1846 ; *m.* 1st. 1872, Elizabeth Edith Denniston, dau. of Alfred Pell. of New York, and by her (who *d.* 1890) had issue,
1. Martin Archer, D.S.O., Major Reserve of Officers, late 19th Hussars, formerly Midshipman R.N., served in S. African War 1899-1902 (dangerously wounded, despatches thrice, Brevet and D.S.O., both medals and six clasps), M.P. Central Finsbury since 1910 (18, *Park Street, W.*), *b.* 5 May, 1873 ; *m.* 14 Oct. 1905, Frances, only dau. of Alfred Pell, of Highland Falls, New York, and by her had issue,
(1) John Pele ARCHER, *b.* 3 Nov. 1906.
(2) Richard Martin, *b.* 11 Oct. 1907.
(1) Edith Frances, *b.* 3 Oct. 1908 \ twins.
(2) Kathleen Winifrede, *b.* 3 Oct. 1908 /
(3) Lucy Mary, *b.* 3 May, 1910.
1. Mary, a nun.   2. Winifrede Theodosia.
He *m.* 2ndly, 1892, Nellie, dau. of the late Thomas Treloar, of Blackheath, and has issue by her,
2. George Archer, *b.* 6 May, 1895.   3. Anna Archer.
(a) Mary Archer, *d.* at Florence 1872.
(b) Harriet, *m.* 1870, Lieut.-Gen. Teonesto Manacorda, of the Italian Army, and has issue.
a. Anna Archer.   *b.* Mary Archer.   *c.* Eliza Jane.

. Marcus. 4. Matthew. 5. Andrew.
The eldest son,
SIR RICHARD SHEE, Knt., of Uppercourt, co. Kilkenny, and of Cloran, co. Tipperary, a Member of Gray's Inn, London, Seneschal of Irishtown 1568, Treasurer of the Regalities of Tipperary 1571, and Deputy to the Lord High Treasurer of Ireland 1576. Sir Richard founded in the year 1582, the hospital in Kilkenny called after his name. He m. 1st, Margaret, dau. of John Sherlock, of Waterford, and had five sons,
1. Robert, d. unm.
2. Lucas, ancestor of the SHEES of Cloran.
3. Thomas, Mayor of Kilkenny, m. Ellen, dau. of Nicholas Dobbyn of Waterford, and d.s.p. Oct. 1636 (Fun. Entry).
4. John, Mayor of Kilkenny, m. Lucy Laborne, and d. 13 Nov. 1633 (Fun. Entry), having had issue,
    1. Richard.
    1. Anne, m. Bryen FitzPatrick, of Gortneclehy, Queen's Co.
    2. Joan.
5. MARCUS, progeni or of the SHEES of Sheestown and Gardenmorris.
Sir Richard Shee m. 2ndly, Margaret, dau. of Christopher Fagan, Alderman of Dublin, but by her, who survived him, he left no issue.
Sir Richard d. 10 Aug. 1608. His 5th son,
MARCUS SHEE, of Sheestown, m. Ellen, dau. of Oliver Grace Baron of Courtstown, and had five sons,
1. RICHARD, his heir. 2. John.
3. Lucas, m. Elizabeth, dau. of Robert Warren, of Castletown, co. Galway, and had a son,
    Nicholas Shee, M.D., who m. Eleonora, dau. of John Purcell, of Borrisoleigh, and had a son,
    Richard, living 1682, from whom claimed descent (as his great-grandson) William Shee, of Camas, co. Limerick, b. 1709, son of Martin Shee, of Camas, by Ellinor, dau. of Edmond Bourke, of Ballinagarde, co. Limerick. He m. 1738, Maria Theresa, dau. of Peter Preponier, of Landreces, Surgeon, and had issue, a son, Henry, Col. of Horse, Knight of St. Louis, Count and Peer of France (father of Françoise, wife of Baron James Wulfraed D'Alton, and mother of Edmond, Count D'Alton-Shee) and a dau., Louisa, who m. Thomas Clarke (a native of co. Kilkenny, and a Col. in the French service), by whom she had a son
    Henry Clarke, Duc de Feltre, Marshal of France, and many years Minister at War to the Emperor NAPOLEON I., b. 1765 ; d. 1818.
4. James. 5. Thomas.
Mr. Shee was s. at his decease by his eldest son,
RICHARD SHEE, of Sheestown, m. Rose, dau. and heir of Peter Rothe, and was s. by his son,
MARCUS SHEE, of Sheestown, m. Mary, dau. of Nicholas Plunkett, of Dunsoghly, and had issue,
1. RICHARD, his successor.
2. Marcus. 3. Nicholas.
4. John, ancestor of the SHEES of Ballyreddan, from whom descended RICHARD SHEE, son of John Shee, of Ballyreddan, Col. of the 35th Regt.
He made his will 16 March, 1664, and was s. at his death by his eldest son,
RICHARD SHEE, of Sheestown, m. the Hon. Dymphna Barnewall, dau. of Robert, 9th Lord Trimlestown, and dying 10 Dec. 1748, left (with a dau. Elizabeth, m. Thomas Power, of Gardenmorris, co. Waterford) four sons,
1. MARCUS.
2. Robert, Col. in Berwick's Regt., and Knt. of St. Louis.
3. Nicholas. 4. James.
The eldest son,
MARCUS SHEE, of Sheestown, m. Thomasina, dau. of Thomas Masterton, of Castletown, co. Wexford, and had, with four daus., who d. unm., two sons,
1. JOHN, his heir.
2. Marcus, a Gen. in the French service, b. 1742 ; m. Victoire Felicité, dau. of Capt. E. P. L. Shee, Knt. of St. Louis, and had a son,
    Alexander, a Capt. in the French service.
Mr. Shee was s. at his decease, 18 Jan. 1750, by his eldest son, who, re-adopting the Irish prefix, became
JOHN O'SHEE, of Sheestown, and served as High Sheriff for the co. of Waterford 1783. He m. 23 Sept. 1767, Elizabeth, dau. and heir of Richard Power, of Gardenmorris, co. Waterford, and had issue,
1. RICHARD POWER, his heir.
2. Arnold, Major in the Waterford Militia, d. unm. 1843.
3. John, a Col. in the Austrian service, d. unm. at Sheestown, 1813.
Mr. O'Shee was s. by his eldest son,
RICHARD POWER O'SHEE, of Gardenmorris and Sheestown, m. 1804, Margaret, dau. of Nicholas Power, of Snowhill, co. Kilkenny, and by her (who d. Nov. 1865) left at his decease, aged 59, in 1827,
1. JOHN POWER, his heir.
2. NICHOLAS RICHARD, successor to his brother, and late of Gardenmorris.
The elder son,
JOHN POWER O'SHEE, of Gardenmorris and of Sheestown, J.P. and D.L., High Sheriff co. Waterford 1832, b. 1810 ; d. 5 July, 1859, and was s. by his brother,
NICHOLAS RICHARD POWER O'SHEE, of Gardenmorris, co. Waterford, and Sheestown, co. Kilkenny, J.P. and D.L. co. Waterford, High Sheriff 1861, b. 1821 ; s. his brother 1859 ; m. 18 April, 1865, Lady Gwendoline Anson, youngest dau. of Thomas William, 1st Earl of Lichfield. She d. 15 March, 1912. He d. 30 March, 1902, leaving issue,
1. RICHARD ALFRED POER, now of Gardenmorris.

2. John Marcus Poer, R.I.C., b. 1869 ; m. 22 Sept. 1900, Myrtle Constance, third dau. of Col. Ynyr Henry Burges of Parkanaur (see that family), and has issue,
    1. Mildred, b. 1901.
    2. Gwendoline Constance, b. 19 April, 1903.
3. George Iver Poer, Capt. Leinster Regt., b. 4 June, 1873 ; m. 11 Sept. 1907, Lady Edith Charlotte Harriett, dau. of 8th Earl of Kingston (see BURKE's Peerage), and has issue,
    Patrick Iver Rivallon Poer, b. 18 Feb. 1909.
    Christine, b. 7 July, 1908.
1. Gwendolen, b. 1866. 2. Aline Angela, b. 1879.
Arms—Quarterly: 1st, per bend indented az. and or, two fleurs-de-lis, counterchanged, the arms of Odoneus O'Shee, 1382 ; 2nd, gu., three swords per fesse arg., hilted or, the centre sword pointing to the sinister side, the arms of William O'Shee, brother of Odoneus; 3rd, sa., three pheons arg., the arms of John O'Shee, brother of Odoneus ; 4th, gu., two swords in saltire arg. point down, surmounted by a third in pale point up, hilted or, the ensign of Edmond O'Shee, brother of Odoneus. Crest—A swan rousant sa. Motto—Vincit veritas.
Seats—Gardenmorris, Kilmacthomas, and Sheestown, near Kilkenny. Club—Army and Navy.

OTWAY-RUTHVEN. See RUTHVEN.

OWENS OF HOLESTONE.

MISS JANE EMILY ORR OWENS, of Holestone, co. Antrim, dau. of the late Rev. James Orr, by his wife Harriet Skeffington, dau. of John Owens, of Holestone (see below). She s. her aunt, Margaret Owens 25 Jan. 1904, and by Royal Licence, 7 Sept. 1904, assumed the name and arms of ORR-OWENS.

Lineage.—The family of Gillilan, from which that of Owens derives the Holestone property, went from Scotland, to Ireland in the reign of CHARLES II.

HENRY OWENS, m. 1724, Jane, eldest dau. of William Gillilan, of Holestone (by which marriage the Gillilan property, for want of heirs male, passed to the OWENS), and by her had (with a dau. Hessie, m. Samuel Ferguson) two sons,
1. WILLIAM, of Holestone, b. 1725 ; d. unm., when the estate devolved upon his nephew. 2. JOHN.
The 2nd son,
JOHN OWENS, of Tildarg, b. 1726 ; m. 7 March, 1769, Anne, dau. of the Rev. George Rogers, Rector of Dunachy, co. Antrim, and d. 1806, having had issue,
1. William Gillelan, d.s.p. 2. John, d.s.p.
3. JAMES, of whom presently.
1. Anne, m. 1796, William Johnson, of Fortfield.
2. Jane, m. George Porter Price.
3. Rachel Margaret Hester, m. Rev. Samuel Smythe, Vicar of Carnmoney, and had issue. 4. Eleanor.
The 3rd son,
JAMES OWENS, of Holestone, J.P., High Sheriff co. Antrim 1838, b. 18 June, 1777. He m. 20 Dec. 1799, Mary, dau. of John Forsythe, of Ballynure, by Sarah his wife, dau. of William Gillilan, of Collin, and by her (who d. 1852) left at his decease, 21 Nov. 1848, a son and successor,
JOHN OWENS, of Holestone, J.P., High Sheriff co. Antrim 1838, b. 30 Jan. 1801 ; m. 4 Feb. 1828, Jane, dau. of James Stewart Moore, of Ballydivity, co. Antrim, J.P. and D.L., and d. 7 Nov. 1874, having had issue,
1. JAMES, late of Holestone.
1. Harriett Skeffington, m. 8 Jan. 1850, the Rev. James Orr, who d. 1902. She d. 14 April, 1855, leaving issue,
    JANE EMILY, who assumed the name of ORR-OWENS, and is now of Holestone.
3. MARGARET, now of Holestone.
4. Jane, d. unm. 23 June, 1902.
5. Elizabeth Anne, m. Jan. 1868, Harry Adair Tracey, Lieut.-Col. R.A., and d. 1872, leaving a son, Harry Owens, b. 11 July, 1869 ; d. Aug. 1895, and two daus.
The only son,
JAMES OWENS, of Holestone, co. Antrim, J.P. and D.L., High Sheriff 1878, b. 3 Aug. 1836 ; m. 1861, Evelyn Margaret, dau. of Robert James Tennent, of Rushpark, co. Antrim, J.P. and D.L., and d.s.p. 22 July, 1900, being s. by his sister,
MISS MARGARET OWENS, of Holestone, co. Antrim, s. her brother 1900, and d. unm. 22 Jan. 1904, being s. by her niece,
Arms—Quarterly: 1st and 4th gu., a boar passant arg., armed collared and chained or to a hollybush on a mount in base ppr., on a cantou of the second, three ravens' legs erased, meeting at the fesse point sa (OWENS); 2nd and 3rd, gu., three piles in point arg., the centre pile charged with a trefoil slipped vert, on a chief or, a torteau between two cross crosslets fitchee of the field (ORR).
Seat—Holestone, Doagh, co. Antrim. Residence—30, Ovington Square, Lennox Gardens, S.W.

PACK-BERESFORD. *See* **BERESFORD.**

PAKENHAM OF LANGFORD LODGE.

LIEUT.-GEN. THOMAS HENRY PAKENHAM, of Langford Lodge, co. Antrim, C.B., J.P. and D.L., formerly M.P. for that county, Lieut.-Gen. in the Army (retired) and Col. East Lancashire Regt., *b.* 26 June, 1826; *m.* 25 Feb. 1862, Elizabeth Staples, eldest dau. of William Clarke, of New York, and has issue,

1. HERCULES ARTHUR, late Capt Grenadier Guards, and Maj. 4th Batt. Royal Irish Rifles Lieut.-Col. Comdg. 18th Batt. County of London Regt., sometime A.D.C. to the Viceroy of India, High Sheriff co. Antrim 1907 (40, *Devonshire Place, W.*), *b.* 17 Feb. 1863; *m.* 16 Nov. 1895, Lilian Blanche Georgiana, dau. of Right Hon. Evelyn Ashley, P.C. (*see* BURKE's *Peerage*, SHAFTESBURY, E.), and has issue,
   1. Hercules Dermod Wilfrid, *b.* 29 July, 1901.
   1. Joan Esther Sybella, *b.* 2 Feb. 1903
   2. Beatrice Constance, *b.* 3 Jan. 1910.
2. Harry Francis, Maj. King's Royal Rifle Corps, served in S. Africa, *b.* 6 Nov. 1864; *m.* 7 Feb. 1905, Gwendoline Beatrice Sanchia May, dau. of the late Lieut.-Col. William Thomas Markham, of Becca Hall (*see* MARKHAM *of Morland*). He *d.s.p.* 11 Feb. 1905. His widow *m.* 2ndly, 20 April, 1910, Brian Mollov.

Gen. Pakenham is the only surviving son of Lieut.-Gen. the Hon. Sir Hercules Robert Pakenham, K.C.B. (who *d.* 7 March, 1850), and Emily his wife (who *d.* 26 Jan. 1875), dau. of Thomas, Baron Le Despencer.

Lineage, *Arms*, &c.—*See* BURKE's *Peerage*, LONGFORD. E.

Residences—Langford Lodge, Crumlin, co. Antrim, and 19, Hertford Street, W. *Clubs*—Carlton, and Army and Navy, S.W.

PAKENHAM. *See* BURKE's PEERAGE, LONGFORD, E.

PAKENHAM-MAHON. *See* **MAHON.**

PALLISER OF ANNESTOWN.

MRS. MARY JANE SYBIL GALLOWAY, dau. of Major Sir William Palliser, C.B., *m.* 3 Nov. 1908, Capt. Harold Bessemer Galloway, Capt. (retired) Seaforth Highlanders, of Blervie, Morayshire, served in Hazara Expedition 1891 (medal and clasp), Relief of Chitral 1895 (medal and clasp), with Lovat's Scouts 1901-2, S. Africa (medal and three clasps), 2nd son of Charles John Galloway, J.P., of Thorneyholme, Knutsford, Cheshire (*see* GALLOWAY *of Blervie*), and has issue,

IAN CHARLES PALLISER, *b.* 25 Jan. 1910.
Sybil Evelyn, *b.* 9 Oct. 1909.

Lineage.—This family paternally descends from that of BURY, Earl of Charleville, extinct, and is now the male representative of that family. JOHN BURY, nephew of WILLIAM BURY, the grandfather of the 1st Earl of Charleville (*see* BURY *of the Little Island*), assumed the surname of PALLISER, upon succeeding to the estates of his maternal grandmother.

JOHN PALLISER, of Newby-upon-Wiske, co. York, *b.* about 1550; *m.* Anne, dau. of Michael Meeke, of Nanby-upon-Swale, same co., leaving issue,

1. THOMAS, his successor.
2. John, of Kirkley, who left, by Elizabeth his wife, a son, John.
   1. Anne, *m.* 1st, Richard Metcalf, of Northallerton, co. York; and 2ndly, Marmaduke Franke, of Knighton, same co.
   2. Jane, *m.* Thomas Pybus, of Fryarsgarth, co. York.
3. Elizabeth, *m.* George Llewellyn, of Danby-upon-Wiske, co. York.
4. Mary, *m.* Robert Wilson, of Thirsk, co. York.

Mr. Palliser *d.* 1623, and was *s.* by his eldest son,
THOMAS PALLISER, of Newby, *b.* 1606; *m.* Joan, dau. of Richard Frankland, of Blobberhouse, co. York, and had issue,

1. JOHN, of Newby, *b.* 1639; *m.* Ursula, dau. of Sir Hugh Bethell, Knt. of Ellerton, co. York, and had, with a dau. Frances, three sons,
   1. THOMAS, of Portobello, co. Wexford, High Sheriff 1700, got a grant of the Great Island, in that co., from James, 2nd Duke of Ormonde, Sept. 1702, *b.* 1661; *d.* Nov. 1756; *m.* Katherine, dau. and heir of William Wogan, of Rathcoffy, co. Kildare, and had issue,
      (1) John, *d. unm.*; *bur.* at Kilmokea, co. Wexford, 7 May, 1728.
      (2) Thomas, of the Great Island, High Sheriff co. Wexford 1729, *m.* Dorothy, dau. of Ven. Robert Elliott, D.D., Archdeacon of Ferns, and *d.s.p.*
      (3) William, *b.* 24 June, 1699; *m.* Mary, dau. of Philip Savage, of Kilgibbon, and *d.v.p.*, having had two sons and three daus.,
         1. Philip, of the Great Island, *m.* Katherine, dau. of James Harvey, of Killiane, and *d.s.p.* 1784.
         2. Bethel, bapt. 28 March, 1722; *d. unm.*
            1. Katherine, heir of her brother, *s.* to the Great Island; *m.* John Wilson, of Scarr, eldest son of Christian Wilson, of Scarr, ancestor of Sir W. H. Wilson-Todd, Bart. (*see* BURKE's *Peerage*). She had issue,
               Christian, of Scarr, *m.* Elizabeth, dau. of Matthew Redmond of Kilgowan, co. Wexford, and had issue,
               (*a*) John, of Scarr, *d.s.p.m.*
               (*b*) Matthew, of the Great Island, who assumed the name of PALLISER, *m.* 12 Aug. 1812, his cousin, Jane, dau. of Christian Wilson, of Sledagb (*see* BURKE's *Peerage*, WILSON-TODD, Bart.), and had issue,
                  1. Christian, of Begerin, J.P., *m.* Mary, dau. of Rodulphus William Ryan, Crown Prosecutor for co. Wexford, and left a dau., *b.* 27 June, 1877.
                  2. Matthew (Rev.), Rector of White Church, *m.* 1855, Sophia, dau. of Rev. Thomas Ottiwell Moore, Rector of Leskinfere, by whom (who *d.* 18 April, 1856) he had a son, Frederick, *b.* April, 1856, *d.s.p.*
               Anne, *m.* Feb. 1785, Richard Waddy, of Clougheast, co. Wexford.
      2. Ursula, *b.* 24 Dec. 1720, *bur.* at Kilmokea, 3 April, 1722.
      3. Mary, *d. unm.* before 1782.
      (4) Walter, of Dublin, *b.* 21 Nov. 1760; *m.* Katherine Cunningham, by whom (who *d.* Aug. 1756) he had a son, Richard, Barrister-at-Law, *d. unm.*; will dated 3 Nov. 1764, and proved 5 June, 1765.
      (1) Juliana Hyde, *m.* 12 April, 1732, Capt. John Orfeur, and had issue,
         1. Dorothea (Mrs. Weston).
         2. Mary, who *m.* George Robinson Walters, R.N.
         3. Catherine Hyde, *m.* Matthew Cavenagh, of Graigue, and *d.* 1814, leaving by him (who *d.* 1819), with other issue, a son, James Gordon, who *m.* Ann, dau. of Odiarne Coates, of Green Court, Herts, and has issue.
   2. Hugh, of North Deighton, co. York, Capt. in the Army, *b.* 1663; *m.* Mary, dau. of Humphry Robinson, of Thicket Priory, co. York, and had issue,
      SIR HUGH PALLISER, 1st bart. of The Vatch, Bucks, Admiral of the White, Governor of Greenwich Hospital, a Lord of the Admiralty, created a bart. by patent 6 Aug. 1773, with special remainder to his nephew, George Robinson Walters, *d. unm.* 19 March, 1796.
      Rebecca, *m.* Major William Walters, who *d.* 28 Feb. 1789, leaving a son, George Robinson Walters, R.N., *m.* (as above) his cousin Mary, dau. of Capt. John Orfeur, and had, with two daus., a son, who, having assumed the surname of PALLISER, and *s.* his great-uncle in the baronetcy, became SIR HUGH PALLISER, 2nd bart. of The Vatch, *b.* 27 Oct. 1768; *m.* 18 Jan. 1790, Mary, dau. of John Yates, of Dedham, Essex, who *d.* 5 Aug. 1823. Sir Hugh *d.* 17 Nov. 1813, leaving issue, 1, SIR HUGH PALLISER, 3rd bart. of The Vatch, *b.* 8 May, 1796; *d. unm.*; 1, Mary Anne Rachel, *b.* 16 March, 1798; *d. unm.* 10 Dec. 1826; 2, Mary Jane, *m.* 1st, 16 April, 1822, William Lockhart, of Gormiston, co. Lanark, and 2ndly, 11 May, 1848, John Manley Arbuthnot, 3rd Lord Keane, and *d.* Oct. 1861.
   3. Walter, of North Deighton, *m.* Elizabeth, Sterne, and had issue,
      Walter (Rev.), Rector of Stokenham, and Vicar of Great Drayton, and Askham, co. Nottingham, *d.* 1778.
      Alice, *m.* Robert Cooper.
2. WILLIAM (Most Rev.), of whom hereafter.
3. George, whose son,
   John (Rev.), D.D., Rector of Rathfarnham, co. Dublin, Chancellor of Cloyne 26 Dec. 1771, *m.* 21 Nov. 1747, Mary Holmes, by whom he left issue, one son and three daus. His will, dated 6 July, 1788, was proved 26 June, 1795.

Mr. Palliser was living 1665, being then aged 59. His 2nd son, MOST REV. WILLIAM PALLISER, Archbishop of Cashel, D.D., entered Trin. Coll. Dublin, 13 Jan. 1660, was elected a Fellow 1668, ordained 1669, consecrated Bishop of Cloyne 5 March, 1693, and translated to the Archbishopric of Cashel, 16 June, 1694. He was *b.* 1645, and *m.* Mary, dau. of Jonah Wheeler, of Greenan, co. Kilkenny, widow of William Greatrakes, of Affane, co. Waterford, by whom (who *d.* 1 June, 1735) he had issue,

WILLIAM, his successor.

Parker.

IRELAND.

Jane, m. John Bury, of Shannon Grove, co. Limerick, by whom he had, with other issue (*see* BURY *of the Little Island*),
1. William Bury, whose grandson, Charles William Bury, was created, 1806, Earl of Charleville.
2. JOHN BURY, who assumed the surname of PALLISER, of whom hereafter, as heir to his maternal uncle.
10 Archbishop *d*. 1 Jan. 1727, and was bur. at St. Andrew's, ublin. He was *s*. by his only son,
WILLIAM PALLISER, of Rathfarnham, *b*. 1695; *m*. May, 1728, ary, dau. of Matthew Pennefather, of Cashel, Accountant-General Ireland, and sister of Elizabeth, wife of Alexander, 5th Earl { Antrim, by whom (who *d*. 7 April, 1769) he had no issue. He *s.p.* Oct. 1768, and was *s*. by his nephew,
JOHN PALLISER (formerly BURY), of Comragh, co. Waterford, ho assumed the name of PALLISER, *m*. 1762 a dau. of Richard aylor, of Cork, and *d*. 1769, and was *s*. by his son,
WRAY PALLISER, of Derryluskan, *m*. Mary, dau. of Ven. Richard haloner, Rector of Fethard, and Prebendary of Kilbragh, Archeacon of Cashel (*see* CHALONER *of King's Fort*), and was father of
JOHN PALLISER, of Derryluskan, High Sheriff co. Waterford 802, *b*. 19 May, 1760; *m*. 1784, Grace, eldest dau. of William 3arton, of Grove, co. Tipperary, and by her (who *d*. 13 March, :844) had issue,
1. WRAY, of Derryluskan, co. Tipperary, High Sheriff 1850, and Comragh, co. Waterford, J.P., High Sheriff 1816, Lieut.-Col. Waterford Militia Artillery, *b*. 1788; *m*. 7 Nov. 1814, Anne (*b*. 1796), dau. and heir of John Jacob Gledstanes, of Annesgift, co. Tipperary. She *d*. 17 Aug. 1851. He *d*. 1863, leaving issue,
1. JOHN, of Comragh, co. Waterford, and Derryluskan, co. Tipperary, J.P. and D.L., C.M.G., F.R.G.S., High Sheriff 1844, Gold Medallist 1589 of Royal Geographical Soc. for his Government Survey of the Rocky Mountains, *b*. 29 Jan. 1817; *d.s.p.* 18 Aug. 1887.
2. Wray Richard Gledstanes, Capt. R.N., of Coolquil, co. Tipperary, *b*. 24 May, 1822; *m*. 1857, Elizabeth, dau. of Richard FitzGerald, of Muckridge House, co. Cork, *d.s.p.* 1891.
3. Frederick Hugh, *b*. 3 July, 1826; *m*. 12 Aug. 1852, Emily, dau. of Sir Charles Price, Bart., and *d*. leaving issue,
(1) Charles Frederick Wray Bury, *b*. 26 July, 1854; *m*. Elizabeth, dau. of Richard Proctor, of "Solitude," Canterbury, New Zealand, and has issue,
1. Wray Cecil.
1. Edith Kathleen. 2. Eileen Bessie.
(2) Farquhar Edward Bury.
(3) Cecil Hunter Bury, *m*.1901, Clara, dau. of Edward Smith, of Throndhjern, Norway.
(1) Edith Charlotte Bury.
4. Edward Mathew, of Annesgift, co. Tipperary, late Capt. 7th Hussars. served in Crimea (medal), Umbeyla Campaign 1863 (medal), and as Staff Officer, Alberta Field Force, in suppression of Riel Revolt in Canada 1885 (medal, services mentioned in Canadian House of Commons, promoted Major Canadian Mil.), *b*. 20 Sept. 1828; *m*. 1st Jane, dau. of Major-Gen. Sir John Rose, of Holme Rose, co. Inverness, H.E.I.C.S., and had issue a son, Edward. He *m*. 2ndly, Ann, dau. of Capt. Preotis, and *d*. 15 March, 1907.
5. William (Sir), C.B., Major 18th Hussars, formerly Rifle Brigade, M.P. for Taunton 1880, inventor of bolts for securing armour plates, chilled shot for piercing armour plating and conversion of smooth bore guns into rifled guns, received C.B. for his inventions in 1868 and knighted 1873, *b*. 18 June, 1830; *m*. 1868, Anne, dau. of George Perham, and *d*. 4 Feb. 1882, leaving issue,
(1) Wray, *d.s.p.*
(2) Hugh Arbuthnot, *b*. 25 Feb. 1879; *m*. 30 May, 1908, Annie Elizabeth, youngest dau. of late J. Brooke Dickenson.
(1) Grace Evelyn.
(2) Mary Ethel, *m*. 25 Jan. 1896, E. A. Joseph, 4th Baron WALLSCOURT (*see* BURKE'S *Peerage*).
(3) MARY JANE SYBIL, now of Annestown.
1. Grace Penelope, *m*. 15 June, 1851, William Fairholme, of Chapel-on-Leader, co. Berwick, who *d*. 1868, leaving issue, four daus., Caroline Grace, now of Comragh and Kilmacthom s; Mary; Louisa; and Catherine.
2. Sarah Elizabeth, *m*. 17 Oct. 1840, George Stephens, 2nd Viscount Gough, and *d.s.p.* Aug. 1841.
3. Anna, *m*. 1846, John Nugent Rose, of Holme Rose, C.B., son of Major-Gen. Sir John Rose, H.E.I.C.S.
4. Mary, *d. unm.*
2. JOHN BURY (Rev.), of whom presently.
3. Richard Bury, of Castle Warden, co. Kildare, J.P. for Sussex, Capt. 12th Lancers, *m*. 8 Aug. 1832, Fanny (*b*. 23 Sept. 1805; *d*. 16 Jan. 1878), dau. of Joseph Maryat, M P., of Wimbledon House, Surrey. He *d*. 1852; she *d*. 16 Jan. 1878, having had issue,
1. John, Capt. 76th Regt., *d.s.p.*
2. Henry, *m*. Beatrice, dau. of Gen. Astell, *d.s.p.* March, 1907.
3. Richard William, late Capt. 8th Hussars, *d.s.p.* 8 Aug. 1906.
4. Joseph, *d*. 8 June, 1898; *m*. and left issue, one son and four daus. 5. Hugh, *d.s.p.*
1. Charlotte, *m*. — Bird.
2. Frances, *m*. 1856, Alexander Robert Campbell Johnston, F.R.S., of Yoxford, Suffolk, J.P., who *d*. 21 Jan. 1888, and has issue.
3. Margaret, *m*. 22 Nov. 1905, Henry Elliott.
1. Elizabeth, *m*. 1810, Charles, 2nd Viscount Gort, *d*. 2 April, 1858, leaving issue.
2. Margaret Jane, *m*. 8 March, 1826, Frederick Charles Phillips, late Lieut.-Col. 15th Hussars, who *d*. 1858 (*see* PHILIPS *of Rhual*).
3. Grace, *d. unm.* 4. Anna, *d. unm.*
Mr. Palliser *d*. 17 Dec. 1833. The 2nd son,

THE REV. JOHN BURY PALLISER, of Annestown, Rector Clonmel, *b*. 4 Feb. 1791; *m*. 10 March, 1830, Julia Phillida, dau. of Capt. John Howe, H.E.I.C.S., and *d*. 8 April, 1864, having had issue. She *d*. 4 June, 1875.
1. WRAY BURY, late of Annestown.
2. John Richard, Lieut. 1st Royal Regt., served in the China War 1860, including taking of Taku Forts (medal and clasp), *b*. 28 March, 1835; *d*. at Tientsin 29 Aug. 1860.
The elder son,
CAPT. WRAY BURY PALLISER, of Annestown, co. Waterford, J.P. and D.L. (High Sheriff 1883), *b*. 9 March, 1831; *m*. March, 1861, Maria Victoria Josephine, younges dau. of the late Joseph Gubbins, of Kilfrush, co. Limerick, and *d*. 4 April, 1906. She *d*. 10 Jan. 1896 having had issue,
Alice Grace, *b*. 12 April, 1863; *d*. 14 Oct. 1878.

Arms (*of* PALLISER)—Confirmed to the descendants of Sir William Palliser, C.B. Quarterly: 1st and 4th, per pale sa. and arg. three lions rampant counterchanged (for PALLISER); 2nd and 3rd, vert, a cross-crosslet or (for BURY). *Crest*—Out of a coronet gu. a demi-eagle wings elevated or charged on the breast with a cross-crosslet vert. *Motto*—Deo volente.

Seat—Annestown, Tramore, co. Waterford. *Residence*—Blervie Morayshire.

ORPEN-PALMER OF KILLOWEN.

CAPT. HAROLD BLAND HERBERT ORPEN-PALMER, 87th Royal Irish Fusiliers, of Killowen, Kenmare, co. Kerry, educated at Pembroke Coll, Camb., B.A., *b*. 8 Sept. 1876; *m*. 5 Oct. 1911, Olga Mary, 2nd dau. of the Colonel W.W. Pemberton, I.S.C., and Adèle his wife, and grand-dau. of the late Hon, John Sandfield Macdonald, Premier of Ontario, Canada.

Lineage.—The family traces its descent from the Rev. Thomas Palmer, Vicar of Clonfert and Tullilease, and Rector of Knocktemple, co. Cork. He was appointed in 1670 to the Crown livings of Kilmare, Kilgarvan, Templenoe, Kilcrohan, and Cahirciveen, in the Diocese of Ardfert and Aghadoe, which he held till his death in 1702. He was a magistrate for the co. Kerry, and Judge of the Admiralty Court of Munster. A prominent incident in his life, set forth in Macaulay's *History of England*, Smith's *History of Kerry* (1756), and Miss Cusack's *History of the Kingdom of Kerry*, was his joint leadership with his son-in-law, Richard Orpen (*see* ORPEN *of Ardtully*), of the Protestant colony of settlers in Kenmare, in their defence of the fort of Killowen, whose ivy-clad ruins still overhang the beautiful river Roughty, commonly called the "Siege of the White House," during the winter 1688-9, against some thousands of the Irish forces of the King, JAMES II. A detailed account of this is given in a pamphlet by the above-mentioned Richard Orpen (a copy exists in the British Museum, G. Greville Coll. 5669, and another in the King's Inn Library, Dublin). Reference is made to the attainder of Mr. Palmer, Mr. Orpen, and many others, by Act of the Irish Parliament, for their loyalty to William of Orange, in Archbishop King's *State of the Protestants of Ireland*, 1730.
THE REV. THOMAS PALMER *m*. 1st, Jane, dau. of Sir Richard Aldworth, of Newmarket, co. Cork (*see that family*), and had issue,
1. THOMAS, of whom presently.
2. George (Rev.), B.A. Dublin 1713, Rector of Killorglin, Knockane, and Kiltallough, co. Kerry, *m*. Margaret, dau. of William White, of Bantry, and had issue (with five daus.),
1. Thomas, *d.s.p.* 2. John, *d.s.p.*
3. George, Governor of the Bank of Ireland, *m*. 26 Aug. 1766, Anne, only dau. and heiress of Daniel Bickerton, of Milestown, Castle Bellingham, and *d*. 1813, leaving issue.
4. Henry, *m*. Miss Bolingbroke.
1. Isabella, *m*. Richard Orpen, of Killowen (*see* ORPEN *of Ardtully*).
2. Mary, *m*. Joseph Taylor, of Dunkerron Castle, co. Kerry, from whom descend the families of TAYLOR *of Clontoo*, of BLAND *of Derriquin*. &c.
3. Cecilia, *m*. Richard, son of Abraham Allen, of Curragbroe, and had issue, 1, Abraham; 2, Philip; 3, Richard; 4, William 5, George; 6, Kyle.
4. Margaret, *m*. Beversham Harman, and had four sons, 1, Thomas; 2, Daniel; 3, George; 4, John; 1, Catherine, *m*. Thomas Hutchins, of Ballylickey, from whom descend the HUTCHINS *of Ardnagashull*, co. Cork.
He *m*. 2ndly, Julia, dau. of the MacCarthy More (from whose family the Killowen property passed into Palmer and Orpen hands), but had no issue by her. His elder son,
THOMAS PALMER, *m*. Mary, dau. of Abraham Coakley, of Curragh, co. Cork, and Mary his wife, dau. and co-heiress of Samuel Pomeroy, of Pallis, co. Cork, and had issue,
1. ABRAHAM, of whom presently.
2. Thomas. 3. George.
1. Margaret. 2. Sarah.
3. Ellen. 4. Martha.
His eldest son,
ABRAHAM PALMER, *m*. Isabella, dau. of William Duckett, and had issue,
1. CALEB, of whom presently.
2. Abraham, *m*. Sarah Wren.

Pack.

Mary. 2. Martha.
3. Sarah. 4. Hannah.

The elder son,
CALEB PALMER, of Milltown and Castlemaine, co. Kerry, m. 1782, Dorcas, dau. of William Twiss, of Ballybeg, co. Kerry, and Avicia Godfrey his wife, and d. 1794, leaving issue,
1. ABRAHAM, of whom presently.
2. William (Rev.), B.A. Dublin 1808, m. Catherine Twiss.
3. George, m. Margaret Giles.
4. Caleb, d. unm.
1. Avicia, m. William Peacock.
2. Isabella, m. James Eagar.
3. Catherine, m. Rev. John Carey.

His eldest son,
ABRAHAM PALMER, of Ashgrove, co. Kerry, and Dublin, m. 1805, Margaret Orpen, of Killowen, and d. 1860, leaving issue,
1. EDWARD ORPEN, of whom presently.
2. Caleb Richard, of Ashbrook, Clontarf, co. Dublin, m. 1st, Anne, dau. of Capt. Ralph Smythe, 7th Dragoon Guards, and by her had issue,
  1. Abraham Smythe (Rev.), D.D., Vicar of Holy Trinity, Hermon Hill, Woodford, b. 23 July, 1844; m. 9 July, 1875, Frances, dau. of Echlin Molyneux, Q.C., and has issue,
    (1) Geoffrey Molyneux, Mus. Bac. Oxon, b. 8 Oct. 1882.
    (1) Gladys Mary. (2) Gwendolen Sylvia.
    (3) Phyllis Audrey. (4) Eileen Stephanie.
  1. Henrietta, d. unm. 2. Sarah, m. Robert Freeman.
  3. Margaret Anna, m. 1st, L. W. King, LL.D., and 2ndly, W. H. Peard, and had issue.
  4. Anna Victoria, m. G. H. King, M.A., and has issue.
  5. Emily Theodora, m. Rev. James Torrens, and has issue.
He m. 2ndly, Harriet Archer, and d. 1889, having by her had further issue,
  2. Herbert Albert, d. an infant.
  6. Kathleen Augusta, m. Arthur Panton, F.T.C.D., and has issue.
  7. Edith Orpen, d. unm. 1903.
3. Henry Orpen, B.L., a learned genealogist, d. unm. 1841.
4. Abraham, d. an infant. 5. Charles, d. an infant.
6. William, of Roxboro', co. Armagh, J.P., m. Emma Margaret Armstrong, and d. 1883, leaving issue,
  1. Abraham William, m. Jane Stitt, and has issue.
  2. Benjamin Armstrong, of Millvale House, Newry, co. Armagh, J.P., b. 30 March, 1852; m. 1 June, 1882, Susan Georgina Browne, and has issue,
    (1) Orpen William, b. 4 March, 1883; d. an infant.
    (1) Isabel Orpen, b. 8 March, 1885.
    (2) Emma Elise, b. 27 April, 1886.
    (3) Sybil Armstrong, b. 26 Feb. 1891.
  3. Richard Armstrong.
  1. Elizabeth, d. young.
  2. Margaret, m. A. J. Turretin.
  3. Isabella, d. unm.
  4. Emma Dorcas, m. J. Cosgrave, and has issue.
  5. Elizabeth Lily. 6. Ida Mary.
  7. Florence, m. C. M'Alpin, and has issue.
7. Abraham Orpen, d. unm.
1. Dorcas Maria, d. unm. 1897.
2. Margaret Lucy, d. unm. 1853.

The eldest son,
EDWARD ORPEN PALMER, of Killowen, co. Kerry, b. 1 May, 1807, m. 5 Oct. 1841, Elizabeth Agnes, 3rd dau. of Capt. Robert Hutchinson Herbert, R.N.,* of Lakeview, Killarney, and d. 13 May, 1883, having by her (who d. 15 March, 1895, aged 74) had issue,
1. Abraham Henry Herbert, late of Killowen.
2. Robert Herbert, d. an infant, 1849.
1. ELIZABETH AGNES, of Killowen, co. Kerry.
2. MARGARET DORCAS, of Killowen, co. Kerry.
3. Agnes Laura, d. 18 March, 1910.

The eldest son,
REV. ABRAHAM HENRY HERBERT ORPEN-PALMER, B.D., M.A., T.C.D., of Killowen, co. Kerry, Vicar of St. Peter's, Cheltenham, assumed the name of ORPEN 1892, b. 29 Jan. 1843; m. 28 Oct. 1872, Eveline Cecilia, 3rd dau. of Evory Carmichael, of Monkstown, co. Dublin, and Elizabeth, his 1st wife, dau. of G. O'Brien (Mr. Carmichael m. 2ndly, Hon. Victoria de Montmorency, dau. of 4th Viscount Mountmorres), and d. 7 June, 1909, having had issue,
1. EDWARD ORPEN HERBERT, late Lieut. R.M.L.I., b. 8 Nov. 1873; d.v.p. unm. 27 May, 1908.
2. HAROLD BLAND HERBERT, now of Killowen.
3. Reginald Arthur Herbert, b. 26 Dec. 1877, educated at Clare Coll. Camb., Capt. Leinster Regt.
4. Geoffrey de Montmorency Herbert, Lieut. The Leinster Regt., b. 1 March, 1883.

Seat—Killowen, Kenmare, co. Kerry.

---

* Capt. R. H. Herbert, R.N. (who m. Elizabeth, dau. of Nathaniel Bland, and was uncle of Philip, 5th Baron Somers), was 5th son of Arthur Herbert, of Brewsterfield, and Barbara Hutchinson his wife, eldest son of Bastable Herbert and Barbara his wife, dau. of Maurice, Knight of Kerry. Bastable Herbert was 6th son of Arthur Herbert, of Currens, co. Kerry, and heir to his brother, Arthur Herbert, of Cahirnane and Brewsterfield, Killarney (see HERBERT *of Currens*).

PALMER OF RAHAN.

CHARLES COLLEY PALMER, of Rahan, co. Kildare and of Clonlost, co. Westmeath, J.P. and D.L. for the former co., High Sheriff 1875, b. 10 March, 1845; m. 4 April, 1866, May Jane, only dau. of Francis Longworth Dames, of Greenhill, King's Co., D.L., by Elizabeth his 2nd wife, dau. of R. Smyth, of Gaybrook, Westmeath (*see those families*), and has had issue,
1. William Francis, b. 30 Aug. 1867; d. unm. 25 Sept. 1895.
2. DUDLEY COLLEY, J.P., Hon. Major (retired) 4th. Batt. Leinster Regt., b. 28 Oct. 1868; m. 5 Aug. 1896, Constance M. A., 2nd dau. of the late Charles Florance Young, of 22, Cranley Gardens, S.W., and has issue,
  Charles Dudley, b. 1897.
3. Charles Nugent, b. 22 Feb. 1870.
1. Mabel Elizabeth, b. 26 March, 1872; m. 3 June, 1896, Thomas Mansel Longworth Dames, son of Capt. Thomas Longworth Dames, D.L., of Greenhill, King's Co. He d. 8 Jan. 1909, leaving issue (*see that family*).

Lineage.—THOMAS PALMER, of Killeskillen, co. Meath, living *temp.* CHARLES II., m. 28 Dec. 1708, Mary, dau. of George Colley, of Monasteroris, King's Co., and sister of Dudley Colley, of Rahan, High Sheriff co. Kildare 1734, and of Charles Colley, who d. 31 Oct. 1771 (will dated 25 April, 1771), nephews of Henry Colley, of Castle Carbury, the ancestor of the Duke of Wellington. They had issue,
1. George. 2. Dudley.
3. John.
4. CHARLES, of whom presently.
1. Susanna.
2. Judith.
3. Mary.
4. Anne.
5. Margaret, m. John Hutchinson, and had issue.

The youngest son,
CHARLES PALMER, of Rahan, co. Kildare, inherited that estate by the will of his maternal uncle, Charles Colley (*see above*). He was b. 1731; m. 2 Jan. 1772, Anne, dau. of William Lambe, of Prospect, co. Wicklow, and d. 1806, having had issue,
1. CHARLES LAMBE, his heir.
2. William Lambe, Capt. 18th Light Dragoons, m. 1797, Augusta, dau. of Sir John Temple, 8th bart. of Stowe, and had issue,
  1. John Temple, d. 1823.
  2. Charles Colley, d. 1858.
  3. Frederick Temple, d. 1901.
  4. William Bowdoin, d. 1889.
  1. Anne Elizabeth, d. 1803.
  2. Augusta Temple, d. 1840; m. 16 Oct. 1823, Rufus Prime, of New York, who left issue, Temple, d. 1903, and Cornelia.
  3. Elizabeth Mary, d. 1875.
3. Thomas, of Ballyhagan, d. unm. 11 Aug. 1825.
1. Eliza, b. 1774; d. 1856.

The eldest son,
THE REV. CHARLES LAMBE PALMER, of Rahan, Vicar of Carbury, m. 1809, Elizabeth, dau. of Hamilton Lowe Lockwood, of Castle Lake, co. Tipperary, by Henrietta his wife, sister of Sir John Craven Carden, 1st bart. of Templemore, and has issue,
1. Hamilton William, d. young.
2. Charles Colley, d. young.
3. WILLIAM LAMBE, his successor.
1. Elizabeth, m. 1839, Thomas Kemmis, of Killeen, Queen's Co., and d. 1893.

The youngest son,
WILLIAM LAMBE PALMER, of Rahan, m. 1841, Elizabeth Emily Anne, 3rd dau. of Col. James Nugent, of Cloolost. She d. 1837. He d. 1849, having had, with three daus., Isabella, Elizabeth, and Henrietta (who d. young),
1. CHARLES COLLEY, now of Rahan.
2. Hamilton William, yonst. Regt., m. 1877, Henrietta Frances, widow of Capt. George Macartney, of Lissanoure Castle, co. Antrim, and 3rd dau. of Robert Smyth, of Gaybrook, co. Westmeath, D.L.
1. Augusta, m. 1870, Capt. William Clarke, of Ballybrittan, King's Co., who d. 1897, leaving issue, Herbert Pascal, b. 1874, and Cecile.

Arms—Quarterly, 1st and 4th, az., on a fess between three palmer's scrips or, two palm branches in saltire vert (PALMER); 2nd and 3rd, or, a lion rampant gu., ducally gorged of the first (COLLEY). **Crest**—Between two palm-branches vert an arm vambraced and gauntleted embowed ppr., garnished, or, the hand grasping a tilting-spear also ppr. **Motto**—Honor virtutis præmium.

Seat—Rahan, Edenderry, co. Kildare, and Clonlost, Killucan, co. Westmeath. **Club**—Kildare Street, Dublin.

PALMER. See BURKE's PEERAGE, **PALMER, Bart.**

PARKE OF DUNALLY.

The late COL. ROGER KENNEDY PARKE, C.B., of Dunally, co. Sligo, commanded 18th Batt. and subsequently a Brigade of Imp. Yeo. in S. Africa, is a Brevet-Col. (retired) late 3rd Dragoon Guards, High Sheriff co. Sligo 1910, b. 1848. He was son of the late Major George Parke, d. 23 Jan. 1911.

Lineage.— SIR WILLIAM PARKE, of Dunally, co. Sligo, J.P. and D.L., High Sheriff 1820 and 1838, Lieut.-Col. and Major 66th Regt., b. 1 March, 1779, eldest son of Roger Parke, of Dunally, who m. 25 Sept. 1775, Alice, dau. of Rev. Thomas Browne, of Riverstown, co. Cork; received the honour of knighthood 1836. He served throughout the campaigns in the West Indies, Egypt, and the Peninsula, and was wounded at Corunna. Sir William m. 13 July, 1813, Louisa Elizabeth, dau. of the late Charles Johnstone, of Ludlow, and niece of the late Sir Richard Johnstone, Bart. of Hackuess Hall, co. York, and by her (who d. 31 March, 1883) had issue,
1. ROGER CHARLES, of Dunally.
2. JOHNSTON WILLIAM ROBERT, late of Dunally.
1. Jemmett, d. 25 Dec. 1866.
2. Louisa Elizabeth, d. unm. 13 Jan. 1902.

Sir William d. 1 Sept. 1851, and was s. by his elder son,
ROGER CHARLES PARKE, Lieut.-Col., of Dunally, co. Sligo, J.P., B.A., High Sheriff 1858, b. 1816; m. Alice, dau. of Rev. Thomas Browne (see BROWNE of Riverstown), and d. 24 Jan. 1889, and was s. by his brother,
JOHNSTON WILLIAM ROBERT PARKE, of Dunally, co. Sligo, High Sheriff for co. Leitrim 1890, b. 20 Dec. 1822; s. his brother 1889; d. 1901, being s. by Col. Roger Kennedy Parke.

Seat—Dunally, Sligo. *Residence*—Chiselhampton, Wallingford. *Clubs*—Army and Navy, S.W., Cavalry.

PARKER OF BALLY VALLEY.

ROBERT GABBBETT PARKER, of Bally Valley, co. Clare, J.P., High Sheriff 1891, M.A. Wadham Coll. Oxford, b. 14 July, 1846; m. 30 July, 1868, Louisa, 2nd dau. of John Whitty of Cotham Lodge, Clifton, son of the Venerable John Whitty, Archdeacon of Kilfenora, and has issue,
1. ANTHONY JOHN, b. 24 March, 1874.
2. Robert Gabbett, Major King's Own Royal Lancaster Regt., of Garry Kennedy, co. Tipperary, and Castle Lake, co. Clare, b. 4 Dec. 1875.
3. Ronald Elphinstone, R.F.A., b. 5 Jan. 1886.
1. Louisa Margaret.
2. Amy Christina, m. 14 July, 1898 F. W. Abbott-Anderson Manchester Regt., and has issue,
 1. Anthony Willoughby, b. 23 Oct. 1900; d. 13 July, 1902.
 2. Derek Glyn Edward, b. 8 Nov. 1904.
3. Mabel Vernon.   4. Eleanor.
5. Edith Gustava, m. 11 Aug. 1909, Robert Arthur Lidwill, of Dromard, co. Tipperary (see that family).

Lineage.—JOHN PARKER, of Dunkipp, co. Limerick whose will is dated 1698, left issue by Abigail his wife,
1. JOHN, his heir.   2. Thomas.
3. Edward.   4. Nicholas.
5. George.

The eldest son,
JOHN PARKER (will dated 1726), m. Alice, dau. of Rev. Anthony Irby, D.D., and had a son,
ANTHONY PARKER, who s. to the Tipperary and Limerick properties, and was High Sheriff for the latter co. 1738. He m. Amy Massy, and d. 1785, having by her (who d. 1784) had issue,
1. ANTHONY, his heir.   2. William.
3. John, of Bonlyglass, co. Limerick.
4. Hugh, of Faha, co. Tipperary.
5. George, of Clahan, co. Limerick.
6. Nicholas, of Limerick.
1. Amy, m. 1759, Charles Conyers.

2. Anne, m. 27 Aug. 1767, Gilbert Purdon, of Belkelly, co. Clare.
3. Alicia.   4. Elizabeth.
5. Mary.

The eldest son,
ANTHONY PARKER, of Castle Lough, High Sheriff co. Limerick 1761, and co. Tipperary 1768. He m. 22 Sept. 1761, Anne, dau. of Standish Grady, of Elton (by Mary Theresa, his wife, dau. of Robert Oliver, of Castle Oliver, M.P. co. Limerick), sister to Mary Theresa, Countess of Ilchester, and d. 1800, having had issue by her (who d. 1825),
1. ANTHONY, his heir.
2. STANDISH GRADY, s. his brother.
3. William, of Bally Valley, co. Clare, Barrister-at-Law, m. Anne, dau. of William Wilson, of Caberconlish, co. Limerick, and d.s.p.
4. Henry Thomas, 9th Lancers, d.s.p.
1. Mary, d. unm.
2. Amy, m. 1793, George Finch, of Kilcoleman.
3. Anne.   4. Eliza.
5. Theresa.   6. Catherine.

The eldest son,
ANTHONY PARKER, of Castle Lough, J.P. and D.L., d. unm. 1837, and was s. by his brother,
REV. STANDISH GRADY PARKER, of Castle Lough, m. 1841, Margaret, dau. of Rev. Robert Gabbett, D.D., of Castle Lake, co. Clare, by whom (who d. 30 April, 1886) he had issue, two sons,
1. ANTHONY, late of Castle Lough, High Sheriff 1876, J.P. cos. Tipperary and Clare, b. 21 Dec. 1841; m. 18 July, 1867, Anna Christiana, dau. of the late John Dawson Hutchinson, of Timoney Park, Roscrea, co. Tipperary, and by her (who d. 18 Oct. 1871) had issue,
 1. STANDISH GRADY JOHN PARKER-HUTCHINSON, now of Castle Lough, of Timoney Park, co. Tipperary, High Sheriff Queen's Co. 1893, and co. Tipperary 1908, b. 9 Jan. 1870; assumed the surname and arms of HUTCHINSON in addition to and after that of Parker, 25 April, 1891 (see PARKER-HUTCHINSON of Timoney); m. 30 Sept. 1902, Mary Eleanor, eldest dau. of Capt. J. Hill Poe, of Riverston, co. Tipperary (see that family).
 1. Anna Christina, b. 20 May, 1868; d. 12 Aug. 1871.
 2. Elizabeth Margaret, m. 3 Oct. 1906, William Andrews Morton, M.D., Birr.
He d. 26 Feb. 1905.
2. ROBERT GABBETT, of Bally Valley (see above).

Arms—Sa., a stag's head caboshed, between two flaunches arg., in the centre chief point a mullet or. *Crest*—A stag salient ppr., charged with a mullet, as in the arms. *Motto*—Fideli certa merces. *Seat*—Bally Valley, co. Clare. *Club*—Kildare Street.

PARKER OF PASSAGE WEST.

LIEUT.-COL. ST. JOHN WILLIAM TOPP PARKER, of Passage West, co. Cork, Lieut.-Col. Army Service Corps, late 56th Essex Regt., b. 20 Sept. 1866; m. 1901, Alice, dau. of late J. Wood, of Harrogate, by whom he has had issue,
1. RICHARD NEVILL HARDING, b. 1906.
1. Barbara Neville, b. 1902; d. 1904.
2. Iris Neville.   3. Mona Nevill.

Lineage.—MICHAEL PARKER, obtained through the interest of the Duke of Shrewsbury a commission (dated 1 April, 1695) as cornet of Dragoons in King WILLIAM's Army, and went to Ireland with his regiment in 1698, and m. 1700, Margaret, only dau. and heiress of Major Hugh Harding, of the Great Island, Queenstown, by whom he had issue, an only son,
HARDING PARKER, of Passage West, co. Cork, High Sheriff 1727, and Mayor 1740, b. 1701; m. 20 Nov. 1728, Catherine, dau. of John Neville. of Furnace, co. Kildare (see NEVILLE of Ahanure), and d. 1776, leaving issue,
1. MICHAEL, of whom presently.
2. William, Comm. H.E.I.C.N.S., m. Elizabeth Banton, and d.s.p.
3. John Nevill, a General in the Indian Army, who was killed 23 April, 1781, at Panwell, near Bombay, in the first Mahrata War.
1. Elizabeth Anne, m. 1st, Major Hayward St. Leger Gillman, by whom she had two sons. She m. 2ndly, Adm. Sir Henry Martin, Bart., Comptroller of the Navy.
2. Anna, m. Norcott d'Esterre, of Limerick, and had issue.

The eldest son,
MICHAEL PARKER, of Passage West, b. 1730; m. 23 Feb. 1761, Anne, dau. of Henry d'Esterre, of Castle Henry, co. Clare, and d. 16 Sept. 1791, leaving issue,
1. Harding, Capt. R.N., m. Catherine, dau. of John Skottowe, of Chesham Park, Bucks, Governor of St. Helena, and d. on service Dec. 1796. From him is descended the Rev. F. H. Parker, of Gleenbrook.
2. RICHARD NEVILLE, of whom presently.
3. William, m. Alicia, dau. of Thomas Townshend Somerville, of Castle Haven and Drishane, and was father of William d'Esterre, of Passage West, co. Cork, m. Sarah Dowman, and left issue,
 (1) Catherine Jane, m. 1st, her cousin, Richard Neville Parker (see below), and 2ndly, 22 Aug. 1900, Samuel Bright Lucas.
 (2) Mabella Anne d'Esterre.
 (3) Mary Townshend, m. J. A. Oakshott, M.D., and has one son, William Albert Neville.

Parker. THE LANDED GENTRY. 552

1. Lucia.
2. Eliza Anne, *m.* Thomas Boland, of Pembrook.
3. Ann, *m.* Jan. 1791, Benjamin Phipps, of Cork.
4. Judith, *m.* William Stammers, of Rock Castle, Innishannon.
5. Mabella, *m.* William Parker d'Esterre.
6. Dorcas.
7. Alicia.
8. Catharine Anne, *d.* 1869, aged 97.

The 2nd son,
RICHARD NEVILLE PARKER, of Passage West, Mayor of Cork 1828, *b.* 17 Jan. 1774; *m.* 1 Oct. 1795, Margaret, younger dau. of John Skottowe, of Chesham Park, Bucks, Governor of St. Helena, &c., and *d.* 30 July, 1832, leaving issue,
1. RICHARD NEVILLE, of whom presently.
2. William Skottowe, *m.* Amelia Hayley, and *d.s.p.*
3. Henry, *m.* Anne Cross, and had issue.
4. John, *m.* Jane Phillips.
5. Nicholas Skottowe, *d.s.p.*
6. Michael, settled in America.
1. Lucia, *m.* Corless Hawkes.
2. Margaret Skottowe, *m.* R. J. Kinsman.
3. Catharine, *m.* Charles Jackson.
4. Anne Langford, *m.* Joseph Reid, of New Zealand.
5. Sarah Honeywood Pollock, *m.* Herbert Gillman.
6. Eliza, *d.* 1840.

The eldest son,
RICHARD NEVILLE PARKER, of Passage West, *b.* 26 July, 1799; *m.* 15 Feb. 1824, Hannah Maria, eldest dau. of John George Newsom, of Cork, by whom he had issue,
1. Richard Neville, *m.* 1st, Henrietta, dau. of Thomas Savage French, of Marino, and 2ndly, Catherine Jane, dau. of William d'Esterre Parker (*see above*), and *d.s.p.*
2. JOHN GEORGE NEWSOM, of whom presently.
3. Thomas Wilson, *d.s.p.*
4. William Henry, *m.* Susan, dau. of Henry Ridgeway of Waterford, and has issue.
1. Anne Newsom, *m.* David Bruce Murray, and has issue.
2. Margaret Skottowe, *m.* Lucius Henry Spooner, son of Archdeacon Spooner, and has issue.
3. Mary Tisdall, *d.* aged 16.
4. Caroline Maria.

The 2nd son,
JOHN GEORGE NEWSOM PARKER, of Passage West, *b.* 5 Sept. 1830; *m.* 5 June, 1862, Sarah Johnson, eldest dau. of John William Topp, of Cork, and grand-dau. of John Topp, of Whitton, co. Salop, and *d.* 26 Jan. 1869, leaving issue,
1. NEVILLE SKOTTOWE, late of Passage West.
2. ST. JOHN WILLIAM TOPP, now of Passage West.
1. Elisabeth Topp, *m.* Surg.-Capt. R. E. Foott, of Cork, and has issue.
 Charles.
 Marjorie.
2. Ethel Hannah Newsom, *d. unm.* 24 June, 1906.

The elder son,
NEVILLE SKOTTOWE PARKER, of Passage West, co. Cork, LL.B. St. John's Coll. Camb. (1887), Barrister-at-Law, *b.* 1860; *d. unm.* 13 Aug. 1901, and was bur. at sea off the W. Coast of Africa. He was s. by his brother,

Seat—Waterview Passage West, co. Cork. Residence—Beech Holme, Curzon Park, Chester.

PARKER-HUTCHINSON. *See* HUTCHINSON.

PARSONS. *See* BURKE'S PEERAGE, ROSSE, E.

PATRICK OF DUNMINNING.

JOHN PATRICK, of Dunminning, co. Antrim, J.P., Capt. late 4th Batt. Royal Irish Rifles, *b.* 31 Oct. 1871; *m.* 15 June, 1897, Annie Florence, youngest dau. of Joseph Clarke Rutherfoord, of Bray, co. Wicklow, and has issue,

JOHN, *b.* 10 June, 1898.
Florence Amy, *b.* 4 April, 1900.

Lineage.—This family is of Scotch extraction, and descends from a younger branch of the Ayrshire Patricks, which joined the expedition to the North of Ireland (under Hugh Montgomery, of Braidstane, in 1606), where they subsequently settled.
JOHN PATRICK, *m.* 1770, Elizabeth Boyle, and *d.* 1773, leaving a son,

JOHN PATRICK, M.D., *m.* 10 Oct. 1795, Anne McKean, by whom (who *d.* 9 Oct. 1859) he had issue,
1. JOHN, of whom presently.
2. James Barnett, *d.* 13 Dec. 1878.
1. Isabella, *m.* 1813, John A. Brown, of Philadelphia; and *d.* 1819, leaving issue.
2. Anne, *d.* 20 Aug. 1860.   3. Eliza, *d.* 12 Dec. 1880.

Mr. Patrick *d.* 23 Sept. 1858, and was *s.* by his son,
JOHN PATRICK, of Dunminning, J.P., *b.* 28 June, 1802; *m.* 28 Jan. 1835, Grace, 4th dau. of William Gihon, of Hilhead, co. Antrim; and *d.* 23 March, 1879, having by her (who *d.* 1 June, 1891) had issue,
1. JOHN, of whom presently.
1. Rose, *d.* 16 Nov. 1861.
2. Isabella, *d. unm.* 31 Dec. 1898.   3. Margaret.
4. Anne, *m.* 1 March, 1871, Richard Davison, of Ballymena, and has issue.

The son,
JOHN PATRICK, of Dunminning, co. Antrim, J.P., *b.* 28 March, 1844; *m.* 6 Nov. 1869, Augusta Mary, dau. of John Davison, of Raceview, Broughshane, co. Antrim, and *d.* 29 June, 1894, leaving issue,
1. JOHN, now of Dunminning.
2. James Alexander, *b.* 21 June, 1876.
3. Norman Cohun, *b.* 13 Aug. 1878; *m.* 17 Aug. 1911, Nina Mary Adelaide only dau. of William Moore, K.C., M.P., of Moore Lodge, co. Antrim (*see that family*).
4. Malcolm William, *b.* 15 Aug. 1882.
1. Augusta Mary Grace, *b.* 19 Sept. 1870; *d.* 23 Jan. 1871.
2. Gertrude Emily, *b.* 5 March, 1874; *m.* 8 April, 1902, Rev. Arthur Thomas Webb (*see* WEBB *of Webbsborough*).
3. Grace Kathleen, *b.* 1 July, 1880.

Arms—Arg., a saltire engr. sa., between in chief a thistle and in base a trefoil slipped, both ppr., on a chief of the second three roses of the first. Crest—A dexter hand erect ppr., charged with a saltire sa., grasping a dagger also erect ppr. Motto—Ora et labora.

Seat—Gledheather (Dunminning), Glarryford, co. Antrim. Clubs—Sackville Street, Dublin; and Ulster, Belfast.

PAUL. *See* BURKE'S PEERAGE, PAUL, Bart.

PEACOCKE OF SKEVANISH.

WARREN THOMAS PEACOCKE, of Skevanish, Innishannon, co. Cork, late Capt. Rifle Brigade, *b.* 2 Oct. 1852; *m.* 19 June, 1888, Ethel Helen, 3rd dau. of Charles R. Fenwick, High Firs, Herts, and has issue,
1. WARREN JOHN RICHARD, *b.* 4 May, 1889.
2. Montagu Thomas, *b.* 19 Aug. 1891; *d.* 1910.
3. Michael Harry, *b.* 20 Oct. 1899.
1. Rachel Frederica de Roll, *b.* 29 April, 1897; *d.* 29 April, 1898.

Lineage.—GEORGE PEACOCKE, of Graige, co. Limerick, purchased an estate in the barony of Poble O'Brien, in that co., *temp.* CHARLES II, which was afterwards confirmed to him by the Crown under letters patent. He *m.* Aphra, sister of John Maunsell, of Ballyvorine, in the same co.; who *d.s.p.* 1678. By his will, lodged for probate 17 Feb. 1687, he devised all his estate to his nephew,
RICHARD PEACOCKE, of Graige, formerly of Rothwell, co. York, who *d.s.p.* By his will, dated 15 March, 3 WILLIAM III and MARY II, and proved 3 April, 1691, he settled all his estate on his brother,
JAMES PEACOCKE, of Graige and Cahir Etna, now Fort Etna, which latter place he leased to his step-son, Thomas Goodricke, 8 April, 1720. He *m.* Mrs. Elizabeth Goodricke, widow, and had issue,
1. Edmond, of Graige, his heir, *m.* Sept. 1718, Alice, dau. of Alderman Thomas Ponsonby, of Cork, and sister of Richard Ponsonby, of Crotto, co. Kerry, and *d.* 1734, leaving two sons, 1. James.   2. Samuel.
2. George, of Barntic, co. Clare, and afterwards of Graige, *m.* 1st (sett. dated 27 and 28 Sept. 1732), Mary, dau. of Joseph

Lavit, Alderman of the City of Cork, which lady d. 1744. He d. 1775, having had issue,
1. JOSEPH (Sir), of Barntic, who was created a bart. 24 Dec. 1802. Sir Joseph m. 1761, Elizabeth, only dau. of Thomas Cuffe, M.P., of Grange, co. Kilkenny, and d. 1; June, 1812, having had issue.
(1) NATHANIEL (Sir), 2nd bart. of Barntic, Lieut.-Col. in the Army, b. 3 Oct. 1769; m. 20 June, 1803, Henrietta, eldest dau. of Sir John Morris, Bart. of Claremont, co. Glamorgan, and by her (who d. 4 June, 1825) he left at his dec. 1 Nov. 1847, with two daus., Elizabeth Henrietta and Frances Emma (who d. 14 May, 1812), an only son,
JOSEPH FRANCIS (Sir) 3rd bart. of Barntic, b. 1 July, 1805; d.s.p., 1877.
(2) William (Rev.).
(1) Grace.
(2) Eliza, m. 1800, Capt. J. O'Beirne, brother of Thomas Lewis O'Beirne, D.D., Bishop of Meath; d. 19 July, 1851, aged 86.
(3) Philippa, d. 1842.
(4) Christiana Emma, m. 1797, Francis Gore, of Derrymore, co. Clare, and d. 14 July, 1855.
(5) Mary, m. Major-Gen. Daniel O'Meara.
(6) Alicia Anne, m. 1815, T. Lawrence, of Bristol.
(7) Georgina, killed by a fall from her horse 16 May, 1811.
2. Marmaduke, of Cork, Capt. in the Army, d.s.p. 1795.
3. William, of Llanfair, co. Anglesey, Col. of the Anglesey Militia, m. 1770, Emma, dau. of Col. William Jones, of Twyny, co. Carnarvon, and d.s.p.
4. Nathaniel, Lieut. R.N., d. in the East Indies.
Mr. Peacocke m. 2ndly, in 1746, Mary, dau. and heir of Thomas Sandford, of Sandford Court, co. Kilkenny, and by her (who d. 1778) had issue,
5. George, Capt. 7th Foot, killed in America.
1. Mary, b. 1748; m. Marmaduke Peacocke, her cousin.
2. Elizabeth, m. William Gardiner, M.D., of Armagh.
3. MARMADUKE, of whom hereafter.
4. William, living unm. 1773.
5. Septimus, of Fort Etna, s. under the will of his half-brother, Thomas Goodricke, dated 24 March, 1741. He was ancestor of the family of Peacocke of Fort Etna, now represented by Goodricke Thomas Peacocke, of Carraig na Greina co. Dublin, J.P. co. Limerick.
James Peacocke was dead in 1747, when his estates were in possession of his oldest son. His 3rd son,
MARMADUKE PEACOCKE, of London, d. at Hackney, co. Middlesex, 1773, leaving with other issue,
MARMADUKE, his successor.
Nancy, m. George Keating, of Moulton Park, co. Northampton.
The son,
MARMADUKE PEACOCKE, of London, m. his cousin, Mary, dau. of George Peacocke, of Barntic, co. Clare, and co-heir of her mother, Mary Sandford, only dau. and heir of Thomas Sandford, of Sandford Court, co. Kilkenny, and had issue,
1. Marmaduke Warren (Sir), K.C.H., K.T.S., a Gen. Officer, d.s.p.
2. George, m. 1st, Rachel, dau. of Sir John Dalling, Bart., which lady d.s.p. 1808, and 2ndly, Jemima, dau. of Lieut.-Col. J. Montagu Durnford, by whom he left at his decease, 1851, a son,
George Montagu Warren Sandford, of Reeves Hall, co. Essex, M.P. for Maldon, J.P. and D.L., M.A., b. 1821, Barrister-at-Law, who assumed by Royal Licence, 1866, the surname and arms of SANDFORD. He m. 1858, Augusta Mary (Reeves Hall, Colchester), dau. of Algernon Greville, Bath King of Arms (see BURKE's Peerage, WARWICK, E.), and d. 19 June, 1879, leaving issue,
(1) Francis Marmaduke Henry, Capt. late Gren. Guards, b. 1860; m. 10 May, 1886, Constance Georgiana, dau. of William George Craven (see BURKE's Peerage), and has issue.
(1) Charlotte Mary. (2) Alice Rose.
(3) Blanche Caroline. (4) Caroline Amabel.
3. Edward, m. Amelia, dau. of Sir T. H. Apreece, Bart.
4. RICHARD, of whom hereafter.
5. Stephen, Lieut.-Col. Scots Fusilier Guards, m. Louisa, dau. and co-heir of Ponsonby Tottenham, M.P., and had issue.
6. Thomas, Gen. in the Army, K.T.S.
7. John, an Officer Scots Fusilier Guards, dec.
The 4th son,
RICHARD PEACOCKE, Vice-Admiral, R.N., m. Martha Louisa, dau. of George Dacre, of Marwell Hall, co. Southampton and had issue,
1. WARREN WILLIAM RICHARD, who s. him.
2. George, Lieut.-Gen. in the Army, d. Sept. 1895.
Admiral Peacocke d. 1846. His eldest son,
WARREN WILLIAM RICHARD PEACOCKE, of Efford Park, co. Southampton, b. 1822; m. 1st, 1850, Cornelia Frederica de Roll, youngest dau. of Rev. Frederick Shallett Lomax, of Netley Park, Surrey, and by her (who d. 1873) had issue,
1. WARREN THOMAS, now of Skevanish, and late of Efford Park.
2. George Richard, b. 1855; d. 1910.
1. Louise Fanny, m. Jules Duplessis, of Newtown Park, Lymington.
2. Emily Augusta, m. Capt. S. Frewen, of 16th Lancers.
3. Maud Frances, m. Harry Pomeroy Bond, of Owermoigne Conibe, Dorchester.
Mr. Peacocke m. 2ndly, 30 Sept. 1875, Georgina Theresa Ellen, eldest dau. of Frederick Richard West, of Ruthin Castle, eldest son of Hon. Frederick West, and grandson of John, 2nd Earl de la Warr. He d. 1877, when he was s. by his son.

Arms—Quarterly, or and az., over all four lozenges conjoined in cross, between as annulets, all countercharged. **Crest**—A cockatrice, wings erect, vert. **Motto**—Vincit veritas.
Seat—Skevanish, Innishannon, co. Cork. **Clubs**—Naval and Military, and Boodle's.

PELHAM-CLINTON. See CLINTON.

PEMBERTON-PIGOTT. See PIGOTT.

PENNEFATHER OF RATHSALLAGH.

FREDERICK WILLIAM PENNEFATHER, of Rathsallagh, co. Wicklow, M.A., LL.D., Barrister-at-Law Lincoln's Inn, and King's Inn, formerly Judge of the Supreme Court of New Zealand, b. 29 April, 1852; s. his brother 1904.

Lineage.—The first of this family who settled in Ireland was

MATTHEW PENNEFATHER, a Cornet in the Army, son of Abraham Pennefather, and younger brother of Abraham Pennefather, of Hanbury-on-the-Hill, co. Stafford. He acquired by patent, 1666, the estates of Clonegoose, Ballylanigan, &c., co. Tipperary; he m. and had (with another son, John, of Compsey) a son and heir,
MATTHEW PENNEFATHER, m. Levina, dau. of William Kingsmill, M.P., of Ballybeg Abbey, co. Cork (see KINGSMILL of Hermitage Park), heir to the estates of Balyowen, afterwards New Park, co. Tipperary, and left three sons,
1. KINGSMILL, his heir.
2. Matthew, Lieut.-Col. in Gen. Sabine's Regt. in Queen ANNE's wars, gallantly distinguished at Oudenarde, subsequently returned to Ireland, and was appointed Auditor of the Irish Revenue in the reign of GEORGE I. and was High Sheriff co. Tipperary 1712, and M.P. for Cashel from 1716 until his decease 1733. Col. Pennefather m. 1697, Catherine, dau. of Sir Randal Beresford, 2nd bart., of Coleraine, and left four daus.
1. Mary, m. William Palliser, of Rathfarnham.
2. Levina, d. unm., 14 May, 1734.
3. Dorothea, m. William Williams, of Mount Williams, co. Meath.
4. Elizabeth, m. 1735, Alexander, 5th Earl of Antrim.
3. William, of Marlow, d. Oct. 1772 (see PENNEFATHER of Marlow).
The eldest son,
KINGSMILL PENNEFATHER, of New Park, Col. of Militia, M.P. for Cashel, and afterwards for Tipperary, High Sheriff 1703 and 1708, m. his cousin, the only dau. and heir of John Pennefather of Compsey, and had (with four daus., the eldest, Mary, m. Hamilton Lowe, of Roc's Green, co. Tipperary; the 2nd, Lavina, m. Sir John St. Leger, Baron of the Exchequer; the 3rd m. Capt. Prince; and the 4th m. Rev. Francis Gore) six sons,
1. RICHARD, his heir.
2. Thomas, on whom the Compsey estates, together with Kilshane and Ballyneira, were settled 1730. He m. in that year, Frances Goodwin, of Island Bridge, near Dublin, and left at his decease, 1764 (with two daus., one of whom, Frances, m. Thomas Oldis, of Ballylanigan), a son,
John Bolton, m. his cousin, the dau. of John Pennefather, of Poulevarla, and d. 12 Feb. 1812, aged 77, leaving (with two daus., Elizabeth and Anne, m. William Latham, of Ballyshenan), one son,
Thomas, of Ballylanigan, Mayor of Cashel, m. Anne, dau. of John Hunt, of Moyne, and d. 25 Dec. 1828, having had issue,
1. William, of 30th Regt., distinguished in India, the Peninsula, and Egypt, and at Waterloo, m. 2 Sept. 1822, Susan, dau. of Anthony O'Dwyer, of Cashel. d.v.p., leaving an only son, William, of Ballylanigan, J.P., b. 16 Aug. 1823; m. 16 Nov. 1852, Kate, 2nd dau. of Richard Scott, Solicitor, and left issue,
a. William, b. 19 Sept. 1853; d.
b. Richard, b. 22 July, 1855; d.
c. John, b. 20 May, 1858; d.
d. George, b. 15 April, 1862, Capt. China Navigation Co.; m. Mary, dau. of M. I. J. Breen, Insp.-Gen. of Hospitals and Fleets, Royal Navy, and has issue,
(a) Thomas Francis.

(b) Ian Kingsmill.
(a) Mary. (b) Kathleen.
a. Mary Susan, m. I. J. Breen, Insp.-Gen. of Hospitals and Fleets, and has issue.
b. Kathleen Ada Susan Mary Aloyisia, m. Col. A. G. Watson, 30th East Lancs. Regt., and has issue.
c. Helen m Joseph Meldon, of Coolname, Athenry, co. Galway.
d. Susan (Daisy), m. Major John J. Cronin, Indian Army, Deputy Commissioner, Burma.
e. Edith
2. Kingsmill, an officer in the Army, d. in the Peninsula.
3. Richard, of Kilshane, m. Miss Going, dau. of Rev. John Going, and had issue, Thomas Bolton, m. Elizabeth Smithwick.
4. Thomas, Mayor of Cashel.
1. Cherry, m. John Smithwick, and had issue.
3. William, of Carrigeen. 4. John, of Poulevarla.
5. Matthew. 6. Frederick, d. 1741.
Mr. Pennefather d. 1735, and was s. by his eldest son,
RICHARD PENNEFATHER of New Park, High Sheriff co. Tipperary, 1724, M.P. for Cashel, d. 11 Oct. 1777; m. Charity, 3rd dau. of Alderman John Graham, of Platten, co. Meath, and had two sons and three daus.,
1. KINGSMILL, High Sheriff co. Tipperary, 1750, M.P. for Cashel 1753, 1761, and 1771, m. 26 June, 1754, Hon. Mary Lysaght, dau. of John, Lord Lisle, and dying v.p. 2 May, 1771, left issue,
1. RICHARD, successor to his grandfather, of New Park, High Sheriff, 1790, M.P. for Cashel, Lieut.-Col. of the Tipperary Militia, m. 1st, 1782, Anna, only dau. and heir of Matthew Jacob, of St. Johnstown, co. Tipperary; 2ndly, 1801, Penelope, relict of John Jacob Gledstanes, of Annesgift, co. Tipperary; and 3rdly, Elizabeth, dau. of Nicholas Mansergh, of Grenane. Lieut.-Col. Pennefather d. May, 1831, and by the 1st wife only he had issue to survive youth, three sons and five daus.,
(1) KINGSMILL, Lieut.-Col. of the Tipperary, Militia, High Sheriff 1819, who d. in the lifetime of his father, 1819. He m. 1st, Maria, dau. of Burton Persse, of co. Galway, by whom he had one dau.,
1. Anna, m. Stephen Moore, of Barne, co. Tipperary.
He m. 2ndly, 1816, Grace, dau. of Thomas Barton, of Grove, and had two daus.,
2. Mary, d. unm. 1895.
3. Catherine, m. 17 Aug. 1840, Hon. Henry Alexander Savile, 2nd son of John, 3rd Earl of Mexborough, and d. 1 Jan. 1843, having by him (who d. 1 March, 1850) had issue, William, Capt. late 9th Lancers, b. 8 Oct. 1841; m. 1865, Emily, dau. of Capt. Delme Seymour Davies, of Highmead, and d. 1903, leaving issue. She d. 1909 (see BURKE'S *Peerage*, MEXBOROUGH, E.).
(2) MATHEW, of New Park, co. Tipperary, J.P. and D.L., High Sheriff 1826, and formerly M.P. for Cashel, b. 1784; m. 1814, his cousin Anna, 4th dau. of Daniel Conner, of Ballybrickem, co. Cork. He d. 1858, leaving issue,
1. Daniel Francis, b. 1816. 2. Richard.
1. Mary. 2. Anna.
(3) WILLIAM, of Lakefield, m. 1819, Charity Maria, dau. of Richard Long, of Longfield, co. Tipperary, and d. 4 Feb. 1872, leaving issue,
1. RICHARD, of Lakefield, J.P., b. 19 Jan. 1826; m. 24 Feb. 1857, Emma Elizabeth, dau. of Robert Darwin Vaughton, of Ashfurlong House, co. Warwick; and d. 1876, leaving issue, 1. WILLIAM VAUGHTON, of Lakefield, b. 14 Jan. 1862; m. 17 Nov. 1891, Louisa Mary, eldest dau. of the late William John Bankes, of Winstanley Hall, and has, with other issue, Richard, b. 1893;
2. Richard Dymoke, b. 1805; 1. Maria Emma; 2. Harriet Lavinia; 3. Anna Louisa.
2. William. 3. Matthew, d. 1859.
4. William John Copley Lyndhurst, d. 1865.
(1) Dorothea, m. 1st, Richard Lockwood, of Cashel, and 2ndly, 1827, Thomas Sadleir, of Castletown, co. Tipperary.
(2) Mary Anne, m. Lieut.-Col. John Lindsay, of co. Tyrone.
(3) Catherine, m. Col. Owen Lloyd, of Rockville, co. Roscommon.
(4) Margaret, m. Ambrose Going, of Ballyphilip, co. Tipperary.
(5) Eliza, m. 1st, Major Acheson Montgomery Moore, of Garvagh, co. Tyrone, by whom she had one dau., and 2ndly, Sir John Judkin Fitzgerald, 2nd bart. of Lisheen.
2. John (Rev.), D.D., Rector of St. John's, Newport, co. Tipperary, m. Elizabeth, dau. of Major Perceval, and had issue,
(1) Kingsmill, Major Limerick Militia, m. 1st, Frances, eldest dau. of Major Townsend Monckton Hall, of the 28th Regt., and had one son, John, and four daus., Elizabeth, Fanny, Caroline, and Clare. He m. 2ndly, 1842, Jane Catherine Patrica, eldest dau. of Thomas de Grenier de Fonblanque, K.H., formerly H.M.'s Consul-General and Chargé d'Affaires in Servia, and grand-dau. of Sir Jonah Barrington, Knt., Judge of the Admiralty in Ireland, by whom (who d. 6 May, 1886) he had issue,
1. Charles Edward de Fonblanque, b. 23 June, 1848, Controller-General of Prisons, Queensland, m. 2 Feb. 1881, Mary Rose, dau. of James Mackay Seward, of Somerset Park, Melbourne, Victoria, and has issue,
1. John William Seward, b. 29 Sept. 1883.
2. Charles Edward de Fonblanque, b. 3 June, 1885.
3. Edward Kingsmill, b. 9 July, 1898.
2. de Fonblanque, J.P. Herefordshire (*Kinnersley Castle, Hereford*), b. 1856; m. 8 April, 1886, Madeline, dau. of Sir Robert Prescott Stewart, Mus.D.

1. Ruth, m. 31 July, 1879, William Nimmo, of Liverpool.
(2) William Westby, Lieut. R.N., m. Elizabeth, dau. of William Harding.
(3) John Lysaght (Sir), K.C.B., Grand Cross of the Legion of Honour, and Commander of the Order of St. Maunce and St. Lazarus of Sardinia, Gen. in the Army, Col. 22nd Foot, and Commander of the Forces at Malta, distinguished in India and the Crimea, m. 1830, Margaret, eldest dau. of John Carr, of Mountrath, and d. 1872.
(4) Joseph Lysaght, Barrister-at-Law, m. Elizabeth, dau. of — Rea, of Barnwood, co. Gloucester, and had one dau., Julia.
(5) Robert Perceval, Lieut. and Adjutant in the 3rd Regt. of Native Cavalry in Bengal, m. Elizabeth Benson, and by her (who d. 28 March, 1887) had one son, Henry, late Capt. 41st Regt., m. 23 Oct. 1860, Margaret Luchesa Jane Maria, widow of Col. Temple West, and only dau. and heir of Sir John George Reeve de la Pole, 8th bart., of Shute House, and d. 9 Aug. 1888, aged 97; and a dau., Laura, m. Dr. George Rae, Bengal Medical Establishment.
(1) Ann, m. William Ryan, of Ballymackeogh, co. Tipperary, and has issue.
(2) Mary Charity, m. 15 May, 1809, Vice-Admiral Henry Vansittart, and had issue (*see* VANSITTART *of Bisham Abbey*).
(3) Clare, m. Thomas Evans, of Asbore, co. Tipperary, Lieut. R.N.
(4) Laura, m. 1840, William Stumbles Philips, of Mount Philips.
3. William, M.P. for Cashel from 1783 to 1797; he was for thirty-eight years Revenue Collector of Athlone and Cork, and for ten years Surveyor-General in Ireland; he m. Frances, 2nd dau. of Francis Nisbett, of Derrycarne, co. Leitrim, and had issue,
(1) William, H.E.I.C.S., d. Aug. 1826.
(2) RICHARD DANIEL, of Kilbracken, co. Leitrim, J.P. and D.L., Col. (retired) East Kent Militia, b. 13 Aug. 1818, *dec.*; m. 7 Oct. 1868, Hon. Sarah Anna de Montmorency, dau. of Very Rev. Hervey, Viscount Montmorres, and had issue,
1. William de Montmorency, b. 27 Aug. 1869.
1. Anna de Montmorency, m. 26 Sept. 1900, Col. George Fleming, C.B., LL.D., of Higher Leigh, Combe Martin, N. Devon. He d. 13 April, 1901.
2. Mary Eva de Montmorency.
(1) Jane, m. Daniel Conner, of Ballybricken, co. Cork, and d. 1869.
(2) Margaret, m. Richard Warren, M.D., of Lisgoold, son of Rev. Robert Warren, of Crookstown, co. Cork.
(3) Elizabeth, m. Phineas Bury, of Curragh Bridge, co. Limerick, and Little Island, co. Cork.
(4) Frances Mary, m. Col. Arthur St. George Herbert Stepney, C.B., Coldstream Guards, and d. 1848.
1. Mary, m. 6 Feb. 1779, Daniel Conner, of Ballybricken, co. Cork, and had issue.
2. Catherine, m. Daniel Mansergh, of Cashel, and had issue.
3. Margaret, m. Robert Warren, son of Sir Robert Warren, 1st bart. of Warrenscourt, and had issue.
2. William, of Knockevan, Major 13th Light Dragoons, M.P. for Cashel 1771, m. Ellen, eldest dau. of the Ven. Edward Moore, D.D., of Mooresfort, co. Tipperary, Archdeacon of Emily, and d. Nov. 1819, having had two sons,
1. Richard, one of the Barons of the Exchequer in Ireland, b. 1773; m. Jane, eldest dau. of John Bennet, Justice of the King's Bench in Ireland, and had three sons and three daus.,
(1) Richard, of Knockeevan, co. Tipperary, J.P., D.L., High Sheriff 1848, Under-Secretary for Ireland, m. 1836, Lady Emily Arabel Georgiana Butler, dau. of Richard, 1st Earl of Glengall, and d. 1849, leaving issue, Richard, b. 13 May, 1837, d. 1863, and Evelyn Henrietta, m. 2 March, 1869, Arthur Philip, 6th Earl Stanhope, who d. 19 April, 1905, leaving issue. His widow m. 1852, Col. H. A. Hankey.
(2) John, Q.C., m. 8 Aug. 1842, Elizabeth Jemima, dau. of MajorHon. Edward Mullins (*see* BURKE'S *Peerage*, VENTRY, B.). He d. April, 1855, having had, with other issue,
1. (A.) Richard (Sir), C.B., J.P. Essex, Receiver Metropolitan Police District 1883–1909 (*Little Waltham Hall, near Chelmsford*), b. 1845; m. 1867, Thomasina C., dau. of T. C. Savory.
(3) William, b. 1816; d. 30 April, 1873; m. 16 Sept. 1847, Catherine, dau. of Admiral the Hon. James King (*see* BURKE'S *Peerage*, KINGSTON, E.).
(1) Ellen, m. John Cromie.
(2) Susan, m. Rev. Robert Jessop.
(3) Dorothea, m. Somerset Richard, Lord Farnham, and d. 30 Nov. 1861.
2. EDWARD (the Right Hon.), Lord Chief Justice of the Court of Queen's Bench in Ireland (of whom we treat).
1. Mary, m. John Croker, of Ballinagard.
2. Eliza, m. 12 July, 1751, Morgan O'Meara, of Toomavara.
3. Charity, m. 26 Feb. 1763, Samuel Alleyn, of Golden.
Mr. Pennefather d. 11 Oct. 1777. His grandson,
THE RIGHT HON. EDWARD PENNEFATHER, Lord Chief Justice of Ireland, one of the most eminent and learned lawyers of his time, 2nd son of Major William Pennefather, 13th Light Dragoons, of Knockevan, co. Tipperary, M.P. for Cashel by Ellen his wife, m. 6 Jan. 1806, Susan, eldest dau. of the late John Darby, of Markly, Sussex, and of Leap Castle, King's Co., and d. 6 Sept. 1847, having by her (who d. 6 April, 1862) left issue,
1. EDWARD, late of Rathsallagh.
2. William (Rev.), Rector of Callan, co. Kilkenny, b. 1811; m. 1846, Anne, eldest dau. and co-heir of the late Gen. Hon. John

Brodrick (youngest son of the 3rd Viscount Midleton), by Anne his wife, dau. of Robert Graham, of Fintry, and had issue,
1. Edward Graham, Lieut.-Col. Inniskilling Dragoons, *b.* 1850, *m.* Mary, dau. of Rev. J. L. Crompton, and has issue,
  (1) William, Lieut. R.N., *b.* 1887.
  (2) John Roderick, *b.* 1890.
  (3) Edward Matthew, *b.* 1895.
  (1) Mary.
  1. Mary Alice.   2. Margaret Susan, *d.* 1905.
  3. Florence Anne, *d. unm.* 5 Dec. 1907.
  4. Ellen Isabella.   5. Agnes Elizabeth.
3. John Edward, *d.* 19 May, 1842.
4. Richard Theodore, Auditor-Gen. of Ceylon, *m.* 1851, Ariana Margaretta, dau. of Col. Shore, and *d.* 1865, leaving two sons,
  1. Edward George, dec.
  2. Richard, *d.* 8 Jan. 1908.
1. Anne, *m.* 1831, the late Wade Browne, of Monkton Farleigh, Wilts, and had issue.
2. Ellen, *m.* 1836, James Thomas O'Brien, D.D., late Bishop of Ossory and Ferns 1842-75, and had issue. She *d.* 30 Aug. 1906.
3. Susan, *m.* 1840, the late Richard Hall, of Finden Place, Sussex, and 92, Eaton Place, London, and had issue.
4. Katherine.
5. Mary, *d.* 8 May, 1909 ; *m.* 5 Aug. 1845, George Le Hunte, of Artramont, co. Wexford, D.L. (Le Hunt *d.* 1891), and had issue, Sir George Ruthven, K.C.M.G. (*see Knighlage*), Governor of Trinidad ; and three daus. (*see* LE HUNTE *of Artramont*).
6. Dorothea, *m.* 1850, the late James Thomas, 4th Earl of Courtown, and *d.* 1859, leaving issue.
The eldest son,
EDWARD PENNEFATHER, of Rathsallagh, Grangecon, co. Wicklow, Barrister-at-Law, Q.C., J.P. and D.L., *b.* 22 Sept. 1809 ; *m.* 30 March, 1841, Harriet, 3rd dau. of the late Richard Hall, of Copped Hall, Totteridge, co. Hertford, and *d.* 22 Feb. 1895, having by her (who *d.* 7 March, 1868) had issue,
1. Edward Wade, *b.* 4 May, 1843 ; *d.* 16 Sept. 1846.
2. Arthur Willoughby, *b.* 19 Feb. 1847 ; *d.* 6 Sept. 1863.
3. CHARLES EDWARD, late of Rathsallagh.
4. FREDERICK WILLIAM, now of Rathsallagh.
1. Susan Mary, *m.* 1862, John Gathorne Wood, eldest son of John Wood, of Thedden Grange, co. Southampton (*see that family*), and *d.* 18 Dec. 1894, leaving issue, two daus.
The 3rd son,
CAPT. CHARLES EDWARD PENNEFATHER, of Rathsallagh, co. Wicklow, late 4th Queen's Own Hussars, J.P., High Sheriff 1890, *b.* 1 May, 1849. He *d.* 4 Dec. 1904, being *s.* by his brother.
Arms—Per fesse or and gu. a bend erm.   *Crest*—A lion sejant arg., sustaining an oval shield per fesse or and gu., charged with a bend erm.   *Mottoes*—I abyde my tyme ; Vivite fortes.
Seat—Rathsallagh, Colbinstown, co. Wicklow.

PENNEFATHER OF MARLOW.

RICHARD PENNEFATHER LLOYD PENNEFATHER, of Marlow, co. Tipperary, J.P., *b.* 1863 ; *m.* 1903, Mary, dau. of Ven. Edward Gabbett, Archdeacon of Limerick, and has issue,
1. KINGSMILL, *b.* 1904.   2. Edward, *b.* 1905.
3. George Lionel, *b.* 1907.   4. Aubrey, *b.* 1908.
1. Emily, *b.* 1911.
Lineage.—The family seated at Marlow descends from William, 3rd son of Matthew Pennefather, of Newpark, who *m.* Lavinia Kingsmill (*see* PENNEFATHER *of Rathsallagh*). This
WILLIAM PENNEFATHER, of Marlow, *d.* Oct. 1772 ; *m.* 1734, Anne, dau. of Lovelace Taylor, of Noan, co. Tipperary, by whom he had two sons,
1. THOMAS, his successor.
2. John, whose only son, Thomas, *s.* to Marlow at the decease of his uncle.
The elder THOMAS PENNEFATHER, of Marlow, dying unmarried, was *s.* by his nephew,
THOMAS PENNEFATHER, of Marlow, *m.* Nov. 1783, Mary, dau. of Ven. Edward Moore, of Mooresfort, co. Tipperary, Archdeacon of Emly, and *d.* 1825, leaving three sons and a dau.,
1. EDWARD, his successor.
2. Thomas, of Maryville, Cashel, *m.* 1818, Mary, dau. of Vere Dawson Hunt of Cappagh, co. Tipperary (*see* HUNT *of Ballisinode*), and had issue,
  1. Thomas (Rev.), Rector of Kiltennell, co. Carlow, Canon of Leighlin, *b.* 1823 ; *m.* 1859, Catherine, dau. of Rev. Henry Preston Elrington, D.D., and *d.* 15 Jan. 1909, having had issue,
    (1) Thomas Henry, *b.* 1861.
    (2) William De Vere, *b.* 1870 ; *m.* dau. of Richard J. Kinkead, whose issue,
      (1) Isabella Mary.
      (2) Charlotte Sophia.
      (3) Ellen Emily Janet.
    1. Frances Mary Dorothy.
  2. Anna, *m.* Col. Hunt.
  3. Matthew, who *m.* and left a son,
    Richard, of Wilford, who *m.* and has issue, a son and 2 daus.,
      (1) Richard, of Wilford, *m.* Mary, dau. of Capt. George Pennefather (*see below*).
        (1) Georgina, *m.* John Millett, of Willmount, co. Tipperary.
        (2) Emily.
    1. Ellen, *m.* Rev. Hugh Brady Hulcatt.
The eldest son,
EDWARD PENNEFATHER, of Marlow, *m.* 1824 Mary, dau. of Daniel Mansergh, of Cashel, and had issue,
1. THOMAS JOHN, of whom hereafter.
2. Daniel, *m.* Miss Kerr, and *d.* 1894, leaving five sons, settled in Australia.
3. Edward, *d. unm.*
4. George, Capt., *m.* Miss Kildahill, and has issue,
  A son,
  Mary, *m.* Richard Pennefather, of Wilford (*see ante*).
5. Nicholas, Col., *m.* and *d.s. p.*
The eldest son,
THOMAS JOHN PENNEFATHER, of Marlow, *b.* 1827 ; *m.* 1859, Catherine, dau. of Richard Pennefather Lloyd (and grand-dau. of Lieut.-Col. Owen Lloyd, of Rockville, co. Roscommon), and *d.* 1892, leaving issue,
1 RICHARD PENNEFATHER LLOYD, now of Marlow.
1. Augusta, *d.* aged 11.
2. Adeline, *m.* Arthur William Radbourne.
3. Hortense Mary, *m.* 1894, Hugh Hamon Massy, of Riverdale, co. Limerick (*see* BURKE'S *Peerage*, MASSY, B.).
Arms—As Pennefather of Rathsallagh.
Seat—Marlow, Goold's Cross.

PENROSE OF WOOD HILL.

JAMES EDWARD PENROSE, M.V.O., of Wood Hill, co. Cork, J.P. cos. Cork, Meath and Waterford ; *b.* 15 Feb. 1850 ; *m.* 30 Dec. 1880, Ethel Charlotte, dau. of Sir John Joscelyn Coghill, 4th bart., and has issue,
1. JOSCELYN DENNIS, *b.* 1882.
2. Nevill Coghill, *b.* 1884 ; *m.* 29 April, 1909, Nellie, elder dau. of late Alfred Clarkson Osler, of Fallowfield, Edgbaston.
3. Evelyn Cooper, *b.* 1885.
1. Katharine St. Aubyn.
2. Ethel Mary Judith Yorke.
3. Honor Ashley Pettitot.
Mr. Penrose is the eldest son of the late Rev. John Dennis Penrose, of Wood Hill (who *d.* 4 Feb. 1894), younger brother of the late Robert Uniacke Penrose-FitzGerald, of Corkbeg and Lisquinlan (*see* BURKE'S *Peerage*, UNIACKE-PENROSE-FITZGERALD, Bart.). They were sons of James Penrose, of Wood Hill (who *d.* 19 April, 1845), and grandsons of Cooper Penrose (*see* PENROSE-WELSTED *of Ballywalter*).
Lineage.—See PENROSE-WELSTED *of Ballywalter*.
Seat—Wood Hill, Cork. *Residence*—Lismore Castle, Lismore, co. Waterford. *Club*—Kildare Street, Dublin.

PENROSE OF LEHANE.

The late WILLIAM HENRY PENROSE, of Low Park, Dedham, Essex, and Lehane, co. Cork, J.P. cos. Essex and Suffolk, *b.* 1810 ; *m.* 1st, 16 July, 1840, Hon. Georgiana Isabella, youngest dau. of John, 1st Lord Keane, G.C.B., G.C.H. (*see* BURKE'S *Peerage and Baronetage*), which lady *d.* 14 April, 1854, leaving issue,
1. HENRY FRANCIS KEANE.
He *m.* 2ndly, 1856, Louise, dau. of John Hyde, of Castle Hyde, co. Cork, which lady *d.s.p.* 1857. He *m.* 3rdly, 1858, Ann Agnes, eldest dau. of Charles Lillingstone, of The Chantry, Ipswich, which lady *d.* 13 May, 1860, leaving one dau.,
1. Elizabeth Harriet Anne Agnes.
He *m.* 4thly, 1863, ELIZABETH WATHERSTON (now of Lehane), youngest dau. of the late Capt. Robert Tait, R.N., of Pirn, Midlothian, and Manderston, Berwickshire, and *d.* 1896, having had issue,
2. William Watherston, *b.* 29 Oct. 1863.
3. Robert Tait, *b.* 29 March, 1865.
4. Edward Samuel, *b.* 13 March, 1868.
5. Arthur Cruden, *b.* 4 Nov. 1870 ; *d.* Dec. 1884.
6. John Ernest, *b.* 18 Nov. 1872.
The late Mr. Penrose was the only son of Samuel Penrose, who *d.* 1811, and Elizabeth his wife (who *m.* 2ndly, Sir Richard Keane, Bart., and *d.* 1842), dau. of Richard Sparrow, of Oaklands, and grandson of William Penrose (*see* PENROSE-WELSTED *of Ballywalter*).
Lineage.—*See* PENROSE-WELSTEAD *of Ballywalter*.
Residence—1, Eton Terrace, Edinburgh.

PENROSE OF RIVERVIEW.

ROBERT WILLIAM HENRY PENROSE, of Riverview, Ferrybank, and Seaville, Tramore, co. Waterford, b. 1827, d. 22 August, 1911; m. 1872, Frances Alice, dau. of the late Rev. William Sandford, M.A., Trin. Coll. Dublin, Rector of Clonmel, Canon of Rossduff and Chancellor of Lismore, and Susan Alice his wife, eldest dau. of John Lyster, of Ballymeelish, and Norefields, Abbeyleix, Queen's Co., J.P., and has issue,

1. WILLIAM ROBERT, Capt. late Waterford Artillery, J.P. cos. Waterford and Kilkenny (Belline, Piltown, co. Kilkenny), b. 1873; m. 1899, Isabel Montserrat Mary, dau. of Edward Nevill, of Bawnmore, New Ross, co. Wexford, and Eleanor his wife, dau. of Alexander Colles, J.P., of Milmount, co. Kilkenny, and has issue,
   1. Robert William Edward, b. 1909.
   1. Frances Isabel Susan Eleanor.
   2. Beatrix Willie.
2. HENRY HERBERT, Lieut. Royal Naval Reserve, b. 1874.
3. Arthur John b. 1875; d. 1892.
4. Edward Alick, b. 1877.
5. John Samuel Sandford, Lieut. R.N., b. 1879; m. 1910, Irène Hester, eldest dau. of Henry Joshua Smith, of Pinehurst, Cape Colony, and Dorathea, his wife, dau. of John le Sueur, of Rosedale Cape Town.
   1. Mabel Frances, d. 30 Sept. 1911; m. 1904, Rev. Edward Nevill, B.A., B.D., Trin. Coll. Dublin, Rector of Fenagh, co. Carlow, eldest son of Edward Nevill, of Bawnmore, New Ross, co. Wexford, and Eleanor his wife, and has one dau.,
     Rhoda Frances.
2. Susan Alice.   3. Sara Elizabeth.
4. Frances Amelia.   5. Emily Kathleen.

Mr. R. W. H. Penrose is the eldest son of the late Capt. Jacob Penrose, 33rd Regt., of Adelphi, Waterford, and Seaville, Tramore, co. Waterford, and Sarah Anne his wife, dau. of Robert Cooke, and grandson of William Penrose (see PENROSE-WELSTED of Ballywalter).

Lineage.—See PENROSE-WELSTED of Ballywalter.
Seat—Riverview, Ferrybank, and Seaville, Tramore, co. Waterford.

PENROSE-WELSTED. See WELSTED.

PEPPER OF BALLYGARTH.

CHARLES PEPPER, of Ballygarth Castle, co. Meath, J.P. and D.L., High Sheriff 1887, Hon. Col. and Lieut.-Col. late Comm. Royal Meath Regt., 5th Batt. Leinster Regt., M.A. Trin. Coll. Camb., b. 1 Nov. 1845; s. 1884.

Lineage.—CAPT. GEORGE PEPPER obtained, 1666, a confirmation of a previous grant of Ballygarth, and other lands, co. Meath, he was J.P. for that co. 1662, High Sheriff 1670, and also a Commissioner. By Hannah his wife, he had issue,
1. SIMEON, of whom presently.
2. Gilbert, of Dublin, m. 1st, a dau. of Justus Otgher, a wealthy Turkey Merchant in London, and 2ndly, Evelyn, dau. of Daniel Parke, Governor and Admiral of the Leeward and Caribbee Islands. By the latter, who took out administration to her husband 30 Dec. 1742 (he d. in 1736), he had issue,
   1. Parke Pepper, Lieut.-Col. 49th Foot, m. twice, and d. 1777. By the 1st wife he had no issue; by his 2nd he had (with other issue),
     Samuel, m. Ann, dau. of — Satur, and had issue, one son and four daus.,
       1. Parke, Lieut. 49th Foot, m. Miss English, and had an only child,
         Jane Evelyn, m. 1794, Simon Whyte.
       1. Anne, m. Dr. Maule, of Leicester.
       2. Evelyn, m. Senior Davis.
       3. Jane, m. 21 Jan. 1775, John Pittar.
       4. Charity, m. Arthur Richard Neville.
   A dau., m. 1st, Major John Plunknett, who d. 1 Jan. 1758; and 2ndly, — Dixon.
   2. George Pepper.
3. John, a Major-Gen., Col. Comm. Pepper's Belted Dragoons, now the 8th Royal Irish Hussars, after the fall of Brigadier-Gen. Killigrew at the battle of Almanza, 25 April, 1707, M.P. for Oban 1715. His will is dated 12 Oct. 1725, and was proved 1 Jan. 1725-26. His only child,
   Hannah Pepper, m. Rev. Ossory Medlicott, Rector of St. George's, Hanover Square.
1. Susannah, m. Brabazon Moore, of Ardee, son of the Hon. Randle Moore, and grandson of Charles, 2nd Viscount Drogheda.
2. Hannah, m. Francis Holder.
3. Mary.

The eldest son,
SIMEON PEPPER, of Ballygarth, was a Commissioner for Meath, under 10 WILLIAM III. cap. 3, to collect the sum charged on that co.; his d.v.p.; his will is dated 18 Nov. 1701, and was proved 5 Dec. following; he m. 15 Aug. 1688, Rose, dau. of the Hon. Oliver Lambart, son of 1st Earl of Cavan, and by her (who m. 2ndly, Christopher Nicholson, of Balrath, co. Meath, and d. 9 Dec. 1737) had issue,
1. GEORGE, of whom presently.   2. Simon.
3. Lambart, m. 1st, Nov. 1730, Jane, dau. of Thomas Otway, of Castle Otway, co. Tipperary, and by her had issue,
   1. George, of Knockalton, co. Tipperary, m. Aug. 1759, Catherine, dau. of Maunsell Andrews, of Millbrook, co. Tipperary, and sister of John Andrews, of Firmount, and d.s.p.
   2. Theobald, whose only child (by his wife Elizabeth Westropp, of Curraghbridge, co. Limerick),
     Lydia Pepper, m. Michael Roberts, of Kilmoney, co. Cork.
   3. Thomas, Major 14th Light Dragoons, afterwards of Laughton, King's Co., m. Mary, dau. of John Ryder, D.D., Archbishop of Tuam, and had a son,
     Thomas Ryder, of Laughton, High Sheriff of King's Co. 1792, b. 1771; m. Anne, dau. of John Bloomfield, of Newport, co. Tipperary, and sister of Benjamin, 1st Lord Bloomfield, but had no issue.
   4. Simon, Capt. 14th Light Dragoons, m. 28 Jan. 1777, Eleanor 2nd dau. of John Andrews, of Firmount, King's Co., and d. Aug. 1821, leaving issue,
     (1) George, b. 1777; d. unm. 1842.
     (2) Lambart, b. 1779; m. 1818, Hannah, dau. of — Westropp, of Fort Anne, co. Clare, and d.s.p. 1825.
     (3) Simon, Capt. 12th Light Dragoon Guards, and Queen's Bays, b. 1781; d. unm. 1813.
     (4) John, d. aged 15.
     (5) Christopher Nicholson, an Officer R.N., d. unm.
     (6) Maunsell, d. unm. 1843.
     (7) Theobald, of Lisaniskea, formerly an Officer in the 3rd Dragoon Guards, b. Sept. 1794; m. Jan. 1823, Margaret, dau. of John Willington, of Castle Willington, co. Tipperary, and d. Oct. 1865, leaving issue by her (who d. 16 June, 1877),
       1. John Willington, now of Lisaniskea.
       2. George Nicholson, Lieut.-Col. (retired) 31st Foot; m. 10 Sept. 1867, Ellen, dau. of John Churchill, and d. 31 Oct. 1901, leaving issue, 1, George Robertson, b. 6 Feb. 1872; 2, another son, b. 22 March, 1877; 1, Kate Ellen, m. 18 July, 1896, Major Walter Tibbits, R.A.M.C.; 2, Margaret Louisa Amyrelda; 3, Mary Churchill, M.B., Ch.B., m. 23 Nov. 1900, Andrew McKaig, M.B., Ch.B. Edin.
       1. Jane Willington, m. the late Percy William Cornwallis Lipyeatt, son of Charles Lipyeatt, of the Priory, Dawlish, Devon, and left issue.
       2. Ellen.
       3. Eliza Charlotte, m. Ralph Bromfield Fisher, of Fisherwick Park, Westmorland, Capt. Cumberland Militia, who d. 24 April, 1869, and had issue. His widow d. 4 Nov. 1877.
     (8) Hampden Nicholson, a retired Lieut.-Col. Bengal Artillery, b. 1790; m. 1847, Penelope Briggs, of Bandon, and had an only child,
       Penelope Susanna, m. 10 Sept. 1869, Charles Edward Tuthill, Barrister-at-Law.
     Mr. H. N. Pepper was drowned at Kilkee 1855.
     (9) John, of Lismore House, Nenagh, b. 1793.
     (10) Thomas, formerly of the Civil Department of the Ordnance in Dublin Castle, b. 17 Dec. 1795; d. 31 Aug. 1862.
     (1) Amelia, d. 21 March, 1855.
     (2) Catherine, m. 1806, David Joyce, of Norwood, co. Tipperary; he d. 31 May, 1861.
Capt. Lambart Pepper m. 2ndly, 24 Aug. 1753, Lydia, dau. of John Preston, of Bellinter, co. Meath, but by her had no issue, His will is dated 8 Aug. 1775, and was proved 25 June, 1776. He d. 22 April, 1776.
1. Elinor, m. Christopher Nicholson, of Balrath, co. Meath.

The eldest son,
GEORGE PEPPER, of Ballygarth, b. 1693; High Sheriff co. Meath 1724, d. 18 June, 1751; m. Anne, dau. of the Right Hon. Sir Thomas Taylour, 1st bart. of Headfort, grandfather of Thomas, 1st Earl Bective, and by her, (who d. 20 April, 1749) left an only child,
   THOMAS PEPPER, M.P. for Kells, 1761 and 1768, b. 1733; m. 29 Aug. 1772, Henrietta, eldest dau. and eventual co-heir of Richard Moore, of Barne, co. Tipperary, and by her (who d. 21 April, 1831, aged 84) had issue,
1. THOMAS, his heir.
2. GEORGE, successor to his brother Thomas.
3. Richard, H.E.I.C.S., afterwards Major co. Meath Militia, b. 12 May, 1778, ; m. Margaret, dau. of Rev. John Aldwell, of co. Tipperary, and d. 27 Dec. 1871, leaving an only child, Henrietta.
4. Henry, C.B., Col. H.E.I.C.S., commanded the 14th Bengal N.I. at the siege and storming of Bhurtpore, b. 1780; d. unm. 4 March, 1828.
5. Hercules, C.B., Col. H.E.I.C.S., commanded 34th Madras N.I., served as Brigadier in Burmah, under Sir Archibald Campbell, and d. unm. in India 25 July, 1826, of wounds received in action in Pegu.

6. Charles Hampden, Lieut.-Col. commanding the 27th Regt. For sixteen years he served in Italy, under the command of Sir John Stuart, and in the Peninsula, under the Duke of Wellington. He was b. 1783, and d. 15 Oct. 1848 ; m. Matilda Mary, dau. of Arthur French St. George, of Tyrone House, co. Galway, and Lady Harriet St. Lawrence his wife, dau. of William, Earl of Howth, and by her (who d. 19 Aug. 1853, aged 46) has surviving issue,
  1. THOMAS ST. GEORGE, late of Ballygarth.
  2. CHARLES, now of Ballygarth.
   1. Harriet Mary.
   2. Matilda Victoria Mary, d. unm. 26 Nov. 1907.
7. Edward (Rev.), Prebendary of Momnohenock, Diocese of Dublin, m. 1st, Elizabeth, 2nd dau. of Rev. William Hales, D.D., which lady d. 8 April, 1860. He m. 2ndly, 16 Aug. 1864, Frances Mary, dau. of William R. Yeilding, J.P., and widow of John FitzGerald, Barrister-at-Law. She d. 5 April, 1872. He d.s.p. 10 May, 1870.
8. Octavius. Lieut. 28th Regt., d. unm. 1835.
  1. Henrietta, d. unm.
  2. Anne, m. Rev. George Hamilton, of Hampton Hall, co. Dublin ; d. 8 Feb. 1849, and was mother of Right Hon. George Alexander Hamilton, M.P.
  3. Charlotte, a. unm. 5 June, 1834.
  4. Harriet, m. 6 Aug. 1801, James Corry Lowry, of Rockdale, co. Tyrone, and d. 18 April, 1834.
The eldest son,
  THOMAS PEPPER, of Ballygarth Castle, Lieut.-Col. Comm. Royal Meath Militia for fifty years (1797-1847), M.P. for Kells at the time of the Union, and High Sheriff of Meath 1802, b. 12 Oct. 1774 ; m. Mary Louisa, elder dau. of Rev. William Hales, D.D., and by her (who d. 9 May, 1862) had no issue. He d. 9 Oct. 1857, and was s. by his brother,
  CAPT. GEORGE PEPPER, of Ballygarth Castle and Mosney, Julianstown, co. Meath, High Sheriff of Meath 1813, b. 15 Sept. 1775 ; d. unm. 10 Dec. 1860, and was s. by his nephew,
  THOMAS ST. GEORGE PEPPER, of Ballygarth, J.P. and D.L., High Sheriff 1866, b. 13 July, 1035 ; d. unm. 21 July, 1884, and was s. by his brother,

Arms—Gu., on a chevron arg., between three demi-lions rampant or, as many grains of pepper ppr., in chief a trefoil slipped of the second. Crest—A demi-lion rampant or. Motto—Semper erectus.
Seat—Ballygarth Castle, Julianstown, co. Meath. Clubs—Carlton ; Sackville Street ; and Kildare Street.

PERCEVAL OF TEMPLE HOUSE.

ALEXANDER ASCELIN CHARLES PHILIP SPENCER PERCEVAL, of Temple House, co. Sligo, Lieut. Irish Guards, b. 29 Dec. 1885.

Lineage. — GEORGE PERCEVAL, b. 15 Sept. 1635, youngest son of Sir Philip Perceval, Knt., the distinguished statesman (great-grandfather of John, 1st Earl of Egmont), by Catherine Usher his wife, dau. of Arthur Usher and granddau. of Sir William Usher, Clerk of the Council, was Registrar of the Prerogative Court, Dublin. He m. Mary, dau. and heir of William Crofton, of Temple House, co. Sligo, and by her (who m. 2ndly, 30 April, 1677, Richard Aldworth, of Newmarket, co. Cork, and d. 15 Oct. 1705) had issue,
  1. PHILIP, his heir.
  2. William, ancestor of PERCEVAL-MAXWELL of Finnebrogue (see that family).
  3. Charles, Major of Brigadier Hunt Wither's Regt. of Dragoons, 1710, served in Portugal with great reputation, was Governor of Denia, in Spain, which he gallantly defended, b. 8 Feb. 1674 ; killed in a duel at Lisbon 6 May, 1713.
  1. Catherine, b. 26 Jan. 1666 ; m. George Brereton, of Carrigslaney, co. Carlow. She d. 10 Jan. 1728.
George Perceval was drowned near Holyhead, on his voyage to England, with the Earl of Meath and other persons of distinction, 25 March, 1675. His eldest son and heir,
  PHILIP PERCEVAL, of Temple House, co. Sligo, b. 3 Aug. 1670 ; m. 1691, Elizabeth, dau. of John D'Aberor, of Wandsworth, Surrey, and dying 1704, left, with other issue, a son and heir,
  JOHN PERCEVAL, of Temple House, b. 1700 ; High Sheriff co. Sligo 1728 and 1742 ; m. 17 Oct. 1722, Anne, dau. of Joshua Cooper, of Markree, co. Sligo, and dying 1754, was s. by his eldest son,
  PHILIP PERCEVAL, of Temple House, b, 18 Oct. 1723 ; High Sheriff, 1775, m. Mary, dau. and co-heir of Guy Carleton, of Rossfad, and dying 1787, was s. by his son,

GUY CARLETON PERCEVAL, who d.s.p. 1792, and was s. by his brother,
  REV. PHILIP PERCEVAL, of Temple House, m. Nov. 1783, Anne, dau. of Alexander Carroll, of Dublin, and had issue, three sons and two daus.,
    1. Philip, m. unm.   2. ALEXANDER, his heir.
    3. Guy, d. unm.
    1. Anne, m. John Drought.   2. Mary, m. John Warburton.
The 2nd son,
  ALEXANDER PERCEVAL, of Temple House, co. Sligo, High Sheriff 1809, M.P. 1831-41, J.P., Lieut.-Col. Sligo Militia. Serjeant-at-Arms to the House of Lords, b. 10 Feb. 1787 ; m. 11 Feb. 1806, Jane Anne, eldest dau. of Col. Henry Peisley L'Estrange, of Moystown, King's Co., and by her (who d. 20 Jan. 1847) had surviving issue,
    1. PHILIP, D.L., High Sheriff 1845, formerly Lieut. Royal Horse Guards, b. 19 March, 1813 ; m. 1st, 1 July, 1843, Frederica Penelope, youngest dau. of Col. Hugh Duncan Baillie, of Red Castle, N.B. She d. 13 June, 1861, leaving issue.
      1. Alexander Glentworth Paul Clifton, Capt. 2nd Life Guards, b. April, 1847 ; d. unm.
      2. Hugh Spencer Dudley, b. 3 April, 1856.
      1. Maria Jane Kathleen, m. 19 July, 1866, Goring Apsley Traherne, 2nd son of M. Traherne, M.P., and left issue.
    He m. 2ndly, 9 Jan. 1868, the Hon. Ernestine Wellington Sydney (who d. 20 Sept. 1910), dau. of Philip Charles, 1st Lord de Lisle and Dudley, and d. 28 March, 1897, leaving issue,
    3. Philip HUNLOKE, who assumed for himself and issue by Royal Licence, 4 Jan. 1905, the name of Hunloke in lieu his patronymic, and the arms of Hunloke quarterly with his own, b. 26 Nov. 1868 ; m. 1892, Silvia, dau. of John Postee Haseltine, of Walhampton, Lymington, and has issue,
      4. Ernest, b. 19 Nov. 1871 ; d. young.
      1. Kathleen Sophy, twin with Philip.
      2. Ernestine, d. 1887.
    2. Henry (Rev.), Rector of Den, co. Cavan, b. 2 Nov. 1819 ; m. 10 Jan. 1850, Elizabeth Letitia, only child of John Hutchinson, and d.s.p. 16 May, 1880.
    3. ALEXANDER, of whom presently.
    4. Charles George Guy, b. 27 May, 1831 ; m. 1 June, 1870, Ellen, 3rd dau. of W. Inglis, H.B.M. Consul at Port Said, Egypt, and d. 16 Oct. 1898, leaving issue, one son, Alexander Charles Guy, b. 17 Oct. 1871.
    1. Elizabeth Dora, m. Aug. 1844, Rev. William N. Guinness, and d.s.p. June, 1845.
    2. Frances, d. unm.
    3. Sophia, m. Rev. William Willoughby Wynne. He d. Sept. 1860. She d. 18 June, 1881.
    4. Georgiana Sarah, d. unm.
    5. Maria Frances, d. unm. 13 Sept. 1894.
    6. Emily Jane, d. 1901.
  Col. Perceval d. 9 Dec. 1858. His 3rd son,
  ALEXANDER PERCEVAL, of Temple House, Barrister-at-Law, b. 25 June, 1821 ; m. 22 July, 1858, Annie E., youngest dau. of George de Blois and widow of Capt. Nye, and by her (who d. 11 April, 1886) had issue,
    1. ALEXANDER, of Temple House.
    2. Robert Jardine, b. 22 Oct. 1860 ; d. 11 Dec. 1862.
    3. Philip Dudley, b. 11 Dec. 1865 ; m. 22 June, 1892, Muriel Caroline Louisa, eldest dau. of Owen Wynne, of Hazelwood, Sligo, and has issue a dau.,
      Dorothy Sophia.
    1. Jeannie, m. 29 Dec. 1831, Sir Charles Larcom, Bart., who d. 23 March, 1892, leaving issue.
    2. Sophie, m. 30 July, 1884, Arthur Larcom, C.B., M.A. (see BURKE's Peerage, LARCOM, Bart.).
  He d. 8 May, 1866, and was s. by his eldest son,
  ALEXANDER PERCEVAL, of Temple House, co. Sligo, J.P. and D.L., High Sheriff co. Sligo 1882, b. 30 Oct. 1859 ; m. 3 Feb. 1881, Charlotte Jane, eldest dau. of Charles William O'Hara, of Annaghmore, co. Sligo, and d. 22 July, 1887, having had issue,
    ALEXNDER ASCELIN CHARLES PHILIP SPENCER, now of Temple House.
    Sibyl Annie, b. 17 July, 1882 ; d. 22 Jan. 1884.

Arms—Arg., on a chief indented gu. three crosses pattée of the field. Crest—A thistle erect, leaved ppr. Mottoes—Over the crest, Yvery ; under the shield, Sub cruce candida.
Seat—Temple House, Ballymote. Clubs—Guards, Pratt's.

PERCEVAL OF BARNTOWN.

JOHN JAMES PERCEVAL, of Barntown, co. Wexford, late Lieut. 17th Foot, b. 22 Nov. 1837.

Lineage.—JOHN PERCEVAL, of Dublin, will proved 1629, who left by Katharine his wife a son and a dau.,
  JOHN, his heir.
  Anne, m. John Wiggat.
The only son,
  JOHN PERCEVAL, of Dublin, who left by Alice his wife (who was bur. in Drogheda, 12 Nov. 1665), two sons,
    1. JOHN, his heir.
    2. David, who left issue, settled at Bristol.
The elder son,
  JOHN PERCEVAL, of Dublin, who left, by Catherine his wife (who was bur. in Wexford, 27 Jan. 1740), two sons,
    1. JOHN, his heir.

Perceval.   THE LANDED GENTRY.   558

2. Robert, of Ardcavan, co. Wexford, *m.* Ann, dau. of — Patterson. She was bur. 9 July, 1717. He *d.* Aug. 1771 (will dated 5 April, 1771), leaving a dau. Mary, bapt. 1 June, 1715.
The elder son,
JOHN PERCEVAL, of Wexford, and previously of Kilcoole, co. Wicklow, bapt. 1 May, 1684; *m.* 8 July, 1710, Frances, dau. of Edward Gregg. She *d.* April, 1735. He *d.* 4 March, 1736 (will dated 23 Feb. 1736, proved 1 July, 1737), having had issue,
 1. William, bapt. 24 Nov. 1712, from whom descended the family of Perceval of Ballytramon, co. Wexford, now extinct.
 2. Edward, of Garrygibbon, co. Wexford, bapt. 17 Oct. 1714; *m.* Jane, dau. of William Charlton. His will was proved 6 April, 1773; hers 29 April, 1775. They left two daus.,
   1. Frances, *m.* Samuel Waddy, of Curraghduff, co. Wexford.
   2. Anne, *m.* Arthur Meadows, of Wexford.
 3. JOHN, of whom presently.
 4. Henry, *d. unm.*
 1. Catherine, bur. 21 July, 1712.
 2. Mary.   3. Frances.
 4. Agnata.
The third son,
JOHN PERCEVAL, of Wexford, bapt. 30 April, 1719; *m.* Martha Martin, and *d.* 1768, having by her (who *m.* 2ndly, Rev. — Leneka) had issue,
 1. EDWARD, his heir.
 2. John, *b.* 1766, *d.* 1769.
 1. Anne, *m.* Edward Wheeler, of Barntown, co. Wexford.
The elder son,
EDWARD PERCEVAL, of Barntown, co. Wexford, J.P., High Sheriff 1798, Deputy Governor of co. Wexford, 1793, Capt. in the County Militia, *b.* 1 Sept. 1763; *m.* 31 Oct. 1788, Mary, dau. of Robert Woodcock, of Killowen, co. Wexford, and widow of Ralph Evans. She *d.* 8 Nov. 1803. He *d.* 21 Oct. 1809 (will dated 29 March, proved 29 Nov. 1809), leaving issue,
 1. JAMES, his heir.
 2. Edward, R.N., *b.* 9 June, 1792; killed on service, 6 Jan. 1813, *unm.*
 3. Charles John, midshipman, R.N., *b.* 8 Sept. 1793; *d. unm.* 1808.
 4. Frederick William, Ensign Wexford Militia, *b.* 8 March, 1795; *d. unm.* Jan. 1814.
 5. George, *b.* 25 June, 1796; bur. 5 Dec. 1801.
 6. Robert, *b.* 10 Nov. 1797; *m.* 4 July, 1829, Sarah, dau. of William Harvey, of Killiane, co. Wexford. She *d.* 3 May, 1880. He *d.* 19 Oct. 1836, having had issue,
   1. Anne Maria, *d.* 1 June, 1831.
   2. Mary, *m.* 1st, Richard Pope Williams, who *d.* Jan. 1868, and 2ndly, Edmund Dimsdale, who *d.* 24 May, 1897. She *d.* 8 July, 1907.
   3. Sarah, *d. unm.* 1891.   4. Anne, *d. unm.* 1901.
 7. Nelson, *b.* 15 Dec. 1799; *d.* 5 July, 1821. Will dated 21 April, 1821, proved in Dublin.
 1. Jane, bapt. 9 Sept. 1789; bur. 27 Aug. 1790.
The eldest son,
JAMES PERCEVAL, of Barntown House, co. Wexford, served in the 95th Regt. (now Rifle Brigade) 1805-25, in Germany 1805, at Copenhagen 1807, at Corunna 1808, at Lisbon 1809, at Vittoria, 1812, at San Sebastian 1813 (severely wounded), in France 1816-17, retired from the army as Major 8th Hussars, 1833, *b.* 13 May, 1791; *m.* 17 Dec. 1831, Jane Jones, dau. of Edward Westby of High Park. She *d.* 1851. He *d.* 26 June, 1843, having had issue,
 1. JOHN JAMES, now of Barntown.
 2. Edward Westby, *b.* 2 March, 1842; *m.* 30 Aug. 1869, Margaret, dau. of Thomas Kerr, and *d.s.p.* 16 Aug. 1883. His widow *m.* George Bennet, of Kelso.
 1. Jane Westby, bur. 26 Feb. 1833.
 2. Martha Westby, *m.* 14 Oct. 1865, Phillips Newton, J.P., of Ballinglen, co. Wicklow, who *d.* 6 June, 1892, leaving issue,
   1. Hibbert Perceval, *b.* 5 March, 1877.
   1. Dorothy Mary Perceval, *d. unm.* 13 Oct. 1903.
   2. Jane Phœbe Westby.
 3. Mary Westby, *m.* 28 Feb. 1866, Rev. Thomas Mooney, Vicar of Heywood, Wilts, who assumed the name of THORNBURGH 1885, and *d.* 2 April, 1889, having had issue,
   1. Perceval Thornburgh, *b.* 17 March, 1877.
   2. Westby Thornburgh, *b.* 6 March, 1879.
   3. Francis Thornburgh, *b.* 6 Jan. 1882.
   1. Mary Thornburgh.   2. Florence Beatrice Perceval.
   3. Amy Thornburgh, *d.* an infant.
   4. Eva Thornburgh.   5. Louise Perceval.
   6. Ella Thornburgh.
 4. Anne Westby, *m.* 14 Oct. 1871, Major George Glascott Newton, J.P., late 12th Foot, of Ballybeg, co. Wicklow (*see that family*), who *d.* 10 June, 1910, leaving issue,
   1. James Hibbe t, *b.* 1 Sept. 1879.
   2. George Perceval, *b.* 29 April, 1884.
   3. Francis Philips, *b.* 6 Sept. 1888.
   1. Anne Catharine.   2. Dorothea Eliza.
   3. Barbara Mary.   4. Martha Westhy.
   5. Araminta.
   6. Jane Frances, *m.* 20 July, 1894, Rev. W. J. M'Combe.
 5. Catherine Westby, *d.* at Toulouse, 14 Sept. 1844.

Seat—Barntown, Wexford.

———

PERCEVAL-MAXWELL.   *See* MAXWELL.

———

PERRY OF WOODROOFF.

WILLIAM PERRY, of Woodrooff, co. Tipperary, late Capt. 3rd Batt. R.I. Regt., *b.* 19 Feb. 1869; *s.* his father 1908; *m.* 3 Feb. 1898, Emily Dorothea Mary Clare, eldest dau. of Col. Henry Arthur Hunt Boyse, of Bannow (*see that family*) and has issue,
 1. HENRY WILLIAM PATRICK, *b.* 7 Dec. 1900.
 2. Arthur John, *b.* 7 May, 1906.
 1. Sylvia Frances Vera, *b.* 17 Oct. 1904.

Lineage.—JOHN PERRY, of Woodrooff, co. Tipperary, whose will bears date 1709, and was proved 1710, *m.* Anne dau. of John Neville, of Newrath, co. Wicklow (*see* NEVILLE *of Ahanare*), and by her (who *m.* 2ndly, 23 Dec. 1723, Rev. Thomas Somerville, *see that family*) had with other children, two sons, JOHN and SAMUEL. The eldest son, JOHN, of Woodrooff, *d.s.p.*, and by his will, which bears date 1 June, 1757, and was proved 1759, devised his estates to his nephew, WILLIAM. The other son,
SAMUEL PERRY, *m.* Phœbe, dau. of William Norcott, and had issue,
 1. WILLIAM, of whom hereafter.
 2. Richard, of Cork, merchant, *m.* 1st, Ellen, dau. of Alderman Lavitt, and had a son,
   1. Samuel, who *m.* and had issue.
 He *m.* 2ndly, 7 March, 1769, Mary, dau. of Adam Newman, of Dromore, and had issue.
   2. Adam.   3. Richard.
   4. William Newman (Rev.). 5. Charles.
   1. Mary, wife of Capt. James Jackson.
 1. Dorcas, *m.* William Warren, 2nd brother of Sir Robert Warren, 1st bart., of Warren's Court.
 2. Elizabeth, *m.* — Kiddell.
The elder son,
WILLIAM PERRY, as nephew and devisee of his uncle John, *s.* to the family estate, and *m.* 13 June, 1764, Anne, dau. of Belchel Peddar, and had issue. Mr. Perry *d.* Oct. 1791, and was *s.* by his eldest son,
SAMUEL PERRY, of Woodrooff, *b.* 12 May, 1765, *m.* March, 1791, the Hon. Deborah Prittie, 2nd dau. of Henry, 1st Lord Dunalley, and by her (who *d.* 20 Aug. 1829) had issue,
 1. WILLIAM, his heir.
 2. Henry Prittie (Rev.), *b.* 16 March, 1798; *m.* 1830, Lady Catherine Bourke, 3rd dau. of the Hon. and Rev. Richard Bourke, Bishop of Waterford, and sister of Robert, 5th Earl of Mayo. She *d.* 12 Sept. 1876, having had, with six daus., two sons,
   1. Samuel William, *b.* 1831, *m.* Elizabeth Jane, dau. of J. Hastings Otway, Recorder of Belfast, and *d.* 14 Aug. 1898.
   2. Henry Robert Prittie, *d.* 24 Aug. 1903.
 3. Samuel, *b.* 22 June, 1804, *m.* Thomasine Isabella, dau. of Horace Townsend, of Woodside, co. Cork, and *d.s.p.* Nov. 1871.
 1. Catherine, *m.* 1815, William Barton, of Grove, co. Tipperary.
 2. Anne, *m.* Mathew Sankey, of Coolmore.
 3. Mary.
 4. Phœbe, *m.* Sampson Towgood French, of Cuskinny, co. Cork.
Mr. Perry *d.* 5 May, 1829. His eldest son,
WILLIAM PERRY, of Woodrooff, J.P. and D.L., High Sheriff 1828, *b.* 13 Feb. 1793; *m.* 12 Oct. 1838, Mary, 3rd dau. of Major Langley, of Brittas Castle, co. Tipperary, and had issue,
 1. SAMUEL, of Woodrooff.
 1. Maria, *d.* 1852.
 2. Mary Anne Deborah Margaret, *m.* 24 Oct. 1867, William Thomas Erskine Bookey, J.P., late Capt. of the Carabiniers.
He *d.* 13 July, 1869.
SAMUEL PERRY, of Woodrooff, co. Tipperary, J.P. and D.L., late of the 12th Lancers, *b.* 15 Sept. 1839; *m.* 25 June, 1867, Mary de la Poer, 2nd dau. of John Power, of Gurteen, co. Waterford (*see that family*), and *d.* 25 March, 1908, leaving issue,
 1. WILLIAM, now of Woodrooff.
 2. John, *b.* 30 Nov. 1875.
 1. Frances Mary, *m.* 1891, Col. John B. Symes Bullen, late 15th Hussars, of Catherston and Marshwood Manor, Dorsetshire, D.L. and J.P., and has issue.
 2. Mary, *m.* 1895, Brig.-Gen. Charles Toler MacMurrough Kavanagh, C.V.O., C.B., D.S.O., late 10th Hussars (*see* KAVANAGH *of Borris*), and has issue,
 3. Edith.
 4. Kathlene, *m.* Major Kenneth Kirke, R.A.
 5. Florence Grace, *m.* 1895, Eric James Walter Platt, of Bryn Mêl, Anglesey, and has issue.
 6. Harriette, *d.* 16 Dec. 1909.
 7. Blanche, *m.* Frank Howard, late 14th Hussars.

Seat—Woodrooff, Clonmel.

———

PERRY OF PERRYMOUNT.   *See* McCLINTOCK OF SESKINORE.

———

PERSSE OF ROXBOROUGH.

CAPT. WILLIAM ARTHUR PERSSE, of Roxborough, co. Galway, J.P. and D.L., High Sheriff 1899, late Capt. R.A., b. 8 Sept. 1863; s. his father 1893; m. 18 Jan. 1894, Katharine Ellen, dau. of Lieut.-Col. Henry John Wolsteyn Gehle, R.E., and has issue,

DUDLEY WILLIAM, b. 31 Dec. 1901.
Kathleen Mary, b. 22 Dec. 1897.

Lineage.—REV. ROBERT PERSSE was Vicar of Carrogh and Downings, co. Kildare, 1605–1612. He d. 1612, and was bur. at Bowdenstown, leaving issue several sons, the seniority of whom is unknown,
1. Francis, of Killadirge, co. Wicklow, Gent., Seneschal of the Manor of Bray, m. Eleanor Walsh, and d. May, 1640 (will dated and proved that month and year) leaving issue, all minors,
  1. George.   2. Henry.   3. Oliver.
  1. Mary.   2. Elizabeth.
2. Edward (Rev.), s. his father as Vicar of Carrogh in June, 1612, also appointed Vicar of Straffan in June, 1612; living, 1642.
3. HENRY, of Clune, co. Kildare, Gent., will dated 26 March, 1672, proved 11 July, 1673; bur. at Bowdenstown. By his wife Elizabeth he left a dau. Sybil, and a son DUDLEY, of whom next.

VERY REV. DUDLEY PERSSE, B.D., Trin. Coll. Dublin, Dean of Kilmachuagh, Archdeacon of Tuam, &c., matriculated at Trin. Coll. Dublin, 14 Feb. 1641–2, aetat 16. Received grants of lands in the cos of Galway and Roscommon in 1677 and 1678; m. Sarah, youngest dau. of John Crofton, of Lisdorne, co. Roscommon, and d. 1699, having had issue, two sons and seven daus.,
1. HENRY, his heir.
2. William, of Spring Garden, co. Galway, High Sheriff 1711, m. Alice, dau. of Charles Fox, of Fox Hall, co. Longford. and had two sons, David, d. 2 Sept. 1745, and Patrick, of Spring Garden, High Sheriff 1762, m. Nov. 1766, the widow of — Lewis, and had a dau., m. Oct. 1799, Rev. Joseph FitzPatrick.

He purchased Spring Garden, co. Galway, and lived there until he purchased Roxborough, in the same co. Dean Persse's daus. were m. as follows: the eldest, Catherine, to Major Hugh Galbraith, of Capard, co. Galway; the 2nd, Alice, to Capt. William Colles, eldest son of Charles Colles, of Magheramore, co. Sligo, Provost Marshal for Connaught, by whom she had issue; the 3rd to Nethercott; the 4th to Ormsby, of Tubbervaddy; the 5th to Hickman, of co. Clare; the 6th, Sarah, to John Blakeney, of Castle Blakeney; the 7th to Walsh, of co. Meath. His eldest son,

HENRY PERSSE, of Roxborough, High Sheriff co Galway 1701, m. 27 June, 1688, Mary, dau. of Robert Stratford, M.P., aunt of John, 1st Earl of Aldborough, and d. 12 Feb. 1733, having had issue two sons and a dau., viz.,
1 ROBERT, his heir.
2. Francis, of Ballymerret, High Sheriff 1734, m. Sarah Skerrett, of Drumgriffin, co. Galway.
1. Grace, m. Col. John Blakeney, M.P., of Castle Blakeney, co. Galway.

The elder son,
ROBERT PERSSE, of Roxborough, d. 15 May, 1781, High Sheriff 1742; m. 1727, Elizabeth, dau. of William Parsons and sister of Sir Laurence Parsons, Bart. of Birr Castle, and had issue by her (who d. Jan. 1768).
1. Henry, d.s.p.   2. WILLIAM, his heir.
3. Robert, m. Ann, dau. of Sir Arthur Brooke, 1st Bart. of Colebrooke, and d.s.p. 1758.
4. Dudley.
5. Parsons, m. 9 June, 1770, Elizabeth, dau. of Robert Fetherston, of White Rock, co. Longford.
6. BURTON, of Moyvode (see that family).
1. Sarah, m. 27 July, 1764, Sir Richard St. George, 1st bart. of Woodsgift, and had issue.

The son and successor,
WILLIAM PERSSE, of Roxborough, High Sheriff 1766, m. about 1750, his cousin, Sarah, dau. of Col. John Blakeney, M.P., of Abbert, co. Galway, and had issue,
1. ROBERT, his heir.
2. William, m. Anne, eldest dau. of Neptune Blood, of Roxton, co. Clare.
3. Parsons.
4. Henry Stratford, m. 1792, Anne Sadleir, and had issue, Matilda, m. 24 Nov. 1825, Burton Persse, of Moyode Castle (see that family).
1. Elizabeth, m. William Worth Newenham, eldest son of Sir Edward Newenham.

Col. Persse d. 1802, and was s. by his eldest son,
ROBERT PERSSE, of Roxborough, and Castleboy, High Sheriff 1814, b. 24 June, 1767; m. 29 May, 1801, Maria, dau. of Samuel Wade of Fairfield, co. Galway, and by her (who d. 1810) had issue,
1. DUDLEY, of Roxborough.
2. Robert Henry, of Castleboy, co. Galway, J.P., b. 7 Dec. 1806; m. 1828, Katherine Isabella, dau. of Col. Seymour, of Somerset, co. Galway, and d. 1884, leaving issue,
  1. Robert, late Capt. Royal Canadian Rifles, m. Anne O'Hara, of Raheen.
  2. William Edward Camden.
  1. Maria Augusta, m. 1855, William Bindon Blood, of Cranagher, co. Clare. She d. 23 June, 1860, leaving issue (see that family).
  2. Katherine Isabella, d. unm. 3 Feb. 1910.
  3. Elizabeth Margaret, d. unm. 21 March, 1910.
  4. Frances.   5. Sarah.   6. Arabella.

3. William, Capt. Queen's Bays, b. 15 Sept. 1809; m. Frances, eld. dau. of Thomas Wade, of Fairfield (see WADE, of Carrowmore). He d. 10 June, 1860. She d. 27 Oct. 1894, leaving issue, Wilhelmina, m. 27 April, 1880, George Charles Ker Mahon, of Ballydonelan (see that family).
1. Sarah, m. Rev. Canon Richard Booth Eyre, Rector of Eyrecourt, and had issue.
2. Maria, m. 1 May, 1825, Denis Arthur, 3rd Lord Clanmorris, and d. 27 Aug. 1899, leaving issue.
3. Eliza, m. 1825, Thomas Warren White, and had issue.
4. Catherine, m. Abel Onge, and had issue.

Mr. Persse d. Jan. 1850, and was s. by his eldest son,
DUDLEY PERSSE, of Roxborough, co. Galway, D.L., High Sheriff, 1835, b. 19 Feb. 1802; m. 1st Nov. 1826, Hon. Katherine O'Grady, dau. of Standish, 1st Viscount Guillamore, and by her (who d. 11 Dec. 1829) had issue,
1. DUDLEY, of Roxborough, of whom hereafter.
1. Katherine Henrietta, m. 9 Jan. 1862, George H. Wale, Comm. R.N. (who d. 1879), 4th son of Gen. Sir Charles Wale, K.C.B., of Shelford, co. Cambridge, and d. 11 Dec. 1899, leaving issue.
2. Maria, d. unm. 1883.

He m. 2ndly, July, 1833, Frances, only dau. of Col. Richard Barry, by Elizabeth O'Grady his wife, sister of the 1st Viscount Guillamore, and by her (who d. 22 March, 1896) had issue,
2. Richard Dudley, Barrister-at-Law, Recorder of Galway, d. 1879.
3. WILLIAM NORTON, s. to his brother.
4. Edward, Col. Madras Staff Corps, m. 1868, Margaret, dau. of Gen. Thomas Clerk, Madras Staff Corps, and has issue,
  1. Dudley Peyton, b. 5 Sept. 1869.
  2. Alexander Annesley, b. 26 Nov. 1871.
  3. George Standish, b. 17 Oct. 1877.
  4. Richard, b. 6 Dec. 1879.
  5. Edward Aubrey, b. 28 June, 1881.
  6. Thomas Beverley, b. 22 June, 1884.
  7. Henry Wilfred, b. 19 Sept. 1885.
  8. Gerard Baldwin, b. 11 July, 1891.
  1. Ethel Frances, m. 6 Aug. 1896, Henry Paul Harvey, C.B., B.A. (Oxon.), Financial Adviser to the Egyptian Government, and has issue.
  2. Marion, m. 27 July, 1909, David Runciman Boyd, D.Sc., Ph.D.
  3. Gertrude.
5. Robert Algernon, of Creg Clare, Ardrahan, co. Galway, High Sheriff 1885, J.P., b. 14 June, 1845; m. 23 July, 1880, Hon. Eleanor Laura Jane, youngest dau. of Viscount Gough, and d. 25 May, 1911, leaving issue,
  1. Rodolph Algernon, b. 12 May, 1892.
  2. Olive Nora, b. 13 Sept. 1887.
  3. Daphne Gertrude, b. 27 June, 1889.
6. Francis Fitz Adelm, of Ashfield, Gort, co. Galway, J.P., b. 26 April, 1854; m. 20 July, 1880, Mary (who d. 27 Nov. 1909), dau. of William Monahan, of Templemartin, co. Galway, and had issue,
  1. John Geoffrey, b. 8 May, 1884.
  2. Dudley Francis, Midshipman R.N., b. 3 Feb. 1892.
  1. May, m. 1905, Matthew O'Byrne White, Dist. Insp., R.I.C.
  2. Gertrude.   3. Alice.
  4. Mildred Rosamond, m. 17 Jan. 1912, John Joseph Stafford, of Grace Dieu, Waterford.
7. Henry, of Loughrea, co. Galway, J.P., b. 14 Oct. 1855; m. 5 July, 1888, Eleanor Ada, dau. of Rev. Frederick Fleming Beadon, of North Stoneham, co. Hants, Rector of Basset, Sussex, and has issue,
  1. Reginald Barry Lovaine, b. 17 May, 1896.
  2. Dermot Beadon, b. 14 Sept. 1898; d. 17 Sept. 1901.
8. Gerald Dillon, b. 23 Sept. 1857; d. unm. 26 March, 1898.
9. Alfred Lovaine, of Rose Park, Gort, co. Galway, b. 9 April, 1859; m. 11 Oct. 1883, Florence Geraldine, dau. of the Rev. Canon Richard Booth Eyre, and has issue,
  1. Dudley Eyre, 4th Batt. Royal Dublin Fus., b. 14 Aug. 1892.
  1. Gwendoline Irene, m. 30 Jan. 1905, Francis eldest son of Capt. Francis Sarsfield-Sampson, Inspector Local Government Board.
  2. Gladys, m. 24 March, 1909, John Alfred Studdert, of Cramoher, co. Clare, and has issue (see STUDDERT, of Bunratty Castle).
  3. Elizabeth, m. 24 Nov. 1864, Walter Taylor Newton Shawe-Taylor, of Castle Taylor, co. Galway, D.L., and d. 24 Aug. 1896, leaving issue.
  4. Frances Adelaide, m. 9 July, 1870, Rev. James William Lane, Rector of Redruth, Cornwall, and d. 8 Feb. 1900, leaving by him (who d. 1910) with other issue a son, Sir Hugh P. Lane.
  5. Gertrude, m. 9 July, 1873, Edmund Beauchamp Beauchamp, D.L., of Trevince, Cornwall, and d. 14 Feb. 1876, leaving issue.
  6. Arabella, m. 18 March, 1891, Robert William Waithman, D.L., of Moyne Park, co. Galway.
  7. Isabella Augusta, m. 4 March, 1880, Right Hon. Sir William Gregory, P.C., K.C.M.G., of Coole Park, co. Galway. He d. 6 March, 1892, leaving issue (see that family).

Mr. Dudley Persse d. 7 Sept. 1878, and was s. by his eldest son,
DUDLEY PERSSE, of Roxborough, co. Galway, D.L., late Capt. 7th Fusiliers, served with that Regt. in the Crimea, and was severely wounded at the Alma, b. 7 Nov. 1829; s. his father Sept. 1878; and d. unm. 13 March, 1892, and was s. by his brother,
MAJOR WILLIAM NORTON PERSSE, of Roxborough, R.A., D.L. co. Galway, b. 10 Sept. 1831; m. 11 Sept. 1860, Rose, and dau. of Rev. Arthur Bennet Mesham, Rector of Wootton, Kent (see MESHAM of Ewloe Hall, and by her (who d. 23 May, 1909) had issue,

Persse.   THE LANDED GENTRY.   560

1. WILLIAM ARTHUR, now of Roxborough.
2. Dudley Jocelyn, b. 24 July, 1873.
1. Rose Charlotte, m. 8 May, 1896, Major Robert Fair Ruttledge Fair, of Cornfield, co. Mayo, and has issue.
2. Kathleen, m. 8 June, 1896, William Creagh Burke, of Cloonee, co. Mayo, and has issue.
3. Millicent, m. 9 Aug. 1890, Douglas L. Foxwell, of Penstone, Lancing, co. Sussex, and has issue.
5. Ione Albertha, m. 12 July, 1898, Col. Adrien Samuel Woods, of Renmore Galway, late commanding 88th Regimental District, and has issue.
Major Persse d. 11 Feb. 1893.

Seat—Roxborough, Loughrea, co. Galway.

PERSSE OF MOYODE.

BURTON WALTER PERSSE, of Mackney, Ballinasloe, co. Galway, J.P., b. Sept. 1854; s. his father 1885.

Lineage.—BURTON PERSSE, youngest son of ROBERT PERSSE, of Roxboro' (see that family), m. 13 Jan. 1770, Sarah Pennefather, of co. Tipperary, and d. 1829, leaving issue,
1. BURTON, of whom presently.
2. William, C.B., Col. 16th Lancers, served in Peninsular War, m. Arabella, dau. of Judge Moore, of Lamberton, Queen's Co., and had issue,
  1. Walter Blakeney, of Bagnalstown, co. Carlow, Capt. 90th L.I., served in the Crimea, m. 1860, Anne Jane, dau. of J. C. Whiteman, of Theydon, Epping, Essex, d. 1889, leaving issue,
    (1) William Horsley, Major late Queen's Bays (Naval and Military Club), b. 16 Oct. 1863; m. 29 June, 1909, Beatrice Mary Ethel, dau. of Major C. Brice Wilkinson.
    (2) John Claremont, b. 1867.
    (1) Anne Madeline, b. 1861.
    (2) Rose Eleanor, b. 1862; m. 7 Jan. 1886, Capt. Arthur Cairnes Daniell, R.A.
    (3) Helen, b. (twin) 1869; m. 1889, Commander W. B. Forbes, R.N.
    (4) Lily, b. (twin) 1869; d. 1869.
  1. Madeline Eliza, m. 22 April, 1852, her cousin, Burton Robert Parsons Persse, of Moyode, and d. 8 July, 1882, having by him (who d. 1885) had issue (see below).
  2. Arabella, m. W. Norton Barry, of Castle Cor, co. Cork (see that family).
1. Maria, m. Kingsmill Pennefather, Lieut.-Col. Tipperary Militia, and had issue.
2. Eliza, m. T. Lambert, of Castle Lambert, and had issue.
3. Sarah, d. unm.
4. Frances, m. Major Graham, and d. 1837.
5. Matilda, d. unm.
6. Grace Anne, d. unm. 1853.
The elder son,
BURTON PERSSE, of Moyode Castle, co. Galway, J.P. and D.L., High Sheriff 1816, m. 1st, 1820, Anchoretta, 3rd dau. of Giles Eyre, of Eyrecourt Castle, co. Galway, and had issue with a son, b and d. 1822, three daus.,
1. Anne, b. 1821; d. 1853.
2. Eliza, b. 1823; m. 1847, Samuel Wade, of Carrowmore, co. Galway, and d. 30 April, 1896, leaving issue.
3. Anchoretta Maria, b. 1824; d. unm. 2 Oct. 1911.
He m. 2ndly, 24 Nov. 1825, his cousin, Matilda, dau. of Henry Persse, of Galway, by his wife Miss Sadleir, of Cork, and d. 31 Aug. 1859, having by her (who d. June, 1862) had issue,
1. BURTON ROBERT PARSONS, of whom presently.
2. William Henry, d.s.p.
3. Henry Sadleir, of Glenarde, co. Galway, and Kiltullagh, same co., J.P., High Sheriff of Galway Town, 1868, b. 17 Nov. 1832; m. 13 June, 1862, Eleanora Alice, dau. of Col. Thomas Seymour, of Ballymore Castle (see that family), and d. 8 March, 1899, having by her (who d. 17 June, 1890) had issue,
  1. William Henry, High Sheriff of Galway Town 1888, b. 27 July, 1863; m. 17 May, 1893, May Paulet, 2nd dau. of Col. Cosby, of Stradbally Hall, Queen's Co. (see that family), and has issue,
    (1) Burton Desmond Seymour, b. 8 March, 1894.
    (2) Sydney Henry, b. 29 June, 1897.
    (1) Eleanor Alice, b. 12 March, 1895.
    (2) Mary Audrey, b. 7 Sept. 1901.
  2. Henry Seymour, b. 1869.
  3. John Beauchamp, b. 1870; d. 1877.
  4. Cecil de Burgh, b. 1875.
  1. Matilda Theodora, b. 1865; d. 16 Aug. 1881.
  2. Sarah Henrietta, b. 1866.
  3. Eleanora Alice, b. 1867.
  4. Violet Seymour, b. 1872; m. 11 Nov. 1896, Ernest Johnson, of Oakhurst, Ambergate.
  5. Helen Parker, b. 1877.
  6. Noel Marjorie, b. 1878; d. 1888.
4. Theophilus, d.s.p.
5. Charles Graham, b. 1836; m. Alice, dau. of Thomas Richardson, of Tyaquin, co. Galway; and d. 1869, leaving a dau.,
  Cora Alicia, m. 24 June, 1896, Charles Lyons, F.R.C.S., of Ledeston, Westmeath.
6. Dudley Thomas, Col. 13th Light Infantry, served in the Zulu war, b. 1839; m. 1880, Mary (Belleville, Athenry, co. Galway), dau. of Stephen W. Creagh, and d. 6 Nov. 1894, leaving issue,

Henrietta, m. 11 July, 1910, Capt. Cyril Darcy Vivien Cary-Barnard, Wilts Regt.
7. De Burgh Parsons, High Sheriff Galway Town 1890, b. 1840; m. Miss Blair, of Limerick, and has issue.
  1. Charles, b. 1873.
  2. De Burgh, b. 1882.
  1. Henrietta, b. 1872; m. Edgar Joyce, and has issue.
  2. Rose Eileen, b. 1875.
  3. Jessie Madeline, b. 1880.
4. Sarah Selina, m. 23 May, 1843, John Charles Robert, 4th Baron Clanmorris, and had issue. He d. 5 April, 187.6 She d. 28 Nov. 1907.
5. Maria Sadleir, m. 1856, Edward Beauchamp Beauchamp, of Trevince, co. Cornwall, and has issue.
6. Matilda, d. unm.
7. Henrietta Burton, d. Oct. 1886.
The eldest son,
BURTON ROBERT PARSONS PERSSE, of Moyode Castle, co. Galway, J.P. and D.L., High Sheriff 1862, b. 4 Nov. 1828; m. 22 April, 1852, his cousin, Madeline Eliza, dau. of Col. William Persse, C.B. (see above), and d. 1885, having by her (who d. 8 July, 1882) had issue,
1. BURTON WALTER, now of Moyode Castle.
2. William Beauchamp, b. Nov. 1857; m. June, 1898, Miss McDonald, of Queensland.
3. Arthur Moore, b. Oct. 1858; d. 1888.
4. Theophylis, b. Feb. 1866; d. 21 Aug. 1883.
1. Arabella Eliza, m. 1882, Francis Joyce, son of Pierce Joyce, of Mervue, co. Galway, and d. 14 May, 1883, leaving a dau., Madeline Eliza Addie.
2. Madeline Beatrice.
3. Frances Moore, m. Jan. 1895, Hon. Burton Percy Bingham, 3rd son of John Charles Robert, 4th Baron Clanmorris. He d.s.p. 10 Dec. 1898.
4. Maria Tucker.

Seat—Mackney, Ballinasloe, co. Galway.

PERY. See BURKE'S PEERAGE, LIMERICK, E.

PERY-KNOX-GORE. See GORE.

PEYTON OF LAHEEN.

JAMES REYNOLDS PEYTON, of Laheen, co. Leitrim, J.P. and D.L., High Sheriff 1879, b. Dec. 1842; s. his brother 1875; m. 4 April, 1894, Alice Mary, dau. of the late Major John Edward Riley, late 88th Connaught Rangers, and has issue,
JOHN REYNOLDS, b. 19 Jan. 1896.
Dorothea Reynolds.

Lineage.—REV. THOMAS PEYTON, 2nd son of Thomas Peyton, of Bury St. Edmunds, by Lady Cecilia Bourchier, dau. of John, 2nd Earl of Bath, matriculated Trin. Coll. Dublin, 1610, B.A. 1614, M.A. 1617, Fellow, Nov. 1617, B.D. 1625, Dean of Tuam 1625, Prebendary of Kinvarra, in the Cathedral of Clonfert, Oct. 1627, and Rector of Ballinrobe, co. Mayo, 5 Nov. 1631, d. 1638. He m. Dorothy, dau. of George Andrewe, Bishop of Ferns and Leighlin, and was father of
JOHN PEYTON, of Boyle, co. Roscommon, m. Catherine, dau. of Humphrey Reynolds, of Loughscur, co. Leitrim, by Russell his wife, dau. of Sir James Ware, Knt., Auditor-Gen. of Ireland, and by her (who d. 19 May, 1664) had issue,
1. HUMPHREY.
2. George, of Streamstown, co. Westmeath, d.s.p. 1698; m. Thomasine, dau. of Sir Robert Pigott, widow of Argentine Hull, and of Col. Prime Iron Rochfort (see PIGOTT of Capard).
3. Oliver.
The eldest son,
HUMPHREY PEYTON, of Boyle, co. Roscommon, d. intestate (administration 10 June, 1669), leaving issue, by his wife Elizabeth,
1. JOHN, his heir.
1. Catherine, of Drincy House, co. Leitrim, m. Catherine, dau. of James Reynolds, of Loughscur Castle, co. Leitrim, and widow of Robert Sandys, and had issue,

1. GEORGE, of Driney House, m. Jane, dau. of Walter Gray, of Tubbercurry, co. Sligo, and d. 1809, having had a son, Walter Peyton, of Driney House, J.P., Deputy-Governor, co. Leitrim, m. Nov. 1789, Alice, eldest dau. of Richard Cunningham, of Portshane, co. Leitrim, and had (with a dau. Alice, m. Laurence Park) one son, Capt. George Hamilton Conyngham Peyton, of Driney House, J.P. and D.L., High Sheriff 1815, b. 9 Nov. 1791; m. 15 Dec. 1818, Elizabeth, dau. of James Duncan, and left issue,
 (1) Rev. Walter Conyngham, of Driney House, M.A., Rural Dean, Incumbent of Billis, co. Cavan, b. 1821; m. 1856, Margaret, dau. of Rev. James M'Creight Rector of Keady, co. Armagh, and grand-dau. of William Foster, Bishop of Clogher, and d.
 (2) James Duncan, of Driney and Wyatt Ville, Ballybrock, d. 8 March, 1908; m. 21 June, 1870, Harriett Elizabeth, youngest dau. of the late Capt. William Cary, 17th Regt., Adjutant Carlow Rifles, and had issue.
  1. William Walter (Rev.), of Driney, co Leitrim, Rector of Toomna, Carrick-on-Shannon, B.A., Trin. Coll. Dublin, b. 21 March, 1871; m. 21 Dec. 1909, Eleanor Charlotte, youngest dau. of the late Rev. Joseph Rawlins, B.A., Rector of Templeport, co. Cavan.
  2. Algernon, b. 2 Jan. 1876.
   1. Mary, b. 13 Oct. 1872; m. 1 Aug. 1906, George Randall Penrose, of Tullylough, Cavan.
   2. Olive Mabel, b. 28 Oct. 1877; m. 14 June, 1911, Henry Craig, of Aberley, Ballybrook, co. Dublin.
   3. Ethel Mildred, b. 9 Oct. 1878.
 (3) George Richard (Rev.), M.A., Rector of Newtownforbes, d. 12 Nov. 1905.
 (4) Henry Alfred, Lieut. Indian Army (retired), formerly H.E.I.C.S., b. 10 June, 1827; m. Ida, dau. of Rev. Joseph Hamilton, Rector of Tara, co. Meath, and has issue,
  1. George Hamilton Alfred, I.C.S., m. Elizabeth Barecroft, and d. 15 Aug. 1905, leaving issue,
   a. Alfred, Capt. 13th Rajputs.
   b. Walter.   c. George Patrick.
   a. Elizabeth.   b. Frances.
   c. Eileen.   d. Beatrice.
  2. Westropp Joseph, C.M.G., Major Ind. Army, b. 1 May, 1860; m. 1890, Eleanor (Driney, Harpenden), dau. of Col. Fenton, Ind. Army. He d. 4 Jan. 1903, leaving issue, Patrick George, b. 19 Jan. 1902.
   Grauuaile Katherine, b. 1900.
  3. Charles Cunningham, b. 3 June, 1874.
  1. Pauline Frances Ada, m. George Winmül, I.C.S.
 (5) Lorenzo Oliver, settled in Australia, m. Emma Bellman.
 (1) Hannah Maria.   (2) Elizabeth Arnold.
2. James, of Cartrons, co. Roscommon, b. 1716; d. 1 March, 1790, leaving, by Hannah, his wife, dau. of Edward Wynne, three sons (John, William, and Wynne) and a dau., Catherine, m. Archibald Fraser.
1. Catherine.
The eldest son,
 JOHN PEYTON, of Laheen, co. Leitrim, High Sheriff 1731, d. 1740; m. a dau. of James Reynolds, sister and co-heir of Christopher Reynolds, of Laheen, co. Leitrim, and had issue,
 1. TOBIAS, of whom presently.
 2. Reynolds.   3. Martin.
 4. Henry.   5. John.
 1. Anne.
The eldest son,
 TOBIAS PEYTON, of Laheen, and Oxhill, co. Leitim, m. a dau. of John Yeadon, of Abbeyboyle, Roscommon, and had issue,
 1. JOHN, his heir.   2. Yeadon, d. unm.
 3. William, m. widow of Capt. Thomas Dunbar, and left a dau., Mary Yeadon.   4. Henry, d. unm.
 1. Jane, m. 17 April, 1751, Lewis Jones, of Tubberpatrick, co. Sligo.
 2. Margaret, m. 12 July, 1754, Robert Phibbs, of Sligo.
 3. Catherine, m. 1st, 8 Feb. 1765, Simon Bradstreet McCalley, and 2ndly, 1767, Robert Holmes.
 JOHN PEYTON, of Laheen, High Sheriff of Leitrim 1751, m. a dau. of Robert Hamilton, of co. Cavan, and had issue,
 1. JOHN, his heir.
 2. Hamilton, m. Susannah, dau. of William Chambers, of Kilboyne, co. Mayo, and relict of Edmond Finn, and by her had a son,
 John Hamilton, High Sheriff co. Leitrim 1817, who m. 1814, Mary, dau. and heir of Bryan Cunningham, of Port; and d. 1863, having by her four sons and six daus.
  (1) Bernard, of Castlebar, co. Mayo, b. 1818; m. 1844, Anne Elizabeth, eldest dau. of the late Major Robert Henry Boughton, and has, with other issue, Robert Henry, b. 1848.
  (2) Hamilton, b. 1822.   (3) John, b. 1823.
  (4) William, b. 1836.
  (1) Susannah.   (2) Jane.
  (3) Mary.   (4) Emily.
  (5) Margaret.   (6) Anne.
The son and heir,
 JOHN PEYTON, of Laheen, High Sheriff 1787, and Lieut.-Col. Leitrim Militia, b. 1759; m. Mary, dau. of George Nugent Reynolds, of Lefferyan, co. Leitrim, and sister and co-heir of George Nugent Reynolds, of same place, and d. May, 1806, having by her who m. 2ndly, Richard McNamara) had issue,
 JOHN REYNOLDS, his heir.
 Jane, m. John Lambert, 2nd son of Walter Lambert, of Castle Lambert, co. Galway, and had issue (see LAMBERT of Aggard).
The son,

I.L.G.

JOHN REYNOLDS PEYTON, of Laheen, High Sheriff 1830, m. 1st, Louisa, eldest dau. of Samuel Scott, of Dublin, and 2ndly, Alicia, dau. of Andrew Ennis, of Roebuck, co. Dublin, by whom he left at his decease, 1850,
1. RICHARD REYNOLDS, late of Laheen.
2. John Reynolds.
3. JAMES REYNOLDS, now of Laheen.
The eldest son,
 RICHARD REYNOLDS PEYTON, of Laheen, co. Leitrim, J.P. and D.L., an Officer 1st Dragoons, b. 2 July, 1838; d. 1875, and was s. by his brother.

Arms—Sa., a cross engrailed or, in the 1st quarter a mullet arg. Crest—A griffin sejant or. Motto—Patior, potior.
Residence—4, Gloucester Street, Portman Square, W. Clubs—Carlton, Turf.

PHELPS OF WATERPARK.

JOHN VANDELEUR PHELPS, of Waterpark, Castle Connell, co. Limerick, and Broadford, co. Clare, J.P., High Sheriff 1889, Lieut. South of Ireland Imp. Yeom., late Capt. 3rd Batt. Royal Warwickshire Regt., b. 26 April, 1866; m. 25 April, 1903, Millicent Douglas, 4th dau. of Thomas Pilkington, of Sandside, Thurso, and has issue,
1. DOUGLAS VANDELEUR, b. 29 Jan. 1904.
2. Harold Vandeleur, b. 27 April, 1907.

Lineage.—THOMAS PHELPS joined in the revolution of 1645, and served under CROMWELL, by whom he was granted considerable estates in the cos. of Tipperary, Kerry, and Down, chiefly in the first-named co., around the Keeper Mountain, with Camaltha. Thomas Phelps settled in the city of Limerick after the revolution, and King CHARLES II. confirmed Mr. Phelps' titles to those estates, with a few exceptions. Mr. Phelps turning, however, his sword into a ploughshare, became a disciple of George Fox. At the age of 45 be m. Susan Fennell (who d. 20 Dec. 1684), dau. of a brother officer, with estates at Cahir, co. Tipperary, and had issue. He m. 2ndly, 20 June, 1687, Anne, widow of Bradford, but had no issue by her (who d. 11 Sept. 1706). His will is dated 15 Dec. 1694. By his first wife he had, with other issue, who q. young,
1. John, b. 1665; m. dau. of John Park, s.p.
2. JOSEPH, of whom presently.
1. Susanna, d. 23 Nov. 1765; m. John Bond.
2. Mary, m. 2 July, 1683, Joshua Fennell, of Kilcommonbeg, co. Tipperary.
The younger son,
 JOSEPH PHELPS, b. in Limerick 30 July, 1665; d. 3 March, 1737; m. 1st, 1710, Hannah, dau. of John Taylor, of London, and had issue by her, who d. 16 Aug. 1713. He m. 2ndly, 2 Aug. 1717, Hannah Henry, who d.s.p. 25 Feb. 1729. He m. 3rdly, 1731, Elizabeth, widow of Cubbage Hillary, but had no issue by her, who m. 2ndly, Abraham Fuller, of King's Co. By the 1st wife he had a son and two daus.,
 1. THOMAS.
 1. Susanna, b. in Limerick 1712.
 2. Anne, b. in Limerick 1712.
The only son,
 THOMAS PHELPS, b. in Limerick 17 July, 1711, was, with others, largely instrumental to the introduction of linen manufactures into the North of Ireland. He moved his residence to his estate in co. Down; m. 26 July, 1741, Sarah, only dau. of Isaachar Willcocks of Dublin, and by her had issue,
 2. Willcocks, m. Sarah Denman, of Bristol, and had issue,
  1. John.   2. Joseph.
  3. William.   4. Charles.
  1. Elizabeth, m. George Fennell.
 3. John, m. Elizabeth, dau. of Archibald Shaw, of Lurgan, and had issue,
  1. Joseph.   2. James, m. in Australia.
  3. Thomas.   4. Henry.
  5. George.
  1. Mary.   2. Louisa.
 4. Joshua.
  1. Hannah.   2. Mary.
 3. Elizabeth, m. Jacob Handcock, of Lisburn.
 4. Sarah.
The eldest son,
 JOSEPH PHELPS, of Moyallon, co. Down, b. 1749; m. Nov. 1771, Mary, dau. of Thomas Christy, of Moyallon (she was b. 9 Jan. 1750), and by her (who d. 1837) he had issue,
 1. THOMAS, m. Charlotte, dau. of Sampson Lloyd, of Bordesley, co. Warwick, and had issue,
  Joseph Lloyd, m. Evisa Smythe, and had,
   1. Thomas.   2. Joseph.
   3. William.   4. Henry.
   1. Charlotte, m. Edward Peyton, 2nd son of Abel Peyton, of Cahirspoole, Worcestershire, and Oakhurst, Edgbaston, and has issue.
   2. Emnia.   3. Mary.
   4. Rachel.
 2. John, d. unm.
 3. Joshua, m. Eliza, dau. of James Greer, of Clonrode, co. Armagh, and had issue,

2 N

Phibbs.

1. Thomas. 2. James.
3. Joseph. 4. Alfred.
1. Henrietta.
2. Caroline, m. George Valentine.
3. Mary Anne.
4. Anne Sophia, m. George Pim, of Belfast.
4. William, d. unm.   5. James, of whom hereafter.
6. George, d. unm.   7. Samuel, d. unm.
1. Sarah, d. unm.   2. Mary, m. Robert Newsom.
3. Hannah, m. George Robinson.
4. Elizabeth, d. unm.

Joseph Phelps d. 1790. His 5th son,
James Phelps, b. 1782, m. 1814, Anne dau. of John Lecky, of Ballykealey, co. Carlow, by whom (who was b. 1788, and d. 3 Sept. 1834) he had issue,
1. John Lecky, late of Waterpark.
2. Joseph James, m. 1877, Mary, dau. of Very Rev. James Hastings Allen, Dean of Killaloe. He left issue,
Thomas Herbert, b July, 1870; d. unm. 18 April, 1906.
3. Robert Lecky, m. Josephine, dau. of Col. Petley, R.A., and has issue,
1. John.
1. Anne Valverde.   2. Mabel Maude.
4. James, d. young.
1. Elizabeth Lecky, m. William H. Harvey, F.R.S., Professor of Botany, Trin. Coll. Dublin. He d.s.p. She d. 26 March, 1908.
2. Mary, d. young.
3. Jane Hannah, m. J. M. Harvey.
4. Lydia Matilda, d. unm. 1902.

Mr. Phelps d. 1839. His eldest son,
John Lecky Phelps, of Waterpark and Broadford, co. Clare, J.P., b. 15 Oct. 1815; m. 4 May, 1864, Rosetta Anne (d. 28 Oct. 1911), 2nd dau. of Col. John Vandeleur, 10th Hussars, of Ballinacourty, co. Limerick, by Alice his wife, dau. of the Right Hon. John Ormsby Vandeleur, of Kilrush House, by Lady Frances Moore, dau. of Charles, 1st Marquess of Drogheda, and d. 28 May, 1881, leaving,
1. John Vandeleur, now of Waterpark.
2. Ernest James, b. 5 Aug. 1867; m. 14 April, 1898, Sara Haughton Ridgway, younger dau. of James E. Murphy, and has issue,
John James, b. 24 July, 1899.
Doreen Mary Vandeleur, b. 22 May, 1902.
3. Edgar Lecky, b. 20 Sept. 1868; m. 7 June, 1899, Helen Louisa, only dau. of Dudley O'Grady, of Ballyhort, co. Limerick (see O'Grady of Aghamarta), and has issue,
Edgar, b. 16 June, 1900.
Helen Rose, b. 4 Aug. 1903.
4. Joseph Harold, b. 12 March, 1874.
5. Lancelot Robert Lecky, b. 19 April, 1878, and d. 15 Dec. 1887.
1. Annie Rosalie, m. 16 June, 1887, Col. and Brig.-Gen. Robert Arundel Ker Montgomery, C.B., D.S.O., R.A., and has issue, 1, Lancelot Alexander, b. 1888; 2, Robin, b. 1889; 1, MaryPipon.
2. Alice Maude, m. 9 April, 1890, Alexander Edmund Bannatyne, of Glenbevard, co. Limerick, and has issue, Edgar Alexander, b. 1891; Rose Mary, b. 1896.
3. Mary Frances, m. 6 July, 1892, Bernard Harvey Randolph, Capt. Worcester Regt., and d. 28 Oct. 1892.
4. Rosalie Emily, m. 9 Oct. 1895, Robert B. Whitehead, and has issue, 1, Thomas Bovil; 1, Mary Frances; 2, Aileen; and 3, Clare.
5. Ethel Agnes Vandeleur, m. 14 July, 1904, Marcus Wyndham Paterson, son of late Col. Marcus Paterson, D.L., of Clifden, Corofin.

Seats—Waterpark, Castle-Connell, co. Limerick; The Lodge, Broadford, co. Clare. Club—Windham, S.W.

PHIBBS OF LISHEEN.

Owen Phibbs, of Lisheen, co. Sligo, J.P. for cos. Roscommon and Sligo, D.L. for co. Sligo, and High Sheriff 1884; late Lieut. 6th Dragoon Guards; b. 25 March, 1842; m. 20 Nov. 1866, Susan, dau. of William Talbot-Crosbie, of Ardfert Abbey, co. Kerry (see that family), and has issue,

1. Basil, of Corradoo, Boyle, High Sheriff co. Sligo, 1905, b. 1867; m. 2 May, 1890, Rebekah Wilbraham, youngest dau. of Herbert Wilbraham Taylor, of Hadley Bourne (see that family), and has issue,
1. Geoffrey Basil, b. 5 April, 1900.
2. Denis William, b. 14 May, 1902.
3. Richard Owen Neil, b. 11 Jan. 1911.
1. Catherine Meave, b. 11 Oct. 1907.
2. William Talbot, LL.D., b. Oct. 1869; m. 11 Oct. 1905, Phyllis Mary, dau. of James Hunter Prinsep, late B.C.S., and has issue, James Owen Talbot, b. 17 Aug. 1908.
Elizabeth Christina, b. 26 July, 1907.
3. Owen Lindsey, C.E., b. 13 Nov. 1870.
4. Darnley, sometime Lieut. Irish Horse, served in S. African War, Willow Grange, Potchefstroom, S. Africa). m. 2 Sept. 1903, Laura, only dau. of George Hewson, of Tubrid, Ardfert, co. Kerry, and has issue,
1. Noel, b. Dec. 1902.
1. Catherine Anne.   2. Patricia.

Lineage.—Of this family two brothers came over to Ireland, as soldiers, about 1590. From records now existing in Trin. Coll. Dublin, they are found in half-pay, 1616 and 1619, under the name of Phipps, a name that some of the younger branches of the family resumed about 1765. Of these two, William settled in co. Cork, in the south-west of which county the name still remains as ffibbs. The elder of the two,
Richard Phipps, who served under Sir Tobias Caulfield, and was pensioned as a maimed soldier in 1619, settled at Kilmainham, Dublin, where he d. in 1629, and was bur. in St. James' Church. He had issue,
1. Richard, of whom presently.
2. John, living in co. Sligo, in 1663.
3. Edward, whose descendants have been traced down to the Rev. Joshua Phipps, b. 1711; m. Mary Mercer, and d. in Carlow, 20 June, 1750.
1. Hester.   2. Jane.
3. Sarah.   4. Rebecca.

The eldest son,
Richard Phipps or ffibs, of Coote's Horse, was granted land in co. Sligo 1659 (name written ffibs and Phibbs in grant): served in Capt. Francis King's troop of horse in Lord Colloney's Regt. He d. in 1670, and was interred in St. John's Church, Dublin. He had issue,
1. Matthew, of Templevaney.
2. William, of Grange, purchased Abbeyville or Ardlahurty, 3 Aug. '1715; m. Anna, dau. of John Fleming, and had issue, three sons and two daus.,

The elder son,
Matthew Phibbs, of Templevaney, afterwards of Rockbrook, co. Sligo, was High Sheriff in 1716, and d. 1738. He had issue, four sons and two daus.,
1. William, of Rockbrook and Rathmullen.
2. Richard, of Lisconney, m. Catherine Knox, of Londonderry, by whom he had issue, five sons and four daus. His will was proved 1753.
3. Robert, b. 1703; entered Trin. Coll. Dublin 1721; Rector of Ardcarne, co. Roscommon, and of Tawnagh, co. Sligo, 1745; m. Marie du Puygebeau, dau. of a Huguenot refugee (name changed in Ireland to Raboteau), and by her had three sons and five daus.; the eldest son, Isaac, Col., was gazetted as Ensign Phibbs 1768, and as Lieut. Phipps 14 March, 1771.
4. Mathew, of Spurtown, co. Sligo, b. 16 April, 1706; m. 1741, Esther, sister of Marie Raboteau, and d. 1769, leaving issue.
1. Anne, m. to Richard Fleming.
2. Margaret, m. to R. Hawkes, of Bushfield, co. Roscommon.

The eldest son,
William Phipps or Phibbs, of Rockbrook and Rathmullen, b. 1696; m. 1717, Mary, only dau. of John Harloe, of Rathmullen, by whom he had twenty-one children. He d. Sept. 1775, leaving issue surviving, three sons and five daus.,
1. Harloe, of Bloomfield, High Sheriff 1769, b. 12 July, 1719; m. 1st, Judith, dau. of Rev. C. Dodd; and 2ndly, July, 1787, Elizabeth, dau. of Mathew Phibbs, of Spurtown, and had issue, with five daus.,
1. William Harloe, of Bloomfield, High Sheriff 1814; m. 20 Jan. 1778, Susan, dau. of John Lloyd, of Croghan, and d. 1827, leaving issue, four sons and three daus.
2. Charles, of Lisconney, m. July, 1787, Sarah, eldest dau. of Thomas Ormsby, of Baltinamore (see that family), from whom descends Charles Phibbs, of Doobeg, co. Sligo.
2. Mathew, b. 1725; d. 1784.
3. William, of Hollybrook, of whom presently.
1. Mary, b. 1722; m. Thomas Trumble, of Kilmorgan.
2. Anne, b. 1724; m. John Johnston, of Dartrey.
3. Joanna, b. 1726; m. 1747, James Knott, of Battlefield.
4. Rebecca, b. 1729; m. 1757, John Irwin, of Camlin, co. Roscommon.
5. Eleanor, m. — Leeche.

The 2nd surviving son,
William Phibbs, of Hollybrook, High Sheriff, 1781, b. 20 May, 1738; m. 21 May, 1768, Jane, dau. of Owen Lloyd, of Rockville, co. Roscommon, and by her (b. 1740; d. 1817) had ten children, of whom
1. William, b. 1771; d. 1772.   2. William, b. 1773; d. 1797.
3. Owen, of whom presently.
2. Susan, b. 1769; m. Lieut. Kitson, 4th Light Dragoons, and d. 1796, leaving issue, a son.
2. Mary, m. A. Carey, of Portarlington, and had issue, four sons and four daus.,

Mr. Phibbs d. 16 July, 1801. His only surviving son,
Owen Phibbs, of Merrion Square, Dublin, High Sheriff 1804, b. 1776; m. 1798, Anne, dau. of Thomas Ormsby, of Baltinamore, co. Mayo (see that family), by whom he had issue,
1. William, of Seafield.
2. Ormsby, Lieut.-Col. 88th Regt., b. 15 March, 1806; d. at Barbadoes, 1848.
3. Owen, of Merrion Square, b. 1811; d. 29 Dec. 1899.
1. Elizabeth, d. young.
2. Jane, b. 1801; d. 1874.
3. Maria, b. 1802; d. 1886.

Mr. Phibbs d. 1829. His eldest son,
William Phibbs, of Seafield, co. Sligo, High Sheriff 1833, sometime 11th Light Dragoons, b. 1803; m. 26 May, 1840, Catherine, dau. of George Meares Maunsell, of Ballywilliam, co. Limerick. She d. 30 Nov. 1903, having had issue,
1. Owen, now of Lisheen.
2. George, Lieut.-Col. 87th Regt., b. 1844; m. Fanny, eldest dau. of Lieut.-Col. Robert Bramston Smith, of Pencraig, Anglesey, and d. 1885, leaving issue,

1. William Griffith Baynes, Major R.I. Fusiliers, b. 12 Jan. 1872.
  1. Maud, m.   2. Kathleen, m.
3. William, Col. Commanding 1st Batt. Dorset Regt., b. 8 Oct. 1845; m. 2 Jan. 1873, Rose Blanche, dau. of Rev. William De Moleyns (see BURKE's *Peerage*, VENTRY, B.), and d. Aug. 1894, leaving issue,
  1. Bertram, Lieut. R.N., m. 5 Jan. 1901, Kathleen, dau. of the late Charles William O'Hara, D.L., of Annaghmore, co. Sligo.
  2. Alured, d. Sept. 1894.
  1. Ethel Rose, m. Charles Boissevain, Amsterdam.
  2. Theodoria Helena, m. 6 Dec. 1907, Charles Reginald Willoughby Bryan, eldest son of Willoughby Bryan, of Haskells, Lyndhurst, and has issue.
1. Catherine, d. 1852.
2. Anne.   3. Edythe Frances.
Mr. Phibbs d. Dec. 1881.
Seat—Lisheen, co. Sligo.

PHIBBS OF DOOBEG.

CHARLES PHIBBS, of Doobeg, co. Sligo, J.P., b. 1 March, 1842; m. 29 June, 1877, Mary Emma, dau. of the late Henry Warburton, of Bray, co. Wicklow, and has issue,

1. CHARLES, b. 27 May, 1878; m. 24 Sept. 1908, Beatrice Gwendoline, 2nd dau. of Walter Lanyon Nickels, of Chenotrie, Cheshire, and has issue,
  Walter Charles Ormsby, b. 1909.
2. Peter Warburton, b. 22 Aug. 1880.
3. Henry Warburton, b. 2 Sept. 1883.
4. John Lynch, b. 4 May, 1885.
5. Thomas Ormsby, b. 2 May, 1890.
1. Elizabeth Anne, b. 9 Feb. 1882.
2. Mary Louisa, b. 26 Jan. 1887.
3. Sarah Mary, b. 8 Oct. 1888.
4. Harriet Margaret, b. 7 Sept. 1890.
5. Charlotte, b. 25 May, 1893.

Lineage.—CHARLES PHIBBS, of Sligo, descended from Harloe Phibbs, of Bloomfield, eldest son of William Phibbs, of Rockbrook, by Mary his wife, only dau. of John Harloe, of Rathmullen (see PHIBBS of *Lisheen*), left issue, a son,

PETER RUTTLEDGE PHIBBS, of Kingstown, co. Dublin, m. 1840, Elizabeth, dau. of — Holmes. She d. 1897. He d. 1881, having had issue,
1. CHARLES, now of Doobeg.
1. Elizabeth Vingorla, m. Rev. John Lynch.
2. Sarah Mary, d. young.

Seat—Doobeg, Ballymote, co. Sligo.

PHILLIPS OF GAILE.

MAJOR SAMUEL PHILLIPS, of Gaile, co. Tipperary, and of Foyle, co. Kilkenny, J.P. and D.L. co. Tipperary, High Sheriff 1902, Major late Royal Irish Regt., b. 11 June, 1849; m. 1885, Helen Clementina, dau. of John Gilchrist, and widow of Colin A. Fraser, and has issue,

1. RICHARD ERNEST GILCHRIST, Lieut. Roy. Irish Regt., b. 2 Nov. 1887.
1. Moira Sydney.
2. Aileen Susie, m. 9 Aug. 1911, Capt. Roland Luker, Lancashire Fus.

Lineage—SAMUEL PHILLIPS, received under the Act of Settlement 1661, a patent of the lands of Foyle, co. Kilkenny. His son,

RICHARD PHILLIPS, of Foyle, b. 1672; m. 28 April, 1697, Alice, dau. of William Despard, of Cranagh, Queen's Co. His son,

SAMUEL PHILLIPS, of Foyle, b. 1698; m. 1732, Sarah, dau. of John Max, of Killough, co. Tipperary. His son,

RICHARD PHILLIPS, of Foyle, b. 1733; m. 1755, Frances Phillips, and had a son,

SAMUEL PHILLIPS, of Foyle, b. 1756; m. 1779, Joan, dau. of John Max, of Gaile, co. Tipperary. His elder son,

RICHARD PHILLIPS, of Foyle and Gaile, b. 1780; m. 1799, Jane, dau. of Thomas Godfrey, of Beechmount, co. Tipperary, and left surviving issue, three sons and four daus. His eldest son,

SAMUEL PHILLIPS, of Gaile, co. Tipperary, b. June, 1800; m. May, 1824, Caroline Anna, dau. of Col. Richard Long, D.L., of Longfield, co. Tipperary. She d. 10 May, 1875. He d. May, 1838, having had issue,
1. Richard, his heir.
2. Samuel William, b. 3 Sept. 1827; d. 1880; m. 1851, Sarah Pilkington, and had issue, four sons and five daus.
3. John, b. 4 July, 1829; d. 1851.
4. Stephen Moore, b. 16 Sept. 1830; d. 7 June, 1906.
5. Edward, of Thurlesbeg House Cashel, co. Tipperary, J.P., b. 3 March, 1832; m. 2 Aug. 1864, Mary Catherina, dau. of John Hopkinson, of Broome House, Derbyshire, and d. 7 June, 1906, leaving issue, a son,
  John Hopkinson, b. 5 April, 1865; m. 13 Dec. 1890, Georgina Violet Masters, only child of George Colthurst Dunscombe, of Mount Desert, co. Cork (see that family), and has issue,
    (1) Edward George Masters.
    (1) Mary Violet Masters.
    (2) Georgina Margaret Masters.
6. Thomas Godfrey, of Parkville, Clonmel, co. Tipperary, b. 14 July, 1836; d. 1902.
7. Henry William Long, Maj. 12th Foot, b. 12 July, 1838; d. 1885; m. Priscilla C. Forbes, and had issue, a son, Henry F. C., m. 24 Oct. —, Elizabeth Maud, dau. of Richard Edward Ram, of Hill House, Messing, Essex.
1. Cherry Louisa, b. 4 July, 1826; dec.
2. Jane Harriet, b. 7 Sept. 1828; d. 1892.
The eldest son,

RICHARD PHILLIPS, of Gaile, J.P. and D.L., b. 1 Aug. 1825; m. 14 July, 1847, Mary Elizabeth, dau. of Fitzmaurice Hunt, of Cappagh House, co. Tipperary. She d. 1885. He d. 1894, having had issue,
1. SAMUEL, now of Gaile.
2. Fitzmaurice, b. 18 March, 1853; d. 30 Sept. following.
3. Richard, b. 17 May, 1859.
4. Henry Fitzmaurice Hunt, b. 21 Jan. 1863, who assumed the additional surname of HUNT (see HUNT of *Ballysoden*).
1. Dorothea, m. 1866, Charles Butler Prior, of Crosiogue, co. Tipperary (see WANDESFORD of *Castle Comer*).
2. Caroline Anna, d. 1902.
3. Mary Elizabeth, d. 1874.
4. Susan, d. 1883.

Seat—Gaile House, Cashel, co. Tipperary. Club—Raleigh, S.W.

PHILLIPS-CONN. See CONN.

PHILLIPS-HUNT. See HUNT.

PIGOTT OF CAPARD.

ROBERT EDWARD PIGOTT, of Capard, Queen's Co., High Sheriff 1888, late Lieut. 5th Batt. Royal Munster Fusiliers, b. 12 Sept. 1862; s. his father 1886.

Lineage.—JOHN PIGOTT, of Dysart, Queen's Co., had a grant of that estate by letters patent dated 28 Feb. 1562, in all which he was s. by his son,

SIR ROBERT PIGOTT, Knt. of Dysart, knighted by Sir Arthur Chichester, Lord Deputy of Ireland, 30 Sept. 1609; had a re-grant of Dysart by patent dated 16 Oct. 1587, and obtained a grant of Corbally, Capard, and other lands in Queen's Co., by patent dated 29 April, 1622. He m. 1st, Anne, dau. of William St. Leger and grand-dau. of Sir Anthony St. Leger, Lord Deputy, by whom (who d. 9 Oct. 1599) he had issue,

1. JOHN, of Grangbeg, s. to Dysart, Major in the Army, slain in battle with the Irish 1646, m. Martha, dau. of Sir Thomas Colclough, Knt. of Tintern Abbey, and had, with other issue,
  1. ROBERT, of Dysart, whose lineal descendant and representative, temp. GEORGE III.,
    REV. RICHARD PIGOTT, D.D., of Dysart, had an only dau. and heir,
      ANNE, m. March, 1783, Robert Shapland Carew, of Castle Boro, co. Wexford, and was mother of ROBERT SHAPLAND, 1st Lord Carew.
  2. Thomas (Right Hon.), of Long Ashton, Somerset.
  3. ALEXANDER, ancestor of PIGOTT, Bart. of *Knapton* (see BURKE's *Peerage and Baronetage*).
  4. John, who m. twice, and left issue by the 1st wife. His 2nd wife was Mary, dau. of Francis Edgeworth, and widow of Pierce Moore (see MOORE of *Cremorgan*).
2. Alexander, of Innishannon, co. Cork.
1. Sibella.
2. Dorothea, m. Andrew Hoult, of Aghenehelly, co. Cork, who d. Dec. 1637.
3. Joan.

Sir Robert m. 2ndly, Thomasine, dau. and co-heir of Christopher Peyton, Auditor at War, and widow of Peter Baptiste, alias Castilion, by whom he had further issue,
8. THOMAS, of whom hereafter.
4. William, of Kilfinny, High Sheriff co. Limerick 1655, 1656 and 1663, m. Anne, dau. and co-heir of Sir John Dowdall, Knt. of Kilfinny, co. Limerick, by Elizabeth his wife, dau. of Sir Thomas Southwell, Knt. of Pollylong, and widow of John Southwell, of Rathkeale, and d. 25 Feb. 1667, leaving issue,
  1. John, of Kilfinny, Barrister-at-Law, m. 1st, Catherine, dau. of Sir Thomas Southwell, 1st bart. of Castle Mattress, by whom (who d. 28 May, 1683) he had issue,
    (1) William, of Kilfinny, who had two sons, John and William, both d.s.p. in 1718.
    (2) SOUTHWELL, who s. to Capard.
    (3) John, d.s.p.   (4) Robert d.s.p.
    (5) Richard, d.s.p.

Pigott. THE LANDED GENTRY. 564

(1) Jane, *m.* Sir Henry Piers, 3rd bart., who *d.* 14 March, 1733, leaving issue.
He *m.* 2ndly, 1696, Margaret, dau. of Sir Cæsar Colclough, 2nd bart. of Tintern Abbey, sister and heir of Sir Cæsar Colclough, 3rd bart. of Tintern Abbey, and widow of Robert Leigh, of Rosegarland, co. Wexford, by whom (who *d.* 23 April, 1723), he had no issue. He assumed the additional surname of COLCLOUGH on his 2nd marriage, and *d.* 8 May, 1717.
1. Martha, *m.* Lieut. George Stamer, of Carnelly, co. Clare.
2. Elizabeth, *m.* Thomas FitzGerald, of Woodhouse, co. Waterford.
5. Arthur. 6. Robert.
4. Thomasine, *m.* 1st, Argentine Hull, of Leamcon, co. Cork, who *d.* Aug. [1637; 2ndly, Col. Prime Iron Rochfort, who was shot by order of Court Martial 14 May, 1652; and 3rdly George Peyton, of Streamstown, co. Westmeath (*see* PEYTON *of Lakeen*).
5. Elizabeth, *m.* Richard Cosby, of Stradbally, Queen's Co., who *d.* Dec. 1631.
Sir Robert made his will 23 May, 1641, which was proved 17 April, 1644. His eldest son by his 2nd wife,
THOMAS PIGOTT, of Capard, s. to that estate, and obtained a re-grant of the same and Corbally by patent dated 6 Dec. 1639, which estates he put into settlement on his son's marriage, 1676, and entailed them on the male descendants of himself and his brother, William Pigott. He was High Sheriff of Queen's Co. 1663, and had two sons, ROBERT and CHIDLEY, who both enjoyed the estate in succession. He *d.* intestate, and administration was granted of his chattels 30 Aug. 1686, and was *s.* by his eldest son,
ROBERT PIGOTT, of Canard, High Sheriff of Queen's Co. 1712, *m.* (settlements dated 26 Feb. 1676) Margaret, dau. of Sir Thomas Southwell, 1st bart. of Castle Mattress, who *m.* 2ndly, Thomas FitzGerald, co. Limerick, and *d.* 1717. He *d.s.p.* 1706, intestate, when he was *s.* by his brother,
CHIDLEY PIGOTT, of Capard, who administered to his elder brother 6 July, 1708, and *d.s.p.* 1718, when the estate reverted under the settlement of 1676 to his cousin,
SOUTHWELL PIGOTT, of Capard. He *m.* Henrietta Wynanda Vandergraff, by whom (who *d.* 31 March, 1747) he had issue,
1. COLCLOUGH, his heir.
2. DOWDALL, *s.* to his father.
3. John, of Rathkeale, *m.* May, 1743, Mary, dau. of William Brownlow, M.P. (ancestor of Lord Lurgan), by Lady Elizabeth Hamilton his wife, eldest dau. of James, 6th Earl of Abercorn, and had a son,
JOHN, heir to his uncles.
1. Cornelia Gertrude, *m.* May, 1739, Sir John Piers, 4th bart. of Tristernagh.
2. Margaret, *m.* Dec. 1741, Edward Riggs, Barrister-at-Law, of the Middle Temple, London.
3. Henrietta, *m.* Mr. Agnew.
Mr. Pigott, whose will, dated 18 May, 1751, with a codicil, dated 20 Feb. 1755, was proved 24 Sept. 1756, was *s.* by his eldest son,
COLCLOUGH PIGOTT, of Capard, *m.* April, 1739, Anne, dau. of Edward Riggs, M.P. for Baltimore 1707-13, Bangor 1715-27, and Newtown-Limavady 1739-41, by Anne his wife, dau. of Thomas Medlycott, M.P. for Milborne, and *d.s.p.* 1779, when he was *s.* by his brother,
DOWDALL PIGOTT, of Capard, whose will, dated 25 Feb. 1785, was proved 20 Feb. 1789. He *d.s.p.* and was *s.* by his nephew,
JOHN PIGOTT, of Capard, *m.* Elizabeth, dau. of Jonathan Lovett, of Liscombe, co. Buckingham, and had issue,
1. JOHN, his heir. 2. Robert, *d. unm.*
3. Thomas Southwell, Capt. in the Army, *b.* 19 Dec. 1793; *m.* 1820, Josephine de Steiger, dau. of Frederic, Baron de Riggisberg, by whom (who was *b.* 24 May, 1798, and *d.* 17 June, 1851) he left at his decease, 24 Oct. 1837, two sons and three daus.,
1. John Rudolph William, *b.* 1 Jan. 1822; *d.* 21 Dec. 1862.
2. HENRY ARMAND ROBERT, late of Capard.
1. Margaret Sophia Elizabeth, *m.* Alfred Zeerleder, and has issue.
2. Frederika Henrietta Mary Fanny, *m.* William de Steiger, and has issue; she *d.* 1878.
3. Henrietta Sophia Eleanor Anna, *m.* Xaver de Merhart, and has issue.
1. Mary, *m.* 15 June, 1807, Rev. Sir Henry Delves Broughton, 8th bart., of Broughton, and *d.* 26 Dec. 1863.
Mr. Pigott *d.* 1828, and was *s.* by his eldest son,
JOHN PIGOTT, of Capard, High Sheriff 1835, *m.* Harriett Eleanor Thorpe Porter, and had issue,
1. John, *d. unm. v.p.* 1846.
2. Henry Perase, High Sheriff 1844, *d. unm. v.p.* 27 May, 1864, accidentally drowned in the lake at Capard.
3. Edward, *d. unm. v.p.*
Mr. Pigott *d.* without surviving issue 3rd March, 1867, and was *s.* by his nephew,
ROBERT HENRY ARMAND PIGOTT, of Capard, Queen's Co., *b.* 2 April, 1830; *m.* 1st, 1861, Julia Theresa Eleanor Ellen, dau. of Edward Baron de Sturler, of Berne, Switzerland, by whom (who *d.* 25 Feb. 1865) he had issue,
1. ROBERT EDWARD, now of Capard.
2. Arthur, *b.* 1 Dec. 1863; *d.* 4 Feb. 1865.
1. Mary Ellen, *b.* 14 Feb. 1865; *m.* Eugende Jenner, of Berne, Barrister, and has issue.
He *m.* 2ndly, 1875, Cecile Adèle, dau. of E., Baron de Sturler, and *d.* 20 July, 1886, and was *s.* by his only surviving son.

Arms—Erm., three fusils conjoined in fesse sa., the centre one charged with a crescent or, for difference. Crest—A wolf's head erased arg., charged with a crescent gu.

Seat—Capard, Rosenallis, Queen's Co.

PIGOTT OF SLEVOY.

COL: EDWARD CHARLES PEMBERTON-PIGOTT, of Slevoy Castle, co. Wexford, and Furzecote, Maidenhead Thicket, served with the 44th Essex Regt. in the Crimea, India, Chinese War 1860 and Nile Expedition 1884-86 (medal and clasps and Khedive Star), *b.* 8 July, 1836; *m.* 1st, 24 Nov. 1859, Eliza Anne, dau. of William Elphinstone Underwood, Madras C.S., and has, with other issue,
1. GEORGE HAMILTON, *b.* 19 March, 1863.
2. Robert Edward, *b.* 6 Oct. 1866.
1. Edith Jessie, *m.* 1st, Stanley Thompson, Madras Police; and 2ndly, Joseph Todhunter, Kingsmore House, Essex.
2. Madeline Florence, *m.* 1 Nov. 1894, George Henry Hunt, eldest son of Col. W. S. Hunt, late Madras Staff Corps.
3. Ethel Christine, *m.* 25 Jan. 1899, Benjamin Edward Todhunter, elder son of Charles Franklin Todhunter, of Christchurch, N.Z.
4. Eileen Ella.

He *m.* 2ndly, 1891, Madeline Louisa, eldest dau. of Rev. Edward Pierce Grant, Vicar of Portsmouth.

Lineage.—JOHN PIGOTT, residing in co. Antrim, *temp.* CHARLES II. and JAMES II., was father of
REV. HARFINCH PIGOTT, Rector of Taghmon, Diocese of Ferns, who was *b.* 1688, entered Trin. Coll. Dublin, 2 April, 1705, became a Scholar 1708, B.A. 1709, and was appointed to the Prebend of Taghmon 1742. In March, 1733, he obtained a lease for ever of the house and lands of Slevoy, co. Wexford, from Charles Tottenham, of Tottenham Green. He had, with a dau. Hester (Mrs. Hutton), two sons,
1. Thomas (Rev.), Vicar of St. James's, Dublin, *s.* his father at Slevoy, which he sold to his brother 1746. His will, dated 16 Aug. 1775, was proved 4 June, 1776; he left an only dau., who *m.* Hardy Pemberton, of the city of Dublin, merchant, eldest son of John Pemberton, of Dublin, merchant, by Sarah his wife, dau. of Thomas Hardy, of Meath Street, Dublin, and had one son,
WILLIAM PEMBERTON, who adopted the surname of PIGOTT upon succeeding to Slevoy, of whom hereafter.
2. WILLIAM, of whom presently.

Rev. Harfinch Pigott *d.* 1746. His 2nd son,
WILLIAM PIGOTT, of Slevoy, purchased that estate from his elder brother. He was High Sheriff co. Wexford 1771, and *m.* Hannah, dau. of Jacob Goff, of Horetown, co. Wexford, by whom (who *d.* 1789) he had no issue. By his will, dated 25 July, 1788, and proved 10 Nov. following, he bequeathed his estates (with an injunction that he should take the surname of PIGOTT) to his grand-nephew,
WILLIAM PEMBERTON-PIGOTT, of Slevoy Castle, already mentioned. He was *b.* 3 Jan. 1773; was High Sheriff 1794, J.P. and Lieut.-Col. Wexford Militia 21 July, 1801. He *m.* 20 Dec. 1794, Ellen, dau. of Henry Thomas Houghton, of Kilmannock, co. Wexford, and by her (who *d.* 1 June, 1862) had issue,
1. William Henry, bapt. 4 Dec. 1796; *d.* 1815, aged 19.
2. GEORGE POWELL, his heir.
3. Thomas (Rev.), *m.* Caroline, dau. of Rev. Mr. Fletcher, of Callington, Cornwall, and left one dau.
4. Charles Cæsar, Capt. in the Indian Army, *m.* March, 1839, Mary Madeline Hannie, of co. Perth, and *d.* 12 April, 1843, leaving issue.
1. Maria Frances, *d.* 1826.
2. Jane, *m.* Rev. Maxwell Phaire, and *d.* 1829.
3. Ellen, *m.* before 1835, Rev. Maxwell Phaire.
4. Anne Eliza, *m.* Jacob W. Goff, of Horetown, co. Wexford.
5. Charlotte. 6. Martha.
7. Mary Anne, *d.* 1842.
8. Emily, *m.* 1839, Rev. Robert Polwhele, Vicar of Avenbury, who *d.* 1877 (*see* POLWHELE *of Polwhele*). She *d.* 1 June, 1907.
Col. Pemberton-Pigott *d.* 10 March, 1854. His son,
GEORGE POWELL PEMBERTON-PIGOTT, of Slevoy Castle, J.P. Capt. Wexford Militia, *b.* 2 Dec. 1802; *m.* 5 July, 1834, Mary, eldest dau. of Edward Beatty, of Healthfield, co. Wexford, and had issue,
1. EDWARD CHARLES, now of Slevoy.
2. George Powell, *m.* 13 Nov. 1869, Jemima Mabel, dau. of Maurice Wilson Knox, of Kilmannock, co. Wexford, and has issue,
1. George Frederick.
1. Elizabeth Mabel. 2. Mary Frances.
3. William Henry Samuel, late Capt. 73rd Regt., of Kyle House, co. Wexford, J.P., *b.* 1839; *m.* 1861, Mary Palmer (*d.* 20 Nov. 1908), dau. of William Taylor, Bengal C.S., and has issue.
1. Skipworth Lockwood, *b.* 1 Nov. 1864; *m.* 1892 Mabel Louise, dau. of the late Thomas James, of Llandaff, co. Glamorgan, and has issue, two daus.
2. Vicars Longley Boyse, *b.* 3 April, 1866.
3. Arthur Frederick, *b.* 10 Aug. 1867.
4. William John Hobhouse, *b.* 18 Dec. 1871; *m.* 17 Sept. 1907, Anna Georgina, dau. of Rev. John Moore, M.A., of Shillelagh.
5. Villiers Graham, *b.* 12 Dec. 1873.
6. Ernest Richard, *b.* 9 Aug. 1875.
1. Jessie Elizabeth, *b.* 4 April, 1862.
2. Mary Charlotte, *b.* 12 Aug. 1863.
3. Violet Ruthven Palmer, *b.* 10 Aug. 1870.
4. Florence Letitia, *b.* 9 Feb. 1877; *m.* 8 July, 1908, George Henry Scott.
4. Richard.
5. John Charles, *m.* 1872, Mary Margaret, dau. of David Beatty, of Borodale, and has issue.

6. Frederick Knollys, m. 12 July, 1884, Amy, dau. of Rev. John Keefe Robinson, Rector of Whitechurch, co. Wexford.
7. Henry Loftus.   8. David William.
1. Elizabeth Eleanor.
2. Olivia Goodall, m. 1st, 24 Sept. 1872, Major-Gen. Arthur Loftus Steele, and 2ndly, 1898, John Edmund Barry, D.L., of Summer Hill, and has issue (*see that family*).
3. Mary, m. 8 July, 1877, William George Williamson, Inspector Royal Irish Constabulary.
4. Emily Maude.
5. Letitia Julia, m. 15 Aug. 1896, Albert Garner Richards, of Macmine Castle, co. Wexford (*see that family*).

PIKE OF GLENDARARY.

RICHARD NICHOLSON PIKE, of Glendarary, co. Mayo, Assistant Resident Northern Nigeria, late R.N., b. 18 May, 1880.

Lineage.— RICHARD PIKE, or PYKE, of Newbury, Berks, b. 1596, had considerable estates in that co., a portion of which he offered to settle on his son, RICHARD PIKE, of Sarsfield Court, co. Cork (b. at Newbury, Berks, 1627), the first of his family who settled in Ireland, provided he returned and resided on the English estate. He m. 1655, Elizabeth, dau. of J. Jackson, of London (whose ancestors were Chief Magistrates in London), and d. in 1668, leaving issue, four sons and two daus. His son,
RICHARD PIKE, of Summerhill, co. Cork, b. 1659 ; m. Sarah, dau. of John Watson, of Kilconnor, co. Carlow, and d. 1739, leaving by her (whose will was dated 20 Aug. 1745) two sons, WILLIAM and Samuel, and four daus.
WILLIAM PIKE, of Summerhill, the elder son, was b. 1695 ; m. Deborah (whose will is dated 3 March, and was proved 28 June, 1766), dau. of John Pim, of Edenderry. He d. 1756, leaving a son,
RICHARD PIKE, of Summerhill, co. Cork, and Fullers Court, co. Kildare, b. 1748 ; m. 1779, Anne, dau. of Jonathan Wilkinson, of Riversview, Cumberland, and d. 1810, leaving a son,
JONATHAN PIKE, of Beechgrove, co. Tyrone, b. 1782 ; m. 1813, Sarah, dau. of James Nicholson, of Grange Lodge, same co. (by Lydia his wife, dau. of James Clibborn, of Hall, co. Westmeath), and had issue,
1. RICHARD, of Beechgrove.
2. James Nicholson, of Derry Vale, Tyrone, d. 1849.
3. WILLIAM, of whom presently.
1. Anne.
2. Lydia Clibborn, m. 10 March, 1841, Ebenezer Pike, of Besborough, co. Cork (*see that family*).
Mr. Pike d. 1860.
WILLIAM PIKE, of Glendarary, co. Mayo, J.P., Barrister-at-Law, m. Marion, dau. of John Watson, of Toxteth Park, co. Lancaster, by his wife Mary Anne, dau. of R. Laming, of Kent, and by her (who d. 1866) had issue,
1. RICHARD JAMES, late of Glendarary.
2. William Watson, D.S.O., F.R.C.S.I., Lieut.-Col. R.A.M.C., b. 10 March, 1860 ; m. 1886, S. L., dau. of E Wheatley.
1. Mary Anne Laming, d. 1859.
2. Sarah Helen Nicholson, d. 1865.
3. Elizabeth Barrington.
4. Marion Watson, d. 1889.
5. Isabella Harriet Wilkinson.
Mr. Pike d. 1881, and was s. by his eldest son,
RICHARD JAMES PIKE, of Glendarary, co. Mayo, Major Suffolk (late 12th) Regt., b. 17 Feb. 1850 ; m. 1879, Mary Emily, dau. of Charles Todd Naylor, and has issue,
1. RICHARD NICHOLSON, now of Glendarary.
2. William, b. 28th Sept. 1881.
3. Frank, b. 13 March, 1886.
1. Kathleen Agnes.
Major Richard James Pike d. 29 Nov. 1891.

Arms—Per pale or and arg., on a chevron az., between three trefoils slipped vert an escallop of the second. *Crest*—An arm embowed in armour, the hand gauntleted, grasping a broken spear all ppr., and charged on the elbow with an escallop az. *Motto*—Vrai à la fin.

Seat—Glendarary, Achill Sound, Westport, co. Mayo.

PIKE OF BESBOROUGH.

JOSEPH PIKE, of Besborough, co. Cork, J.P. and D.L., High Sheriff 1891, High Sheriff of City of Cork, 1898, b. 30 Dec. 1851 ; m. 28 Sept. 1881, Frances Annie, dau. of Walter R. Critchley, late of Salwick Hall, co. Lancaster, and his wife Elizabeth (*née* Dawson), and has issue,

Cecil Francis Montgomery, Lieut. Royal Dragoons, b. 3 Aug. 1882 ; d. unm. 23 Feb. 1937.
Lydia Dorothy Muriel, b. 20 Jan. 1885 ; m. 22 April, 1908, Capt. Lachlan Gordon Duff, eldest son of Thomas Gordon Duff, of Drummuir and Park, Banff, and has issue (*see that family*).

Lineage.—RICHARD PIKE, or PYKE, of Newbury, Berks, b. 1598, had estates in that co., part of which he offered to settle on his son, RICHARD PIKE, of Sarsfield Court, co. Cork, b. at Newbury 1627 (the first of the family who settled in Ireland) provided he returned to reside on his English estate. He m. 1655, Elizabeth, dau. of J. Jackson, of London, and d. 1668, leaving issue, four sons and two daus. (*see preceding Memoir*). His son,
JOSEPH PIKE, b. 15 Jan. 1657 ; d. 7 Nov. 1729 ; m. April. 1682, Elizabeth, dau. of Francis Rogers, and had, with other issue,
RICHARD PIKE, of the city of Cork, merchant, m. 1721, Mary Randall, and had issue.
1. Samuel, of Cork, banker, whose will, dated 26 July, 1775, was proved 15 May, 1797. By Katherine his wife, he left an only dau., Mary, m. Samuel Randall.
2. EBENEZER, of whom hereafter.
3. Richard, of Cork, m. Anne Penrose.
1. Sarah, m. — Wily, and had three sons, Richard, Samuel, and Thomas.
Richard Pike made his will 25 Nov. 1762, which was proved 14 Oct. 1768. His 2nd son,
EBENEZER PIKE, of the city of Cork, banker, m. 1765, Mrs. Anne Pim, widow, née Clibborn, and had issue,
1. Richard.   2. JOSEPH, of whom presently.
1. Mary, m. James Lecky, of Kilnock, co. Carlow.
2. Elizabeth.
Ebenezer Pike made his will 10 May, 1784, which was proved 25 June, 1785. His 2nd son,
JOSEPH PIKE, of Besborough, co. Cork, m. 1803, Lydia Fennell, who d. 1807, leaving issue,
1. EBENEZER, of whom presently.
2. Joseph.
1. Sarah.
Mr. Pike d. 1826. His son,
EBENEZER PIKE, of Besborough, b. 25 March, 1806 ; m. 10 March, 1841, Lydia Clibborn, dau. of Jonathan Pike, of Beechgrove, co. Tyrone (*see that family*), and by her (who d. 22 March, 1900) had issue,
1. JOSEPH, now of Besborough.
2. Ebenezer, of Kilcrenagh, Carrigrohane, co. Cork, J.P., High Sheriff 1905, b. 18 Dec. 1853 ; m. 12 Nov. 1884, Ethel Norah Godfrey, dau. of Godfrey Trevelyan Godfrey Faussett (*see that family*), and has issue,
  1. Ebenezer, b. 22 Oct. 1885.
  2. Godfrey, b. 14 Sept. 1886.
  3. Hubert, b. 31 July, 1890.
  1. Norah Eileen, b. 10 June, 1894.
  2. Hilda Marjorie, b. 13 Feb. 1898.
3. Robert Lecky, of Kilnock, co. Carlow, J.P. and D.L., High Sheriff 1885, B.A. Trin. Coll. Camb. (*Kildare Street Club*), b. 23 Jan. 1858 ; m. 1 Feb. 1883, Catherine Henrietta, dau. of Lieut.-Col. Stanley Howard, of Ballina, co. Wicklow, and has issue,
  1. Ebenezer John Lecky, b. 29 Feb. 1884.
  2. Robert Maxwell, b. 30 Aug. 1886.
  1. Rhoda Vava Mary, b. 3 Feb. 1899.
1. Sarah Louisa, m. Thomas Wilson Strangman, of Shanagarry, co. Cork.
2. Mary Lecky, m. 14 April, 1864, Arthur Pease, D.L., M.P., of Hummershuatt, Darlington, who d. 27 Aug. 1898, leaving issue.
3. Elizabeth Pike, m. 1872, Richard Goodbody, of Clara, King's Co., and has issue.
4. Lydia Josephine, m. John Wilson Walter, of Tring, and d.
5. Henrietta Sophia, m. the late Reginald Ryley, of Lea, Middlesex.
6. Anne Emily.   7. Florence Lilias.
Mr. Pike d. 29 March, 1883

Seat—Besborough, Cork. *Residence*—Dunsland, Glanmire. *Clubs*—Jun. Carlton, S.W., and Kildare Street, Dublin.

PILKINGTON OF TORE.

COL. HENRY LIONEL PILKINGTON, C.B., of Tore, co. Westmeath, late J.P. co. Westmeath, and Orange River Colony, Col. South African Constabulary, and Hon. Lieut.-Col. Commonwealth Military Forces of Australia, served with W. Australian Mtd. Inf. in S. African War, Capt. Reserve of Officers, late 21st Hussars, b. 22 May, 1857 ; m. 23 June, 1896, Louisa Ellice Benedicta Grattan, 2nd dau. of Sir John Esmonde, 10th bart. (*see* BURKE'S *Peerage*), and has issue,
1. Ellice Moira Charity Gertrude, b. 1897.
2. Annette Mina Emily Elizabeth, b. 1903.

Lineage.—RICHARD PILKINGTON, b. 1635, a descendant of the family seated at Rivington, co. Lancaster, was a staunch royalist, and had to compound for his estates. He acquired, before the year 1695, extensive property in Westmeath and King's Co., and settled at Rathgarrett or Tore, in the former co. He d. 10 Oct. 1711, leaving, by Mary his wife, two sons, 1. Richard,

High Sheriff of co. Westmeath 1709, who *d.s.p.*, and **2.** ABRAHAM, and eight daus. The 2nd son,

ABRAHAM PILKINGTON, of Tore, *m.* 2 June, 1701, Elizabeth, dau. of Thomas West, of Corleagh, co. Longford, and *d.* May, 1712, leaving by her, who *d.* 1714,

1. HENRY, his heir.
1. Mary, *m.* Philip Pakenham.
2. Elizabeth, *m.* Phineas Johnston.
3. Anne, *m.* John Walsh.
4. Martha.

The only son,
HENRY PILKINGTON, of Tore, High Sheriff co. Westmeath 1738, *m.* 1st, 4 March, 1726, his cousin, Sarah, dau. of Barakiah Low, of Newtown Low, and by her had a son,
1. ABRAHAM, his heir.

He *m.* 2ndly, 1738, Barbara, dau. of Archdeacon Sampson, and by her had two sons,
2. Edward, who left one dau., Anne Hamilton, *m.* 1789, her cousin, Henry Pilkington, of Tore (*see below*).
3. Thomas, *m.* 4 Oct. 1768, Bridget, only dau. of the Rev. Ephraim Harpur, of Urney, King's Co., and had issue,
 1. Henry, *m.* and had a son,
  Rev. Michael Pilkington, *m.* Anne Orr, sister of George Orr Dunbar, M.P. for Belfast (who *d.* 1876), and *d.* 1827, leaving issue,
   George Dunbar, *d.* 1872.
   Sarah, *d.* 1874.
 2. William, Col. in the Army.
 3. Richard, Capt. 81st Regt.
 4. Thomas, Capt. 3rd West India Regt.
 5. Edward, of Urney, King's Co., *m.* Margaret Nellis, of Upper Canada, and dying 1835, left issue,
  (1) Edward.
  (1) Elizabeth, *m.* June, 1838, Rev. Philip Kelland, late Fellow of Queen's Coll. Camb., and Professor of Mathematics at the University of Edinburgh.
  (2) Mary Anne, *m.* 11 April, 1843, Robert Potter, M.A.
 6. John, Lieut. 3rd Regt. 7. George.
 8. Sampson.
 9. Abraham, Capt. 92nd Highlanders, with which regiment he fought at Waterloo, and Capt. 2nd Life Guards, *d.* 24 May, 1843.
 10. Gammell, *d.* young.
 11. Matthew, 3rd Regt.

Mr. Pilkington *d.* 1777, and was *s.* by his eldest son,
ABRAHAM PILKINGTON, of Tore, *m.* 23 Oct. 1748, Mary Shaw, of Raheen, Queen's Co., sister of Anne, the wife of Col. Low, of Newtown Low, and had issue,
1. HENRY, his heir.
2. William, *m.* Margaret Mills, but *d.s.p.*
3. Abraham.
1. Matilda, *m.* Luke Usher.
2. Sarah, *m.* Philip North.
3. Anne, *m.* Charles North.

Mr. Pilkington *d.* 1799, and was *s.* by his son,
HENRY PILKINGTON, of Tore, J.P., *m.* 1st, 19 May, 1778, Frances Emilia, dau. of Rev. John Mulock, D.D., of Bellair, King's Co., and by her had issue,
1. HENRY, of whom presently.
2. Abraham John, Capt. Londonderry Militia, *m.* 1803, Maria, dau. of — McHugo, of co. Galway, and had issue,
 Homan, *m.* 1st, Jane, dau. of — Lambert, of co. Galway, and by her had issue, Henry, and Anna. He *m.* 2ndly, 1856, Elizabeth, widow of Mathew Baker, Q.C.
 Belinda, *m.* 1829, Isaac North Bomford, of Ferrans, co. Meath, and *d.* 1854.
3. William Lowe, Lieut. R.N., *d.* 1809.
1. Frances, *m.* 1797, John Swift Emerson, by whom she had issue.

Henry Pilkington *m.* 2ndly, 1789, Anne Hamilton, dau. and heir of Edward Pilkington (*see above*), and by her had issue, one son,
4. Edward, *m.* 1818, Eleanor, dau. of Joshua Bereton, M.D., and *d.* in 1836, leaving issue,
 1. Edward, *m.* 26 Sept. 1872, Eliza Mary, eldest dau. of Henry Woodbridge Woodbridge, late of Camberwell, Surrey.
 2. Henry Bereton, *m.* Jane Grubb, and *d.s.p.* 30 April, 1859.
 3. David, *d. unm.* 24 April, 1877.
 1. Katherine Elizabeth, *m.* 4 Aug. 1842, Rev. Canon Hebden, M.A., Church of the Ascension Rectory, Hamilton, Canada, and has issue.

Henry Pilkington *d.* 1810, and was *s.* by his eldest son,
HENRY PILKINGTON, J.P., of Tore, *b.* 3 Nov. 1780; *m.* 24 April, 1806, Barbara, 5th dau. of Rev. John Lang, Rector of Randalstown, co. Antrim. She *d.* 14 April, 1864, leaving issue,
1. HENRY MULOCK, of whom presently.
1. Elizabeth, *d.* 21 Jan. 1888.
2. Emily Frances, *m.* 10 Aug. 1848, Rev. George Phillips, D.D., President of Queen's Coll. Camb., who *d.* 5 Feb. 1892. She *d.* 14 Aug. 1898.

He *d.* 23 Dec. 1865, and was *s.* by his son,
HENRY MULOCK PILKINGTON, of Tore, co. Westmeath, J.P. and D.L., Q.C., LL.D. Trin. Coll. Dublin, M.A. Cambridge, *b.* 24 Sept. 1811; *m.* 12 May, 1855, Wilhelmina Charity, eldest dau. of John McDonnell, M.D., of Murlough, co. Antrim (*see* McDONNELL *of Brackney*). She *d.* 16 July, 1902. He *d.* 23 May, 1899, leaving issue,
1. HENRY LIONEL, now of Tore.
2. Alexander John McDonnell, *b.* 17 May, 1863; *m.* 8 Nov. 1887, Dorothy Mulock, adopted dau. of George L. Craik and Dinah M. Craik. He *m.* 2ndly, 23 Jan. 1912, Margaret Wilhelmina Grimes, younger dau. of late James McDonnell, of Kilsharvan, co. Meath (*see that family*).

3. George Lawrence, B.A. Cambridge, *b.* 4 June, 1865; killed at the storming of Lubwa's Fort, Uganda, 11 Nov. 1897.
4. Robert Rivington, B.A. Cambridge, Barrister-at-Law (*Furnival Chambers, Perth, Western Australia*), *b.* 8 Feb. 1870; *m.* 13 Dec. 1899, Ethel, dau. of Thomas Longworth-Danies, of Greenhill King's Co. (*see that family*), and has issue,
 Eunice Mina, *b.* 17 Oct. 1900.
1. Charity Mary, *d.* 11 Nov. 1911; *m.* 1 Feb. 1894, Sir Harry Rudolph Reichel, only son of the Most Rev. the Bishop of Meath (*see* REICHEL *of Newton House*).
2. Emily Georgina Catherine, *m.* 22 Sept. 1902, Rev. Henry Nathaniel Joly, 2nd son of the late Rev. John Swift Joly, Rector of Athlone.
3. Katharine Anne Isabel, *m.* 18 April, 1892, Rev. William J. Kittson, Rector of Drumconrath, Diocese of Meath, who *d.* 8 Feb. 1897, leaving issue, Wilhelmina Charity Margaret.

Seat—Tore, Tyrrels Pass, co. Westmeath.

PLUMMER, OF MOUNT PLUMMER, CO. LIMERICK.

BRUDENELL PLUMMER, of Mount Plummer, Limerick, *b.* 20 Jan. 1864.

Lineage.— RICHARD PLUMMER, of Donoman, co. Limerick, formerly of Cork, son of Richard Plummer, of Bodwyn, Wilts, who was the first of the family to settle in Ireland, *m.* Sarah Burgess, who *d.* 1715, and by her he left issue,
1. DANIEL, his only son.
1. Rebecca, *m.* Temple Briscoe.
2. Sarah, *m.* M. Corbett.

The only son,
DANIEL PLUMMER, of Castle Quin, co. Limerick, *m.* Mary, dau. of Charles Williams, of Mundilly, co. Limerick. His will was dated 24 Aug. 1728, and proved 17 Jan. 1729. He left issue,
1. Charles Williams, *d.s.p.*
2. Thomas, *d.s.p.*
3. RICHARD, his heir.

The 3rd son,
RICHARD PLUMMER, of Mount Plummer, co. Limerick. He *m.* Ellen, dau. of Frances Brudenell, of Ballinguile, co. Limerick, by his wife, Catherine Ryves. He left issue,
1. BRUDENELL, his only son.
1. Mary, *m.* 1781, Edward Deane-Freeman (*see that family*), of Castle Cor, co. Cork, High Sheriff 1797. He was *b.* 9 Jan. 1760 and *d.* 25 March, 1826. They had issue.
2. Elizabeth, *m.* Rev. Rowland Davies, and had issue.

The only son,
BRUDENELL PLUMMER, of Mount Plummer, co. Limerick, J.P. and High Sheriff 1808. He *m.* Frances, dau. of Thomas FitzGerald, Knight of Glin, of Glin Castle, co. Limerick (*see that family*), by his wife, Mary, dau. of John Bateman, of Oak Park, co. Kerry. He left issue,
1. RICHARD, his eldest son.
2. Brudenell, County Inspector, Royal Irish Constabulary, *m.* Martha, dau. of Rev. Edwin Thomas, of Ballynacourty, co. Kerry (by his wife, Jane Reeves). He *d.* 1860, leaving issue,
 1. Frances FitzGerald. 2. Mary Geraldine.
 3. Martha Edwina.
 4. Jane Louisa, *m.* Major Alexander Boyle, J.P., B.A. (Trin. Coll. Dublin), of Bridge Hill, Limavady, and has issue (*see* BOYLE *of Limavady*).
3. Thomas FitzGerald (Rev.), B.A., Dublin Rector of Mahoonagh, co. Limerick; *m.* Diana, dau. of Rev. Edwin Thomas. He *d.* leaving issue,
 1. Brudenell, *d.s.p.* 2. Edwin, *d.s.p.*
 3. Thomas.
 4. Richard (Rev.), Rector of Cootehill, co. Cavan, D.D. Dublin, *m.* Mary, dau. of Rev. John Campbell Quinn, and has issue, one dau., Mary Geraldine.
 5. Walter, M.D. 6. Charles.
 1. Fannie. 2. Diana.
 3. Jane, *m.* Rev. H. Johnston, and has issue.
4. Charles Williams, *d.s.p.* 5. Edward, *d.s.p.*

The eldest son,
RICHARD PLUMMER (Rev.), B.A. Dublin, Rector of Killury, co. Kerry, *m.* his cousin Alice, dau. of Thomas Lloyd, by his wife, Elizabeth FitzGerald, dau. of Thomas FitzGerald, Knight of Glin. He left issue,
1. BRUDENELL, his eldest son.
2. RICHARD, of whom presently.

The eldest son,
BRUDENELL PLUMMER, of Mount Plummer, co. Limerick. He *d.s.p.*, and was *s.* by his brother,

RICHARD PLUMMER, b. 1 March, 1822, Major in the Kerry Militia; m. 1861, his cousin, Elizabeth, dau. of the Rev. Richard FitzGerald, of Ballydonoghue, co. Limerick, by h's wife, Sarah Georgina Boyd. He left issue.
1. Richard, m. Sybil, dau. of Edward Barnett, of Kenton Court, Sunbury, Middlesex, and d.s.p. 8 Nov. 1904.
2. BRUDENELL, now of Limerick.
3. William FitzGerald, Lieut.-Col. in the Munster Fusiliers, b. 20 May, 1867, served in the South African War 1900-1 (Queen's Medal and four clasps), and in West Africa 1902-4 (mentioned in despatches, medal with two clasps); d.s.p. Koko Town, Southern Nigeria, 19 Dec. 1907.
1. Geraldine, d.s.p. 2 Feb. 1880.
2. Alice, d.s.p. 2 Jan. 1894.
Mr. Richard Plummer d. 31 July, 1895.

Arms.—Vert, a chevron or between three lions' heads erased of the second guttee de sang. *Crest*—A lion's head erased as in the arms. *Motto*—Vincit Veritos.

Residence—Limerick.

PLUNKET. *See* BURKE'S PEERAGE, **PLUNKET, B.**

PLUNKETT OF PORTMARNOCK.

THOMAS LUKE PLUNKETT, of Portmarnock House, co. Dublin, J.P.and D.L., High Sheriff 1897, Barrister-at-Law, late Lieut. Dublin Artillery, Militia, b. 3 April, 1850; m.27 June,1876, Lizzie, dau. of Francis Chadwick, of The Glen, Drogheda, and has three daus.,
1. Lizzie Angela Mary.
2. Caroline.
3. Maude.

Lineage.—HENRY PLUNKETT, Alderman and Mayor of the City of Dublin, 1516, living 1568 (son of RICHARD PLUNKETT, *Visitation of Dublin*,1568), m. Elizabeth, dau. of Sir Robert Dillon, Knt., Chief Justice of Common Pleas in Ireland, and had issue,
1 William.
2. Thomas, Alderman of Dublin, m. 1st, Margaret, dau. of Alderman James Bellew, and 2ndly, Joan, dau. of John Long, of Newry, and widow of Robert Panting. He d. 26 Jan. 1620, leaving issue by his 1st wife only,
  1. Robert, of Rathmore, m. Eleanor, dau. of John Segrave, of Cabragh, co. Dublin, and d. 23 Oct. 1661, leaving isssue,
    (1) John, of Rathmore, m. Elizabeth, dau. of Michael Browne, Sheriff of Dublin.
    (2) Thomas.
    (3) Christopher.
    (4) Ignatius.
    (5) Lawrence.
    (1) Margaret.
    (2) Alison.
    (3) Mary.
    (4) Jane.
  2. Walter, who administered to his brother.
  1. Elizabeth, m. Edward Dowdall, of Athlumney, co. Meath.
  2. Elinor, m. Rowland Chamberlaine.
  3. Anne, m. Richard Jordan, of Dublin, who d. 20 June, 1635.
3. James.
4. LUKE, of whom hereafter.
1. Alice, m. John Rochfort, of Dublin, merchant, and d. 7 Jan. 1623 (*Fun. Entry, Ulster's Office*).
2. Elizabeth.
3. Joan.

His 4th son,
LUKE PLUNKETT, of the City of Dublin, merchant, obtained a grant by patent dated 8 June, 1635, of the castle, town, lands, and hereditaments of Portmarnock, co. Dublin. He m. Ellinor Panting, and d. 1636, leaving, with a dau., Margaret, a son,
WILLIAM PLUNKETT, of Portmarnock, m. Anne, dau. of Sir Theodore Duffe, Knt., by whom (who d. 27 Aug. 1666) he had issue,
1. LUKE, his heir.
1. Lucy.
2. Mary.
3. Teresa.
He d. 2 Dec. 1662, was bur. at St. Andrews, and was s. by his son,
LUKE PLUNKETT, of Portmarnock, m. Josiah, dau. of Michael St. Lawrence, and had issue,
1. William.
2. THOMAS, who eventually s. to the estate, of whom hereafter.
3. John.
4. Ignatius.
1. Elizabeth.
2. Jane.
3. Frances.
4. Anne.
5. Susan.
6. Mabel.

His will, dated 14 Oct. 1682, was proved 2 July following. The 2nd son,
THOMAS PLUNKETT, of Portmarnock, m. Katherine Kennedy, and had issue,
1. LUKE, his successor.
2. William, m. Bridget Caddell (his will, dated 26 May, 1756, was proved 13 Feb. 1770).
3. Walter.
1. Anne (Mrs. FitzSimons).
Mr. Plunkett d. 1728, and was s. by his eldest son,
LUKE PLUNKETT, of Portmarnock, m. Frances Caddell, and had issue,
1. THOMAS, his successor.
2. William.
3. Richard.
1. Margery.
Mr. Plunkett d. April, 1755, and was s. by his eldest son,
THOMAS PLUNKETT, of Portmarnock, who had, with other issue, a dau., Frances, m. Henry Vernon, of Clontarf Castle, and an elder son, his successor,
LUKE PLUNKETT, of Portmarnock, Barrister-at-Law, m. 14 Aug. 1805, Helen, dau. of John Howard, of Willow Bank, co. Dublin, and had issue,
1. JOHN WILLIAM, his heir.
1. Maria, b. 10 April, 1806 ; m. 1828, Rev. James Lawson, of Waterford, and had issue.
2. Helen, b. 26 Jan. 1809 ; m. 1828, William England, of Hindringham, co. Norfolk, and d. 1829, leaving issue.
The son and heir,
JOHN WILLIAM PLUNKETT, of Portmarnock, J.P., m. 7 May, 1849, Caroline, dau. of Lawrence Esmonde White, of Scarnagh, J.P. co. Wexford, and d. 24 Feb. 1862, leaving a son and successor, the present THOMAS LUKE PLUNKETT, of Portmarnock.

Arms—Sa., a bend arg., in chief a tower triple-towered of the last, a border gu. *Motto*—Festina lente.

Seat—Portmarnock House, Baldoyle, co. Dublin. *Clubs*—Hibernian, United Service.

PLUNKETT. *See* BURKE'S PEERAGE, **FINGALL, E., LOUTH, B.,** and **DUNSANY, B.**

POË OF RIVERSTON.

CAPT. JAMES HILL POË, of Riverston, co. Tipperary, M.A. Trin. Coll. Dublin, J.P. and D.L. co. Tipperary, late Capt. 94th Regt., served in Africa (medal), b. 10 July, 1845 ; m. 22 June, 1875, Elinor Mary Anne, 2nd dau. of the late Richard Warburton, of Garryhinch, King's Co., D.L., and has issue,
1. JOHN HUGH LOVETT, Lieut. West India Regt., b. 22 Nov. 1878
1. Mary Eleanor, m. 30 Sept. 1903, Standish Grady John Parker-Hutchinson, of Timoney, and has had issue (*see that family*).
2. Blanche Frances Jane.
3. Ida Maud.

Lineage.—THOMAS and WILLIAM POE, two brothers, were Officers in CROMWELL'S Army, and by the roll of muster it appears were at the siege of Limerick, for which services grants of land in Ireland in fee and freehold were made to them, and confirmed by King WILLIAM III., 1691.
EMANUEL POE, eldest son of Capt. Thomas Poe, d. 1683, having had issue,
1. WILLIAM, of Knock, from whom descended the Donnybrook branch, now extinct in the male line.
2. EMANUEL, of Clonnuck, from whom is descended the Solsborough branch.
3. JAMES, who purchased the Harley Park estate, co. Kilkenny (*see* POE *of Harley Park*).
The 2nd son,
EMANUEL POE, of Solsborough, m. Mary, dau. of Col. Hill, of Derry, who had a command at the siege of Derry, and d. 1727, leaving,
1. JOHN, his successor, d.s.p. 1771.
2. Emanuel, of Movroe, had three sons, who d.v.p. unm., and one dau., m. John Foster Hill Forster.
3. JAMES, heir to his brother John, and of whom presently.
The 3rd son and eventual heir,
JAMES POE, of Solsborough, s. his brother John ; he m. 1772, Blanche, dau. of Samuel Waller, of Newport, by his wife Anne Jocelyn, sister of Robert, 1st Baron Newport, afterwards Viscount Jocelyn, Lord Chancellor of Ireland. (Blanche's sisters, Charlotte, m. John Bloomfield, ancestor to Lord Bloomfield, and Elizabeth, m. Cooke Otway, of Castle Otway.) He d. 1784, having had issue.
1. JOHN, b. 1773 ; m. 1800, Barbara, dau. of Thomas Bernard, of Castle Bernard, King's Co., and d.s.p. 24 April, 1857.
2. JAMES HILL, of whom presently.
3. Samuel Waller, m. Anne Richardson, and d.s.p.
4. Robert Waller, m. 12 Aug. 1817, Anne, dau. of William Harington, Madras C.S., and d. 11 April, 1851, having by her (who d. 15 May, 1827) had issue,
  1. Robert Harington, b. 27 Oct. 1820 ; dec.

Poe. THE LANDED GENTRY. 568

2. William Harington, late of Calcutta, Solicitor, b. 3 Sept. 1822, and d. 23 Sept. 1859.
3. HENRY HARINGTON, of Solsborough, co. Tipperary, J.P. and D.L., late of Calcutta, Solicitor, b. 7 Nov. 1824; m. 20 Nov. 1856, Caroline, youngest dau. of James Ilbery, and widow of Samuel Turner Fearon, M.D., of Hoddesdon, Herts. She d. 9 April, 1888. He d. 19 Aug. 1898, leaving issue,
(1) William Harington, b. 18 May, 1858; d. 7 Nov. 1859.
(2) HENRY ROBERT, b. 2 June, 1860; killed at Listowell, 1902.
(1) Annie Blanche Caroline, m. Capt. Rupert Sullivan, I.S.C.
4. Emanuel Thomas (who has adopted the surname HARINGTON, after his mother), b. 23 March, 1827; m. 6 Oct. 1859, Isabella Jane, eldest dau. of James William Crowdy, late Capt. 47th Regt., and has had issue,
(1) Robert James, b. 11 Aug. 1860; d. 9 June, 1861.
(2) Lawrence Ilbery, b. 14 Dec. 1861; m. 1895, Ianthe, dau. of F. J. Rhodes.
(3) Herbert Henry, Capt. Lincolnshire Regt., b. 14 Aug. 1868.
(4) Charles Harington, Lieut. King's Regt., b. 31 May, 1872.
(1) Eleanor Kathleen.
1. Annie Blanche, m. 24 Nov. 1839, Henry John Childe Shakespear, of the Bengal army (Comm. of the Nagpore Irregular Force), and d. 2 June, 1857, leaving issue.
2. Cecilia, d. in infancy.
3. Eliza Henrietta, d. Sept. 1860.
5. Emanuel Thomas, Major 50th Regt., d. unm. 7 Jan. 1822, at Up Park Camp, Jamaica.
The 2nd son,
REV. JAMES HILL POE, M.A., Rector of Nenagh, b. 19 Oct. 1777; m. 1806, Frances (who d. 7 Feb. 1864), dau. of William Poe, of Donnybrook line, and d. 7 Feb. 1859, leaving issue,
1. JAMES JOCELYN, his heir. 2. John.
3. William Thomas, M.A., Barrister-at-Law, of Curraghmore, co. Tipperary, and Glen Ban, Queen's Co., b. 17 June 1811; m. 1st, 1842, Mary Ellen, dau. of George Leslie, of Donaghadee, by whom (who d. 12 Oct. 1851) he had issue,
1. James Leslie (Rev.), M.A., b. 15 Oct. 1844, Rector of Earsham, Norfolk; d. unm. 19 July, 1886.
2. George Leslie, of Suntry Court, co. Dublin, and of Glen Ban, Abbeyleix, Queen's Co., Capt. R.N. (retired), b. 29 May, 1846; m. 14 Nov. 1877, Mary Caldecott, dau. of the late Edward Charley, of Conway House, Dunmurry, co. Antrim, and has issue,
(1) Charley Vernon Leslie, Capt. King's; Royal Rifle Corps, b. 22 July, 1880.
(2) Leonard Hutcheson, b. 1 Aug. 1888.
(1) Violet Mary, b. 25 Oct. 1878; m. 29 Jan. 1902, Gerald Edward Campbell Maconchy, youngest son of the late George Maconchy, of Rathmore, co. Longford (see that family), and has issue.
(2) Muriel Gladys, b. 28 Feb. 1882.
3. William Hutcheson, C.B., Col. late Royal Marines, b. 20 Sept. 1848 (see POE of Heywood).
4. Edmund Samuel (Sir), K.C.V.O. 1906, K.C.B. (Military) 1908, Admiral, of Black Hill, Abbeyleix, Queen's Co., J.P., was Commodore in Command of the Training Squadron 1897-1900, Rear-Adm. 2nd in Command Home Fleet 1903, Commanded 1st Cruiser Squadron 1904-05, Commander-in-Chief East Indies Station 1905-07, and of Cape of Good Hope Station 1907-08, Commander-in-Chief Mediterranean Fleet 1910, J.P for Queen's Co., A.D.C. to Queen Victoria 1899, and to the King 1901, b. 11 Sept. 1849; m. 1 Sept. 1877, Frances Catherine, eldest dau. of the late Gen. Sir Justin Sheil, K.C.B., formerly H.M.'s Minister in Persia, and has issue,
(1) William Skeffington, Capt. R.M.A., b. 24 June, 1878.
(2) Basil Richard, Lieut. R.N., b. Feb. 1883.
(1) Grace Mary Leonora, b. 1879; m. 14 May, 1907, Commander Howard Keely, R.N.
Mr. W. T. Poë m. 2ndly, 14 June, 1854, Hon. Elizabeth Mary Skeffington, youngest dau. of Thomas Henry, 2nd Viscount Ferrard, by Harriet his wife, 10th Viscountess Massereene. She d.s.p. 19 June, 1878. He d. 14 Feb. 1892.
4. Percy Jocelyn, b. 24 April, 1821; m. Mary Sophia, dau. of W. Roake, of Surrey Villa; d.s.p. 25 March, 1883.
1. Barbara Ellen, m. Rev. Henry Beasely, M.A.
The eldest son,
JAMES JOCELYN POE, of Derrinvohill, co. Tipperary, M.A. Trin. Coll. Dublin, b. 4 Dec. 1807; m. 29 Sept. 1843, Jane Lovett, eldest dau. and sole heir of the late John Bennett, of Riverston, co. Tipperary, and d. 1895, leaving issue,
1. JAMES HILL, now of Riverston.
2. John Thomas BENNETT-POE, who assumed the name of BENNETT 1889, M.A. Trin. Coll. Dublin. b. 22 Sept. 1846; m. 3 June, 1889, Rosetta Mary, widow of Harford Pearson, and dau. of Thomas Sanders, Q.C. She d. 10 March, 1891.
Seat—Riverston, Nenagh, co. Tipperary. Club—Naval and Military, W.

POË OF HEYWOOD.

MARY ADELAIDE POE, of Heywood, Queen's Co., Slaghtfreedan, co. Tyrone, only surviving dau. of the late Sir William Compton Domvile, 3rd bart. (see BURKE's Peerage), b. 26 June, 1855; m. 21 Jan. 1886, Col. WILLIAM HUTCHESON POE, C.B., late Royal Marines, J.P. and D.L. Queen's Co, (High Sheriff 1891), High Sheriff co. Tyrone 1893, 3rd son of William Thomas POË, of Curraghmore, co. Tipperary (see POE of Riverston), and by him has issue,
1. HUGO COMPTON DOMVILE, b. 19 June, 1889.
1. Mary Gwendoline, b. 23 Dec. 1886; d. 22 Oct. 1890.
2. Isabel May, b. 30 July, 1893.

Lineage.—SIR COMPTON POCKLINGTON DOMVILE, of Templeogue, and Santry (see BURKE's Peerage), custos rotulorum of the co. of Dublin, and for eighteen years a Member of the Imperial Parliament, was created a baronet 22 May, 1815. He m. 1st, 21 Oct. 1811, Elizabeth Frances, dau. of the Hon. and Right Rev. Charles Lindsay, D.D., Bishop of Kildare, and cousin of the Earl of Crawford and Balcarres, by whom (who d. 1812) he had a son,
1. Compton Charles, an Officer in the Army, b. 1812; m. 19 April, 1842, Isabella Maria, eldest dau. of Sir Charles Arthur, Bart., and d.s.p. at Nice, 19 March, 1852. His widow m. 2ndly, 18 Feb. 1868, Charles J. Malton, and d. 22 July, 1891.
Sir Compton m. 2ndly, 7 Dec. 1815, Helena Sarah, dau. of Frederick Trench, of Heywood, Queen's Co., by whom (who d. 10 Feb. 1859) he had issue,
2. Frederick Compton Henry, b. 1821; d.s.p. 1828.
3. CHARLES COMPTON WILLIAM, 2nd bart.
4. WILLIAM COMPTON, 3rd bart.
1. Anna Helena, m. 21 June, 1842, Sir Thomas Edward Winnington, Bart., and d. 29 March, 1883.
2. LOUISA ELIZABETH, m. 24 Nov. 1865, His Excellency Torben De Bille, Danish Minister at the Court of St. James, and d. his widow, 26 March, 1888, aged 69.
3. Emily Frances, d. unm. 15 Aug. 1864.
Sir Compton d. 23 Feb. 1857, and was s. by his son,
SIR CHARLES COMPTON WILLIAM DOMVILE, 2nd bart., Hon. Col. 4th Batt. Royal Dublin Fusiliers, b. 24 Dec. 1822; m. 20 June, 1861, Lady Margaret St. Lawrence, 4th dau. of Thomas, 3rd Earl of Howth, K.P. Sir Charles, d.s.p. 10 July, 1884, and was s. by his brother,
SIR WILLIAM COMPTON DOMVILE, 3rd bart., J.P. and D.L., b. 20 May, 1825; m. 12 July, 1854, Caroline, dau. of Gen. Hon. Robert Meade, and by her (who d. 8 July, 1890) had,
1. COMPTON MEADE (Sir), 4th and present bart. (see BURKE's Peerage).
1. MARY ADELAIDE, s. her aunt, LOUISA ELIZABETH, widow of His Excellency Torben De Bille, Danish Minister, 26 March, 1888, and is now of Heywood.
2. Helen Maud, b. 4 July, 1862; d. 10 Jan. 1865.
3. Evelyn Caroline, b. 7 March, 1864; d. 19 Sept. 1884.
Sir William d. 29 Sept. 1884.

Seats—Heywood, Ballinakill, Queen's Co.; Slaghtfreedan Lodge , Cookstown, co. Tyrone.

POE OF HARLEY-PARK.

JAMES PUREFOY POE, of Harley Park, co. Tipperary, J.P. cos. Kilkenny and Tipperary, b. 21 Dec. 1859.

Lineage.—CAPT. JAMES POE, 3rd son of Emmanuel Poe (see POE of Riverston), purchased the Harley Park estate. He m. Mary Cooke, of Kiltinan, and d. 1728, leaving issue,
1. James, of whom presently.
2. Susan, m. 7 Nov. 1729, Purefoy Poe, son of William Poe, of Knock, and d.s.p.
The son,
JAMES POE, of Harley Park, m. Bridget, dau. of the Hon. Richard Power, Baron of the Court of the Exchequer in Ireland, and d. 1756, having had issue (with a dau., Susan) three sons,
1. PUREFOY, his heir.
2. John, m. Miss Barton, of Ballyline, and had three sons,
1. James, of Kilkenny, m. 1820, Harriet Arabella Waters, and d. 1851, leaving issue,
(1) James, Clerk of the Crown, co. Kilkenny, b. 1827; m. 1857, Susan Elizabeth, 2nd dau. of Rev. Jeremiah McCheane, and has issue,
1. Purefoy, d. unm. 17 March, 1910.
2. James, LL.D., m. 1st, Kathleen Sophia (d. 23 March, 1907), 2nd dau. of Thomas Kough, and has issue,
a. Harriet Patricia Kathleen. b. Dorothy.
He m. 2ndly, 24 June, 1911, Agnes Berenice, dau. of John Child Hanyngton, M.C.S.
3. John, Major R.A. Medical Corps, m. Kathleen Goff, and has issue,
John.
Katherine Mary.
1. Ellen, m. 12 April, 1898, William T. Pilsworth.
2. Harriet. 3. Susan.
4. Mary, m. Henry Stoker, M.D., and has, Edward.
(2) Purefoy, m. 1861, Elizabeth Shaw, dau. of Rev. Jeremia McChearne, and has issue,
1. Purefoy (Rev.). 2. James Leonard (Rev.).
2. John William.
1. Bessie William. 2. Georgina Arabella.
(3) John.
(4) Robert.
(5) Richard De Shee.

(1) Mary, m. James Comerford.
(2) Anne, m. William F. Winslow.
(3) Harriet.
(4) Georgiana Susan.
(5) Margaret.
2. Purefoy, m. Miss Izod, d.s.p.
3. John, resided in England.
3. James, d.s.p.
The eldest son,
PUREFOY POE, of Harley Park, m. 3 March, 1769, Martha, eldest dau. of the Hon. George Smyth, one of the Barons of the Exchequer in Ireland, and left at his decease, 15 Feb. 1817, an only son and heir,
JAMES PUREFOY POE, of Harley Park, J.P., b. 23 Oct. 1777; m. 28 Jan. 1818, Catherine, only dau. of Arthur Adams, of Bengerstown, and by her (who d. 26 Feb. 1863) had issue,
1. PUREFOY, his heir.
2. ARTHUR, s. his brother.
3. James, b. 3 Feb. 1830; d. unm. Feb. 1898.
1. Frances, d. young, Feb. 1827.
2. Martha, d. unm. 1887.
3. Kate, m. Rev. George Russell, and d. 1888.
4. Susan, d. unm. March, 1893.
5. Frances, d. unm. Feb. 1891.
Mr. Poe d. July, 1851. His eldest son,
PUREFOY POE, of Harley Park, J.P., High Sheriff of co. Kilkenny 1854, d. unm. July, 1860, and was s. by his brother,
ARTHUR POE, of Harley Park, J.P., for cos. Tipperary and Kilkenny. High Sheriff 1869, b. 1 Nov. 1828; m. 15 Sept. 1858, Olivia Elizabeth, dau. of John Jacob, M.D., of Maryborough, Queen's Co., and d. 1 Oct. 1903, having had issue,
1. JAMES PUREFOY, now of Harley Park.
2. John Julius Evans, b. 16 March, 1864.
3. Arthur Percy, b. 4 Sept. 1866; m. 1903, Ethel Amelia McGibbon, and has issue,
Jeffrey Arthur.
Violet Ethel.
1. Katherine Adelaide.
2. Olive, m. 1901, George Coddington Ball.
Seat—Harley Park, Callan.

POLLARD-URQUHART. See URQUHART.

POLLOCK OF MOUNTAINSTOWN.

JOHN POLLOCK, of Mountainstown, co. Meath, b. 9 Nov. 1896; s. his father 1905.

Lineage.—The estate of Mountainstown was in the possession of the family of Pollock some time prior to 1800. In that year it was left by JOHN POLLOCK to his son,
ARTHUR HILL CORNWALLIS POLLOCK, of Mountainstown, co. Meath, High Sheriff 1809, m. 1811, Jessy, dau. of George Clark, of West Hatch, Middlesex, and d. 1846, leaving issue,
1. JOHN OSBORNE GEORGE, of whom hereafter.
2. George Annesley, of Oatlands, co. Meath, m. 1846, Louisa, eldest dau. of Daniel McKay, of Stephens Green, Dublin, and d. Jan. 1867, leaving, with other issue,
Arthur John Osborne, of Newcastle, Kingscourt, co. cavan, Col. late 21st Royal Scots Fusiliers, b. 1846; m. 1887, Susan, dau. of William Richardson, of Brooklands, co. Antrim. He d. 20 Sept. 1901.
The elder son,
JOHN OSBORNE GEORGE POLLOCK, of Mountainstown, co. Meath, J.P. and D.L., High Sheriff 1854, b. 21 Oct. 1812; m. 18 June, 1856, Maria Louisa, eldest dau. of Henry Darley, of Wingfield, Bray, co. Wicklow, and by her (who m. 2ndly, 1883, Lieut.-Col. John Nicholas Coddington, and d. 25 March, 1886) had issue,
1. ARTHUR HENRY TAYLOR, of whom presently.
2. JOHN NAPER GEORGE, late of Mountainstown.
1. Jessy Frances Elizabeth, b. 6 June, 1857; d. unm. 6 May, 1879,
Mr. J. O. G. Pollock d. 7 March, 1871. His elder son,
ARTHUR HENRY TAYLOR POLLOCK, of Mountainstown, b. 18 Nov. 1858; d.s.p. 23 Feb. 1881, and was s. by his brother,
JOHN NAPER GEORGE POLLOCK, of Mountainstown, co. Meath, J.P. and D.L., High Sheriff 1884-5, b. 19 Jan. 1861; m. 3 June, 1891, Anna Josephine (Mountainstown, Navan, co. Meath), 5th dau. of Sir Croker Barrington, Bart, D.L., of Glenstal, co. Limerick, and d. 13 Feb. 1905, leaving issue,
1. JOHN, now of Mountainstown.
1. Anna Jessy. 2. Hazel Burton.
Seat—Mountainstown, near Navan.

POLLOK OF LISMANY.

ALLAN BINGHAM POLLOK, of Lismany, co. Galway, J.P., Capt. 7th Hussars, b. 3 March, 1874.

Lineage.—ALLAN POLLOK, of Faside, Renfrewshire, m. Jane, dau. of John Coats, of Philips Hill, and Kilbride, and has issue,
1. ALLAN, his heir.
1. Agnes, m. James Crum, of Bushby.

2. Janet, m. Patrick Graham, W.S., of Edinburgh.
Mr. Pollok d. 1851, and was s. by his son,
ALLAN POLLOK, of Lismany, J.P. and D.L., High Sheriff 1871, b. 16 June, 1815, m. Aug. 1839, Margaret, dau. of Arthur Pollok, of Lochliboside, N.B., and had by her (who d. 1861) issue,
1. Arthur, b. 1847; d. 1864. 2. JOHN, of Lismany.
1. Barbara Thompson, m. 1859, John Gardner, of Lisbeg, co. Galway.
2. Mary Thompson, m. 1873, Rev. John N. Ward, of Gressenhall Rectory, co. Norfolk.
Mr. Pollok d. March, 1881. His only surviving son,
JOHN POLLOK, of Lismany, J.P. and D.L., High Sheriff, 1881, b. Dec. 1850; m. 13 April, 1873, Hon. Florence Madeline Bingham, 2nd dau. of John Charles Robert, 4th Lord Clanmorris, and by her (who m. 2ndly, 6 June, 1895, Capt. J. D. Barry, late R.A.) had issue,
1. ALLAN BINGHAM, his heir.
2. Arthur Persse (Grove, Fethard, Tipperary), b. 26 Dec. 1874; m. 11 Sept. 1902, Elizabeth Rose, 2nd dau. of the late William Bassett Holmes, of St. David's, Nenagh, and has issue,
John Traherne, b. 4 May, 1904.
3. Ian Frederick, Lieut. 9th Lancers, b. 19 Sept. 1876, killed in S. Africa, 3 June, 1900.
4. Valentine Robert, Lieut. 15th Hussars, b. 14 Feb. 1884.
1. Zara Eileen, b. 20 Jan. 1879; m. 1 June, 1908, Capt. the Hon. Alexander Gore Arkwright Hore-Ruthven, V.C., son of Right Hon., Baron Ruthven (see BURKE's Peerage).
2. Ruby Irene, b. 23 Sept. 1881; m. 5 Dec. 1905, Louis Fleischmann, of 59, Brooke Street, W.
3. Sheela Maud, b. 7 Oct. 1886; m. 20 Oct. 1910, Capt. Frederick St. John Blacker, of Castle Martin, co. Kildare.
Mr. Pollok d. Aug. 1891.
Seat—Lismany, Ballinasloe. Clubs—Cavalry, and Kildare Street.

PONSONBY OF KILCOOLEY ABBEY.

THOMAS BRABAZON PONSONBY, of Kilcooley Abbey, co. Tipperary, J.P. and D.L., High Sheriff co: Kilkenny 1906, late 10th Hussars, b. 29 Dec. 1878; m. 25 Nov. 1909, Frances Mary, dau. of Major George Paynter, of Gate House, Leek (see that family).

Mr. Ponsonby is the elder son of the late Chambré Brabazon Ponsonby, 10th Hussars, of Kilcooley Abbey, who d. 9 Dec. 1884, and the Hon. Mary Eliza Sophia Plunkett, dau. of Edward, 16th Lord Dunsany, and great-grandson of Chambré Brabazon Ponsonby-Barker, of Kilcooley Abbey, son of Chambré Brabazon Ponsonby, of Ashgrove, by Mary his 3rd wife, dau. of Sir William Barker, Bart., of Kilcooley, and grandson of Major-Gen. the Hon. Henry Ponsonby, of Ashgrove, 2nd son of William, 1st Viscount Duncannon.

Lineage, Arms, &c.—(See BURKE's Peerage, BESSBOROUGH, E.).

Seat—Kilcooley Abbey, Thurles, co. Tipperary.

TALBOT-PONSONBY OF INCHIQUIN.

CHARLES WILLIAM TALBOT-PONSONBY, of Inchiquin, co. Cork, J.P. cos. Cork and Hants, retired Lieut. R.N., b. 29 May, 1843; assumed by Royal Licence 11 Oct. 1866, the additional surname and arms of PONSONBY; m. 15 Jan. 1868, Constance Louisa youngest dau. of F. P. Delmé-Radcliffe, of Hitchin Priory, Herts, and has had issue,
1. William Charles Frances, b. 14 Oct. 1868; d. 6 June, 1870.
2. John Seymour William, Lieut. R.N., b. 1 May, 1870; d. 15 Jan. 1895.
3. EDWARD FREDERICK, Capt. (retired) late R.H.A., b. 21 Oct. 1872; m. 26 Sept. 1899, Marion Theodora, dau. of William Nicholson, of Basing Park (see that family), and has issue,
John Arthur, b. 10 March, 1907.
Marion Constance, b. 19 Jan. 1904.

Ponsonby. THE LANDED GENTRY. 570

4. Charles George, B.A. Oxford, Barrister-at-Law, b. 1 May, 1874.
5. Frederick William, Lieut. R.N., b. 19 Jan. 1879.
6. Arthur Haigh Brabazon, b. 4 Sept. 1885.
1. Evelyn Mary Georgiana, b. 22 Feb. 1876.
2. Constance Emma, b. 18 Nov. 1882.

Lineage.—WILLIAM BRABAZON PONSONBY, 4th Lord Ponsonby, of Imokilly, dying s.p. 10 Sept. 1866, that title became extinct, and his cousin, the present Mr. TALBOT-PONSONBY, s. to the manor of Inchiquin, in the Barony of Imokilly, co. Cork, under the will of William, 3rd Lord Ponsonby, assuming thereupon, by Royal Signmanual, the name and arms of PONSONBY, in addition to those of TALBOT (see BURKE's *Peerage*, SHREWSBURY AND TALBOT, E.).

THE VERY REV. CHARLES TALBOT, Dean of Salisbury (2nd son of the Hon. and Rev. George Talbot, D.D., who was 3rd son of Charles, 1st Lord Talbot, of Hensol, Lord Chancellor of England), 26 Oct. 1769; m. 27 June, 1796, Lady Elizabeth Somerset, dau. of Henry, 4th Duke of Beaufort, and d. 28 Feb. 1823, leaving by her (who d. 5 May, 1836), five sons and six daus. The 2nd son,

ADMIRAL SIR CHARLES TALBOT, K.C.B., b. 1 Nov. 1801; m. 11 Dec. 1838, Charlotte Georgiana, widow of Lieut.-Col. Stapleton, dau. of Major-Gen. the Hon. Sir William Ponsonby, K.C.B., and sister of William, 3rd Lord Ponsonby, of Imokilly, and d. 8 Aug. 1876, having by her (who d. 7 Sept. 1883), had, with other issue (see BURKE's *Peerage*, SHREWSBURY, E.), a son, the present CHARLES WILLIAM TALBOT-PONSONBY, R.N., now of Inchiquin.

Arms—Quarterly: 1st and 4th, gu., a chevron between three combs arg., for PONSONBY; 2nd and 3rd, gu., a lion rampant, within a border engrailed or, for TALBOT. **Crests**—1st, On a ducal coronet or, three arrows, points downwards, one in pale and two in saltire, shafts or, feathered and pointed arg., entwined by a serpent ppr., for PONSONBY; On a cap of maintenance gu., turned up erm., a lion statant, tail extended or, for TALBOT. **Mottoes**—1st, Pro rege, lege, grege; 2nd (over and crest), Prest d'accomplir.
Seat—Inchiquin, near Youghal, and Langrish House, Petersfield, Hants. **Clubs**—Carlton, S.W., and Naval and Military, W.

PONSONBY.
See BURKE's PEERAGE, **BESSBOROUGH, E.**

POOLE OF MAYFIELD.

HEWITT RICHARD POOLE, of Mayfield, co. Cork J.P., b. 18 Jan. 1853; s. his father, 1903; m. 27 April, 1911, Grace French, 4th dau. of James Edward Somerville, M.D. (see SOMERVILLE of Drishane).

Lineage.—THOMAS POOLE purchased the estate of Mayfield, co. Cork. He m. Mary, dau. of Francis Bernard, of Castle Mahon, co. Cork, and was father of
FRANCIS POOLE, of Mayfield, m. Margaret, dau. of Capt. Thomas Hungerford, of The Island, and had a son,
THOMAS POOLE, of Mayfield, m. Miss Hewitt, of Clancoole, co. Cork, and was father of
THOMAS POOLE, of Mayfield, m. Anna, dau. of Henry (or Walter) Baldwin, of Mossgrove, co. Cork, and had a son,
HEWITT BALDWIN POOLE, of Mayfield, m. 1768, Dorothea, dau. of Jonas Morris, of Barley Hill, co. Cork, and had issue,
1. THOMAS, his heir.
2. Jonas Morris (Rev.), m. Mary Anne, dau. of R. Sealy, of Barleyfield, co. Cork, and d. leaving issue,
 1. Hewitt Robert (Rev.), D.D., Fellow of Trin. Coll. Dublin, who d. Nov. 1897, leaving, with other issue, an eldest son and dau.,
  Jonas Sealy, M.D., d. 29 Feb. 1907.
  Henrietta Charlotte, d. unm. 20 June, 1910.
 2. Dorothea.
 2. Harriett, m. Very Rev. George Purcell White, Dean of Cashel.
 3. Mary Anne, d. unm.
1. Anna Baldwin.
2. Dorothea, m. Rev. Robert Cane.
3. Catherine, m. — Meade, M.D.
4. Barbara, m. — Keatinge.
5. Elizabeth, m. Samuel M'Call, of Glyntown.
6. Maria, m. James M. Morgan, of Tivoli, co. Cork.
7. Harriet, m. Rev. Morgan Jellett, and was mother of Rev. J. H. Jellett, Provost of Trin. Coll. Dublin.
8. Jane Morris.
9. Charlotte Sophia.
Mr. Poole d. 1800, and was s. by his eldest son,
THOMAS POOLE, of Mayfield, b. 1773; m. 14 June, 1806, Joanna Meade, dau. of the Rev. Horace Townsend, of Derry Rosscarbery, and by her (who d. 1867) had issue,
1. HEWITT, late of Mayfield.
2. Horace Townsend, b. 6 Jan. 1813; m. 1854, Judith Isabella, eldest dau. of Lionel J. Fleming, of Newcourt, Skibbereen, co. Cork. She d. 1861. He d. 24 March, 1872, having had issue,
  Thomas Hewitt, d. Dec. 1911; m. Mia Emily, dau. of Rev. J. H. Jellett, Provost of Trin. Coll. Dublin, and had issue,
   (1) Horace Hewitt, b. 1885.
   (2) John Hewitt Jellett, b. 1893.
   (1) Hilda Isabel.
   (2) Dorothy. (3) Eva.
  Elizabeth, d. unm. 1898.
3. Thomas, b. 1820; m. Anne, eldest dau. of George Bennett, J.P., of Willaston, Douglas, Isle of Man.

1. Helena Charlotte, d. unm. 1888.
2. Dorothea Morris, d. 1890.
3. Katharine Townsend, m. 1848, Henry Newton, Chief Justice of Bombay, and d. 1865, leaving five daus.
4. Charlotte Meade, d. unm. 1846.
5. Joanna Townshend.
6. Elizabeth Henrietta, m. 1863, William Jackson Cummins, M.D., of Cork, son of Robert King Cummins, of Belmont, Cork, and d. 1868, leaving, with a dau., Lily Poole (who d. 30 April, 1910) a son, Major Henry Alfred Cummins, C.M.G., M.D., Royal Univ., of Ireland, late R. Army Med. Corps, retired 1906, now Professor of Botany and Agriculture University Coll., Cork, b. 8 March, 1864; m. 14 June, 1894, Ethel Percy, dau. of the late Robert Constable Hall, J.P., of Rockcliffe, Cork, and has issue,
 1. Henry Alfred Poole, b. 11 Nov. 1908.
 1. Kathleen Percy.
 2. Joan Poole.
 3. Geraldine Ethel Aylmer Poole.
 4. Elizabeth Patricia Poole.
7. Isabella Susan, m. 1859, John William Perrott, of Castle Lyons, co. Cork, and had a son and a dau.

Mr. Poole filled the office of Sovereign of Midleton for upwards of thirty years. He d. 1854. His eldest son,
HEWITT POOLE, of Mayfield, co. Cork, J.P., Major 3rd Batt. Royal Munster Fus., b. 5 Jan. 1812; m. 1st, 31 May, 1836, Jane, eldest dau. of the late Joseph Deane Freeman, of Castle Cor, co. Cork, D.L., and by her (who d. Feb. 1841) had issue,
1. Thomas, b. 1 Jan. 1840; d. Oct. 1852.
1. Bessie Deane Freeman.
2. Joanna Townsend, m. 17 April, 1879, Horace Townshend, late Capt. 99th Regt. She d. April, 1910.
He m. 2ndly, 17 Nov. 1849, Lucia Anne, eldest dau. of the late Richard Wills Gason, of Richmond, Nenagh, co. Tipperary, D.L. She d. 22 April, 1888. He d. 24 May, 1903, having by her had issue,
1. HEWITT RICHARD, now of Mayfield.
3. Alice Katherine, d. unm. 22 Nov. 1862.
4. Lucia Theodora, d. Aug. 1910.

Seat—Mayfield, near Bandon, co. Cork.

POOLER OF TYROSS.

THE REV. LEWIS ARTHUR TREVOR POOLER, of Tyross, co. Armagh, M.A., D.D., T.C.D., sometime Scholar of Trin. Coll. Dublin, late Minor Canon of Down Cathedral, Chaplain of Hollymount 1889-99, Examining Chaplain to Bishop of Down from 1898, Rural Dean of Lecale East, and Rector of Down with Hollymount since 1899, Canon of St. Patrick's Cathedral, Dublin, Chaplain to the Lord-Lieutenant of Ireland from 1903, b. 29 Jan. 1858; m. Sept. 1885, Augusta, 2nd dau. of the Ven. John Charles Wolfe, Archdeacon of Clogher, and has issue,

JAMES GALBRAITH, B.A. Trin. Coll. Dublin, Curate of Down, late Lieut. 5th Batt. Royal Irish Rifles, b. Feb. 1887.
Isabella Mabel.

Lineage.—In 1689, Robert (eldest son of Robert Pooler, of Tyross and grandson of Capt. Robert Pooler, who settled at Tyross, in the reign of Queen ELIZABETH, 1585, and received a grant of lands) led troops to the relief of Derry. "Pooler," says STUART, in his *Historical Memoirs of Armagh*, "in almost every sortie made by the famous Murray, was always in the thickest of the battle, and yet escaped unhurt. When, however, the garrison had received information that the Irish army had commenced its retreat, Pooler looked through an embrasure in the battlements in hope of witnessing their final departure. As that moment a random shot from one of those who had lingered in the rear struck him on the head, and killed him on the spot, the last man slain at the siege of Derry." In the *Metrical Catalogue of Besiegers and Defenders of Derry*, 1689, published in GRAHAM's *Ireland Preserved*, Pooler is alluded to in the following line—"Cust and Cross and Pooler of Tyross."

CAPT. ROBERT POOLER, b. 1541; m. Maud, only dau. of George Armitage, and left a son,
ROBERT POOLER, of Tyross, co. Armagh, b. 1594; m. Elizabeth, 2nd dau. of Walter Bond, and had a son,
ROBERT POOLER, of Tyross, b. 1626; m. Susanna, sister of John Grindall, Governor of Antigua, and d. 1742, aged 116, leaving a son,
JOHN POOLER, of Tyross, b. Sept. 1700; m. Martha, dau. of William Scott, of Scotsborough, co. Fermanagh, and d. Sept. 1746, leaving a son,

IRELAND. Porter.

ROBERT POOLER, of Tyross, b. 1734; m. Katharine, dau. of John Galbraith, of Roscavy, co. Tyrone, and Katharine his wife, dau. of Samuel Perry, and d. 1823, leaving issue,
1. ROBERT, of whom presently.
2. John, Major in the Army, killed in action.
3. Galbraith, d. unm.
1. Rebecca.   2. Martha.
3. Anne.
4. Katharine, m. William Scott, J.P., of Scottsborough, co. Fermanagh, and d. 22 July, 1813.

The eldest son,
ROBERT POOLER, of Tyross, m. 1812, Frances, dau. of Samuel Reid, of Newry, and d. 1865, having had issue,
1. Robert, d. unm.   2. John, d. unm.
3. Hugh, d. unm.
4. JAMES GALBRAITH, his heir.
5. Isaac, d. unm.
1. Jane.   2. Katherine.
3. Margaret.

The 4th son,
REV. JAMES GALBRAITH POOLER, D.D., Rector of Newtownards, co. Down, Rural Dean of Bangor, Chaplain to the Marquess of Londonderry, Canon of St. Patrick's Cathedral, Dublin, and some time Scholar of Trin. Coll. Dublin, b. 1826; m. 7 June, 1855, Angelica, 5th dau. of the late Rev. Edward Leslie, B.D., Rector of Anahilt, co. Down, and grand-dau. of Charles Powell Leslie, of Castle Leslie, Glasslough, M.P. for co. Monaghan, and d. 5 March, 1896. leaving issue,
1. LEWIS ARTHUR TREVOR, now of Tyross.
2. Charles Francis Knox (Rev.), M.A. Trin. Coll. Dublin, M.R.I.A., b. 7 Jan. 1860; m. Mary, dau. of the late James Thompson, J.P. of Macedon, Belfast.
3. Edward Leslie, M.D., b. 2 Aug. 1861; m. 26 April, 1886, Emma, only dau. of the late Alexander Johns, of Sunnylands, Carrickfergus, and has a dau., Angelica Leslie.
4. James Galbraith George, b. 19 Nov. 1869; d. unm. 1909.
1. Frances May, d. unm. 1879.
2. Ida Frances Margaret.
3. Angelica Katharine, m. 15 Jan. 1894, Rev. Arthur Edward Corner, Rector of Hinderwell, Yorks.

Arms—Per pale, or and arg., a fessse az., between two lions' heads erased in chief gu. and a crescent in base of the third. Crest—A falcon rising ppr., beiled or, and charged on the breast with a lozenge gu. Motto—Vi et virtute.

Seats—Tyross, Armagh, and Bessmount, co. Down. Residence—Downpatrick, co. Down.

PORTER OF BELLE ISLE.

JOHN PORTER PORTER, of Belle Isle, co. Longford, J.P. and D.L. co. Longford. High Sheriff 1879, D.L. and J.P. co. Fermanagh, High Sheriff 1883, b. 3 April, 1853; m. 31 Jan. 1884, Josephine Henrietta, dau. of Col. Jesse Lloyd, of Ballyleck, co. Monaghan, and has issue,
1. JOHN GREY, Lieut. 9th Lancers, b. 1886.
2. Nicholas Henry Archdale, b. 1890.
3. William Wauchope Montgomery, b. 1895; d. 19 Sept. 1910.
1. Coralie Adelaide Mervyn, m. 14 Aug. 1908, Eric Merrik Raymond Burrell, 7th Bart., and has issue (see BURKE's Peerage).
2. Audley Josephine Helen.

Mr. Porter is the 2nd son of the late Nicholas Montgomery Archdale, of Crock na Crieve, co. Fermanagh (who d. 2 Feb. 1877), and Adelaide Mary his wife, 4th dau. of the Rev. John Grey Porter, of Kilskeery and Belleisle, co. Fermanagh (see below), and grand-dau. of the Right Rev. John Porter, Bishop of Clogher. Mr. Porter assumed by Royal Licence, 11 May, 1876, the name and arms of PORTER only in lieu of ARCHDALE.

Lineage (of ARCHDALE).—See ARCHDALE of Castle Archdale.

Lineage (of PORTER).—JOHN PORTER, D.D., Lord Bishop of Clogher, m. 1786, Mary Smith, of Norfolk, and by her (who d. 1830) had
1. JOHN GREY (Rev.), of Kilskerry.
2. Thomas, Capt. R.N.
3. Charles (Rev.), Rector of Rounds, co. Northampton.
4. Henry Edward, Gen. in the Army.
5. William, of Henbury Fort, near Honiton, co. Devon, J.P. and D.L., late Capt. Carabineers, b. 11 Oct. 1802; m. 1830, Elizabeth Gibbs, youngest dau. of Abraham Ludlow, of Heywood House, Wilts, and d. 1887, leaving issue,
1. William Henry, b. 1833; d. 3 Jan. 1911.
2. John Frederic, b. 1837; d. 1852.
3. Edward Endymion, of East Hill, Rodden, Frome, co. Somerset, J.P. for Wilts and Somerset, b. 1843; m. 1871, Alice (who d. 24 May, 1911) only dau. of the late Spencer Graves, of Mayfield, co. Derby, and has, with other issue,
(1) William Endymion Huyshe, b. 1874.
(2) Charles Edward Ludlow, Capt. Worcestershire Regt., b. 1877
(1) Florence Evelyn Greaves, b. 1872.
(2) Lilian Mary, b. 1881.
1. Eliza Gibbs, m. Rev. W. de Quetteville, Rector of Brinkworth, Wilts.
2. Julia Mary Ann, m. 29 Sept. 1864, Rev. Francis Paynter, Rector of Stoke-next-Guildford, Surrey.
3. Agnes Antonia.   4. Florence Susanna.
1. Elizabeth, m. — Carmichael.
2. Margaret, m. Hugh Harris, of Ashfort, co. Armagh.

The Bishop d. 1819, and was s. by his eldest son,
REV. JOHN GREY PORTER, of Kilskeery, co. Tyrone, LL.B. Trin. Coll. Camb., b. 1789; m. 1816, Margaret Lavina, eldest dau. of Thomas Lindsey, of Hollymount, by Lady Margaret, his wife, dau. of the 1st Earl of Lucan, and d. leaving issue,
1. JOHN GREY, late of Belle Isle.
1. Lavinia (dec.), m. Henry Thompson.
2. Louisa, dec.
3. Elizabeth Phoebe, m. 27 May, 1851, John William Ellison Macartney, M.P., of Montjoy Grange (see that family). She d. 22 Dec. 1902. Their 2nd son,
Thomas Stewart, late Lieut. R.N., assumed by Royal Licence the surname and arms of PORTER only (see PORTER of Clogher).
4. Emmy.   5. Frances.
6. Adelaide Mary, m. 27 Jan. 1852, Nicholas Montgomery Archdale, of Crocknacrieve, co. Fermanagh, who d. 2 Feb. 1877, leaving issue (see ARCHDALE of Castle Archdale). Their 2nd son, JOHN PORTER, assumed by Royal Licence, 1876, the surname and arms of PORTER only and is now of Belle Isle.

JOHN GREY VESEY PORTER, of Belle Isle, co. Fermanagh, J.P. and D.L., High Sheriff 1844, b. 1818; m. 1861, Elizabeth Jane, dau. of Richard Hall, of Innismore, co. Fermanagh, and d.s.p. 5 Oct. 1903, being s. by his nephew, John Porter Porter.

Arms—Sa., three bells arg., a canton of the last charged with a portcullis ppr. Crest—A portcullis ppr. therefrom pendent by a chain or a shield of the arms. Motto—Et fide et virtute.

Seats—Belle Isle, Lisbellaw. Residence—Belle Isle, co. Fermanagh. Clubs—Carlton, and Kildare Street.

PORTER OF CLOGHER PARK.

THOMAS STEWART PORTER, of Clogher Park, co. Tyrone, J.P. cos. Tyrone and Fermanagh, late Sub-Lieut. R.N., b. 19 Aug. 1854; m. 28 July, 1892, Mary, dau. of the Right Hon. Frederick Stringer Wrench, P.C., of Killacoona, co. Dublin, and has issue,
1. ALAN GREY, b. 20 Sept. 1894.
2. Arthur Digby, b. 27 June, 1897.
1. Olga Lavinia, b. 18 July, 1893.
2. Guinevere Mary, b. 1 Nov. 1895.
3. Evelyn Kathleen Frances, b. 5 Feb. 1898.
4. Wanda Eleanor Mae, b. 7 Dec. 1901.

Mr. Porter is the 2nd son of John William Ellison-Macartney, of Mountjoy Grange, co. Tyrone, J.P. and D.L., sometime M.P. for Tyrone (see that family), and Elizabeth Phoebe his wife (who d. 22 Dec. 1902), dau. of the Rev. John Grey Porter, of Belleisle, co. Fermanagh, and Kilskeery, co. Tyrone (see PORTER of Belle Isle), and grand-dau. of the Right Rev. John Porter, D.D., Bishop of Clogher. Mr. Porter assumed by Royal Licence. 7 Sept. 1875, the name and arms of PORTER only, in lieu of ELLISON-MACARTNEY, under the will of his maternal grandfather.

Lineage—See ELLISON-MACARTNEY of Mountjoy Grange.

Arms—Sa., three bells arg., a canton of the last charged with a portcullis ppr. Crest—A portcullis ppr. therefrom pendent by a chain or a shield of the arms. Motto—Et fide et virtute.

Seat—Clogher Park, Tyrone.

PORTER-HATTON. See **HATTON.**

POUNDEN OF BALLYWALTER HOUSE.

JOHN COLLEY POUNDEN, of Ballywalter House, co. Wexford, M.D., b. 4 May, 1868; m. 22 Oct. 1903, Alice Caroline, eldest dau. of the late Rev. Henry Townend, M.A., Rector of Swepstone, Leicestershire, and has issue,

1. JOHN COLLEY, b. 29 Oct. 1904.
2. William Dawson, b. 30 April, 1906.
3. George Henry, b. 24 July, 1909.
1. Betanna Caroline.

Lineage.—This family resided, it is stated, originally in Liege, Belgium, where they occupied a highly respectable position. Owing to a fire in 1734, which consumed a great portion of their property, JOHN POUNDEN removed with his family to Ireland, where he had a son born named PATRICK, who m. Jane, dau. of the Rev. Joshua Nunn, Rector of Whitechurch, and was father of

JOHN POUNDEN, of Daphne, b. 1765; m. 1786, Alice, only dau. and heir of John Colley, of Ballywalter House, co. Wexford, and by her (who was b. 7 April, 1772, and d. 16 Dec. 1861) had a son, PATRICK, and a dau., Jane Maria, who d. unm. 17 Dec. 1878, aged 84 years. Mr. Pounden was killed in the Rebellion of 1798, leading a band of Volunteers against the insurgents. His son,

REV. PATRICK POUNDEN, Vicar of Westport, m. 5 Nov. 1822, Elizabeth, dau. and co-heir of Rev. W. Dawson, Rector of Clontibret, co. Monaghan, and by her (who d. 26 Aug. 1847) had issue,

1. JOHN COLLEY, of whom presently.
2. William Dawson (Rev.), b. 7 Sept. 1830.
1. Rosanna, d. 6 March, 1832.

Rev. Patrick Pounden d. 3 April, 1847. His elder son,

JOHN COLLEY POUNDEN, of Ballywalter House, co. Wexford, B.A., J.P., b. 30 Aug. 1827; m. 10 Jan. 1852, Betanna Catherine, only dau. of George Battersby, Q.C., of Lough Bawn, co. Westmeath, and d. 13 Nov. 1898, leaving issue,

1. PATRICK COLLEY, late of Ballywalter.
2. George Battersby, Lieut. 19 Madras N.I., b. 14 Feb. 1863; d. 9 May, 1889.
3. JOHN COLLEY, now of Ballywalter.
1. Charlotte Elizabeth, d. 8 Sept. 1869.
2. Alice Betanna Catherine, m. 4 Feb. 1875, Major-Gen. Robert Beatty, Madras N.I., and has issue.
3. Phillippia Fanny.
4. Elizabeth Dawson, m. 29 April, 1884, Rev. George Patton Mitchell, B.A., Rector of Drumbo, co. Down, and has issue.
5. Jane Wilhelmina, m. 26 July, 1876, Thomas Beatty, C.E., D.P.W., India, and has issue.
6. Louisa Mary.
7. Frances Rosanna.
8. Betanna Octavia.
9. Josephine.
10. Thomasina, m. 28 Sept. 1897, Rev. George Robert Bell, B.A., of Lisburn, and has issue.
11. Margaret Anne, d. 19 Sept. 1893.

His elder son,

PATRICK COLLEY POUNDEN, of Ballywalter House, co. Wexford, B.A., T.C.D., b. 8 Sept. 1861; m. 9 April, 1896, Emma Lucy, only child of Thomas S. Hope, of Ballybane House, Enniscorthy. He d. 26 Feb. 1902.

Seat—Ballywalter House, Gorey, co. Wexford.

POWELL OF BAWNLAHAN.

THE REV. FRANCIS PERY HUTCHESSON POWELL, of Bawnlahan, co. Cork, M.A., late Vicar of Great Bentley, Colchester, b. 7 July, 1843; m. 29 Nov. 1887, Caroline Eleanor, eldest dau. of the late William Uniacke Townsend, and has issue,

1. FITZHENRY TOWNSHEND SCUDAMORE, b. 28 Aug. 1888.
2. William Uniacke Pery, b. 1 June, 1891.
1. Marina Elsie Lilian.

Lineage.—This family derives from the Powells, or Ap Howells, of Penkelly, to which ancient family belonged SIR JOHN POWELL, Judge of King's Bench, who fearlessly defended the bishops brought to trial by JAMES II. From GWYLLIAM, his brother, the existing branch is lineally descended.

THOMAS POWELL, son of Gwylliam, m. Hannah Vaughan, and was father of

WILLIAM POWELL, m. Joanna Scudamore, and had issue. His 3rd son,

REV. ROBERT POWELL, m. Anne Kydley, and d. 1783, leaving a son and a dau.,
EDWARD, of whom presently.
EMMA ANN, m. 1800, THE O'DONOVAN, Lieut.-Col. of the Inniskilling Dragoons, who d.s.p. 1829, having bequeathed Bawnlahan and the ancient O'Donovan estates to his wife absolutely. She d. 1832, leaving the estates to her brother.

The only son,

MAJOR EDWARD POWELL, of Bawnlahan, of the 9th and 10th Regts., m. 1797, Eleanor Buchanan, and d. 1847, leaving issue,
1. EDWARD, his heir.
2. HENRY CLARINGBOLD, s. his brother.
1. Anna Maria.

The elder son,

EDWARD POWELL, of Bawnlahan, m. Anna Mathilda Digby, and d.s.p. 19 Sept. 1867, and was s. by his brother,

HENRY CLARINGBOLD POWELL, of Bawnlahan, co. Cork, J.P., Lieut.-Col. in the Army, served in the 10th Regt., and as Commandant of the Newcastle-on-Tyne District, b. 31 July, 1806; m. 11 July, 1836, Mary Ann, dau. of Lieut.-Gen. Thomas Hutchesson, Col. Comm. R.A. She d. March, 1896. He d. 10 Oct. 1901, leaving issue,

1. EDWARD O'DONOVAN, late Capt. Royal Marine Light Infantry, b. 17 May, 1838; m. 8 Jan. 1873, Mary Elizabeth, dau. of Licut. Jenkin, R.E. She d. 29 Oct. 1901. He d. March, 1902, leaving issue, one son,
HENRY JENKYN, b. 27 Aug. 1878.
2. Harry Hutchesson, d. 1846.
3. Thomas Hutchesson, 10th Regt., d. 1861.
4. FRANCIS PERY HUTCHESSON, now of Bawnlahan.
5. Scudamore Kydley, M.D., b. 7 Nov. 1844; m. 20 Feb. 1877, Ada, dau. of George Seymour, of Clifton Manor, co. York.
1. Elizabeth Jane.
2. Anna Maria Mary, m. 22 Sept. 1875, Sir Francis Langford O'Callaghan, K.C.M.G., C.S.I., C.I.E., late Consulting Engineer of the Indian Government and Secretary to the Public Works Dept. in India, and d. 14 Jan. 1911, leaving issue. He d. 14 Nov. 1909.
3. Eleanor Sarah, m. 14 Oct. 1875, James Gibbons Smyth, Major-Gen. late 1st Dorset Regt.

Arms—Or, two chevronels between three lions' gambs erased gu., in centre chief point a trefoil slipped vert. **Crest**—Out of a ducal coronet or, a demi-griffin vert, charged on the shoulder with a trefoil slipped gold. **Motto**—Edrych i fynu (Look upward).

Seat—Bawnlahan, Union Hall, Cork.

POWER, now DE LA POER, OF GURTEEN LE POER.

EDMOND JAMES DE POHER DE LA POER, of Gurteen Le Poer, co. Waterford, Knight of Justice (Devotion), of St. John of Jerusalem (Malta), formerly Chamberlain to H.H. Pope PIUS IX, and Count of the Roman States, so created 19 Aug. 1864, J.P. and D.L. co. Waterford, H.M.L. for Co. and City of Waterford, and M.P. for that co. 1866-73, High Sheriff 1879, b. 6 March, 1841; m. 1 June, 1881, Hon. Mary Olivia Augusta Monsell, only dau. of William, 1st Lord Emily, and has issue,

1. JOHN WILLIAM RIVALLON DE POHER, Capt. 4th Royal Btt. Leinster Regt., J.P., D.L. co. Waterford, b. 10 March, 1882; m. 2 July, 1907, Muriel, dau. and heir of the late Capt. the Hon. Robert Rainy Best (see WYNFORD, B.), and has issue,
  1. Edmond Robert Arnold, b. 25 Feb. 1911.
  1. Francis. 2. Patricia.
2. Edmond Alain Trémeur de Poher, Lieut. R.N., b. 30 April, 1883.
3. William Stephen Arnold Trémeur de Poher, b. 8 Nov. 1885.
1. Elinor Mary Tréfine de Poher, m. 17 Dec. 1907, Humphry Weld, Esq., Lord of the Manor of Chidcock, and has issue (see that family).
2. Ermyngarde Berthe Frances de Poher, m. 9 June, 1908, Frederick Barnard Elliot, 2nd son of the late Col. Elliot, 18th R.I., and has issue.
3. Mary Frances Yseult de Poher.

Count De La Poer claims as heir male (see Reg. Ped. in Ulster's Office) the Barony of Le Power and Coroghmore, conferred on Sir Richard Le Poer, by patent of 13 Sept. 1535, with remainder to the heirs male of his body.

Lineage.—This family was founded by Sir Robert de Poher, Knt., Marshall and Lord of Waterford in 1179. In 1177 he was joined in commission with the Lord Hugh de Lacy in the Government of Ireland, and from him have descended the Barons of Donoyle, and the Lord Power and Curraghmore.

SIR RICHARD POER, Knt. of Curraghmore, co. Waterford, Sheriff of the co. 1535, whose ancestors had been summoned to attend Parliament as Feudal Barons, was created by patent, dated 13 Sept. 27 HENRY VIII, A.D. 1535, Baron of Le Power and Coroghmore, with remainder to the heirs male of his body. He *m*. Lady Katherine Butler, dau. of Pierce, 8th Earl of Ormonde, by whom (who *d*. 1552) he had issue,
1. PIERS, his successor.
2. JOHN, 3rd Lord.

Lord Power *d*. 10 Nov. 1536-7, and was *s*. by his eldest son,

SIR PIERS, 2nd Lord Power, *b*. 1522, a minor at his father's death, and granted in ward to James, 9th Earl of Ormonde, 1 March, 1540. He took part in the Siege of Boulogne, and *d*. of his wounds at Calais, *unm*. 13 Oct. 1545, and was *s*. by his brother,

SIR JOHN, 3rd Lord Power, *b*. 1527, who was then a minor. He *m*. Lady Elinor Fitzgerald, dau. of James, 15th Earl of Desmond, and had, with three younger sons,
1. RICHARD, his successor, 4th Lord.
2. Piers, of Rathgormycke, who *m*. Margaret, dau. of Piers Butler, and *d*., according to an inq. post mort. taken 10 Oct. 4 JAMES I., 26 May, 1597, leaving a son and heir,
  RICHARD POWER, of Rathgormycke, and Clondonnel, who had livery of his father's lands 3 Feb. 1618, and *m*. Elinor, dau. of William Butler, Lord of the Manor of Ballyboe, and had (with three younger sons, James, a Capt. in the Spanish Army, Edmond and William, and four daus., one of whom, Honora, *m*. Edmond Power, of Curraghkealyl, fitzNicholas) two elder sons,
  (1) JOHN, his successor.
  (2) PIERS, ancestor of the Gurteen line, of whom hereafter.
  Richard Power, of Rathgormycke, *d*. 28 Feb. 1635, was bur. at Mothell, co. Waterford, and was *s*. by his eldest son,
  JOHN POWER, of Rathgormycke, who had livery of his father's lands 12 March, 1635. He *m*. (settlements dated 14 June, 1629) Ellan, dau. of Donold McGrath, of Mountain Castle, co. Waterford, and had issue,
    (1) Piers, of Knocklafala, proprietor of Rathgormycke in 1641, and, according to the survey of the co. Waterford, 1654, held Knocklafala, Clondonnel, and other lands. Transplanted to co. Galway, 1654, and *d*. there at Cregmulgreny, *s.p.*
    (2) Richard, Capt. in the Royal Army, was transplanted to Connaught by OLIVER CROMWELL. He *m*. Hellen, dau. of Capt. David Power, of Kilbolan, co. Cork (who was transplanted to Ballynagran, co. Galway, by OLIVER CROMWELL), and *d*. at Ballindrainny, 5 April, 1705, leaving issue, three daus.,
      1. Bridget, *m*. 14 Sept. 1702, Francis Fitz John Mac-Namara, of Cratloe, co. Clare.
      2. Mary, *m*. as hereafter, John Power, of Gurteen, who was next relative in blood of the male line to her father.
      3. Mercy, *d*. *unm*. 1703.
    His brother,
    PIERS (2nd son of Richard Power, of Rathgormycke), *m*. Margaret, 2nd dau. of Nicholas Lee, and widow of Henry Power, of Adamstown, co. Waterford, and by her (who *m*. 3rdly, Richard Strange, of co. Waterford, whose will is dated 26 March, 1681, and was proved 24 Nov. 1682) had issue, two sons and a dau.,
      (1) John, Lieut.-Col. in the French service, living 1687, and *d*. *unm*.
      (2) EDMOND, of whom presently.
      (1) Katherine, *m*. Garratt Gough, of Ballyvanin, co. Clare, grandson of Sir Thomas Gough, Knt., of Kilmanahan, co. Waterford, and *d.s.p.*
    The 2nd son,
    EDMOND POWER, of Curraghkealy, obtained from the Duke of Ormonde a leasehold of Gurteen, co. Waterford, *m*. Eleanor, dau. of Pierce Power, of Monalargie, and sister of John, 9th Lord Power, and *d*. intestate 1698, leaving issue,
      (1) Pierce, *d.s.p.*
      (2) JOHN, of whom hereafter as representative of the family on the death of Henry, 10th Lord Power, 1742.
      (3) WILLIAM FITZEDMOND, *s*. to his brother.
      (4) Richard FitzEdmond, *m*. Martha, dau. of John Fitz-Gerald, of Ballymalloe, and *d.s.p.* 1717.
      (5) James FitzEdmond, *m*. Mary, dau. of William Higgins, of Gortardagh, co. Waterford, and had issue,
        1. EDMOND, *s*. to his uncle, of whom hereafter.
        2. Richard.
        1. Ellen.   2. Magdalen.

Lord Power *d*. 8 Nov. 1592, and was *s*. by his eldest son,

RICHARD, 4th Lord Power, *b*. 1550 ; *m*. Hon. Katherine Barry, dau. of James, Viscount Buttevant, and had issue,
1. JOHN, *m*. Hon. Helen Barry, dau. of David, Viscount Buttevant, and was killed by Edmond FitzGibbon (the " White Knight ") *v.p.*, leaving by her (who *m*. 2ndly, Thomas, 10th Earl of Ormonde and Ossory) with a dau., Ellen, *m*. David, Viscount Fermoy, an only son,
  JOHN, *s*. to his grandfather, as 5th Lord.
2. Pierce, of Monalargie, who was mentioned by his grandfather in deed of settlement of the Curraghmore estates 14 Feb. 28 Queen ELIZABETH. He was living in 1633, and *m*. Lady Katherine Butler, dau. of Walter, 11th Earl of Ormonde and Ossory, and had a son,
  Pierce, of Monalargie, who was attainted on account of the part he took in the rebellion of 1641. He had a dau., Eleanor, *m*. Edmond Power, of Gurteen, and an only son,

JOHN (attainted for his adhesion to JAMES II), of whom hereafter, as 9th Lord Power, but for the attainder.
3. Thomas, who was also mentioned in his grandfather's deed of settlement 28 Queen ELIZABETH.
4. Edmond, mentioned in the same deed.

Lord Power *d*. 8 Aug. 1607, and was *s*. by his grandson,

JOHN, 5th Lord Power, *b*. 1596, who had livery of his grandfather's lands 30 March, 1639 ; *m*. Ruth, dau. of Robert Phypoe, of St. Mary's Abey, Dublin, and had issue,
1. RICHARD, his successor, 6th Lord.
2. David, *d*. *unm*. 17 Aug. 1661, bur. at St. Michan's.
3. John, *d*. *unm*. 22 Sept. 1656, bur. in Dublin.
4. Pierce, of Killowen, *m*. Hon. Honora Burke, dau. of John, 2nd Lord Brittas ; made his will 1 March, 1668, which was proved 10 May, 1669, and left issue, an only dau.,
  Ruth Judith, *m*. Thomas Duckett, ancestor of DUCKETT *of Duckett's Grove*, co. Carlow.
1. Eleanor, *m*. Thomas Walsh, of Pilltown, co. Waterford.
2. Katherine, *m*. 1658, John Fitzgerald, of Dromana, Lord of the Decies, and *d*. 1660.

Lord Power was excused from transplantation at the hands of OLIVER CROMWELL, as he was bereft of reason, and had been so for twenty years, 18 Jan. 1654. He was *s*. by his eldest son,

RICHARD, 6th Lord Power, who was created, by patent dated 9 Oct. 1673, Viscount Decies and Earl of Tyrone. He *m*. 1654, Lady Dorothy Annesley, dau. of Arthur, 1st Earl of Anglesey, by whom (who was bur in the Cathedral of Waterford) he had issue,
1. Arthur, *d*. *unm*. *v.p.*
2. JOHN, his successor, 7th Lord and 2nd Earl.
3. JAMES, 8th Lord and 3rd Earl.

Lord Power, 1st Earl of Tyrone, was imprisoned in the Tower of London, as a Jacobite, where he *d*. 14 Oct. 1690, and was bur. at Farnborough, Hants, when he was *s*. by his eldest son,

JOHN, 7th Lord Power, 2nd Earl of Tyrone, *b*. 1664, who *d*. *unm*. in Dublin 14 Oct. 1693, and who was bur. at Carrick-on-Suir, when he was *s*. by his brother,

JAMES, 8th Lord Power, 3rd Earl of Tyrone, *b*. 1666 ; *m*. Anne, dau. of Andrew Rickards, of Dangan Spidoge, co. Kilkenny, by whom he had an only dau.,

Lady Katherine Power, *m*. 1717, Sir Marcus Beresford, 4th bart. of Coleraine, and brought her husband the Curraghmore estates. She *d*. 1769. Sir Marcus was created, 18 July, 1746, Earl of Tyrone, and was ancestor of the Marquess of Waterford.

Lord Power, 3rd Earl of Tyrone, *d*. without male issue, 19 Aug. 1704, when his earldom and viscounty became extinct, but his Barony of Power of Curraghmore reverted to his heir male,

JOHN, 9th Lord Power, *de jure* (*see* the descendants of Pierce Power, of Monalargie), who, being a Col. in the army of JAMES II, and attainted and outlawed on account of the Rebellion in 1688, could not take his seat, but he was allowed a pension of £300 per annum by the Crown. He *d*. in Paris, 20 Aug. 1725 (will dated 10 July, 1717), and left, with two daus., Charlotte and Clare, an only son,

HENRY, 10th Lord Power, but for the attainders of his father and grandfather. He took out administration to his father 11 Sept. 1725, and petitioned the Duke of Bolton, Lord Lieutenant of Ireland, for the Curraghmore estate, as heir male, upon which petition the Lords Stanhope and Harrington made a favourable report to his Grace, but the petition never came to a hearing. He *d*. intestate and *unm*. May, 1742, and was bur. at St. Matthew's Church, Irishtown, Dublin. Administration was granted to his sisters, 5 Dec. 1743. Upon his death the whole male descendants of Richard, 4th Lord Power, became extinct, and the representation of the 1st Lord Power devolved on the heir male of Pierce Power, of Rathgormuck, the brother of the 4th Lord,

JOHN POWER, of Gurteen, co. Waterford, and of Grange, co. Galway (*see* descendants of Pierce Power, of Rathgormuck). He served in France under his maternal uncle, Col. John Power, 9th Lord Power, and on his return to Ireland he *m*. 6 Oct. 1703, Mary, dau. and co-heir of Richard Power, of Ballydrimney, co. Galway, at the request of his kinsman, he being the next relation in blood of the male line. By this lady (who *d*. 1726) he had five daus.,
1. Helen, *m*. Hyacinth, Lord Mount Leinster, and *d.s.p.*
2. Mary, *d*. *unm*.   3. Bridget, *d.s.p.*
4. Katherine, *m*. 1733, John Power, of Clashmore, co. Waterford, and had issue.
5. Elizabeth, *m*. 13 April, 1739, her cousin, Edmond Power Fitz-James, of Gurteen.

Mr. Power *d*. at Grange, co. Galway, 1743, and was *s*. by his brother,

WILLIAM POWER (FitzEdmond), of Gurteen, who *d.s.p.* at Gurteen, 5 Aug. 1755, and was bur. at Kilsheelan. His will, dated 22 July, 1755, was proved 18 Sept. following, and he was *s*. by his nephew,

EDMOND POWER, of Gurteen, *m*. 1st, 13 April, 1739, his cousin Elizabeth, dau. and co-heir of John Power (FitzEdmond), of Gurteen, and had issue,
1. WILLIAM, his heir.
2. John, *m*. 1774, Joanna, dau. of Thaddeus O'Meagher, of Ikerrin, co. Tipperary, and by her (who *d*. 1801) he had issue,
  1. EDMOND, who *s*. his uncle.
  2. James, of Ballydine, J.P., Capt. Tipperary Militia, *m*. Katherine, dau. of James Butler, of Wilford, co. Tipperary, and *d*. 11 June, 1854, having had an only son,
    Edmond, *d*. *unm*. at Madeira, 5 Dec. 1838.
  3. William, of Glyn, *d*. *unm*. 1839.
  1. Honora, *m*. 1st, Major Quinn, and 2ndly, William Talbot, of Castle Talbot, co. Wexford.
  2. Elizabeth.   3. Eleanor.
  3. James.   4. Richard.
1. Elizabeth, *m*. Francis Mandeville.
2. Katherine, *m*. William Howley.

Power. THE LANDED GENTRY. 574

Mr. Power *m.* 2ndly, 1753, Mary O'Brien, widow of Capt. Walter de la Mar, of Porterstown, co. Dublin, by whom he had another dau.,
3. Eleanor, *m.* Peter Lynch.
Mr. Power was *s.* by his eldest son,
WILLIAM POWER, of Gurteen, High Sheriff co. Waterford 1784; *m.* 10 Sept. 1765, Mary, dau. and heir of Capt. Walter de la Mar, of Porterstown, co. Dublin, by Mary O'Brien his wife, and *d.s.p.* 1813, when he was *s.* by his nephew,
EDMOND POWER, of Gurteen, *b.* 1775, served in the 8th Light Dragoons (now 8th Hussars) under the Duke of York, during the Flanders Campaign. He *m.* 29 May, 1815, Anastatia, dau. and co-heir (with her sister Mary, who *m.* 1827, Richard Montesquieu Bellew, and *d.s.p.*) of John Lalor, of Long Orchard, co. Tipperary, and had issue by her (who *m.* 2ndly, the Right Hon. Richard Lalor Sheil, M.P., and *d.* at Florence, 3 Aug. 1852) three sons and two daus.,
1. JOHN WILLIAM, his heir.
2. EDMOND JAMES (*see* POWER-LALOR *of Long Orchard*).
3. Richard Francis, *m.* 3 March, 1840, Sara, dau. of Charles Gordon, of Virginia, U.S.A., and *d.* 1880, leaving two daus.,
 1. Anastatia, *d. unm.* 17 Oct. 1895.
 2. Mary, *m.* July, 1883, George Ryan, D.L. of Inch, co. Tipperary, and *d.* 14 Nov. 1894, leaving issue (*see that family*).
1. Mary, *m.* 1846, Henry Petre, of Dunkenhalgh, D.L. co. Lancaster, and *d.* 1880.
2. Ellenor, *m.* 1843, Patrick William Power, of Pembrokestown, co. Waterford, and *d.* 1888, leaving issue.
Mr. Power *d.* 29 May, 1830, and was *s.* by his eldest son,
JOHN WILLIAM POWER, of Gurteen, M.P., J.P. and D.L. co. Waterford, High Sheriff 1841; *b.* 10 Feb. 1816; *m.* 30 April, 1840, Frances, dau. of Sir John Power, 1st bart. of Kilfane, by Harriet his wife, dau. of Gervais Parker Bushe, of Kilfane, and *d.* 12 May, 1851, having by her (who *d.* 28 Jan. 1893) had issue, five sons and four daus.,
1. EDMOND JAMES DE POHER DE LA POER, now of Gurteen le Poer.
2. John, *b.* 1842; *d.* 1851.
3. William, *b.* 2 June, 1843, late Capt. 65th Regt.; *m.* 2 Sept. 1879, Mary Anastatia, eldest dau. of his uncle, Edmond Power Lalor, of Long Orchard. She *d.* 27 Aug. 1908.
4. Raymond, of Kilcronagh, co. Kilkenny, J.P., D.L., High Sheriff 1889, *b.* 6 March, 1846, late 15th Regt.; *m.* 6 April, 1873, Emily Frances Lloyd, 3rd dau. and co-heir of Charles Thomas Warde, of Clopton House, co. Warwick, by Marianne his wife, dau. of John Bennet Lawes, of Rothamsted, Herts.
5. Arnold, *b.* 17 Oct. 1849, late 20th Regt.; *d. unm.* 17 Oct. 1883.
1. Harriette Anastatia, *m.* 17 June, 1860, Gen. Sir Charles John Stanley Gough, G.C.B., V.C. Col. 5th Bengal Cavalry, 2nd son of George Gough, sometime Commissioner of Patna, and has issue.
2. Mary, *m.* 25 June, 1867, Samuel Perry, of Woodroff, D.L., co. Tipperary, and has issue.
3. Anastatia, *m.* 15 July, 1875, Sir John Nugent, bart., of Cloncoskoraine, co. Waterford, and has issue.
4. Frances Vincent, *m.* 5 Sept. 1881, Thomas William Gaston Monsell, 2nd Baron Emly, and has had issue (*see* BURKE'S *Peerage*, EMLY, B.).
A Royal Licence, dated at St. James's, 14 May, 1863, was granted to Frances, widow of John Power, of Gurteen, that she and her issue by her said deceased husband should take and use the surname of DE LA POER in lieu of that of POWER.

Arms—Arg., a chief indented sa. *Crest*—A buck's head caboshed ppr., attired or, between the attires a crucifix of the last. *Motto*—Per crucem ad coronam.

Seat—Gurteen Le Poer, Kilsheelan, co. Waterford.

POWER OF FAITHLEGG.

PATRICK JOSEPH MAHON POWER, of Faithlegg House, co. Waterford, J.P. and D.L., High Sheriff 1855, *b.* 1826; *m.* 1 March, 1859, Lady Olivia Jane Nugent (who *d.* 1903), dau. of Anthony Francis, 9th Earl of Westmeath, and has issue,
1. HUBERT, High Sheriff co. Waterford 1888, *b.* 1860; *m.* 1888, Marie Therese Aimee, youngest dau. of M. Alexis Charles Tousaint Bourges.
1. Maud. 2. Ellen.
3. Catherine, *m.* 20 Aug. 1903, Henry Gallwey, of West Cliff, Tramore.
4. Emily.

Lineage.—NICHOLAS POWER, J.P., *m* 1780, Catherine, dau. of Bartholomew Rivers, of Tramore, co. Waterford, and had issue,
1. PATRICK, of Bellevue, co. Kilkenny, J.P. and D.L., formerly M.P. for Waterford, *m.* Mary, dau. of John Snow, of Larkfield and Kilmurry, co. Kilkenny, and *d.*, having had issue,
 1. NICHOLAS ALFRED, of Bellevue House, co. Kilkenny, J.P. D.L., *b.* 8 Nov. 1813; *d.* 28 March, 1905; *m.* 15 Jan. 1838, Margaret Jane, dau. and only surviving child of Major Cane, 5th Dragoon Guards, by Anne his wife, dau. of John Helsham, of Ormond House, Kilkenny, J.P., and by her (who *d.* 1893) had issue,
  (1) FREDERICK PATRICK WILLIAM, of Bellevue House, near Waterford, late Major 3rd Batt. Royal Irish Regt., *b.* 1843; *m.* 20 June, 1905, Caroline Bate, younger dau. of Henry Palmer Shearman, J.P., of St. Vincent, W.I.
  (2) Alfred Richard, Major King's Own Yorkshire L.I., *b.* 29 Oct. 1857; *d.* in S. Africa 8 June, 1900, having *m.* Agnes Mary Emily, dau. of James Farrell, of Newlawn, co. Dublin,

by Elizabeth Emily, his wife, only dau. of John Farrell, of Moynalty (*see that family*), and left issue,
 1a. Arthur. 2a. Frederick.
 1a. Evelyn.
  (1) Emily, *m.* Edward Middelton, son of the late Peter Middelton, of Myddleton Lodge and Stockeld Park, co. York.
  (2) Augusta, *m.* Walter Gyles, Barrister-at-Law, 2nd son of Rev. Walter Gyles, Vicar of Cahir, co. Tipperary.
  (3) Louisa, *m.* John Baines, late Inniskilling Dragoons, son of H. Baines, of Esher, Surrey.
  (4) Elise. (5) Lucy.
  (6) Annie.
  (7) Margaret Winifred, *m.* 24 Aug. 1880, Alexander Carew Anderson, son of James Anderson, of Grace Dieu, and has issue (*see that family*).
 2. Patrick William. 3. John.
 4. Pierce.
 1. Eliza, *d. unm.*
2. NICHOLAS, of Faithlegg House.
1. Maria, *d. unm.*
Mr. Power *d.* June, 1793. His younger son,
NICHOLAS MAHON POWER, of Faithlegg House, co. Waterford, J.P. and D.L., M.P. for that co. from 1847 to 1859, *b.* 1787; *m.* 23 March, 1818, Margaret, only child of Nicholas Mahon, of Dublin, and had issue,
1. PATRICK MAHON, now of Faithlegg.
2. Albert William, *d. unm.*
1. Margaret Emily, *m.* 31 May, 1841, Denis O'Conor, of Mount Druid, and had issue (*see that family*).
2. Catherine Georgina, *m.* James Archbold, of Davidstown, co. Kildare.
3. Maria Louisa, *m.* Finlay Chester, J.P., of Williamstown, co. Louth. She *d.* 22 April, 1899.
4. Frances Emily Mary.
5. Adelaide Mary Josephine Isabella, *m.* 7 May, 1874, the late John Aloysius Blake, M.P. for Waterford.
He *d.* Feb. 1873.

Seat—Faithlegg House, Waterford.

POWER OF ANNAGHMAKERRIG.

The late SIR WILLIAM JAMES TYRONE POWER, K.C.B., of Annaghmakerrig, co. Monaghan, J.P. and D.L., High Sheriff 1874, *b.* 1819; *d.* 24 July, 1911; *m.* 1859, Martha, dau. of the late Dr. John Moorhead, J.P. and D.L., of Annaghmakerrig, co. Monaghan, and by her (who *d.* 4 June, 1890) has issue,
1. JOHN MOORHEAD, B.A. Camb., *b.* 1862; *m.* 1887, Susan Dewen, dau. of Henry Dennis, of New Hall, co. Denbigh.
1. Susan Gilbert Power.
2. Norah, *m.* D. T. C. Guthrie.

Sir William was Commissary-General in Chief 1864-70, and Director of Supplies and Transport 1870-71, and was acting Agent-General for New Zealand 1877-78. He served in China 1843, in New Zealand 1846, in Kaffir War 1851, in the Crimea 1854, in China 1857-58, and in Canada 1861. He is the son of Tyrone Power, of Waterford, by Anne his wife, dau. of John Gilbert, of Newport, Isle of Wight.

Seat—Annaghmakerrig, Clones, co. Monaghan. *Residence*—Kilmore, Tunbridge Wells.

POWER OF SNOWHILL.

JOHN JOSEPH O'NEILL-POWER, of Power Hall, Snowhill, co. Kilkenny, J.P. cos. Waterford and Kilkenny, formerly Capt. R.F.A. (Special Reserve), *b.* 8 July, 1879, educated at Beaumont Coll.

Lineage.—NICHOLAS POWER, of Snowhill, *m.* 1st, 26 Jan. 1780 the dau. of Edward O'Neill, of Dublin, and 2ndly, Margaret McCarthy, of Spring House, who *d.s.p.* By his 1st wife he had with three daus. (of whom Margaret *m.* 1804, Richard Power O'Shee, of Gardenmorris, *see that family*), an only son,
DAVID O'NEILL POWER, of Snowhill, *m.* Eliza Nash, of Cork. She *d.* 20 Dec. 1819. He *d.* 1863, having had issue,
1. NICHOLAS, of whom presently.
2. Edward.
3. Joseph, who *m.* 15 Aug. 1839, Eleanor, 2nd dau. of Walter Kavanagh, of Borris, Kilkenny, and left issue.
The eldest son,
NICHOLAS O'NEILL POWER, of Snowhill, *b.* 10 Sept. 1809; *m.* 10 Nov. 1830, Jane, dau. of Alexander Sherlock, and *d.* 1869, having had issue,
1. Nicholas Alexander, *b.* 6 Jan. 1835; *d. unm.*
2. Alexander, *d. unm.*
3. JOSEPH EDWARD, of whom presently.
4. Bernard Patrick Irving, 80th Regt., *m.* Helen (*d.* 13 May, 1909), dau. of Pierce Joyce, D.L., of Mervue.

5. Augustine, *d. unm.*
1. Helen, *d. unm.*
2. Elizabeth, *d. unm.*
3. Victoria Jane, *d. unm.*
4. Eliza Mary, *d. unm.*

The 3rd son,
JOSEPH EDWARD O'NEILL POWER, of Power Hall, Snowhill, *b.* 16 June, 1841 ; *m.* 1st, 27 Nov. 1869, Elizabeth Antonia, youngest dau. of the late Sir John Ennis, Bart. She *d.* 20 Oct. 1879, leaving issue,
1. JOHN JOSEPH, now of Snowhill.
1. Anna Maria Gabriel, *m.* 7 Nov. 1894, Dr. Morris, of Clonmore, and *d.* 31 Dec. 1899.

He *m.* 2ndly, 8 Oct. 1881, Marguerite, youngest dau. of David Henry, and by her had issue,
2. Alexander Harold, *b.* 9 Dec. 1882 ; *d.* 19 March, 1888.
2. Violet Marguerite Josephine Mary.

He *d.* 2 Sept. 1897.

Seat—Power Hall, Snowhill, co. Kilkenny. *Clubs*—Bath, Irish Automobile, and Kildare Street, Dublin.

POWER OF GLENCAIRN. *See* BUSHE OF GLENCAIRN.

POWER-LALOR. *See* LALOR.

PRATT OF CABRA CASTLE.

JOSEPH PRATT, Enniscoe, co. Mayo, J.P. and D.L. co. Mayo, J.P. co. Cavan, late the Royal Scots, High Sheriff co. Mayo, 1876, and co. Cavan 1894, *b.* 1 Jan. 1843 ; *m.* 1 Sept. 1870, Charlotte Eliza (who *d.* 9 July, 1910), only dau. of James Hamilton, of Cornacassa, co. Monaghan, and has had issue

1. MERVYN, D.S.O., Capt. (retired) King's Royal Rifle Corps, now of Cabra Castle (*Cabra Castle, Kingscourt, co. Cavan*), J.P. co. Cavan, *b.* 24 April, 1873.
2. Audley Charles, Capt. Royal Scots, *b.* 13 May, 1874.
1. Eglantine Madeline Georgina, *d.* an infant.

Lineage.—The branch of the family of which we are treating was settled in co. Leicester 1641, when three brothers, Joseph, Benjamin, and John Pratt, migrated thence ; Joseph and Benjamin to Ireland, John to Jamaica. Joseph and Benjamin obtained lands in Meath from CROMWELL, which they divided between them. The elder was ancestor of the PRATTS of *Cabra ;* the younger, of the WINTERS *of Agher.*

JOSEPH PRATT, High Sheriff co. Meath 1698, *m.* 1st, Frances, sister and heir of Col. Thomas Coach, of Cabra Castle, co. Cavan, and Covoddly, co. Donegal ; and 2ndly, Elizabeth, dau. of Sir Audley Mervyn, and widow of Nathaniel Poole, and by her had issue,
1. Joseph, *d.* young.
2. Benjamin (Dr.), of Cabra Castle, Provost of Trin. Coll. Dublin, *m.* Lady Phillippa Hamilton, 3rd dau. of James, 6th Earl of Abercorn, but *d.s.p.*
3. John, of Cabra Castle, Constable of Dublin Castle, and Deputy-Treasurer of Ireland : *m.* Honoretta, eldest dau. of Sir John Brookes, of York (by his wife Mary, dau. of Sir Hardress Waller, Knt. by Elizabeth, dau. and co-heir of Sir John Dowdall), and *d.* 1740, having had two sons, drowned in the Phœnix Park 1723, and one dau. Mary, *m.* 1st, Sir George Savile, of Thornhill and Rufford, 7th bart., M.P. for Yorkshire, who *d.* 1743, leaving issue, George (Sir), 8th and last bart., M.P. for Yorkshire, *d. unm.* Jan. 1784 ; Arabella, *m.* 1744, John Thornhagh, of Osberton, took the name of Hewett for Shinoaks estate and had issue ; and Barbara, who *m.* Richard, 4th Earl of Scarborough. Lady Savile *m.* 2ndly, Capt. Wallis, and 3rdly, Dr. Charles Morton, of the British Museum.
4. Thomas, *d.s.p.*
5. MERVYN.
1. Margaret.

The youngest son,
MERVYN PRATT, M.P. co. Cavan, High Sheriff 1722, *m.* 1704, Elizabeth, dau. of Thomas Coote, of Coote Hill, co. Cavan, and sister of the Earl of Bellamont, and *d.* 1751, having had (with three daus., Elizabeth, *m.* Dr. Burleigh ; Anne, *m.* Oct. 1749, John Pratt, of Agher, co. Meath ; and Frances, M. Joseph Methec) a son and successor,

REV. JOSEPH PRATT, of Cabra, *m.* Elizabeth, dau. of Knightley Chetwode, of Woodbrook, Queen's Co., and had issue,
1. Mervyn, *d.* 1798.
2. JOSEPH, of whom presently.
3. James Butler, of Drumsna, co. Leitrim, *m.* Margaret, dau. of William Foster, of Dunleer, and *d.* 1829, leaving issue,
1. William, *b.* 1775 ; *d. unm.* 1864.
2. James, *m.* 1821, Juliana, dau. of Col. John Hallowes, of Glapwell Hall, co. Derby, and had issue,
(1) Henry Hamilton, of Southville, Queen's Co., Col. 94th Regt., *m.* 1860, Anne Blanche, dau. of Rev. J. Bonham, c Ballintaggart, co. Kildare, and has issue,
1. James Bonham, Capt. King's Own Scottish Borderers *b.* 9 Feb. 1862.
2. Harry Arthur, Capt. R.A., *b.* 29 Sept. 1864.
(1) Anne Frances, *m.* Charles Bond.
(2) Louisa Harriet, *m.* 1855, Richard Bond, and has issue three sons and one dau.
3. Henry, *d. unm.*
1. Elizabeth, *m.* 1799, — Bellingham, and *d.* 1810.
2. Anne, *m.* — Donovan.
3. Frances, *m.* — Salvador.
1. Elizabeth, *m.* 1st, Dr. C. Morton, and 2ndly, — Bacon.
2. Ann, *m.* Henry Foster.

The 2nd son,
REV. JOSEPH PRATT, of Cabra Castle, *b.* 1738 ; *m.* 28 March, 1772, Hon. Sarah, dau. of Hervey, Viscount Mountmorres, by Lady Letitia Ponsonby his wife, dau. of Brabazon, Earl of Bessborough, and had issue,
1. JOSEPH, his heir.
2. Mervyn (Rev.), *d.* 1823.
3. Hervey, of Castle Morris, co. Kilkenny, who, upon the death of his father, *s.* his mother in the Kilkenny estates, which she and her sister, the Marchioness of Antrim, had jointly inherited as co-heirs of their brother, Hervey Redmond, 2nd Viscount Mountmorres (*see* DE MONTMORENCY *of Castle Morres*).
1. Mary, *m.* Sir John Piers, Bart.
2. Letitia, dec.

Mr. Pratt *d.* 1831, and was *s.* by his eldest son,
JOSEPH PRATT, of Cabra Castle, Col. of Militia, High Sheriff co. Cavan 1799, *b.* 1775 ; *m.* 1st, 1806, Jemima Roberta, dau. and co-heir of Sir James Stratford Tynte, Bart., of Tynte Park, and by her (who *d.* 1822) had issue,
1. MERVYN, of Cabra Castle.
2. JOSEPH TYNTE, of Tynte Park (*see* TYNTE *of Tynte Park*).
3. Fitzherbert, *d.* 1849.
4. Walter Caulfeild, J.P. and D.L., of Oving House, Bucks, Col. Commanding Royal Bucks Militia, and formerly 67th Regt., *b.* 25 Dec. 1819 ; *m.* 11 March, 1852, Catherine Cecilia, 6th dau. of George, 3rd Lord Boston, and *d.* 9 June, 1900, having by her (who *d.* 25 March, 1894) had issue,
1. Douglas Walter Joseph Caulfeild, *b.* 1853 (dec.).
2. Gerald George Caulfeild, Major 3rd Batt. Oxfordshire L.I., *b.* 1855.
3. Cecil de Montmorency Caulfeild, *b.* 1857.
1. Constance.
5. Fitzmaurice Caldwell Tynte, of Glen Heste, Blessington, co. Wicklow, *b.* 5 Sept. 1822 ; *m.* 1850, Isabella Mary, dau. of Charles Edmund Costello, of Edmondston, co. Mayo, and *d.* 1884, leaving a dau., Josephine, who *d.* 1890.
1, Hannah, *m.* Charles Rochfort.
2. Sarah, *m.* 12 July, 1834, Robert Doyne, of Wells, co. Wexford, and had issue (*see that family*).
3. Elizabeth, Martha, *m.* 4 Feb. 1840, Robert Francis Saunders, of Saunders Grove, co. Wicklow, and had issue (*see that family*).

Col. Pratt *m.* 2ndly, 1826, Nichola Sophia, relict of the late Claud William Cole Hamilton, of Kingsfort, co. Meath, and *d.* 27 Aug. 1863. His eldest son,
MERVYN PRATT, of Cabra Castle, J.P. and D.L., High Sheriff co. Cavan 1841, co. Mayo 1843, and co. Meath 1875, *b.* 2 Aug. 1807 ; *m.* 27 Oct. 1834, Madeline Eglantine, only dau. and heir of Col. William Jackson, of Enniscoe, co. Mayo, and *d.* 1890, leaving issue,
1. JOSEPH, now of Cabra Castle.
1. Louisa Catherine Hannah, *m.* 28 June, 1866, Thomas Rothwell, of Rockfield, co. Meath, D.L. He *d.* 1 March, 1909, leaving issue (*see that family*).
2. Madeline Caroline Mary.
3. Jemima Roberta Emily Tynte.

Arms—Arg., on a chevron sa., between three ogresses, each charged with a martlet of the first, three mascles of the field. *Crest*—A lion's head erased gu. pierced through the back of the neck with a broken spear ppr. *Motto*—Virtute et armis.

Seat—Enniscoe, Crossmolina, co. Mayo. *Club*—Kildare Street.

PRATT OF GAWSWORTH.

HENRY PRATT, of Gawsworth, co. Cork, late Lieut. Royal Munster Fusiliers, *b.* 6 Dec, 1857 ; *s.* his father 1910 ; *m.* 1898, Annie Hamilton, dau. of William Spence, of Alloa, N.B.

Lineage.—THE REV. JAMES PRATT, Prebendary of Kilnaglory, and Rector of Athnowen, co. Cork, Sch. Trin. Coll. Dublin 1766, B.A. 1767, M.A. 1784, Deacon 18 Dec. 1768, Priest 17 Feb. 1771, and Chancellor of Cork 1782-5, left issue a son,

MAJ. HENRY PRATT, of Sundays Well, Cork, *b.* 1787 ; *m.* 23 Dec. 1815, Sarah, dau. of Richard Fitton, of Gawsworth, co. Cork, by Brianna his wife, dau.

Prendergast. THE LANDED GENTRY. 576

of Patrick Bellew, of Ballindiness, near Castlemartyr, co. Cork. She *d*. 7 May, 1876. He *d*. 27 April, 1858, having had issue,
1. James, *b*. 12 June, 1820 ; *d*. 11 April, 1822.
2. Richard, *b*. 5 Oct. 1824 ; *d*. 6 Oct. 1829.
3. Henry, *b*. 7 March, 1827 ; *d*. 6 Oct. 1832.
4. ROBERT, of Gawsworth.
   1. Anne, *m*. 9 April, 1835, Thomas Ware Corker, son of Maj. John Corker, Cork City Militia. She *d*. 6 April, 1842, leaving three daus.
   2. Elinor, *m*. 6 July, 1844, Noblett Dunscombe Parker, M.D., and *d*. 29 Jan. 1883, leaving issue. He *d*. 18 Nov. 1883.
   3. Sophia, *d. unm.* 22 Sept. 1845.
   4. Mary, *m*. 10 Nov. 1887, C. O. K. Smith, and *d*. 30 Nov. 1906. He *d*. 25 Jan. 1907.
   5. Sarah Louisa, *m*. Dec. 1860, Rev. James Clarke, Curate of Kinsale, Cork, and *d*. 22 Feb. 1863.

The 4th son,

ROBERT PRATT, of Gawsworth, co. Cork, J.P., *b*. 9 May, 1835 ; *m*. 29 Nov. 1855, Anna Maria, dau. of Austin Cooper Chadwick, of Damerville, co. Tipperary, by Anne his wife, dau. of Edward Millett, M.D., of Queenstown, co. Cork (*see* CHADWICK *of Ballinard*), and *d*. 24 Nov. 1910, leaving issue,
1. HENRY, now of Gawsworth.
2. Austin Cooper Chadwick, *b*. 13 March, 1859 ; *m*. Lilian Kathleen, dau. of Robert Jenings, of Cork.
3. Robert, *b*. 8 Oct. 1860 ; *m*. 3 Sept. 1902, Jane Adela Pope, youngest dau. of the late Pope Gray, of Woodsgift, Blackrock, co Cork, and has issue,
   1. Robert Pope, *b*. 19 Sept. 1903.
   2. Rowland Davies, *b*. 21 Aug. 1905.
   1. Claire Adela.
4. James Edward, *b*. 22 July, 1870.
5. John, L.R.C.P. and S. (I), 1904, late Midshipman R.N., *b*. 26 Jan. 1880 ; *m*. 12 June, 1906, Mary Mary, dau. of Armoud Bernard, M.D., of 57, Rodney Street, Liverpool, and has issue, John McLeod, *b*. 11 April, 1907.
1. Anna Matilda, *m*. 6 Aug. 1884, Frederick F. Jennings, 3rd son of Robert Jennings, of Cork, by Catherine his wife, dau. of William Harrington, and has issue, two sons and three daus.
2. Sarah Fitton, *m*. 9 Aug. 1887, Charles Haines O'Keeffe, of Clonmel, and has issue, three sons.
3. Maria Emma, *m*. 6 Dec. 1887, Joseph William McMullen, son of J. W. McMullen, of Cork.
4. Mary, *m*. 19 Jan. 1892, Richard Henderson Fetherstonhaugh, 2nd son of Theobald Fetherstonhaugh, of Newtown, Moate, co. Westmeath, and has issue. He *d*. 15 Oct. 1902.
5. Eleanor Sophia Mary, *d.* young, Oct. 1868.
6. Sophia Eliza, *d. unm.* 7 June, 1892.
7. Fanny Louisa, *m*. 3 April, 1902, William Henry Barton, of Ballyline, co. Kilkenny.
8. Elizabeth.

Arms—Gu., on a fesse or three mullets sa. between three elephants' heads erased of the second tusked arg. *Crest*—An elephant's head erased sa. tusked or.

Seat—Gawsworth, Carrigrohane, co. Cork.

PRENDERGAST OF ARDFINNAN.

CAPT. ROBERT JOHN PRENDERGAST, R.N., of Ardfinnan Castle, co. Tipperary, *b*. 9 July, 1864 ; *m*. 1905, Bertha Janet, only child of Capt. John Binnie Mackenzie, 1st Royal Scots, and has issue,

FREDERICK JOHN SENHOUSE, *b*. 4 Feb. 1909.

Lineage—JOHN PRENDERGAST, of Knockane, near Moneygall, co. Tipperary, was in possession of certain lands called Spittle adjoining Ardfinan in 1729, 1742, and 1750. He *m*. Mary, only dau. of John McCaffrey, of Limerick (who assumed the surname, of PRENDERGAST), by his wife Mary, only surviving child and heir of Jeffrey Prendergast, of Newcastle, the son of Edmond Prendergast, of Newcastle (*see* BURKE's *Peerage*, GORT, V.). They had issue,
1. James.
2. Thomas.
3. EDMUND, of whom below.
4. Robert, of Lacken and Greenmount, who *d*. 28 Aug. 1826, aged 96, having *m*. a dau. of Archer Butler, by whom he had issue.

The 3rd son,

EDMUND PRENDERGAST, of Marl Hill, *b*. 1731 ; *d*. 1809 ; *m*. a dau. of Walter Strang, of Coolcagh, by whom he had issue, with a dau. Mary, a son,

ROBERT PRENDERGAST, of Ardfinan Castle and of Marl Hill, both in co. Tipperary, who *d*. 3 Jan. 1838, aged 58. He *m*. 9 July, 1808, Anne, dau. of Robert Keating, of Ballydribid, Cahir, co. Tipperary, who *d*. 21 Jan. 1859. They had issue,

1. EDMOND, of Ardfinnan.
2. ROBERT KEATING, who *s*. his brother.
3. James, *b*. 15 May, 1812 ; *d. unm.*
4. John, *b*. 4 Aug. 1813 ; *d*. 5 June, 1820.
5. Henry, *b*. 5 May, 1817 ; *d. unm.*
6. Leonard, Barrister-at-Law, *b*. 11 Oct. 1818 ; *d. unm.*
7. John, *b*. 25 July, 1820 ; *d.* young.
8. Nicholas, *b*. 1821 ; *d. inf.*
9. Nicholas, *b*. 9 July, 1827.
1. Alicia Anne, *b*. 23 April, 1809 ; *d*. 21 April, 1844 ; *m*. A. Hearn, and had issue.
2. Mary Anne, *b*. 24 Sept. 1814 ; *d. unm.*
3. Margaret, *b*. 22 Jan. 1816 ; *m*. Sir William Mackenzie, K.C.B., C.S.I., Hon. Physician to QUEEN VICTORIA, and had issue.
4. Catherine, *b*. 5 Dec. 1822 ; *d. unm.* in India.
5. Lucy, *b*. 22 June, 1825 ; *d. unm.*

The eldest son,

EDMOND PRENDERGAST, of Ardfinan Castle, *b*. 25 April, 1810 ; *m*. 27 Oct. 1831, Elizabeth Vowel, graud-dau. of Jeffrey Prendergast, of Croane, and widow of — Hunt, of Cappowhite, and had issue,

1. Robert Henry, of Merioola, Edgecliffe, Sydney, N.S.W., J.P. for N.S. Wales, Queensland, and Victoria, *b*. 23 June, 1836 ; *m*. 19 Feb. 1873, Sabina, eldest dau. of Edward Fitzgerald, of Castlemaine, Victoria, and has issue,
   1. Edward Henry, *b*. 22 Nov. 1873.
   2. Desmoud Paul, *b*. 30 June, 1876.
   3. Robert Darcy, *b*. 25 May, 1881.
   4. Kenneth Francis, *b*. 25 June, 1885.
1. Susan, *m*. Col. George Ramsay Alured Denne, late 4th Dragoon Guards.
2. Marian, *m*. Kenneth James Loch Mackenzie, of Amraoti, Berar, Nezam's Dominions.

The 2nd son,

SURGEON-GEN. ROBERT KEATING PRENDERGAST, of Ardfinan Castle, J.P. co. Tipperary, *b*. 13 June, 1811 ; *d*. 25 Nov. 1890, having *m*. 5 Dec. 1860, Julia, dau. of Rev. John Kinahan, M.A. Trin. Coll. Dublin, Rector of Knockbreda, co. Down, by whom he had issue,

1. ROBERT JOHN, now of Ardfinan.
2. Frederick, Capt. and Bt.-Major R.A., *b*. 14 Dec. 1865 ; *d*. 7 May, 1903.
1. Emily Rosana, *b*. Jan. 1869 ; *d. inf.*

Arms—Gu., a saltire engrailed vair, a bordure or, charged with eight trefoils slipped of the field. *Crest*—An antelope's head erased ppr., charged with a trefoil slipped vert. *Motto*—Veritas vincit.

Seat—Ardfinnan Castle, Cahir, co. Tipperary. *Club*—United Service.

PRESTON OF SWAINSTON.

ARTHUR JOHN PRESTON, of Swainston, co. Meath, J.P. co. Durham, B.A. Trin. Coll. Dublin, Major late 33rd Regt., *b*. 31 July, 1841 ; *m*. 29 Nov. 1877, Gertrude Mary, dau. of Richard Knight, of Bobbing Court, Kent, and has issue,
1. Arthur John Dillon, Lieut. Royal Dublin Fus., *b*. 1885.
1. Gertrude Mary.
2. Dorothy Beresford.
3. Edith Florence.

Lineage.—JOHN PRESTON, of Dublin, and of Ardsallagh, co. Meath, M.P. for Navan 1661-66, had a grant of Arms 17 CHARLES II, son of Hugh Preston, of Bolton, Lancashire ; *m*. 1st, Mary, dau. of John Morris, of Bolton, and by her had issue,
1. Phineas, of Ardsallagh, *d*. 1673 ; *m*. Elizabeth, dau. of Robert Hamond, of Chertsey, and by her, who *m*. 2ndly Edward Ford, had an only son,
   John, of Ardsallagh, *b*. 1672, will dated 17 April, 1702, proved 28 April, 1703, *m*. Hon. Mary Stewart, dau. of William 1st Viscount Mountjoy, and by her, who *m*. 2ndly George 3rd, Earl of Granard, left issue,
   Phineas, of Ardsallagh, *d.s.p.*
   Mary, *m*. by licence, 31 May, 1710, Peter Ludlow, M.P., and from her descended the extinct Earls of Ludlow (*see* BURKE's *Extinct Peerage*).
2. Samuel, of Emo, Queen's Co., High Sheriff 1676, *m*. Mary, dau. of Theophilus Sandford, of Moyglare, co. Meath, and *d*. 1692, leaving two daus.,
   1. Anne, *m*. Ephraim Dawson, of Dawson's Grove, and from her descended the Earls of Portarlington (*see* BURKE's *Peerage*).
   2. Mary.

1. Mary, m. 1st, Sept. 1661, Rev. Edward Baynes, of Dublin, and 2ndly, Nehemiah Donellan. She d. 26 Sept. 1684.
He m. 2ndly, lic. 31 Dec. 1660, Katherine, dau. of John Ashburnham, and widow of Sir John Sherlock, Knt., but by her had no issue. He m. 3rdly, lic. 12 June, 1676, Anne, dau. of Alderman Richard Tighe, of Dublin, and widow of Theophilus Sandford, and by her had two sons.
3. John, of Balsoon, M.P. for Meath, b. 23 April, 1677; m. 1st, by licence, 10 Feb. 1698, Lydia, dau. of Joseph Pratt, of Cabra, co. Cavan. She d. 5 Feb. 1714. He m. 2ndly, 25 Oct. 1720, Henrietta, dau. of Sir Thomas Taylor, 1st bart. She d. 15 Jan. 1729. He d. 23 Sept. 1732, and by his first wife was ancestor of the Baron Tara (see BURKE's *Extinct Peerage*) and the PRESTONS *of Bellinter*, now extinct.
4. NATHANIEL, of whom presently.
He d. at Ardsallagh, 13 July, 1686. His youngest son,
NATHANIEL PRESTON, of Swainstown, co. Meath, M.P. for Navan 1713-60, b. circa 1678; m. 1st, by licence, 31 Dec. 1718, Anne, dau. of — Dawson. He m. 2ndly, 2 July, 1739, Alice, dau. of — Lambert, and d. 1760 (will dated 13 June, 1760, proved 3 Dec. 1760). By his first wife he had issue,
1. Joshua, bapt. 17 June, 1722, Major in the Army, d. v. m. 8 March, 1751.
2. NATHANIEL, of whom presently.
3. John, bapt. 14 Sept. 1727; d. unm.
4. Henry, bapt. 11 Feb. 1728-9; d. unm.
5. Arthur, Major 9th Lancers, m. 16 Nov. 1758, Anne, dau. of Edward Noy, of Newbrook, co. Dublin, and d.s.p. 1788. His will, dated 12 May, 1770, was proved 17 Nov. 1788.
1. Anne, bapt. 15 Jan. 1720-1; m. 20 Oct. 1738, Joseph, 1st Earl of Milltown, and d. 17 Jan. 1766, leaving a dau.
The 2nd son,
REV. NATHANIEL PRESTON, of Swainstown, bapt. 21 Jan. 1723-4; M.A. Dublin, 1744; m. 1st, by licence, 22 May, 1751, Alice, dau. of Sir John Dillon, of Lismullen, and by her had issue,
1. NATHANIEL, his heir.
2. Arthur John (Very Rev.), D.D., Dean of Limerick, b. 1760; m. 1st (mar. lic. dated 24 May, 1794) Araminta Anne, dau. of William, 1st Baron Decies, Archbishop of Tuam. She d. 26 Sept. 1816, leaving issue,
(1) Arthur John, now of Swainston.
(2) William Massy, late of Lleinlog Castle, Beaumaris, and Llanlliana, Cemaes, Anglesey, C.C. Anglesey, J.P. co. Cork, b. 9 Feb. 1845; m. 30 Oct. 1895, Blanche Margaret, 2nd dau. of the late Lieut.-Col. James Henry Wyatt, C.B., and Jane Forbes his wife, dau. of William Hogarth, and has issue,
1. William Forbes Amias, b. 23 Oct. 1896.
2. John de la Poer Beresford, b. 10 Feb. 1901.
1. Blanche Mary Gwen, b. 4 Jan. 1898.
(3) John Beresford, d. unm. 27 Aug. 1867.
(1) Araminta, m. 23 Feb. 1865, Arthur Robert Macdonnell, and d. 8 Feb. 1876.
(2) Harriet Frances Beresford, m. 28 Aug. 1876, Robert Dunsromhe, D.L., of Mount Desert, co. Cork, and has issue, George, b. 10 June, 1878, and Araminta Lydia, m. 2 Dec. 1908, Lieut.-Col. Desmond Hartley (see HARTLEY *of Beech Park*).
2. William Richard, General (retired), late 45th Regt., b. 1 Oct. 1808; m. 19 Jan. 1836, Jane (who d. 1900), dau. of John Ingle, D.L., of Sandford Orleigh, and d. 1892, leaving issue,
John Ingle, Maj.-Gen. (retired), late 45th Regt., b. 24 Dec. 1836 (Clubs—*Army and Navy, Junior United Service, Royal Western Yacht*).
The Dean of Limerick m. 2ndly, 1819, Isabella, dau. of Rev. John Shepherd, Rector of Paddington, Middlesex. She d. 23 Dec. 1859. He d. 2 Nov. 1844, having by her had a dau.,
1. Elizabeth, m. 3 Oct. 1844, James FitzGerald Massy, of Stoneville, co. Limerick. He d. 13 June, 1861.
1. Elizabeth, m. Aug. 1781, Charles William Quin, M.D., and d.s.p.
2. Alice, m. Richard Walsh, and left issue
The Rev. Nathaniel Preston m. 2ndly, 27 Oct. 1763, Mary, dau. of Hon. Henry Hamilton, M.P. (see BURKE's *Peerage*, BOYNE, V.), and d. 1796 (his will, dated 2 Sept. 1794, was proved 18 Oct. 1796), having by her had issue,
3. Henry Thomas (Rev.), Rector of Laracon, co. Meath; d. unm. March, 1801.
3. Anne, m. 1797, Sir George Talbot, Bart., and left issue.
4. Mary, m. 25 Aug. 1794, Hon. William Brodrick, and d.s.p. 20 March, 1834. He d. 29 April, 1819.
The eldest son,
NATHANIEL PRESTON, of Swainston, b. 1752; m. Anne, dau. of John Bertridge, of Templemore, and dying 1812, left issue,
1. NATHANIEL, his heir.
2. Arthur John, Capt. Royal Fusiliers, d. unm.
3. John Charles, Capt. 66th Regt., High Sheriff co. Meath 1824, d. unm.
4. Henry, Capt. in the Army, killed in the West Indies.
1. Frances, m. William Battersby, of Freffans, co. Meath, and had issue (see BATTERSBY *of Loughbawn*).
2. Alice, d. unm.
The eldest son,
THE REV. NATHANIEL PRESTON, of Swainston, m. by licence, 17 Dec. 1807, Elizabeth, dau. of John Webb, of Hilltown, co. Westmeath, and dying 1840, left five children,
1. NATHANIEL, his heir.
I.L.G.

1. Elizabeth Anne, m. Rev. St. George Caulfeild Irvine, Rector of Kilmessan (see IRVINE *of Castle Irvine*), and left one dau., Georgina Elizabeth (19, Lansdowne Road, Lee, Blackheath, S.E.), m. 1st, Hull Browning Reid, and by him had issue one son. She m. 2ndly, 1863, Lieut.-Col. George William McNalty, C.B., late R.A.M.C., and by him has issue three sons and two daus.
2. Emily, m. H. D. Mills.
3. Alice, m. Col. Walsh.
4. Georgiana, m. R. D. Massey.
The son and heir,
NATHANIEL PRESTON, of Swainston, b. 1813; m. 1839, Margaret, 2nd dau. of Samuel Pratt Winter, of Oakley, King's Co., and dying 1853, left issue,
1. NATHANIEL FRANCIS, late of Swainston.
2. Frances Elizabeth, m. 1867, Charles Yescombe, 3rd son of the Rev. Morris B. Yescombe, of Truro, Cornwall, and has two daus.
The only son,
NATHANIEL FRANCIS PRESTON, of Swainston, co. Meath, J.P., B.A., Camb., b. 1843; m. 25 July, 1865, Augusta Florence (who d. 1 Dec. 1911) dau. of Lieut.-Col. John Caulfeild, of Bloomfield, co. Westmeath. He d.s.p. 28 June, 1903.

Arms—Ermines, on a chief arg., three crescents gu. *Crest*—A crescent or, between two wings erected az. *Motto*—Virtus sui ipsius praemium.

Seat—Swainston, near Navan.

PRESTON. See BURKE's PEERAGE, GORMANSTON, V.

PRETYMAN-NEWMAN. See NEWMAN.

PRICE OF SAINTFIELD.

MAJOR JAMES NUGENT BLACKWOOD-PRICE, of Saintfield House, co. Down, J.P. and D.L., High Sheriff 1902, has Coronation medal. b. 13 Oct. 1844; Brevet Major late 60th Rifles, served in the Afghan Campaign, &c., accompanied Lord Roberts in his march to the relief of Candahar, mentioned in despatches (medal with two clasps, bronze decoration, and brevet of Major), m. 5 Jan. 1869, Alice Louisa, dau. of the late W. R. Ward, of the Diplomatic Service, and has issue,
1. CONWAY WILLIAM, B.A. Trin. Coll. Camb., b. 28 July, 1872.
2. Edward Hyde (Rev.), Rector of St. Nicholas and Vicar of St. Peter's, Droitwich (Worcs.), M.A. Wadham Coll. Oxford, b. 5 Feb. 1875.
1. Ethelwyn Mary, b. 28 Feb. 1871; m. 27 Aug. 1901, Richard Douglas Perceval, J.P., eldest son of the late Gen. John Maxwell Perceval, C.B., and has issue (see PERCEVAL-MAXWELL).

Lineage.—NICHOLAS PRICE, of Hollymount, co. Down, m. Catherine, dau. of James Hamilton, M.P., and widow of Vere Essex Cromwell, Earl of Ardglass, and had a son,
LIEUT.-GEN. NICHOLAS PRICE, m. Dorcas, 4th dau. of Roger West, of The Rock, co. Wicklow, and had issue,
1. JAMES, m. Frances, natural dau. of Lord Herbert of Chirbury, and had two daus.,
1. Catherine, m. 1st, John Savage, of Portaferry, and 2ndly, 13 Jan. 1738, Edward Baillie, D.D., Dean of Ardfert.
2. Dorcas, m. Dr. Whittle, of Lisburn.
2. Cromwell, M.P. for Downpatrick, High Sheriff, co. Down, 1722, m. 1st, Margaret, dau. of Mr. Anderson, of Belfast, and by her (who d. 1741) had a son, Nicholas Tichborne, b. 1725, who d. young; and two daus., Elizabeth, m. June, 1743, Roger MacNeal, of Tinesk; and Dorcas, m. 21 Nov. 1768, Patrick West, 1st Royal Scots. He d.s.p. Sept. 1770. She d. 1773. He m. 2ndly, March, 1742, Mary, dau. of the late Hugh Willoughby, of Carrow.
3. NICHOLAS.
1. Sophia, d. unm. Oct. 1720.
2. Margaret, m. May, 1718, Rowland Savage, of Portaferry.
3. Anne, m. James Stevenson, of Killeleagh, M.P.
The 3rd son,
NICHOLAS PRICE, of Saintfield, M.P. for Lisburn, High Sheriff co. Down, 1704, m. 1st, Mary, dau. of Francis, 1st Lord Conway, of Ragley, co. Warwick, by whom he had a son, FRANCIS, and 2ndly, 1732, Maria, dau. of Col. the Hon. Alexander Mackenzie, 2nd son of the 4th Earl of Seaforth, by whom he also had issue. He d. 1742, and was s. by his son,

2 O

Prior. THE LANDED GENTRY. 578

FRANCIS PRICE, of Saintfield, many years M.P. for Lisburn, High Sheriff, co. Down, 1753, *m.* Charity, dau. of Matthew Forde, of Seaforde, co. Down, and *d.* 1794, having had issue,
1. NICHOLAS, of Saintfield.
1. Christian Arabella, *m.* William Hoey, of Dangantstown, co. Wicklow.
2. Harriet Jane. 3. Mary, *d.* young.
The only son,
NICHOLAS PRICE, of Saintfield, J.P. and D.L., *t*High Sheriff 1801, *b.* 1 Oct. 1754; *d.* 13 March, 1840; *m.* Nov. 1779, Lady Sarah Pratt, dau. of Charles, 1st Earl Camden, and by her (who *d.* 7 April, 1817) had one dau.,
ELIZABETH ANNE, *m.* 17 June, 1804, James Blackwood (who *d.* 5 June, 1855), of Strangford, co. Down, High Sheriff 1813 (a descendant of the BLACKWOODS *of Ballyleidy*), who assumed the name and Arms of PRICE by Royal Licence 2 Aug. 1847, and *d.* 6 Feb. 1867, having had issue,
1. Nicholas, *b.* 1805; *d.* 1819.
2. JAMES CHARLES, of whom presently.
3. William Robert Arthur, *b.* 22 Jan. 1813; *m.* 1st, May, 1843, Anna Eliza, 2nd dau. of Rev. W. Jex-Blake, of Swanton Abbots, Norfolk, and had one dau., Anna Maria Frances. He *m.* 2ndly, Henrietta, dau. of George Kenyon, of Cefn, co. Denbigh.
4. Townley, *b.* 5 Jan. 1815; *m.* 1st, Feb. 1841, Maria Catherine, eldest dau. of Rev. W. Jex-Blake, and 2ndly, Anne, eldest dau. of Hon. and Rev. Henry Ward, and has issue. He *m.* 3rdly, Sarah, dau. of Hugh Lyle, of Knocktarna, co. Derry, and has issue.
5. Richard Price, Lieut.-Col. R.A., *b.* 12 May, 1818; *m.* Anne, 2nd dau. of Lieut.-Col. Wade, of Clonabraney, co. Meath (*see that family*), and has issue.
1. Sarah, *d.* young. 2. Mary Georgiana.
3. Sarah Elizabeth, *m.* Rev. Henry Archdall, 4th son of Edward Archdall, of Castle Archdall, co. Fermanagh, and has issue.
4. Elizabeth Catherine, *m.* Oct. 1841, Rev. Alexander Orr, and has issue.
His grandson,
JAMES CHARLES PRICE, of Saintfield House, co. Down, J.P. and D.L., High Sheriff 1859, *b.* 17 June, 1807; *m.* 18 March, 1840, Anne Margaret, eldest dau. of Patrick Savage, of Portaferry, Major 26th Foot, and *d.* 23 May, 1894, having by her (who *d.* 14 March, 1877) had issue,
1. Nicholas Price, *b.* 11 June, 1842; *d.* 3 July, 1889.
2. JAMES NUGENT, now of Saintfield House.
3. William Charles, *b.* 17 Oct. 1845; *d.* 8 Nov. 1845.
4. Francis William, *b.* 27 Dec. 1847.
1. Harriet Anna, *b.* 17 Jan. 1847; *d.*
2. Elizabeth Dorcas, *b.* 7 Jan. 1850; *d. unm.* 18 Nov. 1876.
3. Catherine Anne, *b.* 20 Oct. 1851.

Arms—Az., three lions' heads erased within a bordure or. Crest—A lion's head as in the Arms. Motto—Quis timet.
Seat—Saintfield House, Saintfield, co. Down. Clubs—Army and Navy, S.W., and Ulster, Belfast.

PRIOR-WANDESFORDE. *See* WANDESFORDE.

PROBY. *See* BURKE'S PEERAGE, CARYSFORT, E.

PURCELL OF BURTON PARK.

RAYMOND JOHN HUGO PURCELL, of Burton Park, co. Cork, J.P., M.A. Oxford and Lieut. King's Royal Rifle Corps, educated at Beaumont and Christ Church, *b.* 13 May, 1885; *s.* his father 1904.

Lineage.—JOHN PURCELL, of Pulleen, co. Cork, *m.* and had (with other issue),
1. JOHN, of Pullen, co. Cork.
2. RICHARD, of whose descendants we treat.
3. JAMES, ancestor of PURCELL *of Altamira*.
The 2nd son,
RICHARD PURCELL, of Kilbrin, Knockballymore, Rathnagardbeg, and Gortnaconroe, all in co. Cork, *m.* Barbara, youngest dau. of Richard Atkins, of Currykerry West (now Fountainville), co. Cork, and had issue, with three daus., two sons,
1. JOHN, of Temple Mary, co. Cork, whose male line is extinct.
2. THOMAS, of Gortnaconroe, of whom presently.
The 2nd son,
THOMAS PURCELL, of Gortnaconroe, co. Cork, *m.* 1st, a dau. of John Webb, of Cork, and by her had issue,
1. JOHN, his heir.
1. Mary, *m.* 1769, John Atkins, of Straw Hall, co. Cork.
He *m.* 2ndly, a dau. of Fitzgerald, of co. Kerry, and had issue by her,
2. Richard, *m.* Avice, dau. of William Twiss, and had issue a son and a dau., viz.,
Richard, *m.* Barbara, dau. of Robert Crofts, 6th son of William Crofts, of Velvetstown, co. Cork, and had issue.
Avice, *m.* Bartholomew Purdon.
The son and successor,

SIR JOHN PURCELL, of Highfort, co. Cork, knighte. 18 June, 1811, for the gallant defence he made when attacked by a gang of robbers, *m.* Gertrude, dau. of Mathew Franks, of Moreston'n, co. Limerick, and *d.* about 1830, having had three sons
1. MATHEW, of whom presently.
2. John, of Ramaher, co. Cork.
3. Richard, M.D., *m.* his cousin Eliza, dau. of Pierce Purcell, of Altamira (*see that family*).
The eldest son,
REV. MATHEW PURCELL, of Burton, Rector of Churchtown and Dungourney, *m.* 17 July, 1800, Eliza (*d.* 1848), dau. of William Leader, of Mount Leader (by Margaret his wife, dau. of Warham St. Leger, of Heyward Hill), and had issue,
1. JOHN, his heir.
1. Matilda, *d. unm.*
2. Eliza, *m.* 25 Jan. 1830, George Crofts, of Walshestown, co. Cork, 2nd brother of Rev. Freeman Wills Crofts, of Churchtown.
3. Henrietta, *m.* 1836, Richard Labarte, of Clonmel.
4. Margaret, *m.* 1st, 1832, William Purcell, of Altamira (*see that family*), and 2ndly, 1838, Richard Harris Purcell, and had issue by both.
5. Emily, *m.* Francis Sandes Bradshaw, of Tipperary.
6. Louisa, *m.* 1848, John Powell Longfield, of Waterloo, co. Cork.
7. Octavia, *m.* May, 1834, Richard Gibbings, of Gibbings Grove, and had issue (*see that family*).
8. Georgiana, *m.* 1834, William Gumbleton, of Curryglass House, co. Cork.
Mr. Purcell *d.* 1845, and was *s.* by his son,
JOHN PURCELL, of Burton House, D.L., *b.* 1801; *m.* 14 May, 1850, Anna Moore, dau. of M. K. Dempsey, of Kildare, and had issue by her (who *d.* 1872),
MATHEW JOHN, of Burton Park.
Elizabeth Mary, *d. unm.* 1867.
Mr. Purcell *d.* 5 Jan. 1853. His only son,
MATHEW JOHN PURCELL, of Burton Park, co. Cork, J.P. cos. Dublin and Cork, *b.* 30 Nov. 1852; *m.* 29 Aug. 1882, Anne Marie, youngest dau. of Peter Paul Daly, of Daly's Grove, co. Galway, by Anne his wife, dau. of Hubert Thomas Dolphin, of Turoe, co. Galway, and *d.* 21 Dec. 1904, leaving issue,
1. John Mathew Charles, *b.* 11 and *d.* 25 Sept. 1883.
2. RAYMOND JOHN HUGO, now of Burton Park.
3. Charles Francis, of Balliol Coll. Oxford, *b.* 23 April, 1891.
1. Annie Louisa. 2. Margaret Mary.
3. Elizabeth Mary. 4. Louisa Caroline.
5. Matilda Josephine, *d.* in infancy.
6. Angela Mary, *d.* Jan. 1904.

Seat—Burton Park, Churchtown, Buttevant, co. Cork.

PURCELL OF ALTAMIRA.

WILLIAM WILLS PURCELL, of Altamira and Dromore, B.A. Trin. Coll. Dublin, *b.* 22 May, 1860; *s.* his brother 1906; *m.* 1902, Eveline Gertrude, dau. of Thomas Nelson Foster, J.P., of Altdinas, Cheltenham, and has with other issue,
PIERCE WILLS, *b.* 1905.

Lineage.—PIERCE PURCELL, of Altamira, son of William Purcell, of Altamira, co. Cork (by Mary Goold his wife), and grandson of James Purcell, 3rd son of John Purcell, of Pulleen, (*see previous memoir*), *m.* Barbara, dau. of Thomas Harris, of Harrisgrove (by Hannah his wife, dau. of Richard Purcell, of Kilbrin, co. Cork), and had issue,
1. WILLIAM PURCELL, of Altamira, *m.* 1832, his cousin, Margaret, dau. of Rev. Mathew Purcell, of Burton House, and dying 2 Jan. 1837, left an only child, Eliza Augusta, heir of Highfort, *m.* 1857, Henry Longfield, of Seacourt.
2. James, of Dromore, co. Cork, *m.* 17 Nov. 1808, Ellen (who *d.* Feb. 1819), dau. of Usher Philpot Williamson, of Old Dromore, near Mallow, in the aforesaid co., J.P., by Anne his wife, dau. of Col. Thomas Lloyd, of Beechmount, co. Limerick; *d.* 10 Feb. 1830, having had issue, two sons and one dau.,
1. PIERCE, of whom presently.
2. Usher Williamson (Rev.), of Wigginton Vicarage, near Tamworth, co. Stafford, *m.* Susan (who *d.* 17 July, 1876), dau. of the late Rev. William Fell, Rector of Sheepy. He *d.* 9 Nov. 1897.
1. Anne.
3. Richard Harris, now of Annabella, near Mallow, *m.* Louisa, youngest dau. of William Leader, of Mount Leader, co. Cork, and had issue, *inter alios*,
1. Richard Harris Purcell, Barrister-at-Law, *m.* 1832, his cousin, Margaret, dau. of Rev. Mathew Purcell, of Burton House, co. Cork (*see that family*), and has issue by her,
(1) Ferdinand Albert Purcell.
(2) Mio Adolph. (3) Eugene.
2. John Harris, of Copeswood, co. Cork, *m.* Louisa, dau. of Thomas Leader, of Spring Mount, co. Cork, and *d.* leaving issue,
(1) Isabel, *m.* 1894, Charles Owen Starkey, of Woodville, Ballyhooley.
(2) Harriet St. Leger. (3) Florence Meta, a nun.
1. Hannah.
2. Eliza, *m.* her cousin, Richard Purcell, M.D., of Highfort (*see* PURCELL *of Burton Park*).
3. Mary.
4. Lucinda Barbara, *m.* 14 Jan. 1806, John Sandes, of Moyvane, who *d.* 7 March, 1818, leaving issue (*see* SANDES *of Greenville*). She *d.* 31 Dec. 1865.
His grandson,

PIERCE PURCELL, of Dromore and Altamira, co. Cork, J.P., b. 27 May, 1811; m. 7 June, 1856, Alicia Ellen (d. 7 July, 1909), 2nd dau. of the late Richard Wills Gason, J.P. and D.L., of Richmond, near Nenagh, co. Tipperary, by Anne his wife, eldest dau. of the late Charles Henry Leslie, of Wilton, and d. 28 March, 1896, leaving issue,
1. JAMES CHARLES HENRY, of Altamira.
2. WILLIAM WILLE, now of Dromore.
1. Annette Ellen.
2. Georgina Hannah, m. 27 April, 1893, Ludlow Mainwaring Jones, son of the late Rev. A. Armstrong Jones, Rector of Kilmore, Nenagh, co. Tipperary.
The elder son,
JAMES CHARLES HENRY PURCELL, of Altamira and Dromore, co. Cork, b. 31 Jan. 1859, and d. 9 April, 1906, being s. by his brother.
Seats—Altamira, near Buttevant, and Dromore, near Mallow.

PURCELL, late OF GLANNANORE.

JAMES EDWARD PURCELL, of Foxborough House, King's Co. and Donoughmore House, co. Meath, b. 20 April, 1866; s. his father 1911.
Lineage.—RICHARD PURCELL (of the ancient family of Purcell, Barons of Loughmoe) of Kanturk House and Springfort, co. Cork, temp. CHARLES II., m. Miss Butler, and had issue,
1. John, b. 22 Jan. 1687.
2. James, b. 22 Nov. 1692.
3. William, b. 23 Nov. 1694.
4. RICHARD, of whom presently.
1. Sarah, b. 1 Oct. 1696.   2. Mary, b. 3 July, 1698.
The 4th son,
RICHARD PURCELL, of Kanturk House and Springfort, b. 16 June, 1703; m. Jane, dau. of Richard Goodwin, of Coomhooly and Reindesart, co. Cork, and had issue, seven sons and two daus.,
1. RICHARD (Rev.), b. 1728; Scholar Trin. Coll. Dublin, 1747, Rector of Coole 1759; m. 1762, Catherine Grove, of Ballyhimmock, co. Cork, and d.s.p. 12 Aug. 1797.
2. William, b. 20 Sept. 1730; d. at St. Helena 16 June, 1753.
3. Percival, b. 23 Sept. 1731; killed at the storming of Bellisle.
4. James, b. 5 June, 1733; d. 5 Oct. 1801.
5. John, b. 12 May, 1735; d. in Portugal 29 Aug. 1759.
6. Thomas, b. 3 June, 1738; d. 24 July, 1775.
7. GOODWIN, b. 8 Dec. 1739.
1. Catherine, b. 10 July, 1732.
2. Mary, b. 18 May, 1734.
The youngest son,
GOODWIN PURCELL, J.P., of Kanturk House, b. 8 Dec. 1739; m. Mary Allen (whose family had property near Kanturk, co. Cork), and had issue,
1. GEORGE.
2. Richard, Major North Cork Militia.
3. James.
4. Goodwin, Major 31st Regt.
The eldest son,
GEORGE PURCELL, J.P., of Glannanore, Castletown Roche, near Fermoy, co. Cork, m. 1791, Mary, dau. of Rev. Edward Delany, Rector of Whitechurch or Templegall, Diocese of Cloyne, and d. 29 Jan. 1830, having had issue by her (who d. 22 May, 1837) four sons and five daus.,
1. JAMES GEORGE (Rev.).
2. Charles Percival, m. Miss Holmes, of Maiden Hall, Charleville, co. Cork.
3. George, of Kenmare, co. Kerry.
4. Goodwin (Rev.), Vicar of Charlesworth, co. Derby, m. 1st, Sarah, dau. of Joseph Lea, of Davenham, co. Chester, and had two sons and one dau.,
  1. Joseph, who d.s.p.
  2. James, of Carrigmore House, co. Cork, b. 1849; m. 1875, Elizabeth, dau. of John Dickinson, of Wembrick House, Ormskirk, co. Lancaster, and has a son,
    Goodwin, b. 1876.
  1. Anne, m. 24 Aug. 1881, Henry Daniel Conner, K.C., of Manch House, co. Cork (see that family), and has issue.
Rev. Goodwin Purcell m. 2ndly, Elizabeth La Touche. He d. 1877.
1. Mary, m. 5 Aug. 1819, Rev. Joseph Rogerson Cotter, Rector of Donoughmore, co. Cork, Senior Prebendary of Cloyne, and Rural Dean, grandson of Sir James Cotter, of Rockforest, near Mallow, co. Cork, and d. 15 April, 1851, having had issue.
2. Jane, m. William Delany, of Conwaymore, co. Cork, and had issue.
3. Anne, m. Rev. James White, Vicar of Inchegeela, co. Cork, and had issue.
4. Susan, m. Robert Bullen, of Ballythomas House, Mallow, co. Cork, and had issue.
5. Catherine, d. unm.
The eldest son,
REV. JAMES GEORGE PURCELL, of Glannanore, Vicar of Worminghall, co. Buckingham, m. 17 April, 1820, Letitia, dau. of Francis Talbot (of the Wexford Talbots), of Foxboro' House, King's Co., by Mary his wife, widow of Robert Norton, K.C., and dau. of John Eiffe, and by her (who d. 12 Feb. 1868) he had issue,
1. GEORGE, his heir, b. 12 Jan. 1827; m. Eliza Hamilton, and d.s.p. 17 Sept. 1871.
2. FRANCIS TALBOT, now of Edstaston.
1. Bridget Frances, b. 9 Feb. 1821; d. 19 March following.
2. Mary Georgina, b. 11 April, 1822; d. May following.
3. Mary Anne Bridget, b. 4 Aug. 1823; d. 9 Aug. 1850.
4. Frances, b. 20 Oct. 1824; d. May, 1825.

Rev. James George Purcell d. 7 Nov. 1843, and was s. by his only surviving son,
REV. FRANCIS TALBOT PURCELL, Vicar of Edstaston, co. Salop, b. 30 Jan. 1833; m. 5 Oct. 1858, Fanny Jane, dau. of Edward Keane, Capt. R.N., by Sarah Ladd Peake his wife, and grand-dau. of Michael Keane, uncle of the 1st Lord Keane, and d. 8 July, 1911 having had issue,
1. JAMES EDWARD, now of Foxborough House.
2. John Norton, b. 20 Nov. 1870.
1. Letitia Sarah, b. 1 Jan. 1860; m. 3 July, 1883, Rev. Victor Reginald Bomford, Vicar of Wigginton, Staffordshire, who d. 24 Aug. 1900, leaving a dau. (see BOMFORD of Oakley Park).
2. Frances Isabella Mary, b. 25 Feb. 1862.
3. Agnes Taibot, b. 23 April, 1864.
4. Eleanor, b. 13 July, 1868.
5. May Eiffe, b. 22 April, 1873; d. 14 Dec. 1896.
Seats—Foxboro' House, Roscrea, King's Co., and Donoughmore House, Ashbourne, co. Meath.

PURCELL-FITZGERALD. See FITZGERALD.

PURDON OF TINERANA.

ANNIE LOUISA and HELEN, late of Tinerana, co. Clare, sisters and co-heirs of the late W. C. Purdon, of Tinerana, s. their brother 1893. The elder Annie Louisa, m. 6 Oct. 1898, John L. Thomas, of Caeglas, Llandilo, who d. 13 Aug. 1910. The younger Helen m. 14 Jan. 1909, the Rev. Cecil Grafton Norton, son of Rev. D. E. Norton, Rector of Maperton.

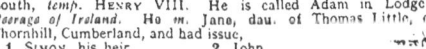

Lineage.—JAMES PURDON, of Kirklington, Cumberland, settled at Lurgan Race, co. Louth, temp. HENRY VIII. He is called Adam in Lodge's Peerage of Ireland. He m. Jane, dau. of Thomas Little, of Thornhill, Cumberland, and had issue,
1. SIMON, his heir.   2. John.
1. Jane, m. Adam Loftus, D.D., Archbishop of Dublin, and Lord High Chancellor. She was bur. in St. Patrick's Cathedral 21 July, 1595.
2. Margaret, m. Thomas Jones, D.D., Archbishop of Dublin.
Mr. Purdon was s. by his elder son,
SIMON PURDON, of Tallagh, co. Dublin, and of Ballynakill, King's Co., m. Miss Arthur, and d. 1596, leaving issue,
1. JOHN, his heir.
2. Richard (see PURDON of Lisnabin).
1. Elizabeth, m. William Conway, and d. 1612. He d. 1663.
2. Mary, m. Robert Conway, D.C.L. He d. 1602.
Mr. Purdon's elder son,
JOHN PURDON, of Tullagh, co. Clare, m. Eleanor, dau. of Sir John Fleming, brother of the then Lord Slane, and had issue, five sons, of whom the youngest, SIR NICHOLAS PURDON, M.P. for Baltimore, was ancestor of the PURDONS of Ballyclogh, co. Cork, now extinct in the male line. The eldest son,
SIMON PURDON, of Tullagh, co. Clare, m. Ellice, only dau. and heir of Edmund Bourke, of Cloghadromond, co. Limerick, and was s. by his eldest son,
JOHN PURDON, of Tullagh, co. Clare, m. Grace, dau. of John Hurley, of co. Limerick, and had issue, Sylvester, m. a dau. of John Magrath, of Derrymore, co. Clare, and had issue, John. His only brother,
GEORGE PURDON, of Tinerana, co. Clare, High Sheriff 1663, m. Mary, dau. of William Lewis, of co. York, and had issue. Mr. Purdon was s. by his eldest son,
SIMON PURDON, of Tinerana, co. Clare, M.P., b. 1655, High Sheriff 1684, and 1696, m. 1st, Mary, dau. of Sir George Ingoldsby, which lady d.s.p.; and 2ndly, Helena, dau. of the Right Rev. Edward Synge, D.D., Bishop of Cork, and d. 4 Nov. 1719, leaving, with several daus.,
1. GEORGE, his heir.
2. SIMON, bapt. 1691, m. Elizabeth eldest dau. and eventual co-heir of Major George Purdon, of Primrose Hill, co. Cork, and had issue,
  1. GEORGE, his heir.
  2. Gilbert, of Ballykelly, m. Anne, dau. of Anthony Parker, of Castle Lough (see PARKER of Bally Valley), and had an only child,
    Amy, m. Charles O'Callaghan.
  1. Jane, m. the Ven. George Massy.
  2. Avarina, m. Richard Ringrose Bowerman, of Moynoe House, co. Clare.
3. Edward (Rev.), b. 1692.   4. Charles.
5. William, of Claremont, co. Dublin. He m. the dau. of Anthony Parker, of Castle Lough, and had an only son,

William John Purdon, who *m.* Jane, dau. of Chidley Coote, of Ash Hill, co. Lmerick, and had an only son,
Simon Purdon. He *m.* Anne, dau. of George Le Hunte, of Artramont, co. Wexford, and had, *inter alios*, a son,
Rev. William John Purdon, of De Vesci Terrace, Kingstown, co. Dublin, M.A. Oxon. He *m.* 1st, 9 Sept. 1824, Charlotte Emily, dau. of Right Hon. Denis Browne, M.P. (*see* BURKE's *Peerage*, SLIGO, M.), by whom (who *d.* 23 April, 1838) he had two daus., Emily Jane, and Anna Maria. He *m.* 2ndly, June, 1842, Katherine Geraldine, dau. of Sir Ross Mahon, Bart., of Castlebar.

6. John, *d.s.p.*
1. Margaret. 2. Barbara.
3. Helena Maria, *m.* as his first wife (setts. dated 9 Jan. 1721) Daniel Toler, of Beechwood, co. Tipperary, ancestor, by his second wife, of the Earls of Norbury.

Mr. Purdon was *s.* by his eldest son,
GEORGE PURDON, of Tinerana, co. Clare, and of Woodfort, co. Cork, M.P. for Clare 1725 and 1727. He *m.* 19 Oct. 1715, Arabella, 3rd dau. and co-heir of Col. William Casaubon, of Carrig, near Mallow, co. Cork, M.P. for Doneraile, by his wife, a dau. of Gore, of Derrymore, dying 1740, and was *s.* by his eldest son,
SIMON PURDON, of Tinerana, High Sheriff co. Limerick 1772, He *m.* Mary Anne, dau. of James Nash, of Kilbroney, co. Cork, and widow of Hugh Ingoldsby Massy, but dying *s.p.* Nov. 1791, was *s.* by his next brother,
WILLIAM CASAUBON PURDON, of Tinerana, b. 26 Dec. 1752, Major 7th Dragoon Guards, *m.* Aug. 1793, Deborah, eldest dau. of Michael Head, of Derry, co. Tipperary, by Margaret his wife, sister of Henry Prittie, 1st Lord Dunalley, and had issue,
1. SIMON GEORGE, his heir.
2. William Casaubon, Vicar of Loxley, co. Warwick, *b.* 1798; *m.* 17 July, 1838, Augusta Louisa, only child of Rev. George F. Tavell, by Lady Augusta Fitzroy his wife, 5th dau. of Augustus Henry, 3rd Duke of Grafton, and *d.s.p.* Aug. 1850. His widow *m.* 2ndly, J. Murray Gartshore, of Gartshore, co. Perth.
1. Arabella Mary Anne.
2. Margaret Elizabeth, *m.* 17 July, 1826, Rev. William Buckner Lewis.
3. Deborah, *m.* 6 Feb. 1835, the Rev. Robert Maunsell Evans, Archdeacon of Cloyne, 2nd son of Eyre Evans, of Ash Hill Towers, co. Limerick.
4. Charlotte, *m.* 1st, 1829, Capt. Michael Stackpole, R.N., and 2ndly, George Harrison, of The Arke, co. Wicklow.

Mr. Purdon dying 1 Feb. 1836, was *s.* by his elder son,
SIMON GEORGE PURDON, of Tinerana, J.P. and D.L., Major Clare Militia, High Sheriff 1829, *b.* 8 May, 1797; *m.* 11 Aug. 1836, Louisa Elizabeth Eleanor, 2nd dau. of the Hon. and Right Rev. Richard Ponsonby, 1st Lord Ponsonby, of Imokilly, and by her who *d.* 10 Aug. 1873) had issue,
1. WILLIAM CASAUBON, his heir.
2. GEORGE FREDERICK ROBERT, of whom presently.
3. Richard Ponsonby, R.N., *b.* 17 Oct. 1842; drowned in H.M.S. *Captain*, Sept. 1870.
4. Simon Godfrey, *b.* 11 Sept. 1844; *d.* 2 Feb 1909.
5. John Molesworth, *b.* 10 April, 1848; *m.* 6 June. 1888, Louisa Alice, dau. of E. M. Clissold, of Fawley Lodge, Cheltenham.
6. Frederick Ponsonby, *b.* 13 Sept. 1849.
1. Frances Harriett, *m.* 18 Aug. 1864, Herbert Lloyd, of Kilybebyll, co. Glamorgan.
2. Deborah Louisa Grace, *m.* 24 Oct. 1867, Robert Bruce Robertson Glasgow, of Mount Greenan, co. Ayr, Lieut. 74th Highlanders, and *d.* 9 Jan. 1887.
3. Emily Charlotte (14, *Hamilton Gardens, N.W.*), *m.* 12 Sept. 1874, Charles W. Howard, late 79th Regt.
4. Augusta Harriet Arabella, *d. unm.* 5 Sept. 1907.
5. Georgina Margaret (*Pontardawe, Glamorgan*), *m.* June, 1883, Major F. E. Lloyd.

Mr. Purdon *d.* 7 Aug. 1862, and was *s.* by his son,
WILLIAM CASAUBON PURDON, of Tinerana, Lieut. Rifle Brigade, *d.* 26 July, 1837; *d.* 10 Jan. 1864, and was *s.* by his brother,
GEORGE FREDERICK ROBERT PURDON, of Tinerana, J.P., Commander R.N., *b.* 11 May, 1840; *m.* 5 Dec. 1867, Annie, only dau. of Gen. Caulfeild, C.B., of Copswood, co. Limerick, and by her (who *d.* 22 June, 1882) had issue,
1. WILLIAM CASAUBON, late of Tinerana.
2. George Muirson, *b.* 10 Dec. 1875; *d. unm.* 1881.
1. ANNIE LOUISA, now of Tinerana.
2. HELEN, now of Tinerana.

Commander Purdon *d.* 15 June, 1882. His son,
WILLIAM CASAUBON PURDON, of Tinerana, *b.* 24 Dec. 1869; *s.* his father 1882, and *d. unm.* 11 May, 1893, when he was *s.* by his two sisters.

Arms—Arg., a leopard's face gu. between a chief and a chevron sa., quartering CASAUBON and BURKE. *Crest*—An arm embowed ppr. holding a broken spear with a banner arg., charged with a leopard's face gu. *Motto*—Pro aris et focis.

Seat—Tinerana, Killaloe, co. Clare.

PURDON (now WINTER) OF LISNABIN.

EDWARD WINTER WINTER, of Agher, co. Meath, and of Lisnabin, co. Westmeath, Lieut.-Col. and Hon. Col. late 6th Batt. Rifle Brigade, *b.* May, 1853; *s.* his father 1910; *s.* his uncle, James Sanderson Winter, of Agher, 1911, and assumed the name of Winter and the arms of Winter quarterly with those of Purdon by Royal Licence dated 2 April, 1912; *m.* May, 1893, Cecilia Albuera Frances, younger dau. of Charles Edward Radclyffe, of Little Park, Hants (*see that family*), and has issue,
1. CHARLES EDWARD, *b.* Feb. 1894.
2. Samuel Francis, *b.* Sept. 1895.
3. George Hardress, *b.* Jan. 1897.
4. Denis James, *b.* 19 May, 1900.

Lineage.—Rev. RICHARD PURDON (*see* PURDON *of Tinerana*), *m.* Margaret, dau. of James Vian (who *d.* 1619), and settled at Killucan. His son,
Rev. HENRY PURDON, of Rathwire, Vicar of Oldcastle, 1639, *m.* Miss Griffin, by whom he acquired Griffinstown, co. Westmeath. His son,
PETER PURDON, of Rathwire, co. Westmeath, *b.* 1569; *m.* 1700, Mary, dau. of Robert Adair, of Hollybrook, co. Wicklow, M.P. for Phillipstown, and *d.* 1734, leaving, with other issue,
EDWARD PURDON, *b.* 1709, who settled at Lisnabin; *m.* 1738, Esther Cooper, and had, with other issue,
CHARLES PURDON, of Lisnabin, *b.* 1746, *m.* 1773, Miss Mary Nugent, of Castle Rickard, co. Meath, and *d.* 1790, leaving issue,
1. EDWARD, his heir.
2. George Rodney, *m.* Mary Macminn, of Donaghadee.
1. Elizabeth, *m.* Charles Marsball.

The elder son,
EDWARD PURDON, of Lisnabin, *b.* 1774; *m.* Jan. 1810, Miss Margaret Eva Moore, of Dublin, and by her (who *d.* 1855) had issue,
1. GEORGE NUGENT, of Lisnabin.
2. Rodney William, *b.* 12 Sept. 1820, *d.* 9 Nov. 1911; *m.* 1850, Angel, dau. of Rev. Charles Rawlins, and has surviving issue,
  1. Frances. 2. Edward.
  1. Eva Mary. 2. Constance.
  3. Another dau.
1. Dorothea Jane, *m.* Rev. George Gough Gubbins, and had issue, six sons and six daus.
2. Maria Martha, *m* Rev. Oliver J. Tibeaudo.
3. Elizabeth Caroline, *m.* Rev. Robert Irwin, and had issue (*see that family*), six sons and six daus.
4. Alicia Fanny, *d. unm.* 5 July, 1899.

He *d.* 1867. The elder son,
GEORGE NUGENT PURDON, of Lisnabin, co. Westmeath, J.P., High Sheriff 1872, *b.* 2 Aug. 1819; *m.* Aug. 1852, Elizabeth Anne, eldest dau. of Samuel Winter, D.L., of Agher, co. Meath. She *d.* 1864. He *d.* 6 March, 1910, leaving issue,
1. EDWARD WINTER, now of Lisnabin.
2. George Richard (Rev.), *b.* 1854.
3. John James, Major, late Royal Inniskilling Fusiliers, *b.* 24 Oct. 1855.
4. Charles Saunderson, M.B., of Lodge Park, Freshford, co. Kilkenny, *b.* 1857; *m.* 2 Sept. 1897, Ethel Emily, dau. of John Millard Lush, of Dorchester, Dorset, and has issue,
  1. John Nugent, *b.* April, 1899.
  2. Edmund Rodney, *b.* Aug. 1901.
  1. Joyce Elizabeth Mary, *b.* Nov. 1903.
5. Samuel Pratt, of Huntingdon, Killucan, co. Westmeath, *b.* 1859; *m.* 8 Sept. 1896, Florence Beatrice, dau. of the late Thomas Richard Peareth, 12th Lancers (*see* PEARETH *of Thorpe Maundeville*), and *d.* 12 June, 1908, leaving issue,
  1. Willoughby Thomas Pancras, *b.* 10 April, 1908.
  1. Beatrice Florence. 2. Irene Cecilia Lucy.
  3. Rosalind Juliet Dorothy.
1. Lucy Helen, *m.* 13 Sept. 1883, Lieut.-Col. James Smyth, of Gaybrook, co. Westmeath, and has issue (*see that family*).

Seats—Lisnabin, Killucan; Agher, Enfield, co. Meath.

PUREFOY OF GREENFIELDS.

WILFRED BAGWELL-PUREFOY, of Greenfields, co. Tipperary, J.P., late Lieut. 3rd King's Own Hussars, *b.* 13 June, 1862.

Lineage. — LIEUT. - COL. EDWARD BAGWELL-PUREFOY, of Greenfields, J.P., Vice-Lieut. of co. Tipperary, High Sheriff for the co. 1856, educated at Harrow, Capt. 3rd Dragoon Guards, Hon. Col. co. Tipperary Artillery Militia, *b.* 2 Aug. 1819; *m.* 1st, 10 July, 1854, Isabella Petronella, youngest dau. of the late Major Langley, 2nd Life Guards, of Brittas Castle, co. Tipperary, but by her had no issue. He *m.* 2ndly, 20 July, 1861, Charlotte, 4th dau. of John Green Wilkinson, D.L. and by her (who *d.* Nov. 1881) had issue,
1. WILFRED, now of Greenfields.
2. Henry John, Capt. late 5th Dragoon Guards, *b.* 26 Aug. 1864.
3. Edward, Capt. late 16th Lancers, *b.* 25 Nov. 1868; *m.* 24 June

1897, Frances Elizabeth, eldest dau. of J. T. Rogers, of River Hill, Sevenoaks. She d. 25 Feb. 1903, leaving issue,
1. John, b. 24 May, 1898.
2. Arthur Edward, b. 30 Jan. 1903.
1. Maude Isabel, d. Jan. 1883.
This gentleman assumed the additional surname of PUREFOY, by Royal Licence, 5 April, 1847, on succeeding to the estate of the late Col. Purefoy, who d. 1846. He was 2nd son of Very Rev. Richard Bagwell, Dean of Clogher, by Margaret his wife, dau. of Edward Croker, of Ballynagarde, co. Limerick (see BAGWELL of Marlfield). He d. 2 July, 1883.

Arms—Quarterly: 1st and 4th, sa., three pairs of hands conjoined one and two or, ruffled arg., for PUREFOY; 2nd and 3rd, paly of six arg. and az., on a chief gu. a lion passant of the first, for BAGWELL. Crest—A hand in armour grasping a broken lance, all ppr. Motto—En bonne foy.

Seat—Greenfields, Tipperary.

PUXLEY OF DUNBOY CASTLE.

HENRY WALLER LAVALLIN PUXLEY, of Dunboy Castle, co. Cork, b. 1898; s. his grandfather 1909.

Lineage.—JOHN PUXLEY, of Galway, J.P., settled about 1700 at Dunboy, co. Cork, with Henry, his brother, who m. a dau. of Capt. Richard Godwin, and aunt of the Rev. Thomas Goodwin, Rector of Achaven. John (shot March 1754), m. Mary, dau. of James Reyes, of Kinsale, and had issue.
1. HENRY, of whom presently.
2. Othwell, m. Mary, dau. of Thomas Shaw and widow of Major Eyre.
3. John, commanded a native Indian Regiment.
1. Mary, d. unm.   2. Anne, d. unm.
3. Ellen, m. J. M'Carthy.

The eldest son,
HENRY PUXLEY, m. July, 1771, Sarah, dau. and co-heir of Philip Lavallin. Mr. Puxley was killed by a fall from his horse, and was s. by his only son,
JOHN LAVALLIN PUXLEY, of Dunboy Castle, D.L. co. Carmarthen, m. Sarah, dau. of S. Hobbs, of the Isle of Wight, and had issue,
1. Henry, d. unm.
2. JOHN LAVALLIN, of whom presently.
1. Sarah, d. unm.   2. Elizabeth, d. unm.
3. Barbara, d. nm.
4. Fanny, m. Rev. Henry Herbert, of co. Montgomery.
5. Henrietta, m. Robert Thomas, 10th Regt.
6. Jane, d. unm.

The only surviving son,
JOHN LAVALLIN PUXLEY, of Dunboy Castle, m. 1830, Frances Rosa Maria, dau. of Simon White, of Glengariff Castle, co. Cork, and niece of Richard, 1st Earl of Bantry, and had issue,
1. JOHN SIMON LAVALLIN, his heir.
2. HENRY LAVALLIN, late of Dunboy Castle.
3. Edward Lavallin (Rev.), late Vicar of Steep, Petersfield, Hants, late Lieut. 4th Dragoons, b. 1835, m. 1864. Maria Winifred, only dau. of Henry Leader, of Clonmoyle (see LEADER of Dromagh Castle), and d. 30 June, 1909, leaving issue, two sons and three daus.
4. Herbert Boyne Lavallin (Rev.), of Llether Llestry, Carmarthen, and Lavallin House, Tenby, Rector of Catton, Yorks, b. 1 July, 1836; m. May, 1869, Catherine, dau. of the late Robert Benson, of St. Helens, Cockermouth, co. Cumberland, great niece of Gen. Richard Benson, and of Rev. Christopher Benson, Master of the Temple, and Canon of Worcester, and d. 20 Jan. 1908, leaving issue,
1. Robert Boyne Lavallin, Lieut. R.A., b. 15 March, 1871; d. unm. Dec. 1894.
2. Herbert Lavallin (Rev.), of Llether Llestry, Carmarthen, and Lavallin House, Tenby, Rector of Westonbirt, Glos., b. 23 Nov. 1872; m. 6 Aug. 1908, Dorothy, eldest dau. of the late Philip Wroughton, of Woolley Park, Berks (see that family), and has issue,
Michael Lavallin, b. 28 Sept. 1909.
Margaret Mary Lavallin, b. 22 Jan. 1911.
3. Harry Othwell Lavallin, late Lieut. Royal Scots Regt., b. 1 Oct. 1874.
1. Sybil Lavallin, m. 27 Dec. 1900, Hugh Lamplugh Brooksbank (see BROOKSBANK of Healaugh).
2. Kate Ierne Lavallin, m. 17 Sept. 1896, her cousin, Herbert Hardress Lavallin Puxley, and has issue (see below).
3. Louise Madeleine Lavallin, m. Aug. 1898, John Townsend Keily, Barrister-at-Law, and has issue.
4. Zoë Hylda Lavallin.
1. Fanny Sarah Eliza Lavallin, m. 1855, the Rev. John Thomas Waller, of Castletown Manor, Pallas Kenry, co. Limerick, eldest son of the Rev. William Waller, of Castletown, co. Limerick, and has issue (see that family).

Mr. Puxley d. 1837, and was s. by his eldest son,
JOHN SIMON LAVALLIN PUXLEY, of Dunboy Castle, Capt. 6th Dragoons, b. 13 July, 1831; d. unm. 1860, and was s. by his brother,
HENRY LAVALLIN PUXLEY, of Dunboy Castle, co. Cork, M.A., J.P. cos. Cork and Carmarthen, High Sheriff co. Cork 1865, and High Sheriff co. Carmarthen 1864, b. 4 April, 1834; m. 1st, 4 June, 1857, Katherine Ellen, dau. of Rev. William Waller, of Castletown, co. Limerick (see that family), and by her (who d. 1872) had issue,
1. John Lavallin, b. 21 Dec. 1859; d. unm.
2. Edward Lavallin, b. 10 June, 1861; d. unm.
3. Henry Edmund Lavallin, b. 14 Feb. 1866; m. 15 Sept. 1897, Jane Eliza, only dau. of Rev. John Halahan, Rector of Berehaven, co. Cork. He d. 1900, leaving by her (who m. 2ndly, 4 Aug. 1909, William Steele Haughton) issue,
1. HENRY WALLER LAVALLIN, now of Dunboy Castle.
2. John Paul Lavallin, b. 1900.
4. William Waller Lavallin, b. 17 Feb. 1867; d. unm.
5. Herbert Hardress Lavallin, of Llangendeirne and Landdaroe Carmarthenshire, b. 26 May, 1868; m. 17 Sept. 1896, his cousin Kate Ierne Lavallin, dau. of Rev. Herbert Lavallin Puxley, and has issue,
1. Robert Lavallin, b. 23 June, 1897.
2. William Lavallin, b. 5 July, 1898.
3. Patrick Lavallin, b. 3 Nov. 1900.
4. Herbert Lavallin, b. 6 Nov. 1907.
1. Ruth Lavallin, b. 4 May, 1904.
1. Maria Frances, m. 20 March, 1884, Robert O'Brien Studdert, J.P., of Cullam, co. Clare (see STUDDERT of Bunratty Castle).
2. Katherine Rosa, m. her cousin Simon White, of Glengariff Castle, co. Cork, and d. leaving issue.
3. Elizabeth Jane.

He m. 2ndly, 9 Dec. 1875, Adeline, youngest dau. of Gen. Charles W. Nepean, grand-niece of the late Sir Evan Nepean, 1st bart., Madras Army, and widow of Col. William Fergusson Hutchinson. He d. 6 Feb. 1909, being s. by his grandson.

Arms—Quarterly: 1st and 4th, gu., on a bend cottised arg. five lozenges conjoined of the first; in the sinister chief point an annulet or, for PUXLEY; and 2nd and 3rd, arg., a fleur-de-lis sa., a chief engrailed az., for LAVALLIN. Crests—An arm in armour embowed ppr., charged with a lozenge between two annulets in pale gu., the hand grasping a dagger, also ppr. Motto—Loyal en tout.

Seat—Dunboy Castle, Castletown, Berehaven, and Llangan co. Carmarthen.

WYNDHAM-QUIN. See BURKE'S PEERAGE, DUNRAVEN, E.

RAINEY-ROBINSON. See ROBINSON.

RAM OF CLONATTIN.

REV. EDWARD DIGBY STOPFORD RAM, of Clonattin, co. Wexford, Rector of Oxted since 1902, M.A. Oxon, b. 29 Dec. 1868; educated at Marlborough and St. John's Coll. Oxford; m. 1st, 17 Sept. 1896, Mabel, 3rd dau. of Rev. W. H. Castleman, Rector of Nuneham Courtney, Oxford, and by her (who d. 9 April, 1898) has issue,
1. Mabel Charlotte, } twins, b. 10 May, 1897.
2. Eileen Isabel,

He m. 2ndly, 11 Oct. 1899, Clara Helen, dau. of the late Sir Henry Flower Every, 11th bart. (see BURKE'S Peerage and Baronetage), and by her has had issue,
1. ABEL JAMES, b. 3 Nov. 1902.
2. Andrew Digby, b. 26 March, 1908.
3. Helen Geraldine, b. 20 July, 1900; d. Feb. 1901.

Lineage.—RIGHT REV. THOMAS RAM, D.D., Bishop of Ferns and Leighlin, b. at Windsor in 1564, was educated at Eton, and as King's Coll., Camb., whence, having taken the degree of Master of Arts, he went to Ireland, as Chaplain to Robert Devereux, Earl of Essex, in 1599. The next year he was made Dean, first of Cork, and then of Ferns. He was consecrated Bishop of Ferns and Leighlin, in Christ Church, Dublin, 2 May, 1605. On the plantation of Wexford in 1615, by JAMES I., he obtained a grant of lands, which descended to his children. He m. 1st, Jane Gifford, widow of Mr. Thompson, and had one son and four daus.,
1. THOMAS (Very Rev.), M.A. Dublin 1624, appointed Dean of Ferns, 11 Feb. 1626; d.s.p.

Ram.

THE LANDED GENTRY

1. Grace, *d.* young.
2. Susan, *m.* Very Rev. Robert Wilson, Dean of Ferns.
3. Jane, *m.* Ven. Richard Jennings, Archdeacon of Ferns.
4. Anne, *m.* John Allen, of Woodhouse, co. Wexford.

The Bishop *m.* 2ndly, Anne, dau. of Robert Bowen, of Bally Adams, Queen's Co., and had further issue,

2. Robert (Rev.), M.A. 1614, and Fellow of Trin. Coll. Dublin 1615, Prebendary of Crosspatrick, or Kilcommon, Diocese of Ferns; *d.s.p.*
3. Abel, of whom hereafter.
4. Henry, *d.s.p.*
5. Elizabeth, *m.* Rev. William Hewetson, Rector of St. Werburgh's, Dublin.
6. Grace.

The Bishop *d.* of apoplexy in Dublin, 24 Nov. 1634, at 70 years of age, during the session of a Convocation there, whence his body was conveyed to Gorey, co. Wexford, and deposited in a "fair marble tomb, in a chapel built by himself." His 3rd son,

Abel Ram, of Ramsfort and Clonattin, s. to the estates, and *m.* Eleanor, dau. of George Andrewes, D.D., Bishop of Ferns and Leighlin, by whom (who *d.* 24 June, 1686) he had issue,

1. Abel (Sir), his successor.
2. Andrew, of Dublin, *m.* 12 Dec. 1678, Jane, dau. of William Hoey, of Ballyeotlane, by whom (who *d.* 24 June, 1681) he had one son,
   Thomas, *d.s.p.* (will proved 8 Nov. 1699).
1. Jane, *m.* Stephen Marmyon.
2. Frideswide, *m.* Charles Buggs.
3. Anne.

Mr. Ram *d.* 11 June, 1676, and was s. by his son,

Sir Abel Ram, Knt., of Ramsfort and Clonattin, Sheriff of Dublin 1673, and Lord Mayor 1684, *m.* 1667, Eleanor, dau. of Stephen Palmer, of Dublin, by whom (who *d.* 31 Oct. 1737) he had issue,

1. Abel, his successor.
2. Stephen, *d.s.p.* Sept. 1746.
3. George, M.A. Dublin 1695, LL.D. 1718, High Sheriff, co. Wexford 1710, *d.* 1729.
4. Joshua, *d.* young.
5. Andrew, *b.* 1684, entered Trin. Coll. Dublin 11 Dec. 1701, B.A. 1706, M.A. 1709.
6. Samuel. 7. Thomas.
1. Ellinor, *d.* young. 2. Elizabeth.
3. Rebecca, *m.* 15 Oct. 1710, Thomas Trotter.
4. Cassandra. 5. Anne.

Sir Abel *d.* 1692, and was s. by his eldest son,

Abel Ram, of Ramsfort, and Clonattin, *b.* 1669, entered Trin. Coll. Dublin 26 April, 1685, M.P. for Gorey 1692, High Sheriff, co. Wexford 1708, *m.* 1702, Sarah, only dau. of Thomas Humfreys, of London, merchant, by whom (who *d.* April, 1747) he had issue,

1. Abel, of Ramsfort and Clonattin, *b.* 1705, entered Trin. Coll. Dublin 10 July, 1722; High Sheriff 1742, *m.* 1 Aug. 1756, Rebecca, dau. of Dr. Thomas Trotter, and had one son,
   Abel, *b.* 11 June, 1757, who *d.* young.

Mr. Ram (whose will, dated 10 July, 1771, was proved 2 Sept. 1778) was s. in the Ramsfort portion of the estates by his nephew.

2. Humfreys, M.P. for Gorey, *m.* 3 May, 1738, the only dau. of William Hawkins, Serjeant-at-Law, and by her (who *d.* in London, 16 Oct. 1769, aged 56) had issue,

1. Stephen, of Ramsfort, M.P. for Gorey 1789; *m.* 16 June, 1774, Lady Charlotte Stopford, 6th dau. of James, 1st Earl of Courtown, and *d.* 1821, having had issue,
   (1) Abel, of Ramsfort, High Sheriff co. Wexford 1829, *m.* 19 Dec. 1818, Eleanor Sarah, only dau. of Jerome Knapp, of Charlton House, Berks, and *d.* 14 Jan. 1832, having had issue,
   Stephen, of Ramsfort, D.L., High Sheriff for co. Wexford 1842, *b.* 15 April, 1819 ; *m.* 7 Aug. 1839, Mary Christian, dau. of James Archbold Casamaijor, Madras C.S., and *d.* 7 March, 1899, leaving issue,
   a. Stephen James, Capt. Scots Fusilier Guards, *b.* 10 April, 1840 ; *d. unm.* 11 April, 1869.
   b. Edmund Arthur, *b.* 1841 ; *m.* 1873, Florence Jane eldest dau. of Charles Richard Harford, and *d.s.p.*
   c. Abel Humphrey, *b.* 1843 ; *m.* 16 July, 1870, Helen Harriet Elizabeth, only dau. of Frederick William Allix, of Willoughby Hall, co. Lincoln (see *that family*). He *d.s.p.* 1897. She *d.* 28 Dec. 1906.
   d. Arthur Archibald, *b.* 1852 ; *m.* 9 Jan. 1899, Blanche Mary, eldest dau. of the late Arthur Loftus Tottenham, of Glenfarne Hall, co. Leitrim (see Tottenham *of Tudenham Park*). She *d.* 28 Feb. 1903. He *d.* 20 Dec. 1905, leaving issue,
      Mary Christina, *b.* 21 Dec. 1902.
   a. Mary Eleanor.
   b. Adela Jane Benedicta Mary, *d. unm.* 21 April, 1901.
   c. Elizabeth.
   Eleanor Anne, *m.* 1849, Archibald James Campbell, and left issue.
   (2) Stephen, *d. unm.* 1820.
   (1) Anne, *m.* Robert Brooke (see Brooke *of Dromavana*).
   (2) Elizabeth, *m.* 1827, Christopher Domvile.
   (3) Charlotte.
2. Abel. 3. George Andrew.
1. Mary, *m.* 1777, Robert Doyne, of Wells, co. Wexford (see *that family*), and *d.* 1826.
3. Andrew, of whom presently.
1. Mary, *m.* 1766, Thomas Cooley.
2. Sarah, *d. unm.*

Mr. Ram's will, dated 1 March, 1735-6, was proved 4 Dec. 1740. His 3rd son,

Andrew Ram, *b.* 1711, entered Trin. Coll. Dublin 15 May, 1728, B.A. 1732, M.P. co. Wexford 1755, s. to the Clonattin portion of the estate by bequest of his eldest brother, Abel. He was *b.* 1711, and *m.* 14 Dec. 1752, Mary, dau. of John Digby (see Burke's *Peerage*, Digby, B.) of Landenstown, co. Kildare by Mary his wife, only dau. of the Very Rev. Jeremy Marsh, Dean of Kilmore, and granddau. of the Most Rev. Francis Marsh, Archbishop of Dublin (see Marsh *of Springmount*), and dying 1793, was s. by his son,

Abel Ram, of Clonattin, Lieut.-Col. Wexford Militia, M.P. for Duleck 1780, and subsequently for the co. Wexford, *m.* 1775, Elizabeth, dau. of Joseph Stopford, brother of James, 1st Earl of Courtown (by Anne his wife, dau. of Knightley Chetwode, of Woodbrook, Queen's Co.), and *d.* 1830, having had issue,

1. Abel John, of whom presently.
2. William Andrew, *b.* 20 May, 1784, Lieut. R.N., killed on board H.M.S. *Victory*, at the battle of Trafalgar, 21 Oct 1805.
3. James Stopford, *b.* 5 Oct. 1785, Lieut. R.N., drowned 2 Feb. 1809, off Bermuda, in the endeavour to save the life of a brother officer.
4. Digby Joseph Stopford (Rev.), of Brookeville, co. Cork, B.A. (Dublin), *b.* Feb. 1790 ; *m.* Penelope, dau. of Christmas Paul Wallis, of Rennie, co. Cork (see Wallis, *late of Drishane Castle*), and by her (who *d.* 1851) had (with a dau., Mary Anne Elizabeth, *m.* 2 June, 1843, Sir Christopher Robert Lighton, 4th bart. of Merville, co. Dublin) a son,
   Stopford James (Rev.), Vicar of Christ Church, Battersea, *b.* 1 March, 1826 ; *m.* 20 March, 1849, Eleanor Mary, dau. of Lieut.-Col. Edward Hawkshaw, 31st Regt., and *d.* 1881, having had issue,
   (1) Ernest Digby, *b.* 25 June, 1856 ; *d. unm.* July, 1903.
   (2) Henry Stopford, *b.* 11 Dec. 1858.
   (3) Nixon Chetwode (Rev.), Rector of Tenby, *b.* 25 Jan. 1861, *m.* 12 Jan. 1910, Judith Evelyn, dau. of Major-Gen. Edward Clive, of Perrystone Court, Herefordshire.
   (4) Stopford Edward, *b.* 7 Dec. 1863 ; *d. unm.* 13 Aug. 1882.
   (5) Andrew Wilmot, *b.* 7 Sept., *d.* 22 Sept. 1864.
   (1) Constance Josephine Stopford, *d. unm.* 25 March, 1877.
   (2) Edith Eleanor, *m.* 1884, Rev. William Ernest Evill, B.A., Vicar of St. Dunstan, Canterbury.
   (3) Augusta Mary, *m.* 22 Nov. 1876, Justyn G. D. Douglas, M.D., who *d.* 1893.
   (4) Dora Janet, *m.* 1881, Rev. Henry Marten Evill, Vicar of St. Martin, Hereford.
1. Mary Anne, *m.* 4 April, 1809, Thomas Hamilton Miller, of Dalswinton, co. Dumfries, and *d.* 10 July, 1819, leaving issue, two sons and one dau.,
2. Elizabeth Frances, *d.* July, 1839.
3. Catherine Henrietta, *m.* 2 April, 1812, Lieut.-Col. Robert Nixon, 1st (Royal) Regt., 4th son of John Nixon, of Carrick, co. Westmeath, and *d.* 30 Jan. 1823, leaving issue, one son and four daus.

The eldest son,

Abel John Ram, of Clonattin, *b.* 26 June, 1776 ; *m.* 11 Aug. 1803, Frances Anne, dau. of John Port, of Ilam Hall, co. Stafford (by Mary his wife, dau. of John D'Ewes, of Wellesbourne, co. Warwick (see Granville *of Wellesbourne*), and *d.v.p.* 3 Nov. 1823, leaving by her (who *d.* 4 Nov. 1860), with two daus. (Harriet Elizabeth Mary and Frances Mary Anne) a son,

Rev. Abel John Ram, of Clonattin, Rector of Rolleston, Burton-on-Trent, co. Stafford, Hon. Canon of Rochester Cathedral, *b.* 20 May, 1804 ; *m.* 11 April, 1833, Lady Jane Stopford, dau. of James George, 3rd Earl of Courtown, K.P. (by Lady Mary Montagu Scott, eldest dau. of Henry, 3rd Duke of Buccleuch, K.G.), and *d.* 18 Aug. 1883, leaving by her (who *d.* 28 Dec. 1873),

1. George Stopford, of whom presently.
2. Abel John, K.C., Bencher of the Inner Temple, of Berkhampstead Place, co. Hertford, and 3, Paper Buildings, Temple, J.P. co. Herts., Knight of Grace of the Order of St. John of Jerusalem, Recorder of Wolverhampton, M.A., Oxford, *b.* 21 Sept. 1842 ; *m.* 23 April, 1871, Hon. Mary Grace O'Brien (who *d.* June, 1912) 3rd dau. of Lucius, 13th Lord Inchiquin (see Burke's *Peerage and Baronetage*), and had issue,
   1. Abel, *b.* and *d.* 12 Oct. 1875.
   2. Lucius Abel John Granville, educated at Eton and Exeter, Coll. Oxford, B.A. 1909, Barrister-at-Law (Inner Temple) 1910, Lieut. Herts Yeomanry, *b.* 24 June, 1885.
   1. Elaine Augusta. 2. Irene Mary Montagu.
3. Robert Digby (Rev.), M.A. Cambridge, Vicar of Hampton, Middlesex, Prebendary of St. Paul's and Rural Dean, *b.* 24 Jan. 1844 ; *m.* 13 Sept. 1877, Mary, only dau. of George Edward Anson, C.B., Keeper of the Privy Purse to the Queen (by Hon. Georgiana Mary Harbord, his wife, dau. of Edward, 3rd Lord Suffield, Bedchamber Woman to the Queen), and grand-dau. of Very Rev. Frederick Anson, D.D., Dean of Chester, brother of Thomas, 1st Viscount Anson, and by her (who *d.* 1889) had issue,
   1. George Edward, Capt. 4th Batt. Staffordshire Regt., *b.* 25 April, 1879 ; *m.* 9 Oct. 1907, Millicent Grace, only dau. of late Commander Augustus Henry Webb, R.N., and has issue,
      Georgiana Mary, *b.* 31 July, 1908.
   2. Frederic Montagu Anson, *b.* 30 Aug. 1885.
   1. Emily Jane, *m.* 1 Oct. 1901, Sir John Home-Purves-Hume-Campbell, 8th bart. of Marchmont, and has issue (see Burke's *Peerage*).
   2. Mary Frances, *d.* 5 Sept. 1875.
   3. Frances Anne Jane, *m.* 8 Jan. 1884, her cousin, John Robert Miller, M.D. (son of Thomas Hamilton Miller, of Dalswinton, co. Dumfries), Surgeon-General and late Inspector-General of Hospitals in the Punjaub, who *d.* 1886.

The eldest son,

Rev. George Stopford Ram, of Clonattin, M.A. Oxford, Vicar

of St. Peter's, Bournemouth, *b.* 18 June, 1838 ; *m.* 23 May, 1866, Hon. Charlotte Anne O'Brien, 2nd dau. of Lucius, 13th Lord Inchiquin, and *d.* 19 Nov. 1889, having had issue,
1. EDWARD DIGBY STOPFORD, now of Clonattin.
2. George Montagu, *b.* 11 May, 1881.
3. Abel Bernard, twin with George, *d.* young.
1. Mary Frances Jane, *m.* 14 Feb. 1902, Francis Charlesworth, M.B., of H.M.'s Agency, Zanzibar.
2. Evelyn Charlotte, *m.* 15 Jan. 1903, Archibald J. T. Aitchison, only son of Gen. Sir John Aitchison, G.C.B.
3. Geraldine Louisa. 4. Kathleen Lucy.
5. Winifred. 6. Dorothy.
7. Marjorie Freda.

Arms—(Confirmed and crest granted 1664 and 1683)—Az., a chevron erm., between three rams' heads erased arg., armed or.
Crest—A ram's head erased arg., charged with a chevron az. *Motto*—Quod tibi vis fieri fac alteri.

Seat—Clonattin, Gorey, co. Wexford. *Residence*—The Rectory, Oxted, Surrey.

RATHBORNE, late OF SCRIPPLESTOWN.

COL. WILLIAM HANS RATHBORNE, of Kilcogy, Co. Cavan, *b.* 21 Dec. 1841, Royal Engineers, was C.R.E. at Gibraltar ; *m.* 3 July, 1879, at St. Luke's, Cheltenham, Bella Grace, dau. of John Donald McNeale, of Charlcote, Cheltenham, and co. Louth, and has issue,
1. WILLIAM DONALD MCNEALE *b.* 8 June, 1884, Lieut. Indian Army.
1. Margaret Grace, *m.* 5 Sept. 1909, Capt. R. B. Graham, Sutherland Highlanders.
2. Gladys Emmeline, *m.* 29 Dec. 1908, Capt. C. M. Vassar Smith, 85th Regt., son of Vassar Smith, J.P., of Charlton Park, Cheltenham.
3. Freda Penelope, *m.* 18 Jan. 1911, Herbert Robin Cayzer, 5th son of Sir Charles Cayzer, Bart., of Gortmore, Perthshire (*see* BURKE's *Peerage*).
4. Evelyn Kathleen. 5. Mary Ella.
6. Adrienne Jean.

Lineage.—JOHN RATHBONE, who came from the north of Wales and settled in the Hundred of Macclesfield East, Cheshire obtained a grant of land at Masefen, *temp.* HENRY III., *circa* 1265-70, was father of,
WILLIAM RATHBONE, of Masefen, *temp.* EDWARD I., 1272-1307, father of,
1. JOHN, of whom presently.
2. Philip, acquired lands at Hampton, 1316.
JOHN RATHBONE, seized of lands of Tressyn-cleam by charter dated at Eaton 1316, was father of,
HENRY RATHBONE, of Masefen, living there 7 RICHARD II. (1383) father of,
WILLIAM RATHBONE, of Masefen, 2 HENRY IV. (1401), father of,
JOHN RATHBONE, of Masefen, living there *temp.* HENRY V. (1410-22) father of,
JOHN RATHBONE, of Masefen, *b.* 13 RICHARD II. (1390), living 11 EDWARD IV. (1471), father of,
HUGH RATHBONE, of Masefen, living *temp.* HENRY VII., father of,
1. WILLIAM, of whom presently.
1. Isabel, *m.* David de Brow, or Brower.
The elder son,
WILLIAM RATHBONE, of Masefen, *temp.* HENRY VII., was father of,
1. Richard. 2. JOHN, of whom presently.
The 2nd son,
JOHN RATHBONE, Sheriff of Chester 1503-04, Alderman 1512, Mayor 1514-15, 1519-20, father of,
WILLIAM RATHBONE, *d.* 1542, father of,
RICHARD RATHBONE, Sheriff of Chester 1582-83, father of,
RICHARD RATHBONE, Alderman of Chester 1590-98, Mayor 1598-99, *m.* Anne, dau. of Joseph Taylor, of Chester, and by her (who *d.* Aug. 1604) had issue,
JOSEPH RATHBONE, *m.* Anne Madden, and by her had, with others,
1. William, settled in Liverpool, ancestor of Rathbone of Green, bank (*see that family*).
2. RICHARD, of whom presently.
The 2nd son,
RICHARD RATHBONE, *b.* 1640, went to Ireland in the reign of CHARLES II. and settled in Drogheda, was Sheriff of Drogheda 1686, *m.* Mary Howard, and by her had, with others,

JOSEPH RATHBONE, of Dublin. *b.* 1679 ; will dated 10 Nov. 1737, proved 29 June, 1738 ; *m.* Catherine, dau. of William Norman of Drogheda, and by her had issue,
1. Rev. Richard, of Ballymore, co. Galway, *b.* 1703, B.A. Trin. Coll. Dublin 1725, M.A. 1729 ; *m.* Mary, dau. of Capt. Jonathan Wilson, R.N., and by her had issue,
1. Richard, of Ballymore, *m.* 1774 (marr. setts. 22 Aug. 1776), Bridget, dau. of Thomas Firman, of Selby, co. York (*see* FIRMAN *of Gateforth*), and had issue,
(1) Richard, of Ballymore, *b.* 1775, *d.* 30 July, 1854 ; Capt. 9th Dragoons, High Sheriff co. Galway, 1815 ; *m.* 1st Eliza, dau. of George Stoney, of Kyle Park, co. Tipperary (*see that family*), issue five daus., of whom Kate *m.* — McCartney ; Mary Anne, *m.* 1857, Capt. John Peter Hall ; and Eleanor, *m.* 1852, Henry Torrens Graham. He *m.* 2ndly, 1825, Anna Maria, 3rd dau. of Walter Lambert, of Castle Lambert, co. Galway (*see* LAMBERT, *of Aggard*), and by her had issue,
1. Richard of Ballymore, Ngarnawahia, New Zealand, J.P., *b.* 1830 ; *m.* Maria, dau. of Capt. L. H. Davy, of H.E.I.C.S., and has issue,
(1) Richard Charles, of Bernardsville, New Jersey U.S.A., *b.* 24 June, 1857, at Carlisle, England ; *m.* 19 Nov. 1896, Grace Reid, dau. of Gavin Hamilton Watson, and had one son, Richard Leyton Davy, *b.* 23 Sept. 1903 ; *d.* 9 Feb. 1911.
(2) Edwin, *b.* 9 Dec. 1859.
(3) Wilson, *d.* an infant, and seven daus., of whom the youngest, Elizabeth, *m.* Robert L. Birks.
2. Wilson, *d.* in New York, Sept. 1860.
3. Charles Lambert, *d.* Dec. 1908, *m.* Bessie Lane, of New York, and has issue,
(1) Charles L. F., of Colorado.
(2) R. William *m.*
(3) Walter Lambert, of New York, *m.*
(1) Frances Josephine, *m.* Joseph W. Cushman, of New York.
(2) Elizabeth N., *m.* Alfred Wendt, of New York.
4. Robert William, of Pelham Manor, New York.
1. Anne.
2. Sarah, *d. unm.* 4 July, 1896.
3. Octavia, *m.* 1853, Major George Percival Drought, 62nd Regt. (*see* DROUGHT *of Lettybrook*, King's Co.).
4. Hester, *m.* Samuel Pierce Holden.
(2) William, Lieut. 46th Regt., *d.* in West Indies, 1805.
(1) Ellen, *d. unm.*
2. Wilson, Rear-Adml. R.N., *b.* 1748. He entered the Navy as able seaman 1763-74, Master of the " Hunter " 1774-80, Lieut. 16 March, 1780, Com. 9 Nov. 1795, lost his eye and left arm 14 March, 1794 at Ferrol, on the " Santa Margarita," commanded the Sea Fencibles of Essex 1808-10, and the Impress Service on the Tyne 1810-13, C.B. 1815, Superintendent of the Ordinary at Chatham 1822-31, Presented with a sword. He *m.* dau. of John French, of Loughrea ; *d.* 1831, having by her had issue,
(1) Anthony Blake, Col. H.E.I.C.S., Barrister-at-Law, *d.* 11 Jan. 1885, having *m.* and had issue, one dau.
(2) Joseph.
(3) Richard.
1. Hester, *m.* 1779, John Croker, Surveyor-General of Ireland, and was mother of the Right Hon. John Wilson Croker, M.P., Chief Secretary, Ireland, 1808, Secretary to the Admiralty 1809-32, &c.
2. WILLIAM, of whom presently.
3. Joseph, *d. unm.*
1. Mary, *m.* Philip Crampton, Alderman of Dublin, grandfather of Sir Philip Crampton, created a Baronet 1839.
2. Catherine, *m.* John Fitzpatrick, of Drumcondra.
3. Dorothy, *m.* Francis Gladwell of Dublin.
4. Alice, *m.* John Marsden, of Dublin.

The 2nd son,
WILLIAM RATHBORNE, of Dublin, will dated 26 Oct. 1778, proved 23 March, 1779, *m.* 1735, Anne, dau. of Robert Billing, and by her had issue,
1. Joseph, B.A. (Dublin) 1768, *m.* June, 1774, Anne, dau. of Robert Madden, of Meadesbrook, co. Meath.
2. WILLIAM, of whom presently.
1. Anne, *m.* 1st 1760, Mungo Campbell, 55th Regt. ; 2ndly, Col. Price.

The younger son,
WILLIAM RATHBORNE, of Scripplestown, co. Dublin. *m.* 8 Nov. 1784, Florence Elizabeth Anne, dau. of William Irvine, M.P., of Castle Irvine, co. Fermanagh (*see that family*), and *d.* 1810, having by her had issue,
1. WILLIAM, of whom presently.
2. Henry, of Dunsinea, co. Dublin, *d.* 1 July, 1836 ; *m.* Jane, 2nd dau. of Rev. Henry Bayly, of Bayly Farm, Nenagh (*see* BAVLY *of Debsborough*), and by her (who *d.* 17 July, 1849) had issue,
1. William Prittie, *d.* 1 Jan. 1833.
2. Henry Bayly, *b.* 1814 Barrister of Dublin ; *d.s.p.* 26 June, 1885, aged 71.
3. John Garnett, *b.* 1820, of Dunsinea, J.P. co. Dublin ; *m.* Eliza, dau. of W. Burnley ; *d.* 23 March, 1895, having by her (who *d.* 12 May, 1867) had issue,
(1) Henry Burnley, of Dunsinea, J.P., *b.* 10 Nov. 1866, M.A. Trin. Coll. Dublin ; *m.* 27 Oct. 1897, Mary Florence, eld. dau. of Charles Robert Barton, D.L., of Waterfoot, co. Fermanagh (*see that family*) and has issue,
1. Henry Barton, *b.* 4 Feb. 1899.
2. John Charles Errol, *b.* 12 Nov. 1902.

4. James (Rev.), M.A. Trin. Coll. Dublin, b. 4 Oct. 1827; m. 8 Sept. 1853, Jane, dau. of William Tanner, of Blacklands Park, Calne; d. 30 June, 1903, having by her had issue,

(1) Ambrose Beatty, b. 20 Jan. 1858; m. 5 Sept. 1894, Florence Ada Monica, only child of Rev. Rowland Buckston, of Sutton-on-the-Hill and Bradborne Hall, Derby, who d. 12 July, 1900, he d.s.p. Feb. 1903.

(2) Mervyn Reginald William, b. 24 Feb. 1864; m. 24 Aug. 1904, Eleanor Maud, dau. of Lewis Davis Little, formerly of Harnhill, Gloucestershire, and has issue one son, Reginald Mervyn St. George, b. 3 June 1905, and twin daus. Eleanor Ambrose and Isabella Maud, b. 19 July, 1911.

(3) Launcelot, St. George Prittie, b 9 Oct. 1869; m. 28 June, 1905, Olivia Mary Yorke, dau. of Roland Yorke Bevan and the Hon. Mrs. Bevan (see BURKE'S *Peerage* KINNAIRD, B.), and has,

Arthur St. George, b. 27 Sept. 1906.

(1) Mary Agnes, m. 15 March, 1894, Capt. George Broughton, U.S. Navy.

(2) Jane Isabella, d. Jan. 1888; m. 27 April, 1878, William Nelthorpe Beauclerk, of Little Grimsby Hall, co. Lincoln (see BURKE'S *Peerage*, ST. ALBANS, D. OF).

(3) Beatrice Maud, m. 21 July, 1900, Arthur Tewdyr Davies Berrington, D.L., co. Monmouth.

(4) Florence, m. 18 March, 1884, Henry Conway Belfield, of Primley Hill, Devon, C.M.G., and has issue.

(5) Helen Evelyn Mabel, m. 20 Sept. 1888, Thomas Hislop Hill.

1. Jane, b. Dec. 1815; d. Sept. 1900; m. June, 1840, Rev. Thomas Luby, D.D., Senior Fellow Trin. Coll. Dublin; d. June, 1870.

2. Isabella, m. 1845, Walter Keating, of Silvan Park, co. Meath.

3. Kate Florence Prittie, b. Sept. 1819; d.s.p. Aug. 1900.

3. St. George, m. 1818, Mary Martha Knipe, and d.s.p. His widow m. 1850, Marcus Geale.

1. Sophia Maria Anne, m. 13 June, 1803, Christopher Edmund John Nugent, of Farren Connell, co. Cavan (see that family), and d. 11 May, 1850.

2. Florence, m. 1808, Robert Johnston, of Oakfield, co. Leitrim.

The eldest son,

WILLIAM RATHBORNE, of Scripplestown, co. Dublin, and Kilcogy, co. Cavan, J.P., High Sheriff co. Dublin 1811, High Sheriff co. Cavan 1834, M.A. Dublin, 1832, m. Penelope Mary, dau. of Rev. Henry Bayly, of Bayly Farm, Nenagh, co. Tipperary (see BAYLY of Debsborough); d. 24 Sept. 1857, and by her (who d. 1845) had issue,

1. WILLIAM HUMPHREY, of whom presently.

2. Robert St. George, b. 3 Oct. 1821; m. 1848, Grace, dau. of — Coffy, of Newcastle, co. Westmeath.

3. Gorges Lowther, b. 30 Oct. 1824, 72nd Highlanders; m. 20 Nov. 1849, Margaret Hettrick, dau. of William Robertson, and has issue,

1. Gorges William, b. 24 Aug. 1850.

2. St. George Henry, b. 25 Dec. 1854; m. 1879, Jessie Fremont, dau. of John A. Conn, and has,

(1) St. George Fremont, b. 23 Feb. 1880; m. 26 Sept. 1907, Mary Irene Peterkin.

(2) Percy Julian, b. 2 Oct. 1884; m. 28 Sept. 1905, Grace Lydia Goddard, and has issue,
 a. Edwin Kermit.
 a. Grace Mildred.   b. Jesse Gladys.

(3) Paul Lewis, b. 11 Oct. 1889.

(1) Jessie Marguerite, b. 11 Jan. 1886.

3 Robert Franklin Lowther, b. 4 July, 1867; m. Pearl Ritchie, and has,

Robert William Ritchie.

1. Jessie Emily, b. 9 Aug. 1852; m. 16 Sept. 1875, Joseph Ashland Baldwin.

2. Fannie, b. 1857; m. 6 Aug. 1891, Beauregarde Faulconer.

3. Margaret Kerr, b. 24 Oct. 1859; m. 21 May, 1891, Herman Betz.

4. Helen Mary, b. 11 Dec. 1861.

5. Grace Maude, b. 12 Nov. 1864; m. Charles Clifford Applegate

4. St. George, b. 21 Nov. 1827, R.N.; d. at Lagos, West Coast of Africa.

1. Jane Florence, b. 23 June, 1815; d. young.

2. Penelope, m. 1849, Richard Coffy, of Newcastle, co. Westmeath.

3. Isabella Sophia, b. 5 Dec. 1826; m. 10 Jan. 1849, Major Longworth, 31st Regt.; d. 1856; she d. 20 May, 1849.

4. Emily Adelaide, b. 21 Oct. 1830; d. 21 May, 1849.

5. Helen, b. 23 March, 1832; m. Thomas Alloway, and d. 11 May, 1872.

The eldest son,

WILLIAM HUMPHREY RATHBORNE, of Scripplestown, b. 16 July, 1819, 50th and 99th Regts.; m. 1839, Elizabeth Allen, dau. of Col. Hans Allen, Royal Artillery. He d. 29 April, 1889, having by her (who d. 24 May, 1902) had issue,

1. WILLIAM HANS, now as above.

2. Hans Robert (Ivy Villa, Weymouth), b. 23 June, 1843, Lieut.-Col. late K.O. Borderers; m. 6 Oct. 1881, Blanche, 2nd. dau. of Thomas Were Fox, Esq. of Hoe House, Plymouth (see Fox of Grove Hill), and by her has issue,

1. Hans Wallace Allen, b. 4 Jan. 1883; d. 22 March, 1884.

2. Francis Hans Bunbury, Lieut. Dorset Regt., b. 10 Aug. 1884; m. 15 Sept. 1909, Agnes Mary Dorothy, dau. of John Sturrock, C.I.E. (see BURKE'S *Peerage*), and has issue,

Francis John Hans, b. 3 Dec. 1910.

1. Blanche Florence Natalie, b. 16 Dec. 1886; d. 4 Jan. 1887.

3. St. George John, Major 66th Regt., b. at Scripplestown, 29 Nov. 1846; m. 22 April, 1889, at British Embassy, Paris, Margaret, dau. of John Donald McNeale, of Charlcote, Cheltenham, and co. Louth, and has issue,

1. St. George Ronald McNeale, b. 19 June, 1892.

2. Ivon Eyre, b. 10 Jan. 1895.

4. Henry Humphrey, b. 30 Jan. 1855; m. 28 Feb. 1885, at Trieste, Bertha Ramann, of Trieste, Austria, and has a son, Charles Edward Henry, b. at Trieste, 17 Feb. 1886, in R.M.L.I.

1. Penelope Katherine Judith, m. 20 June, 1871, Rev. Barry Charles Browne, of Camden Lodge, Cheltenham, Rector of St. John the Baptist, Gloucester, who d. 25 June, 1890.

2. Elizabeth Helen, m. 26 Sept. 1897, John Moore Cooke, of Nanoti, Victoria Co., Natal, son of George Cooke, of Clifton, and has issue.

Arms.—Az., a cross or, between four roses arg., on a chief of the last a lion rampant gu. *Crest*—A rose gu., barbed, seeded and slipped, ppr. *Motto*—Je ne change qu'en mourant.

READE OF WOODPARK. See HIBBERT OF WOODPARK.

REEVES OF BESBOROUGH.

WILLIAM VANDELEUR REEVES, of Besborough, co. Clare, J.P., b. 6 July, 1874, educated at Eton and Trin. Coll. Camb.; m. 23 Nov. 1906, Aileen Jane, dau. of the Ven. John Alexander Long, Archdeacon of Cashel and Rector of Templemore, co. Tipperary.

Lineage.—MAJOR ROBERT REVE or REEVES, son of a very respectable family in Sussex, settled in Ireland temp. CHARLES I, and m. Elinor, dau. of Col. Owny O'Dempsey, eldest son of Sir Terence O'Dempsey, Viscount Clanmalier, by Margaret Nugent his wife, dau. of Lord Delvin, by whom he had (with one dau., who m. Mr. Lodge, ancestor, in the female line, of the Lords Frankfort de Montmorency) a son,

WILLIAM REEVES, m. Bridget Malone, widow, dau. of Richard Neville, of Furness, co. Kildare, and had issue, a son and heir,

ROBERT REEVES, m. Mary Bodley, of Kilkenny, of kin to Sir Thomas Bodley, who founded the library at Oxford. They had issue,

1. ROBERT, his heir.

1. Hester, m. — Haywood.

2. Elizabeth, m. — Beaumont.

3. Rebecca, m. — Savage.

4. Amelia, m. — Stephenson.

The only son,

ROBERT REEVES, m. Grace, dau. of Thomas Spaight, of Bunratty Lodge, and Burrane, co. Clare, and had issue,

1. ROBERT, of whom presently.

2. Joseph, m. 1st, Anna, dau. of Thomas Somerville, and had by her a son and two daus.,

1. Thomas Somerville, of Tramore House, co. Cork, J.P., High Sheriff; m. 1814, Rebecca, dau. of Isaac Morgan, of Buckingham House, Cork, and d. 21 Aug. 1863, in his 83rd year, leaving issue,

(1) Isaac Morgan (Very Rev.), M.A., D.D., Rector of Myross and Dean of Ross, b. 1822; m. 1st, 3 Sept. 1857, Anna Maria Toke, dau. of Rev. Sir Henry Bouchier Wrey, Bart., Rector of Tawstock, and by her (who d. 7 March, 1867) has one dau., Helen Wray, m. Joseph Wrixon Leycester, of Ennismore, co. Cork, and has issue. He m. 2nd May, 1870, Adelaide, dau. of Arthur Ussher, of Ballysaggartmore, co. Waterford. She d. his widow 31 March, 1910, having had, with other issue, Thomas Somerville, b. 1873; m. 28 April, 1903, Olive Susan younger dau. of John Stephen Collins, of Ardnalee, co. Cork, J.P. (see that family).

(2) James Somerville (Rev.), D.D.

(1) A dau., m. Joseph Woodley Lindsay, of Lindville, co. Cork.

1. Maria, m. Samuel Bennett, of Clonakilty, co. Cork.

2. Anne, m. Paul Maylor, of Chipley.

He m. 2ndly, Eliza, dau. of Major Ancram, of the 34th Regt., and had by her,

2. William Ancram, dec.   3. Robert Neville.

3. Catherine Spaight, m. William Parker, of Cork.

3. Thomas, m. Ellen, dau. of Lewis Buckle, of Borden, East Meon, Hants, and had one son,

Lewis Buckle.

4. Edward Hoare, m. 1st, Mary, widow of Arthur Devonshire, of Kilshonnick, co. Cork, but by her had no issue. He m. 2ndly, Dorothea, dau. of John Carleton, of Cork, and niece of Lord Carleton, and had by her two sons and four daus.,

1. Francis, of Ballyglisane, co. Cork, Major H.E.I.C.S., d.s.p. 1862.

2. Edward Hoare, of Castle Kevin, co. Cork, J.P., *m.* 23 Oct. 1838, Elizabeth Mary, dau. of Lieut.-Gen. Bourke, of Prospect Villa, Cork, and *d.* 24 April, 1867, having had, with other issue, EDWARD HOARE, J.P., of Castle Kevin and Ballyglissane, co. Cork, Lieut. 1st Dragoon Guards, served in Zulu War 1879, *b.* Dec. 1840; *m.* 20 July, 1873, Katherine, eldest dau. of William Wrixon Leycester, of Ennismore, co. Cork, and *d.* Sept. 1888, leaving issue,
(1) Edward Hoare, of Castle Kevin, co. Cork, Capt. late 7th Dragoon Guards, served in S. African War (medal with five clasps), *b.* 25 April, 1875 (*Clubs*—Army and Navy, Cavalry).
(2) William Wrixon Leycester, *b.* 21 Nov. 1880.
(3) Victor Charles Methuen, *b.* 30 Nov.1887.
1. Rebecca, *m.* Bernard Shawe, of Cork.
2. Mary, *m.* Sandford Palmer, of King's Co.
3. Dorothea, *m.* Abraham Morris, of Dunkettle, co. Cork.
4. Elizabeth, *m.* George Beresford Poer, of Waterford.
1. Grace, *m.* 1782, William Collins, of Dublin.
2. Mary, *d. unm.*
3. Catherine, *m.* Henry Madder, of Limerick.
4. Jane, *m.* 1798, the Rev. Edwin Thomas, of Ballinacourty, co. Kerry.
5. Eliza, *m.* Francis Hewitt, of Cork.
The eldest son,
ROBERT REEVES, of Platten, co. Meath, of Burrane, co. Clare, and of Merrion Square, Dublin, *m.* Sept. 1782, Mary, dau. of William Maunsell, of Limerick (*see* MAUNSELL *of Spa Hill*), and had issue,
1. ROBERT, of Merrion Square, Dublin, *d. unm.* 13 July, 1860.
2. WILLIAM MAUNSELL, of Burrane.
3. Samuel Spaight, of Platten, co. Meath, and Upper Mount Street, Dublin, *m.* Maria (who *d.* 25 March, 1838), and dau. of Major Randal Stafford, of Tully, co. Cavan, and *d.* 30 Jan. 1875, leaving an only child,
Robert, of 5, Fitzwilliam Place, Dublin, *b.* 1834; *m.* 31 Jan. 1861, Emily, eldest dau. of Edward John Smith, of Rutland Square, Dublin, and *d.* 16 Feb. 1899, leaving an only child, Frances Angel, *m.* 13 April, 1882, Philip Francis Chenevix Trench (who *d.* 6 April, 1911) and had issue (*see* BURKE'S *Peerage*, ASHTOWN, B.).
4. Robert, of Lower Fitzwilliam Street, Dublin, and of Platten, co. Meath, *b.* 1795; *m.* May, 1828, Juliet Matilda, youngest dau. of Rev. Richard Studdert, of Mount Rivers, co. Clare (*see* STUDDERT *of Bunratty*), and *d.* 28 Oct. 1877, leaving issue,
1. Robert Edward, of Morenane, co. Limerick and Skeard, co. Kilkenny, J.P. cos. Limerick and Tipperary and Queen's Co., High Sheriff for the latter 1882, M.A. Dublin, Barrister-at-Law, *b.* 28 March, 1829; *d.* 12 Nov. 1908; *m.* 26 April, 1853, Sophia Louisa, dau. of Rev. James Blacker, Rector of Keady, co. Armagh, and by her (who *d.* 14 May, 1897) had issue,
(1) Paget Edward Stuart, D.S.O., Major Leinster Regt., *b.* 16 Feb. 1862; *m.* 4 June, 1890, Harriet, dau. of Rev. R. R. Cary, of Memfin, co. Wexford, and has issue,
1. Richard Edward Cary, *b.* 13 May, 1891.
1. Mona Lilian.
2. Edith Sherlagh, *d. unm.* 16 May, 1911.
(2) Robert Blacker, *b.* 20 April, 1864; *m.* Annie, widow of — Waters, and *d.s.p.* 1896.
(3) William James, *b.* 8 July, 1866; *m.* 14 Dec. 1892, Annie, only dau. of John Parker, of Brookfield, co. Tipperary, and *d.* 13 June, 1904, leaving an only child,
1. Henry Jack Parker, *b.* 23 Jan. 1894.
2. Robert William George, *b.* 18 April, 1897.
1. Eilleen Violet.
(4) Henry Pigott, *b.* 17 May, 1870; *d. unm.* 25 May, 1893.
(1) Juliet Eliza.
2. Richard Studdert, of Rosedale, Shanhill, co. Dublin, J.P.
1. Maria M'Mahon, *m.* Capt. Arthur Oswald Richards, (3rd son of the Right Hon. John Richards, Baron of the Exchequer (who *d.* 5 May, 1909). She *d.* 20 Feb. 1902, leaving an only child,
John William Richards, *b.* 9 April, 1857; *m.* 26 Dec. 1885, Adelaide Prudentia, dau. of William Roper, of Hazelbrook, co. Roscommon, and has issue (*see* RICHARDS *of Macmine*).
2. Juliet Matilda, *d.* 8 Jan. 1911.
3. Mary Victoria Winthrop, *m.* Jan. 1866, Conolly Marcus Gage, J.P., of Drummond, co. Londonderry, and Carrickmore, co. Tyrone, and has issue,
(1) William Charles, of Willbrook House, Rathfarnham, co. Dublin, *b.* 30 May, 1877; *m.* 28 Nov. 1904, Mary Gurney, eldest dau. of the Right Hon. Hugh Holmes, P.C., Lord Justice of Appeal in Ireland, and has issue,
Conolly Hugh, *b.* 10 Nov. 1905,
Mary Violet.
(1) Juliet Mary, *m.* 1890, Hugh Stewart Olphert. Tel. Dept. I.C.S., and 2nd son of Very Rev. Thomas Olphert, Dean of Derry (*see* OLPHERT *of Ballyconnell*).
(2) Armande Edith Marie, *m.* 21 Nov. 1911, Rev. W. Craig Dixon, M.A.
4. Edith Meta, *m.* Dec. 1875, John Adam Alexander, J.P., of Caw House, co. Londonderry. He *d.* 31 Jan. 1907.
5. Richard, of Magoola, co. Cork, *m.* 1st, Miss Arthur, of co. Clare, who *d.s.p.*, and 2ndly, Mary, youngest dau. of Rev. Robert Conway Dobbs, by whom he has
1. Robert, Q.C., *d.s.p.* 1889.
2. Conway Richard, Lieut. R.A., *d.s.p.* 21 Oct. 1867.
3. William.
1. Wilhelmina Frances, *m.* Capt. Charles Orde Brown, R.A., and *a.s.p.* 1862.
2. Mary Winthrop.

3. Rose Charity, *m.* 18 Oct. 1892, William Dobbs MacDonnell, *d.* 1 Jan. 1911.
6. Joseph Robert, of Athgarvan, co. Kildare, and of 10, Fitzwilliam Place, Dublin, *b.* 1803; *m.* Georgiana Jane, 3rd dau. of Geoffrey Browning, of Carass, co. Limerick. She *d.* 1874. He *d.* 1866, having had issue,
1. Robert. 2. Jeffrey, *d.s.p.* 4 Dec. 1861.
3. Joseph, *d.s.p.*
4. Thomas Browning, of Athgarvan, co. Kildare, B.A. Trin. Coll. Dublin, J.P., *b.* 19 May, 1848; *d.* 5 Feb. 1910; *m.* 21 June, 1883, Elizabeth, eldest dau. of James Edward Medlicott, of Dunmurry, co. Kildare, and had issue,
(1) Robert Henry Medlicott, *b.* 29 Aug. 1885.
(2) Geoffrey Browning, *b.* 6 Sept. 1891.
(3) Arthur James Medlicott, *b.* 22 April, 1893.
(1) Gladys Stuart Georgina.
(2) Hilda Mary Corinna.
5. William Maunsell. 6. Francis, *d.s.p.*
1. Frances, *m.* J. H. Chippendal-Healy, of Little Limber Grange, co. Lincoln, late 11th Regt., and left issue.
2. Mary Winthrop. 3. Georgina, *d.s.p.*
4. Caroline, *m.* C. C. Baker, of Paignton, Devonshire, late 15th Regt., and *d.* 14 July, 1910, having had issue.
1. Bridget, *d. unm.*
2. Grace, *m.* Christopher Tuthill, Lieut. R.N., and has issue.
3. Mary, *d. unm.*
Mr. Reeves *d.* 11 July, 1835. His 2nd son,
WILLIAM MAUNSELL REEVES, of Burrane, co. Clare, J.P., Barrister-at-Law, *b.* Sept. 1788; *m.* 20 Sept. 1828, Rose, eldest dau. of the Rev. Robert Conway Dobbs, 2nd son of Conway Richard Dobbs, of Castle Dobbs, co. Antrim, and by her (who *d.* 4 Oct. 1864) had issue,
1. ROBERT WILLIAM CARY, of Burrane and Besborough.
2. Conway Richard, Ensign 58th Foot, *b.* 20 Dec. 1840; *d. unm.* 1 Jan. 1860.
3. William Maunsell, of Ebbisham House, Epsom, Surrey, *b.* 6 Oct. 1843; *m.* 20 Jan. 1876, Letitia, 2nd dau. of Gen. Thomas Armstrong Drought, of Hill House, Winchester. He was drowned in the wreck of "Berlin" 21 Feb. 1907, and left issue,
1. Robert William Drought, *b.* 15 Oct. 1876; *m.* 1 Nov. 1902, Laura, 2nd dau. of Francis Pedro Fladgate, of Oporto, and has issue,
(1) Laura Joan Letitia, *b.* 23 Oct. 1908.
(2) Sonia.
2. John Maunsell, *b.* 14 Oct. 1878; *m.* 10 Feb. 1909, Hilda Margaret Smith, of Pollokshields, Scotland.
1. Letitia Alice (7, *Campden House Road, London, W.*), *b.* 21 Dec. 1879.
2. Rose Mary, *b.* 14 April, 1883; *m.* June, 1906, Claud Bertram Collier, son of Mortimer Collier, of Foxhams, near Plymouth.
3. Shela, *b.* 10 Jan. 1885.
1. Wilhelmina Josepha, *d. unm.* 30 Sept. 1904.
2. Mary Winthrop, *d. unm.* 26 Sept. 1904.
3. Charity, *d. unm.* 12 July, 1909.
4. Rose Emily, *m.* 4 Feb. 1862, Herbert G. Bainbridge, 2nd son of A. F. Bainbridge, of Putney, Surrey, and has issue.
Mr. Reeves *d.* 16 July, 1857, and was s. by his eldest son,
ROBERT WILLIAM CARY REEVES, of Besborough and Burrane, co. Clare, LL.B. of Trin. Coll. Camb. 1859, called to the Bar at the Inner Temple, 1862, J.P. and D.L. for co. Clare, High Sheriff 1869, *b.* 14 March, 1837; *m.* 19 July, 1866, Grace Dorothea, youngest dau. of Col. Crofton Moore Vandeleur and Lady Grace Vandeleur, of Kilrush, co. Clare, and *d.* 13 June, 1901, leaving issue,
1. WILLIAM VANDELEUR, now of Besborough.
1. Grace Wilhelmina, *m.* 17 April, 1895, Capt. Percy Agnew Bainbridge, R.A., 2nd son of the late Herbert Glendinning Bainbridge and Mrs. Bainbridge, of the Grange, Yardley, to. Worcester, and has issue.
2. Rose Frances, *m.* 17 April, 1895, Ernest Arthur Jelf, Barrister-at-Law, of the Inner Temple, eldest son of Sir Arthur Richard Jelf, of Oak House, Putney, and has issue.
3. Elizabeth Mary, *m.* 4 July, 1900, Rowland William Henry Gray, son of Richard Townsend Gray, of Lotaville, co. Cork, and has issue.
4. Shela Alice, *m.* 18 Aug. 1902, Rev. Richard Hedges Eyre Roberts, of Ardmore, co. Cork (*see that family*).
5. Eileen Rosetta, *m.* 1st, 4 Dec. 1899, James Sandiford Lane Long, Executive Eng. India Public Works Dept., eld. son of the Archdeacon of Cashel. He *d.* 16 Dec. 1900; 2ndly, 1904, Capt. C. J. Pickering, Duke of Wellington's Regiment.

Arms—Quarterly: 1st and 4th, or, on a chevron engrailed between three escallops az. as many caglets displayed of the first, for REEVES; 2nd and 3rd, arg., on a fesse sa. three pheons of the first, for SPAIGHT. Crest—A dragon's head erased or, collared az.; over it an escrol, therein the words "Animum rege." Motto—Virtute et fidelitate.
Club—Carlton, S.W.

REID.

SIR EDWARD REID, Knt. (1868), of Londonderry, J.P. for the city and co. of Londonderry, Alderman of the city, Mayor 1867, 1868, 1880, 1881, and 1882, *b.* 17 May, 1819; *m.* 10 Aug. 1871, Agnes Isabella, (*b.* 16 July, 1847) 3rd dau. of the late Duncan Mon-

Reilly. THE LANDED GENTRY 586

teith, of Belleville Lodge, Blacket Place, Edinburgh, and formerly of Calcutta (who *d.* 28 Nov. 1879), and Margaret his wife (who *d.* Feb. 1874). dau. of Gen. Jonathan Samson Paul, H.E.I.C.S., and has issue,

1. EDWARD MONTEITH, Solicitor (*Aberfoyle, Duppas Hill, Croydon, Surrey*), *b.* 6 Feb. 1876; *m.* 29 July, 1908, Edyth Kate, eld. surviving dau. of the late Allan Evans, of Ross-on-Wye, Herefordshire, and has issue,
   Joan Monteith, *b.* 15 June, 1909.
2. James Seaton (44, *Auckland Road, Upper Norwood, S.E.*), *b.* 6 Feb. 1878; *m.* 3 June, 1899, Muriel Dora Scott Stewart, dau. of Matthew Stewart Murray, and has issue,
   1. Desmond Stewart Murray Seaton, *b.* 13 July, 1904.
   2. Alaster Edward Seaton, *b.* 10 Aug. 1906.
   1. Doreen Monteith Seaton, *b.* 1 Dec. 1901.
3. George Hay (*Glentea, Fleet, Hants*), *b.* 10 Nov. 1879; *m.* 3 Sept. 1902, Agnes Mary, 4th surviving dau. of the late Allan Evans, of Ross, Herefordshire, and has issue,
   Dagmar Isabel Mary, *b.* 30 March, 1904.
1. Margaret Monteith, *b.* 16 Aug. 1873.
2. Isabel Mary, *b.* 10 Nov. 1879; *d.* 1880.

Lineage.—JOHN REID was exiled to Bass Rock during the religious persecutions of the Presbyterians, *temp.* CHARLES II; from there he was banished to Jamaica, but returned to Ireland, and settled in Lurgan, co. Armagh. His son,

JOHN REID, of Lurgan, *b.* 1720; *m.* 1745, Margaret, eldest dau. of James Forrest, and *d.* 1802, having had issue three sons and one dau., of whom

FORREST REID, of Lurgan, *b.* 1751; *m.* 1774, Mary Weir, and *d.v.p.* 1801, having had with other issue a son,

THE REV. EDWARD REID, M.A., of The Manse, Ramelton, co. Donegal, Moderator of The Synod of Ulster 1821, *b.* 1782; *m.* 1st, 21 Sept. 1805, Elizabeth McMurray, and by her (who *d.* 1816) had issue,

1. George Hay, *b.* 1808; *d.* 1828.
2. James Seaton, M.D., M.R.C.S., L.A.C., Professor at Queen's Coll., Belfast, *b.* 1811; *m.* 1850, Elizabeth Montgomery. She *d.* 1895. He *d.* 3 May, 1896, having had issue,
   1. Edward, *b.* 1853; *d. unm.* 1877.
   2. James Seaton, *b.* 1856; *d. unm.* 1877.
   1. Maria, *b.* 1851; *m.* 23 Nov. 1870, O. McCausland, and has issue.
   2. Margaret Elizabeth, *b.* 1862; *m.* 1885, Francis Samuel Gregory Fenton, and has issue.
1. Mary Ann, *o.* 1806; *d.* 1807.
He *m.* 2ndly, 7 July, 1817, Martha, dau. of John Kelso, of Londonderry and Ramelton, and *d.* 11 Feb. 1838, having by her (who *d.* 1836) had issue,
3. John Kelso, *b.* 1818; *m.* 1857, Adelaide Barnsley, and *d.* 1874, having had issue,
   Godfrey Forrest, M.D., M.Ch. Trin. Coll. Dublin, *b.* 1858; *m.* 1881. Marian Gertrude Llewellyn D'Alton. She *d.s.p.* 1895. He died from wounds received at the battle of Tweefontein, South Africa, 26 Dec. 1901.
4. EDWARD (Sir).
5. Forrest, *b.* 1821, Sessional Crown Solicitor, Londonderry, *m.* 1859, Ellen Mackey. She *d.* 1895. He *d.* 1887, having had issue,
   1. John Kelso (*The Elms, Londonderry*), LL.D. Trin. Coll. Dublin, Solicitor, *b.* 1863; *m.* 1892, Ada Meredith, and has issue,
      (1) Forrest, *b.* 1893. (2) Dorothy, *b.* 1894.
   1. Agnes Boomer, *b.* 1860; *d.* 1865.
   2. Martha Kelso, *b.* 1862.
6. Robert, *b.* 1825; *m.* 1st, 1850, Mary M. Mackey, and by her had issue,
   1. Agnes, *b.* 1851; *d.* 1852.
   2. Mary, *b.* 1853; *d.* 1874.
   3. Martha Elizabeth, *b.* 1855; *d.* 1856.
He *m.* 2ndly, 1859, Frances M. Parr, and *d.* 1881, having by her (who *d.* 8 Dec. 1901) had issue.
   1. Robert, (26, *Malone Road, Belfast*), *b.* 1863; *m.* 1895, M. Robb, and has issue, a son and a dau.,
      Francis, *b.* 1896.
      Hilda, *b.* 1898.
   2. Washington Pirrie, *b.* 1865; *m.* 1900, Ellie Moore.
   3. John Kelso, *b.* 1868; *d.* 1873.
   4. Charles Joseph Scott, served in South African War 1900–02, *b.* 1871; *m.* 1904, Edith Aichison.
   5. Seaton, *d.* an infant, 1873.
   6. Forrest, *b.* 1875.
   4. Adelaide, *b.* 1861; *m.* 1891, W. Hind, and has issue.
   5. Frances, *b.* 1864.
   6. Constance Maud, *b.* 1869; *m.* 14 Aug. 1901, Emmanuel, Genohr.
2. Jane, *b.* 1823; *m.* 1847, Joseph Scott, of Castlederg, J.P., who *d.s.p.*
3. Mary, *b.* 1827; *m.* 1850, the late Robert McConnell, of Liverpool. She *d.* his widow 15 Nov. 1901, leaving issue.

Residence—"Tremere," Fleet, Hants.

REILLY OF SCARVAGH.

The late GUSTAVUS MILES O'HARA REILLY, of Scarvagh House, co. Down, *b.* 22 June, 1869; *d.* 28 March, 1909.

Lineage.—This branch of the ancient Milesian House of O'REILLY, Princes of East Brefny, has, for some generations discontinued the prefix O'.

TURLOGH O'REILLY, youngest son of Edmund O'Reilly, of Kilnacroft, Prince of East Brefny (*see* O'REILLY of East Brefny), had two children, BRIAN and John. The elder, BRIAN O'REILLY, had two sons, JOHN O'REILLY, of Belfast, and Miles, a Capt. in the Army. The former was father of

MILES REILLY, of Lurgan, co. Armagh, *b.* 1660; *m.* 19 Aug. 1680, Jane Ackens, and by her (who *d.* at Lurgan 10 Dec. 1715) had issue,

1. James, *d.s.p.* 2. Charles.
3. Marlow. 4. JOHN.

Miles Reilly *d.* 13 May, 1735, and was *s.* by his youngest son,

JOHN REILLY, of Scarvagh, *m.* 1738, Lucy, dau. of Francis Savage, of Ardkeen, co. Down, and was father of

JOHN REILLY, of Scarvagh, Chief Commissioner of Public Accounts, M.P. for Blessington, High Sheriff of co. Down, 1776, and of co. Armagh 1786, *b.* 1745; *m.* 1773, Jane, dau. and co-heir of Col. William Lushington, of Sittingbourne, Kent, and had issue,

1. JOHN LUSHINGTON, his heir.
2. William Edmond, of Tamnagharrie, co. Down, M.P. for Hillsborough, High Sheriff of co. Down 1815, *m.* Harriett, dau. of Robert Hamilton, of Strabane, co. Tyrone, and had issue,
   1. JOHN, *b.* 1808; *m.* Julia, dau. of William Brabazon; *d.* 1847, and had issue,
      (1) William, *m.* 1870, Rosalind, dau. of Hamilton Smythe, and *d.* 1871.
      (2) John. (3) Hamilton.
      (1) Letitia.
   1. Anne, *d. unm.*
   2. Jane, *m.* Rev. James Ford; *d.* 1842.
   3. Harriett, *m.* 1847, Charles Hamilton; *d.* 1869.
3. James Miles, of Cloon Eavin, co. Down, Barrister-at-Law, *m.* Feb. 1817, Emilia Georgina Susanna (who *d.* 1867), 2nd dau. of Rev. Hugh Montgomery, of Grey Abbey, co. Down, by his wife the Hon. Emilia Ward, youngest dau. of Bernard, 1st Viscount Bangor, and *d.* 4 Jan. 1848, having had issue,
   1. JOHN, Barrister-at-Law, Deputy-Keeper of the Rolls in Ireland, *b.* 16 Nov. 1817; *m.* 14 Aug. 1845, the Hon. Augusta Sugden, youngest dau. of Edward, 1st Lord St. Leonards, and *d.* 1 July, 1875, having had,
      (1) Emily.
      (2) Kathleen Matilda, *m.* 7 July, 1870, Matthew John Bell.
      (3) Winifred Ellen, *m.* 1st, 5 May, 1881, Hon. J. M. Stopford, son of James, 4th Earl of Courtown, who *d.* 1885; 2ndly, 29 July, 1889, Arthur Saunders William Charles Fox, 5th Earl of Arran.
   2. James Myles, in the Indian Army, *b.* Feb. 1823; *d.* 11 April, 1844.
   3. Francis Savage (Sir), K.C.M.G., Barrister-at-Law, Q.C., Counsel to the Speaker, *b.* Feb. 1825; *d. unm.* 27 Aug. 1883.
   4. William Edmund Moyses, Major-Gen., Inspector-Gen. of R.A., C.B., Chevalier of the Legion of Honour, *b.* Jan. 1827; *d.* July, 1886.
   5. Hugh Arthur, Capt. R.N., *b.* May, 1828; *d. unm.* 11 July, 1862.
   1. Emilia Maria Catherine, *d.* 1868.
   2. Jane Hester.
   3. Theodosia Harriett, *d. unm.* Sept. 1897.
1. Jane Hester, *d.* 1813.
2. Amelia, *m.* Lieut.-Col. Stacpoole, 45th Regt., and *d.* 1865.
3. Elizabeth, *m.* Francis Hamilton, and *d.* 1836.

Mr. Reilly *d.* 26 July, 1804, and was *s.* by his son,

JOHN LUSHINGTON REILLY, of Scarvagh, High Sheriff of co. Down, 1810; *m.* 9 June, 1807, Louisa, 2nd dau. of Gustavus Handcock Temple, of Waterstown, co. Westmeath, and by her (who *d.* Aug. 1852) had issue,

1. JOHN TEMPLE, of Scarvagh.
2. Gustavus Handcock, an Officer in the Army, *b.* Feb. 1813; *d.* 29 July, 1841.
3. Robert Lushington, Capt. H.E.I.C.S., *b.* 1818; *m.* 1 Jan. 1847, Clementina Janet, dau. of Thomas Andrew, of Edinburgh; *d.* Dec. 1859, leaving issue,
   1. John Temple Charles, 23rd Foot, *b.* 30 June, 1849; *d.* 6 June, 1908.
   1. Louisa Elizabeth, *d.* Feb. 1897.
   2. Flora Christian, *m.* Dec. 1890, Capt. Ruck Keene, R.N. Capt. Reilly's widow *m.* 2ndly, 1862, Robert, 3rd Earl of Roden, K.P.
4. William Charles, *b.* May, 1819; *d.* 19 Dec. 1845.
5. James Myles Townsend, Capt. 45th Madras Infantry; *m.* Feb. 1846, Eliza, dau. of Gen. James Mandeville Hacket, and *d.* Feb. 1856. She *d.* 30 June, 1901, having had a son, Arthur Cecil, *b.* 1850.
1. Isabella Elizabeth, *m.* May, 1834, Rev. John D'Arcy, of Galway, who *d.* 1875, leaving issue. She *d.* 5 March, 1898.
2. Jane Lushington, *m.* 13 Aug. 1830, Rev. J. Hill, and *d.* 21 Dec. 1839, leaving issue.
3. Louisa Mary.
4. Gertrude Harriett, *m.* 17 Feb. 1840, Robert Quin Alexander, of Acton House, co. Armagh, who *d.* 13 Aug. 1887. She *d.* 24 March 1905.
5. Mary Amelia.
6. Frances Lucy.

7. Charlotte Moore, m. 1855, Gen. George F. Moore, late Staff Officer of Pensioners, who d. 8 Sept. 1884, leaving issue.
Mr. Reilly d. 3 Dec. 1842, and was s. by his son,
JOHN TEMPLE REILLY, of Scarvagh, co. Down, J.P. and D.L., High Sheriff 1854, and J.P. co. Armagh, b. 19 Jan. 1812 ; m. 30 Oct. 1865, Elizabeth, dau. of James O'Hara, of Lenaboy, co. Galway, by his wife Anne, dau. of the Hon. Power le Poer Trench, Archbishop of Tuam, and d. 30 Jan. 1903, having had issue,
1. John Temple Miles, b. 21 March, 1867 ; d. 13 Jan. 1868.
2. GUSTAVUS MILES O'HARA, late of Scarvagh.
3. John Temple James, b. 18 May, 1871 ; d. 25 Dec. 1871.
1. Anne Elizabeth.
Arms, &c.—(See O'REILLY of East Brefny.)
Seat—Scarvagh House, Scarva, co. Down.

REYNELL OF KILLYNON.

RICHARD REYNELL, of Killynon, co. Westmeath, b. 14 Aug. 1879 ; s. his father 1911.

Lineage.—EDMUND REYNELL, 2nd son of Edmund Reynell, of Malston, by Anne, dau. of Lewis Hatch, of Allar, Devon, and 14th in direct descent from Sir Richard Reynell, temp. HENRY II, settled in Ireland in the 17th century. He m. Mary, dau. of Hugh Fortescue, and left issue, besides other children,
EDWARD REYNELL, of Malone, co. Antrim, "sove.aigne" of Belfast 1665. By Katherine Dobbin his wife he left (with three daus.
1. Mary, m. Richard Nugent ; 2. Margaret, m. Samuel Moore ; 3. Alice, m. James Brownlow) a son and successor,
EDMUND REYNELL, of Dublin, a Six Clerk in Chancery, who purchased estates in Westmeath, Longford, Leitrim, Roscommon, and Galway, and d. 3 Feb 1698 (bur. in the vaults of St. Michan's, Dublin), leaving issue by Hannah his wife (who d. May, 1723), dau. of — Dobbin, of Carrickfergus, co. Antrim,
1. ARTHUR of Castla Keynell, co. Westmeath, High Sheriff 1718 and 1727, d. 19 Oct. 1735 ; m. 1720, Elizabeth, dau. of Robert Cooke, of Cookesborough, co. Westmeath, and was grandfather of Col. William Reynell, of Castle Reynell, b. Jan. 1762, who m. 1791, Jane, dau. of Sir William Montgomery, Bart., of Macbie Hill, and d. 3 May, 1829, leaving issue,
1. Anne, m. Admiral de Vecknell, of Holland, 2nd Baron de Metitza, of Saxony.
2. Harriet, d. unm.
3. Barbara, m. 5 Sept. 1827, John, 3rd Earl of Donoughmore, and d. at Chiavari, near Genoa, 11 Jan. 1857.
2. RICHARD.   3. Edmund.
1. Mary, m. Hector Payne.
The 2nd son,
RICHARD REYNELL, of Killough, co. Westmeath, Capt. 5th Dragoon Guards, m. circa 1720, Dorcas (who d. Jan. 1776), dau. of Robert Cooke, of Cookesborough, co. Westmeath, and d. 1 May, 1756 (will proved 8 Nov. 1768), leaving, with other issue,
1. Arthur (Rev.), Rector of Churchtown, Killagh, and Clonarny Dioc s·· of Meath, disinherited, m. Eliza Catherine, dau. of James Nugent, of Clonlost, and had a dau., Dorcas, m. Rev. Mr. Madden, and dying 1784, left two sons,
1. Cooke, Reynell, of Woodfort, co. Westmeath. b. 1761 ; m. Catherine Webb, of Webbsboro, co. Kilkenny; she d. 4 Jan. 1838, aged 82, and left an only child, Catherine, m. Walter Nugent, of Dublin, and had issue. He d. 27 Jan. 1841, aged 81.
2. Richard, d. unm.
2. NICHOLAS, of Reynella, co. Westmeath. b. 1722 ; m. 1st, July, 1758, Frances Brush, and 2ndly, Mary, dau. of Francis Winter, of Agher, co. Meath. He d. in March or April, 1768, leaving issue by his 1st m.rriage.
1. RICHARD, his successor, of Reynella, b. 1759 ; m. Feb. 1789, Elizabeth, only child of Arthur Molesworth, of Fairlawn, co. Armagh (eldest son of the Hon. Bysse Molesworth), by Catherine Fletcher Vane, of Cumberland. She d. Nov. 1827. He d. 28 Jan. 1807, leaving issue,
(1) Arthur Molesworth, b. 1790 ; d. unm. 31 May, 1812.
(2) RICHARD MOLESWORTH, of Reynella, High Sheriff 1819, b. Dec. 1791 ; m. May, 1819, Catherine, only dau. of the Hon. Ponsonby Moore, brother of the 1st Marquess of Drogheda. She d. at Bath, 17 Dec. 1859. He d. 13 Sept. 1824, leaving an only child and heir.
ELIZABETH CATHARINE, m. 12 Jan. 1843, at Leamington, Blaney Townley Balfour, of Townley Hall, co. Louth, who d. 2 Sept. 1882, aged 83, leaving issue (see that family).
(1) Frances, m. 14 Feb. 1814, Gen. John Nugent, C.B., and d. 3 April, 1827.
2. Edmund, d. unm.
1. Elizabeth Frances, m. 26 June, 1779, Sir Charles Levinge, 5th bart., of Knockdrin, and d. 19 May, 1828.
3. EDWARD, of whom we treat.
4. Robert, m. Elizabeth, dau. of Ranfurlie Knox, of H.E.I.C.S., and d. Dec. 1794, having had issue,
1. Harriet, m. 23 May, 1795, her cousin, Richard Reynell, of Killynon.

2. Clarissa, m. 1798, Rev. George Leslie Gresson.
5. John, of Ballinaleck, Westmeath, m. Miss Standish, and had issue,
1. John, of Ballenaleck, m. 28 April, 1805, Barbara English. She d. Nov. 1829, he d. Aug. 1846.
1. Matilda, m. Richard English.
2. Francis Elizabeth, m. 8 Feb. 1806, Rev. William Annesley, son of the Hon. and Very Rev. William Annesley, Dean of Down.
6. Cooke, killed in a duel in Germany,
The 3rd son,
THE REV. EDWARD REYNELL, of Killynon, co. Westmeath, m. 1st, his cousin Lettice, dau. of John Reynell, of Castle Reynell. She d.s.p. 19 June, 1760. He m. 2ndly, 24 Jan. 1767, Jane, eldest dau. of Francis Winter, of Agher. She d. 22 Jan. 1777. He d. 28 Jan. 1788, leaving issue,
1. RICHARD, of whom presently.
2. Benjamin Pratt, d. unm. 23 Feb. 1789.
1. Margaret, m. Thomas Barnes, of Donover, co. Meath.
2. Jane, m. Rev. William Kellett, Rector of Moynalty.
3. Elizabet d. unm., March, 1844.
The elder son,
RICHARD REYNELL, of Killynon, co. Westmeath, b. 20 March, 1768 ; m. 23 May, 1795, his cousin Harriett, dau. and co-heir of Robert Reynell, of Edmonton, and d. 1 Nov. 1834, having by her (who d. 21 May, 1828) had issue,
1. Edward, d. unm. 25 Nov. 1828.
2. RICHARD WINTER, of Killynon.
3. Samuel Arthur, of Archerstown, co. Westmeath, b. 15 Dec. 1814 ; m. 13 June, 1836, his cousin Frances Elizabeth, dau. of Major-Gen. John Nugent, C.B., and by her (who d. 30 July, 1856 ; he d. 11 Jan. 1877) left issue, four daus.,
1 Frances.   2. Georgina, d. unm. Feb. 1899.
3. Rosa.   4. Clara.
4. William Knox, d. unm. 8 May, 1856.
1. Martha, m. 12 Dec. 1833, Sir Arthur Percy Aylmer, 11th bart., of Donadea. She d. 5 Feb. 1887, and had issue (see BURKE'S Peerage).
2. Anna Maria, m. 15 Sept. 1837, Rev. John William Fairbrother Drought, of Glencarrig, co. Wicklow, and d. 28 May, 1867.
3. Elizabeth Dorcas, m. 3 Sept. 1846, Rev. Thomas Acton Drought, and d. 14 March, 1852.   He d. 13 Dec. 1892, leaving issue (see DROUGHT of Glencarrig).
The eldest son,
RICHARD WINTER REYNELL, of Killynon, J.P., High Sheriff 1839, b. 5 Nov. 1804 ; m. 10 Feb. 1830, Frances Alexandrina, youngest dau. of James Sanderson, D.L., of Clover Hill, co. Cavan (see that family), and by her (who d. 31 Oct. 1874) had,
1. RICHARD, late of Killynon.
2. James Sanderson, b. 30 May, 1832 ; d. unm. 20 March, 1887.
3. William Alexander (Rev.), B.D., b. 10 March, 1836, d. unm. 3 March, 1906.
1. Harriette Eliza.   2. Frances Charlotte.
3. Eliza Thomasina.
4. Cecilia Jemima, d. unm. 24 July, 1903.
Mr. Reynell d. 3 Feb. 1887. His eldest son,
RICHARD REYNELL, of Killynon, co. Westmeath, J.P., b. 1 Jan. 1831 ; m. 22 July, 1875, Louisa Anna, youngest dau. of Rev. Thomas Smyth, of Coole, co. Westmeath, and sister of Thomas James Smyth, of Ballynegall, co. Westmeath (see that family), and by her (who d. 17 Dec. 1881) had issue,
RICHARD, now of Killynon.
Louisa Anna.
He d. 2 Jan. 1911.

Arms—Arg., masonry sa., a chief indented of the second. Crest—A fox passant or.   Mottoes—Murus aeneus esto ; Indubitata fides.
Seat—Killynon, Killucan, co. Westmeath.

RIALL OF ANNERVILLE.

MRS. DOROTHEA MARIA MONTGOMERY, of Annerville co. Tipperary, dau. of the late Samuel Riall by his wife Maria (who d. 5 Nov. 1888), dau. of George Baker, of Cahir, and widow of Thomas Quin, of Redmondstown ; s. her brother 1904 ; m. 20 Oct. 1874, Thomas Bedford Montgomery, of Government House, Londonderry (see MONTGOMERY of Killee), and has issue,
1. ARTHUR SAMUEL, b. 5 April, 1877.
1. Amy Maria, b. 9 Feb. 1879 ; m. 14 April, 1904, Capt. Thomas A. D. Best, Royal Inniskilling Fusiliers.
2. Violet Aileen Riall, b. 15 Oct. 1897.
Lineage.—PHINEAS RIALL, of Clonmel, co. Tipperary, b. 1 Jan. 1659 ; m. 1692, Elizabeth, dau. of William Vaughan, of Clonmel, and had a son,
WILLIAM VAUGHAN RIALL, of Clonmel, m. 1727, Mary, dau. of John Bagwell, and by her (who d. 1774) had issue,
1. PHINEAS, of whom presently.
2. Samuel (Rev.), m. Elizabeth Miles, sister and heir of Col. Lawford Miles, of Rochestown, and has issue,
John Bagwell, who d.s.p.
Elizabeth, m. Dunbar Barton, of Rochestown, co. Tipperary.
1. Catherine.
2. Elizabeth, m. Simon Newport of Waterford.
The elder son,

PHINEAS RIALL, of Heywood, co. Tipperary, *b.* 16 April, 1729; *m.* 19 Nov. 1768, Catherine, dau. of Charles Caldwell, of Dublin, by Elizabeth his wife, dau. of Benjamin Heywood, of Liverpool, great-grandfather of Sir Benjamin Heywood, 1st bart., of Claremont, co. Lancaster, and dying 15 May, 1797, left issue,
1. WILLIAM, of whom presently.
2. CHARLES (*see* RIALL *of Old Conna Hill*).
3. Phineas (Sir), Gen. in the Army, *m.* Miss Scarlett, and *d.s.p.*
4. Arthur, *m.* twice.
1. Eliza, *m.* Gen. Sir George Cockburn.
2. Mary, *d. unm.*

The eldest son,
WILLIAM RIALL, of Annerville, *b.* 17 Nov. 1769; *m.* 4 Jan. 1798, Dorothea, eldest dau. of Col. Henry Bellingham, of Castle Bellingham, co. Louth, and by her (who *d.* March, 1848) had issue,
1. Phineas, *b.* 1799; *d. unm.* 1827.
2. William Henry, Comm. R.N., *b.* 1803; *m.* 1831, in South America, Miss E. F. Parkinson, and *d.s.p.* 9 Jan. 1886. His widow *d.* 1870.
3. SAMUEL, of Annerville.
1. Elizabeth, *d. unm.* 1825.
2. Catherine, *m.* 1834, James Ramsay Smith.
3. Dorothea, *m.* 1830, Richard Moore, of Clonmel, and *d.* 1862, leaving issue.

Mr. Riall *d.* 2 Nov. 1843, and was *s.* by his eldest surviving son,
SAMUEL RIALL, of Annerville, J.P., *b.* 6 Sept. 1807; *m.* 29 April, 1840, Maria, widow of Thomas Quin, of Redmondstown, and only dau. of George Baker, of Cahir, and by her (who *d.* 5 Nov. 1888) had issue,
WILLIAM ARTHUR, late of Annerville.
DOROTHEA MARIA, now of Annerville.

Mr. Riall *d.* 3 Feb. 1872, and was *s.* by his only son,
WILLIAM ARTHUR RIALL, of Annerville, co. Tipperary, J.P. and D.L., High Sheriff 1895, *b.* 20 April, 1850, and *d.* 10 Nov. 1904, and was *s.* by his sister.

Seat—Annerville, Clonmel.

RIALL OF OLD CONNA HILL.

LEWIS JOHN ROBERTS RIALL, of Old Conna Hill, co. Dublin, J.P. and D.L., High Sheriff 1889, J.P. co. Wicklow, late Capt. 15th Regt., *b.* 15 Jan. 1838; *m.* 16 Feb. 1871, Elizabeth Sophia, eldest dau. of Capt. David Beatty, of Heathfield, co. Wexford, and has issue,
1. Olive Mary.
2. Violet Maud.
3. Elizabeth Rose.

Lineage.—CHARLES RIALL, of Heywood, Clonmel (2nd son of Phineas Riall, of Heywood, *see preceding article*), *m.* 6 April, 1801, Anne, 3rd dau. and co-heir of John Roberts, of Old Conna Hill, co. Dublin, descended from ancient Welsh ancestry, and by her (who *d.* 1837) had issue,
1. PHINEAS, of Old Conna Hill.
2. John, *b.* 15 Sept. 1805; *d.* 9 Dec. 1884.
3. George Charles, *b.* 28 May, 1820; *d.* 7 Aug. 1835.
4. Arthur, *b.* 16 Sept. 1822; *d.* 17 Sept. 1829.
1. Martha, *d. unm.* 26 June, 1887, aged 85.
2. Kate, *m.* Col. George Robert Kennedy, R A., and had issue, two sons and two daus.
3. Anne, *b.* 1816; 1st, John Murray, who *d.* leaving issue, four sons and two daus.; and 2ndly, Richard John Roe, and *d.* 21 Feb. 1903, having by him had issue, two daus.
4. Jane Charlotte, *m.* 1839, George John Beresford, Lieut.-Col. R.A., great-grandson of Marcus, 1st Earl of Tyrone, and *d.* 6 April, 1842.

Mr. Riall *d.* 15 April, 1855, and was *s.* by his eldest son,
PHINEAS RIALL, of Old Conna Hill, J.P. and D.L. for Dublin, and J.P. for Wicklow, High Sheriff for co. Dublin 1863, *b.* 11 May, 1803; *m.* 15 July, 1834, Mary Anne, dau. of John Roe, of Rockwell, co. Tipperary, and by her (who *d.* 16 May, 1861) had issue,
1. LEWIS JOHN ROBERTS, now of Old Conna Hill.
2. Charles Phineas Roberts, *b.* 17 Jan. 1840; *d. unm.* 14 April, 1886.
3. Arthur George Roberts, Comm. R.N. (retired), *b.* 9 Feb. 1842; *m.* 26 Nov. 1874, Selina Florinda, eldest dau. of William Truelock Bookey, of Derrybawn, co. Wicklow, and has issue, four sons and two daus.
4. William Augustus, of Heywood, co. Tipperary, J.P. and D.L., Lieut.-Col. R.A. (retired), *b.* 25 Aug. 1844; *m.* 27 July, 1880, Eleanor Mary, only dau. of Sackville Deane Hamilton, of Beechmont, co. Cork, and has had issue,
  1. Gerald William, *b.* 8 July, 1886.
  1. Marion Eleanor. 2. Helen.
  3. Aileen Maude.
5. Richard Villiers Sankey, late Major 15th Regt., *b.* 30 Aug. 1846; *m.* 4. Jan. 1887, Lily, 3rd dau. of Jonathan S. Harrison, of Brandesburton Hall, East Yorks.

1. Elizabeth Jane, *m.* 17 Sept. 1873, Rev. Ralph A. A. Meredith, M.A., who *d.* 20 Dec. 1878, leaving issue, two sons and one dau.
2. Edith May Marion, *m.* 16 Oct. 1872, Col. Delves Broughton, 15th Regt., and had issue.

Mr. Riall *d.* 15 Aug. 1884, and was *s.* by his eldest son.

Arms—Quarterly: 1st and 4th Arg., on a bend engrailed az. between an eagle displayed sa. and an escallop gu., a pile issuant from the dexter chief point of the first for RIALL; 2nd and 3rd, erm., a mullet, gu., between three rows close sa., each holding its beak an ear of wheat ppr., for ROBERTS. Crest—A lion's head erased or, charged with an escallop gu., in the mouth a trefoil vert. *Motto*—Duw au fendith yw fy ngwenwth.

Seat—Old Conna Hill, Bray. Club—Kildare Street, Dublin.

RICE OF BUSHMOUNT.

RICHARD JUSTICE RICE, of Bushmount, co. Kerry, J.P., High Sheriff 1901, Lieut.-Col. late 4th Batt. Royal Munster Fusiliers, and Reserve of Officers, *b.* 28 Nov. 1852; matriculated London Univ. (1st Div.) 1870; selected Unionist Candidate (N. Kerry) 1892 and 1895.

Lineage.—EDWARD RICE, of Dingle l'Couch, co. Kerry, *temp.* HENRY VIII. He *m.* Anne, dau. of John Wall, co. Limerick, and was father of
ROBERT RICE, of Dingle, *m.* Juliana, dau. of Sir James Whyte, Knt. of Casbel, co. Tipperary, and was father of
STEPHEN RICE, of Dingle, M.P. co. Kerry 1613, who made a deed of settlement of his estates 31 March, 1619, and *d.* 31 March, 1623. He *m.* Helen, dau. of Thomas Trant, of Cahir Trant, co. Kerry, and had two sons, 1. JAMES, M.P. for Dingle 1635, from whom descended RIGHT HON. THOMAS SPRING RICE, M.P., of Mount Trenchard, co. Limerick, created Lord Monteagle, 5 Sept. 1839 (*see* BURKE'S *Peerage*); and 2. Dominick, M.P. for Dingle 1635, *m.* Alice, dau. of James Hussey, Baron of Galtrim, from which marriage descended Sir Stephen Rice, Knt., of Mount Rice, Lord Chief Baron of the Court of the Exchequer in Ireland, 1686.

DOMINICK RICE, of Dingle. He *m.* his cousin-german, Mary Rice, and had issue,
1. DOMINICK, his heir.
2. John, of Dingle (who *d.s.p.* leaving his property by will dated 9 April, 1753, to Thomas Rice-George, appointing him sole executor.
1. Joan, *m.* her cousin, Rice, of Dingle, and had a son, Dominick Rice, Barrister-at-Law.
2. Mary, *m.* John Lawlor, of Lackamore.
3. Barbara, *m.* — Brunton, and had issue.

The eldest son,
DOMINICK RICE, of Taulaght and Racanny, near Dingle, co. Kerry, *b. circa* 1720; will dated 1755. He *m.* Mary, dau. and co-heir of John Collis, of Taulaght, near Tralee, and had a dau. Elizabeth, *m.* Francis Eagar, of Cuel, same co., and a son and successor,
JOHN RICE, of Ballymacawhim Castle, near Causeway, co. Kerry, *b.* 1754; *m.* 1784, Elizabeth, widow of John Payne, of Tralee, and eldest dau. of Monckton Carey, of Dromartin, same co., and granddau. of Lieut. Tristram Carey (by Elizabeth his wife, dau. of Major Nicholas Monckton, of Kilmore, co. Limerick). By this lady (*b.* 1745; *d.* May, 1826) Mr. Rice left at his decease, 1788, an only child,
DOMINICK RICE, of Bushmount, co. Kerry, *b.* 25 Sept. 1785; *m.* 1807, Frances, only surviving child of Justice Griffin, of Larca, same co., and first cousin to Right Rev. Henry Griffin, D.D., Bishop of Limerick and Ardfert 1853-66, by whom (who *d.* 25 May, 1876, aged 92) he had surviving issue,
1. JUSTICE DOMINICK, his heir.
2. John, of Ballyloughrane, J.P., *b.* 1814; *m.* 1847, Susan, dau. of John James, of Snugborough, co. Kerry, and *d.* 28 Feb. 1878, leaving issue. 3. Dominick, *b.* 1820; *d.* 1834.
4. Richard, *b.* 1829; *d.* 1849.
1. Ellen, *b.* 1810; *m.* 1843, Robert McCarthy Hilliard, J.P., of Billerough House, Listowel (dec.), and *d.* 1893, leaving issue.
2. Elizabeth, *b.* 1815; *m.* 1833, Benjamin Jackson (dec.), Inspector R.I.C. co. Galway, and *d.* 1880, leaving issue.
3. Sarah, *b.* 1818; *m.* 1st, 1849, William Pope, of Causeway, co. Kerry, who *d.* 1864; and 2ndly, 1867, Joseph Hamilton, of Tarbert, same co., J.P., and *d.s.p.*
4. Frances, *b.* 1822, a nun in the Order of the Sisters of Mercy, Killarney; *d.* 1854.
5. Mary, *b.* 1824; *m.* 1854, Edward Mulchinock, of Clogher's House, co. Kerry, and Pembroke Road, Dublin, J.P., who *d.* 1880, leaving issue.
6. Anne, a nun in the Order of the Sisters of Mercy, Killarney, *b.* 1827; *d.* 1849.

Mr. Rice *d.* 8 Feb. 1864, and was *s.* by his eldest son,
JUSTICE DOMINICK RICE, of Bushmount, J.P., *b.* 1813, *m.* 1850, Bidelia Mary (who *d.* 17 Dec. 1905), only surviving child of John Geoghegan, of Cork, and had issue,
1. Dominick, *b.* 4 Oct. 1851; *d.* 11 Jan. 1866.
2. RICHARD JUSTICE, now of Bushmount.
3. William Francis, *b.* 10 Sept. 1854; *d.* 21 Dec. 1868.
4. Justice Griffin, of Ivanhoe, Wythe, co. Va., U.S.A., *b.* 15 Dec. 1860; *d.* 5 Jan. 1912; *m.* 1893, Susan Shrader, and had issue,

1. Arthur, *d.* young, 1898.
2. Garland, *b.* 1895.
1. Mary Ethel.
2. Eula Bidelia.
1. Delia Katherine, *m.* 1889, Gerard J. Pierse, M.D., of Causeway, and who *d.* 15 Aug. 1894, leaving a son,
2. Frances Anne, *m.* 1892, Charles Irwin Taylor, of Dublin, and *d.* 11 May, 1912.
3. Ellen Mary, *m.* her brother-in-law, Dr. Pierse, and *d.* 24 Aug. 1900, leaving issue.
Mr. J. D. Rice *d.* 4 Dec. 1888.

Seat—Bushmount, Lixnaw, co. Kerry.

SPRING-RICE. *See* BURKE'S PEERAGE, MONTEAGLE, B.

RICHARDS OF SOLSBOROUGH.

URBAN VIGORS RICHARDS, of Solsborough, co. Wexford, J.P., High Sheriff 1912, Major (ret.) New Zealand Forces, formerly of the 72nd Duke of Albany's Own Highlanders, 33rd Duke of Wellington Regt. and 87th Royal Irish Fusiliers, served with the 33rd Regt. in Abyssinia 1867-8, present with stormers at the assault and capture of Magdala (medal), *b.* 1841 ; *s.* his cousin by will dated 23 Feb. 1903 ; *m.* 4 Sept. 1893, Katharine Faith, dau. of the Rev. W. Michell, Rector and Prebendary of Dinder, Wells, Somerset.

Lineage.—JOHN RICHARDS, who resided at Subinton, co Southampton, *temp.* JAMES I, *m.* Constance, dau. of Ralph Ffawkner, of the co. of Wilts, gent., by Margaret his wife, dau. of William Disney, and grand-dau. of John Disney, and Margaret his wife, dau. of John Fox, of co. Lincoln, the brother and heir of Richard Fox, D.D., Bishop of Exeter 1487, and of Winchester 1501 ; *d.* 1528. By this lady he had issue,
1. John. 2. Thomas.
3. SOLOMON, of whom hereafter. 4. Henry.

The 3rd son,
SOLOMON RICHARDS, *m.* Anne, dau. of John Curle, of Brixton, in the Isle of Wight, gent., and had issue,
1. SOLOMON, his successor. 2. John.
1. Eleanor. 2. Anne.
3. Elizabeth, *m* Samuel Foley, of Clonmel, co. Tipperary, *d.* 1695.

The elder son,
SOLOMON RICHARDS, of Solsborough, co. Wexford, previously of Westminster, Col. of a Regt., was a Commissioner in Ireland and Governor of the town of Wexford during the usurpation of OLIVER CROMWELL. He had a grant of Solsborough and other lands in co. Wexford amounting to over 3,000 acres, which was confirmed under the Act of Settlement, by patent dated 18 Dec. anno 18 and 19 CHARLES II. On the accession of WILLIAM III and MARY II, he raised the 17th Regt., of which he was appointed the first Col. He *m.* 1st, Rhoda, dau. of Samuel Wilson, of London, gent., by whom he had 2 dau., Rhoda, who *m.* (lic. 19 Feb. 1674) William Mercer. He *m.* 2ndly, Abigail, dau. of Henry Goddard, of Deptford and Chatham, co. Kent, and had, with other issue, who *d.* young,
1. Solomon, living 1654, *d.v.p.*
2. John, eldest son at his father's death ; was disinherited, and *d.s.p.* beyond the seas.
3. GODDARD, who carried on the line.
4. Michael, Capt. in his father's regt., and a Brigadier-Gen. in the Army. His father having disinherited his elder sons, bequeath the estates to him, and he dying *unm.* 1721, left them to his elder surviving brother. 5. Nathaniel.
1. Rose, *d. unm.* 2. Anne, *d. unm.*
3. Abigail, *d. unm.*
Col. Richards *d.* Oct. 1691, and was buried at Westminster Abbey the 6th of that month. His third son,
GODDARD RICHARDS, of Solsborough, *b.* 1661 ; *s.* to the estates by the will of his brother, Brigadier-Gen. Michael Richards, 1721. He *m.* by licence 29 March, 1684, Dorothea, dau. of John Jacob, of Sigginstown, co. Wexford, by whom he had issue,
1. JOHN, his heir. 2. Jacob.
3. Goddard. 4. Jonathan.

Mr. Richards was *s.* by his eldest son,
JOHN RICHARDS, of Solsborough, High Sheriff 1728, *m.* and had issue,
1. SOLOMON, his successor.
2. Goddard, ancestor of RICHARDS *of Monksgrange (which see).*
3. Edward, of Enniscorthy, *m.* Judith, dau. of John Bowers, of Monfin, co. Wexford, and had one dau., Katherine, *m.* Arthur Thomas.
4. John, of Askinvillar, *b.* 1718 ; *d. unm.* 1763.
1. Elizabeth, *m.* William Stephens, of Ferns, co. Wexford, and *d.* Sept. 1781.

Mr. Richards *d.* 1749, and was *s.* by his eldest son,
SOLOMON RICHARDS, of Solsborough, High Sheriff co. Wexford 1753, *m.* Frances, dau. of Urban Vigors, of Ballyconnick, co. Carlow, and had issue,

1. SOLOMON, his heir.
2. William, Capt. in the Solsborough and Farmley Yeomanry, *b.* 1769 ; *m.* Louisa, dau. of Col. George Rawson, of Belmont, co. Wicklow, M.P., and *d.* 17 Nov. 1847, having had by her (who *d.* 14 July, 1841) two sons,
1. William Vigors, *b.* 3 Sept. 1805 ; *d.s.p.* in South America 1831.
2. George Rawson, of Farmley, co. Wexford, J.P., *b.* 1 Aug. 1812 ; *m.* Jane, dau. of Richard Huson, of Ballyorrel, co. Wexford, and had two sons, George and William ; both went to America.
3. Edward, bapt. 12 Aug. 1777 ; *d. unm.* 31 Dec. 1801.
1. Frances, *m.* 13 Nov. 1784, Matthew de Rinzy, of Clobemon, co. Wexford.
2. Katherine, *m.* 21 June, 1781, Nicholas Aylward Vigors, of Old Leighlin, co. Carlow, and *d.* 20 March, 1802.

Mr. Richards (whose will was proved 1784) was *s.* by his eldest son, SOLOMON RICHARDS, of Solsborough, LL.B. Trin. Coll. Dublin, High Sheriff 1793, *b.* 1765 ; *m.* 1st, 14 April, 1784, Martha, dau. of Francis Gorman, of Ballynahessan, co. Meath, and had issue,
1. SOLOMON, his heir.
2. Bartholomew Vigors, *b.* Feb. 1788 ; *d. unm.* 1830.
3. Edwin, Capt. R.N., *m.* Sept. 1823, Mary Anne, dau. of the Very Rev. Walter Blake Kirwan, Dean of Killala, and *d.* 28 Sept. 1866, having had issue,
1. Edwin, Capt. 41st Regt., *d. unm.*, killed at the battle of Inkerman, 5 Nov. 1854.
2. Frederick William (Sir), G.C.B., Admiral of the Fleet, Lord of the Admiralty 1882-5, Commander-in-Chief on East Indian Station 1885-8 ; and on the China Station 1890-2, late 1st Naval Lord at the Admiralty, A.D.C. to Queen Victoria 1872-82, *b.* 30 Nov. 1833 ; *m.* 30 Oct. 1866, Lucy, dau. of Fitzherbert Brooke, of Horton, co. Gloucester, and widow of Rev. Edwin Fayle. She *d.s.p.* 1880.
3. Solomon, accidentally drowned at Dunbrody Park, co. Wexford 1847.
4. URBAN VIGORS, now of Solsborough.
1. Julia, *m.* 25 Aug. 1853, Sir William Leeson. Knt., Genealogist to the Order of St. Patrick, and *d.* 22 Dec. 1879. He *d.* 21 April, 1885.
2. Maud, *m.* 3 Jan. 1874, John Stanley Wood, of the Adjutant-General's Office, Bombay, and is dec.
3. Sophia (deceased), *m.* Leland Crosthwaite.
4. Louisa, *m.* Lieut.-Col. John Henry Keogh, of Kilbride, co. Carlow, and *d.* 22 May, 1863.
5. Frances.
6. Anne Vigors, *m.* 1861, the late Rev. Thomas Stack, Sen. Fellow of Trin. Coll. Dublin.
4. William Gorman, *b.* July, and *d.* Aug. 1795.
5. Francis, *d.* young.
1. Sophia, *m.* Mathew O'Brien, of Newcastle, co. Limerick.
2. Frances, *m.* Rev. John Howard Gorges.
3. Martha, *m.* Rev. Henry Barnes.
4. Katherine, *m.* Rev. Richard Fayle.

Mr. Richards *m.* 2ndly, 23 Sept. 1797, Martha, dau. of Col. George Rawson, of Belmont, co. Wicklow, M.P., and had issue,
8. George Rawson, *d. unm.* 1826.
5. Maria, *d. unm.* 1802.

Mr. Richards *d.* 1811, and was *s.* by his eldest son,
REV. SOLOMON RICHARDS, of Solsborough, High Sheriff 1818, who afterwards entered into Holy Orders, and was appointed Rector of Clone, co. Wexford, *b.* 1787 ; *m.* 9 May, 1814, Elizabeth, eldest dau. of Col. Thomas Bermingham Daly Henry Sewell, of Athenry (by Hon. Harriett Beresford his wife, dau. of William, 1st Lord Decies, Archbishop of Tuam), and grand-dau. of Thomas Bailey Heath Sewell, by Lady Elizabeth Bermingham his wife, eldest dau. and co-heir of Thomas, 22nd Lord Athenry and Earl of Louth. By her (who *d.* 26 Jan. 1861) Mr. Richards had issue,
1. SOLOMON, late of Solsborough.
2. William Beresford, County Inspector Royal Irish Constabulary, *b.* 1819 ; *d. unm.* 29 Nov. 1887.
3. John, Lieut. H.E.I.C.S., *m.* 9 Sept. 1852, Eleanor Maria, dau. of Alexander Napper, of New Ross, co. Wexford, and *d.* Sept. 1859, leaving issue,
1. Alfred Beresford, *b.* 17 June, 1853 ; *d. unm.*
2 ROLAND, *b.* 26 Oct. 1854.
3. William James Napper, *b.* 21 May, 1857 ; *m.* 28 Sept. 1887, Amy Elizabeth, dau. of Dr. John Byrne, of Charles Street, New Ross.
1. Harriet, *m.* Richard Howard Gorges. Both are deceased.
2. Louisa, *b.* 1820 ; *d.* April, 1830.
3. Bessie, *m.* 8 Sept. 1854, the late William Donovan, of Tomnalossett, co. Wexford.
4. Isabella.
5. Louisa Martha, *m.* 1st, 8 Dec. 1866, Richard Archibald Gorges, Capt. Royal Marine Artillery, who was lost in the *Captain* turret ship 7 Sept. 1870, and 2ndly, George Jones.

Mr. Richards *d.* 28 Feb. 1866, and was *s.* by his eldest son,
GEN. SOLOMON RICHARDS, of Solsborough, co. Wexford, J.P., entered the Bengal Army as Ensign 8 March, 1836, and had attained the rank of Gen. 22 Jan. 1889, served in the Sutlej Campaign of 1845-6, and was present at the battle of Sobracon (medal), served with the Bhootan expedition 1865-8 (medal), *b.* 26 May, 1817. Gen. Richards was senior co-heir of Lady Elizabeth Bermingham, the eldest dau. and senior co-heir of Thomas, 22nd Lord Athenry, and Earl of Louth, who *d.* 1799. He *d. unm.* 27 Feb. 1905, and devised the Solsborough estates to his cousin.

Seat—Solsborough, Enniscorthy, co. Wexford. *Clubs*—United Service, Dublin, Royal St. George's Yacht, Kingstown.

RICHARDS OF MONKSGRANGE.

The late EDWARD MOORE RICHARDS, late of Monksgrange, co. Wexford, b. 1826; m. 1st. Sarah Elizabeth, dau. of William Tisdale, of Virginia, North America, by whom (who d. 19 Feb. 1860) he had issue,

1. John Evelyn, b. 1852; d. 1858.
1. ADELA ELIZABETH, now of Monksgrange, m. 18 Aug. 1880, Goddard Henry Orpen, B.A., Barrister-at-Law, and has issue (*see* ORPEN *of Ardtully*).
2. Dora, d. 1860.

Mr. Edward M. Richards m. 2ndly, 7 Dec. 1882, Ellen Elizabeth, dau. of Capt. David Aird, R.N., of The Anchorage, Pembroke. Mr. Richards transferred by deed of gift Sept. 1899, the Monksgrange property to his only surviving dau. Mrs. G. H. Orpen, and d. 4 Sept. 1911.

Lineage.—GODDARD RICHARDS, b. 1715, 3rd son of John Richards, of Solsborough (*see that family*), was bequeathed Grange (originally called Monksgrange) and other estates in co. Wexford, by his father, which estates had been purchased between 1718 and 1742, and had formerly belonged to the company formed for "making hollow sword blades." He m. 1756, Anne, dau. of Ven. Nicholas Hewetson, Archdeacon of Killaloe, and had issue,

1. JOHN, his successor.
2. SOLOMON, ancestor of RICHARDS *of Ardamine* (which *see*).
3. Goddard, of Gath, Col. H.E.I.C.S., b. 1764; m. Anne, dau. of Henry Houghton, of Kilmannock, co. Wexford, by whom (who d. 2 Oct. 1855) he had issue,
  1. Goddard Henry, m. Miss Mason, and d. leaving a dau., Katherine, who became a nun. 2. William (Rev.).
  1. Mary Anne.
  2. Elizabeth, m. William Blunt, 3rd son of Sir Charles William Blunt, 3rd bart., of Ringmer, co. Sussex, and had issue.
  3. Ellen, m. 29 March, 1825, William Monckton, of Amherst House, co. Gloucester, grandson of John, 1st Viscount Galway, and had issue.
  4. Maria (Mrs. Burges), 5. Charlotte (Mrs. Whately).
  6. Virginia. 7. Julia.
4. William, called to the Irish Bar 1792, b. May, 1768; d. unm. 1832. 5. Nicholas, b. 1770; d. unm. v.p. July, 1788.
6. Edward, 55th Regt., b. Nov. 1771; d. unm. 1798.
7. Robert Hewetson, of 15, Baggot Street, Dublin, Assistant-Barrister for co. Wexford, b. Nov. 1773; m. 1814, Matilda, dau. of Henry Garnett, of Athcarne, co. Meath, and d. 1829, having had by her (who d. 24 April, 1880, aged 81),
  1. William Henry, d. young.
  2. Robert, Lieut.-Gen. Bombay Staff Corps, m. Maria, dau. of Gen. Nicholas Wilson, younger son of Christian Wilson, of Sledagh, co. Wexford, and d. 13 Nov. 1884, leaving issue,
    (1) Charles Grant.
    (1) Annie Matilda. (2) Alice. (3) Grace.
    (4) Edith. (5) Florence.
  1. Anne Matilda, m. 6 Aug. 1836, Thomas Lewis Roberts, of Dormstown Castle, co. Meath, and had issue (*see that family*).
  2. Mary Anne, m. 30 Dec. 1862, Rev. William Birche-Wolfe, of Wood Hall, Essex. He d.s.p. 1864. She d. 6 Aug. 1897.
8. Henry, b. June, 1780; d. young, bur. 2 March, 1788.
1. Anne, b. 11 July, 1760; m. 28 June, 1780, Richard Donovan, of Ballmore, co. Wexford, and d. 12 July, 1831.
2. Sarah, b. 2 July, 1761, m. Richard William Tighe, M.P. co. Wicklow, 3rd son of William Tighe, of Rossana.
3. Katherine Jane, b. July, 1763; m. Rev. Robert Alexander, LL.D., of New Ross, co. Wexford, and d. 2 March, 1842.
4. Elizabeth, b. 1765; m. 1 April, 1796, Richard Colles, Barrister-at-Law.
5. Wilhelmina, b. 1766; m. 22 Sept. 1798, Very Rev. Walter Blake Kirwan, Dean of Killala, and d. 1832. He d. 27 Oct. 1805, aged 51. 6. Letitia, b. Jan. 1777; d. unm.

Mr. Goddard Richards d. 1 July, 1795, and was s. by his eldest son, REV. JOHN RICHARDS, of Grange (or Monksgrange), b. 6 Sept. 1757; m. March, 1796, Elizabeth, dau. of Sir Joshua Paul, 1st bart., of Paulville, co. Carlow, and Ballyglan, co. Waterford, and by her (who d. 1845) he had issue,

1. GODDARD HEWETSON, his successor.
1. Sarah Elizabeth, b. 11 Jan. 1797; d. unm. 3 Sept. 1847.
2. Anne Dorothea, b. 29 Dec. 1800; d. unm. 17 Oct. 1873.
3. Ellen, b. 20 Jan. 1803; d. 26 Jan. 1810.
4. Dorothea Elizabeth, b. 4 Sept. 1805; d. unm. 9 July, 1884.
5. Elizabeth, b. 27 May, 1807; m. Cope Garnett, of Rhos-y-gar, Monkstown, co. Dublin, and d. 10 Aug. 1875. Mr. Garnett d. 20 April, 1875.
6. Katherine Wilhelmina, b. 4 Sept. 1809; d. unm. 20 Oct. 1818.
7. Ellen Susan Gertrude, b. 7 July, 1813; m. 2 Sept. 1840, John Herbert Orpen, of Stephen's Green, Dublin, LL.D., Barrister-at-Law, and d. 19 Dec. 1855, leaving issue (*see* ORPEN *of Ardtully*).

Rev. John Richards d. 1827, and was s. by his only son, GODDARD HEWETSON RICHARDS, of Grange (Monksgrange) and Pembroke Street, Dublin, Barrister-at-Law, b. 2 Nov. 1798; m. by licence 23 June, 1823, Dorothea Arabella, dau. of Edward Moore, of Mooresfort, co. Tipperary, and by her (who d. 15 Dec. 1886, aged 87 years and 10 months) he left at his decease, Dec. 1829, two sons,

1. JOHN FRANCIS, J.P., b. 1824, who s. his father, and d. unm. 28 Oct. 1860. 2. EDWARD MOORE, late of Monksgrange.
Seat—Monksgrange, Enniscorthy, co. Wexford.

RICHARDS OF ARDAMINE.

ARTHUR WILLIAM MORDAUNT RICHARDS, of Ardamine, co. Wexford, J.P. and D.L., High Sheriff 1906, Major late 2nd Dragoons (Scots Greys), b. Feb. 1860; m. 8 Sept. 1886, Elizabeth, 2nd dau. and co-heir of William Miller Kirk, of Ramsfort, co. Wexford.

Lineage.—SOLOMON RICHARDS, of York Street, Dublin, b. 1758, 2nd son of Goddard Richards, of Grange, and grandson of John Richards, of Solsbroough (*see these families*), was the celebrated Surgeon Richards, President of the Royal College of Surgeons, Member Irish Academy and Royal Dublin Society. He purchased the estate of Roebuck, co. Dublin, from Lord Trimleston, Ardamine, in co. Wexford, from Sir Thomas Roberts, Bart., and other estates in the same co. from Abel Ram, of Clonattin. He m. Elizabeth, dau. of Edward Groome, by whom (who d. 2 March, 1846) he had issue,

1. JOHN GODDARD, his successor.
2. Edward (Rev.), M.A. Trin. Coll. Camb., Rector of Clonallon for forty-seven years, Chancellor of the diocese of Dromore, b. 1797; m. 1824, Emily, dau. of Right Rev. James Saurin, D.D., Bishop of Dromore, and d. 12 Feb. 1883, aged 86, having had issue,
  1. Edward, m. 6 Dec. 1860, Frances Elizabeth, dau. of Edward Willoughby, of Bryan House, Blackheath, and has issue,
    (1) Edward Willoughby, Major Indian Army, b. 27 June, 1865.
    (2) James Saurin, Major Indian Army, b. 6 Dec. 1866; d. 25 March, 1905.
    (1) Amy Frances.
  2. James Saurin, an Officer in the Army, d. unm.
  3. Lewis (Rev.), D.D., Rector of Dungannon, co. Tyrone, resigned 1 Sept. 1907; m. 13 Feb. 1866, Charlotte Georgiana, dau. of Hon. and Rev. Charles Maude, and d. 6 Nov. 1910, leaving issue,
    (1) Charles Maude, b. 1867.
    (2) Lewis Saurin, b. 7 July, 1869; m. 23 Sept. 1903, Lucy Dennes, eldest dau. of Lovell Burchett Clarence, J.P., of Coaxden, Axminster.
    (1) Mary Alice, m. 1906, Rev. Kivas Collingwood Brunskill, Rector of Donaghhendry, Stewartstown, co. Tyrone, and d. 1911, leaving issue.
    (2) Mabel Emily.
  4. Henry Goddard, b. 1833; d. 20 June, 1901.
  5. William Saurin, b. 1886; d. 1889.
  6. Charles Frederick, Brigade Surg. Army Medical Staff (retired 1887), late of the 85th King's L.I., d. 30 Aug. 1906.
    1. Anne Catherine, m. 20 Sept. 1865, Percy Magan, of Kilcleagh Park, co. Westmeath, J.P. He d. 26 Dec. 1903, leaving issue (*see* MAGAN *of Clonearl*).
3. Solomon, of Ounavara, co. Wexford, J.P., b. 1798; m. 1st, Katherine, dau. of Rev. Henry Wynne, Rector of Templeshambo, co. Wexford, who d. 31 Oct. 1848, and 2ndly, 9 June, 1852, Florence, dau. of Rev. Henry Moore, Rector of Ferns, co. Wexford, who d. 1 Feb. 1873. He d.s.p. 14 Aug. 1862.
1. Mary Anne. d. unm.
2. Mary Anne, m. 31 Oct. 1824, Rev. Henry Wynne, Rector of Ardcolm, co. Wexford, and d. 21 April, 1867, leaving issue.

Surgeon Richards d. Oct. 1819, and was s. by his eldest son, JOHN GODDARD RICHARDS, of Ardamine and Roebuck, Barrister-at-Law, J.P. and D.L. co. Wexford, High Sheriff 1824; b. 1794; m. 1st, 16 July, 1821, Anne Catherine, dau. of Hon. Robert Ward, by whom (who d. 10 May, 1835) he had issue,

1. SOLOMON AUGUSTUS, his heir.
2. Robert Edward (Rev.), M.A. Camb., late Principal of the Gloucester, Bristol, and Oxford Training College, and Rector of Little Hinton, b. 1832; m. Oct. 1870, Katharine Maud, dau. of Rev. Edward Hayes Pickering, M.A., of Eton Coll., and d. 17 Oct. 1902, leaving issue,
  1. Robert Charles Pickering.
  2. Arthur Francis, m. Jan. 1903, Muriel, dau. of Col. Ward, of Reading.
  3. George Hamilton, m. April, 1906, Winifred, dau. of Major Garrard, of Ealing.
  4. Walter Hayes Pickering, Lieut. R.M.L.I.
  1. Kathleen Louisa Vere, m. April, 1897, Berkeley William Fairthorne, of The Manor House, Shrivenham, Berks.
3. William Hamilton, Prof. Staff Coll., Col. late 55th Regt. of Foot, formerly Instructor of Military Drawing and Surveying at Sandhurst, afterwards Chief Garrison Instructor at Lucknow, b. 29 Dec. 1833; m. Aug. 1858, Margaret Isabella, dau. of Major Samuel Hill Lawrence, 11th Hussars, V.C., and d. 18 April, 1895, leaving issue,
  1. Hamilton MacDonald, Capt. Border Regt.
  2. Charles de Clare. 3. John Goddard.
1. Louisa Elizabeth, m. April, 1843, George Maconchy, of Rathmore, co. Longford, and d. 1864, leaving issue.
2. Mary Anne, m. 5 Nov. 1850, Samuel Johnson, of Janeville, J.P. co. Wexford. He d. 2 April, 1883, aged 71, leaving issue.
3. Emily Sophia, m. April, 1849, Rev. Philip Walter Doyne, Vicar of Monart, co. Wexford. She d. 31 Dec. 1907. He d. 23 Oct. 1861, leaving issue (*see* DOYNE *of Wells*).

Mr. J. Goddard Richards m. 2ndly, 5 May, 1840, Mary, dau. of Sir William Rawson, by whom (who m. 2ndly, John Billingsley Parry, of Cumberland Street, Hyde Park, London, Barrister-at-Law, Q.C., and Judge of the County Court District No. 36, in England) he had no further issue. He d. 13 April, 1846, and was s. by his eldest son,

IRELAND.   Richards.

SOLOMON AUGUSTUS RICHARDS, of Ardamine, and Roebuck, B.A. Oxford, J.P., High Sheriff 1854, Capt. Wexford Militia, b. Aug. 1828; m. 10 June, 1856, Sophia Mordaunt, dau. of Rev. Bernard John Ward, of Bangor, co. Down, and d. 13 Jan. 1874, having by her (who d. 11 Aug. 1899) had three sons,
1. BERNARD JOHN GODDARD, his heir, b. 10 Aug. 1857; d. unm. 17 April, 1879.
2. ARTHUR WILLIAM MORDAUNT, heir to his brother.
3. Francis Augustus (*Bickenhall Mansions, W.*), b. 9 Aug. 1873; m. 7 July, 1908, Euphrosyne Muriel, dau. of Joshua Whitaker, of Palermo, Sicily, and has issue,
   Arthur Hubert Mordaunt, b. 17 July, 1910.
Seat—Ardamine, Gorey, co. Wexford.   Clubs—Naval and Military, S.W.; Kildare Street, Dublin.

RICHARDS OF MACMINE CASTLE.

JOHN LOFTUS RICHARDS, of Macmine Castle, co. Wexford, late Capt. 6th Batt. Rifle Brigade, formerly Lieut. Leinster Regt., b. 1875.

Lineage.—The ancestors of this family were settled in co. Wexford long previous to the usurpation of OLIVER CROMWELL.

THOMAS RICHARDS, of Park, the ancient seat of the family, had by Edith his wife two sons and four daus.,
1. John, of Park, m. May, 1699, Sarah Duzell, and by her had a dau., Mary, bur. 2 March, 1706. He d.s.p. and was bur. at St. Patrick's, Wexford, 29 Dec. 1712. By his will, dated 7 Oct. 1712, and registered 2 Oct. 1719, he bequeathed his estates to his nephew.   2. THOMAS, of whom below.
1. Mary, m. William Jones.   2. Elizabeth, m. John Morton.
3. Maria, m. Dec. 1680, John Jacob, of Sigginstown, co. Wexford.
4. Frances, m. 30 Oct. 1696, Samuel Crompton, of Polemaloe, now Pilltown, co. Wexford.
Thomas Richards was bur. at St. Patrick's, Wexford. His 2nd son,
THOMAS RICHARDS, of Rathaspick, co. Wexford (*jure uxoris*), m. Oct. 1680, Jane, dau. and co.-heir of Loftus Codd, of Castletown and Rathaspick, and by her (who was bur. 13 Jan. 1743) he had issue,
1. THOMAS, his successor.
2. John, bapt. 13 April, 1687,
3. Nicholas, bapt. 5 Dec. 1696, who had issue,
   1. Loftus, bapt. 3 April, 1729.   2. Thomas.
   1. Mary.   2. Anue.
4. William, hapt. 14 July, 1691,
5. Edward, who had two daus.,
   1. Jane.   2. Mary.
1. Katherine, bur. 30 Aug. 1685.
2. Jane, bapt. 2 April, 1686; m. Philip Hore, of Pole Hore.
3. Edith, m. Henry Hatton, of Clonard.
4. Margaret, m. Patrick Hogan, of Horetown.
5. Sarah, bapt. 17 July, 1689; m. 15 Jan. 1753, Brigadier-Gen. Edward Jones.
6. Mary, bapt. 23 June, 1694; m. Anthony O'Neill.
7. Frances, m. Joshua Tench, of Bryanstown.
Thomas Richards, whose will is dated 16 March, 1716, was bur. in St. Patrick's, Wexford, 20 March same year. His eldest son,
THOMAS RICHARDS, of Rathaspick, b. 1688; s. to Park and other estates under the will of his uncle 1713; m. Elizabeth, dau. of Joseph Orme, of Wexford, and by her (who d. 22 June, 1762) had issue,
1. THOMAS, of Rathaspick, b. 1722; m. 1776, Martha, dau. of Matthew Redmond, of Kilgowan, co. Wexford, and had two daus.,
   1. Martha, who s. to Rathaspick, and m. March, 1802, John Louis Gideon Ernest Von Prebenton, Count Willmsdorf, of the kingdom of Hanover, who assumed by Royal Licence, dated 8 May, 1802, the surname and arms of RICHARDS only. She d. 1855, leaving
      (1) Thomas William Frederick Von Prebenton Willmsdorf-Richards, of Rathaspick, d. unm.
      (1) Henrietta, m. Capt. Frederick Davrolles.
      (2) Anne, m. 1832, John Craven Mansergh, and d. 1844.
      (3) Elizabeth, d. unm. 1898.
   2. Elizabeth, m. 1802, Count van Limburg Stirum, of the Netherlands.
2. JOHN, of whom below.
3. George, m. Elizabeth, dau. of Sheppard French, of Wexford, ancestor of RICHARDS *of Glynn and Ballynahorna*, co. Wexford.
4. Loftus, who m. and had issue,
   (1) John.
   (2) Loftus, of Little Clonard, co. Wexford, Ensign 71st Foot, Capt. 1815, m. (licence dated 23 Feb. 1818) 1st, Elizabeth, widow of — Hatton, of Little Clonard. By his 1st wife he had issue,
      1. Henry, b. 1815; m. Fannie, 2nd dau. of Joseph Wrenfordsley, and had a dau. and an only son, Thomas Henry Hatton Richards, of British New Guinea.
      2. Thomas, officer 8th Hussars.
      1. Isabella.
5. James, ancestor of RICHARDS *of Ballynastud*, co. Wexford.
6. Richard, m. Susan, dau. of John Nunn, of St. Margaret's, co. Wexford, and d. May, 1769, leaving (with a dau. Susan, wife of John Hatchell) a son,
   John Nunn, m. 1st, Dec. 1784, Elizabeth, dau. of Oliver Fitzgerald, Great Britain Street, Dublin, and 2ndly, Frances, dau. of Thomas Gurly, of Carlow; d. 1821, leaving by his 1st wife two sons,

(1) William, Capt. 5th Dragoons, m. Caroline, dau. of Henry Gonne Molony, of Granaban, co. Clare, and d. 17 Sept. 1822, leaving a son, William, and a dau. Caroline.
(2) JOHN (Right Hon.), a Privy Councillor, and one of the Barons of the Court of Exchequer in Ireland, b. 1790; m. 1st, by licence, dated 7 Jan. 1815, Catherine, dau. of Henry Gonne Molony, of Granaban, co. Clare, and 2ndly, 1832, Christiana, dau. of Christopher James O'Brien. He d. 1872, leaving issue by his 1st wife only,
   1. John Henry, late Judge of County Court, Mayo, b. 1817; m. 1853, Lydia Gribble, dau. of Henry Scovell, of Ferny, co. Dublin. He d. 22 May, 1901, leaving issue;
      a. John Berwick, b. 1855; d. 1898.
      b. Henry George (Sir), Kt., K.C., of the Irish Bar, M.A., Chief Justice of the High Court, Allahabad, 1911 (*Residence—Allahabad, India*), b. 22 Sept. 1861; m. 1891, Frances Maud Lyster, dau. of the late Henry Mathew Smythe, of Barbaville, Collinstown, co. Westmeath, and has issue, three sons and three daus.
      c. Hubert O'Kelly, b. 1866; m. 1904, Dorothy Johnston.
      d. Whitmore Lionel, Barrister-at-Law, Lincoln's Inn (*Rathangan, Putney*), b. 1869; m. 1st, 1900, Ethel (who d. 1905), dau. of Right Hon. Joseph Chamberlain, M.P., and had issue,
         (a) Hilda Mary, b. 15 June, 1901.
      He m. 2ndly, 1908, Evelyn Mary, dau. of William B. Eastwood, of Kingswood, Englefield Green, Surrey (*see* EASTWOOD *of Leigh Court*), and has further issue,
         (a) Claud Irvine Whitmore, b. 3 Sept. 1909.
         (b) Lionel Henry, b. 6 Nov. 1910.
      a. Lydia Lestelle Christina Grace.
      b. Mildred, m. 1878, Capt. C. Harding.
      c. Emily Louisa.
      d. Mabel Whitmore, m. 3 March, 1887, Horace Fisher, son of C. Fisher, of Oakfield, Tamworth.
   2. William Frederick, m. Frances Jane, dau. of Joshua Nunn, of St. Margaret's, co. Wexford, and d. 1891, leaving an only dau., Anne, m. March, 1874, E. V. Westmacott.
   3. Arthur Oswald (Capt.), d. 5 May, 1909; m. Maria McMahon, dau. of Edward Reeves, of Platten Hall, co. Meath, and Fitzwilliam Street, Dublin. She d. 20 Feb. 1902. He d. leaving issue, a son,
      John William (7, *Lower Fitzwilliam Street, Dublin; Rath Greystones, co. Wicklow*), J.P., b. 9 April, 1857; m. 26 Dec. 1885, Adelaide Prudentia, dau. of William Roper, of Hazelbrooke, co. Roscommon, and 17, Upper Mount Street, Dublin, and has issue,
         (a) William Reeves, b. 16 Jan. 1891.
         (b) Edward Taylor, b. 13 July, 1900.
         (a) Juliet Adelaide.
         (b) Edith Marie, m. 7 Aug. 1909, Edward Martin Fitzgerald, and has issue.
         (c) Shelah Kathleen.
      1. Henrietta, m. Robert Piers.
      2. Elizabeth, m. Charles Rolleston, Q.C., Judge of County Court, Tipperary.   3. Catherine, m. Thomas Spunner.
      4. Charlotte, m. Thomas Rowley Symes.
Thomas Richards d. 9 Oct. 1768. His 2nd son,
JOHN RICHARDS, of Great Britain Street, Dublin, was called to the Bar in Trinity Term, 1750. He m. by licence, dated 24 Dec. 1767, Mary, dau. of George Lendrum, of Mowfield, co. Tyrone, by whom (who d. 1822) he had,
1. JOHN, m. Elizabeth, dau. of John Saunders, of Saunders Park, co. Wicklow, and d. 1844, leaving
   1. John William, of Baranagh, co. Mayo, and Tempo, co. Fermanagh, J.P., heir male and head of the family of RICHARDS *of Park*, 1810; m. 1846, Susan, dau. of Richard Augustus Saunders, D.L., of Largay, co. Cavan, and by her (who d. 1894) has, with other issue,
      John Richard Harlowen, Major R. West Surrey Regt., b. 4 Oct. 1849; m. Emily Anne, dau. of Edward Saunders, of Ballinderry, co. Tipperary (*see* SAUNDERS *of Kilavalla*).
      1. Mary Anne.   2. Melosina.
      3. Helena.
   2. GEORGE (Rev.), of whom hereafter.
   1. Hannah, m. — Hamilton, of Seaview, co. Donegal.
   2. Frances Anne, m. Rev. Thomas Skeleton.
John Richards (whose will, dated 22 Jan. 1787, was proved 18 Oct. 1788) d. 1788. His 2nd son,
REV. GEORGE RICHARDS, of Coolstuffe, ordained 1805, B.A. Trin. Coll. Dublin, 1802, M.A. Nov. 1832, appointed Prebendary of Coolstuffe, co. Wexford, 1823, b. 1781; m. 31 May, 1806, Margaret Sophia, dau. of James Johnstone, of Fir House, co. Dublin, and by her (who d. 1856) had issue,
1. JOHN, who purchased Macmine.
2. James (Rev.), Rector of Cloydagh, co. Carlow, and Treasurer of Leighlin, b. 8 May, 1810; m. 25 May, 1837, Ellen Sarah Johnston, widow of Mr. Crawford, who d. 30 April, 1869. He d.s.p. Nov. 1871.
3. George, b. 5 March, 1812; d. unm.
4. Francis Stephen, Lieut. Wexford Militia, b. 26 Dec. 1817; m. Oct. 1860, Letitia, dau. of Joshua Nunn, of Dawson Street, Dublin, and d.s.p. 18 Jan. 1870. She d. Aug. 1875.
1. Lucretia, d. unm. 1895.
2. Margaret Sophia Ellinor, d. unm. 1901.
3. Elizabeth Marianne, m. 22 June, 1854, Rev. George Ross, Rector of Killinick, co. Wexford, and d. 1 June, 1872.
4. Georgina, m. Nov. 1855, Rev. Thomas Hamilton, Whitfield, Rector of Ballybuskard, and d. 3 Aug. 1859.
Rev. George Richards d. April, 1873. His eldest son,

JOHN RICHARDS, of Macmine, co. Wexford, J.P., b. 2 Nov. 1808, purchased that property from the King family. He m. 27 June, 1838, Harriett Martha, dau. of Major Gledstanes, and by her (who d. 20 Sept. 1875) had issue,
1. George Gledstanes, Capt. Wexford Militia, b. 6 Aug. 1839; m. 30 June, 1868, Marian, dau. of Loftus Anthony Bryan, of Upton, co. Wexford, and d.v.p. 24 Feb. 1876, leaving issue,
 1. JOHN LOFTUS, heir to his grandfather, after the death of his uncle, Albert Garner Richards, and now of Macmine Castle.
  1. Harriet Marian, m. Capt. G. W. W. D'Arcy-Evans, Bedfordshire Regt., and has issue.
  2. Charlotte Ikon, m. M. A. Nixon.
 2. ALBERT GARNER, late of Macmine.
 3. Hampden Augustus, Capt. 44th Regt., b. 1 Aug. 1849; m. 1875, Dora, dau. of John McGowan, Inspector-Gen. of Lahore, East Indies, accidentally drowned while fishing in the river Slaney, 15 March, 1878.
 1. Anne Margaret Sophia, m. 2 Dec. 1868, Major James Jocelyn Glascott, Manchester Regt., 2nd son of William Madden Glascott, of Pilltown House, co. Wexford (see that family).
Mr. John Richards d. 14 Aug. 1881, and was s. by his second son,
 ALBERT GARNER RICHARDS, of Macmine Castle, co. Wexford, J.P., High Sheriff 1896, formerly Lieut. 22nd Foot, b. 22 Sept. 1840; m. 1869, Isabella Mary, dau. of William Barkus, of Tynemouth, Northumberland, and by her (who d. 14 April, 1888) had issue,
Lilian Garner, m. June, 1892, George Edgar Hughes, A.M. Staff.
He m. 2ndly, 15 Aug. 1896, Letitia Julia, youngest dau. of the late Capt. G. Pemberton-Pigott, of Slevoy Castle, co. Wexford (see that family). He d. 19 Jan. 1911, being s. by his nephew.
Seat—Macmine Castle, Enniscorthy, co. Wexford. Clubs—United Service and Royal St. George Yacht.

RICHARDSON OF ROSSFAD AND RICH HILL.

COL. JOHN MERVYN ARCHDALL CARLETON RICHARDSON, of Rossfad, co. Fermanagh, J.P. and D.L., High Sheriff 186?, Col. (retd) 3rd Batt. Royal Inniskilling Fusiliers, High Sheriff co. Tyrone 1885, and for co. Fermanagh 1888, b. 3 Dec. 1836; m. 22 Sept. 1880, Mildred Harriet, 3rd dau. of the late Gartside Tipping, of Rossferry, co. Fermanagh, and of Bolton-le-Moors, co. Lancaster, and has issue,

1. HENRY SACHEVERELL CARLETON, Lieut. Rifle Brigade, b. 18 Jan. 1883.
2. Guy Carleton, b. 4 May, 1885.
1. Jane Mary.
2. Mildred Cicely Carleton.

Lineage.—This family of RICHARDSON is descended from WILLIAM RICHARDSON, stated by Roberts, Ulster, in a confirmation of arms 22 May, 1647, to be descended from the ancient family of RICHARDSON of Pershore, co. Worcester. His 2nd son, MAJOR EDWARD RICHARDSON, of Legacorry, co. Armagh, M.P. for that co. 1661, High Sheriff 1665, m. Anne, only child and heir of Francis Sacheverell, of Legacorry, and Dorothy his wife (dau. and co-heir of Sir John Blennerhassett, Knt. Baron of the Exchequer). Mr. Francis Sacheverell was son of Francis Sacheverell, of Reresby, Leicestershire, who had a grant of Legacorry, 9 JAMES I (1611). By Anne his wife (who was b. 1632 and d. circa 1706) Major Richardson, who d. 1690, had issue,
1. William, of Legacorry, M.P. for co. Armagh 1689 and 1715, High Sheriff 1690, matriculated at Trin. Coll. Dublin, 22 Oct. 1677, b. in co. Armagh 1658; m. (licence dated 21 Feb. 1694-5) Elizabeth, dau. of the Right Hon. Sir Richard Reynell, Bart., Lord Chief Justice, and d.s.p. 1 June, 1727.
2. JOHN, of whom presently.
The youngest son,
 JOHN RICHARDSON, of Legacorry, alias Rich Hill, an Officer in the Army; b. in that co. 1663; matriculated at Trin. Coll. Dublin, 23 Jan. 1681; m. 1707-8, Anne, dau of William Beckett, Prime Serjeant-at-Law, and d. about 1744 (will dated 14 Sept. 1743), leaving issue,
1. WILLIAM, of Rich Hill, M.P., b. 1709; matriculated at Trin. Coll. Dublin, 13 Jan. 1725; High Sheriff 1737; m. 22 Oct. 1746, Isabella only dau. of Daniel Mussenden, Merchant of Belfast, and d. 16 Feb. 1758 (administration granted to his

only brother, Col. Henry Richardson, owing to the minority of his son, 10 March, 1758), having by her (who d. 29 Dec. 1753) had issue,
 1. WILLIAM, of Rich Hill, High Sheriff 1777, many years M.P. for co. Armagh; m. 1st, 9 May, 1775, Dorothy, dau. of Henry Munro, of Roe's Hall, co. Down, and by her (who d. 14 Sept. 1793) had no issue ; and 2ndly, 20 Oct. 1794, Louisa, dau. of Richard Magenis, of Waringstown, co. Down, and by her (who d. 29 Feb. 1860) had three daus., co-heirs,
  (1) Elizabeth, d. unm. 23 Dec. 1859.
  (2) Isabella, d. unm. 12 Aug. 1860.
  (3) Louisa, of Rich Hill, m. 22 Aug. 1832, Edmund Bacon, eldest son of Sir Edmund Bacon, 10th Bart., of Raveningham Hall, Norfolk, who was High Sheriff of co. Armagh 1835, and d.s.p. 14 April, 1852; she d.s.p. 23 Feb. 1881.
    1. Mary Anne.   2. Isabella, m. Edmund Baun.
    3. Louisa.
 2. HENRY (Col.), of whom hereafter.
 1. Hester, m. Feb. 1745, Rev. James Lowry, of Pomeroy, and d. 1771.
 2. Mary, m. 1740, Archibald, 1st Lord Gosford, and had issue.
His 2nd son,
 COL. HENRY RICHARDSON, of Rossfad, Lieut.-Col. 29th Regt.; entered the Army as cornet 8th Horse, Ligonier's, 1743 (see Historical Record 7th Dragoon Guards, p. 37), m. 1st, Catherine, eldest dau. of Samuel Perry, of Moyloukmore, co. Tyrone, which lady d.s.p. 1765, He m. 2ndly, 26 June, 1766, Jane, dau. and co-heir of Guy Carleton, of Rossfad, co. Fermanagh, and d. circa 1794 (admon. granted 31 May, 1794), having by her had issue a son,
 JOHN RICHARDSON, of Rossfad, Major Tyrone Militia, b. 4 May, 1768; m. 5 Sept. 1807, Angel, dau. of Col. Mervyn Archdall, M.P., of Castle Archdall (see that family), and d. 10 Dec. 1841, leaving by her (who d. 1817) an only son,
 HENRY MERVYN RICHARDSON, of Rossfad, D.L., High Sheriff 1834, b. 13 Dec. 1808; m. 22 Dec. 1834, Mary Jane, widow of John Johnston, of Crockna Crieve, co. Fermanagh, and 2nd dau. of Charles Ovenden, M.D., of Enniskillen, and Mayfield, Sussex, and d. 3 Aug. 1882, having by her (who d. 10 Dec. 1868) had issue,
 1. JOHN MERVYN ARCHDALL CARLETON, his heir.
 2. Charles William Henry, late Lieut. 73rd Regt., b. 2 Dec. 1840; d.s.p. 8 Nov. 1888.
 1. Jane Angel, d. unm. 11 June, 1902.
 2. Angel Catherine Charlotte, d. unm. 13 March, 1906.
 3. Emilie Margaret, m. 9 Feb. 1871, Rev. Robert Rigby Kewley, Vicar of Wingham, Kent, and has issue.
 4. Henrietta Martha Mervyn, m. 1 Aug. 1872, Capt. Charles Robert Barton, of The Waterfoot, J.P. and D.L., co. Fermanagh, and has issue (see that family).
Mr. Richardson s. on the death of his cousin Louisa, Mrs. Bacon, in 1881, to two-thirds of the Rich Hill estate.

Arms—Arg., on a chief sa. three leopards' heads erased of the first, a crescent for difference. Crest—An armed arm, holding in the hand a sword, thereon a bush of thorns ppr., the sword's hilt and pomel sa. Motto—Plus spinis quam ferro.
Seat—Rossfad, Ballinamallard, co. Fermanagh. Clubs—Sackville Street Dublin; and Constitutional, W.C.

RICHARDSON OF POPLAR VALE.

EDWARD JOHN RICHARDSON, of Poplar Vale, co. Monaghan, J.P. and D.L., High Sheriff 1902, Capt. and Hon. Major late 5th Batt. Royal Irish Fusiliers, b. 16 Sept. 1874; s. his father 1883.

Lineage.—SIMON RICHARDSON was granted 30 May, 1667, considerable lands in the cos. of Monaghan, of which he was High Sheriff 1664, Cavan, and Tyrone, part of which was jointly granted to Robert Burgh. By Katherine his wife, dau. of the before-mentioned Robert Burgh, he had issue,
1. Francis, m. Edith Nollcot, who d. 1721. He d. in Dublin, 1682, leaving two daus.,
 1. Katherine, m. 1704, her cousin, Francis Richardson, of Poplar Vale.
 2. Letitia, m. Ferdinand McVeagh, M.D.
2. HENRY, of whom hereafter.
3. EDWARD, m. Miss Coote, and had an only son, FRANCIS, who s. his uncle.
The 2nd son,
 HENRY RICHARDSON, of Poplar Vale, co. Monaghan, High Sheriff 1692 and 1700, attainted by the Parliament of JAMES II, m. 1st, Jane, dau. of Robert Maxwell, of Finnebrogue, co. Down, and had issue,
Edward, d.s.p.
Jane, m. Beaumont Astle, an Officer of Dragoons.
He m. 2ndly, Miss Gibson, of Ballykinlar, co. Down, and had nine daus., two d. unm.; three m. three Mr. Montgomerys; one m. Agmondisham Cuffe, of Castleinch, co. Kilkenny; one m. Mr. Watson; and another m. Rev. Oliver Douglas, Rector of Tigkallon, Diocese of Clogher, who d. 1738. He d. 1730, and was s. by his nephew,
 FRANCIS RICHARDSON, of Poplar Vale, Capt. of Dragoons, High Sheriff 1741; m. 1704, his cousin, Katherine, dau. of Francis Richardson (see above), and had issue,
1. Simon, b. 1705; d. unm. v.p. 1744.
2. EDWARD, his heir.
3. Christopher, b. 1711; d. 1776.

RICHARDSON OF LISBURN.

CHARLES HERBERT RICHARDSON, of Cedarhurst, co. Down, J.P. co. Antrim, b. 4 March, 1855; m. 26 Nov. 1884, Helen Noel, 2nd dau. of the late John Richardson, J.P. (by Emily Margaret his wife, only dau. of the late Rev. George M. Black, of Stranmills, co. Antrim), and grand-dau. of Jonathan Richardson, of Lambeg House, co. Antrim, M.P. for Lisburn (by Margaret his wife, only surviving dau. and heir of Alexander Airth, of Craigs, co. Dumfries), and great grand-dau. of John Richardson, of Lisburn (by Harriet his wife, dau. of James Greer, of Clanrole). He has issue,

1. DEREK CHARLES HOUGHTON, b. 28 June, 1887.
1. Ina Olive Vera, b. 18 Nov. 1885.
2. Violet Mabel, b. 4 April, 1892.

Lineage.—REV. JOHN RICHARDSON, Rector of Warmington, Warwickshire, whose will was proved 11 Feb. 1602, by his wife Margaret, who d. 1611, and whose will was proved 14 July, 1614, had issue,

1. Joseph, of Mollington, m. Joyce Gatestone, and had issue.
2. William.
3. ZACHERY, of Loughall, of whom presently.
4. John (Rev.), M.A., Rector of Loughgall, d. 1634; m. Elinor Foularton, and had issue,
   1. John, murdered 1641.
   2. Samuel, will proved 1660, had issue by his wife Anne, a dau., Elizabeth.
   1. Elizabeth.   2. Anne.
   3. Mary.   4. Elinor.
1. Joan.   2. Margery.

The 3rd son,
ZACHARY RICHARDSON, of Loughgall, had issue with a son, William, and other issue, a son,
JONATHAN RICHARDSON, of Eagarlongher, Loughgall, whose will was proved 1691. He had issue,
1. WILLIAM, of whom presently.
2. Samuel, who by his wife Philadelphia, had several children.

The elder son,
WILLIAM RICHARDSON, m. 1691, Mary Calvert, and d. 1716, having had issue,
1. JONATHAN, of whom presently.
2. William, m. Mary Nicholson, and had issue, Joseph, of Stranmore, d. unm.
1. Isabella, m. Thomas Nicholson.

The elder son,
JONATHAN RICHARDSON, b. 1681; d. 1737; m. Elizabeth Nicholson, and by her had with other issue (of whom Alice m. Nathaniel Richardson), a son,
JOHN RICHARDSON, of Lisburn, b. 1719; d. 1759; m. Ruth Hogg, by whom he had issue, James, d. unm., and a son,
JONATHAN RICHARDSON, b. 1756; m. Sarah Nicholson, and had issue,
1. JAMES NICHOLSON, of whom presently.
2. John, m. Harriet Greer, by whom he had issue,
   1. Jonathan, of Lambeg, J.P. cos. Antrim and Down, M.P. for Lisburn, b. 1804; d. 1894; m. 1828, Margaret Airth, by whom he had three daus., who all m. and had issue, and sons, Alexander, Philip, Smith and Edward, all of whom m. and three of whom had issue, an eldest son,
   John, of Lambeg, J.P. co. Antrim, b. 1833; d. 1899; m. 1862 Emily Black, and had issue,
   (1) Robert Airth, J.P. Warwickshire (*The Wolds, Snitterfield, Stratford-on-Avon*), Warwickshire Imp. Yeo., b. 1864; m. 1888, Evelyn Barbour, and has issue,
      a. Daphne, b. 1889.   b. Phyllis.
      c. Marjorie.   d. Yvonne Patricia.
   (1) Bertha.
   (2) Helen, m. C. H. Richardson, and has issue.
   (3) Laura, m. William Richardson, and has issue.
   (4) Ada, m. H. Mulliner, and has issue.   (5) Norah.
   (6) Kate, m. Dr. R. Shekelton, and has issue.
   2. James J., m. Charlotte Wakefield, and had issue, with three daus., a son,
   John, of Trewmount.
      1. Mary Louisa, m. John Smith, and had issue.
   3. Joseph, m. Mary Strangman, and had with other issue, Jonathan Joseph, who had issue, two daus.,
      (1) Mary, m. W. Christie-Miller.
      (2) Anne, m. A. Smith.
   1. Mary, m. Francis Smith, and had issue.

The eldest son,

---

4. Francis, b. 1720; d. 1733.
1. Dorothy, d. unm.

Capt. Richardson d. 1764, and was s. by his eldest surviving son,
EDWARD RICHARDSON, of Poplar Vale, b. 1707; m. 1732, Catherine, dau. of Thomas Baillie, of Dublin, and by her (who d. 1794) had issue,
1. FRANCIS, his heir.   2. Thomas, d. Aug. 1745.
3. Simon, b. 1742; m. 1779, Frances, dau. of John Clements, and had issue, Edith, m. Col. Shaw; d. 1818.
4. Edward, d. unm. 1785.
5. John, m. 1775, Miss Williams, and had a dau., Katherine; d. 1796.
6. Christopher, m. 1783, Susannah, dau. of Edward Dawson, of Kilcrow, co. Monaghan, and had,
   1. Edward, Lieut. 50th Regt., b. 1784, served during the Peninsular war; d. unm. 1819, of yellow fever, in Jamaica, serving with his Regiment.
   2. Francis, d. young.
   3. Samuel, b. 1787, Lieut. 11th Regt., killed in the Pyrenees, in command of the advanced picquet of his corps, in 1813.
   4. JOHN, who eventually s. to Poplar Vale.
   1. Catherine, d. 1888.   2. Elizabeth Eleanor, d. 1878.
   1. Mary Anne, m. Capt. Williams, R.F.
   2. Elizabeth, m. Rev. Edward Weeks, co. Cork.
   3. Catherine, m. John Bolton.   4. Dorothy, m. Mr. Ashton.
   5. Sarah, m. Pakenham Smyth.

Mr. Richardson d. 1761, and was s. by his son,
FRANCIS RICHARDSON, High Sheriff 1767, who m. 1767, Mary Anne, dau. of Lancelot Fisher, and had issue,
1. EDWARD, his heir.
2. Lancelot, b. 1771; d. 1785.
3. Francis Henry, d. 1785.   4. Henry, b. 1776; d. 1784.
5. George Arthur, b. 1776; d. unm.
6. William, d. 1784.
1. Katherine Elizabeth, d. unm.
1. Harriett Matilda, d. unm.

Mr. Richardson d. Oct. 1782, and was s. by his eldest son,
EDWARD RICHARDSON, of Poplar Vale, High Sheriff 1793, b. 1769; m. 1788, Alicia, dau. of Rev. Francis Lucas, of Coote Hill, and dying s.p. 3 Aug. 1845, was s. by his cousin,
JOHN RICHARDSON, of Poplar Vale. High Sheriff 1846, some time Capt. in the 40th and 83rd Regts.; served with distinction with the 40th Regt. in the Peninsular war; present at the battles of Toulouse, Orthes, Nivelle, Pyrenees, Vittoria, Salamanca, Badajoz, Cuidad Rodrigo, Busaco (medal and nine clasps), Waterloo (medal), also at Redinha, Gonezales, Heights of Vera, Olivinza and Pampeluna, and New South Wales and India; was twice severely wounded in the face and once in the knee. He was presented with a gold snuffbox by the officers of the 83rd, which has the inscription, " From the officers of the 83rd Depôt, to their friend and comrade, Captain John Richardson, in token of their admiration of his services as a soldier and esteem for his character as a man—March, 1840." He was b. 1794; m. 1st, 29 July, 1834, Elizabeth, dau. of James Wood Wright, of Gola, by whom (who d. 1836) he had issue,
1. Elizabeth, d. 1885.

He m. 2ndly, 23 Sept. 1840, Frances, dau. of George Jacson, of Barton, co. Lancaster, by whom (who d. 1854) he had issue,
1. EDWARD, his heir.
2. George Clements Kirkwood, Barrister-at-Law, b. 25 Sept. 1844 m. 1871, Edmundia, dau. of Chief Justice Harding, of Natal, and has a dau., Charlotte Susanna.
3. Henry Francis, b. 13 Dec. 1846; m. 1872, Anne Cecilia, dau. of Chief Justice Harding, of Natal, and has had issue,
   1. John Charles, b. 25 Feb. 1874; d. 18 July, 1876.
   2. George Clements Victor, b. 30 July, 1875; d. 13 June, 1876.
   1. Dorothy Eleanor, m. Stewart Erskine, of Johannesburg.
   2. Kathleen, d. young.
4. Thomas Ferdinand, J.P., Major and Hon. Lieut.-Col. 5th Batt. Royal Irish Fusiliers, b. 19 May, 1849; m. 1876, Victoria, dau. of Major Thomas Coote, J.P. and D.L. co. Monaghan, and d. 20 May, 1894, leaving issue,
   1. Thomas Coote, b. 18 Jan. 1880.
   2. Albert Victor John, b. 4 Sept. 1884.
   3. Henry Francis Edmund, b. 17 May, 1886.
   1. Catherine Horatio Elizabeth, m. 18 Nov. 1905, Capt. R. H. St. C. Coote Robinson.
   2. Rebecca Victoria, d. 1888.
   3. Charlotte Susanna, d. 1872.

Mr. Richardson d. 23 Aug. 1859, and was s. by his eldest son,
EDWARD RICHARDSON, of Poplar Vale, J.P. and D.L., High Sheriff 1871, sometime Lieut. 41st and 80th Regts., b. 26 June, 1843; m. 1873, Anna Charlotte, dau. of Robert Adams, M.D, Surgeon in Ordinary to the Queen in Ireland, by Mary his wife, dau. of Major Alexander Nixon Montgomery, of Bessmount Park, co. Monaghan. She d. 19 March, 1882, leaving issue,
1. EDWARD JOHN, now of Poplar Vale.
2. Robert Adams, b. 19 Dec. 1875; d. unm. in S. Africa, 26 July, 1899.
3. Charles Roger, b. 24 Feb. 1879.
4. George Clements Kirkwood, b. 31 Dec. 1880; accidentally drowned while night fishing on the Umzimkulu River, Natal, S. Africa, 1 Dec. 1910.
1. Frances Dorothy, d. young, 1877.
2. Mary Eleanor.

Mr. Richardson d. 9 July, 1883.

Seat—Poplar Vale, Monaghan.

I.L.G.

Richardson. THE LANDED GENTRY. 594

JAMES NICHOLSON RICHARDSON, of Glenmore, Lisburn, co. Antrim, b. 1782, and d. 1847, leaving by his wife A. Grubb, issue,
1. JONATHAN, his heir.
2. John Grubb, of Moyallon House, co. Down, and Bessbrook, co. Armagh, b. 1815; m. 1st, 1844, Helena, dau. of Richard Grubb, of Cahir Abbey, co. Tipperary, and by her had issue,
  1. James Nicholson, of Mount Caulfeild, Bessbrook, co. Armagh, J.P., M.P. for co. Armagh 1880-5 (*Reform Club*), b. 1845; m. 1st, 1867, Sophia, dau. of William Malcolmson, of Portlaw, co. Waterford, and 2ndly, 1893, Sarah, dau. of Samuel Alexander Bell, of Bellevue, Lurgan.
    1. Susan Helena.
  He m. 2ndly, 1853, Jane Marion (d. 4 Jan. 1900), dau. of Thomas Christy Wakefield, of Moyallon, co. Down, and Burtown House, co. Kildare, and Marianne Wilcox his wife, of Dungannon, co. Tyrone, and d. 1890, leaving issue,
  2. Thomas Wakefield, of Moyallon, co. Down, and Bessbrook, co. Armagh, J.P. cos. Down and Armagh, b. 7 Dec. 1857, m. 27 May, 1891, Hilda Sophie, dau. of the late John Charles Whitty, late Madras Army, and grand-dau. of the Ven. the Archdeacon of Kilfenora, co. Clare.
  2. Marion, d. unm. 1874.
  3. Anne Wakefield.
  4. Sarah Edith, m. 1896, George Williams.
  5. Jane Goff, m. 1891, George Pitt Holland Maynard, of Hawkhurst, co. Kent.
  6. Gertrude, m. 1886, Frederick Leverton Harris, M.P. for Stepney Div. of Tower Hamlets, of Camilla Lacey, Dorking, son of Frederick William Harris, J.P., of Devonshire Place, London.
  7. Ethel J., m. 1897, Henry Stephens Richardson, of Aberdelghy, Lambeg, co. Antrim, and has issue.
  8. Mary Kathleen, m. 30 Aug. 1910, Samuel Alexander Bell, of Belle Vue, Lurgan, youngest son of late Samuel Alexander Bell, J.P., of Lurgan.
3. James Nicholson, of Lissue, Lisburn, co. Antrim, b. 10 Aug. 1818; m. 18 March, 1841, Margaret Maria, dau. of B. Haughton, of Banford, Gilford, co. Down. She d. 4 Feb. 1848. He d. 4 May, 1896, having had issue,
  James Theodore, of Lissue, Lisburn, co. Antrim, J.P., D.L., b. 18 April, 1844; m. 20 Aug. 1873, Sarah Elizabeth, dau. of Edward Walker, of Springfield Mount, Leeds, and has issue,
    (1) James Herbert, b. 6 July, 1874.
    (2) Edward Theodore Haughton, b. 10 June, 1885.
    (1) Kathleen Marguerite, b. 25 Oct. 1875; m. 21 Oct. 1897, James Leslie Findlay, of Muirton, Craigellachie, Banffshire, and 10, Eton Terrace, Edinburgh, and has issue.
    (2) Mary Cecelia, b. 16 June, 1882.
    (3) Dorothy, b. 7 Dec. 1890.
  Annie, b. 5 Jan. 1842; m. Arthur Pim, and d. 23 July, 1894.
4. Thomas, m. and had issue.
5. William, m. and had issue.
6. Joshua, m. and had issue.
7. Joseph, m. and had issue.
The eldest son,
JONATHAN RICHARDSON, of Glenmore, Lisburn, co. Antrim, J.P., b. 26 June, 1811; m. 11 May, 1850, Louisa Jane, dau. of the late Maj. Richard Rollo Houghton, late 3rd Buffs, of Springfield, Lisburn, co. Antrim, and d. 2 Aug. 1869, having had issue,
1. Jonathan, b. 27 March, 1851.
2. Richard Rollo Houghton, b. 22 May, 1853; m. 1883, Anna, dau. of — Ellis, and d. 7 Jan. 1896, having had issue,
  Allan Graham.
3. CHARLES HERBERT, of Cedarhurst.
4. Ivan Owden, Capt. late 4th Hussars, b. 21 July, 1858; m. 1894, Helen, dau. of Edward Franks, and has issue,
  Eileen Louise.
5. Arthur Percy, b. 29 June, 1861; m. 14 Sept. 1887, Ethel Margaret, eld. dau. of Capt. Edmund Stronge, and has issue,
  1. Edmund. 2. Kenneth.
  3. Mervyn.
1. Maria Louisa, b. 4 Nov. 1859; m. 1881, David Henry Crailsheim, son of the late Edward Crailsheim, and has issue.
2. Florinda Maud, b. 27 March, 1861; m. 22 Aug. 1903, Wilson Ranson, F.R.C.S, of Ashburton, S. Devon, 4th son of J. Farrar Ranson, of Ingleby, Norwich.
3. Harriett Mabel, b. 27 Sept. 1865; m. 28 July, 1884, Stephen Perceval Maxwell, 2nd son of Maj. Robert Perceval Maxwell, of Finnebrogue, co. Down, and has issue (*see that family*).

Arms—Arg. on a fess engrailed per saltire az. and gu. between in chief a bull's head couped of the third and in base a galley ppr., four escallops, two in fess and two in pale or. Crest—A lion rampant arg. armed and langued gu., holding between the paws a laurel garland ppr. Motto—Virtute acquiritur honos.

Seat—Cedarhurst, Newtownbreda, co. Down.

STUART-RICHARDSON. *See* BURKE'S PEERAGE, CASTLESTEWART, E.

RIVERSDALE OF LISNEGAR. *See* ALCOCK-STAWELL.

ROBERTS OF ARDMORE.

MAJOR BYAM MARTIN LOVEDAY ROBERTS, of Ardmore, co. Cork, J.P., Major 3rd Batt. Royal Munster Fusiliers (ret.), b. 10 March, 1863; m. 31 August, 1909, Eileen Mary, dau. of Alexander McOstrich, J.P., of Eglantine, Cork.

Lineage.—ROBERTS, of Ardmore, co. Cork, first emigrated to America, and then settled in Ireland. He m. and had issue,
1. JOHN, his heir.
1. Jane, d. unm. 2. Sarah, m. Henry Cheney, M.D., of America.
3. Mary, m. — Bentley, and had Roberts and Mary, who both d. unm.
The son,
JOHN ROBERTS, of Ardmore, m. Sarah, 2nd dau. of John Lake, of co. Durham, and by her (who d. 8 April, 1810, aged 78) had issue,
1. John, d. unm. 2. RICHARD, his heir.
1. Mary, m. 1782, William Atkins, of Fountainville, co. Cork, and had issue.
Mr. Roberts d. 1795, and was s. by his son,
RICHARD ROBERTS, of Ardmore, j.P., b. 1751. m. 1st, Bridget, dau. and co-heir of William Norris, of Old Court, co. Cork, and by her (who d. 1794-5) had no issue. He m. 2ndly, Mary Anne Neville, dau. of Norcott D'Esterre, of Killura and Castle Henry, co. Clare, by his wife, a dau. of Harding Parker, of Hilbrook, and had issue by her,
1. JOHN, his heir.
2. Norcott D'Esterre, of Fitzwilliam Place, Dublin, m. 1841, Cherry, 2nd dau. of Col. Robert Torrens, M.P. for Bolton, by Charity his wife, dau. of Richard Chute, of Roxborough, co. Kerry, and had issue,
  1. Norcott D'Esterre, Lieut.-Col. late Loyal North Lancashire Regt., b. 5 Nov. 1846; d. unm. 7 Dec. 1902.
  2. Richard Torrens, d. unm. April, 1868.
  1. Cherubina Herbert D'Esterre, m. 6 Feb. 1869, Francis B. Chute, of Chute Hall, co. Kerry. He d. 1902, leaving issue (*see that family*).
  2. Jane, m. 4 Jan. 1866, Pearson Hill, only son of Sir Rowland Hill, K.C.B.
  3. Mary Anne, d. unm.
Mr. N. D. Roberts d. 1865, and his widow m. 2ndly, 1866, Gen. R. J. Stotherd, R.E.
3. Richard, Lieut. R.N., m. 1838, Jane, dau. of William Johnson, and sister of Noble Johnson, of Rockenham, co. Cork, and d. 1841, having had issue, one child,
  Richard, Major, late Capt. 9th Foot and Adjt. Kerry Militia, m. 23 Feb. 1867, Lucia Parker, 2nd dau. of Rev. W. Cotter Williamson, and had issue,
    (1) Richard Edwin, Capt. Cork Artillery.
    (2) Ivon D'Esterre, Capt. R.F.A., b. 3 July, 1879.
4. William D'Esterre, m. 1646, Christina M'Call, dau. of M'Call Browne, of Langtine, co. Ayr, and has issue,
  1. William D'Esterre. 2. Norcott D'Esterre.
  3. Richard.
  1. Christina M'Call.
  2. Minnie D'Esterre, m. Norman M'Leod.
  3. Jane. 4. Sarah Green.
  5. Anne Amelia Sherston. 6. Wilhelmina.
5. Abraham, d. unm.
1. Anne Eliza, m. 1816, William FitzWilliam Wentworth, Lieut. R.N.
2. Sarah, m. Sydenham Green, of Bristol, and d. 1869.
3. Marianne, m. William Maitland (son of John Maitland, of Eccles, co. Dumfries, M.P., brother of Lady Roberts, of Britfieldstown).
Mr. Roberts was s. by his son,
JOHN ROBERTS, of Ardmore, b. 1801, m. 1862, Anne, dau. of William Johnson, and sister of Noble Johnson, of Rockenham, co. Cork, and dying 1850, left issue,
1. RICHARD, late of Ardmore.
2. William D'Esterre, m. 21 Dec. 1866, Emily G. Villiers, dau. of Rev. Arthur Leman.
3. Norcott D'Esterre, Paymaster-in-Chief (retired) R.N.
4. John, d.
1. Sarah, d. unm.
2. Mary Anne D'Esterre, m. 1860, R. Hedges Evre White, jun., of Glengariffe Castle, co. Cork, and has issue (*see* WHITE *of Bantry*).
3. Eliza, d. unm.
The eldest son,
RICHARD WILLIAM ROBERTS, of Ardmore, co. Cork, J.P., b. 27 July, 1827; m. 24 April, 1856, Henrietta Sarah Dorman, eldest dau. of Robert Hedges Eyre White, of Glengariffe Castle, co. Cork. (by Charlotte Mary his wife, dau. and heir of Thomas Dorman, of Raffeen House, co. Cork), great-niece of the 1st Earl of Bantry (who d. 14 Feb. 1904). He d. 24 May, 1903, leaving issue,
1. John, b. 1857; d. unm. 19 Feb. 1905.
2. Richard Hedges Eyre (Rev), M.A., Trin. Coll. Dublin, Chaplain of Missions to Seamen, Cork, from 1901, formerly Rector of Ballinadee; m. 18 Aug. 1902, Shela Alice, dau. of R. W. C. Reeves, D.L., of Besborough (*see that family*), and has issue,
  1. Grace Vandeleur. 2. Shela.
3. BYAM MARTIN LOVEDAY, now of Ardmore.
4. Norcott D'Esterre, Capt. A.V.D., b. 9 Oct. 1872; m. 15 Sept. 1909, Eileen Elizabeth, only dau. of Thomas Beamish, M.D., J.P., of Castle View, Passage West (*see* BEAMISH *of Kilmalooda*).
1. Charlotte Frances, d. unm. July, 1891.
2. Anna Maud, d. unm. Feb. 1882.
3. Henrietta Sarah Vereker, d. an infant.
4. Henrietta Sarah Vereker, d. unm. 23 Oct. 1908.
Seat—Ardmore, Passage West, co. Cork.

ROBERTS OF DORMSTOWN CASTLE.

JOHN RICHARDS ROBERTS, of Dormstown Castle, co. Meath, J.P., b. 1838 ; m. 2 January, 1863, Matilda Barbara Eliza, eldest dau. of the late Capt. Richard Nugent Everard, of Randalstown House, co. Meath, and has issue,
1. THOMAS HERBERT EVERARD, b. 1870; d. 1902.
2. JOHN NUGENT.
  1. Grace.   2. Maude.
  3. Alice.
  4. Amy, d. 1909.

Lineage.—HENRY ROBERTS, of Hafodyworn, in Clynnog, m. 1728, Mary, 2nd dau. and co-heir of John Parry, son of Robert Parry, of Penrallt, in Clynnog, who m. Margaret, 2nd dau. and co heir of Thomas Williams, of Glangwna, who was descended from Owen Gwynedd, Prince of North Wales, who d. A.D. 1169. Henry Roberts, by Mary Parry his wife, had a son,

THE VEN. JOHN ROBERTS, Rector of Llanbedrog, co. Carnarvon, Archdeacon of Merioneth, who m. 1761, Katherine, dau. and heir of John Jones, of Tanrallt and Hendre, and had issue,
1. Thomas (Rev.), Rector of Llarmore, m. Anna Diana, dau. of Rev. E. Owen.
2. Henry, a Col. in the Army.
3. William (Rev.), Rector of Llanbulan, m. Margaret, dau. of Capt. Goddard, of Holyhead and Falmouth.
4. JOHN, of whom presently.
5. Richard Worthington, Surgeon-Gen. A.R., Woolwich, m. Sophia Mary, dau. of Sir George Bolton.
  1. Mary, m. Rev. P. Williams.
  2. Catherine, m. Rev. C. Chester.   3. Margaret.
  4. Ann.   5. Ellen.
  6. Jane.

The 4th son,

REV. JOHN ROBERTS, Rector of Rathore, m. Anna Maria, dau. of David Thompson, of Oatlands, co. Meath, and had issue,
1. THOMAS LEWIS, of Dormstown Castle.
2. John.
3. David, m. Miss Nightingale.
4. Anna, m. Dugall Campbell.

His eldest son,

THOMAS LEWIS ROBERTS, of Dormstown Castle, co. Meath, J.P., b. 1808 ; m. 6 Aug. 1836, Matilda, dau. of Robert Hewetson Richards, Assistant-Barrister, co. Wexford (see RICHARDS of Monksgrange), and had issue,
1. JOHN RICHARDS, now of Dormstown Castle.
2. William Edward, of Hendre, Killiney, co. Dublin, Lieut.-Col. late 2nd Batt. Duke of Cornwall's Light Infantry, B.A. Trin. Coll. Dublin, b. 15 April, 1841 : s. in 1897, his aunt Marianne, widow of Rev. William Birch-Wolfe, of Wood Hall, Essex, which property has now been sold.
3. Thomas Herbert, m. 1871, Sarah, dau. of T. M. Daly, Member in the Dominion Parliament of Canada for co. Perth, and has issue,
  1. Thomas Lewis.   2. William.
  3. Howard.
  1. Helen Maude.
1. Anna.

Mr. Roberts d. 1880, and was s. by his eldest son, the present JOHN RICHARD ROBERTS, of Dormstown Castle.

Arms—Vert, on a chevron, between three eagles displayed with two heads or, an estoile sa. Crest—An eagle's head couped or charged with an estoile sa. Motto—Eu ncr a volant.

Seat—Dormstown Castle, near Navan.

CRAMER-ROBERTS OF SALLYMOUNT.

MARMADUKE WILLIAM COGHILL CRAMER-ROBERTS, of Sallymount, co. Kildare, Belmore, co. Westmeath, and Doraville, co. Tyrone, J.P. and D.L., High Sheriff co. Kildare 1889, b. 19 May, 1864 ; m. 22 Sept. 1885, Anna Graves Fetherstonhaugh, only child of the late John Fetherstonhaugh Lowry, of Belmore House, co. Westmeath, and of Lime Hill and Doraville, co. Tyrone (see LOWRY of Pomeroy), and has issue,

Anna Dorothea Alexandra Lowry.

Lineage—BALTHAZAR CRAMER, born in Germany, came to Ireland in 1629 and became col. of a regiment. He had a confirmation of his Arms with an augmentation in consideration of his services from Dr. Roberts, Ulster, in 1646. He d. 23 Nov. 1659 (funeral entry). His will, dated 9 Dec. 1650, was proved 7 Nov. 1660. He left with two daus., three sons,
1. TOBIAS his heir.   2. John.
3. Benjamin.

TOBIAS CRAMER made a free denizen of Ireland 28 May, 1639, Sheriff Dublin 1653, of Ballyfoyle, co. Kilkenny, High Sheriff thereof 1661 ; bur. in St. James' Church, Dublin (will proved 1684. He m. lic. 31 July, 1640, Mary Sterne, and left issue,
1. BALTHAZAR, of whom hereafter.   2. Tobias.
1. Hester, m. Sir John Coghill, of Coghill Hall, co. Dublin, knighted June, 1686. He d. 1699, leaving two sons and a dau.,
  1. Marmaduke (Right Hon.), P.C., M.P., LL.D. Dublin University, Chancellor of the Exchequer, Ireland, 1735-9, d. unm.
  2. James, LL.D. m. Mary Pearson, of Rathmore, co. Meath, and d. 1734, leaving an only child, Hester, who d.s.p., leaving her property to Sir John Cramer, Bart., having m. 1st, 1787, Charles, Earl of Charleville, who d.s.p. ; 2ndly, Major J. Mayne, of Richings, Bucks, M.P., Newport, who, by Royal Licence, assumed the surname of COGHILL, 1779, and was created a baronet of Great Britain 1781, and d.s.p. 1785, when the title became extinct (see BURKE'S Extinct Baronetage).
  1. Hester, m. her cousin, Oliver Cramer (see below).
2. Deborah, m. Capt. Arthur Webb, of Webbsboro', co. Kilkenny.

The elder son,

BALTHAZAR CRAMER, of Ballyfoyle, co. Kilkenny, High Sheriff 1683, b. 1614, matriculated Trin. Coll. Dublin, 4 June, 1660 ; d. 1705 ; m. 1st, Sarah, dau. of Lieut.-Col. Oliver Jones, and had issue, three sons and a dau. He m. 2ndly, Elizabeth, widow of Rev. Hugh Drysdale, D.D., dau. of — Fox, by whom he had no issue. She d. 1723.
1. Tobias, b. 1666, matriculated Trin. Coll. Dublin, 17 June, 1684, d.v.p.
2. OLIVER, of whom presently.
3. Ambrose, High Sheriff of Cork 1723, Mayor 17.. ..usanna Browne, of Cork, a.. ... ...scend the CRAMERS of Rathmore ..

The 2nd se.. ...
OLIVER C......R, of Ballyfoyle, co. Kilkenny, High Sheriff of ... co. 1714, m. 1700, his cousin Hester, mentioned above, and had issue,
1. Balthazar, d. 18 June, 1741, having m. 23 April, 1724, Hon. Judith Butler, only dau. of Brinsley, 1st Viscount Lanesborough, and by her (who d. 13 May, 1749) had issue, three sons and a dau.,
  1. John (Sir), created a baronet 1778, assumed the name of COGHILL, pursuant to the will of his great uncle, Right Hon. Marmaduke Coghill ; m. Maria, dau. of Right Rev. Josiah Hort, Archbishop of Tuam, and had issue (see BURKE'S Baronetage, COGHILL, Bart.).
  2. Oliver Coghill, of Coghill Hall, m. 1st, 1758, Elizabeth Humphreys, who d. 7 Sept. 1758 ; 2ndly, March, 1761, Miss Waring, of Dublin ; and 3rdly, Jane Holland, of Shrewsbury, by whom (who d. 9 Dec. 1771) he had a dau., Jane, sole heir, who m. George Mowbray, of Ford, co. Durham, and left issue.
  3. Marmaduke (Rev.), of Sallymount, co. Kildare, b. 1739 ; m. 24 Aug. 1763, eldest dau. of Thomas Taylor, Alderman of Dublin. His son,
    John (Rev.), of Sallymount, co. Kildare, assumed, by Royal licence, the additional surname and the arms of ROBERTS, 9 Oct. 1801, having m. 2 Jan. 1794, Martha (b. 20 Sept. 1767), eldest dau. of Sir Thomas Roberts, Bart., of Glassenbury, Kent (see BURKE'S Baronetage), and had five sons and a dau.,
      1. Marmaduke Coghill CRAMER-ROBERTS, of Sallymount, co. Kildare, D.L., d. 22 Sept. 1852, having m. 28 Oct. 1834, Georgina, dau. of Benjamin Torin, of Egham, Surrey. She d. 12 March, 1848. He had issue,
        a. Charles Torin, of Sallymount, J.P., Lieut. H.L.I. b. 11 Feb. 1837 ; d. 16 Oct. 1877 ; m. 4 July, 1861, Lizzie, dau. of James Alexander Hamilton, of Kildonan, co. Dublin, and had issue,
          (a) MARMADUKE WILLIAM COGHILL, now of Sallymount.
          (b) Cecil John, b. 6 Jan. 1865 ; d. Aug. 1894.
          (c) Charles Evelyn, b. 21 March, 1866.
          (d) Claud Jocelyn, b. 13 April, 1868 ; d. unm. 11 April, 1901.
        b. Marmaduke Coghill, Lieut. R.N., b. 17 Aug. 1841 ; m. Eliza, dau. of Robert Tooth, of Swift's Park, Cranbrook, Kent, and d.s.p. 13 April, 1877.
        c. Henry Thomas, late Capt. 36th Regt., b. 1 Feb. 1845 ; m. 30 July, 1873, Louisa, only dau. of the late Henry Justice, of Hinstock Hall, Shropshire, D.L., and has issue,
          (a) Francis William Henry, b. 7 April, 1875.
          (b) Henry Justice, b. 22 Feb. 1879.
          (c) Marmaduke Torin, Lieut. 4th Gurkha Rifles, Indian Army, b. 14 Dec. 1880.
          (a) Constance Caroline.
          (b) Amy Isabel.
          (c) Gladys.
        d. John Walter, b. 23 Feb. 1848 ; m. 23 Dec. 1871, Kate Maver, dau. of John Watson Harris, of New York, and by her (who d. 25 March, 1887) has issue,
          (a) John Henry.
          (a) Evelyn Kate.   (b) Kathleen Amy.
          (c) Ethel.   (d) Nora Cavendish.
          (e) Muriel Patricia.   (f) Sybil Hort.

a. Georgina Hester Mary Anne, *m.* 1st, 6 Nov. 1860, her cousin, Frederick Ponsonby Cramer-Roberts, Capt. 2nd Grenadiers, Bombay Infantry, who *d.* 29 June, 1865 leaving an only child, Marian Edith (*see below*). She *m.* 2ndly, Col. William Dundas Couchman, of Bengal L.I.
b. Amy Harriet, *m.* 30 Nov. 1870, William Robert Aylmer Haly, Lieut. 3rd Buffs, son of late Gen. Sir William O'Grady Haly, K.C.B. He *d.s.p.* 12 Feb. 1876.
c. Marian Martha, *m.* 16 Oct. 1873, Edmond Burdoe, 2nd son of Col. Burdoe Wilkinson, and has issue, Dermot, and Claire May, *m.* (as his second wife), 29 June, 1893, Sir William Hollingworth Quayle-Jones (from whom he obtained a divorce, 1905).

2. John, Lieut.-Col. D.I., R.I.C., A.D.C. to Governor of Malta, *b.* 1796 ; *m.* 12 Nov. 1828, Marian, dau. of David Ross (by Marian his wife, dau. of Col. Gall), and *d.* 4 March, 1864, having had issue,
a. John David, *b.* Nov. 1832 ; *m.* Aug. 1858, Elizabeth, dau. of John Beaseley, of Chapel Crampton, and had a son, who *d.* in infancy.
b. Frederick Ponsonby, *b.* 25 May, 1835 ; *m.* his cousin (as above), and has a dau., Marian Edith, *m.* 1889, Capt. Cecil Hornby, of Cheshire, and has issue.
c. Herbert William, *b.* May, 1837 ; *d. unm.* 185-.
d. Francis Alexander Randal (Right Rev.), Bishop of Nassau, 1878, Suffragan Bishop of Manchester. 1887. *b.* 3 Dec. 1840 ; *m.* 1st, 29 July, 1867, Anna Maria Charlotte, dau. of Baron Alexander de Steiger, and *d.* 9 Feb. 1901, having by her (who *d.* 17 April, 1880) had issue,
   (*a*) Herbert Alexander, *b.* 18 May, 1870 ; *m.* Aug. 1893, Muriel, only child of Fielder King.
   (*b*) Eric Charles, *b.* 17 June, 1871 ; *d.* 1879.
   (*a*) Evelyn Emily.
He *m.* 2ndly, Isabel, dau. of Rev. — Faithful. He *d.* 9 Feb. 1901.

3. Thomas, *m.* Mary, dau. of — Gowan, and *d.* 3 Feb. 1847, having had issue, two sons, Francis and Marmaduke, who both *d.s.p.*

4. Walter Randal (Rev.), Vicar of Edwardstone, Suffolk, *b.* 16 Oct. 1802 ; *m.* 8 Aug. 1834, Martha Hewitt, dau. of David Mitchell, of Doon, and *d.* 21 Jan. 1 , having issue, two sons and a dau.,
a. Charles John, of Bicester House, Oxon, Lieut.-Col. 9th Regt., *b.* 28 Aug. 1834 ; *m.* 3 Feb. 1869, Frances Templer, dau. of Richard Duckworth Dunn, late Queen's Bays, and *d.* Sept. 1895, leaving issue,
   (*a*) Walter Evelyn, Capt. Norfolk Regt., served in S. Africa, and wounded at Paardeburg, 1900, *b.* 11 Oct. 1872 ; *m.* 28 Dec. 1899, Geraldine, dau. of late Col. George Webber, C.B. (*see* WEBBER *of Lockfield*), great-grand-dau. of George, 3rd Earl of Kingston, and has issue,
      Judith Amy Fitzgerald, *b.* 13 May, 1910.
   (*b*) Frank William, *b.* 26 June, 1882.
   (*a*) Isabella Catherine, *m.* 24 Sept. 1910, Major George Holme Arbuthnot, Royal Berks Regt., only son of Major-Gen. Henry Thomas Arbuthnot, C.B.
b. Clayton, *b.* 20 March, 1836.
a. Amy Catherine.

5. William Butler, of Thornton, co. Kildare, Col. Bengal Cavalry, *b.* 12 May, 1808 ; *d.s.p.* 28 July, 1870, having *m* 8 July, 1844, Elizabeth, dau. of Robert Borrowes, of Gilltown, co. Kildare.

1. Amy, *m.* 1838, Roger Chambers Walker, Q.C., of Rathcarrick, co. Sligo, who *d.* 1854, leaving issue. She *d.* May, 1874.

1. Catherine, *m.* 4 April, 1748, Ralph Smyth, of Fieldstown, co. Westmeath.
2. Oliver (will proved 1754), *m.* Deborah, dau. of Henry Rudkin, of Tinnegarney, co. Carlow, and had a son and two daus.,
a. Coghill, *m.* 1st, 4 June, 1758, Elizabeth, dau. of Matthew Humphrey ; 2ndly 22 March, 1764, — Waring.
a. Hester, *m.* 1st, 19 Feb. 1754, Charles Tisdall, of Charlesfort ; 2ndly, 1767, as his second wife, Nicholas Forster.
b. Mary.

Arms (of ROBERTS, Royal licence 1801, H. Coll.)—Per chevron sa. and az., on a chevron or, three mullets pean. *Crest*—An eagle erminois, wings elevated arg. each charged with a trefoil slipped vert, gorged with a collar az. Of CRAMER, Ulster's Office, confirmed, to Balthazar, Kramer by Roberts, Ulster, in 1646).—Per fess indented az. and or, in chief two fleur-de-lis of the second, a cantone erm. *Crest*—A fleur-de-lis between a pair of wings expanded or penned arg. *Mottoes*—Over the crest "Mors ultima linea rerum," beneath the arms "Inevitabile fatum."

Seats—Sallymount, Prannockstown, co. Kildare, and Deraville, Broughderg, co. Tyrone.

ROBERTS OF KILMONEY ABBEY.

THE REV. WILLIAM RALPH WESTROPP ROBERTS, Fellow of Trinity Coll., Dublin, M.A., *b.* 6 May, 1850; *m.* 4 July, 1882, Lydia Mary, youngest dau. of George Hodder, of Fountainstown, co. Cork, and has issue,
1. Wilhemina Dorothy Maud.
2. Monica Katherine.

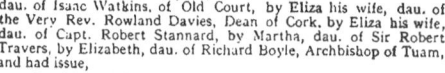

Lineage.—HODDER ROBERTS, of Bridgetown, *b.* 11 Oct. 1693, eldest son, by his 2nd marriage, of RANDAL ROBERTS, of Brightfieldstown (*see* BURKE's *Peerage and Baronetage*, ROBERTS, Bart. *of Brightfieldstown*), *s.* to the Bridgetown and other estates in co. Cork ; *m.* 1718, Jane, dau. of Isaac Watkins, of Old Court, by Eliza his wife, dau. of the Very Rev. Rowland Davies, Dean of Cork, by Eliza his wife, dau. of Capt. Robert Stannard, by Martha, dau. of Sir Robert Travers, by Elizabeth, dau. of Richard Boyle, Archbishop of Tuam, and had issue,

1. Randal, of Bridgetown *m.* 29 Dec. 1739, Mary, dau. of John Kift, and left an only child and heir,
   Catherine, who *m.* Richard Martin, of Clifford, and had an only child and heir, Mary Martin, who *m.* John Southcote Mansergh, whose descendants possess the Bridgetown estates. (*See that family.*)

2. Watkins, of Shanbally, *m.* 29 Dec. 1743, his cousin, Martha, dau. of Rev. George Synge and Elizabeth his wife, dau. of Randal Roberts, and *d.* 7 Jan. 1744, leaving by her (who *d.* 1792),
1. Hodder, of Shanbally, *b.* 15 Aug. 1749, Lieut. in the 4th Black Horse; *m.* 20 July, 1777, Elinor, dau. of Ambrose Mason, by Jane, dau. and heir of Robert Chudleigh and Jane Roberts, and *d.* 1825, leaving two sons,
   (1) Watkins, of Shanbally, *d.* 1841.
   (2) Hodder William, in 85th Regt., *b.* 1785, *m.* 1809, Jane, dau. of the Rev. Michael Fitzgerald and Jane Patterson his wife, niece to Lord Chief Justice Patterson, and *d.* Jan. 1854, having had issue by her,
      1. Michael Hodder, *d. unm.* 1845.
      2. Hodder George, *d. unm.* 1846.
      3. William Watkins Synge, *d. unm.* 1850.
      4. George Synge, Surgeon, R.N., *d. unm.* 1847.
      5. Watkins Charles (Rev.). 6. Ralph.
      7. Charles, Lieut. R.N., *d. unm.* 1851.
      1. Martha, *m.* 8 Aug. 1838, Col. John Jauncey, 10th Regt.
      2. Jane.
      3. Elizabeth Adelaide, *d. unm.* 21 March, 1907.
2. Michael, *d. unm.* 11 Oct. 1769.
3. George Synge, *b.* 13 Oct. 1750 ; *d.s.p.* 1826.
4. William, *d. unm.*
1. Martha, *d. unm.*
2. Elizabeth, *m.* 20 July, 1773, Michael Busteed Westropp, and had issue (*see* WESTROPP *of Attyflin*).
3. MICHAEL, of whom presently.
4. William, Capt. 4th Black Horse, *d.s.p.*
1. Elizabeth, *m.* 19 April, 1742, William Freeman, of Glennanore, co. Cork, and had issue.
2. Martha, *m.* 2 Sept. 1738, William Verling, Recorder of Cork, and had issue.
3. Arabella, *d. unm.*
4. Harriett, *m.* 14 Feb. 1758, Arthur Dillon, of Quartertown, co. Cork.

Mr. Hodder Roberts *d.* 6 March, 1747. His 3rd son,
MICHAEL ROBERTS, of Kilmoney Abbey, *s.* on the death of his uncle, Michael Roberts, of Glanworth, to part of the lands of Glanworth and to other estates in co. Cork, by will dated 1 April, 1741. He *m.* 14 July, 1750, Mary, dau. and heir of Thomas Gabbett Spiers, and had issue,
1. MICHAEL, his heir.
2. William, *m.* Elizabeth, dau. of Rev. Joseph Poulter and *d.* 19 Dec. 1826, leaving by her (who *d.* 29 Jan. 1811),
   1. Michael, of Mount Rivers, co. Cork, J.P., *m.* 31 Aug. 1826, Frances, 2nd dau. of Charles Hill, of St. John's, co. Wexford, and had issue,
      (1) William Poulter, *b.* 7 June, 1827 ; *d.s.p.*
      (2) Charles Hugh, *b.* 11 June, 1829 ; *d.s.p.* 1902.
      (3) Michael Hodder Joseph, *b.* 8 April, 1831.
      (4) Thomas Randal, *b.* Jan. 1835.
      (5) George John, Lieut. R.N., *b.* 6 Feb. 1839.
      (6) Poulter Benjamin, *b.* 28 Sept. 1840.
      (7) Francis Henry Stratford, *b.* 28 March, 1842.
      (8) Stratford Canning, *b.* 10 Nov. 1843.
      (9) Richard Gabbett Spiers (*Oak Mount, Crofts Lea Park, Ilfracombe*), *b.* 31 Dec. 1845 ; *m.* 1st, 20 Feb. 1884, Annie Pelah, dau. of James Kendrick, of Mallow, co. Cork. She *d.s.p.* He *m.* 2ndly, Jemima Aitken, dau. of William Miller, Collector of Customs, H.M.C.S., and has issue,

IRELAND.   Robertson.

1. Michael Rookherst, b. 24 Oct. 1894.
2. Richard Arthur, b. 24 Aug. 1907.
(1) Mary Jane.   (2) Eliza Letitia.
2. Randal, d. young.
1. Elizabeth, m. 28 May, 1811, John Dillon Croker, formerly of Quartertown, co. Cork, and had issue.
2. Letitia Jane, m. 25 May, 1815, George Culloden Frend, and had issue,
3. Abigail, m. 11 Sept. 1821, Rev. Benjamin Williamson, of Old Dromore, co. Cork, and had issue.   4. Mary.
3. Thomas.   4. Hodder.
1. Mary.
2. Jane, m. Hugb Hovell Farmar (see FARMAR of Bloomfield).
Mr. Michael Roberts was s. by his eldest son,
MICHAEL ROBERTS, of Kilmoney Abbey, m. 1 May, 1781, Lydia, dau. and heir of Theobald Pepper, of Moxta, co. Tipperary, by Elizabeth Westropp, of Curraghbridge, his wife (see PEPPER of Ballygarth), and had issue,
1. MICHAEL, his heir.
2. Pepper, of Moxta, m. 19 Aug. 1817, Charlotte Shadwell, and d.s.p.
1. Mary, m. 3 Oct. 1814, Major John Black, a distinguished officer of the 4th Regt.
2. Jane, m. 7 Jan. 1818, Capt. George Garvey, R.N., of Thornvale, King's Co., and had issue.
3. Elizabeth, m. 8 July, 1816, John Halburd.
Mr. Michael Roberts was s. by his eldest son,
MICHAEL ROBERTS, of Kilmoney Abbey, Capt. North Cork Regt., m. 15 April, 1815. Elizabeth, dau. of Rev. William Stewart, of Wellbeld. co. Cork, and had issue,
1. MICHAEL, of Kilmoney Abbey, Senior Fellow of Trin. Coll. Dublin, b. 10 May, 1817 ; m. 1851, Kate, now of Kilmoney Abbey, dau. of John Drew Atkin, of Castle Park, co. Dublin, and Merrion Square, and d. 3 Oct. 1882, having had issue,
1. MICHAEL RANDAL, b. 1861.   2. John Drew, b. 1863.
3. Walter Theobald Pepper, b. 1868.
1. Georgina.   2. Katherine.
3. Lydia.   4. Florence Susan.
2. William (Rev.), Senior Fellow of Trin. Coll. Dublin, b. 10 May, 1817 (twin with his elder brother), m. 7 June, 1849, Wilhelmina Augusta, dau. of Ralph Westropp, of Meadstown, co. Cork (see WESTROPP of Attyflin). She d. 21 June, 1887. He d. 24 Dec. 1884, having had issue,
1. WILLIAM RALPH WESTROPP (Rev.), of Kelston, Stillorgan, co. Dublin.
2. Michael Theodore, b. 21 May, 1851 ; m. April, 1886, Ellen Mary, dau. of the Rev. Dr. Welldon, and sister of Right Rev. Bishop Welldon.
3. Ralph Augustus, b. 14 May, 1854 ; m. Aug. 1889, Julia Isabel, youngest dau. of James Scott, of Ballygannon, co. Wicklow.
4. Charles Westropp (Rev.), b. 1857, m. 16 June, 1885, Cornelia Jane Florence, dau. of Hodder Westropp, of Rookhurst. co. Cork (see WESTROPP of Attyflin). She d.s.p. 7 June, 1898.
3. Henry Pepper.
4. Pepper, formerly Capt. 4th Regt., d.s.p. 1900.
5. John, d. unm.
6. Hodder, Lieut.-Col. in the co. Derby Militia, formerly Lieut. 4th Regt., m. 1854, Jane, dau. of Richard Walker, and had issue,
1. Herbert Hodder.   2. Augustus Stewart, d.s.p.
1. Ada Jane.
2. Agnes, m. 1879, John H. Platt.   3. Evelyn Alice Jane.
4. Helen May, m. 28 May, 1884, Samuel Ratcliffe Platt, of Werneth Park, Lancs., and has issue (see PLATT of Gorddinog).
5. Bessie Helena.   6. Gertrude.   7. Beatrice.
1. Elizabeth Townsend, m. 12 Jan. 1843, George Hodder, of Fountainstown, co. Cork, and had issue (see that family).
2. Lydia Mary, m. 3 Nov. 1842, Ralph Westropp, of Ravenswood, co. Cork, and had issue (see WESTROPP of Attyflin).
Mr. Michael Roberts d. 1862, and was s. by his eldest son.

Arms—Az., on a chevron arg., cotised or, three mullets of six, points pierced sa. Crest—On a mount vert, an eagle displayed az., wreathed round the neck with ivy ppr. Motto—Post funera virtus.
Residence—Kelston, Stillorgan, co. Dublin.

ROBERTSON OF HUNTINGTON CASTLE.

HERBERT ROBERTSON, of Huntington Castle, co. Carlow, and Hasketon Manor, Woodbridge, and 36, Bedford Square, W.C., Barrister-at-Law, of Lincoln's Inn, M.A. Magdalen Coll. Oxford, J.P. cos. London and Carlow, High Sheriff 1899, M.P. for South Hackney 1896-1906, b. 26 April, 1849 ; m. 1 Jan. 1880, Helen Alexandrina Melian, eldest dau. and co-heiress of the late Alex-

ander Durdin, LL.D., J.P., of Huntington Castle, co. Carlow, by Melian Jones his wife, 2nd dau. of the late Matthew Hayman, J.P., of South Abbey, co. Cork, and has issue.
1. MANNING DURDIN, b. 29 May, 1887.
2. Nevill Warham, b. 27 May, 1890.
3. Magnus Storm, b. 11 Oct. 1893.
1. Helen Manning.
2. Brenda Melian Manning, d. young, 7 April, 1884.

Lineage.—ALEXANDER REID, younger son of John Reid, styled 4th Baron of Strathloch, assumed the name of Robertson at the same time as his elder brother, John Reid, styled 5th Baron Rua of Strathloch, who, in 1567, m. his cousin Marjory, dau. of John Robertson, of Lude, and thereupon assumed the name of Robertson, and was ancestor of the succeeding barons Rua (a title which continued to be borne until this, the elder line, became extinct, in 1807), and also of the Robertsons of Cray and of West and East Bleaton, Alexander Reid was of Dounie, in Strathardle, Perthshire, and m. Mary, dau. of Thomas Scott, of Dounie, and had issue, besides a younger son, Walter, who was of Middle Dounie, an elder son,
JOHN REID or ROBERTSON, of East Dounie, who was s. by his son,
ALEXANDER ROBERTSON, of Dounie, b. 1585, who had, with other issue,
1. Alexander, b. 1607, whose descendants remained at Dounis until the end of last century.   2. JAMES, of whom we treat.
The younger son,
JAMES ROBERTSON, b. 1608, migrated to Kirkwall, in the Orkney Islands, in 1630, and settled at Orphir. He had nine sons, who left numerous descendants. His eldest son,
THOMAS ROBERTSON, b. at Ophir, 1642 ; m. a dau. of Magnus Halcro, and had issue,
1. James, of Groundwater.   2. NICOL, of whom presently.
3. John, m. Marjory Velzian, and had issue.
The 2nd son,
NICOL ROBERTSON, b. 1 Feb. 1670, settled in G... ...ter, and left by Catherine his wife, with other issue a son,
GEORGE ROBERTSON, of Upper Groundwater, b. 1706 ; m. Helen, dau. of Magnus Wilson, of Upnouse, and had, with four daus.,
1. JAMES, of whom.   2. Thomas, bapt. 8 July, 1739.
3. George, bapt. 2 Oct. 1741 ; m. Elspet Garvey.
4. Magnus, bapt. 17 April, 1743.
5. John, bapt. 2 Nov. 1746.
6. Andrew, bapt. 1 Aug. 1748 ; m. Jean Sinclair, and left issue.
Mr. George Roberson d. 1780. His eldest son,
JAMES ROBERTSON, of Upper Groundwater, bapt. 18 Aug. 1734 ; m. 12 Oct. 1763, Catherine Heddle, and had issue,
1. THOMAS, of whom hereafter.
2. Robert, bapt. 8 Nov. 1772 ; d.s.p. 1794.
3. James, bapt. 2 March, 1775 ; m. 1806, Barbara Cumming, and left issue, some of whom are still living in the Orkneys.
4, William, bapt. 18 Nov. 1779 ; d. young.
1. Helline.   2. Catherine, m. James Cumming.
The eldest son,
THOMAS ROBERTSON, b. 14 Aug. 1765, was the first of the family to leave Scotland. After having spent his life at sea, he settled in London. He m. 8 Dec. 1807, Maria, dau. of Joseph Howell, of Cheltenham, and widow of James Wilson, R.N., and d. 14 Feb. 1847, having by her (who d. 28 Dec. 1856) had issue an only son,
THOMAS STORM ROBERTSON, M.D., F.R.C.S., b. 5 Feb. 1809 ; m. 1st, 22 Jan. 1843, Annabella, dau. of George Bland ; she d.s.p. 30 March following ; he m. 2ndly, 15 Oct. 1846, Maria Louisa, only dau. of the late Robert Manning, of Clapham (and sister and heiress, in her issue, of Robert Henry Manning, who d. 23 May, 1891), and by her (who d. 9 Feb. 1887) had issue,
HERBERT, now of Huntington Castle.
Maria Louisa, m. 20 Sept. 1864, Col. Thomas William Haines, of Hasketon Manor, Suffolk, and d. 11 July, 1879, leaving issue,
Arthur Manning, b. 15 April, 1867, Major York and Lancaster Regt.
Eveline Constance, m. 5 Aug. 1896, the Hon. Terence Theobald Bourke, youngest son of the 6th Earl of Mayo, and has issue two daus. (see BURKE'S Peerage).
Dr. Robertson d. 6 Aug. 1859.

FAMILY OF DURDIN.

It is stated that this family is a branch of a very ancient Essex family, and that JOHN DURDIN, a Magistrate for that co., d. in the early part of the 17th century and was bur. in Westminster Abbey, where there was until lately a tablet to his memory. His son,
JOHN DURDIN, migrated to co. Cork circa 1639. When the great rebellion broke out, 1641, he was constrained to flee back to England, and in a list of fugitives we find his name recorded as John Durdin, of Glanmire. He resided for a time in Norwich ; and in the registry of St. George's Church in that city is the baptism, 1649, of his youngest child, "Mary, dau. of John Durdin and Mary his wife." On the restoration of tranquillity in Ireland, Mr. Durdin returned Cork, where he d. at the great age 108, and was bur. at Carrigtuohill. His son,
MICHAEL DURDIN, of Ballymagooley, co. Cork, 1663, m. Anne, dau. of Edmund Cotter, of Innismore, co. Cork, and sister of Sir James Cotter, Knt., and dying aged 97, was bur. at Carrigtuohill, being s. by his son,
JOHN DURDIN, of Fortarabia, co. Cork, b. 1676 ; m. Anne, dau. of Alexander Cole, of Innishannon, co. Cork, and had issue. He d. 1772, aged 96, and was bur. at Carrigtuohill. His son,
ALEXANDER DURDIN, b. 1712, was of Shanagary, co. Cork, and of Huntington, co. Carlow. This gentleman was married four times. His 1st wife, whom he m. by a Cloyne licence of 1758, was Anne, dau.

of Richard Heycock. She d. a few days after the birth of her only child.

1. RICHARD; m. 1st, Helen, dau. and heir of Sir John Esmonde, of Huntington Castle, near Clonegal, co. Carlow, the 5th bart, and by her had an only son,
  1. Alexander, who d.s.p.

He m. 2ndly, 1785, Frances, dau. of Sir James Esmonde, 7th bart., and by her (who m. 2ndly, — Lewis) had issue,
  2. Richard Heycock, b. 1790; d. 22 July, 1809.
  1. Frances Maria Esmonde, b. 1788; d. unm. 17 Dec. 1814.

Mr. Alexander Durdin m. 2ndly, at St. Ann's, Dublin, by licence dated 11 May, 1765, Mary, dau. of James Duncan, of Kilmoon House, co. Meath, but she d.s.p.; and 3rdly, 1766, Anne (née Vaux), relict of William Penn, grandson of the founder of Pennsylvania, and with this lady he received a large portion of the Irish as well as of the American estates of the family. She d.s.p. 1767. He m. 4thly, April, 1768, Barbara, 2nd dau. (by his wife Margaret, eldest dau. and co-heir of Robert Atkins, of Waterpark, and Highfield, co. Cork) of Warham St. Leger, of Heyward's Hill, and by her (who d. 1820) he had further issue,

2. Warham of Sunville, Dromadda, and Midleton Lodge, all in co. Cork, b. 1768; m. 27 May, 1792, Anne, eldest dau. of Thomas Garde, of Ballindiniss, co. Cork, and by her (who d. 1847) had issue,
  1. Alexander, b. 1797; d. unm. at Paris, Dec. 1819.
  2. Thomas Garde, of Shanagarry Castle (the old seat of the Penns), an Officer of the 13th Light Dragoons, m. 17 June, 1835, Anne Isabella, dau. of James Lewis, and d. 1867, having by her (who d. 22 Dec. 1889) had issue,
    John Peel, d.s.p. 1898.
    Henrietta, d. unm.
  3. Henry, served in Spain, d.s.p.
  4. Warham, an Officer in the Perth Rifles, d.s.p. June, 1886.
  5. Charles, of Sunbury, co. Cork, m. Miss Bowles, d. 24 Dec. 1875, s.p.
  1. Elizabeth, d. unm.
  2. Barbara, m. John Boston, M.D., of Middleton, co. Cork, and d. 1831, leaving issue.
  3. Anne, m. Stephen Jermyn Masters, and d. 1830.
  4. Jane, m. John Miles, of Ballinvilla.
  5. Louisa, m. William Garde, of Kilberry, and d. 1854, leaving issue.

3. John, Barrister-at-Law, of Ballymagooley, co. Cork, b. 1770; d. unm. 30 March, 1817, and was bur. at Clonegal.
4. Alexander, b. 1773; m. Mary, dau. of Thomas Rhames, of co. Wicklow, by whom he had issue,
Alicia, m. 1842, William Whitton, of Dublin.
He d. 19 May, 1829, and was bur. at Clonegal.

5. Robert Atkins, of Cranemore House, co. Carlow, J.P. and D.L., m. Elizabeth, dau. of Thomas Garde, of Ballindiniss, co. Cork, who d. 1852. He d. 5 Jan. 1841, leaving issue,
  1. Alexander Warham (Rev.), m. 7 Oct. 1847, Lydia, only child of Robert Pitcher, of Kenwick Hall, co. Norfolk, J.P.; d.s.p 18 Aug. 1889.
  2. Thomas Garde (Rev.), m. Charlotte, dau. of Antony Browne, of Rathgar, Dublin, J.P., and d. 27 Oct. 1902, leaving issue,
    (1) Robert Charles, M.D., of Cranemore au Great Eedwyn, Wilts.
    (1) Adelaide, of Kenwick Hall, m. James Love, who d.s.p.
    (2) Charlotte Elizabeth, m. Rev. Wm. Francis Singleton, and d.s.p. 18 May, 1904.
  3. Charles Garde, b. 1814, Barrister-at-Law, d. unm. 1843.
  4. Robert Garde, b. 1818, Lord Mayor of Dublin, 1872; m. Fidelia, only dau. of William Durdin, of Huntington Castle (see below), and d. 19 Oct. 1878, leaving issue, a dau., Fidelia Barbara, m. William Francis Cooke.

6. WILLIAM LEADER, of whom presently.
7. Michael, b. 1782, left issue, Michael St. Leger, Alexander, Barbara, and Eliza.
  1. Margaret, m. Thomas McCarthy, of Heathfield, near Youghal, and of Dublin, by whom she had four sons,
  2. Sarah, m. John Revell, of Ardoyne, co. Carlow, and had issue a son and a dau.
  3. Jane, m. Capt. Roche, but left no issue.
  4. Barbara, m. Henry Beere, of Black Castle, co. Kildare, by whom she had two daus.
  5. Harriette, d. unm. at Huntington Castle, 21 March, 1872.

Mr. Durdin d. 20 Sept. 1807, aged 95. His 6th son,
WILLIAM LEADER DURDIN, of Huntington Castle, co. Carlow, B.A., M.D., b. 18 Dec. 1778; m. April, 1820, Mary Anne, dau. of William Drury, of Ballinderry, co. Wicklow, and by her (who d. 13 April, 1883) had issue,
ALEXANDER, his heir.
Fidelia, m. her cousin, Robert Garde Durdin, and d. 17 Oct. 1896, leaving issue (see above).

Mr. Durdin d. 1 Jan. 1849. His eldest son,
ALEXANDER DURDIN, of Huntington Castle, co. Carlow, and of Albany, Monkstown, co. Dublin, LL.D., J.P., b. 6 March, 1821; m. 6 Sept. 1851, Melian Jones, 2nd dau. of the late Matthew Hayman, J.P., of South Abbey, Youghal, and d. 4 Jan. 1882, leaving issue,
1. HELEN ALEXANDRINA MELIAN, m. as above.
2. Florence Amy, m. 14 Feb. 1893, Alexander Ferrier Beasley, and has issue, Alexander and Winifred St. Leger.
3. Melian Lucy Anne, m. 16 Sept. 1886, Walter Holloway of Charlbury, and d. 3 Nov. 1899, leaving issue, a dau., Melian Eileen Jane, m. Charles Chessman, R.I.C., and has issue.
4. Harriette Emily Hayman, m. R. W. B. Frizell, and d. 13 Dec. 1894, leaving issue, Richard Alexander Fraser, and Ethel Melian.

Arms—(Lyon Office)—Gu., on a fesse between three wolves' heads erased close to the skull arg. a man in chains all ppr. Crest—

A dexter cubit arm erect holding a falchion enfiled with an antique crown all ppr. Motto—Ramis micat radix.
Seats——Huntington Castle, co. Carlow; 36, Bedford Square London. Clubs—Athenæum, Carlton, and Saville.

ROBERTSON-EUSTACE. See EUSTACE.

ROBINSON. See BURKE'S PEERAGE, ROBINSON, Bart.

RAINEY-ROBINSON.

COLONEL ROBERT MAXIMILIAN RAINEY-ROBINSON, late Commanding 62nd Punjabis, Major Indian Staff Corps, b. 26 April, 1861, assumed the surname and arms of ROBINSON in addition to Rainey by Royal Licence 6 Nov. 1897; m. 2 Dec. 1903, Alice Frances, eldest dau. of Arthur Hidding Hildebrand, C.I.E.

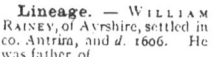

Lineage. — WILLIAM RAINEY, of Ayrshire, settled in co. Antrim, and d. 1606. He was father of
JOHN RAINEY, of Killybegs, co. Antrim, b. 1600; d. 1688, bur. at Antrim. He left three sons and two daus.,
1. WILLIAM, of whom presently.
2. Robert, of Killybegs, will dated 25 Feb. 1722, proved at Antrim, 17 July, 1725; m. and left issue.
3. Hugh, of Magherafelt, will dated 11 April, 1707, proved 9 May, 1709; m. and left issue.
1. Elizabeth, m. William Brown.
2. Mary, m. — Watt.

The eldest son,
WILLIAM RAINEY, of Belfast, b. 1640; m. dau. of — McCormick, and left four sons and four daus.,
1. John, of Belfast, will dated 1 Nov. 1717, proved 2 May, 1718, at Connor, by Elinor his wife, left William, Mary, Jane, Elizabeth and Sara.
2. WILLIAM, of whom presently.
3. Robert, of Newry, will dated 15 March, 1735, proved 26 Nov. 1736; m. Martha, dau. of Francis Sheen, of Cherry Valley, co. Antrim, and had issue,
  1. Francis, M.D., m. and left issue,
    (1) Robert.
    (2) Daniel, M.D., will proved 31 May, 1783; m. Elizabeth Sarah Mitchell, and left Francis, Robert and Mary.
    (3) James.
  2. Daniel, of Newry, d. 1741; m. Jane, dau. of Surgeon William Hamilton, of Dublin, s.p. Her will dated 15 April, 1762, proved 1 Oct. 1771, at Down.
  3. Robert, m. Elizabeth Ronet, and left a son,
    (1) William, of Bellevue, co. Down, d. 1789; m. Margaretta, dau. of James Moore, of Rostrevor, s.p.
4. Daniel (Rev.), Minister of the Church at Amsterdam, will proved 3 Sept. 1746; m. Cornelia Russell, s.p.
1. Jane, m. John Eccles.
2. Mary, m. — McKibbin.
3. Anne, m. Robert Hutcheson.
4. Grizzel, d. unm., will proved 25 May, 1725, at Connor.

The 2nd son,
WILLIAM RAINEY, of Belfast, will dated 15 Nov. 1725, proved 11 Dec. 1725; m. Katherine, dau. of — Shaw, by Elizabeth, dau. of James Maxwell, and sister and co-heir of Arthur Maxwell, of Drumbeg, co. Down, and had four sons and a dau.,
1. Arthur Rainey Maxwell, of Castle Hill, co. Down, assumed the surname of MAXWELL, d. 1754; m. Frances, dau. of Surgeon William Hamilton, of Dublin, and had two sons and a dau.,
  (1) Rainey Maxwell, of The Lodge, Belfast, will proved 28 Jan. 1813, d.s.p.
  (2) Arthur Maxwell, d.s.p.
  (1) Catherine.
2. JOHN, of whom presently.
3. William, d.s.p. before 1742. 4. Patrick.
1. Jane, m. — Andrews.

The 2nd son,
JOHN RAINEY, of Greenville, co. Down, d. 1793; m. Mary, dau. of Surgeon William Hamilton, of Dublin, and had an only son and two daus.,
1. WILLIAM, his heir.
1. Frances, m.
2. Elizabeth, m. John Goddard.

The only son,
WILLIAM RAINEY, of Greenville, co. Down, d. 1803; m. 1st, Henrietta Maria, dau. of Rev. James Hutchinson, by whom he had five sons and two daus. He m. 2ndly, Mary Anne Boyd, and had a son, Boyd, and a dau., Elizabeth. The children of the 1st wife were,

1. John, of Drumbo, co. Down, d.s.p. 1856.
2. WILLIAM HENRY, of whom presently.
3. James, d. 29 Nov. 1816, Major H.E.I.C.S., m. Anne Loring, and had issue,
 1. William Henry Sneyd, d.s.p.
 2. Arthur Crowe (Rev.), Major Indian Army, afterwards in Holy Orders, b. 1810 ; d. 1891 ; m. Louisa Hester Pigou, and left a son,
  John Crofton, b. 3 May, 1853 ; m. 20 March, 1877, Eva Margaret, dau. of Thomas Birkbeck Wakefield, of Hall, Moate, co. Westmeath, and has issue,
   1. Arthur Pigou, b. 21 Feb. 1878 ; m. 1903.
   2. John Wakefield, b. 31 Dec. 1881, Capt. A.V.C.; m. 1 Jan. 1910, Elsie Clare, dau. of Francis Dominic Bowles, J.P., C.C. London.
   3. Edward Holmes, b. 5 April, 1886.
   4. Robert French, b. 19 Dec. 1888.
   1. Eva Marjorie.   2. Ada Madeleine.
   3. Gertrude Sophia.
 3. Henry Garner, C.B. (1869), Major-Gen.; b. 6 Nov. 1813; d.
  1. Matilda Mary.
  4. Francis.   5. Henry, Capt. 82nd Regt.
  1. Martha, m. 1st, George Stewart ; 2ndly, Robert Rowan (see ROWAN of Mount Davys).
  2. Mary, m. James Goddard.

The 2nd son,
WILLIAM HENRY RAINEY, of Mount Panther, co. Down, Major 4th Bengal Cavalry, H.E.I.C.S., J.P. co. Down, b. 1780 ; d. 1830 ; m. Margaret, dau. of Robert Macan, of Carriff, co. Armagh, and had a son and a dau.,
 ARTHUR JACOU MACAN, his heir.
 Elizabeth Ann, m. 1844, Robert Leslie Ogilby, of Ardnargle, co. Londonderry (see that family).
The only son,
MAJOR-GEN. ARTHUR JACOB MACAN RAINEY, b. April, 1826; d. June, 1906; m. Aug. 1854, Caroline Susanna, eldest dau. of Rev. William Robinson, Rector of Bovevagh, co. Londonderry, and sister and co-heir of Henry Jeffery Robinson, of Portrush, and had issue,
 1. William John, d. an infant 1857.
 2. ROBERT MAXIMILIAN, now RAINEY-ROBINSON, of Portrush.
 3. Francis Edward, b. 27 May, 1863.
 4. Edward Flower, b. 9 Nov. 1865, Capt. Indian S.C.
 1. Caroline Susanna.   2. Esther Sophia.

Lineage—of ROBINSON.—REV. WILLIAM FRIEND, D.D., Oxon, Dean of Canterbury 1760, b. 1714 ; d. 26 Nov. 1766 ; m. April, 1739, Grace, youngest dau. of William Robinson, of Rokeby, Yorkshire, and sister of Richard Robinson, Archbishop of Armagh, created Baron Rokeby, and by her (who d. 28 Dec. 1776) had with other issue a son,
REV. SIR JOHN ROBINSON, Bart., Archdeacon of Armagh, who assumed the surname of ROBINSON instead of Friend by Royal licence 20 Nov. 1793, and was created a baronet 14 Dec. 1819. He was b. 15 Feb. 1754 ; d. 16 April, 1832 ; m. 1786, Mary Anne, dau. of James Spencer, of Rathangan, co. Kildare, and had with other issue,
 1. Sir Richard, 2nd bart., on the death of whose younger son, Sir Richard Harcourt Robinson, 5th bart., unm. 26 Feb. 1910 the title became extinct.
 2. William (Rev.), Rector of Bovevagh, b. 20 Dec. 1793 ; d. Dec. 1834 ; m. 21 May, 1824, Hon. Susannah Sophia Flower, dau. of Henry Jeffery, 4th Viscount Ashbrook, and by her (who m. 2ndly William Wilson Campbell, M.D., and d. 6 Nov. 1864) had two sons and two daus.,
  1. John, Capt. 34th Regt., killed at the Redan 18 June, 1855, unm.
  2. Henry Jeffery, of Portrush, 76th Regt., J.P. co. Antrim, d.s.p. 4 April, 1896.
  1. Caroline Susanna, m. Aug. 1854, Major-Gen. Arthur Jacob Macan Rainey (see above).
  2. Helena, m. 21 July, 1888, Sewell Hamilton (see HAMILTON STUBBER of Moyne).

Arms—Quarterly, 1st and 4th, vert, on a chevron or, between three bucks trippant of the last and pelletée, as many quatrefoils gu. (ROBINSON) ; 2nd and 3rd, gu., two flaunches or, over all as many eagles' wings conjoined in base, ppr. (RAINEY). Crests—1. A buck as in the arms (ROBINSON) ; 2. issuant from a mural crown ppr., a lion's head or, guttée-de-larmes. Motto—Sola in Deo Salus (ROBINSON), Fuimus (RAINEY).
Residence—Kilbroney House, Rostrevor, co. Down.

ROCH OF WOODBINE HILL.

The late SAMPSON ROCH, of Woodbine Hill, co. Waterford, Deputy-Surg.-Gen. (retired), M.R.C.S. Eng., Licentiate of King's and Queen's College of Physicians, Ireland, Licentiate of Royal Rotunda Lying in Hospital, Dublin, Member of the Royal Zoological Society, and late Medical Officer of Health for Cheltenham. He was b. 21 June, 1829 ; m. 21 Oct. 1869, Agnes (now of Woodbine Hill), youngest dau. of Bartholomew John Brown, of Moorham Hall, Essex, and d. 9 Nov. 1906, leaving issue,
 1. George Butler, Capt. Royal Waterford Art. (Mil.), b. 1872 ; d. unm. 31 March, 1905.
 2. Harry Leslie, b. 1874.
 3. HORACE SAM, Capt. R.A.M.C., b. 1876.

Surg.-Gen. Roch served in the Crimean war, Indian Mutiny, and Abyssinian Expedition (medals and clasps), and was formerly J.P. co. Waterford.

Lineage.—From JOHN ROCH, of Touriu, b. 1507, son of George Roch, Lord Roch and Fermoy, descended
JAMES ROCH (only son of George Roch, of Tourin and Glyn), Col. in King WILLIAM's Army at the relief of Derry, b. at Kinsale, 29 Sept. 1659. In the Williamite Army he soon attained the rank of Colonel, and at the memorable siege of Derry distinguished himself by an act of Roman heroism. When Kirke, the General sent to the relief of the beleaguered town, arrived off Lough Foyle, he found a strong boom or barricade stretched across the harbour's mouth, so effectually to preclude the passage of his ships. In despair, he would have sailed away without any communications with the defenders of Derry, when Col. Roch offered to swim to the town, bearing despatches. He did so, having attached bullets to the letters, that he might sink them in the event of his own capture, and he returned to his companions, after due performance of his object ; but, from having been repeatedly fired upon by the Irish troops who lined the banks, his jawbone was broken, and three musket-balls were lodged in different parts of his body. For this achievement he was, during the remainder of his life, honourably called "the Swimmer," and he received from the King the more substantial reward of certain ferries of Ireland, along with fifteen of the forfeited estates. The latter were lost to him by the Act of Resumption, and Parliament in lieu voted him a sum of money. Col. Roch m. 1st, 1693, Elizabeth, dau. of William Gough, and grand-dau. of Dr. Francis Gough, Bishop of Limerick, and had issue, a son and a dau., who were named after the King and Queen, and had the honour of having their majesties for sponsors,
 1. William, b. 1695 ; d.s.p. at Glyn Castle 29 July, 1723.
 1. Mary, b. 10 Oct. 1694 ; m. at Churchtown, 17 Nov. 1709, Capt. Benjamin Greene (of the Kilnanahan family) ; she d. 9 Dec. 1727 (see GREENE of Greenville).
He m. 2ndly, 20 July, 1700, Elizabeth, dau. of Benjamin Hamerton, and relict of John Hanbury, and by her (who d. 1 March, 1730-1) had a son,
 2. JAMES, of whom hereafter.
Col. Roch was High Sheriff co. Waterford 1714. He d. 22 Dec. 1722, in his 65th year. His son by his 2nd marriage,
JAMES ROCH, of Glyn Castle, near Carrick-on-Suir, and afterwards of Dungarvan, b. 1702, was twice married. By Anna Maria, his 1st wife (who d. 9 July, 1725), he had issue,
 1. JAMES, his heir.
 1. Susanna.
Mr. Roch m. 2ndly, 3 March, 1730-1, Melian, dau. of Thomas Holmes Pomeroy, and by her (who d. 28 Dec. 1755) had issue,
 2. William, of Lehard, m. Mary, dau. of Ambrose Lane, of co. Tipperary, and had issue, four sons and two daus. The widow of Ambrose, the 3rd son, was Regina Maria, dau. of Col. D'Alton, authoress of The Children of the Abbey.
 3. Luke, Lieut. in the Army, m. Elizabeth Waring, but d.s.p. 1781.
 2. Melian, m. Beverley Usher, of Canty, co. Waterford.
 3. Audriah, m. 18 May, 1757, Matthew Jones, Collector of Youghal, and d. 26 Feb. 1819, leaving two daus.,
  1. Maria, d. unm.
  2. Melian, m. 1782, Samuel Hayman, of Youghal (see HAYMAN of South Abbey), and d. 1835.
He d. at Dungarvan, 28 Jan. 1740-1, and was s. by his eldest son,
JAMES ROCH, of Odell Lodge and Woodbine Hall, High Sheriff 1754, who m. Oct. 1747, Isabella, elder dau. of John Osborne, Odell, of Mount Odell, co. Waterford, and had a dau., Melian, m. Sampson Roch, and three sons. He m. 2ndly, Mary Cotter, relict of Thomas Webb, of Kilonaford, co. Waterford, and left by her at his decease (2 Dec. 1792) one son.
GEORGE BUTLER ROCH, of Woodbine Hill, co. Waterford, J.P. b. 23 May, 1784 ; m. 23 Oct. 1813, Jane, dau. of William Wilkinson, and d. June, 1859, having had issue,
 1. GEORGE, late of Woodbine Hill.
 2. James, b. 12 Sept. 1822 ; m. 24 Feb. 1851, Mary Jane, dau. of John Melen, of Chalford, co. Gloucester, and d. 1859, leaving issue.
 3. SAMPSON, late of Woodbine Hill.
 1. Mary, d. unm. 19 Jan. 1892.
 m. Col. Henry D. Sheppard, 19th N.I., H.E.I.C.S., and d. 3 Nov. 1891.
 3. Selina, m. 1855, John Sheppard, late Comm. Indian Navy, and d. 21 Jan. 1892.
 4. Jane, m. 1849, Henry Peard, of Carrigeen Hall, co. Cork.
 5. Sarah, dec.
His eldest son,
GEORGE ROCH, of Woodbine Hill, co. Waterford, and Rochestown, co. Cork, J.P. and D.L., b. 15 April, 1819 ; m. 18 July, 1874, Harriett St. Leger, of Rochestown Wood, Rochestown, co. Cork, dau. of Richard Harris Purcell, of Annabella and Burnfort Park, co. Cork, and d.s.p. 3 July, 1894.

Seat—Woodbine Hill, Youghal, co. Waterford.

ROCHE OF GRANAGH CASTLE AND RYE HILL.

STEPHEN REDINGTON ROCHE, of Rye Hill, co. Galway, Granagh Castle, co. Kilkenny, and Moyvanine, co. Limerick, J.P. co. Galway, b. 14 Nov. 1859 ; m. 1 Aug. 1903, Lily, youngest dau. of the late George

Washington Brasier-Creagh, of Creagh Castle, Doneraile, and Woodville, Buttevant, co. Cork (see *that family*).

Lineage.—JOHN ROCHE, of Castletown Roche, was a member of the Catholic Parliament or Council held at Kilkenny during the Civil War, and his name appears as such to the declaration of the Irish Roman Catholics, 1641. His eldest son,

ROBERT ROCHE, *m.* Juliana O'Moore, dau. of Alexander O'Moore, and was *s.* by his eldest son,

STEPHEN ROCHE, known by the designation of *Dov* or *Black*, from his complexion, whose estate, already injured by composition in the time of CROMWELL, was entirely forfeited under WILLIAM III. Compelled in consequence to leave co. Cork, he retired to Kilrush, co. Clare, and afterwards took up his abode at Pallas, co. Limerick, in the vicinity of his brother-in-law, William Apjohn. He *m.* Anastasia, elder dau. and co-heir (with her sister Catherine, who *m.* William Apjohn) of Thomas Lysaght, and was *s.* by his son,

JOHN ROCHE, *b.* 1688 ; *m.* Anne, youngest dau. of Philip Stackpole, of Mount Cashel, Kilneen, and Kilconian, co. Clare, and had, with other issue,

1. STEPHEN, his heir.
2. John, *m.* Miss Harold, cousin of Gen. Harold, of the Saxon service, and had a dau.,
 Mary Anne, *m.* John Meade, of Limerick.
3. Philip, of Shannon View, co. Limerick, *m.* Margaret, dau. of John Kelly, of Limerick, and had issue,
 1. John, *m.* Margaret, dau. of Charles Whyte, of Leixlip (*see* WHYTE *of Lourhbrickland*), and *d.v.p.*, having had issue,
  (1) Philip, of Donore, co. Kildare, *m.* the Hon. Anna Maria Plunkett, dau. of Randall, 13th Lord Dunsany, and by her (who *m.* 2ndly, 22 July, 1822, Admiral Ryder Burton, R.N., K.H., and *d.* 26 April, 1856) had issue,
   1. John, Lieut.-Gen. late 2nd Life Guards, *m.* 3 April, 1869, Agnes Jane, dau. of James Mugford. He *d.s.p.*
   1. Margaret Radaliana, *m.* 3 Nov. 1836, Thomas, 16th Lord Trimleston. She *d.* 4 Sept. 1872. He *d.* 4 Aug. 1879, and had issue (*see* BURKE'S *Peerage*).
   2. Anna Maria, *m.* 20 Nov. 1830, Thomas Oliver, 12th Lord Louth. She *d.* 18 Jan. 1878. He *d.* 26 June, 1849, leaving issue.
  (2) Charles Whyte, of Ballygran, co. Limerick, *m.* his first cousin, Letitia, dau. of John Whyte, of Loughbrickland (*see that family*), and by her had issue,
   1. Charles Philip, of Ballygran, Capt. Cavan Militia, *b.* 1819 ; *m.* 1861, his cousin, Louisa, dau. of Nicholas Charles Whyte, D.L., of Loughbrickland, Capt. R.N., and *d.* 10 Nov. 1871, having had issue,
    a. Charles Hugh, *b.* 1863 ; *d. unm.* 1889.
    b. Henry John, Lieut.-Col. Indian Army, *b.* 12 Aug. 1864.
    c. Edward Richard, B.A., A.M.I.C.E., *b.* 1867.
    d. Arthur, *b.* 1870 ; *d.* 1892.
    a. Letitia Mary, *m.* 1886, J. Knox Wight, I.C.S.
    b. Frances, *m.* 1899, R. Bodkin Mahon, F.R.C.S.E.
   1. Letitia Maria, *m.* 18 Oct. 1842, Sir John Nugent, 3rd Bart., of Ballinlough, who *d.* 16 Feb. 1859, leaving issue (*see* BURKE's *Peerage*).
   2. Helena Maria, *m.* 1st, 1845, Richard Barnewall, of Bloomsbury, co. Meath, who *d.s.p.* 3 Feb. 1866. She *m.* 2ndly, Vicomte de Chasteigner.
  (1) Margaret, *m.* John Therry, of Castle Therry, co. Cork, sometime Chairman of the Commissioners of Excise in Ireland.
  (2) Anna, *d. unm.*
  (3) Mary, *m.* 12 Oct. 1803, Major William Skerrett, of Finavara, co. Clare, and *d.* 1821, leaving issue (*see that family*).
  (4) Helen, *d. unm.*
  (5) Fanny, *m.* James Skerrett, of Carnacron, co. Galway.
  (6) Letitia, *m.* 8 May, 1816, Thomas Kelly, of Shannon View, Limerick, and had issue (*see* KELLY *of Rockstown Castle*).
  (7) Rose, *d.* young.
 1. Ellen, *m.* Peter Daly, of Cloncagh, co. Galway.
 2. Mary, *m.* 15 July, 1783, George Ryan, of Inch, co. Tipperary, and had issue (*see that family*).
 3. Margaret, *m.* July, 1787, Standish Barry, of Leamlara, and had issue (*see that family*).
 1. Jane, *m.* John Sheehy, of Cork, and had a dau. *m.* Bryan Keating, by whom she was mother of General Keating.
 2. Christiana, *m.* James Lombard, of co. Cork.

The eldest son,

STEPHEN ROCHE, *b.* 5 Dec. 1724 ; *s.* his father 1760. He *m.* 1st, Margaret, dau. of Richard Meade, and had issue,

1. JOHN, his successor, one of the most eminent merchants in Dublin, who *m.* Mary, dau. of Thady Grehan, of that city, but *d.s.p.* Sept. 1825.
2. Richard (Rev.), who *d.* 1805.
3. George, of Granagh Castle, co. Kilkenny, *d.s.p.*
1. Anne, *m.* Peter Long, of Waterford.
2. Mary, *m.* Peter Grehan, of Dublin, and has issue (*see* GREHAN *of Clonmern*).

Stephen Roche *m.* 2ndly, Sarah, dau. and co-heir of John O'Brien, of Moyvanine and Clounties, co. Limerick, and by her (who *d.* 8 Nov. 1786) had issue,

4. STEPHEN, of Moyvanine and Clounties, *m.* Maria, dau. of John Moylan, of Cork, and had issue,
 1. STEPHEN, of Rye Hill. 2. John.
 1. Mary, a nun.
 2. Sarah, *m.* Sir John Howley, Serjeant-at-Law, and *d.* 1856.
 3. Anne. 4. Helena.
 5. Harriet, *m.* Daniel Cronin.

5. Thomas, of Limerick, *m.* Helen, dau. of John Ankettle, and has issue,
 1. Stephen, *m.* Catherine, dau. and co-heir of Christopher Knight, of co. Limerick.
 2. John.
 3. William, of Dublin, *m.* Eliza, dau. and co-heir of Christopher Knight, of co. Limerick.
 1. Helen, *m.* Daniel Ryan Kane, M.A., Q.C., Chairman of Quarter Sessions, E. R. co. Cork, and had issue.
 2. Sarah.
6. James, of Cork, author of *The Memoirs of an Octogenarian*, *m.* Anne, dau. of John Moylan, by whom he left at his decease, two daus.,
 1. Marianne.
 2. Sarah, *m.* — Collins.
7. William, M.P. for Limerick, *m.* the dau. of — Dillon, and *d.* in Limerick 1850, having by her had issue, with a younger son, Henry, *d.* young, an elder son,
 James, of Limerick and Great Yarmouth, an Officer of the Customs, *m.* Ellen, dau. of John Hogan, of Limerick, and had issue,
  (1) William, *b.* in Limerick ; *d.* at Bury St. Edmunds.
  (2) Henry, *b.* in Limerick ; *d.* at Great Yarmouth.
  (3) James, of Detroit, U.S.A., *b.* 11 Feb. 1843 ; *m.* and has issue, a son and a dau., Helena Mary, *m.* 9 Feb. 1897, John Francis O'Brien.
  (4) John, *b.* at Great Yarmouth ; *d.* in London.
  (1) Anne.
  (2) Julia, a nun at Skipton, Yorks.
  (3) Helena. (4) Mary.
3. Sarah, *m.* Francis French, of Portcarran, co. Galway, who *d.s.p.*
4. Helen, *m.* Denis O'Meagher, of Kilmoyler, co. Tipperary, who is dec.
5. Anastasia, *m.* Edward O'Meagher, of Marl Hill, co. Tipperary.

Stephen Roche *m.* 3rdly, Mary Anne, dau. and co-heir of Richard Ankettle, M.D., but by her (who *d.* Dec. 1821) he had no issue. He *d.* 12 Feb. 1804, and was *s.* by his grandson,

STEPHEN ROCHE, of Granagh Castle, co. Kilkenny, and Rye Hill, co. Galway, *m.* 1832, Eleanor, eldest dau. and co-heir of Thomas Redington, of Rye Hill, co. Galway, and by her (who *d.* 1891) had issue,

1. THOMAS REDINGTON, late of Rye Hill.
2. Stephen, *d. unm.* 1853.
1. Eleanor, *d. unm.* 1855.

Mr. Roche *d.* 4 Sept. 1864, and was *s.* by his eldest son,

THOMAS REDINGTON ROCHE, of Rye Hill, co. Galway, Granagh Castle, co. Kilkenny, and Moyvanine, of Limerick, J.P. and D.L., High Sheriff co. Galway 1869, *b.* 14 July, 1847 ; *m.* 8 Sept. 1858, Jane Elizabeth, 5th dau. of Anthony Cliffe, of Bellevue, co. Wexford, and *d.* 10 May, 1900, leaving issue,

1. STEPHEN REDINGTON, now of Rye Hill.
2. Anthony, *b.* 16 April, 1862.
3. Thomas James, *b.* 25 July, 1863.
4. Charles, *b.* 16 Sept. 1867 ; *d.* 25 May, 1898.
5. George Philip, *b.* 21 Nov. 1869.
1. Eleanor Mary, a nun, *d.* 18 Aug. 1903.
2. Isabella Theresa.
3. Cecilia Jane, *d.* in infancy.

Seat—Rye Hill, Athenry, co. Galway.

ROCHE. *See* BURKE'S PEERAGE, **FERMOY, B.**, and **ROCHE, Bart.**

ROCHFORT OF ROCHFORT BRIDGE.

CONSTANCE EMILY, MURIEL, and ROSE MINDEN ROCHFORT, of Rochfort Bridge, co. Westmeath, *s.* their father 1882. The youngest dau., Rose Minden, *m.* 18 Nov. 1903, Maj. Francis Henley, Oxfordshire L.I., eldest son of Capt. A. Henley, late 52nd L.I.

Lineage.—PRIME IRON ROCHFORT, Lieut.-Col. in the Army of CROMWELL, youngest son of James Rochfort, of Agherry, co. Wicklow, and 9th in descent from Sir William Rochfort, Lord of the Manor of Kill at the commencement of the 14th century, was executed under a court-martial, for killing in a duel Major Turner, 14 May, 1652. By Thomasina his wife, dau. of Sir Robert Pigott (*see* PIGOTT *of Capard*), he left two sons and three daus. The youngest son,

ROBERT ROCHFORT, chosen Speaker of the Irish House of Commons, 27 Aug. 1695, and constituted Chief Baron of the Exchequer

30 June, 1707, b. Dec. 1652 ; m. Hannah, dau. of William Hancock, of Twyford, co. Westmeath, and dying 10 Oct. 1727, left two sons,
1. GEORGE (Right Hon.), his heir.
2. JOHN, of Clogrenane (see that family).

The elder son,
THE RIGHT HON. GEORGE ROCHFORT, M.P., Chief Chamberlain of the Court of Exchequer, m. 24 Jan. 1704, Elizabeth, dau. of Henry, 3rd Earl of Drogheda, and had issue,
1. Robert, created Baron Belfield 16 March, 1737, Viscount Belfield 5 Oct. 1751, and EARL OF BELVEDERE 29 Nov. 1756. His Lordship m. 1736, Mary, eldest dau. of Richard, 3rd Viscount Molesworth, and d. 1772, leaving (with a dau. Jane, m. 1st, to Brinsley, 2nd Earl of Lanesborough (see MARLAY of Belvedere), and 2ndly, John King) three sons ; the two youngest, Richard, Col. in the Army, and Robert, High Sheriff 1777, both d.s.p. ; the eldest, George, 2nd Earl of Belvedere, m. 1st, Dorothea, dau. of John Bloomfield, of Redwood, and 2ndly, Jane, dau. of the Rev. James Mackay, but d.s.p. 1814, when the title became extinct. His lordship's widow m. 2ndly, 1815, Abraham Boyd, King's Counsel, and had by him an only son, the late GEORGE AUGUSTUS ROCHFORT BOYD, of Middleton Park, co. Westmeath.
2. Arthur, LL.D., M.P. for Westmeath, b. 7 Nov. 1711 ; m. Sara, dau. of the Rev. Rowland Singleton, of Drogheda, and had issue (with two daus.), five sons,
1. GEORGE, Gen. of Artillery, whose dau. and heir, Eliza, m. George Clarke, of Hyde Hall, co. Chester.
2. Singleton, an Officer in the Army.
3. Philip, Capt. in the Army, m. 1770, his cousin, Deborah, widow of George Bishop, of Bishop Hall, and younger dau. of John Rochfort, of Clogrenane, and d. Aug. 1771, leaving by her (who d. 1804) an only child, Robert, b. 1771, d. 1823, having m. 1st, Mrs. Sarah Deacon, of Cowes, by whom he had an only child, Sarah, who m. her cousin, Rev. Henry Rochfort ; he m. 2ndly, Mary, dau. of Hugh Carey, of Kilbeccan, and had eight children, of whom, Singleton, Barrister-at-Law, was Public Prosecutor and Government Pleader at Kurrachi, British India, and a District Judge of Napier, N.Z. This Singleton Rochfort m. 30 Jan. 1858, Isabella Mary, eldest dau. of Alexander Shepherd, Colonial Treasurer of New Zealand, and by her has had issue, Robert, who d. young ; Anne Louisa, m. 11 June, 1879, Cecil Greville Horne, Commander R.N. ; Isabella Marie, m. 12 June, 1889, Oswald Robert Younghusband, of Auckland, N.Z., by whom she has issue, Cuthbert Oswald, b. 8 May, 1890.
4. Rowland, an Officer in the Army.
5. Henry, an Officer in the 28th Regt., Assist.-Comm.-Gen. on the Irish Establishment ; m. Henrietta, dau. of John Hill, of Barnhill, co. Carlow, and dying 4 Oct. 1816, left issue,
(1) JOHN, Major 18th Regt., d. unm.
(2) Gustavus Robert, Comm. R.N., b. 1789, a distinguished Naval Officer ; m. 12 Sept. 1814, Maria, dau. of George Leonard, of Dover Castle, Sussex Vale, New Brunswick, North America, and had issue, two daus., 1, Henrietta Caroline, and 2, Sarah Napier, d. unm. 25 Sept. 1839.
(1) Catherine, m. John Rae, Capt. 72nd Regt.
(2) Elizabeth, d. unm. 10 Feb. 1830
3. GEORGE, of whom we treat.
4. William, b. 1713 ; m. 1742, Henrietta, dau. of Col. John Ramsay, and left issue,
Harriet, m. Jan. 1777, John Kilpatrick, M.P. for Granard.
1. Mary, m. Sir Henry Tuite, Bart., of Sonna.
2. Alice, m. Thomas Loftus, of Killyan.
3. Thomasine, m. Gustavus Lambart, of Beau Parc.
4. Anne, m. Henry Lyons, of River Lyons.

The 3rd son of the Right Hon. George Rochfort,
GEORGE ROCHFORT, of Rochfort, b. 1713 ; m. May, 1746, Alice, dau. of Sir Gustavus Hume, Bart., of Castle Hume, co. Fermanagh, and had an only son,
GUSTAVUS ROCHFORT-HUME, M.P. for Westmeath, who sold Rochfort. He m. July, 1779, Frances, dau. of John Bloomfield, of Redwood, and had issue,
1. GEORGE, d. unm. 1809.   2. John, d. unm. 1811.
3. Gustavus, M.P., Col. in the Army, m. 1806, his cousin, Dora, dau. of John Nixon, of Carrick, co. Westmeath ; and dying 1848, left issue, a son, Gustavus Rochfort, Capt. 4th Dragoon Guards, d. unm. 1855. His 2nd dau., Harriet Bloomfield, b. 12 Aug. 1807, m. 25 Sept. 1826, Edmund Wakefield Meade ; and d. 28 Sept. 1838, leaving with other issue, Edmund Waldo Meade-Waldo, of Stone Wall, and Hever, Kent.
4. Richard, late Comptroller of the Customs of Cork, m. 1833, his cousin, Augusta, dau. of Col. John Lyons Nixon, Governor of St. Christopher's, and d. 1842, leaving issue,
George, Capt. 49th Regt., killed at the Redan.
5. Henry (Rev.), Rector of Castletown, co. Westmeath, m. 1829, his cousin, Sarah Rochfort, and d. 1854, leaving a dau.,
Frances, m. Juland Danvers, and has issue.
6. William, Capt. R.N., m. 1833, Arabella, dau. of John Calcraft, M.P., and d. 1847, leaving issue, three daus.
7. Charles, of Rochfort Lodge, co. Donegal, late Rifle Brigade, with which he served at Waterloo, m. 1832, Hannah, eldest dau. of Col. Pratt, of Cabra Castle (she d. 1843) ; and d. 1844, leaving issue, a son, CHARLES GUSTAVUS, the late male representative of the Rochforts, and a dau., Emily Frances.
1. Jane, m. Mervyn Archdale, of Castle Archdale, Gen. in the Army.   2. Alice.
3. Elizabeth, m. Thomas Fane Uniacke.
4. Frances Jocelyn, m. William Dutton Pollard, of Kinturk, and d. 1812.
5. Dorothea, m. 15 Jan. 1813, Thomas Wade, of Carrowmore, co. Galway. She d. 15 June, 1879. He d. 26 Oct. 1863, leaving issue (see that family).

The son of the above-mentioned Charles, of Rochfort Lodge,

CHARLES GUSTAVUS ROCHFORT, of Rochfort Bridge, Capt. 20th Regt., b. 15 March, 1837 ; m. 12 Feb. 1872, Mary, youngest dau. of S. H. May Somerville, D.L., of Whitecroft, co. Dumfries ; and d. 1882, having by her (who m. 2ndly, 12 Nov. 1884, Col. Fortescue Joseph Tynte, C.B., of Tynte Park, J.P. and D.L. co. Wicklow, who d. 24 Sept. 1907 (see that family), and d. 16 April, 1899) had issue,
1. CONSTANCE EMILY,)
2. MURIEL,   } now of Rochfort Bridge.
3. ROSE MINDEN,   )

Arms—Az., a lion rampant arg. Crest—A robin ppr. Motto—De rupe forte.

Seat—Rochfort Bridge, co. Westmeath.

ROCHFORT OF CLOGRENANE.

HORACE COSBY ROCHFORT, of Clogrenane, co. Carlow, b. 16 May, 1877 ; s. his father 1908 ; m. 1906 Violet Ethel, 3rd dau. of the late John Ussher, of Rocklands, co. Galway, and has issue
HILARE FRANCIS.

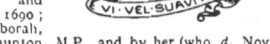

Lineage.—JOHN ROCHFORT, of Clogrenane, co. Carlow, and New Park, co. Dublin, 2nd son of Robert Rochfort, M.P., Speaker of the House of Commons (see preceding memoir), was M.P. for Ballyshannon 1713-27, and Mullingar 1727-39, b. 1690 ; m. 1st, 10 June, 1722, Deborah, only dau. of Thomas Staunton, M.P., and by her (who d. Nov. 1737) had surviving issue,
1. JOHN, his heir.
2. Mary, m. 7 Oct. 1767, Thomas Maunsell.
3. Deborah, m. 1st, 19 Jan. 1754, George Bishop, of Bishop's Hall, co. Kilkenny, and 2ndly, 1770, her cousin, Capt. Philip Rochfort.
He m. 2ndly, 24 May, 1746, Emilia, widow of Rev. William Wilson, and dau. of John Eyre, of Eyre Court, co. Galway, but by her (who d. 23 Aug. 1770) had no issue. He d. 29 Jan. 1771. The only surviving son,
JOHN ROCHFORT, of Clogrenane, High Sheriff co. Carlow 1758, b. 1735 ; m. 25 Feb. 1760, Dorothea, dau. of Thomas Burgh, of Bert House, co. Kildare, and sister of the late Viscountess Ferrard in here own right, and d. Dec. 1812, having by her had issue,
1. JOHN STAUNTON, his heir.
2. Robert (Rev.), d. unm.
1. Anne, m. Sept. 1782, Sir Mathew Blakiston, Bart., and d. in her 102nd year, 27 Nov. 1862.
2. Dorothea Emilia, m. 1804, Francis Turnly, of Richmond Lodge, co. Down, and Cushendall, co. Antrim, and d. 1866, having by him (who d. 1845) had issue (see that family).

The elder son,
COL. JOHN STAUNTON ROCHFORT, of Clogrenane, High Sheriff 1823, m. 1st, 1802, Harriette, 3rd dau. of Sir Horace Mann, Bart. (since extinct), by Lady Lucy Noel his wife, dau. of John, Earl of Gainsborough, and by her (who d. April, 1810) had one son,
1. HORACE WILLIAM NOEL, of Clogrenane.
He m. 2ndly, 1814, Mary, youngest dau. of Thomas Burgh, of Bert House, co. Kildare, and sister of Gen. Lord Downes, K.C.B., and by her (who d. 1866) had a son and two daus.,
2. JOHN DOWNES, of Eaton Place, London, Bawnboy, co. Cavan, and Lisnagree, co. Westmeath, b. 7 July, 1825 ; dec.
1. Dorothea Anne, m. 16 May, 1839, the Hon. Henry Spencer Law, son of Edward, 1st Lord Ellenborough, and d. 25 Nov. 1871. He d. 15 July, 1885, leaving issue (see BURKE's Peerage, ELLENBOROUGH).
2. Anne Margaret, m. 3 May, 1842, T. B. Thornton Hildyard, of Flintham Hall, Notts, M.P., who d. 19 March, 1888.
Col. Rochfort d. 6 May, 1844. His elder son,
HORACE WILLIAM NOEL ROCHFORT, of Clogrenane, B.A., J.P., and D.L., High Sheriff for co. Carlow 1840, and for Queen's Co. 1845, b. 1809 ; m. 1st, 6 Aug. 1837, Frances Elizabeth, eldest dau. of Thomas Phillips Cosby, of Stradbally Hall, Queen's Co., and by her (who d. 25 March, 1841) had issue,
1. JOHN BURGH, late of Clogrenane.
2 Horace William, Capt. R.N. (retired), b. 20 Aug. 1839 ; m. 1882, Elizabeth, only dau. of Marriott R. Dawlay, of Bella Hill, co. Antrim, M.P. for Carrickfergus 1868-80, and has issue,
Horace Marriott Thomas, b. 21 Jan. 1883.
Dorothy Frances Elizabeth, b. 6 Feb. 1886.
3. Thomas Francis Cosby, Col. 4th European Light Cavalry (retired), b. 8 Feb. 1841 ; m. 1889, Alice, widow of the late Col. Daunt, Bengal Army. He d. 14 Oct. 1901.
Mr. Rochfort m. 2ndly, 4 Sept. 1845, Hon. Charlotte Hood, dau. of Samuel, 2nd Baron Bridport, and had issue,
4. William Robert Hood, of Cahir Abbey, Cahir, co. Tipperary, J.P., D.L., Fell. Surveyor's Inst., formerly Lieut. R.A., b. 29 Dec. 1847 ; m. 14 April, 1875, Helen Blanche, dau. of Robert S. Palmer, of Dromquinna, co. Kerry.

5. Alexander Nelson (Sir) K.C.B. (1911), C.B. (1900), C.M.G. (1904), Major-Gen. R.A., Lieut.-Governor of Jersey, 1910, (*Government House, Jersey. Clubs : Naval and Military; Authors*'), *b.* 3 June, 1850.
6. Henry, dec.
1. Amelia Catharine, *m.* 14 Dec. 1871, Thomas Pakenham Law, K.C., of 48, Stephen's Green, Dublin.

Mr. Rochfort, *d.* 16 May, 1891. His eldest son,

JOHN BURGH ROCHFORT, of Clogrenane, co. Carlow, late Lieut. R.H.A., *b.* 28 June, 1838 ; *m.* 29 Dec. 1863, Hilare Charlotte (who *d.* 1 March, 1907), eldest dau. of Henry Hall, of Barton Abbey, co. Oxford, and *d.* 17 Aug. 1908, leaving issue,
1. HORACE COSBY, now of Clogrenane.
2. Oswald John, *b.* 25 Jan. 1883 ; *m.* 2 March, 1910, Ruth Laurie, only dau. of A. Rapaport, of Blackheath.
1. Catherine Frances, *b.* 2 June, 1867 ; *m.* 3 Jan. 1895, Joseph Henry Garratt, of Glenvar, Blackrock, co. Dublin.
2. Eva Blanche, *b.* 10 June, 1871.
3. Hilare Gertrude, *b.* 12 Aug. 1873 ; *m.* 14 Dec. 1910, Raleigh Cooper Payne, of Funchal, Madeira.
4. Grace, *b.* 20 Aug. 1879.

Arms—Az., a lion rampant arg. *Crest*—A robin ppr. *Motto* —Vi vel suavitate.

Seat—Clogrenane, co. Carlow.

ROCHFORT OF CAHIR ABBEY.
See **ROCHFORT OF CLOGRENANE.**

BOYD-ROCHFORT OF MIDDLETON PARK.

GEORGE ARTHUR BOYD-ROCHFORT, of Middleton Park, co. Westmeath, High Sheriff 1904, *b.* 1 Jan. 1880 ; *m.* 3 July, 1901, Olivia Ellis, dau. of late Christopher Ussher, of Eastwell, co. Galway (*see that family*).

Lineage.—THE REV. JAMES BOYD, Rector of Erris, co. Mayo, *b.* 1725 ; *m.* 1752, Mary, dau. of Abraham Martin, and relict of Arthur Vernon, and *d.* 1775, leaving an only son,

ABRAHAM BOYD, Barrister-at-Law and King's Counsel *b* 1760; *m.* July, 1786, Catherine Shuttleworth, relict of John Davies, by whom he had one child, Helena, *m.* Thomas Fenton. He *m.* 2ndly, 1815, Jane, Countess of Belvedere, dau. and eventually sole heiress of the Rev. James Mackay, and by her (who *d.* 1836) left as his decease, 4 Nov. 1822, an only son,

GEORGE AUGUSTUS ROCHFORT-BOYD, of Middleton Park, J.P. and D.L., High Sheriff 1843, *b.* 13 March, 1817 ; *m.* 4 July, 1843, Sarah Jane, eldest dau. of George Woods, of Milverton, co. Dublin, by Sarah his wife, dau. of Hans Hamilton, of Abbotstown, for many years M.P. for co. Dublin, and had issue,
1. ROCHFORT HAMILTON, of Middleton Park.
2. George, *b.* Oct. 1849 ; *d.* an infant.
3. Charles Augustus Rochfort, C.M.G., of Belvedere House, Farnboro, Hants, Col. late R.E. (*United Service and Kildare Street Clubs*), *b.* 4 Oct. 1850 ; *m.* 1st, 4 June, 1874, Adeline Maud Felicia, dau. of the late Mountifort Longfield, D.L., of Castle Mary, co. Cork. She *d.* 6 May, 1902, having had issue,
  1. Robert Mountifort, *b.* 6 April, 1875 ; *d.* 25 June, 1884.
  2. Henry Charles, Capt. R.H.A., *b.* 13 Oct. 1877 ; *m.* 1 June, 1908, Dorothy, dau. of Arthur Nicholson, of Brighton.
He *m.* 2ndly, 26 Nov. 1906, Grace, widow of W. W. Whiston, of Birchwood, Fleet.
4. George Warren Woods, Major Manchester Regt., *b.* 13 Dec. 1854 ; *m.* 6 July, 1882, May, dau. of the late Capt. Thomas Lloyd, 57th Regt., and *d.* 23 Oct. 1891, leaving issue,
  1. Ruth Helen, *m.* 21 Sept. 1904, Lieut. Francis Chilton, R.N., and has issue.
  2. Dorothy May.
  3 Eileen Marjorie.
5. Francis, *b.* 2 Jan. 1857 ; *d.* 1863.
1. Alice Jane, *d.* Aug. 1855.
2. Edith Sarah Hamilton, *m.* 24 July, 1873, Thomas Tighe Chapman, of South Hill (*see* CHAPMAN, Bart., Collateral), and has issue.
3. Florence, *d.* March, 1871.

Mr. Rochfort-Boyd inherited from his mother, the Countess of Belvedere, a great portion of the Rochfort estates situated in co. Westmeath, and assumed, in consequence, the surname and arms of ROCHFORT, in addition to those of BOYD by Royal Licence, dated 16 Nov. 1867. He *d.* 18 Sept. 1887, and was *s.* by his eldest son,

ROCHFORT HAMILTON BOYD-ROCHFORT, of Middleton Park, J.P., High Sheriff 1876, Major West Kent Yeomanry Cavalry, late Capt. 15th Hussars, *b.* 23 Sept. 1844 ; *m.* 1 May, 1875, Florence Louisa, dau. of Richard Hemming, of Bentley Manor and Foxlydiate, co. Worcester, and had issue,
1. GEORGE ARTHUR, of Middleton Park.
2. Harold, Lieut. 21st Lancers, *b.* 18 July, 1882 ; *m.* 7 Jan. 1909,

Winifred, only dau. of John Bathurst Akroyd, of Birdingbury Hall, Rugby, and has issue,
  Diana Nancy, *b.* 13 March, 1910.
3. Cecil Charles, *b.* 16 April, 1887.
1. Ethel Victoria, *m.* 13 Aug. 1898, John Richard Mordred Henry Malone, eld. son of Col. Malone, of Baronston (*see that family*).
2. Alice Eleanor, *m.* 18 Jan. 1900, Percy O'Reilly, eld. son o Philip O'Reilly, D.L., of Colamber, co. Westmeath, and has issue (*see that family*).
3. Winifred Florence.
4. Muriel, *m.* 5 Aug. 1909, John Oloff McCall, of Ballyhooly, co. Cork, and has issue.

Major Boyd-Rochfort assumed the surname of ROCHFORT, by Royal Licence, in 1888, on succeeding to the Rochfort estates left by his grandmother, Jane, Countess of Belvedere. He *d.* 11 Jan. 1891.

Arms—Quarterly : 1st and 4th, az., a fess chequy arg. and gu. between three crescents of the 2nd, for BOYD ; 2nd and 3rd, az., a lion rampant arg. in chief two robin redbreasts ppr., for ROCHFORT.
Crests—1st, Out of a ducal coronet or, a hand erect with the third and fourth fingers folded ppr., for BOYD ; 2nd. On a mural crown or, a robin redbreast ppr., charged with a cross pattée or, for ROCHFORT.
Mottoes—Under arms, Candor dat viribus alas : over 1st crest, Confido.

Seat—Middleton Park, Castletown, co. Westmeath.

ROE OF BALLYCONNELL HOUSE.

SAMUEL BLACK ROE, C.B., of Ballyconnell House, co. Cavan, J.P. and D.L., High Sheriff 1892-93, Deputy Surgeon-Gen. (retired), L.R.C.S., M.B. Trin. Coll. Dublin, served in Crimea 1855, in Indian Mutiny 1858, in Afghan War 1879-80, and in S. African War 1881, *b.* 11 Sept. 1830; *s.* his mother, 1876.

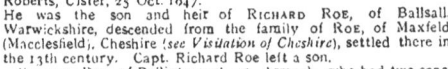

Lineage.—RICHARD ROE, Capt. in Col. Anthony Hungerford's Regt., sent in 1647 to suppress the Rebellion in Ireland, *temp.* CHARLES I; had his arms confirmed by Roberts, Ulster, 25 Oct. 1647.

He was the son and heir of RICHARD ROE, of Ballsall, Warwickshire, descended from the family of ROE, of Maxfeld (Macclesfield), Cheshire (*see Visitation of Cheshire*), settled there in the 13th century. Capt. Richard Roe left a son.

CHARLES ROE, of Ballintaggart, co. Armagh, who had two sons, 1. William, who left no descendants, and 2. THOMAS, of whom we treat. The younger son.

THOMAS ROE, of Mount Roe, co. Armagh, left a son and heir,

THOMAS ROE, of Mount Roe, co. Armagh, who had issue, six sons,
1. Thomas, who had two sons drowned at sea.
2. Charles, *d. unm.*
3. George, who had two daus., 1. Eliza, *m.* Joseph Nicholson, and 2. Charlotte, *m.* — Langtry.
4. Walter, whose issue settled at Baltimore, U.S.A.
5. John, twin with Walter, left issue, who settled also at Baltimore.
6. EDWARD (Rev.), of whom presently.

The youngest son,
THE REV. EDWARD ROE, Rector of the united parishes of Donegore and Kilbride, in the Diocese of Connor, left issue,
1. Samuel, *d unm.*
2. GEORGE, of whom we treat.
3. Edward, *d.s.p.*
4. William, *d. unm.*

The second son,
GEORGE ROE, of Ballyconnell House, co. Cavan, M.D., *b.* 20 Oct. 1788 ; *m.* 23 April, 1829, Eliza, dau. of Maj. Samuel Noble, H.E.I.C.S. She *d.* 7 Sept. 1876. He *d.* 25 July, 1858, having had issue,
1. SAMUEL BLACK, now of Ballyconnell.
2. George Noble, Capt. 3rd Buffs, served in Crimea 1855, and in China 1861, *b.* 11 Oct. 1833 ; *d.* 14 Feb. 1893.
3. Edward Alexander Henry, Lieut.-Col., late Surg.-Maj. A.M.S., formerly Lieut. 10th Foot, and Ass. Surg. 10th Hussars, served in Afghan War 1878-80, *b.* 28 June, 1839.
4. William Alexander Crawford (of Cabragh House, Cootehill, co. Cavan, J.P., Lieut.-Col. (retired) Indian M.S., served in Afghan War 1878-80 with 21st Punjab Infantry, *b.* 4 March, 1847 ; *m.* 9 Nov. 1871, Emma, dau. of William Goodsall, of Gravesend, Kent, and has issue,
  1. Samuel George, Capt. Royal Innis. Fus., *b.* 23 Aug. 1875.
  2. William Edward, Capt. A.S.C., *b.* 25 Oct. 1878.
  1. Eliza Matilda, *b.* 20 Dec. 1872.
  2. Maud Ethel, *b.* 8 Jan. 1874 ; *d* 18 Aug. 1876.
1. Eliza, *b.* 17 Dec. 1831.

2. Anne Mary, b. 11 April, 1835 ; m. Jan. 1877, Lockhart Ramage, and d. 9 July, 1909.
3. Catherine Louise, b. 27 Aug. 1837.
4. Ellen Sarah, b. 29 Sept. 1842.
5. Isabella, b. 12 May, 1844 ; d. *unm.* 5 March, 1886.

Arms—Arg. nine bees volant transversed and a beehive sa., on a canton gu. a rose of the first. Crest—A demi lion rampant erm. armed and langued, gu. holding between his paws a crescent of the east. *Motto*—Duriora virtus.

Seat—Ballyconnell House, Ballyconnell, co. Cavan. *Clubs*—Naval and Military, W., and Hibernian United Service. Dublin.

ROE, OF LORAN PARK.

DEPUTY SURGEON GEN. WILLIAM CARDEN ROE (retired), of Loran Park, co. Tipperary, L.R.C.S.I., L.K. and Q.C.P.I., served in Roy. Irish Fus. during Crimea and Indian Mutiny Campaigns, b. 1834, m. 1864 Emily Louisa, third dau. of Gen. William Twistleton Layard, and has issue,

1. WILLIAM ROBINSON ROBERT (*Loran Park, Roscrea, co. Tipperary. Junior Naval and Military Club*), b. 1872.
1. Annie Kathleen, b. 1865 ; m. 1891, Charles Liesching, of Tiverton, Devon.
2. Margaretta Emily, b. 1870 ; m. 1907, George Theodore Whitfield Hayes, Barrister-at-Law.
3. Emily Georgina, b. 1875 ; m. 1904, Edward Redmond Morres, of Springfield Lodge, Guernsey.

Lineage—THOMAS ROE, of Lismore House, Queen's Co., had issue a son,
WILLIAM ROE, of Lismore House, d. 1844, who by his wife, Margaretta (d. 1873), dau. of John Warren, of Ballyaville, King's Co., had issue,
1. Thomas Warren, d. 1857.
2. John Dalton, b. 1850.
3. WILLIAM CARDEN, now of Loran Park.

Seats—Loran Park, Roscrea, co. Tipperary ; Shackenhurst, Bournemouth. *Club*—Constitutional.

ROLLESTON OF FFRANCKFORT CASTLE.

CHARLES FFRANCK ROLLESTON, R.M., of ffranckfort Castle, King's Co., late Major King's Royal Rifles Militia, b. Feb. 1833; m. 10 Jan. 1873, Mary Dorothea, dau. of John Hutchinson, of Killtorkan, co. Kilkenny, and has issue,

1. JAMES HENRY FFRANCK. b. Nov. 1873.
2. Charles John ffranck, b. April, 1875.
3. Alured ffranck, b. April, 1877.
4. Loftus ffranck, d. 17 Aug. 1881, aged 2 years.
1. Jane Eleanor Daisy ffranck.

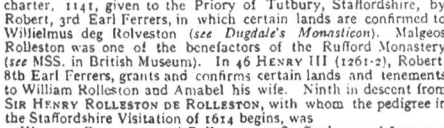

Lineage.—WILLIAM ROLLESTON, son of Sir Henry Rolleston, is mentioned in a charter, 1141, given to the Priory of Tutbury, Staffordshire, by Robert, 3rd Earl Ferrers, in which certain lands are confirmed to Willielmus deg Rolveston (*see Dugdale's Monasticon*). Malgeos Rolleston was one of the benefactors of the Rufford Monastery (*see* MSS. in British Museum). In 46 HENRY III (1261-2), Robert, 8th Earl Ferrers, grants and confirms certain lands and tenements to William Rolleston and Amabel his wife. Ninth in descent from SIR HENRY ROLLESTON DE ROLLESTON, with whom the pedigree in the Staffordshire Visitation of 1614 begins, was
WILLIAM ROLLESTON, of Rolleston, co. Stafford, son of Laurence Rolleston, and Agnes his wife, dau. of John Rollesley, d. 1593, leaving issue five sons and three daus.,
1. Gilbert, d. 1618 ; m. Jane, dau. of R. Sneyd, of Keele, and had issue,
Walter, "son and heir," aged 10, at Staffordshire Visitation, 1614.
Grace, d.s.p.
2. William, d. 1653 ; m. Mary, dau. of William Whatton, of Newtown Linford, co. Leicester, and had issue,
1. William, of Rolleston, Col. d.s.p. 1672 ; mortgaged the estate of Rolleston to Sir Oswald Mosely.
2. Simon, had two daus.
3. RICHARD (Rev.), d. 1636, having had issue,
1. Henry, d.s.p.
2. Edward, murdered by the rebels, 1641.
3. Richard, had one son, John an infant.
4. Ralph, murdered by the rebels, 1641.
5. Thomas, murdered by the rebels, 1641.
6. John, murdered by the rebels, 1641.
1. Susanna, m. Richard Cochrane, d.s.p. 1675.
4. JOHN, d.s.p. 1630.   5. ARTHUR, of whom hereafter.
1. Grace, m. R. Ainsworth.   2. Jane, m. J. Pershall.
3. Elizabeth, m. R. Rolleston.
The above Rev. Richard, John, and Arthur Rolleston went to Ireland A.D. 1610, having received from JAMES I, by patent dated at Westminster, 10 May, 1610, a large grant of land in co. Armagh, in the Barony of Onelan, the manor of Teemore, containing eight and a half townlands, with a proviso that Richard Rolleston should not sell or let any portion of the grant to any Irishman, or other person who did not take the Oath of Supremacy before the Lord Chancellor. Richard and his brothers, in the new year 1618, let all these premises to Sir Francis Annesley, afterwards Lord Baron of Mountnorris, and to Sir John Bourcher and others who had not taken the Oath of Supremacy according to the proviso. Upon an Inquisition being held, Lord Mountnorris took possession of the property. In the year 1637, Thomas, Earl of Strafford, Lord-Deputy of Ireland, attempted to reinstate the heirs of Richard Rolleston, and this matter was made the sixth article of impeachment against him. The youngest son,
ARTHUR ROLLESTON, had issue by Eleanor his wife,
1. FRANCIS, of whom hereafter.
2. Arthur.
3. Richard, who had a dau. Mary, m. John Rolleston.
The eldest son,
FRANCIS ROLLESTON, of Tomlough, co. Tipperary, Col. in the Army of JAMES II, and Governor of Kinsale, co. Cork, m. Eleanor, Fox, and had issue,
1. ARTHUR, his successor.   2. Francis, Capt. in the Army.
1. Katherine, m. Henry Humfrey.
2. Susannah.   3. Mary.
Col. Rolleston made his will 13 June, 1691, and was s. by his son,
ARTHUR ROLLESTON, of Tomlough, Capt. Coldstream Guards, b. 12 July, 1691 ; m. Elizabeth, dau. of Gen. Michael Merritt, of Finnoe, co. Tipperary, and had issue,
1. FRANCIS, his heir.   2. Michael, d.s.p.
3. Stephen (Rev.), of Bridepark, co. Cork, Rector of Knockmorne, m. Eleanor Parr ; d. 1780, having had issue,
1. Stephen.   2. James.
1. Eleanor, m. 1765, her cousin, James ffranck Rolleston, of ffranckfort.
2. Frances, m. Mr. Kilvington.
3. Harriet.   4. Elizabeth, m. — Macbeth.
5. Dorothea, m. — Percival.
6. Katharine, m. W. Swayne.
1. Elizabeth, m. — Walsh, of Walsh Park, King's Co.
2. Susan, d.s.p.   3. Christian, d.s.p.
4. Margaret, m. 1738, Daniel Rogers, of Liskinland, co. Tipperary.
5. Eleanor, m. Capt. James ffranck, of ffranckfort Castle.
Mr. Rolleston d. 1720, and was s. by his eldest son,
FRANCIS ROLLESTON, of ffranckfort, *alias* Coologue, Town Major of Galway and Capt. of Militia Dragoons, b. 1700 ; m. 1740, Frances Everingham, the adopted dau. and heir of Capt. James ffranck, of Coologue, or ffranckfort, and thus acquired that estate. By her he had issue,
1. JAMES FFRANCK, his heir.   2. Arthur, d.s.p.
1. Frances, d. unm.
Mr. Rolleston d. 1779, and was s. by his eldest son,
JAMES FFRANCK ROLLESTON, of ffranckfort Castle, Col. of Volunteer Yeomen 1782, High Sheriff of King's Co. 1784, b. 1742 ; m. his first cousin, Ellen, dau. of Rev. Stephen Rolleston, of Bridepark, and by her had a dau. Frances, who d. an infant. He m-2ndly, 1766, Jane, dau. of Charles Bagge, of Lismore, co. Waterford, and has issue,
1. JAMES FFRANCK, his heir.
2. Charles, of Silver Hills, King's Co., b. 6 March, 1768 ; m. 13 Jan. 1806, Helena Maria, dau. of Richard Maunsell, of Quinsboro', co. Limerick, 2nd son of Richard Maunsell, of Ballywilliam, in said co., and d. 23 Oct. 1820, having by her (who d. 1860) had issue,
1. JAMES FFRANCK, heir to his uncle.
2. Charles Rolleston-Spunner, of Glasshouse, Shinrone, King's Co., Q.C., Chairman Quarter Sessions co. Mayo, assumed for himself only the name of SPUNNER under the will of Thomas Spunner in 1867, b. 2 Nov. 1807 ; m. 22 Oct. 1836, Elizabeth, eldest dau. of Right Hon. John Richards, Baron of H.M.'s Court of Exchequer in Ireland, and d. 1886, leaving issue,
(1) Charles John, late Capt. 74th Regt., b. 1837.
(2) Henry Hugh Barry, b. 1842 ; m. Nicourier Ide Ethel, dau. of Capt. William Richards. He d. 27 July, 1910.
(3) Thomas William, of Hellywood House, Glenealy, co. Wicklow (*Club: Royal Societies, S.W.*), b. 1 May, 1857 ; m. 1st, July, 1879, Edith Caroline (who d. 1896), dau. of Rev. William de Burgh, D.D., Rector of Ardhoe, co. Tyrone, and has issue,
1. Hugh Charles, b. 28 May, 1882.
2. Arthur George, b. 11 Oct. 1883.
3. Charles Henry b. 17 April, 1888.
1. Una Gwynn, b. 17 Dec. 1886.
He m. 2ndly, 8 Oct. 1897, Maud Henrietta, dau. of Rev Stopford Brooke, M.A. (*see* BROOKE *of Dromavana*), and by her had issue,
4. Owen Molony, b. 9 Aug. 1899.
5. Patrick William, b. 22 Oct. 1902.
2. Honor Stopford, b. 21 Jan. 1902.
3. Aideen Maud, 11 Nov. 1904.
(4) Katherine Elizabeth, m. 20 Aug. 1861, Henry Truell, of Clonmannon, co. Wicklow, and d. 12 March, 1890 (*see that family*).

Roper. THE LANDED GENTRY. 604

3. Arthur William, formerly Comptroller of H.M.'s Customs, Sydney, b. 5 June, 1814; m. 1852, Elizabeth, dau. of John O'Connor.
4. Stephen Robert, b. 29 July, 1815.
5. Richard, b. 1811; d.s.p. 1826.
1. Rebecca Elizabeth.
2. Helen Jane, m. Thomas Woods, M.D., of Parsons own, Queen's Co., and d. 1860, leaving issue.
3. Arthur (Rev.), b. 21 May, 1769; m. Feb. 1808, Lucy, dau. of Col. Wemyss, of Danesfort, co. Kilkenny, and d.s.p. 1850.
1. Susan, m. 1793, William Curtis, of Annaghmore, King's Co., and d. 1810.
2. Jane, d. unm. 1847.

Col. Rolleston d. 20 Oct. 1800, and was s. by his eldest son,

JAMES FFRANCK ROLLESTON, of ffranckfort Castle, Major King's Co. Militia, High Sheriff 1804, b. 16 April, 1767; m. 22 May, 1806, Dorothea, eldest dau. of William Minchin, of Greenhills, but d.s.p. 5 April, 1826, when he was s. by his nephew,

JAMES FFRANCK ROLLESTON, of ffranckfort Castle, J.P. and D.L., High Sheriff 1831, b. 11 Oct. 1806; m. 28 May, 1828, Georgiana Elizabeth, dau. of John Bland, of Blandsfort, Queen's Co., and d. Dec. 1875, having had issue,

1. CHARLES FFRANCK, his heir.
2. James ffranck, formerly 50th Queen's Own Regt., d. Nov. 1882.
3. Loftus John, C.M.G., Major Diamond Fields Horse, Griqualand West 1879-84, formerly Royal Sherwood Foresters, b. 1839, m. 1870, Isabella Louise (dec.), dau. of Samuel Stonestreet, of Kimberley, Griqualand West. He d. 1903.
1. Elizabeth Sarah, m. Rev. Knox Homan, Rector of Balteagh, Londonderry.
2. Georgiana Katherine, m. 1864, Edmund Whitney Fetherstonhaugh Whitney, of New Pass, co. Westmeath, 2nd son of Rev. Sir Thomas Fetherstonhaugh, 4th bart., of Ardagh, and has issue.
3. Caroline Rebecca, m. 14 June, 1862, Theobald Richard Wolfe, of Rockford, co. Tipperary, and had issue (see WOLFE of Forenaghts).

Arms—Arg., a cinquefoil az., on a chief gu. a lion passant guardant or. *Crest*—An eagle's head erased ppr. *Motto*—Ainsi et meilleur peute estre.

Seat—ffranckfort Castle, Roscrea, King's Co.

ROPER OF RATHGAR AND LACKAGH.

CHARLES EDWARD ALEXANDER ROPER, of Rathgar, co. Dublin, and Lackagh, co. Kildare, Barrister-at-law of King's Inns, Dublin, b. 20 Jan. 1863; s. his maternal uncle 10 March, 1908.

Lineage.—JOHN FITZGERALD, of Navinstown, co. Kildare, b. 1720, m. 1748, Anne, only dau. and sole heir of John Cusack, of Rathgar, co. Dublin, High Sheriff 1738, by his marriage in 1731 with Elizabeth, dau. of William Armstrong, of Stonestown, 2nd son of Edmund Armstrong, of Gallen, King's Co. Through this marriage, the property of Rathgar passed to the FitzGerald family. It had been granted by the Crown early in the 16th century to Miss Cusack's ancestor, John Cusack, of the City of Dublin, Alderman, son and heir of Nicholas Cusack, of Ballymolgan, co. Meath, as appears by an inquisition taken at Dublin Castle 20 Jan. 1620. John FitzGerald d. 1777, leaving his wife, who d. 1764, a son and heir,

CHARLES FITZGERALD, of Navinstown, Laceagh and Rathgar, b. 1760, m. 1785 (setts. dated 6 Dec. 1785), Elizabeth, dau. of William Hodson of Old Court, co. Wicklow, and Tuitestown, co. Westmeath, and Harriett his wife, dau. of Hartley Hutchinson, of co. Dublin. He d. 1821, leaving two sons,

1. CHARLES, of whom presently.
2. Robert, who s. by will to Navinstown, and d. 1869.

The elder son,

CHARLES FITZGERALD, of Rathgar and Laccagh, b. 1787, m. (setts. dated 26 Oct. 1826) Jane, only dau. of George Walsh, of co. Dublin. She d. 1858. He d. 3 May, 1861, leaving issue,
1. FREDERICK LATTIN, late of Rathgar.
2. Charles Edward Otho, d. unm. 1884.
3. Henry, d. unm. 1855.
1. Geraldine Sophia, m. 1854, Alexander Roper, of Drax, co. Kent. He d. 30 June, 1899. She d. 19 Jan. 1898, leaving surviving issue,
1. CHARLES EDWARD ALEXANDER ROPER, now of Rathgar.
2. Frederick Hamilton De Lacy, b. 14 March, 1877.
1. Alexandra Fanny. 2. Mary Georgina.
3. Lucy Hamilton.
2. Caroline, d. unm. 1856.

The eldest son,

FREDERICK LATTIN FITZGERALD, of Rathgar, co. Dublin, and Laccagh, co. Kildare, late Capt. 63rd Regt. with which he served in the Crimea 1854-5 (medals and clasps), and Capt. Royal Ayrshire Rifles, b. 19 June, 1832; s. his father 1861, and d. 10 March, 1908, being s. by his nephew.

Estates—Lackach, co. Kildare, and Rathgar, co. Dublin.
Residence—55, Leeson Park, Dublin. *Club*—Constitutional, W.C.

ROPER-CALDBECK. *See* **CALDBECK.**

ROSE OF AHABEG AND FOXHALL.

RICHARD DE ROS ROSE, of Ahabeg, co. Limerick, and Foxhall, co. Tipperary, D.L. co. Limerick, High Sheriff 1902, b. May, 1879; m. 16 April, 1902, Gladys Mary, eldest dau. of Rev. F. G. Johnson, of Gosport.

Lineage.—THOMAS ROSE, who went to Ireland from co. Devon, and settled in the co. of Limerick, was elected Sheriff of Limerick 1674, and Mayor 1695, and was attainted by King JAMES 1689. He was seised of the lands of Morgans and others, cos. Limerick, Tipperary, and Clare. He m. and had a son,

GEORGE ROSE, of Morgans and Mount Prospect, co. Limerick, a Grand Juror 1678, m. and had issue, HENRY, GEORGE, Thomas, and three daus. The eldest son,

RT. HON. HENRY ROSE, of Mount Pleasant, co. Limerick, P.C., M.P., 3rd Justice of the King's Bench, Ireland, 1734, m. Anne, dau. of David Crosbie of Ardfert, co. Kerry, and sister of Maurice, 1st Lord Brandon, and aunt of William, Earl of Glandore, and by her (who d. 5 May, 1740) had issue,

1. GEORGE, his heir.
1. Sarah, m. 1st, her first cousin, John Southwell, of Enniscouch, co. Limerick, and had an only child and heir, Agnes Elizabeth, m. 11 Aug. 1750, John Wandesford, Earl Wandesford. Mrs. Southwell m. 2ndly, 30 May, 1739, William Talbot, of Mount Talbot, co. Roscommon.
2. Jane Rose. 3. Elizabeth Anne, m. William Gunn.

Mr. Justice Rose, whose will, dated 13 July, 1740, was proved 25 Feb. 1742, was s. by his only son and heir,

GEORGE ROSE, of Morgans and Mount Prospect, co. Limerick, High Sheriff 1766, m. 1744, his cousin, Catherine, dau. of Launcelot Sandes, of Carrigafoyle, co. Kerry, and by her (who d. 1799) left at his death, prior to 1795, an only child and heir, Elizabeth Rose, m. 2 Oct. 1765, her first cousin, William Talbot, of Mount Talbot, co. Roscommon. We now return to

GEORGE ROSE (2nd brother of the Right Hon. Henry Rose), of Ahabeg, co. Limerick, who m. 1st, 1702, Jane, dau. of Thomas Hickman, of Barntie. co. Clare, and by her had issue,

1. HICKMAN, of whom presently.
1. Agnes, m. 1719, William Gough, of Tureen, co. Limerick, and had issue,
(1) Gertrude, d. unm. Will dated 2 May, 1758.
(2) Jane, m. 1st, Napper; 2ndly, Thomas Keane.

George Rose m. 2ndly (marriage articles, 18 July, 1721), Susanna, widow of Edmund Burgh, of Newcastle, co. Limerick, and dau. of Richard Stephens, of Newcastle, and of Barnstaple, Devonshire, she d. Jan. 1740-1, leaving a son,

2. RICHARD, of whom later.

He d. 17 Nov. 1748, intestate, leaving an elder son (the only son of his first marriage with Jane Hickman).

HICKMAN ROSE, sometime of Ahabeg, and afterwards of Limerick, entered Trinity College, Dublin, 23 April, 1723, but did not graduate, m. at Youghal, 15th June, 1738, Elizabeth, eldest dau. of Jonah Pratt, of Castlemartyr, co. Cork, son of Robert Pratt, of Carrigmashining, near Youghal. She d. July, 1766, having had issue, ten sons and five daus.

1. Robert, b. 30 Jan. 1739-40, buried 2 March following.
2. Henry, o. Patrick's Wall, co. Limerick, b. at the Custom House, Kinsale, 11 Jan. 1740-41, m. Oct. 1775, Alice, dau. of Alexander Hoops, of Tipperary, and d. before 1799, having had by her, whose will was proved 20 Dec. 1728 (with another son, in the navy, drowned from the ship of his uncle Capt. Jonas Rose, and three daus., Margaret, Alicia, and Elizabeth) two sons,
1. Hickman, of Limerick, entered Trinity College, Dublin, 3 Nov. 1794, aged 17, did not graduate, entered Gray's Inn, London, 13 March, 1799, d. 2 Dec. 1810.
2. Alexander, Capt. R.N., of Ballyhandrahan, co. Limerick, m. Mary Elizabeth, eldest dau. of Gerald de Courcy O'Grady, The O'Grady of Kilballyowen, co. Limerick (*see that family*), and had three sons and four daus.
(1) Alexander O'Grady, d. unm., in Melbourne.
(2) Hickman, d. in Melbourne.
(3) Tom, d. Omaha, U.S.A., 1872.
(1) Eliza, m. Wm. Cleburn, and d.s.p.
(2) Alice, d. unm., 24 March, 1910, in her 95th year.
(3) Mary Elizabeth m. Lieut.-Colonel Charles Clement Deacon, C.B., 61st Regiment, and had issue.
(4) Henrietta Dorothea, m. 11 Jan. 1860, Jeremiah Shine, of Ballynacreese, co. Limerick, and d. 29 Jan. 1909, leaving issue.
3. John Tom, d. young. 4. Robert, d. young.
5. George, d. young. 6. George, d. young.
7. Hickman, Paymaster 59th Regt.; b. 22 Oct., 1752: m. 1781, Jane, dau. of Samuel Handy, of Bracca Castle, co. Westmeath; and d. 19 March, 1823, leaving by her (who d. 3 Aug. 1823), three daus.,

IRELAND.   Ross.

(1) Lucinda, *m.* Sept. 1801, John Timothy Kirby, President of the Royal College of Surgeons of Ireland, 1823, and had issue.
2. Elizabeth, *m.* 1816, John Dick, J.P., of Bellefield, co. Wicklow, and *d.s.p.* 13 Oct. 1862.
3. Mary Ann Margaret, *m.* 1814, Michael Daniell, and *d.* 1833, leaving issue.
8. William, Surgeon in the Army, *b.* 3 Nov. 1756; *m.* 28 April, 1789, his cousin Alice, sister of Lieut-General Sir Charles Pratt, K.C.B., and dau. of James Pratt, of Castle Martyn. By her, who *d.* s March, 1799, he had, with Heikman and Elizabeth, who were living at Fethard, co. Tipperary, issue:—
(1) James Pratt Rose, Capt. 66th Regt., bapt. at Castle Martyn, 23 October, 1791 ; *m.* 1st, 11th June, 1818, Elizabeth, dau. of William Davis, of Killeagh, co. Cork, by Margaret, dau. of Roger Green, of Youghal. She *d.* 27th March, 1821, leaving a son, William, who *d.* young ; and Capt. Rose *m.* 2ndly, 1822, Elizabeth, dau. of John Boles, of Springfield, by Anne, only dau. of Thomas Garde, of Dunsfort, both in co. Cork. She *d.* 1840, and he *m.* 3rdly, 16 May, 1843, Aphrasia, youngest dau. of John Gaggin, of Ballybane, co. Cork, who *d.* 20 Sept. 1849, Capt. Rose *d.* 10 June, 1848.
(2) William Hickman, Ensign 2nd Batt. 60th Regt., *d.* at Barbadoes, 12 May, 1811.
(1) Frances Elizabeth.
9. Jonas, Port Capt. R.N., 1801 ; *b.* 26 March, 1759; *d.* 20 July, 1820.
10. James Leslie Rose, *b.* 20 Dec. 1761.
1. Elizabeth, *m.* May, 1770, Capt. Robert Molesworth, 38th Regt., son of the Hon. Byrne Molesworth, M.P., and had issue (for whom see BURKE's *Peerage*, MOLESWORTH, V.)
2. Jane, *d.* young.
3. Gertrude, *m.* 1774, Joseph Rose, M.D., and was grandmother of the late Lieut.-Col. John Rose Holden Rose, 9th and 17th Lancers.
4. Agnes, *m.* Feb. 1777, Simeon Davies, Lieut. 68th Regt., son of the Ven. Michael Davies, Archdeacon of Cloyne.
5. Mary, *m.* Oct 1781, her cousin, Jeremiah Pratt, of Kinsale, co. Cork, and had issue.

We now return to the son of George Rose by his second wife, Susanna Stephen.
RICHARD ROSE, of Limerick, *m.* Mary, dau. of John Anderson, of Foxhall, co. Tipperary, and had issue,
1. THOMAS MAUNSELL, his heir.
2. John, *m.* Anne, dau. of Edward Croker, of Ballinagarde, co. Limerick, and had issue, one son and two daus.,
1. Croker, an Officer in the Army, killed during the Burmese war.
1. Anne, *m.* 1st. John Keating, brother of Lieut.-Gen. Sir Henry S. Keating, and 2ndly. Thomas Westropp, of Ross House, co. Clare, 2nd son of Ralph Westropp, of Attyflyn, co. Limerick.
2. Mary, *m.* Roger O'Callaghan, of Knocknanagh, co. Cork, and had issue.
3. Richard.   4. George.
1. Grace, *m.* Robert King, brother of Sir Gilbert King, Bart.
Richard Rose *d.* 1762, and was *s.* by his son,
THOMAS MAUNSELL ROSE, of Ahabeg and Rathkeale, co. Limerick, *m.* Mary, dau. of Simon Lowe, of Galbally, co. Limerick (see *Low of Kilshane*), and dying 12 Oct. 1831, left issue,
1. RICHARD ANDERSON, of whom presently.
2. Simon, *m.* 29 Sept. 1830, Maria, dau. of Arthur Ormsby, of Ballygrenan and Ballyculleen, co. Limerick, by Maria his wife, 2nd dau. of Thomas Vereker, of Roxborough, and sister of Charles, Viscount Gort, and *d.* 1851, having had issue,
1. HENRY ORMSBY, of Ballyculleen, and Ballygrenan, co. Limerick, and Merrion Square, Dublin, Capt. in the Royal County Limerick Militia. This gentleman *s.* to the estates of the Ormsby family on the decease of his uncle, Henry Ormsby. He *m.* Oct. 1863, Lucy, dau. of Henry Steuart Burton, D.L., of Carrigaholt Castle, co. Clare, and had issue,
Henry, *b.* 1864.
1. Henrietta Ormsby.
2. Mary Ormsby, *m.* 1863, Major Willington, 77th Regt.
3. Thomas, Capt. 32nd Regt.   4. John, Lieut. 98th Regt.
5. Henry, of Ballyclough, co. Limerick.
6. James.   7. William, Lieut. 81st Regt.
The eldest son,
RICHARD ANDERSON ROSE, of Ahabeg and Foxhall, *m.* 1807, Maria, 2nd dau. of Mark A. Tuite, and sister of Sir George Tuite, Bart., of Sonna, co. Westmeath, and dying 4 April, 1820, left issue,
1. RICHARD ANDERSON, his heir.
2. Wellington Anderson, of Foxhall, co. Tipperary, *m.* Julia, dau. of Edward O'Grady, and niece of the 1st Viscount Guillamore, which lady, *m.* 2ndly, Sir Edward FitzGerald, Bart., of Carrigoran.
1. Wilhelmina, *m.* Edward Statuer O'Grady, of Glenagh, co. Clare, and of Merrion Square, Dublin.
The elder son,
RICHARD ANDERSON ROSE, of Ahabeg and Foxhall, J.P. for co. Limerick, *m.* 1st, Eliza Sadlier, grand-dau. of O'Brien Butler, of Dunboyne Castle, co. Meath, and by her he had issue,
ROBERT DE Ros, late of Ahabeg.
Mary.
Mr. Rose *m.* 2ndly, Elizabeth Vereker, dau. of Thomas Jervis, Capt. Carabineers. He *d.* March, 1860. His only son,
ROBERT DE Ros Rose, of Ahabeg, co. Limerick, and Foxhall, co. Tipperary, J.P. co. Limerick, High Sheriff 1882; *b.* Oct. 1851 ; *m.* 1873, Agnes Eliza, 2nd dau. of Benjamin Bunbury Frend, J.P., of Boskill, co. Limerick, and *d.* April, 1900, leaving issue,
1. RICHARD DE Ros, now of Ahabeg.
2. Benjamin Frend, *b.* Sept. 1890.

1. Maud Mary, *m.* 11 April, 1896, Capt. Charles FitzGerald Thomas Cochrane, late Leinster Regt., and has issue (see BURKE's *Peerage*, DUNDONALD, E.)
2. Edith Gladys Jeanette, *m.* 28 June, 1905, Rev. Eyre William Preston Archdall, Rector of Killaloe (see ARCHDALE *of Castle Archdale*).

Arms—Quarterly: 1st and 4th per pale arg. and or, a chevron gu. between three water-bougets sa., for ROSE : 2nd, per chevron arg. and gu. in chief two eag'ets displayed az., for STEPHENS 3rd, arg., a saltire, between two mullets in chief and in base gu. and two boars' heads erased in fesse sa., or ANDERSON. Crests—1st, A demi-lion rampant arg., holding in the dexter paw a rose gu., slipped vert ; 2nd, an eagle, wings elevated sa., preying on a lion's gamb erased ppr. ; 3rd, An oak tree ppr.   *Motto*—Non sine sente rosa.
Seat—Ardhu, co. Limerick.

ROSE-CLELAND. See CLELAND.

ROSS-LEWIN. See LEWIN.

ROSS OF DUNMOYLE.

KATHERINE MARY JEFFCOCK DEANE, only surviving dau. and heir of the late Deane Mann, of Dunmoyle, *m.* 17 Aug. 1882, the Rt. Hon. JOHN Ross, P.C., Judge of the High Court of Justice in Ireland, and a Bencher of King's Inn, LL.B., and M.P. for Londonderry 1892-5, son of Rev. Robert Ross, D.D., and has issue.
1. RONALD DEANE, Lieut. North Irish Horse, *b.* 13 July, 1888.
1. May Margaret Ernestine, *m.* 29 Dec. 1910, Francis Perceval Saunders, Lieut. R.N., eldest son of Lieut.-Col. Saunders, Alton St. Pancras, Dorset.
2. Irene Katherine Douglas, *d.* 27 Dec. 1904.

Lineage.—This family on first coming to Ireland, about the year 1600, received a grant of lands, and settled at Byblox, near Doneraile, co. Cork, and afterwards in Tyrone.
JOHN MANN, a Merchant in Dublin, who received a grant of land, left by will, dated 5 Nov. 1633, his property to his brother,
WILLIAM MANN, who sold his estate in co. Tipperary to Elias Green, of Cashel, and *d.* about 1690, leaving issue, two sons,
1. SAMUEL, of Byblox.
2. William, *b.* 1681 (his son, Charles Mann, of Moy, co. Tyrone, made his will 21 June, 1785).
The elder son,
SAMUEL MANN, of Byblox, near Doneraile, co. Cork, *b.* 1680, *m.* and had issue,
1. THOMAS, his heir.
2. Isaac, Archdeacon of Dublin, and afterwards Bishop of Cork and Ross.
3. Horace, settled at Baltimore, North America.
4. William, an Officer in the Army.
The eldest son,
THOMAS MANN, of Byblox, *b.* 1710 ; *m.* 1744, Frances Henrietta Hamilton, and had issue,
1. HENRY.   2. John.   3. Isaac.
1. Frances.   2. Henrietta.
3. Catherine.   4. Mary.
He *d.* 1780. The eldest son,
HENRY MANN, of Byblox, afterwards of Athenry, co. Tyrone, *b.* 1745 ; *m.* 1772, Jane, dau. of William Smythe, by Anne his wife, dau. of J. Crosbie, of co. Kerry, and by her (who *d.* 1809) had issue,
1. Thomas, *b.* 1774 ; *d.* 1822 ; *m.* 1799, Esther Browne, and had issue.
2. DEANE, of whom presently.
3. William, of Blessingbourne, *b.* 1781 ; *d.s.p.* 1859.
1. Anne Jane, *m.* William Oliver, and had issue. Their son, Henry Oliver, is now of Pittsburgh, U.S.A.
2. Frances, *m.* Charles Mills.   3. Eliza, *m.* Stewart Hall.
Henry Mann *d.* 1 March, 1818. His 2nd son,
DEANE MANN, of Corvey Lodge, co. Tyrone, *b.* 1776 ; *m.* 16 March, 1805, Sarah, dau. of Arthur Mulholland, of Pomeroy, and by her (who *d.* 23 May, 1835) had issue,
1. John Henry, *d.* an infant.
2. DEANE, late of Dunmoyle.
1. Violet, *m.* 1826, Rev. Andrew Christie, M.A., of Termon House, Carrickmoore, and The Parsonage, Six-Mile Cross, Incumbent of Cooley ; *d.* 10 Dec. 1872.
2. Anne Jane, *d.* 5 Feb. 1879.   3. Eliza.
4. Emily, *d.* unm. 22 June, 1898.   5. Sarah, *d.* 3 Aug. 1861.
6. Maria, *m.* 24 July, 1855, her cousin, Thomas Mann, of Stormhill House, co. Tyrone, J.P., and *d.* 1 Jan. 1891, leaving issue,
1. William Henry, LL.B., M.A., Barrister-at-Law, *b.* 11 July, 1856 ; *m.* 10 Oct. 1882, Catherine Egerton Dysart, dau. of Samuel Ewing Porter, of Burt, co. Donegal, and *d.* 1 July, 1897, leaving,
Deane, *b.* 24 Jan. 1884.   Frances Eveleen, *b.* 13 July. 1887.
2. Thomas Deane, *b.* 18 May, 1858 ; *d.* 20 Jan. 1859.
7. Frances Henrietta, *d.* 5 Aug. 1881.
Mr. Mann *d.* 22 Aug. 1844.   His only surviving son,
DEANE MANN, of Dunmoyle and Corvey Lodge, co. Tyrone, J.P. and D.L., Lieut.-Col. late Royal Tyrone Fusiliers, and 4th Batt. Royal Inniskilling Fusiliers (retired with full rank), Lord of the Manor of Corrigan, Killyman, and Patron of the living of Dunmoyle, *b.* 22 June, 1824 ; *m.* 23 Jan. 1856, Mary Stobart, only surviving dau. of the late William Jeffcock, of High Hazles, co. York, J.P.

Ross. THE LANDED GENTRY. 606

West Riding, Major 1st West York Yeomanry Cavalry, 1st Mayor of Sheffield. She d. 19 May, 1903. He d. 1 Dec. 1894, leaving issue,
1. KATHERINE MARY JEFFCOCK DEANE now of Dunmoyle.
2. Emily Frances Henrietta, d. 28 Jan. 1859.
Arms—(of MANN)—Or, on a chevron engrailed ermines, between three lions rampant sa., a trefoil of the first. Crest—A tower or, charged with a trefoil vert, issuant from the battlements five spears ppr. Motto—Virtus vincit invidiam.
Seat—Dunmoyle, near Six-Mile Cross, co. Tyrone. Residence—66, Fitzwilliam Square, Dublin.

ROSS-OF-BLADENSBURG OF ROSSTREVOR.

LIEUT. - COL: SIR JOHN FOSTER GEORGE ROSS - OF - BLADENS - BURG, K.C.B., K.C.V.O., of Rosstrevor, co. Down, J.P. and D.L., Chief Commissioner of the Dublin Metropolitan Police, formerly Major Coldstream Guards, previously Lieut. R.A., A.D.C. to Earl Spencer when Lord Lieutenant of Ireland, A.D.C. to the Earl of Carnarvon when Lord Lieutenant of Ireland, b. 27 July 1848; m. 6 Jan. 1870 Hon. Blanche Amelia, youngest dau. of John, 10th Viscount Massereene and Ferrard, K.P. (see BURKE'S

Peerage). Sir John served in the Soudan Campaign 1885 (medal and Khedive's star), and was Secretary to the Duke of Norfolk's mission to the Holy See 1880, and to Sir Lintorn Simmons' mission to the Holy See 1890.
Lineage—ROBERT ROSS, of Rosstrevor, High Sheriff co. Down 1700, M.P. for Killeleagh 1715-1727, and for Newry 1727 until his death Dec. 1750; m. 1st (marriage licence 21 May, 1700), Anne, eldest dau. and co-heir of Robert King, of Lissenhall, Swords, M.P. (see BURKE's Peerage, KING of Corrard, Bart.), and by her had issue,
1. ROBERT, his heir.   2. Hamill.
1. Mary, m. 1st, 17 May, 1752, Alderman John Mackerell, M.P., of Dublin; 2ndly, 22 Sept. 1758, as his 2nd wife, Charles Gordon, of Killester, co. Dublin, and d.s.p. 4 Dec. 1763.
2. Anne, m. Lucas Savage. He d. 1757, leaving issue.
He m. 2ndly, Jane ——, and by her had further issue.
3. Jane, m. Capt. John Doyne, and had issue (see DOYNE of Wells) The eldest son,
ROBERT ROSS, of Rosstrevor and Dublin, M.P. for Carlingford 1723, 1727, 1761 and 1768, Lord Mayor of Dublin 1748-9, High Sheriff co. Down 1771, had issue by his wife Anne (who d. 22 March, 1741).
1. Robert, Col. in the Army, b. 24 Feb. 1728; d. unm.
2. DAVID, of whom next.
1. Anne, b. 7 June, 1732.
The younger son,
DAVID ROSS, Major in the Army, b. 1 March, 1729, m. Elizabeth, half-sister of James, Earl of Charlemont, and dau. of Thomas Adderley, of Innishannon, by Elizabeth his wife, dau. of Francis Bernard, by Alice Ludlow his wife, and had issue,
1. THOMAS, of whom presently.
2. Robert, Major-Gen. in the Army, who, after serving with the highest distinction in the Peninsula, was appointed Commander-in-Chief of the Army sent against the United States, and after a short career of uninterrupted success, during which he achieved the victory of BLADENSBURG, and possessed himself of the American capital, fell 12 Sept. 1814, whilst advancing to attack the enemy's position near Baltimore. On his widow and his descendants was conferred by the Prince Regent 5 Aug. 1816, the honorary distinction "of Bladensburg," to be added to the family name, and an augmentation of arms. General Ross m. Jan. 1803, Elizabeth Catherine, eldest dau. of William Glassock, and by her (who d. 12 May, 1845) left issue,
1. DAVID ROSS-OF-BLADENSBURG, of whom presently.
2. Robert Ross-of-Bladensburg, d. Nov. 1859.
1. Elizabeth, who d. 1827.
3. James, Lieut. R.M., drowned at sea.
1. Mary, m. Rev. Dr. Blacker.
The eldest son,
REV. THOMAS ROSS, of Rosstrevor, m. 1796, Maria O'Brien, grand-dau. of Sir Edward O'Brien, Bart., of Dromoland, co. Clare, and had issue,
1. DAVID ROBERT, his heir.
2. Edward, m. 31 March, 1833, Anne, dau. of the Right Hon.

Thomas Peregrine Courtenay, brother of the 11th Earl of Devon, and d.s.p. 1840.
1. Charlotte.
Rev. Thomas Ross d. 1818, and was s. by his eldest son,
DAVID ROBERT ROSS, of Rosstrevor, J.P. and D.L., Sheriff 1837, and M.P. for Belfast, b. 22 March, 1797; m. 21 Oct. 1819, Harriet Jane, dau. of the Hon. and Right Rev. Edmond Knox, Bishop of Limerick, and by her (who d. 4 Feb. 1864) had issue,
1. THOMAS, R.N., d. 1847.
2. David, Major, b. 1828; d. 1888; m. 1851, Mary, dau. of Dr. William Austin, Insp. Gen. of Army Hospitals, and had with other issue, an eldest surviving son,
William Levington, L.R.C.S., L.R.C.P.I. (Burslem, Staffs), b. 1855; m. 1896, Laura, dau. of G. M. Felton, and has issue,
(1) Austin Felton, b. 1897.
(2) George Levingston, b. 1898.   (3) David Robert, b. 1900.
(1) Laura Kathleen.
3. Edmond (145, Langdale Road, Thornton Heath), m. 1st, Emily Dalton, and by her had issue.
1. Edmond Augustus, b. 1876.   2. Thomas Hesketh, b. 1878.
3. William Dalrymple, b. 1880.
He m. 2ndly, Emily Augusta Belton, and by her had issue,
4. David Newlyn, b. 1896.
4. Robert, d. unm. 1890.
5. Edward Charles (Sir), C.S.I., Col. late Indian Army, Consul-General for Fars and Khuzistan 1878-91 (8, Beaufort Road, Clifton, Bristol), b. 23 Sept. 1836; m. 1862, Sarah M. C., eldest dau. of Col. Charles S. Whitehill, and has, with other issue, a 3rd son,
George Whitchill, Capt. Indian Army, b. 6 June, 1878; m. 11 April, 1903, Clare Josephine, elder dau. of Major G. A. Welman, Indian Army.
1. Jessie, m. Dr. D. A. Talbot. She d. 1907.   2. Harriet Adèle.
David Ross was Governor of Tobago, and d. 1851. After his death, the part of his property in which is Rosstrevor was purchased by his cousin,
DAVID ROSS-OF-BLADENSBURG, of Rosstrevor, J.P., b. 24 Sept. 1804; m. 1st, 1838, Mary Anne Sarah, only dau. of William Drummond Delap, and by her (who d. 1841) had a dau.,
1. Kathleen Elizabeth, m. June, 1861, Col. Francis J. Oldfield, Political Agent at Kolaporc. He d. 1877. She d. 7 April, 1907.
He m. 2ndly, 9 Dec. 1843, Hon. Harriet Margaretta Skeffington, sister of John, 10th Viscount Massereene and Ferrard, K.P., and by her (who d. 31 Oct. 1883) had issue,
1. ROBERT SKEFFINGTON (Rev.), S.J., late of Rosstrevor.
2. JOHN FOSTER GEORGE (Sir), s. his brother.
3. Edmund James Thomas, Col. late R.E., of Fairy Hill, Rosstrevor, co. Down, J.P., b. 17 Aug. 1849; m. 3 July, 1878, Alexina Frances, youngest dau. of Hon. Colin Lindsay, and by her (who d. 26 Sept. 1897) has issue,
1. Harriet Frances Mary Angela.
2. Olive Margaret Mary.   3. Kathleen Blanche.
4. Mary Josephine.
2. Harriett Margaret, m. 8 May, 1873, William Augustine Ross, of Dunlewy House, co. Donegal. He d. 1883.
He d. 5 Nov. 1866, and was s. by his eldest son,
REV. ROBERT SKEFFINGTON ROSS-OF-BLADENSBURG, S.J., of Rosstrevor, co. Down, M.A. Exeter Coll. Oxford, late Capt. in the Royal South Down Militia, b. 26 Jan. 1847; d. 4 March, 1892, and was s. by his brother.
Arms—Per fesse embattled arg. and or. in chief, the honourable augmentation granted for the services of Major-Gen. Ross, viz., issuant a dexter arm embowed vested gules, the cuff az., encircled by a wreath of laurel, the hand grasping a flagstaff broken in bend sinister, therefrom flowing the colours of the United States of America, ppr. in base, the arms of Ross of Rosstrevor (a chevron embattled counter embattled between three water bougets sa.). On a canton of the third pendant from a ribbon a representation of the gold cross presented by command of His Majesty to the said Major-Gen. Ross. Crests—1st (of honourable augmentation), out of a mural crown or, a dexter arm grasping the colours as in the arms; 2nd, an arm embowed in armour, the hand grasping a dagger all ppr. Motto—Bladensburg.
Seat—Rosstrevor House, Rosstrevor, co. Down. Clubs—Guards', Junior Carlton, S.W.; Kildare Street, Dublin; and St. George's Yacht, Kingstown.

ROTHE late OF MOUNT ROTHE.

COL. GEORGE WALTER CHARLES ROTHE, of Collitrim, co. Cork, Oxfordshire, Colonel (retired) R.H.A., b. 10 May, 1841.

Lineage.—The first of this family to settle in Ireland in 1172 is said to have been JOHN ROTHE, fitz William, 2nd son of William Rothe, of Northon Rothe, Lancashire. He was ancestor of THOMAS ROTHE, sovereign of Kilkenny in 1403, who m. Ellen, dau. of —— Purcell, by Rose, dau. and heir of Adam Waring, and had seven sons. Among the descendants of JOHN ROTHE, the eldest son, were ROBERT ROTHE, M.P. for

IRELAND. Rotherham.

Kilkenny 1585, JOHN ROTHE, M.P. for Kilkenny City 1585, WILLIAM ROTHE, M.P. for Callan 1613, DAVID ROTHE, M.P. for Kilkenny City 1634, PETER ROTHE, M.P. 1639, and JOHN ROTHE, M.P. 1689, for the same place, PETER ROTHE, M.P. for New Ross 1634, DAVID ROTHE, Bishop of Ossory 1613-50, SIR ROBERT ROTHE, knighted while Mayor of Kilkenny 1646, and MICHAEL ROTHE, Captain in the Royal Irish Foot Guards and afterwards Colonel of Rothe's Regiment in the French service 1701, and a Knight of St. Louis, father of CHARLES EDWARD ROTHE, Colonel of Rothe's Regt.

From RICHARD ROTHE, youngest son of the above-mentioned Thomas Rothe and Ellen Purcell, descended

RICHARD ROTHE, of Butler's Grove and Lower Grange, co. Kilkenny, a Burgess of the Corporation of Gowran 1688; *m.* Lettice, dau. of William Connell, of Kilkenny, and *d.* 22 Dec. 1694, having had six sons and four daus.,
1. ABRAHAM, of whom presently.
2. Thomas, *d. unm.*
3. Michael, *b.* 1676; *m.* Anne, dau. of Perkins Vaughan, by Elizabeth his wife, dau. of Sir John Hoey, of Dunganstown, co. Wicklow. She *d.* Aug. 1736. He *d.* May, 1746, having had issue,
   1. RICHARD, *s.* his uncle.
   2. George, Registrar of the Court of Chancery, M.P. for Thomastown 1783-9, *b.* 1729; *m.* May, 1758, Elizabeth, dau. of Rev. William Gore, niece of Arthur, 1st Earl of Arran. She *d.* 1809. He *d.s.p.* 21 Jan. 1789.
   3. William, settled in the West Indies, and left issue, Jeremiah and Mary.
   4. Abraham, *d. unm.* 1779.
   1. Elizabeth, *m.* Jan. 1738, Nuttal Greene, of Low Grange, co. Kilkenny (see GREENE *late of Greenville*).
   2. Lettice, *m.* James Eaton, of Powerstown, co. Kilkenny.
   3. Anne, *d. unm.* 1779.   4. Sarah, *d. unm.*
4. Edmund, who left issue,
   1. Richard, of Cork, *d. unm.* 1768.
   2. Abraham, *d. unm.*   3. Oliver, *d. unm.*
   4. Michael, *d. unm.* in Jamaica.
   1. Judith, *m.* Daniel Ryan.
5. John, of Kilcullen, co. Kilkenny, *b.* 1680; *m.* Elinor, dau. of Henry Houghton, of Balliane, co. Wexford, and *d.* 1746 (will proved 7 March, 1749) having had issue,
   1. Richard, who *m.* twice and *d.* in S. Eustacius, West Indies, leaving a son and a dau.,
      (1) John, *m.* July, 1780, Anne, dau. of — Mason, and had issue,
         1. George. *m.* 5 March, 1827, Damaris, dau. of John Nicholson Constable, of Rock Lodge, co. Tipperary, and *d.s.p.* 21 Sept. 1840.
         2. Abraham, *d. unm.*
         1. Anne, *b.* 1783 ; *m.* 13 March, 1803, Rev. Hans Caulfeild, and *d.* 13 April, 1852, leaving issue (see BURKE'S *Peerage*, CHARLEMONT, V.).
      (2) Elinor.
   2. John, of Kilcullen, *m.* 1755, Mary, dau. of J. Whelan. She *d.* Dec. 1791. He *d.* Dec. 1793, having had issue,
      (1) Patrick, *b.* 1762 ; *d. unm.* 22 Aug. 1783.
      (2) Richard, of Kilcullen, *b.* 1770 ; *d. unm.* 25 Dec. 1824.
      (1) Mary, *b.* 1757 ; *m.* George Bowers, and *d.s.p.* Dec. 1792.
      (2) Catherine, *b.* 1759 ; *m.* Feb. 1784, Peter Burtchaell, of Coolroe, co. Kilkenny, and *d.* 5 April, 1789 (see BURTCHAELL *of Brandondale*).
      (3) Bridget, *b.* 1763 ; *m.* J. Walsh, and *d.s.p.* 26 Jan. 1823.
   3. Michael, of Cappagh, *d.s.p.l.* 25 May, 1782.
   4. Abraham, *d.* at sea *unm.* 1756.
   1. Elizabeth, *m.* June, 1739, William Kenney, of Clonegall, co. Carlow.
   2. Elinor, *m.* July, 1747, John Clarke, of Raheenroche, co. Kilkenny.
6. William, *d. unm.*
1. Mary, *m.* John Mulcahill, of Drumneen, Queen's Co.
2. Ellen, *m.* 1699, Thomas Hewetson, of Cloghruske, co. Carlow
3. Elizabeth, *m.* Capt. Charles Den Roche.
4. Sarah, *m.* Edward Hill, of Graigue, co. Kilkenny.

The eldest son,

ABRAHAM ROTHE, of Butler's Grove, High Sheriff co. Kilkenny, 1728, *b.* 1673 ; *m.* Elizabeth, widow of Perkins Vaughan, and dau. of Sir John Hoey, of Dunganstown, co. Wicklow. She *d.* Jan. 1729. He *d.s.p.* 6 May, 1736, and was *s.* by his nephew,

RICHARD ROTHE, of Butler's Grove and Mount Rothe, High Sheriff co. Kilkenny 1758 ; *m.* 1st, Dec. 1748, Catherine, only dau. of Thomas Cooper, of Graigue, Queen's Co., and niece and heir of Sir William Cooper, Bart., M.P. She *d.* Aug. 1759, leaving an only dau.,
1. Catherine, *b.* 1757 ; *m.* 24 Dec. 1774, Hon. Pierce Butler, M.P. (see BURKE'S *Peerage*, CARRICK, E.), who assumed the additional name of COOPER, and *d.s.p.* 5 May, 1825. She *d.* 20 Feb. 1833.

He *m.* 2ndly, 1765, Catherine, dau. of — Dalton, and by her (who *m.* 2ndly, William Barton, who *d.* 28 April, 1823) had one son and three daus.,
1. GEORGE ABRAHAM, of whom presently.
2. Charlotte, *d. unm.*   3. Anne, *d. unm.* Dec. 1851.
4. Elizabeth, *m.* 3 Sept. 1789, William Moore, of Moore Lodge, co. Antrim (see *that family*).

Mr. Richard Rothe *d.* 28 March, 1771, and was *s.* by his only son,

GEORGE ABRAHAM ROTHE, of Mount Rothe, *b.* 1767, matriculated at Christ Church, Oxon. 17 June, 1784, admitted to Lincoln's Inn 20 Nov. 1784, High Sheriff co. Kilkenny 1804, Mayor of Kilkenny 1810 ; *m.* 5 Dec. 1794, Anne Salisbury, dau. of Laurence Hickie-Jephson, of Carrick House, co. Tipperary. She *d.* 25 May, 1842. He *d.* 10 March, 1846, having had issue,
1. RICHARD JEPHSON, of whom presently.
2. George Walter, Lieut. 13th Regt., *d. unm.* 17 Nov. 1823.

3. Lorenzo, Lieut.-Col. 93rd Regt., *m.* 15 July, 1863, Margaret, dau. of George Stirling, of Glasgow, and *d.s.p.*
4. James, *d.* in infancy.
5. James Abraham, *d.* 4 May, 1823.
1. Dorothea Catherine, *m.* 24 Feb. 1821, John Ladeveze Adlercron, of Moyglare, co. Meath, and *d.* 31 Oct. 1879, leaving issue.
2. Anne Salisbury, *m.* 4 July, 1821, Col. Samuel White, M.P., of Killakee, co. Dublin. He *d.* 1854. She *d.s.p.* 27 Nov. 1880 (see BURKE'S *Peerage*, ANNALY, B.).
3. Katherine, *d. unm.* 31 March, 1889.
4. Frances Elizabeth, *d. unm.* 5 Jan. 1896.

The eldest son,

THE REV. RICHARD JEPHSON ROTHE, Prebendary of Killanully and Rector of Macloneigh and Kilmichael, co. Cork, B.A. Trin. Coll. Dublin, 1820 ; *m.* 1st, 22 Oct. 1830, Letitia, dau. of the Hon. and Right Rev. Thomas St. Lawrence, Bishop of Cork and Ross (see BURKE'S *Peerage*, HOWTH, E.). She *d.s.p.* 1833. He *m.* 2ndly, 18 July, 1848, Harriet, dau. of Lieut.-Gen. Charles Turner. She *d.* 20 Dec. 1879. He *d.* 26 April, 1845, having had issue,
1. GEORGE WALTER CHARLES, present representative.
1. Harriet Salisbury, *m.* 10 Oct. 1881, Col. Cyril Blackburne Tew who *d.* 1890 (see TEW *of Carleton Grange*). She *d.* 24 Feb. 1899.
2. Salisbury Anne Charlotte.

Arms—Or, on a mount in base vert, a stag trippant arg. under an oak tree ppr. *Crest*—On a mount vert a stag lodged arg., attired or. *Motto*—Solo salus servire Deo.

Residence—Neithrop House, Banbury, Oxfordshire. *Club*—Naval and Military.

ROTHERAM OF CROSSDRUM.

EDWARD ROTHERAM, of Crossdrum, co. Meath, J.P., High Sheriff 1906, *b.* 7 April, 1872 ; *m.* 6 Feb. 1907, Jane Mabel, dau. of Sir Robert Gardner, of Ashley, Clyde Road, Dublin, and has issue,
EDWARD, *b.* 18 Jan. 1908.
Jean, *b.* 23 Sept. 1910.

Lineage.—EDWARD ROTHERAM, son of THOMAS ROTHERAM, *m.* Catherine, dau. of John Schoales, of co. Derry, and was father of

GEORGE ROTHERAM, of Triermore, *b.* 1763, who *m.* Sept. 1782, Catherine Margaret, dau. of Jeremiah Smith, of Beabeg, co. Meath (see SMITH *of Annesbrook*), and had issue,
1. EDWARD, of Crossdrum.
2. Thomas, of Triermore, co. Meath, J.P., Lieut. 18th Foot, *b.* 1793 ; *m.* 28 July, 1814, Maria, eldest dau. of Rev. William Cox, Vicar of Lusk, co. Dublin, and *d.* 1861, having had issue,
   1. THOMAS EDWARD, of Triermore, *b.* 1825 ; *m.* Maria Hughes, and *d.s.p.* 1884.
   2. WILLIAM, late of Triermore, *b.* 8 Aug. 1835, *d. unm.*
   1. Maria, *m.* 17 May, 1847, Ferdinand M'Veagh, of Drewstown, co. Meath, and has issue.
3. George Smith, *m.* Jane, only dau. of W. Coates, of co. Kildare, and *d.s.p.* 26 Dec. 1878.
1. Margaret Catherine. *m.* Thomas Battersby, of Newcastle House, co. Meath.
2. Mary Anne, *m.* Feb. 1806, Thomas Gerrard, of Liscarton Castle, co. Meath.
3. Elizabeth Jane, *m.* Francis Battersby, C.B., of Listoke, co. Louth, late Lieut.-Col. 64th Regt.

The eldest son,

EDWARD ROTHERAM, of Crossdrum, J.P., High Sheriff cos. Meath 1852, and Cavan 1855, *b.* 25 March, 1789 ; *m.* 11 April, 1822, Barbara, 3rd dau. of Sir Hugh Crofton, 2nd bart., of Mohill, and by her (who *d.* 1863) had issue,
1. George Augustus, of Kilbride, co. Meath, High Sheriff 1878, *b.* 14 Oct. 1825 ; *m.* 1st, 20 Aug. 1845, Elizabeth, dau. of St. George Smith, of Green Hills co. Louth, by whom he had issue,
   1. George Augustus Edward, of Kilbride, Trim, *b.* 29 Oct. 1851 ; *m.* 189-, Jessie Emily Crampton.
   1. Emily Constance, *m.* Alexander Macauley.
He *m.* 2ndly, 15 April, 1858, Sarah, 6th dau. of Matthew Brinkley, of Parsonstown, co. Meath, and has issue,
   2. Walter Henry, Major R.E., *m.* Nancie MacMillan.
   3. Graham Francis, *m.* Ella E. King.
   2. Minna Georgina, *m.* Rev. Thomas Pearson.
2. EDWARD, late of Crossdrum.
3. Morgan Thomas, *b.* 22 May, 1830 ; *d.* 1893 ; *m.* 18 March, 1857, Isabella Lucinda, 2nd dau. of Francis Hopkins, of Mitchelston, co. Meath, and left issue,
   Edward Crofton, of Belview, Crossakiel, Meath, *b.* 14 March, 1858.
   Mary Countess.
4. Arthur, *b.* 10 Aug. 1831 ; *m.* Ellen G. Forsyth, and *d.* 3 Nov. 1908, leaving issue,
   Eileen, *m.* Robert M'Crory.
5. Henry William, *b.* 10 Feb. 1836 ; *m.* Sarah Ford, and *d.s.p.* 1890.
1. Frances, *m.* William Hopkins, eldest son of Francis Hopkins, of Mitchelstown.   2. Barbara.
3. Jane, *m.* Rev. Ronald MacDonnell.   4. Anne.

Mr. Rotheram *d.* 1881, and his 2nd son,

EDWARD ROTHERAM, of Crossdrum, co. Meath, J.P., High Sheriff 1885, *b.* 25 Nov. 1828 ; *m.* 12 Sept. 1886, Maria Louisa, youngest dau. of Samuel Cooper, of Killcuure Castle, co. Tipperary, and *d.* 4 June, 1904, leaving issue,
1. EDWARD, now of Crossdrum.
2. George Astley, of Sallymount, Castlepollard, co. Westmeath

b. 6 Jan. 1874 ; m. 22 July, 1909, Millicent, dau. of John Radcliff Battersby, of Loughbawn, Collinstown, co. Westmeath (see that family), and has issue,
Clothilde Rosa, b. 2 July, 1910.
3. Austen Morgan, of Castlecor, Oldcastle, High Sheriff co. Cavan 1903, b. 11 June, 1876.
4. Sisson Henry, of Mount Palace, co. Cavan, b. 12 Jan. 1880 ; m. April, 1906, May Jackson.
1. Louisa Barbara, m. 4 April, 1894, Hugh Ponsonby Wilson, of Coolure, co. Westmeath, and has issue (see WILSON of Daramona).
2. Katherine Maria, m. 1897, Capt. A. Law, North Staffordshire Regt., and has issue.

Seats—Crossdrum, Oldcastle, co. Meath, and Sallymount House, Castlepollard, co. Westmeath.

ROTHWELL OF ROCKFIELD.

The late THOMAS ROTHWELL, of Rockfield, co. Meath, B.A. Oxford, J.P. and D.L., High Sheriff 1867, M.A. Mag. Coll. Oxford, late Lieut. Meath Militia, b. 25 June, 1834 ; m. 28 June, 1866, Louisa Catherine Hannah (now of Rockfield, co. Meath), eldest dau. of Mervyn Pratt, J.P. and D.L., of Cabra Castle, Kingscourt, co. Cavan (see that family) and d. 1 March, 1909, leaving issue,
1. Emily Madeline Elizabeth.
2. Louisa Frances, m. 20 Jan. 1904, Rev. J. W. ff. Sheppard, Rector of Wouldham, Kent, and has issue (see SHEPPARD).
3. Florence Isabella. m. 1 Aug. 1894, John Hampden Nicholson of Balrath Burry, co. Meath, and has issue (see that family).
4. Helen Grace.

Lineage.—JOHN ROTHWELL, of Berfordstown, co. Meath, d. intestate 19 Sept. 1714 (Chancery Bill 1714-15), leaving by Mary his wife, four sons and five daus.,
1. JOHN, his heir.
2. Thomas, of Berford, Meath, m. April, 1741, Mary, dau. of Rev. Mr. Jourdon, Rector of Dunshaughlin, a French refugee, and had a son, John. 3. James. 4. Joseph, b. 1711.
1. Elizabeth. 2. Martha. 3. Mary.
4. Anne. 5. Grizel.

The eldest son,
JOHN ROTHWELL, of Cannonstown, Meath, m. shortly before 22 Jan. 1714-15, the dau. of — Barry, and had issue,
1. John, m. his cousin Miss Barry, and d.s.p.
2. Thomas, of Cannonstown, b. 1738 ; m. Elizabeth Shields, of Furze Park, and d. 1798, having had issue,
1. John, of Cannonstown, m. 18 March, 1800, Catherine, dau. of Thomas Prendergast, and sister of Lieut.-Gen. Sir Jeffrey Prendergast. She d. 30 Oct. 1860. He d. 18 May, 1842, having had issue.
(1) Jane, m. 1818, her cousin John Martley, of Ballyfallon, co. Meath (see that family).
(2) Eliza, m. 5 May, 1828, William Woodward Sadleir, and has issue (see SADLEIR of Castletown).
2. Wade, of Cannonstown, Major in the Army, m. Sarah, dau. of James Kellett, of Spandan, Meath, and had a son,
Thomas Wade, of Warwick, whose eld. dau. Sarah Sidney, m. 13 Jan. 1857, P. E. Bucke, son of the Rev. Horatio Walpole Bucke.
3. Thomas, Ensign 46th Regt. ; killed at Albuera, d. unm.
4. Richard, Lieut. in the Army ; d. of wounds.
5. Charles, of Kells and Staffordstown, co. Meath, m. 1st, Mary Jane, dau. of Robert Kellett, of Waterstown, co. Meath, and had a son,
Thomas Robert (Rev.), M.A., Precentor of Lismore, Prebendary of Clashmore, and Rector of Ardmore, Youghal.
He m. 2ndly, Jane, dau. of Rev. Mr. Irwin, and by her had, Georgina Eleanor, m. 1878, Richard John Butler, of Staffordstown, co. Meath, and d. 1888.
6. William.
1. Maria. m. Henry Burrows. 2. Elizabeth.
3. Alicia, m. 1800, Rev. John Boyle Thompson.
4. Sarah, m. Lieut. Thomas Shields, Adjt. N. Recruiting District, and d. 6 Aug. 1864, aged 84.
3. Richard, of whom presently.
1. Anne, m. 1st, Rev. J. Smyth, and 2ndly, Thomas Radcliffe, LL.D., Judge of the Prerogative Court.
2. Mary, m. Samuel Garnett, of Summerseat, co. Meath (see that family).
3. Mathilda, m. Henry Garnett, of Athcarne Castle, co. Meath.

The youngest son,
RICHARD ROTHWELL, of Berford, s. to his uncle's (Thomas Rothwell) estate, and bought the property of Rockfield from his elder brother. He m. 5 April, 1763, Mary, dau. and heir of Hugh Lowther, of Hurlstown, and by her (who d. 14 Sept. 1802) had issue,
1. John, of Staffordstown, b. 1703, m. 1794, Alicia, dau. of N. Forth, and d.s.p. Aug. 1826.
2. THOMAS, of whom presently.
3. Hugh, m. Miss Allevn, and had four sons. 4. Richard, d.s.p.
1. Abigail, m. Dudley St. George Ryder.
2. Martha, m. Rev. R. Butler, D.D.
3. Mary, d. unm. 7 Feb. 1859.
4. Elizabeth, m. 1798 William Martley, of Bailyfallon, co. Meath, and had issue (see that family). 5. Anne, m. Henry Cusack.

Mr. Rothwell d. 1780. His 2nd son,
THOMAS ROTHWELL, of Rockfield, High Sheriff 1794, b. 1765 ; m. 1st, 15 April, 1795, Helena, dau. of C. H. Upton, of Dublin, and by her (who d. 17 Feb. 1800) had issue,
1. RICHARD, his heir.
1. Isabella, m. Rev. James Butler, of Priestown, Meath, who d. March, 1869 ; she d. Nov. 1876.
2. Mary Anne, m. 1772, Samuel Garnett, of Summerseat, co. Meath, who d. Dec. 1862 ; she d. 30 April, 1888, and had issue (see that family).

Mr. Rothwell m. 2ndly, 23 Jan. 1810, Letitia, dau. of James Corry, of Shantonagh, co. Monaghan, by Mary his wife, dau. of John Ruxton, of Ardee House, and had by her a son,
2 THOMAS, of Shantonagh and Black Castle, who assumed the name and arms of FITZHERBERT (see that name).

Mr. Rothwell d. Sept. 1817. and was s. by his son,
RICHARD ROTHWELL, of Rockfield, J.P. and D.L., High Sheriff 1839, B.A. Exeter Coll. Oxford 1820, b. March, 1799, who m. 17 June, 1824, Elizabeth, only child of Rev. Thomas Sutton, Rector of Cloogill, co. Meath, and by her (who d. 24 Nov. 1871) had issue,
1. THOMAS, late of Rockfield.
2. John Sutton, Col. R.A., b. 22 Oct. 1841 ; m. 21 Jan. 1880, Henrietta Camilla, dau. of Vice-Admiral Alexander Boyle, R.N. He d. 13 March, 1893. She d. 28 May, 1902, leaving issue,
1. Richard Sutton, b. 18 Jan. 1882.
2. Mark Sutton, late Lieut. R.N., b. 4 Jan. 1883 ; m. 21 Sept. 1910, Agnes Gertrude, only child of George Reginald Grant.
3. Guy Sutton, b. 22 Jan. 1887.
1. Mary Elizabeth, m. 18 June, 1868, Rev. Edward Butler, who d. 23 Feb. 1877, leaving a dau.,
Katherine May Dorothea, m. April, 1899, Ivor Atkins, Mus. B.
2. Helena, d. 18 Nov. 1906. 3. Elizabeth.
4. Isabella. m. 17 Aug. 1865, Major William D. Hague, son of Barnard Hague, of Micklegate, Yorks : and d. 6 Oct. 1894.
5. Frances Maria. m. 12 July, 1855, Rev. John Richard Brougham, M.A., Canon of Cloyne Cathedral, and has issue, a son,
Richard Henry Vaux (Rev.), b. 14 March, 1870 , m. 24 Sept. 1896, Beatrice Rose, dau. of Maj. Alexander Dickson Burnaby, R.A., and has issue,
John Collingwood, b. 7 Oct. 1897.
6. Catharine Emma, m. 12 Feb. 1863, Very Rev. Horace Townsend Fleming, Dean of Cloyne, and has had issue,
1. Lionel Rothwell (Rev.).
2. Horace Townsend, d. 23 Oct. 1896.
1. Elizabeth Mary.
2. Emma Hildegarde.
3. Catharine Emma Louisa, who d. 8 Jan. 1880.
7. Anne Upton, d. 7 June, 1873.

Mr. Rothwell d. 13 Aug. 1853.

Seat—Rockfield, near Kells, co. Meath. Clubs—Kildare Street and Junior Constitutional.

ROWAN OF MOUNT DAVYS.

JOHN JOSHUA ROWAN, of Mount Davys, co. Antrim, J.P. and D.L., Lieut.-Col. late 4th Batt. Royal Irish Rifles, and served in the 62nd Regt., b. 12 Dec. 1838 ; m. 1st, 1866, May Amelia, eldest dau. of George Wright, sometime Colonial Treasurer of Prince Edward Island, which lady d.s.p. 1879. He m. 2ndly, 1881, Ellen Augusta, dau. of Rev. Edward W. Vaughan, Rector of Llantwit Major, co. Glamorgan.

Lineage.—The family of Rowan is of Scotch descent, and derives from
JOHN ROWAN, of Greenhead, in the parish of Govan, co. Lanark, N.B., b. 1548, who acquired these lands with his 1st wife, the dau. and heir of John Gibson, of Greenhead. His only son by this lady,
JOHN ROWAN, of Greenhead, d. 1614, leaving by Agnes Shanks his wife, an elder son and heir,
JOHN ROWAN, of Greenhead, m. Janet Anderson, of Govan, co. Lanark, and d. 1685, having had, with other issue, an eldest son,
REV. ANDREW ROWAN, who went to Ireland, and was inducted to the Rectory of Dunaghy, Diocese of Connor, co. Antrim, 13 Sept. 1661, and resided at Old Stone, alias Clough, co. Antrim. He m. 1st, about 1660, a dau. of Capt. William MacPhedris, of Camglass, in the same co., and by her had, with two daus., two sons,
1. WILLIAM (Capt.), of Derry, attainted, with his father, by the Parliament held by King JAMES II at Dublin, in 1689 ; m. Mildred Thompson, and left an elder son,
WILLIAM, of Richmond, Surrey, m. Elizabeth, dau. of Edward Eyre, of co. Galway, and left at his decease an only dau. and heir,
Jane, who m. 1st, Tichborne Aston, and 2ndly, Gawen Hamilton, of Killyleagh (see ROWAN-HAMILTON of Killyleagh).
2. John, of whose line we treat.

He m. 2ndly, Alice Dunlop, and by her had, with two daus., three sons,
3. Robert. 4. Archibald.

5. George, of Maghera, co. Down, ancestor of the Kerry family of Rowan.

Rev. Andrew Rowan d. 1717. His 2nd son.

Rev. John Rowan, of Ballinagapog, co. Down, m. Margaret Stewart, of co. Down, and had issue. The 7th son,

Rev. Robert Rowan, of Mullans, co Antrim, Chancellor of the Diocese of Connor, m. Letitia, dau. and sole heir of John Stewart, of Garry (by his wife, a dau. and co-heir of Redmond, of Blaris, co. Down), and had an eldest son and heir,

John Rowan, of Mullans and Garry, b. 18 Feb. 1733, High Sheriff co. Antrim 1755; m. 3 Feb. 1753, Rose, dau. of Capt. Charles Stewart, of Lisburn, co. Antrim, and (: Clunie, N.B., by Rose his wife, dau. of Roger Hall, of Narrow Water, co. Down, and by her (who m. 2ndly, Capt. Phillips) had issue. The eldest son and heir,

Robert Rowan, of Mullans, Garry, and Belleisle, co. Antrim, b. 9 Aug. 1754; m. 6 April, 1777, Eliza, dau. of Hill Willson, of Purdysburn, co. Down, and by her (who d. 1817) had issue,
1. John, his heir.
2. Hill Willson, m. Eliza Jackson, sister to Mr. Justice Jackson.
3. Robert, m. 1st, Martha, eldest dau. of William Rainey, of Greenville, co. Down, relict of George Stewart, and by her had issue,
   1. Charles, dec.   2. John, dec.
   3. Arthur, dec.   4. Henry, Lieut.-Gen., C.B., dec.
   5. Frederick, dec.
   1. Harriet, dec.

He m. 2ndly, Harriet Fulton, dec.; and 3rdly, Henrietta Murphy, dec.
4. James, m. Rose Bristow, both dec.
5. Charles (Sir), K.C.B., Commissioner of Metropolitan Police, Assistant-Adjutant-Gen. Light Division in the Peninsular War, d.s.p.
6. Frederick, m. Sarah Prom, of Norway, and had two daus., Eliza and Frederick, both dec.
7. Edward, Capt. R.N., m. Elizabeth Legge, dec.
8. William (Sir), G.C.B., Field-Marshal and Col. 52nd Foot, a distinguished officer, who served in Sicily, Portugal, France and Belgium (at Waterloo), and commanded the Forces in Canada from 1849 to 1855, b. 1789; m. 1811, Martha, dau. of John Spong, of Mill Hall, Kent, and d.s.p.
   1. Eliza, d. unm.
   2. Elinor, m. John J. Heywood, Dempster of the Isle of Man, and is dec.

Mr. Rowan served as High Sheriff co. Antrim 1779, and d. 12 Sept. 1832. His eldest son,

John Rowan, of Garry and Aboghill, J.P. and D.L., High Sheriff 1814, Major Antrim Militia, b. 30 March, 1778; m. 1st, 25 May, 1800, Eliza Honoria, eldest dau. of Lieut.-Col. Alexander Macmanus, of Mount Davys, co. Antrim, High Sheriff 1782, by Hester Henrietta his wife, 2nd dau. of Mark Kerr O'Neill, of Flowerfield, co. Londonderry, cadet of O'Neill of Shanes Castle, and by her (who d. 18 May, 1819) had

Robert Willson (Rev.), of Mount Davys.

He m. 2ndly, 28 Oct. 1823, Dorothea Shaw Ogilvie, relict of James Blair, of Merville, co. Antrim. Mr. Rowan d. 19 Dec. 1855, and was s. by his son,

Rev. Robert Willson Rowan, of Mount Davys, co. Antrim, J.P., b. 9 March, 1810; m. 26 Sept. 1834, Anna, 2nd dau. of Joshua Minnitt, of Anaghbeg, co. Tipperary (see that family), and d. 31 Jan. 1886, leaving issue,
1. John Joshua, now of Mount Davys.
2. Alexander Macmanus, Lieut. 13th Foot, b. 24 April, 1841, dec.
3. Robert Kerr O'Neill, b. 17 Jan. 1849.
1. Eliza Hester, b. 24 Feb. 1843; m. Capt. T. L. Stack, and has issue,
   Charles Robert Stack.
2. Mary Dorothea Stuart, b. 14 Dec. 1844; m. 31 Aug. 1869, Edmund William Waller, of Ardtona, Drumcoun, co. Dublin, and had issue (see Waller of Prior Park).
3. Anna Villiers, b. 7 March, 1847.

Family of Macmanus.

The Macmanus Sept, an ancient Irish family, formerly possessed of extensive property in counties of Antrim, Fermanagh, Londonderry, and the co. and town of Carrickfergus, descended from Magnus O'Connor, 3rd son of Tirleigh Mor O'Conor, 48th King of Connaught and 181 elected monarch of Ireland. A branch of this sept settled in co. Antrim, of which

Bryan Macmanus, of Ballybeg, m. 1662, Esme McNaghten, of Beardiville, and had issue,

Alexander Macmanus, of Carndonaghay, m. 1708, Honoria, dau. of McGuinness, of Cabra, co. Down, and had

Bryan Macmanus, High Sheriff co. Antrim 1769, m. Alicia, dau. of Adam Stodhard, of Drumbain, co. Down, and had

Alexander Macmanus, High Sheriff co. Antrim 1782, m. Hester Henrietta, dau. of Mark Kerr O'Neill, of Flowerfield, and had a dau.,

Eliza Honoria, m. 25 May, 1809, John Rowan, of Garry and Ahoghill (see above).

Arms—Quarterly: 1st, vert, a fesse chequy or and gu. between a trefoil slipped in chief and three crosses-crosslet fitchée issuant from as many crescents in base of the second, for Rowan; 2nd, or, a fess chequy arg. and az. between two sinister hands couped at the wrist, all within a double tressure, flory counter flory gu., for Stewart; 3rd, gu., three cushions erminois, a crescent for difference, for Redmond; 4th, or, a fess gu. and in chief a boar passant sa., for Macmanus. *Crest*—A naked arm couped at the elbow, grasping a dagger ppr. pommelled or. *Motto*—Cresco per crucem.

Seat—Mount Davys, Cullybackey, co. Antrim.
I.L.G.

ROWLEY OF MOUNT CAMPBELL.

William Rowley, of Mount Campbell, co. Leitrim, J.P. and D.L., High Sheriff 1899, b. 19 May, 1832; s. his brother 1887; m. 26 Dec. 1853, Rosetta, dau. of Richard Goddard, of Colchester, Essex.

Lineage.—Clotworthy Rowley, M.P. for Downpatrick, Barrister-at-Law, 3rd son of Admiral of the Fleet Sir William Rowley, K.B. (who d. 1 Jan. 1768), by Arabella his wife (who d. Feb. 1784), dau. and heir of Capt. George Dawson, and brother of Rear-Admiral of the White Sir Joshua Rowyle, 1st Bart. (see BURKE'S Peerage), b. 1731; m. 1766, Letitia, dau. and co-heir of Samuel Campbell, of Mount Campbell, co. Leitrim. She d. 1776. He d. 1805, having had issue.
1. William, Recorder of Kinsale, co. Cork, and Commissioner of the Customs, d. unm. 1811.
2. Josias (Sir) Bart., G.C.B., G.C.M.G., Admiral R.N., created a Bart. 2 Nov. 1813; d. unm. 10 Jan. 1842.
3. Samuel Campbell, of Mount Campbell, co. Leitrim, J.P., Rear-Admiral of the White, b. 19 Jan. 1774; m. 1st, Mary, dau. of — Thompson, of Whitepark, co. Fermanagh, and 2ndly, 4 Nov. 1830, Mary, dau. of Edmund Cronin, of Newtown, co. Kilkenny, and d.s.p.
4. John, of whom presently.
1. Mary, m. Charles Vigogne, of Wicklow, sometime in the French Service, and had issue.

The youngest son,

Rev. John Rowley, LL.D., Prebendary and Canon of Christ Church, Dublin, Chaplain to the Prince Regent, m. 30 Sept. 1826, Catherine, 2nd dau. of Joseph Clarke, of Kilburne Priory, Middlesex, and left issue,
1. Josias, of Mount Campbell, co. Leitrim, J.P. and D.L., High Sheriff 1851, Commander R.N., b. 2 April, 1829; m. 25 Nov. 1869, Alice Kemmis, youngest dau. of Rev. William Betty, of Kingstown, Queen's Co., and d.s.p. 1887.
2. William, now of Mount Campbell.
1. Sophia, m. 11 Sept. 1846, William Armit Lees. She d. 12 Jan. 1859, leaving issue (see BURKE'S Peerage, LEES, Bart.). He m. 2ndly, 6 Feb. 1861, Mary Louisa, dau. of John Hamilton, of The Grove (see HAMILTON of Ballymacoll). She d.s.p. 4 Jan. 1898. He d. 11 Oct. 1885.
2. Catherine Mary, m. 7 Jan. 1859, Charles Henry James, Official Assignee of the Court of Bankruptcy in Ireland. She d. 21 June, 1873, leaving issue (see BURKE'S Peerage, JAMES, Bart.).
3. Mary.

Arms—Arg. on a bend engrailed between two Cornish choughs sa. three escallops of the field. *Crest*—A mullet pierced or. *Motto*—Ventis secundis.

Seat—Mount Campbell, Drumsna, co. Leitrim.

ROWLEY OF MARLAY GRANGE.

Hercules Douglas Edward Rowley, of Marlay Grange, Rathfarnham, co. Dublin, J.P. and D.L., late Lieut. 5th Batt. Leinster Regt., b. 1 Aug. 1859; m. 7 Oct. 1884, Agnes Mary, only dau. of the late A. Allen, of Devizes, Wilts, and has issue,

1. Ivy Mabel Armine Douglas, b. 9 Nov. 1880; m. 26 Oct. 1910, Reginald Stanley Lewis Boulter, eldest son of Stanley Boulter, J.P., of Garstone Park, Godstone, Surrey.
2. Monica Evelyn Douglas, b. 27 Feb. 1893.

Lineage—Col. the Hon. Hercules Langford Boyle Rowley, of Marlay Grange, co. Dublin, J.P. and D.L. co. Meath, Hi h Sheriff 1859, J.P. co. Dublin, Hon. Col. 5th Batt. Prince of Wales's Own Leinster Regt., formerly Capt. 6th Inniskilling Dragoons, educated at Eton and Sandhurst, the 2nd

2 Q

son of the late Hercules Langford, 2nd Baron Langford (who *d.* 3 June, 1839) (*see* BURKE'S *Peerage*, LANGFORD, B.); *b.* 19 June, 1828; *m.* 3 Nov. 1857, Louisa Jane, sister of 1st Baron Blythswood, and *d.* 20 March, 1904, leaving issue,
1. HERCULES DOUGLAS EDWARD, now of Marlay Grange.
2. Arthur Sholto Langford, Consul at Tahiti from 1909, late Lieut. 5th Batt. Leinster Regt., *b.* 10 Dec. 1870.
1. Armine Charlotte.
2. Gladys Helen Louisa, *m.* 5 May, 1887, Claude Hume Campbell Guinness, and *d.* 23 March, 1891, leaving issue,
Marjory Gladys, *m.* 11 Feb. 1909, Lieut.-Col. Alexander Victor Frederick Villiers Russell, M.V.O., Grenadier Guards, Military Attaché in Berlin from 1910 (*see* BURKE'S *Peerage*, AMPTHILL, B.).
3. Evelyn Augusta, *m.* 19 Jan. 1897, Maj. Edward Milner, Scots Guards (*see* BURKE'S *Peerage*, MILNER, Bart.).

Arms—Arg. on a bend cotised gu. three crescents or. *Crest*—A wolf's head erased arg. collared and langued gu. *Motto*—Bear and forbear.
Seat—Marlay Grange, Rathfarnham, co. Dublin. *Residences*—8, Cambridge Place, Kensington, W. *Clubs*—Junior Carlton, S.W.; Isthmian, W.; Kildare Street, Dublin.

RUSSELL OF GLANMORE.

The late MICHAEL RUSSELL, of Glanmore, co. Cork, *b.* 14 Sept. 1845; *m.* 1st, 29 April, 1876, Wilhelmina, youngest dau. of James Lyons, D.L., of Croom House, co. Limerick (*see that family*). She *d.* 14 March, 1877, leaving a son,
1. Henry, *d.* an infant 1878.

He *m.* 2ndly, 8 Jan. 1880, Alice Gertrude, 2nd dau. of John Morrogh-Bernard, D.L., of Fahagh Court, co. Kerry (*see that family*), by Frances Mary Blount, his wife, and *d.* 13 April, 1912, having by her had issue,
2. MICHAEL MARY, *b.* 18 April, 1882.
1. Frances Mary, a nun.
2. Agnes Mary, *d.* 22 Nov. 1898.

Lineage.—JAMES RUSSELL, *b.* 1687; *m.* Miss Dwane, and *d.* 1779, leaving issue two sons and a dau. The elder son,
MICHAEL RUSSELL, of Mount Russell, co. Limerick, and Ballinaboulia (now Glanmore), co. Cork, *m.* Deborah, dau. of — Sarsfield, and *d.* 1819, having had with eight daus. one son,
PATRICK RUSSELL, of Mount Russell, *b.* 1783; *m.* 1804, Theresa, 2nd dau. of James Morrogh. She *d.* 1835. He *d.* 1828, having had issue,
1. Daniel, *d.* young.
2. James, of Mount Russell, *b.* 1807; *m.* 1834, Maria, dau. of Pierce Shannon, of Limerick, and *d.* 25 April, 1858, having had issue,
  1. Patrick, of Mount Russell, *d. unm.* 20 Sept. 1881.
  2. Michael Alexander, *d. unm.* 1880.
  3. James Albert, *d. unm.* 1895.
  4. Henry, *d. unm.* 1888.
  5. Pierce.   6. George.
  1. Antoinette, *d. unm.*   2. Eliza, *d. unm.* 1887.
  3. Emily, a nun, *d.* 1872. 4. Theresa, a nun.
  5. Alice, a nun, *d.* 1886.
3. George, *b.* 1809; *m.* Miss Lynch, and had with four daus., one son,
Patrick George, *d. unm.* 1889.
4. MICHAEL, of whom presently.
5. Henry, *b.* 1819; *d. unm.* 21 Jan. 1892.
6. Patrick Joseph, *b.* 1822, *d. unm.* 1879.
1. Jane, *m.* Frank Healy-Coppinger, and *d.* 1847, leaving issue.
2. Eliza, *m.* John Clanchy, 2nd son of John Clanchy, of Charleville, and left issue.
3. Delia, *m.* 1835, Thomas Ledwell, and *d.* 1889, leaving four daus.
4. Mary, a nun, *d.* 1866.
5. Theresa, *m.* John Cahill, and *d.* 1898, leaving a dau.

The 4th son,
MICHAEL RUSSELL, of Ballinaboulia (Glanmore), co. Cork, s. his grandfather in that propety 1819, *b.* 20 July, 1812; *m.* 27 June, 1843, Marianne, dau. of Daniel Clanchy, D.L., of Charleville, co. Cork. She *d.* 28 May, 1894. He *d.* 24 March, 1859, having had issue,
1. MICHAEL, late of Glanmore.
2. Daniel Clanchy, *b.* 3 Oct. 1854; *m.* 30 Nov. 1895, Josephine, dau. of Michael Ryan, and *d.s.p.* 19 June, 1907.
1. Anna, *m.* 15 Nov. 1869, Thomas Davys, who *d.* 29 June, 1895, leaving issue,
  1. Francis, *d.s.p.* 1898.   2. Michael.
  3. Edward.   4. Richard.
  1. Pauline, a nun.
2. Theresa, *m.* 1st, 7 Sept. 1874, John Hutchinson, who *d.* 2 May, 1885, leaving issue,
  1. Constance.   2. Violet, a nun.
  3. Evelyn, a nun.
  4. Vera, *m.* 1906, Major Donal McCarthy Morrogh, and has issue.
  5. Gertrude.
She *m.* 2ndly, 2 June, 1887, Capt. Henry Thomas Clanchy, R.N., and by him (who *d.* 16 Feb. 1907) has issue,
  1. John Daniel, *b.* 1889.
  2. Henry, *b.* 1893, R.N.
  6. Mary.   7. Theresa.
Seat—Glanmore, Charleville, co. Cork.

OTWAY-RUTHVEN OF CASTLE OTWAY.

FRANCES MARGARET, MRS. W. C. B. OTWAY-RUTHVEN, of Castle Otway, co Tipperary, only child of Vice-Adm. R. J. Otway, D.L., of Castle Otway, *m.* 12 Oct. 1865, William Clifford Bermingham Otway-Ruthven, of Queensboro', co. Galway, J.P. and D.L., co. Leitrim, High Sheriff 1889, J.P. cos. Tipperary and Galway, who *d.* 24 Aug. 1907, leaving issue,
1. ROBERT MERVYN BERMINGHAM, Capt. late R.G.A., *b.* 2 Aug. 1867:
m. 25 April, 1900, Margaret, dau. of Julius Casement, of Cronroe, co. Wicklow (*see that family*), and has had issue,
  1. Robert Jocelyn Oliver, *b.* 12 March, 1901.
  1. Frances Katherine Margaret, *b.* 4 June, 1908; *d.* 4 Jan. 1909.
  2. Annette Jocelyn.   3. Phœbe Elizabeth.
2. Thomas Ormonde Bermingham, *b.* 12 Feb. 1872.
3. Mervyn Henry Bermingham, *b.* 18 Sept. 1877.
1. Annette Rosabelle Bermingham, *m.* 15 July, 1896, Capt. Richard Meredith, late Warwickshire Regt. She *d.* 31 Oct. 1903, leaving issue.
2. Marguerite Frances Bermingham, *b.* 9 Sept.; *d.* 25 Sept. 1869.
3. Rosabelle Frances Elizabeth Bermingham, *m.* 3 Oct. 1904, George Spencer Webb Bradish.
4. Edith Mary Joseeline Bermingham, *m.* 5 June, 1907, Alexander John Selwyn Willson.
5. Cecil Harriet Beatrice Bermingham, *m.* 1 Oct. 1898, William Heneage Finch, Capt. 3rd Batt. Manchester Regt., only son of Hugh Finch (*see* FINCH *of Tullamore Park*), and has issue.

Mr. W. C. Bermingham Otway-Ruthven, *b.* 14 July, 1840, assumed by Royal Licence, 21 April, 1865, the name and arms of RUTHVEN only, in lieu of TROTTER, and in 1887 the additional name of OTWAY. He was the only son of THOMAS BERMINGHAM TROTTER, of Bermingham, co. Galway (who *d.* 12 Jan. 1844), and Rosabelle Maria Frances his wife (who *d.* 18 Jan. 1843), dau. of Maj. William Stirling St. Clair, of Emma Vale, co. Wicklow, and grandson of CLIFFORD TROTTER, of Charleville, co. Wicklow (who *d.* 24 Oct. 1859), and Lady Mary St. Lawrence his 1st wife (who *d.* 24 Jan. 1825), dau. of William, 2nd Earl of Howth, and the Lady Mary Bermingham his wife, 2nd dau. and co-heir of Thomas, Earl of Louth, and 22nd Baron Athenry (*see* BURKE'S *Extinct Peerage*).

Lineage.—This is a branch of the ancient family of OTWAY, long seated in the co. of Westmorland, of which the Right Hon. Sir Arthur John Otway, Bart., is the head (*see* BURKE'S *Peerage and Baronetage*). The first member of the family in Ireland, JOHN OTWAY had a grant of Castle Otway, co. Tipperary, by patent 10 Oct. 1685; *m.* 1650, Phœbe, dau. of Nicholas Loftus, of Fethard, co. Wexford, descended from Adam Loftus, Archbishop of Dublin and Lord Chancellor of Ireland, *temp.* ELIZABETH. His great grandson,
COOKE OTWAY, of Castle Otway, Capt. in the Life Guards, *m.* Aug. 1766, Elizabeth, dau. of Samuel Waller, of Newport, co. Tipperary, by Anne, his wife, dau. of Thomas Jocelyn, and sister of Sir Robert Waller, 1st bart., of Newport, by whom (who *d.* 1807) he had issue,
1. Thomas, *d.* young.   2. HENRY, his heir.
3. ROBERT WALLER (Sir), created a Bart. 15 Sept. 1831 (*see* BURKE'S *Peerage and Baronetage*).
4. Cooke John, *d. unm.*
5. Samuel Jocelyn (Rev.), *m.* Sept. 1800, Margaret, dau. of Gen. Hart, H.E.I.C.S., who *d.* 22 Jan. 1863. He *d.* 5 Sept. 1855, leaving issue,
  1. Cooke (Rev.), *b.* 1802; *m.* 1841, Caroline Elizabeth, dau. of Rev. John Backhouse, Rector of Deal, Kent, and *d.* 9 March, 1882, having by her (who *d.* 18 Oct. 1884) had issue,
   (1) John Jocelyn, *b.* 16 Jan. 1844; *d.* 1866.
   (2) Robert Cooke, Maj., late Capt. Prince Albert's Somersetshire Light Infantry, *b.* 24 Oct. 1846.
  2. ROBERT JOCELYN, *s.* to Castle Otway under the will of Hon. Robert Otway Cave in 1844.
   1. Margaret Sarah, *m.* Sept. 1835, Rev. Henry George Johnson, youngest son of Sir John Allen Johnson Walsh, 1st bart., of Ballykillcavan, Queen's Co. He *d.* Aug. 1856. She *d.* 12 May, 1879, leaving issue.
   2. Martha Elizabeth Anne, *d.* 1858.

6. Loftus William (Sir), C.B., Lieut.-Gen. in the Army, Col. of the 84th Regt., Knight Commander of CHARLES III. of Spain, *m.* Frances, only dau. of Sir Charles Blicke, Knt., of Caroon Park, Surrey, and *d.* 7 June, 1854, leaving issue, one son and one dau.,
    Loftus Charles, C.B., H.M. Minister Plenipotentiary in Mexico and Consul-Gen. in Milan, D.L. co. Radnor, *m.* Gertrude Marceliana, dau. of His Excellency Don Francisco de Paula Enriquez, Intendente de Manilla ; he *d.s.p.* 26 Sept. 1861.
    Georgina Frances, who became heir of her brother, *m.* 20 Oct. 1837, Capt. William John Majoribanks Hughes, 4th Light Dragoons, D.L., who by Royal Licence, dated 14 Dec. 1873, assumed the surname of LOFTUS-OTWAY, in lieu of his patronymic, and *d.* 19 May, 1885, having had issue.
7. George, Major in the 85th Foot, *d.* in Jamaica, 1804.
1. Martha, *m.* 1st, George Hartpole, of Shrule Castle, and 2ndly, 10 Sept. 1800, Hon. Francis Aldborough Prittie (*see* BURKE's *Peerage*, DUNALLY, B.), and *d.* March, 1802, leaving issue. He *d.* 8 March, 1853.
Mr. Otway *d.* 1800, and was *s.* by his 2nd son,
    HENRY OTWAY, of Castle Otway, bapt. 2 Aug. 1768 ; *m.* 25 Feb. 1790, Sarah, dau. of Sir Thomas Cave, 5th bart., of Stanford, and sister and heir of Sir Thomas, the 6th bart., afterwards BARONESS BRAYE in her own right, who, after her husband's decease, assumed the additional surname of CAVE in 1818. By the Baroness Braye, his wife, who *d.* 21 Feb. 1862 (when her barony fell into abeyance between her daus.), he had issue,
1. Henry, *d.* an infant.
2. George Antony, *d.* an infant.
3. ROBERT, his heir.
4. Thomas, Maj. in the Army, *d. unm.* 19 Jan. 1831, *v.m.*
1. Maria, *d. unm.* 13 May, 1879, when the abeyance of the barony of Braye terminated.
2. Anne, *m.* 1st, 28 Feb. 1828, J. A. Arnold, of Lutterworth, who *d.s.p.* 1844, and 2ndly, 2 Dec. 1847, Rev. Henry Kemp Richardson, Rector of Leire, co. Leicester. She *d.s.p.* 22 May, 1871.
3. Catherine, *m.* 1st, 19 Oct. 1826, Henry Murray (youngest son of Lord George Murray), who *d.s.p.* 26 Nov. 1830, and 2ndly, 11 Feb. 1850, John Reginald, 3rd Earl Beauchamp, who *d.s.p.* 21 Jan. 1853. She *d.s.p.* 4 Nov. 1875.
4. HENRIETTA, BARONESS BRAYE, *s.* 1879 ; *m.* 24 Sept. 1844, Rev. Edgell Wyatt-Edgell. He *d.* 26 Sept. 1888. She *d.* 14 Nov. 1879, having had issue (*see* BURKE's *Peerage*).
Mr. Otway *d.* 13 Sept. 1815, and was *s.* by his eldest son,
    HON. ROBERT OTWAY CAVE, of Castle Otway, co. Tipperary, M.P. for Leicester 1826-30, and for co. Tipperary 1832-44, *m.* 23 Oct. 1833, Sophia, dau. of Sir Francis Burdett, 5th bart., of Foremark, and *d.s.p.* 30 Nov. 1844, *vitâ matris*, when Castle Otway devolved on his widow for life, and at her death, 30 Dec. 1849, it went by will to his cousin,
    VICE-ADM. ROBERT JOCELYN OTWAY, of Castle Otway, co. Tipperary, J.P. and D.L. (2nd son of Rev. Samuel Jocelyn Otway), *b.* 29 Sept. 1808 ; *m.* 17 Aug. 1836, Anne Digby, youngest dau. of Sir Hugh Crofton, 2nd bart., of Mohill House, co. Leitrim, and by her had an only child and heir,
    FRANCES MARGARET, now of Castle Otway, *m.* 12 Oct. 1865, WILLIAM CLIFFORD BERMINGHAM RUTHVEN (afterwards OTWAY-RUTHVEN), and has issue (*see above*).
Admiral Otway *d.* 16 Oct. 1884. His widow *d.* 14 Dec. 1899, and was *s.* by her only child.

Arms—Paly of six arg. and gu., a canton erminois. *Crest*—A goat's head erased arg., attired or, charged with a mullet gu. *Motto* (over the crest)—Deed Shaw.

Seat—Castle Otway, Templemore, co. Tipperary.

RUTTLEDGE OF BLOOMFIELD.

THOMAS HENRY BRUEN RUTTLEDGE, of Bloomfield, co. Mayo, and of Barbersfort, co. Galway, D.L. co. Mayo, High Sheriff 1904, *b.* 7 Sept. 1852 ; *m.* 1st, 22 Dec. 1883, Florence Rose, dau. of John Trant, D.L., of Dovea, co. Tipperary (*see that family*), and by her (who *d.* 2 Jan. 1892) has issue, five daus.,
1. Katherine.
2. Barbara Alice.
3. Harriet.
4. Florence Lillian.
5. Maud Margaret.

He *m.* 2ndly, 6 Oct. 1898, Mary Caroline, eldest dau. of William Browne-Clayton, D.L., of Browne's Hill, co. Carlow (*see that family*), and by her has issue,
1. ROBERT FRANCIS, *b.* 11 Sept. 1899.
2. William, *b.* 22 July, 1901.

Lineage.—REV. FRANCIS RUTTLEDGE (formerly LAMBERT), Rector and Prebendary of Kilnaine, *b.* 1788 (2nd son of Joseph Lambert, of Brookhill, by his 1st wife, Barbara, dau. of Thomas Ruttledge, of Bloomfield) : *m.* 9 June, 1819, Margaret, 2nd dau. of Col. Henry Bruen, of Oak Park, M.P., and had issue,
1. ROBERT, late of Bloomfield.
2. Thomas, of Cornfield, co. Mayo, J.P. and D.L. for co. Mayo, High Sheriff 1865, *b.* 5 April, 1826 ; *m.* Jane, only dau. and heir of Robert Fair, of Bushfield, co. Mayo, and *d.* 1877, leaving issue, four other sons and one dau.,
    John, Capt. 4th Batt. K.O. Royal Lancaster Regt., *m.* 7 Jan. 1904, Charlotte, youngest dau. of late W. J. J. Banky, of Winstanley Hall, Wigan.
Mrs. Ruttledge assumed, by Royal Licence, 28 Aug. 1857, for herself and her issue, the additional surname and arms of FAIR, and *d.* 31 Dec. 1905.
3. Francis, late Mayo Militia, *b.* 20 Aug. 1828 ; *m.* 30 Nov. 1864, Hester Elizabeth Frances, 3rd dau. of Thomas Spencer Lindsey, of Hollymount House, co. Mayo. She *d.* 14 Feb. 1903, leaving issue.
4. John, H.M. 34th Regt., *d.* in India, 1859.
1. Harriet, *d. unm.* 1880.
2. Elizabeth, *m.* 6 Aug. 1851, James A. Lyle, of the Oaks, Londonderry. He *d.* 11 April, 1907, leaving issue (*see that family*).
3. Margaret Maria Anne Harriet, *d. unm.* 1871.
4. Helena Margaret Harriet.

Mr. Lambert assumed, by sign-manual, 7 April, 1819, his maternal name and arms of RUTTLEDGE, instead of LAMBERT, and *s.* his uncle, Robert Ruttledge, of Bloomfield, High Sheriff of Mayo, 1788, who *m.* 1787, Elizabeth, 3rd dau. of Francis Knox, of Rappa Castle, and represented the borough of Duleek for many years in the Irish Parliament. The eldest son,
    ROBERT RUTTLEDGE, of Bloomfield, co. Mayo, J.P. and D.L., High Sheriff 1864, late Lieut.-Col. Commanding South Mayo Militia, *b.* 16 July, 1823 ; *m.* Feb. 1850, Katherine, dau. of Peter Low (by Louisa his wife, dau. of Sir Richard Butler, 7th bart., of Ballintemple), and *d.* 20 Sept. 1900, having by her (who *d.* June, 1856) had issue,
1. THOMAS HENRY BRUEN, now of Bloomfield.
1. Margaret Harriet, *m.* 20 Sept. 1877, Capt. William Henry Field, 8th Hussars, eldest son of Lieut.-Col. W. Field, of Shelton Oak Shrewsbury.
2. Louisa Katherine, *d.* 23 Jan. 1912.

Arms—Arg., a stag trippant ppr., on a chief engrailed az. three estoiles wavy or. *Crest*—An oak tree ppr., pendant from a dexter branch thereof by a riband az. an escutcheon or. *Motto*—Verax atque probus.

Seats—Bloomfield, Hollymount, co. Mayo ; Barbersfort, Tuam, co. Galway. *Residences*—Johnstown House, Enfield, co. Meath ; 42, North Great George's Street, Dublin. *Club*—Kildare Street.

RUTTLEDGE.

DAVID KNOX RUTTLEDGE, of Cahergal House, co. Galway, J.P., *b.* 29 June, 1866 ; *m.* 30 June, 1891, Hon Meta Handcock, 4th dau. of Lord Castlemaine. He *m.* 2ndly, 1 Nov. 1907, Hilda Mary, dau. of H. Charles Gregory, of Westcourt, co. Kilkenny.

Lineage.—DAVID RUTTLEDGE (formerly WATSON) of Barbersfort, co. Galway, M.A., Barrister-at-Law, J.P. for co. Mayo and Galway, High Sheriff 1851, South Mayo Rifles, *b.* Nov. 1811 ; *m.* 1836, Eleanor, youngest dau. of John Knox, formerly of Moyne Abbey, and by her (who *d.* 1889) had issue,
1. David, J.P. for Galway, Hon. Major Connaught Rangers, *b.* 1839 : *m.* 1862, Sarah Knox, 2nd dau. of the Rev. Edward Leet, of Otranto, Kingstown, and *d.* 5 Oct. 1886 leaving issue,
    1. DAVID KNOX, now of Cahergal House.
    2. Percy Edward, *m.* 1902, Eda Fletcher, of Warwick, Queensland.
    1. Eleanor F. M., *m.* Oct. 1902, Richard Edward Thompson, L.R.C.S.I., L.K.Q.C.P.I., L.M., son of the late Rev. Neville Thompson.
    2. Anne Bell, *m.* 1899, Rev. Canon George FitzHerbert McCornick, Rector of Colbooney, co. Sligo.
    3. Eveline Amy, *m.* Oct. 1898, Gerald S. Caldecott, of Highcroft, Rugby.
2. John Knox, late Capt. 2nd Dragoon Guards, *m.* 1878, the only dau. of Col. De Longueville, of Saneby Broom, Bucks.
3. Alfred, Major 14th Regt., *m.* 1888, May, dau. of Ormsby Fulton, and has issue.
1. Eleanor, *m.* 1862, Arthur Rudge, R.A.
2. Elizabeth, *m.* Henry Ernest Stone. She *d.* 15 Jan. 1903.
3. Olivia, *m.* 1874, Christopher Ussher, of Eastwell, co. Galway, J.P., who *d.* 1884.

This gentleman *s.* 1833, to the unsettled estates of his stepfather, Robert Ruttledge, of Bloomfield, and under his will, assumed by Royal Licence, 1st Jan. 1834, the name and arms of RUTTLEDGE only. He *d.* 16 Dec. 1890.

Arms—Arg., a stag trippant ppr., on a chief engrailed az. three estoiles wavy or. *Crest*—An oak-tree ppr., pendant from a dexter branch by a riband az. an escutcheon or. *Motto*—Verax atque probus.

Seat—Cahergal House, Tuam, co. Galway.

Ruxton. THE LANDED GENTRY. 612

RUXTON OF ARDEE HOUSE.

WILLIAM VERNON CHICKERING RUXTON, of Ardee House, co. Louth, b. May, 1891 ; s. his grandfather 1895.

Lineage.—JOHN RUXTON, of Shanboe, co. Meath, b. 1556, whose will was dated 27 April, 1634, m. and left issue (with two daus., Mary, wife of George Proctor, and Elizabeth, Mrs. Manning) three sons,
1. Henry, of Bective, co. Meath.
2. JOHN, of whom we treat.
3. William.

The 2nd son,
CAPT. JOHN RUXTON, of Ardee, co. Louth, was patentee of considerable estates in co. Louth under the Act of Settlement temp. Charles II, and High Sheriff 1659 and 1660. He m. twice ; his 2nd wife, Priscilla, d. his widow, 29 Nov. 1743. aged 87. By his 1st, Capt. John Ruxton had issue,
1. John, b. 1642, M.P. for Ardee, 1671, High Sheriff co. Louth 1673 and 1707, d.s.p.
2. WILLIAM, eventual heir to his father.
3. Charles (Rev.), b. 1661, attainted 1688.
4. MATTHEW, father of John Ruxton, of Ballybonny (see RUXTON of Broad Oak).
1. Jane. 2. Sarah.

The 2nd son,
WILLIAM RUXTON, of Ardee House, was attainted by King James II, 1688. By Anne his wife, he left a dau., Margaret, and a son and heir,
WILLIAM RUXTON, of Ardee House, High Sheriff 1718, M.P. for Ardee 1747. He m. 1718, Mary, dau. of Samuel Gibbons, of Mountainstown, co. Meath, and d. 15 Feb. 1751, aged 54, leaving issue,
1. JOHN, his heir. 2. William, Surg.-Gen.
3. Samuel, d. unm.
4. Charles, M.P. for Ardee. m. Elizabeth, dau. and heir of Robert Parkinson, of Red House, co. Louth, and d. 1806, aged 80, leaving a son and heir,
William Parkinson Ruxton, of Red House, Barrister-at-Law, High Sheriff 1819, and M.P. for Ardee, m. 18 Jan. 1802, Anne Maria, dau. of Thomas Fortescue, of Dromiskeen, M.P., but d.s.p.
5. Gilbert Gibbons, m. 15 Nov. 1770, Elizabeth, dau. of Richard Gason, of Killashallee, co. Tipperary.
1. Anne, m. 1769, Arthur Wolfe, Lord Kilwarden, Lord Chief Justice of Ireland (she was created 30 Sept. 1795, BARONESS KILWARDEN, of Kilteel, in her own right).
2. Mary.

The eldest son and heir,
JOHN RUXTON, of Ardee House, M.P., b. 1721 ; m. Letitia, dau. and eventual co-heir of William Fitzherbert, of Shercock, co. Cavan, by Anne his wife, dau. of Ven. Andrew Carleton, Archdeacon of Kilmore, and grand-dau. of William Fitzherbert, by his wife, the dau. and heir of Sir Henry Piers, Knt., of Piers Court, or Shercock, which last William Fitzherbert was 2nd son of William Fitzherbert, of Swinnerton, co. Stafford, and Norbury, co. Derby (see that family), by Anne, his wife, dau. of Sir Basil Brooke, Knt., of Madeley, and dying 7 March, 1785, left issue,
1. WILLIAM, his heir.
2. John, of Black Castle, co. Meath. m. 27 Aug. 1770, Margaret, dau. of Richard Edgeworth, of Edgeworthstown, co. Longford, and had issue,
 1. Herbert, Capt. 63rd Regt., d. 1799.
 2. RICHARD, of Black Castle, co. Meath, b. 3 Aug. 1775 ; m. 10 Jan. 1807, Elizabeth Selina, 3rd dau. of Sir Robert Staples, 5th bart., of Dunmore, Queen's Co., by the Hon. Jane Vesey, sister of Thomas, 1st Viscount de Vesci.
 1. Sophia. 2. Margaret.
Mr. Ruxton d. July, 1825, aged 80.
3. Samuel, of Swinnerton, co. Meath, who assumed the surname of FITZHERBERT, and d.s.p. 1826.
1. Mary, m. James Corry. 2. Anne.

The eldest son,
WILLIAM RUXTON, of Ardee House, co. Louth, and Shercock, co. Cavan, M.P., m. Anne, dau. of Christopher Henry Upton, by Isabella his wife, dau. of Col. Clarges, Royal Irish Dragoons, son of Sir Thomas Clarges, Bart., and had issue,
1. JOHN FITZHERBERT, his heir.
2. Henry, m. Isabella, dau. of James Carlyle, of Cradoxtown, co. Kildare, and has issue,
 Isabella, m. George A. Grierson, of Rathfarnham House, co. Dublin.
3. William, m. Elizabeth Anne Young, of Rogerstown, co. Louth, and had issue.
4. Robert, d. young.
5. Clarges, m. Mary, dau. of Sir Robert Barnewall, 7th bart., of Crickstown, and d.s.p.
6. Charles, m. Mary Fraser, dau. of William Fraser Tytler, of Belnain, co. Inverness.
7. George, of Rahanna, co. Louth, J.P., High Sheriff 1851, Major in the Army, b. 1804 ; m. Mary, dau. of Hon. William Frankland Odell, Colonial Secretary to New Brunswick ; and d. 18 May, 1869, leaving issue,
 George William, of Rahanna, B.A. Trin. Coll. Dublin, J.P., b. 1837 ; m. 20 Aug. 1865, Arabella Anna (d. 19 Feb. 1910),
2nd dau. of George Bomford, of Oakley, co. Meath (see that family), and d. 25 Dec. 1899. leaving issue a son,
 Cecil, m. 18 June, 1903, Helen Bolton (Lottie), dau. of Peter J. Morris, of Dunluce, Bray, co. Wicklow.
8. Arthur, m. 1st, Christina, dau. of William Fraser Tytler, of Belnain, and 2ndly Emily (decd), dau. of James Forbes, of Kingerloch, co. Argyll, and had issue by each. He d. 28 July, 1894.
1. Isabella, m. Rev. Townley Filgate, Rector of Charlestown, co. Louth.
2. Anne, m. 1812, Right Hon. Edward Lucas, of Castle Shane, co. Monaghan.
3. Helena, d. young. 4. Letitia, d. young.

The eldest son,
JOHN FITZHERBERT RUXTON, of Ardee House and Shercock, High Sheriff for co. Louth 1823, and for co. Cavan 1824, m. 1826, Anna Elizabeth, dau. of Nicholas Coddington, of Old Bridge, co. Meath, by Letitia his wife, dau. of Gaynor Barry, of Beau, co. Dublin (see that family), and d. 1826, leaving issue,
1. WILLIAM, his heir.
2. John Fitzherbert, d. unm. 12 May, 1879.
1. Anna Frances.
2. Elizabeth Henrietta, m. Richard Olpherts, of Dungiven, co. Derry, who d. 1892. She d. in Jan. 1892.

His son,
WILLIAM RUXTON, of Ardee House, co. Louth, J.P. and D.L., Vice-Lieut. co. Louth, and J.P. co. Cavan, High Sheriff 1847, b. 26 April, 1823 ; m. 15 July, 1854, Caroline Diana, younger dau. and co-heiress of Charles Vernon, of Royal York Crescent, Clifton, and d. 10 April, 1895, leaving issue,
1. JOHN FITZHERBERT VERNON, b. 12 Nov. 1863 ; m. Sept. 1887, Mary, dau. of George Harvey Chickering, of Boston, U.S.A., and d. at Brooklyn, U.S.A., 1 June, 1892, leaving issue,
 WILLIAM VERNON CHICKERING, now of Ardee.
 Dorothy Vernon, m. 23 Sept. 1911, Adolphe Boissevain, son of Edward Boissevain, of Amsterdam, Holland.
2. Charles Harcourt Vernon, b. 6 June, 1870 ; m. 9 Oct. 1894, Lauvetta Eliza, eldest dau. of Rev. Ralph Daly Cocking, M.A., Incumbent of Holy Trinity, Brighton, and has issue,
 William Ralph, b. 1895.
1. Georgina Anna, m. Jan. 1880, George Ramsay Alured Denne, Lieut.-Col. late 4th Dragoon Guards, and has issue.
2. Florence Elizabeth (The Seasons, Ballymore Eustace, co. Kildare), m. 5 Oct. 1887, Sir Erasmus Dixon Borrowes, Bart., of Barretstown Castle, co. Kildare, and has issue (see BURKE's Baronetage). He d. 8 Feb. 1898.
3. Caroline Lydia.
4. Helen Vernon, m. Feb. 1881, Lieut.-Col. Walter Clare Savile D.S.O., R.A., and has issue (see that family).
5. Beatrice Geraldine, m. 15 July, 1891, Arthur Ommaney Hill-Lowe, of Court of Hill, Commander R.N. He d. 17 April, 1910, leaving issue (see that family).

Through the female line, Mr. Ruxton, of Ardee, represented a branch of the great and ancient family of FITZHERBERT, of Norbury, co. Derby, and Swinnerton, co. Stafford.

Arms—Quarterly : 1st and 4th, arg., three bulls' heads erased sa., armed or, for RUXTON ; 2nd and 3rd, arg., vaire, or and gu., over all a bend sa., charged with a crescent of the field for difference, for FITZHERBERT. Crest—a bull's head erased sa., armed or. Motto—Jam, jam.

Seat—Ardee House, Ardee, co. Louth.

RYAN OF BALLYMACKEOGH.

CHARLES ARTHUR RYAN, of Ballymackeogh, co. Tipperary, J.P., b. 7 Nov. 1853 ; m. 24 Feb. 1903, Mary, dau. of the late Henry Ormsby Rose, of Ballycullen, co. Limerick.

Lineage.—WILLIAM RYAN, of Ballymackeogh, was s. in that estate by his son, DANIEL RYAN, and the estate was afterwards confirmed to him by grant from CHARLES II., 1667. He m. Honor, dau. of Col. John Ewer, and had issue, three sons and three daus.,
1. WILLIAM, his heir. 2. Anthony.
3. George.
1. Elizabeth, m. Edward Lee, of Barna.
2. Anne, m. Edmund Griffin. 3. Mary.

Mr. Ryan d. 1731, and was s. by his eldest son,
WILLIAM RYAN, of Ballymackeogh, m. 1725, Elizabeth, dau. of Richard Newstead, of Ballyloughane, co. Tipperary, and d. 1765, having had issue,
1. EWER, his heir, of whom presently.
2. Richard. 3. William, m. Miss Bradshaw.
4. George, m. Miss Lysaght. 5. Anthony.
1. Anne, m. John Ewer.
2. Elizabeth, m. Solomon Cambie, of Castletown.

The eldest son and heir,
EWER RYAN, of Ballymackeogh, m. 1754, Elizabeth, dau. of Richard Margrath, of Lisduff, co. Tipperary, and by her (who d. 1791) had issue, six sons and three daus.,
1. WILLIAM, his heir. 2. George.
3. John. 4. Richard, Capt. in the Army.
5. Anthony. 6. Rickard, Major 93rd Regt.
1. Eleanor, m. Bever Smith. 2. Bridget.
3. Elizabeth.

Mr. Ewer Ryan d. 1802, and was s. by his eldest son.

WILLIAM RYAN, of Ballymackeogh, *m.* Sept. 1814, Anne, dau. of the Rev. John Pennefather, D.D., Rector of St. John's, Newport, co. Tipperary, and sister to Lieut.-Gen. Sir John Lysaght Pennefather, K.C.B., and by her (who *d.* Dec. 1863) had issue,
 1. WILLIAM, late representative.
 2. John, *m.* 1843, Louisa Ricarda, dau. of Major Kingsmill Pennefather, of Knockinglass, co. Tipperary, and *d.* Sept. 1873, having had issue,
  1. William Ewer (Rev.), M.A.
  2. John Pennefather, M.D.
  1. Frances Elizabeth, dec.
  2. Louisa Mary, *m.* 1885, Townsend Hall, of Pilton, co. Devon, and is dec.
 3. George Henry, M.D., Surgeon, R.N., dec.
 4. Robert Perceval, dec.   5. Edward, dec.
 1. Elizabeth, dec.   2. Clare, dec.
 3. Mary Anne, *d. unm.*   4. Laura.
Mr. Ryan *d.* 27 Nov. 1835. His eldest son,
 WILLIAM RYAN, of Ballymackeogh, J.P., *b.* 1 Dec. 1815; *m.* 29 Nov. 1842, Jane, dau. of John Grogan, Barrister-at-Law, and sister of Sir Edward Grogan, Bart., late M.P. for the city of Dublin, and *d.* 13 Feb. 1890, having by her (who *d.* 17 Nov. 1895) had issue,
 1. William Edward, R.N., *b.* 24 March, 1851; *d.* 16 March, 1870.
 2. CHARLES ARTHUR, now of Ballymackeogh.
 1. Anne Alicia Susanna, *m.* 8 Jan. 1881, Ringrose Drew, brother of Col. Francis Drew, 7th Hussars, of Drewscourt, co. Limerick, and by him (*d.* 23 Dec. 1895) has issue (*see that family*).
 2. Elizabeth, *d. unm.*   3. Antoinette Jane, *d. unm.*
 4. Jeanette, *m.* 10 Aug. 1886, Edward Herbert Maunsell, of Macleod, Alberta, Canada, son of the late Frederick Maunsell, of Finnetherstown House co. Limerick, and has issue.
Seat—Ballymackeogh, Newport, co. Tipperary.

RYAN OF INCH.

GEORGE EDWARD RYAN, of Inch, co. Tipperary, J.P. and D.L., High Sheriff 1878, *b.* 20 Aug. 1844; *m.* 1st, 18 Aug. 1874, Elizabeth, 2nd dau. of David Sherlock, Serjeant-at-Law, of Stillorgan Castle, co. Dublin, M.P., and by her (who *d.* May, 1878) has issue,
 1 George, *b.* Feb. 1878; *d. unm.* Feb. 1900.
 1. Mary Elizabeth.
 2. Lilian Mary, *d.* young.

He *m.* 2ndly, July, 1883, Mary, dau. of Richard L. Power, of Blackrock, co. Dublin, 3rd son of the late John Power, of Gurteen, co. Waterford (*see* DE LA POER *of Gurteen*). She *d.* 14 Nov. 1894. having had issue,
 2. RICHARD, *b.* Dec. 1888; *m.* 18 Aug. 1910, Kathleen, dau. of Stephen Grehan, of Clonmeen, Banteer, co. Cork (*see that family*).
 3. Mabel, *d.* young, July, 1901.

Lineage.—JOHN RYAN, of Inch House, son of DANIEL RYAN, of Inch House, and Frances his wife, dau. of Patrick Ragget, of Ballycormuck, co. Tipperary, *m.* 1714-15, Mary, dau. of Thomas Mathew, of Annefield, same co., and was father of
 DANIEL RYAN, of Inch House, *m.* 2 Feb. 1737, Elizabeth, dau. of Justin MacCarthy, of Spring Hoưse, co. Tipperary, and had issue. The 3rd son,
 GEORGE RYAN, of Inch House, *m.* 15 July, 1783, Mary, dau. of Philip John Roche, of Limerick (*see* ROCHE *of Granagh Castle*), and had issue,
 1. Daniel, of Inch House, *d.s.p.* 6 April, 1831.
 2. Philip, *d.* 18 March, 1830.
 3. GEORGE, of Inch House.
 4. John Dennis, *m.* 182?, Anna Elizabeth, eldest dau. of Thomas Lenigan, of Castle flogerty, co. Tipperary, and *d.* 1863, leaving by her (who *d.* 28 June, 1865),
  1. George, Lieut.-Col. late commanding 70th Regt.
  2. John Vivian RYAN-LENIGAN, of Castle flogerty, co. Tipperary (*see that family*).
  3. Valentine, Maj.-Gen. in the Army, late Lieut.-Col. North Staffordshire Regt., *b.* 19 Oct. 1833; by Bertha his wife (who *d.* 10 Sept. 1903) has had issue,
   (1) Valentine John Eustace, Lieut. R.A., of Thomaston Park, King's Co., High Sheriff 1910, *b.* 12 Dec. 1882; *m.* 27 March, 1906, Louisa Florence, eldest dau. of Lieut.-Col. N. Gully, R.A.
   (2) Lionel, *d.* in India April, 1903.
  1. Penelope, *d. unm.* 25 Dec. 1887.
  2. Nina.   3. Emma.
  4. Marian.   5. Elizabeth.
 1. Margaret, *m.* May, 1809, Stephen Grehan, of Rutland Square, Dublin, and had issue.
 2. Elizabeth, *m.* 7 Jan. 1824, Valentine Bennett, of Thomastown House, King's Co. She *d.* 1863. He *d.* May, 1839, leaving issue (*see that family*).
Mr. Ryan *d.* 18 Feb. 1805, and was *s.* by his eldest surviving son,
 GEORGE RYAN, of Inch House, J.P. and D.L., High Sheriff 1851, *b.* 17 July, 1791; *m.* 31 May, 1839, Catherine Margaret, eldest dau. of Capt. Edward Whyte, R.N., of Loughbrickland, co. Down (*see that family*), and had issue,
 1. GEORGE EDWARD, now of Inch.

 2. Edward, *b.* 1846; *m.* 6 Nov. 1878, Florence, eldest dau. of Finlay Chester, J.P., of Williamstown House, co. Louth, and has issue.
 3. John, *b.* Aug. 1852; *d. unm.* July, 1884.
 4. Charles, *b.* June, 1854; *d.* April, 1899, leaving issue.
 1. Mary Frances, *m.* 1858, Edmond J. Power-Lalor, of Long Orchard, co. Tipperary, who *d.* 4 Aug. 1873, leaving issue (*see that family*).
 2. Caroline Letitia, *m.* Oct. 1862, John Joseph Whyte, D.L., of Loughbrickland, co. Down, and has issue (*see that family*).
Mr. Ryan *d.* 4 Sept. 1875, and was *s.* by his son, GEORGE EDWARD, now of Inch House.

Seat—Inch, Thurles, co. Tipperary.

RYAN OF SCARTEEN.

JOHN JOSEPH RYAN, of Scarteen, co. Limerick, J.P., High Sheriff 1908, *b.* 25 March 1871; *s.* his father 1905.

Lineage.—THADDEUS RYAN, of Ballyvistea, co. Limerick, *d.* 1740, served in St. Ruth's Horse at Battle of Aughrim and Siege of Limerick 1691, *m.* Katherine Hayes, of Dromkeen, co. Limerick, and had a son,
 JOHN RYAN, of Ballyvistea, *b.* 1699; *d.* 1724, having *m.* Miss O'Brien, of Bansha, co. Tipperary, and had issue,
 JOHN RYAN, of Ballyvistea, *b.* 1722; *d.* 1810; *m.* 1st, Grace, dau. of —— Grady, of Bilboa Court, Cappamore, and had issue,
 1. Thomas, *d. unm.*
 1. Grace, *m.* William Sadleir, of Shronell, co. Tipperary.
He *m.* 2ndly, Eliza, dau. of —— O'Brien, of Abercross, co. Cork, by whom he had issue,
 2. Hugh, *m.* Miss Meagher, of Kilmoyler, and *d.s.p.*
 3. THADDEUS RICHARD, of whom next.
The 3rd son,
 THADDEUS RICHARD RYAN, of Ballyvistea and of Scarteen, Knocklong, co. Limerick, *b.* 1760; *d.* 1813; *m.* Helen Howley, of Rich Hill, co. Limerick, by whom he left issue, a son,
 JOHN RYAN, of Scarteen, J.P. co. Limerick, *b.* 1800; *m.* 1835, Alicia, 2nd dau. of John McKnight Hartigan, of Limerick. She *d.* 1891. He *d.* 1863, having had issue,
 1. THADDEUS RICHARD, late of Scarteen.
 2. John, *b.* 1838; *m.* Josephine, dau. of T. O'Shee, and *d.* 1902, leaving issue.
 3. William, *b.* 1839; *d. unm.* 1901.
 4. Hugh, *b.* 1841; *d.s.p.* 1890.
 5. Clement, *b.* 1845; *m.* Lilian, dau. of Charles Bianconi, and has issue.
 6. Richard, *b.* 1848.
 7. Charles Edward, of Glenlara, co. Tipperary, J.P., F.R.C.S.I., M.R.C.P.I., Knight of the Order of Louis II. of Bavaria, *b.* 11 Feb. 1850; *m.* 9 June, 1880, Mary Vincent, eldest dau. of the late Sir Henry Watson Parker, Kt., and has issue,
  1. Mary Monica, *b.* 1881.   2. Hilda Mary, *b.* 1883.
  3. Philomena Agnes Mary, *b.* 1884; *m.* 3 July, 1906, Capt. John Carlon Markes, Lancashire Fusiliers, only surviving son of Alfred Markes, and has issue.
 4. Moyra Vincent, *b.* 1900.
 8. Arthur, *b.* 1852.
 9. Walter, *b.* 1853; *m.* Alice, dau. of Rev. —— Maul, and has issue.
 1. Alice, *b.* 1843.   2. Helen, *b.* 1855
The eldest son,
 MAJ.-GEN. THADDEUS RICHARD RYAN, of Scarteen, co. Limerick, J.P. and D.L., late R.A., *b.* 25 April, 1837; *m.* 31 May, 1870, Gwendaline Agnes, dau. of Sir James Power, Bart., of Edermine, Enniscorthy, (*see* BURKE's *Peerage*) and *d.* 4 Jan. 1905, leaving issue,
 1. JOHN JOSEPH, now of Scarteen.
 2. James, *b.* 25 Sept. 1872; *d.* 25 May, 1890.
 3. Thaddeus Francis, *b.* 7 Oct. 1873.
 4. William, *b.* 8 March, 1875.
 5. Clement Ignatius, *b.* 23 July, 1876; *m.* 23 April, 1910, Blanche, younger dau. of Col. Maguire, late Essex Regt., of Coolderry, co. Monaghan.
 6. Hugh Joseph, *b.* 7 July, 1879.
 7. Francis Thomas, *b.* 14 Sept. 1883.
 1. Jane Matilda.   2. Alice.
Seat—Scarteen, Knocklong, co. Limerick.

RYAN OF KILHEFERNAN.

JOHN HENRY RYAN, of Kilhefernan, co. Tipperary, M.A., LL.B. Trin. Coll. Dub., M.Inst.C.E., Past Pres. Inst. of Civil Engineers, Ireland, *b.* 5 Jan. 1846; *s.* his father 1905; *m.* 8 Nov. 1887, Henrietta Anne, dau. of William Stewart, of Bellingham, of Ravensdale, co. Kildare, and the Cliffs, Howth, co. Dublin (*see* BELLINGHAM, Bart.), and has issue,
 Muriel Gertrude.

Lineage.—FRANCIS RYAN, of Killaloan, co. Tipperary, descended from William Ryan, or O'Mulryan, of Solloghead, More, co. Tipperary (who surrendered his estate to the Crown and had a re-grant 16 July, 1600, and d. 14 Aug. 1637); b. 1712; m. Margaret, dau. of Thomas Prendergast, of Ballynamasna. He was shot in a duel 15 Dec. 1773. His will, dated 20 July, 1767, was proved 3 Feb. 1774. He had with six daus. two sons,
1. THOMAS, his heir.   2. Francis.

The elder son,
THOMAS RYAN, of Killaloan, b. 1749; m. Elizabeth, dau. of Caleb Going, of Traverston. She d. 19 Sept. 1843. He d. 15 April, 1815, leaving issue,
1. THOMAS, of whom presently.
2. James, m. Catherine, dau. of Oliver Latham, of Helen's Park, co. Tipperary, and d.s.p. She m. 2ndly, Rev. Mr. Biggs.
3. Francis, d. unm.
4. O'Callaghan, murdered 2 Sept. 1852.
5. William, R.M., m. Nanno, dau. of William Quin, of Loughlogher Castle, co. Tipperary. She d. 2 Dec. 1878. He d. 26 Aug. 1850, having had issue,
Thomas, d. unm. 18 May, 1881.
Mary, m. 1836, Thomas Cambridge Grubb, of Suir Island, co. Tipperary (see GRUBB of Ardmayle).
1. Mary, m. Matthew Cooke, of Pointstown, and Ballinastic, co. Tipperary, and d.s.p. 2 Jan. 1846.

The eldest son,
THOMAS RYAN, of Kilhefernan, in parish of Killaloan, co. Tipperary; m. Margaret, dau. of Cornelius Pyne, M.D., of Ballinacarriga, co. Cork. She d. 15 May, 1856. He d. 12 Feb. 1840, having had issue,
1. THOMAS, late of Killefernan.
2. Francis, d. unm.   3. Philip, d. unm.
4. O'Callaghan, d. 21 July, 1905; m. Charlotte, dau. of — Dudley, and had issue, James, Sophie, and Anne.
1. Mary, m. Lewis Watters, of Dungarvan, co. Waterford.
2. Margaret, d. unm.   3. Charlotte, d. unm.
4. Jane, d. unm. 3 Sept. 1850.
5. Kate, d. unm. 1903.

The eldest son,
THOMAS RYAN, of Kilhefernan, co. Tipperary, b. 1815; m. 1st, 7 July, 1841, Mary Grace, dau. of John Hewetson, of Castlecomer, co. Kilkenny, and by her (who d. 25 Dec. 1851) has had issue,
1. Francis Thomas, b. 24 Jan. 1844; d. unm.
2. JOHN HENRY, now of Kilhefernan.
1. Mary Grace Gertrude, m. 1st, Yosif Effendi Shakoor, of Anizahalta, Mount Lebanon, Syria, and 2ndly, Aniceen Shakoor Bey, of Mount Lebanon.

Mr. Ryan m. 2ndly, Sarah, widow of — Hill, and dau. of W. Hawkshaw, of Millbrook, co. Tipperary. She d. 14 Jan. 1905. He d. 4 Jan. 1905, leaving issue by 1st marriage.

Seat—Kilhefernan House, Clonmel, co. Tipperary. Club—University, Dublin.

RYAN-LENIGAN. See LENIGAN.

RYE OF RYECOURT.

JOHN BALLIE TONSON RYE, of Ryecourt, co. Cork, J.P., D.L., b. 1846; m. 10 Aug. 1876, Madeline Charlotte, 3rd dau. of Sir Thomas Dancer, 6th bart., of Modreeny, and has issue,
1. RICHARD BAILIE, J.P. co. Cork, Capt. Reserve of Officers late Lieut. Western Div. R.E., educated at Radley; b. 1877.
2. John Reginald, educated at Radley; b. 1878; m. 1907, Clare de la Roche, eldest dau. and co-heir of the late Mrs. Stopford, of Rathmore, Kinsale, co. Cork, and has issue,
John Richard Coghill, b. 1910.
3. Hubert Bernard, 2nd Lieut. Royal Munster Fus.; educated at Radley; b. 1882; m. 1909, Harriet Emma, eldest dau. of Rev. Courtney Moore, Rector of Mitchelstown, co. Cork, Canon of Cloyne (see BURKE's Peerage, DUFF-SUTHERLAND-DUNBAR), and has issue,
Eudo John, b. 1910.

Lineage.—CHRISTOPHER RYE, one of the Aldermen of the city of Cork, was Sheriff 1661, and Mayor 1667 and 1668. He m. Anne, dau. of George Evans, ancestor of Lord Carbery, and had issue, an only son,

GEORGE RYE, of Ryescourt, J.P., b. 1686, m. Anne, dau. and co-heir of John Bailie, of Castlemore, co. Cork, J.P., and d. 1735, having had by her a son,
JOHN RYE, of Ryecourt, J.P., m. 6 Sept. 1758, Elizabeth Peniel, dau. and sole heir of the Rev. Percy Meade (by Elizabeth his wife, dau. of Henry Tonson, of Spanish Island, co. Cork), son of the Rev. Dominick Meade, Archdeacon of Cloyne, and nephew of Sir John Meade, Bart., ancestor of the Earls of Clanwilliam, and by her left issue at his decease, 1786,
1. RICHARD TONSON, of whom presently.
2. George, of Ryemount and Kilcondy, co. Cork, m. July, 1784, Catherine, dau. of Sir Robert Warren, Bart., and d.s.p.

The elder son,
RICHARD TONSON RYE, of Ryecourt, m. 1st, 6 July, 1791, Anne, dau. of Richard Orpen, of Ardtully. She d.s.p. He m. 2ndly, Anne, dau. of James Badham Thornhill, of Thornhill Lawn, co. Limerick, and had a son,
JOHN TONSON RYE, of Ryecourt, m. his cousin, Mary, dau. of Samuel Godseil, by Sophia his wife, dau. of James Badham Thornhill, and had issue,
1. RICHARD TONSON, now of Ryecourt.
1. Sophia, m. James Richard Moore Corcor, of Cor Castle, Innishannon, co. Cork, who left issue, Chambré, d. unm. 17 Jan. 1867; Richard Rye, Lieut. and Adjt. 24th Regt., d. unm. at Gibraltar 6 March, 1873; Eliza Katherine, m. Henry Slorach, M.D.; Caroline Georgina Sophia, m. Henry Stillington Grey Stephenson, of Lympshum Manor, Somerset; and Georgina Alice, m. Col. T. H. Brock, Royal West Kent Regt.
2. Eliza Anne, m. 23 April, 1844, Thomas Bousfield Hetrick, of Shippool Castle. She d. Nov. 1903. He d. 6 Feb. 1892, leaving issue (see that family)
3. Kate, m. Col. Thomas Quin Meade, late R.M.A., and had issue.
4. Penelope, m. the Rev. Edward Jones, and d.s.p.
5. Georgina, m. 10 Aug. 1858, Col. Richard Hall Lewis, 20th Regt., and had issue (see that family).

The only son,
RICHARD TONSON RYE, of Ryecourt, co. Cork, J.P. and D.L., High Sheriff 1853, formerly Capt. S. Cork Militia, n: 1845, Mary, dau. of Henry Baldwin, of Mount Pleasant, co. Cork, and d. 12 July, 1907, leaving issue,
1. JOHN BAILIE TONSON, now of Ryecourt.
2. Richard, d. 31 Jan. 1869.
1. Elizabeth Tonson, m. Major Arthur Fawkes, late 8th Regt., 6th son of Rev. Ayscough Fawkes, of Farneley Hall and Hawksworth Hall, co. York.

Arms—Quarterly: 1st and 4th, gu., on a bend erm. cotised or, three rye stalks of the last (RYE); 2nd, gu. a chevron erm. between three trefoils slipped arg. (MEADE); 3rd, gu. on a fesse arg. two pellets, in chief a dexter gauntlet erect between two towers of the second (TONSON). **Crest**—A cubit arm erect vested gu., charged with a bar gemel or, cuffed arg. holding in the hand three rye stalks of the second. **Motto**—Fide et amore.

Seat—Ryecourt, Crookstown, co. Cork.

RYND OF RYNDVILLE.

MRS. MARIA JANE ELTON and MRS. ELIZABETH HUME, of Ryndville, co. Meath, daus. of late Robert Fleetwood Rynd, of Ryndville, who d. 1875, by his wife Maria, dau. of Thomas Longworth Dames, of Greenhills, King's Co. The elder dau., Maria Jane, m. 10 June, 1863, the late Lieut.-Col. Frederick Cockayne Elton, V.C., 55th (Border) Regt. and Royal Scots Fusiliers, who d.s.p. (see BURKE's Peerage, ELTON, Bart.). The younger dau. Elizabeth m. Arthur Hume and has issue.

Lineage.—DAVID RYND, of Enniskillen, patentee under the Act of Settlement of Lands in Fermanagh, m. Margaret, dau. of Christopher Irvine (and sister of Sir Gerard Irvine, Bart., and William Irvine, ancestor of the Castle Irvine family—see that family), and widow of Col. Richard Bell and of Capt. Thomas Maxwell. Mr. Rynd, whose will bears date 2 Oct. 1677, and was proved at Clozher, left issue (with a dau. Elizabeth, m. 1669, Capt. Arthur Auchmuty, of Brianstown), a son and heir.

DAVID RYND, of Derryvolan, co. Fermanagh, J.P., High Sheriff 1681, attainted by JAMES II, 1689. He m. Margaret, dau. of William McCullagh, by Jane his wife dau. of Capt. Thomas Maxwell, and had issue,

IRELAND. Sadlei

1. JOHN, of whom hereafter.
2. Thomas, b. 1679. d.s.p. circa 1709.
3. Christopher, of Fenagh, co. Leitrim
1. Jane, m. Mr. Graham.
2. Rebecca, m. Mr. Lowther.
3. Elizabeth, m. William Richardson.

Mr. David Rynd d. about 1723, and was s. by his eldest son,
JOHN RYND, of Derryvolan, J.P., High Sheriff co. Fermanagh 1708, and co. Leitrim 1722, d. Jan. 1746 ; m. Elizabeth Richardson, and had, with other issue,
1. David, of Derryvolan, High Sheriff 1745. m. 2 Oct. 1764, Mary, dau. of Oliver Moore, of Saulstown. co. Meath, and left at his decease an only child and heir,
Mary, m. 20 May, 1769, Edward Denny.
2. Thomas, of whom presently.

The 2nd son,
THOMAS RYND, of the city of Dublin, m. 2 Sept. 1745, Mary Marshall Irvine, and by her (who d. 18 Oct. 1759) had issue. Mr. Thomas Rynd d. circa 1783. His only son,
JAMES RYND, of Dublin, b. 15 Oct. 1748 ; m. 1 Dec. 1776, Mabella, dau. of Thomas Goodlatte, by Mabella his wife, eldest dau. of Rev. Richard Crump, and by her had issue,
1. Thomas, of Ballywilliam, co. Fermanagh, a Major in the Army, b. 13 Dec. 1777 ; m. 16 June, 1816, Jane, dau. of William McKay, of Merrion, and d. 1848, having had issue,
 1. John Goodlatte, Barrister-at-Law, b. 10 March, 1817 ; d. unm. 8 Feb. 1853.
 2. William Richardson, b. 12 July, 1819 ; m. 5 Feb. 1856, Mary Anne, dau. of Henry Blennerhassett Thompson, by Meliora his wife, dau. of John Young, of Philpottstown, co. Meath, and had issue, two daus.,
  (1) Meliora Laura.   (2) Era Ethel, d. unm.
 3. Henry Nassau (Rev.), m. Elizabeth, youngest dau. of Col. Thomas Kennedy, and has issue,
  (1) Frederick Augustus, d. unm.
  (2) Walter, d. unm. 1909.
  (1) Anne.   (2) Beatrice, d. unm. 1910.
  (3) Clara.   (4) Ada.
  (5) Brenda, d. unm.   (6) Constance.
  (7) Amy, m. Charles East, M.D., of Malvern, and has issue.
  (8) Bertha, d. unm. 1909.
 4. Frederick Augustus, d. unm. 22 July, 1857.
 5. McKay, Lieut.-Col., late Major 62nd Foot, m. Eliza Sarah, dau. of C. Twining, and relict of James Claud N. Taylor, Lieut. R.N., and has had issue,
  (1) Arthur Hampden, d. young.
  (2) Frederick Cecil, Lieut.-Col. Ind. Army, b. 24 Sept. 1861; m. 1887, Elizabeth, dau. of John Rowland, of Mont d'Elise, Granada, W.I., and has issue,
   1. Evelyn Cecil McKay, b. (twin) Feb. 1888 ; d. inf.
   2. Patrick Gerald, b. 5 Nov. 1905.
   1. Phyllis Muriel Clare, b. (twin), Feb. 1888 ; d. inf.
   2. Laura Eileen, b. 1889.
   3. Enid Violet, b. 1890.
  (3) Gerald Cleeve, Capt. Manchester Regt. (retired).
   (1) Laura Evelyn.
   (2) Edith.
  1. Eliza Laura.
 2. Goodlatte, killed at the battle of Salamanca.
 3. James, m. Miss Buchanan, and had issue.
Mr. James Rynd m. 2ndly, Sarah, dau. of — Dunn, who d.s.p. He m. 3rdly, Hester, dau. of Robert Fleetwood, of Parkstown, co. Meath (by Catherine Margaret Hopkins his wife) and by her (who d. Dec. 1849) he left issue at his decease, 16 Oct. 1814.
4. ROBERT FLEETWOOD, late of Ryndville.
5. Francis, of 14, Huine Street, Dublin M.D., b. 1800 ; m. Aug. 1831, Elizabeth, dau. of Alderman John Alley, Lord Mayor of Dublin. She d. 1859. He d. 1861, having had issue,
 1. Philip Crampton, Col., late Bengal Staff Corps, b. 23 Oct. 1833 ; m. Phœbe, dau. of the late John Rynd, of Reynella, Killucan, and d. Nov. 1898, leaving issue,
  (1) Francis John.
  (1) Lily.   (2) Norah.
 2. John Nuttall, M.A., C.E. (T.C.D.), b. 1835 ; d. unm. Jan. 1899.
 3. Francis Edward, late Capt. 4th (King's Own) Regt., b. 1838.
 4. Scrope Barnard Christopher, m. Olivia, dau. of Frederick Pilkington, of Newberry Hall, co. Kildare. He d. 5 Aug. 1907,
  1. Hester Matilda, m. 1855, Lieut.-Gen. James Henry Craig Robertson, 42nd Highlanders, who d. May, 1899, leaving issue.
  2. Nannie Louisa, d. unm.
  3. Elizabeth, m. Major Browning Drew, late 75th Regt., who d. 1890, leaving issue.
6. John, J.P., co. Westmeath (dec.), m. Harriet Townshend, dau. of Robert McKerlie, representative of the ancient family of McKerlie, of Craggleton Castle, co. Wigton, Scotland, and left issue.
7. James (Rev.) (dec.), m. Eliza, dau. of Robert Crow Fleming, of Nutfield, co. Clare, and left issue.
8. Christopher, of Mount Armstrong, co. Kildare, J.P. and D.L., m. 8 Feb. 1842, Helena Maria, only surviving dau. and heir of Peter Wolfe, of Blackball, co. Kildare, d. 1882, leaving issue.
 1. Robert Fleetwood, of Blackball, co. Kildare, J.P. Hon. Major Kildare Rifles, late Capt. 22nd Regt., b. 1842 ; m. 1892, Natalie, eldest dau. of the late H. A. Cowper, of Trudder Newtown Mount Kennedy, co. Wicklow.
 2. William Wolfe, Capt. 7th Foot, d. 18 May, 1886, aged 42, having m. 1884, the dau. of —Reid, of The Barn, Carrickfergus.
 3. Fleetwood, of Mount Armstrong, co. Kildare, J.P., m. 1885, Julia, dau. of L. N. Izod, of Chapel Izod, co. Kilkenny (see that family). She d. 17 July, 1901, leaving issue.

Christopher Lorenzo, b. 1894.
4. Theobald Christopher.
1. Maria Elizabeth (dec.), m. William Thomas Briscoe, of Lugga King's Co., and Riversdale, co. Westmeath, and left issue.
2. Hester (dec.), m. 1828, the late Edward Briscoe, of Grangemore, co. Westmeath, High Sheriff 1833 for that co.
3. Catherine (dec.), m. 1816, the late Alexander Andrews, Cap in the Army, eldest son of Thomas Andrews, of Merrion Square Dublin.
Mr. Rynd d. 16 Oct. 1814, and was s. by his son,
ROBERT FLEETWOOD RYND, of Ryndville, J.P., m. Nov. 1832, Maria, dau. of Thomas Longworth Dames, of Greenhills, King's Co., and had issue,
1. JAMES FLEETWOOD, late of Ryndville.
1. MARIA JANE, now of Ryndville, m. Lieut.-Col. Elton, V.C.
2. ELIZABETH, m. Arthur Hume, and has issue.
Mr. Rynd d. 1875, and was s. by his son,
JAMES FLEETWOOD RYND, of Ryndville, co. Meath, B.A., called to the Bar 1853, late Col. 8th Batt. Rifle Brigade, b. 1833 ; s. his father 1875, d. April, 1908, and was s. by his sisters.

Arms—Erm., on a cross gu., a cross-crosslet fitchée or the sinister quarter arg., charged with two mullets in fesse az. on the cross, in the centre chief point a crescent of the third. Crest— A demi-lion rampant gu., holding in the paws a cross-crosslet fitchée or, and charged on the shoulder with a crescent as in the arms. Motto—Fide et fortitudine.

Seat—Ryndville, near Enfield, Meath.

SADLEIR OF CASTLETOWN.

JOHN MARTLEY SADLEIR, of Orchard House, St. Dunstans, Kent, formerly a Lieut. R.M.L.I. and served in the Baltic Expedition under Sir Charles Napier, b. 1835 ; s. to the representation of the family at the decease of his cousin the late Thomas Owen Saunders Sadleir, of Castletown, 13 Oct. 1904 ; m. 18 July, 1859, Amelia Jane, dau. of William Wallace, and by her (who d. 16 Nov. 1907) has an only son,
HENRY ETHELRED WALLACE, b. 12 Feb. 1865.

Lineage.—HENRY SADELEYER, of Hackney, Middlesex, left issue, two sons,
1. RALPH, of whom presently.
2. John, who commanded a company at the siege of Boulogne, 1544, and left issue.

The elder son,
SIR RALPH SADLEIR, of Standon, Herts, Knight Banneret, M.P. for Herts, Lord Lieut. of Herts, Privy Councillor temp. HENRY VIII., EDWARD VI., and ELIZABETH for forty years, sometime Principal Secretary of State, Ambassador to Scotland, and Guardian to MARY, Queen of Scots, Master of the Grand Wardrobe, Chancellor of the Duchy of Lancaster, etc., b. 1507, was a legatee under the will of HENRY VIII., and twice entertained Queen ELIZABETH at Standon ; m. Ellen Mitchell, widow of Matthew Barre, of Sevenoaks, Kent, and d. 30 March, 1587, having had issue,
1. Thomas (Sir), of Standon, Herts, High Sheriff 1588 and 1595, M.P. for Lancaster 1572-83, knighted by JAMES I. 1603, when that King stayed at Standon, m. 1st, Ursula, dau. and co-heir of Sir Henry Sherrington, of Lacock Abbey, Wilts. She d.s.p. May, 1576. He m. 2ndly, Gertrude, dau. of Robert Markham, of Cotham, Notts, and d. 5 Jan. 1606, having by her had issue,
 Ralph, of Standon, High Sheriff 1609, b. 1581 ; m. 11 Sept. 1601, Anne, eldest dau. of Sir Edward Coke, Lord Chief Justice of England (see BURKE's Peerage, LEICESTER, E.) and d.s.p. 12 Feb. 1660. He is the "Noble Mr. Sadler" of WALTON's Compleat Angler.
 Gertrude, m. Walter, 1st Baron Aston, of Forfar, who d. 13 Aug. 1639, whose son the 2nd Baron eventually s. to Standon.
2. EDWARD, of whom presently.
3. Henry, of Everley, Wilts, High Sheriff 1595, M.P. for Lancaster 1571-86, Clerk of the Hanaper 1572-1604, entertained JAMES I. and his Queen at Everley Aug. 1603 ; m. 1st, Mary, dau. of Edward Gilbert, and 2ndly, 12 Aug. 1586, Ursula, dau. of John Gyll, of Wideial Hall, Herts. He d. 17 March, 1618, leaving issue, by both wives.
 1. Anne, m. Sir George Horsey, of Digswell, High Sheriff, Herts, 1572. She d. 1576.

2. Mary, *m.* Thomas Bowles, of Wallington, High Sheriff Herts 1576.
3. Jane, *m.* Edward Baesh, of Stanstead, High Sheriff Herts 1571, M.P. for Rochester. She *d.* 1614.
4. Dorothy, *m.* 6 June, 1567, Edward Elrington, of Birch Hall, Essex, M.P. for Wigan.

The 2nd son,
EDWARD SADLEIR, of Temple Dinsley, Herts, and Aspley Guise, Beds, admitted to the Inner Temple Nov. 1555, *m.* Anne, dau. and co-heir of Sir Richard Lee, of Sopwell, Herts, the famous military engineer, and *d.v.p.* 4 April, 1584, leaving issue by her (who *m.* 2ndly, 1584, Ralph Norwich),
1. Lee, of Temple Dinsley, and Aspley Guise, *b.* 1565; *m.* 1586, Elizabeth, dau. of William Pascall, of Preston, Essex, and *d.* 1588, leaving with a dau., Anne, who *m.* Edward Aston (younger brother of Walter, 1st Lord Aston), a son,
Thomas Lee Sadleir, of Temple Dinsley and Aspley Guise, Serjeant-at-Law, *b.* 1587; *m.* 1612, Frances (who *d.* 1676), dau. of Francis Bury, of Toddington, Beds. He *d.* 1644, leaving issue,
(1) Thomas, *b.* 1619; *d.v.p.* 1630.
(2) Sir Edwin, of Temple Dinsley, Baronet, so created 3 Dec. 1661, *b.* 1620; *m.* 1654, Elizabeth, dau. of Sir Walter Walker, LL.D., and *d.* 1672, having had issue,
 1. Walter, *d.* young.
 2. Ralph, *d.* young.
 3. Sir Edwin, 2nd bart., of Temple Dinsley (which he sold 1712) and Aspley Guise, *b.* 1656; *m.* 1686, Mary, dau. of John Lorymer, and widow of William Croune, of London, M.D. Lady Sadleir, who *d.* 29 Sept. 1706, founded the Sadleirian Lectures in Mathematics at Cambridge. He *d.s.p.* 14 July, 1719, when the baronetcy became extinct.
 4. Thomas, *d. unm.* 1687.
 1. Mary, *m.* 1697, Edward Brereton, of Burhas, Denbighshire.
 2. Elizabeth, *d. unm.* 1691.
(3) Ralph, of Aspley Guise, *d. unm.* 1685.
(4) Lee, of Hadley, Herts, whose great-grandson, George Sadleir, of Aspley Guise, J.P., *d.s.p.* 1752.
(5) Edward, *d.s.p.*
(6) William, of Kempston, Beds, ancestor of Richard Vernon Sadleir, J.P., at whose decease in 1810, the Aspley Guise estate passed to his nephew, Robert Sadleir Moody.
(7) Richard, *d.s.p.*
(8) Robert, of London, *d. unm.* 1668.
(9) Edmund, *d. unm.* 1639.
(10) John, *b.* 1638; *d.* 1684.
(1) Elizabeth.
(2) Frances, *m.* 1635, John Williord.
(3) Anne, *m.* 1648, Robert Barker.
(4) Jane, *m.* William Stone, and *d.* 1689.
(5) Sarah, *m.* Rev. William Joel, Rector of Sarret, Herts.
(6) Mary, *d. unm.* 1669.
2. RICHARD, of whom presently.
3. Edward, of Lotsford, near Standon, *b.* 1571; *m.* 4 April, 1604, Ann, dau. of Roger Birchley, of Hertford, and widow of Richard Fisher, of Standon.
4. Thomas, *d. unm.*
1. Mary, *b.* 1568; *m.* 18 Dec. 1587, Thomas Coningsby, 3rd son of Thomas Coningsby, of Leominster, Herefordshire.
2. Ellen, *d. unm.* 29 May, 1600.
3. Dorothy.

The 2nd son,
RICHARD SADLEIR, of Sopwell, Herts (inherited from his mother), *b.* 1569; *m.* May, 1603, Joyce, dau. of Robert Honeywood, of Charing, Kent, and *d.* 1624, leaving issue,
1. Robert, of Sopwell, J.P., Capt. Herts Militia, admitted to Gray's Inn 23 Oct. 1626, *m.* Ellen, dau. of Thomas Bancroft, of Santonhouse, Norfolk. She *d.* 1640. He *d.* 1669, leaving issue,
 1. Robert, *b.* 1632, admitted to Gray's Inn 24 June 1650, *d.s.p.* 1652.
 2. Edward, *b.* 1633, admitted to Gray's Inn 14 June, 1651, *d.s.p.* 1669.
 3. Thomas, *d.s.p.*
 1. Ellen, *m.* 1662, Thomas Saunders, of Beechwood, Herts, who sold Sopwell to Sir Harbottle Grimston. She *d.* 1699, leaving an only dau. and heir, Anne, *m.* 1st, by licence, 24 March, 1687-8, Sir Edward Sebright, 3rd bart., and had issue (see BURKE'S *Peerage*),
 2. Anne, *d. unm.*
 3. Margaret, *d. unm.*
2. Ralphael, *d.* Nov. 1612.
3. Richard, *d. unm.* 1669.
4. THOMAS, of whom presently.
5. Edward, of London, *m.* Susan, dau. of Francis Underwood, of Whittlesey, Cambs, and *d.* 1692, leaving four daus.
6. Blount, of London, purchased Manor of Betham, Westmorland 1655, appointed a Capt. in the Hon. Art. Company 1656, *m.* Mary (who *d.* 1684) dau. of Thomas Sharpe, and left issue,
 1. Thomas, Member of the Council of Barbados, where he was appointed Chief Baron of the Exchequer in 1696, *m.* the widow of Col. Salter, and *d.* Sept. 1701, leaving issue, two daus.,
 (1) Anne, *b.* 1690.
 (2) Elizabeth, *b.* 1692.
 2. Blount.
 3. Ralph, a sea captain, at Rotherhithe, 1691.
 1. Mary. 2. Judith.
6. Henry, *b.* 1619, *d.s.p.*
1. Mary, *m.* 10 April, 1629, Henry Thompson, of Kentfield, co. Kent.

2. Dorothy, *m.* James Ellis, of St. Albans.
3. Margaret, *m.* James Fincham.

The 4th son,
COL. THOMAS SADLEIR, of Sopwell Hall, co. Tipperary. M.P. for Carlow, Kilkenny, and Wexford in the Parliaments of 1654-5, 1656-8, and M.P. for Galway and Mayo 1658-9, Governor of Wexford and subsequently of Galway, High Sheriff co. Wexford 1652, and M.P. for co. Tipperary 1661-6, High Sheriff 1666, joined the Parliamentary Army in 1643, went to Ireland in command of a regt. of foot and served as Adjutant-Gen. under Cromwell. By Order in Council 18 Sept. 1655, a "Gold Medal and Chain, worth £50" was granted to him "as a gratuity for his faithful service." He obtained estates in Tipperary and Galway including Kilnelagh Castle, in Lower Ormond (which he re-named Sopwell Hall), *m.* 1st, Anne, dau. of Thomas Goodridge, of St. Albans, and widow of John Shadd, and 2ndly, 1662, Mary, dau. of James Salmon, of Glandore, co. Cork, and widow of Vincent Gookin, Surveyor-General of Ireland, and *d.* about 1680, leaving by his first wife,
1. THOMAS, his heir.
1. Elizabeth, *m.* John Briggs, of Castletown, co. Tipperary, and Dunstable, Beds. He *d.* 1694, leaving issue.
2. Sarah, *m.* — Abbott, nephew to Col. Daniel Abbott, of Nenagh, M.P.
3. Alice, *m.* — Foster.

The only son,
THOMAS SADLEIR, of Sopwell Hall, J.P., High Sheriff 1692 and 1695, *m.* Frances, dau. of Capt. Robert Oliver, M.P., of Cloghnodfoy (Castle Oliver), co. Limerick, and *d.* 1716, leaving issue,
1. Thomas, of Sopwell Hall, J.P., *b.* 1680; *m.* 20 Sept. 1701, Catherine, dau. of Thomas Tilson, and grand-dau. of Right Rev. Henry Tilson, Bishop of Elphin, and *d.* 1724, having by her (who *m.* 2ndly, Rev. Thomas Bindon, Dean of Limerick, and *d.* 1771), had issue,
 1. Oliver, *d.v.p.*
 2. Francis (Col.), of Sopwell Hall, Fellow Commoner, Trin. Coll. Dublin 1727, admitted a Freeman of the City of Cashel 29 Sept. 1749, *b.* 1709; *m.* 21 March, 1735, Catherine, dau. of William Wall, M.P. of Coolnamuck, co. Waterford, and niece of the Earl of Bessborough, and *d.* 14 Dec. 1797, leaving issue,
  (1) Mary, *m.* 20 Aug. 1754, Frederick Trench, M.P., of Woodlawn, who *d.* 27 Nov. 1797 (great-grandfather of Capt. the Hon. Cosby Trench, D.L., now of Sopwell Hall).
  (2) Catherine, *m.* 1st, 1761, John Bury, of Shannon Grove, co. Limerick, by whom she had an only child, Charles William 1st Earl of Charleville. She *m.* 2ndly, 6 Jan. 1766, Henry Prittie, M.P. of Kilboy, created 1st Lord Dunalley (see BURKE'S *Peerage*).
 3. Charles, *d.s.p.* 1734, aged 12.
 1. Eliabeth, *m.* 1745, John Bateman, of Altavilla, co. Limerick (4th son of John Bateman, of Oak Park, co. Kerry), and *d.* 1748.
 2. Alice, *m.* 1st, 22 Jan. 1740, Thomas Bateman, of Mount Catherine, co. Limerick (3rd son of John Bateman, of Oak Park, co. Kerry); *m.* 2ndly, — McCarthy.
2. CHARLES, of whom presently.
3. Robert, of Brookfield, co. Tipperary, *b.* 1686, *d. unm.* 1746.
1. Bridget, *d. unm.* 1752.
2. Anne, *m.* 1697, William Vaughan, of Golden Grove, King's Co. She *d.* 12 Dec. 1710, leaving issue (see that family).
3. Elizabeth, *m.* 1707, John Ormsby, of Cloghans, co. Mayo.

The 2nd son,
CHARLES SADLEIR, of Castletown, co. Tipperary, J.P., *b.* 1684; *m.* 1718, Margery dau. of Thomas Baldwin, of Corolanty, King's Co., by Mary his wife, dau. of John Eyre, M.P., of Eyrecourt, co. Galway, and *d.* 1729, having by her (who *m.* 2ndly, 1736, Col. Thomas Crow, 13th Light Dragoons, and *d.* 1776) had an only child,
CHARLES SADLEIR, of Castletown, sometime Cornet 13th Light Dragoons, served in Scotland 1745, taken prisoner at Preston Pans, *m.* 1st, Mary Blair, by whom he had a son,
1. Charles, Lieut. 13th Light Dragoons, M.A. Glasgow, *d. unm.* 1786.
He *m.* 2ndly, 1 Feb. 1750, Abigail, dau. of Rev. Joseph Grave, of Ballycommon, King's Co., Rector of Geashill, by Abigail his wife, dau. of Simon Digby, Bishop of Elphin (see BURKE'S *Peerage*, Digny, B.). He *d.* 26 Oct. 1756, having by her (who *m.* 2ndly, 4 April, 1762, Rev. Ralph Grattan, D.D., and *d.* 2 Nov. 1809, aged 80) had another son,
2. THOMAS, s. to Castletown.

The younger son,
THOMAS SADLEIR, of Castletown, co. Tipperary, and Seapark, co. Dublin, Barrister-at-Law, educated at Glasgow Univ., *b.* 2 Sept. 1753; *m.* 19 Feb. 1773, Rebecca, eldest dau. of William Woodward, of Cloughprior, co. Tipperary, by Rebecca, his wife, dau. of Freeman Rogers, of Ballynavin, co. Tipperary. She *d.* 6 Aug. 1792, leaving issue,
1. THOMAS, of whom presently.
2. Franc (Rev.), D.D., of Mullagh, King's Co., Provost of Trinity Coll. Dublin, a Commissioner of National Education, Vice-Pres. of the Royal Irish Academy, Pres. of the Irish Art Union, etc., *b.* 3 May, 1775; *m.* 17 July, 1801, Letitia Abigail, 3rd dau. of William Grave, of Ballynagar, King's Co. She *d.* 4 Dec. 1850, aged 81. He *d.* 14 Dec. 1851, leaving with three daus., who *d. unm.*
 1. Randal Cæsar, B.A., Trin. Coll. Dublin, *b.* 26 June, 1802; *d. unm.* 27 Feb. 1863.
 2. Francis Ralph (Rev.), D.D., Rector of Raddenstown, co. Meath, *b.* 22 April, 1806; *m.* 15 Sept. 1835, Flora Harriet, (who *d.* 14 Jan. 1874), dau. of Ferdinand McVeagh, of Drewstown, Meath, and *d.* 21 April, 1875, having had issue,
  (1) Ferdinand Francis, Lieut. Tipperary Art., *b.* 12 Sept. 1841; *d. unm.* 8 Nov. 1870.

(2) Franc Digby Henry Wynch, b. 1843; d. unm. 17 Dec. 1887.
(3) William Henry Brooke, b. Feb. 1851; m. 1874, Isabella, dau. of Thomas Burndage, of St. John's, New Brunswick, and has issue,
  1. Ralph Waterbury, b. 1881.
  2. Brooke, b. 1882.
  3. Kenelm Digby, b. 1891.
    1. Gertrude Muriel.
(4) Thomas Otway, b. 1853; d. unm. 1907.
(1) Charlotte, m. 1860, Capt. Thomas Quin, 6th Punjab Rifles.
(2) Flora, m. 17 April, 1861, George Winter Bomford, of Drumlargan, and has issue (see BOMFORD of Oakley Park).
(3) Margery, d. unm. 6 Nov. 1909.
(4) Josephine.   (5) Frances, d. unm.
(6) Anne, d. unm. 1871. (7) Edith, d. unm. 1871.
(8) Isabel.
3. William Digby (Rev.), D.D., Senior Fellow Trin. Coll. Dublin, b. 26 Sept. 1807; m. 1st, 20 June, 1840, Jane, dau. of Rev. Cæsar Otway, and 2ndly, 1857, Georgina, dau. of Hans White, of Aghavoe, Queen's Co. She d. 17 April, 1898. He d.s.p. 7 July, 1858.
4. Thomas Henry, of Mullagh, King's Co., m. 7 Nov. 1848, Anne dau. of Robert Bickerstaff, of Preston, Lancashire. She d. 7 April, 1884. He d.s.p. 2 July, 1875.
1. Letitia Sarah Georgina, m. 1839, her cousin Rev. Ralph Sadleir, D.D.
1. Anna Maria, m. 5 Dec. 1800, Rev. Matthew Jellett, who d. Aug. 1821. She d. 6 Aug. 1831.
2. Sarah, d. unm. 20 May, 1834.
3. Catherine, m. William Munroe Fairlie, and d. 29 March, 1840.

Mr. Thomas Sadleir m. 2ndly, 4 May, 1793, Florence (who d. March, 1819), dau. of Charles Atkinson, and grand-dau. of Anthony Atkinson, M.P., of Cangort, King's Co. He d. 16 July, 1815, having by her had issue,
3. Charles, of Seapark, co. Dublin, sometime R.N., b. 24 Feb. 1798; m. 1822, Emily (who d. Feb. 1824), dau. of Edward Shawe, of Coolcor, co. Kildare. He d.s.p. 3 Dec. 1841.
4. James Edwin, of Cork, b. 29 Sept. 1799; m. 1826, Catherine Christiana, dau. of James Wilmott, and d. 3 April, 1866, leaving issue,
  1 Thomas Willmott, d. unm.
  2. Henry Edwin, emigrated to Australia 1852.
  3. Charles Atkinson. 4. John Ormsby.
  5. James Francis, d. unm.
  1. Jane Henrietta, m. 1850, Capt. Molloy.
  2. Francis Florence, m. 1853, Thomas Horner.
  3. Sarah Maria, m. 1856, Henry Torrens Owen.
5. William Atkinson, b. 11 Nov. 1800; m. 1827, Mary, dau. of Thomas Willan, of Carrick Hill, co. Dublin, and d. 1855, having by her (who d. 4 March, 1873) had issue,
  1. Esther, d. unm. 1853.
  2. Charlotte, d. unm. 1861.
  3. Emily Florence, m. 1857. Rev. William Miler Magrath.
6. Anthony, B.A. Trin. Coll. Dublin, b. 22 June, 1805; d. 1852, leaving a son and a dau. settled in Australia.
4. Mary, m. 1821, John Gumley, LL.D., Barrister-at-Law, and d. 4 Aug. 1868.
5. Anne Henrietta, d. unm. 9 Jan. 1826.
6. Jane Urania, d. unm.
7. Florence, b. 1807; m. 24 Feb. 1835, Rev. Thomas Pentland, Rector of Drumreilly, co. Cavan, who d. 1874.

The eldest son,

THOMAS SADLEIR, of Castletown, Capt. in the Ancient Irish Fencibles 1799, Paymaster 99th Foot 1805-9, Clerk of the Peace for co. Tipperary 1812-42, served in Egypt, where he was wounded, Minorca, and Bermuda, b. 19 Feb. 1774; m. 16 April, 1793, Margaret dau. of John Watson, of Brookwatson, co. Tipperary, and grand-dau. of George Watson, of Garrykennedy, same co. She d. 16 Aug. 1817. He m. 2ndly, 1 Oct. 1827, Dorothea, eldest dau. of Col. Richard Pennefather, D.L., M.P., of Newpark, co. Tipperary, and widow of Richard Lockwood. She d.s.p. 1845. He d. 22 Oct. 1842, having by his first wife had issue,
1. THOMAS, his heir.
2. William Woodward, of Cannonstown, Meath b. 5 Feb. 1803 m. 5 May, 1828, Eliza Isabella (who d. 19 Aug. 1872), dau. of John Rothwell, of Cannonstown. He d. 17 July, 1875, having had issue,
  1. Thomas Rothwell, Lieut. 28th Punjab Infantry, served in the Mutiny with the Madras Rifles, b. 1830; d. unm. 12 April, 1863.
  2. JOHN MARTLEY, present representative.
  3. Francis John, b. 1837; d. unm.
  4. Richard Willoughby, b. 1839; m. 1863; d. 1874, leaving issue,
    (1) Richard. (2) Arthur Willoughby.
    (1) Isabel.
  5. William Martley, b. 1843; m. 1872, Mary, dau. of William Mitchell, by Jane, dau. of Peter Holmes, of Peterfield, co. Tipperary, and has issue,
    (1) William. (2) Lancelot.
    (1) Violet.
  6. Godfrey Fetherstonhaugh, b. 1845; d. unm. 8 Dec. 1874.
  7. Arthur Prendergast, b. 1847; d. unm. 1868.
  1. Isabel, m. 1st, 1848, Capt. Arthur Sewell, Indian Army; 2ndly, Major Elliott Seward Ostrehan, B.S.C., and d. 17 April, 1871.
3. Henry Atlantic (Rev.), Rector of Galbally, co. Tipperary, b. at sea 4 June, 1807; m. 1st, 9 June, 1835, Anne, dau. of Rev.

John Whitty, of Ricketstown, co. Carlow; 2ndly, 1866, Jeannette, sister of Col. John Stanley Howard, of Ballinapark, co. Wicklow; and 3rdly, 1874, Anne (who d. 3 May, 1903), dau. of William Patterson, of Montgomerie Castle, Ayrshire. He d.s.p. 28 Nov. 1880.
4. Edwin, of Oakwood, King's Co., Secretary to the Grand Jury, co. Tipperary, b. 2 April, 1810; m. 2 June, 1837, Jane, dau. of James Willington, of Castle Willington, co. Tipperary, and d. 20 March, 1875, having had issue,
  1. Thomas Vernon, Lieut. North Tipperary Mil., b. 18 March, 1838; d. unm. 1883.
  2. James Willington, sometime Lieut. North Tipperary Mil., b. 26 March, 1842; m. Maria Jane, dau. of Samuel Sheldon Dudley, of Tenderry and Mount Dudley, co. Tipperary, and has issue,
    Edwin William Henry, b. 17 May, 1874.
    Lilian Dudley, m. 7 April, 1904, Rev. James Campbell Lindsay, of St. John's Coll., Oxon, Rector of Carnew, co. Wicklow.
  2. Edwin William Henry, b. 21 May, 1843. d. unm.
  3. Francis Prittie, b. 8 May, 1844; m. 3 May, 1873, Frances, dau. of Sir Edward Synge, 3rd bart., and d. 31 Jan. 1887, having had issue,
    (1) Francis Hutchinson Synge, b. 8 March, 1874; m. 24 July, 1907, Winifred, dau. of Edward Lewis, of Dyserth, Flints, and has issue,
      Frances Winifred Patricia.
    (2) Edward William Follett, b. 2 July, 1879; m. Oct. 1906, Etheldreda, dau. of Samuel Richardson, and has issue,
      Francis Bertram Synge, b. 1907.
      Etheldreda Myra.
    (1) Pauline Annie.
  5. John Willington, b. 23 June, 1845; d. unm. 1895.
  6. Charles, b. 12 March, 1850; d. unm. 1883.
  7. Henry Altantic, b. 1 Dec. 1858; m. 29 Jan. 1889, Anna Violet, dau. of Surg. Thomas Rogers, and d. 30 March, 1908, leaving issue,
    (1) Edwin Henry, b. 14 April, 1892.
    (2) Ralph Vernon, b. 11 Jan. 1906.
    (3) Ruby Violet, m. 5 June, 1911, William R. Lee.
  8. Frederick William, b. 1860; d. unm. 27 Dec. 1883.
  1. Sarah Letitia, m. 16 Oct. 1876, Rev. Richard John Cockburn Richey, Rector of Kilcash.
  2. Margaretta Watson, m. 30 Jan. 1869, Col. John Sadleir Brereton, and has issue (see BRERETON of Rathurles).
  3. Caroline Ada, m. 17 Nov. 1874, James Wilson, son of John W. Wilson, of Harvest Lodge, co. Tipperary.
  4. Elizabeth.
  5. Myra, m. Henry Mills, of Seattle, U.S.A.
5. Ralph (Rev.), D.D., of Carrig, co. Galway, Rector of Castleknock, Canon and sometime Sub-Dean of St. Patrick's, Dublin, Private Chaplain to the Earls of Clarendon and St. Germains during their Viceroyalty, b. 5 Jan. 1815; m. 1st, 6 May, 1839, his cousin Letitia, dau. of Rev. Franc Sadleir, D.D., Provost of Trin. Coll. Dublin. She d. 27 Nov. 1867, leaving a son.
  Franc (Rev.), M.A., Senior Chaplain to the Forces (retired), Rector of Newcastle Lyons, b. 28 May, 1841; m. 24 Jan. 1871, Philippa Elizabeth, elder dau. of Charles Granby Burke, Master of the Common Pleas (see BURKE's Peerage, BURKE, Bart.), and has issue,
    (1) Ralph Granby (Rev.), B.A., Chaplain R.N., b. 1871; m. 1907, Ruth Eleanor, elder dau. of Matthew John Smyly (see SMYLY of Cannus) and has issue,
      Ralph Edward, b. 24 May, 1908.
      Constance Hermione.
    (2) Harold Franc, Lieut. R.N. (retired), (Junior Savage Club), b. 1877.
    (3) Thomas Ulick, M.A., Barrister-at-Law (Junior Conservative Club), b. 1882.
He m. 2ndly, 13 Feb. 1871, Letitia, dau. of Capt. Sewell, and grand-dau. of Gen. Sewell. He d. 28 Sept. 1902, having by her had a dau.,
  Serena Letitia Henrietta, m. 14 April, 1903, Major James Meldon, 4th Batt. Royal Dublin Fus.
1. Rebecca, m. 2 Oct. 1818, Daniel Falkiner, of Beechwood, co. Tipperary, 4th son of Richard Falkiner, of Mount Falcon. She d. 13 Sept. 1878. He d. 23 Feb. 1853, leaving issue (see that family).
2. Maria, m. 1 Dec. 1817, Thomas Brereton, of Rathurles, co. Tipperary. She d. 17 Dec. 1874, leaving issue (see that family).
3. Abigail, m. 14 Feb. 1819. Rev. Ralph Stoney, Rector of Terrysglas. She d. 5 Aug. 1836, leaving issue (see STONEY of Downs).

The eldest son,

THOMAS SADLEIR, of Castletown and Ballinderry, co. Tipperary, J.P., High Sheriff 1859, sometime R.N., b. 21 Dec. 1796; m. 4 April, 1825, Eleanor Elmina, elder dau. of Owen Saunders, of Newtown Saunders, co. Wicklow, and Ballinderry, co. Tipperary, and by her (who d. 1 Aug. 1863) had issue,
1. THOMAS OWEN SAUNDERS, late of Castletown.
1. Jemima, m. 30 June, 1856, Richard Hackett, of Elm Grove, Parsonstown, and d. 27 Feb. 1907, leaving issue (see HACKETT of Riverstown).
2. Mary Ellen Annette, d. unm. 9 Nov. 1906.
3. Adelaide, m. 4 April, 1861, Sir Frederick Richard Falkiner, K.C., P.C., and d. 2 June, 1877, leaving issue (see FALKINER of Mount Falcon).
4. Georgina, m. 26 Oct. 1859, Richard Henry Falkiner, D.L., of Mount Falcon, co. Tipperary, and d. 1891, leaving issue (see that family).

St. George. THE LANDED GENTRY.

5. Eleanor Thomasina, m. 17 Nov. 1868, John Smallman Kenning Masters, of Shrewsbury House, Shooter's Hill, Kent, and d. 21 Feb. 1870, leaving issue.

Mr. Sadleir d. 15 July, 1863. His only son,

THOMAS OWEN SAUNDERS SADLEIR, of Castletown, b. 7 July, 1835; d. unm. 13 Oct. 1904. The estates became vested in his sisters, while the male representation of the family devolved on his cousin, John Martley Sadleir.

Arms—Or, a lion rampant per fesse az. and gu. Crest—A demi-lion az., ducally crowned or. Motto—Servire Deo sapere.

Seat—Castletown, Borrisokane. Residence—Orchard House, St. Dunstans, Canterbury.

ST. GEORGE OF WOOD PARK.

The late ACHESON ST. GEORGE, of Wood Park, co. Armagh, M.A., T.C.D., b. 16 July, 1819; m. 25 Nov. 1890, Jane Rebecca, only surviving child of the late Thomas Knox Armstrong, of Fellows Hall, co. Armagh (see WRIGHT - ARMSTRONG of *Killylea*), and d.s.p. 2 July, 1902.

Lineage.—This family deduces its pedigree from BALDWIN ST. GEORGE, one of the companions-in-arms of the CONQUEROR, whose descendants flourished in England for several centuries, and frequently represented co. Cambridge in Parliament.

SIR RICHARD ST. GEORGE, Clarenceux King of Arms (19th in lineal descent from Baldwin), m. 1575, Elizabeth, dau. of Nicholas St. John, of Liddiard Tregooze, Wilts, by whom he left at his death, 17 May, 1635, three sons,

1. Henry (Sir), Garter King of Arms, m. 1614, Mary, dau. of Sir Thomas Dayrell, Knt. of Lillingstone Dayrell, and d. 5 Nov. 1644, leaving with four daus. (1. Elizabeth, m. Col. P. Bourke; 2. Mary, m. Ferdinand Hastings; 3. Frances, m. George Tucker; and 4. Rebecca, m. George Cook) four sons,
   1. Sir Thomas St. George, Garter King of Arms, d. 6 March, 1703.
   2. William St. George (Col.), a Cavalier, killed at the storming of Leicester.
   3. Sir Henry St. George, Clarenceux King of Arms, d. 1715, aged 91.
   4. Richard St. George, Ulster King of Arms, m. Mary Hastings, d.s.p.
2. George (Sir), of Carrickdrumrush, co. Leitrim, whose son, Sir Oliver, Bart., M.P., m. Olivia, dau. of Michael Beresford, and was father of SIR GEORGE ST. GEORGE, Bart., elevated to the Peerage of Ireland, as LORD ST. GEORGE in 1715. He m. Margaret, dau. of John, 2nd Viscount Massereene, and left at his decease, 4 Aug. 1735, aged 80, a dau., the Hon. Mary St. George, m. John Usher, M.P., by whom she had a dau., Olivia, m. 23 Jan. 1736, Arthur French, of Tyrone, co. Galway, and a son, St. George Usher, who was elevated to the Peerage of Ireland, in 1763, as LORD ST. GEORGE of *Hatley St. George, co. Leitrim*, which dignity expired at his lordship's decease, without male issue in 1775; his only dau., by Elizabeth Dominick his wife, Emilia Olivia, m. William Robert, 2nd Duke of Leinster.
3. RICHARD, of whom we treat.

The 3rd son,

CAPT. RICHARD ST. GEORGE, went over to Ireland in the beginning of the 17th century, in the Royal Army, and was appointed Governor of the town and Castle of Athlone. He was b. at Hatley St. George 27 March, 1590, and m. 20 Feb. 1625, Anne, dau. of Michael Pinnock, of Turrock, co. Roscommon, and left at his death, 24 April, 1667 (with two daus., Mary, m. 1st, Thomas Ash, of St. John's, co. Meath, and 2ndly, Stafford Lightburn, of Adamstown; and Anne, m. Major Wood), an only surviving son,

HENRY ST. GEORGE, of Athlone, M.P., and of Woodsgift, co. Kilkenny, an Officer in the Irish Army of CHARLES II. This gentleman, who was b. 15 Oct. 1638; m. 3 June, 1669, Annie, dau. of Mr. Alderman Ridgeley Hatfield, of the city of Dublin, by whom he left at his decease, 1723, four sons,

1. RICHARD, of Kilrush, a Lieut.-Gen. in the Army, M.P., m. 1696, Elizabeth, dau. of Lord Coloony, and d. in Dublin in 1755, without legitimate issue.
2. Henry, d. unm. 1723.
3. ARTHUR (Very Rev.), D.D., Dean of Ross, of whom presently.
4. George, of Woodsgift, M.P., father of Sir Richard St. George, of Woodsgift, co. Kilkenny, created a baronet 12 March, 1766 (see BURKE'S *Peerage and Baronetage*).

The 3rd son,

THE VERY REV. ARTHUR ST. GEORGE, D.D., Dean of Ross, d. 24 Sept. 1772, aged 91, leaving by his wife Jane, dau. of Sir Thomas McIyneux, 1st bart. of Castle Dillon,
1. Richard, of Kilrush, co. Kilkenny, m. 1763, Sarah, eldest dau. of the Very Rev. Richard Handcock, Dean of Achonry, and had a son,
   Richard, b. 1776; d. unm. June, 1840.
2. THOMAS, of whom hereafter.
3. Capel, Capt. of Grenadiers, d. in West Indies.
4. Arthur, Major 62nd Foot, d. 1769.
5. HOWARD, ancestor of ST. GEORGE of *Kilrush*.
6. Henry (Rev.), m. 1st, Mary, dau. of Philip Perceval, of Temple House, co. Sligo, and had by her one son,
   1. Arthur, b. 1776; d. unm. 1845.
He m. 2ndly, Jane, dau. and co-heir of William Walsh, of co. Limerick (by Elizabeth, dau. of John Flood, of Flood Hall, and sister of Sir Frederic Flood, Bart.), and by her had issue,
   2. Henry (Rev.), d. 1840.
   3. Oliver, Capt. 23rd Fusiliers, m. 1st, 1827, Harriet Susanna, widow of Rev. Frederick Austin, M.A.; and 2ndly, 10 July, 1869, Julia Mary, dau. of Col. Girardot, Coldstream Guards.
   4. Nelson, of Altamont, m. Miss Cash, of Dublin, and d.s.p.
   5. William, of Kildavin House, m. Miss Lovel, and d.s.p. 1871.
   1. Elizabeth, d. unm.
   2. Jane, m. Rev. Mr. Whitty.
   3. Henrietta, d. unm.
   4. Isabella, m. Theophilus Edward, 2nd son of Arthur John St. George, of Kilrush.

1. Catherine, m. Clement Wolseley, 2nd son of Sir Richard Wolseley, 1st bart., and had issue, Wilhelmina, who m. Thomas Belmore St. George (see BURKE'S *Peerage and Baronetage*, ST. GEORGE, Bart.).

The 2nd son,

THOMAS ST. GEORGE, M.P. for Clogher, Commissioner of Barracks, b. Oct. 1738; m. 15 Aug. 1776, the Hon. Lucinda Acheson, 4th dau. of Archibald, 1st Viscount Gosford, and by her (who m. 2ndly, Jeremiah French, Capt. 80th Regt.) he left at his decease, 1 April, 1795,
1. Thomas Baldwin St. George, Capt. 80th Regt., b. 12 May, 1777; m. Miss Eliza Mason, and d. 28 Feb. 1852, having had issue, three sons,
   1. Thomas (Rev.), Vicar of Kilnasalagh, co. Clare, m. Elizabeth, eldest dau. of Joseph Clarke, and d.s.p.
   2. Archibald (Rev.), m. Penelope, dau. of Robert Johnston, Q.C., of Kinbough, co. Leitrim, and d.s.p. His widow m. 2ndly, Rev. — Gully.
   3. Howard, d. unm.
2. ACHESON, of Wood Park, of whom presently.
3. John, of Woodside, co. Chester, Capt. 80th Regt., and Lieut.-Col. Salop Militia, b. 16 Aug. 1779; m. 21 April, 1811, Frances, youngest dau. of Archibald Campbell, M.D., of Stafford, and d. 28 Jan. 1854, having by her (who d. 10 Oct. 1865) had issue,
   1. John (Sir), K.C.B., Gen. Col. Commandant Royal Artillery, commanded the siege train at the fall of Sebastopol, and was subsequently President of the Ordnance Select Committee, Director of Ordnance, b. 18 Jan. 1812; m. 15 Aug. 1860, Elizabeth Marianne, youngest dau. (and co-heir of both father and mother) of Thomas Evans, of Lyminster House, Sussex, J.P., and Margaret his wife, only dau. and heir of William Harris, and had one son,
      Baldwin John, Capt. 4th Dragoon Guards, b. 16 Feb. 1862.
   2. Archibald, of Camma Lodge, Athlone, J.P. co. Roscommon, B.A. Trin. Coll. Dublin, b. 5 June, 1813, m. 22 Dec. 1862, Kate, dau. of Archibald St. George. He d. 14 April, 1902. She d. 13 June, 1902, having had issue, a dau.,
      Frances Milicent, d. 25 Jan. 1890.
   3. William Whitmore, of Clifton Park, Birkenhead, b. 3 Dec. 1814; m. 10 May, 1842, Mary Anne, dau. of David Cram, and d. 10 July, 1890, having by her (who d. 25 Aug. 1863) had issue,
      (1) William Baldwin, Lieut. R.A., b. 11 Sept. 1843; d. 6 Dec. 1876.
      (2) Edward Whitmore, b. 20 May, 1850; d. 14 March, 1853.
      (3) Acheson Whitmore, b. 9 Aug. 1856, Major, late Prince of Wales's Own (West York) Regt., d. 7 Aug. 1901.
      (4) Howard, b. 6 April, 1858; d. unm. 20 Nov. 1908.
      (5) George Herbert, b. 12 March, 1860.
      (6) Charles Henry, b. 12 Jan. 1863.
      (1) Mary Anne Frances.
      (2) Millicent Eleanor, m. 10 July, 1884, Rev. Edward Whitmore Simpson, Vicar of Laxton, co. York.
      (3) Lucy Olivia, m. 26 April, 1881, George Arbuthnot Moore, of Estlands, co. Somerset, and has issue.
      (4) Harriet Louisa.
      (5) Emily Agnes, m. 13 Nov. 1883, Martin Benson Lawford, of Oerley Hall, Oswestry, and has issue.
      (6) Sophia Emma.
   4. George, H.M. Customs, b. 12 June, 1816; m. 19 Aug. 56, Annie, dau. of Richard Bryans, J.P., of Parkfield, Birkenhead, and d. 19 April, 1880, leaving issue,
      (1) George Edward, b. 17 July, 1857.
      (2) Arthur Baldwin, b. 30 July, 1858.
      (3) Archibald Henry, b. 2 Oct. 1859.
      (4) Annie Georgina.
      (5) Frances Aline, m. Horace Stedall, and has issue.
   5. Howard (Rev.), M.A., Vicar of Billinge, co. Lancaster, and J.P., b. 13 Jan. 1819; m. 22 June, 1864, Emilia, 2nd dau. of Andrew Comber, of Stand House, co. Lancaster, and had a son,
      Howard Comber, b. 25 Sept. 1866; m. 30 Dec. 1891, Mary Melicent, dau. of William Latham, M.A., Q.C.; and a dau., Frances Emilia.

1. Millicent, *m.* 21 July, 1853, Frederic William Holder, of Liverpool.
2. Lucy Elizabeth Georgiana, *m.* 7 June, 1849, Rev. William Edward Coldwell, M.A., Vicar of Sandon, and has issue.
4. Archibald, of Camma Lodge and Dublin, *b.* 27 Feb. 1782 ; and *d.* 14 Nov. 1863.
5. William Molyneux, *b.* 17 Feb. 1784, 3rd Lieut. of the *Conqueror*, killed at Trafalgar, 21 Oct. 1805, *s.p.*

The eldest surviving son,

ACHESON ST. GEORGE, of Wood Park, co. Armagh, *b.* 21 June, 1778 ; *m.* 1st, 1810, Eleanor, dau. of Robert Gordon, of Clonmel, and by her (who *d.* May, 1821) had issue,
1. THOMAS GORDON, Lieut.-Col. H.E.I.C.S., *b.* 1812 ; *m.* 23 April, 1861, Sarah Strangham, only child and heir of William Lloyd Caldecot, of Plas Llandegwyn, co. Carnarvon, and had issue,
  1. Acheson William Gordon, *b.* 2 July, 1866 ; *d.* 23 Oct. 1880.
    1. Nora. 2. Ethel Eugenie.
    3. Adela Eleanor.
2. William, H.E.I.C.S., *d. unm.* in India, 2 Sept. 1836.
3. ACHESON, late of Wood Park.
4. John, H.E.I.C.S., *b.* 27 April, 1821 ; killed at the Khyber Pass 2 Nov. 1841.
1. Lucinda Margaret, *d. unm.* 16 April, 1845.
2. Eleanor Mary, *d. unm.* 6 Dec. 1904.
3. Olivia, *d. unm.* 19 June, 1836.

He *m.* 2ndly, 1 Dec. 1824, Jane, 2nd dau. of the Hon. and Very Rev. John Hewitt, Dean of Cloyne, 4th son of Jain s 1st Viscount Lifford, and by her had one dau.,
4. Alicia Hewitt Caroline, *m.* 15 Oct. 1856, Edward Chaloner Knox, of Desertcreat, co. Tyrone. He *d.s.p.* April, 1896.

Mr. St. George *d.* 3 Dec. 1855.

Arms—Arg., a chief az., over all a lion rampant gu., ducally crowned or, armed and langued of the second. *Crest*—A demi-lion rampant gu., ducally crowned or, armed and langued as. *Motto*—Firmitas in cœlo.

Seat—Wood Park, Tynan, co. Armagh.

ST. GEORGE OF TYRONE.

KATHERINE ST. GEORGE and JOSEPHINE BROWNE, daus. and co-heirs of Christopher St. George (*see below*), *s.* their father 1877.

Lineage.—ARTHUR FRENCH, of Tyrone, co. Galway, Mayor of Galway, 1691, son of Christopher French, of Tyrone (who *d.* 1676) left issue by his first wife, with a dau., a son,

CHRISTOPHER, of whom presently.

He *m.* 2ndly, 2 May, 1691, Sarah, only dau. of Ulick Burke, of Clare, co. Galway, and widow of Iriel Farrell, of Cloonyquin, co. Galway, and by her had, with other issue, a son,
ARTHUR, of Cloonyquin, ancestor of the family of FRENCH, of Cloonyquin (*whom see*).

He *d.* 1712. His eldest son,

CHRISTOPHER FRENCH, of Tyrone, co. Galway, conformed 1704, *m.* about 27 Jan. 1699, Margery, 3rd dau. of Iriel Farrell, of Cloonyquin, by Sarah his wife, dau. of Ulick Burke (*see above*). His will, dated 31 July, 1718, was proved 1720. His widow *m.* James Browne, of Galway, who *d.* 1757. Her will, dated 27 June, 1757, was proved 24 May, 1760. Mr. Christopher French left issue,
1. ARTHUR, of whom presently.
2. Patrick, of Brook Lodge, co. Galway, who was father of Christopher, of Brook Lodge, *m.* his cousin, Julia, dau. of Arthur French, of Tyrone (*see below*), and had issue, Patrick and St. George.
3. Christopher.   4. James.
1. Jane.   2. Juliane.
3. Sarah.   4. Mary.
5. Margery.   6. Rosa.

The eldest son,

ARTHUR FRENCH, of Tyrone, co. Galway, appellant in the case of French *v.* Caddell, in the House of Lords 1764-5, *m.* 23 Jan. 1736, Olivia, eldest dau. of John Usher, M.P., of Carrick, by his wife, the HON. MARY ST. GEORGE, only dau. and heir of GEORGE, BARON ST. GEORGE, of Hatley St. George, and dying 8 May, 1779, left issue,
1. CHRISTOPHER, his heir.
1. Olivia, *m.* 25 June, 1772, Anthony Nugent, of Pallas, who *d.* Sept. 1814, leaving issue (*see* BURKE's *Peerage*, WESTMEATH, E.).
2. Julia, *m.* her cousin, Christopher French, of Brook Lodge, and had issue (*see above*).
3. Nicola.

The only son,

CHRISTOPHER FRENCH, of Tyrone, *b.* 13 April, 1754, who assumed 1774, the surname of ST. GEORGE in compliance with the settlement of his great-grandfather, Lord St. George. He *m.* 1778, Anne, eldest dau. of Henry Bingham, of Newbrook, co. Mayo, and left with two daus. (Letitia, *m.* James Kelly, and Olivia, *m.* William Robert Wills, of Willsgrove), a son and heir,

ARTHUR FRENCH ST. GEORGE, of Tyrone, *b.* 8 Aug. 1780 ; *m.* 22 Jan. 1801, Lady Harriet St. Lawrence, eldest dau. of William, Earl of Howth, and co-heir of her mother, Lady Mary Bermingham, 2nd dau. and co-heir of Thomas, 22nd Lord Athenry, Earl of Louth. By her had issue,
1. CHRISTOPHER, of Tyrone.
2. Arthur St. George, of Tyrone, *d. unm.*
1. Mary, *m.* Francis Cuff, of Creagh, co. Mayo.

2. Matilda, *m.* Col. Charles Pepper, of Ballygarth (*see that family*).
3. Louisa, *m.* Col. H. Bingham, 60th Rifles.
4. Anne, dec.   5. Harriet, dec.

Mr. St. George *d.* 1 Jan. 1844, and was *s.* by his eldest son,

CHRISTOPHER ST. GEORGE, of Tyrone, J.P. and D.L., M.P. for Galway from 1847 to 1852, *b.* 15 March, 1810 ; *m.* 16 Dec. 1852, Henoria Kane, and *d.* 12 Nov. 1877, leaving two daus.,
1. KATHERINE, *m.* 5 Feb. 1874, Robert James Ker St. George, of Woodsgift, co. Kilkeanny, and has issue,
  1. Richard Christopher Bligh.   2. Arthur French.
  3. Robert Charles Cecil.
  1. Rosamond.   2. Gladys.
  3. Josephine.
2. JOSEPHINE, *m.* Andrew Browne, of Carnacregg, co. Galway.

Arms—Quarterly: 1st and 4th, arg., a chief az., over all a lion rampant gu., ducally crowned or, for ST. GEORGE ; 2nd and 3rd, quarterly, 1st and 4th, erm., a chevron az., for FRENCH ; 2nd and 3rd, az., a chevron erm., between three billets arg., for USHER. *Crest*—A demi-lion rampant gu. ducally crowned or. *Motto*—Firmitas in cœlo.

Seat—Tyrone House, Oranmore, co. Galway.

SANDERS OF CHARLEVILLE PARK.

ROBERT MASSY DAWSON SANDERS, of Charleville Park, co. Cork, J.P., High Sheriff 1901, M.E., Dublin University, 19 May, 1862 ; *m.* 1 Feb. 1899, Hilda Auguste Katherine, youngest dau. of Francis Henry Beaumont, of Buckland Court, co. Surrey (*see that family*), and has issue,
1. CHARLES CRAVEN, *b.* 8 Dec. 1899.
2. Terence Robert Beaumont, *b.* 2 June, 1901.

Lineage.—The Boyles, by deed of 20 Sept. 1697, conveyed to William Sanders, on a lease for ever, The Park, at Charleville, which has since been the abode of the Sanders family. This

WILLIAM SANDERS, of Charleville, *m.* Tamsine, dau. of Christopher Knight, of Ballynoe, co. Cork, and had (with two daus., Catherine and Tamsine, both *d. unm.*) a son,

CHRISTOPHER SANDERS, of Charleville, *m.* 28 Feb. 1771, Sarah Stevelly, and *d.* 28 Sept. 1810, having had issue,
1. WILLIAM, of whom presently.   2. Robert, *d. unm.* 1833.
1. Sarah, *m.* Joseph Harding.
2. Tamsine, *m.* James Fisher, Capt. 81st Regt.

The elder son,

WILLIAM SANDERS, of Charleville Park, *b.* 2 Aug. 1773 ; *m.* 7 March, 1806, Elizabeth, dau. of Thomas Andrews, Lord Mayor of Dublin 1799, and *d.* 1819, having had issue,
1. CHRISTOPHER, of Deer Park, *b.* 25 June, 1808 ; *m.* Elizabeth Broomhead, and *d.* 22 Nov. 1839, leaving one dau., Francis Kennedy, 3rd son of Sir John Kennedy, 1st bart., of Johnstown, and subsequently to Sir George Ribton, Bart.
2. William Robert, of Charleville Park, *b.* 16 Feb. 1810 ; *d. unm.* 3 Aug. 1851.   3. ROBERT, of Charleville Park.
4. THOMAS, of whom presently.
5. Francis Alexander (Rev.), *b.* 2 Aug. 1818 ; *m.* Margaret Cooper, and has had issue,
  1. Frederick.   2. William.
  3. Francis Alexander, Major Inniskilling Fusiliers, *b.* 30 Dec. 1855, killed in action in South Africa 21 Feb. 1900.
  4. Robert.
  1. Margaret.   2. Penelope.
1. Penelope, *m.* Thomas Wilson, and *d.s.p.* 1829.
2. Maria (dec.), *m.* William F. Darley, LL.B.
3. Eliza Sarah (dec.), *m.* Joseph Stock, LL.D.

The 3rd son,

ROBERT SANDERS, C.B., of Charleville Park, co. Cork, Col. in the Army and Lieut.-Col. 19th Regt., J.P. for the co., *b.* Dec. 1814 ; *s.* his elder brother in 1830, and *d.s.p.* 1 Nov. 1869, and was *s.* by his brother,

THOMAS SANDERS, of Sanders (Charleville) Park, co. Cork, LL.D., Barrister-at-Law, J.P., co. Cork and Limerick, *b.* 10 May, 1816 ; *m.* 14 Aug. 1861, Mary Charlotte, dau. of Richard Duckworth Dunn, Capt. Qeen's Bays, of Surbiton, Surrey, by Isabella Pallmer his wife, dau. of James Hewitt Massy-Dawson, of Ballinacourte, co. Tipperary, and *d.* 1892, leaving issue,
1. ROBERT MASSY DAWSON, now of Charleville Park.
2. William Arthur, *b.* 12 May, 1863 ; *d.s.p.* 1891.

St. Lawrence. THE LANDED GENTRY. 620

3. Evelyn Francis, M.Inst.C.E. (17, *Garden Reach Road, Calcutta*), *b.* 12 July, 1864; *m.* 16 Oct. 1903, Maria Elizabeth Coote, dau. of the late William Uniacke Townsend, J.P. (*ee* TOWNSHEND *of Myross Wood*), and *d.* 31 Dec. 1909, leaving issue,
    Frederick Alvin Oliver, *b.* 16 Nov. 1906.
4. Charles Stewart, *b.* 15 March, 1868.
5. Edmund Duckworth, *b.* 20 Sept. 1868.
6. Alvin Augustus, *b.* 31 March, 1870.
7. Aubrey Thomas, *b.* 26 March, 1873.
1. Isabella Maria, *m.* 27 Oct. 1890, Charles Arthur Webb, of Quartertown House, co. Cork, and has issue.
2. Eliza Benita, *m.* 9 July, 1902, the 6th Baron Hotham, and has issue (see BURKE'S *Peerage*, HOTHAM, B.).
3. Mary Ethel.

Arms—Arg., a chevron gu. between thre elephants' heads erased sa., on a chief az. a sword erect ppr., pommel and hilt or, between two bezants. **Crest**—Out of a mural crown, an elephant's head ppr. charged with a bezant. **Motto**—Nil conscire sibi nulla pallescere culpa.

Seat—Charleville Park, co. Cork.

GAISFORD - ST. LAWRENCE OF HOWTH.

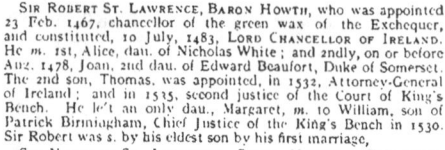

JULIAN CHARLES GAISFORD - ST. LAWRENCE, of Howth Castle, co. Dublin, formerly of Offington, co. Sussex, J.P., late Lieut. R.N., *b.* 28 March, 1862; *m.* 19 Nov. 1889, Bertha Mary, elder dau. of the late Francis H. Riddell, of Cheeseburn Grange, Northumberland, and has issue.

1. Thomas Julian, *b.* 30 Sept. 1890.
2. Stephen Francis, midshipman R.N., *b.* 3 April, 1892.
3. Cyril Hugh, *b.* 18 June, 1893.
1. Margaret Teresa Mary, *b.* 28 Sept. 1896.
2. Dorothy Teresa Mary, *b.* 30 July, 1898.
3. Cecily Mary, *b.* 9 April, 1901.
4. Clare Emily Mary, *b.* 24 Jan. 1903.

On succeeding to the estates of his uncle Ulick Tristram, 4th Earl of Howth, K.P., he assumed by Royal Licence 31 May, 1909, the additional surname and arms of St. Lawrence.

Lineage—(of ST. LAWRENCE).—SIR AMORICUS, or AMORY TRISTRAM, the brother-in-law and companion in arms of Sir John de Courcy, in 1177, effected a landing at Howth, defeated the Irish in a battle at the bridge of Ivora, and obtained the lands and barony by tenure of Howth, as a reward for his distinguished valour during the conflict. After this successful commencement, Sir Amoricus, with Sir John de Courcy, reduced the whole province of Ulster; but in 1189, when Sir John was removed from the Government of Ireland by RICHARD I, Sir Amoricus, who was then in Connaught, being attacked by O'Conor, king of that province, and overwhelmed by numbers, himself and his whole party, consisting of thirty knights and two hundred infantry, perished to a man. By the sister of Sir John de Courcy, Earl of Ulster, Sir Amorey left three sons, the eldest,
  SIR NICHOLAS FITZ AMOREY, of Howth, was obliged to content himself with the lands of Howth, and relinquished to religious houses the conquests of his father in Ulster. His son,
  ALMERICUS DE ST. LAWRENCE, of Howth, was granted by JOHN, Lord of Ireland, afterwards KING JOHN, a charter of confirmation of the lands of Howth, as held by his father, to hold by service of one knight's fee. His son,
  SIR NICHOLAS ST. LAWRENCE, LORD OF HOWTH, acknowledged himself, in 1285, bound to serve suit of Court in the County of Dublin for Howth, and was *s.* by his son,
  ADAM ST. LAWRENCE, LORD OF HOWTH, who by his wife Isabella had a son and heir,
  ADAM ST. LAWRENCE, LORD OF HOWTH, was *s.* by his son and heir Nicholas, who had livery of his father's lands 1342, and was summoned to a Great Council to be held in Dublin 1372. He *m.* Alice, dau. of John Plunket, but *d.s.p.*, being *s.* by his next heir and nearest of kin
  STEPHEN ST. LAWRENCE, whose eldest son was
  CHRISTOPHER ST. LAWRENCE, BARON HOWTH, who was buried in the church of Howth, as appears by the inscription on his monument. He *m.* Anne, dau. of Plunkett, of Rathmore, co. Meath, and was *s.* by his son,
  SIR ROBERT ST. LAWRENCE, BARON HOWTH, who was appointed 23 Feb. 1467, chancellor of the green wax of the Exchequer, and constituted, 10 July, 1483, LORD CHANCELLOR OF IRELAND. He *m.* 1st, Alice, dau. of Nicholas White; and 2ndly, on or before Aug. 1478, Joan, 2nd dau. of Edward Beaufort, Duke of Somerset. The 2nd son, Thomas, was appointed, in 1532, Attorney-General of Ireland; and in 1535, second justice of the Court of King's Bench. He le^t an only dau., Margaret, *m.* to William, son of Patrick Birmingham, Chief Justice of the King's Bench in 1530. Sir Robert was *s.* by his eldest son by his first marriage,
  SIR NICHOLAS ST. LAWRENCE, BARON HOWTH. This nobleman, for his fidelity to HENRY VII., in the affair of Lambert Simnel, was presented by that monarch with three hundred pieces of gold, and confirmed by charter, dated 4 March, 1489, in the lands of Howth, &c. He subsequently attended the Lord-Deputy Kildare at the famous battle of Knocktough, in Connaught, fought against the Irish 19 Aug. 1504, when his lordship headed the billmen on foot. Sir Nicholas was made LORD CHANCELLOR OF IRELAND, 10 June, 1509. He *m.* 1st, Genet, only dau. of Sir Christopher Plunkett, Lord Killeen. He *m.* 2ndly, Anne, widow of Bermingham, and dau. and heir of Thomas Berford, of Kilrowe, co. Meath. He *m.* 3rdly, Alice, dau. of Robert Fitzsimons and widow of Nicholas Cheevers and sister to Walter Fitzsimons, Archbishop of Dublin, 1484-1511. He *d.* 10 July, 1526, and was *s.* by his eldest son by his 1st wife,
  SIR CHRISTOPHER ST. LAWRENCE, BARON HOWTH, *m.* before 1509, Amy, sister and heir of Richard Birmingham of Ballydungan. He *d.* 2 April, 1512, and was *s.* by his eldest son,
  EDWARD ST. LAWRENCE, BARON HOWTH, *b.* 1506; *d.* 2 July, 1549; *m.* 1528, Alison, dau. and co-heir of James Fitz Lyons, of Aucheston, by whom he left issue, two daus. and co-heirs,
1. Anne, *m.* Bartholomew Dillon, of Keppoch.
2. Alison, *m.* John Golding, and had issue.
His brother,
  SIR RICHARD ST. LAWRENCE, BARON HOWTH, *m.* Dame Catharine Fitz Gerald, and *d.s.p.* 1559, at whose decease the Barony of Howth passed to the heir male, his brother,
  CHRISTOPHER ST. LAWRENCE, BARON HOWTH, generally called " the blind lord," who *m.* Elizabeth, dau. of Sir John Plunkett, of Beaulieu, by his wife, Anne, dau. of Robert Barnewall, of Dromenagh. He *m.* 2ndly, Cecilia, dau. of Henry Cusack, Alderman of Dublin, and *d.* 24 Oct. 1589; and was *s.* by his eldest son by his first wife,
  SIR NICHOLAS ST. LAWRENCE, BARON HOWTH, *b.* 1555; *m.* 1st, Alison, 5th dau. of Sir Christopher Barnewall, of Turvey; and 2ndly, Mary, dau. of Sir Nicholas Whyte, of Leixlip, Master of the Rolls, and widow successively of Christopher Darcy, of Plattyn, and of Robert Browne, of Mulranken. He *d.* 14 May, 1606, and was *s.* by his eldest son (by his 1st marriage),
  SIR CHRISTOPHER ST. LAWRENCE, BARON HOWTH. A Colonel of Infantry, commanded the rear of the vanguard, at the Battle of Carlingford, 13 Nov. 1600, under the Lord-Deputy Mountjoy, against Tyrone. His lordship *m.* Elizabeth, dau. of Wentworth of Pickering, co. York, and had issue,
1. NICHOLAS, of whom next.
.2. Thomas, who had issue a son, WILLIAM, Baron Howth, of whom later.
1. Margaret, *m.* 1st, William Fitzwilliam, and 2ndly, Michael Burford.
He *d.* Oct. 1619, and was *s.* by his elder son,
  NICHOLAS ST. LAWRENCE, BARON HOWTH, *b.* 1597; *m.* 1615, Jane, only surviving dau. and heir of Dr. George Montgomery, Bishop of Meath, and had issue. His lordship *d.s.p.m.s.* but leaving four daus. and co-heirs 1643, and was *s.* by his brother,
  THOMAS ST. LAWRENCE, BARON HOWTH, who by his wife Eleanor had a son and heir,
  WILLIAM ST. LAWRENCE, BARON HOWTH, Custos Rotulorum of co. Dublin. This nobleman *m.* Elizabeth, widow of Col. Fitzwilliam and dau. and co-heir of his predecessor. He *d.* 17 June, 1671, was *s.* by his son,
  THOMAS ST. LAWRENCE, BARON HOWTH, *b.* 1659. This peer sat in King JAMES's Parliament, of 1689, as he did in 1692, the first Parliament after the Revolution, and signed the association and declaration (2 Dec. 1697) in defence of the person and government of King WILLIAM, and the succession as settled by Act of Parliament. He *m.* 23 Sept. 1687, Mary, eldest dau. of Henry Barnewall, Viscount Barnewall, of Kingsland, and had issue. His lordship, dying 30 May, 1727, was *s.* by his son and heir,
  WILLIAM ST. LAWRENCE, BARON HOWTH, *b.* 11 Jan. 1688; *m.* 2 Aug. 1728, Lucy, younger dau. of Lieut.-Gen. Richard Gorges, and by her (who *m.* 2ndly, Nicholas Weldon) had issue. He *d.* 4 April, 1748, and was *s.* by his elder son,
  THOMAS, 1ST EARL OF HOWTH, *b.* 10 May, 1730; who was created, 3 Sept. 1767, Viscount St. Lawrence and EARL OF HOWTH. His lordship was sworn, in the following year, of His Majesty's Privy Council in Ireland; and in consideration of his own and his ancestors' services, obtained, 7 June, 1776, a pension of £500 a year. His lordship *m.* 17 Nov. 1750, Isabella, dau. of Sir Henry King, Bart., and sister of Edward, 1st Earl of Kingston, by whom (who *d.* 30 Oct. 1794) he had issue,
1. WILLIAM, his successor. 2. Henry, *d. unm.* 1787.
3. Thomas (Rt. Rev.), *b.* 1755; D.D., Bishop of Cork and Ross; *m.* Frances, eldest dau. and co-heir of the Rev. Henry Coghlan, D.D., and left at his death, 10 June, 18.1,
1. Thomas (Rev.), who *m.* in 1816, Harriet, dau. of Lieut.-Gen. John Gray, and *d.s.p.* in 1833.
2. Edward (Rev.), Archdeacon of Ross, and Prebendary of Cork; *m.* Elizabeth, dau. of Sir Nicholas Colthurst, Bart.; and *d.s.p.* 21 June, 1842.

3. Robert Kingsborough (Rev.), Rector of Moragh, b. 29 Sept. 1797; m. 3 Sept. 1850, Elizabeth Anne, dau. of R. B. Townsend, of Castle Townsend, co. Cork, and d.s.p. June, 1866. Mrs. St. Lawrence d. 13 Jan. 1885, aged 95.
1. Emma, m. 1805, Rev. William Lewis Beaufort, LL.D., and d. in 1865.
2. Isabella, m. 1808, Right Rev. Dr. John Leslie, Bishop of Kilmore; and d. 3 Nov. 1830, leaving issue.
3. Letitia, m. 18 Oct. 1830, Rev. Richard Jephson Rothe; and d. 1833.
4. Frances Elizabeth, m. 9 July, 1836, Robert Morgan Tighe, of Mitchelstown, Westmeath, who d. 1853. She d. 30 Sept. 1871.
1. Isabella, m. 16 Nov. 1773, Dudley Cosby, Lord Sydney.
2. Elizabeth, m. 7 Feb. 1786, Sir Paulus Æmelius Irving, Bart.; and d. 1799.
3. Frances, m. 15 Oct. 1808, Rev. Dr. James Phillott, Archdeacon of Bath; and d. Jan. 1842.

The earl d. 20 Sept. 1801, and was s. by his elder son,
WILLIAM, 2ND EARL OF HOWTH b. 4 Oct. 1752; m. 1 June, 1777, Lady Mary Bermingham, dau. and co-heir of Thomas, Earl of Louth, by whom (who d. 1793) he had,
1. Harriet, m. 22 Jan. 1801, Arthur French St. George, of Tyrone, co. Galway; and d. 1830, leaving issue.
2. Isabella, m. May, 1803, William Richard, Viscount Glerawly (afterwards 3rd Earl Annesley), which marriage was dissolved in 1820. She d. 1827.
3. Matilda, m. Major William Burke, of Quansborough; and d. 1840. He d. 10 July, 1859.
4. Mary, m. Clifford Trotter; and d. 1825.

His lordship m. 2ndly, Margaret, dau. of William Burke, of Kielogues, co. Galway, by whom (who d. 19 Sept. 1856) he left at his decease, 4 April, 1822,
1. THOMAS, 3rd earl.
5. Catherine, m. 1823, Viscount Dungarvan, who d. 1834. She d. 4 April, 1879.
6. Elizabeth, m. 12 May, 1831, Sir Edward Richard Borough, Bart., and d. 4 April, 1863.

His lordship d. 4 April, 1822, and was s. by his only son,
SIR THOMAS, 3RD EARL OF HOWTH, K.P., Vice-Admiral of Leinster; b. 16 Aug. 1803; m. 1st, 9 Jan. 1826, Lady Emily de Burgh, dau. of John Thomas, 13th Earl of Clanricarde, and by her (who d. 5 Dec. 1842) had,
1. WILLIAM ULICK TRISTRAM, 4th earl.
1. Emily, m. 26 Oct. 1850, Thomas Gaisford, of Offington, Sussex (who d. 26 Feb. 1898), and d. 6 Nov. 1868, leaving issue (see below).
2. Catherine Elizabeth, m. 28 Aug. 1850, James Joseph Wheble, of Bulmershe Court, Berks, who d. 1884, leaving issue
3. Mary, d. 15 Nov. 1864.
4. Margaret, m. 20 June, 1861, Sir Charles Compton W. Domvile, 2nd bart., who d. 1884.

The Earl m. 2ndly, 27 Feb. 1851, Henrietta Digby, only child of Peter Barfoot, of Landenstown, co. Kildare, and by her (who d. 5 March, 1884) had issue,
2. Thomas Kenelm Digby, b. 12 Dec. 1855, Capt. 5th Dragoon Guards, one of the pages of the Prince of Wales at H.R.H.'s installation as a Knight of St. Patrick in 1868, d. 8 May, 1891.
5. Henrietta Eliza, m. 6 Sept. 1881, Capt. Benjamin Lee Guinness, late Royal Horse Guards, brother of Lord Ardilaun, and has issue.
6. Geraldine Digby.

His lordship d. 4 Feb. 1874, and was s. by his only son,
SIR WILLIAM ULICK TRISTRAM ST. LAWRENCE, 4TH EARL HOWTH, K.P., Viscount St. Lawrence, and Baron of Howth, in Ireland, Baron Howth, of Howth, co. Dublin, in the United Kingdom, J.P. and D.L. co. Dublin, formerly Capt. 7th Hussars, M.P. for Galway 1863 to 1874; b. 25 June, 1827; s. his father as 4th Earl 1874, and created a Peer of the United Kingdom, 1881. He d. unm. 1909, when all his Peerages are believed to have become extinct, and when he was s. at Howth Castle by his nephew Julian Charles Gaisford, who thereupon assumed the additional surname and arms of St. Lawrence.

Lineage (of GAISFORD).—WILLIAM GAISFORD, of Westbury, m. Elizabeth, dau. of Thomas Hill, of Ditton's Marsh, and by her (who d. 24 June, 1740) had issue,
1. THOMAS, of Bitham.
1. Elizabeth, d. in infancy.
2. Jane, m. Richard Gibbs, of Westbury, and had a son, Gaisford Gibbs, of Heywood.

Mr. Gaisford d. in 1768, and was s. by his son,
THOMAS GAISFORD, of Bitham, Wilts, b. 1701; m. 1st, Mary Blatch, of Bratton, and had issue,
1. Elizabeth, who m. Benjamin Peach, of Westbury.

He m. 2ndly, Sarah Cooke, of Devizes, and had issue,
1. William, b. 1740; d. 1762.
2. JOHN, of Iford.
2. Sarah, m. 1780, William Temple, of Bishopstrow (see that family).

He d. 1774, and was s. by his son,
JOHN GAISFORD, of Iford, of Wilts, J.P., High Sheriff co. Wilts, 1793, b. 1747; m. Elizabeth, dau. of Rev. — Bushell, Rector of Laycock, and by her (who d. 1823) had issue,
1. THOMAS, heir.
2. Charles.
3. John.
4. William, of Worton.
1. Sarah Elizabeth, m. Capt. T. Festing, R.N., and d. 1855.
2. Charlotte, m. Capt. Dewell, of Malmesbury, and d. 1829.

Mr. Gaisford d. 1810, and was s. by his eldest son,
THE VERY REV. THOMAS GAISFORD, D.D., of Iford, Dean of Christ Church, Oxford, Regius Professor of Greek, Oxford, an eminent scholar, m. 1st, 1815, Helen Margaret, dau. of Rev. Archibald Douglas, Rector of Salwarpe, co. Worcester, and by her (who d. 1831) had issue,
1. THOMAS, of whom presently.
2. John William, Lieut.-Col. 72nd Highlanders, b. 1820; m. Nov. 1854, Jane Vaughan, dau. of Very Rev. Henry Cotton, LL.D., Dean of Lismore, and widow of Major George Sheaffe Montizambert, of Montreal, and d. 1889, having had issue,
1. Cecil Henry, b. 27 Sept. 1856; 2nd Lieut. 72nd Highlanders, killed in Afghan War, 1879.
2. Douglas John (Dolly's Grove, c. Meath), b. 17 July, 1860, Capt. South Wales Borderers, m. 20 June, 1892, Elizabeth, dau. of Gen. Sir Archibald Alison, Bart., and has issue,
(1) John William, b. 26 Aug. 1894.
(2) Robert Sandeman, b. 14 Jan. 1896.
(1) Jane Esme, b. 7 May, 1893.
3. Algernon Richard (Fortgranite, Baltinglass), Lieut. late Seaforth Highlanders, b. 4 Dec. 1865; m. April, 1905, Cecily dau. of Col. Farrant, R.E.
1. Helen Kate, m. 1882, Sir Robert Sandeman, K.C.S.I., who d. 1892, leaving issue. 2. Mabel Frances.
3. William, b. 1822; drowned at Oxford, 1843.
4. Douglas, b. 1826; d. 1833.
5. George (Rev.), M.A., Rector of East Lavant, Sussex, b. 30 May, 1827; m. 15 April, 1858, Agnes, dau. of Sir Charles Mills, 1st bart. of Hillingdon Court, and d. 25 June, 1903, having had issue,
1. Francis, b. 6 Nov. 1860; d. unm. 24 Oct. 1902.
2. Reginald, b. 21 March, 1870; d. 1882.
3. Arthur (twin with Reginald), b. 21 March, 1870, Rector of Tangmere, Sussex.
4. Ernest Charles, b. 25 Sept. 1875.
1. Anne Evelyn Agnes, b. 8 May, 1868.

1. Frances, m. 1859, Henry Hobhouse, of Hadspen, Somerset. He d. 1862.
2. Helen, m. Rev. R. Stokes, late Vicar of Staines, and d. 5 June, 1905, leaving issue a dau., Margaret.

Dr. Gaisford, m. 2ndly, Jane Catherine, dau. of Rev. R. Jenkyns, Rector of Evercreech. He d. 1855, and was s. by his eldest son,
THOMAS GAISFORD, of Offington, Sussex, formerly Capt. 79th Highlanders, J.P. and D.L. for cos. Sussex and Wilts, b. 12 Dec. 1816; m. 1st, 1 Jan. 1850, Henrietta Horatia, dau. of Rear-Admiral Charles Feilding (see BURKE's Peerage, DENBIGH, E.), and by her (who d. 8 Aug. 1851) had issue,
1. Horace Charles, b. 26 July, 1851, Capt. Grenadier Guards; d.s.p. 20 Sept. 1899.

He m. 2ndly, 26 Oct. 1859, Lady Emily St. Lawrence, eldest dau. of Thomas, 3rd Earl of Howth, K.P., and by her (who d. 6 Nov. 1868) had issue,
2. Cyril, b. 25 Sept. 1860; d. 1862.
3. JULIAN CHARLES, now of Howth Castle.
4. Basil, St. Lawrence (Rev.), b. 7 Nov. 1867, a priest.
5. Philip, b. 31 Oct. 1868.
1. Teresa Mary, b. 5 Sept. 1863 (Danefold, West Grinstead, Sussex).
2. Mary Emily, b. 20 Aug. 1865 (Danefold, West Grinstead, Sussex).
3. Agatha Mary, b. 30 Sept. 1866 (Danefold, West Grinstead, Sussex).

He m. 3rdly, 20 June, 1870, Lady Alice Mary Kerr, dau. of John, 7th Marquess of Lothian (see BURKE's Peerage), and d. 26 Feb. 1898, having by her (who d. 25 Jan. 1892),
6. Walter Thomas, Major Seaforth Highlanders, b. 7 Oct. 1871.
7. Hugh William, First Sec. Diplomatic Service at Lisbon, b. 18 Aug. 1874; m. 11 May, 1904, Virginia, dau. of the late John P. Bryce, of Bystock, near Exmouth.

Arms—Quarterly: 1 and 4, gu., two swords in saltire points upwards between four roses arg. barbed and seeded of the second (St. Lawrence); 2 and 3. arg., on a chevron gu. between three greyhounds courant sa. as many chaplets of the field (Gaisford). **Crests**—1. a sea-lion erect ppr. (ST. LAWRENCE); 2, on a fern brake, a greyhound courant sa. (GAISFORD). **Motto**—Qui Panse.
Seat—Howth Castle, co. Dublin. **Clubs**—Naval and Military, S.W.; Kildare Street, Dublin.

SANDERSON OF CLOVERHILL.

SAMUEL SANDERSON, of Cloverhill, co. Cavan, J.P. and D.L., High Sheriff 1876, b. 2 May, 1824; m. 1 March, 1860, Anne, dau. of John Armytage Nicholson, of Balrath, co. Meath (see that family). Mr. Sanderson, who is 2nd surviving son of the late Samuel Winter, of Agher, assumed the name of SANDERSON, and the arms of Sanderson quarterly with those of Winter, under Royal Licence 2 Oct. 1873.

Sandes.   THE LANDED GENTRY.

Lineage.—JAMES SANDERSON, of Cloverhill, *alias* Drumcassidy, co. Cavan, son of Alexander Sanderson, and nephew of Col. Robert Sanderson of Castle Sanderson, was M.P. for Enniskillen for thirty years, *temp*. GEORGE II. He *m.* Maria, dau. of Brockhill Newburgh, of Ballyhaise, co. Cavan, and had issue,
1. ALEXANDER, his heir.
2. Francis (Rev.), of Dromearn, co. Cavan.   3. Robert.
   1. Mary, *m.* Charles Atkinson, of Cangort (*see that family*).

Mr. Sanderson made his will 15 April, 1767, which was proved 15 March following, and was *s.* by his eldest son,
ALEXANDER SANDERSON, of Cloverhill, High Sheriff co. Cavan 1775, *m.* Lucy, dau. of Rev. Samuel Madden, D.D., of Manor Waterhouse, co. Fermanagh, " Premium Madden," and had issue,
1. JAMES, his successor.
2. Marv.
3. Charlotte.

Mr. Sanderson made his will 4 June, 1785, which was proved 14 March, 1787, and he was *s.* by his only son,
JAMES SANDERSON, of Cloverhill, D.L., *m.* Elizabeth, dau. of Isaac Walker, of Newry, and had four daus.,
1. Mary Anne, *d. unm.* 1873.
2. Lucy, *m.* 18 Nov. 1826, Samuel Winter, of Agher, co. Meath, and *d.* 11 Nov. 1864, leaving with other issue (*see* WINTER *of Agher*), a 3rd son,
   SAMUEL SANDERSON, now of Cloverhill.
3. Elizabeth.
4. Frances Alexandrina, *m.* 10 Feb. 1830, Richard Winter Reynell, of Killynon, co. Westmeath, and had issue (*see* REYNELL *of Killynon*).

Arms- Quarterly: 1st and 4th, arg., three bends az., the centre one charged with a crescent between two estoiles or, for SANDERSON; 2nd and 3rd, chequy or and az., on a fesse arg. a crescent gu., for WINTER. **Crests**—1st, SANDERSON, On a mount vert, an estoile or, 2nd, WINTER, A martlet or, charged with a crescent gu. **Motto**—Toujours propice.

Seat—Cloverhill, Belturbet, co. Cavan. **Club**—Sackville Street, Dublin.

SANDES OF SALLOW GLEN.

THOMAS WILLIAM SANDES, of Sallow Glen, co. Kerry, J.P., High Sheriff 1885, late Capt. Kerry Militia, educated at Trin. Coll. Cambridge, Barrister-at-Law, *b.* 26 March, 1842; *m.* 8 May, 1873, Amy, dau. of Rawdon Macnamara, M.D., of Dublin, and has issue,
1. Eva Maude, *m.* 14 April, 1904, John Kinahan, of Low Wood, Belfast.
2. Margaret Amy, *m.* 28 June, 1906, Hugh Henengh Finch, of Maryville, co. Limerick.

Lineage.—WILLIAM SANDES went to Ireland in 1649 with Oliver Cromwell, and was granted a portion of the extensive estates forfeited by the House of O'Conor. He *m.* Elizabeth, dau. of — Fernley, and by her (who *d.* 28 Dec. 1656, and was bur. at St. Michan's, Dublin (Funeral entry), had issue,
1. LANCELOT, of whom presently.
2. John, of Kilcavan, Queen's Co., from whom descend the family of Sandes, *of Carrigafoyle.*
   1. Anne, *m.* William Hamilton, of Liscloony, King's Co., who *d.* 13 Oct. 1679, and left issue.
   2. Judith, *m.* Richard Warburton, and had issue.
3. Elizabeth, *m.* Henry L'Estrange, of Moystown, King's Co., and had issue.
4. A dau., *m.* —Stanford.

The elder son,
LANCELOT SANDES, of Carrigafoyle, co. Kerry, M.P. (1661), High Sheriff 1666, *m.* Margaret, dau. of Anthony Stoughton, of Ballyborgan, co. Kerry, and *d.* 1668 (will dated 24 March, 1668, proved 16 Feb. 1669), leaving issue by her (who *m.* 2ndly, Edward Payne, of Limerick),
1. William, of Carrigafoyle, M.P. (1697), *m.* Mary, dau. of Henry Coward, and had issue,
   1. Lancelot, of Carrigafoyle, *m.* 4 May, 1721, Margaret, dau. of David Crosbie, of Ardfert, and had issue,
      (1) Mary Dorothea, *m.* her cousin Lancelot Sandes, of Kilcavan, and had issue, who *s.* to Carrigafoyle.
      (2) Jane, *d.s.p.*
      (3) Catherine, *m.* George Rose, of Morgans, co. Limerick, and had issue.
   2. William, *m.* Dorothea, dau. of Thomas Smith, D.D., Bishop of Limerick, and *d.s.p.* 1721.
   1. Margaret, *m.* Pierce Crosbie, of Rusheen, co. Kerry, and had issue.
   2. Catherine, *m.* Maurice Crosbie, of Ballykealy, co. Kerry, and had issue.
   3. Elizabeth, *m.* Arthur Crosbie, of Tubrid, co. Kerry, and had issue.
2. Lancelot, *d.s.p.*   3. Henry, *d.s.p.*
4. JOHN, of whom presently.
   1. Ellen, *d.s.p.*

The 4th son,
JOHN SANDES, of Cloonbrane, co. Kerry, J.P., *m.* Mary, dau. of Thomas Blennerhasset, of Littor, co. Kerry, and Ellen his wife, dau. of Anthony Stoughton, of Ballyhorgan, and by her had issue,
1. THOMAS, of whom presently.
2. Henry (Rev.), B.A. 1732, Chanter of Ardfert Cathedral, *b.* 1709, and *d.s.p.* 26 Dec. 1773 (will dated 17 Dec. 1773, proved 3 March, 1774).
3. John, of Moyvane, ancestor of SANDES, *of Greenville* (*see that family*).
1. Susannah, *m.* Rev. Thomas Connor, and had issue.
2. Ellen, *m.* Zacharias Johnson, of Carrunas, co. Kerry, and had issue.
3. Martha, *m.* William Hoare, of Ralapane, co. Kerry, and had issue.

The eldest son,
THOMAS SANDES, of Sallow Glen, *m.* Bridget, dau. of Maurice FitzGerald, *The Knight of Kerry*, and Elizabeth his wife, dau. of David Crosbie, of Ardfert, and by her (who *m.* 2ndly, Stephen Creagh, of Limerick) had issue, a dau., Elizabeth, who *d.s.p.*, and a son,
WILLIAM SANDES, of Sallow Glen, J.P., High Sheriff 1775, *b.* 1736; *m.* 1768, Margaret, dau. of Stephen Creagh, of Reens, co. Limerick, and Catherine his wife, dau. of John Burke, of Limerick. She *d.* 1812, leaving issue,
1. THOMAS WILLIAM, his heir.
2. William, of Pyrmont, co. Kerry, Barrister-at-Law, *b.* 1773; *m.* Aphra, dau. of Thomas Wren, of Littor, and *d.* 1852, having had issue,
   1. William, *d.s.p.* 9 March, 1869.
   2. Thomas, *d.s.p.* 1839.
   3. Stephen Creagh, *d.s.p.* 3 Sept. 1855.
   4. John, *d.s.p.* 1874.
   5. Robert Wren (Rev.), *m.* Alicia, dau. of William Carrique Ponsonby, of Crotta, co. Kerry, and *d.s.p.* 26 Jan. 1895.
   1. Margaret, *m.* 1st, 1823, Robert Leslie, of Tarbert, and had issue (*see that family*); she *m.* 2ndly, 20 May, 1841, Col. James Duff MacIver Campbell (formerly Patterson), of Asknish, and had issue (*see that family*).
   2. Alicia, *m.* George Wren, of Littor, and *d.* 7 July, 1885, having had issue.
   3. Aphra, *d.s.p.* 1 Nov. 1893.
3. Stephen Creagh (Right Rev.), D.D., F.T.C.D., Bishop of Cashel, *b.* 1778, *m.* 1819, Mary, dau. of Samuel Dickson, of Ballynaguile, co. Limerick. She *d.* 16 July, 1866. He *d.* 14 Nov. 1842, having had issue,
   1. William Stephen, Capt. 11th Hussars, *d.s.p.* 8 Feb. 1905.
   2. Samuel Dickson (Rev.), (26, *St. Paul's Road, Thornton Heath, Surrey*), *m.* 4 Nov. 1856, Sophia Julia, dau. of John Besnard, J.P., of Cork, and has issue,
      (1) Stephen, *d.s.p.* 4 Dec. 1874.
      (2) John, *b.* 26 Feb. 1863; *m.* 24 Nov. 1897, Clare Louise, dau. of Sir Graham Berry, of Melbourne, Australia, and has issue.
      (3) Samuel Dickson, *b.* 2 Sept. 1865; *m.* 14 May, 1898, Rose Isabella, dau. of Mr. Allison, of Princeton, British Columbia, and has issue.
      (4) William Besnard, *b.* 12 Feb. 1867; *m.* 28 June, 1905, Elizabeth Eva, dau. of Rev. William Wilson, of Templebrady, co. Cork, and has issue.
      (1) Sophia, *m.* Arthur de Chair Baker, of South Croydon, Surrey, and has issue.
      (2) Mary, *m.* John Gerrard Baker, and has issue.
      (3) Fanny Elizabeth, *m.* Benjamin Charles Johnston, of Hong-Kong.
      (4) Flora.
   1. Mary Catherine, *d.s.p.* 1856.
   2. Margaret Eliza, *d.s.p.* 1876.
4. Robert Fitzgerald, Capt. 50th Regt., *d.s.p.* 1813.
5. John Blennerhasset, *d.s.p.* 1807.
   1. Catherine, *m.* 1807, Lawrence Cussen, of Rockhill, co. Limerick, and had issue.

Mr. Sandes *d.* 31 March, 1812, and was *s.* by his eldest son,
THOMAS WILLIAM SANDES, of Sallow Glen, J.P. and D.L., High Sheriff 1804, *b.* 1771, *m.* 1797, Margaret, dau. of Francis Chute, of Chute Hall, co. Kerry (*see that family*), and by her (who *d.* 1855) had issue,
1. WILLIAM, his heir.
2. Francis (Rev.), *d.s.p.* 9 Nov. 1839.
3. THOMAS, *s.* his brother.
4. Stephen Creagh, *m.* Mary Anne, dau. of William Carrique Ponsonby, of Crotta, co. Kerry, and *d.* 10 Dec. 1866, leaving issue,
   1. THOMAS WILLIAM, now of Sallow Glen.
   2. Ponsonby Carrique, Lieut. 102nd Regt., *d.s.p.*
   1. Honoria, *m.* Capt. J. M. Magill, of Churchtown, co. Kerry, and had issue.
   2. Margaret, *m.* Lieut.-Col. C. M. Stockley, Norfolk Regt., and had issue.
   3. Eliza Anne.
   4. Frances.

5. Emily, *m.* Percy Ripley Wilson, of Los Angeles, California, and had issue.
6. Ellen Louisa, *m.* Richard Quain, of Clonsilla, co. Dublin.
7. Kathleen, *m.* Capt. H. H. Were, Lancashire Regt.
5. Richard, *d.s.p.* 5 April, 1874.
6. Maurice Fitzgerald, of Oak Park, co. Kerry, J.P., High Sheriff 1874, Barrister-at-Law, Registrar-General of Calcutta, *b.* 1805; *m.* 8 Jan. 1857, Ellen Louisa, dau. of Thomas Stratford Dennis, of Fort Granite, co. Wicklow (*see that family*). She *d.s.p.* 16 March, 1894. He *d.* 4 March, 1879, leaving his estates to his nephew, Falkiner Sandes Collis (now Collis-Sandes), 6th son of Stephen Edward Collis, of Tieraclea (*see* COLLIS-SANDES *of Oak Park*).
7. Robert, *d.s.p.* 1875.
8. Falkiner Chute, *m.* 19 April, 1860, Amelia, dau. of Sir John Lister-Kaye, Bart., of Denby, co. York, and *d.s.p.* 8 April, 1874. She *d.* 1861.
1. Margaret, *m.* 29 July, 1829, Stephen Edward Collis, of Tieraclea, co. Kerry, She *d.* 25 Aug. 1868. He *d.* 7 Jan. 1880, leaving issue (*see that family*).
2. Elizabeth, *m.* July, 1831, Pierce Crosbie, of Ballyheigue, co. Kerry, and *d.* 25 May, 1835, leaving issue.
3. Anna, *m.* 25 Feb. 1854, Rev. John Nunn Woodroffe, Rector of Glanmire, co. Cork, and *d.* 30 Nov. 1872, leaving issue.

Mr. Sandes *d.* 10 May, 1835. His eldest son,
WILLIAM SANDES, of Sallow Glen, High Sheriff 1828, *b.* 1799; *m.* Dec. 1830, Rupertia, only dau. of Charles Higgs, of Charlton Kings, co. Gloster. He *d.s.p.* 1867, and was s. by his brother,
THOMAS SANDES, of Sallow Glen, J.P. and D.L., *b.* 1802; *m.* 29 April, 1839, Elizabeth, dau. of Francis Bernard Chute, of Rathanny, co. Kerry. Mr. Sandes *d.s.p.* 21 June, 1874, and was s. by his nephew, THOMAS WILLIAM SANDES, now of Sallow Glen.

Arms—Arg., a fess dancettée between three cross-crosslets fitchée gu.

Seat—Sallow Glen, Tarbert, co. Kerry.

SANDES OF GREENVILLE.

JOHN SANDES, of Greenville, co. Kerry, J.P., late Capt. 4th Batt. Royal Munster Fus., educated at Trin. Coll. Dublin, called to the Irish Bar 1893, *b.* 25 Sept. 1868; *m.* 30 April, 1896, Maud Tudor, dau. of Richard Sale, J.P., of The Manor House, Barrow-on-Trent, co. Derby, and has issue,

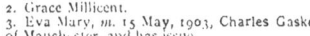

1. JOHN GOUGH, *b.* 12 Dec. 1903.
1. Gladys Maud.
2. Doris Aphra.

Lineage.—This family descends from JOHN SANDES, of Moyvane, co. Kerry, J.P., 3rd son of John Sandes, and Mary Blennerhassett, his wife (*see* SANDES, *of Sallow Glen*). He *m.* Mary, dau. of William Gough, of Toureen, co. Limerick, and Agnes his wife, dau. of George Rose (*see* ROSE *of Ahabeg*). She *d.* 26 Sept. 1793, leaving issue,

1. THOMAS, of whom presently.
2. Thomas, of Woodpark, co. Kerry, *m.* Margaret, dau. of John Kittson, of Derry, co. Kerry, and Sarah, his wife, dau. of Edward Creed, of Ballynanty, co. Limerick. She *d.s.p.* 5 Jan. 1833.
3. Henry, of Glenfield, co. Kerry, *m.* 22 April, 1785, Alicia, dau. of Arthur Browne, of Ventry, co. Kerry, and Alice, his wife, dau. of Thomas Hurley (*see* HURLEY, *of Glenduffe*). She *d.* 1 Oct. 1826. He *d.* 6 Oct. 1808, leaving issue,
 1. Thomas, Capt. 90th Regt., *b.* 1791, and *d.* on board ship returning from India, 13 July, 1839.
 2. Arthur, served in Commissariat Department till the Peace of 1815, present at Waterloo, subsequently joined the forces of Bolivar in South America, *b.* 1793, and *d.s.p.* at Guayaquil, South America, 1 Sept. 1832.
 3. John, Capt. 47th Regt., present at the Siege of San Sebastian and Battle of Vittoria, served in the Mahratta War, subsequently joined the Cape Mounted Rifles, *b.* 1794; *m.* 24 Dec. 1844, Martha Farnall, dau. of Francis William Bowzer, of Neath, Glamorganshire, and *d.s.p.*, being killed in action near Graham's Town, South Africa, 18 April, 1846. She *d.* 18 May, 1855.
 4. Henry, served in Ordnance Department, *b.* 1799, and *d.s.p.* at Trinidad, 3 Sept. 1825.
 5. Goodman, served in Ordnance Store Department, *b.* 26 Aug. 1802; *m.* 3 Oct. 1840, Henrietta, dau. of Walter Hussey Fitton, of Cork. She *d.* 1 Aug. 1897, aged 83. He *d.* 13 Feb. 1882, leaving issue,
   (1) Henry Thomas Thompson, Col. R.A., *b.* 17 Oct. 1841; *m.* 6 May, 1873, Grace Henrietta, dau. of Rev. Edward Warren Caulfeild, of Beechingstoke, Wilts (*see* BURKE'S *Peerage*, CHARLEMONT, V.). He *d.* 2 Dec. 1906, leaving issue,
     1. Edward Warren Caulfeild, Capt. R.E., *b.* 13 Feb. 1880.
     1. Norah Melita.
     2. Grace Millicent.
     3. Eva Mary, *m.* 15 May, 1903, Charles Gaskell Falkner, of Manchester, and has issue.
     4. Elsie Naomi.
   (2) Robert FitzMaurice, *b.* 7 April, 1843; *m.* 28 May, 1867, Catherine Bond, dau. of Richard Peed, of Kinsale, co. Cork and has issue,
     1. Athol Gordon, *d.s.p.* 1887.
     1. Bessie Henrietta.
     2. Nellie Kathleen, *m.* 11 Oct. 1893, Ernest de Courcy Drury, of Hamilton, New Zealand, and has issue.
     3. Alice Mary Helena, *m.* 17 Jan. 1899, John Gwalter Palairet, of Gisborne, New Zealand, and has issue.
     4. Inez Browning.
   (3) Thomas Goodman, *b.* 24 April, 1846; *m.* 20 Aug. 1876, Isabella, dau. of John McGlashan, of Dunedin, New Zealand, and *d.* 6 May, 1897, leaving issue,
     1. Walter Goodman, *b.* 17 Nov. 1879.
     2. Spencer Fitton, *b.* 22 Aug. 1883.
     3. Noel McGlashan, *b.* 4 Jan. 1893.
     4. Tom Trevor, *b.* 2 Nov. 1894.
     1. Bessie Kathleen.
   (4) John Stewart, *b.* 1849; *d.s.p.* 2 June, 1862.
   (5) Walter, *b.* 1850; *d.s.p.* 20 April, 1882.
   (1) Ellen, *m.* 6 Jan. 1872, Charles Cornelius Henshaw, C.E., of Kingston, Canada, and *d.* 11 July, 1886, leaving issue.
   (2) Henrietta.
   (3) Alicia, *m.* 24 June, 1889, John MacDonald Broun, of New South Wales.
 6. George, served in Ordnance Department, *b.* 1805, and *d.s.p.* at Trinidad, 4 Jan. 1834.
   1. Mary, *d.s.p.* 27 Aug. 1862.
   2. Alicia, *d.s.p.* 13 Oct. 1816.
   3. Margaret, *m.* 1834, Frederick Mason, of Kilmore, co. Kerry, and *d.s.p.* 23 Jan. 1881.
   4. Elizabeth Agnes, *m.* 1824, Montagu Griffin, Lieut. R.N., and *d.* 21 Feb. 1861, leaving issue.
4. John, of Moyvane, J.P., *m.* 1st, 17 Dec. 1797, Honoria Maria, dau. of Daniel Harnett, of Kilconlea, co. Limerick, and Mary, his wife, dau. of Daniel Collins, of Abbeyfeale, and by her had issue,
 1. Maria, *b.* 1798; *m.* 11 Sept. 1816, Maurice De Courcy, of Molahiff, co. Kerry, and had issue. She *d.* 10 Nov. 1874.
 2. Agnes, *b.* 1800, *m.* her first cousin John Sandes, and *d.* 30 April, 1858, leaving issue (*see below*).

Mr. Sandes *m.* 2ndly, 14 Jan. 1806, Lucinda Barbara, dau. of Pierce Purcell, and Barbara, his wife, dau. of Thomas Harris, of Harrisgrove (*see* PURCELL *of Altamira*), and by her (who *d.* 31 Dec. 1865) had issue,
 3. Catherine, *b.* 1806; *m.* 4 Nov. 1835, Thomas McDonnell, M.D., and had issue.
 4. Barbara, *b.* 1807; *d.s.p.* 28 Nov. 1872.

Mr. Sandes *d.* 7 March, 1818.
5. Nicholas, *d.s.p.*
1. Agnes, *m.* 10 Dec. 1783, William Hunt Forster, of Dublin, and had issue.

The eldest son,
GEORGE SANDES, of Greenville, B.A. 1772, J.P., High Sheriff 1795; *m.* 1783, Elizabeth, dau. of Major FitzMaurice Connor, 16th Regt. She *d.* 13 Dec. 1806. He *d.* 1 May, 1829, aged 78, having had issue,
1. Henry Moore, *d.s.p.* 11 June, 1820.
2. Edwin, *b.* 1786; *d.s.p.* 1 Nov. 1824.
3. FitzMaurice (Rev.), B.A. 1812, *b.* 1789; *m.* 14 Feb. 1820, Mary, dau. of James Shewell, of Ballygrennan, co. Kerry. He *d.* 1 Feb. 1847. She *d.* 21 Aug. 1874, having had issue,
 1. Martha, *b.* 1823; *d.s.p.* 25 Jan. 1878.
 2. Elizabeth, *b.* 1828; *d.s.p.* 25 June, 1847.
4. JOHN, of whom presently.
5. George, Ensign 17th Regt., *b.* 1795, killed at the seige of Bergenop-Zoom, under Sir Thomas Graham, 9 March, 1814.
6. Thomas, *b.* 1797; *d.s.p.* 21 July, 1856.
7. William Gough, of Greenville, J.P., *b.* 3 Oct. 1801; s. his father 1829; *m.* 14 Oct. 1852, Margaret Elliott, dau. of Francis William Bowzer, of Neath, Glamorganshire, and *d.s.p.* 22 April, 1873. She *d.* 21 Jan. 1883.
1. Agnes, *b.* 1793; *d.s.p.* 15 Aug. 1809.
2. Elizabeth, *b.* 1794; *d.s.p.* 27 April, 1855.

The 4th son,
JOHN SANDES, of Listowel, Capt. Kerry Regt., *b.* 22 March, 1791; *m.* 1820, his first cousin, Agnes, dau. of John Sandes (*see above*). She *d.* 30 April, 1858. He *d.* 31 May, 1845, aged 54, having had issue,
1. GEORGE, of whom presently.
2. John, *b.* 8 March, 1824; *m.* 26 Oct. 1865, Catherine, dau. of John De Renzy Waters, of Dublin, and *d.s.p.* 18 March, 1887.
3. Henry Moore, Major Kerry Regt., *b.* 31 May, 1832; *m.* 10 April, 1876, Mary Wilhelmina, dau. of Hugh Eldon Yielding, of New Park, co. Limerick, and *d.s.p.* 13 Dec. 1883.
4. Thomas William, Capt. Madras Staff Corps, *b.* 20 May, 1842; *m.* 11 Aug. 1887, Marie Louise, dau. of Henry Sheldon, of Staverton House, Gloucestershire, and *d.s.p.* 23 June, 1895.
1. Horonia, *b.* 24 June, 1826; *d.s.p.* 2 Nov. 1834.
2. Elizabeth Agnes, *b.* 1 Oct. 1830; *m.* 30 Aug. 1849, Henry Smith, County Inspector, R.I.C., and had issue. She *d.* 29 Aug. 1889.
3. Maria, *b.* 13 May, 1831; *m.* 20 Nov. 1860, William Alton, M.D., of Tralee, and had issue. She *d.* 2 March, 1890.

The eldest son,

Sandes. THE LANDED GENTRY. 624

GEORGE SANDES, of Greenville, J.P., High Sheriff 1887, b. 12 Oct. 1821; s. his uncle, 1873; m. 16 Dec. 1854, Anna, dau. of Capt. Charles John Whyte, 95th Regt. (see WHYTE, of Loughbrickland), and by her (who d. 8 July, 1894, aged 60) had issue,
1. George, Capt. Kerry Regt, b. 2 Nov. 1851; d.s.p. 3 March, 1887.
2. JOHN, now of Greenville.
  1. Rose, b. 14 Dec. 1855; m. 5 Jan. 1831, William Ra alow, of Wolfsdene, co. Tipp rary, and had issue. She d. 17 March, 1888.
  2. Agnes, b. 5 Aug. 1857; m. 16 Sept. 1889, Robert Butler Moriarty of Millstreet, co. Cork, and had issue.
  3. Josephine, b. 1 Jan. 1859; m. 30 Jan. 1883, Fleet-Surgeon Ingham Hanbury, C.B., R.N.
Mr. Sandes d. 25 Oct. 1895; and was s. by his second son.

Arms—Arg. a fesse dancetty between four cross cross'ets fitchée three in chief and one in base gu. Crest—On a mount vert a griffin segreant or collared fleuretty gu. Motto—Virtus fortunae victrix.

Seat—Greenville Listowel, co. Kerry. Club—United Service, Dublin.

COLLIS-SANDES OF OAK PARK.

MAURICE JAMES COLLIS - SANDES, of Oak Park, co. Kerry, b. 25 July, 1886, s. his father 13 Feb. 1912.

Lineage.—Stephen Edward Collis, of Tieraclea, co. Kerry (who d. 7 Jan. 1880) (see that family), by Margaret, his wife, who d. 25 Aug. 1868, eldest dau. of Thomas William Sandes, D.L., of Sallow Glen, co. Kerry (see that family), had a 6th son,
FALKINER SANDES COLLIS-SANDES, of Oak Park, co. Kerry, J.P. and D.L., High Sheriff 1882, Barrister-at-Law, B.A. Trin. Coll. Dublin 1866, b. 15 Oct. 1844; m. 31 Oct. 1882, Louisa Jane (who d. 24 May, 1905), dau. of Col. James Young, R.A., 3rd son of the late John Adolphus Young, of Hare Hatch House, Twyford, Berks, and d. 13 Feb. 1912, having had issue,
1. MAURICE JAMES, of Oak Park.
1. Margaret Jessie.   2. Doris Rosa.
3. Joan Elizabeth.
Mr. F. S. Collis-Sandes assumed by Royal Licence, 8 July, 1879, the additional name and arms of SANDES in compliance with the will of his maternal uncle, Maurice FitzGerald Sandes, of Oak Park (who d. 4 March, 1879).

Arms—Quarterly 1st and 4th arg., a fesse dancetty gu., between four cross crosslets fitchée three in chief and one in base of the last (SANDES); 2nd and 3rd arg., on a chevron engrailed between three lion's heads erased sa. five cinquefoils of the first (COLLIS) Crests—1. On a mount vert a griffin segreant or collared fleuretty gu. (SANDES); 2. On a rock a sea pie charged on the breast with a fountain and preying on a dolphin all ppr. Motto —Virtus fortunae victrix.

Seat—Oak Park, Tralee, co. Kerry. Clubs—Oriental and Junior Constitutional, London, and Kildare Street, Dublin.

WILLS-SANDFORD OF WILLSGROVE.

THOMAS GEORGE WILLS - SANDFORD, of Willsgrove and Castlerea, co. Roscommon, J.P., High Sheriff 1906, b. 9 Nov. 1870; m. 12 Feb. 1907, Kathleen Fanny, only surviving dau. of the late Capt. Robert James Burrowes, 1st King's Dragoon Guards, of Stradone House, co. Cavan (see that family), and has issue,
WILLIAM ROBERT, b. 3 Feb. 1909.

Lineage.—CAPT. THOMAS WILLS, whose name is among the enrolments for receiving compensation after the wars of King WILLIAM III, m. about 1670, the widow of Alexander Montgomery, and by her left two sons. The elder,

CASPAR WILLS, a Capt. in the Army, purchased (with his brother) the Roscommon estates, part of the forfeited possessions of King JAMES II, and settled at Willsgrove, High Sheriff co. Roscommon 1708. He m. Sarah Cole, of the Enniskillen family, but d.s.p. His brother,
JAMES WILLS, an Officer in the Army, d. 1731. He m. Martha, dau. of John Curtis, of Dublin, and left (besides two daus.) one of whom, Sarah, m. Mr. Lennox, a banker) two sons,
1 GODFREY, his heir.
2. Robert, of Annalee, co. Cavan, who d. unm.
The elder son,
GODFREY WILLS, of Willsgrove, Lieut.-Col. Roscommon Militia, High Sheriff 1755, m. 1st, Sarah, dau. of Robert Montgomery, of Ballyleck, co. Monaghan, by whom he had,
1. THOMAS, his heir.
2. Robert, m. Miss Ousley; d.s.p.
3. Caspar, Capt. Royal Scots, m. 12 Jan. 1765, Catherine Carter, and had issue sons, who d.s.p.
1. Elizabeth, m. 23 June, 175_, Thomas Mitchell, of Castle Strange, co. Roscommon.
2. Martha, m. Charles Wood, of Larkfield. co. Sligo.
3. Sarah, m. Sir Ralp'i Fethers on, 1st bart., of Ardagh.
4. Catherine, m. July, 1767, Samuel Owens, of Longford.
5. Susan, m. William Fetherstone, of Carrick.
Col. Wills m. 2ndly, 1 June, 1771, Charlotte Elizabeth, dau. of Luke Stirling, of Mount Ditton, co. Meath, and by her had,
4. James, of Plâs Bellin, co. Flint.
5. Charles, d. unm.
6. Ann, m. William Berry, of Eglish Castle, King's Co
Col. Wills d. 11 May, 1778, and was s. by his eldest son,
THOMAS WILLS, of Willsgrove, High Sheriff 1771. m. 1st, 1765, Jane, dau. of William Talbot, of Mount Talbot, co. Roscommon, and by her had issue,
1. WILLIAM ROBERT, his heir.
1. Sarah, m. Rev. W. McLoughlin, of Roscommon.
2. Elizabeth, d. unm.
3. Anne, m. W. Dobbs Burleigh, of Burleigh Hill, Carrickfergus,
4. Jane, d. unm.
Mr. Wills m. 2ndly, Miss Browne, dau. of Capt. James Browne, of Moyne, and had issue,
2. Thomas, of Carvozie, or Annalee.
3. James (Rev.), m. Katherine E., dau. of Rev. William Gorman and niece of Lord Chief Justice Bushe, by whom he had issue,
  1. William Gorman, artist and author, b. 1828; d. 14 Dec. 1893.
  2. Thomas Bushe (Rev.), B.A., m. 1 July, 1858, Margaret, dau. of Rev. Percival Banks Weldon.
3. Freeman (Rev.), M.A.
1. Elizabeth.
4. John.
He d. 1792, and was s. by his son,
WILLIAM ROBERT WILLS, of Willsgrove, J.P. and D.L., High Sheriff 1807, m. 1st, Olivia, dau. of Christopher St. George, of Tyrone House, co. Galway, but by her had no issue; and 2ndly, 1816, Mary Grey, dau. of the Rev. William Sandford, of Castlerea, and niece and co-heir (with her sister, Eliza Catherine, wife of the Hon. and Very Rev. Henry Pakenham, D.D.), Dean of St. Patrick's, of Henry, Lord Mountsandford, and by her (who d. 1851) had issue,
1. THOMAS GEORGE, of Castlerea.
2. William Sandford, of Garryglass, Queen's Co., and Compton Castle, Castle Cary, Somerset, J.P. for Somerset, late of the 83rd Regt., b. 26 March, 1822; m. 30 May, 1849, Julia, youngest dau. of William Foster, of Stourton Court, co. Worcester; and d. 8 Feb. 1882, leaving issue,
  1. Harry, b. 13 May, 1850, late Lieut. 60th Rifles; d. 20 Jan. 1872.
  2. Arthur Pakenham, of Garryglass, Queen's Co., and of the Priory House, Sherborne, Dorset (Arthur's Club), b. 7 Jan. 1856.
  3. Reginald, b. 5 May, 1862; m. 1892, Mary, eldest dau. of H. C. Phillips, and has a dau.,
    Georgina.
  1. Florence Mary, m. 8 Feb. 1872, John Graham Carrick Moore, Lieut. Royal Horse Guards, and only son of John Carrick Moore, of Corswall, Stranraer, N.B.
  2. Geraldine, m. 1st, 19 Oct. 1899, Arthur Dendy. She m. 2ndly, 28 Nov. 1908, Loftus Moller Le Champion, only son of Lieut.-Col. H. Moller Le Champion, late Munster Fus.
  3. Maude.
2. Jane Catherine.
2. Elizabeth Sydney, m. 18 July, 1844, Godfrey, 2nd son of James Wills, of Plâs Bellin, co. Flint, and d. 1871, having by him (who d. 1866) had issue,
  Ormond Kingsley, b. 1860.
  Aleine Mary, b. 1862.
3. Ellen Maria Sarah.   4. Caroline Julia.
Mr. Wills who assumed by Royal Licence 12 Aug. 1847, the additional surname and arms of SANDFORD, d. 11 Aug. 1859, and was s. by his elder son,
THOMAS GEORGE WILLS-SANDFORD, of Willsgrove and Castlerea, J.P. and D.L., High Sheriff for co. Roscommon 1844, b. 15 Aug. 1817; m. 20 Sept. 1841, Theodosia Eleanor Blagden, dau. of Robert Blagden Hale, of Alderley, co. Gloucester, by the Lady Theodosia his wife, dau. of Joseph Deane, 3rd Earl of Mayo, and by her (who d. 23 Aug. 1857) had issue,
1. WILLIAM ROBERT, of Willsgrove.
2. George Hale, b. 26 July, 1849; d. 16 Sept. 1882.
3. Edward Wills SANFORD-WILLS, of Cashlieve, Ballinlough, co. Roscommon, J.P., High Sheriff 1904, assumed by Royal Licence, 12 Jan. 1889, the additional name and arms of WILLS, after that of SANDFORD (Kildare Street Club), b. 20 Feb. 1851; m. 28 May, 1889, Amy Henrietta, dau. of Henry Guinness, o'

IRELAND.

Burton Hall, Stillorgan, co. Dublin (see BURKE's *Peerage*, ARDI-LAUN, B.), and has issue,
  1. Lucy Eleanor.   2. Mary Grace.
4. Godfrey Robert, *b.* 5 Oct. 1852.
1. Theodosia Eleanor, *d. unm.* 24 April, 1907.
2. Alice Mary.
3. Evelyn Louisa, *m.* July, 1881, William Frederick Hammersly Smith, and has issue (see SMITH *formerly of Glasshouse*).
Mr. Wills-Sandford *d.* 13 April, 1887, and was *s.* by his eldest son,
  WILLIAM ROBERT WILLS-SANDFORD, of Willsgrove and Castlerea, J.P., Capt. 2nd Dragoons, *b.* 12 April, 1844; *m.* 26 March, 1874, Adelaide Elizabeth, 2nd dau. of the late Henry Jephson, of Glenbrook, co. Wicklow, and grand-dau. of Sir Philip Crampton, Bart., and by her (who *d.* 1880) had issue,
1. THOMAS GEORGE, now of Willsgrove.
1. Charlotte Georgina, *m.* Charles Wood, Fellow of Gonville and Caius Coll. Camb., son of Charles Wood, Lay Vicar of Armagh Cathedral.
2. Mary Adelaide.
Capt. Wills-Sandford *d.* 3 April, 1889.
  Arms—Quarterly: 1st and 4th, SANDFORD, per chevron or and erm. in chief two boars' heads erased sa. langued gu; 2nd and 3rd, WILLS, arg., three griffins passant in pale sa. within a border of the second bezantée. **Crests**—1st, from a ducal coronet a boar's head and neck or, langued gu. (SANDFORD); 2nd, a demi-griffin segreant sa., holding in his claws a battle-axe ppr. (WILLS). **Motto**—Cornunum via una.
  Seats—Castlerea and Willsgrove, co. Roscommon. *Clubs*—White's, S.W.; Kildare Street, Dublin.

SANKEY OF COOLMORE.

The late MATTHEW VILLIERS ELRINGTON SANKEY, of Coolmore, co. Tipperary, late Lieut. 5th Dragoon Guards, and Lieut. P.W.O. Regt., *b.* 1 April, 1846; *s.* his father 1881, and *d. unm.* 26 Oct. 1907.

  Lineage.—HIEROM SANKEY, aged 25 in 1646 (son of Richard Sankey, of Endsworth, Salop, by Anne his wife dau. of Hilary Smolt, of Burford Castle, Dorset, and grandson of Peter Sankey, of Cotton, Salop, who was younger son of Thomas Sankey, of Sankey, co. Lancaster *temp.* Queen ELIZABETH), was Major Commanding the Regt. of Horse of Chester, afterwards Col. of Horse and Commn. of a brigade in Ireland. He became M.P. successively for cos. Cork, Waterford and Tipperary, and also for the borough of Woodstock. He *d.s.p.* and intestate. Administration was granted 4 Feb. 1687, to his nephew,
  RICHARD SANKEY, Col. in the Army of WILLIAM III (son of Robert Sankey, of Hodnet, Salop), *m.* Mary, dau. of William Taylor, of Ballynort, co. Limerick, and dying 1693, left a son,
  JACOB SANKEY, of St. Johnstown, co. Tipperary, *m.* Abigail, dau. of Matthew Jacob, M.P., of Johnstown, and was father of
  MATTHEW SANKEY, of Coolmore. *m.* Elizabeth, dau. and co-heir of George Villiers, of Waterford, and had issue,
1. JACOB, his heir. 2. Matthew.
3. Richard, of St. Kitt's, Member of Assembly.
4. George.
5. William, M.P., of Harcourt Street, Dublin, *m.* Mary, dau. of Stephen Mills, banker of Cork, and had issue,
  1. Matthew of Bawnmore, co. Cork, and Modeshill, co. Tipperary, J.P., Barrister-at-Law, *m.* 1819, Eleanor, dau. of Col. Henry O'Hara, of O'Harabrook, co. Antrim, nephew of Viscount Duncan, of Camperdown, and by her (who *d.* 1 Dec. 1882) had issue,
    (1) William, C.B., of Bawnmore, co. Cork, and Modeshill, co. Tipperary, General, late Lieut.-Col. 62nd Regt., *b.* 15 July, 1822; *m.* 9 Dec. 1852, Hannah Maria, 3rd dau. of John Roe, D.L., of Rockwell, and *d.* 1892, leaving issue,
      1. Matthew Henry Phineas Riall, of Bawnmore, co. Cork, Capt. late R.E., *b.* 9 Nov. 1853; *m.* 5 July, 1876, Elizabeth, dau. of Major-Gen. Pym, and has issue,
        a. Crofton Edward Pym, Capt. R.E., *b.* 17 May, 1877; *m.* 1st, 14 Jan. 1902, Catherine Evelyn, only child of Cecil Coward, of Kensington; *m.* 2ndly, 2 Dec. 1908, Gertrude Marion, dau. of G. A. Keefer, of British Columbia.
        b. Geoffrey Hierom Pym, *b.* 22 April, 1891; *d.* 7 April, 1892.
        a. Celia Katherine Pym, *b.* 6 Nov. 1880.

I.L.G.

        b. Margaret Elizabeth Pym, *b.* 22 May, 1883; *m.* 2 April, 1910, William Johnstone Marshall, 3rd son the late Dr. Marshall, of Greenock.
        c. Joyce Ethel Pym, *b.* 22 May, 1887.
      2. Alfred Robert Mandeville, Lieu.-Col. R.E., *b.* 19 Dec. 1857.
      3. Cyril Charles, Major R.A., *b.* 1 Aug. 1861; *m.* and ha issue, a son, *b.* 29 Jan. 1900.
      1. Agnes Elizabeth, *b.* 9 April, 1859; *m.* 16 Jan. 1912, George Cecil Croxon Crampton, of St. Valerie, co. Wicklow.
    (2) Matthew Henry, of Lurganbrae, Fermanagh, J.P., *b.* 8 Dec. 1823; *m.* 1st, 24 Sept. 1850, Mary Charlotte, only dau. of Rev. William Lennard Roper, of Monaghan, and grand-dau. of the Hon. and Very Rev. Henry Roper, Dean of Clonmacnoise, and by her (who *d.* 7 Oct. 1851) had a son,
      1. WILLIAM ROPER, *b.* 8 July, 1851, dec.
Mr. Sankey *m.* 2ndly, 1 Feb. 1853, Mehitabel, youngest dau. of John Roe, D.L., of Rockwell, co. Tipperary, and *d.* 18 Feb 1876, having had issue,
      2. Matthew Villiers, *b.* 3 Oct. 1853.
      3. Hierom Richard John, *b.* 2 Dec. 1854.
      4. Henry, *b.* 14 Oct. 1856.
      5. Edward Morgan Crofton, *b.* 17 April, 1859.
      6. Charles Arthur.   7. Gerald Lewis.
      1. Emily May Elizabeth. 2. Ethel Eleanor.
    (3) Morgan Crofton, Major Bengal Artillery, *b.* 3 Nov. 1827, *d.* 19 March, 1868.
    (4) Richard Hierom (Sir), K.C.B., Lieut.-Gen R.E., Chairman of Board of Works, Ireland, 1884-96; *b.* 22 March, 1829, entered Madras Engineers 1846, and attained the rank of Lieut.-Gen. (retired) 1884; served in Indian Mutiny campaign (medal with clasps, and recommended for V.C.); *m.* 1st, 1858, Sophia Mary, dau. of William Henry Berson, Bengal Civil Service, and by her (who *d.* 26 Oct. 1882) had surviving issue, two daus. He *m.* 2ndly, 1890, Henrietta (5, *West Halkin Street*, S.W.), dau. of the late Pierse Creagh, of O'Brien's Castle, co. Clare, and widow of E. Browne, of Cooloe, co. Galway. He *d.* 10 Nov. 1908.
      (1) Eleanor, *m.* Sackville Deane Hamilton, of Beechmount, co. Cork, and *d.* 1870. He *d.* 30 July, 1878.
      (2) Marianne, *m.* May, 1844, John M. Abbott, and has issue.
      (3) Eliza Villiers.
      (4) Grace Jane, *m.* Capt. Benson, Madras Army, and *d.* 16 Aug. 1873, having had issue.
  2. William Villiers, M.A., *m.* Sophia, dau. of Robert Mulock, Comptroller-General of the Stamp Office, and had issue,
    (1) William Henry Villiers, *d.* 12 Aug. 1879.
    (2) Robert Stephen Villiers.
    (1) Anna Sophia, *d. unm.* 20 Nov. 1902.
    (2) Maria Sarah, *d. unm.* 16 Jan. 1897.
  1. Hannah Elizabeth, *m.* John Roe, of Rockwell.
  2. Mary.   3. Anne.
The eldest son and heir,
  JACOB SANKEY, of Coolmore (whose will, dated 1783, was proved 1784), *m.* 29 Jan. 1768, Mary Elizabeth Caldwell, of Dublin, sister of Admiral Sir Benjamin Caldwell, and had issue,
1. MATTHEW VILLIERS, his heir.
2. Charles.   3. Jacob.
4. Andrew Hierom, Capt. 57th Foot, killed in Spain, 1814.
5. Benjamin, *d.s.p.*
1. Anne.
2. Eliza, *m.* Benjamin Benyon, M.P. for Stafford.
3. Catherine.
The eldest son,
  MATTHEW VILLIERS SANKEY, of Coolmore, *m.* Sept. 1792, Mary Amelia, sister of Major Elrington, Major of the Tower of London, and by her (who *d.* 1836) had issue,
1. Matthew Villiers, of Coolmore. *m.* Anne, dau. of Samuel Perry, of Woodroffe, co. Tipperary, but *d.s.p.* 1837.
2. John Henry, H.E.I.C.S., *d. unm.*
3. JACOB, of Coolmore.
1. Mary Elizabeth Anne, *m.* Edward Galwey, son of Ven. William Galwey, Archdeacon of Cashel.
2. Ellenor Jane.
3. Catherine, *m.* 12 May, 1820, Rev. James Morton. He *d.* 14 Aug. 1870. She *d.* 24 Sept. 1831, leaving issue (see SANKEY-MORTON *of Little Island*).
4. Dorothea.
Mr. Sankey *d.* 1815, and was *s.* by his son,
  JACOB HIEROM SANKEY, of Coolmore, Tipperary, J.P., Capt. R.N., *b.* 23 July, 1807; *m.* 8 Feb. 1844, Melita Anne, only dau. of Capt. Gawen William Rowan Hamilton, R.N., C.B., of Killyleigh Castle, co. Down (see that *family*), and by her (who *d.* 13 July, 1901) had issue,
1. MATTHEW VILLIERS ELRINCTON, of Coolmore.
1. Catherine Amelia, *m.* July, 1865, David Hart, 2nd son of David Hart, of The Park, Leytonstone, Essex.
2. Mary Elizabeth, *m.* 12 June, 1867, J. Barnett Barker, late Capt. 75th Regt.
3. Evelyn Grace, *m.* Rev. William Smyly, M.A. (see SMYLY of *Camus*).
Capt. J. H. Sankey *d.* 1881.
  Arms—Arg., on a bend sa. three salmon of the field. *Crest*—A cubit arm vested sa., cuffed arg., holding a salmon ppr. *Motto*—Sancta clavis cœli fides.

2 R

SANKEY OF FORT FREDERIC.

HARRY SAMUEL SANKEY, of Billas Grange, co. Cavan, and Fort Frederic, co. Cavan, b. 18—.

Lineage.—EDWARD SANKEY, of Newtown and Kill, King's Co., d. 1698, leaving with other issue a son,
THOMAS SANKEY, of Slyhane, co. Longford, m. Mary, dau. of Luke Nugent, and had with two daus.,
1. EDWARD, of whom presently.
2. John, of New Park, co. Longford, High Sheriff 1761 ; m. Jane, dau. of Abney Parker, of Fermoyle, co. Longford, and d. 1767, having bad issue,
   1. Abney Parker, a unm. (will dated 18 Jan. 1767, proved 10 March, 1768).
   1. Lettice, d. unm.
   2. Jane, m. 11 Oct. 1766, George Kelly, of Kellybrook, co. Roscommon.
The elder son,
EDWARD SANKEY, Alderman of Dublin, and Lord Mayor 1766 ; m. by licence 28 April, 1732, Mary, dau. of George Medlicott, and d. 1780, leaving issue, with one dau., three sons,
1. Thomas, Major in the Army ; m. Deborah, dau. of Richard Jones, of Oaklands, co. Wexford, and had with others, who d.s.p., Richard Jones, of Oaklands, Lieut.-Col. in the Army ; m. Sarah, only dau. of John Smith, of Newcastle, co. Limerick, and d.s.p. 27 Jan. 1839.
2. Henry Gore, of Fort Frederic, co. Cavan, High Sheriff 1813, Alderman of Dublin and Lord Mayor 1791 ; m. by licence 21 May, 1776, Barbara, dau. of Rev. Thomas Sneyd, of Baillieborough, and d. Oct. 1821, having had issue,
   1. Edward, Capt. in the Army, m. Aug. 1807, Frances, dau. of Sir John Cramer Coghill, Bart., and d.s.p.
   2. Henry, d. unm. 1819.
   1. Eleanor, m. 17 March, 1823, Richard Scott.
   2. Mary.   3. Barbara.
3. JOHN, of whom we treat.
The third son,
JOHN SANKEY, Major Dublin City Militia, m. by licence 8 Oct. 1782, Margery, dau. of Rev. Thomas Sneyd, of Baillieborough, and had issue,
1. SAMUEL, of whom presently.
2. John, Barrister-at-Law, m. 12 Dec. 1834, Frances, dau. of the Hon. and Very Rev. George Gore, LL.D., Dean of Killala (see BURKE'S Peerage, ARRAN, E.). She d. 14 Feb. 1898. He d. 2 Jan. 1873, leaving issue,
   1. Richard Jones, now of Fort Frederic, late Capt. 5th D.G., D.L. co. Cavan, m. 27 April, 1905, Alice Maude, 2nd dau. of Gen. W. Saunders-Knox-Gore (see that family).
   1. Anne.   2. Margery Elizabeth.
   3. Frances Sophia, d. 31 Dec. 1907.
3. Henry, d. young.
1. Frances.   2. Elizabeth.
3. Eleanor.
4. Maria, m. 1831, Rev. John Browne.
The eldest son,
MAJOR SAMUEL SANKEY, 9th Foot, m. 1841, Mary, dau. of William Anderson, of Aughnacloy, and d. 1861, having had issue,
1. ALEXANDER WILLIAM JACKSON, late of Fort Frederic.
2. HARRY SAMUEL, now of Fort Frederic.
1. Margery Theodora.
The elder son,
ALEXANDER WILLIAM JACKSON SANKEY, of Fort Frederic, co. Cavan, J.P. and D.L., High Sheriff 1874 ; B.A. Trin. Coll. Camb., b. 1841 ; d. unm. 15 July, 1903.

Seat—Fort Frederic, Virginia, co. Cavan. Residence—70, Merrion Square, Dublin. Club—Junior Carlton, S.W.

SARSFIELD OF DOUGHCLOYNE.

THOMAS RONAYNE SARSFIELD, of Doughcloyne, co. Cork, J.P., Capt. 3rd Batt. Royal Munster Fusiliers, b. 13 April, 1862 ; educated at Cheltenham and at Exeter College, Oxford.

Lineage. — GEOFFREY SARSFIELD, m. Jeanie Martyn, and acquired with her large estates near Cork, and the fishery called Tully Calvy. He was father of THOMAS SARSFIELD, whose son, EDMUND SARSFIELD, is mentioned in the will of Peter " Sarcell." He had two sons,
1. WILLIAM, of whose line presently.
2. Thomas, ancestor of the SARSFIELDS, VISCOUNTS KILMALLOCK.
The elder son,
WILLIAM SARSFIELD, had two sons, THOMAS and James, whose son, Patrick, was ancestor of a branch of the family settled at Johns-town. The former, THOMAS SARSFIELD, presented to the Rectory of Glanman in 1582. He was the father of WILLIAM SARSFIELD, mentioned in the settlements of Sarsfield Court 14 Oct. 1620. This William had (with younger issue) a son, THOMAS SARSFIELD, living in 1633, who was father of
DOMINICK SARSFIELD, who obtained a decree 23 July, 1636, to be re-established in possession of Sarsfield Court, Tempulosky, and other lands, and, 3 July, 1681, letters patent to execute the decree. His son,
DOMINICK SARSFIELD, m. Catherine Ronayne, and had three sons,
1. Dominick, d. unm. in 1767.
2. THOMAS, of whom presently.
3. Edmond, Col. in the Irish Brigade, d. unm. in France.
The 2nd son,
THOMAS SARSFIELD, of Doughcloyne, m. Mary Ronayne, and had an elder son,
DOMINICK RONAYNE SARSFIELD, of Doughcloyne, m. Jan. 1793, Mary Bruce, only dau. of James Bonwell, of Cork, and Mary Bruce his wife, and had issue,
1. THOMAS RONAYNE, of Doughcloyne.
2. James, d. unm.
3. Dominick, Barrister-at-Law, d. 1866.
4. Phillip, m. the dau. of Daniel Egan, and had one son and two daus., d. 1868.
1. Mary, m. William Hastings Greene, of Lota, co. Cork, d. 1872.
The eldest son,
THOMAS RONAYNE SARSFIELD, of Doughcloyne, J.P. and D.L., High Sheriff 1849, b. 10 Dec. 1793 ; m. 20 May, 1820, Angelina, dau. (by Abigail Evans his wife) of the Rev. William Stopford, Rector of Garrycloyne, and by her had issue,
1. DOMINICK RONAYNE PATRICK, of Doughcloyne.
1. Abigail Joseph Anne.   2. Angelina Maria.
Mr. Sarsfield d. 7 Oct. 1865, and was s. by his son,
DOMINICK RONAYNE PATRICK SARSFIELD, of Doughcloyne, J.P. and D.L., High Sheriff 1878, late Capt. North Cork Rifles, b. 9 Sept. 1828 ; m. 17 June, 1858, Mary Mary-Anne Elizabeth Helena, dau. of James de la Cour, of Mallow, by Henrietta Georgiana his wife, dau. and co-heir of James Lombard, of Lombardstown, co. Cork (who was killed in action, when a Major in command of a wing of the North Cork Militia 1798), and had issue by her (who d. 5 Nov. 1911).
1. THOMAS RONAYNE, his heir.
2. James de la Cour, b. 20 Sept. 1864.
3. William Stopford, Major Connaught Rangers, b. 23 Feb. 1868 ; m. 5 July, 1898, Beatrice Lalage Powell, dau. of Percy John Gordon Maynard, of Ratoath, co. Meath, and has issue, Patrick, b. 13 April, 1899.
1. Henrietta Georgina Lombard.
2. Angelina Stopford, m. 1897, Rev. S. H. P. Harman, eldest son of Rev. S. Harman, Rector of Rathcormac, co. Cork.
3. Mary Elizabeth Annie Helena, m. 4 Feb. 1891, Rev. Arthur Wilson, 2nd son of late Rev. P. Wilson.
4. Annie Becher de la Cour.   5. Octavia Violet Angelina.
6. Helena Rose Sophia, m. 30 Jan. 1896, Thomas Jennings, of Brookfield, Cork
7. Flora Patricia.
8. Ethel Hyacinth Mary Josepha.
Capt. Sarsfield d. 4 Feb. 1892.

Arms—Per pale gu. and arg. a fleur-de-lis per pale of the second, and sa. Crest—A leopard's face or. Motto—Virtus non vertitur.

Seat—Doughcloyne, Cork.

SAUNDERS OF SAUNDERS GROVE.

The late ROBERT JOSEPH PRATT SAUNDERS, C.B., of Saunders Grove, co. Wicklow, J.P. and D.L. co. Wicklow, and J.P. co. Kildare, High Sheriff co. Wicklow 1878, late Col. Commanding the Mid-Ulster Artillery, Lieut. R.A. from 1859 to 1868. sometime A.D.C. to the Lord-Lieutenant of Ireland (the Duke of Marlborough) b. 15 Jan. 1841 ; d. 18 March, 1908.

Lineage.—This branch of the family of Pendred, settled in Ireland temp. WILLIAM III. Through an heir of the family of SAUNDERS they acquired estates in the cos. of Wicklow and Kildare, and adopted the surname of SAUNDERS (see SAUNDERS of Largay).
WILLIAM PENDRED, m. Catherine, dau. of Roger Beetch or Beshe (by Mary Anne Butterfield his wife), and grand-dau. of Roger Beshe, of Harnden, co. Northampton, by Sarah his wife, dau. of Roger Garndun, of Warnton, in same co.), and sister of George Beetch, of Broghillstown, co. Carlow, which George Beetch, by his will, dated 26 Jan. 1699, bequeathed Broghillstown to his brother-in-law, and in two years after assigned to him and Katherine his wife, Harnden, co. Northampton, in consideration of £500. The issue of this marriage were, a dau. Elizabeth, m. 16 Jan. 1696, William Bunbury, of Lisnevagh, co. Carlow, and a son,
WILLIAM PENDRED, of Broghillstown, who purchased lands in the Barony of Talbotstown, co. Wicklow, by deeds of 15 Oct. and 30 Nov. 1719, and lands in the Barony of Rathvilly, co. Carlow, by deed of 24 Dec. 1723. He m. Elizabeth Chamney, and d. 1735, leaving issue,
1. WILLIAM, of Broghillstown, b. 1709 ; m. 15 July, 1739, Letitia, dau. of William Peisley Vaughan, of Golden Grove, King's

Co., and *d.* 15 Oct. 1753, leaving (with four daus., 1, Letitia, whose will, dated 26 June, 1765, was proved 4 Nov. 1771; 2, Wilhelmina; 3. Bridget Sadleir, *m.* 1772, Thomas Hume; 4. Martha, *m.* Jan. 1777, Cornelius Heldon, of Dublin) two sons,
   1. WILLIAM, of Broghillstown, *m.* (settlements dated 12 May, 1770) Anne, dau. of Love Thalt, of Dublin, and *d.s.p.*
   2. Vaughan, of Brookfield. Blackrock, co. Dublin, *b.* 1762; *m.* 1st, Charlotte, dau. of Thomas Jones, of Vessington, co. Meath, sister of Frederick Jones, lessee of Crowe Street Theatre, Dublin, and had by her, with an elder son, Frederick, who *d.* aged 17, and two daus., Frances and Letitia, a son,
     VAUGHAN, *m.* Sarah, dau. of John Hamilton Weldon, of Knock and Gravelmount, co. Meath, by Mary his wife, dau. of Thomas Taylour Rowley, and by her (who *d.* 3 Jan. 1884) had issue,
      1. VAUGHAN PENDRED, representative of the family, *m.* Marian, dau. of James Meade Loughnan, of Crohill, J.P. co. Kilkenny, by whom he has,
       a. Vaughan.
       b. Loughnan St. Lawrence.
       c. Berthon Fleming.
       a. Charlotte Berthon.
      2. Hamilton Weldon.   3. William Molesworth.
      4. Morley Edward.
       1. Mary, *d. unm.*   2. Charlotte, *d. unm.*
       3. Eleanor Saunders, *d. unm.*
He *m.* 2ndly, Rosetta, dau. of Thomas Byder, patentee of the Theatre Royal, Dublin, and *d.* 1837, leaving by her one son,
     5. John, executor to his father's will.
   2. GEORGE, of whom hereafter.
   2. Sarah, *d. unm.*; her will was proved 2 July, 1800.
   2. Martha, *d. unm.*; will dated 3 Nov. 1779, proved 1 Jan. 1788.
   3. Elizabeth, *m.* June, 1718, Jonathan Naylor, Gent., of Baltinglass.
   4. Katherine, *m.* Walter Murray.
   5. Mary, *m.* Sept. 1733, John Scott, of Ballygannon, co. Wicklow.
Mr. Pendred's will, dated 16 March, 1735, was proved 6 Jan. 1736. His son,
   GEORGE PENDRED, of Saunders Grove, co. Wicklow, was High Sheriff for that co. 1735. He *m.* Cordelia, dau. and heir of Morley Saunders, of Saunders Grove, LL.D., Second Serjeant-at-Law, by whom he had three sons and one dau.,
   1. MORLEY, his heir.   2. Joseph.
   3. William.
   1. Avis.
George Pendred *d.* 24 April, 1741. His eldest son,
   MORLEY PENDRED, of Saunders Grove, *d.* 20 July, 1772, having inherited his mother's property, adopted the surname of SAUNDERS. He *m.* Lady Martha Stratford, dau. of John, 1st Earl of Aldborough, and had, with other daus.,
   1. MORLEY, his heir.
   2. John Stratford, Lieut.-Gen. in the Army, *m.* Jan. 1822, Jane, dau. of Alderman Mark Bloxham, of Dublin, and had issue,
     1. John Stratford, an Officer in the 56th Regt., *b.* 5 April, 1824; *d. unm.* Dec. 1854.
     2. Morley Caulfield, an Officer in the 12th Regt., *d.* 11 March, 1908, *m.* Miss Henrietta Howard, and had issue, five sons, Morley, Charles, John, Stratford, Arthur, and three daus., Grace, Florence, Lucy.
      1. Martha Elizabeth Jane, *m.* Mark Taylor.
     1. Martha Louisa, *m.* John Lloyd Williams, of Gwernant, co. Cardigan (*see that family*).
     2 Delia Sophia, *m.* Rev. Meade Swift, *alias* Dennis.
The elder son,
   MORLEY SAUNDERS, of Saunders Grove, J.P., High Sheriff co. Wicklow, 1788 *m.* June, 1787, Ellen Katherine, dau. and heir of James Glascock, of Music Hall, co. Dublin, and by her (who *d.* 20 Sept. 1839) had issue,
   1. Morley John Stratford, *d. unm.* 1809.
   2. ROBERT FRANCIS, who *s.* his father.
   3. Edward Henry Conyngham, a Midshipman on board Sir Michael Seymour's frigate, the *Neiman*, killed by the captain of an American prize (the *Purse*), with which he was sent home as Prize-Master, Nov. 1811.
   4. James Thomas Conolly (Rev.), *m.* 11 Dec. 1828, Augusta Sophia, dau. of John Lloyd Williams, of Gwernant, co. Cardigan, and *d.* Aug. 1888, leaving issue,
     1. Morley Benjamin (Rev.), *b.* 6 Jan. 1830; *d.* 17 Dec. 1911; *m.* 26 May, 1860, Maria Frend. She *d.* 2 Dec. 1891.
      1. Louisa Emily, *m.* 12 Jan. 1860, Thomas Tickell, Capt. R.N.
      2. Ellen Oliver, *m.* 17 Feb. 1863, John O. H. N. Oliver, Deputy-Commissioner at Sirsa, in the Punjaub, India.
      3. Augusta Catherine, *m.* 19 July, 1860, James A. M. M. Biggs, H.E.I.C.S.
     5. Albert Wingfield, Ensign 80th Regt., killed at Vittoria.
     1. Katherine Martha, *m.* Thomas Stratford Dennis, of Fort Granite, co. Wicklow, and *d.* 1825.
     2. Ellen, *d. unm.* 1877.
     3. Charlotte Hannah Maria, *d. unm.* 1873.
Mr. Saunders *d.* 25 March, 1825, and was *s.* by his eldest surviving son,
   ROBERT FRANCIS SAUNDERS, of Saunders Grove, co. Wicklow, J.P. and D.L., High Sheriff of the co. 1822, served with the 67th Regt. in the Peninsula (for which he received medal and clasps), and with the 68th in North America, *m.* 4 Feb. 1840, Elizabeth Martha, 3rd dau. of Joseph Pratt, of Cabra Castle, co. Cavan (*see that family*), and had issue,
   1. ROBERT JOHN PRATT, late of Saunders Grove.
   2. HARLOVEN MORLEY, late Lieut.-Col. 58th Regt., *b.* 10 Dec.
1842; *m.* 27 April, 1882, Jane Georgina Janet, dau. of Walter Turnbull, of Fenwick, co. Roxburgh. He *d.* 8 Nov. 1901.
   1. Jemima Sarah, *b.* 1845; *d.* 1847.
Mr. Saunders *d.* March, 1871, and was *s.* by his eldest son,
   Seat.—Saunders Grove, co. Wicklow. *Clubs*—Carlton, Army and Navy, and Kildare Street.

SAUNDERS OF KILAVALLA.

MAJOR OWEN EDGAR MOORE SAUNDERS, of Kilavalla, co. Tipperary, Major 5th Dragoon Guards, *b.* 6 Nov. 1874; *m.* 12 Jan. 1904, Ida Evelyne, younger dau. of Col. Richard Poyser, D.S.O., and has issue,
   1. BASIL HARLOVEN GRANT, *b.* 24 July, 1905.
   2. Henry Owen, *b.* 8 April, 1909.
   Lineage.—ROBERT SAUNDERS, a Col. in OLIVER CROMWELL'S army, was appointed Governor of Kinsale, co. Cork by the Usurper. He got a grant of "The Deeps" and other lands in co. Wexford, amounting to 3,725 acres, by patent dated 7 Feb. 19 CHARLES II., and a lease of several lands and tenements in the barony of Imokilly, co. Cork, dated 15 Feb. 1657. He *m.* Sarah, dau. of Henry Owen FitzHerbert, of co. Stafford, and had issue,
   1. JOSEPH, of Saunders Court, co. Wexford, whose will, dated 1 March, 1681, was proved 11 May, 1682. He *m.* Jane, dau. of Henry Whitfield, of Dublin, by whom (who *m.* 2ndly, Robert Doyne, Lord Chief Justice of the Common Pleas in Ireland—*see* DOYNE *of Wells*) he had, with a dau. Dorothy, a son,
     RICHARD, of Saunders Court, High Sheriff co. Wexford, 1707, M.P. for Taghmon 1703-13, Wexford 1713-14, and Taghmon 1715 till death, who left an only dau. and heir,
      JANE, *m.* 1st, Aug. 1725, William Worth, of Rathfarnham, co. Dublin, and 2ndly, Arthur, 1st Earl of Arran.
   2. Robert, of Dublin, Prime Serjeant-at-Law, 1703, M.P. for Cavan 1692-1708, whose will, dated 8 March, 1707, was proved 14 Dec. 1708. He left, with a dau., *m.* Benjamin Fish, three sons,
     1. Joseph, of Newtown Saunders, co. Wicklow, whose will, dated 6 Oct. 1713, was proved 28 Nov. 1730. He *d.s.p.*
     2. Robert, of Dublin, whose will, dated 25 Oct. 1731, was proved 18 Dec. 1732. He left, by Anne, is wife, a dau. Avis, and two sons,
      (1) Anderson, *b.* 1694, Lieut. in Hawley's Regt. 1723, who left issue.
      (2) Richard, who is mentioned in the will of his uncle, Joseph.
     3. Morley, LL.D., Barrister-at-Law, appointed Second Serjeant-at-Law 29 Oct. 1692, *b.* in co. York, 1671, M.P. for Enniscorthy 1703-13. Purchased Saunders Grove and other estates in co. Wicklow, and left, by Frances Goodwin, his wife, an only dau. and heir,
      Cordelia, *m.* George Pendred, and had a son, Morley Pendred, who adopted the surname of SAUNDERS (*see* SAUNDERS *of Saunders Grove*).
   3. ANDERSON, of whom we treat.
   1. Elizabeth, *m.* John Puckle, of New Ross, co. Wexford.
   2. Mehetabel.   8. Rebecca.
   4. Hannah.   5. Bethia.
   6. Mary.   7. Bathsheba.
   7. Jane.
The 3rd son,
   ANDERSON SAUNDERS, of Newtown Saunders, co. Wicklow, M.P. for Taghmon 1692-1717, *m.* Elizabeth Battersby, and *d.* 1717, leaving an only son,
   ANDERSON SAUNDERS, of Newtown Saunders, M.P. for Enniscorthy, *b.* 1716; *m.* 1st, Lucy, dau. of Owen Wynne, of Hazelwood, co. Sligo, by whom he had issue,
   1. RICHARD, his successor.
   1. Joanna, *m.* Nov. 1759, Thomas Townley Dawson, of Kinscaly, co. Dublin.
Mr. Saunders *m.* 2ndly, Elizabeth Wallbanke Childers, of Cantley Lodge, co. York, and had further issue,
   2. Anderson.   3. William.
   2. Elizabeth.
The eldest son,
   RICHARD SAUNDERS, of Newtown Saunders, *m.* Anne Parker, and had four sons and four daus.,
   1. OWEN, his successor.   2. John Robert.
   3. Anderson.   4. Richard.
   1. Belinda.   2. Anne Mary.
   3. Ellen.   4. Jane.
The eldest son,
   OWEN SAUNDERS, of Largay, *m.* 1799, Mary Anne, dau. of Richard Sadleir, of Sadleir's Wells, co. Tipperary, and *d.* 1831, having had issue,
   1. RICHARD, of Largay, *b.* 27 Jan. 1800; *m.* 1st, 5 Aug. 1821, Miss Day, niece of Sir John Day, Advocate-General of Bengal, and by her (who *d.* Dec. 1834) had issue,
     1. Augustus Richard, Lieut. 60th Rifles, *b.* 1822; deceased.
     2. Henry, Lieut. 82nd Regt., *b.* 1824; *d.* at Carlisle Barracks.
     3. EDWARD, of Largay, late Cornet, 2nd Dragoon Guards (Queen's Bays), *b.* 1824; *m.* Caroline, dau. of John Weldale Knollys, of Reading, Berks, and had issue,
      (1) Edward Francis, of Corolanty, King's Co., *m.* and has issue an only child Francis Grant, *m.* 12 July, 1911, Leonora Dolores, dau. of Don Pedro Juan d'Alemberto, of São Paulo, Brazil.

(1) Ellen, m. 18 Feb. 1898, Richard Falkiner, of Mount Falcon, co. Tipperary, D.L.
(2) Emily, m. Major John R. H. Richards (see RICHARDS of Macmine).
(3) Amy, m. 1879, Robert Jocelyn Waller, of Summerville, Nenagh.
(4) Katherine, m. 1880, Joshua Robt. Minnitt, M.B. (see MINNITT of Annaghbeg).
(5) Lucy Maud, m. 1891, Rev. Charles Corser Langdon.
(6) Mary, m. John Hall Andrews, of Knocknacree, co. Tipperary.
1. Susan, m. John Richards, of Barnagh, co. Mayo.
2. Julienne, m. A. Z. Cox, of Heron Gate and Harwood Hall, Essex.
3. Mary Anne, m. Rev. Mainwaring White.
Mr. Saunders m. 2ndly, Jane, widow of Richard Leigh, of Hawley House, Kent, and d. 1881.
2. HENRY OWEN, of whom presently.
1. Eleanor Elmina, m. 6 April, 1825, Thomas Sadleir, of Castletown, co. Tipperary, and d. 1 Aug. 1863, leaving issue (see that family).
2. Margaret Jemima, m. 16 Feb. 1836, Sir Edward Synge, 3rd bart., of Syngefield, King's Co., and d. 14 Nov. 1845, leaving issue.
The younger son,
HENRY OWEN SAUNDERS, of Greyfort and Kilavalla House, co. Tipperary, b. 1805; m. 1832, Ellen, dau. of Rev. Matthew Moore, of Mooresfort, and d. 1880, having had issue,
1. Robert Harloven, b. July, 1838; d. unm.
2. EDWARD HENRY, late of Kilavalla House
1. Ellen Pauline, d. unm.
The younger son,
EDWARD HENRY SAUNDERS, of Kilavalla, co. Tipperary, J.P. and D.L., High Sheriff 1900, late Capt. 5th Lancers and 8th Hussars, b. 1 Jan. 1839; m. 1866, Ellen, dau. of Henry Robert Edgar, M.D., of Norwich. She d. 21 April, 1909. He d. 21 April, 1911, leaving issue,
1. OWEN EDGAR MOORE, now of Kilavalla
2. Cecil Harloven, late 2nd Lieut. 6th Dragoon Guards (Carabineers), b. 18 May, 1880.

Seat—Kilavalla, Borrisokane, co. Tipperary.

SAUNDERS OF TULLIG.

The late HENRY L'ESTRANGE SAUNDERS, of Tullig, co. Kerry, b. 19 Feb. 1820; m. 28 Jan, 1888, Emma, dau. of Robert Johnston of St. Mary Cray, Kent, and d.s.p. 13 Sept. 1905.

Lineage.—ROBERT SAUNDERS, of Tullyganter, co. Kerry, m. Barbara, dau. of William Meredith, of Dicksgrove, co. Kerry. His will, dated 21 Oct. 1708, was proved 22 Feb. 1808-9. He had issue,
1. WILLIAM, of whom presently. 2. Thomas.
3. Edward. 4. Robert.
1. A dau., m. George Eager.
2. Mary. m. — Fitzmaurice.
The eldest son,
WILLIAM SAUNDERS, of Tullig, co. Kerry, m. his cousin, Margaret, dau. of Arthur Herbert, of Currens (see that family), 3.d son of Thomas Herbert, of Muckross (see that family), and by her had a son,
ARTHUR SAUNDERS, of Currens, co. Kerry, m. Lucy, dau. of — Boulton. His will, dated 24 Aug. 1787, was proved 5 June, 1789. He left issue,
1. WILLIAM HERBERT, of whom presently.
2. John, of Sackville, co. Kerry, m. Frances, dau. of Thomas Lloyd, of Beechmount, co. Limerick, by Ellen his wife, dau. of Thomas Lloyd, of Killodromin, and had issue,
1. Arthur Lloyd.
1. Ellen, m. Rev. Hawtrey Andrews, 2nd son of John Andrews, of Firmount, King's Co.
2. Mary, m. — Durant, of Tonge Castle, Salop, and had issue.
1. Lucy, m. 20 Oct. 1770, her cousin, Richard Meredith, of Annaghmore and Dicksgrove, co. Kerry, who d. 1821, leaving issue (see that family).
2. Barbara, m. 2 Dec. 1783, Peter Dumas.
3. Mary, m. — Joice. 4. Charity, d. unm.
5. Frances, m. 1st, Alexander Haynes, and 2ndly, — Young.
6. Zenobia Anne, m. John Mahony.
The elder son,
REV. WILLIAM HERBERT SAUNDERS, of Tullig, co. Kerry, m. Alice, widow of Robert Lane and dau. of William Freeman, of Glannamore, co. Cork, and Eliza his wife, dau. of Hodder Roberts, of Bridgetown, co. Cork, and Jane his wife, dau. of Isaac Watkins, of Old Court, co. Cork, and Elizabeth Davies his wife, who was great great grand-dau. of John Travers, of Cork, and Sarah his wife, sister of Edmund Spenser, the Poet, of Kilcoleman, co. Cork, author of "The Fairie Queene." She d. Jan. 1791, having had issue,
1. Arthur, of Tullig, co. Kerry, m. Mary Charlotte, dau. of Col. Morgan, H.E.I.C.S., and had issue,
1. Arthur William, of Tullig.
2. George, of Worcester Coll.
1. Jane Whatton.
2. William Herbert, M.D., d. unm.
3. JOHN, of whom presently.
The youngest son,

JOHN SAUNDERS, of Cork, m. Catherine, widow of Michael Morrison and 3rd dau. of Noblett Rogers, of Lota, co. Cork, by Mary his wife, dau. of Archdeacon Michael Davis. She d. 1820. He d. April, 1845, having had issue,
1. William (Rev.), Rector of Carrigtuohill, d. unm. May, 1882.
2. Arthur John, m. the dau. of William Logan. of Cork, and d.s.p.
3. HENRY L'ESTRANGE, late representative.
Residence—19, Montpelier Road, Brighton.

SAUNDERS-KNOX-GORE. See GORE.

SAUNDERSON OF CASTLE SAUNDERSON.

CAPT. SOMERSET FRANCIS SAUNDERSON, of Castle Saunderson, co. Cavan, D.L., J.P. for that co., High Sheriff 1907, Capt. late Rifle Brigade, b. 7 Aug. 1867.

Lineage.—"ALEXANDER SANDERSON, Esq, of Scotland," was made a Denizen of Ireland 26 Sept. 1613, and was High Sheriff co. Tyrone in 1622, and twice subsequently. He was granted Tullylegan, and other lands to the extent of 1000 acres, the whole being erected into the Manor of Sanderson, 30 Nov. 1630. He d. 8 Dec. 1633, leaving three sons.
1. Archibald, of Tullylegan, m. Dorothea Stewart, who was made Denizen of Ireland 27 June, 1634. He d. 1657 (admon. dated 19 Oct. 1657). His son, Alexander. of Tullylegan, and ancestor of the family of that place.
2. Robert, of whom we treat.
3. George, d.s.p. Will dated 14 June, 1664.
The 2nd son,
ROBERT SANDERSON, settled at Portagh, and there built Castle Sanderson. He was Col. in the Army of Gustavus Adolphus, and was High Sheriff co. Cavan 1657; m. Katherine, eld. dau. of James Cunningham, and sister and co-heir of John Cunningham, both of Ballyachen, co. Donegal. He d. 1675 (admon. granted 8 June, 1675), leaving issue,
1. ROBERT, his heir.
2. James, High Sheriff co. Cavan 1679; d. unm.; will dated 22 Dec. 1679, proved 29 Dec. 1680.
3. Alexander, of Drumkeevil, m. Mary, dau. of Thomas Whyte, of Red Hills, co. Cavan, and was bur. at St. Mary's, Dublin, leaving, with other issue,
1. ALEXANDER, s. his uncle.
2. James, of Drumcassidy, alias Clover Hill (see that family).
3. Robert, of Dromkeen, ancestor of that family.
4. William, of Moycashel, co. Westmeath, m. Mabella, widow of Charles Rochfort, of Streamstown, and dau. of Right Hon. Sir Theophilus Jones, and d. 1702 (admon. granted 19 May, 1702), leaving issue.
The eldest son,
ROBERT SANDERSON, of Castle Sanderson, M.P. and Col. of a Regt. in WILLIAM III's Army; m. Jane, dau. of the Right Rev. John Leslie, Bishop of Clogher (see BURKE's Peerage, LESLIE, Bart.). He d.s.p. 1723, and was s. by his nephew,
ALEXANDER SANDERSON, of Castle Sanderson, High Sheriff co. Cavan 1714; m. his cousin Mabella, dau. of William Sanderson, of Moycashel, Westmeath, and was bur. at St. Mary's, Dublin, 15 Aug. 1726. His son.,
FRANCIS SANDERSON, of Castle Sanderson, High Sheriff co. Cavan 1740; m. Anne, eldest dau. of Anthony Atkinson, of Cangort, and d. 11 Aug. 1746 (admon. granted 25 Aug. 1746), leaving two sons and two daus. His son and heir,
ALEXANDER SAUNDERSON, of Castle Sanderson, High Sheriff co. Cavan 1758, changed the spelling of his name. He m. Rose (d. 7 Jan. 1775), dau. of Trevor Lloyd, of Gloster, King's Co., and d. at Cork, March, 1768, and was bur. at Shinrone, King's Co. His will, dated 31 Dec. 1765, was proved 2 June, 1768. He left, with other issue,
1. FRANCIS, his heir.
2. Alexander, Col. in the Army, and Lieut.-Col. 69th Regt., d. unm.
3. Robert (Rev.), Rector of Borrisokane, co. Tipperary, m. dau. of Capt. John Johnston, of Magherameua, and d. 1847, having had one surviving son,
James, of Villa Nova, co. Monaghan.
4. John, m. Miss Hamilton, and had a son and a dau., both dec.
The eldest son,
FRANCIS SAUNDERSON, of Castle Saunderson, M.P. co. Cavan, High Sheriff 1781, b. 15 Sept. 1754; m. 28 Aug. 1779, Anne Bassett, dau. of Stephen White, of Miskin, Glamorgan, and heir of the Bassett estates in that co., and by her (who d. 1845) had issue,
1. ALEXANDER, his successor.
2. Francis (Rev.), M.A., Rural Dean, Rector of Kildallon, co. Cavan, m. 3 May, 1825, Lady Catherine Crichton, sister of John 3rd Earl Erne, K.P., and d.s.p. 22 Dec. 1873. She d. 14 Oct. 1860.
3. Hardress Robert, Lieut.-Col., late of the Grenadier Guards, of Northbrook House, Hants, m. 17 Feb. 1821, Lady Maria Anne Luttrell Olmius (b. 1799), dau. and co-heir of John, 3rd and last Earl of Carhampton, and Baron Irnham. He d. 1865. She d. 14 Nov. 1861, having had issue,

IRELAND.

(1. Hardress Luttrell, Col. Cavan Militia, and late Capt. 66th Regt., b. 1822; m. 20 Dec. 1847, his cousin, Lady Eliza Dawson Damer, sister of Henry John, 3rd Earl of Portarlington, K.P., and d.s.p. 21 June, 1881. She d. 13 Feb. 1897.
2. John Luttrell, Capt. R.A., d. 18 Feb. 1867.
3. Francis Luttrell, late Capt. Durham Light Infantry, d. from an accident 3 Nov. 1911.
1. Maria Anne, m. 3 Aug. 1852, William Stevenson, J.P., late Scots Fusilier Guards, of Fox Lease, Hants, and had issue. She d. 3 Jan. 1907. He d. 16 Oct. 1910.
2. Cecilia Selina Carhampton, m. 17 Aug. 1865, Edward Slater Harrison, of Shelswell Park, Oxon (see that family). She d.s.p. 1 July, 1899. He m. 2ndly, 10 July, 1900, Emma Cecilia, dau. of Richard Aubrey Cartwright, of Edgcote (see CARTWRIGHT of Aynhoe).
3. Lydia Frances Rose, m. Bonham William Carter. He d. 1901. She d. 20 Sept. 1905.
4. Constance Albuera, m. 1860, Charles Edward Radclyffe, of Little Park, Hants, and has issue (see that family).
5. Florence Vittoria, m. 1st, July, 1856, Marmaduke Grimston, of Grimston Garth, co. York, who d. 14 Nov. 1879, leaving issue (see that family). She m. 2ndly, 2 Jan. 1883, Gen. Sir Edmund F. Du Cane, K.C.B., who d. 7 June, 1903.
4. James, Lieut. R.N., m. Selina, dau. of Col. and Lady Anne Fox, of Fox Hall, co. Longford, and grand-dau. of Barry, 2nd Earl of Farnham, and had issue.
5. William Bassett, Lieut.-Col. in the Army.
1. Lydia Waller, m. Very Rev. Gilbert Holmes, Dean of Ardfert.
2. Cecilia, m. James Henry Sclater, of Newick Park, Sussex.
Mr. Saunderson d. 1827. His eldest son,
ALEXANDER SAUNDERSON, of Castle Saunderson, J.P. and D.L. Col. of the Militia, High Sheriff 1818, and M.P. co. Cavan, b. 22 July, 1783; m. 18 March, 1828, Hon. Sarah Juliana Maxwell, eldest dau. of Henry, 6th Lord Farnham, and by her (who d. 17 Dec. 1870) had issue,
1. Alexander de Bedick, b. 18 Feb. 1832; d. 26 Dec. 1860.
2. Somerset Bassett, 11th Hussars, A.D.C., b. 16 Nov. 1834; m. 16 April, 1864, Emily Mary, dau. of Edward Henry Cole, of Stoke Lyne, Oxon, and Lady Henry Moore, and d. 1892, leaving issue,
  1. Henry.   2. Richard.
  3. Charles, m. 22 June, 1909, Esme, dau. of Major-Gen. C. A. Cuningham, of Cheltenham.
  1. Maud.
3. EDWARD JAMES, late of Castle Saunderson.
4. Llewellyn Traherne Bassett, of Dromkeen House, co. Cavan, and of St. Hilary, co. Glamorgan, late Lieut. 11th Hussars, J.P. co. Cavan, High Sheriff 1868, late Capt. Cavan Militia, b. 4 Sept. 1841; m. 3 May, 1866, Lady Rachel Mary Scott (d. 1 Jan. 1911), 3rd dau. of John Henry, 3rd Earl of Clonmell, and has had issue,
  1. Alexander Traherne, d. 8 Jan. 1869.
  2. Llewellyn Traherne, Capt. Rifle Brigade, b. 5 June, 1870; d. unm. of wounds received in action at Stanterton, S. Africa, 24 April, 1902.
  3. Reginald Traherne, b. 23 Nov. 1873.
  4. Maurice Traherne Bassett, 2nd Lieut. 3rd Batt. Norfolk Regt., b. 5 July, 1875.
  5. Robert, b. 30 June, and d. 3 July, 1879.
  6. Samuel, b. 1884.
  1. Mabel Charlotte, b. 9 July, 1867; m. 1 June, 1889, Hon. Alfred John Mulholland, son of the late Lord Dunleath, and has issue (see BURKE'S Peerage).
  2. Ethel Rose, b. 9 March, 1872.
  3. Rachel Cecilia, b. 5 Jan. 1877; m. 1899, Capt. Robert Clements Gore, and has issue (see BURKE'S Peerage and Baronetage, GORE, Bart.).
  4. Esther Eliza, b. 15 Sept. 1881; m. 14 July, 1903, Capt. Hubert Francis Crichton, Irish Guards (see BURKE'S Peerage, ERNE, E.).
  5. Olive Julia, b. 1886. 6. Crista Jeanette, b. 1892.
1. Juliana Harriet, m. 5 Jan. 1860, Rev. Lewis Hogg.
2. Rose Ann.
Col. Saunderson d. Dec. 1857. His 3rd son,
COL. THE RIGHT HON. EDWARD JAMES SAUNDERSON, P.C., of Castle Saunderson, co. Cavan, H.M. Lieutenant for that co., High Sheriff 1859, M.P. co. Cavan 1865-74, and for North Armagh 1885-1906, late Col. Commanding 4th Batt. Royal Irish Fusiliers, b. 1 Oct. 1837; m. 22 June, 1865, Hon. Helena Emily De Moleyns, youngest dau. of Thomas, 3rd Lord Ventry, and d. 21 Oct. 1906, leaving issue,
1. SOMERSET FRANCIS, now of Castle Saunderson.
2. Edward.
3. Armar, m. 14 June, 1906, Anne, youngest dau. of John D. Archbold, of New Bedford, Massachusetts, U.S.A.
4. John Vernon, late Lieut. R.A., b. 21 March, 1878; m. 12 Jan. 1910, Hon. Eva Norah Helen Mulholland, only dau. of Henry Lyle, 2nd Baron Dunleath (see BURKE'S Peerage).
1. Rosa, m. Oct. 1892, Major Henry Nugent Head, The Cameronians (Scottish Rifles), and has issue (see HEAD of Derrylahan Park).

Seat—Castle Saunderson, Belturbet, co. Cavan. **Clubs**—Carlton; Wellington; Kildare Street, Dublin.

SAVAGE. See NUGENT OF PORTAFERRY.

SAVAGE-ARMSTRONG. See ARMSTRONG.

SCOTT OF WILLSBORO'.

WILLIAM EDWARD SCOTT, of Willsboro', co. Londonderry, J.P. and D.L., High Sheriff 1857, Capt. and Hon. Major Londonderry Militia, b. 11 Jan. 1833; m. 1861, Catherine Georgina, dau. of Ven. Alexander Stuart, Archdeacon of Ross, and by her (who d. 1865) has had issue,
1. Thomas George Stuart, d. 1868.
1. KATHERINE ELIZABETH, m. 1896, Edward Loftus Phillips, 4th son of the late Charles P. Phillips, of Berkeley Cottage, Herts, and has issue,
  WILLIAM EDWARD PHILLIPS, b. 1903.
2. Anne Frances Emily, d. 1891.

Lineage.—REV. GIDEON SCOTT, M.A. Oxford, went to Ireland as Chaplain in King WILLIAM's Army in 1688, and purchased the Willsboro' estate 1696. He m. Jane, dau. of Robert McNeill, of Ballintoy, by Margaret his wife, dau. of Sir Thomas Ruthven, and widow of Sir Dougal Stewart, and d. 1724, leaving (with two daus., Anne and Jane) an only son,
WILLIAM SCOTT, of Willsborough, b. 1704, for many years Recorder and M.P. for the city of Londonderry, sometime Prime Serjeant and a Judge of the King's Bench and eventually a Baron of the Exchequer. He m. Hannah, dau. of Thomas Gledstanes, and d. 1776, having by her (who d. the same year) had issue,
1. Thomas, Recorder of Derry 1765; d. 1770.
2. JAMES, of whom presently.
3. Anthony, d. 1770.
The 2nd son,
JAMES SCOTT, of Willsboro', b. 1745; m. 1779, Catharine Elizabeth, dau. of James Leslie, D.D., Bishop of Limerick, and sister of Sir Edward Leslie, of Tarbert House, co. Kerry (see that family), and by her (who d. 1832) had issue,
1. William, d. 1803-4. 2. THOMAS, his heir.
3. Edward, Major in the Army, d. 1821.
4. Richard, m. 17 March, 1823, Eleanor, eldest dau. of Col. Henry Gore Sankey, of Fort Frederic, co. Cavan d. 1856.
5. George (Rev.), Rector of Banagher, m. 1823, Elizabeth J. Richardson, and had issue,
  1. George.
  2. James Bedell (Rev.), m. Ellen, dau. of Hugh Lyle of Knocktarka, co. Derry and d. 1896.
  1. Elizabeth, m. Rev. John Young Ruttledge.
6. Charles, m. Jane, dau. of Mr. Farrell, of Larne, and d. at Trincomalee, in the Island of Ceylon, where he was many years Judge and Magistrate.
7. James Leslie Montgomery (Rev.), Chancellor of Down, and Rector of Portaferry, b. 1795; d. 1885; m. 1823, Elizabeth, dau. of Rev. Edward Lucas, of co. Monaghan, and had issue,
  1. James Edward, M.D., Deputy Surgeon-Gen., b. 1824; m. 1873, Dorothea, dau. of Rev. John Frederick Gordon (see GORDON of Delamont).
  2. Francis Montgomery, Rev., m. 1907, Alice, dau. of Thos. Agmondesham Vesey, and d. 1899, having had issue,
    (1) Francis Lucas Clements, m. 1907, Alice, dau. of Theophilus Lucas-Clements, of Rathkenny, co. Cavan, D.L. (see that family).
    (2) Charles. (3) Vesey.
  3. Richard Leslie (Rev.), Rector of Little Parndon, Essex, m. Isabella, dau. of Wm. Charley, of Seymour Hill, co. Antrim, and d. 1901.
  4. Theophilus Leslie, Major-Gen. b. 1831; m. 1st, Jane, dau. of Wm. Alley, and by her has issue,
    (1) Edward Lucas. (2) Francis Leslie.
    (3) Harold. (4) Arthur.
Gen. Scott m. 2ndly, 1884, Louisa, dau. of Robt. Wm. Parsons and widow of Capt. Bradby, 74th Highlanders.
  5. Walter Henry (Rev.), m. 1874, Katherine, dau. of Samuel Galbraith, of Clanabrogan, co. Tyrone.
  6. Horatio, M.D., m. 1st, Miss Steele, and by her had issue, one son and three daus.,
    (1) Horace, M.D.
    (1) Elizabeth, m. J. Seaman.
    (2) Dorothea, m. Col. Birch.
    (3) Maud.
Dr. Scott m. 2ndly, 1892, Eleanor, 3rd dau. of Fredk. Beresford Molony (see MOLONY of Kiltanon), and d. 1895.
  1. Catherine. 2. Harriot.
1. Joice, m. Robert Ogilby, of Pellipar, co. Derry.
2. Hannah, d. 1806.
3. Maryanne Martha, d. June, 1854.
4. Jane, d. 1867.
Mr. Scott d. 1820, and was s. by his 2nd son,
THOMAS SCOTT, of Willsboro', J.P. and D.L., High Sheriff, 1844, formerly Lieut. Bengal Army, afterwards Brigade Major of Yeo-

manry in Ireland, b. 20 Oct. 1783; m. 1st, 1 Dec. 1823, Hannah, widow of John Campbell, of Newtownlimavady; 2ndly, 1827, Anne (d. 1840), 3rd dau. of Rev. Edward Lucas, of Rathconnell, co. Monaghan; and 3rdly, 1844, Katharine Elizabeth, eldest dau. of Rev. Thomas Richardson, of Somerset, co. Londonderry. He had issue by his 2nd wife,
1. James, d. 1846.
2. WILLIAM EDWARD, now of Willsboro'.
3. Thomas Lucas (Rev.). M.A. Trin. Coll. Dublin, Incumbent of St. George's, Dublin, Canon of St. Patrick's Cathedral, and formerly Rector of Lower Moville, Chaplain to the Lord-Lieut. of Ireland, b. 22 Aug. 1834; m. 4 Feb. 1864, Frances Maria, dau. of the Ven. John Russell, Archdeacon of Clogher, and d. 1 May, 1908, leaving issue,
 1. Thomas Arthur, b. 7 Jan. 1865; d. 1891.
 2. John Russell, b. 16 April, 1866; m. 1905, Amina Gertrude, eldest dau. of the late Rev. Robert Walmsley, Vicar of Aspull, Lancashire.
 3. William Lucas, b. 25 July, 1870; m. 29 Dec. 1909, Mabel Eames, youngest dau. of Rev. George Kirkpatrick.
  1. Frances Elizabeth.   2. Mary Monica.
  3. Norah Leslie.   4. Agnes Geraldine.
 5. Kathleen Varena Story, d. young 1899.
4. Charles Stewart (Right Hon. Sir), P.C., G.C.B., G.C.M.G., Envoy Extraordinary and Minister Plenipotentiary at Berne 1888-92, at Copenhagen 1893-8, and Ambassador to the Emperor of Russia 1898-1904, b. 17 March, 1838; m. 1875, Christian Crawford, dau. of James Macknight, W.S., Edinburgh, and has issue,
 1. Charles Edward Stewart.
 1. Vera Helen.   2. Alice Maud.
 3. Margaret Aimée, m. 16 June, 1903, Herbert William Davis-Goff, only surviving son of Sir William J. Davis-Goff, Bart. (see BURKE's Peerage).
 4. Marie Christian.   5. Eileen Agnes.
5. Henry Richardson, b. 26 Aug. 1850; m. Elizabeth, dau. of W. Gage, of co. Derry, and d. 1875.
 1. Elizabeth, m. 1857, Rev. John Lyle, of Knocktarna, co. Derry, and has issue.
 2. Hannah, m. Ven. Edward Bowen, Archdeacon of Raphoe, and d. 1884.
 3. Annette.
 4. Hatton Thomasina, m. 13 Feb. 1872, Right Rev. Henry Stewart O'Hara, D.D., Bishop of Cashel (see O'HARA of O'Hara Brook).
5. Katharine Emily, d. 1855.   6. Jane Barbara, d. 1850.
Major Scott d. Jan. 1872.

Arms—Or, on a bend az., a mullet between two crescents of the field, a bordure engrailed pean. *Crest*—An escallop shell sa. charged with a trefoil or. *Motto*—Perge.
Seat—Willsboro', co. Londonderry.

SCOTT OF ANNEGROVE ABBEY.

JAMES WILLIAM EDMUND SCOTT, of Annegrove Abbey, Queen's Co., b. 1855.

Lineage.—CAPT. JAMES SCOTT, an Officer in WILLIAM III's Army, settled in Ireland about 1690, and purchased the seat of Annegrove Abbey (then called Cahirdaragh). He m. Sarah Llewellyn, and had a son,
JAMES SCOTT, of Annegrove, Queen's Co., m. Miss Stanley, and had a son,
JAMES SCOTT, of Annegrove, m. Anne, dau. of William Butler, of Park, co. Tipperary, and had an only child,
JAMES EDMUND SCOTT, of Annegrove, J.P., m. Rosetta, dau. of Sir Richard Wheeler Denny Cuffe, Knt., of Leyrath, co. Kilkenny, and sister of Sir J. Denny Wheeler Cuffe, 1st bart. (see BURKE's Peerage), and d. 1853, having had with two daus., who d. unm., one son,
JAMES WILLIAM BUTLER SCOTT, of Annegrove, J.P. Queen's Co., High Sheriff 1870, b. 1811; m. 28 June, 1851, Elizabeth Rosetta, dau. of John Bolton Massy, of Brazille, co. Dublin, Clareville, Black Rock, and Ballywire, co. Tipperary, and d. 1859, having by her had issue,
1. JAMES WILLIAM EDMUND, his heir.
1. Elizabeth Rosetta, m. 1876, Capt. Sir John Hawley Glover, G.C.M.G., R.N., sometime Governor of Lagos, Newfoundland and the Leeward Islands, who d. 1885.
2. Jane, d. unm.
3. Charlotte Annie, m. 9 Sept. 1893, John Buchan Sydserff, eldest son of Thomas Buchan Sydserff, of Ruchlaw, Haddingtonshire, and has issue (see that family).
4. Fannie Catherine, m. Adam William Stafford Delmege, of Ballywire, co. Tipperary, and has issue (see that family).
Seat—Annegrove Abbey, near Mountrath, Queen's Co.

LUCAS-SCUDAMORE OF CASTLE SHANE.

EDWARD SCUDAMORE LUCAS-SCUDAMORE, of Castle Shane, co. Monaghan, and of Kentchurch Court, Hereford, J.P. and D.L. cos. Monaghan and Hereford, High Sheriff co. Monaghan 1879, and J.P. cos. Monmouth and Radnor, late Lieut.-Col. and Hon. Col. 4th Batt. The King's Shropshire L.I., assumed by Royal Licence, 30 Nov. 1900, the additional surname and arms of SCUDAMORE, b. 8 March, 1853; s. his uncle 1874; m. 1 Dec. 1900, Sybil Frances, youngest dau. of the late Col. George Webber, C.B. (see WEBBER of Leekfield), and has issue,

JOHN HARFORD STANHOPE, b. 16 Jan. 1902.
Geraldine Clara, b. 24 Aug. 1903.

Lineage.--THOMAS LUCAS, of Saxham, Suffolk, Secretary to Jasper Tudor, Duke of Bedford, and Solicitor to HENRY VIII. Will proved 12 March, 1531, m. Elizabeth, dau. of R. Kemys, of Raglan, Wales, and had three sons and two daus.
1. Jasper, of Saxham, his heir, m. Margaret, dau. of Robert Geddinge, and left issue.
2. HENRY, of whom presently.
3. John, m. 1st, Mary Abel; 2ndly, Elizabeth Christmas, and left issue by both.
 1. Lettice, m. John Grenfeld, of Exeter.
 2. Anne, m. Sir Thomas Barnardiston.
The 2nd son,
HENRY LUCAS, m. 1st, Mary, dau. of Edward Grene, of Bury St. Edmunds, and had by her nine sons and two daus. He m. 2ndly, Alice, dau. of Simon Bradock, of Horam, Suffolk, and had by her, FRANCIS, Henry, Thomas, and Martha.
FRANCIS LUCAS, of Hollinger, near Bury St. Edmunds, m. Anne, dau. of — Munings, of Monk's Ely, Suffolk, and had a son,
FRANCIS LUCAS, of Elmsett and Grunsborrow, Suffolk, m. Matilda, dau. of Thomas Munings, of Monk's Ely, and had two sons,
1. Thomas, of Colchester, and the Inner Temple, mentioned in the will of his brother Francis, m. Anne, dau. of John Tidd, of Wells, Norfolk, and had a son,
 Thomas, b. 1642.
2. FRANCIS, of whom next.
The younger son,
FRANCIS LUCAS, Cornet in the Army, the first of Castle Shane, whose will, dated 15 Oct. 1657, was proved 8 Dec. 1657, m. Mary Poyntz, and by her (who m. 2ndly, Robert Moore) had issue,
1. FRANCIS.   2. William.
3. Richard.   4. Charles.
1. Lucy, m. by licence, 20 Dec. 1684, Charles Poyntz, son of Sir Toby Poyntz.
The eldest son,
FRANCIS LUCAS, of Castle Shane, High Sheriff 1673, b. 1646; d. 29 March, 1705, having by Mary his wife (will will dated 26 Dec. 1719, proved 28 Nov. 1747) had issue,
1. FRANCIS, of whom presently.
2. EDWARD, s. his brother.   3. Robert, killed in a duel, s.p.
1. Anne, m. — Simes.
2. Lucy, m. Hugh Savage, of Ardkeen, and d. 13 Nov. 1751.
3. Jane, m. Michael Ennis.
The eldest son,
FRANCIS LUCAS, of Castle Shane, High Sheriff 1703, M.P. for the borough of Monaghan from 1713 to 1746. He d. unm. May, 1746 (will dated 27 Aug. 1744, proved 26 May, 1746), and was s. by his brother,
EDWARD LUCAS, of Castle Shane, High Sheriff 1709, m. 1st, by licence, 10 July, 1696, Elizabeth, dau. of Thomas Smyth, of Drumcree, co. Westmeath; and 2ndly, by licence, 10 Sept. 1723, Abigail, widow of Rev. William Brooke, and dau. of Thomas Handcock, of Twyford, Westmeath. She d.s.p. bur. 4 June, 1757, will dated 24 May, proved 18 June, 1757. By the former he had (with three daus.) two sons,
1. Thomas, of Monaghan, b. 1698, m. Feb. 1719, Alice, dau. of William, 6th Lord Blayney. He d.v.p., May, 1726 (will dated 3 March, 1723, proved 27 May, 1727), and by her (admon. 28 May, 1756) had issue,
 1. EDWARD, s. his grandfather.
 2. William, b. 1721, bur. 23 May, 1759, s.p.
 3. Francis (Rev.), Rector of Drumgoon, b. 1723, m. Isabella, dau. of Daniel Eccles, of Fintona. His will dated 31 March, proved 23 May, 1770. He left issue,
  (1) Thomas.
  (2) Daniel Eccles (Rev.), m. Anne, dau. of — Allen. His will dated 28 June, 1827, proved 20 May, 1828. Her will dated 12 Nov. 1845, proved 8 Jan. 1848. They had issue.

Scudamore.

(3) Edward.
(4) Francis, who left issue.
(5) Charles Robert, of Cavan Lodge, co. Tyrone, *m*. Frances, dau. of Daniel Eccles, of Ecclesville. His will dated 2 July, 1845, proved 21 March, 1846. Her will dated 1 April, proved 24 Nov. 1846. He *d.s.p.*
(6) William.
(1) Frances. (2) Anne.
(3) Alice, *m*. 1788, Edward Richardson, of Poplar Vale.
(4) Mary.
1. Elizabeth, *b*. 1721, *m*. William Lee, of Leesborough, co. Monaghan.
2. Sarah, *b*. 1724, *m*. 1752, Rev. Joseph Warren.
3. Thomasina Anne, *b*. 1725, *m*. 1747, Joseph Hammersley.
2. Francis, of Grenon, co. Monaghan, High Sheriff 1748, *m*. Mary, dau. of Hugh Savage, of Ardkeen. He was bur. 23 Aug. 1758. His will, dated 23 Oct. 1757, was proved 2 May, 1759, Her will dated 2 Aug. 1772, proved 5 April, 1782. He left issue,
1. Edward, of Moynalty, co. Monaghan, High Sheriff 1763, *m*. Elizabeth Davis. His will, dated 6 April, 1794, was proved 16 Dec. 1796. He left issue,
(1) Francis, of Clontibret, co. Monaghan, *b*. 1776, *m*. Elizabeth, dau. of Richard Lee, of Leesborough, co. Monaghan. He *d*. 1815 (will dated 24 Feb. 1815, proved 24 April, 1816), leaving issue,
1. Davis, of Clontibret, and Drommargle, co. Armagh, *b*. 1802 *m*. Elizabeth, dau. of Capt. Thomas Hill. She *d*. 1837. He *d*. 1786, leaving issue,
a. Francis, *d. unm.* 1860.
b. Thomas, *m*. Susan, dau. of Gen. John Millet Hamerton, C.B.
c. Edward.
d. Charles Davis, V.C., Rear Adm., retired, J.P. cos. Kent and Argyll, of Great Culverden, Tunbridge Wells, Kent (48, *Phillimore Gardens, W., and Army and Navy Club*), *b*. 19 Feb. 1834; *m*. 22 April, 1879, Frances Russell, only child of Adm. Sir William Hutcheon Hall, K.C.B., F.R.S., and grand-dau. of George, 6th Viscount Torrington, and has issue,
(*a*) Hilare Caroline. (*b*) Frances Byng.
(*c*) Caroline Louisa Byng.
a. Ellen.
b. Elizabeth, *m*. 7 March, 1846, Sir George de la Poer Beresford, 2nd bart. He *d*. 11 Feb. 1873. She *d*. 23 Dec. 1898, leaving issue (*see* BURKE'S *Peerage*, BERESFORD-PEIRSE, Bart.).
c. Charlotte, *m*. John Caulfeild, and has issue.
2. Thomas, *m*. Catherine, dau. of Edward Lucas, and had issue.
1. Mary Anne, *m*. John Reynell.
(2) Edward, Capt. in the Army, who left issue, by Catherine his wife,
1. Edward, of Sarzy Lodge, Rathgar, co. Dublin. Will dated 5 Dec. 1841, proved 11 Jan. 1844.
2. Davis, Asst.-Surg. 68th Regt.
1. Catherine, *m*. Thomas Lucas.
(1) Mary, *m*. William Lucas, Capt. Monaghan Militia.
(2) Margaret, *d. unm.*
(3) Elizabeth, *m*. 1816, Henry Courtney, of Knockbarrow.
2. Thomas, Capt. 20th Regt., of Derryvhalla, co. Monaghan, High Sheriff 1770, *m*. by licence, 13 Dec. 1776, Alice, 2nd dau. of Edward Lucas, of Castle Shane.
3. Francis, Lieut. R.N., lost at sea. Admon. 3 June, 1773.
1. Elizabeth, *m*. by licence, 20 Dec. 1756, George Nugent, of Castlerickard, co. Meath.
2. Lucy, *m*. Matthew Lorinan, of Ardee.
3. Mary, *m*. -- Ley.
1. Mary, *m*. Francis Savage, of Ardkeen. He *d*. July, 1770.
2. Anne, *m*. Rev. Thomas Skelton, Vicar of Newry.
3. Jane, *m*. 1748, Rev. Joshua Pullein, of Clonallon, co. Down. Mr. Lucas was bur. 2 Jan. 1757 (will dated 13 Oct. 1756, proved 26 April, 1757), and was *s*. by his grandson,
EDWARD LUCAS, of Castle Shane, M.P. for co. Monaghan, 1761-5, High Sheriff 1752, *b*. 1720; *d*. June, 1771; *m*. Elizabeth (*d*. 2 Sept. 1775), dau. of Francis Savage, of Ardkeen. His will dated 1 Aug. 1770, was proved 22 Sept. 1775. He left issue,
1. Francis, of Castle Shane, High Sheriff, 1773, *b*. 9 March, 1749; *m*. by licence 27 March, 1781, Florinda, dau. of Thomas Norman, of Lagore, co. Meath, and *d.s.p.* 1789. Will dated 7 May, 1784, proved 28 Dec. 1789. She *m*. 2ndly, Charles Norman.
2. Edward, *b*. Nov. 1752; *d*. an infant.
3. Thomas, *b*. May, 1754; bur. 28 June, 1754.
4. CHARLES, of whom presently.
5. William, *b*. Aug. 1760; *m*. 1782, Mary, eldest dau. of Edward Lucas, of New Grove, co. Armagh, and *d*. of wounds received in a duel with Col. Robert Sparrow, of Tanderagee, Aug. 1797, having had issue Edward and Elizabeth.
6. Robert, of Raconnel, co. Monaghan, High Sheriff 1806, Lieut.-Col. in the Army, *b*. March, 1763; *m*. Olivia, dau. of John Owen, of Raconnel, and widow of Henry Owen Scott, and *d*. 1839, will dated 5 Dec. 1829, proved 3 Sept. 1839, having had issue,
1. Robert, *d*. 1836.
2. John Owen, Capt. 29th Regt., *b*. 1814, killed 22 Dec. 1845, at the battle of Feroeeshah, when Brigade Major to Sir Hugh Gough.
3. Edward William, of Raconnel, *b*. 15 Aug, 1815; *m*. 5 Dec. 1855, Louisa Martha, 3rd dau. of Henry George Johnston, of Fort Johnston (*see that family*), and *d*. 20 Sept. 1862, leaving issue,

(1) Robert William, Barrister-at-law, B.A. Trin. Coll. Dublin.
(1) Emily Maria, *m*. 5 July, 1887, Rev. George W. N. Clark, and has issue, Mary Lucas.
(2) Maria Olivia.
4. Charles.
1. Olivia, *d*. young. 2. Maria, *d*. young.
3. Florinda, *m*. Lieut.-Gen. Andrew T. Hemphill.
4. Jane Elizabeth. 5. Frances. *d*. young.
6. Isabella, *d*. young.
7. Anne, *m*. Rev. William Spencer Walsh, D.D., of Knockboyne, co. Meath (*see* WALSH *of Laragh*).
7. Edward (Rev.), of Cootehill, co. Cavan, *b*. April, 1776; *m*. 1st (setts. dated 25 Aug. 1795), Elizabeth Ann, dau. of Theophilus Clements, of Rathkenny, and by her had issue, who assumed the name of CLEMENTS (*see* CLEMENTS *of Rathkenny*). He *m*. 2ndly, Olivia, dau. of Sir James Hamilton, and by her had a dau., Olivia, *m*. 1st, Henry Smyth, of Mount Henry, Queen's Co.; she *m*. 2ndly, 1840, Robert Hamilton Stubber, of Moyne, Queen's Co. His will dated 21 Dec. 1813, proved 15 Sept. 1815.
1. Mary, *b*. Nov. 1748; *m*. 11 Dec. 1767, Rev. Howard St. George.
2. Alice, *b*. Aug. 1751; *m*. 1st, by licence, 13 Dec. 1776, Thomas Lucas, and 2ndly, Jan. 1783, Robert Hamilton, of Dublin.
3. Abigail, *b*. April, 1756.
4. Elizabeth, *b*. Dec. 1761; *d*. 1784. Admon. 25 Nov. 1784.
5. Hester, *b*. Sept. 1764.
The 2nd son,
CHARLES LUCAS, of Castle Shane, High Sheriff 1795, Barrister-at-Law, *b*. Nov. 1757; *m*. 1st, 1786, Sarah (who *d*. 14 July, 1788), eldest dau. of Sir James Hamilton. Knt., of Monaghan; and 2ndly, Louisa, dau. of Charles Evatt, of Mount Louise. By the former he left at his decease, 13 Dec. 1796, an only child and successor,
THE RIGHT HON. EDWARD LUCAS, of Castle Shane, J.P., High Sheriff 1818, M.P. co. Monaghan 1834-41, and Under-Secretary of State for Ireland 1841-6, sworn of the Privy Council there 1845, *b*. 27 Sept. 1787; *m*. 1812, Anne, 2nd dau. of William Ruxton, of Ardee House, co. Louth, M.P. for Ardee, and by her (who *d*. 15 Aug. 1880) had issue,
1. Francis, formerly Lieut. 46th Regt., *d. unm*. 1846.
2. EDWARD WILLIAM, of Castle Shane.
3. Fitzherbert Dacre, *m*. 24 May, 1852, Laura Adelaide, only surviving child and heir of Lieut.-Col. John Lucy Scudamore, of Kentchurch Court, co. Hereford (*see that family*), and had issue by her (who *m*. 2ndly, 1859, John Donegan, of Carrigmore, co. Cork),
EDWARD SCUDAMORE, now of Castle Shane.
Mr. Lucas *d*. 30 Sept. 1857, of a wound received the previous day at Lucknow, where, as for four months previously, he had acted as a Volunteer.
4. Charles Pierrepoint, Capt. Bengal N.I., *b*. 1825; *d. unm*.
5. Gould Arthur, of Lower Ucomanzi, Natal, Chief Magistrate, Durban, Natal, for ten years, late Capt. 73rd Regt., late R.M. (*Ndhu-Mhlope, Llangian, near Pwllheli, North Wales*), *b*. 1832; *m*. 1st, 1857, Christabella, dau. of William Allen, of Liscongill, to. Cork. He *m*. 2ndly.
1. Catherine Anne, *m*. 1852, Samuel Fitzherbert Filgate, J.P., of Hillsborough, co. Down.
2. Anna Isabella. 3. Isabella Florinda.
The Right Hon. Edward Lucas *d*. 12 Nov. 1871, and was *s*. by his son,
EDWARD WILLIAM LUCAS, of Castle Shane, J.P. and D.L., Lieut. 88th Regt., who was *b*. 1819; *d*. 1874, and was *s*. by his nephew, now of Castle Shane.

Arms—Quarterly 1st and 4th gu., three stirrups leathered and buckled or (SCUDAMORE); 2nd and 3rd arg., a fess between six annulets gu. (LUCAS). *Crests*—1. Out of a ducal coronet or a bear's paw sa. (SCUDAMORE); 2. a demi-griffin arg., beaked and membered or (LUCAS). *Motto*—Stat religione parentum.

Seats—Castle Shane, co. Monaghan; Kentchurch Court, Hereford. *Clubs*—Brooks'; Sackville Street, Dublin.

SCULLY OF MANTLE HILL.

VINCENT SCULLY, of Mantle Hill, co. Tipperary, High Sheriff 1870, B.A., Christ Church, Oxon., b. Aug. 1846; m. 1st, 21 Nov. 1871, Emma Eliza Mary Clare, dau. of Pierce Marcus Barron, of Belmont Park, D.L., co. Waterford, and by her (who d. 7 April, 1890) has had issue,

1. Vincent Bernard, b. 1 Sept. 1872; d. 10 Nov. following.
2. DENYS VINCENT ARTHUR, b. 6 Sept. 1873.
3. Marcus Vincent Barron, b. 2 July, 1881.
1. Katherine Juliet Mary.
2. Manuella Beatrice Mary, a nun.
3. Louise Frances.

He m. 2ndly, 22 July, 1897, Amy, youngest dau. of the late John Netterville Barron of 59th Regt.

Lineage.—JEREMIAH SCULLY, of Ryallstown, or Lyonstown, co. Tipperary, with his brother Roger Scully, settled near Cashel, in that co., subsequent to the Restoration of CHARLES II. Tradition, carefully preserved in the family, says they came from the King's Co. or Longford : the latter, Roger, d. 1704 : the former, Jeremiah, was b. 18 Sept. 1645, and had four sons and two daus. He d. 2 June, 1710. The eldest son,

TEIGE, or TIMOTHY SCULLY, of Barnahilla, co. Tipperary, was b. 8 Aug. 1674 ; m. 1708, Mary, dau. of Roger Ryan, of Kilnemanagh, in the same co., by whom he had nine sons and two daus. ; of the sons, the two elder were,

1. Jeremiah, of Kilconnell and Shanbally, same co., b. 1709 ; m. Katherine Maher, and d. 27 April, 1765.
2. ROGER, of whom hereafter.

He d. 27 July, 1748. His 2nd son,

ROGER SCULLY, of Kilfeacle and Dualla, co. Tipperary, b. 17 Nov. 1713 ; m. 24 Jan. 1734, Mary, dau. of Gilbert Maher, of Tullamaine, same co., by whom (who d. 10 July, 1780, aged 60 years) he had, with ten daus., seven surviving sons,

1. JAMES, of whom hereafter.
2. Edmund, of Cashel, b. 24 Dec. 1739 ; d. 24 Aug. 1806 ; m. Dora, dau. of Roger Ryan, of Kilcloan, by whom (who d. 16 June, 1806) he had a son, Daniel, b. 1 May, 1773 ; d. 17 Dec. 1786, and six daus.,
   1. Mary, m. 1791, Andrew O'Ryan, of Bansha Castle.
   2. Ellen, m. Matthew Moore, son of Rev. Crosbie Moore, of Mooresfort.
   3. Elizabeth, m. 27 Sept. 1800, William Delany, of Castle Durrow.
   4. Margaret, m. Theobald O'Meagher.
   5. Frances, m. William Colles.
   6. Dora, m. Michael Lidwell, of Dromore and Beakstown.
3. Jeremiah, of Silverfort, b. 8 Dec. 1741 ; d. 19 Sept. 1807 ; m. 1768, Barbara, dau. of Daniel Hourigan, of Tantore, by whom (who d. 3 Nov. 1818) he had, with six daus., as many sons,
   1. Roger, of Limerick, b. 1770 ; m. Ellen, dau. of Denis Lyons, of Croom, J.P. co. Limerick, and had a son, Edmund, Capt. in the Imperial Hussars of Austria.
   2. Daniel, Lieut. 7th Dragoon Guards, b. 1772 ; m. Feb. 1779, Elizabeth, dau. of James Aylmer, of Painstown, co. Kildare, and d. 21 Jan. 1802.
   3. Patrick, Capt. 99th Regt., b. 1776 ; d. in West Indies 4 March, 1796.
   4. James, of Tullamaine, b. 21 July, 1779 ; d. 18 May, 1853 ; m. 1st, Katherine, dau. of Denis Moylan (who d. 18 Jan. 1827), and 2ndly, Jan. 1830, Jane Balfe, widow of John Taaffe, of Annahill, co. Mayo.
   5. Jeremiah, of Silverfort, b. 1786 ; m. Jan. 1811, Elenor, dau. of Capt. John Burke, of Limerick. She d. 29 Jan. 1818. He d. April, 1838.
   6. Edmund, of Clonbanane, J.P., b. 1788 ; d.s.p. 18 Dec. 1847.
4. William, of Dually, b. 6 June, 1746 ; m. 1776, Anne, dau. of Robert Roe, and d. 21 Dec. 1828.
5. Timothy, b. 28 April, 1755.
6. Roger, b. 27 June, 1758 ; m. 1798, Elizabeth, dau. of Patrick Curley, of Galway, and d. 1828.
7. Patrick, of Carrick-on-Suir, b. 1764.

Roger Scully d. 8 March, 1783. His eldest son,

JAMES SCULLY, of Kilfeacle. J.P. co. Tipperary, b. 9 Nov. 1737 ; m. 14 July, 1760, Katherine, dau. of Denis Lyons, of Croom House, co. Limerick, by whom (who d. 30 June, 1818) he had (with six daus., 1. Mary, d. 12 Aug. 1831 ; 2. Fanny, m. 1793, Jean Bernard Pasquet, of Bordeaux, and d. 20 Dec. 1795 ; 3. Katherine, m. 9 Nov. 1786, Richard Sausse, of Annesbrook, and d. 14 Aug. 1788 ; 4. Anne, m. 15 June, 1791, Thomas Mahon, d. 28 Oct. 1841 ; 5. Lucinda, m. 1800, Leonard Keating, d. 21 May, 1843 ; 6. Joanna, m. 19 Sept. 1805, Clement Sadleir, d. 25 Dec. 1858) six sons,

1. Roger, b—, Nov. 1772 ; d.v.p. unm. 7 Jan. 1797.
2. DENYS, of whom hereafter.
3. JAMES, of Shanballymore and Tipperary, J.P. co. Tipperary, b. 25 March, 1777 ; m. 17 Jan. 1806, Margaret, dau. of John Wyse, of the manor of St. John, Waterford, and d. 31 Dec. 1846, leaving three sons and one dau.,
   1. James, of Shanballymore, and Mountjoy Square, J.P. co. Tipperary, m. 1st, 1832, Helen, dau. of Alex. Sherlock ; and 2ndly, 1860, Catherine, dau. of Charles Galwey, and d. 4 Dec. 1878, leaving issue.
   2. John, Resident Magistrate, Capt. 80th Regt.
   3. Francis, M.P. co. Tipperary 1847-57.
   1. Eliza, m. 5 June, 1849, John Duff Coghlan, of Kilcop, who d. 21 Oct. 1854, leaving issue.
4. William Timothy, M.D., of Torquay, Devon, b. 15 May, 1778 ; m. 18 Feb. 1796, Margaret Roe, of Rockwell, co. Tipperary, and d. 5 Nov. 1842.
5. Edmund, of Bloomfield, b. 22 Jan. 1779 ; m. 6 March, 1806, Anne, dau. of Con O'Brien, and d. 16 Sept. 1839.
6. Jeremiah, of London, b. 15 Dec. 1872 ; m. 1st, 4 July, 1809, Alice, dau. of Francis Arthur, and 2ndly, Ellen, dau. of Edmund Sexton, of Limerick, and d. 1 March, 1840.

Mr. Scully d. 11 Feb. 1816. His eldest son,

DENYS SCULLY, of Kilfeacle, Barrister-at-Law, author of Statement of the Penal Laws, 1812, b. 4 May, 1773 ; m. 1st, 26 Nov. 1801, Mary, dau. of Ferdinand Huddleston, of Sawston Hall, co. Cambridge, who d.s.p. 12 April, 1806, and 2ndly, 2 Sept. 1808, Katherine, dau. of Vincent Eyre, of Highfield and Newholt, co. Derby, by Katherine his wife, only child of William Parker, of Rainhill, co. Lancaster, by whom (who d. 11 June, 1843) he had issue,

1. JAMES, his successor, b. 13 Sept. 1809 ; d. unm. 26 Nov. 1842.
2. VINCENT, of whom hereafter.
3. Rodolph Henry, b. 12 March, 1812 ; m. Mary, dau. of John Graham Lough, Sculptor, and d. 6 Aug. 1876, leaving four sons,
   1. James Rodolph, of Rickmansworth, Middlesex and Ballyneil, Carrick-on-Suir, Ireland, b. 5 Sept. 1853 ; m. 24 Oct. 1876, Annie, (who d. 2 Feb. 1911) dau. of T. O'Neil, of Beechdale, Kent, by whom he has issue,
      (1) James Rodolph, b. 9 Oct. 1877.
      (2) Vincent Raymond.   (3) Reginald Lough.
      (1) Mary Julia, m. 12 Aug. 1903, William Raymond Connelly, son of the late James Roche Connelly, of the War Office.
      (2) Cecilia Rose.
      (3) Annie.
   2. Rodolph Francis, b. 28 Jan. 1855.
   3. Reginald William, b. 5 July, 1856.
   4. Thomas Vincent, Barrister-at-Law, b. 1 May, 1857 ; m. 8 Aug. 1878, Rosa Victoria, youngest dau. of the late Vincent Scully, of Mantle Hill (see below).
4. Thomas Joseph Denis, b. 12 July, 1817 ; d.s.p. 13 April, 1857.
5. William Francis John, of Ballinaclough, co. Tipperary, and Holland Park, London, b. 23 Nov. 1821 ; m. 1st, 1851, Margaret, dau. of Michael Sweetman, by whom (who d. 20 May, 1861) he had three daus.,
   1. Gertrude.
   2. Julia.
   3. Kathleen.

He m. 2ndly, — Chynoweth, and d. 17 Oct. 1906, having by her had issue.

1. Katherine Julia Mary, m. Prince Antonio Publicola Santa Croce, Duke of Corchiano and Santo Gemine, Grandee of Spain of the First Class, and d. 16 Feb. 1864, leaving three daus.,
   1. Louisa, m. Marquis Rangoni.
   2. Vincenza, m. Count Santa Fiora.
   3. Valeria, m. Marquis Passari.
2. Mary Ann, a nun, dec.
3. Juliana, a nun, dec.

Mr. Scully d. 25 Oct. 1830. His 2nd son,

VINCENT SCULLY, of Mantle Hill, co. Tipperary, and Merrion Square, Dublin, Barrister-at-Law, Q.C., M.P. co. Cork 1852-7 and 1859-65, b. 8 Sept. 1810 : s. his eldest brother 1842 : m. 6 Sept. 1841, Susanna, dau. of John Grogan, of Harcourt Street, Dublin, Barrister-at-Law, and sister of Sir Edward Grogan, Bart., M.P. for the city of Dublin 1841-55, and by her (who d. 3 Sept. 1874) had issue,

1. VINCENT, now of Mantle Hill.
1. Katherine, d. unm. 4 July, 1910.
2. Juliet, a nun.
3. Rosa Victoria, m. 8 Aug. 1878, Thomas Vincent Scully (see above).

Mr. Scully d. 4 June, 1871.

Arms—Vert, a cross boutonné between two mullets in chief and a fleur-de-lis in base or. Crest—Out of a mural crown ppr. a phœnix also ppr., charged on the breast with a cross boutonné as in the arms. Motto—Sine labe resurgens.

Seat—Mantle-hill House, Golden, near Cashel, co. Tipperary. Club—Oxford and Cambridge, S.W.

SEALY OF RICHMOUNT.

JANE STAWELL BERNARD, MRS. KING-SEALY, of Richmount, Bandon, co. Cork, dau. and co-heir of Capt. Sampson Stawell Sealy, 84th Regt. (who d. 1867), with her sister (d. unm. 7 Jan. 1912), s. their uncle, Richard Sealy, of Richmount, co. Cork (who d. unm. 1882). She m. 1853, Charles Lewes King, of Newtown House, Leixlip, co. Kildare, son of Charles King, banker, of Bolton Street, Piccadilly, and Maria Spong his wife. He d. 1869, aged 55, leaving issue,

CHARLES SEALY, J.P. co. Cork, b. 6 Oct. 1860 ; m. 1 June, 1886, Beatrice Ada, dau. of William Jocelyn Bradford, M.D., T.C.D., and has issue,
1. Ludlow Sealy, 2nd Lieut. 4th Royal Munster Fusiliers, b. 3 Sept. 1891.
2. Charles Sealy, 2nd Lieut. 4th Royal Munster Fusiliers, b. 18 Aug. 1894.
1. Esther, m. 16 Jan. 1909, Rev. Walter W. Stewart, B.A., Trin. Coll. Dublin, and has issue.
2. Violet Rose.

Jane Rose Violet, m. 2 March, 1886, William Arthur Mahon, M.D., son of Arthur Mahon, formerly of Cavetown, co. Roscommon, and has issue, two sons, William Ludlow and Charles Hartland.

Mrs. King assumed the additional name of SEALY.

Lineage.—JOHN SEALY settled in Ireland temp. CHARLES II, and was father of

ROBERT SEALY, of Bandon, m. 1699, Elizabeth, sister of Gen. Marsh, and had issue,
1. Armiger, b. 1706.   2. JOHN, of whom presently.
3. George, ancestor of Sealy, of Gortnahorn (see that family).
1. Mary, m. 1750, Francis Travers.

The 2nd son,
JOHN SEALY, of Richmount, co. Cork, J.P., b. 1707 ; m. 1st, 1738, Elinor Fuller, of Downaghmore, co. Cork, and 2ndly, 1751, Mary, widow of — Barter, of Annagh. By his 1st wife he had issue,
1. RICHARD, of whom presently.
2. Robert, d. an infant.   3. William, d. an infant.
1. Elizabeth, m. 1758, Francis Beamish, of Kilmalooda (see that family).
2. Ellinor, m. 1762, Richard Townsend, M.D., of Myross Wood (see that family).

The eldest son,
RICHARD SEALY, of Richmount, m. 1766, Elizabeth, sister of James Bernard, of Bassingbourne Hall, Essex, and Castle Bernard, co. Cork (see BURKE'S Peerage, BANDON, E.). He d. 1789, leaving issue,
1. JOHN, of whom presently.
2. North Ludlow, b. 1770.   3. Francis, b. 1775.

The eldest son,
JOHN SEALY, of Richmount, b. 1769 ; m. 1796, Esther, dau. of Sampson Stawell, of Kilbrittain Castle, co. Cork, and d. 1836, having had issue,
1. RICHARD, of Richmount.
2. Sampson Stawell, Capt. 84th Regt., b. 1800 ; m. 1828, Jane, dau. of Rev. Ambrose Hickey, D.D., Rector of Murragh, co. Cork, and grand-dau. of Falkiner Herrick, of Shippool, co. Cork (see that family), and d. 1867, having had, with a second dau. Esther, who d. an infant, two surviving daus.,
1. JANE STAWELL BERNARD,
2. ROSA ANNA BERNARD STAWELL, } of Richmount.
3. John Ludlow Nelson, Commander R.N., d. unm. 1867.
4. Francis, Capt. 62nd Regt., d. unm. 1876.
5. Jonas, d. unm. 1884.   6. James, d. unm. 1880.
7. William, d. unm. 1885.   8. Ludlow, d. unm. 1894.
1. Esther, d. young.
2. Elizabeth Rose, m. Rev. Abraham Evanson.
3. Melian Charlotte, d. unm.
4. Charlotte, m. Councillor Daly, of Kinsale.

The eldest son,
RICHARD SEALY, of Richmount, b. 1798, s. his father 1836, and d. unm. 1882, when he was s. by his nieces as above. The younger Rosa Anna Bernard Stawell Sealy, d. unm. 7 Jan. 1912.

Arms—Quarterly: 1st and 4th, per pale gu. and or a lion rampant counterchanged, holding between the paws a boar's head erased of the second (KING); and 2nd 3rd, on a fess bretessed az. between three wolf's heads erased sa., as many lozenges arg. (SEALY).

Seat—Richmount, Bandon, co. Cork.

SEALY OF GORTNAHORN.

The late JOHN THOMAS HUNGERFORD SEALY, M.D., of Gortnahorn House, co. Cork, J.P., b. 4 Dec. 1852 ; m. 3 April, 1877, Sarah, dau. of the late Joseph Weightman, of Stainton-le-Vale, co. Lincoln. He d. 29 Dec. 1908.

Lineage.—GEORGE SEALY, of Gortnahorn, b. 1717, 3rd son of ROBERT SEALY, of Bandon (see SEALY of Richmount). He m. Anne, only dau. of Rev. Richard Baldwin, of Ardacrow, Rector of Rathclareen, and had issue,
1. ROBERT, his heir.   2. Richard.
3. Armiger.   4. George.
5. Baldwin.
1. Eliza.   2. Bridget.
3. Jane.

The eldest son,

ROBERT SEALY, of Gortnahorn, m. 1st, Eliza, dau. of Jonas Morris, of Dunkettle, and had a son, JONAS MORRIS SEALY, of Gortnahorn, Barrister-at-Law, Q.C., d.s.p. 1837, and a dau., Mary Anne, m. 1820, Rev. Jonas Morris Poole. He m. 2ndly, Anne, eldest dau. of John Hungerford, of Burren, brother of Col. Thomas Hungerford, of The Island (see that family), and by her had issue,
1. JOHN THOMAS HUNGERFORD, M.D., B.A., b. 26 March, 1804 ; m. 18 Dec. 1829, Sarah, 4th dau. of Rev. Robert Shanly, of Julianstown, co. Meath ; and d. 1850, in California, leaving
ROBERT, b. 13 Sept. 1830, to whom his uncle, Jonas Morris Sealy, bequeathed the estates of Gortnahorn, Kilcoleman, and Garranreagh, after the decease of his widow. He d.s.p. in Australia, 1862.
Alice.
2. WINTHROP BALDWIN, of Gortnahorn.
1. Anna Maria, d. unm.

Mr. Sealy d. 1826. His youngest son,
WINTHROP BALDWIN SEALY, of Gortnahorn, co. Cork, B.A. J.P., b. 1806 ; m. 4 June, 1836, Susan Jane, youngest dau. of the late Richard Hungerford, of The Island, co. Cork, and had issue,
1. ROBERT WINTHROP BALDWIN (Rev.), B.A., b. 1839.
2. Richard Hungerford, b. 1841.
3. Jonas Morris, b. 1844 ; d. 1885.
4. Winthrop Baldwin, b. 1847 ; m. 1875 ; d. 1887.
5. JOHN THOMAS HUNGERFORD, late of Gortnahorn.
6. George Marsh, b. 1854.
1. Frances Eyre, dec.   2. Susan Jane.
3. Henrietta Helena.   4. Letitia Charlotte, dec.
5. Eliza Anne, m. W. H. K. Sandiford.
6. Maria Catherine Becher, m. Thomas Gillman Lakefield.

Mr. Sealy d. 24 Nov. 1887.

Seats—Gortnahorn House, and Barleyfield, Bandon, co. Cork.

SEGRAVE OF CABRA.

MAJOR O'NEILL EDWARD JOHN SEGRAVE, D.S.O., of Kiltimon, co. Wicklow, Cabra, co. Dublin, and of Calla House, co. Galway, formerly a Resident Magistrate in Ireland and Major 18th Batt. Imp. Yeo. in S.A., b. 1856, m. 17 Sept. 1882, Beatrix, dau. of Deputy-Commissary-Gen. William John Jortin Warneford, formerly Commissariat and Transport Dept., and has with other issue,

O'NEILL, late Lieut. Royal Irish Regt., b. 1883.

Lineage.—RICHARD SEGRAVE, Chief Baron of the Exchequer in Ireland A.D. 1404, was father of PATRICK SEGRAVE, living 1445, who m. Mary, dau. and heir of William Wafer, of Killeglan, co. Meath, and was father of RICHARD, whose son, JOHN SEGRAVE, of Killeglan, circa 1500, m. Jenet Dongan, and left two sons, PATRICK, of Killeglan, d.s.p., and

RICHARD SEGRAVE, who d. 1541. He m. 1st, Elizabeth Dowdall, by whom he had
1. PATRICK, of Killeglan, heir to his uncle ; he m. 1st, Joan Beg, and left with two daus., Catharine, wife of Robert Usher, and Anna, wife of Simon Barnewall, of Kilrew, one son,
Richard, a Baron of the Exchequer in Ireland, m. twice, and left issue ; d. 1598.
He m. 2ndly, Mary, dau. of Sir Robert Dillon, of Riverston.
2. Laurence.

He m. 2ndly, Jenet Eustace, by whom he had, with other issue, a 4th son,
WILLIAM SEGRAVE, m. Elizabeth, dau. of William Walsh. of Carrickmaine, and d.v.p., leaving a son,
CHRISTOPHER SEGRAVE, of Dublin, and Bretonstown, co. Meath, Alderman and Mayor of that city 1559. He m. twice. By his 1st wife, Alson, dau. of Nicholas Humphrey, he left at his decease, 2 Oct. 1589, a son and heir,
WALTER SEGRAVE, of Dublin, and Bretonstown, co. Meath, Alderman and Mayor of that city 1588, who m. twice. By Catherine his 1st wife, he had one son, JOHN, his heir ; and by Elinor Ball, his 2nd wife, he had issue, Christopher ; James, to whom his father and uncle gave the dissolved monastery of St. John's, Dublin ; Mary, m. Sir John Tyrrell, Knt. ; Alice, m. John Fagan ; and Jane, m. Robert Kennedy, Alderman of Dublin. Walter Segrave d. 9 Dec. 1621, and was s. by his son,
JOHN SEGRAVE, m. Jane, dau. of Christopher Fagan, Alderman of Dublin, and left a son,

Seymour. THE LANDED GENTRY. 634

HENRY SEGRAVE, of Little Cabra (heir to his grandfather), b. 1599; d. 1662, leaving, by Alice his wife, several children, of whom the eldest son,
JOHN SEGRAVE, of Cabra, co. Dublin, m. Anne, dau. of Sir Neal O'Neil, Bart., of Killelagh, co. Antrim, and was father of
HENRY SEGRAVE, of Cabra, whose will, dated 18 Aug. 1738, was proved 1739. He m. Anne, sister of John Davis, and had issue,
1. NEILL, his heir. 2. John.
3. Richard. 4. Jenico.
5. Arthur, who d. in London, 1817, at a very advanced age.
1. Emelia, m. Gerald Archbold, of Donodea, co. Kildare.
2. Elizabeth. 3. Barbara. 4. Anne.
The eldest son,
NEILL SEGRAVE, of Cabra, d. July, 1777, whose will, dated 8 March, 1769, was proved 16 July, 1777, m. Clara (d. 2 Aug. 1746), dau. and co-heir of Michael Ambrose, of Dublin, and sister of Lady Palmer, "the dangerous Papist," and had issue, two sons, 1. JOHN, his heir, and 2. James, who went abroad, and three daus, 1. Rose, m. Darby O'Grady; 2. Frances, d. 1794; and 3. Eleanor, m. Anthony Brown. The eldest son,
JOHN SEGRAVE, of Cabra, m. Anne, dau. of William Nugent, styled Lord Riverston, and had issue,
1. O'NEILL, his heir. 2. William, d. unm.
3. Thomas, of Dublin, m. Anne, dau. of Peter Greban, by Mary his wife, dau. of Stephen Roche, and d. 1817, leaving issue,
1. John, dec.
2. O'Neill, late Inniskilling Dragoons, m. Frances, 2nd dau. of Ambrose Harbord Stewart, of Stoke Park, Suffolk, and had issue. His eldest surviving son, Francis, d. 7 Jan. 1907.
3. Henry (Rev.), dec.
4. Stephen, b. 1808; m. Isabella, dau. of Lieut.-Gen. J. Birkenhead Gliegg, of Backford and Irbie, co. Chester; and d. 29 Jan. 1889, having had issue. 5. Peter (Rev.).
6. Thomas, Barrister-at-Law, m. Miss Hamilton, dau. of Dr. Hamilton, of Edinburgh; and d. 1846, leaving issue.
7. Patrick, J.P. co. Dublin, m. 1858, Henrietta Cecilia, dau. of Robert Daniell, D.L., of New Forest, co. Westmeath, and has issue,
(1) Thomas Louis, Capt. Royal Irish Regt., b. 20 Dec. 1861.
(2) John O'Neill, b. 31 Dec. 1864.
(3) Henry Francis, b. 1 Oct. 1866.
(1) Anne. (2) Mary Clare. (3) Cecilia.
1. Mary, m. Nicholas Whyte, of Loughbrickland.
2. Anne Frances, m. 1826, Hon. William Browne, and d.s.p.
3. Clara, m. John Lewis More O'Farrall, of Lissard, co. Longford.
4. Margaret, m. Hon. James O'Brien, one of the Judges of the Court of Queen's Bench in Ireland.
1. Henrietta, m. William Kellet, of Great Clonard.
2. Clara, m. Marcus Blake Lynch, of Barna.
3. Anne, m. Capt. Baldwin, R.A.
4. Frances, d. unm.
Mr. Segrave d. 1783, and was s. by his son,
O'NEILL SEGRAVE, of Cabra, m. Margaret, dau. of George Goold, of Cork, and by her (who m. 2ndly, John Agnew Connell), left at his decease, 1793, a son and successor,
HENRY JOHN SEGRAVE, of Cabra, m. 1817, his cousin Anna Frances, dau. of William Kellet, of Great Clonard, co. Wexford, and had issue,
1. O'NEILL, of Cabra. 2. HENRY, late of Kiltimon.
3. William Francis, late Capt. 71st Highlanders, b. 16 Oct. 1826; m. 17 March, 1868, Isabella, dau. of Major Haliburton, 78th Highlanders, and d. 10 April, 1903, leaving issue,
1. John Roderick, Capt. R.N., b. 8 Nov. 1871; m. 15 Jan. 1907, Mary Stephenie, youngest dau. of late Frederick Ricardo, of 40, Onslow Gardens, S.W., and has issue,
William Francis Roderick, b. 2 Nov. 1907.
Rosemary, b. 13 May, 1911.
2. William Henry Eric, D.S.O., Capt. Highland L.I., b. 26 Nov. 1875; m. 1904, Nellie Borlase, dau. of the late Vice-Adm. J. J. Kennedy, C.B., and has issue,
Pamela Frances, b. 8 Oct. 1907.
1. Ivy, b. 12 Sept. 1874; m. 9 Jan. 1906, Gerald Arthur Arundel, and has issue (see BURKE's Peerage, ARUNDELL of Wardour, B.).
4. Thomas, R.M., late Capt. 14th Foot, m. 15 Aug. 1854, Louisa Mary, dau. of Major William Buckley, late 18th Regt., and has issue,
1. Henry John, b. 9 Nov. 1861.
2. Thomas George (The Cottage, Great Warley, Essex), Surveyor of Shipping to the India Office, late Lieut. Commander U.S.N., b. 26 May, 1864; m. July, 1895, Harriet Daly, sister of the late William Daly, of Dunsandle (see that family).
1. Claire Mary, m. 8 May, 1884, James Lombard Cotter, son of Sir James Cotter, 4th bart., who d. 12 April, 1893. She m. 2ndly, 1897, John Francis O'Connor, and d. 2 April, 1910, leaving issue by her 1st marriage, James Laurence (present Baronet), and Thomas Lombard, and by her 2nd husband a son and a dau.
Mr. Segrave d. 1843, and was s. by his eldest son,
O'NEILL SEGRAVE, of Kiltimon and Cabra, D.L., High Sheriff of co. Wicklow 1870, an Officer 7th Dragoon Guards, m. 23 May, 1848, Matilda, 3rd dau. of John Hyacinth Talbot, of Castle Talbot, co. Wexford, M.P.; and d.s.p. 25 June, 1878, and was s. by his brother.
HENRY SEGRAVE, of Kiltimon, co. Wicklow, of Cabra, co. Dublin, and of Calla, co. Galway, J.P. and D.L. cos. Dublin and Wicklow High Sheriff 1893, late Capt. 12th Foot, b. 1823; m. 1850, Mary Elizabeth (now of Cabra and Kiltimon), dau. of Edward Francis Debane, of The Beeches, co. Stafford, and d. 16 Sept. 1906, leaving issue,

1. O'NEILL EDWARD JOHN, now of Kiltimon.
2. Walter Henry, d. 1910.
3. Charles William, J.P. cos. Galway and Tipperary, m. 1st, 27 April, 1893, Mary Lucy, dau. of James K. Harwood, late U.S. Navy, and grand-dau. of the late Right Rev. James Kemp, Archbishop of Maryland, U.S.A.; 2ndly, 11 June, 1901, Jessie Campbell, dau. of John Stone, of Huyton, Lancashire.
1. Frances Emma, m. 1st, 21 Nov. 1876, Sir John Talbot Power, 3rd bart., who d. 4 Dec. 1901, leaving issue (see BURKE's Peerage, POWER of Edermine). She m. 2ndly, 23 July, 1904, Anthony Loftus Cliffe, of Bellevue, J.P. and D.L. (see that family).
2. Mary Clare, m. 31 Jan. 1889, Hon. George Stopford, 3rd son of the Earl of Courtown, and has issue (see BURKE's Peerage, COURTOWN, E.).
3. Edith Blanche, m. 4 Sept. 1890, Henry Close, son of Maxwell Close, J.P. and D.L., of Drumbanagher, Newry, and has issue (see that family).

Arms—Quarterly: 1st and 4th, arg., on a bend gu. three trefoils or (for SEGRAVE); 2nd and 3rd, az., three eagles displayed or (for WAFER). Crest—A demi-lion rampant arg., between the paws a branch of oak ppr., fructed or. Motto—Dieu et mon roi.
Seats—Cabra House, co. Dublin; Kiltimon, Newtownmountkennedy. co. Wicklow, and Calla House, Kilconnell, co. Galway, St. Antoine, St. Servan, France.

SEYMOUR OF BALLYMORE CASTLE.

THOMAS PATRICK DUNBAR SEYMOUR, of Ballymore Castle, J.P. co. Galway, b. 4 Oct. 1865.

Lineage.—During the reign of WILLIAM III, two brothers, Thomas Seymour and John Seymour, went to Ireland as Officers in the English army, and settled in Connaught. From the elder, THOMAS, derive the SEYMOURS of Ballymore Castle, and from the younger, JOHN, the SEYMOURS of Somerset, co. Galway. An elder brother of these d.s.p., leaving his property to his only sister, who m. Col. Sadleir.
THOMAS SEYMOUR, m. 1735, Belinda, dau. of A. O'Madden, of Clare Madden, co. Galway, and had one son, JOSEPH, his heir, and two daus., Catherine, m. Samuel Harrison, of Spruce Hill, co. Galway, and Belinda, m. Robin Cooke, of Galway. The son and heir,
JOSEPH SEYMOUR, m. 1760, Susanna, widow of A. Thomas, and had issue, three sons and two daus.,
1. THOMAS, of whom presently.
2. Charles, Vicar of Kilronan, m. Beata, dau. of Fergus Langley, of Knockanure, co. Tipperary, and was father, inter alios, of William Digby Seymour, Q.C., M.P. for Sunderland 1852-5, and for Southampton 1859-65, m. 1847, Emily, dau. of Joseph J. Wright.
3. Robert, who settled at Clonfert, co. Galway.
1. Eliza, m. Robert Drought, of Ridgemount, King's Co.
2. Charlotte, m. William Bird, M.D., of Birdville, King's Co.
The eldest son,
THOMAS SEYMOUR, of Ballymore Castle, m. 1786, Jane, only dau. and heir of David Thompson, of Banagher, and d. 17 June, 1821, having by her (who d. 1847) had issue,
1. THOMAS, of whom presently.
2. David (Rev.), m. 1st, 1821, Eliza, dau. of S. Bindon, of Cloona, co. Clare, and by her had three sons and a dau. He m. 2ndly, Sarah, dau. of R. Butler, of co. Carlow.
3. Henry, m. Eliza, dau. of Robert Drought, of Ridgemount, King's Co., and has issue.
1. Eleanor, m. 1810, Peter Lambert, of Castle Ellen, co. Galway, and d. 20 Nov. 1828, having by him (who d. 17 Jan. 1844) had issue (see that family).
2. Charlotte, m. 1st, Giles Eyre Blake, of Moorfield, co. Galway, and has had issue. She m. 2ndly, the late William Grome, of Sycamore Hill, co. Galway.
3. Lavinia, m. Richard Galbraith, of Cappard, co. Galway, and of Belgair, co. Stirling, N.B., and d. 1832, having had issue.
His eldest son,
THOMAS SEYMOUR, of Ballymore Castle, Galway, J.P., Barrister-at-Law, Lieut.-Col. co. Galway Militia, High Sheriff King's Co. 1859, b. Dec. 1793; m. July, 1822, Matilda Margaret, dau. of Walter Lawrence, of Lisreaghan, co. Galway, and d. 20 Jan. 1881, leaving issue,
1. WALTER, late of Ballymore Castle.
2. John Thompson, b. Feb. 1826; m. 14 Oct. 1854, Louisa, 2nd dau. of the late John Cuss, of Chisenbury, Wilts, and dying 1868, left issue,
1. Thomas. 2. Allen.
1. Anne. 2. Matilda.
3. David Thompson, late 12th Regt., formerly A.D.C. and Private Secretary to Sir George Bowen, Governor of Queensland, Commissioner of Police in Queensland, b. 5 Nov. 1831; m. in Queensland.
1. Catherine Mary, d. unm. 1843.
2. Margaret Matilda, m. 20 Dec. 1859, Henry Blake Mahon, only son and heir of Major Thomas Mahon, of Belvill, co. Galway, and d. 1871, leaving issue.
3. Eleanora Alice, m. 13 June, 1862, Henry Sadleir Persse, of Glenarde, co. Galway, 2nd son of Burton Persse, of Moyode Castle, co. Galway, and d. 17 June, 1890, leaving issue (see PERSSE of Roxborough).
The eldest son,
WALTER SEYMOUR, of Ballymore Castle, co. Galway, J.P., Secretary to the Grand Jury of co. Galway, b. 3 Nov. 1824; m. 19 Dec. 1859, Belinda Jane Dunbar, only child of Rev A. L. Gordon. She d. 20 Jan. 1887. He d. 3 April, 1892, leaving issue,

1. THOMAS PATRICK DUNBAR, now of Ballymore Castle.
2. William Alexander Robert, M.D., b. 18 Dec. 1866 ; d. 12 Feb. 1893.
3. Walter Gordon, J.P. co. Galway, b. 3 Oct. 1869.
1. Belinda Jane Dunbar, d. 9 April, 1869.
2. Kathleen Mary.   3. Margaret Matilda.
4. Ellen Dunbar.   5. Jane Margaret.
6. Lilias Dun, m. 4 June, 1902, Henry Worsley Gough, Connaught Rangers.

Seat—Ballymore Castle, Ballinasloe.

SEYMOUR OF KILLAGALLY.

CHARLES BARHAM EYRE SEYMOUR, of Killagally Park, King's Co., J.P., B.A. Trin. Coll. Dublin, late Lieut. 1st Batt. Leinster Regt. and 3rd Batt. Connaught Rangers, b. 9 Dec. 1848 ; m. 9 Jan. 1879, Grace Anne Foster, dau. of the late Rev. Richard Foster Carter, Rector of Rowner, Fareham, Hants, of Eastbottom, Deal, Kent, and Bury Grange, Alverstoke, Hants, and has issue,

1. CHARLES RICHARD FOSTER, Captain Indian Army (13th Rajputs), p.s.c. formerly Hampshire Regt., B.A., Trin. Coll. Dublin, b. 9 April, 1880 ; m. the eldest dau. of Col. Leslie Bishop, of Ealing.
2. Henry Bolingbroke, b. 12 Nov. 1881.
1. Florence Mary Clavell.   2. Emily Grace.
3. Helen Eva Elliott.
4. Edith Rowena Dorothy Vaughan.

Lineage.— RICKARD EYRE SEYMOUR, of Lisnacody, Cloughbrack, co. Galway, m. Hannah, dau. of Charles Donelan, of Lisnacody, and had issue,
1. Thomas, of Cloughbrack, m. Miss Bloomfield, and had issue, now extinct in the male line.
2. EYRE, of whom presently.
1. Elizabeth, m. Capt. Thomas Harrison, 62nd Regt. and 110th Regt., Paymaster of the Galway Militia.
2. Jane.   3. Anne.

The 2nd son,
BYRE SEYMOUR, of Lisnacody, co. Galway, m. Kitty, dau. of John Bolingbroke, of Old Castle, co. Mayo, and d. 20 July, 1852, having had issue,
1. DONELAN BOLINGBROKE, of whom presently.
2. Edward.
1. Elizabeth.   2. Kate.

The elder son,
REV. DONELAN BOLINGBROKE SEYMOUR, M.A., T.C.D., Rural Dean of Clonmacnois, b. 18 June, 1815 ; m. 1st, 1840, Harriette, dau. of Lieut.-Col. Sir Joseph Brooke, son of Sir Samuel Brooke (Bart.), and had issue,
1. Edward, settled in Sydney, N.S.W.
1. Louisa, } m., and settled in America.
2. Lizzie,
3. Harriette.
He m. 2ndly, 22 Feb. 1848, Augusta Emily, dau. of Rev. Thomas Shuttleworth Grimshawe, M.A. Cantab., Rector of Burton-Latimer, Northants, and Vicar of Bidenham, Beds, and d. 26 April, 1884, having by her (who d. 14 Oct. 1880) had issue,
2. CHARLES BARHAM EYRE, now of Killagally.
4. Charlotte Anne Caroline Vaughan, m. Sept. 1878, Rev. R. C. Clarke.
5. Georgiana Emily Ida, m. April, 1877, Richard William Foster Carter, M.D.

Seat—Killagally Park, Belmont, R.S.O., King's Co.

SEYMOUR OF LIMERICK.

JOHN NICHOLSON SEYMOUR, b. 11 Sept. 1858, M.B. Dublin (1882), Professor at Tokyo, Japan ; m. 1886, Isuru Nagai, dau. of Mr. Yosuke Nagai, of Yokohama, and has issue,

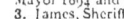

1. CHARLES NICHOLSON, b. 1894.
1. Hannah.
2. Clara Maria, m. 1907, Richard Aylmer Coates.
3. Lily.
4. Eva Botan.

Lineage.—EDWARD SEYMOUR, m. a dau. of William Hartwell, Alderman of Limerick and Mayor 1659, and had issue, a son,
JOHN SEYMOUR, Alderman of Limerick, Sheriff 1708, Mayor 1720 ; d. 1735 ; m. Jane, dau. of Seymour Wroughton, and had issue,

1. JOHN, his heir.
2. William, m. Jane, dau. of Edward Wight, Alderman of Limerick, Mayor 1694 and 1711, and left issue (see CULME-SEYMOUR, Bart.).
3. James, Sheriff of Limerick 1728 ; m. a dau. of Ezekiel Holland, Mayor of Limerick 1718, no surviving issue.
4. Richard, Sheriff of Limerick 1730.
5. Walter, Sheriff of Limerick 1742, m. Margaret, dau. of David Bindon, Sheriff of Limerick 1716, s.p.

The eldest son,
JOHN SEYMOUR, of Dublin, d. 1754 ; m. Frances, elder dau. and co-heir of Aaron Crossley (author of The Peerage of Ireland) by Abigail, dau. of Pierre André Perscheau, of Saumur, and by her (who d. April, 1700) had an only son,
AARON CROSSLEY SEYMOUR, of Castletown, Queen's Co., d. 1787 ; m. 8 June, 1754, Margaret, 2nd dau. of Matthew Cassan, of Sheffield, Queen's Co. (see that family), and by her (who d. 25 Jan. 1812) had issue,
1. JOHN CROSSLEY, his heir.
2. Matthew Cassan, m. 1st, Frances Smith, who d. 1811, and had four sons,
1. Aaron Crossley, H.E.I.C.S., d.s.p.
2. Graves Chamney, H.E.I.C.S., d.s.p.
3. Matthew, d.s.p.   4. John, d.s.p.
He m. 2ndly, Maria, dau. of Rev. Roger Curtis, s.p.
3. Aaron Crossley, d. 1828, H.E.I.C.S., Registrar to the Secretary of the Revenue and Judicial Depts., Bengal ; m. 1st, Maria, dau. of Dr. Hogarth, and by her (who d. 31 July, 1816) had a dau.,
1. Frances Maria, m. her cousin John Crossley Seymour, of Coolnagower.
He m. 2ndly, Margaret Brown, and had two sons and three daus.,
1. Charles Crossley, H.E.I.C.S.
2. Samuel Francis, H.E.I.C.S.
2. Jane Helen.   3. Elizabeth Maria.
4. Margaret Moore.
4. Stephen, Capt. R.N., d. unm.

The eldest son,
REV. JOHN CROSSLEY SEYMOUR, B.A. (Dublin), Vicar of Cahirelly, d. 19 May, 1831 ; m. Jan. 1789, Catherine, dau. of Rev. Edward Wight, Rector of Meelick, co. Limerick, and had eight sons and seven daus.,
1, Aaron Crossley, of Castletown House, Queen's Co., b. 19 Dec. 1789 ; d. 22 Oct. 1870 ; m. 3 April, 1818, Anne, only dau. and heir of John Geale, of Mount Geale, co. Kilkenny, and by her (who d. 28 Feb. 1825) had with two daus., who d. young, a son and a dau.,
John Crossley Geale, b. 11 Nov. 1819 ; d. 14 Jan. 1849 ; m. 19 June, 1845, Caroline Mary Anne, dau. of Capt. Francis Baker, R.N., but had no issue by her, who m. 2ndly, 17 Aug. 1858, Henry Chaytor, of Witton Castle, Durham.
Catherine Elizabeth Frances, m. 21 Sept. 1846, Joseph Seymour Kane.
2. Edward Wight, b. 25 Jan. 1791 ; d. 3 Nov. 1870 ; m. 4 June, 1822, Margaret, dau. of Peter Roe, of Rockville, co. Dublin, and by her (who d. 16 Feb. 1878) had three sons and three daus.,
1. John Wight Hobart, M.A. (Dublin), m. 1st, 3 Oct. 1861, Emma Isabella, dau. of Rev. Charles Marlay Fleury, D.D., and by her (d. 29 Sept. 1870) had a son, Edward. He m. 2ndly, 11 Dec. 1874, Alice Elizabeth, dau. of Laurence Parsons, of Parsonstown, King's Co.
2. Edward Roe (Rev.), M.A. Dublin and Oxon, Precentor Christ Church Cathedral, Dublin, m. 22 Oct. 1874, Annie Frances, dau. of Joseph Seymour Kane, and had issue, three daus.
3. Robert George, m. 1 June, 1866, Georgina Adelaide, dau. of William Henry Birch, of Roscrea, co. Tipperary, and had issue, two daus.
1. Margaret Emily.   2. Henrietta Georgina.
3. Frances Maria Victoria, m. 4 May, 1872, Richard Pennefather, of Milford, co. Tipperary.
3. JOHN CROSSLEY, of whom presently.
4. Matthew Cassan, b. 1794 ; d. 1855, Barrister, King's Inn 1823, m. 1842, Elizabeth, dau. of Admiral Edward O. Osborne, R.N, s.p.
5. Stephen Sheffield, B.A. (Dublin, m. Selina, dau. of Edward Harte, M.D., of Dunow, Queen's Co., s.p.
6. William Hobart, d. unm.
7. Michael Hobart (Rev.), M.A. (Dublin) and Oxon, b. Sept. 1800 ; d. June, 1871 ; m. Jan. 1844, Maria Elizabeth, widow of the Baron Mill, dau. of Gen. Thomas, H.E.I.C.S. She d.s.p. 23 Oct. 1881.
8. Richard Hobart, M.A. (Dublin and Oxon), M.B. (Dublin) m. 21 June, 1848, Frances Nina, dau. of Admiral John Impey.
1. Frances, m. 28 Nov. 1816, Joseph Thomas Kane (see KANE of Drumreaske).
2. Jane, d. unm.
3. Margaretta Eliza, d. unm. 19 June, 1819.
4. Catherine, d. unm.
5. Eliza, d. unm.
6. Mary Anne, m. 2 Nov. 1822, Robert Rundell Guinness, of Stillorgan Park, co. Dublin.
7. Charlotte Alicia, d. unm. 19 April, 1819.

The 3rd son,
JOHN CROSSLEY SEYMOUR, of Coolnagower, Queen's Co., b. 18 Jan. 1793 ; d. 1884, Commander R.N. ; m. 1st, 11 May, 1818, Frances Maria, dau. of Aaron Crossley Seymour, H.E.I.C.S. She d. 4 Dec. 1870. He m. 2ndly, 11 Oct. 1877, Harriet, dau. of Cuthbert Eccles, of Dublin. By his 1st wife he had an only surviving son,
REV. JOHN HOBART SEYMOUR, b. 31 Aug. 1830 ; d. 1897, M.A. (Dublin), Incumbent of Newcastle, co. Down ; m. 1st, 16 May, 1856, Lily Anna Floyer, dau. of Alexander Jaffray Nicholson, M.D., and sister of Brig.-Gen. John Nicholson. She d. 14 Aug. 1862. He m.

andly, 4 June, 1867, Matilda, dau. of William Stevenson, of Belfast. By his 1st wife he had a son and a dau.,
JOHN NICHOLSON, his heir.
Clara.
Arms—Az., a pair of wings conjoined in lure, surmounted by a mural crown or. Crest—Out of a mural crown a phœnix or, in flames ppr. Motto—Foy pour devoir.
Residence—Tokyo, Japan ; 23, Upper Pembroke Street, Dublin.

SHARMAN-CRAWFORD. See CRAWFORD.

SHAWE-TAYLOR. See TAYLOR.

SHELTON OF BRUREE HOUSE.

JOHN WILLINGTON CLARENS ORBY SHELTON, of Bruree House, co. Limerick, b. 1893.
Lineage.—JOHN SHELTON, Capt. 1st Royal Dragoons, of Ireland, temp. Queen ANNE ; d. at Ghent in the Netherlands while serving under the Duke of Marlborough, leaving a son and heir,
ROBERT SHELTON, of Rossmore House, co. Limerick, J.P., m. Margaret, dau. of Giles Powell, of Houndscourt, co. Cork, and left a son and successor,
JOHN SHELTON, of Rossmore House, J.P., m. 1789, Elizabeth, dau. of John Willington, of Castle Willington, co. Tipperary, and had issue,
1. JOHN WILLINGTON, his heir.
1. Mary, m. Thomas Hayes, of Sunbury.
2. Alicia, m. John Chapman, of Castle Mitchell.
The only son,
JOHN WILLINGTON SHELTON, of Rossmore House, J.P., Capt. in the Army, served throughout the Peninsular War with the 28th Foot, and was in the battle of Waterloo, in which he was four times severely wounded, appointed subsequently for his service, Adjutant of the Royal Surrey Militia, b. 1791 ; m. 14 Aug. 1817, Mary, dau. of John Richards, of Blackdown House, co. Southampton, by whom (who d. 16 March, 1874) he had issue,
1. GRANTLEY JOHN WILLINGTON (Rev.), of Rossmore House, b. 1 April, 1820 ; m. 11 Oct. 1847, Rosa (d. 27 July, 1908), dau. of Read Robert Hill, of Cringleford, Norfolk, and d. 8 July, 1882, leaving issue,
GRANTLEY DEANE, of Rossmore House, co. Limerick, formerly Lieut. Royal Limerick Fusiliers (Militia), b. 7 Feb. 1852 ; m. 28 March, 1882, Emma Anne, dau. of Edward Atkinson, J.P., of Glenwilliam Castle, co. Limerick (see that family), and has issue,
(1) Augustus Grantley, b. 15 March, 1883 ; d. 27 Aug. 1883.
(2) DEANE GRANTLEY, b. 19 July, 1886.
(3) Edward Willington, b. 15 Aug. 1889.
(4) Augustus Curlrin, b. 11 Dec. 1890.
(1) Mary Olive Emma, b. 7 March, 1884.
(2) Rosa Kathleen, b. 17 Sept. 1887
(3) Rowena Mary, b. 15 April, 1892.
(4) Emma Nora, b. 11 Dec. 1893.
Mary.
2. George Augustus Frederick, M.B., Surgeon-Gen. in the Army (half pay), formerly of the 60th Rifles and 48th Foot, b. Oct. 1821 ; d. 12 Oct. 1895.
3. JONATHAN ROBERT WILLINGTON, of whom presently.
Mr. Shelton d. 19 July, 1847. His 3rd son,
JONATHAN ROBERT WILLINGTON SHELTON, of Bruree House, co. Limerick, J.P., late Lieut.-Col. Royal Limerick Fusiliers (Militia) sometime Lieut. in the 14th and 28th Regts., b. 19 Nov. 1826 ; m. 4 July, 1848, Emily Mary, dau. of Read Robert Hill, of Cringleford, Norfolk, and d. 1892, leaving issue,
1. WILLINGTON AUGUSTUS DAVID, late of Bruree House.
2. Abbott George, b. 21 Sept. 1853.
The elder son,
WILLINGTON AUGUSTUS DAVID SHELTON, D.S.O., of Bruree House, co. Limerick, Lieut.-Col. (retired) late Major 3rd Batt. Queen's Regt., formerly an Officer 62nd Regt., served throughout S. African War 1899-1902, twice mentioned in despatches, two medals, b. 14 May, 1849 ; m. 1st, 1877, May, dau. of Henry Goodlake, of Benhams, Worcestershire ; 2ndly, Victoria, dau. of John Chancellor ; and 3rdly, 1889, Florence Lockhart, dau. of Edward Campbell, of Stapleton, co. Gloucester. He d. 14 June, 1909. She d. 18 June, 1905, leaving issue,
JOHN WILLINGTON CLARENS ORBY, now of Bruree.
Violet Mary Pauline, b. 1892.

SHELTON OF THE ARGORY.

CAPT. RALPH MACGEOUGH-BOND-SHELTON, of the Argory, co. Armagh, J.P. and D.L., late 12th Royal Lancers and as Cornet in that Regt. was in the wreck of H.M.S. Birkenhead on the 26th February, 1852, off Cape of Good Hope, adopted the name of SHELTON ; m. 21 May, 1873, Caroline (d. 27 Nov. 1907) dau. of Arthur Nepean Molesworth, of Fairlawn, co. Armagh (see BURKE'S Peerage, MOLESWORTH, V.). Capt. R. MacGeough-Bond-Shelton is the 2nd son of the late Walter MacGeough-Bond, of Drumsill, co. Armagh, who assumed the name and arms of BOND by Royal Licence 1824, and d. 17 March, 1866 (see that family), and Anne, his wife, who d. 1892, dau. of Ralph Smyth, of Gaybrook (see that family).
Lineage—See MACGEOUGH-BOND of Drumsill.
Seat—The Argory, Moy, co. Armagh. Clubs—Travellers', Army and Navy, and Kildare Street.

SHEPPARD OF KILCUNAHANBEG (FORMERLY called CLIFTON).

HENRY GODDINGTON SHEPPARD, of Kilcunahanbeg (formerly called Clifton), co Tipperary, J.P., Capt. and Hon. Major late 3rd Batt. Leinster Regt., served in South African War (two medals), b. 17 Jan. 1869 ; m. 9 Jan. 1895, Mabel Frances, dau. of Craven Westenra Doolan, son of Palmer Doolan, J.P., of Derry House, Shinrone, and has issue,
Winifred Agnes, b. 1900.
Lineage.—Two brothers, THOMAS and WILLIAM SHEPPARD, settled in Ireland. The latter was the ancestor of Sheppard of Kilcunahanbeg (see below). The former,
CAPT. THOMAS SHEPPARD, who came over in Cromwell's Army, was Governor of New Ross, co. Wexford, in 1659. He received a grant of 1,439 acres at Castle John, co. Tipperary (Act of Settlement enrolled 12 Dec. 1666), and in his will, dated 1670, proved 1671, he mentions his son, THOMAS, of whom next, his four daus., and his brother, William. The son,
THOMAS SHEPPARD, of Castle John, co. Tipperary, J.P. 1724 ; will dated 3 Dec. 1723, proved 3 June, 1724 ; m. Mary —, and had, with other issue,
THOMAS SHEPPARD, of Castle John, co. Tipperary, m. (sett. 2 May, 1721) Hannah, dau. of Sir John Mason, of Waterford, by whom he had issue with three daus., Mary, m. 1743, Thomas Hackett of Gamlestown, co. Tipperary; Jane, m. 7 Sept. 1748, Henry Alcock of Waterford; Susannah, m.— Paul.
JOHN SHEPPARD, of Castle John and of Loughborough, co. Kilkenny, d. 1786 ; will dated 17 Mar. 1781, pr. 31 May, 1786; m. 1st, Ellen, dau. of William Hore, of Harperstown, co. Wexford, by whom he had issue,
1. THOMAS, of whom next.
2. John, Major 13th Dragoons, d.s.p.
He m. 2ndly (marriage setts. 1755), Anne, dau. of George Read, of Snugborough, co. Kilkenny, and had further issue,
3. George, m. 1789, Mary, dau. of William Alcock, and had issue, William, of Kiltrassy, co. Kilkenny, m. 1823, Dorothea Anne, dau. of William Morris, of Harbour View, co. Waterford, and had issue an only child,
Mary Elizabeth, d. 1834 ; m. 1848, George Sutherland, of Forse, Caithness.
1. Anne, m. 1774, Lieut. Benjamin Morris, 3rd Regiment of Horse.
The eldest son,
REV. THOMAS SHEPPARD, of Castle John, m. 1st (setts. 1770) Hannah, dau. and co-heir of Edward Dawson, of Whitefield, co. Tipperary, and had issue,
1. John, d.s.p.
2. Thomas, of whom next.
He m. 2ndly, Susannah, dau. of — Bull, of Waterford, and by her had issue,
3. Ponsonby, R.N.
The second son,
THOMAS SHEPPARD, of Edwardstown, co. Wexford, M.F.H. Waterford, d. 1865; m. Eliza, dau. of Samuel Meade Hobson, Q.C., of Muckridge, co. Cork, and had issue,
1. Thomas Dawson, Col. late King's Own Royal Lancaster Regt., J.P. cos. Wexford and Gloucester, served in Crimean War 1854-5, present at Alma, Inkerman, Sebastopol, and in Indian Mutiny 1857-8, has fifth class Medjidie (The Grange, Shanklin, Isle of Wight; Army and Navy Club; Kildare Street Club), b. — ; m. 1863, Georgiana, only dau. of George Lees, J.P., of Werneth Hall, Lancs, and has issue,
1. Thomas Dawson Lees, M.V.O., Capt. R.N. (Elm Cottage, Shiplake, Henley-on-Thames), b. 7 April, 1866 ; m. March, 1904, Mona, widow of Major Holden, Berkshire Regt.
2. George Sidney, Major Indian Army, b. 1 Nov. 1867; m. 1896, Constance, dau. of the late Colonel Dickson, R.A.
3. Herbert Cecil, Major R.F.A, b. 23 July, 1869.
1. Marie Georgina, m. Major C. N. Evelegh, who d. Dec. 1907.
2. John, d. in New Zealand ; m. and had issue, a dau., Lily Maud.
3. Henry, Capt. 34th Regt., m. Lily Hamilton, dau. of — Campbell.
4. Ponsonby, Major-General, late Col. 2nd East India Regt., b. 1842 ; d. Feb. 1909 ; m. Miss Levy, of Jamaica, and had issue,

IRELAND. Sherlock.

Ponsonby, D.S.O., Capt. R.F.A., served in S. African War, 1899-1901, action of Nonclweni, *b.* 10 Jan. 1879, *m.* 8 Dec. 1906, Nellie Marion, eldest dau. of Henry Adler, of Dornfontein, Johannesburg. S. Africa.
5. Richard Meade. *m.* Miss Innes, and had issue, a dau.
1. Martha, *m.* John Milward, of Loxley.
2. Hannah, *m.* Col. Alex. Green Grant, 85th Light Infantry.
3. Eliza, *m.* William Michael Ardagh.
4. Victoria Eleanor, *m.* J. E. Tarleton.

We now return to William Sheppard first mentioned, brother of Capt. Thomas Sheppard. This
WILLIAM SHEPPARD, of Ballinageelogue, co. Wexford. He had a son,
JAMES SHEPPARD, settled at Kilcunahanbeg, in the year 1699, *b.* 1678; *m.* 1st, Mary, dau. of R. Asheton, of Cullen, co. Wicklow, and had with a dau., Esther, *b.* 1699, a son,
1. William, of Castle Sheppard, co. Tipperary, *b.* 24 Oct. 1703; *d.* 1762; *m.* Edith, dau. of — Bradshaw, and widow of Thomas Robicson, and mother of Gen. Robert Robinson, and had issue, William, of Castle Sheppard, *b.* 2 Oct. 1739; *d.* 1800: *m.* 1766, Mary, dau. of John Shortt, of Wingfield, Shinrone, and had issue,
(1) Robert Robinson, H.E.I.C.S., Adjutant Madras Regt., *b.* 1765; *d. unm.* in India 10 Nov. 1800.
(2) John, Lieut. 85th Regt., *b.* 1778; *d.* at Port Royal in India 29 July, 1802.
(3) William, of Castle Sheppard, *b.* 1781; *m.* 1809, Eliza, dau. of Capt. Robert Bradshaw, 5th Dragoon Gds., of Aileen, co. Tipperary, and *d.s.p.* 14 Nov. 1852.
(1) Edith, *b.* 1772; *m.* Randal Cooke, and had issue.
(2) Sara Maria, *b.* 1774; *m.* Christopher Abbott.
He *m.* 2ndly, 1711, Mary Robinson, by whom he had issue,
2. JAMES, of whom presently.

The 2nd son,
JAMES SHEPPARD, of Kilcunahanbeg, *b.* 13 Nov. 1712; *m.* Mary, dau. of William Wyllie, of Annagh, co. Westmeath, and had a son,
JAMES SHEPPARD, of Kilcunahanbeg, *b.* 5 Aug. 1755; *m.* 1779, Mary, dau. of John Gilbert, of Cloughane, Holycross, co. Tipperary, and *d.* 1780, leaving a son,
JAMES SHEPPARD (who changed the name of his house to Clifton), *b.* 1780, Capt. in Tipperary Militia; *m.* 1808, Mary, dau. of Thomas Doolan, of Wingfield, Shinrone, by Mary, dau. of Amos Palmer, of Derry House, King's Co., and *d.* 1866, leaving issue, with two sons, Arthur, *b.* 1828, who went to Australia, and Charles, *b.* 1832, who went to Canada, and seven others, who *d.s.p.*
1. William (Rev.), M.A., T.C.D., Rector of Kilgiffen, formerly a Barrister-at-Law, *b.* 1811; *m.* Bithia, dau. of Leonard Watson, of Warrenpoint, and *d.* 1855, leaving issue,
William Harry Cope, of Newstead, Blackrock, *d.s.p.* 1907.
Bithia Mary, authoress of *Pretty Miss Neville, Diana Barrington*, &c., *m.* Lieut.-Col. J. Croker, Munster Fusiliers, of Drumkeen, co. Limerick, and has issue, a dau., Eileen, *m.* Col. Albert Whitaker, of Babworth Hall, Notts.
2. HENRY, of whom presently.
3. Frank, of St. Cronan's, Roscrea, *b.* 1826; *m.* 1856, his 2nd cousin, Sara Maria, dau. of Thomas ffranck Goulding, and *d.* 27 Nov. 1886, leaving issue,
1. John Frank, B.A., T.C.D., Major Royal Dublin Fusiliers, Commandant of Gambaga during Ashanti War (medal), *b.* 26 April, 1859; *d.* 11 June, 1901.
2. James William ffranck (Rev.), M.A. (Dublin), Rector of Wouldham, Kent, author of "A Song of Truth and other verses," *b.* 1866; *m.* 20 Jan. 1904, Louisa Frances, dau. of Thomas Rothwell, J.P. and D.L., of Rockfield (*see that family*), and has issue,
(1) Mervyn Cecil ffranck } twins, *b.* 21 June, 1905.
(2) Francis Baden ffranck }
(3) Raymond Thomas Rothwell, *b.* 5 Nov. 1907.
1. Grace, *b.* 1857, *d.* 1876.
2. Mary Eleanor, *m.* Rev. H. J. Gillespie, D.D., M.A. (Dublin), of Clontara Rectory, and has issue, 3 sons and 3 daus.
1. Maria, *m.* James Kennedy, of Spafield, Roscrea, and had one dau., Mary.
2. Frances Eleanor, *b.* 1816; *d.* 1848; *m.* 1840, John Smith, son of Robert Smith, of Lismacrory, and had issue, Abigail, *m.* Craven Westenra Doolan, son of Palmer Doolan, J.P., of Derry House, Shinrone, and had issue, Mabel, *m.* 9 Jan., 1895, CAPT. HENRY GODDINGTON SHEPPARD, now of Kilcunahanbeg (*see below*).

The 2nd son,
HENRY SHEPPARD, of Clifton, co. Tipperary, J.P., formerly Capt. Tipperary Militia, and Capt. 67th Regt., *b.* 28 July, 1823; *m.* 22 Aug. 1866, Emily Agnes, dau. of Joseph Frederick Ledsam, J.P., D.L., of Chad Hill, Edgbaston, Warwick, by his wife, Elizabeth Ann Ashton Goddington, and *d.* 9 Aug. 1893, leaving surviving issue,
1. HENRY GODDINGTON, now of Kilcunahanbeg.
2. James Frederick, L.R.C.S., L.R.C.P., *b.* 5 Aug. 1870; *m.* 19 Oct. 1891, Emmie, dau. of the late John Hesley, of Eye, Northampton, and has issue,
James Ledsam, *b.* 15 Aug. 1900.
Kathleen Emily Goddington, *b.* 22 May, 1902.
3. Thomas Moreton, Lieut. R.A., *b.* 10 Aug. 1874.
4. John Ashton, *b.* 24 April, 1876; *m.* 1st, 18 Oct. 1905, Patience (who *d.* 1908), dau. of Rev. George Benjamin Sweetman, of Aghadown Rectory, co. Cork. He *m.* 2ndly, 1 Nov. 1911, Alice Stewart, only dau. of Thomas Popham, M.D., of Bantry.

Arms—Az. on a chevron engrailed or, between three fleurs-delys arg., as many estoiles gu. Crest—A cubit arm vested az. cuffed arg., the hand holding a shepherd's crook ppr. Motto—Deus Pastor Meus.
Seat—Kilcunahanbeg, Shinrone, King's Co.

SHERLOCK OF RAHAN.

DAVID SHERLOCK, of Rahan Lodge, King's Co., J.P. and D.L., Barrister-at-Law, *b.* 27 March, 1850; *m.* 12 May, 1873, Mary Elizabeth, 2nd dau. of Edward Murphy, of Castle Connell, co. Limerick, and Elizabeth White his wife, and has issue,
1. DAVID CHRISTOPHER EUSTACE, *b.* 6 Jan. 1879.
2. Gerard Lourdes, *b.* 13 Dec. 1884.
3. Edward Mary, *b.* 8 May, 1886.

Lineage.—CHRISTOPHER SHERLOCK, of Littlerath and Derrindarragh, co. Kildare (son of Richard Sherlock, of Littlerath and Derrindarragh), was M.P. for Naas 1613, 1634, and 1639-42. By Elinor, his first wife, he had a son,
1. John (Sir), *b.* 1603, Gentleman of the Privy Chamber to CHARLES I., knighted 13 Jan. 1635, M.P. for co. Dublin 1642-9, bur. at St. Michan's 18 March, 1652. His will is dated 6 March, 1652. He *m.* 1st, a lady, whose name is unknown, and 2ndly, by licence in London 14 July, 1634, Katherine, dau. of — Ashburnham, but by her had no issue. His widow *m.* 31 Dec. 1660, John Preston, of Dublin, ancestor of PRESTON of *Swainstown*, and *d.* 10 Sept. 1665.
He *m.* 2ndly, Anne, dau. of James FitzGerald, of Osberstown, co. Kildare, and by her had, with other issue, a son,
2. PHILIP, *s.* to Littlerath.

The younger son,
PHILIP SHERLOCK, of Littlerath was decreed "Innocent" by the Court of Claims and restored to his estate 1662. He *m.* Elizabeth. dau. of William Eustace. He *d.* 18 May, 1684 (will dated 16 May, previously), and by her had (who *m.* 2ndly, Nicholas Adams) had issue,
1. CHRISTOPHER, his heir.
2. Laurence, *d.s.p.*
3. Eustace, of Drumlargin, co. Meath; *m.* Hester, dau. of — FitzSimon. His will, dated 16 June, was proved 14 Aug. 1707. He left a dau., Elizabeth.
4. Robert, *d. unm.* 5. Edward, *d. unm.*
6. John, *d. unm.* 7. William, *d. unm.*
1. Helen, *m.* — Bellew. 2. Mary, *d. unm.* 1695.
The eldest son,
CHRISTOPHER SHERLOCK, of Littlerath, Capt. in FitzJames' Regt. of Foot in King JAMES II.'s Army, was attainted in 1691 and his estate forfeited. He left issue,
1. THOMAS, his heir.
2. Eustace, *m.* 29 July, 1734, Jane, widow of — Wallace, and *d.* 14 March, 1762, leaving two daus., Margaret and Mary.
1. Elizabeth.
The elder son,
THOMAS SHERLOCK, of Dundrum, co. Dublin, *d.* 7 June, 1780; *m.* Mary, dau. of David Sutton, of New Ross. His will, dated 5 June, was proved 20 June, 1780. He left issue,
1. Christopher, *m.* Mary, dau. of Hugh O'Connor, of Dublin, and *d.s.p.* 1785.
2. DAVID, of whom presently.
1. Jane, *m.* John Goran Kennedy.
2. Anastasia.
The 2nd son,
DAVID SHERLOCK, of Dundrum, co. Dublin, *m.* Mary, dau. and co-heir of Timothy Mahon, of Dublin, and had issue,
1. THOMAS, his heir. 2. Timothy.
1. Margaret, *m.* Anne.
The elder son,
THOMAS SHERLOCK, of Laurel Lodge, Dundrum, *m.* March, 1808, Isabella, dau. of John Ball, of Dublin, and sister of the Right Hon. Nicholas Ball, Justice of the Common Pleas, and had issue,
1. DAVID, his heir.
2. John, of Rahan, King's Co., High Sheriff 1879, *d. unm.*
1. Isabella. Mary Anne.
3. Cecilia. 4. Anna Maria.
The elder son,
DAVID SHERLOCK, of Stillorgan Castle, co. Dublin, and 15, Harcourt Street, Dublin, Serjeant-at-Law, M.P. for the King's Co. 1868-80, called to the Irish Bar 1837, Q.C. 1855, Bencher of King's Inns 1868-80, *b.* 1816; *m.* 1843, Elizabeth, youngest dau. of John Thierri, and *d.* 16 April, 1884, having had issue,
1. Thomas Thierri, *b.* 1844; *d.* 5 March, 1905; *m.* 17 Feb. 1873, Letitia Mary, eldest dau. of Sir John Nugent, 3rd bart., of Ballinlough, and widow of Maj. Richard Connolly, of Green Park, co. Westmeath, and has issue,
David Thomas Joseph, *b.* 1881, B.A. (Dublin), Barrister-atlaw.
2. DAVID, now of Rahan.
3. John. 4. Charles Eustace.
1. Mary.
2. Elizabeth (Lily), *m.* 18 Aug. 1874, George Edward Ryan, D.L. of Inch, and *d.* 1878, leaving issue (*see that family*).

Arms—Per pale arg. and az., three fleurs-de-lys counterchanged. *Crest*—A pelican in her piety ppr.

Seat—Rahan Lodge, King's Co., and 71, Lower Leeson Street, Dublin.

SHIRLEY OF LOUGH FEA. See SHIRLEY OF ETTINGTON PARK, CO. WARWICK.

SHULDHAM OF BALLYMULVEY.

MOLYNEUX WILLIAM SHULDHAM, of Ballymulvey (Moigh House) and Ballymahon, co. Longford, High Sheriff 1895, b. 24 Aug. 1870; m. 2 Sept. 1896, Augusta Georgina, younger dau. of Col. George Knox, of Prehen, co. Derry (*see that family*).

Lineage.—WILLIAM SHULDHAM, of Shuldham Hall, in co. Norfolk, (3rd son of JOHN SHULDHAM, Lord of Shuldham and Marham). In his will, which is dated 30 April, 1578, he mentions his son and heir,

FRANCIS SHULDHAM, b. 1575, and entered at Caius Coll. Camb. 1589; m. 1st, 1 Oct. 1612 Mary, dau. and heir of Robert Travener, Lord of the Manor of Kettlestone, in co. Norfolk, and settled at Croxton in the adjoining parish of Fulmondeston. He m. 2ndly, Mary, dau. and heir of Robert Thornton, of Hingham, co. Norfolk, and had issue, four sons. His 2nd son,

LEMUEL SHULDHAM, was bapt. at Hingham, 4 April, 1627, and was entered at Caius Coll. Camb., in 1642. He settled at Walsingham, co. Norfolk, and by Eleanor his wife had three sons and two daus., all bapt. at Little Walsingham. After her husband's death, in or about 1638, the widow with her children removed to Dublin, where she died and was bur. in St. Bridget's Church, 11 July, 1703. Lemuel and Eleanor Shuldham had issue,
1. Francis (Rev.), of Dublin, bapt. 3 May, 1667; m. Mary, and had issue, a son and two daus., Mary and Eleanor.
2. LEMUEL (Rev.), of whom later.
3. EDMUND, of whom next.

The 3rd son,

EDMUND SHULDHAM, bapt. at Walsingham 14 Oct. 1669, was of Dublin and Ardtully, co. Kerry, 1708, Crown Solicitor 1713; m. Elizabeth, dau. and heir of Jeremy MacCarthy, of Lisnakelly, co. Limerick. By this lady (who d. in 1760, will at Dublin, and was bur. at St. Bridget's, Dublin, in the same grave as her husband) he had two sons and three daus.,
1. Lemuel, bapt. at St. Bridget's 18 Aug. 1712; bur. at St. Bridget's 2 July, 1713.
2. Edmund, mentioned in his father's will.
1. Helanor, bapt. at St. Bridget's 15 Dec. 1709; d. before 1722.
2. Catherine, bapt. at St. Bridget's 17 Jan. 1714; bur. at St. Bridget's 18 April, 1720.
3. Elizabeth, bapt. at St. Bridget's 11 April, 1720; m. 1745, Beverly Ussher, of Kilmeadon, co. Waterford, M.P.

In 1722 Edmund Shuldham made his will, which is dated 12 Oct. and was proved 4 March, 1723, at Dublin. He desires to be buried in St. Bridget's Church, "on the left side of my dear mother and in which place I have three dear children and a sister (Alice) buried" (15 Sept. 1711). He also mentions his two brothers, Revs. Francis and Lemuel Shuldham, and their children. He was s. by his son,

EDMUND SHULDHAM, m. (sett. 2 Dec. 1749) Judith, 2nd dau. of Capt. Arthur Ussher, of Cappagh, co. Waterford, and had issue by her, who m. 2ndly, John Creagh, of Castle Creagh, co. Cork,
1. Edmund, d.s.p. 1760.
2. ARTHUR LEMUEL, of Dunmanway, of whom below.
3. Thomas, Maj.-Gen. H.E.I.C.S., Bengal, m. Sophia, dau. of Dr. Hume, D.D., Bishop of Salisbury, and the Lady Mary his wife, and d. 1832, having had issue,
  1. John (Rev.), Christ Church, Oxford.
  2. Thomas, Gen. H.E.I.C.S., d. 1874.
1. Mary, m. Chief Justice Mackenzie, of Calcutta.
1. Lucy, m. Very Rev. Richard Bourne, Dean of Tuam.

Mr. Shuldham d. 1758, and was s. by his son,

ARTHUR LEMUEL SHULDHAM, of Dunmanway, co. Cork, and of Pallas Green, co. Limerick, late King's Dragoon Guards, b. May, 1753, who resided for many years at Deerpark, Devon, and was a D.L. for that co. and Lieut.-Col. in the East Devon Yeomanry Cavalry. He m. 1st, Katherine Maria, dau. of Sir William Anderson, 6th bart., of Broughton, and Lea Hall, co. Lincoln, and had by her,
1. EDMUND WILLIAM, his heir.
2. John George Evelyn, Lieut. R.N., dec.
3. Molyneux, Comm. R.N., m. 1820, Frances, dau. of Rev. T. Naunton Orgill Leman, of Brampton Hall, Suffolk, and d. 23 Feb. 1866, having by her (who d. 22 Jan. 1866) had issue,
  1. Arthur James, Col. late 2nd Batt. R. Inniskilling Fusiliers, of Melton, Sylvan Road, Upper Norwood, S.E., b. 13 Sept. 1823; m. 1st, 8 Jan. 1857, Katherine Dora, eldest dau. and co-heir of Rev. C. E. Dukinfield, late 7th Madras Cavalry, afterwards Vicar of Edenhall, co. Cumberland, and niece of Sir H. R. Dukinfield, Bart., and by her had issue,
    (1) Edmund Dukinfield, b. 29 Nov. 1857.
    (2) Molyneux Charles Dukinfield, b. 13 Aug. 1861.
    (3) Herbert Leman Dukinfield, b. 13 Feb. 1863.
    (1) Margaret Evelyn, m. Rev. A. E. Stewart, M.A., and left issue.
    (2) Geraldine Maud, m. 19 Jan. 1901, Henry Walker, eldest son of the late Charles Walker, Barrister-at-Law.
    (3) Eleanor Maria, m. Rev. T. E. F. Cole, Chaplain Bengal Establishment, and has issue.
    (4) Dora Frances Mary Blanche.
  He m. 2ndly, 14 Sept. 1869, Lucy Elizabeth, dau. of Sir William Sidney Thomas, 5th bart., of Yapton, Capt. R.N., and d. 17 Oct. 1905, having by her had issue,
    (4) Sidney Arthur Naunton, b. 26 June, 1870; m. 27 Oct. 1900, Florence Kate, dau. of the late A. Perkins, of Cape Town.
    (5) Harry George, b. 17 Sept. 1871, drowned in South Africa, 8 July, 1899.
    (6) Victor Lemuel, b. 23 Oct. 1872.
    (5) Violet Lucy Hester, m. 11 June, 1901, Henry Manby Colegrave, 2nd son of Edward Colegrave, of Upper Norwood, S.E.
  2. Naunton Lemuel (Rev.), b. 24 Sept. 1831; m. 8 Aug. 1866, Sophia Frances, only dau. of John Mathew Quantock, of Norton Manor, Somerset, and d. 24 July, 1874, having by her (who d. 17 April, 1874) had issue, with twin daus., who d. in infancy, Frank Naunton Quantock, of Norton Manor, Ilminster, co. Somerset, J.P., b. 25 March, 1868; m. 9 April, 1890, Emily, eldest dau. of W. Macalpine Leny, of Dalswinton, and Glencoe, and has issue,
    Walter Frank Quantock, b. 17 June, 1892.
    Evelyn Agnes Quantock, b. 23 Feb. 1891; d. 29 May, 1908.
4. Henry George, Midshipman, R.N., killed at the taking of Surinam.
5. Arthur, Lieut.-Col. H.E.I.C.S., m. Charlotte, sister of Col. Delemain, and d. 1837, leaving one son and two daus., of whom the elder m. Lieut. — Unwin, H.E.I.C.S.
1. Maria Lucy Eliza, m. Rev. Joseph Guerin, of Bagborough and Norton Fitzwarren, Somerset, and is dec.

Mr. Shuldham m. 2ndly, Esther, dau. of H. Preston, and by her (who d. 1832) had two sons and one dau.,
6. William Lemuel, m. 1839, Eleanor, youngest dau. of Rev. Morgan O'Donovan, Chief of the sept of O'Donovan.
2. Catherine, m. Henry Richardson, of Aber Hirnant, co. Merioneth.

He d. 1843, and was s. by his eldest son,

EDMUND WILLIAM SHULDHAM, of Dunmanway, Lieut.-Gen. H.E.I.C.S., for some years Quarter-master-Gen. at Bombay, m. 3 Dec. 1817, Harriet Eliza Bonar, dau. of Dr. Rundell, of Bath, and by her (who d. 31 July, 1847) left at his decease, 17 Nov. 1852, two sons and a dau.,
1. EDMUND ANDERSON, late of Dunmanway.
2. Leopold Arthur Francis, of Phale Court, co. Cork, J.P., b. 1828; d. unm. 28 Jan. 1887.
1. Harriet Maria Catherine, m. 5 Aug. 1852, George Patrick, Lord Carbery, and d. 15 Aug. 1884, leaving issue

The eldest son,

EDMUND ANDERSON SHULDHAM, of Dunmanway, co. Cork, M.A. Ch. Ch. Oxon, J.P., D.L. co. Cork, High Sheriff 1871, Lieut.-Col. late South Cork Mil., formerly A.D.C. to the Earls of Carlisle and Eglinton when Lords-Lieut. of Ireland, b. 12 May, 1826; d. unm. 31 July, 1904.

We now return to the other branch of the family, descending from the 2nd son of Lemuel and Eleanor Shuldham, viz.,

REV. LEMUEL SHULDHAM, of Dublin, m. 1712, Elizabeth, widow of Bryan Kelly, of Ballyforan, co. Roscommon, and dau. of Daniel Molyneux, of Ballymulvey, by Catherine his wife, dau. of Thomas Pooley, of the city of Dublin, and grand-dau. (by Mary his wife, dau. and co-heir of William Dowdall, of Mount-town, co. Meath) of Col. Adam Molyneux, of Ballymulvey, M.P. co. Longford 1661, who was son of Daniel Molyneux, of Newlands, co. Dublin, Ulster King of Arms, M.P. for Strabane 1613, and grandson of Thomas Molyneux, Chancellor of the Exchequer in Ireland *temp.* ELIZABETH, who d. 3 Jan. 1596. By Elizabeth Molyneux, who m. 3rdly, Buckley Butler, of Kilkenny, and was sole heir of her brother, Pooley Molyneux, of Ballymulvey, who d.s.p. 1772. Rev. Lemuel Shuldham, who d. 1719, had issue,
1. Lemuel.
2. MOLYNEUX, Vice-Admiral R.N., and M.P. for Fowey, created BARON SHULDHAM in the Peerage of Ireland, 31 July, 1776. His Lordship m. 4 Oct. 1790, Margaret Irene, relict of John Harcourt, of Ankerwycke Park, Bucks, and dau. of John Sarney, but d.s.p. Oct. 1798. His widow m. 13 July, 1805, Richard, 2nd Earl of Clanwilliam.
1. Rebecca, d. unm. 1785.

The eldest son,

LEMUEL SHULDHAM, of Ballymulvey, *m.* Sarah Hamilton, of Dublin, and *d.* 23 Oct. 1775, having had issue,
1. POOLEY, his heir.
1. Elizabeth, *m.* Folliott Warren, of Lodge, co. Kilkenny.
2. Elinor, *d.s.p.*
he only son,
POOLEY SHULDHAM, of Ballymulvey, *m.* 1768, Mary, dau. of Sampson Brady, of Lakeview, co. Antrim, and *d.* 1793 (will dated 2 Aug. 1790, and proved 2 July, 1793), having had issue,
1. JOHN BRADY, his heir of Ballymulvey, *d. unm.* 1832.
2. Molyneux William, of Ballymulvey, of whom next.
1. Elizabeth, *m.* Edwar¹ Warren.
2. Rebecca, *m.* Rev. Edward Berwick.
3. Elinor, *m.* Rev. T. Henry.
4. Sarah, *m.* Daniel O'Neill.
5. Mary, *m.* Samuel Crawford.
6. Charlotte, *m.* J. Johnston.
The 2nd son,
MOLYNEUX WILLIAM SHULDHAM, of Ballymulvey, J.P., D.L., High Sheriff 1829, *b.* 1784, *m.* 1824, Helen, dau. of Col. Alexander Macnanus, of Mount Davis, co. Antrim (*see* ROWAN *of Mount Davys*), by Hester, his wife, dau. and heir of Mark Kerr O'Neill, of Flowerfield, co. Derry, a branch of the O'NEILLS of *Shane's Castle*, and *d.* 15 Dec. 1846, having by this lady (who *d.* Oct. 1875) had issue,
1. JOHN, of Ballymulvey (Moigh House), co. Longford, and Gortmore, Ballybrack, co. Dublin, J.P. and D.L., High Sheriff 1850, *b.* June, 1826; *m.* Nov. 1867, Frances Helena, eldest dau. of Hermann Robert De Ricci, M.D., of Molesey House, Surrey, and *d.s.p.* 30 July, 1891.
2. Alexander, of Flowerfield, co. Derry, of the 6th Foot, Capt. Derry Militia, High Sheriff co. Londonderry 1873, *m.* 22 Sept. 1863, Letitia Mary, elder dau. of George Knox, of Prehen, co. Derry, and *d.* March, 1876, having by her (who *d.* 29 July, 1883) had issue,
1. MOLYNEUX WILLIAM, now of Ballymulvey.
2. George Knox, of Flowerfield, co. Derry, *b.* 11 Oct. 1871.
1. Anna Maria.
2. Helen, *m.* William Cope, Barrister-at-Law.
3. Molyneux Pooley, *m.* Kate Staples, dau. of Rev. Robert Alexander, of Portglenone. House, co. Antrim, and *d.* 29 July, 1911, having had issue.
1. Helen Kate, *m.* C. Alexander.
2. Hester Grace, *m.* Edward White, Barrister-at-Law.
4. Pooley Francis, 73rd Regt., and Capt. and Adjutant Londonderry Militia, *m.* Mary, dau. of John Ross, of Capetown, and *d.* 12 Sept. 1865, leaving issue, a dau., Kate.
5. Robert, Capt. Longford Militia, *d.* 1870.

Arms—Gu., an eagle displayed or. *Crest*— A griffin passant arg. *Motto*—Post nubila Phœbus.

Seat—Ballymulvey, co. Longford. *Residence*—Ounavarra Gorey, Ireland.

SINCLAIR OF HOLYHILL AND BONNYGLEN.

WILLIAM HUGH MONTGOMERY SINCLAIR, of Holyhill and Bonnyglen, Inver, co. Donegal, educated at Marlborough and Brasenose Coll., Oxford, B.A. 1889, called to the Irish Bar 1897, joined Consular Service 1900, Vice-Consul at Manila 1900-2, and at Boston 1902-4, at Buenos Aires 1904-7, and at Emden 1907-9, appointed Consul for the States of Bahia and Sergipe 1909, *b.* Dec. 1868.

Lineage.—REV. JOHN SINCLAIR, son of James Sinclair, was the first of the family who settled at Holyhill, Ireland; he was appointed Rector of the Parish (Lockpatrick) 1665-6. He was *s.* by, JOHN his son, father of JOHN, whose son,
WILLIAM SINCLAIR, *d.* before his father; he *m.* Isabella, dau. of Thomas Young, of Lough, Eske, co. Donegal, and had issue,
1. JAMES, of Holyhill.
2. Thomas, *m.* Alicia, dau. of Thomas Young, of Lough Eske, and *d.* 1808.
1. Rebecca (who *d.* 1845), *m.* John de Cluzeau.
The eldest son,
JAMES SINCLAIR, of Holyhill, D.L., *b.* 1772; *m.* 1805, Dorothea, dau. and heir of Rev. Samuel Law, and *d.* having had issue,
1. WILLIAM, late of Holyhill.
2. James, *m.* 4 June, 1861, Katherine, dau. of Rev. Robert Alexander, of Agnadoey, co. Derry (*see* ALEXANDER *of Forkhill*). She *d.* his widow, 15 Jan. 1906, leaving issue.
3. Alexander Montgomery.
1. Mary, *d. unm.* Dec. 1890.   2. Dorothea, *d. unm.* Aug. 1871.
3. Marion, *d. unm.* Jan. 1874.
4. Rebecca, *m.* 1847, Lieut.-Col. Sinclair, H.E.I.C.S., and has issue, a dau.; he *d.* May, 1861.   5. Ann.
6. Isabella, *d.* May, 1864.
7. Caroline Elizabeth, *d. unm.* 11 Aug. 1908.
Mr. Sinclair *d.* Feb. 1865. The eldest son,
WILLIAM SINCLAIR, of Holyhill, co. Tyrone, and of Drumbeg, co. Donegal, J.P. and D.L., co. Donegal, High Sheriff 1854, and J.P. co. Tyrone, Barrister-at-Law, *b.* 17 April, 1810; *m.* Dec. 1830, Sarah dau. of James Cranborne Strode, and *d.* 25 Aug. 1896, leaving issue,

1. JAMES MONTGOMERY, his heir.
2. William Frederic, *b.* May, 1843; *d.* Aug. 1843.
3. William Frederic, late Bombay C.S., *d.* 15 May, 1900.
4. Donald Brooke, *d.* June, 1879.
5. Alfred Law, D.S.O., Lieut.-Col. Indian Army, *b.* 30 April, 1853; *d.* 14 Oct. 1911; *m.* 1897, Kate Adèle, dau. of H. P. Rushton, of Calcutta.
1. Jemima Sarah, *m.* 10 Feb. 1897, Capt. Alexander Montgomery Stewart, of Killendarrogh.   2. Dorothea Mary.
The eldest son,
JAMES MONTGOMERY SINCLAIR, of Holyhill and Bonnyglen, Inver, co. Donegal, B.A., J.P., High Sheriff co. Donegal, 1899, *b.* 23 Nov. 1841; *m.* 29 Jan. 1868, Mary Everina (*Holy Hill, Strabane*), youngest dau. of Lieut.-Col. Hugh Barton, late 2nd Life Guards, of the Waterfoot, co. Fermanagh, and *d.* 1899, leaving issue,
1. WILLIAM HUGH MONTGOMERY, now of Holyhill and Bonnyglen.
1. Everina Mary Caroline, *b.* 31 May, 1870; *m.* 1900, C. L. D. Maxwell, and has issue,
2. Rosabel, *b.* Jan. 1884.

Seats—Holyhill. Strabane, co. Tyrone, and Bonnyglen, Inver, co. Donegal. *Clubs*—New Oxford and Cambridge, S.W., Friendly Brothers' House, Dublin, Royal Ulster Yacht and Puritan, Boston, U.S.A.

SINCLAIR OF HOPEFIELD HOUSE.

THE RIGHT HON. THOMAS SINCLAIR, P.C., of Hopefield House, Belfast, J.P. and D.L. cos. Antrim and Belfast, M.A., Hon. D.Lit. Queen's University, Chairman of its Convocations, *b.* 23 Sept. 1838; *m.* 1st, 1876, Mary, dau. of the late Charles Duffin, of Strandtown Lodge, Belfast. She *d.* 1879. He *m.* 2ndly, 1882, Elizabeth Lecky, dau. of William Richardson, of Brooklands, Belfast, and widow of John M. Sinclair, of Belfast, and has issue. His eldest dau., author of the "Soundless Tide," &c., *m.* 9 April, 1906, W. S. Crichton, Liverpool, and his second dau. Elizabeth Dora *m.* 24 Sept. 1908, Capt. Miles Carbery, 87th Royal Fus. Mr. Sinclair is the son of the late Thomas Sinclair, of Hopefield House, Belfast, and Sarah his wife, eldest dau. of William Archer, of Rockshill, Hillsborough, co. Down.

Seat—Hopefield House, Belfast. *Clubs*—Reform, S.W., Ulster and Ulster Reform, Belfast.

SINGLETON OF ACLARE.

The late UVEDALLE CORBET SINGLETON, C.B., of Aclare, co. Meath, J.P., D.L., High Sheriff 1893, Rear Admiral "Retired List," *b.* 14 Sept. 1838; *m.* 1st, 18 Aug. 1877, Matilda, 4th dau. of Edward Beauman, of Furness, co. Kildare (she *d.* 2 June, 1878); 2ndly, 9 April, 1885, Adelaide Mary (*now of Aclare, co. Meath*), 3rd dau. of the late Major-Gen. Lord John H. Taylour (*see* BURKE'S *Peerage*, HEADFORT, M.), and *d.* 14 Feb. 1910 leaving issue,

Monica Virginia Corbet.

Lineage.—THE VERY REV. FRANCIS CORBET, D.D., Dean of St. Patrick's, Dublin, *d.* 1775. He *m.* Anne, dau. of Rev. John Morris, by Sarah his wife, dau. of Edward Singleton, and had by her (with three daus.) four sons. all of whom, *d.* young, except ROBERT CORBET, of Corbet Hill, co. Wexford, *b.* 20 Jan. 1741; *m.* 21 Oct. 1769, Susannah, dau. of ― Woodward, of Drumbarrow co. Meath, and *d.* 27 May, 1804, having had issue,
1. FRANCIS, his heir.
2. ROBERT, *b.* 10 May, 1777, Capt. R.N.; killed in action 13 Sept. 1810.
3. Samuel, *b.* 21 April, 1785, H.E.I.C.S.; *d.* Nov. 1811.
1. Henrietta, *d. unm.*   2. Anne, *d. unm.* 1812.

Singleton.   THE LANDED GENTRY.

3. Sarah, m. 29 July, 1797, Lieut.-Col. William O'Brien, and d. 5 April, 1817.   4. Ellinor Susannah.
5. Elizabeth Margaret. m. 22 Sept. 1810, Rev. Thomas Gore, Rector of Mulrancan, co. Wexford.
The eldest son,
FRANCIS CORBET, b. 14 Oct. 1770; m. 11 Feb. 1806, Frances, dau. of Joseph Deane, of Terenure, co. Dublin, M.P., and relict of Major Anthony Cliffe, of Abbeybraney and New Ross, co. Wexford, and by her (who d. 1860) had issue,
1. HENRY, his heir.
2. Robert Corbet (Rev.), M.A., b. 9 Oct. 1810; d. unm. 7 Feb. 1881.
3. Francis Corbet, R.N. (S. Australia), b. 17 Dec. 1812; m. Louisa, dau. of Rev. T. Gore, Rector of Mulrancan, and d. 10 May, 1887, leaving issue.
4. Samuel Wellington Corbet, b. 18 June, 1815; d. unm. 1854.
1. Frances Susanna, m. June, 1826. John Timothy Kirby, M.D.
Mr. Corbet assumed in compliance with the will of his great grand-uncle, Right Hon. Henry Singleton, sometime Master of the Rolls, and Chief Justice of the Common Pleas in Ireland, the surname and arms of SINGLETON by Royal Licence, dated 9 Nov. 1820. He d. Sept. 1825, and was s. by his eldest son,
HENRY CORBET SINGLETON, of Aclare, co. Meath, J.P. and D.L., High Sheriff 1842, formerly Lieut. 7th Dragoon Guards, b. 27 Dec. 1806; m. 7 Sept. 1833, Jane Perceval Compton, youngest dau. of Gen. William Loftus, by the Lady Elizabeth, his 2nd wife, dau. of George, 1st Marquess Townsend, and by her (who d. 10 Aug. 1884) had issue,
1. HENRY CORBET, of Aclare.
2. UVEDALE CORBET, s. his brother.
3. Francis Corbet, C.B., Lieut.-Col. Bombay Staff Corps, b. 8 June, 1841; m. 14 Oct. 1875, Jane, 2nd dau. of Francis Corbet Singleton, of Adelaide, Australia, and d. 18 Jan. 1886, leaving two daus.,
1. Aclaio, d. unm. 28 Feb. 1894.
2. Yolande Perceval Compton Corbet, m. 5 Feb. 1903, Rev. S. Cooke Collis Smith, son of Maj.-Gen. E. Davidson Smith.
4. Loftus Corbet, Maj. 92nd Highlanders, b. 2 Aug. 1842; m. 6 Dec. 1872, Emmeline, youngest dau. of Thomas de Moleyns, Q.C., and d. of wounds, received in action with Boers, 1 May, 1881, leaving issue,
Henry Townsend Corbet, D.S.O., Capt. Highland L.I., b. 27 Jan. 1874; m. 26 Nov. 1902, Evelyn Elsie, youngest dau. of Gen. Philip H. F. Harris, C.B., Indian Army, and has issue,
(1) Loftus Corbet, b. 30 Nov. 1903; d. 28 Aug. 1904.
(2) Colin Henry Corbet, b. 2 Dec. 1905.
(1) Isoult Violet, b. 15 Dec. 1906.
Violet Theodora, m. 18 Dec. 1907, Rev. L. George Buchanan, M.A., youngest son of the late Robert Buchanan, of Finlona, co. Tyrone.
5. Reginald Corbet, Lieut.-Col. late Comm. 1st Batt. Highland Light Infantry (*Rathmoyle, Abbeyleix*), b. 19 March, 1847; m. 28 April, 1909, Jessica, widow of George William Ferrars Loftus, of Hastings.
1. Annie Elizabeth Harriet Jane.
2. Constance Francis, m. 3 Nov. 1860, Capt. Frederick Radford, late 1st Royal Dragoons.
3. Edith Charlotte Sophia, m. 1st, 12 July, 1864, John Payne Garnett, eldest son of Samuel Garnett, of Arch Hall, co. Meath (who d. Jan. 1872), leaving John Payne. She m. 2ndly, Cicel Gilliat.
4. Alice Cecilia, m. 28 June, 1866, Henry Thomson, of Newry, co. Down, M.P.
Mr. Singleton d. 14 April, 1872, and was s. by his eldest son,
HENRY CORBET SINGLETON, of Aclare, co. Meath, J.P. and D.L., High Sheriff 1877, late Brevet-Major 30th Foot, b. 29 April, 1837, and d. unm. 23 Aug. 1890.

Arms—Quarterly: 1st and 4th arg., three chevronels gu. between as many martlets sa., for SINGLETON; 2nd and 3rd or, a raven close ppr. for CORBET. Crests—1st, An arm embowed in armour grasping a sceptre terminated by an estoile or, for SINGLETON; 2nd, An elephant arg., armed or, on his back a tower of the last, the trappings gu., garnished or, for CORBET. Motto—Bona fide sine fraude.

Seat—Aclare House, Ardee, co. Meath.

SINGLETON OF MELL.

JOHN ROLLAND SINGLETON, of Mell, co. Louth, Piers Court, co. Cavan, and Hazely Heath, Hants, High Sheriff co. Cavan 1895 and for co. Louth 1906, b. 31 July, 1869; m. 1 June, 1893, Frederica Julia (who obtained a divorce 1901), only dau. of the Rev. Julius Henry Rowley (*see* BURKE'S *Peerage*, ROWLEY, Bart.), and has issue,

1. JOHN HENRY PHILIP ARCHIBALD, b. 15 April, 1894.
2. Mark Rodney, b. 14 Sept. 1896.

Lineage.—JOHN FOWKE, of Gonston, Stafford, eighth in descent from William Fowke, of Brewood in co. Stafford, acquired estates in Stepney, Middlesex, by his marriage with Joyce, dau. of Richard Marsh, of Limehouse, Middlesex, Gentleman Usher to King CHARLES I. and CHARLES II. His only son, according to the pedigree registered in Ulster's Office in 1722, was
REV. RICHARD FOWKE, D.D., m. Elizabeth, dau. of Sir Humphrey Sydenham, of Chetworth, Somerset, and had issue,
1. Humphrey, d.s.p.
2. Sydenham (Sir), Knt., d. June, 1748, m. 1st, Catherine Bladen and 2ndly, Frances, dau. and co-heir of Edward Progers, of Wes Stowe, Suffolk.
3. Marsh, d.s.p.   4. Phineas, d.s.p.
5. JOHN, of whom presently.
1. Elizabeth.
The 5th son,
JOHN FOWKE, of Dublin, settled in Ireland during the Viceroyalty of the Earl of Rochester about 1700. He m. Patience, dau. of Edward Singleton, and sister of the RIGHT HON. HENRY SINGLETON, Lord Chief Justice of the Common Pleas, and left a son and heir,
SYDENHAM FOWKE, who s. to a portion of the property of his uncle the Chief Justice, and adopted the surname of SINGLETON in lieu of his patronymic 1759, M.P. for Drogheda 1776-8.3 He m. 30 July, 1753, Elizabeth dau. of Mark Whyte, and by her (who d. Aug. 1797) had issue,
1. Henry, b. 1757, d. 1762.
2. JOHN, his heir.
3. Mark, an officer in the Guards, b. 1762, M.P. for Carysfort 1799-1800; m. 1785, Lady Mary Cornwallis, dau. of Charles, 1st Marquess Cornwallis, Governor General of India, and d. 17 July 1840.
4. Sydenham, b. 1764, d. young.
5. Henry, of Belpatrick, Collon, co. Louth, b. 1769, m. Miss Burke, and had issue,
1. Sydenham, b. d. at Eton School.
2. Edward, of Collon and Belpatrick, J.P., High Sheriff 1864, m. Maria, sister of Sir Claude Martin Wade, and d. 1881, having had issue with two other sons, who d.s.p.,
(1) Edward Cecil, Capt. 51st Light Infantry, m. Jane Josephine Morris, but d.s.p.
(2) Henry, who d. 30 March, 1846, from the result of an accident at Oxford, unm.
3. Charles.   4. James.
5. John Henry, Major-Gen., Col. of the 11th North Devon Regt., m. 1848, Sarah Frances, dau. of John Vance, of Jersey, and d. 10 April, 1877, leaving issue,
(1) Mark, of Collon and Belpatrick, co. Louth, High Sheriff 1900, b. 24 Dec. 1849, formerly of the 87th R.I. Fusiliers, m. 1893, M. B., dau. of Thomas James, and has had issue,
1. Reginald Charles Fowke, d. 22 July, 1899.
2. Edward John Fowke.
(2) James Sydenham Fowke (Rev.), Rector of Theale, co. Somerset, b. 1851; m. 15 Aug. 1881, Mary, dau. of John Norman.
(3) John, b. 14 Oct. 1853.
(1) Mary, d. unm.
(2) Anne Henrietta.
(3) Ada Frances.
(4) Caroline Elizabeth, m. William Herbert Evans, 2nd son of Edward Prichard Evans, J.P., of Temple Bar.
6. George, Col. Indian Army, left issue, Sydenham and Lucy.
7. Richard, of Belpatrick, b. 20 Dec. 1814; d. unm. 3 Feb. 1884.
8. Arthur.
1. Mara, d. unm.
2. Anne, m. John Scott, of Bodono.
3. Caroline Elizabeth, d. unm. 24 Feb. 1905.
4. Lucy Sophia, m. Rev. Henry Francis Mallet, and had issue.
6. James, an officer 7th Light Dragoons, b. 1771; m. 21 Aug. 1804, the Hon. Caroline Upton, dau. of Clotworthy, Viscount Templetown.
1. Elizabeth, b. 1754, d. 1761.
2. Patience, b. 1756, m. Gen. O'Mara.
3. Charity, b. 1760, m. July, 1779, Joshua Spencer, and was drowned 1800.
4. Elizabeth, b. 1766, m. Robert Wynne.
Mr. Singleton d. 1801, and was s. by his son,
JOHN SINGLETON, of Hazeley, Hants, an officer in the army, b. 20 Feb. 1759; m. 12 Oct. 1812, Sarah, dau. of James Moore, and had issue,
1. HENRY SYDENHAM, of Mell.
1. Patience, b. 1813; m. 30 July, 1839, the Right Rev. Lord Arthur Hervey, Bishop of Bath and Wells, 4th son of Frederick William, Marquess of Bristol.
2. Sarah, b. 1814; m. 3 Aug. 1850, Robert Dennet, 6th Lord Rodney.
Mr. Singleton d. 12 Aug. 1849, and was s. by his son,
HENRY SYDENHAM SINGLETON, of Mell, co. Louth, and Hazely Heath, Hants, High Sheriff co. Louth, 1862, and of co. Cavan 1867, b. 14 April, 1819; m. 27 Feb. 1864, Mary Montgomerie, eldest dau. of the late Charles J. S. M. Lamb, and sister of Sir Archibald Lamb, 5th bart., of Beauport, Sussex, and had issue,
1. Henry Montolieu Rodney, b. 12 June, 1867; d.v.p. unm.
2. JOHN ROLLAND, now of Mell.
1. Clara Patience Sarah.   2. Mary Sophie Theresa.
Mr. Henry Sydenham Singleton d. 16 March, 1893. His widow m. 2ndly, 24 Jan. 1894, Philip Henry Wodehouse Currie, Lord Currie. She d. 13 Oct. 1905. He d.s.p. 13 May, 1906.

Arms—(of FOWKE)—Vert a fleur-de-lis arg. Crest—An arm couped above the elbow, sleeved vert, turned up arg. the hand ppr. holding a pheon or, headed and feathered arg.

FAMILY OF SINGLETON.

EDWARD SINGLETON, Alderman of Drogheda, M.P. 1692-1710, the grantee mentioned in the Act of Parliament passed in England, in the second year of Queen ANNE, *d.* between Dec. 1709 and April, 1710, leaving, by his wife, Catherine,
1. ROWLAND (Rev.), *m.* Elizabeth Graham, and *d.* 1741-2, leaving issue,
  1. Patience, *m.* Francis Leigh.
  2. Sarah, *m.* Arthur Rochfort.
  3. Mary, *m.* Philip Tisdall, afterwards Attorney-General, and by him had two daus.,
    (1) Elizabeth, *m.* Col. Hugh Morgan, by whom she was mother of an only child, Catherine, *m.* Robert Stearne Tighe, of Mitchelstown (*see that family*).
    (2) Mary, *d. unm.*
  4. Charity, *m.* 1st, May, 1742, William Cope; and 2ndly, 13 Sept. 1744, Sir William Yorke, Bart., Chief Justice of the Common Pleas; and *d.s.p.*
2. Samuel, M.D., *d.s.p.* 1726.   3. Edward, *d. unm.* 1725-6.
4. John (Rev.), *d. unm.* 1736.
5. Henry (Right Hon.), Recorder of Drogheda, M.P. 1713-40, Prime Serjeant 1726, Lord Chief Justice of the Court of Common Pleas, Ireland, 1740-5 ; Master of the Rolls 1754, *d. unm.* 9 Nov. 1759.
  1. Sarah, *m.* the Rev. John Morris, and had a dau., Anne, *m.* the Very Rev. Francis Corbet, D.D., Dean of St. Patrick's, co. Dublin (see SINGLETON *of Aclare*).
  2. Mary, *m.* John Leigh.
  3. Margaret, *m.* George Hardman, of Drogheda.
  4. Jane, *m.* James Meade.   5. Elizabeth, *m.* Judge Lindsay.
  6. Patience, *m.* JOHN FOWKE, whose son Sydenham Fowke took the surname of SINGLETON (*see above*).
  7. Anne, *m.* — Madders.

Arms—(of SINGLETON)—Arg. three chevronels gu., between as many martlets sa. *Crest*—An armed arm, the hand naked ppr., holding a murdering staff or.
Seats—Mell, Drogheda, co. Louth : Piers Court, Shercock, co. Cavan.

SINGLETON OF QUINVILLE ABBEY.

The late EDWARD NEWPORT SINGLETON, of Quinville Abbey, co. Clare, *b.* 9 Dec. 1829 ; *m.* 1870, Annie May, eldest dau. of George Richardson, of Montreal, and left issue,
1. John, *b.* 28 and *d.* 29 March, 1875.
2. John Edward, *b.* 5 March, 1876 ; *d.* 13 March, 1899.
3. Frederick George, *b.* 21 Sept. 1881 ; *d.* 12 Nov. 1893.
4. Lucy Isabella, *b.* 16 Nov. 1873 ; *d.* 20 Jan. 1877.
5. Susan Ethel, *b.* 13 Dec. 1877.
3. Irene Lily, *b.* 14 Aug. 1889.   4. Annie May Richardson.

Lineage.—JOHN SINGLETON, *m.* Jane Bruffe, and had issue,
1. JOHN, his heir.
1. Anne, *m.* Samuel Cooper, of Cooper Hill, co. Limerick.
2. Sarah, *m.* 1st, Richard Copley, afterwards of Boston, America, and by him had issue. She *m.* 2ndly, Henry Pelham, and by him had issue.
The only son,
JOHN SINGLETON, of Ballygreen, *m.* Marcella, dau. of Michael d'Alton, of Deer Park, and heir of her brother, and had issue,
1. JOHN, formerly of Quinville, co. Clare, and afterwards of the city of Limerick.
2. EDWARD D'ALTON.
1. Jane, *m.* Sir Anthony King, of the city of Dublin.
2. Mary, *m.* 1766, Edward Palmer, of Elen Grove, King's Co.
Mr. Singleton *d.* 1797. His 2nd son,
EDWARD D'ALTON SINGLETON, of Quinville, *m.* 1791, Mary, eldest dau. of Hugh Brady, of the city of Limerick, a member of Tomgreany family of co. Clare, and by her (who *d.* Feb. 1835) had issue,
1. JOHN, of Quinville.
2. Hugh Brady, *m.* Jane, dau. of John Massey, of Doonas, and had three sons and three daus.
3. Edward, *m.* Olivia Margaret, dau. of James David Potts, of Pitville House, Cheltenham, and had issue, one son Edward James, late Maj. 15th Regt., and one dau., Olivia Narney, *m.* 1863, Richard Garnett, C.B., LL.D., of the British Museum, and *d.* 24 June, 1903.
4. Anthony.
1. Marcella, *m.* 1st, Henry Vereker D'Esterre, of Rosemanaher, only son and heir of Henry D'Esterre, Recorder of co. Limerick ; and 2ndly, William Finch, of Kilcolman, co. Tipperary.

2. Anne, *m.* John Brady, of Raheens, co. Clare.
3. Maria, *m.* John Browne Finch, of Clomaken, co. Limerick.
4. Eliza, *m.* James Campbell Patterson, of Tarbert.
Mr. Singleton *d.* 6 Oct. 1814, and was *s.* by his eldest son,
JOHN SINGLETON, of Quinville Abbey, J.P., High Sheriff 1825, *b.* 16 Feb. 1793 ; *m.* 1st, 18 Nov. 1819, Isabella Carew, only child and heir of Michael Creagh, of Laurentinum, co. Cork, by Sarah Dobson his wife, dau. of Robert Shapland Carew, of Castleboro', co. Wexford, and by her (who *d.* May, 1861) had issue,
1. Michael Creagh, *b.* 1 Nov. 1820, late Lieut. 10th Foot ; had medals for Sobraon, and was mentioned in despatches, &c., dec.
2. JOHN, late of Quinville Abbey.
3. EDWARD NEWPORT, late of Quinville Abbey.
1. Sarah Dobson, *m.* Capt. James Butler Staveley, of Croydon Park, co. Dublin.   2. Mary.
3. Susan Anne, *m.* Jan. 1865, Capt. William Walshe, R.I.C., 2nd son of J. Walshe, of Walshe Park, co. Tipperary, who is dec.   4. Isabella, *d. unm.* 8 Jan. 1890.
5. Marcella Elizabeth Carew, *d.* 20 March, 1857.
He *m.* 2ndly, 1867, Emma, widow of Thomas Woodforde, and dau. of Rev. Matthew Phillips, of Myrrtheer, co. Pembroke, and *d.* 5 Aug. 1877. His son,
JOHN SINGLETON, of Quinville Abbey, co. Clare, J.P., Lieut.-Col. R.A., Col. in the Army, and retired Lieut.-Gen., *b.* 4 April, 1826 ; *m.* 4 Jan. 1856 Catherine Marianne, eldest dau. of Major-Gen. Barry, R.E. Major-Gen. Singleton served in the Eastern campaign 1854-5, at the Alma, Balaklava, Inkerman, the siege and fall of Sebastopol, and in India in 1858, commanding the artillery in the repulse of the Sepoys at Mooltan during the Mutiny. He had medals and clasps, the Order of the Medjidie, the Legion of Honour, &c., and was thanked by Lord Raglan for his services 26 Oct. 1854. He *d.s.p.* Aug. 1880, and was *s.* by his brother, EDWARD NEWPORT SINGLETON, late of Quinville Abbey.

SKEFFINGTON. See BURKE'S PEERAGE,
MASSEREENE, V.

SKERRETT OF FINAVARA.

REV. HYACINTH HEFFERNAN SKERRETT, of Finavara, co. Clare, in Holy Orders of the Church of Rome, *b.* 2 Nov. 1845.

Lineage.—HYACINTH SKERRETT, of Finavara, *m.* 20 July 1768, Mary, dau. of George Byrne, of Cabinteely, co. Dublin, by Clare his wife, sister of Robert, Earl Nugent, and left a son and successor,
MAJOR WILLIAM SKERRETT, of Finavara, *m.* 12 Oct. 1803, Mary, dau. of John Roche, of Limerick, and by her (who *d.* 1821) he left at his decease. Aug. 1818, with three daus. (Margaret, *m.* Thomas Comyn, of Hodiwell, co. Clare (see COMYN *of Woodstock and Kilcorney*), Clarinda, *m.* George Comyn, of Holliwell, brother of Thomas, afore-mentioned ; Mary Ann, *m.* Valentine French, of Prospect Hill, co. Galway), one son,
WILLIAM JOSEPH SKERRETT, of Finavara, J.P. and D.L., High Sheriff 1843, *b.* 2 Feb. 1819 ; *m.* 26 Feb. 1840, Anna, dau. of John MacMahon, J.P., of Firgrove, and *d.* 1 Sept. 1874, leaving issue,
1. WILLIAM, his heir.
2. JOHN, heir to his brother.
3. HYACINTH HEFFERNAN (Rev.), now of Finavara.
4. Alfred Thomas, dec.   5. Philip, *b.* 3 Nov. 1850 ; dec.
6. Charles Percival, B.A. Trin. Coll. Dublin, *b.* 30 Aug. 1852 ; *m.* 3 June, 1884, Ada Mildred, youngest dau. of John Hanson Sperling, of Catton House, co. Norfolk, and *d.* leaving one son and two daus.
7. Valentine Joseph, } twins, *b.* 9 Dec. 1854.
8. Robert David,
9. Frederick Thomas, Surg.-Capt. A.M.S., F.R.C.S.I., *b.* 16 Oct. 1858 ; *m.* 31 Aug. 1897, Rose Edith, elder dau. of F. F. Kelly, Vicar of Camberwell, and *d.* 19 Aug. 1899.
10. Patrick de Basterot, Surg.-Capt. A.M.S., *b.* 20 Aug. 1861.
1. Helena, *m.* July, 1864, Stephen Cowan, of Gornamona, co. Galway, J.P., late Capt. Galway Militia.   2. Mary, a nun.
3. Matilda, *m.* George Douglas Williams, of London, and had issue.
4. Elizabeth, *m.* Lieut. G. H. Yonge, R.N.
The eldest son,
WILLIAM SKERRETT, of Finavara, J.P., Capt. 36th Regt., *b.* 11 Feb. 1842 ; *m.* 4 June, 1877, Helena, dau. of John Reilly, of Dublin, and dying 10 June, 1878, was *s.* by his brother,
JOHN SKERRETT, of Finavara, J.P., *b.* 30 Aug. 1844 ; *d. unm.* 1881, and was *s.* by his brother, REV. HYACINTH HEFFERNAN SKERRETT, now of Finavara.

Arms—Arg., three squirrels passant gu. *Crest*—a griffin passant vert, beaked and armed or. *Motto*—Deo adjuvante.

SLACKE, late OF ASHLEIGH.

CHARLES OWEN SLACKE, b. 21 Jan 1872; m. 14 June, 1902, Kate, dau. of Rt. Hon. Sir Daniel Dixon, Bart., P.C., D.L., of Ballymenoch, Holywood, co. Down (see BURKE'S *Peerage*, DIXON, Bart.), and has issue,

RANDAL CHARLES, b. 24 Jan. 1904.
Edith Avril, b. 11 June, 1908.

Lineage.—WILLIAM SLACKE, of Annadale, co. Leitrim, the family seat, m. his cousin Angel Anna Slacke, and d. 1810, having had issue, three sons and four daus.,
1. RANDAL JAMES.
2. James Wilkinson, m. and had a son, the present owner of Annadale.
3. William, m. and had issue.

The eldest son,
RANDAL JAMES SLACKE, who resided in Strokestown, co. Roscommon, m. 1800, Jane, dau. of James Cooper, and d. Aug. 1807, and by her (who survived him till 1849) was father of
REV. WILLIAM RANDAL SLACKE, of Ashleigh, Incumbent of Newcastle, co. Down, b. 2 Feb. 1808; m. 26 Dec. 1834, Mary, dau. of Jacob Owen, and d. 7 Dec. 1877, having by her (who d. 31 Oct. 1888) had issue,
1. OWEN RANDAL, his heir.
2. William Randal, Col. late R.E. (*Newcastle, co. Down*), b. 9 Oct. 1839; m. 6 Dec. 1866, Harriette Earl, dau. of Major-Gen. White, R.E. She d. 14 Sept. 1901, leaving with other issue,
Kathleen Isabel, m. 5 June, 1907, Percy W. F. Le Breton, son of Major de Breton.
1. Margaret Jane, m. F. V. Clarendon, and has issue.

The elder son,
SIR OWEN RANDAL SLACKE, Knt., C.B., b. 15 Aug. 1837, J.P. for co. Waterford, formerly Capt. 10th Royal Hussars, and late Divisional Commissioner for the Northern Division, Ireland ; was made C.B. 1893 ; knighted Jan. 1897 ; m. 1st, 7 Oct. 1863, Katherine Anne, eldest dau. of the late Sir Charles Lanyon, of The Abbey, co. Antrim, and by her (who d. Jan. 1872) has issue;
1. CHARLES OWEN.
1. Helen Marie, m. 23 Aug. 1906, Major A. H. W. Lowndes, late Rifle Brigade, and d. May, 1909.
Sir Owen Slacke m. 2ndly, 17 July, 1875, Fanny Rose (31, *Chesham Street, S.W.*), 3rd dau. of the late Peter Connellan, of Coolmore, D.L. co. Kilkenny (*see that family*), and d. 27 April, 1910, leaving issue,
2. Randal Beresford, b. 31 Oct. 1876; m. 17 Sept. 1903, Edith Mary, dau. of the late John Thwaites, of Troy, Blackburn, Lancashire, and has issue,
Raymond Leslie Randal, b. 3 April, 1908.
Rosamond Prudence, b. 17 Feb. 1905.
3. Roger Cecil, Capt. the Buffs, East Kent Regt., b. 10 Oct. 1880 ; m. 10 Oct. 1910, Violet Mary, dau. of late G. Turner Phillips, of Folkestone.

Arms—Az. a cross pattée throughout per bend sinister erm. and or, a quatrefoil counterchanged, in the centre chief point a mullet gu. Crest—A lion couchant ppr., resting his dexter forepaw on a quatrefoil of the arms. Motto—Lente sed certe.
Residence—Wheatfield, Belfast. Club—Ulster.

WILSON-SLATOR OF WHITE HILL.

HENRY BEVAN WILSON-SLATOR, of White Hill, co. Longford, and Belle Ville, co. Meath, High Sheriff co. Longford 1908, Capt. 4th Batt. Royal Irish Fusiliers, b. 20 Dec. 1884 ; s. his father 1892.

Lineage.— HENRY SLATOR, of Lislea House, co. Longford, m. Nov. 1659, Rebecka, dau. of Crawford, an officer in Cromwell's army, and d. 1714, leaving issue,
1. William, of Lislea, d.s.p. 1746.
2. Henry, of Dublin, who d. 1758, leaving with other issue,
Henry, b. 1725; m. 1755, his cousin Rebecka, dau. of James Slator, of Moniscallaghan, co. Longford, and Kilgarren, co. Carlow.
3. JAMES, of whom presently.

1. Margrett, d. 1730.
2. Rebecka, m. 1st, 28 Oct. 1700, William McKay ; and 2ndly, 2 Aug. 1710, John Whitcraft.

The 3rd son,
JAMES SLATOR, of Moniscallaghan, co. Longford, and Kilgarren, co. Carlow, b. 1677 ; m. 1701, Anne, dau. and co-heiress with her sister,* of Ensign Alexander Graydon, of White Hill, by Jean Crawford his wife, and d. 1757, leaving issue,
1. John, of Tonyn, co. Longford, b. 1704 ; m. 1741, Elizabeth, dau. and co-heiress of William Bevan, of Cootehill, co. Cavan, and had issue,
1. Arthur, d.s.p. 1785.
2. Bevan, of Tonyn, co. Longford, Bruno, co. Cavan, and Prospect, co. Wexford, m. Mary, dau. of Edward Beatty, of Heathfield, co. Wexford, and Lismore, co. Longford, and d.s.p. 1811.
3. Alexander.
4. James (Rev.), of Townend, co. Longford, and Laragh Manor, co. Cavan, Rector of Naas, co. Kildare ; m. Henrietta Dorothea Thomas, and left issue, five daus.,
(1) Jemima, m. Capt. Henry Tucket.
(2) Ellen, d. unm. 1886.
(3) Harriette, m. — Cumming, and d. 1825.
(4) Mary Anne, m. — Fagan, of Fagantown, co. Meath.
(5) Elizabeth, m. Rev. W. Spencer Walsh, of Knockboyne, co. Meath, and left issue (see *WALSH of Laragh*).
1. Anne, m. Henry Montford, of Bawn House, and Newtownbond, co. Longford.
2. Mary, d. unm. 1816.
3. Elinor, m. Thomas Coates, of Newbridge, and Clinan, co. Longford, and had issue, with two daus., one son,
BEVAN COATES SLATOR, of Clinan, co. Longford, and Bruno, co. Cavan, assumed the name of SLATOR 1813, on succeeding to the property of his maternal uncle, Bevan Slator (*see above*), b. 1799, and d. 7 May, 1854, leaving with other issue,
1. Arthur Coates SLATOR, of Cartron, Ballymahon, co. Longford.
2. Bevan Coates SLATOR, of Clinan, co. Longford, and White Heather, Achill Island, m. Anne, dau. of John Robinson, of Lisglassick, co. Longford, descendant of a Cromwellian officer ; d. 19 Oct. 1901, having had issue,
a. Annson John, b. 1871 ; d. 1873.
2. Alexander, of whom presently.
3. Henry, b. 1714, left a dau. Nancy, who d. unm., and a son, James.
4. William, of Moniscallaghan, d.s.p. Aug. 1772.
5. James, of Wood of Oogh, King's Co., m. 1767, Susanna, dau. of Thomas Low, of Bloomhill, King's Co., and left issue,
1. John. 2. Thomas.
3. Nathaniel, Robert, m. Frances Alicia dau. of Robert Berry of Shannon Harbour, King's Co., and left issue,
(1) Frances Alicia, d. unm.
(2) Elizabeth, m. Rev. John Joly, and left, with other issue, a son, Charles J. Joly, D.Sc., F.R.S., F.T.C.D., Astronomer Royal for Ireland, who d. leaving issue, 4 Jan. 1906.
1. Elizabeth, d. unm. 2. Georgina, d. unm.
3. Margaret, m. Fleming Handy, of Cloonagh, co. Westmeath, and Gayville, and left issue, an only dau., Jane, who m. Edward Fetherstonhaugh, of Ballintubber, co. Westmeath.
6. George Slator, of Ballynock, b. 1721 ; m. Rebecka, dau. of Robert Belton, of Ballinamona, King's Co., and d. 12 June, 1772, leaving issue,
1. John, b. 1767, and d.s.p. m. May, 1803.
2. Alexander. 3. James.
1. Jane, b. 1765 ; d. unm. 11 Aug. 1798.
1. Rebecka, b. 17-6; m. 1755, Henry Slator, her cousin, grandson of Henry Slator, of Lislea.

The 2nd son,
ALEXANDER SLATOR, by the will of his maternal grandfather, Ensign Alexander Graydon, s. th White Hill, b. 1707 ; m. 1741, Mary, dau. and co-heiress of William Bevan, of Cootehill, co. Cavan (*see above*), and d. 1772, leaving issue,
1. William Henry, of White Hill, High Sheriff co. Longford 1784, b. 1742, and d.s.p. 1802.
2. Alexander, b. 1750, and d.s.p. 1823.
1. Anne, m. 1771, Thomas Hinds, of Corakain, co. Cavan, and Lismoreville.
2. Elizabeth, m. Lieut. Joseph Ramage, son of L. Ramage, of Craddenstown, co. Westmeath.
3. Rebecka, d. unm.
4. Jane, of White Hill, b. 1750 ; d. unm. 1832.
5. Mary, m. 1784, Thomas Wilson, M.D., of Bruce Hall, co. Cavan, and Proudstown, co. Meath, son of Thomas Wilson, of Obristown, co. Meath, by Elizabeth Whitton his wife, and had issue with three daus., Maryanne, m. Robert Webb, of Lisrine, co. Longford ; Anne Sara,† m. Richard J. Hinds, of New Grove, co. Longford ; Elizabeth Jane, m. Moutray Erskine, of co. Cavan (*see that family*), left issue, an only son,

---

* Her sister, Jean, m. Andrew McClaughery, of Abide and Mosstown, co. Longford, whose descendants Anglicised their name to its equivalent "King's stone." Their tombs lie side by side with those of the Graydons and the Slators in the ruined churchyard of Kilcoinmack, co. Longford, and on one of them is the inscription : "Alexander Kingston, late of Mosstown, Esqre., Gaelic McClaughery of the Highlands."

† Her dau., Euphemia, m. 1850, Bernard William Bagot, Barrister-at-Law, of Carranure, co. Roscommon, son of — Bagot, of Ballymoe, and Aughrane Castle, co. Galway (*see that family*), another dau. m. — Sidney, Barrister-at-Law.

IRELAND. Smith.

HENRY BEVAN WILSON-SLATOR, of White Hill ; Bruce Hall, co. Cavan, and Belle Ville, co. Meath, High Sheriff co. Cavan 1851, High Sheriff co. Longford 1852, J.P., s. to the property of his maternal uncle, and, in pursuance of family settlements, assumed by Royal Licence, 5 May, 1885, the additional surname and the arms of SLATOR, b. 28 March, 1785 ; m. 8 April, 1808, Annabelle, only dau. and heiress of John Hinds, of Mulbussey Castle,* co. Meath, and grand-dau. of William Gerrard, of Dornstown Castle, co. Meath, and d. 25 June, 1857, leaving issue,
1. William Henry, of White Hill, m. Margaret Dillon, and d. 1859, leaving issue,
 1. Alexander, of White Hill, b. 1840 ; d.s.p. 1864.
 2. William Henry, b. 1842.
 3. Bevan Francis, Midshipman R.N., b. 1850, and d.s.p. 1868.
 4. Edward.
  1. Annabelle, b. 1846.   2. Margaret Elizabeth.
2. Henry Bevan, b. 1813 ; d.s.p.
3. Thomas Hinds, b. 1816 ; d.s.p.
4. John Hinds. b. 1819 ; d.s.p. in Ohio, America, 1843.
5. GEORGE WARNER, of whom presently.
1. Maryanne, b. 1809 ; m. 1841, Joseph Montgomery.
The 5th son,
GEORGE WARNER WILSON-SLATOR, of White Hill, and Belle Ville, co. Meath, J.P. co. Meath, J.P. and D.L. co. Longford, High Sheriff co. Longford 1877, b. 8 Jan. 1823 ; m. 4 Nov. 1874, Harriette Vokes, only dau. of James Vokes Mackey, J.P., of Scribblestown, co. Dublin, and 69, Merrion Square, Dublin, by Mariannc Sadlier, only surviving dau. of William Sadlier Bruvere, of Bewick, Northumberland, his wife, d. 16 May, 1892, leaving issue,
1. Henry Bevan Edward, b. March and d. April, 1876.
2. George Warner William, b. 29 March, 1877, and d. March, 1878.
3. HENRY BEVAN, now of White Hill.
1. Marion Harriette Annabelle, m. 2 June, 1909, Sidney Stratton Whitaker, Lieut. 7th Gurkha Rifles,only son of Col. C. J. Whitaker, York and Lancs. Regt., and grand-nephew of Field-Marshal Viscount Wolseley.
2. Bertha Violette, m. 24 Aug. 1908, Mainwaring Ravell Walsh, Capt. Worcestershire Regt., son of Col. T. Prendergast Walsh, of Laragh Manor, co. Cavan, and has issue (see that family).
3. Georgina Beatrice.

Arms—Arg., a saltier az. between four trefoils slipped vert. **Crest**—On a wreath of the colours a lion passant per pale gu. and sa., holding in his dexter paw a trefoil slipped as in the arms. **Motto**—Garde de Loi.
Seats—White Hill, Edgeworthstown, and Belle Ville, Tara, co. Meath.

SMITH OF ANNESBROOK.

FITZHENRY AUGUSTUS SMITH, of Annesbrook, Duleek, co. Meath, and Besborough, cc. Meath, J.P., High Sheriff 1905, b. 17 Sept. 1859 ; s. his uncle Major Michael Edward Smith, 1903 ; m. 1910, Kathleen Muriel, elder dau. of the late Lieut.-Col. Joseph Oates Travers, Leicestershire Regt. and grand-dau. of the late Major-Gen. Sir Henry Marion Durand, R.E., K.C.S.I.
Lineage.—This family was originally from co. York.
JOHN SMITH, living at Bryanstown, co. Louth, will proved, 4 March, 1691, m. Ellinor —, and had issue,
1. JEREMIAH, of whom presently.
2. Walter.
1. Elizabeth, m. Richard Workman.
2. Sarah, m. — Shewell.
3. Anne, m. Henry Baker.
4. Mary.
The elder son,
JEREMIAH SMITH, who possessed the lands of Maine and Coolestown, co. Louth, married three times. By his 1st wife Elizabeth, dau. of Robert Bickerton, of Clantinuff, co. Armagh, and Anne his wife, dau. of Henry Bellingham, of Gernonstown (see BURKE's Peerage BELLINGHAM, Bart.), he had one dau,
1. Anne.
By his 2nd wife Jane (settlement dated 1 Feb. 1695), dau. of Edward Corker, of Ratoath and Castletown, co. Meath, by his wife Esther, dau. of Sir Daniel Bellingham (see BURKE's, Peerage BELLINGHAM, Bart.), he had issue,

* Mulhussey Castle was burnt to the ground in the Rebellion of 1798, the family only escaping through the faithfulness of an old servant, who conveyed them through the Rebel lines.

1. Edward, Capt. in the Battle-Axe Guard (commission dated 18 Aug. 1718), High Sheriff co. Louth 1750, to whom his father gave the estate of Maine, co. Louth. He married Catherine, dau. of Sir Francis Foulke, Commander of Cork, and left issue, Mary, m. 4 July, 1746, Hugh Stafford (see STAFFORD of Maine).
2. Esther.   3. Ellinor.
By his 3rd wife Alice, dau. of Henry Townley, of Aclare Castle, co. Louth, and Mary Hudson his wife, dau. of the Bishop of Elphin (m. lic. dated 22 Dec. 1702), he had issue,
2. Harry, Recorder of Drogheda, 1742.
3. Towuley (Rev.), of Coolistown, Rector of Mansfieldstown, who m. Susanna —, and left a son,
Tennison.
4. JEREMIAH — of whom presently.
5. Tennison — who had issue,
Edward Tyrell Smith, became Admiral 12 Aug. 1812, and m. Maria, dau. of Hon. James Nevin, of New Hampstead, Boston, U.S.A.
Alicia, m. Mr. Tyndall, of The Fort, Bristol.
6. HAMILTON, of Mount Hamilton, d. unm, leaving his Louth estates to his cousin Jeremiah Workman.
4. Mary Anne, m. 1st Charles Sandford, of Sandford Court, Kilkenny ; 2ndly, William Foster, M.P., High Sheriff for Louth 1754.
The 4th son,
JEREMIAH SMITH, m. Margaret, dau. of Adam Schoales, Alderman of Drogheda, and is buried with his wife at St. Peter's, Drogheda. He had issue,
1. HENRY, of whom presently.
2. Jeremiah, Capt. in the Carabineers 13 Oct. 1781.
1. Jane, m. Dr. William Gibbons.
2. Catherine Margaret, m. George Rotheram, of Crossdrum, co. Meath (see that family).
The elder son,
HENRY SMITH, of Beabeg, d. 1817 ; m. March, 1783, Martha, dau. of Laurence Steele, of Rathbride, co. Kildare. and had issue,
1. HENRY, of whom presently.
2. St. George, of Greenhills, co. Louth, who m. Mary Hannah, only dau. of Ralph Smythe, of Barbavilla, co. Westmeath (see that family).
1. Elizabeth Esther.   2. Matilda Jane.
3. Catherine Margaret, m. Capt. Walter Synnott (see SYNNOTT of Ballymoyer).
4. Emily, m. Major James Kynaston Edwards, of Old Court, co. Wicklow.
The elder son,
HENRY SMITH, D.L., of Beabeg and Annesbrook, b. 28 Nov. 1783 ; High Sheriff 1819, m. 1st, 28 Dec. 1802, Margaret, dau. of Henry Osborne, of Dardistown Castle, same co., by Alice his wife, dau. of Francis Dunne, of Brittas, Queen's Co., and had issue,
1. HENRY JEREMIAH, his heir, of Beabeg, b. Oct. 1803 ; m. 1st, 1828, Sarah Maria, dau. of Robert Harrison, of Preston. Kent, and by her had issue, one son,
 1. HENRY JEREMIAH, of Beabeg, co. Meath, b. 14 Sept. 1829 m. 16 July, 1857, Elizabeth, youngest dau. of James Kynaston Edwards, of Old Court, co. Wicklow, and by her (who d 1880) has issue,
  (1) HENRY JEREMIAH.
  (1) Emily Kate.   (2) Lilla Caroline Constance.
  (3) Gertrude Frances Helen.
He m. 2ndly, Oct. 1836, Hon. Henrietta Priscilla Carleton (who d. 20 Oct. 1892), dau. of Lieut.-Col. Hon. George Carleton, and sister of Guy, 3rd Lord Dorchester, and d. 13 March, 1877, having by her (who d. 20 Oct. 1892) had issue,
 2. Carleton, formerly Lieut.-Col. and Hon. Col. comdg. 3rd Batt. East Surrey Regt., late Capt in the Army, m. 12 Oct. 1865, Alice Anna, younger dau. of Charles Kaye Freshfield, late M.P. She d. 27 June, 1902. He d. 3 Oct. 1910.
 3. George.
 4. Dudley Henry Seymour. late Lieut. 64th Foot.
 1. Georgina Sarah, m. W. Davies, Capt. Essex Rifles.
2. Francis Edward. Capt. H.E.I.C.S., d.s.p.
He m. 2ndly, 18 Jan. 1809, Elizabeth, dau. of William Radcliffe, of Tinnekilly, co. Wicklow, by Catherine his wife, dau. of Sir Michael Cox, 3rd bart., and d. 1857, having by her had issue,
3. STEPHEN HENRY, of Annesbrook, J.P., High Sheriff 1861, late Lieut.-Col. Londonderry Militia, b. 1813 ; m. 1st, 2 Nov. 1860, Georgina Barbara, only dau. of Col. Raymond Pelly, 16th Lancers, C.B. and by her (who d. 1874) had issue, three daus. He m. 2ndly, 1876, Francesca Helen Mary, eldest dau. of Col. Henry Bouchier Saville. He d. 1890.
4. St. George William, of Newtown, co. Meath, J.P., d. 1892.
5. MICHAEL EDWARD, of Annesbrook and Newtown, co. Meath, and Killetar, co. Tyrone, Major in the Army, m. 8 Sept. 1847. Jane Grace, 2nd dau. of the late William Ireland Syme, of Ryedale, co. Kirkcudbright, and Lilias his wife, dau. of the Rev. Charles Maitland Babington, M.A., Rector of Peterstow, co. Hereford, and d.s.p. 19 May, 1903.
6. WILLIAM THOMAS, of whom presently.
7. Richard Jeremiah, J.P., m. 18 March, 1858, Adela, youngest dau. of George Archer, Town Clerk of Dublin, and grand-dau. of W. H. Archer, Lord Mayor of Dublin 1811, and had with other issue, a dau., Emily Gertrude, m. 4 Oct. 1899, Rev. Edwin Henry Cock, M.A.
8. Frederick Augustus, Col. (retired), V.C., dec.
9. Kynaston Walter, accidentally killed 1857.
1. Catherine Matilda, m. 16 Aug. 1843, Col. Sir Robert Wallace, K.C.B., H.E.I.C.S., and left issue.
2. Elizabeth, m. 26 June, 1840, Hugh Lyons Montgomery, of Belhavel, co. Leitrim, M.P., and had issue (see that family).

3. Matilda Cox, *m.* 14 Sept. 1865, Francis Macnamara Faulkner. She *d.* his widow 3 April, 1907.
4. Emily, dec.
5. Mary Henrietta, *m.* 1857, Ralph Smyth, J.P., of Newtown House, co. Louth, and *d.* 1876, leaving issue.

The 6th son,
CAPT. WILLIAM THOMAS SMITH, of Besborough, co. Meath, late of the 75th and 22nd Regt., *b.* 1816. *m.* 1st, Caroline Eliza, dau. of William Walman Patterson, of Coggleshall, Essex, and by her (who *d.* 1866) had issue,
1. FITZHENRY AUGUSTUS, now of Annesbrook.
2. Percy R. C., *b.* 1862.
3. Otto William, *b.* 1863.
1. Amina Constance, *m.* 1881, Gustavus Villiers Briscoe, of Bellinter, co. Meath, High Sheriff 1897, and had issue.

He *m.* 2ndly, 1873, Kate Auber Chambers, and *d.* 1884, having by her (who *d.* 1909) had issue,
4. Ernest St. George, Capt. 4th Batt. Royal Dublin Fusiliers, *b.* 20 March, 1878; *m.* 17 Oct. 1910, Kathleen Emily, widow of Avenal Bradford and eldest dau. of Col. Arthur Philpotts, late R.A.
5. Mabel Geraldine Auber, *m.* 1901, Capt. Cecil Savile, 1st Bombay Lancers.

Arms—Arg., on a bend, between two bulls' heads erased az. armed or, three lozenges of the last. *Crest*—A demi-bull salient az. armed and ungulled or. *Motto*—Delectat amor patriæ.

Seats—Annesbrook, Duleek, co. Meath; Besborough, Babrath, co. Meath. *Club*—Sackville Street, Dublin.

SMITH-BARRY. *See* BARRY.

SMITH, FORMERLY OF GLASSHOUSE.

WILLIAM FREDERICK HAMMERSLEY SMITH, *b.* 16 May, 1843, late Resident Magistrate, Ireland; *m.* 20 July, 1881, Evelyn Louisa, 3rd dau. of Thomas George Wills-Sandford, of Willsgrove and Castlerea, co. Roscommon (see that family), and has issue,

Evelyn Eleanor, *m.* 1904, George Hugh Mercer, D.I., R.I.C.

Lineage.—JOSHUA SMITH, of Ballytorcen, Coolroe, Glasshouse, and Gortercan, King's Co., an Officer in the Army in Ireland 1641-1649, *m.* circa 1660, Eleanor Coffey, and had issue, three sons,
1. Thomas, of Kinegad, co. Westmeath.
2. John, of Kilcomin, Ballytorcen and Coolroe, *m.* 1685, Lydia— and had issue,
    1. Joshua, *d.s.p.* 1716.
    2. William, of Ballytorcen, *m.* (sett. 7 March) 1716, Anne, dau. of Joseph Judkin, of Greenhills, Cashel, and had two sons and a dau.,
        (1) Joseph, of Ballytorcen, admon. 29 June, 1756; *m.* (licence 2 Oct.) 1752, Mary, dau. of Edward Symes, of Castlelost, co. Westmeath.
        (2) William, of Borris in Ossory, *m.* — Minchin, and left issue,
            (1) Lydia, *m.* (licence 7 June), 1746, Samuel Harding, of Silvermines.
    3. JOSHUA, of whom next.

The 3rd son,
JOSHUA SMITH, of Glasshouse and Gortercan, *b.* 1665; *d.* 1752; *m.* 1690, Mary, dau. of Cornet John Higham, of Barkwell, King's Co., and by her (who was *b.* 1676 and *d.* 16 Sept. 1714) had issue, three sons and a dau.,
1. Ralph, of Glasshouse, *m.* 1735, Jane, dau. of Aquilla Kent, of Kilderry, co. Tipperary, and had a son,
    Aquilla, of Glasshouse, *m.* 1769, Phœbe, dau. of Jonathan Kent, of Ballylough Castle, and had issue, with others, *d. unm.*,
        (1) Ralph, *m.* Mary, dau. of William Hogg, of Limerick, and left, with other issue,
            1. Aquilla, *m.*—Crampton.
            2. Aquilla, *m.* 1825, Charity, dau. of Richard Daucer (see BURKE'S *Peerage*, DANCER, Bart.).
        (2) Jonathan, *m.* dau. of William End, of Limerick.
        (1) Elizabeth, *m.* Major Ralph Smith (*see below*).
        (2) Judith, *m.* Joshua Dancer, of Shinrone, and *d.* 1840, leaving issue (see BURKE'S *Peerage*, DANCER, Bart.).

2. William, of Gortercan, *b.* 1 Feb. 1700; *m.* Priscilla, dau. of — Kent, of Garry Kennedy, co. Tipperary, and had, with other issue, three sons,
    1. Aquilla, *b.* 1742; *d.* 1810; *m.* — Hastings.
    2. Joshua, *b.* 1744; *d.* 1810; *m.* June, 1774, Frances, dau. of Richard Carroll, of Enmel Castle, and had with other issue, a son,
        William Carroll, of Sora Hill House, Nenagh, *m.* Elizabeth, dau. of William Doolan, of Kilmurry, and left, with other issue,
            1. Joshua, *m.* Elizabeth Doolan.
            2. Thomas, *m.* — Short.
            1. Mary, *m.* John Doolan.
            2. Elizabeth, *m.* — Birch.
    3. William, of Smithville, *b.* 14 April, 1746; *d.* 7 Sept. 1811; *m.* 1st, 16 Feb. 1772, Abigail, dau. of Parsons Poe, of Knock (see POE of *Riverston*), and had,
        (1) Aquilla, *b.* 11 Jan. 1776; *d.* 18 April, 1858; *m.* 19 Feb. 1799, Catherine, dau. of William Doolan, of Kilmurry, and had, with other issue,
            1. William Poe, *b.* 8 Dec. 1799; *m.* — Rainsford.
            2. Aquilla, M.D. Dublin (*Honoris Causa*) 1839, *b.* 28 April, 1806; *d.* April, 1890; *m.* 21 Feb. 1831, Esther, dau. of George Faucett, and left issue by her, who *d.* 18 Feb. 1850.
        (2) Joshua, *m.* 1802, Priscilla, dau. of Amos Palmer.
            (1) Mary, *m.* 1792, John Doolan, of Cloghjordan.
        William Smith, of Smithville, *m.* 2ndly, 30 Dec. 1781, Anne, dau. of William Molloy, and had, with other issue, a dau., Martha, *m.* 1806, George Faucett. He *m.* 3rdly, Alice Poe, *s.p.*
3. JOSHUA, of whom presently.
1. Eleanor, *m.* — Hastings, of Killaloe.

The 3rd son,
JOSHUA SMITH, of Shinrone, *b.* 1711; *d.* 15 Feb. 1766; *m.* (licence 16 June), 1738, Dorothy, dau. of Robert Patten, of Dublin, and by her (who was *b.* 1715 and *d.* 24 Sept. 1794) had issue,
1. Robert, *b.* 8 Dec. 1741; *d.* 1792; Alderman of Dublin 5 May, 1787; *m.* (licence 20 Oct.) 1767, Anne Brown, and had, with other issue,
    Joshua, *m.* 1801, Maria, dau. of Sir Parker Steele, Bart. (*extinct*), and had three sons,
        (1) Robert BRAMSTON SMITH, of Hampstead, co. Dublin, and Pencraig, Anglesey, J.P., D.L., assumed the name of BRAMSTON 1839, *d.* 21 April, 1890; *m.* 4 April, 1839, Elizabeth Charlotte, dau. of Sir Richard John Griffith, Bart. (see BURKE'S *Peerage*, WALDIE-GRIFFITH, Bart.), and by her (who *d.* 4 Nov. 1907) had two daus.,
            Frances Charlotte, *m.* 6 July, 1869, Lieut.-Col. George Phibbs (see PHIBBS of *Lisheen*).
            Matilda Elizabeth, *m.* 17 Aug. 1870, John Adam Richard Newman, of Dromore, co. Cork (see NEWMAN of *Newberry Manor*).
        (2) Francis William (Sir), M.A., M.B. Dublin, Knighted 8 March, 1837, *b.* 1809; *d.* 16 Dec. 1840; *m.* 1833, Sophia Caroline, dau. of John Prendergast, and had a son and a dau.,
            Sydney, *d.s.p.*   Frances, *d.s.p.*
    2. RALPH, of whom presently.
    3. Joshua.
4. John, of Anneville, *b.* 24 Jan. 1745; *m.* — Palmer, and left issue.
5. Patten, *b.* 8 Oct. 1760; *d.* 1837; *m.* 1782, Mary, dau. of Rev. William Birch, and had, with other issue,
    1. Joshua, *b.* 1785; *d.* 1848; *m.* 1818, Elizabeth Crighton, and had issue.
    2. John Sidney, *b.* 1788; *d.* 1851, Anne, dau. of Henry Allen, and had, with four daus., two sons,
        Patten.
        Sidney, *b.* 1858; *m.* 1884, Anna Catherine, dau. of George Birch, of Monaincha.
    3. William, *b.* 1790; *d.* 1840; *m.* 1819, Frances McDowell, and had issue.
        1. Mary, *m.* 1805, William Bridge.
        2. Dora, *m.* Richard Cathcart.
1. Jane, *m.* 1769, Richard Hayes.
2. Mary, *m.* Richard Dancer (see BURKE'S *Peerage*, DANCER, Bart.).
3. Frances, *m.* 14 Feb. 1781, William Goulding.

The 2nd son,
RALPH SMITH, of Cullenwain, *b.* 24 April, 1743; *d.* 26 Jan. 1820; *m.* (licence 2 Jan.) 1769, Jane, dau. of Rev. William Birch, of The Valley House, Roscrea. She was *b.* 1749, and *d.* 25 May, 1807. He *m.* 2ndly, Jane Palmer. The issue of the 1st marriage, who survived childhood, were,
1. HENRY BIRCH, his heir.
2. Ralph, *b.* 30 Sept. 1777, Major in the Army, settled at Montreal; *m.* 1st, 1801, Elizabeth, dau. of Aquilla Smith, of Glasshouse (see *above*), and left issue
3. John, *b.* 26 Aug. 1785; *m.* 1809, Catherine, dau. of Richard Dancer (see BURKE'S *Peerage*, DANCER, Bart.).
1. Mary, *m.* 1801, Vizor Bridge, of Racket Hall, Roscrea.

The eldest son,
HENRY BIRCH SMITH, of Clareen, King's Co. *b.* 26 June, 1776; *d.* 3 June, 1849; *m.* 21 Aug. 1798, Eleanor, dau. and co-heir of George Nuttall, of Sherwood, co. Carlow, and by her (who was *b.* 1774, and *d.* 30 June, 1845) had issue,
1. RALPH, his heir.
2. George Nuttall (Rev.), B.A. Dublin, *b.* 14 April, 1804; *d.* March, 1858; *m.* 1830, Grace, dau. of Richard Hammersley, of Corolanty, King's Co., and by her (who was *b.* 26 April, 1809, and *d.* 1859) had issue,

1. Henry, b. March, 1832; d.s.p.
2. Richard William, of Dunesk, Cahir, b. Sept. 1833; m. 1863, Caroline, dau. of William Going, of Altavilla, co. Tipperary, and by her (b. 20 March, 1840; d. 1896) had issue,
   (1) George Nuttall (Rev.), M.A. Dublin, b. 14 July, 1866; m. 4 May, 1897, Maria Frances Honoria, dau. of Hugh Baker Stoney, M.D., of Abbeyleix (see STONEY of Portland Park), and has,
      1. Ralph Nuttall, b. 2 March, 1898.
      2. Hugh Richard, b. 4 Aug. 1899.
      3. Bindon William, b. 8 Dec. 1900.
      4. George Alexander, b. 24 Feb. 1902.
      5. Frederick Joshua Edward, b. 28 Sept. 1906.
      1. Daisy Mary Caroline.
   (2) Richard William, B.A. Cantab, b. 25 Aug. 1871; m. 15 Jan. 1902, Grace Ellinor, 7th dau. of Frederic Chatfield Smith, D.L., M.P., of Bramcote Hall, Notts (see that family), and has issue,
      1. William Frederic, b. 20 Sept. 1903.
      2. Richard Henry, b. 9 May, 1905.
      3. Alexander George, b. 11 Sept. 1909.
      (1) Wilhelmina.
      (2) Grace Caroline, d. 28 March, 1907.
      (3) Eleanor Matilda.
3. Henry Birch, of Cullenwain, b. 24 April, 1806; m. Frances, dau. of Major-Gen. Richard Stoven.
4. Robert Tottenham, b. 3 May, 1815; d. 6 Dec. 1867; m. Alicia Mary, dau. of John Lawder, of Ashford, co. Roscommon, and had issue by her (who d. 15 April, 1909),
   1. George Henry, B.A.T. Dublin, b. April, 1857; m. Feb. 1889, Kate Matilda, dau. of Rev. Benjamin Nicholson White Spunner, of Miltown Park, Shinrone, and has issue,
      (1) Lawder Benjamin Sandys, b. 1891.
      (2) Zoe Katherine.   (2) Eileen Norah.
1. Mary Anne, d. unm.
2. Jane Barbara, m. 2 Oct. 1838, Amos Palmer Doolan, of Derry House, King's Co.
The eldest son,
RALPH SMITH, of Clareen, J.P. King's Co., b. 27 June, 1799; d. 24 Dec. 1875; m. 1st, Hannah, dau. of Alderman John Exshaw, of Dublin, and had four sons d. unm., and a dau., Eleanor. He m. 2ndly, Alicia, 3rd dau. of Richard Hammersley, of Corrolanty, King's Co., and had,
1. WILLIAM FREDERICK HAMMERSLEY, present representative.
2. Francis George, b. 8 Sept. 1846.
3. Ralph Edward Henry, b. 13 Aug. 1850; m. 1877, Isabella Jane, dau. of Richard Lindsey Bucknall, and has issue,
   1. Ralph Henry Hammersley, b. 7 June, 1880; Lieut. 4th Bengal Lancers; m. 3 June, 1908, Magdalen Frances, 2nd dau. of Henry McDowell, of Oakhurst Park, Weybridge, Surrey.
   2. Frederick Holmes, d.s.p.
   1. Florence Evelyn, m. 20 Aug. 1908, John Wesley Smyth, of Johannesburg.
4. Henry Edward, d. unm.
5. Robert Tottenham, b. 5 Dec. 1857, of Clareen, Berea, Johannesburg, F.R.C.S.I., J.P., m. 5 Dec. 1902, Catherine Margaret, dau. of Henry James Newberry, and has issue,
   Ralph Henry Tottenham, b. 21 Sept. 1893.
1. Isabella Jane, m. George Hammersley Heenan, C.E.

Arms—Arg., on a bend between two unicorns' heads erased vert, corned or, three lozenges of the last. Crest—Out of a crest coronet or, a unicorn's head vert, armed of the 1st. Motto—Exaltabit honore.

SMITHWICK OF BALLYNGAWSEY.

REV. RICHARD FITZGERALD SMITHWICK, of Ballyngawsey, co. Limerick, and Seaforth Vicarage, Liverpool, M.A. Cantab., and Cuddesdon Coll. Oxon, Vicar of Seaforth, Rural Dean of Bootle, Hon. Canon of Liverpool and Proctor in Convocation, b. 31 Aug. 1843; m. 17 Oct. 1883, Sarah Coates, dau. of Walter Hebden Wilson, of Nortonsea, Waterloo, near Liverpool, and has issue,
1. ROBERT FITZGERALD, b. 18 June, 1886.
2. Walter FitzGerald, b. 14 April, 1891.
1. Catherine Elinora, b. 6 Sept. 1884.
2. Geraldine, b. 17 May, 1893.
3. Stella, b. 27 Oct. 1894.

Lineage.—ROBERT SMITHWICK, of Rathjordan, J.P. cos. Limerick and Tipperary (see SMITHWICK of Youghal), b. May, 1760; m. 1st, 1787 Rebecca, dau. of Henry White, J.P., of New Ross, and Mantle Hil co. Tipperary, by Elizabeth his wife, 3rd dau. of Thomas Maunsell, LL.D., K.C., M.P. for Kilmallock, and Dorothea his wife, youngest dau. of Richard Waller, of Castle Waller, co. Tipperary, and had issue, ROBERT, his heir. Mr. Smithwick m. 2ndly, in 1803, Eliza, dau. of Rev. John Madder, Rector of Newport, co. Tipperary, by Dorothea his wife, dau. of George Gough, of Woodstown, co. Limerick (grandfather of Hugh, 1st Viscount Gough), but by her had no issue. His son,

ROBERT SMITHWICK, of Ballyngawsey, R.M., m. 12 March, 1829, Catherine, dau. of Rev. Richard FitzGerald, and by her (who d. 21 Dec. 1870) had issue,
1. RICHARD FITZGERALD, of Ballyngawsey.
2. Robert, d. 22 Dec. 1885.
1. Rebecca, d. 22 Nov. 1859.
2. Ellen FitzGerald, m. 7 May, 1853, William Pidgeon, J.P., of Athlone, co. Westmeath, and Greystones, co Wicklow, and has issue. Mr. Smithwick d. 16 Dec. 1881.

Residence—Seaforth Vicarage, Liverpool.

SMITHWICK OF YOUGHAL.

The late CAPT. WILLIAM FITZWILLIAM SMITHWICK, of Youghal, co. Tipperary, late 47th Foot, b. 1834, d. 7 April, 1909; m. Flora, dau. of J. Lamming.

Lineage.—WILLIAM SMITHWICK was in the Commission of the Peace for co. Tipperary in 1715, and he was probably father of JOHN SMITHWICK, of Abbey Athassel, who d. at an advanced age in 1769. This John Smithwick left two sons,
1. PETER, his heir.
2. Robert, of Barnlough, co. Tipperary, who m. and left numerous issue.
The elder son,
PETER SMITHWICK, of Mount Catherine, co. Limerick, m. Miss Apjohn, of Linfield, co. Limerick, and d. 1780, having had issue,
1. WILLIAM, of whom presently.
2. Peter, who m. Miss Gabbett, and had an only dau., Martha.
1. Margaret, m. — Bradshaw.
The elder son,
WILLIAM SMITHWICK, of Mt. Catherine, m. 1753, Catherine, dau. of William Gabbett, of Caherline, co. Limerick, and d. 29 Sept. 1796, having had issue,
1. Peter, d. unm.
2. John, m. Anne Lloyd, of Dromsalla, and d. leaving issue,
   1. William John, (Rev.)
   1. Maria, m. John Scott.   2. Catherine.
   3. Anna Ogilvie, m. 1818, Peter Broughton, of Tunstal Hall, Shropshire (see that family).
3. Robert, of Rathjordan, co. Limerick (see SMITHWICK of Ballyngawsey).
4. MICHAEL, of Mt. Catherine, of whom later.
1. Margaret.
2. Martha, m. 1866, Francis Wise, of Anne Grove, co. Cork.
The youngest son,
MICHAEL SMITHWICK, of Mount Catherine, co. Limerick, m. 1st, 1797, Alicia, dau. of William Bleasby, of Ballycoree, co. Cork; and 2ndly, Elizabeth, dau. of Ven. Garrett Wall, Archdeacon of Emly. She m. 2ndly 1807, Abram Orpen, M.D., of Cork. By his 1st wife Mr. Smithwick had issue,
1. WILLIAM BLEASBY, of whom hereafter.
2. John, of Rathclogheen, co. Tipperary, m. 1823, Cherry, dau. of Thomas Pennefather, of Ballylanigan, co. Tipperary, and left three daus.,
   1. Anne, m. 1845, William Johnson, of Vostersburg, co. Cork, D.L.
   2. Cherry.   2. Elizabeth, m. — Pennefather.
3. Michael, of Mt. Catherine, m. 1825, Maria, 2nd dau. of Richard Waller, of Castle Waller (see WALLER of Rockvale), and d. 1857, leaving a son,
   William Henry, of Mt. Catherine, b. 1826; d. unm.
4. Peter, of Shanbally, and Tullamore Park, co. Tipperary, b. 1806; m. Mary, dau. of Rev. Robert Gabbett, LL.D., Rector of Castletown, and d. 1894, having had issue,
   1. Robert, of Crannagh, co. Tipperary, b. 1833; m. 1870, Charlotte, dau. of Admiral Webb, R.N., of Milford House, Surrey, and has issue,
      (1) Emily, m. 1904, Thomas Newton Brady.
      (2) Norah, d. unm.
   2. John, of Shanbally, J.P., b. 1836; m. 1866, Emily, dau. of Admiral Webb, of Milford House, Surrey, and has issue,
      (1) Edith, m. Edward Abraham Jones.
      (2) Mary Prolyn.
   3. Frederick Peter, of Monsea, co. Tipperary, b. 1838, d. 9 Oct. 1911.
   4. Standish Poole (Rev.), Rector of Monasterevan, and Chancellor of Kildare Cathedral, b. 1848; m. 1875, Caroline Anna Grant, dau. of George Grant Webb, 6th Foot, of Ballyhay, co. Down, and d. 1909, having had issue,
      (1) Charles Standish, b. 1877; d. unm. 1897.
      (2) Standish George, Capt. Royal Dublin Fusiliers, b. 1878.
      (3) Frederick Falkiner (Rev.), Chaplain to the Forces, b. 1879; m. 1908, Violet Irene, dau. of William Perry Odlum of Huntingdon, Queen's Co.
      (4) Algernon Robert, Lieut. R.N., b. 1887.
      (1) Mary Louisa, m. Norman Fraser Falkiner, of Moira, N.S.W.
5. George Arnold, b. 1852; d. unm.
1. Alicia, m. 1852, Andrew Jackson, of Mt. Pleasant, co. Tipperary.

Smyly. THE LANDED GENTRY. 646

2. Mary Emilia.
3. Elizabeth, *m.* Rev. Edward Synge, Rector of Zockeen, co. Tipperary.
4. Agnes, *m.* 1895, William Evans, of Gilliardstown, co. West Meath.
5. Caroline Maud.
1. Maria, *m.* Samuel Bleasby.

The eldest son,
WILLIAM BLEASBY SMITHWICK, of Youghal, co. Tipperary, J.P., *b.* 1800; *m.* 1827, Anna, dau. of Rev. Robert Gabbett, LL.D. Rector of Castletown (*see* GABBETT *of Caherline*), and *d.* 1891, having had issue,
1. WILLIAM FITZWILLIAM late of Youghal.
2. Robert John, *m.* Miss Laura Vyner, and *d.* leaving issue,
   1. Charles. 2. Vyner.
   3. William.
   1. Laura. 2. Dorothy.
3. Charles Albert, *d. unm.*
4. Mary, *m.* Heber Koe, of the Lodge, Nenagh, co. Tipperary.
2. Annette, *d. unm.* 3. Harriet.
4. Elizabeth.
5. Margaret, *m.* 30 Sept. 1875, James Netterville Atkinson, of Ashley Park, co. Tipperary (*see that family*).
6. Kathleen.

Seat—Youghal, Nenagh, co. Tipperary.

SMYLY OF CAMUS.

His HONOUR JUDGE WILLIAM CECIL SMYLY, of Camus and Castlederg, co. Tyrone, Barrister-at-Law, K.C., County Court Judge at Bow and Shoreditch, *b.* 1840; *s.* his brother 1912, *m.* 1884, Alice, only dau. of Samuel Brooks, of Watford, and has issue,
1. CECIL FERGUSON, *b.* 1884.
2. Alexander Ferguson, *b.* 1886.
1. Alice Eileen, *b.* 23 May, 1889.
2. Sylvia Mary, *b.* 9 Jan. 1891.

Lineage.—JOHN SMYLY came from Scotland, and settled at Carrygullion, near Camus, in 1628. He left three sons: John, *b.* 1634; Robert, *b.* 1636; and Thomas, *b.* 1638. John, the eldest son *m.* and had issue,

ROBERT SMYLY, of Camus, *b.* 1676, who *d.* 1742, leaving issue, two sons,
1. JOHN, his heir.
2. Robert, of Carrygullion, co. Tyrone, *b.* 1701: who *m.* Anne Tredennick, and *d.* 1777, leaving issue, now extinct in the male line.

The elder son,
JOHN SMYLY, of Camus, *b.* 1700; *m.* 1st, 1727, Prudence Williams, and by her (who *d.* 1750) had issue,
WILLIAM, his successor.
Catherine, *m.* Samuel Tagert, of Woodbrook, co. Tyrone.
He *m.* 2ndly, 1752, Margaret Moore, and *d.* 1787. The elder son,

WILLIAM SMYLY, of Camus, *b.* 1730; *m.* 1759, Jane, eldest dau. and co-heir of John Armstrong, of Strabane, by his wife Anne, dau. and co-heir of Robert Conyngham, and *d.* 1812, leaving one son and one dau.,
JOHN, of whom hereafter.
Anne, *m.* Alexander Crawford, of Lisburn, M.D.

The eldest son,
JOHN SMYLY, Barrister-at-Law, K.C., *b.* 1767; *m.* 1796, Belissa dau. of John Crampton, of Merrion Square, Dublin, and sister of Sir Philip Crampton, Bart., the celebrated surgeon. Mr. Smyly *d.* 1821, having had issue, five sons and three daus.,
1. JOHN GEORGE, of whom presently.
2. Cecil (Rev.), Vicar of Carlingford, *b.* 1802; *d.* 28 Dec. 1874; *m.* 31 Oct. 1834, Elizabeth, 5th dau. of Nathaniel Callwell who *d.* 1883, leaving one dau.
   Ellen Frances, *d.* 20 March, 1869; *m.* Rev. Edward Gabbett, Archdeacon of Limerick.
3. Josiah, of Merrion Square, M.D., *b.* 1803; *m.* Ellen, dau. of Matthew Franks, and *d.* 1864, leaving three sons and six daus.,
   1. Philip Crampton (Sir), Knt., M.D., *b.* 1838; *m.* 1 Feb. 1864, Hon. Selina Maria, dau. of 3rd Lord Plunket (*see* BURKE'S *Peerage*), and *d.* 8 April, 1904, having had issue,

(1) Philip Crampton (Sir), Knt., Chief Justice of Sierra Leone, *b.* 1864; *m.* (*his cousin*) 1905, Eileen, dau. of Sir Wm. J. Smyly, M.D. (*see below*).
(2) Josiah Gilbert, Fellow Trin. Coll. Dublin, *b.* 1867.
(3) Wm. Cecil, *b.* 1883.
(1) Charlotte, *m.* Joseph Shaw, K.C., Barrister-at-Law.
(2) Mabel, *m.* 8 March, 1902, Wm. Dermod O'Brien, of Cahirmoyle, co. Limerick, and has issue (*see that family*).
(3) Sylvia. (4) Constance.

2. Matthew John, of Boden Park, co. Dublin, M.A., *b.* 1848; *m.* Katherine, dau. of John Davis Garde, of Mt. Dillon, co. Dublin, and has issue,
   (1) Richard Josiah, Capt. North Lancs. Regt., *b.* 1879; *m.* 1910, Miss Pilkington, and has issue,
   (2) Neville, *m.* Effie, dau. of David Tennent, and has issue, John David, *b.* 1905.
   (3) Gordon, *d. unm.* 1907.
   (4) Percy.
   (1) Ruth Eleanor, *m.* 1907, Rev. Ralph Granby Sadleir, R.N. and has issue (*see* SADLEIR *of Castletown*).
   (2) Louisa, *m.* Percy Harris.

3. Wm. Josiah (Sir), of Merrion Square, Knt., M.D., *b.* 1850; *m.* Eleanor, dau. of Henry Tweedy, M.D., of Dublin (*see* TWEEDY *of Cloonmahon*) and has issue,
   (1) Henry Joscelyn.
   (1) Eileen, *m.* (*her cousin*) 1905, Sir Philip Crampton Smyly Knt. (*see above*).
   (2) Rachel. (3) Phyllis.
   (4) Vivienne.
1. Harriet.
2. Mary, *m.* John Gibson Watson, and *d.* 1906.
3. Ellen.
4. Louisa, *m.* Rev. Robt. Warren Stewart (*see* STEWART *of Summerhill*).
5. Anne. 6. Mildred.

4. William (Rev.), Rector of Aghaulos, *b.* 1799; *m.* Catherine, Charlotte, dau. and co-heir of Right Hon. John Claudius Beresford, M.P., and *d.* 1835, leaving issue,
   1. John Beresford, Maj.-Gen., of Glenmoyle, co. Derry, *b.* 1828, adopted name of BERESFORD in lieu of Smyly; *m.* 1866, Emma, 3rd dau. of Rev. Bourchier Wray Savile, and has, with other issue, a son Rev. John Claudius, *b.* 28 April, 1871.
   2. Wm. Archibald (Rev.), Rector of Kilcullen, *b.* 1834; *m.* Annie Calvert Brown, and has issue,
      (1) Constantia, *d. unm.* (2) Marion, *m.* Alfred Gossett.
      (3) Belissa, *m.* Alfred Ord. (4) Selina, *m.* Spencer Heaven.

5 Philip, Maj.-Gen., *m.* 1849, Mary, dau. of John Dunn, of Heathfield, Hobart, Tasmania, and had issue,
   1. William (Rev.), M.A., Rector of Penge, *m.* Evelyn Grace, dau. of Capt. Jacob Hierom Sankey, of Coolmore, co. Tipperary (*see that family*).
   2. Frederick Philip, Major South Wales Borderers, *b.* 1856; *m.* 1885, Charlotte, dau. of Sir John Frederick Price, K.C.S.I. (*see* PRICE, Bart.).
   3. John George, *m.* Wilhelmina, dau. of James Todd-Thornton, of Westbrook, co. Donegal (*see that family*).
   1. Augusta. 2. Belissa.

1. Belissa, *m.* 1835, Espine Batty, of Ballyhealy, co. West Meath.
3. Anne, *m.* 1842, Rev. Brent Neville.
2. Charlotte, *m.* 1838, Ven. Joseph Thacker, Archdeacon of Ossory.

The eldest son,
JOHN GEORGE SMYLY, Barrister-at-Law, Q.C., D.L., co. Tyrone, *b.* 1797; *m.* 1828, Eliza, dau. and co-heir of Sir Andrew Ferguson, Bart., M.P., of Castlederg, co. Tyrone (by his wife Elizabeth, dau. of Robert Alexander and niece of the 1st Earl of Caledon), and *d.* 1866, having had issue,
1. JOHN GEORGE, of whom next.
2. Andrew Ferguson, (Very Rev.), Dean of Derry, D.D., *b.* 1831; *m.* 1st, 10 Jan. 1856, Eliza, dau. of Rev. Robert Alexander (and sister of Most Rev. William Alexander, Archbishop of Armagh); and *d.* 9 May, 1875, leaving issue three daus.,
   1. Frances, *m.* Major Arthur Smyth of Ballintemple, and has issue,
   2. Jane, *m.* H. B. Lane, of Rush Hall, Limavady, and has issue.
   3. Dorothea, *m.* Rev. Richard King, Rector of Limavady, and has issue.
Dean Smyly *m.* 2ndly, 27 Dec. 1876, Barbara Anne (who *d.* 25 April, 1911), dau. of John Montgomery of Benvarden, co. Antrim, and *d.* 1897 (*see that family*).
3. WILLIAM CECIL, now of Camus.
1. Elizabeth Ferguson, *d. unm.* 1904.
2. Ellen Belissa, *m.* 1867, Rev. Edward Newland, Canon of Derry. He *d.* — and had issue,
   John George, *d. unm.*
   Eliza Ferguson, *m.* 16 Oct. 1900, Major John Alexander Montgomery, of Benvarden, co. Antrim, and has issue (*see that family*).

The eldest son,
MAJOR JOHN GEORGE SMYLY, of Camus and Castlederg, co. Tyrone, late Derry Militia, *b.* 1829; educated at Winchester and Trin. Coll., Dublin, *s.* his father 1866. He *d.* 17 Feb. 1912, being *s.* by his brother.

Arms.—Az., a chevron erm. between three pheons arg. Crest—An armed arm embowed ppr., the hand holding a pheon by the point thereof, gu. Motto—Viribus virtus.

Residence—84, St. George's Square, W.

SMYTH OF MOUNT HENRY.

MAJ. RANDAL CHARLES EDWARD SKEFFINGTON SMYTH, of Mount Henry, Queen's Co., J.P. and D.L., Maj. (ret.) late Coldstream Guards, b. 27 Dec. 1864; m. 27 July, 1888, Beatrix Virginia Louisa Tollemache, dau. of the late Col. the Right Hon. T. Edward Taylor, of Ardgillan, Balbriggan, co. Meath, M.P. for Dublin.

Lineage. — JAMES SMYTH of Lisnegarvy, co. Antrim, m. Frances, dau. of Edward Dowdall, of Mountown, co. Meath, by Margaret, dau. of Sir Henry Piers, Bart., and had issue,
1. John, m. Mary, dau. of William Scott, of Shanganagh, Queen's Co., and had issue, two sons and three daus.
2. EDWARD, of whom presently.
3. William (Rev.), Archdeacon of Connor, will proved 1710; m. Katherine, dau. of Foulk Mastin.
 1. Mary, m. Humphrey Clerk, of Ballinderry, co. Antrim.
 2. Margaret, m. Anthony Harris, D.D.
 3. Elizabeth, d. unm.

The 2nd son,
RIGHT REV. EDWARD SMYTH, D.D., Bishop of Down and Connor, b. at Lisburn, 1662, having been educated at the University at Dublin, was elected a Fellow in 1684, but expelled by JAMES II 1689. He was afterwards Chaplain to WILLIAM III, and was appointed, 1696, Dean of St. Patrick's, and consecrated Bishop of Down and Connor 2 April, 1699, when arms were confirmed to him. He m. 1st, lic. 15 Feb. 1696, Elizabeth, dau. of William Smyth, Bishop of Kilmore, by whom he had
1. Elizabeth, m. 24 Feb. 1726-7, James, 1st Earl of Courtown. He m. 2ndly, April. 1710, Hon. Mary Skeffington, dau. of Clotworthy, 3rd Viscount Massereene, and had issue,
 1. SKEFFINGTON RANDAL, of whom we treat.
 2. James, of Tenny Park, co. Wicklow, M.P. for Antrim, in 1742, Mary, dau. of James Agar, and sister of Ellis, Countess of Brandon in her own right, and d. 23 June, 1771, leaving issue,
  1. Skeffington Edward (Sir), P.C., created a bart. 1776; m. Nov. 1782, Margaret, dau. of Hyacinth Daly, of Dalystown (and heir to her brother, the Right Hon. Denis Bowes Daly, M.P.), by whom he had two daus. and co-heirs,
   (1) Maria, m. 5 March, 1808, James, 1st Lord Dunsandle, and had issue.
   (2) Elizabeth, m. M. G. Prendergast, M.P. for Galway.
  1. Mary, m. 25 April, 1758, John Preston, of Bellinter, and was mother of Lord Tara (see BURKE's Extinct Peerage).
  2. Ellis, m. 6 Sept. 1764, Francis, 1st Earl of Llandaff. She d. 9 Aug. 1782, leaving issue (see BURKE's Extinct Peerage).
  3. Elizabeth, m. 1777, Comte de Jarnac, Vicomte de Chabot.
 2. Rachel, m. 14 Dec. 1738, Francis Burton, and had issue.

The Bishop of Down d. at Bath, 16 Oct. 1720. His elder son,
SKEFFINGTON RANDAL SMYTH, m. 21 Aug. 1735, Mary, dau. of Hon. and Rev. John Moore, D.D., Vicar of St. Katherine, Dublin, and Chaplain to the House of Commons, 4th son of Henry, 3rd Earl of Drogheda, and d. 23 Oct. 1748, leaving a dau., Mary, m. 4 Aug. 1764, Lieut.-Col. Henry Gore, M.P., co. Longford, 2nd Lord Annaly of Tenelick, and a son,
EDWARD SMYTH, of Jubilee Hall, Queen's Co., b. 15 Sept. 1746; m. 1st, Mary Anne Needham; and 2ndly, Letitia, dau. of Very Rev. Arthur Champagné, Dean of Clomacnois, and was s. by his son,
HENRY SMYTH, of Mount Henry, Queen's Co., and Terlicken, co. Longford, m. Olivia, dau. of Rev. Edward Lucas, of Coote Hill, and d. 1838, leaving by her, who m. 2ndly, 1840, Robert Hamilton Stubber, of Moyne, Queen's Co., an only son,
EDWARD SKEFFINGTON RANDAL SMYTH, of Mount Henry, Queen's Co., Vice-Lieut., D.L. and J.P. for that co., and J.P. for King's Co., High Sheriff for the former 1865, and for co. Longford 1893, served as Lieut. 28th Regt. in Crimean campaign 1855, including the siege and fall of Sebastopol, wounded, received medal and clasp, and Turkish medal, b. 27 Sept. 1831; m. 9 Sept. 1862, Hon. Gertrude Valentine Fitz-Patrick, dau. of John, 1st Lord Castletown of Upper Ossory. He d. 25 Dec. 1897. She d. 25 Jan. 1912, having had issue,
1. RANDAL CHARLES EDWARD SKEFFINGTON, now of Mount Henry.
2. Geoffrey Henry Julian Skeffington (20, Hertford Street, W.), D.S.O., Major Army Motor Reserve, late Capt. 9th Lancers, b. 11 Dec. 1873; m. 7 July, 1904, Hon. Violet Frances Monckton, only dau. of the 7th Viscount Galway (see BURKE's Peerage), and has issue,
 1. Terence George Randal, b. 31 May, 1905.
 2. Noel Edward Vere, b. 25 Dec. 1908.
 3. Denys Brian, b. 16 July, 1910.
1. Viola Lilian Heuriette, m. 19 Sept. 1894, Edward Kenrick Bunbury Tighe, of Woodstock, Inistioge, co. Kilkenny, and has issue (see that family).

Arms—Arg., on a bend az., between two unicorns' heads erased sa., three lozenges or. Crest—A unicorn's head couped sa.
Seat—Mount Henry, Portarlington. Club—Guards.

SMYTH OF GAYBROOK.

COL. JAMES SMYTH, of Gaybrook, co. Westmeath, J.P. and D.L., High Sheriff 1892, Col. in the Army, lately commanding the Lancashire Fusiliers (20th Regt.), b. 6 Oct. 1839; s. his brother 1890; m. 13 Sept. 1883, Lucy Helen, only dau. of George Nugent Purdon, of Lisnabin, co. Westmeath (see that family), and has issue,
1. ROBERT, b. 19 Feb. 1885.
2. James, b. 24 Jan. 1886.

Lineage.—WILLIAM SMYTH, of Dundrum, co. Down, settled in Ireland from Rossdale Abbey, co. York, temp. JAMES I, 1630, m. Mary, dau. of John Dowdall, of Glasspistol, co. Louth, by Anne his wife, dau. of Sir Thomas Cusack. He had issue,
1. JOHN, who had a son, JAMES, and three daus., 1. Marjorie, m. Richard Currell; 2. Katherine, m. 1701, Rev. Benjamin Span, Vicar Gen. of Diocese of Armagh, and had issue; 3. Judith, m. Capt. Kelly, of Portadown. The only son,
JAMES SMYTH, m. his cousin, Sarah Dawson, and had, with Richard, Eleanor, Anne, Mary, Eliza, and Marjorie, an elder son,
REV. CURRELL SMYTH, m. 1739, Anne, dau. of Rev. Robert Meares, of the Meares Court family, and had, with a younger son, Currell, who d. at Florence, and two daus., Anne, m. John Hopkins, and Sarah, m. George Slator, of Swiftbrooke, co. Dublin, an elder son,
ROBERT SMYTH, m. Elizabeth Newitt, and had issue,
 1. Currell, m. Katherine, dau. of Charles Kelly, of Glencarra (see that family), and had issue.
 2. Robert.
 3. William Henry, m. Amanda Rooke, and had a son, ROBERT BOLTON, Lieut.-Col. in the Army, m. Miss Atkinson.
 4. Beresford Burston, m. Clemina Kelly.
 5. HENRY, of Allenstown, co. Meath.
 1. Sarah, m. Thomas Houston.
 2. Elizabeth Jane, m. Robert Eyre, of Tarlton, co. Galway
 2. RALPH, of whom hereafter.
 1. Isabel, m. M. Dawson, and had issue.

The 2nd son,
RALPH SMITH, of Ballymacash, co. Antrim, High Sheriff 1680, Capt. in the Army, will proved 1690, m. Elizabeth, dau. of Richard Hawkesworth, of co. York, and had issue,
1. WILLIAM (Right Rev.), his successor.
2. Thomas, ancestor of SMYTH of Drumcree (see that family).
3. Ralph, of Ballingarry, co. Tipperary, m. Mary Jackson, and had a dau., Mary, m. Anthony Walsh, of Grange Carn, co. Down, and a son,
Ralph, of Ballingarry, m. Anne, dau. of — Cornwall, of Ballylusky, co. Tipperary, who had, with a dau., Mary, m. Thomas Johnson, of Lisburn (now Johnson-Smyth), a son,
Thomas Smith, of Ballingarry Castle, co. Tipperary, m. a dau. of Thomas Cooke, of Ardzlin, co. Tipperary, and d. 1754, having had a son,
Ralph, of Lismacrory, m. Anne, dau. of John Drought, of Cappagolan, and The Heath, King's Co., and had a son,
Thomas, of Lismacrory, d. 10 May, 1774, will proved 1774; m. Dorcas, dau. of John Smith, of Violetstown, co. Westmeath, and had three sons,
 1. RALPH, of Milford House, co. Tipperary, m. 2 Feb. 1772, Elizabeth, dau. of George Stoney, of Greyiort, and d. Oct. 1813, having had (with two daus., Rebecca Margaretta, m. 1795, Joseph Bernard of Frankfort, King's Co., whose dau. Elizabeth, m. James W. Cusack, of Abbeyville and Cussington; and Sarah, m. Lieut.-Col. C. A. Bailey, Governor of the Island of Goza) a son and heir,
Ralph, of Milford, co. Tipperary, and of the Co. of Dublin, m. Ellen, dau. of Richard Flood Firman, of Slevoir, co. Tipperary, and d. 1835, having issue (with six daus, the eldest, 1, Ellen, m. Thomas Pierson Firman; 2, Joanna; 3. Horatio; 4, Anne; 5, Margaret; 6, Henrietta); three sons,
  1. Ralph Smith, of Milford, b. 1814; m. Rebecca Margaretta, dau. of Thomas Bunbury, of Lisbryan, and d. at Rock Island, Illinois, U.S.A., 1852, leaving issue,
   a. Richard Flood, d. in London, leaving issue.
   b. Ralph Sydney.
   c. Charles, d. in America.
   d. Francis, of Carter Co., Kentucky, America.
  2. Richard Flood, b. 1815; d.s.p., aged 23.
  3. William Sidney, of Milford House, Christchurch, New Zealand, b. 1822; d. 29 Nov. 1902, m. 1880, Louisa Bagot, dau. of John D'Arcy, of Clifden Castle, and Kiltulla, co. Galway (by his 2nd wife, Louisa Bagot, dau. of Henry Sneyd, son of Ralph Sneyd, of Keele Hall, Staffordshire. She d. 2 April, 1903, leaving issue,
   a. James Henry, m. Mary Eleanor Galwey, and has issue, Sidney O'Carroll.
   Eleanor D'Arcy.
   b. Norman Lionel D'Arcy, Major and late Chief Staff Officer, New Zealand Defence Force.

c. Ralph Sneyd (*Milford Street, Christchurch, New Zealand*).
   a. Louisa, *m.* Philip Henry Cannon, and has issue.
   b. Ellen Sneyd.
   c. Anne Frances, *m.* William Sackville Smythe, and has issue (*see below*).
   d. Joanna Elizabeth.
2. John (Rev.), *m.* Jane, dau. of Thomas Bernard, of Castle Bernard, King's Co. He *d.* 15 Jan. 1813.
3. William, of Gurteen, co. Tipperary, *m.* Sarah, dau. of George Stoney, of Greyfort.
4. Robert (Rev.), Vicar of Ballyloughloe, co. Westmeath, *m.* Miss Arnold, and had issue,
  1. Michael, *m.* Isabella Johnstone, and had issue.
  1. Alice, *m.* Rev. Joseph Travers, and had issue.
  2. Jane, *m.* 1714, Rev. Stephen Radcliffe, and had issue.
1. Alice, *m.* George Lambert, and had issue, of whom was Ralph Lambert, Bishop of Meath 1726-31, and Elizabeth, his sister, *m.* William Brabazon, of Rath House, Louth, and had issue (*see* BURKE's *Peerage,* MEATH, E.).
2. Mary, *m.* Col. Daniel McGenis, and had issue.
3. Margaret.

Capt. Smyth's will is dated 15 Aug. 1688. His eldest son,

RIGHT REV. WILLIAM SMYTH, Bishop of Kilmore and Ardagh, *b.* 1644, was consecrated Bishop of Raphoe, 1682, and translated to Kilmore 1693. He *m.* May, 1672, Mary, dau. of Sir John Povey, Chief Justice of the Common Pleas of Ireland, and had,
1. Ralph, *m.* Anne, dau. of Col. Sir J. Lanier, of the Guards, and *d.s.p.* 1737.   2. JAMES, of whom we treat.
8. WILLIAM, ancestor of SMYTHE *of Barbavilla* (*whom see*).
  1. Elizabeth, *m.* Feb. 1696, Edward Smyth, Bishop of Down and Connor (*see* SMYTH *of Mount Henry*).
  2. Mary, *m.* Thomas de Burgh, of Oldtown, co. Kildare, and had issue (*see that family*).
  3. Frances, *m.* Darby Clarke, of Kildare, and had issue.
  4. Alice, *m.* Rev. John Echlin, nephew of John Vesey, D.D., Archbishop of Tuam.

The Bishop of Kilmore *d.* 24 Feb. 1698. His 2nd son,

VEN. JAMES SMYTH, Archdeacon of Meath, appointed 14 Sept. 1732, *m.* June, 1713, Catherine, dau. of John Vesey, D.D., Archbishop of Tuam, and had issue,
1. RALPH, of whom presently.
2. Edward, High Sheriff, co. Fermanagh, 1747, *m.* Eleanor, dau. and heir of John Ralphson, and had four daus., Catherine, *m.* Joseph Steck, D.D., Bishop of Killala; Anna Maria, *m.* William Newcome, D.D., Archbishop of Armagh; Eleanor, *m.* Henry Palmer, M.A., Archdeacon of Ossory; Jane.
3. James (Rev.), of Bath, *m.* Hannah, dau. of Arthur Reynell, of co. Kildare, and *d.s.p.*
4. William, an Officer of Dragoons, *m.* Charlotte, dau. of Capt. Charles Stewart, of Lisburn, co. Antrim, and of Clunie, co. Perth, by Rose, his wife, dau. of Roger Hall, of Narrow Water, co. Down, and had issue,
  1. James (Rev.), *m.* Joanna Ryan, and had one son,
    William St. John (Rev.), of Ballymoney, co. Antrim, Chancellor of Down, 8 Jan. 1828, Præcentor of Connor, March, 1843, *m.* Mary, dau. of Henry Mant, and *d.* Jan. 1847, leaving a dau., Gertrude Adeline, *m.* Rev. George Webster, D.D., Chancellor of Cork, and five sons,
      1. Henry Mant, *m.* and had issue.
      2. William Nugent, of Royd's Hall, co. York, *b.* 19 Nov. 1831; *m.* 20 Oct. 1863, Catherine Isabel, eldest dau. of Charles Hardy, of Odsall House, co. York, and Chilham Castle, Kent, brother of Gathorne, 1st Earl of Cranbrook (*see* BURKE's *Peerage*), and has issue a son and a dau.,
        Arthur Nugent, of Kyme Lodge, Tadcaster, Yorks, *b.* 7 July, 1864; *m.* 1st, 23 Sept. 1891, Ethel Mary Hague, dau. of Thomas Hague Cook, of Hall Croft, Mirfield, Yorks. She *d.s.p.* 7 Oct. 1892. He *m.* 2ndly, 20 Nov. 1894, Evelyn Duesbery, youngest dau. of Col. W. Wilkinson, of Cottingham, E. Yorks, and has issue by her,
          a. Eileen.
          b. Enid Evelyn.
        Gertrude Catherine Nugent.
      3. Arthur Gaselee, *m.* Miss Lawrence.
      4. Charles Reginald.
      5. Richard Phillott, *m.* Mary Thompson.
  2. Ralph, 30th Regt., *m.* Amelia St. George, dau. of Rev. Thomas Adderley Browne (*see* BROWNE *of Riverstown*), and has issue,
    (1) William Thomas, *m.* Mary Gray, dau. of Richard Chambers, of Whitebourne Court, co. Hertford, and Cradley Hall, co. Worcester, and had issue,
        Edward St. George, 30th Regt., *m.* Marie, dau. of Mons. J. de Lignières, grand-dau. of Charles Dieudonné de Montenach, Patrician of Fribourg.
        Mary St. George, *m.* Rev. William Austin, son of William Piersy Austin, D.D., Bishop of Guiana, and has issue.
    (2) Thomas Graham (Rev.), of La Fouan, near Nice, *b.* 1810; *m.* 1st, Charlotte, dau. of Capt. G. H. Baumgarten, R.N., and 2ndly, Cecilia, dau. of the late W. Gale, of Bardsea Hall, Ulverstone, who *d.* his widow, 26 April, 1901.
    (3) Ralph, of St. George's Lodge, Southampton, Lieut.-Col. in the Army, *m.* 1st, Mary, dau. of J. Gibbon, and had issue,
      1. Ralph Graham, Major R.E., *m.* Lucy, dau. of J. Werge.
      2. Charles Thuillier.
      1. Jemima, *m.* Lieut. Ross, 35th Regt.
      2. Amelia St. George, *m.* William Bayley.
      3. Katherine, *m.* Frederick Higginson, M.D

Col. Smyth *m.* 2ndly, Harriett, dau. of Campbell Cameron, and has further issue,
  3. Ralph Adderley.
  4. Edward Adderley St. George, *m.* and has issue, Male Cameron, *b.* 4 May, 1901.
  5. Hugh Cameron.
  4. Maud.
(4) George Sackville, Lieut. in the Guards of the late King of Hanover, *m.* Maria, dau. of Newburgh, Higginbothom, and left issue,
  1. Newburgh Ralph, *m.*, and has issue.
  2. William Sackville, *m.* Anne Frances, dau. of William Sidney Smith, of Milford, Ch.Ch., N.Z. (*see above*), and has issue,
    a. Alice Louisa.
    b. Eileen St. George.
  1. Amelia St. George Catherine.
  2. Eileen Eva Graham. *m.* Henry Satto.
  3. Alice Harriett. *m.* John Martin.
  4. Katherine, *m.* George Armstrong.
(1) Anne, *m.* J. Thompson, of Sherwood Hall, co. Nottingham, and had issue, of wnom the 3rd son is Sir Ralph Wood Thompson, K.C.B., Permanent Under-Secretary for War.
(2) Elizabeth Katharyne.
(3) Amelia St. George, *m.* Rev. Henry Turton, Vicar of Betley, co. Stafford, and has issue.
(4) Katherine Mary, *m.* Rev. Henry Deane, Prebendary of Salisbury Cathedral, and has issue.
  1. Anne, *m.* Major Philip Stewart, and had issue.
  2. Katherine, *m.* Richard Stewart, of Galgorm, co. Antrim, and *d.* 19 March, 1809, leaving issue.
1. Anne Maria, *m.* William Waller, of Allenstown.

The Archdeacon of Meath *d.* 1759. His eldest son,

RALPH SMYTH, of Fieldstown, co. Westmeath, High Sheriff 1766, *m.* 4 April, 1748, Judith, dau. of Balthazar John Cramer, by Hon. Judith Butler, his wife, dau. of Brinsley, 1st Viscount Lanesborough, and had (with a younger son, James, Capt. R.N., who was killed in action during the American war, 1781), an elder son and heir,

RALPH SMYTH, of Gaybrook, High Sheriff 1790. *b.* 1751; *m.* 1st, Mary, dau. of M. Harrison, by whom he had several children, all of whom *d.* young, except a dau.,
1. Catherine, *m.* Hon. George Cavendish, of Leixlip Castle, co. Kildare.

He *m.* 2ndly, 1799, Hannah Maria, dau. of Sir Robert Staples, 5th bart., of Dunmore, and by her (who *d.* 16 Feb. 1849) had issue,
1. RALPH, his heir.   2. ROBERT, successor to his brother.
2. Mary Jane. *d. unm.* 27 Feb. 1843.
3. Anne, *m.* 1830, Walter MacGeough Bond, of The Argory, co. Armagh, and *d.* 1892, leaving issue.
4. Elizabeth Selina, *m.* 1839, Francis Longworth-Dames, of Greenhill, King's Co., and had issue.

Mr. Smyth *d.* 1817, and was *s.* by his eldest son,

RALPH SMYTH, of Gaybrook, *b.* 1800; *m.* 1821, Georgiana, dau. of Hon. John Thomas Capel, 2nd son of William Anne, 4th Earl of Essex, by whom (who *m.* 2ndly, 18 June, 1831, Pierce O'Brien Butler, of Dunboyne Castle, co. Meath, and *d.* 19 Oct. 1835) he had no issue. He *d.* 1827, and was *s.* by his brother,

ROBERT SMYTH, of Gaybrook, J.P., D.L., *b.* 20 July, 1801, late 7th Hussars, and Capt. 24th Regt., High Sheriff co. Westmeath 1830, and co. Antrim 1852; *m.* 20 May, 1830, Henrietta Frances, youngest dau. of Nathaniel Alexander, D.D., Bishop of Meath, and by her (who *d.* 9 July, 1885) had issue,
1. RALPH, his heir.
2. Nathaniel Alexander, *b.* 5 Dec. 1835; *d.* 1838.
3. Robert Staples, *b.* 21 Dec. 1837; *m.* 24 Aug. 1862, Christina, dau. of Mr. Macpherson, and has with other issue. a son, Ralph.
4. James, now of Gaybrook.
1. Anne, *m.* 20 March, 1859, Charles Pole Stuart, of Woburn Sands, Woburn, Beds., 2nd son of William Stuart, of Aldenham Abbey, Herts, and has issue. He *d.* 1896.
2. Maria Hannah, *m.* 3 Oct. 1865, Samuel Thompson, of Muckamore Abbey, co. Antrim (who *d.* 12 April, 1904), and had issue.
3. Henrietta Frances, *m.* 1st, 3 Oct. 1865, George Travers Macartney, late Capt. 15th Hussars, of Lissanure Castle, co. Antrim, and had *s.* by him (who *d.* 29 Aug. 1874) issue (*see that family*) She *m.* 2ndly, 30 June, 1877, Hamilton W. Palmer, 2nd son of W. L. Palmer, of Rahan, Edenberry, co. Kildare, and has issue.

Mr. Smyth *d.* 28 July, 1878, and was *s.* by his eldest son,

RALPH SMYTH, of Gaybrook, J.P. and D.L., High Sheriff 1879, formerly Capt. 17th Regt., served in the Crimea; *m.* 6 Aug. 1861, Hon. Selina Constance Somerville, 4th dau. of Kenelm, 17th Baron Somerville, Admiral R.N. She *d.s.p.* 15 Jan. 1910. He *d.* 20 Nov. 1890, and was *s.* by his younger brother.

Seat—Gaybrook, Mullingar, co. Westmeath. *Clubs*—Naval and Military, and Kildare Street, Dublin.

SMYTH OF DRUMCREE.

HENRY SMYTH, of Drumcree, co. Westmeath, *b.* 31 Oct. 1827; *s.* his brother 1904; *m.* 20 Sept. 1876, Margaret, dau. of Alexander Cross, of Bendigo, Victoria, Australia, who *d.* 22 July, 1903, leaving issue,

IRELAND. Smyth.

1. HENRY MAXWELL, b. 19 May, 1878.
2. Arthur Hamilton, b. 7 Feb. 1886.
3. Alexander Cross, b. 6 Aug. 1887.
1. Emily Isabella Elizabeth.   2. Mary Louisa.
3. Cecilia Katherine Hamilton.
4. Alicia Margaret, d. 9 Dec. 1894.

Lineage.—THOMAS SMYTH, of Drumcree, Capt. in the Army, High Sheriff co. Antrim 1691, bur. at Drumcree, 30 Oct. 1712, will dated 2 April, 1709; proved 20 Feb. 1712-3, son of Capt. Ralph Smyth, of Ballymacash (see SMYTH of Gaybrook), m. Elizabeth, dau. of Ridgeley Hatfield, and had issue,
1. WILLIAM, his heir.
2. Thomas (Ven.), Archdeacon of Glendalough, m. 1st, Mary Gifford, and 2ndly, Elizabeth Mitchell, and d.s.p.
3. Hawkesworth, m. Evelyn Sherard, and had issue.
1. Mary, m. 1693, Thomas Nugent, of Clonlost, and had issue.
2. Elizabeth, m. Edward Lucas, of Castle Shane, and had issue.
3. Anne, m. Dudley Loftus, of Killyon, and had issue.
4. Alice, m. Richard Berry, of Wardenstown, and had issue.
5. Abigail, m Thomas Judge, of Grangebeg, and had issue.

The son and heir,
WILLIAM SMYTH, of Drumcree, d. April, 1742; m. (setts. 11 Dec. 1713) Mary, 2nd dau. and heir of Robert King, of Lissenhall, Swords. M.P., and ward of William King, Archbishop of Dublin, and d. 30 March, 1742, leaving issue by her (who d. Jan. 1733),
1. THOMAS, his heir.
2. Robert, who s. to his mother's manor of Monea, co. Fermanagh.
3. Ralph, ancestor of SMYTH of Glananea (see that family).
4. William.
1. Alicia, m. 6 Nov. 1749, William Chamberlaine.
2. Mary, m. 25 Oct. 1766, Rev. Coote Mitchell.

The eldest son,
THOMAS SMYTH, of Drumcree, b. 1 Oct. 1714; High Sheriff 1746; m. 1st, 30 Oct. 1742, Alice, dau. of Thomas Nugent of Clonlost, by whom he had
1. WILLIAM, his heir.
1. Frances Maria, m. Rev. Philip Johnson.

He m. 2ndly, Aug. 1761, Miss Purefoy, and 3rdly, 22 March, 1764, Martha, dau. of Ven. Francis Hutchinson, Archdeacon of Down and Connor, by whom he had a son,
2. THOMAS HUTCHINSON, ancestor of SMYTH of Ballynegall (see that family).

The elder son,
WILLIAM SMYTH, of Drumcree, M.P. for 30 years for co. Westmeath, High Sheriff (1770), m. 1st, 1766, Maria, dau. of Mark Synnot, of Drumcondragh, co. Armagh, and sister of Sir Walter Synnot, Knt. of Ballymoyer (see that family), and by her had issue,
1. ROBERT, his heir.
1. Anne, m. 1st, Hon. Robert Rochfort, and 2ndly, Thomas Creaser, M.D., of Bath.

He m. 2ndly, Jan. 1790, Frances, dau. of Hamilton Maxwell, of Drumbee, co. Down, and by her had
2. William Hamilton, of Drumbeg, co. Down, m. May, 1821, Isabella Margaret, dau. of Henry Daniel, of New Forest, Westmeath (see that family). She d. Nov. 1887. He d. April, 1866, having had issue,
1. WILLIAM MAXWELL, late of Drumcree.
2. Arthur, Capt. 14th Foot, b. 17 Dec. 1825; d. unm. Nov. 1857.
3. HENRY, now of Drumcree.
4. Robert Hamilton, b. 16 Jan. 1829; d. May, 1836.
5. Thomas, d. an infant.
1. Isabella Letitia, b. July, 1822; d. unm. Jan. 1884.
2. Frances Alicia, b. Sept. 1830; d. Aug. 1839.
3. Emily Henrietta, b. March, 1832; m. the late Joseph K. Smith, of Bendigo, Australia, and d.s.p. April, 1895.
4. Louisa, b. 14 Feb. 1834.
5. Cecilia Katherine, b. Dec. 1838.
6. Adelaide Elizabeth, b. June, 1841; d. July, 1859.
7. Alicia Frances, b. Aug. 1843.
2. Letitia, m. John Berry, of Middleton, co. Westmeath, and had issue.
3. Alicia, m. J. Gibbons, of Ballynegall, co. Westmeath.
4. Emily, m. Rev. Michael de Courcy, nephew of John, 26th Lord Kingsale, and had issue (see BURKE's Peerage).

Mr. Smyth m. 3rdly, April, 1806, relict of Rev. G. Graydon, and d. May, 1827, and was s. by his son,
ROBERT SMYTH, of Drumcree House, High Sheriff 1823, and M.P. for the co. 1826, b. Jan. 1777; m. 26 Jan. 1835, Elizabeth, widow of Major Snodgrass, and sister of Col. Clunes, H.E.I.C.S., and left at his decease, two daus. his co-heirs,
1. ALICIA MARIA ELIZA, s. her father.
2. Emily Anne.

The elder dau.,
ALICIA MARIA ELIZA SMYTH, of Drumcree, Westmeath, m. 12 Feb. 1866, Gen. the Hon. Sir Leicester Curzon-Smyth, K.C.B., K.C.M.G., J.P. and D.L. Westmeath, High Sheriff 1872, who assumed by Royal Licence 16 Nov. 1866, the name and arms of SMYTH. Sir Leicester was the youngest son of Richard William Penn, 1st Earl Howe, G.C.H. (see BURKE's Peerage). He d.s.p. 27 Jan. 1891. The Hon. Lady Curzon-Smyth d. 13 July, 1898.

WILLIAM MAXWELL SMYTH, of Drumcree, co. Westmeath, J.P. Capt. Turkish Irregular Cav. during Crimean War, b. 10 Nov. 1823; m. Nov. 1873, Agnes Mary, dau. of C. de Queiros, of Calcutta, and d. Nov. 1904.

Seat—Drumcree House, Killucan. Club—Ulster, Belfast.

SMYTH OF BALLYNEGALL.

THOMAS JAMES SMYTH, of Ballynegall, co. Westmeath, J.P. and D.L., High Sheriff 1858, late Capt. Westmeath Rifles, B.A. Trin. Coll. Dublin, b. 7 July, 1833; s. to the property at the decease of James William Middleton Berry, 1855; m. 14 Jan. 1864, Bessie, 4th dau. of Edward Anketell Jones, of Adelaide Crescent, Brighton, and by her (who d. 27 Oct. 1891) has issue,
1. THOMAS GIBBONS HAWKESWORTH, Capt. late East York (15th) Regt., b. 10 June, 1865; m. 22 Aug. 1895, Constance, youngest dau. of Harry Corbyn Levinge, D.L., of Knockdrin Castle, Mullingar (see BURKE's Peerage, LEVINGE, Bart.) and has issue,
1. Thomas Reginald Hawkesworth, Naval Cadet, b. 1897.
1. Marjorie.   2. Constance Gwendoline.
1. Ellinor Marion Hawkesworth, m. 11 Feb. 1893, Capt. Edward Gloster, Adj. 1st East Yorkshire Regt., eldest son of Rev. Thomas Gloster, M.A., of Dublin, and has issue.
2. Maud Emily Abigail Hawkesworth, m. 29 Jan. 1908, Capt. Gerald Scott Tweedie, The Royal Scots, youngest son of James Tweedie, of Quarter, co. Peebles (see that family).

Lineage.—This is a branch of SMYTH of Drumcree.
THOMAS HUTCHINSON SMYTH (only son of Thomas Smyth, of Drumcree, by his 3rd wife, Martha, dau. of Ven. Francis Hutchinson, Archdeacon of Down and Connor, see preceding article), served as High Sheriff 1792, being then described as of "Smythboro," or Coole. He m. 1796, Abigail, dau. of John Hamilton, of Belfast, and d. 1830, leaving issue by her (who d. 1853).
1. THOMAS, his heir.
2. Francis, Capt. R.N., b. 1801; d. 20 Aug. 1879; m. 23 April, 1835, Dorothea, 3rd dau. of William Ireland, of Low Park, co. Roscommon (by Dorothea his wife, only child of Samuel Arnoldi Gardiner, of Robertstown House, co. Kildare), and by her (who d. Oct. 1875) had issue,
1. Horatio Francis, Col. R.A. (retired), b. 1 Sept. 1840.
2. Robert, b. Oct. 1842; d. Jan. 1897.
3. Samuel Gardiner, Col. R.A. (retired), b. 18 Aug. 1844.
1. Florence, d. Sept. 1870.
2. Auna Frances (3, Knapton Terrace, Kingstown, Ireland).
3. John Stewart, d. 1887.   4. Edward, d. 1857.
5. Arthur, M.D., d. 1866.
6. Hamilton, Barrister-at-Law, b. 1859; d. 1883.
1. Anna.   2. Emily.

The eldest son,
REV. THOMAS SMYTH, b. 1796; m. Aug. 1832, Mary Anne, dau. of Adam Tate Gibbons, H.E.I.C.S., and niece of James Gibbons, of Ballynegall, d. 8 March, 1874, leaving issue,
1. THOMAS JAMES, now of Ballynegall.
2. James Gibbons, Major-Gen. (retired), formerly Lieut.-Col. 39th Regt. (15, The Crescent, Alverstoke, Hants., b. 21 Feb. 1837; m. Oct. 1875, Eleanor, dau. of Col. Powell, of Danlahan, co. Cork, and has issue, one dau., Eleanor Mary.
3. William Arthur, Lieut.-Col. 11th Regt., b. 1839; d. Oct. 1885.
4. Albert Edward, Col. 15th Regt., b. 1842; m. 1878, Florence, dau. of Col. Grantham.
1. Elizabeth Abigail Mary Amelia.
2. Mary Anne, m. 1856, Chaworth Joseph Fergusson, J.P., Barrister-at-Law, and has had issue.
3. Louisa Anna, m. July, 1875, Richard Reynell, eldest son of Richard Winter Reynell, of Killynon, and d. 1881, leaving issue (see that family).

Seat—Ballynegall, near Mullingar.

SMYTH OF BALLYNATRAY.

LADY HARRIETTE GERTRUDE ISABELLA SMYTH, of Ballynatray, co. Waterford, and More Park, Kilworth, co. Cork, m. 17 Oct. 1872, Col. John Henry Graham Holroyd Smyth, C.M.G., J.P. co. Cork, and J.P. and D.L. co. Waterford, High Sheriff 1902, Comm. 3rd Batt. Prince of Wales' Leinster Regt., late Capt. 65th Regt., who d. 29 Oct. 1904, leaving issue,
1. ROWLAND HENRY TYSSEN, D.L. co. Waterford, b. 3 Aug. 1874; m. 21 April, 1902, Alice Isabelle, youngest dau. of the late Chambré Brabazon Ponsonby, of Kilcooley Abbey (see BURKE's Peerage, BESSBOROUGH, E.), and has issue,

Smyth.   THE LANDED GENTRY.   650

  1. John Rowland Chambré, b. 4 Oct. 1903.
  2. Henry Horace Digby, b. 12 Dec. 1905.
  3. Bryan Hubert Holroyd, b. 29 April, 1908.
  1. Mary Lavender, b. 14 Oct. 1910.
  2. Charles Edward Ridley, b. 16 Aug. 1882.
  3. William Baker, b. 5 June, 1885.
  1. Isabelle Charlotte Sophie Wilmot, b. 21 July, 1873; m. 14 June, 1894, Col. Herbert Martin, C.B., late 1st Leinster Regt. and has issue.
  2. Helena Anna Mary More, b. 7 March, 1876.
  3. Gwendoline Harriette, b. 4 Nov. 1878; m. 23 April, 1905, Thomas Percy Butler, son of Capt. Henry William Paget Butler of Geraldine, co. Kildare, and has issue (see BURKE's *Peerage*, BUTLER, Bart.).
  4. Sophia Beryl Sheila, b. 29 Sept. 1880.
  5. Penelope Victoria Minna, b. 24 Nov. 1887; m. 5 Feb. 1907, Andrew Hubert Watt, Lieut. 3rd Dragoon Guards, 2nd son of Andrew Alexander Watt, of Thorn Hill, Londonderry, and has issue (*see that family*).

Col. and Lady Harriette Smyth assumed by Royal Licence 3 June, 1892, the surname and arms of SMYTH in lieu of Holroyd. Col. Smyth served in New Zealand 1864-5 (medal) and in Egypt 1883-7 (medals, Medjidie, 3rd class), commanded the Irish Militia Brigade at the Queen's Jubilee 1897 (medal), and served in S. African War 1899-1901 (despatches, Queen's medal with three clasps, C.M.G.). Col. J. H. G. Smyth, C.M.G., was the youngest son of the Rev. James John Holroyd of White Hall, Colchester Essex, Rector of Abberton, Essex, who d. 1876, aged 76 and Sophia, his wife, dau. of Samuel Tyssen, of Narborough Hall, Norfolk, and grandson of Sir George Sonley Holroyd, Judge of the King's Bench.

Lineage.—SIR RICHARD SMYTH, Knt., of Ballynatray, co. Waterford, High Sheriff 1613, and Rathcogan, co. Cork, who flourished in the reign of Queen ELIZABETH, m. Mary, dau. of Roger Boyle, of Preston, Kent, and sister of RICHARD BOYLE, the first and great Earl of Cork, and had one son and three daus.,
  1. PERCY (Sir), his heir.
  1. Catherine, m. 24 April, 1622, William FitzEdmond Supple, of Aghadoe, ancestor of De Capel Brooke, Bart., of Oakley.
  2. Dorothy, m. Arthur Freke, ancestor of Lord Carbery.
  3. Alice, m. 1st, William Wiseman, of Bandon, and 2ndly, Redmond Roche, of Ballyhendon.

Sir Richard commanded as captain in the defeat and expulsion of the Spaniards at Castle-Ny Parke, co. Cork. He was s. by his son, SIR PERCY SMYTH, Knt., of Ballynatray, distinguished for his loyalty and courage in the rebellion of 1641. He raised one hundred men to assist Sir William St. Leger, Lord President of Munster, and obtained at the same time, with Lord Broghill and Capt. Brodrick, his commission as Capt. of Foot. He was knighted 17 Jan. 1629, and was Military Governor of Youghal in 1645. Sir Percy m. 1st, Mary, dau. of Robert Meade, of Broghill, and by her (who d. 27 Nov. 1633) had issue,
  1. Mabella, m. Sir Henry Tynte, M.P. for Youghal, whose dau. Elizabeth, m. Sir Richard Hull, of Leamcon Manor.
  2. Joan, m. Beverley Ussher, whose dau., Mary, m. Francis Smyth, of Rathcourcy, co. Cork.

Sir Percy m. 2ndly, Isabella, dau. of Arthur Ussher (by Judith his wife, dau. of Sir Robert Newcomen), and grand-dau. of Sir William Ussher, Clerk of the Council, by Isabella his wife, dau. of the Most Rev. Adam Loftus, D.D., Archbishop of Dublin, and Lord High Chancellor of Ireland, and left issue,
  1. Boyle, M.P. for Tallow, whose will, dated 15 Aug. 1661, was proved the following year, d. unm. v.p.
  2. Percy, d. unm.
  3. WILLIAM, his heir, ancestor of SMYTH *of Headborough* (*see that family*).
  4. RICHARD, of whom we treat.
  5. John, whose will, dated 15 Aug. 1688, was proved in Dublin, d.s.p.
  3. Margaret, d. unm.
  4. Elizabeth, m. Charles Oliver, of Castle Oliver, co. Limerick.
  5. Isabella, m. Walter Galwey, of Cork.
  6. Maria, m. Very Rev. Arthur Stanhope, Dean of Waterford, and d. 1684.
  7. Catherine, m. Rev. John Rugge, of Ballydaniel, co. Cork.

The 4th son,
  RICHARD SMYTH, of Ballynatray, m. 1st, Susanna, dau. of John Gore, of Clonrone co. Clare, who d.s.p. He m. 2ndly, Alice, dau. (and co-heir with her sister Susanna, wife of Thomas Ponsonby, of Crotto) of Richard Grice, of Ballycullane, co. Limerick, and had with a dau., Isabella, m. Col. William Crosby, of Tubbrid, co. Kerry, a son,
  GRICE SMYTH, of Ballynatray, High Sheriff 1710, m. Gertrude, dau. of William Taylor, of Burton, co. Cork, and had issue, RICHARD, his heir, and Deborah, who m. Robert Blakeney, of Mount Blakeney, co. Limerick, brother of Lord Blakeney. He d. intestate administration to his effects being granted 24 April, 1724, and was s. by his son and heir,
  RICHARD SMYTH, of Ballynatray, b. 1706; High Sheriff 1739, m. 1st, 1764, Jane, dau. and co-heir of George Rogers, of Cork, son of Robert Rogers, of Lotamore, M.P., and by her had one dau. Gertrude, m. William Blakeney, of Mount Blakeney, co. Limerick.

Mr. Smyth m. 2ndly, 1756, Penelope, dau. of John Bateman, of Oak Park, co. Kerry, and by her (who d. Sept. 1789) had issue,
  1. RICHARD, his successor.
  2. GRICE, of whom presently, as heir to his brother.
  3. John, of Temple Michael, co. Waterford, m. 1st, Penelope, dau. of Morley Saunders, of Saunders Grove, by Lady Mary Stratford his wife, and had one son, John, who m. Mary, 2nd sister of Kilner Brazier, of Rivers, co. Limerick. John Smyth, of Temple Michael, m. 2ndly, Barbara, dau. of Carré Williams, of Cork, and by her had a son, Carré, who d. unm. and a dau., Barbara, m. John Willington Brazier, and has a son, Brooke.
  4. Rowland, d. unm.
  1. Elizabeth, m. Sir Henry Hayes, Knt. of Vernon Mount, co. Cork.
  2. Penelope, m. 1st, 1788, Francis Garden Campbell, of Troup House, and Delgaty Castle, co. Banff, and 2ndly, Major-Gen. Bruce.

Mr. Smyth d. April, 1768, and was s. by his eldest son,
  RICHARD SMYTH, of Ballynatray, High Sheriff 1793, who d. unm. and was s. by his next brother,
  GRICE SMYTH, of Ballynatray, High Sheriff 1803, m. June, 1795, Mary Brodrick, dau. and co-heir of Henry Mitchell, of Mitchell's Fort, co. Cork, by Ellen his wife, dau. of Richard Peard, of Coole Abbey, same co., and by her (who m. 2ndly, John Caulfeild Irvine) had issue,
  1. RICHARD, his heir.
  2. Henry Mitchell, ancestor of SMYTH *of Castle Widenham.*
  3. Grice Blakeney (Rev.), d. 18 July, 1864.
  4. Rowland, d. unm. 12 July, 1836.
  5. John Rowland (Sir), K.C.B., Gen. in the Army, and Col. 6th Dragoon Guards, d. 14 May, 1873. He m. Hon. Catherine Alice Abbott, dau. of Charles, 1st Lord Tenterden, and by her (who d. 31 Dec. 1865) had a dau., Penelope Mary Gertrude, m. 2. Aug. 1859, Charles Stuart Aubrey, 4th Lord Tenterden, and d. 30 March, 1879, leaving issue.
  1. Ellen, m. 1827, Henry Wallis, of Drishane Castle, co. Cork, and had issue (*see that family*).
  2. Penelope, m. 5 April, 1836, H.R.H. Charles Ferdinand Borbone, PRINCE OF CAPUA. He d. 22 April, 1862. She d. 13 Dec. 1882. d. 2 Jan. 1871, leaving an only child.
  3. Gertrude, m. 11 April, 1840, William Lewis, 1st Lord Dinorben, and d. 2 Jan. 1871, leaving an only child.

Mr. Smyth d. 18 Jan. 1816, aged 54, and was s. by his eldest son,
  RICHARD SMYTH, of Ballynatray, M.A., J.P. and D.L., and High Sheriff 1821, b. 7 May, 1796; m. 31 Oct. 1821, Hon. Harriet St. Leger, dau. of Hayes, 2nd Viscount Doneraile, by Charlotte his wife, dau. of James Bernard, of Castle Bernard, and sister of Francis, 1st Earl of Bandon, and by her (who d. 29 May, 1846) had an only surviving child.
  CHARLOTTE MARY, of Ballynatray.

Mr. Smyth d. 19 April, 1858, and was s. by his dau.,
  CHARLOTTE MARY SMYTH, of Ballynatray, who m. 18 Jan. 1848, Charles William, 5th EARL MOUNT CASHELL (see BURKE's *Peerage*), who assumed by Royal Licence 9 July, 1858, the additional name and arms of SMYTH, and was High Sheriff of co. Waterford 1862. She d. 15 Jan. 1892, having had issue,
  1. Richard Charles More, b. 26 Sept. 1859; m. 16 Oct. 1884, Helen Stirling, younger dau. of Rev. William Makellar, and d.v.m. 3 Jan. 1888, leaving a son,
    Claude William Stephen Richard, Lord Kilworth, b. 19 Dec. 1887; d. 1 Oct. 1890.
  1. HARRIETTE GERTRUDE ISABELLA, now of Ballynatray.
  2. Helena Anna Mary, d. unm. 6 Nov. 1876.
  3. Charlotte Adelaide Louisa Riversdale.

The Countess Mount Cashell, having no surviving male issue was s. at her death by her eldest dau. The Earl Mount Cashell d. 20 Feb. 1898, when the More Park estates passed to his eldest dau.

Arms—Arg., on a bend, between two unicorns' heads erased az., armed, crined, and tufted or, three lozenges of the last. **Crest**—Out of a ducal coronet or, a demi-bull saliant arg., armed and unguled gold. **Motto**—Cum plena magis.

Seats—Ballynatray, Youghal, co. Waterford, and More Park, Kilworth, co. Cork. **Club**—Army and Navy.

SMYTH OF HEADBOROUGH.

PERCY ROBERT EDWARD SMYTH, of Headborough, and Monatrea, co. Waterford, formerly Lieut. Waterford Artillery, S. Div. R.A., b. 4 Nov. 1870; s. his father 1910.

Lineage.—WILLIAM SMYTH, of Headborough, 3rd son of Sir Percy Smyth, of Ballynatray (see *preceding article*), m. Anne, dau. of Richard Smyth, of Bridgefield, co. Cork, and d. leaving issue, a son and heir,

PERCY SMYTH, of Headborough, Capt. in the Army, m. Elizabeth, dau. of Joseph Jervoise, of Brade, co. Cork and by her had issue.
  1. WILLIAM, his heir.

1. Mary, d. *unm.*
2. **Esther**, *m.* 1st, Robert Gookin, of Carrageen, co. Cork, who d. 1752, leaving issue; and 2ndly, 1755, James Bernard, M.P., of Castle Bernard, and d. 1780, leaving with other issue, Francis Bernard, of Castle Bernard, created 1800, Earl of Bandon (see BURKE'S *Peerage*).
3. **Anne**, *m.* 1747, Hibernicus Scott, of Lisnalcen, or Flaxford, co. Cork, and had issue,
 1. PERCY, of whom presently.
 2. Matthew, Lieut.-Col. 18th Foot, *d. unm.* in the West Indies.
 1. Anne, *m.* Rev. Edward Spread, of Forest, Rector of Youghal, and *d.* leaving an only child, Anne Isabella, who *m.* Rev. Henry Hamilton Beamish of Mountbeamish.

Mr. Smyth was *s.* by his only son,
WILLIAM SMYTH, of Headborough, High Sheriff 1734, *m.* Elizabeth, dau. and co-heir of Digby Fowke, and dying *s.p.* 1794, was *s.* by his nephew Percy Scott, who assumed the name of SMYTH, and became

PERCY SCOTT SMYTH, of Headborough, High Sheriff 1807. He *m.* Sarah, dau. of Samuel Kingston, of Bandon, co. Cork, by the dau. of Robert Gookin (6th in descent from Sir Vincent Gookin), and had issue,
1. WILLIAM his heir.
2. PERCY (Rev.), *s.* his brother.
 1. Elizabeth, *d. unm.* 2. Anne, *d. unm.*
 3. Sarah, *d. unm.*
 4. Esther, *m.* Crofton Uniacke, of Ballyre, co. Cork, and *d.* March, 1868.

Mr. Scott-Smyth *d.* 1826, and was *s.* by his elder son,
WILLIAM SMYTH, of Headborough, High Sheriff 1822, *d. unm.*, and was *s.* by his brother,
REV. PERCY SCOTT SMYTH, of Headborough, and Monatrea, *m.* 4 Sept. 1827, Catherine, dau. of John Odell, of Carriglea, co. Waterford, by Catherine his wife, dau. of Mathew Young, D.D., Bishop of Clonfert, and *d.* 1846, leaving by her (who *d.* 31 May, 1882) an only son and heir.

(By Royal Licence 3 Dec. 1862, Catherine, widow of Rev. Percy Scott Smyth, and her son Percy Smyth were granted permission to continue to use the surname of Smyth in lieu of Scott, and bear the arms of Smyth.)

PERCY SMYTH, of Headborough, and Monatrea, co. Waterford, B.A., J.P., High Sheriff 1872, *b.* 8 Oct. 1839; *m.* 27 June, 1865, Mary (who *d.* 6 March, 1910), eldest dau. of Robert Perceval Maxwell, of Finnebrogue and Groomsport House, co. Down, by Helena Anne, his wife, only dau. of William Moore, of Moore Hill, co. Waterford, and *d.* 9 March, 1910, leaving issue,
1. William Crofton, *b.* 25 Jan. and *d.* 19 Feb. 1868.
2. PERCY ROBERT EDWARD, now of Headborough.
3. Cecil Ernest, *b.* 19 Dec. 1871.
4. Robert Riversdale, *b.* 8 Dec. 1875; *m.* 1906, Emelyn Irene, 2nd dau. of Lieut.-Col. Norton C. Martelli, I.A., of Creg, Fermoy, J.P.
 1. Ethel Maud.
 2. Louisa Mary Kathleen, *d. unm.* 7 Aug. 1906

Arms—Arg., on a bend, between two unicorns' heads, erased az., armed crined and tufted or, three lozenges of the last, a martlet for difference. *Crest*—Out of a ducal coronet or, a demi-bull salient arg., armed and ungulcd of the first and charged with a martlet for difference. *Motto*—Cum plena magis.

Seats—Headborough, Tallow, and Monatrea, co. Waterford.

SMYTH OF MASONBROOK.

JOHN JOSEPH SMYTH, of Masonbrook, co. Galway, High Sheriff 1908, formerly Lieut. 4th Batt. Connaught Rangers, *b.* 1866; *s.* his father 1905; *m.* 7 Aug. 1894, Mary Clare Theresa, youngest dau. of Sir Thomas Burke, 3rd Bart., of Marble Hill, co. Galway (see BURKE'S *Peerage*), and has issue,
1. JAMES JOHN, *b.* 1902.
1. Mary Charlotte. 2. Sylvia Agnes.
3. Hilda Clare. 4. Clare Emily Josephine.
5. Ismay. 6. A dau.

Lineage.—JAMES SMYTH, J.P., of Masonbrook, co. Galway, *m.* Charlotte, 3rd dau. of Major McDermott, of co. Galway, and had by her,
1. JOHN, late of Masonbrook. 2. James, *b.* 1839; *d.* 1876.
3. Anthony, late Capt. Galway Militia, formerly Capt. 28th Foot, *b.* 1842.
1. Annie Josephine, *m.* 17 Feb. 1857, John Martyn, of Tillyra Castle, co. Galway, J.P.
2. Louisa, a nun in the cloisters of the Sisters of Mercy.

Mr. Smyth *d.* 1868, and was *s.* by his eldest son,
JOHN SMYTH, of Masonbrook, co. Galway, J.P., High Sheriff 878, late Capt. 15th Regt., *b.* 1835; *m.* 29 Oct. 1863, Charlotte Frances, dau. of Andrew William Blake, D.L., of Furbough, co. Galway (see DALY of Raford); and *d.* 3 March, 1905, leaving issue,
1. JOHN JOSEPH, now of Masonbrook.
2. Robert Henry, *b.* 1869.
3. Edgar, *b.* 1873, *d.* 20 Aug. 1904.
4. Harold, *b.* 1878.
1. Marion Frances, *b.* 1872; *m.* 21 Aug. 1902, Arthur George Vaughan Chichester, Capt. Connaught Rangers, 4th son of the late Rev. George Vaughan Chichester, brother o. 1st Lord O'Neill. (see BURKE'S *Peerage*). She *d.s.p.* 9 March, 1903.
2 Mildred, *b.* 1875.

Seats—Masonbrook, near Loughrea; Cooliney, Loughrea, co. Galway. *Club*—Stephen's Green, Dublin.

SMYTH OF DUNEIRA.

JOHN WATT SMYTH, of Duneira, co. Antrim, J.P., Barrister-at-Law, Judge of the Supreme Court of the Punjab, Bengal Civil Service 1857-86, *b.* 1 March, 1836; *m.* 14 Sept. 1871, Annabella Charlotte (who *d.* 20 Feb. 1907), dau. of Hon. and Rev. Henry O'Brien (see BURKE'S *Peerage*, INCHIQUIN, B.), and Harriet, his wife, dau. of John Godley, of Killigar (see that *family*), and has issue,
1. HENRY JOHN WATT, B.A. Oxon, *b.* 16 June, 1872.
2. Gerald James Watt, Capt. R.E., *b.* 29 March, 1874.
3. Austin Edward Arthur Watt, M.A. Camb., late fellow of Trin. Coll. Camb., *b.* 28 May, 1877.
1. Norah Aimée Geraldine Watt, *m.* 25 Aug. 1908, C. F. Massy Swynnerton, of Southern Rhodesia.

Lineage.—JOHN SMYTH, of Larne, co. Antrim, left issue, a son,
JOHN SMYTH, of Duneira, Larne, co. Antrim, *b.* 14 Feb. 1795; *m.* 8 Jan. 1830, Agnes, dau. of James Watt, of Ballycraigy, Larne, co. Antrim. She *d.* 27 Dec. 1889. He *d.* 29 June, 1863, having had issue,
1. James Watt, *b.* 8 March, 1833; *m.* 29 Oct. 1874, Elizabeth Ruth, dau. of the late Rev. John Hewson, of Kilmore Glebe, co. Mayo, and *d.* 6 Aug. 1885, leaving issue.
2 JOHN WATT, now of Duneira.
3 Thomas Watt, M.A., I.C.S., Judge of the High Court of the Punjab, *b.* 6 Jan. 1839; *m.* 18 Oct. 1884, Amy Evans, youngest dau. of Maj. Henry William Massy, of Grantstown, co. Tipperary (see *that family*), and has issue a dau.
1. Eliza. 2. Annie Jane.
3. Isabella.

Arms—Arg. on a saltire between three crescents one in chief and two in fess, and a leopard's face in base az. an eastern crown or. *Crest*—A dexter arm couped below the elbow and erect charged with a palm branch and holding in the hand a scimitar all ppr. *Motto*—With thy might.

Seat—Duneira, Larne, co. Antrim. *Club*—E.I. United Service, S.W.

SMYTH OF ARDMORE.

MAJOR ROSS ACHESON SMYTH, of Ardmore House, co. Londonderry, J.P., late Royal Irish Regt., *b.* 3 Sept. 1862, *m.* 11 Feb. 1892, Edith, dau. of Thomas Malcolmson, of Minella, Clonmel, co. Tipperary, and has had issue,
1. Ross Acheson, *b.* 26 Dec. 1892; *d.* 30 June, 1893.
2. JOHN Ross, *b.* 11 June, 1896.
1. Norah Kathleen Ross, *b.* 3 Oct. 1899.

Lineage.—JAMES SMYTH, of Colehill, near Londonderry, *d.* 26 Jan. 1764, leaving issue by Margery his wife (who *d.* 11 May, 1791),
1. JOHN, of whom presently.
2. James, who *d.* 26 Sept. 1815, leaving issue by Rebecca his wife, who *d.* 1796.
3. David, who *d.* 2 March, 1770.
1. Mary. 2. Elizabeth.

The eldest son,
REV. JOHN SMYTH, of Colehill, co. Donegal, Presbyterian Minister at Loughbrickland for 47 years, who was *b.* at Colehill 1728, and *d.* 27 May, 1804, left issue, with a dau. Esther, wife of Capt. Llittle, a son,
JOHN ACHESON SMYTH, of Ardmore, co. Londonderry, J.P. and D.L., *b.* 1769; *m.* 1795 Anne, dau. of William Dysart, of Londonderry (who *d.* 1852, aged 77), and *d.* 30 July, 1847, having by her had issue,

Smyth. THE LANDED GENTRY. 652

1. Ross THOMPSON, of whom presently.
2. John, of Morville, co. Derry, b. 1802 ; m. 1850, Agnes Halford, dau. of Rev. John George Maddison, Rector of West Monkton, co. Somerset, and d. 1868, leaving issue,
3. William Dysart, of Drumahoe, co. Derry, b. 1804 ; m. 1832, Anna Maria, dau. of Charles Armstrong, of Cherry Vale, co. Antrim, and d. 1878, leaving issue.
4. Mitchell (Rev.) of Ballintemple, co. Derry, b. 1806 ; m. 1844, Anne Elizabeth, dau. of Major A. R. Heyland, of Ballintemple, and d. 1894, leaving issue,
5. Hamill, of The Lodge, Coleraine, b. 1808 ; m. 1844, Jane, dau. of Patrick Gilmour, of The Grove, Londonderry, and d. 1890, leaving issue.
   1. Esther, d. 1881.
   2. Elizabeth, m. 1831, Col. Joseph Jones, 12th Regt., and d. 1891, leaving issue.
   3. Georgina.

His eldest son,
ROSS THOMPSON SMYTH, of Ardmore, b. 1797 ; m. 1828, Sarah, dau. of Hugh Lyle, of Jackson Hall, Coleraine (see LYLE of Knocktarna), and d. 14 Jan. 1881, having by her (who d. 22 March, 1871) had issue,
  1. JOHN ACHESON, of Ardmore.
  2. Hugh Lyle, now of Barrowmore Hall, co. Chester (see that family).
  1. Sarah.
  2. Agnes, m. 1st, 16 Aug. 1858, Sir William Mackenzie, Bart. of Coul, who d.s.p. 21 Dec. 1868. She m. 2ndly, Sept. 1881, Baron Grachelli.
  3. Esther, m. 22 April, 1858, Thomas Waring, M.P., of Waringstown, co. Down, and d.s.p. 26 March, 1873.
  4. Elizabeth Eleanor, m. Rev. A. Langtry, of Braynsford, co. Down.

The elder son,
JOHN ACHESON SMYTH, of Larchmont, Londonderry, b. 1 May, 1833 ; d. 24 July, 1874 ; m. 17 April, 1860, Alice, dau. of Robert McClintock, J.P., D.L., of Dunmore, co. Donegal (see that family), by whom he had issue,
  1. Ross ACHESON, now of Ardmore.
  2. Robert McClintock, b. 1864 ; m. Dorothy, dau. of Rev. Canon John Gould Adams, and has issue,
     Ralph McClintock, b. Sept. 1911.
     Dorothy.
  3. Hugh Lyle Waring (Drumchoe, Londonderry), b. 1868 ; m. 14 Nov. 1900, his cousin Una Maud Lyle, dau. of Hugh Lyle Smyth, of Barrowmore Hall (see that family).
     1. Margaret Lyle, b. 1861 ; m. 16 Aug. 1881, Col. W. S. Daniell, 105th Regiment, who d. 8 Nov. 1889, having had issue.
     2. Alice Mabel, b. Aug. 1871 ; m. 19 Dec. 1899, Major Godfrey R. C. Stuart, East Lancashire Regiment, and has issue.

Arms—Arg. on a bend engrailed between two unicorns' heads erased az., three lozenges erminois. *Crest*—Out of a ducal crest coronet a unicorn's head az. charged with a lozenge as in the arms. *Motto*—Exaltabit honore.

Seat—Ardmore House, co. Londonderry.

SMYTH OF GLANANEA.

RALPH ALFRED EDWARD SMYTH, of Glananea, co. Westmeath, Lieut. Antrim Artillery (Special Reserve), and Hon. 2nd Lieut. in the Army, formerly Lieut. Royal Bucks Hussars, educated at Elstree and Uppingham, b. 11 Dec. 1881.

Lineage.—RALPH SMYTH, of Glananea, 2nd son of William Smyth, of Drumcree (see that family), m. 8 Jan. 1757, Jane, dau. and co-heir of Anthony Walsh, of Grange Cairn, co. Down. He d. 1797, leaving an only son,
WILLIAM THOMAS SMYTH, of Glananea, m. 1742, Anne Lucinda, 2nd dau. of Thomas Loftus, of Killyon, co. Meath, and d. 1818, leaving issue,
  1. RALPH, of whom presently.
  2. William Thomas, Capt. 69th Regt., m. June, 1836, Harriet Louisa, dau. of Capt. J. B. Harrison, R.N., and d. 1842, leaving a dau.,
     Carlotta Louisa, m. Capt. Henry A. Williams, 14th Regt.
  1. Maria, d. unm. 1837.
  2. Evelina Anne, d. unm. 1852.

The elder son,
RALPH SMYTH, of Glananea, co. Westmeath, High Sheriff 1813, b. 1786 ; m. 1828, Jane Alicia, elder dau. of Thomas Wrixon Fitzgerald, Barrister-at-Law, and Maria Eleanor his wife, dau. of Thomas Loftus, of Killyon. He d. 1839, leaving a son,
WILLIAM EDWARD SMYTH, of Glananea, co. Westmeath, J.P., High Sheriff 1878, B.A. Trin. Coll. Dublin ; b. 1830 ; m. 3 Dec. 1880, MARGARET ALTHEA MARIA (now of Glananea), elder dau. of the late Henry Matthew Smythe, of Barbavilla (see that family). He d. 15 June, 1890, leaving issue,
  1. RALPH ALFRED EDWARD, now of Glananea.
  2. Abel Edward, served with Inniskilling Dragoons, b. 9 Jan. 1885.
  1. Lucy Jane Loftus, b. 1883.

Seat—Glananea, Drumcree, Killucan. *Club*—Wellington, S.W.

SMYTHE OF BARBAVILLA.

WILLIAM LYSTER SMYTHE, of Barbavilla, co. Westmeath, J.P. and D.L., High Sheriff 1888, Col. Reserve of Officers, late Comdg. Dublin City R.F.A., formerly Assistant Private Secretary to Earl Spencer, K.G., when Lord-Lieutenant of Ireland 1882-5, Gentleman-in-Waiting to the Earl of Aberdeen in 1886, and now A.D.C. to his present Excellency, since 1892, b. 29 Sept. 1859 ; m. 6 Oct. 1885, Agnes Mary Henrietta, only child of Capt. Richard Weld Litton, late 31st Regt., by Mary, his wife, dau. of Sir Hugh Stewart, 2nd bart. of Ballygawley, and has issue,
  1. HENRY INGOLDSBY LYSTER, b. 4 June, 1890.
  2. Cecil St. George Lyster, b. 17 March, 1895.
  3. Richard Litton Lyster, b. 3 July, 1897.
  1. Gladys Mary Lyster.
  2. Elizabeth Olwen Lyster.

Lineage.—This is a branch of SMYTH of Gaybrook, springing from
WILLIAM SMYTHE, of Barbavilla, b. 1693, youngest son of RIGHT REV. WILLIAM SMYTH, Bishop of Kilmore and Ardagh (see SMYTH of Gaybrook), who purchased different estates in Westmeath from Lord FitzWilliam, of Merrion, and others 1670 ; m. 1712, Barbara, dau. of Sir George Ingoldsby, Knt., son of Sir Richard Ingoldsby, of Lethenborough, co. Buckingham, by Elizabeth Cromwell, 1st cousin of the Protector. Mr. Smythe d. 29 April, 1769, leaving a son and heir,
RALPH SMYTHE, of Barbavilla, b. 1716 ; m. Anne (d. 14 Sept. 1771), dau. of Darby Clarke, of co. Kildare, and sister of James Clarke M.P. for Ballyshannon, and had issue,
  1. WILLIAM, his heir.
  2. Ralph, of Drogheda, m. Mary Schoales, and had a son, Ralph (of Newtown House, co. Louth, J.P., who m. Anna, dau. of Rev. Charles Crawford, Vicar of St. Mary's, Drogheda, and had Ralph of Newtown House, J.P., High Sheriff of co. Louth 1869, late Capt. Louth Militia, m. 1st, 1857, Mary Henrietta (d. 2 Jan. 1908), dau. of Henry Jeremiah Smith, of Annesbrook, which lady d. 1876 ; and 2ndly, 1878, Maria Georgina, youngest dau. of James Brabazon, of Mornington, co. Meath, and has a son, Ralph George, b. 1864 ; Mary Frances, m. 1866, Sir Robert Forster, Bart. ; and Sarah, and a dau. Mary Hannah, who m. St. George Smith, of Greenhills.
  1. Frances, m. 4 June, 1787, Sir Hugh Crofton, of Mohill House, co. Leitrim, and had issue (see BURKE's Peerage).
  2. Barbara, m. John Cooke, of Cookesborough, and had issue.

Mr. Smythe d. 1790, and was s. by his eldest son and heir,
WILLIAM SMYTHE, of Barbavilla, b. 1761. High Sheriff 1793. m. 1783, Catherine, dau. and heiress of William Meade Ogle, M.P. for Drogheda, and had issue,
  1. RALPH, his heir.
  2. William Meade, of Deer Park, Devon, M.P. for Drogheda, m. Aug. 1815, Lady Isabella Howard, dau. of William, 3rd Earl of Wicklow, and d. 9 July, 1866, having had three daus.,
     1. Eleanor.
     2. Catherine Stuart.
     3. Isabella.
  3. Henry, of Newtown, co. Louth, m. Frances Barbara (d. 1 March, 1906), dau. of Rev. R. Cooke, of Ballyneal, co. Kilkenny, and d. 1862, having had, with other issue, a son,
     Richard Altamont, of Lauragh, Queen's Co., High Sheriff co. Louth, 1871, late Capt. Salop Militia, b. 1838 ; m. 29 July, 1869, Frances Anne Jane, dau. of Sir Edward Alan Bellingham, 3rd bart. of Castle Bellingham, and has issue,
     (1) Alan Theodore, Capt. R.E. Thames Div., b. 8 Sept. 1873 ; m. 11 March, 1903, Hon. Charlotte Anne Trench, elder dau. of the late Hon. Frederick S. C. Trench (see BURKE's Peerage ASHTOWN, B.), and has issue,
        Kathleen Patricia.
     (2) Eudo Somerset, b. 18 Oct. 1875.
     (3) Rupert Cæsar, b. 1879.
     (1) Agnes Elizabeth, m. 1899, Rev. William Dudley Saul Fletcher, Incumbent of Lissadell, co. Sligo, and has issue.
     (2) Laura Frances, m. 1899, Leslie Edmunds, of Ballaghadareen, co. Mayo, and has issue.
     (3) Olive Mary.
     (4) Frances Victoria Lucy, m. 10 Jan. 1905, Henry Loghan O'Brien, only son of Murrough O'Brien, of Mount Eagle Killiney, and has issue.
     (5) Eileen Barbara.
  4. John (Rev.), of Dromiskin, co. Louth, m. Harriet, dau. of Rev. J. Wyatt, and had issue,
     1. William, d. 1842.   2. James.
     3. Henry.   4. Frederick.
     1. Anne.
  1. Altha Maria, m. Thomas Rice Fosbery, of Clorane, who d.s.p. 1828.
  2. Anne, m. Col. Thomas Wade, Deputy-Adjutant-General of Ireland, and had issue.
  3. Catherine Elizabeth, m. John Hamilton, of The Grove, co. Meath (see HAMILTON of Ballymacoll.)

Mr. Smythe d. 1812, and was s. by his eldest son and heir,
RALPH SMYTHE, of Barbavilla, b. 1786, High Sheriff 1813 ; m. 1808, Eliza, dau. and heiress of Matthew Lyster, of New Park, co. Roscommon, and by her (who d. 1845) left at his decease, 1815,
  1. WILLIAM BARLOW, his heir.

2. HENRY MATTHEW, late of Barbavilla.
3. Frederick, formerly 66th Regt., Staff Officer of Pensioners Major (retired on full pay), *m*. Ellen, dau. of Benjamin Johnson, of Newcastle, co. Northumberland. He *d*. 18 Nov. 1897. She *d*. 28 Dec. 1901, leaving issue,
  1. Henry Gerald.
  2. Ellen.   2. Emma.
  3. Helena.

The eldest son,
  WILLIAM BARLOW SMYTHE, of Barbavilla, J.P. and D.L., High Sheriff 1832, and J.P. co. Meath, *b*. 26 Nov. 1809 ; *m*. 7 Feb. 1837, Lady Emily Monck, dau. of Henry Stanley, Earl of Rathdowne, and by her (who *d*. 25 Nov. 1837) had one dau., Emily, *d*. 3 Dec. 1842. Mr. Smythe *d*. 1886, and was s. by his brother,
  HENRY MATTHEW SMYTHE, of Barbavilla, co. Westmeath, B.A., J.P., co. Roscommon, *b*. 1810 ; *m*. 3 Dec. 1855, Maria, 2nd dau. of the late Robert Carr Coote, Capt. 8th Royal Irish Hussars, brother of Sir Charles Coote, 9th bart. of Ballyfin, and by her (who was murdered in her brother-in-law's carriage at Barbavilla 2 April, 1882) had issue,
  1. WILLIAM LYSTER, now of Barbavilla.
  1. Margaret Althea Maria, *m*. 3 Dec. 1880, W. E. Smyth, of Glananea, who *d*. 15 June, 1890, leaving issue (*see that family*).
  2. Elizabeth Ada Mary, *m*. 1st, 1878, Christopher W. Bailey, of Moorock House, co. Clare, and 2ndly, 21 Dec. 1885, James Hume Dodgson.
  3. Louisa Ellen Lyster.
  4. Lydia Lucy Lyster, *m*. 30 July, 1887, Robert Darley Guinness.
  5. Maud Frances Lyster, *m*. 20 Aug. 1891, Henry Richards.
Mr. H. M. Smythe *d*. 6 Sept. 1893, and was s. by his son.

Seat—Barbavilla, Collinstown, co. Westmeath. *Clubs*—Kildare Street, Dublin, and St. George Yacht.

SOLLY-FLOOD. *See* FLOOD.

SOMERVILLE OF DRISHANE.

COLONEL THOMAS CAMERON FITZGERALD SOMERVILLE, of Drishane, co. Cork, M.V.O. (1911), late Colonel The King's Own Royal Lancaster Regt., Commandant R.M.S.M., Kneller Hall 1910, *b*. 30 March, 1860.

Lineage.—WILLIAM SOMERVILLE, a Church of England Minister, who fled from persecution in Scotland, 1692. He *m*. Agnes, dau. and co-heiress of Sir Patrick Agnew, Bart., and had
1. William, *b*. 1688, who returned to Scotland, and possessed some of the old family estates.
2. THOMAS, ancestor of the branch in Ireland.
1. Judith, *m*. William Cameron, of Lochbar, Dean in the English Church, and was grandmother of Gen. William Cameron.

The 2nd son,
REV. THOMAS SOMERVILLE, Rector of Myross, Braad, and Castlehaven, J.P., co. Cork, *b*. in Galloway, Scotland, 1689, *m*. 23 Dec. 1723, Anne, dau. of John Neville, of Furnace, co. Kildare, granddau. of Edward Riggs, of Riggsdale, co. Cork, and widow of John Perry, of Woodroof, co. Tipperary, and by her had issue,
1. THOMAS, his successor.
2. Edward,
3. James,   who all went to America, founded there the town
4. John,   of Somerville, and all *d.s.p*.
1. Elizabeth. 2. Agnes Agnew, *m*. Dr. Griffin.
3. Margaret, *m*. William Limerick, of Union Hall.
4. Judith, *m*. her cousin, Rev. W. Cameron.
5. Alice, *m*. Major William Ancram.

Mr. Somerville was s. by his son,
THOMAS SOMERVILLE, of Castlehaven, co. Cork, *m*. 1759, Mary, dau. of Capt. Philip Townsend, of Derry, in the same co., and by her (who *d*. 1815) had issue,
1. THOMAS TOWNSEND, his successor. 2. Richard Neville.
3. Philip, of the Prairy, Schull, co. Cork ; *m*. Henrietta, dau. of Richard Townsend, of Point House, Castletownsend, and had issue,
  1. Thomas, *m*. Millicent Becher.
  2. Philip, *m*. Ellen Bright.
  3. Richard, *m*. Elizabeth Benson.
  1. Mary, *m*. Brisbane Warren.
  2. Elizabeth, *m*. Richard Large, and had issue, who assumed by deed poll the surname of SOMERVILLE-LARGE. She had three sons, William Somerville, Philip Townshend, and Brisbane Warren.

He *m*. 3rdly, Isabella, dau. of Redmond Uniacke, of Old Court, and had further issue,

4. Redmond Uniacke, Major 61st Regt., *m*. Mary, dau. of Andrew Mitchell Uniacke, and had an only surviving child, Isabella Myric.
1. Anna, *m*. Joseph Reeves.
2. Mary, *m*. Edward Becher, and *d*. 1848.
3. Catherine, *m*. T. Hungerford, of Farley Cottage, co. Cork.
4. Susan, *d. unm*.
5. Alice, *m*. William Parker, and *d*. 1840.
6. Judith, *m*. Becher Fleming, of New Court, co. Cork.
7. Agnes, *m*. Capt. J. Townsend.   8. Harriet, *d. unm*.

Mr. Somerville *d*. March, 1793, and was s. by his eldest son,
THOMAS TOWNSEND SOMERVILLE, of Drishane, and Castlehaven, co. Cork, J.P., *m*. Nov. 1796, Elizabeth Becher, dau. of John Townsend, M.P., of Shepperton, and by her (who *d*. Feb. 1832) had issue,
1. THOMAS, his heir.
2. John Townsend, Major H.M. Bengal Service, *b*. 1800 ; *m*. May, 1836, Frances Margaret, dau. of Rev. Arthur Herbert, Rector of Myross Wood, co. Cork. He *d*. 1861.
3. Richard, *d*. young.   4. William Henry, *d*. young.
5. Philip Owens Becher Townsend (Rev.), Rector of Doneraile, *d*. 1867.
6. Philip Horatio Townsend, Admiral R.N., *m*. 1849, Mary Stewart, dau. of David Maitland M'Gill Crichton, of Rankeilour, co. Fife, and by her (who *d*. May, 1881) had with other issue,
  1. Thomas Townshend, whose dau., Eleanor Julia, *m*. 27 June, 1905, John Leatham Bright, son of William Leatham Bright.
  2. Maitland Makgill Crichton, *m*. 14 April, 1909, Agnes Jardine younger dau. of the late James Agnew.
7. James Edward, M.D., *m*. 1894, Ellen, dau. of John French, of Rath, co. Cork (of an elder branch of the FRENCHES *of Marino*), and had issue.
8. Morris Townsend, in Australia, *m*. Miss Anketell, and *d*. 1891, leaving issue.
  1. Mary, *m*. Jonas Morris Townsend, of Point (2nd son of Richard Townsend, of Point House).
  2. Elizabeth, *m*. 1831, her cousin, Richard Neville Somerville, of Millfield, Roscarbery, and *d*. 1891. He *d*. 6 Nov. 1909.

Mr. Somerville *d*. June, 1811, and was s. by his eldest son,
THOMAS SOMERVILLE, of Drishane, J.P. and D.L., High Sheriff 1863, *b*. 1797 ; *m*. 12 Oct. 1822, Henrietta Augusta, eldest dau. of Col. Richard Boyle Townsend, of Castle Townsend, and had issue,
THOMAS HENRY, of whom presently.
Henrietta.

Mr. Somerville *d*. 19 May, 1882, and was s. by his eldest son,
LIEUT.-COL. THOMAS HENRY SOMERVILLE, of Drishane, co. Cork, J.P. and D.L., High Sheriff 1888, late Lieut.-Col. 3rd Buffs, *b*. 29 Oct. 1824 ; *m*. 29 June, 1857, Adelaide Eliza, 10th dau. of Admiral Sir Josiah Coghill, 3rd bart., by his wife, Anna Maria, dau. of Chief Justice Bushe, and *d*. 15 March, 1898, having by her (who *d*. 3 Dec. 1895) had issue,
1. THOMAS CAMERON FITZGERALD, now of Drishane.
2. Joscelyn Josiah Coghill, *b*. 1862 ; *d*. 1864.
3. Henry Boyle Townshend, Capt. R.N., *b*. 7 Sept. 1863 ; *m*. 7 April, 1896, Helen Mabel, youngest dau. of the late Sir George Wigram Allen, K.C.M.G., of Toxteth, Sydney, N.S.W. (*see Colonial Gentry*), and has issue,
  1. Raymond Thomas, *b*. 14 March, 1897.
  2. Brian Aylmer, *b*. 27 Jan. 1900.
  3. Michael Fitzgerald, *b*. 13 Sept. 1908.
  1. Diana Marian.
4. Aylmer Coghill, J.P., co. Cork, late Capt. S. of Ireland Imperial Yeomanry (*Penleigh House, Westbury, Wilts*), *b*. 23 Sept. 1865 ; *m*. 1st, 1888, Emmeline Sophia, dau. of Daniel Sykes, of Oaklands, co. Gloucester, and by her (who *d*. 13 Feb. 1900) has issue,
  1. Desmond Henry Sykes, *b*. 6 Aug. 1889.
  1. Gillian Margaret Hope, *m*. 30 June, 1911, Francis Hugh Bonham-Carter, son of Lieut.-Col. Hugh Bonham-Carter, Coldstream Guards.
He *m*. 2ndly, 1901, Nathalie Adah, eldest dau. of William B. Turner, of Ponsonby Hall, Cumberland, and by her has issue,
  2. Thomas Henry Coghill, *b*. 29 April, 1907.
  2. Elizabeth Geraldine Aylmer, *b*. 3 March, 1905.
5. John Arthur Coghill, Major Royal Sussex Regt., Mil. Attaché Japan 1911 (*Naval and Mil. Club*), *b*. 26 March, 1872 ; *m*. 3 Nov. 1910, Vera Cooper, younger dau. of Charles W. Aston Key, 15, Southwick Crescent, London, and has issue,
  Anthony Cameron, *b*. Aug. 1911.
6. Hugh Gualtier Coghill, Commander R.N. (*Jun. Naval and Mil. Club*), *b*. 10 July, 1873 ; *m*. 1900, Mary, dau. of W. Hancock, of Patras, and has issue,
  1. Henry Nugent, *b*. 4 Aug. 1904.
  2. Philip, *b*. 5 Dec. 1906.
1. Edith Anna Œnone.
2. Elizabeth Hildegarde Augusta, *m*. 11 July, 1893, Sir Egerton Bushe Coghill, 5th bart., and has issue (*see* BURKE'S *Peerage*).

Arms—Az. three mullets or, two and one between seven cross crosslets fitchée or, and on a canton of the 2nd a trefoil vert. *Crest*—A dragon vert charged with a trefoil or spouting out fire, behind and behind ppr., and standing on a wheel or. *Motto*—Fear God in life.

Seat—Drishane, Skibbereen, co. Cork. *Club*—United Service S.W.

SOUTHWELL. *See* BURKE'S PEERAGE.
SOUTHWELL, V.

GARTSIDE-SPAIGHT OF DERRY CASTLE.

Mrs. Louisa Dorina Gartside-Spaight, of Derry Castle, co. Tipperary, m. 30 Jan. 1889, Captain Cavendish Walter Gartside-Tipping, and has issue,

1. Irene Maria Louisa.
2. Daphne Dorina Flora.
3. Dorothea Elspeth.

This lady with her husband Major Cavendish Walter Gartside-Tipping assumed by Royal Licence, 6 Aug. 1898, the additional name of Spaight and the arms of Spaight only, in pursuance of the will of Francis Spaight, of Derry Castle, Major Cavendish Walter Gartside-Spaight, *b.* 16 Feb. 1857, is the youngest son of the late Gartside Gartside-Tipping, of Bolton (*see that family*), and has served in the 82nd Regt., the 1st W.I. Regt., and the Army Service Corps, of which he was adjutant 1890-2, served on the Staff as D.A.A.G. in the Boer War of 1899-1902, mentioned in despatches, and promoted, medal with four clasps.

Lineage.—James Spaight, of Woolwich, Kent, afterwards of Coleraine, co. Derry (whose will was proved 1669), was father of

Thomas Spaight, whose son and heir,

Thomas Spaight, of Bunratty Lodge, co. Clare, Seneschal to Henry, 7th Earl of Thomond, was on the Grand Jury of Clare, and signed the address to Charles II. 1683, and was High Sheriff in 1697. He had a grant of arms from Sir Richard Carney, Ulster King of Arms, dated 20 Dec. 1684. He *m.* 1684, Eliza, dau. of Mounteford Westropp, of Bunratty, co. Clare, and by her had issue,

1. Thomas, of Bunratty Lodge, and Burrane, High Sheriff co. Clare, 1725, *m.* 26 Sept. 1725, Grace, dau. of Edward Hoare, M.P., co. Cork, by whom (whose will, dated 1 Feb. 1764, was proved 8 Aug. 1765) he left at his dec. 10 Oct. 1757,
    1. Thomas, of Kinsale, co. Cork, whose will, dated 13 Sept. 1771, was proved 4 July, 1775. He *m.* June, 1752, Prudence, dau. of Francis Hely, of Gortrough, and sister of Right Hon. John Hely-Hutchinson (father of Richard, 1st Earl of Donoughmore), and had issue,
        (1) John, *d.s.p.*
        (1) Prudence, *m.* Edward Ferriter, of co. Kerry, and had issue.
        (2) Mary Grace, *d.s.p.*
        (3) Christian, *m.* Richard Tyrrell, of Barne, and *d.s.p.*
    2. Palmer, *d.s.p.*   3. Joseph, *d.s.p.*
    4. Samuel, High Sheriff co. Clare 1795, *m.* Diana, dau. of John Hickey, of Cappagh, co. Clare, and *d.s.p.*
        1. Catherine, *d. unm.*
        2. Grace, *m.* 1749, Robert Reeves, of Cork, who *d.* 1802, leaving issue.
2. William, of whom presently.
1. Elizabeth, *m.* William FitzGerald, brother of Augustine Fitz-Gerald, of Mov Castle, co. Clare.

The 2nd son,

William Spaight, of Six-mile Bridge, co. Clare, J.P., Barrister-at-Law, *m.* Ann, dau. of Mountiford Westropp, of Attyflin, and widow of Richard Bury, of Mount Pleasant, co. Clare, and by her had issue,

1. William, of whom presently.
2. Westropp.
1. Elizabeth.
2. Mary, *m.* Rev. Francis Morice, of Atterbury, co. Clare, and had issue,

The son and heir,

William Spaight, of Corbally, Capt. 65th Regt. (with which he served at Bunker's Hill), High Sheriff for co. Clare 1791, *m.* 1784, Millicent Anne, dau. of Thomas Studdert, of Bunratty Castle, co. Clare, and by her (who *d.* 1846) had issue,

1. William, a Capt. in the Army, *d.s.p.*
2. Thomas, of Corbally and Ardnataggle, co. Clare, *m.* 1837 Elizabeth, dau. of Rev. Robert Gabbett, LL.D., of Castle Lake, co. Clare, and *d.s.p.* 1869 (see Gabbett *of Caherline*).
3. George (Rev.), of Limerick, B.A., *m.* Mary Ann, dau. of William Smith, of Cherrymount, co. Meath, and had issue,
    George, *d. unm.*
    Ann Millicent, *m.* Wainwright Crowe, of Caherculla, co. Clare, and had issue.
4. Francis, of whom presently.
5. Henry, of Corbally and Affock, co. Clare, an Officer in the 48th Regt., *b.* 1798; *m.* 1838, Constantia, dau. of Rev. Robert Gabbett, LL.D., of Castle Lake, co. Clare, and had issue,
    1. William FitzHenry, of Ardnatagle, co. Clare and Union Hall, co. Cork, J.P., Col. R.E., *b.* 1842; *m.* 1st, 1868, Ellen, dau. of Thomas Crowe, of Dromore, co. Clare, D.L., and by her had,

(1) Ethel.
(2) Ellen Constance.

He *m.* 2ndly, 1878, Lucy, only child of John Limrick, J.P., of Union Hall, and has issue,
(1) Thomas Henry Limrick.
(3) Charlotte Frances Lucy.
(4) Constance Elizabeth, *m.* 5 Nov. 1907, James Molony Spaight (*see below*).

2. Robert, of Affock, co. Clare, J.P., *b.* 1845; *m.* 1875, Alice Maude, dau. of James Molony, of Tulla, co. Clare. She *d.* 22 Nov. 1906. He *d.* 1888, leaving,
    (1) Henry William.
    (2) James Molony, LL.D., *m.* 5 Nov. 1907, Constance Elizabeth, 4th dau. of Col. William FitzHenry Spaight, late R.E., of Ardnataule (*see above*).
    (1) Rebecca Mabel Clare.   (2) Constance Stapleton.
    1. Helen Constance Thomasina.
2. Anna Margaret, *m.* Major Robert G. S. Maunsell, J.P. of Amberd, Bournemouth, and has issue.
3. Gustava Caroline.

1. Maria, *m.* Francis Morice, of Springfield, co. Clare, and has issue.
2. Millicent, *d. unm.*

Mr. Spaight *d.* 1798. His 4th son,

Francis Spaight, of Derry Castle, co. Tipperary, J.P., *b.* 24 June, 1790; *m.* 1812, Agnes, dau. of James Campbell Paterson, of Kilrush, co. Clare, and sister of Duncan Campbell, Laird of Asknish, Lochgair House, co. Argyll, and *d.* 16 Feb. 1861, leaving issue,

1. William, of Derry Castle, J.P. for cos. Clare and Tipperary, High Sheriff Limerick city 1850, *b.* 6 March, 1817; *m.* 18 Sept. 1845, Anne, only dau. of Capt. Marcus Paterson, of Shepperton, co. Clare, and had issue,
    Francis Windham, *b.* at Rome, 12 Feb. 1847; *d.s.p.* 17 July, 1865.
    Caroline Mary Gertrude, *d.* 8 May, 1865.
2. James (Sir), J.P., D.L. co. Tipperary, High Sheriff City of Limerick 1853, M.P. for that city 1859-65, Mayor 1856 and 1877, *b.* 1818; *m.* 1850; Elizabeth Alason (*Guy's Cliffe Lawn, Leamington*), dau. of John Eckford, H.E.I.C.S., and *d.* 1902.
3. Francis, *d.s.p.*
4. George Campbell, of whom presently.

1. Jean, *d.* 1840, *m.* George Julius, M.D., of Richmond, Surrey, and had issue.
2. Agnes, *m.* Col. Lumley, late 31st Regt., and has issue.
3. Harriette Dare, *m.* 17 Aug. 1848. Maj.-Gen. Charles Edward Astell, of West Lodge, Dorchester. She *d.* his widow 30 Dec. 1904, leaving issue.
4. Amelia, *m.* Major John Blood Smyth, of Fedamore House, co. Limerick, and has issue.

The fourth son,

Col. George Campbell Spaight, of Derry Castle, co. Tipperary, J.P. cos. Clare, Tipperary, and Limerick, Col. Commanding Limerick City Artillery, Local Government Inspector 1880-93, *b.* 9 Oct. 1831; *m.* 12 Aug. 1863, Dorina, only dau. of the Chevalier Pierre Beretta, of Corfu, and had issue,

1. Francis Beretta, *b.* 30 May, 1864; *d.* 13 July following.
1. Louisa Dorina, now of Derry Castle.
2. Caroline Mabel, *m.* 1 Dec. 1891, Col. Phillip Ribton Crampton, R.A.

Col. G. C. Spaight began his service in the 91st (Argyllshire) Highlanders, served with the 31st Regt. in the Crimea, and after with the 2nd Batt. 9th Regt. (medal and clasp, and Turkish war medal). He *d.* 10 Jan. 1898, and was *s.* by his dau. Louisa Dorina (Mrs. Gartside-Tipping).

Arms—Arg., on a fesse sa., three pheons of the field. *Crest*— A jay ppr. *Motto*—Vi et virtute.

Seat—Derry Castle, Killaloe.

SPRATT OF PENCIL HILL.

Richard Henry Spratt, of Pencil Hill, co. Cork,, *b.* 1858, *m.* 1900, Eileen Charlotte Martha, eld. dau. of the late Joseph Verling Carpenter, of Eden Hill Mallow, co. Cork.

Lineage.—This family was established in Ireland by Rev. Devereux Spratt (son of Rev. Thomas Spratt, of Stratton-on-Vosse, Somerset, and Elizabeth his wife, dau. of Rev. Robert Cooke), who, after taking his degree at Magdalen Coll. Oxford, settled in the co. of Kerry about 1640, and obtained estates by patent in cos. Wexford and Cork, and the livings of Tipperary, Mitchelstown, and Gallbally. At one period of his life, escaping from the hands of the insurgents during the great rebellion, he took ship from Youghal, but was captured by an Algerine pirate, and detained a slave at Algiers. Whilst at Algiers he officiated as Chaplain to the English captives there, and a record is still preserved of a marriage then celebrated by him. By his wife, Palgrave Cubitt, Devereux Spratt was father of

Devereux Spratt, *b.* at Torbay, near Mitchelstown, 30 May, 1670, who *m.* Martha, dau. of John Bond, of Ballynahilisk, co. Cork, by Elizabeth his wife, dau. and co-heir of Capt. William Harmer, and had issue. The 3rd son,

Harmer Spratt, *m.* Catherine Nash, and had, besides a dau. Margaret, two sons, James (who *s.* his uncle, James, in the family estates, and *d.* without legitimate issue, and by will disinherited his brother) and Harmer. This latter,

Harmer Spratt, *m.* 19 Nov. 1778, Martha, dau. and co-heir of Thomas Foott, of Elmvale and Springfoot, co. Cork, and through this marriage the lands of Baltidaniel and Pencil Hill came into the family. By her Mr. Spratt left at his decease, 2 June, 1830, a son,
Thomas Edward Spratt, of Pencil Hill, *b.* 8 April, 1782; *m.* 1814, Barbara, dau. of Col. Richard Foott, Milfort, co. Cork, and by her (who *d.* 2 May, 1858) had issue,
1. Harmer Devereux, late of Pencil Hill.
2. Richard, *b.* 1822; *m.* 3 July, 1851, Eliza Louisa, eldest dau. of the late Henry Baldwin Foott, of Carrigacunna Castle, co. Cork, and *d.* 1885, having by her (who *d.* 26 Sept. 1893) had issue.
  1. Richard Henry, now of Pencil Hill.
  2. Harmer Devereux, B.A., Barrister-at-Law, served in the S. African War and was killed 9 June, 1902, *unm.*
  3. Henry Baldwin, *m.* 1903, Emma Mary, eldest dau. of Richard Clear, of Bansha, co. Cork.
    1. Evelyn Augusta, *m.* 1902, Carlo Homan Haines, of Sunnyside, co. Cork.
  1. Mary Baldwin, *m.* 1853, Paul Smith.
  2. Margaret Martha, *d. unm.* 1854.
Mr. Spratt *d.* 21 Oct. 1833. The elder son,
Harmer Devereux Spratt, of Pencil Hill, co. Cork, J.P., *b.* 24 Oct. 1815; author of *Juverna*, &c.; *m.* June, 1848, Elizabeth Louisa, only dau. of Edward Townsend Warren, of Belleville, co. Cork, and Penelope his wife, dau. of Rev. Edward Mitchel Carleton, of Woodside, co. Cork. She *d.* 3 April, 1892. He *d.s.p.* 1901.

Seat—Pencil Hill, Mallow, co. Cork.

STACK OF NEDSHERRY, CO. FERMANAGH.

The Right Rev. Charles Maurice Stack, late Lord Bishop of Clogher, of Nedsherry, co. Fermanagh, *b.* 23 Aug. 1825; *m.* 21 Nov. 1859, Margaret Jane Auchinleck, of Crevenagh, co. Tyrone, and has issue,
1. Edward Churchill, J.P., F.R.C.S.I., of Burton-on-Trent, *b.* 25 Nov. 1860; *m.* 1 June, 1887, Susan Masfen, and has issue,
  1. Charles Maurice, *b.* 17 March, 1888.
  2. John Masfen, *b.* 28 Aug. 1889.
  3. William Auchinleck.
2. Charles Maurice (Rev.), M.A., T.C.D., Vicar of Magheracloone, Kells, *b.* 6 Sept. 1865; *m.* 7 May, 1901, Anna Kathleen, dau. of the Rev. T. L. F. Stack, of Mullaghmore, co. Tyrone, and has issue,
  1. Marcia Elizabeth Margaret, *b.* 21 March, 1904.
  2. Kathleen Tempe, *b.* 1 Oct. 1904.
  3. Mary, *b.* 14 May, 1907.
  4. Meta Dorothea, *b.* 19 Sept. 1910.
3. Walter Auchinleck (Rev.), M.A. Trin. Coll. Dublin, Rector of Drumkeeran (*Tubrid, Kesh*), *b.* 28 March, 1869; *m.* 6 May, 1897, Henrietta, dau. of the late Major Francis D'Arcy, of co. Fermanagh (*see Irvine of Castle Irvine*).
4. William Bagot (Rev.), Rector of Magheraculmoney, late Lieut. Royal Irish Fus., *b.* 26 Sept. 1874; *m.* 2 Sept. 1908, Margaret Edith, dau. of Robert Gray, F.R.C.P., Armagh.
  1. Elizabeth Mary, *b.* 1 Feb. 1862; *d.* 26 July, 1879.

This gentleman is son of the Rev. Edward Stack, J.P., by his wife Tempe (*m.* 24 Nov. 1807), dau. of the Rev. Walter Bagot, Rector of Monastervan, co. Kildare.

Residence—Ardess Kesh, co. Fermanagh.

STACPOOLE OF EDENVALE.

Richard John Stacpoole, of Edenvale, and Strasburgh, co. Clare, J.P. and D.L., High Sheriff 1894, late Lieut. Clare Art., *b.* 7 May, 1870; *m.* 19 July, 1894, Geraldine Norah Isabella, only dau. of Robert Hume Crowe, of Toonagh, co. Clare (*see* Crowe *of Dromore*), and Geraldine his wife, dau. of James Foster Vesey FitzGerald, of Moyreisk, Quin, co. Clare, and has issue,

Richard Hassard, *b.* 8 March, 1896.
Norah Dorothy, *b.* 25 April, 1895.

Lineage.—Bartholomew Stacpoole, was Sheriff of Limerick in 1596, and had three sons, of whom,
1. James, a burgess of Limerick, *m.* Christian, dau. of Nicholas Comyn, and *d.* 1626, leaving issue,
Bartholomew, *b.* 1619, who was the Recorder of Limerick at the time of Ireton's siege of that city, and signed the capitulation 1651; *m.* 1641, Mary, dau. of Thomas Arthur, and had issue.
2. Robert, the ancestor of the present family.
Clement Stacpoole, the son of Robert, was transplanted from Limerick to Clare by Cromwell. He *m.* Alice MacMahon, and had issue,

1. George, who *m.* Bridget Woulfe, and was ancestor of George, Count de Stacpoole.
2. William, of whom hereafter.
3. John, *d. unm.*, lost at sea.
The 2nd son,
William Stacpoole, of Annagh, living 1743, *m.* Elinor, dau. of James Forster, of Cloeene, co. Galway, and had (with two daus.) four sons,
1. William, *d.s.p.*   2. George, of whom presently.
3. James, *m.* Elinor Ronayne, and left issue.
4. John, *m.* his cousin, Barbara Stacpoole, and left issue.
  1. A dau., *m.* William Bourke, and had issue.
  2. Mary, *m.* John Brady.
  3. A dau., *m.* William Hogan, and had issue.
The son and heir,
George Stacpoole, of Annagh, *m.* 1739, Mary, dau. of Col. Hugh Massy, of Duntrileague, co. Limerick, and sister of Hugh, 1st Lord Massy, and Eyre, Lord Clarina, and by her had issue,
1. William, his heir, of whom presently.
2. John, of Lifford and Ennis, *m.* Mary MacDonough, and *d.s.p.* 1822.
3. George Massy, of Cragbrien Castle, High Sheriff 1763, Barrister-at-Law, *m.* 1767, Jane, dau. of Andrew Lysaght, of Summerville, and *d.* 1812, leaving issue,
  1. George, *m.* Clara Skerrett, and *d.s.p.* 1816.
  2. Andrew, of Ballyalla, *m.* 1st, 1803, Bridget, dau. of Lawrence Comyn, by whom he had a son, George, *d.* young, and a dau. Jane, *m.* Richard John Delazouche Stacpoole, of Edenvale (*see below*). He *m.* 2ndly, Georgina Maria, dau. of William Stacpoole, of Edenvale, but by her had no issue; and 3rdly, 1826, Diana, 2nd dau. of Daniel Finucane, of Stamer Park, co. Clare, and by her (who *d.* 1849) had issue, 1. William, of Ballyalla, M.P., *b.* 1830; *m.* Mary Anne Catherine Winifred, eldest dau. of Charles Hennessy, of Leamington, and *d.* 1879, leaving issue, a son, Guildford William Jack, *b.* 1868; *m.* Henrietta Jane Stacpoole, dau. of Henry Vereker, and widow of Ralph Hugh Westropp, of Springfort, co. Limerick; 2. Andrew, *d. unm.* 1862: 1. Kate, *m.* Augustine Butler, of Ballyline, co. Clare, and *d.* 1861, leaving two sons; and 2. Diana, *m.* C. M. Parkinson, and *d.* 1862, leaving issue.
  3. Mathias, *m.* 1st, Miss Pilkington, and 2ndly, Miss Louisa Macnamara, and by the latter only had surviving issue, two daus.,
    (1) Sarah.   (2) Mary.
  4. Hugh, Lieut.-Col. 43rd Regt., *d.s.p.* 1840; *m.* Jane Wasey, of Prior Court, Berks.
  5. William Henry (Very Rev.), D.D., of Cragbrien, Clare, Dean of Kilfenora, *b.* 1787; *m.* 1813, Jane, dau. of Robert Marshall, of Sandbrook, co. Carlow, and had issue,
    (1) George Marshall, *b.* 1814, *d.* 1837.
    (2) Robert, *b.* 1817, *d.* 1818.
    (1) Frances, *d. unm.*
    (2) Jane, *m.* 1844, Charles Mahon, of Corbally, co. Clare, and *d.* 1879.
    (3) Wilhelmina, *d. unm.* 5 Feb. 1894.
    (4) Charlotte, *d.* 1881.
  6. Michael, Capt. R.N., *m.* 29 Oct. 1829, Charlotte, dau. of William Cassaubon Purdon, of Tinerana, co. Clare, and *d.s.p.*
  1. Mary, *m.* Michael Furnell, co. Limerick, and had issue.
  2. Eliza, *m.* Rev. Thomas Westropp, and had issue.
  3. Lucinda, *m.* 1st, Walter Lysaght, and 2ndly, William Adams Brew.
  4. Jane, *m.* Rev. George William Gale.
4. Massy, *m.* 1767, Mary, only dau. of Hassard Powell, of Kilkenny, and had issue,
  1. William, of Instow, co. Devon, *m.* Louisa, dau. of Sir Thomas Wentworth, and had issue, two sons and a dau.
  2. George, *d.s.p.* in the West Indies.
  3. Hassard, Capt. R.N., killed in a duel in Jamaica 1814, *m.* Isabella, only dau. and heir of John Leek, of Grosvenor Place, London, and had issue, a son and three daus.
  4. John, Col. in the Army, *m.* and had issue,
    (1) Andrew Douglas (Rev.), Fellow of New Coll. Oxon., and Vicar of Writtle, Essex, *m.* and *d.s.p.* 1884.
    (2) John William.
1. Elizabeth, *m.* 1766, Sir Hugh Dillon Massy, 1st bart. of Donass, and had issue.
2. Elinor, *m.* John Ross Lewin.
3. Mary, *m.* Charles McMahon, of Leadmore, co. Clare, and had issue.
4. Jane, *d. unm.* 1826.
5. Lucy, *d. unm.*
The eldest son,
William Stacpoole, of Annagh and Edenvale, High Sheriff 1784, *m.* 1st, 1773, Dorothea, dau. and co-heir of Thomas Burton, by whom he had issue,
  1. George William, LL.D., *d. unm.* 1822.
He *m.* 2ndly, 1788, Honoria, dau. of William Stamer, of Carnelly, co. Clare, and widow of Temple French, of co. Cork, and *d.* 1796, having by her had issue,
2. Richard John Delazou he, of whom presently.
1. Georgina Maria, *m.* Andrew Stacpoole, of Ballyalla (*see above*), and *d.s.p.* 1824.
The son and heir,
Richard John Delazouche Stacpoole, of Edenvale, J.P. and D.L., High Sheriff 1827, *b.* 21 May, 1792; *m.* 13 March, 1825, Jane dau. of Andrew Stacpoole, of Ballyalla, co. Clare (*see above*), and by her (who *d.* 12 Oct. 1856) had issue,
1. William, *b.* 10 April, 1827; *m.* 1859, Catherine O'Connor (who *d.* 1863), and *d.* 1866, leaving issue,

Stacpoole. THE LANDED GENTRY. 656

Richard George, of Roonard, Alexander Drive, Sefton Park, Liverpool, *b.* 8 May, 1860; *m.* 15 Aug. 1888, Edith Maud, eld. dau. of Sir Edward John Dean Paul, Bart. (*see* BURKE'S *Peerage*), and has issue,
(1) George Eric Guy, *b.* 18 Jan. 1892.
(2) William Aubrey Clement, *b.* 7 April, 1896.
(1) Gladys Edith.   (2) Vera.
Elizabeth Jane, *m.* 13 April, 1885, Hugh Massy Westropp, of Park House, Clonlara (*see* WESTROPP *of Attyflin*).
2. RICHARD, of Edenvale.
3. George William, Lieut.-Col., late 18th Regt., *b.* 18 Nov. 1832 ; *m.* 18 June, 1863, Josephine Julia Helen, dau. of Henry Lloyd, of Farrinrory, co. Tipperary, and widow of the 3rd Lord Rossmore ; and *d.* 19 Nov. 1894.
1. Georgina Maria, *m.* 26 March, 1856, Charles Heaton Armstrong, of Larch Hill, co. Clare, and has issue (*see* HEATON-ARMSTRONG *of Farney Castle*).
2. Honoria, *d. unm.* 24 June, 1843.
3. Jane, *m.* 8 Nov. 1858, Henry Vereker, and *d.* 25 Nov. 1859, leaving a dau. He *m.* 2ndly, 5 July, 1865, Martha Rogers, dau. of Philip MacAdam, of Blackwater, and *d.* 10 July, 1871, leaving issue.
4. Elizabeth, *d. unm.* 1 May, 1857.
Mr. Stacpoole *d.* 9 Oct. 1866. His 2nd son,
RICHARD STACPOOLE, of Edenvale, J.P. and D.L., High Sheriff 1864, *b.* 19 Aug. 1828 ; *m.* 19 Aug. 1868, Alice Julia, youngest dau. of John Westropp, of Attyflin Park, co. Limerick, and by her (who *d.* 12 July, 1907) had issue,
1. RICHARD JOHN, now of Edenvale.
2. George William Robert, D.S.O., Capt. South Staffordshire Regt., *b.* 27 May, 1872.
1. Mary Eva Louisa, *m.* 28 March, 1896, Charles Randal Armstrong MacDonnell, D.L., of New Hall, Ennis, co. Clare, and has issue (*see that family*).
2. Alice Jane.   3. Gwendoline Clare.
Mr. Stacpoole *d.* 16 June, 1891.

Seats—Edenvale and Strasburgh, Ennis, co. Clare.

STACPOOLE. *See* DE STACPOOLE.

STAFFORD OF MAINE.

EDWARD TYTLER STAFFORD HOWARD STAFFORD, of Maine, co. Louth, and Lansdowne, Christchurch, New Zealand, *b.* 24 May, 1862 ; *m.* 22 Dec. 1888, Theresa E. C., dau. of F. Krull, and has issue,

1. RONALD SEYMOUR SEMPILL HOWARD, *b.* 22 Feb. 1890.
1. Carmen Corisande.   2. Valerie Violet.

Lineage.—HUGH STAFFORD, who *m.* 1st, 4 July, 1746, Mary, dau. and heir of Edward Smith, of Maine (*see* SMITH *of Annesbrook*), and by her had issue,
1. EDWARD, his heir.
2. William (Rev.), B.A., *m.* Hannah, widow of Brent Spencer, of Ballycastle, and *d.s.p.*
3. Hugh, Lieut.-Gen. H.E.I.C.S., *m.* 1st, Thomasine, dau. of Rev. H. Sullivan, of Clonakilty, co. Cork, and by her had issue,
1. John, Major-Gen. in H.M.'s service, *m.* Frances, dau. of Francis Whalley, of Winscombe Court and Norton Hill, Somerset, and Hinton House, Hants, and by her (who *d.* Dec. 1847) left issue at his decease, Feb. 1846,
(1) William Joseph Fitzmaurice, C.B., Major-Gen. Bengal Staff Corps (retired), *m.* 1852, Emily Mary (who *d.* March, 1909), dau. of Major Gavin Young, Judge-Advocate Gen. of the Bengal Army. She *d.* 8 March, 1909. He *d.* 20 Aug. 1887, having had issue,
1. William Francis Howard, C.B., Col. R.E., *b.* 19 Dec. 1854 ; *m.* 1884, Edith Mary Culling Carr, dau. of F. C. Carr-Gomm, late of the Madras C.S., and has issue,
a. John Howard, 2nd Lieut. R.E., *b.* 4 March, 1890.
a. Janet Elsie Howard.
b. Lucy Edith Howard, *m.* Dec. 1910, Lieut. C. H. Coode, R.M.L.I.
c. Ursula Howard.
2. Henry Lawrence Caulfeild Howard, Lieut.-Col. and Brevet Col. R.E. (retired), *b.* 20 May, 1859 ; *m.* 1892, Violet Laura Pennefather, dau. of R. L. Warren, of Queenstown, and has issue,
a. Hugh Warren, *b.* 4 Jan. 1893.
a. Ethel Howard.
b. Margaret Emily.
3. Edmund Hyde Whalley Howard, Major R.E., *b.* 26 May, 1868 ; *m.* July, 1902, Christian Elizabeth, only child of Very Rev J. Mitford Mitchell, D.D., Chaplain in Ordinary to the King in Scotland.
1. Florence Howard.
(2) Thomas Sedgwick, *d.* 1853, *unm.*
(3) John Francis, Major-Gen. Bengal Staff Corps (retired), *b.* 1823 ; *d.s.p.* 17 Sept. 1898.
(4) Charles Stewart, *d.* young.
(5) Boyle Torriano, Maj.-Gen. Indian Army (20, *Upper Maze Hill, St. Leonards-on-Sea*), *b.* 1828 ; *m.* 1874, Georgina, dau. of S. Newington, M.D., of Ridgeway, Sussex.

(1) Thomasine, *m.* M. Vadnalle, and has issue, a dau.
(2) Mary.   (3) Anna, *d.* young.
(4) Julia.
2. Edward, Major 31st Regt., *d.* Aug. 1826, *unm.*
1. Eliza.
2. Harriet, *m.* Col. Layton, of Drayton Hall, Norfolk, and had issue, one son and one dau.
3. Letitia, *m.* Major-Gen. Caulfeild, C.B., son of Venerable John Caulfeild, Archdeacon of Kilmore, of Benown, co. Westmeath, and *d.* Aug. 1826, leaving issue, four sons.
4. Frances, *m.* H. S. Mercer, of Edinburgh, and *d.s.p.*
5. Emily, *m.* 1st, John Forbes Paton. Capt. Bengal Engineers, by whom she had issue, three sons and one dau., and 2ndly, John Brown, of co. Roscommon, by whom she had issue, one son.
Gen. Hugh Stafford *m.* 2ndly, Harriet, only child of Lieut.-Col. Spencer, and by her had issue, one son and three daus., all *d.s.p.* He *d.* Jan. 1819.
Hugh Stafford *m.* 2ndly, Catherine, dau. of H. Cumming, of Killowen, co. Down, but by her had no issue. He *d.* 1783, and was s. by his eldest son,
EDWARD SMITH STAFFORD, Colonel in the Army, High Sheriff co. Louth 1777, *b.* 1747 ; *m.* 1st, Frances, dau. of Francis Palmer, of Palmerstown, co. Mayo, and of Rush, co. Dublin, but by her had no issue. He *m.* 2ndly, Mary, 3rd dau. of Robert Agnew, of Howlish, co. Durham, grandson of Sir James Agnew, Bart. by his wife Lady Mary Montgomerie, dau. of Alexander, 8th Earl of Eglinton, and by her had issue,
1. Edward Norton, *b.* and *d.* 1793.
2. BERKELEY BUCKINGHAM, his heir.
1. Augusta Buckingham, *d.* 1807.
2. Clementina Louisa, *d.* 1872.
3. Thomasine Palmer, *m.* Rev. John Hermin Stafford, Incumbent of St. Paul's, Liverpool, and *d.* 1834, leaving issue.
4. Frances, *m.* 19 Jan. 1820, Rev. Patrick Brewster, and *d.* 7 June, 1831, leaving issue.
Col. Edward Stafford *d.* 1802, and was s. by his son,
BERKELEY BUCKINGHAM STAFFORD, High Sheriff co. Louth 1828, *b.* 25 March, 1797 ; *m.* 3 July, 1818, Anne, 3rd dau. of Lieut.-Col. Patrick Duff Tytler, by Isabella Erskine his wife, dau. of the Hon. James Erskine, of Alva, Senator of the College of Justice, and by her had issue,
1. EDWARD WILLIAM (Sir), G.C.M.G., his heir.
2. Berkeley Buckingham de Bohun (Rev.), *d.* 23 Aug. 1822 ; *d.* 5 Dec. 1889.
3. Hugh Henry Tytler de Toeni, *b.* 19 April, 1824 ; *m.* Jan. 1860, Caroline, dau. of William Wood, and left issue at his dec. 28 Nov. 1881,
1. William, *b.* Oct. 1860.   2. Berkeley Buckingham.
3. Hugh Henry Archibald.
1. Isabella Erskine.   2. Emily Margaret.
4. Patrick Plunkett Leslie, Col. Madras Staff Corps (retired), *b.* 13 July, 1826 ; *m.* July, 1887, Letitia, dau. of Henry Taylor, and *d.s.p.* 16 May, 1889.
1. Isabella Erskine, *d.* 18 Oct. 1895.
2. Mary Montgomerie, *d.* 5 June, 1911.
Berkeley Buckingham Stafford *d.* Aug. 1847, and was s. by his eldest son,
THE HON. SIR EDWARD WILLIAM STAFFORD, G.C.M.G., of Maine, co. Louth, and Lansdowne, Christchurch, New Zealand, Prime Minister of New Zealand June, 1856, to July, 1861, Oct. 1865, to June, 1869, and in 1872 ; Member of the House of Representatives of New Zealand uninterruptedly from Oct. 1855, to March, 1878, *b.* 23 April, 1820 ; *m.* 1st, 24 Sept. 1846, Emily Charlotte, only child of Col. William Wakefield, by Emily Elizabeth his wife, dau. of Sir John Shelley Sidney, Bart., and sister of Philip Charles, 1st Lord de L'Isle and Dudley, but by her (who *d.* 18 April, 1857) had no issue. He *m.* 2ndly, 5 Dec. 1859, Mary, 3rd dau. of Thomas Houghton-Bartley, Barrister of the Inner Temple, Speaker of the Legislative Council of New Zealand, and *d.* 14 Feb. 1901, having by her (who *d.* 23 Dec. 1899) had issue,
1. EDWARD TYTLER STAFFORD HOWARD, now of Maine.
2. Humphrey De Bohun Howard, *b.* 31 March, 1864.
3. Berkeley Howard (155, *Sloane Street, S.W.* ; *Club : Whites, S.W.*), *b.* 24 Oct. 1869 ; *m.* 7 April, 1900, Gertrude Howes, dau. of John Edward Banks, of Thames, Auckland, New Zealand, and has issue,
1. Berkeley Buckingham Edward Howard, *b.* 25 Oct. 1901.
2. Hugh Anthony Howard, *b.* 28 Jan. 1906, and *d.* 24 Jan. 1908.
1. Anne Isabella, *m.* 8 Nov. 1892, Major W. Staveley Gordon, R.E., son of Sir Henry Gordon, K.C.B., and has issue,
Gerard Stafford Staveley, *b.* 20 Dec. 1895.
2. Mary Montgomerie.
3. Edith Margaret, *m.* 31 Jan. 1894, Charles Digby Wallington, Capt. Lancashire Fusiliers, son of Sir John Wallington, K.C.B. and has issue,
1. Geoffrey Stafford, *b.* 8 Nov. 1896.
2. Edward Leonard, *b.* 30 Nov. 1900.
1. Marjorie Enid.

STAFFORD-KING-HARMAN. *See* HARMAN.

STANNUS OF CARLINGFORD.

THOMAS ROBERT ALEXANDER STANNUS, of Carlingford, co. Louth, and the Elms, Portarlington, Queen's Co., J.P., Major The Queen's Co. Militia, served in S. Africa (severely wounded, medal), b. 29 Sept. 1870; m. 5 March, 1895, Elizabeth Graydon, only dau. of John Graydon Smith, Capt. 7th Royal Fusiliers, of Baltiboys, Blessington, co. Wicklow, and has issue,

1. GRAYDON GRANT HERVEY TREVOR, b. 26 May, 1900.
2. James Gordon, b. 23 Dec. 1902.
1. Rose Thelma.
2. Edris.

Lineage.—The first mention of the family in Ireland is found in a patent of naturalization (consequent upon the plantation of Ulster by JAMES I), dated 1618, and granted to WILLIAM STANEHOUSE, of Carbolzie, in Scotland, whereby all the rights and privileges of an English subject were fully secured to him and other persons of consideration. The son of this William was

JAMES STANNUS, of Carlingford, the principal part of which town and manor he was seised of, including several townlands. His interment in the church of Knock, co. Down, previous to 1683, is recorded in a very interesting family document. His son,

WILLIAM STANNUS, also styled " of Carlingford," was High Sheriff of Louth 1704. It is to be remarked that on the Sheriff's roll the name is spelt " Stanehouse." He m. Mabella, sister of Ephraim Dawson, of Dawson's Court, M.P. for Queen's Co., whose grandson was created Earl of Portarlington. William Stannus (or Stanehouse) d. 1717, having had issue,

1. James, b. 1686; M.P. for Carlingford 1713–21, High Sheriff of Louth 1721, in which year he died.
2. William, b. 1695, M.P. for Carlingford 1721–27, and M.P. for Portarlington 1730, which last place he continued to represent until his death, 1732. He m. Margaret, dau. of Sir Thomas Hazelwood, Bart. of Wick, co. Worcester, and had issue,
   Ephraim, m. Margaret, dau. of Stephen Sibthorp, of Drogheda, and had a son,
   Ephraim, m. Miss Foster, sister of John Foster, of Dunleer, but d.s.p.
3. Ephraim, b. 1697; d. in Gambia.
4. TREVOR, of whom we treat.
1. Mabella, b. 1690; m. 1708, Thomas Tipping, of Castle Town Castle, co. Louth, and had issue.
2. Anne, b. 1699; d. 1734.
3. Sophia, b. 1706; d. 1713.

The youngest son,

TREVOR STANNUS, styled " of Portarlington," b. 1709, s. to part of the Carlingford estates, and was High Sheriff co. Louth 1744, m. 1728, Jane, dau. of Robert Sibthorp, M.P. for Louth, and d. 19 Oct. 1771, leaving issue,

1. THOMAS, his heir, of whom presently.
2. William, b. 1730; d. 1758.
3. James, b. 1738; d. unm. 1808.
4. Ephraim, b. 1739; m. Susanna, dau. of Joseph Gerrish, of Halifax, North America, and had issue,
   1. Trevor, Major 14th Foot, b. 1781; d. in India, 1812.
   2. Ephraim Gerrish (Sir), Major-Gen., C.B., b. 1784; m. 16 Oct. 1839, Mary Louisa, widow of James Gordon, a younger branch of the GORDONS of Newton, co. Aberdeen. This officer was highly distinguished in the Kattywar and Mahratta campaigns. He filled the office of Private Secretary to the Hon. M. Elphinstone, Governor of Bombay, and was for seventeen years Lieut.-Governor of the Hon. East India Company's College, Addiscombe, where he d. Oct. 1850.
   3. Robert, Major 29th Foot, b. Aug. 1786: served through the Peninsular War, receiving five wounds at the actions of Roleia, Talavera, and Albuera. He m. Clotilda Bona, dau. of Major-Gen. Graves.
      1. Mary, m. 1805, John Fenton, of Bellevue, co. Londonderry, and had issue, (1) John, d. a minor; (2) Trevor Alexander, m. 1855, Charlotte Sarah, dau. of George Oakley, of Rye Gate, Surrey.
      2. Anne Catherine, b. 1856.
      3. Susanna, d. 1819.
   1. Jane, m. Col. Delacour, and had issue, Jane, m. Alexander Carroll, of Hollymount, co. Wicklow.

Mr. Trevor Stannus was bur. in the French church at Portarlington. He was s. by his eldest son,

THOMAS STANNUS, M.P. for Portarlington 1798–99, who served during the American War in the 22nd Regt., and was severely wounded, b. 1736; m. 1784, Caroline, eldest of Hans Hamilton, of Abbotstown, co. Dublin, M.P. for that co., and d. May, 1813, leaving issue,

1. THOMAS, of whom presently.
2. James (Very Rev.), Dean of Ross and Rector of Lisburn, m. 22 April, 1816, Elizabeth, youngest dau. of Sir Erasmus Dixon

I.L.G.

Borrowes, 6th bart. of Gilltown, co. Kildare. She d. 14 May, 1873. He d. 28 Jan. 1876, having had issue.
   1. Thomas Robert, of Maghraleave, Lisburn, J.P. co. Antrim, b. 21 Sept. 1818; m. 1st, 1844, Jane Mary Anne, dau. of Hans Hendrick, of Kerdiffstown, co. Kildare (she d. 1845). He m. 2ndly, 1 Dec. 1869, Margaret Elizabeth, dau. of Thomas Wayne, of Glandare, Aberdare, co. Glamorgan, J.P. cos. Brecon and Glamorgan, and Ann Coffin his wife, of Merthyr Tydvil, and d. 8 Nov. 1907, leaving issue, a dau.,
      Rowena Elizabeth Dorothea, m. 11 Jan. 1894, her cousin Harold William Stannus Gray, of Graymount, co. Antrim, only son of Maj. George Gray, D.L., and has issue (see that family).
   2. Beauchamp Walter (Rev.), M.A., T.C.D., Rector of Arrow, co. Warwick from 1863, m. 23 April, 1857, the Hon. Mabella Geraldine Vesey Fitzgerald (who d. 30 April, 1910), dau. of the 3rd and last Lord Fitzgerald and Vesey, and d.s.p. 18 Aug. 1908.
   3. Henry James (Gen.), C.B., Lieut.-Col. 20th Hussars, commanding at Agra, India, 1870, m. 3 April, 1851, Sarah (who d. 1904), dau. of John Oliver, of Newcastle-on-Tyne, Northumberland, and d. 30 May, 1898, leaving issue,
      (1) Florence, d. unm. 29 Oct. 1898.
      (2) Constance, d. unm.
      (3) Alice Caroline Beauchamp (The Corner Cottage, Wimbledon Common, S.W.), m. 7 Aug. 1866, Capt. Ashley Edmund Mackenzie, late East Yorkshire Regt., son of Col. Mackenzie, 60th Rifles, and has issue.
      (4) Evelyn, m. Joseph B. Diplock.
      (5) Mabella.
      Gen. Stannus was present at the actions of the Khyber Pass, Mamoo Kheil (medal), Maharajpoor (bronze star), Moodkee, Ferozeshah, Aliwal, Ramnugger, Sobraon (medal and three clasps), Chilianwallah, and Goojerat (severely wounded—medal). At the latter action he commanded the personal escort of Lord Gough, the Commander-in-Chief, which command be also held in the Gwalior campaign.
   4. Walter Trevor, of Lisburn, co. Antrim, and Moneymore, co. Londonderry, LL.D., J.P. and D.L. co. Antrim, and J.P. cos. Down, Tyrone, Londonderry, and Antrim, b. 1827; m. 16 Oct. 1856, the Hon. Catherine Geraldine Vesey Fitzgerald, 4th dau. of Henry, 3rd and last Lord Fitzgerald and Vesey. She d. 14 March, 1904. He d. 1895, having had issue,
      (1) Henry Vesey Fitzgerald, d. young.
      (2) Gerald Walter James Fitzgerald, Major late 20th Hussars, of Yatton Court, Leominster, Herefordshire (19, Pont Street, S.W.), b. 4 June, 1868; m. 1904, Evelyn Margaret, elder dau. of Duncan Cameron, of Canterbury, N.Z., and has issue,
      Reginald George Walter FitzGerald, b. 2 April, 1907.
      (1) Louisa Mabel Georgina (Manor House, Lisburn, Ireland).
      (2) Geraldine Maude, d. young.
      1. Harriet Jane, d. unm.
      2. Caroline Mary Anne, d. unm.
      3. Elizabeth Emily Sophia, m. 8 Feb. 1866, George Gray, of Graymount, J.P. and D.L. co. Antrim. He d. 14 March, 1879, leaving issue (see that family).
   3. Trevor, Capt. 97th Regt., for many years Aide-de-Camp to Sir Wilmot Horton, Bart., Governor of Ceylon; b. 1798; m. Caroline, dau. of Charles Hamilton, of Hamwood, and d. May, 1844.
      1. Caroline, dec.
      2. Charlotte, m. Rev. Charles William Doyne, Rector of Fethard; she d. 5 Jan. 1865.
      3. Sophia, m. John Hamilton, of Dunboyne Castle, co. Meath; she d. 21 July, 1863.
      4. Jane, m. Joseph Goff, of Hale Park, Hants.
      5. Harriette, m. W. Magill, of Littleton, co. Westmeath; dec.

The eldest son,

THOMAS STANNUS, of Portarlington and Carlingford, an Officer in the 9th Lancers, m. Oct. 1819, Catherine Sophia, dau. of Robert Hamilton, of Clonsilla, co. Dublin, a branch of the Abbotstown family, and had issue,

1. THOMAS ALEXANDER, his heir.
2. ROBERT TREVOR, late representative.
3. JAMES JOHN, late representative.
4. Catherine, d. unm.

Thomas Stannus d. 28 March, 1840, and was s. by his son,

THOMAS ALEXANDER STANNUS, who, having served for some years in the 14th Madras Infantry, was accidentally drowned Aug. 1851, and was s. by his brother,

ROBERT TREVOR STANNUS, of Carlingford, co. Louth, and of Portarlington, Queen's Co., late Capt. 16th Bengal Grenadiers, present at the actions of Ghuznee (wounded), Maharajpoor, Moodkee, Ferozeshah, and Sobraon (two medals, two clasps, and bronze star), J.P. for Queen's Co., b. 1824; m. 3 March, 1853, Caroline Sophia, dau. of John Hamilton, LL.D., of Dunboyne Castle, co. Meath, and d.s.p. 31 March, 1888.

JAMES JOHN STANNUS, of Carlingford, co. Louth, and The Elms, Portarlington, Queen's Co., J.P., m. 1867, Rose Mary, dau. of John Armstrong, of Graigaverne, Queen's Co., and by her (who d. 1876) has issue,

1. THOMAS ROBERT ALEXANDER, now of Carlingford.
2. Catherine Letitia, m. 25 Oct. 1905, Nicholson Pim, of Lisnagarvey, Lisburn, co. Antrim.

He m. 2ndly, Julia Sophia, dau. of William Blosse Armstrong, late 9th Lancers, of Lisnagrough, co. Tipperary, and d. 17 Sept. 1908, leaving issue,

2. William Trevor, d. unm.

Arms—Arg., on a fesse, between three pigeons rising az. a tiger's face ppr., between two mullets of the first. **Crest**—A talbot's head ppr., collared and lined or, in the mouth a martlet sa. **Motto**—Et vi et virtute.

Residence—The Elms, Portarlington, Queen's Co.

LYNCH-STAUNTON OF CLYDAGH.

CHARLES RUSHWORTH LYNCH-STAUNTON, of Clydagh, co. Galway, Inspector of Local Government Board, Ireland, 1892-1905 (ret.), b. 1854.

Lineage. — GEORGE STAUNTON (2nd son of REGINALD STAUNTON, of Smewen's Grange, Bucks) went to Ireland as a military officer in 1634, and settled in co. Galway, where he acquired considerable landed property. He m. and left three sons, the 2nd of whom,

GEORGE STAUNTON, of Clydagh, co. Galway, m. Eliza, dau. of James Martyn, of Tillyra, by whom he had two sons, on the 2nd of whom,

GEORGE STAUNTON, he settled the castle and lands of Cargin and Clydagh. He m. Anne, dau. of Nicholas Lynch, of Galway, by whom he had five sons and two daus., and was s. by his eldest son,

COL. GEORGE STAUNTON, m. Margaret, dau. of John Leonard, of Carra, co. Galway, and was s. by his son,

GEORGE LEONARD STAUNTON, M.D., b. 1737, who adopted eventually the profession of the Law, was appointed a Member of Council and Attorney-General in the island of Grenada ; he afterwards accompanied Lord Macartney to Madras, and negotiated the peace with Tippoo Sultan 1784, for which service he was created a Bart. of Ireland 31 Oct. 1785. He also accompanied Lord Macartney to China as Secretary of Embassy 1792, was eventually Minister Plenipotentiary, and published a narrative of the mission. He m. 1771, Jane, dau. of Benjamin Collins, of Wilford, Wilts, and dying 14 Jan. 1801, was bur. in Westminster Abbey. He was s. by his only child,

SIR GEORGE THOMAS STAUNTON, Bart., F.R.S. and D.C.L., of Leigh Park, Hants, and Clydagh, co. Galway, the distinguished Oriental scholar and well-known writer on China, b. 26 May, 1781, educated at Trin. Coll. Camb. From 1818 to 1833 he sat in Parliament for St. Michael's and Heytesbury, in 1832 was returned for South Hampshire, and from 1838 to 1854 represented Portsmouth. He d. in London 10 Aug. 1859, and was s. in his English estate of Leigh Park by his cousin, Capt. Henry Cormick Lynch (younger brother of George Staunton Lynch-Staunton, late of Clydagh), who assumed the additional name of STAUNTON, and d. 1859 (see LYNCH of Duras), and in his Irish estate and personal property by his cousin,

GEORGE STAUNTON LYNCH-STAUNTON, of Clydagh, co. Galway, b. 1798 ; m. 1824, Sarah Jane, dau. of Frances Hardwick, of Nottingham, late Capt. 62nd Regt., and had issue,
1. Francis Hardwick, b. 1828 ; m. 1857, Victoire, dau. of G. Corbet, of Kingston, Canada West, and has issue,
  1. George, b. 1858,   2. Alfred, b. 1859.
2. Richard, b. 1846 ; m. 1871, Marion, dau. of A. S. Duncan, of Cheltenham.
1. Mary Anne, m. 1861, John Blake, of Rockville, co. Galway, who d. June, 1880 (see BLAKE of Cregg Castle).
2. Victoire, d. 1857.   3. Fanny.
4. Anna.   5. Eleanor.
6. Lucy.   7. Sarah.

Mr. Lynch-Staunton, J.P. and D.L. co. Galway, and J.P. co. Mayo, High Sheriff co. Galway 1867, was eldest son of Mark Lynch, of Duras, co. Galway (see that family), by his 2nd wife, Victoire, dau. of Richard Wolsley Cormick, of Wolseley Park, in the Island of Grenada, and niece of Sir George Leonard Staunton, Bart. of Clydagh. He assumed 4 Oct. 1859, by Royal Licence, the name and arms of STAUNTON in addition to those of LYNCH, in accordance with the terms of the will of his cousin, Sir George Thomas Staunton, Bart., and d. 4 April, 1882. His eldest son,

MARCUS STAUNTON LYNCH-STAUNTON, of Clydagh, co. Galway, Barrister-at-Law, b. 1826 ; m. 1851, Horatia Anne, dau. of Charles Powlett Rushworth, Commissioner of Inland Revenue, and d. 19 Oct. 1896, having by her (who d. 1859) had issue,

CHARLES RUSHWORTH, now of Clydagh.
Alice.

Arms.—(Heralds' Coll.) Quarterly : 1st and 4th, STAUNTON, arg. two chevronels, sa. ; 2nd and 3rd, LYNCH, az., a chevron between three trefoils slipped or. Crests—1st, STAUNTON, upon a mount vert, a fox statant ppr. ; 2nd, LYNCH, a lynx passant ppr., charged with a mullet gu. Motto,—En Dieu ma foy.
Seat—Clydagh, Headford, Tuam, co. Galway. Club—Union, S.W.

STAWELL OF COOLMAIN, AND OF KILBRITTAIN AND LISNEGAR, CO. CORK.

ESTHER MARY ALCOCK-STAWELL-RIVERSDALE, who, on the death of her last surviving brother in 1907, assumed, by Royal Licence 24 July, 1907, the additional surname of RIVERSDALE on succeeding to the estate of Lisnegar, co. Cork.

Lineage.—The founder of the family in England was a Norman knight who accompanied WILLIAM THE CONQUEROR, and was rewarded by him for his services by a grant of land in Somerset amounting to four knights' fees, which represented the sum of £80 per annum. Three of these fees were held under the Bishop of Winchester as part of his manor of Taunton, and they included the manor of Cothelstone which remained in the possession of the Stawells for over 700 years. The remaining fee, which was held under the Abbot of Glastonbury consisted of five hides (600 acres) at Stawell, in the parish of Moor linch, and of a messuage of land at Glastonbury. For over 100 years the family was known by the names both of DE COVESTON (or DE COTHELSTONE) and DE STAWELL (vide the Red and Black Books of the Exchequer, pp. 205 and 228, and 69 and 88 respectively, wherein it is stated that Galfridus de Coveston held the above-mentioned fees in 1166, and that his father, Adam, and his grandfather Galfridus, had held them before him. Also the entries in Curia Regis Rolls, Nos. 48 and 49, of 9 and 10 JOHN, relating to Galfridus de Stawell, avus, Adam de Stawell, pater, and Galfridus de Stawell plita). Whether the elder Sir Geoffrey mentioned in the Books o the Exchequer, or, as is generally supposed, his father, Sir Adam was the original founder of the family in England, cannot now be definitely stated. It is, however, certain that by the commencement of the 13th century the name of de Coveston was abandoned and the family was known from thenceforth under that of de Stawell In the Curia Regis Rolls above referred to, it is shown that Sir Geoffrey de Stawell II. m. the dau. and heir of Geoffrey Flambard. She brought the property of Flambardeston, co. Wilts, to the Stawells in whose possession it remained until the year 1368 (Fect of Fine for co. Wilts of 42 EDWARD III.). Sir Adam de Stawell II. m. Maud dau. of — Trumpington, and d. in 1230 (Cal. Pat. Rolls). In th Rentalia and Custumale of Abbot Michael, of Glastonbury, 1235-52 is the following entry under the head of Nomina Militum Tenetum de Abbatia Glastonia : " Apud Stalwelle Adam de Stawelle unum feodum, Nunc G. de Stawelle."

This SIR GEOFFREY (III.), who d. circa 1240, left a son and heir,

SIR HENRY DE STAWELL,w hose name frequently appears in the old records of the county. By his marriage with the dau. and heir of Sir Matthew de Stratton, who brought him the manors of Stratton Prestleigh and Evercreech, co. Somerset, Sir Henry, who d. in 1261 left issue a son and heir, SIR GEOFFREY DE STAWELL, who was summoned in 1297 and in 1300-01 to perform military service beyond the seas and against the Scots. He d. circa 1303, leaving issue a son and heir,

SIR MATTHEW DE STAWELL, of Cothelstone, who by his marriage with Anastasia, dau. of — Brent, of Cossington, co. Somerset, left issue, at his death in 1316, a son and heir,

SIR GEOFFREY DE STAWELL, who m. Joan, dau. and heir of John de Columbers, of Nether Stowey, co. Somerset, and dying circa 1325, left issue, besides a dau., Eleanor, who, according to the Register of Ralph of Shrewsbury, Bishop of Bath and Wells, was m in 1333, in the chapel at Cothelstone, to Richard de Stapleton, a son and heir,

SIR GEOFFREY DE STAWELL, who m. Juliana, dau. of Walter Gastelin, and sister and co-heir of Sir William Gastelin, of Pauntor Cotell, co. Gloucester. Sir Geoffrey d. on 13 Dec. 1361 (Inq. p. m.) leaving issue, two sons, SIR MATTHEW, of Cothelstone, and William of Flambardeston.

SIR MATHEW DE STAWELL, who d. in 1379 (Cal. Pat. Rolls), m. Eleanor, dau. and heir of Sir Richard Merton, of Merton, co. Devon who brought that estate, together with the manors of Sutcombe Welcombe, Affordesworthy and Nutley, all in the same county, to the Stawells. By this marriage there was issue, a son and heir,

SIR THOMAS STAWELL, whose arms are given in Atkinson's Roll of Arms, from Harleian M.S., 1408, fol. 105, as follows : " About the time of the Wars of the Roses—He be'rith quart'ly gowlys a cross mascule sylu', and he be'rith sylu iij bendys asure," or, in modern language, " Gules a cross masculy (or lozengy) arg., (for STAWELL), quartering arg. three bends az. (for MERTON)." Sir Thomas, who m. 1stly, Joan, dau. of Sir John Berkeley ; 2ndly, Joan, dau. of Walter Frampton, of Buckland Ripers, co. Dorset ; and 3rdly, Margaret, dau. of Henry Burton, d. in 1439, and was bur. in Glastonbury Abbey. His numerous estates descended to his grandson and heir,

ROBERT DE STAWELL, of Cothelston, whose father, Walter, who d.v.p., Sir Thomas' son by his 2nd marriage, who had m. Joan, dau. and co-heir of John Farway, of Penhallam, co. Cornwall. He m. Elizabeth, dau. of William Wadham, of Merrifield, co. Somerset, and had issue, two sons,
1. Edward, d.v.p. in 1496, who m. Agnes, dau. of John Cheyney, of Pinboe, co. Cornwall, by whom he had issue a son, Robert.
2. David, who is believed to have been the founder of the Devon and Irish families.

Robert Stawell d. on 28 Oct. 1499 (Inq. p. m.), and was bur. in Glastonbury Abbey. His estates descended to his grandson and heir,

ROBERT STAWELL.
The great-grandson of this Robert Stawell, Sir John Stawell, of Cothelstone, was one of the original undertakers for the settlement, by English families, of the forfeited estates of the Earl of Desmond and other Irish rebels in Munster. He was, however, dissatisfied with the amount of land awarded to him and gave up the enterprise (Cal. State Papers, Ire.). Sir John's great-grandson,

RALPH STAWELL, was created, 15 Jan. 1683, Baron Stawell Somerton, in the co. of Somerset, in consideration of the eminent loyalty and sufferings of his father, Sir John Stawell, K.B., of Cothelstone. The Barony became extinct on the death, without male issue, of Edward, 4th Lord Stawell, in 1755, but GEORGE II. " being desirous that the honours of such an old family should be preserved," created his dau.,

MARY, wife of the Right Hon. Henry Bilson Legge, on 21 May, 1760, Baroness Stawell, of Somerton. On the death, without male

issue, of their son, Henry Stawell Bilson Legge, last Lord Stawell, of Somerton, on 25th Aug. 1820, the title finally became extinct. The family estates descended to Lord Stawell's dau., the Hon. Mary Legge, who m. 11 Aug. 1803, John, 2nd Baron Sherborne, of Sherborne House, co. Gloucester (see BURKE's *Peerage*, SHERBORNE, B.).
We now return to,
DAVID STAWELL, 2nd son of Robert Stawell, of Cothelstone, by his marriage, in 1438, with Elizabeth Wadham. David apparently had a son,
THOMAS STAWELL, of Hatherleigh, who d. on 10 Oct. 1516 (*Inq. p. m. E.,* 171, No. 25, of 24 HENRY VIII.), when he was s. by his son and heir,
EDMUND STAWELL of Passaford, in Hatherleigh, who was b. in 1492. He d. on 7 July, 1550 (*Inq. p. m.*), leaving issue, two sons,
1. John, of Hatherleigh, who m. and had issue.
2. EUSTACE, of whom next.
The younger son,
EUSTACE STAWELL, of Chudleigh, co. Devon, by his marriage with Elizabeth, dau. of S. Baker, of co. Monmouth, left issue at his death, on 4 July, 1592, two sons, the younger of whom, Thomas, was of Blandford, Dorset.
WILLIAM STAWELL, of Harcombe, Chudleigh, co. Devon, who d. in Feb. 1592 by his marriage, 16 July, 1572, with Joan, dau. of John Bennet, of Whiteway, Chudleigh, had issue,
1. ANTHONY, of Wraxall, co. Do. set, of whom hereafter.
2. Eustace, who was b. in Sept. 1576, and d. in Jan. 1584.
3. Thomas, of whom later.
4. William, of Herebeare, in Bickington, co. Devon, who was b. in 1589, and m. Joan, dau. and heir of Hugh Wottou, of Herebeare. He was the founder of the Herebeare branch of the family, which included Sir John Stawell, of Parke, Bovey Tracey, co. Devon, who d. on 19 Jan. 1669, and his son, William, who was nine times elected M.P. for Ashburton in that county. He d. in 1702.
The eldest son,
ANTHONY STAWELL, was b. in 1574. He resided for some years at Wraxall, a Dorsetshire manor belonging to the Stawells, of Cothelstone. He was mentioned in the will, dated 10 Jan. 1603, of Sir John Stawell, of Cothelstone, who bequeathed to him the reversion of his estates. In 1593 he m. Helen, dau. of John Ball, of Bridgeland, co. Devon. About the year 1613 he emigrated to Ireland, and it is recorded in *Carew MS.* 629 that he commanded one of the companies of infantry, composed of tenants of Sir Richard Boyle, 1st Earl of Cork, which were reviewed on 30 Aug. 1622, by the King's Commissioners at Bandon Bridge. In the parish church of Ballymoney, co. Cork, there is now in use a silver communion chalice, bearing the Stawell arms, and the inscription : " Ex dono Hellenæ Uxoris Anthony Stawell, gen., ob. mort. August 9th, 1632." By his marriage he left issue,
1. Anthony, of Chudleigh, b. 1605 ; d. unm. 1628.
2. JONAS, of Chudleigh, who was b. in 1612. He m., on 28 Jan. 1630, Elizabeth, dau. of John Bennet, of Whiteway, Chudleigh, by whom he had issue, a son,
Jonas, who was b. in 1632. He migrated to Ireland, and was " sovereign," or Chief Magistrate of Clonakilty, co. Cork, in 1677 and 1685. He became " of Coolmain," in the parish of Ringrone, co. Cork, and d. in 1703. By his marriage with Anne, dau. of ————, he had issue,
(1) EUSTACE, of Coolmain, of whom hereafter.
(2) John (Rev.), who was b. at Coolmain in 1687. He entered at Trin. Coll. Dublin, as " son of Jonas Stawell, Esq.," on 1 Feb. 1703, and took his degrees of B.A and M.A. in 1708 and 1711.
(3) William (Rev.), who, in 1728, was curate of Ringrone.
(1) Anne, who m. — Spiller, and had issue.
EUSTACE STAWELL, of Coolmain, J.P. co. Cork, Barrister-at-Law, was granted, 6 Aug. 1722, administration of the affairs of his mother. His will, dated 20 July, 1755, was proved at Cork in 1761. By his marriage, in 1717, with Elizabeth, dau. of Jonas Stawell, of Kilbrittain, he left issue,
1. WILLIAM, of whom hereafter.
2. Eustace, of Garranfeen co. Cork, who was b. in 1740. He entered at Trin. Coll. Dublin, 29 April, 1755, B.A. in 1760. He m. Sarah, dau. of — Coates, who d. on 1 May, 1809. He d.s.p. 13 April, 1807.
The eldest son,
WILLIAM STAWELL, of Coolmain, by his marriage with Phoebe, dau. of — Scott, he had issue,
1. EUSTACE, of whom hereafter.
2. (Rev.) William, M.A., Trin. Col. Dubin, b. 1761, Rector of Kilmaloda, co. Cork 1786-1811 ; m. 1stly, Mary, dau. of— O'Callaghan, by which marriage there was no issue ; and 2ndly, Eliza, dau. of — Rogers, who d. on 1 March, 1822. He d. 23 Dec. 1837. By his 2nd marriage he had issue,
William, d. unm. 1798.
Elizabeth, d unm. 12 March, 1813.
The elder son,
EUSTACE STAWELL, of Coolmain, J.P., Barrister-at-Law, on 14 Feb. 1786, presented his brother, the Rev. William Stawell, with the living of Kilmaloda, of which he was patron. On 31 Oct. 1796 he was appointed 1st Lieut in the Kilbrittain troop of Cavalry (Yeomanry), of which Sampson Stawell, of Kilbrittain, was the captain. He m. 14 Dec. 1795 Mary Maria, dau. of the Rev. John Griffith, by whom he had issue,
1. Eustace, d. young.
1. Ruth, d. unm. 4 Jan. 1800.
2. Maria Amy, m. 17 March, 1833, St. George Ryder Barry, and had issue.
3. Esther Elizabeth Phoebe, m. 17 March 1832, Alexander William Heard, and had issue, four sons, the 2nd of whom

Alexander Edward Stawell Heard, J.P., is now " of Coolmain (*See* HEARD *of Kinsale*).
4. Catherine, who d. unm.   5. Elizabeth, who d. unm.
6. Melian Georgina, who d. unm.
The Coolmain branch thus became extinct in the male line.
We return to,
THOMAS STAWELL, 3rd son of William Stawell, of Harcombe, Chudleigh, by his marriage with Joan, dau. of John Bennet, of Whiteway. He was b. in 1579 ; m. April, 1600, Joan, dau. of — Isimbone, who d. in Dec. 1601, leaving issue, a son and a dau.,
1. (REV.) JONAS, of whom hereafter.
1. Elizabeth.
Thomas Stawell m. 2ndly, Mary, dau. of Robert Pollard, and shortly afterwards migrating to Ireland he settled at Cork. By his 2nd marriage there was issue, two daus.,
2. Mary, who m. — Williams.
3. Margaret, m. 20 May, 1635, Henry Ussher.
The only son,
REV. JONAS STAWELL, was Vicar of Kinsale, co. Cork 1637, Rector of TAXAX 1639 and of Rincurran 1666, all of which livings he held with the Archdeaconry of Ross, in the same co., to which he was admitted on 15 June, 1644, until his death, *circa* 1669. In his will, which was proved at Cork in 1671, and in which he mentioned, besides his sons, Anthony and Jonas, his " sister, Mary Williams " and his " sister, Ussher," he described himself as " sometime of Chudleigh in Devonshire." By his marriage (wife's name unknown), the Ven. Jonas Stawell left issue, two sons and three daus.,
1. ANTHONY, of whom hereafter.
2. Jonas, *see* STAWELL *of Crobeg*.
1. Eleanor, who m., in 1657, Richard, eldest son and heir of Sir Richard Travers, of Ballinane, co. Cork, and had issue.
2. Frances, m. 1st, 1662, Cornelius Coveney, of Kinsale ; and 2ndly, Thomas Mills, of Ballybeg, co. Cork, by whom she had issue.
3. Joan, who m. in 1665, William Billing, of Kinsale.
The elder son,
ANTHONY STAWELL, of Kinsale, J.P., was " sovereign " of that borough in 1661, 1666, 1675, 1676, 1679, 1680, 1681, 1683 and 1685. He was a Capt. in the Bandon Infantry (Militia), and when the country became settled after the rebellion, he bought considerable property in and about Kinsale and Bandon, including the estate of Kilbrittain. He was appointed a J.P. for co. Cork 9 Dec. 1667. In 1677 he signed at Kinsale an address to King CHARLES II. He d. 18 Oct. 1685. By his marriage with Jane, widow of Walter French (who d. in 1688) he had issue, three sons and two daus.,
1. JONAS of whom hereafter.
2. Edward, sovereign of Kinsale 1697 and 1702, Capt. of the Kinsale Troop of Dragoons (Yeomaury), d. in 1715. By his marriage with Elizabeth, dau. of — Marten, he had issue,
1. Jonas, who d. unm. May, 1 696.
2. William, b. June, 1704, and d. unm. April, 1721.
1. Jane.
2. Lydia, m. 1723, Andrew Symes, of Derrygra, co. Cork.
3. William, b. in 1666, educated at Trin. Coll. Dublin, Capt. in the Militia ; m. 1689, Katherine, dau. of Sir Richard Rooth. He d.s.p. in Nov. 1701.
1. Jane, m. 1st, 1677, Richard, eldest son and heir of Sir Richard Gethin, Bart., of Gethin's Grott, co. Cork, and had issue ; and 2ndly, Dudley Thompson, of Dublin.
2. Elinor, m. 1682, Thomas Chudleigh, of Kinsale, and had issue.
The eldest son,
JONAS STAWELL, of Kilkearns, Kilbrittain, and Madame, co. Cork, b. 1658, matric. at St. Edmund's Hall, Oxford, on 23 Oct. 1674, as " son of Anthony of Kinsale, co. Cork, arm." In 1689, Stawell, of Kilbrittain, co. Cork, Esq.," who was one of the many Protestants who had " before the 5th day of November last, absented themselves from this kingdom." He was appointed Capt. of the Kilbrittain troop of Dragoons (Yeomanry), 16 Aug. 1702. He was mentioned in the will, dated 19 Aug. 1690, of Abigail, Lady Stawell, widow of Ralph, 1st Baron Stawell, of Somerton, as " my kinsman, Mr. Jonas Stawell." On 19 Sept. 1692, he was elected M.P. for Kinsale. In 1705 he was sovereign of Clonakilty. He d. May, 1716. By his 1st marriage with ————, dau. of — Throgmorton, he had issue, a son,
1. Throgmorton, who d. young.
By his 2nd marriage, in 1682, with Sarah, dau. of John Newenham, of Coolmore, co. Cork, who d. Feb. 1688, he had issue,
2. ANTHONY, of whom hereafter.
3. Ralph, who d. unm. in Oct. 1689.
1. Jane, who m., in 1706, John Keefe, of Kinsale, and had issue.
By his 3rd marriage, in 1694, with Katherine, dau. and heir of Robert Honnor, eldest son and heir of Lieut.-Col. John Honnor, of Madame, co. Cork, he had issue,
4. JONAS, of whom hereafter.
2. Katherine, m. 1718, Andrew Ruddock, of Wallstown, co. Cork, and had issue.
3. Elizabeth, m. 1717, Eustace Stawell, of Coolmain, and had issue. She d. 28 Oct. 1769.
4. Anne, who d. unm.
5. Ruth, who m. 1728, Henry Ball, of Youghal, co. Cork, and had issue.
The 2nd son,
ANTHONY STAWELL, of Kilbrittain, b. in 1685, was educated at Trin. Coll. Dublin, and in 1713 he was Adjutant of the Royal Regt. of Foot, of Ireland. He resigned his commission in 1717. In 1724 and 1725, he was sovereign of Kinsale. He d. unm. in Feb. 1730.
By his will he devised his estates to his half-brother,
JONAS STAWELL, of Kilbrittain and Madame, J.P., b. in 1700, M.P. for Kinsale from 1745 until his resignation in 1760. He d. in 1767. By his marriage in 1734 with Melian, dau. and heir of

2 T 2

Alderman John Allin, of Cork, he had issue in addition to five sons, Anthony, Allin, Jonas, John and Edward, all of whom d. young unm.,
1. SAMPSON, of whom hereafter.
2. William, of Kilbrack, co. Cork, J.P., who matriculated at Christ Church, Oxford, on 12 Oct. 1762, as "son of Jonas Stawell, of Cork, arm." He m. 4 April, 1775, Catherine, dau. of John Creagh, of Creagh Castle, co. Cork, and Rachel his wife, who was dau. of Andrew Ruddock, of Wallstown, by his marriage with Katherine, dau. of Jonas Stawell, of Kilbrittain. He d.s.p. 17 Feb. 1830, and Catherine Stawell on 19 July, 1839.
 1. Catherine, d. unm.,
 2. Elizabeth, m. 5 Nov. 1766, George Stawell, of Summerhill and Ballyveniter, and had issue. She d. on 22 Sept. 1821.
 3. Anne, m. Aug. 1793, Kilner Baker, and had issue.
 4. Melian, d. unm.
The eldest son,
 SAMPSON STAWELL, of Kilbrittain, J.P., b. Sept. 1741. He took his degree of B.A. at Trin. Coll. Dublin 1759, and 10 Dec. 1760, matric. at Ch. Ch. Oxford. He was Col. of the Bandon Cavalry in 1782, and on 31 Oct. 1796, was gazetted Capt of the Kilbrittain troop of Cavalry (Yeomanry). He d. 1 Jan. 1819. He m. 2 Dec. 1775, Hester, dau. of James Bernard, of Castle Bernard, co. Cork, and sister of Francis, 1st Earl of Bandon, and by her (who d. on 17 May, 1824) he had issue,
 1. JONAS, of whom hereafter.
 2. Bernard, b. Oct. 1777; d.s.p.
 3. William, b. 1780; d.s.p.
 4. James Ludlow, b. 1783; m. 2 Aug. 1831, Rose Emma, dau. of Francis Scaly, of Woodview, co. Cork, and d.s.p. 30 Oct. 1832.
 5. (Rev.) Francis, of Kilbrack, B.A. Trin. Coll. Dublin, Rector of Templeroan and Doneraile, b. May, 1784; d. unm. 21 July, 1866. He inherited the property of Kilbrack, co. Cork, on the death, without issue, in 1839, of Catherine, widow of his uncle William Stawell.
 6. Sampson, b. 6 Oct. 1785. He served in the Peninsula with the 12th Lancers 1811-14, being present at the sieges and capture of Ciudad Rodrigo and Badajoz, the cavalry action of La Rena, the destruction of the bridge at Almaraz, the Battle of Vittoria, and the siege and capture of San Sebastian. At Waterloo he, though a junior Capt., commanded the regiment and brought it out of action, his superior officers having all been placed hors-de-combat. On 4 June, 1827, he obtained the command of the regiment, which he held for 20 years. In 1832, he was elected M.P. for Kinsale. He d. unm. 21 Aug. 1849.
 7. Charles, Capt. in the Militia, b. Aug. 1787; d. unm. 6 Aug. 1829.
 8. George Eustace, b. 1788; d. March, 1792.
 1. Esther, m. 21 June, 1796, John Sealy, of Richmount, co. Cork, and had issue. She d. Nov. 1856.
 2. Melian Charlotte, m. 17 Jan. 1816, Thomas Quin, and had issue. She d. Nov. 1852.
The eldest son,
 JONAS STAWELL, of Kilbrittain, J.P., b. 24 Sept. 1776; d. 15 Jan. 1835, having m. 9 July, 1816, Hon. Charlotte St. Leger, dau. of Hayes, 2nd Viscount Doneraile, by whom he left issue, a dau. and heir,
 CHARLOTTE HARRIET HESTER, who m., 18 Sept. 1845, her cousin, WILLIAM ST. LEGER ALCOCK, Capt. 23rd Royal Welsh Fusiliers, afterwards Lieut.-Col. of the North Cork Rifles (Militia), J.P. and D.L. of co. Cork. In 1845, Capt. and Mrs. Alcock assumed, by royal licence, the additional surname and arms of Stawell. She d. 27 July, 1882. He d. 5 June, 1905. Of their marriage there was issue,
 1. JONAS WILLIAM, J.P. co. Cork, b. 3 Aug. 1846, ; d. unm. 17 Feb. 1900.
 2. WILLIAM THOMAS JONAS, J.P., b. 20 Jan. 1850. He assumed the additional surname and arms of RIVERSDALE by Royal Licence 7 March, 1871, on succeeding to the estate of Lisnegar, co. Cork, under the will of his relative, the Right Rev. Ludlow Tonson, last Baron Riversdale, Bishop of Killaloe, who d. unm. 13 Dec. 1861. He was a J.P. for co. Cork and lord of the manor of Lisnegar and Rathcormac in that county. He d. 6 May, 1907, having m. 30 Jan. 1889, Caroline Fakes, dau. of Thomas Gray, of Boston, U.S.A., and widow of J. B. T. Davidge, who s to the Kilbrittain estate on the death, without issue, of her husband on 6 May, 1907.
 1. Caroline Emily, d. unm. 1848.
 2. Frances Charlotte Esther, d. unm. 1857.
 3. ESTHER MARY, who on the death of her brother William Thomas Jonas, in 1907, s. to the estate of Lisnegar, and assumed the additional surname of RIVERSDALE.

Arms (of STAWELL)—Gu., a cross lozengy arg., a crescent or, for difference. Crest—On a cap of maintenance gu., turned up erm., a falcon rising arg., in his beak a scroll, thereon the motto "En parole je vis."

Lineage (of Alcock).—WILLIAM ALCOCK, of Raunston, co. Leicester, b. 1723 ; m. Mary, sister of Sir Joseph Mawbey, Bart., of Botleys, Surrey, and dau. of John Mawbey, by Martha his w.fe, dau. of Thomas Pratt, and by her (who d. 1802, aged 76) left at his decease, 3 Sept. 1764, four sons,
 1. Joseph, of the Treasury. 2. William.
 3. John, of the Temple. 4. THOMAS.
The 4th son,
 THOMAS ALCOCK, of Burwood House, Surrey, b. 9 June, 1763, J.P. and D.L., Major H.E.I.C.S., and Lieut.-Col., Commandant 3rd Surrey Local Militia, was for many years Treasurer of the Ordnance. He m. 26 July, 1802, Hon. Caroline Catherine Letitia, dau. of St. Leger, 1st Viscount Doneraile, and by her (who d. 1 Feb. 1840) left at his decease, 15 July, 1856, aged 93, two sons and two daus.,

1. THOMAS, Lieut.-Col. Royal East Middlesex Militia, late Major 95th Regt., d. 7 Aug. 1882.
2. WILLIAM ST. LEGER, late of Kilbrittain Castle (see above).
1. Caroline. 2. Emily Jane, d. unm. 17 July, 1899.

Arms (of ALCOCK-STAWELL)—Quarterly : 1st and 4th gu. seven lozenges in cross, arg., a crescent or difference or, for STAWELL ; 2nd and 3rd sa., a fesse between three cocks' heads erased arg. combed and wattled or, for ALCOCK. Crests—1st, On a cap of maintenance gu., turned up erm., a falcon rising arg, in his beak a scroll, thereon, "En parole je vis," for STAWELL ; 2nd, a cock arg., combed and wattled gu., spurred az., for ALCOCK. Motto—Vigilnert.

Seat—Kilbrittain Castle, near Bandon, co. Cork.

STAWELL OF CROBEG.

SAMPSON STAWELL, of Crobeg, co. Cork, b. 3 Oct. 1848 ; m. 1st, 1 Oct. 1885, Frances Matilda (d.s.p. 16 Oct. 1888), dau. of Charles Cavanagh Murphy, of Streamhill, co. Cork. He m. 2ndly, Susanna Mary, dau. of Spiers Norcott, of Cottage, Doneraile.

Lineage.—JONAS STAWELL, of Mallow and Ballylought, co. Cork, 2nd son of the Ven. Jonas Stawell, Archdeacon of Ross, whose will was proved at Cork in 1671 (vide STAWELL of Kilbrittain) served in the war in Ireland as a Royalist Officer (Inrolments of Adjudications) before 5 June, 1649. He was appointed a J.P. for co. Cork on 20 June, 1671. In 1677 he signed at Kinsale an address to King CHARLES II. On 29 June, 1691, "Lieut.-Col. Jonas Stawell" was elected sovereign of Kinsale. A few years afterwards he settled at Ballylought, in the neighbourhood of Mallow. By his marriage with Anne, dau. of — Crofton, he had issue,
 1. GEORGE, of whom hereafter.
 2. John, d. unm. 3. Eustace, d. unm.
 1. Catherine, m. 1699, John Langford, of Tallaher, co. Limerick.
 2. Elizabeth, m. 1709, Richard Chillingworth.
 3. Bryanna, m. Dodsworth Mitchell.
 4. Mary, m. 1708, Joseph Cooper.
The eldest son,
 GEORGE STAWELL, of Ballylought and Ballyveniter, d. in 1749. He m. 1700, Anne, dau. of Edward Dodsworth, of Maryborough, Queen's Co., by whom he had issue,
 1. ANTHONY, of whom hereafter.
 2. Jonas, of Ballyveniter, d. unm. 1758.
 3. Dodsworth, d. unm. July, 1795.
 1. Mary, m. 1735, John Fowkes, M.D., of Mallow.
 2. Anne, d. unm.
The eldest son,
 ANTHONY STAWELL, of Ballydoolin, co. Cork, d.v.p. July, 1741. He m. 15 June, 1732, Mary, dau. and heir of the Rev. Thomas Cooper, by whom he had issue,
 1. GEORGE, of whom hereafter.
 2. Thomas, b. Feb., d. Oct. 1741.
 1. Sarah, d. unm. 6 June, 1809.
 2. Jane, d. unm. April, 1737.
 3. Mary, d. unm. Nov. 1740.
 4. Anne, m. Samuel Austin, and had issue.
 5. Bryanna, m. 1768, Robert Travers, of Round Hill, co. Cork.
The elder son,
 GEORGE STAWELL of Summerhill Ballylought and Ballyveniter, J.P., B.A. Trin. Coll. Dublin, Barrister-at-Law, J.P. Capt. in the Mallow Independents ; d. 9 May, 1808. He m. 5 Nov. 1766, Elizabeth, dau. of Jonas Stawell, of Kilbrittain (see that family), and by her (who d. 22 Sept. 1821) he had issue,
 1. Anthony, who d. young.
 2. JONAS, of whom hereafter, as "of Oldcourt."
 3. George, of Crobeg, Summerhill and Ballyveniter, B.A. Trin. Coll. Dublin, Barrister-at-Law, J.P. for co. Cork, b. Feb. 1770 ; d. 13 Jan. 1825, having m. 16 Nov. 1801, Elizabeth, 2nd dau. of John Longfield, of Longueville, co. Cork (High Sheriff for co. Cork 1775, and M.P. for Mallow), and by her (who d. 8 Dec. 1823, he had issue, four sons and four daus.,
  1. George, of Crobeg and Madame, J.P., b. 12 Sept. 1808. He d. on 19 Jan. 1879, having m. 10 March, 1834, his cousin, Anna Henrietta, 3rd dau. of Jonas Stawell, of Oldcourt, co. Cork, by whom (who d. in April, 1877) he had issue, four sons and three daus.,
   (1) George Stawell, of Crobeg and Madame, B.A. Trin. Coll. Dublin, J.P., b. 5 Feb. 1836 ; d. unm. 25 March, 1892.
   (2) Jonas William Foster, of Ballynascarthy and Ballyhologue, co. Cork, b. 4 Nov. 1840 ; d. unm. 1 Oct. 1903.
   (3) William, b. March, 1846 ; d. unm. May, 1863.

(4) Sampson, now of Crobeg, *b.* 3 Oct. 1848; *m.* 1st, 1 Oct; 1885, Frances Matilda, dau. of Charles Cavanagh Murphy, of Streamhill, co. Cork, who *d.* without issue 16 Oct. 1888. He *m.* 2ndly, Susanna Mary, dau. of Spiers Norcott, of Cottage, Doneraile.
(1) Anna Letitia, *m.* 1st, 20 July, 1870, Warden Francis Grove Annesley, 5th son of Lieut.-Gen. Hon. Arthur Grove Annesley, of Annesgrove, co. Cork, who *d.s.p.* 19 Sept. 1875. She *m.* 2ndly, Oct. 1878, Rev. J. Rice, who *d.s.p.* 1882. She *m.* 3rdly, 1885, Edward Fitzgibbon.
(2) Katharine Letitia, *m.* Oct 3. 1878, Rev. William Henry Cotter, LL.D., Rector of Buttevant, co. Cork, and *d.* 1894, leaving issue.
2. John Robert, of Summerhill, *b.* 17 July, 1812, Capt. in the 38th Foot; *m.* 14 Dec. 1854, Frances Anne, 3rd dau. of Sir John Allen de Burgho, Bart., of Castle Connell, co. Louth, and had issue,.
(1) John Allen George, *b.* 18 Dec. 1858; *d. unm.* 23 March, 1893.
(2) William Eustace, *b.* 12 Dec. 1859; *d.* 1860.
(1) Anna Maud Katherine, *m.* 1 June, 1880, Henry Bird, who *d.* 20 Feb. 1900, leaving issue.
(2) Mildred Frances Elizabeth, *d.* 1862.
(3) Elizabeth Maria Teresa. *d.* August, 1864.
3. Jonas, *b.* 17 July, 1814. He was a Capt. in the 45th Foot, and afterwards served as Principal Barrack Master at the Cape of Good Hope. He *d.* 16 Nov. 1885, having *m.* 1st, 25 Nov. 1840, Henrietta, 2nd dau. of Thomas Prothero, of Malpas Court, co. Mon., J.P. and D.L., High Sheriff of Monmouthshire 1846, who *d.* on 2 Sept. 1850. He *m.* 2ndly, 14 Feb. 1854, Harriet Innes, dau. of Capt. Thompson, by which marriage there was no issue. By his 1st marriage he had issue, a son,
George Dodsworth, *b.* 14 July, 1849. He served in the Devonshire Regt., and retired from the Army with the substantive rank of Col. Dec. 1902. He *m.* 20 July, 1887, Eleanora Mabel, 3rd dau. of Edward Byrom, of Culver, Exeter, and Kersall Cell, Lancs., D.L. of Devon, and High Sheriff of that co. in 1888, and has issue,
Katharine Eleanora Innes.
4. William, of Kilbrack, J.P., B.A. Trin. Coll .Dublin, *b.* 11 Nov. 1819. He inherited the property of Kilbrack, co. Cork, on the death, without male issue, of the Rev. Francis Stawell in 1866 (see STAWELL of *Kilbrittain*). He *d.* 31 March, 1880. He *m.* 17 April, 1855, Eliza, dau. of the Rev. Thomas Croker, by whom he had issue,
(1) Francis, formerly of Kilbrack, and now of Mitchelstown, co. Cork, J.P., *b.* 14 Jan. 1859.
(2) William, *b.* 5 June, 1862; *m.* 3 July, 1900, Ellen, dau. of — Carre, M.D.
(1) Eliza Emilia Arethusa.
1. Elizabeth, *m.* 20 July, 1825, Nathaniel Webb Ware, of Woodfort, co. Cork, and had issue. She *d.* 9 Jan. 1865.
2. Catherine, *m.* 16 Feb. 1833, Hugh Delacour, of Beareforest, co. Cork. She *d.s.p.* June, 1841. He *d.* March, 1873.
3. Susan Patience, *m.* 6 Aug. 1827, Capt. Robert Vivian, 22nd Foot, who *d.* 18 Dec. 1871, and had issue. She *d.* 1882.
4. Charlotte, *m.* 14 Dec. 1840, Robert Longfield, Q.C., who *d.* in 1868. She *d.s.p.* Aug. 1894.

We now return to the eldest surv. son of George Stawell, of Summerhill, Ballylought and Ballyveniter,

JONAS STAWELL, of Oldcourt, co. Cork, *b.* 8 Jan. 1769, Ensign in the Mallow Independents, B.A. Trin. Coll. Dublin, Barrister-at-Law, J.P. for co. Cork. He *d.* 25 July, 1840, having *m.* 14 Feb. 1805, Anna Elizabeth (who *d.* 15 Nov. 1833), dau. of the Right Rev William Foster, D.D., Bishop of Clogher, whose father, the Right Hon. Anthony Foster, was Lord Chief Baron of the Exchequer, Ireland, and his brother, John, who was Chancellor of the Exchequer and last Speaker of the Irish House of Commons before the Union, was created Baron Oriel in 1821. They had issue, five sons and five daus.
1. George Cooper, of Oldcourt, *b.* 16 Sept. 1809; *m.* 15 May, 1843, Elizabeth, 3rd dau. of George Tandy, of Balrath, co. Meath, and *d.s.p.* 14 Jan. 1862.
2. William, *b.* 1810; *d.* 3 Nov. 1814.
3. (Sir) William Foster, K.C.M.G., of Gurrane, co. Cork, and D'Estaville, Melbourne, B.A. Trin. Coll. Dublin, and Barrister-at-Law, *b.* 27 June, 1815. He emigrated to Australia, where in 1851, he became the first Attorney-General of the newly created colony of Victoria, of which, on 25 Feb. 1857, he was appointed Chief Justice. He was knighted 1857, and in 1873 the degrees of LL.B. and LL.D. were conferred upon him by the University of Dublin. In 1875, 1877 and 1884 he acted as Governor of Victoria, and in 1886 he was created K.C.M.G. In August, 1886, he resigned his office of Chief Justice and was appointed Lieut.-Governor of Victoria. He *d.* 12 March, 1889, having *m.* Jan. 1856, Mary Frances Elizabeth, dau. of William Pomeroy Greene, of Collon House, co. Louth, by whom he had issue,
1. Jonas Molesworth, *b.* 12 July, 1858. He is a Civil Engineer, and resides at Sydney, N.S.W.
2. William (*Melbourne*), *b.* 22 March, 1860. He *m.* 1894, Clara de Castilla, dau. of Charles Lyon, and has issue,
(1) Juliet. (2) Joan.
3. Charles Leslie, B.A., LL.B. (Camb.), Barrister-at-Law (*Perth, W.A.*), *b.* 15 Sept. 1861; *m.* 1902, Mildred, dau. of Robert Kennedy, and has issue,
Richard, *b.* 25 April, 1905.
4. George Cooper, *b.* 23 Dec. 1862. Is in P.W. Dept., India. He *m.* 1894, Kathleen, dau. of Capt. Alan Deane, and has issue,

William Arthur McDonald, *b.* 22 Jan. 1895.
5. Richard Rawdon, M.D., Melbourne (with gold medal), D.P.H., London (*Melbourne*), *b.* 14 March, 1864; *m.* 12 Aug. 1908, Evelyn, dau. of Henry Connolly, and has issue,
(1) Mary Elizabeth.
(2) Anna Evelyn.
6. Rodolph de Salis, B.A., M.B., B.C. Camb., F.R.C.S. (Eng.) (*Castle Gates, Shrewsbury*), *b.* 30 Nov. 1871; *m.* 5 Sept. 1900, Maud, dau. of Admiral Right Hon. Sir Astley Cooper Key, G.C.B., F.R.S.
1. Anne Catherine, *m.* 17 Oct. 1889, Sylvester John Browne, of Whittingham, N.S W., and has issue.
2. Mary Letitia, *m.* 14 May, 1890, Edward Willam Hawker, of Adelaide, South Australia, and has issue.
3. Henrietta.
4. Florence Melian, who was educated at Melbourne University and Newnham Coll. Camb. She was placed in the first division of the first class in the Classical Tripos, Camb. 1892.
4. Jonas Sampson, of Hillsborough, co. Down, and Gurrane, co. Cork, *b.* 19 April, 1817; *d. unm.* 2 Dec. 1887.
5. John Leslie (Rev. Canon), B.A. Trin. Coll. Dublin, late Rector of Aughnamcadle, Toomavara, co. Tipperary, *b.* 16 Oct. 1818; *d.* 25 July, 1911; *m.* 25 Aug. 1848, Frances, dau. of John Wilmot Smith, of Ballynanty House, co. Limerick, by whom he had issue,
1. Jonas Cooper Lloyd, B.A., M.B Trin. Coll. Dublin, *b.* 9 Jan. 1857; *m.* 4 Oct. 1885, his cousin, Charlotte Mary, dau. of Charles Wilmot Smith, of Ballynanty House, co. Limerick, who *d.* on 4 Jan. 1890. He *d.s.p.* 26 Jan. 1901.
1. Mary Anna Grace. 2. Letitia Frances Charlotte.
1. Catherine Elizabeth Anna, *m.* 10 Feb. 1830, George Garnett, J.P., of Williamstown, co. Meath, who *d.* 1856. She *d.* 15 April, 1880, having had issue.
2. Elizabeth Georgianna, *m.* 2 Sept. 1844, Arundell Hill, of Donnybrook, co. Cork, and had issue.
3. Anna Henrietta, *m.* 10 March, 1834, her cousin, George Stawell, of Crobeg (*q.v.*). She *d.* April, 1877.
4. Esther Harriet, *d. unm.* Sept. 1818.
5. Letitia, *d. unm.* 2 Aug. 1894.

Arms—Gu., a cross lozengy arg., a crescent or for difference.
Crest—On a cap of maintenance gu., turned up erm., a falcon rising arg., in his beak a scroll, thereon the motto—En parole je vis.
Seat—Crobeg, Doneraile, co. Cork.

STEELE-NICHOLSON. *See* **STEELE.**

STEPHENS-TOWNSHEND. *See* **TOWNSHEND.**

STEWART OF ARDS.

ENA DINGWALL TASCA, LADY STEWART-BAM, of Ards, co. Donegal, eldest dau. of the late Alexander George John Stewart and his wife, Julia Blanche, dau. of Charles Dingwall; *s.* her grandfather 1904; *m.* 26 July, 1910, Sir Pieter Canzius van Blommestein Stewart-Bam, of Sea Point, Cape Town, Capt. (ret.) Cape Garrison Art., J.P. (son of the late Johannes Andrew Bam), who assumed with his wife by Royal Licence the prefix surname and the additional arms of STEWART on his marriage.

Lineage.—ALEXANDER STEWART, *b.* 26 March, 1746 (2nd son of Alexander Stewart, of Mount Stewart, co. Down, M.P., and younger brother of Robert, 1st Marquess of Londonderry),

Stewart. THE LANDED GENTRY. 662

purchased the estate of Ards from the Wray family, and settled there 1782, High Sheriff 1791. He m. 2 Oct. 1791, Lady Mary Moore, 2nd dau. of Charles, 1st Marquess of Drogheda, by Lady Anne Seymour his wife, dau. of Francis, 1st Marquess of Hertford, and by her (who d. 22 Feb. 1842) had (with other children, who d. young),

1. ALEXANDER ROBERT, his heir.
2. Charles Moore (Rev.), b. 5 March, 1799; m. 1830, Alice, 2nd dau. of the Right Hon. John Ormsby Vandeleur, of Kilrush House, co. Clare, and d.s.p. Feb. 1831. His widow m. 2ndly, Col. John Vandeleur, 10th Hussars.
3. John Vandeleur, of Rock Hill, co. Donegal, J.P. and D.L., High Sheriff 1838, b. 4 Oct. 1802; m. 18 Dec. 1837, Lady Helen Graham-Toler, 3rd dau. of Hector John, 2nd Earl of Norbury, and d. 24 June, 1872, having by her (who d. 22 April, 1883) had issue,

 1. ALEXANDER CHARLES HECTOR, of Rock Hill, Letterkenny, &c. Donegal, and 23, Lennox Gardens, S.W., J.P. and D.L. co. Donegal, High Sheriff 1881, Major Gen. (retired), late Col. commanding 2nd Life Guards, b. 15 Nov. 1838; m. 25 April, 1872, Gertrude Mary, eldest dau. of Eric Carrington Smith, of Ashfold, Sussex, and has issue, a dau.,
  Kathleen, b. 8 Jan. 1875; m. 8 June, 1904, Philip Arthur Macgregor, D.S.O., Capt. Coldstream Guards.
 2. Hector Brabazon, Rear-Admiral (retired) R.N. (13, *Warwick Square, S.W.*), b. 13 Dec. 1841.
 3. Robert Seymour, b. 28 May, 1846, Major (retired) Donegal Militia Artillery, m. 27 Jan. 1885, Frances Lucia, only dau. of Col. O'Hanlon.
 4. Charles John, Barrister-at-Law, Public Trustee (32, *Eccleston Square, S.W.*), b. 1851; m. 11 Oct. 1884, Lady Mary Catherine, eldest dau. of Hector John, 3rd Earl of Norbury, and has issue,
  (1) Gerald Charles, 10th Royal Hussars, b. 29 March, 1888.
  (2) John Maurice, b. 27 April, 1895.
  (1) Helen Margaret, b. 4 April, 1886.
  (2) Eirene Mary, b. 29 Sept. 1890.
  (3) Marjorie Alice, b. 6 Aug. 1893.
 1. Elizabeth Georgiana.
1. Maria Frances, m. 10 June, 1811, Robert Montgomery, of Convoy House, who d. 1846; she d. 1857.
2. Gertrude Elizabeth, dec.

Mr. Stewart d. Aug. 1831, and was s. by his eldest son,

ALEXANDER ROBERT STEWART, of Ards and Laurencetown House, J.P. and D.L., High Sheriff co. Donegal 1830, b. 12 Feb. 1795; m. 28 July, 1825, Lady Caroline Anne Pratt, 3rd dau. of John Jeffries, 1st Marquess Camden, and by her (who d. 7 Oct. 1827) left at his decease, 25 March, 1850, one son,

ALEXANDER JOHN ROBERT STEWART, of Ards. co. Donegal, and Laurencetown House, co. Down, J.P. for cos. Donegal, Down, and Middlesex, and D.L. for Donegal and Down, High Sheriff co. Donegal 1853, and co. Down 1861, b. 5 July, 1827; m. 17 May, 1851, Lady Isabella Rebecca Graham-Toler (22, *St. Aubyn's, Hove, Sussex*), 7th dau. of Hector John, 2nd Earl of Norbury, and d. 30 July, 1904, leaving issue,

1. ALEXANDER GEORGE JOHN, Barrister-at-Law, b. 13 Feb. 1852; m. 10 April, 1883, Julia Blanche, dau. of Charles Dingwall, of Knollys Croft, co. Surrey, and d. 5 Dec. 1897, leaving issue, two daus.,
 1. ENA DINGWALL TASCA, now of Ards.
 2. Muriel Neara.
2. Charles Hector, b. 23 May, 1853; m. 21 Oct. 1910, Minnie, dau. of William Barwell.
3. George Lawrence, b. 6 Sept. 1861; m. 2 May, 1911, Emma May, dau. of Bradford Hardinge, H.M., Bengal C.S. (*see* BURKE'S *Peerage*, HARDINGE, Bart.).
4. Henry Moore, b. 29 March, 1863.
5. Cecil George Graham, b. 14 June, 1868.
1. Caroline Helen Mary, m. 5 July, 1883, Capt. Frederick Thomas Penton, late 4th Dragoon Guards, formerly M.P. for Central Finsbury 1886-91, and has issue,
 1. Henry Alexander.
 2. Cyril Frederick, m. 20 July, 1909, Gladys Lane, 4th dau. of the Rev. Canon Thynne, and has issue,
  John, b. 25 April, 1910.
  1. Kathleen Winifred.
  1. Dorothy Grace.
2. Beatrice Charlotte Elizabeth.
3. Ida Augusta Isabella.

Arms—Quarterly: 1st and 4th, per pale, sa. and or, barry of four counterchanged on a chief erm., a thistle slipped and leaved between two dice ppr. (BAM); 2nd and 3rd, or, a bend counter-compony arg. and az. between two lions rampant gu., a crescent for difference (STEWART of Ards; confirmed to the descendants of the late Alexander John Robert Stewart), and for distinction a canton of the fourth. **Crests**—1. A thistle leaved and slipped ppr. between two ostrich feathers or (BAM). 2. A dragon statant or, charged with a crescent for difference, and (for distinction charged on the wing with a cross-crosslet gu. *Motto*—Metuenda corolla draconis.

Seats—Ards, Letterkenny, co. Donegal, and Laurencetown House, Gifford, co. Down. *Residence*—5, Old Court Mansions, Kensington, W.

STEWART OF HORN HEAD.

CHARLES FREDERICK STEWART, of Horn Head, co. Donegal, B.A., J.P., High Sheriff 1871, b. 10 March, 1845; s. his father 1868; m. 1st, 12 Aug. 1869, Elizabeth Frances, 2nd dau. of Rev. Thomas Lindesay, Rector of Upper Cumber, co. Derry, and by her (who d. 4 March, 1881) has had issue,

1. CHARLES FREDERICK (*Runcleven, Dunfanaghy*), late Capt. 5th Batt. Royal Inniskilling Fus., b. 12 July, 1870; m. 1st, 20 Sept. 1899, Alice Mary Lydia, dau. of the late Capt. John Keys Humfrey, of Cavan a cor (*see that family*). She d. 3 Jan. 1907, leaving issue,
 1. Elizabeth Frances. 2. Alice Humfrey.
He m. 2ndly, 5 Oct. 1910, Hildegarde Ellen Elizabeth, dau. of Frederick Lindesay, of Waverley Road, Liverpool, and has further issue,
 1. Charles Frederick, b. 6 Aug. 1911.
2. Wiliam, b. 2 Aug. 1871; d. 22 Jan. 1895.
3. Thomas Francis (Rev.), Vicar of St. Paul's, Worcester, b. 9 Oct. 1872.
4. Walter Edward, b. 14 June, 1876; d. 1 Oct. 1883.
1. Ann Elizabeth Frances, m. 21 June, 1900, Henry Eliot Howard, and has issue (*see* HOWARD *of Stone*).
2. Nicola Mary, d. April, 1891.
3. Eleanor Louisa. 4. Elizabeth Frances, d. April, 1891.

He m. 2ndly, 6 May, 1884, Georgina Sophia, youngest dau. of Blackwood Hamilton, of Highnam, Bray, by whom he has issue,

5. Bertram Robert, b. 14 Jan. 1886.
6. Richard Arthur, b. 17 Sept. 1888.
5. Georgina Sophia.

Lineage.—CAPT. CHARLES STEWART, an Officer in the Army of King WILLIAM III., and one of those who fought at the battle of the Boyne, had a lease of Doone, in King's Co., but migrating northward in 1700, he purchased from Capt. John Forward and Capt. William Sampson, the Donegal estates of Horn Head, &c., and was High Sheriff 1707. He left issue,
1. FREDERICK, of whom presently.
2. Charles.
3. Gustavus, of Ray, co. Donegal, High Sheriff 1750.
1. Eleanor, m. Benson, of Lumsford.

The eldest son,

FREDERICK STEWART, of Horn Head, High Sheriff 1742, m. 1730, Mary, eldest dau. of George Knox, of Prehen, co. Derry, and had issue. Mr. Stewart made his will 17 April, 1768, which was proved 14 May, 1770. His eldest son,

CHARLES STEWART, of Horn Head, Capt. of Dragoons, High Sheriff 1768, m. 1st, 1762, Elizabeth, dau. of his uncle, Gustavus Stewart, but by her had no issue. He m. 2ndly, 10 Oct. 1772, Nichola Anne, dau. of — Charlton, and by her had issue. Mr. Stewart m. 3rdly, Elizabeth Knox; he made his will 4 Oct. 1799, and it was proved 12 Jan. 1809. His eldest son,

WILLIAM STEWART, of Horn Head, Capt. Donegal Militia, High Sheriff 1805, m. 1799, Elizabeth, dau. of Richard Maxwell, of Birdstown, and by her (who d. 13 July, 1860) had issue,

1. CHARLES FREDERICK, his heir.
2. Richard, Capt. H.F.I.C.S., dec.
3. William, M.D., of Killendarragh, Lifford, co. Donegal, b. 1805; m. 1833, Angel Isabella, dau. of Sir James Galbraith, Bart., and d. Jan. 1851, leaving issue,
 1. William Richard, b. 23 June, 1834; d. Dec. 1857.
 2. James Frederick, b. 3 Aug. 1839; d. Dec. 1882.
 3. Alexander Montgomery, of Killendarragh, Lifford, and Drumbeg, Inver, co. Donegal, b. 23 April, 1842; d. 2 Dec. 1909; m. 10 Feb. 1897, Jemima Sarah, dau. of William Sinclair, of Holy Hill, co. Tyrone.
  1. Dorothea Elizabeth, m. 1863, James Hamilton, of Brown Hall, co. Donegal, and has issue (*see that family*).
  2. Angel Isabella.
4. Peter Benson, Comm. R.N., m. Augusta, dau. of Capt. Foote, R.N., dec.
5. Alexander (dec.), Rector of Tullaghyhobigly, m. Sarah, dau. of Rev. Thomas Gibbings, and had issue.
 1. Anne, d. unm. 2. Nichola Anne Mary, d. unm.
 3. Elizabeth, dec., m. Leonard Cornwall, who is dec.
 4. Emily, dec. 5. Frances, dec.
 6. Charlotte Augusta, d. unm. 7. Georgina, dec.

Capt. Stewart d. 9 March, 1840, and was s. by his eldest son,

REV. CHARLES FREDERICK STEWART, of Horn Head, J.P., m. 9 March, 1831, Anne, only dau. of Col. Robert Stirling, H.E.I.C.S., by his wife, the dau. of Sir William Toone, K.C.B., H.E.I.C.S., and had,

1. William, Capt. 3rd Buffs, d. Sept. 1864.
2. Robert, d. under age.
3. CHARLES FREDERICK, now of Horn Head.
1. Elizabeth Mary, d. 1906.
2. Mary (dec.), m. Michael Becher, of Corriganear, co. Cork.
3. Emily Anne, m. Rev. J. Brodie, M.A.

4. Charlotte, *d.* 4 June, 1905.
5. Ann Louisa, *d.* 1900.
Rev. Mr. Stewart *d.* Oct. 1868.

Arms—Quarterly: 1st and 4th, az., three fleurs-de-lys within a bordure engrailed or; 2nd and 3rd or, a fesse chequy az. and arg., within a bordure gu., charged with eight buckles of the first, over all in the chief centre point a mullet counterchanged. *Crest*—Out of a ducal coronet or, a bull's head sa., vomiting flames ppr., and charged with a mullet or. *Motto*—Avant Darnly.

Seat—Horn Head, Dunfanaghy, co. Donegal.

STEWART OF BALLYMENAGH.

EDWARD MICHAEL STEWART, of Ballymenagh, co. Tyrone, and Corcam, co. Donegal, and Ballytibbot, co. Cork, *b.* 24 March, 1864.

Lineage.—Early in the reign of JAMES VI. of Scotland and I. of England, JAMES STEWART migrated from Scotland, and purchasing Cookstown, co. Tyrone, and the adjacent lands from one Cook, settled himself at Ballymenagh. James had two sisters, Barbara, *m.* Rev. Richard Darroch, Rector of Derrytown, and Grissel, *m.* Richardson, of Clougher, in same co. This James had five daus. (June, *m.* Thomas Goodlott, of Derrygallie; one *m.* Rev. John Cheevers, of Manor Roe; one *m.* her cousin, James Richardson, of Clogher; Sarah, *m.* Barkley, of Magherafelt, co. Derry; and Mary, *d. unm.* 1701) and one son,
WILLIAM STEWART, who moved to Killymoon, which his father, who *d.* in 1679, purchased in 1634. He *m.* 1664, Margaret, eldest dau. of John Shaw, of Ballygellie, co. Antrim, and had issue,
1. JAMES. 2. Alexander, *d. unm.*
3. Henry, High Sheriff of Tyrone 1711, *d. unm.*
4. John, drowned in the River Killymoon whilst yet a boy.
1. Margaret, *m.* Dec. 1706, Clotworthy Upton. M.P. co. Antrim, and *d.s.p.* 1797. 2. Mary, *d. unm.* 1701.
The eldest son,
JAMES STEWART, of Killymoon, *m.* 1709, Helen, dau. of Patrick Agnew, of co. Antrim, and had issue,
1. WILLIAM, his heir.
2. Patrick, *m.* Mary Heywood, of Dublin.
1. Margaret, *m.* her cousin, William Agnew.
The eldest son,
WILLIAM STEWART, of Killymoon and Ballymenagh, High Sheriff 1738, M.P. co. Tyrone 1747-68, *b.* 1710; *m.* 1740, Eleanor, eldest dau. of Sir Henry King, 3rd Bart., of Rockingham, and by her (who *d.* 1811) he left at his decease, 1797,
1. JAMES, of Killymoon, M.P. co. Tyrone 1768, *b.* 1741: *m.* 1774, Hon. Elizabeth Molesworth, dau. and eventually co-heir (with Lady Ponsonby, wife of 1st Lord Ponsonby, and Mrs. Staples, wife of the Right Hon. John Staples, of Lissain, co. Derry) of Richard, 3rd Viscount Molesworth, and by her (who *d.* 30 April, 1835) had, with other issue (James, *b.* 1812; Richard (Rev.), *d. unm.* 24 Feb. 1869), all *dec.*, a son and a dau., viz.,
WILLIAM, of Killymoon, M.P. co. Tyrone, *b.* 1780; *d.* 1850. At his death Killymoon was sold.
Louisa, *m.* Henry John Clements, M.P., of Ashfield Lodge, co. Cavan, and *d.* 1850.
2. HENRY, of whom presently.
3. Edward, of London, *b.* 1750: *m.* Amelia Anne Marler, dau. of John Marler, of Hadley, Middlesex, and *d.* 1834, having had sixteen children.
1. Isabella, *m.* John Hamilton, of Brown Hall, co. Donegal, and had issue (*see that family*).
2. Frances, *m.* Surgeon-Gen. George Stuart (*see* BURKE'S *Peerage*, CASTLE STEWART, E.).
The 2nd son,
HENRY STEWART, of Tyrcallen, co. Donegal, *b.* 10 May, 1749: *m.* Jan. 1793, Hon. Elizabeth Pakenham, eldest dau. of Edward Michael, 2nd Lord Longford, and by her (who *d.* 10 Aug. 1851) had issue,
1. William (Rev.), *b.* 1794, *m.* 1815, Anne Eliza Williams, and *d.s.p.* 1858.
2. EDWARD MICHAEL (Rev.), M.A., of Corcam and Ballymenagh, *b.* 1797; *m.* 1833, Jane Renwick, dau. of John Jeffrey, and by her (who *d.* 1878) had issue,
 1. HENRY WILLIAM (Rev.), late of Corcam.
 2. John Alexander, *b.* 1838, *m.* 1879, Elisa Charlotte, dau. of Rev. B. B. Gough, *d.* 1882.
  1. Charlotte Jane. 2. Elisabeth, *m.* 1861, F. Chadwick.
Mr. Stewart *d.* 1883.

3. Henry, *b.* 1799; *m.* 1st, 1838, Lucy Elizabeth, dau. of John Norris, and 2ndly, 1856, Frances Isabella Anne, dau. of Capt. Style, R.N. By the former he had a son, William, dec.
4. THOMAS, late of Ballymenagh, Mount Blakeney, and Whitegate House, co. Cork, J.P., *b.* 7 July, 1802; *m.* 29 March, 1855, Anne (*d.* 23 Feb. 1885), 5th dau. of James Penrose, of Woodhill, co. Cork, by Louisa Pettitot his wife, dau. of Robert Fitzgerald of Corkbeg. He assumed the surnames of BLAKENEY and LYON before STEWART and the arms of those families quartered with STEWART by Royal Licence 23 June, 1855, and *d.* 1 Jan. 1874.
5. James Robert, of Gortleitragh, Whitegate, and Mount Blakeney (*see* STEWART *of Summerhill*).
1. Catherine, *d.* 1808.
Mr. Stewart *d.* Sept. 1840.

REV. HENRY WILLIAM STEWART, of Ballymenagh, co. Tyrone, and Corcam, co. Donegal, and Ballytibbot, co. Cork, M.A., Rector of Knockbreda, co. Down, Chancellor of the Cathedral Church of Holy Trinity, Dio. Down and Rural Dean, *b.* 24 Sept. 1834; *m.* 10 April, 1860, Fanny (who *d.* 26 Jan. 1911), dau. of Ven. Arthur Palmer, Archdeacon of Toronto, and *d.* 5 Nov. 1910, leaving issue,
1. EDWARD MICHAEL, now of Ballymenagh.
2. Arthur Henry, *b.* 1869; *m.* 30 March, 1891, Alice, eld. dau. of Arthur W. Mosse, of Castletown, co. Kilkenny.
3. Pakenham Thomas, *b.* 1871; *m.* 1901, Mary Dupré, dau. of John George Fennell, of Yara Grange, Melbourne.
4. William (Rev.), B.A., *b.* 1876. 5. James Robert, *b.* 1878.
6. John Alexander, *b.* 1881.
1. Frances Mary.
2. Jane Charlotte, *m.* 1884, Jonas Sealy Poole, M.D.
3. Hester Madeline, *m.* 1894, Lieut. O. H. Daniel, R.N.
4. Katharine Elizabeth Martha, *d. unm.* 1892.
5. Elizabeth Margaret Anne Palmer.

Arms—Or, a fesse chequy arg. and az. between three lions ramp. gu. *Crest*—A griffin's head couped ppr. *Motto*—Forward.

Estates—Ballymenagh, co. Tyrone, Corcam, co. Donegal, and Ballytibbot, co. Cork. *Residence*—8, Mount Charles, Belfast. *Club*—Royal Ulster Yacht.

STEWART OF SUMMERHILL.

GEORGE FRANCIS STEWART, of Summerhill, co. Dublin, J.P. and D.L. co. Leitrim, High Sheriff 1892, *b.* 1 Nov. 1851: *m.* 28 June, 1881, Georgiana Lavinia, dau. of Rear-Admiral Richard Robert Quin, son of Lord George Quin (*see* BURKE'S *Peerage*, HEADFORT, M.), and has issue,

1. CLEMENTS GEORGE, late 2nd Lieut. Royal Inniskilling Fus., *b.* 9 Aug. 1882: *m.* 4 Jan. 1912, Ellen, dau. of late Thomas Eades Walker, M.P., of Lynden House, Lynden Gardens, London.
2. Robert Henry Rynn, educated at Wellington Coll. and Magdalen Coll. Oxford, *b.* 18 Sept. 1883.
1. Mary Selina, *b.* 22 March, 1887; *d.* July, 1908.
2. Ethel Georgiana, *b.* 10 Sept. 1890.

Lineage.—JAMES ROBERT STEWART, of Gortleitragh, co. Dublin, and Mount Blakeney, co. Limerick, J.P. and D.L. co. Dublin, M.A., 5th son of Henry Stewart, of Tyrcallen, co. Donegal (*see* STEWART *of Ballymenagh*), *b.* 1805; *m.* 27 Oct. 1835, Martha Eleanor, dau. of Richard Benson Warren, Serjeant-at-Law (*see* BURKE'S *Peerage*, WARREN, Bart.). She *d.* 5 May, 1865. He *d.* 10 Dec. 1889, having had issue,
1. Henry (Rev.), D.D., of Mount Blakeney, co. Limerick, Rector of Banbridge, co. Down, *b.* 1836; *m.* 1861, Martha Angelina, only dau. of Rev. Edward Michael Hamilton (*see* HAMILTON *of Brown Hall*), and niece of Baron Clermont and Baron Carlingford. He *d.* 1896, having had issue,
 1. Edward Hamilton (Rev.), M.A., of Dronisken, co. Louth, Trin. Coll. Camb., Vicar of Kemsing, Kent, *b.* 13 June, 1862; *m.* 9 Jan. 1896, Constance, eldest dau. of the late John Henry Gilchrist-Clark, of Speddoch, Dumfriesshire (*see that family*), and has issue,
  (1) Henry Robert, *b.* Oct. 1903.
  (1) Emily Hilda, *b.* Oct. 1897.
  (2) Margaret Louisa, *b.* Feb. 1899; *d.* March, 1906.
  (3) Eileen Constance, *b.* April, 1900.
 1. Martha Louisa. 2. Emily Gertrude.
2. Richard Warren, Col. late R.E., *b.* 6 Nov. 1837; *d.* 12 Sept. 1910. His wife Mary *d.* 12 March, 1904.

Stewart. THE LANDED GENTRY. 664

3. James Robert, d. 1891.
4. Edward Pakenham, late Capt. 78th Regt.
5. Augustus Philip, d. 1864.
6. William Thomas.
7. Robert Warren (Rev.), m. Louisa, dau. of Dr. Josiah Smyly, of Dublin (see SMYLY of Camus). Both were massacred in China 1895.
8. GEORGE FRANCIS, of Summerhill.
9. Arthur Blakeney FitzGerald, d. 1879.
1. Elizabeth Martha, d. unm.
2. Emily Lucy.
3. Mary Florence, m. 27 April, 1889, Robert William Norman (see NORMAN of Glengollen).

Arms—Or a fesse chequy arg. and az. between three lions rampant gu. Crest—A griffin's head couped ppr. Motto—Forward.

Seat—Summerhill, Killiney, co. Dublin.

STEWART OF ST. HELEN'S.

JAMES AUGUSTUS STEWART, of Belle Vue, Buncrana, co. Donegal, J.P., b. 7 March, 1835; m. 12 June, 1884, Ann Wilhelmina Jean, dau. of William Wray, of Oak Park, co. Donegal, and has issue,

1. JAMES AUGUSTUS, b. 17 Aug. 1894.
1. Wilhelmina Augusta.
2. Mary Adeline Cecil.
3. Edith Frances.
4. Augusta Anna Blanche.
5. Hester Leonora Sophia.
6. Flora Euphemia.

Mr. Stewart is younger brother of Sir Augustus Abraham James Stewart, 9th bart. (who d. unm. 26 Aug. 1889), and 3rd son of Capt. William Augustus Stewart, 58th Regt. (who d. 23 Aug. 1876), and Anna his wife (who d. 6 June, 1864), dau. of William Molloy, of Blackfort, co. Tipperary, and grandson of Rev. Abraham Augustus Stewart, D.D., Rector of Dunabate, and Chaplain to the Lord Lieutenant of Ireland.

Lineage, Arms, &c.—See BURKE'S Peerage, STEWART, Bart. Club—Sackville Street, Dublin.

STEWART. See BURKE'S PEERAGE, LONDONDERRY, M.

STEWART. See BURKE'S PEERAGE, STEWART, Bart.

STEWART-MOORE. See MOORE.

STOKES OF MOUNTHAWK.

MAJOR-GEN. GEORGE BARET STOKES, of Mounthawk, co. Kerry, Major-Gen. late Royal Inniskilling Fusiliers, b. 31 July, 1833; m. 6 Sept. 1875, Isabella Barbara, only dau. of Robert Law, of Dublin, M.D. (see LAW of Killaloe), by Eleanor Vesey his wife, and by her (who d. 9 July, 1891) had issue,

1. Charles Henry George Vesey, Capt. Royal Inniskilling Fus., b. 20 July, 1876; d. unm. 11 Aug. 1905.
2. Robert Law Day, b. 7 Feb. 1878; d. 16 May, 1884.
3. OLIVER MAURICE FITZGERALD, b. 28 May, 1881.
4. Frank Bertram Vesey, b. 3 Dec. 1883.
1. Eleanor Mary Geraldine.
2. Olive Muriel Kathleen.

Lineage.—The first settler in Ireland was an Officer in the Army, who had considerable property in co. Limerick, Stokesfield, &c., and was buried at Askeaton, in that co. His son,

JOHN STOKES, of Dunmoylan House, co. Limerick, living circa 1622, m. Sarah O'Connell, dau. of Jeffery O'Connell, of Iveragh, co. Kerry, and left a son,

EDWARD STOKES, m. Judith, dau. of Lacy, of Ballingarry, and grand-dau. of Lacy, of Bruree. Of this family was the celebrated Field-Marshal Lacy, in the service of MARIA THERESA. Edward Stokes and Judith Lacy left a son,

JOHN STOKES, m. Honoria, dau. of John Fitzgerald, of Clenglish, co. Limerick, and left a son,

OLIVER STOKES, m. Margaret, dau. of John Creagh, of Ballybunnion House, co. Kerry, and left a son,

GEORGE STOKES, m. 1771, Bridget, dau. of John Cooke, of Skeheneriu, co. Kerry, and grand-dau. of Thomas Cooke, of Paynestown, co.   , by his wife, a dau. of Robert Fitzmaurice, of Ballykealy Castle, co. Kerry, and had a son,

OLIVER STOKES, of Caracraig, co. Kerry, J.P., m. 1795, Elizabeth, dau. of John Day, of Cork, by his wife, Margaret Hewson. John Day and Margaret Hewson were first cousins, and were grandchildren of Maurice Fitzgerald, Knight of Kerry, by Elizabeth Crosbie his wife, dau. of David Crosbie, and sister of Maurice, 1st Lord Brandon. She d. 24 May, 1863. Mr. Stokes d. 1 Jan. 1844, leaving issue,

1. GEORGE DAY, his heir.
2. Robert Day, b. 2 May, 1802; m. 20 Aug. 1826, Eliza, dau. and co-heir with her sister (his brother George's wife) of Robert Day, of Horstead Hall. She d. 11 Sept. 1868. He d. 13 Sept. 1871, leaving surviving issue,
   1. Oliver Robert, Major-Gen. R.A. (retired), of Lassinagh, Tralee, co. Kerry, b. 12 Oct. 1827. His wife Elizabeth d. 31 Dec. 1908.
   2. Robert Baret (Sir), Knt., C.B., of Drumultonmore, co. Kerry, Capt. 54th Foot, Resident Magistrate for Derry, b. 10 Feb. 1833; m. 22 Oct. 1854, Marjorie Augusta, dau. of the late John Simpson, of Oakfield, Ontario, Canada, and d. 5 Sept. 1899, leaving issue,
      (1) Robert Henry Simpson, of Drumultonmore, co. Kerry, Capt. R.N., b. 5 Aug. 1855; m. 16 Sept. 1882, Maude, only dau. of I. Simpson, of Kingston, Canada.
      (2 Leslie Falkiner John de Vere, Capt. King's Own Regt., b. 13 March, 1862; d. unm. 24 Aug. 1903.
   3. John Edward, Rear Admiral, b. 5 June, 1838; m. 4 Oct. 1870, Frances, who d.s.p. 15 June, 1894, dau. of Lieut.-Col. Patrick Day Stokes (see below).
   4. Edward William, of Ellel Hall, Lancaster, J.P., Major Royal Lancaster Regt. (retired) and Capt. 1st Royal Lancashire Militia, Knt. of Grace of the Order of St. John of Jerusalem, b. 14 June, 1841; m. 15 Jan. 1880, Margaret Annie, dau. of William Storey, J.P., of Lancaster, and has issue,
      (1) Gertrude Eveline.
      (2) Phyllis Baret, m. 11 Jan. 1904, Gilbert Augustus Elliot, son of the late Augustus John Elliot, of Bengal C.S.
      (3) Violet (twin), m. 26 June, 1907, Ralph George Elphinstone Mortimer.
      (4) Constance (twin).
      (5) Kathleen Frances.
   5. Maurice Fitzmaurice, b. 18 Nov. 1843, Lieut.-Col. Royal Munster Fusiliers, d. unm. 13 Jan. 1900.
   6. Graham Arthur, b. 20 April, 1849; d. unm.
   1. Elizabeth Valentine, m. Leslie Wren, of Littor, co. Kerry, who left issue.
3. John Day, of Lassinagh, co. Kerry, Major-Gen. in the Army, late British Representative at the Court of Mysore, m. Jane, youngest dau. of Col. Littlejohn, Bengal Army, and d.s.p. 1863. She d. 15 April, 1873.
4. Edward Day, of Farranakilla, co. Kerry, J.P., b. 1809, m. 1832, Anne, dau. of Col. Haldane, R.E., Quartermaster-Gen. of the British forces in India (descended from John Haldane, of Gleneagles, N.B., by Mary Drummond, dau. of David, 3rd Baron Maderty, eldest brother of William, 1st Viscount Strathallan), co-heir (with her sister, Julia) of Gen. Haldane. She d. 5 Oct. 1857. He d. 6 Dec. 1885, leaving issue,
   1. Oliver Haldane, late Capt. R.E., b. 1833, m. Henrietta, dau. of Major Mackintosh.
   2. Edward John, Capt. 39th Regt., d. unm. 17 Sept. 1865.
   3. Henry Haldane, d. unm.
   4. Alexander Haldane, Lieut.-Col. late R.A.M.C., b. 9 Oct. 1843.
   1. Maria Louisa, m. 10 Aug. 1858, Edward Guyon de Moleyns. She d. 15 March, 1862, leaving issue (see BURKE'S Peerage; VENTRY, B.).
   2. Elizabeth Bridget, m. 18 Oct. 1870, Rev. Rowland Bateman, son of Rev. Rowland Bateman, of Kalcara, co. Kerry. She d. 9 Feb. 1881, leaving issue.
   3. Georgina Anne.
5. Oliver Day, of Castle Ballymalis and Caracraig, co. Kerry, J.P., Major late Madras Army, formerly Capt. Kerry Militia, b. March, 1811; m. 1st, 1843, Catherine, only dau. of John Hilliard, of Ballydunled, by his wife, Anne Hickson, of Fermoyle, and by her (who d. 22 June, 1871) had issue,
   1. Henry, Lieut. 38th Regt., d. unm. 26 Dec. 1872.
   2. William Edward, Lieut. 14th Hussars, b. Feb. 1852; d. unm. 27 Sept. 1878.
   3. Oliver Adrian, Capt. R.N. (St. Florence, Cheltenham), b. 14 Dec. 1854; m. 22 Oct. 1908, Lavinia Mary, dau. of late Rev. Joseph Wood.
   1. Annie Jane.
   2. Elizabeth May.
   3. Kathleen Emily, m. 3 Nov. 1883, Col. James White Thurburn, C.S.I., R.E., and has issue.
He m. 2ndly, 3 April, 1872, Hannah, widow of Edward Udale Thompson, and 3rd dau. of John Chapman, of Craggs House, Whitby, co. York, and d. 17 March, 1897.
6. Patrick Day, late Lieut.-Col., b. 1812; m. Dec. 1833, Julia, youngest dau. of Col. Henry Haldane, R.E. Quartermaster-Gen. in India, and co-heir (with her sister) of Gen. Haldane

(*see* HALDANE *of Glencagles*). She *d.* 1868. He *d.* 11 April, 1871, having had issue.
1. Oliver, *d.* young.
2. Charles Patrick, of Farran-a-Killa, Camberley, Surrey, Major-Gen. late 4th The King's Own-Regt. (*United Service Club*), *b.* 11 Aug. 1836; *m.* 15 Sept. 1868, Frances, dau. of Richard Leahy, of Tralee, 2nd son of John Leahy, Southill, Killarney, J.P., served with 4th The King's Own in the Crimea 1854–55, siege and fall of Sevastopol, attack on Cemetery, mentioned in despatches, Indian Mutiny 1857-58, in command of a field force in pursuit of Tantia Topee, attack and capture of Mondetti.
3. John Day, *m.* Jessy, dau. of H. Stephens. He *d.* 1873, having by her (who *m.* 2ndly, C. Tyser) had issue, a son,
Haldane Leo Tresillian.
4. Henry Haldane, Lieut.-Col. late R.A.M.C., M.B. (*Devonshire House, Crowley, Offord*), *b.* 11 Sept. 1846; *m.* Florence, dau. of J. Browne, of Barbados, an dhas issue,
Haldane Day, M.V.O., Lieut. King's Own Regt., *b.* 21 Sept. 1885.
5. Julian Fitzmaurice, *b.* Feb. 1849; *d. unm.* Jan. 1879.
6. Radclyffe Haldane, Major late Army Service Corps and King's Own Yorkshire L.I., *b.* 11 April, 1853; *m.* 27 April, 1882, Alice, dau. of Henry Glasse, Inspector-Gen. of Hospitals in India, and has issue,
(1) Beryl Emily. (2) Violet Alice.
1. Frances, *m.* 4 Oct. 1870, her cousin, Capt. John Edward Stokes, R.N. (*see above*). She *d.s.p.* 15 June, 1894.
2. Olivia Elizabeth, *d. unm.* 1861. 3. Alice, *d. unm.* 1860.
4. Louisa Anne, *m.* 1873, Capt. Colthurst Bateman, and bad issue.
5. Isabella Maria.
1. Margaret, *m.* Maurice Fitzmaurice, of Duagh House, J.P. for co. Kerry.
2. Elizabeth B., *m.* Capt. Henry Bowles, of Mounthawk, J.P. for co. Kerry.
3. Honoria, *m.* 7 July, 1824, Col. David Graham, of Meiklewood, D.L. for co. Stirling. He *d.* 1847, leaving issue.
4. Lucy, *m.* 27 May, 1841, Rowland Eager, of Cullenymore, co. Kerry, and had issue.
The eldest son,
GEORGE DAY STOKES, of Mounthawk, Kerry, J.P., Treasurer of the co. M.A. Trin. Coll. Dublin, *b.* 9 Nov. 1800; *m.* 20 Aug. 1826, Mary Anne, dau. and co-heir (with her sister Eliza) of Robert Baret, of Horstead Hall, Norfolk, and by her (who *d.* 11 April, 1851) had issue,
1. Oliver George, Capt. 1st West India Regt., *b.* 18 Jan. 1830; *d. unm.* 27 March, 1855.
2. Henry Bowles, Capt. 47th Regt. (retired), *b.* 14 July, 1831; *m.* July, 1860, Janet Bryan Stephenson, dau. of John Stephenson, of Fort William, co. Londonderry. She *d.* 25 July, 1873. He *d.* 17 Feb. 1874, leaving a dau., Henrietta Elizabeth, *b.* July, 1863. He served through the Crimean war, and had his name mentioned in Lord Raglan's despatches for bravery at the Quarries.
3. GEORGE BARET, now of Mounthawk.
4. Robert Yallop, Lieut. 8th Regt. (retired), *b.* 1 July, 1836.
5. John George, *b.* 1 April, 1841.
6. Edward George, of Mounthawk, Tralee, *b.* 23 Aug. 1844; *m.* Sept. 1886, Jane, dau. of Charles H. Auster, Solicitor, of Grimlay Hau, Bromsgrove, and grand-dau. of B. Littlewood, D.L., of Clent House, co. Worcester. She *d.* 7 Nov. 1887.
1. Anna Maria Georgina, *m.* 12 Jan. 1847, Col. John Curry Day, 17th Madras N.I., son of Rev. Edward Day, Rector of Kilgobbin. He *d.* 22 April, 1869, leaving issue.
2. Emily, *b.* 9 Oct. 1840; *d.* young.
3. Elizabeth Georgina, *m.* 2 Oct. 1861, William Dickey, son of James Dickey, of Hollybrook, co. Antrim, and has issue.
Mr. Stokes *d.* 22 Nov. 1882.

Seats—Mounthawk, Tralee; and The Priory, Slapton, Kingsbridge, Devon.

BUTLER-STONEY OF PORTLAND PARK.

WALTER CHARLES BUTLER-STONEY, of Portland Park, co. Tipperary, J.P. and D.L., High Sheriff 1907, B.A. Cantab, *b.* 23 Oct. 1846; *m.* 12 Dec. 1872, Ellen Cattley, 3rd dau. of Rev. Charles Kemble, Rector of Bath and Prebendary of Wells. She *d.* 27 Jan. 1912, leaving issue.

1. THOMAS BUTLER, *b.* 20 March, 1875.
2. Charles Kemble, *b.* 13 Jan. 1877.
3. Bowes, *b.* 11 May, 1879.
4. Herbert Brooke, Lieut. R.F.A., *b.* 2 May, 1887.
1. Ellen Cattley, *b.* 6 March, 1891.

Lineage.—THOMAS STONEY (eldest son of GEORGE STONEY, of Kettlewell,* co. York, who *m.* 6 Jan. 1675, Mary, only child and heiress of Thomas Moorhouse,† of Rilston) went to Ireland shortly after the Revolution of 1688, and settled in co. Tipperary, where he acquired considerable property. He was *b.* 17 Dec. 1675; *m.* 1711, Sarah sister of Gen. Andrew Robinson, Equerry to H.R.H. Augusta, Princess-Dowager of Wales (GEORGE III's mother), and grand-dau. of George Robinson, an Officer in Cromwell's Army, and settled at Knockshegowna. By this lady (who *d.* 19 Aug. 1748) he left at his decease, 18 Aug. 1726, three sons,
1. GEORGE, of whom we treat. 2. Andrew, *d.s.p.*
3. Thomas, who *d.* 1764, aged 50, having had issue, by Mary his wife, dau. of Isaac Humphreys,
1. George, Capt. R.N., a distinguished Naval Officer, who was 1st Lieut. of the *Victory*, and was promoted Capt. for his gallant conduct in the engagement with the French fleet, 27 July, 1778. He *d.* whilst commanding the *Fox*, at Jamaica, in 1786, leaving a dau.,
Mary Margaret, who *m.* Sir Charles Morgan. 2nd bart. of Tredegar, co. Monmouth, and *d.* 24 March, 1807 (*see* BURKE's *Peerage and Baronetage*).
2. Isaac, of Frankford, twin with his brother George, *m.* Anne, only child of Thomas Dunne, of Frankford, and left issue,
(1) Thomas, *d.s.p.* Sept. 1845. (2) George, *d.s.p.* 1819.
(3) Robert (Rev.), *d.s.p.*
(4) Andrew, of Frankford, *m.* 1816, Frances, dau. of James Moffat, of Derryfore, Queen's Co., and *d.* 1872, leaving by her (who *d.* 1862) an only son,
Andrew Acres, of Frankford, King's Co., J.P., and Hon. Deputy Surg.-Gen. in the Army, served in 94th Regt. and Scots Greys, *b.* 1826; *m.* 1876, Mary Frances, dau. of Capt. John Alfred Drought, of Whigsborough, King's Co., and *d.* leaving issue, Thomas Drought, *b.* 1877, and Violet Charlotte Josephine.
(5) Isaac, *m.* Elizabeth, dau. of William Loftie, of Tandragee, co. Down, and has issue,
John Henry Loftie, *b.* 6 March, 1840; *m.* Lucy Hester, dau. of Rev. RobertCharles Loftie; and *d.* 26 Aug. 1883; having had issue,
Loftie.
1. Mary, *m.* Henry Howard, dec.
2. Anne, *m.* Ignatius O'Callaghan, of Clonsilla, co. Dublin, both dec., and left issue.
The eldest son,
GEORGE STONEY, of Greyfort and Portland, *b.* 11 Aug. 1713; *m.* 14 Jan. 1745, Eliza, dau. of Capt. James Johnston, of Ballynockane, and sister of Capt. Robert Johnston, 37th Regt., of Emell Castle; and *d.* 1787, aged 74, having by her (who *d.* 1808) had issue,
1. Andrew Robinson, an Officer in the Army, *b.* 19 June, 1747; *m.* 1st, Sept. 1769, Hannah, sole dau. and heir of William Newton, of Newcastle-on-Tyne; and 2ndly, 17 Jan. 1777, Eleanor, Dowager Countess of Strathmore, only dau. and heir of George Bowes, of Streatlam Castle, and Gibside, co. Durham; by the latter he had issue, a dau. Mr. Stoney, on his 2nd marriage, assumed the additional surname of BOWES, was M.P. for Newcastle-on-Tyne, and High Sheriff co. Durham, 1780. He *d.* 16 Jan. 1810.
2. THOMAS, of whom presently.
3. James Johnston, of Oakley Park, *b.* 23 April, 1759; *m.* Catherine, 2nd dau. of William Baker, of Lismacue, co. Tipperary; and *d.* 1824, leaving issue,
1. George, of Oakley Park, *b.* 1792; *m.* 1821, Anne, dau. of Bindon Blood, of co. Clare, and left at his decease,
(1) George Johnstone, F.R.S., late Secretary to the Queen's University, *d.* July, 1911; *m.* 1863, Margaret, second dau. of Robert J. Stoney, of Parsonstown, and had issue, George Gerard, C.E., Robert Bindon, M.D., and three daus.
(2) Bindon Blood, LL.D., F.R.S., C.E., *m.* 1879, Susanna Frances, dau. of J. F. Walker, Q.C., and *d.* 5 May, 1909, leaving with other issue, a son, George Bindon, *d.* 22 Jan. 1909.
(1) Anne, *m.* Right Rev. William Fitzgerald, Bishop of Killaloe. (2) Catherine, *d. unm.*
2. William Baker (Rev.), M.A., Rector of Castlebar, *m.* Fanny, dau. of Rev. John Going, and left, with other issue (of whom Rev. William Stoney *d.* 7 Jan. 1907), a son and a dau.,
Rev. Robert Baker Stoney, M.A., of Alfreton, *m.* Elizabeth Harrison, and *d.* 18 Oct. 1904, being father of Rev. F. Shirley Stoney, B.A. Oxon., Vicar of Waltham Cross, Herts.
Frances Anne, *d. unm.* 25 Jan. 1900.
3. Robert Johnstone, of Parsonstown, *m.* 1831, Anne, dau. of —Smithwick, and had issue,
(1) Johnston George (Rev.), dec.
(2) Charles Baker, M.B., M.D., of Birr, or Parsonstown,

---

* JOHN STONEY, grandson of a younger son of George Stoney, of Kettlewell, emigrated from Ireland to South Carolina about 1770, where he founded an influential family, at present represented by Capt. W. E. Stoney, of Charleston, Ex-Controller-General of South Carolina, who highly distinguished himself, as Assistant Adjutant-General of the Southern Army, at the defence of Charleston 1863–5; and Lieut. George M. Stoney, U.S. Navy, Flag-Lieut. on the Pacific station. Mr. Theodore Stoney, of Charleston, who built, in 1863, the first cigar-shaped torpedo boat, and *d.* 1890, and the Hon. Judge Thomas Stoney, of San Francisco, who *d.* in 1891, were also members of this family.

† This Thomas Moorhouse, *b.* 1613, *m.* 1651, Abigail Windle, and *d.* in 1657, was the eldest son of Richard Moorhouse, who was the son of Thomas Moorhouse, of Rilston, who was *b.* 1576; *m.* 1609, Maria Howson, and *d.* 1658, a descendant, it is presumed, of "Adam de Merehouse," who paid Poll Tax at Rilston, 1379.

Stoney. THE LANDED GENTRY. 666

b. 24 July, 1840; *m.* 15 July, 1868, Ada (*Residence*—7, John's Mall, Birr, King's Co.), youngest dau. of John Studholme, of St. Nicholas and Morton Head, Cumberland, and *d.* 9 April, 1907, leaving issue,
  1. Frances Elizabeth, *b.* 1869.
  2. Constance Anne, *b.* 1872; *m.* Charles Frederick Sealy Allen, son of Francis Sealy Allen, of Elfordsleigh, Devon, and formerly of Dunsland, co. Cork.
  3. Ethel Marion, *b.* 1874; *m.* 3 Jan. 1906, Michael George Head, youngest son of Capt. Edward Head, of Carrig, King's Co., late 38th and 89th Regt.
  4. Alice Dora, *b.* 1877.
  (3) Robert Baker (Rev.), Canon, D.D., of Killiney, *m.* 13 April, 1875, Katherine Mabel, 4th dau. of Richard Atkinson, of Gortmore, co. Dublin (*see* ATKINSON *of Cangort*), and has issue,
  Richard Atkinson, M.B.
  (4) Hugh Baker, M.B., M.D., of The Heath, Abbeyleix, Queen's Co., *m.* Mary Anne, dau. of Bindon Blood, Cranagher, co. Clare (*see that family*), and has issue,
    1. George Bindon, of Volksrust, Transvaal, South Africa, *m.* 19 Dec. 1911, Mabel, dau. of P. H. White, of Durban, South Africa.
    1. Maria Frances Honoria, *m.* 4 May, 1897, Rev. G. Nuttall Smith, M.A., and has issue.
    2. Margaret Eleanor, *m.* 9 Oct. 1901, Richard W. Brew, M.B., of Enniskerrey, co. Wicklow, and has issue.
    3. Mary Hilda, *m.* 9 Nov. 1905, J. B. R. Cough, M.B., of Johannesburg, South Africa, and has issue.
    4. Janet Constance.   5. Anne Florence Susan.
  (1) Margaret, *m.* 1863, George Johnstone Stoney, F.R.S.
  4. James, M.D., of Borrisokane, *m.* Helen, dau. of Capt. Dillon, and had issue,
  (1) James Johnston.   (2) William.
  (3) John.
  (1) Letitia.   (2) Helen.
  (3) Julia.   (4) Catherine.
  (5) Mary.   (6) Eliza.
  1. Eliza, *m.* Capt. Richard Rathborne, of Ballymore, co. Galway, and had issue (*see* RATHBORNE, *formerly of Scripplestown*).
  2. Catherine, *m.* James Sayers, M.D., of Limerick.
  3. Sarah, *m.* Samuel Cusack, D.D.
  4. Letitia, *m.* Charles Going.
  4. Bigoe Armstrong, of Killavalla, House, Major in the Army, *b.* 26 March, 1762; *m.* Mary, dau. of Col. Kyffin; and *d.* 1827, aged 62, leaving one son,
  Robert Johnston, of Killavalla House, co. Tipperary, J.P., *b.* 1792, *m.* 1st, Frances, youngest dau. of Thomas Stoney, of Arran Hill, who *d.s.p.*; and 2ndly, Mary Julian, of the family of Julian, of co. Kerry, by whom he had issue,
  (1) Bigoe Armstrong.   (2) Robert Johnston.
  (3) George Robert.
  (1) Maria.   (2) Alicia.
  (3) Eliza Belinda.
  (4) Emily, *m.* 13 June, 1867, George Francis Stoney, of Kyle Park.
  5. George Robert (Capt.), *b.* 1775; *m.* 1801, Johanna, dau. of Gen. Ellis, and sister of Sir Henry Ellis, killed at Waterloo, and *d.s.p.* 8 Oct. 1808.
  1. Rebecca, *m.* Robert Palmer, of Shrule.
  2. Sarah, *m.* William Smith, of Gurteen, and *d.* 1810.
  3. Elizabeth, *m.* Ralph Smith, of Milford, and *d.* 1829 (*see* SMYTH *of Gaybrook*).
  4. Mary, *m.* Edward Lawrenson, of Capponellan, Queen's Co.
  5. Catherine, *m.* Bladen Swiney.
  6. Frances, *m.* Right Hon. Arthur Moore, of Lamberton, Judge of the Court of Common Pleas in Ireland.

The 2nd son,

THOMAS STONEY, of Arran Hill, and Emell Castle, J.P. and Deputy-Governor co. Tipperary, *b.* 20 July, 1748; *m.* 6 May, 1773, Ruth, dau. of Richard Falkiner, of Mount Falcon; and *d.* 20 Oct. 1826, having had by her (who *d.* 19 Sept. 1810),
  1. George, of Kyle Park, *b.* April, 1774; *m.* 1804, Marianne, his cousin, dau. of William Smith, of Gurteen; and *d.v.p.* 1810, having by her (who *m.* 2ndly, 1818, Francis Goold Morony, of Seaview, co. Clare, and *d.* 29 April, 1867) had an only son,
  Thomas George, of Kyle Park, J.P., *b.* 29 May, 1808; *m.* 12 Sept. 1829, Anna Henrietta (who *d.* 25 May, 1880), only dau. of Thomas Waller, J.P., of Finoe House, Borrisokane, by Margaret Vereker his wife, and *d.* 13 Nov. 1886, having had issue,
    (1) George Francis, of Kyle Park, Capt. Tipperary Light Infantry, *b.* 22 Sept. 1834; *m.* 13 June, 1867, Emily, youngest dau. of Robert Johnston Stoney, J.P., of Killavalla, and *d.* 1 March, 1872, leaving issue,
      1. Thomas George, of Kyle Park, *b.* 27 Aug. 1868.
      2. George, *b.* 1872.
    (2) Thomas Waller, *b.* 17 Nov. 1835.
    (3) Francis Goold, C.E., of Ipswich, Inventor of the "Roller Sluice," without which the barrages on the Nile could not have been accomplished, *b.* 29 April, 1837; *m.* 10 Aug. 1865, Annie Elizabeth, only dau. of Alexander Duncan, C.E., and *d.* 7 Aug. 1897, leaving issue,
      Edward Duncan, *b.* 31 July, 1868; *m.*   , and *d.* 1898, leaving issue, a son and two daus.
    (4) Edward Waller, C.I.E. (1904), M.I.C.E., Chief Enigneer, Madras Railways (retired), M.E. Queen's University, Ireland (*The Gables, Coonoor, Madras, India*), *b.* 10 Feb. 1844; *m.* 7 July, 1875, Sara, 2nd dau. of John Crawford, of Cartron Abbey, co. Longford, and has issue.
      1. Richard Francis, Ex-Engineer Madras P.W.W., *b.* 1 April, 1876; *m.* 1910, Edith Gillon.

  2. Edward Crawford, B.A., M.B., Lieut. R.A.M.C., *b.* 16 Aug. 1883.
    1. Evelyn Waller, *b.* 29 Sept. 1877; *m.* 3 Feb. 1903, Lionel Edward Kirwan, and has issue.
    2. Ethel Sarah, *b.* 18 Nov. 1881; *m.* 1 Oct. 1907, Julius Mattieson Turing, I.C.S., and has issue.
  (5) William Albert, *b.* 27 June, 1845.
  (1) Margaret Henrietta, *d.* May, 1875.
  (2) Frances Elizabeth, *m.* 15 April, 1850, William Fraser, C.E., dec., and *d.* in the East Indies, 28 April, 1856, leaving issue, William John, of Ashburton, Devon, M.D., *b.* May, 1853. Frances Elizabeth, *m.* 26 Sept. 1878, Arthur Saunders, 3rd son of Rev. Canon Gore, and grandson of Hon. and Very Rev. George Gore, Dean of Killala, co. Mayo.
  (3) Marianne Harriett, *m.* 9 July, 1868, Robert Westropp Ellis, late Capt. 52nd Light Infantry, and has issue.
2. Robinson, *d.* 1796.
3. RICHARD FALKINER, of whom presently.
4. Thomas Johnston, of Harvest Lodge, *b.* 1780; *m.* 1st, Eliza, dau. of Richard Going, of Bird Hill; and by her (who *d.* 1843) had issue,
  1. Thomas Going, of Harvest Lodge, *m.* Jane, dau. of Thomas Legge, and *d.* having had issue,
    (1) Thomas Johnston, *d.* young.   (2) George, M.D.
    (1) Margaret.   (2) Eliza.   (3) Jane.
  His widow *m.* 2ndly, Rev. George Frederick Stoney, and are both dec. having had one son, Barry, *d.* 1882, and a dau.
  1. Eliza, *m.* Capt. Colville, and *d.s.p.*
  2. Charlotte, *m.* 1st, Charles Meares, of Dublin, and 2ndly, Capt. Yarde. He *d.* 1844.
  Mr. T. J. Stoney *m.* 2ndly, Eliza Pattison Isaac, and *d.* 11 Aug. 1869.
5. Andrew Robinson, an Officer 44th Regt., *d.* in India, aged 19.
6. Robert Peter Smart, *d.* in India, 1808.
7. RALPH. (*see* STONEY *of the Downs*).
8. James Johnstone, of Emell Castle, Cloughjordan, King's Co., J.P., M.A., Barrister-at-Law, *b.* Nov. 1790; *m.* 1845, Elizabeth, dau. of Rev. Wiliam Minchin, of Greenhills, co. Tipperary; and *d.* 3 Aug. 1849, leaving issue,
  1. Johnstone Thomas, of Emell Castle, Cloughjordan, J.P., *b.* 28 July, 1849; *m.* 1st, 5 Dec. 1872, Rebecca, only dau. of Edward Corker Minchin, of Canterbury, New Zealand, and by her (who *d.* 7 March, 1875) had issue,
    (1) Rebecca Sarah Minchin, *m.* 20 Dec. 1899, Capt. Richard Minchin Minchin, of Busherstown, King's Co., J.P. (*see that family*).
  He *m.* 2ndly, 12 March, 1878, Arabella Louisa, only surviving child of the late Percy William Cornwallis Lipyeatt, of Dawlish, Devon, late 24th Regt., and has issue,
    (1) Johnstone Percy Lipyeatt, Capt. 2nd Batt. Worcester Regt. served in S. African War 1901-2, *b.* 27 April, 1881.
    (2) Raleigh Cecil Watson, *b.* 27 Feb. 1883.
    (3) Gerald Johnstone Lipyeatt, Lieut. 2nd Batt. Worcester Regt., *b.* 17 June, 1884.
    (4) Edward Bowes, *b.* 30 March, 1886.
    (1) Dorothea Ruth, *b.* 20 Jan. 1879.
    (2) Sybil Arabella Lepycatt, *b.* 1 April, 1880; *d.* 1882.
    (3) Olive Arabella, *b.* 30 March, 1886.
  1. Mary Anne Elizabeth, *m.* Oct. 1866, George Thompson Archer, and had issue.
  2. Ruth Georgina, *b.* 1846; *d.* 25 Aug. 1856.
1. Mary Anne, *m.* Rev. John Travers, many years Rector of Kinnitty, King's Co., who *d.* March, 1814.
2. Elizabeth, *m.* Samuel Barry, of Borrisokane.
3. Ruth, *m.* Robert Robinson, of Ballynavan.
4. Frances, *m.* Robert Johnston Stoney, J.P., of Killavalla House, co. Tipperary (*see above*).

The 3rd son,

RICHARD FALKINER STONEY, of Portland, *m.* 10 Feb. 1812, Jane, 2nd dau. of James Butler, of Castlecrine, co. Clare, and had issue,
  1. THOMAS BUTLER, of Portland.
  2. James Butler, of Ross-y-Vera, Newport. co. Mayo, J.P., *b.* 13 May, 1814; *m.* 1838, Mary Frances, eldest dau. of Robert Elwood, of Knockadoo, co. Roscommon, by Anna, eldest dau. of Rev. Dr. Vesey, of Derrabard House, co. Tyrone, and *d.* 1 May, 1897, having by her (who *d.* 30 April, 1902) had, with other issue,
    1. Robert Vesey, of Rosturk Castle, and Inasherkin, co. Mayo, and of Knockadoo, co. Roscommon, J.P. and D.L. for co. Mayo, High Sheriff 1884, and J.P. co. Roscommon, *b.* 27 June, 1841; *m.* 1st, May, 1878, Emily Rose, who *d.* 1893, dau. of Charles Bligh, of Brittas, co. Meath. He *m.* 2ndly, Feb. 1896, Phœbe Editha, 2nd dau. of Robert Truell (*see that family*), and by her has issue,
      Thomas Samuel Vesey, *b.* 1898.
    2. Thomas Butler, of Oakfield Park, Raphoe, co. Donegal, J.P. and D.L., High Sheriff 1887, late Capt. Donegal Art. Militia, *b.* 27 Feb. 1844; *d.* 5 March, 1912; *m.* 11 June, 1873, Annie, dau. of Wybrants Olphert, D.L. of Ballyconnel, co. Donegal, and had issue,
      (1) Cecil Robert Vesey, B.A., Camb., *b.* 10 June, 1875; *m.* 3 April, 1902, Frances Maria, younger dau. of the late Rev. C. H. Mackenzie, Rector of East Harptree, Somerset, and had issue by her (who *d.* 7 Sept. 1911),
        Dorothy Frances Annie.
      (1) May Constance.   (2) Ethel Mary.
      (3) Alice Maude.
      (4) Winnifred Claire.
      (5) Muriel Florence.
    3. Henry Butler, Major 40th Regt., *b.* 1816; *m.* Fanny, dau. of Benjamin Wilson, of Sledagh, co. Wexford, and has issue,
      James Butler.

4. George Butler, Major-Gen., b. 1818; m. Sarah Howard, dau. of Capt. Ormond, 86th Regt., and by her (who d. 28 Aug. 1908) had issue,
   George Ormond, Major King's Own Borderers, m. 27 Sept. 1876, Meylia (who d. 1 April, 1910), dau. of Patrick Sinclair Laing, Deputy Insp.-Gen. of Hospitals, and d. 1890, leaving issue,
   (1) George Butler, Capt. K.O.S. Borderers, b. 18 Aug. 1877.
   (2) Bowes Ormond, C.C.S., b. 4 Dec. 1878; d. 16 Oct. 1910.
   (3) Patrick Sinclair, Capt. Indian Army, b. 9 Jan. 1880.
   (4) Thomas Ramsay, b. 9 July, 1882.
   (5) Henry Howard, Lieut. N. Staffordshire Regt., b. 12 March, 1886.
   (1) Isabella Katherine.
   Wilhelmina Ruth, m. 15 Oct. 1889, Colin McKenzie Smith, of Oakwood Hall, Rotherham, Yorks (see SMITH of *Barnes*).

Mr. Stoney d. 5 June, 1830, and was s. by his eldest son,
THOMAS BUTLER-STONEY, of Portland Park, J.P. co. Tipperary and Galway, and High Sheriff of the former 1855, sometime 19th Regt., b. 22 March, 1813; m. 15 Nov. 1837, Sarah Eliza, eldest dau. and co-heir of Robert Fannin, J.P., of Leeson Street, Dublin, and by her (who d. 7 March, 1897, aged 83) had issue,
1. Robert Fannin, Capt. 53rd Regt., b. 30 Aug. 1838; d.s.p. 1862.
2. Richard Butler, Lieut. R.A., b. 30 Aug. 1839; d 1861.
3. Thomas Bowes, b. 24 Sept. 1843; d. 1870.
4. WALTER CHARLES, now of Portland Park.
1. Mary Sarah, m. 24 July, 1861, John Charles Sheffield, of Carradoyne, co. Mayo, late Capt. 21st Fusiliers, 3rd son of Sir Robert Sheffield, 4th bart. of Normandy Park, co. Lincoln, and had issue. She d. 1899.
2. Emma Sarah, m. 1870, Joseph John Dunnington Jefferson, eldest son of Rev. Joseph Dunnington Jefferson, Canon of York, of Thicket Priory, Yorkshire.
3. Florence Kate, m. 1884, Robert Donald Douglas, only son of Sir Donald Maclean, of Napier, N.Z.
Mr. Butler-Stoney d. 19 March, 1893.

Arms—Or, on a bend cottised az., three escallops of the field. *Crest*—Out of a mural crown ppr., a demi-lion or, holding between the paws a spur erect arg., winged gu. *Motto*—Nunquam non paratus.

Seat—Portland Park, Roscrea, co. Tipperary. *Residence*—17, Elm Park Gardens, S.W.

STONEY OF THE DOWNS.

LIEUT.-COL. FRANCIS SADLEIR STONEY, of Little Heath, Kent, and The Downs, Delgany, co. Wicklow, J.P., late Lieut.-Col. R.A., author of the *Life and Times of Sir Ralph Sadleir, Secretary of State to HENRY VIII*. He was b. 17 Feb. 1834; m. 1st, 31 July, 1867, Catherine Jane, dau. of Robert Lawe,* Banker, of Preston, co. Lancaster, and by her (who d. 31 Aug. 1870) he had issue,

1. Kathleen Sadleir Lawe, m. 7 Jan. 1890, Lieut. John Hamilton Allen, R.N., only son of Col. Allen, of Errol Park, co. Perth, grandson of the 1st Earl of Camperdown. He d. 17 June, 1903, leaving issue, a dau., Stella Ada. She m. 2ndly, 2 Nov. 1905, Ralph Gervase Riddell-Carre, of Cavers Carre, Roxburghshire (see *that family*), and has issue, Gervase Robert, b. 30 Oct. 1906.

He m. 2ndly, 11 June, 1872, Emma Sophia Christina, elder dau. of Christopher Mercer Durrant, M.D., F.R.C.P., J.P. co. Suffolk, and relict of Capt. Alexander Selwyn Gordon Maynard, 20th Regt., and has issue,
1. RALPH DURRANT SADLEIR, Capt. A.P.D., late Capt. 87th Royal Irish Fusiliers, b. 8 April, 1873; m. 26 July, 1900, Amy, only surviving dau. of the Rev. W. Moore Morgan, LL.D., Canon of Armagh Cathedral, and has issue,
   Ralph Francis Ewart, b. 28 June, 1903.
   May Eileen Morgan, b. 18 Sept. 1901.
2. George Franc Woodward, b. 29 March; d. 25 Aug. 1874.
3. Franc Aubrey Sadleir, B.A. Trin. Coll. Dublin, b. 23 May, 1875.
4. Leigh Sadleir, of Forrest, Queen's Co., J.P., High Sheriff 1911, Capt. 4th Batt. Roy. Irish Fus., b. 19 April, 1878; m. 20 Dec. 1896, Anna Theodosia Hester, dau. of John Stuart Eccles, D.L., of Ecclesville (see MCCLINTOCK of *Seskinore*), and has issue,
   Rose Kathleen Rachel.

* Robert Lawe was a lineal descendant of Lawe of Preston, who received a grant of Arms *temp*. CHARLES II.

2. Ruth, d. in infancy, 3 April, 1877.
3. Emma Geraldine, m. 17 Jan. 1905, C. A. Campbell Bentley, Royal Warwickshire Regt., Staff Capt. Trinidad, eldest son of Dr. Bentley, of Kirkliston, Linlithgowshire, and has issue.
4. Mary Moorhouse, b. 13 April, 1883; d. 9 Feb. 1898.

Lineage.—REV. RALPH STONEY, M.A., of Terryglass and Ballynockane, 7th son of Thomas Stoney, of Arran Hill and Emell Castle, co. Tipperary (see STONEY *of Portland Park*). He was b. Oct. 1784; m. 14 Feb. 1819, Abigail, dau. of Thomas Sadleir, of Castletown, co. Tipperary, brother of Dr. Sadleir, Provost of Trin. Coll. Dublin (see SADLEIR *of Castletown*), and d. 27 June, 1856, having by her (who d. 5 Aug. 1836) had issue,
1. Thomas Sadleir, of Ballycapple House, co. Tipperary, and of Grange, co. Dublin, M.A., Barrister-at-Law, J.P. co. Dublin, b. 3 Aug. 1822; m. 1st, Lizzie, dau. of John Shortt, of Pallas, co. Tipperary, by whom he had a dau.,
   1. Alice, d. in infancy.
He m. 2ndly, 12 Aug. 1857, Eleanor (who d. 1904), dau. of Rev. Thomas Luby, D.D., Senior Fellow of Trin. Coll. Dublin, and d. 25 Feb. 1899, leaving issue,
   1. Thomas Johnston, of Ballynockane (*Stradbally House, Castleconnell, co. Limerick*), b. 13 Dec. 1858; m. 16 Feb. 1892, Adelaide Frances, 2nd dau. of John Stephen Dwyer, of Stradbally, J.P.
   2. Frederick Joseph Wetherall, Major R.A.M.C., b. 25 Oct. 1861; m. 15 July, 1897, Gertrude, dau. of Senator Marquetti, and d. 6 March, 1903, leaving issue, a son.
   3. Ralph, M.D., of Gloucester Terrace, Kensington, b. 4 April, 1863; m. 9 Dec. 1893, Stella, dau. of Edmund Charles Morgan, killed by an elephant while shooting in Uganda, 19 Oct. 1905, leaving issue, Irene.
   4. Franc Sadleir (Rev.), Vicar of Tashinny, co. Longford, b. 10 Dec. 1865; m. 22 Aug. 1893, Elizabeth, dau. of Rev. William Noble.
   5. George Frederick, b. 26 Aug. 1869.
   2. Laura Eleanor, m. 2 Oct. 1893, William Egan, and has issue.
   3. Florence Georgina, m. 22 Oct. 1895, Capt. Stuart Ogilvy Boyd, R.A., and has issue.
   4. Frances Elizabeth.
2. George Frederick (Rev.), M.A., of Holly Park, King's Co., b. 2 Jan. 1826; m. 21 June, 1857, Jane, dau. of Thomas Legge, and relict of Thomas Going Stoney, of Harvest Lodge, and d. 18 Aug. 1869, leaving issue,
   Ralph Barry, b. 1860; d. 7 April, 1882.
   Abigail, m. C. Belhouse, of Philadelphia, and has issue.
3. Ralph Francis Feltham Sadleir (Rev.), B.D., Vicar of Wrea Green, co. Lancaster, b. 27 March, 1830; m. 1st, 24 Aug. 1859, Eliza, widow of Robert Lawe, of the Larches, Preston, eldest dau. of John Drinkwater, of Liverpool (brother of Sir George Drinkwater), and sister of Sir William Drinkwater, and had issue, Eliza and Ruth Selina, both d. young. She d. 4 Jan. 1867. He m. 2ndly, 22 July, 1870, Sybilla Frances, 2nd dau. of Rev. William Francis Homan, Rector of Modreeny, and d. 7 June, 1902, having by her had issue,
   1. Ralph Sadleir (Rev.), M.A., Ch. Ch. Oxon., Vicar of St. Peter's, Regent Square, London (*The Manor House, Wrea Green, Lancashire*), b. 1 Sept. 1872.
   2. Travers Strathmore (Rev.), M.A., Exeter Coll. Oxon., Vicar of St. Catherine's, Wigan, b. 15 Feb. 1874; m. 1908, Gertrude, dau. of Rev. J. W. Bardsley, and niece of Dr. Bardsley, Bishop of Carlisle.
   3. Edwin Fazakerley (Rev.), M.A. Trin. Coll. Dublin, Curate-in-charge of St. Luke's, St. Helens (*Lyon House, St. Helens, Lancashire*), b. 26 March, 1875.
4. FRANCIS SADLEIR, of The Downs.
5. Ruth, m. 9 Sept. 1847, Rev. Benjamin Biggs Talbot, of Ashgrove, who d. 28 July, 1878. She d. 24 Jan. 1900, leaving a son, Lieut.-Col. Johnston Stoney Talbot, 53rd Regt.
6. Margaretta, d. unm. 11 March, 1900.
7. Marianne, d. unm. 31 Dec. 1889.
8. Abigail Maria, d. unm. 21 Nov. 1874.
9. Letitia.

Arms—Or on a bend cotised az. three escallops of the field. *Crest*—Out of a mural crown ppr. a demi-lion or holding between the paws a spur erect arg. winged gu. *Motto*—Nunquam non paratus.

Seat—The Downs, Delgany, co. Wicklow.

STOPFORD. See BURKE'S PEERAGE, COURTOWN, E.

STORY OF CORICK.

JOHN BENJAMIN STORY, of Corick, co. Tyrone, High Sheriff 1911, M.B., M.Ch., F.R.C.S.I., b. 31 Aug. 1850; m. 25 June, 1892, Blanche Christabel, dau. of Rev. J. W. Hallowell, and has issue,
1. Eleanor Constance.
2. Joan Blanche.

Lineage.—JOHN STORY, of Bingfield, Hexham, Northumberland, settled in Ireland about 1697. He d. at Corick, near Clogher, 1725, aged 77, leaving issue,
1. THOMAS, of whom presently.
2. Joseph, ancestor of STORY *of Bingfield*, co. Cavan (*see that family*).
3. John, b. 1681.　　　4. Samuel, b. 1683.

The eldest son,
THOMAS STORY, of Corick, Clogher, co. Tyrone. b. 1678, m. 1707, Rebecca —, and had five sons and two daus., of whom,
1. JOHN, of whom presently.
2. Joseph (Rev.), Rector of Monaghan, b. 1711, and d.s.p. 1784.
3. Thomas, b. 1715, d. *unm.* 1744.
4. Benjamin, b. 1718, m. 1750, Anne Theaker, and had two sons, of whom the elder d. young, and the younger, JOHN BENJAMIN, s. his uncle.

The eldest son,
JOHN STORY, of Corick, co. Tyrone, b. 1708; d. unm. 1780, and was s. by his nephew,
REV. JOHN BENJAMIN STORY, of Corick, co. Tyrone, Chancellor of Clogher, b. 1764; s. his uncle 1780; m. 1790, Jane, dau. of Alexander Young, of Coolkeiragh, co. Derry (*see that family*), by Catherine his wife, dau. of Richard Hassard, of Gardenhill, co. Fermanagh. She d. 18 June, 1851. He d. 24 March, 1844, leaving issue,
1. JOHN BENJAMIN, his heir.　　2. Alexander, d. unm.
3. WILLIAM, s. his eldest brother.
1. Anne, m. Oct. 1818, Rev. William Lodge. Rector of Killybegs, co. Donegal.
2. Kate.　　3. Elizabeth, m. Richard Twigg, M.D.
4. Jane.　　5. Letitia.
6. Frances Thomasina, m. 23 Aug. 1831, the Ven. John A. Russell, Archdeacon of Clogher.
7. Maria.

The eldest son,
JOHN BENJAMIN STORY, of Corick, co. Tyrone, m. 9 Jan. 1840, Catherine, dau. of Capt. Valentine Munbee, of Horringer, Suffolk, 43rd L.I., and d.s.p. 1862, and was s. by his only surviving brother,
REV. WILLIAM STORY, of Corick, co. Tyrone, Rector of Aghabog, m. Sarah Bernard, dau. of John Black, and d. 9 Feb. 1888, leaving issue,
1. JOHN BENJAMIN, now of Corick.
2. William George Theaker, b. 1863.
1. Marion Letitia, m. 14 Nov. 1882, Gen. Sir Edmund George Barrow, G.C.B., son of Major-Gen. Joseph Lyon Barrow, C.B., and has two sons and a dau.
2. Alice Gertrude.　　3. Emma Mary Geraldine.

Seat—Corick, Clogher, co. Tyrone. *Residence*—6, Merrion Square, Dublin.

STORY OF BINGFIELD.

LIEUT.-COL. ROBERT STORY, of Bingfield, co. Cavan, J.P., High Sheriff 1909, late King's Royal Rifle Corps, b. 11 July, 1854; m. 1st, 15 May, 1879, Florence Mansfield, eldest dau. of William Harrington Bush, of Helston Villa, Clifton, and by her (who d. 1888) has issue,

1. Vida Hope Carmichael, b. 8 Feb. 1881; m. 6 Jan. 1910, Ponsonby M. L. Carew.

He m. 2ndly, 1896, Mary, 4th dau. of the late Edward Jollie, M.H.R., of Waireka, Taranaki, N.Z., and by her has issue,

1. ARTHUR PATRICK, b. 14 Nov. 1896.
2. Ralph Napier, b. 3 July, 1898.
3. Francis Edward, b. 28 Oct. 1899.
4. Robert Basil Eric, b. 3 April, 1902.
2. Dorothea Vera Caroline, b. 14 June, 1904.
3. Laila May, b. 18 July, 1911.

Lineage.—JOHN STORY, of Bingfield Hall, near Hexham, Northumberland, sold his estates in England, and settled at Corick, near Clogher, co. Tyrone, in Ireland, under the auspices of Bishop St. George Ashe, about 1697. He left (with other issue) three sons,
1. Thomas, of Corick, ancestor of STORY *of Corick*.
2. JOSEPH, of whom we treat.
3. Benjamin.

The younger son,
RIGHT REV. JOSEPH STORY, Bishop of Killaloe, 1740, and afterwards of Kilmore, 1742, was b. 1679, at Bingfield, near Hexham, Northumberland, whence this family appears to have gone over to Ireland. He m. 1st, Deborah Richardson, and had by her two daus., Elizabeth, and Katherine, m. John Irvine, of Rockfield, co. Fermanagh. He m. 2ndly, Sophia, widow of Rev. William Grattan, F.T.C.D., Rector of Tullycleagh, co. Fermanagh, and eldest dau. of Sir William Gore, 3rd bart. of Manor Gore, and sister to Sir Ralph Gore, Speaker of the Irish House of Commons, and had issue, one son, JOSEPH, of Kilmore. Bishop Story was Chaplain to the Irish House of Commons; he d. 1757, and was s. by his son,

VEN. JOSEPH STORY, Archdeacon of Kilmore, who settled in the neighbourhood of Kilmore, and called his residence Bingfield. He m. Frances Arabella Sneyd, of Lisnamandra, co. Cavan, and had issue, eight sons and seven daus. Archdeacon Story d. 1767 (his widow 1809), and was s. by his son,
REV. JOSEPH STORY, of Bingfield, co. Cavan, m. 1788, Sarah, dau. of Robert Bogle Delap, of Kingston, Jamaica, and by her (who d. 1795) had issue,
1. JOSEPH of whom presently.　　2. Samuel, d.s.p.
3. Robert William, Col. R.A., b. Dec. 1791; m. Sarah Ainsworth, dau. of Col. Enery, of Ballyconnell, co. Cavan, and had by her one son,
Robert John, who d. young.
4. James Hamilton, of Relagh Lodge, co. Tyrone, J.P., High Sheriff 1822, Barrister-at-Law, b. 10 April, 1793; m. 1 June, 1826, Sarah Thorpe, only child of Henry Waymouth, of Bryanston Square, and d. 1863, leaving by her (who d. 1878),
1. JAMES, of Ture, co. Cavan, and Errington, co. Tyrone, M.A. Camb. and Dublin, F.Z.S., F.B.S., late Capt. Cavan Militia, M.A., J.P. for cos. Cavan and Tyrone, High Sheriff of the former co. 1860, Knt. Comm. of the Order of CHARLES III of Spain, b. 1828. and d. unm. 4 Feb. 1894, and was s. by his only surviving sister, SARAH MARY ANNE STORY, and his nephew, FRANCIS CORYNDON CARPENTER ROWE, J.P. co. Cornwall, son of the late Sir W. C. Rowe.
1. SARAH MARY ANNE, d. unm. 22 Oct. 1896, and was s. by her cousin, Evelyn James Story (*see below*).
2. Frances Elizabeth, m. Sir William Carpenter Rowe, Chief Justice of Ceylon, and had issue, William Henry Pendarvis, d. 1880, and Francis Coryndon Carpenter, d. 1897.
1. Anna Victoria, m. 1809, Richard Purefoy Jervoise, of Herriard House, Hants, Major 1st Royal Dragoons.
2. Frances Matilda, m. 1st, 1808, Robert Saunderson, of Drumkeen, co. Cavan, and 2ndly, Henry Theophilus Killbee.
3. Mary Anne, m. Rev. John Richardson, of Summerhill, co. Fermanagh.
Mr. Story d. Feb. 1810, and was s. by his eldest son,
REV. JOSEPH STORY, of Bingfield, co. Cavan. b. 23 April, 1788; m. 1812, Louisa, dau. of Sir Peter Rivers, Bart., and d. 1838, having by her (who d. 1852) had issue,
1. JOSEPH, his heir.　　2. William Rivers, d.s.p. 1845.
1. Emilia Henrietta, m. 1850, Christopher Bagot Lane.
2. Ellen Martha Sarah.
3. Frances, m. 17 Oct. 1849, Sir Thomas Gibson Carmichael, 12th bart. of Castle Craig, who d.s.p. 30 Dec. 1855.
4. Louisa Maria Elizabeth, m. 1855, George Luard, of Blyborough Hall, co. Lincoln.
5. Caroline Maria, m. Rev. De Courcy Meade.
6. Agnes Sarah, m. 1856, Lieut.-Col. John Bean, H.M. Madras Engineers.

The eldest son,
JOSEPH STORY, of Bingfield, co. Cavan, J.P., High Sheriff cos. Cavan 1853, and Leitrim 1872, b. 17 March, 1817; m. 13 July. 1852, Caroline Sophia Kenneth, dau. of Nevile Reid, of Runnymede, Berks, by Hon. Caroline Napier his wife, dau. of Francis, 7th Lord Napier, and d. 27 Nov. 1875, leaving issue,
1. ROBERT, now of Bingfield.
2. William Oswald, Rear-Admiral R.N., b. 18 April, 1859; m. 19 Nov. 1893, Olave, dau. of Capt. Baldwin, of Dunedin, N.Z., and has issue,
1. Nevill Edward Oswald, b. 24 Aug. 1898.
2. Andrew Charles Kenneth, b. 15 Dec. 1900.
3. Michael Francis Benedict, d. young 1902.
4. Martin Aloysius, b. 6 Nov. 1906.
1. Janet Olave.　　2. Mary Caroline.
3. Monica Gerard.　　4. Josephine Norah.
5. Norah Cecilia Frances.
6. Ursula Margaret Gwenda, b. 10 June, 1905.
7. Elizabeth Magdalen, b. 26 May, 1908.
3. Edward Joseph, Capt. 3rd Batt. Welsh Regt., b. 13 Feb. 1862; d. on service in South Africa, 1885.
4. Arthur Nevile John, b. 21 March, 1864; d. in India, 27 Nov. 1894.
5. Evelyn James, of Errington, Kilskeery, co. Tyrone, J.P. and D.L., High Sheriff 1908, b. 28 Feb. 1866; m. 29 April. 1897, Hilda Grenside, eldest dau. of the late Richard Brinsley Hooper, of Clifton, and has issue,
1. George Frederick, b. 25 Feb. 1900.
2. Richard James, b. 16 Sept. 1901, twin with his sister.
1. Mary Josephine, b. 19 Sept. 1898.
2. Margery Lillian, b. 16 Sept. 1901, twin with her brother.
6. Francis Napier, b. 11 March, 1867; m. 1900, Edith Rose.
1. Louisa Fanny, m. 23 May, 1882, Edward Maclane Field, H.M. Inspector of Schools.
2. Clara Ellen, d. 1858.　　3. Anna Josephine, d. 1861.
4. Charlotte Eliza.　　5. Florence Emily.

Seat—Bingfield, Crossdoney, co. Cavan.

STOUGHTON OF OWLPEN.

Rose Trent-Stoughton, of Owlpen, co. Gloucester, and Ballyhorgan, co. Kerry, widow of Thomas Anthony Stoughton, of Owlpen, &c., m. 2ndly, Jan. 1889, Col. Harrison Walke John Trent, of Saltwood, co. Kent (eldest son of Francis Onslow Trent, b. 1830, J.P. cos. Gloucester and Kerry, High Sheriff for the latter co. 1896, and formerly Col. 68th Durham Light Infantry, and Inspector-General of Musketry), who thereupon assumed the additional surname and arms of Stoughton, by Royal Licence dated 1 March, 1889. He d. 1 Aug. 1899.

Lineage.—Gilbert Stoughton, of Stoughton, Surrey, whose will is dated 7 April, 1516 ; m. Mariana, dau. of Robert Beardsley, of London, and had four sons,
1. Laurence, his heir, of Stoughton, will dated 10 May, 1577; m.—dau. of—Combes, and had seven sons, of whom the eldest, Thomas, of Stoughton, was ancestor of Sir Nicholas Stoughton, created a Baronet 29 Jan. 1600-1 (extinct 1691-2), and the 6th son was Edward, of Slivellgreen, near Guildford, m. Katherine Henvage, of Milton, Sussex, and had with other issue, an eldest son,
John, of Callan, co. Kilkenny, Commissary of Munster, d. 16 Feb. 1635 (Funeral Entry), having had two sons and two daus.,
(1) Laurence, d. unm. v.p.
(2) John, m. Mory, dau. of George Jones, Alderman of Dublin.
(1) Katherine, m. Walter Bennett, of Kilkenny.
(2) Mary, m. Laurence Warter, of Culkile, co. Kilkenny.
2. Anthony, of whom presently.
3. John, whose issue is extinct.
4. George, d.s.p.

The 2nd son,
Anthony Stoughton, Groom of the Chamber to Henry VIII, m. Jane, dau. and heir of — Jones, of Whitly, Surrey, and had six sons and four daus.,
1. William of Worplesden, Surrey, m. Elizabeth, dau. of William Muschamp, of Kensington, and had six sons and three daus.,
 1. Anthony, of St. John's, Warwick, b. 1587 ; m. Dorothy, dau. and heir of John Brett, of Kemmerton, Kent, and had issue.
 2. Nathaniel, of London, Goldsmith, m. Margaret, dau. of Robert Sibthorpe, of North Cadbury, Somerset, and had three sons,
  (1) Nathaniel, of Dublin, Goldsmith, m.—dau. of—Leman, who d. 12 Oct. 1671 (Funeral Entry).
  (2) John.   (3) George.
 3. William.   4. Jonathan.
 5. Thomas.   6. Timothy.
 1. Elizabeth.   2. Jane.
 3. Mary.
2. Anthony, of whom presently.
3. Thomas, m. Thomasine, dau. of — FitzJames, of Ruttidge, Somerset.
4. John, of Dublin, d. unm. 17 Jan. 1634 (Funeral Entry).
1. Mercy, m. Edward Raymond, of Dunmow, Essex.
2. Jane, m. 1st, Ambrose Belgrave, of Belgrave, Leicester ; 2ndly, Humphrey Davenport.
3. Elizabeth, m. 1st, Thomas Cheney ; 2ndly, — South.
4. Constance, unm.

The 2nd son,
Anthony Stoughton, appointed Clerk of the Castle Chamber in Ireland, 1 April, 1586, acquired the Abbey of Rattoo, co. Kerry, and was M.P. for Askeatou 1613-15. He m. Margaret, dau. of Capt. William Deeringe, Steward of the Household to several Lord Deputies, and d. 5 Sept. 1626 (Funeral Entry), having had by her (who d. 19 May, 1632, Funeral Entry), two sons,
1. Anthony, his heir.
2. Arthur, b. 1603, B.A. Dublin 1622, M.A. 1625, had, with other issue,
 Anthony, bur. 10 Dec. 1698, at St. Michan's, Dublin ; m. (licence 10 Jan.) 1675, Anne, widow of — Ward.
 Cromwell (Rev.), Schol. Trin. Coll. Dublin 1663, B.A. 1665, Rector of Wicklow, d. 1688.
 Richard, d. unm. 14 Jan. 1683-4 (Funeral Entry).

The elder son,
Anthony Stoughton, of Rattoo, co. Kerry, b. 1601, B.A. Dublin 1622, Clerk of the Castle Chamber, M.P. for Ardfert 1639-49, d. 2 Sept. 1667 ; bur. in St. John's, Dublin, his will being dated at Cork 30 Aug. 1644. He m. 1st, Mary, dau. of Henry Mainwaring, Master in Chancery, by whom (who d. 3 Jan. 1631) he had a dau., Elizabeth. He m. 2ndly, Honora, dau. of Dermot, 5th Baron Inchiquin and sister of Murrough, 1st Earl of Inchiquin, and had two sons and four daus.,

1. Henry his heir.
2. William, b. in Cork 1650, matriculated Trin. Coll. Dublin 18 Aug. 1667 ; d. before May, 1698, at Belturbet, co. Cavan.
1. Margaret, m. 1st, Launcelot Sandes, of Carrigaforde, co. Kerry (see Sandes of Sallow Glen) ; and 2ndly, Edward Payne, Dublin (see Moore of Cremorgan).
2. Elizabeth, m. 1667, Col. Roger Moore, of Johnstown, co. Dublin (see Moore of Cremorgan).
3. Ellen, m. Thomas Blennerhassett (see Blennerhassett of Ballyscedy).
4. —, m. — Harding, of Cork.

The elder son,
Henry Stoughton, of Rattoo, m. 1st, Mary, 2nd dau. of John Ponsonby, of Crotto, and had by her an only dau.,
1. Honora, m. Edward Shewell, of Ardfert.
He m. 2ndly, Sarah, dau. of Sir Thomas Crosbie, and had two sons,
1. Anthony, his heir.
2. Thomas. m. Dorothy, dau. of Rev. Archdeacon Bland, and had issue.

The elder son,
Anthony Stoughton, of Rattoo, m. Sarah Lloyd, niece of Mr. Justice Rose, and had (with a dau., Sarah, m. George Bateman, of Dromultin, co. Kerry) a son,
Anthony Stoughton, of Rattoo, High Sheriff, 1747, m. 1748, Elizabeth, dau. of Rowland Bateman, of Killeene, by Elizabeth his wife, dau. and co-heir of Nicholas Colthurst, of Ballyhally, co. Cork, and had issue,
1. Thomas, his heir.   2. Anthony (Rev.), d. unm.
1. Sarah, m. 1765, William Townsend Gun, and had issue, Penelope, m. Maynard Denny.

The eldest son,
Thomas Stoughton, of Ballyhorgan, m. Jane, dau. of Thomas Lewis, of St. Pierre, co. Monmouth, and widow of John Hanbury, of Pontypool, and had issue,
1. Thomas Anthony, of Ballyhorgan.   2. William.
1. Charlotte Elizabeth, m. Sir Charles Ibbetson, Bart.
2. Caroline, m. 1st, Col. Dickson, and 2ndly, Sir Thomas Pelham Hayes, Bart.

The son and heir,
Thomas Anthony Stoughton, of Owlpen, co. Gloucester, Ballyhorgan, co. Kerry, High Sheriff 1839, and Gortigrenane, co. Cork, m. July, 1815, Mary, dau. and sole heiress of Thomas, Daunt, of Owlpen and Gortigrenane (see Daunt of Tracton Abbey), and by her (who d. 8 Dec. 1867) had issue,
1. Thomas Anthony, his heir.
2. Charles William, of Ballynoe, co. Kerry, J.P. and D.L., b. 20 Oct. 1823 ; m. 1854, Percy Georgina Laura, 2nd dau. of George Bagot Gosset, 4th Dragoon Guards, A.D.C. She d. 7 Aug. 1907. He d. 7 Oct. 1889, leaving issue,
 1. Charles Cecil Percy, Major late Capt. 14th Hussars (Marrick, Lansdowne Road, Bournemouth), b. 21 Dec. 1856 ; m. 1890, Alice Eleanor, dau. of John Kirkpatrick, of Monks Horton, Kent, and has a son, b. 25 Dec. 1896 ; d. 12 Jan. 1900 ; Maud Eleanor and Violet Georgina.
 2. Herbert Lionel, b. 1859 ; d. 1905.
 3. William Anthony, b. 1862.
 1. Beatrice Mary, m. 1891, T. M. Jones Tailby, Capt. 11th Hussars, and has issue.
 2. Maud Edith, d. 24 Sept. 1883.
 3. Helen Percy, m. 1889, F. Bulkeley Johnson, Barrister-at-Law, and has issue.
 4. Wilhelmina Rose, m. 24 June, 1897, Major-Gen. Frederick Spencer Robb, C.B., M.V.O. (46, Rutland Gate, Knightsbridge, S.W.), late Durham L.I., and has issue.
1. Mary, d. young.

Mr. Stoughton d. 8 Jan. 1862, and was s. by his son,
Thomas Anthony Stoughton, of Owlpen, co. Gloucester, Ballyhorgan, co. Kerry, and Gortigrenane, co. Cork, J.P. and D.L., High Sheriff co. Gloucester 1873, b. 18 Feb. 1818 ; m. 23 Oct. 1862, Rose, youngest dau. of William Plunkett, Barrister-at-Law, and d.s.p. 2 Dec. 1885, when the estates devolved on his widow for her life, with remainder to his nephew William Anthony Stoughton.

Arms (Heralds' College)—Quarterly : 1st and 4th, Stoughton, az., a cross engrailed erm., in the dexter canton a mullet or, and the cross charged (for distinction) with a cross-crosslet in chief of the field ; 2nd and 3rd, Trent, per saltire arg. and gu. two swords in saltire ppr. pommels and hilts or, between three crowns vallery, one in chief of the second, and two in fesse or, and in base a rose, also of the second, barbed and seeded ppr. **Crests**—Stoughton, A robin-redbreast ppr. charged (for distinction) with a cross-crosslet az. ; Trent, a crescent or, between two roses as in the arms.

Seats—Ballyhorgan, Lixnaw, co. Kerry ; Owlpen, Dursley, co. Gloucester.

VILLIERS-STUART OF CASTLETOWN.

HENRY JOHN RICHARD VILLIERS - STUART, of Castletown and Castlane, co. Kilkenny, D.L., co. Kilkenny, High Sheriff 1887, and J.P. cos. Tipperary, Waterford, and Kilkenny, late Lieut.-Col. Waterford Militia Artillery, formerly Capt. 68th Regt., *b.* 3 March, 1837; *m.* 4 May, 1870, Jane Rigby, eldest dau. of Benjamin Rigby Murray, of Parton Place, co. Kircudbright, and has issue,

1. WILLIAM DESMOND, Capt. Indian Army (5th Gurkha Rifles), *b.* 11 April, 1872.
2. Charles Herbert, Capt. Indian Army (56th Rifles F.F.), *b.* 2 Sept. 1874.
3. John Patrick, Capt. Indian Army (55th Coke's Fiffes F.F.), *b.* 1 March, 1879.
1. Kathleen Jane, *m.* 6 May, 1903, Lieut.-Col. Henry Richmond Gale, R.E., and has issue (*see* GALE *of Bardsea Hall*).
2. Gertrude Elsie.
3. Marie Violet.

Lineage.—LORD HENRY STUART, 5th son of JOHN, 4th Earl and 1st Marquess of Bute, *b.* 7 June, 1777; *m.* 1802, Lady Gertrude Amelia Mason-Villiers, only dau. and heir of George, 2nd and last Earl of Grandison, and has issue,

1. HENRY, created 10 May, 1839, LORD STUART DE DECIES, *b.* 8 June, 1803; *d.* 23 Jan. 1874.
2. WILLIAM, of whom presently.
3. Charles, *b.* 11 Sept. 1808; *m.* Nov. 1830, Elizabeth, dau. of Rear-Admiral John Rouet Smollet, of Bonhill, and *d.* 19 Dec. 1871. She *d.* 27 Jan. 1889.
1. Gertrude Amelia, *d. unm.* 1826.

Lord Henry Stuart *d.* 1809. His 2nd son,

WILLIAM VILLIERS-STUART, of Castletown, co. Kilkenny, J.P. and D.L., High Sheriff 1848, M.P. co. Waterford 1835-47, Capt. 12th Lancers, Lieut.-Col. Waterford Militia Artillery, *b.* 21 Aug. 1804; *m.* 1 June, 1833, Katherine, only dau. of Michael Cox, of Castletown, co. Kilkenny (by Hon. Mary Prittie his wife, dau. of Henry Sadleir, 1st Lord Dunalley), and sister and heir of Sir Richard Cox, 8th bart. of Dunmanway (*see family of Cox below*). She *d.* 14 Sept. 1879. He and his brother and sister assumed the additional surname and arms of VILLIERS by Royal Licence 17 May, 1822, and *d.* 7 Nov. 1873, having had issue,

1. HENRY JOHN RICHARD, now of Castletown.
2. Dudley, formerly of 51st Regt., *b.* 1840.
1. Gertrude Mary, *d. unm.* 8 Jan. 1851.
2. Geraldine, *m.* 25 Aug. 1874, Arthur J. Chichester.
3. Evelyn.

FAMILY OF COX.

SIR RICHARD COX, 1st bart. of Dunmanway, Lord Chief Justice of Common Pleas in Ireland, was appointed, 1703, Lord High Chancellor of Ireland, and was twice one of the Lords Justices during the absence of the Lord-Lieutenant. He was *b.* 1650, knighted 1692, and created a baronet 21 Nov. 1706. He *m.* 26 Feb. 1673, Mary Bourne, by whom (who *d.* 1 June, 1715) he had, with seven daus., five sons,

1. RICHARD, M.P. for Tallaght 1705, and for Clonakilty 1717, *b.* 27 Oct. 1677; *m.* 1st, 5 Sept. 1698, Susannah French, who *d.* 10 Aug. 1716, and 2ndly, 13 March, 1719, Mary, dau. of Very Rev. Arthur Pomeroy, Dean of Cork, and *d.v.p.* 15 April, 1725, leaving issue by his 1st wife only (with four daus.), three sons,
  1. RICHARD (Sir), 2nd bart. of Dunmanway, M.P. for Clonakilty, *b.* 23 Nov. 1702; *m.* 13 Dec. 1725, Mary, dau. of Right Hon. George Evans, and sister of George, 1st Lord Carbery, which lady *d.* Jan. 1768. He *d.* Feb. 1766, having had (with four daus., the eldest of whom, Mary, *m.* Joshua Hamilton, and had a son, Henry Hamilton, who assumed by Act of Parliament the surname of Cox), three sons,
    (1) Richard, *m.* Eliza Turner, dau. of John Becher, of Creagh, co. Cork, and *d.v.p.*
    (2) MICHAEL (Rev. Sir), 3rd bart. of Dunmanway, *m.* 7 Jan. 1762, Hon. Elizabeth Massy, dau. of Hugh, 1st Lord Massy, and widow of John Arthure, of Seafield, co. Dublin, and *d.* July, 1772, leaving (with one dau.) two sons,
      1. RICHARD EYRE (Sir), 4th bart. of Dunmanway, *m.* 7 Jan. dau. of Edward O'Brien, grandson of William, 3rd Earl of Inchiquin, and sister of William and James, and 3rd Marquesses of Thomond, and was accidentally drowned 16 Sept. 1784, leaving by her (who *m.* 2ndly, the Right Hon. William Saurin, Attorney-General for Ireland) an only dau., Maria.
      2. Michael, *d. unm.* before his brother.
    (3) George, *d. unm.*
  2. James, *b.* 13 Dec. 1703; *d.s.p.*
  3. John, of Bandon, *b.* 14 April, 1705, had (with four daus.) three sons, of whom, Richard, the eldest, Capt. 46th Regt., *d.* at the Havannah; John, the 3rd, Major H.E.I.C., *d.s.p.*, and the 2nd,

MICHAEL, Lieut.-Col. in the Guards, *m.* Jan. 1765, Anna Maria, dau. of Daniel Shea, a West Indian planter, and *d.* 4 Feb. 1782, leaving by her (who *d.* Nov. 1793), with four daus., four sons,

1. RICHARD (Sir), 5th bart., *b.* 6 June, 1769, lost in his passage from Bengal, Sept. 1786, *d.s.p.*
2. JOHN (Sir), 6th bart., an Officer in the Life Guards, *b.* 4 April, 1771; *d.s.p.* 23 Dec. 1832.
3. Michael Joseph, Capt. 1st Royal Scotch Regt.; *d.s.p.* at Antigua 1804.
4. GEORGE MATHEW (Sir), 7th bart., Major-Gen. Bombay Army, *b.* 24 Feb. 1777; *d.s.p.* 28 June, 1838.

2. Walter, *b.* 8 Feb. 1679; *d.* 5 June, 1683.
3. John, *b.* 22 April, 1684; *d.* 2 Dec. 1692.
4. William, *b.* 1 Jan. 1686; *d.* Aug. 1693.
5. Michael (Most Rev.), D.D., Archbishop of Cashel, *b.* 2 Nov. 1691; ordained Priest 20 Sept. 1713; Chaplain to James, 2nd Duke of Ormonde, when Lord-Lieutenant: consecrated Bishop of Ossory 29 May, 1743; translated to Cashel 22 Jan. 1754; *m.* 1st, 22 May, 1712, Anne, dau. of Theobald Purcell. She *d.s.p.* He *m.* 2ndly, 23 March, 1744, Anne, dau. of Hon. James O'Brien, M.P. for Youghal, and grand-dau. of William, 3rd Earl of Inchiquin, by whom (who *d.* 19 Jan. 1745) he left at his decease, 28 May, 1779, an only son,

Richard, of Castletown, co. Kilkenny, *b.* 15 Jan. 1745; *m.* 25 Jan. 1766, Mary, dau. of Francis Burton, brother of Sir Charles Burton, 1st bart. of Pollacton, and had (with two daus., 1, Rachel, *m.* Ponsonby Hore; and 2, Anne, *m.* Hon. Price Blackwood) five sons,

(1) Michael, of Castletown, *b.* 14 April, 1768, High Sheriff of co. Kilkenny 1819; *m.* Hon. Mary Prittie, dau. of Henry Sadleir, 1st Lord Dunalley, and had issue,

1. RICHARD (Sir), 8th bart., of Castletown, High Sheriff 1829, *d.s.p.* 7 May, 1846.
2. Henry, *d. unm.*
1. KATHERINE, heir to her brother, *m.* 1 June, 1833, LIEUT.-COL. WILLIAM VILLIERS STUART, M.P. co. Waterford, afterwards of Castletown.

(2) FRANCIS (Sir), 9th bart., *b.* 23 July, 1769; *m.* Aug. 1803, Anne Maria, dau. of Sir John Ferns, and *d.s.p.m.* 6 March, 1856.

(3) Richard (Rev.), Rector of Cahirconlish, *b.* 20 Sept. 1771; *m.* Sarah, dau. of Rev. Ralph Hawtrey, and had

1. HAWTREY (Sir), 10th bart., *b.* 1808; *m.* 1857, Elizabeth, widow of Henry Hore, and *d.s.p.* 12 April, 1872.
2. William Saurin, *m.* Mary, dau. of Major Miller, of co. Derry, and had, Richard, *d. unm. v.p.*; Margaret.
3. MICHAEL (Sir), 11th bart., *d. unm.* 15 June, 1872.
4. FRANCIS HAWTREY (Sir), 12th bart., *m.* 6 March, 1853, Emma Katherine, dau. of Duncan McKellar, and *d.s.p.* 17 Oct. 1873, when the baronetcy became extinct.
1. Maria, *m.* Rev. Matthew Enraght.
2. Anne, *m.* Rev. Thomas Lyon.

(4) William, *b.* 6 Jan. 1773; *d.s.p.* in the West Indies before 1811.

(5) Benjamin, *b.* 20 Jan. 1775; *d.s.p.*

Sir Richard Cox, the 1st bart., Lord Chancellor, *d.* 3 May, 1733, aged 83 years.

Arms (Heralds' College)—Quarterly: 1st and 4th, or, a fesse chequy arg. and az., within a double tressure flory counterflory gu. a martlet for difference, for STUART; 2nd and 3rd arg., on a cross gu. five escallops or, for VILLIERS. **Crests**—1st, a demilion rampant gu. charged on the shoulder with a martlet for distinction (for STUART); 2nd, VILLIERS, a lion rampant arg., ducally crowned or, charged on the shoulder with a crescent. **Motto**—Under arms: Avito viret honore. Over STUART crest: Nobilis ira.

Seat—Castlane, Carrick-on-Suir, co. Kilkenny.

VILLIERS-STUART OF DROMANA.

ION HENRY FITZGERALD VILLIERS-STUART, of Dromana, co. Waterford, *b.* 23 Nov. 1900; *s.* his father 1908.

Lineage.—HENRY WINDSOR VILLIERS-STUART, of Dromana-within-the-Decies, co. Waterford, M.A., J.P. and D.L., M.P. co. Waterford 1873 to 1874, and 1880 to 1885, Vice-Lieut. co. Waterford 1871, 1872, and 1873, High Sheriff 1889, *b.* 13 Sept. 1827; *m.* 3 Aug. 1865, Mary, 2nd dau. of Ven. Ambrose Power, Archdeacon of Lismore, 4th son of Sir John Power, 1st bart. of Kilfane. She *d.* 14 Sept. 1907. He *d.* 12 Oct. 1895, leaving issue,

1. HENRY CHARLES WINDSOR, late of Dromana.
2. Gerald, *b.* 1869; *m.* Maud, dau. of — Hutchinson, and has issue,
  1. Percival.   2. Desmond.
  3. Fitzgerald.
  1. Muriel.
3. Maurice Ambrose, *b.* 1870; *m.* Rose Clark, and has issue, Gerald Ambrose.
4. Horace Gervase, *b.* 8 Dec. 1872.
5. Patrick, Capt. 2nd Batt. Royal Fus. (*Beachamwell Hall, Swaffham, Norfolk*), *b.* 27 April, 1879; *m.* 26 Feb. 1908, Constance

Mary, only child of the late Joshua Fielden, J.P. and D.L., of Beachamwell, Norfolk, and has issue,
  Patricia Frances Mary, Fielden, b. 28 Sept. 1910.
1. **Mary Thérèse**, m. 16 Feb. 1904, Sir John William Pitt Muir-Mackenzie, K.C.S.I., youngest son of Sir John W. P. Muir-Mackenzie, 2nd bart. (*see* BURKE'S *Peerage*).
2. **Gertrude Gwendoline**.
3. **May**, m. 10 July, 1907, Capt. Hugh Taylor, Scots Guards, elder son of Thomas Taylor, of Chipchase Castle, Northumberland, J.P. (*see that family*).
4. **Winifred Frances**, m. Capt. F. Leyland, 7th Hussars.

Mr. Villiers-Stuart s. to the extensive estates of Henry, Lord Stuart-de-Decies, at that nobleman's decease, 23 Jan. 1874. He was the author of *Nile Gleanings, Egypt after the War*, and other works, and was commissioned by the Government in 1882 to visit Egypt, and report upon the condition of the population after the battle of Tel-el-Kebir. His eldest son,

HENRY CHARLES WINDSOR VILLIERS-STUART, of Dromana-within-the-Decies, co. Waterford, J.P. and High Sheriff 1898, His Majesty's Lieut. for co. Waterford, Major S. Irish Horse, late Capt. Waterford Artillery, served in S. Africa 1900 (medal), b. 3 Aug. 1867; m. 20 Aug. 1895, Grace Frances, only dau. of the late J. A. R. Newman, D.L., of Dromore House, co. Cork (*see that family*), and d. 8 Sept. 1908, having by her (who m. 2ndly, 25 July, 1910, Sir Alexander Kay Muir, 2nd bart.) had issue,
1. ION HENRY FITZGERALD, now of Dromana.
1. Geraldine Mary, b. 7 June, 1896.
2. Nesta Mona, b. 17 Nov. 1897.

Seat—Dromana, Cappoquin, co. Waterford.

STUART-FRENCH. *See* FRENCH.

HAMILTON-STUBBER OF MOYNE.

ROBERT HAMILTON HAMILTON-STUBBER, of Moyne and Castle Fleming, Queen's Co., J.P. and D.L., High Sheriff 1873, late Lieut. Royal Dragoons, b. 18 June, 1844, m. 1st. 15 Nov. 1877, Adèle Grainger, dau. of Alexander Duncan, of Knossington Grange, co. Leicester, and by her (who d. 5 April, 1882) has had issue,
1. ROBERT, Capt. 1st Life Guards, served in S. African War, 1900-01, b. 28 Sept. 1879.
1. Olive, b. 2 Sept. 1878; d. Nov. 1881.

He m. 2ndly, 22 Sept. 1885, Georgina Alice Mary, youngest dau. of George Power, 6th son of Sir John Power, Bart., of Kilfane, co. Kilkenny, and has issue,
2. Margery Hamilton.

Lineage.—HUGH HAMILTON settled at Lisbane, near Bangor, co. Down, *temp.* JAMES I, and was made denizen of Ireland 1616. He d. about May, 1655, and was buried at Bangor. He left issue,
1. JOHN, of Ballymenoch, near Hollywood, and of Ballyvernon, near Bangor, living 1673, had a son,
  Alexander, of Ballyvernon, b. 1648; m. Isabella, dau. of John Blackwood, of Ballyleidy. She d. 12 Oct. 1738, leaving a son,
    John, of Ballyvernon, b. 1681, d. 1738, leaving a son,
      Alexander, of Ballyvernon, d.s.p.
2. ALEXANDER, of whom presently.
3. Robert, m. Jane Phillips. She d. 1689, leaving a dau.,
  Ursula, m. John Blackwood, of Ballyleidy, co. Down, and d. 12 Sept. 1741, leaving issue (see BURKE'S *Peerage*, DUFFERIN, M.).

The 2nd son,
ALEXANDER HAMILTON, of Killyleagh, m. Jean, dau. of John Hamilton, of Belfast, and d. 26 Jan. 1676, leaving issue by her, who d. 1699,
  HUGH, his heir.
  Jane, m. William Sloane, of Chelsea, brother of Sir Hans Sloane, Bart., and had issue.

The son and heir,
HUGH HAMILTON, of Ballybrenagh, m. Mary, sister of Robert Ross, of Rosstrevor, and dau. of George Ross, of Portavo, by Ursula his wife, dau. of Capt. Hans Hamilton, of Carnessure, and dying 16 Nov. 1728, was buried at Killyleagh, leaving issue,
1. ALEXANDER, his heir.
2. GEORGE, of Tyrella, co. Down, m. Elizabeth, dau. of John Echlin, of Ardquin, co. Down (*see that family*), elder brother of Sir Henry Echlin, 1st bart. He d. 1770 in his 73rd year, leaving issue,

George, of Tyrella, M.P. for Aucher, Tyrone, 1776-83, d. unm. 6 July, 1796.
Elizabeth, m. her cousin George Hamilton, of Hampton, Baron of the Exchequer, who d. 1793, leaving issue (*see below*).
1. Jane, m. 1720, John Gordon, of Ballinteggart.

The elder son,
ALEXANDER HAMILTON, of Knock, co. Dublin, and Newtown Hamilton, co. Armagh, M.P. for Killyleagh, 1730-61, m. Isabella, dau. of Robert Maxwell, of Finnebrogue, co. Down, by Jane, dau. of Rev. Simon Chichester, Vicar of Belfast (eldest son of Henry Chichester, of Marwood), by Jane, dau. of Robert Maxwell, Bishop of Kilmore. He d. 1768, leaving four sons and three daus.,
1. HUGH (Right Rev.), D.D., F.T.C.D. and F.R.S., of Newtown Hamilton, co. Armagh, sometime Dean of Armagh, Lord Bishop of Clonfert, 21 Jan. 1790, and Bishop of Ossory, from 1798, until his death, b. 26 March, 1729; m. 6 Aug. 1772, Isabella, eldest dau. of Hans Widman Wood, of Rossmead, co. Westmeath, by Frances his wife, twin-sister of Edward, Earl of Kingston; and d. 1 Dec. 1805, having by her (who d. 1834) had,
  1. ALEXANDER, Q.C., Barrister-at-Law, of Newtown Hamilton, co. Armagh, and Oak Lawn, co. Dublin, b. 27 Jan. 1774; m. 29 Jan. 1799, Julia, dau. of Michael Tisdall, of Charlesfort, co. Meath (she d. 1840), and d. Oct. 1852, having had (with other issue who d. unm.),
    (1) Isabella, m. 1816, John Synge, D.L., of Glanmore, co. Wicklow, d. 1830.
    (2) Julia, m. 19 Oct. 1819, Hon. and Rev. John Pratt Hewitt, and d. 1827.
    (3) Catherine, m. Rev. Joseph Wright, d. 1891.
    (4) Alicia, m. Archibald Tisdall, of Clontarf (she d. 1876).
  2. Hans (Rev.), D.D., Prebendary of Kilmanagh, and Rector of Knocktopher and Kilmoganny, b. 22 May, 1776; m. Susanna, dau. of the Right Hon. Silver Oliver, M.P., of Castle Oliver, co. Limerick, and sister of Catherine, Lady Mount Sandford, and d.s.p. 1839.
  3. Henry, of Tullylish House, co. Down, J.P., b. 24 Nov. 1780; m. 1808, Sarah, dau. of Rev. Michael Sandys, Rector of Powerscourt, co. Wicklow (she d. 28 Nov. 1871), and d. 7 Dec. 1834, having had issue,
    (1) Hugh (Rev.), b. 19 March, 1811; m. 19 July, 1838, Mary Charlotte, dau. of Rev. Henry Ormsby (*see* ORMSBY-HAMILTON *of Cabinteely*), and d. 1884, having by her (who d. 1871) had issue,
      1. EDWIN, Barrister-at-Law, M.A., J.P. (*The Crossways, Donaghadee, co. Down*). b. April, 1849; m. 10 Sept. 1891, Helen Vaughan, 2nd dau. of Daniel Delacherois, D.L., and has issue by her (who d. 6 Nov. 1911),
        Hugh Delacherois George, b. 2 Oct. 1900.
      1. Henrietta. 2. Lucy.
      3. Isabella.
    (2) HENRY ALEXANDER, of Hampton, J.P. and D.L. co. Dublin, High Sheriff 1887, b. 5 Oct. 1820; d. unm. 30 March, 1901.
    (3) George Hans (Ven.), D.D., Archdeacon of Northumberland and Prebendary of Durham, J.P., b. 1823; m. 1st, 9 May, 1848, Arabella Sarah, only dau. of John Best, of the H.E.I.C. Civil Service; and by her had issue,
      1. Hans Alfred, b. 27 May, 1849.
      2. Henry Best Hans (His Honour), Barrister-at-Law, County Court Judge, J.P. Lancashire, late Lieut.-Col. Commanding Northumberland Artillery Militia, b. 14 Oct. 1850; m. 22 July, 1875, Margaret Gordon, eldest dau. of late John Bond Cabbell, of Cromer Hall, Norfolk (*see that family*), and has issue,
        (a) Benjamin Henry Noel Hans, b. 25 Dec. 1882; m. 7 July, 1906, Ida, dau. of Percy Mortimer, J.P., of Ashe Park, Overton, Hants, and has issue,
          Hugh.
        (b) George Cecil Hans, B.A., LL.B., Barrister-at-Law, b. 13 Feb. 1888.
        (a) Marguerite Elgiva Hans, b. 8 March, 1890.
      1. Eliza Arabella Sarah, m. 1883, Robert Thornewill, J.P., of Craythorne, Burton-on-Trent.
    He m. 2ndly, 1 June, 1869, Lady Louisa Frances, sister of Robert, 4th Earl of Leitrim (*see* BURKE'S *Peerage*), and d. 23 Sept. 1905, leaving issue,
      3. George Francis Clements, b. 24 March, 1870; d. 1900.
      4. Robert Charles Clements, b. 15 May, 1871; d. 1901.
      5. Collingwood George Clements, b. 1 Nov. 1873.
      1. Louisa Lindisfarne Clements, m. 29 May, 1902, William Maitland, of Loughton Hall, Essex.
)4) William Alfred (Rev.), D.D., Rector of Taney, and Canon of Christ Church, Dublin, b. 19 March, 1824; m. 10 Jan. 1849, Henrietta Katherine, 3rd dau. of Henry St. George Cole, of Annestown, co. Waterford, and d. 13 Feb. 1897, leaving issue,
      1. Henry Balfour (Rev.), M.A., Rector of Normanton-on-Soar, co. Nottingham, b. 18 Dec. 1849; m. 24 Aug. 1875, Hannah Sophia, dau. of John Hubert Moore, and has issue,
        (1) Alfred Henry John, J.P. (*West Leake House, Nottinghamshire*), late Royal Indian Marine, b. 12 Sept. 1877; m. 8 Aug. 1906, Lilian, dau. of George Cope, J.P., and has issue,
          1. Henry Cope. 2. Brian Alfred.
          3. Gerald John.
          1. Joan Elise.
        (2) John Cole.
        (1) Henrietta Cecily Augusta.
      2. Alfred St. George, b. 5 Dec. 1851; m. 1897, Emeline, 4th dau. of John Atkinson, of Gortmore, co. Dublin.

3. William Drummond, of Lennan Bank, Ramelton, co. Donegal, J.P., M.A. (Oxon), b. 4 Aug. 1859; m. 5 Aug. 1891, Alice Josephine, dau. of George Kinahan, D.L., of Roebuck Park, Dundrum, and has issue,
    a. George Alfred Drummond, b. 1892; d. 21 June, 1900.
    a. Margaret Henrietta.   b. Dorothy Alice.
    c. Gertrude Emily, d. young.
4. Willoughby James, b. 9 Dec. 1864.
5. Francis Cole Lowry, b. 26 April, 1869.
6. Blayney, b. 13 June, 1872.
1. Gertrude May, b. 29 April, 1853; m. 1st, 1 Sept. 1875, the late Erskine Wilmot Chetwode; and 2ndly, Rev. Edward Walker, M.A., Fellow of Queen's Coll. Oxon.
2. Florence Eglantine, b. 29 April, 1853; m. 1898, Francis Elrington Ball, 2nd son of Right Hon. J. J. Ball, LL.D., Lord Chancellor of Ireland.
3. Catherine Henrietta, b. 4 May, 1858; m. 26 Oct. 1886, her cousin, Robert Pollock Hamilton (see below).
(5) Alexander, of Inistioge, J.P., co. Kilkenny, b. 4 Jan. 1829; m. 25 Oct. 1851, Emma, dau. of the Right Hon. Sir Frederick Pollock, Bart., Lord Chief Baron of the Court of Exchequer, and by her had issue,
1. Frederick Alexander Pollock, b. 20 Aug. 1852, B.A. Cantab. Barrister-at-Law, d. 9 Sept., 1909.
2. Charles Pollock, b. 9 Oct. 1853; d. 1878.
3. Horace George Pollock, b. 6 Nov. 1854; d. 17 Jan. 1891.
4. Walter Richard Pollock, b. 18 Aug. 1856, V.C., Bengal Staff Corps, killed in the massacre of the British Embassy at Cabul, 3 Sept. 1870, aged 23.
5. Alexander Pollock (Rev.), M.A. Trin. Coll. Dublin, (Grosvenor Road, Norwich), b. 8 July, 1858; m. 1902, Ada, dau. of the late Thomas Anderson.
6. Robert Pollock, b. 31 March, 1860; d. 10 June, 1907; m. 26 Oct. 1886, his cousin, Catherine Henrietta, dau. of Rev. W. A. Hamilton, D.D.
7. Archibald Pollock, b. 17 Sept. 1861, d. 1880.
(1) Sarah, m. 19 Jan. 1854, William Barclay Browne Scriven, M.D., who s. his brother-in-law, Henry Alexander Hamilton, at Hampton 1901. He d. 12 Sept. 1906. She d. 1901, leaving issue, two sons.
(2) Frances Barbara, d. 1877.
(3) Julia, m. 1 Sept. 1840, Right Hon. Henry Wilmot Ormsby. P.C., who d. 17 Sept. 1887, leaving issue (see ORMSBY-HAMILTON of Cabinteely).
4. George (Rev.), Rector of Killermogh, Queen's Co., an eminent Hebrew Scholar, b. 19 Dec. 1784; m. 1st, 31 Oct. 1809, Sophia Dorothea, dau. of George Kiernan, of Blackhall, co. Dublin, and niece of Col. Molesworth Philips, of Belcotton, co. Louth, who accompanied Capt. Cook in his voyage round the world, and by her (who d. 1820) had issue,
(1) Augusta Sophia, m. 1844, Rev. Richard Johnston, of Kilmore, co. Armagh, and d. 30 April, 1860, leaving issue.
(2) Isabella, d. unm. 16 Nov. 1841.
He m. 2ndly, 1825, Frances Anna, dau. and eventually heiress of Admiral Sir Chichester Fortescue, of Dromiskin, co. Louth, Ulster King of Arms, cousin-german of Arthur, Duke of Wellington. She d. 1875. He d. 9 Aug. 1830.
5. Hugh (Rev.), of Innishmacsaint, co. Fermanagh, b. 13 Aug. 1790; m. Elizabeth, dau. of Right Hon. John Staples, P.C., M.P., of Lissan. co. Tyrone, by his 2nd wife, Henrietta, dau. of Richard, 3rd Viscount Molesworth, and d. 1865, having had issue,
(1) Hugh Staples (Rev.), of Manston, Leeds, d. 19 July, 1899, leaving issue.
(2) Richard (Rev.), Rector of Killelagh, co. Derry, d.s.p. June, 1878.
(3) Albert, d. 1842.
(4) Thomas (Rev.), m. 1859, Mary, dau. of Sir John Borlase Warren, 4th bart. of Warrenscourt, co. Cork, and has issue.
(1) Harriet, m. 1852, William Malachy Burke, M.D., Registrar-General for Ireland, and has issue.
1. Frances, b. 2 May, 1775; m. 1802, Rev. Michael Dodgson Madden, Chancellor of St. Canice, Kilkenny (d. 2 Jan. 1809), and d. leaving issue.
2. Isabella, b. 24 Aug. 1777; d. unm. 1845.
2. ROBERT, of whom we treat.
3. GEORGE (see ORMSBY-HAMILTON of Cabinteely).
4. Charles, of Hamwood (see HAMILTON of Hamwood).
1. Isabella, m. 1754, Richard Sheffield Cassan, Barrister-at-Law.
2. Anne, m. 16 May, 1774, Lieut.-Col. Henry Caldwell, 3rd son of Sir John Caldwell, 2nd bart., and d. 28 May, 1810.
3. Elizabeth, m. Rev. Robert Law, D.D., Fellow Trin. Coll. Dublin.

The 2nd son,
ROBERT HAMILTON, of Gloucester Street, Dublin, m. Hester, dau. of Crewe Chetwood, of Woodbrook, Queen's Co., by Anne his wife, dau. of John Holford. He d. July, 1790, having had issue,
1. ALEXANDER CHETWOOD, of whom presently.
2. Robert, m. 1803, Sidney, dau. of Mervyn Archdale, of Castle Archdale, M.P. for Fermanagh (see that family). He d. 26 July, 1830, having had with four daus., five sons,
    1. Maxwell, of Merrion Sq., Dublin, bapt. 17 Aug. 1801; m. 4 May, 1854, Mary John, dau. of John Graves, of Mickleton Manor, co. Gloucester. She d. 4 Feb. 1885. He d. 27 Feb. 1867, leaving issue, an only child,
        Sidney Graves, of Kiftsgate Court, Campden, co. Gloucester, J.P., M.A., Fellow of Hertford Coll., Oxford, 1878-1906, b. 13 June, 1855; m. and has issue (see HAMILTON of Kiftsgate Court).
    2. Mervyn.   3. Robert (Rev.), who left issue.
    4. Chetwood.   5. Dawson.
The elder son,
REV. ALEXANDER CHETWOOD HAMILTON, Rector of Thomastown, co. Kilkenny, m. 1801, Eleanor, dau. and co-heir of REV. SEWELL STUBBER, and assumed, by Royal Licence, 20 Feb. 1824, the surname of STUBBER instead of Hamilton, and the arms of STUBBER only. By her he had issue,
1. ROBERT, of Moyne.
2. Sewell (Rev.), m. 1832, Selina, dau. of Sir John Robinson, 1st bart. of Rokeby Hall, co. Louth, and d. 1863, having by her (who d. 1860) had, with other issue,
    Gertrude Sophia, m. 18 July, 1866, 8th Viscount Ashbrook. She d. 8 Nov. 1911, leaving issue (see BURKE's Peerage).
3. William, of Roundwood, Mountrath, m. 1820, Henrietta, dau. of Charles Powlett Doyne, of Portarlington, and had issue,
    1. Robert, m. his cousin Ethel (who d. 1883), dau. of Sewell Hamilton, and d. 1882, leaving issue.
    2. Charles Paulet, of Roundwood, Mountrath, m. 17 Dec. 1878, Emily Louisa, fourth dau. of Very Rev. William Smyth King, Dean of Leighlin, and d. 24 Jan. 1907, leaving issue,
        (1) Maurice Chetwode, Capt. 4th Batt. Leinsters, b. 1882.
        (2) Hubert Charles, Barrister-at-Law, b. 1886.
        (1) Elinor Frances, m. 1903, Alexander Ian Mitchell, Capt. 3rd Dragoon Guards.
        (2) Kathleen Elizabeth.
        (3) Alice Maud.
        (4) Mary Beatrice.
    1. Elizabeth.   2. Harriet.
    3. Frances, d. 1904.   4. Olivier.
4. Alexander Chetwood, m. Miss Storking.
5. Richard Hugh (Rev.).
1. Hester Maria, m. Abel John Caulfield Warren, of Lowhill, co. Kilkenny.
2. Harriet Anne.   3. Sophia Elizabeth.
4. Anne Matilda, m. Francis Curry, of Lismore.
The son and heir,
ROBERT HAMILTON STUBBER, of Moyne, J.P. and D.L., High Sheriff 1831, b. 1 Oct. 1803; m. 2 May, 1840, Olivia, dau. of Rev. Edward Lucas, of the Castleshane family, and widow of Henry Smyth, of Mount Henry, Queen's Co., and d. 28 Feb. 1863, having by her (who d. 1866) had issue,
1. ROBERT HAMILTON, now of Moyne.
1. Olivia Harriet Florence Hamilton.
2. Eleanor Frances Beatrice Hamilton, m. 3 April, 1879, Richard, 1st Lord Stalbridge, and d. 21 March, 1911, leaving issue (see BURKE's Peerage).

Arms—Quarterly; 1st and 4th, erm. on a pile sa., an heraldic antelope's head erased or, for STUBBER; 2nd and 3rd, arg., on a bend gu. three martlets of the first, for SEWELL. Crest—On a mural crown gu. a martlet arg. Motto—Gladio et arcu.
Seats—Moyne, Durrow, Queen's Co., and Castle Fleming, Ballybrophy. Clubs—Army and Navy, Naval and Military, and Kildare Street, Dublin.

STUBBS OF DANBY.

HENRY STUBBS, of Danby, co. Donegal, M.A., Trin. Coll. Dublin, J.P. and D.L., co. Donegal, High Sheriff 1891, J.P. co. Fermanagh, High Sheriff 1901, b. 30 May, 1846.

Lineage.—JOHN STUBBS, of Eltham, co. Kent (whose will was proved 22 Sept. 1556), left by Margaret his wife, five sons and two daus. The eldest son,
HENRY STUBBS, of Eltham (whose will, dated 14 Dec. 1569, was proved 31 March, 1571), had issue by his wife Katherine, three sons, one of whom was
JOHN STUBBS, of Eltham and Chislehurst, m. 21 Oct. 1605, Alice, dau. of Richard Masters, of Chislehurst, and left (will dated 29 March, 1632), with other issue, a son,
RICHARD STUBBS, of Chislehurst, Clerk of Ye Cheque to Henrietta Maria, Royal Consort of King CHARLES I., b. 1606, m. 1631, Jane, dau. and co-heir of Philip Fowler, of East Wickham, co. Kent, and left an only son,
PHILIP STUBBS, of St. Andrew Undershaft, London, b. 1636; m. 1st, 5 Nov. 1663, Elizabeth, dau. of Thomas Hillier, of St. Dionis, Backchurch, London, by whom he had issue, eight sons and one dau. Elizabeth, who m. Rev. Ambrose Bonwicke, of Headley, Surrey, B.D., and had issue: she d. 3 Dec. 1722; their eldest son, Ambrose Bonwicke, b. 1691, d. 1714, whilst at St. John's Coll. Cambridge, of which college he was a Scholar, and where he suffered loss of preferment on account of his non-juring scruples. His life was written by his father in 1729, entitled, A Pattern for Young Students in the University, set forth in the Life of Mr. Ambrose Bonwicke, sometime Scholar of St. John's College in Cambridge, republished and edited

by Prof. J. E. R. Mayor in 1871 (*see also* Nichols's *Lit. Anecd.* 1. 39 and v. 118–136, Abbey's *The English Church*, 1700–1800, vol. 1. *p.* 66, and *Dict. of Nat. Biog.* vol. v.). Philip Stubbs *m.* 2ndly, 2 Nov. 1680, Mercy, relict of John Sergeant, of London, by whom he had, with other issue, Samuel, of Rotherhithe and St. Clement Danes, *b.* 1689, *m.* 1718, Anne Norton, of Hurstpierpoint, Sussex, and *d.* 1758. The eldest surviving son of the above Philip was,

Rev. Philip Stubbs, B.D., F.R.S., Fell. Wadham Col!. Oxford, Archdeacon of St. Albans, First Chaplain to Royal Hospital, Greenwich, Rector of Launton, Oxfordshire, *b.* 1665; *m.* 1696, Mary, dau. of Rev. John Wyllys, of Brentwood, Essex. To him Dr. Wolfran Stubbe, Vice-Master of Trin. Coll. Cambridge, by his will, dated 1719, left the reversion of his three manors of Scottow Auburys, Felmingham, and Runton, in Norfolk (*see* Wood's *Athenæ Oxonienses, The Spectator*, No. 147, and *Dict. Nat. Biog.* vol. lv.). He *d.* 13 Sept. 1738 (will dated 10 Dec. 1733, proved 31 Oct. 1738). She *d.* 1759, aged 95, leaving issue,
1. Philip, *b.* 1697, *d.* 1698.   2. Lawrence, *b.* 1698, *d.* 1699.
3. John, *b.* 1699, *d.* 1700.
4. William, of Rochester, Proctor and Registrar of St. Albans and Rochester, *b.* 1703, *m.* Mary Gascoigne, of Suffolk, sister of Capt. Edward Gascoigne, R.N., and *d.* 1790 (will dated 17 April, 1789, proved 17 March, 1790). She *d.* 1761, leaving issue,
  1. Thomas, of St. Albans, *m.* 14 July, 1771, Mary Roberts (who *d.* 1836, aged 90), and *d.s.p.* 1776, *v.p.* (will dated 17 Sept. 1772, proved 23 July, 1776).
  2. William, *b.* 1741, *d.* 1742.
  3. Edward, *b.* 1745, *d.* 1745.
  4. William, *b.* 1749, *d.* 1749.
  1. Mary, *d.* 1805.   2. Elizabeth, *b.* 1738; *d.* 1776.
  3. Sarah, *b.* 1740, *m.* 1768, John Dufour, of Stamford Hill, and had issue.
5. Charles, of whom presently.
1. Philippa Maria, *b.* 1701, *d.* 1786 (will dated 3 March, 1772, proved 1 May, 1786).
The 2nd son,
Charles Stubbs, of East Greenwich, *b.* 1705; *m.* 12 May, 1733, Rebecca, dau. of Robert Wallrond, of St. James's, Westminster, and *d.* 1741, having by her (who *m.* 2ndly, John Kerby, of Northampton, and *d.* 1764) had issue,
1. Philip West, *b.* 1734, *d.* young.
2. Charles, of whom hereafter.
1. Ann, *b.* 1737; *m.* 5 March, 1759, Richard Keene, and *d.* 1760, leaving issue,
2. Elizabeth, *b.* 1739, *m.* 1761, Francis Grojan, of St. James's, Westminster, and had issue.
The only surviving son,
Charles Stubbs, of St. James's, Westminster, *b.* 1736; *m.* 17 March, 1761, Elizabeth, dau. and heir of Richard Troubridge, of St. James's, Westminster, grand-uncle of Sir Thomas Troubridge, 1st bart., and *d.* 22 Nov. 1771 (will dated 3 April, proved 3 Dec. 1771), having by her (who *m.* 2ndly, 1781, Joseph Thompson, and *d.* 1 Feb. 1809, leaving no issue by her 2nd marriage) had issue,
1. Charles Errington, *b.* 18 July, 1767; *d.* 10 Oct. 1768.
2. William Troubridge, of whom presently.
1. Mary, *b.* 1 March, 1762; *d.* 10 April, 1762.
2. Ann, *b.* 31 March, 1763; *m.* 1st, 1789, James Mawdsley; 2ndly, Henry Helmsley, and *a.s.p.* 1832.
3. Elizabeth, *b.* 28 Nov. 1764; *m.* John Jackson, and *d.* 1837, leaving issue.
4. Mary, *b.* 13 June, 1766; *d.* 1 March, 1770.
5. Sarah, *b.* 6 Aug.; *d.* 18 Aug. 1769.
The only surviving son,
William Troubridge Stubbs, of Marylebone, London, *b.* 4 Oct. 1770; *m.* 12 Aug. 1801, Ann, dau. and heir of Richard Westgarth, and *d.* 25 Jan. 1835, having by her (who *d.* 7 Sept. 1838) had issue,
1. Thomas Troubridge, of whom presently.
2. Charles Grogan, *b.* 8 April, 1806; *d.* 18 April, 1845, leaving issue.
3. John Willock, *b.* 20 Sept. 1807; *d. unm.* 5 Jan. 1845.
4. James Henry Philipps, *b.* 9 May, 1810; *m.* 29 Aug. 1839, Ann Verrity, and *d.* 23 Aug. 1864, leaving issue.
5. William Stuart Dick, *b.* 25 June, 1812; *d.* June, 1882, leaving issue.
6. Griffith, *b.* 2 March, 1815; *d. unm.* 26 Aug. 1842.
1. Elizabeth Mary Ann, *b.* 21 Dec. 1816; *d.* Aug. 1821.
The eldest son,
Thomas Troubridge Stubbs, of Marylebone, London, and Ballyshannon, co. Donegal, *b.* 28 Sept. 1802, removed to Ireland in 1834; *m.* 8 Nov. 1839, Elizabeth Chinnery, 3rd dau. of Joseph Follingsby, of Belfast and Ballyshannon, by Eleanor, eldest dau. of Sir Broderick Chinuery, Bart., M.P., of Ann's Grove, co. Cork (*see* Chinnery Haldane *of Gleneagles*). Mrs. Stubbs *s.* on the death of her cousin, the Rev. Sir Nicholas Chinnery, Bart., in the railway accident at Abergele 1868, to one-third of the Flintfield estate in co. Cork. She *d.* 15 April, 1887. He *d.* 12 April, 1872, leaving issue,
1. Charles Albert (Rev.), of Salthill, Mountcharles, co. Donegal, J.P., Incumbent of Parish of Camus-juxta-Bann, co. Londonderry, 1884–93, *b.* 20 Nov. 1840; *m.* 1st, 8 Oct. 1872, Phœbe, only dau. of Rev. Walter Riky, Perpetual Curate of Queensborough, co. Kent, and by her (who *d.* 2 Oct. 1886) had issue,
  1. Thomas Troubridge, Lieut. 2nd Batt. Royal Munster Fus., *b.* 20 March, 1876; *m.* 7 Dec. 1907, Grace Winifred, dau. of James Hunter Annandale, of The Vale, Polton, N.B., and has issue,
    Thomas Troubridge, *b.* 17 Nov. 1908.
    Mary Phœbe, *b.* 10 May, 1911.
  1. Emily Chinnery, *b.* 16 April, *d.* 1 May, 1875.
  2. Ethel Elizabeth, *b.* 7 Sept. 1879; *m.* 24 Nov. 1908, Capt. Walter Tyrwhitt Bromfield, Leicestershire Regt., son of Col. Francis W. Bromfield, late Cheshire Regt., and has issue.
I.L.G.

He *m.* 2ndly, 27 Sept. 1894, Lizzie Sarah, dau. of Joseph Betts Horrell, and *d.* 16 April, 1905, having had further issue,
  3. Mary Chinnery, *b.* 23 Oct.; *d.* 5 Nov. 1895.
2. Henry, now of Danby.
3. Alfred, of Portnason, co. Donegal, M.A., and LL.B., Trin. Coll. Dublin, *b.* 6 Jan. 1849.
1. Eleanor, *d.* young.
2. Anna, *b.* 31 May, 1844, *m.* 1 June, 1876, Robert Crawford, D.L. of Stonewold, co. Donegal (*see that family*), and *d.* 11 Dec. 1880, leaving issue, four sons.
3. Emily, *b.* 19 May, 1850; *m.* 26 Nov. 1889, William Alexander Hamilton, J.P. of Coolmore and Coxtown, co. Donegai, and *d.s.p.* 9 Jan. 1891.

Arms—(Herald's Coll.)—Sa., on a bend between three pheons or, as many round buckles, gu., on a chief of the 2nd three stumps of trees eradicated ppr. *Crest*—A stump of a tree eradicated ppr., thereon a demi-eagle displayed or, collared sa., holding in the beak an oak branch also ppr. *Motto*—Dominus exaltatio mea.

Seats—Dauby, Ballyshannon, co. Donegal; St. Ernan's Donegal.

STUBBS OF FORTWILLIAM AND BALLYBODEN.

William Cotter Stubbs, of Fortwilliam, Finglas, co. Dublin, M.A., Trin. Coll. Dublin, F.R.S.A.I., Barrister-at-Law, Examiner of Titles to the Irish Land Commission since 1905, Senior Crown Prosecutor for co. Louth and Jun. Crown Prosecutor for co. Monaghan until 1905. Member of the General Synod, and Vice-President of the Royal Society of Antiquaries of Ireland 1903–6, Sec. to the Trin. Coll. Dublin Estates Commission 1904–5, *b.* 19 Feb. 1862; *m.* 14 May, 1890, Mary, eldest dau. of John George Gibbon, LL.D., Barrister-at-Law (*see* Gibbon *of Sleedagh*), and has issue,
1. John William Cotter, *b.* 30 May, 1891.
1. Elinor Kathleen.
2. Muriel Florence.

Lineage.—Robert Stubbs, migrated from England before 1680 with his brother John, and settled in Ballyboden, near Rathfarnham, co. Dublin, where he held a considerable portion of land, from Lord Wharton, which is still in the possession of the family. He had two sons, William and Robert. The elder son,
William Stubbs, of Ballyboden, whose will, dated 14 June, 1742, was proved 5 April, 1754. He left issue,
1. John, of whom presently.
2. Robert, of Kilbride House, co. Dublin, *b.* 1708, *d.* 1775, leaving by Catherine his wife, a son and a dau.,
  John, who had a dau. Anne.
  Mary, *m.* 7 Jan. 1765, Richard Tilson, of Tomroe, Westmeath, and had a dau. Catherine.
3. Thomas, of Perrystown, *b.* 1711.
The eldest son,
John Stubbs, of Ballyboden, *b.* 1706, *m.* 1743, Margaret, dau. of John Bloomer, of Woodtown. She *d.* 30 July, 1774, aged 66. He *d.* 18 July, 1784, leaving issue,
1. John, *b.* 28 June, 1746; *d.s.p.* 20 Feb. 1786.
2. Robert, of whom presently.
3. William Deane, *b.* 3 Feb. 1750; *d.s.p.* 6 June, 1783.
4. Thomas, *b.* Easter Tuesday, 1752.
5. James (Rev.), B.A., T.C.D., of Edmonstown House, near Rathfarnham, J.P. co. Dublin, for 38 years Curate of St. Catherine's, Dublin, *s.* his younger brother George at Ballyboden. He was *b.* 30 Oct. 1755; *m.* 26 Nov. 1783, Anne, eldest dau. of Rev. Hamilton Morgan, Prebendary of Dunlavin, co. Wicklow. She *d.* 27 Sept. 1795. He *d.* 23 March, 1823 (will dated 15 March, proved 15 May, 1823), leaving issue,
  1. John Hamilton (Rev.), of Ballyboden, M.A., T.C.D., Rector of Dromiskin, co. Louth, for 25 years, *b.* 26 Jan. 1786; *m.* 4 Aug. 1814, Margaret, eldest dau. of John Carleton, of High Park, co. Dublin. He *d.* 25 Oct. 1856, leaving surviving issue,
    (1) Elias Thackeray (Rev.), of Ballyboden, Rector of Charlcombe, Bath, M.A., T.C.D., *b.* 29 April, 1827; *m.* 3 June, 1857, Charlotte, dau. of the late John Hamilton, of the Grove, co. Meath. He *d.* 18 Feb. 1897, leaving issue,
      John Hamilton, of Ballyboden, B.A. Oxon, *b.* 1 May, 1861.
      Catherine Mira.
  (2) Francis William, Major-Gen. late Royal (Bengal) Art., J.P. co. Louth, *d.* 2 Aug. 1911; *m.* 8 Nov. 1865, Caroline Euphemia, dau. of Arthur Kennedy Forbes, of Newstown, co. Meath, and Craigavad, co. Down. She *d.* 25 March, 1901, leaving issue,
    1. Arthur Kennedy, Capt. and Brev. Maj. Worcestershire Regt., *b.* 8 Dec. 1867; killed in action near Colesberg, S. Africa, 12 Feb. 1900.
    2. Edward Carleton, Lieut. R.N., *b.* 9 March, 1881.
    1. Caroline Elizabeth (*Clarence Terrace, Cork*).
    (1) Elizabeth Susanna.

2 U

2. James Morgan (Rev.), M.A., Rector of Rossdroit, co. Wexford, b. 1 Nov. 1791; m. 1st, 29 March, 1815, Elizabeth, dau. of Rev. William Glascott, of Pilltown (see GLASCOTT, of *Alderton*). She d. 28 July, 1847, leaving issue,
    (1) James Williani, Col. Indian Staff Corps, m. 1st, Mary, dau. of George A. Bushby, Bengal C.S. She d. 8 June, 1863, leaving surviving issue,
      1. Arthur George Bushby, Major Army Pay Dep. late Cheshire Regt., b. 11 March, 1856; m. Hope, dau. of Major B. H. Burge.
      2. James William Hill.
He m. 2ndly, Elizabeth Ella, dau. of Charles C. Black. She d. 25 Nov. 1867, leaving a dau.,
      1. Margaret Dora.
He m. 3rdly, Margaret, dau. of the late Major Yule. Col. Stubbs d. 27 Jan. 1873.
    (2) William Glascoti, d. in Australia.
    (3) Warden Flood (Rev.), M.A., Incumbent of St. Columba, Liverpool, 1868-86; m. Cecilia, dau. of Rev. Cecil Russell, and d. 21 March, 1908, leaving issue.
    (4) Edward, Capt. late R.N., m. Anne, only dau. of George Arland, of Cassington, co. Leicester, and d. 18 Feb. 1909, leaving issue.
      (1) Elizabeth Anne.
      (2) Mary Sarah, d. 27 Sept. 1908.
      (3) Lucy Charlotte, d. 10 April, 1907.
      (4) Arabella, m. 22 July, 1865, Rev. Charles Waller, M.A., and has issue.
The Rev. J. M. Stubbs m. 2ndly, Mary, widow of Rev. Alan Morgan. He d. 1 Jan. 1858.
    1. Margaret, m. 18 May, 1823, Rev. William Phelan, D.D., F.T.C.D., and had issue two daus. who d. *unm*.
    2. Maria Katherine, m. 21 June, 1837, Robert Mansfield, but *d.s.p.*
6. George, of Ballyboden, heir to his father, b. 30 March, 1757; d. *unm.* Nov. 1787 (will proved 26 Jan. 1788), and was s. by his brother Rev. James Stubbs (see *ante*).
1. Mary, b. 3 Jan. 1744; m. Richard Hicks, of Kilmacanoge, co. Wicklow, and d. 1837, leaving issue.
2. Jane b. 26 Nov. 1753; m. Robert Eccleston, and d. May, 1883, leaving issue.
3. Margaret, b. 26 Feb. 1759; d. *unm.* 15 Dec. 1785.

The second son,
ROBERT STUBBS, of Stubton, (now Fortwilliam), Finglas, co. Dublin, b. 26 March, 1748; m. 14 Feb. 1777, Susanna, dau. of Robert Smith, of Rolestown House. Swords, co. Dublin. She d. 1803, aged 48. He d. 27 July, 1798, leaving issue,
1. Robert Smith, m. Alicia, dau. of Robert Anderson, and d. 1857, leaving issue,
    1. Susan, m. David Archer, of Corovante, Crobam Road, Croydon, and Gracemere, Rockhampton, Queensland, and had issue. He d. 10 Jan. 1900. She d. 28 March, 1901.
    2. Elizabeth, d. 16 April, 1909.
2. JOHN WILLIAM, of whom presently.
3. William, d. young.
1. Margaret, m. John Sheppard.
2. Eliza Susanna Mary.   3. Mary.

The younger son,
JOHN WILLIAM STUBBS, of Rolestown House and Stubton, J.P., b. 1790; m. 1820, his cousin Anne, dau. of Thomas Smith, of Rolestown. She d. 1871. He d. 1851, leaving issue,
1. JOHN WILLIAM, late of Fortwilliam.
    1. Margaret Emma, d. 12 Nov. 1903.
    2. Susanna Annette. m. her cousin Charles Smith, M.D., Surgeon 67th Regt., and d. 1870.

Thk only son,
REV. JOHN WILLIAM STUBBS, D.D., S.F.T.C.D., of Fortwilliam, Finglas, co. Dublin, a Commissioner of National Education and a member of the Representative Body of the Church of Ireland, Treasurer of St. Patrick's Cathedral, b. 1 Feb. 1821; m. 14 Oct. 1854, Catherine Louisa (who d. 11 May, 1903), dau. of the Rev. Joseph Rogerson Cotter, M.A., Rector of Donaghmore, co. Cork, and Prebendary of Cloyne, grandson of Sir James Cotter, Bart., of Rockforest (see BURKE's *Peerage*). He d. 10 Jan. 1897, leaving issue,
    1. John William, b. 1855, d. 1861.
    2. WILLIAM COTTER, now of Fortwilliam.
    1. Mary Louise Annette, b. 1857, d. 1863.
    2. Anna Margaret Constance, m. 1881, Arthur Wyndowe Willert Baker, M.D., F.R.C.S.I., of Ardeen, Greystones, co. Wicklow, and 59, Merrion Square, Dublin, and has issue.
    3. Louisa Susan Georgina (32, Corrig Avenue, Kingstown).
    4. Florence Josephine, *d.s.p.* 21 April, 1904.
    5. Laura Kathleen (32, Corrig Avenue, Kingstown).

Seat—Fortwilliam, Finglas, co. Dublin. *Town residence*—28, Hatch Street, Dublin. *Club*—Dublin University.

STUDDERT OF BUNRATTY CASTLE.

THOMAS STUDDERT, of Bunratty Castle, co. Clare, educated at Clifton Coll. and Royal Mil. Coll., b. 17 Dec. 1879.

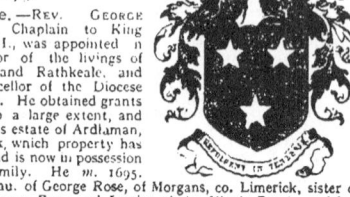

Lineage.—REV. GEORGE STUDDERT, Chaplain to King WILLIAM III., was appointed in 1669. Rector of the livings of Kilpeacon and Rathkeale, and made Chancellor of the Diocese of Limerick. He obtained grants of lands to a large extent, and settled on his estate of Ardlaman, co. Limerick, which property has devolved and is now in possession of the family. He m. 1695, Millicent, dau. of George Rose, of Morgans, co. Limerick, sister of the Hon. Henry Rose, 3rd Justice of the King's Bench, and had (with two daus.) four sons,
1. THOMAS, of whom presently.
2. George, b. 1697, m. Miss Eyre, of co. Galway, and settled in King's Co.
3. Richard, of Clonderalaw, co. Clare, m. 29 June, 1746, Mary, youngest dau. of Jonah Pratt, of Castlemartyr, co. Cork (see BURKE's *Family Records*) and had issue, three sons and one dau.,
    1. George, High Sheriff 1794, m. Elizabeth, dau. of Thomas Studdert, of Bunratty, and was s. by his son, George, of Clonderalaw, High Sheriff 1831, who m. 1828, Ellen, dau. of Rev. John Lloyd, Rector of Cashel, and niece of Thomas Lloyd, M.P., of Beechmount (see *that family*), and d. 1857, and was s. by his son, George Lloyd, of Clonderalaw, co. Clare, J.P., late Capt. 12th Regt., b. 25 Nov. 1828; m. 25 Jan. 1861, Maria Jane, dau. of Dr. Lloyd, of Limerick, and by her (who d. 1872) has issue,
      (1) George, b. 22 May, 1865.   (2) Edward, b. 31 May, 1866.
      (1) Maria, b. 1861.   (2) Ellen, b. 1863.
      (3) Fanny, b. 1867.
    2. Maurice (Rev.), D.D., m. 1777, Margaret, dau. of Rev. Francis Patterson, and had issue, a son,
      Richard (Rev.), m. 1798, Juliet, dau. of Robert Scott, M.P. for Newry, and left issue,
      1. Richard, of Mount Rivers, m. Frances, dau. of Hon. George Massy, and had a son, Richard Massy, of Fort House, co. Clare, J.P., Auditor of the Local Government Board at Belfast, Hon. Lieut.-Col. Clare Militia Artillery.
      2. Robert, of Coolreagh, Bodyke, co. Clare, m. 7 Jan. 1836, Elizabeth Jane Hallam. She d. Jan. 1870. He d. 21 Aug. 1866, having had issue,
        a. Richard, J.P., b. 6 Jan. 1837.
        b. George Hallam, of Hazelwood, Quin, co. Clare, J.P., b. 20 Sept. 1841; m. 26 Oct. 1889, Eva, dau. of Major George S. Studdert (see *below*), and d. 6 Feb. 1905, leaving issue,
          (a) Robert Hallam, Lieut. R.A., b. 21 Nov. 1890.
          (b) Reginald Hallam, b. 31 July, 1892.
          (c) De Clare Hallam, b. 9 April, 1902.
        a. Mary Fitzgerald.
        b. Juliet Maria, m. Jan. 1870, John Norris Russell, eldest son of Thompson Russell, of Faha, co. Limerick, and has issue.
    3. Jonas, m. 1834, Sarah, dau. of John Morgan, of Beverston, co. Clare, and d. 16 March, 1899, having had issue (with a dau. Maria Juliet, m. 1870, Lieut.-Col. Marcus Paterson, of Cliden, co. Clare, D.L., and has issue) an only son,
      Charles Washington (*Cragmoher*, *Corofin*, *co. Clare*), late Major Clare Militia, m. 1st 1856, Catherine Jane, dau. of Rev. Charles Waller, of Trewley, Suffolk. She d. 20 Aug. 1904, having had issue,
        (a) Jonas Waller, Barrister-at-Law, d. 1889.
        (b) Charles William, d. 1860.
        (c) Charles Washington, d. 1861.
        (d) William, d. 1862.
        (e) John Alfred, m. 24 March, 1908, Gladys Eyre, dau. of Alfred Loraine Persse, of Rose Park, co. Galway, and grand-dau. of Dudley Persse, of Roxburgh, co. Galway (see *that family*), and has issue.
        Maurice Eyre Persse, b. 29 March, 1910.
        (f) Thomas Julian, d. 16 May, 1910, m. Miss Alley.
        (a) Catherine Florence, m. Bagot Blood, of Rockforest, co. Clare, and d. 1896, leaving issue.
      Major C. W. Studdert m. 2ndly, 7 Dec. 1908, Mary Louisa, widow of H. S. Maye, and dau. of late E. B. Edwards, of Ullett Grange, Liverpool.
    4. Francis (Rev.), m. 19 July, 1849, Caroline, dau. of Charles Percival, and had issue, Richard, m. Miss FitzMaurice, and d. 1890, leaving issue; and Caroline, m. Robert W. Biddulph, R.N., and has issue.
      1. Alicia, m. Rev. Henry Whitty, and had issue.
      2. Margaret, m. William D. Lawler, M.D., and had issue, a dau., Juliet Mary, m. 1851, William Bentley, of Hurdlestown, co. Clare, and has issue.
      3. Juliet Matbilda, m. May, 1828, Edward Reeves, of Platten, co. Meath, and by him (who d. 28 Oct. 1877) had issue (see REEVES *of Besborough*).
3. Jonas, Barrister-at-Law, m. a dau. of Thomas Crowe, of Dromore House.

1. Anne, *m.* Andrew Welsh, of Newton, J.P. for cos. Clare and Limerick.
4. Maurice, of Elm-Hill.
1. Elizabeth, *m.* 1st, — Freeman, and 2ndly, — Langford, both of co. Limerick.   2. Agnes, *m.* — Southwell.

The eldest son,
THOMAS STUDDERT, *b.* 1696, acquired property in cos. Clare, Limerick, and Kerry, and took up his residence at the Castle of Bunratty. He *m.* 1st, Madame Cusack, by whom the estate of Kilkishen, came into the family; and 2ndly, Miss Parker, of Castle Lough, and had issue,
1. THOMAS, his heir.
2. George, of Kilkishen, High Sheriff 1799, *m.* 1788, Hannah, dau. of John Blood, of Castle Fergus, and had issue,
   1. Thomas, of Kilkishen, his successor, High Sheriff 1809, who *m.* 1807, Milicina, dau. of Robert Ashworth, and sister of Lieut.-Gen. Sir Charles Ashworth, Governor of Oporto, and *d.* 19 July, 1873, having had issue by her (who *d.* Jan. 1850),
      (1) Robert Ashworth, of Kilkishen House, co. Clare, J.P. and D.L., High Sheriff 1847, late Major Clare Militia, *b.* 31 Dec. 1817; *m.* 18 Jan. 1849, Maria, eldest dau. of Rev. William Waller, of Castletown, and *d.* 18 Aug. 1906, leaving issue, a son,
         Thomas, *b.* 1850; *d.* 1869.
      (2) George Frederick, *b.* 28 Dec. 1816; *d.* 12 May, 1846.
   2. George, *m.* Miss Massy, and was father of
      George, of Glenwood and Kilnamona, co. Clare, *m.* Jane, dau. of Hugh Russell, of Limerick, and grand-dau. of Capt. Neptune Blood, of Roxton House, co. Clare, and had issue,
      1. George Hampden de Clare (Rev.), M.A., late Vicar of Edwardstone, Boxford, Suffolk; *d.* 15 June, 1911.
         1. Jane Agnes.
         2. Thomasina Bloomfield, *m.* 4 April, 1866, Sir Reginald R. B. Guinness, son of R. G. Guinness, M.P., and grandson (maternally) of Sir Charles Jenkinson, 10th bart., of Hawkesbury, and has issue.
      3. Richard (Rev.), *m.* Mary, dau. of Lieut.-Gen. O'Meara, and has issue.
      1 Elizabeth, *m.* George Waller, of Prior Park, brother of Sir Robert Waller, Bart. of Lisbrain, and uncle to Lord Bloomfield.
      2. Mary, *m.* George Mansergh, of Riversdale, co. Kildare.
      3. Alicia, *m.* her cousin, Thomas Studdert, of Bunratty.
   4. Elizabeth, *m.* 1787, George Studdert, of Clanderalaw.
   2. Milicent, *m.* William Spaight, of Corbally.

Mr. Studdert, who served as High Sheriff of co. Clare 1727, was s. at his decease by his elder son,
THOMAS STUDDERT, of Bunratty Castle, Deputy-Governor of co. Clare, High Sheriff 1785, *b.* 1748; *m.* 1778, Anne, dau. of James Fitzgerald, of Shepperton, and had issue,
1. THOMAS, his heir.
2. James Fitzgerald, Lieut. 16th Regt., dec.
3. George, *m.* Letitia, dau. of Very Rev. Stewart Blacker, of Carrick-Blacher, co. Armagh (*see that family*), Dean of Leighlin, and by her (who *d.* 8 April, 1831) had issue,
   1. Thomas, Capt. R.E., dec.
   2. Abraham Wellington, *m.* Miss Cooper; *d.* and left issue.
   3. Stewart Blacker, dec.
   4. George (Rev.), M.A., Rector of Ardee, co. Louth, *m.* 8 Oct. 1861, Caroline Amelia, dau. of Major Edward Jonathan Priestley, Deputy-Inspector-General of Constabulary in Ireland, and *d.* 14 April, 1897, having by her (who *d.* 19 March, 1897) had one dau., dec.
      1. Elizabeth, *m.* Dr. O'Flaherty.   2. Anne, dec.
4. Charles Fitzgerald, of Newmarket House, Newmarket-on-Fergus, *m.* 1808, Maria, only dau. of Robert Wogan, of Dublin, Deputy Keeper of the Rolls in Ireland. She *d.* 5 Jan. 1883. He *d.* 27 Nov. 1851, leaving issue,
   1. Robert Wogan, of Cullane, Kilkishen, J.P., *b.* 5 Dec. 1810; *m.* 1840, Katherine Maria, dau. of Admiral O'Brien (*see* BURKE'S *Peerage*, INCHIQUIN, B.). She *d.* 12 April, 1900. He *d.* 27 May, 1897, leaving with other issue,
      (1) Robert O'Brien, of Cullane, Kilkishen, co. Clare, and Arranmore, Miltown Malbay, co. Clare, J.P., D.L. cos. Cork and Clare and High Sheriff co. Clare 1901-2, *b.* 28 Nov. 1848; *m.* 1st, 12 Feb. 1874, Marianne, dau. of Rev. Lord Adam Loftus; and 2ndly, 20 March, 1884, Maria Frances, eldest dau. of Henry Lavallin Puxley, of Dunboy, co. Cork (*see that family*), and has issue, by the former,
         1. Thomas George Herbert, Lieut. R.E. Militia, *b.* 13 April, 1875.
         2. Loftus Adam, *b.* 11 March, 1877, High Sheriff co. Leitrim 1912; *m.* 1 Aug. 1902, Charlotte Isabella, dau. of the late Major Octavius La Touche, of Bellevue (*see that family*).
            1. Rose Mary, *m.* 22 Feb. 1909, Frederick W. Kennedy, M.D., and has issue.
            2. Violet, *m.* 13 July, 1911, Martin E. P. White (*see* WHITE *of Mount Sion*).
         (2) Charles Fitzgerald, *d.s.p.*
         (3) Thomas George, *d.s.p.*
      2. Charles Fitzgerald, of Newmarket House, J.P., Major late 30th Regt., *m.* 1862, Eliza, dau. of Charles Putland, of Bray-head, co. Wicklow, and *d.* 11 Nov. 1887.
      3. Frederick, dec.
      4. William Steele, of Keeper View, O'Brien's Bridge, co. Clare, J.P., *b.* 8 Nov. 1821; *m.* 6 July, 1854, Constance (*d.* 14 Jan. 1911), dau. of Robert George Massy, of Avondale, son of Hon. George Massy, and *d.* 30 July, 1892, leaving issue.

(1) Charles Henry Thompson, *b.* 13 Sept. 1856, dec.
(2) William John Massy, *b.* 16 Dec. 1857, dec.
(3) Hugh Samuel, *b.* 30 April, 1861.
(1) Constance Helen, *m.* 1st, Lucius Arthur, of Glenomara, and 2ndly, William Paumier Ball, of Merrion Square, Dublin, elder son of Right Hon. J. T. Ball, LL.D., Lord Chancellor of Ireland and has issue by the former.
5. George (Major), J.P., of Craggane Tower, co. Clare, late Major Clare Militia, *m.* 1838, Agnes, 2nd dau. of Rev. Charles Waller, of Trimley, Suffolk, and *d.* leaving issue,
   (1) Charles Fitzgerald, *b.* 18 July, 1859; *d.* 16 June, 1884.
   (2) Reginald Waller, M.A., B.C.L., *b.* 27 June, 1862; *d.* 14 May, 1886.
   (3) Frederick Naunton, *b.* 18 June, 1866; *m.* 1897, Isabel M., dau. of Hugh Ballingall, of Dundee, and has issue,
      Claire Dorothy Naunton, *b.* April, 1893.
   (1) Kathleen Agnes.
   (2) Eva, *m.* 26 Oct. 1889, George Hallam Studdert, of Hazelwood, co. Clare (*see above*).
   (3) Ethel Mary, *m.* T. Townsend, M.D., of Cork.
5. John Fitzgerald, Admiral R.N., J.P., of Pella, *m.* 1831, Anne, dau. of Rev. Richard Welsh, of Newtown House, co. Clare, and *d.* 1867, leaving issue, by her (who *d.* 1878),
   1. Thomas, Lieut. R.N., *b.* 1833; *d.* 1863.
   2. Richard Augustine Fitzgerald, of Pella, Kilrush, co. Clare, Major R.M.A., served in Crimea, and China, and as Capt. and Adjutant of London Artillery Brigade, *b.* 1835; *m.* 1860, Maria Isabella, youngest dau. of William Ansdale Leech, of Ratheran, co. Mayo. He *d.s.p.* 20 Nov. 1900.
   3. John Fitzgerald, of Lochnavar, co. Clare, *b.* 1848, *m.* 1869, Mary Catherine, eldest dau. of Capt. Charles Hall, R.N., and has, with a dau. Anne Welsh,
      John Fitzgerald, *b.* 1872.
   1. Jane Anne, *m.* 1857, John Mariner Redmayne, of South Dene, co. Durham.
6. Edward, settled in Canada, *m.* Miss Kilburn, sister of Col. Kilburn, *d.* and had issue.
1. Mary, *m.* Rev. Robert Gabbett, Rector of Castletown, and Vicar-General of Killaloe, dec. (*see* GABBETT *of Caherline*).
2. Elizabeth, *m.* Rev. Edward Eyre Maunsell, of Fort Eyre, dec.
3. Caroline, dec., *m.* 1st, Marcus, son of Marcus Paterson, by Mary his wife, sister of Valentine, 1st Earl of Dunraven, and 2ndly, E. W. Burton, of Clifden House, co. Clare.

Mr. Studdert *d.* 1825, and was *s.* by his eldest son,
THOMAS STUDDERT, of Bunratty Castle, J.P. and D.L., High Sheriff 1805, *b.* 1779; *m.* Alicia, dau. of George Studdert, of Kilkishen, by Hannah his wife, dau. of John Blood, of Castle Fergus, and had issue,
1. Thomas de Clare, *d. unm.* 1866.
2. GEORGE, of Ardlaman, co. Limerick, *d. unm.* 10 June, 1897.
3. RICHARD, late of Bunratty.
4. Robert, *m.* 1st, a niece of Lieut.-Gen. Hawkshaw; and 2ndly, dau. of Rev. J. B. Langton, and settled in Australia; *d.* leaving issue.
5. Charles, *d. unm.* 17 April, 1894.
6. John Fitzgerald, Resident Magistrate for co. Carlow, late 85th King's L.I., *m.* Alice, widow of Arthur Bastable, Barrister-at-Law and *d.* 1870, having had one son and three daus., of whom Gertrude Marie Fitzgerald, *m.* 15 June, 1897, Surg.-Capt. Philip Glover Ievers, A.M.S., who *d.* June, 1909, leaving issue (*see* IEVERS *of Mount Ievers*).
7. Augustine Fitzgerald, *m.* Margaretta, dau. of John Ferguson, of Glenmore, Bute, and has issue,
   1. Thomas de Clare.   2. Augustine Fitzgerald.
   3. Richard.   4. John Ferguson.
   1. Anna.   2. Margaretta.
1. Hannah Maria, *d. unm.* 18 Dec. 1897, aged 91.
2. Alicia, *m.* Gen. Frederick Maunsell, Col. 85th King's Light Infantry, and has issue.
3. Elizabeth.
4. Milicent Anne, *m.* John S. Gabbett, of Castle Lake.

Mr. Studdert *d.* Aug. 1870, and was *s.* by his 2nd surviving son,
RICHARD STUDDERT, of Bunratty Castle, co. Clare, J.P., High Sheriff 1874, Capt. R.N. (retired), *m.* 1877, Helen, dau. of James Denniston, of Greenock, co. Renfrew, and *d.* 1900, leaving issue,
1. THOMAS, now of Bunratty.   2. Richard.
1. Alicia Agnes, *m.* 15 Jan. 1902, Capt. H. T. Russell, R.F.A., eldest son of Edmund M. Russell, of Milford, Limerick, and has issue.
2. Helen Anne Fitzgerald.   3. Jane Fairrie Denniston.

Arms—Per pale az. and gu., three mullets arg. Crest—A demi-horse rampant sa, round the body by a ducal coronet or. Motto—Refulgent in tenebris.

Seat—Bunratty Castle, Bunratty, co. Clare.

STUDHOLME OF BALLYEIGHAN.

LAUNCELOT JOSEPH MOORE STUDHOLME, of Ballyeighan and Kilmaine, King's Co., High Sheriff 1909, *b.* 21 Sept. 1884; *s.* his father 1905.

Lineage.—JOHN STUDHOLME, of Studholme, Abbey Holme, and afterwards of St. Nicholas and Morton Head, Cumberland, sold the last of the family estates. He *m.* Elizabeth Nixon, and had issue,
1. JOSEPH, late of Ballyeighan and Kilmaine.
2. John, resident in New Zealand, *m.* Ellen Moorehouse, of York, and has issue.

Style. THE LANDED GENTRY. 676

3. Michael, resident in New Zealand, m. and has issue.
4. Paul.
1. Fanny. 2. Elizabeth.
3. Ada, m. 15 July, 1868, Charles Baker Stoney, M.D., and has issue.

The eldest son,
JOSEPH STUDHOLME, of Ballyeighan and Kilmaine, J.P. for King's Co., High Sheriff 1861, m. 11 July, 1878, Mary Hastings, only dau. of James Robert Davis, of Bagot Street, Dublin, by Charlotte Elizabeth his wife, dau. of Robert Atkins, of Firville, co. Cork, and d. 1905, having had issue,
1. John, b. 9 June and d. 5 July, 1882.
2. LAUNCELOT JOSEPH MOORE, now of Ballyeighan.
1. Elizabeth Charlotte Anne, d. 13 Nov. 1905, having m. Major Ambrose W. Newbold.
2. Mary Hastings, m. 30 Aug. 1906, Capt. Arthur Granville Vivian, Indian Army, youngest son of Capt. Aylmer Mac Iver-Campbell, of Askinsh (*see that family*).
3. Rosalind.

Seat—Ballyeighan, Parsonstown, King's Co.

STYLE. See BURKE'S PEERAGE, **STYLE**, Bart.

SULLIVAN OF TULLILEASE.

REV. JOHN SULLIVAN, of Tullilease House, co. Cork, b. 1 Nov. 1838; m. 5 June, 1877, Georgina, only dau. of John Cox, J.P., Weston-super-Mare, Somerset, and has had issue,
1. WILLIAM, b. 24 May, 1880.
1. Annie Marion, d. unm.
2. Eliza Adams, d. unm.
3. Mary Georgina, d. unm.
4. Augusta Florence, d. unm.

Lineage.—DANIEL O'SULLIVAN, dropped the prefix "O" to his surname. He m. Margaret Tucker, of co. Kerry, and dying in 1682, left a son,
DARBY SULLIVAN, m. Joanna Taylor, of Kilbolane Castle, and d. 22 Jan. 1718, leaving a son,
JOHN SULLIVAN, m. 1714, Mary Herne, of Hernesbrook, and d. 1737, leaving issue,
1. JEROME, of Kill, co. Kildare, b. 8 Nov. 1716; m Ann Russell, of Dublin, and had (with two daus., Elizabeth and Mary) a son, Maurice Sullivan, b. 9 April, 1757.
2. WILLIAM, of whom hereafter.
3. James, b. 14 June, 1731; m. 1 March, 1764, Margaret, dau. of Mark Conor, of Ballyire, and sister of the late Daniel Conor, and had issue,
   1. John, b. 1765, m. 1789, Elizabeth, dau. of Christopher Knight, of Brickfield, co. Limerick, and sister of Col. Peppard Knight, of Charleville, and d. 1830, leaving issue,
     (1) James, Lieut. 83rd Regt., d. 1821.
     (2) Peppard Knight, d.s.p.
     (1) Margaret, m. Edward Rae.
     (2) Susan, m. John Parker.
   2. James, of Chesterfield, co. Limerick, Major 83rd Regt., J.P., b. 9 Oct. 1778; m. 2 Sept. 1812, Mary Anne, eldest dau. of Rev. William Ashe, Prebendary and Rector of Croagh, in the diocese of Limerick, by Elizabeth his wife, only dau. of Edward Jefferies, of Ludtow, Salop, by his wife, Frances, sister of Rev. Thomas Locke, of Newcastle, co. Limerick, and d. 8 Feb. 1830, having had issue,
     (1) William, d. Dec. 1832.
     (2) Henry White, d. 2 June, 1848.
     (3) James (Rev.), Rector of Askeaton, co. Limerick, b. 1818; m. 23 July, 1856, Georgina Lucie, only dau. of George Annesley Owen, of Ramsgate, co. Wexford, by Lucie Catherine his wife, eldest dau. of Rev. Henry Moore (see BURKE'S *Peerage*, DROGHEDA, E.), Rector of Ferns, and had, with other issue,
       Ponsonby Augustus Moore (Rev.), Vicar of Rangeworthy, Gloucestershire, b. 1857.
     (4) John, d. 29 Sept. 1838.
     (5) Edward, Lieut. in the Army, d. 8 Sept. 1845.
     (6) Thomas, d. 22 March, 1845. (7) Jefferies, dec.
     (1) Eliza, d. unm.
     (2) Marion, m. 14 Aug. 1855, Major Charles Parker, 4th R.S. Middlesex Militia, late 69th Regt., only son of Major Parker, 62nd Regt., and d. April, 1898.
     (3) Margaret, d. Oct. 1853. (4) Fanny, d. Aug. 1846.
     (5) Harriette (dec.), m. 18 Nov. 1852, Col. Charles J. Ellis, Royal Marines, son of Capt. Ellis, R.N.
   3. William, Capt. 30th Regt., b. 1781; a. unm. 1827.
   1. Margaret, m. John Wall.
   2. Eliza, m. Roger Adams, of Rock Abbey, co. Cork, and d.s.p. 1844.
   3. Mary, m. Thomas Green, of Air Hill, co. Cork, and d. leaving a son (James Sullivan, late of Air Hill, M.A., K.C., J.P., m. and has issue) and three daus. (Susan, m. William Sullivan, of Tullilease House, J.P.; Eliza (dec.); and Ann, d. unm. 1850).

The 2nd son,

WILLIAM SULLIVAN, b. 29 Sept. 1729; m. 15 Feb. 1763, Mary dau. of Thomas Morgell, J.P., of Mount Morgell, co. Limerick and sister of Crosbie Morgell, M.P., and d. 22 Feb. 1795, leaving issue,
1. JOHN, his heir. 2. Robert, b. 5 Oct. 1767.
3. Thomas Morgell, b. 11 May, 1771; m. Miss Blennerbasset.
4. Jeremiah, b. 15 Aug. 1773.
5. Melian, m. 1789, George Morgan, of Old Abbey, co. Limerick.

The eldest son,
JOHN SULLIVAN, of Tullilease House, b. 19 June, 1764; m. 10 July, 1794, Anne, sister of Gen. Costley, H.E.I.C.S., and had issue,
1. WILLIAM, of Tullilease House. 2. John (dec.).
3. James, M.D. (dec.), m. Marion Beresford, dau. of Major Tomkins, 27th Regt., of Kilnappy, co. Londonderry, and Richmond Park, co. Limerick, cousin of Viscount Gough, K.P., and had issue,
  1. Beresford, b. March, 1837 (dec.).
  2. Arthur Bunbury, b. 1840 (dec.). 3. James John, b. 1848.
    1. Jane Bunbury Marion Beresford (dec.), m. 22 April, 1869, William White Flint.
    2. Susan Wilhelmina, m. 11 Sept. 1867, Rev. Joseph Barton, of East Leigh, Havant.
4. Thomas, d. 1836.
5. Jeremiah John, of Great Grimsby, co. Lincoln, and afterwards of Middlewich, Chesbire, b. 9 July, 1815; m. 6 May, 1846, Anne Duncuft, eldest dau. of James Ogden, of Hollinwood, near Manchester. She d. 18 Jan. 1861. He d. 18 March, 1878, leaving issue,
  1. Charles Edward (Rev.), M.A., Vicar of St. Michael's, Hulme Walfield, Congleton, Cheshire, b. 7 April, 1847; m. Emily Elizabeth, eldest dau. of Edward Cleaver, of Dalston, London, and grand-dau. of William Canning, of Stratford-on-Avon, and has issue,
    Emily Mary.
  2. Alfred, d. an infant.
  3. Frederick, b. 24 March, 1850; d. unm. 18 June, 1881.
    1. Eliza Anne, d. unm. 24 Dec. 1891.
6. Charles Costley (dec.), m. Belinda, dau. of Major Tomkins, and sister of his elder brother James's wife, and d. 2 Jan. 1869, leaving issue, an only dau., Annie.
1. Anne, d. unm.
2. Melian, m. Jeremiah Sullivan, and had one son, John, of Curramore, co. Limerick (*see next Memoir*).
3. Caroline, m. 1834, Richard Gregg White, and d. 28 Sept. 1893, aged 88, leaving issue (see WHITE *of Kilbyrne*).
4. Eliza (dec.), m. — Dooley (dec.), and had two daus., 1, Annie; 2, Emma (dec.).
5. Mary, m. M. J. Mason, of Glenbrook, co. Limerick, and left issue, 1, John; 2, Edward (dec.); 1, Anne; 2, Melian; 3, Kate.
6. Bridget O'Callaghan (dec.).

Mr. Sullivan d. 30 March, 1836, and was s. by his eldest son,
WILLIAM SULLIVAN, J.P., of Tullilease House, b. 15 April, 1807; m. Susan, dau. of Thomas Green, of Air Hill, co. Cork, and had issue,
1. JOHN (Rev.), now of Tullilease House.
2. James William, b. 1851; d. 1 April, 1876.
1. Maria Eliza, d. 28 Aug. 1870. 2. Eliza Adams.

Mr. Sullivan d. 28 Dec. 1871.

Seat—Tullilease House, Charleville, co. Cork. Residence—Elmfield, Ilfracombe, N. Devon.

SULLIVAN OF CURRAMORE.

HERBERT SULLIVAN, of Curramore, co. Limerick, B.A. Trin. Coll. Dublin, J.P., High Sheriff 1889, b. 22 Oct. 1852; m. 1889, Cecilia Anne, dau. of Frederick Banbury, of Shirley House, Surrey.

Lineage.—(See SULLIVAN *of Tullilease*.) The late JEREMIAH SULLIVAN, m. Melian, dau. of John Sullivan, of Tullilease House, by Ann Costley his wife, and d. June, 1825, leaving an only child,
JOHN JEREMIAH SULLIVAN, of Curramore, co. Limerick, B.A., J.P., b. May, 1825; m. 1st, 1852, Isabel, dau. of Richard Harrison, of Wyton Hall, co. York, and by her (who d. 1863) had issue,
1. HERBERT, now of Curramore.
2. Algernon, b. 1 May, 1854; d. 1866.
3. John Ernest Holt, late Lieut. 73rd Regt., b. 1856; killed in India, 28 Sept. 1880.
1. Adela. 2. Beatrice Isabel.

He m. 2ndly, 4 June, 1867, Caroline Harriet Taylor, only child of Rev. John Fletcher, Rector of Quedgeley, co. Gloucester, and d. 11 Feb. 1891.

Seat—Curramore, Broadford, co. Limerick.

SWEETMAN OF LONGTOWN.

EDMUND CASIMIR SWEETMAN, of Longtown, co. Kildare, J.P. and D.L., High Sheriff 1888, b. 1831; m. 1881, Alice, dau. of Richard Butler, of Suir Vale, co. Tipperary.

Lineage.—PATRICK SWEETMAN, of the city of Dublin, m. Mrs. Mary Thunder, widow, sister of Patrick, Thomas, and George Dodd, whose will, dated 25 Feb. 1782, was proved 21 Sept. 1784. Mr

Sweetman's will, dated 22 Dec. 1770, was proved 14 Jan. following, when he was s. by his grandson,
PATRICK SWEETMAN. of Belvedere, co. Dublin, previously of the city of Dublin. He m. Eleanor, dau. of Michael Thunder, of Ballaly, co. Dublin, who d. 1813. His will, dated 24 March, 1792, was proved 15 Nov. 1793, and he was s. by his son,
MICHAEL SWEETMAN, of Longtown, co. Kildare, b. 1775 ; m. 1st, 1802, Alice, dau. of John Taaffe, of Smarmore Castle, co. Louth, and had issue,
1. PATRICK, his heir.
2. John, of Merrion Square, Dublin, b. 1805 ; m. Honoria O'Connor, and d. 1859, leaving issue,
 1. John, of Drumbarrow, co. Meath, M.P. for E. Wicklow. 1892-1895, b. 1844, is m. and has a dau., b. 3 Nov. 1907.
  1. Honoria. 2. Alice, a nun.
  3. Cecilia, d. unm.
  4. Margaret, Superioress, Sisters of Charity, Stanhope Street, Dublin, d. 13 Nov. 1886. 5. Janette, d. unm.
Mr. Sweetman m. 2ndly, Margaret Gertrude, dau. of Thomas Blackney, of Ballyellen, co. Carlow, by whom he had further issue,
3. Michael James, of Lamberton Park, Queen's Co., J.P., High Sheriff 1852, b. 20 July, 1829 ; m. 1849, Mary Margaret, only child and heir of Michael Powell, of Fitzwilliam Square, Dublin, and d. 1864, leaving issue,
 1. JOHN MICHAEL SWEETMAN-POWELL, of Lamberton Park, J.P. for Queen's Co., High Sheriff 1884, late Capt. Queen's Co. Militia, b. 1 June, 1852 ; assumed by Royal Licence, 1874, the additional surname and arms of POWELL, in compliance with the will of his maternal grandfather ; m. 28 Oct. 1879, Adela Jane, 2nd dau. of Hon. Arthur and Lady Catharine Petre, and d.s.p. 8 March, 1907.
 2. Michael James, b. 28 June, 1864.
  1. Gertrude.
  2. Mary, m. 18 Nov. 1879, Francis Nicholas Blundell, 2nd son of Col. Blundell, of Crosby, and has issue (see that family).
  3. Eleanor.
  4. Agnes, m. 18 June, 1883, Egerton S. Castle, only son of Arthur Castle, of 2, Chapel Street, Park Lane.
4. Walter, of Clohamon, co. Wexford, b. 1831 ; d. 24 June, 1905 ; m. Mary, dau. of Richard Butler, of Suirville, co. Tipperary, and has issue,
 1. Michael James, Major 2nd Batt. East Yorks Regt., b. 31 March, 1865 ; m. 22 Aug. 1907, Adelaide Mary, dau. of Hon. Rev. Charles William Alexander Feilding (see BURKE's Peerage, DENBIGH, E.).
  1. Margaret. 2. Mary.
1. Alice, m. Col. Blackney.
2. Katherine, m. 1851, William Scully, of Ballinaclough, co. Tipperary.
Mr. Sweetman d. 1852, and was s. by his eldest son,
PATRICK SWEETMAN, of Longtown, J.P., D.L., High Sheriff 1862, b. March, 1803 ; m. 1817, Mary, dau. of Edmund Cashin, of Waterford, by Mary Anne Morissy his wife, and had issue,
1. EDMUND CASIMIR, now of Longtown.
2. Hugh, b. 1834 ; m. Gertrude, dau. of Walter Blackney, of Ballyellen, co. Carlow. She d. (his widow 5 Jan. 1912) issue,
 1. Patrick, b. 1871. 2. Hugh, b. 1872.
 3. James, b. 1874.
 4. Roger, b. 1875 ; m. 17 May, 1904, Kathleen Mary, 5th dau. of Thomas Aliaga Kelly, of Dublin.
 5. Walter, b. 1877.
1. Mary Anne, m. Richard Butler of Surville, co. Tipperary.
2. Katherine Mary.
Mr. Sweetman d. 25 Jan. 1885.

Seat—Longtown, Clane, co. Kildare.

SWIFTE OF SWIFTSHEATH AND LIONSDEN.

GODWIN BUTLER MEADE SWIFTE, of Swiftsheath, and Foulksrath Castle, co. Kilkenny, and Lionsden, co. Meath, J.P. and D.L., High Sheriff co. Kilkenny 1892, and co. Carlow 1901, b. 24 March, 1864 ; m. 15 July, 1909, his cousin, Nathalie, dau. of the late Jerome O'Brien, 28th Regt.

Lineage.—BRYAN SWYFTE had a grant from Godfrey de Beaumont, Lord Bishop of Durham (who d. 1333), of part of the lordship of Allergill, co. Durham, to be held of the palatine earldom of the Bishop by service of the eighth part of a knight's fee. He was s. by his son,
SIR HUMPHREY SWYFTE, Knt. of Allergill, who m. a dau. of Alexander, of Beddick, and was s. by his son,

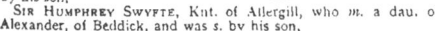

JOHN SWYFTE, of Allergill, who m. Maria, dau. of John Hedworth, and was s. by his son,
EDMOND SWYFTE, of Allergill, who m. Margaret, dau. of Thomas Trollope, of Thornley, and was s. by his son,
ANTHONY SWYFTE, of Allergill, who m. a dau. of Sir Richard Surtees, Knt. of Dinnisdall, and was s. by his son,
ROBERT SWYFTE, of Allergill, and of Rotheram, co. York. This Robert m. twice ; 1st, a dau. of William Hansarde, of Walworth, by which lady he had issue,
1. THOMAS, of whom presently.
He m. 2ndly, Agnes, dau. of Martin Anne, of Frickley, by whom he had two sons,
2. Robert, of Rotheram, b. 1478 ; m. Anne, dau. of William Taylor, of Sheffield, (which lady d. 1539), and to whom and his said wife there is a splendid monument erected in Rotheram Church, 1561, the year of his death. He was s. by his son,
Robert Swifte, of Rotheram, m. Elinor, dau. and sole heir of Nicholas Wickerley, of Wickerley and Broomhall, co. York. They left three daus. only,
 (1) Frances, m. Sir Francis Leake, Knt. of Sutton, co. Derby, ancestor of the Earls of Scarsdale.
 (2) Mary, m. Francis Wortley, of Wortley.
 (3) Anne, m. Richard Jessop, of Broomhall.
3. William, of Rotherham, who m. Margaret, dau. of Hugh Wyrrall, of Loversall, co. York, and dying 1569, was s. by his son,
Sir Robert Swifte, of Rotherham, b. 1551, knighted by King JAMES I at York, 1603. He had the title of "Cavaliero" given him by Queen ELIZABETH, was twice High Sheriff of Yorkshire, "a great swordsman and elegant speaker." In 1609, he entertained Henry, Prince of Wales, at his house. He m. twice, 1st Bridget, dau. and heir of Sir Francis Hastings, of Fenwick, near Doncaster, by whom he was father of Sir Edward Swifte, knighted by King JAMES I at Belvoir, and d.s.p. before his father, having m. Elizabeth, dau. of Edmund Sheffield, Earl of Mulgrave, whose son was afterwards created Duke of Buckingham ; and 2ndly, Ursula, dau. of Stephen Barnham, of Lewes, co. Sussex, and cousin-german of the great Sir Francis Bacon, Viscount St. Albans (which lady d. 1632), by whom, on his death, 1625, he left (with two daus., (1) Penelope, m. William, Viscount Ayr, and Earl of Dumfries, whose dau. Elizabeth, m. Alexander, 8th Earl of Eglinton ; and (2) Mary, m. Sir Robert Anstruther, Ambassador at Copenhagen) an eldest son,
Barnham Swifte, created 1627 Viscount Carlingford, to him and the heirs male of his body, but d. without issue male 1634, when the title became extinct. He m. Lady Mary Crichton, sister to his brother-in-law, the Earl of Dumfries, and left one dau., the Hon. Mary Swifte, who m. the profligate and notorious Robert Fielding, generally known as "Beau Fielding."

The eldest son,
THOMAS SWIFTE, of Allergill, was s. by his eldest son,
HENRY SWIFTE, of Sheffield, co. York. At his death he left two sons, viz., Sir Francis Swifte, knighted 1616, d. 1642, and
THE REV. THOMAS SWIFT, collated 1561 to St. Andrew's, Canterbury, d. 1592, and was bur. in Canterbury Cathedral. He m. Margaret, dau. and heir of Thomas Godwin, D.D., Bishop of Bath and Wells, and left an only son,
REV. WILLIAM SWIFT, b. 1566, Rector of Herbaldown, who afterwards s. to his father's cure. He m. 5 Oct. 1592, Mary Philpott, by whom (who d. 5 March, 1626) he had THOMAS (Rev.), his successor, and two daus., Katherine, m. Thomas Whitenerde, and Margaret, m. Henry Atkinson, of London. He d. 1624, and was s. by his only son,
REV. THOMAS SWIFT, of Goodrich and Bridstow, co. Hereford, distinguished for his active devotion in the cause of CHARLES I., and to the person of his son, Prince Charles (afterwards CHARLES II.), during the latter's protracted wanderings. He m. Elizabeth, dau. of John Dryden, sister of Sir Erasmus Dryden, 1st bart. of Canons Ashby, and grand-aunt of John Dryden, the poet, by which lady he had (with four daus., 1, Emily ; 2, Elizabeth ; 3, Sarah ; 4, Katherine) ten sons, of whom,
1. GODWIN, s. him.
2. Dryden, d.s.p.
3. Thomas, m. the dau. of Sir William Davenant, Knt., and had a son,
 Thomas (Rev.), Rector of Puttenham, Surrey b. 1665, d. 1752, aged 87.
4. William, who had lands in cos. Carlow, Kilkenny, Leitrim, and Roscommon. His will, dated 19 May, 1713, was proved 11 March, 1705. He m. 1st, Frances, dau. of Rev. Ralph King, D.D., by whom he had a son, Thomas, d.s.p., and a dau., Elizabeth, m. her cousin, Godwin Swift, of Dunbrow. He m. 2ndly, Elizabeth, dau. of Capt. Ralph Arrom, by whom (who d. 1716) he had a son,
 William, of Dublin, m. Elizabeth, dau. of William Longfield, and d. 1769, leaving (with a son and a dau., who d. young) a son, William.
5. Jonathan, of Dublin, Solicitor, d. May, 1667 ; m. Abigail Erick, of co. Leicester, by whom (who d. 27 April, 1700) he left (with a dau. Jane) a posthumous son,
 JONATHAN SWIFT (Very Rev.), D.D., the celebrated Dean of St. Patrick's, b. in Hoeys Court, Dublin, 30 Nov. 1667, who has related many anecdotes of his grandfather's loyalty in his account of The Family of Swift, the original M.S. of which is still preserved in the library of Trinity College, Dublin : appointed Dean of the Cathedral Church of St. Patrick, Dublin, by patent, 6 May, 1713 ; d. 19 Oct. 1745.
6. Adam, of Green Castle, co. Down, whose will was proved 26

Swifte.   THE LANDED GENTRY.   678

May, 1704, *m.* Miss Cotterell, and had (with two daus., 1, Anne, *m.* James Perry, of Perrymount, co. Down ; 2, Martha, *m.* 1st, 4 April, 1707, Rev. Theophilus Harrison, and 2ndly, Edward Whiteway, of Dublin) one son,
William, *m.* May, 1685, Mrs. Elizabeth Naylor, widow.
Rev. Thomas Swift *d.* 1658. His eldest son,
GODWIN SWIFT, of Ormond Quay, in the city of Dublin, Barrister-at-Law, Attorney-General to the Duke of Ormonde for the County Palatine of Tipperary, *m.* 1st, Elizabeth Wheeler, by whom he had two sons,
1. Thomas, of Dublin, *m.* Mary, dau. and co-heir of Sir Humphrey Jervis, Knt, Alderman of Dublin. and *d.s.p.* 1679.
2. Willoughby, of Hertford, whose will, dated 27 Jan. 1710, was proved 4 July, 1715, left two daus.,
    1. Hannah, *m.* 30 April, 1714, Rev. Stafford Lightburne, of Trim, co. Meath, and had issue.
    2. Honoria, *m.* Ferdinando Swanton.
Mr. Swift *m.* 2ndly, Katherine, dau. of William Webster, of London, Merchant, by whom (who was bur. at St. Patrick's Cathedral, Dublin, 13 Jan. 1672) he had two sons,
3. GODWIN, his successor.
4. Robert, *d. unm.*
Mr. Swift *m.* 3rdly, May, 1674, Hannah, dau. of Major Richard Deane, and had further issue,
5. Deane, of Castle Rickard, co. Meath, *b.* 20 March, 1670 ; *m.* Elizabeth Lenthall, and *d.* 1713, leaving a dau., Elizabeth, *m.* Godwin Swift, of Tidenton, and a son,
    Deane, of Castle Rickard, *m.* 1739, Mary, dau. of Rev. Theophilus Harrison, and had a dau., Maria, *m.* Rev. Godwin Swift, and a son,
    Theophilus, of Castle Rickard, *m.* Charlotte Maria Pead, and had two sons,
        1. Deane, of Castle Rickard, *m.* Miss Bellew, and had Henry, *d.s.p.* and Christopher.
        2. Edmond Lenthall, Keeper of the Regalia in the Tower of Dublin. *m.* 1st, Mary, dau. of Owen Dalby, and 2ndly, Miss Atkins, and had issue, of whom,
            Mary Ernestine Alexandra, *m.* 13 July, 1874, Major-Gen. Adam Cuppage, Madras Army, who *d.* June, 1890.
6. Joseph, bapt. 7 Aug. 1677.
1. Hannah Maria, bapt. 24 May, 1676.
2. Elizabeth, bapt. 17 June, 1679.
Mr. Swift *m.* 4thly, Ellinor, dau. of Col. William Meade, by whom (who *m.* 2ndly, 13 April, 1702, Very Rev. Theophilus Harrison, Dean of Clonmacnois) he had further issue (with four younger sons, Thomas ; Edward ; William, bapt. 18 Nov. 1684 ; John, *b.* 1691) an elder son,
7. MEADE, of Lynn, J.P., *b.* 29 June, 1682 ; *m.* 1st, Mary, dau. of John L'Estrange, of Keoltown, co. Westmeath, and by her had issue,
    1. JOHN, *m.* Katherine Swanton, and had issue,
        Richard, *m.* Jane, dau. of Alexander Swift, of Lynn, and had issue (with a younger son, John, *m.* Miss Auchmuty, and a dau., Jane Sophia, *m.* 1st, her cousin, Godwin Swift, of Lionsden, and 2ndly, the Comte Lepelletier de Molandé), Benjamin Domville, *m.* July, 1805, Mary, dau. of Godfrey Vaughan, of Dublin, and had (with a younger son, Benjamin Pratt, M.D., Deputy-Inspector of Hospitals) another son,
            REV. RICHARD MEADE SWIFT, B.A., Incumbent of Mountfield. Omagh, *m.* Margaret Julia, dau. of The Mac Dermott Roe, of Alderford, and had issue, Katherine Theresa, *m.* H. Nichol, of Belfast and Sydenham, co. Down ; and Marie Wetzlar, *m.* Rev. Richard Archdall Byrn, B.A., of Braganza, Carlow, Incumbent of Broomfield, Castleblayney, and had issue, Rev. Mervyn Benjamin Archdall Byrn, *m.* 25 July, 1910, Laura Elizabeth, second dau. of Joseph Manley Neale of Newington House (*see that family*).
    2. Thomas, of Lynnbury *b.* 1711 ; *m.* Frances, dau. of John Dennis, of Kinsale, co. Cork, Solicitor, and sister of James Lord Tracton, and had two sons,
        (1) Meade (Rev.), of Union Hill, co. Westmeath, Vicar Choral of Cork ;
        (2) John, Barrister-at-Law, both of whom adopted the surname of DENNIS (*see* DENNIS *of Fort Granite*).
Meade Swift *m.* 2ndly, Frances, dau. of Rev. Alexander Delgarno, of Movlisker, co. Westmeath, and by her had
    3. ALEXANDER SWIFT, of Lynn, *b.* 1712 ; *m.* Elizabeth, dau. of Benjamin Pratt, of Agher, co. Meath, and left (with two daus., Jane, *m.* Richard Swift ; Fanny, *m.* 26 March, 1771, David Jones, of Clonmole, co. Westmeath) a son,
        MEADE SWIFT, *m.* 1773, Anne, dau. of Sir Richard Levinge, 4th bart. of Knockdrin, and left, with three daus., two sons,
        1. Alexander, *b.* 1779, *d.s.p.* 1811.
        2. RICHARD, of Lynn, *b.* 4 April, 1782 ; *m.* 1st, 10 Aug. 1810, Sarah, sister of Sir John Perring, 1st bart. of Membland, Devon, which lady *d.s.p.*, and 2ndly, 17 Oct. 1813. Martha. only surviving dau. of Jacob Bryan, of Dublin, by whom he had issue,
            a. JACOB MEADE, M.D., M.R.C.S.L., *b.* 1814, *m.* 1839, Elizabeth, only surviving child of William Grant Forsyth, of Elgin, and *d.* in New South Wales, 12 Dec. 1865, having had one son, HENRY THOMAS, *b.* Jan. 1848.
            b. Richard Levinge, Barrister-at-Law, and H.B.M. Consul for the Baltic Provinces, *b.* 1821, *m.* 1849, Harriet Frances, only child of Edmund Mills, of Binfield Lodge, co. Berks, and had issue,
                1. Richard Glenelg Levinge, *b.* 15 Oct. 1851 ; 2, Edmund Alexander Levinge, *b.* 26 Sept. 1852 ; 3, Loftus Bryan Levinge, *b.* 7 Dec. 1854 ; 1, Frances Emma Levinge ;

2, Martha Laura Levinge.
c. Charles Alexander, R.N., *b.* 1823.
d. William Alfred, Capt. in the Army, *b.* 1827, *m.* 1853, Amelia, youngest child of James Hulkes, of Little Hermitage, Rochester, Kent, and had issue, 1, Arthur Delgarno, *b.* 1855 ; 2, Richard Gordon Hulkes, *b.* 1857, and 1, Martha Jane.
e. Arthur Delgarno, Lieut. 90th Regt. L.I., *b.* 1834 ; killed in the attack on the Redan, 8 Sept. 1855.
a. Georgina Martha.
Mr. Swift *d.* 7 Dec. 1695, and was bur. at St. Werburgh's Church, Dublin. His eldest surviving son,
GODWIN SWIFT, of Dunbrow, co. Dublin, and of Swiftsheath, co. Kilkenny, *m.* his cousin, Elizabeth, dau. of William Swift, and had (with two daus., Elizabeth, *m.* Folliott Whiteway, and Katherine) four sons,
1. GODWIN, his heir.
2. Michael, of co. Dublin, *d.* 12 Oct. 1777, whose will (dated 23 Dec. 1774) was proved 21 Oct. 1777, left by Mary his wife, a son, Robert, Barrister-at-Law, and six daus.,
    1. Mary, *m.* William Stewart.   2. Anne (Mrs. Bayley).
    3. Katherine.   4. Ellinor.
    5. Maria.   6. Sarah.
3. Jonathan, of co. Dublin, *d.* 1778.
4. William, of co. Dublin, *m.* Elizabeth, dau. of Robert Bor, of Big Butter Lane, co. Dublin, and had two sons,
    1. William.   2. Michael.
Mr. Swift *d.* 1730, and was *s.* by his eldest son,
GODWIN SWIFT, of Tidenton and Swiftsheath, *m.* his cousin of the half-blood, Elizabeth, dau. of Deane Swift, and had two sons,
1. Godwin (Rev.), his heir.
2. Deane, *m.* Anne Hayman, of Youghal, co. Cork, and had a son, Godwin, of co. Dublin, *m.* Mary, dau. of John Swift, and had
    (1) Godwin.
    (1) Mary Jane.   (2) Anna Maria.
Mr. Swift *d.* 21 July, 1770, and was *s.* by his eldest son,
REV. GODWIN SWIFT, of Swiftsheath, and of LionsJen, co. Meath. He *m.* his cousin of the half-blood, Maria, dau. of Deane Swift, of Castle Rickard. co. Meath (grandson of Godwin Swift, by Hannah his 3rd wife, dau. of Richard Deane, of Castle Rickard), by whom he had issue,
1. GODWIN, his heir.
2. Deane, *m.* Isabella, dau. of James Seely.
Mr. Swift *d.* 1815, and was *s.* by his grandson, the eldest son of
GODWIN SWIFT, *d.* 1814 (a year before his father), having *m.* his cousin of the half-blood. Jane Sophia, great-grand-dau. of Godwin Swift, by his 4th wife, Elinor, dau. of Col. William Meade, by whom (who *m.* 2ndly, Count Lepelletier de Molandé, Staff Officer of GEORGE IV.) he left four sons and three daus.
1. GODWIN MEADE PRATT, heir to his grandfather.
2. William Richard, of Whiterhurch Lodge, co. Dublin, and of Dawson's Grove, co. Armagh, *m.* 1830, Elizabeth Catherine, dau. and co-heir of Rev. Daniel Kelly, of Dawson's Grove, co. Armagh, and Killeshall, co. Tyrone, by his wife, Mary Anne, dau. of Peter Gervais, and *d.* 18 Feb. 1890, having had issue,
    (1) Ernest Godwin, K.C., Chief Metropolitan Police Magistrate of Dublin, (18, *Fitzwilliam Square, Dublin*), *b.* 3 June, 1839 ; *m.* 9 Sept. 1869, Fanny, only surviving child (by Henrietta his wife, dau. of Barbazon Morris, of Mulloha, co. Meath) of Robert Coddington, great-grandson of Rev. William Coddington, Vicar of Carrickmacross, who was 4th brother of John Coddington, of Oldbridge, co. Meath, and has issue,
        (1) Ernest Godwin, Barrister-at-Law and Sec. to the Lord Chief Justice of Ireland, *b.* 14 Aug. 1870.
        (2) Latham Coddington, Indian C.S., *b.* 20 Sept. 1871.
        (3) Arthur Meade, Capt. 6th Dragoon Guards (Carabiniers), *b.* 28 Dec. 1874.
        (4) Francis William, Capt. Royal Fus., *b.* 5 May, 1876.
        (5) Charles Barnham, *b.* 14 Oct. 1878 ; *d.s.p.* 4 Aug. 1909.
        (1) Kathleen Mary, *m.* 1 June, 1898, Col. George Ewbank Briggs, Royal Fus., of Catherington, Hants, and Eastwood, Bagenalstown, co. Carlow, and has issue,
            George Swifte Ewbank, *b.* 30 Dec. 1900.
        1. Alice Mary, *d. unm.* 9 April, 1909.
        2. Julia Frances, *d. unm.* 8 March, 1900.
    3. John Pratt, *d. unm.* 1866.
    4. Edward Bulkeley, of Clondalkin, co. Dublin, *m.* 1841, Louisa dau. of Frederick Bourne, of Terenure, co. Dublin, and *d.* 1888, leaving two sons and two daus.
        1. Anne Maria Caroline, *m.* 1833, Capt. Hœner de Mamiel (*d.* 1866) of the Garde du Corps of LOUIS XVIII of France, and *d.* 1849, leaving five sons and two daus.
        2. Jane Christina, *m.* 1835, His Excellency the Chevalier Sergio de Macedo (*d.* 1867), Minister Plenipotentiary of the Emperor of Brazil in London, and *d.* 1853, leaving three sons and two daus.
        3. Maria, *m.* 1830, His Excellency the Chevalier Louis Pereira de Sodré, Minister Plenipotentiary of the Emperor of Brazil at St. Petersburg ; *d.* 1836, leaving a dau., who *d.s.p.*
The eldest son,
GODWIN MEADE PRATT SWIFT, of Swiftsheath and Lionsden, *s.* his grandfather, and revived the ancient spelling of SWIFTE for SWIFT. He *m.* 1st, 1833, the Baroness Marie Fernanda von Wetzlar, dau. and heir of the Baron Franz von Wetzlar, of Schonkirchen, Austria (which lady *d.s.p.* Jan. 1859) ; and 2ndly, Feb. 1863, Mary Jane, dau. of Robert Clark, of Bansha, co. Tipperary, by which lady he left at his decease, 4 July, 1814, a son,
GODWIN BUTLER MEADE SWIFTE, now of Swiftsheath and Lionsden.

Arms—Quarterly : 1st and 4th sa., an anchor in pale or, stock az., the stem entwined by a dolphin, or swift descending arg. ; 2nd and 3rd, or, a chevron vairé between three bucks in full course ppr.

Crest—A sinister arm embowed vested vert, cuffed arg., holding in the hand ppr., a sheaf of four arrows or, feathered arg., barbed az. **Motto**—Festina lente.

Seats—Swiftsheath, Jenkinstown, co. Kilkenny; and Lionsden, Castlerickard, co. Meath, and Foulkrath Castle, co. Kilkenny.

SYNGE OF GLANMORE CASTLE.

ALEXANDER HAMILTON SYNGE, late Lieut. Northumberland Art. Mil., b. 5 Aug. 1856; m. 1887, Georgina Mary, dau. of Rev. Richard Drought Graves, of Cloghan Castle, Banagher, King's Co., Vicar of Hanford, Staffs (see GRAVES of Cloghan Castle), grand-dau. of the late Henry Mussenden Leathes, of Herringfleet Hall, Suffolk (see that family), and has issue,

FRANCIS PATRICK HAMILTON, b. 5 Feb. 1889.
Doreen Hamilton, b. 27 Sept. 1893.

Lineage—RICHARD SYNGE, of Bridenorth, co. Salop, d. 1631; m. Alice, dau. of Roger Rowley, and had with other issue, two sons,
1. George (Right Rev.), Bishop of Cloyne, who d. 1653; m. Anne, dau. of Francis Edgeworth, and left Margaret, m. Michael Boyle, D.D., Archbishop of Armagh.
2. Edward (Right Rev.), Bishop of Cork and Ross, m. Barbara, dau. and co-heir of William Latham, of New Place, co. Donegal, and d. in 1678, leaving issue,
  1. Samuel (Very Rev.), Dean of Kildare.
  2. EDWARD, of whom we treat.

The grandson,
THE RIGHT REV. EDWARD SYNGE, Archbishop of Tuam, d. 23 July, 1741; m. Jane, dau. of Rev. Nicholas Proud, Dean of Clonfert, leaving two sons,
1. Edward (Right Rev.), Bishop of Elphin, who d. 29 Jan. in 1762; m. Jane, dau. of Robert Curtis, of Inane, co. Tipperary, leaving an only child,
  Alicia, m. Right Hon. Joshua Cooper, of Markree (see that family).
2. NICHOLAS.

The younger son,
THE RIGHT REV. NICHOLAS SYNGE, Bishop of Killaloe in 1746, m. Elizabeth, dau. of Frederick Trench, of Garbally, and d. 1 Feb. 1771, leaving (with several daus., of whom the eldest, Elizabeth, d. unm. 1834; and the 2nd, Mary, m. 3 June, 1761, William Peisley Vaughan, of Golden Grove, co. Tipperary) an only son,
THE REV. EDWARD SYNGE, D.D., of Syngefield, King's Co., m. Feb. 1753, Sophia, dau. of the Right Rev. Samuel Hutchinson, Bishop of Killala. She d. 24 Jan. 1799. He d. 9 Oct. 1792, leaving issue,
1. Edward (Rev.), D.D., of Lislee, co. Cork, b. 8 Dec. 1753; d. unm. 1818.
2. Samuel (Sir), 3rd bart., M.A., Archdeacon of Killala, b. 22 April, 1756; s. in 1813 to a baronetcy created 11 Dec. 1782, in favour of his maternal uncle, Sir Francis Hutchinson, 1st bart., of Castle Sallah, co. Wicklow (who d.s.p. 18 Dec. 1807), with a special remainder, and assumed the additional name and arms of HUTCHINSON by Royal Licence 3 April, 1813. He m. 1st, 12 June, 1787, Frances, dau. of Hans Wood, of Rosmead, Westmeath. She d.s.p.m. 12 June, 1788. He m. 2ndly, 3 March, 1801, Dorothy, dau. and co-heir of John Hatch. She was bur. 15 Feb. 1836. He d. 1 March, 1846, leaving issue. This baronetcy became extinct 3 Nov. 1906, at the death of his grandson, the 4th bart.
3. George, of Rathmore, King's Co., b. 24 June, 1757; m. 7 June, 1787, Mary, dau. of Charles Macdonell, of New Hall, co. Clare, and had issue. He d. 1837. She d. 1810.
4. Robert (Sir), created a baronet 12 Aug. 1801; m. 7 May, 1784, Margaret, dau. of Theobald Wolfe, of Newtown, co. Dublin. He d. 1804, leaving issue by her (who d. 1 April, 1838) (see BURKE's Peerage, SYNGE, Bart.).
5. FRANCIS, of Glanmore Castle, co. Wicklow.
  1. Elizabeth, m. — Ormsby, and is dec.

The 5th son,
FRANCIS SYNGE, of Glanmore Castle, M.P. for Swords, b. 15 April, 1761; m. Barbara, dau. and co-heir of John Hatch, of Dublin, and had issue. He m. 2ndly, Elizabeth, dau. of Walter Taylor, of Castle Taylor, and widow of Col. George Stewart, and had issue. His son,
JOHN SYNGE, of Glanmore Castle, m. 1st, 1816, Isabella, dau. of Alexander Hamilton, M.P., Q.C., of Newtown Hamilton, co. Armagh, by whom he had issue,
1. FRANCIS, of Glanmore Castle.

2. Alexander Hamilton (Rev.), of Newtown Hamilton, Armagh, Vicar of St. Peter's, Ipswich, b. 1820; d. 12 March, 1872, having m. 1855, Eugenia Money (d. 1909), dau. of the late Rev. Prebendary Edward Bishop Elliott, of Brighton, and had issue,
  1. ALEXANDER HAMILTON, heir to Glanmore Castle (see above).
  2. Edward Elliott, b. 1868.
  3. Percy Hamilton, b. 1872; m. 14 Dec. 1901, Hon. Ella Campbell Scarlett, M.D., eldest dau. of William Frederick, 3rd Baron Abinger (see BURKE's Peerage).
    1. Eugenia Elliott (twin), b. 17 Oct. 1858; dec.
    2. Isabel Hamilton (twin), b. 17 Oct. 1858; d. 1910.
    3. Annie Frances, b. Feb. 1863.
3. John Hatch, Barrister-at-Law, b. 1824; d. 1872; m. 1856, Kathleen, dau. of Rev. Robert Traill, of Schull, co. Cork, and had issue,
  1. Robert Anthony, b. 1858.
  2. Edward, b. 1859; m. 11 Sept. 1885, Ellen Frances, eldest dau. of James Price, of Knockeevin, Greystone, co. Wicklow.
  3. Samuel, b. 1867.
  4. John Millington, b. 1871; d. 1908.
  1. Julia, d.   Jane, d.
  3. Elizabeth, d.

He m. 2ndly, Fanny, dau. of Sir Richard Steele, Bart., and d. 28 April 1845, leaving by her, who d. 8 June, 1861,
4. Samuel, d.
5. Richard, b. 1835; d. 1874; m. 1866, and had issue,
  Henry.
6. Robert, 90th Regiment, d. at Delhi, 1858.
7. Henry, 52nd Regiment, and Col. Turkish Gendarmerie, d.
8. George.
4. Isabella, m. Arthur Sanders (who d. —) of Fernhill, Isle of Wight, and has with other issue,
  Robert Arthur Sanders, of Barwick House, Yeovil, J.P., Barrister-at-Law, M.P. for Bridgewater, Div. Major R.N. Devon (Hussars). Clubs—Carlton, Arthur's, Garrick); b. 1867; m. 1893, Lucy, dau. of W. H. Halliday, of Glenthorne, Devon.
5. Frances Mary, m. 6 July, 1870, Rev. J. A. Owen, Fellow of Oriel Coll. Oxon, son of W. Owen, of Withybush, co. Pembroke.

The eldest son,
FRANCIS SYNGE, of Glanmore Castle, J.P., D.L. co. Wicklow, High Sheriff 1844, d.s.p. 1878, having m. 7 Nov. 1861, Editha Jane (now of Glanmore Castle), younger dau. of late Robert Holt Truell, J.P., D.L., of Clonmannon, co. Wicklow (see TRUELL of Clonmannon). She m. 2ndly, 20 Nov. 1879, Major Theodore Webber-Gardiner.

Arms—Quarterly: 1st and 4th, az., three millstones ppr.; 2nd and 3rd, arg., an eagle displayed with two heads sa., beaked and legged gu. **Crest**—Out of a ducal coronet an eagle's claw all ppr. **Motto**—Cœlestia caninus.

Residence—7, Albany Mansions, Battersea Park, S.W.

HART-SYNNOT OF BALLYMOYER.

The late MAJ.-GEN. ARTHUR FITZROY HART-SYNNOT, C.B., C.M.G., of Ballymoyer, co. Armagh, J.P., b. 4 May, 1844; m. 22 Dec. 1868, MARY SUSANNA, now of Ballymoyer, eldest dau. of Mark Seton Synnot, of Ballymoyer, D.L., and sister and co-heir of Mark Seton Synnot, of Ballymoyer, J.P., and d. 29 April, 1910, leaving issue,

1. ARTHUR HENRY SETON, D.S.O., Major E. Surrey Regt., b. 19 July, 1870.
2. Ronald Victor Okes, D.S.O., B.Sc. Lond., Lieut. E. Surrey Regt. (retired 1904), b. 24 July, 1879.
1. Beatrice May.   2. Horatia Annette Blanche.

Maj.-Gen. and Mrs. Hart assumed by Royal Licence, 17 Feb. 1902, the surname of SYNNOT in addition to and after that of HART, and the arms of Synnot quarterly with the arms of Hart. Maj.-Gen. Hart Synnot was educated at Cheltenham College, Royal Military College, Sandhurst, and Staff College; appointed an Ensign in the 31st Regt., 23 Dec. 1864; Lieut. 29 May, 1867; Capt. 13 June, 1874; Brevet Major 29 Nov. 1879; Major 1 July, 1881; Brevet Lieut.-Col. 18 Nov. 1882; Col. 18 Nov. 1886, Major-Gen. Commanding 1st Brigade Aldershot 1897-99, and 5th Brigade, &c., South

Synnot. THE LANDED GENTRY. 680

Africa Field Force 1899-1902 ; commanded the 1st Batt. East Surrey Regt. 1891-5. He received the 4th Class of the Order of Osmanieh for his services in Egypt in 1882, was made a Companion of the Bath 1889, and of the St. Michael and St. George 1900.

Lineage (of HART).—THE REV. WILLIAM HART, of the parish of Netherbury, co. Dorset, b. 1668-9, possessed land in Dorsetshire, namely, Corfe in the parish of West Milton, Pomice, Hurlands, Colmer's Estate, Camesworth, Greening's Orchard and Furzeleasc House, in Netherbury. He was bur. 11 June, 1746, at Netherbury, leaving, by Ann, his wife (b.1672-3, dau. of Christopher Travers, of Powerstock, Dorset), who was bur. there 10 Dec. 1735, with other issue, who d. young, a son,

WILLIAM HART, of Netherbury, bapt. there 13 Sept. 1707 ; Inherited his father's estates ; m. 20 April, 1731, Elizabeth, dau. of Richard Henvill, of Hacknolle, Netherbury. She was bur. 25 Oct. 1782. He was bur. 6 May, 1771, at Netherbury, leaving with two daus., Betty and Ann, both d. unm., an only surviving son,

GEORGE HART, of Netherbury, bapt. 12 Oct. 1744 ; possessed lands in Dorsetshire, namely, Corfe, Cape Leazne, and Pomice ; m. Elizabeth Hood, who was bur. 4 April, 1819, at Charmouth. He d. 24 May, 1824, leaving issue,

1. WILLIAM, of whom hereafter.
2. George, Ensign, 2 Sept. 1794 ; Lieut. 35tb (Dorsetshire) Regt. of Foot, 4 Nov. 1795. He held the lands of Pomice, Corfe, &c. ; d. unm. ; bur. 2 Aug. 1806, at Netherbury, aged 35.
1. Maria, d. unm. 1791.

His elder son,

WILLIAM HART, of Netherbury, b. 18 May, 1764 ; entered the Navy as a Midshipman ; afterwards appointed Ensign in the Dorsetshire Militia 13 Dec. 1792 ; Lieut. 28 June, 1793 ; Lieut. 111th Foot, 7 Aug. 1794 ; Cornet 28th Light Dragoons, 15 Aug. 1795 ; Lieut. 8th Light Dragoons, 3 May, 1799 ; Capt. Royal Train, 21 Feb. 1800 ; Major 20 Nov. 1805 ; Major 2nd Garrison Batt., 29 Jan. 1807 ; Brevet Lieut.-Col. 1 Jan. 1812 ; Major 60th Foot Royal Americans), 14 April, 1814 ; retired (by sale of Commission) 21 April, 1814 ; served as Cornet in Royal Wagon Train from 25 May, 1815, in Army of Occupation, Paris ; possessed the lands of Pomice, Hurlands, Colmer's Estate, Greening's Orchard, Ford, Coopers, Camesworth, &c. : m. 18 Jan. 1801, Jane, dau. of Charles Matson, of Wingham, co. Kent. Went to the Cape of Good Hope in 1819 ; he d. at Wynberg 1 Sept. 1848, aged 84. His widow d. 17 May, 1861, having had issue,

1. William, b. 24 Jan. 1805 ; m. and d. without issue, 3 Feb. 1865.
2. George, b. 10 Aug. 1806 ; d. young.
3. HENRY GEORGE, of whom hereafter.
4. Samuel Hood. b. 2 Nov. 1811 ; d. unm. 20 Nov. 1875.
5. Charles, of Loughton, co. Essex, b. 7 Feb. 1813 ; m. 1st, 29 March, 1845, Sophia, dau. of John Hawkes, of Wingham, co. Kent ; she d. 15 June, 1868. He m. 2ndly, 22 Dec. 1866, Caroline, dau. of James Fryer, of Sheffield, co. York, and d.s.p. 16 March,1886.
1. Eliza, m. 1st, Dec. 1821, Capt. George Scott, who d. 5 March, 1822, and 2ndly, 5 April, 1835, Thomas Holt Edward Okes, son of the Rev. Holt Okes, D.D. ; he d. 1861. She d. 28 Jan. 1883, leaving issue by both husbands.
2. Mary Anne, d. young.
3. Emily, d. unm. 1851.

His 3rd son,

LIEUT.-GEN. HENRY GEORGE HART, b. 7 Sept. 1808, Ensign 49th Regt. of Foot, 1 April, 1829 ; Lieut. 19 July, 1832 ; Capt. 1 Dec. 1842 ; Major 15 Dec. 1848 ; Brevet Lieut.-Col. 30 May, 1856 ; Col. 27 Dec. 1860 ; Major-Gen. 6 March, 1868 ; Lieut.-Gen. 4 Dec. 1877 ; m. 7 Jan. 1833, Frances Alicia, dau. of the Rev. Holt Okes, D.D. She d. 24 Dec. 1874. He d. 24 March, 1878, having had issue,

1. Henry Travers Holt. b. 8 May, 1836 ; d. 21 April, 1841.
2. Holt William, b. 27 June, 1838 ; drowned 20 July, 1850.
3. George Okes, b. 20 Jan. 1842 ; d. 19 June, 1851.
4. ARTHUR FITZROY, late of Ballymoyer.
5. Reginald Clare (Sir), V.C., K.C.B., K.C.V.O., b. 11 June, 1848 ; educated at Marlborough and Cheltenham Colleges, Royal Military Academy, Woolwich ; entered the Army as Lieut. Royal Engineers 13 Jan. 1869 ; Capt. 1 July, 1881 ; Brevet Major 18 Jan. 1882 ; Brevet-Lieut.-Col. 18 Nov. 1882 ; Col. 18 Nov. 1886 ; Major-Gen. 9 Dec. 1902 ; Lieut.-Gen. 18 Nov. 1908 ; Brigadier-Gen. Comg. Belgaum District, Madras, 1896-99 ; Maj.-Gen. Comg. Quetta 1899-1902, and Thames District since 1902-6 ; Gen. Comg. at Cape Colony District 1907-9 ; Royal Humane Society's silver medal 1860, silver clasp 1884 ; Medal of Honour, 1st class (French) 1880 ; received the Victoria Cross for gallantry in the Afghan War in 1879 from the Queen, 9 Dec. 1879, the 4th Class of the Order of Osmanieh for services in Egypt in 1882, C.B. in 1896, K.C.B. 1899, K.C.V.O. 1904, m. 6 Aug. 1872, Charlotte Augusta, dau. of the late Mark Seton Synnot, of Ballymoyer, co. Armagh, J.P. and D.L. for Armagh (see below), and has issue,

1. Harold Charles (twin), Capt. Royal Warwickshire Regt., b. 30 March, 1874.
2. Henry (twin), b. 30 March, 1874 ; d. same day.
3. Henry Francis, b. 7 June, and d. 16 Aug. 1876.
4. Reginald Seton, 2nd Lieut. Notts and Derbyshire Regt.. b. 27 June, 1882.
5. Norman Synnot, Lieut. " The Buffs," b. 24 March, 1888.
1. Annie Rosabe Care, d. unm. 4 Oct. 1902.
2. Sylvia Agnes Alicia, b. 31 May. 1885 ; m. 1st Jan. 1912, Capt. Warren Hastings D'Oyly, R.N., third surviving son of Sir Warren Hastings D'Oyly, Bart. (see BURKE's Peerage D'OYLY, Bart.).
6. Horatio Holt, b. 9 Aug. 1850 ; educated at Cheltenham College, Royal Military Academy, Woolwich ; entered the Army as Lieut. of Royal Engineers 23 July, 1870 ; Capt. 23 July, 1882 ;

Major 10 Jan. 1889 ; Lieut.-Col. 22 Oct. 1895 ; Brevet-Col. 22 Oct. 1899 ; m. 1st, 8 Aug. 1872, Emily Aline, dau. of James George Clements, of Redcliffe Square, and by her (who d. 10 March, 1902) has issue,

1. William Cecil, b. 16 Aug. 1877.
2. Laurence George, Capt. 61st Pioneers (Indian Army), twin with his brother ; m. 26 Dec. 1906, Winifred Beatrice Florence, dau. of G. Breithaupt, at Ootacamund, India.

He m. 2ndly, 2 April, 1903, Alice Maud, 4th dau. of H. B. Goodall, Barrister-at-Law, of Belvedere, Mussoorie.

1. Jane Margaret, b. 24 Jan. 1834 ; m. 14 Aug. 1862, James Curtis Leman, of Putney, co. Surrey, M.A. Cambridge, and d. 20 May, 1806, leaving issue. He d. 27 June, 1897.
2. Frances Alicia, b. 20 March, 1840 ; m. 25 April, 1867, Edward Coventry, of Holmleigh, Wandsworth Common, and has issue.
3. Isabel Clara, b. 4 June, 1846 ; m. 22 July, 1868, Francis Mackenzie Salmond, Lieut.-Col. 21st Royal Scots Fusiliers, and has issue (see SALMOND of Waterfoot). He d. 31 Oct. 1900.

Lineage (of SYNNOT).—TOBIAS SYNNOT, of co. Londonderry, gent., was brought up a Protestant, and was in Londonderry during its celebrated siege. His eldest son,

THOMAS SYNNOT, Town Major of the city of Dublin and Capt. in Lucas's Regt. of Foot 1711, whose will, dated 10 March, 1724, was proved 5 July, 1726, d. May, 1725, and left a son and heir,

RICHARD SYNNOT, of Drumcondragh, Registrar of the Diocese of Armagh, whose will, dated 28 March, 1727, was proved May, 1727. He m. April, 1694, Jane, dau. of Edward Bloxham, gent. of Dublin, and had (with a dau. Anne, m. St. John) a son,

MARK SYNNOT, of Drumcondragh, bapt. 8 May, 1696 ; d. 19 Nov. 1754. He m. 1st, Euphemia, dau. of — Rivers ; and 2ndly, 16 Sept. 1769, Anne, dau. of Walter Nugent, of Carpenterstown, co. Westmeath, by whom he had issue,

1. Mark, of Drumcondragb, m. 28 Feb. 1777, Susanna, dau. of James Nugent, of Carpenterstown, co. Westmeath, co-heir, and eventually sole heir, of her only brother, John Nugent,* and by her (who d. 29 March, 1778) had issue, an only son, Mark, his heir. Mr. Synnot served the office of High Sheriff of Westmeath 1778, and dying March, 1789, was s. by his only son,
    Mark Synnot, of Monasteroris House, King's Co., b. 20 Dec. 1777 ; m. June, 1807, Mary, dau. of Robert Wilson, of Monasteroris, and by her (who d. 14 Feb. 1841) had issue,
    (1) John, d. unm. at Madeira, 27 Feb. 1839.
    (2) Richard, d. unm. 17 Feb. 1841, when the male line of the elder branch of Synnot became extinct, and the estates devolved upon the daus. as co-heirs-at-law.
    (1) Susanna, d. unm. 11 March, 1842.
    (2) Maria, m. 4 Aug. 1842, George Woods Maunsell, 2nd son of Richard Maunsell, of Oakly Park, co. Kildare, and has issue (see MAUNSELL of Oakly Park).
    (3) Anne Jane, m. 24 Aug. 1843, Mark Seton Synnot, late of Ballymoyer, and d. 4 Nov. 1898, leaving issue (see below).
    (4) Charlotte Augusta, m. 10 Dec. 1846, Charles Cottingham, only son of James Johnstone, of Drum, co. Monaghan, and left issue,
        Charles Synnot JOHNSTONE, 7th Dragoon Guards, d. at Melbourne, Victoria, March, 1878.
        Florence, m.
    Mrs. Johnstone d. at Teneriffe 16 Nov. 1853, and Mr. Johnstone at Baden-Baden, July, 1870.
    Mr. Synnot d. at Grove House, Clapham, 7 June, 1838.
2. WALTER (Sir), of whom presently.
1. Mary, m. 1766, William Smyth, of Drumcree, co. Westmeath, and by him (who d. May, 1827) bad issue (see that family).

The 2nd son,

SIR WALTER SYNNOT, Knt. of Ballymoyer, High Sheriff co. Armagh 1783, m. 1st, 1770, Jane dau. of John Seton, of Camberwell, representative of SETON of Parbroath, and sister of John Seton, of New York, and by her (who d. 1803) had issue,

1. MARCUS, his heir.
2. Walter, of Ballintate, co. Armagh, Capt. 66th Regt., m. 1st. Catherine, dau. of Henry Smith, of Beabeg, near Drogheda, and by her had an only son,
    1. Walter, b. 12 March, 1807.
  He m. 2ndly, Elizabeth, dau. of George Houston, and by her (who d. 1834) had issue,
    2. Robert, m. 1 July, 1846, Catherine, eldest dau. of — Balintine, d. 1871, leaving issue.
    3. George, of Fernside, Geelong, m. 12 Dec. 1844, Catherine

---

* Richard, 10th Lord Delvin, d. 1450, leaving issue (besides Christopher, his successor · Robert, of Drumcree, and Lavallin, of Dysert) a 4th son, Andrew Nugent, of Donore, who left (besides Walter of Donore) a 2nd son, Andrew Nugent, of Clonlost, who d., leaving Christopher, of Clonlost, who d., leaving James, of Clonlost, who d., leaving Thomas, of Clonlost, m. Ismay, dau. of Theobald Nugent, of Newhaggard, and left issue, James, of Clonlost, and Christopher, of Wardenstown, and Rathfarn. James, the eldest son, had issue (besides Thomas, who s. his father at Clonlost) a son,

Walter Nugent, of Carpenterstown, s. his father in the Clondelinn and Kingsland (now Reynalla) estates, and in 1719 s. also to his cousin, Haytor Nugent, d.s.p., only son and heir of Christopher Nugent, of Wardenstown, in the Higginstown and Rathfarn estates, which had been granted to his father by CHARLES II., for his losses in the Royalist cause. He left besides other issue, an eldest son, James, who m. Deborah, dau. of J. Staunton, of Galway, and bad issue, John and Susanna, m. Mark Synnot. John d. unm. 1776, when all his estates devolved upon his sister, Susanna, in whose descendants, being the descendants of Mark Synnot, of Drumcondragh, they still remain.

IRELAND. Taaffe.

Holmes, 2nd dau. of Joseph Mather, of Maytone House, co. Armagh, and *d.* 1 July, 1871, leaving issue by her, who *d.* 13 Feb. 1881,
  (1) Walter Seton, *b.* 24 May, 1847; *m.* 23 March, 1872, Lucy Emily Nixon, dau. of William Lucas, and has a dau. Anna Lucas, *b.* 16 March, 1873.
  (2) George Nugent, *b.* 29 Oct. 1849.
  (1) Mary Jane Cumberland, *m.* 10 Jan. 1862, David Boswell Reid, and *d.* 4 Jan. 1874, leaving issue.
  (2) Catherine, *m.* 26 Aug. 1873, Travers Adamson, B.L., son of Travers Adamson, of Carn Park, co. Westmeath, and by him (who *d.* 4 April, 1897), had issue, three daus., Mary Synnot Travers, Catherine Fanny Travers, and Janet Adelaide Travers.
4. Marcus, *d.s.p.*   5. Albert Erasmus, *d.* Dec. 1859, *s.p.*
6. Monckton, *m.* and had issue.
7. William, *d.s.p.*
8. Nugent.
  1. Jane, *m.* Thomas Manifold, and had issue.
  2. Mary Anne, *m.* 11 Feb. 1857, Rev. Montagu Williams.
  3. Catherine, *m.* — Cobham.
Capt. Synnot *m.* 3rdly, 8 April, 1836, Mary Jane, youngest dau. of Joseph Mather of Maytone House, co. Armagh, by whom (who *m.* 2ndly, Charles MacArthur, 2nd son of Hannibal Hawkins MacArthur, M.P.) he had no issue. He *d.* 1850.
Sir Walter *m.* 2ndly, 10 Aug.1804, Ann Elizabeth, dau. of Rev. Robert Martin, and had by her a dau., Elizabeth, wife of Rev. Fitzgibbon Stewart, and a son,
3. Richard Walter, *m.* 12 April, 1836, Henrietta, dau. of Henry Thornton, of Battersea Rise (who *d.* 1853), and *d.* 20 April, 1841, leaving a son, Robert Harry Inglis, M.A., Ch. Ch. Oxford, 1863, *m.* Mary, dau. of — Preston, and *d.* 12 April, 1872, *s.p.*, and a dau., Henrietta Louisa.
The son and heir,
MARCUS SYNNOT, of Ballymoyer, J.P., served as High Sheriff co. Armagh 1830, *b.* 21 June, 1771; *m.* 29 June, 1814, Jane, dau. of Thomas Gilson, of Wood Lodge, co. Lincoln, and by her had issue,
1. MARCUS, his heir.
2. MARK SETON, of Ballymoyer, heir to his brother.
3. Parker George, *b.* 1824; *m.* 9 Oct. 1856, Georgiana Thorpe, eldest dau. of William Verrail, of The Manor House, Lewes, Sussex, and had issue,
  1. Marcus, *b.* 22 Jan. 1858.   2. William George.
  1. Georgiana Constance, *d.* 1870.
  2. Jane Seton, *m.* 1887, Rev. James Madden Ford, B.A.
4. William Forbes, Capt. Armagh Light Infantry, *d.s.p.* 29 Feb. 1876.
  1. Mary Marcia, *d.* Aug. 1869.
  2. Maria Eliza, *m.* Sept. 1848, Rev. Alexander Rowley Miller, Rector of Lissan, co. Tyrone, and has issue; he *d.* 1877.
  3. Agnes Jane, *m.* 17 July, 1851, Rev. Francis Crawford, Rector of Derryloran, co. Tyrone, and has issue.
  4. Barbara Cecilia, *m.* 22 Sept. 1869, George Crawhall, of The Priory, Nun-Monkton, co. York.
  5. Juliana Hewitt.
Mr. Synnot *d.* 3 Feb 1855, and was *s.* by his eldest son,
MARCUS SYNNOT, of Ballymoyer House, J.P. and D.L., High Sheriff 1856, *b.* 19 Feb. 1813; *m.* 28 Feb. 1844, Ann, eldest dau. of William Parker, of Hanthorpe House, co. Lincoln, and *d.s.p.* 8 Oct. 1874, when the estates devolved on his brother,
MARK SETON SYNNOT, of Ballymoyer, co. Armagh, J.P., D.L., High Sheriff 1876, *b.* 31 July, 1820; *m.* 24 Aug. 1843, Anne Jane, 2nd dau. and co-heir of Mark Synnoth, of Monasteroris House, King's Co., and Grove House, Clapham, Surrey, and by her (who *d.* 14 Nov. 1898) had issue,
1. MARK SETON, late of Ballymoyer.
1. MARY SUSANNA, now of Ballymoyer.
2. Rosalie Jane.
3. Eva Charlotte, *m.* 22 Jan. 1875, Capt. Corbet Smith, 1st Royal Dragoons, of Walcot House, Lutterworth, co. Leicester, and has issue, Ada Emily Corbet.   4. Cecilia Agnes.
5. Charlotte Augusta, *m.* 6 Aug. 1872, Major-Gen. Sir Reginald Clare Hart, V.C., K.C.B., K.C.V.O., R.E., 2nd son of Lieut.-Gen. Henry George Hart, and has issue (*see* HART *lineage*).
6. Ada Maria.
7. Annette Beatrice, *d.* an infant.
Mr. Synnot *d.* 1890, when he was *s.* by his only son,
MARK SETON SYNNOT, of Ballymoyer, co. Armagh, J.P., formerly Capt. Armagh Light Infantry, *b.* 1847, and *d. unm.* 16 Aug. 1901, when he was *s.* by his eldest sister.

Arms—(H. Coll.)- Quarterly 1st and 4th arg., three swans in pale sa;, ducally gorged or, on a canton gu. a sword in pale ppr. (SYNNOT); 2nd and 3rd sa., a chevron or between two stag's heads caboshed in chief of the last and three swords one in pale surmounted by two in saltire points downwards in base ppr. pommels and hilts gold (HART). Crest—1. SYNNOT: A swan issuant, wings expanded sa., ducally crowned or, and vulned in the breast with an arrow gold, feathered arg.   2. HART: A stag's head between two antlers all ppr.   Mottoes—SYNNOT: Sine macula. HART: Celer atque fidelis.

Seat—Ballymoyer, co. Armagh.

———

TAAFFE OF SMARMORE.

GEORGE JOSEPH TAAFFE, of Smarmore Castle, and Glenkeiran, co. Louth, J.P. and D.L. co. Louth, High Sheriff 1907, J.P. co. Meath, late Capt. 4th Batt. Royal Lancaster Regt., *b.* 29 April, 1866; *s.* his cousin, 1894; *m.* 18 July, 1895, Alice Catherine Trevor, younger dau. of B. T. Griffith Boscawen, D.L., of Trevalyn, co. Denbigh (*see that family*), and has issue,

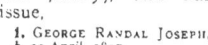

1. GEORGE RANDAL JOSEPH, *b.* 29 April, 1897.
2. Rudolph Trevor Aloysius, *b.* 21 June, 1901.
1. Maureen Helen, *b.* 1 Sept. 1910.

Lineage.—The Taaffes were seated at Smarmore in the 14th century. In 1320 the Prior of Kilmanham sued William Taaffe, of Smarmore, for a coeurcate of land in Coynstown, *see* D'ALTON, *Dublin*). They also held land in many other parts of the present county of Louth. The wills of Sir William Taaffe, of Smarmore, Knight, and Lady Ismay, his widow, were proved in Dublin in 1631. He was High Sheriff of Louth in 1624.
PETER TAAFFE, of Pepparstown and Dromine, co. Louth, brother of Sir William Taaffe, ancestor of the VISCOUNTS TAAFFE (*see* BURKE's *Peerage*), and son of John Taaffe, of Harristown, *m.* and had issue,
1. Jenico, father of John Taaffe, of Carrowstown and Rathmoyle, Roscommon, of which he had a grant 1 May, 30 CHARLES II, 1678.
2. LAWRENCE.
The 2nd son,
LAWRENCE TAAFFE, of Pepparstown, who had a grant of confirmation 1624, was father of
JAMES TAAFFE, of Pepparstown, who was deprived of his estate by the usurping powers under CROMWELL. He *m.* Margaret, dau. of Clement MacDermott Roe, of co. Roscommon, and had, with other issue,
1. John Taaffe, *m.* and had issue.
2. GEORGE, of whom presently.
3. Peter, Major of Dillon's Regt. of the Irish Brigade, *m.* a dau. of Garvey, by his wife, a Plowden, and had issue, Mary and Frances.
4. Lawrence (Rev.).
The elder son,
GEORGE TAAFFE, of Corballis, co. Meath, *m.* Miss Fleming, of the Slane family, and had issue,
1. JOHN, his heir.
1. Alicia, *m.* James Lynch, of Drogheda.
2. Elizabeth, *m.* Randal Kernan, of Dublin.
3. Mary, *m.* Luke Teeling, of Lisburn.
The son and heir,
JOHN TAAFFE, of Smarmore, co. Louth, *b.* 1746, *m.* 1st, Miss Plunkett, of Portmarnock, co. Dublin, and by her had issue,
1. Elizabeth, *m.* Patrick Thunder, of Lagore.
2. Mary, *d. unm.*
3. Alicia, *m.* Michael Sweetman, of Longtown, and *d.* leaving issue.
He *m.* 2ndly, Catharine, dau. and co-heir of Robert Taaffe, of Ardmulchan, co. Meath, and *d.* 16 Sept. 1825, having by her (who *d.* 1 Oct. 1823) had issue,
1. John, Knight of St. John of Jerusalem, *m.* 1st, Catherine, dau. of Andrew Fitzgerald, Gen. in India, and had a son, John, Knight of St. John of Jerusalem, late Capt. of Dragoons in Piedmont and Major Louth Rifles. He *m.* 2ndly, Adriana Ferro, Marchesa Gabucini, Comtessa Ferretti Villa Nova, Boccacio Pausneci, of Fano, in the Papal States, and *d.* at Fano, in Italy, 28 Sept. 1862.
2. ROBERT, of Ardmulchan, co. Meath, *m.* 30 April, 1827, Catharine Isabella, only dau. of Theobald Mackenna, Dublin, and *d.* 12 June, 1854, leaving issue,
   JOHN ROBERT, of Ardmulchan, J.P., *b.* 31 March, 1829; *m.* 4 Nov. 1857, Catalina Aliaga, dau. of Patrick William Kelly, of Kingstown, co. Dublin, by Rosita Manuela Aliaga, his wife, dau. of Juan de Aliaga, Marquis of Lurigarcho, in Spain, and *d.* 1886, leaving issue,
     (1) ROBERT JOSEPH, of Ardmulchan, *b.* 18 Oct. 1858, dec.
     (2) Theobald Joseph, *b.* 10 Aug. 1861, dec.
     (3) John Joseph, *b.* 26 Aug. 1864, dec.
     (1) Rosita Mary.   (2) Mary Catalina.
   Frances, *d. unm.* 4 Feb. 1908.
3. GEORGE, of whom presently.   4. Stephen, *d. unm.*
4. Catharine, *m.* John McDonnell, and *d.* leaving a son, John Randal.
5. Achsah Elinor, a nun, dec.   6. Mary Jane, *d. unm.*
7. Anne, *m.* Count Luigi Burgogeli, of Fano, in the Papal States, dec.
8. Rose, dec.   8. Frances, dec.

10. Martha, dec.
11. Julia, m. Theobald Mackenna, Assistant Under-Secretary, Dublin Castle, and had a son, John Mackenna, and other issue.

The 3rd son,

GEORGE TAAFFE, of Smarmore Castle, m. 1814, Elizabeth Anne, dau. of Randall McDonnell, of Fairfield, co. Dublin, and by her (who d. 1856) had issue,

1. Randall, d. unm. 1848.   2. MYLES, his heir.
3. George, Capt. 1st Royals, d. unm. at sea 1861.
4. JOHN, of Smarmore, of whom presently.
5. Stephen, of Glenkeiran, co. Meath, J.P., b. 1828, m. 1865, Mary Aliaga, dau. of Patrick William Kelly, of Kingstown, co. Dublin (see above), and d. 4 April, 1894, leaving issue,
   1. GEORGE JOSEPH, now of Smarmore.
   1. Mary.   2. Rosita Mary.
3. Elizabeth Mary, m. April, 1899, F. F. Kilkelly, who d. April, 1901, leaving a dau., Stephanie Mary.
4. Catalina Mary.   5. Georgina Mary.
1. Anna, d. unm. 1877.   2. Catherine
3. Bridgett, d. unm. 1837.   4. Mary, d. unm. 1846.
5. Elizabeth, d. unm. 1875.   6. Georgina, d. unm. 1903.

Mr. Taaffe d. 1848, and was s. by his 2nd son,

MYLES TAAFFE, of Smarmore, J.P. and D.L., High Sheriff 1856-7, b. April, 1824 ; d. unm. 1872, and was s. by his brother,

JOHN TAAFFE, of Smarmore, J.P. and D.L. for Louth, J.P. for King's Co., High Sheriff co. Louth, 1878 ; m. 1867, Olivia Mary, dau. of John Joseph Blake, of Garbally, King's Co. (see BLAKE of Ballyglunin Park), and had issue,

GEORGE ROBERT, late of Smarmore.

Mr Taaffe d. 1890. His only son,

GEORGE ROBERT TAAFFE of Smarmore, b. 1871, d. unm. 1894, and was s. by his cousin.

Arms—Gu., a cross arg., fretty az. Crest—A dexter arm in armour embowed, brandishing a sword ppr., hilt and pommel or. Motto—In hoc signo, spes mea.

Seats—Smarmore Castle, Ardee, and Glenkeiran, co. Meath.

TABUTEAU-HERRICK. See HERRICK.

TALBOT OF CASTLE TALBOT.

JOHN HYACINTH TALBOT, of Castle Talbot, of co. Wexford, J.P. and D.L., High Sheriff 1894, b. 13 Dec. 1851 ; m. 23 July, 1896, Emily, dau. of Heffernan Considine, D.L., of Derk, co. Limerick (see that family).

Lineage.—WALTER TALBOT, Clerk of the Crown for co. Wexford, was a party in a suit in Chancery 1586. He m. Joane, dau. and co-heir of Jasper Bolane, of Talbotstown, co. Wexford, and left issue,

Francis, of whom presently.

Elinor, wife of Patrick Walsh, of Ballyclonecranell.

The only son,

FRANCIS TALBOT, of Ballynamony, who was granted that estate now called Castle Talbot, in the territory of O'Morchoe's county and co. Wexford, by patent dated 20 Feb. 1617. He m. Anne, dau. of Sir William Synnott, Knt. of Ballyfarnoge, co. Wexford, and had, with two daus. (Joan, m. Col. John Synnott, and Margaret, m. Mark Synnott), a son,

WALTER TALBOT, of Ballynamony, High Sheriff co. Wexford 1649. He m. Elinor, dau. of William Esmonde, of Johnstown, co. Wexford, and had,
1. WILLIAM, his heir.
2. Charles, of Curraghcloe, m. Anne Wallis.
3. Elinor, m. James Sherlock, of Ballyna.

Mr. Talbot was s. by his eldest son,

WILLIAM TALBOT, of Ballynamony, M.P. for Wexford in King JAMES II.'s Parliament 1689, killed at the siege of Derry, on King JAMES'S side ; he m. Margaret, dau. of Richard Masterson, of Castletown, co. Wexford, by whom he left issue,
1. ROGER, his heir.
2. Gabriel (Rev.), Superior of the College of Oporto.
3. Richard, of Ballynagore.   4. James, in the Spanish Army.
1. Mary, m. James Byrne, of Coolnehorney.
2. Elinor, m. Walter Butler, of Tullow, co. Carlow.
3. Anne, m. Capt. Mayo, R.N.

Mr. Talbot was s. by his eldest son,

ROGER TALBOT, of Ballynamony, m. 1st, Margaret, dau. of Robert Walsh, of The Walsh Mountains, co. Kilkenny, and had issue,
1. WILLIAM, his heir.

He m. 2ndly, Elizabeth, dau. of Patrick Fitzpatrick, of Ballybooden, Queen's Co., by whom he had issue,

2. MATHEW, successor to his brother.
1. Catherine, m. Dominick Ford, of Ballyfad.
2. Margaret, m. Edmund Loghlin, of Durrow.

Mr. Talbot was s. by the son of his 1st marriage,

WILLIAM TALBOT, of Castle Talbot, m. Teresa, dau. of John Smith, of Dama, co. Kilkenny, and had issue,
1. ROGER, d.v.p.
2. Jane, m. April, 1763. Edward Masterson, brother of Luke Masterson, of Castletown.
2. Elizabeth, m. Laurence O'Toole, of Buxtown, and had issue, Bryan O'Toole, Lieut.-Col. of the 7th Portuguese Regt. of Cacadores, C.B., Knt. of St. Louis of France, d. 1824.
3. Margaret, m. Edward Sutton, brother of Count Sutton de Clonard, of France.

Mr. Talbot, whose will was dated 22 June, 1750, d. that year and was s. by his half-brother,

MATHEW TALBOT, of Castle Talbot, m. 1st, Juliana, dau. of Richard Donovan, of Camolin (see DONOVAN of Ballymore), and widow of Richard, 6th Earl of Anglesey, and had by her (who d. 20 Nov. 1776, and was buried with her 1st husband, at Rossminoge, co. Wexford) a son,
1. WILLIAM, his heir.

He m. 2ndly, 11 July, 1783, a dau. of John D'Arcy, of Kiltullagh, co. Galway, and widow of Count D'Arcy, of France, and dying 27 Oct. 1795, left
2. Mathew Roger D'Arcy, Capt. co. Stafford Militia, b. 1786 ; d. unm. 1850.
3. JOHN HYACINTH, who eventually s. to Castle Talbot.
4. James, of Knockmullen, co. Wexford. J.P., Lieut. in the 1st Regt. of Foot Guards, present at the Battle of Waterloo, b. 1794, m. 1824, Mary, dau. of Edward Sutton, of Summer Hill, co. Wexford, and d. 1852, having had issue,
   1. George, of Knockmullen, C.B., J.P. co. Wexford, Chief Commissioner of the Dublin Metropolitan Police from 1871 to 1882, formerly Capt. 13th Light Infantry, served throughout the first Afghan Campaign (medal), b. 1823, m. 1852, Mary (d. 25 Feb. 1908), dau. of Francis O'Beirne, of Jamestown, co. Leitrim, and has issue,
      (1) George James Francis, Major late R.A., served in S. African Campaign (medal, despatches), b. 3 Jan. 1857 ; m. Mary, dau. of Henry Schlesinger, and has issue,
         Roger, b. 14 July, 1898.
      (1) Augusta, d. unm. 8 May, 1884.   (2) Gwendoline.
   2. Mathew Edward, d. unm. 20 March, 1869.
   3. Henry John, d. unm. 1876.
   1. Margaret Matilda, m. 27 March, 1843, Hon. John Charles Dundas, 2nd son of Lawrence, 1st Earl of Zetland. He d. 14 Feb. 1866. She d. 8 Dec. 1907, leaving issue (see BURKE'S Peerage, ZETLAND, M.).
   2. Mary Anne.
1. Margaret Matilda, d. unm. in Paris, bur. at Père la Chaise.
2. Anne, Canoness of the Order of Bavaria, d. unm.

Mr. Talbot d. 1795, and was s. by his eldest son,

WILLIAM TALBOT, of Castle Talbot, b. 19 Jan. 1765 ; m. 1st, 30 Jan. 1785, Mary, dau. of Laurence O'Toole, of Buxtown, co. Wexford and by her (who d. 19 May, 1796) had issue,
1. Matthew, b. 7 March, 1787 ; m. Anne, dau. of Laurence O'Rourke, of Bluebell, co. Dublin, and d. 15 Nov. 1838, having had issue,
   Matthew St. Lawrence, d.v.p. Feb. 1832.
   Elizabeth, d. at Brussels, 19 June, 1839.
2. WILLIAM, heir to his father.
3. Laurence, R.N., d. at sea, 8 Nov. 1813.
1. Maria, m. 27 June, 1814, John, 16th Earl of Shrewsbury and Waterford ; d. 4 June, 1856.
2. Julia, m. 7 Sept. 1815, Patrick Bishop, of Bishop's Court, co. Waterford ; d. Feb. 1820.
3. Margaret, m. 20 March, 1820, George Bryan, of Jenkinstown, co. Kilkenny, and had issue,
   George Bryan, late of Jenkinstown.
   Augusta Mary, wife of Edward, 2nd Lord Bellew (see BURKE'S Peerage).

Mr. Talbot m. 2ndly, 24 Aug. 1796, Anne, dau. of Robert Woodcock, of Killown, co. Wexford, and by her (who d. 11 March, 1808) had issue,
4. Robert, Lieut. in the Royal Guard of France, b. 1799 ; d.s.p.
5. John, Lieut. in the Royal Guard of France ; b. 1800, d. in Bombay.
6. Charles, b. 1801 ; d. in Jamacia.
7. George, b. 1804 ; d. at Richmond, in Virginia, North America, 1829.
4. Anne, d. 30 Nov. 1865.
5. Catharine, m. 11 June, 1835, Henry Lambert, of Carnagh, D.L. co. Wexford, and had issue (see that family).

Mr. Talbot m. 3rdly, 11 Sept. 1808, Anne, dau. of John Beaumont, of Hyde Park, co. Wexford. He was s. by his eldest surviving son,

WILLIAM TALBOT, of Castle Talbot, J.P., Capt. 27th Regt., and Major in the Queen of Spain's service, b. 29 Jan. 1789 ; m. 1st, Honora, dau. of John Power, sister of Edmund Power, of Gurteen, co. Waterford, and widow of Major Quin, Scots Fusiliers and 2ndly, Sept. 1859, Charlotte, dau. of Macarius John Kennedy, and d.s.p. 3 Jan. 1861, when he was s. by his uncle,

JOHN HYACINTH TALBOT, of Castle Talbot, Talbot Hall, and Ballytrent, J.P., D.L., M.P., m. 1st, 10 May, 1822, Anne Eliza, only dau. and heir of Walter Redmond, of Ballytrent, co. Wexford, and by her (who d. 1826) had three daus. (co-heirs of their mother),
1. Anne Eliza Mary, m. 30 Aug. 1824, Sir Thomas N. Redington, K.C.B., of Kilcornan, co. Galway, who d. 1862.
2. Jane Anne Eliza, m. 26 Jan. 1843, Sir James Power, 2nd bart. of Edermine, co. Wexford, who d. 30 Sept. 1877.

3. Matilda Anna Eliza, *m.* 23 May, 1848, O'Neill S grave, of Cabra House, co. Dublin, and Kiltimon, co. Wicklow, who *d.* 1878.
He *m.* 2ndly, 25 Feb. 1851, Eliza, 5th dau. of Sir John Power, 1st bart. of Edermine, and by her, who *d.* 1892, had issue,
1. JOHN HYACINTH, now of Castle Talbot.
4. Emily Mary, *m.* 8 Jan. 1880, Sir Heffernan James Fritz Joseph John Considine, C.B., D.L., B.A. Oxon, eldest son of Heffernan Considine, J.P., of Derk, co. Limerick. She *d.* 1903, leaving issue (see that family).

Arms—Gu., a lion rampant within a bordure engrailed or.
Crest—On a chapeau gu., turned up erm., a lion statant or.
Motto—Prêt d'accomplir.
Seats—Castle Talbot, Blackwater, co. Wexford ; and Ballytrent, Broadway. **Club**—Stephen's Green, Dublin.

TALBOT OF MOUNT TALBOT.

WILLIAM JOHN TALBOT, of Mount Talbot, co. Roscommon, J.P. and D.L. co. Roscommon, J.P. co. Galway, High Sheriff for co. Roscommon, 1886, and for Armagh, 1903, late Capt. 7th Brigade South Irish Division R.A., *b.* 1 July, 1859 ; *m.* 14 Aug. 1895, Julia Elizabeth Mary, only child of Sir Capel Molyneux, Bart., D.L., Castle Dillon, co. Armagh.

Lineage.—RICHARD TALBOT, of Templeogue, co. Dublin, 2nd Justice of the Court of Common Pleas in Ireland 1557. *d.* 1577, son of William Talbot, a younger son of Talbot of Malahide, *m.* Alice, dau. of John Burnel, of Balgriffin, and was father of
JOHN TALBOT, of Templeogue, whose will was proved in 1584, father of
ROBERT TALBOT, of Templeogue, *d.* 1616 ; *m.* Eleanor, dau. of Sir Henry Colley, of Castle Carbury (see BURKE's *Peerage,* WELLINGTON, DUKE OF), and had two sons,
1. John, of Templeogue, *d.s.p.* 1627.
2. Henry, who succeeded.
The younger son,
Sir HENRY TALBOT, of Templeogue, Knt., *m.* Margaret, dau. of Sir William Talbot, Bart., of Carton, co. Kildare, and sister of Richard, Duke of Tyrconnell, and by her (who *d.* 14 Dec. 1603) had two sons and six daus.,
1. James, his heir, of Templeogue, and Mount Talbot, co. Roscommon, a Col. in JAMES II.'s Army, killed at the Battle of Aughrim 12 July, 1691. He *m.* Hon. Bridget Bermingham, dau. of Francis, 17th Baron Athenry, and by her (who *m.* 2ndly, Capt. Thomas Burke, and *d.* 20 March, 1699) had two daus.,
1. Mary, *m.* Oct. 1684, John, Lord Bophin, afterwards 9th Earl of Clanricarde.
2. Bridget, *m.* Valentine Browne, of Mount Browne, co. Mayo (see SLIGO, MARQUESS OF).
2. WILLIAM, who s. his brother.
1. Elizabeth, *m.* Col. John Talbot, of Belgard, co. Dublin.
2. Bridget, *m.* Garret Dillon, of Manin, co. Mayo.
3. Mary, *m.* Theobald, 7th Viscount Mayo (see BURKE's *Peerage*).
4. Alice, *m.* Edmund Moore, of Clonbrany, co. Mayo.
5. Ellen, *m.* Laurence Cruise, of Cruisetown, co. Meath.
6. Barbara, *m.* Dominick Browne, of Breaghwy, co. Mayo (see that family).
The younger son,
WILLIAM TALBOT, of Mount Talbot, *d.* 1692 ; *m.* Lucy, widow of George Holmes, dau. and co-heir of William Hamilton, of Lischoony, King's Co. (see HOLMES of *St. David's*), and had a son,
HENRY TALBOT, of Mount Talbot, High Sheriff 1713, *d.* 1729 ; *m.* Isabella Forward, and had two sons,
1. WILLIAM, his heir.
2. John (Rev.), Rector of Kirklington, York, *d.* June 1773, leaving by Mary his wife (who *d.* Dec. 1768) a son,
Henry Herbert, *b.* 1765.
The eldest son,
WILLIAM TALBOT, of Mount Talbot, High Sheriff 1753, *d.* May, 1787 ; *m.* 30 May, 1739, Sarah, widow of John Southwell, and dau. of Mr. Justice Rose (see ROSE *of Ahabeg*), and by her (who *d.* 9 Dec. 1778) had two sons and a dau.,
1. Henry Rose, *d.s.p.* 29 Dec. 1759.
2. WILLIAM JOHN, who s.
1. Bridget, *m.* Henry La Rive.
2. Jane, *m.* 1765, Thomas Wills of Willsgrove (see WILLS-SANDFORD).
The younger son,
WILLIAM JOHN TALBOT, of Mount Talbot, *d.* Aug. 1787 ; *m.* 1st,

2 Oct. 1765, Elizabeth Margaret, dau. of George Rose of Moyvane, co. Limerick, and had a dau.,
1. Jane, *m.* Aug. 1786, Sir Edmund Stanley.
He *m.* 2ndly, 24 May, 1775, Lady Anne Crosbie, dau. of William, 1st Earl of Glandore, and had issue,
1. William, of Mount Talbot, High Sheriff 1819, *d.s.p.* 1851 ; *m.* 20 Dec. 1802, Susanna, dau. of Thomas Kemmis (see KEMMIS *of Shaen*).
2. JOHN, of whom presently
3. Charles, Capt. 5th Fusiliers, killed at Walcheren.
2. Theodosia, *m.* 1802, Commodore Thomas Gordon Caulfeild, of Curraghmore, co. Roscommon, who *d.* 23 June, 1825, leaving issue (see BURKE's *Peerage*, CHARLEMONT, V.).
The 2nd son,
REV. JOHN TALBOT, assumed the name and arms of CROSBIE, in pursuance of the will of his uncle, John, last Earl of Glandore, by Royal Licence, 14 Feb. 1816. He *m.* Sept. 1811, Jane, dau. of Lieut.-Col. Thomas Lloyd, of Beechmount, co. Limerick, and had issue,
1. WILLIAM, the late WILLIAM TALBOT CROSBIE, of Ardfert Abbey, co. Kerry. 2. JOHN, of Mount Talbot.
1. Anne, *m.* 27 June, 1839, Rev. M. A. Cooke.
2. Diana, *m.* 6 Aug. 1835, Edward Thomas Coke, of Debdale, Notts, and of Trusley, co. Derby, Hon. Col. 1st Derbyshire Militia, and has issue.
Mr. Talbot Crosbie *d.* Jan. 1818. His 2nd son,
JOHN TALBOT, of Mount Talbot, co. Roscommon, J.P. and D.L. High Sheriff 1857, formerly of the 35th Regt., assumed by Royal Licence 23 Sept. 1851, the name and arms of Talbot instead of Crosbie ; *b.* 4 Oct. 1818 ; *m.* 1st, 2 Jan. 1845, Marianne, eldest dau. of Marcus McCausland, of Fruit Hill, co. Londonderry, and by this marriage (which was dissolved by Act of Parliament, 20 July, 1856) he had an only dau. Marianne Jane Theodosia, *m.* 21 Oct. 1869, Arthur Rickard Lloyd, son of Thomas Lloyd, D.L., of Beechmount, co. Limerick, and *d.* 3 Jan. 1894. Mr. J. Talbot *m.* 2ndly, 15 Oct. 1858, Gertrude Caroline, dau. of Lieut.-Col. Bayly, of Ballyarthur, co. Wicklow, and by her (who *m.* 2ndly, 18 Aug. 1864, Hon. F. G. Crofton, and *d.* 19 Aug. 1867), had a son, WILLIAM JOHN, now of Mount Talbot. Mr. John Talbot *d.* 16 July, 1895.

Arms—Quarterly : 1st and 4th, arg., a lion rampant within a bordure engrailed gu., for TALBOT ; 2nd, arg., a lion rampant sa., armed and langued gu. ; in chief two dexter hands apaumée of the third, for CROSBIE ; 3rd, gu., three cinquefoils, two and one, erm., for HAMILTON. **Crests**—1st, on a cap of maintenance az., turned up erm., a lion passant gu., for TALBOT ; 2nd, three swords, one in pale with point upwards and two in saltire with points downwards, entwined with a serpent, all ppr., for CROSBIE. **Motto**—Prêt d'accomplir.
Seat—Mount Talbot, co. Roscommon. **Clubs**—White's, S.W., Kildare Street, Dublin, and Royal St. George's Yacht Club, Kingstown.

TALBOT. See BURKE'S PEERAGE, **TALBOT DE MALAHIDE, B.**

TALBOT-CROSBIE. See **CROSBIE.**

TALBOT-PONSONBY. See **PONSONBY.**

TARLETON OF KILLEIGH.

JOHN WILLIAM FRANCIS TARLETON, of Killeigh and Fenter, King's Co., *b.* 2 Aug. 1875, late Capt. Inniskilling Dragoons.

Lineage.—GILBERT TARLETON, of Hazlewood, near Liverpool, settled in Ireland in the 16th century. He is recorded in Ulster's Office as being present at the funeral of Thomas Ruish, eldest son of Sir Francis Ruishe, at St. Audeon's, Dublin, 21 Nov. 1629. He *d.* July, 1656, and was buried at Geashill, King's Co. By his wife, Muriel (who *d.* 25 March, 1673, and was bur. at Geashill) he had three sons and a dau.,
1. Kildare, of Killeigh, King's Co., J.P. for co. Kildare 1672, *d. unm.* 2 Feb. 1675, and was bur. at Geashill.
2. Edward, bur. at Geashill, 28 Feb. 1664 ; will dated 6 May. 1694 ; proved 20 April, 1695 ; *m.* Mary, sister of George Johnson, of Roscrea, and left issue, three sons and four daus.
3. JOHN, who follows.
The 3rd son,
JOHN TARLETON, of Killeigh, *d.* 20 Dec. 1700 ; will dated 14 Dec., proved 21 Dec. 1700 ; *m.* Anne, dau. of — Brereton, and grand-dau. of Sir William Gilbert, of Kilminchy, Queen's Co., and had with a dau., a son,

Digby Tarleton, of Killeigh, entered Trin. Coll. Dublin, 10 July, 1606, aged 15, B.A. 1701. His will dated 24 Sept. 1741, was proved 1 March, 1742. He *m.* 28 June, 1705, Arabella, dau. of William Weldon, of Rahinderry, Queen's Co., M.P. for Athy 1661-66 (*see* Weldon, *Bart.*, Burke's *Peerage*), and by her had, with daus., three sons,
1. John, his heir.
2. Digby, will dated 13 Nov. 1753; proved 26 June, 1755; *m.* 1737, Mary, dau. of Mark Tew, of Culmullin, co. Meath, *s.p.*
3. Weldon, *d.* 1775; *m.* and left issue.

The eldest son,
John Tarleton, of Killeigh and Fenter, *d.* 2 April, 1758, aged 47; *m.* (licence 22 May) 1740, Barbara, dau. of Adam Mitchell, of Rathgibbon, King's Co. (co-heir with her sisters, Jane, wife of Thomas Bernard, of Castle Bernard, King's Co., and Susanna, wife of John Drought, of Whigsborough, in same county (*see those families*), and by her (who *d.* 2 Aug. 1753) had, with two daus., five sons,
1. Digby, *d.* young, 1740. 2. Digby, *d.* young, 1750
3. Adam, *d.* young, 1750. 4. Mitchell, *d.* 16 July, 1758, aged 6.
5. John Weldon, who succeeded.

The 5th son,
John Weldon Tarleton, of Killeigh and Fenter, *d.* 1824; *m.* 4 Dec. 1779, Margaret, dau. of General George Scott, Governor of Bengal, and step-dau. of George Armstrong, of Castle Armstrong) King's Co., and had, with six daus., five sons,
1. John William, his heir
2. George Matcham, 6th Foot, mentioned in Wellington's despatches after Echalar, *m.* Louisa, dau. of George Best, of Chilston Park, Kent, M.P. for Rochester 1790-1796 (*see* Best *of Park House*, Burke's *Landed Gentry of Great Britain*).
3. Robert Weldon, *b.* 1795; *d.* 1885; *m.* Charlotte, dau. of Nicholas Gamble, of Killooly, King's Co. (*see that family*).
4. Digby.
5. Drought Blakely, *m.* Elizabeth, dau. of Matthew Weld, and left issue.

The eldest son,
John William Tarleton, of Killeigh and Fenter, *d.* 26 Dec. 1865; *m.* 1831, Anne, dau. of Richard Fothergill, of Lowbridge House, Westmorland (*see that family*, Burke's *Landed Gentry of Great Britain*), and Carleon, Monmouthshire, and by her (who assumed the name and arms of Fothergill, of Hensol Castle, Glamorganshire, in 1887, and *d.* 1895) had four sons and four daus.,
1. John William, his heir.
2. Rowland, Capt. King's Co. Militia, *d. unm.*
3. Thomas Weldon, Lieut. 5th Fusiliers, *d. unm.*
4. Drought Blakely, Lieut. 39th Regt., *d. unm.*
1. Mary Anne, *m.* 28 Aug. 1873, P. Hamlet Thompson, of Stonestown, King's Co. (*see* Thompson *of Clonfin*).
2. Henrietta, *m.* 3 April, 1872, David Dunlop Urquhart, of Strawberry Hill, King's Co. (*see that family*).
3. Isabella, *m.* 3 June, 1877, Sir Rose Lambart Price, Bart. (*see* Burke's *Peerage*, Price, *Bart.*).
4. Elizabeth Constance, *d. unm.* 1862.

The eldest son,
John William Tarleton, of Killeigh, *b.* 1833; *d.* 1896; *m.* 3 June, 1874, Isabella Sarah, younger dau. of Francis Moony Enraght-Moony, of The Doon, King's Co. (*see that family*), and had two sons and two daus.,
1. John William Francis, now of Killeigh.
2. Francis Rowland, of Hunstanton, King's Co., *b.* 24 Jan., 1877, Capt. The Black Watch (Royal Highlanders).
1. Kathleen Muriel.
2. Isabella Rosemary Anne, *m.* 22 Feb. 1911, Capt. James Augustine Ryan, 15th United States Cavalry.

Arms—Or, on a bend gu., a fleur-de-lys between two lozenges of the field. Crest—A dragon's head erased vert, collared and chained or. Motto—Pro fide, rege, et patria pugno.
Seat—The Abbey, Killeigh, King's Co.

TAYLOR OF ARDGILLAN CASTLE.

Capt. Edward Richard Taylor, of Ardgillan Castle, co. Dublin, J.P. and D.L., Capt. late Grenadier Guards, *b.* 21 Sept. 1863; *s.* his father 1883 Capt. Taylor is the eldest son of the Right Hon. Thomas Edward Taylor, P.C., of Ardgillan Castle, who *d.* 3 Feb. 1883, by Louisa, Harrington his wife, 2nd dau. of the Hon. and Rev. Hugh Francis Tollemache, Rector of Harrington (*see* Burke's *Peerage*, Dysart, E.), and grandson of the Hon. and Rev. Henry Edward Taylor, 4th son of Thomas 1st Earl of Bective.

Lineage.—(*See* Burke's *Peerage*, Headfort, M.).
Arms—Erm., on a chief gu. a fleur-de-lis, between two boars' heads couped and erect or. Crest—A naked arm embowed, holding an arrow all ppr. Motto—Prosequitor quodcunque petit.
Seat—Ardgillan Castle, near Balbriggan. Clubs—Guards', Carlton and Wellington.

TAYLOR OF BALLINURE.

Godfrey Lovelace Taylor, of Ballinure, co. Tipperary, J.P. co. Wexford, *b.* 11 April, 1839; *m.* 1871, Dorothea Marie, eldest dau. of Karl Brüün, of Bergen, Norway, and has issue,
1. Godfrey, Staff Surgeon R.N., *b.* 6 Oct. 1873.
2. Nathaniel, *b.* 5 May, 1875.
3. Otto Carl, *b.* 5 July, 1878.
4. Charles, Lieut. 3rd. Batt. Royal Irish Regt., *b.* 5 Feb. 1882.
1. Florence, *m.* 6 Aug. 1903, Hon. Cecil Thomas, eldest surviving son of the Right Hon. Lord Atkinson, and has issue (*see* Burke's *Peerage*, Atkinson, B.).
2. Inga Lilian, *d.* 20 March, 1885.
3. Helena Violet.
4. Ethel Mary.

Lineage.—The Ven. Rowland Taylor, Archdeacon of Exeter, and Chaplain to Archbishop Cramer, commonly known as Taylor the Martyr, *b.* 1415, was burned for his defence of Protestantism at Hadleigh 8 Feb. 1554. His son,
Edmond Taylor, *d.* in 1607, having had issue a son,
Nathaniel Taylor, whose name occurs in a list of churchwardens of Cambridge Parish in 1589, *m.* 3 Oct. 1605, Mary Dean, and had issue,
1. Edmond, *b.* 3 Aug. 1606; *d.* 22 Sept. 1607.
2. Nathaniel, of whom presently.
3. Jeremy (Right Rev.), the Celebrated Divine, Bishop of Down and Connor, P.C., *b.* 6 Aug. 1613, left by Joanna, his second wife, a dau., Mary, *m.* the Most Rev. Francis Marsh, Archbishop of Dublin. Bishop Taylor *d.* 1673.
4. Thomas, *b.* 21 July, 1616.
5. John, *b.* 13 April, 1619.
1. Mary.

The 2nd son,
Nathaniel Taylor, of Noan, co. Tipperary, an officer in Cromwell's Army, obtained a grant from Charles II., 1666, of the lands of Noan, Ballygreheny and Roanmoley, near Cashel, *b.* 8 Dec. 1611; *m.* Susannah, dau. of — Lovelace, of Galway, and *d.* 16 Dec. 1675, having had issue,
Robert, his heir.
Mary, *m.* Samuel Brocas, or Brockhus.

The only son,
Robert Taylor, of Noan, *m.* Elizabeth, dau. of Gyles Cook, of Thurles, and had issue,
1. Lovelace, his heir.
2. Gyles.
3. Nathaniel, *d.* in Dublin, will dated 26 March, 1752.

The eldest son,
Lovelace Taylor, of Noan and Ballinure (which he purchased in 1742), J.P. co Tipperary, High Sheriff 1731, *m.* Anne. dau. of Rev. Robert Hackett, of Thurles. He *d.* 1760 (will dated 1759), leaving issue,
1. Nathaniel, his heir.
2. Godfrey, *s.* his brother.
3. Thomas, Lieut. North Cork Militia, *d.* 1748.
1. Ellen, *m.* Benjamin Prince.
2. Anne, *m.* 1734, William Pennefather, second son of Matthew Pennefather, of Newpark, and Lavinia Kingsmill his wife.
3. Elizabeth, *m.* Robert Low, of Mallards, co. Tipperary.

The eldest son,
Nathaniel Taylor, of Noan and Ballinure, *b.* 1714; *m.* 1744, Susannah, dau. of — Hackett, but *d.s.p.* 7 March, 1775. His brother,
Godfrey Taylor, of Noan and Ballinure, *b.* 1723; *m.* 1st, 25 Feb. 1756, Anna Maria, dau. of Archdeacon Daniel Hearn, of Dublin, and 2ndly, 1758, Lydia, dau. and co-heir of Edward Bacon, of Rathkenny. He *d.* 9 Sept. 1799, having had issue,
1. Lovelace, *d. unm. v.p.*
2. Edward, of Noan, *m.* Elizabeth, dau. of Wallace Hewetson, of Kilkenny, and *d.* 1801, having had issue,
  1. Nathaniel, of Noan, J.P. co. Tipperary, High Sheriff 1818; *m.* 1808, Anne Alicia, only child of Samuel Jacob, of Mobarnan, Fethard. H. *d.s.p.* 28 April, 1828, and was *s.* by his nephew, son of his sister.
  2. Edward. 3. Godfrey.
  1. Anne, *m.* 1819, John Bagwell, of Kilmore, co. Tipperary, who adopted the name of Taylor, and had a son, John Bagwell Taylor, *b.* 1820, *s.* his uncle at Noan, which was sold in 1853.
3. Nathaniel, of whom presently.
4. Robert, *d.* young.
1. Lydia, *m.* 1798, Jeremiah Langley, of Lisunden.
2. Anne, *m.* 1787, Richard Levinge, of Lurgo, 2nd son of Sir Richard Levinge, 4th Bart.
3. Elizabeth, *m.* 1806, John Barton.
4. Susannah, *m.* Laurence Grace Langley, of Brittas Castle.
5. Frances, *d.* unm.

The 3rd son,
Nathaniel Taylor, of Ballinure, *m.* 1798, Helena, dau. of Rev. Patrick Hare, of Deerpark, Cashel, and *d.* 1830, leaving issue,

1. GODFREY, his heir.
1. Mary, *m.* 1822, John Langley, of Parkstown, Thurles.
2. Lydia, *m.* 1833, Robert William White, of Springmount, Golden.
3. Helena, *m.* Gen. Frederick Scargill, of Cashel.

The only son,
GODFREY TAYLOR, of Ballinure, J.P. co. Tipperary, Lieut. North Cork Militia, *b.* 1 Oct. 1803 ; *m.* 2 Nov. 1830, Anna, dau. of John Hare, of Deerpark, Cashel, and *d.* 5 April, 1850, leaving issue,
1. NATHANIEL, his heir.
2. GODFREY LOVELACE, now of Ballinure.
3. John Hare, *b.* 25 Nov. 1841 ; *d.* in New Zealand, 26 July, 1894.
4. Charles Edward, *b.* 25 July, 1843.
5. Edward, of Bessmount Park, co. Monaghan, *b.* 6 Dec. 1844 ; *m.* Anna, dau. of Robert T. Atkins, and has issue, Edward, *b.* 13 Oct. 1898.
1. Elizabeth Anna, *m.* Rev. Richard Deverell.
2. Helena Frances, *d. unm.* 19 Feb. 1899.
3. Anna Maria, *m.* Rev. Mahony Vincent Watson.
4. Charlotte.

The eldest son,
NATHANIEL TAYLOR, of Ballinure, J.P. co. Tipperary, Capt. 3rd Royal Westminster Regt., *b.* 5 May, 1835 ; *d. unm.* 27 July, 1872, and was *s.* by his brother.

Residence—Grangeville, Fethard, co. Wexford.

SHAWE-TAYLOR OF CASTLE TAYLOR.

The late WALTER TAYLOR NEWTON SHAWE-TAYLOR, of Castle Taylor, co. Galway, J.P. and D.L., High Sheriff, 1868, *b.* 31 March, 1832 ; *d.* 29 May, 1912 ; *m.* 24 Nov. 1864, Elizabeth, dau. of Dudley Persse, of Roxborough, and by her (who *d.* 24 Aug. 1896) had issue,

1. JOHN, J.P., Galway, formerly A.D.C. to G.O.C. Southern District, Capt. Reserve of Officers, late Cheshire Regt., *b.* 3 Jan. 1866 ; *d.v.p.* 30 June, 1911 ; *m.* 12 July, 1905, Amy Eleonora, only child of the late Gerard Norman, B.C.S., of Bromley, Kent, and had issue,
Walter Michael, *b.* 21 Dec. 1906.
Eleonora Elizabeth Aileen.
2. Francis Manley, *m.* 1 June, 1901, Agnes Mary Eleanor, eldest dau. of the late Christopher Ussher, of Eastwell, co. Galway (see that family), and has issue,
A dau., *b.* 4 Jan. 1903.
1. Frances Elizabeth, *m.* 7 Sept. 1893, the Hon. William Cosby Trench, of Clonodloy Castle, co. Limerick, 2nd son of the late Hon. Frederick Trench (see BURKE's *Peerage*, ASHTOWN, B.).

Lineage.—WALTER TAYLOR (son of John Taylor, by Anne his wife, dau. of Walter Tavlor, of Ballymacragh, and grandson of Walter Taylor and Catherine Staunton his wife, *m.* 1st, Lady Anne Barry, dau. of James, 4th Earl of Barrymore, and 2ndly, Oct. 1766, Hester Trench, sister of William, 1st Earl of Clancarty, and left at his decease one son and four daus.,
1. John (Sir), of Castle Taylor, co. Galway, K.C.B., Lieut.-Gen. and Col. of the 88th Regt., High Sheriff co. Galway 1804, *b.* 29 Sept. 1771 ; *m.* 24 April, 1798, Albinia Frances, widow of Lieut.-Col. Stephen Francis William Fremantle (see BURKE's *Peerage*, COTTESLOE, B.), and dau. of St. John Jeffreys, of Blarney Castle, co. Cork, and left at his decease, Dec. 1843, two daus. The younger, Cecilia Agnes, *m.* the Hon. Henry Cavendish Butler, youngest son of the Hon. Augustus Butler Danvers and grandson of Brinsley, 2nd Earl of Lanesborough : she *d.s.p.* The elder dau., Albinia Hester, *m.* 28 March, 1825, FRANCIS MANLEY SHAWE (younger son of William Cunliffe Shawe, of Southgate House, Herts, by Philippa Pole his wife), and had issue,
1. WALTER TAYLOR NEWTON, of Castle Taylor.
1. Cecilia Fhilippa, *m.* 8 June, 1848, Robert Wright Cope Cope, of Loughgall Manor, co. Armagh.
2. Sophia Frances, *m.* Rev. W. C. Templer.
3. Albinia Letitia, *d. young.*
4. Geraldine, *m.* Robert Baron Templer, of Armagh, and *d.* 22 Nov. 1905.
Francis Manley Shawe, who was *b.* 29 Aug. 1797, *s.* to Castle Taylor on the death of his father-in-law Dec. 1843, and assumed in consequence, by Royal Licence, 15 March, 1844, the additional surname of TAYLOR. He was J.P. and High Sheriff for co. Galway, and formerly Capt. Coldstream Guards. He *d.* 1863, and was *s.* by his only son, the present WALTER TAYLOR NEWTON SHAWE-TAYLOR.
1. Frances, *m.* Robert O'Hara, of Raheen, co. Galway, and had issue.
2. Elizabeth, *m.* 1st, Lieut.-Col. Stewart, 35th Regt., and 2ndly, Francis Synge, of Glanmore Castle, co. Wicklow.   3. Hester.
4. Anne, *m.* the Hon. and Most Rev. Power Le Poer Trench, Archbishop of Tuam, son of the 1st Earl of Clancarty.

Seat—Castle Taylor, Ardrahan, co. Galway.

TEMPLE OF WATERSTON.

ARTHUR REGINALD HARRIS-TEMPLE, of Waterston, co. Westmeath, J.P. and D.L., *b.* 1 Aug. 1874 ; *s.* his father 1906 ; *m.* 28 Oct. 1898, Clare, dau. of Alan Cameron, A.I.G., Royal Irish Constabulary, and has issue,

1. ARTHUR TEMPLE, *b.* 15 March, 1904.
1. Nilah Clare, *b.* 25 Nov. 1899.
2. Dita Helena, *b.* 7 June, 1901.

Lineage.— CAPT. THE HON. ARTHUR ERNEST TEMPLE, of Waterston, co. Westmeath, J.P., late 43rd Foot, *b.* 31 Jan. 1835 ; *m.* 25 July, 1871, Jane, dau. of the late Richard Butler Bryan, and widow of Capt. Arthur Chaigneau, of Benown House, Westmeath, and *d.* 12 Aug. 1906. She *d.* 11 May, 1891, leaving a son,
ARTHUR REGINALD, now of Waterston.
Capt. the Hon. A. E. Temple was the 2nd son of William George, 2nd Lord Harris (who *d.* 30 May, 1845), by Isabella Helena, his 2nd wife (who *d.* 1 Jan. 1861), only child of Robert Handcock Temple, of Waterston, co. Westmeath. He *s.* his only brother, the Hon. Reginald Robert Temple, D.L., of Waterston (who *d. unm.* 4 Feb. 1900), and assumed, by Royal Licence, 25 April, 1900, the name of TEMPLE, in lieu of HARRIS, and the arms of TEMPLE quarterly with his own arms of HARRIS (see BURKE's *Peerage*, HARRIS, B.).

Arms—Quarterly 1st and 4th arg. two bars sa. each charged with three martlets or a crescent gu. for difference (TEMPLE), 2nd and 3rd vert on a chevron embattled erminois between three hedgehogs or as many bombs sa. fired ppr. on a chief of augmentation a representation of the gates and fortress of Seringapatam, all ppr. (HARRIS). *Crest*—Out of a ducal crest coronet a martlet or charged with a crescent gu. for difference. *Motto*—Templa quain dilecta.

Seats—Waterston, Athlone, co. Westmeath.

TENISON OF LOUGHBAWN.

COL. WILLIAM TENISON, of Lough Bawn, co. Monaghan, J.P. and D.L., High Sheriff 1896, Lieut.-Col. commanding (Hon. Col.) 4th Batt, Royal Irish Fusiliers, late Major Manchester Regt., *b.* 26 April, 1856 ; *m.* 30 Dec. 1882, Marion Angela, youngest dau. of Thomas Huggins, of Buxted Lodge, Sussex, and has issue,

1. WILLIAM PERCIVAL COSNAHAN, Lieut. R.F.A., *b.* 25 June, 1884.
2. Thomas Michael Greville. *b.* 27 Aug. 1891.
3. Gerald Evan Farquhar, *b.* 10 Jan. 1897.
1. Marguerite Angela.

Lineage.—THOMAS TENISON, of Carrickfergus, of which town he was Bailiff or Sheriff in 1645 ; a kinsman of Archbishop Tenison, had issue,
1. RICHARD, who follows.
2. William, living in Carrickfergus, 1682, who had a son, Richard, a legatee under his uncle Richard's will, 1705.
3. Robert, of Carrickfergus, 1682, who had issue,
1. Robert, of Trim, co. Meath, will (not proved) dated there 29 March, 1722. He *m.* Anne and *d.s.p.*
2. Dudley, *b.* at Trim about 1669, being aged 18 when he matriculated at Trin. Coll. Dublin, 4 May, 1687. He *d.* intestate, administration 1719, 1721 and 1726.
The eldest son,
THE MOST REV. RICHARD TENISON, D.D., *b.* 1642, matriculated Trin. Coll. Dublin 1659, Master of the Diocesan School at Trim, Rector and Vicar of Laracor 4 Feb. 1671-2 (Royal Presentation), J.P. co. Meath, Rector and Vicar, Augher Palace, Chaplain to the Earl of Essex, Lord Lieut., Rector of Louth and Dean of Clogher 1575, Vicar of Donoughmore, near Navan, and of St. Peter's, Drogheda, Bishop of Killala and Achonry, consecrated 1682 D.D. 1682, went to London in 1688, and became Minister of St. Helen's, Bishopsgate, Bishop of Clogher 1690-1, sat in House of Lords 1692, Bishop of Meath 1697, a Privy Councillor, Vice-Chancellor, Dub. Univ., 1698 ; *d.* 29 July, 1705 ; will dated 28 July and proved 26 Aug. 1705. He *m.* 1st ——, and had issue,
1. Henry, of Dillonstown, Louth, *b.* 1666, B.A., Barrister-at-Law 1690, M.P. for co. Monaghan 1695 (elected for Clogher but sat for Monaghan), and for Louth 1703, *m.* 1695, Anne (*b.* 1670 ; *d.* 10 Jan. 1708), dau. and co-heir of Thomas Moore, of Knockballymore, co. Fermanagh, and Mellifont, co. Louth, by whom he had issue,
1. Richard, *b.* 7 Sept. 1704 ; *d.* before 1709.
2. Thomas, *b.* about 1706, Barrister-at-Law 1731, Prime Serjeant 1759, Justice of Common Pleas 1761, M.P. for Dunleer 1728-61, a Commissioner for Revenue Appeals 1753 ; *m.* 6 July,

1732, Dorothy (who d. 1795), dau. of Thomas Upton, M.P., uncle of 1st Lord Templetown, and d. 6 July, 1732, leaving issue,

(1) Richard, b. 1734, admitted to Middle Temple 1756, a Commissioner of Revenue, and d. 1759.
(2) Henry, bapt. 17 Jan. 1735; d. an infant.
(3) Thomas, bapt. 20 March, 1736; m. Mary Norton, and d.s.p.
(1) Sarah, bapt. 4 Sept. 1733; d. in infancy.

1. Elizabeth, b. 1697.
2. Mary, b. 1699; m. 14 July, 1722, Nicholas Coddington (who d. Nov. 1737), ancestor of Coddington, of Oldbridge, co. Meath, and d. 1785, having issue (see that family).
3. Anne, b. 1700; d. unm. 1722.

1. Mary, m. 1686, Samuel Raymond. She was living 1705, having had a son.

The Bishop m. 2ndly, Anne (who d. 1696) by whom he had issue,

2. Richard, of Thomastown, co. Louth, M.P. for Dunleer, 1713, admitted to Middle Temple 1684; m. about 1705, Margaret, dau. of William Barton, of Thomastown, and d. 29 Nov. 1725, leaving by her (who m. 2ndly, 1732, Rev. Patrick Delany,* D.D.), one son and two daus.,

1. William, of Philipstown, b. about 1706; M.P. Dunleer 1727; d. intestate and s.p. 6 May, 1728; m. 1727, Maria, dau. of Hamilton Townley, of Townley Hall and Millifont. She remarried 30 Nov. 1734, Blayney Townley, and d. July, 1754.
1. Elizabeth, m. 16 Dec. 1731, Robert Rochfort, afterwards Earl of Belvedere, and d.s.p. 5 June, 1732.
2. Margaret, b. 21 Aug. 1723; d. unm. 11 Jan. 1742, will proved Feb. 1742-3.

3. John, b. 1686; d.s.p. 1725.
4. Norbury, of whom presently.
5. Thomas, of Finglas, co. Dublin, b. 1692; m. before 1730, Alice, dau. of the Rev. William Mosse, M.A., Rector of Maryborough, Queen's Co., and d. 4 May, 1764, leaving by her (who d. 17 Aug. 1775) two daus. (Mary Jane, m. 1759, Hon. and Rev. Richard Henry Roper, 2nd son of Henry, 8th Baron Teynham; Ann, m. 1750, James Edwards, of Old Court, co. Wicklow) and one son,

1. Thomas, b. about 1730, High Sheriff co. Leitrim 1763, then of Drumkirk, M.P. for co. Monaghan 1776-83; m. 30 May, 1758, Mary Anne (who d. 1764), 2nd dau. of Col. John Daniel Desgenes, of Portarlington, Queen's Co., and d. 5 April, 1808, leaving an only son,

(1) Thomas, of Castle Tenison (now Kilronan Castle), b. about 1759, High Sheriff co. Roscommon 1791, and for co. Leitrim 1792, M.P. for Boyle 1792, and afterwards Lieut.-Col; Roscommon Militia. m. 1st, 1803, Lady Frances Anne King, dau. of Edward, 1st Earl of Kingston, and by her (who d. May, 1812) had two sons,

1. Thomas, of Castle Tenison, b. 1804; d. unm. 5 Nov. 1843.
2. Edward King, of Kilronan Castle, co. Roscommon, M.A. Cantab. Lieut.-Col. Roscommon Mil., H.M.'s Lieut. and Custos Rotulorum of that co. 1856, served as High Sheriff cos. Roscommon and Leitrim, M.P. for the latter co. from 1847 to 1852, and J.P. for cos. Roscommon, Leitrim, and Sligo, b. 21 Jan. 1805; m. 26 Nov. 1838, Lady Louisa Mary Anne Anson, eldest dau. of Thomas William, 1st Earl of Lichfield, and d. 19 June, 1878, having by her (who d. 27 Aug. 1882) had two daus.,

a. Louisa Frances Mary, m. 14 June, 1866, John Baptiste Joseph, 12th Lord Dormer, and d. 9 Sept. 1868, leaving issue (see Burke's Peerage, Dormer, B.).
b. Florence Margaret Christina, m. 23 Jan. 1872, Henry Ernest, 8th Earl of Kingston, and has issue (see Burke's Peerage).

Lieut.-Col. Thomas Tenison m. 2ndly, 7 July, 1815, Mary Anne (who d. 1847), dau. of Lieut.-Col. Coore, of Golder's Hill, Middlesex, and Scrutton and Hanswell, co. York, and d. 1835, leaving by her an only dau.,

Thomasine Sophia, m. 1st, 1837, Robert Saundersoun, and 2ndly, 1848, Rev. Henry Peisley Herbert Stepney, and d. 1850.

(1) Frances, d. unm. 1830, aged 62.
1. Anne, m. 1754, Lieut.-Col. James Edwards, of Old Court, Wicklow, High Sheriff 1758 (b. 1708; d. 1780), and had with other issue,

Tenison, m. Charity, dau. of John Barrington, and had issue, a dau.,
Annabella, b. 1761; m. 11 May, 1808, Henry Hartstonge, Viscount Glentworth, and had issue (see Burke's Peerage, Limerick, E.).

2. Mary Jane, m. 1759, as his 2nd wife, the Hon. and Rev. Richard Roper, son of the 8th Lord Teynham, and d. 16 Feb. 1765, leaving issue (see Burke's Peerage, Teynham, B.).

6. William, of Finglas, b. 1696; m. Harriett, dau. of Robert Percy, of Dublin, and d. Jan. 1758, leaving issue,
1. Richard, B.A. Trin. Coll. Dublin 1758.
1. Harriet. 2. Elizabeth. 3. Anne.
1. Elizabeth, m. 1705-6, as his 2nd wife, Michael Cole, of Derry, co. Tipperary, 3rd son of Sir John Bart., and brother of Arthur Cole, 1st Lord Ranlagh.

The Bishop of Meath d. 29 July, 1705, and was bur. at the college.
His 4th son,

Norbury Tenison, of Carrickmacross, co. Monaghan (legatee with his brother Thomas under the will of Dr. Tenison, Archbishop of Canterbury), b. 19 June, 1661; m. 7 Dec. 1709, Elizabeth (d. soon after 23 Oct. 1771), dau. of William Eccleston, of Drumshallon, co.

---

* This eminent preacher m. 2ndly, 1743, as his second wife Mary Granville, the celebrated Mrs. Delany, the friend of Swift.

Louth, by whom (whose will, dated 1 Jan. 1770, was proved 21 May, 1772) he had issue,
William, his heir.
Anne, m. about 1734, William Fitch, of Carrickmacross and by him (who d. 1738) left issue.

The only son,
William Tenison, of Priorland, co. Louth, b. 1715, m. Margaret, dau. of John Woods, of Lisanisk, by whom (who m. 2ndly, William Richards, of Coolderry, co. Monaghan) he had

1. William Barton, his successor.
1. Elizabeth. 2. Anne. 3. Charity.

He d. 2 April, 1750, and was s. by his only son,

William Barton Tenison, of Monally, co. Monaghan, Lieut. in Armstrong Regt., High Sheriff 1772, b. 8 Jan. 1743-4, who m. 1st, 1765, Charity, dau. of Adam Noble, of Longfield, same co., High Sheriff, 1772, and by her had issue,

1. Elizabeth, b. 16 Dec. 1765.
2. Anne. 3. Margaret, b. 15 April, 1770.
3. Dorothy, b. 30 Aug. 1771; m. before 1817, John Spittall, of Douglas, and d.s.p.
4. Mary, b. 30 Nov. 1772.

He m. 2ndly, 1783, Margaret Cosnahan (who d. 25 May, 1836), of Douglas, in the Isle of Man, and d. before 1818, leaving by her,

1. William Barton, late of Loughbawn.
2. Thomas, b. 28 July, 1785; d. 14 June, 1786.
3. Henry, b. 19 July, 1789.
4. Michael, b. 1791; d. unm. 1853.
5. Barton, of Douglas, Capt. 10th Foot, Brevet Major 1844, b. 1793; m. Emily, dau. of George Byne, and d. 1848, leaving issue.
1. Elizabeth, m. Robert Cochrane, of Strabane, co. Tyrone, and has issue.
6. Margaret, m. 1819, as his 2nd wife, Col. Richard Murray (who d. 1843), son of Lord Henry Murray, and grandson of the 3rd Duke of Atholl, and d. 8 Nov. 1864, leaving issue (see Burke's Peerage, Atholl, D.).

The eldest son,
William Barton Tenison, of Loughbawn, Capt. 72nd Foot 1816, 1st Foot 1823, b. 7 July, 1784; m. 13 Jan. 1803, his cousin Isabella (who d. 22 Aug. 1855), dau. of Hon. John Cosnahan, Deemster of the Isle of Man, and d. 1 March, 1840, having had, with three sons (William, b. 19 Dec. 1803, d. 17 March, 1819; John, b. 17 Feb. 1808, d. 12 April, 1832; Joseph, b. 8 July, 1809, d. 23 Sept. 1831), surviving issue,

1. William, late of Loughbawn.
1. Margaret, b. 21 July, 1811; d. 3 Dec. 1814.
2. Catherine Georgina, b. 5 Jan. 1815; m. Robert Lloyd, who d. 22 Jan. 1881. She d. 18 Oct. 1881.
3. Isabella Dorothy, b. 21 April, 1817; d. 23 Dec. 1870.
4. Margaret, b. 18 Nov. 1819; m. L. Paulet, and d. 1886.

His only son,
William Tenison, of Lougbbawn, co. Monaghan, J.P., b. 28 Sept. 1828; m. 1850, Flavia, dau. of Signor Fundelli, of Florence. She d. 26 March, 1896. He d. 20 Sept. 1901, having had issue,
1. Michael George. 2. William, now of Loughbawn.
1. Isabella, d. unm.
2. Marguerite, m. 1873, Evan Mackenzie, of Genoa, and has issue.

Seat—Loughbawn, Ballybay, co. Monaghan. Residence—4, Stanhope Gardens, S.W.

THACKWELL OF AGHADA HALL.

Charlotte, Mrs. Thackwell, of Aghada Hall, co. Cork, and Wynstone Place, Gloucestershire, younger dau. of Rev. Henry Tomkinson, of Reaseheath Hall, Cheshire (see that family); m. 1864, Major - Gen. William de Wilton Roche Thackwell, C.B., of Wynstone Place and of Aghada Hall, who d. 16 June, 1910, leaving issue (see below).

Lineage.—Lieut.-Gen. Sir Joseph Thackwell, G.C.B., K.H., of Aghada Hall, co. Cork, Coueragh, co. Waterford, and Norman's Land and Woodend, co. Gloucester, was the 4th son of Johnman Thackwell, J.P. and D.L., of Wilton Place, co. Gloucester, and Rye Court and Moreton Court, co. Worcester, by his wife, Judith Daffy, of Mavsington, a descendant of the Egyoke family (see Thackwell of Wilton Place). Sir Joseph, who was b. 1 Feb. 1781, entered the Army in April, 1800, as a Cornet in the 15th King's Light Dragoons, and during a career of nearly sixty years rose to the highest distinction. He served in that regiment for thirty-two years, during twelve of which he held the command. He was with Sir John Moore in Spain (1808-9) and at Corunna. He also shared in the glories of the campaign of 1813-4 in the Peninsula, and was engaged at Vittoria (seriously contused on right shoulder), the Pyrenees, Orthes, Tarbes, and Toulouse. At Granada, he boldly attacked and forced back upwards of 280 French troopers, though he was aided by only forty-five of the 15th Hussars, making several prisoners. Was also at Quatre Bras and at Waterloo, where he received several wounds, and had two horses shot under him while charging squares of infantry, his left arm having to be amputated close to the shoulder. When wounded he seized the bridle with his mouth, and dashed on at the head of his men to charge the enemy. During the above services, it appears from *The Records of the 15th Hussars*, he frequently greatly distinguished himself, and was several times specially recommended for promotion. Sir Joseph's subsequent brilliant career was in India. In 1837 he was appointed to the command of the 3rd (King's Own) Light Dragoons, and proceeding with his regiment to India, he was promoted to Major-Gen. (local) the same year, and held important and distinguished commands in the first Afghan campaign of 1838-9, the campaign in Gwalior (1843), and on the Sutlej in 1846, in one of which he commanded the cavalry division. He bore a conspicuous part in the actions of Ghuznee (23 July, 1839), Maharajpoor (29 Dec. 1843); and Sobraon (10 Feb. 1846); in the last, his leading the cavalry with such effect against the Sikh batteries is most memorable, his conduct being strongly commended in Lord Gough's despatch. Sir Joseph Thackwell headed the cavalry division in the Punjaub campaign (1848-9), in which he was second in command of the Army under Lord Gough. He there, while leading the left wing, made some splendid charges at Chilianwallah and Goojerat; and with a small British detachment, which he commanded, he gained the important victory of Sadoolapoor over the Sikh Army, headed by Shere Sing in person (3 Dec. 1848). For these achievements he thrice received the thanks of Parliament and of the East India Company. He was created K.H. Feb. 1834, C.B. July, 1838, K.C.B. 20 Dec. 1839, and G.C.B 9 June, 1849, was made Col. of the 16th Lancers in the latter year, and Inspector-Gen. of Cavalry in 1854. He had the silver war medal and three clasps, besides many other medals and clasps, and the Order of the Dooranee Empire. Sir Joseph m. 29 July, 1825, Maria Audriab, eldest dau of Francis Roche, of Rochemont, co. Cork (see BURKE'S *Peerage*, FERMOY, B.), by whom (who d. 1 June, 1874) he had issue,

1. EDWARD JOSEPH, of whom presently.
2. William de Wilton Roche, C.B., of Wynstone Place, co. Gloucester and Aghada Hall, co. Cork, Major-Gen., Col. of the Dorsetshire Regt., J.P. cos. Gloucester and Cork, High Sheriff co. Cork 1900, late Lieut.-Col. 38th Regt., Hon. Col. 4th Vol. Batt. Liverpool Regt., Knight of the Medjidie (Third Class); served in the Crimea in 1855, including siege and fall of Sebastopol, b. 5 Sept. 1834; m. 29 June, 1864, Charlotte, now of Wynstone Place, Gloucs., and Aghada Hall, co. Cork, youngest dau. of Rev. Henry Tomkinson, of Reascheath Hall, co. Chester (see that family), and d. 16 June, 1910, leaving issue,
   1. Edward Francis, b. 16 Nov. 1868; m. 3 Feb. 1894, Catherine, dau. of Sir H. Low, G.C.M.G., and widow of Sir John Pope Hennessy, K.C.M.G., of Rostellan Castle.
   1. Katherine Harriet, formerly of Birtsmorton Court, Worcestershire, m. 29 Oct. 1891, Col. Edward Rawdon Penrose, B.S.C., assumed the name of PENROSE-THACKWELL by Royal Licence 20 Oct. 1904, and the arms of THACKWELL quarterly with those of PENROSE, 4th son of Rev. J. D. Penrose, of Woodhill, co. Cork, and has issue,
      (1) William John Rawdon, b. 17 Jan. 1900.
      (2) Geoffrey Joseph Elliot, b. 28 March, 1904.
      (1) Mary Geraldine Harriet.
      (2) Elinor Maude Charlotte.
      (3) Marjory Helen Florence.
   2. Florence Mary, d. unm. 12 Feb. 1903.
   3. Ethel Maria, m. 24 April, 1907, Capt. Francis Herbert English Torbett, Loyal North Lancashire Regt., only son of Rev. J. E. Torbett, and has issue,
      James William English, b. 4 Dec. 1908.
3. Osbert Dabitot, Lieut. Bengal Army, killed at Lucknow, 1858, during the Indian Mutiny.
4. Francis John Roche, Capt. 5th Royal Irish Lancers, d. from tiger wounds in India, 24 June, 1869.
   1. Elizabeth Cranbourne, d. unm. 17 Feb. 1911.
   2. Anne Maria Esther, m. 1860, Rev. Thomas Palling Little, M.A., Vicar of Edge, co. Gloucester, and d. 1902.
   3. Maria Roche, m. 1875, James Bennett, Lieut.-Col. late Royal Wilts Militia.

Sir Joseph d. 8 April, 1859, and was s. by his eldest son,

EDWARD JOSEPH THACKWELL, of Norman's Land, Dymock, co. Gloucester, Barrister-at-Law. Entered the Army in 1845 as Cornet in the 3rd (King's Own) Light Dragoons, served on the staff of Sir Joseph Thackwell during the Punjaub campaign of 1848-9, and was present at the battles of Ramnuggur, Sadoolapoor, Chilianwallah, and Goojerat, being frequently mentioned in despatches. Subsequently served as Capt. in the 48th and 50th Regts., author of *The Second Sikh War*, b. 4 Sept. 1827; m. 24 Feb. 1852, Charlotte Price (who d. 13 May, 1910), dau. and co-heir of Capt. Lucas, Bengal Army, by his wife, Charlotte Loftie, and step-dau. of Gen. Mossom Boyd. He d. 27 Dec. 1903, leaving issue,

1. JOSEPH EDWARD LUCAS, late of Aghada Hall.
2. Edward Loftus Roche, Col. Army Pay Dept., late Capt. 7th Royal Fusiliers, b. 8 Feb. 1856; m. 19 March, 1879, Emily, only dau. of Lestock Reid, Indian C.S. Commissioner N.D. Bombay, and has issue,
   Monica de Wilton Roche, b. 26 Sept. 1881; m. 1st. 1902, George Burrows, Lieut. E. Lancashire Regt., son of General G. R. S. Burrows, Bombay Army, and had issue. She m. 2ndly, 15 June, 1907, Adrian Francis Hugh Sibbald Simpson, late Indian Army, son of Sir Benjamin Simpson, K.C.I.E.
3. Colquhoun Grant Roche, D.S.O., Col. Indian Army, late Lieut. South Yorkshire Regt., b. 8 Dec. 1857; served in the Afghan Campaign of 1879-80 (medal), specially mentioned in despatches, and in the Egyptian war of 1882 (medal with clasp and Khedive's star), and in Tirah Campaign 1897 (mentioned in despatches). He m. Lilian, dau. of George Spencer, and has had issue, a son,
   Colquhoun George Spencer, d. 3 Nov. 1900.
4. Osbert Montagu Roche, Col. R.E., b. 7 Sept. 1860; m. 29 Aug. 1905, Florence Theophile, dau. of C. E. Palmer, and has issue,
   Denys Edward Osbert, b. 18 March, 1909.
1. Charlotte Barbara Roche, m. 22 May, 1877, Lieut.-Col. Frederic Graham, late 2nd Batt. Middlesex Regt., eldest son of Major-Gen. Stuart Frederick Graham, Commissioner at Moo'tan, and grandson of Sir Robert Graham, 8th bart. of Esk, co. Cumberland (see BURKE'S *Peerage*), and has issue.

The eldest son,

JOSEPH EDWARD LUCAS THACKWELL, of Aghada Hall, co. Cork, and Coneragh, co. Waterford, J.P. co. Cork, Lieut.-Col. 3rd Brigade South Irish Division, R.A., and formerly Lieut. 5th Royal Irish Lancers, b. 23 Jan. 1853; m. 2 Dec. 1874, his cousin, Caroline Matilda Georgina, only child and heir of Gen. Edmund Roche, 3rd Hussars, of Ballymonis, co. Cork (see BURKE'S *Peerage*, FERMOY, B.), and had issue,

1. WALTER JOSEPH DE RUPE, late of Aghada Hall, and Coneragh, co. Waterford, Capt. Tipperary R.G.A., b. 12 July, 1876.
2. Noel Edmund Osbert, Lieut. R.G.A., b. 16 Dec. 1878.
3. Edward Hillyar Roche, of Coneragh, near Youghal, co. Waterford, Capt. 3rd Batt. Royal Irish Regt. formerly of the E. Lancashire Regt., served in the South African War and West African Benue Expedition, b. 15 Nov. 1879.
4. Arthur Charles Austen, Capt. Indian Army, late Lieut. Middlesex Regt., b 17 Nov. 1881.
1. Violet Caroline Josephine, m. 3 June, 1902, Major Sinclair Francis Kirkwood, R.F.A. (Special Reserve), (see KIRKWOOD of Chongonagh).

Lieut.-Col. Thackwell d. 16 Dec. 1886, and was s. by his eldest son.

Arms (H. Coll.)—Quarterly: 1st and 4th paly of six or and gu., a maunch arg., semée of fleur-de-lis az., for THACKWELL; 2nd and 3rd, per pale az., and gu., a cross engrailed ermine; in the 1st and 4th quarters, a water bouget arg., for CAM. Crests—1st, Out of a mural crown arg. a dexter hand embowed, vested in the uniform of the 15th King's Hussars from the wrist pendant by a riband gu., fimbriated az., a representation of the silver medal for Waterloo, the hand grasping and in the attitude of striking with a sword ppr., pommel and hilt or, between two branches of laurel, issuant in like manner from the mural crown, also ppr., and above, on an escrol, the motto "Frappe fort" (this crest, having been specially granted to Sir Joseph Thackwell for his military services, is limited to his descendants); 2nd, within a chaplet of oak ppr., a dragon's head erased, paly of six or and gu., the neck transpierced by an arrow, barbed and flighted, also ppr. Motto—Mihi solicitudo futuri.

Seats—Aghada Hall, Rostellan, co. Cork, and Wynstone Place Brookthorpe, co. Gloucester.

THOMPSON OF CLONFIN.

JOHN FREDERICK WENSLEY THOMPSON, of Clonfin, co. Longford, b. 1862; s. his father 1908.

Lineage.—The first of this family who settled in Ireland was CAPT. WILLIAM THOMPSON, b. 1655, who accompanied King WILLIAM III. to that country 1688. His son, PETER THOMPSON, was father of

WILLIAM THOMPSON, of Clonfin, co. Longford, m. — dau. of Peter Metge, of Athlumney Castle, co. Meath, and had five sons and five daus.,

1. PETER, his heir.
2. Arthur, m. Miss Goff, of co. Roscommon, and had a dau. Mary, m. John Young, of Philipstown, co. Meath.
3. Henry, d. unm.
4. William, d. unm.
5. David, of Oaklands, co. Meath, b. 1738; m. Anne, 4th dau. of George Higginbotham, of Larghy, co. Cavan, by Anne his wife, dau. of Robert Acheson, and d. circa, 1816. leaving seven sons and three daus.,
   1. William, b. 1767, m. Anne Elizabeth, dau. of Rev. Henry Wright, and d. 1851, leaving issue,
      (1) David William, m. Mary, dau. of Rev. George Horan, and d. 1840, having had issue, (1, William, m. Jane, dau. of Henry Watson ; 2, George : 3, Horan, m. Maria Theresa, dau. of Thomas Thompson, of Springfield, co. Wicklow ; 1, Anne ; 2, Elizabeth Emily : and 3, Ellen Margaret, m. Marcus Charles Magrath).   (2) Henry.
      (1) Martha, m. James Haig, one of H.M.'s Judges in India.
      (2) Elizabeth, m. Henry Kyle, J.P., of Laurel Hill, Coleraine.
      (3) Frances.

Thompson. THE LANDED GENTRY. 688

2. George, of Clonskeagh Castle, co. Dublin, b. 16 Aug. 1769; m. 1st, Eleanor, 2nd dau. of John Wade, and by her had issue,
(1) David, d. 1875.
(2) Thomas Higginbotham, of Clonskeagh Castle, co. Dublin, and of Mayne, co. Meath, J.P. cos. Galway and Dublin, b. 1808, m. 1836, Martha, dau. of the late Thomas Wallace, K.C., M.P. for Carlow, of Belfield, Donnybrook, co. Dublin. She d. 30 Oct. 1900. He d. 27 May, 1886, leaving issue,
1. Robert Wade, of Clonskeagh Castle, co. Dublin, J.P., B.A. Trin. Coll. Dublin, Barrister-at-Law, late Capt. Dublin Art. Mil., b. 22 April, 1815; m. 10 March, 1876, Edith Isabella, dau. of Rev. William Jameson, and Eliza his wife, dau. of the late Arthur Guinness, of Beaumont, co. Dublin, and has issue,
  a. Thomas William, B.A., Camb., C.E. b. 4 Jan. 1877.
  b. Hamlet George, b. 5 May, 1878.
  c. William Jameson, B.A. Camb., b. 27 Oct. 1885.
  d. Edith Eliza, b. 11 Nov. 1879; m. 17 Nov. 1908, Rev. Oliver H. Knight, M.A. (Oxon), Missionary, Matsuy-, Japan.
  b. Frieda Katherine, b. 26 May, 1883.
  c. Madeline Geraldine, b. 24 March, 1889.
  d. Alice Isabella, b. 15 April, 1891.
  e. Olive Lillian, b. 16 June, 1894.
2. Arthur William, Lieut.-Col. late Dublin City Artillery, B.A., T.C.D. (*Jun. United Service Club*), b. 5 Aug. 1849.
  1. Katherine, m. 1859, Col. Rowan, of Belmont, co. Kerry, who d. 1876, leaving issue.
  2. Annie, m. 22 Aug. 1863, Major Oloff G. de Wet, Indian Army, who left issue.
3. Louisa Elizabeth, m. 1876, Capt. O'Sullivan de Terdeck.
4. Ellen Wade, m. 13 Oct. 1864, Rev. Walter T. Turpin, and has issue.
(3) George William, d. 1904.
(1) Anne Mary, m. 1828, David Peter Thompson.
(2) Louisa Elizabeth, m. Edmund ffloyd Cuppage, of Claregrove, co. Dublin, and d. 1840.
George Thompson m. 2ndly, Catherine, dau. of Gen. Robert Alexander, of co. Derry, and 3rdly, Jeanett, 4th dau. of Wm. Butler, of Drom, co. Tipperary, by Hon. Caroline Massy, 6th dau. of Hugh, 1st Lord Massy, and by her had a son,
(4) Massy Wade, b. 17 March, 1843.
He d. May, 1860.
3. Robert Acheson, m. Hannah, dau. of John Griffith, and d. 14 May, 1860.
4. David, b. 1774; m. Anne, dau. of Ffolliot Magrath, of co. Kerry, and d. 1852, leaving issue,
(1) David.   (2) Robert, d. 1862.
(1) Anne.
(2) Ellen, m. Rev. George Irwin, and d. 1848.
5. Peter, of Tralee, Treasurer of co. Kerry, b. 1775; m. Oct. 1800, Anne (who d. 13 Aug. 1856), dau. of Thomas Blennerhassett, of Annadale, co. Kerry, son of Conway Blennerhassett, whose father, Conway Blennerhassett, m. Elizabeth, dau. of Wentworth Harman, of Bawne, co. Longford, by Mary his wife, dau. of Garrett Wellesley, of Dangan, co. Meath, great-granduncle, of Arthur, 1st Duke of Wellington. Peter Thompson purchased Lord Glandore's estate in King's Co., and d. 3 Jan. 1850, leaving issue,
(1) David Peter, of Stonestown and Park, King's Co., J.P. b. 1803; m. 2 Dec. 1838. his cousin Anna Maria, eldest dau. of George Thompson, of Clonskeagh Castle, and d. 7 Jan. 1845, leaving issue,
  1. Peter Hamlet, of Stonestown and Park, King's Co., High Sheriff 1875, J.P., m. 28 Aug. 1873, Mary Anne, eldest dau. of John W. Tarleton, of Killeigh, King's Co., and d. 1883.
  2. George Irwin Thompson, Capt. 96th Regt., d. Jan. 1867.
  3. Blennerhassett David, of Claremont, co. Westmeath, d. 6 Oct. 1890, aged 52.
  1. Ellen Wade, m. Jan. 1866, Lieut.-Col. Henry Alexander Little, C.B., (Indian Army, who d. 7 Sept. 1908, leaving issue (*see* LITTLE *of Stewartstown*).
  2. Hannah Gerrald, m. June, 1866, H. W. Cuppage, 49th Light Infantry, and d. July, 1868.
(2) Thomas Blennerhassett, b. 1804 : m. 1828, Meliora, dau. of John Young, of Philpotstown, and d. 1853, leaving a son, Peter Henry, Lieut. 88th Regt., d. 1854, and a dau., Mary Anne, m. 5 Feb. 1856, William Rynd, of Messina.
(3) William.
(4) Henry, Capt. 74th Highlanders, d. unm.
(5) Robert, of Sandville, co. Kerry, m. 1843, Christina Frances, dau. of Francis Christopher Bland, of Derryquin, co. Kerry, and has had issue,
  1. Peter, b. 9 Aug. 1845, dec.
  2. Robert Acheson, b. 5 Sept. 1848, dec.
  3. Edward Herbert Bland, b. 21 Nov. 1851, dec.
  4. William, b. 18 Jan. 1854.
  1. Lucy Anne.
  2. Clara, m. 21 Sept. 1871, George Anthony, son of William Denny, J.P. and D.L., and d. 8 Oct. 1873, leaving a dau., Ethel.
  (6) Alice, d. young.
  (7) Alicia, m. 1820, the Ven. Arthur Blennerhassett Rowan, Archdeacon of Ardfelt, who d. 14 Aug. 1861.
5. Thomas, of Springfield, co. Wicklow, m. Anne, dau. of Thomas Brennan, of Kingston Lodge, co. Dublin, and had,
(1) Robert, m. Anne, dau. of R. Montgomery, and is dec.
(2) Thomas.
(3) George, dec.

(4) Philip.
(1) Anne, m. Robert Day, son of Rev. John Day, Rector of Kiltallagh, co. Kerry.
(2) Elizabeth Rachel.
(3) Maria Theresa, m. George Horan Thompson.
(4) Charlotte.
7. Henry, d. unm.
1. Hannah, d. unm.
2. Anna Maria, m. Rev. John Roberts, of Anglesea, N.W.
3. Penelope Jane, m. Thomas Herbert Orpen, M.D.
1. Mary, m. John Beatty.
2. Margaret, m. John Garnet, of Hollywoodrath, co. Dublin.
3. Isabella.
4. Jessica.
5. Anne.
The eldest son,
PETER THOMPSON, of Clonfin, m. Hannah, dau. of James Webster, of Longford, and had issue,
1. WILLIAM, his heir.
1. Margaret, m. William Slacke, of Annadale, co. Leitrim.
2. Mary, d. unm.
The son and heir,
WILLIAM THOMPSON, of Clonfin, Major Longford Militia, and J.P., m. 1793, his cousin, Mary, dau. of John Garnet, of Hollywoodrath, and had issue,
1. JOHN, his heir.
2. William, d. unm.
3. George (Rev.), d. unm.
4. David, Col. H.E.I.C.S., m. Sept. 1843, Harriette, dau. of — Montgomery, and has had issue,
  1. Cajeton, b. 1853.
  2. Cyrilla Jemima.
5. Thomas, J.P. and D.L., m. 2 Aug. 1839, Linda Mary Jane, dau. of Lieut.-Gen. Cobbe, R.A., 2nd son of Charles Cobbe, of Newbridge, co. Dublin, and d. Sept. 1868, having had issue,
  1. William Thomas, of Hollywoodrath, co. Dublin, J.P., B.A. Trin. Coll. Dublin, late Capt. 42nd Highlanders, b. April, 1840.
  2. George Ivan, late Capt. 99th Regt., b. June, 1842.
  3. Henry Bourke, b. Dec. 1844.
  4. Charles, b. June, 1847; m. 12 Sept. 1874, Alice Emily, only child of Lieut.-Col. Fetherstonhaugh, of Denahiney, late of 14th Hussars.   5. Arthur Trench, b. Sept. 1852.
    1. Linda Catherine Azele Frances.   2. Emma Harriette.
1. Mary, m. Sir William Osborne, 12th bart., of Ballintaylor.
Mr. Thompson d. 1850, and was s. by his son,
JOHN THOMPSON, of Clonfin, J.P. and D.L., High Sheriff 1820, m. June, 1826, Catherine, dau. of Robert Blackall, of Coolamber Manor, co. Longford. and by her (who d. Jan. 1862) had issue,
1. William Robert, an Officer in the Army, b. Oct. 1828; d.v.p. 4 June, 1860.   2. JOHN EDWARD, late of Clonfin.
1. Katherine Maria, m. 14 April, 1847, Hon. Robert Le Poer Trench. Capt. R.N., youngest son of Richard, 2nd Earl of Clancarty, and d. Sept. 1874.   Capt. Trench d. April, 1867.
2. Elizabeth, d. unm.
Mr. Thompson d. March, 1861.
JOHN EDWARD THOMPSON, of Clonfin, co. Longford, J.P., High Sheriff 1865, b. Jan. 1841; m. 1861, Emily Grace, eldest dau. of Rev. John James Fox, of Kinawley, co. Fermanagh (by Harriett Louisa his wife, dau. of Rev. Charles Cobbe Beresford, of Termon, co. Tyrone), and d. 8 May, 1908, having had issue,
1. JOHN FREDERICK WENSLEY, now of Clonfin.
2. Frederick Thomas Edward, b. April, 1864.
3. Beresford Osborne, b. Aug. 1865.
4. Guy Robert Maxwell, b. 1867.
5. Francis St. John, b. March, and d. Sept. 1868.
6. Richard Hercules, b. 1871.
1. Harriette Catherine.

Arms—Or, a fesse indented az., charged with three estoiles gold, on a canton of the second a sun in glory and in the centre base point a trefoil vert. **Crest**—An arm embowed in armour ppr., holding in the hand, also ppr., five ears of wheat or, the arm charged with a trefoil vert. **Motto**—In lumine lucem.

Seat—Clonfin, Granard, co. Longford. **Club**—Kildare Street, Dublin.

THOMPSON OF KILCOKE.

CHARLES HERBERT THOMPSON, of Kilcoke, Queen's Co., M.A., M.D., Trin. Coll. Dublin, Member of the Royal Coll. of Physicians of London, and Member of the Royal Coll. of Surgeons of England, b. 16 April, 1857; s. his father Jan. 1895.

Lineage.—RICHARD THOMPSON was settled at Cuddagh, Queen's Co., in 1737. His will, which is dated 4 May, 1766, was proved 22 Feb. 1767. He left issue by his wife, Jane, an only son,
RICHARD THOMPSON, of Ralish, Queen's Co., m. 1742, Mary McNeill. She d. 17 March, 1776. He d. 23 Aug. 1788, leaving issue, a son,
RICHARD THOMPSON, of Dublin, a lawyer, m. 1st (setts. dated 9 Feb.), 1776, Mary, dau. of Thomas White, of Ballybrophy, Queen's Co. (*see* WHITE *of Charleville*), and by her (who d. 1804) had issue,
1. Richard White, Barrister-at-Law, d. 1826.
2. Thomas, Capt. 53rd Regt., d. unm. circa 1807.
3. ALEXANDER, of whom presently.
Mr. Thompson m. 2ndly, Anne, widow of Henry Craven Holland, and dau. of Edward Lawrenson, of Rathmoyle, Queen's Co., and d. 1814. He was s. by his son,

/ .EXANDER THOMPSON, of Fitzwilliam Street, Dublin, and of he Queen's Co., in early life an officer 53rd Regt., *b*. 7 Nov. 17¦ ; *m*. 18 Jan. 1810, his cousin Elizabeth, dau. of Charles W¦ te, of Ballybrophy, and by her (who *d*. 22 Oct. 1843) had issu ,
 1 Richard, M.A. Trin. Coll. Dublin, Barrister-at-Law, *b*. 3 March, 1 11 ; *m*. Mary A. Heatly, and *d.s.p.* 19 Dec. 1875. She *d*. 1891.
 2 Robert, *b*. 10 Feb 1813 ; *d. unm*. 21 Jan. 1842.
 3 CHARLES, of whom presently.
 4 Alexander, *b*. 7 Feb. 1819 ; *d*. 7 April, 1835.
 1 Jane Maria, *b*. 28 March, 1815 ; *d. unm*. 8 March, 1889.
 2 Sarah, *d*. young.
Mr. Thompson *d*. 16 March, 1845, and was *s*. by his 3rd son,
CHARLES THOMPSON, of Harristown and Kilcoke, J.P. Queen's Co., B.A. Trin. Coll. Dublin, *b*. 10 Jan. 1818 ; *m*. 29 March, 1855, Thomasine Elizabeth, dau. of the Rev. Henry Herbert, Rector of Rathdowney, and half-sister of Sir John Blunden, Bart., of Castle Blu¦den, co. Kilkenny (*see* HERBERT *of Muckruss*), and had issue,
 1 CHARLES HERBERT, now of Kilcoke.
 2 Alexander Richard, *b*. 14 June, 1858.
 3 Henry Arthur, B.A. Trin. Coll. Dublin, Priv. Sec. to the Governor of the Straits Settlements 1884, and a Magistrate in the Colonial Civil Service, *b*. 10 Dec. 1859 ; *d*. at Penang, *unm*. 1 July, 1889.
 4 Edward Robert, *b*. 31 July, 1870 ; *m*. 9 March, 1903, Ellen Mary Charlotte, dau. of Sir Robert Dundas, Bart., of Arniston, and widow of Lieut.-Col. Gerald L. J. Goff, of Hale Park, Hants, late Argyll and Sutherland Highlanders.
 1. Harriet Elizabeth, *b*. 12 March, 1856 ; *d. unm*. 15 June, 1887.
 2. Thomasine Sophia.
 3. Sophia Jane, *m*. 31 May, 1894, Willoughby James Hamilton, son of the Rev. Canon Hamilton, Rector of Taney, Dundrum, co. Dublin (*see* HAMILTON *of Hampton*).
 4. Alice Olivia.
Mr. Thompson *d*. 28 Jan. 1895, and was *s*. by his eldest son.

Residence—Kilcoke, Ballybrophy, Queen's Co. *Club*—Junior Constitutional. W.

THOMPSON OF RATHNALLY.

FRANCIS D'ARCY THOMPSON, of Rathnally and Ross, co. Meath, J.P., M.A. Queens' Coll. Cambridge, *b*. 7 Oct. 1865 ; *m*. 3 Sept. 1908, his cousin, Annie Eleanor, only dau. of the late William Thompson, J.P. of Rathnally (*see below*).

Lineage.—JOHN THOMPSON, of Muckamore, whose will dated 18 Dec. 1705, was proved 1706, (Connor) bur. 28 Dec. 1705, and left issue, with three daughters, as many sons,
 1. William, of Muckamore, whose will dated 31 March, 1754, was proved 2 Sept. following. He *m*. 5 Aug. 1703, Elizabeth Blair, and had issue.
 2. SAMUEL, of whom presently.
 3. John.
He and one son,
SAMUEL THOMPSON, of Muckamore, left issue,
 1. John. 2 Samuel, bapt. 28 May, 1709.
 3. THOMAS, of whom presently.
 4. George, bapt. 29 June, 1718.
 1. Mary, bapt. 7 Oct. 1705.
The 3rd son,
THOMAS THOMPSON, of Greenmount, in the parish of Muckamore, bapt. 12 April, 1713. His will dated 28 Feb. 1799, was proved Nov. 1802. He *d*. 2 March, 1802, aged 89, having *m*. by licence, Jan. 1741, Eleanor Kinnier, whose will dated 13 Aug. 1804, being then of Cromore, co. Londonderry, was proved 25 April, 06. She *d*. 11 March, 1806, aged 89. They had issue,
 1. Samuel, of Belfast, and sometime of the Island of St. Croix, in the West Indies, who *d*. 9 April, 1794. His will dated 14 April, 1785, was proved 23 May, 1794 and 24 Nov. 1796. By his wife, Anne, widow of Bozen de Lance (marr. sett. dated 26 Nov. 1777), he left issue,
  1. Thomas, *b*. about 1780.
  1. Anne. 2. Eliza.
  3. Mary. 4. Louisa.
 2. John Kinnier, of Copenhagen, who *d*. before 1799.
 3. SKEFFINGTON, of whom presently.
 4. Robert Stewart, of Greenmount, J.P., *b*. 1755 ; *d*. 8 April, 1822. By his wife, Anne, he had issue,
  1. Caroline Beekman. 2. Margaret Beekman.
 1. Elizabeth, *d*. 13 March, 1786.
 2. Margaret. 3. Elenor.
 3. Mary, *m*. William Dunn, of Dublin.
 4. Anne, *m*. John Cromie.
The 3rd son,

I.L.G.

SKEFFINGTON THOMPSON, of Rathnally, co. Meath, *b*. 1742 ; *m*. 1779, Anna Maria, only child and heiress of Thomas Carter (*see* CARTER *of Shaen Manor*), of Rathnally, M.P. for Old Leighlin (or Loughlin), by Anna Maria, dau. of Sir Samuel George Armytage, Bart., of Kirklees, co. York (*see* BURKE'S *Peerage*, ARMYTAGE, BART.). He *d*. 5 Jan. 1810, having by his wife (who was *b*. 1764, and *d*. 27 March, 1813) had issue,
 1. Thomas, *d. unm*.
 2. John, *b*. 1792 ; D.L. of co. Meath, 1837, *d. unm*. 1858.
 3. Robert (Rev.), M.A. (Dublin), Rector of Navan, *d.s.p.* 10 Jan. 1857, having *m*. Louisa Cole, dau. of John Metgé, of Athlumney (*see that family*).
 4. William, of Rathnally and of Ross, J.P., *b*. 1801 ; *d*. 5 Dec. 1802, having *m*. 1st, 1830, Maria, 2nd dau. of Samuel Thompson, of Greenmount, co. Antrim, by whom he had no issue ; 2ndly, 1860, Annie Wharfe, dau. of William Paterson, of Surbiton, by whom he had issue,
  William, of Rathnally, J.P. and High Sheriff of co. Meath 1896, *b*. 1865 ; *d.s.p.* 5 Nov. 1901 ; *m*. 1896, Rebecca May, dau. of James Basten.
  Annie Eleanor, *m*. 1st, His Honor Judge Richard Mart in Dane, K.C., who *d*. 22 March, 1903, and by whom she had issue (*see* DANE *of Küllyhevlin*), and 2ndly, 3 Sept. 1908, her cousin, Francis d'Arcy Thompson (*see above*).
  He *m*. 3rdly, Lydia, dau. of Robert Macklin, of Carlton House, Maida Vale, London, but had no further issue.
 5. SKEFFINGTON, of whom below.
 1. Anna Maria, *b*. 1779 ; *d.s.p.* 5 July, 1859, having *m*. Jules Regnault, the French scientist.
 2. Eleanor, *b*. 1781 ; *m*. May, 1811, Sir Francis Hopkins, 1st bart. (extinct), by whom she had issue.
 3. Caroline, *d. unm*. 4. Amelia, *d. unm*.
 5. Fanny, *m*. James Somerville, of Ross, co. Meath (*see* BURKE'S *Peerage*, ATHLUMNY, B.), and had issue.
 6. Elizabeth, *b*. 4 June, 1786, and *d*. 8 March, 1876, having *m*. 1811, Sir John Gibney, Kt. M.D., of Brighton, Physician to George IV, by whom she had issue.
 7. Louisa, *b*. 1796 ; *d. unm*. 1872. 8. Octavia.
The 5th son,
REV. SKEFFINGTON THOMPSON, B.A. (Dublin), held curacies of Dunboyne and Drumcondra, of Tully, co. Antrim, 5. 11 July, 1803 ; *d*. 13 Feb. 1892 ; *m*. 11 Feb. 1834, Elizabeth Margaret, eld. dau. of Rev. Joshua d'Arcy, Rector of Lacka, and of Killalon, co. Kildare (*see* D'ARCY *of Hyde Park, co. Westmeath*), and by her (who was *b*. 1814 and *d*. 24 Sept. 1860) he had issue,
 1. Skeffington, of Ross, co. Meath, late Capt. Antrim Artillery Militia, *b*. 27 Nov. 1835 ; *d*. 1907 ; *m*. 30 June, 1890, Zara, widow of John Huston, formerly widow of — Dubedat, 3rd dau. of Isaac Corry, J.P., D.L. cos. Down and Armagh.
 2. FRANCIS DANIEL, of whom below.
 3. Thomas Carter, *b*. 6 Feb. 1838 ; *d. unm*. 6 Sept. 1868.
 4. John Edward, late Capt. 2nd Royal Lancashire Regt., *b*. 26 June, 1839 ; *m*. 17 May, 1862, Sarah Jane, dau. of — Spanton, and has issue.
 5. William (twin with Louisa), *b*. 2 Feb. 1849 ; *d*. young.
 6. William Henry, *d*. young.
 7. William Armytage, *b*. 12 Nov. 1852.
 1. Anna Maria, *m*. 31 Dec. 1870, Thomas Arthur d'Arcy, and has issue.
 2. Frances, *m*. 1866, Wm. H. O. Jackson, and has issue.
 3. Elizabeth, *m*. 16 July, 1867, B. B. Ussher, M.D., younger son of Capt. Beverley Ussher, and has issue.
 4. Louisa (twin with William), *b*. 2 Feb. 1849 ; *d*. 23 Aug. 1869.
 5. Eleanor, *m*. 25 Sept. 1869, J. d'Arcy Morton, son of Pierce Morton, Astronomer Royal, Capetown, and has issue.
 6. Sarah, *d*. young, 1856.
The 2nd son,
REV. FRANCIS DANIEL THOMPSON, M.A., Trin. Coll. Dublin, Vicar of Everton, Bawtry, Notts, *b*. 28 Nov. 1836 ; *m*. 10 Aug. 1860, Kate, 4th dau. of Jonathan Roose, of Liverpool, and has issue,
 1. FRANCIS D'ARCY (twin), now of Rathnally.
 2. Arthur Wellington (Rev.), M.A., Emm. Coll., Camb., R.D., and Rector of Christchurch, Salford, Manchester (twin), *b*. 7 Oct. 1865 ; *m*. 1895, Maude E., dau. of — Peirce, of Northampton.
 3. George de Roos (*New Reitfontein, Transvaal, South Africa*), *b*. 19 Nov. 1867 ; *m*. 1905, Katherine Carmichael, dau. of James Georgeson, of East London, S. Africa.
 4. Ernest Pelham Percy Lea (Rev.), M.A. Emm. Coll., Camb., Vicar of St. Matthew's, Nottingham, *b*. 30 Aug. 1869 ; *m*. 1898, Lilian Augusta, dau. of Capt. Alderson, and has issue,
  1. D'Arcy Perceval Pelham, *b*. 9 Oct. 1899.
  2. Westby R. d'Arcy, *b*. 22 Aug. 1902.
  1. Irene A. d'Arcy, *b*. 31 July, 1905.
 5 James Walter (*Quebec Chambers, Quebec Street, Leeds*), *b*. 14 June 1873.
 6. Norman d'Arcy, Assist. Paymaster R.N., *b*. 31 Oct. 1883.
 1. Kate Lucy, *m*. 1891, H. Russell Thomas, J.P., of Heucage Court, Falfield, Glos.
 2. Mabel, *m*. 1902, G. Wallace Allen.
 3. Helen, *m*. 1900, Vivian H. King (13, *Eton Road, N.W.*).
 4. Mary Beatrice, *m*. 1905, Charles Yates Luson.
 5. Elizabeth. 6. Ethel Armytage.

Arms—Quarterly, 1st and 4th, Per pale or and az., on a fess dancettée three estoiles all counterchanged, for a quarter of the 2nd, a sun in splendour of the 1st (for THOMPSON) ; 2nd and 3rd, Arg., two lions combatant sa. (for CARTER). Crest —A dexter cubit arm couped vested gu., charged with an estoile or, cuffed arg., the hand holding five ears of wheat ppr. Motto—In lumine luce.

Seats—Rathnally and Ross, co. Meath.

THOMSON OF ALTNAVEIGH.

Henry Thomson, of Altnaveigh, co. Down, J.P. and D.L. co. Down, High Sheriff 1910, J.P. co. Armagh and for Newry, M.P. for Newry 1880-5, b. 1840; m. 28 June, 1866, Alice Cecilia, dau. of Henry Corbet Singleton, of Aclare, co. Meath, D.L. (*see that family*).

Lineage.—Henry Thomson, of Downshire House, Newry, co. Down, m. Anne, dau. of the late Rev. William Henry, of Tassagh, co. Armagh, and had issue,
1. Henry, his heir.
2. William, of Cloondavin, Newry, late Capt. 78th Highlanders, m. 25 Aug. 1869, Alice, dau. of the late Capt. William Broughton, R.N. (see Burke's *Peerage*, Broughton, Bart.), and d. 1893, leaving issue.
1. A dau., m. Eastwood Bigger, of Falmore Hall, Dundalk.
2. Nicolina (*Downshire House, Newry*).

Seat—Altnaveigh, Newry; and Ballyedmond, Killowen, co. Down. **Club**—Carlton.

TODD-THORNTON OF WESTBROOK.

James Henry Brooke Todd-Thornton, of Westbrook, co. Donegal, late Capt. Sherwood Foresters, Derbyshire Regt., b. 11 July, 1855; m. 1880, Ada, dau. of Dr. L. Huntley, Brighton.

Lineage.—The family of Todd, seated for a considerable time in the north of Ireland, is of ancient Scottish descent.

William Thornton Todd, of Buncrana Castle, co. Donegal, son of Daniel Todd, by Letitia Thornton his wife, aunt of Sir William Thornton, and grandson of John Todd, by Elizabeth Patterson, m. 12 Jan. 1799, his cousin, Wilhelmina, dau. and heir of Daniel Patterson, of The Farm, Londonderry, and of Fox Hall, co. Donegal, by Jane his wife, sister and co-heir of Henry Vaughan Brooke, for many years M.P. for that co., and had issue,
1. Daniel, his heir.
2. William. Capt. 85th Light Infantry, d. 1849.
3. James Henry, late of Westbrook.
4. Andrew Thornton, m. 1st, Miss Fitzgerald, dau. of Major Butler Fitzgerald, of Toronto, and 2ndly, Miss Evans, dau. of Rev. George Evans, of Dungannon, and has issue, a dau., Mary Georgina, m. 10 May, 1899, Charles Edgar Byron.
1. Jane Wilhelmina, m. Rev. Hamilton Stuart, of Drumasple, co. Tyrone, and Rockfort, co. Donegal.
2. Angel, m. Arthur Darley, Capt. R.N., of Fern Hall, co. Dublin.
3. Mary, d. 1867.
4. Eliza, m. Hamilton Lane, 2nd son of Wiley Lane, of Lane's Park, co. Tipperary, and d. 1840.

The eldest son,
Daniel Todd, of Buncrana Castle, J.P. and D.L., b. 4 July, 1804; m. Miss Lloyd; d. 1863, and was s. by his brother,
James Henry Todd-Thornton, of Westbrook, co. Donegal, J.P. and D.L., High Sheriff co. Donegal, 1867, and co. Armagh 1879, late Capt. 40th Regt., subsequently Major and Hon. Lieut.-Col. Donegal Militia (Prince of Wales's Own), m. 12 Sept. 1850, Anna Letitia, only child of Capt. Daniel Geale, R.N., and had surviving issue,
1. James Henry Brooke, now of Westbrook.
2. Frederick Geale, Asst. District Commissioner, late Capt. Dorset Regt., b. 24 March, 1861, and d. at Benin 13 March, 1897.
3. Daniel Bickley Thornton, Capt. Donegal Artillery, Hon. Major, J.P. co. Kerry 1888, b. 12 Sept. 1863; m. Elizabeth Pennefather Francis, eldest dau. of Wm. Phineas Bury, of Little Island, co. Cork.
1. Wilhelmina, m. John George Smyly, son of Gen. Smyly, of Drayton Lodge, Monkstown, co. Dublin (*see* Smyly *of Camus*).
1. Mary.
3. Alice Elizabeth, m. 2 June, 1886, Sydney Hoare, son of Thomas Rolls Hoare, of Ennismore Gardens, and has issue.
4. Clara. 5. Edith Letitia, d. 28 Dec. 1870.

This gentleman was authorised by Royal Licence, dated 8 Sept. 1866, to take the surname of Thornton, in addition to and after the surname of Todd, and to bear the arms of Thornton and Todd quarterly, in consequence of the Thornton estates being centred and united in his person. Lieut.-Col. Todd-Thornton d. 1889, and was s. by his eldest son.

Family of Thornton.

There were two brothers of Yorkshire ancestry, Rev. Thomas Thornton, M.A., and William Thornton, of Bentham, near Settle, Craven. Of these brothers, the elder, Rev. Thomas Thornton, M.A., was Rector of Sutton, Sussex, 1663, and was bur. there 4 Feb. 1681. By Elizabeth, his wife, who was also bur. at Sutton, 8 Sept. 1687, he left three sons and one dau.,

1. George, of Petworth, whose will was proved 4 Oct. 1709, an was bur. at Sutton 14 June, 1709.
2. Thomas, executor to his brother George 1709, bur. at Sutton 30 Aug. 1715.
3. Joshua (Rev.), M.A., Rector of Sutton for 54 years, m. (article dated 15 Sept. 1724) Penelope, dau. of John Pery, and was bur 30 Sept. 1735.
1. Elizabeth, m. Richard Hargrave, and was bur. at Sutton 1 Sept. 1709.

The younger brother,
William Thornton, of Bentham, near Settle, Craven, West Riding, co. York, was father of
George Thornton, of Petworth, Sussex, where he was bur. 1 Feb. 1726, leaving issue,
1. Thomas, who d. before 1733, leaving, by Catherine his wife (wh afterwards m. James Stevens), one son and three daus.,
1. George.
1. Sarah. 2. Mary.
3. Anne.
2. William, of whom we treat.

The 2nd son,
William Thornton, of Muff, near Londonderry, was the first o the family who settled in Ireland. He proved the will of his cousin Rev. Joshua Thornton, Rector of Sutton, 30 Sept. 1736, and m about 1726, the dau. of Col. MacNeill, by whom he left issue,
1. William, his heir.
1. Catherine, m. Hon. and Rev. John Skeffington, 3rd son o Clotworthy, 4th Viscount Massereene.
2. Sarah, m. Spencer Huey.
3. Letitia, m. Daniel Todd, and was mother of William Thornto Todd, of Buncrana Castle, father of the late Col. Todd-Thornto of Westbrook.

The son and heir,
William Thornton, of Muff, near Londonderry, and of Armagh whose will, dated 12 March, 1792, was proved in the same year, d and was bur. at Bath, aged 51. He m. Anne, dau. of Perrott Jame of Magilligan, and had two sons,
1. William (Sir), K.C.B., Lieut.-Gen. in the Army, a very distin guished military officer, d. unm. 30 March, 1840.
2. Robert Innes Thornton, Capt. 15th Foot and of 21st Ligh Dragoons, d.s.p.

Lieut.-Col. James Henry Todd-Thornton, mentioned abov as grandson of Daniel Todd, by Letitia Thornton his wife, s. to the estates in cos. Antrim and Donegal of his cousin, Lieut.-Gen. Si William Thornton, K.C.B., at the death of his eldest brother, Danie Todd, 1863, and to the estates of his cousin, Major Robert Inne Thornton, in co. Armagh, 1866, consequent on the death of hi cousins, Col. Henry Huey and Capt. Huey.

Arms—Quarterly: 1st and 4th arg., on a bend gu., between two cinquefoils sa., three escarbuncles or, for Thornton; 2nd and 3rd arg., a chevron, between three foxes' heads erased gu., a mulle or, for Todd. **Crests**—1st, A griffin's head erased sa., beaked and collared or, charged on the neck with an escarbuncle of the last for Thornton; 2nd, A fox passant ppr., charged on the shoulder with a torteau (*Motto* over, Faire sans dire), for Todd. **Motto**— Nec temere nec timide.

Seats—Westfield, Buncrana, co. Donegal; Granitefield, co Dublin.

THUNDER OF LAGORE.

Patrick Thunder, of Lagore, co. Meath, and Ballay, of Dublin, J.P. and D.L. co. Meath, J.P. co. Dublin, b. 21 Jan. 1838; m. 1871, Mary Anne, youngest dau. of Peter de Penthony O'Kelly, of Barretstown, co. Kildare, and has issue,

Michael Penthony, b. 1874; m. 1900, Mary Christina (who d. 1908), only child of the late Patrick Sullivan, and has issue,
Patrick George, b. 1904.
Mary Anne Charlotte.

Lineage. — Michael Thunder, of Ballay, co. Dublin, m. Ellen O'Rorke, and was father of
Patrick Thunder, of Lagore, co. Meath; m. 1798, Elizabeth, eldest dau. of John Taaffe, of Smarmore Castle, c Louth, and had issue,
1. Michael, his heir.
2. Patrick, dec. 3. John.
4. George, m., 1837, Eliza Pauline (d. 1878), dau. of Alexand Mansfield, of Morristown Lattin, co. Kildare, and d. 1877, leavir issue,
Lattin, of Kingston Lodge, co. Meath, J.P., b. 1838.
5. Henry.
1. Anne, m. Francis Bernard Haly, of Boulogne-sur-Mer.
2. Ellen, dec.

His eldest son,

MICHAEL THUNDER, of Lagore, J.P. and D.L., High Sheriff 1850, 28 Oct. 1802 ; *m.* 2 Sept. 1834, Charlotte Mary, dau. of Col. Denis D'Alton, H.E.I.C.S. She *d.* 16 July, 1889. He *d.* 20 Nov. 79, leaving issue,
1. PATRICK, now of Lagore.
2. Michael Harman D'Alton of Seneschalstown, co. Meath, J.P., late Lieut. 58th Regt. (*United Service Club, Dublin*), b. 17 Feb. 1842 ; *m.* 19 June, 1878, Mary, eldest dau. of Sir Stuart Knill, Bart., and by her (who *d.* 25 Nov. 1893) has issue,
   1. Stuart Harman Joseph, Capt. Northamptonshire Regt. (*Junior Naval and Military Club*), b. 23 March, 1879 ; *m.* 6 Sept. 1910, Ethel Mary, eldest dau. of David Tidmarsh, of Lota, Limerick.
   2. Francis Dalton, *d.* young 8 March, 1887.
   3. Leo, *b.* 5 Feb. 1891.
   1. John Charles, *b.* 4 Aug. 1893.
   1. Charlotte, *b.* 20 Jan. 1882.
   2. Margaret Mary, *b.* 27 March, 1889.
3. John Albert, *d.* young.
4. James William Thomas, late of Bellewstown House, Drogheda, J.P., *b.* 1848 ; *m.* 1873, Laura, 4th dau. of the late William Plowden, of Plowden Hall, Salop (*see that family*), and has issue,
   1. Cyril Joseph, *b.* 27 July, 1875 ; *d.* 17 Jan. 1908, having *m.* 24 April, 1906, Ethel Georgina Emily, dau. of Thomas Everard Upton, of Ashburton, N.Z.
   2. Bernard William, *b.* 15 Aug. 1877 ; *m.* 2 Jan. 1907, Mabel Penelope Minchin Eckersley.
   3. Wilfrid Michael, *b.* 15 Nov. 1881.
      1. Hilad Mary, *b.* 28 July, 1879 ; *m.* 7 Oct. 1907, Gerard Thomas Manby-Colegrave, only son of the late Thomas Manby Colegrave, of 24, Onslow Square.
      2. Constance Maria, *b.* 29 June, 1885 ; *d.* 26 Oct. 1898.
      3. Mary Annette, *b.* 10 Nov. 1887.
5. George Francis, Major late 38th Regt. and 7th Royal Fusiliers, *m.* the relict of — Purcell, of Bombay. He *d.* 18 June, 1904, leaving issue, James and Michael.
6. Robert, *d.* young.
7. Francis, *m.* 1885, Louisa, dau. of the late John Maher, of Ballinkeele, co. Wexford.
   1. Charlotte Mary, *m.* Thomas Boylan, J.P., of Hilltown, co. Meath, and had issue,
      Thomas, *b.* 8 Aug. 1865 *m.* 1893, Cecilia Mary, eldest dau. of Charles E. Cary, of Follaton, Devon.
   2. Elizabeth, a nun of the Sacré Cœur, Roehampton, *d.* 24 Sept. 1875.
   3. Mary Jane.
   4. Julia, *m.* 2 Aug. 1863, Hugh O'Connor, of Dublin, and left issue.
   5. Helena, a Sister of Mercy.
   6. Rose, a nun of the Sacré Cœur, Roehampton.
   7. Mary, *d.* young.

Arms—Arg, on a chevron engrailed, between three trumpets fesseway sa., a mullet of the first.   *Crest*—A cubit arm ppr., grasping a trumpet sa.   *Motto*—Certavi et vici.

Seats—Lagore, near Dunshaughlin, co. Meath ; Ballalley, Lusk, co. Dublin.

TICKELL OF CARNOLWAY.

LIEUT.-COL. EDWARD JAMES TICKELL, D.S.O., of Carnolway, co. Kildare, J.P., Maj. 14th Hussars, served in Uganda 1897 and 1899 (despatches, medal and clasp, D.S.O), and in S. African War (despatches, medal and 4 clasps) *b.* 9 Feb. 1861 ; *m.* 12 Feb. 1902, Eliza, dau. of Lieut.-Col. Thomas Maxwell, Resident Magistrate, Natal.

Lineage.—THOMAS TICKELL, living *temp.* ELIZABETH, whose family had for many generations been settled in co. Cumberland, held landed property at Ullock in that co., which he transmitted by will, dated 23 May, 1617, to his eldest son,

RICHARD TICKELL, who *m.* Katherine, dau. of Rev Dr. Henry Fairfax, and grand-dau. of Sir Thos. Fairfax, 1st Baron of Cameron. He had, with two daus., three sons,
1. THOMAS.   2. William.
3. John.
The eldest son,

THOMAS TICKELL, bapt. at Crosthwaite Church 6 May, 1623, left a son,

RICHARD TICKELL (Rev.), appointed Vicar of Egremont, co. Cumberland, 7 June, 1673, and of Bridekirk in 1680, and again inducted to Egremont 2 Jan. 1686. He *m.* Mary Gale, of Whitehaven, and had issue,
1. Richard, Sec. at War in Ireland 1724-9 ; *m.* at Whitehaven, Elizabeth — ; he was heir general of the family, but sold the property to his brother Thomas by deeds of 23 and 24 Feb. 1721.
2. THOMAS, of whom we treat.
The 2nd son,

THOMAS TICKELL, *b.* 17 Dec. 1685, bapt. 19 Jan. 1686, at Bridekirk, M.A. Queen's Coll. Oxford 1708, Fellow in 1710, was the author of a small volume of poems published in Dr. Johnston's collection, and a friend of Addison, who procured him the post of Under-Sec. of State in 1717. In 1725 he was made Sec. to the Lords Justices of Ireland, which post he held till his death, which occurred at Bath 23 April, 1740. He *m.* 23 April, 1726, at St. Ann's, Dublin, Clotilda, dau. and co-heir of Sir Maurice Eustace, of Harristown, co. Kildare, and thus became entitled to that family's estate at Carnolway. She *d.* at Dublin 16 July, 1792, aged 92, and was bur. with her husband at Glasnevin. Her will, dated 16 Aug. 1772, was proved by her grandson, Thomas Tickell. They left issue,
1. JOHN, of whom presently.
2. Thomas, Capt. 11th Dragoons, *b.* 1735 ; *d.s.p.* at Dublin 9 March, 1765.
   1. Margaret, *b.* 1732 ; *m.* Major Bladen Swinny.
   2. Clotilda, *b.* 1734, *d.* 1737.   3. Philippa, *b.* 1738, *d.s.p.* 1740.

The elder son,

JOHN TICKELL, of Glasnevin, *b.* 23 Nov. 1727 ; *m.* 8 May, 1748, at St. Cigbi's, Holyhead, Esther, dau. of Thomas Pierson, of Glasnevin. He sold the Cumberland property in 1781, and after holding a civil appointment at Windsor for a time went abroad, and *d.* at Aix-la-Chapelle, his mother surviving him. He left issue,
1. THOMAS, of whom presently.
2. Richard, *b.* 1751, a well-known political writer in his day, appointed Commissioner of Stamps by Lord North 1779. He *m.* twice, 1st, in 1780, Mary Linley, of Bath, sister to Mrs. Sheridan, and 2ndly, Mrs. Sarah Leigh, a widow. He *d.* 4 Nov. 1793, by a fall from one of the parapets of Hampton Court Palace, where he was in the habit of sitting and reading. He had, with a dau., Elizabeth Anne, *b.* 1781, *d.* 1862, two sons,
   1. Richard, *b.* 1782, Lieut. R.N. ; killed in action on H.M.S. *Phœbe*, off Sardinia, May, 1805.
   2. Samuel Richard, Capt. 8th Bengal N.I., *b.* 1785 ; *m.* 1810, Mary, dau. of Capt. Morris, 3rd Bengal N.I. ; *d.* 5 Oct. 1827, at Berhampoor (M.I.), leaving issue,
      (1) Samuel Richard, Col. H.M. Bengal Army, *b.* 1811 ; *m.* 1844, Maria, dau. of J. W. Templer ; *d.* 20 April, 1875, leaving a son, George Templer, and two daus., Mary Louisa, *m.* William Marsh Cooper ; and Ada Elizabeth, *m.* George Scott.
      (2) Edward Lawrence, *b.* 1817, *d.s.p.* 1883.
      (1) Mary Rose, *b.* 1815 ; *m.* 1st, 1834, Col. Hodson, Bengal Artillery, and 2ndly, 1840, Lumsden Strange.
3. John Ambrose (Rev.), Rector of Wells, Norfolk, *b.* 1753, *m.* 1783, Sarah Cumberland ; *d.* 26 March, 1835, leaving two sons,
   1. Thomas, *b.* 1784 ; *m.* 4 Oct. 1809, Maria Quartermain Trotter, and had, with eight daus., one son,
      Thomas Quartermain, who *d.s.p.*
   2. John, *d.s.p.*
1. Elizabeth Clotilda, *b.* 1754 ; *m.* 30 Nov. 1788, at Ghent, Sir Robert Barclay, Bart., and left issue.
2. Helena Maria, *b.* 1755 ; *m.* 1773, Samuel Wood, and left issue, Samson Tickell, *b.* 1774.

The eldest son,

THOMAS TICKELL, of Carnolway, *b.* 1749 ; Capt. 5th Royal Irish Dragoons, served as Major in the Kildare Militia during the Irish Rebellion, High Sheriff of Kildare 1803 ; *m.* 1771, Sarah, only dau. of Luke Sparks, H.E.I.C.S. ; *d.* s. to the estates on the death of his grandmother Clotilda, in 1792 ; *d.* 30 Dec. 1831, at Bath, and was bur. with his wife in Carnolway Churchyard. His will, dated 14 Feb. 1825, was proved by his son Edward. He had issue,
1. Thomas, Capt. 70th Surrey Regt., *b.* 1772, *d.s.p.* 1802, at Trinidad.
2. Edward, Q.C., *b.* 1779, many years chairman of co. Armagh ; *s.* to the estates on the death of his father in 1831, and added to them by purchases from the Duke of Leinster. He *d.s.p.* at Dublin 18 July, 1863 ; bur. at Mount St. Jerome Cemetery, leaving the estates to his nephew, Thomas Tickell, R.N.
3. John (Rev.), *b.* 1783, *d.s.p.*
4. RICHARD, of whom presently.   5. Robert, *b.* 1789, *d.s.p.*
1. Sarah, *b.* 1775, *d.s.p.*

The 4th son,

LIEUT.-GEN. RICHARD TICKELL, C.B., *b.* 10 Sept. 1785, served from 1804 to 1839 in the Bengal Engineers ; *m.* 1st, 1 Feb. 1808, at Cawnpore, Mary Anne, dau. of Richard Procter, and by her (who *d.* 27 Sept. 1833, at Calcutta), had issue,
1. Richard Samuel, Major H.E.I.C.S., *b.* 28 June, 1809, in India ; *m.* Jessey Eliza, dau. of Maj.-Gen. Sir Robert Bartley, K.C.B. ; *d.s.p.* at Brighton 24 Oct. 1860 ; bur. in Kensal Green. She *d.* 27 April, 1901.
2. George, *b.* 12 Dec. 1815 ; took Holy Orders in the Church of Rome, and *d.* at Stonyhurst, 6 April, 1893.
3. THOMAS, late of Carnolway.
4. Edward Arthur (Rev.), *b.* 1819, Vicar of Ulrome, Yorkshire ; *d.* 2 Aug. 1897.
5. James, Col. I.C.S., *b.* 15 Aug. 1821 ; *m.* 10 Oct. 1853, Sophia Victoria, 2nd dau. of Col. George W. Moseley, and *d.* 25 Oct. 1895, leaving issue,
   1. James Robert, *b.* 25 Nov. 1855 ; P.W.D. India.
   2. Richard Hugh, *b.* 1 Aug. 1860 ; P.W.D. India.
   1. Sophia Margaret.   2. Alice Georgiana, *d.* 5 July, 1888.
1. Sarah, *b.* 1811, *m.* 1828, Arthur Lang, Bengal C.S. ; *d.* 12 June, 1880, having had six sons and three daus.

Gen. Tickell *m.* 2ndly, 18 June, 1840, at St. George's, Bloomsbury, Margaret Scott, 2nd dau. of Adam Walker ; she *d.* 15 Feb. 1882, at Cheltenham. They had issue,
6. Robert Procter, Major R.E., *b.* 20 March, 1841, at Reading ; *d.s.p.* 10 July, 1884, at Movar, India.
7. Arthur Lang, Lieut.-Col. 77th Regt., *b.* 4 April, 1844, at Reading ; *m.* 7 Dec. 1871, at St. Philip's, Cheltenham, Henrietta Margaret, dau. of Sir Richard Green-Price, Bart., and has issue,
   1. Arthur Claud Powlett, *b.* 24 June, 1875 ; *d. unm.* 21 Jan. 1894.

2. Hugh Richard, b. 23 Oct. 1879.
1. Laura Margaret, m. Major Ernest Bellers, Middlesex Regt.
2. Ellenor Forbes.   3. Nora Constance.
4. Violet.
8. John Larkins, P.W.D. India, b. 7 Nov. 1845, at Cheltenham.
9. Eustace Ashburner, Capt. 68th Regt., b. 8 March, 1851, at Cheltenham; d.s.p. 2 July, 1877, bur. with his father at Cheltenham.
10. Charles, P.W.D. India, b. March, 1853; m. 1st, 16 April, 1887, Ella Buck. She d. 30 April, 1887. He m. 2ndly, 2 April, 1891, Alice Esther, dau. of the late Charles Wordley Francis, of Southchurch, Essex.
2. Eliza Anne Minor, m. 18 June, 1863, at St. Luke's Cheltenham, Joseph Christian Corbyn, Deputy Surgeon-Gen. Bengal Army, She d. 7 April, 1910, leaving issue.
3. Fanny Ellen, m. 26 April, 1866, Col. Sir Edward Stock Hill, K.C.B., M.P., who d. 17 Dec. 1902, leaving issue.
Gen. Tickell d. 3 Aug. 1855, at Cheltenham, and was bur. in Leckhampton Churchyard. His 3rd son,
THOMAS TICKELL, of Carnolway, co. Kildare, Commander R.N., retired 14 Jan. 1854, b. 28 Feb. 1817; m. 12 Jan. 1860, Louisa Emily, eldest dau. of Rev. James T. C. Saunders. She d. 29 April, 1907. He d. 4 April, 1898, leaving issue,
1. EDWARD JAMES, now of Carnolway.
2. Richard Eustace, b. 29 April, 1864.
3. Henry Maurice, M.A. Trin. Coll. Camb., b. 14 Aug. 1866.
1. Mary Louisa, m. 5 July, 1887, Charles E. F. Mouat-Biggs, 2nd son of Col. John Peter Mouat-Biggs, and has issue.

Arms—Quarterly: 1st and 4th, gu., a maunche arg.; 2nd, sa. on a bend arg., three escaliops gu.; 3rd, gu., a saltire or, for EUSTACE, and also quarters PARSONS, COOKE, PEYTON, GERNON, COLVILL, SUTTON, and FRANCIS. Crest—An arm couped below the elbow and erect vested gu., charged with three fleurs-de-lis or, cuffed arg., holding in the hand ppr. a fleur-de-lis gold. Motto—Vita posse priore frui.
Residence—The Lypiatts, Cheltenham. Clubs—Naval and Military, S.W.; Cavalry, W.; Kildare Street, Dublin.

TIGHE OF WOODSTOCK.

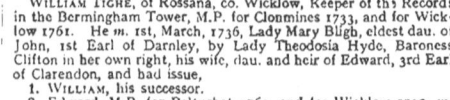

EDWARD KENRICK BUNBURY-TIGHE, of Woodstock, co. Kilkenny, educated at Harrow and Trin. Coll. Camb., J.P. and D.L., High Sheriff co. Kilkenny 1895, co. Westmeath 1903, late Lieut. Grenadier Guards, and formerly Rifle Brigade, b. 24 Aug. 1862; s. his father 1891; m. 19 Sept. 1894, Viola, only dau. of Edward Skeffington Randal Smyth, of Mount Henry, Queen's Co. (see that family), and has had issue,
1. FREDERICK EDWARD FOWNES, b. 1904; d. 8 Aug. 1911.
1. Kathleen Augusta Louisa.
2. Oonah Frances Geraldine.
3. Moira Gertrude Florence.

Lineage.—RICHARD TIGHE (son of William Tighe, of Market Deeping, by Mary his wife, dau. of Tobias Houghton, of Kelthorpe, Rutland) went over to Ireland, and settled there. He was Sheriff of Dublin 1649, Col. Dublin Militia, Mayor of Dublin 1651, 1652, 1655, and Member for the same city in CROMWELL'S Parliament 1656. He acquired considerable estates in cos. Carlow, Dublin, and Westmeath, during the reigns of CHARLES I and CHARLES II, and m. Mary, dau. of Newman Rooke, of London, and d 20 Feb. 1673, leaving issue,
1. WILLIAM, his heir.
1. Anne, m. 1st, Theophilus Sandford, ancestor of Lord Mount Sandford (extinct); 2ndly, John Preston; and 3rdly, Hon Oliver Lambart, 3rd son of Charles, 1st Earl of Cavan.
2. Rebecca, m. Hugh Lecson, ancestor of the Earl of Milltown.
3. Mary, m. 1670, Francis Wheeler.
Richard Tighe was s. by his son,
WILLIAM TIGHE, b. 1657; m. Anne, dau. of Christopher Lovett (see LOVETT of Liscombe), and by her (who m. 2ndly, Thomas Coote, a Judge of the King's Bench) had issue,
RICHARD, his heir.
Mary, m. 1694, Capt. Hon. Alexander Stewart, 2nd son of William, 1st Viscount Mountjoy.
Mr. Tighe d. 1679, and was s. by his only son,
RIGHT HON. RICHARD TIGHE, P.C., temp. GEORGE I, M.P. for Belturbet 1703, for Newton 1715, and for Augher 1727. He m. Barbara, dau. and co-heir of Christian Bor, of Drinagh, co. Wexford (by Ellen his wife), and had, besides two daus., a son and successor,

WILLIAM TIGHE, of Rossana, co. Wicklow, Keeper of the Records in the Bermingham Tower, M.P. for Clonmines 1733, and for Wicklow 1761. He m. 1st, March, 1736, Lady Mary Bligh, eldest dau. of John, 1st Earl of Darnley, by Lady Theodosia Hyde, Baroness Clifton in her own right, his wife, dau. and heir of Edward, 3rd Earl of Clarendon, and had issue,
1. WILLIAM, his successor.
2. Edward, M.P. for Belturbet 1763, and for Wicklow 1790, m. Miss Jones, of co. Westmeath, and left one son,
George William, m. Margaret, widow of Stephen, 2nd Earl Mountcashel, and dau. of Robert, 2nd Earl of Kingston, and d.s.p.
3. Richard William, M.P. for Wicklow 1768, m. Sarah, dau. of Goddard Richards, of Grange, co. Wexford, and had, with other issue, who d. unm., two sons,
1. Edward, m. Lucy, youngest dau. of Richard Newton King, of Macmine Castle, co. Wexford, d.s.p.
2. Robert Richard, m. 1st, Sarah Frances, dau. of Rev. John Cleland, and 2ndly, Louisa Joan, dau. of Hon. George Jocelyn, and widow of Hon. and Rev. Edward Wingfield, and d.s.p. 20 July, 1873.
1. Theodosia, m. Rev. Richard Blachford, and had one son, John Blachford, of Altadore, co. Wicklow, and one dau., Mary, wife of her cousin, Henry Tighe.
Mr. Tighe m. 2ndly, Margaret, eldest dau. and co-heir of Capt. Thomas Theaker, M.P., by whom he had a son, Thomas, m. and had issue, and a dau., Barbara, m. 1 Aug. 1776, Rev. Michael Sandys, Rector of Powerscourt. He d. 1766, and was s. by his son,
WILLIAM TIGHE, of Rossana, M.P. for Athboy 1761, and subsequently for Wicklow, m. 23 May, 1765, Sarah, only child of the Right Hon. Sir William Fownes, Bart., of Woodstock, co. Kilkenny, by Lady Elizabeth Ponsonby his wife, dau. of Brabazon, 1st Earl of Bessborough, and had issue,
1. WILLIAM, his heir.
2. Henry, M.P. for Inistioge, m. his first cousin, Mary, dau. of Rev. Richard Blachford, and d.s.p. 1836. Mrs. Henry Tighe gained distinction as a poetess. She d. 1810.
3. John Edward, d. unm.
1. Elizabeth, m. Rev. Thomas Kelly, of Kellyville, Queen's Co.
2. Marianne Caroline, m. Charles Hamilton, of Hamwood.
Mr. Tighe d. 1782, and was s. by his eldest son,
WILLIAM TIGHE, of Woodstock, co. Kilkenny, b. 1766, Member for the borough of Wicklow in the Irish, and for the co. in the Imperial Parliament. This gentleman, as patron of the boroughs of Wicklow and Inistioge, returned four members to Parliament, and was at the time of the Union one of the most influential commoners in Ireland. He m. 1793, Marianne, dau. and co-heir of Daniel Gahan, of Coolquil, co. Tipperary, M.P. for Fethard, by his wife Hannah, sister and co-heir of Matthew Bunbury, of Kilfeacle, co. Tipperary, and by her (who d. 1853) he had issue,
1. WILLIAM FREDERICK FOWNES, his heir.
2. Daniel, of Rossana, co. Wicklow, J.P. and D.L., High Sheriff 1827, formerly in the Grenadier Guards, assumed by Royal Licence, 2 May, 1872, the additional surname and arms of BUNBURY; m. 3 March, 1825, Hon. Frances Crofton, 3rd dau. of Hon. Sir Edward Crofton, 3rd bart., of Moate, by Lady Charlotte Stewart his wife, dau. of John, 7th Earl of Galloway, and d. 26 March, 1874, having had issue by her (who d. 20 Dec. 1881),
1. FREDERICK EDWARD, of whom presently.
2. JAMES STUART, of Rossana, Ashford, co. Wicklow, J.P. and D.L., High Sheriff 1876, Lieut.-Col. (half-pay) late 8th Madras Cavalry, b. 1 March, 1831; m. 21 Oct. 1857, Charlotte, youngest dau. of Very Rev. Thomas John de Burgh, of Oldtown, co. Kildare, Dean of Cloyne (see that family), by the Lady Anna Louisa Hely-Hutchinson his wife, sister of John, 3rd Earl of Donoughmore. He d. 3 July, 1904, having by her (who d. 18 Aug. 1904) had issue,
(1) Walter Stuart, of Rossana, b. 26 July, 1861; m. 1894, Adelaide Margaret, dau. of Major David Philip Browne, 7th Hussars.
(2) Wilfred, b. 8 June, 1868; m. 21 April 1898, Lucy Emily, dau. of Frederick Thomas Lewin, of Castlegrove, co. Galway (see that family).
(1) Louisa, } twins, b. 25 Oct. 1859.
(2) Flora,
(3) Charlotte Frances, d. 6 April, 1876.
(4) Una Emily, b. June, 1864.
(5) Maud May, b. June, 1866.
3. Arthur Francis, R.N., b. 1837; d. 1870.
4. Richard William, b. 1839; d. 1843.
5. Francis Robert Spencer, b. 1845; d. 1855.
1. Frances Marianne, m. 7 Aug. 1852, Hon. Frederick A. H. Chichester, 3rd son of Arthur, 1st Lord Templemore, and by him (who d. 18 May, 1863) had issue.   2. Louisa Elizabeth.
3. Theresa Augusta, m. 19 Oct. 1864, Hon. Charles St. George Crofton, R.N., and d. 14 Aug. 1867, leaving issue.
4. Georgiana Harriet, m. J. Hargrave Bridgford, and d. 9 Jan. 1900.
5. Susan Diana.   6. Gertrude Fanny, d. unm.
1. Hannah, m. 1818, Lord Patrick James Herbert Crichton Stuart, M.P., only brother of John, 2nd Marquess of Bute, and had issue.
Mr. Tighe d. 1816, and was s. by his eldest son,
RIGHT HON. WILLIAM FREDERICK FOWNES TIGHE, of Woodstock, J.P. cos. Wexford, Westmeath, and Carlow, High Sheriff co. Kilkenny 1823 and co. Carlow 1837, Lord-Lieut. and Custos Rotulorum of Kilkenny, Col. Kilkenny Fusiliers, and one of H.M.'s Most Hon. Privy Council, b. 17 March, 1794; m. 18 April, 1825, Lady Louisa Madelina Lennox, 5th dau. of Charles, 4th Duke of

Richmond and Lennox, and by her (who d. 2 March, 1900), had an only dau.,
Charlotte Frances, who d. an infant 1827.
Mr. Tighe d. 1878, and was s. by his nephew,
FREDERICK EDWARD BUNBURY-TIGHE, of Woodstock, co. Kilkenny, J.P. co. Wicklow, formerly in the 53rd and 32nd Regts., and late Lieut.-Col. Comm. Kilkenny Militia, b. June, 1826; s. his uncle 1878; m. 10 Aug. 1858, Lady Kathleen Louisa Georgina Ponsonby dau. of John William, 4th Earl of Bessborough, and by her (who d. 9 July, 1863) had issue,
 1. William Frederick, Lieut. Grenadier Guards, b. 17 June, 1860; d. unm. 19 April, 1887.
 2. EDWARD KENRICK, now of Woodstock.
Col. Tighe d. 6 Jan. 1891, and was s. by his only surviving son.
Arms—Per chevron, embattled arg. and sa., five crosses-crosslet in chief, four in base counterchanged. Crest—A wolf's head erased ppr., with a collar az., charged with a cross-crosslet between two studs or. Motto—Summum nec metuam diem nec optem.
Seat—Woodstock Park, Inistioge, co. Kilkenny. Town Residence—25, Norfolk Street, Park Lane, W. Clubs—Guards', Naval and Military, Brooks', Bachelors', and Kildare Street, Dublin.

TIGHE OF MITCHELSTOWN.

ROBERT HUGH MORGAN TIGHE, of Mitchelstown, co. Westmeath, late Lieut. 5th Batt. P.W.O. Leinster Regt., b. 8 Dec. 1874; s. his father 1895; m. 12 Feb. 1903, Florence, eldest dau. of Charles Ebenezer Trefry, of Place Fowey, Cornwall, and widow of Capt. Hewlett Charles Perkins, Duke of Cornwall's Lt. Inf.

Lineage.—RICHARD TIGHE, of The Haymarket and of Kilpatrick, co. Westmeath, b. 1645, m. Mabella, dau. of Robert Stearne, of Tullynally, co. Westmeath, sister of Major-Gen. Robert Stearne, Governor of Kilmainham, and first cousin of John Stearne, D.D., Bishop of Clogher, and d. 1699 (will dated 28 April, proved 6 May that year), leaving issue,
 1. Richard, bapt. 2 May, 1678; d. young.
 2. William, bapt. 17, d. 19 July, 1681.
 3. Richard, bapt. 14 Aug. 1682 (will dated 27 Sept. 1751, proved 13 Feb. 1753). He left issue.
 4. William, bapt. 10 Jan. 1684; d. young.
 5. ROBERT, of whom presently.
 6. John, bapt. 19 Dec. 1688; bur. 24 Sept. 1689.
 7. Stearne, of Carrick, co. Westmeath, bapt. 21 Jan. 1690; ancestor of the TIGHES of Carrick, co. Westmeath, and Clonlee, co. Meath.
 8. Stephen, bapt. 16 May, 1694; bur. 17 Dec. 1698.

The 5th son,
ROBERT TIGHE, who s. his father in his estates in cos. Westmeath and Carlow, purchased the estates of Mitchelstown, Castletowndelvin, Scurlogstown, and other lands in co. Westmeath, from his kinsman, Richard Tighe. He was bapt. 7 May, 1686; m. 1715, Mary, sister of the Right Hon. Nathaniel Clements, father of the 1st Lord Leitrim, and by her (who d. 1780) had issue,
 1. Richard Stearne, M.P. for Athy, b. 1717; d.v.p. 23, Dec. 1761. He m. 25 Sept. 1759, Arabella, dau. of Sir John Osborne, 6th bart., of Ballintaylor, co. Waterford, and had issue,
  1. ROBERT STEARNE, heir to his grandfather.
  2. William Fitzgerald, b. 22 June, 1762, d. 1770.
  1. Mary Ann, b. 1761, d. 1770.
 2. Robert, of South Hill, co. Westmeath, M.P. for Carlick, who s. to his father's co. Carlow estate, d. 1799. He m. Isabella, dau. of Gilbert King, of Charlestown, co. Roscommon, and sister of Sir Gilbert King, 1st bart., and by her had issue,
  1. Robert, Major Westmeath Militia, M.P. for Carlow at the period of the Union, m. 1st, Frances, dau. of Robert Wade, of Clonebrany, co. Meath, and 2ndly, Charlotte, dau. of James Fetherston, of Bracklyn Castle, co. Westmeath. By his 1st wife he had one dau., and by his 2nd, two sons,
   (1) ROBERT, of Fitzwilliam Square, Dublin, J.P., Chairman of co. Limerick, m. 1st, Hester Catherine (who d.s.p. 1872), eldest dau. of the late Right Hon. T. B. Cusack-Smith, Master of the Rolls in Ireland. He m. 2ndly, 3 April, 1879, Jane, dau. of Michael Dobbyn Hassard, M.P. He d.s.p. 15 June, 1881. His widow m. 2ndly, 25 Aug. 1888, Frank Woodward Tonge.
   (2) Richard.
   1. Anne, m. Francis Hopkins, of Newtown.
   2. Isabella, m. Henry Daniel, of Newforest.
   3. Eliza, m. Joseph Morgan Daly, of Castle Daly.
   4. Louisa, m. Robert Handcock Temple, of Waterstown, co. Westmeath, and had one dau., Isabella, wife of William George, 2nd Lord Harris.
  3. Richard, killed at the siege of Gibraltar.
  1. Anne, m. Benjamin Chapman, of Killua, co. Westmeath, and was mother of Sir Benjamin Chapman, and of Sir Thomas Chapman, 1st and 2nd barts., of Killua Castle.
Mr. Tighe d. 1766, and was s. by his grandson,
ROBERT STEARNE TIGHE, b. 3 March, 1760; m. 1st, 18 March, 1785, Catherine, only dau. and heir of Col. Hugh Morgan, of Cottlestown, co. Sligo, and of Cork Abbey, co. Wicklow, by Elizabeth his wife, dau. and heir of the Right Hon. Philip Tisdall, Attorney-General of Ireland, by Mary Singleton his wife, niece and co-heir of the Right Hon. Henry Singleton, Lord Chief Justice of the Common Pleas, Ireland, and by her (who d. 18 Feb. 1819) had issue,
 1. ROBERT MORGAN his successor.
 2. William Stearne. b. 6 Feb. 1793; lost on board H.M.S. Ajax Dec. 1806.
 3. Hugh Usher (Very Rev.), Dean of Derry, s. 1833, to the estate of Carrick, co. Westmeath, under the will of Stearne Tighe, grandson of Stearne Tighe, of Carrick, b. 27 Feb. 1802; d. 11 Aug. 1874; m. 21 April, 1828, Anne Florence, dau. of John M'Clintock, of Drumcar, co. Louth, by his wife, Lady Elizabeth French, dau. of William, 1st Earl of Clancarty, and by her (who d. 21 Feb. 1893) had issue,
  1. Robert Hugh Morgan, b. Feb. 1829; d. unm. May, 1867.
  2. Charles Moland Morgan, d. April, 1843.
  1. Elizabeth Lætitia Morgan, m. 22 June, 1853, Edward Stopford Blair, of Penninghame (see BURKE'S Peerage, COURTOWN, E.). He d.s.p. 17 Sept. 1875. She d. 25 Feb. 1896.
  2. Catherine Florence Morgan, m. 6 July, 1858, J. E. Severne, M.P., of Wallop Hall and Thenford.
 1. Catherine, m. July, 1807, William Henry Worth Newenham, of Coolmore, co. Cork, who d. Sept. 1842. She d.s.p. Feb. 1858
Mr. Tighe m. 2ndly, Anna, dau. of Major-Gen. Dilkes, and siste of Lieut.-Gen. Dilkes, Lieut.-Governor of Quebec, and by her (who d. May, 1823) had no issue. He d. 21 May, 1835, and was s. by his eldest son,
ROBERT MORGAN TIGHE, of Mitchelstown, J.P. co. Westmeath, b. 1 July, 1790; m. 9 July, 1830, his cousin, Frances Elizabeth, youngest dau. (and eventual sole heir of her brothers) of Hon. and Right Rev. Thomas St. Lawrence, Bishop of Cork and Ross, by Frances his wife, dau. and co-heir of Rev. Henry Maule Coghlan, D.D., and by her (who d. 30 Sept. 1871) had issue,
 1. ST. LAWRENCE ROBERT MORGAN, his heir.
 2. Marcus Anthony, b. 9 Aug. 1839; d. 16 Oct. 1855.
He d. 19 Jan. 1853. His only surviving son,
ST. LAWRENCE ROBERT MORGAN TIGHE, of Mitchelstown, co. Westmeath, D.L., b. 20 Feb. 1838; s. his father 9 Jan. 1853; m. 5 Feb. 1874, the Hon. Laura Allanson Winn, now of Ashgrove, Flintshire, eldest dau. of Charles Allanson, 4th Lord Headley (see BURKE'S Peerage), and d. 2 April, 1895, having had issue,
ROBERT HUGH MORGAN, now of Mitchelstown.
Margaret Catherine Hume Morgan, m. 25 March, 1909, Francis R. Wood, Lieut. R.N., son of Charles Wood.
Residences—Ashgrove, Ellesmere, Shropshire, and 121, Belsize Road, N.W. Club—Windham.

TIGHE OF THE HEATH.

THOMAS ALOYSIUS TIGHE, of The Heath, co. Mayo, J.P. and D.L., High Sheriff 1879, and J.P. co. Galway, M.P. for co. Mayo 1874, b. 1829; m. 29 April, 1875, Marie Antoinette, eldest dau. and co-heir of the late Peter Hubert Dolphin, J.P., of Danesfort, co. Galway (see DOLPHIN of Turoe), and has issue,
 1. THOMAS ALOYSIUS, Capt. 3rd Batt. Connaught Rangers, b. 10 May, 1876.
 2. Robert Dolphin, of Danesfort, co. Galway, Barrister-at-Law b. 20 Sept. 1877.
 3. Peter Hubert Joseph, late Lieut. 5th Batt. Connaught Rangers, b. 21 April, 1880.
 1. Marie Antionette.

Lineage.—ROBERT TIGHE, of The Heath, and of Ballinrobe, co. Mayo, J.P. (whose father m. Annie, dau. of John Patton, an officer in a Dragoon Regt.), b. 1800, m. 1st, 1828, Catherine, dau. of Thomas Kelly. She d. 1817, having had issue,
 1. THOMAS ALOYSIUS, now of The Heath.
 2. Robert Henry, late Maj. 3rd Batt. East Surrey Regt., b. 1833, m. 1867, Julia, dau. and co-heir of James Clarke, of Melbourne, Australia, and has issue,
  1. Maude.   2. Eileen.
 3. James, late Capt. Hants. Art., b. 1835; d. unm. 12 Aug. 1888.
 1. Ellen, d. young.
 2. Mary, d. young.
He m. 2ndly, 1838, Joanna, dau. of Joseph Gleeson. She d. 1845. He d. 1872, having by her had issue,
 4. Joseph, b. 1841, d. unm. 1857.
 5. John Patton, Lieut. 1st Batt. Devonshire Regt., b. 1843, accidentally shot in S. Africa 1872.
 3. Annie, m. 1869, Henry de Blaquiere, J.P., of Fiddane House, co. Galway, who d. 1883, leaving five sons and four daus.
Seat—The Heath, Claremorris, co. Mayo.

TILLIE OF DUNCREGGAN HOUSE.

MARSHALL TILLIE, of Duncreggan House, co. Londonderry, J.P. and D.L., and J.P. co. Donegal, b. 18—; s. his brother 1908; m.   , dau. of   , and has issue, of whom his 2nd dau. Nora, m. 15 June, 1910, Claud John Low, of Holt House, Redhill.

Tisdall. THE LANDED GENTRY. 694

Lineage.—JOHN TILLIE, of Crookston Mains, Midlothian, had issue, a 2nd son,
WILLIAM TILLIE, of Duncreggan House, o. Londonderry, J.P. and D.L. for that co., High Sheriff 1872, and H.M. Lieutenant for Londonderry, b. 1823; d. 1904; m. Agnes Marshall, dau. of William Lee, of Fernichurst, Midlothian, and by her (who d. 4 Sept. 1900) had issue,
1. WILLIAM JOHN, b. 1855; m. 1 Feb. 1888, Alice Pilling, elder dau. of Benjamin Gibbons, of Woodleigh, Cheshire.
2. Charles Reid Tillie, of Duncreggan House, co. Londonderry, Solicitor, d. 1908.
3. MARSHALL, now of Duncreggan House.

Residence—Duncreggan, Londonderry.

TISDALL OF CHARLESFORT.

CHARLES ARTHUR TISDALL, of Charlesfort, co. Meath, Captain Irish Guards, b. 22 April, 1875; s. 1892; m. 1904, Gwynneth May, only child of Charles Adshead, and has issue 2 daus., of whom one was b. 15 Dec. 1907.

Lineage.—The first of the family in Ireland was MICHAEL TISDALL, who had a sister, Catherine, m. — FitzSymons. This Michael Tisdall was of Castle Blaney, co. Monaghan; he had by his wife Ann (née Singleton), seven sons and two daus., viz.,
1. MICHAEL, of whom presently.
2. James, J.P., who purchased Bawn, co. Louth, 16 July, 1690; M.P. for Atherdee 1695, 1701, and 1713; m. Feb. 1682, Elinor, dau. of Mathew French, of Belturbet, co. Cavan, High Sheriff 1677, and had issue,
James, of Bawn, m. Rose, dau. of Oliver McCausland, and d. 1 Oct. 1757, aged 63, leaving a son and a dau.,
James, of Bawn, m. 1787, Catherine Maria, dau. of Thomas Townley Dawson (see BURKE'S *Peerage*, DARTREY, E.). His will, dated 18 Oct., was proved 14 Dec. 1797. He left by her, who m. 2ndly, 4 June, 1798, Charles, 3rd Earl of Charleville, two children,
James Thomas Townley, of Bawn, d. 15 Dec. 1851.
Catherine Louisa Augusta, m. 1828, Lieut.-Col. George Marlay, C.B., and had issue (see MARLAY of *Belvedere*).
Rachel, m. Edward Bond, of Bondville, co. Armagh, and had issue. She m. 2ndly, Rev. Robert Gorges, Rector of Termonfeckin.
3. Thomas, of Bawn, co. Louth, d. 1681-2, who had issue,
1. William, of Charles Street, Dublin, who, by Elizabeth his wife, was father of the Rev. Thomas, M.A., Rector of Atherdee, who m. Lætitia, dau. of Chichester Fortescue, of Dromiskin.
2. Richard, Registrar of the Court of Chancery in Ireland, M.P. for Dundalk 1707, and for co. Louth 1713 and 1715, and who, by Mary Boyle, his wife, was father of the Right Hon. Philip Tisdall, P.C., M.P. for Dublin University 1739, 1761, and 1768. Solicitor-General 1751; Attorney-General 1760; Principal Secretary for Ireland, and Keeper of the Privy Seal. 1763. He d. 11 Sept. 1777. He m. Mary, 3rd dau. of the Rev. Rowland Singleton, D.D., and niece and co-heir of the Right Hon. Henry Singleton, Lord Chief Justice of the Common Pleas, and had issue, Elizabeth, m. Col. Hugh Morgan, of Cottelstown, co Sligo.
2. Michael, d. 9 Jan. 1702-3.
3. Richard.
1. Anne.
2. Mary.
4. John, of Teltown, co. Meath, d. 1693-4, leaving issue.
5. Richard, d. unm. 1683.
6. George.
7. William, of Carrickfergus b. 1641; by Anna his wife, he was father to Rev. William Tisdall, D.D., Rector of Dromcree, who m. Eleanor, dau. of Hugh Morgan, of Cottlestown, co. Sligo, and was father to Rev. William Tisdall, B.A., Vicar of St. James', Dublin, who m. Lady Mary Brabazon, dau. of Chambre, 5th Earl of Meath, and had issue (see BURKE'S *Peerage*, MEATH, E.).
1. Catherine, m. Andrew Harvey.
2. A dau., m. Christopher Caldwell, of Dublin.

The eldest son,
MICHAEL TISDALL, of Mount Tisdall, purchased in 1668 the manor of Martry, co. Meath (wherein the mansion of Charles fort stands). He was Secondary of the Court of King's Bench in Ireland, and J.P. for co. Meath in 1679, whom arms were granted 27 May, 1679, to him and his brother James by Richard St. George, Ulster. He m. 18 April, 1666, Anne, dau. of Rev. William Barry, Rector of Killucan, brother of Sir James Barry, Knt., 1st Lord Santry, Chief Justice of the King's Bench in Ireland, and had issue,
1. WILLIAM, of whom presently.

2. Michael, b. 1671, Barrister-at-Law, Military Advocate-General and Commissioner for Appeals in Ireland; who had issue, Michael, b. in Dublin 1723.
1. Catherine, b. 1670; m. Charles Campbell.
2. Elizabeth, bapt. 21 Sept. 1671.

The elder son,
WILLIAM TISDALL, of Mount Tisdall, b. Feb. 1668; is supposed to have d. in 1725. He m. Frances, 3rd dau. of the Hon. Robert Fitzgerald, and sister of Robert, 19th Earl of Kildare, and by her (who d. 26 Aug. 1719) had issue,
1. MICHAEL, his heir.
2. George (Rev.), D.D., Rector of St. Mary, Shandon, Cork, bapt. 19 June, 1707; d. 28 March, 1772; m. 17 March, 1727, Frances, dau. of Lieut.-Col. George Canning, of Garvagh, co. Londonderry (see BURKE'S *Peerage*, GARVAGH, B.), and had issue,
1. Michael (Ven.), Archdeacon of Ross, m. 8 Aug. 1754, Elizabeth, dau. of Ald. Thomas Farran, of Cork, and d. 1788, leaving issue,
Fitzgerald (Rev.), M.A., Rector of Kilmore, co. Cork, J.P.; m. Aug. 1788, Mary, dau. of William Jameson, and was murdered on Easter-day 1809, leaving issue,
1. Michael, of Rockhouse, Clifton.
2. FitzGerald, d.s.p.
3. George Canning, d.s.p.
1. Jane, m. Abraham Chatterton, and was mother of the Right Hon. Hedges Eyre Chatterton, Vice-Chancellor of Ireland.
2. Mary, m. — Devereux.
Frances, b. 1769.
1. Frances.   2. Letitia, m. — Bayley.
3. Catherine.

Mr. Tisdall was s. by his elder son,
MICHAEL TISDALL, of Mount Tisdall, M.P. for Atherdee 1713 and 1715, m. Catherine, dau. of the Right Hon. William Palmer, Principal Secretary in Ireland, Secretary for War, and Commissioner for Appeals, M.P. for Kildare 1695, and for Castlebar 1723, and by her (who m. 2ndly, Rev. Edward Hudson, D.D.) had issue,
1. CHARLES, his heir.   2. Michael.
1. Catherine, m. 1st, 17 April, 1750, Arthur Hamilton-Maxwell, of Drumbeg, co. Down; and 2ndly, — Caulfeild.
2. Frances, m. Emanuel Bayly.

He d. Dec. 1726 (his will, dated 25 Jan. 1724, was proved 18 Jan. 1727), and was s. by his son,
CHARLES TISDALL, of Mount Tisdall, b. 29 Oct. 1719, who built a new house on his manor of Martry, and called it CHARLESFORT, which has since been the designation of the family. He m. 19 Feb. 1754, Hester, dau. of Oliver Cramer, 2nd son of Oliver Cramer, of Ballyfoyle, co. Kilkenny, by Hester his wife, dau. of Sir John Coghill, Knt., LL.D., Master in Chancery. He d. 27 June, 1757, having by her (who m. 2ndly, 1767, Nicholas Forster, of Coolderry) had issue,
1. MICHAEL, his heir.
2. Charles, b. 31 Oct. 1756; m. Maria, dau. of Edward Croker, and d. 1816, leaving an only son,
Charles, of Dublin, who d. 28 July, 1834; he m. 1st, Susanna, dau. of Harman FitzMaurice, of Spring Hill, co. Carlow. She d. 1823, leaving an only son,
(1) Charles Edward (Rev.), D.D., Chancellor of Christ Church Cathedral, Dublin, and late Rector of Dolough, Dublin, b. 19 May, 1821; d. 28 Aug. 1905; m. Frances Caroline, youngest dau. of John Barton, and has had issue,
1. Sidney Fitzmaurice, d. 28 Jan. 1868.
2. Henry Cusack Wilson, Royal Hibernian Academician, b. 14 Nov. 1861.

Charles Tisdall m. 2ndly, Anna, dau. of Capt. Lodge, of Ballinahone, co. Armagh, and had a son,
(2) Richard.
Charles Tisdall m. 3rdly, Catherine Elizabeth, dau. of Major W. Stirling St. Clair, and had issue,
(3) William St. Clair, of the Deanery, Auckland, New Zealand, Audit Inspector to the New Zealand Government, served in 15th and 47th Regts., and was afterwards Major 2nd Waikato Regt., b. 8 Nov. 1831; m. Maryanne Josephine Caulfeild, and d. 8 April, 1892, having had issue,
1. William St. Clair Towers (Rev.), M.A., D.D., of Ispahan, Persia, b. 19 Feb. 1859; m. 1st, Bertha Alice, dau. of Benjamin Maclean, of Cornwall, and afterwards of Auckland, N.Z., and by her has issue,
(1) Charles William St. Clair, b. 11 Dec. 1881.
(1) Bertha Annette St. Clair, b. 16 June, 1884; m. 22 March, 1911, Ralph Howard Tatton, son of Rev. D. Tatton, of Bushey, Herts.
He m. 2ndly, Marian Louisa, eldest dau. of Rev. William Gray, M.A., Secretary, Church Missionary Society, London, and by her has issue,
(2) Arthur Walderne St. Clair, b. 21 July, 1890.
(3) John Theodore St. Clair, b. 9 Oct. 1893.
(4) Edward Gordon St. Clair, b. 25 April, 1895.
(5) Francis Royston St. Clair, b. 17 Feb. 1901.
(2) Irene Mary St. Clair, b. 1 Feb. 1888.
(3) Edith Rosabelle St. Clair, b. 11 March, 1889.
(4) Ruth Noel St. Clair, b. 25 Dec. 1896.
(5) Violet Marian St. Clair, b. 23 Feb. 1899.
2. Charles Edward Gordon, of Singapore, m. Cissie, dau. of — Robinson, of Queensland, Australia, and has issue,
(1) Arthur, b. 11 Aug. 1906.
(2) Charles.   (3) Vernon.
1. Mary Catharine Louisa, d. unm.
2. Frances Alice.
3. Ethel Adelaide Elizabeth.   4. Edith Annie Isabelle.

IRELAND. Torrens.

(4) Gordon Charles Vernon, b. 24 Feb. 1835; m. Annie, dau. of the Rev. — Harden, and left a son,
Charles Archibald (Rev.), M.A., of Auckland, N.Z.
(1) Rosabella Catherine Maria, b. 5 July, 1833; d. 14 June, 1844.

The elder son,
MICHAEL TISDALL, of Charlesfort, b. 2 Dec. 1755, served as High Sheriff of Meath 1788. He m. 15 April, 1779, Juliana, dau. and coheir (with her sister Jane, m. George, 1st Lord Headley) of Arthur Blennerhassett, of Ballyseedy, co. Kerry, M.P. for Tralee 1743-60 (see BLENNERHASSETT of Ballyseedy), and by her (who d. 24 Oct. 1789) had issue,
1. CHARLES ARTHUR, his heir.
2. James (Rev.), Rector of Ballinderry, b. 20 May, 1784; m. Sarah Eyre, dau. of Thomas Jackson, of Tullydoey, co. Tyrone, and d. 16 Nov. 1851, leaving issue,
   1. Thomas, d. unm. 1871.   2. James, d. unm.
   3. Archibald, of Sunnyside, Clontarf, b. 2 Oct. 1822; d. 1 April, 1885, having m. Alicia, dau. of Alexander Hamilton, Q.C., by whom he had,
      (1) James Archibald, b. 1855, d. 1862.
      (2) Anne Catherine, m. William Neville Ward.
   (2) Juliana, m. 14 Feb. 1899, Richard Deane-Freeman, son of the late Rev. Richard Deane-Freeman, Rector of Ardnageehy, co. Cork, and grandson of Edward Deane-Freeman, D.L., late of Castlecor, co. Cork.
   4. Benjamin (Rev.), B.A., of Ballinderry, m. 19 Aug. 1880, Jane Mackinnon (Beechwood, Ballinderry, co. Antrim), dau. of W. H. Sefton, of Beechwood, Ballinderry, and d. 7 Feb. 1895.
   5. William Alexander, d. unm.
      1. Juliana, d. unm.
3. Archibald, Rear-Admiral R.N., b. 5 Sept. 1786; d. unm. 28 April, 1854. Served in the action off St. Domingo 1806, and in the reduction of Java 1811, as A.D.C. to Gen. Gillespie.
   1. Juliana, m. 29 Jan. 1799, Alexander Hamilton, of Newtown Hamilton, co. Armagh, Q.C. (son of Hugh, Lord Bishop of Ossory), and d. 1840.
   2. Catherine, m. 16 March 1807, Rev. Francis Gervais, of Cecil, co. Tyrone (see that family).

Mr. Tisdall m. 2ndly, widow of Rev. Crow. She d. 1 April, 1800. He d. 9 March, 1794, and was s. by his son,
CHARLES ARTHUR TISDALL, of Charlesfort, High Sheriff 1811, b. 7 Nov. 1782; m. 30 March, 1807, Elizabeth, dau. of John Vernon, of Clontarf, co. Dublin (see VERNON of Clontarf Castle), and had issue,
1. JOHN, late of Charlesfort.
2. William, of Balbray, J.P., Treasurer of Meath, b. 1817; m. Frances, dau. of Rev. George O'Connor, and has had issue,
   1. George, J.P., Barrister-at-Law, b. 12 March, 1860; m. 1887, Margaret Stedman, 3rd dau. of Andrew Armstrong, J.P., of Kylemore House, co. Galway, and has issue, a dau., Winifred.
   2. Richard John, b. 1862; d. unm.
   1. Frances Elizabeth.   2. Elizabeth Martha.
   3. Isabella Charlotte.   4. Henrietta.
   5. Georgina Florence.
3. Archibald, Major-Gen., commanded Royal Sussex Regt., and Brigade Depôt, Aberdeen, b. 31 Aug. 1822; m. 1 Jan. 1856, Anna Claire, eldest dau. of Major Henry Walter Bellew, Bengal Army (see BURKE'S Extinct Peerage), granted a reward for distinguished and meritorious services 1880. She d. 3 July, 1887. He d. 30 July, 1896, leaving issue,
   1. Archibald Walter Bellew, M.A., LL.B., b. 15 Aug. 1858; d. 4 March, 1910; m. 3 Aug. 1892, Elizabeth Amy, only dau. of the Rev. James Pratt, D.D., son of Col. Pratt, of Stoneville, and has issue,
      (1) Archibald James, b. 9 Sept. 1893.
      (2) Charles Henry, b. 24 Feb. 1897.
      (1) Claire Elise, b. 5 Oct. 1895.
   2. Arthur Lance, Lieut.-Col. R.A., b. 25 Nov. 1860; m. 4 April, 1893, Katharine Maude, dau. of John Gordon Bowen, of Burt House, co. Donegal (see that family), and widow of A. B. Gzowski, Major 69th Welsh Regt.
      1. Ismay Frances, m. Rev. John Anderson Brown, M.A., of Beawar, Rajputana, son of G. Brown, of Galashiels, N.B.
      2. Anna Claire, m. 23 Oct. 1888, Major William Wilfrid Webb, M.D., F.S.A., Ind.Med.S. (see WEBB of Oddstock).
      3. Sarah Sophia, m. William Stewart Harrison.
4. James, b. 1826; d. unm. 9 June, 1879.
   1. Juliana, m. 22 March, 1838, James Noble Waller, of Allenstown, co. Meath (see that family), and d. 1847.
   2. Henrietta, m. 1835, Richard Chaloner, of Kingsfort, co. Meath (see that family). She d. 22 Nov. 1890.
   3. Elizabeth, d. unm.   4. Maria, d. unm.
   5. Frances, m. 1845, Alexander Montgomery, of Kilmer, co. Meath, who d. 1863, leaving issue (see MONTGOMERY of Kilmer).

Mr. Tisdall d. 22 July, 1835, and was s. by his eldest son,
JOHN TISDALL, of Charlesfort, co. Meath, J.P. and D.L., b. 23 July, 1815; m. 3 Oct. 1837, Isabella, dau. of the late Hon. George Knox, D.C.L., by Harriet his 2nd wife, dau. of Thomas Fortescue (see BURKE'S Peerage, RANFURLY, E.), and had issue,
1. Charles Arthur, Capt. 18th Hussars, b. 28 June, 1838; d. unm. 22 Jan. 1869.
2. John Knox, Capt. R.E., b. 10 June, 1839; m. 23 April, 1874, Jane Elizabeth, only dau. of Robert Adams, and d. 16 July, 1885, leaving issue,
   1. CHARLES ARTHUR, now of Charlesfort.
   2. William George Robert, b. 18 Dec. 1876; m. 13 Feb. 1899, Elsie Beatrice, eldest dau. of William Gardiner, of Rockshaw, Merstham, and had issue,

Michael William Knox, b. 13 June, 1903.
   1. Kathleen Isabel.   2. Elizabeth Violet.
   3. Mary.
3. George William, Lieut. R.E., b. 9 Oct. 1844; d. unm. at Missourie, 7 June 1872.
4. Henry Chichester, J.P., b. 21 Jan. 1849; d. 6 Aug. 1908; m. 24 June, 1875, Isabella Frances, eldest dau. of John E. Vernon, of Erne Hill, co. Cavan (see that family).
5. Vernon Archibald, Commander R.N., b. 2 Sept. 1850.
6. Richard Louis, b. 13 April, 1855; m. 24 July, 1896, Rita, dau. of J. Wilson, of Montevideo, and d.s.p. 4 Dec. 1896.
7. Arthur James, b. 15 June, 1856; m. 24 Feb. 1896, Frances Katherine, dau. of Capt. G. R. Harriott, of St. Andrews, N.B., and d.s.p. 8 April, 1898.
8. Alfred Oliver (Rev.), M.A. Oxon. Chaplain of St. Saviour's, Belgrano, Hon. Canon Anglican Pro-Cathedral at Buenos Aires, b. 7 July, 1859; m. 13 Jan. 1887, Evelyn Susan, 4th dau. of Rev. Arthur John Empson, M.A., Rector of Eydon, co. Northampton, and has issue,
   1. Michael Henry, b. 15 March, 1888.
   2. John Denis, b. 10 June, 1889.
   3. Walter Brian, b. 23 Sept. 1890.
   4. Charles Richard, b. 22 Feb. 1893.
   5. Oliver Rafael, b. 2 April, 1899.
   1. Monica Isabel, b. 19 May, 1894.
1. Harriet Elizabeth, m. 17 April, 1873, Rev. A. H. Cole-Hamilton, Rector of Scaldwell, co. Northampton, who d. Dec. 1889 (see BURKE'S Peerage, ENNISKILLEN, E.).
2. Isabella Maria, m. 7 Dec. 1876, Arthur R. Nugent, who d. 1896 (see NUGENT of Portaferry).
3. Anne Charlotte.

Mr. Tisdall s. his father 22 July, 1845, served as High Sheriff 1841, and d. 7 March, 1892, and was s. by his grandson.

Arms—Sa., a thistle or, between three pheons arg., quartering BLENNERHASSETT. Crest—An armed hand erect, charged with a trefoil or, and holding an arrow ppr. Motto—Tutantur tela coronam.
Seat—Charlesfort, Kells, co. Meath. Club—Guards', S.W.

TODD-THORNTON. See THORNTON.

TOLER-AYLWARD. See AYLWARD.

TORRENS OF ROSSTULLA.

The late JOHN TORRENS, of Rosstulla, co. Antrim, J.P., B.A. Worcester Coll. Oxford, b. 20 Oct. 1849; m. 17 Oct. 1876, Florence (now of Rosstulla), dau. of Robert Stewart Lepper, J.P., of Trainfield, Belfast, and d. 21 Feb. 1908, leaving issue,
1. JAMES ROBERT, late Lieut. 21st Lancers, and Capt. 4th Batt. Royal Irish Rifles (Cavalry Club, W.; b. 20 Oct. 1877; m. 5 March, 1902, Enid Maude (whom he divorced in 1908), dau. of the late Hon. William Forster, Agent-General of New South Wales, and has issue,
   JOHN BASIL HUGHES, b. 1902.
1. Florence Muriel, b. 10 Nov. 1881; d. 22 Feb. 1893.
2. Eileen, b. 20 Jan. 1886; m. 16 May, 1911, Capt. Herbert Frederick Spence, Duke of Cambridge's Own (Middlesex Regt.).

Mr. John Torrens was the elder son of the late JAMES TORRENS, J.P. cos. Antrim and Donegal, of Edenmore, co. Antrim (who d. 7 Aug. 1884, aged 68), by Sarah Hughes his wife (who was m. 11 May, 1848, and d. 7 July, 1893), dau. of Samuel Gelston, J.P., of Rosstulla, co. Antrim, and Eliza his wife, dau. of Thomas Hughes.
Seat—Rosstulla, Whiteabbey, co. Antrim.

TORRENS OF EDENMORE.

THOMAS HUGHES TORRENS, of Edenmore, co. Antrim, J.P., High Sheriff 1903, D.L. for the City of Belfast, educated at Cheltenham Coll., b. 4 Sept. 1851, younger son of the late JAMES TORRENS, of Edenmore, co. Antrim (who d. 7 Aug. 1884) (see TORRENS of Rosstulla).
Seat—Edenmore, Whiteabbey, co. Antrim. Clubs—Junior Carlton, S.W., and Ulster, Belfast.

Torrens. THE LANDED GENTRY. 696

TORRENS OF SOMERSET.

MAJ. JOHN ARTHUR WELLESLEY O'NEILL TORRENS, of Somerset, co. Londonderry, J.P. and Vice-Lieut., High Sheriff 1898, Major Reserve of Officers, Maj. (retired) Scots Greys, b. 2 Feb. 1856; son of Rev. Thomas Henry Torrens (who d. 1858) by Barbara Maria his wife, elder dau. and co-heir of the late Thomas Rumbold Richardson, of Somerset, co. Londonderry (who d. 7 March, 1868), by Hatton Elizabeth his wife, dau. of Rev. Gardiner Young.

Seat—Somerset, Coleraine, co. Londonderry. Club—Naval and Military, W.

TOTTENHAM OF TOTTENHAM GREEN AND WOODSTOCK.

CHARLES ROBERT WORSLEY TOTTENHAM, of Tottenham Green, co. Wexford, Woodstock, co. Wicklow, and Plâs Berwyn, co. Denbigh, J.P. for cos. Denbigh, Merioneth, and Wicklow, D.L. co. Merioneth, High Sheriff co. Wicklow 1888, M.A. Ch.Ch. Oxford, late Major 3rd Batt. Royal Welsh Fusiliers, b. 21 Feb. 1845; m. 1st, 5 Nov. 1874, Dorothea Anne (who d. 1903) dau. of the late Leonard Cornwall, of Brownstown House, co. Meath, and by her (who d. 8 Jan. 1903) has issue,

1. CHARLES LOFTUS WATKIN, M.A., b. 28 Nov. 1876; m. 28 April, 1906, Ethel Frances, youngest dau. of the late Henry A. Cowper, of Trudden, co. Wicklow.
2. George Leonard, b. 20 April, 1879.
3. Sophia Dora Elizabeth, m. 30 April, 1902, Major Peter La Touche, of Bellevue, co. Wicklow (see that family). He d. 13 March, 1904. She m. 2ndly, 17 Jan. 1907, Frederick Cowper, of Trudden, co. Wicklow.
4. Amy Maude.

He m. 2ndly, 1905, Eleanor Cockburne, dau. of Major Alexander John Lindsay, late R.A.

Lineage—WILLIAM TOTTENHAM, of Barrington, co. Cambridge, is named in the Subsidy Rolls, 14 and 15 HENRY VII. (anno 1523), as one of the two principal persons in that parish. By Margery his wife, he had two sons and four daus., the elder being William, Lord of the Manors of Wyllyen, Herts, and Skelton Bedfordshire, m. Elizabeth, widow of Robert Castell, and d.s.p. May, 1600. Mr. Tottenham's will, dated 20 May, was proved June, 1557. His 2nd son,
JOHN TOTTENHAM, of Barrington, is named in the Subsidy Rolls of 1566, 1571, and 1597. By Alice his wife, he left three sons, and two daus.,
1. JOHN, his heir.
2. Humphrey (Rev.), M.A., Vicar of Wooton, co. Bedford, 1599 to 1638; m. two wives, and had four sons and five daus.
3. James, of Barrington, m. Agnes Titchmarsh, and had issue.
1. Beatrice, m. John Hancock, of Shepreth, and had a 4th son, Barnabas Hancock, b. 1601, who settled in Ireland, acquired the estate of Ballyduffe, near Lismore, co. Waterford, and adopted the surname of TOTTENHAM. He m. 1630, Mrs. Martha Harman, widow, and d.s.p. 1632. His widow re-married Sir Erasmus Borrowes, 1st bart., of Giltown.
2. Eleanor, m. Thomas Gunston, and left issue.
Mr. Tottenham d. June, 1599, and was s. by his eldest son,
JOHN TOTTENHAM, of Barrington, m. 11 Oct. 1608, Agnes Mustell; and d. Aug. 1611, having had by her (who m. 2ndly, Matthew Scott) two sons,
1. JOHN, his heir. 2. Humphrey, d.s.p.
Mr. Tottenham d. Aug. 1611, and was s. by his eldest son,
JOHN TOTTENHAM, of Youghal, co. Cork, bapt. 14 June, 1609, settled in Ireland, and was named in his cousin, Barnabas Hancock, alias Tottenham's, will. He m. Aug. 1632, Margaret, dau. of Sir Robert Tynte, Knt. of Ballycrenan, cc. Cork, and had two sons,
1. JOHN, his heir.
2. EDWARD, of Cheddar, Somerset, d. 28 Dec. 1702, leaving issue by his 2nd wife, Sarah Spencer, two sons and a dau.
The eldest son,

JOHN TOTTENHAM, of Tottenham Green, alias Ballyloskernan (which estate he purchased from Charles Collins), in co. Wexford. He m. 1st, Catherine, dau. of John Atkin, of Polemore, co. Cork, by whom (who d. 24 Aug. 1661) he had issue, and 2ndly, 30 July, 1671, Anne, dau. of John Clarke, of Hardingstone, co. Northampton, by whom (who d. 1716-7) he had three children, all of whom d. young. Mr. Tottenham d. 14 Oct. 1700, and was s. by his only surviving child,
EDWARD TOTTENHAM, of Tottenham Green, J.P., b. 7 Sept. 1659; m. 1st, 3 May, 1683, Elizabeth, dau. of Samuel Hayman, of Youghal (his will was proved 20 Feb. 1712-13 by his widow, Jane), and d. 1712, when he was s. by his only child,
CHARLES TOTTENHAM, of Tottenham Green, High Sheriff co. Wexford 1737, M.P. for New Ross temp. GEORGE II. He m. Ellinor, dau. of John Cliffe, of Mulrancan, co. Wexford, by whom (who d. 5 June, 1745) he had issue,
1. JOHN (Sir), of whom presently.
2. CHARLES, ancestor of TOTTENHAM of Ballycurry.
3. Edward (Rev.), of Ballinaboun, b. 1717; m. 1st, July, 1756, Bridget, dau. of Rev. Jasper Cox, and 2ndly, Aug. 1780, Dorothy, dau. of John Cox, of Coolcliffe, co. Wexford, and d.s.p. 1793.
4. Loftus Anthony, Gen. in the Army, Col. 55th Regt., b. 1723; d. 16 March, 1811; m. Katherine, dau. and heir of Mr. Millard, of Wakefield, by whom (who d. 7 Nov. 1793, aged 72) he had an only child, Kitty, who d. unm. 7 Nov. 1810, aged 54.
5. Cliffe, an Officer in Gen. Bragg's Regt., afterwards of Cork, d.s.p. 1773; m. 10 April, 1756, Frances, dau. of Rev. Joshua Thomas, Rector of Ferns.
6. Synge, Lieut. 28 Foot, d.s.p. 1793; m. 1st, 1765, Henrietta Jones, and 2ndly, Mary, dau. of William Kingston, which lady d. 1797.
1. Eleanor, m. Maurice Howlin-D'Arcy, of Coolure, co. Wexford, and left issue.
2. Barbara, m. May, 1746, Ephraim Carroll, of Stephen's Green, Dublin; and d. 21 Nov. 1767, leaving issue.
Mr. Tottenham m. 2ndly, 1746, Mary, dau. of John Grogan, of Johnstown (widow, 1st, of Major Andrew Knox, of Rathmacnee, and 2ndly, of William Hore, of Harperstown), but by her (who d. 1777, aged 83) had no issue. This gentleman was well known in the political circles of Ireland by the name of " Tottenham in his boots."
He d. 20 Sept. 1758, and was s. by his eldest son,
SIR JOHN TOTTENHAM, 1st bart., of Tottenham Green, so created 18 Dec. 1780, M.P., High Sheriff co. Wexford 1749, b. 6 July, 1714; m. 31 Dec. 1736, Hon. Elizabeth Loftus, dau. of Nicholas, 1st Viscount Loftus, and sister and co-heir of Henry, 3rd Earl of Ely, and by her (who d. June, 1747) had surviving issue,
1. CHARLES, of whom presently.
1. Anne, m. 8 Dec. 1756, Joseph Rogers, of New Ross, and left issue.
2. Ellinor, m. 29 May, 1766, Rev. John Orr, and left issue.
3. Mary, m. 5 Dec. 1766, Richard Annesley, of New Ross, who was murdered by the rebels at The Rower, co. Kilkenny, 5 June, 1798, leaving issue.
Sir John d. 29 Dec. 1786, and was s. by his son,
SIR CHARLES TOTTENHAM, 2nd bart., of Tottenham Green, created MARQUESS OF ELY (see BURKE's Peerage), b. 23 Jan. 1738; m. 11 June, 1766, Jane, dau. and co-heir of Robert Myhill, of Killarney, co. Kilkenny, by whom (who d. 21 Feb. 1807) he had issue,
1. JOHN LOFTUS, 2nd Marquess of Ely (see BURKE's Peerage).
2. ROBERT PONSONBY (Right Rev.), of whom presently.
1. Mary Elizabeth, d. unm. 1 March, 1769.
The Marquess of Ely d. 22 March, 1806. His 2nd son,
LORD ROBERT PONSONBY TOTTENHAM, D.D., of Tottenham Green, s. to the Tottenham Estates, was consecrated Bishop of Killaloe 1804, translated to Leighlin and Ferns 1820, and to Clogher 1822, b. 5 Sept. 1773; m. 28 May, 1807, Hon. Alicia Maude, dau. of Cornwallis, 1st Viscount Hawarden. She d. 21 Dec. 1866. He d. 26 April, 1850, having had with other issue (see BURKE's Peerage, ELY, M.), an eldest son,
CHARLES JOHN TOTTENHAM, of Tottenham Green, and Woodstock, and of Plâs Berwyn, co. Denbigh, Hon. Col. of co. Denbigh Hussars, Capt. and Regt. of Life Guards, B.A., D.L., and J.P., High Sheriff cos. Merioneth 1855, Wicklow 1859, Denbigh 1861, and Wexford 1871, b. 27 June, 1808; m. 11 Sept. 1839, Hon. Isabella Jane Maude, dau. of Cornwallis, 3rd Viscount Hawarden, and d. 17 Dec. 1878, leaving by her (who d. 11 July, 1892),
1. CHARLES ROBERT WORSLEY, his heir.
1. Adelaide Alicia, m. 10 Aug. 1875, Lieut.-Col. Edward Richard Bayly (see BAYLY of Ballyarthur), and has issue.
2. Emily Anne, m. 1st, 11 Nov. 1880, Lieut.-Col. Latham C. Browurigg, 60th Rifles, who d. 20 Oct. 1882; and 2ndly, 12 April, 1887, Henry Barker, eldest son of Canon Barker, Rector of Thornton-le-Moors, Chester. She d. 23 April, 1902.
3. Florence Isabella Maude, m. 27 Oct. 1896, Rev. Mordaunt Elrington, Bisset (see BISSET of Lessendrum), and d. 30 Sept. 1909.

Arms—Gu., three bars dancettée arg., quartering LOFTUS, CHETHAM, and CREWKERNE. Crest—A lion rampant gu. Motto—Ad astra sequor.

Seats—Woodstock, Newtown-Mount-Kennedy, co. Wicklow; and Plâs Berwyn, Llangollen, North Wales.

TOTTENHAM OF BALLYCURRY.

CHARLES GEORGE TOTTENHAM, of Ballycurry, co. Wicklow, J.P. and D.L. for that co., High Sheriff 1881, and J.P. co. Wexford, High Sheriff 1874, M.P. for New Ross 1864-8 and 1878-80, Hon. Col. 7th Brigade North Irish Division R.A. (Wicklow Militia), formerly Capt. and Lieut.-Col. Scots Fusilier Guards, has medal and clasp for the Crimea, and Medjidie (Fifth Class) and Turkish Medal, *b*. 11 April, 1835; *m*. 19 Jan. 1859, Catherine Elizabeth (who *d*. 18 March, 1905), dau. of Hon. and Rev. Sir Francis Jarvis Stapleton, 8th bart., of Grey's Court, and grand-dau. of Thomas, 22nd Lord Le Despencer, by whom he has issue,

1. CHARLES BOSVILE, D.S.O., late Major 14th Hussars, *b*. 19 Oct. 1869; *m*. 27 July, 1907, Ruby, dau. of Piercy Benn, of Folkestone. He *d*. 11 Feb. 1911.
2. George Robert, *d*. young.
   1. Catherine Isabelle, *m*. 30 Aug. 1898, Major Roger Casement R.A., son of Julius Casement, of Cronroe, co. Wicklow (*see* CASEMENT *of Magherintemple*).
   2. Florence Margaret.   3. Lillian Emma.
   4. Mary Talbot Augusta.

Col. Tottenham is the sixth Charles Tottenham who has sat in Parliament in regular succession for the borough of New Ross from father to son.

Lineage.—This is a branch of TOTTENHAM *of Tottenham Green*.

CHARLES TOTTENHAM, of New Ross, M.P., Surveyor-General of the Province of Leinster, 2nd son of Charles Tottenham, of Tottenham Green, M.P. (*see preceding Memoir*), *b*. 1716; *m*. 1st, Hon. Anne Loftus, 2nd dau. of Nicholas, 1st Viscount Loftus, and by her (who was *b*. 8 Nov. 1718, and *d*. 10 Nov. 1768) had issue,

1. CHARLES, his heir.
2. NICHOLAS LOFTUS, ancestor of TOTTENHAM *of Glenfarne*.
3. Ponsonby, M.P. for Fethard, Clerk of the Ordnance, *b*. 1746; *m*. 1 June, 1782, Arabella, dau. of Robert Leigh, of Rosegarland, co. Wexford, M.P., and by her (who *d*. 2 Aug. 1806, aged 50) had issue. He *m*. 2ndly, Oct. 1807, Caroline Draper, dau. of Thomas Neville, of The Lodge, Brighton, and widow of Col. Symes, and by her (who *d*. Nov. 1818) had no issue. He *d*. 13 Dec. 1818.
4. Edward, *d*. young.
   1. Ann, *d. unm*. 9 Nov. 1775.
   2. Elizabeth, *m*. 15 June, 1772, Ven. Sir James Hutchinson, 2nd bart., of Castle Sallah, Archdeacon of Achonry, and *d*. 28 April, 1827, aged 75.

Mr. Charles Tottenham *m*. 2ndly, 1770, Jane, dau. of John Cliffe, and widow of Rev. Joshua Tench, of Bryanstown, co. Wexford, but by her (who *d*. 1798) had no issue. He *d*. 10 Nov. 1795, and was *s*. by his eldest son,

CHARLES TOTTENHAM, of New Ross, M.P., *b*. 19 April, 1743; *m*. 23 June, 1766, Frances, dau. and heir of Robert Boswell, of Ballycurry, co. Wicklow, and by her (who *d*. 11 March, 1821, aged 84) had issue,

1. CHARLES, his heir.   2. Robert Boswell, *d*. young.
3. Henry Loftus, of Mac Murrough, co. Wexford, *b*. 29 Oct. 1770; *d*. 21 Nov. 1826; *m*. 1 March, 1802, Sarah, dau. of Rev. John Cliffe, of New Ross, and by her (who *d*. 12 Dec. 1839, aged 58) had issue,
   1. Charles, of Mac Murrough, Barrister-at-Law, M.A., *b*. 12 Jan. 1803; *m*. 21 May, 1834, Margaret, dau. of Lieut.-Gen. Sir James Kearney, K.C.H., and by her (who *d*. 27 Feb. 1852) had issue,
      (1) James Henry Loftus, of Mac Murrough, *b*. 17 Oct. 1836; *d. unm*. 29 March, 1880.
      (2) Charles, of Mac Murrough, *b*. 13 Sept. 1837; *d. unm*.
      (3) Loftus Ponsonby, *b*. 27 July, 1847; *d. unm*. 22 May, 1877.
      (1) Margaret Anne.   (2) Sarah De Cliffe.
      (3) Constance Emmeline, *d. unm*. 9 Jan. 1903.
      (4) Edith Amelia, *d*. 14 Nov. 1865.
   2. John Loftus, Major Bengal Light Cavalry, *b*. 24 May, 1804; *d*. 29 May, 1847; *m*. 14 Oct. 1833, Isabella, dau. of Alexander Gordon, of Edinburgh, and had by her (who *d*. 26 June, 1875), one son,
      Henry Loftus Alexander, Col. Bengal Staff Corps, *b*. 15 July, 1836; *m*. 1863, Helen Winifred Brown, and has issue,
         1. Alfred, *b*. 1871.   2. Gordon, R.E.
         1. Ella.   2. Edith.
   3. Robert Boswell Horatio Nelson, *b*. 22 Nov. 1805; *d*. 21 Jan. 1822.
   4. Henry Loftus, B.A., Barrister-at-Law, *b*. 16 Jan. 1814; *m*. 1 Oct. 1851, Joice, dau. of James Lowry (*see* LOWRY *of Rockdale*), and widow of Edward Leslie Colvill. She *d*. 27 Sept. 1892. He *d*. 26 April, 1896, leaving issue,
      (1) Henry Loftus, *b*. 3 July, 1852; *m*. 16 Dec. 1886, Mary Elizabeth, only dau. of Rev. Edward Lowry Barnwell, M.A., of Melksham, Wilts, and has had issue,
         Charles Edward, *b*. 29 Oct. 1887.
      (2) Lowry Cliffe Loftus, District Inspector Royal Irish Constabulary, *b*. 12 April, 1858; *m*. 18 Sept. 1888, Isabella Ogle, only child of Ven. William Creek, D.D., Archdeacon of Kilmore, and Rector of Kildallon, co. Cavan, and has, with other issue,
            Harry Leslie William, *b*. Oct. 2 1889.

(3) Charles Francis Bosvile (Rev.), *b*. 10 May, 1863; *m*. 11 Sept. 1889, Josephena Florenda, dau. of the late Richard Bolton, J.P., of Castle Ring, co. Louth (*see that family*), and has issue,
   1. Raymond Charles, *b*. 5 Aug. 1890.
   2. Clive Gordon, *b*. 6 Nov. 1891.
   3. Edward Loftus, *b*. 12 May, 1896.
   4. Leonard Bolton, *b*. 28 July, 1901.
   1. Joice Marjorie, *b*. 22 July, 1893.
   2. Sidney Josephine, *b*. 25 Aug. 1897.
   3. Maude Lowry, *b*. 5 Sept. 1898.
   4. Zoe Mary Bolton, *b*. 30 Jan. 1900.
(1) Henrietta Elizabeth, *d*. 31 March, 1872.
(2) Georgina Mary, twin with her elder sister.
(3) Mary Louisa Joice.
5. Francis Robert, *b*. 18 Oct. 1822; *m*. 28 July, 1857, Caroline, dau. of Solomon Speer, of Granitefield, co. Dublin. She *d*. 8 Sept. 1888, leaving issue,
   (1) Henry Loftus Speer Gordon, *b*. 23 Aug. 1858.
   (2) William Edward, *b*. 11 May, 1860.
1. Frances Anne, *d. unm*. 22 Jan. 1822.
2. Elizabeth, *d. unm*. 17 June, 1875.
3. Anne, *d. unm*. 11 Nov. 1887.
4. Sarah Caroline, *d. unm*. 18 Aug. 1892.
5. Mary Harriet, *m*. 17 March, 1842, Lieut.-Col. James Gordon, 3rd Bengal Light Cavalry, and *d.s.p*. 24 Oct. 1869. He *d*. 15 Sept. 1875.
6. Charlotte Irvine, *m*. 26 Nov. 1845, Major George Frederick Long, 50th Foot, who *d*. 10 June, 1864, leaving issue. She *d*. 15 May, 1906.
4. Edward William, of Woodville, co. Wexford, *b*. 26 April, 1779; *m*. 23 Sept. 1807, Henrietta, dau. and co-heir of Sir John Alcock, Knt., of Waterford (*see* ALCOCK *of Wilton*), and dying 24 March, 1860, left issue by her (who *d*. 5 Jan. 1861) an only dau. and heir, Sarah, *m*. 18 June, 1835, William Denis, of Waterford, who, by Royal Licence, dated 1835, assumed the additional surname and arms of TOTTENHAM, and by him (who *d*. 24 Oct. 1869) had an only surviving son,
   JOHN DENIS-TOTTENHAM, of Ashfield, Rathfarnham, *b*. 22 Oct. 1837.
She *d*. 5 May, 1822, aged 74.
1. Frances Anne, *d. unm*. 8 Jan. 1795.
2. Eliza Jane, *m*. 29 April, 1816, St. George Knudson, *d.s.p*. 11 Feb. 1858, aged 83.
3. Anne Caroline, *m*. 16 March, 1809, John David La Touche, and *d*. 16 June, 1852, leaving issue.

Mr. Charles Tottenham *d*. 13 June, 1823, and was *s*. by his eldest son,

CHARLES TOTTENHAM, of Ballycurry, M.P., High Sheriff co. Wicklow 1812, and Wexford 1827, *b*. 1 March, 1768; *m*. 21 Oct. 1803, Catherine, dau. of Sir Robert Wigram, 1st bart. of Walthamstow, and by her (who *d*. 22 Sept. 1865, aged 90) had issue,

1. CHARLES, his heir.
2. Robert, of Anamult, co. Kilkenny, B.A., Barrister-at-Law, *b*. 11 April, 1810; *m*. 2 May, 1844, Mary Bids, dau. of Lieut.-Col. Charles Synge, of Mount Callan, Inagh, co. Clare. She *d*. 20 Sept. 1889. He *d*. 22 Aug. 1858, having had issue,
   1. Charles Robert, *b*. 23 Jan. 1846; *d*. 18 Nov. 1855.
   2. Frederick St. Leger, of Mount Callan, co. Clare, J.P. and D.L. High Sheriff 1899, *b*. 9 Aug. 1850; Lieut.-Col. late 7th Fusiliers; *m*. 17 July, 1888, Mabel Caroline, dau. of Very Rev. Thomas Garnier, Dean of Lincoln, by Lady Caroline Keppel his wife, dau. of William Charles, 4th Earl of Albemarle, and has issue,
      (1) Robert Garnier, Lieut. Royal Fusiliers, *b*. 16 Oct. 1889.
      (2) George Richard Frederick, *b*. 18 Nov. 1890.
      (3) Edward Synge, *b*. 21 Sept. 1893; *d*. 13 March, 1903.
   3. Arthur Ely Heathcote, *b*. 18 Nov. 1852, Major late Argyll and Sutherland Highlanders, and *d*. 9 June, 1908.
   1. Mary Louisa, *m*. 25 Feb. 1865, John Holy-Hutchinson, of Seafield, co. Dublin, and has issue.
   2. Blanche Catherine, *d. unm*. 15 Jan. 1899.
   3. Georgiana Isabella.   4. Florence Sophia.
   5. Grace, *d*. young.   6. Alice Rose.
   7. Gertrude Annie, *m*. 16 Aug. 1887, John Arthur Maconchy, Barrister-at-Law, and has issue.
   8. Amy Beatrice.
3. William Heathcote, Lieut.-Col. 12th Royal Lancers, bapt. 7 June, 1815; *m*. Mary Louisa (who *d*. 1909), 2nd dau. of Rev. William Crofton, Rector of Skreene, co. Sligo, and *d*. 6 July, 1857, leaving a posthumous dau.,
   Wilhelmina Heathcote.
1. Eleanour Frances, *d. unm*. 11 March, 1876.
2. Frances Maria, *d. unm*. 2 July, 1829.

Mr. Charles Tottenham *d*. 6 July, 1843, and was *s*. by his eldest son,

CHARLES TOTTENHAM, of Ballycurry, M.P. for New Ross, D.L. and J.P., High Sheriff of Wicklow 1845, of Wexford 1846, *b*. 14 Nov. 1807; *m*. 14 Jan. 1833, Isabella Catherine, dau. of Lieut.-Gen. Sir George Airey, K.H. (by Catherine his wife, dau. of the Baroness Talbot de Malahide), and sister of Gen. Lord Airey, G.C.B. (*see* BURKE'S *Family Records*), and by her (who *d*. 5 April, 1863) had issue,

1. CHARLES GEORGE, his heir.
2. Loftus Richard, late Justice of the Supreme Court, Calcutta, *b*. 31 Aug. 1836; *m*. 20 May, 1860, Georgina Emily, dau. of Arthur Littledale, of Stoke Hill House, Guildford, Bengal C.S., and has issue,
   1. Loftus Charles, *b*. 10 Nov. 1861; *d. unm*. 23 June, 1900.
   2. Charles Frederick, *b*. 20 June, 1865.
   3. Henry Crawford, *b*. 24 Sept. 1867; *m*. 27 Dec. 1901, Maud

Tottenham. THE LANDED GENTRY. 698

Annie, only child of the late William Pitt, of Kimberley, Cape Town.
4. George Bertie, b. 1 July, 1872; d. 1894.
1. Evelyn Christina Charlotte, m. 29 Jan. 1908, Jardine Giesson, of Hong-Kong and Birlingmon House, Worcestershire.
3. Julius Airey, b. 5 Oct. 1839; m. Miss Gibson, of Queensland, and d. in Queensland 1891, leaving issue,
   1. Charles Loftus, b. 26 Sept. 1883.
   2. Arthur Talbot, b. 7 Nov. 1887.
   1. Katherine Isabel, b. 5 Nov. 1877.
   2. Julia Eleanor, b. 31 May, 1879.
   3. Blanche Agnes, b. 30 June, 1882.
   4. Margaret Mary, b. 7 Aug. 1885.
   5. Mildred Amy, b. 4 Sept. 1889.
1. Catherine, m. 1st, 25 Nov. 1871, Capt. Harry Maxwell Howard, 18th Hussars, who d. 11 Feb. 1875. She m. 2ndly, Sept. 1897, Admiral Sir William Hornby, K.C.B., who d. 28 June, 1899.
2. Isabella Eliza, m. 22 April, 1868, Rev. George J. Cowley-Brown, and is dec.

Mr. Charles Tottenham d. 1 June, 1886, and was s. by his eldest son, CHARLES GEORGE TOTTENHAM, now of Ballycurry.

Arms, *Crest*, and *Motto*—Same as TOTTENHAM of *Tottenham Green*.

Seat—Ballycurry, Ashford, co. Wicklow. *Clubs*—Carlton, S.W., Kildare Street, Dublin.

TOTTENHAM OF TUDENHAM PARK.

CHARLES GORE LOFTUS TOTTENHAM, of Tudenham Park, co. Westmeath. J.P., D.L., High Sheriff co. Leitrim 1898, late Lieut. Rifle Brigade, b. 25 Aug. 1861; m. 30 April, 1888, the Hon. Georgina Alice Somerville, 2nd dau. of late Lord Athlumney, and has issue,
1. HAROLD WILLIAM LOFTUS, b. 26 Feb. 1889.
2. Desmond Frank Charles Loftus, b. 1896.
1. Dorothy Loftus. 2. Aileen Loftus.
3. Angela Francis Diane Loftus.

Lineage.—This is a branch of TOTTENHAM of *Tottenham Green*, co. *Wexford*, springing more immediately from TOTTENHAM of *Ballycurry*.

NICHOLAS LOFTUS TOTTENHAM, 2nd son of CHARLES TOTTENHAM, of New Ross, by Hon. Anne Loftus his wife (*see preceding Memoir*), M.P., b. 1745; m. June, 1778, Mary, dau. and co-heir of Sir James May, 1st bart. of Mayfield, co. Waterford, and by her (who d. Feb. 1836) had issue,
1. CHARLES HENRY, his heir.
2. Loftus Anthony, of Glenade, co. Leitrim, High Sheriff 1824, b. 1788; m. Aug. 1815, Mary, dau. and heir of Hon. Abraham Creighton, and d. 30 Aug. 1850, leaving by her (who d. 29 Sept. 1819), with a dau., Charlotte Mary, m. 1836, Nathaniel Pryce Cameron (son of Col. Nathaniel Cameron, of Danygraig, near Swansea), an only son,
Loftus Abraham, of Glenade, J.P., High Sheriff 1848, b. 28 Dec. 1818; m. 3 March, 1851, Constance, and dau. of Isaac Newton Wigney, of Brighton, M.P., and has
(1) Beresford Granville Stuart, b. 29 June, 1856, formerly an Officer in 106th Foot and 10th Hussars.
(1) Ida Constance Pauline Creighton, m. 15 July, 1869, Capt. Charles Hanbury, 5th Lancers.
(2) Victoria Augusta Wharncliffe, d. Nov. 1853.
1. Anne, m. June, 1812, Col. Thomas Challoner Bisse Challoner, of Portnal Park, Surrey, and d.s.p. 3 Oct. 1857, aged 82.
2. Mary, d. unm. 7 Dec. 1865, aged 83.
3. Letitia, m. 1824, Lieut.-Col. John Nicholas Lucas, of Stout Hall, co. Glamorgan.

Mr. Nicholas Loftus Tottenham d. 11 March, 1823, and was s. by his eldest son,

CHARLES HENRY TOTTENHAM, of Glenfarne Hall, High Sheriff 1820, b. 1786; m. Sept. 1814, Dorothea (who d. 23 June, 1869), dau. and heir of George Crowe, of Nutfield, co. Clare, and by her had issue,
1. NICHOLAS LOFTUS, his heir.
2. Charles Henry, formerly 50th Regt., b. Nov. 1818; m. 10 Jan. 1850, Marion Sarah Bransby, dau. and co-heir of Rev. Robert Rede Rede, of Ashmans, Suffolk, and d. 11 April, 1871, leaving issue,
   1. Charles Loftus Henshaw Rede, b. 26 Dec. 1851; d. young.
   2. Henry Rede, b. 13 April, 1856, Fellow of St. John's Coll. Camb.
   1. Marian Louisa.
   2. Maude Loftus Henshaw Rede, m. 27 Dec. 1894, Willoughby Dreyer Wade, of St. Heliers, Jersey.
3. Algernon, b. Nov. 1827; d. unm. 1870.
4. Anne, d. unm. Aug. 1866.
2. Sarah Maria, d. unm. 22 May, 1828.

Mr. Charles Henry Tottenham d. 29 Feb. 1836, and was s. by his eldest son,

NICHOLAS LOFTUS TOTTENHAM, of Glenfarne Hall, J.P. and D.L., High Sheriff 1841, b. Sept. 1815; m. 17 Aug. 1835, Anna Maria, dau. of Sir Francis Hopkins, 1st bart., of Atbboy, M.P., and heir of her brother, Sir Francis Hopkins, 2nd bart., and by her (who d. 7 March, 1906) had issue,
1. ARTHUR LOFTUS, his heir.
2. George Charles Loftus, late of Glenade, co. Leitrim, J.P. and D.L., High Sheriff 1888, B.A. and Scholar Trin. Coll. Camb. b. 9 March, 1844; d. 28 May, 1910.

3. Francis Loftus, formerly 10th Foot and Capt. Westmeath Rifle Militia (*The Garden House, Mildmay Park*), b. 17 Nov. 1847; m. 29 Aug. 1871, Cicell, dau. of Charles Grimston, of Grimston Garth and Kilnwick, co. York, and had issue,
   1. Percy Marmaduke, b. 17 Aug. 1873; m. Aug. 1909, Angel, dau. of E. M. Archdale, of Riversdale, Ballinamallard, co. Fermanagh, and has issue,
      Frank Mervyn Loftus.
   2. Francis Loftus, R.N., b. 1; Aug. 1880.
   1. Anna Maude, m. 2 July, 1907, Major-Gen. Henry Wylie, C.S.I., son of the late Macleod Wylie, Barrister-at-Law.
   2. Mabel Gertrude, m. 5 Oct. 1907, Dudley W. Carnalt Jones, F.R.C.S., Edin., son of late T. W. Carnalt Jones, F.R.C.S.
   3. Edith Leonora. 4. Grace Marguerite.
4. Henry Loftus, b. 1 Jan. 1851; d. unm. 8 June, 1899.
1. Eleanor Loftus, m. 23 Sept. 1864, Lieut.-Col. Alleyne Fitz-Herbert Fenton Bloomfield, Madras Staff Corps, and d. Aug. 1909 leaving issue.
2. Anna Loftus, m. 27 July, 1869, Charles James Bury, of St. Leonards, Nazing, Essex, J.P., and has issue.
3. Mary Loftus, d. unm. 4 July, 1861.

Mr. Nicholas Loftus Tottenham d. 25 March, 1851, and was s. by his eldest son,

ARTHUR LOFTUS TOTTENHAM, of Glenfarne Hall, co. Leitrim, J.P. and D.L., High Sheriff 1866, M.P. for Leitrim 1880-5, and for Winchester 1885-7, formerly Capt. Rifle Brigade, b. 5 April, 1838; m. 14 June, 1859, Sarah Anne, dau. of George Addenbrooke Gore, of Barrowmount, co. Kilkenny, and d. 4 Dec. 1887, having by her (who d. 23 June, 1895) had issue,
1. CHARLES GORE, now of Tudenham Park.
2. Ralph George, b. 15 Feb. 1864; m. July, 1888, Margaret, eldest dau. of John Taaffe, of Louth.
3. Henry Arthur Leicester, b. 11 Oct. 1868; d. 29 May, 1876.
4. Frederick William, b. 2 Jan. 1870; m. 31 July, 1897, Roberta Guadalupe, dau. of the late Joseph Barron, of Almeria, Spain, and Pau, France, and d. 8 Dec. 1905, leaving issue,
   1. Frederick Joseph Loftus, b. 4 May, 1898.
   2. Edmund Loftus, b. 28 June, 1903.
5. Herbert Ponsonby GAUSSEN, of Brookman's Park, North Mimms, Herts, b. 21 Feb. 1871, late R.N.; m. 21 June 1898 Emilia Christian, dau. of the late Capt. Robert George Gaussen, of Brookman's Park (*see that family*). He assumed by Royal Licence, 17 Sept. 1906, the surname and arms of GAUSSEN, and has issue,
   1. Arthur Robert Loftus, b. 22 July, 1900.
   2. Charles Casamajor, b. 12 Nov. 1901.
   3. Herbert Patrick, b. 17 March, 1904.
   4. Frederic Michael, b. 16 Oct. 1907.
   5. Peter William, b. 29 July, 1909.
   1. Christian Nickola.
   2. Emilia Rachel.
6. Arthur Gore, b. 19 Sept. 1874, formerly Sub-Lieut. R.N., served with Imperial Yeomanry in S. African War.
7. Reginald Stuart, b. 18 Aug. 1877; d. 3 Nov. 1883.
1. Blanche Mary, m. 9 Jan. 1899, Arthur Archibald Ram, 4th son of Stephen Ram, of Ramsfort. She d. 28 Feb. 1903. He d. 20 Dec. 1905, leaving issue (*see RAM of Clonattin*).
2. Edith Emily.
3. Violet, m. 25 July, 1897, John Morris Post, of Pau, son of John Post, of New York, and has issue, a dau.

Arms, *Crest*, and *Motto*—Same as TOTTENHAM of *Tottenham Green*, quartering MAY.

Seat—Tudenham Park, co. Westmeath. *Club*—Carlton.

TOWNLEY-BALFOUR. *See* BALFOUR.

TOWNSHEND, late OF CASTLE TOWNSHEND·

MAURICE FITZGERALD STEPHENS-TOWNSHEND, late of Castle Townshend. co. Cork, b. 4 Nov. 1865.

Lineage.—The first who settled in Ireland was a Col. RICHARD TOWNSEND, TOWNESENDE, or TOWNSHEND, an officer in the Army of the Parliament during the wars previous to the Commonwealth. In 1646 he was present at the surrender of Pendennis Castle, Cornwall, and (his regiment having been ordered to Ireland in June, 1647, by the House of Commons) he commanded the main body of the Army, under Lord Inchiquin, at the battle of Knocknoness, near Mallow, co. Cork, Cols. Grey and Blunt heading the left and right wings respectively during the temporary revolt from the Parliament at Mallow, 3 April, 1848. Inchiquin and his principal officers there received Lord Ormonde as Lord-Lieutenant for Ireland, in Sept. 1648. After the King's execution in the following year, the garrison of Cork, declaring the question no longer to be between the King and Parliament, revolted back to the Lord Protector, and Col. Townsend subsequently presented the keys of the city of Cork into OLIVER CROMWELL's hands at Dungarvan. Col. Townsend made several large purchases of land from time to time, for which he got three several patents, viz., in 1666, 1668, and 1679; the first being for Castle Townsend (afterwar s the seat of the head of the family), which he had purchased some time before. He was elected M.P. for Clonakilty 10 April, 1661, and was appointed to command a troop of (Carbery) Militia in 1666 by the Duke of Ormonde, at Lord Orrery's instance. He was appointed High of the co. 1671. He d. July, 1692, having had issue, nine sons and three daus. The 2nd son and eventual heir,

BRYAN TOWNSEND, of Castle Townsend, Commander of H.M.S. *Swiftsure*, M.P. for Clonakilty 1695, *m.* 1680, Mary, dau. of Edward Synge, D.D., Bishop of Cork and Ross, and by her had issue,
1. RICHARD, of whom presently.
2. Edward, *b.* 17 Sept 1685; *d. unm.*
3. Brian, *b.* 4 Feb. 1686–7; *d. unm.*
4. John, of Skirtagh, co. Cork, Barrister-at-Law, *b.* 26 May, 1691; *m.* Katherine, dau. of Col. Barry, of Rathcormack, co. Cork, and had three sons.
5. SAMUEL, *b.* 23 Sept. 1689; *m.* Dorothea, dau. of Sir Edward Mansel, 2nd bart., of Muddlescombe, co. Carmarthen, and had four sons and a dau. *(see TOWNSHEND of St. Kames Island).*
6. Francis, *b.* 1694; *d. unm.*
7. William, *b.* 1699; *d. unm.*
8. PHILIP, of Derry, co. Cork, ancestor of the Myross Wood and Derry Branches *(which see).*
9. HORATIO (Rev.), Rector of Donoughmore, co. Cork, *b.* 1 Sept. 1706; *m.* 1730, Mary, dau. of Thomas Hungerford, of The Island, and had issue *(see TOWNSHEND of Garryeloyne).*
1. Mary, *m.* Dr. George Hough, of Castle Townsend.
2. Katherine, *d. unm.*
3. Helena, *m.* Very Rev. William Meade, of Ballymartle, Dean of Cork.
4. Barbara, *m.* Thomas Hungerford, of Cahirmore, co. Cork.

The eldest son,

RICHARD TOWNSEND, of Castle Townsend, High Sheriff co. Cork 1671 and 1672; *b.* 15 July, 1684; *m.* 1st, 1706, Mary, dau. of Very Rev. Samuel Synge, Dean of Kildare, and by her had one son, 1. Samuel, who *d.* a minor about 1725, and one dau., 1. Mary, *m.* 5 Sept. 1746, Rev. Thomas Daunt, of Fahalea, co. Cork. Mr. Townsend *m.* 2ndly, Elizabeth, dau. of Henry Becher, of Affadown, co. Cork, and by her (who *d.* 1743) had three sons and three daus.,
2. RICHARD, his successor.
3. John, of Shepperton, co. Cork, Member of the Irish Parliament for many years, *m.* 1769, Mary, dau. of Jonas Morris, of Barley Hill, co. Cork, and *d.* 4 Aug. 1810, having had, besides other issue, who *d.* young or *unm.*,
1. Richard, J.P., of The Point, afterwards of Ballinatona, Collector of Excise, *m.* 1st, 5 July, 1790, Barbara, dau. of David Mellifont, of Dublin, and by her had issue,
(1) RICHARD MELLIFONT TOWNSEND, of Dunbeacon, *m.* 24 May, 1819, Eliza, dau. of Gen. David Mellifont, which lady *d.* at Nice 27 Nov. 1868, and her widower assumed by Royal Licence the prefix surname of MELLIFONT.
(2) Jonas Morris, *m.* 1827, Mary, dau. of Thomas Somerville, of Drishane, co. Cork, and *d.* in Australia 1862, having had issue,
1. Richard, of Dunbeacon Lodge, J.P. co. Cork, *d.* 12 Feb. 1912.
2. Thomas Somerville, *m.* in Australia, and has, Thomas Richard, and two daus.
1. Elizabeth Henrietta.
2. Victoria.
3. Mary Beecher.
(3) John Henry, J.P., *m.* 28 Dec. 1842, Mary, dau. of Rev. Arthur Herbert, of Myross Wood, co. Cork, and has a son, Richard Arthur Herbert, *b.* 1853, late 13th Regt.
(1) Henrietta Anna Margaretta, *m.* Aug. 1816, Philip Somerville, of Prairie, Skull, co. Cork.
(2) Barbara Mellifont, *d. unm.* 1832.
(3) Elizabeth Hildegardis, *m.* 15 Dec. 1835, William Warren, of Prospect Villas, Monkstown.
He *m.* 2ndly, Katherine, dau. of Major Ancram, and by her had issue,
(4) William Richard, *d. unm.* 1849.
(5) Henry Owen Becher, *d. unm.* 1849.
(4) Catherine Helena, *m.* Oct. 1837, William Baldwin, of Gurteenakillagh, who *d.* July, 1854, leaving issue.
Mr. Townsend *m.* 3rdly, *circa* 1822, Anne, dau. of Edward Mansel Townsend, of Whitehall, and widow of Thomas Warren, of Prospect Villas, Monkstown, co. Cork.
2. Jonas Morris, of Shepperton, near Rosecarberry, co. Cork, *m.* 24 May, 1815, Jane, eldest dau. of Richard Digby, of Cork, and *d.* 1844, having had issue,
(1) John, *b.* 1827; *d. unm.* 1853.
(1) Frances, *m.* 1st, 10 June, 1840, John Digby, of Landenstown, co. Kildare; 2ndly, 1848, the Hon. Cecil Lawless, and 3rdly, Andrew Browne, of Mount Hazel, co. Galway, and *d.* 1890.
(2) Louisa, *m.* 1843, John Hamilton de Burgh, eldest son of John Hussey de Burgh, of Donore, co. Kildare.
3. Henry Owen Becher, J.P., *m.* 1st, Frances, dau. of — Fenwick, of Mohonagh, near Dunmanway, co. Cork, and relict of Richard Hodnett, and 2ndly, Anne, dau. of Rev. Philip Homan, of Sarock, co. Westmeath, and *d.* 18 March, 1847, having by her (who *d.* Sept 1817) an only child,
John FitzHenry, of Seafield, Castletownshend, LL.D., Judge of the High Court of Admiralty, *b.* 1 Jan. 1811; *m.* 24 March, 1840, Ellen, dau. of Rev. George Armstrong, of Cork. She *d.* 21 April, 1878. He *d.* 2 Feb. 1893, leaving issue a son and a dau.,
Henry FitzJohn, of Seafield, Castletownshend, co. Cork, J.P., late Maj. and Hon. Lieut.-Col. 4th Batt. Scottish Rifles, formerly in the 26th Regt. Cameronians, *b.* 18 Feb. 1841; *m.* 1st, 15 Nov. 1870, Mary (who *d.* 21 Feb. 1890), eldest dau. of Arthur Bushe, Master of the Queen's Bench, by whom he has issue a son and a dau.,
Arthur FitzHenry, Capt. 4th Batt. Cameronians Scottish Rifles, late Lieut. 1st Batt., *b.* 19 May, 1874.
Sylvia Rosalie, *m.* 3 July, 1900, Lieut.-Col. Edward Howard Gorges, D.S.O., 1st Manchester Regt., son of the late Major Richard James Martin, King's Dragoon Guards, of Charville, co. Galway.
Lieut.-Col. H. F. Townshend *m.* 2ndly, 27 Sept. 1900, Elizabeth, widow of Major Sawyer and elder dau. of the late Major Richard James Martin, King's Dragoon Guards, of Charville, co. Galway.
Charlotte.
4. Abraham Morris, *d. unm.* 13 April, 1830.
1. Elizabeth, *m.* Nov. 1796, Thomas Somerville, of Drishane, co. Cork.
2. Harriet, *m.* 24 Nov. 1802, Beresford Gahan, of Waterford.
3. Katherine Helena, *d. unm.* 1848.
4. Henry, Capt. R.N., *d. unm.*
2. Elizabeth, *m.* Capt. Gwynne, R.N.
3. Harriet, *m.* Rev. David Freeman, Rector ot Castlebaven, co. Cork, and *d.s.p.*
4. Helena, *m.* Rev. Arthur Herbert, of Cahirnane, co. Kerry, who *d.* 30 Sept. 1760.
Mr. Townsend *d.* 1742, and was *s.* by his son,
RICHARD TOWNSEND, of Castle Townsend, M.P. for co. Cork, High Sheriff 1753, and Col. of its Militia. He *m.* 1752, Elizabeth, dau. and eventual heir of John Fitzgerald, of Dingle, Knt. of Kerry, and had (with an only dau., Elizabeth, who *d.* young) one son,
RICHARD BOYLE TOWNSEND, of Castle Townsend, High Sheriff 1785, *b.* 1756, *m.* 1784, Henrietta, dau. of John Newnham, of Maryborough, co. Cork, and had issue,
1. Richard, *d. unm.*   2. JOHN, his successor.
3. MAURICE FITZGERALD, successor to his brother.
4. Henry, R.N., *d. young.*
5. Abraham Boyle (Rev.), Rector of Easthampstead, Berks, *d. unm.* 5 Feb. 1860.
1. Henrietta Augusta, *m.* 1824, Thomas Somerville, of Drishane.
2. Elizabeth Anne, *m.* 1850, Rev. Robert St. Lawrence, of Moragh, co. Cork, 3rd son of Hon. and Right Rev. Thomas St. Lawrence, Bishop of Cork and Ross.
Mr. Townsend *d.* 26 Nov. 1826, and was *s.* by his son,
COL. JOHN TOWNSEND, of Castle Townsend, Lieut.-Col. 14th Light Dragoons, A.D.C. to the Queen, *b.* 11 June, 1786, who, dying *unm.* 23 April, 1845, was *s.* by his next brother,
REV. MAURICE FITZGERALD STEPHENS TOWNSEND (afterwards TOWNSHEND), of Castle Townsend, co. Cork, J.P. and D.L. for co. Gloucester,Vicar of Thornbury, *m.* 16 May, 1826, Alice Elizabeth, 3rd dau. of Richmond Shute, of Iron Acton, co. Gloucester, and heir of her maternal uncle, Henry Stephens, of Chavenage House, co. Gloucester, and by her had issue,
1. Henry John, 2nd Life Guards, J.P., *b.* 1 Nov. 1827; *m.* 29 Sept. 1864, Jane Adeliza Clementina, eldest dau. of John Hamilton Hussey de Burgh, J.P., of Kilfinnan Castle, co. Cork *(see DE BURGH, of Dromkeen),* and *d.v.p.* 7 Sept. 1869, leaving issue,
1. MAURICE FITZGERALD STEPHENS, present representative.
2. Hubert de Burgh Fitzgerald, J.P. co. Cork, late Capt. 4th Batt. Essex Regt., served in S. African War 1901–2 (medal with four clasps), *(Shepperton Park, Leap, co. Cork. Clubs—Cork, Royal Cork Yacht, Royal Munster Yacht, Public Schools, Alpine, Sports), b.* 4 April, 1867.
1. Geraldine Henrietta, *m.* 30 April, 1870, Major-Gen. P. H. Mundy, son of Gen. Godfrey Basil Mundy, of Shipley, co. Derby, and the Hon. Sarah Brydges Rodney his wife, dau. of George Brydges, 1st Lord Rodney.
2. Alice Gertrude, *m.* 25 March, 1856, Hon. and Rev. Courtenay John Vernon, son of Robert, 1st Lord Lyveden.
The Rev. M. F. S. Townsend altered the spelling of his name to Townshend, in 1870, and *d.* 2 March, 1872, and was *s.* by his grandson.

Arms—Per chevron az. and sa., chevron erminois between three escallops arg., quartering FITZGERALD, Knight of Kerry and STEPHENS. **Crest**—On a mount vert. a stag trippant ppr., attired, hoofed, and charged on the side with an escallop or. **Motto**—Haec generi incrementa fides.

Residence—Riviera Lodge, Glandore, co. Cork.

TOWNSHEND OF MYROSS WOOD.

CAPT. WILLIAM TOWER TOWNSHEND, of Myross Wood, and Derry, co. Cork, J.P., late Capt. Queen's Own Royal West Kent Regt., *b.* 26 Aug. 1855; *m.* 28 Feb. 1901, Hon. Geraldine Emily Curzon 5th dau. of Lord Scarsdale, and has had issue,
1. Alfred Curzon, *b.* 2 July, *d.* 8 July, 1903.
1. Blanche Hermione, *b.* 15 Dec. 1901.
2. Marjorie, *b.* 5 Oct. 1905.
3. Eveline Mary Curzon, *b.* 12 Oct. 1910.

Townshend. THE LANDED GENTRY. 700

Lineage.—PHILIP TOWNSEND, of Derry (which was purchased in 1686 by his father), Capt. in the Army, *b.* 5 Aug. 1700, 8th son of BRYAN TOWNSEND, of Castle Townsend (see *that family*); *m.* 28 Nov. 1733, Elizabeth, dau. of Thomas Hungerford, and had issue,
1. RICHARD, of whom presently.
3. Thomas Hungerford, *b.* 1737-8, Captain of the Battle-axe Guards at Dublin Castle; *d. unm.*
2. Horatio (Rev.) (see TOWNSHEND *of Ballinagorna*).
4. William, *d. unm.* 1821.
1. Susannah, *m.* Michael French, of Rath, co. Cork.
2. Mary, *m.* Thomas Somerville, of Castlehaven, co. Cork.

The eldest son,
RICHARD TOWNSEND, of Dublin, M.D., *b.* 12 Jan. 1736-7; *m.* 1st, Eleanor, dau. of Dr. Sealy, of Bandon, co. Cork, and by her had (besides two sons, *d.* young),
1. JOHN SEALY, of Myross Wood.
2. Richard, Barrister-at-Law, *d. unm.*
3. Thomas, of Clyda, near Mallow, *b.* 1770; *m.* 1799, Martha, dau. of Redmond Uniacke (see UNIACKE *of Mount Uniacke*), and *d.* 13 April, 1847, having by her (who *d.* 31 May, 1839) had issue,
 1. Richard, M.D., *m.* 1st, 4 July, 1826, Katherine, dau. of J. Mackinnon, of London, which lady *d.* 1828. He *m.* 2ndly, 22 Sept. 1829, Mary, dau. of Adam Newman, of Dromore, co. Cork, and by her left issue,
  (1) Thomas. (2) Adam Newman.
  (3) Samuel. (4) Richard.
  (5) Robert Uniacke Fitzgerald, *d.* 16 April, 1911; *m.* Gertrude, dau. of Rev. Thomas Uniacke Townsend, and had issue,
   (1) Katherine.
 2. Thomas Uniacke (Rev.), Vicar of Inistiogue, co. Kilkenny, *m.* Elizabeth, dau. of Edward Carr, of Arnestown, co. Wexford, and has issue,
  (1) Edward Carr.
  (2) Richard, *m.* Antoinette, dau. of Rev. Henry Denny, of Churchill, co. Kerry.
   (1) Gertrude, *d.* 29 April, 1885; *m.* Robert Uniacke Fitz-Gerald Townsend.
  (2) Helen, *m.* Henry J. Meares, 21st Fusiliers.
  (3) Eleanor, *m.* 1st, Henry Moore, 4th Regt., and 2ndly, J. P. Devereux, of Rocklands.
  (4) Martha, *m.* Rev. J. R. Corbett. (5) Maria.
 3. Horatio Uniacke, of Rathmoyle, Abbeyleix, *b.* 1826; *m.* 16 June, 1841, Louisa Jane, dau. of John Clarke, of Wilfield, co. Dublin, and *d.* 15 Feb. 1897, leaving issue,
  (1) Thomas Courtney, *b.* 4 Feb. 1845; *m.* 4 Feb. 1875, Adelaide Helen, dau. of the late Edward Brown, and has issue,
   1. Horace Montagu Dimock, M.B. Dublin, *b* 10 June, 1878.
    1. Mabel.
    2. Eva.
  (2) Horace, *b.* 23 Feb. 1852.
  (3) John, *b.* 10 July, 1853; *m.* Maye, dau. of J. McCullagh.
  (4) William, *b.* 7 Aug. 1854; *m.* 1st, Henrietta, dau. of Rev. J. Fraser: She *d.s.p.* He *m.* 2ndly, Annie, dau. of T. Mason, M.D., and by her has issue,
   (1) Godfrey, *b.* 1890. (2) Horace, *b.* 1892.
   (1) Muriel. (2) Gladys.
  (5) James Richard, *b.* 22 April, 1861.
   (1) Maria. (2) Martha.
  (3) Janet, *m.* 1870, Charles R. Galwey, son of the Ven. Archdeacon of Derry, and has issue.
  (4) Louise. (5) Susan.
  (6) Grace. (7) Mary.
4. Sealy Uniacke, *m.* Elizabeth Dyke, and by her (who is deceased) has one son, Thomas Dyke.
5. Philip Uniacke.
6. William Uniacke, J.P., *m.* 1856, Mary Anne Harriet, dau. of late Charles Eyre Coote (see COOTE *of Mount Coote*), and *d.* 1888, leaving issue,
 (1) Charles Eyre Coote, *b.* 1856; *m.* 1887, Ida Dalrymple, dau. of Theodore Billing, of Dublin, and has issue.
 (2) Thomas Crofton Croker, *b.* 1870.
  (1) Caroline Eleanor, *m.* 1887 Rev. Francis Percy Huchesson Powell, of Bawnlahan, Union Hall, co. Cork, and has issue.
  (2) Martha Attilia, *m.* 1881, Rev. Robert Wilkes Gosse, who *d.* 1899 leaving issue. She *m.* 2ndly, 1901, G. E. Norton, and has issue.
  (3) MaryAnne Elizabeth, *m.* 1894, George Melmonth Scott, M.D., and has issue.
  (4) Maria Elizabeth Coote, *m.* 16 Oct. 1903, Evelyn Francis Sanders, M.Inst.C.E. (see SANDERS *of Charleville Park*), and has issue.
  (5) Eleanor, *m.* H. Kenning.
  (6) Alicia Uniacke, *m.* 1895, Hermann Gundert Harris, and has issue.
7. Charles Uniacke, of Burlington Road, Dublin, *m.* 1st, 17 Oct. 1854, Anna Maria Sarah, eldest dau. of Rev. Robert Loftus Tottenham (see BURKE's *Peerage*, ELY, M.), and by her (who *d.* 8 April, 1873) had issue,
 (1) CHARLES LOFTUS UNIACKE, of Castle Townshend (see TOWNSHEND *of Castle Townshend*).
 (2) Thomas Loftus Uniacke (7, *Palmerston Park, Dublin*), *b.* 31 Aug. 1864; *m.* 1st, 14 July, 1891, Maud Ogilvie (who *d.* 6 Feb. 1907), dau. of E.D.S. Ogilvie, of Yulgilbar, N.S.W. (see *Colonial Gentry*), and has issue;
  Theodosia Madeline Cecilia. *b.* 17 July, 1893.
He *m.* 2ndly, 8 June, 1910, Harriett Hickley, dau. of the late Gen. Walter Weldon of Forenaghts, Kildare (see BURKE'S *Peerage*, WELDON, Bart.).
 (3) Robert Ponsonby Loftus, *b.* 8 Feb. 1866.
 (1) Anna Maria Eleanor. (2) Maud Alicia.
 (3) Caroline Mary. (4) Madeline.
 (5) Emilie Frances, *d.* young.

Mr. Charles Uniacke Townshend *m.* 2ndly, 7 July, 1875, Anna Maria, eldest dau. of the late Samuel Ussher Roberts, C.B., of Burlington Road, Dublin, and *d.* 21 June, 1907, having by her had issue,
 (4) George, *b.* 14 June, 1876.
 (5) Philip Ernest Uniacke, Lieut. R.N., *b.* 16 Dec. 1885.
 (6) Hildegarde Isabella.
 (7) Mildred Ethel.
 (8) Geraldine Audrey.
 (9) Kathleen Cecile.
 (10) Dorothy Uniacke.
1. Elizabeth, *m.* Samuel Harrison, of Cork.
2. Eleanor.
3. Mary, *m.* Edward Bryan Molloy, of Kiltra, Enniscorthy, co. Wexford.
1. Eleanor, *m.* John Townsend, Recorder of Clonakilty.
2. Elizabeth, *d. unm.* 3. Susan, *d. unm.*

Mr. Townsend *m.* 2ndly, Margaret, dau. of Horatio Townsend, of Bridgemount, co. Cork. She *d.s.p.* He *d.* 1817. His eldest son, JOHN SEALY TOWNSEND, of Myross Wood, for many years one of the Masters in the Irish Court of Chancery, *m.* 1795, Anne, dau. of John Hancock, Lieut.-Governor of Charles Fort, Kinsale, and *d.* 1852, leaving issue,
 RICHARD, High Sheriff co. Cork 1834, *b.* 1800, *m.* 1826, Helena, dau. of Very Rev. Thomas Trench Dean of Kildare, brother of Frederick, 1st Lord Ashtown, and *d.v.p.* 29 Nov. 1839, leaving two sons and two daus.,
  (1) JOHN HANDCOCK, of Myross Wood.
  (2) Frederick Trench, Col. late Commanding 2nd Life Guards; Knight of the Imperial Ottoman Order of the Osmanieh (4th class).
   (1) Helen, *m.* Col. Charles Holder, late Scots Guards.
   (2) Anna Jane, *m.* 1858, John Croasdaile, of Rynn, Queen's Co. (see CROASDAILE *of Rynn*).
 Elizabeth Susanna, *m.* April, 1832, William Steuart Trench (see BURKE'S *Peerage*, ASHTOWN, B.), and had issue.

Mr. Townsend *d.* 18 March, 1852, and was *s.* by his grandson, JOHN HANDCOCK TOWNSHEND, of Myross Wood, J.P., *b.* 30 Oct. 1829; *m.* 19 March, 1853, Katherine Emma (*d.* 26 March, 1907), 2nd dau. of Rev. William Tower, of How Hatch, Essex, and niece of Christopher Thomas Tower, of Weald Hall (see *that family*), and had issue,
1. RICHARD HARVEY, late of Myross Wood.
2. WILLIAM TOWER, *s.* his brother.
3. Ernest, Major R.E. (retired), of Rose Vale, co. Wexford, *b.* 2 March, 1860; *m.* 29 Dec. 1898, Agnes Mary, 2nd dau. of the late William Routledge, of Yarra Yarra, Eastbourne.
4. Arthur Edward, *b.* 10 Feb. 1863.
5. Christopher, *b.* 5 April, 1869; *d.* 25 Jan. 1874.
1. Caroline Edith, *b.* 30 Sept. 1856; *m.* 3 June, 1890, George W. Hutt, of Appley Towers, Isle of Wight, who *d.* 4 Jan. 1910.
2. Mildred Louisa.
3. Honoria Maria, *b.* 27 Sept. 1861; *m.* 4 Aug. 1881, James Alexander Whitla, of Beneaden, co. Antrim. She *d.* 9 Jan. 1908, leaving issue (see *that family*).
4. Mary, *b.* 11 March, 1865; *d. unm.* 1 Feb. 1901.
5. Florence, *d.* 17 Jan. 1874. 6. Ellen Beatrice, *b.* 19 July, 1870.
7. Alice Katherine, *b.* 10 Jan. 1873; *m.* 10 Feb. 1898, Edward James Morgan Chaplin, of Lincoln's Inn, Barrister-at-Law (13, *Addison Gardens, W.*; 2, *Pump Court, Temple*), eldest son of the late Edward Chaplin, of Hamburg.

Mr. Townsend *d.* 26 Oct. 1889. His eldest son,
RICHARD HARVEY TOWNSHEND, of Myross Wood, co. Cork, J.P., sometime Lieut. Connaught Rangers and Capt. 3rd Batt. Royal Munster Fus., *b.* 23 Feb. 1854; *d. unm.* 30 Aug. 1899.

Seat—Myross Wood, Leap, co. Cork. *Residence*—Derry, Rosscarbery, co. Cork.

TOWNSHEND OF BALLINAGORNA.

GEORGE CHAMBRÉ WILMOT TOWNSHEND, of Ballinagorna, co. Cork, *b.* 26 Nov. 1863; *m.* 1894, Eliza Susan, dau. of French Gray, Ceylon C.S., and has issue,
1. BASIL WILMOT OLIVER, *b.* 22 April, 1898.
1. Ruth Catherine.
2. Janet Gray.
3. Caroline French.

Lineage.—THE REV. HORATIO TOWNSEND, of Derry, 3rd son of Capt. Philip Townsend, of Derry, who was 8th son of Bryan Townsend, of Castle Townsend (see *that Memoir*), became Rector of Clonakilty and of Cartigaline, and was seated at Derry, near Rosscarbery, co. Cork. He was *b.* 5 Nov. 1750; *m.* 1st, Helena, dau. of the Rev. Robert Meade, of Ballintober, and by her had one dau.,
1. Joanna, *m.* Thomas Poole, of Mayfield, co. Cork.
He *m.* 2ndly, Katherine, dau. of Ven. Chambre Corker, of Lota, co. Cork, Archdeacon of Ardagh, and by her had issue, three sons and seven daus.,
1. CHAMBRE CORKER, of whom presently.

2. Horatio (Rev.), Rector of Carragaline; *m.* 1st, 3 June, 1829, Anne, dau. of Rev. Edward Kenney, of Kilmeen, co. Cork, which lady *d.s.p.* 2 April, 1830. He *m.* 2ndly, Jane Florence, dau. of Justin MacCartie, of Carrignavar, and *d.* 19 Dec. 1837, leaving by the latter one son, Horatio.
3. Richard William, C.E., *m.* Aug. 1850, Laura, dau. of Henry Hebbert, of Bromley, Kent. He *d.* 1855, leaving issue,
  1. Mary Henrietta, *m.* Rev. Charles Eustace Boultbee, M.A. Camb., Vicar of Chesham, Bucks, and has issue.
  2. Katherine Isabella, *m.* Joseph Arnuitage, of New Coll. Oxon. and has issue.
  3. Laura Provence, *m.* Rev. Bernard Keene Bourdillion, M.A. Oxon., Rector of Trinity Church, Cape Town; *d.* 1888, and has issue.
2. Eliza, *m.* Lionel Fleming, of New Court, and *d.* 1863, leaving issue.
3. Katherine, *d. unm.* 1873.
4. Maria, *m.* Philip Somerville, *d.s.p.*
5. Isabella, *m.* Major Edward Townsend, and *d.* 1865.
6. Susan, *m.* Edward Hume Townsend, formerly Revenue Commissioner, Bombay C.S., and left issue.
7. Harriet, *d. unm.* 1887.   8. Caroline Charlotte, *d. unm.*
Mr. Townsend purchased his elder brother's interest in the family estate, added considerably thereto, and built a new mansion-house. Mr. Townsend *d.* 26 March, 1837, and was *s.* by his eldest son,

Rev. Chambre Corker Townsend, of Derry, Rector of Kilmacabea, co. Cork. He *m.* 1st, 1824, Frances Vere, dau. of Edward Stewart, son of William Stewart, of Killymoon, M.P. co. Tyrone, and by her (who *d.* Nov. 1824) had one son,
1. Horace, late of Derry.
He *m.* 2ndly, 18 Aug. 1831, Eliza, dau. and heir of Major-Gen. N. Wilmot Oliver, R.A., and by her (who *d.* 17 Aug. 1906) had issue, three sons and eight daus.,
2. Nathaniel Wilmot Oliver, late of Ballinagorna.
3. Chambre Corker, M.A. Camb., *b.* 1838; *m.* Emily, dau. of J. Gibson, and left issue,
  1. Brian.
  2. George.
  1. Carolina.
  2. Rachel Susannah, *m.* 15 May, 1909, Frederic Hillersdon Keeling, eldest son of the late Frederic John Keeling, of Colchester.
4. Richard Baxter, joint editor of "An Officer of the Long Parliament," and author of several works, Sch. and M.A. Trin. Coll. Camb. and also M.A. of Wadham Coll. Oxon. (117, *Banbury Road, Oxford*), *b.* 1846; *m.* 28 July, 1881, Letitia Jane Dorothea, dau. of Rev. Ralph Bourne Baker, of Hasfield Court, co. Gloucester, grand-dau. of Dr. Singer, Bishop of Meath.
  1. Marianne Oliver, *m.* John Townshend, Comm. R.N., who left issue.
  2. Katherine Corker.   3. Eliza Susan.
  4. Caroline Charlotte, *m.* 14 Dec. 1865, Rev. Thomas Miller, Fellow of Queen's Coll. Camb., and *d.* Feb. 1868, leaving issue.
  5. Anne.
  6. Susan, *m.* April, 1869, Brian Houghton Hodgson, F.R.S., D.C.L., of Alderley, Bengal C.S. (retired list).
  7. Isabella Frances Vere, *d. unm.* 1882.
  8. Alicia Hewitt, *m.* Edward Strachan Morgan, M.A. of Monte Fiano, Florence, and has issue.
Mr. Townsend *d.* 30 July, 1852, and was *s.* by his eldest son,

Horace Payne-Townshend, of Derry, co. Cork, J.P. and D.L., Barrister-at-Law, *m.* 20 Oct. 1855, Mary Susanna, eldest dau. and co-heir of Lieut.-Col. Thomas Cox Kirby, and devisee under the will of Thomas Payne, of Edstaston House, Wem, Salop, of his estates situated in Salop and co. Gloucester. In obedience to the directions contained in Mr. Payne's will, Mr. Townshend, upon succeeding to the estates in right of his wife, obtained in 1863 a Royal Licence to use the name of Payne in addition to and before the name of Townshend. He *d.* 2 Feb. 1885, leaving two daus.,
1. Charlotte Frances, of Derry, co. Cork, which she sold, *m.* George Bernard Shaw, Literary and Dramatic Critic (*see* Burke's *Peerage*, Shaw, Bart.).
2. Mary Stewart, *m.* 24 March, 1885, Col. Hugh Cholmondeley, C.B., Rifle Brigade, son of Col. Hon. T. G. Cholmondeley, and has issue (*see* Burke's *Peerage*, Delamere, B.).
His half brother,
Nathaniel Wilmot Oliver Townshend, of Ballinagorna, co. Cork, *b.* Feb. 1836; *m.* June, 1862, Maria, 4th dau. of Geo. Smith Strawson, C.E., of Cardiff, and *d.* 1896, having had issue,
1. George Chambre Wilmot, present representative.
2. Horatio Baxter, R.N., *b.* 18 Aug. 1871; *m.* Alice Kühlet, and has issue.
3. William Pearson, P. & O. and R.N., *b.* 14 June, 1875; *m.* Blanche Strawson, and has issue.
4. Dudley Ryder, M.A. (Oxon.), *b.* 6 July, 1877.
5. Herbert Oliver, *b.* 20 June, 1880.
1. Harriet Elizabeth Barrington.   2. Katherine Disney.
3. Helena Strawson.   4. Florence Maria.

Residence—41, Ashburton Road, Croydon.

TOWNSHEND OF ST. KAMES ISLAND.

Samuel Edward Townsend, of St. Kames Island, co. Cork, LL.B., *b.* 29 June, 1885; *s.* his uncle 1910.

Lineage.—Samuel Townsend, 5th son of Bryan Townsend of Castle Townsend (*see* Townshend, *late of Castle Townshend*), *b.* 23 Sept. 1689; *m.* Dorothy, dau. of Sir Edward Mansel, 1st bart., of Trimseran, and had issue,
1. Edward, his heir.
2. John, *d. unm.*
3. Samuel, Lieut.-Gen. in the Army, *m.* Elizabeth, dau. of — Aikenhead, of Lanark, and widow of Gilbert Ford, of Northaw, Herts, Att.-Gen. of Jamaica, and *d.* 27 May, 1794, leaving issue a son,
  Samuel Irwin, Capt. in the Guards, *m.* Katherine, dau. of David Thomas, of Wellfield, Brecknockshire, and left issue,
    Samuel Thomas (Rev.), Rector of Chicheley, *m.* 1st, 18 Feb. 1828, Catherine Lousia, dau. of Anthony Butler St. Leger, of Park Hill, Yorks, and 2ndly, Eliza, dau. of H. Cadogan, and *d.s.p.* 1874.
      Elizabeth Trelawny.
  1. Dorothea, *m.* 1st, Rev. T. Robinson, of Coronea, co. Cork, and 2ndly, Richard Wright, of Cloverhill, same co.
The eldest son,
Edward Mansel Townsend, bapt. 23 July, 1727; *m.* 1st, Helena, dau. of Henry Becher, of Creagh, co. Cork, and by her had a dau.,
1. Dorothea, *m.* Rev. Arthur Kelley, of Bellevue, co. Cork.
He *m.* 2ndly, Anne, dau. of Walter Baldwin, of Curraghvody (now Mount Pleasant), and by her had issue,
1. Samuel, of whom presently.
2. Edward Mansel, *m.* Dorothea, dau. of Rev. William Robinson, of Coronea, co. Cork, and *d.s.p.*
3. Anne, *m.* 1st, Thomas Warren, of Prospect, and 2ndly, Richard Townsend, of the Point.
The elder son,
Samuel Townsend, of Whitehall, co. Cork, J.P. and D.L., High Sheriff 1798, *b.* 1768, *m.* Mercy, dau. of Henry Baldwin, of Curraghvody, and *d.* 19 June, 1836, having had issue,
1. Edward Henry, of Whitehall, J.P., *b.* 1798, *m.* Mary Carré, dau. of Thomas Warren, of Prospect, and *d.* 1857, having had issue,
  1. Samuel Richard, of Whitehall, J.P., *b.* 12 July, 1833; *d. unm.* Feb. 1879.
  1. Charlotte Frances, *m.* 1st, 1859, Rev. Henry Paine Procter, and 2ndly, 22 Nov. 1866, G. W. Hughes, and by him had a son, Piers Edward, *b.* 9 July, 1868, who *s.* to Whitehall, and assumed the name of Townsend.
  2. Anna Mary, *d. unm.*
  3. Augusta Amelia, *m.* Richard L. Warren.
2. Samuel, of whom presently.
3. Henry, *b.* 1801, *m.* 1838, Belle, dau. of Robert Westropp, of Fort Anne, and had issue,
  1. Samuel Henry, *d. unm.*
  1. Henrietta, *m.* 1864, Henry Morgan Earbury Crofton, of Inchinappa, co. Wicklow.
  2. Annabella.   3. Jane.
  4. Elizabeth.
4. Walter, *b.* 1803, *m.* 1839, Alice, dau. of Benjamin Sweete, and *d.* 1869, leaving issue,
  1. Marion, *m.* H. F. Sneyd.
  2. Alice.
5. William, *d.s.p.* 1869.
1. Mercy, *d. unm.* 1833.
2. Anne, *m.* Edward Becher, of Rock Castle, co. Cork.
3. Henrietta, *d. unm.*   4. Georgiana.
5. Anna Maria, *d. unm.*
The 2nd son,
Samuel Townsend, of St. Kames Island, Dereeny, and Blackrock, all co. Cork, J.P., *b.* 1800; *m.* Feb. 1844, Charlotte Augusta, dau. of Edward Becher, of Rock Castle, and Hare Island, co. Cork. She *d.* 1881. He *d.* 11 Dec. 1865, having had issue,
1. Samuel Nugent, of St. Kames Island.
2. Edward Becher, *b.* 1857; *m.* 22 Dec. 1883, Elizabeth Ellen White, of N.S.W. and was drowned in Australia 18 Aug. 1886, leaving an only child,
  Samuel Edward, now of St. Kames Island.
3. Lionel Becher, *b.* 1859.
4. Henry Becher, *b.* 1861, *d.s.p.* 1881.
1. Mary Alice, *m.* Nov. 1865, Edward Townsend, of Australia, brother of Professor Townsend, F.R.S., Sen. Fellow T.C.D.
2. Mercy.
3. Charlotte, *m.* 1873, Francis Joseph Edward Spring, C.I.E.
4. Annie Johnson, *m.* Rev. J. T. Jones, Rector of Baltimore co. Cork.
5. Alice, *d. unm.*
The eldest son,
Samuel Nugent Townsend, of St. Kames Island, co. Cork, J.P., *b.* 7 Dec. 1844; *m.* 12 Oct. 1886, Henrietta, dau. of the late Anthony Morgan, of Prospect Hill, and Bunalun, co. Cork, and widow of Capt. George Lane, of H.M. Corps of Gentlemen-at-Arms. He *d.* Dec. 1910.

Seat—St. Kames Island, Skibbereen, co. Cork. *Residence*—Selwood, Allison Road, Randwick, near Sydney, N.S.W.

TOWNSHEND OF GARRYCLOYNE CASTLE.

Samuel Philip Townshend, of Garrycloyne Castle, co. Cork, *b.* 1869; *m.* 1895, Blanche, dau. of — Richardson, and has issue,
1. Philip Mervyn Maunsell.
1. Hiddagardis Catherine.   2. Mildred Muriel.

Townshend. THE LANDED GENTRY. 702

Lineage.—REV HORATIO TOWNSEND, Rector of Donoughmore, co. Cork, 9th son of Bryan Townsend, of Castle Townsend (see TOWNSHEND, *late of Castle Townshend*), *b.* 1 Sept. 1706; *m.* 1739, Mary, dau. of Thomas Hungerford, of the Island, and *d.* Oct. 1772, having had issue,
1. Edward Synge (Rev.), Rector of Clondrohid and afterwards of Kilcorney, *b.* 18 Jan. 1741; *m.* 2 Oct. 1766, Elizabeth, 3rd dau. of Horatio Townshend, of Bridgemount, and *d.* 2 Jan. 1819, leaving issue.
2. Horatio, *d. unm.*
3. Thomas, *d. unm.*
4. RICHARD, of whom presently.
5. Samuel Philip, of Firmount, co. Cork, *m.* April, 1782, Helena, dau. of Rev. Thomas Robinson, of Coronea, co. Cork, and had issue. From him descended the TOWNSHENDS *of Woodside*.
   1. Susan, *m.* Rev. John Meade, of Ballymartle, co. Cork, and *d.s.p.* 18 March, 1820.
   2. Mary, *m.* 1768, Adam Newman, of Kinsale.
   3. Barbara, *d. unm.*

The 4th son,
RICHARD TOWNSEND, of Pallastown, co. Cork, *m.* 29 Sept. 1772, Mildred, dau. and co-heir of Achilles Daunt, of Gortigrenan, co. Cork, and Owlpen, Glos., and *d.* 8 April, 1805, leaving issue,
1. Horatio, *b.* 1775, *d. unm.*   2. Richard, *b.* 1776, *d. unm.*
3. SAMUEL PHILIP, of whom presently.
   1. Anne, *b.* 1773; *d. unm.* 22 Oct. 1822.
   2. Mary, *b.* 1778, *d. unm.*   3. Mildred, *b.* 1780, *d.* 1783.
   4. Elizabeth, *d. unm.*   5. Susan, *d. young*.
6. Helena, *m.* Sept. 1808, William McDermott, of Dublin, and *d.s.p.* 1809.
7. Mildred, *m.* Webber Carleton, of Rock Ladge, co. Cork, and has issue.
8. Jane, *m.* Rev. Rowland Davies Gray, Curate of Garrycloyne.

The youngest son,
SAMUEL PHILIP TOWNSEND, of Garrycloyne, co. Cork, purchased 1837, the estate of Garrycloyne from John Travers ; *m.* 1836, Frances Helena, dau. of Adam Newman, of Dromore, and *d.* 7 Sept. 1864, having had issue,
1. RICHARD HORATIO, his heir.
2. Samuel Philip, *b.* 16 Oct. 1840 ; *d. unm.* Oct. 1888.
3. Edward Synge, *b.* 21 Sept. 1843 ; *d. unm.* Aug. 1908.
4. Horatio Adam, *b.* 22 Aug. 1846 ; *d. unm.*
5. Thomas Achilles, M.E., R.U.I. (8, *St. Augustine's Road, Bedford*), *b.* 1847 ; *m.* 1884, Eveline Victoria, 2nd and only surviving dau. of Evory Carmichael, M.D., and has issue,
   1. Philip Achilles Kingston, Lieut. Royal Berkshire Regt., *b.* 7 Dec. 1885.
   2. Francis Horatio Evory, Lieut. R.E., *b.* 10 May, 1887.
   3. Richard Samuel Hungerford, Lieut. North Staffordshire Regt., *b.* 12 Dec. 1888.
6. George Robert, Col. R.A., *b.* 13 April, 1856; *m.* 9 Oct. 1886, Petrie, dau. of T. H. Wisdom, and has issue,
   Hugh, *b.* 17 Nov. 1890.
   Dorothy Petrie, *b.* 8 May, 1895.
1. Frances Dorothea, *b.* 17 Aug. 1839; *m.* 1869, John Crewe Chetwode Townsend, Capt. North Cork Rifles, and had issue. He *d.* 1873.
2. Emily Mildred, *b.* 1849 ; *m.* 20 Feb. 1873, Rev. Thomas Allin, and *d.* 12 Feb. 1898.
3. Mary Hungerford, *b.* 3 Aug. 1850.
4. Alice Maud, *b.* 20 April, 1854; *m.* 1884, William Hare Maunsell, Lieut. R.N., who *d.* Dec. 1907.

The eldest son,
RICHARD HORATIO TOWNSEND, B.A., of Garrycloyne, co. Cork, Lieut. 31st E. Surrey Regt., *s.* his father 1864 ; *b.* 9 July, 1838 ; *m.* 1868, Frances Maria, eldest dau. of William Hare Mauns-ll. She *d.* 1882. He *d.* 1879, leaving issue,
1. SAMUEL PHILIP, now of Garrycloyne.
   1. Mary Helena Maunsell, *m.* Sidney Ernest Langdon, son of Capt. Charles Henry Clark Langdon, R.N., and had issue.
   2. Hildagardis Maud Leigh, *m.* Francis Hemingway, son of James Hemingway, C.E. ; *d.* 1903 and has issue.
   3. Katherine Granville Eyre, *d. unm.*
   4. Emily Mabel, *m.* Wm. Townsend, eldest son of Prof. Edward Townsend, Queen's Coll. Galway, and has issue.

Seat—Garrycloyne near Blarney.

TOWNSHEND OF CASTLE TOWNSHEND.

CHARLES LOFTUS UNIACKE TOWNSHEND, of Castle Townshend, co. Cork, late Capt. 5th Batt. Royal Irish Rifles, *b.* 7 Jan. 1861 ; *m.* 27 April, 1895, Beatrice Margaret, only child of the late Carl von Bunsen, of Mein Genügen, Biebrich, Germany, of the German Diplomatic Service, and grand-dau. of Baron von Bunsen, sometime Prussian Minister at the Court of St. James, and has issue,
1. CHARLES RICHARD DE BUNSEN LOFTUS, *b.* 4 April, 1896.
2. Frederick William Chisholm Loftus, *b.* 19 Nov. 1897.
3. Charles Maurice Waddington Loftus, *b.* 30 Jan. 1899.
4. Edward Arthur Penderell Loftus, *b.* 20 June, 1901.
5. Walter Bevil Granville Loftus, *b.* 8 Nov. 1902.
6. Bernard Hugo Uniacke Loftus, *b.* 19 Dec. 1905.

Mr. C. L. U. Townshend purchased this property in 1897 from his kinsman. He is the eldest son of Charles Uniacke Townshend, of Dublin (see TOWNSHEND, *of Myross Wood*), by Annie his wife, eldest dau. of the Rev. Robert Loftus Tottenham (see BURKE'S *Peerage*, ELY, M.).

Seat—Castle Townshend, co. Cork. **Residence**—46, Lansdowne Road, Dublin. **Clubs**—Sackville Street, Dublin, and Royal St. George Yacht, Kingstown.

TRAILL OF BALLYLOUGH.

ANTHONY TRAILL, of Ballylough House, co. Antrim, J.P., High Sheriff 1882, LL.D. and M.D. M.Ch., D.L., Provost of Trin. Coll. Dublin, Hon. F.R.C.S.I., Hon. F.R.C.P.I., Hon. LL.D. Glasgow University, Hon. LL.D. Aberdeen University, Hon. LL.D. St. Andrew's University, Commissioner of Educational Endowments (Ireland) 1885–92, Member of Royal (Fry) Commission on Irish Land Acts 1897-8, Commissioner of National Education 1901, *b.* 1 Nov. 1838 ; *m.* 25 June, 1867, Catherine Elizabeth (*d.* 19 Dec. 1909), 2nd dau. of James Stewart Moore, D.L., a Waterloo Veteran, of Ballydivity, co. Antrim, by Fanny his wife, dau. of Rev. Thomas Richardson, of Somerest, co. Londonderry, and has issue,
1. WILLIAM STEWART, *b.* 28 March, 1868, Major R.E. ; *m.* 7 Nov. 1896, Selina Margaret, dau. of Charles Frizell, of Castle Kevin, co. Wicklow, and has issue,
   Anthony O'Brien, *b.* 19 Sept. 1897.
2. James Anthony, *b.* 7 Aug. 1870 ; *m.* 20 Dec. 1898, Annie Isabel, dau. of Capt. J. O. Gage, R.M. He *d.* 11 Nov. 1901. His widow *m.* 10 Aug. 1911, Rev. F. R. M. Hitchcock.
3. Robert Thomas, *b.* 3 Jan. 1872 ; *d.* 17 March, 1873.
4. Henry Edward O'Brien, Capt. R.G.A., *b.* 3 Nov. 1876 ; *m.* Dec. 1906, Ella Kerr.
5. Edmund Francis Tarleton, Capt. A.S.C., *b.* 9 May, 1878 ; *m.* 27 June, 1911, Grace Ethel, dau. of — Harvey, of Bush Hall, Melton Constable.
6. Alexander Frederick, *b.* 2 May, 1891.
1. Frances Catherine, *m.* 10 Aug. 1898, Leslie Denny, of Dumbarton, N.B.
2. Harriet Agnes, *m.* 14 April, 1896, Alfred Edward Brett, elder son of Sir Charles H. Brett, of Gretton, Malone, Belfast.
3. Annie Margaret, *m.* July, 1905, Hugh Lecky, Junr., of Beardiville, co. Antrim (*see that family*).

Lineage.—COL. ANDREW TRAIL, younger brother of ALEXANDER TRAIL, Laird of Blebo, co. Fife, ancestor of the Trails in co. Fife, and of the Traills of Orkney, served the Confederate States of Flanders as well as HENRY IV of France with reputation. On his return, he was made Gentleman of the Privy Chamber to Prince Henry, eldest son of JAMES I. He *m.* Helen, dau. of Thomas Myrton, of Cambo, and was father of
JAMES TRAILL, of Denino, who *d.* 1635, leaving by his first wife, Matilda, dau. of Melville, of Cambee, three sons,
1. James, *b.* 1600, Col. in the Parliamentary Army, settled at Tallachin, co. Down, where he *d.* in 1663. He *m.* 1647, Mary, dau. of James Hamilton, Viscount Claneboy, and had issue, four sons and eight daus., of whom the 6th, Eleanor, *m.* her cousin, William Trail.
2. ROBERT, of whom presently.   3. Andrew, *d. unm.*

The 2nd son,
REV. ROBERT TRAIL, *b.* 1603, Minister of Elie, co. Fife, and afterwards of the Grey Friars, Edinburgh, was taken prisoner by CROMWELL ; he assisted afterwards at the coronation of CHARLES II, and was banished to Holland for nonconformity ; he returned, however, in 1674, and *d.* at Edinburgh 10 July, 1676. He *m.* 23 Dec. 1639, Jane Allen, dau. of Alexander Annan, Laird of Auchterallen, and by her (who *d.* Dec. 1680) had issue. His eldest son,
REV. WILLIAM TRAIL, Minister of Borthwick, *b.* Sept. 1640 ; *m.* 1st, 15 Sept. 1671, Euphan, 2nd dau. of Provost Sword, of St. Andrews, and by her (who *d.* 1677) left an only dau., Mary. He *m.* 2ndly, 25 March, 1679, his cousin, Eleanor, 6th dau. of James Trail, and by her (who *d.* 4 Jan. 1695) had issue,
1. James (Rev.), *d.* 1723, leaving two daus.
2. William (Rev.), *b.* in Ireland 13 Oct. 1683 ; *m.* 1st, Isabel, 4th dau. of John Haldane, of Myrton, near Stirling, and had, with other issue who *d.s.p.*, an eldest son,
   William, Minister of Logie and Pet, *m.* his cousin, Mary, eldest dau. of his uncle, Rev. Robert Trail, and had issue.
He *m.* 2ndly, Marion, dau. of Alexander Hamilton, by whom he had no issue.
3. ROBERT (Rev.), of whom presently.
1. Sarah, *d. unm.* 1685.   2. Jean, *d. unm.*
3. Margaret, *m.* Robert Alison, Writer in Edinburgh.
4. Eleanor, twin with Margaret, *d.* young, 1692.
5. Elizabeth, *m.* Mr. Stevenson.

The 3rd son,

703 IRELAND. Tredennick.

Rev. Robert Trail, Minister of Panbride, co. Forfar, b. 20 Nov. 1687; m. 10 April, 1718, Jane, 8th dau. of John Haldane, of Myrton, and by her (who d. 1776) had issue,
1. Robert, of whom presently.
2. John, b. 25 April, 1721; d. unm.
3. William, b. 23 March, 1723; d. 12 March, 1729.
4. James (Right Rev.), Bishop of Down and Connor, b. 9 Feb. 1725; m. 31 May, 1766, Margaret Black, of Edinburgh, and d.s.p. 1 Nov. 1783.
1. Mary, m. her first cousin, Rev. William Trail.
2. Margaret, m. 1st, Aug. 1768, — Webster, of Dundee, and 2ndly, 4 March, 1794, William Dow, brother of Mrs. R. Trail.
Rev. Robert Trail d. 7 Nov. 1752. His eldest son,
Rev. Robert Trail, Minister of Panbride, b. 10 July, 1719; m. Jane, dau. of Rev. Anthony Dow, of Fettercairn, and by her (who d. 2 June, 1805) had issue,
1. Robert (Rev.), Rector of Ballintoy, b. 29 Aug. 1754; d. unm.
2. Anthony, of whom presently.
3. James, Minister of St. Cyrus, or Ecclesgraig, co. Kincardine, b. 7 May, 1767; m. Anne, dau. of Rev. David Burns, of Largo, co. Fife. 4. John.
5. Thomas, Merchant in Montrose, b. 18 Jan. 1764; m. 9 Feb. 1795, Mary, dau. of Robert Airth, of Mains of Dun, and d. 11 Feb. 1822, having had issue.
6. David, Minister of Panbride, b. 27 June, 1765; m. 23 June, 1795, Elizabeth, dau. of John Biss, of Deptford, co. Durham, and had issue.
1. Catherine Jane, m. Alexander Airth.
2. Margaret Black, m. her cousin, James Dow.
The Rev. Robert Trail d. 7 April, 1798. His 2nd son,
Rev. Anthony Trail, of Ballyloug, Prebendary of St. Andrews, Archdeacon of Connor, and Rector of Skull, b. 25 Nov. 1755; m. 3 Jan. 1788, Agnes, dau. of William Watts Gayer, LL.D., Chief Clerk of the House of Lords in Ireland, and by her (who d. 30 Nov. 1838) had issue,
1. James, b. 26 July, 1789; d. unm. 27 June, 1810, in Madeira.
2. William, of whom presently.
3. Robert (Rev.), Rector of Skull, co. Cork, b. 15 July, 1793; m. 11 Feb. 1829, Anne, eldest dau. of Sir Samuel Hayes, and bart., of Drumboe, and d. 1847, having had issue. His dau., Kathleen, m. 1856, John Hatch Synge (see Synge of Glanmore). His youngest dau., Harriette Adelaide, m. 29 Oct. 1861, R. Cathcart Dobbs, eldest son of Major-Gen. Richard Stewart Dobbs.
1. Catherine, d. unm. 23 March, 1823.
Archdeacon Trail d. 16 Nov. 1831. His 2nd son,
William Trail, of Ballylough, B.A. Trin. Coll. Dublin, and M.D. Edinburgh, b. 3 Aug. 1791; m. 1st, 11 Nov. 1824, Louisa Ann, dau. of Rev. Thomas Lloyd, of Castle Lloyd, by Elizabeth Fitzgerald his wife, dau. of the Knight of Glin, and by this lady had issue, two daus.,
1. Elizabeth Catherine, m. William Dunne. She d. 28 Dec. 1901.
2. Agnes, d. 1833.
He m. 2ndly, 28 July, 1836, Louisa Henrietta, dau. of Robert French, of Monivea Castle, co. Galway, by Nichola his wife, sister of Sir Edward O'Brien, 4th bart., of Dromoland, co. Clare, and by her had issue,
1. Anthony, now of Ballylough.
2. Robert Gayer, Major late P.W.O. Yorks Regt., Barrister-at-Law, b. 21 Nov. 1839; d. 4 March, 1908; m. Alice Campbell, of Sydney; d. Dec. 1908.
3. William Aeneson, b. 2 Sept. 1844; m. 1st, Harriett Jane Wrigley; m. 2ndly, Elizabeth Greer, and has issue.
8. Maria Nichola.
4. Agnes Victoria, m. 23 Jan. 1867, Rev. John Joseph Jackson, of Ballinderry Rectory, eldest son of Very Rev. James Jackson, Dean of Armagh, and has issue. 5. Louisa Henrietta, d. 1850.
Seat—Ballylough House, Bushmills, co. Antrim. Town address—Provost's House, Dublin.

TRANT OF DOVEA.

The late Fitzgibbon Trant, of Dovea, co. Tipperary, J.P. and D.L., High Sheriff 1889, late Lieut. 72nd Highlanders, and Lieut.-Col. 4th Batt. Royal Irish Regt., b. 19 Oct. 1849; d. 12 April, 1912; m. 6 Dec. 1882, Georgina Emily, youngest dau. of Phillip Jocelyn Newton, of Dunlckney Manor, co. Carlow, and had issue,
1. Laurence Dominick, b. 29 March, 1887.
2. John Philip, b. 23 Dec. 1889.
1. Irene, m. 31 Aug. 1910, Major William Cautley Olpherts, late Royal Scots, only son of late Gen. Sir William Olpherts, V.C., G.C.B.
2. Hope Minnie. 3. Ruth Mary.
Lineage.—The great-grandfather of the present representative was Dominick Trant (John), of Dingle, co. Kerry, who was father of Dominick Trant, of Dunkettle, co. Cork, m. Eleanor Fitzgibbon, sister of John, 1st Earl of Clare, Lord Chancellor of Ireland, and had issue,
1. John Frederick, of whom presently.
2. William Henry, m. Charlotte, dau. of — Lumsden.
1. Maria, m. Henry, and Lord Dunalley.
The eldest son,
John Frederick Trant, of Dovea, J.P. and D.L., Capt. 10th Royal Hussars, m. Caroline, dau. of Francis Brooke, of Colebrooke, co. Fermanagh (brother of the Right Hon. Sir Arthur Brooke, Bart.), by Hannah his wife (dau. of Henry Prittie, of Dunalley Castle, and Killboy, co. Tipperary, and sister of the 1st Lord Dunalley), and had issue,
1. John, late of Dovea.
1. Caroline, m. Nov. 1833, James Hans Hamilton, of Abbotstown, co. Dublin, M.P. for that co.; d. 9 March, 1845.
2. Louisa Anne. 3. Selina, m. A. B. Cane; d. 5 Nov. 1859.
He d. 21 Nov. 1838, and was s. by his only son,
John Trant, of Dovea, co. Tipperary, J.P., D.L., High Sheriff 1846, b. 23 May, 1819; m. 3 Nov. 1842, Sarah Sophia, 2nd dau. of Sir Henry Robert Carden, 3rd bart., of Templemore, and by her (who d. Aug. 1893) had issue,
1. Fitzgibbon, now of Dovea.
2. Frederick Ion, b. 17 Sept. 1856; m. 1889, Alice Mottershead, and has issue,
1. Frederick.
2. John Francis.
3. Patrick Harold.
4. Ion Hans.
3. John Francis, Capt. in the Army, b. 14 April, 1858.
4. Hans Arthur, b. 4 Feb. 1864; d. 1885.
1. Caroline Frances.
2. Sara Louise, m. 9 Aug. 1864, Francis Wise Low, of Kilshane, co. Tipperary.
3. Eleanor Nina, m. 15 Oct. 1878, Rev. R. W. Nash, M.A., Rector of Kilmanagh, co. Kilkenny.
4. Emily Henrietta.
5. Alice Sophia, d. unm. 16 Jan. 1900.
6. Florence Rose, m. 22 Dec. 1883, Thomas Bruen Ruttledge, only son of Robert Ruttledge, of Bloomfield, co. Mayo (see that family), and d. 3 Jan. 1892.
7. Arabella Maud.
8. Mabel, d. 15 Sept. 1861.
Mr. Trant d. 11 May, 1887, and was s. by his eldest son.
Seat—Dovea, Thurles, co. Tipperary.

TREDENNICK OF CAMLIN.

The Rev. George Nesbitt Haydon Tredennick, M.A., of Camlin, co. Donegal, Vicar of Sparbrook, Birmingham, b. 1860; m. 19 Nov. 1889, Alice Jane, eldest dau. of the Ven. Robert Phair, Archdeacon of Rupert's Island, N.W.A., and has issue,
1. John Nesbitt Ernest, b. 23 Sept. 1892.
2. George Hugh Percival Phair, b. 30 June, 1899.
Lineage.—William Tredennick had two sons, John, his heir; William; and nine daus. The elder son,
John Tredennick, of Camlin, m. 1st, Elizabeth Crozier, by whom he had issue,
1. William, of Camlin, his heir, m. Elizabeth, dau. of John Jones, and d.s.p.
1. Margaret. 2. Jane.
He m. 2ndly, Sarah Hamilton, of Eden, and by her (who d. 1801) left issue,
2. James, d. unm. 3. George, d. unm.
4. Archibald, d. unm. 5. Galbraith, his heir.
He d. 1778. The 5th son,
Galbraith Tredennick, of Camlin, b. 1757; s. to his estates on the death of his eldest brother, William, who d. 30 June, 1816. He m. 19 April, 1793, Anne, dau. and, in her issue, heir of George Nesbitt, of Woodhill, co. Donegal, and by her (who d. 20 Sept. 1851) had issue,
1. John Arnold, late of Camlin.
2. George Nesbitt (Rev.), of Woodhill, Ardara, co. Donegal, Vicar of Kilbarron, diocese of Raphoe, b. 25 May, 1796; m. June, 1827, Lydia, 6th dau. of William Magee, D.D., Archbishop of Dublin (she d. 1865), and had issue,
1. John Galbraith, of Camlin.
2. George Nesbitt (Rev.), Incumbent of St. John's, Devonport, subsequently Rector of Lismore, B.A., b. 3 Dec. 1840; m. Blizabeth Moulson, dau. of Rev. T. H. C. Finny, of Freechurch, co. Cork (see Finny of Leixlip).
3. James Richard Knox, Major-Gen. 57th Regt., b. 4 Oct. 1842; m. Katherine Stephens.
4. William Magee, M.D., b. 5 July, 1844; d. 26 Feb. 1876; m. Marie Pryor.
1. Elizabeth Moulson, m. Rev. John Taylor Coffy, Rector of Magorban.
2. Anne Nesbitt, m. March, 1851, Lieut.-Col. Robert Abraham Logan, 57th Regt., and has issue; d. 12 Aug. 1887.
3. Lydia, m. Charles King Colquhoun, Capt. Tyrone Militia.
4. Jane, d. young. 5. Maria, d. young.
6. Margaret Sarah, d. unm. 24 Jan. 1899.
3. William Richard, of Fortwilliam, co. Donegal, b. 1802; d. 7 Nov. 1885; m. 1832, Maria, 7th dau. of William Magee, D.D., Archbishop of Dublin, and by her (who d. Dec. 1851) had issue,
1. William Richard, late Capt. 27th Regt., d. 4 July, 1911; m. 1874, Millie Letitia, dau. of James Johnstone, of Laputa, co. Donegal, and had issue.
2. Charles, m. 1 March, 1887, Elizabeth, youngest dau. of J. G. Willans, of Bayswater.
1. Elizabeth.
2. Annette Catherine, m. 1856, St. George Robert Johnston 3rd son of Robert Johnston, of Kinlough (see that family).
3. Wilhelmina, d. unm. 1801.
4. Marcia, m. 1st, Rev. W. Dalby; m. 2ndly, John Beattie.

Trench. THE LANDED GENTRY. 704

  5. Jane, *m.* Rev. Martin Bradshaw.
  6. Arabella, *m.* Alexander Kingstone.
  7. Charlotte.   8. Maria.
1. Elizabeth Jane, *m.* Capt. Coyne Reynolds, of Coolbeg, co. Donegal, 39th Regt., and had a dau., Anna Maria.
2. Annabella, *m.* Capt. William Atkinson, of Devonport, 30th Regt., and *d.s.p.*
Mr. Galbraith Tredennick *d.* 17 June, 1817, and was *s.* by his eldest son,
JOHN ARNOLD TREDENNICK, of Camlin, J.P. cos. Donegal, Fermanagh, and Roscommon, High Sheriff co. Fermanagh 1821, *b.* 21 May, 1795 ; *m.* 25 Jan. 1819, Elizabeth, dau. of Joseph Johnston, of Summer Hill, co. Donegal, and *d.s.p.* His nephew,
JOHN GALBRAITH TREDENNICK, of Camlin, Col. Donegal Militia, *b.* 8 April, 1828 ; *m.* 3 March, 1859, Emily Dodsworth, dau. of Joseph Haydon, of Guildford, and by her (who *d.* 10 Dec. 1893) had issue,
1. GEORGE NESBITT HAYDON, now of Camlin.
2. John Magee (Rev.), M.A., T.C.D., Vicar of Langdale, Westmorland, *m.* 3 Oct. 1890, Alice Maud, only dau. of J. C. Robins, of London, and has issue,
  1. John Edwin Foster, *b.* 15 Nov. 1906.
  1. Evelyn Florence Haydon, *b.* 9 July, 1902.
3. Arthur Heywood (Rev.), M.A., Vicar of Hatfield St. Mary's, Hertford, *m.* 17 July, 1900, Florence Elizabeth, eldest dau. of Rev. P. R. Sleeman, of Clifton, Bristol, and has issue,
  Mona Florence Heywood, *b.* 13 March, 1907.
4. Trevrand Galbraith, *d.* 24 Sept. 1908.
5. Percival Dodsworth Foster, *d. unm.* 20 Aug. 1893.
6. Galbraith William.   **7.** Charles Joseph Haydon.
1. Sophia Harriett.
Col. Tredennick *d.* 22 Feb. 1884.

Seat—Camlin, Ballyshannon.

TRENCH OF CLONFERT.

CHARLES O'HARA TRENCH, of Clonfert, co. Galway, J.P., late 14th Regt., *b.* 19 March, 1846 ; *s.* his brother Dec. 1867 ; *m.* 14 April, 1874, Elizabeth Olivia, 3rd dau. of Robert St. George, and grand-dau. of Sir Richard Bligh St. George, Bart., of Woodsgift, co. Kilkenny, and has issue,
1. JOHN ARTHUR BURDETT, *b.* 24 Aug. 1884.
2. Charles Frederick, Lieut. 7th Hariana Lancers, *b.* 29th July, 1885.
1. Grace Eulalie St. George, *m.* 29 Oct. 1902, Hubert William Crane, C.I., R.I.C., eldest son of Rev. Canon Crane, of Manchester, and has issue.
2. Violet Madeline Maud, *d.* 1905.
3. Moira Sophia.

Lineage.—EYRE TRENCH, of Ashford, co. Roscommon, 2nd surviving son of Frederick Trench, of Garbally, M.P. for co. Galway (*see* BURKE'S *Peerage*, CLANCARTY, E.), by Elizabeth his wife, dau. of John Eyre, of Eyrecourt Castle, *m.* 1768, Charlotte, only child of Kean O'Hara, of Dublin, and grand-dau. of Kean O'Hara, of Annaghmore, co. Sligo, and *d.* 1775, leaving an only son,
REV. FREDERICK EYRE TRENCH, Rector of Kellistown, co. Carlow, *b.* 1769 ; *m.* 1795, Catherine, dau. of Michael Head, of Derry Castle, co. Tipperary, and had issue,
1. JOHN EYRE, his heir.
2. William Eyre, *b.* 1800 ; *d.s.p.* 1861.
Rev. Mr. Trench *d.* 1848, and was *s.* by his eldest son,
JOHN EYRE TRENCH, of Clonfert, co. Galway, purchased the old Episcopal Palace and See lands of Clonfert, co. Galway, on the abolition of the Bishopric in 1834. He was *b.* 1798 ; *m.* 1834, Grace, 3rd dau. of Rev. John Burdett, Rector of Banagher, King's Co. and Ballygarth, co. Meath, and by her (who *d.* Jan. 1889) had issue,
1. FREDERICK AUGUSTUS EYRE, his heir.
2. CHARLES O'HARA, now of Clonfert.
1. Margaret Matilda, *d.* 1874.
2. Catherine Maria Louisa, *d.* 1871.
3. Grace Florinda, *m.* 1862, Arthur Burdett, of Coolfin, King's Co. ; and *d.* 1863, leaving issue (*see that family*).
4. Charlotte Henrietta.
Mr. Trench *d.* Feb. 1864, and was *s.* by his eldest son,
FREDERICK AUGUSTUS EYRE TRENCH, of Clonfert, co. Galway, *b.* 1836 ; *s.* his father in 1864 ; *d. unm.* Dec. 1867, and was *s.* by his brother, the present
CHARLES O'HARA TRENCH, of Clonfert.

Arms, &c.—(*See* BURKE'S *Peerage*.)

Seat—Clonfert, Eyrecourt, co. Galway. Club—Hibernian United Service, Dublin.

TRENCH OF SOPWELL HALL.

THE HON. COSBY GODOLPHIN TRENCH, of Sopweil Hall, co. Tipperary, J.P. and D.L., High Sheriff 1886, and J.P. co. Waterford, late Capt. 1st Royal Dragoons, *b.* 6 Jan. 1844 ; *m.* 19 June, 1873, Maria, eldest dau. of Sir Richard Musgrave, Bart., and has issue,
1. CHARLES SADLEIR MUSGRAVE, Capt. late Northumberland Fus., (*Club,* Bachelors'), *b.* 15 April, 1874.
2. Edward Cosby (*Seat: Lanagour, Cowichan Bay, Vancouver Isl., B.C.; Club: St. James'*), *b.* 2 May, 1881 ; *m.* 5 Feb. 1910, Evelyn eldest dau. of Col. de Courcy Daniell, late R.A.
3. Clive Newcome, *b.* 7 July, 1884 ; *m.* 27 Jan. 1910, Kathleen Maud Marion, dau. of the late Major Ivan MacIvor, C.S.I., and has issue.
4. Hubert Roland, *b.* 3 Feb. 1887 ; *d.* Dec. 1911.

Capt. Trench is the 2nd and only surviving son of Frederick Mason, 2nd Baron Ashtown (who *d.* 12 Sept. 1880), by Harriette Georgiana his 1st wife (who *d.* 25 Feb. 1845), dau. of Thomas Cosby, of Stradbally Hall, Queen's Co.

Lineage.—*See* BURKE'S *Peerage*, ASHTOWN, B.

Arms—Arg. a lion pass. gu. between three fleurs-de-lys az., on a chief of the last a sun in splendour or. *Crest*—A dexter arm embowed in armour, the hand grasping a sword all ppr. *Motto*—Virtutis fortuna comes.

Seat—Sopwell Hall, Cloughjordan, co. Tipperary. Clubs—Naval and Military and Kildare Street.

TRENCH OF REDWOOD.

The late WILLIAM THOMAS TRENCH, of Redwood, co. Tipperary, J.P. and D.L. for that co. and J.P. King's Co., High Sheriff 1885, B.A. Trin. Coll. Camb., Barrister-at-Law, unsuccessfully contested in the Unionist interest the Birr Division of King's Co. 1892, *b.* 5 Sept. 1843 ; *d.* 18 Dec. 1911; *m.* 10 Jan. 1877, Elizabeth Ida, eldest dau. of Colin G. Campbell, of Stonefield, Argyllshire. Mr. Trench was the 2nd son of the late Henry Trench, of Cangort Park, King's Co., J.P. and D.L. (who *d.* 7 March, 1881), by Georgiana Mary Amelia his wife (who *d.* 13 Jan. 1893), dau. of Benjamin, 1st Lord Bloomfield, and grandson of William Trench, of Cangort, younger brother of Frederick, 1st Lord Ashtown.

Lineage.—*See* BURKE'S *Peerage*, ASHTOWN, B.

Arms—Arg. a lion passant gu. between three fleurs-de-lys az. on a chief of the last a sun in splendour or. *Crest*—A dexter arm embowed in armour, the hand grasping a sword, all ppr. *Mottoes*—1. Virtutis fortuna comes. 2. Dieu pour la Tranche qui contre?

Seat—Redwood, Birr, co. Tipperary.

TRENCH OF GLENMALYRE.

THOMAS SANDES TRENCH, of Glenmalyre, Queen's Co., J.P., D.L., and J.P. co. Cork, B.A. Trin. Coll. Dublin, late Capt. 4th Batt. Leinster Regt., *b.* 29 March, 1840. Mr. Trench is the eldest son of the late Henry Trench, of Glenmalyre, Queen's Co., J.P. and D.L. (who *d.* 28 Feb. 1888), by Elizabeth

Anne Caroline his wife (who d. 1898), eldest dau. of Charles Lancelot Sandes, of Indiaville, Queen's Co., and grandson of the Very Rev. Thomas Trench, of Glenmalyre, Dean of Kildare, younger brother of 1st Baron Ashtown.
Lineage, Arms, &c.—See BURKE's *Peerage*, ASHTOWN, B.
Seat—Glenmalyre, Ballybrittas, Queen's Co.

TRENCH. See BURKE'S PEERAGE, **ASHTOWN, B.,** and **CLANCARTY, E.**

TRENT-STOUGHTON. See **STOUGHTON.**

TRUELL OF CLONMANNON.

THE REV. WILLIAM HENRY AUGUSTUS TRUELL, of Clonmannon, co. Wicklow, B.A. Trin. Coll. Camb., late Vicar of Wall, co. Stafford, b. 21 May, 1843; m. 29 July, 1873, Lady Cornelia Stuart, dau. of Rev. Edmund Luttrell Stuart (see BURKE'S *Peerage*, MORAY, E.), and has issue,

1. ROBERT HOLT STUART, a Master at Dover Coll., b. 6 Dec. 1875.
2. Edmund Gray Stuart, Capt. Connaught Rangers, b. 14 Aug. 1878.
3. William Henry Stuart, b. 28 Feb. 1880.
1. Mary Louisa, m. 3 Sept. 1903, John Milne, M.B., only son of J. Milne, J.P., of Heyside, near Oldham, and has issue.
2. Cornelia Isabel, m. 14 June, 1900, Frank Mortimer Rowland, M.D. of Lichfield, and has issue.
3. Kathleen Augusta.
4. Gertrude Margaret.
5. Constance Elizabeth.

Lineage.—REV. HOLT TRUELL, b. 1701, was for many years J.P. co. Wicklow; he m. 1st, about 1724-5, Catherine, dau. of Abraham Yarner and widow of Richard Stone, but by her had no issue. He m. 2ndly, Rachel, dau. of Rev. Michael Symes, Rector of Kilcommon, co. Wicklow, and had issue, several sons and daus., all of whom d. unm., except
REV. ROBERT TRUELL, D.D., of Clonmannon, b. 10 March, 1754; m. 21 Oct. 1791, Editha, only dau. and heir of Edward Jones, of Dublin, and of Bramley, co. Southampton, and by her (who d. 21 March, 1843) had issue,
1. ROBERT HOLT, of whom presently.
2. Henry, b. 1803; d. unm. 1820.
3. William (Rev.), Rector of Tyueham, Dorset, b. 25 May, 1804; m. 8 Feb. 1834, Jane, dau. of John Hawkesworth, of Forest, Queen's Co., and d. 12 July, 1885, having by her, who d. 1890, had
 1. Robert Holt, Major-Gen. (ret.) 53rd Regt., b. 30 Sept. 1837; m. 1st, 1884, Elizabeth, dau. of the Rev. Charles Onslow. She d. 1889. He m. 2ndly, 1890, Harriet, dau. of George Churchill, of Alderholt Park, Dorset, and d. Sept. 1900.
 2. WILLIAM HENRY AUGUSTUS, now of Clonmannon.
 1. Eleanor Mary Florentina.
4. George, b. 1808; d. unm. 1824.
1. Jane, d. unm. 1832. 2. Edith, d. 1807.
3. Patience, d. unm. 1828.
4. Elizabeth, m. Hon. Henry Pomeroy, 5th son of John, 4th Viscount Harberton. 5. Sarah, d. unm. 1833.
He d. 26 June, 1830, and was s. by his son,
ROBERT HOLT TRUELL, of Clonmannon, J.P. and D.L., High Sheriff 1824, b. 15 Nov. 1797; m. 18 Aug. 1824, Phœbe, 4th dau. of Rev. George Vesey, D.D., of Derrabard House, co. Tyrone, and by her had issue,
1. Robert, Capt. Wicklow Rifles, b. 10 Jan. 1828; m. 1st, 7 Nov. 1858, Frances Emily, 4th dau. of Rev. William Knox, of Clonleigh, co. Donegal, and had issue,
 1. Louisa, d. unm.
 2. Phœbe Editha, m. July, 1896, Robert Vesey Stoney, D.L., of Rosturk Castle, co. Mayo, and has issue (see that family).
He m. 2ndly, Feb. 1866, Henrietta, dau. of Very Rev. Ogle William Moore, Dean of Clogher, and d. 27 Feb. 1867, having by her had issue,
 1. Robert Holt, who d. an infant.
I.L.G.

2. George Vesey, an Officer 28th Regt., b. 1 May, 1831; d. 10 March, 1849.
3. HENRY POMEROY, late of Clonmannon.
 1. Barbara Anna, d. unm. Aug. 1848.
 2. Editha Jane, m. 1st, 7 Nov. 1861, Francis Synge, of Glanmore Castle, co. Wicklow (see that family), and 2ndly, 20 Nov. 1879, Major Theodore Webber-Gardiner.
Mr. Truell d. 7 March, 1870. His 3rd son,
HENRY POMEROY TRUELL, of Clonmannon, co. Wicklow, M.B., J.P. and D.L., High Sheriff 1871, b. 19 March, 1836; m. 20 Aug. 1861, Katherine Elizabeth, only dau. of Charles Rolleston-Spunner, Q.C., Chairman of co. Tipperary (see ROLLESTON, of *Franckfort Castle*). She d. 12 March, 1890. He d.s.p. 8 July, 1902.

Arms—Arg., a lion rampant, and in chief two hearts gu. **Crest**—A heart gu. between two palm-branches vert. **Mottoes**—Above the crest, Semper fidelis; below, Diligentia fortior.
Seat—Clonmannon, Rathnew, co. Wicklow. **Club**—Junior Conservative.

TUITE OF KILLEEN AND CLOONE.

ROBERT STRATFORD TUITE, of Killeen, co. Longford, and Cloone, co. Cavan, J.P. for co. Longford, late Major 4th Batt. Royal Irish Fusiliers, b. 27 July, 1852; m. 15 May, 1888, Georgina Phelps, eldest surviving dau. of the late Major George Roche Smith, 2nd Queen's Royals, and 99th Regt., by Grace Elizabeth his wife, eld. dau. of Major Robert Hedges Eyre Maunsell, 39th Regt., of Plassey, co. Limerick, and Beakstown, co. Tipperary, and has issue,

1. THOMAS MARK HARDRESS STRATFORD, b. 17 April, 1891.
2. Norman Eric Maunsell Stratford, b. 25 April, 1892.
3. Evelyn Morgan Aubrey Stratford, b. 1 Aug. 1894.
4. Maurice John Southwell Law, b. 15 Jan. 1902.
1. Gladys Grace Dawson-Damer Stratford.

Lineage.—SIR RICHARD DE TUITE accompanied the Earl of Pembroke into Ireland 1172, and was killed in Athlone 1211, while holding a Court. He erected the famous abbey of Lara, near Granard, co. Longford, in 1205, long the burial place of the Princes of Annally, and where he himself was buried. Sir Richard left two sons,
1. Sir Richard de Tuite, surnamed *The Black*, Baron of Moycashell.
2. Maurice Tuite, ancestor of TUITE *of Sonagh* (see BURKE's *Peerage and Baronetage*).
A branch of the family of TUITE *of Sonagh*, possessing lands in the cos. of Longford, Cavan, and Meath, descends from Sir Edmund Tuite, Knt., m. Alice, dau. of James Fitzgerald, of Laccagh, co. Westmeath, and had a son, EDWARD TUITE, of Tuitestown, co. Westmeath. In 1612, High Sheriff 1642, who, while sheriff, raised the county against His Majesty's Army, and was killed in a battle near Ticroghan; in consequence of which, his estates of Tuitestown, Ledwithstown, Carolstown, Coblestown, and others, became forfeited, and were granted to Philip, Lord Wharton, and were claimed by THOMAS TUITE, son of Edward Tuite, in 1664, but the "Act of Explanation" of 1666 excluded the claims of Innocents (see *Report of Carte Papers*, 1869, at the Bodleian Lib. Oxford).
THOMAS TUITE, grandson of Edward Tuite, settled at Carragh, Granard, co. Longford, in 1700, and m. 1720, Kathleen, dau. of James Major, of Higginstown, in that co., and d. 1772, aged 92, leaving two sons, FRANCIS; James, b. 1732; and one dau. surviving. The elder son,
FRANCIS TUITE, b. 1730; m. 1752, Rachel, dau. of Rev. Edward Groome, M.A., of Eyre Court, co. Galway, and d. 3 May, 1813, having by her (who d. July, 1799) had issue,
1. THOMAS, his heir.
2. Edward, d. April, 1792.
The elder son,
THOMAS TUITE, of Rockfield, Granard, b. 10 April, 1756, was a very extensive land agent, and held, with other agencies, that of his kinsman, Sir Henry Tuite, 8th bart., of Sonagh. He m. 23 June, 1790, Mary, dau. of Edward Reid, J.P., of Galmoylestown, co. Meath, and by her (who d. 23 Aug. 1827) had issue.
1. THOMAS, his heir.
2. Edward, d. 15 May, 1876.
1. Alice Palles, d. 11 Aug. 1830.
2. Jane, d. June, 1831.
3. Matilda Maconchy, d. 1870.
4. Maria, d. 1868.
5. Rachel Groome, d. 4 July, 1822.
Mr. Tuite d. 26 June, 1827, and was s. by his eldest son,
THOMAS TUITE, of Granard, co. Longford, b. 11 March, 1806; m. 10 Nov. 1842, Eleanor, dau. of Capt. Robert Stratford, of Annsgrove, co. Westmeath, and by her (who d. 25 Feb. 1901) had issue,
1. Thomas Groome, b. 21 April, 1845; d. 11 July, 1858.
2. ROBERT STRATFORD, of Killeen and Cloone.
1. Mary, d. 29 Sept. 1843.
2. Annie Jane, d. unm. 31 March, 1888.
Mr. Thomas Tuite d. 29 Sept. 1893.

Seats—Killeen, Granard, co. Longford; and Cloone Gowna co. Cavan. **Residence**—27, Herbert Place, Dublin.

2 Y

TUITE OF SONNA.

Henry Maurice Tuite, of Sonna, co. Westmeath, J.P., b. 15 Oct. 1856; s. his father 1910; m. 8 March 1886, Constance Edith, dau. of Henry Murray Campbell, of Halston, Westmeath.

Lineage.— See Burke's *Peerage*, Tuite, Bart. Hugh Morgan Tuite, M.P., D.L., of Sonna (who d. 16 Aug. 1868), by Mary his 1st wife (who d. 14 March, 1863), dau. of Maurice O'Connor, of Mount Pleasant, and grandson of Capt. Hugh Tuite, of Sonna, 4th son of Sir Henry Tuite, 6th bart., had issue, an only son,

Joseph Tuite, of Sonna, co. Westmeath, J.P. for that co., High Sheriff 1868, D.L. co. Longford, late Lieut. 15th Regt., b. 15 Oct. 1828; m. 1st, 8 Jan. 1852, Ellen Mary, dau. of Rev. Charles Fox Chawner, Rector of Bletchingley. She d. 2 Dec. 1863, leaving issue,

1. Henry Maurice, now of Sonna.
2. Marian Charlotte Mary, m. 1879, Brook Pakenham Bridges Taylor, a Gentleman Usher to H.M. the King.

He m. 2ndly, 4 June, 1868, Ellen, youngest dau. of James B. Boothby, of Twyford Abbey, and d. 21 Feb. 1910. She d.s p. 26 April, 1898.

Arms—Quarterly arg. and gu. *Crest*—An angel vested arg., holding in her dexter hand a flaming sword ppr., the sinister resting on a shield of the arms. *Motto*—Alleluiah.

Seat—Sonna, Westmeath.

FRANCE-LUSHINGTON-TULLOCH OF SHANBOOLARD.

Kate Mary, Mrs. France-Lushington-Tulloch, of Shanboolard, co. Galway, dau. of Charles Hugh Lushington, of Rodmersham, Kent, only surviving son of William John Lushington, of Rodmersham (see Lushington, *of Park House*); s. her aunt, Jane Ann, widow of James Tulloch and dau. of William John Lushington. She m. 1st, Oct. 1881, William Cairns Armstrong-Lushington-Tulloch (b. 10 April, 1848), son of the late John Armstrong, of Graigaverne, Queen's Co. (who d. 1888), by Letitia Pratt his wife (who d. 1881), 2nd dau. of Major Harvey Randall Saville Pratt de Montmorency, of Castle Morres, co. Kilkenny (see that family), and grandson of Capt. Elliot Armstrong, of the Dragoon Guards, and Mary Carleton his wife. They assumed (by Royal Licence, 1884) the additional surnames of Lushington and Tulloch. He d. 10 Jan. 1901, leaving issue,

1. Graham de Montmorency, b. Nov. 1886.
2. Kinmount Willie, b. March, 1889.
3. Eric, b. April, 1893; d. July, 1900.
1. Edna de Montmorency, m. 2 Sept. 1908, Walter Marchant, of Matfield House, Kent, and Weston Bank, Salop.

She m. 2ndly, 17 Dec. 1901, James Geoffrey Cave France, Royal Irish Constabulary, youngest son of William Hanmer France, by Frances Emily, his wife, dau. of Thomas Cave-Browne-Cave, of Cliff House, co. Warwick (see Burke's *Peerage*), and grandson of Richard France, of Plealey, Salop. They assumed by Royal Licence, 25 Feb. 1902, the surnames and arms of Lushington-Tulloch, in addition to and after France. He d. 17 April, 1903.

Arms—Quarterly 1st and 4th or, on a fess invected plain cottised gu., three estoiles arg., in chief as many cross crosslets fitchée of the 2nd, and for distinction in the dexter canton a cross crosslet sa. (Tulloch); 2nd and 3rd arg., two lions passant reguardant az., between three bars gu., an orle of fleurs-de-lys of the last (France); on an escotcheon of pretence, quarterly 1st and 4th or, on a fess invected plain cottised gu. three estoiles arg., in chief as many cross crosslets of the 2nd (Tulloch); 2nd and 3rd or, on a fess wavy between three lions' heads erased vert langed gu. as many ermine spots of the field (Lushington). *Crests*—1st, a demi-lion gu., grasping a battle-axe the head to the dexter and charged on the shoulder with three cross crosslets fitchée two and one all or,

and for distinction on the neck with a cross crosslet arg. (Tulloch); 2nd, on a mount vert, a lion sejant regardant az. collared or, therefrom a shield of the last charged with a fleur-de-lys of the 2nd (France).

Seat—Shanboolard, Letterfrack, co. Galway.

TURNLY OF DRUMNASOLE.

Francis John Seymour Turnly, of Drumnasole, co. Antrim, J.P. cos. Antrim, Galway and Mayo, b. 22 Nov. 1862; s. his father 1909; m. 14 March, 1896, Hessie Metcalfe McNeill, dau, of Charles Higginson of Springmount, co. Antrim, and has issue,

1. John Francis, b. 1 Oct. 1898.
2. Archibald Gordon Edward, b. 27 June, 1902.
1. Mary Dorothea Rochfort.

Lineage.—Francis Turnly, of Downpatrick, J.P. for co. Down, whose father was also a J.P. for Downpatrick, b. 1735; m. 1760, Catherine Black, of Bordeaux, and by her (who d. 1795) left at his decease, 10 March, 1801, landed property to his children. He had issue with four daus., three sons, 1. John, d.s.p.; 2. Francis, of whom presently; and 3. Alexander, who left issue. The 2nd son,

Francis Turnly, of Drumnasole, co. Antrim, and Richmond Lodge, co. Down, b. 1765, H.E.I.C.C.S., spent his early life in China; he m. 1804, Dorothea Emilia, dau. of John Rochfort, of Clogrenane, co. Carlow (see that family), and grand-dau. of Robert Burgh, of Birt, and d. 1845, having by her (who d. 1866) had issue,

1. John, d. an infant. 2. Francis, d. unm. 1820.
3. Robert Alexander, of Drumnasole, b. 1805; d. unm, 6 Nov. 1885. 4. Joseph, d. unm.
5. John, of Drumnasole. 6. Charles Horace, d. 1885.
1. Dorothea Anna, d. 1885. 2. Catherine, d. unm. 26 Nov. 1906.

The 5th son,

John Turnly, of Drumnasole, co. Antrim, B.A., J.P., and D.L., b. 17 Sept. 1819; m. 2 July, 1850, Charlotte Emily (who d. 20 Oct. 1909), dau. of the late Right Hon. Edward Litton, Q.C., a Master in Chancery, Ireland, and d. 9 May, 1909, having had issue,

1. Francis John Seymour, now of Drumnasole.
2. John Edward Litton Alexander, b. 1869.
1. Sophia Dorothea, m. Percy A. E. Wood, late an Officer in the Army.
2. Dorothea Vescina, m. William Eames, M.D., R.N., and d. 16 Oct. 1889.
3. Charlotte Augusta Anne. 4. Flora Eugenie.
5. Catherine Beatrice.
6. Nina Rochfort, m. Frank Graham.
7. Gertrude, m. James Young.
8. Hilda, m. 11 Jan. 1894, Frederick Taylor Bagwell.

Arms—Arg., a fritillaria meleagris, stalked and leaved ppr., on a canton gu. a cross pattée or. *Crest*—On a mount vert, an oak-tree ppr., supporting on the sinister side a shield gu. charged with a cross pattée or. *Motto*—Perseverando.

Seat—Drumnasole, Glenarm, co. Antrim.

TUTHILL, FORMERLY OF KILMORE.

Phineas Barrett Villiers - Tuthill, Lieut. - Col. late R.A.M.C., F.S.A., M.D., D.S.M. Univ Dub., F.R.C.S.I.; assumed the name of Villiers, prefixed to his patronymic of Tuthill by Deed Poll dated 15 Dec. 1908, enrolled in H.M. High Court of Justice in Ireland (Chancery Division); m. 16 Dec. 1908, at the Chapel Royal, Dublin, Mary Wilhelmina Constance, widow of Capt.

John North-Bomford, of Ferrans, Kilcock, co. Meath (*see that family*), eldest dau. of the late Sir William Kaye, C.B., K.C., LL.D., Knt., Assistant Under-Secretary for Ireland.

Lineage—WILLIAM TOTHILL, Alderman of the City of Exeter, High Sheriff of Exeter 1549, Mayor 1552, will dated 24 Aug. 1557, *m.* Elizabeth, dau. of Geoffrey Matthew, of Vorganwg, in Pembrokeshire. She *d.* 2 May, 1584, and was bur. at St. Martin's, Exeter. They had issue,
 1. Geoffrey Tothill, eld. son and heir, of Peamore, near Exeter. Recorder of Exeter 1563-74, during which time he represented the City of Exeter in Parliament. He *d.* 15 Sept. and was bur. 20 Sept. 1574, in Exminster Church. Will dated 29 June, 1574; proved 10 Nov. 1574. He *m.* Joan, dau. of Robert Dillon, of Chymwell, in co. Devon, and had issue,
  1. Henry, eldest son and heir of Peamore, co. Devon, *b.* 1561; High Sheriff of Devon in 1623 and 1624; *d.* 9 Dec. 1640, aged 78 years; bur. in Exminster Church 22 Dec. 1640, M.I. They had issue, two daus.,
   (1) Joan, *m.* Robert Northleigh, of Matford, co. Devon.
   (2) Grace, *m.* William Tothill, of Peamore.
   Henry Tothill's will, dated 23 Nov. 1640, was proved 12 Feb. 1640-41, in the P.C.C., by his son-in-law, William Tothill, sole executor. Mary Tothill's will, dated 5 Oct. 1646, proved 30 April, 1647, by Henry Northleigh, in the P.C.C.
  2. Robert Tothill, matriculated Broadgate Hall, Oxford, 8 Nov. 1583, aged 18 years, *d. unm.* and was bur. 16 Aug. 1589 in Exminster Church; will dated 9 Aug. 1589, proved (P.C.C.) 24 Nov. 1590, by Henry Tothill, his brother, sole executor.
  3. Arrys Tothill, *d. unm.*
  1. Joan Tothill *d.* 1567.
  Geoffrey Tothill *m.* 2ndly, Elizabeth, dau. of Bartholomew Fortescue, of Filleigh, co. Devon, widow of Louis Hatche, of North Molton, mar. licence 24 Nov. 1569, Exeter, but had no further issue; she *d.* and was bur. 1587, in Exminster Church.
 2. John, of Mary Major, Exeter; administration granted 19 April, 1583, Exeter; *m.* Alice, dau. and heir of—Parlebien, of Heavitree, near Exeter, and had issue,
  1. WILLIAM, of whom presently.
  2. Haise, *d.s.p.*   3. Thomas, *d.s.p.*
  1. Elizabeth, *d.s.p.*
 3. Richard, J.P., of Castle Gwys, or Wiston, in Pembrokeshire, *d.* St. Michaelmas Day, 1593, at Wiston; *m.* Joan, dau. of Richard Grafton, the celebrated Antiquary, and had issue, four sons and seven daus.,
  1. William, an eminent Lawyer, appointed one of the six Clerks in Chancery, compiled one of the earliest Reports in Chancery, known as *Tothill's Reports*. He purchased Shardeloes, near Amersham, Bucks., where, as Lysons says, he had the honour of entertaining the Queen in one of Her Royal Progresses. He *d.* and was bur. in Amersham Church in 1626, M.I. He *m.* Katherine, sister to Sir John Denham, Knt., Baron of the Exchequer, and had issue, two daus.,
   (1) Joan, *m.* Francis Drake, P.C., of Ashe, co. Devon, 3 March, 1602, at St. Dunstan's-in-the-West, Middlesex. She *d.* 18 April, 1625; bur. at Amersham.
   (2) Katherine.
  2. James, *m.* Ellen, dau. of William Gooch, of Grysvswacht, and had a son,
   Edward, born in or before 1591.
  3. Richard is believed to have sailed with his wife Mary and three children from London, April, 1635, in the ship "Plantar" for America, and settled in Boston, Mass., where she died and was buried in the Granary Burial Ground there. Her tombstone bears the Tothill Coat of Arms of Devonshire.
  4. John, is believed to have sailed with his wife and four children, in the ship "Plantar," from London for America, and settled in Boston, Mass. He came over from Boston to Ireland on business; during his absence his wife, Joanna, managed his affairs in Boston. He *d.* at Carrickfergus, in Ireland, 30 Dec. 1656; will dated 27 Dec. 1656, proved 16 April, 1657, Prerog. Dublin; *m.* Joanna Lawrence, widow, and left issue,
   (1) Simon.   (2) John.
   (1) Sarah, *m.* Richard Martin, of Boston.   (2) Hannah.
  1. Jane, *m.* Roger Bourne, of Wells.
  2. Alice, *m.* Thomas Kowldhurst.
  3. Mary, *m.* Jesse Snides, of Ireland.
  4. Susan, *m.* 1624, James Hawley, of co. Middlesex.
  5. Elizabeth, *m.* William Bradshaw.
  6. Anne.   7. Judith.
 4. Robert.
 1. Joan, *m.* 1st, John Halse, of Kennedon, co. Devon; *m.* 2ndly, Richard Hockley.
 2. Grace, *m.* 1st, James Walker, of Exeter; 2ndly, Thomas Bruerton.
 3. Alice, *m.* William Parsons.
 4. Julyan, *m.* Richard Burnby, of Burnby, co. Devon. She was bur. 29 March, 1579, and he 25 Sept. 1603, both at Bratton, Clovelly.
 5. Amy, *m.* — Sted.
 6. Elizabeth, *m.* Thomas Stukely, of Ireland.
 7. Katherine, *m.* 1st, William Kingsley, of Chorley, co. Lancaster. He *d.* at Rosehall, co. Herts. She *m.* 2ndly, Nicholas Drake, 6th son of Robert Drake, of Wiscombe, a pensioner of JAMES I. His will dated 3 October, 1640; administration granted (P.C.C.) 2 June, 1641 (Evelyn 72). She *d.* 18 June, 1662; bur. in Canterbury Cathedral.

WILLIAM TOTHILL, son and heir, of Kingsbridge and of Exeter, appears in Subsidy Roll 101-420, Nov. 22, Elizabeth, 1580, parish of St. Kerrians, Exeter, as owning land; *d.* 9 June, 1636; bur. 11 June, 1636, at Exminster, M.I. He *m.* Anne, dau. of — Wood of Merton, co. Devon, and had issue,
 1. William, eldest son and heir, admitted to Middle Temple 4 March, 1612; inherited Peamore on the death of his father-in-law, Henry Tothill, who also appointed him sole executor of his will. He *d.* 26 April, 1645; bur. at Exminster. Will dated 27 April, 1643; proved 16 May, 1645, at Exeter by his widow, Elizabeth. He *m.* 1st, his cousin, Grace, dau. and co-heir of Henry Tothill, of Peamore; she *d.* 24 Feb. 1623, aged 18 years; bur. 29 Feb., in Exminster Church, M.I., leaving issue,
  1. Henry, son and heir, bapt. 15 April, 1623, at Exminster Church; matric. 4 June, 1641, Exeter Coll., Oxford, aged 18 years; bur. 29 Oct. 1641, at Exminster, *unm.*
  William Tothill *m.* 2ndly, 19 Dec. 1626, at Exeter, Elizabeth, dau. of Sir George Southcote, of Dartmouth Castle, co. Devon, Knt. She *d.* 12 Dec. 1647; bur. at Exminster, leaving issue.
  2. George, *d.* 30 May, 1629; bur. at Exminster, *unm.*
  3. John, mentioned in his father's will of 27 June, 1643; *d.* 1647, *s.p.*, so Peamore went to the Northleighs.
   1. Elizabeth, *m.* 22 July, 1658, at Yarnscomb, co. Devon, Christopher Wood, of North Tawton.
   2. Anne, *m.* 14 July, 1663, at Yarnscomb, John Hale, son of John Hale, of Borings-Leigh, in the parish of West Alvington, co. Devon.
 2. CHRISTOPHER, of whom presently.
 3. John, was Churchwarden of Alphington Church, bur. 1 June, 1638, at Exminster.
 4. Richard, of St. Davids, Exeter, *b.* 1604; *d.* 11 May, 1676; bur. at All Hallows Church, Goldsmith Street, Exeter; will dated 10 April, 1676, proved July, 1676 at Exeter. He left issue,
  1. Thomas.   2. John.   3. Robert.
  1. Sara.   2. Alice, *m.* — Attwell.
 1. Elizabeth, *m.* Crispin Hopar.
 2. Anne, bur. 30 June, 1639, at Exminster.

The 2nd son,
CHRISTOPHER TOTHILL, was bur. 24 Aug. (St. Bartholomew's Day), 1637, in the New Cemetery of the Friernhay, Exeter, called St. Bartholomew's Cemetery, which was consecrated and opened on that day by Bishop Joseph Hall. He *m.* Alice, dau. of ————. She was bur. 22 Oct. 1644, in Exeter Cathedral; issue, two sons,
 1. GEORGE, of whom presently.
 2. ————, whose widow, Joan, is mentioned in her brother George's will of 20 June, 1654.

The elder son,
GEORGE TUTHILL, of Minehead, Somersetshire, to whom George Searle, by deed of assignment dated 26 May, 1654, assigned the Bathpoole Estates for 5,000 years, which George Tuthill, by will, left to his two sons in equal shares. He *d.* 24 June, 1654, and was bur. in West Monkton Churchyard. Will dated 20 June, 1654; proved (P.C.C.), 15 May, 1655. He *m.* Joan, youngest child of —White, of Vurley, in the parish of Membury, near Chard, Somersetshire. She *d.* 31 Dec. 1698, at Minehead, and was bur. there, being 90 years of age. Administration granted 2 June, 1699, at Wells, Somersetshire; had issue,
 1. CHRISTOPHER, of whom presently.
 2. George, of West Monkton, Somersetshire, *d.* 1707. Administration granted 15 May, 1707, to his widow, Grace, and to his eldest son, Thomas; he left issue,
  1. Thomas.   2. Christopher.   3. John.
  1. Anna, mentioned in her uncle Christopher Tuthill's will of 11 June, 1712.

The elder son,
CHRISTOPHER TUTHILL, *b.* 24 June, 1650, at Minehead. He came to Ireland, embarking in the "Happy Return" at Minehead, and landing on Sunday, 30 Aug. 1685, at Youghal, co. Cork, where he settled. A lease dated 11 Sept. 1691, of the lands called the Blackbog of Youghal, for the term of thirty-one years was assigned and made over to Christopher Tuthill 1 Oct. 1692, which he assigned on 30 Dec. 1697, to his two sons. He also took a lease of Faha, co. Limerick, in 1697, from Mrs. Osborne, which he settled on his sons, John and George equally. Christopher Tuthill took a lease of Kilmore, Ballylinev, and Doorless, all in the co. of Limerick, 15 Jan. 1694, from Nicholas Monkton. He *d.* 11 June, 1712, at Youghal; bur. there with his wife, Mary. Will dated 11 June, 1712; proved 14 July, 1712, Prerog. Dublin. He *m.* 19 May, 1685, at the parish church of Northwood, Isle of Wight, by the Rev. Dr. Smith, Mary, dau. of John Hall, of Swainston, near Newport, Isle of Wight. She *d.* 30 Jan., and was bur. 1 Feb. 1695, at St. Mary's Church, Youghal, aged 40 years. Issue,
 1. John, of Newtown, co. Limerick, *b.* 11 Feb. 1686, at Youghal; bapt. there 22 Feb. 1686, in St. Mary's Church. He *m.* 1st, 27 March, 1707, Deborah, dau. of John Patfield, of Hillsborough, co. Clare, by whom he had issue two sons,
  1. Christopher, son and heir, *d.v.p.* 15 Sept. 1738.
  2. John, *d.v.p.* August, 1750.
  He *m.* 2ndly, Jane Sabatier, of Rathfeston, King's Co., and had issue.
 2. GEORGE, of whom presently.
 Christopher Tuthill *m.* 2ndly, Hannah Rule, widow, dau. and heir of Capt. Thomas Lucas, of Limerick (brother of Abraham Lucas, of Bury St. Edmunds) and Anne, his wife; mar. sett. 14 Sept. 1698. Hannah's will dated Nov. 1737, was proved August, 1745, Prerog. Dublin. She left issue,
  Anna, will dated 18 Dec. 1780; proved 21 July, 1791, Prerog. Dublin; *m.* John Scott, of the City of Limerick, and of Emmel, King's Co., and had issue.

The younger son,
GEORGE TUTHILL, of Kilmore and Faha, *b.* 25 May, 1693, at Youghal, bapt. there 27 May, 1693. Under his father's will he inherited the lease of Kilmore, Ballylinev and Doorless, which places he purchased on 22 Nov. 1737, from Edward Monkton. He also

purchased John's share of Faha. He d. 13 March, 1771, at Faha; bur. in the vestry of Kilkeedy Church, co. Limerick. Will dated 21 May, 1768 ; lodged in the Prerog. Court, Dublin, with memorial, 12 Nov. 1771. He m. 1st, 30 May, 1727, Jane, dau. and co-heir of Capt. John Armstrong, of Lisnamuck, co. Limerick (she d. at Newtown, co. Limerick, 21 Jan. 1732 ; bur. in Kilkeedy Church). Issue,

1. Palmes, d. unm.
1. Elizabeth, d. unm.   2. Mary, d. unm.

George Tuthill m. 2ndly, 9 Nov. 1740, Dorothea, dau. of John Villiers, of Ballinabolie, co. Kilkenny. She d. 3 June, 1784 ; bur. in the Vestry of Kilkeedy Church, leaving issue,

1. JOHN, of whom presently.
2. Christopher, of Faha, b. 10 June, 1750 ; d. 11 June, 1817 ; will dated 26 Oct. 1816, proved 18 Nov. 1817, Prerog. Dublin. He m. 1st, 22 Feb. 1775, Barbara, dau. and co-heir of Anthony Hickman, of Ballyket, otherwise Elm Green, co. Clare (she d.s.p. and was bur. at Kilkeedy ; will dated 26 Nov. 1783, proved 6 Dec. 1808). He m. 2ndly, Dec. 1784, at Limerick, Mary Anne, dau. of Hugh, 2nd Lord Massy (she d. at Faha ; bur. in Kilkeedy Church), leaving issue,
  1. George, only son, of Faha, m. 31 Dec. 1812, at Cork, his cousin, Catherine, dau. of Maj. William Greene, H.E.I.C., of Lota, co. Cork, M.P. for Dungannon, and Hon. Jane Massy, 3rd dau. of Hugh, 2nd Baron Massy. She d.s.p. 13 Aug. 1845, at Faha ; administration granted 1846.
  2. Catherine, m. 5 Sept. 1815, at Kilkeedy Church, Richard Taylor, of Holly Park, co. Limerick. She d. 1873 ; bur. at Askeaton Churchyard, and left issue.
  3. Frances, m. Robert Harrison, of Garruragh, co. Clare.
  4. Anna, d. 22 Aug. 1838, at Annaghbeg, aged 91 years ; m. Oct. 1776, at Limerick, Joshua Minnitt, of Anaghbeg, co. Tipperary (see that family).

The elder son,

JOHN TUTHILL, of Kilmo e, Ballyliney and Doorlass, b. 1 Jan. 1744, at Faha, co. Limerick. In March, 1794, he assumed the name of VILLIERS in lieu of his patronymic of TUTHILL, in accordance with the will of his uncle, Edward Villiers, of Kilpeacon. He d. 20 July, 1814, at his house, 50, Stephen's Green, Dublin, and was bur. 24 July, 1814, at Rathcoole Cemetery, co. Dublin, M.I. ; will dated 29 June, 1811 (signed J. Villiers), proved 10 Aug. 1814. He m. 29 Dec. 1769, Elizabeth, dau. of Jeremiah Jackson, of Fanningstown. She d. 16 May, 1826, aged 77, at 50, Stephen's Green, and was bur. 20 May, 1826, at Rathcoole Cemetery ; will dated 31 Dec. 1823 (signed Elizabeth Villiers), proved 13 June, 1829. Issue,

1. GEORGE, of whom presently.
2. Jeremiah, b. 15 April, 1772, at Limerick, B.A. Dublin, 1792, of Ardenadague, co. Limerick ; d. unm. April, 1854, at Limerick.
3. John, of St. Thomas Island, co. Clare, and of Kilmore House, co. Limerick, b. 26 Sept. 1774, at Limerick, contested Limerick as an Independent in 1816 ; d. 24 Nov. 1835 ; bur. at Ballingarry, co. Limerick ; administration 16 Jan. 1841 ; m. May, 1798, Margaret, dau. of Robert Cripps, of Edwardstown, co. Limerick (who d. July, 1810 ; bur. 8 July, 1810, at Cahernary Church, aged 28 years), and had issue,
  1. John, of St. Thomas Island, b. 1804 ; d. 10 Sept. 1850, admon. 12 Aug. 1852 ; m. Emily Rodgers, s.p.
  2. George, d. 9 March, 1848, s.p.
  3. Robert, bapt. 6 July, 1806 ; d. 24 Aug. 1828, unm.
  1. Margaret, m. 5 March, 1839, the Rev. Joseph Gabbett, M.A., of Ardvullen and Shelbourne House, Limerick, had had an only child, Margaret, m. Thomas Dickin, of Loppington (see DICKIN of Loppington).
  2. Elizabeth Dorothea, m. Major William Jones, 61st Regt., afterwards Gen. Sir William Jones, G.C.B., d. without issue.
4. Christopher Devonsher (Rev.), of Upper Ballinastona, co. Limerick, and of Webbville, Blackrock, near Cork, b. 26 Jan. 1781, at Limerick ; matric. 11 Dec. 1798, St. Edmund's Hall, B.A. Oxford, 1802 ; d. 5 Feb. 1846 ; M.I. in St. Michael's, Blackrock ; will dated 4 Dec. 1843, proved 12 March, 1846 ; m. 22 May, 1804, Arabella, dau. of Benjamin Frend, of Boskel, co. Limerick (see FREND of Kootiagh), and had issue,
  1. John Benjamin, d. unm.   2. Charles, d. unm.
  3. Capt. William, of Moyglare, co. Kildare, late K.D.G., b. 11 May, 1815 ; d. 7 May, 1885 ; m. 17 Jan. 1852 ; Alicia (who d. 24 April, 1887), dau. of John Fitzgerald Gabbett, of Strand House, Limerick, and had issue,
    (1) Christopher Devonsher Villiers, of Moyglare, co. Kildare, Capt. 14th Hussars, b. 3 Jan. 1853 ; d. 26 Sept. 1900 ; m. 23 March, 1887, Ada Kathleen, widow of Col. John Knox, 14th Hussars, and eldest dau. of Edward Tipping, of Bellurgan Park, co. Louth.
    (2) John Fitzgerald, of Esker, co. Dublin, and of Moyglare, Capt. Devon. Militia, b. 13 June, 1856 ; m. 1 Jan. 1880, Lily, dau. of William Foster, of Shewbridge Hall, Nantwych, and has issue.
    (3) William, of Auckland, N.Z., b. 1857 ; m. 27 Sept. 1888, Mary Hannah, dau. of Thomas G. Anderson, of Jesmond, Kati Kati, N.Z., and has issue.
    (4) Daniel Fitzgerald, b. 17 Oct. 1862 ; d. unm. 27 April, 1884.
    (5) Charles Fitzgerald, of Moyglare, Le Puke, Auckland, N.Z., b. 20 May, 1864 ; m. 12 Nov. 1895, Mary Wilhelmina, dau. of William Norris Lee, and has issue.
    (6) Alfred, of Parkstone, co. Dorset, M.D., M.Ch. Dublin, b. 10 March, 1866 ; m. 24 Oct. 1895, Catherine Grace, dau. of Rev. David Watkin-Davies, of Hendredochydd, Wales.
    (1) Anastasia.
    (2) Arabella Mary, m. 11 June, 1883, Capt. Jacob Sherrard, Kildare Militia, and has issue.
    (3) Catherine Jane.   (4) Alicia Christina.   (5) Maud.
  1. Jane, d. unm.

2. Arabella, m. D. P. LeGrice, of Treifes.   3. Elizabeth.
5. Thomas Edward Villiers, of Rathgar Mansion, Dublin, and of Lower Ballinastona, b. 9 July, 1783, at Limerick, B.A. Cantab 1803 ; d. 2 June, 1859, at Rathgar Mansion ; bur. 6 June, in Mount Jerome Cemetery ; will dated 27 April, 1859, proved 2 July, 1859 ; m. April, 1805, at Askeaton Church, co. Limerick, Anne, dau. of John Stack, of Ballyconry, co. Kerry. She d. 29 July, 1854, at Rathgar Mansion ; bur. 1 Aug. in Mount Jerome Cemetery. Issue,
  1. Jackson Villiers, Capt. Queen's Bays (2nd D.G.), m. 1840, Jane Eyre, dau. of Dr. Porter, Inspector-General of Hospitals, of 9, Upper Seymour Street, and had issue.
  2. Elizabeth, m. Rev. John Studdert, Precentor of Killaloe.
  3. Bridget, m. Rev. Henry Hickman Harte, F.T.C.D.
  4. Isabella Anne, m. Thomas Neville, J.P., D.L. for co. Kilkenny (see NEVILLE of Ahanure and Rockfield).
1. Catherine, m. Hon. Edward Massy, of Ballynort, co. Limerick (see MASSY, B.).
2. Dorothy, d. unm. ; bur. at Hope Chapel, Clifton, Somersetshire.

The eldest son,

GEORGE TUTHILL, of Kilmore, Ballyliney, Doorless and Ballyteigue, co. Limerick, and of 14, Fitzwilliam Square, Dublin, b. 14 Feb. 1771, at Kilmore, B.A. (Dublin) 1791, M.A. 1832 ; d. 11 Aug. 1842, at his house, 14, Fitzwilliam Square ; bur. 15 Aug. in his vault at Mount Jerome Cemetery ; will dated 19 Aug. 1841, proved 10 Sept. 1842 ; m. 23 Feb. 1792, at Killenaule Church, Catherine, dau. of Henry Langley, of Lisnamrock Castle, co. Tipperary (see LANGLEY of Coalbrook) ; mar. setts. 18 May, 1793. She d. 25 March 1854, at 2, Salem Place, Dublin ; bur. in the family vault, Mount Jerome Cemetery ; will dated 13 Oct. 1851, proved 13 April, 1854. Issue,
  1. JOHN, of whom presently.
  2. George, b. 29 Oct. 1795 ; Ensign 10th Regt. of Foot, 20 April, 1815 ; d. unm. 15 June, 1826, at Clifton, Somersetshire ; bur. in Hope Chapel.
  3. Henry, b. 12 Nov. 1800, at Tullamaine Castle, co. Tipperary ; d. 1 Oct. 1827, at Baltimore, U.S.A. ; administration 15 Nov. 1887 ; m. Elizabeth Henderson, of Baltimore, U.S.A.
  4. Christopher Jeremiah, M.D., of Lower Ballyteigue, co. Limerick, b. 31 Aug. 1812, at 14, Fitzwilliam Square, Dublin ; d. 23 July, 1860, at Waterloo Road, Dublin ; bur. in the family vault, Mount Jerome Cemetery ; will dated 10 Sept. 1841, proved 15 Sept. 1860 ; m. 28 July, 1841, at Ballingarry Church, co. Tipperary, Margaret Isabella, dau. of Ambrose Going, of Ballyphillip, co. Tipperary (see that family). She d. 12 June, 1858, at Rock Vale, near Newport, co. Tipperary ; bur. in the family vault, Mount Jerome. Issue,
    1. George, of Lower Ballyteigue, b. 26 June, 1843 ; Ensign 96th Regt., 19 Aug. 1862 ; d. unm. 22 Oct. 1867, at Poonah ; administration, 25 March, 1868.
    2. Ambrose Going, b. 10 Oct. 1846 ; d. 25 Sept. 1889 ; bur. in Mount Jerome Cemetery ; will proved 25 Oct. 1889 ; m. 21 March, 1877, at St. Peter's, Dublin, Grace, dau. of Rev. Benjamin Wilson Eames, Rector of Swinford, co. Mayo, s.p.
    5. Charles Langley of Upper Ballyteigue, co. Limerick, b. 17 Aug. 1817, at 14, Fitzwilliam Square, B.A. (Dublin) 1839 ; d. 1 March, 1873, at Ballyteigue ; bur. in Mount Jerome ; will dated 14 Oct. 1848, proved 29 April, 1873 ; m. 28 Jan. 1847, Helena Mary, dau. of Daniel Litton, of Waterloo Road, Dublin. She d. 3 April, 1865, at Dublin ; bur. in Mount Jerome. Issue : George, and nine daus.
  1. Elizabeth Dorothea, m. Harry Langley, of Coalbrook and Lisnamrock Castle (see that family).
  2. Hannah, m. Charles Atkinson, of Rehins, co. Mayo.
  3. Frances, d. unm.   4. Anna, d. unm.
  5. Mary, d. unm.   6. Catherine, d. unm.   7. Margaret, d. unm.

The eldest son,

JOHN TUTHILL, of Kilmore, Ballyliney and Doorless, and of Rapla, co. Tipperary, b. 3 June, 1793, at Lisnamrock Castle ; admitted 19 May, 1815, Middle Temple ; d. 13 Feb. 1876, at Birr ; bur. at Clonoghil Cemetery ; [will dated 12 Feb. 1876, proved 25 March, 1876 ; m. 1st, 12 May, 1815, at St. Peter's, Dublin, Anna Strettell dau. of Strettel Jackson, of Peterborough, near Cork, and sister of Mr. Justice Jackson, sometime M.P. for Bandon. She d. 20 March, 1844, at Rapla. Issue,
  1. George, b. 22 Jan. 1822, at Annaghbeg, co. Tipperary ; d. 13 June, 1857 ; bur. in the family vault in Mount Jerome ; administration granted to John Tuthill, his father.
  2. Strettel Jackson, b. 6 Sept. 1826, at Riverview, co. Tipperary ; went to Australia in 1851, where he d. in 1873 v.p.
  3. Joseph Devonsher, b. 4 Sept. 1829, at Riverview ; went to America in 1852.
  4. John, b. 30 Oct. 1830, at Riverview ; went to America in 1852 d. 23 June, 1874, at Lockport, U.S.A., v.p.
  5. Charles Langley, b. 6 Dec. 1832 ; went to America in 1852 ; d. 1873 v.p.

John Tuthill m. 2ndly, 15 Dec. 1846, at St. Peter's Dublin, Margaret, eldest dau. of Robert Lloyd, M.D. (see LLOYD of Lossett) (b. 10 March, 1812, at Clare Street, Dublin · d. 21 Oct. 1895, at 27, Northbrook Road, Dublin, and bur. at Clonoghil Cemetery ; will proved 24 Jan. 1896). Issue,

6. PHINEAS BARRETT.
  1. Catherine Hannah, m. 11 Nov. 1875, John Louis Emil Dreyer, M.A., Ph.D., of the Observatory, Armagh, and has issue.
  2. Charlotte Elizabeth, m. 12 Aug. 1875, Lieut.-Col. Richard William Woods, son of Maj. Richard Woods, 3rd Regt., "The Buffs," and has issue.
  3. Mary Maria, d. unm. 11 Jan. 1876.
  4. Margaret Dartnell, m. 24 Jan. 1885, Maj.-Gen. Henry Wellington Palmer, C.B., and has issue.
  5. Susan Penelope, m. 16 Sept. 1884, Rev. Henry Brownrigg Hewson, Rector of Clonaslee, and has issue.

Arms—Az. on a bend. arg., cotised or, a lion passant sa. Quartering: VILLIERS, COOKE, PEYTON, GERNON, COLVIL, SUTTON, LANGLEY OF KNOWLTON, ATBRIG, ATLESS, LANGLEY OF SUTTON FOLFIELD, FISHER, LUCY, CHAMBERLAINE, FRANCIS, WOODCOCKE, KINGE, RAWSON, CRAFORD, COLMAN, GAYNSFORD, DE LA POYLE, WIRLEY, STOPFORD, ALSEN and LLOYD. **Crest**—On a mount vert. a turtle dove ppr. holding in its beak an olive branch vert, fructed or. **Motto**—Pacis ac legis jure.

Seat—The Slopes, Kingstown. **Clubs**—Junior United Service, Royal St. George Yacht.

TWEEDY OF CLOONAMAHON.

HENRY COLPOYS TWEEDY, of Cloonamahon, co. Sligo, M.D. Dublin, F.R.C.S.I., *b.* 3 April, 1847; *m.* 2ndly, 26 Aug. 1882, Alice Maude (who *d.* 1896), only dau. of Capt. Thomas James Meredith, 90th Light Infantry, of Cloonamahon, and sister and heir of Herbert Willoughby Meredith, Lieut. R.N., of Cloonamahon. She *d.* 30 April, 1896, and was *s.* by her husband. He has issue,

1. MAURICE WILLOUGHBY, *b.* 24 May, 1887.
2. Owen Meredith, *b.* 22 Oct. 1888.
1. Elizabeth Margaret, *m.* 23 April, 1908, Ernest Percival Beard, 2nd son of Steyning Beard, of Rottingdean, Sussex.
2. Sydney Alice Rose.
3. Mary Eleanor.

Lineage.—THOMAS TWEEDY, Alderman of the City of Dublin, High Sheriff 1788-9, *m.* July, 1779, Jane, dau. and co-heir of Robert Johnston, of Stoneville, co. Fermanagh. He left an only son,

Rev. HENRY TWEEDY, M.A. Dublin, sometime Lieut. 7th Dragoon Guards, *m.* Dec. 1808, Mary, dau. and co-heir of Thomas Delahunty, of Ballyostler, co. Clare, by Susanna his wife, only dau. and heir of James Colpoys, of Crusheen, co. Clare, and had an only surviving son,

HENRY COLPOYS, of Crusheen, co. Clare, and Rutland Square, Dublin, *b.* 1810; *d.* 21 Sept. 1906; *m.* 1843, Elizabeth, dau. of Lieut.-Geo. Owen, late Quartermaster-General in Ireland, and had issue an only son,

HENRY COLPOYS, now of Cloonamahon.

Arms—Quarterly 1st and 4th arg., a saltire engrailed gu. on a chief az. three fleames or (TWEEDY); 2nd arg. on a saltire sa. five trefoils slipped or, on a chief gu. three cushions of the thidr (JOHNSTON); 3rd arg. a maunch ermines (COLPOYS); over all on an escutcheon of pretence az. a lion rampant per pale arg. and or (MEREDITH). **Crest**—A pewit volant arg. **Motto**—Fais ce que doit advienne que pourra.

Seat—Cloonamahon, Collooney, co. Sligo. **Clubs**—University, Dublin, Royal Societies, S.W., and County, Sligo.

TWIGG, FORMERLY OF THORNDALE.

COL. ROBERT HENRY TWIGG, *b.* 4 April, 1860, Brevet Colonel Indian Army.

Lineage. — This family settled in co. Cavan in the early part of the 17th century, as appears from the Muster Rolls of Ulster. Two brothers left the following descendants

1. THOMAS, of whom presently.
2. Charles, *b.* in co. Cavan, in garrison at Carrickfergus at the beginning of the rebellion 1641, was promoted to be Captain, and given the command of a Foot Company in 1661 in consideration of his services and those of his father-in-law. He *m.* 1st, Miriam, widow of Henry Worrall, and dau. of William Ireland, of Liverpool, and had two sons. He *m.* 2ndly (*lic.* 9 Oct. 1677) Letitia widow of Henry Martin, and previously of Robert Hall, by whom he had no issue. He *d.* Dec. 1680. The sons were,

1. William (Rev.), M.A. (Dub.), *b.* at Carrickfergus 1657, *d.* 1725, Archdeacon of Limerick, *m.* Diana, dau. and co-heir of Sir Drury Wray, Bart., of Rathcannon, co. Limerick, and by her, who died 1780, left two daus. and co-heirs,
 (1) Jane, *m.* 1716, Rev. Stacpole Pery, M.A., and had issue (see BURKE's *Peerage*, LIMERICK, E. OF).
 (2) Anna, *m.* 1725, Thomas Maunsell, of Thorp Malsor (see *that family*).
2. John (Rev.), M.A. (Dub.), *b.* 1659, *d.* 1731, Rector of Castle Knock and Canon of St. Patrick's, Dublin, left three sons,
 (1) John, *m.* 1731, Margaret Price.
 (2) Thomas, B.A. (Dub.) 1718, *m.* — Higgins.
 (3) Paul (Rev.), M.A. (Dub.), 1721, Minor Canon of St. Patrick's 1731, Rector of Carlingford 1740, *m.* 1733, Hannah, dau. of Roger Tuthill, and had issue,
  a. Thomas Tuthill, father of Richard Elliott Twigg, Commander R.N.
  b. Hugh (Rev.), B.A. (Dub.) 1757, *d. unm.* 1790.
  c. Michael.   *d.* Paul, M.D., *d. unm.*
  e. Roger of Carlingford, *m.* and left issue.

THOMAS TWIGG, of St. Kevins, Dublin, *d.* 1672, leaving by Maria his wife, two sons,
1. THOMAS, of whom presently.
2. Robert, Sheriff of Dublin 1693-94, Alderman of Limerick and Mayor 1709, *d.* 1727; *m.* (*lic.* 13 Sept.) 1692, Maria Taylor, and had issue,
 1. Thomas, bapt. at St. John's, Dublin, 15 Nov. 1694, *d.* young.
 1. Margaret, bapt. at St. John's 1 Oct. 1693; *m.* 1720, George Wilkinson, of Ballyvalley, co. Clare.
 2. Elizabeth, *m.* Randall Holland, Alderman of Limerick.
1. Maria, *m.* Isaac Ambrose.

CAPT. THOMAS TWIGG, of Donnybrook Castle, and Puckstown, co. Dublin, on which the house of Thorndale was built, admitted to the King's Inns as an Attorney 18 July, 1674, Town Clerk of Dublin 30 June, 1693, resigned 18 April, 1702, and *d.* same year. He *m.* (*lic.* 27 July, 1678) Alice, dau. of Richard Neville, of Furnace, co. Kildare (see NEVILLE *of Ahanure*), and had five sons and a dau.,

1. Francis, *b.* 1681, matric. Trin. Coll. Dub. 26 March, 1699, *d. unm.* 1702.
2. Thomas, *b.* 1682, matric. Trin. Coll. Dub. 26 March, 1699, *d.* 1728; *m.* (*lic.* 30 March) 1714, Anne, dau. of Gamaliel Purefoy, of Clonbullock, King's Co., and by her, who *d.* Nov. 1718 (*Funeral Entry*), had issue, with two sons, Thomas and Purefoy, who *d.* young, an only dau. and heir,
 Elizabeth, *m.* 18 Feb. 1737, Robert Downes, M.P. for Kildare, who had a son, William Downes, Lord Chief Justice of Ireland, created Baron Downes 1822 (see BURKE's *Extinct Peerage*).
3. JAMES, of whom presently.
4. John, Sheriff of Dublin 1735-36, Alderman 2 Nov. 1736, *d. unm.* 1739.
5. Richard, *d. unm.* after 1724.
1. Mary, *m.* Raleigh Colpoys, Sheriff and Mayor of Limerick.
2. Margaret, *m.* Richard Maunsell, M.P. for Limerick 1740-61 (see MAUNSELL *of Limerick*).

JAMES TWIGG, of Bettystown, co. Meath, *b.* 1685, *d.* 1742; *m.* (*lic.* 15 July) 1730, Barbara, dau. of Stewart Blacker, of Carrickblacker, co. Armagh (see *that family*), and by her, who *d.* 1784, had four sons and four daus.,
1. Thomas, of Thorndale, *b.* 1731, *d.* 1800; *m.* (*lic.* 18 June) 1763, Mary Betty, dau. of Rev. Thomas Carr, D.D., *s.p.*
2. Stewart, *b.* 1733, *d. unm.* 1755.
3. James, *b.* 1740, *d. unm.* 1833.
4. JOHN, of whom next.
1. Elizabeth, *b.* 1731, *d. unm.*
2. Alice, *b.* 1735; *m.* 1773, Thomas Winder, Secretary to the Board of Revenue.
3. Barbara, *d.* young.   4. Mary, *d.* young.

JOHN TWIGG, of Roughan, co. Tyrone, *b.* 1741, *d.* 1818; *m.* 1785, Anne, dau. of William Despard, of Donore, Queen's Co., and by her, who *d.* 1816, had seven sons and four daus.,
1. THOMAS, his heir.
2. George, *d.* an infant.
3. James, *b.* 1793, *d.* 1875; *m.* Gertrude Despard, and had with four daus., two sons,
 1. Robert H., *b.* 1839; *m.* Mary Gorringe, and had a dau., Gertrude, *m.* Rev. George Stuart.
 2. James Burton, *b.* 1847.
4. John, *b.* 1794, *d.* 1866, Capt. 3rd Buffs; *m.* 1st, 1831, Deborah Sandes, and 2ndly, 1836, Elizabeth, dau. of Samuel Knox, and had two sons,
 1. John Thomas, Major-General R.E., *d.* 1909.
 2. Samuel Knox, *m.* Frances Vance, and had,
  (1) Mabel, *m.* Charles Johnson, of Vancouver.
  (2) Sidney, *m.* 1910, John A. Kenworthy.
5. Richard Stewart, *b.* 1796, *d.* 1888, M.D.; *m.* Elizabeth, dau. of Rev. John Benjamin Story, of Corick, co. Tyrone (see *that family*), and had,
 1. John Benjamin, *b.* 1830, B.A. (Dub.); *m.* 1866, Wilhelmina, dau. of James Hamilton, of Fintra, co. Donegal, and had,
  (1) Richard Hamilton, *b.* 1867, Solicitor; *m.* 1899, Leila, dau. of William Brown.
  (2) Lewis.
  (1) Caroline, *m.* 11 Sept. 1895, Col. Robert Hugh Wallace, C.B., of Myra Castle, co. Down (*whom see*).
 2. James, *d. unm.*   3. Richard, *d. unm.*
 4. William, M.D., *d.* 11 Sept. 1911; *m.* Jane, dau. of Thomas Smith, R.I.C., and had seven sons and three daus.,
  (1) Arthur, *d.s.p.*
  (2) Herbert, C.E., British Colombia.
  (3) William, M.D., Cape Colony.

Twiss. THE LANDED GENTRY. 710

(4) James Stewart, R.A.M.C., killed in S. Africa 1901.
(5) Harold Despard, solicitor, Vancouver.
(6) Charles Blacker, C.E., British Colombia.
(7) Theaker Austin.
6. William, *b.* 1797, *d.* 1820, Lieut. Bombay Native Infantry.
7. Samuel (Rev.), M.A. (Dub.), *b.* 1801, *d.* 1869, Rector of Tamlaght, co. Londonderry; *m.* 1838, Annie Hill, dau. of Capt. Henderson Boyle, and had issue,
   1. John Hill, B.A. (Dub.), I.C.S., *b.* 1841; *m.* 1896, Alice, dau. of Edward Hull, F.R.S.
   2. Henderson J., of Petane, Napier, N.Z., J.P., *b.* 1843; *m.* 1871, Elizabeth Torr, of Napier, N.Z., and has, with two daus.,
      (1) Samuel.   (2) Frank.
      (3) Ernest.   (4) Garnet.   (5) Despard.
   3. Thomas Samuel, *b.* 1848 (*Rare-an-Ilen, Dalkey, co. Dublin*).
   4. William Robert, *b.* 1851; *m.* 1884, Matilda, dau. of Rev. John Lee, and has, with three daus.,
      (1) Robert.   (2) Francis.
      (3) Giles.   (4) Thomas.
   5. George Despard, *b.* 1853, Surgeon, R.N., Deputy Inspector-Gen.; *m.* 1882, Mary Anne Edith, dau. of Lieut.-Col. W. J. Morris, Bombay Army, and has, with one dau.,
      (1) Francis Walter Despard, *b.* 1883, Lieut. R.N.
      (2) Ala i George Despard, *b.* 1884, Lieut. R.N.
   1. Anne.
   2. Lucy, *m.* 1872, Surgeon-Major Henry Seymour Smith, Bengal Army, and has issue, W. Brownlow Smith, M.D., and Muriel.
1. Gertrude, *b.* 1788, *d.* 1864; *m.* Samuel Wright, of Desertlyn, co. Londonderry.
2. Barbara, *d. unm.* 1870.
3. Mary Anne, *d. unm.* 1879.
4. Jane, *d.* an infant 1790.
REV. THOMAS TWIGG, M.A. (Dub.), *b.* 1786; *d.* 1872, Rector of Pomeroy, co. Tyrone; *m.* Sarah, dau. of Frederick McCausland, of Bessbrook, co. Londonderry (*see McCAUSLAND of Drenagh*), and had three sons and two daus.,
   1. THOMAS, his heir.
   2. John James, M.A. (Dub.), K.C., Bencher of the King's Inns 1889-1906, *b.* 1825; *m.* 1868, Eliza, dau. of James Corry Lowry, Q.C., of Rockdale, co. Tyrone (*see that family*).
   3. Conolly, B.A. (Dub.), I.C.S., *d.s.p.*
   1. Elizabeth, *m.* Henry E. Stuart.
   2. Anne, *m.* Finch White, Q.C.
REV. THOMAS TWIGG, M.A. (Dub.), *b.* 1822, *d.* 18 Sept. 1903, Canon of Swords in St. Patrick's National Cathedral; *m.* 1852, Margaret, dau. of George Bolton, and had issue, with four daus.,
   1. ROBERT HENRY, present representative.
   2. Conolly, *b.* 1861.
   3. Richard C., M.B., B.A., B.A.O. (Dub.), *b.* 1863.
   4. Marcus Fitzgerald, B.A. (Dub.), Solicitor, *b.* 1867.
   5. Arthur, *b.* 1867.
   6. Edward Francis, *b.* 1868, Major, Indian Army.

Arms—Gules, a cross vair in the dexter canton a cinque'oil or.
Crest—A cubit arm erect, the hand grasping a laurel wreath, all ppr. **Motto**—Honor sit virtuti.

TWISS OF BIRDHILL.

ROBERT GEORGE EDWARD TWISS, of Birdhill House, co. Tipperary, High Sheriff 1896, late 6th Dragoon Guards, served with his regiment in the three Afghan campaigns 1878, 1879, 1880, and was present at the battle of Dacka, and took part in the expeditions against Wazier Kail (medal and clasp), *b.* 7 Sept. 1856; *m.* 16 Nov. 1881, Alice Elizabeth, eldest dau. of Major Edward Henry Drake, late Northumberland Fusiliers, of Falfield, co. Gloucester.

Lineage.—The first of this family who settled in Ireland at the close of the reign of CHARLES I. was
RICHARD TWISS, of Killintierna, J.P. co. Kerry, and, as agent to Herbert, Earl of Powis, lived in the castle of Castle Island. He *m.* Frances Broderick, a cousin of the Earl of Powis, and had issue,
1. FRANCIS, his heir.
2. Robert, *m.* Dorah Parsons (of the Cragbeg family), co. Limerick.
3. George, *m.* Arabella Cooper, co. Limerick.
4. Richard.
1. Jane, *m.* Francis Radley, of Knockerown, co. Cork.
The eldest son,
FRANCIS TWISS, of Killintierna, *m.* Jane Parsons, of co. Limerick, and had (with two daus.) a son,
MARTIN TWISS, of Killintierna, *m.* Catherine, dau. of John Williams, of Gortaclea, in the same co., and had issue,
1. Francis, *d. unm.*; will dated 29 April, 1734.
2. ROBERT, his heir.
3. William, *m.* Avice, dau. of John Godfrey, of Ballingamboon, co. Kerry, and had issue,
   1. William, *m.* his first cousin, Henrietta Godfrey.

1. Catherine, *m.* David Fitzgerald, of Adrival, co. Kerry, and had issue.   2. Dorcas, *m.* Caleb Palmer.
3. Jane, *d. unm.* 1841.
4. Avice, *m.* Richard Purcell, of Gurtnaconroe, co. Cork.
4. George, *m.* Eliza, dau. of Maurice Day, of The Manor, co. Kerry, and had issue, two sons, Francis and Edward, and two daus., *m.* Mason and Shewell.
5. Richard, *m.* 2 July, 1756, Eliza, 2nd dau. and co-heir of Thomas Radley, of Knockerown, co. Cork, and had one son, Martin, *m.* Eliza, dau. of — Nugent.
6. John, *m.* Eliza, dau. of Arthur Bastable, of Mohaliffe Castle, co. Kerry, and had a son,
William.
1. Ellen, *m.* John Marshall, of Riverville, co. Kerry.
2. Mary, *m.* — Williams.
Mr. Twiss (whose will, dated 4 Nov. 1742, was proved in Tralee 1745) was *s.* by his 2nd, but eldest surviving son,
ROBERT TWISS, of Killintierna, *m.* Dorcas, dau. of John Godfrey, of Ballingamboon, co. Kerry, by Dorcas his wife, dau. of Henry Blennerhasset (aunt of Sir Rowland Blennerhasset, 1st bart., of Blennerville), and *d.* 29 Jan. 1771, leaving (with two daus. Catherine, *m.* William Hilliard, and Avice, *m.* Thomas Marshall, of Riverville, co. Kerry) one son,
GEORGE TWISS, of Cordell House and Anna, co. Kerry, *m.* 11 Jan. 1773, Honoria, dau. of William Meredith, of Dicksgrove, co. Kerry, by Marian, dau. of Maurice Fitzgerald, Knt. of Kerry, and niece of Maurice Crosbie, 1st Lord Brandon, and had issue,
1. ROBERT, his heir.
2. William Meredith, Capt. Kerry Militia, *m.* his cousin, Letitia, eldest dau. of Col. James Crosbie, of Ballyheige Castle, co. Kerry, M.P., and Governor of that co. Mrs. Twiss *d.* March, 1838, and he *d.s.p.* 28 Aug. 1844.
3. Francis, *b.* 1784; *m.* Margaret Ruth, dau. of Edward Collis, of Lismore, co. Kerry, and had issue, a son, Francis, dec., and four daus.
   1. Marion, *m.* William Hunt Forster.
   2. Dorcas, *m.* Arthur Blennerhassett, of Ballyseedy, co. Kerry, and had issue.
   3. Margaret, *m.* James Hilliard, of Ballyhogan, co. Kerry.
   4. Lucinda, *m.* Basil Bromfield, of Ievy, Queen's Co.
Mr. Twiss *d.* 2 April, 1802, during his shrievalty of co. Kerry, and was *s.* by his eldest son,
ROBERT TWISS, of Cordell House and Anna, co. Kerry, and latterly of Parteen, co. Tipperary, *b.* 26 Sept. 1777, J.P. co. Kerry, and High Sheriff of that co. 1802-3; *m.* 5 June, 1804, Elizabeth, dau. of Robert Atkins, of Firville, co. Cork, by whom (who *d.* 1865) he had issue,
1. GEORGE, his heir.
2. Robert Atkins, of Parteen, co. Tipperary, M.D., *m.* Jan. 1841, Frances, dau. of Richard Phillips, of Mount Rivers, co. Tipperary, and great-niece of Henry Deane Grady, and *d.* Feb. 1848, leaving issue, one dau.,
   Frances Margaret, who *d. unm.* July, 1864.
3. HASTINGS, successor to his brother.
4. Arthur Ormsby (Rev.). *d. unm.* June, 1848.
1. Maria Hastings, *d.* 23 June, 1869.
2. Diana Sackville, *d.* 1815.
3. Dorcas Georgiana, *d. unm.* 1899.
4. Letitia Crosbie, *d. unm.* 1896.
5. Margaret Ormsby, *m.* 1858, Richard R. Fulton, eldest son of the late Col. James Forrest Fulton, K.H., by Frances Penelope his wife, dau. of Richard Bowyer Atkins, of Braywick Grove, Berks (*see FULTON of Braidinjle*). She *d.* his widow 17 Feb. 1909.
Mr. Twiss *d.* May, 1851, and was *s.* by his eldest son,
GEORGE TWISS, of Birdhill, co. Tipperary, *b.* 1807; who became possessed of Birdhill by deed of gift from his aunt, Margaret, 4th dau. of the late Robert Atkins, of Firville, co. Cork, and widow of Arthur Ormsby, of Birdhill, who left her that estate at her sole disposal. He *d. unm.* 26 Nov. 1878, and was *s.* by his only surviving brother,
HASTINGS TWISS, of Birdhill House, co. Tipperary, M.D., J.P., *b.* 1817; *m.* 27 Sept. 1855, Sarah, dau. and co-heir of Capt. Stirton, H.E.I.C.S., of Earlswood House, Surrey. She *d.* 7 March, 1906. He *d.* 13 Sept. 1897, leaving issue,
1. ROBERT GEORGE EDWARD, now of Birdhill.
2. Hastings Stirton, *d.* young.
3. Arthur Ormsby, *d.* young.   4. William, *d.* young.
1. Sarah Elizabeth Letitia, *m.* 25 July, 1895, Henry FitzPatrick Berry, I.S.O., Litt.D., M.A., Trin. Coll. Dublin, Assist. Keeper of the Records, son of the late Parsons Berry, M.B.
2. Emily Alice Moore, *m.* 14 April, 1891, Rev. Alexander Thomas. Rector of Nenagh, co. Tipperary, and *d.* 10 Feb. 1892, leaving a son, Robert Alexander Hastings, *b.* 2 Feb. 1892.

Seat—Birdhill House, co. Tipperary.

TYNDALL OF OAKLANDS.

ROBERT TYNDALL, of Oaklands, co. Wexford, J.P. and D.L. for that co., High Sheriff 1898, and J.P. co. Kilkenny, *b.* 21 April, 1837; *m.* 19 March, 1872, Emily Thomasina Mary Hunt, dau. of Henry Samuel Hunt Boyse, of Bannow, Capt. R.N., D.L. for co. Wexford, and has had issue,

1. ROBERT, Capt. Durham Light Infantry, b. 12 Sept. 1874; m. 22 Jan. 1908, Isabel, dau. of Thomas Young Bramwell, of Tynemouth, Northumberland, and has issue, a son,
   Robert, b. 14 Nov. 1908.
2. Henry Samuel, b. 5 March, 18676; m. 8 Nov. 1911, Violet, dau. of W. Sayer, of Melbourne, Australia, widow of J. S. Stewart, of Sydney.
3. Edward Boyse, b. 11 Oct. 1879; d. 31 May, 1881.
4. William Harman, b. 15 Nov. 1883.
1. Emily Grace Sophia Cora.
2. Maude Margaret, m. 19 July, 1899, John Sharp Dawson, of Haullwishairn, co. Montgomery, 4th son of the late Joseph Sharp Dawson, of Royds Hall, Yorks.

Lineage.—JOHN TYNDALL came from Gloucestershire to Ireland during the wars of the Rebellion, and had a grant of land confirmed to him in 1668. He m. Isabella de Rinzy, of the Wexford family, and had one son,
— TYNDALL, who m. Ellen Dean, and had three sons,
1. ROBERT, of whom presently. 2. Isaac, m. Ellen Whitfield.
3. Edward, who left issue.
The eldest son,
ROBERT TYNDALL, of Bellevue Park, co. Dublin, and Oaklands, co. Wexford, b. 1769; m. 1st, 1799, Elizabeth, dau. of Rev. William Bolton, by whom (who d. 30 June, 1807, and was bur. at St. Michan's, Dublin) he had (with three children, who d. young and were bur. at the same place) a son and a dau.,
1. ROBERT, his heir.
1. Elizabeth, m. 1827, Alexander Richard Pope, of Rocksbire, co. Waterford, who d. 1848, leaving issue.
Mr. Tyndall m. 2ndly, Elizabeth, dau. of Michael Lewis, of Ballinderry and Myrtle Grove in King's Co., and by her, who d. 9 March, 1840, aged 65, aud was bur. at St. Michan's, he had (with four other children, who d. young and are bur. at the same place) a dau.,
2. Francis Isabella, m. William Hales Carroll, of Harcourt Street, Dublin, and d. 14 Jan. 1842, aged 27, leaving issue.
Mr. Tyndall d. 25 May, 1834, aged 65, and was bur. at St. Michan's, when he was s. by his son,
ROBERT TYNDALL, of Oaklands, J.P. cos. Wexford and Kilkenny, High Sheriff for the latter co. 1844, b. 1800; m. 3 June, 1833, Grace Sophia, only dau. of Rev. Thomas Harman, of Palace, co. Wexford (see that family), and by her (who d. 21 Nov. 1883) had issue,
1. ROBERT, now of Oaklands.
2. Thomas Harman, P.W.D., India, b. 7 April, 1840; m. 12 Nov. 1867, Cecilia Lucy, dau. of Charles Webb, M.D., of Exeter, and d. 1902, having had issue,
   1. Charles Cecil Robert (Rev.), Rector of Washford Pyne, Devon, b. 8 Nov. 1868.
      1. Muriel, b. 30 Sept. 1871; d. 1872.
      2. Aileen Olive Napier.
3. Samuel William, of Ballyanne, co. Wexford, Col. Durham Light Infantry, b. 15 Nov. 1842; d. unm. 15 July, 1888.
4. ALBERT HENRY, of Ballyanne (see next article).
5. Arthur Isaac, b. 23 Dec. 1846; d.s.p. 1 Dec. 1911; m. 2 June, 1909, Emily Frances, only dau. of Joseph Edward Deane-Drake, of Stokestown (see that family).
1. Sarah, d. unm. 12 Nov. 1877.
2. Elizabeth, d. March, 1908.
3. Sophia Grace, d. unm. 14 Feb. 1909.
4. Hannah Jane.
Mr. Tyndall d. 1880, and was s. by his eldest son.

Seat—Oaklands, New Ross, co. Wexford. Club—Kildare St., Dublin.

TYNDALL OF BALLYANNE.

ALBERT HENRY TYNDALL, of Ballyanne House and Berkeley Forest, co. Wexford, J.P., High Sheriff 1903, b. 27 Aug. 1844; m. 6 April, 1892, Katherine Cecilia, only dau. of John St. George Deane, D.L., of Berkeley Forest (see DEANE of Glendaragh). Mr. A. H. Tyndall is the fourth son of Robert Tyndall, of Oaklands, who d. 1880, by Grace Sophia his wife, who d. 21 Nov. 1883, only dau. of the Rev. Thomas Harman, of Palace, co. Wexford. He s. his brother, Col. Samuel William Tyndall, Durham L.I., of Ballyanne, who d. unm. 15 July, 1888.

Lineage.—See TYNDALL of Oaklands.

Seats—Ballyanne House, New Ross, and Berkeley Forest, Wexford. Club—Kildare Street.

TYNTE OF TYNTE PARK.

MERVYN ARTHUR TYNTE, of Tynte Park, and Saunders Grove, co. Wicklow, and Tynte Lodge, co. Leitrim, b. 3 Nov. 1878 late Capt. Royal Munster Fusiliers.

Lineage. — EDWARD TYNTE, of Wraxhall, Somerset, m. Anne Parmenter and had a son,
EDMUND TYNTE, of Wraxhall, m. Elizabeth, dau. of John Panther, of Kenysham, Somerset, and had with other issue,
1. Edward, of Chelvey, Somerset, m. Anne, dau. of Sir Edward Gorges, of Wraxhall, and had with other issue,
   John, of Chelvey, M.P. for Bridgewater 1661, m. Jane, dau. and heir of Hugh Halsewell, of Halsewell, co. Somerset, and left a son,
   (Sir) Halsewell Tynte, created a Baronet 26 Jan. 1673-4, which title became extinct on the death of the 5th Bart., 25 Aug. 1785.
2. ROBERT, of whom next.
The younger son,
SIR ROBERT TYNTE, of Ballycrenane, co. Cork, 5th and youngest son of Edmund Tynte was bapt. at Wraxhall, 31 March, 1571, Knighted in Ireland 4 July, 1620. His will is dated 10 May, 1643. H. m. 1st, s.p.; 2ndly, 3 March, 1612, Elizabeth, widow 1st of EDMUND SPENSER, the Poet; 2ndly, of Roger Seckerston, dau. of — Boyle, and had three sous and four daus.,
1. ROBERT, his heir.
2. John, of Kilcredan, co. Cork, admitted to Gray's Inn, 29 Oct. 1628.
3. William, of Cahirmony, co. Cork, d.s.p. 5 Oct. 1669; m. 1664, Anne, widow of Anthony Atkinson, of Cangort, King's Co. (see that family), dau. of Sir Robert Newcomen, Bart. She m. 3rdly, William Digby, of Newtown, King's Co.
1. Catherine, m. 1st, William Hyde, of Carrigoneda, co. Cork (see HYDE of Castle Hyde); 2ndly, Edmund Magrath.
2. Bridget, m. William Bowen, of Ballyadams, Queen's co.
3. Mary, m. Gyles Workinan, of Leough, co. Tipperary.
4. Margaret, m. 1632, John Tottenham (see TOTTENHAM of Tottenham Green).
The eldest son,
ROBERT TYNTE, of Ballycrenane, will dated 28 June, 1644, pr. 10 Sept. 1646; m. Phillis, eldest dau. of Sir Edward Harris, of Dromny, a Justice of the King's Bench, Ireland, and had six sons and six daus.,
1. Robert, b. 1620, matric. Trin. Coll Dub. 7 March, 1638; d. unm. 5 Sept. 1645.
2. Edward, d. before his brother Robert.
3. HENRY, who succeeded.
4. John. 5. William.
6. Thomas.
1. Elizabeth. 2. Phillis.
3. Mary.
4. Jean, m. 1st, 1647, Edward Browne, of Ballinvoher, co. Cork; 2ndly, 1671, Walter Yelverton.
5. Anne.
6. Bridget, m. Sir Thomas Crosbie, of Ardfert, co. Kerry (see CROSBIE of Ballyheigue).
The 3rd son,
SIR HENRY TYNTE, of Ballycrenan, Knighted 30 Dec. 1660, M.P. for co. Cork 1661; d. 26 Oct. 1661; m. Mabell, dau. of Sir Percy Smyth, of Ballynatray, co. Waterford (see that family), and by her who m. 2ndly, Col. Roger Osborne (see OSBORNE, Bart.), had an only son, and six daus.,
1. HENRY, his heir.
2. Elizabeth, m. Sir Richard Hull, of Leamcon, co. Cork.
3. Mary, m. 1st, William Maynard, of Curryglass, co. Cork; 2ndly, Rev. William FitzGerald, Dean of Cloyne, afterwards Bishop of Clonfert.
3. Isabel, m. Richard Pyne, of Waterpark, co. Cork, afterwards Chief Justice of the Common Pleas, Ireland, and Knighted 5 Nov. 1692.
4. Mabella, m. William Worth, a Baron of the Exchequer, Ireland, 1681-86, and had a son,
   JAMES, who assumed the name of TYNTE, of whom hereafter.
5. Catherine, m. Lawrence Clayton, of Moyallow, co. Cork.
6. Margaret, m. John Cooke, of Youghal.
The only son,
HENRY TYNTE, of Ballycrenane, b. 1661, matriculated Trin. Coll. Dublin 3 Jan. 1678-9. His will dated 20 March, 1689, proved 13 May, 1691. Dying unm. he was s. by his cousin,
JAMES WORTH, who assumed the name of TYNTE, on succeeding to Ballycrenane, High Sheriff co. Cork 1711, M.P. for Rathcormack 1715-1727 and for Youghal 1727 till his death in 1758. He was also a Privy Councillor, Ireland. He m. 1st, 15 April, 1702, Hester dau. and heir of John Bulkeley, of Old Bawn, co. Dublin, and Dunlavan, co. Wicklow, and had by her (who d. 9 Aug. 1723) with other issue, d. young, a son,
ROBERT, his heir.

He m. 2ndly, Elizabeth Kelly, whose will dated 3 Aug. 1758, was proved in 1761, but had no issue by her. His only son,
ROBERT TYNTE, of Old Bawn and Dunlavan, B.A. Dublin 1745, M.A. 1748, High Sheriff co. Dublin 1759, d. June, 1760. He m. 18 May, 1758, Lady Elizabeth Stratford, 2nd dau. of John, 1st Earl of Aldborough, and had a posthumous son,
SIR JAMES STRATFORD TYNTE, Bart., so created 24 Aug. 1778; b. Aug. 1760, B.A. Dublin 1779, High Sheriff co. Wicklow 1785, d. 10 Nov. 1785, when the title became extinct. He m. Nov. 1781, Hannah, dau. of Morley Saunders, of Saunders Grove, co. Wicklow, and by her (who m. 2ndly, March, 1790, Fitzmaurice Caldwell, and d. 21 March, 1840) had issue,
1. James, d. an infant v.p.
1. Elizabeth, d. 1816.   2. Martha, d. 1791.
3. JEMIMA ROBERTA, who succeeded.

The 3rd dau.,
JEMIMA ROBERTA TYNTE, m. 1806, Col. JOSEPH PRATT, of Cabra Castle, co. Cavan (see that family), and d. 1882, leaving with other issue a 2nd son,
JOSEPH PRATT TYNTE, of Tynte Park, co. Wicklow, J.P., D.L., High Sheriff 1842, assumed the name and arms of TYNTE instead of Pratt by Royal Licence 26 July, 1836, b. 1815; d. 1896; m. 1840, Geraldine, dau. and co-heir of William Richard Hopkins-Northey of Oving House, Bucks, by Anne Elizabeth, dau. and heir of Gerald Fortescue, Ulster King of Arms 1787, and by her (who d. 12 Jan. 1888) had issue,
1. FORTESCUE JOSEPH, his heir.
2. MERVYN CHALLONER STEPHEN, who s. his brother.
1. Hannah Elizabeth, m. 3 Aug. 1865, Henry Edward Moore, of Moorefield, co. Kildare, and had issue (see BURKE'S *Peerage*, DROGHEDA, E. of).
2. Madeline.
3. Alice Geraldine, m. 2 April, 1873, Lieut.-Col. Richard St. Leger Moore, C.B., of Killashee, co. Kildare (see that family).

The elder son,
FORTESCUE JOSEPH TYNTE, of Tynte Park, C.B. (1898), Col. 3rd Batt. Royal Dublin Fusiliers, J.P., D.L. co. Wicklow, High Sheriff 1892, b. 18 June, 1841; d.s.p. 24 Sept. 1907; m. 12 Nov. 1884, Mary, widow of Charles Gustavus Rochfort, of Rochfort Bridge, co. Westmeath (see that family), dau. of T. H. May Somerville, of Whitecroft, Dumfries. She d. 16 April, 1899.
MERVYN CHALLONER TYNTE, of Tynte Park, and Saunders Grove, co. Wicklow, and Tynte Lodge, co. Leitrim, retired Lieut.-Col. 4th Dragoon Guards, Resident Magistrate co. Londonderry, J.P. co. Wicklow, High Sheriff 1910, b. 1 Sept. 1846; d. 23 April, 1910; m. 17 June, 1876, Alice Elise, dau. of Arthur Lathain, of Weaste Hall, Manchester, and had issue,
1. MERVYN ARTHUR, now of Tynte Park, &c.
2. Audley Fortescue, Lieut. R.G.A., d. unm. 20 April, 1910.
1. Elise Geraldine Katie, m. 1 Oct. 1903, Hardress E. Waller, of Troy, Londonderry.
2. Nora Ina Olive Violet.

Arms—Gu., a lion dormant between six cross crosslets arg. Crest—A unicorn sejant arg., armed and crined or.
Seats—Tynte Park, Dunlavan; Saunders Grove, Baltinglass co. Wicklow; Tynte Lodge, Tullaghan, co. Leitrim.

UNIACKE OF MOUNT UNIACKE.

NORMAN COMPTON FITZGERALD UNIACKE, of Mount Uniacke, co. Cork, retired Lieut. R.N., b. 14 Dec. 1848; s. his father 12 Sept. 1877; m. 21 Nov. 1882, Louisa, dau. of William Garde, of Bilberry, co. Cork.

Lineage.—THOMAS UNACK or UNIACK, of Ballyhobbert, near Youghal, living in the year 1500, was an Alderman and twice Mayor of Youghal in 1556 and 1560. By Margaret his wife, he had two sons,
1. JAMES, his heir.
2. Edmund, of Youghal, living in 1578. He had issue, a son and heir,
THOMAS, who s. to the property on the death of his cousin, John Uniacke, in 1623.

The elder son,
JAMES UNIACK, of Ballyhobbert, a Burgess of Youghal, m. Margaret, dau. of Edmund FitzGerald, of Ballymartyr, and sister to the famous John FitzEdmond, the Earl of Desmond's last Seneschal of Imokilly; by whom, who survived him, he left issue, an only son, JOHN, and two daus., Ellen and Christian.   His will is dated 27 Feb. 1577, and dying 1578 (Inq. p.m.), he was s. by his son and heir,
JOHN UNIACKE, of Ballyhobbert, a Burgess of Youghal, a minor at his father's death, granted in ward to Henry Sheffelde, Gent., 23 April, 1586; and had livery of his lands of Ballyhobbert, Moke-rishe, Ballyvergyn, Barnageehy, and Vanchymore, with other property in Youghal, 1 Dec. 1602. He m. (settlement dated 22 Jan. 1591) Johanna, dau. of Thomas Coppinger, of Youghal, an Alderman and four times Mayor of Youghal; but by her (whose will is dated 10 Feb. 1635) he had no issue, and dying before 1623 (Inq. p.m.), he was s. by,
THOMAS UNIACKE, of Youghal, his cousin and heir male, son of Edmund Uniacke, and grandson of Thomas Uniacke, of Youghal aforesaid, father of James Uniack, of Ballyhobbert. He is mentioned as kinsman in the curious will of Sir John FitzGerald of Ballymaloe, 1 Sept. 1640, who bequeathed to him considerable property near Youghal. By Margaret his wife, a dau. of one of the FitzGeralds, of Glenane, co. Cork, he had issue,
1. MAURICE, his heir.
2. Edmond, living 1649; one of the Overseers of his brother's will.
1. Christian, living 1649.
2. A dau., m. Nicholas Miagh, of Youghal, Gent.

He was s. by his elder son,
MAURICE UNIACKE, of Ballyvergyn, near Youghal, an Alderman and Mayor of Youghal 1639, and Mayor of the Staple 1640. His will is dated 10 April, 1646, with a codicil 9 Feb. 1648. He m. Margrett, dau. and sole heir of Richard Kearney, of Youghal, Burgess, by whom (who survived him) he had issue,
1. THOMAS, his heir.
2. JAMES, of Dublin, of whom presently.
3. Edmond, of Youghal, Gent., living in 1632; m. and had issue a son and a dau.,
James, of Cappagh, co. Tipperary, Counsellor-at-Law m. 1st, his cousin, Ann, dau. of James Uniacke, of Dublin, Gent., and 2ndly, Barbara, dau of John Power, of Clashmore, co. Waterford; and d. 1732, leaving issue, an only dau. and heir,
Katharine, m. her cousin, Maurice Uniacke, of Woodhouse, co. Waterford.
Anstance, m. John Colpoys, Attorney-at-Law, 2nd son of Thomas Colpoys, of Rathfoland, and had a son, Adm. Sir John Colpoys, K.C.B.
4. Richard, entered at Gray's Inn, London, 6 July, 1669.
5. John, of Curreheen, co. Cork, an Alderman of Youghal, m. Phillis, dau. of Alderman Pierce Miagh, of Youghal, by whom (who d. 1684, and is bur. at Youghal) he had issue, two children, who both d. young. His will is dated 13 March, 1729.
1. Anstance, m. Theobald FitzGerald, of Clonea, co. Waterford, Gent.
2. Joane, living 1649.

Mr. Maurice Uniacke d. 1649, and was s. by his son and heir,
THOMAS UNIACKE, of Ballyvergyn, and Barnageehy, co. Cork: his estates were confiscated by Cromwell in 1658, for his adherence to the Royal cause, but were restored to him in 1663, by a Decree of Innocence under the Acts of Settlement. He was an Alderman, and M.P. for Youghal in King JAMES' Irish Parliament of 1689; m. Ellinor, dau. of Garret FitzGerald, of Lisquinlan, co. Cork (and co-heir of her brother, Robert FitzGerald, who d.s.p. 1718), by whom he had issue,
1. THOMAS, his heir.
2. James, of Corneveagh, co. Cork; m. (settlement dated 2 Aug. 1703) Anstace, dau. of Philip FitzJames Ronayne, of Ronayne's Court, co. Cork; his will is dated 7 May, 1712, and dying the same year, he left issue,
1. Maurice, b. 1705.
2. James, settled at Port Morant, Jamaica; m. and had issue.
3. Philip, of Youghal, living 1737.
1. Helen, m. — Prendergast.
1. Margaret, b. 1672.
2. Elinor, d. 1680, bur. in the South Abbey, Youghal.

Mr. Thomas Uniacke d. 1708, and was s. by his son and heir,
THOMAS UNIACKE, of Ballyvergyn, and Barnageehy, co. Cork, and of Woodhouse, co. Waterford, which latter estate he purchased from Maj. Richard FitzGerald in 1725. He was an Alderman, and Mayor of Youghal 1723; m. (licence dated 3 March, 1707) Helena, dau. and co-heir of Christian Bor, of Bor Mount, co. Wexford, a General in King William's Army (by Ellen his wife, an heiress of the family of Hore, of co. Wexford), by whom he had issue,
1. BOR, his heir.
2. Robert, of Lisquinlan and Corkbeg, co. Cork, which estates he inherited under the will of his maternal great-uncle, Robert FitzGerald, of Lisquinlan, assuming, in compliance with testator's wishes, the names and arms of FITZGERALD. He m. 1750, Frances, dau. of John Judkin, of Ballymore, co. Tipperary, and had issue,
1. Robert Uniacke FitzGerald, M.P. for co. Cork, from whom descend the family of UNIACKE PENROSE FITZGERALD, Bart. of Corkbeg (see BURKE's *Peerage*, FITZGERALD, Bart.).
2. Thomas Judkin FitzGerald, of Lisheen, co. Tipperary, created a baronet 5 Aug. 1801, from whom descend the JUDKIN FITZGERALDS of Lisheen (see BURKE'S *Peerage and Baronetage*)
3. Maurice, of Woodhouse, co. Waterford, in which estate he had a life interest under his father's will; m. Katherine, dau. and sole heir of Counsellor James Uniacke, of Cappagh, and d. 2 Feb. 1743, leaving issue, an only dau. and heir, Barbara, m. Walter Atkins, of Leadington, co. Cork.
1. Clotilda, m. 16 Oct. 1738, William Wallis, of Ballycrenane, co. Cork.

Mr. Thomas Uniacke, of Woodhouse (whose wil is dated 21 June, 1733), d. 1734, and was s. by his son and heir,
BOR UNIACKE, of Ballyvergyn and the Red House, Youghal, and of Woodhouse, co. Waterford, b. 1710, Bailiff of Youghal 1736; m. (licence dated 3 April, 1742) Anne, dau. of Frederick Trench, of Moate co. Galway, and d. 25 April, 1777, having had issue,
1. Robert, of Woodhouse, M.P. for Yough l, Col. Waterford

Militia, and Surveyor-Gen. of the Ordnance; *m.* 1790, Annette Constantia, dau. of the Right Hon. John Beresford, brother to George, Marquis of Waterford, and *d.* 1802, leaving issue (with a son, James, who *d. unm.*, and six daus.), a son and heir,
   Robert John, of Woodhouse, J.P., D.L., an Officer 7th Hussars, served in the Peninsular and at Waterloo; *m.* 1821, the Lady Mildred Bourke, sister to Robert, 5th Earl of Mayo, and *d.* 1851, leaving issue (with four daus.), an only surviving son, Robert Bor Uniacke, who *d. unm.* in 1853, when the male line of the Woodhouse Uniackes became extinct, the property devolving upon Col. George Beresford, R.A., in right of his wife, Frances Constantia, eldest dau. of Col. Robert John Uniacke, above mentioned.
2. Frederick, *d.* young.
1. Helena, *b.* 1744; *m.* Richard Uniacke, of Ahadda, co. Cork.
2. Mary, *b.* 1748; *d.* young.
3. Elizabeth, *b.* 1754; *m.* Crofton Uniacke, of Ballyre, co. Cork.

We now return to
   JAMES UNIACKE, of the city of Dublin, Gent.; 2nd son of Maurice Uniacke, of Ballyvergyn; entered at Trin. Coll. Dublin, 28 Jan. 1661, and adopted the law as his profession; *m.* (licence dated 10 May, 1665) Mary Neale, of St. Warburgh's, Dublin, by whom he had issue,
1. John, *b.* 1669; *d.* young.   2. JAMES, his heir.
3. Norman, of Curreheen, co. Cork, M.D., *b.* 1678, entered at Trin. Coll. Dublin, 8 Aug. 1695; *m.* (settlement dated 6 Jan. 1713) Elizabeth, dau. of William Supple, of Aghadoe, co. Cork, and *d.* 5 Dec. 1727, leaving issue,
   1. James, of Youghal, an Alderman and Mayor of Youghal, 1755 and 1757; *m.* 23 April, 1747, Jane, dau. of Alderman John Lucas, of Youghal, and had issue,
      (1) Norman William.   (2) Arthur Hyde.
      (3) James Tonson.   (4) Richard.
      (5) Jasper, of Araglyn, co. Cork, *m.* Maria, dau. of Joshua Andrews, of Kilworth, co. Cork, by whom he had, with other issue, a son, James, Maj. R.M., killed at the storming of Chin-Keang-foo in China, 21 July, 1842, leaving issue by Emma his wife, dau. of Edmond Roche, an only dau., Jane, *m.* 1st, Capt. Nuttaw Stephens, 87th Regt., and 2ndly, Col. Donald Frazer, R.E. Mr. Jasper Uniacke was murdered in his own house, together with Col. Mansergh St. George, in the Irish Rebellion of 1798.
   2. William, of Cork, *m.* Elizabeth Morris; killed in a duel at Cork, 1760.
   3. John, of Cottage, co. Cork, J.P.; *m.* Frances, dau. and co-heir of Roger Mainwaring, of Kerminchain, Cheshire, and by her (who *d.* Dec. 1796), he left issue at his decease 9 Sept. 1793.
      (1) John Mainwaring, of Cottage and Kermincham, Lieut. 66th Regt.; *m.* Mary, dau. of the Very Rev. Dixie Blundell, D.D., Dean of Clontarf, by whom he had (with a dau., Mary, *m.* Henry C. MacVeagh, of Drewstown, co. Meath) an only son,
         John, of Cottage and Kermincham, and of Broughton House, Cheshire, Mayor of Chester 1837 and 1838; *m.* 3 June, 1823, Anne, dau. of Vice-Admiral Pierrepont, and had issue,
         a. William Pierrepont, bur. in Chester Cathedral.
         b. Henry Turner, of Laywell House, co. Devon, Capt. 19th Foot, present at the battle of Alma, siege of Sebastopol, and storming of the Redan; *m.* 1861, Isabella Louisa (who *d.*   ), dau. of George Fortescue, of Newton Abbot, co. Devon, and *d.* 19 Aug. 1907, having had issue,
            (a) Henry Percy, Major Gordon Highlanders, *b.* 13 Sept. 1862; *m.* 22 July, 1896, Flora Alexandra Lucy, dau. of Samuel Leo Shuster, of the Grange, Leatherhead, Surrey, by Lady Isabella FitzMaurice his wife, dau of the 5th Earl of Orkney, and had issue,
            'Evelyn Pierrepont.
            (b) John Mainwaring, *d.* 13 July, 1906.
            (c) Frederick FitzGerald, *d.* young.
            (d) Evelyn Pierrepont, Lieut. 11th Foot.
            (e) Charles Fortescue, Cheshire, *b.* 29 Aug. 1875; *m.* Feb. 1909, Annie Christine Cecilia, younger dau. of Ashcroft S. O. B. ffrench, of Monivea Castle, Athenry (*see that family*), and has issue,
            John Herbert Fortescue, *b.* 3 June, 1910.
            (a) Kathleen, *m.* 1st, St. John Blackett; and 2ndly, Bernard Wezuclin, of Coombe End.
            (b) Isabel Alice.
            (c) Juliana Fortescue, *m.* Sept. 1901, Maj. Victor Frederick William Augustus Paget, R.H.A., eldest son of the late Right Hon. Sir Augustus Berkeley Paget (*see* BURKE'S *Peerage*, ANGLESEY, M.). She *d.s.p.* 22 May, 1906.
            (d) Geraldine, *d.* young.
         a. Mary Frances, *m.* the Rev. R. N. Wood, M.A., and *d.*
         b. Maria, *m.* 1st, Col. Dorman Macleod; 2ndly, Frederick Wright, and *d.*
      (1) Catherine, *m.* John R. Parker, of Green Park, Youghal, and Upper Harley Street, London.
      (2) Frances, *m.* Henry Turner, of Bath.
      (3) Margaret, *m.* 12 Nov. 1770, William Power, of Drumraghill, co. Waterford.
         1. Mary, living 1754.   2. Mabella, living 1754.
      3. Elizabeth, *m.* Edmond Browning, of the city of Dublin, Gent.
   4. Kearney, *b.* 1681; *d.* young.

1. Margaret, *b.* 1668; living in 1727.
2. Mary, *b.* 1673; living 1730, *d. unm.*
3. Ann, *b.* 1674; *m.* her 1st cousin Counsellor James Uniacke, of Cappagh; she *d.* 1711, and is bur. at Youghal.
4. Grace, *b.* 1679; *d.* young.

Mr. James Uniacke's will is dated 29 June, 1687, and dying 10 Aug. following, at Tunbridge Wells, co. Kent, he was *s.* by his son and heir,
   JAMES UNIACKE, of Coolegorragh, co. Cork, J.P., *b.* 12 Oct. 1671; an Officer in Col. Conyngham's Regt. of Dragoons (commission dated 16 March, 1692); purchased the estate of Coolegorragh from James FitzGerald, of Glenane, co. Cork (son of Sir William FitzGerald, Knt.), and built there the house called Mount Uniacke. He *m.* (settlement dated 31 Jan. 1705) Mary, dau. of William Mathews, of Templelyon, co. Wicklow, by whom (who *d.* 1762) he left issue,
1 RICHARD, his heir.
2. John, of Carrigyower, co. Cork, M.D., entered at Trin. Coll. Dublin, 17 Jan. 1726; *m.* Judith, dau. of Redmond Barry, of Ballyclough, co. Cork, and had issue,
   Redmond of Old Court, co. Cork, *m.* 1782, Elizabeth, dau. of Lionel Fleming, of Green Park, Skibbereen, co. Cork, and *d.* 3 Jan. 1803, leaving issue,
      (1) John, Capt. 95th Regt. (Rifle Brigade); killed at the storming of Ciudad Rodrigo, 1812, *unm.*
      (2) Lionel, *m.* Elizabeth, dau. of George Crotty, and had issue.
      (3) Thomas Fane, of Lymbury Lodge, co. Westmeath, an Officer in the Rifle Brigade, *m.* Elizabeth, dau. of Gustavus Rochfort, M.P., and had issue.
         1. Redmond Rochfort, Ensign 71st Highland Light Infantry, accidentally shot by a brother Officer 1842.
         2. Gustavus, *d.* young.
         3. John Rochfort, Ensign 71st Regt.
         1. Frances, *m.* Capt. Lionel Smith, 54th Regt.
         2. Jane Jocelyn, *d. unm.* 2 Dec. 1906.
         3. Catherine Rochfort, *m.* Rev. Canon John Allen. She *d.* his widow, 28 April, 1908.
      (1) Martha, *m.* Thomas Townsend, of Clyda, co. Cork.
      (2) Elizabeth, *m.* Capt. Arthur Molloy, 32nd Regt.
      (3) Judith, *m.* General Richard Uniacke.
      (4) Isabella, *m.* Philip Somerville, of the Prairie Schull.
      (5) Henrietta, *m.* Capt. Edward Coxon, Rifle Brigade.
   Mary, *m.* Major Henry Ffolliott, of Hollisbrook, co. Sligo.
3. NORMAN, of Castletown (*see that family*).
1. Mary, *m.* James Lombard, of Craig, co. Cork.
2. Elizabeth, *m.* 1740, the Ven. Perkins Crofton, Archdeacon of Aghadoe, Vicar-General of Cork and Ross.

Capt. James Uniacke's will is dated 1 May, 1730, and dying June, 1733, he was *s.* by his son and heir,
   RICHARD UNIACKE, of Mount Uniacke, co. Cork; *m.* (settlement dated 4 Nov. 1735) Ann, dau. of John Longfield, of Castle Mary, co. Cork, J.P. (*see* LONGFIELD, *of Longueville*), by whom (who *d.* July, 1787) he had issue,
1. JAMES, his heir.
2. John, Cornet 14th Dragoons, 4 March, 1760; *d. unm.* 1763.
3. Richard, of Dublin, and of Abadda, co. Cork, Mayor of Youghal 1777 and 1781; *m.* Helena, dau. of Bor Uniacke, of Woodhouse, by whom (who *d.* 16 Sept. 1779) he had issue,
   Richard, *d.* young.
   Mary Elizabeth Helena, only dau. and heir, *m.* John Bayley, of Debsborough, co. Tipperary.
4. Robert, Col. 58th Regt., served at the siege of Gibraltar, and in the Irish Rebellion of 1798; *m.* 1777, Mary, dau. of Arthur Baynes, M.D., Surgeon-General at Gibraltar, and *d.* 1832, leaving issue,
   1. Richard, of Seaview, co. Cork, General Royal Irish Artillery; *m.* Judith, dau. of Redmond Uniacke, of Old Court, by whom he had issue,
      (1) Redmond, Deputy Commissary-General (retired), *d. unm.* 25 Sept. 1910.
      (2) Richard, of Brisbane, Queensland, *m.* 1st, Margaret, dau. of Lieut. Thomson, and had issue,
         1. Richard, *d.* young.
         2. Norman, *d.* young.
         3. Redmond FitzGerald, of Queensbayen, Victoria, *m.* Mary, dau. of William J. Higgs, of Victoria, and has issue,
            a. Redmond.
            a. Florence.   *b.* Rosa.
         4. Arthur Reibey, of Williamia, New South Wales, *m.* Lucy, dau. of John Law, and has issue,
            a. Arthur.
            a. Lucy.   *b.* Rosa.   *c.* Ida.
         1. Celia Constance Maude, *m.* Hon. George Thorn, Premier of Queensland, and had issue.
      He *m.* 2ndly, Fanny, dau. of John Whitworth, and by her had issue,
         5. Victor, *d. unm.*
         2. Nathalie Isabel, *m.* 18 May, 1896, Alexander Cumming Hutton Potts.
         (3) Lambert, of Monkstown, co. Cork., Maj. Royal North Lincoln Militia.
            (1) Elizabeth, *d. unm.*   (2) Mary, *d. unm.*
            (3) Judith, *d. unm.*   (4) Anne, *d. unm.*
            (5) Jane Lambert, *d. unm.*   (6) Caroline, *d. unm.*
      2. Robert, Capt. 18th Royal Irish, and Paymaster 10th Foot, *d. unm.*
         1. Anne, *d. unm.*   2. Caroline, *d. unm.*
         3. Harriet, *m.* Capt. John Armstrong, 88th Connaught Rangers.
         4. Mary, *d. unm.*   5. Catherine, *d. unm.*

Uniacke. THE LANDED GENTRY. 714

 6. Amy, *d. unm.*   7. Jane, *d. unm.*
 1. Elizabeth, *m.* John Swayne, of Youghal.
 2. Harriet, *m.* Capt. Mathew Nash, Royal Irish Artillery.
 3. Ann, *d. unm.*   4. Mary, *d. unm.*
Mr. Richard Uniacke's will is dated 19 March, 1761, and dying the same year, he was *s.* by his son and heir,

JAMES UNIACKE, of Mount Uniacke; entered at Trin. Coll. Dublin, 20 Feb. 1753; M.P. for Youghal. 1776-96; *m.* 1st, 17 Sept. 1760, Caroline, dau. of Charles Coote, of Coote Hill, co. Cavan, and sister to Charles, last Earl of Bellamont, by whom (who *d.* 1792), he had an only dau.,
 1. Prudence, *b.* 1764; *d.* an infant.
He *m.* 2ndly, Mary Higgins, by whom, who survived him, he left at his decease, 1803,
 1. George Richard, *d.* young.   **2.** NORMAN, his heir.
 2. Ann, *m.* Patrick Lawler, Attorney-at-Law.
 3. Elizabeth.
His son and heir,

NORMAN UNIACKE, of Mount Uniacke, commonly called "the Minor," *b.* 1796; *m.* 7 Oct. 1818, Eleanor, dau. of George Lax, of Wells, co. Somerset, by whom (who *d.* 1876) he left at his decease, 19 April, 1861,
 1. NORMAN JAMES BIGGS, his heir.
 2. George Lax, *d. unm.* 1875.
 3. Robert FitzGerald, *d.* 13 Dec. 1862, in Australia.
 4. Crofton Bernard, *m.* 1880, Josephine, widow of — Meredith, of Bristol; *d.s.p.* 1891.
 1. Eleanor, *d. unm.*
 2. Florence Elizabeth, *m.* 1854, Robert Uniacke FitzGerald Uniacke, of Castletown, and has issue (*see next article*). He *d.* 6 Jan. 1903.
 3. Marianne. *d. unm.*   4. Caroline, *d. unm.*
 5. Susan Helena, *m.* the late George Morris.
The eldest son,

NORMAN JAMES BIGGS UNIACKE, of Mount Uniacke, an Officer in the Denbighshire Cavalry; *m.* 10 Sept. 1844, Mary Elizabeth. dau. of Col. Drinkwater Bethune, of Balfour, co. Fife, by whom, who *d.* 10 Nov. 1863, he left issue at his decease, 12 Sept. 1877,
 1. NORMAN COMPTON FITZGERALD, now of Mount Uniacke.
 1. Eleanor Georgina.   2. Geraldine Cecilia.

Arms—Arg., a wolf passant ppr. a chief gu. **Crest**—A dexter cubit armed arm erect, gauntletted ppr., holding a hawk's lure, or. **Mottoes**—" Unicus est," and " Fortis et Fidelis."
Seat—Mount Uniacke, Killeagh, co. Cork.

UNIACKE late OF CASTLETOWN.

ROBERT UNIACKE FITZ- GERALD UNIACKE, late of Castletown, co. Cork, *b.* 23 March, 1858.

Lineage.—NORMAN UNIACKE, of Castletown, 3rd son of Capt. James Uniacke, of Mount Uniacke (*see preceding article*), *m.* Alicia, dau. and co-heir of Bartholomew Purdon, of Garrane James, co. Cork, the 2nd son of Capt. Thomas Purdon, of Drinagh, co. Cork, and grandson of Sir Nicholas Purdon, Knt., of Ballyclough, by whom he had issue,
 1. JAMES, his heir.
 2. Bartholomew, Ensign 60th Foot, *d. unm.*
 3. Norman. Lieut. 40th Foot, *m.* Mary Anne, dau. of Simon Dring, of Rock Grove, co. Cork, *d.s.p.*
 4. Richard John, of Mount Uniacke, Halifax, B.N.A., *b.* 22 Nov. 1753, settled at Halifax 1781; Solicitor-General for the province of Nova Scotia 1782, Attorney-General 1797, and Member of His Majesty's Council, 1808. He *m.* 1st, 3 May, 1775, Martha Maria, dau. of Moses de Lesdernier, of Canton Geneva, Switzerland, by whom he had issue,
  1. Norman FitzGerald, of Lincoln's Inn, H.M. Attorney-General and Judge of the Supreme Court of Lower Canada, *b.* 1778; *m.* Sophia de Lesdernier, and *d.s.p.* 11 Dec. 1846.
  2. Crofton, of Lincoln's Inn, Judge of the Vice-Admiralty Court, Nova Scotia, *b.* 1783; *d.* 26 Oct. 1852; *m.* 1805, Dorothea, dau of Capt. Jones Fawson, and had issue,
   (1) Richard John (Rev.), B.A. Oxon,1832, Rector of Sydney, Nova Scotia, *m.* 1 June, 1847, Anne, dau. of the Ven. Archdeacon Willis, and *d.* 1888 having had issue,
    1. Richard (Rev.), *d. unm.* 1888.
    2. FitzGerald.   3. Crofton.
    1. Dorothea, *m.* 1872, Alvin Morton Cady, C.E.
   (2) Crofton, *d. unm.* 1817.
   (3) Norman FitzGerald, *d.* 1896.

   (1) Martha Maria, *b.* 4 Feb. 180' ; *d. unm.*
   (2) Elizabeth, *d. unm.*   (3) Alicia, *d. unm.*
  3. Richard John, H.M. Attorney-General, of Cape Breton, and Judge of the Supreme Court in British America ; *m.* Mary Anne. (who *d.* 10 Jan. 1857), dau. of the Hon. Charles Hill, of Halifax ; and *d.* 21 Feb. 1834, leaving issue,
   (1) Charles Hill, Maj. 2nd Dragoons, served in Crimea and Indian Mutiny, and *d. unm.* 30 Jan. 1878.
   (2) Richard John Norman, *d.* 1844.
   (1) Helen Maria, *d. unm.* 21 Dec. 1845.
   (2) Mary Mitchell, *d.* 27 Oct. 1860 ; *m.* 1851, C. W. Watkins, of Badby House, Northants.
  4. Robert FitzGerald (Rev.), Rector of St. George's, Halifax *m.* Elizabeth Frankyn (who *d.* 23 Dec. 1874), and *d.s.p.* 1 June, 1870.
  5. James Boyle, H.M. Attorney-General, and Commissioner of Crown Lands, Nova Scotia, *b.* 1799; *d.* 1858 ; *m.* Rosina (*d.* 1858), dau. of the Hon. William Black, and had issue,
   (1) William FitzGerald, Barrister-at-Law, *b.* 1 Dec. 1833 ; *d. unm.* 1871.
   (2) Rupert, *b.* 4 Sept. 1835 ; *d.*
   (3) Richard, *b.* 1838.
   (4) James Boyle (Rev.), of Mount Uniacke, Halifax, *b.* 1840 ; *d.* 26 Feb. 1901; *m.* 1st, 19 Sept. 1865, Saidie (who *d.* 10 July, 1866), dau. of Judge Wilkins, and had issue, an only child,
    1. Saidie, *m.* 6 Feb. 1901, Sidney Rutherford, younger son of John Buckley Rutherford, of Blackwater, I. of Wight.
He *m.* 2ndly, Mary Merkle, by whom he had issue,
    1. James Boyle, *b.* 1875 ; *d.* 1878.
    2. Franklyn FitzGerald, Capt. Royal Canadian Regt., *b.* 25 Feb. 1878 ; *d.* 13 Jan. 1906.
    3. James Boyle, Lieut. King's (Liverpool) Regt., *b.* 26 Aug. 1879.
    4. Redmond, *b.* and *d.* 1887.
    2. Mary Geraldine.   3. Helena Elizabeth.
    4. Mildred Alice.
   (1) Florence, *b.* 1847
  1. Mary, *b.* 1782 ; *m.* 3 May, 1805, Rear-Admiral Sir Andrew Mitchell, K.B. She *d.* 25 Feb. 1825.
  2. Martha Maria, *m.* 3 May, 1805, Thomas N. Jeffery, Collector of H.M. Customs at Halifax.
  3. Alicia, *m.* William Scott, of Sunderland Hall, co. Roxburgh.
  4. Anne Margaret, *b.* 9 May, 1794 ; *d.* 26 Feb. 1871, having *m.* 30 Oct. 1817, Capt. Kevan Izod Leslie, 60th Rifles, of Wilton, co. Cork.
  5. Elizabeth, *d. unm.* 1849.
  6. Eleanor Rebecca, *d.* 1849, having *m.* William Hacket, Inspector-General of Military Hospitals, who *d.* 29 May, 1854.
Mr. Richard John Uniacke *m.* 2ndly, 14 Jan. 1808, Elizabeth, dau. of Maj. Philips Newton, 48th Regt., and dying 11 Oct. 1830, left issue by her (who *d.* 16 April, 1849), an only son,
  6. Andrew Mitchell, of Halifax, Barrister-at-Law, D.C.L., Judge Advocate-General, and Custos Rotulorum, Chief Commissioner for Nova Scotia at the International Exhibition, London, 1862, *b.* 9 Nov. 1808 ; *m.* 6 Feb. 1834, Elizabeth McLean (*d.* 6 June, 1886), dau. of John Fraser, Barrister-at-Law, formerly an Officer in the Fraser Fencibles (who became co-heir of her brother John, who *d. unm.*). He *d.* at Dover, 26 July, 1895, leaving issue,
   (1) Robie, of Gorsebrook, Halifax, Barrister-at-Law, *b.* 3 Dec. 1834; *d.* 4 July, 1904; *m.* 1st, 9 June, 1863, Georgina Harriet, dau. of Sir Edward Archibald, K.C.M.G., C.B., and by her (who *d.* 20 Oct. 1867) had issue,
    1. Elizabeth Robie, *b.* 1864.
    2. Catherine, *b.* 1866 ; *d.* 1885.
He *m.* 2ndly, 23 Nov. 1870, Frederika Marion Douglas, dau. of Arthur Woodgate, by whom he has
    1. Cecil Dudley Woodgate, Lieut. R.A., *b.* 22 May, 1876 ; *m.* 21 Feb. 1905, Evelyn Catherine, dau. of Lieut.-Col. Arthur Harry Clark Kennedy, and has issue,
     Robie Dennis Woodgate, *b.* 21 Jan. 1906.
     Diana Evelyn.
   (2) Norman FitzGerald, an Officer in the 60th Rifles, *b.* 11 April, 1836 ; *m.* 18 Aug. 1862, Mary Augusta, widow of Capt. C. Molyneux-Seel, and dau. of Capt. James Winsloe Phillipps, 7th Hussars. She *d.* 30 March, 1909. He *d.* 12 April, 1872, leaving issue,
    1. Andrew Louis Cary, *b.* 8 Aug. 1863 ; *d. unm.* 8 July, 1899.
    2. Norman James Fyfe, Lieut. 19th Hussars, *b.* 24 Feb. 1865 ; *m.* 29 Nov. 1893, Kathleen, dau. of the late James Cassidy, of Monasterevan, co. Kildare. He *d.s.p.* 29 April, 1899.
    3. Lucius George Preston (*Sultana, Tulare co., California, U.S.A.*), *b.* 7 Nov. 1866 ; *m.* 15 Oct. 1890, Jennie M., dau. of Edward Cox, of Currie, Minnesota, U.S.A., and has issue,
     a. Norman Edward, *b.* 5 April, 1899.
     b. Desmond Bernard, *b.* 31 Dec. 1901.
     c. Kathleen (twin), *b.* 7 Aug. 1907.
     a. Mary Geraldine, *b.* 20 Oct. 1891.
     b. Frances Evelyn, *b.* 30 April, 1893.
     c. Carmen Inez, *b.* 5 March, 1896.
     d. Kathleen Patricia, *b.* 4 May, 1904.
     e. Bernardine (twin), *b.* 7 Aug. 1907.
    4. Edmund Fitzgerald, *b.* 1870 ; *d.* young.

5. Francis Phillipps, *b.* 5 Sept. 1872; *m.* 1 Sept. 1897, Meta, dau. of Surg. Carbery, 14th Foot, and has issue,
   a. Norman Loman William, *b.* 7 Feb. 1909.
   a. Geraldine, *b.* 6 June, 1898.
   b. Mary Elizabeth, *b.* 18 June, 1900.
   c. Catherine Andrea, *b.* 29 Sept. 1906.
  1. Geraldine Leslie, *b.* 24 Feb. 1868; *m.* 29 Oct. 1889, Arthur Levick, of Tezpore, Assam.
(3) Andrew Elliot Molyneux, of the War Office, London, *b.* 19 April, 1837; *d.* 13 Nov. 1900.
(4) Robert FitzGerald (Rev.), M.A., late Vicar of Tandridge co. Surrey, *b.* 15 March, 1840; *m.* 3 April, 1866, Hannah, dau. of Thomas Salmon, of St. Hilda's, co. Durham, and has issue,
  1. Richard Gordon FitzGerald, of Fox Hall, Upminster, Essex, B.A. Trin. Coll. Oxon, F.R.S.A. Ireland, *b.* 19 Aug. 1867; *m.* 31 Aug. 1892, Cecilia Monica, dau. of Frederick Lambert, of Garratts Hall, Banstead, co. Surrey, and has had issue,
   a. Bernard Lambert FitzGerald, *b.* 30 Aug. 1894; *d.* 26 Nov. 1898.
   b. Desmond Percival FitzGerald, *b.* 18 Dec. 1895.
   c. Richard Heygate FitzGerald, *b.* 18 Oct. 1898.
   a. Helen Monica Geraldine, *b.* 30 Aug. 1893; *d.* 7 Nov. same year.
   b. Gwladys Patricia, *b.* 27 May, 1901.
  2. Robie FitzGerald Capt. Royal Inniskilling Fusiliers (*Woodleigh, Sunning Hill, Berks*), *b.* 8 June, 1869; *m.* 3 March, 1894, Jane, only dau. of the late John R. Cuthbert, formerly Capt. 10th Hussars.
  3. Andrew FitzGerald (*Gorsley House, Upper Hardres, Kent*), *b.* 1874; *m.* 5 Oct. 1904, Hilda Byng, dau. of George Marshall, of Hardres Court.
(5) Crofton James, Lieut.-Col. Army Service Corps (4, *Alhambra Road, Southsea*), *b.* 9 June, 1841; *m.* 1865, Fanny, dau. of Col. John Campbell, late 60th Rifles, and has issue,
  1. Herbert Crofton Campbell, Major Royal Artillery, *b.* 4 Dec. 1866; *m.* 21 March, 1899, Minnie Mary, dau. of Thomas Wild, of Maidenhead, and has issue,
   a. Herbert Caryl, *b.* 1900.
   b. Richard John, *b.* 4 Feb. 1909.
  2. Andrew Gore, D.S.O., District Superintendent of Police, N. Nigeria. Capt. 21st Batt. Imperial Yeomanry, *b.* 9 Sept. 1872.
  3. Gerald Lawrence, Capt. Royal Lancaster (K.O.) Regt. *b.* 31 Aug. 1877.
  1. Helen Fanny.
(6) Gordon, *d.* young.
(1) Helen Elizabeth, *b.* 1838; *m.* 1859, Brenton Halliburton Collica, of Dunorlan, Tunbridge Wells, J.P.
(2) Maria Jeffery, *m.* 25 June, 1868, Col. George W. Stockley, R.E.
(3) Alicia Harriot, *m.* 6 Feb. 1868, Rev. W. H. L. Cogswell, D.D.
(4) Mary McCawley, *m.* 21 May, 1872, Maj. Redmund Uniacke Somerville, 61st Regt.
5. Crofton, of Ballyre, co. Cork, J.P., *m.* Elizabeth, dau. of Bor Uniacke, of Woodhouse, and had issue,
  1. Crofton, of Ballyre, *m.* 1835, Esther, dau. of Percy Smyth, of Headborough, and *d.s.p.*
  1. Anne.   2. Alicia.
1. Mary, *m.* Simon Dring, of Rock Grove.
Mr. Norman Uniacke's will is dated 17 March, 1774, and, dying 1776, he was s. by his eldest son and heir,
JAMES UNIACKE, of Castletown, *m.* (settlement dated 13 Feb. 1777) Elizabeth, dau. of Simon Dring, of Rock Grove, and *d.* 1835, having had issue,
1. NORMAN, his heir.
2. James, of Glengarra, co. Cork, Major North Cork Rifles, *m.* Alicia, dau. of Simon Dring, and *d.s.p.*
1. Mary, *m.* 1799, William Crawford, of Lakelands, co. Cork.
The elder son,
NORMAN UNIACKE, of Castletown, Lieut.-Col. North Cork Rifles, *m.* 1821, Eleanor, dau. of Col. Robert Uniacke FitzGerald, of Corkbeg, M.P. (co-heir of her brother Robert, who *d.s.p.* 1832), and *d.v.p.* 1835, leaving issue,
1. ROBERT UNIACKE FITZGERALD, late of Castletown.
2. James FitzGerald, M.D., *d.s.p.*
1. Louisa. *d.* young.   2. Elizabeth Frances.
The elder son,
ROBERT UNIACKE FITZGERALD UNIACKE, of Castletown, co. Cork, *b.* 1822; *m.* 1854, Florence Elizabeth, dau. of Norman Uniacke of Mount Uniacke (*see that family*), and *d.* 6 Jan. 1903, leaving a son,
ROBERT UNIACKE FITZGERALD, present representative.

Arms *and* **Crest**—Same as UNIACKE *of Mount Uniacke* (quartering KEARNEY, PURDON, and FITZGERALD). **Motto**—Fortis et Fidelis.
Residence—

UPTON OF COOLATORE.

HENRY ARTHUR SHUCKBURGH UPTON, of Coolatore, Moate, co. Westmeath, J.P., High Sheriff, 1897 *b.* 3 March, 1870; *m.* 1897, Victoria Florence Emma, dau. of Col. George Hibbert Anchitel Kinloch, 13th Somerset L.I.

Lineage.—ARTHUR UPTON, of L'UPTON, elder brother of the Chevalier John Upton, Knight of Malta, and grandson of John Upton, of Lupton, Devon, by Joan his wife, dau. and heir of Sir Wincombe Raleigh, Knt. John Upton, of Lupton, was 4th in descent from John Upton (and Agnes his wife, sister and heir of John Peniles, of Lupton), younger son of John Upton, of Trelaske, co. Cornwall. Arthur Upton *m.* Gertrude, dau. of Hugh Fortescue, of Filleigh, and had with other issue,
1. JOHN, of whom presently.
2. HENRY, from whom derive the Viscounts Templetown (*see* BURKE's *Peerage*).

The eldest son,
JOHN UPTON, of Lupton, co. Cornwall, 1620, B.A. Lincoln Coll. Oxon, M.P. for Clifton, Dartmouth, and Hardness, *b.* 7 April, 1590; *m.* 23 Feb. 1601, Dorothy, dau. of Sir Anthony Rous. She was bur. 20 Feb. 1643. He *d.* 11 Sept. 1641, leaving issue,
1. Arthur, of Lupton, ancestor of the family of Upton of Ingmire Hall (*see* UPTON-COTTRELL-DORMER *of Ingmire*).
2. John, of London and Hadley, merchant, bapt. 22 Sept. 1616; *m.* 1st, Elizabeth, dau. of John Bence, of London. She *d.s.p.* He *m.* 2ndly, Jane, dau. of Sir John Lytcott, of Moulsey, Surrey. She was bur. 8 Aug. 1672. He was bur. 10 Dec. 1689.
3. AMBROSE, of whom presently.
4. Anthony, of Seville and Cadiz, *b.* 1621; bur. 1 Sept. 1669.
5. Gilbert, of London, *m.* Dorcas Smith. Will dated 11 Dec. 1693, proved 28 Feb. 1693-4.
6. Hugh, of London, bapt. 1 Jan. 1632; *d.* before 31 Oct. 1688, leaving issue by Anne his wife.
7. Thomas (Rev.), Rector of East Lockinge, Berks, bapt. 7 Sept. 1634; *m.* 26 May, 1673, Dorothy Lambe. Will dated 13 May, 1684, proved 4 Nov. following.
1. Elizabeth, *m.* 9 Oct. 1638, John Vaughan.
2. Dorothy.
3. Anne, *m.* 19 July, 1642, John Champness.
4. Rebecca.   5. Bridget.
6. Eleanor.
7. Phillippa, *m.* 28 June, 1653, Samuel Thomas.
8. Gertrude, bapt. 5 June, 1631.

The 3rd son,
REV. AMBROSE UPTON, M.A., All Soul's Coll. Oxon, Canon of Christchurch, *b.* 1621; *m.* Mary, dau. of Francis Charleton, of Apley Castle, Salop, and *d.* 1686, leaving issue,
1. AMBROSE, of whom presently.
2. Francis, B.A. Pembroke Coll., L.R.C.P., *b.* 1658; *m.* Sarah, dau. of Robert Norman, and *d.* 3 Sept. 1711, leaving issue.
3. Arthur, of Barbados, merchant, *m.* Sarah, dau. of Clement Heirne, of Norfolk, and had issue.
1. Mary, *m.* 1st, 20 Dec. 1667, Charles Vermuyden, and 2ndly, Sir John Maynard, and 3rdly, 22 Nov. 1691, Henry, Earl of Suffolk. She *d.* Jan. 1720-1.
2. Margaret, *m.* Thomas Norman.
3. Rebecca.   4. Arabella.

The eldest son,
AMBROSE UPTON, of Dublin, Deputy-Consul in Andalusia, *m.* 17 Nov. 1687, Jane, dau. of William Wright, of Oxford. Her will, dated 20 April, 1752, was proved 26 Nov. 1755. They had issue,
1. AMBROSE, of whom presently.
2. William.
3. Richard, of Trin. Coll. Dublin, *b.* 1692.
4. Arthur, of Ealing.   5. Thomas.
1. Jane, *m.* Jonathan Wilson.

The eldest son,
REV. AMBROSE UPTON, M.A. Camb., Rector of Kilnaboy, Kilrush, and Killimur, Treasurer of Kilfenora 1711-52, *b.* 1688; *m.* Anna, dau. of Boleyn Whitney, of Newpass, co. Westmeath. He *d.* 1752, leaving issue,
1. Francis, of Limerick, *m.* the dau. of — Burke. Will dated 4 July, 1785, was proved 7 Feb. 1786. He left issue,
  1. Ambrose Whitney, *d. unm.* May, 1790.
  2. Henry, Capt. in the Army, *d. unm.*
  1. Anna, *m.* John Dwyer, of Singland, co. Limerick.
  2. Frances, *d. unm.*
2. Ambrose, of Hermitage, co. Dublin, High Sheriff co. Fermanagh, 1789, Maj. 13th Dragoons, *m.* June, 1768, Margaret, dau. of James Gledstanes, of Fardross, co. Tyrone. She *d.* 1804, leaving issue, from whom descend the family of GLEDSTANES *of Fardross* (*see that family*).
3. HENRY, of whom presently.
1. Anna, *d. unm.*

The youngest son,

Upton.   THE LANDED GENTRY.   716

HENRY UPTON, *m.* 2 Aug. 1764, Isabella, dau. of Lieut.-Col. Christopher Clarges, Royal Irish Dragoons, youngest son of Sir Thomas Clarges, Bart., and had issue,
1. SHUCKBURGH WHITNEY, of whom presently.
2. Clarges, Capt. 43rd Regt., *d. unm.*
   1. Anna, *m.* 4 July, 1785, William Ruxton, of Ardee House, and had issue (*see that family*).
   2. Helen, *m.* 14 April, 1795, Thomas Rothwell, of Rockfield, and *d.* 17 Feb. 1800, leaving issue (*see that family*).
The elder son,
REV. SHUCKBURGH WHITNEY UPTON, B.A. Trinity Coll. Dublin 1790, Rector of Kilmoon, co. Meath, *m.* 9 March, 1795, Margaret, dau. of Lewis Francis Irwin, of Tanragoe, co. Sligo. She *d.* 1836. He *d.* 1807, leaving issue,
1. Henry, *b.* 1797 ; *d. unm.* 17 April, 1824.
2. Lewis, of whom presently.
3. Arthur Shuckburgh, of Coolatore, Moate, co. Westmeath, J.P., late Maj. Westmeath Militia, *b.* 1807 ; *m.* 1869, Alice Plunkett, eldest dau. of Rev. Robt. Hedges Plunkett Dunne, of Brittas (*see that family*). She *d.* 11 March, 1870. He *d.* 1889, leaving an only son,
HENRY ARTHUR SHUCKBURGH, now of Coolatore.
1. Elizabeth Beatrice Isabella, *m.* 22 Sept. 1829, Theophilus Edward Lucas Clements, of Rathkenny, co. Cavan, who *d.* 1852, leaving issue (*see that family*).
2. Isabella, *d. unm.*
The 2nd son,
LEWIS UPTON, of Glyde Court, co. Louth, and Stanstead Bury, Herts, formerly 4th Hussars and 9th Lancers, late Capt. Louth Rifle Militia, J.P. co. Louth, High Sheriff 1846, *b.* 3 Dec. 1805 ; *m.* 14 Aug. 1844, Isabella Sophia Georgiana, only child of William Henry Feilde, of Netherfield House, Herts. She *d.* 1865. He *d.* 1889.

Arms—Sa. a cross moline arg. ; quartering for CARNOTHER, az. three covered cups arg. ; for MULES, Arg. two bars gu. in chief three torteaux ; for TRELAWNEY, larg. chevron sa. in chief a trefoil slipped torte ; for MOHUN or a cross engrailed sa. a crescent for difference ; and for PENELLS, arg. on a chevron a fish haurient between two others chevronwise of the first. *Crest*—On a ducal coronet or a war horse courant sa. caparisoned or. *Motto*—Semper paratus.

Seat—Coolatore, Moate, co. Westmeath. *Club*—Kildare Street.

UPTON. *See* BURKE'S PEERAGE, **TEMPLETOWN, V.**

POLLARD-URQUHART OF CRAIGSTON AND CASTLE POLLARD.

LIEUT.-COL. FRANCIS EDWARD ROMULUS POLLARD URQUHART, of Craigston, co. Aberdeen, and Castle Pollard, co. Westmeath, J.P. and D.L. for both cos., and D.L. for Banffshire, High Sheriff 1901, co. Westmeath, late R.A., *b.* 8 Sept. 1848 ; *m.* 28 Nov. 1888, Louisa Henrietta (who *d.* 1 Oct. 1908), 2nd dau. of the late Garden Duff, of Hatton Castle, co. Aberdeen (*see that family*).

Lineage.—JAMES URQUHART, of Knockleigh, 3rd son of Patrick Urquhart, of Meldrum (*see that family*), *m.* Margaret, dau. of Fraser Tyrie, and was *s.* by his only son,
CAPT. JOHN URQUHART, of Craigston, who purchasing the estate of Cromarty, was designated by either title. He *m.* his cousin, Jean, dau. of William Urquhart, of Meldrum, and had issue,
1. WILLIAM, his heir.
2. James, a General Officer, who *d.s.p.*
3. John, who *d. unm.*
1. Mary, *m.* Robert Arbuthnot, of Haddo.
2. Elizabeth.
3. Jean, *m.* the Chevalier Urquhart, of Blyth.
4. Margaret, *m.* Robert Clerk, of Mavisbank.
Capt. Urquhart *d.* 1756, and was *s.* by his son,
WILLIAM URQUHART, of Craigston, who sold the estate of Cromarty. He *m.* 1st, Margaret, dau. of George Irvine, of Artamford, and had issue,
1. JOHN, his heir.
1. Jane, *m.* Francis Gregor, of Trewarthenick, Cornwall.
2. Eleanor.
Mr. Urquhart *m.* 2ndly, Margaret, dau. of A. Ogilvie, of Auchiries, and had,
2. Adam, *m.* Mary, dau. of the Right Rev. Edward Maltby, Bishop of Durham.
3. Elizabeth, *m.* J. C. Champion, Maj. 21st Regt.

4. Frances, *m.* G. Green, Capt. 21st Regt.   5. Rebecca.
He was *s.* by his elder son,
JOHN URQUHART, of Craigston, *m.* Isabella, dau. of Alexander Moir, of Scotstown, and had issue,
1. WILLIAM, his heir.   2. George, *d. unm.* in India.
3. Francis Gregory, Maj.-Gen. in the Army, C.B., *m.* 1848, Rachel Louisa, dau. of Henry David Forbes, of Balgownie (*see that family*), and *d.* 1889, leaving issue, two daus.
1. Margaret, *m.* 1825, Col. Jonathan Forbes Leslie, of Rothie Norman, late of the 78th Regt. (*see that family*), and *d.* 1882, leaving issue.
2. Eleanor, *m.* John Ardine Clegg, who *d.* 1869. She *d.* 1883.
Mr. Urquhart *d.* 1821, and was *s.* by his eldest son,
WILLIAM URQUHART, of Craigston, J.P. and D.L., *m.* Mary, dau. of Alexander Fraser, of Fraserfield, and dying March, 1847, left an only dau. and heir.
MARY ISABELLA URQUHART, of Craigston, *m.* 20 Aug. 1846, William Pollard, of Castle Pollard, co. Westmeath, J.P. and D.L., M.P. for that co., who assumed by Royal Licence the additional surname of URQUHART, and *d.* 11 Dec. 1873, leaving issue (*see* POLLARD *family below*).

Lineage (*of* POLLARD).—This ancient family was established in Ireland by CAPT. NICHOLAS POLLARD, who accompanied Robert, Earl of Essex, to Ireland, and had a grant of the castle and lands of Mayne. He is supposed to have been a younger son of Sir Lewis Pollard, of King's Nympton, co. Devon, Judge of the King's Bench, His son,
NICHOLAS POLLARD, of Castle Pollard, co. Westmeath, *b.* 1567, who built the castle of Rathyoung, since called Castle Pollard, was father of
WALTER POLLARD, of Castle Pollard, living 1637, *m.* Ismay, dau. of Richard Nugent, of Cargeen, co. Roscommon, and by her (who *m.* 2ndly, Thomas Nugent, of Clonlost, and *d.* 1685) had a son,
WALTER POLLARD, of Castle Pollard, M.P., High Sheriff co. Westmeath 1692, whose lands were erected into the Manor of Castle Pollard by letters patent, dated 36 CHARLES II. He *m.* Elizabeth, eldest dau. of Arthur Dillon, of Lismullen, co. Meath, and had one son and one dau. Mr. Pollard *d.* 1718. His only son,
DILLON POLLARD, of Castle Pollard, Barrister-at-Law, M.P. for Westmeath, *d.s.p.* His sister and heir,
LETITIA POLLARD, *m.* 1696, CHARLES HAMPSON, of Achecreevy, co. Cavan, Maj. in the Army, and High Sheriff of co. Cavan 1698 and 1715, and co. Westmeath 1729, who assumed the name and arms of POLLARD, and *d.* 1 Aug. 1729. The eldest son of this marriage,
DILLON POLLARD, of Castle Pollard, *m.* 1 Sept. 1734, Anna Maria, dau. of James Naper, of Loughcrew, co. Meath, and had an only son,
WILLIAM POLLARD, of Castle Pollard, *m.* 1st, July, 1763, Isabella, dau. and heir of John Morres, of Bodentown, co. Meath, and had by her,
1. DILLON, his heir.   2. John.
He *m.* 2ndly, 10 June, 1782, Sophia, dau. of William Bull, sister and co-heir of Rev. William Bull, of Dalkey, co. Dublin, and by her (who *d.* 1835) had issue,
3. WILLIAM DUTTON, *s.* to his brother.
1. Sophia, *m.* John Hill Forster, of Forest, co. Dublin, and *d.* 1876.
2. Anna Maria, *m.* Mathias Kenny, and *d.* 1868.
Mr. Pollard *d.* 1790, and was *s.* by his eldest son,
DILLON POLLARD, High Sheriff 1798, *d. unm.* Sept. 1803, and was *s.* by his brother,
WILLIAM DUTTON POLLARD, of Castle Pollard, Lord of the Manor of Castle Pollard, J.P. and D.L., High Sheriff 1812, *b.* 10 Oct. 1789 ; *m.* 1st, 10 May, 1811, Frances Jocelyn, 3rd dau. of Gustavus Hume Rochfort, of Rochfort, M.P. co. Westmeath, but by her had no issue ; and 2ndly, 1 Sept. 1814, Louisa Anne, eldest dau. of Admiral the Hon. Sir Thomas Pakenham, G.C.B., and by her had issue,
1. WILLIAM, late of Castle Pollard.
2. Thomas Edward, Capt. 72nd Highlanders, *b.* 1816 ; *d.* 1848.
3. Walter James, Capt. R.N., *b.* 1817 ; *m.* Jane, dau. of F. V. Keane, of Hermitage, Ennis, co. Clare, and *d.* 1879, having had issue,
    (1) Thomas Edward Pakenham, *b.* 1862 ; *d. unm.* 1905.
    (2) Charles William Dutton, Major Ordnance Dept. late Leinster Regt., *d.* 20 Feb. 1906.
    (3) Walter Marcus Louis (*Bournemouth Club, Bournemouth*), *b.* 26 April, 1870.
    (4) George Embleton Fox, *m.* Florence Glenn, of Hampstead.
4. Gustavus Dillon, Maj.-Gen., *m.* Rebecca Dysart, and *d.* 1893, leaving issue.
5. George Augustus, *m.* Annie, dau. of J. Smyth, of Leicester, and has issue ; *d.* 1866.
6. John Lucas Romulus, of H.M. 31st Regt., killed at the Battle of Moodkee, Dec. 1845.
7. Richard, *b.* 1825.
8. Charles, Lieut.-Gen. Bengal Engineers, *b.* 1826, *d.* 24 July, 1911 ; *m.* Miss Maria Cole, and has issue.
Mr. Pollard *d.* 25 Sept. 1839, and was *s.* by his eldest son,
WILLIAM POLLARD, of Castle Pollard, and of Craigston Castle, co. Aberdeen, M.A., J.P. and D.L., High Sheriff 1840, M.P. co. Westmeath from 1852-7, and 1859-71, *b.* 19 June, 1855 ; *m.* 20 Aug. 1846, Maty Isabella, only dau. and heir of William Urquhart, of Craigston Castle, co. Aberdeen, assumed, by Royal Licence, 11 June, 1847, the additional surname and arms of URQUHART, and had issue,
1. WALTER WILLIAM DUTTON, late of Castle Pollard.
2. FRANCIS EDWARD ROMULUS, now of Castle Pollard and Craigston.

3. Arthur de Capel Broke (Rev.), b. 1 April, 1850.
4. Michael Bruce, b. 25 Dec. 1851; m. June, 1875, Florence Adelino, dau. of — Billings, and d. 29 April, 1879, leaving issue, Michael Bruce, b. 15 Aug. 1879.
5. Montagu Alexis, b. 9 May, 1859; m. July, 1882, Honora Elizabeth, dau. of Rev. E. Buckley, Rector of Alderford, and has issue,
  1. William Edward, 2nd Lieut. 1st Batt. Royal Sussex Regt.
  2. Arthur Lewis.
    1. Norah, m. Jan. 1906, Lieut. A. H. Loughborough, R.A., and d.s.p. Sept. 1909.
    2. Ada.
6. Ralph Louis John, b. 29 Aug. and d. 3 Dec. 1868.
  1. Adah Mary Louisa, m. Oct. 1882, Dudley Billings, who d. Dec. 1910.
  2. Leonora Anna Maria Helen.
  3. Octavia Harriet, m. July, 1888, Charles Humphreys, M.D.
He d. 1 June, 1871; his widow, 12 Dec. 1873. The eldest son,
  WALTER WILLIAM DUTTON POLLARD-URQUHART, of Castle Pollard, co. Westmeath, J.P. and D.L., High Sheriff 1873, b. 10 July, 1847; d.s.p. 29 Dec. 1892, and was s. by his brother.

Arms—Quarterly: 1st and 4th, or, three boars' heads erased gu., armed and langued az., a mullet of the first for difference, for URQUHART; 2nd, arg., a chevron between three escallops az., for POLLARD; 3rd, arg., three hemp-brakes sa., for HAMPSON. *Crests*—1st, URQUHART, A demi-otter rampant ppr., crowned with an antique crown or, collared of the last, charged with three crescents gu.; 2nd, POLLARD, A stag trippant arg., horned or; 3rd, HAMPSON, Out of a mural coronet arg., a greyhound's head sa. collared gu., charged with three plates. *Motto*—Will well.

Seats—Castle Pollard, co. Westmeath; and Craigston Castle, Turriff, N.B. *Clubs*—United Service, Boodle's, and Junior Carlton.

USSHER OF EASTWELL.

WILLIAM ARLAND USSHER, of Eastwell, co. Galway, late Lieut. 3rd Batt. The Cameronians, b. 1876; s. his father Feb. 1884; m. 24 April, 1910, Mary Caulfeild, and has issue,
A child b. 15 Jan. 1911.

Lineage.—A voluminous pedigree of this family, and all the various branches, compiled by Sir William Betham, Ulster King of Arms, commences with
ARLAND USSHER, Bailiff of Dublin 1460-2, and Mayor 1469-71, of whom notices remain connected with the years 1462-71. He m. 1st, Alsone Taylor, by whom he had a dau., Margaret, and an only son, Thomas, who m. Elizabeth Cheevers, of Macetown, and had an only dau. and heir, Alsone, m. 1st, William Bath, of Athcarne, and 2ndly, John Bellew, of Bellewstown. Mr. Ussher m. 2ndly, Anne Berford, and had issue, four sons,
1. JOHN, Sheriff of Dublin 1524, m. Johanna, dau. of William Foster, of Killeigh, and was ancestor of USSHER *of Santry*, HENRY USSHER, Archbishop of Armagh, ROBERT USSHER, Bishop of Kildare, and JAMES USSHER, Archbishop of Armagh, the illustrious scholar and divine. 2. Robert, d.s.p.
3. Philip, d.s.p.
4. CHRISTOPHER, of whom hereafter.
The 4th and youngest son,
CHRISTOPHER USSHER, Mayor of Dublin 1518 and 1524, d. 30 Jan. 1526. He m. 1st, Maud Darcy, who d.s.p. 1523, and 2ndly, Alison, dau. of Thomas Fitzwilliam, of Merrion, by whom, who m. 2ndly, James Fitzsimons, of Dublin, merchant, and 3rdly, Alderman James Segrave, of Dublin, he had a son,
JOHN USSHER, Mayor of Dublin 1561, collector of the customs of Dublin, *Michaelmas* 1564, d. 1 May, 1600. He m. Alison, dau. of William Newman, Mayor of Dublin, by whom (who d. 1601) he had, with a son, Christopher, who d. young, a successor,
SIR WILLIAM USSHER, Knt., of Donnybrook, b. 1588, Clerk of the Council, knighted by Sir George Cary, Lord Deputy of Ireland, 25 July, 1603. He m. 1st, Isabella, dau. of Adam Loftus, Lord Chancellor of Ireland, and Archbishop of Dublin, who d. 11 Nov. 1597, and 2ndly, Margaret, dau. of Edward Cludde, of Orleton, co. Salop, widow of George Goodman, of St. John's, who d.s.p. 8 Sept. 1603. By his 1st wife he had issue,
1. ARTHUR, his heir.
2. Adam, Ulster King of Arms 1632, d. 1 July, 1633.
1. Mary, m. William Crofton, of Temple House, co. Sligo.
2. Jane, d. 17 May, 1674, m. Daniel Molyneux, Ulster King of Arms, who d. 13 June, 1632.
3. Margaret, m. Sir Beverley Newcomen, Knt., of Moystown.
4. Alice, d. 1 April, 1671; m. Sir Thomas Phillips, Knt., of Newtownlimavady.
5. Elinor, m. Charles Forster, Mayor of Dublin.

6. Anne, d. 12 May, 1669; m. Sir Robert Meredith, Chancellor of the Exchequer, who d. 17 Oct. 1668.
Sir William, whose will is dated 28 Dec. 1657, was s. by his grandson, son of his eldest son,
ARTHUR USSHER, of Donnybrook, m. Judith, dau. of Sir Robert Newcomen, Knt., of Moystown, by whom (who d. 1652) he had issue,
1. WILLIAM (Sir), his heir. 2. James, d.s.p.
3. John, d.s.p. 4. Adam, d.s.p.
5. Beverley of Kimeadon, co. Waterford, d. 1683; m. 1st, Joan, dau. of Sir Percy Smith, Knt., of Ballynatray, by whom he had a dau., Mary, m. Francis Smyth, of Rathcourcy; and 2ndly, Grace, dau. of Sir Richard Osborne, 1st bart., of Ballyntaylor, co. Waterford, by whom he had issue,
  1. Beverley, M.P. for Waterford, d. 1756; m. 1st, 26 March, 1733, Mary, dau. of Nicholas Lysaght, and had a son, Beverley of Kilmeadon, who d. 1756, and a dau., Mary, m. April, 1758, John Congreve, of Mount Congreve (*see that family*). He m. 2ndly, Elizabeth, sister of Edmond Shuldham, and had a dau., Elizabeth Katherine, m. 6 Sept. 1766, Henry Alcock, of Wilton.
  2. James, of Ballyntaylor, m. Jane, dau. of Edmund Donellan, and had issue,
    (1) John, M.P. for Dungarvan, d.s.p. 1747.
    (2) Arthur (Rev.), went to America.
    (3) Beverley, m. 1750, 1st, Melian, dau. of James Roche, of Glynn, and had,
      1. John, of Canty, m. Susanna, dau. of John Hearne, and had issue,
        1. Melian (Mrs. Hearns).
      2. Jane, m. John Boate, of Duckspool.
      3. Isabella, m. Roger Dalton.
      4. Anne, m. Thomas Grant, of Kilmurry.
      5. Jane, m. John Osborne Odell, of Mount Odell.
      6. Isabella, m. Jonas Blackall.
      7. Susan, m. Christopher Musgrave, of Tourin.
He m. 2ndly, Mary, dau. of Ambrose Congreve, of Mount Congreve, and had another dau.,
    8. Rebecca, m. Ambrose Power, of Barretstown.
  3. John, M.P. for Carrick, d. 1741; m. Hon. Mary St. George, and had issue,
    St George Usher, ST. GEORGE, Lord St. George, m. Elizabeth, dau. of Christopher Dominick, and had a dau., Emily, m. 4 Nov. 1775, William Robert, 2nd Duke of Leinster, and had issue (*see* BURKE's *Peerage*, LEINSTER, D.).
    Olivia, m. 1736, Arthur French, of Tyrone, co. Galway, and had issue.
  4. ARTHUR, ancestor of USSHER *of Camphire*.
    1. Judith, m. Robert Taylor, of Ballynort, co. Limerick.
    2. Isabel, m. Edmund Hubbart, of Waterford.
    3. Anne, m. 1st, Sir Thomas Osborne, 4th bart., of Ballyntaylor, and 2ndly, Francis Skiddy, of Dublin.
6. Christopher, d. young. 7. Philip, d. young.
1. Margaret, m. Sir Paul Davys, Knt., Clerk of the Council, 2nd d. 20 July, 1633.
2. Catherine, d. 2 Jan. 1681; m. Sir Philip Perceval, Knt., ancestor of the Earl of Egmont.
3. Isabella, m. 1635, Sir Percy Smyth, Knt., of Ballynatray.
4. Alice, d. 1684; m. Sir Theophilus Jones, Knt., of Osberstown.
Mr. Ussher was drowned in the river Dodder, 2 March, 1628, v.p., when he was s. by his eldest son,
SIR WILLIAM USSHER, Knt., of Portrane, co. Dublin, and of the Castle of Grange, co. Wicklow, knighted 26 May, 1636. m. 1st, Elizabeth, dau. of Sir William Parsons, Bart., Lord Justice of Ireland, and by her (who d. 29 Nov. 1638) had issue,
1. Arthur, d.s.p.
2. Christopher, of Dublin, d. Jan. 1706; m. Martha, dau. of Thomas Pigott, of Long Ashton, and had issue,
  1. William, d. 1718; m. Lettice, dau. and co-heir of Sir Henry Waddington, Knt., of Clostokin, co. Galway, and had four sons (1) William; (2) Henry; (3) Christopher; (4) John, all of whom d.s.p., and two daus. (1) Martha, m. Anthony Marlay, of Dublin, and (2) Dorothy.
  2. Henry, Barrister-at-Law, m. 1739, Frances, dau. of William Waring, of Waringstown, and d.s.p.
    1. Martha, d. July, 1751; m. 1st, Nehemiah Donellan, Chief Baron of the Exchequer, and 2ndly, Philip Perceval, brother of John, 1st Earl of Egmont.
    2. Florence. 3. Elizabeth. 4. Mary Anne.
1. Margaret, m. Richard Neville.
2. Judith, m. Sir James Wemyss, Knt., and d. 11 Oct. 1674.
3. Elizabeth, d. unm. 1675.
Sir William m. 2ndly, 14 May, 1645, Ursula, dau. of Capt. George St. Barbe, of the House of White Parish, Wilts, and had issue,
3. JOHN, of whom presently. 4. William, d. 25 Nov. 1647.
5. Adam (Rev.), Archdeacon of Clonfert, m. Rebecca Wye, who d. 8 Aug. 1695, and had issue; Frederick (Rev.), m. Martha Cope, and d. in 1766; and eight other children.
6. Arthur. 7. Henry, d. 1658.
4. Mary, m. 1674, Henry Colley, of Castle Carberry, and was mother of Richard, 1st Lord Mornington.
5. Frances, d. young.
Sir William d. April, 1671. His 3rd son, but the eldest of his 2nd marriage,
JOHN USSHER, of Mount Ussher, Master-in-Chancery, m. 13 Oct. 1681, Alice, dau. of Samuel Molyneux, 3rd son of Daniel Molyneux, Ulster King of Arms, by whom his wife, dau. of Sir William Usher, Knt., of Donnybrook, and had issue,
1. CHRISTOPHER, his heir. 2. John.
3. Samuel (Rev.), Rector of Dungarstown, co. Wicklow, b. 1694, entered Trin. Coll. Dublin, 9 July, 1714, aged 20, M.A. 1722; m.

Frances Walsh, and had, with three daus. (Frances, *m.* Thomas Ball, of Seapark, co. Wicklow; Alicia, *m.* William West, co. Wicklow; Katherine, *m.* 1st, — Sheppard, and 2ndly, William Phillimore), four sons,
  1. William, Capt. R.N., lost at sea off Scilly.
  2. Thomas, Capt. 16th Regt. of Foot, *m.* Rebecca, dau. of Rev. William Walsh, and *d.s.p.*
  3. John (Rev.), *m.* May, 1764, Katherine, dau. of Rev. John Humble, and had three sons,
    (1) John (Ven.), D.D., Archdeacon of Raphoe, 30 Aug. 1818, *d.s.p.* 1835.   (2) Cornelius.
    (3) Henry (Rev.), D.D., Fellow of Trin. Coll. Dublin, *m.* his cousin, Rebecca, dau. of Rev. Henry Ussher, D.D., and had, 1, Henry ; 2, Thomas ; 3, William ; 4, Samuel ; 5, James ; 1, Frances ; 2, Maria.
  (4) Henry (Rev.), D.D., Senior Fellow Trin. Coll. Dublin, Astronomer-Royal, Ireland, *m.* Mary Burne, and had, with five daus., 1, Frances ; 2, Margaret ; 3, Sarah ; 4, Rebecca ; 5, Alicia ; and two younger sons, John, and Henry, who both *d.s.p.*, an elder son,
  SIR THOMAS USSHER, Knt., C.B., K.C.H., Rear-Admiral of the Blue, *b.* 1779 ; Midshipman R.N. 27 Jan. 1791, Capt. of the *Redwing*, 18 guns, 18 Oct. 1806, and of the *Undaunted*, 38 guns, 2 Feb. 1813, in which ship he conveyed NAPOLEON I to Elba 28 April, 1814. Sir Thomas *m.* Elizabeth, dau. of Thomas Foster, of Grove House, co. Buckingham, and *d.* 6 Jan. 1848, having had issue,
    a. Thomas Neville, H.M. Chargé d'Affaires and Consul-General at Hayti, *m.* Eliza, dau. of Capt. Fawsett, and *d.* 13 April, 1885, leaving a son, Herbert Taylor, whose dau. *m.* Major Charles Talbot Davenport ; and two daus., Adelaide Juliana Lucinda, *m.* Gen. Robert Hughes ; and Haitiana, *m.* Col. Augustus Staveley Murray.
    b. Sydney Henry, Capt. R.N. 23 Nov. 1846, served on the North American and West Indian stations, *d. unm.*
    c. Edward Pellew Hammett, Major Royal Marines, served in Scinde 1839, and in the wars in China 1840–2, and with the Baltic Fleet (Russian war) 1854–5 ; *m.* Charlotte Maria, dau. of Rev. E. Duke, of Lake House, Wilts, and *d.s.p.* His widow *m.* 2ndly, Col. R. S. Cole, 1st Argyll and Sutherland Highlanders.
    d. William, R.N., *m.* Miss Clarke, and *d.* leaving two sons.
      a. Caroline, *m.* Rev. Neville Parry, and *d.* 1 March, 1884.
      b. Elizabeth, *m.* Rev. I. St. George Williams.
      c. Frances, *d.* young.
    4. William, *d.* young.
  4. Thomas, *b.* 4 Nov. 1704 ; *d.s.p.*
  1. Mary, *b.* 9 Oct. 1691.   2. Alice.
  3. Letitia, *b.* 1693.
  4. Jane, *m.* Ross Mahon, of Castlegar, co. Galway.
Mr. Ussher *d.* 10 March, 1745. His eldest son,
CHRISTOPHER USSHER, of Mount Ussher, co. Wicklow, *d.* Sept. 1763 ; *m.* 22 Feb. 1715, Elizabeth, dau. of Benjamin Chedwode, M.P. for Harristown and had issue,
  1. JOHN, his heir.   2. William, *d.s.p.*
  3. Christopher, of Eastwell, co. Galway, *d.* 1772 ; *m.* Margaret Bailie, and had issue,
    1. CHRISTOPHER, of whom hereafter.
    2. John, Capt. in the Army, settled in Canada, *m.* Mary, dau. of — Street, and had issue,
      (1) John.   (2) Edgeworth.
      (3) Samuel.
      (1) Margaret, *m.* Thanet Thompson.
      (2) Harriet, *m.* George Mitchell.
      (3) Mary, *m.* 1831, her cousin, John Ussher, of Eastwell, and had issue (*see below*).
    1. Katherine.   2. Alice.
    3. Martha, *m.* Robert Edgeworth, of Firmount, co. Longford.
    4. Jane, *m.* 18 June, 1753, George Rowan, of Drumbeg, co. Wicklow.
Mr. Ussher *d.* 1756, and was *s.* by his eldest son,
JOHN USSHER, of Mount Ussher, and of Eastwell, co. Galway, M.P. for Inistioge 1783–90, who *d.s.p.* 1796. High Sheriff co. Wicklow 1764. His nephew,
CHRISTOPHER USSHER, of Eastwell, inherited that estate, and *m.* July, 1797, Ellis, dau. of James Browne, of Browne Hall, co. Mayo, by whom (who *d.* 1820) he had issue,
  1. JOHN, his heir.
  2. Christopher (Rev.), *d.* 1859 ; *m.* Elizabeth, dau. of Richard Crane Brush, of Gill Hall, co. Down, and had issue,
    1. Arland.   2. Christopher James.
    1. Caroline.   2. Ada.
  3. William, *d.s.p.*
  1. Ellis, *m.* 25 Oct. 1817, Xaverius Blake, of Orane Castle, co. Galway.
  2. Honoria, *m.* John Donellan, of Ballydonellan Castle, co. Galway.
Mr. Ussher was *s.* by his eldest son,
JOHN USSHER, of Eastwell, *m.* 1831, his cousin Mary, dau. of Capt. John Ussher, of Canada (*see above*), and had issue,
  1. CHRISTOPHER, his heir.
  2. John, *d.* 1878 ; *m.* Isabella, dau. of Capt. Dillon, of Johnstown, and *d.* 1878, having had issue, two sons and three daus.
  3. Edmund Augustus, *d.* young.
  4. William Augustus Edmund.
  1. Mary, *m.* Stewart Johnston, M.D.
  2. Ellis Belinda' *d. unm.* March, 1825.
Mr. Ussher *d.* 24 April, 1851, and was *s.* by his eldest son,

CHRISTOPHER USSHER, of Eastwell, *b.* 1832 ; *m.* 1873, Olivia, dau. of David Ruttledge, of Barbersfort, co. Galway, and had issue,
  1. WILLIAM ARLAND, now of Eastwell.
  2. Christopher, *d.* 10 Sept. 1880.
  3. Henry Ingham, *b.* 10 Feb. 1879.
  1. Agnes Mary Eleanor, *m.* 1 June, 1901, Francis Manley Shawe-Taylor, younger son of Walter T. N. Shawe-Taylor, of Castle Taylor, and has issue (*see that family*).
  2. Olivia Ellis, *m.* July, 1901, George Arthur Boyd-Rochfort, of Middleton Park, Westmeath (*see that family*).
  3. Alison, *m.* 7 July, 1902, Frederick Charles Maitland Freake, only surviving son of Sir Thomas G. Freake, 2nd bart. (*see* BURKE's *Peerage*).
Mr. Ussher *d.* 21 Feb. 1884.

Arms—Az., a chevron erm. between three batons or. Crest—An arm couped below the elbow and erect, vested bendy or and az., holding in the hand ppr. a baton or. Motto—Ne vile velis.
Seat—Eastwell, Kilrickle, Loughrea, co. Galway.

USSHER OF CAPPAGH.

RICHARD JOHN USSHER, of Cappagh House, co. Waterford, J.P. and D.L., High Sheriff 1901, *b.* 6 April, 1841 ; *m.* 20 Jan. 1866, Elizabeth Owen, eldest dau. of Rev. John W. Finlay, J.P., of Corkagh House, co. Dublin (*see that family*), and has had issue,
  1. BEVERLEY GRANT, *b.* 19 Feb. 1867 ; *m.* 15 Oct. 1898, Emily Horseley, eldest dau. of the late Arthur Trevor Jebb, of The Lyth, Ellesmere, Salop, and has issue,
    Perceval Arland, *b.* 9 Sept. 1899.
  2. Percy John, *b.* 28 Aug. 1868 ; *d.* Dec. 1903.
  3. Arthur Hamilton, *b.* 14 Sept. 1869 ; *d.* 13 Dec. 1906.
  4. Neville Osborne, *b.* 23 Aug. 1873 ; *d.* 5 March, 1880.
  5. Isabella Mary Grant, *b.* 20 May, 1871 ; *m.* 23 March, 1901, Capt. William Odell, late Innis. Fus., son of the late Edward Odell, of Carriglea, co. Waterford, and has issue,
    1. Isabel Mary, *b.* 11 Aug. 1902.
    2. Ruth Violet, *b.* 6 July, 1904.

Lineage.—This family is a branch of USSHER *of Mount Ussher* (*see preceding memoir*).
ARTHUR USSHER, of Cappagh and Camphire (4th son of BEVERLEY USSHER, of Kilmeadon, and grandson of ARTHUR USSHER, of Donnybrook, by Judith Newcomen his wife), *m.* Lucy, dau. of Berkeley Taylor, of Askeaton, co. Limerick, and left, with other issue, two daus., Sarah, *m.* Richard Keily, of Strancally, whose grandson, Arthur Keily, assumed by Royal Licence, 1843, the surname of USSHER ; Judith, *m.* 1st, 1 49, Edmund Shuldham; 2ndly, John Creagh ; and a son,
JOHN USSHER, of Cappagh, *b.* 1743 ; *m.* 1st, 8 June, 1761, Elizabeth, dau. of Christopher Musgrave, of Ballyin, and sister of Sir Richard Musgrave, 1st bart., of Tourin, and had by her,
  1. Arthur, of Camphire, *b.* 30 March, 1764 ; *m.* 3 Jan. 1788, Margaret, dau. of the Rev. John Hewetson, J.P., of Suirville, and left at his decease nine daus. and three sons, the eldest of whom, Christopher Musgrave Ussher, of Camphire, co. Waterford, *m.* 7 Dec. 1833, Eleanor, dau. of Thomas O'Grady, and niece of Standish, 1st Viscount Guillamore, and *d.* 2 Dec. 1880, having by her (who *d.* 22 March, 1897) had issue,
    (1) Arthur Edward, of Camphire, J.P. co. Waterford, *b.* 1835 ; *m.* 1st, 25 April, 1861, Annie Julia, dau. of William Henry Hassard, Recorder of Waterford ; 2ndly, 15 Feb. 1876, Kate Emilie, dau. of George Henry Adams, and *d.* 15 May, 1903, leaving issue.
    (2) Thomas O'Grady, of Flower Hill, co. Waterford, *b.* 28 June, 1838 ; *d.* 27 March, 1908 ; *m.* 14 Jan. 1869, Henrietta Mary, only dau. of Thomas Harris, Q.C., and by her (who *d.* 1902) had issue, Christopher Arthur, *b.* 25 Feb. 1872 ; Thomas Harris, *b.* 30 Sept. 1878 ; Gertrued Elizabeth, *d.* 5 Dec. 1907 ; Eleanor Melian ; and Henrietta Anne.
  1. Sarah, *m.* Dec. 1790, Ussher Boate, of Duckspool, and *d.s.p.*
Mr. Ussher *m.* 2ndly, 26 Aug. 1770, Elizabeth, dau. of Alderman William Paul, and *d.* 8 March, 1789, leaving (with other issue) by her,
  2. RICHARD KEILY, of Cappagh.
  3. John, of Landscape, co. Wexford, *m.* Lucy, dau. of the Rev. William Glascott, of Pilltown, co. Wexford, and *d.* 16 Feb. 1844, leaving issue by her (who *d.* 30 March, 1863),
    1. John Glascott, of Landscape, Barrister-at-Law, J.P. co. Wexford, *d. unm.* 12 June, 1863.
    2. Richard, of Landscape, *b.* 1818 ; *m.* 1st, 1849, Charlotte, dau. of Rev. James Metge, and widow of Robert Livingstone, and by her (who *d.* 1875) had a son, John Richard, *b.* 1851, and *d.* young, and a dau., Lucy Cassandra, *b.* 1856 ; *d.* 25 March, 1867. He *m.* 2ndly, 5 Aug. 1876, Mary, dau. of William Hales Carroll, of Harcourt Street, Dublin, and by her has issue, Richard Neville, *b.* 7 Oct. 1882.
    3. Arthur Beverley, settled in Australia.
    4. William Neville, *m.* Maryanne, dau. of Jasper Grant, and has issue. Their son William settled in New Zealand. Their 2nd dau., Lucy Glascott, *d.* 9 Jan. 1885.
      1. Elizabeth, *d. unm.* 15 Aug. 1861.   2. Sarah.
      3. Lucy Arabella, *d. unm.*   4. Mary.
      5. Susan Emily, *m.* 8 Aug. 1849, Adam Glascott, 4th son of John Glascott, of Killowen.

6. Charlotte, *d.* 23 June, 1910; *m.* 13 July, 1867, Rev. J. F. Metge ffrench.
7. Isabella, *d. unm.*
2. Elizabeth.
3. Lucy.
4. Judith.
5. Susanna.

The eldest surviving son of the 2nd marriage,
RICHARD KEILY USSHER, of Cappagh, *b.* 4 Feb. 1778; *m.* 1st, Martha, dau. of Rev. John Hewetson, J.P., of Suirville, and 2ndly, 2 Feb. 1836, Isabella (who *d.* 20 July, 1881), dau. of Col. Jasper Grant, 41st Regt., Governor of Upper Canada and Lieut.-Governor of Carlisle (of the Grants of Kilmurry, co. Cork). By the latter, he left at his decease, 25 Feb. 1854, a son and successor, the present RICHARD JOHN USSHER, of Cappagh.

Arms and *Crest*—Same as USSHER *of Eastwell. Motto*—*Amor vincit omnia.*

Seat—Cappagh House, Cappagh, S.O., co. Waterford.

VANDELEUR OF KILRUSH.

ALEXANDER MOORE VANDELEUR, of Kilrush, and Cahiracon, co. Clare, J.P., Capt. 2nd Life Guards, *b.* 25 Dec. 1885; *s.* his father 1909; *m.* 3 Nov. 1910, Hon. Violet Ethel Meyscy-Thompson, eldest dau. of Henry Meysey, 1st Lord Knaresborough (see BURKE'S *Peerage*), and has issue,
GILES ALEXANDER MEYSEY, *b.* 2 Sept. 1911.

Lineage.—GILES VANDELEUR, settled at Rathlahine, co. Clare, 1660, and was one of the commissioners for aplotting quit-rents in Ireland. He *m.* a dau. of Col. John Jephson, of Mallow, M.P., and Bridget his wife, dau. of Richard Boyle, Archbishop of Tuam, and had issue,
1. James, of Blane, who left issue.
2. JOHN, of whom presently.
3. Boyle, High Sheriff 1706, *m.* Miss Spaight, of Lodge, co. Clare, and had issue,
  1. Thomas, *m.* 20 Dec. 1754, Elizabeth, dau. of Odell Conyers, of Castletown.
  2. Giles, of Rathlahine, co. Clare, *d.* 12 June, 1762; *m.* Alice, sister of Col. Edward Fitzgerald, of Carrigoran, co. Clare, and had issue,
    Boyle, of Rathlahine, co. Clare, Col. in the Army, *m.* Diana, dau. of John Scott, of Cahircon, and had issue, two sons and four daus.,
    1. John Scott, *m.* Emily, dau. of Arthur Maloy of Woodstock, and by her had issue,
      a. Boyle.
      b. Arthur, Maj. R.A., of Rathlahine, *m.* 3 Jan. 1856, Mary, dau. of James Molony of Kiltanon (see that *family*). He *d.* 1860, leaving issue,
        (a) Lucy, *d.* 19 Dec. 1911; *m.* 1881, A. B. Stoney, LL.D., Barrister-at-Law, and has issue.
        (b) Emily Harriet, *m.* 29 April, 1884, Lord George Herbert Loftus, and *d.* 27 Nov. 1886, leaving issue (see BURKE'S *Peerage*, ELY, M.).
      a. Louisa Selina, *m.* James Maximillan Gordon, and had issue.
      b. Diana.
      c. Emily.
    2. Bindon.
    1. Elizabeth.
    2. Mary Diana, *m.* her cousin, the Rev. William Vandeleur, and had issue (see *post*).
    3. Hannah Villiers, *m.* William Boyd, M.D., and had issue.
    4. Jane, *m.* John Carrol Peach, and had issue.
    Anne, *m.* 1776, James Creagh, of Cahirbane, and has issue (see that *family*).
  3. Boyle, *m.* May, 1754, Catherine Arthur, and had issue,
    (1) Walter, R.N.
    (2) William, Lieut.-Gen. late 16th Regt., *m.* Euphemia, dau. of Col. William Caulfeild, of Benown (see BURKE'S *Peerage*, CHARLEMONT, V.), and by her (who *m.* 2ndly, J. Cary) had issue.
    Grace Anna Maria, *d. unm.* May, 1883.
    (3) Thomas.
    (1) Eleanor.
    (2) Anna Maria, *d. unm.* 1831.

The 2nd son,
REV. JOHN VANDELEUR, M.A., of Cragg, co. Clare, Rector of Kilrush, seated himself at Kilrush 1687, *m.* Elizabeth, dau. and co-heir of Thomas Crofton, of Inchirourke, co. Limerick, by whom (who *d.* 1703) he left (his will was dated 19 Aug. 1726, and proved 13 March, 1727), besides a younger son, Thomas, who *m.* Miss Cophson, and *d.s.p.*, an eldest son,
JOHN VANDELEUR, of Kilrush, *m.* Frances, dau. of John Ormsby, of Cloghans, co. Mayo, and *d.* 1754. His will dated 9 April, was proved 9 Nov. 1754. He had issue,

1. CROFTON, his heir.
2. John Ormsby, of Maddenstown co. Kildare, *m.* June, 1766, Frances Pakenham, dau. of Thomas, Lord Longford, and dying 1777, left two sons,
  1. John Ormsby, Lieut.-Col. 5th Dragoon Guards, of Maddenstown, Kildare, and of Ballinamona, co. Limerick, *m.* Rosetta Beattie, and had issue,
    (1) John, of Mannister, co. Limerick, Col. 10th Hussars, *m.* Alice, widow of the Rev. Charles Moore Stewart, and dau. of Right Hon. J. O. Vandeleur, of Kilrush, P.C. (see *below*), and had issue by her (who *d.* 21 Dec. 1884),
      1. Crofton, C.E., *d. unm.*
      2. John Ormsby, of Ballinacourty, C.B., late Capt. Rifle Brigade, Col. Commanding 4th Vol. Batt. Hampshire Regt., *b.* 1839; *m.* 15 Nov. 1870, Frederica Jane, 4th dau. of Charles William Beauclerk, grandson of the 5th Duke of St. Albans (see BURKE'S *Peerage*). He *d.* 9 June, 1900, having had issue,
        a. John Beauclerk, 2nd Lieut. Durham Light Infantry, *b.* 1887.
        a. Alice Caroline, *m.* 17 Nov. 1896, Thomas Frederic Wodehouse, of Hunstrete House, Pendsford, Somerset, He *d.* 9 Dec. 1908, leaving issue (see BURKE'S *Peerage*, KIMBERLEY, E.).
        b. Marie Frederica.
        c. Evelyn Rose.
        d. Janetta.
      1. Rosetta Anne, *m.* 4 May, 1864, John Lecky Phelps, of Waterpark, co. Limerick, who *d.* 28 May, 1881, leaving issue (see that *family*).
      2. Frances Dorothea, *m.* 12 Nov. 1861, Dawson Westropp, of Mellon, co. Limerick (see that *family*).
      3. Emily, *m.* 12 Oct. 1876, Col. James Hay Fraser, Bengal Staff Corps, brother of 17th Baron Saltoun (see BURKE'S *Peerage*).
      4. Alice, *m.* — Gubbins, and is deceased.
      5. Elizabeth Agnes, *m.* 1876, John Ulick Bourke, son of Richard Bourke, of Thornfields (see that *family*).
    (2) Robert, of Springfort, co. Cork, Lieut.-Col., *m.* Penepole Hill, and had issue,
      1. John Ormsby, C.B., Maj.-Gen. late Royal Sussex Regt., *b.* 5 April, 1832, and *d.* 1908.
      2. Francis, *d.* young.
      1. Penelope, *d. unm.*
      2. Mary Elizabeth, *d. unm.* 10 June, 1904.
      3. Alice, *m.* Capt. Philip Douglas.
    (3) Edward, 12th Lancers, left issue by Mary, his wife,
      1. Edward, 2nd Dragoon Guards, *m.* 1904, Catherine Stewart, dau. of Stewart Charles Dixon.
      2. David Roche, Lieut.-Col. late 30th Regt., *b.* 26 April, 1840.
      1. Mary.
    (4) Thomas Pakenham, Capt. 21st Regt., *m.* 1st, 1827, Mary, dau. of Sir Fitzwilliam Barrington, Bart. She *d.* 1829. He *m.* 2ndly, 26 Aug. 1854, Frances Lucy, dau. of the Ven. William Wray Maunsell, Archdeacon of Limerick (see MAUNSELL *of Thorpe Malsor*). She *d.* 1891. He *d.* 1875, leaving surviving issue,
      1. Frank Edward, *m.* 1875, Emily, dau. of Edward N. Conant, of Lyndon, co. Rutland, and *d.* 1900, leaving issue,
        a. Thomas Pakenham, *b.* 1878.
        a. Evelyn, *m.* 1 Feb. 1906, Charles Harold, son of Charles Francis Tetley, M.A., J.P. West Riding of Headingly, Leeds.
        b. Sheila.
      2. Frederick Edmund, *m.* 1877, Caroline, dau. of Rev. J. Henderson, and has issue,
        Ormsby, *b.* 1879.
        Tara.
      3. Cecil Ernest, *m.* 1st, 1887, Eva Alice, dau. of William Roche (see BURKE'S *Peerage*, ROCHE, Bart.). She *d.* 1893. He *m.* 2ndly, 1895, Gertrude, dau. of the late Thomas Borron Myers, of Porter's Park, Herts, and has issue,
        Cecil Ronald Pakenham, *b.* 1896.
      1. Edith Lucy, *m.* 1892, William Daubeny, of Bath, who *d.* 1902.
      2. Adelaide Louisa, *m.* 1874, Wilton Allhusen, of Pinhay, co. Devon, and has issue (see that *family*).
      3. Alice Gertrude, *m.* 19 Aug. 1875, Augustus Edward Burdon, of Hartford House, Northumberland. He *d.* 29 Dec. 1908, leaving issue (see that *family*).
      4. Georgina, *m.* 1885, Lieut.-Col. George Goring Sutton Jones, Indian Staff Corps, who *d.* Oct. 1900.
    (5) George, of Ballynamona, co. Limerick, sometime Inniskilling Dragoons, *m.* Augusta (*d.* 9 Nov. 1883), dau. of Robert Holden, of Nuttall Temple (see that *family*). He *d.* 19 March, 1884, having had issue,
      1. Ormsby, *d.* 1883.
      2. Gerald Ormsby (Rev.), of Ballynamona, M.A., Chaplain to the Forces, Rector of Revenstone, Ashby-de-la-Zouche, *m.* 6 July, 1868, MaryCharlotte (*d.* 28 March, 1911), dau. of the Hon. Henry Martley, Q.C., Judge of the Landed Estates Court, Ireland (see that *family*), and *d.* 24 May, 1903, leaving issue,
        a. Gerald Claude, late of Ballynamona, B.A., *b.* 9 Nov. 1869; *m.* 9 Oct. 1900, Edith Banner, dau. of John Forshaw, of Hurst Grange, Preston.
        b. Henry Martley, Capt. R.A., *b.* 12 Dec. 1875.
        a. Mabel Alice Mary.
        b. Emmeline Augusta.
      2. George Crofton Ormsby, *d.* 1873.

3. Edward Pakenham Ormsby, d. 1873.
4. Arthur Ormsby, d. 1886.
1. Rosa Augusta, m. 16 March, 1858, James Henry Brabazon, of Mornington House, co. Meath, and had issue (see BURKE's *Peerage*, MEATH, E.). She d. 24 Feb. 1859.
2. Ellen, d. 1857.   3. Florence, d. 1885.
4. Kathleen, d. unm. 28 March, 1901.
5. Constance Eva, m. 5 Jan 1886, Henry Frederick Martley, son of Henry Martley, Judge of the Land Court, Ireland (see that family).
(1) Frances, m. 14 Feb. 1825, Sir David Roche, Bart., and d. Sept. 1841, leaving issue (see BURKE's *Peerage*).
(2) Elizabeth, m. 8 June, 1826, William Cox, of Ballynoe, and had issue (see that family). She d. 5 Feb. 1872. He d. 19 April, 1879.
2. Thomas Pakenham, Maj.-Gen.: killed at Delhi.
3. Richard, of Rutland, Queen's Co., Capt. 9th Lancers, m. Elinor, dau. of John Firman, of Firmount, and d. 1772, leaving issue,
1. John Ormsby (Sir), Gen., G.C.B., b. 1763, m. 1829, Catherine, dau. of Rev. John Glasse, and d. 1849, leaving issue,
(1) Richard, d. unm.
(1) Mary.
(2) Ellen, m. Col. Greaves.
1. Elizabeth, m. — Moore, and d.s.p.
4. Ellen, m. William Armstrong, and had issue.
1. Mary, m. 13 May, 1771, John Meares, of Meares Court, who d.s.p. 1790 (see that family).

His eldest son,

CROFTON VANDELEUR, of Kilrush, m. 28 March, 1765, Alice, dau. of Thomas Burton (uncle of Francis Pierpoint Burton, 2nd Lord Conyngham), by Dorothy his wife, dau. of the Right Hon. John Forster, Chief Justice of the Common Pleas in Ireland, and by her had issue,
1. JOHN ORMSBY, his heir.
2. Thomas Burton, one of the Judges of the King's Bench in Ireland, d.s.p. 1835.
3. Crofton, Major-Gen. in the Army, m. 1803, Elizabeth, 2nd dau. of Col. Richard Croasdaile, of Rhyn, Queen's Co. She d. Jan. 1860. He d. at Antigua, Oct. 1806, leaving an only son,
Crofton Thomas Croasdaile, of Wardenstown, co. Westmeath, late Capt. 34th Regt., m. 11 Nov. 1835, Elizabeth Emily, eldest dau. of the Right Hon. Maurice FitzGerald, Knight of Kerry. She d. 10 April, 1860. He d. 13 Aug. 1876, leaving an only child,
Crofton Thomas Burton, of Wardenstown, Killucan, co. Westmeath, and Moyville, Athenry, co. Galway, late Capt. 12th Lancers, J.P. co. Westmeath, High Sheriff 1880, b. 20 Feb. 1842; m. 7 Oct. 1868, Hon. Mary Letitia (Maletta) Yelverton (who d. 15 March, 1910), dau. of Barry John, 3rd Viscount Avonmore, and d.s.p. 13 June, 1881.
4. Richard, Major 88th Regt., d. unm.
5. Frederick, Capt. 87th Regt., killed at the battle of Vittoria.
6. William Richard (Rev.), Rector of Julianstown, b. 1787, m. 1827, Mary Diana, dau. of Col. Boyle Vandeleur, of Rahaline, co. Clare (see ante). She d. 1881. He d. Aug. 1843, leaving issue,
1. Thomas Burton, Major 7th Fus., b. 1 April, 1836; killed at Kandahar, 26 Aug. 1880.
2. Boyle, Col. late 5th Lancers, of Moyville, Athenry, co. Galway, b. 13 March, 1837; m. 8 Feb. 1876, Sarah Christiana, only dau. of Major Henry Peach Keigley, of Idlicote, and widow of Capt. the Hon. Lucius Cary, only son of 10th Viscount Falkland. He d.s.p. 12 April, 1898. She d. 4 Oct. 1902.
3. William Richard, of Moyville, co. Galway, Col. late 9th Regt., s. his brother; b. 26 Aug. 1841 (18, *Salisbury Road, Brighton*); m. 10 June, 1868, Emma Susan Hotham, 2nd dau. of the late B. B. Williams, and by her (who d. 16 Nov. 1903) has issue,
(1) William Mount Charles, Capt. Essex Regt., b. 29 May, 1870.
(2) John Frederick, Electric Engineer, Toronto, Canada, b. 10 Oct. 1881; m. 30 Dec. 1909, Mary Theodora, dau. of William Owen, and grand-dau. of Sir Richard Owen.
(1) Florence Mary (18, *Salisbury Road, Hove*).
4. Ormsby, of Rathlahine, Greystones, co. Wicklow, J.P., b. 7 May, 1843; m. 12 Nov. 1869, Georgiana Isabella, only dau. of Capt. Laurence Tallan, and has issue,
(1) William Elder George Ormsby (Rev.), M.A. T.C.D., Rector of Kilkea Glebe, co. Kildare, b. July, 1874.
(2) Thomas Boyle, Capt. Royal Irish Regt., b. 27 July, 1877.
(1) Mary Isabella Christiana.
1. Alice Francis, m. 24 Aug. 1854, Rev. G. R. Handcock, and had issue.
1. Dorothy.   2. Alice.
3. Emily.   4. Frances, d. unm.

The eldest son,

THE RIGHT HON. JOHN ORMSBY VANDELEUR, of Kilrush, P.C., Commissioner of the Customs for Ireland, m. 17 Nov. 1800, Lady Frances Moore, youngest dau. of Charles, 1st Marquess of Drogheda, and by her (who d. 5 Oct. 1833) had issue,
1. CROFTON MOORE, his heir.
2. Henry Seymour Moore, d. unm. 19 March, 1875.
1. Anna Frances.
2. Alice, m. 1st, Rev. Charles Moore Stewart, 2nd son of Alexander Stewart of Ards, co. Donegal, and 2ndly, Lieut.-Col. John Vandeleur, 10th Hussars (see ante).
The Right Hon. J. O. Vandeleur d. 28 Nov. 1828, and was s. by his elder son,

CROFTON MOORE VANDELEUR, of Kilrush, co. Clare, J.P. and D.L., Col. of the Clare Regt. of Militia, High Sheriff 1832, M.P. for co. Clare 1859 to 1874, b. 9 Dec. 1808; m. 23 April, 1832, Lady Grace Toler, 2nd dau. of Hector John, 2nd Earl of Norbury, and by her (who d. 3 May, 1872) had issue,
1. HECTOR STEWART, of Kilrush.
2. Crofton Toler, late Capt. 7th Dragoon Guards, b. 7 March, 1840; m. 18 Oct. 1864, Charlotte Mary, youngest dau. of Rev. R. Bury, of Carrigrenane, co. Cork, and has with other issue,
1. Crofton Bury, Major, formerly Capt. and Brevet Maj. the Cameronians, b. 28 March, 1867; m. 11 Feb. 1903, Evelyn Mary Hamilton, dau. of the late Gen. T. Conor O'Leary, R.H.A., and has issue,
John Ormsby Evelyn, b. 14 Nov. 1903.
2. Robert Seymour, Capt. Seaforth Highlanders, b. 6 June, 1869; m. 7 July, 1900, Hester Caroline, dau. of Maj.-Gen. George de la Poer Beresford (see BURKE's *Peerage*, DECIES, B.), and has issue,
Beatrice.
3. John Ormsby Moore, Lieut.-Col. Gordon Highlanders (retired), b. 5 July, 1841; d. unm. 26 Feb. 1901.
1. Elizabeth Frances, m. 1855, St. John Blacker Douglas, of Elm Park, co. Armagh, of Tullahennel, co. Kerry, and of Grace Hall, co. Down. He d. 26 Sept. 1900, leaving issue (see that family).
2. Frances Letitia.
3. Grace Dorothea, m. 1866, Robert Cary Reeves, of Besborough, co. Clare.

Col. Vandeleur d. 9 Nov. 1881. His eldest son,

HECTOR STEWART VANDELEUR, of Kilrush, co. Clare, H.M.'s Lieut. of co. Clare, High Sheriff 1873, late Capt. Rifle Brigade, b. 18 Jan. 1836; m. 18 July, 1867, Charlotte, eldest dau. of William Orme Foster, M.P., of Apley Park, co. Salop (see that family). He d. 3 Oct. 1909, having had issue,
1. Cecil Foster Seymour, D.S.O., b. 11 July, 1869, Maj. and Brevet Lieut.-Col. Irish Guards, formerly Scots Guards, served in Unyoro Expedition 1895 (despatches, medal), in Nandi Expedition 1895-6 (despatches, D.S.O.), in the Niger Soudan Campaign 1897 (despatches, Brevet of Maj., medal with clasp), in Nile Expedition, 1898 (slightly wounded at Khartoum (despatches, Medjidie medals with two clasps), in Nile Expedition 1899 (clasp), and in South African War 1899-1901 (medal with six clasps, severely wounded). He was killed in action near Waterval, S. Africa, 31 Aug. 1901, d. unm.
2. ALEXANDER MOORE, now of Kilrush.
1. Isabel Grace, m.
2. Evelyn Norah, m. 14 July, 1904, Sydney R Christie-Miller of Britwell, and has issue (see that family).

Arms—Or, a trefoil vert between three mullets pierced two and one purp. *Crest*—A martlet purp. holding in the beak a trefoil or. *Motto*—Virtus astra petit.

Seat—Kilrush and Cahircon, Ennis, co. Clare. *Residence*—50, Rutland Gate, S.W.

BAYLY-VANDELEUR OF WARDENSTOWN.

CROFTON TALBOT BAYLY-VANDELEUR, of Wardenstown, co. Westmeath, assumed the name and arms of Vandeleur by Royal Licence 26 April, 1911, on succeeding to the estate of his cousin Crofton Thomas Burton Vandeleur, of Wardenstown (see VANDELEUR *of Kilrush*).

Lineage.—THE RIGHT HON. MAURICE FITZGERALD, Knight of Kerry (see FITZGERALD, Bart.), who d. 6 March, 1849, had with other issue by his 1st wife, Maria, dau. of the Right Hon. David Digues La Touche, two daus.,
1. Elizabeth Emily, d. 10 April, 1860; m. 11 Nov. 1835, Crofton Thomas Croasdaile Vandeleur, of Wardenstown, co. Westmeath, (see VANDELEUR *of Kilrush*), who d. 13 Aug. 1876, and had an only child,
Crofton Thomas Burton Vandeleur, of Wardenstown, Capt. 12th Lancers, High Sheriff co. Westmeath 1880, d.s.p. 13 June, 1881; m. 7 Oct. 1868, Hon. Maletta Yelverton, dau. of Barry John, 3rd Viscount Avonmore; on her death, 15 March, 1910, the estate passed to the present owner.
2. Catherine, d. 1898; m. 20 June, 1835, Edward Symes Bayly, of Ballyarthur, co. Wicklow (see that family), and had by him (who d. 26 Nov. 1884) with other issue, a son,
Maurice Spring Rice Bayly, b. 17 June, 1850; d. 9 Dec. 1900; m. 19 March, 1880, Jeanie Theodora, 2nd dau. of Capt. Hayes, 44th Regt., and left a son,
Crofton Talbot Bayly, now BAYLY-VANDELEUR, of Wardenstown.

Arms—Quarterly 1st and 4th, Or, a trefoil vert, between three mullets pierced purpure, on a canton erm, a saltire gu., charged with a cross formée arg. (for VANDELEUR); 2nd and 3rd, Gu., a chevron vair, between three martlets or (for BAYLY). *Crests*—1st, A martlet purpure, holding in the beak a trefoil or, and charged on the breast with a cross formée arg. (for VANDELEUR); 2nd, An antelope sejeant vert, gorged with a ducal coronet, and chained and armed or (for BAYLY). *Motto*—Virtus astra petit.

Seat—Wardenstown, Killucan, co. Westmeath.

LLOYD-VAUGHAN OF GOLDEN GROVE.

WILLIAM PEISLEY HUTCHINSON - LLOYD - VAUGHAN, of Golden Grove, King's Co., J.P. and D.L. King's Co., High Sheriff 1878, J.P. co. Tipperary, and High Sheriff co. Carlow 1897, *b.* 28 April, 1844; *m.* 5 Aug. 1869, Elizabeth Henrietta, dau. of William Henry Darby, of Leap Castle, King's Co. Mr. Lloyd-Vaughan is heir-general and representative of LLOYD *of Gloster* and VAUGHAN *of Golden Grove.*

JOHN VAUGHAN, of St. Dowells, co. Pembroke, was seised in fee before 1640 of certain lands and tenements in that co. By Jane Bullen his wife he had, with a son, Richard, mentioned in his brother's will 1710, a son,

HECTOR VAUGHAN, of Dromoyle and Knocknamease, King's Co., who had a grant of a fourth part of the estate of Terence Coghlan (attainted of treason), by patent dated 30 Dec. 1668, and a grant of Tristan and Clonmacpoer, dated 5 Feb. 1670. He was High Sheriff of King's Co. 1698, and *m.* 1st, 10 May, 1664, Mary, only dau. and heir of Capt. William Peisley, of Knocknamease, King's Co., grand-dau. of Bartholomew Peisley, of Punchestown, co. Kildare, Comptroller to Thomas, Viscount Wentworth, afterwards Earl of Strafford, Lord Deputy of Ireland, by Katherine de la Moore his wife, of Moore and Walton, co. Oxford, and great-grand-dau. of George Peisley, of Ascott, co. Oxford, by whom he had issue,

1. WILLIAM PEISLEY, his heir.
2. John, of Dromoyle, *b.* 15 Aug. 1698, whose will is dated 17 May, 1718. He *m.* Mary Hatwell, and had a son, Hector, of Fancroft, King's Co., whose will, dated 3 June, 1779, was proved 18 Nov. the next year. He *m.* his cousin, Bridget, dau. of William Peisley Vaughan, of Golden Grove (who was *b.* 8 Nov. 1706).
    1. Frances, *m.* Col. Robert Hedges, of Macroom, co. Cork.
    2. Jane, *m.* Jasper Grant, of Kilmurry, co. Cork.
    Mr. Vaughan *m.* 2ndly, 1685, Anne Webster, by whom he had a dau., Anna, *m.* Kilner Brazier, of Lizard, co. Limerick. He *d.* 18 Nov. 1710, and was *s.* by his eldest son,

WILLIAM PEISLEY VAUGHAN, of Golden Grove, alias Knocknamease, *b.* 4 Feb. 1666; *m.* 1st (articles dated 8 April, 1697) Anne, dau. of Thomas Sadleir, of Sopwell Hall, co. Tipperary (descended from the Right Hon. Sir Ralph Sadleir, Knt. Banneret, the illustrious warrior and statesman) (*see that family*), and had by her (who *d.* 12 Dec. 1710) two sons and six daus.,
1. Hector Bullen, *b.* 29 Oct. 1701; *d. unm.*
2. WILLIAM PEISLEY OLIVER SADLEIR, his heir.
1. Frances, *b.* 15 Aug. 1698; *m.* (articles dated 17 May 1718). Ralph Wallis, of Springmount, Queen's Co., and had issue.
2. Mary, *b.* 25 June, 1700; *d. unm.* 7 Jan. 1723.
3. Anne, *b.* 17 Nov. 1702; *d. unm.* 1723.
4. Jane, *b.* 10 Feb. 1708; *d. unm.*
5. Letitia, *b.* 2 Dec. 1710; *m.* 14 July, 1739, William Pendred, of Broghillstown, co. Carlow.
6. Bridget, *b.* 8 Nov. 1706; *m.* Hector Vaughan, of Fancroft.
Mr. Vaughan was High Sheriff of King's Co. 1738. His son,

WILLIAM PEISLEY OLIVER SADLEIR VAUGHAN, of Golden Grove, *b.* 29 Jan. 1703; *m.* 5 Oct. 1738, Mary, dau. of Rev. John Trench, of Dublin, and by her (who *d.* 22 Nov. 1742) he left at his decease, *v.p.* 1746 (with a dau., Mary, *b.* 10 July, 1741; *d. unm.* 1764) a son,

WILLIAM PEISLEY VAUGHAN, of Golden Grove, High Sheriff King's Co. 1766, *b.* 15 Oct. 1739; *m.* 3 June, 1764, Mary, dau. of Nicholas Synge, D.D., Bishop of Killaloe, and by her (who *d.* 27 Dec. 1808) he had issue,
1. WILLIAM PEISLEY, his heir.
2. Richard (Rev.), *m.* Catherine, dau. and heir of Oliver Latham, of Killenall; and *d.s.p.* 30 June, 1841.
   1. Martha, *b.* 11 Sept. 1781; *m.* May, 1822, JOHN LLOYD, youngest son of John Lloyd, of Gloster, King's Co. (*see Pedigree of LLOYD*), and *d.* 26 Jan. 1849, bur. at Fancroft, leaving an only child, MARY, *s.* her uncle, William Peisley Vaughan, 1842.
   2. Elizabeth, *d. unm.*   3. Sophia, *d. unm.*
Mr. Vaughan *d.* 14 June, 1809, and was *s.* by his eldest son,

WILLIAM PEISLEY VAUGHAN, of Golden Grove, High Sheriff King's Co. 1805, *b.* 4 July, 1774; *d. unm.* 4 Dec. 1842, and was *s.* by his niece,

I.L.G.

MARY VAUGHAN LLOYD, of Golden Grove, *b.* 3 May, 1823; *m.* 14 Aug. 1843, SAMUEL DAWSON HUTCHINSON, of Mount Heaton, King's Co. (*see* HUTCHINSON *of Timoney*) who assumed, by Royal Licence, dated 26 July, 1843, the names and arms of VAUGHAN and LLOYD. She *d.* 31 Jan. 1845. He *d.* 1855, having had an only son,

WILLIAM PEISLEY HUTCHINSON LLOYD - VAUGHAN, now of Golden Grove.

FAMILY OF LLOYD OF GLOSTER.

TUDOR AP IENEN, 3rd son of IEVAN AP LLEWELLYN, descended from CADROD HARDD, or CADROD the Handsome, a Welsh Prince, (seated in the Isle of Anglesey, in the 10th century), by Mabli his wife, dau. and heir of Grono ap Tudor, derived from Marchweithain, Lord of Is-Aled, Founder of the eleventh Noble Tribe of North Wales and Powys, *m.* Mabli, dau. and heir of Griffith ap Ievan Gethin (ancestor of the MEREDITHS *of Abertanat*), derived from Einion Efell, Lord of Cynllaeth (*see* EDWARDS *of Ness Strange*) From him descended,

DAVID LLOYD, *m.* Mali, dau. and heir of Grono ap Ievan, derived through Eledyr ap Rhys Sais, from Tudor Trevor, Lord of Hereford, and had issue,

TUDOR LLOYD, of Bodidris-yn-Yale, co. Denbigh, *m.* Catherine, dau. of John Edwards, of Plas Newydd, and was *s.* by his son,

JOHN LLOYD, of Bodidris, *m.* Catherine, dau. of Henry Salusbury, and was father of

SIR EVAN LLOYD, Knt., of Bodidris, *m.* Elizabeth, dau. of Thomas Mostyn, of Mostyn, co. Flint, and relict of John Yale, of Plâs yn Yale, co. Denbigh, and had, with a dau. Catherine, *m.* Cadwalader Price, of Rhiwlas, co. Merioneth, a son and heir,

SIR JOHN LLOYD, Knt., of Bodidris, *m.* Margaret, dau. of John Salusbury, of Rug, co. Merioneth (*see* BURKE's *Peerage and Baronetage*, SALUSBURY, Bart., *of Llanwern*), and was father of

EVAN LLOYD, of Bodidris, J.P. and D.L., co. Denbigh, Capt.-Gen. in the service of CHARLES I in Ireland, *m.* Mary, dau. and co-heir of Sir Richard Trevor, Knt., of Allington, co. Denbigh, derived from Tudor Trevor, Lord of Hereford, and had, with other issue,

1. John, of Bodidris, J.P. and D.L. co. Denbigh, *m.* 1st, Margaret, dau. of Sir Bevis Thelwall, Knt.; and 2ndly, Eleanor, dau. of Sir William Jones, Knt., of Castelmarch, one of the Judges of the King's Bench, and widow of John Price, of Rhiwlas, co. Merioneth. By his 1st wife he had a son and heir,
   SIR EVAN LLOYD, 1st bart., of Bodidris, so created 1646. He *m.* Anne, dau. of Sir Charles Williams, Knt., of Llangibby, and was *s.* by his son,
   SIR EVAN LLOYD, 2nd bart., of Bodidris, *m.* Mary, dau. and co-heir of Rees Tanat, and *d* 6 April, 1700, leaving an only dau. and heir (*see* BURKE's *Extinct Baronetage*),
      MARGARET LLOYD, *m.* Richard VAUGHAN, of Corsygedol, co. Merioneth, and was mother of CATHERINE VAUGHAN, who *m.* Rev. Hugh Wynn, D.D., Prebendary of Salisbury, and left a dau. and heir, MARGARET WYNN, *m.* Sir Roger Mostyn, Bart., of Mostyn, co. Flint, and had (with other issue, who *d.s.p.*) ELIZABETH MOSTYN, *m.* Edward Pryce Lloyd, Lord MOSTYN, and ANNA MARIA MOSTYN, *m.* Sir Robert Williames Vaughan, Bart. of Nannau, co. Merioneth.
2. Roger, *m.* Miss Nightingale, and had issue.
3. TREVOR, of whom presently.

Mr. Lloyd *d.* 17 April, 1637, at Presaddfyd, in the Isle of Anglesey. His youngest son,

TREVOR LLOYD, a Capt. in the Army of CHARLES I, *m.* 1639, Rose, dau. and heir of Francis Medhop, of Tonagh, King's Co., by whom he acquired estates in King's Co. and co. Tipperary, and *d.* 1685, leaving (with another son, Trevor) a son and successor,

MEDHOP LLOYD, of Gloster, *m.* Mary, dau. of Christopher Lovett, Lord Mayor of Dublin, and had fourteen children, all of whom *d.s.p.* with the exception of

TREVOR LLOYD, of Gloster, King's Co., *m.* Henrietta, dau. of James Waller, of Castletown, co Limerick (a descendant of Sir Hardress Waller, Governor of Limerick during the Commonwealth), and had, with other issue,

1. JOHN, his heir.   2. Hardress, *d.s.p.*
3. Waller, *m.* Lovat Ashe, of Ashgrove, co. Tipperary.
1. Rose, *m.* Alexander Saunderson, of Castle Saunderson, co. Cavan (*see that family*).

Mr. Lloyd, whose will, dated 13 Jan. 1733, was proved 16 Jan. 1747, was *s.* at his decease by his eldest son,

JOHN LLOYD, of Gloster, M.P. for King's Co. from 1678 until 1790, and subsequently for the borough of Inistiogue. Mr. Lloyd *m.* 7 June, 1777, Jane, youngest dau. and heir (with her sisters, Anne, wife of Rev. Abraham Symes, D.D., and Alice, wife of Samuel Hayes, of Avondale) of Thomas Le Hunte, who *d.* in 1775, 5th son of George Le Hunte, of Artramont, co. Wexford, and had issue,
1. HARDRESS, his heir.   2. Trevor, *d.* at Cambridge 1706.
3. Thomas, Lieut.-Col. in the Army, killed at the passage of the Nivelle, 10 Nov. 1813, at the head of his Regt. (the 94th), *unm.*
4. Evan, *d. unm.*
5. John, *m.*, as above stated, May, 1822, Martha, dau. of William Peisley Vaughan, of Golden Grove, and had an only dau. and heir,
   MARY VAUGHAN LLOYD, of Golden Grove, *s.* her uncle 1842, *b.* 3 May, 1823; *m.* 14 Aug. 1843, Samuel Dawson Hutchinson, of Mount Heaton (*see* HUTCHINSON *of Timoney*), who assumed the surname of LLOYD-VAUGHAN. She *d.* 31 Jan. 1845, leaving an only son,
   WILLIAM PEISLEY HUTCHINSON LLOYD-VAUGHAN, of Golden Grove, present heir-general and representative of LLOYD *of Gloster.*

1. Alice, *m.* 5 April, 1797, Laurence, 2nd Earl of Rosse.
2. Harriet, *m.* 5 June, 1821, Rev Henry King, of Ballylin, and had issue (*see that family*).

Mr. Lloyd was *s.* at his decease by his eldest son,

Vaughan.

HARDRESS LLOYD, of Gloster, J.P. and D.L., M.P. King's Co 1807-16, Lieut Col. South Down Regt. of Militia, *d. unm.* 1860, and was *s.* in the representation of his family by his grand-nephew, WILLIAM P. H. LLOYD VAUGHAN, now of Golden Grove.

Arms—Quarterly of nine: 1st quarterly, 1st, sa., a chevron between three boys' heads couped at the shoulders arg., crined or, round the neck of each a snake entwined ppr., for VAUGHAN; 2nd, paly of eight arg. and gu., a border or pellettée for LLOYD of Gloster; 3rd, erminois, a lion rampant az., ducally crowned arg., for MEDHOP; 4th, quarterly gu. and az. crusily fitchée or, a lion rampant arg. for HUTCHINSON; 2nd, quarterly gu. and az. crusily fitchée or, a lion rampant arg., for HUTCHINSON; 3rd, paly, of eight arg. and gu., for LLOYD of Bodidris; 4th, gu., a lion rampant arg., for GRONO AP IEVAN; 5th, per bend sinister erm. and ermines a lion rampant or, for TREVOR; 6th, erm., a lion rampant az., ducally crowned arg., for MEDHOP; 7th, vert, a saltire or, an annulet of the last for difference, for LE HUNTE; 8th, sa., a chevron arg. between three boys' heads couped at the shoulders, round the neck of each a snake entwined, all ppr., for VAUGHAN; 9th, gu., a lion rampant or, ducally crowned of the last, in the dexter chief point a cross-crosslet arg. for PEISLEY. Crests—1st, VAUGHAN, a boy's head couped at the shoulders, crined or, round the neck a snake entwined ppr.; 2nd, LLOYD of Gloster, a lion rampant arg., holding in the dexter fore-paw a snake ppr.; 3rd, HUTCHINSON, on a ducal coronet or, a cockatrice, wings addorsed, ppr. Motto—Vitæ via virtus.

Seat—Golden Grove, Roscrea, King's Co. Club—Royal St. George Yacht, Kingstown.

VAUGHAN OF QUILLY.

THE REV. GEORGE HENRY VAUGHAN, of Quilly, co. Down, M.A. St. Peter's Coll. Camb. Rector of St. Michan's Dublin, *b.* 11 Feb. 1854; *m.* 7 July, 1909, Evelyn Isabel Myra dau. of James Duncan Long, Esq., LL.D., of Inglebrook, co. Wicklow and Castlebar Road, Ealing, W.

Lineage.—The first of this family on record in Ireland was

REV. GEORGE VAUGHAN, *b.* 1634, who resided for some time near Ardee. He was first appointed Curate of Dundalk, and afterwards Treasurer of Dromore Cathedral. He *d.* leaving a son.

REV. JOHN VAUGHAN, son of the preceding Rev. George Vaughan, was *b.* 1675, B.A. Trin. Coll. Dublin 1701, and was appointed Rector of the united parishes of Dromore and Anaclone, co. Down. He purchased an estate in the parish of Donoughmore, and other property in co. Down; *m.* 23 May, 1710, Anne, sister of Right Rev. Ralph Lambert, D.D., Bishop of Dromore, and had issue,
1. RALPH, *b.* 13 Feb. 1711; *d. unm.*
2. GEORGE, of whom hereafter.
  1. Alice, *m.* 1st, Rev. John Corry, of Newry, and had issue, and 2ndly, Robert Lambert, of Dunleady, co. Down, by whom she had an only dau.,

Anne, heir to her father, *m.* 25 Sept. 1771, Richard, 2nd Earl of Annesley, and had issue (*see* BURKE's *Peerage*).

Rev. John Vaughan, whose will is dated 2 Sept. 1742, *d.* Jan. 1745. His 2nd son,

REV. GEORGE VAUGHAN, B.A. Trin. Coll. Dublin 1732, *b.* 3 Jan. 1713; *s.* his father as Rector of Dromore and Anaclone. He *m.* Margaret Smith, of Clontibret, co. Monaghan, an heir, and had issue,
1. RALPH, *s.* to the property of his uncle, Ralph, *m.* Miss Montgomery, co. Monaghan (cousin of Ann, wife of his brother, George), and had one dau.,

Anne, *m.* her cousin, George Vaughan, of Quilly (*see below*).
2. GEORGE, of whom hereafter.
3. Rebecca, *m.* William McDowell Johnstone, of Ballywillwill, co. Down, and had a son,

Rev. George Henry McDowell Johnstone, of Ballywillwill, *b.* 1775; *m.* 1811, his cousin, Lady Anna Maria Annesley, dau. of Richard, 2nd Earl of Annesley, and *d.s.p.* 1864.

Rev. George Vaughan *d.* 14 May, 1794. His 2nd son,
GEORGE VAUGHAN, of Villa, co. Down, Col. of Dromore and Donaghclony Volunteers 1793 (A very interesting proclamation of the volunteers appears in the *Belfast Newsletter* of 8 Jan. 1793, signed by George Vaughan, Col., and Thos. Dowglass, Capt.), *m.* Anne Montgomery, of Bessmount, co. Monaghan, and had issue,
1. John, of Villa, *d. unm.* 2. GEORGE, of whom hereafter.
3. Ralph, *d. unm.*
1. Margaret, *d. unm.* 21 Aug. 1828.

The 2nd son,
GEORGE VAUGHAN, of Quilly, *b.* 1768; *m.* 1st, his cousin, Anne, only dau. of his uncle, Ralph Vaughan (*see above*), by whom he had no issue; and 2ndly, 1824, Mary, dau. of George Tyrrell, co. West-

---

THE LANDED GENTRY. 722

meath, by his wife, Catherine, dau. of Very Rev. Wensley Bond, Dean of Ross, and sister of Very Rev. James Forward Bond, also Dean of Ross, and *d.* 7 Feb. 1840, having by her (who *d.* 6 Jan. 1892) had issue,
1. GEORGE MONTGOMERY, late of Quilly. 2. John, *d. unm.*
  1. Katharine, *d. unm.* 10 March, 1900.
  2. Margaret, *m.* 1850, Mitchell Henry, of Kylemore Castle, co. Galway, M.P., and *d.* 1874, leaving issue.

The elder son,
GEORGE MONTGOMERY VAUGHAN, of Quilly, co. Down, J.P., B.A. Trin. Coll. Dublin, *b.* 1825; *m.* 1st, Oct. 1850, Frances St. Lawrence, dau. of Gen. Hon. Arthur Grove-Annesley, of Annes Grove, co. Cork, 3rd son of Richard, 2nd Earl Annesley, and by her (who *d.* 17 Sept. 1871) had issue,
1. GEORGE HENRY, now of Quilly.
2. John Montgomery, *b.* 12 Jan. 1857; educated at Lausanne and R.I.E. Coll. Cooper's Hill; *d.* June, 1883.
3. Francis Warden Arthur Annesley, *b.* 6 Sept. 1863.
4. Ernest Llewellyn, *b.* 26 March, 1866, in I.C.S.; *m.* 19 Sept. 1894, Ethel Ada Helen, dau. of Thomas Thornton, fifth son of Thomas Thornton, of the Lund (*see* THORNTON *of High Cross*), and has issue,
5. Charles Annesley, *b.* 16 June, *d.* 18 Sept. 1871.
1. Frances Mary, *b.* 19 Sept. 1852; *d.* 21 Feb. 1862.
2. Elizabeth Mary, *b.* 20 Aug. 1855; *d.* 3 May, 1867.
3. Priscilla Georgiana, *b.* 29 Aug. 1858; *d.* 1 Nov. following.
4. Alice Katherine, *m.* 29 July, 1896, Rev. Joseph Quin, M.A., Rector of Annalong, co. Down.
5. Margaret Beatrice, *m.* 1 Dec. 1898, Ralph De Seton Dudgeon, Major 25th Bombay Rifles.

Mr. Vaughan *m.* 2ndly, Oct. 1872, Jane, dau. of Col. Wall, of Leamington, and widow of Capt. Denis Koenig, of Paris. She *d.s.p.* 1876. He *m.* 3rdly, June, 1884, Caroline Anne, eldest dau. of J. Wykeham Dickenson. She *d.* 4 March, 1901. He *d.* 8 Jan. 1902, having by her had issue,
6. Ralph Montgomery, Inniskilling Fusiliers.
6. Frances Mary.

Arms—Per pale sa. and az., on a chevron engrailed arg. between three boys' heads couped at the shoulders and entwined round the necks with snakes, all ppr., a cross of Ulster gu. Crest—a boy's head as in the arms, charged on the neck with a cross of Ulster gu. Motto—Honeste audax.

Seat—Quilly House, Dromore, co. Down. Residence—43, Wellington Place, Clyde Road, Dublin.

WHYTE-VENABLES. *See* WHYTE.

VERNON OF CLONTARF CASTLE.

EDWARD VENABLES VERNON, of Clontarf Castle, co. Dublin, J.P. and D.L., High Sheriff 1904, and J.P. co. Kerry, Lieut.-Col. and Hon. Col. late 5th Batt. Royal Dublin Fusiliers, 1885-96, *b.* 31 Jan. 1838; *m.* 27 March, 1862, Jane, dau. of Mathew Brinkley, of Partonstown, co. Meath, son of Rev. John Brinkley, D.D., Bishop of Cloyne, and has issue,

1. EDWARD KINGSTON, *b.* 24 March, 1870; *m.* 15 Nov. 1911, Margaret Sophia, youngest dau. of Edward Elwin, of Dover.
2. Granville, *b.* 1874; *d.* 1876.
3. John Cuthbert Avenal, *b.* 28 July, 1882; *m.* 28 Aug. 1905, Margaret, 2nd dau. of the Right Hon. Sir Andrew Marshall Porter, 1st Bart., P.C., Master of the Rolls in Ireland (*see* BURKE's *Peerage*).
1. Louisa Constance, *m.* 12 July, 1892, Henry Edward Cusack, 4th son of Sir Ralph Smith Cusack, of Furry Park, Raheny, co. Dublin (*see* CUSACK *of Gerardstown*).
2. Edyth Agnes, *m.* Sept.1890, Walter Calverley Blades-Calverley, and has issue.
3. Kathleen Louisa, *m.* Capt. W. Wright, A.S.C.
4. Dorothy Mabel, *m.* 6 Feb. 1896, Walter Summers, son of the late John Summers, of Sunnyside, Ashton-under-Lyne.
5. Muriel Maud, *m.* 14 July, 1900, Capt. Mathew Connolly, 1st Batt. Yorkshire L.I., only son of Adm. Connolly, of Bath.

Lineage.—SIR EDWARD VERNON, of Houndshill, *b.* 14 Dec. 1584; *m.* 23 July, 1613, Margaret, dau. and heir of Henry Vernon, of Hilton, co. Stafford. She *d.* 3 Jan. 1656. He *d.* 15 June, 1657, having had issue,

IRELAND. Vernon.

1. HENRY, of Sudbury, Houndshill, &c., *m.* 21 Sept. 1634, Muriel, dau. and sole heir of Sir George Vernon, of Haslington, and was ancestor of the VERNONS *of Sudbury* (now LORDS VERNON), the VERNONS *of Hilton Park, Harefield,* &c.
2. Edward (Col.), of North Aston, co. Stafford, had a grant of the castle and lands of Clontarf, co. Dublin. He *m.* a sister of Joseph Guldeford, and had issue,
  1. Mary, *d. unm.* 1729.   2. Elizabeth, *d.* young.
  3. John, whose line we treat.
  1. Ann, *m.* George Harper, of Twyford, co. Derby.
  2. Ma[r]y Catherine Grace Elizabeth, *d. unm.*
The 3rd son,
JOHN VERNON, of Clontarf, co. Dublin, Quartermaster-General of the Army of Ireland, 1655 bapt. 22 May 1622; *m.* 1st, Anne, dau. of John H[...], of Sand, Devon, and had a son, John, who *d.* in London, *unm.*   *m.* 2ndly, Elizabeth, dau. of Fulke Walwyn, of Much Marcle[,] [H]ereford, and *d.* intestate 13 March, 1670, leaving issue.
The son and heir,
REV. EDWARD VERNON, of Redmile, co. Leicester, *m.* Lettice, dau. of John Bankes, of Uttoxeter, co. Stafford, and had issue,
  1. JOHN, his heir.
  2. Edward, D.D., Rector of St. George's, Bloomsbury, Middlesex, *d. unm.* 1765.
  1. Catherine, *m.* — Yeates.
The elder son,
JOHN VERNON, a Capt. in the Army, afterwards of Clontarf Castle, co. Dublin, *m.* Dorothy, sister of Hans Otto Grahn, a Hanoverian nobleman, by whom (who *d.* 7 May, 1773) he had issue,
  1. GEORGE, his heir.
  2. Edward, of Dublin, Capt. 4th Dragoons, High Sheriff of Dublin 1768; *m.* 1 Jan. 1760, his cousin, Caroline Catherine Yeates, and *d.* 14 Aug. 1805, having had issue,
    1. John Frederick, *b.* 21 Oct. 1760; *d.* 18 Dec. 1760.
    2. George William, Barrister-at-Law, *b.* 16 Jan. 1762; *d. unm.* 1792.
    3. Francis, R.N., *b.* 20 Feb. 1765; *d.s.p.* 1796.
    4. Charles Hawley (Sir), Chamberlain to H.E. the Lord-Lieut. of Ireland, *b.* 22 July, 1766; *d. unm.* 24 June, 1835.
    5. Brabazon Deane, Lieut.-Col. in the Army, and Major 16th Regt., *b.* 27 Nov. 1778; *m.* Helen, dau. of Harmet Bond, of Ballynahillick, near Rockmills, co. Cork, and *d.* 1814, leaving two sons,
      (1) Charles, of Clifton, co. Gloucester, *b.* 21 May, 1802; *m.* 14 Aug. 1828, Georgina Katherine, only child of Nathaniel Evans, of Oldtown, co. Cork, and *d.* 13 April, 1874, having by her (who assumed by Royal Licence, 1876, the additional surname of GORE) had issue (*see* VERNON-GORE *of Derryluskan*).
      (2) Harcourt, Capt. 95th Regt., *d. unm.*
    6. Henry, *b.* 10 May, 1771; *m.* 1796, Frances, dau. of Thomas Plunkett, of Portmarnock, and had issue,
      George Edward (Rev.), Rector of Carlow, *m.* 1st, Jane, dau. of Archdeacon Thomas Kingsbury, and by her had no issue. He *m.* 2ndly, Harriet, dau. of Lieut.-Col. Henry Bruen, of Oak Park, co. Carlow, M.P. She *d.* 5 Feb. 1866. He *d.* 16 March, 1870, leaving a son,
        John Bruen Venables, *b.* 20 Feb. 1836; *m.* 20 Aug. 1861, Catharine Louisa, dau. of Edward W. Whellen, and *d.* 10 May 1873, having by her (who *m.* 2ndly, 7 July, 1877, William Fowler) had issue,
          George Edward, *b.* 22 Dec. 1864; *d.* 15 July, 1880.
          Louisa Harriett Diana.
    7. Harcourt, in the Army, *b.* 18 March, 1775; *d. unm.*
  1. Charlotte, *m.* Thomas Wright, of Houghton, co. Derby.
The eldest son,
GEORGE VERNON, of Clontarf Castle, Barrister-at-Law, whose will is dated 1 May, 1785, and proved 5 May, 1787, *m.* Elizabeth Hughes, widow, and had issue,
  1. JOHN, his heir.   2. George, *d. unm.* 10 May, 1802.
  1. Frances Dorothy, *b.* 17 Nov. 1755; *m.* 22 Oct. 1776, James Crawford, of Auburn, co. Dublin, and *d.* 20 July, 1844.
  2. Diana, *m.* Sir Brodrick Chinnery, Bart.
The eldest son,
JOHN VERNON, of Clontarf Castle, Barrister-at-Law 1778, *m.* 1780, Elizabeth, dau. of Henry Fletcher, of Newtown Park, co. Dublin, and had issue,
  1. GEORGE, his heir.
  2. John Fane (*see* VERNON *of Erne Hill*).
  1. Frances, *m.* Bertram Mitford, Barrister-at-Law.
  2. Elizabeth, *m.* Charles Arthur Tisdall, of Charlesfort, co. Meath, and had issue (*see that family*).
  3. Maria, *m.* 1st, the Hon. and Rev. Pierce Butler, brother of the 3rd Earl of Carrick; and 2ndly, Walter Fawkes, of Farnley, co. York.
The eldest son,
GEORGE VERNON, of Clontarf Castle, Barrister-at-Law, *m.* 1808, Henrietta Maria, dau. of Wilson Gale-Braddyll, of Conishead Priory, near Ulverston, co. Lancaster, and *d.* 1822, having had issue,
  1. GEORGE BRADDYLL, his successor.
  2. JOHN EDWARD VENABLES, late of Clontarf Castle.
  3. Charles Pierce, *d. unm.* about 1838.
  4. Walter Fawkes, *d. unm.*   5. Braddyll Francis, *d. unm.*
  6. Henry Townley, Lieut. R.N., *d. unm.*
  1. Henriett Jane, *m.* 1836, William Waldegrave Pelham Clay, D.L., of Burgage Hill, co. Nottingham, son of Gen. Clay. He *d.s.p.* 1873.
  2. Elizabeth Charlotte, *m.* 8 Feb. 1853, the Right Hon. John Parker, M.P., who *d.s.p.* 5 Sept. 1881.
  3. Maria Frances, *m.* 1st, George Colman; and 2ndly, William Napier, Lieut.-Governor of Labuan, Borneo.
The eldest son,

GEORGE BRADDYLL VERNON, of Clontarf Castle, *d. unm.* about 1833, and was *s.* by his next brother,
JOHN EDWARD VENABLES VERNON, of Clontarf Castle, co. Dublin, B.A., J.P. and D.L., High Sheriff 1847, *b.* 10 Jan. 1813; *m.* 1st, 20 Aug. 1836, Louisa Catharine, only dau. of Charles Proby Bowles, of Park Lane, London, and by her (who *d.* 12 Aug. 1853) had issue,
  1. EDWARD VENABLES, now of Clontarf Castle.
  2. Charles Albert, late 20th Regs., *b.* 17 Jan. 1840; *m.* 1879, Mary, dau. of Duncan McTavish, of the Isle of Islay, N.B., and *d.* Oct. 1906, having had issue,
    1. Albert Archibald, *b.* Feb. 1880; *d.*
    2. Charles Henry Townley, *b.* Dec. 1884.
    1. Violet Mary.
  3. Forbes George, Member Executive Council, and Comm. of Lands and Works, British Columbia, and Agent-Gen. for that Colony 1895-8, *b.* 21 Aug. 1843; *m.* 1877, Kate, dau. of R. Branks, of Oldshields, Lanarkshire, and *d.* 20 Jan. 1911, having had issue,
    1. Gladys Louise, *b.* 1878, *d.* 1892.
    2. Beatrice Alma Ashley, *m.* Capt. Furleer, Royal Irish Rys.
  4. Granville William, Col. late Comm. 2nd Batt. Bedfordshire Regt. and West India Depot, Jamaica. *b.* 2 July, 1845; *m.* 30 Nov. 1882, Emma Rosalie Pender, dau. of Stephen Francis Sharp, of St. Max, St. Leonards, and has issue,
    1. Charles Edward Granville, *b.* 29 Sept. 1883.
    2. Henry St. George Venables, *d.* an infant.
  5. John Francis Henry, late R.N., *b.* 31 Jan. 1848; *m.* 11 Dec. 1873, Jane Agnes, eldest dau. of J. Treherne, of Chelsea; and *d.s.p.* 14 March, 1884.
    1. Louisa Emily, dec., *m.* 2 June, 1863, George William Cuppage, son of E. F. Cuppage, of Clare Grove, co. Dublin. He *d.* 7 Aug. 1908, leaving issue (*see that family*).
Mr. Vernon *m.* 2ndly, 25 Sept. 1856, Hon. Rosa Gertrude Harriet Daly, dau. of James, 1st Lord Dunsandle, which lady *d.s.p.* 31 Aug. 1859. Mr. J. E. Vernon *d.* 29 April, 1890.

Arms—Arg., a fret sa. a mullet az. for difference (with sixty-three quarterings.) Crest—A boar's head erased sa., ducally gorged and charged on the neck with a mullet or. Motto—Vernon semper viret. Seat—Clontarf Castle, near Dublin. Clubs—Carlton, S.W. United Service, S.W.; Kildare Street, Dublin.

VERNON OF ERNE HILL.

JOHN FANE VERNON, of Erne Hill, co. Cavan, J.P. and D.L. for that co., High Sheriff 1890, and J.P. co. Dublin, M.A. Christ's Coll. Camb., Barrister-at-Law, *b.* 5 July, 1849; *m.* 11 May, 1882, Thomasina Georgiana, dau. of Rev. Henry Joy Tombe, D.D., Canon of Christ Church Cathedral, Dublin, and has with other issue,
JOHN EDWARD, Lieut. Royal Dublin Fus., *b.* 1888.

Lineage.— REV. JOHN FANE VERNON, of Aulawn, co. Cavan, *b.* 6 May, 1790, 2nd son of John Vernon, of Clontarf Castle, co. Dublin (*see that family*): *m.* Dec. 1812, Frances, dau. of Right Rev. John Kearney, D.D., Bishop of Ossory, and *d.* 7 June, 1843, having had issue,
  1. JOHN EDWARD, of whom presently.
  1. Anna, *m.* 27 March, 1843, Rev. Sir Nicholas Chinnery, 3rd Bart. This lady and her husband were killed in the railway accident at Abergele, 20 Aug. 1868, leaving an only dau.
  2. Frances.
The only son,
JOHN EDWARD VERNON, of Erne Hill, co. Cavan, J.P. and D.L., High Sheriff 1864, M.A., one of the Irish Land Commissioners, *b.* 12 Aug. 1816; *m.* 1st, 6 July, 1846, Harriet, youngest dau. of the Right Rev. John Leslie, D.D., Bishop of Kilmore, and by her (who *d.* 23 March, 1853) had issue.
  1. JOHN FANE, now of Erne Hill.
  2. Edward Saunderson, *b.* 6 March, 1851, dec.
  1. Isabella Frances, *m.* 24 June, 1874, Henry Chichester Tisdall, son of John Tisdall, of Charlesfort, co. Meath (*see that family*). He *d.* 6 Aug. 1908.
He *m.* 2ndly, 17 Nov. 1857, Maria Esther, eldest dau. of the Hon. George Francis Colley, of Ferney, co. Dublin (*see* BURKE'S *Peerage*, HARBERTON, V.) He *d.* 7 March, 1887, having by her (who *d.* 8 May, 1899) had issue,
  3. George Arthur Pomeroy, *b.* 19 Sept. 1863.
  4. Walter Pomeroy, *b.* 23 May, 1867, dec.
  2. Anna Lilian.

3. Helen Rose, *m.* 27 Nov. 1907, John Thomas Gibbings, of Carrickmacross, son of late Rev. Canon Richard Gibbings (*see* GIBBINGS *of Gibbing's Grove*).
4. Blanche.

Arms—Arg., a fret sa. *Crest*—A boar's head erased sa., ducally gorged or. *Motto*—Vernon semper viret.

Seat—Erne Hill, Belturbet, co. Cavan. *Residence*—1, Wilton Place, Dublin.

VERSCHOYLE OF KILBERRY.

ARTHUR ROBERT VERSCHOYLE, of Kilberry, co. Kildare, and of Mountown, co. Westmeath, J.P., F.R.G.S., formerly Lieut. 4th Batt. Lincoln Regt., *b.* 7 July, 1859 ; *m.* 1st, 28 Sept. 1886, Mary, dau. of Frederick Brown, of the Manor House, Langley, Bucks, and by her (who *d.* 29 July, 1899) has issue,

TERENCE, *b.* Jan. 1894.

He *m.* 2ndly, 3 July, 1904, Mabel Mary dau. of the late Capt. Frederic Sayer, Royal Welsh Regt.

Lineage.—The family of VERSCHOYLE came from Holland on account of religious persecution in 1568. Early in the 17th century two of the name were resident in Dublin, HENRIK and WILLIAM, said to have been brothers. The elder brother, HENRIK VERSCHUYL, of Thomas Street, Dublin, *d.* 1623 ; by his will he devised all his goods to his wife Judith, and their two children. The younger brother, WILLIAM VERSCHOYLE, of the city of Dublin (1634), *d.* 1648, leaving a will in which he mentions his wife Catherine van Pilkam, his nephew Henry Verschoyle, and his niece Catherine Verschoyle, afterwards Catherine Cotton. His nephew, HENRY VERSCHOYLE, was admitted a freeman of Dublin in 1659, and was father of ROBERT VERSCHOYLE, admitted a freeman in 1676, and grandfather of Katherine, *m.* Sir Robert Newcomen, Bart., and of HENRY VERSCHOLYE, of Dolphin's Barn and Donore, co. Dublin, admitted a freeman in 1718, his will, dated 1731, was proved 1734. He *m.* 21 Aug. 1703, Martha Eskrige, of Dublin, by whom he had issue,

1. JOSEPH, his heir. 2. William.
3. Thomas.
1. Hannab, *m.* — Carmichael.
2. Elizabeth, *m.* 1739, James Cartland, of Dublin.

His eldest son,
JOSEPH VERSCHOYLE, of Donore, co. Dublin, J.P., *b.* 1708 ; B.A. Trin. Coll. Dublin ; admitted a freeman 1746 ; senior master of Trinity Guild, and a Governor of Bluecoat Hospital 1759 ; *m.* 8 Dec. 1744, Margaret Mottley, of Dublin, and *d.* May, 1796, having had issue,

1. JAMES, of whom presently.
2. Richard, of Mount Merrion, co. Dublin, High Sheriff 1819 ; *m.* Harbara Fagan, and *d.s.p.* Aug. 1827.
3. JOHN (*see next Memoir*).
4. Joseph. 5. William, *d.* 1785.
1. Elizabeth, *m.* Feb. 1787, William Dickinson.

The eldest son,
THE RIGHT REV. JAMES VERSCHOYLE, of Kilberry, co. Kildare, Bishop of Killala and Achonry, *b.* 1750 ; LL.B. Trin. Coll. Dublin (1776) ; LL.D. (1798) ; minor canon of St. Patrick's Cathedral 1780 ; Archdeacon of Glendalough 1788; Dean of St. Patrick's 1794; Bishop of Killala 1810 ; *m.* (licence dated 8 April) 1790, Frances Walsh, sister of Rev. Henry Lomax Walsh, Prebendary of Swords, and *d.* 13 April, 1834, having had issue,

1. ROBERT, of whom presently.
2. Joseph (Rev.), of Roundwood, Queen's Co., M.A. Trin. Coll. Dublin, Prebendary of Ballysodare, Precentor of Achonry, Rector of Kilmoremoy, co. Mayo, *b.* 1797 ; *m.* July, 1827, Catherine, eldest dau. of Lorenzo Hickie Jephson, of Carrick House, co. Tipperary, by his wife, Hon. Martha Prittie, dau. of Henry, 1st Lord Dunally ; and *d.* 24 Jan, 1867, having by her (who *d.* 23 Jan. 1871) had issue,
 1. Henry Prittie, *b.* Nov. 1828 ; *d.* 1830.
 2. James Lorenzo, of Roundwood, Capt. 66th Regt., *b.* 12 Feb. 1832 ; *m.* 24 Feb. 1868, Caroline Elizabeth, dau. of the Marquis d'Asserèto di Serravalle, of Vianilla, Spain, and *d.* Sept. 1875, having by her had issue,
  (1) Louis Charles Hamilton Massey, *b.* 1868 ; *d.* 1870.
  (2) Robert, *b.* and *d.* 1870.
  (3) Theodore Robert Stuart, of Mountainy, Mountrath, Queen's Co. (*Estates : Roundwood and Clara Hill, Queen's Co.*), Lieut. 3rd Batt. Royal Dublin Fusiliers (Kildare Mil.), Medal, Royal Humane Soc. 15 Jan. 1894, *b.* 16 Dec. 1871 ; *m.* 27 June, 1895, Emily Margaret Pierce, elder dau. of the Rev. John B. McClellan, M.A., Principal of the Royal Agricultural College, Cirencester, and has issue,
   Brian Stuart Verschoyle, *b.* 14 May, 1898.
  (4) James Joseph, *b.* 12 May, 1873 ; *d. unm.* 5 Jan. 1894, being drowned whilst endeavouring to save life (Certificate, Royal Humane Soc.).
  (5) George Montray, *b.* 15 April, 1875 ; *d. unm.* 14 Sept. 1897.
 3. Robert Henry, of Springfield, co. Hereford, J.P. and D.L., late Capt. 11th Hussars, *b.* 20 Aug. 1835 ; *m.* 23 Nov. 1872, Gertrude Mary, dau. of Capt. Edgar Walker, of Quarry, Northam, co. Devon, and by her has issue,
  (1) Ainslie Holford, *b.* 23 July, 1875 ; *m.* 1 Sept. 903, Eleanor Stratford, youngest dau. of the late S. Collins of Cubberley, Ross.
  (2) Henry Cosby Prittie, *b.* 24 Nov. 1887.
  (1) Catherine Mildred. (2) Lucy Caroline.
 4. Richard Jephson *b.* 1837, Ensign 60th Rifles ; *d.* 1857
 1. Martha Mildred, *d. unm.* 1905.
 2. Emily Salusbury, *d. unm.* 3 Jan. 1885.
1. Frances, *m.* 1813, Ven. Joseph Verschoyle (*see* VERSCHOYLE *of Cashelshanaghan*).

The eldest son,
ROBERT VERSCHOYLE of Kilberry, co. Kildare, *b.* 1792 ; *m.* 20 Aug. 1822, Catherine, dau. and heiress of Thomas A. Curtis, of Mountown, co. Meath, and *d.* 1866, having by her (who *d.* 1882) had issue,

1. Henry, *d.* young, about 1835.
2. Augustus, *d.* at Eton, aged 16.
3. HENRY WILLIAM, of whom presently.
1. Georgina, *d. unm.*
2. Catherine, *m.* Rev. — Fuller.
3. Augusta, *m.* 5 July, 1878, Capt. Alfred Manners Drummond, late Rifle Brigade (*see* BURKE'S *Peerage*, PERTH, E.). She *d.s.p.* 2b April, 1908.

The 3rd son,
HENRY WILLIAM VERSCHOYLE, of Kilberry, Lieut.-Col. Grenadier Guards (Crimean medal), *b.* 1835 ; *m.* 18 Dec. 1856, Lucy Clarissa, dau. of Ambrose Goddard, D.L., of The Lawn, Swindon, Wilts, M.P. for Cricklade, and *d.* 20 Aug. 1870, having by her (who *d* 30 March, 1901) had issue,

1. ARTHUR ROBERT, now of Kilberry.
2. Edward Greville, Capt. Grenadier Guards, *b.* 5 Nov. 1866 ; *d.* of wounds received in action at Thabanchu, S. Africa, 6 May. 1900.
 1. Theresa Blanche, *m.* 6 June, 1905, Sir Basil Templer Graham-Montgomery, 5th Bart. (*see* BURKE'S *Peerage*).
 2. Sybil Mary, *m.* 4 Sept. 1902, Charles Garden Duff-Assheton-Smith, of Vaynol.
 3. Kathleen, *m.* 5 Jan. 1907, George Compton, of Pennerley Lodge, Beaulieu, Hants, and has issue.

Arms—Quarterly 1st and 4th, arg. on a chevron between three boar's heads couped gu. langued az. a cross patée or (VERCHOYLE) ; 2nd and 3rd, barry of six or and az. on a fess chequy arg. and sa. three martlets of the first (CURTIS). *Crest*—A boar's head couped gu. langued az. charged with a cross patée or. *Motto*—Temperans et constans.

Seats—Kilberry, co. Kildare ; Mountain, co. Westmeath ; **The Grange**, Chalfont St. Peter's, Bucks ; Holme Park, Rotherfield. *Clubs*—Carlton, Arthur's, Wellington, and Royal Yacht Squadron.

VERSCHOYLE OF CASHELSHANAGHAN.

REV. HAMILTON STUART VERSCHOYLE, of Cashelshanaghan, and of Ballybodonnel and Dunkineely co. Donegal, M.A. Trin. Coll. Dublin 1868, received the Cross of the Crown of Italy in recognition of public services 1888, *b.* 19 Sept. 1844 ; *m.* 15 Dec. 1873, Frances Frederika Dorothea, youngest dau. and co-heiress of the Ven. Frederick Faulkener Goold, of Rosbrien and Dromadda, co. Limerick, Archdeacon of Raphoe (*see* GOOLD VERSCHOYLE *of Dromadda*), and by her has issue,

HAMILTON FREDERICK STUART GOOLD-VERSCHOYLE, of Dromadda and Athea, co. Limerick (*see that family*).

Lineage.—JOHN VERSCHOYLE, of Cashelshanaghan, co. Donegal, and Stillorgan Park, co. Dublin (3rd son of Joseph Verschoyle, of Donore, *see preceding Memoir*), *b.* 1752 ; *m.* 1st, 16 July, 1782, Henrietta, dau. of William Preston, by his wife, Angel, dau. of William Archdall, and by her had issue,

1. Joseph (Ven.), M.A., Archdeacon of Achonry, bapt. 20 May, 1783 ; *m.* 14 July, 1813, his cousin, Frances, only dau. of the Right Rev. James Verschoyle, Bishop of Killala (*see preceding article*), and *d.* 1862, having had issue,

1. James, M.A. Trin. Coll. Dublin, called to the Bar 1840, d. *unm.*
2. Richard John, of Tanrago, co. Sligo, J.P., High Sheriff 1875, b. 14 Dec. 1824; m. 22 Sept. 1858, Eliza Louisa, dau. of Rev. James Peed, Rector of Wexford, and by her had issue,
 (1) Joseph Richard, b. 1861; d. 12 Dec. 1910.
 (2) Robert Henry, m. 27 April, 1905, Mary E., dau. of Dudley Beaumont.
 (3) Charles John, M.A. Oxon, m. 8 June, 1910, Enid, 2nd dau. of late Major Taylor, 85th Rest. of Grovelands, Southgate.
 (4) William Danham. (5) Edward George.
 (1) Louisa Margaret, m. 18 Aug. 1880, Sir Malby Crofton, Bart., of Longford House, co. Sligo, and has issue (*see* BURKE'S *Peerage*).
 (2) Frances Mabella, m. 30 April, 1884, Capt. Charles Ellis Ogle, Royal Dublin Fusiliers.
2. William, bapt. 27 Jan. 1786; d. *unm.*

Mr. Verschoyle m. 2ndly, 2 June, 1802, Margaret, dau. of Hamilton Stuart, of Dromesmill, co. Tyrone (and heiress of her mother, Margaret, dau. and co-heiress of Rev. Albert Nesbitt, of Cashelshanaghan, co. Donegal), grand-dau. of Alexander Stuart (by his wife Sarah, dau. and heiress of William Hamilton, of Dromespill), and great-grand-dau. of George Stuart, of Termon, co. Tyrone, 2nd son of Hon. Robert Stuart, of Irry, 3rd son of Andrew, 1st Lord Castle Stewart, descended in the direct male line from Robert, Duke of Albany, 3rd son of ROBERT II, King of Scotland (*see* BURKE'S *Peerage*, CASTLE STEWART, E.). By this marriage Mr. Verschoyle (who d. 28 June, 1840) had further issue,
3. HAMILTON (Right Rev.), of whom afterwards.
4. John James, of Tassagart, co. Dublin, J.P., b. 20 July, 1805; m. 12 March, 1849, Catherine Helen, dau. of Rev. William Foster, of Belle Isle, co. Donegal, Rector of Loughgilly, co. Armagh, and grand-dau. of Right Rev. William Foster, Bishop of Clogher (brother of Right Hon. John Foster, Lord Oriel, last Speaker of the Irish House of Commons), and d. 2 Aug. 1891, having by her had issue,
 1. John Stuart (Rev.), of Tassagart, Rector of Huish-Champflower, Wiveliscombe, Taunton, M.A., Cantab., b. 3 Nov. 1853.
 2. William Henry Foster, J.P. co. Dublin, b. 1858; m. 16 June, 1888, Frances Harriet Hamilton, youngest dau. of Edward James Jackson, of Upwell, co. Norfolk, and of The Priory, St. Andrews, N.B., and widow of Capt. W. Unett, 21st Hussars, and has issue,
  1. George. 2. Arthur.
  1. A dau.
 1. Helen Catherine, m. 14 Jan. 1874, Moutray Gledstanes, of Fardross, co. Tyrone, and has issue.
 2. Margaret Stuart, m. 1883, Rev. Duncan John Brownlow, Rector of Ardbraccan, co. Meath, and has issue.
 3. Lily Sarah, m. 1880, Very Rev. Richard Stuart Dobbs Campbell, M.A., Rector of St. Mary's, Athlone, Dean of Clonmacnoise and has issue.
 4. Catherine Matilda Frances, m. 1802, Shuldham Henry Shaw.
 5. Matilda Anna Helen, m. July, 1902, Rev. Rathbone Supple.
5. Richard (Rev.), M.A., of Tullydonnell, co. Donegal, Canon of Clogher, Rector of Derryvollen, and Prebendary of Kilsberry. b. 9 June, 1839; m. 1st, 13 July, 1841, Marv Davenport, dau. of Rev. Bartholomew Lloyd, Provost of Trin. Coll. Dublin, and by her had issue,
 1. Richard Lloyd.
He m. 2ndly, 15 April, 1853, Emily (d. 15 March, 1906), dau. of Major James Kynaston Edwards, of Old Court, co. Wicklow, and d. 11 Sept. 1865, having by her had,
 2. John Hamilton, Lieut.-Col. Commanding Duke of Cornwall's Light Infantry (clasp and Khedive's star for Egyptian campaign), b. 1 June, 1854; m. 2 July, 1882, Florence Lyla, dau. of the late Thomas Williams, of Yarth House, Hampstead. She d. 23 April, 1902, leaving issue, two daus.
  (1) Gladys Louise.
  (2) Florence Emily Beryl.
 3. James Kynaston Edwards, C.M.G., B.A. Trin. Coll. Dublin 1881, Inspector-General of Irrigation, Upper Egypt, b. 9 Aug. 1858; m. 27 Sept. 1899, Edith, dau. of Matthew Wilson Armour, of Liverpool. He d. 17 March, 1907, having by her (who m. 2ndly, 23 May, 1910, Capt. Ernest Elborough Woodcock, Indian Army), had issue,
  Harold Denis Edwards, b. 16 July 1900.
 4. Stuart Joseph, b. 24 June, 1860, m. Feb. 1893, Enid Norah, dau. of J. Perry Worgan, and his issue,
  Terence Trevor Hamilton, b. 9 Sept. 1894.
 5. Beresford St. George, b. 14 July, 1863; m. 14 June, 1900, Ethel Janet, fourth surviving dau. of the late T. R. M. Plews, of The Woodlands, Darlington, and has issue,
  Richard Plews, b. 26 July, 1901.
 1. Eleanor. 2. Emily Margaret Elizabeth.
 1. Margaret, d. *unm.* 2. Sarah Elizabeth, d. *unm.*
 3. Matilda Mary, m. 10 May, 1844, Rev. Rawdon Griffith Greene, Rector of Sandgate, co. Kent, and d., his widow, 15 Dec. 1903.

The 3rd son,

THE RIGHT REV. HAMILTON VERSCHOYLE, D.D., of Cashelshanaghan, Lord Bishop of Kilmore, Elphin, and Ardagh, b. 6 April, 1803; Chancellor of Christ Church 1855, Dean of Ferns 1862, and Bishop of Kilmore 1862; m. 1833, Catherine Margaret, dau. and eventually co-heiress of the Very Rev. Thomas Hawkins, of Ballybodonnell, and Dunkineely, co. Donegal, Dean of Clonfert, and d. 29 Jan. 1870, having by her (who d. 19 Nov. 1883) had issue,
1. HAMILTON STUART (Rev.), now of Cashelshanaghan.
2. John, b. 1846; d. 1849.
3. John Thomas Samuel, B.A. Univ. Coll. Oxon, b. 7 April, 1851; m. 1875, Alicia, dau. of Col. Newbolt, and d. 1882, leaving issue, Catherine Stuart.
4. Frederick Thomas, of Castle Troy, co. Limerick, J.P., Capt. late 2nd Brig. South Irish Div. R.A., B.A. Trin. Coll. Camb. (Clubs: Junior United Service, S.W.; Kildare Street, Dublin), b. 9 June, 1854; m. 26 Oct. 1891, Hilda Caroline Hildyard, youngest dau. of Robert Blair, of Blackdales, Ayrshire, and has issue,
 1. Frederick Hildyard Hawkins Stuart, b. 21 Nov. 1894.
 1. Hilda Caroline Gwendoline.
 2. Movra Hamilton.
1. Catherine, d. *unm.* 2. Sarah Matilda, d. *unm.* 1862.
3. Matilda Mary, d. *unm.* 1861.
4. Thomasina, m. 1866, Rev. Dawson Frances Chapman, M.A., Vicar of St. Peter's, Preston, and d. 1905.
5. Margaret Emily.

Arms—Quarterly: 1st and 4th grand quarters, arg., on a chevron between three boars' heads couped gu. langued az. a cross patée or, for VERSCHOYLE; 2nd grand quarter, arg. a chevron gu. between three boars' heads erased sa. langued of the second, for NESBITT; and on a canton the arms of STUART, namely, quarterly, 1st, or, a lion rampant within a double tressure flory counterfloty gu. for SCOTLAND; 2nd, or, a fesse chequy az. and arg. in chief a label of three points gu., for STUART; 3rd, arg., a saltire between four roses gu., for LENNOX; 4th, or, a lion rampant gu., the whole within a bordure compony az. and arg.; 3rd, grand quarter, per chevron arg. and vert three hinds trippant ppr., for HAWKINS; over all on an escutcheon of pretence the arms of GOOLD, namely, az. on a fesse or between five goldfinches three in chief and two in base ppr., three mullets of the field, in the centre chief point a crescent of the second for difference, quartering QUIN and O'RIORDAN. Crest—A boar's head couped gu. langued az. charged with a cross patée or. Motto—Temperans et constans.
Estates—Cashelshanaghan, and Dunkineely, co. Donegal. Residences—Manor House, Dunkineely, co. Donegal; Killadreenan, Newtownmountkennedy, co. Wicklow.

GOOLD-VERSCHOYLE OF DROMADDA AND ATHEA.

HAMILTON FREDERICK STUART GOOLD-VERSCHOYLE, of Dromadda and Athea House, co. Limerick, J.P. cos. Donegal and Limerick, B.A. New Coll. Oxon, b. 6 Oct. 1874; m. 30 Aug. 1900, Sibyl Mary, younger dau. of Col. Frederick Augustus Le Mesurier, C.B., R.E., LL.D., and Louisa Anne his wife, dau. of the late John Denis Brown, M.P. (*see* BURKE'S *Peerage*, SLIGO, M.), and has issue,
1. Hamilton Neil Stuart, b. 19 Dec. 1904.
2. Denis, b. 21 Sept. 1910.
1. Eileen May, b. 17 May, 1902.
2. Sheila Dorothea, b. 28 Aug. 1903.

Mr. H. F. S. Goold-Verschoyle assumed by Royal Licence, 14 March, 1900, the additional surname and arms of GOOLD.

Lineage (*of* VERSCHOYLE).—*See* VERSCHOYLE *of Cashelshanaghan*.

Lineage (*of* GOOLD).—This is a branch of the very ancient family of GOOLD, or GOULD, of the city of Cork, and descends immediately from a common ancestor with the family of Goold, baronets.

FRANCIS GOOLD, of Cork, whose will, dated 6 July, 1770, was proved 26 Jan. 1771, was brother of HENRY GOOLD, whose grandson, FRANCIS, was created a baronet 8 Aug. 1801 (*see* BURKE'S *Peerage and Baronetage*). Francis Goold had by Elizabeth his wife, two daus, 1. Mary, m. Edmond Morony; 2. Barbara, m. Connell O'Connell, and two sons, one of whom,

JOHN GOOLD, of Cork, m. circa 1762, Mary, dau. of Valentine Quin, of Rosbrien, and sister and eventual heiress of John Quin, of Rosbrien (who m. Mary, dau. of Sir Edward O'Brien, Bart., of Dromoland, and left an only child, Mary Quin, of Rosbrien, m. to Matthew O'Brien, and d.s.p.). Valentine Quin was the son of John Quin, of Rosbrien, by Mary Anne his wife, dau. of Sir Walter Blake, Bart., of Menlough, co. Galway, and nephew of Valentine Quin, of Adare, ancestor of the Earl of Dunraven. By Mary Quin his wife, John Goold had issue,
1. Francis, Capt. Carabiniers, d. *unm.* 1815.
2. THOMAS, of whom presently.
3. Valentine, d. *unm.* 18 Dec. 1854.

The 2nd son,

THOMAS GOOLD, of Dromadda and Rosbrien, co. Limerick, M.P., a Master in Chancery, m. July, 1801, Elizabeth, dau. of Rev. Brinsley Nixon, M.A., Rector of Painstown, co. Meath, son of Andrew Nixon, of Cavan, and had issue,

Vesey. THE LANDED GENTRY. 726

1. FRANCIS, of Dromadda, co. Limerick, High Sheriff 1848, accidentally drowned in Sligo Bay 31 Aug. in that year.
2. FREDERICK FALKINER, of whom presently.
3. Wyndham, M.P. co. Limerick, *d. unm.* 27 Nov. 1854.
   1. Emily Mary, *m.* 19 Jan. 1831, the Rev. John George Wynne, Rector of Lorum, co. Carlow, and nephew of the late Owen Wynne, of Hazelwood, and had issue (*see that family*).
   2. Caroline Susan. *m.* 2 April, 1830, Sir Robert Gore Booth, Bart., of Lissadell, co. Sligo, and *d.* 16 Jan. 1855, leaving issue.
   3. Augusta Charlotte, *m.* 18 Aug. 1836, Edwin Richard Wyndham, 3rd Earl of Dunraven, K.P., and *d.* 25 Nov. 1866, leaving issue.

Master Gold *d.* 16 July, 1846. His 2nd son,

The VEN. FREDERICK FALKINER GOOLD, of Rosbrien, Ballygeale, Dromadda, and Athea, co. Limerick, Archdeacon of Raphoe and Rector of Raymochy, co. Donegal, *b.* May, 1808 ; *m.* 16 June, 1830, Caroline, dau. of Charles Newcomen, of Clonabard, co. Longford, and had issue,
1. Thomas Francis, *b.* 2 May, 1837 ; *d. unm.* 1861.
2. Augusta Jane, *d. unm.* 11 June, 1893.
3. Caroline Mary, *m.* 30 June, 1864, Brinsley de Courcy Nixon, son of Capt. Horatio Stopford Nixon, R.N. She *d.s.p* 10 May, 1875. He *m.* 2ndly, 6 Oct. 1877, Frances Evelyn, dau. of Thomas Inglis Hampton.
4. Emily Marianne, of Rosbrien, *m.* 1860, Henry Le Poer Wynne, Bengal Civil Service (*see* WYNNE *of Hazlewood*), and *d.* 21 Dec. 1868, having by him (who *d.* 1874) had a dau., Anne Le Poer, now of Rosbrien.
5. Elizabeth Jessie, *d. unm.* 18 June, 1862.
6. FRANCES FREDERIKA DOROTHEA,of Ballygeale, Limerick, *m.* 15 Dec. 1873, Rev. Hamilton Stuart Verschoyle, of Cashelshanaghan, co. Donegal (*see that family*), and has an only son,

HAMILTON FREDERICK STUART, *s.* his maternal grandfather at Dromadda.

The Ven. F. F. Goold *d.* 1877, and was *s.* by his grandson.

Arms—Quarterly of six, 1st grand quarter quarterly 1st and 4th arg. on a chevron between three boars' heads couped gu. a cross patée or (VERSCHOYLE); 2nd and 3rd, az., on a fesse or between five goldfinches, three in chief and two in base ppr. three mullets of the field, in the dexter chief point a crescent of the second for diff. (GOOLD) ; 2 GOOLD as before ; 3. arg., a chevron gu. between three boars' heads erased sa. (NESBITT) on a canton, within a bordure compony arg. and az. quarterly : 1st, or, a lion rampant gu. within a double tressure flory counterflory of the last (SCOTLAND) ; 2nd, or, a fesse chequy arg. and az. in chief a label of three points gu. (STUART); 3rd, arg., a saltire between four roses gu. (LENNOX) ; 4th, az., a lion rampant arg. (MACDUFF) ; 4th, Per chevron arg. and vert three hinds at gaze ppr. (HAWKINS) ; 5th, vert a pegasus pass. erm. a chief or (QUIN) ; 6th, quarterly : 1st and 4th, gu. out of clouds in the sinister a dexter arm fessewise ppr. holding a dagger in pale arg. pomel and hilt or, 2nd and 3rd, arg., a lion rampant gu. supporting a tree eradicated in the dexter ppr. (O'RIORDAN). Crests—1, a boar's head couped gu. charged with a cross patée or, VERSCHOYLE ; 2, A demi-lion rampant or charged on the shoulder with a crescent gu., GOOLD. *Motto*—Temperans et constans.

Seat—Athea House, Athea, co. Limerick.

VESEY OF DERRABARD.

ISABELLA ; WALLER ; and ZARA VESEY (who *d.* 11 July, 1909), of Derrabard, co. Tyrone, *s.* on the death of their brother, 1887.

Lineage. — GEORGE VESEY, of Hollymount, co. Mayo (5th son of the Most Rev. John Vesey, D.D., Archbishop of Tuam), (*see* BURKE'S *Peerage*, DE VESCI V.), *m.* Frances, dau. of Archibald Stewart, of Ballintoy, co. Antrim, and *d.* 5 July, 1737, having had (with four daus., 1. Anne, *d. unm.* ; 2. Letitia, *m.* her cousin, George Vesey, of Lucan (*see* COLTHURST-VESEY, *of Lucan*); 3. Frances, *m.* Thomas Lindsay ; and 4. Mary, *m.* John Ladaveze) issue,
1. FRANCIS, Barrister-at-Law and Master-in-Chancery, *m.* 22 Oct. 1756, Elizabeth, dau. of William Kenrick. She *d.* 1778. He *d.* 1804. having had issue,
   1. George, Barrister-at-Law, *b.* 24 Jan. 1760 ; *m.* 31 Dec. 1796, Margaret, dau. o John Arbuthnot, of Rockfleet, co. Mayo. She *d.* 2 Jan. 1853. He *d.* 30 May, 1841, having had issue,
      (1) George, of Derrynabuie, co. Galway, Capt. 9th Lancers, *b.* 21 May, 1802 ; *m.* 26 May, 1832, his cousin Harriet, dau. of Lewis Cockran, and *d.* 1886, having had issue,
         1. Charles Cynric Wellesley, of Derrynabuie, late Capt. and Brevet Maj. 72nd Highlanders, *b.* 28 May, 1833.
         2. Arthur Cyril, *b.* 14 Dec. 1834 ; *m.* 26 June, 1877, Fanny, dau. of Rev. Andrew Corbett, and has issue,

   a. George Andrew, *b.* 5 July, 1880.
   a. Blanche Mary.
   b. Margaret Elizabeth.
   3. George Francis, Col. late 43rd Regt., *b.* 2 March, 1839.
      1. Gertrude Frances, *m.* 23 Nov. 1876, Rev. John William Hawtrey, and has issue.
         (1) Anne Phoebe, *m.* 4 Aug. 1829, Nicholas Garry, and had issue.
         (2) Elizabeth Margaret, *d. unm.* 2 Oct. 1882.
         (3) Alicia Anne, *d. unm.* 29 April, 1852.
   2. Francis, Barrister-at-Law, *m.* Maria Lloyd, and *d.s.p.* 1845. She *d.* 1843.
      1. Matilda.   2. Eliza.
   2. JOHN, of whom presently.
   3. Thomas (Rev.), Rector of Dungannon, who by Mary his wife had issue,
      1. George, of Hollymount, *d.s.p.*
      2. Thomas Agmondisham (Rev.), Rector of Magherafelt, *b.* 1759 ; *m.* 30 Jan. 1793, Anna Maria, dau. of Rev. William Murray, D.D. She *d.* Sept. 1837. He *d.* 1844, leaving issue,
         (1) William (Rev.), of Clarinda Park, Kingstown, *b.* 11 June, 1800 ; *m.* 1st, Ann D'Absac, and 2ndly, Sept. 1862, Mary Anne, dau. of Richard Darling. She *d.* May, 1877. He *d.s.p.* 5 May, 1875.
         (2) George (Rev.), Rector of Inniscarra, *b.* 13 Aug. 1808 ; *m.* 21 March, 1839, Kate Marion, dau. of J. McDonnell, of Cork, and *d.* 22 May, 1842, having had issue,
            1. Thomas Agmondisham, of Knapton, Rosstrevor, co. Down, late Surg.-Maj. Royal S. Down Mil., *b.* 7 April, 1840 ; *d.* 31 Aug. 1909 ; *m.* 19 Sept. 1865, Frances, dau. of John Blakeney, and has issue,
               a. George Agmondisham (Rev.), M.A., *b.* 30 March, 1867 ; *d. unm.* 25 July, 1904.
               b. John Richard Murray, *b.* 26 June, 1871.
               a. Edith Frances, *m.* Herbert Mitchell.
               b. Kathleen Marion, *d. unm.*
               c. Elizabeth Mary, *d. unm.*
            2. Richard Murray, M.D., H.E.I.C.S., *b.* 25 Dec. 1843 *d. unm.*
               1. Anna Maria.
               2. Elizabeth Mahatabel.
         (3) Thomas Agmondisham, of Cookstown, co. Tyrone, *b.* 23 Aug. 1812 ; *m.* 28 Nov. 1838, Jemima Belford, dau. of James Gregg, of Londonderry, and *d.* 1895, leaving issue,
            1. Thomas Agmondisham (Rev.), Rector of Marske, Richmond, Yorks, *b.* 10 Jan. 1848 ; *m.* 1st, 2 Jan. 1873 Kathleen Hannah Murray, only child of the late John Alexander, of Caw, Londonderry, and by her (who *d.* June, 1887) has issue,
               a. Eustace de Burgh Agmondisham, *b.* 8 April, 1875.
               b. Douglas John Agmondisham, *b.* 30 March, 1878 ; *d.* 14 Sept. 1894.
               c. Yvo Agmondisham, *b.* 16 June, 1881 ; *d.* 15 Oct. 1897.
               a. Maude Murray, *m.* 24 Jan. 1906, Robert Sidney Hudson, of Ivy Cottage, Richmond, Yorks, eldest son of late Rev. Albert Hudson, and has issue.
               b. Geraldine Ethel Georgina Beatrice, *m.* 17 May, 1904, John Lees Casson, of 22, Elm Park Gardens, and has issue.

The Rev. T. A. Vesey *m.* 2ndly, 9 Oct. 1888, Adelaide Ann, only child of the late James Strain, C.I., R.I.C., and by her has issue,
            d. Norman Agmondisham, *b.* 20 July, 1889.
               1. Anna Matilda, *m.* 17 June, 1876, the late Rev. Francis Montgomery Scott, M.A., and has issue (*see* SCOTT *of Willsborough*).
               2. Elizabeth Frances, *m.* 6 June, 1867, Commander William Grant Douglas, R.N., who *d.* 16 Dec. 1898. leaving issue (*see* BURKE'S *Peerage*, MORTON, E.).
               3. Frances Letitia, *m.* Rev. W. P. Evans.
            (4) John Stuart, M.D., *b.* 22 May, 1815 ; *m.* 21 Dec. 1847, Lucy Elizabeth, dau. of Capt. Henderson Boyle, and *d.* 8 Oct. 1874, having had issue,
               1. Agmondisham Blathwayt, M.D., of Bellview, Magherafelt, co. Down, *b.* 24 Sept. 1848.
               1. Anna Frances Georgina, *m.* 7 Feb. 1871, Charles John Hives, R.N., and *d.* 2 Nov. 1882.
               2. Elizabeth Mary, *m.* 29 Jan. 1878, William Moore Armstrong, and has issue.
               3. Charlotte Amelia Grace Lucy.
            (1) Elizabeth Frances, *m.* 6 Oct. 1828, Rowley Miller, of Moneymore.
            (2) Mary Anne, *m.* 21 Jan. 1822, Col. George William Blathwayt, of Dyrham Park, co. Gloucester. He *d.* 14 Nov. 1871. She *d.* 25 Sept. 1875.

The 2nd son,

JOHN VESEY, of Cross, co. Galway, *d.* 3 June, 1779 ; *m.* Jane, dau. of Poole Hickman, of Kilmore, co. Clare, and had issue,
1. William, of Farnhill, co. Mayo, *m.* Oct. 1778, Phoebe, dau. of George Bingham, and by her, who *m.* 2ndly, James Kirkland, had issue, a dau.,
   Susan, *m.* 1801, her cousin, Gen. Sir Robert Arbuthnot, K.C.B. He *d.* 6 May, 1853. She *d.* 15 July, 1821, leaving issue.
2. GEORGE, of whom presently.
3. Poole Hickman, Lieut.-Col., *m.* 1st, Frances Transe ; and 2ndly, 1810, his cousin, Mary, dau. of James Irwin, and *d.* 9 Sept. 1834, having by his 1st wife had issue, a dau., Frances, *m.* 30 March, 1813, Rear-Adm. William Holt. She *d.* 1 July, 1839, leaving with other issue, Vesey Weston Holt.

4. John Agmondisham, Gen. in the Army, m. 25 June, 1795, Margaret, dau. of Henry Reynett, D.D. She d. 31 July, 1859. He d. 2 Dec. 1811, having had issue,
  1. Edward Agmondisham, b. 9 April, 1807 ; d. unm. 15 Oct. 1830.
  1. Augusta Elizabeth, m. 10 May, 1819, Sir John Kirkland. She d. 5 Aug. 1834. He d. 13 Jan. 1871.
  2. Margaret Anne, m. 22 July, 1817, John Southwell Brown, of Mount Brown, co. Limerick, and d. 13 Jan. 1853, leaving issue.
  3. Mary Sydney, d. unm. 29 Jan. 1878.
  4. Phoebe Susannah, m. Maj. George Rose, 15th Hussars.
5. Poole Francis, Capt. R.N., m. the dau. of —— Lloyd, of Carmarthen.
  1. Frances, m. Robert Marsball. 2. Letitia.
  3. Maria, m. Capt. Lindsay, co. Sligo.

The 2nd son,
REV. GEORGE VESEY, D.D., of Derrabard and Merrion Square, Dublin, Rector of Manfieldstown, co. Louth, Reader at the Royal Hospital, Kilmainham, and Chaplain of the Garrison, Dublin, m. Oct. 1789, Barbara, dau. and heir of Samuel Taylor, of Grange, Swords, co. Dublin, and by her (who d. 19 Dec. 1832, aged 70), left at his decease, 29 Feb. 1845, aged 84,
  1. SAMUEL, his heir.
  1. Anna Jane, m. (licence dated 30 March, 1814) Robert Ellwood, of Knockaboo, co. Roscommon.
  2. Sarah, m. 26 July, 1813, Rev. Christophilus Garstin, Rector of Ballyroney, co. Down, 2nd son of Christophilus Garstin, of Bragganstown, co. Louth, and d. 26 Aug. 1842, leaving issue (see GARSTIN of Bragganstown).
  3. Frances, m. 1 June, 1822, Mervyn Stewart, of Martray.
  4. Phoebe, m. 18 Aug. 1824, Robert Holt Truell, of Clonmannon, co. Wicklow (see that family).
  5. Eleanor, m. Robert Law, M.D., of Upper Merrion Street, Dublin, and d. 21 Oct. 1889, leaving issue (see LAW of Killaloe).

The son and heir,
SAMUEL VESEY, of Derrabard, J.P. and D.L., High Sheriff 1826, b. Nov. 1795 ; m. 10 Feb. 1816, Waller, 3rd dau. of the Right Rev. John Kearney, D.D., Bishop of Ossory, previously Provost of Trin. Coll. Dublin, and by her (who d. 21 July, 1876) had issue,
  1. John Agmondisham, b. 1819 ; d. unm. 1861.
  2. George Waller, of Derrabard.
  3. Mervyn Trevor, b. 1826 ; d. unm. 28 Nov. 1877.
  1. Anne, m. 2 Nov. 1843, James Lendrum, D.L., of Magheracross, co. Fermanagh, and had issue (see that family).
  2. Frances, m. 1846, William Woolsey, of Castle Bellingham, and d.s.p. 4 Oct. 1865 (see WOOLSEY of Milestown).
  3. ISABELLA,
  4. WALLER, co-heiresses of their brother, and now of Derrabard.
  5. ZARA,

Mr. Vesey d. 12 Dec. 1876, and was s. by his eldest surviving son,
GEORGE WALLER VESEY, of Derrabard, co. Tyrone, J.P. and D.L. co. Tyrone, High Sheriff 1879 and J.P. co. Cavan, Major late 5th Dragoon Guards, b. 1 July, 1821 ; d. 28 Feb. 1887, and was s. by his three sisters and co-heiresses.

Arms—Or, on a cross sa. a patriarchal cross of the field. Crest—A hand in armour, holding a laurel-branch, all ppr. Motto—Sub hoc signo vinces.

Seat—Detrabard, Omagh.

COLTHURST-VESEY OF LUCAN.

CHARLES NICHOLAS COLTHURST-VESEY, of Lucan House, co. Dublin, J.P. and D.L., High Sheriff 1908, late Capt. 8th Hussars, b. 11 Aug. 1860.

Lineage.—THE RIGHT HON. AGMONDISHAM VESEY, eldest son of the Most Rev. John Vesey, Archbishop of Tuam, and Lord Justice of Ireland (see BURKE's Peerage, DE VESCI, V.), by Anne, his second wife, dau. of Col. Agmondisham Muschamp. He m. 1st. Charlotte, dau. and sole heir of William Sarsfield, of Lucan, co. Dublin, eldest brother of Patrick, Earl of Lucan, and by her had issue, two daus.,
  1. Anne, m. Sir John Bingham, Bart., who d. 21 July, 1749, leaving issue (see BURKE's Peerage, LUCAN, E.).
  2. Henrietta, m. 18 July, 1721, Caesar Colclough, of Tintern Abbey, who d. 15 April, 1766, leaving issue (see that family).

Mr. Vesey m. 2ndly, Jane, dau. of Capt. Edward Pottinger, and relict, 1st, of John Reynolds, of Killabride, and 2ndly, of Sir Thomas Butler, Bart., by which lady (who d. 1746) he had issue,
  1. AGMONDISHAM, his heir. 2. Edward.
  3. Charles, R.N.
  4. George, m. 1754, his cousin, Letitia, dau. of his uncle, the Rev. George Vesey, and had a son,
    GEORGE, of whom presently, as heir to his uncle.

3. Jane. 4. Letitia, m. — Meredyth.
5. Catherine, m. Anthony Jephson, of Mallow, M.P.
6. Semira.

Agmondisham Vesey (whose will, dated 18 March, 1733, was proved 7 May, 1739) was s. by his son,

AGMONDISHAM VESEY, of Lucan, M.P., Accountant-General of Ireland, m. Elizabeth, dau. of Sir Thomas Vesey, Bart., Bishop of Ossory, and widow of William Handcock, of Twyford, co. Westmeath, M.P., but by this lady, who was the accomplished Mrs. Vesey, the friend of Dr. Johnson, he had no issue. His will bears date 19 Sept. 1772, and was proved 20 Dec. 1785. His nephew and heir,

COL. GEORGE VESEY, of Lucan, m. Emily, dau. of the Right Hon. David La Touche, and had issue, an only child and heir,

ELIZABETH VESEY, m. 11 Nov. 1819, Sir Nicholas Conway Colthurst, 4th bart. (see BURKE's Peerage). He d. 22 June, 1829, leaving issue. Their 2nd son,

CHARLES VESEY COLTHURST-VESEY, of Lucan, J.P. co. Kildare, J.P. and D.L. co. Dublin, High Sheriff 1858, Col. Dublin Light Infantry Militia, b. 13 June, 1826 ; m. 20 July, 1858, Annie (d. 19 March, 1911), dau. of Col. David Fraser, and had issue,
  1. GEORGE, late of Lucan House.
  2. CHARLES NICHOLAS, now of Lucan House.
  3. Edward Robert, b. 30 April, 1862.

This gentleman assumed by Royal Licence, bearing date 21 Nov. 1860, the additional surname and arms of VESEY, and d. 11 May, 1885. His eldest son,

GEORGE COLTHURST-VESEY, of Lucan House, co. Dublin, Capt. King's Shropshire Light Infantry, b. 27 April, 1859, and d. unm. 1894.

Arms—Quarterly: 1st and 4th, or, on a cross sa. a patriarchal cross of the field, for VESEY ; 2nd and 3rd, arg., on a fesse, between three colts courant sa., as many trefoils slipped or, for COLTHURST. Crests—1st, a hand in armour, holding a laurel-branch, all ppr. for VESEY ; 2nd, a colt statant sa., for COLTHURST. Motto—Sub hoc signo vinces.

Seat—Lucan House, Lucan. Clubs—Naval and Military, S.W. Kildare Street, Dublin.

VESEY. See BURKE's PEERAGE, DE VESCI, V.

VESEY-FITZGERALD. See FITZGERALD.

VIGORS OF BURGAGE.

EDWARD CLIFFE VIGORS, of Burgage, co. Carlow, a Clerk in the House of Lords, b. 9 Oct. 1878 ; s. his father 1908.

Lineage.—REV. LOUIS VIGORS, of Hollodon, Bridgerule, North Devon, b. 1578, was the first of the family who settled in Ireland. He matriculated at Exeter Coll. Oxford, 5 May, 1598. In the Irish records, he appears as Vicar of Kilfaughnabeg and Kilcoe, co. Cork, 1615 and 1634 ; Vicar of Templequinlan, Diocese of Ross, 2 Feb. 1616 ; Treasurer of the Cathedral of Ross, 28 March, 1631, installed 7 May same year. He m. Thomasine, only dau. of Thomas Call, Gent., of Hollodon and Bridgerule, and widow of — Veo, of Bridgerule (marriage licence dated 18 April, 1610), and d. at Bideford, North Devon, 9 Oct. 1642, aged 64, and his widow, Thomasine, d. at Holsworthy, Devon, in March 1651. "He was seised in fee of the demesne lands of Hallacton of the value of £300 per annum, and divers other lands and tenements, etc." (Chancery Proceedings, CHARLES I.) His son and heir,

REV. URBAN VIGORS, was Rector of Ardnageehy, co. Cork, Sept. 1634, and Vicar of Kilworth and Kilcrump, co. Cork, 1635 to 1639, also Chaplain to Roger, Lord Broghill, 1st Earl of Orrery, during the Rebellion of 1641. He m. about 1635-6, Catherine, dau. of Rev. Thomas Boyle, sister of Richard Boyle, D.D., Bishop of Ferns and Leighlin, and of Roger Boyle, D.D., Bishop of Clogher (see BURKE's Peerage and Baronetage, CORK, E.), and had issue,
  1. URBAN, of whom presently.
  2. Thomas, of co. Kildare (1700), and of Taghmon, co. Wexford (1707). He m. in 1674, Elizabeth Gilbert, widow, of Castledermot.

Vigors. THE LANDED GENTRY. 728

co. Kildare, and had, with two daus. (Mary, *m.* Rev. Joshua Thomas, Rector of Ferns, Prebendary of Kilrush, co. Wexford, son of the Rev. Thomas Thomas, Prebendary of Clone 1705, and Kilrush 1714 ; the Rev. Joshua Thomas, *d.* 1738 ; and Martha, *m.* April, 1711, Rev. James Burrowes, Rector of Fethard, co.Wexford), a son,

ROGER (Rev.), *b.* 1683, ordained by his uncle, Bartholomew Vigors, Bishop of Ferns and Leighlin, 22 March, 1708, Rector of Barrah, co. Carlow, Dec. 1710 ; and also Rec or of Ballyconnock, and Mulrankin, co. Wexford ; his will is dated 9 Jan. 1734, and he *d.* soon after, leaving, by Elizabeth his wife, dau. of John Harvey, of Killiane, co. Wexford, and widow of Richard Rowe, of Ballyharty, same co., with two younger sons, Bartholomew, *b.* 1705, and William, and two daus., Meek, *m.* 1736, John Vickers (marriage licence dated 16 Feb.), and Martha, living *unm.* 1725, an elder son,

URBAN, of Ballyconnick, and New Ross, co. Wexford, *m.* the dau. of Rev. Joshua Thomas, Prebendary of Kilrush, co. Wexford, and had issue,
1. ROGER, *m.* 2 March, 1766, Esther, widow of—Grainger, of New Ross, and dau. of Boyd, of Rosslare.
2. Urban, *b.* 1747, a Lieut.-Gen. in the H.E.I.C.S (Madras Presidency) 1770 ; *m.* Elizabeth, widow of Thomas Constable of Dublin, and dau. of Joseph Smith, of Bristol; she *d.* Aug. 1817, aged 79 ; be *d.* in London, 10 April, 1815, *s.p.* and was buried in Marylebone Church, where there is a handsome monument erected to his memory.
3. Bartholomew, a Major in the H.E.I.C.S. (Madras Presidency) 1770 ; he *m.* in India. 4. Joshua.
1. Margaret, *m.* Oct. 1671, John Squires, of New Ross ; she *d.* April, 1794.
2. Frances, *m.* (licence dated 12 July, 1760) Solomon Richards, of Solsborough, co. Wexford (*see* RICHARDS *of Solsborough*).
3. Mary, *m.* Major John Cotgrave, Madras Engineers, who *d.* 13 April, 1825, leaving issue.
4. Martha, *m.* Gen. Hewett, C.B., who *d.* 16 April, 1825, and had issue, one son and two daus.

* RICHARD VIGORS, of Old Leighlin (eldest son of Urban Vigors, of Old Leighlin), cornet in Capt. Pierce Butler's troop of Dragoons, 1702, High Sheriff co. Carlow 1714 ; *m.* 1st, Mary, grand-dau. of Samuel and Mary Green, by whom (who *d.* 2 March, 1704) he had no issue. He *m.* 2ndly, 1705, Jane, dau. of John Cliffe (Cromwell's Secretary at War in Ireland) and sister of John Cliffe, of Mulrancan (*see* CLIFFE *of Bellevue*), by whom (who was *b.* 16 June, 1682, and *d.* Nov. 1768) he had issue,
1. BARTHOLOMEW (Very Rev.), his heir.
2. JOHN, successor to his brother.
3. Thomas, *d. unm.* 3 Dec. 1779.
1. Ellinor, *b.* 1710 ; *m.* Feb. 1736, William Cliffe, of New Ross, and *d.* 9 Nov. 1806.

Mr. Vigors *d.* intestate 1723 ; administration was granted to his widow 2 March, 1724, and he was s. by his eldest son,

VERY REV. BARTHOLOMEW VIGORS, of Old Leighlin, Dean of Leighlin, *b.* 3 Aug. 1707, appointed Chancellor of Leighlin 27 Aug. 1740, Rector of Wells, co. Carlow, 20 Jan. 1740, and Dean of Leighlin, 16 Jan. 1749 ; Rector of Shankhill, co. Kilkenny, 1749 ; Rector of Aghada, co. Carlow, 1741-50 ; *m.* 1732, Frances, dau. of Stephen Deane, of Dublin, and niece of Arthur Price, D.D., Archbishop of Cashel. She *d.* intestate, and admon. was granted to her niece, Mary Bradford, 8 Nov. 1785. He *d.s.p.* 17 Nov. 1753, and was bur. in the Earl of Cork's tomb at St. Patrick's, when he was s. by his brother,

JOHN VIGORS, of Old Leighlin, *b.* 19 Aug. 1709, High Sheriff co. Carlow 1766, Freeman of Ross 22 Feb. 1731. He *m.* 6 Nov. 1751, Anne, eldest dau. of Nicholas Aylward, of Shankhill Castle, co. Kilkenny, and had by her (who *d.* March, 1802), three sons and two daus.,
1. Bartholomew, *b.* 19 Sept. 1752 ; *d. unm. v.p.* 11 Sept. 1771.
2. NICHOLAS AYLWARD, his heir.
3. Richard (Rev.), *b.* 28 July, 1760, B.A. Trin. Coll. Dublin 1783 ; *d. unm.* 1819.
1. Catherine, *b.* 15 July, 1755 ; *d. unm.* 18 March, 1790 ; will dated 7 Feb. 1790.
2. Jane, *b.* 26 March, 1762 ; *m.* 12 March, 1784, Philip Doyne, Barrister-at-Law, son of Very Rev. Charles Doyne, D.D., Dean of Leighlin, and had issue.

Mr. John Vigors *d.* 6 Oct. 1776, and was s. by his eldest surviving son, NICHOLAS AYLWARD VIGORS, of Old Leighlin and Belmont, co. Carlow, Capt. H.M. 29th Regt., served in the American War, *b.* 3 Nov. 1755 ; *m.* 1st, 17 June, 1781, Catherine, dau. of Solomon Richards, of Solsborough, co. Wexford, and by her (who *d.* 15 March, 1802) had issue,
1. NICHOLAS AYLWARD, his heir.
1. Frances, *b.* 5 May, 1782 ; *d.* 3 May, 1786.
2. Anne, *b.* 3 June, 1782 ; *d. unm.* 26 March, 1869, bur. at Old Leighlin.
3. Frances Richards, bapt. at Old Leighlin 22 Dec. 1788 ; *m.* Casemir Pierre Adrian d'Herisson, Chef d'Escadron of the Garde du Corps of CHARLES X., King of France, and settled at the Château de Brac, near Toulouse. She *d.* 24 June, 1877, aged 79.
4. Matilda, *b.* July, 1793 ; *m.* William Richards Derinzy, of co. Wexford, and *d.s.p.* 27 Nov. 1870, bur. at Old Leighlin.

Mr. Vigors *m.* 2ndly, 5 Dec. 1803, Mary Jane, dau. of Col. Hon. John Browne, 13th Light Dragoons, by his wife Elizabeth, youngest dau. of Hon. Richard Allen (brother of Lord Allen), by whom (who *d.* 20 Oct. 1828, aged 49) he had issue,
2. THOMAS TENCH, of Erindale, co. Carlow, *b.* 10 Sept. 1804, J.P. and D.L. for co. Carlow, and High Sheriff 1843 ; *m.* 1 Oct. 1832, Jane, dau. and heir of Gilbert Pickering Rudkin, of Wells,

3. George, living July, 1715.
4. BARTHOLOMEW, *b.* at Tawton (Bishops Tawton), Devon, bapt. there 18 Feb. 1643, M.A. and LL.B., J.P., Rector of St. Mary's, Wexford, 1681. In 1668, he was made Chancellor of Ferns, and was for many years Vicar-General of the diocese. He was promoted Dean of Armagh 29 June, 1681, and was consecrated Bishop of Ferns and Leighlin 8 March, 1691. He *m. circa* 1674, Martha, dau. of Constantine Neale, of New Ross, co. Wexford, and sister of Ven. Benjamin Neale, Archdeacon of Leighlin. The Bishop (who left by his will a farm value £548, and £300 to enrich the See of Leighlin, and build a manse house), *d.* 3 Jan. 1721, aged 76, and was bur. in the Earl of Cork's tomb, in St. Patrick's Cathedral, Dublin, as was also his widow, 19 July, 1729. Their children were,
1. Richard, bapt. in Wexford, 3 April, 1679 ; bur. in the Earl of Cork's tomb, St. Patrick's, 21 Feb. 1690-1.
2. Roger, bapt. 16 Jan. 1680.
1. Mary, *m.* Rev. Robert Elliott, D.D., of New Ross, and bad issue.
2. Katherine, *b.* in Wexford 29 Dec. 1675 ; *m.* John Beauchamp, of Ballyloughane, co. Carlow, M.P., and had issue.
3. Susanna, bapt. in Wexford 2 Sept. 1677 ; *m.* St. Leger Gilbert, of Kilminchy, Queen's Co. She was bur. in the Earl of Cork's tomb, in Dublin, 20 Sept. 1713, leaving issue.
4. Martha, *m.* Sir Thomas Burdett, 1st bart. (*see* BURKE's *Peerage and Baronetage,* WELDON).

Rev. Urban Vigors *d.* at Bishops Tawton, Devon, intestate, 1652, and administration was granted to his widow 11 Sept. that year. His eldest son,

URBAN VIGORS, of Old Leighlin, J.P. co. Carlow and High Sheriff 1700, and a Commissioner for that co. under the Act 10 WILLIAM III. cap. 3, *b.* 1636. He *m.* Bridget, dau. of Allen Tench, of Staplestown, co. Carlow (youngest son of — Tench, of Nantwich, co. Chester, who came to Ireland about 1645, and was granted by King CHARLES II estates in the cos. of Wexford and Carlow), and sister of John Tench, of Mullinderry, co. Wexford, and had two sons,
1. RICHARD, his heir, of Old Leighlin, ancestor of the senior line of the family.* 2. THOMAS, of whom we treat.

co. Carlow, by whom (who *m.* 2ndly, June, 1852, Patrick Murphy, Q.C., Assistant Barrister, co. Cavan, and *d.* Boulogne, 29 Oct. 1879, aged 80) he left at his decease 20 Feb. 1840,
HENRY RUDKIN, s. his uncle.
Mary Jane, *b.* 1833 ; *d. unm.* 3 Sept. 1850.
3. Joshua Allen (Col.), bapt. at Old Leighlin 23 Dec. 1805, served in H.M. 52nd Light Infantry in the West Indies, Canada, and in India during the Mutiny. He commanded the storming party of his regt. at the capture of Delhi in 1857 ; *m.* 1 Sept. 1863, at Wintertown, co. Dublin, Mary (who *d.* 21 Jan. 1911), 2nd dau. of the late William Cary, of co. Carlow. He *d.s.p.* 30 March, 1865.
4. Horatio Nelson Trafalgar (Gen.), *b.* 11 March, 1807, commanded H.M. 13th Light Infantry, and afterwards the St. Helena Regt., and was acting Governor of that island. Served in the Cabul campaign 1838-9 ; was sent in pursuit of the Ruler of Candahar, and led the storming party of his regt. at the storming and capture of Ghuznee ; was present at the capture of Cabul, and received the pension for "distinguished service." He *m.* 24 Dec. 1839, Clara Matilda, dau. of Samuel Butler, and by her (who *d.* at Landour, Bengal, 9 Nov. 1842) had issue,
Horace Butler, *b.* 23 Oct. 1842 ; *d.* at Sukkur, in Scinde, 8 Feb. 1844.
Clara Georgina, *d. unm.* in Carlow, 5 May, 1883.
Gen. Vigors *d.* in Paris 21 June, 1864, aged 57, and was bur. in Père-la-Chaise.
5. Charles Henry Fitzroy Stanhope, *b.* 3 May, 1810, served as Lieut. in H.M. 87th Royal Irish Fusiliers ; he was killed by a fall when riding the Garrison Steeplechase, at the "Moor of Meath," near Dublin, 9 April, 1844, *unm.,* aged 34, bur. at Old Leighlin.
6. John Urban, *b.* 14 Dec. 1811, served in H.M. 9th Regt. in India in the campaign of 1842, in Afghanistan, and in the Sutlej campaign, present at the battles of Moodkee, Ferozeshah (in which he was wounded), and Sobraon (medal and two clasps) ; *m.* Sophie Mary Anne, dau. of Capt. John Braham, Ceylon Rifles, by whom (who *d.* 1853) he had issue,
Richard Fitzroy Stanhope Vigors, settled in New South Wales.
Dorothea Eleanor.
He *d.* 20 Aug. 1865, in New South Wales.
5. Dorothea Elizabeth, *m.* Henry Cary, of Carlow, who *d.s.p.* 9 April, 1863. She *d.* in Dublin, 2 March, 1886.

Mr. N. A. Vigors *d.* 3 March, 1828, and was bur. at Old Leighlin. He was *s.* by his eldest son,

NICHOLAS AYLWARD VIGORS, of Old Leighlin, *b.* 1785, D.C.L. Trin. Coll. Oxford, July, 1832, Capt. in the Foot Guards, and served in the Peninsula war, and was severely wounded at the battle of Barossa, 5 March, 1811. He was D.L. co. Carlow, and M.P. for that co. from 1832 until his death. He *d. unm.* in London 26 Oct. 1840, in his 55th year, and was bur. in the nave of the Cathedral of Old Leighlin, when the representation of the family devolved on his nephew,

HENRY RUDKIN VIGORS, of Erindale, Capt. in the Carlow Rifles, formerly Capt. in H.M. 10th Regt., *m.* 20 Aug. 1862, Mary Harriet, eldest dau. of John Campbell (one of the Campbells of Barbeck, N.B.), Civil Commissioner and Resident Magistrate, Cape of Good Hope, and had issue,

THOMAS NICHOLAS, *b.* at Boulogne 2 May, 1863 ; *d. unm.* 19 Nov. 1879.

Capt. H. R. Vigors *d.* at Kingstown, co. Dublin, 20 March, 1883, aged 48. His widow *m.* 2ndly, 23 Sept. 1885, Lieut.-Col. Edward Holme Butler (*see* BURKE's *Peerage,* BUTLER, Bart.) commanding the Carlow Rifles, and *d.* 21 Nov. the same year.

Mr. Urban Vigors was attainted by the Parliament of James II., and was subsequently a Commissioner for co. Carlow under the Act of 10 William III. He d. 7 May, 1716, aged 80. His younger son, Thomas Vigors, of Heywood and Derryfore, Queen's Co., 1714, of Soldon, Devon, 1725, and of Corres, co. Carlow, 1729, b. 1684, Capt. of the Black Horse (Ligonier's Dragoons), J.P. for Queen's Co., and High Sheriff 1714. By Margaret his 1st wife, he had four sons and one dau.,
1. Urban, b. 14 July, 1704, living June, 1729.
2. Bartholomew, b. 3 Aug. 1705; d. 20 Jan. 1766.
3. John, of Youghal. co. Cork, b. 24 June, 1709 (bond dated 5 June, 1746), Anne, dau. of James Hogan, of Youghal.
4. Bourke, b. 13 July, 1715.
1. Lucy, b. 14 Dec. 1707; m. 1st, Sept. 1728, Michael Hewetson, of Dublin (and son of Christopher Hewetson and his wife Ursula Wallis, M.P. for Thomastown, co. Kilkenny, 1695, and great-grandson of Christopher Hewetson, Treasurer of Christ Church Cathedral, Dublin, 1596-1604), and 2ndly, Jan. 1735, Samuel Carpenter, and d April, 1751.
He m. 2ndly, Dec. 1735, Elizabeth Naylor, widow, by whom (who d. 1737) he had no issue. He m. 3rdly, Nov. 1737, Elizabeth, dau. of Edward Mercer, of The Lodge, Bagenalstown, co. Carlow, by whom he had further issue. two sons and as many daus.,
5. Richard, of Orchard, co. Carlow, b. 1739; d. unm. 1760.
6. Edward (Rev.), of whom hereafter.
2. Mary, d. young.
3. Bridget, m. Nov. 1768, William Dawson, of Noghoval, co. Westmeath.
Capt. Vigors d. Oct. 1750. His youngest son,
Rev. Edward Vigors, of Burgage, co. Carlow, Rector of Shankill, co. Kilkenny, 1781, b. 1747, M.A. T.C.D.; m. Dec. 1773, Mary, dau. of Edward Low, of Lissoy, co. Westmeath, and d. 27 June, 1797 (will dated 2 June, 1794), leaving issue,
1. Thomas Mercer, his heir.
1. Elizabeth, d. unm. 27 July, 1828.
2. Maria, m. 4 Sept. 1805, Rev. George Alcock, Rector of Ullard, co. Kilkenny, and d. 5 March, 1854, leaving issue.
The only son,
Rev. Thomas Mercer Vigors, of Burgage, Rector of Powerstown, co. Kilkenny, 1817, until his death in 1850, b. 23 Oct. 1775, B.A. Trin. Coll. Dublin 1796, M.A. 1832, ordained 26 March, 1797; m. 27 Aug. 1810, Anne, dau. of Rev. John Cliffe, of New Ross, and co-heir of her brother, John Cliffe. She d. 1 Oct. 1861. He d. 7 April, 1850, leaving issue,
1. Edward, b. 21 Oct. 1811; d. unm. at Toulouse, 16 Dec. 1828.
2. John Cliffe, b. 14 Jan. 1813.
3. John Cliffe, M.A. T.C.D., J.P. co. Carlow, late Major in the Carlow Rifles, b. 22 June, 1814; d. unm. 9 Jan. 1881, at Burgage. He bequeathed his estates to his brother, Thomas Mercer, for his lifetime, and after his death to his nephew, Thomas Mercer Cliffe, who s. to them in Sept. of the same year through the death of his uncle, Thomas Mercer
4. Bartholomew Urban, B.A. Trin. Coll. Dublin, 1839, b. 24 May, 1817; m. 3 June, 1852, at Perth, Western Australia, Charlotte Elizabeth, eldest dau. of Col. John Bruce, and d. at Perth 15 March, 1854, where he was acting Advocate-General of the colony, leaving by his wife (who m. 2ndly, 15 June, 1865, Charles Leathley, of Roseville, Hampton, Middlesex, and d. 1 Oct. 1877), one son,
Thomas Mercer Cliffe, late of Burgage.
5. Thomas Mercer, M.I.C.E., b. 19 Sept. 18.9, B.A Trin. Coll. Dublin, Superintending Engineer Northern Railway, Nattore, Bengal. "During the Sonthal insurrection he received the thanks of the Governor-General and Council of India, for having given the first check to that rebellion." He m. 13 Jan. 1857, Sophia, youngest dau. of Rev. Charles William Doyne, Prebendary of Fethard, co. Wexford (see Doyne of Wells), and d. 7 Sept. 1881, at Burgage, leaving issue by her (who d. 5 Nov. 1865),
1. Charles Thomas Doyne, Ceylon C.S., b. 11 Dec. 1857; m. 22 April, 1882, at Colombo, Ceylon, Robina Margaret, 2nd surviving dau. of William Ferguson, F.L.S., of Kelvin Grove, Colombo, and has issue,
(1) Mervyn Doyne, Lieut. 5th Bengal Lancers (Hodson's Horse), b. 19 Nov. 1886.
(1) Esmee Innes, b. 22 June, 1885.
(2) Elinor May, b. at Colombo, 29 July, 1892.
2. Thomas Mercer, Major (Retired) A.P.D., formerly Capt. 4th (King's Own) Regt., b. 24 Oct. 1859; m. 17 Dec. 1892, at Malta, Nellie Josephine, dau. of J. Rhattigan, and d. 9 Jan. 1910, leaving issue,
Allen Doyne, b. 11 March, 1908.
3. Philip Urban Walter, D.S.O. (Cromwell Road, Basingstoke), Maj. late 11th (Devon) Regt., gazetted Devonshire Regt. 1882, served in Burmah, 1891 (medal and clasps), S. Africa 1899-1902, twice, wounded at the relief of Ladysmith, March, 1900 (mentioned in despatches, Queen's medal, five clasps, King's medal, two clasps, awarded D.S.O.), b. 8 Feb. 1863; m. 21 Oct. 1891, Anna Louisa Hyacinth, 3rd dau. of the late Rev. Hyacinth Talbot D'Arcy, of Clifden Castle, co. Galway, and has issue,
(1) Urban Cliffe Vigors, b. 31 Aug. 1904; d. 22 April, 1908.
(1) Hyacinth D'Arcy, b. 24 Jan. 1894.
(2) Evelyn Maude, b. 31 Oct. 1897.
4. Cliffe Henry, Major (retired) 18th Royal Irish Regt., b. 10 June, 1864.
6. Percy, b. 28 Dec. 1820, B.A. Trin. Coll. Dublin, 1848, High Sheriff of the colony of the Cape of Good Hope for many years, d. unm. in London, 5 Feb. 1889.
7. Richard William (Rev.), b. 20 Nov. 1823, M.A. Trin. Coll. Dublin, 1867, ordained 17 Oct. 1852, Curate of Westbury, co. Gloucester, 1859, of Henbury 1861-9; Rector of Littleton-on-Severn 1869-75, of Eridge, Sussex, 1875-9, and Rector of Llanwenarth, Diocese of Llandaff, 1879. He m. 1 Nov. 1866, Emily,

dau. of Philip Vaughan, of Redland House, co. Gloucester, and has issue,
1. Thomas Mercer de Cliffe, b. 18 Dec. 1870.
2. Richard Percy Littleton, D.S.O., Capt. (retired) Connaught Rangers, served in S. Africa with 2nd Regt. Mounted Infantry 1899-1902 (mentioned in despatches, Queen's medal, six clasps, and King's medal, two clasps, awarded D.S.O.), b. 25 Jan. 1873; m. 16 March, 1911, Olive Muriel, dau. of Col. H. J. O. Walker, of Buldeigh, Salterton, Devonshire.
3. Philip Urban, M.V.O., Capt. (retired) Royal Irish Regt., served in S. Africa with 1st Batt. Mounted Infantry 1899-1902 (mentioned in despatches, Queen's medal, five clasps, King's medal, two clasps) (Club : Isthmian), b. 7 July, 1875.
1. Emily Edith, m. 29 Sept. 1897, Rev. Fred. H. Aldrich-Blake, Vicar of Bishopswood, Hereford, and has issue (see that family).
2. Eva Alice Maude, d. unm. 25 March, 1894.
8. Philip Doyne, of Holloden, co Carlow, J.P., High Sheriff 1894, served on the Staff in Ireland 1862-3, and with the 11th and 19th Regts. in Australia, Burmah, and India, Col. late commanding 19th (the Princess of Wales's Own) Regt., retired on full pay 12 Jan. 1881; b. 23 Dec. 1825; m. 19 July, 1882, Margaret Caroline, 3rd dau. of Major Henry Joseph Plumridge Woodhead, of Heathfield House, Sussex, and 12, Norfolk Terrace, Brighton, and d. 30 Dec. 1903, leaving issue, Esther Alice, m. 7 June, 1911, Major Standish de Courcy O'Grady, R.A.M.C. (see O'Grady of Kilballyowen).
1. Sarah, b. 1816; d. unm. 18 Sept. 1894.
2. Anne Maria, b. 29 Oct. 1829; d. 18 Jan. 1830.
Thomas Mercer Cliffe Vigors, of Burgage, co. Carlow, J.P. co. Carlow, s. his uncle, Thomas Mercer Vigors, 7 Sept. 1881, b. 13 March, 1853; m. 4 April, 1877, Mary Louisa Helen, eldest dau. of Col. the Hon. Robert French Handcock, R.A. (see Burke's Peerage, Castlemaine, B.), and d. 30 Jan. 1908, leaving issue,
1. Edward Cliffe, now of Burgage.
2. Ludlow Ashmead Cliffe, b. 23 Jan. 1884.
1. Kathleen Mary, b. 4 Feb. 1880; m. 21 Aug. 1909, Hon. Wilfred Gilbert Thesiger, D.S.O., H.M., Envoy Extraordinary and Minister Plenipotentiary at Addis Abeba, Abyssinia, and has issue (see Burke's Peerage, Chelmsford, B.).
2. Eileen Edmée, b. 15 May, 1881; m. 19 Nov. 1909, Rev. Arthur Evelyn Ward, Vicar of Lemsford, Hertfordshire, son of Col. Ward, R.E., of Aubrey House, Milford-on-Sea, and has issue.

Arms (Confirmed to Rev. Richard William Vigors and Philip Doyne Vigors and their descendants only)—Quarterly: 1st and 4th, arg., three stags' heads erased gu., attired or, for Vigors; 2nd, erm. on a fess between three wolf's heads erased sa., a trefoil between two mullets or, for Cliffe; 3rd, az., a chevron between three estoiles arg., for Carr. Crest A stag's head erased, as in the arms. Motto—Spectemur agendo.

Seat—Burgage, Leighlin Bridge, co. Carlow. Residence—18, Buckingham Palace Mansions, London, S.W.

VILLIERS-STUART. See STUART.

VILLIERS-TUTHILL. See TUTHILL.

VINCENT OF SUMMERHILL.

Arthur Hare Vincent, of Summerhill, co. Clare. J.P., High Sheriff 1890, Col. late Commanding 3rd (King's Own) Hussars, b. 19 Feb. 1861; m. 1st, 1 Feb. 1871, Elizabeth Rose, dau. of David Davidson Manson, of Spynie, co. Moray, N.B., and by her (who d. 17 Dec. 1879) has issue,
1. Berkeley, Major 6th Inniskilling Dragoons, late Capt. R.H.A., b. 4 Dec. 1871; m. 18 Sept. 1906, Lady Kitty Edith Blanche Ogilvy, eldest dau. of the 8th Earl of Airlie (see Burke's Peerage, Airlie, E.), and has issue,
John Ogilvy, b. 25 March, 1911.
2. Arthur Rose, B.L., Barrister-at-Law, served as Judge under the Foreign Office at Zanzibar, Bangkok and Shanghai, b. 9 June, 1876; m. 30 March, 1910, Maud, only child of William Bowers Bowen, of Empire Cottage, San Francisco, California, U.S.A.
1. Helena Marion Stewart Mackenzie, m. 7 Oct. 1896, Capt. William Gardiner Eley, 14th Hussars, eldest son of the late William Thomas Eley, of Oxley Grange, Herts.
He m. 2ndly, 1 Dec. 1883, Gertrude Mary, only child of Richard Birley Baxendale, of Blackmore End, Herts. and 35, Portman Square, W., and has further issue,
3. Arthur Birley Patrick Love.
2. Aileen Mary, m. 17 Oct. 1905, Henry Kellerman Hamilton-Wedderburn, Lieut. Scots Guards, son of Col. H. B. Hamilton, late 14th Hussars (see Hamilton of Ballymacoll).
3. Angela Clare Gertrude.
4. Ailsie Noreen Cynthia.
5. Azalea Rosemary Grania.

Lineage.—This branch of the Vincent family has been established in the cos. of Limerick and Clare since the reign of William III.

Wade. THE LANDED GENTRY. 730

John Vincent, Sheriff of Limerick 1696, and Mayor 1703 and 1727, *m.* Phœbe Brown, widow of John Higginbotham, Chancellor of Limerick, and left issue,
1. John, whose will was proved in 1766. 2. Richard.
3. Thomas, Mayor of Limerick 1736 and 1740, from whom descend the Vincents *of Boston Lodge*, co. York.
4. Arthur, of whom hereafter.
1. Anne, *m.* Ven. John Brown, Archdeacon of Limerick.
2. Alice, *m.* George Roche, M.P. for Limerick 1713-15.
3. Elizabeth, *m.* John Davies.
4. Phœbe, *m.* Matthew MacNamara.

John Vincent's will was proved 1735. His 4th son,
Arthur Vincent, Mayor of Limerick 1728 (whose will was proved 1761) *m.* Blanche, sister of George Waller (of the Castle Waller family), and had a son,
John Vincent, of Limerick, who *m.* 1st, 1754, Catherine, dau. of John Love, of Castle Saffron, co. Cork, and by her had, with three daus., three sons,
1. Arthur, his heir.
2. William, Col. 62nd Regt., *b.* 1762; *m.* Fanny Hoare, and *d.s.p.*
3. John, Gen. in the Army, Col. 69th Regt., *b.* 1764; *d. unm.* 1848.

He *m.* 2ndly, Lucy, dau. of Thomas Westropp, of Ballysteen, co. Limerick, and widow of Capt. Lindsay, and by her had, with four daus., three sons,
4. Thomas, *b.* 1769.
5. George (Rev.), *b.* 1772, Rector of Shanagolden.
6. Berkeley, Lieut. 19th Regt.

The eldest son,
Arthur Vincent, of Summerhill, co. Clare, *b.* 1761; *m.* 1783, Mary, dau. of Berkeley Westropp, and had issue,
1. William, Col. 82nd Regt., *b.* 1786; *m.* Frances Blood, and *d.s.p.* 1834.
2. George, of Erinagh, co. Clare, *m.* Henrietta, dau. of John Massy, of Waterpark, co. Clare, and had issue,
1. Arthur William, *m.* Dorothea, dau. of Blood Smyth, of Castle Fergus, co. Clare, and has issue, one dau.,
Fanny, *m.* Capt. Nugent, R.A.
2. John Berkeley, Lieut. 57th Regt., *d. unm.* 1865.
1. Ellen, *m.* 14 Dec. 1853, Col. Jesse Lloyd, of Ballyleck, co. Monaghan.
2. Mary, *m.* Matthew Smyth, Q.C., of Castle Fergus.
3. Berkeley, of Summerhill.

The third son,
Berkeley Vincent, of Summerhill, Lieut. 49th Regt., *b.* 21 Jan. 1803; *m.* 26 Feb. 1835, Helena, dau. of John Hare, of Deer Park, co. Tipperary, and by her (who *d.* 25 April, 1882) had issue,
1. Arthur Hare, now of Summerhill.
2. John Love, Col. late Northumberland Fusiliers, *b.* 15 Aug. 1842; *m.* 22 Nov. 1882, Edith Mabel, only child of the late William R. Croker, of Alston, co. Limerick, and *d.* 15 Sept. 1894.
1. Elizabeth Westropp, *m.* Chichester Hartigan.
2. Mary Frances, *m.* 12 June, 1862, James Smyth O'Grady, of Erinagh, co. Clare.
3. Helena Hare, *m.* 26 Feb. 1868, Dudley O'Grady, J.P., of Ballynort, co. Limerick. He *d.* 25 Feb. 1883. She *d.* 3 May, 1907, having had issue (*see* O'Grady *of Aghamarta Castle*).

Mr. Vincent *d.* 19 Jan. 1882.

Seats—Summerhill, Castle Connell, co. Clare; and Pleasaunce Court, East Grinstead. *Residence*—35, Portman Square, W. *Clubs*—Army and Navy and Marlborough.

WADE OF CLONEBRANEY.

The late Craven Henry Clotworthy Wade, of Rockfield, co. Wicklow, and Clonebraney, co. Meath, J.P. co. Wicklow, High Sheriff 1906, *b.* 1845, and *d.* 5 May, 1911.

Lineage.—Henry Wade, of Clonebraney, co. Meath, High Sheriff 1669, got a grant of Clonebraney, part 1,490 acres in that co. by patent dated 3 Nov. 1684. He *m.* 1st, Anne O'Brien, and had issue,
1. John, his heir.
2. Charles, of Athglassan and Herbertstown, co. Meath, adhered to the cause of James II, and forfeited all his lands; *m.* Anne, dau. of Alexander Plunkett, co. Meath, and had a son,
Richard, of Ballinglare, co. Wexford, *m.* Mary, dau. of John Keogh, co. Wicklow, and had issue,
(1) John, of Dublin, M.D., who claimed Herbertstown at Chichester House 1700, *m.* Jane, dau. of John Butler, of Polestown, co. Kilkenny, and had two sons,
1. Walter, of Dublin, M.D., *m.* Mary Kennedy, and had four sons,
a. John, a Gen. in the Russian Service.
b. Joseph, Lieut.-Col. E.I.Co., *m.* 9 May, 1793, Maria dau. of Lieut.-Col. Robert Ross, and *d.* 1809, leaving Sir Claude Wade, C.B., Knt. of the Doranee Empire, and of the Auspicious Star of the Punjaub.
c. John Peter, M.D., E.I.Co.
d. Charles, M.D., Physician to the Court of Portugal.
2. John, of Dublin, whose son, John, of Dublin, *d.* 1799, leaving, by Katherine his wife, a son, Walter, Professor of Botany, Royal Dublin Society.
(2) Charles, *d.s.p.* (3) Redmond, *s.p.*
(1) Mary, *m.* — Maude.
1. Dorothy, *m.* Michael Sheilds, of Wainstown, co. Meath, son of Capt. Robert Sheilds, of Wainstown (the bearer of despatches

from the Lord Deputy Sir Arthur Chichester from Belfast to Charles I. at Edinburgh, 24 Oct. 1641), by Elizabeth his wife, dau. and co-heir of Michael Beresford, brother of Sir Tristram Beresford, 1st bart., of Coleraine. He *d.* intestate (administration 12 May, 1708), leaving by his wife (who *d.* 1708), with other issue, two sons,
1. Robert Sheilds, of Wainstown, who *d.* 1744, leaving by Anne his wife, with other issue, two sons and a dau.,
(1) Robert, his heir, whose only son, Robert Ford, *d.s.p.* 19 Feb. 1772.
(2) John Sheilds, of Wainstown, who *s.* his nephew in the estate, which he sold 27 June, 1792. He *m.* Sarah, dau. of Robert Wentworth, of Fyanstown, co. Meath (grand-dau. of George Wentworth of same place, who was eldest son of D'Arcy Wentworth, of Argreagh, co. Meath, and Athlone, co. Roscommon, descended from Wentworth *of Elmshall*, co. York), and had a surviving son,
Rev. Wentworth Sheilds, Rector of Kilbeg and Newtown, co. Meath, *b.* 1758; *d.* June, 1829. He *m.* 12 Dec. 1805, Isabella, dau. of Richard Plunkett, of Mount Plunkett, co. Roscommon, and Hollybrook Park, co. Dublin, by whom (who *d.* 12 May, 1832) he left, with other issue, *d. unm.*, two surviving sons,
a. John Gore Wentworth-Sheilds, of Fitzwilliam Street, Dublin, who assumed, with his brother, by Royal Licence, 27 Jan. 1877, the name of Wentworth, *b.* 28 Jan. 1809; *m.* 27 Oct. 1860, Sarah Charlotte, dau. of Rev. William Eames, Rector of Castle Pollard, co. Westmeath, and *d.* 16 May, 1889, having had two daus.,
(*a*) Helen Gore, *b.* 13 May, 1862; *m.* James Henry Wharton.
(*b*) Frances Gore, *b.* 20 Oct. 1863.
b. Francis Webb Wentworth-Sheilds, of Vanbrugh Park, co. Kent, and Delahay Street, Westminster, *b.* 8 Oct. 1823; *d.* 1906; *m.* 24 July, 1860, Adelaide, dau. of John Baker, of Tinnacurra House, Dalkey, co. Dublin, and had issue,
(*a*) Wentworth Francis (Rev.), M.A., Rector of St. James, Sydney (*St. James Rectory, Sydney*, N.S.W.), late Archdeacon of Wagga, N.S.W., *b.* 2 April, 1867; *m.* 3 April, 1902, Annie, dau. of Right Rev. William Boyd Carpenter, late Bishop of Ripon, and has issue,
1. Wentworth Francis Keith M'Neill, *b.* 1904.
2. Francis William, *b.* 1906.
(*b*) Francis Ernest, M.I.C.E. (*Polygon House, Southampton*), *b.* 16 Nov. 1869; *m.* 9 Jan. 1906, Mary, dau. of Right Rev. William Boyd Carpenter, late Bishop of Ripon.
(*a*) Ada Margaret, *b.* 13 July, 1861.
(*b*) Jessie Isabel, *b.* 29 April, 1864.
(*c*) Mabel Adelaide, *b.* 29 April, 1865.
(1) Esther, *m.* her cousin, John Daniel (or Wade), of Clonebraney (*see below*).
2. Clotworthy Sheilds, who assumed the surname of Wade on succeeding to the estates of his maternal uncle, of whom hereafter.
2. Katherine, *m.* 1st, Bridges Daniel, of Dublin, whose will, dated 31 July, 1740, was proved 18 Feb. following. By him she had (with four daus., Mary, Dorothy, Elizabeth, and Katherine), as many sons,
1. John Daniel, who *s.* to Clonebraney on the death of his cousin, Clotworthy (Sheilds) Wade, and assumed the surname of Wade, of whom hereafter.
2. William Daniel, who had four sons, (1) Thomas; (2) Richard, father of Capt. Richard, 21st Regt.; (3) William, Receiver General of the Stamp Office, *d.s.p.*; (4) Michael (Rev.), Rector of Kils Keer, co. Meath, father of William, an Officer in the 17th Dragoons.
3. Richard, *d.s.p.*
4. Michael, ancestor of Daniel, of New Forest.

Mrs. Daniel *m.* 2ndly, Thomas Sheilds, brother of Michael Sheilds, of Wainstown.
3. Elizabeth, *m.* William Beckett, and had issue.
4. Arabella, whose will, dated 22 Oct. 1750, was proved 14 Dec. 1753, *d. unm.*

Mr. Wade, whose will, dated 19 May, 1685, was proved 7 June, 1789, had no issue by his 2nd wife, Joane, who survived him and made her will 26 June, 1702, which was proved 17 March, 1704. He was *s.* by his eldest son,

John Wade, of Clonebraney, who *d.s.p.* He made his will 17 Sept. 1730, which was proved 1 Nov. 1735, under which he was *s.* by his nephew,

Clotworthy Sheilds, of Clonebraney, who assumed the name of Wade, High Sheriff co. Meath 1737. He *m.* Dorothy Winslow, by whom he had no issue. He was killed by a fall from his horse, 6 Jan. 1745, when the estates devolved on his cousin,

John Daniel, *alias* Wade, of Clonebraney, High Sheriff 1748, who, as before stated, took the name of Wade, *m.* 1739, his cousin, Esther, dau. of Robert Sheilds, of Wainstown, and had issue,
1. Robert, his heir. 2. Benjamin.
3. Daniel. 4. Charles.
1. Esther. *m.* Rev. Charles Woodward.
2. Anne. 3. Elizabeth.
4. Catherine. 5. Alice.

Mr. Wade *d.* 1776, and was *s.* by his eldest son,
Robert Wade, of Clonebraney, High Sheriff 1772, *m.* Oct. 1771, Frances, dau. of William Leigh, of Drogheda, and had issue,
1. William Blaney, his heir.
2. Edward (Rev.), *m.* Miss Fox, and *d.* 1868, leaving issue.
3. Charles Taylor (Rev.), M.A. Trin. Coll. Dublin, *b.* 6 Sept. 1793; *m.* 6 June, 1818, Isabella Rebecca, dau. of Henry Hamil-

ton, of Ballymacoll, co. Meath (*see that family*), and *d.* 20 Dec. 1857, leaving, with other issue, a dau.,
Frances Charlotte'Alicia Henrietta, *b.* 29 May, 1831 ; *m.* 3 Sept. 1853, Charles Mayo, of Illinois, son of Rev. Joseph Mayo. M.A. (*see* MAYO *of Cheshunt*), and *d.* 16 Oct. 1868, leaving issue.
4. **Thomas**, C.B., Col. in the Army, Deputy Adj.-Gen. in Ireland, *m.* Anne, dau. of William Smythe, of Barbavilla, co. Westmeath, and *d.* 1846, having had issue,
  1. Thomas Francis (Sir), G.C.M.G., K.C.B., Envoy Extraordinary and Minister Plenipotentiary in China from 1871 to 1883, *b.* 1818; *m.* 28 July, 1868, Amelia, dau. of Sir John Frederick William Herschel, 1st bart., of Collingwood House, and *d.* July, 1895, leaving issue,
    (1) Thomas Stewart Herschel, Major Lanc. Fus., *b.* 22 May, 1869.
    (2) Alexander Price Conolly Herschel, Lieut. E. Yorks Regt., *b.* 6 Aug. 1870, killed in action at Spion Kop, South Africa, 24 Jan. 1900.
    (3) Edward Bruce Herschel, *b.* 1872.
    (4) Harry Amyas Leigh Herschel, Capt. R.A., *b.* 12 Nov. 1873 ; *m.* 3 Dec. 1908, Kathleen Adelaide, elder dau. of late Cecil Lowry Wade, of North Hall, Preston Candover.
  2. Richard Blayney, *m.* Adelaide, dau. of Sir Launcelot Shadwell, Vice-Chancellor of England, and had issue.
    1. Frances, *m.* 1858, Robert Craven Wade, of Clonebraney (*see below*).
    2. Anne, *m.* Lieut.-Col. Richard Price Blackwood, R.A. (*see* PRICE *of Saintfield*).
The eldest son,
WILLIAM BLANEY WADE, of Clonebraney, J.P. and D.L., High Sheriff 1812, *m.* Frances, dau. of Sir John Craven Carden, 1st bart., of Templemore, and *d.* 1849, leaving issue,
  1. ROBERT CRAVEN, late of Clonebraney.
  2. John, *m.* Deborah, dau. of William Barton, D.L., of The Grove, co. Tipperary, and has issue,
    1. William Barton, Army Pay Dept., *b.* 11 July, 1840 ; *m.* and has issue. 2. John.
      1. Catherine Villiers, *m.* 1874, Sir William Fitzmaurice Josiah Horton, 4th bart., of Castle Strange.
      2. Grace Eleanor, *m.* 1874, Lieut.-Col. Norman Macdonald, 5th Regt.
  1. Frances Elizabeth, *m.* 30 March, 1835, Sir John Power, 2nd bart., of Kilfane, who *d.* 8 Aug. 1873, leaving issue (*see* BURKE'S *Peerage and Baronetage*).
The eldest son,
ROBERT CRAVEN WADE, of Clonebraney, co. Meath, J.P. and D.L., High Sheriff co. Meath 1840, and co. Wicklow 1847, *b.* 1809 ; *m.* 1st, 1840, Frances, dau. and co-heiress of Francis Hoey, of Dunganstown, co. Wicklow, by Anne his wife, dau. of Matthias Forde, of Seaforde, co. Down, and by her (who *d.* 1856) had issue.
  1. William George Clayton, *b.* 1842 ; *m.* 12 Jan. 1869, Olivia Blanche, dau. of Anthony O'Reilly, of Baltrasna, co. Meath, and *d.* 1882, having by her (who *m.* 2ndly, 1885, Frederick Parker Dixon (*see* DIXON *of Astle*) and *d.* 20 Oct. 1910) had issue, three daus.,
    1. Olive Frances, *m.* 1 Aug. 1894, Graham Wood, son of W. R. Wood, of the Glebe, Champion Hill, London.
    2. Mabel Alice. 3. Nora Edith Annie.
  2. Francis Hoey, Lieut. 55th Regt., *b.* 1843 ; *d.* 1872.
  3. Craven Henry Clotworthy, of Rockfield, Wicklow.
  4. Henry Meredyth, Lieut.-Col. late 8th Regt., *b.* 5 Aug. 1850.
  5. Edward John Power, *b.* 1846.
  6. Thomas Richard, *b.* 1853 ; *d.* 1886.
    1. Anne Frances, *d. unm.* 28 June 1908.
  2. Kathleen Elizabeth, *m.* 1876, Capt. Henry John Beckwith, 53rd Regt.   3. Isabella Henrietta Charity, *b.* 1854 ; *d.* 1857.
Mr. Wade *m.* 2ndly, 1858, Frances, dau. of Col. Thomas Wade, C.B. (*see above*). and *d.* 1898, leaving further issue,
  7. Robert Blayney, *b.* 1863.
  4. Frances Annie.
Sent—Rockfield, co. Wicklow.

WADE OF CARROWMORE.

ROBERT ROCHFORT WADE, of Carrowmore, co. Galway, J.P., educated at Harrow, *b.* 8 Jan. 1852 ; *m.* 26 Jan. 1886, Marian Olivia, dau. of Thomas Trouton, of Dublin, and has issue,
1. JOHN ROCHFORT, *b.* 6 March, 1887.
2. Mabel Elizabeth.   2. Gladys Rochfort.
3. Marjorie Rochfort.   4. Olivia Dorothy Rochfort.

Lineage.—MAJ. WILLIAM WADE, of a Dragoon Regt. in Cromwell's Army, obtained in 1653 a grant of lands near Tyrrel's Pass, Westmeath, and at Philipstown, King's Co., and lived at the former place. He *m.* the dau. of Rev. Henry Stonestreet, Rector of South Heighton, Sussex, and *d.* 1683, having had issue, a son, JEROME WADE, of Killevalley, co. Westmeath, who had issue,
1. William (Rev.), Canon of Windsor, *b.* 1670 ; *d. unm.* 1 Feb. 1732.
2. JEROME, of whom presently.
3. George, Field-Marshal in the Army, Commander-in-Chief 1745-8, *b.* 1673 ; *d.* 14 March, 1748, having had a son,
George, Capt. 3rd Dragoon Guards, killed in Scotland, 1746.
  1. Christina, *b.* 1672 ; *m.* Robert Cooke, of Kiltinane, co. Tipperary, and had issue.
The 2nd son,
JEROME WADE, of Killevalley, Westmeath, *b.* 1671, left issue, one son,

WILLIAM WADE, of Killevally, Westmeath, *m.* the dau. of William Osbrey, of Dublin (her will was proved 1757), and had issue,
1. THOMAS, of whom presently.
2. George, *m.* Mary, dau. of Capt. Thomas Nugent, and had issue.
1. Hester, *m.* — Sayers.
The elder son,
THOMAS WADE, of Killavally, Westmeath, which he sold 1756, and later of lands in co. Galway, which he purchased, *b.* 1719 ; *m.* 1st, Elizabeth, dau. of Col. Low, of Newtown, and by her had issue,
1. A dau., *m.* — Wakefield.
2. Elizabeth, *m.* John Doolittle, of Slane.
He *m.* 2ndly, 1747, Margaret De Foe, and by her (who *d.* 1 April, 1766, aged 39), had issue,
1. SAMUEL, his heir.
2. Jerome, *b.* 15 July, 1751 ; *d. unm.* 14 May, 1800.
3. Thomas, *b.* 1 Oct. 1753, *m.* Anne, dau. of Samuel Handy, of Coolyclough, co. Westmeath, and had issue.
4. John, Major 36th Regt., *b.* 1 Nov. 1763 ; *m.* Alice, dau. of Thomas Davies, of Newcastle, co. Galway, and *d.* 30 Oct. 1827, leaving issue.   She *d.* 5 May. 1829.
Thomas, *d.* 12 Aug. 1814.
Maria, *m.* 1818, Richard Galbraith, of Cappard, and *d.s.p.* 1819.
3. Margaret, *d. unm.*
4. Anne, *b.* 1761 ; *m.* Henry Whitestone, and *d.* 29 March, 1826. He *m.* 3rdly, Ann, dau. of Jonathan Walshe, of Walshe Park, co. Tipperary, and had by her one child *d.* aged 13. He *d.* 24 July, 1790, aged 71.   His eldest son,
SAMUEL WADE, of Carrowmore, co. Galway, *b.* 16 Feb. 1749 ; *m.* Catharine, dau. of Thomas Davies, of Newcastle, co. Galway, and *d.* 17 Aug. 1826, leaving issue,
1. THOMAS, his heir.
1. Marai, *m.* 1801, Robert Persse, of Roxborough. She *d.* 29 Nov. 1810. He *d.* Jan. 1850, leaving issue (*see that family*).
2. Anne, *m.* 8 Oct. 1807, William Robinson, of Anneville, co. Westmeath, and *d.* 11 June, 1830, leaving issue. He *d.* 1 Oct. 1856.
3. Margaret, *m.* Charles Seymour, of Somerset, co. Galway, and had issue.   She *d.* 5 Dec. 1871, aged 84.
The only son,
THOMAS WADE, of Fairfield House, or Carrowmore, co. Galway, *b.* 9 March, 1788 ; *m.* 15 Jan. 1813, Dorothea, dau. of Gustavus Hume Rochfort, M.P., of Rochfort, co. Westmeath (*see that family*). She *d.* 15 June, 1879.   He *d.* 25 Oct. 1865, having had issue,
1. Samuel, *b.* 14 Sept. 1814 ; *m.* 1847, Eliza, dau. of Burton Persse, of Moyode.   She *d.* 30 April, 1896.   He *d.v.p.* 19 Oct. 1862, having had issue,
  1. ROBERT ROCHFORT, now of Carrowmore.
  2. Thomas, *b.* Sept. 1854 ; *d.* 19 April, 1858.
  3. Burton Persse, of Maryville, Galway, *b.* 29 July, 1859 ; *m.* 20 June, 1902, Helen Geneva, dau. of Bennington Gill Blanchard, U.S.A.
    1. Anchoretta Maria.   2. Dorothy Matilda Elizabeth.
  2. Gustavus Rochfort, *b.* 27 May, *d.* 22 June, 1817.
  3. Gustavus William Rochfort, of Dublin, *b.* 10 June, 1818 *m.* 3 Jan. 1856, Mary (*b.* 10 Dec. 1830), dau. of Rev. Edward Mayne.   She *d.* 15 Oct. 1899.   He *d.* 28 March, 1897, having had issue,
    1. Gustavus Rochfort HYDE, who has assumed the name of HYDE (*see* HYDE *of Lynnbury*).
    2. Thomas George, *b.* 24 April, 1859 ; *m.* 8 Sept. 1899, Martha, dau. of Thomas Irwin, and *d.* 9 Oct. 1903, leaving issue.
      Thomas Gustavus Rochfort, *b.* 3 June, 1901.
      Minna Florence.
    3. Sedborough Mayne (Rev.), M.A., Corpus Christi Coll. and Ridley Hall, Camb., Vicar of Stonegate, Ticehurst, Sussex, *b.* 11 Jan. 1863 ; *m.* 26 April, 1892, Louisa Jane Elibank, dau. of the late George Reade, Madras Army.
    4. William Henry Rochfort, M.A., of Belcamp Hutchinson, Raheny, co. Dublin ; Rochfort, Greystones, co. Wicklow, *b.* 25 April, 1864 ; *m.* 12 March, 1898, Christiana Sophia, dau. of the late Rev. Gervase Thorp, M.A. (Camb.), Vicar of Wealdstone, Harrow, and has issue,
      (1) William Gervase Rochfort, *b.* 26 May, 1900.
      (2) Henry Claud Rochfort, *b.* 13 July, 1905.
      (3) Armigal George Disney Rochfort, *b.* 11 Dec. 1909.
      (1) Mary Mayne Rochfort, *b.* 1 Nov. 1902.
      (2) Margaret Christiana Rochfort.
    5. Edward Hyde Robert Wybrants, late of the Government Railway, Ceylon (*Faircroft, Heene Road, Worthing*), *b.* 14 Feb. 1867.
    6. Rowland Henry Rochfort, of the Chinese Imperial Customs, *b.* 20 Aug. 1869 ; *m.* 22 July, 1899, Charlotte Jane Jones, dau. of Major John FitzThomas Dennis, and has issue,
      (1) Gustavus Fitz Rowland, *b.* 20 June, 1900 ; *d.* 28 Aug. 1902.
      (2) Rowland Henry Dennis, *b.* 26 Aug. 1904.
      (1) Annie Dennis, *b.* 4 March, 1903.
      (2) Kathleen Rose Dennis.
    7. George Frank Graham Rochfort (Rev.), M.A. Trin. Coll; Dublin, Vicar of Rye Harbour, Sussex, *b.* 20 Dec. 1870 ; *m.* 22 April, 1902, Mary, dau. of Richard Wilkinson, J.P., of Dublin, and Balcorris.
      1. Louisa Dorothea, *b.* 26 Oct. 1856.
      2. Mary Harriet Rochfort, *b.* 11 Feb. 1861 ; *d. unm.* 13 June, 1898.
      3. Fanny Maria, *b.* 22 Jan. 1862.

4. Kathleen Alice Rochfort, b. 5 Oct. 1865 ; m. 29 Aug. 1900, Walter Culpepper Stauser Inglis, Deputy Surveyor-General of the Government Survey Department, Ceylon, son of Walter Lawrence Inglis, Major 16th Regt., and has issue.
4. John Rochfort, b. 26 May ; d. 20 June, 1827.
5. Thomas Uniacke, b. 15 Sept. 1833 ; d. 7 June, 1834.
1. Frances, m. her cousin, Capt. William Persse. He d. 10 June, 1860. She d. 27 Oct. 1894, leaving issue (see PERSSE of Roxborough).
2. Jane Alicia, d. unm. 4 April, 1890.
3. Letitia Catherine, m. Major Charles Clements Brooke. He d.s.p. 14 Jan. 1898. She d. 22 July, 1878.
4. Dorothea, m. 1861, Rev. John Henry Moran, who d. 12 May, 1892. She d. 24 Dec. 1905, leaving an only dau., Dora Bloomfield Thomasina Rochfort, b. 20 Dec. 1863.
5. Catherine.
6. Maria Anne, of Hatherley Brake, Cheltenham, m. 20 Dec. 1855, Edward Hyde Clarke, of Hyde Hall, Cheshire. He d.s.p. 25 Dec. 1873.

Seat—Carrowmore, Aughrim, co. Galway.

WAITHMAN OF MOYNE.

ROBERT WILLIAM WAITHMAN, of Moyne Park, co. Galway, and of Moyvannon Castle, co. Roscommon, J.P. for cos. Galway, Roscommon, the West Riding of co. York, and co. Lancaster, and D.L. for the West Riding of co. York, High Sheriff co. Roscommon 1870, of the town of Galway 1882, and of co. Galway 1885, b. 1828 ; m. 1st, 1851, Melicent, 3rd dau. of William Sharp, J.P., of Linden Hall, co. Lancaster, and by her (who d. 1887) has issue,

1. WILLIAM SHARP, of Merlin Park, Galway, and of Gawsworth Old Hall, Cheshire, J.P. co. Cheshire, J.P. and D.L. co. Galway, High Sheriff 1902, J.P. Galway, High Sheriff 1883, b. 1853 ; m. 6 Sept. 1883, Lady Leicester Philippa Stanhope, 2nd dau. of Charles Wyndham, 7th Earl of Harrington, and has issue,
  Henry William Wyndham Arthur Stanhope Sharp, b. 15 June, 1887.
  Eva Pansy Melicent Philippa Stanhope, m. 19 Aug. 1908, Richard Page Croft, J.P. and D.L. for Hertfordshire, High Sheriff 1912, Capt. and Hon. Major 4th Batt. Bedfordshire Regt., and has issue (see CROFT of Fanham's Hall, Ware).
1. Eleanor Jane Sharp.
2. Beatrice Augusta Melicent Sharp, m. 1 June, 1876, Albert H. Bencke, M.A. Oxon, Barrister-at-Law, of Oliva, West Derby, co. Lancaster, and has issue, two sons and a dau.

Mr. Waithman m. 2ndly, 18 March, 1891, Arabella, dau. of the late Dudley Persse, D.L., of Roxboro, co. Galway.

Lineage.—WILLIAM WAITHMAN, of Lindeth, co. Lancaster, b. 1625 ; d. 20 April, 1694, and was s. by his heir,
ROBERT WAITHMAN, of Lindeth, b. 14 Dec. 1668 ; d. 13 Sept. 1729, and was s. by his heir,
WILLIAM WAITHMAN, of Lindeth, b. 9 Dec. 1711 ; m. 10 Feb. 1739, Dorothy, dau. of Anthony Wilson, of High Wray, co. Lancaster ; d. 12 Aug. 1772, and was s. by his son,
JOSEPH WAITHMAN, of Yealand Conyers, b. 3 Aug. 1759 ; m. 11 July, 1797, Grace, dau. of John Spence, of Birstwith, co. York, and aunt of Grace, wife of Sir A. T. C. Campbell, Bart., and had issue,
1. WILLIAM, his heir.
2. John, of Yealand Conyers, b. 19 Nov. 1809 ; m. 8 Feb. 1844, Hannah, dau. of W. Wilson, of Kendal.
  1. Marianne, d. unm.
  2. Sarah, d. unm.
  3. Rachel, d. unm. 1836.
4. Hannah, m. 31 Jan. 1843, Daniel Elletson, of Parrox Hall, co. Lancaster, J.P. for that shire.

Mr. Waithman d. 6 Sept. 1836, and was s. by his son,
WILLIAM WAITHMAN, of Westville, co. Lancaster, b. 4 June, 1799 ; m. 18 Aug. 1825, Eleanor, only dau. of John Armistead, of Leeds ; and d. 4 Sept. 1869, leaving issue,
1. ROBERT WILLIAM, now of Moyne Park.
2. Joseph, of Hurst View, Chudleigh, Devon, J.P. cos. Lancaster and York, b. 7 Jan. 1831 ; m. 1854, Elizabeth (who d. 1889), dau. of William Sharp, J.P., of Linden Hall, co. Lancaster, and has issue,
  Hubert Waithman de Lindeth, b. 1859 ; m. 1887, Grace Gertrude (who d. 1891), dau. of N. W. Winton, of Oaklands, California, U.S.A., and had issue,
    (1) Joseph de Lindeth.
    (1) Maud Victoria.
    (2) Elizabeth Grace de Lindeth.
3. Arthur, of Manchester, J.P., b. 27 May, 1846 ; m. 23 April, 1872, Louisa M., dau. of T. A. Hanson, of Northwood, co. Lancaster.
  1. Sarah Grace, m. 18 May, 1852, John Thomas Rice, J.P., of Grove Hill, Bentham, co. York, d. Dec. 1919.
  2. Dorothea Anne, m. 1865, Walter Caddell, of The Polygon, Cheetham Hill, Lancashire, and Linwood, Torquay, Devon, and had issue, Walter Waithman De Vipont, Capt. Reserve of Officers, late Manchester Regt., b. 1867 ; m. 21 Oct. 1912, Eugénie

Fleming, née Chabaud ; Eleanor Dora ; Marion Houston, m. 1900, Conte Giovanni Giordano Orsini dei Duchi di Bracciano, Capt. 44 Regt. Italian Army.
3. Catherine, d. 13 Nov. 1899.

Seat—Moyvannon Castle, Athlone. Residence—Dominick Street, Galway.

WAKELY OF BALLYBURLY.

HIS HONOUR JUDGE JOHN WAKELY, of Ballyburly, King's Co., D.L. J.P. K.C. M.A. Trin. Coll. Dublin, called to the Bar 1884, Q.C. 1899. Bencher King's Inn 1902 to 1904. County Court Judge and Chairman of Quarter Sessions. cos. Roscommon and Sligo, b. 30 Sept. 1861 ; m. 31 July, 1888, Rebecca Low Montserrat, eldest dau. of the Rev. Morgan Woodward Jellett, LL.D., Rector of St. Peter's and Canon of Christ Church, Dublin, and has issue,
1. Nina Catherine.
2. Raby Clare Jellett.
3. Olive Ivan Montserratt.

Lineage.—JOHN WAKELY, of Navan. M.P. for Navan 1559, and Oliver Nugent had a patent of lands in Meath dated 20 June, 1547 ; another in Louth and Meath, fiant for lease 19 Sept. 1550 ; another for lands in King's Co., including Ballyburly, fiant 15 Feb. 1550. John Wakely m. 1st, Catherine, dau. of — Rawson, and had issue,
1. GEORGE, wardship granted to Hercules Rainsford, 1570, d.s.p.
2. THOMAS, of whom presently.
He m. 2ndly, Anne, 2nd dau. of Oliver, 1st Baron Louth, by his wife Catherine, dau. and heir of John Rochfort, of Carrick, co. Kildare, and d. 2 Nov. 1570. having by her (who m. 2ndly, Gerald Wellesley, of Dangan) had further issue,
3. Christopher.
1. Ellis, m. William Wellesley, of Dangan.

The 2nd son,
THOMAS WAKELY, M.P. for Navan 1585. He had licence to alien and grant Ballyburly to the use of his son John's wife, Mary Luttrell, for jointure, 21 May, 1597. Sir James (Earl of Roscommon) of Moymet, 10 Dec. 1605, conveyed 120 acres in Ladicrath to Sir William Taaffe, who, 24 April, 1608, assigned same to John Wakely, who " suffered a common recovery " in 1608 to Christopher Lewis. He m. 1st, Maud, dau. of William Handcock, Alderman of Dublin, and by her (who d. 3 May, 1617) had issue,
1. John, m. 1597, Mary, dau. of — Luttrell, and d.v.p. leaving two sons,
  1. THOMAS, heir to his grandfather.
  2. James, m. Elizabeth, dau. of Sir John Moore of Croghan, King's Co.
2. Gerald. 3. Martin.
1. Catherine. 2. Margaret.
3. Anne.
He m. 2ndly, Grace, dau. of Richard Coleman, Chief Remembrancer of the Exchequer, and by her (who m. 2ndly, George King) had further issue,
4. Patrick.
4. Mary, m. Luke Sankey, of Ballylackin, King's Co.
Thomas Wakely d. 26 June, 1623 (Fun. Entry, Ulster's Office), and was s. by his grandson (Inq. p.m.).
THOMAS WAKELY, of Ballyburly, b. 1598, m. Thomasine, dau. of Sir John Moore, of Croghan (cousin-german to Sir Garret Moore, ancestor of the Marquis of Drogheda), by his wife Dorothy, dau. of Adam Loftus, Archbishop of Dublin, and d. 18 April, 1634, leaving by her (who m. 2ndly, 1635, Anthony Coughlan) two sons and three daus.,
1. John, his heir. 2. Thomas.
1. Dorothy. 2. Jane.
3. Mary.
The elder son,
JOHN WAKELY, of Ballyburly, was granted in ward to his uncle, Thomas Moore (fine £346 13s. 4d.), High Sheriff King's Co. 1667, m. 1650, Cecilia, dau. of Edward Birmingham, of Grange, by his wife Catherine, dau. of Gerald, Earl of Kildare, and by her (will dated 1661) had issue,
1. John, his heir. 2. Robert, d.s.p.
3. James, b. 1657, ent. Trin. Coll. Dublin, 16 Feb. 1675.
1. Anne.
The eldest son,
JOHN WAKELY, of Ballyburly, M.P. for Kilbeggan 1692, High Sheriff for King's Co. 1695, built Ballyburly Church in 1686 (his

arms and those of his wife are on a slab over the doorway) ; b. 1655, ent. Trin. Coll. Dublin 13 Feb. 1675 ; m. Elizabeth, dau. of the Hon. Oliver Lambart, of Painstown, brother of the Earl of Cavan, and by her (whose will, dated 30 April, 1723, was proved 19 Jan. 1735) he had issue,
1. THOMAS, of Ballyburly.   2. Lambart, d.s.p
3. George, m. by licence 4 March, 1765, Mary, dau. of — Judge.
4. Francis, twin with George.
5. John.   6. Robert.   7. James.
8. William, d. 17 Sept. 1710.
5. John.   6. Robert.   7. James.   8. William.
1. Catherine, m. 17 Dec. 1705, John Meares, of Meares Court.
2. Elizabeth, m. by licence 3 Oct. 1716, Hugh Wilton.
3. Anne, m. Rev. Robert Meares.
4. Henrietta, m. by licence 21 Jan. 1735, Benjamin Everard, of Dublin, and had issue.
5. Mary.
6. Arabella, d Nov. 1722.   7. Rose.
8. Martha, m. by licence 22 Dec. 1740, Thomas Dames, of Rathmoyle.
Mr. Wakely, whose will was proved 24 Nov. 1713, was s. by his eldest son,
THOMAS WAKELY, of Ballyburly, High Sheriff King's Co. 1726, ent. Trin. Coll. Dublin 15 July, 1705, B.A. 1710, b. 1688 ; m. by licence 13 Dec. 1733, Lydia, dau. of — Page, of Barberstown, co. Kildare, and niece of Alderman John Page, and by her (whose will, dated 17 Jan. 1759, was proved 29 Jan. 1762) had issue,
1. John, of Ballyburly, High Sheriff King's Co. 1763, m. by licence 6 Nov. 1764, his cousin Henrietta, widow of Rob rt Gilbert, of Humphreystown, co. Wicklow, and dau. of Benjamin Everard, of Three Castles, co. Wicklow, and by her had issue,
1. John, of Ballyburly, High Sheriff King's Co. 1796, m. Dec. 1788, Mary Anne, dau. of Francis Longworth, of Creggan Castle, co. Westmeath, and d.s.p. 1842. She d. 1847.
2. William George (Rev.), B.A. Dublin 1788, M.A. 1810, Rector of Ballyburly, m. 1789, Anne, dau. of — Plunkett, and d.s.p. 1836.
2. James, d. unm.
3. FRANCIS, of whom presently.
1. Lydia.
Mr. Wakely d. 9 Aug. 1751. His will, dated 5 Aug. 1751, was proved 14 Aug. in that year. His 3rd son.
FRANCIS WAKELY, m. Miss Bowen, and by her (who d. March, 1796) had two sons,
1. Henry, m. Priscilla, dau. of — Widenham, and d.s.p
2. JAMES, of whom presently.
The 2nd son,
JAMES WAKELY, of Dublin, m. 1811, Elizabeth, dau. of George Heron, of Dublin, and d. 28 July, 1826, having had issue,
1. JOHN, of whom presently.   2. Thomas, d. March, 1826.
1. Emma Frances, m. 1839, William Henry Astle, M.B., and had issue.
2. Elizabeth, m. 1853, John Lucas, and had issue.
The only surviving son,
JOHN WAKELY, M.A., of Ballyburly, King's Co., J.P. and D.L., High Sheriff 1853, b. 8 Sept. 1820 ; s. his cousin 1842; m. Aug. 1855, Mary Catherine, dau. of Rev. Richard George, Rector of Kentstown, co. Meath. She d. 10 May, 1899. He d. 13 July, 1896, leaving issue.
1. JOHN, now of Ballyburly.   2. James, b. 18 Nov. 1862.
3. William George, of Rosario, Temple Gardens, Dublin, Secretary of the Incorporated Law Society of Ireland, b. 20 June, 1865 ; m. Eliner, dau. of Charles Thomson, of Dublin, and has issue,
1. Ion, b. 4 May, 1892.
1. Vera.   2. Phyllis.
3. Eileen.
4. Henry Hapsburg, b. 4 April, 1870 ; d. April, 1890.
5. Gustavus, b. 19 Jan. 1873.
1. Frances Elizabeth, m. Richard Welsted Day, of Ballyburly, Nelson, British Columbia.
2. Mary Catherine.   3. Emma Frances
4. Helen Maude.   5. Elizabeth.
6. Henrietta. m. J. Marshall.   7. Harriett.
8. Grace Edith.

Arms—Gu., a chevron between three cross crosslets arg., on a chief of the last a stag's head caboshed of the first.
Seat—Ballyburly, Edenderry, King's Co. Club—University, Dublin.

WALDRON-HAMILTON OF ASHFORT HOUSE.

HUBERT FRANCIS WALDRON-HAMILTON, of Ashfort House, co. Roscommon, b. 14 March, 1854 ; m. 30 April, 1890, Elizabeth Jemima, 4th dau. of James Roberton, D.L., of Lauchope, Lanarkshire, and has issue.
1. HUBERT JOHN, b. 2 June, 1894.
1. Anastatia Catherine, b. 21 Jan. 1893.
2. Victoria Grace, b. 2 Dec. 1895.
3. Minna Barbara Ruby, b. 31 March, 1898.

Lineage.—HENRY WALDRON, of Dromellan Castle, or Farnham, co. Cavan, which had been granted to his ancestor, Sir Richard Waldron, Knt., of Charley Hall, in Charnwood Forest, co. Leicester, in which shire the family had been long seated. He was one of the gentlemen of co. Cavan who was attainted by JAMES II in 1688, and deprived of his estate, which was restored to him, however, by WILLIAM III in the following year. In 1697 he settled at Cartron, Killukin, near Carrick-on-Shannon, and sold his property of Farnham or Dromellan to the Maxwells. He m. Dorothy, dau. of Thomas Farnham, of Quornolon, and was s. by his son,
FRANCIS WALDRON, of Cartron, m. Jane, dau. of Rev. Henry Roycroft, of Danesfort, and left a son,
FRANCIS WALDRON, of Cartron, m. 1710, Mary, dau. of Thomas Jones, of Ardnaree, co. Sligo, and had issue,
1. Arthur, of Ashfort, m. 1774, his cousin Jane, dau. of Charles Jones, of Ardnaree, and had issue, an only son,
Francis, Major 75th Regt., of Ashfort, m. his cousin Sarah, dau. of Capt. Thomas Mainwaring, son of Thomas Mainwaring, M.P. for Lincolnshire, and had one son and three daus.,
(1) Vaughan, of Ashfort, m. 1st, Barbara, only dau. of Thomas Waldron, of Rocksavage, co. Roscommon, and Elizabeth Baldwin his wife, and by her had issue, a dau.,
ELIZABETH BARBARA, heiress of Ashfort, m. Sept. 1816, her cousin Hubert Kelly Waldron, of Drumsna (see below).
Mr. Vaughan Waldron m. 2ndly, Frances Buck, and by her had issue, Francis, Arthur, Vaughan, Andrew, Rebecca, and Catherine. He d. 27 Sept. 1828.
(1) Catherine.
(2) Rebecca, m. Capt. Armstrong, of Caramable, co. Mayo, and had issue.
(3) Mary.
2. THOMAS, of whom presently.
3. Charles, of Cartron, m. Jane, dau. of Edward Simpson, of Mount Campbell and Drumsna, and had issue,
1. Frank, settled in America.
1. Anne.
2. Mary, m. Arthur Lauder, of Bonnybeg, and had issue.
1. Mary, m. Matthew Nesbitt, of Derryearn.
2. Jane, m. James Armstrong, of Annaduff.
The 2nd son,
THOMAS WALDRON, of Drumsna, co. Leitrim, m. Elizabeth, dau. of Col. Thomas Blakeney, of Feigh, co. Galway (see BLAKENEY of Abbert), and left (with a dau., m. Thomas Irwin) an only son,
FRANCIS WALDRON, of Drumsna, m. 1st, Mary, dau. of Hubert Kelly, of Charleville, co. Westmeath, and by her had issue,
1. Thomas, of Lismoyle, co. Leitrim, d.s.p.
2. Edward, J.P., High Sheriff co. Leitrim, m. Jane, dau. of Gilbert Hogg, of Moyglass, and had issue an only son,
Francis, of Lismoyle, m. his cousin Mary, dau. of Joseph Caddy, and had issue,
(1) Edward Francis, m. Emily Yates, and had issue,
Francis, d. young.
Mabel.
(2) Francis, m. his cousin Anne Jane Cullen.
(3) George Nugent, m. Janet Douglas, dau. of John Graham, of Kittockside, co. Lanark.
(4) Andrew, settled in Australia, m. Margaret Templeton and has issue.
(1) Mary Frances, m. William Houstoun, of Lismoyle, co. Leitrim, and Wester, Rossland, Renfrewshire.
(2) Jane, m. Gerald Walsh, J.P. Belmont, Drumsna.
(3) Margaret, m. J. C. Lloyd, Capt. Carlow Rifles.
3. Francis, R.N., lost at sea, circa 1800, d. unm.
4. HUBERT KELLY, of whom presently.
5. Michael, m. 1st, Frances Cox, and 2ndly, Mary Cox, and left issue.
1. Arabella, m. Thomas Watkins, of Summerset House, and had issue.
2. Eliza, m. James Hogg, of Gilstown, and had issue.
3. Maria, d. unm.
4. Anne, m. Joseph Caddy.   5. Jane.
Mr. Francis Waldron m. 2ndly, the widow of John Conroy, and by her had a dau.,
6. Emma, m. 1st, Terence Connelly, and 2ndly, Carden Terry.
The 4th son,
HUBERT KELLY WALDRON, of Drumsna, co. Leitrim, and Ashfort House, co. Roscommon. J.P. and D.L., High Sheriff co. Leitrim 1832, b. 10 Sept. 1795 ; m. 1st, Sept. 1816, his cousin Elizabeth Barbara, heiress of Ashfort, dau. of Vaughan Waldron, of Ashfort House (see above), and by her had issue,
1. Arthur, d. young.   2. Frank, d. young.
1. BARBARA ELIZABETH, of whom presently.
2. Mary Kelly, m. Robert Potterton, LL.D.
3. Sarah Mainwaring, m. William Potterton, of Balatallion, and has issue.
4. Rebecca Elizabeth, m. Wm. Parke Cullen.
Mr. H. K. Waldron m. 2ndly, Dec. 1831, Eleanor, dau. of the Rev. Francis Johnstone, of Travinount, and by her had a son,
3. Hubert Kelly Johnstone, Capt. 31st Regt., b. 14 Oct. 1832 ; m. Margaret Plews, and had issue,
1. Hubert Johnstone Kelly.
2. Vaughan.
1. Beatrice.   2. Lilian.
3. Kathleen Ellen, m. her cousin Henry Martley Giveen, son of the Rev. Lockwood Giveen, and has issue.
The eldest dau.,
BARBARA ELIZABETH WALDRON, of Ashfort House, m. 15 Feb. 1852, JOHN HAMILTON, b. 17 Feb. 1818, 2nd surviving son of Patrick Hamilton, of Brachead and Greenfield, co. Lanark, and Elizabeth his wife, dau. of John Graham, of Kittockside, co. Lanark. She d. 5 Sept. 1899, having had issue,
1. HUBERT FRANCIS, now of Ashfort.
2. John, d. young.
1. Elizabeth Barbara, d. young.
2. Jane Waldron, m. 26 Jan. 1898, Robert G. Patterson, of Holmes and Gaude Hall, co. Lanark.

Seat—Ashfort House, Drumsna, co. Roscommon.

WALDRON OF HELEN PARK.

MAJ. PATRICK JOHN WALDRON, of Helen Park, co. Tipperary, J.P. and D.L. for that co., High Sheriff co. Louth 1896, B.A. Ch. Ch. Oxford, late Maj. 15th Hussars, b. 31 May, 1850.

Lineage.—LAURENCE WALDRON, of Helen Park, co. Tipperary, J.P. and D.L. and M.P., High Sheriff co. Louth 1860, Kilkenny 1867, and co. Tipperary 1868, b. 1811; m. 1842, Anne, dau. of Francis White, and d. 1875, having had issue,
1. PATRICK JOHN, now of Helen Park.
2. Francis, C.B., Col. (retired) R.A., was Assistant Quartermaster-Gen. Irish Command 1905-7, and Brigadier-Gen. Comm. 5th Divisional Artillery, Irish Command 1907-10, b. 12 Sept. 1853; m. 5 May, 1884, Helen, youngest dau. of Thomas FitzGerald, and has issue,
Francis, b. 1890.
3. John, b. 1854, d. 1890.
4. Laurence Ambrose (Right Hon.), M.P. Dublin, St. Stephen's Green Division 1904-10, P.C. Ireland 1911. b. 1858.
1. Anne, m. 1888, Wilfred Fitzgerald.

Seat—Helen Park, co. Tipperary. Clubs—Naval and Military, and Kildare Street.

WALKER OF TYKILLEN.

THOMAS JOSEPH WALKER, of Tykillen, co. Wexford, J.P. and D.L. for co. Wexford, High Sheriff 1881, late Capt. Royal Dragoons, b. 14 April, 1839; m. 20 Sept. 1888, Blanche Louisa, youngest dau. of Col. Stephen Henry Smith, 64th Regt., of Annesbrook, Drogheda, co. Meath, and has issue,
1. CHARLES ARTHUR STEPHEN, Lieut. Irish Guards, b. 9 July, 1889.
2. Thomas Kynaston, b. 4 Nov. 1896.
3. Cecil Raymond, b. 2 June, 1900.
1. Muriel Eleanor Blanche.

Lineage.—CHARLES WALKER, admitted to Lincoln's Inn 7 May, 1744, and to King's Inns 25 Nov. 1749, for thirty-six years one of the Masters of the Court of Chancery in Ireland, 1754-1790, when he resigned. He d. 1795, having m. 4 Dec. 1756, Caroline, eldest dau. of the Hon. Bysse Molesworth, son of Robert, 1st Viscount Molesworth, and had issue, three sons and two daus.,
1. THOMAS.
2. Peter, who left two sons, Charles Edward (Rev.) and Frederick.
3. Charles.
1. Elizabeth, m. Major-Gen. Sir Thomas Blyth St. George.
2. Caroline, m. 1786, Henry Gonne Molony.
The eldest son,
THOMAS WALKER, of Tykillen, co. Wexford, for fifteen years one of the Masters of the Court of Chancery in Ireland, 1790-1806, m. May, 1783, Maria, dau. of William Acton, of West Aston, by Jane Parsons his wife, grand-dau. of Sir William Parsons, 2nd bart., of Birr Castle, and had issue,
1. CHARLES ARTHUR, late of Tykillen.
2. Thomas, a Major in the Army, dec.
1. Caroline, m 1817, Col. William Acton, of West Aston, co. Wicklow, M.P. for that co.
Mr. Walker d. 28 Feb. 1837, and was s. by his eldest son,
CHARLES ARTHUR WALKER, of Tykillen, J.P. and Vice-Lieut. of co. Wexford, M.P. for Wexford from 1830 to 1843; m. 10 Feb. 1836, Eleanor, eldest dau. of Joseph Leigh, of Tinnekelly House, co. Wicklow (brother of Francis Leigh, of Rosegarland), and d. 1873, leaving issue,
1. THOMAS JOSEPH, now of Tykillen.
2. Charles Stephen, of the Deeps, Wexford, late Col. 3rd Hussars (Naval and Military, and Kildare St. Clubs), b. 13 May, 1840.
1. Mary Jane.
2. Eleanor Arabella Caroline, m. 29 April, 1868, William Alex. Dobie, late Capt. 12th Lancers.
3. Elizabeth Mary Anne, m. 9 Feb. 1870, Crosbie W. Harvey, of Bromley, co. Wexford, and had issue (see HARVEY of Bargy Castle).

Seat—Tykillen House, Wexford. Clubs—Army and Navy, London, and Kildare Street, Dublin.

WALLACE OF ARDNAMONA.

The late SIR ARTHUR ROBERT WALLACE, C.B., of Ardnamona, co. Donegal, J.P. and D.L., High Sheriff 1907, B.A. Trin. Coll. Dublin, late Principal Clerk, Chief Secretary's Office in Ireland, b. 1837; d. 9 April, 1912; m. Georgiana Lawrell, dau. of Major George Augustus Frederick Quentin, 10th Royal Hussars, and had issue,
1. ARTHUR WILLIAM BAILLIE, Capt. Durham Light Inf., b. 1876.
2. A son, b.
3. A son, b.
1. Annie Margaret, m. 4 Jan. 1906, Arthur Herbert Empson, elder son of late Christopher Empson, Yorks.
2. A dau., b.

Sir A. R. Wallace was son of the late William Baillie Wallace, by Margaret, his wife, 2nd dau. of John Donnelly, of Blackwatertown, co. Armagh.

Seat—Ardnamona, Lough Eske, co. Donegal. Club—Royal St. George Yacht, Kingstown.

WALLACE OF RAVARA.

WILLIAM FRANCIS ANNESLEY WALLACE, of Ravara, co. Down, late Capt. 53rd Shropshire Regt. (Egyptian medal and Khedive's star), educated at Harrow and Trinity Hall, Camb., b. 18 July, 1858; m. 15 April, 1896, Cecily Mary Poulet, only dau. of the late Col. Poulet Somerset, C.B., Coldstream Guards, M.P. for Monmouth (see BURKE'S Peerage, BEAUFORT, D.), and had issue,
Catherine Cecily.

Lineage.—HUGH WALLACE, m. Eliza Anne, dau. of William Nevin, and by her (who d. 1830) had a son,
WILLIAM NEVIN WALLACE, of Downpatrick and Waterfoot House, co. Down, J.P. and D.L., High Sheriff 1891, and J.P. co. Antrim, m. 12 June, 1856, Catherine Mary, dau. of Capt. the Hon. Francis Charles Annesley, R.N., 4th son of Richard, 2nd Lord Annesley (see BURKE'S Peerage), and d. 14 Jan. 1895, having by her (who d. 30 Dec. 1877) had issue,
1. WILLIAM FRANCIS ANNESLEY, now of Ravara.
2. ROBERT HUGH, of Myra Castle (see next article).

Residence—Black Birches, Hadnall, Salop. Clubs—Naval and Military, and Boodle's, S.W., Hurlingham, and Royal St. George Yacht.

WALLACE OF MYRA CASTLE.

COL. ROBERT HUGH WALLACE, C.B., of Myra Castle, co. Down, High Sheriff 1908, Lieut.-Col. and Hon. Col. 5th Batt. Royal Irish Rifles, educated at Harrow and Brasenose Coll. Oxon., M.A., commanded his battalion in S. Africa 1901-2 (despatches, medal and clasps, C.B.), b. 14 Dec. 1860; m. 11 Sept. 1895, Caroline, dau. of John B. Twigg, of Cookstown, co. Tyrone, and has issue,
HUGH ROBERT, b. 1899.

Col. Wallace is 2nd son of William Nevin Wallace, of Downpatrick, who d. 14 Jan. 1895 (see WALLACE of Ravara), and Catherine Mary, his wife (who d. 30 Dec. 1877), dau. of Capt. the Hon. Francis Charles Annesley, R.N. (see BURKE'S Peerage, ANNESLEY, E.).

Lineage.—See preceding article.

Seat—Myra Castle, Downpatrick, co. Down. Clubs—Isthmian, W., and Ulster, and Royal Ulster Yacht, Belfast.

WALLER OF CASTLETOWN.

WILLIAM WALLER, of Castletown and Castle Grey, co. Limerick, J.P. and D.L., High Sheriff 1884, b. 1857; m. 1886, Louisa Mary, 2nd dau. of the late Samuel Hanna, and has issue,
1. JOHN THOMAS, Lieut. Leicestershire Regt., b. 1889.
2. William Hardress, b. 1891.
1. Elizabeth Grace.

Lineage. — WILLIAM WALLER, of Groombridge, High Sheriff of Kent, son of JOHN WALLER, of Groombridge, and grandson of RICHARD WALLER, of Groombridge (see WALLER of Farmington), m. 1537, Anne Fallemar, of Eastney, co. Southampton, and left two sons,
1. WILLIAM (Sir), his successor.
2. JOHN, ancestor of WALLER of Allenstown (see that family).
He d. 1555, and was s. by his elder son,

WILLIAM WALLER, of Groombridge, *m.* Alice, dau. and co-heir of Sir Walter Hendley, and was father of
SIR WALTER WALLER, Knt., of Groombridge, who *m.* Anne, dau. of Philip Choute, and had two sons,
1. GEORGE, his successor.
2. Thomas (Sir), ancestor of Waller, Bart., *of Braywick* (see BURKE's *Peerage and Baronetage).*

The elder son,
GEORGE WALLER, of Groombridge, *m.* 1st, Eliza, dau. of Michael Sondes, *s.p.*; 2ndly, Mary, widow of Sir William Asheuden, and dau. of Richard Hardress, and had a son,
SIR HARDRESS WALLER (one of the Judges who sat at the trial of King CHARLES I. for which he was afterwards tried and banished), *b.* 1604. Sir Hardress retired to Ireland, settled at Castletown, co. Limerick, and became a Member of the Irish Parliament. He *m.* Elizabeth, dau. and co-heir of Sir John Dowdall, Knt., of Kilfinny, co. Limerick, and by her (with whom he acquired the Manor of Castletown), and who *d.* 15 April, 1658 *(Funeral Entry),* he had issue,
1. John, Governor of Fort Limerick.
2. JAMES, of whom hereafter.
1. Elizabeth, *m.* 1st, Sir Maurice Fenton, Bart., and 2ndly, Sir William Petty. She was created Baroness Shelburne, and was mother of Henry, 1st Earl of Shelburne.
2. Bridget, *m.* Henry Cadogan, of Lismullen, and had a son, William, 1st Earl of Cadogan.
3. Mary, *m.* Sir John Brookes, of York, Bart.
4. Anne, *m.* Sir Henry Ingoldsby, Bart.

Sir Hardress's 2nd son,
JAMES WALLER, of Castletown, Lieut.-Governor of Kinsale, and M.P. for that Borough, *m.* Dorothy, dau. of Col. Rondall Clayton, of Moyaloe, co. Cork, and had (with four daus., 1. Elizabeth, *m.* Maurice Keatinge, of Narraghmore, co. Kildare; 2. Dorothy, *m.* Robert Gookin, of Courtmashen, co. Cork; 3. Mary, *m.* Col. Thomas Evans, of Milltown, co. Cork, brother of George, 1st Lord Carbery; and 4. Henrietta, *m.* Trevor Lloyd, of Gloucester, King's Co.), a son and successor,
JOHN WALLER, of Castletown, M.P. for Doneraile, Lieut.-Col. in the Army, described by Swift as "Jack, the grandson of Sir Hardress." He *m.* Elizabeth, dau. of Thomas Dickson, of Ballybracken, co. Cork, by Elizabeth his wife, heiress of Edward Bolton, of Clonrush, Queen's Co., grandson of Chief Baron Bolton, and had with other issue, a son and successor,
JOHN THOMAS WALLER, of Castletown, High Sheriff co. Limerick 1762, *m.* 4 Nov. 1762, Elizabeth, dau. of the Rev. Richard Maunsell, Rector of Rathkeale, and had issue,
1. JOHN, his heir. 2. BOLTON, successor to his brother.
1. Elizabeth, *m.* De Courcy, The O'Grady, of Kilballyowen, co. Limerick.
2. Katherine, *m.* Standish O'Grady, Lord Chief Baron of the Court of Exchequer in Ireland, 1st Viscount Guillamore.
3. Dorothea, *m.* Rev. Josiah Crampton, Rector of Castle Connell, co. Limerick, brother of Sir Philip Crampton, Bart., M.D.

The elder son and heir,
JOHN WALLER, of Castletown, M.P. co. Limerick, *m.* Isabella Sarah, dau. of Right Hon. Silver Oliver, of Castle Oliver, co. Limerick, M.P., by whom he had one son, John Thomas, who *d. unm.* Mr. Waller *d.* 14 Nov. 1836, and was *s.* by his brother,
BOLTON WALLER, of Castletown and Shannon Grove, Barrister-at-Law, J.P., High Sheriff 1799, *b.* 31 July, 1769; *m.* 5 Dec. 1791, Elizabeth, dau. of William Henn, of Paradise, co. Clare, and had issue,
1. John Thomas, Lieut. 27th Regt., *d. unm.*
2. WILLIAM, his successor.
3. Richard Maunsell, Lieut. R.N., *d. unm.*
4. John, Barrister-at-Law, of Shannon Grove, Pallaskenry, co. Limerick, *m.* Mary, dau. of Matthew Franks, of Merrion Square, Dublin, and had issue,
  (1) Hardress John (50, *Cornwall Gardens, S.W.*), *b.* 24 Jan. 1867; *m.* 26 Jan. 1899, Hon. Margaret Georgina Curzon, youngest dau. of Lord Scarsdale, and has issue,
    1. Hughe Bolton, *b.* 27 March, 1908.
    1. Joyce Margaret, *b.* 20 July, 1900.
    2. Alisson Dorothea, *b.* 30 Nov. 1905.
  (1) Harriet Mary, *m.* 16 Sept. 1903, Col. Herbert Anthony Sawyer, late I.S.C.
  (2) Dorothea Jane.
3. Matthew Hardress, *d. unm.*
3. John Edmund, Maj.-Gen. late Indian Army; *m.* 22 Nov. 1881, Hon. Harriette Mary Ward, dau. of 5th Viscount Bangor.
4. Richard Maunsell, Indian C.S., *m.* Fanny, dau. of Sir Richard McCausland, and has issue.
  1. Mary Harriet, *m.* Oct. 1856, Richard John Mahony, of Dromore Castle, and had issue (*see that family*).
  2. Elizabeth. 3. Ellen. 4. Isabella.
5. Bolton Edmund, *d. unm.*
6. Hardress, Ensign 22nd Regt., *d. unm.*
1. Bidsey, *m.* Rev. Richard Jones Hobson, Rector of Connor.
2. Elizabeth, *m.* Rev. John Beresford Johnstone, Rector of Tullow.
3. Katherine, *d. unm.* 4. Jane Anne, *d. unm.*
5. Isabella, *d. unm.* 6. Anne, *m.* Rev. John Samuel Monsell.
7. Jane Mary, *m.* Hugh Faulkner, of Castletown, co. Carlow.
Mr. Waller *d.* Jan. 1854. His son,
REV. WILLIAM WALLER, of Castletown, co. Limerick, J.P., *m.* 30 Aug. 1820, Maria, 2nd dau. of James O'Grady, brother of Standish, 1st Viscount Guillamore, and had issue,

1. Bolton, *d. unm.* 1853. 2. James O'Grady, *d. unm.*
3. JOHN THOMAS, who *s.* to Castletown.
4. William, *d.s.p.*
5. Richard, *d.s.p.*
6. Hardress Edmund, Maj.-Gen., late 40th Regt. Bengal Native Infantry, wounded at Arrah, *m.* 1857, Charlotte, dau. of John Mackenzie, and has issue,
  1. William Bolton. 2. John. 3. Hardress.
  4. Edmund, Lieut.-Col. Indian Army, *b.* 18 Aug. 1864.
  5. Richard.
7. Walter de Warrene, Lieut. 57th Regt. *d.s.p.*
8. Standish O'Grany, Barrister-at-Law, *d.s.p.*
9. Edmund, Royal Artillery, killed at the taking of Dalimkote Fort, Bhotan, India, *s.p.* 10. Robert de Mortimer, *d.s.p.*
1. Maria, *m.* 1849, Robert Ashworth Studdert, of Kilkishen House, co. Clare. 2. Elizabeth, *d.s.p.*
3. Katherine Ellen, *m.* 4 June, 1857, Henry Lavallin Puxley, of Dunboy Castle, and has issue (*see that family*). She *d.* 1872. He *d.* 6 Feb. 1909.
4. Julia Anna, *d.s.p.* 26 March, 1866.
The Rev. William Waller *d.* 16 Feb. 1863. His son,
REV. JOHN THOMAS WALLER, of Castletown, co. Limerick, Rector of Kilcornan, B.A. Trin. Coll. Dublin, *b.* 1827; *m.* Aug. 1855, Frances, dau. of John Lavallin Puxley, of Dunboy Castle, co. Cork, and *d.* 22 Dec. 1911, having had issue,
1. WILLIAM, now of Castletown.
2. Edward Hardress (Rev.), Rector of Athy, Canon of Christ Church Cathedral, Dublin, M.A., T.C.D.; *m.* 20 July, 1885, Florence Mary Butler, eldest dau. of the late Lucius Deering, and has issue,
  1. Hardress William Lucius, Lieut. R.F.A., *b.* 1886.
  2. Edmund Standish, *b.* 1889.
3. Bolton (Rev.), Rector of St. Munchins, Limerick; *m.* 1889, Jane Dorothea, dau. of Charles Garitt, of Queenstown, and left issue,
  Bolton Charles.
  Dorothy Catherine.
4. John Thomas (Rev.), Rector of St. Lawrence and Trinity Church, Limerick, M.A., T.C.D., *b.* 1869; *m.* 7 June, 1899, Alice Evelyn, dau. of Maxwell C. Close, of Drumbanagher, D.L. (*see that family*).
5. Henry.
1. Rosa Maria. 2. Elizabeth.
3. Kate, *m.* 31 Aug. 1898, Rev. Robert Pulleine, Vicar of Bingley, Yorks, eldest son of Right Rev. John James Pulleine, Bishop of Richmond, and has issue (*see PULLEINE of Crake Hall*).
4. Mary Isabella. 5. Frances Winifred. 6. Grace.

Arms—Sa., three walnut leaves or, between two bendlets arg. *Crest*—On a mount vert a walnut tree ppr. fructed or. *Motto*—Hic fructus virtutis.

Seat—Castletown Manor, Pallaskenry, co. Limerick.

WALLER OF PRIOR PARK.

GEORGE ARTHUR WALLER, of Prior Park, co. Tipperary, and Luska, Nenagh, co. Tipperary, J.P. co. Leitrim and for Tasmania, M.A. Dublin, *b.* 1 Sept. 1835; *m.* 11 May, 1865, Sarah Harriett, dau. of Guy Atkinson, D.L., of Cangort, King's Co. (*see that family*), and has issue,

1. RICHARD FITZARTHUR, M.I.C.E. and M.E., *b.* 19 March, 1867; *m.* Lucie, dau. of C. J. Collier, K.C.
2. William Benjamin FitzArthur, *b.* 30 June, 1868; *d.* 9 Feb. 1869.
3. Guy FitzArthur.
4. George Arthur de Warrenne, Government Geologist, Tasmania, *b.* 7 April, 1872; *m.* Edith Margaret (*d.* 16 Nov. 1908), dau. of Lieut.-Col. Cruickshank, R.E.
5. Henry Trench de Warrenne, F.C.S. and A.R.C.M., *d.* 28 Nov. 1911; *m.* 15 May, 1906, Beatrice Edith, dau. of Rev. Arthur Wayn, leaving issue 2 daus.
6. William Jocelyn De Warrenne, of Prior Park, Nenagh, co. Tipperary, J.P., *b.* 1877; *m.* 12 Jan. 1911, Elizabeth Frances, dau. of Robert Devenish, of Donnana House, co. Leitrim (*see* DEVENISH *of Mount Pleasant*).
7. Robert Studdert de Warrenne, Lieut. R.A., *b.* 27 Feb. 1879; *m.* Feb. 1912, Emily, dau. of Rev. G. F. Streatfield.
8. Arthur Octavius de Warrenne, *d.* 1881.
9. Edward Guinness de Warrenne, of Maple Cresk, Canada.
10. James Hardress de Warrenne.
1. Guudred Anne de Warrenne, *d.* 1878.

Lineage.—SAMUEL WALLER, of Newport, co. Tipperary, Barrister-at-Law, 4th son of William Waller, of Cully (*see* WALLER, *late of Rockvale*), *b.* 1705; *m.* 20 June, 1730, Anne, dau. of Thomas Jocelyn (*see* BURKE's *Peerage,* RODEN, E.), and had by her (who *d.* June, 1800),

Waller. THE LANDED GENTRY. 736

1. ROBERT, 1st bart., of Newport (see BURKE'S *Peerage and Baronetage*).
2. William (Rev.), d. without issue.
3. Jocelyn, d. *unm.* 4. GEORGE, of whom hereafter.
1. Charlotte, *m.* John Bloomfield, of Newport, and was mother of 1st Lord Bloomfield.
2 Elizabeth, *m.* Cooke Otway, of Castle Otway.
3. Blanche, *m.* James Poe, of Solsborough.

Mr. Waller *d.* 1 May, 1762. His 4th son,
GEORGE WALLER, of Prior Park, co. Tipperary, *m.* 1st, 16 Oct. 1782, Jane, dau. of Benjamin Gault, by whom he had issue, one son,

1. BENJAMIN (Rev.), Rector of Rossdroit, co. Wexford, *m.* 1823, Esther, dau. of William Digges La Touche, of Dublin, Banker; and *d.* 13 June, 1868, leaving issue,
  1. GEORGE (Rev.), M.A. Rector of St. John's, Stamford, Lincoln, *m.* 5 Jan. 1882, Charlotte Matilda Elizabeth, dau. of George Finch, of Burley-on-the-Hill, co. Rutland.
  2. James, *m.* Marion, dau. of John Burkitt, of St. Kilda, Australia, and has issue,
    (1) Grace Marian. (2) Ethel La Touche.
  1. Esther, *m.* Rev. Henry Hatton, Vicar of Monart.
  2. Grace.

He *m.* 2ndly, 8 Oct. 1801, Elizabeth, dau. of George Studdert, of Kilkishen, co. Clare, by whom (who *d.* April, 1869, aged 93) he had further issue, four sons and three daus.,
2. George Studdert, *b.* 1809; *m.* Charlotte Falkiner, and had issue,
  1. George Studdert, of The Grange, Wallarobba, N.S.W., J.P., *b.* 1832; *m.* 1861, Johanna Moore, and has issue,
    (1) James Hardress FitzGerald, J.P., *b.* 1865; *m.* 1806, Fannie C., dau. of Abel J. Colcroft.
    (2) George Broomfield, of Wallaringa, N.S. Wales, J.P., *b.* 1871; *m.* 1905, Ethel Maud, dau. of E. Norton, of Tiara, N.S. Wales, and has issue,
      1. Guy Bloomfield, *b.* 1907.
      2. Lewis de Warrenne, *b.* 1908.
      (1) Johanna, *b.* 1869.
    2. John Thomas. 3. Robert Jocelyn.
    1. Elizabeth, *m.* Professor Leadbetter, of Melbourne University.

3. ROBERT, Col. Bengal Horse Artillery, who served with much distinction under Lord Gough, through the Punjaub campaign, *m.* Annie Caroline (who *d.* 24 March, 1905), dau. of Col. Griffiths, Indian Army, and had issue, with five daus.,
  1. Robert Jocelyn, *m.* 1st, Margaret, dau. of Capt. Brawell, and had issue, one son, Jocelyn. He *m.* 2ndly, Mary, dau. of — Tenison, and had two sons and one dau.
  2. Edmund Augustus, Col. R.E., *b.* 15 Dec. 1853.
  3. John Dawson Hutchinson, Major R.A., *b.* 14 June, 1858.
4. WILLIAM THOMAS, late of Prior Park.
5. Richard, R.N., *d.* at sea
1. Elizabeth Hannah, *m.* 1st, 1832, William Henry Hutchinson, of Knockbally Magher, who *d.* 21 Nov. 1842, leaving issue. She *m.* 2ndly, 22 Oct. 1844, John Dawson Hutchinson, of Timoney, and by him had issue (see *that family*).
2. Selina Maria, *m.* 28 March, 1828, Sir Edmund Waller, 4th bart., of Newport.
3. Georgiana Frances, *m.* Caleb Powell, of Clonshavoy, M.P.

Mr. Waller *d.* 16 July, 1833, and was *s.* in his estates by his son,
WILLIAM THOMAS WALLER, of Prior Park, J.P., *b.* 29 Jan. 1811; *m.* 1st, 28 Oct. 1834, Eliza Augusta, dau. of Rev. Hosea Guinness, LL.D., Chancellor of St. Patrick's, Dublin. She *d.* 1873, leaving issue,
1. GEORGE ARTHUR, now of Prior Park.
2. Robert Jocelyn, of Summerville, Nenagh, J.P. co. Tipperary, *b.* 25 Sept. 1838; *m.* 1st, 24 Aug. 1864, Georgina Eliza, dau. of John Andrews, of Rathenny, King's Co. (see *that family*). She *d.* 6 Aug. 1877, leaving issue,
  1. William Arthur de Warrenne, Maj. 4th Batt. R. I. Regt., *b.* 26 May, 1865; *d.* 8 March, 1904; *m.* 12 Jan. 1894, Anna Selina, dau. of E. W. Waller, of Artona, Dundrum, and Elsinore Bray (see *below*) [his widow *re-m.* Richard Edmond Bayly (see BAYLY *of Debsborough*)], and had issue,
    (1) Hardress de Warrenne, *b.* 1898.
    (2) Edmund de Warrenne, *b.* 1902.
    (1) Mary Dorothea, *b.* 1904.
  1. Eliza Georgina, *b.* 26 June, 1873; *m.* 28 Aug. 1902, John Dennis Wills Harrison, C.E., son of George Dennis Harrison, C.E., of 6, Lansdown Place, Clifton, Bristol.

He *m.* 2ndly, 30 Jan. 1879, Amy Margaret, dau. of Edward Saunders, J.P., of Ballinderry Park, co. Tipperary, and by her has issue,
  1. Edgar Hardress, *b.* 10 Jan. 1887.
  2. Ellen Knollys, *b.* 28 April, 1881; *m.* 12 June, 1907, Volkert de Villeneuve Boult, son of Robert Boult, late of Ransworth, Norfolk, and has issue,
3. Edmund William, of Ardtona, Dundrum, co. Dublin, *b.* 21 Jan. 1839; *m.* 31 Aug. 1869, Mary Dorothea Stuart, dau. of Rev. Robert Wilson Rowan, of Mount Davys, co. Antrim (see *that family*), and had issue (he *d.* July, 1893; she *d.* 13 Jan. 1891),
  1. Edmund Robert de Warrenne, *b.* 15 April, 1873; *d.* 21 Sept. 1873.
  2. William Rowan de Warrenne, *b.* 26 May, 1874; *d.* 13 July, 1875.
  3. Arthur Edmund de Warrenne, of Mill Park, Roscrea, co. Tipperary, *b.* 30 Aug. 1879; *m.* 5 Feb. 1907, Eleanor Kate *b.* 20 Aug. 1884), 2nd dau. of Walter May Barton, of Guild Hall, Dereham, Norfolk, and has issue,
    William Rowan de Warrenne, *b.* 16 March, 1909.

Elizabeth Gundred *b.* 11 Nov. 1907.
4. Robert Jocelyn Rowan, *b.* 24 Oct. 1882.
1. Anna Selina, *b.* 24 Dec. 1870; *m.* 12 Jan. 1894, her cousin, Major William Arthur de Warrenne Waller (see *above*).
2. Mary Georgina, *b.* 7 Feb. 1872; *m.* Henry Annesley Coxwell-Rogers, and has issue.
3. Eliza Augusta, *b.* 27 May, 1875; *m.* 1906, Major George O'Bigge, son of Gen. Bigge, and has issue.
4. Olive Rowena, *b.* 19 Dec. 1876; *m.* 17 April, 1904, Henry Mellor Braybrooke, of Tates Hawkhurst, Kent, and has issue.
5. Ada Maud, *b.* 23 Oct. 1880.
6. Marjory Eleanor, *b.* 19 Dec. 1890.
4. William, *b.* 25 June, 1845; *d.* 21 July, 1862.
5. Francis Albert, *b.* 23 Oct. 1846; *m.* 7 Sept. 1872, Frances, dau. of Cæsar George Otway, and has issue,
  1. C. J. L. Otway, *m.* 27 April, 1909, Muriel, youngest dau. of John Bourne, of Hiderstone Hall, Staffs.
  2. William. 3. Robert Gregory.
  1. Georgina. 2. Eva. 3. Frances.
  4. Elizabeth Hannah. 5. Dorothy. 6. Kathleen.
8. Richard Hardress Studdert, *b.* 11 Sept. 1849; *d.* 29 Jan. 1864.
1. Jane Selina. 2. Georgina Eliza Augusta, *d. unm.*

Mr. Waller *m.* 2ndly, 15 Dec. 1873, Eliza Matilda (*d.s.p.* 26 Nov. 1900), dau. of Philip MacAdam, of Blackwater House, co. Clare (see *that family*), and *d.* 10 March, 1898.

Arms—Granted 1809 to George Waller and the other descendants of his ancestor Richard Waller, an officer in the Army, who settled in Ireland c. 1642)—Chequy or and arg. on a canton gu. a lion rampant, double queued of the front. Crest—Out of a ducal crest coronet or an eagle's leg and thigh erect gu. in front of five ostrich feathers alternately arg. and az. Motto—Honor et veritas.

Seats—Luska, Nenagh, and Prior Park, Borrisokane, co. Tipperary.

WALLER OF ALLENSTOWN.

EDMUND NOBLE WALLER, of Allenstown, co. Meath, *b.* 11 June, 1846; *s.* his brother 1909; *m.* 7 April, 1877, Marie Louisa, dau. of Rev. Robert Noble.

Lineage.—This family descends in the female line from WALLER *of Groombridge*. They spring from
JOHN WALLER, *m.* Joan, dau. of William Wettenhall, and had two sons,
1. WILLIAM WALLER, of Groombridge, High Sheriff of Kent, *m.* Anne Fallenar (see WALLER *of Castletown*), and left a son, WILLIAM, *m.* Alice Hendly, and from whom descended WALLER, Bart. (see *Peerage and Baronetage*), and the WALLERS *of Castletown*.
2. John, *m.* Elizabeth Farnefold, and was father of RICHARD WALLER, whose son,
ROBERT WALLER, *m.* Elizabeth Duncombe, and had two sons, William and
EDMUND WALLER, of Coles Hill, Herts, who *d.* 1602, and was bur. in Agmondesham (now Amersham, Bucks) Churchyard, leaving a son,
ROBERT WALLER, of Agmondesham, Bucks, *m.* Anne, dau. of Griffin Hampden, of Hampden, and aunt of Col. John Hampden, the famous Republican, by whom he had eleven children, whose baptisms are to be found in Amersham Church Registry as follows,
1. EDMUND, the celebrated Poet. *b.* 1605; *m.* 1st, Anna Banks; and 2ndly, Mary Bresse (see WALLER *of Farmington*, Bucks).
2. Gryffin, *b.* 1607.
3. ROBERT THOMAS, ancestor of WALLER, of Allenstown, co. Meath. 4. Stephen, *b.* 1610.
1. Elizabeth, *b.* 1601. 2. Anne, *b.* 1602.
3. Cecilia, *b.* 1603; *m.* Mr. Tomkins, Clerk of Queen's Council, who was executed for being concerned in the "Waller Plot," 1643 (see CLARENDON'S *History*).
4. Dorothy, *b.* 1604; *d.* 1604, bur. in Amersham Churchyard.
5. Mary, *b.* 1608. 6. Urfely, *b.* 1613. 7. Ellen, *b.* 1614.

The 3rd son,
ROBERT THOMAS WALLER, bapt. 1609, went to Ireland and was killed in the massacre of 1641, leaving by his wife, a niece of John Brambhall, Archbishop of Armagh, a son,
JOHN WALLER, of Kilmainham Castle, near Kells, co. Meath, *b.* 1641; *m.* Hannah, dau. of William Coddington, of Holmpatrick, co. Dublin, and had four sons and eight daus. He *d.* 6 Feb. 1715, and was bur. in Martry Churchyard. One child only survived him,
ROBERT WALLER, *b.* 1672, High Sheriff co. Meath 1720; *m.* Anna Maria Hughes, and *d.* 1731, having had issue,
1. Robert, of Rookwood, *b.* 1701; *m.* Jane Ormsby; his issue is extinct. 2. WILLIAM, of whom presently.
1. Hannah, *m.* Dixie Coddington, of Athlumney.
2. Mary, *m.* Francis Meredyth, of Dollordstown.
3. Jane, *m.* 1st, Col. Eyre, of Eyrecourt Castle; and 2ndly, Col. William Congreve.

The younger son,

WILLIAM WALLER, of Allenstown, co. Meath, High Sheriff 1750, *b.* 1710, bought most of the property, and built the present house. He *m.* 1733, Anna Maria Smyth, dau. of Ven. James Smyth, Archdeacon of Meath, by Katherine Vesey his wife, dau. of Most Rev. John Vesey, Archbishop of Tuam, and had issue,
1. ROBERT, his heir.
2. James, *b.* 1737; *d.s.p.* 1757, in India.
3. William, *b.* 1749; killed by a fall while hunting 16 Jan. 1781.
1. Catherine, *b.* 1734; *m.* 1755, James Noble, of Glasdrummon, co. Fermanagh (*see that family*), and had issue, several sons and daus., all of whom *d. unm.*, except MUNGO HENRY, of whom presently; Anna Maria, *m.* Dean Browne, and had issue; and Mary Martha, *m.* Rev. Thomas Sutton, and had issue. Mrs. Noble *d.* 19 March, 1791.
2. Anne, *m.* John Young, and *d.* 1806.
3. Mary, *b.* 1739; *m.* 1767, Rev. Daniel Augustus Beaufort, and *d.* 1831.
4. Jane, *b.* 1746; *m.* 1st, Edward Nangle; and 2ndly, Rev. Robert Highland; *d.* 1790.
5. Leonora, *b* 1752; *m.* Capt. Maine, and *d.* 1834.
6. Elizabeth, *b.* 1753; *d.* 1835.
Mr. Waller *d.* 2 Oct. 1796, and was *s.* by his eldest son,
ROBERT WALLER, of Allenstown, High Sheriff 1789, *b.* 1735; *m.* 14 July, 1767, Mary Shirley, and had two sons, both of whom *d.* infants. He *d.* 1809, when his property devolved upon his nephew,
REV. MUNGO HENRY NOBLE, Rector of Clongill, co. Meath (*see* NOBLE *of Glassdrummond*), in right of his mother, whereupon he assumed by Royal Licence, 5th May, 1809, the surname and arms of WALLER. He *m.* 21 Jan. 1794, Maria, eldest dau. of William Newcome, D.D., Archbishop of Armagh, and Primate of all Ireland, by Susanna D'Oyly his wife, and by her (who *d.* 12 April, 1858) had issue,
1. William Henry, *b.* 1 June, 1795 ; *d. unm.* 17 June, 1837.
2. ROBERT, of Glassdrummond (*see* NOBLE *of Glassdrummond*).
3. JAMES NOBLE, of whom presently.
4. Mungo, *b.* 5 Oct. 1805; *d.s.p.* 4 July, 1824.
5. John (Rev.), *b.* 11 July, 1809; *d.* 1835.
1. Susannah, *d.* an infant, 17 Nov. 1797.
2. Maria, *d. unm.* 17 May, 1857.
Mr. Noble Waller *d.* 16 June, 1831. His 3rd son,
JAMES NOBLE WALLER, of Allenstown, J.P. and D.L., High Sheriff 1846, *b.* 28 July, 1800; *m.* 1st, 22 March, 1838, Julia, dau. of Charles Arthur Tisdall, of Charlesfort, co. Meath, and by her (who *d.* 17 April, 1848) had issue,
1. WILLIAM NEWCOME, late of Allenstown.
2. James Henry, *b.* 25 March, 1845; *d.* 13 March, 1884.
3. EDMUND NOBLE, now of Allenstown.
1. Julia Elizabeth, *d. unm.* 3 July, 1900.
He *m.* 2ndly, 25 May, 1858, Anna Marie, 5th dau. of Rev. James A. Burrowes, and by her (who *d.* 17 Sept. 1891) had issue,
2. Catherine Maria.   3. Florence Mary, *d.* 10 Feb. 1889.
Mr. Waller *d.* 18 Dec. 1874 His eldest son,
WILLIAM NEWCOMBE WALLER, of Allenstown, co. Meath, J.P. and D.L., High Sheriff 1880, *b.* 13 Aug. 1839, and *d.* 7 Jan. 1909.

Arms—Arg. a bend voided sa. charged with three walnut leaves ppr. Crest—Pendent from an oak tree ppr. an escutcheon charged with a saltire gu. Motto—"Haec fructus virtutis."

Seat—Allenstown, Kells, co. Meath.

WALLER OF ROCKVALE.

JOHN EDWARD HOPKINS WALLER, late of Rockvale, co. Tipperary, M. Inst. C.E., *b.* 31 Dec. 1856; *m.* 11 Dec. 1887, Annette Elizabeth, dau. of Adolphe Naudé, and has issue,
1. LAWRENCE ARTHUR, *b.* 28 Oct. 1888.
2. Horace Edmund, *b.* 16 April, 1891.
1. Mabel Selina Grace.
2. Eileen Annette.

Lineage.—WILLIAM WARREN, *alias* WALLER, *m.* Elizabeth Hammond, and had issue two sons, Henry, who *d.* 27 Oct. 1631, without male issue, and
EDWARD WALLER, of Ashwell, Herts, and Symond's Inn, Chancery Lane, London, *m.* 1st, Margaret, dau. of Thomas Gray, by whom he had issue,
1. Edward, executor to his father, *d. unm.*
2. William, *d. unm.*
3. Jonathan, of Ashwell, Herts (will dated 3 Nov. 1662, proved 27 Nov. 1663), had issue,
I.L.G.

1. Jonathan Edward, executor to his father.
2. Humberston.   3. John.
1. Mary.   2. Elizabeth.
3. Susan.
4. Joshua.
Mr. Waller *m.* 2ndly, Margaret, dau. of Richard Glascoke, of Downe Hall, Essex, and had further issue four sons,
5. RICHARD, of whom hereafter.   6. Philip.
7. Thomas.   8. John.
Mr. Waller's will, dated 12 Oct. 1639, was proved 19 June, 1640. His 5th son,
RICHARD WALLER, held a commission in CROMWELL's Army in Ireland, 1641, and obtained numerous and extensive grants of land in co. Tipperary. He discontinued the use of the name of Warren, but retained the family arms. He resided at Cully, and became possessed, by marriage, of a portion of Lord Carlingford's Tipperary property. Mr. Waller made his will 6 Oct. 1676. By Dorothy his wife, he left two sons, RICHARD and WILLIAM, the elder of whom,
RICHARD WALLER, of Cully, *m.* Elizabeth Redmond, and by her had three sons and three daus.,
1. Edward, *d. unm.* 1711.   2. WILLIAM, of whom hereafter.
3. Jonathan, *d. unm.*
1. Dorothy, *m.* Joseph Gason, of Killinshallow, ancestor to GASON *of Richmond*.
2. Anne, Mrs. Moody.
Mr. Waller made his will 3 Oct. 1702. His 2nd son,
WILLIAM WALLER, of Cully, *m.* Blanche, dau. of Mark Weeks, His will dated 21 Oct. 1731. He *d.* 1731, leaving issue,
1. RICHARD, of whom presently.
2. Mark.   3. William (Rev.).
4. Samuel, of Newport, ancestor of WALLER, Bart., of Newport (*see* BURKE's *Peerage*), and of WALLER of Prior Park (*see that family*).
5. Edward, *m.* the dau. of Alderman Richard White, Lord Mayor of Dublin, and had a son,
    Richard, of Kimmage, co. Dublin, *m.* Letitia, dau. of Abrabam Augustus Nickson, of Munny, co. Wicklow, and had issue,
    (1) Richard, *m.* Eliza Horsfall, of London, and left issue.
    (2) Edward Augustus, *m.* Anne, dau. of Henry Coddington, of Oldbridge, Meath (*see that family*), and had issue.
    (1) Mary,   (2) Letitia, *m.* Maj. Lorenzo Nunn.
    (3) Jane, *m.* Joshua Nunn, of Dublin.
6. George, *d. unm.*
1. Jane, *m.* Richard Maunsell, ancestor of Maunsell, of Limerick,
The eldest son,
RICHARD WALLER, of Cully (afterwards Castle Waller), *m.* Elizabeth, dau. of Adm. Holland, and had issue,
1. William, *d. unm.*
2. Richard, of Castle Waller, *m.* Anne, dau. of Kilner Brazier, and left two sons,
    1. Richard, *m.* Maria Theresa, dau. of Capt. Theobald Bourke, and had issue. His eldest son, Henry Waller, sold Cully (Castle Waller) and went to America, and had issue. The other sons *d.s.p.* Of his daus., Anne Matilda, *m.* Sir John de Burgho, Bart., and Blanch, *m.* William de Rythee.
    2. Kilner, of Limerick, *m.* Deborah Newton, and had, with other issue,
        Edward, Capt. 87th Regt., *m.* 1810, Anna Maria Percy, and had issue,
            Kilner, of Spring Grove House, Middlesex, who, with all his family, were lost in the *Dunbar*, near Sydney.
3. EDWARD, of whom presently.   4. Mark.
1. Jane, *m.* 13 Nov. 1752, Robert Coppinger.
2. Elizabeth, *m.* George Gough, ancestor of Viscount Gough.
The 3rd son,
EDWARD WALLER, *m.* Constance, dau. of — Gabett, and had issue, four sons and two daus.,
1. John, of Rockvale, *d.s.p.* 1842.
2. Samuel, *m.* Katherine Doherty, and *d.s.p.m.*
3. Edward, *d.s.p.*
4. THOMAS MAUNSELL, of whom presently.
1. Eliza. *m.* Capt. Bolton.
2. Constance, *m.* Capt. Braddell.
The youngest son,
THOMAS MAUNSELL WALLER, of Finoe House, co. Tipperary. *m.* 1802, Margaret, dau. of John Vereker, and *d.* 20 Nov. 1843, having had issue,
1. EDWARD, his heir.   2. Thomas, *d.s.p.* 6 Nov. 1836.
3. JOHN FRANCIS, *s.* his brother.
1. Anna, *m.* Thomas George Stoney, of Kyle Park, co. Tipperary, and *d.* 1880.
The eldest son,
EDWARD WALLER, of Finoe House, J.P., Barrister-at-Law, *m.* 3 Aug. 1829, Mary, dau. of Henry Crossle, of Annahoe, co. Tyrone. She *d.* 1877. He *d.s.p.* 14 Feb. 1873. His only surviving brother,
JOHN FRANCIS WALLER, of Finoe House, LL.D., J.P., Barrister-at-Law, writer and poet, *b.* 1809; *m.* 1835, Anna, dau. of William Hopkins. She *d.* 5 March, 1894. He *d.* 19 Jan. 1894, having had issue,
1. THOMAS FRANCIS, late of Finoe, co. Tipperary, late Sydney Harbour Trust Commissioner, J.P., Sydney, *b.* 29 April, 1844 ; *m.* 17 Jan. 1874, Caroline Jane, dau. of Aimé Cuénod Churchill, of Vevey, Switzerland, Banker, and widow of James Hester, M.D., and by her (who *d.* 2 July, 1898) has issue,
    Francis Aimé, *b.* 23 Oct. 1874; *m.* 15 May, 1901, Marguerite Amelie, dau. of Maxime Labat de Lambert, of Paris, and has issue,
        Marguerite Caroline de Varrenne, *b.* 24 Feb. 1902.
    Edith Selina Eastermorn, *b.* 9 April, 1882.
2. JOHN EDWARD HOPKINS, of Rockvale.

3 A

1. Jane Eleanor, m. 1864, Rev. Canon Thomas Teignmouth Shore, M.A., LL.D., Chaplain in Ordinary to the King (who d. 3 Dec. 1911), and has issue.
2. Margaret Lucy, m. 1 Dec. 1870, Frederick W. Chaplin, and has issue.
3. Harriet Elizabeth, m. 10 April, 1869, Rev. James Robinson, B.A., who d. Sept. 1874, leaving issue. She d. Dec. 1879.
4. Selina Elizabeth, m. 17 Dec. 1872, James Clarke Lane, K.C., and d. 2 Dec. 1873.
5. Anna Cecilia, m. July, 1880, Rev. H. T. Lane, and has issue.
6. Constance Mary, d. unm. 5 May, 1872.

Arms—(Confirmed to the descendants of Thomas Mannsell Waller)—Quarterly: 1st and 4th, sa. three walnut leaves or, between two bendlets arg.; 2nd and 3rd, chequy or and az., on a canton gu. a lion rampant double queued of the first, over all in the centre point a mullet enn. Crest—Out of a ducal crest coronet or an eagle's leg and thigh erect gu. in front of a plume of five ostrich feathers alternately arg. and az. Motto—Honor et veritas. [N.B.—See also note as to arms, sub WALLER of Prior Park.]

Residences—The Nook, Westgate-on-Sea, and 172, Cromwell Road, S.W. Clubs—St. Stephen's, S.W., and Royal Automobile.

WALLIS, late OF DRISHANE CASTLE.

HENRY AUBREY BEAUMONT WALLIS, late of Drishane Castle, co. Cork, J.P., now of Roskrow-Penryn, Cornwall, b. 4 July, 1861; m. 1st, 1 March, 1883, Elizabeth Caroline, eldest dau. of Hon. Albert Yelverton Bingham, 5th son of the 3rd Lord Clanmorris (see BURKE'S Peerage), and by her has issue. From him she obtained a divorce by Act of Parliament 1906.

HENRY DIGBY, late Lieut. Scots Guards (Guards' Club), b. 3 June, 1885.
Audrey Beatrice Jean, b. 23 Jan. 1888; m. 5 Jan. 1909, Francis Ivan Oscar Brickmann, 119th Infantry, Indian Army.

He m. 2ndly, 11 Feb. 1907, Julia Mary Catharine Curteis, widow of Edward Witherden Curteis, Capt. 24 Regiment, and only dau. and heir of Mrs. Wright (see WRIGHT of Mottram Hall, Cheshire).

Lineage.—In 1595, THOMAS WALLYS resided at Curryglass, co. Cork; he d. previous to 1630, leaving a widow and two sons. The elder son,
THOMAS WALLYS, of Curryglass, left at his decease two sons,
1. THOMAS, of Curryglass, of whom hereafter.
2. Peter, of Shangary, co. Cork, living 1630, High Sheriff 1660, had a large grant of land under the Act of Settlement, m. Audrey, dau. of Barachias Baker, of Carrigrohan, co. Cork, and d. 1679, leaving by her (who d. 1685) four daus. (viz., 1. Margaret, m. Col. Edward Corker, of Ballymaloe, co. Cork, and d.s.p. 17 July, 1721; 2. Katherine, m. 1679, Ebenezer Low, and d. 8 July, 1697; 3. Mehetabel, m. Francis Foulke, and d. 1 July, 1703; 4. Mary, m. Benjamin Glascott, of New Ross, who d. 6 Oct. 1723) and two sons,
  1. John, of Carrigrohan, J.P., whose dau. and heir, Mary, m. Charles Gookin.
  2. Barachias, of Ballycrenan, m. 1688, Ellen Cross, of Ballybrazil, co. Wexford, and d. intestate (adm. 7 July, 1711) leaving two daus. (viz., (1) Susan, m. William Corker, of Kilbrenan, co. Cork: (2) Eleanor, m. Jan. 1730, Sylvester Cross, of Passage co. Cork, who d. 1767) and a son,
    William, of Ballycrenan, m. Clotilda, dau. of Thomas Uniacke, of Woodhouse, co. Waterford, and had
      1. Barachias, of Ballycrenan, m. 1763, Anne, dau. of Emanuel Pigott, and d.s.p. Jan. 1765.
      1. Helena, m. John Colthurst.
      2. Clotilda, m. 24 Sept. 1771, Sir Edward Hoare, 2nd bart., of Annabella, and d. 3 Sept. 1816, leaving issue (see BURKE'S Peerage).
The eldest son,
THOMAS WALLIS, of Curryglass, mentioned in will of his uncle Peter, 1630, party to a deed in 1640, had issue,
1. Boyle, b. 1644.
2. THOMAS, of Curryglass, of whom hereafter.
3. Henry, of Drishane, co. Cork, m. Penelope, dau. of John Nettles, of Toureen, and left,
  1. Thomas, d.s.p.   2. Henry, b. 1697; d.s.p. 1749.
  3. John, of Reddy, called to the Bar 1754, High Sheriff of Cork 1772; d.s.p. 1787.
  1. Mary, m. George Jackson, of Grangebeg, co. Cork.
  2. Elizabeth, m. George Wallis, of Curryglass.
The eldest surviving son,
THOMAS WALLIS, of Curryglass, m. 1st, 1679, Jane Ludyman, and by her had issue, Thomas and Grace, who both d. unm. Mr. Wallis had in the time of JAMES II to fly to England with his wife and two children. He m. 2ndly, Persis, dau. of Holmes, and had issue, four daus. (viz., Anne, m. Thomas Moore, of Gregg, co. Cork; Elizabeth, m. Samuel Meade; Arabella, m. Michael Webber; Persis; and Jane, m. Digby Cooke) and two sons,
1. GEORGE, his heir.   2. Thomas.
Mr. Wallis purchased considerable landed property in the co. of Cork, in 1703, from the trustees of Forfeited Estates. His son and heir,

GEORGE WALLIS, of Curryglass, m. 1721, his cousin, Elizabeth, dau. of Henry Wallis, of Drishane, and had two daus. (viz., Penelope, m. John Parker, of Cherrymount, co. Waterford; and Elizabeth, m. Samuel Adams) and as many sons,
1. HENRY, his heir.   2. George, d.s.p.
The elder son,
HENRY WALLIS, of Curryglass and Drishane, under the limitations in the will of his maternal grandfather, Henry Wallis, became entitled to the Drishane and other estates; he m. 1758, Elizabeth, dau. of Christmas Paul, of Paulville, co. Carlow, by Ellen his wife, dau. of Robert Carew, of Ballynamona, co. Waterford, and had four sons and two daus.,
1. JOHN, his heir.
2. Christmas Paul (Rev.), B.A., m. 1st, Elizabeth, dau. of Rev. James Stopford, Fellow Trin. Coll. Dublin, and sister of Edward Stopford, Bishop of Meath, and had three sons and six daus.,
  1. John, an Officer 52nd Regt., d. unm.
  2. Henry, an Officer 52nd Regt., d.s.p.   3. James, d.s.p.
  1. Elizabeth, d. unm.   2. Catherine.
  3. Penelope, m. Rev. Digby Joseph Stopford Ram, and had issue (see RAM of Clonattin).
  4. Ellen, m. William Lombard, of Danestort, co. Cork, son of the Rev. Edmond Lombard, of Lombardstown, co. Cork.
He m. 2ndly, Hannah Fitzgerald, and had further issue,
  4. George.
  5. Thomas, Barrister-at-Law, m. Miss MacDermot, and had a dau., Anne.
  6. Christmas Paul, m. Blessing (d. 23 April, 1910), dau. of Thomas Browning Gardner, of Youghal, co. Cork, and had,
    (1) Christmas Paul, d. unm.   (2) Thomas Henry Gardner.
    (1) Christiana Augustus.   (2) Georgina Blessing.
    (3) Frances.   (4) Penelope Croker.
    (5) Anne, d. unm.
3. Thomas, m. Miss Cooke, and had issue,
  1. Harry, an Officer 52nd Foot, m. Miss Justice, and had three daus.,
    (1) Mary, m. Thomas Crofts.
    (2) Ellen, m. John Moriarty, M.D.   (3) Dora, d. unm.
  2. John Cooke, of Minchill, co. Cork, m. 1846, Elizabeth, dau. of Major Beresford Gahan, 4th Dragoon Guards, and had, with others who d. young, issue,
    (1) Thomas Henry, b. 1847; d. 1886.
    (2) Beresford Gahan, Supt. Engineer, Indian P.W. Dept.; b. 1849; m. 1882, Harriet Florence, dau. of Alfred Gahan, of Cavan, and has issue,
      Beresford Herbert, b. 1888.
    (3) John Cooke, Capt. Imperial Lt. Horse, S. Africa, b. 1854.
    (1) Elizabeth.
  1. Rebecca, m. H. Sherlock.
  2. Elizabeth, d. unm.
  3. Mary, m. J. E. Herrick.
  4. Ellen, m. the Rev. A. Sergeant, of Waterford.
  4. Harry, m. Helen, 2nd dau. of James M'Call, of Braehead, co. Lanark, and had three sons, Harry, drowned; James and John, d.s.p.; and seven daus. of whom the eldest, Sarah, m. William Smith, of Carbeth Gutherie; and the 5th, Margaret, m. George Dennistoun.
1. Ellen, m. Charles Bolton, of Curraghduff, co. Waterford.
2. Elizabeth, m. Sir Joshua Christmas Paul, 2nd bart., of Ballyglan, co. Waterford, and d.s.p. 16 April, 1836.
The eldest son,
JOHN WALLIS, of Drishane Castle, m. 1st, Patience, eldest dau. of John Longfield, of Longueville, co. Cork, and by her had one dau.,
1. Patience, m. James Hauning, of Kilcrone, co. Cork.
He m. 2ndly, Sept. 1787, Marianne, dau. of John Carleton, of Woodside, co. Cork, and by her had issue,
1. HENRY, his heir.
2. Penelope, m. Samuel Adams, of Kilbree, co. Cork, J.P., and had a dau.,
  Marianne Caroline, m. 8 Oct. 1844, John Allin, of Monabeg, nephew of Gen. Sir Thomas Kenah, K.C.B.
3. Elizabeth, m. the Rev. Charles Morgan.
4. Marianne, m. Simon Newport, J.P., of John's Hill Villa, Waterford.
The son and heir,
HENRY WALLIS, of Drishane Castle, co. Cork, J.P. and D.L., High Sheriff, 1814, Lieut.-Col. South Cork Rifles, m. 1st, Miss Forster, by whom he had one son, dec.; and 2ndly, 1827, Ellen, dau. of Grice Smyth, of Ballynatray, co. Waterford, and sister of the Princess of Capua, and of Lady Dinorben (see that family), and had,
JOHN RICHARD SMYTH, of Drishane Castle.
Mary Gertrude, d. unm. 5 May, 1857.
Mr. Wallis d. 6 Jan. 1862, and was s. by his son,
JOHN RICHARD SMYTH WALLIS, of Drishane Castle, J.P., High Sheriff, 1857, Capt. 4th Dragoon Guards, b. 5 June, 1828; m. 1 Sept. 1853, Octavia Willoughby, and by her (who m. 2ndly, 4 April, 1872, Sir G. H. Beaumont, 9th bart., of Cole Orton Hall, co. Leicester, and d. 10 June, 1901) had issue,
1. Digby Henry Willoughby, b. 2 June, 1854; d. 18 July, 1858.
2. HENRY AUBREY BEAUMONT, now of Drishane Castle.
1. Eva Octavia Augusta, d. 28 March, 1860.
2. Eva Violet Amelia Gwen Willoughby, m. 29 June, 1888, Maj. Edgar St. John Christophers, D.S.O., and has issue.
Mr. Wallis d. 27 Oct. 1868.

Seat—Roskrow, Penryn, Cornwall.   Club—Carlton.

WALSH OF MUL HUSSEY.

VALENTINE JOHN HUSSEY WALSH, of Mul Hussey, co. Roscommon, b. 17 Feb. 1862, Barrister-at-Law Middle Temple, Private Secretary to Postmaster-General 1900-1902; m. 19 Oct. 1907, Elizabeth Jeanne Thérèse Marie Duchesse de la Mothe-Houdancourt, Grandee of Spain 1st Class, dau. of Comte Artus de Cossé-Brissac, son of 10th Duc de Brissac by his marriage with Alix, dau. of Olivier Louis Robert Marquis de Walsh Serrant, Duc de la Mothe-Houdancourt, grandee of Spain 1st Class, and widow of Count Renaud de Moustiers, who d. 3 Jan. 1904.

Lineage.—The first members of this family to settle in Ireland were PHILIP, DAVID and GEOFFREY WALSH, nephews of Rees ap Griffith, Prince of South Wales. They accompanied their uncle Robert FitzStephen, who was one of the thirty-three knights who followed the leadership of Richard Strongbow, Earl of Pembroke, in his invasion of Ireland in 1170. David was the ancestor of Walsh of Carrickmines. Philip, known in Irish as Brenagh, the ancestor of this family, m. 1174, Eleanor, dau. of Maurice de Burgh, and had a son,

HOYLE WALSH, or Brenagh, built Castle Hoel in the parish of Kilmagany, co. Kilkenny. He m. Katherine, dau. of Griffin Fitzwilliam. His heir,

GRIFFIN WALSH, or Brenagh, of Castle Hoel, m. and had a son,
HOWELL WALSH, or Brenagh, of Castle Hoel, m. and had a son,
NICHOLAS WALSH, or Brenagh, of Castle Hoel, m. and had a son,
THOMAS WALSH, or Brenagh, of Castle Hoel, m. Mary, dau. of O'Connor Faly, M.I., and d. circa 1300, leaving a son,
GEOFFREY WALSH, or Brenagh, of Castle Hoel, described in Deed dated Thursday after Feast of St. John the Baptist, 48 EDWARD III, as "Galfridus filius Thomæ filii Nicholai filii Howelli Walshe," m. and had a son,
RICHARU WALSH, of Brenagh, of Castle Hoel, suæ nationis capitaneus described as "Richard Gesticysou Walshe." He was an outlaw in Iverke 5 HENRY VI, pleads pardon 8 HENRY IV, appointed Keeper of the Peace for co. Kilkenny 30 July, 1410, m., and had a son,
EDMUND WALSH, or Brenagh, of Castle Hoel, m. Joan Butler, dau. of the Baron of Poulickery, and d. (bur. at Jerpoint) 1476, leaving a son,
ROBERT WALSH, or Brenagh, Baron of Shancahir, m. Catherine Power, of Donhill, and d. 8 Dec. 1501 (M.I.), leaving issue,
1. WALTER, who follows. 2. James (see footnote)*.

* 2. James Walsh, of Ballincowle, who had issue,
1. ROBERT FITZJAMES, who follows.
2. Oliver Fitzjames, of Killaspuck, pardoned 1549, father of Thomas, of Killaspuck, who was living 1653.
3. Edmund of Benanycoyle, pardoned 1549.
ROBERT FITZJAMES WALSH, of Ballincowle, pardoned 1549; m. 1st, Ellen, dau. of Power, of Donelly, whom he divorced 10 Nov. 1540, by whom he had issue,
1. James FitzRobert, of Ballincowle, pardoned 1567, 1571, 1579; m. in Kilfecaragh about 1570, Ellice Forstall; killed at Lismateige Bridge in 1600, and had issue.
Robert Walsh, of Ballynacooly, who was 8 years old Monday after feast of St. Barnabas (June 11), at Fayle., m. 24 Sept. 1597, Mary, dau. of Geoffrey Power, of Moghorban, and had issue,
James, who forfeited Ballynacooly in 1655.
Robert Fitzjames Walsh m. 2ndly, Katherine Gall, and had issue,
2. RICHARD FITZJAMES, who follows.
The 2nd son,
RICHARD FITZJAMES WALSH, pardoned 1575, part owner of Ballynacooly with his brother James, living 1 May, 1638; m. Elizabeth, dau. of Thomas Sutton, and had issue
1. Robert Fitz Richard, of Dunkitt, living 1620.
2. JOHN, who follows.
JOHN WALSH, living 1 May, 1638; m. Mary, dau. of Thomas Scattick, and had issue,
1. Patrick. 2. JAMES, who follows.
3. Philip, settled at St. Malo before 1652, m. Margaret, dau. of William Hore, of Harperstown, co. Wexford. His descendants were the Walsh's Sieurs de Valois, of St. Malo, now represented by the Ronin's, Le Joliffe's and Desfontaines' of St. Servan.
JAMES WALSH, Capt. R.N., conveyed JAMES II. in his vessel from Ireland to France. He m. Margaret, dau. of Thomas Walsh, of the Carrickmines family, and had issue,
PHILIP WALSH, of St. Malo, bapt. 8 Dec. 1666; m. 11 Jan. 1695, Anne, dau. of James Whyte, of Waterford, and d. 11 Sept. 1708, leaving issue,

WALTER WALSHE, or Brenagh. suæ nationis capitaneus, m. Katherine, dau. of Butler, Baron of Poulickery. He signed protest of Kilkenny freeholders against taxation 9 Aug. 18 HENRY VIII, and Presentment of Jury 5 Oct. 1537, and was bur. at Jerpoint (M.I.), leaving 1. EDMUND; 2. Robert; 3. Richard; 1. Onoria, m. John Grace, Baron of Courtstown, and d. 1568 (M.I. Kilkenny Cathedral); and 2. Eleanor, m. Laurence Esmonde, of Johnstown, co. Wexford. The eldest son,
EDMUND WALSH, or Brenagh, of Castle Hoel, Baron of Shancahir, m. 1st, Grany, dau. of Garrett Kavanagh, of Garahill, whom he repudiated, and 2ndly, Margaret, dau. of Rowland FitzGerald, Baron of Burnchurch, She d. 1560. He d. 1550, leaving issue,
1. ROBERT, his heir. 2. Oliver, of Ballyteskin.
3. Philip, of Courtboyle, co. Wexford, father of William, who had a son, Lewis, father of Patrick Walsh.
The eldest son,
ROBERT WALSH, of Castle Hoel, who had livery of seizin 15 May, 1550, m. Helen, dau. of James Tobin, of Cumshinagh. He d. 10 Oct. 1557, leaving issue,
1. WALTER, of whom presently.
2. Edmund.
3. John.
1. Margaret, m. Alexander Redmond, of the Hall, co. Wexford, who d. before 1590. She m. 2ndly, Richard Devereux, of Hooke.
The eldest son,
WALTER WALSH, of The Mountains, Baron of Shancahir, High Sheriff co. Kilkenny, 4 Jan. 1580 and 1585, m. Ellice, dau. of the first Viscount Mountgarrett, and d. 9 May, 1619, leaving issue,
1. ROBERT, of whom presently.
2. Edmund, of Owney, m. Agnes, dau. of Walsh of Pilltown, and had issue. Their last male descendant was Pierce Walsh Porter, of Allarthing, Surrey, and Owney, co. Kilkenny, who d.s.p. 1820.
3. James.
4. William, m. a dau. of —Purcell, of Ballyfalgas.
5. John, b. 1580; d. 1660, M.P. for Waterford, known as Shawn MacWawlthagh, the Gaelic poet of the Welsh Mountains, m. Magdalen, dau. of — Strange, of Waterford, and had issue.
1. Joan, m. Philip Devereux, eldest son of Sir James Devereux, of Ballymagire, who d. 21 Sept. 1635.
2. Margaret, m. William Furlonge, of Horestown, co. Wexford, who d. Jan. 1636.
3. Onor, m. 1st, Leonard Colclough, and 2ndly, the Hon. James Butler, of Knockloftie, who d. 17 April, 1630.
4. Ellen, m. David Grant, of Corlody.
5. Catherine, m. William Wale, of Coolinamuckie, who d. 13 May, 1636.
6. Ellen, m. 20 April, 1614, Thomas Comerford, of Ballinamuck.
The eldest son,
ROBERT WALSH, of Ballingowne, pardoned 1600, m. Eleanor, dau. of Sir John FitzEdmund FitzGerald, of Cloyne, and d. 1603, and by her (who d. 13 Feb. 1611) had a son,
WALTER WALSH, of Castlehoyle, Baron of Shancahir, M.P. co. Kilkenny 1639-40, a Capt. in Lord Castleconnel's Regt., in the army of Confederated Catholics, b. 1601, had livery of seizin 12 Feb. 3 JAS. I; m. 1625, Magdelen, dau. of Sir John Sheffield, K.B., eldest son of the 1st Earl of Mulgrave, and d. 1647, leaving issue,
1. Edmund, b. 1626; m. (setts. dated 8 Oct. 1642) Margaret, dau. of Oliver Grace, M.P., of Inchmore, and was slain at Dissertmoon, near New Ross, about 1647, leaving issue,
Robert, of Cloonassy, M.P. co. Kilkenny 1689, Capt. in Grace's Regt. of Horse in JAMES II's army, b. 1645; m. 15 Jan. 1672, Mary, widow of George Sherlock, and dau. of Peirce Walsh, 2nd son of Sir James Walsh, Bart., of Ballygunner, co. Water,
1. Jacques, b. 6 Jan. 1697; d. young.
2. Patrick, bapt. 13 Oct. 1701; m. 22 Nov. 1723, Mary Anne, dau. of Mark Cranisborough, of Morlaix, and d. 19 Nov. 1790. He was ancestor of the families of Walsh de Chassenon and Walsh, of Cadiz.
3. AntoineVincent, representative of CHARLES EDWARD at Courts of France and Spain, who escorted CHARLES EDWARD to Scotland on his vessel, the Du Teillay, and was consequently created Earl Walsh by the Chevalier St. George, 20 Oct. 1745, and a count by Louis XV, bapt. 22 Jan. 1703; m. 9 Jan. 1741, Mary, dau. of Luke O'Sheill, of Nantes, and d. 2 May, 1763, having had issue, from whom descended the Counts Walsh.
4. FRANCIS JOSEPH, of whom presently.
5. Philip, b. 5 March, 1706; living 1754.
The 3rd son,
FRANCIS JOSEPH WALSH, of Cadiz, afterwards of the Chateau de Serrant in Anjou, created by Louis XV Count de Serrant, in March, 1755, b. 31 March, 1704; m. 26 April, 1743, Mary, dau. of Thomas Harper. He d. 23 Aug. 1782, leaving issue,
1. ANTOINE JOSEPH PHILIPPE, his heir.
2. Charles Edward, Vicomte de Serrant, of the Château de Bouillé-Mesnard, b. 6 Feb. 1746; m. 25 Sept. 1771, Julie, dau. of Jean Paqué, Baron de Lugé, of the Island of St. Domingo, and d. 27 Dec. 1820, leaving issue,
1. Charles, b. 19 Dec. 1771; d. 1786.
2. Jean Joseph, Vicomte de Serrant, b. 25 July, 1773; m. 22 Oct. 1822, Caroline, dau. of Comte de Quéhillac, and d. 23 Sept. 1841, leaving issue,
(1) Albert, 7th Count de Serrant, b. 29 Sept. 1823; d.s.p. 28 June, 1895.
(1) Berthe, b. 6 Nov. 1824; d. 1 May, 1879; m. 23 April, 1849, Comte de Guerdavid.
(2) Robertine, b. 25 March, 1828; m. 18 Nov. 1851, her first cousin, Vicomte Paul de Serrant (see below), and d. May, 1903.

3 A 2

ford (who *d.* 3 Oct. 1710), was attainted 20 April, 3 W. and M., was killed at the siege of Limerick 1691, leaving issue,
    (1) Walter, of Dunkitt, co. Kilkenny, *d.* in France, 13 Feb. 1737.
    (1) Margaret, *b.* 21 Dec. 1673; *m.* John Daly, of Cork. She was declared by judgment of the Court of Chancery, 13 Feb. 1748, to be co-heir (with her sister Magdalen) of the undevised property of Edmund Sheffield, 2nd Duke of Buckinghamshire and Normanby. She *d.s.p.* 27 July, 1754.
    (2) Elizabeth, *d.* young.
    (3) Magdalen, *b.* 1684; *d.* 2 Sept. 1747, bur. in Westminster Abbey, 5 Sept. following.
2. Hoyle, of Ardery (settled upon him by his father, 6 Sept. 1638), Col. in the army of Confederate Catholics, *m.* Anne, dau. of Sieur de Cartault. His estates were forfeited 1657, but restored by CHARLES II.
3. Robert, Capt. in the French Service, *b.* 1632, *d.* of his wounds at the battle of Landerseien in Flanders, 1655.
4. RICHARD, of whom presently.
1. Elizabeth, *m.* John Grace, of Courtstown, M.P. co. Kilkenny.
2. Ursula, *m.* 1st, John Bryan, of Bawnmore, and 2ndly, Edmund Blancheville, of Blanchevillestown.
3. Letitia, *m.* 1st, John Tobin, and 2ndly, Harvey Morres, of Castlemores.
The 4th son,
RICHARD WALSH, settled in the Barony of Athlone, co. Roscommon. He *m.* about 1652, Margaret, dau. of Bryan O'Conor, of Beagh, and granddau. of Sir Hugh O'Conor Don, and was father of
WILLIAM WALSH, of Cranagh, *m.* Winefred, dau. of Bryan Kelly, of Beagh. His son,
WALTER WALSH, of Cranagh, forfeited most of his estates in the penal times, *m.* about 1695, Giles, dau. of Mac Laughlin, of Hall, co. Westmeath, and *d.* 19 March, 1729 (M.I.), leaving issue,
1. William, of Feakle, living 1771.
2. PATRICK, of whom hereafter.
3. James, of Dublin, living 1737.
4. Thomas, of Dublin, living 1737.   5. John, living 1737.
1. A dau., *m.* 1717, Edmund Kelly, of Beagh.
2. Winefred, *m.* William Keogh.
3. Giles, *d.* before 1737.
4. Ellis, *m.* John Donelly, and *d.* 18 June, 1729 (M.I.).
5. Una, *m.* James Keogh.
The 3rd son,
PATRICK WALSH, of Cranagh, *m.* (setts. 12 Dec. 1728), Ellis, dau. of Mathew Tully, of Muckland, and *d.* Dec. 1745, leaving issue,
1. RICHARD, of whom presently.
2. William, of Athlone, *m.* Rebecca, dau. of Francis Flood, of Newtownflood, made will 19 July, 1780, had issue,

3. Charles William, Vicomte de Serrant, *b.* 15 Aug. 1792; *m.* 20 March, 1813, Mathilde Marie Madeleine, dau. of Comte Phillipe Walsh, and *d.* 23 Aug. 1869, having had issue,
    (1) Charles, *b.* 23 Jan. 1814; *m.* 19 Nov. 1839, Sidonie Marie (*b.* 29 Aug. 1827), dau. of Alexandre Guillaume Coustard de Souvré, and had issue, Céline, *b.* 25 June, 1841; *m.* 1867, Count de Carcaradec. He *d.* 9 May, 1905. She *d.* 24 Aug. 1905.
    (2) Raoul, *b.* 25 June, 1819; *d.s.p.* 25 Feb. 1839.
    (3) Gustave, Vicomte de Serrant, *b.* 10 Oct. 1827; *m.* 1st, 1 June, 1858, Caroline, dau. of Louis Gaston d'Arlanges, and had issue, Gustave, of the Chateau de Bouillé Mesnard, (*b.* 9 Jan 1859; *d.* 23 Oct. 1884). He *m.* 2ndly, 23 Sept. 1875, Caroline, dau. of Charles, Marquis de la Jaille (who *d.* 21 July, 1905), and *d.* 24 March, 1876, leaving issue,
    Henry, 8th Count de Serrant, of Le Chêne, near Chateau Gontier, Mayenne, *b.* 5 Oct. 1876; *m.* 21 May, 1901, Victoire Françoise Ghislaine Andrée, dau. of François Benoit Paul Geoffroy, of the Chateau de Baubigné (Mayenne), and has issue,
    Gerard, *b.* 1 Oct. 1903.
    Edwige Marie Céline, *b.* 13 Oct. 1902.
    (4) Paul, *b.* 10 Oct. 1827; *m.* 18 Nov. 1851, Robertine, dau. of Jean Joseph, Vicomte de Serrant (*see above*) (who *d.* May, 1903), and had issue,
    Edgar, Vicomte de Serrant, *b.* 5 Oct. 1856; *m.* 5 Oct. 1885, Marie Anne, dau. of Alexandre Robert de Boistossé, and has issue,
    a. Patrick, *b.* 6 Oct. 1887.
    b. Alberic, *b.* 15 Oct. 1892.
    a. Anne, *b.* 1889.   *b.* Mathilde, *b.* 1898.
    Mathilde, *b.* 14 Sept. 1853; *m.* 1876, Count Charles de Gouvello de la Porte, and *d.* 1 June, 1897.
3. Philippe François Joseph, Count Walsh, Maréchal des camps et armées du Roi, *b.* 13 Jan. 1753; *m.* 24 Dec. 1784, Isidore dau. of Antoine Isidore Lotin de Lagerie, Conseiller du Roi en tous des conseils, and had issue,
Alfred, assumed name of FREEMAN 1823, *m.* 26 June, 1819, Stella, dau. of Philip Dormer Stanhope, and *d.* 19 Dec. 1862, leaving issue,
    (1) Emma, *b.* 27 Feb. 1820; *m.* 2 Feb. 1859, Baron de Méneval, and *d.* 22 Nov. 1899.
    (2) Caroline, *b.* 3 Sept., bapt. 6 Oct. 1821; *m.* 1st, 30 Sept. 1847, Baron de Taintignies; and 2ndly, Count Alfred Walsh, and *d.* March, 1903.
    (3) Mathilde, *b.* 1822; *m.* 2 July, 1846, Count von Diesbach, and *d.* 1904.
1. Marie Dorothée, *b.* 7 Feb. 1748; *m.* 28 Oct. 1765, Antoine Jean Baptiste Pauline, 2nd Earl Walsh, and *d.* 18 June, 1785, leaving issue.

1. William, of Cranagh Mill, *m.* Johanna, dau. of Nicholas Moran, of Drumrany, co. Westmeath, and *d.* Nov. 1827, leaving issue,
    (1) William, of Cranagh Mill, *b.* 1786; *m.* 24 June, 1815, Maria, dau. of Walter Walsh, and *d.* 13 April, 1849, leaving issue,
    1. William, of Cranagh Mill, *b.* 28 Sept. 1817; *m.* 1845, Anne, dau. of Terence Sweeny, of Clonbrush, and *d.* 1 Aug. 1902, leaving issue,
    a. William, of Keelogues bapt. 1 Jan. 1850; *m.* 1 Aug. 1885, Charlotte, dau. of Nicholas Walsh. She *d.* 3 July, 1896, leaving issue, John and Anna Maria.
    b. Francis, bapt. 20 Nov. 1851; *d.* 11 May, 1883.
    c. Terence, of Cranagh Mill, bapt. 12 Jan. 1854; *m.* 30 Jan. 1886, Julia, dau. of William Corrigan. She *d.* 21 Sept. 1909, leaving issue,
    (a) Mary Frances, *b.* 30 April, 1892.
    (b) Elizabeth, *b.* 5 Nov. 1893.
    (c) Maude Josephine, bapt. 8 Dec. 1897.
    d. John, *b.* 12, bapt. 17 Nov. 1855; *m.* 19 Aug. 1879, Maria, dau. of John O'Donnell, and *d.* 12 Feb. 1903, leaving issue,
    (a) William, *b.* 31 Aug. 1880.
    (b) Walter, bapt. 5 Oct. 1888.
    (c) Patrick Joseph, bapt. 5 Jan. 1890.
    (d) Maria Agnes, bapt. 20 Oct. 1881.
    (e) Elizabeth Clare, *b.* 5 Sept. 1888.
    e. Patrick, bapt. 22 Jan. 1857; *d.* in the United States 1898.
    a. Margaret, bapt. 8 Aug. 1847; *m.* 25 Feb. 1867, Hubert O'Brien.
    b. Elizabeth, bapt. 2 Sept. 1848; *m.* 31 Jan. 1877, Luke Donnelly.
    c. Alice, bapt. 13 Nov. 1852.
    d. Norah, bapt. 12 June, 1859; *m.* 13 Feb. 1889, Patrick Murray, and *d.* 24 Dec. 1889.
    e. Anne, *b.* 25 March, 1862.
    2. Richard, of Dundas, Ontario, Canada, *b.* 27 May, bapt. 3 June, 1831; *m.* 1845, Eliza, dau. of Anthony Milligan, of Dundas, Ontario, and *d.* 1853, leaving issue,
    a. William, of Chicago, *b.* 1853.
    a. Alicia, *b.* 30 Nov. 1846; *m.* 1861, John Sarsfield Murray, of Gordon, Nebraska.
    b. Eliza Cecilia, *b.* 6 March, 1848; *m.* 1865, Byron James Mc Cleary, of Chicago.
    c. Mary Jane, *b.* 12 Aug. 1850; *m.* 1871, Franklin Murray, of Gordon, Nebraska.
    d. Maria Louisa, *b.* 22 Feb. 1852; *m.* 1904, Andrew MacVenn, of Galt, Canada.

2. Anne, *b.* 15 Oct. 1753; *m.* 1st, 12 June, 1771, Baron de la Haye, who *d.* 15 Sept. 1790, and 2ndly, 18 Oct. 1791, Vicomte de Scépeaux.
3. Sophie Marie Josepha, *b.* 1 Jan. 1757; *m.* 7 Nov. 1774, Viscount Southwell, and *d.* 6 Jan. 1796, leaving issue (*see* BURKE's *Peerage*)
4. Françoise, *b.* 15 Oct. 1758; *m.* 16 March, 1775, Marquis de Choiseul Beaupré, and *d.* 1793.
ANTOINE JOSEPH PHILIPPE WALSH, 2ND COUNT DE SERRANT, Lieut.-Gen. in the French Army, commanded the Walsh Regt. of the Irish Brigade, *b.* 17 Jan. 1744; *m.* 1st, 15 June, 1766, Renée, dau. of the Marquis de Choiseul Beaupré, and by her had issue,
1. Charles Phillip, *b.* 31 July, 1768; *d.* 13 Oct. 1770.
2. Edouard, 3rd Count de Serrant, *b.* 15 Nov. 1771; *d.* 8 Jan. 1825.
He *m.* 2ndly, 22 Jan. 1795, Louise, dau. of the Marquis de Vaudreuil, and widow of the Marquis de Valady, and by her had issue,
3. Theobald Gautier, 4th Count de Serrant, *b.* 28 Feb. 1796; *m.* 16 Sept. 1823, Sophie, dau. of Jean François le Grand, and *d.* 17 Aug. 1836, leaving issue,
    1. Gaston, 5th Count de Serrant, *b.* 17 July, 1824; *d.s.p.* 9 Aug. 1845.
    2. Robert, *b.* July, 1827; *d.* 5 May, 1829.
    3. Ludovic, 6th Count de Serrant, *b.* 15 May, 1831; *d.s.p.* 11 April, 1894.
    Marguerice, *b.* 17 Dec. 1825; *d.* 3 May, 1839.
4. Louis, Marquis de Walsh Serrant, and *jure uxoris*, Duc de la Mothe Houdancourt, and a grandee of Spain, *b.* 27 Aug. 1797; *m.* 26 March, 1824, Elise Honorée, dau. of the Marquis d'Héricy, and *d.* 17 Nov. 1842, having had issue,
    1. Raoul, *b.* Feb. 1825; *d.* 18 April, 1826.
    1. Leontine, *d. unm.* 31 May, 1849.
    2. Melanie, a nun, *d.* 16 Aug. 1866.
    3. Alix, *m.* 31 May, 1859, the Comte Artus de Cossé Brissac, son of the 10th Duc de Brissac, and *d.* 22 Jan. 1895, leaving issue,
    (1) Marie Augustine Elizabeth, *b.* 22 Feb. 1860; *m.* 3 July, 1889, Baron de Valsuzenay, who *d.* March, 1908.
    (2) Elizabeth Jeanne Thérèse Marie, *b.* 27 July, 1861, now representing the elder branch of the Walsh's de Serrant, *m.* 27 June, 1883, Count Renaud de Moustiers, *jure uxoris*, Duc de la Mothe-Houdancourt, and a grandee of Spain, who *d.* 3 Jan. 1904; 2ndly, 19 Oct. 1907, Valentine John Hussey Walsh, of Mul Hussey, co. Roscommon.
1. Valentine Marie, *b.* 7 March, 1810; *m.* 14 Sept. 1830, Charles, 9th Duc de la Tremoille, and had a son, Louis Charles, 10th Duc de la Tremoille, of the Chateau de Serrant, which he inherited under the will of Count Ludovic Walsh de Serrant, *b.* 26 Oct. 1838; *m.* 2 July, 1862, Margaret, dau. of Count Duchâtel, and *d.* July, 1911, leaving issue.

e. Margaret, *b.* 1855 ; *m.* 1879, George Rockliffe Knight.
3. Nicholas, *b.* 3, bapt. 9 March, 1823 ; *m.* 23 Sept. 1850, Mary, dau. of George Clarke, and *d.* 17 June, 1883, leaving issue,
  a. Richard, *b.* 16 Jan. 1855 ; *m.* 27 Nov. 1893, Orine, dau. of Patrick Hughes, and has issue,
    (a) John, *b.* 23 Dec. 1894.
    (b) William, *b.* 12 June, 1901.
    (c) Patrick Francis, *b.* 27 July, 1909.
    (a) Mary Ann, *b.* 10 Nov. 1895.
    (b) Elizabeth, *b.* 25 Nov. 1897.
  b. John Nicholas, bapt. 4 June, 1866 ; *m.* 28 Feb. 1895, Elizabeth, dau. of Michael Hughes, and has issue.
  a. Anne Mary, bapt. 3 Oct. 1851 ; *d.* 1852.
  b. Anne Mary, bapt. 28 Dec. 1852 ; *d.* 9 Jan. 1900.
  c. Alice, bapt. 20 Feb. 1857, Sister Mary Seraphine, O.S.B. at Chicago, *d.* 27 July, 1889.
  d. Maria Teresa, bapt. 18 June, 1859 ; *d.* 13 Feb. 1831.
  e. Victoria Mary (Sister Mary Nolasco, Order of Mercy, Chicago), bapt. 23 Aug. 1861.
  f. Charlotte, bapt. 30 July, 1864 ; *m.* 1 Aug. 1885, William Walsh.
  g. Jane, bapt. 3 May, 1868, Sister Mary Melchior (Poor Clares, Chicago), *d.* 16 Sept. 1886.
4. Francis Flood, bapt. 13 Feb. 1825 ; *d.* young.
5. Patrick Joseph, of Rochester, U.S.A., *b.* 27 July, bapt. 1 Aug. 1828 ; *m.* Eliza, dau. of Robert Maclean, of Rochester, U.S.A., and *d.* 27 Sept. 1897, leaving issue,
  a. Francis, of Sodus Point, U.S.A., *b.* 11 Feb. 1855 ; *d.* 1 Sept. 1911.
  b. De Forest, *m.* 1 Jan. 1879, Harriet, dau. of Sheffield, of Brighton, Canada.
  c. Walter.   *d.* Richard.
  a. Alicia, *m.* 2 March, 1807, Francis D. Pulver, of Sodus Point, N.Y. State.
  b. Louisa.
6. John, bapt. 30 June, 1830 ; *d.* 1861, during Civil War in U.S.A.
7. Patrick Joseph, of Wisconsin, U.S.A., bapt. 7 Feb. 1837 ; *m.* 19 Nov. 1862, Mary, dau. of Mulligan, and has issue,
  a. Walter, *b.* 1 June, 1869 ; *m.* 4 Jan. 1893, Eva Elmira, dau. of — Fisher, and has issue,
    (a) Marietta, *b.* 25 Oct. 1893.
    (b) Lucila, *b.* 23 Dec. 1895.
    (c) Kathleen, *b.* 17 March, 1898.
    (c) Evelyn, *b.* 7 July, 1901.
  b. William Joseph, *b.* 1 Sept. 1880 ; *m.* 29 June, 1898, Ethel, dau. of — Allen, and has issue,
    (a) Wallace, *b.* 13 Oct. 1904.
    (b) Allen, *b.* 5 Aug. 1907.
    (a) Gladys Luwella, *b.* 2 May, 1899.
    (b) Drusilla, *b.* 11 March, 1901.
    (c) Alice, *b.* 5 Aug. 1907.
  a. Eliza, *b.* 22 Aug. 1863 ; *m.* 16 May, 1883, Herbert N. Northrupp.
  b. Maria, *b.* 19 Nov. 1865 ; *m.* 13 May, 1885, John Wirie.
  c. Drusilla, *b.* 3 Oct. 1867 ; *m.* 1 Aug. 1888, William Rowe, and *d.* 19 Feb. 1891.
  d. Margaret, *b.* 13 July, 1872 ; *m.* 27 June, 1900, Matthias Merlet.
  e. Minnie, *b.* 29 Aug. 1875 ; *m.* 14 Aug. 1904, Ezra F. Priest.
  f. Agnes, *b.* 2 Jan. 1878 ; *m.* 9 Jan. 1907, John L. Murphy.
  g. Celia, *b.* 15 Nov. 1886.
8. Walter R., Government Inspector, Chicago, U.S.A., *b.* 14 July, 1839 ; *m.* 10 July, 1861, Margaret, dau. of — Donoghue, of Lawrence, Mass., U.S.A., and has issue,
  a. William, of Hamilton, Indiana, U.S.A., *b.* 6 Dec. 1870 ; *m.* 24 Jan. 1892, Daisy, dau. of Burton Hudson, and has issue,
    (a) Walter, *b.* 11 Oct. 1895.
    (b) William, *b.* 15 Feb. 1897.
    (c) Bernard, *b.* 9 Dec. 1900.
    (d) Joseph, *b.* 13 April, 1902.
    (e) Francis, *b.* 19 July, 1904.
    (f) George, *b.* 25 May, 1909.
    (a) Helen, *b.* 24 May, 1893.
    (b) Margaret, *b.* 18 Jan. 1907.
  b. Walter James, of Hammond, Indiana, *b.* 23 May, 1880 ; *m.* 21 April, 1903, Minnie, dau. of William Domms, and has issue,
    (a) Margaret, *b.* 29 Aug. 1904.
    (b) Blanche, *b.* 12 Aug. 1906.
  a. Maria Esther, *b.* 24 April, 1862.
  b. Margaret, *b.* 9 May, 1864 ; *m.* 9 Nov. 1887, John M. Fabrig.
  c. Elizabeth, *b.* June, 1866 ; *m.* 1 May, 1893, John Spafford.
  d. Anna, *b.* 1868 ; *d.* 1869.
  e. Honora, *b.* 6 April, 1872 ; *m.* 11 June, 1902, Joseph Farrell.
  f. Julia, *b.* 29 April, 1874 ; *d.* 7 Dec. 1878.
1. Mary, *b.* 21 May, 1816 ; *m.* 1 June, 1837, William Madden of Thumrock.
2. Loetitia, *b.* 13 Sept. 1819 ; *d.* Feb. 1821.
3. Anne, bapt. 18 May, 1832 ; *m.* 1857, John E. Cotter, of Iobir, Illinois, U.S.A.
4. Alice Bidilio, bapt. 7 Feb. 1837.

(2) Patrick Walsh, of Sallymount, *b.* 1788 ; *m.* 17 Feb. 1824, Marcella, dau. of Edmund Dowling, of Ballagh, and *d.* 31 March, 1849, *sp.*, M.I.
(3) Michael, bapt. 20 May, 1791.
(1) Elizabeth, *m.* Dominick Lennon.
(2) Mary, bapt. 28 June, 1789 ; *m.* James Doyle.
(3) Jane, bapt. 20 Dec. 1794 ; *m.* 19 Feb. 1820, Robert Maclean, and *d.* 1838.
(4) Rebecca, bapt. 22 Jan. 1804 ; *m.* 22 Feb. 1826, Michael Caine.
2. James.   3. Richard.
4. Sullivan.   5. George.
1. Anne, *m.* Ignatius Kelly.
1. Ellinor.
2. Ellis, *m.* 10 Nov. 1750, Bryan Naghten, of Killeen, son of Laughlin Naghten, of Firagh, and *d.* 17 Aug. 1753, having had a son.
The elder son,
RICHARD WALSH, of Cranagh, *b.* 1739 ; *m.* Sept. 1759, Mary, dau. of Walter Walsh, of Mount Talbot, by Mary his wife, dau. of John Kelly, of Coolegarry, and by her had
  1. PATRICK, his heir.
  2. William, of Kilmore, *m.* Oct. 1797, Mary Anne, dau. of Michael Cuffe, of Jamaica. She *d.* 12 Feb. 1837. He *d.* 4 Nov. 1839, M.I.
  3. Joseph, *b.* 1764, *d.* 1800.   4. Walter.
Richard Walsh *d.* 19 April, 1790, and was *s.* by his eldest son,
PATRICK WALSH, of Cranagh, *b.* Nov. 1760 ; *m.* 27 Sept. 1787, Margaret, dau. of John Hussey, of Mul Hussey (*see post*). He *d.* 9 Aug. 1798, M.I., leaving issue,
  1. Richard Hussey, *b.* 22 Oct. 1788 ; *d.* Dec. 1804.
  2. JOHN, of whom hereafter.
  3. Patrick Joseph, sometime Capt. Foreign Legion in Grenada, *b.* 3 Nov. 1795 ; *d.* at Rome 22 April, 1849.
  4. William Burke, *b.* 18 Oct. 1796 ; *d.* 17 July, 1816.
  5. Walter Ffrench (Rev.), a Jesuit, *b.* 4 May, 1798 ; *d.* 29 June, 1819.
  1. Lætitia Margaret, *b.* 15 Oct. 1789 ; *d.* 15 July, 1868.
The 2nd son,
JOHN HUSSEY WALSH, of Cranagh and Mul Hussey, and of Kilduff, King's Co., *b.* 11 Feb. 1791 ; *m.* 18 Aug. 1817, Maria, dau. of Michael Henley, of La Mancha, co. Dublin, and *d.* 19 July, 1863, having by her had
  1. William Patrick, *b.* 8 June, 1818 ; *d.* 16 Aug. 1820.
  2. Michael Henry, Barrister-at-Law, *b.* 30 Jan. 1820 ; *d.* 29 Jan. 1843, from a fall out hunting.
  3. John, Barrister-at-Law, *b.* 9 Oct. 1821 ; *d.* 19 July, 1853, from a fall from a horse.
  4. William Charles, of Kilduff, King's Co. and Cranagh, *b.* 2 Sept. 1823 ; *d.* from a fall out hunting, 24 April, 1874.
  5. Richard, Whateley Professor of Political Economy, T.C.D. Superintendent of Government Schools in Mauritius, Barrister-at-Law, *b.* 25 July, 1823 ; *d.* at Port Louis, 30 Jan. 1862.
  6. WALTER, late of Cranagh and Mul Hussey.
  7. Patrick Charles, *b.* 25 May, 1831 ; *d.* in France, 31 May, 1843.
  8. Charles, Maj. late 44th Regt., Assistant Quartermaster-Gen. Rangoon, Burmah, and afterwards Col. in the Egyptian Gendarmerie, *b.* 2 Oct. 1832 ; *d.* 1 Jan. 1893.
  1. Margaret Lætitia, *b.* 25 Nov. 1829 ; *d.* 20 Nov. 1910.
The 6th son,
WALTER HUSSEY WALSH, of Cranagh and Mul Hussey, co. Roscommon, J.P., *b.* 1827 ; *m.* 1860, Ellen, eldest dau. of Valentine O'Brien O'Connor, of Rockfield, co. Dublin, D.L. He *d.* 17 Jan. 1904, having by her (who *d.* 20 Oct. 1911) had issue,
  1. VALENTINE JOHN, now of Mul Hussey.
  2. William, Maj. 4th Batt. Essex Regt., and South African Constabulary, late Capt. Cheshire Regt., *b.* 16 Dec. 1863 ; *m.* 14 Jan. 1892, Mary Frances Angela, only dau. of Rev. Everard Evered, by Isabella his wife, only surviving child and heiress of the late Henry Hawarden Gellibrand Fazakerley, of Fazakerley, and Gellibrand Hall, co. Lancaster, and has issue, Charles William, *b.* 22 Nov. 1892 ; *d.* 25 Aug. 1911. Maude Marie.
  3. Walter Patrick, *b.* 8 March, 1866, Major Leicestershire Regt., late H.B.M. Vice-Consul at Beira, East Africa, *d.* 3 Sept. 1906.
  1. Mary Margaret Elizabeth Vincentia, *b.* 26 Dec. 1874.
  2. Eileen Josephine Mary Bridget, *b.* 6 Feb. 1877 ; *m.* 1 Oct. 1901, Col. Ernest Travlor, A.S.C., son of Rev. Fitzwilliam Taylor, and grandson of Maj.-Gen. T. W. Taylor, C.B., of Ogwell House, Devon, Lieut.-Gov. of the Royal Military College, Sandhurst and has issue.

FAMILY OF HUSSEY.

The Husseys of Mulhussey are a younger branch of the Husseys, Barons of Galtrim (*see* HUSSEY *of Rathkenny*). Matthew Hussey was licensed by HENRY IV to settle the Manor of Mulhussey on Nicholas, his younger son (Patent Roll, 8 HENRY IV). This property seems to have been in the possession of the Baron of Galtrim, *temp.* RICHARD II, when it was held by Edmund Hussey, Baron of Galtrim, under Roger, Earl of March.
NICHOLAS HUSSEY, living 15 May, 1 HENRY VI, *m.* Susanna Plunket, dau. of the Lord of Dunsany. His son,
GERALD HUSSEY, of Mulhussey, *m.* and had a son,
CHRISTOPHER HUSSEY, of Mulhussey, *m.* and had a son,
GERALD HUSSEY, of Moyle Hussey, *m.* and had a son,
WALTER HUSSEY, of Moyle Hussey, *m.* and had issue,
  1. MEYLER, of whom hereafter.
  2. Hubert, of Castle Gregory, co. Kerry, *d.* 3 Feb. 1610. He was ancestor of the HUSSEYS *of Castle Gregory, Dingle, Edenburn, &c.*
  3. Gerald, pardoned 14 Aug. 1578.
The eldest son,

Walsh. THE LANDED GENTRY.

MEYLER HUSSEY, of Moyle Hussey, commissioned to execute martial law in Meath, 21 March, 1553, Commissioner and Keeper of Peace and Sessions 10 Nov. 1555, Commissioner of Array 1559, pardoned 21 July, 1559, *m.* 1st, 20 May, 1544, Alienore, dau. of Robert Barnewall, of Rowston, widow of Patrick Kynton, of Lispopell; and 2ndly, Mary —. He *d.* 7 April, 1582, leaving issue,

1. WALTER, of whom presently. 2. Patrick.
3. Martyn, of Culmullen, *m.* Margaret, dau. of Sergison, of Ballyheslicks, co. Kerry; *d.* 10 May, 1626, leaving issue,
   1. Peter, of Culmullen, *b.* 1596; *m.* Margaret, dau. of Nelson, of Grimston, Yorks, and *d.* 28 Aug. 1666, leaving,
      (1) Edward, *d.* 9 April, 1640.
      (2) Thomas, of Culmullen, *d.* 24 Feb. 1689.
      (3) Meyler of Culmullen, *m.* Marie, dau. of Francis Coghlan, and had issue,
         John, of Courtstown, *m.* 1696, Mary, dau. of Right Hon. Sir Thomas Newcomen, Bart., and widow of Right Hon. Charles Whyte, of Leixlip, and *d.* 10 April, 1734, having had issue,
         a. Meyler, of Derclea, conformed to Church of Ireland, *d.* Nov. 1754. *b.* Thomas.
         a. Mary, *m.* 1717, Edward Edgworth, of Kilshrewly.
2. John, of Glenbegh, co. Kerry.
3. Christopher, *d.* before 1626, leaving by Elizabeth, his wife (who *m.* 2ndly, Thomas Birmingham), a son, Christopher, *b.* 1623.
   1. Margaret, *m.* John Dromgoole, of Walshestown.
   2. Elinor, *m.* Valentine Berford, of Wrightson.
4. Edward.
   1. Katherine, *m.* Robert Dillon, of Clonbrock, who *d.* 1628.
   2. Joan, *m.* Lawrence Delahyde, of Moyglare; *d.* 20 Nov. 1610.

The eldest son,
WALTER HUSSEY, of Moyle Hussey, *b.* 1547; *m.* Ellis Plunket, dau. of 2nd Lord Louth. She *d.* 11 April, 1610. He *d.* 1614, leaving

1. THOMAS, of whom hereafter.
2. John, of Mullahoughterillah, *m.* Giles, dau. of William Birmingham, of Ardkill; *d.* 18 Nov. 1574.
3. Matthew. 4. Meiler. 5. Nicholas.
1. Katherine, *m.* Thomas Lynam, of Adamstown.
2. Rose. 3. Elinor.
4. Elizabeth, *m.* 1609, Nathaniel Fox, of Rathreogh, co. Longford, who *d.* 2 Feb. 1644, M.I.
5. Margaret.

The eldest son,
THOMAS HUSSEY, of Mulhussey, *m.* Anne Plunket, dau. of 9th Lord Killeen, and sister of 1st Earl of Fingall, and widow of William Wogan, of Rathcoffey. She *d.* 31 Dec. 1616. He *d.* 15 Sept. 1629, leaving issue,

1. EDWARD, of whom hereafter. 2. Walter.
1. Eleanor, *m.* John Ayhner, of Ballykenan, who *d.* 27 June, 1620.
2. Mary, *m.* Robert Caddell.
3. Anne, *m.* Francis Makewy, of Ballynestreagh.
4. Margaret, *m.* — Barnewall.

The elder son,
EDWARD HUSSEY, of Mulhussey, co. Meath, *b.* 1607, who submitted to the Peace of 1642, was appointed Recciver-General of the contributions of the co. of Meath, and was restored to his property 1660. He *m.* 1st, Ismay, dau. of Sir John Draycott, of Mornington, and 2ndly, Anne, dau. of Christopher Barnewall, of Turvey, and had issue,

1. THOMAS, of whom hereafter.
2. Walter, of Donore, *m.* Mary, eldest dau. of Matthew Russell, of Drynam, and had issue,
   1. Edward, of Donore, *m.* 1704, Frances, dau. of Robert Arthur, of Hackettstown, *d.* 17 Aug. 1760, leaving issue,
      John, *b.* 1 July, 1705, entered as page of Louis XV 13 March, 1723, Cadet Regt. d'O, in French Service 1 April, 1727; *m.* Mary, dau. of Daniel Dunne, of Brittas, and *d.s.p.*
      Mary, *m.* 21 May, 1737, Thomas Dillon, of the Château of Chevaux in the Orleanais, who assumed the name of Hussey. She *d.* 23 July, 1762, leaving issue,
      1. Edward Patrick Joseph Dillon Hussey.
      2. Count Theobald Dillon, Knight of St. Louis, *b.* 22 July, 1745, Colonel Commanding Dillon Regiment of the Irish Brigade, 10 March, 1788, Maréchal de Camp, 25 Aug. 1790; assassinated by his own soldiers at Lille, 29 April, 1792.
      3. Robert Arthur Dillon Hussey.
      1. Christina.
      2. Mary, *m.* 7 July, 1766, Michael Joseph Langton, of Cadiz.
      3. Frances.
   2. Thomas, of Walterstown, *m.* June, 1716, Anne, dau. of Nicholas Gaynor, of Blackcastle, and had a son, John of Loghboy.
   3. Ignatius, who conformed to the Protestant religion, entered Gray's Inn 3 March, 1704, called to Bar, M.T., 27 Nov. 1719; *m.* 1st, a dau. of William Bursey, of Plummersfarm, Hects, and 2ndly, Elizabeth, dau. of Thomas de Burgh, of Oldtown, M.P., and had issue (*see* DE BURGH *of Drumkeen*).
   4. Peter, of Belgart, *m.* Jane, dau. of Meyler Hussey, of Mulhussey, and *d.* 1748 (will dated 8 Feb. 1748, proved 28 May, 1749), leaving issue,
      (1) Walter, settled at Montignac in Perigord, Capt. in the Berwick Regt. of the Irish Brigade, *b.* 24, bapt. 25 Sept. 1724; *d.* 4 Sept. 1788.
      (2) Miles, of Montignac, Knt. of St. Louis, Capt. Lally's Regt. Irish Brigade, bapt. 29 Nov. 1725; *m.* Margaret Constance,

dau. of Thomas Etienne Dempster, of Abbeville, and *d.* 14 Feb. 1802, leaving issue,
1. Pierre, *b.* 10 May, 1760, Lieut.-Col. Berwick, then 58th Regt., killed at the head of his regt. with the Army of the Rhine, 2 July, 1793.
2. Walter, Maj. Dillon Regt., Irish Brigade, *b.* 6 April, 1760; *m.* 31 Aug. 1795, Helène, dau. of Capt. William Dalton, Irish Brigade, Knt. of St. Louis, and *d.* 4 Sept. 1796, at Fort Augusta, Jamaica, leaving issue,
   Catherine Helen, *b.* July, 1796; *m.* Desiré Lemire, and *d.s.p.* 30 Oct. 1825.
3. William, Capt Berwick Regt., *d.* 23 Aug. 1796, at Fort Augusta, Jamaica.
4. Ignatius, Capt. Dillon Regt., *b.* 12 May, 1769; *d.* 5 Sept. 1796, at Fort Augusta, Jamaica.
   1. Catherine, *m.* 26 July, 1785, Pierre des Veaux, Capt. Gardes du Corps to Louis XVI, Knt. of St. Louis, and *d.* 28 Sept. 1838, leaving issue.
(3) John, Capt. Bulkeley Regt. Irish Brigade, *b.* 24 June, 1729; *d.* 16 June, 1802.
(1) Mary, *m.* FitzGerald, of Yeomanstown.
(2) Catherine, *m.* Williams Wolfe, Lieut. R.N., 9th son of John Wolfe, of Forenghts (*see that family*). Her will, dated 29 Aug. 1806, was proved 22 March, 1810.
(3) Bridget.
4. Michael, living 13 July, 1705.
   1. Clare, *m.* (setts. dated 6 July, 1693) Hugh Geogbegan, of Castletown, Westmeath. 2. Mary.
   3. Elizabeth, *m.* Moore, of Naas.
3. John. 4. Martin.
1. Mary. 2. Elinor, *m.* Robert Caddle.

The eldest son,
THOMAS HUSSEY, of Mul Hussey, *m.* (setts. dated 16 Nov. 1652) Ismay, dau. of Gerald Lynch, of Knock, co. Westmeath, by Ismay, dau. of Christopher Plunket, Lord Killeen. He *d.* 1689 will dated 25 July, 1689), leaving issue,
1. MEYLER, of whom hereafter. 2. Garrett.
1. Clare. 2. Ismay, *d.* before 25 July, 1689.

His elder son,
MAJ. MEYLER HUSSEY, first of Mulhussey, co. Meath, then of Mayne, co. Louth, afterwards of Baltrasney, co. Kildare, Maj. in JAMES II's Army, pardoned 21 July, 1698, *m.* Catherine, dau. of Christopher Dromgoole, of Walshestown. His son,
THOMAS HUSSEY, of Baltrasney, co. Kildare, afterwards of Mul Hussey, co. Roscommon, *m.* 17 Jan. 1723, Jane, dau. of John Moore, of Cranaghmore, co. Roscommon, son and heir of Melchior Moore, of Croyanstown, co. Meath, transplanted to Moynure (now Mulhussey), co. Roscommon, 1656, and *d.* 1761, leaving, with a dau., *m.* James Dillon, of Bellard, and an eldest son, Myles, *d.s.p.* in France, a 2nd son,
JOHN HUSSEY, of Mul Hussey, *b.* 1731; *m.* 20 Nov. 1760, Letitia, dau. of Rickard Burke, and grand-dau. of Sir John Burke, 4th bart., of Glinsk, and *d.* 25 Jan. 1797, having had a dau.,
MARGARET, *m.* 27 Sept. 1787, PATRICK WALSH, of Cranagh.

Arms—Quarterly 1. Arg., a chevron gu. between three broad arrow-heads points upwards, sa. (*for* WALSH). 2. Barry of six erm. and gu. on a canton of the second, a cross or (*for* HUSSEY). 3. Sa., two bars arg (*for* MOORE). 4. Arg., an oak-tree eradicated ppr. in base three lizards passant to the sinister barwise vert (*for* O'CONNOR). **Crests**—1. A swan pierced through the back and breast with a dart all ppr. (WALSH). 2. Upon a mount vert, a hind passant under an oak-tree ppr. *Motto*—Transfixus sed non mortuus.

Seats—Mul Hussey, Athlone, co. Roscommon; Le Fayel, Oise. *Town Residences*—24, Ennismore Gardens, S.W.; 10, Avenue Marceau, Paris. *Clubs*—Athenæum; Cercle del'Union.

WALSH OF FANNINGSTOWN.

The late PETER WALSH, of Fanningstown, co. Kilkenny, J.P. cos. Kilkenny, Mayo, Tipperary, and Waterford, *b.* 20 Feb. 1826; *m.* 13 May, 1884, Mary, dau. of Finlay Chester, J.P. of Williamstown House, co. Louth, by Mary Louisa his wife, dau. of Patrick Mahon Power, of Faithleg, M.P., and D.L. co. Waterford. He *d.* 20 July, 1909.

Lineage.—ROBERT WALSH, of Ballybrushin, and Knockmeilan, is stated to have been son of Philip Walsh, by Eleanor Butler his wife. He *m.* Eleanor, dau. of Gerald Blanchville, of Blanchvillestown, and was father of

PHILIP WALSH, who forfeited his lands. He *m.* a dau. of John Tobin, of Cumsinagh, and *d.* about 1665. His great-grandson,

JOHN WALSH, of Fanningstown, b. 1710 (son of John Walsh, by Margaret Lee, of Dublin, his wife, and grandson of John Walsh, by Katherine Hughes his wife), m. 1st, Katherine Butler, of Knocktopher, by whom he had issue,
1. Peter, of Belline, J.P. co. Kilkenny, m. Eliza, dau. of Matthew Hughes, of Drinagh, co. Wexford.
2. PHILIP, of Fiddown, co. Kilkenny, and Limerick, m. Mary Smith, and had (with four daus., 1. Katherine, m. John Browne, of Dublin; 2, Mary, m. 1st, Christopher Blunden, Capt. R.N., and 2ndly, Robert Smith, Lieut. 26th Regt.; 3. Anne, m. Thomas Philips Vokes, of Limerick; 4. Margaret, m. William Smith, of Derinclare) a son,
PETER, of Waterford and Belline, b. 10 Feb. 1781; m. 1st, Sarah, dau. of John Hughes, of Liverpool, by whom he had issue,
(1) Philip, of Rochestown, m. Maria Smith, and d. 1871.
(2) John Peter, b. 20 July, 1807; m. 1829, Katherine, dau. of John Power, of Carrick-on-Suir; and d. 24 Oct. 1833, leaving,
  1. Peter, of Carrick-on-Suir, d. 1871.
  2. John Peter, m. Alice Cumming, niece of Most Rev. Patrick F. Moran, Roman Catholic Bishop of Ossory, and grand-niece of His Eminence Paul, Cardinal Cullen, and had a dau., Kathleen.
  3. Margaret, m. Medhope Nicholson, of Kilmacoline.
  4. Mary, m. Very Rev. Michael Keatinge, Dean of Kilfenora.
(1) Eliza, b. 4 June, 1805; d. 8 Nov. 1824.
Peter Walsh m. 2ndly, 12 May, 1825, Anne Griffith, and d. 21 Nov. 1859, having had by her further issue,
(3) PETER, late of Fanningstown.
(4) William Thomas b. 12 Nov. 1827; d. 2 July, 1855.
(5) James (Rev.), b. 22 June, 1829, ordained Priest, 10 June, 1859.
(6) Walter, b. 22 June, 1829; d. 28 April, 1858.
(7) Thomas, b. 16 July, 1833; d. 16 April, 1834.
(8) John Peter, b. 15 June, 1835.
(2) Anne Mary, b. 11 June, 1830, professed a Nun in the Presentation Convent, Tralee, 1855; d. 4 March, 1860.
John Walsh m. 2ndly, Katherine Connell, and d. 1793, leaving two other sons,
3. THOMAS, of Fanningstown, b. 1760; m. Barbara, only dau. of Cornelius O'Meagher, of Orchardstown, co. Tipperary, and d. 1827, leaving issue,
  1. JOHN, of Fanningstown, J.P. cos. Kilkenny, Tipperary, and Waterford, b. Feb. 1799; m. Aug. 1836, Elizabeth, dau. of Richard Power, of Ballindesert, J.P. co. Waterford; and d.s.p., when he was s. by his cousin, PETER WALSH, late of Fanningstown.
  2. Peter, b. 1802; d. unm.
  1. Katherine, m. Pierce Francis Garvey, of Brownsford Castle, co. Kilkenny.

Arms—Arg. on a chevron between three pheons gu. an annulet of the field. Crest—A swan pierced through the neck with an arrow all ppr., and charged with an annulet gu. Motto—Dum spiro spero.
Seat—Fanningstown, Piltown.

WALSH OF LARAGH.

LANGTON PRENDERGAST WALSH, C.I.E. 1890, of Laragh, co. Cavan, of the Indian Political Service, Political Agent Sawant Wadi, and Commandant S.W. Loca. Infantry Corps (retired) 1903, J.P. Bombay Presidency, served in Egyptian Campaign 1882, at Tel-el-Kebir and Kassassin (medal with clasp and Khedive's Bronze Star, mentioned in despatches), for many years Asst. Resident, Aden, and from 1884 to 1893 British Agent, Administrator and H.B.M.'s Vice-Consul Berbera, Zeila, Somaliland, N.E. Africa, b. 29 Feb. 1856; m. 1st, 21 March, 1891. Clementina Annie, youngest dau. of the late Major R. G. Macgregor, R.A., of Glengyle, N.B. She d 6 March, 1894, having had issue,
1. Alexa Annie, d. 1893.
He m. 2ndly, 30 April, 1902, Laura, only child of the late John Forbes, K.C., of Forbesfield, Aberdeen, and by her has issue,
1. David Langton Prendergast, b. 23 Nov. 1907.
2. Inez Euphemia Elizabeth.
3. Catherine Laura, b. 6 June, 1905.

Lineage.—THE REV. PHILIP WALSH, M.A., Chaplain to Archbishop Michael Boyle, Primate and Chancellor of Ireland, appointed Vicar of Blessington, Rector of Ballymore Eustace, co. Wicklow, and other parishes, Prebendary of Tipperkevin 1697. He was b. 1655, and m. Catherine, dau. of Rev. John Eastwick, M.A. Camb., Prebendary of Aghold,* by his wife Jane, dau. of Edward Davis, of Moone, co. Kildare. She d. 1769, aged 95. He d. 1740, aged 85 (will dated 13 Dec. 1736, proved 15 July, 1740), and left issue,

---

* The Rev. John Eastwick, son of Alderman Stephen Eastwick, Sheriff of London 1652, by his wife Sarah, dau. of Sampson Sheffield of Seaton, co. Rutland, whose son, Col. Sampson Sheffield in 1647 offered to Parliament his regiment for "The Irish Service."

1. John (Rev.), Rector of Kilcooly, co. Tipperary, and several other parishes, and Prebendary of Fenour, entered Trin. Coll. Dublin 23 Feb. 1714, b. 1698, m. 1st, 1724, Anne, eldest dau. and co-heir of Richard Murphy, of Blessington, and by her had a son, Richard. He m. 2ndly, 1731, Mary, dau. of William Despard, of Donore, Queen's Co. His will, dated 3 April, 1756, was proved 6 Jan. 1757. He left issue, by his second wife,
  1. Philip (Rev.), Rector of Kilcooly, The Park, Kilcooly, co. Tipperary, m. 1758, Barbara, dau. of Gorges Hely, of Foulks. Court, High Sheriff co. Kilkenny (see HELY of Foulks Court).
  2. Samuel, of Kilcooly, will proved 29 July, 1774, unm.
  3. William, unm.
  1. Mary, m. 15 March, 1766, Edmund Butler, of Newtown, co. Kilkenny.
2. Philip, entered Trin. Coll. Dublin 25 May, 1716, King's Inns. Michaelmas, 1724, Bencher King's Inn, and K.C. 1742, b. 1699, m. 1st, 1730, Elizabeth Cox widow, and 2ndly, 10 March, 1739, Mary, dau. of William Roe, of Roesgreen, co. Tipperary, by his wife Jane, dau. of Samuel Green, of Greystown, and Burn Church, co. Tipperary. Her will, dated 10 April, 1758, was proved 20 Dec. 1763. He d. 30 Aug. 1745 (will dated 29 April, 1745, proved 11 Oct. 1745), and left issue,
  (1) Philip, Maj. 12th Lt. Dragoons, d.s.p. unm.
  (2) William, d.s.p., will dated 25 Oct. 1783, proved 16 Feb. 1785, unm.
  (1) Jane, m. by licence 29 Oct. 1762, Capt. Robert Bunbury, 12th Light Dragoons, co. Carlow.
3. Jeremiah (Rev.), of Stedalt, co. Meath, Rector of Killiah, entered Trin. Coll. Dublin 11 May, 1719, B.A. 1724, M.A. 1727, b. 1702, m. 1st, by licence, 30 Jan. 1730, Dorcas, dau. of — Lloyd; 2ndly, by licence, 31 Aug. 1778, Ann, dau. of Col. Cook and widow of Thomas Eyre, M.P., who d.s.p. (see EYRE of Eyre Court). His will, dated 10 June, 1774, was proved 23 March, 1789. By his 1st wife he had issue,
  1. Andrew, of Stedalt, m. 1768, Jane, dau. of James Cane, of Ratoath, co. Meath, and from him descends Mathilde Sophie dau. of Henry T. Blount, of Nantes (see BLOUNT of Orleton, co. Hereford) by his wife Sophia, dau. of James Walsh, J.P., of Stedalt, co. Meath, who m. 1868, Robert T. Tunstall-Moore, J.P. for co. Meath. He d. 6 Dec. 1904, leaving issue. Mrs. Tunstall-Moore's maternal uncle, William Henry Walsh, J.P. and Lord of the Manor of Stedalt, d. 1885. Sophie H. Blount (sister of above Mathilde Sophie) m. 1874, the Vicomte de Kersabiec, and dying in 1897 left issue.
  1. Elizabeth, unm.
  2. Catherine, m. by licence 23 April, 1768, Henry Brownrigg, of Wingfield (see BROWNRIGG, Bart.). 3. Anne, unm.
4. WILLIAM, of whom presently.
1. Elizabeth, m. 1st, 1715, Isaac Finemore, of Ballyward, co. Wicklow; and 2ndly, 1727, Rev. Valentine Goddard.
2. Anne Rebecca, m. 1745, Dudley Ryves, Trin. Coll. Dublin 1736, B.A. 1738, M.A. 1741, LL.D. 1746, of Rathsallagh, co. Wicklow.
3. Frances, m. 1728, Rev. S. Ussher, Rector of Dunganstown, of Eastwell, co. Galway (see USSHER of Eastwell).
4. Jane, m. 1732, William Despard, of Donore, Queen's Co.
5. Catherine, m. 1739, Nathaniel Smith.

The 4th son,
THE REV. WILLIAM WALSH, Vicar of Blessington, Rector of Ardnurcher, Meath, and of Kill and Lyons, co. Kildare, b. 1710, entered Trin. Coll. Dublin 17 April, 1723, B.A. 1728, M.A. 1731, m. 1st, by licence, 8 March, 1736, Mary, dau. of Capt. Robert Stewart, of Coleraine, and sister of Rev. Richard Stewart, D.D., Dean of Leighlin, d. 1781, and by her had a dau.,
1. Rebecca, m. 1779, Capt. Thomas Ussher, 16th Regt. of Foot, of Eastwell, co. Galway (see USSHER of Eastwell).
He m. 2ndly, 1747, Elizabeth, dau. of J. Ravell, and d. 1781, having by her had issue,
1. JOHN RAVELL, of whom we treat.
2. William, of Blessington, Capt. Royal Marines, and Major Wicklow Mil.; m. 1791, Jane, dau. of Rev. Hill Benson, by his wife ——, dau. of — Griffen; d. 1827, and had issue,
  1. William, of Willfield, Blessington, Lieut. 7th Royal Fusiliers, b. 1798; m. 1826, Augusta Junietta, dau. of Major J. W. G. Thwaites by his wife Hannah, dau. of William Everard, of Sunbury; d. 1839, and had issue,
    William, D.D. Oxford (Residence: The Precincts, Canterbury) b. 1836, Bishop of Dover, Canon and Archdeacon of Canterbury (see BURKE's Peerage); m. 1865, Catharine Banchory, dau. of Gen. W. H. Pickering, R.A., by his wife, Agnes, dau. of T. Norris, Governor of Cape Coast Castle, and has issue,
      1. William Trevor Hayne, b. 26 June, 1866, M.A. Oxon (Club: Athenæum); m. 1907, Eva Catherine, dau. of C. N. Wareing.
      2. Leslie Herbert, M.D. (Pulteney Street, Bath), b. 4 Aug. 1867.
  2. Hill, R.M., b. 1802; d. unm.
  3. Arthur Sandys Stawell, C.B., of Blessington, Major-Gen. Royal Marines, served in China War, Commanded a Battalion of Marines at taking of Canton (medal with clasp) 1857, b. 1807; m. 1836, Emma Henrietta, dau. of Col. Edmund Hooper, 3rd Buffs; d. 1880, and had issue,
    (1) Arthur Huntly Hill Major-Gen. Royal Marines, at Blockade of Cronstadt 1855, Baltic medal 1854-5, b. 1837; m. 1877, Georgina, dau. of Henry Cole, of Brent, S. Devon; d. 1898, and had issue,
      1. Huntly, Lieut. R.N., b. 1880.
      2. Philip, Lieut. R.N., b. 1882.
      1. Ellis Emma, m. 1902, Rev. J. Annesley Prendergast, Vicar of Sidbury, Devon, and has issue,

2. Katherine. 3. Margery.
4. Georgina.
(2) John Frederick Benson (Rev.), late Vicar of St. Anne's, Bermondsey, S.E., b. 1844; m. 1877, Alice, dau. of Rev. A. W. Snape, Vicar of Bury St. Edmund's, and has issue,
1. Frederick Huntly Benson, b. 1882.
1. Alice Mary Audrey.
2. Stella Constance.
(3) Henry William Duffield (*Marlborough Road, Exeter*), b. 1854, Fleet Surgeon R.N., served in H.M.S. *Cygnet* 1882, Egypt, Bombardment of Alexandria (medal with clasp, Khedive's Bronze Star).
1. Georgiana. 2. Fanny.
3. Emily Martha. 4. Euphemia.
5. Jane.
3. Ponsonby, d. unm.
2. Martha, d. unm. 3. Jane, d. unm.
The eldest son,
THE REV. JOHN RAVELL WALSH, of Blessington, B.A. Trin. Coll. Dublin, 1776, M.A. 1782, Rector of Tubber and Giltown, and other parishes, b. 10 Jan. 1754; m. 31 May, 1792, Euphemia, dau. of Thomas Prendergast, by his wife Jane, dau. of Samuel Gordon (*see* BURKE's *Peerage*, GORT, V.), Registrar of the Court of Chancery, Ireland, and d. 5 Feb. 1856) had issue, twelve children, of whom the following survived,
1. William Spencer (Rev.), of Knockboyne, co. Meath, D.D. Trin. Coll. Dublin, Rector of Clonard, and Vicar of Balsoon and Assey, co. Meath, b. 1797, m. 1st, Elizabeth, dau. of Rev. James Slator, of Tonyn and Moniscallaghan, co. Longford, by his wife Henrietta Dorothea, dau. of the Rev. Lewis Thomas, Rector of Naas, St. David's Castle, Naas, co. Kildare, and of Brookhill, co. Kilkenny.
1. A dau. d. young.
2. Euphemia Frances Elizabeth, m. 8 Jan. 1853, her cousin, Col. Thomas Prendergast Boles Walsh, of Laragh (*see below*). He m. 2ndly, Anne, dau. of Col. Robert Lucas, of Raconnel, co. Monaghan (*see* LUCAS-SCUDAMORE *of Castle Shane*), and d. 1880, having by her (who d. 21 Oct. 1903) had issue,
3. Olivia Lucas. 4. Annie Jane.
2. JOHN PRENDERGAST, of whom presently.
3. Jeffrey, Lieut. Royal Marines, d. unm.
4. Thomas Prendergast, Lieut.-Col. Madras Army, one of the hostages Afghan War 1842, b. 1804; m. 1855, Alice (who d. 185-), dau. of N. Preston, of Swainston, co. Meath. He d. 1861, leaving issue (*see* PRESTON *of Swainston*),
Thomas Preston, Lieut. 38th Regt., b. 1856, m. (Louisa), Charlotte, dau. of John Metge, of Sion, co. Meath (*see* METGE *of Athlumney*). She d. 1897. He d.s.p. 1903.
Alice Euphemia.
1. Jane, m. 1836, Capt. Joseph Tyndall, of the Bombay Army, and d. 1867, leaving issue.
2. Sarah, d. unm. 1897.
The 2nd son,
THE REV. JOHN PRENDERGAST WALSH, M.A., of Blessington, co. Wicklow, an officer of the Rifle Brigade (old 95th Regt.), served at Waterloo (medal), lost a leg. After twenty years' service he took Holy Orders. He was patron of Kittisford, Somerset; b. 31 May, 1798; m. 10 Feb. 1825, Isabella Christiana Francis, dau. Major James Langton, D.L., of Bruree, co. Limerick, High Sheriff 1786, by his 1st wife ——, dau. of —— Marshall, of co. Wicklow, and by her (b. 9 Dec. 1800, d. at Ealing, 10 July, 1886) had issue,
1. Charles Greenwood, Lieut. 75th Regt., b. 27 March, 1826; d. 1856, unm.
2. John Langton, b. 5 Oct. 1827, } d. in infancy.
3. James Langton, b. 19 Nov. 1828, }
4. Spencer George, Capt. North Cork Rifles, b. 19 Jan. 1830; d. 1805 unm.
5. THOMAS PRENDERGAST BOLES, late representative.
6. John Prendergast, Lieut. 4th West York Militia, b. 16 Sept. 1836; supposed to have d. in New Zealand in 1879.
7. Walter Philip, J.P., Capt. H.M. Indian Forces (retired), and formerly Duke of Cornwall's L.I., Governor of Gaols, Bombay, b. 3 May, 1838; d. unm. 6 June, 1911.
8. Langton, b. 13 June, 1840; d. 1842.
1. Mary Boles, b. 20 April, 1833; d. 1851.
2. Euphemia Isabella, m. 1872, Capt. E. H. T. Tyndall, Bombay Army, who d. 1875, leaving only one son, who d. 1900 unm.
The Rev. John Prendergast Walsh d. 15 Dec. 1867. His 5th son, THOMAS PRENDERGAST BOLES WALSH, of Laragh, co. Cavan Col. Bombay Army, J.P. for Bombay Presidency, b. 20 April, 1831; m. 1st, 8 Jan. 1853, his cousin, Euphemia Frances Elizabeth, dau. of the late Rev. Spencer William Walsh, D.D. (*see above*), and by her (who d. March, 1862) had issue,
1. Spencer John George, b. 24 May, 1854; d. 20 Aug. 1855.
2. LANGTON PRENDERGAST, present representative.
3. George Inverarity, b. 7 Oct. 1857; d. 23 May, 1859.
1. Euphemia Anna Houlton (75, *Longridge Road, Earl's Court, London, S.W.*).
2. Elizabeth Ellen Gordon (75, *Longridge Road, Earl's Court, London, S.W.*).
Col. Walsh m. 2ndly, 8 Nov. 1863, Isabel, dau. of the late Francis Nicholas, D.C.L., Wadham Coll. Oxford, and of the Mansion, Ealing, and by her had issue,
4. George Inverarity, Major 1st Batt. Leicestershire Regt., retired 1908, employed Special Service Staff of Sir Richard Martin, operations Rhodesia 1897 (medal and despatches), served as D.A.A.G. VIII Div. S.A.F.F. Staff of Lieut.-Gen. Sir Leslie Rundle (medal, four clasps and despatches), Coronation medals 1902, 1911, b. 13 Dec. 1866; m. 24 April, 1902, Ethel Parker, younger dau. of M. Dobson, of Kensington Gore, W (*Residence*: *Newnham Manor, Newnham Murren, Oxon.* *Clubs*: *Naval and Military, and Carlton, S.W.*), and has issue,
1. Philip Warrington, b. 11 Jan. 1903.
2. George Charles Nepean, b. 9 Dec. 1910.
1. Elizabeth Isabel, b. 28 June, 1905.
5. Francis Nicholas de Walno, b. 29 March, 1868; d. unm. 16 July, 1899.
6. Mainwaring Ravell, Capt. Worcestershire Regt. (*Club*: *Naval and Military*), b. 29 May, 1876, served as Lieut. Royal Berkshire Regt., S. African War, (1899-1902, specially promoted Capt. Worcestershire Regt. 18 Dec. 1901 (Queen's medal and three clasps, King's medal and two clasps); m. 24 Aug. 1908, Bertha Violette, 2nd dau. of the late George W. Wilson-Slator, of White Hill, co. Longford, and Belle Ville, co. Meath, J.P., D.L., and High Sheriff 1877, co. Longford (*see* WILSON-SLATOR *of White Hill*), and has issue,
Isabel Slator.
3. Isabel, d. 3 Jan. 1866.
Col. T. P. B. Walsh d. 1 Aug. 1893.

Arms (confirmed to the descendants of the Rev. John Ravell Walsh)—Az., a lion rampant arg. debruised by a fesse per pale of the second and gu., charged with three crosses humettée counter-changed. *Crest*—Out of a ducal crest coronet or, charged with a cross humettée az., a demi-lion rampant of the last. *Motto*—Noli irritare leonem.
Seat—Laragh, co. Cavan. *Residence*—16, Grange Park, Ealing. *Clubs*—Carlton and Conservative, S.W.

JOHNSON-WALSH.

See BURKE's PEERAGE, **JOHNSON-WALSH, Bart.**

WANDESFORDE OF CASTLECOMER AND KIRKLINGTON.

RICHARD HENRY PRIOR - WANDESFORDE, of Castlecomer, co. Kilkenny, and Kirklington, Hipswell, and Hudswell, co. York, J.P. and D.L., High Sheriff co. Kilkenny 1894, B.A., b. 15 Sept. 1870; s. his grandmother 1892, and obtained a Royal Licence 16 May, 1894, to continue to bear the name and arms of Wandesforde in addition to those of Prior; m. 17 March, 1896, Florence Jackson von Schwartz, dau. of the late Rev. Ferdinand Pryor, M.A., Rector of Dartmouth, Halifax, Nova Scotia, and has issue,

1. CHRISTOPHER BUTLER, b. 15 Dec. 1896.
2. Ferdinand Charles Richard, b. 23 Oct. 1897.
3. Richard Cambridge, b. 14 Jan. 1902.
1. Vera.
2. Florence Doreen.

Lineage.—JOHN DE WANDESFORDE, of Westwick, near Ripon, m. 1368, Elizabeth, 2nd dau. and heir of Sir Henry de Musters, Knt. of Kirklington, co. York, and widow of Alexander Mowbray, and d. 1396. He was direct ancestor of
THOMAS WANDESFORDE, of Kirklington, in 1503, who m. Margaret, dau. of Henry Pudsey, and d. 1518, having had four sons and two daus.,
1. CHRISTOPHER, his heir.
2. William, of Woodel, co. Bedford.
3. Michael, of Pickhill, whose son, Sir Rowland Wandesforde, Knt., of Pickhill, co. York, was Attorney at the Court of Wards and Liveries in 1637. His dau., Elizabeth, m. Philip, 4th Lord Wharton, and their only dau., ELIZABETH WHARTON, m. Robert Bertie, 3rd Earl of Lindsey.
4. John (Rev.), Rector of Kirklington.
1. Ellen, m. Ambrose Lancaster, of Westmorland.
2. Elizabeth, m. Robert Claxton, of co. Durham.
The eldest son,
CHRISTOPHER WANDESFORDE, of Kirklington, m. Anne, dau. of John Norton, of Norton Conyers, and d. 1540, having had issue,
1. FRANCIS, his heir.
2. Christopher, who married twice, and d.s.p.m.s.
The elder son,
FRANCIS WANDESFORDE, of Kirklington, m. Anne, elder dau. and co-heir of John Fulthorpe, of Hipswell, and had by her, who m. 2ndly, Christopher Nevill, younger son of Ralph, Earl of Westmorland,

IRELAND. Wandesforde.

1. Christopher (Sir). **2.** John, d.s.p.
1. Jane, d. young.
He d. 1559, and was s. by his elder son,
Sir Christopher Wandesforde, Knt., of Kirklington, who was knighted 1586, and served as Sheriff co. York 1578. He m. Elizabeth, dau. of Sir George Bowes, of Streatlam, and dying 11 July, 1590, was s. by his elder son,
Sir George Wandesforde, Knt., of Kirklington, b. 20 May, 1572, and knighted by King James I, 1607. He m. 1st, Catharine, dau. and co-heir of Ralph Hansby, of Beverley, and had issue,
1. Christopher, his successor. **2.** John.
3. Michael (Very Rev.), successively Dean of Limerick and Derry, b. 1597; d. 1637.
1. Anne, m. 4 March, 1621-2, Mauger Norton, of St. Nicholas, near Richmond, co. York.
Sir George m. 2ndly, Mary, dau. of Robert Pamplin, and by her had a dau., Margaret, wife of James Blanchard, and one son, William, Citizen of London, to whom and his heirs his eldest brother, 30 June, 1637, gave £20 per annum, issuing out of the Manor of Castlecomer, and payable upon Strongbow's tomb in Christ Church, Dublin. He d. 1690, aged 85.
Sir George d. 4 Sept. 1612, and was s. by his eldest son,
Christopher Wandesforde, of Kirklington, b. 1592, being upon close habits of intimacy and friendship with Sir Thomas Wentworth, Earl of Strafford, accompanied that eminent and ill-fated nobleman into Ireland when he was constituted Chief Governor of that kingdom, was sworn of the Privy Council, and was appointed in 1623 Master of the Rolls; of this office, he had soon after a grant by patent for life. He was one of the Lords Justice in 1636 and 1639, and was appointed 1 April, 1640, Lord Deputy; but the fate of his friend Lord Strafford had so deep an effect upon him that he d. 3 Dec. in that year. He m. 1614, Alice, dau. of Sir Hewet Osborne, of Kiveton, Yorks, and by her (who d. 10 Oct. 1659) had issue,
1. George, his heir.
2. Christopher, successor to his brother.
3. John, d. unm. 2 Dec. 1655.
1. Catherine, m. 1620, Sir Thomas Danby, Knt. of Farnley, near Leeds, and d. in childbed of her fifteenth child, 1645, aged 30.
2. Alice, b. 13 Feb. 1626; m. William Thornton, of East Newton, co. York.
He was s. by his eldest son,
George Wandesforde, of Kirklington, b. 14 Sept. 1623; d.s.p. 31 March, 1651, and was s. by his brother,
Sir Christopher Wandesforde, of Kirklington, co. York, b. 2 Feb. 1627-8, created a baronet 5 Aug. 1662; m. 30 Sept. 1651, Eleanor, dau. of Sir John Lowther, 1st bart., of Lowther Hall, co. Westmorland, and had issue,
1. Christopher, his heir.
2. George, who m. Elizabeth, widow of Garrett Foulkes.
3. Charles (Rev.), d s p 1695.
1. Mary, d. unm. 1726.
2. Eleanor, m. Amias Bushe, of Kilfane, co. Kilkenny.
3. Catherine, m. Sir Richard Pyne, Chief Justice of the King's Bench, and d. 1731, aged 64.
4. Elizabeth, m. 1691, Edmund Swettenham, of Somerford, Cheshire.
5. Alice, m. Henry Bosville.
6. Frances, m. Robert Maude, of Ripon, co. York, and Kilkenny; d. 5 Jan. 1690.
7. Christiana, m. Richard Lowther, of Leeds, 2nd son of Sir William Lowther, Knt., of Swillington.
Sir Christopher, who was M.P. for Ripon, d. 23 Feb. 1686, and was s. by his eldest son,
Sir Christopher Wandesforde, 1st Viscount Castlecomer, was sworn of the Privy Council William III, and again in 1702, by Queen Anne, who advanced him to the peerage of Ireland 1706, as Baron Wandesforde and Viscount Castlecomer. He m. 20 April 1683 Elizabeth, dau. of George Montagu, of Horton, co. Northampton, and by her (who d. 13 Nov. 1731) had issue,
1. Christopher, 2nd Viscount.
2. George, 4th Viscount.
3. John (Rev.), Rector of Kirklington and Catterick, d.s.p. March, 1747-8.
4. Richard, d. unm. 1719.
1. Henrietta, m. William Maynard, of Curryglass, co Cork, M.P., and d. 19 April, 1736.
His Lordship d. in London, 13 Sept. 1707, and was s. by his eldest son,
Sir Christopher Wandesforde, 2nd Viscount Castlecomer, Member in the Parliament of Great Britain in 1710 for Morpeth, and in 1714 for Ripon. In the latter year he was sworn of the Privy Council to George I, and next year appointed Governor of the co. Kilkenny. In 1717 he was constituted Secretary-at-War, and d. 23 June, 1719, having m. 1715, Hon. Frances Pelham, dau. of Thomas, 1st Lord Pelham, and sister to Thomas, Duke of Newcastle. By her he had an only child,
Sir Christopher Wandesforde, 3rd Viscount Castlecomer, b. 1717, who d. in London of the small-pox, unm., 8 May, 1736, and was s. by his uncle,
Sir George Wandesforde, 4th Viscount Castlecomer, who m. Susannah, dau. of Ven. John Griffith, Archdeacon of Killaloe, and by her (who d. 10 Sept. 1757) he had several children, of whom but three survived,
1. John, 5th Viscount.
1. Susannah, m. Thomas Newenham, of Coolmore, co. Cork.
2. Elizabeth, d. unm. 9 Oct. 1806, aged 80.
His Lordship d. 25 June, 1751, and was s. by his son,
Sir John Wandesforde, 5th Viscount Castlecomer, who took his seat in the Irish House of Lords in 1751, and was created in 1758 Earl of Wandesforde, co. Kilkenny. He m. 11 Aug. 1750, Agnes Elizabeth, dau. and heir of John Southwell, of Enniscouch, co. Limerick, and had issue,
John, Viscount Castlecomer, b. 23 April, 1753; d. young v.p.
Anne, m. 13 Feb. 1769, John Butler, of Garryricken, to whom the Earldom of Ormonde was restored by the House of Lords in 1791. There were four sons and two daus. issue of this marriage; the 3rd son, James, became by the death of his eldest brother 19th Earl of Ormonde; and the 4th son succeeding to the estates of Wandesforde, assumed the surname and arms of Wandesforde, and was the late Hon. Charles H. Butler-Clarke-Southwell-Wandesforde, of Castlecomer and Kirklington.
His Lordship d. 12 Jan. 1784, and his son having predeceased him, all his honours, including the baronetcy, became extinct, and his estates devolved on his only dau.,
Lady Anne Wandesforde, who m. 25 Feb. 1769, John Butler, of Garryricken, who was restored, as 17th Earl of Ormonde and Ossery, 1791 (see Burke's Peerage). Her 4th, but 2nd surviving son,
Hon. Charles Harward Butler-Clarke-Southwell-Wandesforde, of Castlecomer and Kirklington, b. 1780, inherited his mother's estates, and assumed, by Royal Licence 1820, the additional surname of Clarke after Butler, and by another Royal Licence, June, 1830, the additional surnames of Southwell-Wandesforde after Butler-Clarke. He m. 1812, Lady Sarah Butler, dau. of Henry Thomas, 2nd Earl of Carrick, by whom (who d. 7 July, 1838) he had issue,
1. John, b. 2 Sept. 1813; m. 16 Nov. 1841, Emily Selina Frances, dau. of John McClintock, of Drumcar, co. Louth, sister of John, Lord Rathdonnell, and d.s.p.v.p. 26 June, 1856. She d. 29 Jan. 1909.
2. Henry Butler-Clarke-Southwell-Wandesforde, of Ulcombe, b. 3 Oct. 1815; d. unm.
3. Walter, b. 1 Aug. 1825; d.v.p. 15 June, 1853, leaving Charles, of Kirklington and Castlecomer.
1. Sarah, of Castlecomer, and Kirklington (see below).
Hon. Charles H. B. C. S. Wandesforde d. 7 Nov. 1860. His grandson,
Charles Butler-Clarke-Southwell-Wandesforde, of Castlecomer and Kirklington, High Sheriff co. Kilkenny 1879, d. unm. July, 1881, and was s. by his aunt,
Sarah Prior Wandesforde, of Castlecomer, and of Kirklington, Hipswell, and Hudswell, co. York, b. 23 July, 1814; m. 13 Sept. 1836, Rev. John Prior, of Mount Dillon, co. Dublin, Rector of Kirklington, Yorks, son of the Rev. Thomas Prior, D.D., Vice-Provost of Trinity College, Dublin, and Anna Maria his wife, dau. of H. Wray, of Wraymount, co. Dublin, and by him (who d. 21 Dec. 1867) had issue,
1. Charles Butler, of Crossogue House, co. Tipperary, J.P. and D.L., b. 31 Aug. 1840; m. 28 Feb. 1866, Dora, dau. of Richard Phillips, of Gaile, co. Tipperary, J.P. and D.L. (see that family), and d. 7 Jan. 1875, leaving issue,
  1. Richard Henry, now of Castlecomer and Kirklington,
  2. Charles Butler Prior, b. 9 June, 1872; m. and has issue,
    (1) Charles.
    (2) Francis.
    (3) Robert Richard John Henry.
    (1) Dora.
  3. Harold Astley Somerset Prior, b. 25 July, 1874; m. and has issue,
    Charles, b. 1 March, 1902.
    Dorothy.
  1. Mary Caroline Wandesforde. 2. Sarah Emily Edith.
2. Henry Wallis, B.A., J.P. Glos. and Worcestershire, late Lieut. 81st Regt., of Kirklington Hall, Bedale, Yorkshire, and Oakhurst, Leamington, b. 13 March, 1844; m. 4 June, 1878, Mary Anne, 3rd dau. of late Richard Phillips, J.P., of Mount River, Newport, co. Tipperary, and widow of R. H. Collis, of Millbrook, co. Tipperary, and has had issue,
  1. John Wandesford Wallis, b. 20 May, 1882; d. 1897.
  1. Sarah Maude Butler.
  2. Gertrude Anne Ormonde.
1. Sarah Butler, d. unm.
2. Sophia Elizabeth, m. 8 July, 1864, Major-Gen. Henry Frederick Winchilse Ely, of Copse Dale, Cloughjordan, co. Tipperary, and has issue.
Mrs. Prior-Wandesforde s. to the Castlecomer and Kirklington estates on the death of her nephew, 1 July, 1881, and in accordance with the provisions contained in her father's will, assumed by Royal licence, dated 30 Aug. 1882, for herself and her issue the additional surname and arms of Wandesforde. She d. 21 Dec. 1892, and was s. by her grandson, Richard Henry Prior-Wandesforde.

Arms—Quarterly: 1st and 4th, or, a lion rampant double queued az. armed and langued gu., for Wandesforde; 2nd and 3rd, vert., on a bend erm. three chevronels gu., for Prior. Crests—1st, Wandesforde: A church ppr. spire az.; 2nd, Prior: An estoile vert. Mottoes—Wandesforde: Tout pour l'Eglise; Prior: Quis audeat luci aegredi.

Seats—Castlecomer House, co. Kilkenny; The Hall, Kirklington, co. York. Clubs—Royal Automobile Club, London; Kildare Street, Dublin.

WARBURTON OF GARRYHINCH.

RICHARD WARBURTON, of Garryhinch, King's Co., D.L. and J.P. King's and Queen's Cos., High Sheriff Queen's Co. 1869 and King's Co. 1872, b. 1846; m. 18 July, 1867, Georgina Wilhelmina Henrietta, dau. of William Henry Hutchinson, of Rockforest, co. Tipperary, and by her (who d. 1891) has issue,

1. RICHARD HUTCHINSON DUTTON JOHN, b. 1877; d. 1894.
    1. Jessie Georgina Hutchinson, m. 1st, 3 Jan. 1894, H. Goldsmith Whitton, and has issue,
       Doreen Goldsmith, b. Nov. 1895.
       Desmond Cedric, b. Nov. 1897.
       She m. 2ndly, 10 Sept. 1901, Percy Walton Heanly (Clodagh, Palewell Park, East Sheen), second son of Frank E. J. Heanly, late of Hambrook House, Hants, and Ceylon, and has further issue,
       Ivan Bryan Warburton, b. July, 1902.
       Beryl Yolanda Warburton.
    2. Mary Anne, d. 1871.

Mr. Warburton m. 2ndly, 1892, Bridget Mary, dau. of John McNamara, and by her has issue,

2. Richard Henry Haskell, b. 29 May, 1910.
3. Olga Victoria.
4. Vera Irene.
5. Violet Lycinda.

Lineage.—RICHARD WARBURTON, of Dublin, living there in 1622, left three sons and a dau.,
1. RICHARD, his heir.
2. George, of Aughrim, co. Galway, d. 14 Nov. 1709, M.P. for Gowran, 1692-95, Portarlington 1695-99, Postmaster-General, m. and left issue,
3. John, d. 1703, one of the six clerks in Chancery 1669-1700, M.P. for Belturbet 1692-93 and 1695-99, m. July, 1672, Mary, dau. of Matthew French, of Belturbet, and left issue,
   1. Susanna, m. 1st, Capt. Thomas Aske, of Thurles; 2ndly, Daniel Gahan, of Coolquil, co. Tipperary.

The eldest son,
RICHARD WARBURTON, b. 1636, was a junior Clerk of the Council, Ireland, 1654, and afterwards Clerk-Assistant to the Irish House of Commons. He is styled of "Garryhinch," 1662, and was M.P. for Ballyshannon from 1697-99, and 1703-13, High Sheriff King's Co. 1701. He m. April, 1656, Judith, dau. of William Sandes, of Dublin (see SANDES of Sallow Glen), and d. Feb. 1717, having had (with five daus., of whom the eldest, Susannah, m. Henry Warren, of Grangebeg, co. Kildare; the 2nd, Elizabeth, m. Frederick Trench of Garbally, ancestor of the Earl of Clancarty; the 3rd, Anne, m. Very Rev. John Trench, Dean of Raphoe), a son,
RICHARD.

The only son,
RICHARD WARBURTON, of Garryhinch, b. 1664, M.P. for Portarlington from 1692 so 1715, m. (licence 9 Jan.) 1695, Elizabeth, dau. of John Pigott, and had issue,
1. RICHARD, of Garryhinch, b. 6 Dec. 1696, M.P. for Queen's Co. 1729-61; he d. unm. 1771, having devised Garryhinch and other estates to his 4th brother, Peter.
2. John, d. unm.
3. George, of whom presently.
4. PETER, devisee of his brother Richard, d. 29 Sept. 1784.
5. William, m. Barbara, dau. of Lytton Lytton, of Knebworth, Herts, and had a son, RICHARD WARBURTON-LYTTON, m. Elizabeth, dau. of Paul Jodrell, of Lewknor, and left an only dau. and heiress, ELIZABETH BARBARA, heiress of Knebworth, m. 1798, WILLIAM, EARL BULWER, of Wood Dalling and Heydon, Norfolk, Brigadier-Gen. (see BULWER).
   1. Gertrude, m. June, 1719, William Carden, of Lismore, Queen's Co.
2. Judith, m. June, 1727, Emanuel Pigott.
3. Jane, m. George Pigott, of Knapton.
Richard Warburton d.v.p., Jan. 1715. His 3rd son,
GEORGE WARBURTON, of Dublin, m. Jane, dau. of Richard le Hunte, of Artramont, co. Wexford, and was father of
JOHN WARBURTON, of Garryhinch, M.P. for Queen's Co. 1779 to 1794. High Sheriff King's Co. 1786. This gentleman was heir to his uncle Peter. He served in early life as a military officer, and was at the taking of Quebec, under Gen. Wolfe. He m. Martha, dau. of Bowes Benson, and had issue,
1. RICHARD, his heir.
2. Peter, Major H.M.S., m. Elizabeth, dau. of Edmund Malone, and d. 1827, leaving issue,
   1. John. 2. Peter, d. 1838.
   1. Anne. 2. Martha.
   3. Elizabeth.
1. Martha, m. William Augustus Le Hunte, of Artramont.
Col. Warburton d. 1806, and was s. by his son,
RICHARD WARBURTON, of Garryhinch, b. 1778, J.P. and D.L., High Sheriff Queen's Co. 1801, m. 1800, Anne, dau. of Thomas Kemmis, of Dublin, and had issue,
1. John, of Garryhinch, High Sheriff Queen's Co. 1829, d.s.p. 1839.
2. RICHARD, his successor.
3. George, b. 1805; m. a dau. of John Toole.
4. William (Very Rev.), D.D., Dean of Elphin 1848-94, b. 22 Oct. 1806; m. 1st, 18 May, 1835, Emma Margaret, youngest dau. of Major-Gen. Richard Stovin, by Frances Acland his wife, sister of Sir John Palmer Acland, Bart., of Fairfield, and by her had issue,
   1. Richard Stovin, J.P. for Roscommon, b. 28 Feb. 1836; m. 17 Sept. 1874, Rosa, only dau. of Sir William Leeson, by his 2nd marriage. She d. 24 Feb. 1910, leaving issue a son, Stovin.
   2. Joseph William, in the Foreign Office, b. 2 April, 1837; m. 30 July, 1862, Lady Frances Isabella Anne King, only dau. of Robert, 6th Earl of Kingston. She d. 8 Oct. 1890. He d. 1891, leaving issue,
      (1) William Francis Henry, b. 1879.
      (1) Florence Beatrice, m. 3 Oct. 1882, William Blundell Thornhill, eldest son of Rev. William Thornhill, of Huntingdon, and has issue.
      (2) Emma Frances.
      (3) Augusta Maye, m. 22 Dec. 1906, Cyril Vyvyan Hawkesford, of Clifton, Jersey.
      (4) Evelyn Mary.
      (5) Norah Muriel, m. 8 Jan. 1907, George Bull, Leinster Regt., youngest son of R. G. Bull, of Altnaveigh, Newry.
   3. Frederick Tynte, Capt, R.E., b. 22 March, 1839.
      1. Emma Lydia, d. unm. 2 June, 1864.
Dean Warburton m. 2ndly, March, 1878, Elizabeth Emily, elder dau. of the late Loftus Bland, of Blandsfort, Queen's Co., Q.C., Chairman co. Tyrone. She d. 21 July, 1901 (see that family). He d. 3 May, 1900.
5. Peter, b. 1807; d. unm.
6. Henry, m. a dau. of the late Dr. Hume, and d. 1889, leaving issue by her, who d. 1891.
7. James, who emigrated to Prince Edward's Island, m. there the dau. of — Green, of that island, and d. 1892.
8. Robert, Lieut.-Col. Bengal Artillery, served in the Afghan campaign 1839 to 1842, m. an Indian Princess, and d. Nov. 1863, leaving a son, Robert, Lieut. R.A.
9. Arthur, m., and d. Feb. 1896, leaving two sons.
10. Thomas, settled in Australia, and is m.
1. Anne. 2. Martha, m.
3. Susan, m., and d. 1890, leaving issue.
4. Mary, m. James Birch, of Birchgrove, near Roscrea, and has issue.

The 2nd son,
RICHARD WARBURTON, of Garryhinch, J.P. and D.L., High Sheriff of King's Co. 1845, and of Queen's Co. 1849, b. March, 1824, m. 6 Sept. 1844, Mary Ellinor, dau. and heir of Lieut.-Col. Kelly, of Millbrook, King's Co., and d. 1862, having by her (who d. Nov. 1862) had issue,
1. RICHARD, now of Garryhinch.
2. Hugh Dutton, b. 1862, late 11th Hussars; m. 28 July, 1886, Ethel Louisa Alberta, only dau. of Lieut.-Col. O. Williams, of Beenham Lodge, Berks, late Royal Dragoons.
1. Catherine Janette, m. 1st, Charles Lockhart Hamilton, 2nd Highlanders, who d. 1874, leaving issue, three sons; and 2ndly, Capt. Crosbie Barton, 19th Regt.
2. Ellinor, Mary Anne, m. Capt. J. Hill Poe, of Riverstown, Nenagh, co. Tipperary, and has issue.
3. Jessie Isabelle, m. 15 Sept. 1896, Right Hon. Dodgson Hamilton Madden, P.C., of Nutley, co. Dublin (see MADDEN of Hilton Park).
4. Frances Sophia, m. Robert Olphert, and has issue.
5. Ada Blanche, m. 25 June, 1887, Major Henry Walter Trench, 2nd Queen's Regt., and has issue. 6. Maude Alyne.

Arms—Arg. a chev. between three cormorants sa. Crest—A Saracen's head affrontée, couped at the shoulder ppr., round the temples a wreath arg. and gu., issuing therefrom three ostrich feathers or.

Seat—Garryhinch, near Portarlington.

WARD OF BANGOR CASTLE.

The late ROBERT EDWARD WARD, of Bangor Castle, co. Down, J.P. and D.L., High Sheriff 1842, late 10th Hussars, b. 10 Nov. 1818; m. 30 April, 1857, Harriette (who d. 4 March, 1881) dau. of the Hon. and Rev. Henry Ward, Rector of Killinchy, co. Down, brother of the 3rd Viscount Bangor. He d. 29 Nov. 1904, leaving an only child,

MATILDA CATHERINE, *m.* 27 June, 1878, the 5th and present Lord Clanmorris, and has issue (*see* BURKE'S *Peerage*, CLANMORRIS, B.).

Mr. Ward is the only son of Michael Edward Ward, of Bangor Castle, Minister Plenipotentiary at Dresden, who *d.* 12 Sept. 1832, and Matilda his wife, who *d.* 3 Oct. 1842, dau. of Robert, 1st Marquess of Londonderry, and grandson of the Right Hon. Robert Ward, 3rd son of Bernard, 1st Viscount Bangor.

Lineage.—*See* BURKE'S *Peerage*, BANGOR, V.
Arms—Az., a cross-patonce or. Crest—A Saracen's head affrontée, couped below the shoulders ppr. *Motto*—Sub cruce salus.
Seat—Bangor Castle, Bangor, co. Down.

———

WARD. *See* BURKE'S PEERAGE, BANGOR, V.

———

WARING OF WARINGSTOWN.

HOLT WARING, of Waringstown, co. Down, J.P., Capt. North of Ireland Imperial Yeomanry, *b.* 26 May, 1877.

Lineage.—This family became established in Ireland *temp.* JAMES I, when JOHN WARING settled in co. Antrim, and *m.* Mary, dau. of the Rev. Mr. Peers, of Derriaghy, in that co., by whom he had three sons. WILLIAM, John, and Paul; and several daus. The eldest son,

WILLIAM WARING, *b.* 1619, *d.* 1703; became possessed (by purchase from the soldiers of Mr. Deputy Fleetwood's Regt. of Horse) in 1656, of the district of Clanconnell (of which the Waringstown estate is a part), and shortly after built the present mansion and the church adjoining; he served as High Sheriff co. Down 1669. He *m.* 1st, 26 May, 1656, Elizabeth, dau. of William Gardiner, of Londonderry, and by her had issue,
1. SAMUEL, his heir.
1. Mary, *m.* Richard Close.
He *m.* 2ndly, Jane, dau. of John Close, and by her (who *d.* 5 May, 1724) had issue (with six daus., Jane, Mrs. Houston; Rebecca, Mrs. Montgomery, of Convoy; Elizabeth, *m.* Rev. John Cuppage, A.M.; Sarah, *m.* Robert Maxwell, of Falkland; Anne; and Frances) seven sons, of whom the eldest,
2. THOMAS, High Sheriff co. Down 1724, *m.* 1st, Miss Lawrence, by whom he had two sons,
 1. William, *d. unm.* 2. Samuel, *d. unm.*
He *m.* 2ndly, Mary Blacker, and had two other sons,
3. Thomas (Rev.), Rector of Moira, co. Down, *m.* Hester, dau. of Jasper Lucas, of Rickfordstown; and *d.* 1777, leaving with a dau., Mary, *m.* John Holmes, five sons,
 (1) Thomas, of Newry, *b.* 1736; *m.* Anne, dau. of Robert Thompson, and had
  1. THOMAS, *b.* 11 Oct. 1761, J.P. cos. Down and Armagh, High Sheriff co. Down 1797; *d.* 4 March, 1841. He *m.* 11 April, 1792, Mary, 2nd dau. of John Goddard, and by her (who *d.* Jan. 1803) had issue,
   a. Thomas, *b.* July, 1793, Rector of Bright, Diocese of Down, killed by a fall from his horse, Jan. 1823.
   b. HENRY, of Waringstown, of whom presently.
   c. Richard, J.P., Seneschal of Newry, *b.* 3 Sept. 1799; *d.* 31 Aug. 1875.
   a. Anne, *m.* 12 Jan. 1836, Breon Charles Bordes, Lieut. 27th Regt., and *d.* May, 1844.
  2. William. 3. Jasper.
  4. James. 5. John, Lieut. 23rd Light Dragoons.
  1. Hester, *m.* Rev. John Goddard.
  2. Jane. 3. Selina.
 (2) Jasper. (3) William.
 (4) John.
 (5) Lucas (Rev.), Rector of Kilkeel, co. Down, *m.* Ellen, dau. of Charles Douglas, of Grace Hall, co. Down, and had issue,
  1. THOMAS, of Waringfield, co. Down, *m.* Louisa, dau. of Peter Low, of Lowtown, co. Limerick (by Louisa his wife, dau. of Sir Richard Butler, 7th bart., of Garryhundon, co. Carlow), and *d.* 1877, having had issue,
   a. SAMUEL, late Capt. 62nd Regt., who *d.* 1872.
   b. Thomas, killed in New Zealand.
   c. Lucas, of Waringfield, *d. unm.*
   d. Robert Perceval Maxwell, *d.* leaving an infant son.
   e. Henry Low, *d.* 1872.
   a. Louisa, *m.* Capt. George Douglas, of Mount Ida, co. Down.
  2. Charles (Rev.), M.A., Rector of Eglish, co. Armagh, who left with other issue a dau.,
   Harriet, *m.* 15 Dec. 1868, George Brush, of Gill Hall, co. Down.
  3. John, *m.* Geraldine, dau. of Nathaniel Montgomery, Solicitor, of Swalinbar, co. Cavan, and Drominck Street, Dublin, and had two daus.,
   a. Anne. *b.* Eleanor.
  4. Lucas.

4. Richard, of Waringstown, co. Down, *m.* about 1747, Sarah, eldest dau. of Archdeacon John Maxwell, D.D., of Falkland, and left issue,
 (1) John Charles Frederick WARING-MAXWELL, M.P. for Downpatrick, Lieut.-Col. in the Down Militia, who assumed the name of MAXWALL, but *d.* before applying for a Royal Licence. He *m.* Dorothea, dau. of Robert Maxwell of Finnebrogue, co. Down, High Sheriff 1743, and by her (who by Royal Licence 9 April, 1803, assumed for herself and the heirs general of her husband the name and arms of MAXWELL) had issue,
  1. John, of Finnebrogue, M.P. for Downpatrick, *m.* 29 Aug. 1817, Modeline Martha, dau. of David Ker, of Portavo, and *d.s.p.*
  2. Robert, of Killyfaddy, Cornet 19th Light Dragoons and Capt. Monaghan Militia, *b.* 23 June, 1790; *m.* 1820, Isabella, dau. of John Corry Moutray, D.L., of Favour Royal, co. Tyrone, and *d.s.p.* 16 Dec. 1855. His estate passed by his will to FitzAmeline Maxwell Ancketill (*see that family*).
   1. Anne, *m.* 9 Sept. 1809, Rev. William Perceval, of Kilmore Hill, co. Waterford. She *d.* 5 May, 1861. He *d.* 20 April, 1880, leaving issue (*see* PERCEVAL-MAXWELL *of Finnebrogue*).
   2. Sarah, *m.* 23 June, 1809, William Anketill, D.L., of Ankctill Grove. She *d.* 2 April, 1874. He *d.* 23 April, 1851, leaving issue (*see* ANCKETILL *of Ancketill Grove*).
   3. Dorothea Maria, *m.* 6 Jan. 1819, Richard Hunter, D.L. of Straidarran, co. Londonderry. She *d.* about 1870. He *d.* March, 1855.
  (1) Mary, *d. unm.*
  (2) Sarah, *m.* Rev. Thomas Kennedy Bailie, D.D., Rector of Dromore, and had issue.

The eldest son,
SAMUEL WARING, of Waringstown, High Sheriff 1690, M.P. for Hillsborough from 1703 to 1715, *m.* 1696, Grace, dau. of Rev. Samuel Holt, co. Meath, and *d.* 1739, having had issue,
1. SAMUEL, his heir. 2. Richard, *d. unm.*
3. Holt, Major in the Army, served at Dettingen, Fontenoy, and Colloden, *m.* 1746, Anne, dau. of Very Rev. William French, Dean of Elphin, son of John French, of French Park, co. Roscommon, and *d.* 1806, having had issue,
 1. Samuel, Capt. in the Army, killed in action, *unm.*
 2. William, *d.* young. 3. Richard, *d. unm.*
 4. Robert, *d. unm.*
 5. HOLT (Very Rev.), who *s.* to Waringstown.
 1. Frances Arabella, *m.* Rev. William Boyd.
 2. Mary, *m.* William Archer, and *d.* 8 Aug. 1844, aged 83.
1. Jane, *m.* Alexander M'Naghten.
2. Sarah, *m.* 1st, Ralph Lambert; and 2ndly, Rev. James Hamilton, D.D.
3. Frances, *m.* Henry Usher.
4. Alice, *m.* Conway Spencer.

The eldest son,
SAMUEL WARING, of Waringstown, High Sheriff 1734, *d. unm.* 1793, and was *s.* by his nephew,
VERY REV. HOLT WARING, of Waringstown, Dean of Dromore, *b.* 2 Jan. 1766; *m.* 1793, Elizabeth Mary, dau. of Rev. Averell Daniel, Rector of Lifford, co. Donegal, and had issue,
1. Eliza Jane, *m.* James Wapshare. 2. Anne, *d. unm.*
3. Louisa, *m.* 1st, Rev. John Michael Brooke; she *m.* 2ndly, St. John Augustus Clerke, K.H., Lieut.-Gen. in the Army, and Col. 75th Regt., who *d.* 1869, leaving issue.
4. Frances Grace, *m.* Henry Waring, of Waringstown (*see below*).
5. Jane, *m.* Henry Samuel Close, a Banker in Dublin, who *d.* March, 1867; she *d.* Jan. 1877.

The Dean's cousin and son-in-law,
HENRY WARING, of Waringstown, J.P., Major in the Army, *b.* 26 March, 1795; *m.* 14 Jan. 1824, Frances Grace, 4th dau. of Very Rev. Holt Waring, of Waringstown, Dean of Dromore, and by her (who *d.* 1860) had (with three other sons, who *d.* in infancy) issue,
1. THOMAS, of whom presently.
2. Holt, Resident Magistrate in Ireland, formerly Capt. 88th Connaught Rangers, *b.* 25 May, 1835; *m.* 20 May, 1862, Margaret Elizabeth, dau. of Robert McClintock, of Dunmore, co. Donegal (*see that family*), and has issue,
 1. Henry, Lieut.-Col. A. O.D., *b.* 6 March, 1863.
 1. Grace. 2. Margaret.
 3. Mary. 4. Susan.
3. Henry, Lieut.-Col. (retired) The Queen's R.W. Surrey Regt., late Governor of the Military Prison, Gosport, formerly Assistant Adjutant-Gen. Bombay; *b.* 13 Feb. 1840; *m.* 8 July, 1869, Mary Letitia, dau. of Lieut.-Gen. Hutchinson, of Wellesbourne, Bideford, Devon, and has issue,
 1. Richard, Capt. R.A., *b.* 21 April, 1871; *m.* 27 Nov. 1901, Elizabeth Eckley, only dau. of Col. M. F. H. McCausland, late R.A., and has issue,
  Walter Hamilton, *b.* 6 Sept. 1902.
 2. Edmund Henry, Lieut. Indian Army, *b.* 25 March, 1875; *m.* 5 Feb. 1898, Anna Frances Mary, dau. of S. P. Bussell, of Sydney, N.S.W., and has issue,
  Edmund Francis, *b.* 28 Aug. 1899.
  Muriel.
 3. John, Lieut. R.A., *b.* 21 Oct. 1881.
 1. Mary. 2. Esther.
1. Mary Louisa, *m.* 14 Jan. 1853, Rev. Alexander Matthew Pollock, M.A., who *d.* Feb. 1865; she *d.* 18 July, 1873.
2. Elizabeth Mary, *d. unm.* 3 Jan. 1904.
3. Frances Jane, *m.* 20 Oct. 1858, Rev. William Henry Overstreet Fletcher, *d.* 1 Jan. 1880.

Warren. THE LANDED GENTRY. 748

4. Anne, *d.* 1860.   5. Susan, *d.* 1847.
6. Selina Grace, *m.* 18 July, 1867, Robert Henry Martley, eldest son of the Hon. Henry Martley, Judge of the Landed Estates Court, Dublin. He *d.* 6 April, 1878.
Mr. Henry Waring *d.* 6 April, 1866. His eldest son,
   THOMAS WARING, of Waringstown, co. Down, J.P., Barrister-at-Law, M.P. for Northern Division co. Down, Hon. Col. 5th Batt. Royal Irish Rifles, High Sheriff 1868-9, *b.* 17 Oct. 1828; *m.* 1st, 22 April, 1858, Esther, 3rd dau. of Ross Thompson Smyth, of Ardmore, co. Derry. She *d.s.p.* 26 March, 1873. He *m.* 2ndly, 6 Aug. 1874, Fanny, 4th dau. of Admiral John Jervis Tucker, of Trematon Castle, Cornwall, and by her (who *d.* 13 Nov. 1883) had issue,
1. HOLT, now of Waringstown.
2. Ruric Henry, Lieut. R.N., *b.* 16 Aug. 1879.
1. Esther Marian, *b.* 10 Feb. 1876.
2. Mary Theresa, *b.* 8 Dec. 1880; *m.* 12 March, 1906, Samuel Barbour Combe, of Donaghcloney House, co. Down.
3. Frances Joan Alice, *b.* 8 Nov. 1883.
He *m.* 3rdly, 1 July, 1885, Geraldine, 3rd dau. of Alex. Stewart, of Bally Edmond, and *d.* 12 Aug. 1898.

Seat—Waringstown House, Lurgan, co. Down.

WARREN OF RATHFARNHAM PARK.

The late GRAVES SWAN WARREN, of Rathfarnham Park, co. Dublin, and Ballydonarea; co. Wicklow, *b.* 27 March, 1822; *m.* 17 June, 1852, Sarah, only dau. of John Davis, of the Park, Rathfarnham. He *d.* 6 Aug. 1907.

Lineage. — ROBERT WARREN, of Carson, co. Monaghan, 3rd son of Humphrey Warren, by Susanna his wife, dau. of William Davenport, *m.* Margaret, dau of Thomas Wilkinson, of Ballydonarea, co. Wicklow, and *d.* 15 Oct. 1748, leaving two sons,
1. JOHN, of whom presently.
2. James, *m.* Miss Bourke, of the family of Bourke, Viscounts Mayo, and by her had issue,
1. Peter, of Henrietta Street, Dublin, *m.* 1st, Elizabeth, dau. of Francis Paravsol, and had issue,
(1) Francis James, Capt. of Dragoons, *m.* Miss Hardwick, and *d.s.p.*   (2) John.
(3) Robert, Capt. in the Buffs, *d.s.p.*
(1) Caroline, *m.* John Aumuty, Chief Judge of the Supreme Court of Calcutta.
He *m.* 2ndly, July, 1830, Susan Jervis, dau. of Arthur Meredith White, by Jane Lea his wife.
2. Robert (Rev.), *m.* Elizabeth, sister of Sir Gore Ouseley, Bart., and had issue,
(1) Richard,
(2) William, who all *d.s.p.*
(3) Robert,
(1) Elizabeth, *m.* 13 Nov. 1809, Robert Moore, of Lansdown. Lieut.-Col. Kildare Militia, nephew of the 1st Marquess of Drogheda.   (2) Caroline, *m.* Mr. Chambers.
(3) Fanny, *m.* Dr. Kennedy.   (4) Louisa, *m.* H. French.
1. Eliza, *m.* Robert Sandys, of Creveagh, co. Longford.
2. Catherine.   3. Margaret, *m.* Mr. Davis.
The elder son,
   JOHN WARREN, of Ballydonarea, co. Wicklow, *b.* 1719; *m.* 1st, 6 Oct. 1747, Susanna, dau. of Martin Horrish, of Corballis (by Eliza Bryne his wife), and had issue, five sons, 1. William; 2. ROBERT, of whom hereafter; 3. Peter; 4. John; and 5. William; and three daus., 1. Elizabeth; 2. Eleanor, *m.* W. Whitton; and 3. Susanna (Mrs. Davis). Mr. Warren *m.* 2ndly, 1759, Mary, dau. of Thomas Gates, of Great Connell, and by her had issue, 6. Thomas; 7. Francis William, *m.* Anne Caldbeck, and had issue; 8. Ralph, R.N.; 9. William; 10. John, *m.* Miss E. R. Chamney, and had issue; and 4. Sarah. The 2nd son of the 1st marriage,
   ROBERT WARREN, of Ballydonarea, Examiner of the Court of Chancery, *b.* 29 April, 1752; *m.* 10 May, 1781, Barbara, dau. of Joseph Swan, of Tombrean; and by her (*b.* 22 Jan. 1756, and *d.* 18 June, 1831) had issue,
1. John, dec.
2. ROBERT, of Killiney Castle, of whom presently.
3. Joseph St. Lawrence.   4. Thomas.
1. Barbara, *m.* Sandham Symes, of Dominic Street, Dublin.
2. Catherine.
3. Susanna, *m.* Richard McNally, and *d.* 30 March, 1877.
4. Margaret, *d.* 6 Oct. 1877.   5. Ellen, *m.* R. Dowse.
6. Mary, *m.* W. Goodman.
Mr. Warren *d.* 24 May, 1814. His 2nd son,
   ROBERT WARREN, of Ballydonarea, co. Wicklow, and Killiney Castle, co. Dublin, *b.* 6 July, 1787; *m.* 4 Feb. 1819, Alicia, dau. of Athanasius Cusack, of Laragh, and *d.* 20 June, 1869, having by her (who *d.* 21 Feb. 1879, aged 82) had surviving issue,
1. ROBERT, of Ballydonarea, co. Wicklow, Annaghmore, co. Cork, and Killiney, co. Dublin, M.A., Barrister-at-Law, High Sheriff co. Dublin 1873, and for the city 1875, J.P. and D.L. co. and city of Dublin, and J.P. co. Cork, *b.* 14 Feb. 1820; *m.* 27 May, 1846, Anne Elizabeth, dau. of Cadwallader Waddy, of Kilmacow, M.P. co. Wexford, and *d.* 19 April, 1894. She *d.* 22 Nov. 1880.
2. GRAVES SWAN, late of Rathfarnham Park.
3. Samuel Perceval (Rev.), Incumbent of Balbriggan, *b.* 15 April, 1828; *m.* 8 March, 1859, Judith Frances, dau. of T. Somerville Fleming, of Derry Lea, co. Kildare. She *d.* 9 Feb. 1892. He *d.* Oct. 1902, leaving issue,
1. Robert Somerville, *b.* 23 March, 1865; *d.* 14 Feb. 1911.
2. Percy Becher, *b.* 9 April, 1871.
1. Frances Alicia, *m.* 25 April, 1885, Richard John Baker, I.M.S., and *d.* 4 April, 1898, leaving issue.
2. Alicia Judith Dagmar.
3. Judith Pitcairn.
4. Athanasius Cusack, *b.* 8 June, 1834; *d.* 5 Feb. 1873.
5. James William, *b.* 10 Feb. 1836; *d.* 14 July, 1896.
6. John Thomas, *b.* 11 May, 1838.
7. Edward George, *b.* 6 May, 1839; *d.* 2 Sept. 1895.
1. Anna Martha, *d.* 30 May, 1882.

Arms—Chequy or and az., on a canton erm. a trefoil vert. *Crest* —On a chapeau gu. turned up erm. a wyvern arg. wings expanded chequy or and az., on the breast a trefoil ppr. *Motto*—Be just and fear not.

Seats—The Park, Rathfarnham, co. Dublin, and Ballydonarea, co. Wicklow.

WARREN, late OF LODGE PARK.

EMILY ZOE WARREN, late of Lodge Park, co. Kilkenny, *s.* her father 1898, and sold the estate 1905.

Lineage.—THE VERY REV. EDWARD WARREN, Dean of Ossory, B.A. Trin. Coll. Dublin 1608, Fellow and M.A. 1612, Dean of Emily 1620-7, and of Ossory from 1647. He *d.* before 1661, having had, with other issue,
   MAJOR ABEL WARREN, of Balleen Lodge (now Lodge Park), co. Kilkenny, which he purchased from Benjamin Worsley, was Mayor of Kilkenny 1656, M.P. for the city 1661-5, *b.* 19 May, 1623; *m.* 1st, Mary, dau. of Samuel Price, of Keenaugh, co. Longford. She *d.* 24 Dec. 1655 (*Funeral entry*), leaving issue,
1. Abel, *d.u.p.*   2. EDWARD, his heir.
1. Elizabeth.
He *m.* 2ndly, Dec. 1657, Sarah, dau. of Richard Godfrey, of Wye, Kent, M.P. for New Romney 1623-6, and by her (who *m.* 2ndly, 24 Dec. 1655, John Bourden, and *d.* 28 Feb. 1679) had issue,
3. EBENEZER, *s.* his half brother.   4. Thomas.
5. John.   6. Abel.
2. Mary, *m.* George Bradshaw.
Maj. Warren's will is dated 5 Aug. 1667. His eldest surviving son,
   EDWARD WARREN, of Lodge, obtained a patent under the Act of Settlement, 23 Oct. 20 CHARLES II, enrolled 2 April, 1669, confirming the lands acquired by his father. He *d.s.p.*, and was *s.* by his half brother,
   EBENEZER WARREN, of Lodge, M.P. for Kilkenny 1695-9 and 1715-20, Mayor of Kilkenny 1694, 1695, and 1696, High Sheriff for the co. 1694, *b.* 1658; *m.* 1st, 12 July, 1679, Katherine, dau. of John Bourden. She *d.s.p.* 6 June, 1680. He *m.* 2ndly, 29 July, 1680, Mary, dau. of Josias Haydock, M.P. for Kilkenny 1692-3, and *d.* 20 Nov. 1720, having by her had, with several daus., who *d.* young,
1. EDWARD, his heir.
2. Henry, *b.* 17 July, 1688; *d. unm.*
3. Abel, of Lowhill, co. Kilkenny, Maj. in Otway's Foot, *b.* 1 March, 1691; *m.* 6 Aug. 1726, Olivia, dau. of Col. the Hon. Toby Caulfeild, of Clone, and *d.* 28 Feb. 1763, leaving issue, five sons and two daus. His son,
   John, of Lowhill, *m.* Dec. 1789, Sarah, dau. of Arundel Best, of Bestville, co. Carlow. She *d.* 1833. He *d.* 1815, leaving issue,
(1) Abel John Caulfeild, of Lowhill, *m.* 10 Jan. 1824, Hester Maria, dau. of Rev. Alexander Chetwode Hamilton-Stubber, and *d.s.p.* 23 Oct. 1868.
(1) Olivia, *m.* 10 Sept. 1827, Luke Flood.
(2) Rebecca Elizabeth, *d. unm.* 10 Jan. 1868.
4. Algernon, Mayor of Kilkenny 1736, *b.* 9 Dec. 1698; *m.* Aug. 1730, Lettice, dau. of Rev. John Burdett, Dean of Clonfert, and *d.* 2 April, 1763, having had, with other issue, a son,
   Algernon, Capt. 66th Foot, settled in Jamaica, *b.* 1731; *m.* 1767, Dorothy, dau. of Col. Philip Prioleau. She *d.* 1811. He *d.* 1801, leaving ten children. His 4th son, Thomas, was grandfather of Thomas Herbert Warren, M.A., Pres. of Magdalen Coll., Oxford.
5. Honywood, *b.* 12 Feb. 1702; *d.* 25 July, 1703.
1. Elizabeth, *m.* 7 Dec. 1704, Thomas Sandford, of Sandford's Court.
2. Susannah, *m.* 23 April, 1715, Euseby Stratford, of Corbally, Queen's Co.
3. Anne, *m.* Capt. Robert Wolseley.
The eldest son,

EDWARD WARREN, of Lodge, High Sheriff co. Kilkenny 1720, M.P. for Kilkenny 1721-7, Mayor of Kilkenny 1724, 1731, and 1733, b. 20 Feb. 1681; m. 9 Feb. 1714, Isabella, dau. of Folliott Sherigley, of Dublin, and d. 25 April, 1743, having by her had, with four daus. who d. unm.,
1. FOLLIOTT, his heir.
2. Ebenezer, b. 8 March, 1720; m. 12 Jan. 1766, Mary, dau. of Laurence Nowlan. She d. Feb. 1828. He d. 4 Nov. 1779, leaving issue,
 1. Ebenezer, B.A. Dublin 1792, b. 19 Dec. 1772; m. Sept. 1795, Elizabeth, dau. of Rev. John Cary. He d.s.p. 17 March, 1799. She d. 1827.
 1. Mary, m. 18 Nov. 1786, Rev. John Lewis.
 2. Isabella, m. 30 April, 1795, John White, Barrister-at-Law.
 3. Sarah Eliza, d. unm.
The elder son,
FOLLIOTT WARREN, of Lodge, High Sheriff 1753, b. 16 Nov. 1719; m. 1st, 7 Jan. 1745, Mary, dau. of Sir John Staples, Bart. She d.s.p. Oct. 1764. He m. 2ndly, Oct. 1765, Elizabeth, dau. of Lemuel Shuldham, of Ballymulvey, co. Longford. She d. 20 Oct. 1777. He d. 15 Aug. 1788, leaving issue,
1. EDWARD, his heir.
2. Folliott, B.A. Dublin, Lieut. 56th Foot, b. 2 April, 1769; d. unm. July, 1794.
3. Lemuel, b. 15 Sept. 1771; m. June, 1804, Elizabeth, dau. of John Bolton, of Donnybrook, and d. 29 Oct. 1833, having had issue,
 Edward.
 Elizabeth.
1. Anna Isabella, m. 6 July, 1796, William Barton, of Clonelly.
The eldest son,
EDWARD WARREN, of Lodge, b. 1 Oct. 1767; m. 9 April, 1791, his cousin, Elizabeth, dau. of Pooley Shuldham, of Ballymulvey, and d. 20 March, 1816, leaving issue,
POOLEY ABEL, his heir.
Elizabeth, m. 1812, Rev. Henry Lucas St. George.
The only son,
POOLEY ABEL WARREN, of Lodge, b. 22 May, 1806; m. 18 April, 1828, Jessy Ann, dau. of Thomas Bryan, and d. 25 June, 1834, leaving issue,
EDWARD LEWIS, his heir.
Lucy Florence, d. unm. 20 March, 1837.
The only son,
EDWARD LEWIS WARREN, of Lodge, J.P. and D.L., High Sheriff 1861, b. 24 Nov. 1830; m. 17 Sept. 1857, Marianne Emilie (d. 22 April, 1909), dau. of Col. Charles Garraway, and d. 9 Aug. 1894, having had issue,
1. Edward George Shuldham, b. 1 Jan. 1860; d.v.p. 9 Aug. 1891, s.p.
1. EMILY ZOE, late of Lodge.
2. Lucy Jessy, m. 15 Dec. 1888, Maj. Ernest Frederick Smith, R.A.M.C. She d. Aug. 1898.
3. Helen Anne.
Arms—Chequy or and az., on a canton gu. a lion rampant arg. Crest—A plume of four ostrich feathers arg., in front thereof an eagle's leg erect sa. armed gu. Motto—Ero quod spero.

WARREN. See BURKE'S PEERAGE, WARREN, Bart.

WATSON OF BALLINGARRANE.

LIEUT.-COL. SOLOMON WATSON, of Ballingarrane, co. Tipperary, J.P., D.L., High Sheriff 1909, Lieut.-Col. (retired) Royal Field Artillery, b. 31 Oct. 1849; m. 25 Sept. 1888, Hon. Elnith Georgina Isabel de Beauchamp Roper-Curzon, dau. of Henry George, 17th Baron Teynham (see BURKE'S Peerage), and has had issue,
1. William Henry Wyndham, b. 1889; d. 1891.
2. Wilfred Francis Herbert, b. 1892.
3. Sidney Frederick, b. 1893.
4. Reginald Murray, b. 1896.
1. Elnith Irene Harriet Ellinor, b. 1898.
Lineage.—JOHN WATSON, of Crosted, Cumberland, settled at Kilconner, co. Carlow, in 1658. He m. Jane West, and d. 1675, having had issue,
1. John of Kilconner.
2. SAMUEL, of Clonbrogan.
The younger son,
SAMUEL WATSON, of Clonbrogan, co. Tipperary, m. 1676, Elizabeth, dau. of Oliver Thompson, of Penrith, and had issue,
SOLOMON WATSON, of Clonbrogan, m. Abigail, dau. of John Boles (or Bowles), of Woodhouse, co. Tipperary, and had issue,
JOHN WATSON, of Clonbrogan and Summerville, co. Tipperary, who d. 1783, having issue by his wife, Sarah,

SOLOMON WATSON, of Summerville, who m. 1769, Mary, dau. of James Hill, of Limerick, by whom he had issue,
1. Solomon, of Summerville, b. 1777; d. unm. 1854.
2. WILLIAM, of Summerville.
The younger son,
WILLIAM WATSON, of Summerville, b. 1779; m. 1801, Eliza, dau. of George Newenham, of Summerhill, co. Cork, and had issue,
SOLOMON WATSON, of Summerville, now called Ballingarrane, b. 1811; d. 1900; m. 1841, Ellinor, dau. of Henry Sargent, by whom he had issue,
1. William, Major 34th Border Regt., b. 1844; d. unm. 1890.
2. SOLOMON, now of Ballingarrane.
1. Eliza Newenham, m. Col. F. J. P. Hill, Royal Scots Regt. She d. 1897.
2. Ellen Beresford, m. Col. Francis Roberts, R.A.
3. Mary Totenham.
Seat—Ballingarrane, co. Tipperary.

WATT OF THORN HILL.

ANDREW ALEXANDER WATT, of Thorn Hill, co. Londonderry, J.P. and D.L. co. Donegal, High Sheriff co. Londonderry 1886, b. 4 Nov. 1853; m. 7 Oct. 1875, Violet Flora, only dau. of George de Burgh, of Millbank House, co. Kildare (see DE BURGH, of Oldtown), and Constance his wife, dau. of Wellesley Matthews, and has issue,
1. SAMUEL ALEXANDER, b. 27 July, 1876; m. 2 June, 1900, Blanche Moore, only dau. of Alfred Moore Munn, of Westbank, Londonderry.
2. Andrew Hubert, Capt. 3rd Dragoon Guards, b. 26 Feb. 1881; m. 5 Feb. 1908, Penelope Victoria Minna, 5th dau. of the late Col. John Henry Graham Holroyd-Smyth, C.M.G., J.P., of Ballynatray (see that family), and has issue,
 Phyllis Constance Harriet, b. 2 Nov. 1908.
3. Maurice, b. 6 Feb., d. 6 March, 1884.
4. Gerald Allingham, b. 28 Oct. 1888.
1. Constance, b. 14 Feb. 1878; m. 15 April, 1903, Capt. Henry Stern, late 13th Hussars, of Bective, co. Meath, eldest son of the late James Stern, of 25, Princes Gate, S.W.
2. Violet Evelyn, b. 3 Aug. 1879; m. 7 Aug. 1902, Thomas Pryse Arthur Holford, late 10th Hussars, 2nd son of Thomas Holford, D.L., of Castle Hill, Dorset (see that family).
Lineage.—ANDREW ALEXANDER WATT, of Shipquay Street House, Londonderry, d. Feb. 1851, and left issue a son,
SAMUEL WATT, of Thornhill, co. Londonderry, b. 14 Sept. 1817; m. 21 Dec. 1852, Jane, dau. of Capt. Robert Newman, 56th Regt. and Hester Moody his wife. She was b. 29 Oct. 1827, and d. 2 May, 1899. He d. 31 Jan. 1872, having had issue,
1. ANDREW ALEXANDER, now of Thornhill.
2. Samuel, b. 29 May, 1860; d. unm. 3 Feb. 1882.
3. David, b. 1 July, 1872; d. 1909.
1. Hester, b. 22 May, 1856; m. 2 Oct. 1873, Hume Babington, J.P., of Creevagh, Londonderry.
Seat—Thornhill, Londonderry. Clubs—Kildare Street, Dublin, and Northern Counties, Londonderry; Ulster, Belfast; Boodles, S.W.

WEBB OF WEBBSBOROUGH.

RICHARD HENRY WEBB, of Webbsborough, co. Kilkenny, J.P., b. 21 Feb. 1843; m. 7 Dec. 1889, Mary Elizabeth, dau. of Charles Sloane, M.D., F.R.C.S.I., of Clonmel.
Lineage.—CAPT. HENRY WEBB, of Ballinrobe, co. Mayo, in 1667, of Ballylarkin, co. Kilkenny in 1668, and later of Webbsborough in that county, High Sheriff 1678, went, it is said, from Devizes, Wilts., to Ireland, and obtained a grant, by letters patent, under the Act of Settlement, of 5,000 acres in cos. Kilkenny, Mayo, and Sligo. He m. Anne, dau. of Henry Stotesbury, of Corbettstown, co. Kilkenny, and by her had issue,
1. ARTHUR, his heir.
1. Sarah, m. 12 March, 1692, Francis Yarner, of Dublin.
2. Rebecca. 3. Anne.
4. Rachael, m. — Bell.
Capt. Webb's will, dated 7 March, 1679 was proved 8 July, 1680. In this he mentions his nephews Richard and John Webb, and his brother Cramer. His only son,
ARTHUR WEBB, of Webbsborough, co. Kilkenny, attainted by JAMES II 1689, but was appointed Parliamentary Commissioner of Revenue by WILLIAM III, 1695, 1697, and 1698, High Sheriff 1707; m. 1st, Deborah, youngest dau. of Tobias Cramer, of Ballyfoyle, co. Kilkenny, and aunt of Marmaduke Coghill, and by her had issue,

1. ARTHUR, his heir.
2. Tobias, b. 1690; m. March, 1774, Margaret Fitzpatrick, and d. the same month. Will dated 13 March, 1773.
3. Peter, d. 1775, will dated 18 April, 1770, leaving, by Catherine his wife, a son Marmaduke Arthur, d. unm. 1794, and a dau., Frances, d. unm.
4. Oliver.   5. Henry.
6. Marmaduke.
1. Mary, m. 1733, James McClaine.
2. Grace, m. Thomas Crompton.
3. Anne, m. — Handcock.
4. Elisha, m. — Parker, and had issue.

Arthur Webb's will, dated 26 April, 1733, was proved that year. His eldest son,

ARTHUR WEBB, of Webbsborough, b. 1683; m. 18 May, 1706, Elizabeth, 3rd dau. of Sir Henry Wemys, of Danesfort, co. Kilkenny, by Elizabeth his wife, eldest dau. of Sir George Blundell, Bart., and d. 16 Sept. 1748 (will dated 9 Sept., proved 5 Nov. 1748), having by her had issue,
1. ARTHUR, his heir.
2. Henry, d. young.
3. Patrick, Cornet of Dragoons, Gen. Bligh's Regt., 1749, b. 1726; m. by licence, 27 Sept. 1757, Eliza, 3rd dau. and co-heir of Capt. William Waldron, and d. 23 Nov. 1813. having had issue,
 1. Robert, b. 14 May, 1777; m. 29 April, 1808, Dorothea, dau. of Joseph Gabbett, of High Park, co. Limerick (by Mary his wife, dau. of Rev. Rickard Lloyd, of Castle Lloyd, co. Limerick, and grand-dau. of W. Gabbett, of Caherline (see that family), and Dorothea his wife, 3rd dau. of Rev. Richard Burgh, and had issue,
  (1) Patrick Robert, of Herbert Place, Dublin, Barrister-at-Law, b. 29 Jan. 1809; m. 16 Aug. 1837, Elizabeth, eldest dau. of William Woodrooffe, of Stephen's Green, Dublin, and niece of Rev. Samuel Woodrooffe, Rector of Luckington, and left issue,
   1. William Robert, Lieut. 8th King's Regt., b. 16 June, 1838; d. of wounds at Delhi, 15 Sept. 1857, unm.
   2. Henry North, Major Bengal Cavalry, b. 4 March, 1849; m. 17 July, 1894, Alice, dau. of D. M. Fox, and has issue.
    1. Grace.   2. Dorothea.
   3. Isabella Maria.
  (2) Joseph Gabbett, settled in S. Australia, b. 11 March, 1810; d. unm. 16 March, 1854.
  (3) William Thomas, b. 7 June, 1811; m. 9 Nov. 1843, his cousin, Lydia, dau. of John S. Newman, and d. 17 April, 1863, leaving issue.
  (4) Arthur Wellington, b. 25 March, 1813; m. 9 Nov. 1843, Olivia, dau. of — Beasly, of Dublin, and d. 20 April, 1877, leaving issue.
   1. Lydia, m. June, 1785, Ven. William Galway, Archdeacon of Cashel, and had issue.
   2. Isabella.
   3. Elizabeth, m. John Spiller Newman, of Kinsale, co. Cork, and had issue.

The eldest son,
REV. ARTHUR WEBB, of Webbsborough, Rector of Kells 1768, b. 1708; m. 3 April, 1735, Elizabeth, dau. of Richard Reade, of Rossanarragh, co. Kilkenny, and d. 4 Dec. 1784, having had issue,
1. ARTHUR, of whom presently.
2. Richard Henry, b. 1747, m. (setts. dated 13 Oct. 1778) his first cousin, Elizabeth Reade, and d. Oct. 1839, having had issue,
 1. Henry Arthur, d.s.p.
 2. Richard Henry, b. 1784; m. 5 Feb. 1830, Sarah West, and d. 7 July, 1845, having had issue,
  Arthur Nugent, b. 18 Nov. 1830; m. 9 June, 1869, Marian, dau. of T. Cheevers, M.D., and d. 4 Feb. 1902, having had issue,
  (1) Arthur Thomas (Rev.), b. 9 Oct. 1870; m. 8 April, 1902, Gertrude, dau. of John Patrick, of Gledheather (see PATRICK of Dunminning).
  (2) George Stubbs, of Prospect, Shinrone, Roscrea, b. 1874.
1. Elizabeth, m. 30 Dec. 1761, Joseph Matthews, of Bonnettstown, co. Kilkenny.   2. Frances.
3. Kate.   4. Mary.

The eldest son,
ARTHUR WEBB, of Webbsborough, b. 1737, m. Jan. 1773, Dorothea, dau. of Richard Gore, of Sea View, co. Wicklow, and d. 28 July, 1786, having had issue,
1. Henry, d. young.
2. Arthur, d. young, 30 April, 1788.
3. RICHARD HENRY, of whom presently.
4. WILLIAM, s. his brother, 1807.
5. George Oliver, m. Sarah, dau. of — Harrison, and d. 14 May, 1831, leaving with other issue,
 Richard Henry, b. 1817, m. 1836, Frances, dau. of Dowling Wall, of Leighlinbridge, co. Carlow. She d. July, 1891. He d. 4 March, 1843, having had issue,
 (1) GEORGE OLIVER, s. his great uncle, 1852.
 (2) RICHARD HENRY, now of Webbsborough, s. his brother, 1885.
  (1) Caroline, b. 17 July, 1837; d. April, 1853.
  (2) Sarah, b. Aug. 1839; d. Aug. 1849.
  (3) Agnes, b. 29 March, 1841; d. Oct. 1851.
1. Anne.
2. Elizabeth, m. Charles Benson, of Dublin, Barrister-at-Law.

The eldest son,
RICHARD HENRY WEBB, of Webbsborough, b. 1777, m. Aug. 1797, Frances Harrison, but d.s.p. 9 May, 1807, and was s. by his brother,

CAPT. WILLIAM WEBB, of Webbsborough, b. 13 Oct. 1778; d.s.p. 25 April, 1852, and was s. by his great nephew,
GEORGE OLIVER WEBB, of Webbsborough, b. 29 March, 1811, and d.s.p. 16 Aug. 1885, and was s. by his brother, RICHARD HENRY, now of Webbsborough.

Seat—Somerton, near Webbsborough, Jenkinstown, co. Kilkenny.

WEBB OF KILMORE.

CHARLES CALEB COOTE WEBB, of Kilmore, Nenagh, co. Tipperary, and Knocktoran, Knocklong, co. Limerick, J.P. and D.L. co. Tipperary, High Sheriff 1910, b. 18 Nov. 1859; m. 18 Nov. 1885, Amy Simla, 2nd dau. of Lieut.-Gen. Charles Edward Parke Gordon, C.B., and has had issue,
1. STUART NAPIER CHARLES, South Wales Borderers, b. 2 Aug. 1886.
2. Marshall William Traherne, R.E., b. 19 Nov. 1888.
3. Daniel James Gordon, b. 25 July, 1898.
1. Anna Elizabeth.   2. Eva Louisa Oglander.
3. Amy Frances, d. 12 June,

Lineage.—DANIEL WEBB, o Maidstown Castle, co. Limerick. m. Dorothea, dau and heir of M. Leake, of Castle Leake. co. Tipperary, and had issue,
1. DANIEL m. 1st, Jane Lloyd; 2ndly, Elizabeth Creed, but d.s.p. 3 Aug. 1798.
2. Thomas, Dean of Kilmore, d. unm. Dec. 1796.
3. Richard, R.N., d.s.p.   4. JAMES, of whom we treat.
1. Frances, m. Richard Burke, who was created a bart., and assumed the name of DE BOURGHO.

The 4th son,
JAMES WEBB, a Major in the Army, m. 1779, Elizabeth, dau. of Sir John Oglander, Bart., of Nunwell, Isle of Wight, and relict of Sir Gerald Napier, of More Critchell, and Middlemarsh Hall, Dorset, and by her had issue, a son and successor,
DANIEL JAMES WEBB, of Maidstown Castle, co. Limerick, and of Woodville, co. Tipperary, J.P., b. 1 Oct. 1780; m. 22 Oct. 1812, Hon. Ann Wilhelmina, dau. of Charles Stanley, Viscount Monck, and d. 24 Oct 1850, having had issue,
1. JAMES NAPIER, of Knocktoran, co. Limerick, M.A., J.P. co. Limerick, b. 7 Sept. 1813; m. 1st, May, 1841, his cousin, Anne, dau. of Charles Joseph Kelly, 3rd Viscount Monck, which lady d. 23 Sept. 1853; and 2ndly, 29 March, 1855, Anna Thomasina, dau. of Joseph Gubbins, of Kilfrush, co. Limerick (see that family), and d.s.p. 1888. She d. 5 April, 1906.
2. CHARLES DANIEL HENRY, late of Woodville.
1. Elizabeth Anne, d. 1824.

The 2nd son,
CHARLES DANIEL HENRY WEBB, of Woodville, co. Tipperary, J.P., b. 9 Oct. 1825; m. 6 March, 1856, Elizabeth Lucy, dau. of Rev. M. Lloyd Apjohn, of Linfield House, co. Limerick, and Rector of Ballybrood, same co., and d. 1894, leaving issue,
1. Daniel James Napier, 88th Connaught Rangers, b. 24 Nov. 1857; d. in India, 25 Oct. 1886.
2. Michael Marshall Charles, b. 18 Nov. 1858; d. 24 May, 1881.
3. CHARLES CALEB COOTE, now of Kilmore.
4. John William Monck, Lieut. R.N., b. 10 Dec. 1861; m. 18 Feb. 1896, Alice Beatrice, dau. of George Atkins, Barrister-at-Law.

Arms—Erminois, a cross couped sa. charged with a mullet arg. on a chief gu. a heron between two crosses-crosslet fitchée of the third. Crest—A demi-eagle displayed gu. wings erminois, in the beak a cross-crosslet fitchée or, on the breast a mullet arg. Mottoes—Quid prodest.

Seats—Kilmore, Nenagh, co. Tipperary; Knocktoran, Knocklong, co. Limerick.

WEBBER OF LEEKFIELD AND KELLAVIL.

WILLIAM DOWNES WEBBER, late of Leekfield, co. Sligo, and now of Kellavil, Queen's Co., and Mitchelstown Castle, co. Cork, J.P. for Queen's Co. and co. Cork, B.A. Trin. Coll. Dublin, *b.* 19 July, 1834; *m.* 29 July, 1873, Anna (who *d.s.p.* 29 Oct. 1909), Countess of Kingston, Lady of the Manor of Mitchelstown, co. Cork, widow of James, 5th Earl of Kingston, and dau. of Matthew Brinkley, of Parsonstown, co. Meath.

Lineage.—MICHAEL WEBBER, of Cork (whose will was proved at the Consistorial Court, Cork, in 1666), had, with other issue, a son, MICHAEL WEBBER, of Cork, whose will was proved 1669. He left by Elizabeth his wife, a son,
 MICHAEL WEBBER, of Cork, *m.* Elizabeth Farmer, and dying 1749, left a son,
 MICHAEL WEBBER, of Glanbane, co. Limerick, *m.* Isabella, dau. of Thomas Wallis, of Curryglass, co. Cork, and had a son,
 THOMAS WEBBER, Capt. of the 4th Horse, *m.* 28 July, 1754, Letitia, dau. of Col. John Irwin, of Tanragoe, co. Sligo, and Susanna Cadden his wife, and was father of
 DANIEL WEBB WEBBER, Q.C., M.P. for Armagh 1816, and Chairman of the Board of Inquiry, *b.* 1757 ; *m.* Sarah Wood, of Leekfield, an heiress, and *d.* 1847, leaving issue,
 1. THOMAS CHARLES, of whom presently.
 2. Charles Tankerville, Barrister-at-Law, Q.C., *b.* 1803 ; *m.* 1834, Lady Adelaide King, 2nd dau. of George, 3rd Earl of Kingston, and by her (who *d.* Aug. 1854) had issue,
  1. George, Col. in the Army, C.B. and Comm. 10th Brigade Depot, co. York, carried the colours at Kimburn, Crimea, 17th Regt. (medals), and served in Ashanti War 1876 (medals and clasps, and C B.), *m.* 1865, Charlotte, eldest dau. of Major W. H. Jeffery, of Newhurst Grange, Richmond, P.Q. He *d.* 1883, and left issue, three daus.,
   (1) Edith Kingston Tankerville.
   (2) Geraldine Fitzgerald, *m.* 28 Dec. 1899, Capt. Walter Evelyn Cramer-Roberts, Norfolk Regt., son of Col. Charles John Cramer-Roberts, and has issue (*see that family*).
   (3) Sybil Frances, *m.* 8 Dec. 1900, Col. Edward S. Lucas-Scudamore, of Castle Shane, co. Monaghan, and Kentchurch Court, co. Hereford, and has issue (*see that family*).
  2. Charles Philip, J.P., of Gerib, co. Sligo, *m.* 18 Feb. 1868, Marian, eldest dau. of James Johnston, D.L., of Magheramena, co. Fermanagh, and *d.* 1894, having had issue,
   Charles Kingston Webber.
  3. Daniel Thomas, Lieut. R.A., *d.* 27 Feb. 1868.
  4. Robert Tankerville, Major late 23rd R. W. Fusiliers, Chief Constable of Flintshire, *b.* 27 Sept. 1845 ; *m.* 28 July, 1871, Isabella, 2nd dau. of the Hon. and Rev. William Wingfield, Vicar of Abbey Leix. He *d.* 4 May, 1909, having had issue,
   (1) James, R.N., *d.* on service, 1903.
   (2) Mervyn Robert Howe, Lieut. Indian Army, *b.* 4 Nov. 1876.
   (3) Arthur, Lieut. 2nd Vol. Batt. Royal Welsh Fus
   (1) Adelaide, *m.* 18 Aug. 1909, Capt. Ambrose Gledstanes, Indian Army, of Fardross, Clogher, co. Tyrone (*see that family*).
   (2) Norah.
   (3) Elizabeth, *m.* 22 Nov. 1911, Capt. George Philip Morris (*see* MORRIS *of Ballinaboy*).

The elder son,
 REV. THOMAS CHARLES WEBBER, of Leekfield, co. Sligo, Rector of Castle McAdam, co. Wicklow, *b.* 1801 ; *m.* 1832, Frances, 2nd dau. of REV. THOMAS KELLY, of Kellyville, Queen's Co., by Elizabeth his wife, dau. of William Tighe, of Woodstock, co. Kilkenny, and grand-dau. of the Right Hon. Thomas Kelly, one of the Judges of the Common Pleas in Ireland, who was a younger son of Edmond Kelly, of Fedane, derived from the Athleague, the senior, branch of the great Irish family of O'KELLY, chiefs of Hymany. She *d.* 1877. He *d.* 1845, leaving issue,
 1. WILLIAM DOWNES, now of Leekfield and Kellavil.
 2. Thomas Wingfield, of Kellavil, Queen's Co., J.P. and D.L., B.A. Trin. Coll. Dublin, late India Forest Dept., *b.* 10 May, 1836 ; *m.* 22 Sept. 1869, Mathilda Emily, 4th dau. of Thomas Barstow, D.L., of Garrow Hill, co. York, and Anne, his wife, dau. of L. Jones, of Fortland and Ardnaree, co. Sligo, and has issue,
  1. Oswald Thomas O'Kelly, Capt. (retired) late R.E., served in Hong Kong and in S. Africa, *b.* 14 July, 1870 ; *m.* 15 April, 1903, Annie Teresa, elder dau. of Trevor Wheler Calverly Rudston, D.L., of Hayton and Allerthorpe Hall, E. R. Yorks. (*see that family*), and has with other issue,

   (1) Evelyn Charles, *b.* 6 Nov. 1904.
   (2) William Rudston, *b.* 27 May, 1907.
  1. Everilda Caroline, *m.* 2 Sept. 1897, George Harold Gibbs, of Ablington Manor, co. Gloucester, and has issue (*see* BURKE's *Peerage*, ALDENHAM, B.).
  2. Alice Mary, *m.* 12 April, 1904, Ralph Algernon Coote, Capt. 17th Lancers, eldest son of Sir Algernon Charles Plumptre Coote, Bart., H.M. Lieut. Queen's Co., of Ballyfin, Queen's Co., and has issue (*see* BURKE's *Peerage*, COOTE, Bart.).
 3. Charles Edmund, C.B., Major-Gen. Royal Engineers, Indian Mutiny, 1857-9 (frequently mentioned in despatches, medal, Central India clasp), Cape 1879, Egypt 1882, and Soudan 1884-5, medals and 3rd class Medjidie, C.B. for services in War, one of the founders of the Institute of Electrical Engineers, *b.* 5 Sept. 1838 ; *m.* 1st, 28 May, 1861, the Hon. Alice Augusta Gertrude Hanbury Tracy, 4th dau. of Thomas Charles, Lord Sudeley, and by her (who *d.* 25 Feb. 1877) has issue,
  1. Evelyn Francis, *d.* 1877.
  2. Raymond Sudeley, *b.* 16 June, 1865, Capt. and Brevet-Maj. Royal Welsh Fusiliers, served in Burmah 1886 (medal), Egypt 1894-8 (medal, 4th class of Medjidie), 4th class Osmanieh, and in S. Africa, 1889-1901 (despatches, brevet, medals), *m.* 31 Dec. 1903, Sybil Aimée Geraldine, dau. of the late Charles Magniac, M.P., and Hon. McMagniac, of Colworth, Beds, and has issue,
   Cynthia Kathleen Augusta, *b.* 8 Nov. 1904.
  3. Henry O'Kelly, of Johannesburg, South Africa, *m.* 26 July, 1900, Mary Margaret, only dau. of Professor E. C. Clark, LL.D., of Newenham House, Cambridge, and has issue, two daus., *b.* 7 March, 1902.
  4. Lionel Hanbury, A.I.M.M., late R.N. Imperial Yeomanry, H.M. Inspector Mines, S.A. (*Club*—Brooks'), *b.* 24 Jan. 1869; *m.* 1909, Lily Battersby, widow of E. Valle Pope, M.A. and has issue,
   Charles Hanbury, *b.* 10 April, 1910.
 He *m.* 2ndly, 1878, Sarah Elizabeth, dau. of John Gunn, late of Purneah, East Indies, and widow of Richard Stainbank.
 4. Francis John, Capt. Royal Scots Fusiliers and Comm. of the Southern Submarine Miners' Headquarters, Gosport, *b.* 1840 ; *m.* 2 April, 1866, Mary Louisa, 2nd dau. of Rev. William Crofton, Rector of Skreen, co. Sligo, and relict of Lieut.-Col. William Heathcote Tottenham, 12th Lancers, and *d.s.p.* 1888.

Arms.—Arg., on a chevron engrailed az. between three hurts as many annulets of the field, in the centre chief point a trefoil slipped vert. *Crest*—A wolf's head couped per pale arg. and gu. charged with an annulet counterchanged. *Motto*—Esperance.

Seats.—Leekfield, co. Sligo ; and Kellavil (Kellyville), Athy, Queen's Co. *Residence*—Mitchelstown Castle, Mitchelstown, co. Cork.

WEIR, late of HALL CRAIG.

GERALD WEIR, *b.* 4 July, 1857, present representative of the WEIRS of Hall Craig.

Lineage.—BALTREDUS DE VERE, who was witness to a charter of King WILLIAM, who *s.* King MALCOLM in 1165, was *s.* by his eldest son,
 WALTER DE VERE, whose son,
 RADULPHUS or RALPH DE VERE *d.* in the end of the reign of ALEXANDER II., leaving a son,
 THOMAS DE VERE, a witness in a charter of a donation to the monastery of Kelso, by Henricus de St. Clau, anno 1266. He was father of
 RICHARDUS DE WERE, mentioned in a donation to the monastery of Kelso, anno 1294 ; his son,
 THOMAS DE WERE, proprietor of the lands and barony of Blackwood, in the shire of Lanark, *d.* in the reign of David Bruce, leaving a son,
 BUAN WERE, who *d.* in the beginning of the reign of King ROBERT III. His son,
 ROTALDUS WERE, of Blackwood, got a charter from Patrick, Abbot of Kelso, dated 1404. He *d.* in the reign of King JAMES II, leaving a son,
 THOMAS WERE, of Blackwood, who was father of
 ROBERT VEVR, of Blackwood, who got a charter of confirmation from Robert, Abbot of Kelso, dated 1479, and *d.* soon after. His son,
 THOMAS WEIR, of Blackwood, *d.* in the beginning of the reign of Queen MARY, leaving by his wife Ægidia, dau. of John, 3rd Lord Somerset, a son,
 JAMES WEIR, of Blackwood, who lived to a great age, and *d.* anno 1595. By his wife Eupheam Hamilton, he had issue,
 1. James, *m.* Mariotte Ramsay, dau. of George, Lord Dalhousie, and was ancestor of the Veres of Craigie Hall and Blackwood.
 2. William, of Stanebyres. 3. ROBERT, of whom we treat.
 4. John. of Pownell.

The 3rd son,
 ROBERT WEIR, of Craighead, on the river Clyde, sold or assigned his estate about 1610, and settled at Monaghan (now called Hall Craig), co. Fermanagh : *m.* a sister of Sir David Lindsay, and *d.* 1633, having by her had issue,
 ALEXANDER WEIR, who *d.v.p.* 1632. He *m.* 1614, Anne, dau. of Sir John Dunbar, of Derrygonelly, co. Fermanagh, by whom he had issue.

1. John, who fell in the civil wars of 1641.
2. ALEXANDER, of Hall Craig.
1. Jane; and two other daus.

The younger son,
ALEXANDER WEIR, of Hall Craig, fought in the battle of Worcester 1651. In Nov. 1688, he raised, jointly with James, son of Sir John Hume, an independent troop of Horse in support of the Prince of Orange, and (Mr. Hume having d.) routed a party of King JAMES's adherents at Ballyshannon, in June, 1689, and had part in the victory of Newtown Butler; after this he was slain at Boyle, and was there bur. within the Abbey; a monument was erected by Lord Kingston on the spot where he fell at Poherboy. By Sarah Goodwin his wife, he had issue John, who d. young, and
ROBERT WEIR, of Hall Craig, b. 1676; fought at the battle of the Boyne, and at Athlone, Aghrim, and Limerick, and d. 1743. He m. Anne, dau. of Capt. Christopher Carleton, of Market Hill, co. Fermanagh, by whom he had, with several younger children (from one of whom has descended a branch that settled in co. Sligo, and is represented there by the Weirs of Lake View, near Boyle), a son,
ALEXANDER WEIR, of Hall Craig, Capt. in the Fermanagh Militia in 1745; m. 1745, Barbara, dau. of John Crozier, of Magheradunbar, co. Fermanagh, and by her (who d. April, 1779) had issue,
1. JOHN, of Hall Craig.
2. John, Lieut. 43rd Foot, A.D.C. to H.R.H. the Duke of York, nominated one of the esquires to Sir Guy Carleton, upon his installation to the Knighthood of the Bath 1779. He afterwards served in the American War, where (having lost a leg) he d. as Capt. in the 41st Regt. of Invalids in 1811.
1. Barbara, m. Aug. 1776, John Johnston, of Brookhill, co. Leitrim.

Mr. Weir d. Oct. 1784, and was bur. with his wife at Devenish Church. He was s. by his elder son,
ROBERT WEIR, of Hall Craig, J.P. and D.L. co. Fermanagh, and served as High Sheriff 1796, m. July, 1779, Mary, dau. of Thomas Rynd, of Ballywhillin, co. Fermanagh, and by her had (with five other daus.),
1. JOHN, of Hall Craig.
2. Alexander.
1. Mary, m. John Phillips, of Edstone, Stratford-on-Avon, who d. Jan. 1836, leaving two daus., the eldest of whom m. Darwin Galton, son and heir of Samuel Tertius Galton, of Duddeston House, co. Warwick, by Frances Anne Violetta his wife, dau. of Dr. Erasmus Darwin, equally celebrated as a physician and a poet.

Mr. Weir d. 1818, and was s. by his son,
JOHN WEIR, of Hall Craig, m. Caroline Mary, dau. of John Chomley, of Belcamp, co. Dublin, and had, with other issue,
1. Robert, J.P. co. Fermanagh, Lieut. Fermanagh Militia, b. 1822; m. 14 July, 1857, Wilhelmina, dau. and eventual heir of John Brien, of Castletown, co. Fermanagh, and d.s.p. 6 Dec. 1857.
2. John (Rev.), Vicar of Little Horkesley, Essex, b. 6 Oct. 1825; m. 30 July, 1856, Clara Sophia, dau. of Major George Sadler, West Essex Militia, of Horkesley Grove, near Colchester, and d. 24 Nov. 1896, leaving issue,
1. GERALD, present representative.
2. John, b. 18 June, 1859.
3. Robert Darwin, b. 5 Jan. 1861; d. 8 Oct. 1874.
4. Alexander Harcourt, b. 7 Dec. 1862; lost at sea 10 Oct. 1883.
5. Harry, b. 18 Feb. 1865.
6. Octavius, of Valley House, Stratford St. Mary, Suffolk, b. 20 Sept. 1870; m. 26 April, 1897, Flora, dau. of the late Rev. Henry Collison, Rector of East Bilney, Norfolk, and has issue,
(1) Terence John Collison, b. 14 Sept. 1898.
(1) Enid Monica Collison.
(2) Brenda Mary Collison.
(3) Bryda Hope Collison.
7. Thomas Lindsay, b. 28 Nov. 1872.
8. Edmund Palmer, b. 22 Sept. 1878; d. unm. 21 Jan. 1903.
1. Clara Louisa, b. 21 June, 1867.
2. Ella Caroline, b. 1 April, 1869; m. 10 Nov. 1908, The Rev. F. H. Lang, 3rd son of the late Rev. R. Lang, of Old Warden, and has issue.
3. Mary, b. 21 May, 1874; m. 1st, 15 Nov. 1893, George Campbell, eldest son of Sir George Campbell, K.C.S.I., and 2ndly, Major L. Nicholson, 8th King's Regt.
3. Alexander, of Kaiapoi, New Zealand, b. 1832; d. 4 Aug. 1910.
4. Henry, b. 1834; m. Mary Jane, dau. of Thomas Barrett, and d. 20 Dec. 1883, leaving issue.
5. Thomas, of Hall Craig, co. Fermanagh, d. unm. 18 March, 1896.
6. Edmund Malone (Rev.), Rector of Tydavnet, co. Monaghan, m. 1st, Isabella, dau. of John Murray, of Marlfield, co. Tipperary, and had issue. He m. 2ndly, Charlotte, dau. of Rev. William S. Burnside, D.D., Chancellor of Clogher, and d. 1886, leaving issue.
1. Mary, m. 3 Oct. 1855, Rev. Loftus Reade, Rector of Devenish, co. Fermanagh.
2. Harriet, d. 16 Sept. 1888.
3. Louisa.
4. Caroline.

CORNWALL-BRADY-HARTSTONGE-WELD, OF RAHINBAWN AND MYSHALL HOUSE.

EDMOND CORNWALL - BRADY - HARTSTONGE - WELD, of Rahinbawn, co. Carlow, J.P., nominated High Sheriff of Carlow for 1893-4, 1901-3, but excused on account of ill-health, b. 1846; m. 1882, GEORGIANA ELIZABETH, now of Myshall House, co. Carlow, elder dau. and only surviving child and heir of John Cornwall Brady, of Myshall House, co. Carlow. Mr. and Mrs. Cornwall-Brady-Hartstonge-Weld have assumed, by Royal Licence, 15 Aug. 1898, the additional names and arms of CORNWALL and BRADY.

Lineage (of WELD)—THE REV. THOMAS WELD, took his degrees at Trin. Coll. Camb. 1613-1618, was Vicar of Terling, Essex, 1624, and was deprived by Laud, then Bishop of London 1632. He went to Boston with his wife, Margaret, and sons, John, Thomas and Edmond, and took a prominent part in the affairs of the New England colonies. He returned to England on State business in 1641, and went to Ireland the following year with Lord Forbe's expedition. In 1649 he became Vicar of Gateshead, Durham, and d. 1661. His 3rd son,
REV. EDMOND WELD, graduated at Harvard 1650, and soon afterwards came to Ireland as a Chaplain in Cromwell's Army. He was at Blarney Castle 1660, and d. 1668. His son,
REV. NATHANIEL WELD, of Dublin, b. 1660; d. 1730, and left among other issue,
1. EDMOND, of whom hereafter.
2. Isaac (Rev.), m. 1736, Anne, dau. of Jonathan Darby, of Leap Castle, King's Co. He was grandfather of Isaac Weld, of Ravenswell, co. Dublin, Vice-President of Royal Dublin Society, and of Charles Richard Weld, of London.

The elder son,
EDMOND WELD, m. Margaret, dau. of Joseph Kane, of Dublin. He, d. 1751, leaving issue,
MATTHEW WELD, m. 1737, Elizabeth, dau. of Nathaniel Kane, of Drumreaske, co. Monaghan (see that family), and d. 1772, leaving issue,
1. EDMOND (afterwards EDMOND WELD - HARTSTONGE), m. Anne, relict of John Agmondisham Vesey, and d. 1815, having had issue, four sons and two daus., who all d. unm.
2. Nathaniel, an officer in the Army.
3. Matthew, Lieut. R.N., of Lodge, co. Carlow.
4. Richard, of Lodge, co. Carlow, Capt. in the Army, m. Hannah, dau. of Thomas Litton, of Oldtown, co. Kildare, and Ballyfirmot, co. Dublin. He d.s.p. 1824.
5. JOSEPH (Rev.), of whom hereafter.
1. Martha, m. Rev. John O'Connor, Prebendary of Castleknock and Clonsilla, Dublin, and Rector of Donoughpatrick, Meath.
2. Esther, m. Right Rev. John Brinkley, Astronomer Royal of Ireland, Lord Bishop of Cloyne.
3. Elizabeth, m. Rev. Hugh O'Neill, Rector of Chapel Izod, Dublin, and Chaplain to the Forces.
4. Sarah, m. Major Bayley.
5. Margaret, unm.

The 5th son,
THE VEN. JOSEPH WELD, Archdeacon of Ross 1777, m. 1775, Susannah Maria Mann, niece and adopted dau. of the Right Rev. Isaac Mann, D.D., Bishop of Cork and Ross. He d. 1781, having had issue,
1. MATTHEW, of whom hereafter.
1. Anne, m. Rev. Samuel Downing, Rector of Fenagh, Leighlin.
2. Esther, m. Rev. James Adam Ker, Rector of Listerlin, Ossory.

The only son,
MATTHEW WELD, of Lodge, co. Carlow, m. 1810, Mary Izod, dau. of Lorenzo Izod Nickson, of Chapel Izod House, co. Kilkenny. He d. 1832, having had issue,
1. Joseph, m. Isabella, dau. of Capt. James Woodright, of Golah, co. Monaghan, and had issue, with three daus.,
1. Matthew Richard, Ind. Civil Service.
2. Charles James.
2. LORENZO (afterwards Lorenzo Weld Hartstonge), of whom hereafter.
3. Matthew Richard, m. Dora, dau. of Capt. S. J. Ardagh and had issue, with four daus.,
Matthew Richard.
1. Elizabeth, m. Drought Blakely Tarleton (see TARLETON of Killeigh).
2. Mary, m. Arthur Matthew Downing.

The 2nd son,
LORENZO WELD-HARTSTONGE, of Lodge and Rahinbawn, co.

arlow, assumed by Royal Licence 19 Dec. 1849, the additional ame and arms of HARTSTONGE on inheriting the property of the /eld-Hartstonge family, b. 1812; m. 1839, Elizabeth Charlotte etavlere, eldest dau. of Thomas Litton, of Ballyfermot, co. Dublin, nd 70, St. Stephen's Green, Dublin. She d. 1887. He d. 1880, ;aving issue,
1. EDMOND, now of Rahinbawn.
2. Lorenzo (Rev.) M.A., Rector of Farley Chamberlayne, Hants, b. 1856; m. 1900, Edith Mary, eldest dau. of Evans Charles Johnson, of Burgage, co. Carlow, late Madras Civil Service, and has issue,
 1. Lorenzo Charles Edmond, b. 1902.
 1. Beatrix Elizabeth Eveleen.
 2. Edith Agnes, d. an infant.

Lineage (of BRADY).—HUGH BRADY, first Bishop of Meath after the Reformation, and P.C. Ireland. The Bishop m. 1st, Anne, dau. of — Irby. She d.s.p. He m. 2ndly, Alice, dau. of Robert Weston, Lord Chancellor of Ireland, and d. 1584, leaving a son,
 LUKE BRADY, m. 1621, Agnes Evans, and had a son,
 LUKE BRADY, b. 1623, matriculated Trin. Coll. Dublin, 19 May, 1640, who left a son,
 HENRY BRADY, of Raheens, co. Clare, and Tongrany, m. his cousin, Miss Brady, and had with other issue a younger son,
 HUGH BRADY, of Kilkony, co. Galway, whose will, dated 5 Feb 1732-3, was proved 19 Nov. 1748. He m. Dilliana, dau. of Henry van Cruyskersken, of Limerick, who was of Dutch descent. They had issue,
1. HENRY, of whom next.
1. Olivia. 2. Catherine, m. Sargent.
The only son,
 HENRY BRADY, of Kilcorney and Bemskea, co. Galway, whose will dated 14 March, 1760, was proved 16 March, 1770, m. Mary, dau. of James Molony, of Kiltanon and Cragg, co. Clare (see that family), by whom he had issue,
1. HUGH, of whom next.
2. William, of Williamstadt, Mountshannon, co. Clare, who d. 14 Sept. 1790, having had issue by his wife Harriott (who re-m. William Apjohn),
 1. Henry, d. unm. 15 Jan. 1815.
 2. William, of Williamstadt, m. 16 Nov. 1806, a dau. of Edmond Power, of Waterpark, and d. Aug. 1817, leaving issue,
  Mary, m. 30 Nov. 1833, Dr. Francis Cornelius Sampson.
3. James.
1. Olivia, d. 2 Aug. 1803, having m., as his 2nd wife, Cornelius O'Callaghan, of Kilgorey, co. Clare, who d. 29 Nov. 1793, and by whom she had issue,
2. Mary, m. her cousin John Brady, of Bellfield, co. Clare, who d. 21 Jan. 1809. She d. 16 Aug. 1814, having had issue.
3. Dilliana, who d. 20 June, 1806, having m. (mar. sett. 4 July, 1771) her cousin John Molony, of Cragg (see that family), and had issue.
The eldest son,
 HUGH BRADY, of Limerick, High Sheriff of that City 1782, d. 27 April, 1803, having m. Eliza Beauchamp by whom he had issue,
1. HENRY, who is his father.
2. John, Capt. 93rd Regt., killed in a duel at Martinique 27 June, 1796.
3. Hugh, Capt. 57th Regt. and 21st Light Dragoons, m. 27 Nov. 1800, Barbara, dau of Gibbon FitzGibbons, of Ballyseoda, co. Limerick, and d. 17 Feb. 1819, leaving issue,
  Barbara, d. Feb. 1834, having m. Hugh Frederick Finch, of Maryville (see FINCH of Tullamore Park), by whom she had issue.
1. Mary, m. 1 Dec. 1790, Edward D'Alton Singleton, of Ballygrenan and Quinville, who d. 6 Oct. 1814. She d. 29 April, 1835, leaving issue (see SINGLETON of Quinville Abbey).
2. Dilliana, m. 13 June, 1795, John Daxon, of Strasburg, co. Clare, who d. June, 1809, and by whom she had issue.
The eldest son,
 HENRY BRADY, of Limerick, m. 4 Aug. 1791, Sarah, dau. of John Pearson, of Clondalkin. He d. 12 Dec. 1802. She d. Nov. 1813. They had issue.
1. Hugh, b. 1795, d. 1807.
2. JOHN CORNWALL, of whom presently.
1. Jane, m. 1810, her cousin Major John Cornwall, of Myshall, co. Carlow, and d.s.p.
2. Eliza, m. 4 Sept. 1817, Sir Francis Ford, 2nd bart. He d. 13 April, 1839. She d. 29 May, 1875, leaving issue (see BURKE'S Peerage).
3. Sarah, d. young, 1816.
The 2nd son,
 JOHN BEAUCHAMP BRADY, of Myshall House, co. Carlow, J.P., High Sheriff 1853. b. July, 1797; m. 28 Dec. 1825, Jane Harriet, 3rd dau. of Sir Rupert George, Bart. She d. Feb. 1842. He d. 6 Jan. 1874, having had issue,
1. JOHN CORNWALL, of whom presently.
2. Henry Beauchamp, b. 25 July, 1828; m. 1861, Frances Louisa, dau. of Adolphus von Hinüber, and d. 3 May, 1872 leaving issue.
3. Rupert George, b. 1831; d. 16 Jan. 1873.
1. Frances, m. 28 July, 1853, John Frederick Lecky, D.L., of Ballykealy, only son of John James Lecky, D.L. of Ballykealy, co. Carlow, and had issue (see that family).
The eldest son,
 JOHN CORNWALL BRADY, of Myshall, J.P., High Sheriff co. Carlow 1870. b. March, 1827; m. Oct. 1853, Elizabeth Susan, youngest dau. of Thomas Henry Watson, of Lumclone, co. Carlow. She d. 25 Sept. 1902. He d. 27 Dec. 1897, having had issue,
 1. John Beauchamp, b. 1855, d. 1885.

I.L.G.

2. Thomas Henry Cornwall, b. 1857, d. an infant.
3. Rupert George Inglis, b. 1859; d. 1896; m. 14 Feb. 1888, Mary Louisa, dau. of Robert Watson, of Ballydarton, co. Carlow, and had one dau., Mona, b. 5 Nov. 1890. His widow m. 2ndly, 1899, Hon. Ralph Bowyer Norton, eldest son of the 2nd Baron Norton (see BURKE'S Peerage, NORTON, B.).
1. GEORGIANA ELIZABETH, now of Myshall.
2. Florence Clare, d. unm. 1898.

Arms—Quarterly 1 and 4 grandquarters quarterly 1st and 4th vert a fesse nebuly erm. between two crescents in chief arg. and a trefoi slipped in base or (WELD); 2nd and 3rd per chevron invected or and sa. in chief three pellets and in base a stag trippant of the first (HARTSTONGE). 2nd and 3rd grandquarters quarterly 1st and 4th arg. a saltire engrailed or between four doves arg. on a chief gu., three dishes each holding a boar's head couped all of the second (BRADY); 2nd and 3rd arg. a lion rampant gu. crowned or within a bordure engrailed sa. bezantée (CORNWALL). **Crests**—1. (WELD)— A wyvern displayed vert. 2. (HARTSTONGE)—A demi savage, ppr. on his head a cap arg. holding in his dexter hand a sword, point downwards, ppr. hilted or, and in his sinister hand a battleaxe or, hilt ppr. Motto over this crest, Sub libertate quietem. **Motto**— Verum atque decens.

Seats—Myshall House, Myshall, and Rahinbawn, co. Carlow. Residence—Bruff Lodge, Parkstone, Dorset.

WELDON. See BURKE'S PEERAGE, WELDON, Bart.

PENROSE-WELSTED OF BALLYWALTER.

REV. SAMUEL PENROSE-WELSTED, of Shandangan and Ballywalter, co. Cork, M.A. Oxon., Incumbent of Rincurran, co. Cork, since 1890, b. 1829; m. 1857, Mary Elizabeth (who d. 1904) dau. of Henry Davies O'Callaghan, of Nadrid, co. Cork, J.P., and has issue,
1. SAMUEL QUAYLE, b. 1861; m. 1888, Eleanor Grace, dau. of Rev. Canon Thomas H. Fleming, of Ballinakill, co. Galway, and has issue,
 1. Samuel Richard, Lieut. Royal Irish Regt., b. 1889.
 2. Reginald Hugh, b. 1891.
2. Harry Hugh, b. 1862; m. 1889, Mary Elizabeth, dau. of H. Lewis, and has a son,
  Claude Quayle Lewis.
3. Frank Philip, b. 1864; m. 14 May, 1891, Henrietta Mary, dau. of Very Rev. Philip Tibbs, D.D., Provost of Kilmacduagh and Rector of Ballinasloe.

Lineage (of WELSTED).—THOMAS WELSTEAD obtained, 1667, a grant of lands in cos. Cork and Kerry, under the Act of Settlement, comprising therein the present family estates, in which he was s. by
 JOHN WELSTEAD, m. Mary Wilkinson, of co. Limerick, and by her (who m. 2ndly, William Parker, and 3rdly, Bate French) had issue one son and one dau., Mary, m. John Sullivan. The son,
 JOHN WELSTEAD, of Milbourne, co. Cork, was possessed of the estates 1709. He was b. 1684; m. Catherine, dau. of Capt. John Wakeham, by Catherine his wife, dau. of Henry Pyne, and sister of Sir Richard Pyne, Chief Justice of Ireland, and had one son,
 JOHN WELSTED, of Ballywalter, m. 1st, Miss Thornhill, dau. of Edward Thornhill, of Castlekevin, co. Cork, and had by her two daus (one m. Edward Norcott, and the other — Dease) and two sons,
1. QUAYLE, of whom presently.
2. William Welsted, m. his cousin, Miss Thornhill, and left issue, an only dau.
Mr. Welsted m. 2ndly, Mary, 2nd dau. of William Philpot, of Dromagh Castle, co. Cork, and had an only son,
3. Nicholas Boyle, m. Miss Whitestone, and had issue.
The eldest son,
 QUAYLE WELSTED, of Ballywalter, m. Barbara, dau. of George Foott, of Milford, by Julian his wife, dau. of Cornelius O'Callaghan, of Dromskeley, co. Cork, and had issue (besides three daus., Frances, m. 1782, Cornelius O'Callaghan; Harriett, m. David Murphy, of co. Kerry; and Charlotte, d. unm.) an only son,
 JOHN WELSTED, of Ballywalter, m. 11 Jan. 1791, Bridget, dau. of John Hawkes, of Sirmount, co. Cork, and had issue,
1. Quayle, d. unm. 2. RICHARD, late of Ballywalter.
1. Bridget, m. Devonsher Penrose. 2. Barbara.
3. Mary Anne. 4. Frances, m. Eyre Coote Croker.
5. SARAH, m. 1st, Samuel Penrose, and 2ndly, Hugh Lawton, and had issue (see below).
The 2nd son,
 RICHARD WELSTED, of Ballywalter, co. Cork, J.P., b. 10 Dec. 1806; m. 28 May, 1835, Honoria Sarah, eldest dau. of George Sandes, of Dunowen, co. Cork, d.s.p. Oct. 1896, and was s. by his nephew, REV. SAMUEL PENROSE (see below).

Lineage (of PENROSE).—The family of PENROSE of Penrose, in Cornwall, and Alverton, Whildrake, in Yorkshire, was descended, according to a pedigree in the British Museum, beginning about 1350, from Barnard Penrose, of Methela, in Cornwall, whose great-great-great-grandson, Richard Penrose, was Sheriff of Cornwall 1525, and d. 1539, from whom descended Thomas Penrose, who signed the Visitation 1620. The Penrose family went from England to Ireland at an early period; one branch settled in Waterford, the other in co. Wicklow.

3 B

West. THE LANDED GENTRY. 754

RICHARD PENROSE, of Ballycane, co. Wicklow, b. 1630, m. Anne, dau. of John Story, of Churchtown, co. Dublin, and left issue, a son, WILLIAM PENROSE, of Waterford, b. 1676; m. 1701, Margaret, dau. of John Godfrey, of Waterford, and d. about 1746 (will dated 1745, proved 1746), leaving issue,
1. John, b. 1706; m. 12 Aug. 1732, the dau. of Edward Cooper, of Cooper's Hill (formerly Sragh), Queen's Co., by Ann his wife, dau. of John Inglefield, of Dublin, and had issue,
  1. Cooper, b. 1736, m. Elizabeth, dau. of John Denniss, of Cork, by Sarah his wife, dau. of Thomas Newenham, of Maryborough, co. Cork, and had issue, James, of Woodhill, Cork, m. 12 July, 1794, Louisa Pettitot, eldest dau. of Robert Uniacke-Fitzgerald, of Corkbeg and Lisquinlan, co. Cork, M.P., and sister and heir of Lieut.-Col. Robert Uniacke-Fitzgerald, and d. 19 April, 1845, having by her (who d. 28 Oct. 1854) had issue (see PENROSE of Wood Hill, and BURKE'S Peerage and Baronetage, PENROSE-FITZGERALD, Bart.).
  2. William.
    1. Anne, m. Richard Pike, of Cork.
  2. SAMUEL, of whom presently.
  3. Francis, b. 1710, m. Susanna, dau. of John Pim, and had issue,
    1. John.
    2. Thomas, m. Oct. 1782, Jane Spiller Thomas.
    3. William, m. and had issue.
      1. Mary, m. Thomas Barcroft.
      2. Elizabeth, m. — Cherry.
  1. Elizabeth, m. Joseph Boyle, of Cork.
The 2nd son,
SAMUEL PENROSE, of John's Gate, Waterford, b. 1708; m. 1749, Anne, dau. of Thomas Beale, of Cork, and d. about 1765 (will dated 9 Jan. 1764, proved 10 May, 1765), leaving issue,
1. SAMUEL, of whom presently.
2. William, b. 1758; m. 1st, Margaret, dau. of George Randall, of Barnhill, co. Cork, and had issue,
  1. Samuel, b. 1782; m. Elizabeth, dau. of Richard Sparrow, of Oaklands, d. 1811, having by her (who m. 2ndly, 1814, Sir Richard Keane, Bart. of Cappoquin, co. Waterford, and d. 1842, leaving an only son (see PENROSE of Lehane),
    2. George, b. 1785; d.s.p.   3. John, b. 1787; d.s.p.
    1. Elizabeth, b. 1780; d. unm.   2. Anne, b. 1781; d. unm.
    3. Maria, b. 1783; m. — Jacob, and d.s.p.
    4. Margaret, b. 1788; d. unm.
He m. 2ndly, Feb. 1790, Anne, dau. of Jacob Goff, of Horetown co. Wexford (see that family), and Elizabeth his wife, and by her had issue,
  4. William Henry, b. 1791; d. in infancy.
  5. Jacob, of Adelphi, Waterford, and Seaville, Tramore, co. Waterford, Capt. 33rd Regt. Waterford Light Infantry Militia, b. 1792; m. 1826, Sarah Anne, dau. of Robert Cooke, of Waterford, and had issue,
    (1) Robert William Henry, of Riverview, Ferrybank (see PENROSE of Riverview).
    (2) Henry, b. 1830; d. unm. 1860.   (3) Jacob, b. 1831; d. 1868,
    (1) Anne, d. 1881.   (2) Maria, d. 1894.
  6. Henry, b. 1794; d. unm. 1826.
  1. Anne.
The elder son,
SAMUEL PENROSE, b. 1754; m. 1775, Mary, dau. of George Randall, of Barnhill, co. Cork, by Margaret his wife, dau. of Abraham Devonsher, of Kilshanick, and d. 1812, leaving issue,
1. SAMUEL, of whom presently.
2. George Randall, b. 1777; m. about 1818, Margaret, dau. of Samuel Pim, of Waterford, and d. 1864, leaving with other issue, who d. in infancy,
  1. John Pim, b. 1822; m. 1853, —, dau. of — Robinson, and d.s.p. 1889.   2. Devonsher George, b. 1824; d. unm. 1870.
    1. Margaret Maria.
3. Abraham Devonsher, m. Bridget, dau. of John Welsted, of Ballywalter, co. Cork, and had issue.
4. William, of Cork, m. the dau. of Alexander Percy, of Ballinamore, co. Leitrim, and had issue,
  George Devonsher (Sir), b. 1822, Mayor of Cork 1876, Knighted 1876, Sheriff 1884; m. 1st, 1850, Mary (d. 1884), eldest dau. of Keiran Mollov; 2ndly, 1887, Mary Gertrude, dau. of late Jeremiah Dunne, J.P., of 31, Fitzwilliam Square, Dublin. He d. 1902.
    1. Margaret, d. unm.
    2. Elizabeth, m. William Hawkes.   3. Anne.
    4. Sarah, m. Samuel Hawkes.
The eldest son,
SAMUEL PENROSE, of Shandangan, co. Cork, J.P., b. 24 June, 1776; m. June, 1799, Mary, youngest dau. of John Hawkes, of Sirmount, co. Cork, and d. 3 March, 1869, leaving issue,
1. SAMUEL, of whom presently.
2. John, b 1805; m. Hester, dau. of Thomas Gollock, of Elmglyn, and d.s.p.
  1. Bridget, m. Massy Hutchinson Warren, and d. 9 Dec. 1858, leaving issue, two sons, John and Frederick, both dec.
  2. Mary, d. unm.
The elder son,
SAMUEL PENROSE, b. 1804; m. 1827, Sarah, dau. of John Welsted, of Ballywalter, co. Cork (see above), and had issue, a son, SAMUEL, now of Shandangan and Ballywalter; s. 1896, his uncle, Richard Welsted, of Ballywalter.

Seats—Shandangan and Ballywalter, co. Cork. *Residence*—The Cottage, Scilly Kinsale, co. Cork.

WEST OF WHITE PARK.

ERSKINE EYRE WEST, Barrister-at-Law, of the King's Inns, Dublin, late Capt. Londonderry R.G.A., b. 19 May, 1868; m. 3 Aug. 1899, Annette Aileen Maude, elder dau. of Cuthbert Henry Cooke Huddart, B.A., M.B., Trin. Coll. Dublin, of Shoyswell Manor, Sussex, and Brynkir, co. Carnarvon (see HUNT of Danesfort), and has issue,
1. AUGUSTUS CUTHBERT ERSKINE, b. 29 July, 1900.
2. Dudley Somerset Erskine, b. 19 May, 1904.

Lineage.—GEORGE WEST, of Blessington, co. Wicklow, b. Aug. 1716, leaving by his wife Jane, with other issue a son, JACOB WEST, of Quinsborough, and Hutton-Read, co. Kildare, bapt. at Blessington 5 Sept. 1703; m. Mary dau. of Matthew Pretious, of Quinsborough, and Purefoy's Place, co. Kildare, and had issue,
1. Pretious, settled in London.
2. John, of Dublin, m. 21 April, 1763, Elizabeth Austin, and had issue.
3. MATTHEW, of whom presently.
The youngest son,
MATTHEW WEST, of Dublin, b. 2 July, 1747; m. 26 Aug. 1770, Mary Ann, dau. of Thomas Roan, of Kildare. She d. 21 Feb. 1781. He d. 29 Jan. 1806, leaving with other issue,
1. Jacob West, of Loughlinstown House, co. Dublin, High Sheriff for Dublin 1813-14, Alderman 29 Oct. 1821, Lord Mayor 1829, Capt. in the Dublin Yeomanry, b. 11 Sept. 1772; m. 26 June, 1801, Sarah, dau. of William Fry, of Dublin, and d. 17 March, 1859, having had issue,
  1. William, M.B. Trin. Coll. Dublin, Fellow K. and Q. Coll. of Physicians, b. 7 Feb. 1803; m. 17 Sept. 1829, Belinda Annabella Hickman, and d. 8 Oct. 1837, leaving issue,
    (1) William (Rev.), B.A. Trin. Coll. Dublin, formerly Rector of Nairn, N.B., and of Rendlesham, Suffolk, b. 21 March, 1831; m. 16 Sept. 1856, Alice Cordelia, dau. of Robert Mallet, F.R.S., of Dublin, and has issue,
      1. William Wilfrid, b. 8 Nov. 1857.
      2. Francis Robert Leighton, of Waterloo, Liverpool, b. 23 July, 1859; m. 4 May, 1887, Florence Alice, dau. of Archibald Hamilton Jacob, M.D., of Dublin, and has issue,
        a. Reginald Francis, of Trin. Coll. Dublin, b. 29 June, 1891.
        b. Robert Douglas, b. 22 April, 1893.
        c. Gerald Archibald, b. 7 Sept. 1903.
        a. Muriel Winifred.
        b. Constance Rachel.
      3. Frederick Malcolm, b. 26 Feb. 1862.
      4. Arthur Gerald, b. 26 Nov. 1863; m. Nov. 1891, Maud Medora Martin, and has issue,
        Foster, b. 20 Aug. 1892.
        Garnet.
      5. John Henry, b. 10 May, 1878; m. 20 June, 1908, Edith Robertson, and has issue,
        Geoffrey, b. 15 Jan. 1911.
        1. Constance Geraldine, m. 15 April, 1890, Capt. Robert Reynolds, R.N.R., and has issue.
        2. Amy Lilian.
    (2) Augustus, b. Aug. 1835, d. unm.
    (3) Edward William, Col. Bombay Staff Corps, Asst. Political Agent for Kolapore and Southern Mahratta, b. 23 March, 1838; m. 23 March, 1867, Charlotte (who d. 18 Jan. 1911), dau. of George Maxwell, of Broomholm, Dumfries, and d. at Naples, 23 Dec. 1885, leaving issue surviving,
      1. George William Maxwell, 27th Inniskillings and 3rd Gurkhas, b. 18 Jan. 1868; m. 10 Sept. 1895, Catherine Janet, dau. of William Gibson, and fell in action in Chitral 13 Dec. 1897, leaving issue,
        Edward Maxwell, b. 10 June, 1896.
      1. Ethel Rose, m. 14 Sept. 1895, Baron Theodor Von Kranc, of the Prussian Hussars. He d.s.p. 1 Nov. 1896.
      2. Lilian Maxwell, m. 16 Feb. 1901, William Wallach, of Allahabad, Barrister-at-Law, and has issue.
      3. Rediviva Maxwell, m. 30 April, 1902, Lieut.-Col. Ferdinand Von Kaltenborn, of the Military Cabinet and General Staff, Vienna.
    (1) Sarah Frances, m. 1856, William Henry James, M.D., and with her husband d.s.p. during the Indian Mutiny 1857.
    (2) Emily, m. Harley Langley, Surgeon-Col. Indian Army, and d. 7 Nov. 1906, leaving issue.
  2. James West, of Shanganagh Grove, co. Dublin, High Sheriff for Dublin in 1856, b. 11 June, 1805; m. 1st, 2 Sept. 1829, Brillianna, dau. of John Clarke, of Willfield, co. Dublin, and by her (who d. 3 July, 1851), had with numerous other issue, who d. young,
    (1) William Henry, of Farmley, Ferns, co. Wexford, b. 25 Dec. 1846; m. 15 July, 1869, Jane, only dau. of William Bolton, of the Island, co. Wexford, J.P., D.L., and has issue an only child,
      Susan Ismay, m. 26 Jan. 1892, Capt. Henry James Lermitte, Royal Scots Fusiliers (see LERMITTE of Knightons), and has issue.
    (1) Jauet Alice, m. 2 Sept. 1868, Major Robert Callwell Smith, Royal Artillery, and had issue.
  Mr. James West m. 2ndly, 1852, Ismenia Euphemia Catherine, (who d. 2 March, 1890), dau. of Major Edward Archer Langley, 3rd Madras Cavalry, and widow of Stamford Watson, 5th Madras Cavalry, and d. 6 Oct. 1868, leaving further issue,

(2) Langley Archer, of Mount Offaly, Greystones, co. Wicklow, b. 15 June, 1853; m. 18 Aug. 1880, Caroline Lydia, dau. of William Beauchamp Clayton, and has had issue,
  1. Archer Beauchamp, b. 8 June, 1881, Capt. Royal Munster Fusiliers.
  2. Cecil Harley L'Estrange, b. 20 Nov. 1890, Royal Dublin Fusiliers.
  3. Herbert Kenelm, b. 23 July, 1892.
  1. Ismé Ada, b. 15 July, 1882 ; d. Dec. 1897.
3. George West, M.D., of London, b. 19 Aug. 1806 ; m. Sarah Jeffs, and had issue, a dau., dec. unm.
4. Henry West, of Loughlinstown House, co. Dublin, Q.C. and County Court Judge, b. 21 April, 1809 ; m. 3 Aug. 1854, Charlotte Anastasia, dau. and co-heir of Denis Henry Kelly, of Castle Kelly, co. Roscommon, J.P., D.L., M.P. for co. Roscommon, and by her (who d. 14 May, 1859) had issue,
  (1) Henry Seton, of Loughlinstown House, co. Dublin, b. 1855 ; d. unm. Feb. 1899.
  (1) Julie Mary. m. 29 April, 1885, Frederic William Soames, of Bryn Estyn, Wrexham, co. Denbigh, and has issue.
Mr. Henry West m. 2ndly, 23 Oct. 1862, Harriette Elizabeth, dau. of Rev. John Trench (vide BURKE's Peerage, CLANCARTY, E.), and d. 21 April, 1881, leaving further issue by her, who d. 2 Jan. 1891.
  (2) Ernest Lionel, b. 29 Oct. 1863 ; m. 14 Sept. 1904, Mabel, dau. of Richard Edmondson, Barrister-at-Law, and has issue,
    1. Phyllis Muriel.
    2. Eva Lalage.
  (3) Charles Edward, d. 1871, aged 5.
  (4) John Trench, d. 1871, aged 3.
  (2) Eva Florence, m. 16 Oct. 1886, William George Edward, son of Lord Charles Amelius Hervey (vide BURKE's Peerage, BRISTOL, M.), and has issue.
  (3) Frances Helen, m. 8 April, 1893, Col. Henry William Newton Guinness, C.B., 18th Royal Irish Regt., and has issue.
  (4) Lalage Emily, m. 9 July, 1907, Theophilus Edward Lucas-Clements, of Rathkenny, co. Cavan (see that family).
  (5) Dorothea Maud.
5. Charles Matthew, of Mount Avon and Ballyshemane, co. Wicklow, b. 29 March, 1818 ; m. 1849, Dorothea Aylmer, dau. of — Kempston, and d.s.p. 10 Oct. 1883.
  1. Frances, d. unm.
  2. Amelia, d. unm. 4 Feb. 1826.
  3. Anna Maria, m. 20 July, 1836, Robert Dickenson, Clerk of Peace for the City of Dublin, and had issue.
  4. Louisa, m. 1854, James John Young, of Lissanymore, co. Cavan, and had issue.
  5. Harriett Sarab, m. 1850, Rev. William Bourke, of Heathfield, co. Mayo, and d. July, 1886, leaving issue.
  6. Julia, d. unm. 3 June, 1873.
  7. Charlotte, m. 1851, Rev. James Little, and d.s.p.
2. MATTHEW, of whom presently.
3. James LYSTER, of Fort William, co. Roscommon, b. 27 Feb. 1780 ; m. 23 July, 1805, Margaret, dau. of William Lyster, of Athleague, and widow of Richard Rumbold. She d. 1809. He assumed the name and arms of LYSTER on his marriage, but d.s.p.
  1. Rebecca, m. 3 Nov. 1792, William Henry Archer, High Sheriff for Dublin 1798, Lord Mayor 1812, and d. 12 March, 1808, leaving issue.

The 2nd son,
MATTHEW WEST, of Ederney, co. Fermanagh, and Harcourt Street, Dublin, Alderman of the City of Dublin, High Sheriff 1810-11, Lord Mayor elect for 1821, sometime Ensign 16th Foot, b. 13 March, 1777 ; m. 21 July, 1802, Maria Louisa, younger dau. of Jean Jasper Joly, of Charlemont Mall, co. Dublin, and Carton, co. Kildare. He d. 15 Nov. 1820, leaving issue,
1. Charles Matthew, b. 1803 ; d. unm. 2 May, 1823.
2. Henry Jasper, b. 1804 ; d. unm. 7 July, 1829.
3. WILLIAM JAMES, of whom presently.
4. Augustus William (Very Rev.), M.A. Trin. Coll. Dublin, Dean of Ardagh, Chancellor of Kildare, Minor Canon of St. Patrick's, Domestic Chaplain to the Duke of Leinster, J.P. co. Longford, b. 1813, m. 1842, Lucinda, dau. of Henry Digby Brooke, of Prosperous, co. Kildare, and Coolock House, co. Dublin. She d. 28 April, 1883. He d. 3 March, 1893, having had issue,
  1. Fitzwilliam Henry (Rev.), M.A., LL.D. Dublin, b. 12 March, 1845.
  2. Digby Brooke de Blaisy, of Berryville, Arkansas, U.S.A., late Capt. Longford Rifles, J.P. co. Roscommon, b. 14 June, 1846 ; m. 23 Sept. 1868, Frances Louisa, dau. of John George Swindell, of Kilburn Priory, Middlesex, and d. 13 June, 1902, leaving issue,
    (1) Digby John, b. 22 April, 1871 ; m. Frances, dau. of Maj. Clark, late Confederate Army, and has issue,
      Digby Clark, b. 8 July, 1903.
      Helen Maude, b. 27 Oct. 1900.
    (2) Augustus Sydney Colin, b. 31 Aug. 1874 ; m. Mabel Louise, dau. of John Hicklin, Barrister-at-Law, and has issue,
      Stella May, b. 13 July, 1902.
    (3) William Woodville Guinness, b. 14 Nov. 1875 ; d. 29 May, 1876.
    (4) Charles George Fitzgerald, b. 13 June, 1877.
    (5) Heyrick Cole, b. 13 Aug. 1878.
    (6) Frederick Benjamin, b. 23 Nov. 1879.
    (7) John Francis, b. 9 May, 1882 ; m. 23 Aug. 1903, Rowena, dau. of James Nunllay, and has issue,
      Winifred Carroll, b. 15 July, 1904.
    (8) Herbert Swindell, b. Aug. ; d Sept. 1883.

(1) Frances Augusta Louisa.
(2) Maude Mary Kathleen, d. unm. 10 Sept. 1896.
(3) Lucy Annie, m. 20 July, 1899, Eugene Victor Weir, M.D.
(4) Constance Ellen Oldfield, d. unm. 30 Dec. 1905.
(5) Gladys Ellinor Norman, d. young.
3. John George Claude, b. June, 1848 ; d. unm. 16 March, 1886.
4. Augustus Pakenham Fitzgerald (Rev.), M.A. Dublin, late Capt. Royal Longford Rifles, Vicar of Edwardstone, Boxford, Suffolk, b. 10 Nov. 1853 ; m. 25 Sept. 1889, Nora Stewart, 4th dau. of Major Dugald Stewart Miller, late 7th Royal Fusiliers, and has issue,
  (1) Laura Emily Mary Pakenham.
  (2) Amy Rowena Lucinda Pakenham.
1. Lucy Agnes, m. Aug. 1865, William Carroll, C.E., who d.s.p. 27 July, 1897.
2. Maria Louisa Augusta, m. June, 1872, Capt. Colin Hugh Thomson, of Salruck, Connemara, late 74th Highlanders, eldest surviving son of Gen. Alexander Thomson, C.B., and by him (who d. 24 April, 1905) has had issue.
3. Emily Alice Josephine, m. 2 June, 1877, James Cole Sheane, of The Grange, Queen's Co., and by him (who d. 1884) had issue. She m. 2ndly, April, 1894, Rev. Edward Carl Unmack, Rector of West Horseley, and has issue.
4. Wilhelmina Mary Joly.
5. George White, of Ardenode, co. Kildare, J.P., Barrister-at-Law, M.A. Dublin, b. 1815 ; m. 20 Aug. 1840, Georgiana Grove, dau. of Lieut.-Gen. the Hon. Arthur Grove-Annesley, of Annesgrove, co. Cork (see BURKE's Peerage, ANNESLEY, E.). She d. 7 Jan. 1898. He d. 1860, leaving issue,
  1. Matthew Richard, Col. late Royal (Bengal) Artillery, b. 13 Nov. 1841 ; m. July, 1874, Eveline Augusta, dau. of the late John Lucas, of Walton, co. Leicester, and widow of Capt. W. R. Elliott, 29th Regt., and has issue,
    George Evelyn John Annesley, late Capt. R.F.A., b. 9 May, 1875.
    Violet Augusta, m. 21 June, 1900, Charles Watson Low.
  2. Arthur Annesley, M.D., M. Ch. Dublin, F.R.C.S.I., b. 14 June, 1848 ; m. 1872, Mary E. Parker, and d. 1886, leaving issue,
    (1) George White, b. 1877.
    (2) William Parker, b. 1879.
    (3) Arthur Annesley, b. 1883.
    (1) Elizabeth Charlotte.
    (2) Emily Parker.
  3. George Wolfe, of Lismore, N.S.W., Inspector of the Lands Department, b. 3 Feb. 1853 ; m. 4 Sept. 1883, Alice Dunbar, dau. of John O'Hara, of Orange Grove, Duval, N.S.W., and has issue,
    (1) Arthur O'Hara, b. 23 June, 1885 ; d. 20 Jan. 1886.
    (2) George Annesley, b. 4 Aug. 1888.
    (3) John Cecil Darley, b. 12 Jan. 1899.
    (1) Laurie Annesley.
    (2) Ellen O'Hara.
    (3) Mona Jess.
  4. Charles Henry Darley, b. 9 Oct. 1856 ; d. 21 Jan. 1861.
  5. William Augustus, L.R.C.S.I., L.K.Q.C.P.I., and L.M., b. 24 Nov. 1859 ; m. Amy Taylor, of Terrible Vale, N.S.W., and d. 11 Dec. 1905, leaving issue,
    Arthur Lind Annesley, b. 5 Feb. 1891.
    Gwendoline Lind Annesley.
  1. Elizabeth Charlotte, m. 1860, H. O'H. Moore, B.L., and d.s.p. 1866.
  2. Maria Louisa, m. 1st, 16 April, 1874, Marescoe Lloyd Frederick, R.N., who d. 1886, leaving issue (see BURKE's Peerage). She m. 2ndly, 10 April, 1905, Gladwin Cloves Cave, son of the late Thomas Saunders Cave, of Rossbrin Manor, co. Cork, and d. 12 Oct. 1907.
  3. Emily Alicia, m. 15 April, 1875, William Henry Colley-Grattan, of Farm Hill, Kildare, who left issue,
    4. Georgina Augusta, d. an infant, 1855.
  5. Georgiana Augusta, m. 23 July, 1899, her cousin, John Loftus Bland, D.L., of Blandsfort, Queen's Co., late Capt. 6th Inniskilling Dragoons. He d. 3 Jan. 1908.
  6. Charlotte Henrietta Annesley, d. an infant, 1865.
  7. Lilian Annesley.
  8. Marian Stuart O'Hara, m. 1888, Capt. George Lionel Brackenridge Killick, late 60th Rifles, and has issue.
  9. Evelyn Grattan.
1. Maria Louisa, m. 1829, Henry Darley, of Wingfield, co. Wicklow, and d. 1873, leaving issue (see BURKE's Colonial Gentry).
2. Emily Matilda, m. 1834, Isaac Manders, of Castle Size, Kildare, and d. 28 April, 1841, leaving issue.

The third son,
REV. WILLIAM JAMES WEST, M.A., Dublin, of Ederney, co. Fermanagh, and Balix and Legcloghfin, co. Tyrone, Rector of Delgany, co. Wicklow, b. 9 June, 1809 ; m. 3 Aug. 1838, Elmina, dau. and co-heir of Alexander Erskine, of Balhall, co. Forfar, and Longhaven, co. Aberdeen (see ERSKINE of Dun). She d. 30 Nov. 1886. He d. 22 Oct. 1859, having had issue,
1. William Alexander Erskine WEST-ERSKINE, of Ederney, co. Fermanagh, and Hindmarsh Island, Lake Alexandrina, South Australia, M.L.C., Min. of Public Works 1875-6, M.A. Ch. Ch. Oxon., d. unm. 22 Oct. 1892, having assumed, by Royal Licence, the additional name and arms of ERSKINE (see BURKE's COLONIAL Gentry).
2. AUGUSTUS GEORGE, late of White Park.
3. Henry Matthew (Rev.), M.A. Dublin, of Folly Court, Wokingham, Bucks, late Rector of Templemichael, co. Longford, and of Sacombe, Herts, b. 27 Dec. 1842 ; m. 8 May, 1874, Helen Mary, dau. of Robert Foster Dunlop, of Monasterboice, co. Louth, and has issue,

Westby. THE LANDED GENTRY. 756

1. William Robert, b. 11 April, 1875; d. 27 Feb. 1891.
2. Alexander Henry Delap, Capt. R.H.A., b. 27 Dec. 1877.
3. Harry Erskine, b. 22 Aug. 1879; d. 23 May, 1891.
4. Charles Skeffington, late Sub-Lieut. R.N., b. 22 April, 1886.
1. Anne Elmina Blanche.
2. Helen Susan Dorothea, d. 7 Oct. 1884.
3. Jessie Georgiana Rachel.
4. Kathleen Violet.   5. Eileen Myrtle.

4. Alexander, of Balhall, co. Forfar, B.A., C.E., Dublin, b. 13 June, 1844; m. Oct. 1867, Katherine, dau. of Benjamin Darley, and d. 9 Aug. 1871, leaving issue,
   1. Donald Alexander Erskine, d. an infant.
   1. Evelyn Maude, m. 16 April, 1895, Redmond Reali, and has issue.
   2. Constance Kate, m. 25 July, 1894, Henry Crowe, Barrister-at-Law, B.A. Dublin, son of the late Francis Wainwright Crowe, of Cahircalla, co. Clare.

5. Frederick John, late of Glenelg, S. Australia, b. 10 Aug. 1848; m. 1877, Laura Mary, dau. of Charles Swinden, and d. 1 Sept. 1895, leaving a son,
   William Alfred Augustus, b. 1878.

6. Arthur Fitzgerald, b. 13 May, 1850; d. 6 Feb. 1851.
7. Alfred Edward, of Kilcroney, co. Wicklow, late Lieut. Wicklow Rifles, b. 13 Aug. 1851; m. 24 May, 1877, Florence, dau. of Charles E. Levey, of Cataraqui, Quebec, and has issue,
   1. Cyril Charles, Capt. Black Watch, b. 4 Dec. 1878.
   2. Harold Richard Alfrey, b. 6 May, 1884.
   3. Aubrey Fenton, b. 31 March, 1888.
   1. Hazel Valerie, m. 7 July, 1908, Capt. Herbert Curling Laverton, the Black Watch.
1. Elmina Eliza, d. unm. 27 Aug. 1866.
2. Amelia Louisa (Nina), d. unm. 24 April, 1875.

The 2nd son,
AUGUSTUS GEORGE WEST, of White Park, co. Fermanagh, and of Balix and Legcloghfin, co. Tyrone, late Lieut. 76th Foot, b. 19 Jan. 1841; m. 31 July, 1867, Sara (now of White Park), 4th dau. of Rev. Canon Richard Booth Eyre, of Eyre Court, co. Galway, by his 1st wife, Sarah, dau. of Robert Persse, of Roxborough, J.P., D.L. (see that family). He d. 30 June, 1911, having had issue,
1. ERSKINE EYRE (see above).
2. Augustus William, of Leixlip House, co. Kildare, Assistant Land Commissioner, Ireland, Member Royal Agricultural Coll. Cirencester, b. 5 May, 1871; m. 13 Nov. 1900, Fanny Madeline Jane, only dau. of the late Thomas Hanmer, of Bodnod, co. Denbigh (see BURKE's Peerage, HANMER, Bart.), and widow of Lieut.-Col. George Leonard Thomson, 35th Foot, and has issue,
   1. Denys Maida Hanmer.
   2. Joan Valerie.
3. Dudley Alexander, of Salisbury, Rhodesia, F.R.G.S., Member Royal Agricultural Coll., b. 13 July, 1874; d. unm. at Vera Cruz, Mexico, 26 June, 1904.
4. Richard Annesley, late Lieut. 2nd Kitchener's Fighting Scouts, b. 26 Sept. 1878; m. 16 July, 1909, Maude Ethel, 2nd dau. of Henry William Cushing.
1. Adeline Elizabeth.
2. Sara Elmina Erskine.
3. Georgiana Geraldine de Blaisy.

Arms—Arg., a fesse dancetté between three leopards' faces sa. a crescent qu. for difference. **Crest**—Out of a crest coronet or charged with a crescent as in the arms a gryphon's head arg. **Motto**—Jour de ma vie.
Residence—Shoyswell, Cowper Gardens, Dublin.

WESTBY OF ROEBUCK CASTLE.

FRANCIS VANDELEUR WESTBY, of Roebuck Castle, co. Dublin, and Kilballyowen and Rosroe, co. Clare, J.P. and D.L. co. Clare, High Sheriff 1895, J.P. co. Dublin, b. 15 June, 1859; s. his father 1893; m. 28 Jan. 1888, Janet Louisa, 2nd dau. of George Orme, late of Abbeytown, co. Mayo, and has issue,

1. PERCEVAL ST. GEORGE CHARLES, b. 20 Nov. 1888.
2. Horace William Turner, b. 22 Dec. 1891.
3. Granville Nicholas Francis, b. 18 March, 1894.

Lineage.—The founder of this family, in Ireland, is presumed to have been
THOMAS WESTBY, son of Major Westby, of Rawcliffe, co. Lancaster, who settled in Clonmel. His eldest son, the first authenticated ancestor of the family,
NICHOLAS WESTBY, of Ennis, co. Clare, Collector of the Customs of that port, m. 1698, Frances, dau. of John Stepney, of Durrow, Queen's Co., and acquired, as the marriage portion of his wife, the estate of High Park, co. Wicklow. By her (who d. 29 March, 1732) he left at his decease, 19 Oct. 1716, a dau., Jane, m. Robert Perceval, of Knightsbrooke, co. Meath, and a son,
WILLIAM WESTBY, of High Park, co. Wicklow, b. 3 Nov. 1702; m. 1743, Mary, dau. of Brigadier-Gen. Jones, by Mary, dau. and sole heiress of Richard Neville, of Furnace, co. Kildare, and had issue, with three other daus.,
1. Nicholas, of High Park, b. 28 March, 1751, M.P. for Tulsk, as well as co. Wicklow, served as High Sheriff 177-, and d. unm. 30 Nov. 1800. His will was proved 1801, under which the mansion and estate of High Park passed to the younger of his two surviving brothers.
2. WILLIAM, of whom presently.
3. Edward, Master-in-Chancery in Ireland, b. 11 Sept. 1755, who became of High Park, and served as High Sheriff 1807; m. 1st, 1787, Anne, eldest dau. and co-heiress of Richard Palmer, of Glannacurragh Castle, King's Co., and by her (who d. 22 June, 1791) had issue,
   1. Frances, m. 18 Oct. 1816, Richard Donovan. of Ballymore, co. Wexford.
   2. Mary, m. 1817, Joshua Nunn, of St. Margarets, co. Wexford, Mr. Westby m. 2ndly, Phœbe, 3rd dau. of Richard Palmer, of Glannacurragh Castle, and d. 8 Oct. 1838, having by her,
      1. William Jones, late of High Park, J.P. and D.L., High-Sheriff 1827, b. 23 Nov. 1802; m. 9 June, 1828, Catherine, 2nd dau. of Col. George Grogan, of Seafield, co. Dublin, and by her (who d. 11 Oct. 1882) had issue,
         (1) William Henry, now of High Park, late 66th Regt., b. 3 July, 1831.   (2) Thomas Jones, b. 3 Jan. 1838.
         (1) Maria Palmer.   (2) Anne.
         (3) Jane Malvina.   (4) Isabella Frances.
         (5) Martha, m. 19 July, 1877, Rev. William H. Godfrey, of Parkgariffe, co. Kerry, and d. 1 Feb. 1910, leaving issue (see BURKE's Peerage, GODFREY, Bart.). He d. 1909.
      2. Nicholas Henry Jones, b. 17 July, 1805, a Lieut. in the 2nd Regt. of Foot, and subsequently in the 1st Royal Dragoons; m. and had issue.
      3. Henry Humbertson Jones (Rev.), b. 9 July, 1809, Canon of St. Patrick's and Prebendary of Vagoe; m. 5 March, 1835, Mary Georgina, eldest dau. of Col. Cash, of Belville, co. Dublin, and d. 17 Aug. 1887, having by her (who d. 8 Jan. 1900) had issue.
      3. Martha Jones, d. unm.
      4. Anne Palmer, m. 2 Aug. 1831, Parsons, 5th son of Sir Hugh Crofton, Bart., of Mohill House, co. Leitrim: She d. 12 March, 1884.
      5. Jane Jones, m. 17 Dec. 1831, James Perceval, of Barntown House, co. Wexford, a Major in the Army.
      1. Mary, m. Thomas Browne, of New Grove.

Mr. Westby, High Sheriff co. Wicklow 1733, d. 12 Oct. 1754. His 2nd son,
WILLIAM WESTBY, of Thornhill, co. Dublin, b. 18 June, 1753; m. 1st, 18 April, 1781, Mary, dau. of George Fletcher, of Tottenham, and by her (who d. 17 May, 1797) had issue,
1. NICHOLAS, his heir.
2. George, Lieut. 95th or Rifle Regt., b. 2 June, 1790; killed 5 May, 1811, at Fuentes D'Onore, Spain. He d. unm.
3. Edward, Cornet 2nd North British Dragoons, b. 25 Aug. 1794; killed at Waterloo 18 June, 1815. He d. unm.
1. Mary.   2. Louisa.
3. Wilhelmina, m. Right Hon. Richard Moore, late one of the Justices of the Court of King's Bench in Ireland.

Mr. Westby m. 2ndly, 28 Aug. 1809, Elizabeth, dau. of George Boleyn Whitney, of Newpass, co. Westmeath, but by her had no issue. He d. 5 Nov. 1835. The eldest son,
NICHOLAS WESTBY, of Kilballyowen, co. Clare, and 9, York Gate, Regent's Park, b. 23 Oct. 1787; m. 26 Aug. 1815, the Hon. Emily Susan Valdegrave, eldest dau. of William, late Lord Radstock, and d. 24 Aug. 1860, having had by her (who d. 12 April, 1870),
1. EDWARD PERCEVAL, late of Roebuck Castle.
1. Emily Elizabeth, m. Rev. F. Braithwaite.
2. Erina Laura, d. 1 March, 1834.
3. Caroline Mary, m. 6 Nov. 1861, Rev. George Edward Prescott, Rector of Digswell, Herts, grandson of Sir George William Prescott, Bart., and d. 1895.
4. Louisa Isabella, m. 9 Nov. 1847, Marcus Keane, J.P., of Beech Park, co. Clare (see that family), and d. 3 Oct. 1804. He d. 29 Oct. 1883.
5. Horatio Caroline, m. Lieut.-Col. Baron de Teissier, who d. 17 Aug. 1884. She d. 25 Nov. 1900.

The only son,
EDWARD PERCEVAL WESTBY, of Roebuck Castle, co. Dublin, and Kilballyowen and Rosroe, co. Clare, D.L., High Sheriff 1854; b. 1830; m. 1st, 13 Oct. 1853, Elizabeth Mary, dau. of the late Right Hon. Francis Blackburne, Lord Chancellor of Ireland, and by her (who d. 1863) had issue,
1. William Francis Perceval, b. 17 Nov. 1854; d. 23 June, 1870.
2. FRANCIS VANDELEUR, now of Roebuck Castle.
1. Emily Jane Laura.

Mr. Westby m. 2ndly, 16 June, 1864, Susan Elizabeth, dau. of John Davis Garde, and d. 23 April, 1893. She d. 25 Dec. 1904.

Arms—Quarterly: 1st and 4th arg. on a chevron az., three cinquefoils pierced of the first; 2nd, arg. on a chief indented gu. three cross-crosslets fitchée of the field; 3rd, or three garbs vert, over all in the centre of the shield a mullet also gu. **Crest**—a martlet sa. holding in its beak a stalk of wheat ppr. with three ears or, charged on the breast with a mullet of the last. **Motto**—Nec volenti nec volanti.
Seats—Roebuck Castle, Dundrum, near Dublin; and Kilballyowen, co. Clare. **Club**—Kildare Street, Dublin.

WESTENRA.

See BURKE'S PEERAGE, **ROSSMORE, B.**

WESTROPP OF ATTYFLIN.

JOHN MASSY - WESTROPP, of Doonass and Clonmoney, co. Clare, C.M.G., J.P. co. Limerick, Lieut.-Col. and Hon. Col. 5th late Comm. Batt. Royal Munster Fus., formerly Capt. 12th Lancers, *b.* 28 April, 1860; *m.* 16 June, 1890, Georgina, dau. of Frederick William Kennedy, and has issue,

1. JOHN FRANCIS RALPH, *b.* 6 April, 1891.
2. Ralph Frederick Hugh, *b.* 2 Sept. 1892.

Lineage.—The Westropps appear as living in Northern Lincolnshire in 1277, Thomas, son of Nicholas de Westhorp, and his wife Alicia de Boleby, being defendants in a lawsuit (*Cal. Geneal.* vol. i. p. 245). In 1282, John (son and heir of Edward de Westhorp, and Johan de Manby his wife), was living at Brompton, near Scarborough, and in 1321, William de Westhorp witnessed a charter founding chantries in the chapel of Wickham, near Brompton.

THOMAS DE WESTHORPE, son of the above John Westropp, was executor to the will of Rev. Robert de Plays, of Brompton, in 1345; *m.* a dau. of Thomas Linaker. Their son,

JOHN DE WESTHORPE, of Brompton, *m.* Jane, dau. of John FitzEdmond Thweng (who *d.* 1369, *Inq. p.m.*), of Cornborough, near Sheriffhutton, and eventual heiress of her brother Marmaduke Thweng, of Cornborough (who *d.* 1426). John de Westhorpe and his wife were taxed 1381. He *d.* at Brompton 1430 (will proved at York 9 Jan. 1430). He had issue,

1. WILLIAM, his heir.
2. Anthony, of Whitby.
3. James, *m.* the dau. of Gerard Salvyn.
4. Thomas (Rev.), Rector of Newton, exor. of his father 1430, Member of the Guild of Corpus Christi in York 1444. His will, dated 12 Nov. 1466, was proved at York, 15 June, 1467.

The son and heir,

WILLIAM WESTHORPE, of Brompton, one of a jury that tried a claim of Whitby Abbey to certain lands 1421; *m.* Isabei, dau. of Thomas Wentworth, and had issue, 1. ROBERT, his heir; 2. John, priest of St. Andrew's, Newton, living 1452 (his will dates 19 Dec. 1490, proved Jan. 1491), and three daus., 1. Isabella, wife of Thomas Greene, of Stansale; 2. Johan, wife of Robert Morson, of Babrie; their dau. is legatee in will of Rev. Thomas Westhorp, 1466; and 3. Anna, wife of William Palmes, of Naburne. The elder son,

ROBERT WESTHORPE of Brompton, *m.* Anna Meynell, and had a son,

RICHARD WESTHORPE. *b.* 1456, legatee in wills of Thomas Wytham, 1474, Agnes Thweng 1490, and Robert Witham, 1481; proved his descent from Jane, dau. of John Thweng, and wife of John Westhorp, in 1495 (*Inq. p.m.*) and obtained one third of Cornborough; *d.* 1497 (admon. at York, 6 Oct. 1497), leaving issue by his wife Jane, dau. of John Witham, of Brettonby, co. York (she was blind in 1474). Their son,

RALPH WESTHORPE, Gent., of Brompton and Cornborough, was father of

HUGH WESTROPP, Gent., of Brompton, *m.* 1st, a dau. of John Conyers, of Hutton-on-Wyske. She *d.s.p.*; he *m.* 2ndly, 1522, Jane, 2nd dau. of John Sayer, of Worsall-on-Tees, in whose will, 1530, they are legatees. Hugh Westropp *d.* 1545 (admon. at York, 3 Feb. 1545). They had issue,

1. JAMES, of whom presently.
2. Thomas, Capt. in the Army 1568-89, got a pension from ELIZABETH for the loss of his right arm, and for services in the Irish war, *m.* 1591, Anna, widow of — Gowerley. His will dates 9 April, 1604, proved at York same month; *d.s.p.*, and was bur. at Sutton.
3. Ralph, Serjeant-at-Arms, patent 18 May, 1590; he by his report to the Archbishop of York, saved Clifford Tower, York, from demolition, July, 1596. His will dates 7 June, 1605; *d. unm.* 25 June, 1606, bur. in York Minster, where his tomb long remained.
1. Agnes, *d. unm.* at Marrick, 1606 (will dated 16 May, 1606, proved that month).

The eldest son,

JAMES WESTROPP, of Cornborough, served at his own cost in the wars of the Tudors; his will dates at Darnecome, Brompton, 18 Jan. 1579. He *d.* 1580 and was bur. at Brompton, where his tomb remains. He *m.* 1569, Elizabeth, eldest dau. of Christopher Lepton, of Kepwick. (She *m.* 2ndly, Edward Fairfax). They left issue,

1. Ralph, *d.-young.*
2. WILLIAM, of whom presently.
1. Agnes, *m.* Richard Askwith, of Berowby.
2. Elizabeth, *m.* John Laycock, of Brompton.
3. Isabella, *m.* John Jeffryson.
4. Jane, *m.* William Wasse.

His 2nd son,

WILLIAM WESTROPP, aged 14 at the Visitation of 1586, when his pedigree from John Thweng, 1369, and arms were registered. He *m.* 1595, Elizabeth Witham, and *d.* 1603 (*Inq. p.m.*), leaving issue,

1. Ralph, *b.* Dec. 1599; *d.* 1610 (*Inq. p.m.*).
2. THOMAS, of whom presently.
1. Anne, bapt. Aug. 1598; *d.* before 1606.
2. Elinor, *m.* April, 1612, Sir Richard Osbaldeston, Attorney Gen. in Ireland; and *d.* at Dublin 1 Aug. 1638, leaving issue.
3. Gertrude.
4. Elizabeth.

The 2nd son,

THOMAS WESTROPP, legatee in wills of his grand-uncles 1604, 1606, *s.* his brother in Cornborough; he entered into a bond with Sir Frederick Cornwallis, for bail of John Alured, of Charterhouse, in 1638. His will dates at Newham, co. York, 27 Nov. 1656, proved in London 30 Jan. 1657. He left issue,

1. EDWARD, of Newham, Stainesby, summoned by Sir W. Dugdale, 1665, to register his arms and descent.
2. MONTIFORT, of whom presently.
1. Anna, bapt. at Brompton 9 Aug. 1632; *m.* Symon Peacock.
2. Ellen, *b.* March, 1633; *d.* before Nov. 1656.
3. Elizabeth, left to care of her brother Montifort, 1656.

The 2nd son,

MONTIFORT WESTROPP, executor to his father 1657, in which year he settled at Limerick, Comptroller of its port 18 Feb. 1660, purchased successively, Ballynameau, Kilkerin, in the barony of Clonderlaw, 1671, and Dromline and Bunratty, co. Clare. He was High Sheriff of Clare 1674 and 1698. His horses and arms were confiscated for use of JAMES II., 10 April, 1690. He was one of the Commissioners for Clare by an Act of Irish Parliament 1697. His will, dated at Bunratty, 14 Aug. 1698, was proved at Dublin, 15 Oct. 1698. He *m.* Frances, 2nd dau. of John Taylor, of Ballinort, co. Limerick, by Gertrude his wife, dau. and heiress of Sir Francis Berkeley, of Askeaton, and Catherine his wife, dau. of Adam Loftus, Archbishop of Dublin and Chancellor of Ireland (her will, dated 12 Oct. 1705, was proved at Killaloe, 8 May, 1706). They had issue,

1. JOHN, of Killard, co. Clare, 1688, and Cahirduggan, co. Cork, *m.* and had issue an only child, *m.* (as his 1st wife) Charles Atkins, of Currakerry West (now Fountainville), co. Cork, Sheriff of Limerick in 1694, and *d.s.p.* Mr. Westropp was *s.* at Cahirduggan by his brother Ralph.
2. MONTIFORD, of whom hereafter.
3. Ralph, of Cahirduggan, co. Cork, and Clonmoney, co. Clare [1712], J.P. co. Cork, to which he *s.* on the decease of his eldest brother, John, without surviving issue. He *m.* Aug. 1701, Hanna, dau. of Randall Roberts, of Britfieldstown, co. Cork. His will, dated 17 Oct. 1735, was proved April, 1741. He had issue, with three daus. (Martha, *m.* 1733, Randal Roberts, of Britfieldstown; Hannah, *m.* Rev. Cecil Westropp; and Anne, *m.* 1721, John Watkins), five sons,

1. JOHN, of Limenehane (Maryfort), co. Clare, J.P. 1730, High Sheriff co. Clare 1744; *m.* 1728, Jane, eldest dau. of Thomas Roberts, of Britfieldstown, and *d.* 1780 (M.I. at Tulla), leaving issue,

(1) RALPH, of Lismehane, of whom hereafter as successor to Attyflin, at the death of his cousin John, 1781.

(1) Hannah, *m.* 1748, Harrison Ross Lewin, of Fortfergus, co. Clare.

(2) Anne, *m.* 1752, Edmund Morony, of Milltown Malbay, co. Clare, and *d.* 31 July, 1764 (M.I. at Tulla).

2. Robert, of Fort Anne, High Sheriff co. Clare 1746, *m.* 1737, his cousin, Elizabeth, dau. of Poole Hickman, of Kilmore, and *d.* 1776, having had issue,

(1) POOLE, of Fort Anne, J.P. 1770, High Sheriff 1776, Capt. Royal Regt. of Artillery in Ireland, *m.* 1767, Mary, dau. of Henry Hickman, of Kilmore, and *d.* 1803, having by her (who *d.* 1836) had issue,

1. Thomas, *d.s.p.*

2. Robert, of Fort Anne, High Sheriff co. Clare 1804, *m.* 1798, Dorcas, dau. of John Keily, of Strancally Castle, co. Waterford, and *d.* 1826, having had issue,

a. Poole, *d. young.*

b. JOHN, of Fort Anne, J.P., *m.* 1828, Maria, dau. of Francis Macnamara, of Arran View, co. Clare, and *d.* 1850, having by her (who *d.* 1879) had issue,

(*a*) Robert Macnamara, of Fort Anne, J.P., *d.s.p.* 1857.

(*b*) Francis Macnamara, of Fort Anne, J.P., Major Clare Militia, *d.s.p.* July, 1874.

(*c*) John Townsend, *d.s.p.* 1872.

(*d*) William Nugent, *b.* 1838; *m.* 1880, Mary Molony, dau. of Donough Sampson of Garruragh and *d.* Aug. 1893, leaving a son,

Francis Sampson, *b.* Aug. 1881; *m.* 10 April, 1909, Caroline Grace Bolton, of Fairfield.

(*e*) Arthur George, *d.s.p.* April 1878.

(*a*) Dorcas, *m.* John Harrison Moreland, J.P., of Raheen Manor, co. Clare, and had issue.

(*b*) Wilhelmina Jane, *d. unm.* 1886.

(*c*) Maria Victoria.

c. Robert, *b.* 1810; *m.* 27 Jan. 1836, Anne, dau. of William Colclough, of Clonmel, and *d.* 22 Aug. 1849, having by her (who *m.* 2ndly, March, 1854, James Scott, who *d.* 1894, and *d.* 14 Oct. 1879) had issue,

(*a*) Robert Arthur Henry, *b.* 27 Jan. 1837; *d.s.p.* 26 April, 1902.

(*b*) William Keily, Major *h.p.* 68th the Durham Light Infantry, served in Bhotan and Afghanistan; Hon. Lieut.-Col. 1882; J.P. Folkestone, *b.* 21 Oct. 1839, *m.* 6 Oct. 1882, Marie Ione, dau. of Adolphus B.

Westropp. THE LANDED GENTRY. 758

Sutherland, M.D., of Richmond, Virginia, and widow of Harry Thornhill, of Stanton-in-Peak, co. Derby. He d. 28 Nov. 1905.
(c) John, b. 23 July, 1841; d. 24 April, 1854.
(a) Dorcas Frances, m. 1886, L. F. Maberly, and has issue.
   d. Arthur, d.s.p.
a. Jane, m. John Piercy.
b. Mary, m. George O'Callaghan, of Mary Fort, co. Clare.   c. Dorcas, m. John F. Kiernan.
d. Sarah, m. Capt. Hugh Brin White, R.N.
e. Frances, m. Rev. H. W. Crofton, of Inchinappa, co. Wicklow.
f. Annabella, m. Henry Townsend, of Whitehall, co. Cork.
3. Henry Hickman, Capt. 9th Light Dragoons (retired 1816), served at Copenhagen and Monte Video, m. Frances Swift, and d.s.p. 1839.
4. Ralph, Lieut. (51st) the King's Light Infantry, killed at the siege of Badajos 9 May, 1811.
5. John (Rev.), Rector of Ballyvaughan, co. Clare, m. Anne, dau. of Augustine Fitzgerald, of Tureen, co. Clare, and d.s.p.
(2) John, d.s.p.
(1) Margaret, m. 1769, Thomas Gabbett, of Castle Lake (see GABBETT of Caherline).
(2) Jane.
3. Randall, of Cork, Mayor 1743; m. 1737, Peniel, 2nd dau. of Lionel Becher, of Sherkin, and d. 1777, leaving issue,
(1) Michael Roberts, Capt. 18th Royal Irish and 63rd Regts., served in America and West Indies, Major Cork True Blues 1782, Commandant of Cork Volunteers 1803, Sheriff of Cork 1775, Mayor 1801; b. 1737; m. 1773, Jane, eldest dau. of Amos Godsell, of Sunville, co. Limerick, and d. 23 Feb. 1830, having by her (who d. 4 May, 1819) had issue,
1. Michael, b. 2 April, 1778; d. 1790.
2. Henry Bruen, Capt. 7th Dragoon Guards, J.P. and Sheriff of Cork 1818, b. 18 March, 1781; m. 8 May, 1814, Maria Wallis, youngest dau. of Edmond Armstrong, of Lismoher, co. Clare, and d. 9. Dec. 1857, having by her (who d. 20 Oct. 1840) had issue,
a. Michael Roberts (Sir), Knt., B.A., T.C.D. 1838, Advocate-General Bombay 1856, Puisne Judge of High Court of Bombay 1863, and Chief Justice 1870, b. 29 June, 1817; m. 1st, 17 Jan. 1857, his cousin, Elizabeth, eldest dau. of John W. Anderson, of Fermoy, co. Cork, brother of Sir James Anderson, Bart., of Buttevant, and by her (who d. 13 June, 1861) had issue,
(a) Henry Charles Edward, Lieut.-Col. 1st Manchester Regt., served in S. Africa 1901-2 (Queen's medal and two clasps), b. 26 May, 1861; m. 8 Nov. 1894, Mary Frances Anne, dau. of Lieut.-Col. Lowndes, of Eastfield, co. Northampton, and has issue,
1. Lionel Henry Mountifort, b. 20 Feb. 1896.
2. Victor John Eric, b. 24 May, 1897.
3. A son, b. 29 May, 1910.
(a) Cornelia Emily, m. 25 Nov. 1879, Edward McGildowney Hope Fulton, of Braidujle, co. Antrim, and by her (who d. 14 Aug. 1900) has issue (see that family).
He m. 2ndly, 3 Jan. 1865, his cousin, Eliza (who d. 28 May, 1910), eldest dau. of Lieut.-Col. Lionel John Westropp (see below), and d. 14 Jan. 1890, leaving issue,
(b) Lionel Erskine, b. 26 Aug. 1866.
b. Edward Henry, Capt. 29th Regt., fought in the Sutlej Campaign, b. 30 March, 1819; d. 19 Feb. 1895.
c. Henry Bruen, Lieut. 51st Light Infantry, b. 22 April, 1827; d. at Madras, 23 Jan. 1853.
a. Hannah Maria, d. unm. 22 Aug. 1884.
b. Penelope Maria, d. unm. 9 Sept. 1897.
c. Jane Maria, d. unm. 24 July, 1905.
d. Henrietta Maria, d. unm. 16 Jan. 1887.
e. Dora, d. 10 March, 1830.
3. Amos Freeman, Capt. R.N., fought at Camperdown, in Egypt, at Trafalgar, Copenhagen; conveyed the Duke of Wellington to Lisbon, was also at the capture of Guadeloupe, escorted Napoleon to St. Helena. He was b. 26 April, 1782; m. 22 Feb. 1822, Catherine, dau. of the Ven. James Kenny, Archdeacon of Kilfenora, and d. 1 Feb. 1844, having by her (who d. 13 Aug. 1849) had issue,
a. Roberts Michael, of Southwood, Cork, Major-Gen. Bombay Army, b. 19 Nov. 1824; m. 7 Aug. 1852, Eliza, dau. of Gen. George Twemlow, Bengal Army. He 10 d. Feb. 1910.
b. James Edward, Major-Gen. Bombay Army, b. 25 July, 1826; m. 7 May, 1855, Sarah, dau. of William Winstanley Hall, and d.s.p. 4 Sept. 1874. She d. 8 Oct. 1875.
c. Nathaniel William, b. 1827; d. 1828.
d. Amos Robinson, b. and d. 1830.
e. Henry Amos, b. 1831; d. 1847.
f. Richard Henry, b. and d. 1833.
g. George Ralph Collier, Major-Gen. Indian Army, Political Resident at Court of the Rajah of Sawant Waree, served in Indian Mutiny, b. 23 May, 1834; m. 25 May, 1857, Ellen Blanche, dau. of George Bell, of Kelvedon, Essex, and has issue,
(a) Henry Amos (Rev.), B.A., T.C.D., Rector of Chillesford, Suffolk, b. 26 April, 1858; m. 15 Nov. 1894, Mary Charlotte, dau. of Robert Woodman, M.D. She d.s.p. 31 Oct. 1898.
(b) George Ralph Collier, Col. Indian Army, served in Afghanistan 1880 (medal and clasp), Zob Valley

and Chin Lusbai Expeditions, b. 21 June, 1859; m. 27 June, 1899, Ethel Frances, dau. of the late Brig.-Gen. I. A. Tytler, V.C., C.B., and widow of Rear-Adm. J. C. Byng, R.N
(c) Roberts Michael, b. and d. 1864.
(d) Simpson Hackett, Lieut. Indian Staff Corps, b. 11 March, 1868; d. 24 March, 1893.
(e) John Gibbings, Lieut. 15th Regt., Assistant Political Agent at Kathiawar, b. twin with Simpson Hacket; d. 13 June, 1892.
(f) Frederick Malcolm, Major, R.E., served Samana and Tirah Expeditions (medal and three clasps), b. 6 Feb. 1870; m. 7 Nov. 1903, Mabel Jane, dau. of the late Hodder Michael Westropp (see below), and has issue,
Frederick George Michael, b. 17 Jan. 1905.
(g) Alexander Sligo Anderson, of the Indian Civil Service, b. 11 April, 1872; m. 8 Dec. 1904, Helen Mary, only child of the late Edward Shotton, of Preston Tower, North Shields, and has issue,
Edward Ralph Shotton, b. 17 Oct. 1908.
Aileen Dorothy, b. 18 Oct. 1905.
(a) Emily McMahon, b. 1860; d. 1864.
a. Jane, b. 1823; m. 25 Jan. 1844, John Thomas Cuthbert Gibbings, D.L., of Glenburne, Cork, and had issue. He d. 23 Aug. 1858. She d. 21 Oct. 1907.
b. Catherine Stretton, d. unm. 17 July, 1906.
4. Lionel John, Lieut.-Col. 58th Regt., served in the Peninsular War, at Maida 1806, Salamanca 1812, Vittoria 1813, wounded at the taking of the Heights of Eilbellar Pyrenees 1813, and again at Plattsburgh, America, 1814, Brigade-Major at the occupation of Paris 1815 (medal and clasps), Sheriff of Cork 1820, and Mayor 1838. He was b. 25 Jan. 1785; m. 17 Sept. 1819, Eliza, dau. and co-heiress of Philip Splaine, of Rosemount, co. Cork, and d. 5 Nov. 1862, having by her (who d. 15 Sept. 1838) had issue,
a. Michael Lionel, Capt. 58th Regt., served in New Zealand, b. 1820; d. 7 Oct. 1854.
a. Eliza, m. 3 Jan. 1865, her cousin, Sir Michael Roberts Westropp, and by him had issue (see above). He d. 14 Jan. 1890. She d. 28 May, 1910.
b. Sarah Jane, d. 12 March, 1856.
c. Maria, d. unm. 28 Jan. 1904.
d. Penelope Clarina, m. 1st, 1849, Capt. James Spens, Bengal Engineers, who d. Nov. 1856, leaving issue (see SPENS of Craig Sanquhar); she m. 2ndly, 31 Dec. 1863, Rev. Edward James Rhoades, and had issue by both. She d. 14 April, 1897.
e. Emily McMahon, m. 24 Oct. 1857, Capt. Walter Need, R.N., of Woodhouse Castle, Notts. He d. 1901. She d. 29 March, 1910, leaving issue (see that family).
1. Jane, m. 1st, 1797, Bernard Shaw, of Monkstown, co. Cork, who d. 1808, leaving issue; and 2ndly, William Hockin, and left issue. She d. 7 May, 1820.
2. Penelope, m. 29 May, 1796, Major-Gen. Lord Clarina; and d. 26 Nov. 1843, leaving issue.
3. Emily Anne, m. 27 Aug. 1808, Gen. Sir Thomas MacMahon, Bart., G.C.B., and d. 11 May, 1866, leaving issue (see BURKE's Peerage and Baronetage).
(2) Lionel Beecher, Capt. Madras Army, d. unm. 1791.
(1) Hannah, m. 1767, Edmond Armstrong, of Lismoher, co. Clare, and had issue.
(2) Katherine, legatee of her uncle John's will.
(3) Hannah, m. John Exham, and d.s.p.
(4) Mary, m. James Atkins, and had issue.
(5) Jane, m. William Cary, and had issue.
(6) Peniel, m. Capt. Hans Stewart, 61st Regt., and had issue.
(7) Martha, m. Capt. William Lane Hughes, and had issue.
(8) Dora, m. Capt. Edmund Beattie, R.M.
4. Mountiford, d. unm.
5. Ralph, M.D., m. 1745, Mary, 3rd dau. of Michael Bustead, of Meadestown, co. Cork, and d. 1771, leaving issue,
(1) Michael Bustead, Barrister-at-Law, of Cork, b. May, 1746; m. July, 1773, his cousin, Elizabeth, dau. of Watkins Roberts, of Shanballymore, and d. 22 Dec. 1790, leaving issue,
1. Ralph, of Waterpark, co. Cork, b. 1774; m. 1803, Jane, dau. of Hodder Roberts, of Bridgetown, and d. 1822, having by her (who built Rookhurst, co. Cork) had issue,
a. Roberts, of Ravenswood, Cork, b. 1813; m. 3 Nov. 1842, Lydia Mary, dau. of Michael Roberts, of Kilmoney (see that family), and d. 1896, leaving issue,
(a) Ralph, d. unm. 1871.
(b) Michael Hodder, b. 1850; d. unm. 10 Jan. 1889.
(a) Eliza, m. Capt. C. B. Saunders, 77th Regt.
(b) Jane, m. Dr. Ross Lewin Morgan. (c) Lydia.
(d) Constance. (e) Nina.
b. Hodder Michael, of Rookhurst, co. Cork, B.A., Dublin, the well-known Antiquary, m. 1st, Cornelia, dau. of J. W. Anderson, of Fermoy, and by her had issue,
(a) Cornelia Florence, m. 16 June, 1885, Rev. Charles Roberts, and d.s.p. 1898 (see ROBERTS of Kilmoney Abbey).
(b) Eva.
He m. 2ndly, Jane, dau. of Robert Seymour Drought, of Ridgemount, King's Co., and had issue,
(a) Michael Seymour Dudley, M.R.I.A., late Lieut. 1st Batt. Royal Irish Rifles, b. 2 April, 1868; m. 10 June, 1902, Elizabeth Hyde, dau. of John Lanyon, J.P., of Lisbreen, Belfast, and has issue,

Dorothy Elizabeth Mary.
Ralph Michael Lanyon, b. 24 Feb. 1907.
(c) Mabel Jane, m. 7 Nov. 1903, Major Frederick Malcolm Westropp, and has issue (see above).
(d) Eleanor, m. Roger Adams.
(e) Elizabeth Jane, m. Richard Saunders.
(f) Anna, d. unm.
(g) Wilhelmina Augusta, m. 7 June, 1849, Rev. William Roberts, S.F.T.C.D., and d. 21 June, 1887. He d. 24 Dec. 1884, having had issue (see ROBERTS, of Kilmoney Abbey).
2. Watkins Roberts, b. 1778; m. Martha, dau. of — Roberts, and had issue,
a. Elizabeth, m. Richard Odell Westropp, of Ballysteen.
b. A dau.
3. Michael Bustead, b. 1779; m. Jane, dau. of Robert Atkins St. Ledger, of Waterford, and had issue, a dau., Julia, m. R. Wilkinson.
(2) Richard, b. 1753, Lieut. 9th Foot, served in the American War, and was killed at Skenesborough, 8 July, 1777.
(3) Thomas, M.D., of Cork, b. 1759, Provincial Grand Master of Masonic Body of Munster, d. 31 Oct. 1808.
4. Thomas, of Mellon, co. Limerick, purchased Ballysteen from the Chichester House Commissioners 12 June, 1703, m. Elizabeth, dau. of — Bury, of Shannongrove, co. Limerick, by Albinia his wife, dau. of Sir Drury Wray, Bart., and d. 1743-4, leaving issue,
1. Thomas, of Ballysteen, m. 22 July, 1729, Sara, dau. of Berkeley Taylor, of Ballinort, and had issue, with two daus. and a son, Col. Berkeley Westropp (who d. 177–, having m. and had issue, John Berkeley, m. and had issue), an eldest son, THOMAS, who m. Jane, dau. of Thomas Browne, of Newgrove, co. Clare; and d. Dec. 1780, leaving issue (besides three children who d. young), General John Westropp, of Ballysteen, High Sheriff of co. Limerick 1794 d.s.p. 1825, when estates reverted to the issue of his sister, Sara, wife of Thomas Odell, of Ballingarry, co. Limerick, who assumed the name of WESTROPP, and are now of Ballysteen.
2. Mountiford, of Mellon, m. 1744, Martha, dau. of Thomas Roberts, of Britfieldstown, co. Cork, and had issue,
(1) John, of Mellon, and of Rockfield, m. 1776, Susannah, dau. of Thomas Lewin, of Cloghans, co. Mayo, grand-dau. of John Ross Lewis, of Fort Fergus, co. Clare, and d. 3 Nov. 1793, his wife dying 1823, having had, with two daus.,
1, Barbara, m. Howell Powell Clough, 20th Regt., and d.s.p. 1863; and 2, Susanna, m. Charles Whitehead Dunbar Massey, son of Sir H. D. Massey, Bart. (she d. 6 Jan. 1817, and he d. 14 June the same year, leaving a dau., Susanna, m. 9 March, 1843, Samuel H. Bindon, County Court Judge of Gippsland, Victoria, Australia), a son,
Mountiford, of Mellon and Westbury Lodge, 17th Light Dragoons, b. 1781; m. 1815, Jane, dau. of Charles Dawson, of Charlesfort, co. Wexford, and d. 1843, having by her (who d. 1859) had issue,
a. John, d. unm. 1850.
b. Charles Richard, d. unm. 1845.
c. Dawson, of Mellon, co. Limerick, and Westbury Lodge, co. Clare, J.P. Limerick, High Sheriff 1885, b. 26 Feb. 1823, 30th Bengal N. Infantry; m. 12 Nov. 1861, Frances Dorothea, eldest dau. of the late Col. John Vandeleur, 10th Hussars, and grand-dau. of the Right Hon. J. O. Vandeleur, and Lady Frances his wife, 4th dau. of Charles Moore, 6th Earl and 1st Marquess of Drogheda. She d. April, 1901. He d. 7 July, 1893, leaving,
(a) Charles, d. an infant. (b) Dawson, d. an infant.
(c) Mountiford, of Mellon and Cartown, co. Limerick, and of Westbury Lodge, co. Clare, b. 20 July, 1864, Capt. Limerick City Artillery; m. 15 Feb. 1896, Emma Meliora, dau. of William Doyle Hobson, of Mylars Park, Wexford, and widow (m. 20 July, 1886) of Capt. Cecil Ruggles-Brise, and has issue,
1. Mountiford, b. 6 Sept. 1902.
1. Grace More. 2. Rose Vandeleur.
(a) Alice Jane, m. 17 April, 1888, Capt. Francis Welch, R.M., of Yaxley Hall, Sussex. She d. 9 Oct. 1905.
(b) Frances Susan, m. 16 Nov. 1887, Surgeon Francis John Jencken, Army Medical Staff, and d. 11 March, 1889, leaving issue.
(c) Emily Caroline, m. 18 May, 1895, Henry Vernon, of Battle, Sussex.
(d) Rosetta Anna. (e) Agnes Dorothea.
(f) May Vandeleur, m. 30 April, 1903, Frederick St. Clair Hobson, of Lanahrone, Limerick, elder surviving son of the late William Doyle Hobson, of Meylars Park, co. Wexford.
d. Walter Montiford Westropp-Dawson, of Charlesfort, co. Wexford (see WESTROPP-DAWSON of Charlesfort).
a. Ann m. Major Richard Low, who d. 1868, leaving issue. She d. July, 1858.
b. Susan, m. 1843, William Bolton, of The Island, co. Wexford, J.P., High Sheriff 1856, and had issue.
c. Jane, m. 1855, Major George Gavin, M.P., of Kilpeacon House, co. Limerick, 16th Lancers, who d. 1880. and has issue.
(1) Jane, m. Edward Galwey, of Lota, co. Cork, and had issue.
(2) Elizabeth, m. 9 March, 1771, Rev. Richard Collis, Chanter of the Cathedral of Limerick, and had issue.
3. Robert, d. unm.

4. Cecil (Rev.), M.A. Dublin 1737, of Ballydoole, Incumbent of Ardcanny, m. his cousin, Hannah, 2nd dau. of Ralph Westropp, of Cahirdowgan, and d. 1788, leaving an only son,
Thomas, of Curraghbridge, m. Aug. 1771, Frances, 2nd dau. of William Minchin, of Greenhills, co. Tipperary, and had, with four daus., two sons,
1. Thomas (Rev.), Rector of Doonass, co. Clare, B.A., m. Elizabeth, 2nd dau. of George Stacpoole, of Cragbrien, co. Clare, and d. 1843, aged 71, leaving issue,
a. Thomas (Rev.), M.A., Rector of Ardcanny, and Prebendary of Limerick, m. 1st, 1825, Maria Frederica, dau. of William Minchin, of Greenhills, by whom he had two sons,
(a) Thomas, d. unm. Oct. 1871.
(b) William, d. unm. 1859.
He m. 2ndly, Helena, 3rd dau. of Daniel Gabbett, of Strand House, by whom he had issue,
(c) Daniel Gabbett (Rev.), M.A. Dublin, of Killoscully Glebe, Newport, Limerick, b. 14 Nov. 1848; d. 15 March, 1908; m. 6 Feb. 1877, Maria Amelia, dau. of Major Matthew Pennefather Lloyd, 59th Regt. (see LLOYD of Rockville), and has issue,
1. Thomas John (Rev.), B.A. Dublin, b. 13 Dec. 1879.
2. Anna Maria, d. unm.
2. Helena, m. 17 June, 1903, Rev. Victor F. Lindsay.
3. Mary. 4. Alice. 5. Eliza.
(d) Cecil George, Physician, m. Bessie (who d. April, 1903), dau. of Henry Gresham, and d. 3 Nov. 1893, leaving issue,
Charles Henry Gabbett, m. 1905, Jane, dau. of R. O'Reilly.
Emily.
(a) Alicia, m. 1883, Frederick Finch. She d.s.p. 24 May, 1898.
(b) Eliza, d. 1909.
(c) Helena, m. 1869, Hugh Massy Westropp, and d. 1880, leaving issue.
He m. 3rdly, Maria Frederica, dau. of Henry Ross Lewin, of Kilkee, and widow of Capt. Lowe, R.N. She d.s.p. 1896. He d. 12 Jan. 1876.
b. William, M.D., of Limerick, m. Bessy, dau. of John Gabbett, of Shepperton, co. Clare, and d.s.p. Dec. 1887.
c. George, m. Emma, dau. of Michael Furnell, and d. 1858, having had issue, William Stacpoole Westropp, of Lisdoonvarna, M.R.I.A., who d. unm. 16 Feb. 1900.
a. Jane, m. Rev. James Bennett.
2. Ralph, Lieut. R.N., d. unm.
5. Palmes, Sheriff of Cork 1757. Mayor 1778, m. 1749, Susannah, dau. of John Ross Lewin, of Fort Fergus, co. Clare, and d. 23 Oct. 1793, leaving (with a son, Palmes (Col.), father of the late Gen. John Westropp, of Dublin) a son, Henry, of Richmond, Limerick, whose son, Henry Sheares, m. Elinor Winthrop Jones, and had issue, the late Henry Westropp, of Green Park, B.A., High Sheriff of Limerick 1866, M.P. for Bridgwater, who d. unm. 1888.
6. Robert, of Fort Anne, co. Clare, J.P. 1716; m. Anna Smith, and d.s.p., settling estates on his nephew Robert, 1735.
1. Elizabeth, m. 1st, in 1684, Thomas Spaight, of Burrane, co. Clare; and 2ndly, Arthur Ward, of Lodge, and had issue by both.
2. Frances.
3. Susannah, m. Henry White, of Knocksentry, co. Limerick, and had issue.
Montiford Westropp d. 24 Aug. 1698, and was s. by his 2nd (but eldest surviving) son,
MOUNTIFORD WESTROPP, of Kilkerin, J.P. 1709 for Clare. He purchased from the Commissioners at Chichester House, 23 June, 1703, the lands of Attyflin, co. Limerick. He m. 1684, Elizabeth. She d. 1756. His will, dated 25 Jan. 1722, was proved 12 May 1726. He had issue,
1. JOHN, his heir, of whom hereafter.
1. Elizabeth.
2. Mary, m. 1715, Poole Hickman, of Kilmore, co. Clare, and had issue.
3. Frances, m. W. Lavitt, of Cork.
4. Jane, m. 1726, Thomas Browne, of Newgrove, co. Clare.
5. Gertrude, m. 1728, Luke Hickman, of Fenloe, co. Clare.
6. Anne, m. 1st, Richard Bury, of Mount Pleasant, co. Clare; and 2ndly, William Spaight, of Six Mile Bridge.
7. Susannah, m. 21 Sept. 1738, John Longfield, of Longueville, co. Cork, and had issue.
The only son,
JOHN WESTROPP, of Attyflin, J.P., High Sheriff co. Limerick 1745; m. 1734, his 1st cousin, Mary, dau. of Berkeley Taylor, of Ballinort, co. Limerick, and d.s.p. 1781. He devised Attyflin to his cousin,
RALPH WESTROPP, of Lismehane and Clonmoney, afterwards of Attyflin, High Sheriff of co. Clare 1772 (son of John Westropp, of Lismehane, co. Clare, see above); m. 1759, Mary, 2nd dau. and co-heir of William Johnson, of Lizard, co. Limerick, and Ballylegan, co. Cork, by Amy his wife, 2nd dau. of Col. Hugh Massy, of Duntryleague, sister of Hugh and Eyre, the 1st Lords Massy and Clarina, and niece of George Evans, 1st Lord Carbery, and dying 18 June, 1806, had issue,
1. JOHN, of Attyflin, his heir.
2. William Johnson, of Roxborough, m. Anna, dau. of Darby O'Grady, and had issue, William and Ralph, d. young, and seven daus. He d. June, 1818.
3. RALPH, Mayor of Limerick 1800-1801, m. 1795, Harriet Vereker, sister of Charles, 2nd Viscount Gort, and d. March, 1838, leaving issue,

Westropp. THE LANDED GENTRY. 760

1. Ralph, his heir, of Coolreagh, J.P., bapt. 8 Nov. 1800; d.s.p. 11 July, 1883, leaving his estates to Capt. George O'Callaghan, now O'Callaghan-Westropp (*see* O'CALLAGHAN *of Maryfort*).
2. John, *m.* Miss Abby Gabbett, of Corbally, and had,
 (1) Ralph, *m.* Catherine O'Callaghan, of Maryfort, and *d.* 1876, leaving a son John, drowned 1887. (2) John, *d.* 1884.
 (1) Harriet. (2) Mary.
 (3) Anne. (4) Abby.
1. Julia, *m.* 1st, Capt. Ormsby; and 2ndly, Rev. J. B. M'Cree, and had issue.
2. Mary, *m.* Col. George Stamer, of Carnelly, and *d.* Jan. 1883, leaving issue.
3. Henrietta, *m.* Ralph Evans, of Carker, co. Cork, and had issue (*see that family*).
4. George, Lieut. 5th Foot, d.s.p. 14 Nov. 1793.
5. Thomas, of Ross House, co. Clare, Sheriff of Limerick 1807-10, *m.* Anne (who *d.* 186-), dau. of John Rose, and widow of John Keating, and had issue,
 Thomas Johnson, *d. unm.* 1838, aged 20 (M. I. in St. Mary's Cathedral, Limerick).
1. Jane, *m.* 1st, William Stamer, of Carnelly, co. Clare, and had issue; and 2ndly, 1789, Charles Vereker, 2nd Viscount Gort, and had issue.
2. Eliza, *m.* 10 March, 1793, Arthur Brereton, of Ballyadams, and had issue.
3. Emma, *m.* Edward Jameson, and had issue.
4. Anne, *m.* Nov. 1790, Nicholas Green Evans, of Carker, and had issue (*see that family*).

Ralph Westropp was s. by his son,
JOHN WESTROPP, of Attyflin, High Sheriff co. Limerick 1798, *b.* 12 Aug. 1762; *m.* 1799, his cousin Anna, dau. of Major James Burdett Ness, of Osgodby, co. York, and by her (who *m.* 2ndly, 12 Nov. 1842, Peter Warburton Jackson, and *d.* 3 Feb. 1850) had issue in all 23 children, of whom survived,
 1. JOHN, his heir.
 2. George, *b.* 28 Feb. 1819; *m.* 1st, 31 March, 1841, Thomasina Julia, who *d.* 1855, youngest dau. of Ralph Evans, of Carker, co. Cork, by whom he has issue, a son, John, *d.* 1879, and five daus., and 2ndly, 2 Aug. 1865, his cousin, Henrietta, dau. of William Johnson Westropp. She *d.* 8 May, 1903. He *d.* 4 June, 1900.
 1. Mary Johnson, *m.* 26 Jan. 1818, Sir Hugh Dillon Massy, Bart., of Doonass, co. Clare, and *d.* 26 Jan. 1890.
 2. Jane Anne, *m.* 28 Jan. 1829, Capt. William Peacock, and *d.* 14 Jan. 1830.
 3. Charlotte Eliza, *m.* 1st, 2 Nov. 1823, Henry Westby Brady, and had issue, four sons and three daus.; and 2ndly, 5 Feb. 1842, Alphonse, Count Danileski, and *d.* July, 1881, leaving issue.
 4. Georgina, *m.* 1st, 9 Oct. 1835, George Green, Lieut. 37th Regt., who *d.s.p.* 1837. She *m.* 2ndly, 27 Feb. 1841, Henry Thomas Chapman, M.D., and had issue, one son and one dau. She *d.* 22 March, 1897.
 5. Julia, *m.* 7 Jan. 1843, Richard Wilme, M.D., and had issue, one son. She *d.* 9 Jan. 1910.
 6. Cecilia, *m.* 5 April, 1842, William Henry Jackson, of Inane, Roscrea, co. Tipperary, and had issue, five daus. and three sons. She *d.* 31 March, 1858.

Mr. Westropp *d.* 10 April, 1839, and was *s.* by his son,
JOHN WESTROPP, of Attyflin, J.P., *b.* 14 Feb. 1814; *m.* 1st, 18 May, 1836, Georgina Wilhelmina, dau. and co-heiress of Col. George William Stamer, of Carnelly, co. Clare, and by her (who *d.* 3 June, 1852) had issue, with three daus., who *d.* in infancy,
 1. JOHN THOMAS, late of Attyflin.
 2. George William, of Opihi, New Zealand, 11th Regt., *b.* 17 Jan. 1838; *m.* Anna Barry (who *d.* 1886), and had issue, five sons and three daus. He *d.* 16 Aug. 1888.
 3. Ralph Hugh, of Springfort, co. Limerick, *b.* 26 Aug. 1844, B.A., Dublin, 1868, F.R.S.A.I.; *m.* 2 Oct. 1879, Henrietta Jane Stacpoole, dau. and heir of Henry Vereker. He *d.* 31 Oct. 1902. She *m.* 2ndly, Guildford William Jack Stacpoole.
 4. Hugh Massy, of Park House, Clonlara, co. Limerick, J.P. co. Clare, *b.* 23 May, 1847; *m.* 1st, 3 March, 1869, Helena (who *d.* 12 July, 1880), youngest dau. of Rev. Thomas Westropp, Prebendary of Ardcanny, and has issue,
 1. John Ralph, *m.* and has issue. He *d.* 26 July, 1909.
 2. Dr. Hugh Gerald, *m.* and has issue.
 3. Thomas George.
 1. A dau.
He *m.* 2ndly, 13 April, 1885, Elizabeth Jane, dau. of William Stacpoole, of Edenvale, and by her (who *d.* 15 Sept. 1901), had issue, two daus. He *d.* 12 July, 1909.
 1. Mary Herman, *m.* 24 March, 1859, Col. John O'Callaghan, of Maryfort, co. Clare, and has issue (*see that family*).
 2. Elizabeth Anna, *d. unm.* 9 Feb. 1889.
 3. Alice Julia, *m.* 19 Aug. 1868, Richard Stacpoole, D.L. of Edenvale, co. Clare, and *d.* 14 July, 1907, leaving issue (*see that family*). He *d.* 16 June, 1891.

He *m.* 2ndly, 31 July, 1856, Charlotte Louisa, eldest dau. of Lieut.-Gen. Sir Thomas Whitehead, K.C.B., of Uplands Hall, co. Lancaster, by Charlotte his wife, dau. of Maj. James Burdett Ness, of Osgodby, and had by her (who *d.* 31 Oct. 1891),
 5. Thomas Johnson, M.I. at Tulla, *b.* 16 Aug. 1860, M.A. Dublin 1885, M.R.I.A., F.R.S.A.I. and Vice-President 1902-5; author of several works on Irish antiquities.
 4. Louisa, *d.* an infant 20 Nov. 1858.

He *d.* 2 March, 1866. His eldest son,
JOHN THOMAS MASSY-WESTROPP, of Attyflin, co. Limerick, and Clonmoney and Doonass, co. Clare, J.P. for Limerick, B.A. Dublin 1860, Col. 1st Nat. Batt. King's Own Royal Lancaster Regt., and formerly Capt. 3rd Batt. King's Own Regt., *b.* 8 March, 1837; *m.* 6 June, 1859, Margaret, youngest dau. of Thomas Robert Wilson ffrance, of Rawcliffe Hall, co. Lancaster. She *d.* 1 Jan. 1885. He *d.* 17 Dec. 1903, having had issue,
 1. JOHN, his heir.
 2. Ralph Henry, C.E., of Kilkee, co. Clare, *b.* 23 April, 1864; *m.* 1894, Rose, dau. of H. R. Barker, and widow of James Crawley.
 3. Francis Stamer, *b.* 10 Feb. 1867; *m.* 1890, Margaret, dau. of — Montague, and settled in Temora, Australia. He has issue, with two daus., a son, Montague, *b.* Aug. 1891.
 1. MARY GEORGINA, now of Attyflin, *m.* 17 May, 1905, Arthur White, eldest son of Edward White, of Fort Etna.
 2. Margaret *d.* young, 16 June, 1870.
 3. Anna Cecilia Dillon.

Arms—Quarterly: 1st and 4th, sa., a lion rampant erm., ducally crowned or (for WESTROPP); 2nd and 3rd, arg. on a fess gu. between three popinjays vert collared and membered of the second, as many escallops of the field (for THWENGE). Crest—An eagle's head ppr., issuing from a ducal coronet or. Motto—Je me tourne vers l'Occident.

Seats—Attyflin, Patrick's Well, co. Limerick; and Clonmoney and Doonass, co. Clare.

O'CALLAGHAN-WESTROPP. *See* **O'CALLAGHAN of MARYFORT.**

WESTROPP-DAWSON. *See* **DAWSON.**

DE COURCY-WHEELER OF ROBERTSTOWN.

HENRY ELIARDO DE COURCY-WHEELER, of Robertstown House, co. Kildare, M.A. Dublin 1903, called to the Bar at King's Inns, Dublin 1896, Freeman of Dublin, Capt. late 8th Batt. the King's Royal Rifle Corps, Hon. Captain in the Army, J.P. co. Kildare, High Sheriff 1906, *b.* 17 March, 1872; *m.* 19 April, 1904, Selina Maud Beresford, youngest dau. of Hercules Francis Knox, of Rosslare, co. Sligo (*see* KNOX *of Rappa Castle*), by Harriett Elizabeth, his wife, dau. of Rev. John James Fox (*see* Fox *of Fox Hall*) and Harriett Louisa his wife (who *d.* 24 Sept. 1871) dau. of Rev. Charles Cobbe Beresford (*see* BURKE'S *Peerage*, WATERFORD M.), and has issue,

WIGSTRÖM HERCULES BERESFORD, *b.* 10 Nov. 1908.
Elizabeth Dorothea Maxwell, *b.* 26 Dec. 1909.

Lineage.—JOSEPH WHEELER, of Stamcarty, co. Kilkenny, High Sheriff 1634 (brother of Jonas Wheeler, Bishop of Ossory 1613-1640, *see* BURKE'S *Peerage and Baronetage*, WHEELER-CUFFE, Bart.) was *s.* by his son,
JOSEPH WHEELER, of Stamcarty, living in 1673, left with a dau., who *m.* Patrick Welch, of Newtown, co. Kilkenny, two sons,
 1. JOSEPH, his heir.
 2. Jonas, of Ballyreddin, *d.* in 1717, leaving an only dau. and heir, Sarah, *m.* John Shee (*see* O'SHEE OF GARDENMORRIS).

JOSEPH WHEELER, of Stamcarty, d. 16 Sept. 1702; will dated 12 Sept. 1702; proved 25 Nov. following; m. about 1690, Catherine, dau. of Robert Myhill (d. about 1680) of Killarney, co. Kilkenny, and had issue by her, who m. 2ndly, in June, 1703, Wheaton Bradish,
1. ROBERT, his heir.
2. Joseph, d. 14 March, 1725, by Dorothy his wife who d. Sept. 1768, left one son and six daus.,
   1. Robert, of Ballyreddin, 1747, m. July, 1738, Jane, dau. of Henry Brownrigg, of Ballinglare, co. Wicklow, and had two sons,
      (1) John, b. 1740, admitted an Attorney of the King's Bench 1763; d. 1795.
      (2) Henry.
   1. Catherine, m. June, 1747, Rev. James Myhill, b. 1706, 2nd eldest son of James Myhill, of Killarney (who d. 1 Dec. 1737). He m. 2ndly, 1756, Jane, dau. of John Flood, of Flood Hall, co. Kilkenny, and d. 1760 (see SOLLY FLOOD of Ballynaslaney House), she m. 2ndly, 1761, John Murray Prior, of Rathdowney.
   2. Mary.   3. Jane.
   4. Elizabeth, m. 1762, Henry Brownrigg.
   5. Dorothea.
3. John.   4. Jonas.
1. Mary.   2. Jane.
The eldest son,
ROBERT WHEELER, of Stamcarty, d. 1714; m. June, 1713, Sarah, dau. of Rev. William Hull, of Finoul, co. Cork (she m. 2ndly 27 Aug. 1727, William Colles. of Abbeyvale, co. Kilkenny, and d. 29 Sept. 1738), and had an only son,
REV. ROBERT WHEELER, of Stamcarty, b. posthumous, entered Trin. Coll., Dublin, 12 May, 1733. B.A. 1737, M.A. 1740; m. Elizabeth, dau. of — Wheeler, of Tullowherin, co. Kilkenny, and had issue,
   1. Rev. Joseph, of Stamcarty and Wildfield, co. Kilkenny, entered Trin. Coll. Dublin, 4 June, 1765, B.A. 1770; will dated 24 July, 1794; proved 15 May, 1795; m. Jan. 1769, Mary, dau. of John Murray Prior of Rathdowny, Queen's Co., and left with three daus. two sons,
      1. Robert m. Helen, dau. of James Ellis, of Wingfield, co. Kilkenny.
      2. Joseph, an officer of Kilkenny Militia, m. — widow of — Palmer.
   2. Oliver, of the Ordnance Office, Dublin, m. Mary, dau. of — Holmes, s.p.
   3. BRODERICK.
The 3rd son,
BRODERICK WHEELER, of Dublin, d. 6 Aug., 1805; m. Eliza, dau. of George Walker, of Belgriflu co. Dublin. She d. 18 Sept. 1837. Issue,
1. GEORGE, of whom presently.   2. John.
3. Henry, an officer in the Army.
1. Elizabeth, m. 1793, George Russell.
2. Anne, m. 1798, Patrick Murray.
3. Bridget, m. 1818, David Kearney.
The eldest son,
GEORGE WHEELER, of Dublin and Talbotstown, co. Wicklow, Freeman of Dublin, Sheriff 1817-18, Alderman 1818, b. 28 Feb. 1778; d. 3 Dec. 1819; m. 5 May, 1803, Elizabeth (who d. 16 Jan. 1829), dau. of Robert Meade, of Killany, Kinsale, co. Cork, and had issue,
1. GEORGE NELSON, his heir.
2. Henry, b. 5 Dec. 1806; d. 25 Nov. 1829, unm.
3. Robert, Freeman of Dublin, M.R.C.S. Ireland, M.A. Trin. Coll. Dublin, M.A. Univ. Melbourne, called to Australian Bar 1864, b. 29 Nov. 1809; d. 1894, unm.
4. Thomas, M.A. Trin. Coll. Dublin, called to the Irish Bar 1838, b. 22 Aug. 1811; d. unm. 1881.
1. Anna Maria, m. 1825, Richard Bennett.
2. Emily Sophia, d. 16 Sept. 1814.
3. Matilda, m. 1833, James Moore Bennett.
4. Adeline, m. 1835, George Bott.
The eldest son,
GEORGE NELSON WHEELER, of Annesborough, co. Kildare, Freeman of Dublin, b. 9 Dec. 1805; d. 22 Dec. 1867, from effects of gunshot wound when out shooting; m. 22 Jan. 1827, Williamza Florence (who d. 13 Nov. 1880), dau. of William Ireland (who d. 3 March, 1853), of Low Park, co. Roscommon (descended from William Ireland, who m. Hon. Margaret de Courcy, sister and heir of Almericus, 23rd Baron of Kingsale (see BURKE'S Peerage, KINGSALE, B.)), by Dorothea (who d. 18 May, 1859), only child of Samuel Arnoldi Gardiner, of Blackwood Castle, and of Robertstown House, co. Kildare (d. 1 Oct. 1801), and had with other issue, who d. young,
1. WILLIAM IRELAND, his heir.
2. Henry Eliardo, b. 13 May, 1846; d. 26 Feb. 1867, unm.
1. Elizabeth Henrietta, d. 22 April, 1855, unm.
2. Dorothea Anjane, d. 17 May, 1874, unm.
3. Williamza Florence, d. 2 Oct. 1892, unm.
4. Annjin, m. 1865, J. M. Neale (d. 17 Feb. 1911), of Newington House, co. Kildare, and has issue (see NEALE of Newington).
The eldest son,
WILLIAM IRELAND DE COURCY-WHEELER, of Robertstown House, co. Kildare, Freeman of Dublin, M.D., M.Ch. Trin. Coll. Dublin, F.R.C.S.I., President 1884 (Centenary Anniversary), M.R.C.P.I., J.P. co. Kildare, High Sheriff 1892, b. 29 Feb. 1844, d. 25 Nov. 1899, assumed the name of DE COURCY-WHEELER by Royal Licence 9 April, 1897; m. 30 Dec. 1869, Frances Victoria (who d. 24 Oct. 1897), dau. of Henry Shaw (who d. 28 Jan. 1884), of Tullamain, co. Dublin, and grand-dau. of Bernard Shaw (who d. 3 Feb. 1826), of Sandpitts, co. Kilkenny (see BURKE'S Peerage and Baronetage,

SHAW, Bart.), by Martha (d. 24 March, 1861), dau. of Rev. James Cockaine, Vicar of Clifton, co. of Gloucester, d. 8 Jan. 1826, and had issue,
1. George Nelson, b. 28 Jan. 1871, B.A. Trin. Coll. Dublin; m. 5 March, 1900, Christina Jane, dau. of Christopher Oliverson, of Southport.
2. HENRY ELIARDO, now of Robertstown House.
5. Samuel Gerald, b. 8 July, 1877, B.A. Trin. Coll. Dublin, B.A.I., Capt. 2nd R. Dublin Fusiliers, served in South Africa 1899-1902, Queen's Medal five clasps, King's Medal two clasps; m. 5 Dec. 1908, Margaret, dau. of Col. Edward Napoleon L'Estrange, late comdg. 21st Royal Scots, by his 1st wife Margaret Innes, and has issue,
   Gerald George, b. 6 Oct. 1910.
4. William Ireland, b. 8 May, 1879, B.A., M.D. Trin. Coll. Dublin, F.R.C.S.I.; m. Feb. 1909, Hon. Elsie, eldest dau. of Lord Shaw (see BURKE's Peerage).
5. Robert Cecil, b. 28 Jan. 1884, B.A., M.B. Trin. Coll. Dublin, m. 6 Sept. 1911, Hilda Mabel, only child of R. Hunter Craig, Knock Castle, Largs.
6. Horatio Francis, b. 21 May, 1888, B.A., Trin. Coll. Dublin.
1. Williamza Florence, m. 1901, Henry Seymour Murphy, M.D., of Lisburn, co. Down.
2. Martha Kathleen, d. May, 1876.
3. Frances Guinevieve, m. 1 Jan. 1910, Edward Darley Powell, B.E., Trin. Coll. Dublin.
4. Hilliare Frances Elizabeth, m. 12 Feb. 1910, Capt. Edward Bomford L'Estrange, Indian Army, son of Col. Edward Napoleon L'Estrange (who d. 26 June, 1890), by his 2nd wife, Belinda Emily, dau. of Isaac North Bomford (see BOMFORD of Gallon Ferrans).

Arms — Or, a chevron between three leopards faces sa. **Crest** — On a coronet or an eagle displayed gu. **Motto** — Facie tenus.
Seat — Robertstown House, co. Kildare. **Clubs** — Junior United Service Club, S.W.; Hibernian United Service Club, Dublin.

WHITE OF KILBYRNE.

COL. JAMES GROVE WHITE, of Kilbyrne, co. Cork, J.P. for cos. Cork and Waterford, D.L. co. Waterford, High Sheriff for co. Waterford 1910, Col. in the Army and late A.Q.M.G. 2nd Div. 1st Army Corps, late Lieut.-Col. Commanding 1st Batt. Duke of Cambridge's Own Middlesex Regt., served in the Zulu War, etc., b. 21 Oct. 1852; m. 1 July, 1880, Constance, dau. of Abraham FitzGibbon, of the Rookery, Stanmore, co. Middlesex (see FITZGIBBON of Crohana), and has issue,

1. Pierce Grove, Lieut. 1st Batt. Duke of Cambridge's Middlesex Regt., served in S. African War 1901, b. 13 Oct. 1882.
2. Maurice FitzGibbon Grove, Lieut. Royal Engineers, b. 7 Dec. 1887.
3. Eustace Grove, b. 11 April, 1892.
4. Terence Grove, b. 5 July, 1901.
1. Constance Geraldine Grove, m. 16 May, 1904, Major Chas. Sidney Collison, 5th Batt. Duke of Cambridge's Own Regt., late Capt. 2nd Batt. Duke of Wellington's Regt., 2nd son of late Charles Stoughton Collison.

Lineage. — ION GROVE, of Hendon, Middlesex, resided at Cahirduggan Castle, near Doneraile, co. Cork, which he rented from Lord Roche 1603, and d. 1617, leaving by his wife Barbara (who d. 5 May, 1609), issue,
1. Henry, of Cahirduggan, m. Grissell (who m. 2ndly, Richard Williamson), d. 1630, leaving a son Charles, and two daus.
2. WILLIAM, of whom presently.
3. Thomas, of Pharihey and Roscike, near Kildorrey, co. Cork.
4. Ion, d.s.p. before 1633.
5. John, of Kilmacome, Cahirduggan, co. Cork.
1. Dorothy.
The second son,
WILLIAM GROVE, of Cahirduggan in 1628, purchased Ballyhemock (now Annesgrove), co. Cork, and d. 1669, leaving by Grace his wife, two sons,

1. Ion, ancestor of the family of GROVE, of Ballyhemock (Annesgrove).*
2. JOHN, of whom we treat.

The younger son,

JOHN GROVE, of Kilbyrne, co. Cork, which he acquired by deed of gift 17 April, 1667, from his brother, Major Ion Grove, of Lissgriffin Castle, near Butterant, co. Cork. He made his will 18 July, 1707. By Margaret his wife he had an only child,

GRACE GROVE, of Kilbyrne, m. by licence 2 Nov. 1694, JAMES WHITE, jun., of Dromanagh, co. Waterford, son of James White, Seneschal and one of the King's Coroners for co. Waterford, and by him had a son,

JOHN WHITE, of Kilbyrne, co. Cork, to which place he s. under the will of his maternal grandfather, dated 18 July, 1707. He m. (setts. dated 15 April, 1725) Anne, dau. of John Fowlke, of Ballinbrittick now Cecilstown), co. Cork. He was buried 24 May, 1754 (will dated 18 May, 1754, proved 9 July in that year), having by her (who d. 12 June, 1745) had issue,

1. James, b. 14 Feb. 1726; d. young.
2. John, b. 29 May, 1727; bur. 26 July, 1741.
3. JAMES, of whom presently.
4. Grove, of Elm Grove (Ballyellis), co. Cork, b. 10 Sept. 1730; d. 1768.
5. Yelverton, of Dromdeer, near Doneraile, b. 14 Feb. 1732-3, living 1754.
6. Francis, b. 4 Nov. 1736.
7. A son, b. 27 Oct. 1742.
8. Robert, b. 14 March, 1743-4.
1. Sarah, b. 29 Oct. 1731; m. 14 July, 1764, William White, of Hogstown, co. Cork, and was bur. 24 Dec. 1811, leaving issue.
2. Annie, b. 2 May, 1735, m.(setts. 15 Nov. 1771) Matthew Seward, of Nursetown, near Mallow, and d. 6 Jan. 1828, having had issue.
3. Grace, b. 14 Aug. 1738. 4. Marie, b. 28 March, 1740.

The eldest surviving son,

JAMES WHITE, of Kilbyrne, or Kilburne, co. Cork, b. 11 Feb. 1728-9; m. 1756, Sarah, dau. of John Garde, of Glyn, co. Waterford, and was bur. 16 Nov. 1780, having by her (who d. 19 Feb. 1821) had five sons and one dau.,

1. JOHN GROVE, his heir.
2. Thomas, Midshipman R.N. 1783, m. Sarah Collis (b. circa 1765). He d. 5 Feb. 1853, and had issue, three sons and a dau.,
  1. William Grove, Lieut. R.N., m. 15 May, 1822, Rebecca, (she d. Aug. 1826), dau. of Roger Green, of Youghal, co. Cork, and sister of the Ven. T. W. Green, Archdeacon of Ardagh, and d. 20 Nov. 1835, leaving (with a dau., Jane Fell, who d. young), an only child,
    Thomas Fell, of Dublin, b. 5 Oct. 1824; m. Juliet Marie (she d. Sept. 1860), dau. of George Cullin, of Dublin; and d. 11 March 1872, leaving issue,
    1. William James Grove, Crown Solicitor for co. Kildare, B.A., LL.B. Trin. Coll. Dublin (18, Elgin Road, Dublin, and St. Helen's, Lucan, co. Dublin), b. 20 Oct. 1852; m. 12 April, 1877, Emily, dau. of William Wilson, of Dublin, and has had issue,
      a. William Ernest Grove, B.A., T.C.D., b. 13 Feb. 1878; d. 24 Oct. 1900.

* MAJOR ION GROVE, of Lissgriffin Castle, near Buttevant, co. Cork, an officer in 1649, obtained 1666, under the Act of Settlement, a grant of the lands of Ballyhemock, Kilbyrne, West Drinagh, Keatingstown, Ballynemongree, Ballytolosy, Ballytrasna, and Ballymacmurragh, all in co. Cork. By deed of gift 1667 he conveyed Kilbyrne to his brother John (see above). He m. Jane, 3rd dau. of John Piggot, of Dysart, Queen's Co., and d. 1692, having by her had (with a dau., Jane, m. 1679, William Hodder, of Bridgetown, co. Cork, and had issue) a son,

ALEXANDER GROVE, of Ballyhemock, m. 1st, 1681, Dorothy, 2nd dau. of James Mansergh, of Macrony Castle, and by her had a son Ion, his heir. He m. 2ndly, Mary Bruce, and d. 1706-7, having by her had Thomas, Robert, John, and Christian, all living 1707. The eldest son,

ION GROVE, of Ballyhemock, b. 1687, m. 1710, Arabella Blennerhasset, and d. 1730 (will dated 1728, proved 1730), leaving issue,
1. ROBERT, his heir.
2. James, of Kilcummer, near Castletownroche, co. Cork, m. 1756, Catherine Wilson, dau. of Ralph Warter Wilson, of Bilboe, co. Limerick. His will, dated 1773, was proved 1783.
3. Arthur, d.s.p. 1754. 4. Ion.
5. Blennerhasset, of London, m. Martha, dau. of Rev. Edward Fanning, and d. 1773, leaving a dau. Elizabeth, living 1793.
1. Arabella, m. 1st, 1733, Edward Smith, of Kilpatrick, co. Cork, who d. 1754, leaving issue. She m. 2ndly, Daniel Swayne.
2. Ellinor, m. John FitzGibbon, of Mountshannon. Their eldest son, John, was created Earl of Clare (see BURKE'S Extinct Peerage).
3. Catherine, m. 1762, Rev. Daniel Purcell, Rector of Kilcummer, and d.s.p.
4. Dorothy, m. 1749, William Minchin, of Greenhills, co. Tipperary, and had issue.
5. Alice, d. young.

The eldest son,
ROBERT GROVE, of Ballyhemock, m. 1741, Mary, dau. of Richard Ryland, of Dungarvan, co. Waterford, and by her (who d. 1 June, 1758) had an only child,

MARY GROVE, of Ballyhemock, m. 8 Feb. 1766, Francis Charles, 1st Earl Annesley. He d. 19 Dec. 1802. She d.s.p. 1791, devising the Ballyhemock estate (now called Annesgrove), to her husband's, the Annesley, family.

b. Ion Alexander Grove, B.A., T.C.D., b. 24 Dec. 1879.
c. Robert Grove, B.A., T.C.D., Barrister-at-Law, b. 9 Sept. 1881.
d. Gerald Edward Grove, B.A., T.C.D., Solicitor, b. 8 Oct. 1883.
e. James Herbert Grove, B.A. Trin. Coll. Dublin, b. 23 Nov. 1889.
a. Juliet Beatrice Grove, b. 24 Dec. 1885.
2. Richard Blair, of Ashton Park, Monkston, co. Dublin, b. 19 Jan. 1857; m. 25 Sept. 1886, Emily Maud, 2nd dau. of the late Charles Nichols, of Dunedin, N.Z., and has issue,
  a. Charles Thomas Blair, b. 19 Dec. 1889.
  b. Arthur Blair, b. 3 July, 1891.
  c. John Henry Blair, b. 18 Feb. 1894.
  d. Cyril Walter Blair, b. 21 Feb. 1902.
  a. Emily Beatrice, b. 23 Nov. 1888.
  b. Maude Eileen, b. 26 Nov. 1896.
1. Juliet Maria, m. 19 May, 1886, Rev. J. E. Grassett, Vicar of Allensmore, Hereford, and has issue.
2. Rebecca, m. 29 Aug. 1889, Herbert Sessions, of Gloucester, and has issue.
2. Edward James, Col. 70th Regt., served in the Peninsular War, b. 2 Oct. 1792; m. 13 Dec. 1830, Henrietta Dobrée, dau. of Thomas Carey, of Rozel, Guernsey. She d. 29 April, 1875. He d. 17 June, 1865, leaving issue, an only child,
  Amelia Carey, b. 19 Oct. 1831; m. 8 Jan. 1852, her cousin, Major H. T. F. White, of Kilbyrne. He d. 17 May, 1876, leaving issue (see below).
3. John (Dr.), b. 29 Sept. 1803.
1. Rebecca, b. 2 April, 1802; m. — Holland, of Cork, and d.s.p.
8. James (Rev.), Chaplain R.N., m. 1st, 5 Jan. 1801, Ann Dennis; 2ndly, a dau. of Thomas Garde, of Ballynecurra, co. Cork, by whom he had a son, James Garde, b. 1803; d. unm. 28 Aug. 1883. His 3rd wife Abigail was bur. 5 June, 1807. He m. 4thly, 24 May, 1809, Ann, dau. of Richard Drapes, of Waterford; and 5thly, Catherine, dau. of Sir Edward Hoare, 2nd bart., of Annabella, and widow of Henry Prendergast Garde, of Youghal. He d. about 1825.
4. Robert Grove, b. Feb. 1772; m. 24 April, 1799, Mary, dau. of Richard Gregg, of Curraghkerry, near Buttevant, co. Cork, and d. 7 May, 1847, having by her (who d. 24 June, 1838) had issue,
  1. James Garde, b. 1800; m. 29 April, 1826, Prudence, dau. of William Gardiner, of Youghal, and d. Jan. 1841, leaving issue. His widow and family settled in America.
  2. William Fell, bapt. 15 July, 1803; Ensign 47th Regt., d. 2 April, 1828.
  3. Richard Gregg, b. 11 Nov. 1808; m. 7 June, 1834, Caroline, 3rd dau. of John Sullivan, of Tullilease (see that family), and d. 2 Feb. 1891, having by her (who d. 28 Sept. 1893) had issue,
    (1) Robert William Costley, b. 3 Sept. 1840; m. 12 Sept. 1872, Jessie Maria, dau. of Thomas Arnold Marten, J.P., of Swansea, and d. 7 Nov. 1898, leaving issue,
      1. Ernest Costley, B.A. Oxon. Civil Service, Resident Magistrate, Fort Johnston, Nyasaland, B.C.A., b. 9 Aug. 1874.
      2. Kenneth Costley, b. 22 April, 1876; m. 28 April, 1906 Gwendoline Roberts, and has issue,
        Margaret Elizabeth, b. 22 March, 1907.
      3. Cyril Costley, C.E. Cape Colony, b. 9 July, 1877; m. 31 July, 1906, Marguerite, dau. of G. Reitz, of Riversdale, C.C., and has issue,
        William Henry, b. 20 Jan. 1909.
      4. Harold Costley (Rev.), M.A. Oxon, Head Master, Bradfield Coll., b. 9 Nov. 1878.
      1. Jessie Gladys Costley, b. 31 Oct. 1880; m. 11 Oct. 1906, Thos. Camden, youngest son of Robt. McClelland, of Hertford, and has issue.
    (2) John Richard, b. 30 April, 1843; m. 29 June, 1871, Mary Campbell Ricketts, only child of James Alder, of Cheltenham, and d. 6 Nov. 1889, leaving issue,
      1. Sydney Alder Campbell, b. 19 May, 1872. He m. and has issue.
      2. Edwin Stanley Campbell, b. 5 Dec. 1874; m. 16 Sept. 1899, Blanche Welch, dau. of — Compton, and has issue,
        John Vernon, b. 3 April, 1906.
        Doris Kathleen, b. 19 Feb. 1903.
      3. John Dondas Campbell; b. 15 July, d. 5 Aug. 1877.
      4. John Leslie Campbell, b. 13 Dec. 1888.
      5. Arthur Llewellyn Campbell, b. 26 May, 1890.
      1. Florence Kathleen Campbell, b. 10 Sept. 1880.
      2. Violet Lilian Ernestine Campbell, b. 19 June, 1886.
    (1) Annie, of Ballintemple, near Cork.
    (2) Melian Sullivan, d. 29 April, 1906.
    (3) Carrie, m. 20 June, 1872, Rev. Henry Heineken Marten, Rector of St. Paul's, Hobart, Tasmania. She d. 11 Oct. 1904, in Tasmania. He m. 2ndly, Miss Morley, of Tasmania.
  4. Robert Fell, b. 1815; d. unm. Feb. 1853.
  1. Sarah, bapt. 2 Feb. 1810.
  2. Rebecca, b. 14 Feb. 1812; m. 1832, John Fitzsimons, of Cork. He d. 14 May, 1868. She d. 17 April, 1855, leaving issue.
5. William Grove, C.B., Lieut.-Col. 48th and 94th Regts., served in Peninsular War, 2 July, 1799, Elizabeth Chinchen. She d. 10 June, 1846. He d. 3 March, 1844, leaving issue,
  1. William Grove, b. 12 May, 1800, Lieut. and Adjutant 48th

and 94th Regts., *m.* 11 June, 1829, Sarah Talbot, and *d.* 9 Jan. 1884, having by her (who *d.* 30 Jan. 1887) had issue,
   Nathan Chinchen, *b.* 20 Dec. 1832; *m.* 26 Feb. 1884, Maria Hardy.
   Sarah Chinchen, *m.* 15 Oct. 1862, George Holloway, and had issue. She *d.* 1906.
2. Thomas Garde, *b.* 1805; *d.* young.
3. John Grove, *d.* young.
4. Francis Fane, *b.* 5 Sept. 1811; *d. unm.* 19 Sept. 1840.
1. Ann Bullen, *m.* Robert Dugdale Marshfield, and *d.* 21 July, 1868, leaving issue. He *d.* 20 Aug. 1883.
2. Elizabeth, *m.* July, 1850, her cousin, Charles Tuckey White, and *d.* 11 May, 1889, leaving issue (*see below*).
3. Louisa, *m.* William Smith, and *d.* 1880, leaving issue. She *d. circa* 1880.
1. Rebecca, *m.* by licence 23 Jan. 1792, John Denis, Alderman of Waterford, and had issue. She *d.* Nov. 1834.

The eldest son,
JOHN GROVE WHITE, of Kilburne, J.P., Ensign 101st and 36th, and Lieut. 73rd Regts., and Capt. and Adjutant of the Doneraile Yeomanry Cavalry, Deputy-Governor of co. Cork, 13 Aug. 1803, *b. circa* 1758; *m.* 27 Jan. 1791, Mary (*b.* 8 May, 1765), dau. of Anthony Chearnley, of Salterbridge, co. Waterford (*see that family*). She *d.* 8 Sept. 1849 (will dated 25 Oct. 1844). He *d.* 27 Aug. 1825, leaving by her one son,

JAMES (GARDE) GROVE WHITE, of Kilburne, *b.* 15 Nov. 1791; *m.* 3 Oct. 1815, Phœbe, 4th dau. of Rev. Charles Tuckey, LL.D., of Parsons Green, co. Tipperary. She *d.* 5 May, 1879, leaving issue,
1. John Grove, B.A. Trin. Coll. Dublin, *b.* 31 Oct. 1817; *m.* 25 Sept. 1872, Mary Anne (*b.* 8 Oct. 1835), dau. of Hiram Camp, of Newhaven, Connecticut, U.S.A., and settled in America. He *d.s.p.* 23 April, 1891.
2. Charles Tuckey, of Kingstown, co. Cork, Barrister-at-Law, *b.* 20 June, 1820; *m.* July, 1850, his cousin, Elizabeth, dau. of Lieut.-Col. William Grove White, C.B., and *d.* 12 July, 1863, having by her (who *d.* 11 May, 1889) had issue,
  1. James Grove, *b.* 5 Sept. 1851; *d.* young, 22 June, 1857.
  2. Charles Leonard Jackson, C.E., bapt. 19 May, 1853; *m.* 1877, Nina Emily, dau. of William Craig Baynes, of Montreal, Canada, and has issue,
    (1) Francis Alfred, Lieut. 4th Batt. Suffolk Regt.; served in S. African War; *b.* 18 June, 1881; drowned 7 Aug. 1905.
    (2) John Grove, *b.* 30 Aug. 1882.
    (1) Isabella Kathleen Dudley, *m.* 9 Oct. 1901, Richard Waterfield, eld. son of Sir Henry Waterfield, G.C.I.E., C.B., and has issue.
3. HANS THOMAS FELL, of whom hereafter.
4. Henry Grove, *b.* 26 Feb. 1828; *d.* aged three years.
1. Elizabeth, *b.* 26 Aug. 1824; *m.* 16 Feb. 1843, Wills George Crofts. He *d.* March, 1857. She *d.* 16 March, 1892, leaving issue.
2. Mary, *d.* young, 1829.

Mr. White *d.* 13 Jan. 1866. His 3rd son,
HANS THOMAS FELL WHITE, of Kilburne, Major 40th Regt., *b.* 16 Nov. 1821; *m.* 8 Jan. 1852, his cousin, Amelia Carey (*Kilbyrne Doneraile*), only child of Col. Edward James White, 70th Regt. (*see above*), and *d.* 17 May, 1876, leaving issue,
1. JAMES GROVE, now of Kilbyrne.
2. Hans Thomas Fell, of Springfort Hall, Mallow, co. Cork, Comm. (Retired) R.N., was at Suakim 1885 (medal and Egyptian Star), *b.* 7 May, 1856; *m.* 16 July, 1885, Mary Beatrice, eldest dau. of late Charles Nichols, of Dunedin, New Zealand, and has issue,
  1. Hans Grove, *b.* 8 Sept. 1890.
  2. Ion Whiteford Grove, Midshipman R.N., *b.* 29 July, 1894.
  3. Dermot Grove, *b.* 22 Sept. 1905.
  1. Mirabel Grace Grove, *b.* 6 Oct. 1886; *m.* 17 March, 1909, Herbert George, son of Thos. Large, of Terenure, co. Dublin.
  2. Beatrice Mary Grove, *b.* 16 Dec. 1887.
  3. Kathleen Whiteford Grove, *b.* 15 March, 1893.
3. John (Ion) Grove, Capt. 16th Bengal Cavalry, and Adjutant Viceroy's Body Guard, *b.* 1 June, 1869; *d. unm.* 26 March, 1900.
1. Mirabel Bladen Neil, *m.* 17 Dec. 1881, Maj. Alexander Towers-Clark, the Duke of Cambridge's Own Middlesex Regt., and has issue, a son and three daus. 2. Henrietta Cecilia.

Arms—Quarterly: 1st and 4th, arg. on a chevron gu. between three roses of the last barbed vert seeded gold a cross patée or (WHITE); and 2nd and 3rd, erm. on a chevron engrailed gu. three escallops arg. (GROVE). **Crest**—An arm in armour embowed holding in the hand a dagger all ppr. the arm charged with a cross patée or. **Motto**—Nourissez l'espérance.

Seats—Kilbyrne, Doneraile. co. Cork; Rockfield, Cappagh, co. Waterford. **Club**—Army and Navy.

WHITE OF CHARLEVILLE.

HENRIETTA MARGARET WHITE, LL.D. (1905) of Trin. Coll. Dublin and Principal of Alexandra Coll. Dublin; CAROLINE ELIZABETH, MRS. BIRCH, *m.* 1901, Charles Sayce Birch; SOPHIA CHARLOTTE, MRS. GIBSON, *m.* 10 Sept. 1910 as his second wife, Capt. William Gibson, late 40th Regt., formerly of Rockforest, co. Tipperary, J.P. and D.L. (High Sheriff 1879) and a J.P. Queen's Co. (*see that family*); The above ladies, daus. of late Henry White, of Charleville who *d.* 1903 (*see below*), *s.* their brother, 1906.

Lineage.—This family has been settled in the Queen's Co. since the middle of the 17th century. About the year 1657, CHARLES WHITE went from Oxford to Ireland, and settled at Kilmartin, near Borris-in-Ossory. He *m.* Miss Lyons, of co. Meath, and had issue,
1. Edward, of Kilmartin, *m.* Miss Lidwill, of Dromard, co. Tipperary, and had issue, an only son.
  Charles, served in the Black Horse (Ligonier's Dragoons), *m.* Dorothea, widow of John White, of Kilpurcet, and had issue,
   Thomas, of Killadooley, *m.* Miss Flood, of Roundwood, and had issue, a dau., Fannie, *m.* Daniel Dillon.
2. ROBERT, of whom presently.
3. Charles, of Kilpurcet, Queen's Co., who had issue, two sons,
  1. John, of Kilpurcet, *m.* Dorothea Bailey, and *d. circa* 1747, leaving issue,
   (1) John.   (2) Charles.
   (1) Elizabeth.
  2. Thomas, of Ballybrophy, Queen's Co., *m.* 1st, 21 April, 1739, Ann Steele, of Kyle, and by her (who *d.* 1741) had issue, a dau.,
   (1) Elizabeth, who *m.* William Smith, of Golden Bridge, co. Dublin, and was great-grandmother of Garnet, Lord Wolseley (*see* BURKE'S *Peerage*, WOLSELEY, V.).
  He *m.* 2ndly, 1 Jan. 1743, Charitie Baldwin, of Rosenallis, and by her (who *d.* Aug. 1744) had issue,
   (1) Charles, who *d.* young.
   (2) Alicia, *m.* Daniel Nugent, of Barrackstown, co. Meath, and had issue.
  Mr. White *m.* 3rdly, 2 Aug. 1747, Charitie Tydd, and *d.* Jan. 1774, having had issue by her,
   (2) Charles, of Ballybrophy, *b.* 19 May, 1753; *m.* 1775, Sarah, dau. of Charles White, of Aghavoe. She *d.* 13 Feb. 1833. He *d.* 3 Sept. 1828, leaving issue,
    1. Thomas, of Ballybrophy, *b.* 14 Sept. 1780, J.P., B.A. Trin. Coll. Dublin, Capt. Queen's Co. Militia; *m.* April, 1830, Constantia Maria, dau. of the Rev. Robert Mills. She *d.* 1866. He *d.* 16 Nov. 1853, leaving (with a dau., accidentally drowned in 1863) one son,
     Thomas Augustus, settled at Territet, Switzerland. *b.* 8 May, 1831, M.R.C.S. Eng.; *m.* Justa Honoria Villanueva, dau. of William Bigoe Armstrong, of Garry Castle, King's Co. (*see* ARMSTRONG *of Garry Castle*). He *d.* 25 May, 1897, leaving issue,
      1. Thomas Armstrong, B.A. Hertford Coll. Oxford, and of the Inner Temple, Barrister-at-Law, *b.* 25 Feb. 1866; *m.* 29 July, 1897, Gertrude Millicent, dau. of the Rev. W. H. Temple (*see* BURKE'S *Peerage*, TEMPLE, Bart. *of the Nash*).
      2. William Bigoe, *b.* 15 Sept. 1867; *m.* 21 Dec. 1903, Eleanor Fridiswide Mary, dau. of Thomas Douglas Crawford (*see* SHARMAN-CRAWFORD *of Crawfordsburn*), and has issue,
       Charles Thomas Bigoe, *b.* 1 Jan. 1905; *d.* 12 Sept. 1905.
       Joyce Eleanor Honoria.
      3. Charles Francis, *b.* 17 Jan. 1874; *d.* Aug. 1881.
      4. Carteret Le Marchant, *b.* 2 Nov. 1879; *d.* Aug. 1881. 5. Arthur Crawford, *b.* 22 Feb. 1881.
      1. Constantia Elizabeth.
      2. Ellen Honoria, *d.* Aug. 1881.
    2. Charles, *b.* 23 Sept. 1788; *m.* Barbara (*née* Ruttledge), widow of — Knox, and *d.s.p.* 1855.
    3. Richard, of Coleraine, Queen's Co., *b.* 11 Oct. 1789; *m.* Eleanor, dau. of Capt. Joseph Palmer, of Middlemount, and *d.s.p.* 1838.
    4. Samuel, *b.* 5 Oct. 1793; *m.* Elizabeth (*d.* 1875), dau. of Robert White, of Scotchrath, Queen's Co., and *d.* 1849, leaving issue, a son,
     Robert, of the Queen's Co., and Scotchrath, Dalkey, co. Dublin, *b.* 1835; *m.* Adelaide, dau. of Peter Roe, of Gortnaclea, and *d.* 3 March, 1909, leaving issue, one son,
      Samuel Robert Llewellyn, D.S.O.; Maj. Leinster Regt., *b.* 4 June, 1863; *m.* 10 July, 1895, Dorothy Hey, widow of Charles Macdowell, M.D., and dau. of the Rev. B. Fearnley Carlyle, Vicar of Cam, Gloucestershire. She *d.* 22 April, 1903, leaving issue,
       Robert Carlyle Llewellyn, *b.* 27 Jan. 1898.
    1. Elizabeth, *b.* 28 Dec. 1778; *m.* 18 Jan. 1810, Alexander Thompson, of Dublin, and *d.* 1843, having had issue.
    2. Catharine, *b.* 14 April, 1786; *m.* 26 April, 1821, Jonathan Nugent, of Killarkin, co. Meath, and *d.s.p.* 1857.
   (3) Thomas, of Garryduff, Queen's Co., *b.* 23 March, 1759; *m.* Sarah (*d.* 1856), dau. of Joseph Palmer, of Cuffesborough, and *d.s.p.* 9 April, 1827.
   (4) Francis, of Spring Hill, Queen's Co., *b.* 23 Nov. 1762; *m.* Aug. 1790, Sara, only dau. of John Barton, of Goslingstown, co. Kilkenny, and *d.s.p.* 29 Oct. 1824.
   (3) Charitie, *b.* 13 Oct. 1748; *m.* Marmaduke Grace, of Dublin, and had issue.
   (4) Anchoretta, *b.* 26 Aug. 1761; *m.* 1770, Francis Freeman, of Summer Hill, King's Co., and had issue.
   (5) Mary, *b.* 5 March, 1755; *m.* 1776, Richard Thompson, of Dublin, and had issue.
   (6) Anne, *b.* 19 Aug. 1756; *m.* 1776, Edmond Beasley, of Dublin, and *d.* 1789.
4. Humphrey, of Mahanascagh, *m.* the dau. of Samuel Steele, of Castletown, and had issue,

White. THE LANDED GENTRY. 764

1. Samuel, who had issue, a son, Humphrey, and three daus. (Mrs. Marshall, Mrs. Odlum, and Mrs. Galbraith).
2. Humphrey, who *d.s.p.*
3. Edward, who had issue, a son,
Samuel, of Abbeyleix, who *d.* 1844, leaving issue, one son, Edward, of Abbeyleix, who *d.s.p.* 25 Aug. 1851, and three daus. (1) Elinor, *m.* 1810, William Foster, and had issue; (2) Elizabeth, *d. unm.* 1848 ; and (3) Sarah Anne.
5. John, who left issue.
The 2nd son,
ROBERT WHITE, of Raheen (now Charleville), *b.* 1674 ; *m.* Margaret, dau. of Samuel Steele, of Castletown, and *d.* 1750, leaving issue,
1. CHARLES, of whom presently.
2. George, of Scotchrath, Queen's Co., *m.* Jane Mitchell, of the King's Co., and had issue,
1. Robert, of Scotchrath, *m.* Elizabeth, dau. of Charles White, of Aghavoe, and *d.* Aug. 1820, having had issue,
(1) Robert, of Scotchrath, *m.* 28 May, 1824, Mary, dau. of Peter Roe, of Kildellig, and *d.* about 1853, having had issue.
(1) Sarah Catharine, *d. unm.* (2) Clarissa Mary, *d. unm.*
(3) Jane Cecilia, *m.* George Roe, of Loran Park, co. Tipperary, and *d.* 1826, having had issue.
(4) Elizabeth, *m.* Samuel White, of Ballybrophy, and *d.* 25 June, 1875, having had issue.
2. Samuel, *d. unm.* 3. Thomas Mitchell, *d. unm.*
4. George, who had issue, one son, George, who *d. unm.*, and two daus., Mrs. Graham and Mrs. Whitaker.
5. Charles, *m.* by licence, 1786, Mary Llewellyn, and had issue,
(1) George Robert, Solicitor, *m.* Miss Ford, and had issue.
(1) Susannah, *m.* Peter Roe, of Gortnaclea, and had issue.
(2) Elizabeth, *m.* T. Haslam. (3) Ellen, *d. unm.*
1. Elizabeth, *m.* — Alley. 2. Margaret, *m.* — Brereton.
3. Ellinor, *m.* John Roe, of Beckfield.
4. Mary Ann, *m.* Dr. Haslam, of Frankford.
5. Susan, *m.* — Mitchell, of Birr.
3. Samuel, of Raheen (now Charleville), who *d.s.p.* 22 Sept. 1771. By his will, proved 2 Dec. 1771, he bequeathed Raheen to his nephew, Charles White, son of his brother, Charles White, of Aghavoe.
4. Edward, *d.s.p.*
The eldest son,
CHARLES WHITE, of Aghavoe, Queen's Co., *b.* 1706 ; *m.* Elizabeth, dau. of Charles Spunner, of Milltown, King's Co., and *d.* about 1771, having had issue,
1. CHARLES, of whom presently.
2. Robert of Aghavoe, *b.* 8 July, 1748 ; *m.* March, 1779, Charlotte, dau. of James Hamilton, of Sheephill and Holmpatrick, co. Dublin (see BURKE's *Peerage*, HOLMPATRICK, B.), and *d.* 1814, having had issue,
1. Charles, a cornet in the 17th Light Dragoons in 1805, *d. unm.*
2. James, of Aghavoe, Lieut. 42nd Highlanders, High Sheriff for Queen's Co. 1816, *d. unm.* 1825.
3. Robert, of Old Park (Grantston Manor), J.P., High Sheriff for Queen's Co. 1818, *m.* Anne, dau. of Capt. Charles Powlett Doyne, of Portarlington (see DOYNE *of Wells*), and *d.* 1862, aged 75, having had issue,
(1) Robert Philip, of Woodview, Stillorgan, co. Dublin, and of the Queen's Co., *b.* 28 Feb. 1818, B.A. Trin. Coll. Dublin, late Capt. Queen's Co. Militia ; *m.* 3 Oct. 1860, Olivia, dau. of the Rev. Henry Herbert, Rector of Rathdowney, Queen's Co. (see HERBERT *of Muckruss*), and *d.* 31 May, 1904, having had issue,
1. Robert Vicars, *b.* 25 Sept. 1866 ; *d. unm.* 24 June, 1908.
1. Harriet Anne, *m.* 25 Jan. 1894, the Rev. J. Berkeley Bristow, M.A., Rector of Dunluce, and *d.s.p.* 1 Nov. 1903.
2. Annette Charlotte. 3. Olivia Constance.
(2) Charles Paulet, of Erkindale, Queen's Co., J.P., *b.* 21 July, 1821 ; *m.* Joanna Boys, and *d.s.p.* 10 June, 1895.
(3) Hans, *b.* 1823, Lieut. 12th Regt. ; *d. unm.* 1864.
(4) James, *d.* young.
(1) Charlotte, *m.* 1 Oct. 1840, Thomas James Hamilton, and *d.* 1875, having had issue.
4. Hans, of Aghavoe, J.P., *m.* Anne (*d.* 1891), dau. of John Armit, and was accidentally killed 5 March, 1829, having had issue,
(1) Robert (Sir), K.C.B., of Aghavoe and Coulnagour, J.P. and D.L. Queen's Co., Gen. in the Army, Col. 21st Hussars, formerly Lieut.-Col. 17th Lancers, *b.* 21 Feb. 1827 ; *m.* 1868, Charlotte, dau. of the Rev. John Meara, of Headfort, co. Galway. He *d.* 17 Sept. 1902, leaving issue,
1. Hans Stannard, Lieut.-Col. Royal Artillery, *b.* 12 April, 1862 ; *m.* June, 1895, Mabel, dau. of Capt. Allen Mackay, Royal Artillery, and has issue, (1) a son, *b.* 25 June, 1902, (1) Mabel, (2) a dau., *b.* 6 Dec. 1898.
2. Henry Ernest, *b.* May, 1864 ; *m.* 2 Sept. 1893, Frances Mary, dau. of the Hon. Robert Flower (see BURKE's *Peerage*, ASHBROOK, B.), and has issue, Robert Llowarch, *b.* 19 Jan. 1896.
3 Robert F. H., High Sheriff Queen's Co. 1908, *b.* 14 Nov. 1868.
4. Ion Hamilton G., *b.* 29 Sept. 1874.
1. Hope Alice Georgina, *m.* Oct. 1891, Gerard Lawrence, and has issue. 2. Cerise Elinor.
(2) Hans, J.P. Queen's Co., *m.* Mary, dau. of — Saunders, of Tunbridge Wells, and *d.s.p.* 18 April, 1887.
(1) Georgina, *m.* the Rev. Dr. Sadler, F. T.C.D., and *d.s.p.*
1. Caroline, *m.* Charles White, of Charleville, and had issue.
2. Hannah, *m.* Francis Butler, of Castletown, and had issue.

3. Sophia, *m.* Rev. John Isaac Beresford, Rector of Donaghmore, and had issue (see BURKE's *Peerage*, WATERFORD, M.).
3. Edward, *b.* 10 Aug. 1751 ; *d.* young.
4. Samuel, *b.* 13 May, 1754 ; *d.* young.
5. Thomas, *b.* 1 May, 1755 ; *d.* young.
1. Margaret, *b.* 15 Oct. 1749 ; *m.* 1775, John Kemmis, and *d.* 1827, having had issue (see KEMMIS *of Shaen*).
2. Sarah, *b.* 23 Feb. 1753 ; *m.* 1775, Charles White, of Ballybrophy, and *d.* 1833, having had issue.
3. Elizabeth, *b.* 9 March, 1755 ; *m.* Robert White, of Scotchrath, and *d. circa* 1837, having had issue.
4. Catharine, *b.* 28 July, 1759 ; *m.* — Jones, of Nutgrove, co. Dublin, and had issue.
5. Mary, *m.* Dr. John Franck, of Forest, Queen's Co., and had issue.
The eldest son,
CHARLES WHITE, of Charleville, *b.* 12 May, 1747 ; *s.* to Raheen under the will of his uncle, Samuel White, and changed the name to Charleville. He was Colonel of the Kyle Volunteers. He *m.* 1 Sept. 1778, Sophia Alice (who *d.* 1795), dau. of Sir Roger Palmer, Bart., and *d.* 1802, leaving issue,
1. CHARLES, of whom presently.
2. Thomas John, of Borris-in-Ossory, *b.* about 1785 ; *m.* Anne Carroll, and *d.* 1856, having had issue,
1. William, M.D., *b.* 1807 ; *m.* Mary Anne, dau. of D. Mansergh, and had issue, a son, William. 2. Charles, *d.* 1861.
1. Sophia, *d. unm.* 2. Anne, *d. unm.*
The eldest son,
CHARLES WHITE, of Charleville, *b.* about 1783, High Sheriff for Queen's Co. 1815 ; *m.* Caroline, dau. of Robert White, of Aghavoe ; she *d.* about 1846. He *d.* 1833, having had issue,
1. Thomas, *d.* young.
2. James, *d.* young.
3. HENRY, late of Charleville.
4. Hans Robert, *b.* 1825, Major 89th Regt. ; *m.* Mary, dau. of Hubert Moore, of Shannon Grove, co. Galway, and *d.* 1888, having had issue,
1. Hubert Butler Moore, *b.* 1865.
2. Charles Lennox Moore, *b.* 1863 ; *d.* 1874.
1. Harriet Selina Moore, *m.* William G. McIvor, and has issue.
2. Guendoline Alice Moore.
3. Violet Moore. 4. Mary Caroline Moore, *d. unm.* 1891.
1. Charlotte, *d. unm.*
2. Caroline, *m.* Barker Thacker, and *d.s.p.* 1869.
The 3rd son,
HENRY WHITE, of Charleville, Queen's Co., J.P. and D.L. for that co., and J.P. for King's Co., *b.* 1818 ; *m.* 1855, Elizabeth, dau. of Richard Rossall, of Lancaster, and *d.* 9 July, 1903, having by her (who *d.* 1870) had issue,
1. HENRY CHARLES, late of Charleville.
1. HENRIETTA MARGARET, now of Charleville.
2. CAROLINE ELIZABETH, now of Charleville.
3. SOPHIA CHARLOTTE, now of Charleville.
The only son,
HENRY CHARLES WHITE, of Charleville, Queen's Co., J.P. co. Tipperary and King's and Queen's Cos., High Sheriff 1905, *b.* 1861, B.A. Trin. Coll. Dublin, late Lieut. 4th Batt. Leinster Regt. He *d.* 4 Aug. 1906.

Seat—Charleville, Roscrea. *Residence*—4, Earlsfort Terrace, Dublin.

WHITE OF CLOONE GRANGE.

GEORGE WHITE, of Cloone Grange, co. Leitrim, J.P., High Sheriff 1907, *b.* 1881 ; *m.* 11 Sept. 1907, Chisogona Constantia Barbara Beresford, 4th dau. of Charles Cecil Beresford Whyte, of Hatley Manor, co. Leitrim (see *that family*).

Lineage.—LUKE WHITE, of Woodlands, co. Dublin, High Sheriff 1804, M.P. for Leitrim, High Sheriff co. Longford 1806, *m.* 1st, Eliza, dau. of Andrew Maziere, of Dublin, and by her had issue,
1. Thomas, of Woodlands, J.P., High Sheriff 1839, an officer, co. Dublin Mil., *m.* 31 Aug. 1819, Julia, dau. of Charles, 2nd Viscount Gort. She *d.* 14 Feb. 1866. He *d.s.p.* 4 May, 1847.
2. Samuel, of Killakee, co. Dublin, Lieut.-Col. County Dublin Militia, M.P. for Leitrim, High Sheriff 1809, *m.* 4 July, 1821, Salisbury Anne, dau. of George Rothe, of Mount Rothe, co. Kilkenny (see *that family*). She *d.* 27 Nov. 1880. He *d.s.p.* 1854.
3. Luke, of Rathcline, M.P. for Longford, High Sheriff 1821, *d. unm.* 1854.
4. Henry, created BARON ANNALY (see BURKE's *Peerage*).

1. Anna Maria, *m.* 27 Nov. 1807, Charles Trench. He *d.* 6 April, 1840. She *d.* 19 Dec. 1847, leaving issue (*see* BURKE's *Peerage*, ASHTOWN, B.).
2. Eliza, *d. unm*
3. Matilda, *m.* 22 June, 1826, Hugh, 4th Lord Massy. He *d.* 27 Feb. 1836. She *d.* 27 Feb. 1883, leaving issue.
He *m.* 2ndly, 1800, Arabella, dau. of Henry Fortescue, of Cork, and by her (who *d.* Feb. 1853) had issue,
5. WILLIAM, of whom we treat.
Mr. White *d.* 1824. The youngest son,
WILLIAM WHITE, of Shrubs, co. Dublin, *b.* 1801 ; *m.* 2 Oct. 1824, Isabella, dau. of Rev. Henry Bayly, Rector of Nenagh. She *d.* 20 Jan. 1866. He *d.* 14 Feb. 1857, having had issue,
1. GEORGE, of whom presently.
2. Luke, of Chandos, co. Longford, *b.* 3 May, 1832 ; *m.* 19 May, 1859, Elizabeth Mary, dau. of Alexander Richey, of Mount Temple, co. Dublin, and *d.* 1890, having had issue,
  1. William Alexander, of Chandos, co. Longford, J.P. co. Longford, High Sheriff 1891, Capt. 6th Batt. Rifle Brigade, B.A. Trin. Coll. Dublin 1887, *b.* 8 Aug. 1864 ; *m.* 21 Dec. 1891, Adelaide Gray, dau. of Rev. J. J. Newbold, Vicar of Clonbrony, co. Longford, and had issue. He *d.* 30 Oct. 1910.
    Luke William Newbold, *b.* 30 June, 1894.
  1. Maude Helen Elizabeth, *m.* 1893, Lieut.-Col. James Henry Dopping (*see* DOPPING-HEPENSTAL *of Derrycassan*).
  2. Lucie Mary, *m.* Henry Webster, C.E., B.E.
3. Samuel.
4. Henry William, of Southwell, co. Longford, sometime 11th Hussars, High Sheriff, co. Longford, 1866, *b.* 23 June, 1843 ; *m.* 12 Jan. 1864, Alice Clarinda, dau. of Edmund Floyd Cuppage, of Clare Grove, co. Dublin (*see* CUPPAGE *of Mount Edward*). He *d.s.p.* Dec. 1882. She *m.* 2ndly, 16 Jan. 1884, Capt. Alfred Crofton French, 43rd Regt. (*see* FRENCH *of Castle Bernard*).
1. Matilda Emma, *m.* 1851, John Leahy, Q.C., of South Hill, co. Kerry, who *d.* 13 Oct. 1874, leaving issue.
2. Emily, *m.* 17 Dec. 1857, Joseph Bennett Little, of Knockadoo, co. Roscommon, and had issue.
3. Arabella Penelope, *m.* 9 Aug. 1839, John Knight Fitz-Herbert, 5th son of Sir Henry FitzHerbert, 3rd Bart. He *d.* 29 July, 1894. She *d.* 1896, leaving issue (*see* BURKE's *Peerage*, FITZ-HERBERT, Bart.).
4. Helen Maria, *m.* 17 March, 1863, Right Hon. Hugh Law, Lord Chancellor of Ireland. He *d.* 1883. She *d.* 12 Nov. 1875, leaving issue.
The eldest son,
GEORGE WHITE, of Cloone Grange, co. Leitrim, J.P. and D.L., High Sheriff 1861, *b.* 28 Nov. 1828 ; *m.* 25 April, 1854, Mary Charlotte, dau. of Henry Hill, and *d.* 24 Oct. 1874, leaving an only son,
WILLIAM HENRY WHITE, of Cloone Grange, J.P. and D.L., High Sheriff 1883 ; *b.* 31 Jan. 1855 ; *m.* 1st, 6 July, 1876, Audley Harriett, youngest dau. of John Reynolds Dickson, of Woodville, co. Leitrim (*see that family*). She *d.* 6 May, 1887, having had issue,
1. GEORGE, now of Cloone Grange.
1. Audley Mary.
2. Alice, *m.* 24 Oct. 1908, Frederick MacLeod Warre.
3. Helen, *m.* 21 Jan. 1909, Rev. Herbert F. G. Dickinson, Glanhondher, Brecon, S. Wales.
He *m.* 2ndly, 1888, Marion Charlotte, dau. of W. H. Hayes. He *d.* May, 1892. His widow *m.* 1893, John Weston.

Arms—Arg. on a chevron engrailed gu. between three roses of the last a cross-crosslet or. Crests—A cubit arm erect ppr., holding a sprig also ppr., bearing three roses gu. ; on the arm a chevron engrailed of the last charged with a cross crosslet or.
Motto—Vi et virtute.

Seat—Cloone Grange, Mohill, co. Leitrim.

WHITE OF WHITE HALL.

The late FIELD MARSHAL SIR GEORGE STUART WHITE, V.C., G.C.B., O.M., G.C.S.I., G.C.M.G., G.C.I.E., G.C.V.O., of White Hall, co. Antrim, J.P. and D.L. co. Antrim, Col. of the Gordon Highlanders and Hon. Col. 2nd Vol. Batt. Somersetshire L.I., LL.D. Camb. and Dublin, and D.C.L. Oxford, *hon. causâ*, *b.* 6 July, 1835 ; *m.* 1874, Amelia Maria, Lady of the Imperial Order of the Crown of India, dau. of Ven. Joseph Baly, Archdeacon of Calcutta, and has issue,

JAMES ROBERT, D.S.O., Capt. Gordon Highlanders, served in S. African War 1899-1901 (despatches, D.S.O.), *b.* 22 May, 1879 ; *m.* 24 April, 1907, Mercedes, eldest dau. of Alexander Mosley, C.M.G.

Sir George served in the Indian Mutiny 1857-9, in Afghan War 1879-80, in Soudan Expedition 1884-5, in Burmese Expedition 1885-9, in Zhob Field Force 1890, and in South African War 1899-1900 (commanded during siege of Ladysmith). Sir George was Commander-in-Chief in India 1893-8, Quarter-Master-Gen. of the Forces 1898-9, Lieut.-Gen. in Natal 1899-1900, and Governor and Commander-in-Chief at Gibraltar 1900-1905, Governor of the Royal Hospital, Chelsea, from 1905-1912. He *d.* 23 June, 1912.

Lineage.—REV. FULKE WHITE, of White Hall, co. Antrim, 1716, father of
REV. JAMES WHITE, of White Hall, *d.* 1761, father of
JOHN WHITE, of White Hall, *d.* 1770, father of
JAMES WHITE, of White Hall, Deputy-Governor of co. Antrim 1793, *d.* 1804. Had issue two sons,
1. JOHN, his heir.
2. JAMES ROBERT, who *s.* his brother.
JOHN WHITE, of White Hall, High Sheriff co. Antrim 1845, *d.* 18 Feb. 1857, and was *s.* by his brother,
JAMES ROBERT WHITE, of White Hall, barrister, *d.* 9 Jan. 1872 ; *m.* Frances, dau. of George Stuart, of Donaghey, co. Tyrone, Surgeon-General of the Army in Ireland, and had two sons and two daus.,
1. GEORGE STUART (Sir), late of White Hall.
2. John, C.B. (1902), of Innispollin, co. Antrim, *b.* 1830, *d.* 11 Jan. 1912, Fellow Queen's Coll. Oxon, Barr. Lincoln's Inn, Principal Ass. Sec. Board of Education, 1900-3.
1. Frances Avone.   2. Jane.

Arms—Per fesse arg. and gu., in chief six roses three and three of the second barbed and seeded ppr., and in base an eagle displayed or. Crest—A dexter arm embossed, vambraced ppr., charged on the elbow with a four-leaved shamrock slipped ou. holding in the hand a sprig of three roses slipped and leaved ppr.
Motto—Honeste parta.

Seat—White Hall, Ballymena, co. Antrim.

WHITE OF LOUGH ESKE CASTLE.

HENRY HERBERT RONALD WHITE, of Lough Eske Castle, co. Donegal, J.P., High Sheriff, 1912, Capt. late King's Royal Rifle Corps, served in South African War 1901-2 and in Somaliland Campaign 1903-4, *b.* 9 Feb. 1879 ; *m.* 24 June, 1906, Florence Geraldine, dau. of the late Sir John Arnott, 1st Bart. (*see* BURKE's *Peerage*) and Lady FitzGerald Arnott, and has issue,
1. HENRY GEORGE RONALD, *b.* 17 April, 1907.
2. John Maxwell, *b.* 12 July, 1909.

Lineage.—CHARLES NICHOLAS WHITE, of Datchet House, Windsor, Bucks, H.E.I.C.S., Chief Secretary to the Government of Madras, and Judge of the High Court, son of Capt. John White, R.N., and Joanna his wife, dau. of — Dormer, of Alphington, co. Devon, *b.* 18 June, 1754 ; *m.* 28 Feb. 1792, Letitia Mytton, dau. of Edward Owen Williams, of Eaton Mascott Hall, Salop, by Letitia his wife, dau. of John Mytton, of Halston Park, Salop, She *d.* 12 March, 1822. He *d.* 20 Feb. 1839, having had issue,
1. Charles, Col. Gren. Guards, Knt. of the Order of Leopold of Belgium, of St. Anne of Russia, and Medjidie, sometime Equerry to H.R.H. the Duke of Cambridge, *b.* 16 Jan. 1793 ; *m.* 21 Aug. 1821, Marie Adèle, dau. of George Blackshaw, of Ashurst, Tunbridge Wells, Kent. She *d.* 24 Jan. 1872. He *d.* 23 Oct. 1861, having had issue,
  Charles Henry, of Gladwyn, co. Denbigh, J.P., Lieut.-Col. Cheshire Mil., sometime Coldstream Guards, *b.* 28 July, 1822 ; *m.* 24 May, 1849, Elizabeth, dau. of Col. John Potter Hamilton, of Hildersham Hall, Cambs., by Charlotte his wife, dau. of John Fane, of Wormsley, co. Oxford, and *d.* 7 Nov. 1877, leaving a dau.,
    Marie Adèle Cecile, *m.* 9 July, 1891, John Bolton Hamilton, son of Col. Digby St. Vincent Hamilton, of Bath, and *d.s.p.* 8 Nov. 1891.
2. Frederic, Maj. 90th Light Infantry, *b.* 1802 ; *m.* Harriet, dau. of Rev.Thomas French Cooke,of Thomastown,co. Kilkenny. She *d.* 22 Sept. 1858. He *d.s.p.* 1 May, 1856.
3. HENRY, of whom presently.
4. Raymond, Lieut.-Col. 6th Inniskilling Dragoons, *b.* 1808 ; *m.* his cousin Emma, dau. of Richard Williams, of Eaton Mascott Hall, co. Salop. She *d.* 28 April, 1884. He *d.* 13 Jan. 1844, having had issue,
  1. Raymond Herbert, Maj.-Gen. late Scots Guards, *b.* 23 Sept. 1832 ; *m.* 24 Sept. 1885, Hon. Laura Jane Edwardes, dau. of William, 3rd Lord Kensington. He *d.s.p.* 13 July, 1894.
  2. Edward Hubert, Post Capt. R.N., Commodore West Indian Station, served in Baltic 1854-5 (medal with clasp), *b.* 6 Feb. 1835 ; *d. unm.* 6 Aug. 1882.
  3 Walter, Barrister-at-Law, *b.* 22 June, 1842 ; *d. unm.* 6 Jan. 1887.
  1. Fanny, *m.* 25 Nov. 1890, Maj. Horace Durrant, late 8th Hussars.
The 3rd son,
THE REV. HENRY WHITE, of Almington Hall, Salop, sometime Lieut. Coldstream Guards, *b.* 6 July, 1804 ; *m.* 1st, 18 Sept. 1834, Sarah Ford, dau. of George Stevens, R.N., by Sarah his wife, dau. of John Ford. She *d.* 27 Oct. 1870, having had issue,
1. HENRY GEORGE, late of Lough Eske Castle.
1. Ada Letitia, *b.* 31 Dec. 1836 ; *m.* 15 Sept. 1856, Rev. Rowland German Buckston, M.A., of Bradborne Hall, co. Derby, Vicar of Sutton-on-the-Hill. She *d.* 11 Dec. 1892, leaving issue.
2. Edith, *b.* 31 Aug. 1846 ; *d.* 15 Sept. 1852.

He m. 2ndly, Florence, dau. of Rev. Thomas Luby, D.D., S.F.T.C.D. He d. 26 Jan. 1885. She m. 2ndly, 17 Oct. 1896, the Right Hon. Sir George Ferguson Bowen, P.C., G.C.M.G., son of the Rev. Edward Bowen. Sir George d. 21 Feb. 1899. His only son,

MAJ.-GEN. HENRY GEORGE WHITE, of Lough Eske Castle, co. Donegal, J.P. and D.L., Maj.-Gen. in the Army, retired, late Col. Royal Scots Lothian Regt., served in Crimea 1854-6, on field service under Sir Hugh Rose, in Central India 1857-9, in Cyprus 1878-9, and in Bechuanaland 1884-5, b. 22 Sept. 1835; m. 19 Dec. 1874, Frances Cromwell, widow of Capt. Henry Raymond Pelly, R.E., son of Col. Raymond Perry, C.B., 16th Lancers (see BURKE's *Peerage*, PELLY, Bart.), and dau. of Capt. George Ferguson, of Houghton Hall, co. Cumberland, by Elizabeth his wife, dau. of Charles Hill, of Halifax. He d. 24 June, 1906, having had issue,

HENRY HERBERT RONALD, now of Lough Eske Castle.

Sybil Georgina, m. 17 Nov. 1910, Arthur Osmond Barnes, son of John Henry Barnes, of Chorley Wood House, Herts.

Seat—Lough Eske Castle, co. Donegal. *Clubs*—Army and Navy, Royal Automobile, W.

WHITE OF GRACEFIELD.

CAPT. JOSEPH HENRY LACHLAN WHITE, of Bredfield House, Suffolk, and Gracefield, Queen's Co., J.P. and D.L. for Queen's Co., High Sheriff 1904 and J.P. Suffolk, late Capt. 5th (Northumberland) Fus., B.A. Trin. Coll. Camb., b. 7 Jan. 1859; m. 5 Oct. 1886, Frances Mary Josephine (Pansy), dau. of the late Richard Joseph Grace, D.L., of Bruff, co. Limerick, and grand-dau. and co-heir of Oliver Dowell John Grace, V.L., of Mantua, co. Roscommon, and Gracefield, Queen's Co. (see that family).

SEDULE ET PROSPERE

Lineage.—JOSEPH WHITE, of Sutton Hall, Cheshire, b. 1736. m. 1775, Mary, dau. of J. Hough, and d. 30 Dec. 1818, having had issue,

1. JOSEPH, of whom presently.
2. George, b. 1788; m. Mary, dau. of W. Bateman, and d. 30 March, 1848.
   1. Mary, m. Rev. Thomas Scutt, and had issue.
   2. Ellen, m. Dideric Holme.

The elder son,

JOSEPH WHITE, of Sutton Hall, b. 1783; m. 1817, Susan, dau. of Robert Pretyman, of Belstead, Suffolk, and d. 1 March, 1845, having by her had issue,

1. JOSEPH, of whom presently.
2. Robert (Rev.), B.A., B.N.C. Oxford, Vicar of Little Budworth, 1853-98, b. 1820; m. Isabella Ker, dau. of William Johnstone Dobie, of Gresford, and had issue,
   Arthur Pretyman, M.I.M.E., b. 1861; m. 1886, Lucy Murray, dau. of Murdo Mackenzie, and has issue,
   1. Cecil Dobie Murray, b. 1896.
   2. Doris Mary Pretyman.
3. James, M.R.C.S., b. 1823; m. Mary, dau. of R. Prosser, and d. 1897, leaving issue,
   Robert Prosser, b. 1855; m. 1907, Clarice, dau. of Rev. H. Le Rougetel, and has issue,
   Robert Le Rougetel, b. 1908.
4. William, b. 1825; d. Nov. 1851, unm.
5. Richard (Rev.), B.A. Trin. Coll. Camb., b. 1826; m. Emma, dau. of J. Phillips, and d. 1891, leaving five sons and two daus.
6. Thomas, b. 1829; d. 1860, unm.
7. George, b. 1836; m. Mary Elizabeth, dau. of W. Bilham; d. 1902, leaving issue.
   1. Susan, d. 1897, unm.
   2. Mary, m. Rev. R. Shea, and d. 1896, leaving issue.
   3. Minnie, m. W. Gibson, and d. 1893, leaving issue.
   4. Emma, d. 1898, unm.
   5. Fanny, m. W. Bilham, and has issue.
   6. Elizabeth, m. Rev. R. Wilkinson, and has issue.

The eldest son,

JOSEPH WHITE, of Bredfield House, Woodbridge, Suffolk, b. 21 Feb. 1819; m. 1856, Emily, dau. of the late Robert Lachlan, of Gloucester Gardens, Hyde Park, London. She d. 14 May, 1908. He d. 14 March, 1885, having had issue,

JOSEPH HENRY LACHLAN, his heir.

Cecilia Pretyman, b. 14 Nov. 1862; m. 1st, 1888, Herbert Penfold Preston, of Eaton Place, London, who d. 1891, leaving a dau., Ruth. She m. 2ndly, 1893, Kenneth Parish Kingsford, of Queen's Gate Terrace, London, and has issue by him a dau., Grace, b. 1894.

Arms—(H. COLL.)—Arg, two escallops in fess sa. and in base a buck trippant ppr., attired or on a chief az. a bezant between two bees volant also ppr. *Crest*—On a mount vert, a buck trippant per pale arg. and ppr., attired or the dexter foreleg bearing a flagstaff in bend sinister also ppr., thereon hoisted a banner gold fringed and charged with an escallop gu. *Motto*—Sedule et prospere.

Seats—Bredfield House, Woodbridge, Suffolk; Gracefield Athy, Queen's Co. *Clubs*—Naval and Military, and Kildare Street, Dublin.

JERVIS-WHITE OF FERNS.

The late LIEUT.-COL. HENRY JERVIS JERVIS-WHITE, of Ferns, and Healthfield, co. Wexford, J.P. cos. Dublin and Wexford, D.L. co. Wexford, High Sheriff for the latter 1895, M.A. Trin. Coll. Dublin, Lieut.-Col. (retired) Duke of Cambridge's Own Middlesex Regt. (77th), b. 21 June, 1841; m. 9 June, 1887, Marion Eleanor, now of Ferns and Healthfield, dau. of Sir Francis William Brady, 2nd Bart. (see BURKE's *Peerage*). He d. 6 June, 1909.

Lineage.—THOMAS JERVIS JERVIS-WHITE, of Ferns, co. Wexford, next brother to Sir John Jervis White-Jervis, 1st bart. of Ballyellis, and 2nd son of John Jervis-White, of Ballyellis (who d. 12 July, 1793) and Elizabeth his wife (who d. 10 Oct. 1783), dau. of George Whitthorn (see BURKE's *Peerage*, JERVIS-WHITE-JERVIS, Bart.), m. Frances, dau. of Sir John Meredyth, 1st bart., of Carlandstown. He had issue,

1. John, of Ferns, LL.D., Barrister-at-Law, m. Mary, dau. of Thomas Bradford, of Sandbach, Cheshire, and widow of Sir John Jervis-White-Jervis, 1st bart. She d. 15 July, 1879. He d.s.p. 1873.
2. HUMPHREY, of whom presently.
3. Thomas (Rev.), M.A. Trin. Coll. Dublin, Rector of Middlewick, co. Armagh, b. 9 April, 1801; d. unm. 26 July, 1881.
4. Henry, Capt. 77th Regt., d. unm. 1856.
1. Helena, m. Robert Sandys, of Dargle, co. Wicklow, J.P. He d. May, 1875, leaving issue.

The 2nd son,

COL. HUMPHREY JERVIS-WHITE, H.E.I.C.S., 50th Bengal N.I., b. 25 Dec. 1797; m. 1835, Elizabeth, dau. of Maj. —— Bury, 35th Regt. She d. 15 Jan. 1879. He d. 15 Dec. 1849, leaving issue,

1. HENRY JERVIS, late of Healthfield Manor.
2. Thomas, d. unm.
1. Alicia Frances, m. 30 April, 1868, William Anton Doorley, 24th Regt. She d. 1876, leaving issue.
2. Helen Elizabeth, m. 10 April, 1866, Charles Frederick Oakes, M.D. She d. Nov. 1883, leaving issue.

Arms—Quarterly, 1st and 4th sa., a chevron erm. between three martlets or (JERVIS); 2nd and 3rd gu., a chevron vair between three lions rampant or armed and langued az. (WHITE). *Crest*—1. (JERVIS), A martlet or. 2. (WHITE), Three arrows, two in saltire points downwards, the other in fess, point to the dexter, gu. beaded or flighted arg.

Seat—Healthfield Manor, Wexford.

LEIGH-WHITE OF BANTRY.

EDWARD EGERTON LEIGH-WHITE, of Bantry House, co. Cork, J.P. and D.L., High Sheriff 1903, B.A. Merton Coll. Oxford, b. 23 June, 1876, assumed, by Royal Licence, 26 July, 1897, the additional name and arms of WHITE; m. 27 April, 1904, Arethusa Flora Gartside, eldest dau. of the late Peter James Duff Hawker, of Longparish House, Hampshire, and has issue,

1. Clodagh Elizabeth Maude, b. 8 April, 1905.
2. Rachel Veronica Rose, b. 9 Oct. 1906.

Lineage.—RICHARD WHITE, of Bantry, co. Cork, son of Richard White, of Bantry, m. 1734, Martha, dau. of the Very Rev.

IRELAND. White.

Rowland Davies, of Dawston, co. Cork, Dean of Cork and Ross, and had issue,
SIMON, his heir.
Margaret, m. 8 Nov. 1756, Richard, Viscount Longueville, son of Robert Longfield, of Castle Mary (see that family). He d.s.p. 23 May, 1811, when his peerage became extinct. She d. April, 1809.
The only son,
SIMON WHITE, of Bantry, m. 1760, Frances Jane, dau. of Richard Hedges Eyre, of Mount Hedges, co. Cork, by Helena his wife, dau. of Thomas Herbert, of Muckross Abbey, co. Kerry, and d.s.p., having by her (who d. 1816) had issue,
 1. RICHARD, of whom presently.
 2. Simon, Col. in the Army, m. 1801, Sarah, dau. of John Newenham, of Maryborough, and d. 1838, having had issue,
  1. Robert Hedges Eyre, of Glengariffe Castle, co. Cork, late Capt. Rifle Brigade, b. 1809 ; m. 1834, Charlotte Mary, only dau. and heir of Thomas Dorman, of Raffeen House, co. Cork, and had issue,
   Robert Hedges Eyre, of Raffeen House, co. Cork, b. 23 Feb. 1836 ; m. 1860, Mary Anne d'Esterre, dau. of John Roberts, of Ardmore, co. Waterford, and has issue,
    1. Robert Hedges Eyre, b. 1862.
    2. Simon, b. 1863.   3. Edward, b. 1869.
    1. Anna Mary.
    2. Frances Dorothy, m. 7 July, 1883, Robert William Delacour.
   Henrietta Sarah Dorman, m. 24 April, 1856, Richard William Roberts, of Ardmore, co. Cork, and has issue (see that family).
  2. Edward Richard, Capt. 10th Regt., m. 17 Feb. 1863, Margaret, dau. of George Dudley, and has issue,
   Edward Simon, late 4th Batt. Leinster Regt., b. 1869.
   Fanny Sarah Alicia Katherine, m. 1885, Maj. Charles William Bowlby, Connaught Rangers, and has issue.
   1. Fanny Rosa Maria, m. 1830, John Lavallin Puxley, of Dunboy, co. Cork, who d. 1837, leaving issue.
   2. Harriet, d. unm.
 3. Hamilton, m. 1800, Lucinda, dau. of — Heaphy, and d. 7 Dec. 1804, leaving issue,
  1. Richard.
  2. John Hamilton, of Dromore, m. 22 June, 1843, Alicia, only child of Charles Daly, M.D.
 1. Helen, m. R. D. Newnham, of Maryborough, co. Cork, who d. 1835.
 2. Martha, m. 1800, Michael Goold-Adams, of Jamesbrook, co. Cork, who d. 1817. She d. 1847, leaving issue (see that family).
 3. Frances, m. 28 July, 1801, Gen. Edward Dunne, of Brittas. She d. 1864.   He d. 12 Nov. 1844, leaving issue (see that family).
The eldest son,
RICHARD, 1st EARL OF BANTRY and Viscount Berehaven (so created 22 Jan. 1816), Viscount Bantry (so created 29 Dec. 1800). and Baron Bantry (so created 24 March, 1797), all in the Peerage of Ireland, b. 6 Aug. 1767 ; m. 25 Nov. 1799, Lady Margaret Anne Hare, dau. of William, 1st Earl of Listowel. She d. 19 Jun. 1835. He d. 2 May, 1851, having had issue,
 1. RICHARD, 2nd Earl.
 2. WILLIAM HENRY HARE, 3rd Earl.
 3. Simon, an Officer in the Army, b. March, 1807 ; d. unm. 1837.
 4. Robert Hedges, J.P. co. Cork, b. 31 March, 1810, who left issue, now extinct. His son, Richard, d. 18 May, 1886, aged 22.
 1. Mary, b. 10 Nov. 1805 ; d. June, 1807.
The eldest son,
RICHARD, 2nd EARL OF BANTRY, b. 16 Nov. 1800 ; m. 11 Oct. 1836, Lady Mary O'Brien, dau. of William, 2nd Marquess of Thomond (see BURKE's Peerage, INCHIQUIN, B.). She d. 19 July, 1853.   He d.s.p. 16 July, 1868, and was s. by his brother,
WILLIAM HENRY HARE, 3rd EARL OF BANTRY, D.L., Col. West Cork Art., a representative peer, assumed, by Royal Licence, the additional name and arms of HEDGES, b. 10 Nov. 1801 ; m. 16 April, 1845, Jane, dau. of Charles John Herbert, of Muckross, co. Kerry. She d. 7 July, 1898. He d. 15 Jan. 1884, having had issue,
 1. WILLIAM HENRY HARE, 4th AND LAST EARL OF BANTRY, b. 2 July, 1854 ; m. 18 Feb. 1886, Rosamond Catherine, dau. of Hon. Edmund George Petre, and d.s.p. 30 Nov. 1891, when his titles became extinct. She m. 2ndly, 7 Dec. 1897, Arthur, 2nd Lord Trevor.
 1. ELIZABETH, of whom presently.
 2. Emily Anne, d. young, 5 Sept. 1860.
 3. Olivia Charlotte, b. 25 Aug. 1850 ; m. 16 Feb. 1871, Arthur Edward, Baron Ardilaun (see BURKE's Peerage).
 4. Ina Maude, b. 20 May, 1852 ; m. 24 Oct. 1885, Sewallis Edward 10th Earl Ferrers (see BURKE's Peerage).
 5. Jane Frances Anna, b. 2 Aug. 1857 ; m. 6 Jan. 1876, Edward Maxwell Kenney-Herbert, and has issue (see KENNEY-HERBERT, of Castle Island).
The eldest dau.,
LADY ELIZABETH MARY GORE HEDGES-WHITE, b. 29 Jan. 1847 ; m. 5 Aug. 1874, EGERTON LEIGH, of High Leigh, Cheshire (see that family), and d. 1 Oct. 1880, having by him (who m. 2ndly, 7 May, 1889, Violet Cecil May, dau. of Col. Alfred Tipping, and has issue by her) had issue,
 EDWARD EGERTON, now of Bantry.
 Margaret Elizabeth Egerton, m. 4 April, 1899, Richard Oliver Marton, D.S.O., Capt. R.A., son of Col. G. B. H. Marton, of Capenwray, and has issue (see that family).

Arms—Quarterly, 1st and 4th gu., an annulet or within a bordure sa., charged with estoiles of the second on a canton erm. a lion rampant of the third (WHITE); 2nd and 3rd, or, a lion rampant gu. (LEIGH). Crest—1. (WHITE) : A stork arg. beaked and membered or. 2. (LEIGH) : A cubit arm vested paly of five or and sa. cuffed arg., the hand ppr. grasping the upper and lower fragments of a broken tilting spear, the point downwards ppr. Mottoes—1. (Over the second crest) : Force avec vertu. 2. (Under the arms) : The noblest motive is the public good.
Seat—Bantry House, and Glengarriff Lodge, Bantry, co. Cork. Clubs—Windham, Wellington, Garrick, and Kildare Street.

WHITE OF MOUNT SION.

WILLIAM JASPER JOSEPH WHITE, of Mount Sion, co. Limerick, J.P., High Sheriff 1901, b. 1866 ; m. 27 Jan. 1904, Florence Edith, 2nd dau. of the late William Francis Taylor, of Moseley and Moor Green, Worcestershire, and has issue,
 1. A dau.   2. A dau.

Lineage.—RICHARD WHITE, of Ballinity (or Whitestown), co. Limerick in 1413, and afterwards of Ballynanty, same co., m. Catharine Butler, and had issue, a son,
DOMINICK WHITE, of Ballynanty, who built the family mansion there, m. Maria, dau. of Thomas S. rich, of Limerick, and had a son,
RICHARD WHITE, of Ballynanty, m. Margaret, dau. of Nicholas Arthur, of Limerick, and had a son,
NICHOLAS WHITE, of Limerick, m. Eugenia Gough, and had a son,
RICHARD WHITE, of Limerick, m. Helen, dau. of Pierce (or Peter) Creagh, of Clare, and had two sons. The elder,
JOHN WHITE, of Ballynanty, who was restored to the estates of his ancestors, m. Mary O'Brien, and had a son,
JOHN WHITE, of Ballynanty, m. Margaret, dau. of William Sarsfield, and had an elder son,
JOHN WHITE, of Ballynanty, m. Mary, dau. of William Lysaght, and had a son,
WILLIAM WHITE, of Ballynanty, m. Eleanor O'Riordan, of Limerick, and had with a younger son, Robert, settled in America, an elder son,
JOHN WHITE, of Limerick, m. Alice Sexton, and had issue, a son,
WILLIAM WHITE, of Limerick, whose pedigree was certified by Hawkins, Ulster in 1740, but is not recorded in Ulster's Office ; m. 1st, Catherine, dau. of Henry O'Rourke, of Limerick, and 2ndly, Mary, dau. of John Long, of Limerick, and had issue,
 1. John, of Limerick, m. Mary Creagh.   He d.s.p. Will proved 1763, by his nephew, William.
 2. JASPER, of whom we treat.
The younger son,
JASPER WHITE, of Fairy Hill, Parteen, co. Limerick, m. Helen Creagh, of Dangan, co. Clare, and d. 1808, having had issue,
 1. WILLIAM, of whom presently.
 2. Jasper, of Allacanta, Spain, d. unm.
 3. John, of Belmont and Nantenan, co. Limerick (see WHITE of Nantenan).
  1. Helen, m. 1807, Robert McAulay, of Red Hall, co. Antrim.
The eldest son,
WILLIAM WHITE, of Shannon Dale, Castle Connell, co. Limerick, J.P., and 71, George's Street, Limerick, m. Martha, eld. dau. of Hugh Crawford, D.L., of Orangefield, co. Down, and d. 1842, having had issue,
 1. William, Capt. and Adj. of the Buffs, East Kent Regt., d.v.p. in India.
 2. HELENUS, of whom presently.
 3. Jasper, d. unm.
 1. Elizabeth, m. Edward Murphy, of Carelly, and had issue.
 2. Mary, a nun.   3. Martha, d. unm.
 4. Jane, m. Paul Rochfort.
The elder surviving son,
HELENUS WHITE, of Shannon Dale, and Mount Sion, co. Limerick, J.P. and D.L., High Sheriff 1861, sometime Lieut. West India Regt., b. 1812 ; m. 1st, Elizabeth, dau. of John McMahon, of Firgrove, co. Clare, and 2ndly, 1865, Maria, only dau. of the late Peter Blake, of Holly Park, co. Galway, and d. 5 May, 1874, having by his 2nd wife had issue,
 1. WILLIAN, now of Mount Sion.
 2. Helenus Peter Blake, b. 1868, now of Holly Park, co. Galway, and has adopted the surname of BLAKE.
 3. Martin Edward Patrick, of Mulkear Lodge, co. Limerick, b. 1870 ; m. 1st, 1897, Clare, eld. dau. of Thomas Moriarty, of Abbeytown House, co. Roscommon, late Commissioner R.I.C., Belfast, and has issue,
  Helenus Martin, b. 1901.
He m. 2ndly, 13 July, 1911, Violet, youngest dau. of Robert O'Brien Studdert.
 1. Kathleen Mary Josephine.

Seat—Mount Sion, Dromkeen, co. Limerick. Town Residence—71, George's Street, Limerick.

WHITE OF NANTENAN.

CAPT. JOHN JOSEPH WHITE, of Nantenan, co. Limerick, D.L., High Sheriff 1910, Capt. 85th Shropshire Light Infantry, served in S. African War (despatches, medal with six clasps), B.A. Trin. Coll. Oxford (1885), b. 21 Oct. 1863.

Lineage.—LIEUT.-COL. JOHN WHITE, of Belmont Castle, Connell, and Nantenan, Ballingrane, co. Limerick, J.P., High Sheriff 1856, Lieut.-Col. West India Regt., 3rd son of Jasper White, of Fairy Hill, co. Limerick (see WHITE of Mount Sion), m. 1835, Eleanor Mary, dau. of Richard Irwin, of Rathmoyle, co. Roscommon (see that family). She d. 1863. He d. 1858, having had issue,

1. Jasper, Ensign 4th Dragoon Guards, d. 1866..
2. JOHN PATRICK, of whom presently.
3. Richard, d. 1872.
4. William, Col. late 15th King's Hussars, b. 9 Oct. 1846; d. 1909.
    1. Helen, m. 1861, Col. John Howley, and has issue.
    2. Mary, m. P. Bauon-Newell, and has issue.
    3. Ellen.   4. Jane.
    5. Josephine, d. unm. 1910.

The 2nd son,
JOHN PATRICK WHITE, of Nantenan, co. Limerick, J.P. and D.L., High Sheriff 1867, b. 25 March, 1840; m. 21 Nov. 1861, Emily, dau. of John MacMahon, of Stoneball, co. Clare, and d. 18 Oct. 1892, having had issue,

1. JOHN JOSEPH, now of Nantenan.
2. Jasper, Barrister-at-Law, b. 16 June, 1868.
3. Thomas, b. 4 Feb. 1871.
4. William Michael Joseph, Lieut. the Cameronians Scottish Rifles, served in South African War (despatches, medal with five clasps), b. 29 Sept. 1876, killed in action 12 March, 1901, d. unm.
    1. Mary.   2. Aileen.
    3. Emily.

Seat—Nantenan, Ballingrane, co. Limerick. Clubs—Naval and Military, W., and Kildare Street, Dublin.

BARRINGTON-WHITE OF TEMPLE DINSLEY AND ORANGE HILL.

JAMES BARRINGTON-WHITE, of Temple Dinsley, Hitchin, Herts, and Orange Hill, co. Armagh, J.P. for both cos., High Sheriff for Armagh 1898, late Lieut. Herts Imp. Yeom., b. 21 Sept. 1856; m. 3 June, 1884, Mary, dau. of John Kane Boyd, of Cultra House, co. Down, and has issue.

IVAN BARRINGTON, Grenadier Guards, b. 11 Oct. 1886.

He assumed the additional name of BARRINGTON, 1893.

Lineage.—EDWARD WHITE, of Sowlgrave, Northants, whose will was dated 25 Aug. 1631, proved 1 Oct. that year, left by Marianne his wife, an eldest son,
SAMUEL WHITE, of New Garden, co. Carlow, m. Raines Gough. She survived him, and was bur. 23 Dec. 1681, having had issue three sons. The eldest son,
DANIEL WHITE, of Donore, co. Carlow, b. 1642; m. Elizabeth, only dau. of Thomas Andrews, of Dugganstown, co. Carlow. She d. 21 Sept. 1698. He d. 13 April, 1707, leaving issue five sons and three daus. The eldest son,
THOMAS WHITE, of Donore, co. Cork, b. 30 Jan. 1681; m. 30 Jan. 1711-12, Dorothy, dau. of Walter Mason, of Moone, co. Kildare. She d. 20 Feb. 1759. He d. 3 June, 1764, leaving issue five sons and ten daus. The eldest son,
DANIEL WHITE, of Bandon, co. Cork, b. 17 Jan. 1713; m. 30 May, 1745, Anne Taylor. She d. 6 Feb. 1792. He d. 5 April, 1784, leaving issue three sons and six daus. The eldest surviving dau.,
HANNAH WHITE, b. 16 May, 1753; m. 4 June, 1776, THOMAS WHITE, of Cork, son of James White, of Cork, and Sarah Eustace his wife. She d. 30 July, 1805. He d. 10 Aug. 1790, leaving issue. His eldest son,
JAMES TAYLOR WHITE, of Orange Hill, co. Armagh, b. 9 Nov. 1778; m. 1st, 14 Sept. 1806, Lydia, dau. of Abraham Shackleton, of Ballytore. She d.s.p. 1811. He m. 2ndly, 12 Feb. 1818, Mary, dau. of Richard Pike, of Ballytore. She d. 10 April, 1865. He d. 26 Oct. 1847, having by her had issue,
THOMAS HENRY WHITE, of Orange Hill, co. Armagh, J.P., b. 11 March, 1822; m. 28 Dec. 1853, Mary Jane, 2nd dau. of Edward Barrington, D.L., of Fassaroe, co. Wicklow, and sister of Sir John Barrington, of Glenvar, co. Dublin, and has issue,

1. JAMES, now of Temple Dinsley and Orange Hill.
2. Thomas Henry, b. 1876.
1. Sarah Elizabeth.   2. Selina.

Arms—Or, three chevronels sa., between in chief two roses vert and in base a castle flamant ppr. Crest—A crown vallary or, charged on the band with three pommes, issuing therefrom a demi-hermit with the dexter arm elevated vested paly gu. and arg., the hand ppr., grasping three roses gu., on one stem slipped barbed and seeded ppr., on the head a cowl also paly gu. and arg. Motto—Ung durant ma vie.

Seat—Temple Dinsley, near Hitchin, Herts. Town House—15, Prince's Gate, S.W. Clubs—Carlton, Wellington, Cavalry, and Garrick.

WHITE. See BURKE'S PEERAGE, **ANNALY, B.**

WHITELOCKE-LLOYD. See **LLOYD.**

WHITLA OF BEN EADAN.

JAMES ALEXANDER WHITLA, of Ben Eadan, co. Antrim, Major (retired) 4th Batt. Royal Irish Rifles, late Lieut. 2nd Batt. Royal Inniskilling Fusiliers, and 5th Dragoon Guards, b. 4 April, 1859; m. 4 Aug. 1881, Honoria Maria, 3rd dau. of the late John Handcock Townshend, of Myross Wood (see that family). She d. 9 Jan. 1908, leaving issue,

1. GEORGE TOWNSHEND, Lieut. 4th Batt. Royal Irish Rifles, b. 7 June, 1882.
1. Edith Constance.   2. Norah Kathleen.
3. Alice Mildred.

Lineage.—This family is of Scotch origin, the founder of the Irish branch having migrated to Ireland from Ayrshire, during the plantation of Ulster, and settled at Gobrana, Glenavy, co. Antrim, where the family continued to reside till 1860.

WILLIAM WHITLA, of Glenavy, co. Antrim, b. 1655, had issue by his wife Elizabeth, three sons,
1. GEORGE.   2. James.
3. Valentine.

His eldest son,
GEORGE WHITLA, of Gobrana, Glenavy, b. 1689; m. 1727, his cousin, Elinor Whitla, by whom (who d. 25 Dec. 1774) he had four sons and three daus.

1. William, of Derrichrin, co. Antrim, b. 1729; d. 1794.
2. John, of Lisburn, b. 1732; m. Miss Arthur, and d. 12 May, 1790, having had issue, a dau., Rebecca, and two sons,
    1. William, b. 1764.
    2. George, b. 1765; m. 1792, Margaret Allan-Carleton, by whom (who d. 25 Dec. 1842) he had issue, a dau., Elinor, who d. young, and three sons,
        (1) William, of Lisburn, b. 1 Feb. 1793; m. 5 Nov. 1830, Elizabeth, 3rd dau. of James Buchanan, British Consul at New York, and by her had eight sons and five daus.,
            1. George, Surg.-Gen. late R.H.A., b. 1832; m. 1st, Miss Goodden, by whom he had issue,
                a. George, d. 1885.
                a. Susan.
            He m. 2ndly, 9 June, 1868, Catherine Barbara Gould, eldest dau. of the late Capt. Hamilton L. Jackson (who assumed the name of GOULD by Royal Licence on succeeding to the estate of Upwey, Dorset, 1871) (see that family), by whom he has two daus.,
                b. Helena Catherine Georgina, m. 12 Sept. 1899, Major George A. Moore, R.A.M.C., son of William Moore, of Moore Lodge, co. Antrim (see that family).
                c. Ernesta Carlotta Nina, m. 2 Feb. 1899, James Butler Ievers, of Glanduff Castle (see IEVERS of Mount Ievers).
            2. James Buchanan, b. 1834, late Capt. 88th Connaught Rangers; m. Elizabeth Matilda, eldest dau. of the late Capt. Charles Forbes, 17th Regt. She d. 26 March, 1899.
            3. John, b. 1835; d. young.
            4. William, b. 1840, late Col. Comm. 10th (Lincolnshire) Regt.   5. Sidney, b. 1843; d. young.
            6. Seymour Conway, b. 1845; d. young.
            7. Francis, b. 1849.   8. Valentine, b. 1853.
            1. Elizabeth, m. Capt. Carr, R.I.C.
            2. Eleanor Margaret, m. 1862, Col. Lewis Mansergh Buchanan, C.B., 4th Batt. Royal Inniskilling Fusiliers. She d. 1877. He d. 23 April, 1908, leaving issue (see that family).
            3. Emma Hardcastle, m. 6 Sept. 1864, Major Henry Lucas, late 45th Regt., of Rathealy, co. Cork.
            4. Jane Alicia, m. 24 April, 1872, Charles Cotton Bridges.
            5. Ada, m. 1871, Col. Theophilus Higginson, C.B., 4th son of Henry Theophilus Higginson, M.A., J.P., of Carnalea House, co. Down, and d. 30 Aug. 1903, leaving issue (see that family).

(2) John, *b.* 10 Sept. 1795, Lieut. 14th Light Dragoons; *m.* 24 May, 1820, Eleanor, youngest dau. of J. Haines, of Alcester, co. Warwick, and *d.s.p.* 21 March, 1821.
(3) George, *b.* 1803; *d.* young.
3. Francis, of Glendona, Glenavy, co. Antrim, *b.* 1733; *m.* 9 Sept. 1783, Anne Close, of Aghalee, co. Antrim, and by her (who *d.* 8 Oct. 1796) had issue,
1. William, of Glendona, *d.* 1829.   2. George, *d.* 1844.
3. James, *d.* young.
1. Eleanor, *m.* (as *below*) her cousin, Valentine Whitla, of Ben Eadan.
4. VALENTINE, of whom presently.
1. Elizabeth, *m.* J. Wilson.   2. Eleanor.
3. Jane, *m.* J. Oakman, of Glenavy.
Mr. George Whitla *d.* 17 Aug. 1762, and was *s.* by his youngest son,
VALENTINE WHITLA, of Gobrana, *b.* 1735; *m.* 1779, Jane, dau. of John Bashford, by whom (who *d.* 12 April, 1803) he had five sons and a dau.,
1. GEORGE, of Inver Lodge, Larne, J.P. co. Antrim, *b.* 1780; *m.* Mary, eldest dau. of Alexander Gunning, of Carrickfergus, and had issue,
1. Alicia, *d.* 23 Feb. 1883.
2. Jane, *m.* Hugh Crawford-Smith (*d.* 1862), and *d.s.p.* 2 Feb. 1883.
2. JAMES, of whom hereafter.
3 Francis, *b.* 1783; *d.s.p.* 15 March, 1855.
4. William John, *b.* 1784; *d.s.p.* 21 Aug. 1822.
5. Valentine, of Ben Eadan, J.P. co. Antrim, *b.* 1786; *m.* his cousin, Eleanor (*d.* 14 April, 1860), dau. of Francis Whitla, of Glendona, co. Antrim, and *d.s.p.* 12 Aug. 1865.
1. Jane, *d. unm.* 1858.
Mr. Whitla *d.* 17 Jan. 1802, and was *s.* by his 2nd son,
JAMES WHITLA, of Gobrana, co. Antrim, J.P., *b.* 17 Feb. 1781; *m.* 25 Aug. 1806, Catharine, 3rd dau. of Alexander Gunning, J.P., of Carrickfergus, and by her (who *d.* 5 June, 1875) had issue,
1. GEORGE ALEXANDER, of Ben Eadan.
2. Valentine, *bapt.* 16 June, 1821; *d. unm.* 1 Oct. 1857.
3. William John, *b.* 1824; *d.* young.
4 Francis, *d.* young, May, 1810.
1. Alicia Jane, *d. unm.* 8 Aug. 1835.
2. Katherine, *d. unm.* 19 March, 1835.
3. Anne, *d.* young.   4. Susannah, *d.* young 1 Sept. 1826.
5. Frances, *d. unm.* 18 Sept. 1839.
Mr. Whitla *d.* at Dunmurry, co. Antrim, 12 March, 1862, and was *s.* by his eldest son,
GEORGE ALEXANDER WHITLA, of Ben Eadan, co. Antrim, J.P., Capt. Royal Antrim Rifles, *b.* Feb. 1818; *m.* 1 June, 1858, Isabella Frances, youngest dau. of Rev. John Hammond, of Priston Rectory, Bath, D.L. Somerset, and grand-niece of George Hammond, of Portland Place, London, Under-Sec. of State for Foreign Affairs and first British Minister to America, and had issue,
1. JAMES ALEXANDER, now of Ben Eadan
2. Valentine George, *b.* 12 March, 1863, Major 3rd Hussars (late R.N.).
1. Mary Isabel Hammond, *m.* 10 Sept. 1890, Charles Reginald Sidney Douglas-Hamilton, Capt. Gordon Highlanders, 3rd son of Gen. Octavius Douglas-Hamilton, and has issue (*see* BURKE's *Peerage*, HAMILTON, D.).
2. Ellen Constance, *m.* 1 June, 1882, James Swanzy Glenny, of Glenville, near Newry, J.P. co. Down, and has issue, 1, Valentine William, *b.* 14 Jan. 1886; 2, Arthur Willoughby Falls, *b.* 2 March, 1897; 1, Dorothy Marianne; 2, Norah Isabel; and 3, Joan Frances.
3. Isabella Frances Alexandra, *m.* 19 April, 1887, Major William Frederick Anstey, late Highland Light Infantry, son of George Alexander Anstey, of Harley Street, London, and has issue, 1, George Alexander; 2, Chisholm; 3, Audrey.
Capt. Whitla *d.* 3 Aug. 1867. His widow *m.* 2ndly, 5 July, 1869, Sheffield Grace Phillip Fiennes Betham, Cork Herald of Arms (2nd son of the late Sir William Betham, Ulster King-of-Arms), and *d.* 5 June, 1870, having had issue, a dau., Clementina.

Seat—Ben Eadan, near Belfast.

WHITNEY OF BRAYFORT.

SIR BENJAMIN WHITNEY, Knt., of Brayfort, Bray, co. Wicklow, Clerk of the Crown and Clerk of the Peace, and Registrar of Titles for co. Mayo, J.P. co. Roscommon, *b.* 23 Dec. 1833; *m.* 12 April, 1860, Annabella, 2nd dau. of Isaac North-Bomford, of Ferrans House, and Gallow, co. Meath (*see that family*). She *d.* 16 Jan. 1899, leaving surviving issue,
1. Belinda.   2. Mabel Rosamond.
I.L.G.

Lineage.—THOMAS WHITNEY, of Moneytucker, co. Wexford, made his will 11 Feb. 1725, which was proved 9 Jan. 1726. He left, by Rebecca, his wife,
1. James, of Moneytucker.
2. John, of Moneytucker, *m.* Oct. 1750, Alice Pooley, and left issue.
3. Richard, left a son, Thomas, living 1725.
4. Luke, of Mistereen, co. Wexford, whose will, dated 7 April, 1771, was proved 18 April following. He left, by Margaret his wife,
1. Thomas, of Merton, co. Wexford, *m.* 1790, Alithea, dau. of Thomas Whitney, of Bush Park, and widow of Nicholas Whitney, of Old Ross. She *d.* 13 Oct. 1835. He *d.* 4 Feb. 1831, leaving issue,
(1) Luke, *d.s.p.* 1816, admon. 9 Jan. 1818.
(2) John, Lieut. German Legion, killed at Albuera 1811.
(3) Thomas Annesley, of Merton, *b.* 25 Oct. 1794; *m.* 16 March, 1825, Julia, dau. of Luke Gaven. She *d.* 14 Aug. 1363. He *d.* 28 April, 1876, leaving issue,
1. Mary Elizabeth, *m.* Col. Alexander William Gordon, and *d.* 14 Dec. 1862.
2. Alice Julia, *m.* 1848, Rev. Arthur Eden. She *d.* 1897.
3. Amelia Sarah, *m.* 1859, Col. Henry Alexander Hewetson, and *d.* 1893.
2. John, *m.* Anne, sister of Andrew Whitney. His will, dated 22 July, 1783, was proved 14 Aug. 1784. He left issue,
(1) Luke.
(1) Elizabeth.   (2) Margaret.
1. Mary, *m.* 11 May, 1778, John Cullimore.
2. Margaret, *d. unm.*, and was bur. 31 Dec. 1803. Her will, dated 18 Jan. 1800, was proved 29 March, 1804.
5. Thomas, of Bush Park, who left issue,
1. Annesley, of Bush Park, *d.* April, 1843.
1. Alithea, *m.* 1st, Nicholas Whitney, of Old Ross, and 2ndly, Thomas Whitney, of Merton. She *d.* 13 Oct. 1835, leaving issue (*see above*).
2. Martha, *m.* 11 May, 1796, Thomas Whitney, of Old Court (*see below*).
3. Rebecca, *d. unm.* Oct. 1844.
6. BENJAMIN, of whom presently.
The youngest son,
BENJAMIN WHITNEY, of Old Ross, *m.* the sister of Nicholas King, of Faigh, co. Wexford. He *d.* before 31 May, 1782, leaving issue,
1. BENJAMIN, of whom presently.
2. Nicholas, of Old Ross, *m.* by licence, 19 May, 1750, Catherine, dau. of Nicholas Gore, of Tullecanna, co. Wexford. His will, dated 10 Dec. 1771, was proved 4 Nov. 1794. He left issue,
1. Nicholas, of Old Ross, *m.* Alithea, dau. of Thomas Whitney, of Bush Park. He *d.* before 28 June, 1788 (admon.), having by her (who *m.* 2ndly, Thomas Whitney, of Merton (*see above*), and *d.* 13 Oct. 1835), had an only child, Nicholas, Lieut. 66th Regt., *d. unm.* 1816. Will dated 2 Nov. 1808, proved 20 Dec. 1820.
2. Thomas, of Old Court, *b.* 1765; *m.* by licence, 11 May, 1796, Martha, dau. of Thomas Whitney, of Bush Park, and had issue,
(1) Nicholas, *b.* 26 June, 1806.
(1) Catherine.   (2) Alice.
(3) Mary.
3. BENJAMIN, of whom presently.
1. Catherine.
2. Dorothy, *m.* 1773, William Lett, of Kilgibbon.
3. Mary, *m.* 1793, George Allen.
4. Sarah.   5. Elizabeth.
6. Rebecca.
1. Rebecca.
The elder son,
BENJAMIN WHITNEY, of Old Ross, *d. unm.* May, 1792. By his will, dated 13 May, proved 26 May, 1792, he devised his property to his nephew,
BENJAMIN WHITNEY, of Castleview, Old Ross, *b.* 1766; *m.* 29 April, 1801, Alicia, dau. of Thomas Kough, of New Ross. She *d.* 5 Dec. 1825, aged 45. He *d.* 24 April, 1852, having had issue, five sons and three daus. His eldest son,
NICHOLAS WHITNEY, bapt. 13 March, 1805; *m.* 21 March, 1833, Mary Gore, dau. of Thomas Jones. She *d.* 20 March, 1895, aged 85. He *d.v.p.*, and was bur. at Old Ross, 8 March, 1834, having had an only child,
BENJAMIN (Sir), present representative.

Arms—Az. a cross chequy or and sa., in the dexter quarter a cross crosslet arg. Crest—A bull's head couped sa. armed arg., the horns tipped gu. gorged with a collar chequy or and sa., and charged on the neck with a cross crosslet arg. Motto—Magnanimiter crucem sustine.
Residences—Brayfort, Bray, co. Wicklow, and 29, Upper Fitzwilliam Street, Dublin. Clubs—Constitutional, W.C., and Friendly Brothers, Dublin.

3 C

FETHERSTONHAUGH-WHITNEY OF NEW PASS.

HENRY ERNEST WILLIAM FETHERSTONHAUGH - WHITNEY, of New Pass, co. Westmeath, J.P. and D.L., High Sheriff 1887, B.A. Trin. Coll. Dublin, late Capt. and Hon. Maj. 7th Batt. King's Royal Rifle Corps, formerly Lieut. 60th Rifles, b. 2 Nov. 1847; m. 1st, 17 Aug. 1876, Jeannie, dau. of Edward Atkinson, of Seafield Hall, Donabate. She d.s.p. 14 Nov. 1880. He m. 2ndly, 5 Aug. 1885, Alice Marion Caroline, dau. of Col. Robert Caulfeild, of Camolin House, co. Wexford (see BURKE's *Peerage*, CHARLEMONT, V.). Major Fetherstonhaugh-Whitney is the youngest and only surviving son of the Rev. Sir Thomas Francis Fetherston, 4th bart., who d. 28 Aug. 1853, by Anne, his 2nd wife, who d. 20 Nov. 1872, dau. of Edmund L'Estrange, of Hunstanton, King's Co. and grandson of Sir Thomas Fetherston, 2nd bart., who d. 19 July, 1819, and Elizabeth his wife, dau. of George Boleyn Whitney, of New Pass. Major, Fetherstonhaugh-Whitney is uncle and heir presumptive to the Rev. Sir George Ralph Fetherston, 6th bart., and s. his brother, John Henry Fetherston-Whitney, of New Pass, in 1881, and thereupon assumed the additional name and arms of WHITNEY by Royal Licence.

Lineage.—See BURKE's *Peerage*, FETHERSTON, Bart.

Arms—Quarterly 1st and 4th az. a cross chequy or and sa., in the 1st quarter a crescent of the 2nd (WHITNEY); 2nd and 3rd gu. on a chevron between three ostrich feathers arg. a pellet (FETHERSTON). Crests—1. (WHITNEY): A bull's head couped sa. horned arg. tipped gu. gorged with a collar chequy or and sa. 2. (FETHERSTON): An antelope, statant arg. armed or. Motto—Volens et valens.

Seats—New Pass, Rathowen, co. Westmeath, and Furry Raheny, co. Dublin. Club—Junior United Service.

WHYTE OF LOUGHBRICKLAND

JOHN JOSEPH WHYTE, of Loughbrickland, co. Down, J.P. and D.L., High Sheriff 1862, b. 4 Sept. 1826; m. 1st, 1855, Ellen Mary, last surviving dau. of Thomas Laffan Kelly, of Dublin, and by her (who d. 1857) has issue,

1. Mary Jane Elizabeth, m. 9 June, 1892, Major Robert Blount, late 20th Regt., younger son of M. Blount, of Maple Durham, co. Oxford (see that family). He d. 15 April, 1902.

He m. 2ndly, Oct. 1862, Caroline Letitia, dau. of George Ryan, of Inch House, co. Tipperary (see that family), and has issue,

1. John Nicholas, D.S.O., Major Lancashire Fus., b. 24 Dec. 1864; d. 29 April, 1908.
2. Charles Edward, b. 1866; d. 1883.
3. George Thomas, b. 1868.
4. Henry Marcus, b. 1869; d. 1880.
5. Thomas Aloysius, Lieut. R.A., b. 5 April, 1876.
6. Edward, b. 1878; d. 1894.

7. William Henry, Lieut. Royal Dublin Fus., b. 11 March, 1880.
8. Marcus Francis, Lieut. 62nd Punjabis, b. 18 Jan. 1883; d. 8 Jan. 1905.
9. Maurice Ignatius, b. 1888.
2. Caroline Mary, m. 10 Oct. 1894, Charles E. MacDermot, The MacDermot, and has issue (see that family).
3. Letitia Mary, m. 5 Jan. 1898, Major Stephen Eaton Lamb, of West Denton, Northumberland (see that family).
4. Anna Mary, m. 26 April, 1908, Louis William, younger son of Matthew James Corbally, Rathbeale Hall, co. Dublin (see that family).
5. Kathleen.

Lineage.—NICHOLAS WHYTE, m. the sister of Thomas Butler, Prior of Kilmainham, and a Knight Hospitaller of St. John of Jerusalem, and by her was father of MAURICE WHYTE the Lancastrian, so called from his having served under the three kings of the House of Lancaster. In 1418 Maurice, with the Prior of Kilmainham, led 2,000 Irish to assist at the siege of Rouen, and was afterwards Governor of Montaire, under HENRY VI. His son BARTHOLOMEW WHYTE, m. Anne Cusack, and was father of NICHOLAS WHYTE, of King's Meadows, co. Waterford, who m., Elizabeth, dau. of — Power, of co. Waterford, and had a son, JAMES WHYTE, of King's Meadows, who d. 1546, and who (by his wife Margaret Walsh, of co. Waterford), was father of SIR NICHOLAS WHYTE, of Leixlip, seneschal of co. Wexford, and of Whyte's Hall. He was also Governor of the Castle of Wexford, and became Master of the Rolls of Ireland 1572. By his wife, a dau. of Sherlock, Sir Nicholas (who d. in England) left a son,

ANDREW WHYTE, of Leixlip, m. Margaret, dau. of Patrick Finglass, and d. 31 July, 1599, leaving a son,

SIR NICHOLAS WHYTE of Leixlip, aged 16 in 1599; Inq. p.m. He m. Ursula Moore, dau. of Garret, 1st Viscount Moore, of Drogheda, and d. 1654. His 4th son,

CHARLES WHYTE, of Leixlip, was Col. in Spain, and afterwards Governor co. Kildare, 1689, and M.P. for Naas. By his 2nd wife Mary, 5th dau. of Sir Thomas Newcomen, Kt., of Sutton, co. Dublin, and Frances his wife, dau. of Sir William Talbot, Bart., of Cartown, co. Dublin, he left a son,

JOHN WHYTE, of Leixlip, m. Mary, dau. of Nicholas Purcell, Baron of Loughmoe, co. Tipperary, by Rose his wife, dau. of Mark Trevor, Viscount Dungannon, and left a son,

CHARLES WHYTE, of Leixlip, m. 24 Dec. 1751, Anastatia, dau. of Edward Dunne, of Brittas, by Margaret his wife, dau. of Francis Wyse, of the Manor of St. John, Waterford, and left issue,

1. John, his heir. 2. Nicholas (Sir), Knight of Malta.
1. Margaret, m. 24 Oct. 1776, John Roche, of Limerick.
2. Rose.

The elder son and heir,

JOHN WHYTE, of Leixlip, m. 15 Feb. 1776, Letitia, dau. of the Hon. Thomas de Burgh, son of John, 9th Earl of Clanricarde, and had eight sons and two daus.,

1. CHARLES JOHN, Capt. in the Army, b. 1777; m. 1794, Anna, eldest dau. of John Ross-Lewin, of Fort Fergus, co. Clare (by his wife Eleanor, dau. of George Stacpoole, of Edenvale, co. Clare); and d. Nov. 1803, having issue by her, a posthumous son,

CHARLES JOHN, of Strandfield House, co. Clare, Capt. 95th Regt., b. 12 Feb. 1804; m. 1st, 1 Sept. 1832, Rose, relict of John Reeves, of Charleville, co. Cork, and 2nd dau. of George Dartnell, of Limerick, by whom (who d. 1864) he had issue,

(1) John Lewis Auriol, Major Royal South Down Militia, J.P., b. 12 June, 1833; m. 8 Dec. 1864, Rosina Alice, dau. of William Pegge, of Birchgrove, Swansea, and d. 4 Oct. 1885, leaving issue,
 1. John William Charles, b. 11 July, 1866; m. 5 Aug. 1902, Elizabeth Ellen, dau. of Charles Hills, of Norwich.
 2. Walter Cecil, b. 23 Nov. 1876.
 3. Joseph Ormonde, b. 21 Sept. 1880.
 1. Rose Alice, m. William Ranalow, of Tipperary, and has issue.
 2. Maud de Wyte, m. Charles Adams, M.D., of Dublin, and has issue,
 3. Mary Amicie.
(2) George Lewis, Capt. 55th Regt., b. 22 Aug. 1834; m. Frances, only dau. of Henry Whitcombe, Lieut. R.N., and d. 21 May, 1884, leaving issue,
 1. Fanny, m. July, 1876, John O'Dwyer, of Glenhurst, Deal, Kent, and has issue.
 2. Maria Louisa, m. 13 April, 1888, Walter Frank Redknap, of Rutland, St. Andrew's Road, Deal, and has issue.
(3) Charles, Capt. 6th Royal Regt., b. 21 Aug. 1836; m. 20 July, 1871, Gertrude Minna, elder dau. of John Shiell, of Kelly Castle, Arbroath, and Smithfield, Dundee, and d. 7 March, 1889, leaving issue,
 William John de Burgh, b. 5 Dec. 1875.
 Maud Alexandrine, b. 13 Dec. 1872; d. unm. 6 Jan. 1893.
(4) Edward Henry, b. 15 Feb. 1839, Paymaster R.N.; d.s.p. 5 Aug. 1884.
(5) Joseph, b. 12 Oct. 1840, R.N., H.M.S. *Sappho*, perished with all on board, 1858.
(6) Benjamin de Burgh, b. 8 July, 1850; m. 7 Sept. 1875, Isabella, 2nd dau. of William Middleton, M.D., of Mullingar, co. Westmeath, and d. 31 Dec. 1884, leaving issue,
 1. Cecil de Burgh, b. 28 Aug. 1878.
 2. Henry Lewis, b. 3 Dec. 1879.
 3. Lucas, b. 18 April, 1881.
(7) Frederick, b. 8 July, 1852; d.s.p. 1897, drowned at sea.
(1) Anna, m. 16 Dec. 1854, George Sandes, of Greenville. He d. 25 Oct. 1895. She d. 8 July, 1894, leaving issue (see that family).

(2) Rose, m. 20 Feb. 1872, Col. Thomas Challoner Martelli, R.A., and has issue.
(3) Letitia Adelaide, m. 4 Aug. 1870, Robert Stacke, of Dublin, and has issue.
Capt. Whyte m. 2ndly, 23 Oct. 1873, Susan Isabella, eldest dau. of Humphrey Graham, Writer to the Signet, Edinburgh, and d. 18 Nov. 1885.
2. John, E.I.C.S., d.s.p.
3. Thomas, killed in action in Spain, unm.
4. Francis, in the Army, d. unm. in the West Indies.
5. NICHOLAS CHARLES, of whom presently.
6. Edward, Capt. R.N., m. Mary, dau. of Capt. Sober Hall, of Durham, and by her (who d. 1861) left at his decease, 1837, four sons and four daus.,
  1. John Charles, Barrister-at-Law, Acting Judge at Hong Kong, d. unm. 1870.
  2. Edward, in Holy Orders of the Church of Rome.
  3. William, Rear-Admiral 1881, appointed second in command of the Channel Squadron 1884 (5, Cheniston Gardens, W.), b. 1829; m. 1880, Katherine Mary, younger dau. of Thomas Segrave (see SEGRAVE of Cabra), and has issue.
  4. Henry, m. 1859, Mary, dau. of Thomas Comyn, and has issue; d. 1883.
    1. Catherine Margaret, m. 31 May, 1839, George Ryan, of Inch House, co. Tipperary; d. 1884, and had issue (see that family).
    2. Letitia.   3. Frances, d. unm.
    4. Ellen, m. 1865, E. Gorman, of East Bergholt, Suffolk, and d. 1867.
  7. Marcus, Vice-Consul of Lima, dec.
  8. Henry, R.N., d. in the West Indies.
  1. Letitia, m. Charles Whyte Roche, of Ballygran, co. Limerick.
  2. Margaret, m. Col. Charles O'Ferrall, of Ballyna, co. Kildare (see MORE-O'FERRALL, of Balyna), Equerry and Chamberlain to the King of Sardinia.
The 5th son,
NICHOLAS CHARLES WHYTE, of Loughbrickland, J.P. and D.L., Capt. R.N., b. 18 Jan. 1783; m. 10 June, 1825, Mary Louisa, dau. of Thomas Segrave, of Cabra, co. Dublin, and by her (who d. 29 June, 1877) had issue,
1. JOHN JOSEPH, of Loughbrickland.   2. Nicholas, d. 1863.
3. Edward, Major late Royal Canadian Rifles, m. 1st, 1863, Jesse, dau. of E. Rutherford, of Hamilton, Canada (she d. 1877); and 2ndly, 1878, Katherine (who d. 1909), dau. of the late F. Codd, of Dublin, and d. 1904.
1. Anna Maria, a Nun.   2. Letita, a Nun.
3. Louisa, m. 1861, Charles Philip Roche, of Ballygran.
Capt. Whyte, who served as High Sheriff co. Down in 1830, d. 1845.

Arms—Arg., a chevron engrailed between three roses gu. seeded or barbed vert. Crest—A demi-lion rampant gu. holding between the paws a flagstaff ppr., a flag arg. thereon the cross of St. George.
Motto—Uchiel y Goring.
Seat—Loughbrickland, co. Down.

WHYTE-VENABLES OF REDHILLS.

REV. ARTHUR THELLUSSON WHYTE-VENABLES, of Redhills, co Cavan, M.A. Camb. b. 1851; m. 1886, Alice Blair, second dau. of Rev. George Thomas Palmer, Rector of Newington, London, S.E., and Hon. Canon of Rochester, and has issue,

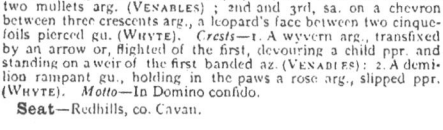

1. HAROLD ARTHUR, b. 1891.
1. Dorothy Alice.
2. Gladys Caroline.

He is the 2nd son of Rev. George Augustus Oddie, Rector of Aston, Herts, b. 1820; d. 1877), by his wife (m. 1848), Ann, youngest dau. of Rev. James Venables, M.A., R.D., Vicar of Buckland Newton, and Prebendary of Wells. He assumed the surname and arms of WHYTE-VENABLES by Royal Licence, 21 Jan. 1905, on succeeding to Redhills, by devise of the late Georgiana Mary Whyte-Venables. She was the dau. of Capt. Samuel Enderby, 5th Dragoon Guards, by his wife Mary, dau. of Francis Whyte, of Redhills, and married 1847 Rev. Edmund Burke Venables, 2nd son of Rev. James Venables, of Buckland Newton and adopted the name of Whyte-Venables. He d.s.p. 24 April, 1894. She d. 3 Sept. 1904.

Arms—Quarterly 1st and 4th, az., two bars and in chief two mullets arg. (VENABLES); 2nd and 3rd, sa. on a chevron between three crescents arg., a leopard's face between two cinquefoils pierced gu. (WHYTE). Crests—1. A wyvern arg., transfixed by an arrow or, fighted of the first, devouring a child ppr. and standing on a weir of the first banded az. (VENABLES): 2. A demi-lion rampant gu., holding in the paws a rose arg., slipped ppr. (WHYTE). Motto—In Domino confido.
Seat—Redhills, co. Cavan.

WHYTE OF NEWTOWN MANOR.

CHARLES CECIL BERESFORD WHYTE, of Newtown Manor and Hatley Manor, co. Leitrim, J.P. and D.L., High Sheriff 1877, and J.P. for Roscommon, b. 18 July, 1845; m. 1874, Petronella Hallberg, dau. of Herr Magnus Hallberg Riksdagsman, of Tyäragarren Tyärely, Sweden, and by her (who s. to the estates of Charles Manners St. George, J.P. and D.L., and Madame Ingri Christina St. George, in the cos. of Leitrim and Roscommon) has issue,

1. CECIL HARMAN BALDWIN ST. GEORGE, Hon. 2nd Lieut in the Army, late Capt., 5th Batt. Connaught Rangers, High Sheriff Leitrim 1911, b. 24 July, 1881.
2. John Theodore Marcus.
  1. Maryanne Christina de Montenach St. George, m. 1st, 2 June, 1900, William E. Barron, of Biarritz, France, who d.s.p. 1902. She m. 2ndly, 17 Oct. 1907, Fernando Quinones de Leon Marqués de Mos and de Valladares.
  2. Ingri Melesina Beatrice Gertrude, d. unm.
  3. Mona Selina Petronella, m. 12 Oct. 1899, Enrique, Comte O'Brien, of Montausey, Bayonne, and has a son, Antonio.
  4. Chisogona Constantia Barbara Beresford, m. 11 Sept. 1907, George White, of Cloone Grange, co. Leitrim (see that family).
  5. Frances May Olga de Longueuil, m. 1st, 19 April, 1898, George Pim, of Brenanstown, Cabinteely, co. Dublin, who d. 15 Sept. 1902, leaving issue, Cecil George and Dorothy Helen. She m. 2ndly, 21 March, 1908, Capt. Richard Alexander Lyonal Keith, A.D.C., Capt. 3rd Seaforth Highlanders, Cork Herald of Arms.
  6. Florence Hulda Medora.
  7. Lucille Theodora Gwendoline, d. unm.
  8. Ebba Harline d'Iberville Le Moyne, m. 16 June, 1911, Sir Everard Alexander Hambro, K.C.V.O.
  9. Edith Estelle Ermyntrude le Poer.

Lineage—JAMES WHYTE (son of Mark Whyte, by Elizabeth his wife, dau. of John Edwards, of Old Court, co. Wicklow), m. 1st, 1783, Gertrude, dau. of James Gee, grandson of William Gee, of Bishop Burton, and by her had issue,
1. JAMES, his heir.   2. Robert, who took the name of Moyser. He m. 2ndly, the dau. of Sir Thomas Hildyard, and had a dau., Anne Catherine, who s. to the Hildyard estates, and m. Col. Thomas Thoroton, who took the name of HILDYARD.
Mr. Whyte d. 1807, and was s. by his son,
JAMES WHYTE, of Pilton House, Barnstaple, m. 9 July, 1805, Frances Honoria, dau. of the Right Hon. John Beresford, brother of the 1st Marquess of Waterford, and d. 24 March, 1852, leaving issue,
1. JOHN JAMES, of Newtown Manor.
2. James Richard (Rev.), m. 4 June, 1844, Louisa Lucy, dau. of Sir John Courtenay Honywood, Bart.
3. Robert Charles, m. Janet Preston.
4. Mark Beresford, m. Emily, widow of J. W. Hinds, 15th Hussars, and has issue, Nina Kathleen Garland, m. 1896, Capt. Arthur Thomas Stuart, M.V.O., R.N., who d. 11 July, 1908.
5. Charles, m. Emily Gardener.
6. William Thomas, m. Emma Heard.
1. Selina Catherine Harriet, m. Felix Ladbroke.
2. Frances Honoria, dec.   3. Mary, m. Rev. Bourchier Savile.
4. Barbara Henrietta, m. 19 March, 1844, Col. William Honywood.
The eldest son,
JOHN JAMES WHYTE, of Newtown Manor, J.P. and D.L. co. Leitrim, High Sheriff 1854, Col. in the Army, late Lieut.-Col. 7th Hussars, b. 7 May, 1806; m. 7 Oct. 1842, Mary Ann Jesse de Montenach, dau. of Charles Dieudonné de Montenach, Patrician of Fribourg, by Mary Elizabeth his wife, dau. of David Grant, by his wife, Charlotte Le Moyne, Baronne de Longueuil, and by her (who d. 1874) had issue,
1. CHARLES CECIL BERESFORD, now of Newtown Manor.
2. Theodore William, b. 7 Oct. 1846; m. 1st, Miss Webster, and 2ndly, 12 Oct. 1886, Lady Maude Ogilvy, dau. of David, 10th Earl of Airlie, and d. 29 March, 1903, leaving issue,
  1. Felix, b. 1889.
  2. Mariott, b. 1895.
  1. Madeleine.
1. Marie Elizabeth Frances Medora, dec.
2. Marie Gertrude, m. 1st, S. Sheil, and 2ndly, J. Doherty.
3. Emma Frances Honoria, m. Charles Bell.
4. Florence Alma Julia, dec.

Seats—Newtown Manor, viâ Sligo; Hatley Manor, near Carrick-on-Shannon, co. Leitrim. Clubs—Kildare Street, Dublin; and Arthur's, S.W.

WILLINGTON OF ST. KIERANS.

James Thomas Cambie Willington, of St. Kierans, co. Tipperary, J.P., M.A. Trin. Coll. Dublin, Barrister-at-Law, b. 18 March, 1863; m. 8 Nov. 1892, Alice Augusta, younger dau. of the late Capt. Francis John Venner, of Dilston House, Upper Norwood, and has issue,
1. Frederick Harold Peel, b. 28 Oct. 1893; d. 20 Dec. 1901.
2. James Vernon Yates, b. 3 Dec. 1894.
3. Robert Malcolm Venner, b. 14 Nov. 1895.
1. Ivy Alice Peel.

Lineage.—Charles Willington, of Ballymoney, Seirkieran, near Birr, King's Co., m. Mary Bonham, and had issue,
1. Thomas King. 2. Charles.
3. William Mite.
1. Jane Berry. 2. Elizabeth Davis.
3. Mary Duffield. 4. Anne Hill.

His will is dated 28 April, 1721. His brother,
James Willington, of Killoskehane Castle, m. Mary Carden, and d. 6 Feb. 1750, aged 104, leaving issue,
1. John, of Killoskehane Castle, co. Tipperary, m. 1st, 1740, Elizabeth, dau. of John Eyre, of Woodfield, co. Galway, and by her had issue,
   1. James, d. unm. Nov. 1754.
   2. John, of Killoskehane Castle, J.P., High Sheriff 1773-5 m. 1st, 23 Oct. 1767, Alicia, dau. of Jonathan Willington, of Castlewillington, by whom (who d. 28 June, 1783, aged 34) he had issue,
      (1) John, of Killoskehane Castle, J.P., m. 23 Jan. 1815, Sarah, dau. of Christopher Ormsby, of Ballinamore, co. Mayo. She d. 5 July, 1870, aged 87. He d. 15 April, 1835, leaving issue,
         1. John James, of Killoskehane Castle, b. 26 Nov. 1815; d. unm. Jan. 1862.
         2. Ormsby, b. 26 Oct. 1816; d. unm. 8 March, 1855.
         3. Jonathan Richard, b. 20 June, 1821; d. unm.
         1. Jane Anne, d. unm. 17 March, 1822.
         2. Alicia Harriet Marmyon, m. 1 July, 1843, John Willington, of Castlewillington, and had issue (see below).
         3. Mary, m. 4 Feb. 1845, Edward Savage, of Glastry, co. Down.
         4. Sarah, d. unm. Oct. 1847.
         5. Elizabeth, d. unm.
      (2) Jonathan, Major in the Army, b. 1773; d. unm. 29 Nov. 1835, aged 62.
      (3) James, Lieut. 43rd Regt., served in the Peninsular war, b. 1781; d. unm. 11 Oct. 1812, aged 31.
      (1) Mary, m. 29 July, 1787, George Bennett, of Richmond House, Templemore, and d. 28 Dec. 1823.
      (2) Elizabeth, m. 29 July, 1789, John Shelton, of Rossmore, co. Tipperary. (3) Priscilla, d. unm.
      (4) Alicia, m. Ringrose Drew, of Drews Court, co. Limerick and d. 11 June, 1868.
   Mr. Willington m. 2ndly, 27 Feb. 1785, Bridget, dau. of Theobald Butler, of Knocka Castle, co. Tipperary, and by her (who d. 22 Feb. 1838, aged 83) he had further issue,
      (4) Theobald Butler, of Templemore, m. Miss Woods, and d. 1861, leaving issue, with two other sons,
         1. Robert Butler, Major 77th Regt., served in Crimea b. Dec. 1833; d. at Murree, India, 1 Sept. 1868, aged 36; m. 1863, Mary Ormsby, dau. of Simon L. Rose, of Ballykisteen, co. Limerick, by whom he left issue,
            a. Richard Henry Rose, of Oldbridge, Pallasgreen, co. Limerick, J.P., b. 1 March, 1864.
            b. Theobald Ernest Woods, Maj. 4th Batt. Leinster Regt., served in S. African War, b. 1865.
         2. Thomas, d.s.p. in Canada.
         1. Maria, m. Rev. George Chute, M.A., Vicar of Drayton-in-Hales, Salop. and d. 3 Feb. 1903.
      (5) Richard, Col. of the 84th Regt., b. 1792; d. unm. 12 July, 1870, aged 78.
      (5) Bridget, m. 29 Nov. 1817, Charles Joseph Kelly, 3rd Viscount Monck, and d. 22 Jan. 1843, aged 53.

He m. 2ndly, Mary Duffield, and d. Jan. 1767, leaving by her, who survived until 1783, further issue,
3. Jonathan, of Rapla, co. Tipperary, m. Mary Disney, and d. 13 Aug. 1818, leaving three sons, John; Robert; and James, Lieut.-Col. 3rd Regt. (the Buffs), all of whom d. unm.; and two daus., Elizabeth, m. John Walsh, of Walshpark, co. Tipperary; and Sophia, m. Morgan Clifford, of Perriston, co. Hereford, and Llatillo, co. Monmouth, by whom she left issue, an only child, Marion, who m. 12 June, 1860, James Fitzwalter Clifford-Butler, 24th Baron Dunboyne.
2. James, of Newhouse, m. 1742, Rebecca, dau. of Nicholas Toler, of Graige, co. Tipperary, who left with a dau., Mrs. Hastings, of Fort Henry, co. Tipperary, two sons,
   1. John, of Drummond, co. Kildare, m. the dau. of Sir Edward Peckevin, and was killed by a fall from his horse, s.p.
   2. Daniel, drowned in the river Shannon, 25 Aug. 1774.
3. Jonathan, of whom presently.
1. Priscilla.

The third son,
Jonathan Willington, of Castlewillington, d. 1767; m. Mary Drought, and had, with four daus. (Anne, m. 1st, Richard Kyffin, of Cashel, and 2ndly, John Minchin; Alicia, m. John Willington, of Killoskehane; Mary, m. Thomas Bernard, of Castle Bernard; Priscilla, d. unm.; and other issue), three sons,
1 James, of Castlewillington, d. unm. 1778.
2. Jonathan, Barrister-at-Law, b. 1758; m. 22 July, 17

Elizabeth, dau. of Nicholas Biddulph, of Borris-a-Leigh, co. Tipperary; and d. 14 Jan. 1791, aged 33, having had an only dau., who d. young. She m. 2ndly, 1806, Sir Robert Waller Bart., and d. 1851. He d.s.p. 1826.
3. John, of whom presently.

The third son,
John Willington, of Castlewillington and Ballintotty, J.P. co Tipperary, m. 21 Feb. 1788, Jane, dau. of Thomas Going, of Travers ton, co. Tipperary, and d. Feb. 1821, having had issue,
1. James, of whom presently.
2. Frederick, b. 30 May, 1800; d. unm. 1832.
1. Mary, m. Theobald Pepper, of Lisaniskea, and d. 15 June, 1877.
2. Charlotte, m. William Jackson.
3. Eliza, d. unm. 5 April, 1869.

The eldest son,
James Willington, of Castlewillington, b. 4 Aug. 1790; m. 14 July, 1817, Sarah, dau. of Thomas Mark, of Limerick, and d. May, 1862, leaving issue,
1. John, M.A., Barrister-at-Law, J.P., b. 1819; m. 1 July, 1843 Alicia Harriett Marmyon, dau. of John Willington, of Killoskehane, and d.v.p. 1861, leaving issue,
   1. James Waldyve Champernowne, of Castlewillington, D.L. co. Dublin, J.P. co. Tipperary, b. 14 July, 1846, and d.s.p. Jan. 1895.
   2. John Ormsby Bracebridge, b. 29 Oct. 1847; d. 15 July, 1878.
   3. Frederick Arthur Carminow, of Castlewillington, b. 12 Aug. 1849.
   4. Ormsby Augustus Mohun, b. 2 June, 1854; m. 24 Dec. 1886, Marie Lefevre, and has with other issue,
      James Waldyve Plumpton, b. 12 June, 1890.
   5. Richard Butler Monck, b. 15 Sept. 1861.
   1. Alice Charlotte, m. 17 June, 1877, Charles Creagh, 2nd son of Richard Coplen Langford, of Kilcosgriff, co. Limerick, and has issue three daus. (see that family).
   2. Florence Matilda Priscilla, m. 18 Sept. 1878, William J. Molony. 3. Mary Louisa Augusta Ormsby.
2. James Jonathan, m. Penelope Wilson, and d.s.p. in Australia, 1855.
3. Frederick, of whom presently.
4 Thomas, drowned in the river Ganges, India.
5. Robert Going, m. 30 April, 1869, Mary Dorothea Webb, of Hilltown, co. Westmeath, and d. at Coolagower, Cloghjordan, 2 June, 1884, in his 45th year, leaving issue,
   James Arthur, Capt. W.I.R., b. 3 May, 1870.
1. Jane, m. 2 June, 1837, Edwin Sadleir.
2. Sarah, m. John M. Wilson, of Harvest Lodge, co. Tipperary, and had issue.
3. Elizabeth, m. 12 Aug. 1868, William Irvine, of Prospect, co. Fermanagh.
4. Charlotte, m. 12 June, 1866, Rowin Francis Cashel, M.D.

The third son,
Frederick Willington, of St. Kierans, co. Tipperary, formerly Lieut. 70th Foot and 18th Regt. Royal Irish, served in ndia, b. 1823; m. 26 April, 1856, Margaret Catherine Lane, dau. of Solomon Richards Cambie, and d. 12 Dec. 1889, leaving issue,
1. James Thomas Cambie, now of St. Kierans.
2. Richard William Camac, b. 9 Oct. 1867; m. 25 Jan. 1893, Emily Cheetham, only dau. of Thomas Shaw, of St. Chad's, Saddleworth, co. York, and has issue,
   1. Audrey Emily. 2. Vivienne Jane.
3. Frederick Francis Clare, b. 12 Sept. 1876; m. 13 Aug. 1908, Mary Agnes, 4th dau. of Henry Warren-Darley, and has issue, Sheila Lucy.
1. Margaret Sarah.
2. Katherine Elizabeth, m. 1886, Richard Huggard, LL.D., of Lismore, Tralee.
3. Jane Read. 4. Charlotte Roberta.

Seat—St. Kierans, co. Tipperary.

WILLS-SANDFORD. See SANDFORD.

WILMOT-CHETWODE. See CHETWODE.

WILSON OF DARAMONA.

John Granville Wilson, of Daramona House, co. Westmeath, J.P., High Sheriff 1911, s. his father 1908, b. 8 Sept. 1887.

Lineage—John Wilson, of Rashee, co. Antrim, is supposed to have landed at Carrickfergus, in the suite of William III. He m. Barbara, dau. of Andrew Porter, and d. 1692, leaving issue,
1. Francis, of Rashee (will dated 19 June, 1705), m. Jane, sister of Thomas Taggart, and left issue,
   1. John.
   2. Nathaniel.
   3. Francis.
   1. Margaret.
   2. Susanna. 3. Jane.

2. Hugh, of whom we treat.
4. Thomas.
1. Janet.
3. Robert.
5. James.
2. Susan.

The 2nd son,
Hugh Wilson, of Rashee (will dated 20 June, 1737), *m.* 1st, Jane Ramsay, and by her had issue,
1. William, of whom presently.
2. John, of Derry.
3. Hugh.
1. Barbara, *m.* — Douglas.
2. Jane, *m.* P. Ramsay.
3. Susan.

He *m.* 2ndly, Jane White. His eldest son,
William Wilson, of Rashee, co. Antrim, *m.* Elizabeth Dobbin, of Carrickfergus, and had issue,
1. Hugh, of whom presently.
2. William Dobbin, *m.* and left issue.
3. James Dobbin, of Asp Mill.
1. Elizabeth, *d. unm.*
2. A dau., Mrs. Moorhead.
8. A dau., Mrs. Milford.

Mr. Wilson *d.* 1769. His eldest son,
Hugh Wilson, of Rashee, *m.* 19 Jan. 1773, Jane Craig, and by her (who *d.* 12 Aug. 1823) had issue,
William, of whom we treat.

Mr. Wilson *d.* 27 Dec. 1822. His son,
William Wilson, of Daramona and Larkhill, co. Dublin, *b.* 10 July, 1787; *m.* 23 Oct. 1815, Rebecca Dupré, dau. of John Mackay, of Elagh, co. Tyrone, and Prospect, co. Londonderry, and by her (who *d.* 2 Nov. 1846) had issue,
1. John, late of Daramona.
2. Robert Mackay, of Coolcarrigan, co. Kildare, J.P., High Sheriff 1887, *b.* 21 March, 1829; *m.* 25 May, 1858, Elizabeth, dau. of Murray Suffern, of Belfast, and has issue,
  1. Robert Mackay, LL.B., *b.* 10 Feb. 1864; *d. unm.* 18 Dec. 1887.
  2. Thomas Hughes Murray, *b.* 6 July, 1870; *d.* 29 Jan. 1884.
  1. Jane Georgina, *b.* 6 Dec. 1860; *m.* 8 Jan. 1889, Professor Sir Almroth Edward Wright, and has issue.
  2. Rebecca Dupré, *b.* 28 July, 1865.
  3. Matilda Edith Ethel, *b.* 7 April, 1867, *dcc.*
3. George Orr, of Dunardagh, co. Dublin, High Sheriff 1884, *b.* 25 Dec. 1830; *m.* 24 March, 1863, Annie Dupré, dau. of Col. Ponsonby Shaw, and *d.* 13 Aug. 1902, leaving issue,
  1. Hugh Ponsonby, of Coolure, co. Westmeath, High Sheriff 1907, J.P. co. Longford and Westmeath, *b.* 6 Feb. 1864; *m.* 4 April, 1894, Louisa Barbara, dau. of Edward Rotheram, of Crossdrum, co. Meath, and has issue,
    (1) George Edward, *b.* 1 Aug. 1897; *d.* 18 April, 1907.
    (1) Kathleen Edith.
    (2) Louisa Gertrude.
  2. William Perceval, C.E., *b.* 17 Feb. 1866.
  3. George Ernest, Lieut. Norfolk Regt., *b.* 15 June, 1870; *d. unm.* 23 June, 1902.
  4. Herbert Stanley, Capt. R.H.A., *b.* 26 March, 1873; *m.* 30 April, 1903, Helena Margaret Floyd, youngest dau. of the late Henry Darvill, of Elmfield, Windsor.
  5. Walter Gordon (*The Manor House, Farningham, Kent*), *b.* 21 April, 1874; *m.* Miss Gray, and has issue.
  6. Frederick Dunbar (*The Old House, Wickham, Hants*), *b.* 24 Aug. 1876.
  1. Helen Dupré, *b.* 22 March, 1868; *m.* 30 April, 1902, Charles Andrew Boughton-Knight, eldest son of Andrew John Rouse-Boughton-Knight, of Downton Castle (see Burke's *Peerage*, Boughton, Bart.).
  2. Annie Eveline, *b.* 22 June, 1869; *m.* Capt. A. J. Chapman, and has issue.
4. James, of Currygrane (see that family).
1. Jane, *b.* 27 May, 1817; *m.* Rev. Canon W. McIlwaine, D.D., and has issue, eight sons and two daus.

The eldest son,
John Wilson, of Daramona House, co. Westmeath, J.P., High Sheriff 1864, M.A. Trin. Coll. Dublin, High Sheriff co. Longford 1851, *b.* 19 June, 1826; *m.* Sept. 1850, Frances, dau. of Rev. Edward Nangle. He *d.* 7 April, 1906, having had issue,
1. William Edward, of Daramona.
1. Elizabeth Dupré, *m.* 22 Oct. 1878, Thomas N. Edgeworth, of Kilshrewly, co. Longford, D.L., and has issue (see that family).
2. Matilda Dorothea, *m.* 11 Aug. 1875, Capt. Henry Loftus Lewis, late R.E., of Violetstown, co. Westmeath, who *d.* 5 Sept. 1898, leaving issue, one dau.
3. Beatrice Frances, *m.* April, 1889, Joseph Lister Pim, of Glenageragh, co. Dublin, and *d.* 23 May, 1899, leaving issue, two sons.

The only son,
William Edward Wilson, of Daramona, F.R.S., D.Sc., J.P. co. Westmeath, High Sheriff 1894, *b.* 19 July, 1851; *m.* 10 Nov. 1886, Ada, dau. of Capt. Granville, and *d.* 6 March, 1908, having had issue,
1. John Granville, of Daramona.
1. Caroline Patience Nangle, *b.* 5 Oct. 1889.
2. Blanche Ada de Vivefay, *b.* 20 July, 1892; *m.* 1 March, 1911, Nugent Winter Humphrys (see Humphrys of *Ballyhaise*).

Arms—Arg., a wolf rampant az. on a chief indented of the first three estoiles of the field. Crest—A demi-wolf rampant per pale indented arg. and az. Motto—Pollet virtus.
Seat—Daramona House, co. Westmeath. Club—Kildare Street, Dublin.

WILSON OF CURRYGRANE.

James Mackay Wilson, of Currygrane, co. Longford, J.P. and D.L., High Sheriff 1887, *b.* 7 Jan. 1863; *s.* his father 1907; educated at Harrow and Trin. Coll. Dublin, B.A. 1885, High Sheriff co. Longford 1887; *m.* 27 Sept. 1894, Amy Alice, 2nd dau. of the late Sir John Senhouse Goldie-Taubman, J.P., Speaker of the House of Keys, of The Nunnery, Isle of Man, by Amy his wife, 2nd dau. of Capt. Grove Ross, 25th Regt., of Invercharron, Ross-shire, and has issue,
Bridget Senhouse Constant, *b.* 28 Sept. 1903.

Lineage—The 4th son of William Wilson, of Daramona, co. Westmeath, and Larkhill, co. Dublin (see Wilson *of Daramona*), was,
James Wilson, of Currygrane, co. Longford, J.P. and D.L., High Sheriff 1864, *b.* 11 July, 1832; M.A. Trin. Coll. Dublin 1856; *m.* 2 Oct. 1861, Constant Grace Martha, eldest dau. of the late James Freeman Hughes, of The Grove, Stillorgan, co. Dublin, by Martha his wife, 4th dau. of William Redfern, of Churchfield House, co. Warwick. He *d.* 12 Aug. 1907, having had issue,
1. James Mackay, now of Currygrane.
2. Henry Hughes, C.B., D.S.O., Brig.-Gen., Director of Military Operations, Army Headquarters (36, *Eaton Place, S.W. Club*—White's), *b.* 5 May, 1864; *m.* 3 Oct. 1891, Cecil Mary, dau. of George Cecil Gore Wray, of Ardnamona, co. Donegal.
3. Arthur John de Courcy, *b.* 10 Jan. 1867; *m.* 8 Dec. 1892, Norah, dau. of Hammon Paine, of The Paragon, Blackheath, Kent, and has issue,
  Cyril John, *b.* 1899.
  Margaret de Courcy, *b.* 30 April, 1895; *d.* 1905.
4. Cecil William, of Lyddington Manor, Swindon, Wilts (*Clubs*—Army and Navy, Royal St. George Yacht), D.S.O., Major late King's Royal Rifle Corps, *b.* 5 June, 1870; *m.* 30 Jan. 1906, Winifred Aline, 7th dau. of Sir Richard Sutton, 4th bart. (see Burke's *Peerage*).
1. Florence Grace, *d. unm.* 16 Dec. 1869.
2. Ada Dupré Martha, *m.* 10 Sept. 1894, Capt. Henry George Powell, Loyal North Lancashire Regt., and son of the late Capt. Grabam Powell, Queen's Bays, and the late Mrs. Graham Powell, of Southwold, Suffolk, and has issue,
3. Eileen Geraldine Edith, *m.* 8 Aug. 1906, Capt. Llewelyn Alberic Emilius Price-Davies, V.C., D.S.O., son of Lewis Richard Price (see Price-Davies *of Marrington Hall*).

Lineage and Arms—See preceding Article.
Seat—Currygrane, Edgeworthstown, co. Longford. Clubs—Athenæum and Brooks', S.W.; Kildare Street, Dublin; Royal St. George Yacht.

WILSON OF MARYVILLE.

Alexander George Wilson, of Maryville and Cranmore, co. Antrim, J.P. co. Down, Lieut. Army Motor Reserve, educated at Harrow, *b.* 7 Aug. 1876; *s.* his father 1904.

Lineage.—Thomas Wilson, of Croglin, said to have been son of John Wilson of Croglin, of an old-established family in Dumfriesshire, had a sister, Christian, *m.* Gilbert Grierson. Thomas Wilson *m.* Agnes Grierson, and *d.* 1571, leaving issue,
1. Matthew, of Croglin.
2. Michael.
1. Janet.
2. Katherine.
3. Malic.
4. Christian.

The elder son,
Matthew Wilson, of Croglin, *d.* about 1612, leaving two sons,
1. John, his heir.
2. Thomas, a merchant burgess of Edinburgh.

The elder son,
John Wilson, of Croglin, J.P. Dumfriesshire, *m.* 1st, 1610, Margaret, dau. of Robert, Lord Dalzell (see Burke's *Peerage*, Carnwath, E.), and *d.* before 1641, having had issue by her,
1. John, his heir.
1. Susanna, *m.* 1626, John Sitlington, of Stanehouse.
2. Anne, *b.* 1619, *m.* John Stewart, of Drumbeg, co. Antrim, and *d.* 1682, leaving issue.

He *m.* 2ndly, Helen Maxwell (sasine 1632), and by her had issue,
2. James, of whom presently.
3. George.
4. Robert.
3. Jean, *m.* Rev. George Clelland, M.A., Minister of Morton.

The eldest son,

Wilson.   THE LANDED GENTRY.   774

JOHN WILSON, of Croglin, Commissioner of War for Dumfriesshire 1643-49, *m.* 1st, — Halliday, and 2ndly, the dau. of — Gordon, and had a son,
  WILLIAM WILSON, of Croglin, *m.* 1643, Sarah, dau. and co-heir of Thomas Grierson, the younger, of Barjarg. He *d.s.p.* and was *s.* by his uncle,
  JAMES WILSON, of Croglin, J.P., *m.* 1657, Helen, dau. of Robert Creichton, and *d.* about 1683. His son,
  WILLIAM WILSON, of Croglin, J.P. Dumfriesshire, left issue at his decease, a son,
  JAMES WILSON, of Croglin, Commissioner of Supply for Dumfriesshire, *m.* the dau. of — Gordon, and *d.* 1735, having had issue,
  WALTER WILSON, of Croglin, *b.* 1705, *m.* 1761, Isabel, dau. of George Gordon, of Troquhain (cadet of Lochinvar). She *d.* 1772. He *d.* 1781, having had issue,
  1. James, *b.* 1767, *d.* an infant.
  2. Walter, *b.* 1771, *d.* an infant.
  3. WALTER, of whom presently.
  1. Margaret, *b.* 1762, *d. unm.* 1822.
  2. Elizabeth, *b.* 1764, *d.* young.
  3. Ann, *b.* 1765, *m.* 1790, John Thompson, of Jennymount, near Belfast, and *d.* 1824, leaving issue, three sons and a dau.
  4. Isabel, *b.* 1769, *d. unm.* 1805.
His only surviving son,
  WALTER WILSON, of Croglin, which was sold owing to losses sustained through the failure of the Bank of Ayr, *m.* 1795, his cousin Jane, dau. of Robert Stewart, of Drumbeg (*see above*), and through her became possessed of Maryville, co. Antrim. She *d.* 1849. He *d.* 1807, having had issue,
  1. Robert Gordon, *b.* 1796, *d.* young.
  2. ALEXANDER GEORGE, his heir.   3. Walter, *d.* young.
  1. Mary Isabella, *b.* 1798, *d. unm.* 1900.
The only surviving son,
  ALEXANDER GEORGE WILSON, of Maryville, co. Antrim, *b.* 1797, *m.* 1837, Emily Lawrence, dau. of Rev. Charles Boyd, M.A., Rector of Magheradroll, by Emilia Juliana Theresa, his wife, dau. of Col. Thomas Dawson Lawrence, of Lawrencetown, co. Down. She *d.* 1899. He *d.* 1856, having had issue,
  1. WALTER HENRY, of Maryville and Cranmore.
  2. Alexander Basil, M. Inst. C.E. (*Maryville, Malone, Belfast; Royal Societies and Ulster Clubs*), *b.* 1845, *m.* Elizabeth Lauder, dau. of Joseph Richard Garrett, of Rialto, Holywood, and has issue,
    1. Josephine Ricarda.   2. Emily Lawrence.
  1. Emily Lawrence, *m.* W. J. Marshall, M.D. of Greenock, who *d.* 1901, leaving issue, four sons and six daus.
The elder son,
  WALTER HENRY WILSON, of Maryville, and Cranmore, co. Antrim, J.P. co. Down, *b.* 15 Nov. 1839; *m.* 30 Sept. 1875, Sarah Elizabeth, eldest dau. and co-heir of James Owen Wynne (*see* WYNNE *of Hazelwood*). He *d.* 14 May, 1901, having had issue,
  1. ALEXANDER GEORGE, now of Maryville.
  1. Marion Emily.   2. Lilian Lawrence, *d.* an infant.
  3. Florence Stewart.   4. Dorothy Gladys.
  5. Mary Wynnefred Kathleen.

  Arms—(MATRIC. LYON OFFICE)—Arg. a chevron between three mullets gu. *Crest*—A demi-lion rampant gu. *Motto*—Semper vigilans.
  Seats—Maryville, and Cranmore, co. Antrim. *Residence*—Belvoir Park, Newtownbreda, co. Down. *Club*—Ulster.

WILSON-FITZGERALD. *See* FITZGERALD.

WILSON-SLATOR. *See* SLATOR.

WINGFIELD.
See BURKE'S PEERAGE, POWERSCOURT, V.

WINN. *See* BURKE'S PEERAGE, HEADLEY, B.

WINTER OF AGHER.

EDWARD WINTER WINTER, of Agher, co. Meath, and Lisnabin, co. Westmeath, Lieut.-Col. and Hon. Col. late 6th Batt. Rifle Brigade, *b.* May, 1853, *s.* his father 1910, *s.* his uncle the late James Sanderson Winter 1911, and assumed the surname of WINTER and the arms of that family quarterly with those of Purdon by Royal Licence dated 2 April, 1912. He *m.* May, 1893, Cecilia Albuera

Frances, younger dau. of Charles Edward Radclyffe, of Little Park, Hants, and has issue,
  1. CHARLES EDWARD, *b.* Feb. 1894.
  2. Samuel Francis, *b.* Sept. 1895.
  3. George Hardress, *b.* Jan. 1897.
  4. Denis James, *b.* 19 May, 1900.

Lineage—CHRISTOPHER WINTER, a younger son of Thomas Winter, co. Oxford, removed to Balshal, co. Warwick, and was father of
  SAMUEL WINTER, D.D., *b.* at Balshal, 1603; *m.* Anne Beeston, of Boston, co. Lincoln, and had a son, SAMUEL, his heir. In 1650, Dr. Winter was obliged to resign the living of Cottingham, York, of which he was Rector, being ordered by the then Government to proceed to Ireland with the commissioners appointed for the settlement of that country, as their Chaplain, and was soon after constituted Provost of Trin. Coll. Dublin, which the preceding troubles had left almost desolate. In this office he exerted himself, with great zeal and success, to re-assemble the surviving members, and re-establish the discipline of the University. He appears to have been removed from the Provostship at the Restoration. Dr. Winter acquired property in King's Co., Meath, and Westmeath, and dying 1666, was *s.* by his eldest son,
  SAMUEL WINTER, who was confirmed in the estates of his father by the letters patent of CHARLES II, 1668. He *m.* Elizabeth, dau. or sister of Col. Sankey, an officer of considerable note under the Commonwealth, and dying 1670, was *s.* by his son,
  SAMUEL WINTER, *m.* Mary, dau. of Francis Pywell, of Possiekstown, co. Kildare, and dying 1692, left a son and successor,
  THE VERY REV. SANKEY WINTER, Archdeacon of Killala and Dean of Kildare, *m.* Elizabeth, dau. of Right Rev. Dr. William Lloyd, Bishop of Killala, but dying *s.p.* 1736, was *s.* by his brother,
  FRANCIS WINTER, *m.* Margaret, eldest dau. of Benjamin Pratt, of Agher, co. Meath, by Jane his wife, dau. of James Nugent, of Clonlost, co. Westmeath, and his wife, Jane, dau. of John Cooke, of Cookesborough, same co. By this lady Mr. Winter left at his decease, 1743, one son and two daus.,
  1. SAMUEL, his heir.
  1. Jane, *m.* Rev. Edward Reynell.
  2. Mary, *m.* Nicholas Reynell, of Reynella, and *d.s.p.*
His only son and successor,
  SAMUEL WINTER, of Agher, High Sheriff co. Meath 1778, *m.* 4 Dec. 1762, Margaret, youngest dau. of Joseph Robbins, of Ballyduff, co. Kilkenny, by Margaret his wife, dau. of Sir Henry Piers, Bart., of Tristernagh, and by her (who *d.* 1814), had issue,
  1. JOHN PRATT, his heir.
  2. Francis Pratt (Rev.).
  3. Samuel Pratt, *m.* Frances Rosa, dau. and co-heiress of Trevor Bomford, youngest son of Stephen Bomford, of Rabinstown, co. Meath, and left at his decease three sons and five daus.,
    1. GEORGE, of Oakley Park, King's Co., *m.* Elizabeth, dau. of James Cox, of Clarendon, Tasmania, and had issue
      (1) Francis Pratt (Sir), C.M.G., M.E.C. and M.L.C. of B. New Guinea, and chief Judicial officer 1888-1903, *b.* 23 Feb. 1848; *m.* 1903, Edith, dau. of Hon. George Moore, of Fiji.
      (2) St. Leonards Crosbie, *b.* 1853.
      (3) Ernest, *b.* 1856.
      (1) Georgina.
    2. Samuel Pratt, of Murndal, Victoria, Australia, dec.
    3. Trevor, dec.
    1. Mary, *m.* her cousin, John Winter, and had issue (*see below*).
    2. Margaret, *m.* Nathaniel Preston, of Swainston, co. Meath, and had issue.
    3. Frances Jane, *m.* Samuel Bomford, Capt. Royal North Gloucester Militia, son of George Bomford, of Drumlargan, co. Meath, and has issue. She *d.* 1910.
    4. Arabella, *m.* Cecil Pybus Cooke, of Lake Condah, Victoria, Australia, eldest son of William Cooke, of Cheltenham, and had issue.
    5. Anna Maria Sarah, *m.* Charles Gustavus Walsh, Col. H.M. Indian Army, 2nd son of John Walsh, of Dundrum Castle, co. Dublin, and had issue.
  1. Anna Maria.
  2. Arabella, *m.* George Bomford, of Drumlargan, and Oakley Park, Kells, co. Meath.
Mr. Winter *d.* 1811, and was *s.* by his eldest son,
  JOHN PRATT WINTER, of Agher, *b.* 31 May, 1768; *m.* 4 Aug. 1794, Anne, youngest dau. of Capt. Arthur Gore, of the E.I.C.S., youngest son of William Gore, of Barrowmount, co. Kilkenny, and by her (who *d.* Aug. 1848) had issue,
  1. SAMUEL, of Agher.
  2. Arthur, *d.* in Greece when taking part in Lord Byron's expedition.
  3. John, *m.* his cousin, Mary, dau. of Samuel Pratt Winter, and had issue, two daus.,
    1. Frances.   2. Ann.
  4. Francis, Major H.E.I.C.S., 59th Bengal Infantry, *m.* 18 April, 1850, Anna Julia (*d.* 29 Jan. 1909), eldest dau. of Col. John Caulfeild, of Bloomfield, co. Westmeath (*see* BURKE'S *Peerage*, CHARLEMONT, V.).
  5. Benjamin Pratt, *d.* in Australia 1844.
  1. Anna Maria, *m.* William Humphrys, of Ballybaise House, co. Cavan, and *d.* 1837, leaving issue.   2. Margaret, dec.
  3. Eliza, *m.* Rev. Thomas Gordon Caulfeild, of Mount Temple, co. Westmeath.
  4. Arabella, *m.* her cousin, George Bomford, of Oakley Park, co. Meath.
Mr. Winter, High Sheriff 1806, *d.* 31 Aug. 1846, and was *s.* by his son,
  SAMUEL WINTER, of Agher, co. Meath, J.P. and D.L., *b.* 2 Aug. 1796; *m.* 18 Nov. 1826, Lucy, 2nd dau. of James Sanderson,

of Cloverhill, co. Cavan, J.P. and D.L., and by her (who d. 11 Nov. 1864) had issue,
  1. John Pratt, Capt. 17th Lancers, fell leading the 2nd squadron of his regt. in the charge of the Light Cavalry Brigade at Balaclava, 25 Oct. 1854.   2. James Sanderson, late of Agher.
  3. Samuel, of Clover Hill, co. Cavan, J.P. and D.L., High Sheriff 1876; b. 1834, assumed by Royal Licence 20 Oct. 1873, the surname and arms of Sanderson; m. 1 March, 1860, Anne, 2nd dau. of John A. Nicholson, of Balrath, co. Meath.
  4. Francis Alexander, b. 1836, Barrister-at-Law; d. 26 Aug. 1883.
  1. Elizabeth Anne, m. 3 Aug. 1852, George Nugent Purdon, of Lisnabin, co Westmeath; she d. 6 Nov. 1864, leaving issue (see that family). The eldest son, Edward Winter Purdon, now of Agher, has assumed the name and arms of Winter.
  2. Lucy Adelaide, d. unm. 22 Jan. 1906.
  3. Mary Anne, d. unm. 16 Dec. 1906.
Mr. Winter was High Sheriff of Meath 1837, and of Cavan 1851. He d. 6 Nov. 1867. His 2nd son,
  James Sanderson Winter, of Agher, co. Meath, J.P. and D.L., High Sheriff co. Meath 1872, and of co. Cavan 1871, M.A., late Royal Meath Militia, b. 15 Feb. 1832, and d. 10 July, 1911, having devised his estate to his nephew, Edward Winter Purdon, conditional on his assuming the name and arms of Winter.

Arms—Qrly. 1 and 4, Chequy, or and sa., a fess arg. (Winter), 2 and 3 (Purdon). Crests—1. A martlet or (Winter), 2. Purdon. Seats—Agher, Enfield, co. Meath, Lisnabin, Killucan, co. Westmeath. Club—Kildare Street, Dublin.

WOGAN-BROWNE. See BROWNE.

WOLFE OF FORENAGHTS.

George Wolfe, of Forenaghts and Bishopsland, co. Kildare, and Acomb Priory, co. York, J.P. co. Kildare, High Sheriff 1900, County Councillor, Ranger of the Curragh, late Lieut. 8th (King's Royal Irish) Hussars, formerly Lieut. in the 87th, Princess Victoria's Royal Irish Fusiliers (medal and clasp and bronze star for Tel-el-Kebir), retired from the Army 29 July, 1890, b. 16 Dec. 1859; m. 25 Oct. 1888, Emily Maud Mary (who d. 5 June, 1910), widow of J. J. Leeman, D.L., sometime M.P. for York, and only child of the late Richard Smethurst, J.P. and D.L., of Ellerbeck Hall, Chorley, High Sheriff of Lancashire 1874 (see Smethurst of Chorley), and has issue,

Emily Maud Charlotte.

Lineage.—Richard Wolfe, the first of the family who settled in Ireland, went there from England about 1658. In a common pleas judgment in 1665, he is described as "lately of the city of Dublin," gent., and in a Chancery suit, dated 12 April of same year, he is shown as of Huttonread, parish of Oughterard, co. Kildare. His will, dated 7 Dec. 1678, was proved 27 Feb. following, and he was bur. in Oughterard Church. By Ann his wife, who survived him, he had,
  1. John, his heir.
  1. Jane, b. circa 1636; m. Hugh Banner, of Punchestown.
  2. Dorothy, m. William Brunton, of Bishopscourt, co. Kildare.
  3. Ann Katharine.   4. Eleanor, m. William Burgoyne.
The elder son,
  John Wolfe, of Baronrath, b. about 1645, was appointed, Act 10 William III, one of the Commissioners for ascertaining the mode of raising the proportion of a Land Tax of £120,000 to be paid by co. Kildare. He m. 1668, Mary Cooper, widow of the Rev. — Colclough, and by her (who d. 1725) had,
  1. Richard, his heir.
  2. John, b. 5 Aug. 1681; m. 31 Aug. 1704, Alice, dau. of James White, of Ballinatray, co. Wexford, and d. 1751, leaving Mary, d. unm. 24 June, 1758.
  1. Elizabeth, b. 1 April, 1669; m. Thomas Blood, of Lady Castle co. Kildare, and had issue.
  2. Ann, b. 1 March, 1670; m. Richard Fletcher, of Rathmore, co. Kildare, and had issue.
  3. Mary, b. 1 March, 1675; m. — King, of Dublin, Merchant, and had issue.
  4. Alice, b. 1 Sept. 1678; m. Samuel Page, of Barbristown, co. Kildare, and d. Sept. 1766, having had issue.
Mr. Wolfe d. 1715. His eldest son,
  Richard Wolfe, of Forenaghts and Baronrath, b. 11 Nov. 1673, Freeman of Dublin 1706; m. 13 April, 1699, Lydia (b. 5 May, 1668; d. 24 Aug. 1715), dau. of Patrick Page, of Forenaghts, by Mary his wife, dau. of Sir William Sandys, Bart., and by her (who

d. 24 Aug. 1715) had, with seven daus. (viz., 1. Mary, b. 6 April, 1701; m. William Sherlock, of Carrick, co. Westmeath; 2. Alice, b. 9 Aug. 1702; m. Fleetwood Cahill, Barrister-at-Law, and d. 9 July, 1764; 3. Elizabeth, b. 24 Aug. 1703; d. unm. 25 March, 1790; 4. Anne, b. 3 Oct. 1706; m. Rev. Thomas Bullen; 5. Lydia, b. 4 Jan. 1708; m. Thomas White, of Ballinatray, co. Wexford, and d. 17 Jan. 1738; 6. Catherine, b. 12 March, 1711; d. unm. 3 April, 1730; 7. Jane, b. 29 July; d. 19 Aug. 1715), five sons,
  1. John, his heir.
  2. Thomas, of Blackhall, co. Kildare, b. 12 June, 1705, Freeman of Dublin 1733; m. 1733, Margaret Lombard, and d. 25 March, 1787, having had a dau., Mary, m. 1st, 1758, Charles Hendrick, and 2ndly, 1767, John Wetherall, and an only son,
    Theobald, of Blackhall, b. 1739, Freeman of Dublin 1769; m. Aug. 1771, Frances, dau. of Rev. Peter Lombard, of Cloncorrig. co. Leitrim, and d. 8 Oct. 1799, having had by her (who d. 15 July, 1811), three daus. (viz. (1) Mary, b. 8 June, 1773, m. Capt. George Mansergh, of Greenane, co. Tipperary; (2) Frances, b. 7 March, 1793; d. unm. ; (3) Margaret, b. 11 May, 1796; m. Lieut. Richard Wall, R.N.), and eight sons,
    (1) Thomas (Rev.), b. 11 Dec. 1774, Freeman of Dublin 1792; d. unm. 1797.
    (2) Peter, of Blackhall, High Sheriff co. Kildare 1815, b. 9 Aug. 1776; m. 1804, Isabella Patrickson, niece of Sir Thomas Clarges, Bart., and d. 28 May, 1848, having had,
      1. Theobald John, b. 4 July, 1806; d. unm. 30 May, 1869.
      2. William Clarges, b. 28 Oct. 1810; Col. in the Army, served in the 39th Regt. in the Crimean War; d. unm. 29 Sept. 1868.
      3. Peter, b. 5 Sept. 1813; Capt. 65th Regt.; d. unm. at Wellington, New Zealand, about 1858.
      4. John Edward, of Blackhall, b. 12 May, 1815; d. unm. 31 Aug. 1870.   5. Christopher, d. young.
      1. Frances Mary, b. 9 April, 1805; d. unm.
      2. Isabelle, b. 25 Aug. 1812; d. unm.
      3. Helena Maria, of Blackhall, m. 8 Feb. 1842, Christopher Rynd (see Rynd of Ryndville).
    (3) James, Major Kildare Militia, b. 16 April, 1778; m. 1 May, 1813, Eliza Walker, and d. 12 July, 1840, having had four daus. (1, Mary Ann, b. 10 May, 1814; d. unm. 9 June, 1884; 2, Margaret, d. unm. 1 March, 1894; 3, Frances Isabella, m. 19 Feb. 1846, Rev. John Murray, Rector of Edenderry, King's Co., who d. 7 June, 1887; d. 1901; and 4, Elizabeth, d. unm. 1 May, 1903), and three sons,
      1. Theobald George Samuel, of whom hereafter, as successor to Forenaghts.
      2. John Charles (Ven.), D.D., Rector of Clontibret, co. Monaghan and Archdeacon of Clogher, b. 10 Feb. 1817; m. 28 Nov. 1855, Sarah Emilie., dau. of Isaac Higgin, of Cave Valley, Jamaica, and d. 30 Aug. 1871, leaving issue,
        a. James Charles, b. 5 Nov. 1856; m. 6 Sept. 1882, Mary Alicia, dau. of Robert Adams, M.D., of Dublin, Surgeon-in-Ordinary to the Queen in Ireland, and widow of Thomas Coote, J.P. and D.L., of Rathconnell House, co. Monaghan, and had issue,
          (a) John Charles, b. 14 June, and d. 26 Aug. 1883.
          (b) James Charles, b. 20 Oct. 1884.
          (c) Richard Straubenzie, b. 6 Dec. 1886; d. 28 Sept. 1888.
          (a) Nora Dorothy, b. 26 Sept. 1885; d. 11 Sept. 1883.
          (b) Eileen, b, 14 Nov. 1888.
        b. Edward John (Rev.), Vicar of St. Thomas, Streatham Hill, Surrey, formerly Vicar of Mulvallally, Tandragee, co. Armagh, b. 4 Aug. 1858; m. 9 Aug. 1883, Henrietta Mary, dau. of Ussher William Alcock, 83rd Regt., and grand-dau. of the late Harry Alcock, of Wilton Castle, co. Wexford (see Alcock of Wilton), and has issue,
          (a) Mona Aphra.
          (b) Vera Dorothy.
          (c) Stella Marjorie.
        c. Thomas, b. 2, d. 3 March, 1860.
        d. Arthur Theobald (1, Priory Gardens, Bedford Park, W.), b. 13 July, 1870; m. 27 April, 1900, ffrida Augusta, 2nd dau. of the late Capt. William Charles Robinson, late Bombay Europeans, and grand-dau. of the late Romney Robinson, D.D. F.T.C.D., and has issue,
          (a) Joan Deirdre, b. 14 March, 1901.
          (b) Maeve Audrey, b. 13 Aug. 1902.
        a. Mary Emilie, b. 19 Sept. 1861; m. 9 Aug. 1882, Albert Augustus Eyre Coote, late Capt. 3rd Batt. Royal Irish Fusiliers, son of Major Coote, D.L. and J.P., Brandrum House, co. Monaghan, and has issue.
        b. Augusta, b. 12 Feb. 1864; m. 2 Sept. 1885, Rev. Lewis Arthur Hill Trevor Pooler, Canon of St. Patrick's, Dublin, and Chaplain to the Lord Lieutenant of Ireland, and has issue (see Pooler of Tyross).
      3. Charles (Rev.), British Chaplain at Havre, b. 10 Sept. 1825; m. Gould Ruxton (see Ruxton of Ardee), and d.s.p. 9 Nov. 1866. She d. March, 1885.
    (4) Theobald, b. 25 Feb. 1780; d. unm.
    (5) Edward, b. 16 Sept. 1781, Major in the Army; d. unm. 20 Feb. 1875.
    (6) Richard, b. 18 Nov. 1782, Ensign 68th Regt. 30 March, 1800; d. 2 July, 1801, in the Leeward Islands.
    (7) Charles, b. 19 Aug. 1784; d. young.
    (8) Charles (Rev.), the Poet, author of the Elegy on the death of Sir John Moore at Corunna, b. 13 Dec. 1791; d. 21 Feb. 1823.

3. Theobald, Barrister-at-Law, b. 10 March, 1710, Freeman of Dublin 1749; m. 1st, 1733, Eliza, dau. of Capt. Charlton, of Curraghtown, co. Meath, and 2ndly, 1745, Elizabeth (who d. Jan. 1772), dau. of Surgeon-General William Dobbs, and d. 1784, having had issue,
  1. Theobald, b. 29 Sept. 1761; d. 25 March, 1770.
  2. William, b. 25 Dec. 1765; d. 21 Nov. 1771.
  1. Mary, m. 10 Nov. 1770, Cuthbert Fetherston, of Mosstown, co. Westmeath, and d. 12 Aug. 1809, having had issue.
  2. Lydia, m. Rev. James Jones, son of Right Hon. Theophilus Jones, and d. 1793, having had issue.
  3. Anne, m. Rev. H. Lomax Walsh, D.D., and d. 25 Dec. 1806, leaving issue.
  4. Charlotte, m. 9 April, 1777, her cousin, Col. John Wolfe, of Forenaghts (see below).
  5. Margaret, m. 7 May, 1784, Sir Robert Synge, 1st bart., of Lislee, and had issue.
4. Richard, of Baronrath, co. Kildare, and of St. Margaret's, co. Dublin, b. 13 Oct. 1712, Freeman of Dublin 1735; m. Alicia, dau. of James Standish, of Dublin, and d. April, 1779, leaving by her (who d. 1754) three daus. (viz., 1, Elizabeth, b. 1750, d. 30 Aug. 1816; 2, Anne, b. 1752, m. Robert French, and d. 14 March, 1805; 3, Lydia) and an only son,
  William Standish, of Baronrath, co. Kildare, and St. Margaret's, co. Dublin, b. 1752, Freeman of Dublin 1775; m. 4 March, 1779, Elizabeth (who d. 1814), dau. of Gilbert Toler and Anne Gason his wife, and d. 1810, having had (with three younger sons, James General, b. 1798; James Walter, b. 1800, both d. young; Arthur Wills Crofts, b. 1804, d. unm. 1856, and six daus., (1) Anna Maria, d. 1842; (2) Mary, d. young; (3) Alicia, b. 23 Oct. 1790; m. E. Cusack; (4) Elizabeth Lydia, b. 16 April, 1792; m. 4 Jan. 1815, Rev. James Metge (b. 1790, d. 9 Jan. 1827), and d. 27 April, 1874, leaving issue; (5) Araminta, b. 8 Dec. 1796; d. 16 May, 1832; (6) Anne French, b. 1807, d. young) the following sons,
  (1) Richard, b. 17 Dec. 1780; d. aged 9 years.
  (2) Theobald, b. 1782, Queen's Co. Militia; d. 16 Jan. 1805.
  (3) William Standisb, of Baronrath, and of St. Margaret's, b. 26 March, 1784, Freeman of Dublin 1813; m. 1808, Jane, sister of Mr. Phillips, Barrister-at-Law, and d. 18 March, 1869, having had,
    1. William, b. 1811; d. an infant.
    2. Richard, b. 1817; d. aged 9 years.
    3. Robert, b. 1819; d. aged 7 years.
    1. Elizabeth, d. aged 16.   2. Lydia, d. aged 14.
    3. Isabella, d. Jan. 1895. 4. Charlotte, d. 1 Jan. 1895.
    5. Jane, d. aged 6.
  (4) Robert, b. 1786, Ensign 59th Regt., killed 26 Aug. 1811, in Java, at storming of French lines of Cornelius, near Batavia.
  (5) John, of Upper Gloucester Street, Dublin, and Rockford, Nenagh, co. Tipperary, b. 6 May, 1787; m. 24 April, 1823, Frances, dau. of William Kingsley, of Rockford, Nenagh, and d. 15 July, 1858, having had by her (who d. 2 Jan. 1878) with two daus. (viz., 1, Frances Elizabeth, b. 7 June, 1825; m. 12 Jan. 1848, William Courtenay, and d.s.p. 26 Feb. 1849; 2, Lucy Ellen, m. 13 July, 1859, Benjamin Towers, of Castleton, co. Tipperary, and d. 15 Feb. 1893, having by him (who d. 28 Sept. 1881) had issue; and two elder sons (Robert French, b. 6 March, 1824; d. young; and John, b. 18 May, 1827; d. unm. 22 Oct. 1850), four sons,
    1. Toler Kingsley, of St. Margaret's, co. Dublin, and Rapla, co. Tipperary, b. 29 Dec. 1829; m. 10 Sept. 1853, Letitia, dau. of Major George Jackson, of Mount Pleasant, co. Tipperary, by Letitia his wife, dau. of Richard Townsend Herbert, of Cahirnane, co. Kerry (see HERBERT of Cahirnane), and d. 27 Sept. 18-8, having had,
      a. John Standish, b. 15 Feb. 1855; m. 22 July, 1879, Mary Toler, dau. of Joshua Robert Minnitt (see MINNITT of Anaghbeg), and d. 4 Feb. 1901, leaving one dau., Marie, who d. 13 June, 1901.
      b. George, of Chicago, U.S.A., late Capt. 4th Batt. R.I. Regt. (Militia), b. 10 May, 1857.
      c. Toler Kingsley, of Milwaukie, U.S.A., b. 26 Sept. 1858; m. 30 Nov. 1881, Mary Ellen Lyster, and has issue, nine children.
      d. Richard Herbert, of Provincial Bank of Ireland, b. 3 Nov. 1864.
      e. William Theobald Butler, b. 20 Feb. 1871; m. 27 April, 1900, Louisa Maude Talbot, of Westport, co. Mayo, and has issue,
        (a) Ernest William Toler, b. 1 July, 1901.
        (b) Richard Herbert, b. 27 April, 1904.
        (a) Vera Kathleen, b. 4 Feb.
      f. Robert French, b. 4 Dec. 1873; m. Mrs. Annie Oliver, née Leate.
      a. Frances Elizabeth, b. 16 May, 1860; m. 3 July, 1876, Lewis Sparrow, of Ivybridge, Devonshire. He d. 1902. She d. 7 Dec. 1907, having had issue, one son and one dau.
      b. Letitia, m. 13 Jan. 1885, Henry Allington, eldest son of Bridges Harvey, of Plymstock, Plymouth, and of Halstead, co. Essex, J.P., and has issue.
      c. Mary Toler, m. Henry Prince, of Cromford, co. Derby, and has issue.
      d. Lucy Ellen, d. 1 Sept 1883.
      e. Louisa, of Milwaukie, U.S.A., m. about 1902, — Kleiner, and has issue.
    2. William Standish, b. 18 May, 1832; m. 12 Feb. 1858, Frances Jackson, of Rapla, and d. at St. Kilda, Melbourne, Australia, 21 March, 1867.

3. Arthur, b. 18 Feb. 1834; d. young.
4. Theobald Richard, of Rockford, Nenagh, J.P., b. 29 Sept. 1839; m. 14 June, 1862, Caroline (who d. 24 Dec. 1908), dau. of James ffranck Rolleston, D.I. (see ROLLESTON of Ffrankfort Castle), and d. 10 Oct. 1911, having had,
  a. John Rolleston, Hon. Lieut.-Col. 3rd Batt. Royal Irish Regt., J.P. co. Tipperary, b. 21 July, 1867; m. 4 Feb. 1910, Lucinda Elizabeth, only dau. of the late Frederick Hugh Finch, of Kilcolman, Nenagh (see that family).
  b. James ffranck Rolleston, b. 20 Aug. 1881; d. 20 Nov. 1907.
  a. Georgiana Lucy, m. 1st, 9 Dec. 1890, James Henry Deacon, of Hoo Meavy, Yelverton, S. Devon (he d. 12 June, 1900) by whom she had a dau. She m. 2ndly, 26 April, 1902, Richard Beiginton Johns, of Bickleigh, Devon, and has issue, one son.
  b. Frances Elizabeth.
  c. Ricarda Alice.
  d. Caroline Blanche.
(6) Richard Thomas, Major in the Army, and Sub-Inspector of Militia of the Ionian Isles, served in the 59th and 98th Regts., Commandant of Robben Island, Cape Colony, 1834, Civil Commissioner and Resident Magistrate of the District of Wynberg 1847, Acting Judge of Police, Capetown, 1854, b. 23 Jan. 1794; m. 1st, 25 Oct. 1818, Anna Maria, dau. of Dr. George Burleigh, M.D., and 2nd Ceylon Rifle Regt. (she d. 12 Feb. 1837), and had two daus. (viz., 1, Alicia Mary, b. 31 Dec. 1820; m. 16 Nov. 1841, Lieut.-Col. Thomas Percipal Touzel, of Jersey, 27th Regt., Assistant Inspector and Chief Instructor of Musketry Jersey Militia, and A.D.C. to the Governor, and d. 25 Sept. 1887; 2, Elizabeth, b. 20 Dec. 1831; d. 2 Aug. 1837) and seven sons,
  1. William George, b. 23 Jan. 1820; d. 27 Jan. 1820.
  2. Charles Henry, of the Colonial Civil Service, Cape Colony, b. 15 Aug. 1822; m. 1st, 13 Dec. 1848, Amelia Long (she d. 25 Feb. 1866), and had issue,
    a. Richard Burleigh, b. 1 May, 1851; d. 7 Nov. 1895.
    b. William Kilwarden, b. 20 March, 1852; d. young.
    c. Charles Henry, of the Colonial Civil Service, Cape Colony, b. 4 July, 1858; d. 19 Sept. 1894.
    a. Charlotte Alicia Burleigh.
  Mr. C. H. Wolfe m. 2ndly, 6 Jan. 1881, Antoinette Elizabeth, dau. of Helperous Ritzima von Lier Kuys, formerly Asst.-Surveyor-General Cape Colony; d. 12 April, 1893, at Kalk Bay, Cape Colony, and had further issue.
  3. Mildmay William Fane, of Port Elizabeth, South Africa, b. 14 Aug. 1824; m. 2 July, 1849, Fanny Sophia Terry, and d. 22 April, 1863, having had
    a. Arthur Kilwarden, b. 24 March, 1851; d. 31 March, 1854.
    b. Arthur Kilwarden, b. 23 June, 1855; d. unm. 2 Jan. 1899.
    c. Mildmay Tindall William, b. 1 May, 1862; d. 28 Nov. 1862.
    a. Cecilia Burleigh.
    b. Alicia Frances, m. 1st, 8 Dec. 1868, Alphonzo Taylor, of Port Elizabeth, South Africa, and of Boston, America, by whom she had issue, and 2ndly, Thomas Hutchinson, by whom also she had issue, and d. Dec. 1889.
    c. Fanny Mildmay, m. 10 July, 1884, George Piers, R.M., and son of Charles Piers, R.M., Cape Colony, and has issue.
    d. Ellen Travers, m. 3 Dec. 1879, Charles Edward Shelly, of Fore Street, Hertford, M.A. and M.D. Cantab.
    e. Millicent Mary Fane, d. young.
  4. George Douglas Dunlevie, Major-Gen., late Assistant British Commissioner to the Basutos, served successively in the 39th, 87th, and 2nd Regts., and as Staff Officer of Pensioners at Northampton, Sheffield, Plymouth, and Northern Division, London, b. 23 April, 1826; m. 4 Jan. 1853, his cousin, Louisa Elizabeth Metge. She d. 18 Jan. 1889. He d. 10 June, 1902, leaving issue.
    a. Richard Cecil Burleigh, b. 30 Nov. 1853; d. 12 July, 1854.
    b. George Cecil Burleigh, b. 18 Aug. 1863, Capt. late Royal Marine Light Infantry.
    a. Elizabeth Lydia Anna [Amatola], b. 8 Feb. 1856; d. 25 Jan. 1867.
    b. Alicia Cecilia Burleigh, b. 2 July, 1858; d. 7 Oct. 1859.
    c. Louisa Alicia Burleigh, m. 23 Dec. 1885, Henry Thomas Perkins, son of Thomas Perkins, of Norbiton, Surrey, and has issue.
  5. ROBERT THOMAS, Lieut.-Col. late Army Pay Department, b. in the Castle, Cape Town, 28 May, 1828, Freeman of Dublin 1875; m. at Graham's Town, South Africa, 24 Jan. 1856, Isabella Sarah, dau. of George Stow, of Nuneaton, co. Warwick (see BURKE's Peerage, PHILIPSON-STOW, Bart.), son of George Stow, of London, by Ann his wife, dau. and co-heir of Humphrey Winter. She d. 25 Dec. 1895. He d. 10 April, 1908, having had issue, Robert Tennant Stow, formerly Lieut. 4th Batt. the King's Liverpool Regiment, of Codglogon, near Killenbourne, Western Australia, b. 20 Aug. 1858; m. 1st, 7 Oct. 1891, Veronica Vivyan Maud (div. 29 Nov. 1900), 2nd dau. of J. J. Whyte, of S. Australia. He m. 2ndly, 6 Sept. 1900, Catherine Wilkinson, dau. of Richard John Harper, widow of John William West, Alicia Mary Stow.

IRELAND. Woodley.

6. Richard Edward, formerly of the Colonial Civil Service, Cape Colony, b. 26 June, 1833; m. 19 June, 1856, Ada McGowan (who d. 27 Jan. 1900), and d. 1 Dec. 1873, having had,
  a. Richard Edward Maclear, b. 27 July, 1857; d. 6 Dec. 1858.
  b. Charles Henry, b. 23 Oct. 1860; m. 31 Jan. 1893, Jessie Wilhelmina Maud, dau. of the late Arthur Smyth, formerly Resident Magistrate of Wynberg, and Civil Commissioner of Humansdorp, Cape Colony, and has issue,
    (a) Cecil Burleigh, b. 16 Dec. 1893.
    (b) Standish Smyth, b. 22 July, 1897.
    (c) Coryn Smyth, b. 30 Aug. 1899.
    (d) Mildmay Smyth, twin with his brother.
    (e) Robert Smyth, b. 16 Dec. 1904.
    (a) Kathleen Smyth, b. 19 June, 1901.
  c. Arthur Kilwarden, late of the Civil Service, Cape Colony, b. 24 June, 1866; m. 1st, 29 Sept. 1891, Ida Willis (div.), dau. of A. Willis Cole, Barrister-at-Law, Cape Colony, and had issue,
    (a) Richard Standish, b. 21 Oct. 1892.
He m. 2ndly, 15 Jan. 1902, at St. Margaret's, Fifeshire, Scotland, Mary Segler, eldest dau. of John Hutchinson, of Peterhead, and has further issue,
    (b) Arthur Kilwarden, b. 12 July, 1903.
    (a) Sheilah Mary, b 27 Oct.
  a. Anna Maria.
  b. Kathleen Mary, m. 19 July, 1888, James Peter Hopkins, C.S. Cape Colony, son of Lieut. Robert Hopkins, R.N., of Hatwell, Berks (see HOPKINS of Tidmarsh), and has issue.
  c. Edith Emily, m. 26 Sept. 1890, Henry Edward Davis, son of James Frederick Davis, C.E., Cape Colony. He d 17 March, 1898.
  d. Lillie Margaret May, m. 20 March, 1902, William James Crowhurst, and has issue.
7. Henry Thomas, b. 26 July, 1836; d. 5 Oct. 1839.
Major Richard Wolfe m. 2ndly, Maria Anna, dau. of Benjamin Grayson, of Rose Hill, Camp Ground, Rondesbosch, and d. 13 May, 1855, having had by her (who d. 23 Aug. 1876),
  1. Anna Maria de Lorentz, m. 21 Sept. 1865, William Mortimer Maynard Farmer, Merchant, of Maynards Ville, Wynberg, Cape Colony, and 18, Bina Gardens, South Kensington, and by him (who d. 30 Sept. 1899) had issue,
  2. Mary, d. 28 June, 1845.   3. Fanny Richmond.
  4. Georgina.   5. Maria Henrica Smith.
  6. Jessy, d. 23 Jan. 1852.
5. William, b. 13 March, 1714, Freeman of Dublin 1736; d. unm. 1742.
Mr. Wolfe d. 2 Dec. 1732, and was s. by his eldest son,
JOHN WOLFE, of Forenaghts, b. 7 April, 1700, Freeman of Dublin 1730, Capt. Kildare Militia 1745; m. 10 June, 1725, Mary, dau. of Williams Philpot, and by her (who d. Feb. 1763) had three daus. (viz., 1. Lydia, b. 21 May, 1728; m. Dr. William Patten, and d.s.p. 19 May, 1793; 2. Mary, b. 7 Jan. and d. 6 Feb. 1745; 3. Jane, b. 7 Jan. 1745; m. Thomas Landy, and is dec.), and nine sons,
1. PHILPOT, his successor.
2. Richard, of Athy, co. Kildare, b. 13 July, 1730, served in the 48th Regt. and 5th Dragoons, Collector of Kilkenny; m. 1st, about 1748, Barbara, dau. of Col. Charles Bucknall, Dep.-Adj.-Gen. of the Forces in Ireland, and had issue,
  1. Williams, b. 1750, Capt. 40th Regt.; d. unm. 20 Sept. 1777, killed in a night attack in the American war.
  2. Charles Bucknall, Lieut. 38th Regt., m. the dau. of — Griffith, Port Surveyor of New York, and d. 17 Oct. 1790; having had by her,
    Richard Straubenzie (Rev.), Rector of Kilbeggan, b. 7 Oct. 1779, and d. 23 July, 1803, killed with his great-uncle, Arthur, Lord Kilwarden, by the rebels in Thomas Street, Dublin.
Mr. Richard Wolfe (whose will, dated 25 Feb. 1778, was proved 22 Nov. 1788) m. 2ndly, Jane Mathews, of Bonnetstown, co. Kilkenny, by whom he had,
  3. Philpot Rogerson, Lieut. 100th Regt., of Belcamp Cottage, Balbriggan, Secretary to Board of Works, and Inspector-General of Barracks in Ireland, m. Martha Thompson, of Coleraine, and d. 21 Dec. 1821, having had issue,
    (1) Richard Arthur, Lieut. 47th Regt., bapt. 23 March, 1790; d. 1808 on his passage from Bombay to Madras.
    (2) Arthur Philpot, bapt. 21 Jan. 1792; d. young.
    (1) Anne Jane, bapt. 14 Jan. 1788; m. Thomas S. Croker, son of Abraham Croker, of Ballynegarde, co. Limerick.
    (2) Charlotte, bapt. 15 May, 1794; d. unm.
    (3) Elizabeth, bapt. 1 Feb. 1801, and d. aged 29.
3. John, of Bishopsland, b. 20 March, 1732, Freeman of Dublin 1753 (will dated 21 May, 1784, and proved 27 Feb. 1786).
4. Thomas, b. 25 June, 1733; d. 7 Oct. 1744.
5. Theobald, of Castle Warden, co. Kildare, b. 21 Dec. 1734, Freeman of Dublin 1756; m. 1762, Anne, dau. of Rev. George Ward, and d. 25 June, 1771, leaving a dau.,
  Elizabeth, m. Rev. Arthur Lord.
6. William, b. 30 May, 1736; d. 17 June, 1737.
7. Isaac, b. 23 Dec. 1737; d. 25 Dec. 1742.
8. ARTHUR, VISCOUNT KILWARDEN, b. 19 Jan. 1738, Freeman of Dublin 1761, entered the Middle Temple, London, Oct. 1761, admitted to the Irish Bar, Michaelmas, 1766, appointed King's Counsel 3 April, 1778, Solicitor-General 11 May, 1787, and Attorney-General 12 Aug. 1789, having been a few days before sworn of the Privy Council, and Lord Chief Justice, King's Bench, 1796. He was a member for Coleraine 1784, and in the succeeding Parliament for James Town and for co. Dublin 1798. He m. 7 Jan. 1769, Anne (who d. 23 Aug. 1804), dau. of William Ruxton, of Ardee (see RUXTON of Ardee). She was created 30 Sept. 1795, BARONESS KILWARDEN of Kilteel, and he, on his elevation to the Bench, was created BARON KILWARDEN of Newlands, 3 July, 1798, and VISCOUNT KILWARDEN, 29 Dec. 1800. He was killed on the night of 23 July, 1803, by the rebels in Thomas Street, Dublin. He had issue,
  1. JOHN, 2nd Viscount Kilwarden, b. 11 Nov. 1769; d.s.p. 16 May, 1830, when the title became extinct.
  2. William, b. 11 Oct. 1770; d. 30 Dec. 1782.
  3. Arthur, Col. in the Army, b. 26 June, 1773; d. unm. 29 June, 1805.   4. Richard, d. young.
  1. Marianne, b. 10 Sept. 1776; m. June, 1809, Hardwicke Shute, and d. 8 Feb. 1814, leaving issue.
  2. Elizabeth, b. 31 Aug. 1778; d. unm. 24 May, 1806.
9. Williams, b. 29 May, 1741, Lieut. R.N., Freeman of Dublin 1764; m. Katharine Hussey, and d.s.p. 4 Aug. 1770.
Mr. Wolfe d. 30 July, 1760, and was s. by his eldest son,
PHILPOT WOLFE, of Forenaghts, b. 10 Sept. 1726, Freeman of Dublin 1751, Capt. Kildare Militia 1756, High Sheriff 1756, Collector of Revenue, Naas, 1758, Sub-Commissioner of Excise 1761, J.P. 1784; m. 10 Feb. 1753, Mary, dau. of Thomas de Burgh, of Droinkeen, co. Limerick, M.P. for Naas (see DE BURGH of Oldtown), and had issue,
1. JOHN, his successor.
2. Richard, b. 17 Dec. 1757; d. 24 June, 1770.
3. Thomas Philpot, b. 10 Aug. 1760; d. 11 July, 1770.
4. Williams Philpot, b. 5 Oct. 1762; d. 6 June, 1770.
5. Arthur, b. 7 Feb. 1764; d. 29 March, 1764.
1. Mary Burgh, b. 4 July, 1755; d. 19 June, 1756.
2. Lydia, b. 5 Aug. 1756; d. 5 Jan. 1761.
Mr. Wolfe d. 20 May, 1775, and was s. by his eldest son,
JOHN WOLFE, of Forenaghts, Col. Kildare Militia, b. 9 Feb. 1754, Freeman of Dublin 1775, High Sheriff 1779, Capt. Forenaghts Cavalry, 31 Oct. 1796, M.P. for Kildare, appointed in conjunction with William Robert, 2nd Duke of Leinster, K.P., Governor of the co. Kildare 12 March, 1803; m. 9 April, 1777, Charlotte (who d. 1787), dau. of his great-uncle, Theobald Wolfe, and had issue,
1. JOHN, his successor.
2. Theobald, b. 12 July, 1780; d. unm.
3. Arthur, Major Kildare Militia, b. 18 Sept. 1786; m. 1811, Margaret, dau. of James Hamilton, of Dunboyne Castle, co. Meath, M.P., and d. 27 Aug. 1813, having had issue,
  John, b. 14 May, 1812; d. 5 April, 1829.
  Elizabeth, b. 20 Sept. 1813; d. 30 May, 1822.
4. RICHARD, heir to his brother John.
1. Elizabeth, b. 18 May, 1779; d. 3 June, 1779.
2. Mary, b. 26 July, 1781; d. 24 Dec. 1826.
3. Elizabeth, b. 25 Jan. 1783; d. 7 May, 1836.
4. Charlotte, b. 4 May, 1785; d. unm.
Col. Wolfe d. 18 April, 1816, and was s. by his eldest son,
JOHN WOLFE, of Forenaghts, b. 26 Feb. 1778, Capt. Forenaghts Cavalry 4 Jan. 1800, Freeman of Dublin 1802, Deputy-Governor co. Kildare 9 Dec. 1803; d. unm. 22 June, 1816, and was s. by his brother,
REV. RICHARD WOLFE, of Forenaghts, b. 10 Oct. 1787; m. 12 April, 1831, Lady Charlotte Sophia Hutchinson, sister of John, 2nd Earl of Donoughmore, and d.s.p. 20 July, 1841, leaving the reversion of his estates to his kinsman,
THEOBALD GEORGE SAMUEL WOLFE, of Forenaghts and Bishopsland, J.P. (known as George Wolfe, of Bishopsland—refer to issue of Thomas Wolfe, of Blackhall), b. 7 Oct. 1815; m. 18 June, 1852, Elizabeth Henrietta (who d. 3 Feb. 1910), dau. of Henry Moreland Ball, of Kersichank House, co. Stirling, and of Tipperkevin, co. Kildare. This lady was descended from Edward I. through the marriage of Lady Elizabeth Plantagenet to Humphrey de Bohun. He s. to Forenaghts and other estates on the death of Lady Charlotte Wolfe in 1870, and d. 12 Jan. 1872, having had issue,
1. RICHARD, his successor.
2. GEORGE, heir to his brother.
1. Elizabeth Caroline, m. 14 April, 1884, Col. William John Read Rainsford, C.I.E., R.A.M.C., of Craddoxtown House, Naas, eldest son of Capt. William Ryland Rainsford, of Craddockstown, and has issue.
Mr. Wolfe was s. by his eldest son,
RICHARD WOLFE, of Forenaghts and Bishopsland, Lieut. 2nd Dragoons, Royal Scots Greys, M.A. and LL.B. Trin. Coll. Dublin, b. 6 July, 1855; killed at the battle of Abu Klea, Upper Soudan, Egypt, 17 Jan. 1885, d. unm., and was s. by his brother.

Seats—Forenaghts, Naas; Bishopsland, Ballymore Eustace, co. Kildare; and Acomb Priory, York. Clubs—Army and Navy, S.W.; Naval and Military, W.

WOODLEY OF LEADES HOUSE.

RICHARD NASON WOODLEY, of Leades House, co. Cork, Capt. R.A.M.C., L.R.C.P. and L.R.C.S. (Edin.), b. 1875; s. his father 1905.

Lineage.—FRANCIS WILLIAM WOODLEY, of Leades House, co. Cork, J.P. and D.L., High Sheriff 1893, late West Cork Artillery Militia, b. 1850; m. 1873, Jane, dau. of the late Richard Nason, of Newtown, co. Cork, and d. 23 May, 1905, having had issue,
  RICHARD NASON WOODLEY, now of Leades House.

Seat—Leades House, Aghinagh, co. Cork.

WOOD-MARTIN. *See* **MARTIN.**

WOODS OF MILVERTON HALL.

EDWARD GEORGE WOODS, of Milverton Hall, co. Dublin, Capt. 8th Hussars, served in S. African War 1900–2 (two medals with five clasps), *b.* 25 Jan. 1880; *s.* his father.

Lineage.—JOHN WOODS, of Yorkshire ancestry, who went to Ireland on military service at the time of the Revolution, *m.* Isabella Bruce, and had a son,
THOMAS WOODS, of Kilmeague, co. Kildare. *m.* Margaret O'Hara, and *d.* 9 Aug. 1745, leaving with a dau., Araminta, a son,
GEORGE WOODS, of Dunshaughlin, co. Meath, and of the city of Dublin, *m.* 22 Dec. 1737, Mary, dau. and co-heiress of John Hogan, of Buddore, co. Dublin (by Isabella his wife, dau. of Cornelius Hamlin), and by her (who *d.* 18 Feb. 1778) had issue,
1. JOHN, who *s.* him.
2. Thomas, of Great Meadow, Isle of Man, and The Bolies, co. Meath, formerly Midshipman H.M.S. *Centaur*, afterwards Capt. 58th Regt., served throughout the sieges of Quebec, the Havannah, and Gibraltar; *b.* 13 May, 1743; *m.* 1st, Elizabeth, dau. of Capt. Maxwell, of The Carabiniers, and by her (who *d.* 2 Jan. 1785) had
  1. George Augustus Maxwell, *b.* 29 Nov. 1784; *d.* March, 1786.
He *m.* 2ndly, Charlotte, eldest dau. and co-heiress of Richard Ambrose Stephenson, of Balladoole, Isle of Man, and by her (who *d.* 30 July, 1838) had, with other issue,
  2. George Augustus, Lieut. R.M., *m.* 1st, 22 June, 1816, Anna Maria, eldest dau. of Rev. William Coney, and had, with other issue,
    WILLIAM BARING, who assumed the name of STEVENSON (*see* STEVENSON *of Balladoole*), and *d.* 2 Feb. 1905, aged 83.
He *m.* 2ndly, 28 Nov. 1839, Charlotte Heptinstall, and *d.* 4 April, 1853.
3. George, R.N., *b.* 8 July, 1752; *d.* 6 March, 1784.
1. Catherine, *b.* 6 Nov. 1739; *m.* 20 April, 1776, Richard Cooban Carr, Barrister-at-Law, and left issue, one son, George.
2. Maria Isabella, *b.* 22 Jan. 1741; *m.* May, 1782, Williams Barry, of Reynoldstown, co. Dublin, and left issue.
3. Hester, *b.* Nov. 1744; *d. unm.* 31 May, 1769.
4. Elizabeth, *b.* 23 June, 1747; *d. unm.*
5. Harriet, *b.* 23 June, 1747; *d.* 31 Oct. 1747.
Mr. George Woods *d.* 30 May, 1781, and was *s.* by his eldest son,
JOHN WOODS, of Winter Lodge, co. Dublin, *b.* 2 Nov. 1738; *m.* 31 March, 1783, Hannah, eldest surviving dau. and co-heiress of Joshua Warren, of Galtrim, co. Meath, by his wife, Frances Coddington, of Turvey, co. Dublin, and by her (who *d.* 16 March, 1829, aged 71) had issue,
1. GEORGE, his heir.
1. Maria, *b.* 29 Dec. 1783; *m.* 1 June, 1807, Richard Maunsell, of Oakley Park, co. Kildare, and had issue. She *d.* 2 March, 1850. 2. Frances, *b.* 13 March, 1785; *d. unm.* 22 April, 1806.
3. Hannah, *b.* 2 May, 1791; *d.* 23 April, 1803.
Mr. John Woods *d.* 7 Jan. 1826, aged 88, and was *s.* by his only son,
GEORGE WOODS, of Milverton Hall, co. Dublin, J.P. co. Dublin, High Sheriff 1822, *b.* 1 Aug. 1786; *m.* 7 Jan. 1812, Sarah, eldest dau. of Hans Hamilton, of Abbotstown, co. Dublin (M.P. for that co. for 30 years), by his 1st wife, Sarah, dau. of Joshua Lynam, and by her (who *d.* 10 June, 1829, aged 37) had issue,
1. John, *b.* 10 June, 1813; *d.* 9 May, 1819.
2. HANS HAMILTON, who *s.* him.
3. George, *b.* 18 Jan. 1816; *d.* 5 Sept. 1836.
1. Sarah Jane, *m.* 4 July, 1843, George Augustus Rochfort-Boyd, of Middleton Park, co. Westmeath, J.P. and D.L. co. Westmeath, and had issue. He *d.* 18 Sept. 1887.
2. Hannah Maria, *b.* 26 June, 1820; *d.* 10 Jan. 1909.
3. Frances Sophia, *b.* 8 Sept. 1822; *d.* 16 Feb. 1905.
4. Jane Law, *b.* 16 Sept. 1824; *d.* 27 Oct. 1824.
Mr. George Woods *d.* 6 Sept. 1876, aged 90, and was *s.* by his only surviving son,
HANS HAMILTON WOODS, of Whitestown House, and Milverton Hall, co. Dublin, J.P. and D.L., High Sheriff co. Dublin 1854, and J.P. co. Meath, High Sheriff co. Meath 1851, *b.* 22 Oct. 1814; *m.* 16 June, 1840, Louisa Catherine, 3rd dau. of the Hon. and Rev. Edward Taylor, of Ardgillan Castle, co. Dublin (4th son of Thomas, 1st Earl of Bective, and brother of the 1st Marquis of Headfort) by his wife Marianne, eldest dau. of the Hon. Richard St. Leger, son of the 1st Viscount Doneraile, and by her (who *d.* 26 March, 1898) had issue,
1. George John, late Lieut. 13th Hussars and 81st Regt., *b.* 27 Dec. 1842; *d.* 25 May, 1885.
2. EDWARD HAMILTON, late of Milverton.
3. Warren St Leger, of Whitestown House, and Winter Lodge, co. Dublin, J.P., M.A. Trinity College, Dublin, *b.* 4 Feb. 1849, and *d.* 3 Oct. 1908.
4. Hans Charles Maunsell, Herts, Col. late Royal Artillery, served in the Egyptian War of 1882 and was present at the Battle of Tel-el-Kebir (medal with clasp and Khedive's bronze star). He was *b.* 29 Dec. 1850; *m.* 9 Oct. 1894, Isabel Thomson, dau. of James Clark, of Kirkland Park, co. Lanark.
5. Richard Taylor, of Whitestown House and Winter Lodge, J.P. co. Meath, Col. 5th Batt. Leinster Regt. (Royal Canadians), *b.* 4 July, 1855.
1. Marianne Sarah.
2. Louisa Harriet, *m.* 10 Aug. 1865, Lieut.-Col. Henry Robert Carden, of Fishmoyne, co. Tipperary, late 77th Regt., J.P. and D.L. co. Tipperary, and has issue. He *d.* 15 Dec. 1880.
Mr. Hans Hamilton Woods *d.* 12 June, 1879, aged 64. His 2nd son,
EDWARD HAMILTON WOODS, of Milverton Hall, co. Dublin, J.P. and D.L. co. Dublin, High Sheriff 1883, J.P. co. Meath, High Sheriff 1888, B.A. Christ's College, Cambridge, late Lieut. Royal Meath Militia, *b.* 7 April, 1847; *m.* 30 April, 1879, Katherine Margaret, 4th dau. of the late Capt. Richard Everard, of Randlestown, co. Meath, by his wife, Mathilde Arabella, dau. of le Marquis d'Amboise, and by her (who *d.* 16 March, 1894) had issue,
1. EDWARD GEORGE, now of Milverton Hall.
2. Arthur Hans Hamilton, *b.* 28 Feb. 1881; *d.* 7 May, 1882.
3. Reginald Everard, *b.* 5 March, 1883; *d.* 1 March, 1896.
4. Charles John, *b.* 28 June, 1884.
1. Kathleen May Ethel, *d.* 28 Oct. 1882.
2. Violet Amy. 3. Eileen Sylvia.

Seats—Milverton Hall, Skerries, co. Dublin. *Clubs*—Cavalry, and Kildare Street, Dublin.

WOOLSEY OF MILESTOWN.

ALICE WOOLSEY-BUTLER, of Milestown, co. Louth, *m.* 21 April, 1887, Cecil Butler (who *d.* 6 Dec. 1901), Barrister-at-Law, 4th son of the late Hon. Charles Lennox Butler (who *d.* 6 Dec. 1901), son of James, 22nd Lord Dunboyne (*see* BURKE'S *Peerage*), and has an only dau.,
CECILIA FRANCES.

Mrs. Woolsey-Butler assumed for herself and her issue, the additional surname of Woolsey by Royal Licence 16 April, 1910.

Lineage.—THE REV. WILLIAM WOOLSEY, M.A., was Chaplain to Primate Boulter, and became successively Vicar of Dundalk 1709–28, and Rector of Faugbart 1728 to his death in 1738. He acquired Priorland, near Dundalk. He *m.* Isabella, dau. of John Walker, of Dundalk, eldest son of Rev. Dr. George Walker, the defender of Derry, and left two sons,
1. JOHN, of whom presently.
2. Thomas (Rev.), Rector of Faughart 1754–75, and of Forkhill 1775 to his death in 1779, who *m.* 1st, a sister of Ephraim Stannus, of Carlingford, and 2ndly, June, 1777, Jane, 3rd dau. of Isaac Read, of Dundalk.
The elder son,
JOHN WOOLSEY, of Priorland, entered the Temple before 1733, *m.* Lucy, dau. of the Rev. Richard Palmer, and *d.* at an early age, July, 1752, leaving an only child,
REV. WILLIAM WOOLSEY, of Priorland, M.A. of Cambridge, *b.* about 1750; was sometime Lieut. 61st Regt., became Rector of Kilsaran (Castle Bellingham) in 1794; *m.* May, 1777, Mary Anne, dau. of Col. Alan Bellingham, of Castle Bellingham, co. Louth (and sister to Sir William Bellingham, 1st bart.), by whom he had issue,
1. JOHN, of whom presently.
2. Thomas, of the Civil Service (Admiralty), *b.* 1784; *m.* Elizabeth, 3rd dau. of William Gibson (who *d.* 1866), leaving issue by him (who *d.* Sept. 1834).
3 William, *b.* 1785, became Commander of H.M.S. *Papillon*, supposed to have been lost about Sept. 1805, with that vessel.
4. O'Bryen Bellingham, sometime Accountant-General of the Admiralty, *m.* Emily, dau. of William Holt, of Enfield; he *d.s.p.* Jan. 1874, aged 82, his wife dying in the same year.
1. Alice, *m.* Richard Moore, of Summerhill, co. Tipperary, *d.* leaving issue by him, who *d.* 1826 (*see* MOORE *of Barne*).
2. Lucy, *d. unm.*
3. Frances, *m.* her cousin, Richard Palmer and *d.* July, 1870, leaving issue by him.
4. Mary Anne, *m.* William Cairnes, of Stameen, co. Meath, and *d.* 24 Sept. 1865, leaving issue by him.
5. Elizabeth Sophia, *m.* 28 Sept. 1815, James Jameson, of Winfield, co. Galway, and Montrose, co. Dublin, brother of her sister-in-law, and *d.* leaving issue.
Rev. William Woolsey, who was subsequently *m.* a 2nd time, *d.* Sept. 1832, aged about 82, his widow surviving to Oct. 1884, aged 86, and was *s.* by his eldest son,
JOHN WOOLSEY, of Priorland, *b.* 6 Jan. 1782, became Capt. 82nd Regt. 8 Jan. 1802, and after retiring from that regt. was appointed on 6 Dec. 1808, 1st Lieut. in the Castle Bellingham Infantry, a Yeomanry Corps; High Sheriff of co. Louth 1826; *m.* 30 March, 1812, Janet, youngest dau. of John Jameson, of Alloa, N.B. (*see* JAMESON), and by her had issue,
1. John, *b.* 12 May, 1815; *d.s.p.* 18 May, 1819.
2. WILLIAM, his successor.
3. Robert Jameson, *b.* 1 Sept. 1821; *d.s.p.* 6 March, 1838.
4. O'BRIEN BELLINGHAM, late of Milestown.
5. John, of Castle Cosey, Castle Bellingham, *b.* 21 Aug. 1830; *m.* in 1865, his cousin, Elizabeth Lucy, 2nd dau. of Rev. Henry de Laval Willis, Rector of Bradford, Yorkshire; she *d.* 10 Nov. 1870, aged 26, and he *d.s.p.* 23 May, 1887.
1. Mary Anne, *b.* 16 Jan. 1813; *m.* 25 Oct. 1836, Major John Woolmore Simmons Smith, 14th King's Light Dragoons, and *d.* 3 April, 1881, leaving issue.

2. Margaret, *b.* 12 July, 1816; *m.* Charles Thornhill, late Capt. 14th King's Light Dragoons (afterwards the Rev. Charles Thornhill), 2nd son of George Thornhill, M.P. of Diddington, Huntingdonshire, and *d.* 6 July, 1877, leaving issue by him, who *d.* 31 Aug. 1881, aged 69 (*see* THORNHILL).
3. Helen Jameson, *b.* 10 Nov. 1819; *m.* Rev. William Thornhill, Rector of Offord D'Arcy, Huntingdonshire, 4th son of George Thornhill (*see above*). He *d.* 17 Sept. 1872, aged 49. She *d.* 10 May, 1908, having had issue.
4. Frances Hester Bellingham, *b.* 16 Aug. 1823; *d.* 28 Sept. 1838.
Mr. Woolsey *d.* 1 Aug. 1853, aged 71 (his widow surviving till 10 April, 1861, aged 72), and was *s.* by his eldest surviving son,
WILLIAM WOOLSEY, of Priorland and Milestown, *b.* 30 Aug. 1818, J.P. for co. Louth, High Sheriff 1868; *m.* 1st, 1846, Frances Rose, 2nd dau. of Samuel Vesey, of Derrabard House, co. Tyrone (*see that family*), who was drowned 4 Oct. 1865, aged 40; and 2ndly, in 1868, Mary Elizabeth Heath, younger dau. of William Heath Jary, of Blofield Lodge, Norfolk (*see* JARY). He *d.s.p.* 11 May, 1887, and was *s.* by his brother,
O'BRIEN BELLINGHAM WOOLSEY, of Milestown and Priorland, co. Louth, J.P. and D.L. for co. Louth, High Sheriff 1889, Maj.-Gen. (retired) Royal Artillery, *b.* 26 Aug. 1827; *m.* 20 May, 1855, Anna (who *d.* 18 Aug. 1905), eldest dau. of the late Sir John Walsham, Bart., of Knill Court, co. Hereford (*see* BURKE'S *Peerage*). He *d.* 14 Jan. 1910, having had issue,
ALICE, now of Milestown.

Seat:—Milestown, Castle Bellingham, co. Louth. *Residence*—Whitehall Court, S.W.

WOULFE OF TIERMACLANE.

The late STEPHEN ROLAND WOULFE, of Tiermaclane, co. Clare, J.P. cos. Clare and Down, High Sheriff of the latter co. 1874, and of the former 1876, served in the 7th Regt. Fusiliers, afterwards Capt. Hunts Militia, *b.* 1822; *m.* 1st, 9 June, 1853, Hon. Isabella Letitia Graves, dau. of Thomas North, 2nd Lord Graves (she *d.* 26 Oct., 1870): he *m.* 2ndly, 1881, ALICE MAUD (now of Tiermaclane), youngest dau. of Edward Blackburn, of Haine, Devon, and *d.* 1 Oct. 1899, leaving issue,

Stephen Harold, *b.* 15 Feb. 1883; *d.* 1888.
Hylda Maud, *b.* 1882.

Lineage.—This family was settled in Limerick at a very early date; the name appears in the records of Limerick during the reigns of the Plantagenet Sovereigns. A pedigree of the family, registered in Ulster's Office, commences with

THOMAS WOULFE, of Ballyphilip, co. Limerick, *m.* Mary, dau. of Daniel Creagh, of Limerick, and was father of

THOMAS WOULFE, Sheriff of Limerick 1470; *m.* Ellen, dau. of Edmond Harrold, of Limerick, and was father of

JOHN WOULFE, *m.* Mary, dau. of Nicholas Bourke, of Limerick, and had a son,

RICHARD WOULFE, a Burgess for the city of Limerick, *temp.* Queen ELIZABETH. He *m.* Mary, dau. of Andrew Creagh, of Limerick, and was *s.* by his son,

JAMES WOULFE, of Corbally, a Merchant in Limerick, *m.* Ellis, dau. of Thomas Arthur, of Ballygrenane, co. Limerick, and had five sons,

1. Patrick, of Corbally, who was joined with his father in deeds relating to houses and land in Limerick, *m.* Ellis, dau. of James Arthur, of Kilmallock, co. Limerick, and had two sons,
    1. James (fitzPatrick), party to a deed of 1 March, 1648, *d.s.p.*
    2. Richard, of Corbally, *s.* his brother, and forfeited that and all his father's property after the Rebellion of 1641, *m.* his kinswoman, Katherine, dau. of Patrick Woulfe, Burgess of Limerick, by Katherine his wife, dau. of Francis White, and grand-dau. of Richard Woulfe, the possessor of large estates in co. Limerick, by Sleganne Bonfield his wife, and had a son,
        Patrick, *b.* 1668; *d.* in Paris, bur. in the Church of St. Eustace, 12 Feb. 1747, aged 79; *m.* his cousin, Mary, dau. of James Woulfe, of Ennis, co. Clare, by whom (who *d.* in Paris 1744) he had a son,
            James Lawrence Woulfe, *b.* in Paris, 16 April, 1743.
2. James (Rev.), a Dominican Friar, murdered by order of Ireton, OLIVER CROMWELL'S General, 1651.
3. STEPHEN, of whom presently.

Mr. Woulfe was living in 1627, as appears from a deed of 3 Nov. of that year, to which his eldest son was a party. His 5th and youngest son,

STEPHEN WOULFE, of Crenagh, co. Clare removed into that co. and settled there. He *m.* Mary, dau. of Thomas Stritch (fitzPatrick), Mayor of Limerick 1650, and had two sons,
1. NICHOLAS, his successor.
2. Patrick, of Ennis, *m.* Mary, dau. of Theobald Fitzgerald, of Gortmore, co. Clare, by whom (who was bur. at Ennis 1697) he had a son,
    James, of Ennis, who went to Paris, *d.* there, and was bur. in the Church of St. Roche, 28 Dec. 1749. He *m.* Alice, dau. of Andrew Woulfe, Burgess of Ennis, by whom (who was bur. at Ennis, 11 Dec. 1748) he had a son and a dau.,
        Lawrence, *m.* Mary, dau. of Brien O'Brien, of Corbally, co. Clare.
        Mary, *m.* her cousin, Patrick Woulfe, of Paris.

Mr. Woulfe, who was bur. at Ennis, was *s.* by his eldest son,
NICHOLAS WOULFE, of Tiermaclane, co. Clare, who obtained that estate from Henry, 7th Earl of Thomond, by deed dated 9 Aug. 1684, and other lands in co. Limerick, 24 Aug. 1708. He had, with four daus. (1. Phillis, *m.* William Trant, of Cork, Merchant, who *d.* 1725; 2. Jane, Mrs. Waters; 3. Margaret, *m.* Thomas Sexton, of Limerick, Merchant; 4. Alice, Mrs. Cantillon), three sons,
1. STEPHEN, his successor.
2. David, who was living in 1765.
3. Patrick, of Emlagh, co. Clare, who *d.v.p.* His will, dated 3 June, 1718, was proved 2 May, 1719. He *m.* Eleanor, sister of Ignatius Casey, and had, with two daus., Mary, and Katherine (Mrs. Butler), eight sons,
    1. Nicholas. 2. Stephen.
    3. Anthony, of Lifford, co. Clare, whose will, dated 6 Aug. 1748, was proved 9 March, 1754. By Anstace his wife, he left a son, James, and a dau., Margaret. 4. Andrew.
    5. Francis. 6. Michael.
    7. Ignatius, of Emlagh, whose will is dated 5 Jan. 1778. He left an only son, Michael.
    8. James, of Cahirash, co. Clare, whose will dated 22 July, 1755, with a codicil 12 May, 1758, was proved 2 June following; *d.* without legitimate issue.

Mr. Woulfe, whose will, dated 9 Oct. 1725, was proved 26 Jan. following, was *s.* by his eldest son,
STEPHEN WOULFE, of Tiermaclane, who, by Bridget his wife, had two sons,
1. NICHOLAS, his successor.
2. Peter, of Bernard's Inn, Holborn, London, Surgeon-Gen. in H.M.'s service, who was guardian to his minor nephew, in 1765.

Mr. Woulfe, who was living in 1737, *d.* intestate, and was *s.* by his eldest son,
NICHOLAS WOULFE, of Tiermaclane, *m.* Alice Maria Harrold, of Pennywell, co. Limerick, and had two sons,
1. STEPHEN, his heir. 2. John, was dead in 1761.

Mr. Woulfe, whose will dated 22 Aug. 1761, was proved 2 Feb. 1765, and was *s.* by his elder son,
STEPHEN WOULFE, of Tiermaclane, *m.* 15 Feb. 1772, Honora, dau. of Michael McNamara, of Dublin, grand-dau. of John McNamara, of Crinagh, co. Clare, and sister of Admiral James McNamara, and Col. John McNamara, of Llangoed Castle, co. Brecon, by whom (who *m.* 2ndly, Balthazar Nihill, Field-Marshal in the service of the King of Naples) he had issue,
1. PETER, his heir.
2. STEPHEN (Right Hon.), Lord Chief Baron of the Court of Exchequer in Ireland, appointed Solicitor-General 1836, Attorney-General and Sworn of the Privy Council 1837, and *s.* Right Hon. Henry Joy, as Lord Chief Baron, 20 July, 1838; *m.* Frances, dau. of Roger Hamill, of Dowth Hall, co. Meath; and *d.* 1840, leaving issue,
    STEPHEN ROLAND, late of Tiermaclane.
    Mary, *m.* 1847, Sir Justin Sheil, K.C.B.
3. Nicholas, *d. unm.*
1. Joanna, *m.* May, 1813, Terence Flanagan, of St. Katherine's Park, Leixlip, co. Dublin, by whom (who *d.* Jan. 1846) she left at her decease, Jan. 1837, three sons (*see* FLANAGAN *of Rathternon*).

Mr. Woulfe, whose will was proved 4 April, 1794, *d.* at Liege, in the Netherlands, and was *s.* by his eldest son,
PETER WOULFE, of Tiermaclane, who *d. unm.* April, 1865, when he was *s.* by his nephew,
STEPHEN ROLAND WOULFE, late of Tiermaclane.

Arms—Per fess arg. and az. in chief on a mount vert a wolf passant in front of an oak tree all ppr. in base two salmon naiant in pale of the last. *Crest*—A stork wings elevated sa. *Motto*—Cuilean uasal.

Seats—Tiermaclane, Ennis, co. Clare; Strangford House, Strangford, co. Down. *Town Residence*—74, Knightsbridge, S.W.

WRENCH OF KILLACOONA.

THE RIGHT HON. FREDERICK STRINGER WRENCH, P.C., of Killacoona, co. Dublin, J.P. cos. Monaghan, Fermanagh, and Cavan, Irish Land and Estates Commissioner and Vice-President of the Royal Dublin Society, educated at Haileybury College, and at Exeter Coll., Oxford, *b.* 4 Nov. 1849; *m.* 8 Feb, 1872, Charlotte Mary, 3rd dau. of Sir Alan Bellingham, Bart., and has had issue,

1. Frederick Arthur Cavendish, Lieut. Central India Horse, *b.* 22 June, 1877; *d. unm.* 13 Oct. 1902.

2. JOHN EVELYN LESLIE, b. 29 Oct. 1882 (*Residence:* 30, *Lower Belgrave Street, S.W. Clubs:* Marlborough; Bath; Beefsteak).
  1. Mary, b. 26 Jan. 1874 ; m. 28 July, 1892, Thomas Stewart Porter, of Clogher Park, co. Tyrone, and has issue (*see that family*).
  2. Winifride, b. 10 Aug. 1880.

Mr. Wrench is the only son of the Rev. Frederick Wrench, Rector of Stowting, near Hythe (who d. 20 April, 1880), and Eliza his wife (who d. Aug. 1869), dau. of Capt. Stringer, Scots Greys, and grandson of Jacob George Wrench and Mary Buxton, his wife.

Residences—Killacoona, Ballybrack, co. Dublin ; Bally Philip, Kilcool, co. Wicklow ; 24, Upper Merrion Street, Dublin. *Clubs*—Kildare Street, Dublin ; Carlton ; and Royal St. George's Yacht, Kingstown.

WRIGHT OF KILNACLOY.

The late JOSEPH WRIGHT, of Kilnacloy, co. Monaghan, D.L., m. 1888, Anne Campbell (now of Kilnacloy), dau. of the late James Campbell Christian, of Sligo, and d.s.p. 23 May, 1908. Mr. Wright was son of the late Henry Wright, of Kilnacloy.

Seat—Kilnacloy, Monaghan. *Club*—Constitutional.

WRIGHT-ARMSTRONG. *See* ARMSTRONG.

WRIXON-BECHER. *See* BECHER.

WYNNE (now PERCEVAL) OF HAZLEWOOD.

MURIEL CAROLINE LOUISA, MRS. PERCEVAL, of Hazlewood, co. Sligo, eldest dau. and heiress of the late Owen Wynne, of Hazlewood, s. her father 21 Nov. 1910 ; m. 22 June, 1892, Philip Dudley Perceval, 2nd son of the late Alexander Perceval, of Temple House, co. Sligo (*see that family*) and has issue,

DOROTHY SOPHIE, b. 8 Oct. 1905.

Lineage.—LEWIS GWYNNE AP CADWALLADER AP RYDDERCA AP DAVID, of Bala, who m. Sidney, dau . of Robert Wynne, of Maesmochnant, co. Denbigh (of the Gwydyr family), and had issue,
  1. OWEN, of whom presently.   2. Cadwallader.
  1. Catherine, m. Edward Wynne, of Nantymerchied, son of Richard Wynne, of Maesmochnant.   2. Margaret.
The elder son,
  OWEN WYNNE, the first who settled in Ireland, High Sheriff cos. Leitrim and Roscommon 1659, m. Catherine, widow of James Hamilton, son of Sir Frederick Hamilton, and dau. of Claud, 2nd Baron Strabane, by Lady Jane his wife, 4th dau. of George, Marquess of Huntly, and the Lady Henrietta Stewart, dau. of Esme, Duke of Lennox, and by her (who m. 3rdly, John Bingham, of Castlebar) had issue,
  1. James, Brigadier-Gen. in the Army, who raised the 5th Dragoons, High Sheriff co. Leitrim 1686. He m. Catherine, dau. of John Bingham, and was killed at Malplaquet, having had issue,
    1. James, d. unm.   2. Sidney.
    1. Dorothy.   2. Jane.
    3. Mary.
  2. LEWIS, of whom presently.
  3. Owen, M.P., Lieut.-Gen. in the Army, and Commander-in-Chief in Ireland. He raised the 9th Dragoons.
  4. John, d. unm.
  1. Catherine, m. John Dunbar, son of Sir John Dunbar.
  2. Lucy, m. John Holliott, of Hollybrook, co. Sligo.
  3. Dorothy, m. Gerald Cuffe, grandfather of Lord Tyrawley.
The 2nd son,
  LEWIS WYNNE, m. Rebecca, dau. of John Bingham, and was father of
  OWEN WYNNE, M.P., of Hazlewood, High Schriff co. Sligo 1723 and co. Leitrim 1724; m. Catherine, (d. 15 Jan. 1778, aged 92), dau. of John Ffolliot, and had (with two daus., Lucy, m. Anderson Saunders, and Hannah, m. June, 1743, William Ormsby) three sons,
  1. James, m. Susanna, dau. of Sir Arthur Shaen, Bart.
  2. OWEN, of whom we treat.
  3. John, d. unm. Jan. 1778.
The 2nd son,

THE RIGHT HON. OWEN WYNNE, of Hazlewood, M.P., High Sheriff co Sligo 1745 and 1758, m 1754, Anne, sister of Robert, Earl of Farnham, and by her (who d. 16 Feb. 1813) had issue,
  1. OWEN, his heir.
  2. John, d. unm.
  3. Henry (Rev.), Rector of Killucan, Westmeath, m. Katherine, dau. of John Eckersall, of Claverton House, near Bath, and had issue,
    1. Henry (Rev.), Rector of Ardcolm, co. Wexford, b. 1799 ; m. Marianne, dau. of Solomon Richards, of Roebuck, near Dublin. She d. 1863.   He d. Sept. 1847, leaving issue,
      (1) Henry Eckersall, m. Aug. 1856, Elizabeth, dau. of Henry Alcock, of Wilton, and d.s.p. 1895.
      (2) Frederick Richards (Right Rev.), D.D., Bishop of Killaloe, b. 19 June, 1827; m. 10 April, 1860, Theodosia Susan, dau. of Rev. John Darley, Fellow Trin. Coll. Dublin, by Susan his wife, dau. of Arthur Guinness, both d. Nov. 1896, leaving issue,
        1. Henry (Rev.), Vicar of St. Mary, Bearwood, Birmingham, M.A., Christ's Coll., Camb., b. 11 Feb. 1861 ; m. 1st, 29 Dec. 1891, Frances Alice, eldest dau. of Alfred Henry Wynne (*see below*), and by her (who d. 1893) has issue,
          a. Henry Francis Devereux, b. 1893.
        He m. 2ndly, 14 April, 1909, Constance Harriet, youngest dau. of late Rev. W. P. Crawley, M.A., Vicar of Walberton, Sussex, and has further issue,
          b. John Frederick, b. 3 Feb. 1910.
          c. Michael William, b. 9 April, 1911.
        2. John Darley, b. 25 March, 1862; m. 10 Sept. 1891, Lucy, dau. of Rev. Thomas Woollen Smith, M.A., and has issue,
          1. Wilfred.
          1. Audrey.   2. Kathleen.
        3. Arthur Eckersall (Rev.), Vicar of Rottingdean, M.A., T.C.D., b. 13 June, 1863; m. 25 June, 1895, his cousin, Constantia Agnes, dau. of the late Rev. Canon Eckersall Nixon, M.A., Rector of Ettagh, Killaloe, and has issue,
          Edward Eckersall, b. 1901.
          Ruth Mary, b. 1897.
        4. Frederick Edward, b. 13 May, 1870 ; m. 1894, his cousin, Agnes, dau. of the late Rev. Robert Hannay, Vicar of Belfast, and has issue,
          a. Robert Frederick.
          b. A son.   c. A son.
        5. Llewellyn, Charles, b. 14 Nov. 1878 ; m. March 1904, Evelyn, 2nd dau. of A. W. I. Oke, of Redruth, Cornwall, and has issue, two daus.
        1. Adelaide Susan, m. 1889, her cousin Rev. James Owen Hannay, and has issue.
        2. Amy Theodosia, m. 1896, Rev. Walter Hugo Harper. She d. 10 March, 1903, leaving issue.
        3. Florence Anna, m. 3 Sept. 1902, Philip Mainwaring Johnston, 5th son of the late John Brookes Johnston, of Denmark Hill, and has issue, one dau.
        4. Mabel Agnes.
      (3) Albert Augustus, of Tigroney, Ovoca, and Glendalough Cottage, Rathdrum, J.P. co. Wicklow, b. 1833 ; m. 15 March, 1870, Alice Katharine, dau. of Rev. John George Wynne (*see below*), and has issue,
        1. John Brian, b. 28 July, 1876.
        2. Charles Wyndham, b. 29 May, 1895.
        1. Emily Adelaide.
        2. Winifred Frances.
        3. Alice Clara Veronica.
      (4) Charles Edward, b. 1835 ; d. unm. 1858.
      (5) Owen Llewellyn, b. 1839 ; d. unm. 1860.
      (1) Elizabeth Agnes, m. 9 Jan. 1856, Richard Donovan, of Ballymore, co. Wexford, and d. 1901.
      (2) Adelaide, d. unm. 1863.
    2. John George (Rev.), Rector of Lorum, co. Carlow, m. 19 Jan. 1831, Emily, dau. of Thomas Goold, M.P., Master in Chancery. She d. Aug. 1874.   He d. 1854, leaving issue,
      (1) Wyndham Henry, of Corris, Baginalstown, co. Carlow, J.P., b. 8 Aug. 1840 ; m. 5 July, 1893, his cousin, Sophie Sarah, dau. of George Wynne, late Scots Greys (*see below*), and d.s.p. 19 May, 1910.
      (1) Clara Frances.   (2) Fanny Stella.
      (3) Alice Katharine, m. 15 March, 1870, her cousin, Albert Augustus Wynne, of Tigroney, co. Wicklow, and has issue (*see above*).
    3. George, General, R.E., b. 1804 ; m. 1st, 16 Dec. 1834 Anne, dau. of Sir Daniel Toler Osborne, 12th bart. She d. 29 May, 1864, leaving issue,
      (1) Henry Le Poer, Bengal C.S., b. 1836, m. 1869, Emily Sarah, 3rd dau. and co-heir of Ven. Frederick Faulkner Goold, of Rosbrien and Dromadda, co. Limerick (*see 'GOOLD-VERSCHOYLE of Dromadda*).   She d. 21 Dec. 1898. He d. 1874, leaving a dau.,
        Anne Elizabeth Le Poer, of Rosbrien, co. Limerick, m. 13 Aug. 1904, Sir Alexander Waldemar Lawrence, 4th Bart., and has issue (*see* BURKE's *Peerage*).
      (2) Edward Toler, Lieut.-Col. R.E., b. 1837 d. unm. 1889.
      (3) Francis George, C.E., b 1846   Dora, dau. of Gen. Frome, R.E.
        (1) Lucy Harriet, m. 10 Aug. 1871, Major Aubrey Stephen O'Brien, 60th Rifles, who d. 18 Dec. 1898, leaving issue (*see* BURKE's *Peerage*, INCHIQUIN, B.).
      Gen. Wynne m. 2ndly, Henrietta, youngest dau. of Lieut.-Col. Darrah, 97th Regt. and d. 27 June, 1890, having by her had no issue.

4. Charles, Lieut.-Col. Fifeshire R.A., *m.* Isabella, dau. of James Nugent, of Clonlost, and *d.s.p.* 1893.
1. Lucy Catherine, *m.* 1 Jan. 1828, Rev. Edward Nixon, M.A., Rector of Castletown, co. Meath, son of the Rev. Brinsley Nixon, Rector of Painstown, co. Meath. He *d.* 30 April, 1847. She *d.* 31 Aug. 1883, leaving issue (*see* BURKE'S *Family Records*).
2. Clara, *m.* 6 Oct. 1836, George Wynne, and had issue (*see below*).
3. Katherine, *m.* Solomon Richards, of Ounavarra, and *d.* 31 Oct. 1848. He *d.s.p.* 14 Aug. 1862 (*see* RICHARDS *of Ardamine*).
4. Mary Anne, *m.* Edmond Wynne (*see below*).
4. Robert, of Rathmines Castle, Dublin, Lieut. 12th Dragoons, afterwards Commissioner of the Customs, and at one time on the staff of the Vice-Regal Household, Dublin Castle. *b.* 1760; *m.* 1791, Elizabeth, dau. of Sydenham Singleton, of Portman Square, London, and *d.* 1838, having had issue,
1. Sydenham, dec. 2. Robert (Rev.), *d.* 1826.
3. James, dec.
4. John, Capt. R.A., of Wynnstay, Roebuck, near Dublin, *b.* July, 1884; *b.* June, 1799; *m.* 31 May, 1838, Anne, dau. of Admiral Sir Samuel Warren, K.C.B., K.C.H. She *d.* 27 Nov. 1874. He *d.* July, 1884, leaving issue,
(1) Robert Maxwell, *b.* March, 1839; *d.* July, 1856.
(2) Warren Richard Colvin, Major R.E., *b.* 1843; *m.* 1st, Eleanor, dau. of James Turbett, of Owenstown, co. Dublin, and by her had issue,
1. Arthur Algernon Warren, *b.* 1873.
He *m.* 2ndly, Lucy, dau. of Capt. A. Parish, and *d.* 1879, having by her had issue,
2. Henry Ernest Singleton, Capt. R.A., *b.* 4 Jan. 1877.
3. Charles Meredith, *b.* 1878.
(3) Arthur Singleton (Sir), K.C.B., Gen. late King's Own L.I., Keeper of the Jewel House, Tower of London (*Haybergill, Warcop, Westmorland*), *b.* 5 March, 1846; *m.* 1886, Emily Mary, dau. of Charles Colville Turner and Mrs. Turner, of Warcop, Westmorland, and has issue,
1. Arthur Colvin, Lieut. R.E., *b.* 1887.
2. Graeme Charnley, K.O. Yorks. Light Infantry, *b.* 1889.
3. Arthur Meredyth, *b.* 1893.
(4) Skeffington John, Colonel, late Capt. Royal Dublin Fusiliers, *b.* 1 Jan. 1849; *m.* 1875, Emily Janet, dau of Bartholomew Clifford Lloyd, Q.C. (*see* LLOYD *of Lossett*), and has issue,
Warren Skeffington, *b.* 6 March, 1876; *m.* 4 Aug. 1904, Elizabeth, eldest dau. of Rev. T. B. Paterson, of Taighstone Hall, Hamilton. N.B., and has issue.
(5) Sydenham Henry, of Milebrook House, Radnorshire, I.C.S., retired, *b.* 15 Feb. 1851; *m.* 4 March, 1899, Mary Kate, dau. of James Hall Lee, of Helstead, Essex, and has issue,
Robert Henry Skeffington, *b.* 14 Dec. 1899.
(6) Charles, *b.* April, 1856; *d. unm.* Dec. 1889.
(1) Katharine, *d.* 1856. (2) Florence Anne.
(3) Frances, *m.* 1881, Maj. Albert Robertson, R.A., and has issue.
5. Charles, dec.
6. William, *d.* 1890.
7. George, 2nd Dragoons (Scots Greys), *b.* 16 Feb. 1806; *m.* 6 Oct. 1836, his cousin, Clara, dau. of Rev. Henry Wynne (*see above*). She *d.* 31 Jan. 1895. He *d.* 30 Oct. 1894, leaving issue,
(1) George Robert (Ven.), D.D., Archdeacon of Aghadoe, *b.* 6 March, 1838; *m.* 3 June, 1863, Ellen Lees (who *d.* May, 1907), dau. of Rev. G. Sidney Smith, D.D., F.T.C.D., and has issue,
1. George Robert Llewellyn (Rev.), *b.* 23 Oct. 1873; *m.* 1900, Alice, dau. of J. C. Deane, and has issue,
a. George Geoffrey Llewellyn, *b.* 3 Jan. 1905.
b. John Lionel Langford, *b.* 30 March, 1906.
c. Robert Edward, *b.* 25 June, 1909.
1. Helen Mary, dec.
2. Florence Maud.
3. Charlotte Sydney, dec.
4. Maria Cerise, *m.* 1896, Rev. H. C. Deane.
5. Edith Gladys.
(2) Alfred Henry, of Collon House, co. Louth, J.P., *b.* 14 March, 1839; *m.* 22 April, 1865, Maria, dau. of Rev. Nicholas Devereux, D.D., of Baliyrankin, and *d.* 27 April, 1908, having had issue,
1 Owen William Singleton. *b.* 1867; *d.* 1885.
1. Frances Alice, *m.* 29 Dec. 1891, Rev. Henry Wynne, eldest son of Rt. Rev. F. R. Wynne, Bishop of Killaloe, and *d.* 1893, leaving issue (*see above*).
2. Effie Florence, *d. unm.* 1888.
3. Edith Clara.
4. Maria Jessop.
(3) Edward Nixon, of Wentworth House, Wicklow, J.P., B.A. Trin. Coll. Dublin, *b.* 1847; *m.* 3 Nov. 1898, Evelyn Caroline Annesley, eldest dau. of the late Col. Charles Ball Acton, C.B. (*see* ACTON *of Kilmacurragh*), and has issue,
Charles Acton, *b.* 13 June, 1900.
Emily Evelyn.
(1) Katharine Florence, *m.* Richard H. Fetherstonhaugh, who *d.s.p.* 1895.
(2) Sophia Sarah, *m.* 5 July, 1893, her cousin, Wyndham Henry Wynne, of Corris House, co. Carlow (*see above*), who *d.* May, 1910.
(3) Edith Clara.
8. Mark, dec. 9. Owen, dec.
1. Harriett, *m.* Marcus Aaronson, and *d.* 2. Emily, dec.
3. Lucy, dec. 4. Fanny Louisa, dec.

5. Caroline, dec. 6. Mary, dec.
5. Richard (Rev.), Rector of Drumcliff, co. Sligo, *m.* Catherine Beavor, dau. of Col. Richard Beavor Brown and Catherine his wife, dau. of John, Lord Mountflorence, and sister of 1st Earl of Enniskillen, and had issue,
1. Richard Beavor, of Hermitage, Sligo, *b.* 12 Dec. 1795; *m.* 1833, Hannah Matilda, 2nd dau. and co-heir of Capt. Jones Taaffe Irwin. She *d.* 19 Dec. 1898. He *d.* 24 Oct. 1851, leaving issue,
(1) Richard, of Perth, Western Australia, *b.* 15 June, 1834.
(2) Arthur Beavor, *b.* 15 Oct. 1835; *m.* 1864, Margaret, dau. of Standish H. Harrison, of Castle Harrison, co. Cork, and has issue. He *d.* 22 Dec. 1906.
1. Richard John Arthur, Cape Forests, *b.* 1870.
1. Florence Isabella, *m.* 1894, Maj. Edward W. Dun, D.S.O., eldest son of Maj.-Gen. Dun. He *d.s.p.* 1895.
2. Esa Geraldine, *m.* 1898, Charles Raymond Dun, younger son of Major-Gen. Dun, and has issue, a son, Edward Beavor, *b.* 1899.
(3) Owen Lowry WYNNE-MARRIOTT, of Avonbank, co. Worcestershire, assumed the additional name and arms of MARRIOTT by Royal Licence, 5 Oct. 1908, formerly R.N., and afterwards Marshal of the High Court of Admiralty of Ireland, *b.* 27 Dec. 1840; *m.* 3 July, 1895, Harriott Julia Catherine, eld. dau. and heir of Major Henry Christopher Marriott, late 82nd Regt., of Avonbank, co. Worcester (*see that family*).
(4) Willoughby Robert, *b.* 16 June, 1842; *d. unm.* 30 June, 1887.
(5) Edward Joshua, *b.* 20 Nov. 1845; *d. unm.* 21 Nov. 1868.
(1) Anna Matilda, *b.* 3 Jan. 1838.
(2) Catherine Marion, *b.* 17 Sept. 1839; *m.* 13 Feb. 1872, Rev. Robert Y. Lynn, B.A., and has issue, one son and three daus.
(3) Florence, *b.* 25 Dec. 1844.
(4) Elizabeth Sarah, *b.* 1 Jan. 1848; *m.* 1888, Thomas S. Murray, L.R.C.S.I.
(5) Henrietta Frances, *b.* 9 July, 1849.
(6) Emily, *b.* 23 June, 1851.
2. Arthur (Rev.), Precentor of Waterford, *m.* Amelia Teresa, dau. of Rev. Francis Law (*see* LAW *of Killaloe*). She *d.* 25 Oct. 1868. He *d.s.p.*
3. Lowry William Montgomery, Lieut. R.A., *m.* Elizabeth, dau. of Lieut.-Col. Richard Paine, R.A., and left issue,
(1) Arthur, R.A. (2) Frederick. (3) Lowry, *d.* young.
(1) Kate, *d.* young.
1. Marion Catherine Florence, *m.* her cousin, James Wynne, Barrister-at-Law, and had issue (*see below*).
6. William, Barrister-at-Law, M.P., *m.* Eleanor, dau. of Sir Samuel Bradstreet, Bart., and *d.* 1855, leaving issue,
1. Owen, of Ardaghowen, co. Sligo, *b.* 1800; *m.* 1829, Susan, dau. of Samuel Thompson, of Liverpool. He *d.* 1839, leaving issue,
(1) John Henry Cole, *m.* 1st, 1861, Georgina L'Estrange, and 2ndly, 1867, Charlotte Fox. He *d.* 1873, having by his second wife had issue,
1. Owen, *b.* 1868.
2. Lionel, Lieut.-Col. (retired), Sligo R.F.A., *b.* 1871.
1. Stella Harriett Beresford, *m.* 1898, George R. Lawless, F.R.C.S.I., and has issue.
(2) Charles Bradstreet, of Clogherevagh, co. Sligo, J.P., Maj. late 99th L.I. and Sligo Rifles, Clerk of the Peace for Sligo, *b.* 1835; *m.* 26 June, 1861, Emily Frances Graham, eldest dau. of the late Sir Robert Gore-Booth, 4th bart. He *d.* 1890, leaving issue,
1. Graham Owen Robert, of Clogherevagh, Capt. late 18th Royal Irish Regt., J.P., *b.* 22 July, 1862; *m.* 7 July, 1897, Maud, dau. of the late Lord Morris and Killanin (*see* BURKE'S *Peerage*, KILLANIN, B.), and has issue,
a. Sydney Michael, *b.* 12 May, 1898.
b. Brigid, *b.* 20 April, 1901.
c. Zundrede Mary, *b.* 17 Nov. 1905.
2. Henry Edward, J.P. of Lakeview, co. Leitrim, *b.* 7 May, 1865; *m.* April, 1898, Emily Phillipa, dau. of Col. Mansfield, D.L., of Castle Wray, co. Donegal (*see that family*), and has issue,
a. Gerard, *b.* 16 March, 1899.
b. Ronald, *b.* 28 Aug. 1900.
1. Caroline Susan Augusta, *d. unm.* April, 1892.
(3) Edward, Capt. 52nd Regt., *m.* 1867, Rosina Benson, *d.* 1888, leaving issue,
Emily Georgina, *m.* 1892, Rev. Richard Fleming, and has issue.
(1) Mariana, *b.* 1836; *m.* 1858, Francis Montgomery Olpherts, J.P., of Mount Shannon, co. Sligo. He *d.* 1897.
(2) Susan Georgina, *b.* 1839; *d. unm.* 1870.
2. James, Barrister-at-Law, *m.* 1st, his cousin, Marion Catherine Florence, only dau. of Rev. Richard Wynne, Rector of Drumcliff (*see above*), and had issue,
(1) William, dec.
(1) Catherine Marion, *d. unm.*
He *m.* 2ndly, the dau. of — Blake, of Castlegrove, co. Galway, and had issue,
(2) James, dec. (3) John, dec.
(4) Owen, *m.* 1887, Phoebe Mary, dau. of James Young, of Harristown, co. Roscommon, and *d.* 23 Oct. 1898, having had issue, two sons.
(2) Emily, *d. unm.* (3) Florence.
3. William (Rev.), *m.* a dau. of James Saurin, D.D., Bishop of Dromore, and had issue,

(1) James Owen, m. Maria Knox, and d. 1865, leaving issue,
  1. Sarah Elizabeth, m. 30 Sept. 1875, Walter Henry Wilson, of Belvoir Park, Belfast. He d. 14 May, 1904, leaving issue (see that family).
  2. Frances, m. 1897, Rev. Henry R. Anderson, M.A.
  3. Eleanor Beatrice, m. 1894, William Langford Symes, M.D., F.R.C.P.I.
(2) Watkin, d. young.
(3) |William, b. 1833; m. Agnes Davis; and has issue, 1, William Henry; 2, Charles Edward; 3, Robert Saurin; 1, Catherine; and 2, Ruth Agnes.
(4) Mark Saurin, Maj. 81st Regt. (retired), b. 29 April, 1839; m. 1881, Susannah Frances Giffard (dec.), and has issue,
  1. William Giffard, b. 1882.
  2. James, b. 1884.
  3. Francis George, b. 1886.
  1. Mary Saurin.
(5) Henry, d. unm.
(1) Elizabeth, d. unm.
(2) Cornelia, m. — Berwick, and is deceased.
(3) Emily, m. Rev. Robert Hannay (dec.), Vicar of Belfast, and has issue.
4. Edmond, m. 1st, 1829, Mary Phillips, of Mount Rivers, co. Tipperary, and had issue,
  (1) William Richard, b. 1830, m. 1st, Charlotte Lydia, sole child and heiress of Major Charles Loftus, nephew of the Marquess of Townshend. He m. 2ndly, Elizabeth, dau. of Rev. M. J. Shaw. He d.s.p. 1897.
  (2) Edmund, dec.
  (1) Fanny Eleanor, d. young.
He m. 2ndly, his first cousin, Mary Anne, dau. of Rev. Henry Wynne. She d.s.p. 1877. He d. 1872.
5. Augustus Frederick, m. Charlotte, dau. of Sir Robert Shaw, 1st bart. (see BURKE's Peerage), and had issue. He d. 1859. She d.
  1. Frederick, dec.
  2. William.
  1. Augusta, d. 1878.
6. Lewis, m. Maria Jones, and d.s.p. His widow m. 2ndly, William Hopkins, of Blackall, co. Meath.
  1. Elizabeth Anne, m. Richard Fowler Butler, of Barton Hall, co. Stafford, and had issue, both dec.
  2. Kate Emily, m. 14 Dec. 1833, Sir Charles John James Hamilton, 3rd bart.,C.B. (see BURKE's Peerage), and d. 25 May, 1879. He d. 23 Jan. 1892.
  3. Eleanor, dec. m. — Prince, of Warburton House, Sussex.
1. Catherine, m. Euseby Cleaver, D.D., Archbishop of Dublin, and had issue, both dec.
The Right Hon. Owen Wynne d. 10 March, 1789. His eldest son,
OWEN WYNNE, M.P., of Hazlewood, High Sheriff co. Sligo 1819 and 1833, m. Jan. 1790, Lady Sarah Elizabeth Cole, eldest dau. of William, 1st Earl of Enniskillen, and by her (who d. 14 March, 1833) had issue,
1. John Arthur, late of Hazlewood.
2. William Willoughby (Rev.), b. 6 Sept. 1802; m. Sophia, dau. of Alexander Perceval, and d.s.p. Sept. 1860.
1. Anne, m. 1 Sept. 1811, Somerset Richard, 3rd Earl of Carrick, and d. 22 Oct. 1829, leaving issue.
2. Sarah Frances, m. Edward Joshua Cooper, of Markree Castle, co. Sligo, and d. 1862. Mr. Cooper d. 23 April, 1863, leaving issue (see that family).
3. Elizabeth, m. 10 Feb. 1825, Rev. Luke Fowler, son of Robert Fowler, D.D., Bishop of Ossory and Ferns. She d. 1855, leaving issue (see FOWLER of Rahinston).
4. Florence, d. unm. 12 April, 1812.
Mr. Wynne, d. 12 Dec. 1841. His eldest son,
THE RIGHT HON. JOHN ARTHUR WYNNE, of Hazlewood, M.P. for Sligo, Under-Secretary to the Lord-Lieutenant of Ireland 1852, J.P., served as High Sheriff for the cost of Sligo (1840) and Leitrim (1834) b. 20 April, 1801; m. 7 April, 1838, Lady Anne Wandesforde Butler, dau. of James, 1st Marquess of Ormonde, K.P., and by her (who d. 27 Nov. 1849) had issue,
1. Owen, late of Hazlewood.
2. James, b. 24 Nov. 1847; d. young.
1. Sarah d. unm. 26 Dec. 1903.
2. Grace Florence.
Mr. Wynne, d. 19 June, 1865. The elder son,
OWEN WYNNE, of Hazlewood, co. Sligo, J.P. and D.L. for that co. and High Sheriff 1875, and J.P. co. Leitrim, High Sheriff for that co. 1881, late Lieut. 61st Foot, b. 5 Feb. 1843; m. 1 Nov. 1870, Stella Fanny, youngest dau. of Sir Robert Gore Booth, 4th bart. He d. 21 Nov. 1910, having by her (who d. 1 March, 1887) had issue,
1. MURIEL CAROLINE LOUISA, now of Hazlewood.
2. Evelyn Mary, m. 24 July, 1901, Henry George l.'Estrange, youngest son of the late Christopher Carlton L'Estrange, of Kevensfort, co. Sligo, and has issue one son and two daus.
3. Madeline Mary, twin with Evelyn Mary.
4. Dorothy Adelaide.

Seats—Hazlewood, Sligo; and Lurganboy Lodge, Manor Hamilton.

WYSE OF THE MANOR OF ST. JOHN'S.

ANDREW NICHOLAS BONAPARTE WYSE, of the Manor of St. John's, co. Waterford, b. 1870, M.A., London University, Inspector of National Schools; m. 16 Sept. 1896, Marie, eldest dau. of the Count de Chripounoff, of Bielevetz Eletz, Orel, Russia, and has issue,

WILLIAM LUCIEN, b. 1908.
Helen Victoria, b. 1897.

Lineage.—The ancestor of this ancient house was a younger son of the family of Wyse, originally of Greston, Cornwall (1167), and subsequently of Sydenham, Devon (1320). He accompanied Richard, Earl of Pembroke, into Ireland, 1171, with the rank and title of knight, and immediately after the Earl's landing and taking possession of co. Waterford (one of the first conquests of the English) was rewarded with large possessions (part of which near Dungarvan retains the name of "Wyse's Point," as marked in the oldest sea charts), in capite, at two knight's fee, and the usual condition of military service. King JOHN, when he visited Waterford as Earl of Moreton, granted, 1195, a charter to the priory, now Manor of St. John's, afterwards confirmed by EDWARD I, 1281, by which it was exempted from all tolls and other charges, with power to hold a court for the trial of minor offences within its jurisdiction, whilst the right to all tithes, great and small, was granted by Walter, Bishop of Waterford, and confirmed by his successors. From 1452 to 1690, when the city surrendered to King WILLIAM, there were (besides several members of Parliament) thirty six Mayors and High Sheriffs of this family. The Mayor, THOMAS WYSE, on signing the capitulation of the city, as Governor, to WILLIAM,1690, paid out of his private purse £1,530, the sum required by the King to save the citizens from an immediate levy, which sum was never repaid to him. The Wyses were amongst the heaviest sufferers by confiscation. In 1647 the entire of their property was seized and possessed by the usurping powers, and it was not until 1663, after the restoration of CHARLES II, that they were restored to its enjoyment by a decree of the Court of Chancery, with large deductions, however, such as Chapelizod, co. Dublin, one hundred houses within the city of Waterford, retained by CROMWELL's soldiers, or those who purchased from them.

The chief line of the English Wyses were those seated at Sydenham, Devon, for details of whom refer to WISE of Clayton Hall. A junior branch, as already mentioned, was established in the sister kingdom so far back as the 12th century by
SIR ANDREW WYSE, Knt., who passed over to Ireland with the first band of warriors that, under the command of Strongbow, sought a settlement in that country. He had issue, WILLIAM and Robert. The former,
WILLIAM WYSE, s. his father, and was progenitor of the Wyses, of whom we are about to treat. His descendants, as well as those of his brother Robert, soon extended their name and possessions in co. Waterford.
ANDREW WYSE, the son of William, was father of
PHILIP WYSE, mentioned in the deed of feoffment of 1323. He had two sons, WILLIAM and John. The elder,
WILLIAM WYSE, had by the aforesaid feoffment, temp. EDWARD II, a confirmation of certain lands in co. Waterford. His son and successor,
WILLIAM WYSE, m. a dau. of the Aylward family, and was father of
PHILIP WYSE, whose son,
JOHN WYSE, m. a dau. of the Madans (one among the first alliances of the English gentry with the native Irish), and left a son and successor,
WILLIAM WYSE, who was father of four sons, George, Walter, Richard, and Galfrid. The 3rd son,
SIR RICHARD WYSE, was father of Andrew and JAMES. The latter,
JAMES WYSE, married into the distinguished family of the Waddings (from whom was the celebrated Franciscan monk, Luke Wadding, an eminent writer of the 17th century), and was father of
JOHN WYSE, whose son,
MAURICE WYSE, was Mayor of Waterford 1452, and was living 1495. In four years afterwards JOHN WYSE and James Sherlock were appointed Justices to hold assizes in the adjacent districts (Patent Roll, 14 HENRY IV, in Chancery, Ireland). This
JOHN WYSE, of the Manor of St. John, the son of Maurice, inherited, by descent, those lands of Island-i-Kane, Ballydermody, &c., which had been the subject of the family settlement of 1325 amongst the Wyses. In 1553,
SIR WILLIAM WYSE, son of John, by his wife, a dau. of Henry Sherlock, being then Mayor of Waterford, wrote to Cromwell, the King's Secretary, an official letter on the state of Ireland, which is preserved in the British Museum, in which he alleges certain correspondence between the Emperor CHARLES V, and the Earl of

Desmond, the object of which he infers was an "invasion of the cities and towns by the sea coast of this land." It is to be here observed, that during his mayoralty occurred the memorable Geraldine rebellion, when Waterford, under his government and control, adhered so firmly to HENRY VIII, that the loyalty of its citizens was acknowledged by three royal letters of thanks, and Wyse himself, having gone to England 1536, was made Esquire of the King's body, and subsequently received the honour of knighthood as "an honourable gift for their renowned fidelity," and returned to Waterford with a cap of maintenance and gilt sword, presented by the King to the Corporation, to be borne thenceforth before the Mayor on all state occasions, which practice is still continued. Sir William d. about 1556, leaving issue, when various inquisitions post mortem were taken to ascertain his estates and possessions in the co. and city of Dublin, cos. Cork and Tipperary, and above all. in the co. and city of Waterford.

HENRY WYSE, of the Manor of St. John, the eldest son of Sir William, m. Joan Clarke, of Bristol, and d. circa 1564. It is also recorded that this Henry Wyse had an exemption to him and his heirs from all tolls and grist at Watkin's mill, on the remarkable condition of defending the granter's title and enjoyment of the watercourse "from St. Catherine's to Ship's or Sheep's Bridge, according to the charter of King JOHN to the House of St. John." This Henry d.s.p., and was s. by

JAMES WYSE, the son of his next brother John, by Maryanne Walshe, of co. Dublin. As heir to his uncle, Queen ELIZABETH granted him by patent, in the 2nd year of her reign, 1563, all and singular the manors, lordships, castles, &c., of which his said uncle died seised. This James m. Alisonne, of the family of Chief Baron Finglass, author of the Breviate of Ireland, dau. and heir of Finglass, of co. Dublin, and d. 1596, leaving issue,
1. JOHN.
2. Andrew, appears to have been Knight of Malta, Prior of England, Privy Councillor to King PHILIP of Spain, in the kingdom of Naples, &c.
3. Henry, of Monkstown, co. Cork, followed Lord Baltimore to America, and was the founder of a family in Virginia, represented by the celebrated Confederate Orator and Statesman, Lieut.-Gen. Henry Wise. 4. Thomas, Mayor of Waterford.
5. Nicholas, Sheriff of Waterford 1605.

The eldest son,
JOHN WYSE, of the Manor of St. John, aged 24 at his father's death, 1596, m. Mary, dau. of Bartholomew Lincolne. He d. 1625, and left three sons. The eldest,
ROBERT WYSE, Sheriff of Waterford 1630; m. Mary Wadding, but d.s.p. 1632. He made a settlement of the family estates in 1631. His brother,
FRANCIS WYSE, of the Manor of St. John, m. Genette, dau. of Robert Walsh, Mayor of Waterford 1602, was his heir-at-law. By his will, 1647, he left very large bequests to the charitable institutions of Waterford, and five shillings to each of its citizens. His heir male,
THOMAS WYSE, eldest son of Andrew, Sheriff of Waterford 1632, 3rd son of John Wyse, by Mary Lincolne his wife, m. the only child and heiress of Thomas Synnell, of Cuddagh, Queen's Co., and was s. by his nephew,
ROBERT WYSE, m. Anstace Le Poer, of Guilcah, co. Waterford, and had (with a dau., Zaveria, m. Edward Fitzgerald, ancestor of the Fitzgeralds of the Little Island, near Waterford), several sons, among whom,
FRANCIS WYSE, of the Manor of St. John, m. Mary, dau. of Thomas Masterson (descended from Sir Thomas Masterson, Knt. of Ferns, seneschal of the co. Palatine of Wexford 1588), of Castletown and Monaseed, co. Wexford, by Thomasine his wife, dau. of John Walshe, of Philltown, co. Kilkenny and by her (who m. 2ndly, Laurence Esmonde, of Ballinastra) had issue,
1. THOMAS.
1. Catherine, a nun. 2. Anstane, a nun.
3. Margaret, m. Edward Dunne, of Brittas, Queen's Co. (see DUNNE of Brittas).

Mr. Wyse d. 1717, and was s. by his son,
THOMAS WYSE, of the Manor of St. John, m. 1st, 1720, Mary Bourne, of London, and by her had issue,
1. FRANCIS, his heir. 2. John.
3. Richard.
1. Anne, m. John M'Carthy, of Spring House, co. Tipperary, and was maternal grandmother of Peter, Count D'Alton, and the Right Hon. Richard Lalor Shiel, M.P. 2. Charlotte, a nun.
3. Margaret, m. Thomas Houghton, of Kilmannock, co. Wexford. Mr. Wyse m. 2ndly, 1740, Dame Hester Edwards, née Dacon, of Norfolk, widow of Sir Francis Edwards, Bart. (Her dau., Hester, heiress of Sir Francis Edwards, m. Viscount Malpas, eldest son of the 3rd Earl of Cholmondeley.) By Dame Hester he had no issue. His eldest son,
FRANCIS WYSE, of the Manor of St. John, d. uam., and was s. by his nephew, Thomas, son of his brother,
JOHN WYSE, m. Mary Ann, dau. of Walter Blackney, of Ballyellin, co. Carlow, by Mary his wife, dau. of John Byrne,* of Cabinteely, by Maryann his wife, dau. of Dudley Colclough, of Duffrey, and had, with other issue,
1. THOMAS. his heir. 2. Walter.
3. James, m. but d.s.p.
4. Francis, m. Mary, dau. of — Scally, and had issue,
1. Francis. 2. James.

* This John Byrne, of Cabinteely, was son of John Byrne, of the same place, by Mary his wife, dau. of Walter Chevers, of Monkstown, by Alson his wife, dau. of Nicholas, 1st Viscount Netterville (see BYRNE of Cabinteely).

3. Thomas, County Inspector, R.I.C., of Galway East, m. 1857, his cousin, Frances, dau. of Francis Wyse, of Rathkullen, and was drowned at Loughrea, co. Galway, 1879, leaving issue,
(1) James Edward, Master Mariner, Mercantile Marine, of The Grove, Great Crosby, near Liverpool, m. 23 Dec. 1907, Mary Elizabeth Lucy, dau. of the late Samuel Sharman, Solicitor, of Liverpool.
(2) Thomas Francis, L.R.C.S., m. 1893. Elizabeth (who d. 4 Dec. 1907), dau. of Charles Lynch, of Killester, co. Dublin.
(3) Alfred William, m. 1890, Mary, dau. of I. Mahon, of Buenos Ayres.
(1) Alice, m. W. M. Crealock.
(2) Mary, m. 23 Nov. 1882, Charles Brenan, of Dublin.
(3) Frances Maria, m. 1885, Henry Forbes Montagu Watson, of Lumelone, co. Carlow, who d.s.p. Jan. 1891.
1. Mary, m. Richard Hore, and had issue.
2. Elizabeth Frances, m. Maurice Hore, nephew of Richard, aforesaid.
1. Eliza, m. John Snow, of Snow Hill, co. Kilkenny, and left four sons and two daus.
2. Mary, m. Anthony Galwey, of Carrick-on-Suir.
3. Catherine, m. her first cousin, Walter Blackney, of Ballyellin.
4. Margaret, m. James Scully, of Tipperary.

The son and successor,
THOMAS WYSE, of the Manor of St. John, m. 6 Jan. 1791, Francis Maria, only dau. and heir (by Fanny Barron his wife) of George Bagge, of Dromore, co. Waterford, and by her had issue,
1. THOMAS, his heir.
2. George, b. 1793, first an Officer in the 6th Regt. of Foot, afterwards a Barrister-at-Law, and Senior Police Magistrate of the City of Dublin, m. 1822, Winifred, 3rd dau. of John Flanagan, of St. Katherine's Park, Leixlip, and of Od Castle, co. Roscommon, and by her (who d. 27 April, 1856) left at his decease, 4 Nov. 1867,
1. John, b. 18 Dec. 1825, formerly an Officer 57th Regt., and Aide-de-Camp to Lieut.-Gen. Sir Harry G. W. Smith, Bart., G.C.B., now in holy orders.
2. Arthur George, Resident Magistrate, Castlebar, co. Mayo, b. 7 Aug. 1830, formerly an Officer in the 48th Regt., and d. Jan. 1891.
1. Winifrede Mary, d. unm. 15 April, 1908.
3. Francis, of Rathcullen, m. Mary, dau. of John Hay, of Ballinkeele, of an ancient co. Wexford family (a branch of which, represented by Count Hay de Slade, is established in Brittany since the time of James II.), and d. 1855, leaving issue,
1. Thomas, d. Oct. 1886.
2. John, an Officer 34th Regt., m. 1861, a lady of the Onslow family.
1. Eleanor.
2. Frances, m. (as above) 1857, her cousin, Thomas Wyse.
3. Mary, a nun.
1. Harriett, d. 1866.
2. Mary Ann, m. Lorenzo Power, of Bonmahon, and had issue, Thomas Power, J.P., Capt. Waterford Artillery, d. 1865.
3. Frances, a nun, d. 1849.

The eldest son,
THE RIGHT HON. SIR THOMAS WYSE, K.C.B., of the Manor of St. John, co. Waterford, D.L., Her Britannic Majesty's Envoy Extraordinary at the Court of Athens, b. Dec. 1791; m. 1821, Letitia, dau. of Lucien Bonaparte, Prince of Canino, brother of NAPOLEON I, Emperor of the French, and had issue, two sons,
1. NAPOLEON ALFRED, J.P. and D.L. co. Waterford, High Sheriff 1870, a Knt. Commander of the Order of St. Maurice and Lazarus, also of that of the Nichan Iftichar, of Tunis, author of Notes sur la Russie, Paris 1854, and of the Flores Pictavienses, Perigeux 1869; b. Jan. 1822.
2. William Charles, late Capt. Waterford Militia, J.P., was High Sheriff 1855; author of numerous poetical works in Provençal and English; b. Feb. 1826; m. 1864, Ellen Linzee, dau. of W. G. Prout, of St. Mabyn, Cornwall, and d. 3 Dec. 1892, leaving issue,
1. LUCIEN WILLIAM BONAPARTE, late of the Manor of St. John's.
2. ANDREW NICHOLAS BONAPARTE, now of the Manor of St. John's.
3. Lionel Harry Bonaparte, b. 1874.
4. Napoléon Gerald Bonaparte, Lieut. Waterford Artillery, b. 1876; m. 2 April, 1910, Gertrude, dau. of John Crowther, of Grove Park, Chiswick.

Sir Thomas Wyse, formerly M.P. co. Tipperary, and subsequently M.P. for Waterford, held office under Lord Melbourne's administration as one of the Lords of the Treasury, and as Joint Secretary of the Board of Control, and was distinguished as a Statesman, Scholar, and Orator. As representative of this very ancient family, he held his estates direct from the Crown, and as lineal descendant of the original grantee he inherited the rights of the Prior of St. John, and was, in that capacity, still subject to visitations of the Lord Bishop of the Diocese. He d. 1862, and was s. by his grandson,
LUCIEN WILLIAM BONAPARTE WYSE, of the Manor of St. John's, co. Waterford, J.P. and D.L., High Sheriff 1900, Capt. Waterford Artillery, b. 27 June, 1868; d. unm. 18 Jan. 1903.

Arms—Quarterly: 1st and 4th, sa., three chevrons erm., for WYSE; 2nd and 3rd, arg., a chevron between three Cornish choughs sa. Crest—A demi-lion rampant gu. gutté d'eau, holding in the dexter paw a mace ppr. Motto—Sapere aude.
Seats—Manor of St. John's, Waterford; Palazzo Bonaparte, Viterbo, Italy. Residence—Herbert Lodge, Sydney Avenue, Blackrock, co. Dublin.

Young. THE LANDED GENTRY. 784

YOUNG OF COOLKEIRAGH.

RICHARD ASHMUR BLAIR YOUNG, of Coolkeiragh, co. Londonderry, Capt. Army Pay Dept. formerly Royal Inniskilling Fusiliers, served in the South African War 1899-1901 (despatches, Queen's medal with six clasps), *b.* 15 May, 1877; *m.* 8 Oct. 1902, Julia Sydney, 4th dau. of the late Conolly T. McCausland, D.L. of Drenagh, Limavady, co. Londonderry (*see that family*), and Laura his wife, dau. of St. Andrew, 14th Baron St. John of Bletsoe (*see* BURKE'S *Peerage*), and has issue,

Margaret Lettice Elizabeth, *b.* 14 May, 1909.

Lineage.—REV. JOHN YOUNG, Rector of Urney, co. Tyrone, *m.* Elspa Douglas, and by her had a numerous family, of whom the eldest son,

JAMES YOUNG, settled in co. Donegal, was present in Derry during the siege 1688-9, and was attainted by JAMES II. His will is dated 1684. He left issue nine sons and several daus. The eldest son,

JOHN YOUNG, of Coolkeiragh (deed dated 1725), *m.* Catherine, sister of Thomas Knox (whose will was proved 1721), and granddau. of the Right Rev. Andrew Knox, Bishop of Raphoe (*see* KNOX *of Prehen*), and *d.* about 1730, having had issue,
1. WILLIAM, of whom presently.
2. Thomas, of Lough Esk, co. Donegal, *m.* 1740, Rebecca, dau. of Oliver Singleton, of Fort Singleton, co. Monaghan, and was ancestor of the late Lord Lisgar, and the Youngs, Baronets of Bailieborough (*see* BURKE'S *Peerage*).
1. A dau. *m.*, Johnston Mansfield, 5th son of George Mansfield, of Castle Wray, co. Donegal, and had issue.

The elder son,
WILLIAM YOUNG, of Coolkeiragh, *m.* 18 Oct. 1732, Letitia, dau. of the Rev. William Hamilton, Rector of Strabane, co. Tyrone, 1734-65, and of Killatee 1716-65. His will is dated 27 March, 1760. He left issue,
1. ALEXANDER, of whom presently.
1. Ann, *m.* 1 Nov. 1770, James Lendrum, of Magheracross, co. Fermanagh, and had issue.
2. Catherine, *m.* 9 May, 1777, Robert Hanna, of Dublin.
3. Letitia, *m.* Robert Johnston, of Stoneville and Crocknacreive, co. Fermanagh, and had issue.

The only son,
ALEXANDER YOUNG, of Coolkeiragh, J.P., *m.* 1st, 27 Nov. 1771, Catharine, dau. of Richard Hassard, of Garden Hill, co. Fermanagh, J.P., and by her (who *d.* 12 Dec. 1782) had issue,
1. William Hamilton, *b.* 16 Jan. 1777; *d. unm.* 25 Sept. 1793.
2. RICHARD, his heir.
3. Thomas, *b.* 27 Nov. 1780; *d. unm.* 8 July, 1835.
1. Jane, *m.* 1790, Rev. John Benjamin Story, of Corick, Clogher, co. Tyrone, and had issue.
2. Letitia, *m.* 1795, Capt. Valentine Munbee, of Horringer Hall, Suffolk, and *d.* 1850, leaving issue.
3. Anne, *d. unm.* 1860.

Mr. Young *m.* 2ndly, 21 Aug. 1791, Elizabeth, relict of John Cunningham, of Londonderry, by whom he had issue,
4. James, *b.* 22 Nov. 1795; *d.* in East Indies 1820, *unm.*
5. Alexander, *b.* 20 Aug. 1800; *d.* 24 Feb. 1828, *unm.*

He *d.* 15 Dec. 1819, and was *s.* by his eldest surviving son,
RICHARD YOUNG, of Coolkeiragh, J.P., Major 19th and 39th Regts., *b.* 10 Aug. 1778; *m.* 25 Feb. 1817, Eliza, only dau. of John Carlwell, M.D., of Londonderry, and Mary, his wife, dau. of Hugh Lecky, of Agivy. She *d.* 16 June, 1847, having had issue,
1. ALEXANDER THOMAS, J.P., *b.* 4 June, 1821; *m.* 13 Feb. 1844, Frances Mary, youngest dau. of Rev. James Ashmur Johnston, of Coalisland, co. Tyrone. She *d.* 8 Dec. 1876. He *d.v.p.* 19 Aug. 1851, leaving issue,
 1. RICHARD JAMES CALDWELL, heir to his grandfather.
 2. Alexander Thomas, *b.* 25 Oct. 1849; *d. unm.* 25 Feb. 1878.
 3. Ashmur Johnston, *b.* 1 Oct. 1850; *d. unm.* 8 Jan. 1868.
 4. Francis Alexander, *b.* 9 Oct. 1851; *d. unm.* 18 April, 1886.
 1. Anne Catherine Frances, *m.* 11 June, 1896, William Irvine, K.C., of Prospect Hill, Carrickmines, co. Dublin, eldest son of William Irvine, of Prospect Hill, Enniskillen.
 2. Elizabeth Emily Charlotte, *d. unm.* 26 April, 1869.
 3. Inez Alexa, *m.* 6 April, 1880, Sir Robert Newman Chambers, 2nd son of Thomas Chambers, of Aberfoyle, and has issue, Thomas Brooke Winsley, *b.* 27 Nov. 1882; and Inez Mary Muriel.
2. Richard John, *b.* 17 Dec. 1825; *d.* 21 Jan. 1837.
1. Mary Elizabeth, *d.* 23 March, 1824.
2. Catharine Jane, *m.* 24 Sept. 1842, George Tomkins, J.P., of Mobuoy, co. Londonderry. She *d.* 5 Dec. 1890.
3. Eliza Letitia, *m.* 19 May, 1859, James Forsyth, M.D., of Templeard Culmore, co. Londonderry, and *d.* 3 Sept. 1893, leaving issue a dau., Eliza Letitia Young.
4. Anne, *m.* 23 Oct. 1860, Edward Augustus Williamson, R.N., and *d.* 5 March, 1892, leaving issue, three sons and a dau., 1. Edward Augustus, *b.* 10 Sept. 1862; 2. Richard Edward, *b.* 17 Dec. 1864; *d.* 1880; 3. William Alexander Finiston, Maj. A.S.C., *b.* 15 May, 1867; 1. Anne Susan Elizabeth.

Major Young *d.* 4 Dec. 1858, and was *s.* by his grandson,
RICHARD JAMES CALDWELL YOUNG, of Coolkeiragh, J.P., Lieut. 14th Regt. and 6th Inniskilling Dragoons, *b.* 2 Dec. 1845; *m.* 22 May, 1872, Catherine Elizabeth, 2nd dau. of Thomas Cochrane, of Singland, co. Limerick, and by her had issue,

RICHARD ASHMUR BLAIR, now of Coolkeiragh.
Beatrice Frances Elizabeth.

Mr. Young *d.* 25 Jan. 1885.

Seat—Coolkeiragh House, Eglinton, co. Londonderry.

YOUNG OF CULDAFF HOUSE.

ROBERT GEORGE YOUNG, of Culdaff House, co. Donegal, J.P., M.A. Trin. Coll. Dublin, *b.* 30 Nov. 1834; *m.* 23 Sept. 1858, Letitia, youngest dau. of Rev. Robert Staveley, of St. Munchins, Limerick, and has issue,
1. GEORGE LAWRENCE, of Millmount, Randalstown, co. Antrim, and Caratra Lodge, Culdaff, co. Donegal, J.P. cos. Donegal, Londonderry, and Antrim, *b.* 1 Oct. 1859; *m.* 22 June, 1883, Annie, youngest dau. of Lieut.-Col. Gardiner Harvey, of Islandnahoe, co. Antrim, and has issue,
 1. Robert Chichester, Barrister-at-Law, Ireland, 1910, *b.* 4 July, 1887.
 2. George Neville Gardiner, *b.* 17 March, 1893.
 3. Guy Owen Lawrence, *b.* 1 Jan. 1896.
 1. Rosetta Mary, *b.* 7 Aug. 1884; *d.* an infant.
 2. Dorothy Gage, *b.* 11 Dec. 1889.
2. Robert Staveley, *b.* 26 March, 1862; *d. unm.* 7 Dec. 1898.
3. Henry Crofton, *b.* 27 Sept. 1867; *m.* 10 Oct. 1910, Frances Edith, 2nd dau. of William Hart, of Kilderry, and has issue William Staveley, *b.* 19 Aug. 1911.
4. John Ffolliott, *b.* 13 March, 1870; *m.* 1899, Ethel, dau. of Rev. C. H. Pelly, and has issue,
 1. Charles.
 1. Kathleen. 2. Rosalie.
 3. Marjorie Angel. 4. Ethel Mabel Valdeck.
1. Mary Anne, *b.* 1 Aug. 1863.
2. Frances Sarah, *b.* 22 June, 1865.

Lineage.—REV. ROBERT YOUNG, who was ordained Presbyter by Andrew Knox, Bishop of Raphoe in 1632, instituted Rector of Cloncha 1640, and of Culdaff 1661, came it is said from Devonshire, and settled in Ireland. His son,

REV. ROBERT YOUNG, Rector of the Parish of Culdaff and Cloncha 1668, *m.* 1st, about 1667, Anne Cary, and had issue (with five daus.), two sons,
1. Robert, *b.* 18 Oct. 1673. 2. Thomas, *b.* 16 Oct. 1675.

He *m.* 2ndly, 1679, Elizabeth Hart, of Kilderry, and had issue by her one son, 3. GEORGE, and four daus. He *d.* 1705. His son by his 2nd wife,

GEORGE YOUNG, *b.* 11 April, 1680; *m.* 1702, Elizabeth, sister of Rev. Daniel McLaughlin, Rector of the Parish of Errigal, and Elizabeth Skipton his wife, and *d.* 1728, leaving, with other issue, an elder son,

ROBERT YOUNG, of Culdaff, High Sheriff 1734; *b.* 23 Sept. 1703; *m.* 1731, Hatton, dau. of Alderman Thomas Hart, of the city of Londonderry, and *d.* about 1747, having had issue,
1. Robert, *m.* Mary, dau. of — Moor, and *d.* 1783, leaving issue.
2. Thomas, *d.* 1781.
3. Gardiner, *m.* Catherine, dau. of — Richardson.
4. GEORGE, of whom presently.
1. Mary, *d.* 1795.
2. Elizabeth, *m.* 16 Oct. 1766, Rev. John Harvie, of Malin Hall (*see that family*).

The youngest son,
GEORGE YOUNG, of Culdaff, High Sheriff 1766, *b.* 1731; *m.* 1760, Rebecca Lamy (of French origin, and nearly related to the Croftons, Whalleys, and other Dublin families), and *d.* Dec. 1789, leaving issue,
1. John. 2. Thomas.
3. ROBERT, of whom presently.
4. George, *m.* Mary, dau. of — Williams.
5. Ralph, *m.* Susan, dau. of Rev. Philip Homan, of Surock, co. Westmeath.
1. Hatton, *m.* Rev. C. Nesbitt.
2. Rebecca, *m.* her cousin, Rev. Edward Harvey (*see* HARVEY *of Malin*). 3. Susan, *m.* John Harvey.
4. Elizabeth, *m.* Rev. William Smith.
5. Anne, *m.* Rev. George Homan, of Surock, co. Westmeath.

The 3rd son,
ROBERT YOUNG, of Culdaff, High Sheriff 1792, *b.* 1761; *m.* 20 Sept. 1790, Marcia, dau. of George Nesbitt, of Woodhill, co. Donegal, and by her (who *d.* 28 May, 1839) had issue,
1. GEORGE, his heir. 2. Robert James, *d. unm.* 7 Aug. 1827.
3. James William, *m.* 1824; *d.* 30 Nov. 1839, leaving issue, five sons and one dau.
1. Catherine, *m.* 23 April, 1812, Rev. Edward Chichester, Rector of Culdaff and Cloncha, and *d.* 15 April, 1875, having had issue, three sons (*see* BURKE'S *Peerage*, O'NEILL, B.).
2. Marcia, *m.* 1817, Lieut.-Col. Brooke Young, and *d.* 11 Jan. 1869, having had issue, one son, George, *d. unm.* 1849.
3. Anne Angel, *d.* 1885.

Mr. Young *d.* 11 Oct. 1823, and was *s.* by his eldest son,

GEORGE YOUNG, of Culdaff House, J.P. and D.L., *b.* 12 Aug. 1792; *m.* 17 Jan. 1832, Mary Anne, eldest dau. of John Ffolliott, of Hollybrook, co. Sligo, and had issue
  ROBERT GEORGE, now of Culdaff.
  Frances, *b.* 12 July, 1833, and *d.* same year.
Mr. Young *d.* 31 May, 1877, and was *s.* by his only son, now of Culdaff House.

Seat—Culdaff House, Culdaff, co. Donegal.

YOUNG OF HARRISTOWN.

OWEN WALLER O'GRADY YOUNG, of Harristown, co. Roscommon, J.P., *b.* Feb. 1864; *m.* 1904, Annie Matilda Victoria, dau. of William Insley, of Castlerea.

Lineage.—The first of this family of whom mention is made in Ireland was OWEN YOUNG, *b.* 1682, a member. It is stated, of a Yorkshire family of that name. He went to Ireland with three brothers, and settled at Castlerea, co. Roscommon, 1706. His sons became possessed of property in the cos. of Sligo and Roscommon. Owen Young *m.* Bridget, dau. of Very Rev. James Wilson, Dean of Tuam, and had issue,
  1. OWEN, *m.* Olivia Bell, 1726, and became ancestor of the elder branch of the family. Amongst his descendants was Matthew Young, the eminent Natural Philosopher and Mathematician, consecrated Bishop of Clonfert in 1799.
  2. JOHN, of whom presently.
  3. Mathew, *m.* Phœbe, dau. of Gen. Robinson. 4. Nicholas.
  1. Eleanor, *m.* Thomas Daly, of Mornington, co. Westmeath.
  2. Bridget, *m.* Rev. Nathaniel Barton.

The 2nd son,
JOHN YOUNG, became proprietor of Harristown, near Castlerea, and settled there in 1744. He *m.* Rebecca Gonne, and had issue,
  1. Owen, *m.* Rebecca, dau. of George Brabazon, of Brabazon Park, co. Mayo. He was High Sheriff for co. Roscommon in 1795, and *d.* without issue. 2. Robert, *d.* young.
  3. MATHEW, of whom presently.
  1. Rebecca, *m.* John Parton, of Castlerea.
  2. Dorothea, *m.* Gen. Bettesworth.
  3. Bridget, *m.* 25 Jan. 1777, George Miller, of Ballinue, co. Mayo.
  4. Letitia, *d. unm.* 5. Phœbe, *d. unm.*

The 3rd son,
MATHEW YOUNG, of Harristown, *s.* his brother Owen. He was appointed Cadet in the Royal Irish Artillery 1762, and afterwards Capt. in that Regt. He *m.* Elizabeth, dau. of William Finch, of Kincolman, co. Tipperary, and had issue,
  1. OWEN, of whom presently.
  2. Mathew, an Officer in the 53rd Regt., *m.* Miss Bushe, and had issue, a son, Finch, *d. unm.*
  3. William (Rev.), *m.* Rebecca, dau. of William Minchin, of Greenhills, co. Tipperary, and had issue,
    1. William, Capt. in the 49th Regt., *m.* Anna, dau. of Rev. William Jelly, of Portarlington.
    2. John Owen, Capt. 60th Regt., *d.* 12 May, 1910; *m.* Anne Catherine, dau. of Augustus Hartford, J.P., of Portarlington, late Capt. 59th Regt.
  4. John, *d.* young.
  1. Rebecca, *m.* her cousin, John Young, of Castlerea.
  2. Anne. *d. unm.* 3. Elizabeth, *d. unm.*

The eldest son,
OWEN YOUNG, of Harristown, *m.* 1st, Rachel, dau. of William Hunter, and by her had issue,
  1. Mathew, *d. unm.* 2. John Barton, *d. unm.*
  1. Jane, *m.* Humphrey Minchin. 2. Elizabeth, *d.* young.
Mr. Young *m.* 2ndly, Marianne, dau. of James Atkinson, of Rathangan, and by her had issue,
  3. JAMES, of Harristown, of whom presently.
  3. Mary, *m.* Godfrey George Massy, of Ballynakill, co. Limerick, and has issue.
He *d.* Sept. 1842, and was *s.* by his only surviving son,
JAMES YOUNG, of Harristown, J.P., A.B. of Trin. Coll. Dublin, *b.* 1834; *m.* 1863, Grace Elizabeth, dau. of Hon. Waller O'Grady,
I.L.G.

Q.C., of Castlegarde, co. Limerick, 2nd son of Standish, 1st Viscount Guillamore, by Grace Elizabeth his wife, dau. of Hugh, 3rd Lord Massy, and had issue,
  1. OWEN WALLER O'GRADY, now of Harristown.
  2. William Mathew O'Grady, *b.* March, 1872.
  1. Rosa Julia Maria Victoria, *m.* 1893, Surg.-Col. Charles Augustus Young, A.M.S., and has issue,
    1. Charles Owen James, *b.* 1894.
    2. Eric William, *b.* 1896.
    1. Grace Edythe Muriel.
  2. Grace Elizabeth Massy (*Elsmere, Carrickmines, co. Dublin*).
  3. Phœbe Mary Dorothea, *m.* 1887, Owen Wynne, D.I. R.I.C., who *d.* Oct. 1898, leaving issue,
    1. Owen Waller James, *b.* 1888. 2. Mervyn Llewelyn, *b.* 1891.
  4. Constance Katherine Matilda.
  5. Ida Ethel Isabella, *m.* 1902, Charles Herbert Thompson, B.A., M.B., B.Ch., T.C.D., and has issue,
    Neville Herbert, *b.* 1903.
  6. Evelyn Maud Henrietta.
Mr. Young was shot in his own demesne, June, 1877.

Arms—Gu., a fess or, charged with a trefoil vert in chief three lioncels rampant of the second. *Crest*—Out of a ducal coronet or, an ibex's head arg. horned and tufted gold and charged on the neck with a trefoil vert. *Motto*—Victoria fortitudo virtus.

Seat—Harristown, near Castlerea.

YOUNG OF BROCKLEY PARK.

JOHN WILLIAM YOUNG, now of Brockley Park, Stradbally, Queen's Co., J.P., B.A. Trin. Coll. Oxford, *b.* Jan. 1861; *s.* his father 1910.

Lineage.—The Youngs of the North of Ireland are of Scottish ancestry. They settled in the co. of Londonderry, afterwards in the co. of Antrim, in the 17th century.
SAMUEL YOUNG, of Portglenone, co. Antrim, 1700 to 1750, was father of
WILLIAM YOUNG, M.D., of Portglenone, *m.* in 1756, Elizabeth, dau. of J. MacRory, of Carmegrim, co. Antrim, and by her (who *d.* in 1839) left at his decease in 1830 (with other issue) a son and heir,
JOHN YOUNG, J.P. Queen's Co., who *m.* in 1826, Jane, dau. of David Brown, of Belfast, and by her (who *d.* in 1870) had one son and two daus., viz.
  1. WILLIAM, late of Brockley Park.
  1. Elizabeth, *d. unm.* 1886. 2. Jane.
Mr. Young *d.* in 1869, and was *s.* by his son, WILLIAM YOUNG, late of Brockley Park.
WILLIAM YOUNG, of Brockley Park, Stradbally, Queen's Co., and Doohulla Lodge, Clifden, co. Galway, *b.* 4 April, 1851; *m.* 22 Dec. 1859, Margaret Emily, dau. of William Kirk, of Tatham House, co. Durham, and has issue,
  JOHN WILLIAM, B.A., now of Brockley Park.
  Jane Agnes Emily.
Mr. Young, who was a Magistrate and Deputy-Lieut. for the Queens' Co., and a Magistrate for the co. of Galway, served as High Sheriff of the former co. 1875. He *d.* 14 April, 1910.

Arms—Arg., three piles sa. each charged with a rose or, on a chief engrailed az. an annulet of the third. *Crest*—A cubit arm erect ppr. charged with an annulet or, the hand grasping an arrow, point downwards also ppr. *Motto*—Press through.

Seat—Brockley Park, Stradbally, Queen's Co. *Club*—Sports.

3 D

YOUNG OF GALGORM.

THE RIGHT HON. JOHN YOUNG, P.C., of Galgorm Castle, co. Antrim, J.P. and D.L., High Sheriff 1863, M.A. Trin. Coll. Dublin, b. Dec. 1826; m. 1st, Jan. 1855, Grace Charlotte, 2nd dau. of Lieut.-Col. Patrick Savage, 13th Light Dragoons, and by her (who d. 1876) has issue,

1. WILLIAM ROBERT, b. 1856; m. 28 Aug. 1893, Mary, elder dau. of Sir Francis Macnaghten, Bart.
2. Patrick Savage, b. 1859; m. 1st, 1884, Flora, youngest dau. of Sir Charles Lanyon, of The Abbey, Belfast, and 2ndly, Emily, dau. of William Walter, and has issue, a son, b. 25 Sept. 1902.

3. Henry George, Capt. 10th Bengal Lancers, b. 7 March, 1870; m. 9 July, 1908, Adelaide Mary Glencairn, dau. of late Colin Glencairn Campbell, of Lower Belgrave Street, London, S.W.
4. John William Alexander, b. 1873.
5. George Charles Gillespie, b. 1876.
1. Anne Charlotte Maria, d. unm. 17 April, 1900.
2. Maria, m. 1892, John Casement, Post Capt. R.N.
3. Grace Cottenham, m. 25 July, 1890, Ogilvie Blair Graham (see GRAHAM of Larchfield). 4. Charlotte.
5. Rose.
6. Jane, m. 12 Sept. 1900, Alexander Miller, son of Sir Alexander Edward Miller, C.S.I.
7. Ethel Margaret, m. 8 March, 1902, John Stevenson, son of John Stevenson, of Middlesborough.

He m. 2ndly, July, 1878, Rose, 2nd dau. of Alexander Miller, of Ballycastle. She d. 11 June, 1894.

Lineage.—WILLIAM YOUNG, of Galgorm, M.D. (son of William Young, by his wife Jane Hunter), m. 1823, Anne, dau. of William Gihon, and by her (who d. 1835) had issue,
1. JOHN, of Galgorm Castle.
2. William Alexander, m. Margaret Gihon, and has issue, one son and three daus.
Mr. Young d. 1854.

Arms—Or, three piles sa., each charged with a fountain. Crest—A cubit arm erect charged with a fountain the hand grasping an arrow all ppr. Motto—Press through.

Seat—Galgorm Castle, Ballymena. Clubs—Junior Carlton and Ulster.

www.ingramcontent.com/pod-product-compliance
Lightning Source LLC
Chambersburg PA
CBHW071307150426
13191CB00007B/536